SUPERFORM

Races &

Racehorses

Flat Edition

> **Results, Ratings and Commentaries
> for Flat Racing, Turf and All Weather
> from Nov 8th 1999 - Nov 4th 2000**

Fifty Second Annual

www.superform.com

Foreword

With the fixture list continually expanding we again present our largest ever annual. Most racing professionals struggle to keep on top of the wall-to-wall racing throughout the summer months and it is difficult to maintain an accurate grasp of the form without specialising in certain types of race. With next season's fixture list larger still, we at Superform will endeavour to do the "leg work" for you and make form study as straightforward as possible.

The 2000 season proved a vintage year in the three and four year old divisions.

Dubai Millennium (134) started the season with emphatic wins in the Dubai World Cup and the Prince Of Wales Stakes at Royal Ascot, by an impressive 8L. Both of those victories were over 10f and connections were reportedly reluctant to attempt 12f again. A serious gallop injury to the Godolphin colt, soon after Ascot, deprived us of a much anticipated clash with last season's Champion 3yo Montjeu (134). Montjeu's finest moment came with a facile victory in the King George. The emergence of John Oxx's dual Derby winner Sinndar (134) added extra spice to the middle distance department and his memorable Arc defeat of Montjeu means that it is difficult for us to split this trio of top-class performers. The Aga Khan's decision to retire Sinndar is a shame as it deprives us from assessing him as a more mature four year old.

Giants Causeway (126) landed a remarkable five consecutive Group 1 races, surely the toughest racehorse seen for many a year. His claims for the top mile honours were there for all to see, but Observatory (126) quietly progressed throughout the season and his battling defeat of the "Iron Horse" at Ascot in September marked him down as Giants Causeway's equal. Then there is the almost forgotten Kings Best (127), whose contemptuous defeat of Giants Causeway in the 2,000 Guineas looks exceptional in light of that colt's subsequent achievements. His turn of foot in the 2,000 Guineas was breathtaking and without his sad injury in the Irish Derby we would surely have been looking at an outstanding Champion.

Kayf Tara (125) took the staying honours for the third successive season. He was deservedly retired after recapturing the Ascot Gold Cup and his departure leaves a big gap in the staying ranks.

Namid (125) took the sprinting honours with a ready win in the Prix de L'Abbaye in October.

For the second successive year the Tabor/Magnier/O'Brien partnership produced the Champion juvenile. Their strength in depth continues to amaze. Along with Minardi (122) they have Beckett, Hemingway, Mozart and Honours List all rated 113 or higher. Minardi defeated high-class fields in the Heinz 57 and Middle Park to come out ahead of Bad As I Wanna Be (119) and Tobougg (119) in our ratings. Tobougg landed the Group 1 Dewhurst in some style and jets off for some winter sun in Dubai as a leading 2,000 Guineas contender. Nayef (119) is a half brother to Champion performer Nashwan and Marcus Tregoning's colt really caught the eye with an impressive 6L Listed win at Ascot. He is to the fore in both the 2,000 Guineas and Derby ante-post betting and looks a potential star for 2001.

Riding honours, too, are shared. Johnny Murtagh had a season to lift anybody's spirits, landing a staggering 10 European Group 1's. No lesser an achievement was that of Kevin Darley. From journeyman of the northern circuit to Champion Jockey!

Sir Michael Stoute turned the trainers Championship into a procession with over £1,000,000 win and place prize money in hand over his nearest rival. As we go to press, Europe's sole Breeders' Cup winner Kalanisi capped a memorable season for the master of Freemason Lodge. Mark Johnston's achievement in topping the trainers list numerically also merits note. Sprint handicap specialist "Dandy" Nicholls had another fine season winning numerous valuable races.

Contents

Foreword	2
Superform Top Prize Winners in 2000	4
Introduction	5
Key To Reading Superform	7
Superform Best Horses of 2000	8
Index To Race Meetings	10
A to Z Index To Horses & Ratings	1423
Trainers Record Full Season	1702
Top Owners	1705
Top Trainers	1707
Top Trainers of Two Year Olds	1708
Top Jockeys	1709
Top Sires	1710
Using The Ratings	1711
Time And Going Figures	1712
Compiling The Ratings	1713
Official Ratings	6, 1713
Racecourse Guide	1714
Abbreviations List	1717
Scale of Age, Weight And Distance	1720

Publisher Kevin Gilroy thanks the following for their tremendous help in the compilation of this annual.

P Champion	D Mitchell
J Craven	T Mummery
K Ducie	M Olley
M Green	P O'Sullivan
P Innocenzi	J Dicker
J Jenkins	P Towning
R Johnson	V Towning
J Limb	C Woods

Photographs by Alec Russell, Huttons Ambo, York.

Front cover (paperback only)
HH Aga Khan's top class middle distance performer, SINNDAR (J P Murtagh) winning the DERBY at Epsom.

Printed In Finland
Published by Furlong Press, High St, Shoreham, West Sussex.
Copyright Furlong Press 2000

SUPERFORM TOP PRIZE WINNERS

4yo+		3yo		2yo	
£ 2386694	4 DUBAI MILLENNIUM	£ 1746694	3 SINNDAR	£ 246850	2 MOZART
1164573	4 FANTASTIC LIGHT	1483950	3 GIANTS CAUSEWAY	192713	2 SUPERSTAR LEO
960911	4 MONTJEU	417290	3 CRIMPLENE	189735	2 MINARDI
731707	6 BEHRENS	380404	3 EGYPTBAND	169618	2 TOBOUGG
731707	4 RHYTHM BAND	373075	3 SAKHEE	163486	2 GOGGLES
494309	6 RUNNING STAG	371568	3 PETRUSHKA	142970	2 NOVERRE
490380	4 KALANISI	322581	3 SAMUM	125913	2 CRYSTAL MUSIC
481733	5 HIGH RISE	295244	3 OBSERVATORY	119100	2 BECKETT
470313	4 MUTAFAWEQ	292200	3 MILLENARY	117195	2 OKAWANGO
445372	7 BIG JAG	286985	3 LOVE DIVINE	116140	2 COUNT DUBOIS
370378	4 DALIAPOUR	279536	3 CIRO	114990	2 INNIT
365854	6 PUBLIC PURSE	273637	3 BACHIR	113600	2 PRETTY GIRL
297742	6 CAITANO	268001	3 HOLDING COURT	107275	2 SEQUOYAH
247492	5 DIKTAT	267001	3 VOLVORETA	106973	2 KINGS COUNTY
243902	4 EASAAR	247166	3 BEAT HOLLOW	106512	2 DILSHAAN
231461	4 KINGSALSA	210544	3 KALLISTO	106146	2 BLUE GODDESS
225235	5 MUHTATHIR	194418	3 BEST OF THE BESTS	98612	2 ENDLESS SUMMER
223864	5 GREEK DANCE	189970	3 AIR MARSHALL	95397	2 ATLANTIS PRINCE
211318	5 NUCLEAR DEBATE	187150	3 GLYNDEBOURNE	92128	2 BAD AS I WANNA BE
206827	4 GOLDEN SNAKE	184485	3 REVE DOSCAR	86314	2 ENTHUSED
206321	4 INDIAN LODGE	182927	3 CHINA VISIT	85100	2 TURNBERRY ISLE
200100	6 KAYF TARA	181700	3 KINGS BEST	84580	2 DIM SUMS
193210	4 PIPALONG	165952	3 GIVE THE SLIP	83512	2 REGAL ROSE
192261	4 TIMBOROA	146925	3 LAHAN	79309	2 BOUNCING BOWDLER
182927	6 PUERTO MADERO	141210	3 LORD FLASHEART	76849	2 AMONITA
179334	4 CATELLA	138455	3 MEDICEAN	75146	2 BANNISTER
175976	4 BERTOLINI	136743	3 LADY UPSTAGE	73437	2 REEL BUDDY
167381	4 ELA ATHENA	131169	3 WINDSOR BOY	73032	2 CD EUROPE
162400	6 ARCTIC OWL	129219	3 BLUEMAMBA	69897	2 HONOURS LIST
159830	5 LEAR SPEAR	129250	3 PRINCESS ELLEN	66795	2 HOTELGENIE DOT COM
157264	4 DANSILI	121750	3 MILETRIAN	62780	2 BERLIN
152425	5 MURGHEM	118533	3 TIMI	61246	2 ELSIE PLUNKETT
146574	8 YAVANAS PACE	101923	3 EL GRAN PAPA	59615	2 KARASTA
144508	5 KABOOL	100980	3 SOBRIETY	58364	2 SUMMER SYMPHONY
141734	4 SAMPOWER STAR	98700	3 KALYPSO KATIE	57742	2 GOODIE TWOSUES
140611	4 ROYAL REBEL	98511	3 PAWN BROKER	57352	2 PERFECT PLUM
134295	5 ARKADIAN HERO	90965	3 MELIKAH	56739	2 MISTY EYED
129387	5 FRUITS OF LOVE	89399	3 SAILING	53491	2 ZIETUNZEEN
127556	4 NAMID	88899	3 SUBTLE POWER	51697	2 TAMBURLAINE
126750	5 AGNES WORLD	87414	3 KUTUB	51119	2 ATMOSPHERIC
126430	6 TAYSEER	86662	3 VALENTINO	51011	2 ROMANTIC MYTH
120985	4 ENDLESS HALL	82500	3 BERNSTEIN	50250	2 IMAGINE
116261	4 INDIAN DANEHILL	81401	3 DUKE OF MODENA	50241	2 DORA CARRINGTON
115290	7 PERSIAN PUNCH	80008	3 LAST RESORT	49019	2 AUTUMNAL
110544	5 CARIBBEAN MONARCH	78604	3 BARATHEA GUEST	44842	2 PAN JAMMER
107641	4 SENDAWAR	77942	3 DANCEABOUT	43556	2 BONNARD
107575	4 SUMITAS	77534	3 KIND REGARDS	42494	2 LADY LAHAR
106858	4 CLAXON	77382	3 MOON SOLITAIRE	42268	2 IRON MASK
99899	5 BAHAMIAN PIRATE	75252	3 CHIANG MAI	41455	2 ASCENSION
98944	4 DARING MISS	73932	3 ATLANTIC RHAPSODY	41307	2 ROLLY POLLY
98486	4 KATY NOWAITEE	73718	3 FORBEARING	40655	2 TORTUGUERO
98150	5 PERSIANO	72490	3 ALSHAKR	38926	2 RED MILLENNIUM
96924	5 ALBARAHIN	71900	3 DISTANT MUSIC	38881	2 IMPERIAL MEASURE
96830	4 AMILYNX	71775	3 JAMMAAL	38729	2 ZILCH
94475	4 ALJABR	71439	3 PAOLINI	38589	2 RED CARPET
93772	5 CRISOS IL MONACO	70350	3 ROMANTIC AFFAIR	38509	2 BRAM STOKER
91463	4 CONFLICT	69275	3 CAPE TOWN	38425	2 SAGACITY
91463	5 CRAIGSTEEL	69063	3 WATCHING	38000	2 SWEET DILEMMA
88366	4 TILLERMAN	68975	3 PACINO	37959	2 FREEFOURRACING
88256	6 RIGHT WING	66891	3 EKRAAR	37907	2 PALATIAL
85011	6 SAN SEBASTIAN	66037	3 BLUE GOLD	37280	2 NO EXCUSE NEEDED

Introduction

The race results in this book include every horse in each race in Britain. The principal foreign races are also included. The results and commentaries are published in weekly parts throughout the season under the title of "Superform".

WHY IS SUPERFORM DIFFERENT?
Our mission at Superform is not simply to report the results but to interpret them. Race results/form have little meaning unless the reader can grasp the value or worth of the form. Why is the form of one handicap, maiden or stakes race likely to prove better than another? Superform performance ratings, calculated on at least the first ten in every race, pin-point the likely worth of the form. Superform performance ratings are printed horse by horse, race by race. **These ratings are revised daily throughout the season** by five professional handicappers who strive to provide the most accurate ratings possible.

There are other vital aspects of form study which the bare results do not reveal. If a horse runs badly, our comment writers search for the likely cause, when it runs well they pin-point the conditions which favour success. Without a lot of page thumbing (sometimes through more than one book) race results give no indication of where or when a horse has won in the past. Superform lists all wins in the past two years for each horse within each detailed commentary. The optimum going, distance and track preferences for each horse are written up in full and we make particular note of long absences from the track. The bare results do not indicate whether a horse is likely to be suited by a longer distance or whether a newcomer is closely related to high class performers. Only a study of breeding can reveal this potential. Such research is time consuming and the tools of reference are costly. Superform comment writers do all this to save you valuable time!

CHARACTER COMMENTARIES
To obtain a character summary simply refer to the horse's last race. This race will either provide the summary or point out where the latest summary is printed with the reference "see ---".

RACE TIMES
A single race time reveals little. It's meaningful only when compared with some standard or average. Consistent methods must then be used to evaluate the condition of the track. Superform produces **pace and going figures** which pin-point fast run races and reflect the condition of the track, on the day. Often our "going" figures differ from the official going report supplied by the racecourse. More information on pace and going figures appear on page 1712.

STARTING PRICES
Starting prices are included not for the purpose of settling bets, but as a **guide** to the relative chance of each horse, expressed by the bookmakers at the track, on the day.

RATINGS
The Superform ratings published here reflect the judgement of our own handicappers, and the ratings are presented on the international 0-140 scale, as used by the official BHB handicappers. In the A-Z style index at the back of the book, you can see at a glance the Superform performance rating, race by race for each horse, for the whole of last season. For future races we normally base our calculations on the best rating the horse achieved in it's last three races. Often you discover a higher rating when searching back through a horse's form. The successful use of ratings often involves pin-pointing just which rating to

use for your calculations. For example, with a seasoned handicapper, it may be prudent to use an earlier, higher rating, if the ground suddenly alters in the horse's favour or the horse returns to form. However, ratings achieved within the previous 35 days are the most reliable. Full information on how to use Superform ratings appears on page 1711.

OFFICIAL RATINGS
In handicaps, the official rating off which the horse ran, is printed in brackets after the horse's weight. In the race title in handicap races, in the right hand margin, the figure in brackets represents the official rating of a horse set to carry 10-0. If the figure is 70, the horse carrying 10-0 is rated officially 70. A horse carrying 8-8 is rated 50 officially, since it carries 20lb less than 10-0 - and so on. This has been a feature of Superform since 1984 and gives some guide to the "class" of the race.

FAST TIME HORSES "+ -"
Horses which win in a fast time of **10 Fast** or more are marked with a **+ sign** instead of the usual asterisk. Second placed horses, beaten 2 lengths or less in a similarly fast time are marked --. These symbols are placed after the race reference number. Fuller explanation of the pace and going figures can be found on page 1712.

COURSE REQUIREMENTS
In the race results we describe the type of race and note the prize money for the winner. The distance of each race, the prevailing going and the pace of the race are also noted. At the beginning of each race meeting there is a brief comment on the course characteristics. Many sharp tracks like Chester and Epsom produce real course specialists.

WEIGHTS__"ex__ow__oh" AND APPRENTICE ALLOWANCES
Regarding the weights shown in the results, these are the weights (plus overweights) allotted to the horse by the race conditions or the handicapper. We do not subtract riders' allowances. The rider's allowance is however, noted in brackets. Penalties are marked **ex: ow** signifies overweight and **oh** notes that the horse was carrying more than the long handicap weight originally set by the handicapper.

LONG HANDICAP WEIGHTS__"oh"
Handicaps are compiled from the highest rated horse downwards. The topweight is usually set to carry 10-0. As the minimum weight in a Flat handicap is normally 7-10, any horse rated more than 32 pounds below the topweight must still carry the minimum weight of 7-10 - not the weight originally allotted by the handicapper. It is the originally allotted weight which is known as the **long handicap weight.** A horse may originally be set 7-0 by the handicapper, but on the day must carry the minimum weight of 7-10 and is therefore said to be **10lbs out of the handicap.**

Reading Superform

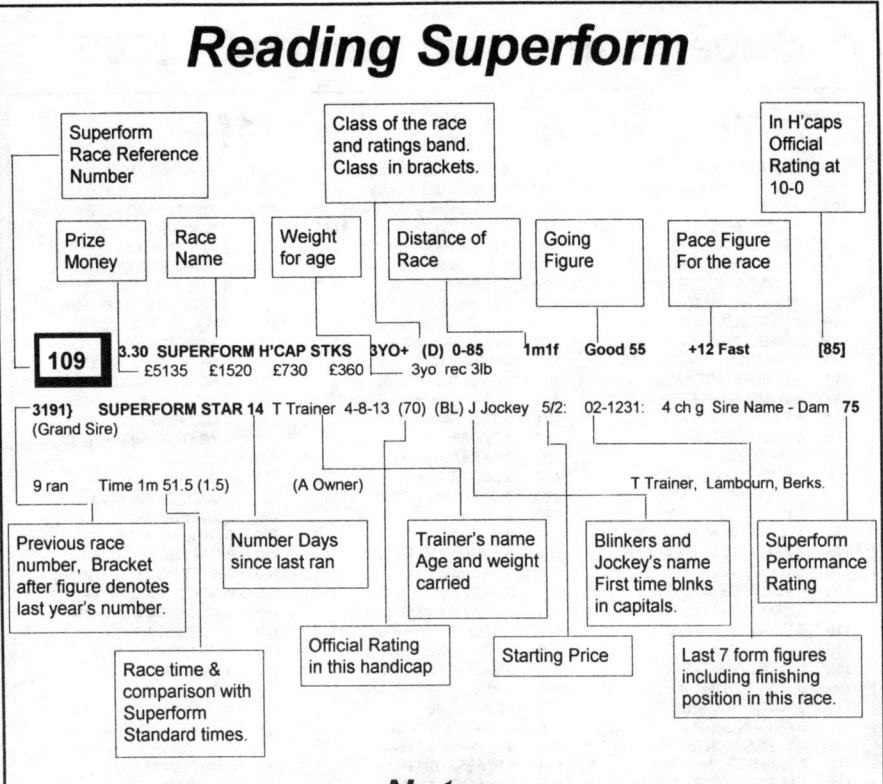

Superform Race Reference Number

Class of the race and ratings band. Class in brackets.

In H'caps Official Rating at 10-0

Prize Money | Race Name | Weight for age | Distance of Race | Going Figure | Pace Figure For the race

109 3.30 SUPERFORM H'CAP STKS 3YO+ (D) 0-85   1m1f   Good 55   +12 Fast   [85]
       £5135   £1520   £730   £360   3yo rec 3lb

3191} SUPERFORM STAR 14 T Trainer 4-8-13 (70) (BL) J Jockey 5/2: 02-1231: 4 ch g Sire Name - Dam 75
(Grand Sire)

9 ran   Time 1m 51.5 (1.5)   (A Owner)   T Trainer, Lambourn, Berks.

Previous race number, Bracket after figure denotes last year's number.

Number Days since last ran

Trainer's name Age and weight carried

Blinkers and Jockey's name First time blnks in capitals.

Superform Performance Rating

Race time & comparison with Superform Standard times.

Official Rating in this handicap

Starting Price

Last 7 form figures including finishing position in this race.

Notes:
GOING FIGURES And PACE FIGURES:

For each race meeting, from the race times we calculate a "going allowance" which gives a fairly accurate picture of what the ground was like - this sometimes differs from the official going description! A pace figure is also calculated which indicates the pace at which each race was run. Fast and slow run races can be seen at a glance. There is a full explanation of the going and pace calculations at the back of the annual.

PREVIOUS RACE REFERENCE:

If the horse is running for the first time in the current season, the race reference in Superform from last season is printed with a } after the number.

NUMBER OF DAYS SINCE RAN:

We believe this feature is most important. You are immediately aware how long the horse has been off the track since it's last run. Any period over 40 days usually needs some explanation. The horse might have had a problem in training or the going might have been unsuitable.

FORM FIGURES:

The last seven form figures are shown for each runner, the last figure being the finishing position in the current race. When assessing form you can see quickly whether the winner beat consistent, improving types, previous winners, or horses with strings of "duck eggs" .

OFFICIAL RATING IN HANDICAPS:

This is the official rating awarded by the BHB handicapper going into the race. It's usually referred to as the mark the horse "runs off". The higher the rating, the better the horse. 140 is the top of the ratings range and 40 and below, the bottom.

Superform's Best Horses Of 2000

5 - 7f

125	4	NAMID 4261*
124	4	INDIAN LODGE 4395*
123	5	NUCLEAR DEBATE 3598*
121	6	SUPERIOR PREMIUM 2115*
120	5	BOLD EDGE 4395
120	5	ARKADIAN HERO 3933
120	4	AGNES WORLD 2615*
120	5	LEND A HAND 3212
118	4	BERTOLINI 4261
118	6	GAELIC STORM 4581
118	3	LINCOLN DANCER 4495
117	6	SUGARFOOT 4395
117	4	SAMPOWER STAR 4125 +
117	5	EASTERN PURPLE 3982-
116	6	RUDIS PET 3982
116	4	PIPALONG 4261
116	4	SUPER LOVER 1746
116	8	TEDBURROW 4125
116	3	AUENKLANG 3784
116	8	PERRYSTON VIEW 4495
116	6	TOMBA 4395
115	4	VISION OF NIGHT 3784
115	3	UMISTIM 4465*
115	3	BERNSTEIN 4266*
115	5	GORSE 3212
115	5	TERTULLIAN 4317*
115	3	LAST RESORT 4352*
115	3	WATCHING 4261
114	5	AREION 2403*
114	3	THREE POINTS 3724*
114	4	TARRY FLYNN 4056
114	5	LORD KINTYRE 3982
114	3	ROSSINI 2115
114	3	PRIMO VALENTINO 4261
114	4	COBOURG LODGE 4398*
114	3	KIER PARK 1172
113	6	SOCIAL HARMONY 4056*
113	6	TAYSEER 4125-
113	3	TRINCULO 4125
113	4	MAIDAAN 4352
113	6	ANDREYEV 4581*
112	3	BLU AIR FORCE 2087
112	4	TILLERMAN 3452
112	5	HARMONIC WAY 4346
112	7	REPERTORY 4495*
112	6	WARNINGFORD 4544
112	3	SIR NICHOLAS 3212
112	4	ASTONISHED 4182-
112	4	IMPERIAL BEAUTY 2065
112	3	CAP LOZ 2226
112	3	CONORMARA 4266
112	5	DIABLENEYEV 2226
112	3	NICOBAR 3995
111	6	ONE WON ONE 4078
111	4	CASSANDRA GO 3059*
111	3	DANGER OVER 4052*
111	3	MOUNT ABU 4352
111	5	BAHAMIAN PIRATE 4346*
111	4	HOT TIN ROOF 3503
111	3	FATH 3610
110	5	LATE NIGHT OUT 4266

8 - 10f

134a	4	DUBAI MILLENNIUM 2089*
127	3	KINGS BEST 2409
126	3	OBSERVATORY 4111*
126	3	GIANTS CAUSEWAY 4111
125	4	KALANISI 4355*
125	4	SENDAWAR 3544
125	5	MUHTATHIR 3933
123	4	DANSILI 4395
122	3	MEDICEAN 4111
122	4	ALJABR 3087
122	4	INDIAN LODGE 4395*
121	5	GREEK DANCE 4355
121	4	ENDLESS HALL 2720 +
121	5	SHIVA 4355
120	3	CRIMPLENE 4111
120	3	EKRAAR 3903 +
120	5	DIKTAT 4111
120a	3	CHINA VISIT 2066
120	4	SLICKLY 4355
120	3	LAHAN 1185*
120	5	ARKADIAN HERO 3933
120	3	BACHIR 3647
120	3	BEAT HOLLOW 2225*
120	3	DISTANT MUSIC 4355
119	3	BEST OF THE BESTS 4111
119	3	ARISTOTLE 1848
119	3	VALENTINO 4111
119	3	REVE DOSCAR 4493
119	3	CIRO 3549*
119	3	SUANCES 1753*
119	5	ALBARAHIN 4544*
119	6	RIVIERA 3933*
118	5	KABOOL 4352
118	4	SLIP STREAM 2573*
118	3	PREMIER PAS 2736
118	5	ZOMARADAH 4064
118	4	FABERGER 4319*
118	4	INDIAN DANEHILL 4355
118	3	BERINES SON 1753
117	4	STATE SHINTO 3071
117	5	FLY FOR AVIE 4399*
117	4	CAPE TOWN 4352
117	4	SUMITAS 4319
117	4	KINGSALSA 4259
117	3	KUTUB 4050
117	3	ADILABAD 4238
117	3	LADY OF CHAD 4211
117	4	AGOL LACK 4050*
117	5	TRANS ISLAND 4395
116	6	FLY TO THE STARS 3847
116	4	ALRASSAAM 3370
116	4	CHELSEA MANOR 4050
116	4	SWALLOW FLIGHT 4180
116	3	SHIBBOLETH 2066
116	3	SOBIESKI 4238
116	3	UMISTIM 4465*
116	6	SUGARFOOT 4395
115	4	RHYTHM BAND 3641
115	4	DOUBLE HEART 1458
115	5	ELLE DANZIG 3071
115	3	SARAFAN 3647
115	3	PRINCESS ELLEN 3151

11f+

134	3	SINNDAR 4262*
134	4	MONTJEU 4355
127	3	EGYPTBAND 4262
126	3	SAKHEE 2497
125	6	KAYF TARA 2114*
124	4	FANTASTIC LIGHT 4316
123	4	AMILYNX 4494*
122	5	FRUITS OF LOVE 3849
122	3	VOLVORETA 4262
122	3	SAMUM 4262
122	3	PETRUSHKA 4263*
122	3	HOLDING COURT 4394
122	7	PERSIAN PUNCH 4351 +
122	4	MUTAFAWEQ 4400*
121	5	WILLIAMS NEWS 4400
121	3	HIGHTORI 4262
121	4	DALIAPOUR 4400
121	3	LOVE DIVINE 4355
120	5	ENZELI 4264
120	5	FAR CRY 3106
120	5	CRAIGSTEEL 4316
120	3	BEAT HOLLOW 2225*
120	4	GOLDEN SNAKE 4493*
120	6	SAN SEBASTIAN 4494
119	5	BORDER ARROW 4355
119	6	ARCTIC OWL 4055*
119	3	MILLENARY 3898*
118	6	CAITANO 1321
118	4	COMPTON ACE 2114
118	3	GLYNDEBOURNE 2409
118	4	ROYAL REBEL 4494
118	4	MUTAMAM 4109*
118	5	CHURLISH CHARM 4351
118	6	TAJOUN 4494
117	5	BLUEPRINT 2149
117	4	FIRST MAGNITUDE 1902
117	5	SAGAMIX 2406
117	4	CATELLA 4147
117	5	RUSSIAN HOPE 4262
117	3	AIR MARSHALL 3898
117	3	WELLBEING 4469*
117	3	CRIMSON QUEST 4394*
116	5	HIGH RISE 767
116	4	ELA ATHENA 4316
116	3	KATHMANDU 3929
116	3	KALYPSO KATIE 2739
116	4	RAMRUMA 4130
116	4	DARING MISS 4262
116	4	BEAT ALL 4109
116	8	ORCHESTRA STALL 4494
116	3	SOBIESKI 4238
116	3	LORD FLASHEART 1752
116	4	ISLAND HOUSE 4469
116	8	YAVANAS PACE 4147
115	3	QUEZON CITY GER 2911
115	5	RAINBOW HIGH 4351
115	5	MONT ROCHER 4050
115	3	CHIMES AT MIDNIGHT 4057
115	7	LE TINTORET 4264
115	4	LITTLE ROCK 4055
115	3	EPITRE 4239*
115	5	CAPRI 3479

Superform's Best Horses Of 2000

2 Year Olds

122 2 MINARDI 4181+	107 2 AUTUMNAL 4356	103 2 SLIGO BAY 4556
119 2 TOBOUGG 4354*	107 2 CHOC ICE 4260	103 2 DARWIN 4463
119 2 BAD AS I WANNA BE 4181	106 2 ATMOSPHERIC 4298*	103 2 WOODEN DOLL 4054
119 2 NAYEF 4296*	106 2 OZONE LAYER 3066	103 2 VICIOUS KNIGHT 3882
118 2 BECKETT 4058*	106 2 GHAYTH 4181	103 2 IMPERIAL DANCER 4455
118 2 OKAWANGO 4320*	106 2 KHULAN 4159	103 2 SILVER JORDEN 3722
117 2 SUPERSTAR LEO 4261	106 2 GREEN MINSTREL 4260	103 2 WORTHILY 4543*
116 2 DILSHAAN 4463*	106 2 KATHERINE SEYMOUR 4356	102 2 CANDICE 3876
115 2 KINGS COUNTY 4492	106 2 JUNIPER 3566	102 2 WINTER SOLSTICE 4556
115 2 NOVERRE 4354	106 2 FROMSONG 4454	102 2 BARKING MAD 4219
114 2 ENDLESS SUMMER 4181-	106 2 CELTIC SILENCE 2091*	102 2 OVERSPECT 4072
114 2 REGAL ROSE 4159*	106 2 SOPRAN GLAUMIX 4492	102 2 LINEA DOMBRA 4401
114 2 ENTHUSED 4159	105 2 POTARO 4455	102 2 SIGN OF NIKE 4488*
114 2 TEMPEST 4354	105 2 FREEFOURRACING 3659+	102 2 CRAZY LARRYS 3361*
113 2 AMONITA 4260*	105 2 ATTACHE 4492	102 2 SOFTLY TREAD 3067*
113 2 VACAMONTE 4354	105 2 EMINENCE 4158	102 2 BRAVADO 2850
113 2 HONOURS LIST 4320	105 2 BAARIDD 4181	102 2 MERSEY SOUND 3983
113 2 MOZART 4354	105 2 PEACEFUL PARADISE 3722	102 2 MARINE 4375
113 2 HEMINGWAY 3537*	105 2 MEDIA MOGUL 3566	102 2 WHEN IN ROME 4127
112 2 COUNT DUBOIS 4492*	105 2 ZILCH 4575*	102 2 FLIGHT OF FANCY 3748*
112 2 TURNBERRY ISLE 4397*	105 2 DIM SUMS 4219+	102 2 DERIVATIVE 3719
112 2 RED CARPET 4181	105 2 CHIANTI 4354	102 2 ECOLOGY 3882
112 2 ATLANTIS PRINCE 4127*	105 2 PANIS 4237*	102 2 CAUVERY 4463
111 2 TAMBURLAINE 4463	105 2 RELISH THE THOUGHT 4467+	102 2 LONGUEVILLE LEGEND 3372
111 2 FREUD 4463	105 2 PERFECT PLUM 4401*	102 2 MODIGLIANI 3844
111 2 CRYSTAL MUSIC 4110*	105 2 KINGS IRONBRIDGE 4354	102 2 SHEPPARDS WATCH 3482
111 2 RUMPOLD 3000*	105 2 TEMPTING FATE 4356	101 2 LIPICA 4467
111 2 EQUERRY USA 3926*	104 2 RESONATE 3067	101 2 LONDONER 3882
111 2 IRON MASK 4261	104 2 STORMING HOME 4196	101 2 GHAZAL 4209*
110 2 BONNARD 4463	104 2 HOTELGENIE DOT COM 4110	101 2 BLUE STELLER 4556
110 2 CLEARING 4455*	104 2 PERIGEE MOON 4557*	101 2 BRING PLENTY 4260
110 2 SPETTRO 4492	104 2 FAIR QUESTION 3983	101 2 DISTINCTLY DANCER 2485
110 2 SEQUOYAH 4159	104 2 BERLIN 4058	101 2 BERMUDA GRASS 4237
110 2 SAGACITY 4556*	104 2 ROMANTIC MYTH 4454	101 2 PIRATE OF PENZANCE 3372
110 2 HURRICANE FLOYD 3996	104 2 KING CHARLEMAGNE 4196*	101 2 CAFETERIA BAY 4455
110 2 MIZZEN MAST 3926	104 2 PRIZEMAN 4455	101 2 REEL BUDDY 4454
109 2 ASCENSION 4401	104 2 THE TRADER 4454	101 2 TUDOR REEF 4572*
109 2 LADY LAHAR 4401	104 2 PATSYS DOUBLE 4196	101 2 AFFIANCED 3845
109 2 BOUNCING BOWDLER 3996*	104 2 LA VIDA LOCA 4260	101 2 SHADOWLESS 3983
109 2 IMAGINE 4356	104 2 RASOUM 4468+	101 2 SANTOLINA 4159
109 2 TOROCA 4159	104 2 PALACE AFFAIR 4454	101 2 TORTUGUERO 4158
109 2 MISTY EYED 3996	104 2 PRETTY GIRL 4158	101 2 LEOPARD SPOT 4556
109 2 CD EUROPE 4463	104 2 ROLLY POLLY 3550	101 2 EURIBOR 3210
109 2 DANEHURST 4454*	104 2 BORN SOMETHING 4260	101 2 HEJAZIAH 2486*
108 2 MARCH KING 4058	104 2 CEEPIO 4462	101 2 FORWOOD 4196
108 2 CERTAIN JUSTICE 1290*	103 2 PAN JAMMER 3996	100 2 GREENGROOM 4320
108 2 DORA CARRINGTON 3372	103 2 PICCOLO PLAYER 4462	100 2 LADY OF KILDARE 3844*
108 2 REDUIT 4556	103 2 FRENCHMANS BAY 4455	100 2 DR BRENDLER 4557
108 2 PYRUS 3550	103 2 SENIOR MINISTER 3567	100 2 SURE MARK 2408
108 2 MALA MALA 4159	103 2 CRYSTAL CASTLE 3210*	100 2 PROCEED WITH CARE 4286
108 2 SUMMER SYMPHONY 4110	103 2 VINNIE ROE 4397	100 2 GIVE BACK CALAIS 3980
108 2 NO EXCUSE NEEDED 4127	103 2 ENRICH 4240	100 2 GOGGLES 3862*
108 2 POMFRET LAD 4181	103 2 INNIT 4318*	100 2 ZAZA TOP 4318
108 2 SAYEDAH 4356*	103 2 GRANDERA 4463	100 2 STRANGE DESTINY 3482*
108 2 SHAARD 4462*	103 2 BLACK MINNALOUSHE 4060*	100 2 MAMMAS TONIGHT 4449
107 2 HILL COUNTRY 4296	103 2 BLUSHING BRIDE 4546	100 2 LILIUM 4356
107 2 BANNISTER 4181	103 2 KEATS 4315	100 2 LUNASALT 3716*
107 2 GALILEO 4554*	103 2 DAYGLOW DANCER 4572	100 2 CONEY KITTY 4315*
107 2 DOWN TO THE WOODS 4462	103 2 SILKY DAWN 4356	100 2 WEST ORDER 4344*
107 2 BRAM STOKER 4181	103 2 TRIPLE BLUE 4455	100 2 SEASONS GREETINGS 4051*
107 2 KARASTA 4260	103 2 AMEERAT 4356	100 2 RED MILLENNIUM 4454
107 2 BLUE GODDESS 3720*	103 2 LUNAR CRYSTAL 4543	100 2 INSPECTOR GENERAL 4345

Index To Race Meetings By Race Number

ASCOT 1107, 2064, 2087, 2112, 2148, 2167, 2674, 2952, 2995, 3014, 3301, 3338, 4109, 4124, 4296,

AYR 1628, 1653, 2136, 2161, 2717, 2873, 3137, 3363, 3957, 3987, 4008, 4303, 4322,

BATH 1088, 1435, 1666, 1993, 2327, 2550, 2784, 2939, 3204, 3513, 3620, 3815, 4137, 4429,

BEVERLEY 973, 1274, 1443, 1758, 1918, 2218, 2479, 2513, 2730, 2879, 3050, 3393, 3406, 3651, 3670, 3949, 4041,

BRIGHTON 891, 1124, 1208, 1330, 1462, 1507, 1647, 1930, 2039, 2423, 2723, 2891, 2903, 3239, 3258, 3525, 3557, 3732, 4116, 4170, 4415, 4537,

CAPANNELLE 11, 1117, 1321, 1618, 4396,

CARLISLE 1252, 1719, 2014, 2239, 2277, 2821, 3079, 3192, 3570,

CATTERICK 777, 1659, 1678, 1813, 2417, 2435, 2741, 2926, 3198, 3437, 4001, 4252,

CHANTILLY 1231, 1619, 1747, 1752, 1900, 2398, 2401, 2485, 2913, 3065, 3843, 3934, 4051, 4144,

CHEPSTOW 1552, 1794, 1968, 2447, 2488, 2656, 2971, 3251, 3678, 3866,

CHESTER 1214, 1220, 1245, 1776, 2245, 2662, 2668, 3168, 3425, 3507, 4068,

CURRAGH 770, 862, 1120, 1621, 1624, 1899, 2400, 2404, 2407, 2738, 3067, 3554, 3719, 3844, 4055, 4057, 4240, 4397,

DEAUVILLE 2572, 2574, 2736, 3069, 3210, 3211, 3212, 3369, 3544, 3374, 3545, 3546, 3550, 3716, 3722, 4401, 4488

DONCASTER 699, 712, 730, 1048, 1067, 1513, 1838, 2315, 2348, 2575, 2607, 2753, 3156, 3859, 3874, 3888, 3895, 4445, 4460, 4566, 4574,

EPSOM 1028, 1825, 1845, 2429, 2626, 2790, 3400, 3412, 3684, 3760, 3852,

FOLKESTONE 958, 2290, 2619, 3038, 3443, 3582,

GOODWOOD 1449, 1468, 1481, 1634, 1807, 1956, 2124, 2303, 2354, 3058, 3085, 3104, 3130, 3149, 3644, 3657, 3881, 3902, 4061, 4075,

HAMILTON 843, 1189, 1239, 1358, 1905, 1936, 2093, 2233, 2392, 2638, 2778, 2796, 3375, 3531, 3801, 3822,

HAYDOCK 808, 986, 1163, 1488, 1533, 1788, 1819, 1832, 2441, 2453, 2500, 2699, 3264, 3283, 3320, 3475, 3766, 3782, 4089, 4103,

KEMPTON 724, 993, 1012, 1075, 1526, 1924, 2081, 2258, 2581, 2747, 2867, 3073, 3357, 3789, 3795, 4034,

LEICESTER 789, 828, 1545, 1571, 1731, 2026, 2506, 2772, 2914, 3092, 3214, 3332, 3836, 4027, 4309,

LEOPARDSTOWN 14, 947, 1314, 1620, 1756, 2070, 2399, 2570, 2909, 3371, 3923, 4554, 4557,

LINGFIELD 1, 22, 52, 90, 100, 108, 147, 155, 163, 203, 219, 234, 240, 262, 285, 312, 332, 353, 371, 398, 419, 438, 457, 483, 503, 523, 543, 570, 591, 615, 628, 649, 690, 771, 835, 878, 1259, 1281, 1394, 1540, 1672, 1739, 1911, 2181, 2212, 2321, 2587, 2650, 2759, 3277, 3488, 3576, 3754, 3828, 4095, 4186, 4267, 4328, 4482,

LONGCHAMP 864, 1025, 1034, 1114, 1317, 1379, 1456, 1617, 2072, 2224, 3847, 3851, 3926, 4053, 4236, 4259, 4320, 4394, 4489, 4494,   **MAISONS-LAFFITTE** 9, 94, 99, 98, 122, 820, 945, 1897, 2737, 3066, 4049,

MUSSELBURGH 795, 898, 1143, 1429, 1684, 2045, 2200, 2373, 2532, 3098, 3589, 3740, 4131, 4516, 4559,

NEWBURY 911, 1371, 1400, 1589, 1782, 1942, 2705, 2808, 2847, 3174, 3449, 3481, 3980, 3994, 4453, 4467,

NEWCASTLE 755, 1006, 1475, 1764, 2271, 2309, 2333, 2520, 2983, 3032, 3245, 3601, 3703, 4402, 4422,

NEWMARKET 950, 966, 979, 1150, 1168, 1182, 1690, 1852, 2130, 2284, 2341, 2563, 2594, 2613, 2802, 2854, 2958, 3020, 3117, 3162, 3295, 3313, 3456, 3607, 3626, 4015, 4157, 4178, 4194, 4209, 4336, 4343, 4351, 4530, 4541,

NOTTINGHAM 783 1019 1081, 1266, 1364, 1407, 1641, 1870, 2007, 2187, 2680, 3002, 3111, 3519, 3972, 4408, 4503,

PONTEFRACT 871, 938, 1101, 1495, 1698, 1864, 2174, 2360, 2556, 2828, 3220, 3500, 4082, 4229, 4372,

REDCAR 1130, 1294, 1558, 1577, 1890, 2142, 2154, 2861, 2989, 3307, 3326, 3632, 4216, 4496,

RIPON 821, 1595, 1858, 2099, 2105, 2538, 2834, 3008, 3180, 3462, 3697, 3710,

SAINT CLOUD 10, 140, 665, 861, 944, 1123, 1313, 1378, 1461, 2406, 4314, 4491, 4556,

SALISBURY 1175, 1343, 1882, 2020, 2227, 2264, 2467, 2686, 2977, 3289, 3387, 3418, 3747, 4163,

SAN SIRO 1227, 1459, 2073, 2486, 4145, 4242, 4318, 4492,

SANDOWN 761, 1041, 1055, 1564, 1584, 1962, 1986, 2473, 2494, 2526, 2920, 2933, 3227, 3431, 3468, 3942, 4202,

SOUTHWELL 30, 44, 68, 83, 124, 176, 195, 211, 246, 278, 297, 324, 338, 365, 384, 412, 425, 451, 470, 496, 510, 535, 555, 584, 598, 641, 667, 682, 692, 737, 801, 855, 865, 1202, 1301, 1415, 1501, 1601, 1801, 1974, 2118, 2297, 2379, 2632, 2815, 2945, 4149, 4364,

THIRSK 904, 924, 1157, 1351, 1381, 1713, 2057, 2964, 3123, 3143, 3344, 3614, 3775,

WARWICK 812, 884, 1000, 1059, 1520, 1706, 2033, 2251, 2459, 2840, 3691, 3909,

WINDSOR 743, 849, 932, 1095, 1196, 1288, 1423, 1725, 1876, 2051, 2206, 2367, 2544, 2711, 2885, 3044, 3186, 3350, 3638, 4288, 4524,

WOLVERHAMPTON 38, 60, 76, 116, 132, 141, 170, 187, 226, 254, 270, 291, 305, 318, 346, 359, 378, 391, 404, 431, 445, 464, 477, 489, 516, 529, 549, 562, 576, 607, 622, 635, 658, 675, 706, 718, 749, 918, 1035, 1136, 1233, 1388, 2075, 2601, 3271, 3494, 3769, 4021, 4223, 4244, 4358, 4379, 4437, 4548,

YARMOUTH 1609, 1770, 1949, 2194, 2386, 2411, 2765, 2897, 3026, 3233, 3381, 3664, 3917, 3935, 3964, 4387, 4475, 4510,

YORK 1307, 1324, 1337, 1980, 2000, 2644, 2692, 3537, 3563, 3595, 3725, 3807, 4275, 4281, 4297,

ALSO

Arlington 2912, 3549	Baden-Baden 1746,3849	Belmont 1616,3932, 4316	Bordeaux 2487,4490
Cagnes 606	Churchill Downs 1226	Clairefontaine 3718	Cologne 1322, 4146
Cork 1232,1898,4266, 4315	Dielsdorf 1119, 3553, 4148	Dortmund 4265	Dusseldorf 1229, 2910
Fairyhouse 3548	Frauenfeld 1903	Galway 3072	Gowran 818,1896
Gulfstream 16	Hamburg 2403	Hannover 3930	Hoppegarten 2573
Jagersro 1323	Klampenborg 3213	Kranji 656, 1230	Lucerne 3850
Mulheim 13	Munich 3071, 4317	Naas 1750	
Nad Al Sheba 655, 666,764	Sha Tin 184	Suffolk Downs 1749	Taby 3931
Tokyo 123, 1755	Woodbine 3933, 4399		

LINGFIELD (Equitrack) MONDAY NOVEMBER 8TH Lefthand, V Sharp Track

Official Going STANDARD. Stalls: 1m - Outside, Rem - Inside.

1 **12.20 CLASS STKS DIV I 3YO+ 0-60 (F) 1m2f aw Going 18 -21 Slow**
£1798 £503 £244 3 yo rec 4 lb

4443} **IMPREVUE 19** [1] R J O'Sullivan 5-9-2 (bl) S Sanders 5/4 FAV: 211311: 5 ch m Priolo - Las Bela (Welsh Pageant) Al handy, rdn 3f out, led ins last, styd on well, rdn out: well bckd: earlier in '99 won here at Lingfield (h'cap, rtd 55a), Brighton (amat riders h'cap) & Nottingham (class stks, rtd 64): back in '97 won at The Curragh (mdn): eff at 10f, stays 12f on firm, hvy, equitrack & any trk: eff with/without blnks: in great heart. **60a**
4328} **TIGHTROPE 27** [6] N P Littmoden 4-9-3 M Fenton 14/1: 0-1022: 4 b g Alzao - Circus Act (Shirley Heights) Dwelt, sn rdn into mid-div, kept on well for press from 2f out, not pace of wnr: op 12/1: earlier in '99 with Sir Mark Prescott, won at Yarmouth (seller, gamble, rtd 56): disapp fav all 3 '98 starts (h'caps, rtd 56): '97 Leicester wnr (h'cap, rtd 83 & 62a): eff at 1m/10f on fast, gd/soft & both AW's: runs well fresh. ¾ **59a**
4504} **KAFIL 14** [5] J J Bridger 5-9-1 P Doe (3) 16/1: 002253: 5 b g Housebuster - Alchaasibiyeh (Seattle Slew) Led, rdn 2f out, hdd ins last & no extra: rnr-up sev times earlier in '99 (rtd 59a, stks, rtd 40 at best on turf, h'cap): '98 Lingfield wnr (class stks, rtd 64a, also rtd 38 on turf): '97 Lingfield wnr again (mdn, rtd 65a): eff at 7f/10f: handles fast & gd/soft, enjoys equitrack/Lingfield: will enjoy a return to 1m. 1¾ **55a**
3908} **HENRIETTA HOLMES 55** [8] Mrs L Richards 3-8-10 O Urbina 11/2: 032214: Rear & rdn halfway, prog over 2f out, no extra fnl 1f: tchd 7/1, 8 wk abs: AW bow today, prev with J R Fanshawe. ½ **53a**
4258} **MASTER LODGE 34** [7] 4-9-1 (t) G Carter 20/1: 5505: Cl-up 9f, fdd: AW bow. 1 **53a**
4503} **HAYDN JAMES 14** [4] 5-9-1 (vis) A Culhane 3/1: 302326: Rdn/towards rear, mod gains: op 7/2. 1½ **51a**
3146} **APPYABO 96** [12] 4-9-1 R Brisland (5) 66/1: 640067: Trkd ldrs 7f: 3 month absence. 3 **47a**
4403} **MARKELLIS 21** [9] 3-8-11 R Fitzpatrick (3) 50/1: 056068: Prom 7f. nk **46a**
4307} **MARTHA REILLY 28** [11] 3-8-8 A Mackay 50/1: 000409: Sn rdn/rear, nvr factor. 1½ **41a**
3914} **AIX EN PROVENCE 54** [10] 4-9-1 A Nicholls (3) 14/1: 010500: Dwelt/rear, nvr on terms: 10th: 8 wk abs. 3 **40a**
1835} **Moss Rose 99** [3] 3-8-8 M Hills 16/1: 4455} **Yalail 18** [2] 3-8-11 G Faulkner (3) 12/1:
12 ran Time 2m 06.71 (3.91) (Mrs Barbara Marchant) R J O'Sullivan Epsom, Surrey.

2 **12.50 2000 NURSERY HCAP DIV I 2YO 0-75 (E) 6f aw rnd Going 18 -25 Slow** **[78]**
£2290 £641 £311

4490} **WELCOME SHADE 16** [2] R Hannon 2-8-13 (63) R Hughes 7/1: 0001: 2 gr g Green Desert - Grey Angel (Kenmare) Led after 1f, pressed fnl 2f, styd on well ins last, drvn out to hold on: tchd 15/2, h'cap/AW bow: rtd 69 at best from 3 mdn starts earlier in '99: dam a decent miler in S Africa: eff at 6f, tried 7f, may yet suit: acts on a sharp trk: improved for forcing tactics on equitrack. **70a**
4404} **ILLUSIVE 21** [7] H J Collingridge 2-9-1 (65)(bl) R Cochrane 9/4 FAV: 005102: 2 b g Night Shift - Mirage (Red Sunset) Chsd ldrs, smooth prog to chall from 2f out, ev ch ins last, rdn/just held nr line: well bckd: prev with W Jarvis, earlier in '99 won here at Lingfield (C/D, h'cap, first time blnks, rtd 69a, rtd 49 at best on turf): eff at 6f, 7f+ may suit in time: handles gd/soft, enjoys equitrack/Lingfield: cld win similar. hd **71a**
4432} **TATTENHAM STAR 20** [8] M J Haynes 2-9-4 (68) S Drowne 8/1: 00563: 2 b c Mistertopogigo - Candane (Danehill) Chsd ldrs, rdn & kept on fnl 2f, not pace of front pair: op 6/1: AW/h'cap bow: rtd 72 on turf earlier in '99 (auct mdn): eff at 6f, return to 7f+ will suit: handles equitrack & gd: likely type for similar over further. 3 **67a**
4425} **SEMIRAMIS 20** [1] Sir Mark Prescott 2-8-13 (63) S Sanders 6/1: 46004: Cl-up 4f: AW bow. 1½ **59a**
4360} **SWYNFORD ELEGANCE 25** [4] 2-7-13 (49) A Mackay 20/1: 0605: Rear/wide, mod prog: hcap/AW bow. 2 **40a**
4279} **CEDAR GUVNOR 31** [6] 2-8-7 (57) S Whitworth 9/2: 360066: Led 1f, btn 2f out: op 3/1. 2 **43a**
4440} **BEDOUIN QUEEN 19** [5] 2-9-7 (71) A Nicholls (3) 7/1: 0037: Rear, nvr factor: op 5/1, AW/h'cap bow. hd **56a**
4430} **SAFARASIKNOW 20** [3] 2-8-10 (60) D Sweeney 15/2: 00008: Cl-up 2f, btn/eased fnl 1f: op 5/1, AW bow. shd **45a**
8 ran Time 1m 12.98 (2.58) (The Queen) R Hannon East Everleigh, Wilts.

3 **1.20 CLASS STKS DIV II 3YO 0-60 (F) 1m2f aw Going 18 -09 Slow**
£1798 £503 £244 3 yo rec 4 lb

1605} **BAAJIL 99** [7] D J S Cosgrove 4-9-1 N Callan (3) 12/1: 224001: 4 b g Murju - Arctic River (Arctic Tern) Cl-up, al trav well, led over 2f out, clr over 1f out, styd on strongly, pushed out cl-home: op 10/1, abs, first win: rnr-up twice over C/D earlier in '99 (mdn, rtd 63a, rtd 24 on turf, h'cap): rtd 68 at best in '98 (plcd, mdn): rtd 88 sole '97 start (mdn, L Cumani): suited by 10f on fast, enjoys equitrack/Lingfield: runs well fresh. **61a**
4276} **FEEL NO FEAR 31** [9] B J Meehan 6-9-2 J Weaver 7/2 CO FAV: 210012: 6 b m Fearless Action - Charm Bird (Daring March) Held up, prog from halfway, chall 2f out, sn outpcd by wnr: op 2/1: earlier scored twice here at Lingfield (sell h'cap & seller, rtd 55a, rnr-up on turf, rtd 54, clmr): rtd 59 for R Simpson in '98: stays 11f, suited by 1m: acts on fast, loves equitrack/Lingfield: best without blnks: apprec 1m back in a seller. 4 **55a**
4502} **TAPAGE 14** [5] Andrew Reid 3-8-11 S Sanders 14/1: 000003: 3 b g Great Commotion - Irena (Bold Lad) Led, rdn/hdd over 2f out, no impress after: op 20/1: rnr-up twice earlier in '99 (rtd 69, clmr, W R Muir, also rtd 48a): '98 wnr here at Lingfield (med auct mdn, Delcan Gillespie, rtd 78a): eff at 7f/1m: acts on firm, fast, equitrack: handles a sharp/gall trk: tried blnks, best without: eff forcing the pace: apprec a return to 1m. 4 **48a**
4402} **FOREST ROBIN 21** [4] Mrs L Stubbs 6-9-1 Kristin Stubbs (7) 7/1: 440064: Chsd ldrs, btn 2f out: op 5/1: rnr-up twice earlier in '99 (rtd 53 & 51, h'caps): '98 h'cap wnr at Redcar (2) & Newmarket (rtd 61, Mrs J R Ramsden, also rtd 43a): plcd in '97 (rtd 64): eff at 6f/1m, stays 10f: acts on firm, gd, both AW's, prob handles gd/soft: handles any trk, likes Redcar: has run well fresh: runs well for a lady rider: a return to h'caps/1m shld suit. 2 **45a**
4579} **COLONEL CUSTER 7** [10] 4-9-1 G Bardwell 7/2 CO FAV: 015605: Rear, eff 3f out, mod gains: tchd 9/2. ½ **44a**
4499} **ROGER ROSS 14** [6] 4-9-1 D Sweeney 12/1: 000006: Rdn towards rear early, no impress: tchd 14/1. 6 **35a**
4443} **WILMORE 19** [1] 3-8-11 M Tebbutt 7/2 CO FAV: 363607: Cl-up, ch 3f out/wknd: op 9/4, AW bow. ½ **34a**
4548} **SKY CITY 10** [3] 3-8-8 A McCarthy (3) 12/1: 260008: Chsd ldrs 7f: tchd 14/1. ¾ **30a**
4553} **SASEEDO 10** [2] 9-9-1 S Carson (5) 12/1: 060069: Slowly away, al rear: tchd 14/1. 6 **24a**
4502} **SWAN LAKE FR 14** [8] 3-8-8 P Doe (3) 25/1: 605600: Struggling halfway: 10th. 11 **5a**
4463} **MAYLAN 18** [11] 4-8-12 R Havlin 33/1: /00000: Al rear: 11th. 1½ **3a**
11 ran Time 2m 05.52 (2.72) (Crown Pkg & Mailing Services Ltd) D J S Cosgrove Newmarket.

4 1.50 2000 NURSERY HCAP DIV II 2YO 0-75 (E)   6f aw rnd   Going 18 -29 Slow   [77]
£2278 £638 £310

4149} **QUEEN OF THE MAY 40** [8] M R Channon 2-9-7 (70) Paul Cleary (7) 6/1: 440441: 2 b f Nicolotte - 77a
Varnish (Final Straw) Prom, led over 2f out, styd on strongly ins last, pushed out cl-home: op 4/1: AW bow:
earlier in '99 made a winning debut at Brighton (fill med auct mdn, rtd 79): eff at 5f, suited by 6f on firm,
gd & equitrack: has run well fresh & likes a sharp/undul trk: likes to race with/force the pace.
4167} **KIRSCH 39** [2] C A Dwyer 2-9-1 (64) L Newman (7) 9/4 FAV: 561402: 2 ch f Wolfhound - Pondicherry 1¼ 66a
(Sir Wimborne) Trkd ldrs, rdn/chsd wnr ins last, kept on tho' al held: nicely bckd: earlier in '99 scored at
Lingfield (clmr, rtd 68, plcd on fibresand, nov auct, rtd 70a): eff at 5f, suited by 6f, may stay further: acts on
firm, gd, both AW's: handles any trk, likes a sharp/undul one: shld win again this winter.
4517} **WHERES CHARLOTTE 13** [4] R Hannon 2-8-0 (49) P Fitzsimons (4) 7/1: 020003: 2 b f Sure Blade - 1 49a
One Degree (Crooner) Cl-up, led after 2f till over 2f out, no extra ins last: tchd 10/1: rnr-up earlier in '99
(4 rnr nov med auct, rtd 70, prob flattered): eff at 6f, tried 7f: handles equitrack & prob soft grnd.
4589} **GREY FLYER 5** [6] Mrs L Stubbs 2-8-12 (61) P McCabe 10/1: -61064: Keen/chsd ldrs, held 1f out: op 8/1. 3 54a
4409} **DAKISI ROYALE 21** [5] 2-8-0 (49)(vis) Dale Gibson 12/1: 300065: Prom 4f, fdd: AW bow. 3 35a
4279} **PYJAMA GIRL 31** [7] 2-9-2 (65) R Perham 10/1: 604506: Held up, rdn/btn 2f out: op 7/1. 1½ 47a
4508} **ZOENA 13** [3] 2-9-0 (63) A Nicholls (3) 13/2: 403047: Led 2f, btn 2f out: op 5/1, AW bow. ½ 43a
4517} **RIDGECREST 13** [1] 2-8-10 (59) P Doe (3) 7/2: 0038: Dwelt/rear, btn 2f out: op 3/1, hcap/AW bow. 2 34a
8 ran   Time 1m 13.21 (2.81)   (Miss Maggie Worsdell & Mrs Carolyn Wood)   M R Channon Upper Lambourn, Berks.

5 2.20 TAUBER MDN 2YO (D)   6f aw rnd   Going 18 -21 Slow
£3501 £1060 £517 £246

4390} **BHUTAN PRINCE 23** [1] J Noseda 2-9-0 J Weaver 13/8: 253221: 2 b c Robellino - Seal Indigo (Glenstal) 85a
Made all, rdn/pressed fnl 1f, styd on well & pushed out cl-home: hvly bckd, tchd 2/1: fin rnr-up on 5 occasions
earlier in '98 (rtd 84 at best, mdn): eff forcing pace at 6f, stays a stiff 1m well: acts on equitrack, firm & soft
grnd: handles a sharp or stiff/undul trk: tough & consistent, deserved this.
4310} **LICENCE TO THRILL 28** [2] D W P Arbuthnot 2-8-9 R Price 25/1: 02: 2 ch f Wolfhound - Crime Of ¾ 77a
Passion (Dragonara Palace) Keen/trkd ldrs, chsd wnr 2f out, ev ch ins last, held nr fin: op 14/1, AW bow: rtd
38 when well btn on sole turf start in '98 (mdn): half-sister to sev wnrs, dam a Gr 2 winning juv: eff at 6f,
7f+ may suit in time: acts on equitrack: left debut bhd, clr of rem here & could find compensation in similar.
4500} **BRANSTON FIZZ 14** [5] M Johnston 2-8-9 M Hills 8/11 FAV: 223: 2 b f Efisio - Tuxford Hideaway 4 67a
(Cawston's Clown) Rear, rdn after 2f out, kept on fnl 2f, nvr a threat to front pair: hvly bckd: AW bow: rnr-up on
both turf starts earlier in '99 (rtd 85, mdn): half-sister to sev wnrs, incl tough 6/7f performer Branston Abbey:
eff at 6f, further cld suit: acts on gd & soft, below best on equitrack here: handles a sharp or stiff/undul trk.
4250} **KATIES VALENTINE 34** [3] R A Fahey 2-8-9 P Hanagan (7) 20/1: 04: Dwelt/rdn rear, mod gains: AW bow. 5 55a
4507} **BETTINA BLUE 14** [4] 2-8-9 A Clark 14/1: 5065: Keen, struggling after 2f: op 10/1, AW bow. ½ 53a
4549} **AZIRA 10** [6] 2-8-9 S Whitworth 25/1: 56: Cl-up 4f, wknd qckly/eased fnl 1f: AW bow. 2½ 46a
6 ran   Time 1m 12.76 (2.36)   (Lucayan)   J Noseda Newmarket.

6 2.50 GPA RI-DRY HCAP 3YO+ 0-70 (E)   2m aw   Going 18 +04 Fast   [69]
£2854 £802 £392   3 yo rec 9 lb

4590} **VIRGIN SOLDIER 5** [8] M Johnston 3-8-5 (55)(6ex) R Ffrench 1/1 FAV: 002111: 3 ch g Waajib - Never 62a
Been Chaste (Posse) Cl-up, went on halfway, rdn/in command over 1f out, styd on strongly, pushed out cl-home:
gd time: hvly bckd, tchd 6/4: earlier in '99 won h'caps here at Lingfield & Musselburgh (rtd 52a & 58), prev
with T Etherington (tried blnks): plcd in '98 (mdn, rtd 62): eff at 12f/2m: acts on gd, gd/soft & equitrack:
handles a sharp or galt trk, likes Lingfield: looks well h'capped for new connections, can win again.
4503} **ANOTHER MONK 14** [12] B R Johnson 8-8-7 (48) A Clark 11/2: /20332: 8 b g Supreme Leader - Royal 1½ 52a
Demon (Tarboosh) Keen/trkd ldrs, rdn/chall 2f out, kept on onepace: nicely bckd: plcd 3 of 4 starts earlier in
'99 (rtd 51a & 44, h'caps): missed '98: '97 wnr at Lingfield (2, h'cap & amat h'cap, rtd 52a, R Ingram):
eff at 12f/2m: acts on both AW's, likes sharp trk, esp Lingfield: runs v well fresh.
4484} **LEGAL LUNCH 16** [1] P W Harris 4-9-13 (68) A Culhane 11/2: 006523: 4 b g Alleged - Dinner 1¼ 71a
Surprise (Lyphard) Towards rear, prog halfway & chsd front pair fnl 3f, kept on tho' al held: clr rem: AW bow:
acts on firm & soft grnd, equitrack: eff with/without a visor: on a fair mark, but only one win in 24 starts.
4442} **LEGGY LADY 19** [4] J A R Toller 3-8-0 (50) A Nicholls (3) 33/1: -0604: Rear, prog halfway, sn held. 5 48a
3040} **HIGHLY PRIZED 99** [13] 5-10-0 (69) S Drowne 14/1: 504425: Cl-up 11f, eased fnl 1f: jmps fit, AW bow. 12 52a
4577} **KATIES CRACKER 7** [5] 4-7-10 (37)(7oh) R Brisland (5) 50/1: 420006: Prom 13f. 1½ 23a
4478} **MISS PIN UP 17** [1] 10-9-5 (60) R Cochrane 33/1: 422007: Csd ldrs 4f out, sn held/eased fnl 2f. 9 37a
3480} **RED RAJA 80** [9] 6-8-13 (54)(VIS) G Carter 12/1: 1U4568: Led 1m, sn btn: op 8/1, vis/jmps fit. 3½ 28a
1837} **ROBANNA 99** [14] 4-8-6 (46)(1ow) S Whitworth 20/1: 2-3409: Chsd ldrs 4f out/sn btn: 5 mth abs/AW bow. hd 21a
4407} **ALHESN 21** [7] 4-10-0 (69) J Weaver 14/1: 161250: Rear, bhd 4f out: 10th: op 12/1. ½ 42a
4502} Piaf 14 [10] 3-7-10 (46)(2oh) J Lowe 33/1:   4447} Raed 19 [2] 6-9-10 (65) A Polli (3) 20/1:
2521} Padauk 99 [3] 5-9-1 (56)(bl) S Carson (5) 25/1:
13 ran   Time 3m 22.25 (2.25)   (J David Abell)   M Johnston Middleham, N.Yorks.

7 3.20 ARENA LEISURE HCAP 3YO+ 0-85 (D)   1m aw rnd   Going 18 +04 Fast   [84]
£3763 £1144 £558 £265   3 yo rec 2 lb

4357} **SECRET SPRING 25** [4] Mrs L Richards 7-9-10 (80) O Urbina 13/2: 324401: 7 b g Dowsing - Nordica 84a
(Northfields) Mid-div, prog over 2f out, switched over 1f out & strong run for press ins last to lead line: gd time:
plcd twice earlier in '98 (rtd 85, 4 rnr stks, also rtd 85a, C/D h'cap): '98 Kempton wnr (h'cap, rtd 90 at best, P R
Hedger), subs unplcd over hdles: '97 Brighton wnr (ltd stks, rtd 80): eff at 1m/10f, tried 12f: acts on firm &
equitrack, handles hvy & any trk: likes a sharp/undul one, esp Lingfield: best held up for late run: can win again.
4562} **VOLONTIERS 9** [9] P W Harris 4-9-9 (79) A Culhane 14/1: 300002: 4 b g Common Grounds - Senlis nk 81a
(Sensitive Prince) Sn prom, led over 2f out, rdn/clr over 1f out, hdd line: tchd 20/1: AW bow: rtd 93 at best
earlier in '99 (tumbled down h'cap): '98 wnr at Haydock (mdn) & Epsom (List, rtd 101): '97 nnr-up (rtd 85): eff
at 7f, stays a sharp/undul 1m well: acts on fast, gd/soft, equitrack: loves to dominate: can find compensation.
4501} **KAYO 14** [6] M Johnston 4-9-10 (80) M Hills 9/4 FAV: 511103: 4 b g Superpower - Shiny Kay (Star nk 81a

12

LINGFIELD (Equitrack)   MONDAY NOVEMBER 8TH   Lefthand, V Sharp Track

Appeal) Rdn mid-div, kept on fnl 2f for press, not pace wnr nr fin: hvly bckd, tchd 11/4: earlier in '99 completed a quick fire h'cap hat-trick at Redcar, Newmarket & Newcastle (rtd 95, current trainer), earlier with T J Etherington (tried blnks): '98 wnr at Southwell (2, rtd 81a), Newbury & Warwick (h'caps, rtd 95): eff at 6/7f, stays a sharp 1m well: acts on fast, hvy, both AW's, any trk: eff weight carrier: has run well fresh: well h'capped on sand.

1919} BE MY WISH 99 [3] W A O'Gorman 4-9-0 (70) R Cochrane 8/1: 004004: Rear, rdn/bhd halfway, styd on strongly from 2f out, nrst fin: op 14/1, 5 month abs: prev with S P C Woods.	1½	68a
4206} TEMERAIRE 37 [10] 4-9-13 (83) M Fenton 5/1: 052105: Keen/cl-up, held fnl 1f: nicely bckd.	1¼	79a
3927} DILKUSHA 54 [8] 4-9-7 (77) J Weaver 9/1: 503066: Rear, eff halfway, mod gains: 8 wk abs/AW bow.	2	69a
4553} APOLLO RED 10 [12] 10-9-12 (82) A Clark 14/1: 323027: Led 6f, sn btn: op 10/1.	¾	73a
4527} BUTRINTO 12 [5] 5-9-1 (71) R Price 33/1: 000008: Rear, nvr able to challenge.	3	56a
4297} SARI 30 [1] 3-9-4 (76) C Rutter 12/1: 040109: Dwelt/mid-div, btn 2f out: op 8/1, AW bow.	1	59a
4206} TOPTON 37 [2] 5-10-0 (84)(bl) T Williams 10/1: 030000: Chsd ldrs 6f: 10th: op 7/1, topweight.	½	66a
4342} EASTERN CHAMP 26 [11] 3-9-1 (73)(t) N Callan (3) 7/1: 142020: Prom 6f: 11th: tchd 9/1.	1½	52a
4522} RAYIK 13 [7] 4-9-2 (72) S Sanders 33/1: 000000: Al bhd: 12th.	½	50a
12 ran Time 1m 37.31 (1.11) (M K George) Mrs L Richards Funtington, W.Sussex.		

---

8   3.50 10 YEARS MDN 3YO (D)   7f aw rnd   Going 18 -15 Slow
      £2814   £852   £416   £198

4541} ROYAL ARTIST 11 [2] W J Haggas 3-9-0 M Hills 11/8 FAV: 04231: 3 b g Royal Academy - Council Rock (General Assembly) Trkd ldrs, briefly no room halfway, pushed into lead over 1f out, in command fnl 1f, readily: hvly bckd: plcd twice on turf earlier in '99 (rtd 73, Yarmouth mdn): dam styd 10f: eff at 7f, 1m shld suit: acts on fast, gd/soft & equitrack: handles a sharp: plenty in hand here, can rate more highly.		66a
4405} SING CHEONG 21 [3] G C H Chung 3-9-0 R Cochrane 12/1: 530002: 3 b c Forest Wind - Lady Counsel (Law Society) Rear, bhd halfway, prog wide from over 2f out, styd on well to take 2nd ins last, no threat wnr: op 10/1: plcd earlier in '99 (rtd 68, 7 rnr mdn, also rtd 38a): eff at 7f, has tried 9f & a return to 1m+ will suit on this evidence: acts on equitrack: eyecatching late hdwy, could find a h'cap.	2	57a
4405} CITY REACH 21 [10] P J Makin 3-9-0 D Sweeney 15/2: -00653: 3 b g Petong - Azola (Alzao) Prom, rdn from 2f out, outpcd over 1f out: tchd 9/1: rtd 75 & 46a at best earlier in '99 (mdns): rtd 77 when rnr-up on sole start in '98: eff at 7f, tried 1m, could suit in time: handles equitrack & hvy: handles a gall or sharp/undul trk.	1¼	54a
4435} GHAAZI 20 [9] Miss Gay Kelleway 3-9-0 P Fredericks (5) 40/1: 0-6004: Rdn chasing ldrs, kept on for press fnl 2f: tried 10f earlier in '99, AW bow today.	½	53a
4548} WHY WORRY NOW 10 [13] 3-8-9 (BL) R Hughes 7/2: 334065: Led 6f: clr rem: blnks/op 5/2, AW bow.	1	46a
3806} LADY BREANNE 62 [4] 3-8-9 S Sanders 7/2: -46026: Chsd ldrs, btn 3f out: op 9/2: 2 mth abs/AW bow.	6	34a
4502} BALLYMORRIS BOY 14 [6] 3-9-0 Dean McKeown 33/1: 000007: Sn rdn/towards rear, nvr factor.	shd	39a
4426} BLACK ROCKET 20 [5] 3-8-9 G Faulkner (3) 11/1: 0-0068: Mid-div, btn 3f out: op 10/1.	nk	33a
4405} PRINCESS KALI 21 [1] 3-8-9 (bl) R Fitzpatrick (3) 10/1: 060539: Prom 5f: op 8/1.	2	29a
4434} HIGHFIELDER 20 [12] 3-9-0 (vis) N Callan (3) 14/1: 060030: Chsd ldrs, btn/eased 2f out: 10th: op 10/1.	16	2a
-- Betchworth Sand [11] 0-9-0 P McCabe 25/1: 570} Dorothy Allen 99 [7] 3-8-9 A Clark 33/1:		
-- Paulines Star [8] 3-8-9 S Carson (5) 33/1:		
13 ran Time 1m 25.11 (2.31) (Tony Hirschfeld) W J Haggas Newmarket.		

MAISONS-LAFFITTE   FRIDAY NOVEMBER 5TH   Left & Righthand, Sharpish Track

Official Going   HEAVY.

9   1.10 GR 2 CRITERIUM DE M-LAFFITTE 2YO   7f   Heavy
      £37675   £15070   £7535   £3767

-- TOUCH OF THE BLUES [8] C Laffon Parias 2-8-11 D Boeuf 82/10: 125231: 2 b c Cadeaux Genereux - Silabteni (Nureyev) -:		114
-- BLU AIR FORCE [8] B Grizzeth 2-8-11 M Demuro 8/1: 121112: 2 b c Sri Pekan - Carillon Miss (The Minstrel) -:	¾	112
4290 COMPTON BOLTER 27 [1] G A Butler 2-8-11 T Jarnet 22/1: -32123: 2 b c Red Sunset - Milk And Honey (So Blessed) -:	nk	112
4016 AKEED 46 [7] P F l Cole 2-8-11 S Guillot 12/1: -144: -:	½	111
8 ran Time 1m 29.8 (Maktoum Al Maktoum) C Laffon Parias France		

SAINT-CLOUD   SATURDAY NOVEMBER 6TH   Lefthand, Galloping Track

Official Going   HEAVY.

10   2.15 GR 3 PRIX PERTH 3YO+   1m   Heavy
      £23681   £8611   £4306   3 yo rec 2 lb

4418 DANZIGAWAY 20 [1] Mme C Head 3-8-8 D Bonilla 22/10 FAV: 401141: 3 b f Danehill - Blushing Away (Blushing Groom) -:		114
4375 SOSSUS VLEI 22 [4] G Wragg 3-8-11 T Thulliez 24/1: 02-162: 3 b c Inchinor - Sassalya (Sassafras) -:	3	110
4249 MISS BERBERE 34 [5] D Smaga 4-8-10 T Gillet 29/10: 632423: 4 ch f Bering - Miss Afrique (African Song)	¾	106
8 ran Time 1m 51.8 (Wertheimer Brothers) Mme C Head France		

CAPANNELLE   SUNDAY NOVEMBER 7TH   Righthand, Flat, Galloping Track

Official Going   HEAVY.

11   2.25 GR 2 PREMIO RIBOT 3YO+   1m   Heavy
£27187   £12480   £7032   3 yo rec 2 lb

*3840 **ORIENTAL FASHION 60** [10] Saeed bin Suroor 3-8-12 L Dettori : -33211: 3 b f Marju - Wijdan 110
(Mr Prospector) -:
*1008 **ALABAMA JACKS 99** [4] R Feligioni 3-9-1 M Tellini : 1-1112: 3 ch c Magical Wonder - Oh   2¾ 108
Jemima (Captain James) -:
4324 **MIDYAN CALL 28** [3] O Pessi 5-9-2 O Fancera : 126133: 5 b h Midyan - Early Call (Kind Of Hush)   3½ 102
9 ran   Time 1m 42.7   (Godolphin)   Saeed bin Suroor Newmarket

12   2.55 GR 1 PREMIO ROMA 3YO+   1m2f   Heavy
£70259   £33557   £20914   £10457   3 yo rec 4 lb

4249 **ELLE DANZIG 35** A Schutz 4-9-0 A Starke : 124141: 4 b f Roi Danzig - Elegie (Teotepec)   115
4399 **HANDSOME RIDGE 22** [6] J H M Gosden 5-9-3 K Darley : 550002: 5 ch c Indian Ridge - Red Rose   1½ 117
Garden (Electric) -:
+4489 **SIGNORINA CATTIVA 15** [2] J L Dunlop 3-8-12 Pat Eddery : 401113: 3 b f EL Gran Senor -   5½ 110
Assez Cuite (Graustark) -:
*4238 **FAIRY QUEEN 36** [4] Saeed bin Suroor 3-8-12 L Dettori : 011414: -:   1½ 108
7 ran   Time 2m 07.0   (Gestut Wittekindshof)   A Schutz Germany

MULHEIM (GERMANY)   SUNDAY NOVEMBER 7TH   --

Official Going   VERY SOFT

13   2.50 LISTED BUCHMACHER DER RUHR 3YO+   2m1f   V Soft
£7220   £2888   £1444   3 yo rec 9 lb

4397 **SPIRIT OF LOVE 22** [6] M Johnston 4-9-0 J Fanning : -40001: 4 ch c Trempolino - Dream Mary (Marfa)   108
--   **DONOSTIA** [1] M J Grassick 3-8-1 E Ahern : 2: 3 b f Unfuwain - Alys (Blakeney)   12 93
--   **MONTINI** [4] Germany 4-9-0 P A Johnson : 3: 4 ch c Platini - Mantova (Escalvo)   6 92
7 ran   Time 3m 54.2   (A W Robinson)   M Johnston Middleham, N Yorks

LEOPARDSTOWN   SUNDAY NOVEMBER 7TH   Lefthand, Galloping Track

Official Going   Str - SOFT/HEAVY; Rnd - SOFT.

14   1.10 LISTED DAVENPORT STKS 2YO   1m1f   Soft
£16250   £4750   £2250

--   **CHIANG MAI** [5] A P O'Brien 2-8-9 J P Spencer 7/1: -11: 2 b f Sadler's Wells - Eljazzi (Artaius)   106
--   **HOMER** [7] A P O'Brien 2-8-12 P J Scallan 9/10 FAV: -312: 2 b c Sadler's Wells - Gravieres (Saint   ¾ 107
Estephe) -:
--   **QUALITY TEAM** [3] D K Weld 2-8-12 (tBL) P Shanahan 25/1: -5603: 2 b c Diesis - Ready For Action   4½ 100
(Riverman) -:
9 ran   Time 2m 05.9   (Mrs David Nagle)   A P O'Brien Ballydoyle, Co Tipperary

15   1.30 LISTED HOTEL STAKES 3YO+   7f   Soft/Heavy
£16250   £4750   £2250   £750   3 yo rec 1 lb

2044 **ONE WON ONE 99** [10] Mrs J Morgan 5-8-12 J P Murtagh 8/1: 003621: 5 b g Naevus - Havard's Bay   108
(Halpern Bay) -:
4030 **WRAY 49** [6] L Browne 7-8-12 J P Spencer 7/1: 032142: 7 ch g Sharp Victor - Faye (Monsanto)   1 106
4418 **MAJOR FORCE 21** [3] D K Weld 3-9-6 P J Smullen 4/5 FAV: -11163: 3 b c Woodman - Ready For Action   ½ 114
(Riverman) -:
10 ran   Time 1m 37.7   (Ms Joanna Morgan)   Mrs J Morgan Ireland

GULFSTREAM PARK   SATURDAY NOVEMBER 6TH   Lefthand, Sharp, Oval Track

Official Going   Turf Crse - GOOD; Dirt Crse - FAST.

16   7.20 GR 1 BREEDERS' CUP MILE 3YO+   1m rnd   Good
£313253   £120482   £72289   £33735

--   **SILIC** [12] J Canani 4-9-0 C Nakatani 72/10: -41511: 4 b c Sillery - Balletomane (Sadler's Wells)   123
--   **TUZLA** [10] B Baffert 5-8-11 D Flores 137/10: 112152: 5 b m Panoramic - Turkeina (Kautokeino)   nk 119
2992} **DOCKSIDER 99** [2] J W Hills 4-9-0 G Stevens 84/10: 121263: 4 ch c Diesis - Pump (Forli)   hd 122
4396 **LEND A HAND 21** [7] Saeed bin Suroor 4-9-0 L Dettori 134/10: -10124: -:   nse 121
2992} **JIM AND TONIC 99** [6] 5-9-0 G Mosse 43/10: 312629: -:   4 115
4396} **SUSU 21** [13] 6-8-11 K Fallon 526/10: 543110: -:   1¾ 108
14 ran   Time 1m 34.26   (Lanni, Poslosky & Schiappa)   J Canani USA

17	**7.53 GR 1 BREEDERS' CUP SPRINT 3YO+** 6f rnd dirt Fast
	£344578 £132530 £79518

--	**ARTAX** [5] L Albertrani 4-9-0 J Chavez 37/10 JT FAV: 225111: 4 br c Marquetry - Raging Apalachee (Apalachee) -:	**124a**
2}	**KONA GOLD 99** [2] B Headley 5-9-0 A Solis 77/10: -12222: 5 b g Java Gold - Double Sunrise (Slew O'Gold) ½	121a
--	**BIG JAG** [3] T Pinfield 6-9-0 J Valdivia 101/10: 145113: 6 br g Kleven - In Hopes (Affirmed) 2¾	114a
3456}	**STRAVINSKY 79** [7] A P O'Brien 3-8-12 (vis) M J Kinane 48/10: -24116: -: 1	109a
14 ran	Time 1m 07.89 (Paraneck Stable) L Albertrani USA	

18	**8.24 GR 1 BREEDERS' CUP F & M TURF 3YO+** 1m3f Good
	£339754 £130675 £78405 £33263 3yo rec 4lb

--	**SOARING SOFTLY** [12] J J Toner 4-8-11 J D Bailey 36/10 FAV: 111511: 4 ch f Kris S - Wings Of Grace (Key To The Mint) -:	120
--	**CORETTA** [14] C Clement 5-8-11 J Santos 162/10: 51P322: 5 b m Caerleon - Free At Last (Shirley Heights) -:	¾ 118
4126}	**ZOMARADAH 42** [6] L M Cumani 4-8-11 L Dettori 92/10: 011213: 4 b f Deploy - Jawaher (Dancing Brave) hd	118
--	**CAFFE LATTE** [3] J Canani 3-8-7 C Nakatani 117/10: 112024: -: hd	118
4247}	**BORGIA GER 34** [8] 5-8-11 K Fallon 68/10: 455205: -: nse	118
14 ran	Time 2m 13.89 (J & J Phillips) J J Toner USA	

19	**8.57 GR 1 BREEDERS' CUP JUVENILE 2YO C&G** 1m110y rnd dirt Fast
	£339754 £130675 £78405 £33263

--	**ANEES** [9] A Hassinger Jr 2-8-10 (vis) G Stevens 303/10: -6131: 2 b c Unbridled - Ivory Idol (Alydar)	**122a**
--	**CHIEF SEATTLE** [1] J Kimmel 2-8-10 E Prado 44/10: -1422: 2 br c Seattle Slew - Skatingonthinice (Icecapade) -:	2½ 115a
--	**HIGH YIELD** [2] D Wayne Lukas 2-8-10 J D Bailey 68/10: 231133: 2 ch c Storm Cat - Scoop The Gold (Forty Niner) -:	¾ 113a
3437}	**MULL OF KINTYRE 80** [5] A P O'Brien 2-8-10 M J Kinane 292/10: -1214: -:	2½ 108a
4398}	**BRAHMS 21** [14] 2-8-10 (vis) O Peslier 543/10: 212327: -:	6½ 96a
14 ran	Time 1m 42.29 (The Thoroughbred Corp) A Hassinger Jr USA	

20	**9.30 GR 1 BREEDERS' CUP TURF 3YO+** 1m4f Good
	£626506 £240964 £144578

4247}	**DAYLAMI 34** [3] Saeed bin Suroor 5-9-0 L Dettori 16/10 FAV: 211101: 5 gr h Doyoun - Daltawa (Miswaki)	136
3899}	**ROYAL ANTHEM 56** [2] W Mott 4-9-0 G Stevens 87/10: -22152: 4 b c Theatrical - In Neon (Ack Ack)	2½ 131
4}	**BUCKS BOY 99** [5] P Noel Hickey 6-9-0 G Gomez 64/10: 11-123: 6 b g Bucksplasher - Molly's Colleen (Verbatim) -:	2 128
3899}	**DREAM WELL 28** [1] P Bary 4-9-0 (bl) C Asmussen 119/10: 331325: -:	4¾ 118
4422}	**COURTEOUS 20** [7] 4-9-0 K Fallon 105/1: 20-137: -:	1 116
14 ran	Time 2m 24.73 (Godolphin) Saeed bin Suroor Newmarket	

21	**10.10 GR 1 BREEDERS' CUP CLASSIC 3YO+** 1m2f Fast
	£1253012 £418928 £289157 £134940 3yo rec 4lb

1}	**CAT THIEF 99** [6] D Wayne Lukas 3-8-10 (bl) P Day 196/10: 612031: 3 ch c Storm Cat - Train Robbery (Alydar) -:	**127a**
--	**BUDROYALE** [9] T West 6-9-0 G Gomez 265/10: 124112: 6 b g Cee's Tizzy - Cee's Song (Seattle Slew) 1¼	124a
3704}	**GOLDEN MISSILE 69** [4] J Orseno 4-9-0 (bl) K Desormeaux 75/1: 441323: 4 ch c A P Indy - Santa Catalina (Seattle Slew) -: hd	124a
3405}	**CHESTER HOUSE 81** [12] R J Frankel 4-9-0 C Nakatani 64/1: 114434: -:	2 121a
4026}	**ALMUTAWAKEL 27** [7] 4-9-0 J D Bailey 66/10: -10235: -:	½ 120a
14 ran	Time 1m 59.52 (Overbrook Farm) D Wayne Lukas USA	

Official Going STANDARD Stalls: Inside, Except 1m - Outside

22	**12.20 APPR HCAP DIV I 3YO+ 0-75 (G)** 1m2f aw Going 45 -13 Slow	**[75]**
	£1542 £430 £207 3 yo rec 4 lb	

4585} **FORTY FORTE 9** [4] K R Burke 3-9-3 (68) P McGann (7) 14/1: 100001: 3 b g Pursuit Of Love - Cominna (Dominion) Keen, led after 1f, clr halfway, wide on bend over 1f out & hdd ins last, rallied gamely for vigorous pushing to lead on line: op 12/1: earlier won at Nottingham (sell, M Channon) & Beverley (h'cap, rtd 78, rnr-up on sand, rtd 64a, mdn): prev eff at 7.5f/1m, stays a sharp 10f well: acts on firm, hvy, both AWs: likes to dominate: handles a gall or sharp trk: inexperienced rider did not carry a whip today & rode well. **71a**

4519} **SPACE RACE 16** [6] C A Cyzer 5-10-0 (75) G Faulkner 9/2: 402502: 5 b g Rock Hopper - Melanoura (Imperial Fling) Prom, chsd wnr halfway, rdn fnl 3f, drvn/led ins last, hdd line: op 4/1: earlier in '99 won here at Lingfield (h'cap, rtd 78a, subs rnr-up on turf, rtd 68, stks): rtd 88 in '98 (rnr-up, 4 rnr h'cap): eff at 1m/10f, stays a sharp 12f well: acts on firm, gd/soft, both AW's: has run well fresh: likes to race with/force the pace. hd **77a**

3716} **SAMMYS SHUFFLE 71** [10] Jamie Poulton 4-8-6 (50) (bl) (3ow) N Callan 13/2: 406043: 4 b c Touch Of Grey - Cabinet Shuffle (Thatching) Mid-div, prog halfway, chsd front pair fnl 3f, styd on well ins last, post came too sn: nicely bckd, tchd 8/1: jumps fit (mod form): place form in '99 (rtd 51a, h'cap, & 37, h'cap): '98 wnr at Brighton (2, h'caps, rtd 48) & here at Lingfield (C/D, h'cap, rtd 44a): stays 12f on firm, equitrack, in blnks. ¾ **54a**

4465} **FAMOUS 21** [11] J J Bridger 6-7-11 (44) P Doe 10/1: 201004: Rear/wide, prog/chsd ldrs 2f out, held fnl 1f. 　2　42a

4335} **HERR TRIGGER 30** [5] 8-9-8 (69)(ebl) R Smith (5) 9/4 FAV: 513405: Slowly away/rdn, mod gains fnl 4f, no threat: op 7/4: earlier in '99 won at Lingfield (C/D, stks, rtd 72a, plcd on turf, rtd 53, h'cap): '98 wnr here at Lingfield (h'cap, rtd 82a, also rtd 63): eff at 10/12f on firm, fast, loves equitrack/Lingfield: best in blnks.　3　63a

2416} **COLONEL NORTH 99** [2] 3-9-8 (73) A McCarthy 10/1: 001166: Led 1f, sn restrained, held 3f out: abs.　1¾　65a

4548} **MALCHIK 13** [7] 3-7-10 (47)(12oh) A Polli 33/1: 653007: Mid-div at best.　¾　38$

4564} **MIGWAR 12** [9] 6-8-13 (60) P Fredericks (5) 12/1: 000008: Prom, wknd 3f out: tchd 14/1.　nk　50a

4574} **OUR PEOPLE 10** [1] 5-8-1 (48) R Fitzpatrick 4/1: 00-069: Mid-div, btn fnl 2f: op 5/1.　1¾　36a

-- **ESTOPPED** [3] 4-7-13 (46) J Mackay (7) 25/1: 0000-0: Bhd halfway: 10th: long abs, mdn.　21　3a

10 ran　Time 2m 08.58 (5.78)　(Nigel Shields)　K R Burke Newmarket, Suffolk

---

23　12.50 APPR HCAP DIV II 3YO+ 0-75 (G)　1m2f aw　Going 45　-02 Slow　[75]
£1542　£430　£207　3 yo rec 4 lb

4020} **JUST WIZ 52** [4] R Hannon 3-9-8 (73)(bl) R Smith (5) 6/1: 200231: 3 b g Efisio - Jade Pet (Petong) Trkd ldrs going well halfway, rdn/prog to lead over 1f out, styd on well ins last, rdn out: op 9/1, 7 wk abs: earlier in '99 won at Southwell (h'cap, rtd 54 & 61a in '98 (h'caps): eff at 7f, suited by 1m/sharp 10f: acts on firm & gd/soft, both AWs & any trk: eff in blnks/visor: runs well fresh: op to further improvement.　80a

4472} **ARDENT 20** [6] Miss B Sanders 5-8-0 (47) P Fitzsimons (3) 6/1: 066202: 5 b g Aragon - Forest Of Arden (Tap On Wood) Trkd ldr, led going well 4f out till 3f out, briefly outpcd over 1f out, kept on ins last: tchd 7/1: earlier in '99 won at Kempton (h'cap, rtd 49): '98 Brighton wnr (h'cap, rtd 52, also rtd 43a, C Benstead): eff at 1m/9f, stays sharp 10f: acts on firm, gd/soft, equitrack: best without blnks: enjoys a sharp/undul or easy trk.　1¼　51a

1645} **JAVA SHRINE 99** [1] D J Wintle 8-9-12 (73)(bl) Joanna Badger (7) 9/2 FAV: 630003: 8 b g Java Gold - Ivory Idol (Alydar) Rear halfway, stdy prog 3f out, styd on well ins last, nrst fin: tchd 7/1: 5 mth abs: earlier in '99 rattled off a hat-trick here at Lingfield (clmr, P Eccles, class stks & clmr, A Reid, rtd 75a, subs rtd 38 on turf): '98 Warwick & Lingfield wnr (sell h'caps, rtd 65 & 65a): suited by 10/11f, stays 12f: acts on firm/fast, fibresand, loves Lingfield/equitrack: best in blnks: runs well fresh: encouraging run for new connections.　1　76a

4156} **ERITHS CHILL WIND 43** [10] G L Moore 3-7-12 (49) R Brisland (5) 11/2: 223104: Cl-up halfway, led 3f out, hdd over 1f out & fdd fnl 1f: op 7/2, abs, A/W bow.　½　51a

4211} **FAILED TO HIT 40** [3] 6-9-9 (70)(vis) P Fredericks (5) 7/1: 260035: Led, rdn/hdd 4f out, sn outpcd, styd on again fnl 1f, no threat: 6 week abs, tchd 9/1.　1¼　70a

1751} **CONFRONTER 99** [5] 10-9-2 (63) P Doe 6/1: 415506: Mid-div, held fnl 2f: op 4/1, 5 month abs.　1½　61a

4463} **TWOFORTEN 21** [7] 4-7-10 (43)(bl) (9oh) A Polli 12/1: 240337: Rear, prog/ch 2f out, fdd: AW bow.　1　40a

4579} **CASHIKI 10** [9] 3-7-10 (47)(1oh) Claire Bryan (5) 14/1: 042008: Towards rear, btn 3f out: op 10/1.　1¼　42a

4402} **ULTRA CALM 24** [2] 3-8-11 (62) T Eaves (7) 8/1: 126509: Mid-div, btn 2f out: op 10/1.　3½　52a

4276} **DURHAM FLYER 34** [11] 4-7-10 (43)(5oh) M Baird 50/1: 000000: Prom 5f: 10th.　7　23a

3　**SASEEDO 3** [8] 9-8-7 (54) N Callan 25/1: 600600: Slowly away, wide/al bhd: 11th: quick reapp.　1¾　32a

11 ran　Time 2m 07.49 (4.69)　(Peter M Crane)　R Hannon East Everleigh, Wilts

---

24　1.20 GOLF CLAIMER 2YO (F)　6f aw rnd　Going 45　-17 Slow
£2137　£600　£292

4517} **OTIME 16** [4] M R Channon 2-8-7 S Drowne 14/1: 140051: 2 b g Mujadil - Kick the Habit (Habitat) Chsd ldrs, rdn/chsd ldr 2f out, styd on well to lead ins last, rdn out: tchd 16/1: AW bow, claimed for £5,000: earlier in '99 won at Bath (sell, rtd 62): eff at 5f, stays a sharp 6f on firm & equitrack.　72a

4149} **PERLE DE SAGESSE 43** [5] Julian Poulton 2-8-4 D Sweeney 8/1: 001052: 2 b f Namaqualand - Pearl Of Dubai (Red Ransom) Trkd ldrs going well halfway, rdn/wide on bend 2f out, styd on well ins last, not reach wnr: 6 wk abs: prev with P Cole, earlier in '99 scored at Windsor (sell, rtd 65, also rtd 52a): eff at 5f, stays a sharp 6f well, 7f may suit: acts on firm, gd, equitrack & any trk: enjoys sell grade, worth a try in headgear.　1　65a

4457} **THE BULL MACABE 21** [6] R Hannon 2-9-3 T Sprake 15/8 FAV: 6013: 2 ch c Efisio - Tranquillity (Night Shift) Prom, led over 3f out, rdn/clr over 1f out, hdd ins last & no extra: well bckd: AW bow, claimed for £10,000: earlier in '99 won at Nottingham (mdn, rtd 80): eff at 5f, stays 6f on gd/soft & equitrack, any trk.　nk　77a

4388} **WELCHS DREAM 26** [3] J Berry 2-8-12 R Lappin 5/2: 144344: Cl-up, wkng/hmpd 2f out: nicely bckd.　3½　63a

4345} **LEA VALLEY EXPRESS 29** [2] 2-8-4 (vis) P Doe 20/1: 540305: Led 3f, sn held.　hd　54a

4404} **SUPREMELY DEVIOUS 24** [7] 2-8-2 (vis) P Fessey 15/2: 426006: Chsd ldrs, held/stly hmpd 1f out.　¾　50a

4549} **DINKY 13** [9] 2-7-12 M Baird (3) 33/1: 0007: Sn rdn/bhd: AW bow.　14　18a

4570} **RIOS DIAMOND 10** [8] 2-8-6 (VIS) A Daly 16/1: 003008: Chsd ldrs 4f: op 10/1: 1st time visor.　1　24a

3979} **LATE NIGHT LADY 33** [1] 2-7-12 Dale Gibson 8/1: 062009: Sn outpcd/bhd: op 5/1.　10　0a

9 ran　Time 1m 14.13 (3.73)　(Ken Lock Racing)　M R Channon Upper Lambourn, Berks

---

25　1.50 SKY TV MDN 3YO+ (D)　6f aw rnd　Going 45　-17 Slow
£3146　£952　£465　£221

4471} **AUBRIETA 20** [6] D Haydn Jones 3-8-9 (bl) A Mackay 13/2: 000601: 3 b f Dayjur - Fennel (Slew O'Gold) Mid-div halfway, rdn/prog & switched over 1f out to lead ins last, styd on strongly, rdn out: tchd 9/1: AW bow: blnks reapplied: plcd earlier in '99 (fill h'cap, rtd 62): plcd 3 times in '98 (rtd 79, C Brittain): eff at 6f, tried 1m: acts on equitrack: handles any trk: AW bow.　59a

4541} **MAAS 14** [10] P J Makin 4-9-0 A Clark 11/4 FAV: 2-0002: 4 br c Elbio - Payne's Grey (Godswalk) Rdn/towards rear & prog 3f out, styd on well ins last, no threat to wnr: op 9/4: rtd 53 on turf earlier in '99 (mdn): rnr-up twice over C/D in late '98 (mdns, rtd 66a): eff at 6f, step up to 7f will suit on this evidence: acts on equitrack & a sharp trk: could find compensation in a similar contest.　3　55a

4553} **MAGIQUE ETOILE 13** [5] M P Muggeridge 3-8-9 (vis) R Ffrench 11/2: 525033: 3 b f Magical Wonder - She's A Dancer (Alzao) Prom, rdn/outpcd over 2f out, kept on well fnl 1f: tchd 8/1: visor reapplied: plcd twice earlier in '99 (rtd 55, clmg h'cap, also rtd 55a, h'cap): plcd in late '98 on sand (rtd 63a, nurs h'cap, rtd 64 on turf): eff at 6/7f, tried 1m: acts on fast & gd/soft, equitrack: eff in a vis, tried blnks: handles any trk.　½　48a

4280} **CARMARTHEN 34** [12] K R Burke 3-9-0 N Callan (3) 6/1: 000304: Cl-up/led 1f out, hdd ins last/fdd.　1¾　49$

4554} **LEVEL HEADED 13** [9] 4-9-0 (BL) T Sprake 33/1: -00005: Mid-div/nvr pace to chall: blnks/AW bow.　½　42$

4541} **SISAO 14** [4] 3-9-0 (bl) S Whitworth 14/1: 0006: Prom, ch over 1f out, no extra: op 10/1, AW bow.　¾　45a

4541} **NEELA 14** [1] 3-8-9 P Dobbs (5) 4/1: 047: Bhd halfway, mod late gains: nicely bckd, AW bow.　hd　39a

4385} **FARAWAY MOON 26** [3] 3-8-9 M Tebbutt 9/1: 300308: Cl-up, led over 1f out till 1f out, wknd qckly.　hd　38a

4219} **BEVELED CRYSTAL 40** [7] 5-8-9 P Doe (3) 25/1: /00069: Dwelt, rdn/rear, mod prog: 6 wk abs/AW bow.　3　31$

-- **ZOES NEWSBOX** [13] 5-8-9 P Fessey 25/1: 0: Wide/mid-div, btn 2f out: 10th: debut.　4　21a

3926} **GALLANT FELLOW 57** [8] 4-9-0 R Brisland (5) 33/1: 500300: Wide/al bhnd: 11th: jmps fit.　shd　26a

---

4371} **ROYAL HUSSAR 27** [2] 3-9-0 T Williams 16/1: 0500: Led 5f, wknd qckly/eased: 13th: op 12/1.   **0a**
4541} **Lady Balla Calm 14** [11] 3-8-9 G Bardwell 33/1:   --   **Good Whit Son** [14] 3-9-0 A McCarthy (3) 25/1:
14 ran   Time 1m 14.09 (3.69)   (Hugh O'Donnell)   D Haydn Jones Efail Isaf, Rhondda C Taff

---

26	**2.20 EBF MDN 2YO (D)** **1m aw rnd Going 45 +13 Fast**
	£3501 £1060 £517 £246

4185} **SAFARI BLUES 41** [1] R Hannon 2-8-9 T Sprake 6/4 FAV: 443521: 2 b f Blues Traveller - North Hut   **84a**
(Northfields) Led after 1f, clr 2f, rdn out: well bckd, 6 wk abs, AW bow, gd time: rnr-up twice earlier in
'99 (nurs h'cap, rtd 77): eff at 7f, stays a sharp 1m, further may suit: acts on firm, soft & equitrack: handles
any trk, likes a sharp one: likes to race with/force the pace: runs well fresh: plenty in hand here.
4569} **INVER GOLD 10** [7] M Johnston 2-9-0 M Hills 15/8: 62: 2 ch c Arazi - Mary Martin (Be My Guest)   7 **77a**
Prom, rdn halfway, outpcd 2f out, kept on ins last, no ch wnr: hvly bckd: AW bow: earlier in '99 showed promise
at Redcar (mdn, rtd 79): half brother to sev wnrs: prob stays 1m, handles equitrack & gd/soft grnd.
4048} **THATS ALL FOLKS 50** [9] P J Makin 2-9-0 A Clark 10/1: 063: 2 b c Alhijaz - So It Goes (Free State)   2 **73a**
Mid-div, prog to chase wnr over 1f out, sn rdn/no extra fnl 1f: op 6/1: 7 wk abs/AW bow: rtd 73 earlier in '99
(auct stks): this 1m trip shld suit: will apprec h'caps.
4462} **BOLD EWAR 21** [8] C E Brittain 2-9-0 R Cochrane 6/1: 053004: Mid-div/nvr on terms: AW bow/op 4/1.   5 **63a**
4550} **SPIRIT OF TENBY 13** [2] 2-9-0 P Doe (3) 12/1: 355005: 199 Trkd ldrs 6f: op 10/1, AW bow.   hd **62a**
4591} **ON CREDIT 8** [10] 2-9-0 (bl) N Callan (3) 33/1: 006: Dwelt, towards rear, btn 3f out: AW bow.   5 **52a**
4149} **FOX STAR 43** [4] 2-8-9 (BL) O Urbina 20/1: 304067: Led 1f, chsd wnr till 3f out, fdd/eased fnl 1f: 1st   5 **37a**
time blnks, 6 wk abs, prev with R Hannon, now with Julian Poulton.
4600} **YES COLONEL 7** [11] 2-9-0 T G McLaughlin 50/1: 08: Dwelt, sn bhd: AW bow.   4 **34a**
4599} **UBITOO 7** [6] 2-9-0 S Drowne 50/1: 09: Mid-div, btn halfway: AW bow.   4 **26a**
4452} **NO REGRETS 21** [5] 2-9-0 A Culhane 25/1: 034600: Chsd ldrs 5f, eased fnl 1f: 10th: AW bow.   ¾ **25a**
--   **FOOLS PARADISE** [3] 2-9-0 A Morris 33/1: 0: Dwelt/sn t.o.: 11th: debut: with C Cyzer.   15 **0a**
11 ran   Time 1m 38.72 (2.52)   (T J Dale)   R Hannon East Everleigh, Wilts

---

27	**2.50 COND STKS 3YO+ (D)** **1m4f aw Going 45 +11 Fast**
	£3820 £1156 £564 £268 3 yo rec 6 lb

3981} **ALBERICH 54** [7] M Johnston 4-8-13 M Hills 4/7 FAV: 200311: 4 b g Night Shift - Tetradonna (Teenoso)   **92a**
Made all, styd on well fnl 2f, pushed out: hvly bckd, AW bow, 8 wk abs, gd time: earlier in '99 won at Newbury
(val h'cap, rtd 95): '98 York wnr (h'cap, rtd 93): eff at 12/13f on firm, gd & equitrack, prob handles hvy:
runs well fresh: loves to dominate: handles a sharp or stiff/gall trk: in gd form.
3060} **CHINA CASTLE 99** [6] P C Haslam 6-9-4 M Tebbutt 11/2: 050102: 6 b g Sayf El Arab - Honey Plum   4 **91a**
(Kind Of Hush) Rcd wide in rear, rdn & styd on well fnl 2f, nrst fin: op 3/1, 3 mth abs: earlier in '99 won at
Southwell (4), W'hampton (3), & Hamilton (h'caps, rtd 52 & 107a at best): '98 Southwell (ltd stks) & W'hampton
wnr (h'cap, rtd 87a): v eff at 11/12f on firm & equitrack, loves fibresand & sharp trks: smart sand performer.
4552} **TALLULAH BELLE 13** [3] N P Littmoden 6-8-13 T G McLaughlin 8/1: 000003: 6 b m Crowning Honors - shd **86a**
Fine A Leau (Youth) Trkd ldrs, chsd wnr over 1f out, no extra fnl, caught for 2nd cl-home: op 6/1, jockey
given 5 day ban for dropping his hands: earlier in '99 won at Lingfield (stks), W'hampton (rtd 86a) & Hamilton
(h'caps, rtd 73): '98 wnr at Lingfield (rtd 75a), Goodwood & Yarmouth (h'caps, rtd 70): eff at 9f/12f on firm,
gd/soft & on both AWs, likes Lingfield: return to h'cap company may suit.
4571} **CRACKLE 10** [2] B W Hills 3-8-2 P Fessey 9/1: 430334: Chsd wnr 7f, held 2f: op 6/1, AW bow.   ¾ **80a**
4511} **CASHMERE LADY 16** [1] 7-8-8 A Mackay 11/1: 100065: Chsd ldrs 9f: op 7/1.   3 **76a**
--   **APADI** [4] 3-8-7 T Sprake 25/1: 000066: Keen in tch, wknd fnl 2f: 4 mth abs/ex-French.   ½ **80a**
4497} **REINE DE LA CHASSE 17** [5] 7-8-8 A Clark 100/1: 067: Bhd 4f out: AW bow.   dist **0a**
7 ran   Time 2m 33.31 (4.11)   (J David Abell)   M Johnston Middleham, N Yorks

---

28	**3.20 HCAP DIV I 3YO+ 0-75 (E)** **7f aw rnd Going 45 -07 Slow**	[75]
	£2528 £764 £372 £176 3 yo rec 1 lb	

4504} **DARYABAD 17** [8] R McGhin 7-9-3 (64)(bl) R Cochrane 7/2 FAV: -00011: 7 b g Thatching - Dayanata   **69a**
(Shirley Heights) Trkd ldrs, prog to lead dist, pushed out cl-home: well bckd: earlier in '99 won here at Lingfield
(class stks, rtd 68a), no turf form: '98 Catterick wnr (stks, rtd 66): eff at 1m, suited by 7f: acts on firm,
gd/soft & fibresand, loves equitrack/Lingfield: eff in blnks: has run well fresh: goes well for R Cochrane.
3879} **RAINBOW RAIN 61** [14] S Dow 5-8-13 (60) R Smith (5) 6/1: 101402: 5 b g Capote - Grana (Miswaki)   1 **62a**
Toward rear/wide, styd on well fnl 2f, nrst at fin: tnchd 7/1, 2 month abs: earlier in '99 won at Brighton (2),
h'caps, rtd 68 & 60a): '98 Lingfield wnr (AW h'cap, rtd 69a & 59): eff btwn 6f/1m, stays a sharp 10f: acts on
firm, gd & equitrack: suited by a sharp/undul trk, loves Brighton: on a fair AW mark.
3751} **BIG BEN 69** [3] R Hannon 5-9-7 (68) M Hills 10/1: 356003: 5 ch h Timeless Times - Belltina (Belfort)   1¼ **67a**
Toward rear, styd on stdly fnl 2f, nrst fin: tchd 12/1, 10 wk abs: plcd sev times earlier in '99 (rtd 63a & 69):
'98 wnr at Folkestone (h'cap), Newmarket (ltd stks, rtd 76) & here at Lingfield (h'cap, rtd 70a): eff at 7f: acts
on fast, hvy & both AWs, prob handles firm: likes Lingfield & to race with/force the pace: not given hard time.
4604} **PRIX STAR 7** [5] C W Fairhurst 4-8-6 (53)(vis) A Culhane 5/1: 006024: Trkd ldrs, rdn/no room over   ½ **51a**
1f out, styd on ins last, no room to chall: nicely bckd.
4471} **DAYNABEE 20** [7] 4-7-11 (44) J Mackay (7) 16/1: 200005: Trkd ldrs, no room over 1f out/no extra fnl 1f.   4 **41a**
--   **JUST LOUI** [11] 5-10-3 (78) N Callan (3) 12/1: 1010-6: Cl-up/ch 1f out, wknd cl-home: op 8/1, long abs.   1 **73a**
4576} **TEMPRAMENTAL 10** [1] 3-7-13 (47)(bl) A Mackay 12/1: 034007: Rear, mid-div 2f out, no further prog.   ¾ **41a**
4131} **PARISIAN LADY 44** [6] 4-8-9 (56) S Whitworth 12/1: 000408: Rear/wide, mod late gains: 6 wk abs.   hd **49a**
3847} **BALANITA 63** [9] 4-8-13 (60) T Sprake 16/1: 6-2009: Led, edged right/hdd over 1f out, fdd: 2 mth abs.   ½ **52a**
4518} **FLITE OF LIFE 16** [13] 3-9-3 (65) M Tebbutt 20/1: 0-0000: Towards rear, nvr factor: 10th: AW bow.   2½ **52a**
3565} **JUST DISSIDENT 78** [10] 7-8-10 (57) D Sweeney 9/1: 000010: Cl-up 6f, fdd: 11th: op 6/1, 11 wk abs.   ¾ **43a**
3805} **ROISIN SPLENDOUR 65** [12] 4-9-10 (71) P Doe (3) 14/1: 605000: Mid-div/wide, btn 1f out/eased: 12th, abs.½ **56a**
4479} **PALERIA 20** [4] 3-9-6 (68) R Lappin 10/1: 5-0000: Mid-div, hmpd halfway, sn btn: 14th: AW bow.   **0a**
4581} **Brave Vision 16** [16] 3-7-12 (44)(bl) (2ow) Dale Gibson 25/1:
4518} **Miss Dangerous 16** [15] 4-8-2 (49) A McCarthy (3) 20/1:
--   **Shades Of Jade** [2] 11-7-10 (43)(13oh) R Brisland (5) 50/1:
16 ran   Time 1m 26.46 (3.66)   (The Three Amigos)   R McGhin Newmarket, Suffolk

LINGFIELD (Equitrack)   THURSDAY NOVEMBER 11TH   Lefthand, V Sharp Track

29 | 3.50 HCAP DIV II 3YO+ 0-75 (E)   7f aw rnd   Going 45   -05 Slow   [75]
£2515   £760   £370   £175   3 yo rec 1 lb

4472} **SCISSOR RIDGE 20** [3] J J Bridger 7-8-5 (52) G Bardwell 6/1: 005441: 7 ch g Indian Ridge - Golden **58a**
Scissors (Kalaglow) Trkd ldrs, led 2f out, styd on well ins last, drvn out: plcd numerous times earlier in '99 (rtd
62a & 47): '98 wnr at Folkestone (h'cap, rtd 56 & 70a): suited by 6/7f, prob stays a sharp 1m: acts on firm, gd/
soft & on both AWs: best without blnks: likes to race with/force the pace: on a fair mark, could win again.
4527} **PENGAMON 15** [7] D T Thom 7-8-1 (48) A Mackay 100/30 FAV: 60/002: 7 gr g Efisio - Dolly Bevan ½ **53a**
(Another Realm) Rear, stdy prog 4f out, styd on well for press, post came too sn: morning gamble from 10/1: prev
with H Collingridge, no form earlier in '99: missed '98: prev term won here at Lingfield (AW h'cap, rtd 77a & 76):
eff at 7f/1m: acts on fast, gd/soft & equitrack: shld sn recoup losses.
4504} **NOBALINO 17** [13] Mrs V C Ward 5-8-13 (60)(vis) R Havlin 11/2: 200033: 5 ch h Sharpo - Zipperti Do 4 **57a**
(Precocious) Trkd ldrs, ev ch when fly-jumped & lost action/place over 2f out, styd on well fnl 1f, no threat front
pair: visor reapplied: rnr-up earlier in '99 (rtd 66 & 63a): rtd 75 & 62a in '98 (Mrs M Macauley): '97 Southwell
wnr (h'cap, rtd 66a & 73): eff at 5f, now seems suited by 7f: acts on firm, gd/soft & on both AWs: likes a sharp
trk, handles any: eff with/without a vis: shade unlucky, a likely type for similar.
3912} **SOUND THE TRUMPET 58** [1] R C Spicer 7-7-10 (43)(t) (4oh) J Mackay (7) 20/1: 600504: Mid-div, styd 1 **38a**
on under hands & heels riding fnl 2f, no threat to ldrs: op 16/1, 2 month abs, stiffish task.
3923} **SPRINGTIME LADY 57** [6] 3-8-12 (60) P Doe (3) 20/1: 500405: Rear, mod gains fnl 3f: abs/AW bow. nk **54a**
3751} **ROBO MAGIC 69** [5] 7-9-12 (73) R Cochrane 4/1: 540306: Cl-up, led 3f out till 2f out, wknd fnl 1f: 3 **61a**
jockey suspended for 2 days for careless riding: op 10/1, 10 wk abs: topweight.
4384} **DONE AND DUSTED 26** [11] 3-9-6 (68) T Sprake 8/1: 150007: Mid-div, nvr pace to chall: tchd 10/1. hd **55a**
4565} **ELLWAY PRINCE 12** [2] 4-9-3 (64)(vis) Dean McKeown 11/1: 060008: Led 2f, cl-up 6f: tchd 14/1. 1¾ **48a**
4504} **LIVELY JACQ 17** [8] 3-8-9 (57) N Carlisle 20/1: 455409: Cl-up 5f: op 14/1. 3½ **34a**
4585} **STYLE DANCER 9** [14] 5-9-3 (64)(vis) D Sweeney 14/1: 440000: Rear/wide, nvr factor: 10th: op 12/1. nk **40a**
4554} **SWYNFORD WELCOME 13** [15] 3-8-8 (56) A Polli (3) 10/1: 000010: Mid-div/wide, btn 3f out: 11th, AW bow.1¼ **29a**
3976} **OUT LIKE MAGIC 54** [4] 4-7-12 (45)(2ow)(3oh) T Williams 14/1: 600050: Led aft 2f, rdn/hdd 3f out, **0a**
btn/hmpd 2f out, eased ins last: 14th: 8 wk abs.
4298} **Lucayan Beach 33** [10] 5-8-13 (60) O Urbina 20/1:   4342} **Violet 29** [12] 3-9-8 (70)(VIS) P Fredericks (5) 16/1:
3790} **Sharp Imp 66** [9] 9-8-0 (45)(bl)(2ow) A Daly (5) 7/1:
15 ran   Time 1m 26.31 (3.51)   (Donald J Smith)   J J Bridger Liphook, Hants

SOUTHWELL (Fibresand)   FRIDAY NOVEMBER 12TH   Lefthand, Sharp, Oval Track

Official Going   STANDARD Stalls: 5f - Outside; Rem - Inside - Outside, Rem - Inside.

30 | 12.05 CARNATION CLAIMER DIV 1 3-5YO (F)   6f aw rnd   Going 44   -14 Slow
£1850   £518   £251

8   **PRINCESS KALI 4** [6] D Carroll 3-8-8 (bl) R Fitzpatrick (3) 25/1: 605301: 3 ch f Fayruz - Carriglegan **54a**
Girl (Don) Mid-div, rdn to chall fnl 2f, drvn ins last, led nr line, all out: qck reapp, first win: earlier
in '99 plcd here at Southwell (C/D, auct mdn, rtd 41): ex-Irish, mod form: eff at 6f on fibresand.
4481} **SEVEN 20** [2] Miss S J Wilton 4-9-4 (bl) T G McLaughlin 3/1: 243262: 4 ch g Weldnaas - Polly's hd **60a**
Teahouse (Shack) Dwelt, sn chasing ldrs, rdn to lead over 1f out, duelled ins last, just hdd nr line: op 7/2: earlier
in '99 won here at Southwell (clmr, B Smart, rtd 68a, subs plcd on turf, rtd 59, h'cap): '98 rnr-up at Lingfield (auct
mdn, rtd 67): eff at 6/7f: acts on gd/soft, likes fibresand/Southwell: best in blnks: handles any trk: enjoys clmrs.
4510} **BEWARE 17** [7] D Nicholls 4-8-11 O Pears 5/2 FAV: 002003: 4 br g Warning - Dancing Spirit 2 **51a**
(Ahonoora) Mid-div halfway, rdn/chsd ldrs fnl 2f, kept on tho' not pace to chall: nicely bckd, AW bow: rnr-up
earlier in '99 (rtd 76, class stks): plcd on a couple of starts in '98 (h'caps, rtd 77): '97 Newbury wnr (nurs h'cap,
rtd 84, R Armstrong): eff at 5/7f: acts on gd & fibresand: handles any trk: has run well fresh.
4405} **GROESFAEN LADY 25** [14] B Palling 3-8-4 T Sprake 12/1: 606424: Led, rdn/hdd over 1f out/no extra. nk **43a**
2884} **DAHLIDYA 99** [11] 4-8-2 P Doe (3) 11/1: 000005: Dwelt/towards rear, mod gains fnl 2f: 4 month abs. 2 **36a**
4363} **GUNNER SAM 29** [12] 3-9-3 Dean McKeown 20/1: 210006: Prom 5f: AW bow, op 14/1. shd **51a**
3655} **TAZ MANIA 75** [4] 3-8-9 (tbl) S Finnamore (7) 66/1: 000007: Cl-up 4f: 11 wk abs. 2½ **36$**
4479} **LAMENT 21** [13] 3-8-4 S Whitworth 12/1: -21608: Mid-div, nvr on terms: op 10/1. hd **30a**
4581} **RA RA RASPUTIN 11** [8] 4-9-1 G Duffield 14/1: 060209: Rear/rdn, nvr factor: op 12/1. 3 **34a**
3770} **PALACE GREEN 69** [9] 3-8-8 A Culhane 7/1: 6-1200: Chsd ldrs 4f: 10th: 10 wk abs, op 5/1. ¾ **23a**
4586} **STUTTON GAL 10** [1] 3-7-13 (1ow)(bl) Martin Dwyer 33/1: 450400: Dwelt, hmpd after 2f/sn btn: 11th. nk **15a**
4586} **Sing For Me 10** [10] 4-8-6 Stephanie Hollinshea 50/1: 2302} **Running Bear 99** [5] 5-8-11 T Williams 66/1:
4252} **Unlikely Lady 38** [3] 3-8-0 Kimberley Hart (5) 33/1:   4479} **Wellow 21** [15] 3-8-5 (tBL) L Newton 20/1:
15 ran   Time 1m 16.8 (3.5)   (Matthew Lee)   D Carroll Southwell, Notts

31 | 12.35 TULIP NURSERY HCAP 2YO 0-75 (E)   7f aw rnd   Going 44   -13 Slow   [79]
£2822   £792   £386

4563} **PHOEBUS 13** [1] W R Muir 2-8-12 (63) Martin Dwyer 10/1: 00041: 2 b c Piccolo - Slava (Diesis) **69a**
Made all, rdn/prsd fnl 2f, styd on gamely ins last, drvn out: first win: jockey given a 2 day ban for misuse of
whip: rtd 69a & 66 earlier in '99: apprec this return to 7f, 1m shld suit: acts on fibresand: likes to dominate.
4461} **MISS WORLD 22** [12] C N Allen 2-8-9 (60)(t)) M Hills 11/2: 414462: 2 b f Mujadil - Great Land nk **65a**
(Friend's Choice) Prom, rdn/ch fnl 2f, styd on well, just held: earlier in '99 won at W'hampton (sell, 1st success,
rtd 60a, rtd 65 at best on turf): eff at 7f, shld stay 1m: acts on both AWs & fast grnd: handles a sharp or
stiff/gall trk: best without blnks, wears a t-strap: can find similar.
4305} **SPRINGS ETERNAL 32** [4] Sir Mark Prescott 2-9-4 (69) G Duffield 5/1 FAV: 004203: 2 b f Salse - Corn ¾ **73a**
Futures (Nomination) Al prom, rdn/ch fnl 2f, kept on well tho' just held nr fin: op 6/1, AW bow: earlier in 99
rnr-up on turf (rtd 72, h'cap): eff at 7f on fibresand, gd & gd/soft: has shown enough to win over further.
4406} **GYMCRAK FIREBIRD 25** [3] G Holmes 2-8-4 (55) T Sprake 11/2: 006024: Chsd ldrs, onepace fnl 2f. 3 **53a**
4476} **PICOLETTE 21** [6] 2-8-5 (56) A Culhane 14/1: 045005: Chsd ldrs 5f: op 12/1. 1½ **51a**
3876} **WILL IVESON 62** [5] 2-8-13 (64) M Tebbutt 7/1: 456056: Mid-div at best: 2 month abs, op 8/1. nk **58a**
4514} **LISA B 17** [2] 2-8-9 (60)(bl) N Callan (3) 14/1: 300007: Prom 5f: tchd 16/1. 2 **50a**

18

3928} **WILEMMGEO** 58 [8] 2-8-9 (60) T Eaves (7) 16/1: -04238: Mid-div, nvr factor: 2 mth abs, op 14/1.   **6**   **38a**
4575} **CRACK DANCER** 11 [10] 2-8-8 (59) S Whitworth 25/1: 000609: Mid-div, btn 2f out.   **1½**   **34a**
4575} **GAIN TIME** 11 [11] 2-9-4 (69)(bl) G Carter 7/1: 006230: Rdn/mid div, nvr factor: 10th, lngr trip.   *shd*   **44a**
4344} **BOSS TWEED** 30 [7] 2-8-6 (57) S Drowne 12/1: 0650: Al towards rear, 11th: h'cap bow, op 10/1.   *nk*   **31a**
4616} Chiko 6 [15] 2-9-0 (65)(vis) R Fitzpatrick (3) 14/1:   3587} **Rainworth Lady** 77 [16] 2-8-5 (56) P Doe (3) 33/1:
4476} **Inch Pincher** 21 [9] 2-8-13 (64) A McCarthy (3) 14/1:   4383} **City Princess** 27 [13] 2-8-10 (61) C Teague 25/1:
15 ran   Time 1m 30.6 (4.0)   (Duncan J Wiltshire)   W R Muir Lambourn, Berks.

---

32   1.05 CARNATION CLAIMER DIV 2 3-5YO (F)   6f aw rnd   Going 44   +01 Fast
     £1850   £518   £251

4481} **VICE PRESIDENTIAL** 20 [11] J G Given 4-8-5 Dean McKeown 20/1: 000001: 4 ch g Presidium - Steelock   **61a**
(Lochnager) Led after 1f, clr 2f out, styd on strongly ins last, rdn out: gd time: op 16/1: mod form on turf
earlier in '99 (rtd 54, h'cap): in '98 trained by T J Etherington to win at Warwick & Musselburgh (clmrs, rtd 65,
also rtd 74a): eff at 6f/sharp 7f: acts on fibresand, gd/soft & soft grnd: has run well fresh: likes claimers.
4553} **WILD THING** 14 [13] R Hannon 3-8-11 P Fitzsimons (5) 4/5 FAV: 302152: 3 b c Never So Bold - Tame   **2**   **62$**
Duchess (Saritamar) Mid-div, prog/switched to chase wnr fnl 2f, kept on tho' al back: clr rem: nicely bckd: earlier
in '99 scored here at Southwell (C/D, auct mdn, rtd 68a, rnr-up on turf, rtd 56, h'cap): eff at 6f, stays a sharp 1m:
acts on both AWs & gd/soft grnd: handles a sharp/turning trk: return to 7f+ may suit.
2833} **EMMAJOUN** 99 [2] W G M Turner 4-8-4 D Sweeney 13/2: 420003: 4 b f Amarati - Parijoun (Manado)   **5**   **43a**
Led 1f, remained handy, outpcd by front pair fnl 2f: op 5/1, 4 month abs: earlier in '99 won on reapp at Lingfield (AW
mdn, rtd 56a, subs rnr-up on turf, rtd 57, clmr): plcd in '98 (h'cap, rtd 65): eff at 5f, stays stiff 6f well, tried
further: acts on gd, firm, equitrack & prob handles fibresand: handles any trk: has run well fresh.
3777} **LEMON STRIP** 69 [5] B Palling 3-8-6 L Newman (7) 25/1: 420304: Prom, no extra over 1f out: 10 wk abs.   ¾   **43$**
4481} **DAINTY DISH** 20 [10] 3-8-2 (BL) P Fessey 20/1: 003305: Mid-div, nvr on terms: 1st time blnks.   **3**   **32a**
--   **SUPERAPPAROS** [8] 5-8-9 S Finnamore (7) 50/1: 4/40-6: Cl-up 4f: long abs.   ¾   **37$**
4303} **OFF HIRE** 32 [12] 3-8-9 (VIS) J Tate 15/2: 006007: Prom/wide 4f: 1st time visor, op 11/2.   **3**   **30a**
4568} **SEVEN SPRINGS** 13 [1] 3-9-0 A Culhane (7) 41/1: 000008: Rdn mid-div, btn 2f out: op 10/1.   ¾   **33a**
4261} **QUAKERESS** 38 [14] 4-7-12 A Polli (3) 25/1: 000009: Sn rdn/al bhd: AW bow.   **2**   **12a**
3431} **IMPERIAL HONEY** 86 [9] 4-8-2(2ow) G Duffield 11/1: 203340: Dwelt/al rear: 10th: 3 month abs.   **1**   **14a**
4449} Go Sally Go 23 [3] 3-8-4 T Williams 16/1:   4496} **Linksman** 18 [7] 4-9-1 O Pears 66/1:
2878} **Magic Glow** 32 [4] 3-8-6 P Doe (3) 66/1:
13 ran   Time 1m 15.9 (2.6)   (A Clarke)   J G Given Willoughton, Lincs

---

33   1.40 LADBROKE HCAP DIV 1 3YO+ 0-85 (D)   7f aw rnd   Going 44   -10 Slow   **[84]**
     £1138   £554   £262   3 yo rec 1 lb

4402} **SEA YA MAITE** 25 [5] S R Bowring 5-7-10 (52) G Bardwell 7/4 FAV: 050021: 5 b g Komaite - Marina   **55a**
Plata (Julio Mariner) Dwelt, rdn into mid-div halfway, stdy run frm press to lead on line, all out: rnr-up twice
earlier in '99 (rtd 64a, C/D, h'cap, rtd 30 on turf): '98 Southwell wnr (h'cap, rtd 68a, plcd on turf, rtd 48, h'cap):
eff at 6f/1m, 7f prob suits best: acts on fast, gd/soft grnd, loves fibresand/Southwell: likes a sharp trk: has run
well fresh: best without blnks: tough gldg, well h'capped, shld win again this winter.
1585} **RONS PET** 99 [7] K R Burke 4-9-2 (72)(t) N Callan (3) 6/1: 460002: 4 ch g Ron's Victory - Penny   *hd*   **74a**
Mint (Mummy's Game) Mid-div, prog/drvn to chall & narrow lead ins last, hdd line: jockey given 3-day whip
ban: tchd 8/1, 6 month abs: earlier in '99 rnr-up at W'hampton (2, clmr & h'cap, rtd 74a, subs rtd 60 on turf):
mod form over hdles prev: '97 Brighton wnr (R Hannon): eff at 1m, suited by 7f: acts on firm & soft, fibresand:
likes a sharp/undul trk, loves W'hampton: has run well fresh: eff in a visor & t-strap, has tried blnks.
3609} **ROYAL CASCADE** 76 [9] B A McMahon 5-9-12 (82)(bl) G Duffield 12/1: 110003: 5 b g River Falls -   **1½**   **81a**
Relative Stranger (Cragador) Led 1f, remained handy & led again over 1f out, hdd ins last & no extra cl-home: abs,
op 10/1: topweight: earlier in '99 rattled off a hat-trick at Southwell (2, clmr & h'cap) & W'hampton (h'cap,
rtd 86a at best, rtd 38 on turf, h'cap): '98 wnr again at Southwell (2, clmr & sell, 1st time blnks) & W'hampton (2,
clmrs): eff at 6/7f, stayed 1m: fibresand specialist, loves W'hampton & Southwell: best in blnks: runs well fresh.
4479} **CRYSTAL LASS** 21 [8] J Balding 3-9-0 (71)(bl) J Edmunds 12/1: 010404: Mid-div/not pace to chall.   **3½**   **63a**
4604} **MARENGO 8** [4] 5-7-11 (52)(1ow) P Doe (0) 9/2: 503405: Led after 1f/clr 3f out, hdd over 1f out/fdd.   **2**   **41a**
437} **ELTON LEDGER** 99 [6] 10-8-11 (67)(vis) R Fitzpatrick (3) 20/1: 431406: Prom 5f: 9 month abs, op 16/1.   **4**   **47a**
4553} **KINGCHIP BOY** 14 [10] 10-8-7 (63)(vis) M Baird (3) 20/1: 504107: Handy 5f: op 16/1.   **1**   **41a**
4456} **RIVERBLUE** 22 [11] 3-9-10 (81) Joanna Badger (7) 10/1: 500008: Mid-div at best: AW bow, op 9/1.   **1**   **57a**
4394} **MARJAANA** 27 [3] 6-8-2 (58) P Fitzsimons (5) 50/1: 20/009: Sn rdn/al outpcd.   **4**   **26a**
4565} **SO WILLING** 13 [12] 3-8-8 (65) C Teague 20/1: 002000: In clr 4f: 10th.   **1**   **31a**
4572} **ERRO CODIGO** 11 [2] 4-8-8 (64) J Tate 9/1: 004100: Slowly away & al rear: 11th: op 6/1.   **2½**   **25a**
3815} **TIME OF NIGHT** 66 [1] 6-7-12 (54) T Williams 12/1: 110400: Dwelt, rdn/towards rear, hung right &   **1**   **13a**
btn 2f out, eased ins last: 12th: op 8/1, 2 month abs: jockey looking down at his mount, something amiss?
12 ran   Time 1m 29.4 (3.8)   (S R Bowring)   S R Bowring Edwinstowe, Notts

---

34   2.15 ORCHID MDN AUCT 2YO (F)   5f aw str   Going 44   -06 Slow
     £2284   £642   £313

4353} **JAMES STARK** 29 [9] N P Littmoden 2-8-11 (bl) G Carter 7/1: 051: 2 b c Up And At 'Em - June Maid   **84a**
(Junius) Chsd ldrs, prog/led over 1f out, styd on well, rdn out: AW bow, op 10/1: rtd 64 earlier in '99 (sell, 1st
time blnks): apprec this drop to 5f, return to 6f+ may suit in time: acts on fibresand, handles gd: eff in blnks.
4081} **CHRISTOPHERSSISTER** 49 [10] N Bycroft 2-8-0 P Doe (3) 9/1: 66452: 2 br f Timeless Times - Petite   **3**   **64a**
Elite (Anfield) Bumped/slowly away, styd on well fnl 2f for press, nrst frn: 7 wk abs, op 5/1: AW bow: earlier in
'99 rtd 69 at best on turf (Redcar fill mdn): eff at 5f, return to 6f shld suit: handles firm & fibresand: acts
on a gall or sharp trk: tardy start cost him dear here, could find a similar contest.
4547} **KIND EMPEROR** 14 [1] M J Polglase 2-8-11 T G McLaughlin 100/30: 000203: 2 br c Emperor Jones -   *shd*   **75a**
Kind Lady (Kind Of Hush) Led, rdn/hdd over 1f out, no extra nr frn: tchd 4/1: rnr-up numerous times earlier in
'99 (rtd 83 at best, mdn, rtd 65a on sand, h'cap): stays 6f, loves to force the pace at 5f: acts on firm,
gd/soft & fibresand: handles any track: shown enough to win similar this winter.
--   **MISS SKICAP** [3] T D Barron 2-8-6 G Duffield 14/1: 4: Dwelt, styd on fnl 2f, nrst fin: debut, op 10/1   *shd*   **69a**
4563} **JANICELAND** 13 [2] 2-8-6 A McGlone 5/2 FAV: 350202: Cl-up 3f, fdd: op 3/1: rnr-up sev times earlier   **2½**   **62a**
in '99 (rtd 67a, h'cap & 75, fill auct mdn): eff at 6f, acts on fast, gd, fibresand: likes a sharp/turning trk.
3319} **DRAGON STAR** 91 [6] 2-8-0 Martin Dwyer 6/1: -366: Chsd ldrs, onepace fnl 2f: 3 month abs/AW bow.   ½   **54a**
4517} **PERTEMPS STAR** 17 [7] 2-8-5 R Perham 33/1: AW bow.   **1½**   **55a**

SOUTHWELL (Fibresand)FRIDAY NOVEMBER 12THLefthand, Sharp, Oval Track

4589} SERGEANT SLIPPER 9 [13] 2-8-5 P Fitzsimons (5) 16/1: 250048: Dwelt, nvr on terms.hd54a
4508} SKYE 17 [12] 2-8-3 J Edmunds 16/1: 0009: Went right start, sn outpcd: AW bow.¾50a
4575} MADEMOISELLE PARIS 11 [11] 2-8-0 (BL) J Tate 14/1: 030060: In tch 3f: 10th: AW bow, blnks.3½38a
4360} BLUE SAPPHIRE 29 [8] 2-8-0 Kimberley Hart (5) 33/1: 600000: Prom 5f: 11th.331a
3354} COLLEGE GALLERY 90 [4] 2-8-8 S Drowne 25/1: 000: Sn outpcd: 12th.¾37a
-- ARANUI [5] 2-8-11 A Culhane 20/1: 0: Soon bhnd: 13th: debut, with R Hollinshead.528a
13 ran   Time 1m 0.3 (2.5)   (Richard Green (Fine Paintings))   N P Littmoden Newmarket, Suffolk

| 35 | 2.50 LADBROKE HCAP DIV 2 3YO+ 0-85 (D)   7f aw rnd   Going 44   +05 Fast | [84] |
£3746   £1132   £551   £260   3 yo   rec 1 lb

4620} FIRST MAITE 6 [1] S R Bowring 6-10-0 (84)(bl) S Finnamore (7) 11/4 FAV: 210001: 6 b g Komaite -91a
Marina Plata (Julio Mariner) Prom, drvn to chall fnl 1f, styd on gamely, led nr line, rdn out: gd time: well bckd:
blnks reapplied: earlier in '99 scored at York (rtd h'cap), Haydock (h'cap) & Ascot (rtd h'cap, rtd 103, rtd 77a on
sand): '98 wnr at Ripon, Ascot & here at Southwell (rtd 83a & 91): suited by 5/6f on turf & a sharp 7f on sand,
stays 1m: acts on firm, loves gd/soft, soft & fibresand: handles any trk: eff with/without blnks/visor: often
wears a t-strap: tough/useful gldg who could well follow up under a penalty, well h'capped on sand.
4368} TAKHLID 28 [5] D W Chapman 8-9-10 (80) A Culhane 13/2: 141002: 8 b h Nureyev - Savonnerie (Irish¾85a
River) Led after 2f, rdn/prsd 1f out, styd on well, just hdd nr fin: op 9/2: earlier in '99 won thrice here at
Southwell (clmrs/h'caps), Lingfield (2, h'caps) & thrice at W'hampton (clmrs, rtd 84a & 64 at best): '98 scorer
at Hamilton & Thirsk (h'caps, rtd 74 & 64a): v eff btwn 6f & 8.4f: acts on firm & soft, loves both AWs: tough.
4342} ALMAZHAR 30 [6] J L Eyre 4-8-8 (64) T Williams 4/1: 000263: 4 b g Last Tycoon - Mosaique Bleue2½64a
(Shirley Heights) Prom, drvn fnl 2f, onepace: tchd 5/1: earlier in '99 rattled off a hat-trick at Redcar (ladies
amat h'cap) & twice here at Southwell (h'caps, rtd 66a & 52 at best): eff at 6f/1m, tried 10f: acts on fast,
loves fibresand/Southwell: best without blnks/visor: handles any trk, likes a sharp one.
4384} KEEN HANDS 27 [7] Mrs N Macauley 3-8-12 (69)(vis) R Price 16/1: 600364: Led 2f/no extra over 1f out.265a
4499} MR BERGERAC 18 [4] 8-9-3 (73) T Sprake 16/1: 512065: Rdn chasing ldrs, held fnl 2f: op 12/1.1½66a
4510} ONLY FOR GOLD 17 [9] 4-8-1 (57) Iona Wands (5) 5/1: 202336: Sn rdn mid-div/nvr on terms: AW bow.1½47a
4131} MAI TAI 45 [2] 4-7-11 (53)(vis) Kimberley Hart (5) 12/1: 000037: Dwelt/nvr on terms: op 14/1, 6 wk abs.141a
4565} MUTABARI 13 [8] 5-8-3 (59)(vis) P Doe (3) 12/1: 550568: Prom 5f: op 14/1.nk46a
4572} ABBAJABBA 11 [11] 3-8-7 (64) S Whitworth 14/1: 606669: Mid-div at best: op 12/1, AW bow.149a
2737} HEVER GOLF GLORY 99 [12] 5-9-1 (71) N Carlisle 20/1: 060040: Al outpcd: 10th: 4 month abs.350a
4565} C HARRY 13 [10] 5-8-9 (65) N Callan (3) 14/1: 216050: Rdn mid-div, btn 2f out: 11th: op 12/1.shd44a
4472} ROI DE DANSE 21 [3] 4-7-10 (52)(4oh) G Bardwell 33/1: 006000: Sn rdn/struggling halfway: 12th.619a
12 ran   Time 1m 29.3 (2.7)   (S R Bowring)   S R Bowring Edwinstowe, Notts

| 36 | 3.25 LILY SELLER 2YO (G)   1m aw rnd   Going 44   -19 Slow |
£2029   £569   £277

4567} TOWER OF SONG 13 [8] M R Channon 2-8-11 Paul Cleary (7) 8/1: 053501: 2 ch g Perugino - New71a
Rochelle (Lafontaine) Held up, smooth prog/led over 2f out, sn in command, styd on strongly, pushed out: op
6/1: sold to Mr D Chapman for 5,000 gns: 1st success: rnr-up on debut earlier in '99 (auct mdn, rtd 72): eff
at 7f/1m, prob stays 10f: acts on firm & gd, fibresand, prob handles soft & any trk: likes selling grade.
4567} HEATHYARDS MATE 13 [4] R Hollinshead 2-8-11 P M Quinn (5) 15/8 FAV: 005422: 2 b g Timeless Times 8 58a
- Quenlyn (Welsh Pageant) Chsd ldrs, rdn/chsd wnr over 1f out, nvr any impress: well bckd, tchd 100/30: rnr-
up earlier in '99 (sell h'cap, rtd 57a, plcd on turf, rtd 72, prob flattered, auct mdn): eff around 1m/8.5f:
handles fast, gd/firm & fibresand: caught a tartar here but clr of rem, has shown enough to win similar.
4454} GENTLE ANNE 22 [14] Ronald Thompson 2-8-6 A Daly 7/1: 506663: 2 b f Faustus - Gentle Stream445a
(Sandy Creek) Prom, drvn 2f out, sn outpcd by wnr: tchd 9/1: AW bow: clr of rem: rtd 65 at best in '98 (mdn):
prob stays 1m, tried 9f & further shld suit in time: sell h'caps could suit best.
3345} FRENCH MASTER 91 [9] P C Haslam 2-8-11 (vis) T Eaves (7) 5/1: 463364: Dwelt, sn chsd ldrs, held640a
fnl 2f: 3 month abs/AW bow, visor reapplied.
4567} DR DUKE 13 [12] Dean McKeown 20/1: 200055: Prom 6f.¾39a
4557} CHURCH FARM FLYER 13 [15] 2-8-6 L Newman (7) 10/1: 0066: Chsd ldrs 3f out/sn held: AW bow.1½30a
3971} SEASAME PARK 55 [11] 2-8-11 T Sprake 8/1: 214027: Prom 6f: op 7/1, 8 wk abs.330a
4570} ROCK ON ROBIN 11 [3] (vis) A Culhane 14/1: 656008: Dwelt/bhd, late gains/no threat: op 12/1.819a
4184} NO COMMITMENT 42 [5] 2-8-11 K W Marks 25/1: 0009: Chsd ldrs 5f: tchd 33/1, 6 wk abs/AW bow.215a
-- SCARLET TANAGER [13] 2-8-6 S Drowne 16/1: 0: Wide/mid-div at best: 10th: op 10/1, debut.nk9a
4570} RED KING 11 [16] 2-8-11 G Carter 20/1: 000000: Al rear: 11th: tchd 25/1: AW bow.2½9a
4229} FORTHECHOP 39 [1] 2-8-11 J Tate 50/1: 600: Dwelt, rdn to lead after 2f, hdd over 2f out/wknd: 12th.½8a
4517} SALLY ANN 17 [10] 2-8-6 P Doe (3) 20/1: 000500: Led 2f, cl-up 5f: 13th: AW bow.nk2a
4454} Bandolera Boy 22 [6] 2-8-11 A McGlone 50/1:   4454} Cool Location 22 [2] 2-8-6 (BL) Martin Dwyer 50/1:
4406} K Ace The Joint 25 [7] 2-8-11 (BL) S Finnamore (7) 50/1:
16 ran   Time 1m 43.4 (5.0)   (M G St Quinton)   M R Channon Upper Lambourn, Berks

| 37 | 3.55 IRIS AMAT HCAP 3YO+ 0-80 (G)   1m6f aw   Going 44   -21 Slow | [51] |
£1976   £554   £269   3 yo   rec 8 lb

*6 VIRGIN SOLDIER 4 [12] M Johnston 3-9-10 (55)(5ex) Mrs C Williams (3) 10/11 FAV: 021111: 3 ch g Waajib - 73a
Never Been Chaste (Posse) Led/dsptd lead, al travelling well, went on over 4f out, in command fnl 2f, unchal/easily:
well bckd: recent Lingfield wnr (h'cap): earlier in '99 scored again at Lingfield (AW h'cap) & Musselburgh (h'cap,
rtd 51 & 58), earlier with T J Etherington: plcd in '98 (mdn, rtd 62): eff at 12f/2m: acts on gd & gd/soft, both
AWs: handles a sharp or gall trk: best without blnks: runs well for an amat: effortless success, shld win again.
3822} BUSTLING RIO 65 [10] P C Haslam 3-9-10 (55) Miss A Armitage (5) 20/1: 414342: 3 b g Up And At 'Em- 7 61a
- Une Venitienne (Green Dancer) Dwelt/bhd, styd on well fnl 3f, nrst fin: op 14/1: 2 month abs: earlier in '99
scored here at Southwell (h'cap, rtd 60a) & Pontefract (h'cap, rtd 61): eff at 11/12f, stays 14.7f well: acts on
gd & fibresand: runs well fresh: handles a sharp or gall trk: caught a tartar here, should be winning soon.
4179} NOUKARI 42 [9] P D Evans 6-11-3 (68) Miss E Folkes (5) 9/2: 145013: 6 b g Darshaan - Noufiyla (Top 5 67a
Ville) Chsd ldrs, rdn 3f out, kept on, nvr pace to chall: op 6/1: jumps fit, recent Stratford & Wincanton wnr (h'cap
hdles, rtd 104h eff at 2m on firm & gd): earlier in '99 scored at Lingfield (AW h'cap), Chester (clmr), Newmarket,
Catterick (amat h'cap), Pontefract (stks) & Lingfield (AW stks, rtd 74 & 73a at best): '98 Southwell & Lingfield wnr
(h'caps, rtd 63a & 63): eff at 10/14.7f on firm, soft & both AWs: handles any trk: most tough & genuine gldg.
4577} GRAND CRU 11 [13] J Cullinan 8-9-10 (47)(vis)(14oh) Miss L Vollaro (7) 33/1: 000034: Bhd, late gains.1¼44$
20

SOUTHWELL (Fibresand) FRIDAY NOVEMBER 12TH Lefthand, Sharp, Oval Track

4397} **JAMAICAN FLIGHT** 27 [8] 6-11-7 (72) Mr S Dobson (5) 14/1: 256505: Led 12f, fdd: recent jmps rnr.   **3 65a**
4577} **ST LAWRENCE** 11 [14] 5-9-10 (47)(4oh) Mr Nicky Tinkler (7) 20/1: 040206: Prom 12f.   **¾ 39a**
4095} **PALAIS** 48 [2] 4-10-11 (62) Mr S Walker (5) 40/1: 405007: Rear, mod gains: jumps fit.   **¾ 53a**
4577} **LANCER** 11 [6] 7-9-10 (47)(vis)(3oh) Mrs L Pearce 9/1: 200428: Nvr on terms: op 7/1.   **5 31a**
4231} **LE SAUVAGE** 39 [15] 4-9-10 (47)(7oh) Miss J Lindley (7) 66/1: 000569: Mid-div at best: jumps fit.   **10 20a**
4571} **SANTA LUCIA** 11 [16] 3-9-12 (57) Mr I Mongan 9/1: 666020: Al towards rear: 10th: AW bow.   **7 21a**
--   **Sefton Blake** [5] 5-10-0 (51)(4ow)(9oh) Mr J Owen (0) 50/1:
4587} **Swift 10** [3] 5-12-0 (79) Mr T Best (5) 12/1:
--   **Sudden Spin** [4] 9-10-4 (55) Miss Diana Jones 40/1:
4577} **Westminster 11** [7] 7-11-1 (60)(6ow) Mr M Jenkins (0) 25/1:
3970} **Castle Secret** 55 [1] 13-9-10 (47)(12oh) Mr G Richards (1) 50/1:
4231} **Almamzar** 39 [11] 9-10-7 (58)(11ow)(35oh) Mrs R Howell (0) 100/1:
16 ran   Time 3m 08.9 (9.1)   (J David Abell)   M Johnston Middleham, N Yorks

WOLVERHAMPTON (Fibresand) SATURDAY NOVEMBER 13TH Lefthand, V Sharp Track

Official Going   STANDARD. Stalls: 7f - Outside, Rem - Inside

38   7.00 JAZZ HCAP 3YO+ 0-65 (F)   1m100y aw   Going 50   +03 Fast   [63]
£2347   £660   £322   3 yo rec 2 lb

4513} **KASS ALHAWA** 18 [2] D W Chapman 6-9-1 (50) D Mernagh (5) 9/2: 006431: 6 b g Shirley Heights - Silver **56a**
Braid (Miswaki) Prom, rdn fnl 2f, edged left/led ins last, rdn out: gd time, tchd 5/1: earlier in '99 won at
Beverley (h'cap, rtd 73 & 50a): '98 wnr at Southwell (rtd 41a) & Beverley again (2, h'caps, rtd 72): eff btwn
6f & 8.5f, stays 10f: acts on firm, gd/soft & both AWs: eff weight carrier, runs well fresh: loves Beverley.
2781} **ARC** 99 [11] F Jordan 5-9-13 (62) N Callan (3) 16/1: 622102: 5 b g Archway - Columbian Sand **1¼ 65a**
(Salmon Leap) Chsd ldrs, ev ch ins last, rdn/held nr fin: op 10/1, a 4 month abs: earlier in '99 won here at
W'hampton (mdn h'cap, rtd 67a) & Carlisle (stks, rtd 64): eff over 7f/8.5f, stays 10f: acts on firm, gd & f/sand:
handles any trk: tough & consistent, best held up for late run: shld win more races on sand.
4568} **BLUSHING GRENADIER** 14 [7] S R Bowring 7-9-7 (56) R Lappin 8/1: 235003: 7 ch g Salt **1¼ 52a**
Dome - La Duse (Junius) Cl-up, led over 2f out till ins last, rdn/no extra: tchd 14/1: earlier in '99 won at
Redcar & Carlisle (clmrs, rtd 67 & 55a): '98 W'hampton (sell, rtd 55a), Warwick (clmr, M J F Godley), Haydock
(sell h'cap) & Newcastle (h'cap, rtd 63): eff btwn 5f/8.5f, all wins at 6f: acts on fast, both AWs: wears binks
or visor: likes to dominate: handles any trk: tough gldg, spot on back at 6/7f.
4593} **LEGAL ISSUE** 10 [9] B S Rothwell 7-9-7 (56) T Sprake 8/1: 030054: Dwelt/rear, styd on fnl 2f, nrst fin. **1¼ 55a**
4581} **DAVIS ROCK** 12 [10] 5-9-9 (58) Martin Dwyer 3/1 FAV: 203515: Dwelt, rdn/towards rear, prog fnl 4f, **4 49a**
nvr pace to chall: tchd 7/2: earlier in '99 scored at Nottingham (h'cap, rtd 49 & 46a): '98 wnr at Lingfield (fill
h'cap) & W'hampton (sell, rtd 63a & 60): '97 Folkestone wnr (h'cap, rtd 68): eff at 7f/1m: acts on firm & soft,
both AWs: eff weight carrier: handles any trk: on a fair mark, could win again
4521} **GRANNYS RELUCTANCE** 18 [12] 3-8-13 (50) T Sprake 8/1: 653626: Led 6f, fdd: op 6/1. **1¾ 38a**
4576} **MARGARETS DANCER** 12 [1] 4-8-13 (48)(t) Dale Gibson 16/1: 006557: Mid-div, btn fnl 2f: op 12/1. **nk 35a**
4593} **ADOBE** 10 [4] 4-9-0 (49)(t) T G McLaughlin 11/2: 533008: Held up, nvr factor: tchd 10/1. **3 30a**
4387} **THE STAGER** 28 [8] 7-9-10 (59)(t) S Whitworth 14/1: 010069: Dwelt/al rear: op 10/1. **8 28a**
4615} **STONE OF DESTINY** 7 [3] 4-9-6 (55) J Bosley 25/1: 01-000: Trkd ldrs 5f: 10th: AW bow. **6 14a**
4593} **RIVERSDALE** 10 [13] 3-9-2 (53) T Williams 11/2: 340020: Prom 5f: 11th: op 9/2: AW bow. **½ 11a**
3441} **Clear Night** 87 [6] 3-9-4 (55) P Fredericks (3) 33/1:   4501} **Flame Tower** 19 [5] 4-9-9 (58)(t) R Studholme (5) 33/1:
13 ran   Time 1m 50.2 (4.0)   (J B Wilcox)   D W Chapman Stillington, N Yorks

39   7.30 BLUES MDN 3YO+ (D)   1m100y aw   Going 50   -00 Slow
£2801   £848   £414   £197   3 yo rec 2 lb

4519} **POLAR FAIR** 18 [3] J Noseda 3-8-9 M Tebbutt 6/1: 000301: 3 ch f Polar Falcon - Fair Country (Town And **65a**
Country) Handy, went on halfway, rdn/edged right ins last, styd on well, rdn out: op 5/1, AW bow: plcd earlier
in '99 (rtd 58, mdn): mod form prev: eff arnd 1m/9f on fibresand & soft: acts on a sharp/undul trk.
4334} **HEATHYARDS JAKE** 32 [11] R Hollinshead 3-9-0 P M Quinn (5) 15/2: 232002: 3 b c Nomination - Safe **1¼ 67$**
Bid (Sure Blade) Held up, rdn & kept on fnl 3f, not pace to chall: op 6/1: plcd numerous times earlier in '99
(rtd 60 & 67a): plcd sev times in '98 (rtd 72 & 78a): eff btwn 7f/9f, poss stays 12f: acts on firm, soft &
fibresand: handles any trk: still a mdn, headgear may help.
4585} **HAYMAKER** 11 [9] B S Rothwell 3-9-0 R Lappin 5/4 FAV: 632023: 3 b g Thatching - Susie Sunshine **1¾ 64a**
(Waajib) Prom, chsd wnr 3f out, ch 2f out, kept on fnl 1f: well bckd, AW bow, clr of rem: rnr-up earlier in '99
(h'cap, rtd 74, I A Balding): eff at 7f, tried 1m: handles firm, soft & f/sand: handles a sharp or stiff/gall trk.
4603} **SADDLE MOUNTAIN** 9 [5] Lady Herries 3-8-9 T Sprake 9/4: 64-: Led 1f, btn 2f out: AW bow. **11 43a**
4198} **ABOVE BOARD** 42 [7] 4-9-2 T G McLaughlin 50/1: 006005: Dwelt, nvr on terms: 6 wk abs. **4 40$**
4496} **ALEANBH** 19 [6] 4-9-2 B McHugh (7) 50/1: 0-06: Held up, mid-div at best: AW bow. **1¼ 38a**
--   **TWO STEP** [1] 3-8-9 Dale Gibson 20/1: 7: Nvr factor: debut. **1½ 30a**
--   **JUST FOR YOU** [1] 3-9-0 G Faulkner (3) 11/2: 8: Cl-up, led 7f out till 4f out, fdd: tchd 10/1, debut. **½ 34a**
--   **KATIE JANE** [8] 4-8-11 N Callan (3) 20/1: 9: Al towards rear: Flat debut, jumps fit. **shd 29a**
4504} **SUPERCHIEF** 19 [12] 4-9-2 (t) S Sanders 20/1: 0-0000: Chsd ldrs 5f: 10th. **4 26a**
4598} **WOOLLY WINSOME** 9 [13] 3-9-0 J Bosley (7) 7/1: -24300: Held up, nvr factor: 11th: op 5/1. **5 16a**
4566} **Barann** 14 [10] 3-9-0 Claire Bryan (7) 50/1:   4496} **Camerosa** 19 [2] 3-9-0 D Griffiths 50/1:
13 ran   Time 1m 50.4 (4.2)   (Sir Gordon Brunton)   J Noseda Newmarket, Suffolk

40   8.00 NEW ORLEANS HCAP 3YO+ 0-75 (E)   5f aw rnd   Going 50   +04 Fast   [73]
£2762   £836   £408   £194

4518} **ECUDAMAH** 18 [6] Miss Jacqueline S Doyle 3-9-1 (60) T Sprake 16/1: 000041: 3 ch g Mukaddamah - Great **67a**
Land (Friend's Choice) Cl-up, led halfway, styd on strongly, rdn out: gd time, op 12/1, AW bow: rtd 75 earlier in
'99 (mdn, reapp), subs tumbled down h'cap (earlier with K Bell): trained by R Phillips in '98 & plcd numerous
times (rtd 78, incl h'caps): eff at 5/6f, tried 7f: acts on fast & soft grnd: handles a sharp/gall trk.
4586} **TORRENT** 11 [9] D W Chapman 4-8-13 (58)(bl) Lynsey Hanna (7) 4/1 JT FAV: 032022: 4 ch g Prince **1¾ 60a**
Sabo - Maiden Pool (Sharpen Up) Held up, prog fnl 2f, kept on tho' not pace wnr: AW bow: earlier in '99 won at

WOLVERHAMPTON (Fibresand)   SATURDAY NOVEMBER 13TH   Lefthand, V Sharp Track

Beverley (class stks, rtd 75): '98 Catterick (mdn) & Thirsk wnr (h'cap, rtd 83, with T D Barron): eff at 5/6f,
tried 7f: acts on firm, gd/soft & f/sand, handles soft: handles any trk: has tried a t-strap, wears blnks.
4267} **RUSSIAN ROMEO 38** [10] B A McMahon 4-9-10 (69)(bl) L Newton 13/2: 112303: 4 b g Soviet Lad -   ¾   **69a**
Aotearoa (Flash Of Steel) Trkd ldrs, rdn/edged left ins last, kept on: op 8/1: earlier in '99 scored at W'hampton
(h'cap) & Southwell (class stks, rtd 69a & 64): '98 Chester wnr (clmr, rtd 72 & 73a): eff at 6f, tried 7f: acts
on fast & f/sand, prob gd/soft: eff in blnks/visor, can front run or come from bhd: runs well fresh.
4604} **SANTANDRE 9** [2] R Hollinshead 3-10-0 (73) P M Quinn (5) 14/1: 100304: Sn outpcd, styd on fnl 2f,   1¼   **70a**
nrst fin: tchd 16/1, top weight: prob appreciate a return to further.
4572} **HEAVENLY MISS 12** [3] 5-8-6 (51)(bl) D Mernagh (5) 4/1 JT FAV: 502105: Chsd ldrs, hmpd/lost place   ¾   **46a**
before halfway, kept on fnl 1f, no threat: tchd 5/1.
4450} **PIGGY BANK 24** [12] 3-9-1 (60) T Lucas 11/1: 000046: Chsd ldrs 4f: AW bow.   ½   **53a**
4568} **BAPTISMAL ROCK 14** [7] 5-8-10 (55) S Whitworth 7/1: 366307: Held up, nvr on terms: tchd 8/1.   1¼   **45a**
4261} **SAMWAR 39** [11] 7-9-13 (72)(bl) R Fitzpatrick (3) 14/1: 100608: Dwelt, nvr factor: op 12/1.   1½   **58a**
3422} **MISS BANANAS 87** [13] 4-8-12 (57) D Meah (7) 8/1: 050019: Chsd ldrs 4f: op 6/1: 12 wk abs.   ½   **41a**
4538} **DIVINE MISS P 16** [4] 6-9-11 (70) D Sweeney 8/1: 020000: Prom 3f: 10th: tchd 10/1.   1¼   **51a**
4565} **CONSULTANT 14** [5] 3-9-6 (65) R Thomas (7) 11/1: 060000: Chsd ldrs, btn 3 out: 11th: op 8/1.   shd   **46a**
2687} **AA YOUKNOWNOTHING 99** [1] 3-9-13 (72) S Finnamore (7) 20/1: 003000: Led 1f/sn held: 12th: abs.   ½   **51a**
2687} **LEGAL VENTURE 99** [8] 3-9-0 (59)(vis) T G McLaughlin 10/1: 060200: Dwelt/al rear: 13th: op 7/1, abs.   2½   **31a**
13 ran   Time 1m 02.5 (2.3)   (Sanford Racing)   Miss Jacqueline S Doyle Upper Lambourn, Berks

---

41 **8.30 SAXOPHONE MDN 2YO (D)   7f aw rnd   Going 50   -26 Slow**
£2749   £832   £406   £193

4210} **JOELY GREEN 42** [4] N P Littmoden 2-9-0 T G McLaughlin 8/1: 263061: 2 b c Binary Star - Comedy   **69a**
Lady (Comedy Star) Chsd ldrs, kept on gamely for press to lead nr line: op 6/1, 6 wk abs: plcd form earlier in
'99 (rtd 66a, h'cap): eff at 5/6f, stays 7f well: acts on f/sand: tried a visor, best without: runs well fresh.
4549} **ISABELLA R 15** [1] Sir Mark Prescott 2-8-9 S Sanders 4/5 FAV: 2532: 2 ch f Indian Ridge - Sun Screen   hd   **63a**
(Caerleon) Chsd ldr, rdn/led ins last, hdd nr line: well bckd tho' op 4/9, clr rem, AW bow: earlier in '99 2nd at
Catterick (mdn, debut, rtd 71): eff at 5/7f: acts on f/sand, gd/soft & soft grnd: likes a sharp/undul trk.
4431} **BONDI BAY 25** [5] A T Murphy 2-8-9 Dean McKeown 25/1: 000003: 2 b f Catrail - Sodium's Niece   4   **55$**
(Northfields) Rdn in rear, styd on fnl 2f, no threat to front pair: op 16/1: rtd 62 & 45a earlier in '99 (mdns,
tried t-strap & visor): half brother to 3 wnrs: prob stys 7f & handles fibresand.
4582} **SHAYZAN 11** [8] W R Muir 2-9-0 Martin Dwyer 3/1: 004: Keen/led, rdn/hdd ins last: op 9/2, AW bow.   ¾   **59a**
5   **KATIES VALENTINE 5** [3] 2-8-9 P Hanagan (7) 6/1: 045: Chsd ldrs 5f: tchd 10/1: quick reapp.   4   **46a**
4607} **MARITUN LAD 8** [6] 2-9-0 N Callan (3) 40/1: 06: Dwelt, sn prom, btn 3f out: AW bow.   7   **40a**
4132} **CROMABOO COUNTESS 46** [2] 2-8-9 J Bramhill 66/1: 0007: Al rear: 6 wk abs.   6   **25a**
4310} **EARLEY SESSION 33** [7] 2-9-0 Dale Gibson 25/1: 008: Bhd halfway: AW bow.   3   **24a**
8 ran   Time 1m 31.5 (5.3)   (Paul J Dixon)   N P Littmoden Newmarket, Suffolk

---

42 **9.00 DIXIELAND SELLER 2YO (G)   5f aw rnd   Going 50   -06 Slow**
£1850   £518   £251

4212} **DIMMING OF THE DAY 42** [1] B J Meehan 2-8-6 (bl) Dean McKeown 7/4: 220421: 2 ch f Muhtarram -   **63a**
Darkness At Noon (Night Shift) Made all, clr over 1f out, pushed out: sold for 5,600gns, nicely bckd, 6 wk abs:
rnr-up thrice earlier in '99 (rtd 63a & 57): eff at 5f on firm & f/sand: handles a stiff/gall or sharp trk:
eff in blnks, runs well fresh: enjoys sell grade.
4589} **SHOULDHAVEGONEHOME 10** [2] P D Evans 2-8-11 (vis) T G McLaughlin 12/1: 300002: 2 ch f Up And   3   **59$**
At'Em - Gentle Papoose (Commanche Run) Chsd wnr, rdn & kept on fnl 2f, al held: op 8/1, visor reapplied: earlier
in '99 scored at Musselburgh (sell, rtd 68 & 58a): eff at 5f, tried 6f: acts on fast, soft & fibresand: handles
any trk, likes a sharp one: eff with/without a visor: has run well fresh: enjoys sellers.
4517} **PETRIE 18** [4] M R Channon 2-8-11 S Drowne 6/5 FAV: 055423: 2 ch g Fraam - Canadian Capers   2½   **52a**
(Ballacashtal) Chsd ldrs, rdn/outpcd fnl 2f: well bckd, tchd 11/8, AW bow: rnr-up earlier in '99 (sell, rtd 60):
eff at 5/5.7f, tried 7f, return to 6f+ cld suit: handles gd/soft & fibresand.
1177} **LADY SANDROVITCH 99** [3] R A Fahey 2-8-6 B McHugh (6) 9/1: 544: Nvr on terms: op 6/1, 6 mth abs.   ¾   **45a**
4514} **MIKE THE SPUD 18** [5] 2-8-11 G Parkin 7/1: 030505: Chsd ldrs 3f: op 5/1, AW bow.   1½   **46a**
4409} **DIAMOND ISLE 26** [6] 2-8-6 D Mernagh 25/1: 630006: Chsd ldrs 3f: AW bow.   hd   **40a**
4212} **FAL N ME 42** [7] 2-8-6 T Williams 66/1: -007: Al bhd: 6 wk abs.   19   **0a**
7 ran   Time 1m 03.00 (2.8)   (Geoff Howard Spink & Lindy Regis)   B J Meehan Upper Lambourn, Berks

---

43 **9.30 B HOLLIDAY HCAP 3YO+ 0-60 (F)   1m4f aw   Going 50   -12 Slow**   **[60]**
£2379   £669   £327   3 yo rec 6 lb

4615} **INCH PERFECT 7** [11] R A Fahey 4-9-11 (57) P Hanagan (7) 3/1 FAV: 111131: 4 b g Inchinor - Scarlet   **63a**
Veil (Tyrnavos) Held up, prog 4f out, rdn ins last & styd on well to lead nr line: nicely bckd: earlier in '99 won at
Southwell (reapp, sell, rtd 56a), Redcar (sell h'cap, J Hetherton), Pontefract, Newcastle & Bath (h'caps, rtd 63):
eff at 10/12f: acts on gd/soft & fibresand, any trk: has run well fresh: in fine form.
4522} **FOREST DREAM 18** [2] Lady Herries 4-9-9 (55) P Doe (3) 4/1: 100222: 4 b f Warrshan - Sirenivo (Sir   hd   **60a**
Ivor) Prom, led over 2f out, clr over 1f out, hdd nr line: tchd 5/1: earlier in '99 won at Lingfield (mdn h'cap,
rtd 57), rnr-up on sand (h'cap, rtd 56a): rtd 63 & 53a in '98: eff at 1m, suited by 10/12f: acts on firm, gd/soft &
fibresand: handles a sharp one: a likley type for similar.
4522} **DARE 18** [8] P D Evans 4-9-8 (54) Joanna Badger (7) 7/1: 111153: 4 b g Beveled - Run Amber Run   1¼   **57a**
(Run The Gantlet) Held up/rcd keenly, led 3f out till 2f out, not qckn cl home: clr of rem: earlier in '99 won at
Hamilton, Salisbury, Southwell & Leicester (h'caps, rtd 55a & 53): unplcd over hdles prev & mod Flat form (E
James): eff at 1m/12f on gd/soft, soft & f/sand: runs well fresh: best without vis & runs well for an apprentice.
4592} **CAEROSA 10** [7] M Johnston 4-8-10 (42)(bl) Dean McKeown 100/30: 512154: Held up, eff halfway,   7   **36a**
held fnl 2f: op 4/1: met some in-form rivals here tonight.
4564} **COUNT DE MONEY 14** [5] 4-9-11 (57) S Finnamore (7) 13/2: 545125: Chsd ldrs, held fnl 3f.   2½   **47a**
4503} **WESTERN COMMAND 19** [3] 3-9-8 (60) R Price 16/1: 024206: Keen/prom, led 4f out, sn hdd & fdd.   ¾   **49a**
4579} **MY LEGAL EAGLE 12** [6] 5-9-7 (53) P Fitzsimons (5) 12/1: 213047: Chsd ldrs 10f: op 9/1.   1   **41a**
4566} **DOBERMAN 14** [10] 4-9-0 (46)(vis) T G McLaughlin 20/1: 403648: Held up, btn 2f out: op 14/1.   2½   **30a**
4519} **REPTON 18** [4] 4-9-7 (53) J Bosley (7) 12/1: 300069: Dwelt, al towards rear: op 7/1.   5   **30a**
4503} **KI CHI SAGA 19** [9] 7-9-3 (49)(bl) P McCabe 25/1: 001000: Keen/prom, led 9f out, hdd 4f out/fdd: 10th.   3   **22a**
4392} **DESIRES GOLD 28** [1] 4-8-8 (40) D Mernagh (5) 40/1: -00050: Led 3f, btn 3f out: 11th: AW bow.   nk   **12a**

22

WOLVERHAMPTON (Fibresand)   SATURDAY NOVEMBER 13TH   Lefthand, V Sharp Track

1599} **NORTHERN SUN 99** [12] 5-9-12 (58) Lisa Somers (7) 16/1: 532030: Sn bhnd: 12th: 6 mth abs.   *dist*   0a
12 ran   Time 2m 41.00 (7.4)   (Tommy Staunton)   R A Fahey Butterwick, N Yorks

SOUTHWELL (Fibresand)   MONDAY NOVEMBER 15TH   Lefthand, Sharp, Oval Track

Official Going   STANDARD. Stalls: Outside.

44	12.05 ROWAN HCAP DIV I 3YO+ 0-85 (D) 6f aw rnd Going 39 +09 Fast [85]
	£3343 £1008 £489 £229

4604} **CARLTON 11** [6] D R C Elsworth 5-7-11 (54) P Fessey 10/11 FAV: 312311: 5 ch g Thatching - Hooray   70a
Lady (Ahonoora) Sn tracking ldrs, smooth prog to lead over 1f out, pulled clr ins last, pushed out, readily: hvly
bckd: fast time: earlier in '99 won at Doncaster (subs disqal), Epsom (h'caps, G Lewis) & Windsor (2, h'caps,
rtd 77): '98 wnr again at Windsor & Newbury (h'caps, rtd 69 & 52a): eff at 7f, stays 1m, suited by 6f on firm,
hvy & fibresand: handles any trk, likes Windsor: has run well fresh with/without blnks: well h'capped on sand.
4134} **ALJAZ 48** [9] Miss Gay Kelleway 9-8-7 (62)(2ow) N Callan (0) 10/1: 002022: 9 b g Al Nasr - Santa   6   63a
Linda (Sir Ivor) Handy, led over 2f out, rdn/hdd over 1f out & sn no ch with wnr: op 8/1: 7 wk abs: earlier in
'99 won here at Southwell (C/D, h'cap, rtd 63a): '98 wnr for Mrs N Macauley at W'hampton (3, clmr & 2 h'caps, rtd
73a): stays 7f, suited by 5/6f: acts on hvy, equitrack, loves fibresand/W'hampton: likes to race with/force the pace.
4538} **BLACK ARMY 18** [2] J M P Eustace 4-9-3 (74) J Tate 14/1: 005303: 4 b g Aragon - Morgannwg (Simply   2½   66a
Great) Sn handy, ch 2f out, rdn/no extra fnl 1f: op 10/1: earlier in '99 scored at Beverley (h'cap, rtd 72 & 74a):
rtd 74 in '98 (mdn): eff at 6f, poss just best at 5f: acts on fast, hvy & fibresand, any trk: apprec return to 5f.
4604} **SWINO 11** [1] P D Evans 5-7-13 (56)(bl) M Henry 12/1: 054034: Rear, rdn & hung left 2f out/mod gains.   nk   47a
28   **PRIX STAR 4** [3] 4-8-1 (58)(vis) G Bardwell 14/1: 060245: Led 4f, fdd: op 10/1, qck reapp.   hd   48a
4572} **MALLIA 14** [11] 6-9-4 (75)(bl) T Sprake 9/1: 000046: Rear, wide over 2f out, mod gains: op 7/1.   1   63a
4267} **BRUTAL FANTASY 40** [8] 5-8-11 (68) A McCarthy (3) 16/1: 260007: Cl-up 4f: op 12/1, 6 wk absence.   1¾   52a
4604} **POLLY MILLS 11** [4] 3-10-0 (85)(vis) Joanna Badger (7) 25/1: 054008: Rdn/towards rear, nvr factor.   2½   62a
4394} **INCHALONG 30** [7] 4-8-0 (57)(vis) T Williams 9/1: 061029: Sn rear/rdn, no impress: op 6/1.   ¾   32a
4572} **YOUNG BIGWIG 14** [5] 5-9-3 (74) G Parkin 9/1: 101250: Cl-up 4f: op 6/1, capable of better.   2½   42a
4297} **YABINT EL SHAM 37** [10] 3-8-9 (66)(t) L Newton 25/1: 000000: Mid-div, btn 2f out: 11th: AW bow.   hd   33a
11 ran   Time 1m 15.10 (1.8)   (City Slickers)   D R C Elsworth Whitsbury, Hants.

45	12.35 ASH SELLER DIV I 3YO+ (G) 1m aw rnd Going 39 -22 Slow
	£1605 £448 £216 3 yo rec 2 lb

4449} **RAMBO WALTZER 26** [6] D Nicholls 7-9-5 Iona Wands (5) 4/1: 000001: 7 b g Rambo Dancer - Vindictive   62a
Lady (Foolish Pleasure) Sn handy, led over 2f out, styd on gamely ins last, op 9/4: mkt drifter, op 9/4:
earlier in '99 won at Catterick, Thirsk, Edinburgh (h'caps, rtd 71) & Southwell (clmr, rtd 75a): '98 W'hampton & Southwell
wnr (2, h'caps, rtd 91a & 72): eff at 7f/9.5f: acts on fast, soft & fibresand: sharp trk specialist tho' handles
any: runs well fresh: enjoys sell/claiming grade & can be placed to win more of these this winter.
4213} **APPROACHABLE 44** [2] Miss S J Wilton 4-9-5 C Rutter 11/2: 311662: 4 b c Known Fact - Western Approach   ½   60a
(Gone West) Keen/trkd ldrs, ch & kept on fnl 1f, held by wnr nr fin: jumps fit (mod form): earlier in '99 scored
thrice at W'hampton (mdn h'cap for R Phillips & 2 clmrs for current connections, rtd 65a): unplcd for J Gosden
in '98 (tried blnks): eff btwn 7f & 10f on both AWs, loves W'hampton: enjoys claim grade, win again.
4496} **LILANITA 11** [5] B Palling 4-8-9 T Sprake 20/1: 005043: 4 b f Anita's Prince - Jimlil (Nicholas Bill)   hd   49a
Led/dsptd lead 6f, no extra well ins last, op 16/1: plcd earlier in '99 (rtd 52, h'cap, rtd 42 at best on turf, clmr):
'98 Chepstow wnr (sole win, seller, rtd 56): eff at 7f/11f: acts on fast, gd/soft & both AW's, likes a sharp/undul trk.
4276} **WAIKIKI BEACH 38** [9] G L Moore 8-9-5 (bl) S Whitworth 11/2: 533034: Dwelt, prog halfway/nvr threat.   2½   54a
4481} **SHOTLEY MARIE 23** [7] 4-8-9 (bl) Martin Dwyer 100/1: 000005: Dwelt/bhd, styd on fnl 2f, nrst fin.   5   34$
4463} **NERONIAN 25** [3] 5-9-0 (vis) N Callan (3) 14/1: 004506: Nvr on terms: AW bow.   7   28a
4449} **PRINCESS BELFORT 26** [8] 6-8-9 (vis) J Bramhill 50/1: 000007: Mid-div at best: modest.   1¼   21a
4496} **TIME ON MY HANDS 21** [10] 3-9-3 (t) S Finnamore (7) 20/1: 100008: Sn drvn/mid-div, btn 3f out.   ¾   30a
3655} **SOUNDS SWEET 78** [13] 3-8-7 L Newton 25/1: -00039: Held up, nvr factor: 11 wk absence.   ½   19a
2919} **GODMERSHAM PARK 99** [4] 7-9-0 G Parkin 7/2 FAV: 333460: Led 6f, fdd: 10th: op 3/1: 4 month abs: nk   23a
rnr-up earlier in '99 (rtd 71a, h'cap, tried blnks), subs tumbled down the weights: '98 wnr thrice here at
Southwell (h'caps) & once at W'hampton (h'cap, rtd 78a & 57): eff at 7f/1m on fast & gd, loves fibresand &
Southwell: best without visor/blnks: likes to force the pace on a fair mark.
4548} Bayard Lady 17 [11] 3-8-7 T Williams 20/1:   --   Croft Sands [12] 6-9-0 G Carter 25/1:
616} Amber Regent 99 [14] 4-9-0 R Price 66/1:   1998} Genius 95 [15] 4-9-5 P Fessey 33/1:
4118} Gathering Cloud 49 [1] 3-8-7 S Drowne 25/1:   4564} Ace Of Trumps 16 [16] 3-9-3 (tbl) Dale Gibson 25/1:
16 ran   Time 1m 44.3 (4.9)   (W G Swiers)   D Nicholls Sessay, N.Yorks.

46	1.05 POPLAR MED AUCT MDN 2YO (F) 6f aw rnd Going 39 -18 Slow
	£2253 £633 £309

4507} **FEAST OF ROMANCE 21** [5] Miss Gay Kelleway 2-9-0 S Whitworth 20/1: 0051: 2 b c Pursuit Of Love -   77a
June Fayre (Sagaro) Handy, led 3f out, duelled with rnr-up ins last, styd on gamely, all out: op 14/1, AW bow:
rtd 68 at best from 3 turf starts earlier in '99 (Lingfield stks): apprec this step up to 6f, 7f shld suit:
acts on a sharp trk & much improved on first start on fibresand.
4600} **KATHOLOGY 11** [2] D R C Elsworth 2-9-0 P Fessey 1/2 FAV: 04222: 2 b c College Chapel - Wicken   hd   76a
Wonder (Distant Relative) Cl-up, rdn to chall & ev ch over 1f out, drvn/just held line: well clr of rem, hvly bckd:
rnr-up twice earlier in '99 (mdns, rtd 86): eff at 6/7f on gd/soft, fibresand & any trk: shld win a race.
--   **CLOPTON GREEN** [8] J W Payne 2-9-0 A McGlone V/L: 3: 2 b g Presidium - Silkstone Lady   10   54a
(Puissance) Chsd ldrs, prog/ch 2f out, sn outpcd by thrret pair: tchd 20/1, debut: Feb foal, 11,000gns 2yo,
dam unrcd sister to 3 wnrs: sire a decent miler: shld improve for this.
4508} **FOR HEAVENS SAKE 20** [9] C W Thornton 2-9-0 Dean McKeown 25/1: 04: Bhd, prog/hmpd over 1f   nk   53a
out, kept on fnl 1f, nvr plcd to chall: AW bow, kind ride: will improve over 7f/1m+.
4508} **MARSHALL ST CYR 20** [4] 2-9-0 T G McLaughlin 5/1: 025: Led 3f, btn over 1f out: op 4/1, AW bow.   ¾   51a
4607} **BULAWAYO 10** [3] 2-9-0 L Newton 33/1: 06: Sn rdn/nvr on terms: AW bow.   1½   47a
4582} **PRESTO 13** [10] 2-9-0 K W Marks 20/1: 007: Slowly away, nl towards rear: AW bow.   1½   43a
4569} **DIAMOND VANESSA 14** [7] 2-8-9 R Lappin 50/1: 08: Chsd ldrs 3f: AW bow.   nk   37a

23

4490} **SKYE BLUE** 23 [1] 2-9-0 Paul Cleary (7) 10/1: 59: Bhd 3f out: op 12/1, AW bow.   5 33a
4058} **LAMMOSKI** 53 [6] 2-9-0 M Tebbutt 50/1: 500000: Cl-up 3f: 10th: 7 wk abs/AW bow.   6 22a
10 ran   Time 1m 16.7 (3.4)   (K & W Racing Partnership)   Miss Gay Kelleway Lingfield, Surrey.

---

47   **1.40 ROWAN HCAP DIV II 3YO+ 0-85 (D)**   **6f aw rnd** Going 39 -08 Slow   **[82]**
£3343   £1008   £489   £229

4471} **GARNOCK VALLEY** 24 [10] J Berry 9-8-8 (62) G Carter 10/1: 000211: 9 b g Dowsing - Sunley Sinner   67a
(Try My Best) Towards rear/wide, stdy prog for press fnl 2f, led well ins last, rdn out: op 8/1: earlier in '99 won
at W'hampton (clmr), Lingfield (clmr), here at Southwell (class stks) & Newbury (h'cap, rtd 52 & 62a at best): '98
Musselburgh wnr (h'cap, rtd 57 & 57a): eff btwn 5f & 7f: acts on fast, soft & both AWs: eff with/without blnks:
runs well fresh: eff weight carrier & handles any trk: tough 9yo, can win again.
4296} **TOM TUN** 37 [1] Miss J F Craze 4-9-6 (74) T Williams 100/30: 423002: 4 b g Bold Arrangement - B Grade 1 76a
(Lucky Wednesday) Led, rdn 2f out, styd on well, hdd well ins last: nicely bckd: earlier in '99 won twice here
at Southwell (h'caps, rtd 75a), Newcastle (h'cap) & Doncaster (2, h'cap & stks, rtd 82): '98 wnr at Newcastle &
Southwell (h'caps, rtd 62a & 65): eff at 5/6f on firm, soft & both AW's: handles any trk, likes Southwell &
Doncaster: loves to race with/force the pace: fine effort, likely to be winning again this winter.
4565} **BLUE KITE** 16 [3] N P Littmoden 4-8-12 (66) J Tate 10/1: 012233: 4 ch g Silver Kite - Gold And Blue   ¾ 66a
(Bluebird) Prom, rdn 2f out, just held nr fin: op 7/1: earlier in '99 won at W'hampton (h'cap, rtd 66a, rnr-up
on turf earlier, rtd 65, stks): rtd 78 & 78a in '98: '97 W'hampton wnr (auct mdn, rtd 85a): eff btwn 5/7f on fast
& soft, loves fibresand/W'hampton, handles any trk: best without headgear, has tried a t-strap: nicely hcapped.
4620} **OCKER** 9 [2] Mrs N Macauley 5-9-10 (78) R Fitzpatrick (3) 11/4 FAV: 300554: Cl-up, rdn/edged right   ¾ 76a
over 1f out & held nr fin: nicely bckd: earlier in '99 scored at Thirsk (h'cap), Nottingham (cond stks) & Haydock
(class stks, rtd 102 & 77a at best): '98 Nottingham, Haydock, Newbury & Doncaster wnr (h'caps, rtd 80 & 74a): best
at 5/6f, stays 7f: acts on firm, soft & fibresand, any trk: has run well fresh: best without a visor: tough/prog.
4131} **GENERAL KLAIRE** 48 [7] P M Quinn (5) 12/1: 025215: Held up, kept on well fnl 2f,   nk 72a
nvr able to chall: op 9/1, 7 wk absence: sound effort & a return to 7f will suit.
4573} **JENNELLE** 14 [9] 5-9-2 (70)(e) S Drowne 14/1: 240036: Chsd ldrs wide 4f: op 10/1, eye-shield/AW bow. 2 62a
4610} **MALADERIE** 10 [6] 5-8-7 (61)(BL) Dale Gibson 25/1: 000007: Prom 4f: AW bow.   3 46a
4610} **DEMOLITION JO** 10 [8] 4-8-11 (65)(vis) T G McLaughlin 5/1: 003328: Bhd, hung left/nvr factor: op 4/1. 1¾ 46a
4471} **KHALIK** 24 [5] 5-8-10 (64)(t) S Whitworth 14/1: 100209: Al outpcd rear: op 12/1, AW bow.   5 36a
--   **PALO BLANCO** [4] 8-8-2 (56) G Arnolda (2) 50/1: 5286-0: Chsd ldrs 3f: 10th: long absence. 10 9a
10 ran   Time 1m 16.1 (2.8)   (Robert Aird)   J Berry Cockerham, Lancs.

---

48   **2.10 HAWTHORN AUCT MDN 2YO (F)**   **1m aw rnd** Going 39 -35 Slow
£2368   £666   £325

36   **HEATHYARDS MATE** 3 [14] R Hollinshead 2-8-11 P M Quinn (5) 3/1 FAV: 054221: 2 b g Timeless Times - 71a
Quenlyn (Welsh Pageant) Chsd ldrs, rdn to lead over 2f out, held on gamely ins last, all out: jockey received a
two-day whip ban, hvly bckd, first win, qck reapp: rnr-up earlier in '99 (sell h'cap, rtd 57a, plcd on turf,
rtd 72, auct mdn): eff around 1m/8.5f: acts on fast, gd & fibresand, prob handles any trk.
3561} **SOFISIO** 82 [1] W R Muir 2-9-0 Martin Dwyer 11/2: 0402: 2 ch c Efisio - Legal Embrace (Legal Bid)   hd 73a
Handy, led 4f out, rdn/hdd over 2f out, rallied strongly for press, just held: clr rem: op 9/2: AW bow/12 wk abs:
rtd 70 earlier in '99: styd lngr 1m trip well, further could suit: acts on fibresand: has tried a t-strap.
4582} **RING MY MATE** 13 [7] W R Muir 2-8-5 Sophie Mitchell 6/1: 63: 2 ch c Komaite - My Ruby Ring (Blushing 4 56a
Scribe) Led till halfway, ch fnl pace front pair over 1f out: op 9/2: AW bow: rtd 61 on debut earlier
in '99 (auct mdn): styd this longer 1m trip & handles fibresand.
4616} **GLENWHARGEN** 9 [8] M Johnston 2-8-6 G Bardwell 5/1: 205304: Mid-div, prog/wide 2f out, hung left 3½ 50a
& btn fnl 1f: plcd twice earlier in '99 (rtd 65 & 54a, h'caps): eff btwn 6f/8.4f: handles gd/soft & fibresand:
handles a stiff/undul or sharp trk: best without blnks.
--   **WEST END DANCER** [9] 2-8-9 T Sprake 8/1: 5: Chsd ldrs halfway, sn held: op 4/1, debut.   1 51a
3581} **EXUDE** [2] 2-8-0 P Fitzsimons (3) 20/1: 06: Cl-up 6f: tchd 33/1, 12 wk abs/AW bow.   1½ 39a
4059} **ODYN DANCER** 53 [15] 2-8-0 G Baker 7/1: 025407: Wide/cl-up 6f: op 8/1, 8 wk absence.   hd 38a
4557} **ACTUALLY** 16 [10] 2-8-3 G Arnolda (3) 33/1: 00508: Sn rdn/bhd, mod gains: AW bow.   5 31a
4570} **MIST OVER MEUGHER** 14 [3] 2-8-0 T Williams 50/1: 00009: Chsd ldrs 5f: AW bow.   5 18a
4386} **RITA MACKINTOSH** 30 [11] 2-8-3 P Doe (3) 10/1: 304030: Dwelt/al rear: 10th: op 7/1, with R Brotherton. 2½ 16a
4367} Flight Eternal 31 [6] 2-8-11 P McCabe 50/1:   4338} Niciara 34 [13] 2-8-9(4ow) R Price 50/1:
3928} Gilfoot Breeze 61 [4] 2-8-5 Dale Gibson 33/1:   4446} Mikes Wife 26 [12] 2-8-0 A Mackay 50/1:
4312} Charlotte Russe 35 [5] 2-8-0 (VIS) N Carlisle 33/1:
15 ran   Time 1m 45.3 (5.9)   (L A Morgan)   R Hollinshead Upper Longdon, Staffs.

---

49   **2.40 TOTE TRIFECTA HCAP 3YO+ 0-95 (C)**   **1m aw rnd** Going 39 -01 Slow   **[95]**
£7165   £2170   £1060   £505   3 yo rec 2 lb

4615} **KING PRIAM** 9 [3] M J Polglase 4-8-7 (74)(bl) T G McLaughlin 5/1: 1352D1: 4 b g Priolo - Barinia 82a
(Corvaro) Dwelt, stdy prog fnl 4f, rdn/led ins last, rdn out: op 9/2: earlier in '99 won here at Southwell (AW
h'cap, rtd 74a), Leicester (class stks), Haydock & York (h'cap, rtd 80): '98 Newmarket wnr (clmr, rtd 70, M
Pipe): eff at 1m/12f: acts on firm, enjoys gd, soft & f/sand: handles any trk: eff in blnks: tough gelding.
4615} **WEETMANS WEIGH** 9 [6] R Hollinshead 6-9-13 (94) N Callan (3) 10/1: 434222: 6 b h Archway -   ¾ 99a
Indian Sand (Indian King) Chsd ldrs, rdn & ev ch fnl 2f, kept on well, just held nr fin: earlier in '99 won at
Southwell & W'hampton (h'caps, rtd 96a & 80): '98 W'hampton, Newcastle & Newmarket wnr (h'caps, rtd 78 & 86a):
eff at 7f/8.5f on firm & gd/soft, loves fibresand & W'hampton: handles any trk: gd weight carrier & runs well fresh.
35   **TAKHLID** 3 [1] D W Chapman 8-8-13 (80) T Sprake 5/1: 410023: 8 b h Nureyev - Savonnerie (Irish   ¾ 85a
River) Led, rdn 2f out, edged right & hdd ins last, no extra: well bckd: qck reapp: see 35.
4488} **ZANAY** 23 [10] Miss Jacqueline S Doyle 3-8-13 (82) A Daly 25/1: 2-3104: Rdn in rear, styd on well   3 81a
fnl 2f, nrst fin: AW bow: earlier in '99 scored at Nottingham (mdn, rtd 86): rnr-up on fnl 2 '98 starts for
R Phillips (mdn, rtd 81): eff at 7f/1m: acts on gd & fibresand: handles a stiff/gall & sharp trk.
*35   **FIRST MAITE** 3 [7] 6-9-9 (90)(bl)(6ex) S Finnamore (7) 15/2: 100015: Cl-up 7f: tchd 8/1: see 35 (7f). 1 87a
33   **RONS PET** 3 [8] 4-8-5 (72)(tvi) Dean McKeown 10/1: 600026: Mid-div, rdn/nvr pace to chall: qck reapp. 4 68a
*7   **SECRET SONG** 7 [14] 7-9-5 (86)(6ex) O Urbina 11/1: 244017: Wide/rear, nvr factor: see 7 (eqtrk). 1 80a
4615} **ITALIAN SYMPHONY** 9 [5] 5-10-0 (95)(vis) Joanna Badger (7) 20/1: 252108: Rdn mid-div, nvr on terms. 2 85a
4562} **GULF SHAADI** 16 [15] 7-9-2 (83) P Fredericks (5) 20/1: 000609: Dwelt/towards rear, mod gains.   ¾ 72a
4216} **LOCOMOTION** 44 [4] 3-8-5 (74) P Doe (3) 20/1: 120200: Chsd ldrs 6f: 10th: 6 wk abs, with S Dow.   ¾ 62a

24

SOUTHWELL (Fibresand)   MONDAY NOVEMBER 15TH   Lefthand, Sharp, Oval Track

7   **KAYO** 7 [2] 4-8-13 (80) M Tebbutt 4/1 FAV: 111030: Sn struggling: 14th: op 7/2: jockey reported   0a
gelding had a breathing problem: see 7.

4562} **Diplomat** 16 [11] 3-8-11 (80) R Price 14/1:		4295} **Final Dividend** 37 [16] 3-8-5 (74) J Tate 25/1:	
4357} **Arterxerxes** 32 [13] 6-8-12 (79) S Drowne 25/1:		2217} **Oddsanends** 99 [12] 3-8-8 (77) L Newman (7) 40/1:	
15 ran Time 1m 42.6 (3.2) (Ian Puddle)		M J Polglase Southwell, Notts.	

---

50   3.10 ASH SELLER DIV II 3YO+ (G)   1m aw rnd   Going 39   -32 Slow
£1605   £448   £216   3 yo rec 2 lb

3955} **SHEER NATIVE** 59 [7] B W Hills 3-8-12 T Sprake 7/4 FAV: -13001: 3 b f In The Wings - Native Magic   57a
(Be My Native) Chsd ldrs, prog/sltly hmpd 3f out, switched & led over 1f out, rdn clr ins last, readily: sold for
9,000gns: well bckd, 2 month abs: earlier in '99 scored at Lingfield (mdn, rtd 75a): rtd 78 on turf in '98: eff
at 1m/10f, poss stays sharp 12f: acts on both AW's: runs well fresh: likes a sharp trk: enjoys sell grade.

2297} **SHARP STEEL** 99 [15] Miss S J Wilton 4-9-0 C Rutter 8/1: -35002: 4 ch g Beveled - Shift Over (Night   3 50a
Shift) Trkd ldrs, prog/ev ch fnl 2f, not pace wnr ins last: op 7/1: 5 month abs: plcd earlier in '99 (rtd 57a, stks):
'98 Southwell wnr (7f seller, rtd 57a): eff at 7f, stays sharp 1m: acts on fibresand: has run well fresh.

4451} **PRINCIPAL BOY** 26 [6] Miss J F Craze 6-9-0 N Carlisle 12/1: 604653: 6 br g Cyrano de Bergerac -   ½ 49$
Shenley Lass (Prince Tenderfoot) Chsd ldrs halfway, hung left 3f out, kept on for press tho' not pace to chall:
tchd 14/1: recent jumps rnr (mod form): plcd numerous times earlier in '99 (rtd 49 & 39a): '98 Southwell wnr
(appr h'cap, rtd 43a, J Glover): eff at 6f/9f on firm, hvy & fibresand: best without a visor.

4481} **LEOFRIC** 23 [10] M J Polglase 4-9-5 (bl) T G McLaughlin 12/1: 100004: Handy, led after 3f/clr halfway,   5 44a
rdn/hdd over 1f out & fdd: a drop back to 6/7f should suit on this evidence.

4502} **SHABAASH** 21 [14] 3-9-3 A McCarthy (3) 20/1: 430005: Chsd ldrs 6f.   1 42a
4463} **BARRIER RIDGE** 25 [5] 5-9-5 R Brisland (5) 10/1: 020046: Dwelt/rear, mod gains fnl 2f: op 8/1.   2½ 37a
3016} **MR ROUGH** 99 [1] 8-9-0 M Tebbutt 14/1: 434007: Towards rear, mod gains: op 16/1, 4 month abs.   1½ 29a
4581} **ADIRPOUR** 14 [11] 5-9-5 P M Quinn (5) 14/1: 040008: Wide/mid-div, nvr factor: tchd 16/1.   2½ 29a
4576} **NORTH ARDAR** 14 [13] 9-9-5 P Doe (3) 15/2: 123009: Dwelt/al towards rear: op 12/1.   3½ 22a
4479} **NEEDWOOD MERLIN** 24 [12] 3-8-12 Dean McKeown 16/1: 530000: Sn bhd: 10th: op 12/1.   6 5a
2262} **FRENCH GINGER** 99 [2] 8-8-9 (t) K Hodgson 50/1: 050000: Al rear: 11th: 5 month abs.   hd 0a
3850} **HANDSOME BEAU** 67 [16] 4-9-0 (bl) A Mackay 50/1: 66-00: Led 3f: 12th: 2 mth abs/AW bow.   ½ 0a
3535} **ROYAL FUSILIER** 84 [8] 3-9-3 R Fitzpatrick(3) 11/2: -1025F: Prom 5f, fdd & fell 3f out: sadly died.   0a
--   **Fanny Parnell** [9] 3-8-7 T Williams 20/1:   4553} **Lambson Katoosha** 17 [3] 4-8-9 G Bardwell 50/1:
--   **Brathay Majic** [4] 5-8-9 P Fessey 50/1:
16 ran   Time 1m 45.1 (5.7)   (R J Arculli)   B W Hills Lambourn, Berks.

---

51   3.40 BEECH HCAP 3YO+ 0-75 (E)   2m aw   Going 39   -66 Slow   [75]
£2691   £756   £369   3 yo rec 9 lb

37   **BUSTLING RIO** 3 [10] P C Haslam 3-7-13 (55) Dale Gibson 6/4 FAV: 143421: 3 b g Up And At 'Em -   61a
Une Venitienne (Green Dancer) Held up, prog to lead over 2f out, styd on well ins last, drvn out: hvly bckd, qck
reapp: earlier in '99 scored here at Southwell (rtd 60a) & Pontefract (h'caps, rtd 61): eff at 11/12f, stays
2m well: acts on gd & f/sand: has run well fresh: handles a sharp or stiff/undul trk: op to further imrovement.

4397} **LITTLE BRAVE** 30 [2] J M P Eustace 4-10-0 (75) J Tate 11/2: 611002: 4 b g Kahyasi - Littlemisstrouble   1½ 79a
(My Gallant) Held up, prog over 4f out, rdn/ch over 1f out, kept on well tho' held nr fin: tchd 15/2, topweight,
clr reapp: earlier in '99 won at Lingfield (class stks, rtd 70a), Warwick & Yarmouth (h'caps, rtd 61): '98 Southwell
wnr (mdn, rtd 69a & 62): eff at 2m/2m2f: acts on fast, soft & both AWs: has run well fresh, handles any trk.

4590} **NETTA RUFINA** 12 [11] M Johnston 4-8-12 (59)(vis) M Tebbutt 9/1: 002533: 4 ch g Night Shift -   5 58a
Age of Elegance (Troy) Led, hdd over 2f out & no extra: op 8/1: earlier in '99 scored at Musselburgh (h'cap,
first time visor, rtd 72 & 48a): '98 Lingfield wnr (mdn, rtd 76a), Ripon (h'cap, rtd 75) & again at Musselburgh
(subs disqual): eff at 12f/2m: acts on fast, soft & both AWs: likes a sharp trk tho' handles any: eff with/
without a visor: likes to race with/force the pace: nicely h'capped on sand, spot on back at 14f.

4618} **TORY BOY** 9 [4] Ian Williams 4-8-2 (49) P Fessey 9/1: 032604: Chsd ldr, rdn & kept on for press fnl   shd 48a
2f, not pace front pair: clr rem, op 7/1: plcd twice earlier in '99 (rtd 60a & 64): '97 Warwick wnr (auct mdn,
rtd 75 at best): eff at 11f/2m: acts on firm, soft & fibresand, likes a sharp/turning trk: best without blnks.

4467} **ROYAL EXPRESSION** 24 [9] 7-9-9 (70) N Callan (3) 16/1: 146205: Bhd 3f out: op 12/1.   25 50a
4458} **NATURAL EIGHT** 25 [8] 5-8-3 (50) A Daly 14/2: 641326: Chsd ldrs 1m: AW bow.   7 23a
4503} **LITTLE FOX** 21 [5] 4-8-13 (60) O Urbina 6/1: 40247: Prom 12f, op 8/1.   18 20a
4587} **IRELANDS EYE** 13 [3] 4-8-7 (54) Paul Cleary (7) 8/1: 002368: Bhnd 5f out: op 6/1, AW bow.   16 2a
4587} **SWEET PATOOPIE** 13 [7] 5-9-9 (70) Claire Bryan(7) 16/1: 132509: Sn bhd: op 14/1.   5 13a
4438} **DANNY DEEVER** 26 [1] 3-7-10 (52)(20oh) M Baird(0) 40/1: 504000: Sn bhd: t.o. in 10th.   6 0a
4393} **DROWNED IN BUBBLY** 30 [1] 3-7-10 (52)(22oh) P M Quinn(0) 40/1: 400000: Sn bhd, t.o.: 11th.   dist 0a
11 ran   Time 3m 42.8 (16.8)   (Rio Stainless Engineering Ltd/R Tutton)   P C Haslam Middleham, N.Yorks.

LINGFIELD (Equitrack)   TUESDAY NOVEMBER 16TH   Lefthand, V Sharp Track

Official Going   STANDARD. Stalls: Inside, except 5f/1m - Outside.

52   12.20 AMAT RDRS HCAP 3YO+ 0-80 (G)   1m4f aw   Going 29   -23 Slow   [50]
£1873   £526   £256   3 yo rec 6 lb

37   **NOUKARI** 4 [10] P D Evans 6-11-4 (68) Miss E Folkes (5) 6/4 FAV: 450131: 6 b g Darshaan - Noufiyla   78a
(Top Ville) Prom, led over 3f out, styd on strongly ins last, rdn out: hvly bckd: qck reapp: recent jumps wnr at
Stratford & Wincanton (h'cap hdles, rtd 104h), eff at 2m on firm & gd): earlier in '99 scored on the level at
Lingfield (AW h'cap), Chester (clmr): Newmarket, Catterick (amat h'cap), Pontefract (stks) & here at Lingfield again
(AW stks, rtd 74 & 73a at best): '98 Southwell & Lingfield wnr (h'caps, rtd 63a & 63): eff at 10/14.7f, acts on firm,
soft & both AWs: handles any trk: loves Lingfield: runs well for an amat/appr: most tough & genuine performer.

4281} **INDIGO BAY** 39 [4] S Dow 3-10-10 (66) Mr R Guest (5) 12/1: 120002: 3 b g Royal Academy - Cape   3½ 71a
Heights (Shirley Heights) Prom, rdn/ch over 1f out, outpcd by wnr fnl 1f: op 10/1 clr rem, 6 wk abs: earlier in '99
scored at Brighton (sell h'cap) & Lingfield (h'cap, rtd 72, mdn, rtd 47a): rtd 71 in '98 for A Stewart: eff at
11/12f on firm, fast & equitrack: eff with/without blnks: likes to race with/force the pace: likes a sharp/undul trk.

4223} **ESHTIAAL** 43 [8] G L Moore 5-11-6 (70)(bl) Mr A Quinn (7) 14/1: 0-0033: 5 b h Riverman - Lady   7 65a

25

Cutlass (Cutlass) Wide/rear, prog/handy halfway, no impress over 1f out: op 12/1: 6 wk abs: AW bow: lightly rcd earlier in '99 (rtd 57, h'cap, rtd 98h over timber): unplcd on sole '98 start, prev term won at Ayr (first time blnks, mdn): Haydock, Beverley & Pontefract (h'caps, rtd 100, J Dunlop): eff at 10f, 12f may yet suit: acts on fast, gd/soft & prob soft: handles any trk: likes to force the pace & suited by blnks.
8 **HIGHFIELDER 8** [2] J S Moore 3-9-4 (46) Mrs S Moore (5) 25/1: 600304: Led 9f, fdd: op 16/1: *6* **32a**
longer 12f trip today: plcd twice earlier in '99 (rtd 53 & 48a): rtd 60 at best in '98 (mdn): eff around 7f/1m: acts on gd, gd/soft & equitrack: has run well in a visor: will apprec a drop in trip & sell grade.
3716} **FOURDANED 76** [3] 6-9-3 (39)(9oh) Mrs K Hills (4) 33/1: 400005: Rear/mod gains: 2 mth jmps abs. *2½* **21a**
1 **HENRIETTA HOLMES 8** [9] 3-10-4 (60) Mr T Best (5) 11/2: 322146: Mid-div, held fnl 3f: op 3/1. *¾* **41a**
4577} **PROTOCOL 15** [5] 5-10-2 (52)(t) Mr S Dobson (5) 5/1: 252517: Rear, nvr a factor: nicely bckd. *4* **27a**
3078} **PREMIER LEAGUE 99** [7] 9-9-6 (42)(3ow)(7oh) Mr M Allen (0) 25/1: 000458: Nvr in it: 3 mth abs. *hd* **17a**
4602} **GREENSTONE 12** [6] 3-11-7 (77) Mr C B Hills (3) 11/2: 034059: Prom 7f: op 5/1: topweight: AW bow. *4* **46a**
4179} **ROMAN REEL 46** [11] 8-10-3 (53) Mrs J Moore 9/1: 000040: Chsd ldrs 1m: 10th: jumps fit. *nk* **21a**
4535} **LANDICAN LANE 19** [1] 3-9-8 (50) Mr T Radford (7) 14/1: 000030: Chsd ldrs 6f: 11th: with T Jones. *8* **9a**
11 ran Time 2m 35.4 (6.2) (J E Abbey) P D Evans Leighton, Powys.

53 — 12.50 CHRISTMAS SELLER 2YO (G) 7f aw rnd Going 29 -38 Slow
£1928 £541 £264

24 **PERLE DE SAGESSE 5** [4] Julian Poulton 2-8-6 A Daly 2/1 FAV: 010521: 2 b f Namaqualand - Pearl Of Dubai (Red Ransom) Unseated rdr sev times bef start, cl-up, led 3f out, rdn clr: no bid, well bckd, qck reapp: earlier in '99 won at Windsor (sell, rtd 65 & 52a, P Cole): eff at 5/7f: acts on firm, gd & equitrack: likes sharp trks. **63a**
31 **INCH PINCHER 4** [3] P Howling 2-8-11 A McCarthy (3) 6/1: 306002: 2 ch c Inchinor - Cutpurse Moll *3* **62a**
(Green Desert) Prom, led 4f out till 3f out, not pace wnr: qk reapp: earlier in '99 won at Sandown (sell nurs, rtd 66): eff at 7f, tried 1m, shld suit: acts on firm, gd & equitrack: handles any trk: eff with/without visor in sells.
4537} **CROSS DALL 19** [9] R Ingram 2-8-6 (VIS) T Ashley 14/1: 0003: 2 b f Blues Traveller - Faapette (Runnett) *½* **56a**
Dwelt/rdn in rear, styd on fnl 2f, nrst fin: tchd 20/1, first time visor: AW bow: rtd 68 at best earlier in '99 (Windsor mdn): eff at 7f, return to 1m+ will suit: handles equitrack & a sharp trk: eff in a visor, tried blnks.
4 **RIDGECREST 8** [1] R Ingram 2-8-11 S Drowne 7/1: 00304: Cl-up, outpcd over 2f out: op 6/1: plcd *1½* **58a**
earlier in '99 (seller, rtd 55): eff at 5.7f, prob stays a sharp 7f: handles equitrack & gd/soft grnd.
2223} **KIGEMA 99** [11] 2-8-6 Martin Dwyer 6/1: 044155: Cl-up, fdd fnl 2f: 5 month abs, op 5/1. *1* **51a**
4433} **RONNI PANCAKE 28** [2] 2-8-6 T Sprake 8/1: 020606: Prom, wknd fnl 3f: op 7/1. *1½* **48a**
4567} **CYBER BABE 17** [6] 2-8-6 (vis) Dean McKeown 20/1: 04D007: Chsd ldrs, nvr able to chall. *nk* **47$**
4588} **WISHEDHADGONEHOME 13** [10] 2-8-6 G Carter 6/1: 000058: Slowly away & well bhd, mod late gains. *3* **41a**
4549} **SHARAVAWN 18** [8] 2-8-7(1ow) T G McLaughlin 25/1: 00009: Wide/towards rear, no impression. *10* **27a**
36 **BANDOLERA BOY 4** [7] 2-8-11 (BL) P Doe (3) 40/1: 000000: Chsd ldrs, strugg halfway: 10th: blnks. *7* **20a**
24 **DINKY 5** [5] 2-8-6 M Baird (3) 33/1: 00000: Sn bhd: 11th: qck reapp. *11* **0a**
11 ran Time 1m 27.5 (4.7) (Russell Reed & Gerald West) Julian Poulton Lewes, E.Sussex.

54 — 1.20 NURSERY HCAP 2YO 0-85 (E) 1m aw rnd Going 29 -20 Slow [83]
£2804 £788 £385

+26 **SAFARI BLUES 5** [6] R Hannon 2-9-13 (82)(6ex) P Dobbs (5) 10/11 FAV: 435211: 2 b g Blues Traveller - **93a**
North Hut (Northfields) Chsd ldrs/wide, rdn/led over 1f out, sn in command: hvly bckd, qck reapp/6lb pen: recent wnr here at Lingfield (C/D, mdn): prev rnr-up twice in '99 (nurs h'cap, rtd 77): eff at 7f, suited by a sharp 1m: acts on firm, soft, loves equitrack, any trk, loves Lingfield: best up with the pace: has run well fresh: progressive.
4386} **MAID TO LOVE 31** [9] G A Butler 2-8-2 (57)(bl) C Rutter 14/1: 330022: 2 ch f Petardia - Lomond *2* **62a**
Heights (Lomond) Chsd ldrs, drvn/prog wide over 2f out, styd on ins last, no threat to wnr: op 7/1: plcd thrice earlier in '99 (rtd 74, auct mdn & 58a, seller): eff at 6f, now suited by 1m, may get further: handles gd & both AWs: eff in blnks: handles a sharp or stiff/gall trk: creditable h'cap bow, caught a tartar, cld win soon.
31 **MISS WORLD 4** [2] C N Allen 2-8-5 (60)(t) Martin Dwyer 7/1: 144623: 2 b f Mujadil - Great Land *1¾* **62a**
(Friend's Choice) Sn handy, outpcd by wnr over 1f out: tchd 8/1, qck reapp: styd longer 1m trip: see 31 (7f).
4616} **CASTLE SEMPILL 10** [7] R M H Cowell 2-9-0 (69)(VIS) Dale Gibson 12/1: 433104: Cl-up, led halfway, *3* **65a**
rdn/hdd over 1f out & fdd: first time visor, op 10/1: AW bow: earlier in '99 scored at Newmarket (seller, J R Fanshawe, rtd 74): eff at 6/7f: acts on firm, handles soft & equitrack.
2 **TATTENHAM STAR 8** [4] 2-8-13 (68) S Drowne 12/1: 005635: Chsd ldrs, not pace to chall: clr rem. *1* **62a**
4601} **BOX CAR 12** [10] 2-8-1 (56) T Williams 33/1: 00066: Sn bhd/wide, nvr factor: AW bow. *10* **35a**
2 **CEDAR GUVNOR 8** [8] 2-8-2 (57) P Doe (3) 25/1: 600667: Chsd ldrs 4f. *½* **35a**
4616} **DATURA 10** [1] 2-9-5 (74) G Carter 7/1: 032408: Dwelt, sn rdn/led after 1f, hdd halfway/fdd: AW bow. *¾* **51a**
2 **BEDOUIN QUEEN 8** [11] 2-9-2 (71) Pat Eddery 16/1: 00309: Al rear: op 12/1. *¾* **47a**
4353} **SHAMAN 33** [5] 2-8-6 (61) G Parkin 20/1: 410300: Prom 5f: 10th: op 14/1, AW bow. *1* **35a**
4498} **SALLY GARDENS 22** [3] 2-8-10 (65) S Sanders 20/1: 051500: Led 1f, struggling halfway: 11th. *11* **22a**
11 ran Time 1m 40.08 (3.88) (T J Dale) R Hannon East Everleigh, Wilts.

55 — 1.50 COND STKS 3YO+ (B) 1m2f aw Going 29 +09 Fast
£9103 £3406 £1665 £716 3 yo rec 4 lb

4560} **BRILLIANT RED 17** [10] Mrs L Richards 6-9-0 (t) O Urbina 5/1: 300021: 6 b g Royal Academy - Red **104a**
Comes Up (Blushing Groom) Chsd ldrs wide halfway, hard rdn & styd on well fnl 1f to lead line: fast time: op 4/1: tough & consistent earlier in '99, won h'caps at Ascot & Sandown (rtd 104 at best): '98 wnr at Lingfield (2, rtd 92a) & Newbury (h'caps, rtd 94, P Hedger): eff at 1m/10f: acts on firm, soft & equitrack, poss fibresand: gd weight carrier: handles any trk, loves Lingfield: wears a t-strap: best up with/forcing the pace: tough/v useful.
4026} **RUNNING STAG 59** [5] P Mitchell 5-9-0 Pat Eddery 1/3 FAV: 215142: 5 b h Cozzene - Fruhlingstag *nk* **103a**
(Orsini) Held up & sev positions bef switched rail & rdn to lead 1f out, hard rdn/hdd line: hvly bckd at long odds on: 2 month abs: earlier in '99 won twice in the US at Belmont & Saratoga (Gr 2 h'caps, rtd 118a): '98 wnr here at Lingfield (stks, rtd 107a) & Deauville (Gr 3, rtd 117): suited by 9/10f: acts on firm, gd/soft, loves equitrack & dirt: runs well fresh: handles any trk, likes a sharp one: tough & v smart entire at best.
4488} **PAS DE MEMOIRES 24** [7] K R Burke 4-9-5 Dean McKeown 20/1: 264563: 4 b g Don't Forget Me - Bally *1½* **106$**
Pourri (Law Society) Led, rdn/hdd 1f out, no extra cl-home: op 14/1: earlier in '99 won at W'hampton (h'cap) & here at Lingfield (stks, rtd 97a), subs scored at Carlisle (val h'cap, rtd 91 at best): plcd in '98 (h'caps, rtd 73 & 83a): eff at 1m/10f: acts on firm, soft & both AWs: likes to race with/force the pace: handles any trk.
4176} **LAMERIE 46** [2] R Hannon 3-8-10 T Sprake 20/1: 021124: Prom, rdn/onepace fnl 2f: 6 wk absence. *1½* **99$**
49 **ITALIAN SYMPHONY 1** [3] 5-9-3 (vis) J P Spencer 33/1: 521005: Towards rear, rdn/nvr able to chall. *5* **95$**

3915} **SICK AS A PARROT 62** [6] 4-9-0 (e) N Callan 12/1: W50056: Prom 6f: op 10/1, 2 mth abs/with K Burke.   5   85a
4602} **CALLDAT SEVENTEEN 12** [11] 3-8-10 S Sanders 33/1: 163047: Prom 1m: stiff task.   3½   80a
27   **APADI 5** [4] 3-8-10 Martin Dwyer 50/1: 000668: Chsd ldrs 6f: qck reapp: no worthwile form.   2½   76a
4470} **DYNAMISM 25** [1] 4-9-0 (VIS) A Culhane 33/1: 045009: Chsd ldrs, btn 2f out: visor.   3½   71a
22   **SPACE RACE 5** [9] 5-9-0 G Faulkner 33/1: 025020: Prom 7f: 10th: qck reapp: see 22 (h'cap).   8   62a
4560} **RAHEEN 17** [8] 6-9-0 G Carter 14/1: 054540: Wide/rear, btn 4f out: 11th: op 10/1.   ¾   61a
11 ran   Time 2m 04.79 (1.99)   (Mrs M J George)   Mrs L Richards Funtington, W.Sussex.

---

56   **2.20 SPONSOR A RACE MDN 3YO+ (D)   1m2f aw   Going 29   -31 Slow**
£2879   £872   £426   £203   3 yo rec 4 lb

4598} **BRAZILIAN MOOD 12** [3] C E Brittain 3-9-0 S Sanders 11/2: 021: 3 b c Doyoun - Sea Mistress   74a
(Habitat) Chsd ldrs, led over 1f out, styd on well: tchd 7/1: AW bow: rnr-up 2nd of 2 starts earlier in '99
(mdn, rtd 75): apprec step up to 10f, 12f may suit: acts on equitrack & gd/soft grnd: likes a sharp trk: imprvg.
2614} **SPANKER 99** [1] B W Hills 3-8-9 A Eddery (5) 10/1: 546342: 3 ch f Suave Dancer - Yawl (Rainbow Quest) 3½   63a
Towards rear, rdn & prog from halfway, kept on ins last, not trouble wnr: op 8/1, 4 month abs, AW bow:
rtd 78 earlier in '99 (Newmarket mdn): eff at 10f, return to 12f+ will suit: handles equitrack & gd grnd.
39   **SUPERCHIEF 3** [7] Miss B Sanders 4-9-4 (t) C Rutter 50/1: -00003: 4 b g Precocious - Rome Express   nk   67$
(Siberian Express) Cl-up, led halfway till rdn/hdd over 1f out, no extra: qck reapp: rtd 50a & 32 at best earlier
in '99: rtd 53 at best in '98 (h'cap, tried visor, J E Banks): offic rtd 38, treat this rating with caution.
4502} **ROYAL FLAME 22** [6] J W Hills 3-8-9 S Whitworth 10/1: 544264: Chsd ldrs, rdn/ch 3f out, sn no extra.   2   59a
4603} **FINAL LAP 12** [14] Pat Eddery 4/1 JT FAV: 04245: Rdn/towards rear, mod gains fnl 2f: nicely   ¾   62a
bckd: clr rem, AW bow: earlier rnr-up in a Nottingham mdn (rtd 78): eff at 1m, stays 10f: handles gd/sft & soft.
8   **BLACK ROCKET 8** [12] 3-8-9 G Faulkner (3) 33/1: -00606: Cl-up 5f, fdd: v stiff task.   6   49$
--   **CEDAR FLAG** [2] 5-9-4 P Doe (3) 25/1: 7: Prom, outpcd fnl 4f: Flat debut, jumps fit.   5   47a
4115} **FIRST CUT 50** [4] 3-8-9 M Henry 5/1: 243458: Mid-div, btn 3f out: ab/AW bow: stablemate of 4th.   1   41a
4455} **DUCK OVER 26** [13] 3-8-9 T Sprake 5/1: 040349: Prom 1m, op 4/1: AW bow.   nk   41a
4564} **FORTUNE COOKIE 17** [5] 3-8-9 Dale Gibson 40/1: 000000: Chsd ldrs 7f: 10th.   23   16a
--   **MALAKAL** [10] 3-9-0 J P Spencer 4/1 JT FAV: 4420: Dwelt, wide/al twds rear: 11th: op 7/4, AW bow: 16   3a
Brit bow: ex-Irish, rnr-up on fnl start over 4 months ago (10f mdn, handles fast & soft): cost B Curley 17,000gns.
2407} Lautrec 99 [11] 3-9-0 R Studholme (5) 20/1:   --   Micky Dee [9] 3-9-0 Dean McKeown 33/1:
13 ran   Time 2m 08.75 (5.95)   (C E Britain)   C E Brittain Newmarket.

---

57   **2.50 CONTACT HCAP 3YO+ 0-60 (F)   5f aw rnd   Going 29   -36 Slow**   [58]
£2148   £603   £294

3727} **CHEMCAST 75** [6] J L Eyre 6-9-1 (45)(bl) Pat Eddery 7/1: 000201: 6 ch g Chilibang - Golden October   48a
(Young Generation) Chsd ldrs, rdn 2f out, styd on strongly for press ins last to lead line: op 7/2: 11 wk abs: rnr
-up earlier in '99 (rtd 41, h'cap): plcd form in '98 (rtd 67a & 60 at best): '97 Musselburgh scorer (h'cap, rtd 73):
eff at 5f, tried further: acts on firm, soft & both AWs: loves a sharp/turning trk: eff in blnks: runs well fresh.
3783} **BOWCLIFFE GRANGE 71** [2] D W Chapman 7-8-13 (43) A Culhane 5/1: 040012: 7 b g Dominion Royale   hd   45a
- Cala Vadelia (Mummy's Pet) Sn led, clr over 1f out, rdn & wknd ins last, hdd line: op 4/1: 10 wk abs: prev in
'99 won here at Lingfield (C/D h'cap, rtd 43a), & Hamilton (appr h'cap, rtd 40): plcd in '98 (rtd 46a & 46): loves
to force the pace at 5f: acts on firm, gd/soft & both AWs: without blnks: can find compensation.
394} **OK JOHN 99** [7] G P Enright 4-9-12 (56) O Urbina 25/1: 2-2443: 4 b g Mac's Imp - Ching A Ling   hd   57a
(Pampapaul) Rdn/towards rear, styd on strongly fnl 1f, just held: top-weight: mod recent form in Ireland:
earlier rnr-up in '99 with J Akehurst, (Lingfield h'cap, rtd 60a): rnr-up in '98 (rtd 54a & 52 at best): handles
gd/soft, likes both AWs: eff at 5/6f: mdn 4yo but a likely type for similar back at 6f.
25   **CARMARTHEN 5** [3] K Burke 3-9-3 (47) N Callan (3) F FAV: 003044: Chsd ldrs/kept on well fnl 1f.   ½   46a
3855} **MISTER RAIDER 68** [10] 7-8-12 (42)(bl) D Kinsella (7) 12/1: 060405: Rear, rdn/kept on well fnl 1f: abs.   ½   39a
4554} **WHATTA MADAM 18** [5] 3-9-5 (49)(t) S Whitworth 10/1: 030006: Chsd ldrs, nvr pace to chall: op 8/1.   ½   44a
3944} **ANOTHER NIGHTMARE 61** [9] 7-9-4 (48) T Williams 9/2: 601207: Led 1f, chsd til clr, wknd fnl 1f: abs.   3   36a
2107} **CELTIC VENTURE 99** [1] 4-9-11 (55) P Doe (3) 11/1: 2/1008: Stumbled/nrly fell leaving stalls, al bhd.   nk   42a
4471} **CLARA BLUE 25** [8] 3-8-12 (42) A Mackay 33/1: U00009: Sn rdn/bhd: AW bow.   ½   27a
4227} **DANCING JACK 43** [4] 6-8-8 (38) G Bardwell 14/1: 000300: Sn rdn/bhd, wide/held 2f out: 10th: abs.   7   6a
10 ran   Time 1m 0.55 (2.75)   (Neil Midgley)   J L Eyre Sutton Bank, N.Yorks.

---

58   **3.20 LADBROKE HCAP DIV I 3YO+ 0-70 (E)   7f aw rnd   Going 29   +02 Fast**   [69]
£2489   £752   £366   £173   3 yo rec 1 lb

4226} **MISTER TRICKY 43** [11] P Mitchell 4-9-7 (62) Pat Eddery 9/2: 650311: 4 ch g Magic Ring - Splintering   69a
(Sharpo) Sn cl-up trav well, led 2f out, styd on well for press: op 3/1, 6 wk abs: earlier in '99 won at Lingfield
(2, AW stks, rtd 64a & a turf h'cap), Windsor & Goodwood (h'caps) & Brighton (class stks, rtd 66): '98 wnr again
at Lingfield (2 h'caps, rtd 68a): eff at 6/7f, stays a sharp 1m: acts on firm, gd/soft & loves equitrack/Lingfield.
29   **PENGAMON 5** [8] D T Thom 7-8-7 (48) A Mackay 11/10 FAV: 0/0022: 7 gr g Efisio - Dolly Bevan   ½   54a
(Another Realm) Trkd ldrs wide halfway, rdn/chsd ldr over 1f out, kept on tho' al held: hvly bckd: qck reapp,
clr rem: deserves to find similar and a return to 1m could suit: see 29.
1924} **FRANKLIN D 99** [9] J R Jenkins 3-8-4 (46) S Drowne 33/1: 0-0003: 3 ch g Democratic - English Mint   3   46a
(Jalmood) Led 5f, no extra fnl 1f: op 20/1: 5 month abs: AW bow: rtd 40 at best earlier in '99 (h'cap): rtd 67
at best in '98 (mdn, subs tried visor): stays sharp 7f, drop back to 6f could suit: handles equitrack.
28   **DAYNABEE 5** [5] A J McNae 4-8-3 (44) P Fitzsimons (5) 6/1: 000054: Trkd ldrs, not pace front pair   ½   43a
fnl 2f: nicely bckd, tchd 15/2: qck reapp: plcd sev times earlier in '99 (rtd 47, h'cap): '98 wnr at Windsor
(h'cap, rtd 56, plcd on sand, rtd 45a): eff at 5/6f, stays 7f well: acts on firm, soft & both AWs: nicely h'capped.
28   **BIG BEN 5** [1] 5-9-13 (68) L Newman (7) 4/1: 560035: Chsd ldrs, outpcd 2f out: bckd, won this in '98.   ¾   66a
4576} **BUNTY 15** [3] 3-7-10 (38) A Polli (3) 14/1: 160016: Towards rear/sn rdn, nvr factor: op 7/1.   7   22a
4576} **SHONTAINE 15** [3] 6-7-13 (40) A Daly 16/1: 002007: Dwelt, rear, rdn halfway/no impress: op 12/1.   1½   21a
3321} **ELEGANT DANCE 95** [4] 5-9-1 (56) P Fredericks (5) 25/1: 300008: Dwelt/rear & wide, no prog: abs.   ½   36a
1478} **SQUARE MILE MISS 99** [10] 6-7-10 (37)(1oh) R Brisland (5) 40/1: 200009: Prom/wide 3f: 6 mth abs.   nk   16a
35   **MUTABARI 4** [6] 5-9-4 (59)(vis) A Culhane 12/1: 505600: Bhd/wide halfway: 10th: qck reapp.   17   4a
10 ran   Time 1m 24.66 (1.86)   (The Magicians)   P Mitchell Epsom, Surrey.

LINGFIELD (Equitrack) TUESDAY NOVEMBER 16TH Lefthand, V Sharp Track

---

59 3.50 LADBROKES HCAP DIV II 3YO+ 0-70 (E)   7f aw   Going 29 -10 Slow   [69]
£2476 £748 £364 £172 3 yo rec 1 lb

29   **NOBALINO 5** [8] Mrs V C Ward 5-9-5 (60)(vis) S Drowne 7/2: 000331: 5 ch h Sharpo - Zipperti Do **68a**
(Precocious) Prom, led over 2f out, styd on strongly & went clr: well bckd, qck reapp: rnr-up earlier in '99 (rtd 66 &
63a): rtd 75 & 62a in '98 (Mrs N Macauley): '97 Southwell wnr (h'cap, rtd 66a & 73): eff at 5f, best over a sharp
7f now: acts on firm, gd/soft & both AWs: likes a sharp trk, handles any: eff with/without vis: cld defy a penalty.
643} **BEST QUEST 99** [11] K R Burke 4-9-9 (64)(t) N Callan (3) 8/1: 004032: 4 b c Salse - Quest For The   4 **64a**
Best (Rainbow Quest) Cl-up trav well/wide halfway, kept on fnl 1f, no ch wnr: 8 mnth abs: rtd 72a at best earlier
in '99 (h'cap): '98 wnr at Doncaster (clmr, rtd 65, J Gosden) & here at Lingfield (h'cap, rtd 72a, current
connections): eff at 6/7f, stays 1m: acts on fast, gd, likes equitrack/Lingfield, without vis: sharper for this.
*29   **SCISSOR RIDGE 5** [9] J J Bridger 7-9-3 (58)(6ex) G Bardwell 100/30 FAV: 054413: 7 ch g Indian Ridge   ¾ **57a**
- Golden Scissors (Kalaglow) Mid-div, sltly hmpd halfway, kept on for press, not able to chall: hvly bckd: qck
reapp under a 6lb pen: bt today's wnr in 29 (C/D).
562} **MUSTANG 99** [2] J Pearce 6-8-5 (46) A Polli (3) 14/1: 6-4044: Prom, led after 3f till over 2f out, no extra   1 **43a**
fnl 1f: op 10/1: 9 month abs: rtd 49a at best earlier in '99 (h'cap, 1st time vis): rnr-up sev times in '98 (h'caps,
rtd 52 & 54a, C Thornton): '97 scorer at W'hampton & here at Lingfield (mdn h'cap & h'cap, rtd 49a): eff at 6f/1m,
suited by 7f: acts on gd/soft, both AWs: eff in blnks/visor, neither worn today: sharper for this, on a fair mark.
4436} **AL MABROOK 28** [7] 4-9-11 (66) G Faulkner (3) 10/1: -40505: Nvr trbld ldrs: rtd 65a & 60 earlier in '99: shd **63a**
(h'caps): late '98 wnr here at Lingfield (mdn, rtd 70a, h'cap, rtd 77): eff at 6/7f, tried 10f: acts on fast & equitrack.
4472} **DELIGHT OF DAWN 25** [3] 7-8-4 (45)(bl) S Carson (5) 15/2: 060466: Rear, mod gains wide: tchd 9/1.   1 **40a**
4502} **QUEEN OF THE KEYS 22** [10] 3-7-12 (40) P Doe (0) 20/1: 0-0007: Chsd ldrs halfway, sn held: op 14/1.   nk **34a**
4372} **CHRISMAS CAROL 32** [5] 3-8-2 (44) L Newman (7) 25/1: 000008: Led 4f, sn btn: qck reapp.   3 **32a**
4604} **THE THIRD CURATE 12** [1] 4-8-12 (53) J P Spencer 9/1: 000009: Mid-div at best: op 9/2: AW bow.   2 **37a**
2683} **SPECIAL PERSON 99** [4] 4-8-8 (49) Pat Eddery 11/1: 006000: Al rear: op 8/1: 10th: 4 mth abs.   4 **25a**
4598} **KIDNAPPED 12** [6] 3-8-7 (49) T G McLaughlin 7/1: 0-0000: Prom 2f, sn btn: 11th: op 8/1: AW bow. 16 **1a**
11 ran   Time 1m 25.5 (2.7)   (Two Out & Hard Held)   Mrs V C Ward Aisby, Lincs.

WOLVERHAMPTON (Fibresand) WEDNESDAY NOVEMBER 17TH Lefthand, V Sharp Track

Official Going STANDARD. Stalls: 7f - Outside; Rem - Inside.

60 1.05 TOULOUSE HCAP DIV 1 3YO+ 0-65 (F)   1m1f79y Going 24 -31 Slow   [65]
£1945 £545 £265   3 yo rec 3 lb

4402} **THE BARGATE FOX 30** [11] D J G Murray Smith 3-8-7 (47) S Whitworth 7/1: 00051: 3 b g Magic Ring - **55a**
Hithermoor Lass (Red Alert) Waited with, hdwy halfway, led 2f out, rdn out to hold on: op 5/1: unplcd earlier (mdns,
rtd 64a & 51a): eff at 9.3f: acts on fibresand & a sharp trk: stewards interviewed trainer about 'imprvd performance'.
4579} **SILVERTOWN 16** [2] B J Curley 4-9-2 (53) J P Spencer 11/2: 310002: 4 b g Danehill - Docklands   ¾ **59a**
(Theatrical) Led, hdd 2f out, rall ins last, just held: earlier in '99 won at Epsom (h'cap) & York (appr h'cap,
rtd 56): plcd in '98 (h'cap, rtd 61): stays 11.5f, best at 10f: acts on firm, gd/soft & f/sand, runs well for an appr.
4503} **GOLDEN LYRIC 23** [4] J Pearce 4-8-3 (40) A Polli (3) 33/1: 600003: 4 ch g Lycius - Adjala (Northfields)   1 **44a**
Settled, gd hdwy 3f out, chall over 1f out, onepcd: early in '99 won at Southwell (AW mdn h'cap, rtd 43a): plcd
in '98 (h'caps, rtd 36a & 44, G Wragg): eff at 9.3f, suited by 11/12f: acts on firm, loves fibresand, without blnks.
4581} **SABOT 16** [8] John A Harris 6-9-7 (58) L Newman (7) 6/1: 400554: Prom, rdn/not pace of ldrs 1f out.   1¾ **59a**
4437} **WESTMINSTER CITY 29** [7] 3-8-13 (53)(vis) G Carter 33/1: 050005: Bhd, prog 5f out, no extra fnl 2f.   ¾ **53a**
4581} **INTERNATIONAL AFFAIR 16** [12] 4-10-0 (65) Lynsey Hanna (7) 4/1 JT FAV: 061546: Waited with, hdwy fnl 2f,   ½ **64a**
no threat: top weight: 4 wks ago won here at W'hampton (h'cap, rtd 67a): sprinter in '98, won again at W'hampton
(mdn auct, rtd 79a): eff at 5f/8.5f, stays a stiff 9f: acts on hvy, handles fast, loves fibresand & W'hampton.
4593} **ERUPT 14** [13] 6-8-4 (41) T Williams 4/1 JT FAV: 061546: Handy, brief effort 2f out, no dngr: 1½ **37a**
earlier in '99 scored at Newcastle (h'cap, rtd 52): '98 Musselburgh wnr (h'cap, rtd 58): best at 7f/1m:
acts on fast & soft grnd, handles fibresand & any trk: has tried a visor, best without.
3   **FOREST ROBIN 9** [5] 6-9-1 (52)(vis) A Culhane 10/1: 400648: Al in rear.   6 **38a**
4535} **MY DARLING DODO 20** [3] 3-8-8 (48) T Sprake 15/2: 0569: Cl-up, lost tch final 2f: h'cap/AW bow.   1½ **31a**
4521} **TEMESIDE TINA 22** [9] 3-8-3 (43) M Henry 25/1: 06060: Prom, wknd final 2f: 10th: AW bow.   1¼ **24a**
33   **KINGCHIP BOY 5** [10] 10-9-12 (63)(bl) P McCabe 12/1: 041000: Prom, fdd fnl 3f, eased: 11th. 15 **24a**
--   **REGALITY** [1] 3-8-13 (53) J Fanning 12/1: -00000: Al bhd: fin 12th: ex-Irish, British/AW bow.   1¼ **12a**
12 ran   Time 2m 03.3 (5.1)   (Mrs Jill McNeill)   D J G Murray Smith Gumley, Leics.

---

61 1.40 MARSEILLE SELLER DIV 1 3YO+ (G)   7f aw rnd Going 24 -32 Slow
£1595 £445 £215   3 yo rec 1 lb

4402} **SHARP SHUFFLE 30** [10] Ian Williams 6-9-5 R Fitzpatrick (3) 9/4 JT FAV: 040201: 6 ch g Exactly Sharp - **60a**
Style (Homing) Sn outpcd, gd hdwy over 2f out, led appr final 1f, rdn out: no bid: recently t.o. over hdles (2m nov):
rnr-up twice in '99 (sell/clmr, rtd 62a): '98 wnr at Newmarket (2, sell & clmr, rtd 70, R Hannon): eff at 7f/1m,
stays a sharp 10f: acts on firm, gd/soft & both AWs: handles any trk, likes Newmarket: best in sellers/claimers.
4496} **NOBLE PATRIOT 23** [4] R Hollinshead 4-9-5 A Culhane 33/1: 040002: 4 b g Polish Patriot - Noble Form   2 **55$**
(Double Form) Prom, rdn to impr over 2f out, not pace of wnr inside last: placed earlier in '99 (mdn h'caps,
rtd 39a & 33): eff at 5/7f: acts on firm, gd/soft & both AWs: surely flattered at the weights (officially 33).
4586} **PALACEGATE TOUCH 15** [2] J Berry 9-9-11 (bl) G Carter 4/1: 560063: 9 gr g Petong - Dancing Chimes   1 **59a**
(London Bells) Dsptd lead, hdd over 2f out, no extra final 1f: early in '99 scored at Lingfield (2, clmrs, rtd 75a
& 62): '98 wnr again at Lingfield (clmr, rtd 76a), Warwick, Hamilton & Catterick (2, clmr/sell, rtd 60):
won 5 in '97: eff at 5/6f, stays 7f: acts on firm, gd/soft & both AWs: eff with/without blnks or visor.
29   **SOUND THE TRUMPET 6** [7] R C Spicer 7-9-5 (t) J Mackay (7) 14/1: 005044: Rdn in tch, late gains.   1 **51$**
4341} **OVER THE MOON 35** [1] 5-9-0 C Rutter 5/1: 630045: In tch, late gains, nvr a threat: best in clmr.   nk **46$**
4568} **TROJAN HERO 3** [8] 8-9-5 Dale Gibson 9/4 JT FAV: 032026: Dsptd lead, led over 2f out, hdd appr   1¾ **48a**
final 1f, wknd: plcd sev times in '99 (clmrs & h'cap, rtd 65a), modest form on turf: '98 Warwick wnr
(classified stks, rtd 63 & 69a): eff at 6f/1m: acts on fast, gd/soft & fibresand: has tried blnks, best without.
4511} **FLYING HIGH 22** [6] 4-9-5 (bl) J Fanning 33/1: /00007: Led, hdd over 3f out, sn lost tch.   2½ **43$**

28

WOLVERHAMPTON (Fibresand)   WEDNESDAY NOVEMBER 17TH   Lefthand, V Sharp Track

4361} LAKE ARIA 34 [11] 6-9-0 J Edmunds 50/1: 004008: Al in rear: v stiff task. — 6 — 28$
4568} PRIDE OF BRIXTON 18 [9] 6-9-5 S Whitworth 20/1: 000009: Sn outpcd. — 5 — 25a
4131} REBECCA JAY 50 [5] 3-8-13 S Drowne 20/1: 000000: Handy, btn halfway: 10th: 9 wk abs, new stable. — 2 — 16a
4598} BICTON PARK 13 [8] 5-9-5 T G McLaughlin 50/1: 000600: Slow to start, al well bhd: fin 11th. — 20 — 0a
11 ran   Time 1m 30.1 (3.9)   (G A Gilbert)   Ian Williams Alvechurch, Worcs.

62   2.10 LYON CLAIMER 2YO (F)   6f aw rnd   Going 24   -25 Slow
£2190   £615   £300

4612} BRANSTON PICKLE 12 [2] T J Etherington 2-8-13 S Drowne 7/4 JT FAV: 614101: 2 ch c Piccolo - — 80a
Indefinite Article (Indian Ridge) Made all, all-out to repel rnr-up: earlier in '99 scored here at W'hampton (sell,
rtd 69a) & Catterick (nursery, rtd 80): eff at 5/6f on gd/soft, soft & fibresand: likes sharp trks, esp W'hampton.
24   WELCHS DREAM 6 [8] J Berry 2-8-6 G Carter 6/1: 443442: 2 b f Brief Truce - Swift Chorus (Music Boy) hd 72a
Cl-up, hdwy to chall over 1f out, styd on well, just failed: op 5/1: qck reapp: '99 wnr at Ripon (mdn, rtd 86):
best up with/forcing the pace at 5/6f: acts on fast & fibresand, handles equitrack: clr rem, win similar.
4   KIRSCH 9 [6] C A Dwyer 2-8-5 L Newman (7) 7/4 JT FAV: 614203: 2 ch f Wolfhound - Pondicherry — 5 — 59a
(Sir Wimborne) Struggled to go pace till gd hdwy over 2f out, no extra appr final 1f: op 6/4: see 4.
4065} BOMBELLINA 54 [7] J M P Eustace 2-8-3 J Tate 9/1: 225604: Sn outpcd, nvr with ldrs: AW bow — 3 — 49a
rnr-up twice in '99 (fillies sell & fillies nursery, rtd 63): eff arnd 6f, has tried 7f: handles fast & gd/soft grnd.
4607} EMMA AMOUR 12 [5] 2-8-7 G Parkin 9/1: -205: Handy, no extra final 2f: Aw bow, op 6/1: debut ½ 52a
rnr-up in '99 (auct mdn, rtd 74, J Fanshawe), cost current connections 5,500gns: eff at 6f: handles fast grnd.
3887} PARDY PET 65 [3] 2-8-5 S Carson (5) 33/1: 014006: Cl-up, wknd final 2f: 9 wk abs. — 4 — 41a
24   RIOS DIAMOND 6 [4] 2-8-3 A Daly 25/1: 030007: Al outpcd: qck reapp. — 2½ — 33a
4065} LANDFALL LIL 54 [1] 2-8-2 G Bardwell 20/1: -02608: Dwelt, al well in rear: 8 wk abs. — 6 — 20a
8 ran   Time 1m 15.7 (2.9)   (J David Abell)   T J Etherington Norton, Nth Yorks.

63   2.40 NORMANDY MDN 3YO+ (D)   6f aw rnd   Going 24   +02 Fast
£2788   £844   £412   £196

4527} CHERISH ME 21 [2] J G Given 3-8-9 A Culhane 10/11 FAV: 52301: 3 b f Polar Falcon - Princess Zepoli — 69a
(Persepolis) Cl-up, led 4f out, clr 2f out, v easily: val 10L+ on AW bow, well bckd, gd time: plcd twice early in '99
(mdns, rtd 28): eff arnd 6f, has tried 7f: acts on fibresand, handles fast & gd: easy wnr today, follow up in a h'cap.
32   LEMON STRIP 5 [13] B Palling 3-8-9 L Newman (7) 14/1: 230042: 3 ch f Emarati - Lon Isa (Grey — 7 — 47a
Desire) Cl-up, lost place over 2f out, kept on, no ch with wnr: qck reapp: plcd twice in '99 (h'caps,
rtd 37a & 44 at best): stays 5/6f, handles firm & fibresand.
25   SISAO 6 [4] Miss Gay Kelleway 3-9-0 (bl) S Whitworth 14/1: 00063: 3 ch c College Chapel - Copt Hall 1½ 48a
Princess (Crowned Prince) Mid-div, prog 2f out, sn outpcd: qck reapp: unplcd prev (mdns, rtd 54, tried blnks).
4566} SOVEREIGN ABBEY 18 [5] Sir Mark Prescott 3-8-9 G Duffield 5/2: 033-54: Prom, hdwy over 2f out, wknd 1½ 40a
4096} MISS PIPPIN 53 [10] 3-8-9 P M Quinn (5) 16/1: 4405: Bhd, some late gains: 8 wk abs. — 1 — 37a
4252} KUWAIT ROSE 43 [9] 3-9-0 G Faulkner (3) 12/1: 036: In tch, wknd final 2f: 6 wk abs, AW bow. 1½ 39a
4252} KUWAIT SAND 43 [8] 3-9-0 S Drowne 6/1: 407: Al outpcd: AW bow, 6 wk abs. 1½ 36a
4554} TONG ROAD 19 [6] 3-9-0 P McCabe 33/1: 000608: Al well in rear: stiff task. — 7 — 20a
25}   FAN TC GEM 99 [12] 3-8-9 J Edmunds 33/1: -004-9: Al outpcd: long abs. hd 15a
3886} HOT LEGS 65 [3] 3-8-9 L Newton 40/1: 060600: Led, hdd 4f out, sn wknd: 10th: 9 wk abs. ¾ 13a
--   Lady Nairn [11] 3-9-0 G Carter 40/1:   --   Kings Chambers [1] 3-9-0 (bl) T G McLaughlin 50/1:
12 ran   Time 1m 14.1 (1.3)   (J R Good)   J G Given Willoughton, Lincs.

64   3.10 LADBROKE HCAP STKS 3YO+ 0-95 (C)   5f aw rnd   Going 24   +12 Fast   [95]
£7002   £2120   £1035   £492

4538} IVORYS JOY 20 [10] K T Ivory 4-8-13 (80) G Duffield 14/1: 012001: 4 b g Tina's Pet - Jacqui Joy (Music — 87a
Boy) Prom, hdwy to lead fnl 1f, drvn out: last time, AW bow: earlier in '99 won at Thirsk & Haydock (h'caps,
rtd 82): plcd sev times in '98 (h'caps, rtd 79): prev term won at Goodwood (2 sell) & Newbury (nursery, rtd 73):
eff at 5/6f: acts on firm & fibresand, loves gd/soft & hvy grnd: best without blnks/vis: tough filly.
4610} JUWWI 12 [2] J M Bradley 5-8-8 (75) Claire Bryan (7) 13/2: 000262: 5 ch g Mujtahid - Nouvelle Star ¾ 80a
(Luskin Star) Dwelt & sn outpcd, strong hdwy over 1f out, styd on, nrst fin: earlier in '99 won at Carlisle
& Chepstow (h'caps, rtd 79 at best): '98 wnr at W'hampton (sell) & Lingfield (h'cap, rtd 80a & 70): eff at 5/6f,
stays 7f: acts on firm, hvy & both AWs: handles any trk, gd weight carrier: best coming late off a strong pace.
4572} CLASSY CLEO 16 [1] P D Evans 4-9-12 (93) Joanna Badger (7) 9/2: 523213: 4 b f Mujadil - Sybaris 1½ 93a
(Crowned Prince) Handy, drvn & not pace of ldrs inside last: '99 wnr at Redcar (h'cap, rtd 99a & 100 at best):
'98 scorer at Chester (2) & Redcar (h'caps, rtd 96): '97 wnr at Beverley, Pontefract, Haydock (R Hannon),
Yarmouth, Southwell & Lingfield (current trainer, rtd 100a & 86): eff at 5/6f on any grnd/trk: on a fair mark.
4356} AFAAN 34 [4] R F Marvin 6-8-13 (80)(bl) T G McLaughlin 5/1: 505504: Led, sn clr, wknd/hdd ins last. ¾ 78a
4052} DIL 56 [9] 4-10-0 (95) R Fitzpatrick (3) 12/1: 000005: Prom, not pace of ldrs over 1f out: top-weight, abs. ½ 92a
47   OCKER 2 [3] 5-8-11 (78) R Price 7/1: 005546: Cl-up, wknd final 2f: op 5/1, qck reapp. hd 75a
4573} DANCING MYSTERY 16 [6] 5-8-13 (80) S Carson (5) 4/1 FAV: 240017: Mid-div at best: earlier in '99 hd 77a
won a h'cap (h'cap), Southwell (AW h'cap, rtd 82a), Warwick (h'cap) & Redcar (classified stks, rtd 78): '98
wnr at Windsor & Goodwood (h'caps, rtd 57 & 74a): stays 7f, best at 5f: acts on fast, gd/soft & both AWs: acts
on any trk, likes a sharp one: was eff with blnks, poss best without now: can runs well fresh: better than this.
4620} DANIELLES LAD 11 [5] 3-9-4 (85) T Sprake 14/1: 002508: Nvr a threat: op 12/1. 1½ 78a
4015} MUKARRAB 58 [11] 5-9-4 (85) A Culhane 16/1: 530359: Chsd ldrs, wknd final 2f: 8 wk abs. 1¾ 73a
4538} PURE COINCIDENCE 20 [8] 4-8-11 (78) N Callan (3) 7/1: 013600: Dwelt, al rear: fin 10th: op 5/1. — 2 — 60a
3483} MANGUS 89 [7] 5-8-9 (76) G Carter 14/1: 302020: Al outpcd: fin 11th: 3 mth abs. ¾ 56a
11 ran   Time 1m 00.8 (0.6)   (K T Ivory)   K T Ivory Radlett, Herts.

65   3.40 MARSEILLE SELLER DIV 2 3YO+ (G)   7f aw rnd   Going 24   -34 Slow
£1595   £445   £215   3 yo rec 1 lb

3368} BROUGHTONS TURMOIL 95 [11] B R Millman 10-9-11 T Sprake 4/1: 506001: 10 b g Petorius - Rustic Stile 67a
(Rusticaro): Handy, hdwy over 3f out, led nist, rdn clr: no bid: 3 mth abs: earlier wnr at Windsor (clmr,
rtd 70): '98 Southwell wnr (h'cap, rtd 73a & 77), prev term scored at Ascot (h'cap, rtd 75): eff between 6f & 1m:
acts on fast, gd & both AWs, handles soft: runs well fresh on any trk: gd weight carrier: now best in sells/clmrs.

30   **SEVEN 5** [10] Miss S J Wilton 4-9-11 (VIS) C Rutter 11/8 FAV: 432622: 4 ch g Weldnaas - Polly's 3½ 60a
Teahouse (Shack) Cl-up, led over 1f out, sn hdd, onepace: nicely bckd, qck reapp: first time visor, usually blnkd.
30   **RA RA RASPUTIN 5** [12] B A McMahon 4-9-5 G Duffield 9/2: 602003: 4 b g Petong - Ra Ra Girl (Shack) 2 50a
In tch, hdwy 2f out, styd on, nvr nrr: op 3/1, qck reapp: rnr-up earlier in '99, here at W'hampton (h'cap, rtd 62a):
won here at W'hampton in '97 (rtd 83a): eff at 7f, stays 1m on fast, hvy & fibresand: has tried blnks, best without.
3285} **DREAM ON ME 98** [3] H J Manners 3-9-5 J Bosley (7) 14/1: 001304: Mid-div, late gains: unplcd in 4 ¾ 50a
recent hdle starts: early in '99 won at Lingfield (AW h'cap, rtd 60a) & Leicester (sell, rtd 64, G L Moore):
'98 wnr at Lingfield (sell, rtd 68a): eff at 7f/1m: acts on firm, gd/soft & equitrack: likes Lingfield.
4581} **MIKES DOUBLE 16** [5] 5-9-5 (vis) R Price 20/1: 050605: In tch, hmpd 3f out, onepcd after. hd 49$
3766} **PAGEBOY 74** [9] 10-9-5 T Eaves (7) 20/1: 005006: Nvr a factor: 10 wk abs. 3½ 43a
4331} **NADDER 36** [4] 4-9-5 J Tate 20/1: 505007: Cl-up, wknd over 3f out: stiff task.. ½ 42$
30   **LAMENT 5** [1] 3-9-5 (VIS) S Whitworth 12/1: 216008: Led, hdd dist, wknd qckly: qck reapp, visor. 1 41a
132} **ROWLANDSONS STUD 99** [2] 6-9-5 (t) A Morris 20/1: 0000-9: Chsd ldrs, wknd final 2f: long abs. 1 38$
4118} **FENCERS QUEST 51** [6] 6-9-5 Dale Gibson 16/1: /00040: Al bhd: fin 10th: 7 wk abs. 1 36a
45   **GENIUS 2** [8] 4-9-11 A Culhane 25/1: 000000: Al well in rear: 11th: qck reapp. 9 27a
4521} **RIVERDANCE 22** [7] 3-9-4 (vis) T G McLaughlin 10/1: 620600: Sn in rear: fin 12th: recent jumps rnr. 5 13a
12 ran   Time 1m 30.3 (4.1)   (B R Millman)   B R Millman Kentisbeare, Devon.

---

66 **4.15 CONNEALLY HCAP 3YO+ 0-60 (F)**   2m46y aw Going 24 -38 Slow   **[59]**
          £2358   £663   £324   3 yo rec 9 lb

*37   **VIRGIN SOLDIER 5** [1] M Johnston 3-9-12 (66)(6ex) J Fanning 1/3 FAV: 211111: 3 ch g Waajib - Never 78a
Been Chaste (Posse) Cl-up going well, led after halfway, sn clr, eased ins last, v easily: well bckd: recent
wnr at Lingfield & Southwell (h'caps): earlier in '99 scored again at Southwell (h'cap, rtd 51a) & Musselburgh
(h'cap, rtd 58): plcd in '98 (mdn, rtd 62, T Etherington): v eff at 12f/2m, even further could suit: acts on
gd, gd/soft & both AWs: handles a sharp or gall trk: best without blnks: most progressive for new connections.
4458} **CHILDRENS CHOICE 27** [6] J Pearce 8-8-7 (38) A Polli (3) 8/1: 013502: 8 b m Taufan - Alice Brackloon 1¾ 40a
(Melyno) Bhd, prog 1m out, styd on well final 3f tho' no ch with easy wnr: well clr rem: earlier in '99 won
at Brighton (sell h'cap) & Redcar (sell, rtd 46): '98 Newmarket wnr (fillies h'cap, first time visor, rtd 55 at
best): eff at 12f/2m: acts on firm & soft grnd, handles fibresand: eff with/without a visor.
3586} **PAWSIBLE 83** [4] D W P Arbuthnot 3-8-7 (47) R Price 12/1: 003163: 3 b f Mujadil - Kentucky Wildcat 14 38a
(Be My Guest) Cl-up, rdn & wknd final 3f: 12 wk abs: earlier in '99 won here at W'hampton (appr h'cap, rtd 47a):
well btn in auct mdns in '98 (rtd 63): eff arnd 14f, may get 2m in time: acts on fibresand & a sharp trk.
4407} **TIME CAN TELL 30** [2] A G Juckes 5-9-13 (58) N Callan (3) 16/1: 126064: Sn rdn in tch, wknd final 4f: 10 41a
top weight: earlier in '99 won here at W'hampton (h'cap, rtd 62a): '98 Lingfield wnr (h'cap, rtd 62a): '98 Lingfield
wnr (clmr, rtd 66a, J Payne): eff between 13f & 2m: acts on both AWs, handles fast & gd/soft, without blnks/vis.
4546} **BROUGHTONS LURE 19** [8] 5-8-7 (38) G Carter 16/1: 0-0005: Held up, eff halfway, sn lost tch. 1¾ 19a
4458} **SILVER GYRE 27** [5] 3-9-2 (56) Dean McKeown 16/1: 214006: Al in rear. 6 32a
1   **YALAIL 9** [7] 3-9-6 (60) S Drowne 33/1: 406007: Cl-up, lost tch final 5f: wide early. 15 14a
4519} **DALLACHIO 22** [13] 8-8-13 (44)(t) S Whitworth 33/1: 100/08: Nvr on terms: t-strap. 4 4a
4590} **CHASKA 14** [10] 4-8-7 (38) D Kilcourse (7) 20/1: 505309: Al bhd: op 14/1. 1 0a
4223} **SLAPY DAM 44** [3] 7-9-1 (46) S Carson (5) 20/1: 110050: Led, hdd 7f out, sn lost tch: 10th: jmps rnr. 2½ 36a
4578} **Frisky Fox 16** [9] 5-8-9 (40) A Culhane 50/1:   4587} **Classic Referendum 15** [12] 5-9-12 (57) J P Spencer 12/1:
1442} **Albemine 99** [11] 10-8-9 (40) Dale Gibson 14/1:
13 ran   Time 3m 39.3 (10.1)   (J David Abell)   M Johnston Middleham, Nth Yorks.

---

67 **4.45 TOULOUSE HCAP DIV 2 3YO+ 0-65 (F)**   1m1f79y Going 24 -21 Slow   **[65]**
          £1945   £545   £265   3 yo rec 3 lb

4564} **MYSTERIUM 18** [1] N P Littmoden 5-8-4 (41) R Thomas (7) 8/1: 315041: 5 gr g Mystiko - Way To Go 53a
(Troy) Well bhd, plenty to do 3f out, strong run for press to lead dist, going away: early '99 wnr at Yarmouth (h'cap,
rtd 44): unplcd in '98 (tried visor, N Littmoden): '97 W'hampton wnr (auct mdn, rtd 61a): eff at 9.3/11.5f:
acts on fast, gd & fibresand: best on a sharp trk, likes W'hampton: qck follow up?
3972} **AREISH 60** [9] J Balding 6-9-0 (51) J Edmunds 14/1: 132302: 6 b m Keen - Cool Combination (Indian 6 51a
King) Bhd, hdwy halfway, chsd wnr in vain final 1f: op 8/1, 8 wk abs: earlier in '99 won here at W'hampton (sell)
& Southwell (fill h'cap, rtd 53a): '98 Southwell (h'cap, D Nicholls) & W'hampton wnr (sell h'cap, rtd 44a, M
Pipe): eff at 1m/12f: acts on fibresand, prob equitrack, loves sharp trks: best without blnks: can go well fresh.
*22   **FORTY FORTE 6** [3] K R Burke 3-9-11 (65) N Callan (3) 13/8: 000013: 3 b g Pursuit Of Love - Cominna ¾ 64a
(Dominion) Prom, ev ch until wknd over 1f out: nicely bckd from 11/4, qck reapp: better expected, see 22 (10f).
1248} **KILLARNEY JAZZ 99** [5] G C H Chung 4-9-12 (63) S Carson 20/1: 442044: Bhd, fnl 2f gains: abs: 1 60a
plcd earlier in '99 (h'caps & clmr, rtd 63a): prev with N Littmoden, won 3 at Southwell in '98 (mdn h'cap/clmrs,
first 2 for J Wharton, rtd 75a): eff at 7f/1m: handles gd/soft grnd, loves fibresand/Southwell, with/without blnks.
3073} **BLACK WEASEL 99** [13] 4-8-3 (40) G Duffield 33/1: 000005: Mid-div at back: long abs. ½ 36a
4444} **POLAR ECLIPSE 28** [2] 6-8-13 (50) Dean McKeown 10/1: 220406: Led, hdd over 1f out, wknd: op 8/1. shd 39a
4458} **DANKA 28** [11] 5-8-7 (44) J Bosley (7) 33/1: 0W0047: Al rear, modest late gains. 2 31a
4581} **SWYNFORD PLEASURE 16** [10] 3-8-0 (40) N Carlisle 33/1: 030008: Nvr a threat: AW bow. ¾ 36a
23   **CASHIKI 6** [4] 3-8-6 (46) T Sprake 20/1: 512600: Al bhd: 10th, AW bow, op 12/1. hd 31a
4592} **AJJAE 14** [7] 3-8-1 (41)(bl) G Bardwell 16/1: 512600: Al bhd: 10th, AW bow, op 12/1. nk 31a
3682} **PERCHANCER 79** [6] 3-9-1 (55) Dale Gibson 14/1: 312000: Cl-up, lost tch final 3f: 11th: op 10/1. ¾ 42a
43   **DARE 14** [12] 4-9-3 (54) Joanna Badger (7) 6/4 FAV: 111530: Fly jumpd start, nvr in it: 12th, ignore. 14 23a
3   **TAPAGE 9** [8] 3-8-13 (53) S Whitworth 20/1: 000030: Handy, lost tch 4f out: fin 13th: see 3.
13 ran   Time 2m 02.4 (4.2)   (Alcester Associates)   N P Littmoden Newmarket.

SOUTHWELL (Fibresand)   FRIDAY NOVEMBER 19TH   Lefthand, Sharp, Oval Track

Official Going   STANDARD. Stalls: Inside, except 5f - Outside.

68 | 12.10 DUDLEY HCAP DIV 1 3YO+ 0-60 (F)   1m4f aw   Going 36 -24 Slow   [57]
£2008   £563   £274   3 yo rec 6 lb

1936} **SOUHAITE 99** [3] W R Muir 3-8-5 (40) Martin Dwyer 25/1: 0061: 3 b g Salse - Parannda (Bold Lad) **46a**
Keen/trkd ldrs, rdn/led over 1f out, styd on well ins last, rdn out: 5 month abs, AW/h'cap bow: rtd 43 at best
earlier in '99 (Sandown mdn, t-strap, showed temperament, subs gelded): apprec this step up to 12f, further cld
suit: acts on fibresand: likes a sharp trk: runs well fresh: lightly raced and open to further improvement.
4437} **MEILLEUR 31** [7] Lady Herries 5-9-11 (54) P Doe (3) 10/1: 221502: 5 b g Nordico - Lucy Limelight 1½ **57a**
(Hot Spark) Chsd ldrs halfway, prog/rdn & led over 2f out, hdd over 1f out, onepace: earlier in '99 scored at
Newbury (ladies h'cap, rtd 53): '98 Hamilton scorer (mdn h'cap, rtd 50a): p.u. on hdles bow in 98/99: eff at
11/12f, stays a sharp 2m: acts on firm, gd/soft grnd & both AWs: eff weight carrier: runs well for an amat.
4402} **SUPREME MAIMOON 32** [13] M J Polglase 5-9-6 (49) T G McLaughlin 14/1: 033103: 5 b h Jareer - 1¾ **50a**
Princess Zena (Habitat) Chsd ldrs towards outer, prog/led over 4f out, hdd/hdd over 2f out, onepace: op 12/1:
earlier in '99 scored here at Southwell (clmr, rtd 49a, mod turf form, rtd 26, h'cap): missed '98: rtd 75a in
'97 (stks): eff at 1m, best at 11/12f: acts on both AW's, no turf form: likes a sharp trk.
4403} **LOST IN LUCCA 32** [4] J W Hills 3-9-3 (52) M Hills 1/1: 516034: Mid-div, prog & ch over 1f out/no extra. 1½ **51a**
4284} **KENT 41** [2] 4-9-0 (43) T Sprake 20/1: 000005: Cl-up, outpcd over 2f out: 6 wk absence. 2½ **38a**
1   **MARKELLIS 11** [14] 3-8-6 (41) R Fitzpatrick (3) 25/1: 560606: Rear, stdy gains fnl 3f, no threat. 1½ **34a**
4509} **MANFUL 24** [12] 7-8-8 (37) F Norton 12/1: 604037: Wide/in tch, btn 2f out: now with R Brotherton. 8 **20a**
34}   **DESERT SPA 99** [11] 4-9-11 (54) A Clark 20/1: 0103-8: Cl-up, brief led 5f out, btn 2f out: op 16/1: 3 **33a**
reapp: prev with P Harris, now with P Makin: should prove sharper for this.
4571} **BOLT FROM THE BLUE 18** [6] 3-9-2 (51) Kim Tinkler 14/1: 502249: Cl-up 9f, fdd: op 12/1: AW bow. 14 **14a**
4546} **NEEDWOOD MYSTIC 21** [9] 4-9-5 (48) J Tate 16/1: 215000: Towards rear, nvr factor: 10th: AW bow. shd **11a**
1568} **MOONSHIFT 99** [15] 5-7-13 (28)(tvi) G Bardwell 12/1: 00-010: Rear/wide early, nvr on terms: 11th, abs. ½ **0a**
3978} **JAMORIN DANCER 62** [1] 4-9-8 (51) Alex Greaves 9/1: 060350: Led 7f, sn btn: 12th: abs/AW bow, **0a**
op 5/1: now with D Nicholls, prev with W Jarvis.
43   **CAEROSA 6** [17] 4-8-13 (42)(bl) J Fanning 100/30 FAV: 121540: Wide/bhd early, eff halfway, sn held: **0a**
16th: disapp, connections unable to offer explanation: earlier in '99 scored at Hamilton (h'cap, first win), York
(appr h'cap) & Bath (h'cap, rtd 62 & 24a at best): rtd 71 at best in '98 (J FitzGerald, mdn, debut): eff at 10/12f,
stays 14f: acts on firm & hvy, poss handles fibresand: handles any trk: eff in blnks/visor: well h'capped on sand.
4592} **HILL FARM DANCER 16** [8] 8-8-1 (30) L Newman (6) 7/1: 06054R: Ref to race: op 9/1. **0a**
4037} **Royal Dolphin 59** [16] 3-8-3 (38) L Newton 25/1:   4225} **Garbo 46** [5] 4-8-11 (40) Dale Gibson 40/1:
4403} **Lion Cub 32** [10] 3-8-9 (44) J Fanning 20/1:
17 ran   Time 2m 42.7 (8.4)   (J Beinstein)   W R Muir Lambourn, Berks.

69 | 12.40 PONTON HCAP DIV 1 3YO+ 0-60 (F)   7f aw rnd   Going 36 -03 Slow   [60]
£2018   £566   £275   3 yo rec 1 lb

4133} **BOUND TO PLEASE 52** [11] P J Makin 4-9-2 (48) A Clark 33/1: 600501: 4 b g Warrshan - Hong Kong Girl **61a**
(Petong) Handy, led 3f out, styd on well fnl 2f, rdn out: 7 wk abs: unplcd earlier in '99 (rtd 55 & 26a): missed
'98: back in '97 fin rnr-up (juv auct mdn, rtd 79 & 6a): prev eff at 5/6f, stays a sharp 7f well: acts on
fibresand, handles fast: likes to race with/force the pace: enjoys a sharp trk & runs well fresh: can win again.
*44   **CARLTON 3** [2] D R C Elsworth 5-10-0 (60)(6ex) P Fitzsimons (5) 1/2 FAV: 123112: 5 ch g Thatching - 1½ **69a**
Hooray Lady (Ahonoora) Chsd ldrs, hmpd/lost pl after 2f, switched right & prog to chase wnr fnl 2f, kept on
tho' held ins last: well bckd at odds on, clr of rem: qck reapp under 6lb pen: eff at 7f, best at 6f.
38   **LEGAL ISSUE 6** [5] B S Rothwell 7-9-10 (56) R Lappin 16/1: 300543: 7 b h Contract Law - Natuschka 3½ **58a**
(Authi) Mid-div, sltly hmpd after 2f, styd on stdly fnl 3f, nrst fin: qck reapp: tchd 20/1: earlier in '98 scored
at Thirsk & Beverley (h'caps, rtd 76 & 42a on sand): '98 wnr at Pontefract & again at Beverley (h'caps, rtd 69 &
50a): eff at 7f/10f, suited by 1m: acts on firm, hvy & both AWs: best without a visor: handles any trk, likes
Beverley: nicely h'capped on sand, relish a return to 1m+ next time.
35   **MAI TAI 7** [10] D W Barker 4-9-7 (53)(vis) Kimberley Hart (5) 25/1: 000304: Chsd ldrs, kept on for 1½ **52a**
press fnl 2f, no threat: qck reapp: earlier in '99 scored at Southwell (C/D auct mdn, rtd 57a) & Redcar (fill
h'cap, rtd 55): plcd form in '98 (h'cap, rtd 58a, Mrs Dutfield): eff at 6/7f on firm, gd/sft & fibresand:
tried blnks, has run well in a visor.
4510} **ORIOLE 24** [6] 6-8-13 (45) Kim Tinkler 33/1: 500045: Mid-div, mod gains fnl 2f. ½ **43a**
60   **ERUPT 2** [12] 6-8-9 (41) T Williams 14/1: 210006: Sn prom, wknd over 1f out: op 10/1, qck reapp. 2½ **34a**
4133} **WISHBONE ALLEY 52** [7] 4-8-13 (45)(bl) C Teague 25/1: 030307: Cl-up/led over 4f out till 3f out/fdd: abs. 1½ **35a**
*33   **SEA YA MAITE 7** [1] 5-9-12 (58)(6ex) S Finnamore (7) 8/1: 500218: Chsd ldrs/hmpd after 2f, sn held. ¾ **47a**
38   **GRANNYS RELUCTANCE 6** [4] 3-9-3 (50) T Sprake 25/1: 536269: Led 2f, sn btn: qck reapp. 5 **29a**
29   **SWYNFORD WELCOME 8** [8] 3-9-9 (56) A Polli (3) 000100: Chsd ldrs, btn 3f out: 10th. 1 **33a**
3910} **Nice Balance 66** [2] 4-8-8 (40) M Dwyer 66/1:   4449} **Westwood View 30** [9] 3-8-7 (40) J Lowe 66/1:
4331} **San Michel 38** [13] 7-9-4 (50)(bl) A Mackay 25/1:   4565} **Flush 20** [14] 4-10-0 (60) G Faulkner (3) 50/1:
4402} **Brandonville 32** [16] 6-8-12 (44) Dean McKeown 25/1:4576} **Mybotye 18** [15] 6-9-6 (52)(t) N Callan (3) 40/1:
16 ran   Time 1m 29.3 (2.7)   (Mrs P J Makin)   P J Makin Ogbourne Maisey, Wilts.

70 | 1.10 DUDLEY HCAP DIV 2 3YO+ 0-60 (F)   1m4f aw   Going 36 -31 Slow   [57]
£2008   £563   £274   3 yo rec 6 lb

4410} **HOMESTEAD 32** [11] R Hannon 5-9-9 (52) L Newman (7) 8/1: 240061: 5 ch g Indian Ridge - Bertrade **56a**
(Homeboy) Chsd ldrs, rdn/prog to lead 3f out, clr 2f out, styd on strongly, rdn out: op 7/1: earlier in '99 won
h'caps at Pontefract, Leicester & W'hampton (rtd 65 & 53a): rtd 45a at best in '98 (h'cap): missed '97
(rtd 52½): eff at 1m/10f, stays a sharp 12f well: acts on firm, hvy & both AWs: handles any trk: runs well
for an apprentice: progressive earlier this year, looks nicely h'capped on sand, can win again.
43   **WESTERN COMMAND 6** [16] Mrs N Macauley 3-9-11 (60) R Fitzpatrick (3) 5/1 FAV: 242062: 3 b g 2 **61a**
Saddlers' Hall - Western Friend (Gone West) Mid-div/wide, prog/chsd wnr fnl 2f, kept on tho' not able to
chall: clr of rem, qk reapp: earlier in '99 won here at Southwell (2, h'caps, rtd 76a, Sir M Prescott):
rnr-up in '98 (mdn, rtd 69a): suited by 12f, stays 14f on both AWs, likes Southwell: best without blnks/visor.
1   **MARTHA REILLY 11** [7] Mrs Barbara Waring 3-9-1 (50) A Mackay 20/1: 004003: 3 ch f Rainbows For Life 4 **45a**
- Debach Delight (Great Nephew) Chsd ldrs, eff 3f out, kept on onepace: earlier in '99 scored here at Southwell
(fill seller, rtd 58a) in '98: eff at 1m, stays 12f on fibresand, handles equitrack: tried blnks.

31

43 **KI CHI SAGA 6** [2] P Burgoyne 7-9-6 (49)(bl) P McCabe 20/1: 010004: Rear, gains fnl 4f/nrst fin. 3½ **39a**
4587} **IRSAL 17** [3] 5-8-1 (30) Kimberley Hart (5) 25/1: 506005: Cl-up, led over 4f out till over 3f out, fdd. 2½ **16a**
3232} **FRONTIER FLIGHT 99** [13] 9-7-13 (28) J Bosley (1) 50/1: 0/0056: Rdn/rear, mod gains: jmps fit. 6 **5a**
3199} **NUBILE 99** [4] 5-8-3 (32) F Norton 12/1: 000167: Rear, mod late prog: op 8/1, 3 month absence. ¾ **8a**
-- **TALECA SON** [15] 4-8-9 (38) R Lappin 16/1: 063058: Rear/rdn, mod prog: op 12/1, AW bow/Brit debut. 5 **7a**
4519} **PREMIERE FOULEE 24** [17] 4-8-8 (37) A Culhane 12/1: 460209: Mid-div, prog wide to lead over 5f out, hdd over 4f out & fdd: op 10/1. 1½ **4a**
4403} **JOHNNIE THE JOKER 32** [14] 8-9-5 (48)(bl) Dean McKeown 8/1: 065000: Cl-up 10f: 10th: jmps fit. 5 **8a**
4592} **ROMA 16** [5] 4-9-2 (45) M Tebbutt 12/1: 001200: Cl-up 9f, 11th: op 8/1. 4 **0a**
4346} **GROOMS GOLD 37** [9] 7-9-4 (47) A Polli (3) 8/1: 634330: Rear, nvr factor: 12th. ¾ **0a**
4576} **LOBUCHE 18** [1] 4-8-5 (34) T Sprake 33/1: 600000: Led 7f, fdd: 13th: jumps fit. 6 **0a**
4502} **ELSIE BAMFORD 25** [8] 3-8-10 (45) J Fanning 8/1: 66U300: Cl-up, btn 4f out: 15th: op 7/1. **0a**
4424} **Aquatic King 31** [12] 4-8-13 (42) N Callan (3) 16/1: 4424} **Delciana 31** [10] 4-8-6 (32)(3ow) G Carter 12/1:
4437} **Set And Match 31** [6] 3-8-13 (48) S Whitworth 16/1:
17 ran Time 2m 42.3 (8.0) (G H Shoemark) R Hannon East Everleigh, Wilts.

71 — 1.45 DUNSTON CLAIMER 3YO+ (F) 5f aw str Going 36 +10 Fast

£2232 £627 £306 Raced centre to stands side.

40 **SAMWAR 6** [8] Mrs N Macauley 7-8-10 (vis) R Fitzpatrick (3) 7/1: 006001: 7 b g Warning - Samaza (Arctic Tern) Chsd ldrs, rdn/led over 1f out, styd on strongly ins last, rdn clr: qck reapp, fast time: earlier in '99 won twice at W'hampton (sell & h'cap) & here at Southwell (h'cap, rtd 72a & 54): plcd form in '98 (rtd 74 & 71a, with Miss G Kelleway): eff at 6/7f, best nowadays at 5f: acts on firm, soft & both AW's, fibresand specialist: has run well fresh: eff in blnks/visor: handles any trk, loves a sharp one: eff weight carrier. **74a**
4568} **SOUTHERN DOMINION 20** [4] Miss J F Craze 7-8-4 (bl) T Williams 14/1: 020002: 7 ch g Dominion - Southern Sky (Comedy Star) Led 3f, edged right fnl 1f, kept on for press: blnks repplied: op 12/1: rnr-up earlier in '99 (rtd 54, h'cap): '98 wnr at Musselburgh (2 h'caps, rtd 63), rnr-up twice on sand (rtd 57a): eff at 5/6f on firm, soft & both AWs: suited by blnks, tried a visor: loves Musselburgh: on a fair AW mark, h'caps suit. 3 **59a**
40 **AA YOUKNOWNOTHING 6** [6] Miss J F Craze 3-8-6 (VIS) T Lucas 12/1: 030003: 3 b g Superpower - Bad Payer (Tanfirion) Cl-up, rdn/ch over 1f out, no extra ins last: op 10/1: qck reapp, first time visor: plcd form earlier in '99 (rtd 75a, AW h'cap & 64, h'cap): '98 Musselburgh wnr (auct mdn, M W Easterby) & Thirsk (auct stks, rtd 81): eff at 5f, tried 6f: acts on firm & soft grnd, both AW's: handles any trk, likes a sharp one: best up with/forcing the pace: has tried blnks & a t-strap: stablemate of rnr-up. hd **60a**
4471} **LORD HIGH ADMIRAL 28** [2] C G Cox 11-8-4 (vis) S Drowne 10/1: 203004: Cl-up, wknd fnl 1f: op 12/1. 1 **56a**
4586} **CZAR WARS 17** [3] 4-8-10 (bl) J Bramhill 25/1: 000035: Dwelt/towards rear, late gains, no threat. 3½ **53$**
4610} **NIFTY NORMAN 14** [17] 5-9-0 F Norton 7/2 FAV: 400406: Chsd ldrs, outpcd fnl 2f: tchd 9/2: earlier in '99 scored twice here at Southwell (h'caps, rtd 73a at best) & once at Chester (h'cap, rtd 69 at best): '98 wnr again at Southwell (h'cap, rtd 58a): eff at 5/6f, tried 7f: acts on fast, loves gd/soft, hvy, fibresand & Southwell. hd **56a**
30 **PALACE GREEN 7** [1] 3-8-5 A Culhane 14/1: -12007: Chsd ldrs 3f: op 16/1. ¾ **45a**
4198} **SWYNFORD DREAM 48** [9] 6-9-0 G Carter 12/1: 600608: Chsd ldrs 3f, sn btn: op 16/1: 7 wk abs. 1¾ **50a**
4573} **TINKERS SURPRISE 18** [14] 5-8-6 J Edmunds 33/1: 204509: Sn rdn, nvr on terms. hd **41a**
4586} **SUE ME 17** [13] 7-8-6 (bl) Clare Roche (7) 16/1: 301000: Prom 4f: 10th: stablemate of 6th. 11 **21a**
30 **SING FOR ME 7** [7] 4-8-5 Stephanie Hollinshead (6) 66/1: 600500: Al outpcd: 11th. nk **0a**
4198} **RING OF LOVE 48** [15] 3-9-5 J Fanning 10/1: 611050: Al outpcd: 13th: abs, top-weight, now with J L Eyre. **0a**
40 **DIVINE MISS P 6** [5] 6-9-3 N Callan (3) 8/1: 200000: Dwelt, al bhd: 15th: qck reapp. **0a**
30 **Groesfaen Lady 7** [16] 3-8-5(2ow) T Sprake 12/1: 3855} **Divide And Rule 71** [12] 5-8-8 P M Quinn (5) 50/1:
32 **Linksman 7** [10] 4-8-4 L Newton 66/1:
16 ran Time 59.10 (1.3) (A Peake) Mrs N Macauley Melton Moubray, Leics.

72 — 2.20 GRANTHAM NURSERY HCAP 2YO 0-75 (E) 5f aw rnd Going 36 -12 Slow [81]

£2814 £852 £416 £198 Majority raced centre to stands side.

2 **ILLUSIVE 11** [5] H J Collingridge 2-8-12 (65)(bl) F Norton 3/1 FAV: 051021: 2 b c Night Shift - Mirage (Red Sunset) Chsd ldrs, rdn/hung right over 1f out, led just ins last, styd on well, rdn out: tchd 7/2: earlier in '99 with W Jarvis, won at Lingfield (h'cap, first time blnks, rtd 69a, rtd 49 at best on turf): eff at 5/6f, handles gd/soft, enjoys both AW's: likes a sharp trk: best in blnks. **73a**
4589} **PARKSIDE PROSPECT 16** [3] M R Channon 2-7-11 (50) P Fessey 7/2: 050212: 2 b f Piccolo - Banner (Known Fact) Handy, rdn/sltly hmpd over 1f out, kept on ins last: op 11/4: earlier in '99 won at Newcastle (seller) & Musselburgh (sell h'cap, rtd 68, rnr-up on sand, rtd 46a, clmr): eff at 5/6f: acts on firm, gd & fibresand: likes to race with/force the pace: handles any trk: suited by sell grade. 1¾ **53a**
4599} **SMOKIN BEAU 15** [9] J Cullinan 2-9-7 (74) N Callan (3) 5/1: 0433: 2 b c Cigar - Beau Dada (Pine Circle) Led, rdn/hdd just ins last, kept on for press: h'cap bow: op 6/1: AW bow, top-weight: plcd on fnl turf start earlier in '99 (rtd 76, Windsor mdn): eff at 5f, tried 6f, shld suit in time: handles gd/soft & fibresand. shd **77a**
34 **MADEMOISELLE PARIS 7** [1] A W Carroll 2-7-10 (49) P M Quinn (5) 16/1: 300604: Rcd towards far side, late gains for press, no threat. 1½ **48a**
4230} **PAPAGENA 46** [6] 2-8-7 (60) Dean McKeown 14/1: 620305: Chsd ldrs/nvr on terms: op 8/1: abs/AW bow. hd **58a**
4616} **PADDYWACK 13** [2] 2-7-10 (49)(bl)(5oh) Joanna Badger (7) 11/2: 300106: Rear, mod prog: tchd 7/1. 1½ **43a**
31 **LISA B 7** [10] 2-8-7 (60)(bl) L Newman (7) 16/1: 000007: Cl-up till halfway: op 14/1. 1¾ **50a**
4082} **GEM OF WISDOM 56** [4] 2-8-2 (55)(vis) T Williams 10/1: 153608: Prom 4f: op 8/1: 8 wk absence. 1¾ **41a**
34 **PERTEMPS STAR 7** [7] 2-7-10 (49)(18oh) A Polli (3) 33/1: 000009: Cl-up till hlafway. 3½ **26a**
4612} **GREAT WHITE 14** [8] 2-8-13 (66) P Dobbs (5) 10/1: 530000: Sn rdn, bhd fnl 2f: tchd 14/1: AW bow. 3½ **34a**
10 ran Time 1m 00.2 (2.4) (J B Com) H J Collingridge Newmarket.

73 — 2.50 BRIDGTOWN MDN 3YO (D) 7f aw rnd Going 36 -04 Slow

£2853 £864 £422 £201

39 **HAYMAKER 6** [2] B S Rothwell 3-9-0 R Lappin 2/1: 320231: 3 b g Thatching - Susie Sunshine (Waajib) Led, rdn/hdd over 1f out, duelled with rnr-up ins last & asserted again nr fin, drvn out: qck reapp, op 6/4: rnr-up earlier in '99 on turf (h'cap, rtd 74, I Balding): eff at 7f, tried 1m, will suit in time: acts on firm, soft & fibresand: handles a sharp or stiff/gall track: proving tough. **71a**
63 **KUWAIT ROSE 2** [6] K Mahdi 3-9-0 S Drowne 14/1: 0362: 3 b c Inchinor - Black Ivor (Sir Ivor) Cl-up, rdn/narrow lead over 1f out, hdd well ins last & no extra: qck reapp: op 10/1: plcd on turf earlier in '99 (Catterick mdn, rtd 61): eff at 6/7f: acts on soft & fibresand: handles a sharp/turning trk: fin well clr of rem. 1¼ **68a**

SOUTHWELL (Fibresand) FRIDAY NOVEMBER 19TH   Lefthand, Sharp, Oval Track

8   **GHAAZI 11** [1] Miss Gay Kelleway 3-9-0 S Whitworth 5/1: -60043: 3 b g Lahib - Shurooq (Affirmed)   10 53a
Chsd ldrs, rdn/outpcd by front pair fnl 2f: rtd 56 at best earlier in '99 (Brighton class stks, t-strap): plcd in
'98 (rtd 75, mdn): eff around 7f, handles firm grnd.

4234} **EL SALIDA 46** [4] J G FitzGerald 3-9-0 T Williams 13/8 FAV: 4344: Cl-up, no impress fnl 2f: well bckd: 6 43a
AW bow/7 wk absence: plcd on turf earlier in '99 (rtd 79 at best, mdn): stays 1m, this drop back in trip may not
have suited: acts on firm & gd/soft grnd & a stiff/undul trk: h'cap company may suit.

4548} **HOT POTATO 21** [10] 3-9-0 N Callan (3) 33/1: 560005: Prom, btn 3f out.   9 30a

4598} **HIDDEN ENEMY 15** [?] 3-9-0 A Culhane 11/1: 046: Sn rdn, al towards rear: AW bow.   ¾ 29a

4603} **HONEY HOUSE 15** [9] 3-8-9 P Mundy (7) 40/1: 07: Dwelt/al rear: AW bow.   nk 23a

35} **WHATSITSNAME 99** [3] 3-9-0 J Fanning 33/1: 0-8: Prom 4f: reapp.   hd 28a

32   **GO SALLY GO 7** [8] 3-8-9 Kimberley Hart (5) 33/1: 050009: Chsd ldrs 4f.   12 5a
9 ran   Time 1m 29.90 (2.8)   (B Valentine)   B S Rothwell Musley Bank, N.Yorks.

---

74 **3.20 MANSFIELD SELLER 2YO (G)**   6f aw   Going 36 -26 Slow
£1913   £536   £260

4589} **CALKO 16** [6] T D Barron 2-8-11 (bl) N Callan (3) 9/2: 300631: 2 ch g Timeless Times - Jeethgaya   61a
(Critique) Sn chsd ldrs, led over 3f, styd on strongly ins last, rdn out: no bid: op 4/1: rnr-up twice earlier
in '99 (rtd 69, mdn, subs plcd in first time blnks): eff at 5f, suited by 6f, may stay further: acts on fibresand,
fast & gd grnd: eff in blnks: likes a sharp trk: enjoys sell grade: fine AW bow, op to further improvement.

42   **PETRIE 6** [14] M R Channon 2-8-11 Paul Cleary (7) 11/2: 554232: 2 ch g Fraam - Canadian Capers   3 54a
(Ballacashtal) Cl-up, rdn/kept on onepace fnl 1f: qck reapp: op 7/2: shown enough to win similar: see 42 (5f).

48   **NICIARA 4** [3] M C Chapman 2-8-11 R Fitzpatrick (3) 40/1: 00003: 2 b g Soviet Lad - Verusa   1¼ 51a
(Petorius) Handy, kept on onepace fnl 2f: qck reapp: apprec this drop to 6f, only mod form earlier in '99
(mdns): eff at 6f, return to 7f+ may suit in time: acts on fibresand: apprec drop to sells, encouraging AW bow.

34   **JANICELAND 7** [11] S E Kettlewell 2-8-6 A McGlone 13/8 FAV: 502254: Dwelt/wide, late gains,   2½ 39a
nrst fin: well bckd: 7f+ may now suit: see 34 (5f).

4367} **NATSMAGIRL 35** [9] 2-8-11 G Carter 20/1: 630005: Chsd ldrs, onepace fnl 2f: visor: tchd 25/1:   ½ 42a
earlier in '99 scored at Thirsk (sell, rtd 62): eff at 6f, stays a stiff 7f: acts on firm & gd grnd, prob fibresand:
handles any trk: some encouragement on AW bow with headgear applied.

42   **MIKE THE SPUD 6** [4] 2-8-11 G Parkin 10/1: 305056: Mid-div, held fnl 2f: qck reapp: op 8/1.   3½ 33a

4575} **UNFORTUNATE 18** [12] 2-8-6 (BL) N Carlisle 33/1: -00607: Bhd, mod gains: first time blnks.   4 18a

4589} **BARRYS DOUBLE 16** [5] 2-8-11 (VIS) T Williams 6/1: 400308: Slly hmpd start, chsd ldrs 4f: visor.   3 16a

4557} **BLAZING PEBBLES 20** [8] 2-8-6 L Newman (7) 40/1: 0009: Cl-up 4f: AW bow.   ¼ 9a

--   **CARDINAL FAIR** [10] 2-8-6 R Lappin 33/1: 0: Drvn/mid-div, no terms: debut, with B Baugh.   3½ 0a

46   **LAMMOSKI 4** [7] 2-8-11 M Tebbutt 40/1: 000000: Cl-up 4f: 11th: qck reapp.   1 3a

--   **JENNY WEST** [1] 2-8-6 P Fessey 33/1: 0: Led till over 3f out, sn btn: 13th: debut.   0a
--   Rolleston Rocket [2] 2-8-6 Joanna Badger (7) 33/1: -- Blazing Rock [13] 2-8-11 A McCarthy (3) 33/1:
14 ran   Time 1m 17.00 (3.7)   (T Calver)   T D Barron Maunby, N.Yorks.

---

75 **3.50 PONTON HCAP DIV 2 3YO+ 0-60 (F)**   7f aw rnd Going 36 -05 Slow   [60]
£2008   £563   £274   3 yo rec 1 lb

4511} **OUT OF SIGHT 24** [11] B A McMahon 5-10-0 (60) T Sprake 6/1: 650001: 5 ch g Salse - Starr Danias   67a
(Sensitive Prince) Trkd ldrs, led over 3f out, drvn/clr 2f out, styd on well for press, eased nr line: op 7/1, AW bow:
rtd 72 earlier in '99 (rtd h'cap): lightly rcd in'98 (rtd 75, reapp, h'cap): '97 wnr at York (h'cap, rtd 80): eff at
1m: acts on firm, gd & fibresand, handles hvy & any trk: eff weight carrier: well h'capped, win again this winter.

4341} **CHALUZ 37** [10] N P Littmoden 5-9-4 (50)(t) T G McLaughlin 5/1: 564522: 5 b g Night Shift -   3 51a
Laluche (Alleged) Prom, rdn & kept on fnl 2f, no threat to wnr: op 4/1: earlier in '99 won at W'hampton (clmr,
K R Burke, rtd 62a at best): '98 Southwell wnr (2, h'caps, rtd 60a): eff btwn 6f/1m: handles equitrack, loves
fibresand: best up with/forcing the pace on a sharp trk, Southwell specialist: eff weight carrier: enjoys clmrs.

4341} **SHES A GEM 37** [14] Mrs V C Ward 4-9-9 (55)(vis) L Newman (7) 10/1: 055403: 4 b f Robellino - Rose   2 52a
Gem (Taufan) Prom, rdn/chsd wnr 2f out, kept on fnl 1f: well bckd: op 8/1: rtd 47a & 58 at best earlier in '99: '98 wnr
at W'hampton (h'cap) & Southwell (sell & h'cap, rtd 70a & 52, Mrs Macauley): eff at 6f, suited by 7f: acts on
fibresand & gd grnd, prob handles gd/soft & fast: likes to race up with/force the pace: off in a claimer.

4521} **FOREIGN EDITOR 24** [6] R A Fahey 3-9-2 (49) P Hanagan (7) 14/1: 006654: Rdn/rear, late gains fnl 2f.   6 36a

8   **BALLYMORRIS BOY 11** [1] 3-8-9 (42) A Polli (3) 20/1: 000005: Dwelt, mod gains.   1½ 26a

--   **PUPPET PLAY 3** [3] 4-9-9 (55) A Culhane 16/1: 620006: Prom, no impress fnl 2f: 10 wk abs, Brit bow.   ¾ 38a

4402} **STRAVSEA 32** [12] 4-8-13 (45) Dean McKeown 16/1: 100607: Dwelt, rdn/mod gains fnl 2f: op 12/1.   2½ 23a

4504} **SURE TO DREAM 25** [9] 6-9-6 (52) R Perham 10/1: 100009: Prom 5f: op 7/1.   7 19a

2919} **NITE OWLER 99** [2] 5-9-12 (58) J Edmunds 4/1 FAV: 012109: Led 2f, sn lost pl/btn: 4 mth abs: op 7/2:   4 17a
earlier in '99 won twice here at Southwell (h'caps) & W'hampton (h'cap, rtd 61a): '98 wnr again at Southwell
(h'cap, rtd 58a & 32): eff at 6/7f: handles any trk: acts on AW bow: loves Southwell: bhd prove sharper for this.

4541} **SOLLYS PAL 22** [5] 4-9-11 (57) A Clark 16/1: 00-00: Dwelt/keen, bhd halfway: 10th: AW bow.   nk 15a

1050} **SCOTLAND BAY 99** [7] 4-9-6 (52) L Newton 20/1: 540000: Handy/led over 4f out till over 3f out/fdd: 11th.   1¾ 7a

--   **LADYS HEART** [8] 4-9-2 (48) R Fitzpatrick (3) 20/1: 035400: Prom 5f: 12th: 3 mth abs/Brit & AW bow.   2½ 0a

1511} **MUNASIB 99** [13] 4-8-11 (43)(BL) A McGlone 33/1: 60-000: Bhd: 13th: blnks: jmps fit, with G Brown.   1½ 0a

4581} **OAKWELL ACE 18** [15] 3-8-8 (41) N Callan (3) 8/1: 000030: Prom 5f: 14th: AW bow.   hd 0a

3630} Astral Rhythm 83 [16] 4-8-13 (45) G Carter 20/1: -- 3650} Sounds Cool 82 [4] 3-8-5 (38) Dale Gibson 20/1:
16 ran   Time 1m 29.5 (2.9)   (D J Allen)   B A McMahon Tamworth, Staffs.

WOLVERHAMPTON (Fibresand) SATURDAY NOVEMBER 20TH   Lefthand, Very Sharp

Official Going   STANDARD Stalls: 7f - Outside, Rem - Inside

76 **1.10 CLASS STKS DIV 1 3YO+ 0-60 (F)**   6f aw   Going 35 +03 Fast
£1903   £533   £259

69   **CARLTON 1** [7] D R C Elsworth 5-9-8 Pat Eddery 4/6 FAV: 231121: 5 ch g Thatching - Hooray Lady   70a
(Ahonoora) Rdn/mid-div early, prog fnl 2f, rdn to chall/drifted left ins last, led nr line: good time: well bckd:
quick reapp, rnr-up yesterday (7f), earlier won at Southwell (h'cap): earlier in '99 won at Doncaster (subs disq),

Epsom (h'caps, G Lewis) & Windsor (2, h'caps, rtd 77): '98 wnr again at Windsor & Newbury (h'caps, rtd 69 & 52a): eff at 7f/1m, suited by 6f on firm, hvy & fibresand: likes a sharp trk: has run well fresh: eff with/without blnks.
4604} **DIAMOND GEEZER 16** [2] R Hannon 3-8-13 P Fitzsimons (5) 12/1: 502502: 3 br c Tenby - Unaria (Prince Tenderfoot) Prom, led over 3f out, rdn fnl 1f, hdd nr line: op 8/1: clr rem: earlier in '99 scored at Lingfield (AW h'cap, rtd 57a) & twice at Windsor (h'caps, rtd 67): '98 Sandown wnr (clmr, rtd 69): eff at 5/6f, stays 7f: acts on firm, gd/soft & both AWs: eff without blnks: handles any trk, likes Windsor: tough & genuine, win again. *½* **58a**
33 **MARENGO 8** [10] M J Polglase 5-8-13 T Sprake 10/1: 034053: 5 b g Never So Bold - Born To Dance (Dancing Brave) Held up, prog fnl 3f, kept on tho' no threat to front pair: op 8/1: rnr-up earlier in '99 (Redcar clmr, J Berry, rtd 66, rtd 52a at best on sand): won 1st 3 '98 starts, at Southwell, W'hampton & Epsom (h'caps, rtd 69a & 68, J Akehurst): eff at 6f, tried 7f: acts on firm, soft & fibresand: likes a sharp trk: on a fair mark. *5* **46a**
4610} **FRILLY FRONT 15** [12] T D Barron 3-8-10 N Callan (3) 11/2: 623034: Prom, no extra fnl 1f: op 4/1: place form earlier in '99 (rtd 61, h'cap): '98 wnr on debut at Musselburgh (med auct mdn, subs rtd 83 at best): eff at 5/6f: acts on fast, soft & fibresand: handles any trk: has run well fresh: best without blnks. *hd* **42a**
141} **YOUNG IBNR 99** [8] 4-8-13 L Newton 50/1: 0000-5: Led 3f, fdd: long abs, with B A McMahon. *2* **40a**
4331} **GOLDEN BIFF 39** [11] 3-9-2 R Lappin 25/1: 620106: Rdn/mid div, nvr on terms. *½* **41a**
*30 **PRINCESS KALI 8** [6] 3-8-13 (bl) R Fitzpatrick (3) 14/1: 053017: Towards rear, mod gains: op 10/1. *hd* **37a**
-- **MADAME JONES** [9] 4-8-10 Dean McKeown 12/1: 561088: Prom 3f: tchd 14/1: long abs. *1½* **30a**
38 **STONE OF DESTINY 7** [1] 4-8-13 M Tebbutt 50/1: 1-0009: Al rear. *1¾* **29a**
44 **SWINO 5** [5] 5-8-13 (vis) M Henry 12/1: 540340: Al bhd: 10th: op 8/1, quick reapp. *1¼* **26a**
30 **GUNNER SAM 8** [3] 3-8-13 A Culhane 20/1: 100060: Sn outpcd: 11th: op 14/1. *1¾* **22a**
32 **SEVEN SPRINGS 8** [4] 3-8-13 G Duffield 50/1: 000000: Prom 3f: 12th. *4* **12a**
12 ran Time 1m 14.7 (1.9) (City Slickers) D R C Elsworth Whitsbury, Hants

77 **1.45 BIRMINGHAM MDN 2YO (D)** **5f aw** **Going 35 -03 Slow**
£2788 £844 £412 £196

4600} **WAFFLES OF AMIN 16** [1] R Hannon 2-9-0 T Sprake 7/2: 526231: 2 b c Owington - Alzianah (Alzao) Chsd ldrs, rdn over 2f out, switched & styd on well for press to lead nr line, all out: tchd 11/2, AW bow: rnr-up twice earlier in '99 (rtd 79, Redcar mdn): apprec this drop to 5f, stays 6f well: acts on gd, gd/soft & fibresand, any trk: fine sand debut, open to further improvement on this surface. **82a**
4376} **DANCING EMPRESS 36** [5] M A Jarvis 2-8-9 M Tebbutt 11/1: 232302: 2 b f Emperor Jones - Music Khan (Music Boy) Chsd ldr, rdn/led 1f out, styd on well for press, hdd nr line: op 8/1: AW bow: plcd 4 times earlier in '99 (rtd 78): eff at 5/6f on firm, gd/soft, fibresand & any trk: can find a similar on the a/w. *shd* **76a**
46 **KATHOLOGY 5** [2] D R C Elsworth 2-9-0 Pat Eddery 4/6 FAV: 042223: 2 b c College Chapel - Wicken Wonder (Distant Relative) Chsd ldrs, rdn/switched when ch ins last, held nr fin: hvly bckd at odds-on: see 46 (6f). *1¼* **78a**
4607} **MANTILLA 15** [4] R Hollinshead 2-8-9 A Culhane 8/1: 534: Rdn/towards rear, styd on well from over 1f out, nrst fin: op 5/1: AW bow: plcd earlier in '99 (Doncaster mdn, rtd 81): eff at 5f, stays 6f & a return to further looks sure to suit: acts on gd/soft, hvy & fibresand: one to note in mdns/hcaps this winter at 6f+. *nk* **72a**
5 **LICENCE TO THRILL 12** [6] 2-8-9 R Price 7/1: 025: Prom 4f, no extra ins last: op 11/2. *¾* **70a**
4612} **DANCE LITTLE LADY 15** [3] 2-8-9 R Lappin 50/1: 006006: Led 4f, fdd: AW bow. *3* **63$**
-- **GERONIMO** [7] 2-9-0 Dean McKeown 40/1: 7: Dwelt/al rear: debut: Efisio colt: with C W Thornton. *2* **63a**
-- **ARPELLO** [10] 2-8-9 G Duffield 14/1: 8: Dwelt/al bhd: op 8/1, debut: Unfuwain filly: with Sir M Prescott. *6* **43a**
-- **POP THE CORK** [8] 2-9-0 J Fanning 40/1: 9: Dwelt/al rear: debut: Clantime colt: with R Whitaker. *shd* **49a**
4386} **KERRIDGE CHAPEL 35** [9] 2-8-9 A Polli (3) 66/1: 005000: Sn outpcd: 10th. *5* **32a**
10 ran Time 1m 02.1 (1.9) (Sheikh Amin Dahlawi) R Hannon East Everleigh, Wilts

78 **2.20 EBF FILLIES HCAP 3YO+ 0-85 (D)** **1m100y aw** **Going 35 -04 Slow** **[85]**
£8286 £2508 £1224 £582 3 yo rec 2 lb

4615} **MY TESS 14** [3] B A McMahon 3-8-5 (64) Dean McKeown 16/1: 053061: 3 br f Lugana Beach - Barachois Princess (Barachois) Made all, rdn/in command fnl 1f, styd on strongly, pushed out cl-home: op 12/1: earlier in '99 scored at Nottingham (fill mdn, rtd 74): rtd 81 in '98 (plcd, mdn): eff around 1m, stays 10f: acts on gd/soft, soft & fibresand, prob hvy: handles a gall or sharp trk: suited by front running tactics: nicely h'capped. **70a**
4101} **SONG OF SKYE 55** [1] T J Naughton 5-9-1 (72) P Doe (3) 10/1: 354302: 5 b m Warning - Song Of Hope (Chief Singer) Rear, rdn/prog fnl 3f, chsd wnr ins last, kept on tho' al held: op 7/1, AW bow abs: earlier in '99 won h'caps at Sandown & Lingfield (rtd 73 at best): plcd in '98 (h'cap, rtd 75): eff at 6f/1m, suited by 7f on firm, gd/soft & fibresand: handles any trk, likes a stiff/gall one, best without blnks: spot on back at 7f. *2* **73a**
4499} **BOBBYDAZZLE 26** [4] Dr J D Scargill 4-8-1 (58)(ebl) F Norton 25/1: 300003: 4 ch f Rock Hopper - Billie Blue (Ballad Rock) Chsd wnr, no extra fnl 1f: AW bow: plcd earlier in '99 (rtd 72, Chepstow class stks): '98 Newcastle scorer (h'cap, rtd 86): '97 wnr again at Newcastle (val nurs h'cap): suited by a stiff 1m: acts on fast, soft & fibresand, poss handles hvy: likes to force the pace: best without blnks: likes Newcastle. *3* **53a**
4382} **RIVER ENSIGN 35** [2] W M Brisbourne 6-7-10 (53)(3oh) P M Quinn (5) 20/1: 341004: Prom/onepace fnl 2f. *1¾* **45a**
7 **BE MY WISH 12** [11] 4-8-13 (70)(bl) G Duffield 5/1: 040045: Held up, wide bend after 1f/nvr factor. *1¾* **59a**
27 **TALLULAH BELLE 9** [5] 6-10-0 (85) T Sprake 11/2: 000036: Chsd ldrs 6f: topweight: see 27. *shd* **74a**
8 **WHY WORRY NOW 12** [7] 3-7-13 (58) P Fitzsimons (3) 10/1: 340657: Chsd ldrs 5f: op 8/1, blnks omitted. *5* **37a**
29 **VIOLET 9** [6] 3-8-6 (65) J Mackay (7) 33/1: 000008: Prom, struggling fnl 3f. *3½* **37a**
4289} **LADY GEORGIA 42** [9] 3-9-12 (85) P Dobbs (5) 12/1: 5-3109: Al rear: op 8/1, AW bow/6 wk abs. *12* **39a**
*39 **POLAR FAIR 7** [12] 3-7-13 (58) Dale Gibson 8/1: 003010: Wide on bend after 1f, al rear: 10th: op 6/1. *4* **4a**
4552} **DARK ALBATROSS 22** [8] 3-9-3 (76) Pat Eddery 3/1 FAV: 543620: Sn rdn/bhd: 11th: tchd 4/1, AW bow: jockey reported filly would not face kick-back. *10* **7a**
4511} **CARAMBO 25** [10] 4-9-4 (75) N Callan (3) 12/1: 130400: Sn bhd: 12th. *2½* **1a**
12 ran Time 1m 49.5 (3.3) (J D Graham) B A McMahon Hopwas, Staffs

79 **2.50 LADBROKE HCAP 3YO+ 0-85 (D)** **7f aw** **Going 35 -08 Slow** **[84]**
£4162 £1260 £615 £292 3 yo rec 1 lb

35 **ALMAZHAR 8** [10] J L Eyre 4-8-8 (64) T Williams 7/1: 002631: 4 b g Last Tycoon - Mosaique Bleue (Shirley Heights) Prom, rdn/chsd ldr 2f out, led ins last, asserted nr fin, rdn out: op 5/1: earlier in '99 rattled off a hat-trick at Redcar (ladies amat h'cap) & twice at Southwell (h'caps, rtd 66a & 52 at best): eff at 6f/1m, tried 10f: acts on fast, loves fibresand/Southwell: best without blnks/visor: handles any trk, loves a sharp one. **73a**
4565} **ROUGE 21** [5] J P Leigh 4-9-2 (72) Pat Eddery 4/1 CO FAV: 602312: 4 gr f Rudimentary - Couleur de Rose (Kalaglow) Led, rdn/hdd ins last, kept on tho' held nr fin: tchd 5/1: earlier in '99 scored here at W'hampton (C/D, h'cap, 1st success, rtd 71a, rtd 49 on turf): promise in '98 (mdns, rtd 58a, p.u. over *1½* **77a**

hdles): eff at 7f/1m: likes to race up with/force the pace: likes a sharp trk & loves fibresand: win again.

29   **STYLE DANCER** 9 [6] R M Whitaker 5-8-4 (60) J Fanning 20/1: 400003: 5 b g Dancing Dissident -   2½   60a
Showing Style (Pas de Seul) Prom, rdn/held fnl 1f: earlier in '99 won at Haydock (h'cap, rtd 68 at best):
'98 York wnr (h'cap, rtd 74): stays 1m, suited by 7f: acts on firm, gd/soft & fibresand: handles any trk, likes
a gall one: tried blnks, suited by a visor, not worn today: fairly h'capped, can find similar in headgear.

35   **C HARRY** 8 [3] R Hollinshead 5-8-6 (62) Dean McKeown 14/1: 160504: Mid-div, kept on fnl 2f, not   ½   61a
pace to chall: op 12/1: earlier in '99 won at Southwell, W'hampton (clmrs), Leicester (sell h'cap) & twice here at
W'hampton (h'cap & clmr, rtd 71a & 60 at best): '98 wnr again here at W'hampton (2, h'caps & sell, rtd 56a & 56):
eff at 6/7f: acts on firm, gd/soft & fibresand: handles any trk, loves W'hampton: best without a visor: tough.
33   **ROYAL CASCADE** 8 [4] 5-9-13 (83)(bl) G Duffield 5/1: 100035: Cl-up, outpcd over 2f out: see 33.   1¼   79a
47   **GENERAL KLAIRE** 5 [2] 4-9-5 (75) P M Quinn (5) 4/1 CO FAV: 252156: Towards rear/mod gains: op 3/1.1¾   68a
3368} **POLAR ICE** 98 [1] 3-9-7 (83) N Callan (3) 12/1: 211307: Dwelt/al rear: op 10/1: abs, D Cosgrove.   5   66a
3474} **MARMADUKE** 92 [8] 3-9-6 (77) S Whitworth 10/1: 553408: Dwelt, chsd ldrs 5f: op 9/1: abs/AW bow.   ¾   59a
4464} **SCHNITZEL** 30 [7] 3-9-4 (75) G Faulkner (3) 4/1 CO FAV: 010049: Al rear: tchd 5/1.   4   49a
7   **SARI** 12 [9] 3-9-2 (73)(BL) T Sprake 11/1: 401000: Chsd ldrs 5f: 10th: 1st time blnks: tchd 12/1.   ¾   46a
10 ran   Time 1m 29.2 (3.0)   (Sunpak Potatoes)   J L Eyre Sutton Bank, N Yorks

---

80   **3.20 HOLIDAY INN SELLER 2YO (G)   1m100y a Going 35 -31 Slow**
£1924   £539   £262

31   **WILEMMGEO** 8 [1] P C Haslam 2-8-6 Dale Gibson 5/1: 042301: 2 b f Emarati - Floral Spark (Forzando)   55a
Trkd ldrs, led 1f out, styd on well, drvn out: no bid: op 4/1: plcd twice earlier in '99 (rtd 62, Thirsk sell, also
rtd 63a on sand, sell): apprec this step up to 8.5f, further may suit in time: acts on firm, gd/soft & fibresand:
handles a stiff/undul or sharp trk: enjoys sell grade.
4567} **SAMARARDO** 21 [6] N P Littmoden 2-9-2 J Tate 7/2: 050612: 2 b g Son Pardo - Kinlet Vision (Vision)   ½   63$
Led, rdn/hdd 1f out, kept on well for press, just held nr fin: tchd 4/1: earlier in '99 scored at W'hampton (C/D,
h'cap, rtd 54a, rtd 60 at best on turf): eff at 8.5f: acts on fibresand: has run well fresh: best without a visor.
4557} **CUPIDS DART** 21 [5] B J Meehan 2-8-11 Pat Eddery 13/8 FAV: 066303: 2 ch g Pursuit Of Love -   1½   55a
Tisza (Kris) Rdn chasing ldrs, kept on fnl 2f for press, not pace to chall: clr rem: clmd for £5,000 by P Howling:
jockey given a 5-day ban for excessive use of whip: tchd 2/1: place form earlier in '99 (rtd 85 & 73a): stays 8.5f,
further may suit: handles firm & fibresand: handles a stiff/gall or sharp trk: has tried blnks, best without.
4597} **IRISH DANCER** 16 [8] Miss Gay Kelleway 2-8-6 (BL) S Whitworth 6/1: 546004: Chsd ldrs 6f: AW bow.   13   30a
4058} **PRICELESS SECOND** 58 [7] 2-8-11 (bl) N Callan (3) 11/1: -0605: Prom 5f: blnks, changed stable.   8   23a
4569} **DOUBLE VISION** 19 [9] 2-8-11 Dean McKeown 14/1: 006: Rear, mod gains: op 20/1: AW bow.   1¼   20a
4   **DAKISI ROYALE** 12 [10] 2-8-6 A Culhane 14/1: 000657: Mid-div at best: op 10/1.   3   9a
4114} **KAHYASI MOLL** 54 [2] 2-8-6 L Newman (7) 33/1: 004508: Al towards rear: 8 wk abs/AW bow.   2½   4a
53   **CYBER BABE** 4 [4] 2-8-6 (vis) G Arnolda (7) 25/1: 4D0009: Nvr factor: quick reapp.   ¾   3a
48   **ACTUALLY** 5 [11] 2-8-6 (BL) T Sprake 33/1: 005000: Sn bhd: 10th: quick reapp/blnks.   2½   0a
4613} **JOYRENA** 14 [3] 2-8-6 G Duffield 33/1: -0000: Al bhd: 11th.   hd   0a
11 ran   Time 1m 51.8 (5.6)   (M J Cunningham)   P C Haslam Middleham, N Yorks

---

81   **3.50 LIVERPOOL HCAP 3YO+ 0-75 (E)   1m4f aw Going 35 -15 Slow**   [74]
£2804   £788   £385   3 yo rec 6 lb

4522} **BODFARI QUARRY** 25 [6] B W Hills 3-9-9 (75)(t) Pat Eddery 9/1: 001001: 3 b f Efisio - Last Quarry   81a
(Handsome Sailor) Rear, stdy prog wide from 2f out, styd on well for press ins last to lead nr line, all out: op 5/1:
earlier in '99 won at Ayr (h'cap) & here at W'hampton (h'cap, rtd 78 & 77a at best): '98 Beverley wnr (debut, fill mdn,
rtd 79, Mrs Ramsden): eff at 7f/9f, well suited by this step up to 12f, may stay further: acts on fast, gd/soft &
fibresand: runs well fresh: suited by waiting tactics: eff in a t-strap: tried blnks, best without.
706} **ROBELLITA** 99 [4] B Smart 5-9-2 (62) T Sprake 11/2: 232112: 5 b g Robellino - Miellita (King Emperor)   hd   67a
Prom, chsd ldr halfway, led 3f out, kept on well for press, hdd nr line: op 9/2: 8 month abs: earlier in '99
scored at Southwell (mdn, rtd 68a) & Nottingham (h'cap, rtd 55): mod form over jumps prev: eff at 12/14f:
acts on hvy & both AWs: likes to race with/force the pace: handles a sharp or gall trk: can win more races.
2299} **QUINTRELL DOWNS** 99 [3] R M H Cowell 4-10-0 (74) M Tebbutt 3/1: 140113: 4 b g Efisio - Nineteenth   1   78a
Of May (Homing) Held up, prog fnl 4f & ch ins last, kept on tho' just held nr fin: op 5/2, 4 month jumps abs (July
'99 W'hampton wnr, nov h'cap, rtd 85h, eff at 2m on fast): earlier in '99 scored at Southwell (2, appr h'cap & h'cap)
& here at W'hampton (h'cap, rtd 74a & 40 at best): ex-Irish: eff at 11/12f: acts on fast, loves fibresand & handles
gd/soft: likes a sharp/easy trk, esp Southwell & W'hampton: runs well for an appr: clr of rem, win again this winter.
43   **FOREST DREAM** 7 [2] Lady Herries 4-9-0 (60) P Doe (3) 6/4 FAV: 002224: Held up, eff 3f out, sn held: 8   55a
op 5/4: more expected after latest: see 43 (C/D).
43   **MY LEGAL EAGLE** 7 [7] 5-8-1 (47) P Fitzsimons (5) 8/1: 130405: Al towards rear: op 5/1.   2   39a
7   **RAYIK** 12 [5] 4-9-7 (67) A Culhane 10/1: 000006: Chsd ldrs 9f: op 7/1.   3½   54a
3782} **LOST SPIRIT** 75 [8] 3-8-11 (63) Dean McKeown 33/1: 530007: Led/ldrs 5f, wknd 3f out/fdd: jmps fit.   2½   46a
38   **FLAME TOWER** 7 [1] 4-8-8 (54)(t) R Studholme (0) 33/1: 0-3008: Chsd ldr 4f, sn btn: longer trip.   21   14a
8 ran   Time 2m 39.6 (6.0)   (Bodfari Stud Ltd)   B W Hills Lambourn, Berks

---

82   **4.20 CLASS STKS DIV 2 3YO+ 0-60 (F)   6f aw rnd Going 35 +03 Fast**
£1892   £530   £257

4568} **PURPLE FLING** 21 [7] A J McNae 8-9-2 T Sprake 6/1: 003131: 8 ch g Music Boy - Divine Fling   64a
(Imperial Fling) Trkd ldrs, switched & rdN to chall ins last, led nr line, all out: op 5/1: gd time, top-weight:
earlier in '99 won at Southwell (h'cap, rtd 62a, plcd on turf, rtd 54 h'cap): mod form in '98 (rtd 63, slipped
down h'cap): eff at 6/7f on any grnd & trk: well h'capped & holding form well this year, can win more races.
61   **TROJAN HERO** 3 [3] M A Buckley 8-8-13 Dale Gibson 10/1: 320262: 8 ch g Raise A Man - Hulleness   nk   60a
(Northfields) Chsd ldr, rdn/led 1f out, hard rdn/hdd line: op 8/1 quick reapp: see 61 (7f).
40   **TORRENT** 7 [1] D W Chapman 4-8-13 (bl) Lynsey Hanna (7) 3/1 FAV: 320223: 4 ch g Prince Sabo -   1¼   57a
Maiden Pool (Sharpen Up) Led, hdd 1f out, kept on: tchd 4/1, clr rem: see 40 (5f).
4133} **FEATHERSTONE LANE** 53 [5] Miss L C Siddall 8-8-13 N Callan (3) 33/1: 604604: Mid-div, styd on   4   47$
for press fnl 2f, not reach front trio: 8 wk abs: plcd sev times earlier in '99 (rtd 54a & 50 at best): '98 wnr 4
times here at W'hampton (2 clmrs, sell & a h'cap, rtd 72a, plcd on turf, rtd 49, h'cap): eff at 5/6f: acts on fast
& gd/soft, loves both AW, W'hampton specialist: eff with/without a visor: not disgraced, will apprec return to h'caps.
44   **PRIX STAR** 5 [11] 4-8-13 (vis) A Culhane 10/1: 602455: Towards rear, mod late gains: op 8/1,   1½   43a
quick reapp: earlier in '99 scored at Catterick (h'cap, rtd 63): plcd in '98 (h'caps, rtd 84 at best): eff at 6f,

WOLVERHAMPTON (Fibresand)   SATURDAY NOVEMBER 20TH   Lefthand, Very Sharp

stays a sharp 7f: acts on firm, soft & fibresand: handles any trk: eff with/without a visor: on a fair mark.

4504} **DOLPHINELLE** 26 [10] 3-8-13 (bl) R Smith (5) 4/1: 254046: Twds rear/mod gains: op 6/1.		2	38a
4471} **NIGHTINGALE SONG** 29 [4] 5-8-13 Pat Eddery 4/1: D10607: Mid-div at best: op 3/1.		¾	36a
788} **PRESS AHEAD** 99 [9] 4-8-13 (bl) G Duffield 8/1: 1-6028: Prom 4f: op 7/1: 8 month abs.		6	24a
40 **MISS BANANAS** 7 [12] 4-8-10 D Meah (7) 12/1: 500109: Speed 3f: tchd 14/1.		hd	20a
4573} **DISTANT KING** 19 [8] 6-8-13 Clare Roche (7) 20/1: 006000: Sn bhd/t.o.: 10th.		18	0a
4385} **PRINCESS FOLEY** 35 [6] 3-8-10 M Tebbutt 25/1: 002600: Sn bhd/t.o.: 11th.		hd	0a
2229} **VIE INDIENNE** 99 [2] 3-8-10 (BL) S Whitworth 10/1: -0030: Sn t.o.: 12th: blnks, op 8/1: AW bow.		hd	0a
12 ran Time 1m 14.7 (1.9) (A J McNae) A J McNae Headley, Surrey			

SOUTHWELL (Fibresand)   MONDAY NOVEMBER 22ND   Lefthand, Sharp, Oval Track

Official Going   STANDARD. Stalls: Inside.

83   12.40 AMAT HCAP DIV 1 3YO+ 0-60 (G)   1m aw rnd   Going 65   -18 Slow   [39]
£1626   £454   £219   3 yo   rec 2 lb

67   **DARE** 5 [3]   P D Evans 4-11-4 (57) (vis) Miss E Folkes (5) 3/1 FAV: 115301: 4 b g Beveled - Run Amber   **64a**
Run (Run The Gantlet): Handy, led 2f out, styd on well inside last, rdn out: qck reapp: earlier in '99 won at
Hamilton, Salisbury, Southwell & Leicester (h'caps, rtd 55a & 53): unplcd over hdles prev & mod Flat form (E James):
eff at 1m/12f on gd/soft, soft & fibresand: runs well fresh: eff with/without a vis: runs well for an appr/amat.

38   **CLEAR NIGHT** 9 [9]   J J Sheehan 3-10-7 (48) Mr D Slattery (7) 33/1: 106002: 3 b c Night Shift - Clarista   ¾   **53a**
(Riva Ridge): Handy, led after 2f till rdn/hdd 2f out, kept on for press: earlier in '99 scored at Chepstow
(sell, R Hannon, rtd 63): place form in '98 (rtd 82, Newbury mdn): eff at 1m: acts on fast, gd/soft & fibresand:
best without blnks, has tried a t-strap: likes to race with/force the pace, can find similar.

4572} **GADGE** 21 [7]   A Bailey 8-10-11 (50) Miss Bridget Gatehou 13/2: 000603: 8 br g Nomination - Queenstyle   5   **45a**
(Moorestyle): Chsd ldrs, kept on final 2f, not pace front pair: place form earlier in '99 (rtd 57a, AW h'cap, also
rtd 49 on turf, h'cap): '98 Brighton wnr (classified stks, rtd 70, also rtd 58a): won 6 h'caps in '97 (rtd 55a & 85 at
best): eff at 6/7f, stays 1m well: acts on firm, hvy & both AWs: best without hdgr: likes to race with/force the pace.

4565} **MAGICAL SHOT** 23 [11]   D Carroll 4-11-7 (60) Mrs C Williams 16/1: 006004: Prom, rdn/wide on bend   1¼   **52a**
over 2f out, kept on tho' al held final 1f: tchd 20/1, jumps fit (mod form): earlier in '99 scored at W'hampton (mdn,
rtd 68 at best): ex-Irish, plcd in mdns for D Weld in '98 (7f/1m, fast & gd/soft): eff at 1m/11f: acts on fibresand,
handles fast & gd/soft grnd: likes a sharp trk: best without blnks.

50   **MR ROUGH** 7 [8]   8-10-0 (38) (vis)(1ow) Mr Paul J Morris (0) 16/1: 340005: Mid-div, effort/wide 2f out   2½   **26a**
kept on tho' held inside last.

3307} **REGAL SPLENDOUR** 99 [4]   6-10-8 (47) Mr J Roe (7) 9/1: -56266: Rdn/towards rear, mod gains: abs.   ¾   **33a**

*60   **THE BARGATE FOX** 5 [16]   3-10-12 (53) (6ex) Miss Alex Wells (7) 9/2: 000517: Wide/rear, late gains   hd   **38a**
final 2f, no threat: tricky high draw: quick reapp: see 60.

4153} **PARK ROYAL** 54 [5]   4-10-0 (39) Mr R Lucey Butler (7 33/1: 000-08: Rear, mod prog: jumps fit.   7   **13a**

45   **WAIKIKI BEACH** 7 [12]   8-11-3 (56) (bl) Mrs J Moore 13/2: 330349: Chsd ldrs 5f.   nk   **29a**

69   **BRANDONVILLE** 3 [13]   6-10-5 (44) Mr Nicky Tinkler (7) 33/1: /0-000: Dwelt/al rear: 10th: qck reapp.   1¾   **14a**

32   **QUAKERESS** 10 [10]   4-9-11 (36) Mr M Murphy (5) 25/1: 000000: Led 2f, btn final 3f: 11th.   1½   **3a**

52   Highfielder 6 [14] 3-10-1 (42) (vis) Mrs S Moore (5) 20/1:

61   Bicton Park 5 [6] 5-9-10 (35) Miss Leigh Hogben (7) 50/1:

45   Neronian 7 [1] 5-9-10 (35) (bl) Miss K Warnett (2) 12/1:

4598} Southbound Train 18 [15] 3-10-9 (50) Mr R Emmett (7) 25/1:

390} Anchor Venture 99 [2] 6-9-13 (38) Mr T Best (3) 33/1:

16 ran   Time 1m 46.00 (6.6)   (J E Potter)   P D Evans Leighton, Powys.

84   1.10 GOLF CLUB MDN Y3O+ (D)   1m4f aw   Going 65   -06 Slow
£2918   £884   £432   £206   3 yo   rec 6 lb

4546} **SHARP STEPPER** 24 [7]   J H M Gosden 3-8-7 M Hills 1/2 FAV: 563321: 3 b f Selkirk - Awtaar (Lyphard):   **78a**
Keen, chsd ldrs, smooth prog to lead over 2f out, sn in command, easily: value for 10L+: well bckd at odds-on:
AW bow: rnr-up earlier in '99 (Newmarket h'cap, rtd 78): eff at 10/12f, further may suit in time: acts on gd,
gd/soft & fibresand: found this a straightforward task, could win more races on sand.

4590} **PRASLIN ISLAND** 19 [9]   A Kelleway 3-8-12 J Tate 16/1: 002062: 3 ch c Be My Chief - Hence   5   **67a**
(Mr Prospector): Led till over 2f out, kept on for press tho' no ch with wnr: op 10/1, had rest well covered:
rnr-up thrice earlier in '99 (rtd 76, Yarmouth mdn & 64a, AW h'cap): eff at 12f, stays stiff/undul 2m1f well:
handles fast grnd & fibresand: best without blnks or t-strap: could find similar this winter.

1813} **MORGANS ORCHARD** 99 [11]   A G Newcombe 3-8-12 G Sparkes 50/1: 053: 3 ch g Forest Wind -   4   **61a**
Regina St Cyr (Doulab): Wide/rear, prog halfway, kept on final 3f, no threat from pair: clr of rem: lngr 12f
trip/AW bow: 6 mth abs: no form from 2 starts on turf earlier in '99.

--   **GUTTERIDGE** [12]   P D Evans 9-9-4 P McCabe 50/1: 4: Held up, effort halfway, btn final 3f: Flat   17   **42a**
debut, 8 wk jumps abs (98/99 wnr of 3 nov chases, rtd 114c at best, best at 2m4f, stays 3m on firm & soft).

4546} **BONNES NOUVELLES** 24 [3]   3-8-7 Pat Eddery 9/2: 55-305: Prom 7f: op 3/1: AW bow.   5   **30a**

4351} **BEAUCHAMP NYX** 40 [1]   3-8-7 C Rutter 66/1: 0-006: Rear, nvr on terms: 6 wk abs, AW bow.   ¾   **29a**

50   **NEEDWOOD MERLIN** 7 [2]   3-8-12 Dean McKeown 50/1: 30007: Sn bhd: lngr 12f trip.   11   **22a**

2219} **KPOLO** 99 [10]   4-9-4 P Doe (3) 33/1: 406068: Chsd ldrs 7f: 5 mth abs.   nk   **22a**

39   **KATIE JANE** 9 [6]   4-8-13 L Newton 50/1: 09: Cl-up 3f.   9   **7a**

4598} **MOLY** 18 [8]   3-8-7 T Sprake 7/1: 450: Prom 7f: 10th: op 6/1: AW bow/lngr 12f trip.   nk   **7a**

3503} Skiffle Man 93 [4] 3-8-12 S Drowne 25/1:   849} Nisibis 99 [5] 3-8-7 G Bardwell 33/1:

12 ran   Time 2m 40.0 (5.7)   (Mrs Diane Snowden)   J H M Gosden Newmarket, Suffolk.

85   1.40 AMAT HCAP DIV 2 3YO+ 0-60 (G)   1m aw rnd   Going 65   -15 Slow   [37]
£1616   £451   £218   3 yo   rec 2 lb

4394} **TROJAN WOLF** 37 [6]   P Howling 4-11-6 (57) Miss S Pocock (7) 8/1: 242051: 4 ch g Wolfhound - Trojan   **70a**
Lady (Irish River): Made virtually all, clr halfway, styd on strongly inside last, rdn out: op 7/1, first win:
earlier in '99 with D Sasse, rnr-up twice (rtd 58 & 56a, h'caps): rtd 76 in '98 (mdn, N Tompkins): eff at 6/7f,
stays 10f, well suited by forcing tactics & 1m today: acts on firm, gd & both AWs: handles a stiff/gall or sharp

trk: best without a t-strap: runs well for an amat: plenty in hand here for new trainer, can win again.
3427} **WESTERN RAINBOW 96** [5] P D Evans 3-10-7 (46) Miss E Folkes (5) 14/1: 0-0002: 3 b g Rainbows For Life - Miss Galwegian (Sandord Lad): Held up, kept on final 3f, no threat to wnr: tchd 16/1, 3 mth abs/AW bow: prev with H Akbary, rtd 34 at best earlier in '99 (h'cap): mod form in Ireland prev: stays 1m & handles fibresand. *6* **53a**
3158} **MYTTONS MOMENT 99** [15] A Bailey 3-10-12 (51)(bl) Miss Bridget Gatehou 11/2 JT FAV: 054633: 3 b g Waajib - Late Swallow (My Swallow): Rear, drvn & kept on final 2f, nvr pace to chall: AW bow, jmps fit (recent Uttoxeter wnr, juv nov hdle, rtd 110h, eff at 2m on firm & gd/soft in blnks): earlier in '99 won at Newmarket (sell, rtd 62 at best): eff at 1m, poss stays 10f: acts on fast, gd/soft & fibresand, any trk: best in blnks. *1* **56a**
4509} **QUALITAIR SURVIVOR 27** [13] J Hetherton 4-10-1 (38) Mrs S Bosley 33/1: 400004: Cl-up 6f: AW bow. *2½* **38a**
39 **ABOVE BOARD 9** [7] 4-9-12 (35) Mrs M Morris (3) 25/1: 060055: Rear, prog/wide over 2f out, sn held. *1½* **32a**
50 **ADIRPOUR 7** [12] 5-10-0 (37) Mr T Best (5) 12/1: 400006: Held up, rdn/no room over 2f out, kept on. *1½* **32a**
2549} **MOONLIGHT FLIT 99** [10] 4-10-10 (47) Miss Diana Jones 6/1: 133007: Chsd ldrs 6f: op 5/1, 5 mth abs. *2½* **37a**
4128} **NEPTUNE 55** [11] 3-9-13 (38) Miss Leigh Hogben (7) 16/1: 060548: Rdn/rear, mod prog: abs/new stable. *½* **27a**
4578} **GENUINE JOHN 21** [14] 6-10-3 (40) Mr D O'Meara 8/1: 000309: Chsd ldrs, held final 2f: op 6/1. *1½* **26a**
78 **RIVER ENSIGN 2** [8] 6-10-13 (50) Miss K Rockey (5) 7/1: 410040: Cl-up 6f: op 5/1: 10th: qck reapp. *nk* **35a**
68 **MARKELLIS 3** [3] 3-10-2 (41) Mrs C Williams 12/1: 606060: Chsd ldrs 6f: 11th: op 14/1: qck reapp. *¾* **25a**
4156} **WRY ARDOUR 54** [1] 3-9-13 (38) Miss C Hannaford (5) 11/2 JT FAV: 000050: Dwelt/reluctant to race, nvr a factor: 12th: 8 wk abs: AW bow. *4* **14a**
4363} **Archello 39** [9] 5-10-6 (43) Mr W Fearon (7) 20/1: -- **Barossa Valley** [2] 8-11-7 (58) Mr R Lucey Butler (7) 50/1:
4372} **Blue Line Angel 38** [16] 3-10-9 (48) Mr S Edgar (7) 20/1:
1206} **Ciel De Reve 99** [4] 5-11-4 (55) Dr A Kimber (7) 40/1:
16 ran Time 1m 45.8 (6.4) (Max Pocock) P Howling Newmarket, Suffolk.

86 2.10 BOX MED AUCT MDN 2YO (F) 1m aw rnd Going 65 -04 Slow
£2295 £645 £315

4613} **SERVICE STAR 16** [5] M A Jarvis 2-9-0 (BL) M Tebbutt 5/1: 442201: 2 b c Namaqualand - Shenley Lass (Prince Tenderfoot): Chsd ldrs, rdn/led 2f out, styd on strongly inside last, rdn out: op 4/1, first time blnks: rnr-up twice earlier in '99 (rtd 77, York auct mdn, rtd 68 on sand, mdn): eff at 1m, mid-dists may yet suit: acts on firm, fast grnd & fibresand: handles a stiff/gall or sharp trk: sharpened up by headgear today. **80a**
4614} **ROYAL CAVALIER 16** [9] R Hollinshead 2-9-0 P M Quinn (5) 6/4 FAV: 43422: 2 b g Prince Of Birds - Gold Belt (Bellypha): Wide/cl-up, ev ch/hung left over 2f out, held final 1f: hvly bckd, tchd 5/2: AW bow: rnr-up earlier in '99 (Doncaster auct mdn, rtd 87): eff at 1m, mid dists should suit: acts on gd/soft, hvy & fibresand: *6* **70a**
-- **EL ZITO** [4] B J Meehan 2-9-0 Pat Eddery 5/2: 23: 2 b g Mukaddamah - Samite (Tennyson): Led till 2f out, kept on for press: op 6/4: British debut/AW bow: rnr-up earlier in '99 Italy (8.5f, soft): eff arnd 1m, mid-dists should suit in time: prob handles fibresand & soft grnd. *½* **69a**
4601} **LE CAVALIER 18** [3] C N Allen 2-9-0 M Hills 20/1: 503004: Chsd ldrs, no extra over 1f out: AW bow. *1¾* **66a**
4607} **COSMIC SONG 17** [2] 2-8-9 Dean McKeown 40/1: -005: Held up, effort 3f out, sn held: AW bow. *4* **53$**
-- **BLUE CAVALIER** [12] 2-9-0 P Doe (3) 25/1: 6: Dwelt, sn handy, fdd over 2f out: debut. *5* **48a**
4528} **OPEN GROUND 26** [6] 2-9-0 A McCarthy (3) 40/1: 07: Chsd ldrs 5f: AW bow, now with P Howling. *5* **38a**
4588} **UNICORN STAR 19** [7] 2-9-0 A Culhane 9/1: 048: Chsd ldrs 5f: op 6/1: AW bow. *3* **32a**
4452} **WILD FLIGHT 32** [11] 2-9-0 T Lucas 40/1: 09: Prom 4f: AW bow. *3½* **25a**
-- **BARTON LEA** [1] 2-8-9 P Hanagan (7) 40/1: 0: Dwelt/nvr a factor: 10th: debut, with R Fahey. *hd* **19a**
4606} **St Georges Boy 17** [10] 2-9-0 F Norton 100/1: -- **Importune** [8] 2-9-0 Kim Tinkler 33/1:
12 ran Time 1m 44.9 (5.5) (N S Young) M A Jarvis Newmarket, Suffolk.

87 2.40 MEMBERS FILL HCAP 3YO+ 0-70 (E) 6f aw rnd Going 65 +07 Fast [61]
£2814 £852 £416 £198

3639} **HAUNT THE ZOO 85** [4] J L Harris 4-8-7 (40) J Bramhill 14/1: 405461: 4 b f Komaite - Merryhill Maid (M Double M) Chsd ldrs, stdy run fnl 2f to overhaul ldr well ins last, rdn out: best time of day, 3 mth abs, first success: place form earlier in '99 (rtd 46 & 47a): missed '98: rtd 75 at best in '97 (juv mdn): eff at 6/7f & has tried 1m: acts on fast grnd & f/sand: handles a sharp or gall trk: runs well fresh: op to further improvement. **48a**
4586} **TANCRED TIMES 20** [9] D W Barker 4-8-6 (39) Kimberley Hart (5) 12/1: 26W502: 4 ch f Clantime - Mischievous Miss (Niniski) Led, rdn fnl 2f, hdd well ins last & no extra: tchd 14/1: rnr-up twice earlier in '99 (rtd 48 & 40a): '98 wnr at Carlisle (h'cap, rtd 65 & rtd 47a): eff at 5/6f, stays 7f: acts on firm, soft & f/sand, prob handles equitrack: handles any trk, likes a sharp one: likes to race with/force the pace: best without blnks. *1½* **42a**
30 **DAHLIDYA 10** [13] M J Polglase 4-8-12 (45) P Doe (3) 7/1: 000053: 4 b f Midyan - Dalawise (Caerleon) Slowly away & rdn, prog wide fnl 3f, held ins last: op 5/1: place form earlier in '99 (rtd 54a, sell): '98 wnr at W'hampton & Southwell (h'caps, rtd 52a): eff at 5/6f, stays 7f & has tried further: acts on fibresand, prob handles equitrack & gd/soft grnd: runs well for an appr: best without blnks: likes a sharp trk. *1½* **44a**
40 **HEAVENLY MISS 9** [7] D Shaw 5-9-2 (49)(bl) Pat Eddery 7/1: 021054: Mid-div, no room 2f out, kept on for press inside last, nvr pace to chall: op 5/1: stays 6f well but poss best suited by 5f. *¾* **46a**
4227} **STRATS QUEST 49** [8] 5-8-11 (44)(vis) S Whitworth 7/1: 260045: Mid-div, nvr pace to chall: op 6/1, abs. *1¾* **37a**
76 **PRINCESS KALI 2** [3] 3-9-10 (57)(bl) R Fitzpatrick (3) 8/1: 530106: Chsd ldrs, nvr factor: tchd 9/1, qck reapp: topweight: see 30 (clmr). *½* **48a**
4331} **PETITE DANSEUSE 41** [2] 5-8-6 (39) P Fessey 13/2: 354267: Chsd ldrs 4f: op 7/1, 6 wk abs. *1¼* **27a**
63 **MISS PIPPIN 5** [1] 3-9-7 (54) L Newton 20/1: 44058: Cl-up 5f: qck reapp. *2½* **35a**
3165} **MAKE READY 99** [10] 5-9-10 (57) L Newman (7) 4/1 FAV: 641509: Chsd ldrs/wide, drvn/held final 2f: op 3/1: earlier in '99 won at W'hampton (h'cap, rtd 50a), Chepstow & Newmarket (fillies h'caps, rtd 71 at best): eff at 5f, suited by 6f: acts on firm, gd & fibresand: handles any trk: best forcing the pace without a visor. *7* **25a**
61 **LAKE ARIA 5** [6] 6-7-13 (32)(bl)(3ow)(11oh) N Carlisle 50/1: 040000: Chsd ldrs 3f: 10th: qck reapp. *1¼* **0a**
45 **Sounds Sweet 7** [12] 3-7-12 (31)(bl) P M Quinn(5) 40/1: 4405} **Compton Amber 35** [11] 3-9-0 (47) G Carter 20/1:
4303} **Red Symphony 42** [5] 3-9-7 (54) R Lappin 12/1:
13 ran Time 1m 16.8 (3.5) (R Atkinson) J L Harris Eastwell, Leics.

88 3.10 MINSTER SELLER 2YO (G) 7f aw rnd Going 65 -17 Slow
£1924 £539 £262

4582} **SIRENE 20** [3] M J Polglase 2-8-6 (1ow) Pat Eddery 14/1: 0001: 2 ch f Mystiko - Breakaway (Song) Made most, styd on gamely ins last, drvn out: no bid, AW bow, rider reportedly given a 2-day whip ban: no form from 3 turf starts earlier in '99: suited by front running tactics at 7f, further may suit: acts on fibresand: apprec drop to selling grade: ever-green Pat Eddery completed record 26th century of winners. **54a**

SOUTHWELL (Fibresand) **MONDAY NOVEMBER 22ND** **Lefthand, Sharp, Oval Track**

74 **PETRIE 3** [9] M R Channon 2-8-11 Paul Cleary (7) 7/4 FAV: 542322: 2 ch g Fraam - Canadian Capers *1* **56a**
(Ballacashtal) Chsd ldrs, rdn to chall fnl 2f, hung left/held nr fin: well bckd: qck reapp: styd lngr 7f trip.
36 **CHURCH FARM FLYER 10** [1] C N Allen 2-8-6 L Newman (7) 12/1: 00663: 2 b f College Chapel - Young *1¾* **48a**
Isabel (Last Tycoon) Chsd ldrs, rdn halfway, kept on ins last tho nvr a threat: op 10/1: rtd 53 on turf earlier in '99 (Newmarket sell): stays 7f, has tried 1m, may suit in time: handles fibresand.
36 **GENTLE ANNE 10** [7] Ronald Thompson 2-8-6 A Daly 4/1: 066634: Prom, effort/hung left over 1f out & *1½* **45a**
sn held: nicely bckd, tchd 9/2: clr of rem: see 36.
48 **EXUDE 7** [11] 2-8-6 G Carter 16/1: 065: Rear, mod gains: op 12/1. *5* **35a**
36 **FORTHECHOP 10** [6] 2-8-11 J Tate 50/1: 6006: Cl-up 5f. *nk* **39a**
3971} **ALL ROSES 65** [8] 2-8-6 R Fitzpatrick (3) 7/1: 02007: Dwelt/rdn & rear, mod prog: op 6/1, 2 mth abs. *hd* **33a**
4567} **SHEERNESS ESSITY 23** [2] 2-8-11 D Griffiths 6/1: 024108: Prom 3f: op 9/2. *5* **28a**
3810} **PEPPERCORN 76** [4] 2-8-6 G Baker (7) 25/1: 50509: Dwelt/al rear: 11 wk abs. *1½* **20a**
4132} **TONGA 55** [10] 2-8-6 Dean McKeown 33/1: 000: Chsd ldrs 3f: 10th: 8 wk abs. *3* **14a**
62 **LANDFALL LIL 5** [5] 2-8-6 G Bardwell 12/1: 026000: Sn bhd: 11th: op 10/1, qck reapp. *1½* **11a**
11 ran Time 1m 32.7 (6.1) (Mark Bury) M J Polglase Southwell, Notts.

89 **3.40 GREAT DAY HCAP 3YO+ 0-75 (E)** **1m6f aw** **Going 65** **+01 Fast** **[75]**
£2696 £756 £368 3 yo rec 8 lb

*66 **VIRGIN SOLDIER 5** [4] M Johnston 3-9-2 (71)(6ex) M Hills 4/6 FAV: 111111: 3 ch g Waajib - Never Been **84a**
Chaste (Posse) Al travelling well in tch, led 6f out & clr 4f out, eased down nr fin, v cmftbly: value for 10L+, gd time, nicely bckd, qck reapp: recently won at Lingfield, Southwell & W'hampton (h'caps): earlier in '99 scored again at Lingfield (h'cap, rtd 51a) & Musselburgh (h'cap, rtd 58): plcd in '98 (mdn, rtd 62, T Etherington): eff at 12f/2m on gd, gd/soft & both AWs: handles any trk, loves a sharp one: best without blnks: tough & progressive.
4618} **IL PRINCIPE 16** [5] John Berry 5-9-4 (65)(e) F Norton 11/4: 341012: 5 b g Ela Mana Mou - Seattle *5* **67a**
Siren (Seattle Slew) Chsd ldrs, chsd wnr fnl 3f, no impress: wore an eye-shield: earlier in '99 won at Haydock, Musselburgh, York & Doncaster (h'caps, rtd 80 & 61a): '98 scorer at Redcar (h'cap, rtd 67 & 65a): eff at 14f/2m on fast, both AWs, loves gd/soft & hvy: handles any trk: best without a visor: met a fast improving rival.
6 **LEGAL LUNCH 14** [3] P W Harris 4-9-7 (68)(vis) Pat Eddery 4/1: 065233: 4 b g Alleged - Dinner Surprise *16* **52a**
(Lyphard) Cl-up, led halfway till 6f out, sn held & eased ins last: tchd 9/2: btr 6 (equitrack).
1566} **CRASH CALL LADY 99** [1] C N Allen 3-7-10 (51)(15oh) J Mackay (7) 66/1: 000254: Led to halfway, sn *8* **26a**
btn: 6 mth abs: earlier in '99 scored at W'hampton (auct mdn, rtd 55a): plcd in '98 (rtd 45 & 47a): eff at 12f, stays 14.8f on fibresand, poss handles gd/soft & soft: eff with/without blnks or vis: likes a sharp trk.
37 **ALMAMZAR 10** [6] 9-7-10 (43)(20oh) Kim Tinkler 100/1: 640005: In tch till halfway: rtd 37 at best *½* **17a**
earlier in '99 (h'cap): mod form over hdles in 95/96: back in '92 won at Yarmouth (1m mdn, Sir M Stoute): prob stays a stiff/undul 2m1f & handles fast grnd: has tried a t-strap.
-- **ONYOUROWN** [2] 6-10-0 (75)(vis) Sarah Robinson (7) 50/1: 3141/6: In tch 4f: long Flat abs/jmps fit. *dist* **0a**
6 ran Time 3m 08.8 (9.0) (J David Abell) M Johnston Middleham, Nth Yorks.

LINGFIELD (Equitrack) **TUESDAY NOVEMBER 23RD** **Lefthand, V Sharp Track**

Official Going STANDARD Stalls: 5f/1m - Outside, Rem - Inside

90 **11.35 FAUCETS APPR HCAP 3YO+ 0-85 (G)** **1m2f aw** **Going 36** **-22 Slow** **[85]**
£1797 £510 £252 3 yo rec 4 lb

4429} **FARMOST 35** [1] Sir Mark Prescott 6-10-0 (85) M Worrell (7) 9/4: 111W01: 6 ch g Pharly - Dancing Meg **89a**
(Marshua's Dancer) Made virtually all, rdn/prsd fnl 3f, styd on well ins last & in command cl-home, rdn out: nicely bckd tho' op 6/4: earlier in '99 won at Chepstow (2, h'caps) & Redcar (class stks, rtd 79): unplcd in '98, prev term won at Bath (ltd stks), Brighton & W'hampton (3, incl Listed, rtd 98a & 85): suited by 9/10f: acts on gd/soft, likes gd & firm, both AWs, any trk: eff weight carrier: v tough (15 wins from 35 starts).
23 **JAVA SHRINE 12** [4] D J Wintle 8-9-2 (73)(bl) Joanna Badger (5) 6/4 FAV: 300032: 8 b g Java Gold - *1½* **74a**
Ivory Idol (Alydar) Cl-up halfway, rdn/ev ch fnl 2f, kept on tho' held nr fin: nicely bckd: clr rem, see 23.
*50 **SHEER NATIVE 8** [2] Miss Gay Kelleway 3-9-1 (76)(6ex) T Eaves (5) 100/30: 130013: 3 b f In The Wings *3½* **72a**
- Native Magic (Be My Native) Chsd wnr 2f, rdn/lost place halfway, kept on fnl 2f, no threat to front pair: op 11/4: prev with B W Hills: see 50 (sell, 1m).
22 **COLONEL NORTH 12** [3] Andrew Reid 3-8-9 (70) G Arnolda (5) 14/1: 011664: Chsd wnr after 2f till *nk* **65a**
halfway, btn 3f out: op 8/1: earlier in '99 scored at Newmarket (clmr, W R Muir) & Carlisle (h'cap, current connections, rtd 75): unplcd sole '98 start: eff at 1m, 10f+ may yet suit: acts on firm, poss handles equitrack.
22 **FAMOUS 12** [5] 6-7-10 (53)(11oh) Claire Bryan 12/1: 010045: Rear, rdn 3f out, sn held: tchd 14/1: *11* **32a**
earlier in '99 scored at Brighton & Sandown (appr h'caps, rtd 45, rnr-up on sand, stks, rtd 57a): plcd in '98 (rtd 50a & 45): eff at 1m/10f, stays a sharp 12f: acts on fast, hvy & equitrack: handles any trk, likes a sharp/undul one: best without blnks/visor: runs well for an appr.
5 ran Time 2m 08.58 (5.78) (W E Sturt - Osborne House II) Sir Mark Prescott Newmarket, Suffolk

91 **12.05 GROHE HCAP 3YO+ 0-75 (E)** **5f aw rnd** **Going 36** **+01 Fast** **[75]**
£2788 £844 £412 £196

4384} **SHARP HAT 38** [7] D W Chapman 5-8-10 (57) A Culhane 20/1: 000001: 5 b g Shavian - Madam Trilby **62+**
(Grundy) Towards rear/wide, strong run for press fnl 1f to lead nr line: op 14/1: earlier in '99 with T J Etherington (rtd 74 & 39a, tumbled down h'cap): plcd in '98 (rtd 87, stks, R Hannon): '97 Newbury wnr (h'cap, rtd 93): eff at 5f, suited by 6f, stays 7f: acts on firm, soft, equitrack & any trk: best without blnks: extremely well h'capped, yet another to be revitalised having left T J Etherington: type to run up a sequence, esp with a return to 6f.
*40 **ECUDAMAH 10** [6] Miss Jacqueline S Doyle 3-9-6 (67) T Sprake 7/2: 000412: 3 ch g Mukaddamah - *shd* **70a**
Great Land (Friend's Choice) Chsd ldrs, drvn & kept on well ins last, briefly led nr fin, just held: tchd 4/1: acts on both AW's, fast & soft grnd: in gd heart: see 40 (fibresand).
4610} **DOUBLE O 18** [5] W Jarvis 5-9-12 (73)(bl) F Norton 7/1: 001003: 5 b g Sharpo - Ktolo (Tolomeo) *½* **74a**
Rdn/outpcd early in mid-div, strong run for press fnl 1f, just held nr fin: op 5/1: recent brief spell with D Nicholls, earlier in '99 scored at Brighton for current connections (h'cap, rtd 73, plcd on sand, rtd 73a h'cap): '98 W'hampton wnr (2 h'caps, rtd 83a): eff at 5/6f, tried 7f: acts on gd, gd/soft, loves both AWs & a sharp trk, esp W'hampton: eff with/without blnks: fairly h'capped, a likely type for similar back at W'hampton.

LINGFIELD (Equitrack)   TUESDAY NOVEMBER 23RD   Lefthand, V Sharp Track

28   JUST DISSIDENT 12 [1] R M Whitaker 7-8-10 (57) L Dettori 5/1: 000104: Cl-up, rdn/ev ch ins last, no ½ 56a
extra cl-home: op 9/2: earlier in '99 won here at Lingfield (h'cap, rtd 56a, rtd 41 at best on turf): rnr-up in '98
(AW h'cap, rtd 58a, rtd 59 on turf, stks): '97 wnr at Pontefract & Lingfield (h'caps, rtd 62 & 57a): eff at 5f, stays
a sharp 7f well: loves to force the pace: acts on gd, firm & equitrack, any trk, likes Lingfield: best without a visor.
4586} PALACEGATE JACK 21 [2] 8-8-6 (53)(bl) D Allan (7) 16/1: 063405: Led, rdn/2L clr 1f out, wknd qckly 2½ 45a
qckly well ins last & hdd nr fin: op 12/1.
4573} LA DOYENNE 22 [3] 5-8-11 (58) S Whitworth 8/1: 425056: Cl-up, rdn/no extra over 1f out: op 6/1. ¾ 48a
3082} LIGHT BREEZE 99 [8] 3-7-10 (43)(60h) R Brisland (4) 50/1: 650007: Rdn/outpcd, nvr factor: 4 mth abs. hd 32a
57   BOWCLIFFE GRANGE 7 [4] 7-7-10 (43) P M Quinn (5) 9/4 FAV: 400128: Dwelt, sn cl-up, ev ch 2f out, 1½ 28a
wknd qckly ins last: nicely bckd, tchd 5/2: speedy gldg who hampers ch occasionally with tardy start: see 57.
57   CELTIC VENTURE 7 [10] 4-8-8 (55) P Doe (3) 16/1: /10009: Al outpcd/bhd. 1½ 36a
3926} SPENDER 69 [9] 10-10-0 (75) A Clark 25/1: 000000: Dwelt, sn bhd: 10th: topweight. 8 36a
10 ran   Time 59.54 (1.74)   (Mrs N F Thesiger)   D W Chapman Stillington, N Yorks

---

92   **12.35 GROHE CLAIMER DIV I 3YO+** (F)   **1m aw rnd   Going 36   -02 Slow**
£1787   £500   £242   3 yo rec 2 lb

4552} NIGHT CITY 25 [7] K R Burke 4-9-7 P Doe (3) 11/4: 001511: 8 b g Kris - Night Secret (Nijinsky) 77a
Prom, chsd ldr halfway, rdn/chall fnl 2f, styd on well for press to lead well ins last, all out: nicely bckd tho' op
7/4: earlier in '99 scored at Hamilton, York (clmrs) & Brighton (h'cap, rtd 74 & 82a at best): won 4 times here
at Lingfield in '98 (2 a/w clmrs & h'cap, also a turf h'cap) & Hamilton (2, h'cap & clmr), Thirsk, Catterick,
Brighton & York (clmrs, rtd 80 & 86a): eff at 1m/13f: acts on any grnd/trk, loves Lingfield: loves to dominate.
61   PALACEGATE TOUCH 6 [4] J Berry 9-8-9 (bl) G Carter 10/1: 600632: 9 gr g Petong - Dancing Chimes hd 64$
(London Bells) Led, rdn/strongly prsd fnl 2f, hdd well ins last, styd on gamely, just held: op 6/1: quick reappr:
eff at 5/6f, now stays a sharp 1m well: loves to force the pace, a return to h'caps could suit: see 61 (sell).
29   LUCAYAN BEACH 12 [5] B Gubby 5-8-5 C Rutter 20/1: 000003: 5 gr g Cyrano de Bergerac - Mrs Gray 1¼ 57a
(Red Sunset) Dwelt, sn chsd ldr, rdn & kept on well fnl 2f, not pace to chall nr fin: op 14/1: rtd 50 earlier in '99
(appr h'cap): '98 Kempton wnr (clmr, reappr): rtd 81 at best from 3 starts in '97: eff at 6f, now stays a sharp 1m
well: acts on fast, gd/soft & equitrack: best without blnks: has run well fresh: handles a stiff/gall or easy trk.
3984} LAKE SUNBEAM 66 [1] G L Moore 3-9-5 L Dettori 8/11 FAV: 053604: Sn rdn/mid-div, no impress 2½ 68a
front trio fnl 2f: hvly bckd, tchd 5/4: AW bow, abs: AW bow: connections reported colt would not face the kick-
back: prev with R Hannon, won at Salisbury earlier in '99 (stks, rtd 92): rtd 93+ on sole juv start in '98 (mdn):
eff at 7f, stays 1m well: likes a stiff/gall trk: has run well fresh: eff forcing the pace.
28   TEMPRAMENTAL 12 [9] 3-8-2 (bl) A Mackay 20/1: 340005: Mid-div, nvr able to chall: op 10/1. hd 50a
4553} TITAN 25 [2] 4-8-5 A Clark 33/1: 205006: Bhd/wide, mod gains fnl 3f, nvr a threat: AW bow: prev 9 37a
with S Dow, now with N Berry: connections reported to stewards that gelding resented the kick-back.
1   AIX EN PROVENCE 15 [6] 4-8-9 Pat Eddery 11/1: 105007: Dwelt/sn rdn rear, no impress: op 6/1: 5 31a
reportedly broke a blood vessel.
373}   SUPER SAINT 99 [3] 5-8-3 (t) G Bardwell 20/1: -51648: Prom 3f: op 12/1, abs: Belgian raider. 1¾ 22a
--   LITTLE PILGRIM [8] 6-8-3 A Daly 66/1: 4506-9: Prom 2f, sn btn: jumps fit. 3 16a
9 ran   Time 1m 39.29 (3.09)   (Nigel Shields)   K R Burke Newmarket, Suffolk

---

93   **1.05 GROHE CLAIMER DIV II 3YO+** (F)   **1m aw rnd   Going 36   +01 Fast**
£1787   £500   £242   3 yo rec 2 lb

58   BIG BEN 7 [2] R Hannon 5-9-3 T Sprake 9/2: 600351: 5 ch h Timeless Times - Belltina (Belfort) 69a
Towards rear, prog from halfway, switched & rdn to lead ins last, drvn out: tchd 11/2: plcd sev times earlier in
'99 (rtd 63a & 69): '98 Folkestone wnr (h'cap), Newmarket (ltd stks, rtd 76) & here at Lingfield (h'cap, rtd 70a):
eff at 7f/sharp 1m on fast, hvy & both AWs: loves Lingfield: given a well judged ride by T Sprake here.
4499} PHILISTAR 29 [6] K R Burke 6-9-7 Dean McKeown 5/2: 553552: 6 ch h Bairn - Philgwyn (Milford) hd 72a
Trkd ldrs going well, prog/led over 1f out, rdn/hdd ins last, kept on for press, just held: well bckd: clr rem:
earlier in '99 scored here at Lingfield (appr h'cap, rtd 76a & 63): '98 wnr here at Lingfield (2, ltd stks & h'cap,
rtd 74a) & Epsom (h'cap): eff btwn 7f & 10f on fast, gd/soft, loves equitrack: eff with/without blnks.
4552} BARBASON 25 [4] G L Moore 7-9-3 L Dettori 9/4 FAV: 410603: 7 ch g Polish Precedent - Barada 4 60a
(Damascus) Rdn/towards rear early, prog fnl 3f, no impress front pair ins last: op 6/4: earlier in '99 scored
at Lingfield (C/D, clmr, h'cap), Newbury (amat h'cap), Sandown & Brighton (clmrs, rtd 76 & 73a): '98 wnr at Lingfield &
Brighton (h'caps): eff at 7f/10f on firm, gd/soft & equitrack: loves Lingfield: eff with/without blnks.
1923} HARPOON LOUIE 99 [5] Alex Vanderhaeghen 9-8-3 A McCarthy (3) 7/1: -41044: Towards rear & rdn, nk 45a
prog/chsd ldrs over 2f out, sn no extra: op 5/1: 7 wk abs, Belgian raider, earlier in '99 won here at Lingfield
(C/D, clmr, rtd 56a at best): rtd 53a sole start in Britain '98 (sell): '97 wnr again here at Lingfield (sell,
rtd 56a): prolific wnr in homeland: eff at 7f/9f: acts on firm & soft, loves equitrack/Lingfield.
3175} FRANKLIN LAKES 99 [9] 4-8-5 (vis) P Doe (3) 50/1: 600505: Handy, led over 3f out, rdn/hdd over 1f 1½ 44$
out & fdd: AW bow, 4 month abs.
3   FEEL NO FEAR 15 [3] 6-8-7 Pat Eddery 7/1: 100126: Led 3f/rem handy, eased/btn fnl 1f: op 6/1: see 3. 6 37a
4276} SPEEDY CLASSIC 46 [5] 10-8-9 A Clark 10/1: 000047: Prom, led 5f out till over 3f out, wknd: 7 wk abs. 7 28a
644}   BOLDLY CLIFF 99 [8] 5-9-1 R Brisland (5) 20/1: 510548: Keen, prom 6f: Belgian raider, 7 wk abs. 16 10a
4553} LITTLE WHITE HEART 25 [1] 4-8-3 A Morris 66/1: 00009: Chsd ldrs, bhd fnl 3f: AW bow. ¾ 0a
9 ran   Time 1m 39.00 (2.8)   (Lady Davis)   R Hannon East Everleigh, Wilts

---

94   **1.40 EUROCO MED AUCT MDN 2YO** (F)   **7f aw rnd   Going 36   -23 Slow**
£2127   £597   £291

48   SOFISIO 8 [10] W R Muir 2-9-0 Pat Eddery 2/1 FAV: 04021: 2 ch c Efisio - Legal Embrace (Legal Bid) 74a
Prom, led going well over 2f out, rdn/clr 1f out, in command nr fin, pushed out cl-home: well bckd tho' op 6/4:
rtd 70 earlier in '99: eff at 7f/1m on both AW'ss: tried a t-strap, best without: likes a sharp trk.
4583} PUDDING LANE 21 [7] R F Johnson Houghton 2-8-9 L Dettori 4/1: 00302: 2 b f College Chapel - Fire 1¾ 65a
Of London (Shirley Heights) Led 2f, remained cl-up & led again 3f out till over 2f out, not pace of wnr over 1f
out: op 3/1: AW bow: plcd on turf earlier in '99 (rtd 69, Redcar fill mdn): eff at 6f, styd this sharp 7f
well, further may suit: handles fast grnd & equitrack, sharp/gall trk: fin clr of rem, shld win a race.
2700} CACOPHONY 99 [1] S Dow 2-9-0 P Doe (3) 20/1: 004603: 2 b g Son Pardo - Ansellady (Absalom) 5 60$
Prom, chsd ldrs 2f out, held fnl 1f: w 4mth abs, rtd 56 at best earlier in '99, no sand form: this longer 7f trip
shld suit: has tried blnks prev: prob handles firm & equitrack.
4181} MASTER JONES 53 [9] Mrs L Stubbs 2-9-0 A Culhane 9/1: -00064: Chsd ldrs, onepcd fnl 2f: op 10/1: 1¼ 57a

39

8 wk abs/AW bow: rtd 62 earlier in '99: poss handles equitrack & soft grnd.
-- **CRUISE** [3] 2-9-0 T Sprake 100/30: 5: Prom, no impress fnl 2f: op 5/2, debut: clr rem. *1* **55a**
4500} **FOSTON FOX 29** [12] 2-8-9 S Whitworth 20/1: 0006: Rdn/bhd, mod gains: op 14/1, AW bow. *9* **36a**
26 **UBITOO 12** [4] 2-9-0 F Norton 25/1: 007: Sn bhd, no ch fnl 3f. *¾* **40a**
53 **SHARAVAWN 7** [8] 2-8-9 (BL) J Tate 33/1: 000008: Dwelt, al towards rear: blnks. *hd* **34a**
34 **COLLEGE GALLERY 11** [11] 2-9-0 S Drowne 33/1: 0009: Prom 5f. *1* **37a**
26 **FOX STAR 12** [5] 2-8-9 (bl) A Daly 16/1: 040600: Cl-up, led after 2f till over 3f out, fdd: 10th. *shd* **32a**
4461} **ARROGANT 33** [2] 2-9-0 A Clark 33/1: 004000: Keen/held up, sn outpcd: 11th: AW bow. *3* **31a**
4556} **RECOLETA 24** [6] 2-8-9 G Bardwell 8/1: 000: Dwelt/al bhd: 12th: AW bow. *6* **17a**
12 ran Time 1m 26.93 (4.13) (North Farm Stud) W R Muir Lambourn, Berks

95 — 2.15 PAUL HAIGH MDN 3YO (D) 6f aw rnd Going 36 -13 Slow
£3783 £1144 £558 £265

3789} **CHARGE 78** [10] B Smart 3-9-0 (t) Pat Eddery 6/4 FAV: -04341: 3 gr g Petong - Madam Petoski (Petoski) Trkd ldrs travelling well, not much room 2f out, switched over 1f out & styd on strongly to lead nr fin, rdn out: hvly bckd: 11 wk abs: rtd 70 at best when plcd earlier in '99: eff at 5/6f, 7f+ may suit: acts on fast, gd & equitrack: handles a gall or sharp/undul trk: runs well fresh: eff in a t-strap: op to improvement. **64a**
63 **SISAO 6** [1] Miss Gay Kelleway 3-9-0 (bl) S Whitworth 11/2: 000632: 3 ch c College Chapel - Copt Hall Princess (Crowned Prince) Led, rdn/clr over 1f out, hdd well ins last & no extra: op 9/2: prob handles both AWs: eff in blnks: sells would suit: see 63 (fibresand). *1* **60$**
63 **KUWAIT SAND 6** [2] K Mahdi 3-9-0 J Tate 9/2: 4003: 3 b c Lugana Beach - Soon To Be (Hot Spark) Trkd ldr, rdn/ch over 1f out, no extra ins last: nicely bckd, tchd 5/1: quick reapp: rtd 67 at best earlier in '99: eff at 6f: handles gd & equitrack. *2* **55a**
4598} **CORN DOLLY 19** [9] R F Johnson Houghton 3-8-9 L Dettori 13/2: 0004: Rdn/chsd ldrs, onepace fnl 2f: op 5/1: AW bow: rtd 59 when unplcd earlier in '99 (Windsor mdn). *¾* **48a**
3789} **PRESELI MAGIC 78** [6] 3-8-9 S Drowne 16/1: 006555: Trkd ldrs, fdd fnl 2f: abs/AW bow: op 14/1. *3* **41a**
485} **FRENCH SPICE 99** [8] 3-8-9 S Sanders 10/1: 606: Dwelt/rear & wide, mod prog: op 7/1, 9 month abs. *5* **32a**
25 **GOOD WHIT SON 12** [11] 3-9-0 A McCarthy (3) 33/1: 07: Sn bhd, nvr factor: no form. *¾* **35a**
-- **WINNIPEG** [3] 3-8-9 C Rutter 20/1: 8: Dwelt/bhd, no impress: debut. *1* **28a**
4502} **TWO PACK 29** [5] 3-9-0 (bl) R Brisland (5) 25/1: 000609: Cl-up 2f, sn btn. *7* **20a**
4042} **QUEENS SIGNET 63** [4] 3-8-9 R Price 33/1: 000: Cl-up 2f, sn bhd: 10th: AW bow. *19* **0a**
-- **HOPEFUL HENRY** [7] 3-9-0 F Norton 10/1: 0: Dwelt/al bhd: 11th: op 6/1, debut: with G L Moore. *11* **0a**
11 ran Time 1m 13.35 (2.95) (D Lacey & N Buckham) B Smart Lambourn, berks

96 — 2.50 LADBROKE HCAP DIV I 3YO+ 0-75 (E) 1m aw rnd Going 36 -05 Slow [72]
£2437 £736 £358 £169 3 yo rec 2 lb

3367} **NAUTICAL WARNING 99** [3] B R Johnson 4-9-11 (69)(t) T Sprake 9/2: 120141: 4 b g Warning - Night At Sea (Night Shift) Cl-up, led before halfway, rdn/clr 2f out, styd on well fnl 1f, drvn out: nicely bckd: 3 mth abs: earlier in '99 won thrice here at Lingfield (AW h'cap & stks, rtd 70a at best & turf h'cap, rtd 56): '98 wnr again at Lingfield (appr h'cap, rtd 62a & 54, J Noseda): eff at 7f/1m: acts on firm, hvy, loves equitrack/Lingfield: eff in a t-strap: runs well fresh: likes to race with/force the pace. **78a**
29 **SPRINGTIME LADY 12** [7] S Dow 3-8-13 (59) P Doe (3) 13/2: 004052: 3 ch f Desert Dirham - Affaire de Coeur (Imperial Fling) Towards rear, rdn/kept on well fnl 2f, no threat to wnr: rnr-up earlier in '99 (rtd 68, Folkestone mdn): prev eff at 6f, now stays a sharp 1m well: handles fast, gd & equitrack: can find similar. *2½* **62a**
4521} **BORDER GLEN 28** [2] D Haydn Jones 3-9-1 (61)(bl) A Mackay 10/1: 000543: 3 b g Selkirk - Sulitelma (The Minstrel) Trkd ldrs, rdn & kept on fnl 2f, held ins last: op 8/1: blnks reapplied: earlier in '99 scored at Southwell (AW h'cap) & Musselburgh (h'cap, rtd 63a & 59 at best, Sir M Prescott): plcd 5 juv starts in '98: eff at 1m: acts on gd, gd/soft & both AW's: eff in blnks, has run well in a visor: likes a sharp trk, prob handles any. *1½* **61a**
4504} **MELLOW MISS 29** [1] R M Flower 3-8-8 (54) S Drowne 25/1: -05004: Towards rear/rdn, prog wide fnl 2f, styd on well ins last, nrst fin. *½* **53a**
3420} **PAGAN KING 97** [9] 3-10-0 (74) S Whitworth 10/1: 042D15: Trkd ldrs 6f: op 8/1, abs/AW bow. *1½* **70a**
4527} **GUILSBOROUGH 27** [4] 4-9-11 (69) M Tebbutt 9/1: 162606: Trkd ldrs, rdn/ch 2f out, wknd fnl 1f. *1½* **62a**
4504} **FUSUL 29** [5] 3-8-4 (50) R Brisland (5) 11/1: 400007: Chsd ldrs 6f: thcd 14/1. *3* **37a**
4554} **MYTTONS MISTAKE 25** [8] 6-9-0 (58) G Faulkner (3) 25/1: 015008: Chsd ldrs 6f: jumps fit (mod form) *4* **37a**
3805} **MYSTIC RIDGE 77** [6] 5-9-8 (66) L Dettori 10/11 FAV: 111319: Led 3f, sn rdn & lost place 3f out, btn/eased fnl 1f: hvly bckd: 11 wk abs: earlier in '99 won h'caps at Brighton, Leopardstown, Galway & Lingfield (rtd 75 & 17a at best): place form in '98 (h'cap, rtd 55): suited by 7f/1m, stays 12f: acts on firm & gd grnd: eff with/without blnks: handles any trk, likes a sharp one: best dominating, unable to do so today. *3½* **38a**
4481} **CAPTAIN LOGAN 31** [10] 4-9-7 (65) A Proud 25/1: 0-0000: Sn bhd: 10th: AW bow, now with A Kelleway. *5* **27a**
10 ran Time 1m 39.46 (3.26) (The Twenty Five Club) B R Johnson Epsom, Surrey

97 — 3.25 LADBROKE HCAP DIV II 3YO+ 0-75 (E) 1m aw rnd Going 36 +05 Fast [72]
£2437 £736 £358 £169 3 yo rec 2 lb

61 **SOUND THE TRUMPET 6** [4] R C Spicer 7-7-10 (40)(1oh)(t) J Mackay (7) 14/1: 050441: 7 b g Fayruz - Red Note (Rusticaro) Chsd ldrs, prog & rdn to lead ins last, styd on well, pushed out cl-home: op 10/1: best time of day: place form earlier in '99 (rtd 35, Ripon h'cap, rtd 45a on sand, clmr): '98 Lingfield wnr (reapp, h'cap, rtd 49a, subs rtd 37 on turf): eff at 5/6f, now stays a sharp 1m well: acts on fast, gd/soft & both AWs: has run well fresh: likes a sharp trk, esp Lingfield: runs well for an appr: eff in a t-strap: nicely h'capped, can win again. **48a**
67 **FORTY FORTE 6** [8] K R Burke 3-9-10 (70) Dean McKeown 11/4: 000132: 3 b g Pursuit Of Love - Cominna (Dominion) Led, clr 3f out, drifted right over 1f out, rdn/hdd ins last, not pace of wnr: well bckd, gd run. *2½* **72a**
79 **STYLE DANCER 3** [9] R M Whitaker 5-9-2 (60) J Fanning 8/1: 000033: 5 b g Dancing Dissident - Showing Style (Pas de Seul) Towards rear, kept on for press fnl 2f, no threat: clr rem: acts on firm, gd/soft & both AW's. *3* **56a**
8 **SING CHEONG 15** [5] G C H Chung 3-8-12 (58) Pat Eddery 2/1 FAV: 300024: Towards rear/drvn halfway, mod late gains: hvly bckd, tchd 11/4: more expected on return to h'caps: see 8 (7f, mdn). *10* **39a**
28 **FLITE OF LIFE 12** [1] 3-9-1 (61) M Tebbutt 12/1: -00005: Prom 6f: op 10/1: rtd 64 earlier in '99: rnr-up in '98 (nurs, rtd 81): eff at 6f, a return to that trip may suit: acts on firm & soft grnd. *1¾* **39a**
44 **INCHALONG 8** [2] 4-8-13 (57)(vis) T Williams 12/1: 610206: Chsd ldr, wknd over 2f out: tchd 14/1: earlier in '99 scored at Pontefract (fill h'cap, made all, rtd 65, rtd 39a on sand): '98 wnr at Windsor (1st time vis) & Ripon (h'caps, rtd 77): eff at 6/7f: acts on fast, gd/soft grnd, any trk: best visored: likes to race with/force the pace: well h'capped, tough & worth another ch when dropped in trip. *¾* **34a**

LINGFIELD (Equitrack) TUESDAY NOVEMBER 23RD Lefthand, V Sharp Track

59 **AL MABROOK 7** [10] 4-9-8 (66) J Tate 9/1: 405057: Sn towards rear/wide, nvr factor. 2½ **38a**
3 **ROGER ROSS 15** [6] 4-8-5 (49)(bl) S Drowne 25/1: 000068: Dwelt, rear/nvr in it. 1¾ **18a**
28 **ROISIN SPLENDOUR 12** [3] 4-9-11 (69) R Smith (5) 14/1: 050009: Chsd ldrs/strugg halfway: op 12/1. ½ **37a**
4548} **LOVE DIAMONDS 25** [7] 3-9-12 (72) G Carter 10/1: 253000: Mid-div, wknd fnl 2f: 10th: op 8/1. 4 **32a**
10 ran Time 1m 38.67 (2.47) (Mrs J A Nichols) R C Spicer West Pinchbeck, Lins

MAISONS-LAFFITTE WEDNESDAY NOVEMBER 24TH Left & Righthand, Sharpish Track

Official Going HEAVY

98 **2.30 LISTED PRIX CONTESSINA 3YO+ 6f Heavy**
£15070 £5167 £3599

4620} **TWO CLUBS 11** W Jarvis 3-8-8 M Dwyer : 421021: 3 br f First Trump - Miss Cindy (Mansingh) **103**
3208} **MATIN DE PRINTEMPS 99** H Van De Poele 5-8-11 S Guillot : 062002: 5 ch h Kendor - Zarzaya (Caro) 2 **101**
1165} **LEVER TO HEAVEN 99** R Collet 3-8-8 T Gillet : 4-5003: 3 b f Bluebird - No Rehearsal (Baillamont) nk **97**
4620} **QILIN 11** M H Tompkins 4-8-8 S Sanders : 103435: -: 1¾ **95**
4469} **THE FUGATIVE 26** 6-8-8 M Tebbutt : 1035D8: -: 8 **81**
9 ran Time 1m 17.6 (Stephen R Hobson) W Jarvis Newmarket

MAISONS-LAFFITTE MONDAY NOVEMBER 22ND Left & Righthand, Sharpish Track

Official Going HEAVY.

99 **1.10 LISTED PRIX ZEDDAAN 2YO 6f Heavy**
£15070 £5167 £3599

-- **ZEITING** [4] R Collet 2-8-8 D Bonilla : 1: 2 b f Zieten - Belle de Cadix (Law Society) **99**
4491} **AWAKE 30** [5] M Johnston 2-8-11 J Fanning : 2112D: 2 ch c First Trump - Pluvial (Habat) 1½ **98**
1251} **WALNUT LADY 99** [3] France 2-8-8 S Guillot : 5612: 2 ch f Forzando - Princess Tateum (Tate Gallery) 1½ **92**
4599} **SCARLETT RIBBON 18** [2] P J Makin 2-8-8 S Sanders : 18: -: 6 **80**
4561} **GIRLS BEST FRIEND 23** [10] 2-8-8 T Quinn : 021049: -: 5 **70**
11 ran Time 1m 17.2 (B P Hayes) R Collet France

LINGFIELD (Equitrack) WEDNESDAY NOVEMBER 24TH Lefthand, V Sharp Track

Official Going STANDARD. Stalls: 1m - Outside, Rem - Inside

100 **12.10 PARTY HCAP DIV I 3YO+ 0-60 (F) 1m2f aw Going 40 -24 Slow [60]**
£1861 £521 £253 3 yo rec 4 lb

4576} **ETISALAT 23** [3] J Pearce 4-8-10 (42) A Polli (3) 16/1: 006001: 4 b g Lahib - Sweet Repose (High Top) **47a**
Led after 1f & clr halfway, kept on gamely ins last, drvn out: AW bow: earlier in '99 won at Yarmouth (sell h'cap, rtd 53): unplcd in 3 '98 starts for R Armstrong (rtd 61): eff at 1m, stays 10f: acts on fast, gd & equitrack.
23 **ARDENT 13** [4] Miss B Sanders 5-9-4 (50) A Clark 5/1: 662022: 5 b g Aragon - Forest Of Arden (Tap On Wood) Prom in chasing grp, rdn/kept on to chase wnr fnl 1f, not able to chall: op 7/2: see 23 (C/D). 1½ **53a**
1045} **HURGILL DANCER 99** [5] R J O'Sullivan 5-8-7 (39) L Newman (7) 10/1: 515043: 5 b g Rambo Dancer - Try Vickers (Fuzzbuster) Prom, kept on for press fnl 2f, not able to chall wnr: clr rem, op 16/1, abs: earlier in '99 won here at Lingfield (h'cap, rtd 40a), plcd on turf (h'cap, rtd 41): plcd in '98 (h'cap, rtd 62): '97 Ripon wnr (J Watts, h'cap, rtd 74): eff at 10f, suited by 12f: acts on firm, gd/soft & both AWs: on a fair mark. ¾ **41a**
23 **ERITHS CHILL WIND 13** [1] G L Moore 3-8-12 (48) F Norton 9/4 FAV: 231044: Prom, chsd ldr over 2f out, wknd fnl 1f: nicely bckd: earlier in '99 scored at Brighton (h'cap, rtd 52): rtd 66 at best in '98: eff arnd 10f: acts on firm, soft & equitrack: likes a sharp/easy trk: shapes as if a drop to 1m will suit. 7 **40a**
4220} **CAPTAIN MCCLOY 53** [11] 4-8-12 (44)(bl) R Brisland (5) 16/1: 264005: Towards rear/rdn, prog 3f out, no further prog fnl 1f: op 14/1: 8 wk abs. 2½ **32a**
1 **KAFIL 16** [6] 5-9-9 (55) P Doe (3) 8/1: 022536: Led 1f, remained prom 1m, fdd: op 6/1: see 1. 5 **36a**
3966} **HAWKSBILL HENRY 68** [13] 5-10-0 (60) G Carter 6/1: 255307: Wide/mid-div halfway, no prog: abs. 3½ **36a**
1450} **ABLE PETE 99** [7] 3-8-8 (44) Dean McKeown 12/1: 000008: Sn bhd: abs, now with A G Newcombe. nk **19a**
50 **NORTH ARDAR 9** [2] 9-9-0 (46) M Tebbutt 20/1: 230009: Sn rdn, mid-div, btn 3f out & eased fnl 1f. 1¾ **19a**
4276} **JUBILEE SCHOLAR 47** [8] 6-9-8 (54)(bl) A Culhnae 10/1: 450050: Rear, nvr factor: 10th, 7 wk abs. 6 **18a**
4499} **Missile Toe 30** [9] 6-8-11 (43) J Tate 16/1: 4604} **Pipe Dream 20** [14] 3-9-2 (52) P McCabe 33/1:
3 **Sky City 16** [12] 3-8-11 (47) A McCarthy (3) 20/1: 3718} **Little Tumbler 84** [10] 4-9-1 (47) T Sprake 10/1:
14 ran Time 2m 09.17 (6.37) (Mrs E M Clarke) J Pearce Newmarket, Suffolk

101 **12.40 PRIVATE BOXES CLAIMER 3YO+ (F) 1m4f aw Going 40 -09 Slow**
£2158 £606 £295 3 yo rec 6 lb

23 **FAILED TO HIT 13** [10] N P Littmoden 6-9-5 (vis) J Tate 4/1: 600351: 6 b g Warrshan - Missed Again (High Top) Al handy, led over 1f out, styd on gamely, all out: op 3/1: earlier in '99 scored at W'hampton (h'cap, rtd 74a), no turf form: '98 wnr at Lingfield (3, h'caps & ltd stks) & W'hampton (3, clmr & h'caps, rtd 68a): eff at 1m/12f: handles fast grnd, AW specialist: eff in blnks/visor: likes a sharp trk, esp Lingfield/W'hampton. **65a**
52 **ESHTIAAL 8** [8] G L Moore 5-9-9 (bl) A Culhane 9/2: -00332: 5 b h Riverman - Lady Cutlass (Cutlass) Chsd ldrs halfway, drvn to chall fnl 1f, just held nr fin: tchd 11/2: acts on fast, gd/soft & e/track, prob soft. ½ **68a**
83 **HIGHFIELDER 2** [7] J S Moore 3-8-7 L Newman (7) 33/1: 030403: 3 b g Unblest - River Low (Lafontaine) Prom, led 7f out, rdn/hdd over 1f out, no extra ins last: clr rem: quick reapp: stays 12f: see 52 (C/D). 1¼ **56$**
6 **HIGHLY PRIZED 16** [11] J S King 5-9-9 S Drowne 9/2: 044254: Trkd ldrs, rdn/ev ch 2f out, sn no 5 **59a**

extra: tchd 11/2: rnr-up earlier in '99 (h'cap, rtd 70): '98 Salisbury wnr (h'cap, rtd 73): eff at 12/14f, tried 2m+: acts on firm, hvy & equitrack: handles any trk, likes a stiff/gall one: eff weight carrier.

1522}	**PRINCE DANZIG 99** [3] 8-9-9 S Whitworth 6/1: 453025: Bhd, mod prog halfway, sn held: op 4/1: 6 month abs: earlier in '99 scored here at Lingfield (clmr, rtd 71a): '98 wnr again here at Lingfield (h'cap, rtd 73a), rtd 45 on turf: suited by 12/13f: acts on firm, soft, fibresand & loves equitrack/Lingfield: sell grade shld suit.		10	48a
56	**CEDAR FLAG 8** [2] 5-8-13 P Doe (3) 25/1: 06: Towards rear, mod gains: longer 12f trip.		1½	36a
4276}	**WITHOUT FRIENDS 47** [5] 5-8-13 (vis) A Clark 40/1: 600407: Mid-div, btn 3f out: 7 wk abs.		8	27a
60	**WESTMINSTER CITY 7** [9] 3-8-13 (vis) G Carter 25/1: 500058: Dwelt/wide, mod factor.		1¾	31a
22	**ESTOPPED 13** [6] 4-8-9 J Mackay (7) 50/1: 000-09: Al bhd.		9	11a
901}	**HENRY ISLAND 29** [1] 6-9-3 Pat Eddery 2/1 FAV: 04-300: Cl-up, led after 2f till 7f out, sn lost place, eased: 10th, hvly bckd, AW bow: jumps rt (has ref to race): plcd earlier in '99 (h'cap, rtd 85): '98 Goodwood wnr (G Wragg, rtd h'cap, rtd 92): eff at 10f, stays 2m2f well: acts on fast & soft: wld not face kickback today.		3½	14a
6	**KATIES CRACKER 16** [4] 4-8-8 F Norton 50/1: 200060: Led 2f, sn lost place/bhd: 11th.		2	2a

11 ran   Time 2m 35.1 (5.9)   (M C S D Racing)   N P Littmoden Newmarket, Suffolk

---

102 1.10 PARTY HCAP DIV II 3YO+ 0-60 (F)   1m2f aw   Going 40   -28 Slow   [60]
£1850 £518 £251   3 yo   rec 4 lb

97	**ROGER ROSS 1** [7] R M Flower 4-9-3 (49) S Drowne 25/1: 000601: 4 b g Touch Of Grey - Foggy Dew (Smoggy) Prom, led over 3f out, clr 2f out, styd on gamely, drvn out: qck reapp: rtd 54 at best earlier in '99 (h'cap), subs tried blnks: '98 wnr at Salisbury (h'cap), Sandown & Ascot (h'caps, rtd 76): eff at 1m/10f on fast & e/track, loves soft: handles any trk, runs well fresh: suited by switch to forcing tactics, well h'capped.			55a
*67	**MYSTERIUM 7** [2] N P Littmoden 5-9-1 (47)(6ex) R Thomas (7) 100/30 FAV: 150412: 5 gr g Mystiko - Way To Go (Troy) Rdn/bhd after 2f, prog wide from halfway, styd on strongly ins last, not rch wnr: 6lb pen: acts on fast, gd & both AWs, in gd heart, can win again: see 67.		2½	49a
22	**SAMMYS SHUFFLE 13** [12] Jamie Poulton 4-9-7 (53)(bl) O Urbina 5/1: 060433: 4 b c Touch Of Grey - Cabinet Shuffle (Thatching) Prom, rdn/chsd wnr 3f out, no extra ins last: nicely bckd tho' op 7/2: see 22 (C/D).		nk	54a
4579}	**KING OF TUNES 23** [10] J J Sheehan 7-9-10 (56) A Clark 8/1: 600004: Towards rear, prog halfway, kept on fnl 2f, tho' no threat to wnr: nicely bckd, op 14/1, topweight: plcd earlier in '99 (h'cap, rtd 72): rnr-up in Lincoln h'cap at Doncaster in '98 (rtd 89): '97 Newmarket wnr (h'cap, rtd 83, M J Haynes): eff at 1m/10f: acts on any trk: has run well fresh: acts on fast, soft & e/track: best without blnks: well h'capped, cld find similar.		1¼	55a
22	**OUR PEOPLE 13** [11] 5-8-11 (43) J Fanning 8/1: 0-0605: Towards rear, mod gains for press fnl 3f: rtd 52 at best earlier in '99 (h'cap, lightly rcd): '98 Carlisle & Redcar wnr (h'caps, rtd 63): eff at 1m/12f: acts on firm & soft, poss handles equitrack: handles any trk, likes a stiff/gall one: best without blnks/vis: nicely h'capped.		3	38a
35	**ROI DE DANSE 12** [6] 4-8-12 (44) Martin Dwyer 20/1: 060006: Led/dsptd lead 7f, fdd.		7	29a
4564}	**SIR WALTER 25** [14] 6-8-6 (38)(BL) Dean McKeown 16/1: 440067: Dwelt, wide & mid-div halfway, btn 2f out: op 14/1, blnks: recent jumps rnr.		1½	21a
60	**GOLDEN LYRIC 7** [3] 4-8-8 (40) A Polli (3) 11/2: 000038: Trkd ldrs, ch 3f out/fdd: op 4/1: btr 60 (f/sand).		7	13a
4598}	**SALORY 20** [4] 3-8-12 (48) T Sprake 20/1: 0-0009: Led/dsptd lead 5f, sn btn: AW bow.		6	12a
50	**BARRIER RIDGE 9** [9] 5-8-11 (43) A Culhane 14/1: 200460: Dwelt & rear/wide, nvr factor & position accepted fnl 2f: 10th: op 12/1: not given a hard time, can do better.		½	6a
4574}	**BADRINATH 23** [13] 5-8-13 (45) F Norton 5/1: 420350: Wide chasing ldrs early, rdn/prom halfway, sn wknd & eased: 12th: struggled from awkward high-draw, worth another look.			0a

4554} **Ok Babe 26** [1] 4-9-9 (55) P Doe (3) 25/1:   3380} **Billichang 99** [5] 3-9-0 (50) A McCarthy (3) 12/1: 1
Moss Rose 16 [2] 3-8-9 (45) M Hills 12/1:
14 ran   Time 2m 09.62 (6.82)   (H Lawrence)   R M Flower Jevington, E Sussex

---

103 1.40 SPONSOR MDN 2YO (D)   1m aw rnd   Going 40   +05 Fast
£2892 £876 £428   £204

4607}	**FORBEARING 19** [9] Sir Mark Prescott 2-9-0 S Sanders 13/8 FAV: 561: 2 b c Bering - For Example (Northern Baby) Dwelt, sn prom, rdn & styd on gamely to overhaul ldr nr fin, drvn out: fast time, well bckd, AW bow: rtd 80 earlier in '99 on turf (mdn): apprec step up to 1m, 10f+ looks sure to suit: acts on equitrack, poss handles gd/soft & hvy: handles a sharp or gall trk: sure to win more races, esp when stepping up in trip.			88a
4605}	**WARNING NOTE 19** [11] R Hannon 2-9-0 T Sprake 15/2: 02: 2 b c Zieten - Caunton (Warning) Handy, led halfway, rdn/clr 2f out, caught cl home: clr rem, AW bow: well bhd on sole turf start earlier in '99 (mdn, rtd 59): apprec this step up to 1m, further may suit: acts on equitrack: lks nailed on for similar.		nk	86a
4605}	**DR COOL 19** [5] W Jarvis 2-9-0 F Norton 11/2: 03: 2 b c Ezzoud - Vayavaig (Damister) Trkd ldrs, eff/outpcd by ldrs fnl 2f: op 3/1: AW bow: rtd 68 earlier in '99 (mdn): lngr 1m trip will suit in time.		10	71a
26	**INVER GOLD 13** [4] A G Newcombe 2-9-0 S Whitworth 4/1: 624: Prom, rdn/outpcd by front pair fnl 2f: nicely bckd: prev with M Johnston: h'cap company could now suit: see 26.		½	70a
41	**BONDI BAY 11** [12] 2-8-9 Dean McKeown 33/1: 000035: Keen/prom, outpcd fnl 3f: see 41 (7f).		¾	64$
--	**KUWAIT TROOPER** [1] 2-9-0 G Carter 5/1: 6: Dwelt, sn chasing ldrs, held fnl 3f: debut.		8	57a
3672}	**RATIFIED 86** [2] 2-9-0 C Rutter 33/1: -0007: Led till halfway, sn btn: AW bow, 12 wk abs.		5	47a
4542}	**CROWN MINT 26** [6] 2-9-0 A Clark 33/1: 008: Sn bhd: AW bow.		16	23a
4606}	**ANGELLO 19** [3] 2-9-0 A Culhane 25/1: 009: Dwelt/sn bhd: AW bow.		3½	16a
--	**CASTLEBRIDGE** [8] 2-9-0 M Tebbutt 25/1: 0: Dwelt/al bhd: 10th: debut.		2	12a
--	**FOREON** [7] 2-8-9 G Parkin 33/1: 0: Slowly away, sn well bhd: 11th: debut.		9	0a

11 ran   Time 1m 38.97 (2.77)   (Eclipse Thoroughbreds - Osborne House IV)   Sir Mark Prescott Newmarket

---

104 2.10 INSIDE CLASSIFIED STKS 3YO+ 0-85 (D)   7f aw rnd   Going 40   +04 Fast
£3747 £1133 £552 £262   3 yo   rec 1 lb

7	**TEMERAIRE 16** [5] D J S Cosgrove 4-9-2 G Carter 3/1: 521051: 4 b c Dayjur - Key Dancer (Nijinsky) Made all, rdn/clr over 1f out, styd on gamely, drvn out: gd time, hvly bckd, AW bow: 9/2 earlier in '99 scored at Newbury (h'cap, rtd 85): 98/99 jumps rnr (rtd 89h, Gr 2 juv hdle): '98 Windsor (mdn) & Lingfield wnr (Mrs A J Perrett, rtd 91, class stks): eff at 7/8.3f: acts on firm, gd & equitrack: has tried a visor: well h'capped.			90a
7	**TOPTON 16** [4] P Howling 5-9-13 (bl) A McCarthy (3) 14/1: 300002: 5 b g Royal Academy - Circo (High Top) Chsd ldrs, kept on well fnl 2f, not rch wnr: op 10/1: earlier in '99 won here at Lingfield (AW h'cap, rtd 86a), Doncaster (2) & Yarmouth (h'caps, rtd 80): '98 wnr again at Doncaster (rtd 72), Southwell & Lingfield (h'caps, rtd 75a): stays 1m, suited by 7f: acts on firm, gd/soft & both AWs: handles any trk: eff in blnks/visor.		1¼	84a
4560}	**ASTRAC 25** [6] A J McNae 4-8-13 T Ashley 12/1: 164003: 8 b g Nordico - Shirleen (Daring Display) Trkd ldrs, chsd wnr 2f out, rdn/no extra ins last: earlier in '99 scored at Catterick (appr stks, rtd 87), rtd		3½	77a

60a on sand (h'cap): '98 wnr at Ayr (h'cap) & Hamilton (stks, rtd 103): eff at 5/7f, suited by 6f: acts on
gd/soft, hvy & equitrack, handles fast: runs well for an appr: spot on back at 6f.

4341} WHITE PLAINS 42 [8] K R Burke 6-8-13 Dean McKeown 14/1: 366054: Slowly away & bhd, rdn & kept on 4 fnl 2f, nrst fin: op 10/1: 6 wk abs: not disgraced here, spot on back at 1m+.		69a
7 VOLONTIERS 16 [9] 4-8-13 Pat Eddery 11/10 FAV: 000025: Prom, chsd wnr 4f out till 2f out going well, sn rdn/btn: hvly bckd: ahead of today's wnr in 7, when able to lead.	2½	64a
7 APOLLO RED 16 [3] 10-8-13 R Brisland (5) 12/1: 230206: Bmpd/sn towards rear, nvr factor: op 8/1.	1	62a
79 MARMADUKE 4 [1] 3-8-12 S Whitworth 20/1: 534007: Al towards rear: quick reapp.	3	56a
4585} SILCA BLANKA 22 [7] 7-8-13 R Perham 8/1: 400008: Chsd wnr, wknd 2f out/eased fnl 1f: op 6/1.	1	54a
4356} CROWDED AVENUE 41 [2] 7-8-13 A Clark 9/1: 3-2049: Held up, btn 2f out: op 7/1: abs/AW bow.	7	43a

9 ran   Time 1m 25.33 (2.53)   (P M Mooney)   D J S Cosgrove Newmarket, Suffolk

---

105   2.40 NURSERY HCAP 2YO 0-85 (E)   6f aw rnd Going 40 -15 Slow   [87]
£2703   £759   £370

*34 JAMES STARK 12 [1] N P Littmoden 2-9-7 (80)(bl) G Carter 11/4 FAV: 0511: 2 b c Up And At 'Em - June Maid (Junius) Made all, rdn/clr over 1f out, rdn out: hvly bckd, tchd 9/2, h'cap bow: recent Southwell wnr (auct mdn): eff at 5/6f: acts on both AWs, handles gd: suited by blnks: enjoyed forcing tactics today.		85a
4599} WATERGRASSHILL 20 [8] N A Callaghan 2-7-11 (56) R Brisland (5) 6/1: 0002: 2 b f Terimon - Party Game (Red Alert) Dwelt, wide/outpcd early, strong run fnl 2f, nrst fin: op 7/1, AW/h'cap bow: rtd 64 earlier in '99 on turf: eff at 6f, return to 7f+ sure to suit: acts on equitrack: spot on similar over 7f+.	1¼	57a
*4 QUEEN OF THE MAY 16 [6] M R Channon 2-9-2 (75) Paul Cleary (7) 4/1: 404413: 2 b f Nicolotte - Varnish (Final Straw) Sn prom/sltly wide, kept on fnl 2f tho' held ins last: op 3/1: see 4 (C/D).	¾	74a
4302} JEPAJE 44 [3] A Bailey 2-8-3 (62) F Norton 10/1: 004204: Cl-up, outpcd 3f out, kept on fnl 2f, not pace to chall: op 7/1, 6 wk abs/AW bow: rnr-up earlier in '99 (nurs h'cap, rtd 62): eff at 5/6f, has tried 7f: handles gd/soft & equitrack: likes a sharp/undul trk.	2	56a
34 DRAGON STAR 12 [7] 2-7-12 (57) Martin Dwyer 12/1: -3665: Dwelt, chsd ldrs, nvr pace to chall: tchd 14/1: h'cap bow: rtd 58 when plcd on turf earlier in '99: step up to 7f+ & similar company may suit.	2	46a
*77 WAFFLES OF AMIN 4 [2] 2-9-13 (86)(7ex) P Dobbs (5) 7/2: 262316: Prom, rdn when no room 2f out till over 1f out, kept on: rdn 7lb pen, op 3/1: quick reapp: see 77 (mdn, fibresand, 5f).	1	73a
*53 PERLE DE SAGESSE 8 [10] 2-8-9 (68)(7ex) A Daly 12/1: 105217: Mid-div at best: op 6/1: see 53 (7f).	2½	48a
4588} SIMBATU 21 [9] 2-8-3 (62) J Fanning 16/1: 5308: Trkd ldrs 4f: op 12/1: AW/h'cap bow.	hd	41a
4222} TALENTS LITTLE GEM 51 [4] 2-7-12 (57)(2ow) N Carlisle 16/1: -60039: Dwelt, al rear: abs.	1½	32a
4 WHERES CHARLOTTE 16 [5] 2-7-10 (55)(5oh) P Fitzsimons (0) 16/1: 200030: Chsd wnr 4f, wknd: 10th.	1¼	27a

10 ran   Time 1m 13.7 (3.3)   (Richard Green (Fine Paintings))   N P Littmoden Newmarket

---

106   3.10 LADBROKE HCAP DIV I 3YO+ 0-75 (E)   7f aw rnd Going 40 -12 Slow   [74]
£2450   £740   £360   £170   3 yo rec 1 lb

4472} BLAKESET 33 [10] T G Mills 4-10-0 (74)(bl) A Clark 10/1: 002601: 4 ch c Midyan - Penset (Red Sunset) Made all, clr 3f out, hard rdn ins last to hold on, all out: AW bow: prev with R Hannon & 2nd twice earlier in '99 (rtd 85, class stks): plcd sev times in '98 (rtd 88, h'cap): '97 Newmarket wnr (mdn, rtd 88): eff at 7/7.5f: acts on firm & in blnks, tried a t-strap: eff weight carrier, well h'capped for new connections.		79a
58 DAYNABEE 8 [9] A J McNae 4-7-12 (44) Martin Dwyer 5/1: 000542: 4 b f Common Grounds - Don't Wary (Lomond) Al prom in chasing group, kept on fnl 2f, edg left, nrst wnr: tchd 6/1: see 58.	¾	47a
*59 NOBALYO 8 [8] Mrs V C Ward 5-9-6 (66)(vis)(6ex) L Newman (7) 13/8 FAV: 003313: 5 ch h Sharpo - Zipperti Do (Precocious) Dwelt & rcd wide, styd on strongly despite drifting right fnl 1f, nrst fin: well bckd under 6lb pen: not able to secure crucial prominent position, came home strongly, worth another look: see 59.	1	67a
83 GADGE 2 [7] A Bailey 8-8-4 (50) F Norton 7/1: 006034: Prom, onepace fnl 2f: tchd 8/1, quick reapp.	¾	50a
59 MUSTANG 8 [6] 6-8-0 (46) A Polli 12/1: -40445: Rear, rdn halfway, mod gains: op 10/1: see 59.	1¾	43a
25 MAAS 13 [4] 4-9-0 (60) Pat Eddery 4/1: -00026: Prom, outpcd over 2f out: op 3/1: see 25 (6f, mdn).	1½	54a
4216} MAPLE 53 [4] 3-9-5 (66) P Doe (3) 20/1: 006007: Towards rear, mod prog & eased when btn ins last: 8 wk abs, earlier in '99 with D R C Elsworth, plcd (h'cap, rtd 88): '98 Newbury wnr (mdn, rtd 90): eff at 5/6f, stays 7f on firm & gd/soft: handles any trk: nicely h'capped & shaped with promise under a kind ride.	1	58a
35 KEEN HANDS 12 [1] 3-9-7 (68)(vis) R Price 12/1: 003648: Chsd wnr, btn 3f out/eased fnl 1f: op 10/1: earlier in '99 scored at W'hampton (sell) & Southwell (3, 2 sells & h'cap, rtd 75a & 45): rtd 56a in '98: eff at 5/7f: fibresand/Southwell specialist: best in a visor: apprec 6f back at Southwell.	5	50a
32 WILD THING 12 [13] 3-9-2 (63) T Sprake 16/1: 021529: Prom 5f: op 14/1, now with J J Bridger.	2	41a
29 SHARP IMP 13 [11] 9-8-0 (45)(bl)(1ow) A Daly 25/1: 400000: Bhd, no ch halfway: 10th.	9	10a
58 ELEGANT DANCE 8 [12] 5-8-10 (56) G Faulkner (3) 20/1: 00000: Slowly away/bhd, sn btn: 11th.	nk	19a

11 ran   Time 1m 26.45 (3.65)   (Epsom Downs Racing Club)   T G Mills Headley, Surrey

---

107   3.40 LADBROKE HCAP DIV II 3YO+ 0-75 (E)   7f aw Going 40 -02 Slow   [74]
£2450   £740   £360   £170   3 yo rec 1 lb

58 PENGAMON 8 [9] D T Thom 7-8-6 (52) F Norton 6/4 FAV: /00221: 7 gr g Efisio - Dolly Bevan (Another Realm) Trkd ldrs going well halfway, rdn to lead over 1f out, styd on well, rdn out: well bckd: earlier in '99 with H Collingridge, mod form: missed '98: '97 wnr here at Lingfield (AW h'cap, rtd 77a & 76): eff at 7f/1m: acts on fast, gd/soft, likes equitrack/Lingfield: deserved this win.		57a
47 BLUE KITE 9 [5] N P Littmoden 4-9-6 (66) C Cogan (5) 7/1: 122332: 4 ch g Silver Kite - Gold And Blue (Bluebird) Towards rear, prog halfway, rdn to chall over 1f out, kept on tho' just held nr line: nicely bckd, tchd 9/1: acts on both AWs, loves W'hampton: on a fair mark, could find similar: see 47 (6f).	½	69a
28 RAINBOW RAIN 13 [6] S Dow 5-9-2 (62) P Doe (3) 5/2: 014023: 5 b g Capote - Grana (Miswaki) Towards rear, prog wide from halfway, kept on fnl 1f, not reach front pair: nicely bckd, op 11/4: see 28 (C/D).	3	59a
91 JUST DISSIDENT 1 [10] R M Whitaker 7-8-11 (57) Dean McKeown 10/1: 001044: Led till dist, fdd: qck reapp, cl-up 4th over 5f here yesterday: see 91.	1	52a
82 DOLPHINELLE 4 [4] 3-8-13 (60)(bl) T Sprake 9/1: 540465: Chsd ldr, rdn/fdd fnl 1f, qck reapp: earlier in '99 scored at Brighton (h'cap, rtd 75 & 61a at best): rtd 74 at best in '98: eff at 5/7f on firm, soft & equitrack: handles any trk, likes a sharp/undul one: drop to 6f shld suit in similar company.	1½	52a
29 DONE AND DUSTED 13 [8] 3-9-5 (66) F Norton 14/1: 500006: Mid-div, no impress fnl 2f: tchd 10/1: earlier in '99 scored here at Lingfield (h'cap, rtd 69a) & Windsor (h'cap, rtd 72): '98 Southwell (sell, J Berry) & here at Lingfield wnr (clmr, rtd 65a & 57): eff at 6/7f, tried 1m: acts on both AWs & firm grnd.	2½	53a
57 DANCING JACK 8 [1] 6-7-10 (42)(4oh) A Polli (2) 33/1: 003007: Rear, mod gains: plcd earlier in '99	4	21a

(rtd 32 & 34a): '95 wnr here at Lingfield (nurs, rtd 55): eff at 5/6f on fast & equitrack: tried blnks.
28 **MISS DANGEROUS 13** [2] 4-7-12 (44) Martin Dwyer 20/1: 502008: Prom 2f, sn btn. *hd* **22a**
4019} **ENTROPY 65** [7] 3-8-2 (49) G Bardwell 25/1: 500009: Prom 5f: 2 month abs, now with B A Pearce. *1* **25a**
4604} **VASARI 20** [3] 5-9-10 (70) Pat Eddery 14/1: 000060: Dwelt & taken wide/bhd, eased over 1f out: *nk* **45a**
10th, op 10/1: may have resented the kickback and was given a considerate ride.
4554} **RAMBOLD 26** [11] 8-8-4 (50) R Brisland (5) 25/1: 060000: Chsd ldrs 4f: 11th. *shd* **25a**
4206} **TRUFFLE 53** [12] 3-9-4 (65) P McCabe 14/1: 1-0000: Dwelt, sn bhd: 12th: AW bow/8 wk abs. *shd* **39a**
12 ran Time 1m 25.75 (2.95) (Miss Arabella Smallman) D T Thom Exning, Suffolk

LINGFIELD (Equitrack) FRIDAY NOVEMBER 26TH Lefthand, V Sharp Track

Official Going STANDARD. Stalls: Inside, Except 1m - Outside

108

12.10 ANTIQUE NOV STKS 2YO (D) 7f aw rnd Going 53 - 29 Slow
£3566 £1080 £527 £251

4616} **INSIGHTFUL 20** [3] R Hannon 2-9-2 Pat Eddery 4/6 FAV: 102531: 2 b g Desert Style - Insight (Ballad **87a**
Rock) Made all, clr over 1f out, pushed out, cmftbly: well bckd: earlier in '99 scored at Newmarket (sell), subs
plcd in 2 nurs h'caps (rtd 80): eff over 7f/1m: acts on firm, hvy & equitrack: handles a stiff/gall or sharp trk.
4376} **RISK FREE 42** [4] N P Littmoden 2-9-0 G Carter 11/4: 102002: 2 ch c Risk Me - Princess Lily (Blakeney) *4* **73a**
(Blakeney) Chsd wnr till halfway, rdn/btn 2f out, kept on ins last to regain poor 2nd nr line: abs, op 9/4: earlier
in '99 won at Southwell (auct mdn, rtd 91a & 87): eff at 5f, poss stays 7f: handles both AWs.
*24 **OTIME 15** [1] Mrs N Macauley 2-9-2 Dean McKeown 11/2: 400513: 2 b g Mujadil - Kick The Habit *nk* **74a**
(Habitat) Chsd wnr halfway, rdn/no extra fnl 1f & lost 2nd nr line: op 4/1, changed stables: return to 6f shld suit.
4616} **LA TORTUGA 20** [2] P D Evans 2-9-2 P McCabe 10/1: 014404: Chsd ldrs 5f: op 6/1, AW bow: earlier *2* **69a**
in '99 won at Carlisle (auct mdn, rtd 86): eff at 5f, 6f+ may suit: acts on firm & gd: best without a visor.
4 ran Time 1m 28.56 (5.76) (Mrs B Burchett) R Hannon East Everleigh, Wilts

109

12.40 SOUTHRIVER MDN DIV I 3YO (D) 1m aw rnd Going 53 -05 Slow
£2411 £728 £354 £167

73 **GHAAZI 7** [7] Miss Gay Kelleway 3-9-0 S Whitworth 3/1: 600431: 3 ch g Lahib - Shurooq (Affirmed) **57a**
Cl-up halfway, led over 3f out, styd on gamely ins last, drvn out: nicely bckd: plcd earlier in '99 (rtd 56a):
plcd in '98 (rtd 75, mdn): eff at 7f/1m, has tried 10f: acts on equitrack & firm grnd: has tried a t-strap.
25 **FARAWAY MOON 15** [2] Lady Herries 3-8-9 M Tebbutt 5/1: 003002: 3 gr f Distant Relative - Moon Magic *nk* **51a**
(Polish Precedent) Trkd ldrs, switched/prog to chase wnr fnl 2f, kept on tho' held nr fin: op 4/1: plcd earlier in
'99 (rtd 70, fill mdn): rtd 57 in '98: eff at 6f, stys a sharp 1m: handles firm, gd & equitrack.
8 **LADY BREANNE 18** [9] G L Moore 3-8-9 Pat Eddery 7/1: 460263: 3 b f Woods Of Windsor - Tootsie Roll *2* **47a**
(Comedy Star) Mid-div, rdn 3f out, kept on fnl 2f, nvr pace to chall: op 4/1: rnr-up earlier in '99 (rtd 65, mdn):
eff at 7f/1m: handles firm & equitrack: h'cap company may suit best.
4598} **ABSOLUTE FANTASY 22** [8] E A Wheeler 3-8-9 (BL) T Sprake 16/1: 0004: Cl-up halfway, ch 2f out, *½* **46a**
no extra fnl 1f: AW bow, 1st time blnks: no form from 3 starts on turf earlier in '99: stays a sharp 1m on equitrack.
4283} **MABROOKAH 49** [1] 3-8-9 J Tate 5/2 FAV: 006245: Rdn/rear in tch, mod late gains, nvr pace to chall: *¾* **45a**
AW bow, 7 wk abs, well bckd: rnr-up on turf earlier in '99 (mdn, rtd 68): eff at 1m/9f, tried 10f & a return to
further shld suit: handles equitrack & soft grnd: h'cap company may suit.
39 **WOOLLY WINSOME 13** [4] 3-9-0 (VIS) J Bosley (7) 7/1: 243006: Cl-up 6f: 1st time visor. *½* **49a**
4603} **BRIGHT BLADE 22** [3] 3-9-0 S Drowne 20/1: 007: Nvr a factor: AW bow. *10* **34a**
3940} **RAIN RAIN GO AWAY 71** [6] 3-9-0 N Callan (3) 12/1: 3-0008: Struggling halfway: 10 wk abs, AW bow. *shd* **34a**
25 **LADY BALLA CALM 15** [5] 3-8-9 G Bardwell 40/1: 00-009: Dwelt, bhd halfway. *30* **0a**
9 ran Time 1m 40.8 (4.6) (A P Griffin) Miss Gay Kelleway Lingfield, Surrey

110

1.10 LOYALTY SELLER DIV I 3YO+ (G) 1m2f aw Going 53 -17 Slow
£1532 £428 £207 3 yo rec 4 lb

2309} **THOMAS HENRY 99** [9] J S Moore 3-9-5 Pat Eddery 9/4 JT FAV: 344041: 3 br g Petardia - Hitopah **65a**
(Bustino) Mid-div, prog 2f out, styd on well for press to lead nr fin: abs, op 5/4: earlier in '99 won here at
Lingfield (mdn, rtd 63a & 70): rtd 78 at best in '98 (visor): eff at 7/10f on equitrack & firm: runs well fresh.
4335} **HIGH SHOT 45** [1] G L Moore 9-9-4 S Whitworth 4/1: 020-02: 9 b g Darshaan - Nollet (High Top) *¾* **58a**
Dwelt, held up, smooth prog to lead 2f out, hdd well ins last & no extra: 6 wk abs, AW bow, op 3/1: lightly rcd
earlier in '99: rnr-up in '98 (h'cap, R Rowe): ex-French, back in '95 won at Evry: eff at 1m/10f: acts on firm,
soft & equitrack: has reportedly choked prev: could find similar.
3716} **RAWI 86** [2] Mrs A J Perrett 6-9-4 T Sprake 14/1: 050503: 6 ch g Forzando - Finally (Final Straw) *2* **55a**
Led till 2f out, hard rdn & rallied ins last: 3 month abs: rtd 34a & 32 at best earlier in '99: missed '98 on the
level: '97 wnr here at Lingfield (appr h'cap) & Folkestone (clmr, rtd 60 & 55 at best, Miss G Kelleway): eff at
6f/1m, stays sharp 10f well: acts on fast & both AWs: eff with/without blnks.
-- **WILD RICE** [8] P Winkworth 7-9-4 S Drowne 12/1: 00/0-4: Chsd ldrs, rdn/ch 2f out, no extra: long abs. *1¾* **53$**
83 **NERONIAN 4** [3] 5-9-4 P Clarke (7) 14/1: 450605: Cl-up halfway, wknd 3f out: op 10/1, qck reapp. *7* **43a**
-- **RUSH** [5] 6-9-9 (t) P Roberts 9/4 JT FAV: -13106: Mid-div halfway, sn rdn/held: Belgian raider. *1½* **46a**
3940} **CRUISE AHEAD 71** [4] 3-9-0 R Studholme (5) 16/1: 00507: Rdn/bhd early, mod gains: AW bow, abs. *2½* **37a**
22 **MALCHIK 15** [10] 3-9-0 A McCarthy (3) 16/1: 530008: Wide/bhd early, prog to chase ldrs halfway, fdd. *6* **28a**
4598} **ARANA 22** [11] 4-8-13 C Cogan (5) 50/1: 000009: Wide/bhd early, nvr factor. *14* **8a**
2520} **QUEENS HAT 99** [6] 4-8-13 G Bardwell 50/1: 000000: Prom early, bhd halfway: 10th: 5 month abs. *2* **5a**
2503} **ARAB GOLD 99** [7] 4-9-4 J Mackay (7) 20/1: 360500: Prom 4f, sn btn: 11th: 5 month abs. *shd* **10a**
11 ran Time 2m 09.80 (7.0) (Ernie Houghton) J S Moore East Garston, Berks

LINGFIELD (Equitrack)   FRIDAY NOVEMBER 26TH   Lefthand, V Sharp Track

111   1.40 LOYALTY SELLER DIV II 3YO+ (G)   1m2f aw   Going 53 -17 Slow
£1532   £428   £207   3 yo rec 4 lb

4504} **BECKON 32** [8] B R Johnson 3-8-9 T Sprake 7/2 JT FAV: 630001: 3 ch f Beveled - Carolynchristensen 53a
(Sweet Revenge) Trkd ldrs halfway, smooth prog to lead 4f out, sn clr, unchall: val for 15L+, hvly bckd, gamble
from 10/1, bt in for 6,400gns: plcd earlier in '99 (rtd 62 & 53a): rtd 57 on fnl of 3 '98 starts (auct mdn):
apprec this step up to 10f, further may suit: acts on equitrack: apprec drop to sell grade.

4463} **KINNINO 36** [3] G L Moore 5-9-4 A Mackay 11/2: 050502: 5 b g Polish Precedent - On Tiptoes 10 43a
(Shareef Dancer) Rdn/chsd ldrs halfway, kept on for press fnl 2f, no ch wnr: op 4/1: rtd 55a & 45 at best earlier in
'99 (tried blnks): unplcd in '98 (rtd 67 & 57a): prob stays a sharp 1m: handles fast, gd & equitrk.

50   **SHABAASH 11** [2] P Howling 3-9-5 A McCarthy (3) 9/1: 300053: 3 b c Mujadil - Folly Vision (Vision) hd 47a
Cl-up, lost pl over 3f out, rallied wide dist, no ch wnr: op 7/1: earlier in '99 won here at Lingfield (clmr,
rtd 61a), subs plcd on turf (nurs, rtd 56, sell): '98 Folkestone wnr (nurs, rtd 67, G Lewis): suited by 7f/1m on firm,
gd & equitrack: handles any trk, likes a sharp/undul one: has run well fresh.

43   **DOBERMAN 13** [7] P D Evans 4-9-4 (vis) P McCabe 7/1: 036404: Prom, briefly led over 4f out, rdn/ hd 41a
no extra fnl 2f: never jumps rnr (unplcd, sell).

25   **GALLANT FELLOW 15** [5] 4-9-4 L Newman (7) 25/1: 003005: Mid-div at best. 5 34a

4434} **PERUGINOS MALT 38** [10] 3-8-9 Dean McKeown 9/2: 143006: Mid-div halfway, sn btn: AW bow, op 3/1. 1½ 27a

4443} **THE WILD WIDOW 37** [4] 5-9-4 (bl) N Callan (3) 7/2 JT FAV: 410007: Led, rdn/hdd 4f out, wknd: op 3/1. nk 31a

1   **APPYABO 18** [6] 4-9-4 J Mackay (7) 20/1: 400608: Rdn towards rear, no impress. 2 28a

1151} **KAZZOUD 39** [1] 3-8-9 P Doe (3) 25/1: 0-009: Sn bhd: 7 month abs, bhd rnr. 18 0a

4479} **END OF STORY 35** [9] 3-9-0 J Tate 10/1: 065000: Bhd halfway: 10th: op 8/1, AW bow, now with P Butler. 15 0a

56   **MICKY DEE 10** [11] 3-9-0 (t) Joanna Badger (7) 50/1: 0-00: Bhd halfway: 11th. dist 0a
11 ran   Time 2m 09.76 (6.96)   (B A Whittaker)   B R Johnson Epsom, Surrey

112   2.10 BHUBANESWAR NURSERY HCAP 2YO 0-85 (E)   7f aw rnd   Going 53 -42 Slow   [83]
£2703   £759   £370

4563} **PERUVIAN CHIEF 27** [8] N P Littmoden 2-9-7 (76) J Tate 7/4 FAV: 00211: 2 b c Foxhound - John's 89a
Ballad (Ballad Rock) Trkd ldrs, rdn/led over 1f out, drifted left nr fin, rdn out: hvly bckd: earlier in '99 won
at W'hampton (auct mdn, rtd 80a): eff at 6/7f: acts on both AWs & a sharp trk: open to further improvement.

4491} **TYCANDO 34** [1] K R Burke 2-9-1 (70) N Callan (3) 4/1: 620102: 2 ch c Forzando - Running Tycoon 3 77a
(Last Tycoon) Led, hard rdn/hdd over 1f out, no extra well ins last: op 5/2, clr of rem: earlier in '99 won at
W'hampton (clmr, rtd 74a with R Hannon), also rnr-up on turf (rtd 78, clmr): eff at 6/7f on firm, gd & both AWs.

4461} **MR GEORGE SMITH 36** [5] G L Moore 2-8-2 (57) F Norton 10/1: 00003: 2 b c Prince Sabo - Nellie's 5 54a
Gamble (Mummy's Game) Rdn in rear, mod gains fnl 2f, no threat: op 8/1, AW bow: unplcd earlier in '99 (auct
mdn, rtd 61): prob handles equotrack, runs as though 1m will suit: may improve.

*36   **TOWER OF SONG 14** [5] D W Chapman 2-8-12 (67) A Culhane 5/1: 535014: Hmpd & dropped rear after 2 60a
2f, mod gains break fnl 2f, ch had gone: op 3/1: no luck in running, best forgotten: prev with M R Channon.

*31   **PHOEBUS 14** [3] Pat Eddery 9/2: 000415: Chsd ldr, rdn/no extra 2f out: op 3/1: see 31. 1¾ 58a

41   **SHAYZAN 13** [4] 2-8-7 (62) Martin Dwyer 11/1: 0046: Chsd ldrs halfway, btn 2f out: op 14/1. 1¾ 49a

4279} **BROWNS DELIGHT 49** [4] 2-8-8 (63) P Doe 7/1: 00027: Al towards rear: 7 wk abs, op 5/1. 1 48a

2   **SEMIRAMIS 18** [2] 2-8-6 (61) S Sanders 10/1: 460048: Mid-div, rdn/btn 3f out: op 7/1: btr 2 (6f). 1¾ 43a
8 ran   Time 1m 29.46 (6.66)   (M C S D Racing)   N P Littmoden Newmarket, Suffolk

113   2.40 WATCHROD HCAP 3YO+ 0-80 (D)   6f aw rnd   Going 53 +01 Fast   [80]
£3947   £1195   £583   £277

76   **DIAMOND GEEZER 6** [12] R Hannon 3-8-5 (57) P Fitzsimons (5) 9/2: 025021: 3 br c Tenby - Unarla 61a
(Prince Tenderfoot) Cl-up, rdn/led dist, styd on gamely, all out: op 7/2: earlier in '99 won here at Lingfield
(rtd 57a) & Windsor (2, h'caps, rtd 67): '98 Sandown wnr (clmr, rtd 69): eff at 5/6f, stays 7f: acts on firm,
gd/soft & both AWs: eff without blnks: handles any trk, likes Windsor & Lingfield: likes to force the pace.

4610} **EMPEROR NAHEEM 21** [13] B J Meehan 4-9-10 (76) M Tebbutt 14/1: 400602: 4 b g Imperial Frontier - nk 79a
Desert Gale (Taufan) Chsd ldrs/wide, kept on well for press ins last, just held: AW bow: op 10/1: rnr-up 1st 2
starts in '99 (rtd 84, h'cap): '98 wnr at Sandown (h'cap), Pontefract (clmr) & Newmarket (ladies amat h'cap, rtd
83): eff at 5/6f, tried blnks: acts on firm, gd/soft & equitrack: likes a stiff trk: best without blnks.

64   **AFAAN 9** [10] R F Marvin 6-10-0 (80) S Righton 6/1: 055043: 6 ch h Cadeaux Genereux - Rawaabe nk 82a
(Nureyev) Chsd ldrs, hard rdn/ch ins last, just held: rtd 106 at best earlier in '99 (List): '98 wnr at Catterick &
Newmarket (h'caps, rtd 94 & 72a): '97 wnr at Southwell (rtd 72a), Redcar (2) & Pontefract (rtd 80, h'caps): eff
at 5/7f: acts on firm, gd/soft & both AWs: handles any trk, loves a gall one, esp Newmarket: eff with/without blnks.

820} **KRYSTAL MAX 99** [6] T G Mills 6-9-12 (78) L Carter 15/2: 132224: Sn trkd ldrs going well, ev ch ins hd 79a
last, no extra cl-home, tchd 12/1, abs: earlier in '99 won here at Lingfield (3) & W'hampton (clmrs,
rtd 79a): '98 Lingfield (2) & Southwell wnr (h'caps, rtd 80a): eff at 5/6f on fast, poss gd/soft, AW specialist.

258} **MEADOW LEADER 99** [7] 3-9-8-12 (64) P Roberts 20/1: 05-15: Dwelt, towards rear, styd on well over ½ 63a
1f out, nrst fin: 7 wk abs, Belgian raider.

3352} **REDOUBTABLE 99** [5] 8-9-6 (72) J Fanning 10/1: 504306: Dwelt/towards rear, keeping on well ins last nk 70a
when no room cl-home, nrst at fin: tchd 12/1, 3 month abs: shld prove sharper in similar next time.

4472} **KILMEENA LAD 35** [8] 3-9-13 (79) T Sprake 4/1 FAV: 010107: Dwelt/towards rear, mod gains: op 3/1. 3½ 68a

29   **ELLWAY PRINCE 15** [9] 4-8-9 (61)(vis) Dean McKeown 14/1: 600008: Led 5f, fdd: tchd 16/1. nk 49a

44   **YOUNG BIGWIG 11** [2] 5-9-8 (74) A Culhane 10/1: 012509: Chsd ldrs/hmpd after 2f, sn lost place/no ch. 1¼ 59a

29   **ROBO MAGIC 15** [1] 7-9-5 (71) Martin Dwyer 6/1: 403060: Chsd ldrs/hmpd after 2f, no ch after. 10th. shd 56a

4610} **BRIMSTONE 21** [3] 4-9-2 (68) A Morris 33/1: 40-000: Mid-div at best: 11th: AW bow. 1¼ 50a

44   **BRUTAL FANTASY 11** [11] 5-9-2 (68) A McCarthy (3) 14/1: 600000: Prom, ch 2f out, sn wknd/eased fnl 11 30a
1f: 12th: jockey reported that he thought gelding had gone lame: op 12/1:

3033} **KAYO GEE 99** [4] 3-10-0 (80)(bl) A Clark 16/1: 110000: Chsd ldrs/badly hmpd after 1f, dropped rear 11 22a
& no ch after: 13th: op 14/1: 4 month abs: no luck in running, this best forgotten.
13 ran   Time 1m 13.51 (3.11)   (J B R Leisure Ltd)   R Hannon East Everleigh, Wilts

LINGFIELD (Equitrack) FRIDAY NOVEMBER 26TH Lefthand, V Sharp Track

114 3.10 SOUTHRIVER MDN DIV II 3YO (D) 1m aw rnd Going 53 -13 Slow
£2411   £728   £354   £167

3940) **UNCHAIN MY HEART** 71 [9] B J Meehan 3-8-9 (bl) Pat Eddery 5/1: 224201: 3 b f Pursuit Of Love - **58a**
Addicted To Love (Touching Wood) Made all, rdn/clr 2f out, styd on well, rdn out: AW bow, 10 wk abs: plcd num
times earlier in '99 (rtd 70, h'caps): plcd fnl of 3 '98 starts (rtd 70, auct mdn): eff at 7f/1m, stays 10f:
acts on firm, soft & equitrack: handles any trk: best in blnks: runs well fresh.

25   **MAGIQUE ETOILE** 15 [2] M P Muggeridge 3-8-9 S Drowne 13/2: 250332: 3 b f Magical Wonder - She's 3½ **50a**
A Dancer (Alzao) Rdn chasing ldrs early, took 2nd 1f out, kept on/al held: op 4/1: stays 1m: see 25 (6f).

4455) **ROTHERHITHE** 36 [6] T J Naughton 3-9-0 F Norton 25/1: 003: 3 ch g Lycius - Cariellor's Miss 3 **49a**
(Cariellor) Bhd, styd on fnl 3f, nrst fin: AW bow: no turf form earlier in '99: shaped as if 10f will suit.

--   **DANCING SEA** [5] J S Bolger 3-8-9 K J Manning 7/4: 232504: Cl-up, rdn/grad fdd fnl 2f: AW bow/Brit 1 **42a**
debut: well bckd: plcd 4 times earlier in '99 in native Ireland: stays 7f: acts on fast & soft grnd.

4520) **PASSE PASSE** 31 [7] 3-8-9 (BL) Pat Eddery 5/1 FAV: 433205: Chsd ldrs wide, btn 2f out: blnks, hvly 5 **32a**
bckd: plcd on turf earlier in '99 (rtd 83, fill mdn): eff at 10/12f: handles fast & gd & a stiff/undul trk.

60   **TEMESIDE TINA** 9 [3] 3-8-9 P McCabe 25/1: 060606: Chsd ldrs 5f. 3 **26a**

4603) **WILOMENO** 22 [4] R Price 33/1: 07: Dwelt/al bhd: no form, AW bow. 20 **0a**

4492) **POLISH FALCON** 34 [1] 3-9-0 G Carter 16/1: 08: Slowly away/al rear: AW bow, op 10/1. 29 **0a**
8 ran   Time 1m 41.46 (5.26)   (Mascalls Stud)   B J Meehan Upper Lambourn, Berks

---

115 3.40 BUY LINGFIELD APPR HCAP 3YO+ 0-70 (G) 1m4f aw Going 53 +06 Fast [70]
£1982   £557   £272   3 yo rec 6 lb

*52   **NOUKARI** 10 [3] P D Evans 6-10-3 (73)(6ex) Joanna Badger (5) 12/1: 501311: 6 b g Darshaan - Noufiyla **80a**
(Top Ville) Chsd ldrs, rdn to lead dist, styd on gamely, all out: op 6/1: recent wnr here at Lingfield (amat
h'cap): earlier won twice over hurdles (rtd 104h, eff at 2m on firm & gd): earlier in '99 won at Lingfield (2,
AW h'cap & stks), Chester (clmr), Newmarket, Catterick (amat h'cap) & Pontefract (stks, rtd 74 & 73): '98 wnr at
Southwell & Lingfield (h'caps, rtd 63a & 63): eff at 10/15f on firm, soft & both AWs: loves Lingfield.

*89   **VIRGIN SOLDIER** 4 [9] M Johnston 3-9-9 (71)(6ex) P Dobbs 1/3 FAV: 111112: 3 ch g Waajib - Never hd **77a**
Been Chaste (Posse) Towards rear, switched wide & prog fr 3f, styd on well ins last, post came to sn: hvly
bckd at odds-on under a 6lb pen: quick reapp: shld win more races: see 89.

4437) **VANTAGE POINT** 38 [11] K McAuliffe 3-8-0 (48) R Brisland 20/1: 313403: 3 b c Casteddu - Rosie 1¼ **52a**
Dickins (Blue Cashmere) Chsd ldrs, prog to lead 3f out till dist, no extra: op 10/1: earlier in '99 won at
Folkestone (h'cap, rtd 51): mod form in '98: eff at 12f, has tried 15f+: handles firm, gd/soft & equitrack.

70   **KI CHI SAGA** 7 [6] P Burgoyne 7-8-1 (43)(bl) Paul Cleary (5) 16/1: 100044: Chsd ldrs, led 4f out till 4 **41a**
3f out, no extra fnl 2f: op 20/1: earlier in '99 scored here at Lingfield (sell, rtd 55a & 57): '98 wnr here at
Lingfield (3, sells & amat h'cap, rtd 63a & 34, G L Moore): suited by 1m/12f: handles gd & soft, loves equitrack/
Lingfield: best in blnks/visor: enjoys sell/clmg grade.

23   **TWOFORTEN** 15 [12] 4-7-10 (38)(40h) J Newman 20/1: 403305: Chsd ldrs, onepace fnl 3f. ¾ **35a**

81   **LOST SPIRIT** 6 [10] 3-9-1 (63) J Bosley (5) 33/1: 300006: Prom, rdn/btn 3f out: quick reapp. 4 **54a**

56   **BLACK ROCKET** 10 [7] 3-8-3 (48)(3ow) P Clarke 50/1: 006067: Prom 1m. 10 **31a**

4458) **BEAUCHAMP MAGIC** 36 [13] 4-7-12 (40) G Baker (7) 33/1: 600008: Sn rdn/bhd: AW bow, jmps fit. 1¼ **18a**

56   **SUPERCHIEF** 10 [2] 4-7-10 (38)(t) P Fitzsimons 12/1: 000039: Led 5f out till 4f out, fdd: btr 56 (10f). 3½ **11a**

4459) **JOIN THE PARADE** 38 [8] 3-8-10 (58) C Cogan 14/1: 023100: Al bhd: 10th: op 10/1, AW bow. ¾ **30a**

66   **YALAIL** 9 [4] 3-8-5 (53) R Thomas (3) 40/1: 060000: Nvr on terms: 11th. ¾ **24a**

52   **INDIGO BAY** 10 [5] 3-9-4 (66) R Smith 10/1: 200020: Sn rdn/rear, nvr factor: 12th: op 8/1: btr 52. nk **36a**

1   **MASTER LODGE** 18 [1] 4-8-11 (53)(t) D McGaffin 25/1: 55050: Led 7f, sn btn: 13th: lngr 12f trip. 7 **13a**
13 ran   Time 2m 34.89 (5.69)   (J E Abbey)   P D Evans Leighton, Powys

---

WOLVERHAMPTON (Fibresand) SATURDAY NOVEMBER 27TH Lefthand, Oval, Sharp

Official Going   STANDARD. Stalls: 7f-1m6f166y - Outside, Rem - Inside

116 7.00 RAMSDENS HCAP 3YO+ 0-60 (F) 5f aw rnd Going 42 -01 Slow [60]
£2316   £651   £318

76   **FRILLY FRONT** 7 [7] T D Barron 3-9-8 (54) N Callan (3) 4/1 JT FAV: 230341: 3 ch f Aragon - So So **58a**
(Then Again) Chsd ldrs, rdn/led well ins last, just held on, all out: op 3/1: plcd sev times earlier in '99 (rtd 61,
h'cap): '98 wnr on debut at Musselburgh (med auct mdn, subs rtd 83 at best): eff at 5/6f on fast, soft & fibresand:
handles any trk: has run well fresh: best without blnks: can win more races this winter.

71   **SOUTHERN DOMINION** 8 [4] Miss J F Craze 7-9-8 (54)(bl) T Williams 8/1: 200022: 7 ch g Dominion - nk **57a**
Southern Sky (Comedy Star) Chsd ldrs, rdn/outpcd 2f out, styd on well for press ins last, just held: tchd 9/1:
on a fair mark, can find a similar contest: see 71 (clmr).

76   **YOUNG IBNR** 7 [13] B A McMahon 4-9-0 (46) L Newton 9/1: 000-53: 4 b g Imperial Frontier - Zalatia ½ **47a**
(Music Boy) Prom, led over 2f out, hdd ins last & no extra cl-home: op 5/1: unrcd earlier in '99: rnr-up twice
in '98 (clmr, P D Evans, rtd 68a & 67): '97 Pontefract wnr (auct mdn, rtd 74): eff at 5f, tried 6f: handles firm,
soft & fibresand: tried blnks/visor, prob best without.

57   **ANOTHER NIGHTMARE** 11 [10] D W Barker 7-9-1 (47) Kimberley Hart (5) 10/1: 012004: Led 3f, no 2 **43a**
extra: op 8/1: earlier in '99 won at W'hampton, Lingfield (rtd 50a) & Hamilton (2, h'caps, rtd 50): plcd form in
'98 (h'caps, rtd 41 & 40a): best at 5/6f, stays 7f: acts on firm, soft & both AWs: handles any trk, likes W'hampton
& Hamilton: likes to race with/force the pace: has run well fresh: best without blnks.

87   **HEAVENLY MISS** 5 [9] 5-9-3 (49)(bl) J Fanning 4/1 JT FAV: 210545: Chsd ldrs, kept on ins last, shd **45a**
not pace to chall: tchd 5/1, quick reapp: see 87.

71   **TINKERS SURPRISE** 8 [5] 5-9-0 (46)(bl) M Tebbutt 20/1: 045006: Chsd ldrs, nvr able to chall: earlier in 1 **40a**
'99 scored here at W'hampton (h'cap, rtd 51a), subs rnr-up twice on turf (rtd 42, h'cap): rnr-up in '98 (rtd 47
& 40a): eff at 5f on firm, gd/soft & both AWs: likes a sharp trk: eff with/without blnks: on a winning mark.

1052) **JACK TO A KING** 99 [1] 4-9-5 (51)(tBL) J Edmunds 33/1: 0-0057: Rdn/rear, mod gains: blnks, abs. ½ **43a**

71   **CZAR WARS** 8 [6] 4-8-13 (45)(bl) J Bramhill 12/1: 000358: Rdn/bhd, mod late gains: op 10/1. 1 **35a**

71   **GROESFAEN LADY** 8 [3] 3-9-2 (48) G Faulkner (3) 16/1: 642409: Nvr on terms: op 12/1. 1½ **34a**

46

33 **ERRO CODIGO 15** [2] 4-10-0 (60) J Tate 16/1: 041000: Prom 3f: 10th: op 14/1. *6* **35a**
40 **LEGAL VENTURE 14** [12] 3-9-9 (55)(bl) T G McLaughlin 9/1: 602000: Prom, btn 2f out: 11th. *½* **28a**
*57 **CHEMCAST 11** [8] 6-9-2 (48)(bl) A Culhane 5/1: 002010: Al towards rear: 12th: op 6/1: see 57. *1½* **17a**
4172} **ROSES TREASURE 58** [11] 3-9-4 (50)(ebl) J Bramhill 25/1: 500000: Al bhd: 13th: 8 wk abs, AW bow. *1* **17a**
13 ran Time 1m 02.3 (2.1) (M Dolby) T D Barron Maunby, N Yorks

117

7.30 COWBOY CLAIMER 3YO+ (F) 1m6f166y aw Going 42 -32 Slow
£2116 £594 £289 3 yo rec 8 lb

4478} **NOUFARI 36** [7] R Hollinshead 8-9-9 P M Quinn (5) 8/15 FAV: 215001: 8 b g Kahyasi - Noufiyla (Top Ville) Held up, prog to lead over 3f out, edged left ins last, just held on, all out: well bckd: earlier in '99 scored at Nottingham & Thirsk (h'caps, rtd 76 & 83a): '98 wnr at Southwell (2), W'hampton (2) & Newcastle (h'caps, rtd 81a & 71): eff at 14f/2m, stays 2½m on firm & gd/sft, loves fibresand: handles any trk, runs well fresh. **64a**
51 **ROYAL EXPRESSION 12** [1] F Jordan 7-9-9 N Callan (3) 7/1: 462052: 7 b g Sylvan Express - Edwins' Princess (Owen Dudley) Trkd ldrs, led 5f out, hdd over 3f out, styd on well for press ins last, just held: clr rem, op 11/2: earlier in '99 won at Nottingham (h'cap, rtd 71 at best): missed '98: eff btwn 12f & 2m: acts on firm, gd/soft & fibresand: eff weight carrier, handles any trk: on a fair mark & a return to h'caps shld suit. *nk* **63a**
89 **CRASH CALL LADY 5** [5] C N Allen 3-8-0 J Mackay (7) 8/1: 002543: 3 b f Batshoof - Petite Louie (Chilibang) Rear, kept on fnl 3f, no threat to front pair: quick reapp, tchd 9/1: see 89. *13* **34a**
68 **HILL FARM DANCER 8** [2] W M Brisbourne 8-8-6 Martin Dwyer 10/1: 605404: Rear, prog 4f out, rdn/no impress fnl 3f: earlier in '99 won at Southwell (appr sell, rtd 54a), subs plcd on turf (rtd 30): '98 Musselburgh wnr (fill h'cap, rtd 59): eff at 12f, prob stays 2m on firm, gd/soft & both AWs: likes W'hampton: enjoys sell grade. *nk* **31a**
27 **REINE DE LA CHASSE 16** [3] 7-8-6 L Newman (7) 20/1: 0605: Rear, bhd 4f out: op 12/1. *25* **12a**
6 **RAED 19** [4] 6-9-5 A Polli (3) 14/1: 200006: Led after 3f till 5f out, sn btn: op 10/1. *2* **23a**
45 **AMBER REGENT 12** [6] 4-8-9 (VIS) T Sprake 33/1: -60007: Keen, led 3f, sn btn: t.o.: visor. *dist* **0a**
7 ran Time 3m 20.5 (10.9) (Ed Weetman) R Hollinshead Upper Longdon, Staffs.

118

8.00 D NOBLE MDN 2YO (D) 6f aw rnd Going 42 -10 Slow
£2866 £868 £424 £202

4616} **THE PROSECUTOR 21** [3] B A McMahon 2-9-0 L Newton 13/2: 260301: 2 b c Contract Law - Elsocko (Swing Easy) Prom, led over 2f out, styd on gamely for press ins last, all out: tchd 8/1: rnr-up twice earlier in '99 (rtd 65a & 66, mdns): eff at 5/6f, tried 7f, may suit in time: acts on fibresand & gd/soft grnd, prob handles fast: handles a sharp or stiff/gall trk: open to further improvement in h'cap company. **74a**
4599} **TWICE BLESSED 23** [1] R Hannon 2-9-0 Martin Dwyer 3/1 FAV: 002: 2 ch c Thatching - Fairy Blesse (Fairy King) Prom, led over 3f out till over 2f out, styd on well for press ins last, just held nr fin: clr of rem, nicely bckd, AW bow: unplcd in 2 starts earlier in '99 (rtd 57): eff at 6f, 7f+ may suit, acts on fibresand. *1* **71a**
-- **NIGHT AND DAY** [7] W Jarvis 2-8-9 M Tebbutt 9/1: 3: 2 ch f Anshan - Midnight Break (Night Shift) Mid-div, kept on fnl 2f, no threat to front pair: op 7/1: debut: May foal, dam a 5/6f wnr: sire a high-class 7f/1m performer: can improve over 7f+ in similar contests. *9* **50a**
-- **CUIGIU** [5] Noel T Chance 2-9-0 R Fitzpatrick (3) 4/1: 050254: Twds rear/mod gains: op 3/1, Brit bow. *1* **53a**
4381} **JOHN COMPANY 43** [8] 2-9-0 (t) T Sprake 7/2: 4625: Chsd ldrs 4f: abs/AW bow, with R M Beckett. *hd* **52a**
4452} **ATALYA 37** [10] 2-9-0 N Callan (3) 16/1: 06: Towards rear, mod gains: op 14/1, AW bow. *3½* **43a**
105 **JEPAJE 3** [13] 2-9-0 P McCabe 7/1: 042047: Chsd ldrs 5f: tchd 8/1, quick reapp. *½* **41a**
4607} **XANIA 22** [4] 2-8-9 J Fanning 16/1: 008: Nvr factor: op 12/1: AW bow. *hd* **35a**
4132} **BASIC INSTINCT 60** [11] 2-8-9 Dean McKeown 20/1: 0359: Prom 4f: abs, now with R Brotherton. *2* **30a**
4613} **MERCEDE 21** [6] 2-8-9 T G McLaughlin 16/1: -000: Al towards rear: 10th: op 14/1, AW bow. *½* **28a**
77 **ARPELLO 7** [9] 2-8-9 S Sanders 16/1: 00: Dwelt/al rear: 11th: op 10/1. *1¾* **24a**
46 **CLOPTON GREEN 12** [2] 2-9-0 A McGlone 15/2: 30: Led 3f, sn btn: 12th. *1½* **25a**
4599} **WYCHWOOD CHARMER 23** [12] 2-8-9 A Daly 33/1: 00: Cl-up 3f: 13th. *14* **0a**
13 ran Time 1m 15.9 (3.1) (Mrs Rita Gibson) B A McMahon Hopwas, Staffs

119

8.30 L'POOL HCAP 3YO+ 0-85 (D) 1m1f79y aw Going 42 +10 Fast **[85]**
£3837 £1160 £565 £267 3 yo rec 3 lb

78 **TALLULAH BELLE 7** [4] N P Littmoden 6-9-12 (83) T G McLaughlin 5/1: 000361: 6 b m Crowning Honors - Fine A Leau (Youth) Held up, prog fnl 2f, styd on well for press to lead nr line: fast time, tchd 7/1: earlier in '99 won at Lingfield (stks), W'hampton (rtd 86a) & Hamilton (h'caps, rtd 73): '98 wnr at Lingfield (rtd 75a), Goodwood & Yarmouth (h'caps, rtd 70): eff at 9/12f: acts on firm, gd/soft & on both AWs: handles any trk, loves a sharp one: eff weight carrier: tough/genuine mare, a credit to connections. **88a**
4060} **PRODIGAL SON 65** [6] Mrs V C Ward 4-9-2 (73) L Newman (7) 7/1: 252262: 4 b g Waajib - Nouveau Lady (Taufan) Prom, rdn/led ins last, hdd nr line: jumps fit (rtd 78h, unplcd): earlier in '99 won at W'hampton (2), Lingfield & Nottingham (h'caps, rtd 72a & 72 at best): plcd sev times in '98 (rtd 51 & 55a, tried blnks, with R Williams): eff at 7/10f: acts on fast, gd & both AWs: handles any trk, loves W'hampton: has run well fresh. *nk* **77a**
*23 **JUST WIZ 16** [5] R Hannon 3-9-3 (77)(bl) R Smith (5) 6/1: 002313: 3 b g Efisio - Jade Pet (Petong) Handy, led over 2f out, hdd ins last & no extra: well clr rem: see 23. *½* **80a**
38 **ARC 14** [2] F Jordan 5-8-7 (64) N Callan (2) 8/1: 221024: Led, hdd over 2f out & sn fdd: see 38 (8.5f). *11* **51a**
35 **MR BERGERAC 15** [8] 8-8-13 (70) A Culhane 20/1: 120655: Held up, nvr mount chall: op 12/1: earlier in '99 won at Bath (h'cap, rtd 64): plcd sev times in '98 (h'cap, rtd 82): '97 wnr at Leicester & Newmarket (h'caps, rtd 84), plcd on AW (rtd 77a): eff at 5/6f, suited by 1m: acts on firm, gd/soft & fibresand, handles soft: runs well fresh: eff with/without blnks: handles any trk, likes a stiff/gall one: fairly h'capped. *shd* **57a**
39 **HEATHYARDS JAKE 14** [3] 3-8-0 (60) P M Quinn (5) 12/1: 320026: Chsd ldrs 6f: op 7/1: see 39. *1¼* **44a**
4585} **QUEENS PAGEANT 25** [7] 5-9-13 (84) T Sprake 25/1: 000057: Sn bhd: op 12/1: earlier in '99 scored on reapp at Thirsk (h'cap, rtd 76): '98 York wnr (h'cap, rtd 75, also rtd 84a): eff at 7f/8.5f: acts on fast, soft & fibresand: has run well fresh: eff weight carrier. *4* **60a**
35 **HEVER GOLF GLORY 15** [9] 5-8-12 (69) N Carlisle 25/1: 600408: Al rear. *1¼* **42a**
8 ran Time 2m 01.2 (3.0) (Trojan Racing) N P Littmoden Newmarket, Suffolk

WOLVERHAMPTON (Fibresand) SATURDAY NOVEMBER 27TH Lefthand, Oval, Sharp

120 9.00 COUNTRY & WESTERN SELLER 2YO (G) 5f aw rnd Going 42 -22 Slow
£1829 £512 £248

74 **JANICELAND** 8 [5] S E Kettlewell 2-8-8(1ow) S Sanders 11/10 JT FAV: 022541: 2 b f Foxhound - Rebecca's **66a**
Girl (Nashamaa) Chsd ldr, rdn/led ins last, in command when eased nr fin: bckd, no bid, 1st success: rnr-up
sev times earlier in '99 (rtd 67a & 75): eff at 5/6f, 7f+ may suit: acts on fast, gd & fibresand: enjoys sell grade.
1800} **FOXY BROWN** 99 [2] Miss I Foustok 2-8-7 N Callan (2) 9/2: 202: 2 b f Factual - Miltak (Risk Me) 1½ **59a**
Rdn/chsd ldrs, keeping on when short of room ins last, not rch wnr: nicely bckd, abs: rnr-up on 1st of 2 starts
earlier in '99 (rtd 66a, fill auct mdn): eff at 5f, step up to 6f+ will suit: handles fibresand: cld find similar.
*42 **DIMMING OF THE DAY** 14 [4] A T Murphy 2-8-12 Dean McKeown 11/10 JT FAV: 204213: 2 ch f nk **63a**
Muhtarram - Darkness At Noon (Night Shift) Led, hung left 1f out & hdd, no extra: bckd: prev with B Meehan.
4432} **BABY ROCKET** 39 [1] R Hannon 2-8-7 T Sprake 25/1: 0004: Bhd halfway: AW bow: mod form. 13 **34a**
4 ran Time 1m 03.4 (3.2) (Cable Media Consultancy Ltd) S E Kettlewell Middleham, N Yorks

121 9.30 FILLIES HCAP 3YO+ 0-65 (F) 7f aw rnd Going 42 -17 Slow [61]
£2263 £636 £310 3 yo rec 1 lb

4527} **SWING ALONG** 31 [11] C F Wall 4-9-12 (59) M Tebbutt 7/2 JT FAV: 530531: 4 ch f Alhijaz - So It Goes **68a**
(Free State) Dwelt, prog halfway to lead over 1f out, sn in command, rdly: tchd 4/1, AW bow, first success: plcd
thrice earlier in '99 (rtd 70, mdn): rnr-up on 1st of 2 starts in '98 (rtd 91, mdn): eff at 7f/1m: acts on gd,
hvy & fibresand: handles a sharp or stiff/gall trk: has run well fresh: can win again.
4568} **DAYS OF GRACE** 28 [10] L Montague Hall 4-10-0 (61) Martin Dwyer 9/2: 341312: 4 gr f Wolfhound - 3 **62a**
Inshirah (Caro) Prom, led 2f out till dist, kept on tho' held by wnr: op 7/2: earlier in '99 won at Southwell &
W'hampton (h'caps, rtd 62a & 56): eff at 5/7f on firm, hvy & f/sand: handles a sharp or stiff trk: gd weight carrier.
69 **MAI TAI** 8 [4] D W Barker 4-9-4 (51)(vis) Kimberley Hart (5) 8/1: 003043: 4 b f Scenic - Oystons 3 **46a**
Propweekly (Swing Easy) Mid-div, prog fnl 2f, kept on tho' not pace wnr: tchd 10/1: see 69.
63 **LEMON STRIP** 10 [2] B Palling 3-8-13 (47) Claire Bryan (7) 9/1: 300424: Led 5f, no extra: see 63 (6f). 1½ **39a**
4593} **LANGUAGE OF LOVE** 24 [3] 3-9-6 (54) J Fanning 11/1: 002005: Chsd ldr, btn fnl 1f: tchd 12/1: AW ¾ **45a**
bow: rnr-up earlier in '99 (mdn, rtd 60): earlier with B Meehan: eff at 7f, handles soft, poss fibresand.
63 **SOVEREIGN ABBEY** 10 [6] S Sanders 12/1: 33-546: Chsd ldrs 5f: op 8/1. 1 **49a**
4568} **MUJAS MAGIC** 28 [9] 4-9-12 (59)(vis) R Fitzpatrick(3) 7/2 JT FAV: 165347: Twds rear, nvr factor: op 5/1. shd **48a**
78 **WHY WORRY NOW** 7 [8] 3-9-8 (56)(bl) T Sprake 7/1: 406508: Chsd ldrs 6f: op 6/1. 1¼ **42a**
63 **HOT LEGS** 10 [7] 3-8-10 (44) L Newton 33/1: 606009: Al rear. 10 **15a**
76 **MADAME JONES** 7 [12] 4-9-8 (55) Dean McKeown 16/1: 100-00: Sn bhd: 10th: op 12/1. 1 **24a**
4603} **SILVER SKY** 23 [1] 3-8-13 (47) J Tate 33/1: 0000: Dwelt, nvr factor: 11th: AW bow. 14 **0a**
11 ran Time 1m 30.3 (4.1) (W G Bovill) C F Wall Newmarket, Suffolk

MAISONS-LAFFITTE FRIDAY NOVEMBER 26TH Left & Righthand, Sharpish Track

Official Going HEAVY

122 3.10 LISTED PRIX ETOILE 3YO FILL 1m2f110y Heavy
£15070 £5167 £3599

-- **DANGEROUS MIND** H Blume 3-9-2 A Starke : 1: 3 b f Platini - Desert Squaw (Commanche Run) 105
4609} **LIMELIGHTING** 21 J H M Gosden 3-8-9 K Darley : 221212: 3 b f Alleged - Stealthethunder (Lyphard) shd 97
-- **ASCENSIONNA** France 3-8-9 A Junk : 3: 3 b f Acteur Francais - Ma Colombe (Don Roberto) 2½ 94
3840} **MARAMBA** 36 P W Chapple Hyam 3-8-9 T Jarnet : -41049: -: 9½ 80
13 ran Time 2m 24.1 (Gestut Sommerberg) H Blume Germany

TOKYO SUNDAY NOVEMBER 28TH Lefthand Track

Official Going FIRM

123 6.20 GR 1 JAPAN CUP 3YO+ 1m4f Firm
£1071545 £425666 £268782 £159322 3 yo rec 5 lb

100} **SPECIAL WEEK** 99 [13] T Shirai 4-9-0 Y Take 24/10: 112011: 4 br c Sunday Silence - Campaign Girl 123
(Maruzensky) -:
2912} **INDIGENOUS** 99 [7] I Allan 6-9-0 D Whyte 83/1: 122602: 6 b g Marju - Sea Port (Averof) 1½ 120
4399} **HIGH RISE** 43 [12] Saeed bin Suroor 4-9-0 L Dettori 19/1: 0-0263: 4 b c Hgh Estate - High Tern nse 120
(High Line) -:
4247} **MONTJEU** 56 [14] J E Hammond 3-8-9 M J Kinane 17/10 FAV: 211114: -: ¾ 119
18 **BORGIA GER** 22 [15] 5-8-9 O Peslier 15/1: 552058: -: 5 107
4422} **FRUITS OF LOVE** 42 [11] 4-9-0 M Roberts 20/1: 161329: -: hd 112
14 ran Time 2m 25.5 (Hiroyoshi Usuda) T Shirai Japan

SOUTHWELL (Fibresand) TUESDAY NOVEMBER 30TH Lefthand, Sharp, Oval Track

Official Going STANDARD Stalls: Inside, Except 5f - Outside

124 **12.00 AMAT CLASS STKS 3YO+ 0-65 (G) 1m6f aw Going 53 -43 Slow**
£1934 £542 £263 3 yo rec 8 lb

37 **GRAND CRU 18** [11] J Cullinan 8-11-3 (vis) Miss L Vollaro (7) 12/1: 000341: 8 ch g Kabour - Hydrangea (Warpath) Held up, smooth prog/chsd ldrs from halfway, led over 1f out, drifted left/rdn ins last, post came in time: op 10/1: unplcd earlier in '99 (rtd 49a & 41): rtd 63 & 54a at best in '98 (unplcd): '97 Newbury wnr (h'cap, rtd 66) & twice here at Southwell,(clmr, Mrs Reveley & sell R Craggs, rtd 66a): eff at 12f/2m on gd/soft, soft & fibresand. **56a**
67 **BLACK WEASEL 13** [16] A Bailey 4-11-3 Miss Bridget Gatehou 25/1: 000052: 4 br c Lahib - Glowlamp (Glow) Prom, rdn/led 2f out, sn hdd, kept on well ins last: clr rem: unplcd earlier in '99 (Miss J Craze, rtd 31a): '98 Pontefract wnr (stks, rtd 70 at best, 1st time blnks, J Dunlop): eff at 1m/12f, now stays sharp 14f well: acts on fast, gd & fibresand: eff in blnks, has tried a visor: handles a stiff/undul or sharp trk. ¾ **54$**
3824} **PIPE MUSIC 83** [13] P C Haslam 4-11-3 (vis) Miss A Armitage (5) 2/1: 050023: 4 b g Mujadil - Sunset Cafe (Red Sunset) Mid-div, chsd ldrs 4f out, kept on onepace: clr rem: op 6/4, 12 wk abs: earlier in '99 won here at Southwell (h'cap, rtd 70a & 54): '98 wnr again at Southwell (h'cap, 1st time vis, rtd 66a & 69): eff at 14f/2m, tried further: acts on gd, gd/soft, prob firm, likes both AWs: eff with/without vis or blnks: loves Southwell. 4 **48a**
89 **IL PRINCIPE 8** [14] John Berry 5-11-11 (e) Mr M Murphy (5) 7/4 FAV: 410124: Dwelt, sn chsd ldrs, led 6f out, rdn/hdd 2f out & sn btn: nicely bckd, tchd 5/2: btr 89 (h'cap, C/D). 9 **46a**
66 **TIME CAN TELL 13** [12] 5-11-3 Mr A Evans 12/1: 260645: Mid-div, btn 2f out: op 10/1: see 66. 14 **22a**
4127} **LAKE DOMINION 63** [5] 10-11-3 Miss A Elsey 50/1: -00006: Nvr a factor: 2 month abs. 13 **8a**
37 **ST LAWRENCE 18** [4] 5-11-3 Mr Nicky Tinkler (7) 25/1: 402067: Chsd ldrs 11f. 1¼ **6a**
85 **MARKELLIS 8** [7] 3-10-9 (BL) Miss C Hannaford (5) 25/1: 060608: Led/sn clr, hdd 6f out/sn btn: blnks. 4 **0a**
3695} **MOON COLONY 91** [10] 6-11-3 Mr P Pritchard Gordo 8/1: 030659: Chsd ldrs 11f: op 6/1, AW bow, abs. 8 **0a**
4577} **TURGENEV 29** [15] 10-11-3 Miss R Bastiman (7) 33/1: 000000: Wide/al rear: 10th. 15 **0a**
798} **Ajdar 99** [8] 8-11-3 Mr S Dobson (5) 33/1: 4578} **Go Too Moor 29** [9] 6-11-3 Miss Michelle Saunde 50/1:
3657} **Fly Home 92** [6] 4-11-0 Mr M Dobson (7) 50/1: 67 **Danka 13** [3] 5-11-3 Miss Leigh Hogben (7 25/1:
85 **Barossa Valley 8** [2] 8-11-3 Mr R Lucey Butler (7 50/1: 2664} **Milnes Dream 99** [17] 3-10-6 Mr M Little (7) 50/1:
16 ran Time 3m 13.2 (13.4) (Alan Spargo Ltd Toolmakers) J Cullinan Quainton, Bucks

125 **12.30 NURSERY HCAP DIV I 2YO 0-75 (E) 1m aw rnd Going 53 -43 Slow [80]**
£2402 £672 £326

26 **BOLD EWAR 19** [4] C E Brittain 2-9-4 (70)(bl) P Doe (3) 14/1: 530041: 2 ch c Persian Bold - Hot Curry (Sharpen Up) Led after 1f & al travelling well, styd on well ins last, drvn out: tchd 20/1: 1st success: blnks reapplied: rnr-up earlier in '99 (rtd 86, mdn): eff at 7f/1m, shld get further: acts on fast, gd & fibresand: handles a sharp or stiff/gall trk: likes to race with/force the pace: best in blnks. **76a**
112 **TOWER OF SONG 4** [8] D W Chapman 2-9-1 (67) A Culhane 7/4 FAV: 350142: 2 ch g Perugino - New Rochelle (Lafontaine) Chsd ldrs, rdn to chall/hung left over 1f out, kept on for press tho' al held: hvly bckd: qck reapp: shld win more races: see 112, 36 (sell, C/D). 1½ **69a**
4404} **SIGN OF THE TIGER 43** [13] P C Haslam 2-8-4 (56) Dale Gibson 16/1: -00043: 2 b g Beveled - Me Spede (Valiyar) Mid-div/wide, styd on for press fnl 2f, nrst fin: op 14/1: 6 wk abs: unplcd earlier in '99 (rtd 52a & 54): apprec this step up to 1m, further could suit: acts on fibresand: ran well from a tricky high draw, can find similar. ½ **57a**
4414} **JUST BREMNER 43** [2] T D Easterby 2-8-10 (62) R Winston 14/1: 3P1004: Chsd ldrs, kept on for press fnl 2f: tchd 16/1: 6 wk abs/AW bow: earlier in '99 scored at Newcastle (clmr, rtd 70 at best): eff at 1m, further is likely to suit in time: acts on fast, gd & fibresand: handles a stiff/gall or sharp trk. hd **63a**
31 **PICOLETTE 18** [5] 2-8-1 (53) Martin Dwyer 10/1: 450055: Dwelt/rdn in rear, mod gains fnl 2f: op 14/1. 3½ **47a**
4567} **CHICAGO BLUES 31** [9] 2-7-10 (48)(2oh) G Sparkes (5) 8/1: 050646: Rear/rdn, mod gains: op 6/1. nk **41a**
86 **LE CAVALIER 8** [1] 2-8-9 (60)(1ow) M Tebbutt 16/1: 030047: Handy, hard rdn/no extra fnl 2f: op 14/1. 3 **48a**
4588} **HI BUDDY 27** [6] 2-8-11 (63)(bl) O Urbina 10/1: 030428: Chsd ldrs 6f: op 9/1: AW bow. 1 **48a**
36 **NO COMMITMENT 18** [10] 2-7-12 (50)(2ow)(12oh) A Mackay 33/1: 00009: Bhd/sltly hmpd 2f out, no dngr. 4 **27a**
48 **ODYN DANCER 15** [7] 2-7-11 (49) G Baker (7) 33/1: 254000: Rdn mid-div, btn 3f out: 10th. 6 **17a**
80 **SAMARARDO 10** [12] 2-8-11 (63) T G McLaughlin 15/2: 506120: Wide/prom, wknd 3f out: 11th: btr 80. ½ **30a**
4616} **BESCABY BLUE 24** [14] 2-8-13 (65) F Norton 10/1: 501060: Prom wide 5f: 12th: op 9/1. 6 **23a**
4550} **VILLA ROMANA 32** [3] 2-9-7 (73) G Carter 8/1: 434150: Led 1f, cl-up 5f: 13th: nicely bckd: AW bow. 3½ **24a**
80 **DOUBLE VISION 10** [11] 2-7-12 (50) T Williams 33/1: 0060: Chsd ldrs 5f: 14th: h'cap bow. 5 **0a**
14 ran Time 1m 47.1 (7.7) (A J Richards) C E Brittain Newmarket, Suffolk

126 **1.00 HCAP DIV I 3YO+ 0-60 (F) 1m3f aw Going 53 -03 Slow [60]**
£1871 £524 £254 3 yo rec 5 lb

*85 **TROJAN WOLF 8** [16] P Howling 4-10-3 (63)(6ex) A McCarthy (3) 13/2: 420511: 4 ch g Wolfhound - Trojan Lady (Irish River) Made all, pshd out cl-home: recent wnr here at Southwell (amat h'cap): earlier rnr-up twice in '99 (D Sasse, rtd 58 & 56a, h'cap): rtd 76 in '98 (M Tompkins): eff at 1m/11f: loves to race with/force the pace: acts on firm, gd & both AWs: handles any trk, loves Southwell: best without a t-strap: runs well for an amateur. **75a**
43 **COUNT DE MONEY 17** [14] S R Bowring 4-9-8 (54) S Finnamore (7) 5/1 FAV: 451252: 4 b g Last Tycoon - Menominee (Soviet Star) Rdn/mid-div, stdy prog fnl 3f, nrst fin tho' nvr a threat: clr rem: earlier in '99 won 4 times here at Southwell (h'cap, 2 clmrs & class stks) & also W'hampton (clmr, rtd 67a at best & 35): '98 wnr at Southwell (amat h'cap, rtd 54a): eff at 11f/14f: handles firm & fast, fibresand/Southwell specialist. 2½ **61a**
81 **MY LEGAL EAGLE 10** [15] R J Price 5-8-9 (41) T Sprake 10/1: 304053: 5 b g Law Society - Majestic Nurse (On Your Mark) Chsd ldrs, rdn/chsd wnr 3f out, held fnl 1f: earlier in '99 scored at Salisbury (appr h'cap, rtd 54 & 28a at best): '98 Thirsk wnr (mdn h'cap, J Hills, rtd 51 & 48a at best): eff around 10f, stays 12f: acts on fast, soft & both AWs: eff with/without blnks: handles any trk: best held up for a late run. 6 **39a**
22 **MIGWAR 19** [8] N P Littmoden 6-9-10 (56) T G McLaughlin 11/1: 000004: Chsd ldrs, ch 2f out, sn held: tchd 12/1: earlier in '99 scored twice here at Southwell (sells, rtd 65a, no turf form since useful dual wnr in '96): eff at 10/12f on fast, gd, fibresand, handles firm: handles any trk, likes Southwell: best without a visor. 1 **53a**
85 **QUALITAIR SURVIVOR 8** [5] 4-8-6 (38) Dale Gibson 20/1: 000045: Chsd ldrs, btn 3f out: tchd 33/1. 13 **21a**
67 **PERCHANCER 13** [13] 3-9-1 (52) T Eaves (7) 14/1: 120006: Dwelt, prog/chsd ldrs 4f out, sn held: op 12/1. ½ **34a**
4564} **SHANGHAI LIL 31** [4] 7-9-4 (50) Joanna Badger (7) 9/1: 406107: Mid-div at best: op 13/2. 5 **25a**
68 **JAMORIN DANCER 11** [3] 4-9-5 (51) A Culhane 20/1: 603508: Mid-div, btn 2f out. nk **25a**
995} **DOMINO FLYER 99** [12] 6-9-13 (59) N Callan (3) 20/1: 002459: Chsd ldrs 7f: tchd 33/1, 7 month abs. 17 **14a**
83 **REGAL SPLENDOUR 8** [9] 6-9-1 (47) G Carter 16/1: 562660: Rear/mod gains: 10th: longer 11f trip. nk **0a**

SOUTHWELL (Fibresand)   TUESDAY NOVEMBER 30TH   Lefthand, Sharp, Oval Track

68   **SUPREME MAIMOON** 11 [10] 5-9-3 (49) M Tebbutt 13/2: 331030: Chsd ldrs, btn 3f out/eased fnl 1f: 11th. 1½   0a
60   **Regality** 13 [1] 3-8-9 (46) Dean McKeown 33/1:   69   **Sea Ya Maite** 11 [11] 5-9-9 (55) G Bardwell 14/1:
83   **Magical Shot** 8 [2] 4-10-0 (60) R Fitzpatrick (3) 11/1:   102   **Golden Lyric** 6 [7] 4-8-8 (40) A Polli (3) 16/1:
4576} **Welcome Heights** 29 [6] 5-9-7 (53) A Mackay 25/1:
16 ran   Time 2m 27.5 (6.2)   (Max Pocock)   P Howling Newmarket, Suffolk

---

127   1.30 UNIVERSAL MDN 2YO (D)   5f aw str   Going 53   +07 Fast
£2822   £792   £386

72   **SMOKIN BEAU** 11 [9] J Cullinan 2-9-0 A Culhane 2/1 FAV: 04331: 2 b g Cigar Dada - Beau Dada (Pine   81a
Circle) Al prom, led over 1f out & rdly asserted, pshd out: fast time, well bckd: plcd on turf earlier in '99
(mdn, rtd 76): eff at 5f, tried 6f, shld suit: acts on fibresand, handles gd/sft: plenty in hand, shld follow up.
1077} **RED REVOLUTION** 99 [6] T D Barron 2-9-0 T Sprake 5/2: -32: 2 ch c Explosive Red - Braided Way   1¼   72a
(Mining) Prom, ev ch 2f out, kept on ins last, not pace nwr: well bckd, op 4/1: AW bow/7month abs: plcd on
sole prev start (auct mdn, rtd 72): eff at 5f, 6f+ shld suit in time: acts on gd & fibresand.
4315} **DIAMOND RACHAEL** 50 [8] Mrs N Macauley 2-8-9 (VIS) R Fitzpatrick (3) 50/1: 03: 2 b f Shalford - Brown   1½   63a
Foam (Horage) Led, rdn/hdd over 1f out & no extra cl-home: AW bow/7W abs: 1st time visor: no turf form
prev in '99 (7f): eff at 5f: handles fibresand: left debut bhd in headgear today.
--   **PACK A PUNCH** [7] Miss L A Perratt 2-8-9 Dale Gibson 20/1: 4: Chsd ldrs, held fnl 1f: op 11/1, debut: 1¾   59a
Up And At 'Em filly, Mar foal, cost 4,400 IRgns: dam unrcd, sire produces speedy 2yos: eff at 5f, handles fbrsnd.
41   **MARITUN LAD** 17 [11] 2-9-0 N Callan (3) 50/1: 065: Prom, no extra fnl 1f.   2   59a
46   **FOR HEAVENS SAKE** 15 [5] 2-9-0 Dean McKeown 9/1: 046: Rdn/towards rear, kept on fnl 2f, nrst fin: shd   59a
op 6/1: h'cap company & a return to 6f+ will suit: eye-catching in 46.
4542} **SKYLARK** 32 [10] 2-8-9 G Carter 14/4: 233007: Sn rdn, mid-div at best: op 2/1, AW bow.   1¾   50a
4607} **LIONS DOMANE** 25 [1] 2-9-0 M Tebbutt 50/1: 008: Rdn/mid-div, nvr factor: AW bow.   2   50a
4369} **EPONA** 46 [13] 2-8-9 R Winston 20/1: 09: Dwelt, nvr on terms: AW bow.   1   43a
4589} **SOUNDS CRAZY** 27 [3] 2-8-9 S Finnamore (6) 50/1: 005000: Prom, wknd 2f out: 10th.   1½   40a
--   **Bold Emma** [2] 2-8-9 P McCabe 20/1:   3311} **Miss Roxanne** 99 [12] 2-8-9 R Lappin 50/1:
4445} **Magical Jack** 41 [15] 2-9-0 P Fessey 50/1:   --   **Mr Stickywicket** [4] 2-9-0 T G McLaughlin 20/1:
74   **Jenny West** 11 [14] 2-8-9 G Parkin 50/1:
15 ran   Time 1m 0.10 (2.3)   (Alan Spargo Ltd Toolmakers)   J Cullinan Quainton, Bucks

---

128   2.00 NURSERY HCAP DIV II 2YO 0-75 (E)   1m aw rnd   Going 53   -40 Slow   [79]
£2402   £672   £326

*48   **HEATHYARDS MATE** 15 [5] R Hollinshead 2-9-0 (65) P M Quinn (5) 6/1: 542211: 2 b g Timeless Times -   74a
Quenlyn (Welsh Pageant) Towards rear, smooth prog to lead 2f out, in command & eased nr line: recent wnr here
at Southwell (C/D auct mdn, 1st win): rnr-up earlier in '99 (sell h'cap, rtd 57a, auct mdn, rtd 72): eff at 1m/8.5f,
acts on firm, gd & fibresand: plenty handles any trk, loves Southwell: plenty in hand here, imprvg, can win again.
4514} **MERRYVALE MAN** 35 [12] J G Given 2-8-7 (58) Dean McKeown 25/1: 035002: 2 b c Rudimentary - Salu   1¾   60a
(Ardross) Chsd ldrs, no room 2f out, switched & kept on for press, al held: tchd 33/1, AW bow: plcd earlier in '99
(auct mdn, rtd 73): appear step up to 1m, shld get further: handles fibresand & gd/soft: gd run from high draw.
74   **NICIARA** 11 [10] M C Chapman 2-8-0 (50)(1ow) P Doe (0) 14/1: 000033: 2 b g Soviet Lad - Verusa   2½   48a
(Petorius) Dwelt, prog halfway/chsd ldrs, kept on ins last tho' al held: op 12/1: stays 1m: can win a sell: see 74.
4373} **JONLOZ** 46 [4] G Woodward 2-7-12 (49) P Fessey 33/1: 60004: Rear, prog/wide 3f out, kept on fnl 2f   3   40a
tho' no threat: AW bow/abs: h'cap bow: unplcd earlier in '99 (mdn, rtd 57): prob stays 1m, handles fibresand.
31   **WILL IVESON** 18 [13] 2-8-10 (61) M Tebbutt 13/2: 560565: Prom, no extra fnl 2f: op 7/1: unplcd   3   46a
earlier in '99 (rtd 74 & 63a at best): return to 7f shld suit: prob handles firm, gd/soft & fibresand.
4575} **AISLE** 29 [14] 2-8-10 (61) R Fitzpatrick (3) 9/2 JT FAV: 300116: Cl-up, wknd fnl 2f: tchd 6/1: earlier   5   36a
in '99 scored here at Southwell & Nottingham (h'caps, rtd 62a & 60): return to 6f shld suit: acts on soft &
fibresand, handles firm: handles a sharp or gall trk: worth another look when dropped in trip.
4256} **PURE BRIEF** 56 [9] 2-8-11 (62) N Callan (3) 33/1: 300077: Mid-div/wide, nvr factor: AW bow/8 wk abs   shd   37a
31   **SPRINGS ETERNAL** 18 [1] 2-9-7 (72) G Duffield 9/2 JT FAV: 042038: Rdn early, led 1f & cl-up 6f,   ½   46a
eased/held fnl 1f: tchd 11/2: btr 31 (7f).
88   **PEPPERCORN** 8 [7] 2-7-10 (47)(2oh) G Baker (7) 25/1: 505009: Mid-div at best.   ¾   20a
4570} **CROSBY DONJOHN** 29 [11] 2-8-12 (63)(BL) S Drowne 33/1: 450500: Prom 6f: 10th: blnks/AW bow.   2½   31a
72   **MADEMOISELLE PARIS** 11 [8] 2-7-10 (47)(1oh) R Brisland (2) 12/1: 006040: Al rear: 11th.   3   9a
*88   **SIRENE** 8 [3] 2-8-5 (56)(6ex) T Sprake 7/1: 00010: Led after 1f, hdd 2f out/wknd: 12th: btr 88 (7f, sell).   4   10a
72   **PADDYWACK** 11 [2] 2-7-10 (47)(bl) (3oh) Joanna Badger (7) 14/1: 001060: Al rear: 13th: tchd 16/1.   ¾   0a
*41   **JOELY GREEN** 17 [6] 2-9-3 (68) T G McLaughlin 13/2: 630610: Handy, ch 2f out, wknd/no room & btn   2½   16a
1f out: 14th: not stay longer 1m trip?: btr 41 (7f, mdn).
14 ran   Time 1m 46.8 (7.4)   (L A Morgan)   R Hollinshead Upper Longdon, Staffs

---

129   2.30 LADBROKE HCAP 3YO+ 0-90 (C)   6f aw rnd   Going 53   -05 Slow   [90]
£7100   £2150   £1050   £500

-64   **JUWWI** 13 [7] J M Bradley 5-9-3 (79) Claire Bryan (7) 8/1: 002621: 5 ch g Mujtahid - Nouvelle Star   85a
(Luskin Star) Rear/rdn, stdy prog for press fnl 2f to lead on line: op 7/1: earlier in '99 scored at Carlisle &
Chepstow (h'caps, rtd 79 & 58a at best): '98 wnr at W'hampton (sell) & Lingfield (h'cap, rtd 80a & 70): suited by
5/6f, stays 7f: acts on firm, hvy & both AWs: handles any trk, well weight carrier: best held up off a strong pace.
*79   **ALMAZHAR** 10 [12] J L Eyre 4-8-8 (70) N Callan (3) 12/1: 026312: 4 b g Last Tycoon - Mosaique Bleue   hd   75a
(Shirley Heights) Chsd ldrs wide, rdn & strong run ins last to chall, just held: op 10/1: tough eff: see 79 (7f).
104   **ASTRAC** 6 [6] A J McNae 8-9-8 (84) T Ashley 16/1: 640033: 8 b g Nordico - Shirleen (Daring Display)   1¾   85a
Handy, led over 1f out, rdn/hdd well ins last & no extra: op 12/1: quick reapp: on a fair mark: see 104.
49   **FIRST MAITE** 15 [9] S R Bowring 6-10-0 (90)(bl) S Finnamore (7) 8/1: 000154: Chsd ldrs/wide, kept   1½   87a
on fnl 2f for press: op 12/1: top weight: gd eff from tricky high-draw: see 35 (7f).
79   **GENERAL KLAIRE** 10 [13] 4-8-11 (73) R Winston 16/1: 521565: Rear, wide, switched & no room over 1f   hd   69a
out, styd on: op 12/1: earlier in '99 won here at Southwell (fill h'cap, rtd 77a & 52): '98 W'hampton wnr (auct
mdn, rtd 67a & 65): eff at 6f/1m, best at 7f: acts on gd, soft, loves fibresand: handles any trk: fairly h'capped.
47   **TOM TUN** 15 [1] 4-9-0 (76) T Williams 100/30 FAV: 230026: Dwelt, sn rdn/chsd ldrs, styd on fnl 1f,   hd   71a
unable to chall: hvly bckd: missed crucial break, ran well in circumstances, don't discount: see 47 (C/D).
91   **DOUBLE O 7** [5] 5-8-11 (73)(bl) F Norton 12/1: 010037: Led 4f, no extra: see 91 (5f).   nk   67a
44   **BLACK ARMY** 15 [8] 4-8-11 (73) J Tate 20/1: 053038: Cl-up, briefly led 2f out, sn held: see 44.   2½   60a

SOUTHWELL (Fibresand) TUESDAY NOVEMBER 30TH Lefthand, Sharp, Oval Track

4573} **PIPS SONG 29** [3] 4-9-1 (77) J Lowe 9/1: 060229: Chsd ldrs, btn over 1f out: op 7/1: earlier in '99   nk **63a**
won h'caps at W'hampton & Leicester (rtd 77 & 78a at best): '98 W'hampton wnr (auct mdn, rtd 77a, plcd on
turf, rtd 73, h'cap): eff at 6f: acts on firm, loves fibresand, gd/soft & hvy: has run well fresh.

79   **ROYAL CASCADE 10** [10] 5-9-6 (82)(bl) S Righton 20/1: 000350: Rdn/bhd, mod gains: 10th: see 33 (7f).½ **66a**
44   **MALLIA 15** [14] 6-8-12 (74)(bl) T Sprake 16/1: 000460: Al bhd: 11th: prev in '99 won at W'hampton   nk **57a**
(2, clmr & h'cap, rtd 76a) & Haydock (h'cap, rtd 76): '98 wnr at Southwell, W'hampton & Ripon (h'caps, rtd 78a &
71): eff at 5/6f: acts on firm, hvy & fibresand, any trk, unbtn at W'hampton: eff in blnks/visor, best held up.

64   **OCKER 13** [11] 5-9-0 (76) R Price 10/1: 055460: Chsd ldrs, held fnl 2f: 12th: see 47 (C/D).   nk **58a**
+64   **Ivorys Joy 13** [2] 4-9-10 (86) M Tebbutt 12/1:   4572} **Tartan Lass 29** [4] 4-8-13 (75)(t) G Duffield 20/1:
79   **Rouge 10** [15] 4-8-13 (75) Dean McKeown 14/1:   64   **Mukarrab 13** [9] 5-9-7 (83) A Culhane 20/1:
16 ran   Time 1m 16.8 (3.5)   (J M Bradley)   J M Bradley Sedbury, Glos

---

130   3.00 TIM & CATHERINE SELLER 3YO+ (G)   7f aw rnd Going 53 -40 Slow
£2018   £566   £275   3 yo rec 1 lb

79   **C HARRY 10** [4] R Hollinshead 5-9-6 N Callan (3) 6/1: 605041: 5 ch h Imperial Frontier - Desert Gale   **67a**
(Taufan) Chsd ldrs, rdn/lost place halfway, prog over 2f out to lead over 1f out, styd on well ins last, rdn out:
tchd 7/1: no bid: earlier in '99 won here at Southwell & W'hampton (clmrs), Leicester (sell h'cap) & twice again
at W'hampton (h'cap & clmr, rtd 71a & 60 at best): '98 wnr again at W'hampton (2, h'caps & sell, rtd 56a & 56):
eff at 6/7f: acts on firm, gd/soft, loves fibresand & Southwell/W'hampton: best without a vis: enjoys clmrs/sells.

87   **PRINCESS KALI 8** [9] D Carroll 3-9-0 (bl) R Fitzpatrick (3) 12/1: 301062: 3 ch f Fayruz - Carriglegan   1 **59a**
Girl (Don) Towards rear, styd on for press fnl 2f, not threaten wnr: tchd 14/1: eff at 6/7f: see 30 (6f).
*65   **BROUGHTONS TURMOIL 13** [10] B R Millman 10-9-6 T Sprake 9/4 FAV: 060013: 10 b g Petorius -   3 **58a**
Rustic Stile (Rusticaro) Keen/trkd ldrs, ch 2f out, rdn/onepace: hvly bckd from 7/2: see 65 (C/D).
*45   **RAMBO WALTZER 15** [7] D Nicholls 3-9-0 T Sprake 4/1: 000014: Trkd ldrs, held/no room 1f out: op 3/1.nk **57a**
92   **PALACEGATE TOUCH 7** [15] 9-9-6 (bl) G Carter 6/1: 006325: Handy, led over 2f out, sn hdd/onepace.   1 **55a**
76   **GUNNER SAM 10** [16] 3-9-5 Dean McKeown 20/1: 000606: Led 5f, fdd: prev in '99 won at Catterick (mdn,   3 **49a**
, rtd 63, B Hills): plcd in '98 (auct mdn, rtd 74): eff forcing it over a sharp 6/7f on gd & soft, prob fibresand.
4341} **DARK MENACE 48** [1] 7-9-6 (bl) D Kinsella (7) 16/1: 360237: Dwelt, mod late gains: 7 wk abs: prev   ¾ **48a**
in '99 won at Brighton (h'cap, rtd 47, plcd on sand, rtd 53a): '98 wnr here at Southwell (h'cap, rtd 41a, clmr,
rtd 47): eff at 6/7f, stays 1m: acts on firm, fast & both AWs: likes sharp/undul trks, esp Brighton: wears blnks.
50   **PRINCIPAL BOY 15** [12] 6-9-0 N Carlisle 25/1: 046538: Rdn/wide, mid-div at best: see 50.   1½ **39a**
1321} **ABSOLUTE MAJORITY 99** [3] 4-9-6 A McCarthy 20/1: 500039: Nvr in it: op 12/1, abs: prev in '99   6 **36a**
won at W'hampton (mdn, rtd 66a, B Curley): eff at 9.4f, tried 12f: acts on fibresand, sharp trk: best forcing it.
50   **LEOFRIC 15** [6] 4-9-6 T G McLaughlin 20/1: 000040: Nvr factor: 10th: tchd 25/1.   shd **36a**
2338} **Jato Dancer 99** [13] 4-8-9 P M Quinn (5) 33/1:   71   **Palace Green 11** [2] 3-9-0 A Culhane 12/1:
4372} **Encounter 46** [5] 3-9-5 R Lappin 25/1:   2531} **Petit Palais 99** [11] 3-9-5 (vis) P McCabe 25/1:
14 ran   Time 1m 33.1 (6.5)   (D Coppenhall)   R Hollinshead Upper Longdon, Staffs.

---

131   3.30 HCAP DIV II 3YO+ 0-60 (F)   1m3f aw Going 53 -26 Slow   [60]
£1861   £521   £253   3 yo rec 5 lb

69   **LEGAL ISSUE 11** [8] B S Rothwell 7-9-9 (55) R Lappin 12/1: 005431: 7 b h Contract Law - Natuschka   **62a**
(Authi) Trkd ldrs, smooth prog/no room & switched 2f out, sn led & styd on well, rdn out: earlier in '99 scored at
Thirsk & Beverley (h'caps, rtd 76 & 42a): '98 wnr at Pontefract & again at Beverley (h'caps, rtd 69 & 50a):
eff at 7f, suited by 1m/11f: acts on firm, hvy & both AWs, without vis: likes Beverley: shld follow up.
70   **WESTERN COMMAND 11** [9] Mrs N Macauley 3-9-8 (59) R Fitzpatrick (3) 5/1: 420622: 3 b g Saddlers'   2½ **61a**
Hall - Western Friend (Gone West) Sn handy, led briefly 2f out, no extra ins last: eff at 11/12f, stays 14f.
*68   **SOUHAITE 11** [13] W R Muir 3-8-9 (46) Martin Dwyer 4/1 FAV: 00613: 3 b g Salse - Parannda (Bold   5 **41a**
Lad) Dwelt & held up/wide, prog/chsd ldrs 4f out, held nr line: op 7/2: see 68 (12f, h'cap bow).
102   **MYSTERIUM 6** [11] N P Littmoden 5-9-4 (50) R Thomas 5/1: 504124: Held up, styd on fnl 3f.   3 **41a**
6   **PIAF 22** [1] 3-8-5 (42) T Sprake 20/1: 000305: Led 9f, fdd: plcd earlier in '99 (rtd 43a, AW h'cap, rtd   2 **30a**
59 on turf, h'cap): rtd 72 in'98 (mdn): eff at 10f, has tried 2m: handles firm, gd & eqtrk: best without blnks.
85   **GENUINE JOHN 8** [14] 6-8-8 (40) J Bramhill 25/1: 003006: Nvr on terms: earlier in '99 won at   2½ **24a**
Beverley (sell, rtd 54 & 31a): '98 wnr at Musselburgh, Hamilton (h'caps) & Ripon (sell, rtd 60 & 47a): eff at
7f/9f, tried further: acts on firm, gd/soft & both AWs, has run well fresh: eff with/without blnks, tried t-strap.
3947} **CLARINCH CLAYMORE 75** [7] 3-9-1 (52) R Winston 7/1: 341427: Chsd ldrs, btn 3f out: AW bow,   shd **36a**
11 wk abs: earlier in '99 scored at Beverley (amat h'cap, rtd 55 at best): rtd 60 in '98 (auct mdn): eff at
8.5f/11f: acts on fast & soft grnd: handles a stiff/undul or gall track: with J Jefferson.
1   **TIGHTROPE 22** [4] 4-10-0 T G McLaughlin 12/1: -10228: Dwelt/towards rear, no impression.   nk **43a**
*83   **DARE 8** [12] 4-10-3 (63)(vis)(6ex) Joanna Badger (7) 15/2: 153019: Cl-up/btn 2f out: op 6/1: see 83 (1m). ½ **45a**
67   **AREISH 13** [3] 6-9-4 (50) J Edmunds 11/1: 323020: Rear, nvr factor: 10th: tchd 12/1: btr 67 (9f).   ¾ **31a**
45   **TIME ON MY HANDS 15** [2] 3-8-12 (49)(tBL) S Finnamore (7) 25/1: 00000P: Chsd ldrs, saddle sn   **0a**
slipped & bhd, p.u. 5f out: blnks.
67   **Polar Eclipse 13** [16] 6-9-2 (48) M Tebbutt 20/1:   1712} **Carequick 99** [10] 3-8-8 (45) G Carter 33/1:
3   **Colonel Custer 22** [6] 4-9-12 (58) G Bardwell 14/1:   3604} **Blow Me A Kiss 94** [5] 4-9-6 (52) Dean McKeown 25/1:
4403} **River Captain 43** [15] 6-9-11 (57) N Callan (3) 14/1:
16 ran   Time 2m 30.0 (8.7)   (B Valentine)   B S Rothwell Musley Bank, N.Yorks.

WOLVERHAMPTON (Fibresand)   WEDNESDAY DECEMBER 1ST   Lefthand, Sharp Track

Official Going   STANDARD. Stalls: Inside.

132   12.50 ROSES CLAIMER DIV I 3YO+ (F)   6f aw rnd Going 39 -04 Slow
£1808   £506   £245

49   **TAKHLID 16** [6] D W Chapman 8-9-11 A Culhane 1/2 FAV: 100231: 8 b h Nureyev - Savonnerie (Irish   **86a**
River) Sn prom, rdn/led over 1f out, edged right ins last & asserted, readily: nicely bckd at odds on: earlier in
'99 won thrice at Southwell (clmrs/h'caps), Lingfield (2, h'caps) & 4 times here at W'hampton (clmrs, rtd 84a & 64
at best): '98 scorer at Hamilton & Thirsk (h'caps, rtd 74 & 64a): eff btwn 6f & 8.4f: acts on firm & soft, loves
both AWs, esp W'hampton: tough/genuine & useful AW performer who relishes claiming grade.

1365} **ELITE HOPE 99** [2] N Tinkler 7-8-8 S Finnamore (6) 6/1: 432342: 7 ch m Moment Of Hope - Chervil (Greenough) Towards rear, rdn & kept on fnl 2f, no threat to wnr: 7 mth abs: earlier in '99 scored twice at Southwell (h'cap & clmr, rtd 70a): '98 wnr at W'hampton (4, h'cap & clmrs, disqual once, rtd 72a): eff at 6f, suited by 7f: acts on fast, gd/soft, real fibresand/W'hampton/Southwell specialist: best without blnks: win sn. *2½* **62a**
4586} **THATS LIFE 29** [12] R Bastiman 4-8-11 G Parkin 11/2: 641003: 4 b g Mukaddamah - Run Faster (Commanche Run) Led, rdn/hdd over 1f out, onepace : tchd 13/2: earlier in '99 scored twice at Lingfield (sell & clmr, with T G Mills, rtd 72a, unplcd on turf, rtd 62, clmr): '98 Folkestone wnr (auct mdn, rtd 73 & 72a): best at 5/6f, does stay 1m: acts on firm, gd & both AW's: has run well fresh: enjoys sellers/claimers. *shd* **65a**
29 **LIVELY JACQ 20** [5] C N Allen 3-8-2 (VIS) N Carlisle 14/1: 554004: Mid-div, rdn & kept on fnl 2f, not pace to chall: op 10/1: first time visor: plcd earlier in '99 (rtd 69, h'cap, unplcd on sand, rtd 55a, h'cap): '98 winning juv at Yarmouth (2, sell & nurs h'cap, rtd 75 at best): eff at 6f, prob stays sharp 7f: acts on firm, gd & prob handles both AW's: has run well fresh: handles any trk, likes Yarmouth: best without blnks. *2½* **49a**
82 **FEATHERSTONE LANE 11** [4] 8-8-7 Dean McKeown 25/1: 046045: Rdn/towards rear, no room ins last & switched, nvr able to chall: a return to h'cap company will suit: see 82. *hd* **53$**
69 **SAN MICHEL 12** [10] 7-8-5 (bl) R Winston 33/1: 000506: Cl-up 5f: looks flattered. *½* **49$**
76 **MARENGO 11** [8] 5-9-3 T G McLaughlin 16/1: 340537: Prom 4f, op 12/1: looks flattered: see 76. *¾* **59$**
4604} **WHITE EMIR 27** [1] 6-8-13 T Sprake 14/1: 304008: Prom 4f: op 12/1: AW bow. *¾* **53a**
82 **PRINCESS FOLEY 11** [3] 3-8-2 A Daly 50/1: 026009: Prom, struggling halfway. *11* **22a**
4134} **NEEDWOOD MINSTREL 64** [9] 3-8-3 J Tate 33/1: 050600: Prom 2f, sn btn: 10th: 2 mth abs. *hd* **22a**
71 **DIVIDE AND RULE 12** [11] 5-8-11 P M Quinn (5) 33/1: 000000: Al rear: 11th. *1¾* **26a**
-- **QUIET MISSION** [7] 8-8-5 J Bosley (7) 66/1: 0000/0: Bhd halfway: 12th: v long absence. *2½* **13a**
12 ran Time 1m 15.4 (2.6) (S B Clark) D W Chapman Stillington, N.Yorks.

133

1.20 100 YEARS MDN 3YO+ (D) 1m aw rnd Going 39 -17 Slow
£2696 £756 £368 3 yo rec 1 lb

115 **BLACK ROCKET 5** [2] K Mahdi 3-8-9 J Tate 16/1: 060601: 3 br f Perugino - Betelgeuse (Kalaglow) Chsd ldrs, rdn/briefly outpcd 2f out, styd on well for press ins last to lead nr line, all out: op 14/1: qck reapp: unplcd earlier in '99 (rtd 59, no sand form): eff at 8.5f: acts on fibresand & a sharp trk. **54a**
119 **HEATHYARDS JAKE 4** [1] R Hollinshead 3-9-0 P M Quinn (5) 10/1: 200262: 3 b c Nomination - Safe Bid (Sure Blade) Held up, prog halfway, drvn to chall/narrow lead ins last, hdd line: op 5/1, qck reapp, mdn. *hd* **58a**
4566} **ABLE MILLENIUM 32** [4] R W Armstrong 3-9-0 R Price 7/2: 333: 3 ch g Be My Guest - Miami Life (Miami Springs) Prom, led over 6f out, just hdd over 1f out, styd on well ins last, just held: tchd 9/2: plcd both starts earlier in '99 (rtd 70a, C/D mdn): eff at 7f/8.5f, further may suit: acts on fibresand & a sharp trk. *shd* **58a**
75 **PUPPET PLAY 12** [6] E J Alston 4-8-10 A Culhane 16/1: 200064: Prom, rdn to chall fnl 2f, briefly led 1f out, styd on well, just held: clr of rem: op 8/1: ex-Irish, rnr-up earlier in '99: eff at 8.5f on fibresand. *hd* **52a**
73 **WHATSITSNAME 12** [8] 3-9-0 R Winston 50/1: 0-05: Chsd ldrs halfway, held fnl 2f: longer 8.5f trip. *8* **45a**
39 **TWO STEP 18** [3] 3-8-9 Dale Gibson 40/1: 06: Led 2f, wknd fnl 2f. *2½* **35a**
59 **KIDNAPPED 15** [7] 3-9-0 P Fitzsimons (5) 50/1: -00007: Mid-div, btn 3f out. *½* **39a**
4602} **BORN FREE 27** [5] 3-8-9 D Sweeney 8/15 FAV: 2-0238: Prom, wide on bend after 1f, sn cl-up till drvn/ wknd 3f out: hvly bckd at odds on: AW bow: connections reported filly unsuited by surface: plcd twice earlier in '99 (rtd 75, h'cap): stays a sharp 10f, acts on firm & gd grnd. *14* **13a**
4603} **AUTUMN LEAVES 27** [10] 3-8-9 T G McLaughlin 33/1: 009: Dwelt/al rear: AW bow. *½* **12a**
4371} **LADY LAUREN 47** [9] 3-8-9 R Lappin 66/1: 000000: Bhd halfway: 10th: 7 wk abs, AW bow. *3* **6a**
25 **LEVEL HEADED 20** [11] 4-8-10 (bl) T Sprake 25/1: 000050: Bhd 3f out, broke blood vessel: 11th. *22* **0a**
11 ran Time 1m 51.00 (4.8) (Hamad Al Mutawa) K Mahdi Newmarket.

134

1.50 ROSES CLAIMER DIV II 3YO+ (F) 6f aw rnd Going 39 -08 Slow
£1798 £503 £244

4471} **NINEACRES 40** [4] J M Bradley 8-8-5 (bl) Claire Bryan (7) 16/1: 000041: 8 b g Sayf El Arab - Mayor (Laxton) Led after 1f, styd on well ins last, rdn out: op 10/1: 6 wk abs: plcd earlier in '99 (rtd 42, h'cap): missed '98: last won in '95 at Lingfield (AW h'cap, rtd 60a, D Nicholls): eff at 5/6f, stays a gall 7f: acts on firm, fast & likes both AWs: eff in blnks/visor: handles any trk, likes a sharp one: runs well fresh. **57a**
44 **POLLY MILLS 16** [8] P D Evans 3-8-12 (bl) T G McLaughlin 9/2: 540002: 3 b f Lugana Beach - Danseuse Davis (Glow) Chsd ldrs, rdn & kept on fnl 2f, not pace wnr: op 4/1, blnks reapp: earlier in '99 scored at Southwell (h'cap, rtd 86a, subs plcd on turf, rtd 69, h'cap): '98 wnr at Windsor (seller, rtd 75) & again at Southwell (nurs h'cap, rtd 82a at best): suited by 5/6f, stays sharp 7f: acts on firm, gd/soft & both AWs: handles any trk, likes Southwell: eff in blnks/visor: spot on in similar back at Southwell. *1¼* **62a**
113 **EMPEROR NAHEEM 5** [3] B J Meehan 4-9-11 M Tebbutt 5/2 FAV: 006023: 4 b g Imperial Frontier - Desert Gale (Taufan) Chsd ldrs, ev ch 2f out, no extra ins last: op 2/1: acts on firm, gd/soft & both AW's. *1¾* **71a**
71 **RING OF LOVE 12** [11] J L Eyre 3-9-2 R Winston 16/1: 110504: Chsd ldrs, ch 2f out, onepace: op 12/1: earlier in '99 scored twice at Musselburgh (h'caps, rtd 70): '98 Chester wnr (mdn, rtd 76): all 3 wins at 5f, stays a sharp 6f: acts on firm, soft & fibresand: handles any trk, likes Musselburgh: tried a visor. *¾* **60$**
95 **PRESELI MAGIC 8** [9] 3-8-5(1ow) S Drowne 25/1: 065555: Chsd ldrs, kept on tho' nvr able to chall. *¾* **47$**
32 **EMMAJOUN 19** [10] 4-8-2 A Daly 14/1: 200036: Cl-up 4f: op 12/1: see 32. *shd* **44a**
71 **SING FOR ME 12** [12] 4-8-8 Stephanie Hollinshea 50/1: 005007: Rear, mod gains. *5* **38a**
30 **BEWARE 19** [6] 4-8-9 F Norton 4/1: 020038: Dwelt, al towards rear: btr 30. *2* **34a**
25 **ZOES NEWSBOX 20** [1] 5-8-2 P Fessey 66/1: 09: Led 1f, sn btn. *2½* **20a**
*32 **VICE PRESIDENTIAL 19** [7] 4-8-11 Dean McKeown 4/1: 000010: Dwelt/rear, hmpd by loose horse 3f out, sn btn: 10th: tchd 5/1, btr 32 (made virtually all, Southwell). *2½* **22a**
30 **UNLIKELY LADY 19** [2] 3-8-2 Kimberley Hart (5) 66/1: 46000: Prom 4f: 11th. *1¾* **3a**
65 **MIKES DOUBLE 14** [5] 5-8-9 (vis) R Price 25/1: 50605U: Mid-div/rdn, stumbled & u.r. 3f out: op 14/1. **0a**
12 ran Time 1m 15.6 (2.8) (J M Bradley) J M Bradley Sedbury, Gloucs.

135

2.20 CRIMEAN HCAP 3YO+ 0-85 (D) 2m46y aw Going 39 -29 Slow [82]
£3720 £1124 £547 £258 3 yo rec 8 lb

6 **ALHESN 23** [1] C N Allen 4-8-11 (65) M Tebbutt 12/1: 612501: 4 b g Woodman - Deceit Princess (Vice Regent) Prom, led over 3f out, sn hard rdn, styd on well ins last: op 10/1: earlier in '99 won twice at Yarmouth (mdn h'cap & h'cap, rtd 45), subs scored at Lingfield & W'hampton (AW h'caps, rtd 70a at best): suited by 14f/2m: acts on firm, fast & both AWs: likes a sharp/fair trk, esp W'hampton & Yarmouth: best without a visor. **70a**
51 **NETTA RUFINA 16** [2] M Johnston 4-8-3 (57)(vis) G Bardwell 7/2: 025332: 4 ch g Night Shift - Age Of *¾* **61a**

Elegance (Troy) Rdn early, chsd ldrs, led after 3f till over 3f out, kept on well tho' held nr fin: clr rem, op 5/2.
51 **TORY BOY** 16 [4] Ian Williams 4-7-11 (51)(bl)(1ow)(4oh) P Fessey 3/1: 326043: 4 b g Deploy -   7   **48a**
Mukhayyalah (Dancing Brave) Led, drvn/hdd over 3f out & sn held: op 11/2, blnks reapp: bhd today's rnr-up in 51.
51 **LITTLE BRAVE** 16 [5] J M P Eustace 4-9-10 (78) J Tate 6/5 FAV: 110024: Held up, rdn halfway, no   1½   **73a**
impress fnl 3f: well bckd: topweight: ahd of todays' rnr-up in 51.
*101 **FAILED TO HIT** 7 [6] 6-9-6 (74)(vis)(6ex) T G McLaughlin 9/1: 003515: Rear/btn 3f out: op 6/1: see 101 (12f).5   **64a**
4374} **MAKARIM** 47 [3] 3-9-1 (77) T Sprake 20/1: 461006: Trkd ldrs halfway, btn 3f out: 7 wk abs, AW bow: 19   **53a**
prev with N Graham, earlier in '99 scored at Bath (mdn, rtd 80, subs disapp in blnks): half-brother to 2 wnrs: eff at
11.6f: acts on firm grnd & has run well fresh: now with P Eccles.
6 ran   Time 3m 40.2 (11.0)   (J T B Racing)   C N Allen Newmarket.

---

136   2.50 COD SELLER DIV I 3YO+ (G)   **1m100y aw**   Going 39   -22 Slow
        £1574   £439   £212   3 yo rec 1 lb

83 **WAIKIKI BEACH** 9 [3] G L Moore 8-9-3 (bl) N Callan (3) 6/1: 303401: 8 ch g Fighting Fit - Running   **55a**
Melody (Rheingold) Mid-div, rdn/briefly outpcd 3f out, styd on well for press fnl 2f to lead nr line, all out: no bid:
earlier in '99 scored at Lingfield (amat h'cap, rtd 67a, unplcd on turf, rtd 41): '98 wnr at Southwell & again at
Lingfield (h'cap & seller, rtd 66a, subs rtd 44 on turf): eff at 7f/10f: acts on fast, gd/soft & both AWs: handles
any trk, loves Lingfield: best in blnks nowadays: enjoys sell grade.
45 **LILANITA** 16 [13] B Palling 4-8-7 T Sprake 4/1: 050432: 4 b f Anita's Prince - Jimlil (Nicholas   shd   **45a**
Bill) Led, rdn/edged left ins last, hdd nr line: clmd for £5,000: op 7/2: deserves similar: see 45.
45 **GODMERSHAM PARK** 16 [2] P S Felgate 7-8-12 G Parkin 7/1: 334603: 7 b g Warrshan - Brown Velvet   ¾   **49a**
(Mansingh) Mid-div, rdn halfway, prog/ev ch ins last when edged right, no extra cl-home: op 6/1: see 45.
38 **BLUSHING GRENADIER** 18 [11] S R Bowring 7-9-3 (bl) S Finnamore (7) 4/1: 350034: Chsd ldrs wide,   1¾   **51a**
kept on onepace fnl 2f: stays 1m, all wins at 6f: see 38 (h'cap).
92 **TEMPRAMENTAL** 8 [10] 3-8-6 A Mackay 7/1: 400055: Prom, no extra fnl 1f: op 11/2: plcd earlier in   1   **39a**
'99 (rtd 47, rtd 45a on sand, h'caps): '98 Chepstow wnr (nurs, rtd 62, first time visor): eff at 5f, prob stays sharp
1m: acts on firm, gd & prob handles both AW's: eff in a visor, has tried blnks: prob handles any track.
61 **OVER THE MOON** 14 [8] 5-8-7 C Rutter 7/2 FAV: 300456: Towards rear, kept on for press fnl 3f, nvr   hd   **38a**
pace to chall: clr rem: nicely bckd: earlier in '99 scored at W'hampton (C/D, clmr, rtd 57a): won thrice here at
W'hampton in '98 (3 clmrs, rtd 61a, N Littmoden): eff at 7f/8.5f: fibresand/W'hampton specialist: loves claimers.
4449} **AMAZING FACT** 42 [6] 4-8-12 S Drowne 50/1: -00007: Rdn/rear, nvr factor: jumps fit.   10   **28a**
61 **NOBLE PATRIOT** 14 [1] 4-8-12 A Culhane 9/1: 400028: Held up, eff 3f out, sn btn: btr 61 (7f).   3   **22a**
4402} **IMBACKAGAIN** 44 [5] 4-8-12 (t) T G McLaughlin 10/1: 236009: Prom 6f: op 8/1: 6 wk absence.   2   **18a**
2973} **BODFARI SIGNET** 99 [9] 3-9-2 (bl) R Lappin 20/1: 001550: Handy/btn 3f out: 10th: jmps fit.   8   **11a**
3175} Flashfeet 99 [7] 9-8-12 N Carlisle 50/1:   4405} Adornment 44 [12] 3-8-6 Dean McKeown 33/1:
12 ran   Time 1m 51.4 (5.2)   (Mrs J Moore)   G L Moore Woodingdean, E.Sussex.

---

137   3.20 LADBROKES HCAP 3YO+ 0-100 (C)   **1m100y aw**   Going 39   +12 Fast   **[100]**
        £7035   £2130   £1040   £495   3 yo rec 1 lb

*49 **KING PRIAM** 16 [12] M J Polglase 4-8-8 (80)(bl) T G McLaughlin 11/4 FAV: 352D11: 4 b g Priolo -   **88a**
Barinia (Corvaro) Chsd ldrs, rdn to chase ldr 3f out, stdy run for press to lead well ins last, rdn out: well bckd:
fast time: earlier in '99 scored here at Southwell (2, h'cap, rtd 74a), Leicester (class stks), Haydock & York
(h'caps, rtd 85a): '98 Newmarket wnr (clmr, rtd 70, M Pipe): eff at 1m/12f: acts on firm, gd/soft & fibresand:
handles any trk: eff in blnks: tough & v progressive gelding.
55 **SICK AS A PARROT** 15 [2] N Callan (3) 10/1: 500562: 4 ch g Casteddu -   ½   **95a**
Sianiski (Niniski) Prom, led 6f out, rdn clr over 2f out, hdd well ins last, just btn: clr of rem: first time blnks:
op 8/1: earlier in '99 with C Dwyer, plcd sev times (rtd 81, h'cap & 97a, list stks): '98 Beverley & Redcar wnr
(h'caps, rtd 86): eff at 1m/11f: acts on firm, gd & both AWs: handles any trk, likes Yarmouth: eff weight carrier:
has run well fresh: has worn a visor, ran well in blnks here: wears an eye-shield on sand: v useful, win again.
4560} **CHEWIT** 32 [4] G L Moore 7-10-0 (100) C Rutter 10/1: 06-003: 7 gr g Beveled - Sylvan Song (Song)   6   **97a**
Dwelt/rear, prog/chsd front pair 2f out, no extra fnl 1f: lightly rcd earlier in '99 (rtd 80, Lincoln h'cap): '98 wnr
at W'hampton (stks, rtd 98a) & Goodwood (h'cap, rtd 93 at best): eff at 7f, stays 8.5f, poss 10f: runs well fresh:
acts on firm, gd & both AWs: handles any trk, loves Lingfield & W'hampton: runs well fresh: spot on at 7f.
55 **ITALIAN SYMPHONY** 15 [5] P D Evans 5-9-6 (92)(vis) Joanna Badger (7) 10/1: 210054: Held up/kept   3½   **82a**
on fnl 2f, no threat: tchd 12/1: earlier in '99 won at Lingfield (stks) & W'hampton (h'cap, rtd 97a at best), subs
scored on turf at Newmarket, Warwick, Catterick & Musselburgh (h'caps, rtd 58 at best): '98 Southwell (2), Lingfield
(2) & W'hampton (5, clmrs/h'caps, rtd 89a & 40) wnr: eff at 7f/1m, stays 9f: acts on firm, gd/soft, loves both AWs:
eff in visor, tried blnks: genuine sort: likes mkt applr jockeys, handles any trk, loves a sharp one: v tough/useful AW performer.
27 **CHINA CASTLE** 20 [8] 6-10-0 (100) M Tebbutt 12/1: 501025: Rear, mod gains: op 10/1: see 27 (12f).   nk   **89a**
93 **PHILISTAR** 15 [1] 6-8-3 (75) T Sprake 10/1: 535526: Led till 6f out, no extra fnl 1f: op 9/1: see 93.   3   **58a**
64 **DIL** 14 [3] 4-9-7 (93) R Fitzpatrick 20/1: 000057: Trkd ldrs, lost pl/hmpd 3f out, sn btn: prefers 5/6f.   ½   **75a**
4580} **WEET A MINUTE** 30 [9] 6-9-12 (98) A Culhane 7/2: 602228: Mid-div, btn 2f out: op 4/1.   2   **76a**
4615} **TONY TIE** 25 [6] 3-8-1 (74) P Fessey 9/1: 000219: Prom 6f: op 6/1: AW bow.   1   **50a**
-- **LAKE MILLSTATT** 10 [4] 4-8-0 (72) T Williams 20/1: 112000: Dwelt/rear, nvr factor: 10th: Brit/AW bow.   9   **35a**
*56 **BRAZILIAN MOOD** 15 [11] 3-8-3 (76) P Doe (3) 9/1: 0210: Handy 6f, eased/btn fnl 1f: 11th: op 7/1,   6   **30a**
h'cap bow: btr 56 (10f, mdn, equitrack).
4375} **YAKAREEM** 47 [7] 3-9-11 (98) J Tate 9/1: 620000: Keen/prom, rdn/btn 2f out & eased over 1f out: nk   **51a**
12th: bit progressively slipped: op 7/1: 7 wk absence.
12 ran   Time 1m 48.50 (2.3)   (Ian Puddle)   M J Polglase Southwell, Notts.

---

138   3.50 COD SELLER DIV II 3YO+ (G)   **1m100y aw**   Going 39   -28 Slow
        £1574   £439   £212   3 yo rec 1 lb

*61 **SHARP SHUFFLE** 14 [12] Ian Williams 6-9-3 R Fitzpatrick (3) 13/8 JT FAV: 402011: 6 ch g Exactly   **59a**
Sharp (Homing) Held up, prog fnl 3f to lead over 1f out, all out to hold on cl-home: nicely bckd, tchd
2/1: sold to J Pointon for 8,000gns: recent wnr here at W'hampton (sell): rnr-up twice in '99 (sell/clmr, rtd
62a): '98 wnr at Newmarket (2, seller & clmr, rtd 70, R Hannon): eff at 7f/1m, stays sharp 10f: acts on firm,
gd/soft & both AWs: handles any trk, likes Newmarket & W'hampton: enjoys sellers/clmrs.
83 **MR ROUGH** 9 [2] D Morris 8-8-12 (vis) M Tebbutt 16/1: 400052: 8 b g Fayruz - Rheinbloom   shd   **53$**
(Rheingold) Mid-div, chsd ldrs halfway, drvn & kept on well fnl 2f, just held: op 14/1: plcd earlier in '99 (rtd
52a, seller & 51 clmr): '98 Brighton wnr (seller, rtd 49 at best): '97 Yarmouth wnr (sell h'cap, rtd 56): eff

WOLVERHAMPTON (Fibresand)   WEDNESDAY DECEMBER 1ST   Lefthand, Sharp Track

around 1m, prob stays 10f: acts on firm, gd/soft & both AWs: handles any trk, likes Brighton: eff in blnks/vis.

65	**DREAM ON ME 14** [7] H J Manners 3-8-11 J Bosley (7) 8/1: 013043: 3 b f Prince Sabo - Helens Dreamgirl (Caerleon) Rear, rdn 3f out, styd on fnl 2f, not pace to chall: op 5/1: acts on both AWs, firm & gd/sft.	¾	52a
45	**APPROACHABLE 16** [1] Miss S J Wilton 4-9-3 C Rutter 13/8 JT FAV: 116624: Handy, drvn 2f out, no extra fnl 1f: nicely bckd, tchd 5/2: all 3 wins here at W'hampton: see 45.	1½	54a
30	**RUNNING BEAR 19** [6] 5-8-12 T Williams 50/1: -00005: Led till over 1f out, no extra: unplcd earlier in '99 (rtd 34, seller): well btn sole '98 start for Miss S E Hall: stays a sharp 8.5f & handles fibresand.	1	47$
65	**PAGEBOY 14** [4] 10-8-12 T Eaves (7) 25/1: 050066: Held up, eff 2f out, held fnl 1f: rnr-up twice earlier in '99 (rtd 54a, also rtd 46): '98 Lingfield wnr (h'cap, rtd 73a, rtd 43 on turf): likes to race with/force the pace at 6f, stays a sharp 7f: acts on fast & fibresand, enjoys equitrack/Lingfield: has run well fresh: tried a visor, prob best in blnks, not worn today: a return to Lingfield/h'caps may suit.	1¼	44a
85	**ADIRPOUR 9** [10] 5-9-3 P M Quinn (5) 20/1: 000067: Held up, mod gains.	1¼	46$
2645}	**WARRIOR KING 99** [9] 5-8-12 C Teague 50/1: -06008: Dwelt/rear, nvr factor: 4 month jumps absence.	5	31a
4208]	**CANTGETYOURBREATH 60** [11] 3-8-11 (bl) R Lappin 20/1: 000009: Chsd ldrs halfway, sn btn/eased fnl 2f: 2 month abs, now with B Baugh.	¾	30$
4553}	**WINLEAH 33** [8] 3-8-11 P Fessey 50/1: 0-0000: Bhd halfway: 10th.	17	4a
--	**DON FAYRUZ** [13] 7-8-12 V Slattery 11/1: 41/0: Chsd ldrs 4f: 11th: op 5/1, AW bow/7 mth jmps abs.	hd	3a
3959}	**CLADANTOM 75** [5] 3-8-11 A Culhane 8/1: 021000: Prom till halfway: 12th: op 5/1/abs: AW bow.	1	1a
130	**PETIT PALAIS 1** [3] 3-9-2 (bl) T G McLaughlin 50/1: 000000: Prom 4f: 13th: unplaced yesterday.	30	0a
13 ran	Time 1m 51.9 (5.7) (G A Gilbert) Ian Williams Alvechurch, Worcs.		

139	**4.20 PUNIC HCAP 3YO+ 0-70 (E) 5f aw Going 39 +01 Fast [70]** £2738 £768 £374

*71	**SAMWAR 12** [1] Mrs N Macauley 7-9-13 (69) (vis) R Fitzpatrick (3) 8/1: 060011: 7 b g Warning - Samaza (Arctic Tern) Rdn/chsd ldrs, prog to lead 1f out, styd on well, rdn out: gd time: tchd 10/1: recent Southwell wnr (clmr), earlier in '99 won twice here at W'hampton (seller & h'cap) & again at Southwell (h'cap, rtd 72a & 54): plcd form in '98 (rtd 74 & 71a, Miss G Kelleway): eff at 6/7f, best nowadays at 5f: acts on firm, soft & equitrack, fibresand specialist: has run well fresh: eff in blnks/visor: loves W'hampton & Southwell: eff weight carrier.		76a
82	**TORRENT 11** [9] D W Chapman 4-9-4 (60) (bl) Lynsey Hanna (7) 4/1: 202232: 4 ch g Prince Sabo - Maiden Pool (Sharpen Up) Held up, prog halfway & ev ch in last, kept on well: tchd 5/1: ahead of this wnr in 40.	½	64a
71	**AA YOUKNOWNOTHING 12** [7] Miss J F Craze 3-9-4 (60) (vis) T Lucas 11/2: 300033: 3 b g Superpower - Bad Payer (Tanfirion) Chsd ldrs & ch 1f out, kept on ins last: clr of rem: see 40 (C/D).	1¼	61a
91	**ECUDAMAH 8** [3] Miss Jacqueline S Doyle 3-9-11 (67) T Sprake 2/1 FAV: 004124: Rdn/towards rear, kept on fnl 2f, no threat front trio: nicely bckd, op 7/2: ahd of today's wnr & rnr-up in 40 (C/D).	4	58a
121	**LEMON STRIP 4** [11] 3-8-5 (47) L Newman (7) 10/1: 004244: Rdn/towards rear, kept on for press fnl 2f, no threat: ddhtd for 4th: tchd 11/1, qck reapp: see 63 (6f, mdn).	dht	38a
71	**NIFTY NORMAN 12** [6] 5-10-0 (70) (BL) Alex Greaves 14/1: 004066: Chsd ldrs 4f: blnks: see 71.	hd	60a
95	**KUWAIT SAND 8** [12] 3-8-13 (55) J Tate 14/1: 40037: Towards rear, mod gains: op 12/1: see 95 (eqtrk).	1¼	42a
65	**RIVERDANCE 14** [10] 3-8-6 (48) (BL) Joanna Badger (7) 25/1: 206008: Towards rear, styd on fnl 2f, no threat: first time blnks, recent jumps rnr (mod form): rnr-up earlier in '99 (rtd 57, mdn h'cap): rtd 85 in '98 (flattered, subs tried visor, K McAuliffe): eff at 1m, handles soft grnd: needs a return to further.	nk	34a
116	**ANOTHER NIGHTMARE 4** [2] 7-8-5 (47) T Williams 15/2: 120049: Led, hdd 3f out & fdd: op 6/1.	hd	32a
91	**BOWCLIFFE GRANGE 8** [5] 7-8-3 (45) Kimberley Hart (5) 12/1: 001200: Prom, led over 3f out till 1f out, wknd qckly: 10th: op 10/1: see 57.	2½	23a
57	**MISTER RAIDER 15** [4] 7-7-13 (41) (bl) D Kinsella (7) 16/1: 604050: Dwelt/al rear: 11th: op 14/1: unplcd earlier in '99 (rtd 48 & 42a at best): plcd form in '98 (rtd 54a, h'cap, also rtd 27): '97 Leicester wnr (sell h'cap, rtd 46, plcd on AW, rtd 68a): eff at 5/6f on fast, gd/soft, loves equitrack, not fibresand: eff with/without blnks: handles any trk, likes Lingfield: subs tried visor, K McAuliffe): will be suited by a return to equitrack.	8	4a
3934}	**BLACKFOOT 77** [8] 3-9-9 (65) (bl) J Edmunds 33/1: -20200: Sn bhd: 12th: 11 wk abs: rnr-up twice earlier in '99 (rtd 69a & 62, mdns): eff at 5f on fibresand & gd grnd: eff in blnks: h'cap bow today.	6	17a
12 ran	Time 1m 02.1 (1.9) (Andy Peake) Mrs N Macauley Sproxton, Leics.		

SAINT CLOUD   TUESDAY NOVEMBER 30TH   Lefthand, Galloping Track

Official Going   HEAVY

140	**1.55 LISTED PRIX DENISY 3YO+ 1m7f Heavy** £15070 £5167 £3599 3 yo rec 8 lb

4397}	**SINON 45** [1] M Johnston 4-9-2 J Fanning : 144-01: 4 ch g Ela Mana Mou - Come In (Be My Guest)		109
4237}	**DIVINATION 59** [4] F Head 4-9-2 T Gillet : 125332: 4 ch f Groom Dancer - Devalois (Nureyev)	5	107
--	**ROLI ABI** [7] France 4-9-2 S Guillot : 3 : 4 b c Bering - All Found (Alleged)	nse	106
4618}	**SEREN HILL 24** [3] G A Butler 3-8-6 K Darley : 233137: -:	18	87
9 ran	Time 3m 39.4 (Ridings Racing) M Johnston Middleham, N Yorks		

WOLVERHAMPTON (Fibresand)   SATURDAY DECEMBER 4TH   Lefthand, Sharp Track

Official Going   STANDARD. Stalls: Inside, except 7f - Outside.

141	**7.00 TAMLA HCAP 3YO+ 0-65 (F) 2m46y aw Going 35 -32 Slow [65]** £2358 £663 £324 3 yo rec 8 lb

115	**BEAUCHAMP MAGIC 8** [5] M D I Usher 4-7-10 (33) G Baker (7) 40/1: 000001: 4 b g Northern Park - Beauchamp Buzz (High Top) Rdn rear, prog to lead well ins last, styd on well, rdn out: unplcd earlier in '99 (h'cap, rtd 54, t-strap, tried blnks): plcd form in '98 (rtd 69, h'cap): rtd 66 in '97 (mdn, J Dunlop): eff arnd an easy 2m: acts on fibresand, handles firm & gd grnd: best without a visor/blnks.		37a
126	**MY LEGAL EAGLE 4** [11] R J Price 5-8-4 (41) Claire Bryan (7) 14/1: 040532: 5 b g Law Society - Majestic Nurse (On Your Mark) Rdn rear, prog to chase ldr over 2f out, briefly led ins last, no extra: op 10/1,	1¼	43a

qck reapp: eff at 10/12f, stays a sharp 2m well: fairly h'capped: see 126 (11f).
115 **VANTAGE POINT 8** [6] K McAuliffe 3-8-4 (49) J Tate 10/1: 134033: 3 b c Casteddu - Rosie Dickins *nk* **51a**
(Blue Cashmere) Led 4f out till ins last, no extra: jockey given 3-day whip ban: eff at 12f/2m on both AWs.
124 **BLACK WEASEL 4** [10] A Bailey 4-8-0 (37) Dale Gibson 7/2: 000524: Trkd ldrs, kept on for press fnl ½ **38a**
3f, not pace to chall: op 9/2, qck reapp: stays an easy 2m, handles fibresand: see 124.
*135 **ALHESN 3** [4] 4-10-6 (71)(6ex) J Bosley (7) 7/1: 125015: Held up, eff 4f out, not pace to chall: ½ **71a**
tchd 8/1, qck reapp, fin clr of rem: 6lbs pen for 135 (C/D).
66 **CHILDRENS CHOICE 17** [2] 8-8-5 (42) A Polli (3) 4/1: 135026: Twds rear/eff 4f out, sn held: op 3/1. *13* **32a**
4293} **ABOO HOM 56** [3] 5-9-4 (55)(t) P Doe (3) 33/1: 035/07: Dwelt, rear, eff 5f out, sn btn: jmps fit *1¾* **43a**
(no form): rtd 52 on sole start on the level earlier in '99 (h'cap): 97/98 Haydock hdles wnr (mdn, rtd 129h,
eff at 2½m/2m6f on gd/soft & soft, without blnks): plcd in a mdn in '97 (A Stewart, rtd 79): AW bow today.
6 **ANOTHER MONK 26** [9] 8-8-12 (49) T Sprake 9/4 FAV: 203328: Chsd ldr, led 11f out till 4f out, rdn & *25* **19a**
btn 2f out: nicely bckd: recent jumps rnr (well btn, rtd 75h, Ascot nov): btr 6 (equitrack).
117 **ROYAL EXPRESSION 7** [12] 7-9-11 (62)(VIS) N Callan (3) 9/1: 620529: Chsd ldrs 12f: op 7/1, visor. *6* **26a**
124 **TIME CAN TELL 4** [13] 5-9-4 (55)(bl) D Sweeney 25/1: 606450: Prom 11f: 10th: qck reapp: see 66. *6* **13a**
4412} **BLACK ICE BOY 47** [1] 8-7-12 (33)(vis)(2ow)(4oh) T Williams 16/1: 60010P: Led 5f, wknd qckly halfway, **0a**
p.u. 4f out: recent jumps rnr (mod form): earlier in '99 scored at Pontefract (h'cap, rtd 45, no sand form): '98
Pontefract wnr again (h'cap, rtd 44): loves to force the pace around 2m/2m5f: acts on fast, loves gd/soft & hvy,
handles fibresand: handles a sharp trk, likes a gall/undul one, esp Pontefract: eff in blnks/visor.
101 **Westminster City 10** [8] 3-8-2 (47)(vis) R Fitzpatrick (2) 33/168 **Caerosa 15** [7] 4-8-3 (40)(bl) G Bardwell 12/1:
13 ran Time 3m 40.00 (10.8) (M D I Usher) M D I Usher Kingston Lisle, Oxon.

142

7.30 MOTOWN CLAIMER 3YO+ (F) 7f aw rnd Going 35 -01 Slow
£2305 £648 £316

*132 **TAKHLID 3** [8] D W Chapman 8-9-10 T Sprake 4/6 FAV: 002311: 8 b h Nureyev - Savonnerie (Irish **84a**
River) Made all, edged right dist, in command & eased nr fin: hvly bckd, qck reapp: recent wnr here at W'hampton
(clmr): earlier in '99 won at Southwell (3), Lingfield (2) & here at W'hampton (4, clmrs/h'caps, rtd 84a & 64):
'98 Hamilton & Thirsk wnr (h'caps, rtd 74 & 64a): eff btwn 6/8.4f on firm & soft, loves both AWs: tough & genuine.
49 **ODDSANENDS 19** [6] C N Allen 3-9-0 L Newman (7) 20/1: 3-4602: 3 b c Alhijaz - Jans Contessa (Rabdan) *2* **66a**
Cl-up, rdn/not pace of wnr fnl 2f: op 14/1: unplcd from 2 starts earlier in '99 (rtd 77a, C/D h'cap): '98 Ascot
wnr (nurs h'cap, rtd 77), also plcd on sand (rtd 83a): eff at 6/7f, has tried 1m: acts on firm, fast & fibresand.
*130 **C HARRY 4** [7] R Hollinshead 5-8-10 N Callan (3) 6/1: 050413: 5 ch h Imperial Frontier - Desert *nk* **61a**
Gale (Taufan) Trkd ldrs, rdn 1f out, no extra nr fin: op 8/1, qck reapp: clr of rem: see 130 (seller).
132 **ELITE HOPE 3** [2] N Tinkler 7-8-9 S Finnamore (7) 5/1: 323424: Dwelt, sn rdn to go prom, held fnl *5* **50a**
2f: clr of rem, op 9/4, qck reapp: also bhd today's wnr in 132 (6f).
130 **PRINCESS KALI 4** [12] 3-8-3 (bl) R Fitzpatrick (3) 12/1: 010625: Chsd ldrs 5f: tchd 14/1, qck reapp. *9* **30a**
134 **MIKES DOUBLE 3** [9] 5-8-10 (vis) A Polli (3) 33/1: 0605U6: Towards rear/rdn, nvr factor: qck reapp: *hd* **36a**
plcd sev times earlier in '99 (rtd 64a & 49): '98 wnr here at W'hampton (2, h'caps, rtd 63a) & Thirsk (h'cap, rtd
62): eff at 6/7f on fast, soft & both AWs, loves W'hampton: eff with/without blnks or visor: on a fair mark.
65 **RA RA RASPUTIN 17** [3] 4-9-0 (bl) S Righton 20/1: 020037: Mid-div at best: blnks reapp: see 65. *1½* **37a**
87 **SOUNDS SWEET 12** [10] 3-7-11 Joanna Badger (7) 50/1: 003008: Chsd ldrs 4f: plcd earlier in '99 *3* **14a**
(clmr, rtd 39, unplcd on sand, rtd 26a): rtd 50 & 24a in '98 (unplcd, J J O'Neill): stays 7f, handles gd.
130 **JATO DANCER 4** [11] 4-8-3 R Lappin 50/1: 000009: Al outpcd rear. *7* **9a**
4580} **CONORA 33** [1] 6-9-8 V Slattery 50/1: 020-00: Sn struggling: 10th: jumps fit. *3½* **21a**
39 **CAMEROSA 21** [4] 3-8-4 (BL) T Williams 50/1: 0000: Dwelt/sn struggling: 11th: blnks. *18* **0a**
11 ran Time 1m 28.7 (2.5) (S B Clark) D W Chapman Stillington, N.Yorks.

143

8.00 SOUL HCAP 3YO+ 0-90 (C) 7f aw rnd Going 35 -04 Slow [90]
£6494 £1967 £961 £458

129 **ALMAZHAR 4** [1] J L Eyre 4-8-8 (70) T Williams 100/30 FAV: 263121: 4 b g Last Tycoon - Mosaique **77a**
Bleue (Shirley Heights) Chsd wnr, styd on gamely for press to lead nr line: jockey given a 2-day whip ban, nicely
bckd, op 9/2, qck reapp: recent W'hampton scorer (h'cap): earlier in '99 won at Redcar (amat h'cap) & Southwell (2,
h'caps, rtd 66a & 52): eff at 6f/1m, tried 10f: acts on fast, loves fibresand: best without blnks/visor.
*96 **NAUTICAL WARNING 11** [8] B R Johnson 4-8-13 (75)(t) T Sprake 7/2: 201412: 4 b g Warning - Night ¾ **80a**
At Sea (Night Shift) Chsd ldrs, led over 3f out, clr over 1f out, hdd nr line: nicely bckd, tchd 6/1: acts on firm,
hvy & both AWs tho' is a Lingfield specialist: see 96 (equitrack, 1m).
4560} **INDIAN BLAZE 35** [6] D R C Elsworth 5-8-5 (67) L Newman (7) 4/1: 640103: 5 ch g Indian Ridge - *hd* **71a**
Odile (Green Dancer) Rear, kept on well fnl 2f, not pace to chall: nicely bckd: earlier in '99 won at Folkestone,
Kempton (2) & Newmarket (h'caps, rtd 86 & 53a): '98 Brighton & W'hampton wnr (h'caps, rtd 61 & 65a): eff at 7f/
1m, prob stays 10f: acts on firm, hvy & fibresand: handles any trk.
*78 **MY TESS 14** [12] B A McMahon 3-8-8 (70) S Righton 12/1: 530614: Chsd ldrs, rdn over 2f out, kept *1* **72a**
on tho' nvr able to chall: op 10/1: return to 1m shld suit: see 78 (made all).
40 **SANTANDRE 21** [4] 3-8-10 (72) P M Quinn (5) 20/1: 003045: Prom, wknd fnl 1f: op 14/1: earlier in *1½* **71a**
'99 scored here at W'hampton (h'cap, rtd 73a), plcd on turf (rtd 60, h'cap): '98 Thirsk wnr (nurs h'cap, rtd 78 &
64a at best): eff at 5f, suited by 6/7f: acts on firm, soft & fibresand.
107 **BLUE KITE 10** [5] 4-8-8 (70) C Cogan (5) 8/1: 223326: Rdn towards rear, mod gains: see 107, 47. *3½* **62a**
*104 **TEMERAIRE 10** [2] 4-10-0 (90) G Carter 5/1: 210517: Chsd ldrs, rdn/btn & eased over 1f out: top- *1½* **79a**
weight, tchd 6/1: btr 104 (made all, equitrack, stks).
96 **GUILSBOROUGH 11** [10] 4-8-6 (68) J Tate 12/1: 626068: Nvr on terms: Southwell wnr earlier in '99 *2* **53a**
(h'cap, rtd 68a & 57): eff at 7f, tried 1m: acts on fast, gd/soft & fibresand: handles a gall/sharp trk.
97 **FORTY FORTE 11** [3] 3-8-10 (72) N Callan (3) 9/1: 001329: Led till halfway/sn btn: op 6/1: btr 97, 22. *6* **48a**
49 **LOCOMOTION 19** [11] 3-8-11 (73)(t) P Doe (3) 25/1: 202000: Nvr factor: 10th. *13* **29a**
79 **POLAR ICE 14** [9] 3-9-5 (81) M Tebbutt 25/1: 113000: Al bhd: 11th. *6* **28a**
28 **JUST LOUI 23** [7] 5-9-0 (76)(vis) D Sweeney 10/1: 010-60: Held up/btn 3f out: 12th: vis reapp. *1¾* **20a**
12 ran Time 1m 28.9 (2.7) (Sunpak Potatoes 2) J L Eyre Sutton Bank, N.Yorks.

WOLVERHAMPTON (Fibresand) SATURDAY DECEMBER 4TH Lefthand, Sharp Track

144 **8.30 SATURDAY MDN 3YO+ (D) 1m4f aw Going 35 -05 Slow**
£2696 £756 £368 3 yo rec 5 lb

84 **PRASLIN ISLAND 12** [8] A Kelleway 3-9-0 J Tate 13/8 FAV: 020621: 3 ch c Be My Chief - Hence (Mr Prospector) Led 2f, remained cl-up, led again over 4f out, styd on gamely, all out nr fin: nicely bckd, op 5/2: rnr-up thrice earlier in '99 (rtd 76, mdn & 64a, h'cap): eff at 12f, stays stiff/undul 2m1f well: handles fast grnd & fibresand: best without blnks or t-strap: likes to race with/force the pace. **76a**
4584} **ROSEAU 32** [6] J H M Gosden 3-8-9 Dale Gibson 5/2: -402: 3 b f Nashwan - Fair Rosamunda (Try My Best) Chsd ldrs, drvn 4f out, rdn/ev ch fnl 1f, kept on well, just held: clr rem: op 7/4, AW bow: 4th at Sandown (fill mdn, rtd 74) earlier in '99: stays an easy 12f, further could suit: acts on fibresand. *hd* **70a**
56 **SPANKER 18** [7] B W Hills 3-8-9 T Sprake 5/2: 463423: 3 ch f Suave Dancer - Yawl (Rainbow Quest) Held up/keen, cl-up 4f out, rdn/no extra fnl 2f: nicely bckd tho' op 2/1: well clr of rem: btr 56 (10f, equitrack). *6* **61a**
70 **TALECA SON 15** [1] D Carroll 4-9-5 R Fitzpatrick (3) 40/1: 630504: Bhd 4f out: ex-Irish, placed in a Down Royal h'cap earlier in '99: eff arnd 7f/1m on fast & soft grnd. *27* **36$**
68 **LION CUB 15** [5] 3-9-0 (BL) R Perham 33/1: 000405: Cl-up, led 10f out till over 4f out, wknd: blnks: unplcd earlier in '99 (rtd 45a & 39): prob stays 12f & handles fibresand: has tried a t-strap. *6* **27a**
39 **SADDLE MOUNTAIN 21** [9] 3-8-9 M Tebbutt 7/1: 046: Trkd ldrs, btn 5f out: op 5/1: btr 39 (8.5f). *hd* **22a**
111 **KAZZOUD 8** [2] 3-8-9 P Doe (3) 50/1: 0-0007: Al rear: mod form. *14* **7a**
84 **KATIE JANE 12** [3] 4-9-0 N Callan (3) 50/1: 008: Bhd halfway: mod form. *1¼* **0a**
-- **SPARTAN HEARTBEAT** [4] 6-9-5 Joanna Badger (7) 14/1: 0/02-9: Sn bhd: op 9/1: long abs. *13* **0a**
9 ran Time 2m 38.4 (4.8) (Kevin Hudson) A Kelleway Newmarket.

145 **9.00 RESCUE ME SELLER 2YO (G) 5f aw rnd Going 35 -19 Slow**
£1819 £509 £247

34 **SERGEANT SLIPPER 22** [2] C Smith 2-8-11 (vis) R Fitzpatrick (3) 10/1: 500401: 2 chc Never So Bold - Pretty Scarce (Handsome Sailor) Dwelt, prog halfway & led ins last, styd on well, rdn out: op 8/1, no bid, visor reapplied: rnr-up earlier in '99 (rtd 60a), plcd on turf (rtd 48, sell h'cap): eff at 5f, has tried 6f: acts on fibresand & gd grnd: eff in a visor: likes a sharp trk & sell grade. **63a**
74 **UNFORTUNATE 15** [4] Miss J F Craze 2-8-6 T Williams 16/1: 006002: 2 ch f Komaite - Honour And Glory (Hotfoot) Rdn rear, styd on well ins last, nrst fin: tchd 20/1: blnks omitted: unplcd earlier in '99 (rtd 47a & 35): eff at 5f, return to 6f+ will suit on this evidence: handles fibresand. *2½* **51a**
120 **DIMMING OF THE DAY 7** [3] A T Murphy 2-8-11 M Tebbutt 11/4: 042133: 2 ch f Muhtarram - Darkness At Noon (Night Shift) Led, rdn over 1f out, hdd/fdd nr fin: op 2/1: see 42 (C/D, blnks). *½* **54a**
77 **DANCE LITTLE LADY 14** [6] J Berry 2-8-6 R Lappin 6/4 FAV: 060064: Cl-up, onepace fnl 2f: nicely bckd: unplcd earlier in '99 (rtd 63, auct mdn): eff at 5f, has tried 6f, shld suit in time: prob handles fibresand. *nk* **48a**
4406} **PONTIKONISI 47** [1] 2-8-11 (BL) T G McLaughlin 20/1: 00005: Sn rdn, nvr on terms: blnks, abs. *4* **43a**
118 **CLOPTON GREEN 7** [7] 2-8-11 (t) N Callan (3) 9/4: 306: Chsd ldrs 4f: nicely bckd/t-strap: btr 46 (6f). *¾* **41a**
74 **BLAZING PEBBLES 15** [5] 2-8-6 A McCarthy (3) 20/1: 00007: Cl-up 3f: mod form. *6* **25a**
7 ran Time 1m 02.9 (2.7) (C Smith) C Smith Temple Bruer, Lincs.

146 **9.30 CAN'T STOP HCAP 3YO+ 0-85 (D) 5f aw rnd Going 35 +11 Fast** **[78]**
£3740 £1130 £550 £260

64 **MANGUS 17** [7] K O Cunningham Brown 5-9-10 (74) N Callan (3) 16/1: 020201: 5 b g Mac's Imp - Holly Bird (Runnett) Made all, styd on well ins last, rdn out: gd time: plcd sev times earlier in '99 (rtd 78a & 64, h'caps): '98 Lingfield & W'hampton wnr (h'caps, rtd 74 & 76a): '97 Warwick wnr (h'cap): eff at 5/6f on firm, gd & both AWs, prob handles gd/soft: has run well fresh: likes to force the pace: back to form here. **81a**
113 **KRYSTAL MAX 8** [4] T G Mills 6-10-0 (78) L Carter 5/1: 322242: 6 b g Classic Music - Lake Isle (Caerleon) Chsd wnr, rdn/held ins last: tchd 6/1: see 113 (6f). *1¾* **79a**
*91 **SHARP HAT 11** [1] D W Chapman 5-8-10 (60) T Sprake 9/4 FAV: 000013: 5 b g Shavian - Madam Trilby (Grundy) Held up, rdn & kept on fnl 2f, not pace to chall: nicely bckd tho' op 6/4: acts on firm, soft & both AWs. *¾* **59a**
4554} **FACILE TIGRE 36** [8] S Dow 4-8-10 (60) P Doe (3) 10/1: 002004: Chsd ldrs, no extra fnl 1f: op 16/1: 2nd earlier in '99 (rtd 51 & 55a): '98 Brighton wnr (2 h'caps, rtd 69): eff at 5/6f on firm, soft & f/sand. *1* **57a**
*139 **SAMWAR 3** [6] 7-9-11 (75)(vis)(6ex) R Fitzpatrick (3) 5/2: 600115: Dwelt, kept on fnl 1f, not pace to chall: nicely bckd: 6lb pen, qck reapp: see 139 (C/D). *nk* **71a**
2677} **SWEET MAGIC 99** [5] 8-8-10 (60)(t) Joanna Badger (7) 33/1: 051056: Chsd ldrs 4f: 5 month abs: earlier in '99 scored here at W'hampton (sell) & Catterick (h'cap, rtd 62 & 65a): lightly rcd on turf in '98 (rtd 58): eff at 5f on firm, soft & both AW's: handles any trk, likes a sharp one: eff in a t-strap. *9* **40a**
40 **RUSSIAN ROMEO 21** [2] 4-9-5 (69)(bl) S Righton 7/2: 123037: Al outpcd: tchd 4/1: btr 40. *1¾* **45a**
113 **KAYO GEE 8** [3] 3-10-0 (78)(bl) T G McLaughlin 20/1: 100008: Prom 2f, sn btn: earlier in '99 won at Lingfield (h'caps, rtd 82a & 64): '98 wnr again at Lingfield (auct mdn, rtd 64a): eff over a sharp 5f, tried further: loves equitrack & Lingfield: suited by blnks. *14* **28a**
8 ran Time 1m 01.4 (1.2) (Danebury Racing Stables Ltd) K O Cunningham Brown Stockbridge, Hants.

LINGFIELD (Equitrack) MONDAY DECEMBER 6TH Lefthand, V Sharp Track

Official Going STANDARD. Stalls: Inside, except 1m - Outside.

147 **12.10 GATWICK FILL HCAP DIV 1 3YO+ 0-70 (E) 1m aw rnd Going 32 -09 Slow** **[66]**
£2303 £645 £313 3 yo rec 1 lb

121 **MAI TAI 9** [2] D W Barker 4-8-12 (50)(vis) Kimberley Hart (5) 9/2: 030431: 4 b f Scenic - Oystons Propweekly (Swing Easy) Chsd ldrs going well halfway, switched & rdn to lead ins last, asserted nr fin, pushed out: op 11/4: earlier in '99 scored at Southwell (auct mdn, rtd 57a) & Redcar (fill h'cap, rtd 55): plcd form in '98 (h'cap, rtd 58a, Mrs Dutfield): eff at 6/7f, stays a sharp 1m well: acts on firm, gd/soft & both AW's: tried blnks, eff with/without a visor: handles any trk, likes a sharp one. **56a**
59 **DELIGHT OF DAWN 20** [6] E A Wheeler 7-8-5 (43)(bl) D Kinsella (7) 7/2 FAV: 604662: 7 b m Never So Bold - Vogos Angel (Song) Chsd ldrs, rdn/ch 2f out, kept on onepace: nicely bckd: earlier in '99 scored *2* **44a**

here at Lingfield (C/D, h'cap, rtd 46a) & Windsor (h'cap, rtd 57): '98 Warwick & Leicester wnr (h'caps, rtd 55
& 40a): eff at 7f/8.3f: acts on firm, soft & both AW's: best in blnks: has run well fresh: on a fair mark.
59   **QUEEN OF THE KEYS 20** [7] S Dow 3-7-13 (38) P Doe (1) 8/1: -00003: 3 b f Royal Academy - Piano   nk 38a
Belle (Fappiano) Dwelt, rdn/rear & wide, rapid prog for press to lead 3f out, drvn/hdd ins last & no extra cl-
home: op 7/1: wore eye-shield: unplcd on 4 starts earlier in '99 (rtd 33 & 28a): well btn both juv starts in
'98: eff at 1m, tried 10f: acts on equitrack: lightly raced & a likely type for similar.
4576} **DAPHNES DOLL 35** [10] Dr J R J Naylor 4-8-11 (49) N Callan (3) 11/1: 032004: Prom, rdn/onepace   hd 48a
fnl 2f: op 8/1: earlier in '99 with Miss G Kelleway, plcd twice (rtd 53, h'cap, rtd 50a on sand): '98 Lingfield
wnr (mdn, rtd 65a, plcd on turf, rtd 74, mdn): eff at 6f/8.5f, suited by 7f: acts on fast, soft, equitrack &
prob fibresand: likes to dominate: handles any trk, likes a sharp one: now with Dr J Naylor.
107   **ENTROPY 12** [11] 3-8-4 (43) G Bardwell 33/1: 000005: Rear/rdn, prog/chsd ldrs 3f out, sn no extra.   ¾ 41a
4565} **DIM OFAN 37** [9] 3-9-9 (62) T Sprake 7/1: 000046: Prom, led over 3f out, sn hdd/fdd fnl 1f: ingr trip.   1¼ 57a
4521} **ANNIE APPLE 41** [1] 3-9-1 (54) T Ashley 9/2: 242307: Held up, btn 2f out: tchd 11/2, 6 wk absence.   6 40a
2435} **TRAWLING 99** [4] 3-9-12 (65) A McGlone 11/2: -13008: Prom 6f: 5 month abs, now with C Dwyer.   8 39a
1688} **PEARL BUTTON 99** [5] 3-8-13 (52) G Faulkner (3) 20/1: 00009: Prom 4f: AW bow, 6 mth abs.   nk 25a
1373} **PURNADAS ROAD 99** [3] 4-8-10 (48)(BL) P Dobbs (4) 33/1: 50-000: Led 5f: blnks, now with H Haynes.   1 19a
121   **SILVER SKY 9** [8] 3-8-1 (40) G Baker (7) 40/1: 00000: Prom 3f, sn bhd: 11th.   ½ 10a
11 ran   Time 1m 39.46 (3.26)   (L H Gilmurray & T J Docherty)   D W Barker Scorton, N.Yorks.

---

148   12.40 COPTHORNE HCAP DIV 1 3YO+ 0-60 (F)   6f aw rnd Going 32 -01 Slow   [60]
£1840   £515   £250

*87   **HAUNT THE ZOO 14** [2] J L Harris 4-9-1 (47) J Bramhill 10/1: 054611: 4 b f Komaite - Merryhill Maid   54a
(M Double M) Sn chsd ldrs, rdn/chsd ldr over 1f out, duelled with rnr-up ins 1f, just prevailed, all out: op 8/1:
recent Southwell wnr (fill h'cap, first success): plcd form earlier in '99 (rtd 46 & 47a): missed '98: AW path,
has tried 1m: acts on fast grnd & both AW's: handles a gall trk, loves a sharp one: has run well fresh: in gd heart.
*113   **DIAMOND GEEZER 10** [1] R Hannon 3-10-0 (60) P Fitzsimons (5) 4/1: 250212: 3 br c Prince - Unaria   hd 66a
(Prince Tenderfoot) Sn cl-up, led over 3f out, rdn/duelled with wnr ins last, hdd nr line, just held: clr of rem:
nicely bckd: possesses vital early pace for this trk, will win more races: loves Lingfield, see 113 (C/D).
132   **SAN MICHEL 5** [9] J L Eyre 7-8-12 (44) R Winston 33/1: 005063: 7 b g Scenic - The Top Diesis (Diesis)   5 41a
Rdn/chsd ldrs wide, kept on fnl 1f to take 3rd, no threat front pair: qck reapp: plcd once earlier in '99 (rtd
56, h'cap, unplcd on sand, rtd 40a): ex-Irish, 1st out in '98, back in '96 won a Leopardstown h'cap: eff at 5/6f,
tried 7f: acts on gd, hvy & prob handles both AW's: eff with/without blnks.
107   **JUST DISSIDENT 12** [3] R M Whitaker 7-9-11 (57) D Sweeney 10/1: 010444: Led 3f/cl-up till fdd fnl 1f.   nk 53a
106   **DAYNABEE 12** [5] 4-9-0 (46) T G McLaughlin 8/1: 005425: Rdn/chsd ldrs, outpcd 2f out: see 58 (7f).   1 40a
87   **TANCRED TIMES 14** [10] 4-8-10 (42) Kimberley Hart (5) 10/1: 6W5026: Chsd ldrs, no extra over 1f out.   ½ 34a
3348} **GOLD EDGE 99** [12] 5-8-2 (34) T Williams 33/1: 000057: Towards rear, nvr pace to chall: 4 month abs: 2 21a
unplaced earlier in '99 for N Tinkler & D E Incisa, (rtd 44 & 26a): '98 rnr-up (fill h'cap, rtd 52): '97 Chepstow wnr
(h'cap, rtd 58, M Channon): eff at 5/6f on firm & soft grnd: prob handles any trk: best without a vis: on a gd mark.
91   **LIGHT BREEZE 13** [8] 3-8-5 (37) N Carlisle 10/1: 500008: Towards rear, nvr on terms: op 8/1:   hd 23a
earlier in '99 scored here at Lingfield (C/D, seller, rtd 51a, G Moore, unplcd on turf rtd 39): ex-Irish, plcd in
'98 (5f, firm): eff at 5/6f: acts on firm & both AWs: likes a sharp track & sellers.
*134   **NINEACRES 5** [6] 8-9-4 (50)(bl) (7ex) Claire Bryan (7) 7/1: 000419: Prom wide 4f, wknd: qk reapp: ¾ 34a
much btr 134 (fibresand, claimer).
65   **ROWLANDSONS STUD 19** [7] 6-8-6 (38)(t) J Bosley (5) 33/1: 000-00: Al outpcd: 10th.   ¾ 20a
146   **SHARP HAT 2** [11] 5-10-0 (60) T Sprake 11/4 FAV: 000130: Dwelt, twds rear/wide & rdn, btn 2f out: 10th: nk 41a
qck reapp: hvly bckd, tchd 4/1: pos too soon after latest: btr 146, 91.
121   **Madame Jones 9** [4] 4-9-3 (49) A McGlone 25/1:   25   **Beveled Crystal 25** [14] 5-7-12 (30)(BL) P Doe (0) 33/1:
95   **Queens Signet 13** [13] 3-7-13 (30)(1ow) C Rutter 50/1:
14 ran   Time 1m 12.36 (1.96)   (R Atkinson)   J L Harris Eastwell, Leics.

---

149   1.10 NURSERY HCAP 2YO 0-75 (E)   7f aw rnd Going 32 -14 Slow   [80]
£2791   £784   £383

112   **MR GEORGE SMITH 10** [2] G L Moore 2-8-2 (54) F Norton 9/1: 000031: 2 b c Prince Sabo - Nellie's Gamble   61a
(Mummy's Game) Chsd ldrs halfway, rdn/chsd ldr 2f out, led over 1f out & in command ins last, rdn out: op 6/1:
first success: rtd 61 at best earlier at '99: eff at 7f, 1m+ shld suit: acts on equitrack: improving.
4327} **ROYAL IVY 55** [8] B W Hills 2-9-4 (70) T Sprake 4/1 FAV: 454032: 2 ch f Mujtahid - Royal Climber   1 74a
(King's Lake) Handy, chsd ldr 3f out, rdn & kept on fnl 2f, not pace wnr: nicely bckd: AW bow, 8 wk abs:
plcd twice earlier in '99 (h'caps, rtd 70): eff at 7f/1m: handles firm, soft & equitrack, handles any trk:
still a mdn but a fine introduction to sand & can prove spot on with a return to 1m.
54   **CASTLE SEMPILL 20** [6] R M H Cowell 2-9-0 (66)(vis) Dale Gibson 9/4 JT FAV: 331043: 2 b c Presidium 3½ 63a
- La Suquet (Puissance) Prom, led 4f out, rdn/hdd over 1f out & no extra: nicely bckd tho' op 6/4: see 54 (1m).
4539} **SONBELLE 39** [7] B Palling 2-9-6 (72) D Sweeney 16/1: 156064: Rdn/wide & rear, mod gains for   4 61a
press: op 12/1: AW bow: earlier in '99 scored on debut at Bath (nov auct stks, rtd 80): eff at 5/6f, 7f shld
suit in time: acts on firm, gd & poss handles equitrack: has run well fresh: shld learn from this sand intro.
4498} **DIRECT REACTION 42** [4] 2-9-6 (72) P Fredericks (5) 10/1: 420505: Rear/in tch, brght wide 2f out,   ¾ 60a
mod gains: op 7/1, 6 wk abs: rnr-up earlier in '99 (AW mdn, rtd 77a, rtd 81 on turf, prob flattered, stks, subs
tried blnks): eff at 5f, shld stay further: handles gd & equitrack: not given a hard time, improve in similar.
72   **PAPAGENA 12** [5] 2-8-6 (58) J Fanning 10/1: 203056: Led 1f, btn 2f out: op 8/1: longer 7f trip.   1¼ 43a
108   **OTIME 10** [3] 2-9-7 (73) A Clark 7/1: 005137: Rear/in tch, chsd ldrs over 2f out, sn wknd: tchd 12/1.   nk 57a
94   **CACOPHONY 13** [1] 2-8-7 (59)(E) P Doe (3) 8/1: 046038: Led after 1f till 4f out/fdd: eyeshield, op 5/1.   2½ 38a
8 ran   Time 1m 26.05 (3.25)   (George Smith Ltd)   G L Moore Woodingdean, E.Sussex.

---

150   1.40 ST PIERS SELLER 2YO (G)   1m aw rnd Going 32 -25 Slow
£1891   £531   £259

88   **CHURCH FARM FLYER 14** [9] C N Allen 2-8-6 L Newman (7) 9/1: 006631: 2 b f College Chapel - Young   57a
Isabel (Last Tycoon) Dwelt/rdn in rear, prog halfway & chsd ldr over 1f out, led ins last, styd on well/rdn out: bght
in for 3,400gns: op 7/1: first success: unplcd on turf earlier in '99 (rtd 53a, seller): eff at 7f, appreciated this
return to 1m, 10f+ may suit in time: handles both AWs & likes a sharp trk: enjoys sell grade.
53   **RIDGECREST 20** [3] R Ingram 2-8-11 S Drowne 4/1: 003042: 2 ch c Anshan - Lady Sabo (Prince Sabo)   ¾ 60a
Sn chsd ldrs, prog to lead over 2f out, rdn/hdd ins last & no extra cl-home: clr rem: op 5/2: eff at 7f/1m.

57

125 **ODYN DANCER 6** [5] M D I Usher 2-8-6 D Sweeney 15/2: 540003: 2 b f Minshaanshu Amad - Themeda (Sure Blade) Rdn/rear early, mod gains for press fnl 2f, no threat to front pair: op 6/1: qck reapp: rnr-up earlier in '99 (auct mdn, rtd 59a, unplcd on turf, rtd 55): eff at 7f, bred to apprec mid-dists: prob handles both AWs. *7* **44a**
145 **PONTIKONISI 2** [11] K McAuliffe 2-8-11 (bl) G Carter 25/1: 000054: Led till over 2f out, wknd fnl 1f: unplcd earlier in '99 (rtd 62): trying longer 1m trip today, similar tactics at 7f could suit. *nk* **48a**
53 **INCH PINCHER 20** [1] 2-9-2 A McCarthy (3) 5/2 JT FAV: 060025: Cl-up, outpcd 2f out: btr 53 (7f). *8* **41a**
125 **PICOLETTE 6** [4] 2-8-6 P Doe (3) 5/2 JT FAV: 500556: Chsd ldrs 5f: nicely bckd: qck reapp: unplcd earlier in '99 (rtd 63, auct mdn & 50a, h'cap). *nk* **30a**
4549} **BLAYNEY DANCER 38** [8] 2-8-11 O Urbina 40/1: 067: Rear/sn rdn, nvr factor: AW bow. *shd* **35a**
103 **CASTLEBRIDGE 12** [6] 2-8-11 J Tate 50/1: 08: Towards rear/rdn, btn 3f out. *½* **34a**
94 **SHARAVAWN 13** [2] 2-8-6 (bl) C Cogan (5) 40/1: 000009: Cl-up, struggling halfway, longer 1m trip. *¾* **28a**
4386} **VICKY VETTORI 51** [12] 2-8-6 G Sparkes (7) 40/1: 00600: Wide/rear, btn 3f out: 10th: 7 wk absence. *5* **18a**
74 **Blazing Rock 17** [10] 2-8-11 G Bardwell 40/1: 127 **Miss Roxanne 6** [7] 2-8-6 A Polli (3) 25/1:
12 ran Time 1m 40.77 (4.57) (Felix Snell) C N Allen Newmarket.

151 2.10 DOUGLAS AND CO HCAP 3YO+ 0-85 (D) 1m4f aw Going 32 +07 Fast [85]
£3837 £1160 £565 £267 3 yo rec 5 lb

*115 **NOUKARI 10** [1] P D Evans 6-9-6 (77) R Fitzpatrick (3) 9/4 FAV: 013111: 6 b g Darshaan - Noufiyla (Top Ville) Sn trkd ldrs, rdn & kept on stdly for press fnl 2f to lead ins last, asserted nr fin, rdn out: best time of day: hvly bckd, tchd 11/4: recent wnr twice here at Lingfield (C/D, h'caps): earlier won twice over timber (rtd 104h, eff at 2m on firm & gd): earlier in '99 won again at Lingfield (2, AW h'cap & stks), Chester (clmr), Newmarket, Catterick (amat h'cap) & Pontefract (stks, rtd 74 & 73): '98 wnr at Southwell & Lingfield (h'caps, rtd 63a & 63): eff at 10/15f: acts on firm, soft & both AWs: handles any trk, loves Lingfield: ultra tough, genuine & progressive. **84a**
55 **SPACE RACE 20** [6] C A Cyzer 5-9-5 (76) G Faulkner (3) 8/1: 250202: 5 b g Rock Hopper - Melanoura (Imperial Fling) Trkd ldrs wide, rdn/led 2f out, hdd ins last & no extra nr fin: op 6/1: can find similar: see 22. *2½* **77a**
3454} **BE GONE 99** [5] C A Dwyer 4-10-0 (85) A McGlone 25/1: 300503: 4 ch g Be My Chief - Hence (Mr Prospector) Rear/in tch, rdn/outpcd 4f out, styd on fnl 2f, no threat front pair: op 14/1, topweight: AW bow: jumps fit (no form): earlier in '99 plcd on turf for H R A Cecil (rtd 99, stks, subs disapp in visor & blnks): '98 wnr at Newcastle (mdn, rtd 85): eff at 9f/12f, further may suit: acts on gd & equitrack, prob handles firm: handles any trk: on a fair mark for new connections, will know more about the sand next time. *1¾* **84a**
3378} **STEAMROLLER STANLY 99** [8] K R Burke 6-9-1 (72) N Callan (3) 100/30: 203664: Led after 2f, rdn/ hdd over 2f out & no extra ins last: nicely bckd, tchd 4/1: 4 month abs earlier in '99 scored at W'hampton (h'cap) & Southwell (clmr, rtd 93a at best, no turf form): with C Cyzer in '98, won here at Lingfield (2, stks, rtd 100a), subs rtd 78 on turf (stks, first time blnks): eff at 10f/2m: acts on firm, fast, relishes both AW's & prob handles hvy: handles any trk, loves a sharp one: has run well fresh: likes to dominate: on a fair mark. *shd* **71a**
92 **LAKE SUNBEAM 13** [4] 3-9-1 (77) P Doe (3) 16/1: 536045: Cl-up 10f: op 10/1, now with W R Muir. *2* **73a**
81 **ROBELLITA 16** [3] 5-8-10 (67) T Sprake 5/2: 321126: Rdn/rear halfway, btn 3f out: well bckd: btr 81. *hd* **62a**
81 **RAYIK 16** [2] 4-8-7 (64) J Fanning 12/1: 000067: Held up rear in tch, outpcd/btn fnl 3f: tchd 14/1: rnr-up earlier in '99 (h'cap, rtd 81a): '98 Lingfield wnr (mdn, N Berry, unplcd on turf earlier for R Armstrong, rtd 76): eff at 10/12f: acts on both AW's. *½* **58a**
2299} **TRAGIC DANCER 99** [7] 3-8-11 (73) G Carter 10/1: 451208: Bhd 4f out, t.o.: op 8/1, 5 mth abs. *19* **47a**
8 ran Time 2m 32.17 (2.97) (J E Abbey) P D Evans Leighton, Powys.

152 2.40 GATWICK FILL HCAP DIV 2 3YO+ 0-70 (E) 1m aw rnd Going 32 -13 Slow [65]
£2303 £645 £313 3 yo rec 1 lb

28 **PARISIAN LADY 25** [3] A G Newcombe 4-9-2 (53) S Whitworth 4/1: 004001: 4 b f Paris House - Mia Gigi (Hard Fought) Rear/rdn, styd on well fnl 3f & strong run ins last to lead nr line: hvly bckd: unplcd earlier in '99 (tumbled down h'cap, rtd 59 & 56a): plcd in '98 (list, rtd 92, rtd 85 in h'caps): '97 wnr at Salisbury (2, auct mdn & stks, rtd 98 at best): eff at 6/7f, now stays a sharp 1m well: acts on firm, fast & equitrack, prob handles fibresand: tried blnks, best without: handles a stiff/gall or sharp trk: well h'capped, shld win again. **58a**
96 **SPRINGTIME LADY 13** [6] S Dow 3-9-8 (60)(E) P Doe (3) 11/4: 040522: 3 ch f Desert Dirham - Affair de Coeur (Imperial Fling) Dwelt, towards rear/wide, prog/chsd ldr over 1f out, led ins last, hdd nr line: eye-shield. *½* **63a**
*114 **UNCHAIN MY HEART 10** [10] B J Meehan 3-9-10 (62)(bl) A Clark 5/2 FAV: 242013: 3 b f Pursuit Of Love - Addicted To Love (Touching Wood) Led/dsptd lead till drvn/hdd ins last, no extra: hvly bckd: see 114. *1¼* **62a**
96 **MELLOW MISS 13** [9] R M Flower 3-9-0 (52) S Drowne 15/2: 050044: Rdn/bhd & wide, kept on fnl 2f for press, nrst fin: op 6/1: lightly rcd & unplcd earlier in '99 (rtd 60 & 53a): trained by E Dunlop & unplcd in 2 '98 starts (rtd 68): eff at 1m & handles equitrack: has tried blnks. *1¼* **49a**
85 **MOONLIGHT FLIT 14** [4] 4-8-8 (45) R Winston 12/1: 330005: Chsd ldrs halfway, rdn/no extra over 1f out: op 8/1: earlier in '99 scored at Southwell (appr fill h'cap, rtd 47a, plcd on turf, rtd 40, h'cap): '98 Pontefract wnr (seller, J G FitzGerald, rtd 41): eff at 1m/10f on firm, gd & fibresand: eff with/without blnks. *1½* **39a**
109 **LADY BREANNE 10** [5] 3-8-12 (50) F Norton 15/2: 602636: Rdn/chsd ldrs, held/eased fnl 1f: op 5/1. *2½* **39a**
58 **SQUARE MILE MISS 20** [8] 6-7-12 (33)(2ow) N Carlisle 25/1: 000007: Chsd ldrs 5f, sn btn: tchd 33/1. *hd* **21a**
8 **DOROTHY ALLEN 28** [7] 3-8-2 (40) Dale Gibson 50/1: 30-008: Rdn/wide chasing ldrs, btn 3f out. *12* **10a**
69 **SWYNFORD WELCOME 17** [2] 3-8-12 (50) A Polli (3) 14/1: 001009: Led/dsptd lead, hdd 3f out/wknd. *¾* **19a**
4604} **SWEET ROSIE 32** [1] 4-8-5 (42) C Rutter 50/1: 0/6000: Sn bhd: 10th. *29* **0a**
10 ran Time 1m 39.76 (3.56) (Advanced Marketing Services Ltd) A G Newcombe Huntshaw, Devon.

153 3.10 MED AUCT MDN 2YO (F) 6f aw rnd Going 32 -19 Slow
£2095 £588 £286

94 **CRUISE 13** [7] R Hannon 2-9-0 T Sprake 5/6 FAV: 51: 2 ch c Prince Sabo - Mistral's Dancer (Shareef Dancer) Prom, led over 1f out, rdn clr: hvly bckd: left debut bhd: half brother to wnrs at 7f/12f: eff at 6f, return to 7f shld suit: acts on equitrack: clrly going the right way, could rate more highly. **72a**
4549} **TOLDYA 38** [6] E A Wheeler 2-8-9 S Drowne 33/1: 0002: 2 b f Beveled - Run Amber Run (Run The Gantlet) Prom, rdn/led over 1f out, sn hdd & no ch with wnr fnl 1f: AW bow: unplcd earlier in '99 (rtd 51). *5* **50a**
-- **SMOGAR** [2] P J Makin 2-9-0 A Clark 11/4: 3: 2 ch c Catrail - Piney River (Pharly) Cl-up, led over 3f out, sn pressed & rdn/hdd over 1f out, no ch wnr ins last: op 2/1: Mar foal, cost 25,000gns: half-brother to a 5f juv wnr & a 1m 3yo wnr: sire a high-class 6/7f performer. *shd* **55a**
-- **TEA FOR TEXAS** [5] H Morrison 2-8-9 C Rutter 14/1: 4: Wide/rear, kept on fnl 2f: op 10/1, debut. *¾* **48a**
4575} **SKY HOOK 35** [4] 2-9-0 T G McLaughlin 6/1: 050305: Rdn/chasing ldrs, held fnl 2f. *½* **51a**
4221} **DAMASQUINER 63** [1] 2-8-9 P Doe (3) 25/1: 000066: Led till over 3f out, sn btn: 2 mth abs/AW bow. *13* **22a**

LINGFIELD (Equitrack) MONDAY DECEMBER 6TH Lefthand, V Sharp Track

-- **CEDAR BOSS** [3] 2-9-0 S Whitworth 8/1: 7: Al rear: op 6/1: debut: with R J O'Sullivan.   7   14a
7 ran   Time 1m 13.43 (3.03)   (Heathavon Stables Ltd)   R Hannon East Everleigh, Wilts.

154   3.40 COPTHORNE HCAP DIV 2 3YO+ 0-60 (F)   6f aw rnd   Going 32   -05 Slow   [60]
£1840   £515   £250

139   **TORRENT** 5 [10] D W Chapman 4-10-0 (60)(bl) Lynsey Hanna (7) 15/8 FAV: 022321: 4 ch g Prince   71a
Sabo - Maiden Pool (Sharpen Up) Sn chsd ldrs wide, smooth prog to chall over 1f out, led 1f out & asserted ins
last, pushed out: hvly bckd, tchd 5/2: qck reapp: earlier in '99 won at Beverley (class stks, rtd 75): '98
Catterick (mdn) & Thirsk wnr (h'cap, rtd 83, T D Barron): eff at 5/6f, tried 7f: acts on firm, gd/soft & both
AWs, prob handles soft: handles any trk, likes a sharp one: eff in blnks, has tried a t-strap: tough & in-form.
69   **WISHBONE ALLEY** 17 [5] M Dods 4-8-9 (41)(vis) A Clark 5/1: 303002: 4 b g Common Grounds - Dul Dul   2   45a
(Shadeed) Rdn early to chase ldr, ev ch over 1f out, kept on tho' not pace of wnr: visor reapplied: earlier in
'99 scored at Newcastle (h'cap, rtd 55, unplcd on sand, rtd 27a): '98 Thirsk wnr (h'cap, rtd 64): eff at 5f,
suited by 6f: acts on fast, soft & equitrack, poss handles firm & hvy: eff in blnks or visor: handles any trk.
139   **ANOTHER NIGHTMARE** 5 [13] D W Barker 7-8-13 (45) T Williams 9/1: 200403: 7 b m Treasue Kay -   1¾   45a
Carange (Known Fact) Led & clr after 1f, rdn/hdd 1f out & no extra: op 6/1: apprec return to 5f: see 116.
57   **WHATTA MADAM** 20 [11] G L Moore 3-9-1 (47)(t) S Whitworth 12/1: 300064: Towards rear/wide,   1   45a
prog/chsd ldrs over 1f out, kept on tho' nvr able to chall: op 8/1: plcd sev times earlier in '99 (rtd 62, h'cap,
mod claim form): plcd 4 of 5 starts in '98 (rtd 65, auct mdn): eff at 5/6f, tried 7f: handles firm & soft, equitrack:
tried blnks/visor, best without.
661}   **REAL TING** 99 [7] 3-7-12 (30)(vis) M Henry 40/1: 00-005: Sn outpcd/bhd, switched wide over 2f   shd   28a
out & styd on well ins last, nrst fin: 9 month abs: lightly rcd & mod form at 5/6f prev (rtd 40, seller): prob
handles equitrack & shld apprec a step up to 7f on this evidence.
4050}   **SUPERLAO** 75 [12] 7-8-1 (33) G Bardwell 40/1: 000406: Rdn/bhd, late prog wide for press: abs.   hd   30a
116   **CHEMCAST** 9 [8] 6-9-1 (47)(bl) R Winston 15/2: 020107: Chsd ldrs 4f: op 6/1: see 57 (5f).   1¾   40a
57   **OK JOHN** 20 [1] 4-9-11 (57) O Urbina 4/1: 000038: Squeezed out after 1f, towards rear & mod gains   nk   49a
when no room over 1f out, nvr factor: well bckd: no luck in running, eye-catching in 57 (5f).
75   **SURE TO DREAM** 17 [6] 6-9-4 (50)(bl) R Perham 9/1: 000009: Sn rdn mid-div, btn 2f out.   shd   42a
4227}   **PRINCESS MO** 63 [9] 3-8-6 (38) R Lappin 33/1: -00000: Mid-div, held fnl 2f: 10th: AW bow, abs.   hd   29a
82   Miss Bananas 16 [2] 4-9-5 (51) D Meah (7) 14/1:   173} Speckled Gem 99 [6] 3-8-4 (36) A Polli (3) 50/1:
12 ran   Time 1m 12.62 (2.22)   (Mrs J Hazell)   D W Chapman Stillington, N.Yorks.

LINGFIELD (Equitrack) WEDNESDAY DECEMBER 8TH Lefthand, V Sharp Track

Official Going   STANDARD. Stalls: 1m - Outside: Rem - Inside.

155   12.10 CELEBRATE CLAIMER 2YO (F)   7f aw rnd   Going 30   -07 Slow
£2179   £612   £298

105   **PERLE DE SAGESSE** 14 [6] Julian Poulton 2-8-4 A Daly 2/1 FAV: 052101: 2 b f Namaqualand - Pearl   63a
Of Dubai (Red Ransom) Chsd ldrs, led over 3f out, clr 2f out, pushed out: nicely bckd: earlier won at
Windsor (seller, rtd 65, P Cole) & here at Lingfield (seller): eff at 5/7f, 1m could suit in time: acts on
firm, gd & equitrack: likes a sharp trk, esp Lingfield: best in blnks/claim prade.
24   **SUPREMELY DEVIOUS** 27 [11] R M H Cowell 2-8-0 (vis) Dale Gibson 7/1: 260062: 2 ch f Wolfhound -   7   49a
Clearly Devious (Machiavellian) Keen in tch, rdn to impr over 3f out, no threat to ldrs fnl 2: op 6/1: rnr-up
once prev in '99 (nurs, rtd 63): eff at 6f, stays 7f: acts on fast, handles equitrack: now wears a visor.
4557}   **CROESO ADREF** 39 [5] S C Williams 2-7-10 P M Quinn 16/1: 0003: 2 ch f Most Welcome - Grugiar   1   43a
(Red Sunset) Cl-up, hdwy 3f out, outpcd fnl 2f: first time in the frame today, well btn in 3 starts earlier
in '99: half-sister to a mid-dist/staying wnr: 1m+ shld suit in time.
54   **SHAMAN** 22 [8] G L Moore 2-8-11 J Parkin 10/1: 103004: Sn well bhd, plenty to do 3f out, styd   1¾   55a
on strongly over 1f out, nvr nrr: earlier in '99 scored at Folkestone (seller, rtd 71 at best, M Channon):
eff at 6f, suited by 7f, 1m+ sure to suit on this showing: acts on fast & gd grnd, any track.
150   **PONTIKONISI** 2 [13] 2-8-9 (VIS) T G McLaughlin 12/1: 000545: Prom, outpcd fnl 2f: op 8/1: visored.   1   51a
3183}   **WICKED** 99 [4] 2-8-4 (VIS) G Carter 20/1: -0606: Led to over 3f out, fdd: long abs, visor, new stable.   shd   46a
53   **KIGEMA** 22 [10] 2-8-6 L Newman (7) 7/1: 441557: Handy, lost pl 3f out, no ch after: op 5/1.   shd   48a
4071}   **QUICKTIME** 75 [7] 2-8-6 S Drowne 8/1: -0048: Nvr better than mid-div: 10 wk absence.   shd   48a
4150}   **STORM SONG** 70 [3] 2-8-1 P Doe (3) 8/1: 606059: Bhd, eff over 3f out, nvr a threat: op 6/1, 10 wk abs.   6   33a
53   **WISHEDHADGONEHOME** 22 [2] 2-8-4 R Fitzpatrick (3) 7/1: 000500: Dwelt, al bhd, fin 10th.   ½   35a
105   **WHERES CHARLOTTE** 14 [9] 2-8-8 P Fitzsimons (5) 10/1: 000300: Cl-up, wknd qckly 3f out, fin last.   0a
105   Talents Little Gem 14 [12] 2-8-4 T Sprake 20/1:   4597} Bauget Jouette 34 [1] 2-7-10 D Kinsella (7) 33/1:
13 ran   Time 1m 25.42 (2.62)   (Russell Reed & Gerald West)   Julian Poulton Lewes, E.Sussex.

156   12.40 TRADE SELLER DIV I 3YO+ (G)   7f aw rnd   Going 30   -20 Slow
£1532   £428   £207

104   **APOLLO RED** 14 [10] G L Moore 10-8-12 A Clark 8/13 FAV: 302061: 10 ch g Dominion - Woolpack   58a
(Golden Fleece) Led 6f out, rdn clr appr fnl 1f, cmftbly: well bckd at odds on: no bid: plcd 4 times at Brighton
earlier in '99 (h'caps & clmrs, rtd 74 & 76a): '98 wnr at Brighton (h'cap, rtd 74, also rtd 72a): '97 wnr again
at Brighton (rtd 75) & Lingfield (rtd 71): stays 1m, well suited by 6/7f: acts on firm, soft & e/track:
loves to force the pace on a sharp trk, loves Brighton/Lingfield: eff with/without blnks/visor: simple task today.
134   **EMMAJOUN** 7 [6] W G M Turner 4-8-13 T Sprake 9/1: 000362: 4 b f Emarati - Parijoun (Manado)   3   50a
Led to 6f out, hdwy to chall 2f out, not pace of ldrs appr fnl 1f: op 7/1: qck reapp: eff at 5/7f: gd run: see 32.
75   **BALLYMORRIS BOY** 19 [2] J Pearce 3-8-12 T G McLaughlin 25/1: 000503: 3 b c Dolphin Street -   nk   49$
Solas Abu (Red Sunset) Cl-up, rdn to impr 2f out, kept on, no ch with wnr: mkt drifter: plcd twice earlier
in '99 (mdn h'caps, rtd 58 at best): eff at 6/7f: acts on firm grnd, handles equitrack.
130   **ABSOLUTE MAJORITY** 8 [9] P Howling 4-9-4 A McCarthy (3) 12/1: 000304: Rdn in tch, onepcd fnl 2f.   3½   48a
138   **RUNNING BEAR** 7 [8] 5-8-12 T Williams 25/1: 000055: Keen & cl-up, wknd fnl 2f: op 10/1, qck reapp.   2   38$
138   **CLADANTOM** 7 [1] 3-8-13 R Lappin 11/1: 210006: Dwelt, well bhd till kept on late, nvr nrr: nk   39a
op 8/1, qck reapp: earlier in '99 scored at Thirsk (mdn, rtd 68 at best), prev with W Jarvis: with Mrs
J Cecil in '98 (rtd 68 at best): eff at 7f, 1m+ shld suit: acts on firm/fast & an easy track.

93	**FRANKLIN LAKES** 15 [11] 4-8-12 (vis) P Doe (3) 10/1: 005057: Cl-up, rdn/no threat 2f out: op 5/1.	1¼	36a
111	**GALLANT FELLOW** 12 [5] 4-8-12 L Newman (7) 20/1: 030058: Prom, lost tch over 2f out.	½	35a
101	**CEDAR FLAG** 14 [12] 5-8-12 S Whitworth 25/1: 069: Sn well bhd, modest gains: op 14/1, inadequate trip today, shld improve over further into h'capped.	½	34a
110	**ARAB GOLD** 12 [7] 4-8-12 S Drowne 33/1: 605000: Bhd, nvr a threat, fin 10th.	4	27a
75	**SCOTLAND BAY** 19 [4] 4-8-7 (VIS) J Bramhill 11/1: 400000: Prom, fdd fnl 3f: 11th: op 8/1, visor.	hd	22a
95	**Winnipeg** 15 [3] 3-8-7 C Rutter 14/1:	3158} **Prime Surprise** 99 [13] 3-8-7 Kimberley Hart (5) 20/1:	
13 ran	Time 1m 26.31 (3.51) (A Moore) G L Moore Woodingdean, E.Sussex.		

---

157   1.10 CALL SALES STKS 3YO+ (D)   1m2f aw   Going 30   +06 Fast
£3820   £1156   £564   £268   3 yo rec 3 lb

49	**ZANAY** 23 [4] Miss Jacqueline S Doyle 3-9-2 T Sprake 14/1: -31041: 3 b c Forzando - Nineteenth Of May (Homing) Chsd ldrs, hdwy to lead over 2f out, sn clr, styd on well, rdn out: best time of day: won at Nottingham (mdn, rtd 86): rnr-up on fnl 2 '98 starts for R Phillips (mdn, rtd 81): eff at 7f/1m, stays 10f well: acts on gd, soft & both AW's: acts on a stiff/gall or sharp trk: progressive & lightly rcd, win again.		97a
49	**SECRET SPRING** 23 [3] Mrs L Richards 7-9-1 O Urbina 5/1: 440107: 7 b g Dowsing - Nordica (Northfields) Cl-up, rdn to impr over 1f out, kept on but no threat to wnr: gd run: see 7.	4	86a
137	**ITALIAN SYMPHONY** 7 [9] P D Evans 5-9-7 (vis) R Fitzpatrick (3) 12/1: 100543: 5 b g Royal Academy - Terracotta Hut (Habitat) Waited with, hdwy 5f out, sn chasing wnr, no extra appr fnl 1f: qck reapp: see 137 (h'cap).	2½	88a
137	**CHINA CASTLE** 7 [1] P C Haslam 6-9-5 Dale Gibson 6/1: 010254: Sn well bhd, ran on strongly for press fnl 2f, nvr nrr: op 4/1, qck reapp: best at 11/12f & 16 of 17 a/w wins have come on fibresand: see 27.	3½	80a
+119	**TALLULAH BELLE** 11 [7] 6-9-0 T G McLaughlin 11/2: 003615: Prom, rdn/outpcd fnl 3f: op 4/1: see 119.	1¼	73a
4619}	**PUNISHMENT** 32 [8] 8-9-1 (tVIS) P Doe (3) 8/1: 300306: Cl-up, hdwy to chall 4f out, sn led, hdd over 2f out, sn rdn & no extra: first time visor: plcd sev times earlier in '99 (h'caps & stks, rtd 92a & 98 at best): '98 wnr at Leiceseter (rtd h'cap), also rnr-up in a Gr 3 (rtd 104): '97 wnr at Deauville & St-Cloud: eff at 9/10f, stays 12f: acts on fast, soft & both AW's: v well h'capped if returning to form.	nk	74a
-137	**SICK AS A PARROT** 7 [6] 4-9-1 (ebl) N Callan (3) 5/4 FAV: 005627: Led 1m out, rdn & hdd appr fnl 3f, wknd qckly: well bckd, qck reapp: disapp effort, something amiss?: much btr 137 (h'cap, fibresand).	6	65a
4602}	**DAUNTED** 34 [5] 3-9-0 (bl) P Dobbs (3) 33/1: 506408: Prom, rdn & wknd 4f out: earlier in '99 won at Lingfield (clmr, rtd 85a), also rtd 73 on turf (h'cap): '98 wnr again at Lingfield (2, mdn & stks, rtd 83a & 72): eff around 1m, handles gd/soft & acts on both AW's: likes a sharp trk, esp Lingfield: eff with/without blnks.	½	66a
55	**APADI** 22 [2] 3-8-12 Sophie Mitchell 25/1: 006609: Led early, with ldrs till lost tch halfway.	8	52a
4270}	**TRIBAL PEACE** 62 [10] 7-9-1 C Rutter 50/1: 000500: Prom, wknd qcky 5f out, t.o, 10th: 9 wk abs: plcd here at Lingfield prev in '99 (clmr, rtd 55a, rtd 41 at best on turf): back in '97 won here at Lingfield (h'cap, rtd 68a) & Goodwood (h'cap, rtd 64): eff at 1m/10f on firm, soft & equitrack: runs well fresh, likes Lingfield.	18	27a
10 ran	Time 2m 05.19 (2.39) (Sanford Racing) Miss Jacqueline S Doyle Upper Lambourn, Berks.		

---

158   1.40 J CLARKE NURSERY HCAP 2YO 0-85 (D)   1m aw rnd   Going 30   -29 Slow   [84]
£2640   £741   £361

4537}	**WELSH PLOY** 41 [6] K McAuliffe 2-9-3 (73) T G McLaughlin 12/1: 325051: 2 b f Deploy - Safe House (Lyphard) Cl-up, rdn 4f out, hdwy to chall 2f out, drvn out to lead cl-home: op 8/1, 6 wk abs: AW/h'cap bow: plcd form earlier in '99 (fill mdns, rtd 86): eff at 7f/1m: runs well fresh: acts on gd, hvy & equitrack.		79a
54	**MISS WORLD** 22 [1] C N Allen 2-8-6 (62)(t) L Newman (7) 6/1: 446232: 2 b f Mujadil - Great Land (Friend's Choice) Prom, dsptd lead 4f out, hdd right appr fnl 1f, styd on, hdd cl-home: op 4/1: in fine form.	nk	67a
54	**MAID TO LOVE** 22 [8] G A Butler 2-8-4 (60)(bl) G Carter 6/1: 300223: 2 ch f Petardia - Lomond Heights (Lomond) Chsd ldrs, outpcd 3f out, rallied & styd on well ins last, no threat: op 7/2: 10f shld now suit.	1	63a
*94	**SOFISIO** 15 [5] W R Muir 2-9-2 (72) T Sprake 3/1: 040214: Dsptd lead, ev ch till no extra ins last: tchd 4/1: see 94 (7f, auct mdn).	hd	75a
105	**WATERGRASSHILL** 14 [3] 2-8-2 (58) P Doe (3) 9/4 FAV: 00025: Dsptd lead, hdd 3f out, not pace of ldrs: well bckd, up in trip: prob not get this longer 1m trip: btr 105.	3½	55a
4570}	**MYTTONS AGAIN** 37 [2] 2-9-7 (77)(bl) J Fanning 10/1: 100426: Dsptd lead 4f, sn btn: op 6/1: AW bow: earlier in '99 scored at Chester (nurs, rtd 74 at best): eff at 7f, stays 1m on gd & hvy: eff in blnks.	3½	68a
4550}	**DONT WORRY BOUT ME** 40 [7] 2-8-11 (67) A Clark 20/1: 263007: Sn well bhd: op 10/1: plcd 3 times earlier in '99 (mdns, rtd 84 & 63a): stays 6f, handles fast & gd grnd.	1¾	55a
*80	**WILEMMGEO** 18 [4] 2-7-12 (54) Dale Gibson 8/1: 423018: Cl-up, btn 3f out: much btr 80 (equitrack, slr).	5	33a
8 ran	Time 1m 40.91 (4.71) (G E Amey) K McAuliffe Lambourn, Berks.		

---

159   2.10 TRADE SELLER DIV II 3YO+ (G)   7f aw rnd   Going 30   -19 Slow
£1523   £426   £206

130	**DARK MENACE** 8 [1] E A Wheeler 7-9-4 (bl) D Kinsella (7) 3/1 FAV: 602301: 7 br g Beveled - Sweet And Sour (Known Fact) Handy, hdwy to lead 4f out, sn clr, rdn no bid: earlier in '99 won at Brighton (h'cap, rtd 47, plcd on AW, rtd 53a): '98 wnr at Southwell (h'cap, rtd 41a, also rtd 47): suited by 6/7f, stays 1m: acts on firm, fast & both AWs: likes a sharp/undul trk, esp Brighton: eff in blnks.		52a
1241}	**CAIRN DHU** 99 [4] D W Barker 5-8-12 Kimberley Hart (5) 20/1: 000-02: 5 ch g Presidium - My Precious Daisy (Sharpo) Dwelt & bhd, rdn to impr over 2f out, styd on well, nvr nrr: long abs: well btn sole prev '99 start (rtd 27): modest form since winning at Nottingham in '97 (seller, rtd 59, Mrs J Ramsden): eff at 6f, stays 7f, further could suit: acts on gd & equitrack, handles fast: has tried blnks, been without.	5	38a
91	**SPENDER** 15 [6] V Soane 10-8-12 A Clark 11/2: 000003: 10 b g Last Tycoon - Lady Hester (Native Prince) Cl-up, chall 4f out, no extra fnl 2f: op 7/2: unplcd earlier in '99 (h'caps, rtd 78a & 56): plcd once in '98 (rtd 69, P Harris), prev term won at Brighton, Bath & Yarmouth (h'caps, rtd 81): best at 5/6f, has tried 7f: acts on gd, firm/fast & equitrack, esp Lingfield: well h'capped but reportedly now be retired.	½	37a
109	**RAIN RAIN GO AWAY** 12 [12] D J S Cosgrove 3-8-12 N Callan (3) 10/1: -00004: Handy, hdwy to chall 3f out, no extra appr fnl 1f: tchd 14/1: unplcd on turf earlier in '99 (rtd 50): plcd sole '98 start for E Dunlop (mdn, rtd 79): stays 7f & handles soft.	hd	37a
110	**MALCHIK** 12 [10] 3-8-12 A McCarthy (3) 16/1: 300005: Cl-up, outpcd over 3f out, rallied & late gains ins last: plcd sev times earlier in '99 (h'caps, rtd 49), modest form on turf: eff btwn 7f & 10f, has tried up to 2m: acts on gd grnd & both AWs.	nk	37a
4496}	**OARE KITE** 44 [7] 4-8-13 (bl) G Parkin 7/1: 400366: Prom, rdn to impr over 2f out, wknd: op 6/1, abs.	2½	34a
107	**DANCING JACK** 14 [3] 6-8-12 L Newman (7) 12/1: 100426: In tch till wknd fnl 2f.	½	32a
110	**WILD RICE** 12 [9] 7-8-12 S Drowne 7/2: 0/0-48: Prom, no extra fnl 3f: now with L A Dace.	nk	32a

LINGFIELD (Equitrack)   WEDNESDAY DECEMBER 8TH   Lefthand, V Sharp Track

106	**SHARP IMP** 14 [5] 9-8-12 (bl) O Urbina 12/1: 000009: Dwelt, al rear.	6 22a
3850}	**IRISH MELODY** 90 [2] 3-8-7 P Fitzsimons (5) 16/1: 000000: Al bhd, fin 10th: 3 month absence.	2½ 13a
95	**TWO PACK** 15 [11] 3-8-12 (e) Sophie Mitchell 20/1: 006000: Rdn/rear, well bhd in 11th.	6 8a
4463}	**LADY CAROLINE** 48 [8] 3-8-7 (BL) J Fanning 8/1: 000000: Led, hdd over 4f out, wknd qckly, t.o.	22 0a

in 12th: op 7/1: disapp effort in first time blnks: recent jumps rnr.
12 ran   Time 1m 26.29 (3.49)   (M V Kirby)   E A Wheeler Whitchurch On Thames, Oxon.

---

160   2.40 ARCHITON HCAP DIV I 3YO+ 0-80 (D)   1m2f aw   Going 30 -12 Slow   [80]
£3401   £1027   £499   £235   3 yo rec 3 lb

4574} **ANEMOS** 37 [7] M A Jarvis 4-9-5 (71) J Fanning 8/1: 006201: 4 ch g Be My Guest - Frendly Persuasion   80a
(General Assembly) Cl-up, led going well 3f out, clr 2f out, tired ins last & rdn out: op 7/1: earlier in
'99 scored at Nottingham (stks, rtd 84 at best): rnr-up in '98 (mdn, rtd 77): eff at 10f on fast, hvy &
equitrack: acts on a gall or sharp trk & eff with/without blnks.

2336} **CAERNARFON BAY** 99 [6] G L Moore 4-7-12 (50) P Fitzsimons (0) 12/1: 120262: 4 ch g Royal Academy 1¾ 54a
- Bay Shade (Sharpen Up) Dwelt, bhd, short of room halfway, hdwy over 2f out, styd on, nrst fin: long abs:
prev in '99 scored at Lingfield (amat h'cap, rtd 53a) & Brighton (h'cap, rtd 48a): plcd in '98 (rtd 61 & 68a, P
Cole): eff at 10f, stays a sharp/undul 12f: acts on firm, gd/soft & both AW's: runs fresh, without blnks.

4429} **FAHS** 50 [10] N Hamilton 7-9-12 (78) T Ashley 6/1: 223603: 7 b g Riverman - Tanwi (Vision)   ½   81a
Held up rear, outpcd 4f out, ran on strongly for press over 1f out, nvr nrr: 7 wk abs: earlier in '99 won at
Yarmouth (h'cap), also rnr-up twice (h'caps, rtd 77): late '98 scored at Lingfield (amat h'cap, rtd 80a), plcd
on turf (h'cap, rtd 81): '97 wnr at Sandown & Yarmouth (h'caps, rtd 80, R Akehurst): eff at 10/12f, stays 14f:
acts on fast, gd & equitrack: handles soft: acts on any trk, likes Yarmouth: best held up: spot on next time.

*1 **IMPREVUE** 30 [2] R J O'Sullivan 5-8-10 (62)(bl) P Doe (3) 5/2 FAV: 113114: Cl-up, led 6f out till   2   61a
3f out, no extra ins last: nicely bckd on hat-trick bid: see 1 (C/D, stks).

137 **PHILISTAR** 7 [8] 6-9-6 (72) N Callan (3) 13/2: 355265: Prom, imprvd 3f out, wknd fnl 2f: op 5/1.   3½   65a

90 **JAVA SHRINE** 15 [9] 8-9-7 (73)(bl) R Havlin 6/1: 000326: Rcd wide cl-up, wknd fnl 3f: op 5/1.   13   48a

*102 **ROGER ROSS** 14 [5] 4-8-3 (55) S Drowne 7/1: 006017: Prom, rdn/wknd 3f out: much btr 102.   1   28a

-119 **PRODIGAL SON** 11 [3] 4-9-10 (76) L Newman (7) 3/1: 522628: Handy, lost tch halfway: nicely bckd.   ¾   48a

69 **FLUSH** 19 [4] 4-8-0 (52) J Bramhill 33/1: 10-009: Al bhd: well btn sole prev Flat start in   ½   23a
'99: 98/99 hdle scorer at Warwick (juv nov, hdles bow, rtd 100+, eff at 2m on hvy, M Pipe): '98 Flat wnr
for J Hills at Leicester (clmr, rtd 74 at best): eff at 1m on firm & hvy grnd, any track.

78 **VIOLET** 18 [1] 3-8-5 (60) A Morris 33/1: 000000: Led, hdd 6f out, sn wknd, 10th: new stable.   3½   26a
10 ran   Time 2m 07.07 (4.27)   (Andreas Michael)   M A Jarvis Newmarket

---

161   3.10 ARCHITON HCAP DIV II 3YO+ 0-80 (D)   1m2f aw   Going 30 -25 Slow   [80]
£3401   £1027   £499   £235   3 yo rec 3 lb

119 **JUST WIZ** 11 [9] R Hannon 3-9-10 (79)(bl) R Smith (5) 11/2: 023131: 3 b g Efisio - Jade Pet (Petong)   86a
Cl-up, hdwy to lead over 4f out, clr 2f out, rdn out: earlier in '99 won at Southwell (h'cap, rtd 71a, also
rtd 64) & recently here at Lingfield: rtd 54 & 61a in '98 (h'caps): eff btwn 7f & 10f: acts on firm, gd/soft
& both AWs: acts on any trk, likes Lingfield: eff in blnks/visor & runs well fresh: tough & improving.

102 **SAMMYS SHUFFLE** 14 [4] Jamie Poulton 4-8-1 (53)(bl) N Carlisle 7/1: 604332: 4 b c Touch Of Grey -   2   56a
Cabinet Shuffle (Thatching) Prom, not pace of wnr ins last: eff at 10/12f: gd run, see 22.

*97 **SOUND THE TRUMPET** 15 [6] R C Spicer 7-7-10 (48)(t) (1oh) G Baker (7) 8/1: 504413: 7 b g Fayruz -   2½   47a
Red Not (Rusticaro) Held up, hdwy 3f out, styd on, nvr nrr: prob styd this longer 10f trip: see 97 (1m).

23 **CONFRONTER** 27 [2] S Dow 10-8-8 (60)(e) P Doe (3) 10/1: 155064: Bhd, short of room 5f out,   4   53a
eff 2f out, no extra ins last: op 8/1: earlier in '99 scored here at Lingfield (h'caps, rtd 63a): plcd on
turf in '98 (h'caps, rtd 56, also rtd 49a): '97 Bath wnr (rtd 59) & Lingfield (h'caps, rtd 55a): eff at 1m/10f
on fast, hvy & equitrack: loves Lingfield: prev eff in blnks/visor, now wears an eye-shield.

4502} **COMPTON ANGEL** 22 [7] 3-9-5 (74) G Carter 9/2 JT FAV: 446105: Handy, hdwy to trk ldrs over   ½   66a
2f out, hung badly left & no extra over 1f out: earlier in '99 won here at Lingfield (h'cap, first win,
rtd 70a, also rtd 67): 4th at best in '98 (fill mdn, rtd 74): eff at 10f, acts on gd/soft & equitrack,
poss not hvy: best forcing the pace on a sharp track.

96 **PAGAN KING** 15 [10] 3-9-2 (71) S Whitworth 10/1: 42D156: Mid-div, prog 3f out, no extra fnl 2f.   3   58a

4615} **CONSORT** 32 [3] 6-9-9 (75) T Sprake 13/2: 460007: Bhd, hdwy 5f out, rdn/btn fnl 2f: 2   58a
op 5/1, A/W bow: prev with Mrs A Perrett, now with A J McNae.

114 **PASSE PASSE** 12 [8] 3-8-5 (60)(bl) A Clark 12/1: 332058: Trkd ldrs, rdn & wknd 4f out.   ¾   42a

*92 **NIGHT CITY** 15 [1] 8-10-0 (80) N Callan (3) 9/2 JT FAV: 015119: Set fast pace, hdd 4f out &   1   60a
wknd: nicely bckd: btr 92 (clmr).

100 **ARDENT** 14 [5] 5-7-13 (51) C Rutter 7/1: 620220: Sn well bhd, fin 10th: op 6/1, much btr 100.   14   12a
10 ran   Time 2m 08.31 (5.51)   (Peter M Crane)   R Hannon East Everleigh, Wilts.

---

162   3.40 LADBROKE HCAP 3YO+ 0-80 (D)   7f aw rnd   Going 30 +01 Fast   [78]
£3929   £1419   £580   £276

4401} **SALTY JACK** 53 [8] V Soane 5-9-10 (74) T Sprake 13/2: 000201: 5 b h Salt Dome - Play The Queen   81a
(King Of Clubs) Cl-up, hdwy to chall 2f out, led well ins last, drvn out: op 5/1, 8 wk abs: gd time: rnr-up
twice in '99, incl val Bunbury Cup h'cap at Newmarket (rtd 89): '98 wnr at Doncaster, Folkestone (ltd stks),
Epsom & Newmarket (rtd 89 & 75a at best): prev term won here at Lingfield (h'cap, rtd 66a): suited by
7f on firm, hvy & equitrack: handles any trk, likes Lingfield: runs well fresh: eff weight carrier: v tough.

3756} **CANTINA** 95 [7] A Bailey 3-9-2 (66) G Carter 9/1: 304502: 5 b m Tina's Pet - Real Claire (Dreams   nk   72a
To Reality) Led, pressed fnl 2f, edged right & hdd well ins last: 3 month abs: prev in '99 won at Redcar (amat
stks, rtd 73): '98 Chester wnr (2, h'caps, disqual once, rtd 80), '97 Catterick wnr (mdn, rtd 71): loves to force
the pace around 7/7.5f: acts on firm, gd/soft & equitrack: handles any trk, likes a sharp one, esp Chester.

113 **REDOUBTABLE** 12 [11] D W Chapman 8-9-8 (72) J Fanning 7/1: 043063: 8 b h Grey Dawn II - Seattle   3   72a
Rockette (Seattle Slew) Dwelt & rear, hdwy halfway, short of room 2f out, styd on well, nvr nrr: earlier in
'99 won at Thirsk (h'cap, rtd 81 at best, also rtd 74a): '98 Lingfield, Ayr & Newcastle wnr (h'cap, rtd 79 &
78a at best): '97 scorer at W'hampton (h'cap, rtd 62, also rtd 49): suited by 6/7f, stays a sharp 1m: acts on
firm, soft & both AWs: has tried blnks, best without: unlucky in running today, keep in mind.

*147 **MAI TAI 2** [2] D W Barker 4-8-6 (56)(vis)(6ex) Kimberley Hart (5) 15/2: 304314: Held up, hdwy   shd   56a
over 3f out, short of room 2f out, kept on ins last, no threat to ldrs: op 5/1, qk reapp: wants 1m now?

106 **NOBALINO** 14 [6] 5-9-4 (68)(vis) L Newman (7) 6/1: 033135: Mid-div, trkd ldrs 2f out, no extra ins last.   2½   63a

LINGFIELD (Equitrack)   WEDNESDAY DECEMBER 8TH   Lefthand, V Sharp Track

*28	**DARYABAD 27** [1] 7-9-5 (69)(bl) Dale Gibson 9/2 FAV: 000116: In tch, short of room & lost pl 5f out, drvn/styd on fnl 2f, no threat: well bckd: unlucky in running & reportedly resented kick-back, forget this: see 28.	3½	58a
107	**RAINBOW RAIN 14** [10] 5-8-12 (62)(E) P Doe (3) 9/1: 140237: Mid-div at best: first time eye-shield.	nk	51a
113	**BRIMSTONE 12** [9] 4-8-10 (60) A Morris 33/1: 0-0008: Nvr a threat: well btn in 3 prev '99 starts: rnr-up on '98 reapp for R McGhin (h'cap, rtd 87): '97 wnr at Sandown (auct mdn, rtd 83 at best, D Elsworth): eff over a stiff 5.7f, 6/7f shld suit: acts on firm & gd grnd: well h'capped.	½	48a
59	**BEST QUEST 22** [3] 4-9-0 (64)(t) N Callan (3) 10/1: 040329: Chsd ldrs, wknd fnl 2f: btr 59.	2	48a
59	**SCISSOR RIDGE 22** [14] 7-8-7 (57) Claire Bryan (7) 10/1: 544130: Nvr a factor, 10th: btr 59, 29.	1¼	38a
3789}	**DEMOCRACY 93** [5] 3-10-0 (78)(bl) S Drowne 20/1: 342210: Cl-up, lost tch fnl 3f: 11th: 3 month abs, top-weight: prev R Hannon, now with P G Murphy.	2½	54a
106	**WILD THING 14** [16] 3-8-11 (61)(BL) G Bardwell 33/1: 215200: Bhd, hdwy over 3f out, wknd, 12th: blnks.	¾	36a
--	**An Lu Abu** [4] 3-8-4 (54) D McGann (6) 33/1:	4186} **Shady Deal 68** [15] 3-8-4 (54) A Clark 33/1:		
113	**Robo Magic 12** [13] 7-9-5 (69) P Dobbs (5) 16/1:	4527} **Ursa Major 42** [12] 5-9-6 (70) O Urbina 16/1:		
16 ran	Time 1m 24.83 (2.03)	(Salts Of The Earth)	V Soane East Garston, Berks.

LINGFIELD (Equitrack)   FRIDAY DECEMBER 10TH   Lefthand, Very Sharp Track

Official Going   STANDARD. Stalls: 5f & 1m - Outside; Rem - Inside.

163   12.10 APPR CLASS STKS 3YO+ 0-70 (G)   1m2f aw   Going 16   -12 Slow
£1864   £523   £255   3 yo   rec 3 lb

93	**BARBASON 17** [7] G L Moore 7-8-10 P Dobbs (5) 7/4 FAV: 106031: 7 ch g Polish Precedent - Barada (Damascus) In tch, smooth prog to lead appr fnl 1f, qknd clr, easily: well bckd: earlier in '99 won here at Lingfield (clmr, rtd 73a), Newbury (amat h'cap), Sandown & Brighton (clmr, rtd 76): '98 wnr at Lingfield & Brighton (h'caps): eff at 7f/10f: acts on firm, gd/sft grnd & equitrack: Lingfield/clmr specialist: eff with/without blnks: v tough.		68a
135	**FAILED TO HIT 9** [5] N P Littmoden 6-8-12 (vis) C Cogan (5) 11/2: 035152: 6 b g Warrshan - Missed Again (High Top) Bhd till kept on strgly fnl 2f, wnr long gone: op 7/2: needs 12f nowadays: see 135.	6	62a
102	**ROI DE DANSE 16** [6] M Quinn 4-8-10 R Studholme (3) 50/1: 600063: 4 ch g Komaite - Princess Lucy (Local Suitor) Cl-up, led halfway till 2f out, same pace: earlier in '99 rnr-up twice here (h'cap, rtd 58a): '98 Brighton wnr (class stks, rtd 71): eff at 7f/10f: acts on gd grnd & equitrack: likes a sharp trk.	5	50$
*3	**BAAJIL 32** [1] D J S Cosgrove 4-8-12 N Callan 11/4: 240014: Prom, led 2f out, sn hdd, fdd: bckd.	1¼	50a
2338}	**SHAMWARI SONG 99** [8] 4-8-10 P Fredericks (5) 50/1: 000065: Chsd ldrs till 2f out: 5 mnth abs: failed to reach the frame earlier in '99 (h'caps, rtd 41a & 41): '98 wnr at Beverley (clmr) & Newcastle (h'cap, rtd 75 & 71a, for J Glover): eff at 7f/1m: acts on firm, gd, prob soft, without visor: likes a stiff trk.	1¾	45$
*110	**THOMAS HENRY 14** [4] 3-8-9 L Newman (5) 7/1: 440416: Prom, rdn/outpcd fnl 2f: see 110 (sell)	1¼	45a
90	**COLONEL NORTH 17** [3] 3-8-7 R Winston 10/1: 116647: Led till halfway, sn btn: op 6/1: better at 1m.	½	42a
110	**ARANA 14** [2] 4-8-7 (BL) P Fitzimons (5) 100/1: 000008: Al bhd: blinkered, modest.	14	19a
8 ran	Time 2m 05.64 (2.84)	(A Moore)	G L Moore Woodingdean, E Sussex

164   12.40 WINTER WARMER MDN 2YO (D)   7f aw rnd   Going 16   -23 Slow
£2703   £759   £370

118	**TWICE BLESSED 13** [12] R Hannon 2-9-0 T Sprake 1/1 FAV: 0021: 2 ch c Thatching - Fairy Blesse (Fairy King) Broke well & led, rdn out fnl 1f: confirmed AW bow promise, well bckd: unplcd in 2 turf starts earlier in '99 (rtd 57): eff at 6/7f: best forcing the pace, acts on both AW's, sharp trks: progressing well.		72a
4305}	**BUGGY RIDE 60** [4] Miss Gay Kelleway 2-9-0 S Whitworth 25/1: 035002: 2 b c Blues Traveller - Tambora (Darshaan) Cl-up, eff 2f out, kept on but al held: 2 month abs, AW bow: plcd earlier in '99 for R Charlton (mdn, rtd 74): eff at 7f, tried 1m, shld stay: acts on fast grnd & equitrack, without visor: acts on any trk.	1½	68a
--	**PORTLAND** [9] Declan Gillespie 2-9-0 J P Spencer 5/2: 0263: 2 ch c Mujtahid - Princess Dixieland (Dixieland Band) Dwelt, mid-div by halfway, styd on for press, nvr nr ldrs: 2 month abs, AW bow, Irish raider, rnr-up in a hvy grnd mdn at Listowel earlier in '99 (1m): handles equitrack, return to 1m sure to suit.	4	60a
48	**RING MY MATE 25** [1] W R Muir 2-9-0 Sophie Mitchell 8/1: 634: Prom, outpcd appr fnl 2f: back in trip, forced the pace over 1m in 48 (fibresand).	½	59a
54	**BEDOUIN QUEEN 24** [7] 2-8-9 (BL) A Daly 20/1: 003005: Handy till onepace 3f out: earlier in in '99 3rd of 6 on turf (nov auct, rtd 73): stays 6f on fast grnd: tried blnks today.	2½	49a
86	**OPEN GROUND 18** [10] 2-9-0 A McCarthy (3) 33/1: 006: Nvr on terms: no worthwhile form.	6	44a
4605}	**ASH BOLD 35** [2] 2-9-0 D Sweeney 20/1: 007: Rear, struggled to handle bend, nvr dngrs: AW bow.	hd	44a
4614}	**GOLD KRIEK 34** [8] 2-9-0 A Clark 25/1: 08: Sn struggling: AW bow.	2	40a
--	**BEACH BABY** [6] 2-8-9 G Bardwell 33/1: 9: Prom till halfway: debut: Mizoram half sister to a 1m/10f wnr, dam unrcd: with J J Bridger.	hd	35a
118	**ARPELLO 13** [11] 2-8-9 C Nutter 16/1: 000: Nvr a factor: 10th, op 12/1: see 77.	hd	35a
4071}	**Tic Tac Mac 77** [5] 2-9-0 A Morris 66/1:	94 **Ubitoo 17** [3] 2-9-0 S Drowne 33/1:		
12 ran	Time 1m 25.53 (2.73)	(J C Smith)	R Hannon East Everleigh, Wilts

165   1.10 LYNHURST NURSERY HCAP 2YO 0-75 (E)   6f aw rnd   Going 16   -36 Slow   [80]
£2615   £734   £358

149	**OTIME 4** [1] Mrs N Macauley 2-9-7 (73)(VIS) A Clark 11/1: 051301: 2 b g Mujadil - Kick The Habit (Habitat) Led, repelled sev challs fnl 2f, gamely: qck reapp: earlier in '99 won at Bath (sell, rtd 62) & Lingfield (clmr, rtd 70a, M Channon): eff at 6f on firm & equitrack, any trk, likes Lingfield: sharpened up by visor.		78a
2514}	**PRINCESS VICTORIA 99** [5] N A Callaghan 2-8-7 (59) P M Quinn (5) 11/1: 102: 2 b f Deploy - Scierpan (Sharpen Up) Chsd ldrs, ran on to chall dist, held nr fin: 5 mnth abs: gd AW bow: earlier in '99 won debut at Beverley (auct, rtd 65): eff at 5/6f, tried 7f, shld suit on sand: acts on gd grnd & equitrack: shld win a race.	nk	62a
72	**PARKSIDE PROSPECT 21** [7] M R Channon 2-7-13 (51) J Tate 11/4: 502123: 2 b f Piccolo - Banner (Known Fact) With ldrs, ev ch 2f out, rdn & not much room below dist: ran well, acts on firm, gd & both AW's.	1¼	51a
*2	**WELCOME SHADE 32** [3] R Hannon 2-9-3 (69) T Sprake 7/4 FAV: 00014: Prsd ldr, switched & ch appr fnl 1f, sn onepce: hvly bckd: shade btr 2 in 2 (C/D)	½	67a
*74	**CALKO 21** [6] 2-8-8 (60)(bl) N Callan (3) 3/1: 006315: Outpcd: much btr 74 (fibresand, seller).	5	46a
4277}	**ANGELAS PET 63** [2] 2-7-11 (48)(1ow) G Bardwell 20/1: 600006: Al bhd: AW bow, flattered prev (rtd 65).	1½	31a
6 ran	Time 1m 13.53 (3.13)	(Miss F V Cove)	Mrs N Macauley Sproxton, Leics

166   1.45 CATHEDRAL HCAP 3YO+ 0-60 (F)   5f aw rnd   Going 16 -08 Slow   [60]
£2211   £621   £303

93   **BOLDLY CLIFF** 17 [9] Andre Hermans 5-8-13 (45)(bl) L Newman (7) 10/1: 105401: 5 b h Never So Bold - **53a**
Miami Beach (Miami Springs) Cl-up, led 3f out, rdn clr, rdly: Belgian raider: won at Chantilly earlier in '99
(h'cap): both wins at 5f, tried 1m: acts on soft & equitrack, up with/forcing the pace: wears blnks.

3936} **FRENCH GRIT** 85 [5] K A Ryan 7-9-0 (46) A Daly 10/1: 423002: 7 b g Common Grounds - Charbatte   2½ **47a**
(In Fijar) Chsd ldrs, outpcd halfway, rall to go 2nd towards fin: 12 wk abs: dual rnr-up earlier in '99 (h'caps,
rtd 56, 66$ & 53a, D Barker): last won in '97, at Ripon (reapp) & Pontefract (h'caps, rtd 79): eff at 5f, suited
by 6f: acts on fast/firm, handles gd/soft, both AWs, goes on any trk: can run well fresh, best held up.

116   **YOUNG IBNR** 13 [4] B A McMahon 4-9-1 (47) N Callan (3) 5/1: 00-533: 4 b g Imperial Frontier -   1¼ **45a**
Zalatia (Music Boy) Prsd lead 3f, kept on same pace fnl 1½f: op 3/1: handles equitrack, best on f/sand: see 116.

113   **ELLWAY PRINCE** 14 [8] Mrs N Macauley 4-9-1 (58)(vis) A Clark 9/1: 000004: In tch, headway pace   ½ **55a**
before str, ran on late: rnr-up earlier in '99 (h'cap, rtd 67a & 45): '98 wnr here at Lingfield (mdn, rtd 72a):
eff at 6f, tried 1m: acts on firm, gd grnd, both AWs, best on equitrack: usually forces the pace, in visor, not blnks.

148   **JUST DISSIDENT** 4 [7] 7-9-11 (57) D Sweeney 5/1: 104445: Outpcd, some hdwy in str, nvr dngrs.   1 **51a**
107   **MISS DANGEROUS** 16 [1] 4-8-8 (40)(BL) S Drowne 20/1: 020006: Al around same place: blnkd.   1½ **30a**
116   **SOUTHERN DOMINION** 13 [2] 7-9-11 (57)(bl) T Williams 4/1 FAV: 000227: Nrly u.r. leaving stall, nvr   2½ **41a**
in it, ran wide ent str: op 9/4: prob worth forgiving: see 71 (forced it).
139   **BOWCLIFFE GRANGE** 9 [6] 7-8-12 (44) J Fanning 5/1: 012008: Led till 3f out, wknd qckly: tchd 8/1.   3 **20a**
139   **MISTER RAIDER** 9 [10] 7-8-9 (41)(bl) D Kinsella (9) 14/1: 040509: Al bhd: see 139.   4 **7a**
116   **LEGAL VENTURE** 13 [3] 3-9-6 (52)(bl) T G McLaughlin 16/1: 02000U: U.r. in stalls.   **0a**
10 ran   Time 59.01 (1.21)   (E C Denderland)   Andre Hermans Belgium

167   2.20 AJAX HCAP DIV I 3YO+ 0-70 (E)   1m5f aw   Going 16 -08 Slow   [67]
£2353   £659   £320   3 yo rec 6 lb

4437} **ZORRO** 52 [10] Jamie Poulton 5-8-11 (50) O Urbina 7/1: 224-51: 5 gr g Touch Of Grey - Snow Huntress   **57a**
(Shirley Heights) Towards rear, trkd ldrs & not much room 3f out, hdwy to lead 2f out, rdn clr, eased cl-home:
7 wk abs: ran just once earlier in '99 (h'cap, rtd 51): rnr-up thrice in '98 on sand (h'cap, rtd 51a, R Flower):
'97 Yarmouth wnr (appr h'cap, rtd 67): eff at 10f/13f: acts on firm grnd & equitrack, any trk: goes well fresh.

141   **VANTAGE POINT** 6 [11] K McAuliffe 3-8-4 (49) J Tate 3/1 FAV: 340332: 3 b c Casteddu - Rosie Dickins   2 **52a**
(Blue Cashmere) Mid-div, prog to lead 3½f out, hdd 2f out, same pace: bckd: proving tough: see 141, 115.
4502} **MAKNAAS** 46 [2] T G Mills 3-8-4 (47)(2ow) A Clark 4/1: 003453: 3 ch c Wolfhound - White Wash (Final   nk **52a**
Straw) Mid-div, chsd ldrs 3f out, onepace: op 7/1, abs: clr rem: plcd on turf earlier in '99 for R Armstrong
(mdn h'cap, rtd 49 & 44a): eff at 1m, stays 13f: acts on soft & equitrack, with/without blnks.
101   **ESHTIAAL** 16 [4] G L Moore 5-9-12 (65)(bl) P Dobbs (3) 7/2: 003324: Cl-up, keen, eff & btn when   13 **58a**
hmpd appr str: nicely bckd: stays 13f?: see 101, 52.
3808} **ANOTHER RAINBOW** 94 [7] 3-9-4 (63) P Fredericks (5) 10/1: 453625: Chsd ldrs till 3f out: op 6/1:   5 **51a**
3 month abs, AW bow: dual rnr-up on turf earlier in '99 (fill mdn, rtd 73): rnr-up in '98 (mdn, rtd 73):
eff at 10f, stays 12f: acts on firm & gd grnd, any trk: with Miss G Kelleway.
110   **NERONIAN** 14 [3] 5-7-10 (35)(2oh) M Henry 40/1: 506056: Front rank, led halfway till 3½f out, wknd.   14 **11a**
111   **APPYABO** 14 [6] 4-7-10 (35) R Brisland (3) 25/1: 006007: In tch 14f out: up in trip.   1¾ **10a**
115   **INDIGO BAY** 14 [1] 3-9-9 (68) R Smith (5) 10/1: 000208: Led 7f, lost pl: op 7/1: see 52 (12f, amat).   1 **42a**
115   **KI CHI SAGA** 14 [5] 7-7-13 (38)(bl) G Bardwell 10/1: 000449: Sn niggled, al bhd: op 5/1: see 115.   5 **7a**
100   **SKY CITY** 16 [9] 3-7-10 (41)(1oh) A McCarthy (3) 50/1: 000000: Dwelt, prog halfway, wknd 5f out: 10th.   13 **0a**
10 ran   Time 2m 45.4 (3.1)   (Mrs G M Temmerman)   Jamie Poulton Telscombe, E Sussex

168   2.55 AJAX HCAP DIV II 3YO+ 0-70 (E)   1m5f aw   Going 16 00 Fast   [67]
£2353   £659   £320   3 yo rec 6 lb

51   **NATURAL EIGHT** 25 [9] Jamie Poulton 5-8-6 (42)(3ow) O Urbina 15/2: 413261: 5 b g In The Wings - Fenny   **53a**
Rough (Home Guard) Mid-div, hdwy to lead appr fnl 3f, sn clr, rdly: op 6/1, fair time: earlier in '99 won
at Bath (mdn h'cap, rtd 49 at best): lightly rcd in '98 (h'cap, rtd 61): '97 rnr-up (mdn, rtd 87, B Hills):
eff at 13f, stays 2m: acts on firm, gd/soft grnd & equitrack, any trk: best without blnks/vis: qk follow-up?

*144   **PRASLIN ISLAND** 6 [11] A Kelleway 3-9-12 (71)(6ex) J Tate 3/1 FAV: 206212: 3 ch c Be My Chief -   3 **76a**
Hence (Mr Prospector) Cl-up, led ent fnl 5f till before 3f out, not pace of wnr: nicely bckd, quick reapp
& pen: ran to best back in h'cap company: acts on both AWs, handles fast grnd: shld be wng again this winter.
101   **HIGHLY PRIZED** 16 [6] J S King 5-9-5 (58) S Drowne 11/2: 442543: 5 b g Shirley Heights - On The Tiles   ½ **62a**
(Thatch) Towards rear, prog before halfway, ev ch 4f out, same pace: op 7/2, clr rem: another sound run.
100   **HURGILL DANCER** 16 [3] R J O'Sullivan 5-8-0 (39) L Newman (4) 4/1: 150434: Chsd ldrs, no extra 4f   10 **34a**
out: better at sltly shorter?: see 100.
52   **HENRIETTA HOLMES** 24 [10] T Sprake 3-8-10 (55)(e) T Sprake 10/1: 221465: Prom till appr fnl 3f: drifted   nk **50a**
from 7/1, wore eye-shield: earlier in '99 scored at Yarmouth (clmr, rtd 68, J Fanshawe), subs clmd for £10,000
& rtd 55a on AW bow: eff at 1m/11.5f on firm & fast grnd, handles equitrack, without visor: with Mrs Richards.
101   **PRINCE DANZIG** 16 [4] 8-9-12 (65) S Whitworth 13/2: 530256: Nvr going pace: tchd 10/1, won this   1¾ **59a**
last term off same mark: see 101.
101   **KATIES CRACKER** 16 [8] 4-7-10 (35)(12oh) R Brisland (3) 25/1: 000607: Well plcd 7f: stiff task: 20 **14a**
earlier in '99 won here at Lingfield (sell h'cap) & Southwell (class clmr, rtd 46a): '98 Southwell & Nottingham
wnr (h'caps, rtd 61a & 52): eff btwn 12f & 2m: goes on fast, soft, both AWs, sharp or gall trk: can force the pace.
3   **MAYLAN** 32 [5] 4-7-10 (35)(7oh) G Bardwell 33/1: 000008: Al bhd: stiff task.   2 **12a**
101   **HIGHFIELDER** 16 [7] 3-8-8 (53) N Callan (3) 9/1: 304039: Led till appr fnl 4f, sn lost place: ¾ **30a**
op 7/1, tchd 11/1: flattered 101 (in front of today's 3rd).
118} **SHELTERED COVE** 99 [2] 8-7-13 (38) T Williams 20/1: 2140-0: Sn struggling: 10th, new stable.   dist **0a**
45   **CROFT SANDS** 25 [1] 6-7-10 (35)(10oh) M Henry 33/1: 000-00: Nvr in it, virtually p.u.: last.   dist **0a**
11 ran   Time 2m 44.43 (2.13)   (Michael Siu)   Jamie Poulton Telscombe, E Sussex

LINGFIELD (Equitrack)　FRIDAY DECEMBER 10TH　Lefthand, Very Sharp Track

169	3.30 LADBROKE HCAP QUAL 3YO+ 0-85 (D)　1m aw rnd　Going 16　+06 Fast	[84]
	£3947　£1195　£583　£277　3 yo rec 1 lb	

157　**SECRET SPRING** 2 [6] Mrs L Richards 7-10-0 (84) O Urbina 9/4 FAV: 401021: 7 b g Dowsing - Nordica **91a**
(Northfields) Mid-div, prog 2f out, led dist, rdn out: nicely bckd, fair time, ran 48hrs ago: earlier in '99 won
here at Lingfield (h'cap, rtd 84a, turf plcd, stks, rtd 85): '98 Kempton wnr (h'cap, rtd 90, P Hedger): eff at
1m/10f on firm & equitrack, handles hvy, any trk, likes Lingfield: best held up: useful & improving.

78　**SONG OF SKYE** 20 [4] T J Naughton 5-9-4 (74) C Rutter 7/1: 543022: 5 b m Warning - Song Of Hope 2½ **75a**
(Chief Singer) Prom, led 2f out till 1f out, outpcd by wnr: op 5/1: taken very well to sand, acts on firm,
gd/soft, both AW's: must win soon, poss back at 7f: see 78.

104　**TOPTON** 16 [9] P Howling 5-10-0 (84)(bl) A McCarthy (3) 6/1: 000023: 5 b g Royal Academy - Circo hd **85a**
(High Top) Early ldr & again 4f out till 2f out, wide into str, styd on towards fin: ran to best: see 104.

4368}　**MAWINGO** 56 [8] G Wragg 6-8-6 (62) J Tate 10/1: 300354: Held up, hdwy under press 2f out, onepace 2 **59a**
dist: tchd 12/1, 8 wk abs: plcd earlier in '99 (h'caps, rtd 65): last won in '96 at Newmarket (2, h'caps, rtd 80)
& Warwick: eff at 7f/1m, tried 10f: acts on firm, hvy, handles equitrack & any trk: tried blnks: well h'capped.

100　**KAFIL** 16 [10] 5-7-11 (53) G Bardwell 20/1: 225365: Prom, feeling pace 4f, wide into str, no impress. 1 **48a**
106　**MAPLE** 16 [3] 3-8-5 (62) A Clark 14/1: 060006: Front rank till lost pl emf fnl 3f: best sprinting? 3 **51a**
97　**STYLE DANCER** 17 [2] 5-8-3 (59)(vis) L Newman (7) 5/1: 000337: Led 2f till halfway, btn 2f out: shd **48a**
nicely bckd tho' op 4/1, visor reapplied, better without last twice: see 29.
*93　**BIG BEN** 17 [7] 5-8-12 (68) T Sprake 11/2: 003518: Nvr in it: found this tougher than 93 (C/D clmr). 1¾ **54a**
49　**GULF SHAADI** 25 [1] 7-9-10 (80) S Whitworth 12/1: 006009: Dwelt, nvr troubled ldrs: dual trf 5 **56a**
rnr-up earlier in '99 (h'caps, rtd 89): '98 wnr at W'hampton (h'cap, rtd 92a & 96, E Alston): eff at 7f/9.4f,
stays 10f: acts on firm, soft grnd, both AWs: with Miss G Kelleway.
4075}　**MY BOLD BOYO** 77 [5] 4-8-5 (61) J Fanning 14/1: 650000: Bhd halfway: 10th, 11 wk abs, AW bow. 3½ **31a**
10 ran　Time 1m 37.01 (0.81)　(M K George)　Mrs L Richards Funtington, W Sussex

WOLVERHAMPTON (Fibresand)　SATURDAY DECEMBER 11TH　Lefthand, Sharp Track

Official Going　STANDARD Stalls: 7f & 1m6f - Outside, Rem - Inside

170	7.00 FESTIVE FUN HCAP 3YO+ 0-60 (F)　1m4f aw　Going 35　-26 Slow	[60]
	£2389　£672　£328　3 yo rec 5 lb	

131　**WESTERN COMMAND** 11 [7] Mrs N Macauley 3-9-12 (63) R Fitzpatrick (3) 11/2: 206221: 3 b g Saddlers' **69a**
Hall - Western Friend (Gone West) Chsd ldrs, rdn halfway, styd on stdly for press fnl 2f to lead nr line: op 9/2:
earlier in '99 won twice at Southwell (h'caps, rtd 76c, Sir M Prescott), mod turf form subs: rnr-up in '98 (rtd 69a,
mdn): suited by 12f, stays 14f: acts on both AWs, likes Southwell: best without blnks/vis: tough/consistent.

68　**DESERT SPA** 22 [3] P J Makin 4-9-3 (49) A Clark 20/1: 103-02: 4 b g Sheikh Albadou - Healing Waters 1 **54a**
(Temperence Hill) Trkd ldr, led 5f out, rdn/hdd nr fin: tchd 25/1: back to form, on a fair mark: see 34 (C/D).

4578}　**SOLE SINGER** 40 [5] D Haydn Jones 3-8-13 (50) N Callan (3) 14/1: 000323: 3 b g Slip Anchor - Singer 1¼ **53a**
On The Roof (Chief Singer) Towards rear, smooth prog from halfway, ev ch/rdn & hung left fnl 1f, held cl-home:
clr rem, op 12/1, AW bow: 6 wk abs: plcd twice earlier in '99 (rtd 59, sell): rtd 71 in '98 (I Balding, mdn):
eff arnd 10/12f: handles fast, soft & fibresand: has worn a t-strap, lkd a tricky ride here.

68　**MEILLEUR** 22 [4] Lady Herries 5-9-11 (57) T Sprake 100/30 FAV: 215024: Ev ch till 2f out: clr rem. 4 **54a**
102　**OUR PEOPLE** 17 [6] 5-8-8 (40) J Fanning 16/1: -06055: Rear, mod prog/no threat: op 10/1: see 102. 10 **26a**
115　**LOST SPIRIT** 15 [1] 3-9-6 (57) J Bosley (7) 20/1: 000066: Keen/led 7f, fdd: earlier in '99 scored at 1 **42a**
Southwell (clmr) & here at W'hampton (C/D, h'cap, rtd 66a, plcd on turf, rtd 49, h'cap): rnr-up in '98 for B Hanbury
(sell, rtd 55): loves to dominate over 12f: acts on firm, gd/soft & loves fibresand: eff with/without blnks.

141　**MY LEGAL EAGLE** 7 [11] 5-8-10 (42) Claire Bryan (7) 6/1: 405327: Dwelt, mid-div at best: btr 141 (2m). ½ **26a**
*131　**LEGAL ISSUE** 11 [9] 7-10-3 (63) R Lappin 7/2: 054318: Held up, eff halfway, btn 3f out: tchd 5/1: 1¾ **45a**
topweight: ahead of today's wnr latest: see 131 (11f, Southwell).

4546}　**ACEBO LYONS** 43 [8] 4-9-3 (49)(vis) S Drowne 25/1: 260409: Prom 9f: 6 wk abs: rnr-up earlier in '99 6 **22a**
(rtd 57a, h'cap): '98 Haydock wnr (stks, rtd 70): eff at 10/12f on fast & gd/soft: tried a vis, prob best without.

--　**DR EDGAR** [2] 7-9-9 (55) R Winston 16/1: 2222-0: Rear, bhd 4f out: 10th: broke a blood vessel: 16 **10a**
tchd 20/1, long abs: last rcd in '98, rnr-up 4 times (rtd 61a, h'cap): back in '95 won at Folkestone & Windsor
(h'caps, rtd 68, G Wragg): eff at 9f/12f on firm, gd/soft & both AWs: best without blnks: prob handles any trk.

126　**SHANGHAI LIL** 11 [10] 7-9-2 (48) T G McLaughlin 20/1: 061000: Dwelt/al rear: 11th. 5 **0a**
60　**SILVERTOWN** 24 [12] 4-9-9 (55) J P Spencer 7/1: 100020: Chsd ldrs till halfway, sn bhd: 12th: op 5/1. 13 **0a**
12 ran　Time 2m 40.9 (7.3)　(Andy Peake)　Mrs N Macauley Sproxton, Leics.

171	7.30 TURKEY NOV STKS 2YO (D)　1m100y aw rnd　Going 35　-11 Slow	
	£2822　£792　£386	

+103　**FORBEARING** 17 [9] Sir Mark Prescott 2-9-5 T Sprake 1/2 FAV: 5611: 2 b c Bering - For Example **95a**
(Northern Baby) Cl-up, led over 3f out & sn clr, in command fnl 1f & eased down, val 8L: hvly bckd, tchd 5/4:
recent Lingfield scorer (mdn): rtd 80 earlier in '99 (nov mdn): eff at 1m, 10f + looks sure to suit: acts on
both AWs, poss handles gd/soft & hvy: handles a sharp/gall trk: plenty in hand, prog/useful colt, win again.

3957}　**YOURE SPECIAL** 85 [10] P C Haslam 2-8-12 T Eaves (7) 20/1: -55202: 2 b g Northern Flagship - Pillow 4 **75a**
Mint (Stagedoor Johnny) Held up, prog/chsd wnr fnl 2f, kept on tho' nvr a ch: op 10/1: AW bow, 12 wk abs:
rnr-up earlier in '99 (auct mdn, rtd 81): stays 1m, mid-dists shld suit: handles gd, gd/soft & fibresand.

*86　**SERVICE STAR** 19 [11] M A Jarvis 2-9-0 (bl) N Callan (3) 4/1: 422013: 2 b c Namaqualand - Shenley 2½ **73a**
Lass (Prince Tenderfoot) Prom, rdn 3f out, sn outpcd by wnr: op 5/2: see 86 (1st time blnks, Southwell).

*128　**HEATHYARDS MATE** 11 [2] R Hollinshead 2-9-4 P M Quinn (5) 7/1: 422114: Nvr dngrs: tchd 11/1. hd **75a**
108　**LA TORTUGA** 15 [3] 2-9-2 (BL) J P Spencer 16/1: 144045: Chsd ldrs 7f: op 12/1, blnks: see 108 (7f). 3½ **67a**
31　**GYMCRAK FIREBIRD** 29 [3] 2-8-7 R Winston 20/1: 060246: Led 5f, sn btn: rnr-up earlier in '99 (sell, 1¼ **55a**
rtd 57a, unplcd on turf, rtd 61): eff at 7f, 1m+ may suit in time: handles fibresand: apprec a return to stalls.

118　**ATALYA** 14 [6] 2-8-12 A Clark 33/1: 067: Rear, mod gains: mod form prev, longer 8.5f trip tonight. 3 **54a**
4500}　**THIRTY SIX CEE** 47 [12] 2-8-7 S Whitworth 25/1: 546008: Held up, btn 2f out: abs/AW bow: unplcd ¾ **48a**
earlier in '99 (rtd 70, nov fill stks): eff around 5/6f on gd/soft: has worn a t-strap.

48	**WEST END DANCER** 26 [11] 2-8-7 S Carson (5) 16/1: 59: Dwelt/al rear: op 10/1.		5	38a
118	**CUIGIU** 14 [4] 2-8-12 R Fitzpatrick (3) 14/1: 502540: Bhd halfway: 10th: see 118 (6f).		10	28a
86	**BLUE CAVALIER** 19 [1] 2-8-12 R Smith (5) 50/1: 60: Al bhd: 11th.		8	16a
--	**ESPERE DOR** [8] 2-8-12 R Lappin 50/1: 0: Mid-div, bhd 4f out: 12th: debut.		7	5a
12 ran	Time 1m 50.1 (3.9) (Eclipse Thoroughbreds - Osborne House IV) Sir Mark Prescott Newmarket, Suffolk			

---

172   8.00 XMAS TREE HCAP 3YO+ 0-95 (C)   1m1f79y   Going 35   +07 Fast   [90]
£6320   £1910   £930   £440   3 yo rec 2 lb

+137	**KING PRIAM** 10 [8] M J Polglase 4-9-10 (86)(bl) T Sprake 6/4 FAV: 52D111: 4 b g Priolo - Barinia			94a
	(Corvaro) Mid-div, smooth prog to lead over 1f out, styd on strongly, rdn out: hvly bckd tho' op evens: fast time:			
	qck hat-trick after wins at Southwell & here at W'hampton (h'caps), earlier in '99 won again at Southwell (h'cap,			
	rtd 74a), Leicester (class stks), Haydock & York (h'caps, rtd 80): '98 Newmarket wnr (clmr, rtd 70, M Pipe): eff			
	at 1m/1f, stays 12f on firm, enjoys gd, soft & progressive: loves W'hampton: wears blnks: very tough & progressive.			
131	**TIGHTROPE** 16 [6] N P Littmoden 4-7-10 (58) C Cogan (2) 10/1: 102202: 4 b g Alzao - Circus Act	1¼		63a
	(Shirley Heights) Led after 1f, rdn/hdd over 1f out, kept on ins last: clr rem: on a handy a/w mark: see 1.			
104	**WHITE PLAINS** 17 [1] K R Burke 6-9-4 (80)(t) N Callan (3) 6/1: 660543: 6 b g Nordico - Flying	5		75a
	Diva (Chief Singer) Chsd ldrs, rdn/outpcd 2f out, kept on ins last, no threat to front pair: op 12/1: earlier in '99			
	scored at Lingfield (stks, rtd 89a at best), subs rtd 60 on turf, stks): '98 Southwell wnr (stks, rtd 93a at best):			
	eff at 1m/10f, stays 12f: acts on firm, gd & both AWs: handles any trk, likes Lingfield: wears a t-strap.			
157	**ITALIAN SYMPHONY** 3 [9] P D Evans 5-10-0 (90)(vis) Joanna Badger (7) 6/1: 005434: Rear, eff 4f out,	4		77a
	held fnl 2f: quick reapp: a drop to 7f/1m in simialr contests could prove ideal: see 138 (sell).			
138	**DREAM ON ME** 10 [10] 3-7-10 (60)(7oh) G Baker (7) 25/1: 130435: Chsd ldrs 7f: see 138 (sell).	4		39a
119	**MR BERGERAC** 14 [3] 8-8-5 (67)(bl) D Sweeney 20/1: 206556: Rear, mod gains: blnks reapplied.	4		38a
836}	**STILL WATERS** 99 [2] 4-8-3 (65) T Williams 16/1: 0-1007: Mid-div, rdn 3f out: 8 month abs: op 12/1:	14		16a
	prev with K Bell, earlier in '99 scored at Southwell (h'cap, rtd 66a, 1st success): plcd in '98 (R Charlton,			
	mdn, rtd 66): eff at 1m, tried 12f: acts on firm, gd & both AWs: handles any trk, likes Southwell: now with I Wood.			
--	**FEARSOME FACTOR** [5] 4-9-4 (80) J P Spencer 14/1: 1-3008: Keen, led 1f, btn 2f out: op 5/1, 6 mth	5		21a
	abs, AW bow: Brit debut: ex-Irish, '98 wnr at Leopardstown (mdn, 10f): eff around 9/10f on hvy: with B Curley.			
157	**TALLULAH BELLE** 3 [4] 6-9-11 (87) T G McLaughlin 5/1: 036159: Mid-div, btn 4f out: quick reapp.	8		16a
4435}	**KARAKUL** 53 [7] 3-8-1 (65) M Henry 20/1: 110000: Al rear: 10th: abs/AW bow: now with R Brotherton.	hd		0a
10 ran	Time 2m 0.8 (2.6) (Ian Puddle) M J Polglase Southwell, Notts			

---

173   8.30 HOLLY & IVY MDN 3YO+ (D)   7f aw rnd   Going 35   -08 Slow
£2654   £744   £362

4133}	**SAND HAWK** 74 [2] D Shaw 4-9-0 (bl) N Callan (3) 11/2: 000451: 4 ch g Polar Falcon - Ghassanah (Pas			54a
	de Seul) Prom, led over 2f out, easily: 10 wk abs, tchd 7/1: rnr-up earlier in '99 (h'caps, rtd 47 & 42a): plcd in			
	'98 (h'caps, rtd 51 & 50a): eff at 7f/1m: acts on fast, gd/soft & fibresand: wears blnks, likes sharp trks.			
--	**WELCOME GIFT** [9] W J Haggas 3-9-0 K W Marks 100/30: 2: 3 b g Prince Sabo - Ausonia (Beldale	8		40a
	Flutter) Dwelt, mid-div halfway, kept on fnl 2f, no threat to wnr: op 3/1, debut: Irish 37,000 gns yearling purchase.			
136	**NOBLE PATRIOT** 10 [8] R Hollinshead 4-9-0 R Lappin 10/1: 000203: 4 b g Polish Patriot - Noble	1¼		37a
	Form (Double Form) Prom, led 4f out till over 2f out, sn held: op 8/1: see 61 (C/D, sell).			
4371}	**ANNADAWI** 57 [4] C N Kellett 4-9-0 N Carlisle 20/1: 06004: Rdn/bhd, mod late gains: AW bow, jumps	2½		32a
	fit (mod form): unplcd on turf earlier in '99 (mdn, rtd 46).			
131}	**JAZZNIC** 99 [7] 3-8-9 A Clark 6/4 FAV: 0422-5: Chsd ldrs 5f: hvly bckd tho' op 5/4: 12 month abs:	7		16a
	rnr-up twice in '98 (rtd 66a, clmr, rtd 66 on turf earlier, clmr): eff around a sharp 6/7f on equitrack, handles soft.			
159	**IRISH MELODY** 3 [6] 3-8-9 (bl) T Sprake 33/1: 000006: Sn outpcd: quick reapp: blnks reapplied.	6		7a
4451}	**MARIANA** 52 [1] 4-8-9 (vis) T G McLaughlin 20/1: 040007: Led 1f, sn struggling: 7 wk abs.	½		6a
56	**MALAKAL** 25 [5] 3-9-0 J P Spencer 4/1: 44208: Led after 1f till 4f out, sn btn: op 6/4: see 56 (10f, eqtrk).	1¼		8a
8 ran	Time 1m 29.2 (3.0) (J C Fretwell) D Shaw Averham, Notts			

---

174   9.00 PARTY FEVER SELLER 3YO+ (G)   1m6f166y   Going 35   -37 Slow
£1924   £539   £262   3 yo rec 7 lb

*117	**NOUFARI** 14 [7] R Hollinshead 8-9-7 P M Quinn (5) 5/6 FAV: 150011: 8 b g Kahyasi - Noufiyla (Top			74a
	Ville) Rear, prog 5f out, led over 2f out, easily: hvly bckd, bght in for 3,400 gns: recent wnr here at W'hampton			
	(clmr, C/D), earlier in '99 won at Nottingham & Thirsk (h'caps, rtd 76 & 83a): '98 wnr at Southwell (2), W'hampton			
	(2) & Newcastle (h'caps, rtd 81a & 71): eff at 14f/2m, stays 2½m: acts on firm & gd/soft, loves fibresand.			
4525}	**SWAN HUNTER** 45 [3] D J S Cosgrove 4-9-3 N Callan (3) 5/2: -00002: 6 b h Sharrood - Cache (Bustino)	12		55a
	Held up, prog halfway, led over 3f out, rdn/hdd over 2f out & sn held: op 7/4: 6 wk abs: rnr-up earlier in '99			
	(h'cap, rtd 91a): '98 wnr at W'hampton (h'cap, rtd 82a, unplcd on turf, rtd 74): eff btwn 12f & 2m: acts on gd,			
	hvy & equitrack, loves fibresand/W'hampton: gd weight carrier.			
--	**MR SPECULATOR** [8] J L Spearing 6-9-3 (tbl) T Sprake 6/1: 00/0-3: 6 ch g Kefaah - Humanity	8		47a
	(Ahonoora) Led/dsptd lead 11f, fdd: op 10/1: long Flat abs, jumps fit (mod recent form, Aug/Oct wnr 4 times			
	over timber, rtd 96h): last rcd on the Flat in '97, won at W'hampton (1st time blnks, h'cap, rtd 55a, J Banks):			
	eff at 12/14f on fast & fibresand: likes a sharp trk: likes to race with/force the pace.			
--	**CHAHAYA TIMOR** [4] Miss S J Wilton 7-9-3 S Whitworth 10/1: 1164-4: Prom 10f: op 8/1: long abs:	6		41a
	last rcd on the Flat in '98, scored twice here at W'hampton (sells, rtd 73a, first one with R Simpson): mod form			
	over timber in '97: eff at 12/15f: acts on gd & fibresand: likes a sharp trk: enjoys sells.			
4438}	**CREME DE CASSIS** 52 [6] 3-8-5 A Clark 16/1: 0R0035: Prom 10f: op 12/1: 7 wk abs/AW bow.	2½		34a
3571}	**FLORA DREAMBIRD** 99 [2] 3-8-5 Joanna Badger (7) 50/1: -65266: Bhd halfway: jumps fit.	19		20a
70	**DELCIANA** 22 [1] 4-8-12 A McCarthy (3) 25/1: 032407: Keen, led/dsptd lead 1m, sn btn: longer 14.8f trip.	8		12a
3657}	**FIELDGATE FLYER** 99 [5] 4-8-12 R Lappin 50/1: 66-08: Sn bhd: abs/AW bow: now with M Mullineaux.	27		0a
84	**NISIBIS** 19 [9] 3-8-5 G Bardwell 50/1: 009: Dwelt/al bhd: longer 14.8f trip.	6		0a
9 ran	Time 3m 20.3 (10.7) (Ed Weetman) R Hollinshead Upper Longdon, Staffs			

WOLVERHAMPTON (Fibresand)   SATURDAY DECEMBER 11TH   Lefthand, Sharp Track

175 9.30 SANTA CLAUS HCAP 3YO+ 0-70 (E)   6f aw rnd   Going 35   +10 Fast   [70]
£2316   £651   £318

*63   **CHERISH ME** 24 [7] J G Given 3-10-0 (70) T Sprake 3/1 FAV: 523011: 3 b f Polar Falcon - Princess   **83a**
Zepoli (Persepolis) Made all, clr 2f out, pushed out, rdly: hvly bckd, tchd 5/1: fast time: recent wnr here at
W'hampton (C/D mdn, easily): plcd twice earlier in '99 (mdns, rtd 71): eff at 6f, has tried 7f, may suit:
handles fast & gd, taken v well to fibresand: eff weight carrier, sharp trks: one to follow at present.
106   **KEEN HANDS** 17 [2] Mrs N Macauley 3-9-10 (66)(vis) R Fitzpatrick (3) 8/1: 036402: 3 ch g Keen -   3 **69a**
Broken Vow (Local Suitor) Prom, rdn/chsd wnr fnl 1f, kept on tho' al held: op 10/1: caught a tartar, on
a fair mark & could find similar, likes Southwell: see 106.
44   **ALJAZ** 26 [12] Miss Gay Kelleway 9-9-11 (67) T Eaves (7) 8/1: 020223: 9 b g Al Nasr - Santa Linda   2½ **63a**
(Sir Ivor) Chsd ldrs, onepace over 1f: loves this trk, could find similar this winter: see 44.
146   **FACILE TIGRE** 7 [4] S Dow 4-9-1 (57) R Smith (5) 10/1: 020044: Mid-div/not pace to chall: see 146 (5f).   hd **52a**
134   **RING OF LOVE** 10 [6] 3-9-2 (58) R Winston (5) 6/1: 105045: Held up, eff halfway, sn onepace: tchd 9/1.   shd **54a**
*82   **PURPLE FLING** 21 [3] 8-9-7 (63) M Pattinson (7) 11/2: 031316: Rdn/rear, mod gains: op 4/1: see 82.   1½ **54a**
2035} **THAAYER** 99 [8] 4-9-3 (59) D Sweeney 14/1: 200037: Mid-div at best: op 12/1: 6 month abs, earlier   ¾ **48a**
in '99 with K Bell, won at Southwell (stks, rtd 65a at best, no turf form): plcd in '98 (rtd 60a, h'cap, rtd 74 at
best on turf) & gd grnd: prob flattered): eff at 6f, tried 7f: acts on fibresand: now with I Wood.
107   **DONE AND DUSTED** 17 [1] 3-9-7 (63) T Williams 16/1: 000068: Dwelt, al outpcd: op 12/1: see 107 (7f).   7 **39a**
4568} **GRASSLANDIK** 42 [10] 3-9-0 (56) S Whitworth 16/1: 200059: Dwelt/al towards rear: 6 wk abs: rnr-up   ¾ **30a**
twice earlier in '99 (h'caps, rtd 68a & 55): '98 wnr at Southwell (sell, debut, rtd 59a): eff at 5f: acts on
fibresand & gd grnd: likes a sharp/turning trk: has run well fresh: with A Newcombe.
40   **CONSULTANT** 28 [9] 3-9-4 (60) T G McLaughlin 5/1: 600000: Al outpcd: 10th: op 7/1: rnr-up earlier   1 **32a**
in '99 (h'cap, rtd 73a, unplcd on turf, rtd 47, h'cap): '98 wnr twice here at W'hampton (sell & now auct, rtd 80a,
rnr-up on turf, rtd 71, nov): eff over 5/6f, has tried 7f: handles firm/fast & equitrack, loves fibresand/W'hampton.
3770} **BLUNDELL LANE** 98 [11] 4-9-11 (67)(vis) S Drowne 12/1: 600000: Chsd ldrs 5f/wknd qckly: 11th: abs.   3½ **30a**
4471} **CATCHTHEBATCH** 50 [13] 3-9-9 (65) S Carson (5) 14/1: 500300: Chsd ldrs 4f: 12th: op 16/1, abs.   11 **8a**
96   **MYSTIC RIDGE** 18 [5] 5-9-6 (62) J P Spencer 7/1: 113100: Stmbld start, al bhd: 13th, op 4/1.   3½ **0a**
13 ran   Time 1m 14.3 (1.5)   (J R Good)   J G Given Willoughton, Lincs

SOUTHWELL (Fibresand)   MONDAY DECEMBER 13TH   Lefthand, Sharp, Oval Track

Official Going   STANDARD. Stalls: Inside, except 5f - Outside.

176 12.00 LAWRIE HCAP DIV I 3YO+ 0-60 (F)   1m aw rnd   Going 25   -34 Slow   [60]
£1882   £527   £256   3 yo rec 1 lb

75   **STRAVSEA** 24 [16] R Hollinshead 4-8-11 (43) P M Quinn (5) 25/1: 006001: 4 b f Handsome Sailor -   **49a**
La Stravaganza (Slip Anchor) Mid-div halfway, switched left & prog to lead ins last, styd on strongly, rdn out: op
20/1: earlier in '99 won here at Southwell (C/D, fill mdn h'cap, rtd 50a, unplcd on turf, rtd 36, h'cap): plcd form
in '98 (auct mdn, rtd 53a & 44): eff at 7f, suited by 1m: acts on gd/soft, enjoys fibresand/Southwell.
85   **WESTERN RAINBOW** 21 [13] P D Evans 3-8-12 (45) S Drowne 6/1: -00022: 3 b g Rainbows For Life -   2 **46a**
Miss Galwegian (Sandford Lad) Rdn/towards rear, styd on well for press fnl 2f, not pace of wnr: mdn h'cap suit.
4110} **BLOOMING AMAZING** 78 [3] G Woodward 5-9-9 (54) N Callan (3) 9/1: 000053: 5 b g Mazillier - Cornflower ¾ **54a**
Blue (Tyrnavos) Prom, hard rdn/led over 2f out, hdd ins last & no extra: op 7/1: 7 wk jumps abs (mod form):
earlier in '99 with J L Eyre, plcd on turf (rtd 76, h'cap, unplcd on sand, rtd 47a, h'cap): '98 wnr at Beverley (amat
h'cap) & Pontefract (h'cap, rtd 85 & 60a): eff on firm, gd/soft & fibresand: handles any trk,
likes Beverley: eff weight carrier: has run well fresh: eff with/without a visor: potentially v well h'capped.
75   **SOLLYS PAL** 24 [14] P J Makin 4-9-6 (52) A Clark 20/1: 00-004: Trkd ldrs going well halfway, rdn/ev ch   4 **44a**
1f out, no extra: tchd 25/1: unplcd earlier in '99 (rtd 53, mdn): stays 1m & handles fibresand.
38   **DAVIS ROCK** 30 [2] 5-9-9 (55) R Winston 12/1: 035155: Led after 2f till over 2f out, no extra: op 7/1.   ¾ **46a**
4527} **KIRISNIPPA** 47 [17] 4-9-10 (56) O Urbina 33/1: 4P3006: Dwelt/rear, late gains: abs/AW bow.   3½ **40a**
156   **ABSOLUTE MAJORITY** 5 [9] 4-9-9 (55) A McCarthy (3) 20/1: 003047: Chsd ldrs 6f: qck reapp: see 156.   shd **39a**
*38   **KASS ALHAWA** 30 [8] 6-9-8 (54) J Fanning 7/2 FAV: 064318: Led 1f, cl-up 6f: well bckd: btr 38.   4 **30a**
126   **SEA YA MAITE** 13 [1] 5-9-8 (54) S Finnamore (7) 8/1: 021009: Chsd ldrs btr 33 (7f).   nk **29a**
4535} **LADY ODDJOB** 46 [11] 3-9-3 (50)(bl) T G McLaughlin 25/1: 350000: Prom 6f: 10th: 6 wk absence.   3 **19a**
*138   **SHARP SHUFFLE** 12 [12] 6-10-0 (60) R Fitzpatrick (3) 9/1: 020110: Sn towards rear, no impress: 11th: 1 **27a**
op 7/1: prev with I Williams, now with Miss S J Wilton: best in claimers/sellers: see 138 (seller).
*100   **ETISALAT** 91 [6] 4-9-0 (46) A Polli (3) 8/1: 060010: In tch till halfway: 12th: btr 100 (10f, equitrack).   9 **0a**
3886} Positive Air 91 [4] 4-9-5 (51) Kimberley Hart (5) 33/1: 4479} Royal Wave 52 [7] 3-9-11 (58) G Carter 14/1:
495} Julies Jewel 99 [5] 4-9-6 (52) S Righton 20/1: P
15 ran   Time 1m 44.10 (4.7)   (E Bennion)   R Hollinshead Upper Longdon, Staffs.

177 12.30 LAWRIE HCAP DIV II 3YO+ 0-60 (F)   1m aw rnd   Going 25   -18 Slow   [60]
£1871   £524   £254   3 yo rec 1 lb

97   **FLITE OF LIFE** 20 [8] W R Muir 3-9-10 (57) N Callan (3) 20/1: 000051: 3 gr g Forzando - Frighten The   **68a**
Life (King's Lake) Trkd ldrs going well halfway, led 2f out, styd on strongly & asserted ins last, rdn out:
op 14/1: rtd 64 earlier in '99 (unplcd): rnr-up in '98 (nurs, rtd 81): eff at 6f, suited by 1m now: acts
on firm, soft & fibresand: likes a sharp trk: first success today, could win again whilst in this form.
3950} **NOBLE CYRANO** 88 [15] G Woodward 4-9-10 (56) R Lappin 10/1: 501002: 4 ch g Generous - Miss   3½ **62a**
Bergerac (Bold Lad) Prom, led over 4f out, rdn/hdd over 2f out, held by wnr ins last: head rest well covered:
op 8/1: 12 wk abs/AW bow: earlier in '99 scored at Haydock (h'cap, rtd 59): plcd on '98 debut for
G Wragg (mdn, rtd 70): eff at 1m: acts on fast, gd & fibresand: handles a sharp/gall trk: has run well fresh.
*69   **BOUND TO PLEASE** 24 [10] P J Makin 4-9-9 (55) A Clark 7/4 FAV: 005013: 4 b g Warrshan - Hong Kong   3 **55a**
Girl (Petong) Prom, led after 2f till over 4f out, held over 1f out: well bckd, tchd 9/4: return to 7f shld suit.
83   **THE BARGATE FOX** 21 [6] D J G Murray Smith 3-9-3 (50) S Whitworth 5/1: 005104: Rdn/towards rear,   2½ **45a**
prog wide over 2f out, nvr threat to ldrs: op 5/1: return to 9f+ should suit: see 60.
142   **PRINCESS KALI** 9 [2] 3-9-7 (54) R Fitzpatrick (3) 16/1: 106255: Chsd ldrs 3f out, held over 1f out.   1 **47a**

66

102 **KING OF TUNES 19** [3] 7-9-9 (55) P Fredericks (5) 14/1: 000046: Dwelt/towards rear, mod gains: op 8/1. *3* **42a**
136 **GODMERSHAM PARK 12** [13] 7-9-4 (50) G Parkin 7/1: 346037: Prom 5f: see 136, 45. *nk* **36a**
76 **SWINO 23** [2] 5-9-6 (52)(vis) S Drowne 20/1: 403408: Prom 5f, fdd: plcd sev times earlier in 99 (rtd 71, h'cap): '98 wnr at Thirsk & Haydock (h'caps, rtd 85): eff over 5/6f: acts on firm & soft grnd, poss handles fibresand: eff in a visor, tried blnks: v well h'capped, return to sprint trips will suit. *3* **32a**
152 **MOONLIGHT FLIT 7** [16] 4-8-13 (45)(VIS) R Winston 12/1: 300059: Chsd ldrs wide 6f: op 10/1: vis. *5* **15a**
111 **SHABAASH 17** [12] 3-8-10 (43) A McCarthy (3) 14/1: 000530: Mid-div at best: 10th: see 111 (equitrack). *hd* **12a**
142 **RA RA RASPUTIN 9** [1] 4-9-8 (54) S Righton 20/1: 200300: Led 2f, sn btn: 15th: op 12/1: blnks omitted. **0a**
65 **Genius 26** [5] 4-9-6 (52) Kimberley Hart (5) 33/1: 4284} **A Chef Too Far 65** [11] 6-9-5 (51)(t) Dale Gibson 12/1:
60 **Kingchip Boy 26** [14] 10-9-13 (59)(bl) K W Marks 16/1:
131 **Time On My Hands 13** [4] 3-9-2 (49)(tbl) S Finnamore (7) 20/1:
100 **Pipe Dream 19** [7] 3-8-12 (45) T G McLaughlin 20/1:
16 ran Time 1m 42.8 (3.4) (Mrs Irene White) W R Muir Lambourn, Berks.

178

1.00 APPR CLASSIFIED CLAIMER 3YO+ 0-60 (G) 1m3f aw Going 25 -45 Slow
£1829 £519 £257 3 yo rec 4 lb

4438} **BOBONA 54** [8] M D I Usher 3-8-5 G Baker (4) 14/1: 003401: 3 b c Interrex - Puella Bona (Handsome Sailor) Held up, prog to chall over 2f out, led over 1f out, asserted ins last, pushed out cl-home: op 10/1, first win, 8 wk abs: plcd earlier in '99 (rtd 28a, mdn h'cap, rtd 45 when unplcd on turf, clmr): eff around 10/12f: acts on fibresand & fast grnd: best without blnks: likes a sharp trk: runs well for an appr: runs well fresh. **31a**
100 **NORTH ARDAR 19** [7] R Brotherton 9-8-11 Paul Cleary 9/2: 300002: 9 b g Ardar - Langwaite (Seaepic) Chsd ldrs halfway, prog & rdn to chall over 1f out, not pace wnr ins last: op 6/1: earlier in '99 scored here at Southwell (C/D, seller, rtd 50a, unplcd on turf, rtd 42, h'cap): '98 Lingfield wnr (2, h'caps, rtd 48a): eff at 1m/12f: acts on firm, soft & likes both AWs: handles any trk, likes a sharp one: enjoys sell grade. *1½* **34a**
138 **ADIRPOUR 12** [6] R Hollinshead 5-8-13 Stephanie Hollinshea 16/1: 000603: 5 gr g Nishapour - Adira (Ballad Rock) Chsd ldrs halfway, prog/ev ch over 1f out, no extra ins last: op 14/1: earlier in '99 scored at Leicester (seller) & Newcastle (clmr, rtd 66, unplcd on sand, rtd 45a): rnr-up in '98 (rtd 47a, N Chance): eff at 6f/11f, both wins at 7f: acts on fast, soft & fibresand: enjoys sell/claim grade & could find similar around 1m. *½* **35a**
124 **MARKELLIS 13** [4] D Carroll 3-8-5 Joanna Badger (4) 10/1: 606004: Chsd ldrs, outpcd halfway, mod gains fnl 2f: op 7/1: blnks omitted. *2½* **27a**
68 **MOONSHIFT 24** [5] 5-9-1 (tvi) W Hutchinson 20/1: 0-0105: Held up, mod gains fnl 3f: op 12/1. *3½* **28a**
4336} **LUCKY NEMO 62** [10] 3-8-11 D Allan (7) 7/1: 000206: Towards rear, mod gains: tchd 8/1, 2 month abs. *2½* **24a**
136 **OVER THE MOON 12** [3] 5-8-12 D Kinsella (4) 6/1: 004567: Prom/led over 2f out, hdd/wknd 1f out: op 4/1. *½* **20a**
4134} **EMPERORS GOLD 76** [2] 4-9-5 D McGann (4) 16/1: 000-08: Sn prom, fdd fnl 2f: op 10/1: 11 wk abs. *shd* **27a**
2920} **WAITING KNIGHT 99** [1] 4-8-13 (vis) Sarah Robinson (7) 4/1 FAV: 605029: Led after 2f till over 2f out, sn btn & eased ins last: op 5/2: 5 month abs: earlier in '99 scored at Lingfield (mdn, rtd 62a): plcd in '98 (rtd 76, mdn, B Hanbury): eff at 7f/9f, tried further: acts on fast, soft & both AWs: eff in a vis: likes a sharp trk. *1½* **19a**
75 **SOUNDS COOL 24** [9] 3-8-9 S Finnamore 16/1: 300000: In tch 1m: 10th: op 12/1. *4* **13a**
83 **Quakeress 21** [16] 4-8-6 (Et) D Williamson (7) 25/1: 60 **Forest Robin 26** [11] 6-9-7 Kristin Stubbs (7) 11/1:
142 **Jato Dancer 9** [14] 4-8-8 A Hawkins (4) 33/1: 174 **Delciana 2** [12] 4-8-8 J Bosley (4) 14/1:
1725} **Sea God 99** [15] 8-8-13 R Farmer (2) 20/1: 1993} **Chameli 99** [13] 4-8-8 D Meah (6) 14/1:
16 ran Time 2m 29.00 (7.7) (Mrs J Black) M D I Usher Kingston Lisle, Oxon.

179

1.30 VIPER AUCT MDN 2YO (F) 5f aw str Going 25 +01 Fast
£2158 £606 £295

77 **DANCING EMPRESS 23** [2] M A Jarvis 2-8-7 N Callan (2) 11/8 FAV: 323021: 2 b f Emperor Jones - Music Khan (Music Boy) Sn prom, rdn over 1f out & edged right, led ins last, styd on well, rdn out: gd time: hvly bckd: plcd 4 times on turf in '99 (rtd 78): eff at 5f/6f: acts on firm, gd/sft & fibresand: likes a sharp trk. **80a**
34 **MISS SKICAP 31** [3] T D Barron 2-8-4 R Winston 4/1: 42: 2 b f Welsh Captain - Miss Nelski (Most Secret) Sn cl-up, rdn/ev ch when hmpd/briefly lost momentum over 1f out, switched & kept on for press tho' not pace wnr: op 11/4: eff at 5f on fibresand: a likely type for similar & 6f shld suit. *1½* **71a**
120 **FOXY BROWN 16** [14] Miss I Foustok 2-8-0 M Henry 14/1: 2023: 2 b f Factual - Miltak (Risk Me) Sn pushed along/cl-up, briefly led over 1f out, kept on onepace: op 10/1: see 120 (seller). *shd* **67a**
127 **DIAMOND RACHAEL 13** [12] Mrs N Macauley 2-8-2 (vis) R Fitzpatrick (2) 6/1: 034: Led, rdn/hdd over 1f out, no extra: tchd 8/1: see 127. *1* **67a**
4582} **STAND BY 41** [1] 2-8-4 L Charnock 33/1: 005: Rdn chasing ldrs, nvr able to chall: 6 wk abs/AW bow: unplcd both turf starts earlier in '99 (rtd 40): return to 6f+ & h'cap company shld suit. *3* **62a**
127 **PACK A PUNCH 13** [11] 2-8-2 Dale Gibson 10/1: 46: Cl-up, ch 2f out, rdn/hung left & wknd: op 7/1. *1¾* **56a**
34 **CHRISTOPHERSSISTER 31** [13] 2-8-0 G Bardwell 7/1: 664527: Sn rdn/towards rear, mod gains: op 5/1. *1¼* **51a**
2 **SWYNFORD ELEGANCE 35** [8] 2-8-0 A Polli (3) 33/1: 06058: Chsd ldrs 3f: unplcd on turf earlier in '99 (rtd 58, auct mdn): dam a winning miler: with J Hetherton. *¾* **49a**
-- **BILLYS BLUNDER** [6] 2-8-0 (t) Joanna Badger (7) 25/1: 9: Dwelt/al towards rear: op 10/1, debut. *½* **47a**
46 **DIAMOND VANESSA 28** [10] 2-8-0 N Carlisle 33/1: 000: Dwelt/al rear: 10th: stablemate of 8th. *½* **45a**
1921} **Diamond Georgia 99** [9] 2-8-2 (E) J Fanning 20/1: 74 **Lammoski 24** [5] 2-8-9 S Drowne 50/1:
-- **Just The Job Too** [7] 2-8-7 T Eaves (7) 25/1: 128 **Niciara 13** [4] 2-8-5 S Carson (3) 25/1: P
14 ran Time 59.00 (1.2) (The C H F Partnership) M A Jarvis Newmarket.

180

2.00 LADBROKE HCAP DIV I 3YO+ 0-85 (D) 6f aw rnd Going 25 -01 Slow [84]
£5017 £1516 £738 £349

87 **DAHLIDYA 21** [3] M J Polglase 4-7-12 (54)(2ow)(9oh) A McCarthy (0) 10/1: 000531: 4 b f Midyan - Dahlawise (Caerleon) Slowly away & rdn/bhd, stdy prog for press over 2f out, strong run ins last to lead line: op 14/1: stiff task: plcd form earlier in '99 (rtd 54a, seller): '98 wnr at W'hampton & Southwell (h'caps, rtd 52a): eff at 5/6f, stays 7f & has tried further: acts on fibresand, prob handles equitrack & gd/soft grnd: runs well for an appr: best without blnks: likes a sharp trk, esp Southwell: gd ride from A McCarthy today. **59a**
*106 **BLAKESET 19** [4] T G Mills 4-9-8 (78)(bl) A Clark 6/1: 026012: 4 ch c Midyan - Penset (Red Sunset) Cl-up & clr with ldr after 2f, led halfway & still clr over 1f out, rdn/hdd line: had the rest well covered: eff at 6/7.5f: acts on firm, gd & both AWs: front running tactics well suited to sand, shld win more races: see 106. *hd* **82a**
116 **ERRO CODIGO 16** [6] S E Kettlewell 4-7-13 (55) L Charnock 33/1: 410003: 4 b g Formidable - Home Wrecker (Affiliation Order) Chsd ldrs, kept on onepace fnl 2f, no threat: earlier in '99 scored at Lingfield (h'cap, rtd 56): '98 wnr here at Southwell (mdn, rtd 70a at best, rtd 65 on turf, h'cap): eff at 6/7f, tried 9f: acts on *3* **52a**

firm, gd/soft & fibresand: handles any trk: best without a visor: on a fair mark.
121 **DAYS OF GRACE 16** [1] L Montague Hall 4-8-6 (62) L Newman (5) 4/1: 413124: Dsptd lead till halfway, btn fnl 1f: op 3/1: see 121 (7f, fill h'cap). *hd* **58a**
*47 **GARNOCK VALLEY 28** [9] 9-8-11 (67) G Carter 4/1: 002115: Towards rear/wide, mod gains for press. *1¼* **60a**
*129 **JUWWI 13** [5] 5-10-0 (84) Claire Bryan (7) 7/2 FAV: 026215: Dwelt, mod gains fnl 2f: ddhtd for 5th. *dht* **77a**
78 **CARAMBO 23** [7] 4-9-0 (70) N Callan (3) 16/1: 304007: Chsd ldrs 4f, eased/btn fnl 1f: earlier in '99 scored at Nottingham (first time blnks, fill h'cap, J L Eyre): dual rnr-up in '98 (h'caps, rtd 82): '97 W'hampton wnr (2, h'caps, rtd 86a): eff at 6f/1m: acts on fast, gd/soft & fibresand: eff in blnks, not worn today: with T D Barron. *13* **39a**
129 **OCKER 13** [2] 5-9-4 (74) R Fitzpatrick (3) 9/2: 554608: Unruly in stalls, slowly away, nvr factor: appeared to lose chance today in preliminaries: see 47 (C/D). *2½* **36a**
2106} **HIBAAT 99** [8] 3-8-8 (64) S Carson (5) 50/1: 0-0509: Chsd ldrs 3f, sn btn: 6 month abs/AW bow: h'cap debut: unplcd earlier in '99 on turf (rtd 64, mdn, P T Walwyn): rtd 79 on sole start in '98: now with M C Chapman. *3* **19a**
9 ran Time 1m 14.8 (1.5) (The Lovatt Partnership) M J Polglase Southwell, Notts.

181

2.30 STAG SELLER 2YO (G) 6f aw rnd Going 25 -32 Slow
£1840 £515 £250

145 **UNFORTUNATE 9** [2] Miss J F Craze 2-8-7 N Carlisle 4/1: 060021: 2 ch f Komaite - Honour And Glory (Hotfoot) Held up, prog over 2f out, rdn to lead ins last & asserted, pushed out cl-home: op 5/1: bght in for 3,800gns: unplcd on turf earlier in '99 (rtd 35): eff at 5f, suited by 6f on fibresand: tried blnks. **53a**
80 **PRICELESS SECOND 23** [7] J A Glover 2-8-12 (bl) N Callan (3) 16/1: -06052: 2 b g Lugana Beach - Early Gales (Precocious) Led, rdn/edged left 2f out, hard rdn/hdd ins last & no extra: op 20/1: unplcd on turf earlier in '99 (rtd 54, P Calver): eff at 6f, has tried 1m: acts on fibresand: eff in blnks. *1¼* **54a**
42 **LADY SANDROVITCH 30** [4] R A Fahey 2-8-7 R Winston 4/1: 5443: 2 b f Desert Style - Mauras Pride (Cadeaux Genereux) Held up in tch, rcd keenly, switched & prog to chall 1f out, onepace ins last: op 3/1: unplcd earlier in '99 (rtd 50 & 51a): eff at 5/6f: prob handles soft grnd & fibresand & a sharp/turning track *1* **47a**
74 **BARRYS DOUBLE 24** [5] C W Fairhurst 2-8-12 (vis) J Fanning 13/2: 003004: Chsd ldrs, rdn/ch 1f out, onepace: op 5/1: plcd earlier in '99 (nurs, rtd 61a, unplcd on turf, rtd 67): eff at 6f on fibresand: wears a vis. *shd* **52a**
88 **PETRIE 21** [3] 2-8-12 Paul Cleary (7) 13/8 FAV: 423225: Held up, prog to chall 1f out, onepace: clr rem. *nk* **51a**
127 **EPONA 13** [1] 2-8-7 L Charnock 9/1: 006: Chsd ldr, btn fnl 2f: op 7/1. *7* **33a**
2533} **MOSAIC TIMES 99** [8] 2-8-12 S Whitworth 14/1: 27: Dwelt, sn chsd ldrs wide, btn 2f out: op 8/1, abs. *3½* **29a**
3345} **COOL JUDGE 99** [6] 2-8-12 S Drowne 33/1: 230008: Chsd ldrs, btn over 2f out: 4 month abs/AW bow. *5* **20a**
8 ran Time 1m 16.7 (3.4) (P Walton) Miss J F Craze Elvington, N.Yorks.

182

3.00 VANTAGE HCAP 3YO+ 0-75 (E) 1m6f aw Going 25 -07 Slow [73]
£2794 £784 £382 3 yo rec 7 lb

168 **PRASLIN ISLAND 3** [5] A Kelleway 3-9-4 (70) P Fredericks (5) 3/1: 062121: 3 ch c Be My Chief - Hence (Mr Prospector) Ran in snatches & prom, led after 5f, rdn clr 3f out, styd on well ins last, rdn out: op 5/2, qck reapp: recent W'hampton wnr (mdn): rnr-up thrice earlier in '99 (rtd 76, mdn & 64a, h'cap): eff at 12/14f, stys stiff/undul 2m1f: handles fast, likes both AWs: best without blnks or t-strap: likes to race with/force the pace. **82a**
126 **COUNT DE MONEY 13** [7] S R Bowring 4-8-12 (57) S Finnamore (7) 11/4 FAV: 512522: 4 b g Last Tycoon - Menominee (Soviet Star) Prom, chsd wnr 3f out, rdn & kept on in last tho' al held: clr rem. *4* **63a**
4525} **URGENT SWIFT 47** [4] A P Jarvis 6-9-8 (67) W Ryan 8/1: 050523: 6 ch g Beveled - Good Natured (Troy) Held up, prog 5f out, no impress front pair over 2f out: op 6/1: 6 wk abs: AW bow: earlier in '99 scored at Salisbury & Haydock (h'caps, rtd 78): plcd over hdles in '98 (2m, gd & hvy, rtd 101h): unplcd in '98 (rtd 54, h'cap): eff at 12/14f: enjoys firm & gd, handles gd/soft: best without blnks: handles any trk. *11* **61a**
70 **MARTHA REILLY 24** [11] Mrs Barbara Waring 3-7-10 (48)(4oh) G Bardwell 14/1: 040034: Held up, eff halfway, btn 4f out: op 10/1: see 70 (12f). *8* **33a**
37 **SUDDEN SPIN 31** [3] 9-8-3 (48) J Fanning 16/1: 0/0-05: Chsd wnr 5f out, btn 3f out: no form on sole start earlier in '99: well bhd sole start in '98 (h'cap): '97 wnr here at Southwell (h'cap, J Norton, rtd 66a, subs unplcd on turf): eff at 12f/2m: acts on fast, hvy & fibresand: best without a visor: likes Southwell. *1¼* **31a**
124 **PIPE MUSIC 13** [8] 4-9-4 (63)(vis) Dale Gibson 6/1: 500236: Sn rdn, al twds rear: op 4/1: btr 124. *1¼* **44a**
4519} **FLETCHER 48** [6] 5-9-10 (69) C Rutter 14/1: 023007: Trkd ldr, led after 2f till 9f out, sn btn: op 10/1: topweight: abs/AW bow: plcd form earlier in '99 (rtd 73, stks): '98 Ascot wnr (amat h'cap, rtd 79): eff at 12f/2m: acts on firm & gd, relishes soft grnd: best coming late: handles any trk, likes a stiff one. *14* **35a**
3636} **DALWHINNIE 99** [2] 6-7-10 (41)(6oh) P M Quinn (5) 14/1: 000508: Bhd halfway: op 10/1, jumps fit. *5* **0a**
4148} **DOUBLE RUSH 75** [1] 7-8-13 (58) G Carter 14/1: 543069: Led 2f, btn 5f out: op 20/1: 8 wk jmps abs. *24* **0a**
9 ran Time 3m 04.3 (4.5) (Kevin Hudson) A Kelleway Newmarket.

183

3.30 LADBROKE HCAP DIV II 3YO+ 0-85 (D) 6f aw rnd Going 25 +05 Fast [84]
£5017 £1516 £738 £349

132 **MARENGO 12** [2] M J Polglase 5-7-10 (52)(2oh) G Bardwell 9/1: 405301: 5 b g Never So Bold - Born To Dance (Dancing Brave) Made all, rdn fnl 2f & duelled with rnr-up ins last, styd on gamely, all out: fast time: op 7/1: won first 3 '99 starts at, Southwell, W'hampton & Epsom (h'caps, rtd 69a & 68, J Akehurst, also rnr-up for J Berry, rtd 66): eff at 6f, tried 7f: acts on firm, soft & fibresand: loves to force the pace on a sharp trk. **58a**
*143 **ALMAZHAR 9** [1] J L Eyre 4-9-4 (74) S Drowne 9/4 FAV: 631212: 4 b g Last Tycoon - Mosaique Bleue (Shirley Heights) Trkd ldrs/sn rdn, prog to chall over 1f out, hard rdn ins last, just held nr fin: jockey given a 2-day ban for misuse of whip: well clr rem: op 5/2: tough & progressive, lost little in defeat: just best at 7f? *½* **78a**
129 **GENERAL KLAIRE 13** [7] B A McMahon 4-9-3 (73) R Winston 100/30: 215653: 4 b f Presidium - Klairover (Smackover) Chsd ldrs, rdn/outpcd over 2f out, kept on to take 3rd, no ch front pair: see 129. *7* **64a**
4342} **MUTAHADETH 61** [3] D Shaw 5-8-5 (61)(bl) N Callan (3) 10/1: 200404: Chsd ldrs, sn rdn, kept on onepace fnl 2f, no threat: 2 month abs: earlier in '99 scored at W'hampton (clmr) & here at Southwell (h'cap, rtd 63a at best): '98 wnr again here at Southwell (clmr, rtd 71a, also rtd 46): eff at 6/7f, suited by 1m: handles gd & firm, fibresand/sharp trk specialist: eff with/without blnks: enjoys claimers, apprec return to 1m. *2* **47a**
129 **ASTRAC 13** [8] 8-10-0 (84) T G McLaughlin 100/30: 400335: Chsd ldrs, rdn/held fnl 2f: op 5/2. *3½* **61a**
-- **MY TYSON** [5] 4-8-12 (68) G Parkin 33/1: 0000-6: Held up in tch, outpcd over 2f out: op 16/1, long abs: last rcd in '99 (unplcd, rtd 54 & 45a, h'caps, K Mardi): '97 Lingfield wnr (mdn, rtd 68a, rtd 66 on turf): eff at 5f, has tried 1m: acts on equitrack & poss handles fast grnd: likes a sharp trk: with J Ryan. *1½* **41a**
33 **SO WILLING 31** [4] 3-8-6 (62) Dale Gibson 20/1: 020007: Cl-up, wknd fnl 2f: op 14/1: earlier in '99 scored here at Southwell (C/D, auct mdn, subs rnr-up in h'caps, rtd 66 & 66a): plcd in '98 (rtd 66 & 64a): eff at 6f, tried 7f: acts on fibresand & hvy grnd, prob handles gd/soft: handles a sharp or stiff/undul track *2* **30a**

SOUTHWELL (Fibresand)   MONDAY DECEMBER 13TH   Lefthand, Sharp, Oval Track

4604} **SNAP CRACKER 39** [6] 3-8-10 (66) J Fanning 14/1: 040408: Al rear: op 10/1: now with D Chapman.   8   19a
8 ran   Time 1m 14.5 (1.2)   (Ian Puddle)   M J Polglase Southwell, Notts.

SHA TIN   SUNDAY DECEMBER 12TH   Righthand Track

Official Going   GOOD/FIRM

184   7.10 GR 2 HONG KONG MILE 3YO+   1m   Good/Firm
£314973   £119472   £54306   £25524   3 yo rec 1 lb

16   **DOCKSIDER 36** [8] J W Hills 4-9-0 O Peslier 23/20 FAV: 212631: 4 ch c Diesis - Pump (Forli)   122
Led after 2f, kicked clr ent str, ran on strgly: earlier in '99 won at Newmarket (stks), Baden-Baden (Gr 3) &
Hoppergarten (Gr 2), also rnr-up in the Sussex Stks & plcd in the Breeders Cup (Gr 1's, rtd 122): '98 Sandown
wnr (stks, rtd 115): v eff at 1m, stays 10f & loves firm & gd grnd: tough & high-class colt.
4418} **FIELD OF HOPE 56** [10] P Bary 4-9-0 S Guillot 10/1: 511612: 4 ch f Selkirk - Fracci (Raise A Cup)   1¾   116
--   **RESFA** [9] D Hayes 5-9-3 B Marcus 64/10 FAV: 351463: 5 b h Fitzcarraldo - Bethel (Good Manners)   nk   118
4324} **MUHTATHIR 63** [11] Saeed bin Suroor 4-9-3 L Dettori 68/10: -25414: -:   nk   118
4168} **WALLACE 73** [5] 3-8-13 R Hughes 43/1: 314200: -:   21   0
12 ran   Time 1m 34.7   (Gary A Tanaka)   J W Hills Upper Lambourn, Berks

185   8.20 GR 2 HONG KONG VASE 3YO+   1m4f   Good/Firm
£314973   £119472   £54306

123   **BORGIA GER 14** [2] A Fabre 5-9-0 O Peslier 293/10: 520501: 5 b m Acatenango - Britannia (Tarim)   120
3701} **BIMBOLA 99** [7] J Bertran de Balanda 5-8-11 T Gillet 49/1: 611252: 5 br m Bikala - Agnes Lily   hd   116
(Raise A Cup) -:
2479} **SEA WAVE 99** [11] Saeed bin Suroor 4-9-0 L Dettori 68/10: U0-343: 4 b c Sadler's Wells - Three Tails ½   118
(Blakeney) -:
4420} **SILVER PATRIARCH 56** [10] J L Dunlop 5-9-3 Pat Eddery 37/10: 441320: -:   7   0
11 ran   Time 2m 30.1   (Gestut Ammerland)   A Fabre France

186   9.00 GR 1 HONG KONG CUP 3YO+   1m2f   Good/Firm
£449961   £170675   £84104   £36462

16   **JIM AND TONIC 36** [8] F Doumen 5-9-0 G Mosse 73/20: 126201: 5 ch g Double Bed - Jimka (Jim French)   126
55   **RUNNING STAG 26** [12] P Mitchell 5-9-0 S Sellers 25/1: 151422: 5 b h Cozzene - Fruhlingstag (Orsini) 3¾   120
4399} **LEAR SPEAR 57** [5] D R C Elsworth 4-9-0 T Quinn 13/1: 110103: 4 b c Lear Fan - Golden Gorse (His   1½   118
Majesty) -:
4399} **KABOOL 57** [4] Saeed bin Suroor 4-9-0 L Dettori 78/10: 422334: -:   1¼   116
12 ran   Time 2m 01.4   (J D Martin)   F Doumen France

WOLVERHAMPTON (Fibresand)   WEDNESDAY DECEMBER 15TH   Lefthand, Oval, Sharp

Official Going   STANDARD. Stalls: Inside, except 7f - Outside.

187   12.50 AVON HCAP DIV I 3YO+ 0-60 (F)   7f aw rnd   Going 40   -30 Slow   [58]
£1934   £542   £263

121   **MUJAS MAGIC 18** [1] Mrs N Macauley 4-10-0 (58)(vis) R Fitzpatrick (3) 10/1: 653401: 4 b f Mujadil -   64a
Grave Error (Northern Treat) Bhd, imprvd after halfway, led dist, rdn out: op 8/1: earlier in '99 won at Beverley
(h'cap, rtd 51 & 59a, K Ivory): '98 Brighton wnr (h'cap, rtd 59): eff at 5f-7f: acts on firm, soft grnd & fibresand:
best winner og or blnkd, suited by sharp trks, handles any: reportedly in season when disapp last time.
8   **CITY REACH 37** [3] P J Makin 3-9-10 (54) D Sweeney 8/1: 006532: 3 b g Petong - Azola (Alzao)   1¼   57a
Trkd ldrs, led 2½f out till 1f out, stayd on for press: drifter from 11/2, clr rem: acts on hvy grnd & both AWs.
3321} **CHURCHILLS SHADOW 99** [11] B A Pearce 5-9-5 (49) O Urbina 11/2: 012453: 5 b h Polish Precedent -   5   42a
Shy Princess (Irish River) Dwelt, stdy prog halfway, rdn bef fnl 1f, same pace: tchd 8/1, hdles fit (no form):
earlier in '99 wnr at Cheptsow (sell h'cap, rtd 53 at best): '98 wnr at Doncaster (appr h'cap, rtd 50): dual '97
wnr at Lingfield (h'cap, rtd 57a): eff at 7f/1m on fast & gd grnd & equitrack, worth another try on fibresand.
107   **DOLPHINELLE 21** [8] R Hannon 3-9-13 (57)(VIS) R Winston 10/1: 404654: Led till 2½f out, no extra.   ¾   49a
75   **CHALUZ 26** [12] 5-9-7 (51)(t) T G McLaughlin 7/2 JT FAV: 645225: Prom, onepce appr fnl 2f: op 5/2.   2½   38a
132   **LIVELY JACQ 14** [5] 3-9-7 (51)(vis) P M Quinn (5) 12/1: 540046: Al same pl: tchd 16/1: see 132.   3   32a
136   **LILANITA 14** [9] 4-9-3 (47) Joanna Badger (7) 7/2 JT FAV: 504327: Nvr a factor, hung left in str: ½   27a
tchd 16/1: new stable, now with P D Evans: unsuited by drop back to 7f2: see 45 (1m).
59   **THE THIRD CURATE 29** [10] 4-9-4 (48) J P Spencer 9/2: 000008: Chsd ldrs halfway: tchd 7/1: no   shd 28a
worthwhile form since coming over from Ireland, June '99 wnr at The Curragh (7f h'cap, gd): has tried blnks.
139   **LEMON STRIP 14** [2] 3-9-1 (45) L Newman (5) 9/1: 042449: Keen, chsd ldrs till 3f out: Ingr trip, see 63.   1½   22a
134   **PRESELI MAGIC 14** [14] 3-8-13 (43) S Drowne 20/1: 655550: Nvr trbld ldrs: 10th, op 14/1: unplcd earlier 2½   16a
in '99 (fill h'cap, rtd 41): plcd in '98 (auct mdn, rtd 60): stays 6f, handles firm grnd, without visor.
87   **Compton Amber 26** [6] 3-8-11 (41) L Charnock 25/1: 69   **Mybotye 26** [7] 6-9-0 (44)(tbl) R Lappin 25/1:
12 ran   Time 1m 31.6 (4.9)   (Miss P Phillips)   Mrs N Macauley Sproxton, Leics.

188   1.20 THAMES NURSERY HCAP 2YO 0-85 (D)   7f aw rnd   Going 40   -29 Slow   [82]
£3566   £1080   £527   £251

*150 **CHURCH FARM FLYER 9** [9] C N Allen 2-7-12 (52)(6ex) P M Quinn (5) 5/1: 066311: 2 b f College Chapel -   62a
Young Isabel (Last Tycoon) Dwelt, grad imprvd, hung left under press ent fnl 2f, led below dist, ran on strgly:
tchd 8/1: recent Lingfield wnr (sell): unplcd on turf (sell, rtd 53): eff at 7f/1m: acts on both AWs, sharp trks.

128   **CROSBY DONJOHN** 15 [4]   E Weymes 2-8-2 (56)(bl)   F Norton 33/1: 505002: 2 ch c Magic Ring - Ovidea (Domynsky) Cl-up, led after 3f, kicked 3L clr turning from home, hdd ent fnl 1f, kept on: promise prev in '99 (mdn, rtd 73, nurs, rtd 64): eff at 7f: goes on fibresand, handles fast: eff in blnks, up with the pace.   1¼   63a

26   **THATS ALL FOLKS** 34 [11]   P J Makin 2-9-4 (72)   A Clark 8/1: 0633: 2 b c Alhijaz - So It Goes (Free State) Outpcd, kept on fnl 2f, nvr on terms: op 9/2: prob handles fibresand, return to 1m likely to suit: see 26.   3½   73a

158   **SOFISIO** 7 [10]   W R Muir 2-9-4 (72)   N Callan (3) 7/2: 402144: Well plcd, eff appr fnl 2f, same pace.   shd   73a

4498}   **SPECIAL PROMISE** 51 [7]   2-8-1 (55) L Charnock 20/1: 66005: Bhd, some late hdwy: 7 wk abs, AW bow: unplcd in 4 starts on turf earlier in '99 (5f clmr, rtd 61): with P Haslam.   3½   50a

127   **FOR HEAVENS SAKE** 15 [3]   2-8-7 (61) J Fanning 2/1 FAV: 0466: Led till after 3f, under press bef 2f out, fdd: nicely bckd tho' tchd 6/4: more expected on h'cap bow stepped up to 7f: better last twice at Southwell.   2½   51a

4514}   **DUN DISTINCTLY** 50 [1]   2-8-0 (54) Dale Gibson 20/1: -40007: Nvr dngrs: AW bow, 7 wk abs, stablemate 5th: well btn all 4 earlier starts on turf: half-brother to a 5f juv wnr.   1¼   42a

171   **LA TORTUGA** 4 [8]   2-9-7 (75)(bl) Joanna Badger (7) 14/1: 440458: Chsd ldrs wide for 4f: tchd 20/1.   ¾   62a

128   **AISLE** 15 [5]   2-8-5 (59) R Fitzpatrick (3) 10/1: 001169: Prom 3f: op 6/1: see 128.   9   30a

128   **MADEMOISELLE PARIS** 15 [2]   2-7-10 (50)(4oh) M Henry 33/1: 060400: Handly till 2f out: 10th.   1¼   19a

41   **ISABELLA R** 32 [6]   2-8-9 (63) D Sweeney 25/1: 25320: Well plcd till wknd qckly 3f out: 11th, nicely bckd from 4/1: surely something amiss on h'cap bow after 41 (C/D mdn).   9   17a

11 ran   Time 1m 31.0 (4.8)   (Felix Snell)   C N Allen Newmarket.

---

189   **1.50 RIVER IDLE MDN 3YO+ (D)   1m1f79y aw   Going 40   +04 Fast**
£2801   £848   £414   £197   3 yo rec 2 lb

1647}   **TROIS** 99 [10]   G Woodward 3-9-0 T G McLaughlin 25/1: 5-4001: 3 b g Efisio - Drei (Lyphard) Dwelt, mid-div, eff to lead ent fnl 2f, rdn clr ins last: best time of day, 7 month abs, AW bow: modest prev for L Cumani: apprec step up to a sharp 9.3f on fibresand: goes well fresh.   67a

133   **HEATHYARDS JAKE** 14 [9]   R Hollinshead 3-9-0 P M Quinn (5) 5/1: 002622: 3 b c Nomination - Safe Bid (Sure Blade) Dwelt, trkd ldrs wide 4f out, kept on for press being dist, no ch wnr: op 6/1: due a win: see 39.   3½   60a

56   **ROYAL FLAME** 29 [13]   J W Hills 3-9-0 M Henry 7/2: 442643: 3 b f Royal Academy - Samnaun (Stop The Music) Rear, prog after halfway, led 2½f out till bef dist, same pace: op 5/1: rnr-up on turf earlier in '99 (mdn, rtd 70): eff at 9f on soft grnd, prob handles both AWs.   nk   55a

114   **POLISH FALCON** 19 [5]   R Hannon 3-9-0 P Dobbs (5) 20/1: 004: Early ldr, chall 2f out, fdd appr fnl 1f: drifter from 12/1: first sign of form for this 32,000gns yearling: fibresand bow, drop back to 1m?   3   55a

4426}   **DENS JOY** 57 [3]   3-8-9 M Tebbutt 5/2: 35: In tch, niggled 4f out, kept on tho' nvr able to chall: 8 wk abs, AW bow: plcd on turf sole prev start (mdn, rtd 65): eff at 7f, worth another try at 9f: handles fast grnd.   1¼   48a

3721}   **AZZAN** 99 [1]   3-9-0 V Slattery 25/1: 404006: Bhd ldrs, not much room appr str, sn no extra: op 16/1, clr rem, 15 wk abs, AW bow: cl-up 4th of 13 on reapp earlier in '99 for J Dunlop (h'cap, rtd 76): rtd 77 at best in '98 (mdn): stays 1m on gd grnd, without blnks & t-strap: now with T Keddy.   1½   51a

4496}   **SWAMPY** 51 [8]   3-9-0 S Righton 12/1: 006U27: Chsd ldrs till wknd ent fnl 3f: 7 wk abs, op 8/1: thrice rnr-up earlier in '99 on turf (mdn h'cap, rtd 66 & 56a, N Callaghan): prob flattered to a '98 mdn for K McAuliffe (rtd 79): eff at 1m/9.5f on gd/soft & hvy grnd, poss handles fibresand?   9   39a

114   **ROTHERHITHE** 19 [2]   3-9-0 F Norton 9/1: 0038: Led after 2f till 2½f out, wknd: lngr trip, f/sand bow.   12   23a

144   **SPANKER** 11 [11]   3-8-9 (BL) M Hills 2/1 FAV: 634239: Well plcd till 3f out: nicely bckd, blnkd.   3½   13a

--   **PREDOMINANT** [12]   3-9-0 K W Marks 8/1: 0: Al bhd: 10th, op 4/1 on debut: related to sev wnrs.   1   17a

4330}   **Occam** 64 [6]   5-9-2 S Drowne 100/1:   --   **Royal Mount** [4] 3-9-0 A Daly 16/1:
133   **Two Step** 14 [7]   3-8-9 Dale Gibson 25/1:

13 ran   Time 2m 04.0 (5.8)   (Mrs Jo Hardy)   G Woodward Brierley, S.Yorks.

---

190   **2.20 CUCKMERE HCAP DIV I 3YO+ 0-65 (F)   2m46y aw   Going 40   -53 Slow**   [62]
£1913   £536   £260   3 yo rec 8 lb

141   **ROYAL EXPRESSION** 11 [13]   F Jordan 7-9-10 (58)   N Callan (3) 7/2: 205201: 7 b g Sylvan Express - Edwins' Princess (Owen Dudley) Held up, prog after 1m, rdn to lead ent fnl 2f, pshd well clr: top-weight, slow time, visor omitted: earlier in '99 won at Nottingham (h'cap, rtd 71): missed '98, '97 Redcar wnr (clmr, rtd 78): has won over hdles: eff at 12f/2m: acts on firm, gd/soft & f/sand, without visor: gd weight carrier, handles any trk.   64a

117   **CRASH CALL LADY** 18 [12]   C N Allen 3-7-10 (38)(4oh) P M Quinn (5) 8/1: 025432: 3 b f Batshoof - Petite Louie (Chilibang) Rear, imprvd after halfway, styd on for 2nd ins last, no threat to wnr: op 6/1: gd run 4lbs o/h: prob worth another try at 2m with more positive tactics: see 89.   10   36$

4407}   **SCONCED** 58 [1]   Martyn Wane 4-7-12 (32)(VIS) L Charnock 12/1: 400533: 4 ch g Affirmed - Quaff (Raise A Cup) Cl-up, led after 1m till ent fnl 2f, fdd: visored, clr rem: well btn in 2 recent hdles: well btn on turf earlier in '99, incl on sand (btn 22L, h'cap, rtd 31a at best): '98 Hamilton wnr (mdn, rtd 64, h'cap, rtd 71, G Wragg), subs joined current connections for 21,000gns: eff at 9/10f on fast & soft grnd.   1   29a

182   **DALWHINNIE** 2 [10]   J G Given 6-8-1 (35)(bl) F Norton 11/2: 005004: Held up, prog to chase ldrs 6f out, btn 3f out: run 48hrs ago, blnks reapp: in Oct '99 plcd over timber (mdn, 2m6f on gd/soft grnd, rtd 85h): no worthwhile Flat form since '98 wnr at Southwell (auct mdn, rtd 51a) & Yarmouth (clmr, rtd 55 at best, J Wharton): eff at 12/14f on firm, soft grnd & fibresand, any trk: eff with/without blnks.   17   19a

124   **DANKA** 15 [6]   5-8-4 (38) J Bosley (6) 8/1: 004005: Handy till outpcd 6f out: earlier in '99 won at Southwell (sell, rtd 49a): plcd in '98 (mdn, rtd 53a): eff at 11/12f: acts on both AWs, with/without vis (not worn).   1   21a

2005}   **ALAKDAR** 99 [2]   5-8-12 (46) S Drowne 12/1: 0-0026: Led for 1m, lost pl 5f out: op 10/1, hdles fit, plcd in 98/99 (nov, rtd 91h, R Champion): 2nd of 4 earlier in '99 (AW clmr, rtd 59$, B Meehan): back in '97 won at Catterick (rtd mdn, rtd 74, A Stewart): eff at 12f/2m on fast, soft & fibresand.   1¼   28a

131   **SOUHAITE** 15 [3]   3-8-3 (45) J Fanning 7/4 FAV: 006137: Keen, trkd ldrs, going well 4f out, sn rdn, wknd qckly: nicely bckd from 9/4: lkd a non-stayer over lngr 2m trip: well worth another chance back at 12f.   nk   27a

3978}   **MUSALSE** 88 [4]   4-9-5 (53) T Eaves (7) 8/1: 006008: Nvr in it, t.o.: op 5/1, 3 month abs.   20   19a

70   **FRONTIER FLIGHT** 26 [7]   9-7-11 (31)(1ow)(7oh) A McCarthy (0) 25/1: /00569: Nvr trbld ldrs.   6   0a

70   **IRSAL** 26 [9]   5-7-10 (30)(7oh) M Henry 20/1: 060050: Prom 1m, t.o.: 10th, stiff task.   25   0a

66   **CLASSIC REFERENDUM** 28 [11]   5-9-2 (50) J P Spencer 8/1: 000000: Chsd ldrs till halfway: 11th.   dist   0a

11 ran   Time 3m 44.3 (15.1)   (Mrs A Roddis)   F Jordan Risburh, H'forshire.

191	2.50 LADBROKE HCAP 3YO+ 0-85 (D) 5f aw rnd Going 40 00 Fast	[83]
	£4045 £1224 £597 £283	

44	**YABINT EL SHAM** 30 [5] B A McMahon 3-8-5 (60) L Newman (5) 25/1: 000001: 3 b f Sizzling Melody - Dalby Dancer (Bustiki) Chsd ldrs, rdn ent str, ran on well to lead towards fin: t-strap omitted, 2nd AW start: well btn earlier in '99 (h'cap, rtd 74): juv wnr at Leicester (mdn, rtd 87): eff at 5f, poss stays 6.5f, tried 7f: acts on fast grnd & fibresand, stiff or sharp trk: looks on a handy mark & is capable of following up.	66a
91	**PALACEGATE JACK** 22 [1] J Berry 8-7-11 (52)(bl)(1ow)(2oh) L Charnock 14/1: 634052: 8 gr g Neshad - Pasadena Lady (Captain James) Tried to make all, worn down well ins last: earlier in '99 won at Newcastle (sell, rtd 58, clmr, rtd 62a): '98 Catterick wnr (clmr, rtd 60): won 5 times in '97 (rtd 68 & 70a): 5f specialist on any grnd/trk: wears blnks: forces the pace & is a genuine 8yo.	1¼ 54a
113	**AFAAN** 19 [6] R F Marvin 6-9-12 (81)(bl) T G McLaughlin 4/1 FAV: 550433: 6 ch h Cadeaux Genereux - Rawaabe (Nureyev) Prom, ev ch ent str, onepace ins last: well bckd, blnks reapp: ran to best.	nk 82a
+146	**MANGUS** 11 [3] K O Cunningham Brown 5-9-11 (80) N Callan (3) 5/1: 202014: Cl-up, outpcd ent str, late rally: consistent sort on sand tho' shade btr 146 (C/D, made all).	1 78a
4288}	**AURIGNY** 67 [2] A Clark 9/1: 510005: Front rank, ch ent fnl 2f, no extra: op 7/1, AW bow, 10 wk abs: earlier in '99 nrw at Goodwood (3 rnr class stks, rtd 91 & 95$): back in '97 won at Brighton (mdn) & Newbury (List, rtd 104): eff at 5f on firm & soft grnd, prob handles fibresand, any trk: can force the pace.	½ 80a
129	**MUKARRAB** 15 [8] 5-9-12 (81) A Culhane 16/1: 035006: Wide, nvr going pace: op 12/1: earlier in '99 nrw at Lingfield (4 h'caps, rtd 87a & 54): '98 wnr again at Lingfield (2, h'caps, rtd 55a) & Thirsk (mdn h'cap, rtd 53): eff at 5/6f on fast, soft grnd, fibresand, equitrack/Lingfield specialist: best without blnks, can carry big weights: back on a winning mark, watch out for him at Lingfield.	nk 77a
146	**SAMWAR** 11 [7] 7-9-6 (75)(vis) R Fitzpatrick (3) 7/2: 001157: Slow away, nvr in it: see 139 (C/D).	nk 71a
*116	**FRILLY FRONT** 18 [4] 3-8-3 (58) Lynsey Hanna (7) 4/1: 303418: Dwelt, last when edged into rails after 2f, nvr nr ldrs: op 3/1: stewards inquired into what appeared to be tender riding in fnl 1f: jockey reported that the filly had nothing left to give & hung left thr'out: well worth another look when reunited with a stronger jockey.	1½ 50a
8 ran	Time 1m 02.2 (2) (G S D Imports Ltd) B A McMahon Hopwas, Staffs.	

192	3.20 SEVERN SELLER 2YO (G) 7f aw rnd Going 40 -44 Slow	
	£1945 £545 £265	

4589}	**COME ON MURGY** 42 [11] A Bailey 2-8-6 J Bramhill 20/1: 000601: 2 b f Weldnaas - Forest Song (Forzando) In tch, hdwy to lead appr fnl 1f, hung left ins last, rdn out: op 10/1, no bid, slow time: 6 wk abs: unplcd all prev starts (rtd 53 & 48a at best, tried blnks): apprec step up to a sharp 7f on fibresand: runs well fresh.	54a
155	**WISHEDHADGONEHOME** 7 [5] P D Evans 2-8-6 (VIS) Joanna Badger (3) 16/1: 005002: 2 b f Archway - Yavarro (Raga Navarro) In tch, rdn to impr over 2f out, styd on well, post came too soon : op 12/1, clr rem: qck reapp: 4th at best prev in '99 (cond stks, rtd 74): eff at 7f on fibresand: galvanized by first time visor.	½ 52a
125	**SAMARARDO** 15 [2] N P Littmoden 2-9-2 T G McLaughlin 3/1: 061203: 2 b g Son Pardo - Kinlet Vision (Vision) Cl-up, rdn & not pace of ldrs appr fnl 1f: drop in trip: btr in 80 (8.5f).	3 56a
150	**RIDGECREST** 9 [1] R Ingram 2-8-11 S Drowne 5-4 FAV: 030424: Chsd ldrs, rdn & outpcd ins last: well bckd: more expected back in trip: btr 150 (1m sell, equitrack).	nk 50a
74	**CARDINAL FAIR** 26 [9] 2-8-6 R Lappin 33/1: 05: Bhd, gd hdwy over 2f out, no extra ins last: see 74.	½ 44a
155	**KIGEMA** 7 [6] 2-8-11 L Newman 14/1: 415506: Led, hdd over 1f out, wknd for press ins last: op 8/1, qck reapp: earlier in '99 scored at Brighton (seller, rtd 66): eff over a sharp/undul 6f on fast grnd.	hd 49a
118	**BASIC INSTINCT** 18 [7] 2-8-6 F Norton 16/1: 03507: Chsd ldrs, lost tch fnl 2f: op 7/1: plcd once for M H Tompkins earlier in '99 (seller, rtd 52a at best): eff at 7f on fibresand.	3½ 38a
74	**NATSMAGIRL** 26 [10] 2-8-11 (vis) G Carter 20/1: 300058: Wide, sn with ldrs, wknd fnl 2f: see 74.	3 37a
4089}	**TALLYWHACKER** 81 [8] 2-8-6 G Bardwell 33/1: 09: Al bhd: 12 wk abs, AW bow.	nk 31a
145	**BLAZING PEBBLES** 11 [1] 2-8-6 A McCarthy (3) 50/1: 000000: Al outpcd, fin 10th: modest form.	nk 31$
36	**K ACE THE JOINT** 33 [4] 2-8-11 R Winston 33/1: 000: Cl-up, wknd qckly fnl 2f, 11th: no form.	2 32a
4597}	**IMARI** 41 [3] 2-8-6 J Fanning 2/1: 444640: Prom, wknd fnl 2f, 12th: 6 wk abs: AW bow, can do better.	¾ 26a
12 ran	Time 1m 32.1 (5.9) (K W Weale) A Bailey Little Budworth, Cheshire.	

193	3.50 AVON HCAP DIV II 3YO+ 0-60 (F) 7f aw rnd Going 40 -04 Slow	[58]
	£1934 £542 £263	

75	**FOREIGN EDITOR** 26 [6] R A Fahey 3-9-2 (46) R Winston 16/1: 066541: 3 ch g Magic Ring - True Precision (Presidium) Made all, clr 2f out, rdn to hold on: op 12/1, first win: unplcd earlier in '99 (h'caps, rtd 54 & 41a, tried blnks): plcd in '98 (mdn, rtd 67): eff at 5f/7f: acts on gd/soft & fibresand: qk follow-up?	58a
*173	**SAND HAWK** 4 [5] D Shaw 4-9-5 (49)(bl)(6ex) N Callan (3) 3/1: 004512: 4 ch g Polar Falcon - Ghassanah (Pas de Seul) Dwelt, sn handy, hdwy over 2f out, hung right over 1f out, hung left for press ins last, styd on strongly, just held: nicely bckd, well clr rem: qck reapp: in fine heart, can win again soon: see 173.	nk 59a
4075}	**ABERKEEN** 82 [4] M Dods 4-9-10 (54) A Culhane 10/1: 520603: 4 ch g Keen - Miss Aboyne (Lochnager) Bhd, gd hdwy 2f out, no extra over 1f out: op 8/1, 12 wk abs: earlier in '99 won at Doncaster (appr h'cap, rtd 61, also rtd 55a): plcd in '98 (h'cap, rtd 82): '97 Pontefract scorer (nov stks, rtd 81 at best): eff at 6/7f, has tried 10f: acts on firm, gd/soft & fibresand: acts on a stiff/gall track.	5 54a
4566}	**INVIRAMENTAL** 46 [12] D Haydn Jones 3-9-4 (48)(BL) F Norton 20/1: 0504: Cl-up, lost pl over 2f out, sn no extra: op 12/1, 6 wk abs: tried in blnks on h'cap bow: unplcd prev in '99 (mdns, rtd 53 & 60).	3 43a
138	**CANTGETYOURBREATH** 14 [7] 3-9-0 (44)(bl) A McCarthy (3) 25/1: 000005: Cl-up, lost tch fnl 2f: plcd once for Mrs N Macauley earlier in '99 (h'cap, rtd 66a, modest form on turf): late '98 scorer at Southwell (seller, rtd 71a): eff at 6f: acts on fast, soft & both AWs: eff in blnks/visor, the former suit.	2 35a
139	**RIVERDANCE** 14 [10] 3-8-13 (43)(bl) Joanna Badger (7) 14/1: 060006: Nvr better than mid-div.	½ 33a
*148	**HAUNT THE ZOO** 9 [8] 4-9-9 (53)(6ex) J Bramhill 9/4 FAV: 546117: Held up, eff halfway, nvr a threat: nicely bckd, back up in trip: below par here on at-hat-trick bid: much better up in trip (6f, equitrack).	1¼ 41a
133	**ABLE MILLENIUM** 14 [1] 3-9-13 (57) G Carter 9/1: 3338: Sn in rear: btr 133 (8.5f).	1 43a
136	**BLUSHING GRENADIER** 14 [3] 7-9-7 (51)(bl) S Finnamore (7) 11/2: 500349: Chsd ldrs, wknd fnl 2f.	nk 37a
106	**GADGE** 21 [2] 8-9-5 (49) D Hayden (7) 11/4: 060340: Handy, short of room & wknd 3f out: 10th: nicely bckd (8/1 - 11/4): poss prefers equitrack or Southwell fibresand: btr 106, 83.	1¼ 33a
147	**ENTROPY** 9 [9] 3-8-11 (43) G Bardwell 16/1: 000050: Well plcd, lost tch fnl 3f: 11th.	9 12a
136	**IMBACKAGAIN** 14 [11] 4-8-11 (41)(t) T G McLaughlin 14/1: 360000: In tch, wknd qckly fnl 2f: 12th.	3½ 5a
12 ran	Time 1m 29.4 (3.1) (Pride Of Yorkshire Racing Club) R A Fahey Butterwick, N.Yorks.	

WOLVERHAMPTON (Fibresand) WEDNESDAY DECEMBER 15TH Lefthand, Oval, Sharp

194 **4.20 CUCKMERE HCAP DIV II 3YO+ 0-65 (F)** **2m46y aw Going 40 -33 Slow** **[60]**
£1913 £536 £260 3 yo rec 8 lb

167 **MAKNAAS 5** [5] T G Mills 3-8-7 (47) A Clark 6/4 FAV: 034531: 3 ch c Wolfhound - White Wash (Final Straw) Chsd ldr in clr 2nd, hdwy to lead 5f out, styd on strongly: nicely bckd from 7/2, qck reapp: up in trip, first win: plcd on turf earlier in '99 for R Armstrong (mdn h'cap, rtd 49 & 44a): eff at 1m/13f, apprec this step up to 2m: acts on soft grnd & both AWs: has run well in blnks, prob best without. **52a**
4438} **MEDELAI 56** [10] Mrs A E Johnson 3-7-11 (37)(1ow)(4oh) A McCarthy (0) 20/1: 500502: 3 b f Marju - No Islands (Lomond) Waited with, gd hdwy 4f out, no extra ins last: 9 wk abs: new stable: unplcd on turf earlier in '99 (h'caps, rtd 47 at best, J Bethell): '98 Nottingham wnr (seller, rtd 59): eff at 1m/10f, stays 2m well: acts on gd, soft & fibresand: likes a stiff/gall track, handles any. *2* **39a**
141 **ABOO HOM 11** [8] S Dow 5-9-3 (49)(t) O Urbina 12/1: 35/003: 5 b h Sadler's Wells - Maria Waleska (Filiberto) Bhd, gd hdwy 4f out, styd on, nrst fin: stays 2m on fibresand: see 141. *1* **50a**
170 **MY LEGAL EAGLE 4** [12] R J Price 5-8-10 (42) Claire Bryan (7) 7/2: 053204: Rear, gd hdwy 5f out, not pace of ldrs fnl 2f: qck reapp: see 141. *nk* **42a**
3305} **KAID 99** [2] 4-8-6 (38) A Daly 9/1: 060005: Waited with, prog 5f out, hung right & no extra appr fnl 1f: op 7/1: 4 month abs, AW bow: unplcd prev in '99 for Mrs B Waring (h'caps, rtd 51 at best, tried blnks): plcd on the level in '98 for E Dunlop (mdn, rtd 67): stays 10f, poss 2m on gd grnd & fibresand. *2* **36a**
*141 **BEAUCHAMP MAGIC 11** [1] 4-8-4 (36) G Baker (7) 6/1: 000016: Rear, hdwy over 5f out, wknd 2f out. *1¾* **32a**
68 **MANFUL 26** [6] 7-8-0 (32)(bl) F Norton 9/1: 040307: Nvr better than mid-div: op 6/1: up in trip: earlier in '99 scored at Ayr (h'cap, rtd 61, Miss L Perratt): '98 wnr again at Ayr (h'cap, rtd 64 at best): eff at 10/12f, poss not stay 2m: acts on fast & both AWs, likes soft grnd: wears blnks: well h'capped on old form. *3* **25a**
4535} **LADY IRENE 48** [7] 3-7-10 (36)(1oh) Gary Bardwell 16/1: 040428: Chsd ldrs, wknd 5f out, t.o.: abs. *dist* **9a**
144 **SPARTAN HEARTBEAT 11** [9] 6-9-10 (56) Joanna Badger (7) 20/1: /02-09: Al bhd, t.o.: up in trip. *5* **0a**
4412} **DANGER BABY 58** [3] 9-9-5 (51)(bl) V Slattery 8/1: 3/3140: Settled rear, rdn & lost tch 5f out, t.o.: 10th: tchd 12/1: AW bow: jumps fit (2m3.5f h'cap chase, refused 4 out): temperamental character. *shd* **0a**
4458} **MUSKETRY 55** [11] 3-7-10 (36)(BL)(4oh) A Polli (3) 6/1: -00000: Led, 15L clr halfway, wknd & hdd 5f out, qckly lost tch: 11th: op 25/1: AW bow: 8 wk abs, tried in blnks: no form: with N Graham. *20* **0a**
4045} **Talib 85** [13] 5-7-12 (30)(t)(2ow)(10oh) L Charnock 50/1:
2503} **Lugana Lady 99** [4] 3-7-10 (36)(VIS)(6oh) J Lowe 33/1:
13 ran Time 3m 41.1 (11.9) (Travel Spot Ltd) T G Mills Headley, Surrey.

SOUTHWELL (Fibresand) FRIDAY DECEMBER 17TH Lefthand, Sharp, Oval Track

Official Going STANDARD. Stalls: 5f - Outside; Rem - Inside.

195 **11.45 BRUNEI CLAMIER DIV 1 3YO+ (F)** **1m aw rnd Going 28 -22 Slow**
£1882 £527 £256 3 yo rec 1 lb

4449} **PIPPAS PRIDE 58** [5] S R Bowring 4-8-6 R Winston 25/1: 140401: 4 ch g Pips Pride - Al Shany (Burslem) Chsd ldrs, rdn to lead over 3f out, hdd 2f out, rallied for press & drvn out to lead cl-home: 8 wk abs: earlier in '99 scored at Lingfield (h'cap, rtd 41a, with M Fetherston Godley): no worthwhile form in prev 2 seasons: eff arnd a sharp 1m, has tried 10f: likes to race up with or force the pace on both AWs: runs well when fresh. **57a**
142 **ODDSANENDS 13** [11] C N Allen 3-8-13 L Newman (5) 6/1: -46022: 3 b c Alhijaz - Jans Contessa (Rabdan) Cl-up, hdwy to lead over 2f out, drvn & hdd cl-home: clmd by T D Barron for £9,000: eff at 6f/1m. *½* **62a**
136 **TEMPRAMENTAL 16** [8] D Haydn Jones 3-8-2 F Norton 14/1: 000553: 3 ch f Midhish - Musical Horn (Music Boy) Prom, rdn over 2f out, styd on, no threat to ldrs: clr rem: off rtd 41: see 136. *1¾* **48$**
130 **PRINCIPAL BOY 17** [6] Miss J F Craze 6-8-2 N Carlisle 16/1: 465304: Dwelt, v keen & short of room 5f out, rdn to impr over 2f out, sn outpcd: nicely bckd: lost ch at start today: see 50. *5* **39a**
-- **MONICAS CHOICE** [1] 8-8-6 R Fitzpatrick (3) 16/1: 6145-5: Rear, late gains no threat: op 12/1: jumps fit, rnr-up at Huntingdon (claim hdle, rtd 92h, eff at 2m/2½m on gd & hvy, any trk): missed '99 on the Flat, prev term won for Mrs M Reveley at Carlisle (clmr, rtd 72 at best): eff at 7f/10f on gd & hvy: with Mrs N Macauley. *1¾* **40a**
*142 **TAKHLID 13** [2] 8-9-8 A Culhane 4/9 FAV: 023116: Led, rdn/hdd over 3f out, wknd: drifted from 1/3: prolific wnr in this grade but something obviously amiss today: much btr 142. *3½* **50a**
2053} **PARLEZ MOI DAMOUR 99** [9] 4-7-13 L Charnock 66/1: 400007: Mid-div at best: jumps fit (mod form): mod form on the level in '99 (rtd 37a at best, tried blnks): poss stays 12f on fibresand. *hd* **27a**
102 **OK BABE 23** [3] 4-8-9(5ow) O Urbina 33/1: 000008: Al in rear: unplcd on the level prev in '99 (rtd 49 at best, tried visor), '98 wnr here at Southwell (h'cap, rtd 72a, J Akehurst): eff at 6f on fast, likes fibresand. *9* **23a**
126 **MIGWAR 17** [4] 6-9-2 T G McLaughlin 14/1: 000049: Cl-up, lost tch fnl 3f: op 10/1: btr 126 (11f). *1* **28a**
3655} **FOURTH TIME LUCKY 99** [7] 3-8-4(3ow) G Parkin 33/1: 200060: Nvr a factor, fin 10th: long abs. *1½* **14a**
-- **Pretty Fly Guy** [12] 3-8-7 S Whitworth 50/1: 83 **Bicton Park 25** [10] 5-8-8 J Bosley (7) 50/1:
193} **Giniski Park 99** [13] 3-8-0 A Polli (3) 66/1:
13 ran Time 1m 43.4 (4.0) (Roland M Wheatley) S R Bowring Edwinstowe, Notts.

196 **12.15 MAURITIUS MED AUCT MDN 3-4YO (F)** **1m3f aw Going 28 -46 Slow**
£2116 £594 £289 3 yo rec 4 lb

4435} **PLURALIST 59** [4] W Jarvis 3-9-0 M Tebbutt 4/11 FAV: 265621: 3 b c Mujadil - Encore Une Fois (Shirley Heights) Made all, easily went clr 2f out, hard held: won with any amount in hand: nicely bckd tho' op 1/4, 8 wk abs: rnr-up twice earlier in '99 (auct mdn & h'cap, rtd 77): rnr-up at York & Epsom in '98 (rtd 76+, mdns): eff at 9/11f & further could suit: acts on firm, gd & f/sand: impressive AW bow, can rate more highly. **58+**
4520} **TOY STORY 52** [6] Miss Gay Kelleway 3-9-0 S Whitworth 5/1: 0602: 3 b g Fijar Tango - Grundygold (Grundy) Mid-div, hdwy to chall halfway, kept on appr fnl 2f, no threat to easy wnr: op 4/1, 7 wk abs: unplcd in 3 turf mdns prev in '99 (rtd 60 at best): eff at 11f on fibresand: caught a tartar here, win a mod event. *3* **46$**
144 **TALECA SON 13** [3] D Carroll 4-9-4 R Fitzpatrick (3) 16/1: 305043: 4 b g Conquering Hero - Lady Taleca (Exhibitioner) Cl-up, rdn to impr 3f out, sn not pace of ldrs: treat rating with caution, off 31: see 144. *1½* **44$**
69 **WESTWOOD VIEW 28** [10] Ronald Thompson 3-8-9 A Clark 33/1: 000004: Rcd wide mid-div, eff over 3f out, onepcd over 2f out: up in trip on AW bow: plcd twice earlier in '99 (h'caps, rtd 54, tried visor/blnks, with J J Quinn): eff at 5/6f, poss styd this longer 11f trip: acts on fast & hvy grnd: off rtd just 33. *2* **36$**

70}	**TANTISPER** 99 [1] 3-9-0 G Bardwell 25/1: -500-5: Cl-up, drvn & outpcd appr fnl 2f: long abs: up in trip: unplcd in 3 starts in late '98 (rtd 60 & 22a, auct mdn): treat rating with caution.		5	34$
45	**SHOTLEY MARIE** 32 [2] 4-8-13 (bl) A Culhane 20/1: 000056: Bhd, prog 5f out, btn 3f out: mod jmps form.		9	15a
3498}	**MOLLYTIME** 99 [8] 3-8-9 R Brisland (5) 33/1: 000507: Mid-div, hdwy 3f out, sn lost tch: long abs.		2½	11a
3371}	**DEVILS NIGHT** 99 [9] 4-9-4 D Sweeney 33/1: -0-008: Al bhd: long abs, no form.		¾	15$
63	**KINGS CHAMBERS** 30 [5] 3-9-0 (bl) S Righton 33/1: 0-09: In tch, wknd halfway, t.o.: no form.		20	0a
917}	**ELENII** 99 [7] 3-8-9 O Urbina 50/1: -0500: Prom, wknd over 3f out, t.o. in 10th: long abs, new stable.		23	0a
10 ran	Time 2m 29.5 (8.2)	(The Pluralist Partnership)	W Jarvis Newmarket.	

---

197   12.45 BRUNEI CLAIMER DIV 2 3YO+ (F)   **1m aw rnd Going 28 -05 Slow**
£1871   £524   £254   3 yo rec 1 lb

130	**RAMBO WALTZER** 17 [13] D Nicholls 7-8-8 F Norton 4/1: 000141: 7 b g Rambo Dancer - Vindictive Lady (Foolish Pleasure) Chsd ldrs, hdwy to lead over 3f out, strongly pressed ins last, drvn out to hold on: recently won here at Southwell (sell): earlier in '99 scored at Catterick, Thirsk (h'caps, rtd 71) & again at Southwell (clmr, rtd 75a): '98 W'hampton & Southwell wnr (2, h'caps, rtd 91a & 72): eff at 7/9.5f on fast & soft, loves f/sand: sharp trk specialist, loves Southwell: runs well fresh & best in sell/claim grade: tough & genuine.			66a
60	**INTERNAL AFFAIR** 30 [7] T D Barron 4-8-12 Lynsey Hanna (7) 11/2: 615462: 4 b g Nicholas - Gdynia (Sir Ivor) Dwelt, gd hdwy over 2f out, ran on strongly ins last, just held: gd effort, win similar this winter.		½	67a
96	**BORDER GLEN** 24 [5] D Haydn Jones 3-9-1 S Drowne 8/1: 005433: 3 b g Selkirk - Sulitelma (The Minstrel) Cl-up, rdn to impr 2f out, not pace of ldrs fnl 1f: gd effort, clr rem: see 96 (h'cap, equitrack).		1¾	68$
129	**ROUGE** 17 [9] J P Leigh 4-9-1 D Sweeney 4/1: 231204: Cl-up, no extra fnl 2f: op 3/1: better expected at the weights today: btr 79 (h'cap).		3½	61a
131	**CAREQUICK** 17 [8] 3-8-6 G Carter 33/1: 000005: Led, hdd over 3f out, wknd over 1f out: unplcd prev in '99 (mdn & h'cap, rtd 53 & 33a at best, tried blnks): rtd 67 at best in '98 (mdn): off rtd 39.		¾	51a
101	**WITHOUT FRIENDS** 23 [10] 5-8-5(1ow) A Clark 33/1: 004006: Rdn in tch, mod gains fnl 2f, no dngr: earlier in '99 scored here at Southwell (h'cap, rtd 55a): '98 Lingfield wnr (3, sell/h'caps, rtd 67a, with J F Heyes): eff at 1m/10f on firm, gd/soft & both AWs: eff in a visor, has tried blnks: likes Lingfield.		3	44$
138	**APPROACHABLE** 16 [1] 4-8-8 (VIS) C Rutter 15/2: 166247: Prom, no dngr fnl 3f: op 13/2, visor.		1¼	45a
1036}	**JIBEREEN** 99 [6] 7-9-2 S Whitworth 7/2 FAV: 435208: Sn rdn in rear, nvr a factor: op 11/4, long abs: wnr here at Southwell early in '99 (clmr, rtd 84a): turf rnr-up (h'cap, rtd 51): '98 wnr at Southwell (amat h'cap, rtd 77a & 56): eff at 7f/1m, stys 9.4f: acts on gd, soft & fibresand: sharper next time.		8	41a
138	**WARRIOR KING** 16 [3] 5-8-2 L Charnock 50/1: 060009: Al in rear.		1¼	25a
156	**RUNNING BEAR** 9 [2] 5-8-6 T Williams 33/1: 000550: Sn outpcd: fin 10th: see 138.		2	25a
156	**PRIME SURPRISE** 9 [4] 3-8-1(1ow) N Carlisle 50/1: 000000: Sn bhd, fin 11th: stiff task.		3	15a
4125}	**Polar Refrain** 81 [12] 6-7-11 P M Quinn (5) 50/1:	3517} **Major Morris** 99 [14] 4-8-6 J Fanning 50/1:		
13 ran	Time 1m 42.0 (2.6)	(W G Swiers)	D Nicholls Sessay, N.Yorks.	

---

198   1.15 BELIZE MDN 2YO (D)   **1m aw rnd Going 28 -19 Slow**
£2794   £784   £382

4210}	**ELEGANT ESCORT** 76 [11] Mrs G S Rees 2-9-0 S Whitworth 9/2: 31: 2 b c Take me Out - Get With It (King Pellinore) Settled in tch, gd hdwy to lead 2f out, rdn clr ins last: 11 wk abs: showed promise on sole prev start in '99 (6f mdn, fibresand): half-brother to sev wnrs in the USA: eff at 1m, further cld suit: runs well fresh on fibresand: impressive wnr today, can rate more highly & win again.			73a
4582}	**SEA SQUIRT** 45 [10] M Johnston 2-9-0 J Fanning 1/1 FAV: 622: 2 b c Fourstars Allstar - Polynesian Goddess (Salmon Leap) Cl-up, led 4f out, hdd 2f out, styd on but not pace of wnr: op 8/11, 6 wk abs, AW bow, clr rem: rnr-up earlier in '99 (auct mdn, rtd 79): eff at 7f/1m on soft grnd & fibresand: met an improving rival.		3½	67a
149	**DIRECT REACTION** 11 [7] Miss Gay Kelleway 2-9-0 P Fredericks (5) 11/2: 205053: 2 b g College Chapel - Mary's Way (Night Shift) Prom, onepcd fnl 2f: tchd 7/1: prob stays 1m: handles gd grnd & both AWs.		3	62a
4588}	**CANNY HILL** 44 [1] D Moffatt 2-9-0 Darren Moffatt 16/1: 064: Led, hdd over 4f out, no extra fnl 2f: 6 wk abs: up in trip on AW bow: unplcd in 2 turf starts prev in '99 (mdn, rtd 55 at best).		nk	62a
88	**GENTLE ANNE** 25 [2] 2-8-9 A Clark 25/1: 666345: In tch, outpcd fnl 2f: see 36.		5	49a
80	**CUPIDS DART** 27 [14] 2-9-0 A McCarthy 20/1: 663036: Keen in tch, wknd fnl 2f: op 8/1, new stable.		3½	49a
--	**ROYAL CZARINA** [5] 2-9-0 D Dineley 50/1: 7: Cl-up, wknd fnl 3f: M Salaman newcomer.		11	28a
179	**JUST THE JOB TOO** 4 [3] 2-9-0 P Goode (5) 25/1: 08: Prom, wknd over 2f out: modest form.		shd	33a
86	**BARTON LEA** 25 [6] 2-8-9 R Winston 50/1: 09: Nvr a threat: looks poor.		1¾	25a
127	**MAGICAL JACK** 17 [4] 2-9-0 T G McLaughlin 33/1: 000: Sn bhd, fin 10th: no form.		4	24a
--	**SUBADAR MAJOR** [9] 2-9-0 Angela Hartley 33/1: 0: Green, al bhd, 11th: stablemate of wnr.		nk	24a
128	**Jonloz** 17 [8] 2-9-0 M Tebbutt 20/1:	4606} **Flight Refund** 42 [13] 2-9-0 A Culhane 25/1:		
4081}	**Capacoostic** 84 [12] 2-8-9 Dale Gibson 20/1:			
14 ran	Time 1m 43.2 (3.8)	(Times Of Wigan)	Mrs G S Rees Sollom, Lancs.	

---

199   1.45 SOLOMAN SELLER DIV 1 3YO+ (G)   **6f aw rnd Going 28 -07 Slow**
£1574   £439   £212

193	**CANTGETYOURBREATH** 2 [2] B P J Baugh 3-8-12 (bl) J Bosley (7) 8/1: 000051: 3 ch g College Chapel - Cathy Garcia (Be My Guest) Prom, hdwy to lead over 1f out, rdn out: op 7/1, qck reapp: no bid: plcd once for Mrs N Macauley earlier in '99 (h'cap, rtd 66a, modest form on turf): late '98 scorer at Southwell (sell, rtd 71a): eff at 6f: acts on fast, soft & both AWs: off in blnks/visor, the former suits.			55a
177	**PRINCESS KALI** 4 [9] D Carroll 3-9-0 (bl) R Fitzpatrick (3) 4/1 JT FAV: 062552: 3 ch f Fayruz - Carriglegan Girl (Don) In tch, ran on well fnl 1f, nrst fin: nicely bckd, qck reapp: a return to 7f cld suit.		3	49a
--	**READY TO ROCK** [1] J S Moore 3-8-12 A Clark 14/1: 000003: 3 b g Up And At'Em - Rocklands Rosie (Muscatite) Led, hdd over 2f out, rallied briefly appr fnl 1f, no extra ins last: 8 wk abs: ex-Irish, failed to make the frame prev in '99: prob stays 6f on fibresand: apprec drop to sell grade for new connections.		2½	41a
116	**CZAR WARS** 20 [6] P T Dalton 3-9-0 (bl) D Sweeney 7/1: 003504: Handy, no extra fnl 2f: plcd once earlier in '99 (clmr, rtd 43 & 45a): plcd in '98 (rtd 58, h'cap), prev term won at Warwick (auct mdn, rtd 70): eff at 7f, stys 1m/11f: acts on gd/soft & soft.		shd	41a
156	**EMMAJOUN** 9 [10] 4-9-0 M Tebbutt 9/2: 003625: In tch, rdn & no extra fnl 1f: btr 156.		1¾	39a
71	**SUE ME** 28 [7] 7-9-5 F Norton 4/1 JT FAV: 010006: Cl-up, hdwy to lead over 2f out, hdd 1f out & wknd: earlier in '99 scored here at Southwell (clmr, rtd 63a) & Ayr (h'cap, rtd 62): '98 scorer at Southwell (3, h'caps, rtd 61a), Pontefract & Doncaster (appr h'caps, rtd 72): prob stays 1m, best over 5/6f on fast, soft/hvy & e/track, loves fibresand & Southwell: handles any trk: eff with/without blnks & can go well fresh.		2	39a

148 **SAN MICHEL 11** [3] 7-8-12 R Winston 5/1: 050637: Prom, lost tch fnl 2f: btr 148. ½ **31a**
-- **THATCHING LAD** [11] 6-8-12 T Williams 20/1: 8: Sn outpcd: t.o. in bmprs previously. 1¼ **28a**
148 **ROWLANDSONS STUD 11** [8] 6-8-12 (t) T G McLauchlin 33/1: 00-009: Bhd, nvr a factor. *shd* **28a**
134 **SING FOR ME 16** [12] 4-8-7 Stephanie Hollinshead (7) 20/1: 050000: Dwelt, al bhd, fin 10th. *nk* **22a**
187 **PRESELI MAGIC 2** [4] 3-8-7 (BL) S Drowne 14/1: 555500: Cl-up, wknd fnl 3f, 12th: qck reapp, blnks. **15a**
4509} **Time And Again 52** [5] 3-8-7 J Fanning 33/1: 83 **Anchor Venture 25** [13] 6-8-12 (BL) A Culhane 50/1:
13 ran Time 1m 15.4 (2.1) (M J Lyons) B P J Baugh Audley, Staffs.

200

2.15 LADBROKE HCAP 3YO+ 0-90 (C) 1m4f aw Going 28 +06 Fast [90]
£6377 £1931 £943 £449 3 yo rec 5 lb

*81 **BODFARI QUARRY 27** [5] B W Hills 3-8-13 (80)(t) M Hills 4/1: 010011: 3 b f Efisio - Last Quarry **88a**
(Handsome Sailor) Held up, hdwy to chall 2f out, led dist, rdn out: gd time: recent wnr at W'hampton (h'cap): prev in '99 won at Ayr (h'cap) & again at W'hampton (h'cap, rtd 77 & 77a at best): '98 Beverley wnr (debut, fill mdn, rtd 79, Mrs Ramsden): eff at 7/12f, further could suit: acts on fast, gd & fibresand: runs well fresh: suited by waiting tactics: eff in a t-strap, has tried blnks, best without: useful & progressive, can complete hat-trick.
81 **QUINTRELL DOWNS 27** [6] R M H Cowell 4-9-1 (77) M Tebbutt 6/4 FAV: 401132: 4 b g Efisio - *2* **80a**
Nineteenth Of May (Homing) Cl-up, hdwy to lead over 2f out, hdd appr fnl 1f, not pace of wnr: nicely bckd: clr rem: in gd form, can win similar this winter: see 81.
151 **STEAMROLLER STANLY 11** [4] K R Burke 6-8-10 (72)(ebl) D Sweeney 11/2: 036643: 6 b g Shirley Heights *3* **70a**
- Miss Demure (Shy Groom) Led, rdn/hdd 2f out, sn outpcd: ran well today with blnks reapplied: see 151.
170 **LEGAL ISSUE 6** [1] B S Rothwell 7-8-3 (63)(2ow) R Lappin 11/1: 543104: Prom, kept on onepcd *1¾* **61a**
fnl 2f: qck reapp: poss just stays 12f: see 131 (11f).
*172 **KING PRIAM 6** [3] 4-10-2 (92)(bl)(6ex) T G McLaughlin 4/1: 2D1115: In tch, ev ch till fdd appr fnl 2f: *3½* **83a**
qck reapp: 4 timer bid: stays 12f but much better at 1m/10f: see 172 (9.4f, W'hampton).
55 **DYNAMISM 31** [7] 4-9-4 (80) A Culhane 40/1: 450006: Handy, no extra fnl 2f: lkd a useful prospect *2* **68a**
when plcd on '99 reapp (List, rtd 103), disapp subs: trained by H Cecil to win at Ripon in '98 (mdn, rtd 91+): eff at 10f, 12f shld suit in time: acts on fast grnd & runs well fresh: now with Mrs L Stubbs.
4359} **FERNY HILL 64** [8] 5-10-0 (90) J Fanning 10/1: 0-0607: Handy, wknd fnl 2f: recently unplcd over *3* **74a**
hdles (2m Gr 2 nov): unplcd in 3 prev Flat starts in '99 (h'caps, rtd 92 at best): '98 wnr at Windsor (stks, rtd 103): eff over 12/14f on firm, gd & fibresand: can go well fresh.
151 **BE GONE 11** [10] 4-9-9 (85) G Bardwell 10/1: 005038: Dwelt, nvr a threat: btr 151 (equitrack). *nk* **69a**
3214} **SUDEST 99** [9] 5-9-9 (85) S Whitworth 25/1: 122009: Al rear: long abs, new stable. *11* **55a**
9 ran Time 2m 36.9 (2.6) (Bodfari Stud Ltd) B W Hills Lambourn, Berks.

201

2.45 SOLOMAN SELLER DIV 2 3YO+ (G) 6f aw rnd Going 28 -10 Slow
£1563 £436 £210

82 **TROJAN HERO 27** [6] K C Comerford 8-8-12 T G McLaughlin 100/30: 202621: 8 ch g Raise A Man - **60a**
Helleness (Northfields) Chsd ldrs, hdwy to lead dist, drvn out: no bid, declared to run with a t-strap but was unable to be fitted: plcd sev times in '99 (claims & h'cap, rtd 65a, with M Buckley), mod turf form: '98 Warwick wnr (class stks, rtd 63 & 69a): eff at 6f/1m on fast, gd/soft & f/sand: has tried blnks, best without.
1783} **JOHN BOWDLER MUSIC 99** [2] Miss S J Wilton 4-9-5 C Rutter 13/2: 231332: 4 b g Soviet Star - Arianna *1* **65a**
Aldini (Habitat) Prom, ev ch till not pace of ldrs ins last: op 9/2, long abs: earlier in '99 won at Lingfield (h'cap) & here at Southwell (sell, rtd 70a at best): '98 rnr-up (mdn, rtd 67): eff btwn 6f & 8.5f: acts on gd/soft & both AWs: likes to race up with or force the pace on sharp trks: encouraging reapp, spot on next time in similar.
154 **OK JOHN 11** [1] G P Enright 4-8-12 O Urbina 3/1 FAV: 000303: 4 b g Mac's Imp - Ching A Ling *2* **52a**
(Pampapaul) Rdn in mid-div, late gains, nrst fin: see 57.
177 **GENIUS 4** [3] D W Chapman 4-9-5 Lynsey Hanna (7) 33/1: 000004: Dwelt, late gains fnl 2f, nrst fin: *½* **58$**
qck reapp: earlier in '99 won at Lingfield (h'cap, rtd 70a): '98 Lingfield wnr (2, h'caps, rtd 72a & 63): best dominating over 1m, poss stays 10f: acts on both AWs, loves equitrack/Lingfield, handles gd/soft: has tried blnks.
130 **GUNNER SAM 17** [9] 3-9-5 (BL) L Newman (5) 20/1: 006065: Led to over 1f out, wknd: op 10/1, blnks. *¾* **56$**
85 **ABOVE BOARD 25** [8] 4-8-12 S Righton 12/1: 600556: Rdn in rear, modest late gains: unplcd *1¼* **46$**
earlier in '99 (rtd 50a & 42 at best): modest form prev (incl blnkd): treat rating with caution, off just 32.
4385} **TAPAUA 62** [5] 3-8-12 (bl) J Fanning 14/1: 030047: Dwelt, nvr a threat: 9 wk abs: plcd once *1½* **42a**
earlier in '99 (seller, rtd 61 & 60a at best, tried blnks): stays a stiff 7f on firm & fast grnd.
130 **PALACE GREEN 17** [4] 3-9-0 A Culhane 14/1: 200008: Cl-up, no room over 2f out & sn wknd: op 9/1. *nk* **44a**
4133} **VOSBURGH 80** [12] 3-8-12 (bl) R Fitzpatrick (3) 10/1: 002349: Prom, wknd fnl 3f: abs, new stable. *2* **36a**
159 **CAIRN DHU 9** [10] 5-8-12 Kimberley Hart (5) 16/1: 00-020: Al rear, fin 10th: see 159 (7f). *2* **30a**
4328} **THE BLUE BRAZIL 66** [7] 3-8-12 L Charnock 50/1: 500000: Mid-div at best: 11th: jumps fit (no form). *3½* **22a**
130 **BROUGHTONS TURMOIL 17** [11] 10-9-5 S Drowne 7/2: 600130: Prom, wknd 2f out, 12th: btr 65 (7f). *¾* **27a**
12 ran Time 1m 15.6 (2.3) (G J Sargent) K C Comerford Brill, Bucks.

202

3.15 TONGA NURSERY HCAP 2YO 0-85 (E) 5f aw str Going 28 +06 Fast [92]
£2668 £748 £364

4529} **CAXTON LAD 51** [5] P J Makin 2-9-0 (78) A Clark 5/1: 360161: 2 b c Cyrano de Bergerac - Urania **88a**
(Most Welcome) Hmpd start, hdwy to lead over 2f out, rdn & sn clr: op 4/1, gd time, 7 wk abs, AW bow: earlier in '99 scored at Haydock (nurs, rtd 78): eff at 5f, poss stays 6f: acts on gd, soft & fibresand: acts on a sharp or gall trk: won well today, can follow up.
128 **SIRENE 17** [8] M J Polglase 2-7-10 (60)(BL)(7oh) Joanna Badger (7) 14/1: 000102: 2 ch f Mystiko *3½* **61a**
- Breakaway (Song) Cl-up, kept on but not pace of wnr over 1f out: blnks: a return to 7f shld suit: see 88 (7f).
*46 **FEAST OF ROMANCE 32** [6] Miss Gay Kelleway 2-8-8 (72) S Whitworth 2/1: 00513: 2 b c Pursuit Of *1* **70a**
Love - June Fayre (Sagaro) Cl-up, drvn & outpcd ins last: nicely bckd tho' op 6/4: btr 46 (6f, auct mdn).
*165 **OTIME 7** [4] Mrs N Macauley 2-9-2 (80)(vis)(7ex) R Fitzpatrick (3) 10/1: 513014: Prom, rdn & no *¾* **77a**
extra fnl 1f: qck reapp: a return to 6f & equitrack shld suit: see 165.
3742} **TING 99** [1] 2-7-12 (62) Dale Gibson 20/1: -0055: Sn outpcd, late gains fnl 2f: long abs, AW bow: *¾* **58a**
unplcd in 3 prev turf starts in '99 (5/6f mdns, rtd 64 at best).
*105 **JAMES STARK 23** [7] 2-9-7 (85)(bl) G Carter 15/8 FAV: 05116: Dsptd lead, outpcd fnl 1f: top- *¾* **80a**
weight: hat-trick bid: prob needs 6f now: see 105 (equitrack).
1703} **CAUTIOUS JOE 99** [3] 2-9-0 (78) R Winston 8/1: 107: Led, hdd halfway, wknd: long abs, AW bow: *¾* **72a**
prev in '99 won at Newcastle (debut, auct mdn, rtd 76): eff over a gall 5f, 6f shld suit: runs well fresh on fast.
72 **GEM OF WISDOM 28** [2] 2-7-12 (62)(vis)(2ow)(10oh) L Charnock 16/1: 536008: Handy, wknd fnl 2f: *8* **40a**

SOUTHWELL (Fibresand) FRIDAY DECEMBER 17TH Lefthand, Sharp, Oval Track

stiff task: earlier in '99 won twice here at Southwell (sellers, rtd 68a, rtd 59 on turf): eff forcing the pace at 5f, has tried 6f: acts on fast & fibresand: eff in a visor, has tried blnks: a return to sell grade shld suit.
8 ran Time 58.9 (1.1) (Four Seasons Racing Ltd) P J Makin Ogbourne Maisey, Wilts.

LINGFIELD (Equitrack) SATURDAY DECEMBER 18TH Lefthand, V Sharp Track

Official Going STANDARD Stalls: 5f/1m - Outside, Rem - Inside

203 **11.55 TRIDENT HCAP DIV 1 3YO+ 0-60 (F) 1m2f aw Going 18 -15 Slow [60]**
£1882 £527 £256 3 yo rec 3 lb

163 **ROI DE DANSE 8** [3] M Quinn 4-8-8 (40) F Norton 20/1: 000631: 4 ch g Komaite - Princess Lucy (Local Suitor) Made all, rdn fnl 2f, styd on well ins last: rnr-up twice earlier in '99 (h'cap, rtd 58a): '98 Brighton wnr (class stks, rtd 71): eff at 7f, now suited forcing the pace at 10f: acts on gd grnd & equitrack, sharp/undul trks. **45a**
38 **THE STAGER 35** [2] J R Jenkins 7-9-11 (57)(t) S Whitworth 16/1: 100602: 7 b g Danehill - Wedgewood Blue (Sir Ivor) Sltly hmpd 1f, chsd ldrs halfway, rdn/chsd wnr 2f out, kept on tho' held ins last: op 12/1: earlier in '99 won at Southwell (h'cap, rtd 60a & 36): '98 wnr again at Southwell (h'cap, rtd 55a): eff at 7f/1m, stays a sharp 10f: acts on firm, gd & both AWs: handles any trk, likes Southwell: best without blnks/visor. *1½* **59a**
*111 **BECKON 22** [5] B R Johnson 3-9-2 (51) L Newman (5) 4/1 FAV: 300013: 3 ch f Beveled - Carolynchristensen (Sweet Revenge) Mid-div, rdn & kept on fnl 2f, nvr pace to chall: well bckd from 9/1: see 111 (sell). *¾* **52a**
96 **FUSUL 25** [4] G L Moore 3-8-10 (45) G Parkin 20/1: 000004: Towards rear/rdn halfway, switched wide & styd on fnl 2f, no threat to ldrs: unplcd earlier in '99 (rtd 72 & 50a, with B Hanbury): promise in 2 '98 starts (mdns, rtd 72): styd this longer 10f trip today, handles equitrack. *2½* **42a**
161 **SAMMYS SHUFFLE 10** [12] 4-9-9 (55)(bl) O Urbina 5/1: 043325: Chsd ldrs 9f: tchd 7/1: see 161, 22. *1¼* **50a**
161 **ARDENT 10** [14] 5-9-5 (51)(H) S Carson (5) 14/1: 202206: Prom wide 1m: eyehood, op 12/1: see 23. *1* **45a**
90 **FAMOUS 25** [8] 6-8-10 (42) G Bardwell 20/1: 100457: Rdn towards rear, nvr factor: see 90, 22 (C/D). *¾* **35a**
152 **MELLOW MISS 12** [10] 3-9-1 (50) S Drowne 10/1: 500448: Prom 7f: op 12/1: btr 96 (1m). *3½* **38a**
160 **CAERNARFON BAY 10** [1] 4-9-10 (56) A Culhane 9/2: 202629: Trkd ldrs 1m, sn btn: well bckd. *1¼* **42a**
131 **MYSTERIUM 18** [13] 5-9-3 (49) R Thomas (7) 6/1: 041240: Mid-div, btn 2f out: 10th, op 4/1: see 67 (fbrsnd). *½* **34a**
3071} **Mogin 99** [7] 6-8-11 (43) C Rutter 20/1: 110 **Rawi 22** [9] 6-8-13 (45) A Clark 12/1:
81 **Forest Dream 28** [11] 4-10-0 (60) T G McLaughlin 12/1: 78 **Polar Fair 28** [6] 3-9-6 (55) M Tebbutt 14/1:
14 ran Time 2m 06.08 (3.28) (Miss A Jones) M Quinn Sparsholt, Oxon

204 **12.25 A GORRIE MDN 2YO (D) 1m2f aw Going 18 -18 Slow**
£2840 £860 £420 £200

4318} **DOUBLE BANGER 68** [4] M Johnston 2-9-0 J Fanning 1/1 FAV: 341: 2 b c Ela Mana Mou - Penny Banger (Pennine Walk) Trkd ldrs halfway, led 3f out & sn clr, easily: val for 15L+, hvly bckd: AW bow/10 wk abs: unplcd in 2 starts earlier in '99 (rtd 77, stks): eff at 10f, 12f+ will suit: acts on equitrack, prob handles good/soft grnd: likes a sharp trk & runs well fresh: plenty in hand here, could win again on sand. **73a**
54 **BOX CAR 32** [5] G L Moore 2-9-0 F Norton 25/1: 000662: 2 b c Blues Traveller - Racey Naskra (Star de Naskra) Chsd ldrs, rdn/kept on to take 2nd over 1f out, nvr a ch with wnr: clr rem: unplcd earlier in '99 (rtd 64, auct mdn): this longer 10f trip shld suit, prob handles equitrack: will apprec h'cap company. *10* **58a**
164 **OPEN GROUND 8** [3] P Howling 2-9-0 A McCarthy (3) 33/1: 0063: 2 ch c Common Grounds - Poplina (Roberto) Mid-div, rdn halfway, kept on fnl 2f to take 3rd, no threat: longer 10f trip, mod form prev. *5* **51a**
94 **FOSTON FOX 25** [8] C B B Booth 2-8-9 S Whitworth 20/1: 00064: : Prom 6f: op 25/1: longer 10f trip. *8* **37a**
36 **DR DUKE 36** [14] 2-9-0 A Clark 33/1: 000555: Chsd ldrs halfway, sn btn: longer 10f trip, stiff task. *7* **32a**
80 **KAHYASI MOLL 28** [1] 2-8-9 L Newman (5) 50/1: 045006: Mid-div at best: modest form. *11* **15a**
164 **BEACH BABY 8** [2] 2-8-9 G Bardwell 50/1: 07: Prom 5f: longer 10f trip. *2* **12a**
103 **KUWAIT TROOPER 24** [9] 2-9-0 (t) G Carter 5/1: 68: Dwelt, nvr factor: tchd 7/1, t-strap: btr 103 (1m). *¾* **16a**
150 **SHARAVAWN 12** [12] 2-8-9 (bl) T G McLaughlin 50/1: 000009: Sn bhd, longer 10f trip. *shd* **11a**
164 **TIC TAC MAC 8** [11] 2-9-0 A Morris 50/1: -00000: Al rear: 10th: longer 10f trip. *7* **6a**
125 **NO COMMITMENT 18** [10] 2-9-0 K W Marks 33/1: 000000: Bhd 4f out: 11th: longer 10f trip. *nk* **5a**
94 **MASTER JONES 25** [6] 2-9-0 A Culhane 16/1: 000640: Led 6f, sn btn: btr 94 (7f). *3½* **0a**
164 **PORTLAND 8** [7] 2-9-0 D Sweeney 5/2: 0263P: Handy, led 6f out-3f out, broke leg fatally dist. **0a**
13 ran Time 2m 06.44 (3.64) (R W Huggins & P H Wilkerson) M Johnston Middleham, N Yorks

205 **12.55 SEALIFE HCAP 3YO+ 0-70 (E) 5f aw rnd Going 18 -16 Slow [68]**
£2640 £741 £361

*154 **TORRENT 12** [2] D W Chapman 4-9-13 (67)(bl) Lynsey Hanna (7) 9/4 FAV: 223211: 4 ch g Prince Sabo - Maiden Pool (Sharpen Up) Sn cl-up, led 1f out, pshd out to assert: well bckd: recent wnr here at Lingfield (h'cap): earlier in '99 scored at Beverley (class stks, rtd 75): '98 Catterick (mdn) & Thirsk wnr (h'cap, rtd 83, T D Barron): eff at 5/6f, tried 7f: acts on firm, gd/soft & both AWs: prob handles soft: handles any trk, likes Lingfield: eff in blnks: tried a t-strap, best without: runs well for an appr: in fine form, can win again. **73a**
113 **BRUTAL FANTASY 22** [8] P Howling 5-9-9 (63) A McCarthy (3) 12/1: 000002: 5 b g Distinctly North - Flash Donna (Well Decorated) Chsd ldrs wide, rdn & kept on ins last, not pace to chall: op 10/1: earlier in '99 scored at Lingfield (h'cap, P Murphy), subs won for current connections at Ascot (h'cap, rtd 72 at best): rtd 67a & 79 at best in '98 (h'caps, J Eyre): eff at 5f, stays 6f: acts on firm, gd/soft & both AWs: has run well fresh: handles any trk: tried blnks/visor, best without: likes to race with/force the pace: well h'capped, find similar. *1¼* **65a**
162 **WILD THING 10** [4] J J Bridger 3-9-5 (59)(bl) G Bardwell 14/1: 152003: 3 b c Never So Bold - Tame Duchess (Saritamer) Rear/wide & rdn, kept on well fnl 2f, nrst fin: op 10/1: eff at 5f, return to 6f+ will suit. *1* **59a**
139 **AA YOUKNOWNOTHING 17** [6] Miss J F Craze 3-9-8 (62)(vis) T Lucas 6/1: 000334: Led, hdd 1f out, no extra ins last: op 9/2: shade closer to this wnr in 139 (fibresand). *shd* **62a**
166 **FRENCH GRIT 8** [7] 7-8-8 (48) G Parkin 7/2: 230025: Trkd ldrs, onepace over 1f out: see 166 (C/D). *shd* **47a**
139 **ECUDAMAH 17** [1] 3-10-0 (68) T G McLaughlin 6/1: 041246: Rdn/towards rear, nvr on terms: top-weight: acts on both AWs but poss best suited by fibresand: see 40. *1¼* **64a**
166 **ELLWAY PRINCE 8** [10] 4-9-2 (56)(vis) A Clark 10/1: 000047: Cl-up 4f: op 8/1: see 166. *1¼* **49a**
4015} **FAUTE DE MIEUX 89** [3] 4-10-0 (68) S Carson (5) 13/2: 200008: Dwelt, al rear: bckd from 9/1: 3 mth abs, AW bow: earlier in '99 won at Windsor (stks, rtd 77 at best, h'cap, D Morris): rnr-up twice in '98 (rtd 71, mdns, A Jones): eff at 5/6f: acts on firm & hvy grnd, prob handles any trk: tried a t-strap: with E Wheeler. *3* **54a**

LINGFIELD (Equitrack) SATURDAY DECEMBER 18TH Lefthand, V Sharp Track

4280} ROYAL ORIGINE 71 [5] 3-9-1 (55) (tBL) A Culhane 25/1: 006009: Outpcd: blnks: jumps fit, new stable.   5 32a
9 ran   Time 59.52 (1.72)   (Mrs J Hazell)   D W Chapman Stillington, N Yorks

206   1.25 BCS NOV STKS 2YO (D)   7f aw rnd   Going 18 -04 Slow
£3468   £1050   £512   £243

4524} STAYIN ALIVE 52 [6] G A Butler 2-8-12 (t) G Carter 11/2: -441: 2 b c Sword Dance - Marilyn's   90a
Mystique (Dearest Doctor) Trkd ldrs al going well, led over 2f out & sn clr, easily: val 9L+: nicely bckd, tchd 7/1:
8 wk abs/AW bow: unplcd earlier in '99 for P C Hyam & A Foster (mdn, rtd 83): eff over a sharp 7f, stays 1m: acts
on equitrack & gd/soft grnd: runs well fresh: suited by application of t-strap: plenty in hand, looks useful.
*108   INSIGHTFUL 22 [1] R Hannon 2-9-9 P Dobbs (5) 2/1: 025312: 2 b g Desert Style - Insight (Ballad 6 89a
Rock) Led, hdd over 2f out, kept on tho' no ch with wnr: well bckd, op 11/4: caught a tartar: see 108 (C/D).
*112   PERUVIAN CHIEF 22 [2] N P Littmoden 2-9-4 T G McLaughlin 6/5 FAV: 002113: 2 b c Foxhound - shd 84a
John's Ballad (Ballad Rock) Chsd ldrs, rdn 2f out, kept on tho' not able to chall: hvly bckd: see 112 (C/D h'cap).
164   BUGGY RIDE 8 [8] Miss Gay Kelleway 2-8-12 S Whitworth 10/1: 350024: Trkd ldrs, weakened fnl 2f: op 6/1. 1¾ 75$
94   PUDDING LANE 25 [3] 2-8-8 (VIS) (1ow) A Culhane 10/1: 003025: Prom, wknd fnl 1f: op 7/1, visor. 2 67a
4460} LUCKY STAR 58 [5] 2-8-7 D Dineley 50/1: -0666: Trkd ldrs, nvr able to chall: AW bow, 2 month 1¾ 63$
abs: unplcd earlier in '99 (rtd 62, nov stks): stiff task: with D Marks.
54   TATTENHAM STAR 32 [7] A-8-12 S Drowne 25/1: 056357: Chsd ldrs 4f: op 16/1: btr 2 (6f). ½ 67a
164   GOLD KRIEK 8 [4] 2-8-12 W Ryan 33/1: 008: Al towards rear: highly tried. 8 55a
8 ran   Time 1m 24.37 (1.57)   (Gary Seidler)   G A Butler Blewbury, Oxon

207   1.55 THAMESWEY CLAIMER 2YO (F)   6f aw rnd   Going 18 -12 Slow
£2085   £585   £285

165   PARKSIDE PROSPECT 8 [6] M R Channon 2-8-4 J Fanning 9/4: 021231: 2 b f Piccolo - Banner (Known 62a
Fact) Made all, rdn over 1f out, styd on strongly & pulled clr ins last: well bckd, tchd 4/1: claimed for £6,000:
earlier in '99 scored at Newcastle (sell) & Musselburgh (sell h'cap, rtd 68, rnr-up on sand, rtd 46a, clmr): eff
at 5/6f on firm, gd & both AWs: likes to race with/force the pace: handles any trk, likes a sharp one: improving?
4   GREY FLYER 40 [1] Mrs L Stubbs 2-8-11 A Culhane 13/2: 610642: 2 gr g Factual - Faraway Grey (Absalom) 6 58a
Chsd wnr, rdn 2f out, kept on ins last tho' sn held: op 5/1: 6 wk abs: earlier in '99 scored at Musselburgh (clmr,
rtd 66, also rtd 35a): eff at 5f, prob stays sharp 6f: acts on fast, handles equitrack: has run well fresh.
149   CACOPHONY 12 [2] S Dow 2-8-3 F Norton 8/1: 460303: 2 b g Son Pardo - Ansellady (Absalom) ¾ 48a
Held up, rdn & kept on fnl 2f, not pace to chall: op 4/1: see 94.
*181   UNFORTUNATE 5 [3] Miss J F Craze 2-8-4 N Carlisle 11/2: 600214: Rdn/rear, mod gains fnl 2f. 1¼ 46a
4454} EMMAS HOPE 58 [4] 2-7-12 (BL) Joanna Badger (7) 33/1: 000005: Chsd ldrs 4f: blnks: 2 month abs: 3½ 31a
mod form/unplcd earlier in '99 for B Baugh (tried visor, rtd 45 at best): now with P Evans.
165   PRINCESS VICTORIA 8 [5] 2-8-4 P M Quinn (5) 6/4 FAV: 1026: Trkd ldrs, btn 2f out: nicely bckd: 1½ 33a
connections unable to offer explanation, poss best cght fresh: much closer to today's wnr in 165.
6 ran   Time 1m 12.22 (1.82)   (Mrs Jean Keegan)   M R Channon West Isley, Berks

208   2.25 CONDITIONS STKS 3YO+ (D)   1m aw rnd   Going 18 +02 Fast
£3765   £1139   £555   £263   3 yo rec 1 lb

*169   SECRET SPRING 8 [2] Mrs L Richards 7-8-12 O Urbina 5/2: 010211: 7 b g Dowsing - Nordica (Northfields) 86a
Trkd ldrs, rdn to lead ins last, ran on well: nicely bckd tho' op 2/1: gd time: recent wnr here at Lingfield
(2, h'caps, C/D): unplcd on turf earlier in '99 (rtd 85, stks): '98 Kempton wnr (h'cap, rtd 90, P Hedger):
eff at 1m/10f on firm & equitrack, handles hvy: handles any trk, likes Lingfield: tough & progressive.
4216} ELMHURST BOY 77 [3] S Dow 3-9-2 (BL) W Ryan 25/1: 231002: 3 b c Merdon Melody - Young Whip 1 88$
(Bold Owl) Chsd ldrs, rdn/narrow lead over 2f out, hdd ins last & no extra cl-home: op 20/1, 1st time blnks: 11 wk
abs: earlier in '99 scored at Epsom (4 rnr mdn, rtd 80): plcd in '98 (rtd 83, nov): eff at 6f/1m on any trk:
acts on firm, hvy & equitrack: eff with/without visor/blnks: fine AW bow, can find compensation.
161   CONSORT 10 [4] A J McNae 6-8-12 R Winston 16/1: 600003: 6 b h Groom Dancer - Darnelle (Shirley nk 82$
Heights) Dwelt, rear, styd on well form press fnl 2f, nrst fin: op 10/1: plcd earlier in '99 for Mrs A J Perrett
(rtd 82, h'cap): rnr-up thrice in '98 (rtd 94): '97 Newmarket wnr (val h'cap, rtd 90): eff at 7f/9f: handles
gd/soft, likes fast, firm & equitrack: handles any trk, likes Newmarket: suited by a fast run race: well h'capped.
172   ITALIAN SYMPHONY 7 [8] P D Evans 5-9-5 (vis) Joanna Badger (7) 10/1: 054344: Sn trkd ldrs, ev ch ¾ 88a
over 1f out, kept on onepace: op 7/1: clr of rem: see 172, 137.
137   CHEWIT 17 [9] 7-8-12 C Rutter 7/4 FAV: 6-0035: Dwelt & held up in rear, smooth prog wide halfway, 6 72a
ch 2f out, sn wknd: hdly bckd tho' op evens: needs a return to 7f: see 137.
403} HUGWITY 99 [7] 7-8-12 M Hills 4/1: 1-2216: Led 6f, fdd: op 7/2: reapp: earlier in '99 won here at 2 68a
Lingfield (h'cap), '98 wnr at Yarmouth (h'cap, rtd 80), Southwell (clmr) & Lingfield (h'cap, rtd 86a at best): eff at
7f/1m, stays 10f: acts on fast grnd & both AWs, esp Lingfield: best up with/forcing pace.
4553} SERGEANT IMP 50 [1] 4-8-12 M Tebbutt 100/1: 000607: Al towards rear: 7 wk abs. ½ 67$
--   MAX [6] 4-8-12 G Bardwell 16/1: -12118: Cl-up 5f: AW bow/Brit debut: Belgian raider. 9 53a
8 ran   Time 1m 37.47 (1.27)   (M K George)   Mrs L Richards Funtington, W Sussex

209   3.00 TRIDENT HCAP DIV 2 3YO+ 0-60 (F)   1m2f aw   Going 18 -18 Slow   [60]
£1882   £527   £256   3 yo rec 3 lb

147   DAPHNES DOLL 12 [5] Dr J R J Naylor 4-9-2 (48) M Henry 12/1: 320041: 4 b f Polish Patriot - Helietta 54a
(Tyrnavos) Prom, led 3f out, rdn out: tchd 16/1: plcd earlier in '99 for Miss G Kelleway (rtd 53, h'cap, rtd 50a
on sand): '98 mwr here at Lingfield (mdn, h'cap, rtd 65a, plcd on turf, rtd 74, mdn): prev eff at 6f/8.5f, now gets 10f
well: acts on fast, soft, equitrack: likes to race with/force the pace: likes Lingfield.
110   HIGH SHOT 20 [3] G L Moore 9-9-10 (56) A Culhane 9/1: 20-022: 9 b g Darshaan - Nollet (High Top) 1½ 58a
Towards rear, prog fnl 3f, kept on ins last tho' no threat to wnr: op 6/1: see 110 (C/D, sell).
115   SUPERCHIEF 22 [12] Miss B Sanders 4-8-8 (40) (tBL) C Rutter 12/1: 000303: 4 b g Precocious - Rome 1¾ 40a
Express (Siberian Express) Led 7f, no extra over 1f out: blnks, op 7/1: stays 10f on equitrack: see 56 (mdn).
106   MUSTANG 24 [2] J Pearce 6-8-10 (44) A Polli (3) 14/1: 404454: Trkd ldrs, onepace 2f out: see 59 (7f). ½ 43a
161   CONFRONTER 10 [1] 10-9-12 (58) W Ryan 11/2 FAV: 550645: Towards rear, mod gains: see 161. 1 56a
169   KAFIL 8 [4] 5-9-5 (51) G Bardwell 11/1: 253656: Chsd ldrs, onepace fnl 2f: see 1 (C/D). 1¼ 47a
100   CAPTAIN MCCLOY 24 [11] 4-8-10 (42) R Brisland (5) 14/1: 640057: Rear, late prog: prev in '99 1 37a

76

scored at Warwick (sell h'cap, rtd 48 at best): plcd in '98 (rtd 45a & 50): eff at 1m, suited by 10f, tried further: acts on fast, gd & equitrack: eff in blnks/visor (not worn): handles any trk, likes a sharp/turning one: best in sells.
161 **SOUND THE TRUMPET 10** [6] 7-9-0 (46)(t) G Baker (7) 6/1: 044138: Chsd ldrs 1m: op 4/1: see 97 (1m). ¾ 40a
147 **PEARL BUTTON 12** [7] 3-8-11 (46) G Faulkner (3) 20/1: 000009: Held up, nvr factor: mod form prev. 6 31a
2565} **FUERO REAL 99** [9] 4-8-8 (40) O Urbina 15/2: 602240: Al rear: 10th: tchd 11/1: AW bow, jumps fit 1 24a
(mod form): rnr-up twice earlier in '99 (rtd 42, h'cap): former Flat wnr in the French provinces: eff arnd 10/12f on fast.
100 **HAWKSBILL HENRY 24** [13] 5-9-12 (58) A Clark 8/1: 553000: Dwelt/al rear: 13th: tchd 12/1: rnr-up 0a
thrice earlier in '99 (stks, rtd 61a, turf h'cap plcd, rtd 50): '98 Lingfield wnr (C/D h'cap, rtd 56a, plcd on turf, rtd 49): eff at 9/10f on fast & gd, likes equitrack, any trk, likes a sharp one: has run well fresh, without visor/blnks.
100 **JUBILEE SCHOLAR 24** [10] 6-9-3 (49)(bl) F Norton 11/1: 50050P: Rear, bhd/p.u. lame 3f out. 0a
4435} **Redouble 60** [14] 3-9-8 (57) S Whitworth 12/1: 160 **Roger Ross 10** [8] 4-9-9 (55) S Drowne 12/1:
14 ran Time 2m 06.36 (3.56) (Mrs S P Elphick) Dr J R J Naylor Shrewton, Wilts

210 **3.35 LADBROKE HCAP QUAL 3YO+ 0-70 (E) 1m aw rnd Going 18 +02 Fast [70]**
£2957 £896 £438 £209 3 yo rec 1 lb

-- **RESIST THE FORCE** [5] R Rowe 9-9-4 (60) M Hills 9/2: 3140-1: 9 br g Shadeed - Countess Tully 67a
(Hotfoot) Prom, rdn/led 1f out, rdly asserted: nicely bckd from 10/1, fair time, reapp: unrcd since '98, won at Folkestone (h'cap) & Epsom (stks, rtd 87, C Cyzer): '97 wnr at Brighton (2) & Lingfield (h'caps, rtd 63a): eff at 6f/1m on fast, gd & equitrack: likes to race with/force the pace: loves sharp/undul trks: runs v well fresh: gd weight carrier: has broken blood vessels: credit to new connections.
*107 **PENGAMON 24** [12] D T Thom 7-9-1 (57) F Norton 13/8 FAV: 002212: 7 gr g Efisio - Dolly Bevan 2 57a
(Another Realm) Held up, rdn & kept on fnl 2f, no ch with wnr: hvly bckd: see 107 (C/D).
*163 **BARBASON 8** [10] G L Moore 7-9-10 (66) P Dobbs (5) 4/1: 060313: 7 ch g Polish Precedent - Barada 1½ 63a
(Damascus) Held up, rdn & hdwy fnl 2f, nvr trbld wnr: nicely bckd: see 163 (stks, 10f).
162 **URSA MAJOR 10** [8] C N Allen 5-9-8 (64)(bl) R Studholme (5) 7/1: 410004: Led till halfway, led again 1½ 58a
over 3f out till 1f out, no extra: tchd 10/1: earlier in '99 scored at York (h'cap, made all, rtd 64 at best): '98 wnr at Southwell (2, clmrs, A Kelleway), subs won twice here at Lingfield (h'caps, current connections, rtd 90a): eff at 6f, suited by 7f/1m, tried 10f: acts on firm & soft, loves both AWs: handles any trk: likes to force the pace.
4576} **COUGHLANS GIFT 47** [4] 3-9-4 (61) R Smith (5) 14/1: 000125: Towards rear, rdn & late gains for nk 54a
press: op 7/1: AW bow: 7 wk abs: earlier in '99 scored at Bath (h'cap, rtd 63 at best): plcd on fnl '98 start (rtd 57): eff at 6f, suited by 7f/1m: acts on gd & soft, prob handles equitrack: likes a turning trk.
162 **BRIMSTONE 10** [2] 4-9-0 (56) A Morris 20/1: -00006: Prom 6f: op 12/1: see 162 (7f). 1 47a
119 **HEVER GOLF GLORY 21** [3] 5-9-9 (65) N Carlisle 25/1: 004007: Rdn/towards rear, mod prog. 1¾ 53a
152 **SPRINGTIME LADY 12** [7] 3-9-5 (62) W Ryan 8/1: 405228: Mid-div at best: op 6/1: btr 152, 96. 2½ 45a
4372} **RAYWARE BOY 64** [9] 3-9-8 (65)(bl) J Fanning 20/1: 000009: Al rear: op 12/1, 2 month abs. nk 47a
131 **DARE 18** [6] 4-9-7 (63)(vis) S Drowne 11/1: 530100: Trkd ldrs 5f: 10th: op 7/1: btr 83 (fibresand). shd 45a
152 **UNCHAIN MY HEART 12** [1] 3-9-5 (62)(bl) M Tebbutt 8/1: 420130: Cl-up, led 5f out till over 3f out, 16 20a
sn btn: 11th: op 6/1: btr 152, 114 (mdn).
11 ran Time 1m 37.46 (1.26) (Mrs Barbara Hogan) R Rowe Storrington, W Sussex

SOUTHWELL (Fibresand) TUESDAY DECEMBER 21ST Lefthand, Sharp, Oval Track

Official Going SLOW Stalls: Inside, Except 5f - Outside

211 **11.45 DECEMBER HCAP DIV 1 3YO+ 0-60 (F) 1m4f aw Going 31 -28 Slow [57]**
£1861 £521 £253 3 yo rec 5 lb

182 **COUNT DE MONEY 8** [12] S R Bowring 4-10-0 (57) S Finnamore (7) 5/2 FAV: 125221: 4 b g Last Tycoon - 67a
Menominee (Soviet Star) Chsd ldrs, rdn 4f out, led over 1f out, asserted ins last, rdn out: earlier in '99 won 4 times here at Southwell (h'cap, 2 clmrs & class stks) & also W'hampton (clmr, rtd 67a at best & 35): '98 wnr at Southwell (amat h'cap, rtd 54a): eff at 11/14f: handles firm & fast, fibresand/Southwell specialist: tough.
167 **VANTAGE POINT 11** [14] K McAuliffe 3-9-1 (49) J Tate 4/1: 403322: 3 b c Casteddu - Rosie Dickins 4 53a
(Blue Cashmere) Chsd ldrs halfway, kept on for press fnl 2f, not pace of wnr: op 3/1: see 141, 115.
190 **SOUHAITE 6** [15] W R Muir 3-8-11 (45) Martin Dwyer 6/1: 061303: 3 b g Salse - Parannda (Bold Lad) 3 45a
Pulled hard early, chsd ldrs halfway, briefly led over 2f out, rdn/kept on onepace after: see 190, 68 (C/D).
196 **TALECA SON 4** [6] D Carroll 4-8-2 (31) Joanna Badger (7) 14/1: 050434: Chsd ldrs wide 4f out, shd 31a
kept on for press tho' not pace to chall: quick reapp: eff around 11/12f: handles fibresand, fast & soft.
1956} **EVEZIO RUFO 99** [9] 7-8-13 (42) R Thomas (7) 16/1: 160455: Rdn/towards rear halfway, stdy gains 3½ 37a
wide fnl 3f, nrst fin: op 14/1: 6 month abs: earlier in '99 scored twice at W'hampton (sell & h'cap, rtd 47a, unplcd on turf, rtd 34): '98 wnr at Lingfield, Southwell & W'hampton (sell h'cap/h'caps, rtd 61a & 55): eff at 11f/14.8f: acts on fast, hvy, loves both AW & sharp trks: eff in blnks/visor: enjoys sell grade.
182 **MARTHA REILLY 8** [3] 3-8-10 (44) A Clark 16/1: 400346: Mid-div halfway, nvr able to chall: see 70. 1½ 37a
4525} **WELLCOME INN 55** [11] 5-7-12 (27)(t) F Norton 14/1: 020507: Cl-up, led halfway, rdn/hdd over 2f hd 19a
out, fdd: op 20/1: jumps fit (mod form): AW bow: t-strap: rnr-up earlier in '99 (clmr, rtd 42): stays a stiff 12f, tried 2m: acts on firm, gd/soft & prob handles fibresand: ran well for a long way, 10f could prove ideal.
4424} **ALBERKINNIE 63** [1] 4-8-2 (31) J Bramhill 16/1: 644028: Nvr a factor: op 12/1, 2 mnth abs: rnr-up 3½ 18a
twice earlier in '99 (rtd 33, h'cap): unplcd in '98 (appr h'cap, rtd 43 & 31a): acts on fast, prob handles gd/soft.
170 **OUR PEOPLE 10** [4] 5-8-7 (36)(t) J Fanning 16/1: 060559: Al towards rear: t-strap: see 102. 11 11a
4592} **AMBIDEXTROUS 48** [8] 7-8-6 (35) L Charnock 14/1: 556200: Twds rear/mod gains: 10th: jumps fit. shd 10a
170 **LOST SPIRIT 10** [16] 3-9-4 (52) Dean McKeown 25/1: 000660: Led 6f, btn 4f out: 14th: see 170. 0a
3452} **Geegee Emmarr 99** [13] 6-8-8 (35)(2ow) T G McLaughlin 25/1:
117 **Hill Farm Dancer 24** [5] 8-8-1 (30) A McCarthy (3) 12/1:
131 **Colonel Custer 21** [2] 4-9-10 (53) G Bardwell 16/1:
4147} **Chayanees Arena 83** [10] 4-7-13 (28) G Sparkes (7) 33/1:
-- **Missed May** [7] 5-8-4 (30)(tBL)(3ow) R Lappin 33/1:
16 ran Time 2m 41.4 (7.1) (Roland M Wheatley) S R Bowring Edwinstowe, Notts

SOUTHWELL (Fibresand) TUESDAY DECEMBER 21ST Lefthand, Sharp, Oval Track

212 12.15 HAPPY XMAS HCAP DIV 1 3YO+ 0-75 (E) 6f aw Going 31 -02 Slow [74]
£2374 £664 £322

143 **BLUE KITE 17** [12] N P Littmoden 4-9-9 (69) J Tate 8/1: 233261: 4 ch g Silver Kite - Gold And Blue (Bluebird) Trkdkd ldrs, led over 2f out & rdn clr, kept on well: prev in '99 won at W'hampton (h'cap, rtd 66a, stks, rtd 65): plcd in '98 (rtd 78 & 78a): eff btwn 5/7f on fast & soft, loves fibresand: likes sharp trks, without headgear. **76a**
177 **SWINO 8** [6] P D Evans 5-8-6 (52)(vis) S Drowne 16/1: 034002: 5 b g Forzando - St Helena (Monsanto) Rdn/towards rear halfway, switched & styd on well fnl 2f, nrst fin: op 12/1: looks nicely h'capped: see 177. ¾ **56a**
*73 **HAYMAKER 32** [13] B S Rothwell 3-9-7 (67) R Lappin 11/2: 202313: 3 b g Thatching - Susie Sunshine (Waajib) Slowly away & bhd/wide, styd on well for press from over 2f out, nrst fin: eff at 6/7f: lost chance at start today, a likely type for similar off this mark with a level break: see 73 (7f, mdn). *nk* **70a**
199 **CZAR WARS 4** [1] P T Dalton 4-7-11 (43)(bl) J Bramhill 12/1: 035044: Chsd ldrs halfway, kept on fnl 2f tho' not pace to chall: quick reapp: eff at 6f, return to 7f+ could suit: acts on fibresand, gd/soft & soft. *1* **44a**
3394} **XSYNNA 99** [2] 3-9-3 (63) M Tebbutt 16/1: 300435: Chsd ldrs, no extra fnl 1f: op 12/1: 4 month abs: plcd earlier in '99 (h'caps, rtd 68a & 55, S Williams): '98 Lingfield scorer (nurs h'cap, rtd 64a, turf plcd, rtd 76): eff at 5f, suited by 6f, tried 7f: acts on firm, gd/soft & equitrack, prob fibresand, without blnks: likes sharp trks. *4* **54a**
175 **FACILE TIGRE 10** [9] 4-8-10 (56) Dean McKeown 9/1: 200446: Mid-div at best: op 7/1: see 146 (5f). *2* **42a**
3936} **LIFT THE OFFER 96** [7] 4-9-11 (71) R Winston 25/1: 520007: Towards rear, no impress: 3 month abs: rnr-up earlier in '99 (rtd 48, h'cap): plcd in '98 (h'cap, rtd 68, R Hannon): '97 wnr at Leicester (auct mdn, rtd 71) & twice at Lingfield (nurs & stks, rtd 81a): eff at 6f/1m: acts on fast, gd/soft & equitrack: best without a visor. *1* **55a**
4261} **DEKELSMARY 77** [3] 4-7-12 (44)(t) A Polli (3) 20/1: 010008: Chsd ldrs 4f: 11 wk abs: earlier in '99 won at Thirsk (appr h'cap, rtd 46, plcd on sand, rtd 47a, h'cap): '98 Southwell wnr (h'cap, rtd 53a, turf plcd, rtd 52): eff at 5/7f, stays 1m: acts on fast, firm & fibresand: best without blnks, wears a t-strap: runs well for an apprentice. ¾ **24a**
75 **SHES A GEM 32** [10] 4-8-8 (54)(vis) L Newman (5) 9/2: 554039: Led 1f, cl-up till outpcd fnl 2f: op 7/2. *shd* **34a**
*183 **MARENGO 8** [11] 5-8-11 (57)(7ex) T G McLaughlin 5/2 FAV: 053010: Led after 1f, clr halfway, rdn/ hdd over 2f out & sn btn: 10th, nicely bckd under a pen: btr 183 (C/D, made all). *shd* **36a**
183 **MUTAHADETH 8** [4] 5-9-1 (61)(bl) J Fanning 14/1: 004040: Sn outpcd/al rear: 11th: see 183. *nk* **39a**
183 **MY TYSON 8** [5] 4-9-8 (68) C O'Donoghue (5) 33/1: 000-60: Al rear: 12th: see 183. *3½* **37a**
12 ran Time 1m 15.3 (2.0) (T Clarke) N P Littmoden Newmarket, Suffolk

213 12.45 FESTIVE NURSERY HCAP 2YO 0-85 (E) 1m aw Going 31 -13 Slow [83]
£2668 £748 £364

158 **MISS WORLD 13** [7] C N Allen 2-8-9 (64)(t) L Newman (5) 9/2: 462321: 2 b f Mujadil - Great Land (Friend's Choice) Chsd ldrs, rdn 3f out, led over 1f out & styd on strongly: earlier in '99 scored at W'hampton (sell, rtd 60a & 65): eff at 7f/1m: acts on both AWs & fast grnd: handles a sharp or stiff/gall trk: best without blnks, wears a t-strap: v consistent filly, deserved this. **72a**
*158 **WELSH PLOY 13** [11] K McAuliffe 2-9-7 (76) T G McLaughlin 13/2: 250512: 2 b f Deploy - Safe House (Lyphard) Prom, rdn/briefly led over 1f out, kept on ins last: op 9/2: acts on both AWs, gd & hvy: see 158. *4* **77a**
171 **HEATHYARDS MATE 10** [9] R Hollinshead 2-9-6 (75) P M Quinn (5) 11/2: 221143: 2 b g Timeless Times - Quenlyn (Welsh Pageant) Towards rear/wide, late gains tho' no threat to wnr: tchd 13/2: see 128 (C/D). *2* **72a**
149 **PAPAGENA 15** [3] C W Thornton 2-8-1 (56)(BL) F Norton 14/1: 030564: Cl-up, led after 2f, rdn/hdd 2f out & no extra: blnks, op 12/1: rnr-up earlier in '99 (rtd 62, 4-rnr auct mdn): eff at 6f, this longer 1m trip shld suit in time: handles firm & gd/soft grnd, prob fibresand. *2½* **48a**
128 **WILL IVESON 21** [10] 2-8-2 (57) L Charnock 7/1: 605655: Keen/prom, briefly led 2f out, no extra. *½* **48a**
3160} **COLOMBE DOR 99** [4] 2-8-4 (59) Dale Gibson 25/1: 0006: Chsd ldrs, rdn/outpcd halfway, no impress on ldrs after: h'cap/AW bow: 5 month abs: unplcd from 3 starts earlier in '99 (rtd 59): longer 1m trip today. *1½* **47a**
128 **PURE BRIEF 21** [6] 2-8-2 (57) A McCarthy (3) 20/1: 500007: Led 2f, btn over 1f out: unplcd earlier in '99 (rtd 66, debut, auct mdn): bred to apprec mid-dists, has tried 10f. *3½* **38a**
179 **NICIARA 8** [8] 2-7-10 (51) Joanna Badger (7) 12/1: 0033P8: Dwelt, bhd halfway/mod gains: tchd 14/1. *hd* **31a**
125 **TOWER OF SONG 21** [5] 2-9-0 (69) A Culhane 7/2 FAV: 501429: Trkd ldrs, btn 2f out: btr 125, 36 (sell). *3½* **42a**
181 **BARRYS DOUBLE 8** [2] 2-8-2 (57)(vis) J Fanning 14/1: 030040: Chsd ldrs 3f: 10th: see 181 (6f). *19* **2a**
158 **MYTTONS AGAIN 13** [1] 2-9-5 (74) G Carter 10/1: 004260: Sn bhd: 11th, op 8/1: see 158. *8* **3a**
11 ran Time 1m 42.9 (3.5) (Bernard Butt) C N Allen Newmarket, Suffolk

214 1.15 BOOK A TABLE CLAIMER 3YO+ (F) 5f aw str Going 31 -01 Slow
£2158 £606 £295

191 **SAMWAR 6** [9] Mrs N Macauley 7-9-3 (vis) R Fitzpatrick (3) 5/1: 011501: 7 b g Warning - Samaza (Arctic Tern) Trkd ldrs, smooth prog to lead over 1f out, rdn out: op 4/1: recent wnr here at Southwell (clmr) & W'hampton (h'cap): earlier in '99 won at W'hampton (2, 1 sell) & again at Southwell (h'caps, rtd 72a, unplcd on turf, rtd 54): plcd in '98 (rtd 74 & 71a, Miss G Kelleway): eff at 6/7f, suited by 5f nowadays: acts on firm, soft & equitrack, fibresand specialist: has run well fresh: eff in blnks/visor: handles any trk, loves W'hampton/Southwell. **74a**
148 **NINEACRES 15** [4] J M Bradley 8-8-5 (bl) Claire Bryan (7) 12/1: 004102: 8 b g Sayf El Arab - Mayor (Laxton) Rdn chasing ldrs, kept on ins last, not pace of wnr: op 9/1: eff at 5f, return to 6f shld suit: see 134. *1½* **57a**
32 **OFF HIRE 39** [6] C Smith 3-8-7 (vis) J Tate 25/1: 060003: 3 b g Clantime - Lady Pennington (Blue Cashmere) Led, rdn/hdd over 1f out, kept on for press: rnr-up earlier in '99 (rtd 58, stks, unplcd on sand, rtd 68a, h'cap): '98 Musselburgh wnr (sell nurs, rtd 42, plcd on sand, rtd 63a, nurs): eff at 5/6f: acts on gd/soft, soft & fibresand: likes a sharp/turning trk: eff with/without a visor: enjoys sell grade. ¾ **57a**
166 **SOUTHERN DOMINION 11** [3] Miss J F Craze 7-8-7 (bl) T Williams 10/1: 002204: Sn chsd ldrs, kept on for press fnl 1f, nvr able to chall: back to form after nrly u.r. last time: see 71. *1½* **54a**
139 **NIFTY NORMAN 20** [12] 5-8-9 (bl) F Norton 7/1: 040665: Chsd ldrs, no extra fnl 1f: see 71. ¾ **54a**
116 **JACK TO A KING 24** [10] 4-8-3 (tbl) J Edmunds 20/1: -00506: Chsd ldrs, held over 1f out: unplcd earlier in '99 (rtd 36a, stks): mod form in '98 (rtd 62, mdn): wears a t-strap & blnks: with J Balding. *nk* **47a**
134 **POLLY MILLS 20** [2] 3-8-12 (bl) N Callan (3) 6/1: 400027: Sn rdn, nvr on terms: see 134. ¾ **54a**
*201 **TROJAN HERO 4** [11] 8-8-5 C Cogan (5) 8/1: 026218: Towards rear/rdn early, nvr pace to chall. *1½* **43a**
2189} **AVONDALE GIRL 99** [7] 3-8-8 J Fanning 16/1: 306109: Chsd ldrs 3f, sn outpcd: 6 mth abs: earlier in '99 scored at W'hampton (sell, C Dwyer, rtd 63a), & Thirsk (amat h'cap, current connections, rtd 71): '98 Yarmouth wnr (sell, rtd 72 at best): eff at 5/6f on firm, soft & fibresand, sharp trks: gd weight carrier. *3* **39a**
116 **ROSES TREASURE 24** [8] 3-8-0 (ebl) J Bramhill 40/1: 000000: Nvr going pace: 10th. *3½* **22a**
-146 **KRYSTAL MAX 17** [13] 6-9-1 A Clark 6/4 FAV: 222420: Towards rear/rdn halfway, btn/eased fnl 1f: *2½* **30a**

11th: hvly bckd: jockey reported that the gelding had lost its action: btr 113 (6f, equitrack).
30 **TAZ MANIA 39** [1] 3-8-9 (tbl) R Winston 33/1: 000000: Bhd halfway: 12th. 3½ 15a
12 ran Time 59.4 (1.6) (Andy Peake) Mrs N Macauley Sproxton, Leics

215

1.45 DECEMBER HCAP DIV 2 3YO+ 0-60 (F) 1m4f aw Going 31 -42 Slow [57]
£1861 £521 £253 3 yo rec 5 lb

178 **MARKELLIS 8** [16] D Carroll 3-8-2 (36) Joanna Badger (7) 16/1: 060041: 3 b g Housebuster - Crimsonscontender (Monsieur Champlain) Cl-up wide halfway, led 3f out, held on well ins last, rdn out: 1st success: only mod form prev: eff around 11/12f on fibresand: best without blnks: runs well for an apprentice. 41a
66 **BROUGHTONS LURE 34** [12] W J Musson 5-8-5 (33)(1ow) G Carter 5/1: -00052: 5 ch m Archway - Vaal Salmon (Salmon Leap) Chsd ldrs halfway, rdn & kept on well fnl 2f, not reach wnr: op 7/1: lightly rcd/unplcd earlier in '99 (rtd 35, fill h'cap): '98 Warwick wnr (amat h'cap, rtd 52 & 36a at best): eff at 11/12.5f, has tried further: acts on fibresand, gd & gd/soft grnd: handles a sharp/gall trk: well h'capped on old turf form. ¾ 36a
131 **GENUINE JOHN 21** [6] J Parkes 6-8-7 (36) R Fitzpatrick (3) 25/1: 030063: 6 b g High Estate - Fiscal Folly (Foolish Pleasure) Towards rear halfway, styd on well for press fnl 2f, nrst fin: eff at 7f/9f, stays 12f. nk 37a
178 **NORTH ARDAR 8** [9] R Brotherton 9-8-12 (41) Paul Cleary (7) 11/2: 000024: Mid-div, prog/chsd ldrs 3f out, kept on ins last, unable to chall: fin clr of rem: see 178 (clmr). nk 41a
4581} **A DAY ON THE DUB 50** [1] 6-9-4 (47) A Clark 11/4 FAV: 021125: Chsd ldrs, rdn halfway, held 2f out: 7 wk abs, bckd tho' op 2/1: prev in '99 won here at Southwell (auct mdn, rtd 44a), Newcastle (clm h'cap) & Redcar (clmr, rtd 56): stays 2m on gd/soft over hdles (rtd 74h): eff at 1m/12f on fibresand, fast & gd/soft grnd. 10 36a
70 **ELSIE BAMFORD 32** [7] 3-8-8 (42) J Fanning 11/1: 6U3006: Led 3f, btn 2f out: tchd 12/1: plcd earlier in '99 (rtd 58 & 48a, h'caps): unplcd in '98 (rtd 62): eff at 7f, stays 12f: acts on firm, soft & fibresand. 3 27a
43 **REPTON 38** [14] 4-9-7 (50) J Bosley (7) 12/1: 000607: Cl-up wide halfway, briefly led over 3f out, sn held. 4 29a
178 **MOONSHIFT 8** [5] 5-7-13 (28)(tvi) Dale Gibson 15/2: -01058: Mid-div at best. 2½ 3a
3716} **PINE RIDGE LAD 99** [8] 9-9-4 (47)(bl) Dean McKeown 25/1: 263059: Handy 9f: 4 month abs. 1 21a
124 **AJDAR 21** [17] 8-8-13 (42) Sarah Thomas (7) 25/1: 440000: Dwelt, al towards rear: 10th: jumps fit. 1½ 14a
117 **RAED 24** [13] 6-9-11 (54) T G McLaughlin 12/1: 000060: Led halfway, hdd over 3f out & fdd: 11th. 5 19a
2025} **PIMPINELLA 99** [11] 3-8-2 (36)(eBL) J Bramhill 33/1: 60000: Led 9f out till halfway/sn btn: 15th: blnks. 0a
39 **Aleanbh 38** [10] 4-8-6 (35) R Winston 14/1: 133 **Whatsitsname 20** [2] 3-8-10 (44) A Culhane 16/1:
39 **Barann 38** [15] 3-7-10 (30) G Bardwell 50/1: 85 **Wry Ardour 29** [3] 3-7-13 (33) T Williams 14/1:
16 ran Time 2m 43.1 (8.8) (Mark Barrett) D Carroll Southwell, Notts

216

2.15 TOTE CREDIT HCAP 3YO+ 0-95 (C) 7f aw rnd Going 31 +08 Fast [91]
£7132 £2160 £1055 £502

208 **ITALIAN SYMPHONY 3** [10] P D Evans 5-9-11 (88)(vis) S Drowne 12/1: 543441: 5 b g Royal Academy - Terracotta Hut (Habitat) Chsd ldrs, led over 1f out, rdn out: gd time: earlier in '99 won at Lingfield (stks), W'hampton (h'cap, rtd 97a at best), Newmarket, Warwick, Catterick & Musselburgh (h'caps, rtd 58): '98 Southwell (2), Lingfield (2) & W'hampton (5, clmrs/h'caps, rtd 89a & 40) wnr: eff at 7f/1m, stays 9f: acts on firm, gd/sft, loves both AWs: eff in a visor, tried blnks: goes well for appr jockeys, any trk, loves sharp ones: tough/useful. 95a
169 **TOPTON 11** [2] P Howling 5-9-7 (84)(bl) A McCarthy (3) 10/1: 000232: 5 b g Royal Academy - Circo (High Top) Sn handy, rdn/ch 2f out, kept on onepace: op 8/1: proving consistent up with the pace now: see 104. 3 86a
137 **DIL 20** [6] Mrs N Macauley 4-10-0 (91) R Fitzpatrick (3) 25/1: 000503: 4 b g Primo Dominie - Swellegant (Midyan) Led, rdn 2f out, hdd over 1f out & no extra: earlier in '99 scored here at Southwell (h'cap) & W'hampton (h'cap, rtd 96a, unplcd on turf, rtd 82): '98 wnr at Doncaster (2, auct mdn & h'cap, rtd 83, B Hanbury) & Leicester (h'cap): eff at 5/6f, stays a sharp 7f: acts on firm, gd/soft & fibresand, any trk: has run well fresh. 1½ 90a
143 **INDIAN BLAZE 17** [4] D R C Elsworth 5-8-6 (69) J Fanning 5/1 JT FAV: 401034: Mid-div halfway, switched & rdn over 1f out, kept on onepace: btr 143. 1 66a
180 **JUWWI 8** [11] 5-9-7 (84) Claire Bryan (7) 14/1: 262155: Towards rear, late gains, nrst fin: see 129 (6f). ¾ 80a
183 **ALMAZHAR 8** [9] 4-8-11 (74) T Williams 6/1: 312126: Chsd ldrs, no extra fnl 1f: op 9/2: see 143. hd 69a
*180 **DAHLIDYA 8** [1] 4-7-10 (57)(6ex)(2oh) Joanna Badger (7) 10/1: 005317: Slowly away & bhd, prog wide fnl 3f, nrst fin: tchd 12/1, 6lb pen for latest: habitual slow starter: see 180 (6f). 1½ 51a
142 **C HARRY 17** [13] 5-8-2 (65) P M Quinn (5) 16/1: 504138: Chsd ldrs halfway, held over 1f out: op 14/1. hd 56a
49 **RONS PET 36** [14] 4-8-9 (72)(t) N Callan (3) 12/1: 000269: Chsd ldrs, btn 2f out: op 10/1: see 33 (C/D). 2 59a
176 **BLOOMING AMAZING 8** [12] 5-7-10 (59)(5oh) J Bramhill 20/1: 000530: Mid-div at best: 10th, see 176. nk 45a
4005} **WINDSHIFT 93** [7] 3-9-1 (78)(vis) R Winston 25/1: 504300: Nvr in it: 11th: 3 month abs: prev in '99 scored here at Southwell (2, h'caps, rtd 79a at best) & Warwick (h'cap, rtd 83): '98 wnr again at Southwell (nurs h'cap, rtd 58a & 57): eff at 7f, 1m suits, tried further: acts on gd/soft, soft & fibresand: wears a visor. 2 60a
129 **FIRST MAITE 21** [8] 6-9-13 (90)(bl) S Finnamore (7) 5/1 JT FAV: 001540: Chsd ldrs wide 5f: 12th. 1 70a
4562} **GIFT OF GOLD 52** [3] 4-8-1 (64) G Bardwell 15/2: 003040: Dwelt/al rear: 16th: 7 wk abs: earlier in '99 scored at Goodwood (h'cap, rtd 85, unplcd on sand, rtd 59a): '98 Lingfield wnr (h'cap, rtd 83 at best, A Kelleway): stays 1m, all 3 wins at 7f: acts on fast, soft & poss handles both AWs: handles any trk. 0a
162 **Best Quest 13** [15] 4-7-13 (62) F Norton 20/1: *152 **Parisian Lady 15** [16] 4-7-10 (59)(3oh) M Henry 14/1:
97 **Al Mabrook 28** [5] 4-7-13 (62) J Tate 25/1:
16 ran Time 1m 28.2 (1.6) (J E Abbey) P D Evans Leighton, Powys.

217

2.45 COME JUMP RACING SELLER 2YO (G) 5f aw str Going 31 -29 Slow
£1850 £518 £251

*145 **SERGEANT SLIPPER 17** [10] C Smith 2-9-3 (vis) R Fitzpatrick (3) 4/1: 004011: 2 ch c Never So Bold - Pretty Scarce (Handsome Sailor) Dwelt, prog halfway, rdn/led over 1f out, styd on well ins last, rdn out: no bid: recent W'hampton wnr (seller, first success): rnr-up earlier in '99 (rtd 60a, plcd on turf, rtd 48, sell h'cap): eff at 5f, tried 6f: acts on fibresand & gd grnd: eff in a visor: likes a sharp trk & is at home in sellers. 61a
4367} **NOWT FLASH 67** [6] B S Rothwell 2-8-12 R Lappin 14/1: 600602: 2 ch c Petardia - Mantlepiece (Common Grounds) Prom, rdn/ch over 1f out, kept on for press: op 12/1: 10 wk abs: unplcd earlier in '99 (rtd 49 & 43a, tried blnks): eff at 5f on fibresand: could find a race in this grade. ½ 53$
4589} **APRILS COMAIT 48** [5] Miss J F Craze 2-8-7 N Carlisle 12/1: 400003: 2 br g Komaite - Sweet Caroline (Squill) Chsd ldrs, rdn & kept on fnl 1f, not pace to chall: op 10/1: 7 wk abs: unpld earlier in '99 (rtd 52a & 54): eff at 5f, has tried 6f: handles fibresand. 1½ 44a
181 **PRICELESS SECOND 8** [7] J A Glover 2-8-12 (bl) N Callan (3) 6/4 FAV: 060524: Dwelt & rdn/rear, hung left halfway, not able to chall: well bckd: btr 181 (6f). ½ 47a
179 **LAMMOSKI 8** [4] 2-8-12 (VIS) M Tebbutt 14/1: 000005: Chsd ldr, no extra over 1f out: visor: tchd 2 42a

SOUTHWELL (Fibresand)   TUESDAY DECEMBER 21ST   Lefthand, Sharp, Oval Track

20/1: unplcd earlier in '99, tried up to 7f (flattered in a mdn, rtd 64): with M Chapman.

181	**MOSAIC TIMES 8** [2] 2-8-12 S Whitworth 12/1: 206: Mid-div at best: op 7/1.	½	40a
179	**BILLYS BLUNDER 8** [1] 2-8-7 (tVIS) S Drowne 12/1: 07: Prom 4f: op 10/1, visor.	hd	34a
2238}	**XENOS 8** [9] 2-8-12 A McCarthy (3) 12/1: 0008: Chsd ldrs 4f: 6 mnth abs, AW bow, new stable.	1½	35a
127	**SOUNDS CRAZY 21** [3] 2-8-7 (bl) R Winston 33/1: 050009: Led till over 1f out, fdd.	2½	23a
2301}	**SKI FREE 99** [8] 2-8-7 (t) L Charnock 9/1: -5360: In tch 3f: 10th: op 6/1, 6 month absence.	1	21a

10 ran   Time 1m 00.8 (3.0)   (C Smith)   C Smith Temple Bruer, Lincs.

---

218   **3.15 HAPPY XMAS HCAP DIV 2 3YO+ 0-75 (E)**   6f aw rnd   Going 31   -04 Slow   [74]
£2374   £664   £322

175	**THAAYER 10** [4] I A Wood 4-8-11 (57) D Sweeney 12/1: 000301: 4 b g Wolfhound - Hamaya (Mr Prospector) Chsd ldrs trav well, smooth prog to lead 1f out, readily: earlier in '99 with K Bell, won here at Southwell (stks, rtd 65a at best, no turf form): plcd in '98 (rtd 60a, h'cap, rtd 74 at best, prob flattered): eff at 6f, tried 7f: fibresand specialist, loves Southwell: plenty in hand here, qck follow-up on the cards.		68a
180	**GARNOCK VALLEY 8** [6] J Berry 9-9-7 (67) G Carter 9/2: 021152: 9 b g Dowsing - Sunley Sinner (Try My Best) Towards rear, rdn & kept on wide fnl 2f, no ch with wnr: op 5/1: see 47 (C/D).	3	68a
143	**SANTANDRE 17** [5] R Hollinshead 3-9-10 (70) P M Quinn (5) 11/2: 030453: 3 ch g Democratic - Smartie Lee (Dominion) Chsd ldrs, rdn to lead 2f out, hdd 1f out & sn outpcd by wnr: see 143.	nk	70a
175	**KEEN HANDS 10** [9] Mrs N Macauley 3-9-8 (68)(vis) R Fitzpatrick (3) 5/1: 364024: Towards rear, kept on fnl 2f, nrst fin: op 4/1: see 175, 106.	1	66a
199	**SAN MICHEL 4** [12] 7-7-13 (44)(VIS)(1ow) T Williams 20/1: 506305: Chsd ldrs, not able to chall: visor.	3½	34a
73	**KUWAIT ROSE 32** [2] 3-9-5 (65) J Tate 9/2: 03626: Mid-div at best: op 7/2: see 73 (7f, mdn).	4	44a
183	**SO WILLING 8** [3] 3-9-2 (62)(VIS) A Clark 25/1: 200007: Chsd ldr, btn 2f out: visor: see 183.	1½	37a
2035}	**ICE AGE 99** [7] 5-8-7 (53)(bl) F Norton 3/1 FAV: 040608: Led, clr halfway, rdn/hdd 2f out & wknd qckly: 6 month abs: prev with R J R Williams, earlier in '99 scored here at Southwell (C/D, seller, rtd 57a, rtd 38 on turf): '98 wnr here at Southwell (2, h'cap & seller, rtd 68a) & Yarmouth (h'cap, rtd 49): likes to race with/force the pace at 5/6f: acts on fast, gd/soft & loves fibresand/Southwell: wears blnks: handles any trk: enjoys sell grade.	3	21a
116	**HEAVENLY MISS 24** [11] 5-8-2 (47)(bl)(1ow) J Fanning 9/1: 105459: Wide/mid-div, nvr on terms: earlier in '99 scored at Thirsk & W'hampton (fillies h'caps) & Bath (h'cap, rtd 52 & 54a at best): plcd form in '98 (rtd 50): eff at 5/6f on fast, soft & both AWs: eff in blnks: prob handles any trk, likes a sharp one.	hd	15a
148	**GOLD EDGE 15** [8] 5-7-11 (43)(1ow)(12oh) M Henry 50/1: 000500: Al towards rear: 10th.	1½	6a
113	**YOUNG BIGWIG 25** [10] 5-9-11 (71) A Culhane 12/1: 125000: Chsd ldrs 4f: 11th: op 10/1.	3	27a
3175}	**TAYOVULLIN 99** [13] 5-8-11 (57) G Parkin 12/1: -01230: Al rear: 12th: 5 month abs, with K Ryan.	8	0a

12 ran   Time 1m 15.4 (2.1)   (Mrs Joyce Wood)   I A Wood Upper Lambourn, Berks.

LINGFIELD (Equitrack)   WEDNESDAY DECEMBER 22ND   Lefthand, V Sharp Track

Official Going   STANDARD. Stalls: Inside.

219   **12.35 XMAS APPR HCAP 3YO+ 0-80 (G)**   1m5f aw   Going 41   -14 Slow   [78]
£1776   £504   £249   3 yo rec 6 lb

160	**FAHS 14** [2] N Hamilton 7-10-0 (78) J Bosley 11/10 FAV: 236031: 7 b g Riverman - Tanwil (Vision) Held up, prog to lead over 4f out, rdn/clr 2f out, in command when eased nr fin: hvly bckd: earlier in '99 won at Yarmouth (h'cap, rtd 77): '98 Lingfield wnr (amat h'cap, rtd 80a), plcd on turf (h'cap, rtd 81): eff at 10/13f, stays 14f: acts on gd & equitrack, handles soft: acts on any trk, likes Yarmouth & Lingfield: best held up.		82a
167	**KI CHI SAGA 12** [4] P Burgoyne 7-7-7 (46)(bl)(10oh) G Baker 20/1: 004402: 7 ch g Miswaki - Cedilla (Caro) Held up in tch, rdn/chsd wnr fnl 2f, kept on tho' al held: op 12/1: stays 13f: see 115 (12f).	1¼	46a
161	**NIGHT CITY 14** [3] K R Burke 8-10-0 (78) Beatrice Patisi 11/2: 151103: 8 b g Kris - Night Secret (Nijinsky) Led, sn clr, hdd over 4f out & sn held: mkt drifter, op 5/2: see 92 (1m, clmr).	3	74a
4340}	**COCO GIRL 70** [5] Mrs A E Johnson 3-7-10 (52)(10oh) G Sparkes 66/1: 000404: Held up in tch, rdn/btn fnl 2f: 10 wk abs: unplcd earlier in '99 (rtd 63 & 38a, early on with I Balding): rtd 75 in '98 (unplcd, mdn).	7	38a
619}	**BIGWIG 99** [1] 6-7-10 (46)(bl) Joanna Badger 6/4: 461145: Chsd ldr, rdn/held fnl 3f: nicely bckd, tchd 7/4: jumps fit, recent rnr-up (rtd 94h, h'cap, eff at 2m/2m4f on firm & soft): earlier in '99 scored twice here at Lingfield (C/D amat h'caps, rtd 48a): eff arnd 13f on equitrack: eff in blnks: runs well for an amateur.	1¼	30a

5 ran   Time 2m 49.51 (7.21)   (City Industrial Supplied Ltd)   N Hamilton Epsom, Surrey.

---

220   **1.05 EASAL HCAP DIV 1 3YO+ 0-70 (E)**   1m2f aw   Going 41   -15 Slow   [67]
£2391   £670   £326   3 yo rec 3 lb

203	**SAMMYS SHUFFLE 4** [8] Jamie Poulton 4-9-2 (55)(bl) O Urbina 7/1: 433251: 4 b c Touch Of Grey - Cabinet Shuffle (Thatching) Chsd ldrs, rdn to lead dist, styd on gamely, drvn out: jockey given a 4-day whip ban: mod form over hdles earlier: plcd form in '99 (rtd 51a & 37, h'caps): '98 Brighton (2, h'caps, rtd 48) & here at Lingfield wnr (h'cap, rtd 44a): eff at 10/12f on firm, loves equitrack/Lingfield: suited by blnks.		58a
163	**FAILED TO HIT 12** [7] N P Littmoden 6-9-13 (66)(vis) J Tate 7/2 FAV: 351522: 6 b g Warrshan - Missed Again (High Top) Sn handy, rdn 4f out, ev ch fnl 2f, kept on well for press tho' not pace of wnr: jockey referred to Jockey Club for whip use: top-weight, well bckd: eff at 10f, suited by 12f: see 101.	¾	67a
537}	**HALF TIDE 99** [11] P Mitchell 5-8-3 (42) F Norton 5/1: -22133: 5 ch h Nashwan - Double River (Irish River) Keen/chsd ldrs halfway, briefly no room dist, kept on ins last: op 7/2, abs: earlier in '99 won here at Lingfield (h'cap, rtd 52a): rnr-up in '98 (rtd 43a & 54): eff at 10f, suited by 12f on equitrack: win soon.	1	42a
209	**SUPERCHIEF 4** [6] Miss B Sanders 4-8-10 (tvi) C Rutter 10/1: 003034: Led, rdn/hdd over 1f out, kept on ins last tho' held nr fin: qck reapp: visor reapplied: see 209, 56.	hd	40a
4410}	**ADMIRALS PLACE 65** [1] 3-9-2 (58) G Carter 13/2: 261205: Chsd ldrs halfway, briefly no room 2f out, kept on onepace ins last: abs: earlier in '99 won at Lingfield (h'cap, rtd 59a) & Beverley (h'cap, rtd 65, R W Armstrong): eff at 1m/10f, tried 12f: acts on gd, soft & both AWs, handles any trk: tough & genuine colt.	½	57a
163	**BAAJIL 12** [4] 4-9-7 (60) M Hills 13/2: 400146: Held up in tch, prog/chsd ldrs over 2f out, rdn/held ins last & eased nr fin: op 7/1: see 3 (C/D, stks).	nk	59a
159	**MALCHIK 14** [3] 3-7-10 (38)(3oh) R Brisland (0) 25/1: 000057: Chsd ldrs, btn 3f out: see 159 (sell).	5	30a
111	**KINNINO 26** [5] 5-7-13 (38) A Mackay 10/1: 505028: Mid-div halfway, btn 2f out: see 111 (seller, C/D).	6	21a
4387}	**UTAH 67** [2] 5-8-12 (51) A Culhane 14/1: -52009: Bhd/wide, nvr factor: tchd 16/1, 6 wk jumps abs	5	27a

LINGFIELD (Equitrack)   WEDNESDAY DECEMBER 22ND   Lefthand, V Sharp Track

(rtd 76h, nov): earlier in '99 with L Montague Hall, rnr-up (rtd 52a, h'cap): well btn sole '98 start for B Gubby:
eff arnd 8.4f on fibresand: best without blnks: now with G L Moore.
209 **KAFIL 4** [2] 5-8-12 (51) G Bardwell 12/1: 536560: Prom, rdn halfway/sn btn: op 10/1, qck reapp.   5 20a
4502} **ROOKIE 58** [10] 3-8-5 (47) P M Quinn (5) 10/1: 005020: Chsd ldrs wide halfway, btn 3f out: 11th: hd 15a
tchd 12/1, 2 month abs: prev with C A Cyzer, now with Mrs A E Johnson.
11 ran   Time 2m 08.43 (5.63)   (Mrs G M Temmerman)   Jamie Poulton Telscombe, E.Sussex.

221 1.35 BEST WISHES MDN 2YO (D)   6f aw rnd Going 41 -24 Slow
£2703   £759   £370

4430} **DACCORD 64** [5] E A Wheeler 2-9-0 S Carson (5) 6/1: 04431: 2 ch g Beveled - National Time (Lord   80a
Avie) Cl-up trav well, led over 1f out, pushed out: op 7/2, AW bow, 2 month abs: plcd earlier in '99 (auct mdn,
rtd 76): eff at 6f, 7f+ may suit: acts on gd, AW equitrack: likes a sharp/undul trk: runs well fresh.
206 **BUGGY RIDE 4** [4] Miss Gay Kelleway 2-9-0 S Whitworth 7/2: 500242: 2 b c Blues Traveller -   1¼ 76a
Tambora (Darshaan) Sn cl-up, led over 3f out till hdd over 1f out, kept on tho' al held by wnr: nicely bckd.
4364} **JUST MAC 69** [8] Mrs L Stubbs 2-9-0 A Culhane 12/1: 63: 2 br c Dayjur - Play On And On (Stop The   3 69a
Music) Rdn/chsd ldrs halfway, kept on fnl 2f, no threat to front pair: op 10/1: 10 wk abs/AW bow: unplcd on
sole start earlier in '99 (rtd 70, mdn, J Noseda): eff at 6f: handles equitrack & prob fast grnd.
2815} **SHAMSAN 99** [1] M Johnston 2-9-0 J Fanning 11/2: 064: Led till over 3f out, held fnl 2f: op 10/1,   nk 68a
fin clr of rem: 5 month abs/AW bow: unplcd in 2 starts earlier in '99 for B Hanbury (rtd 60, mdn).
-- **LADYWELL BLAISE** [7] 2-8-9 J Tate 11/2: 5: Dwelt/bhd, late gains, no threat: op 3/1, debut.   7 50a
165 **ANGELAS PET 12** [6] 2-8-9 R Smith (5) 40/1: 000066: Chsd ldrs 4f.   2½ 43a
3300} **BAHAMIAN PRINCE 99** [3] 2-9-0 M Hills 3/1 FAV: 07: Dwelt & towards rear, nvr factor: AW bow/   3½ 39a
4 month abs: slowly away & fin last on sole start earlier in '99 (mdn, H Cecil): with J Noseda.
3623} **CAPPUCINO LADY 99** [9] 2-8-9 G Bardwell 40/1: 0R3068: Sn bhd: 4 month abs, AW bow.   6 23a
-- **TIME** [2] 2-9-0 A Clark 10/1: 9: Slowly away/al rear: debut, op 8/1.   1¾ 24a
9 ran   Time 1m 14.3 (3.9)   (Dagfell Properties Ltd)   E A Wheeler Whitchurch On Thames, Oxon.

222 2.05 HAPPY NURSERY HCAP 2YO 0-85 (E)   6f aw rnd Going 41 -07 Slow   [84]
£2640   £741   £361

149 **CASTLE SEMPILL 16** [3] R M H Cowell 2-8-8 (64)(vis) P M Quinn (5) 5/1: 310431: 2 b c Presdium -   69a
La Suquet (Puissance) Sn trkd ldrs, switched 1f out & stdy run ins last to lead nr fin, rdn out: op 4/1: earlier
in '99 scored at Newmarket (seller, J Fanshawe, rtd 74): eff at 6f/7f, tried 1m: acts on firm, equitrack & handles
soft grnd: handles a stiff/gall or sharp trk: eff with/without a visor.
112 **TYCANDO 26** [1] K R Burke 2-9-6 (76) N Callan (3) 5/2 JT FAV: 201022: 2 ch g Forzando - Running   nk 80a
Tycoon (Last Tycoon) Led, drvn ins last, hdd nr line: hvly bckd: see 112.
4616} **BOADICEA THE RED 46** [7] B S Rothwell 2-9-1 (77) J Fanning 11/2: 256203: 2 gr f Inchinor - Kanika 1½ 71a
(Be My Chief) Handy, rdn & kept on onepace fnl 1f: op 4/1: 6 wk abs/AW bow: rnr-up twice earlier in '99
(rtd 72, auct mdn): eff at 6f, stays 7f & a return to that trip shld suit: handles gd, hvy & equitrack, any trk.
158 **WATERGRASSHILL 14** [2] N A Callaghan 2-8-2 (58) R Brisland (5) 9/2: 000254: Handy/onepace fnl 1f. nk 57a
+127 **SMOKIN BEAU 22** [4] 2-9-7 (77) A Culhane 5/2 JT FAV: 043315: Handy, ch over 1f out, hard rdn/no nk 75a
extra ins last: hvly bckd: stays sharp 6f, best at 5f: acts on both AWs, handles gd/soft: see 127 (5f, fibresand).
181 **PETRIE 9** [6] 2-7-12 (54) P Fessey 16/1: 232256: Bhd halfway: op 14/1: btr 88, 74 (fibresand).   13 20a
6 ran   Time 1m 13.3 (2.9)   (Mrs J M Penney)   R M H Cowell Six Mile Bottom, Cambs.

223 2.35 FESTIVE FEELING HCAP 3YO+ 0-95 (C)   6f aw rnd Going 41 +07 Fast   [95]
£6406   £1940   £947   £451

*58 **MISTER TRICKY 36** [9] P Mitchell 4-8-0 (67) F Norton 11/4 FAV: 503111: 4 ch g Magic Ring -   72a
Splintering (Sharpo) Trkd ldrs, rcd keenly, briefly no room over 2f out, hard rdn ins last to lead nr line, all
out: hvly bckd, fast time: recent wnr here at Lingfield (h'cap), earlier in '99 won again at Lingfield (2, rtd
64a), Windsor, Goodwood (h'caps) & Brighton (class stks, rtd 66): '98 wnr at Lingfield (2 h'caps, rtd 66a): eff
at 6f/1m: acts on firm, gd/soft & loves equitrack/Lingfield: tough & progressive gelding, keep on the right side.
64 **CLASSY CLEO 35** [7] P D Evans 4-9-12 (93) Joanna Badger 9/1: 232132: 4 b f Mujadil - Sybaris   nk 97a
(Crowned Prince) Cl-up halfway, hard rdn & styd on well ins last, just held: op 7/1: see 64.
148 **DIAMOND GEEZER 16** [3] R Hannon 3-7-13 (66) Martin Dwyer 9/2: 502123: 3 br c Tenby - Unaria   hd 69a
(Prince Tenderfoot) Cl-up, rdn/led over 2f out, hdd nr line, just held: nicely bckd, tchd 11/2: see 113 (C/D).
113 **KILMEENA LAD 26** [4] E A Wheeler 3-8-12 (79) S Carson (5) 8/1: 101004: Chsd ldrs halfway, kept on 2½ 75a
fnl 1f, nvr pace to chall: earlier in '99 scored at Newmarket & Lingfield (h'caps, rtd 75 & 81a): '98 scorer at
Newbury (mdn, rtd 85): suited by gd, tried 7f: acts on firm, hvy & equitrack: handles any track.
191 **AURIGNY 7** [8] 4-9-2 (83) W Ryan 12/1: 100055: Chsd ldrs, kept on fnl 1f, nvr pace to chall: op 10/1. ¾ 77a
*95 **CHARGE 29** [5] 3-8-2 (69)(t) C Rutter 14/1: 043416: Cl-up, led 3f out till over 2f out, fdd: tchd 20/1. 2½ 56a
4413} **ZIGGYS DANCER 65** [2] 8-8-8 (75) A Polli (3) 16/1: 654007: Led till over 3f out, hard rdn/fdd: op 14/1: ½ 60a
plcd numerous times earlier in '99 (rtd 104, List stks, prob flattered): '98 wnr at Southwell (clmr, rtd 68a), subs
rtd 88 on turf (h'cap): suited 5/6f on firm, gd & both AWs: handles any trk, loves Chester: has run well fresh.
191 **AFAAN 7** [12] 6-9-0 (81)(bl) S Righton 10/1: 504338: Prom wide halfway, btn fnl 2f: see 113.   ¾ 64a
4172} **PRINCE PROSPECT 83** [6] 3-9-7 (88) A Culhane 20/1: 136409: Sn outpcd, mod late prog: op 14/1:   hd 70a
earlier in '99 won at Sandown (h'cap, rtd 81 & 91a): '98 Lingfield scorer (mdn, rtd 82a), plcd on turf (rtd 87,
J Noseda): eff at 5/6f on firm, gd/soft & e/track: handles any trk: best without a visor & with forcing tactics.
180 **BLAKESET 9** [11] 4-8-11 (78)(bl) A Clark 13/2: 260120: Chsd ldrs wide halfway/held fnl 2f: 10th: op 4/1. hd 59a
134 **EMPEROR NAHEEM 21** [10] 4-8-11 (78)(bl) M Tebbutt 10/1: 060230: Mid-div, btn halfway: 11th: 6 48a
op 8/1: blnks reapplied: see 134, 113.
4144} **BOLD EFFORT 84** [1] 7-10-0 (95)(bl) G Carter 16/1: 064000: Sn bhd: 12th: op 12/1: 12 wk abs: 25 20a
earlier in '99 scored here at Lingfield (C/D h'cap, rtd 97a), unplcd on turf subs (rtd 83, h'cap): '99 wnr at Sandown
& Kempton (h'caps, rtd 96 & 87a): eff at 5/6f, stays 1m: acts on firm, gd/soft & both AWs: suited by blnks.
12 ran   Time 1m 12.43 (2.03)   (The Magicians)   P Mitchell Epsom, Surrey.

81

LINGFIELD (Equitrack) WEDNESDAY DECEMBER 22ND Lefthand, V Sharp Track

224 **3.05 EASAL HCAP DIV 2 3YO+ 0-70 (E) 1m2f aw Going 41 -32 Slow [67]**
£2391 £670 £326 3 yo rec 3 lb

195 **MIGWAR 5** [3] N P Littmoden 6-9-1 (54)(vis) C Cogan (5) 16/1: 000401: 6 b g Unfuwain - Pick Of The Pops (High Top) Held up, rdn to lead ins last, styd on well, rdn out: visor reapplied: earlier in '99 won at Southwell (2, sells, rtd 65a): eff at 10/12f on fast, gd & both AWs: likes Southwell: eff with/without a visor. **58a**
203 **FAMOUS 4** [9] J J Bridger 6-8-3 (42) G Bardwell 14/1: 004502: 6 b g Tropular - Famous Horse (Labus) Held up, prog over 2f out, led over 1f out, rdn/hdd ins last & no extra: op 16/1: qck reapp: see 90. *1½* **43a**
169 **MAPLE 12** [5] S Dow 3-9-3 (59) A Clark 12/1: 600063: 3 ch g Soviet Lad - Little Red Rose (Precocious) Chsd ldrs, rdn & kept on onepace fn 2f: eff at 5/6f, now stays a sharp 10f: see 106. *1¼* **58a**
4522} **INKWELL 57** [1] G L Moore 5-7-13 (38)(bl) A Mackay 12/1: 002204: Towards rear, rdn & kept on fnl 2f, nrst fin: tchd 16/1, 8 wk abs: rnr-up twice earlier in '99 (rtd 40, h'cap): '98 Brighton (2, h'cap & clmr) & Bath wnr (h'cap, rtd 56): eff at 7f/1m, poss best arnd 10f: acts on firm, enjoys gd & soft grnd, handles e/track: handles any trk, likes Brighton: has run well fresh: well h'capped, could win this winter. *2½* **33a**
154 **PRINCESS MO 16** [10] 3-7-10 (38)(5oh) A Polli (3) 50/1: 000005: Chsd ldrs wide 3f out, sn held: earlier with T Powell, unplcd on turf (rtd 54, mdn): unplcd in 3 '98 mdns (rtd 63, Pat Mitchell): has tried blnks & a visor: this longer 10f trip could suit: now with B R Johnson. *1* **32a**
168 **HIGHFIELDER 12** [8] 3-8-5 (47)(BL) Martin Dwyer 8/1: 040306: Handy, led after 2f till over 1f out, fdd. *1* **40a**
210 **BARBASON 4** [4] 7-9-13 (66) R Brisland (5) 4/5 FAV: 603137: Chsd ldrs halfway, rdn/btn over 1f out: well bckd at odds on: qck reapp, topweight: btr 210, 163 (C/D, stks). *2½* **55a**
210 **DARE 4** [6] 4-9-10 (63) Joanna Badger (7) 10/1: 301008: Trkd ldrs 1m: op 7/1: see 83 (1m, fbrsnd). *2½* **48a**
4472} **EI EI 61** [11] 4-8-1 (40) F Norton 50/1: 000009: Rear, nvr factor: AW bow/abs: unplcd earlier in '99 (rtd 44, h'cap): '98 Folkestone wnr (mdn, rtd 84, B Hills): eff at 7/7.5f: acts on fast & hvy: has run well fresh. *1¾* **23a**
167 **ANOTHER RAINBOW 12** [7] 3-9-2 (58) P Fredericks (5) 14/1: 536250: Chsd ldrs, ch 4f out, sn fdd: 10th. *hd* **40a**
157 **TRIBAL PEACE 14** [2] 7-8-10 (49) C Rutter 20/1: 005000: Led 2f, btn 3f out: 11th: see 157 (C/D). *3* **27a**
11 ran Time 2m 10.05 (7.25) (Avon & West Racing Club Ltd) N P Littmoden Newmarket.

225 **3.35 GREETINGS MDN 3YO+ (D) 7f aw rnd Going 41 -28 Slow**
£2691 £756 £369

95 **CORN DOLLY 29** [12] R F Johnson Houghton 3-8-9 G Carter 9/2 CO FAV: 00041: 3 ch f Thatching - Keepers Lock (Sunny's Halo) Held up, prog/led over 3f out, styd on well ins last, drvn out: nicely bckd, tchd 7/1: rtd 59 when unplcd earlier in '99 (Windsor mdn): eff at 6/7f: acts on equitrack: op to further improvement. **54a**
133 **PUPPET PLAY 21** [5] E J Alston 4-8-9 A Culhane 9/2 CO FAV: 000642: 4 chf Broken Hearted - Fantoccini (Taufan) Sltly hmpd start & bhd, styd on well fnl 2f tho' al held by wnr: op 5/2: eff at 7f/8.5f: acts on both AWs & h'caps shld suit: see 133. *2* **49a**
159 **RAIN RAIN GO AWAY 14** [6] D J S Cosgrove 3-9-0 N Callan(3) 9/1: 000043: 3 ch g Miswaki - Stormagain (Storm Cat) Prom, briefly no room 2f out, onepace: bckd at long odds: handles soft & equitrack: see 159. *1¾* **51$**
156 **BALLYMORRIS BOY 14** [9] J Pearce 3-9-0 T G McLaughlin 6/1: 000534: Towards rear/rdn, styd on fnl 2f, nrst fin: bckd at long odds, tchd 12/1: see 156 (C/D, seller). *shd* **51$**
109 **WOOLLY WINSOME 26** [2] 3-9-0 (vis) J Bosley (7) 8/1: 430065: Prom 6f: rnr-up earlier in '99 (rtd 56a, mdn): plcd in '98 (rtd 55a, mdn, unplcd on turf, rtd 74): eff arnd 7f/1m on equitrack & fast: tried vis/blnks. *nk* **50$**
189 **ROTHERHITHE 7** [4] 3-9-0 F Norton 9/1: 00306: Held up, eff 2f out, sn held: see 114. *nk* **49$**
177 **PIPE DREAM 9** [1] 3-9-0 M Tebbutt 33/1: 000007: Led 4f, fdd over 1f out: mod form prev. *1¼* **46$**
156 **FRANKLIN LAKES 14** [11] 4-9-0 (vis) G Baker (7) 33/1: 050508: Wide/rear, nvr factor: unplcd earlier in '99 (rtd 38, ladies h'cap): mod form in '98 (C Horgan): eff at 7f, handles firm & fast: best efforts in blnks. *6* **37$**
-- **AMBUSHED** [8] 3-9-0 J Fanning 9/2 CO FAV: 9: Trkd ldrs 4f: nicely bckd tho' op 5/2: debut. *¾* **36a**
1212} **WILD NETTLE 99** [7] 5-8-9 R Smith (5) 25/1: 422460: Al rear: 10th: 8 month abs. *2½* **26a**
-- **HUNAN SCHOLAR** [10] 4-9-0 J Tate 8/1: 000500: Held up, nvr factor: 11th: op 14/1: Brit/AW bow. *8* **19a**
3098} **LATCH LIFTER 99** [3] 3-9-0 S Whitworth 20/1: 0-0000: Prom 4f: 12th: 5 mth abs/now with Miss G Kelleway. *½* **18a**
12 ran Time 1m 27.62 (4.82) (Bob Lanigan) R F Johnson Houghton Blewbury, Oxon.

WOLVERHAMPTON (Fibresand) MONDAY DECEMBER 27TH Lefthand, Sharp Track

Official Going STANDARD Stalls: Inside.

226 **1.10 BRANDY BUTTER HCAP DIV 1 3YO+ 0-65 (F) 6f aw rnd Going 29 -08 Slow [64]**
£1892 £530 £257

175 **DONE AND DUSTED 16** [2] R Brotherton 3-9-9 (59) C Carver (5) 9/1: 000601: 3 ch f Up And At 'Em - Florentink (The Minstrel) Prom, led over 1f out, styd on well ins last, rdn out: earlier in '99 scored at Lingfield (h'cap, rtd 69a) & Windsor (h'cap, rtd 72): '98 Southwell wnr (seller, J Berry) & again at Lingfield (clmr, rtd 65a & 57): eff at 6/7f, tried 1m: acts on both AWs & firm grnd: likes a sharp trk: nicely h'capped, score again. **66a**
175 **GRASSLANDIK 16** [12] A G Newcombe 3-9-2 (52) S Whitworth 10/1: 000502: 3 b c Ardkinglass - Sophisticated Baby (Bairn) Held up, rdn/chsd wnr over 1f out, kept on tho' held nr fin: eff at 5/6f: see 175. *1½* **53a**
216 **C HARRY 6** [11] R Hollinshead 5-10-0 (64) P M Quinn (5) 7/1: 041303: 5 ch g Imperial Frontier - Desert Gale (Taufan) Rdn/rear, styd on fnl 2f, not pace to chall: op 6/1, qck reapp: see 130 (7f, seller). *½* **63a**
180 **ERRO CODIGO 14** [6] S E Kettlewell 4-9-3 (53) J Tate 9/2 FAV: 100034: Held up, kept on fnl 2f/no threat. *3* **45a**
4450} **AMARO 68** [9] 3-8-9 (45) G Carter 16/1: 204005: Mid-div, not pace to chall: 10 wk abs: rnr-up twice earlier in '99 (rtd 61, auct mdn, unplcd on sand, rtd 42a): eff at 5f, stays 6f: handles fast & a stiff/gall track. *2* **32a**
212 **FACILE TIGRE 6** [10] 4-9-6 (56) P Doe (3) 11/1: 004466: Mid-div at best: qck reapp: see 146 (5f). *½* **41a**
154 **MISS BANANAS 21** [3] 4-8-10 (46) D Meah (6) 25/1: 010007: Prom 4f: earlier in '99 scored at Leicester (amat riders h'cap, rtd 41, rnr-up on sand, C/D h'cap, rtd 57a): '98 Lingfield wnr (h'cap, rtd 63a): eff up with the pace at 5/6f, tried 7f: acts on gd & both AWs: handles a sharp or stiff/undul track. *5* **22a**
147 **PURNADAS ROAD 21** [8] 4-8-5 (41)(bl) J Bramhill 33/1: 0-0008: Nvr on terms: lightly rcd & mod form for J Toller earlier in '99: rtd 61 at best in '98 (mdn): now with H Haynes. *2* **12a**
214 **TROJAN HERO 6** [5] 8-9-9 (59) T G McLaughlin 6/1: 262109: Nvr pace to chall: op 7/1: see 201 (sell). *2* **25a**
175 **BLUNDELL LANE 16** [1] 4-9-13 (63)(vis) D Sweeney 8/1: 000000: Led after 1f till over 1f out, fdd: 10th. *1¼* **26a**
4471} **LIVE TO TELL 66** [4] 3-9-1 (51) R Price 5/1: 622100: Led 1f, btn 2f out: 11th: op 4/1: 10 wk abs. *5* **5a**

199 **Ready To Rock** 10 [13] 3-8-9 (45) A Clark 11/1:   957} **Weetrain** 99 [7] 3-8-12 (48) Dean McKeown 25/1:
13 ran   Time 1m 15.00 (2.2)   (Paul Stringer)   R Brotherton Elmley Castle, Worcs.

227   1.40 W & S HCAP DIV 1 3YO+ 0-60 (F)   1m100y aw rnd   Going 29 -18 Slow   [60]
£1976   £554   £269   3 yo rec 1 lb

95 **FRENCH SPICE** 34 [2] Sir Mark Prescott 3-8-7 (40) D Sweeney 6/1: 6061: 3 b f Cadeaux Genereux - **48a**
Hot Spice (Hotfoot) Mid-div, switched over 1f out & rdn/styd on strongly to lead ins last, rdn
out: op 4/1: h'cap bow: unplcd/mod form earlier in '99 (rtd 41, mdn): apprec this step up to 8.5f, further
will suit on this evidence: acts on fibresand & a sharp trk: lightly raced, type to win again.
*203 **ROI DE DANSE** 9 [10] M Quinn 4-8-12 (44) C Rutter 5/1 FAV: 006312: 4 ch g Komaite - Princess Lucy   2 **46a**
(Local Suitor) Sn led, clr over 1f out, rdn/hdd ins last & rdn out: op 8/1 on both AWs & gd grnd.
187 **LILANITA** 12 [1] P D Evans 4-8-13 (45) T G McLaughlin 9/1: 043203: 4 b f Anita's Prince - Jimlil   ¾ **46a**
(Nicholas Bill) Sn chsd ldr, kept on onepace fnl 2f: op 8/1: gd run: see 187, 45 (seller).
*109 **GHAAZI** 31 [6] Miss Gay Kelleway 3-9-13 (60)(BL) S Whitworth 7/1: 004314: Chsd ldrs briefly 2f out,   2½ **56a**
sn no extra: acts on both AWs & firm: not disgraced on return to h'caps tried in blnks: see 109 (mdn, equitrack).
162 **RAINBOW RAIN** 19 [5] P Doe (3) 10/1: 402305: Chsd ldrs, onepace fnl 2f: acts on both   ¾ **55a**
AWs, firm & gd grnd: fairly h'capped on sand & all wins at shorter trips: see 28 (equitrack).
85 **RIVER ENSIGN** 35 [7] 6-9-2 (48) P M Quinn (5) 10/1: 100406: Led 1f out, remained prom, onepace over   shd **43a**
1f out: op 7/1: earlier in '99 scored at W'hampton (clmr, rtd 53a) & Chepstow (h'cap, rtd 47): '98 Southwell
& Nottingham wnr (h'cap, rtd 44a & 44): eff at 5/10f on gd, hvy & fibresand: acts on any trk, runs well fresh.
195 **TEMPRAMENTAL** 10 [8] 3-8-8 (41)(bl) A Mackay 8/1: 005537: Chsd ldrs, btn/eased fnl 1f: blnks reapp.   8 **24a**
172 **DREAM ON ME** 16 [3] 3-9-6 (53) J Bosley (7) 8/1: 304358: Mid-div, nvr threat: see 138 (seller).   ¾ **35a**
193 **GADGE** 12 [9] 8-9-1 (47) G Carter 9/1: 603409: Rear, nvr factor: see 193, 83.   ¾ **28a**
92 **TITAN** 34 [11] 4-8-8 (40) A Clark 12/1: 050060: Dwelt/al rear: 10th: see 92 (equitrack).   6 **12a**
178 **WAITING KNIGHT** 14 [4] 4-9-10 (56)(vis) R Price 9/1: 050200: Chsd ldrs 6f: 13th: see 178.   **0a**
4442} Red Wolf 68 [13] 3-9-7 (54) Dean McKeown 20/1:   162 An Lu Abu 19 [12] 3-9-3 (50) N Callan (3) 25/1:
13 ran   Time 1m 50.2 (4.0)   (J Morley)   Sir Mark Prescott Newmarket.

228   2.15 PUDDING CLAIMER 2YO (F)   6f aw rnd   Going 29 -23 Slow
£2284   £642   £313

-179 **MISS SKICAP** 14 [2] T D Barron 2-8-12 N Callan (3) 5/2: 421: 2 b f Welsh Captain - Miss Nelski   **70a**
(Most Secret) Chsd ldr halfway, rdn to lead over 1f out, asserted ins last, rdn out: clmd by J Pointon for £10,000:
first success: apprec this step up to 6f, further could suit in time: acts on fibresand: enjoys claim grade.
125 **BESCABY BLUE** 27 [4] J Wharton 2-8-6 C Cogan (5) 11/1: 010602: 2 b f Blues Traveller - Nurse Tyra   3½ **54a**
(Dr Blum) Rdn/rear, kept on fnl 2f for press & al held: op 9/1: earlier in '99 scored on debut at Southwell
(auct mdn, rtd 68a at best) & Redcar (clmr, rtd 64 at best): eff at 5/7f, 1m + may suit in time: acts on fast,
hvy & fibresand: handles a sharp & gall trk: runs well fresh: a likely type for similar at 7f.
207 **CACOPHONY** 9 [3] S Dow 2-8-3 P Doe (3) 20/1: 603033: 2 b g Son Pardo - Ansellady (Absalom)   hd **50a**
Rdn/bhd, kept on fnl 2f for press: op 14/1: handles both AWs, firm grnd & a sharp trk: see 94.
62 **WELCHS DREAM** 40 [6] J Berry 2-8-10 G Carter 2/1 FAV: 434424: Chsd ldrs 5f: nicely bckd, 6 wk abs.   3 **50a**
4221} **DIAMOND PROMISE** 84 [1] 2-8-8 N Carlisle 6/1: 021235: Led till over 1f out, no extra: 12 wk abs: 1¼ **45a**
earlier in '99 scored at Thirsk, Leicester & Lingfield (clmrs, rtd 75, rnr-up on sand, rtd 70a, C/D seller): eff at
5/6f: acts on gd, soft & fibresand: loves to force the pace & handles any trk: tough/consistent, loves claim grade.
155 **SUPREMELY DEVIOUS** 19 [5] 2-7-13 (vis) Dale Gibson 13/2: 600626: Chsd ldr 3f, sn held: op 5/1.   1¼ **33a**
42 **SHOULDHAVEGONEHOME** 44 [7] 2-8-2 (BL) J Tate 9/1: 000027: Chsd ldrs 5f: blnks: 6 wk abs.   nk **35a**
7 ran   Time 1m 15.9 (3.1)   (Messinger Stud Limited)   T D Barron Maunby, N.Yorks.

229   2.50 BREAD SAUCE MDN 3YO+ (D)   1m100y aw rnd   Going 29 -30 Slow
£2801   £848   £414   £197   3 yo rec 1 lb

189 **HEATHYARDS JAKE** 12 [4] R Hollinshead 3-8-13 P M Quinn (5) 11/4: 026221: 3 b c Nomination - Safe   **58a**
Bid (Sure Blade) Rear, rdn/prog to lead ins last, all out nr line: op 2/1, first win on 36th start: plcd num
times earlier in '99 (rtd 60 & 67a): eff btwn 7f/9f, poss stays 12f: acts on firm, soft, fibresand & any trk.
225 **PUPPET PLAY** 5 [12] E J Alston 4-8-9 (bl) A Culhane 9/4 FAV: 006422: 4 ch f Broken Hearted -   nk **52a**
Fantoccini (Taufan) Trkd ldrs 3f out, ev ch going well 1f out, hard rdn ins last, just held: op 3/1: jockey given
a 2-day whip ban: found less than expected off the bit here: see 133.
225 **RAIN RAIN GO AWAY** 5 [7] D J S Cosgrove 3-8-13 C Rutter 8/1: 000433: 3 ch g Miswaki - Stormagain   1½ **54$**
(Storm Cat) Prom, led halfway, rdn to lead & no extra: qck hangup: stays 8.5f: acts on soft & fibresand.
173 **ANNADAWI** 16 [1] C N Kellett 4-9-0 N Carlisle 33/1: 060044: Chsd ldrs, onepace ins last: see 173.   4 **46$**
4449} **KHATTAFF** 68 [8] 4-9-0 (bl) G Bardwell 50/1: -00065: Chsd ldrs 6f: 10 wk abs/AW bow: unplcd   2½ **41$**
earlier in '99 (rtd 35, clmr, tried blnks): mod form in '98.
133 **AUTUMN LEAVES** 26 [2] 3-8-8 C Cogan (5) 40/1: 0006: Rear, mod gains: unplcd on turf earlier in '99.   shd **36$**
215 **ALEANBH** 6 [9] 4-9-0 P Hanagan (7) 40/1: 0-0607: Rear, mod gains: qck reapp: mod form.   2 **37a**
65 **NADDER** 40 [13] 4-9-0 T G McLaughlin 40/1: 050008: Nvr factor: 6 wk absence: unplcd earlier in '99   7 **26a**
(rtd 49 & 39a at best): no form over timber previously.
3376} **MAJOR ATTRACTION** 99 [11] 4-9-0 J Fanning 14/1: -64349: Chsd ldrs 6f: op 20/1: 4 month absence.   2½ **21a**
-- **NOTIONAL** [10] 3-8-8 (t) N Callan (3) 5/1: 423300: Bhd, nvr factor: 10th: op 4/1: AW bow/jmps fit.   4 **8a**
-- **TATTOO** [5] 4-8-9 J Tate 8/1: 0: Sn rdn to lead, hdd 5f out & sn btn: 13th: debut.   **0a**
-- Little Lottie [3] 3-8-8 R Lappin 25/1:   -- Envy [1] 3-8-8 Dean McKeown 40/1:
13 ran   Time 1m 51.2 (5.0)   (L A Morgan)   R Hollinshead Upper Longdon, Staffs.

230   3.20 LADBROKE HCAP 3YO+ 0-100 (C)   1m1f79y aw   Going 29 -02 Slow   [97]
£6775   £2050   £1000   £475

137 **WEET A MINUTE** 26 [5] R Hollinshead 6-9-13 (96) A Culhane 6/1: 022201: 6 ro h Nabeel Dancer -   **103a**
Ludovica (Bustino) Sn handy, led 3f out, clr 2f out, kept on well ins last: earlier scored here at
W'hampton (C/D h'cap, rtd 101a, plcd num times on turf subs, rtd 94, h'cap): '98 wnr at W'hampton (h'cap, rtd 97a,
this race), also plcd on turf (rtd 104): eff at 1m/10f, prob stays 12f: acts on firm & hvy, fibresand/W'hampton
specialist: handles any trk, runs well fresh: eff weight carrier: tough/genuine & useful AW performer.
200 **KING PRIAM** 10 [1] M J Polglase 4-9-10 (93)(bl) T G McLaughlin 11/4 FAV: D11152: 4 b g Priolo -   ¾ **98a**

- Barinia (Corvaro) Held up, rdn/chsd wnr over 1f out, kept on tho' not pace to chall: apprec return to 9f: see 172.
172 **WHITE PLAINS 16** [2] K R Burke 6-8-10 (79)(t) N Callan (3) 9/2: 605433: 6 b g Nordico - Flying Diva (Chief Singer) Led 1f & remained handy, onepace over 1f out: also bhd today's wnr in 172. *3* **78a**
172 **TIGHTROPE 16** [6] N P Littmoden 4-7-10 (65)(1oh) C Cogan (1) 4/1: 022024: Dwelt, rdn/led after 1f, hdd 3f out & held over 1f out: op 7/2: ahd of today's 3rd latest: see 172, 1. *½* **63a**
*216 **ITALIAN SYMPHONY 6** [8] 5-9-8 (91)(vis)(6ex) D Sweeney 11/2: 434415: Held up, rdn/chsd ldrs over 1f out, sn held: 6lb pen, qck reapp: stays 9f, best at 7f/1m: see 216. *3* **83a**
216 **PARISIAN LADY 6** [7] 4-7-10 (65)(9oh) G Baker (7) 25/1: 400106: Bhd halfway, mod gains: see 216. *2½* **52a**
160 **JAVA SHRINE 19** [3] 8-8-4 (73)(bl) J Tate 14/1: 003267: Nvr factor: op 10/1: see 23 (10f, equitrack). *½* **59a**
197 **INTERNAL AFFAIR 10** [4] 4-7-10 (65) L Charnock 5/1: 154628: Chsd ldrs 7f: see 197, 60. *12* **33a**
8 ran Time 2m 01.1 (2.9) (Ed Weetman, Haulage & Storage Ltd) R Hollinshead Upper Longdon, Staffs.

231 3.50 TURKEY SELLER 3YO+ (G) 1m4f aw Going 29 -40 Slow
£1945 £545 £265

211 **COLONEL CUSTER 6** [2] J Pearce 4-9-8 G Bardwell 12/1: 605001: 4 ch g Komaite - Mohican (Great Nephew) Chsd ldr halfway, led 3f out, rdn clr 2f out, unchall/easily: op 10/1: bght in for 5,000gns: qck reapp: earlier in '99 scored at Southwell (h'cap, rtd 62a, unplcd on turf, rtd 51, h'cap): plcd in '98 (rtd 66a, also rtd 50a, C W Thornton): suited by 11/12f: acts on fibresand, has disapp on equitrack. **50a**
211 **AMBIDEXTROUS 6** [6] E J Alston 7-9-8 L Charnock 20/1: 562002: 7 b h Shareef Dancer - Amber Fizz (Effervescing) Rear, kept on for press fnl 2f tho' no ch wnr: op 14/1: qck reapp: recent mod jumps form: earlier in '99 scored at Chester (amat h'cap) & Carlisle (clmr, rtd 48, plcd on sand, rtd 37a, h'cap): plcd in '98 (rtd 55 & 43a): eff at 10f, best at 12f: acts on firm, soft & fibresand: best without blnks/visor. *9* **40$**
211 **HILL FARM DANCER 6** [10] W M Brisbourne 8-8-13 C Cogan (5) 33/1: 540403: 8 ch m Gunner B - Loadplan Lass (Nicholas Bill) Slowly away/well bhd, kept on for press fnl 2f, nearest fin: qck reapp: jockey given a 2-day ban for careless riding: continues to hamper chance with slow starts: see 211, 117. *nk* **30a**
4564} **BANNERET 58** [7] Miss S J Wilton 6-9-8 P M Quinn (5) 11/4: 011534: Twds rear, mod gains fnl 2f: jumps fit (plcd, sell hdle, rtd 64h): earlier in '99 scored at Southwell (class clmr) & here at W'hampton (C/D h'cap, rtd 66a, no turf form): '98 wnr at W'hampton (2, seller & auct mdn, G Woodward, rtd 71a) & Southwell suited by 10f/12f on fast, loves fibresand & Southwell/W'hampton: best without blnks: enjoys sell/claim grade. *1* **38a**
174 **SWAN HUNTER 16** [8] 6-9-4 N Callan (3) 15/8 FAV: 200025: Chsd ldrs, onepace 2f out: well bckd. *1½* **32a**
215 **NORTH ARDAR 6** [12] 9-9-8 C Carver (5) 7/1: 000246: Held up, nvr factor: qck reapp: see 178. *3½* **31a**
102 **SIR WALTER 33** [11] 6-9-4 (bl) Dean McKeown 25/1: 400607: Keen/sn clr, hdd 3f out & sn held. *3* **23a**
-- **SOME MIGHT SAY** [9] 4-9-4 M Tebbutt 6/1: 2312-8: Chsd ldrs, btn fnl 2f: jumps fit. *¾* **22a**
178 **ADIRPOUR 14** [3] 5-9-8 Stephanie Hollinshea 16/1: 006039: Al towards rear: see 178. *5* **19a**
168 **KATIES CRACKER 17** [4] 4-9-3 C Rutter 40/1: 006000: Chsd ldr 6f, sn btn: 10th: see 168. *4* **8a**
219 **KI CHI SAGA 5** [5] 7-9-8 (bl) G Baker (7) 11/1: 044020: Wide/al rear: 11th: tchd 14/1: qck reapp. *1¾* **11a**
11 ran Time 2m 41.9 (8.3) (D Leech) J Pearce Newmarket.

232 4.20 BRANDY BUTTER HCAP DIV 2 3YO+ 0-65 (F) 6f aw rnd Going 29 +09 Fast [64]
£1892 £530 £257

*193 **FOREIGN EDITOR 12** [3] R A Fahey 3-9-2 (52) P Hanagan (7) 5/2 FAV: 665411: 3 ch g Magic Ring - True Precision (Presidium) Led after 1f, clr halfway, rdn out, unchall: op 7/2: fast time: recent wnr here at W'hampton (h'cap, first success): unplcd earlier in '99 (h'caps, rtd 54 & 41a): plcd in '98 (mdn, rtd 67): eff at 7f, suited by drop to 6f: acts on gd/soft & loves fibresand/W'hampton: plenty in hand here, shld win again. **71a**
148 **DAYNABEE 21** [12] A J McNae 4-8-10 (46) P Doe (3) 10/1: 054252: 4 b f Common Grounds - Don't Wary (Lomond) Led 1f, chsd wnr thr'out tho' btn fnl 2f: op 8/1: see 58 (7f, equitrack). *9* **48a**
212 **MARENGO 6** [1] M J Polglase 5-9-8 (58) G Bardwell 10/1: 530103: 5 b g Never So Bold - Born To Dance (Dancing Brave) Chsd ldrs, hit rail over 3f out, kept on fnl 2f tho' no ch wnr: qck reapp: see 183 (made all). *¾* **58a**
*218 **THAAYER 6** [11] I A Wood 4-10-0 (64)(7ex) D Sweeney 4/1: 003014: Chsd ldrs/onepace fnl 2f: op 7/2. *½* **62a**
187 **CHALUZ 12** [13] 5-9-1 (51)(t) T G McLaughlin 15/2: 452255: Chsd ldrs, not pace to chall: see 75 (7f). *1* **47a**
187 **LIVELY JACQ 12** [9] 3-8-12 (48)(vis) N Carlisle 16/1: 400466: Towards rear, mod gains: see 132. *nk* **43a**
2919} **NERO TIROL 99** [8] 3-9-13 (63)(bl) P Fredericks (5) 25/1: 050007: Prom 4f: 4 month jumps abs (rtd 65h, juv nov): earlier in '99 scored twice at Southwell (auct mdn & h'cap, rtd 76a, unplcd on turf, rtd 58, h'cap): unplcd 3 '98 starts (rtd 75): suited by 6f, tried 1m: acts on fibresand, loves Southwell: eff in blnks. *2½* **51a**
132 **FEATHERSTONE LANE 26** [5] 8-8-12 (48) Dean McKeown 20/1: 460458: Twds rear, mod prog: see 82. *½* **34a**
142 **MIKES DOUBLE 23** [4] 5-8-5 (41)(vis)(1ow) R Price 20/1: 605U69: Chsd ldrs 4f: see 142. *nk* **26a**
175 **CONSULTANT 16** [2] 3-9-6 (56) M Tebbutt 12/1: 000000: Al towards rear: 10th: now with C Kellett. *¾* **39a**
148 **SHARP HAT 21** [6] 5-9-9 (59) A Culhane 4/1: 001300: Dwelt, hampered after 2f, chsd ldrs 4f, sn btn: 11th: nicely bckd tho' op 3/1: btr 91 (5f, equitrack). *2* **37a**
152 **Swynford Welcome 21** [10] 3-8-9 (45) A Polli (3) 20/1: 4343} **Baritone 75** [7] 5-8-8 (44)(vis) J Tate 33/1:
13 ran Time 1m 14.00 (1.2) (Pride Of Yorkshire Racing Club) R A Fahey Butterwick, N.Yorks.

233 4.50 W & S HCAP DIV 2 3YO+ 0-60 (F) 1m100y aw rnd Going 29 -35 Slow [60]
£1976 £554 £269 3 yo rec 1 lb

177 **THE BARGATE FOX 14** [6] D J G Murray Smith 3-9-3 (50) S Whitworth 3/1 FAV: 051041: 3 b g Magic Ring - Hithermoor Lass (Red Alert) Rdn/rear, styd on well fnl 2f to lead nr fin, rdn out: tchd 9/2: earlier scored here at W'hampton (h'cap): unplcd earlier (mdns, rtd 64 & 51a): eff at 8.5f/9.3f, likes fibresand/W'hampton. **54a**
2098} **HANNIBAL LAD 99** [3] W M Brisbourne 3-9-13 (60) T G McLaughlin 16/1: -10042: 3 ch g Rock City - Appealing (Star Appeal) Prom, rdn 3f out, led 1f out, rdn/hdd nr fin: op 14/1: 6 month abs: earlier with P D Evans, scored here at W'hampton (seller, rtd 66a, unplcd on turf, rtd 44): '98 Southwell wnr (seller, rtd 67a & 69): eff at 7f, suited by 1m/9.3f: acts on firm & fibresand: runs well fresh: enjoys sell grade. *¾* **62a**
197 **CAREQUICK 10** [2] A Bailey 3-8-6 (39) G Carter 9/1: 000053: 3 ch f Risk Me - Miss Serlby (Runnett) Led till over 2f out, ev ch 1f out, held nr fin: eff around 8.5f: acts on fibresand: see 197. *¾* **40a**
197 **BORDER GLEN 10** [7] D Haydn Jones 3-10-0 (61)(bl) A Mackay 11/2: 054334: Chsd ldr, led over 2f out till 1f out, onepace: topweight: blnks reapp: see 96 (equitrack). *1* **60a**
177 **GODMERSHAM PARK 14** [9] 7-9-2 (48) G Parkin 12/1: 460305: Towards rear, mod gains: op 10/1. *1* **45a**
147 **QUEEN OF THE KEYS 21** [11] 3-8-6 (39) P Doe (3) 8/1: 000036: Rear, mod prog: acts on both AWs. *1½* **33a**
*133 **BLACK ROCKET 26** [10] 3-9-6 (53) J Tate 4/1: 606017: Held up, btn 2f out: see 133 (C/D, mdn). *5* **37a**
60 **MY DARLING DODO 40** [4] 3-8-9 (42) D Sweeney 33/1: 05608: Prom 5f: 6 wk abs: unplcd earlier in '99 (rtd 57, mdn): has tried up to 10f previously: with B Palling. *1¼* **23a**

WOLVERHAMPTON (Fibresand) MONDAY DECEMBER 27TH Lefthand, Sharp Track

3947} **DANESTAR 99** [1] 4-8-10 (42) P M Quinn (5) 14/1: 0-5009: Al rear: op 10/1: 3 month abs/AW bow: 2 **19a**
unplcd in Britain earlier in '99 (rtd 41, fill h'cap): ex-Irish, lightly rcd & modest form in native country.
201 **GENIUS 10** [13] 4-9-8 (54) A Culhane 7/1: 000040: Sn bhd: 10th: op 5/1: see 201 (seller). 15 **8a**
176 **KIRISNIPPA 14** [12] 4-9-6 (52)(VIS) Dean McKeown 14/1: P30060: Al rear: 11th: visor: op 10/1. 1¼ **3a**
2097} **GEEFORCE 99** [8] 3-8-11 (44) N Carlisle 9/1: 0-0010: Chsd ldrs 4f: 12th: op 12/1: 6 month abs. 27 **0a**
12 ran Time 1m 51.6 (5.4) (Mrs Jill McNeill) D J G Murray Smith Gumley, Leics.

LINGFIELD (Equitrack) WEDNESDAY DECEMBER 29TH Lefthand, V Sharp Track

Official Going STANDARD. Stalls: Inside, except 5f/1m - Outside.

234 1.15 GOLF & RACING NURSERY HCAP 2YO 0-75 (E) 5f aw rnd Going 34 -14 Slow [78]
£2590 £727 £354

*221 **DACCORD 7** [3] E A Wheeler 2-10-0 (78)(7ex) S Carson (5) 1/2 FAV: 044311: 2 ch g Beveled - National **86a**
Time (Lord Avie) Made all, styd on strongly ins last, in command cl-home, pushed out: hvly bckd at odds on: 7lb pen: recent wnr here at Lingfield (mdn): plcd earlier in '99 (auct mdn, rtd 76): eff at 5/6f, 7f+ could suit acts on gd, soft & equitrack: likes a sharp trk, esp Lingfield: runs well fresh: eff forcing the pace: fast improving.
4430} **WILLOW MAGIC 71** [5] S Dow 2-8-12 (62) P Doe (3) 7/1: 6002: 2 b f Petong - Love Street (Mummy's 1¼ **65a**
Pet) Cl-up, rdn/outpcd 2f out, kept on ins last, not pace of wnr: h'cap/AW bow: 10 wk abs: unplcd earlier in '99 (rtd 68, mdn): eff at 5f, return to 6f shld suit: acts on equitrack, prob handles fast, gd & a sharp trk.
4221} **ITSGOTTABDUN 86** [2] K T Ivory 2-8-11 (61) C Catlin (7) 7/1: 550203: 2 b g Foxhound - Lady Ingrid 2½ **57a**
(Taufan) Dwelt, sn rdn/chsd ldrs, onepace over 1f out: bckd at long odds, tchd 14/1: 12 wk abs/AW bow: rnr-up here in '99 (seller, rtd 62): eff at 5f, tried 6f: handles soft & equitrack: handles a sharp/undul trk: tried blnks.
3820} **POWER AND DEMAND 99** [1] D Shaw 2-8-1 (51) F Norton 33/1: 00604: Cl-up, ch 2f out, wknd ins last: shd **47a**
op 16/1, 4 month abs: unplcd earlier in '99 (rtd 65 & 42a): eff at 5f & handles equitrack.
217 **SKI FREE 8** [7] 2-7-10 (46)(1oh) P M Quinn (5) 33/1: -53605: Wide/al outpcd: now with J L Harris. 6 **31a**
4184} **FOXKEY 89** [6] 2-9-3 (67)(BL) S Whitworth 9/1: 211006: Cl-up, btn/sltly hmpd 2f out: op 5/1, blnks: shd **52a**
3 month abs, prev with A J McNae, now with Miss Gay Kelleway.
4430} **POLLYOLLY 71** [4] 2-7-10 (46)(5oh) R Brisland (1) 33/1: 50007: Keen/prom, hmpd 2f out/sn btn: abs. 20 **9a**
7 ran Time 1m 0.20 (2.4) (Dagfell Properies Ltd) E A Wheeler Whitchurch On Thames, Oxon.

235 1.45 FURLONGS HCAP 3YO+ 0-75 (E) 5f aw rnd Going 34 -02 Slow [75]
£2615 £734 £358

205 **AA YOUKNOWNOTHING 11** [6] Miss J F Craze 3-9-1 (62)(tvis) S Finnamore (7) 8/1: 003341: 3 b g **71a**
Superpower - Bad Payer (Tanfirion) Made all, in command 1f out, styd on strongly, rdn out: plcd form earlier in '99 (rtd 75a & 64, h'caps): '98 Musselburgh wnr (auct mdn, M W Easterby) & Thirsk (auct stks, rtd 81): eff at 5f, tried 6f: acts on firm, soft & both AWs: handles any trk, likes a sharp one: likes to race with/force the pace: suited by visor & a t-strap, has tried blnks: speedy gelding.
154 **WISHBONE ALLEY 23** [4] M Dods 4-7-10 (43)(vis) Dale Gibson 100/30: 030022: 4 b g Common Grounds 1¼ **47a**
- Dul Dul (Shadeed) Chsd ldrs, rdn & kept on ins last, not pace to chall: nicely bckd: return to 6f shld suit.
*205 **TORRENT 11** [3] D W Chapman 4-9-12 (73)(bl) Lynsey Hanna (7) 7/4 FAV: 232113: 4 ch g Prince Sabo 2½ **70a**
- Maiden Pool (Sharpen Up) Hmpd after 1f, trkd ldrs halfway, sn onepace: well bckd tho' op Evens: topweight.
57 **CARMARTHEN 43** [7] K R Burke 3-8-0 (47) F Norton 9/1: 030444: Chsd ldrs 4f: 6 wk abs: op 6/1: 1 **42a**
plcd form earlier in '99 (rtd 55, h'cap): rnr-up on racecourse bow in '98 (mdn, rtd 70, I Balding): eff at 5f, has tried 6f: acts on firm, gd & equitrack, prob handles soft: likes a sharp/turning track.
205 **BRUTAL FANTASY 11** [5] 5-9-4 (65) A McCarthy (3) 5/1: 000025: Cl-up, rdn/outpcd over 1f out, shd **60a**
kept on ins last, not pace to chall: nicely bckd: see 205 (C/D).
159 **DANCING JACK 21** [1] 6-7-10 (43)(13oh) R Brisland (1) 50/1: 300006: Bhd, mod late prog: see 107. 1 **36a**
183 **SNAP CRACKER 16** [2] 3-8-12 (59) A Culhane 20/1: 404007: Al outpcd rear: plcd form earlier in '99 1 **50a**
(rtd 69, h'cap, H S Howe): '98 wnr at Sandown (debut), Leicester & Chester (med auct & nov stks, rtd 84, for M Quinn): eff at 5f: acts on fast, enjoys gd/soft & hvy: handles any trk: has run well fresh: well h'capped.
7 ran Time 59.6 (1.8) (T Marshall) Miss J F Craze Elvington, N.Yorks.

236 2.15 TEES & STALLS SELLER 2YO (G) 1m aw rnd Going 34 -18 Slow
£1889 £531 £259

155 **SHAMAN 21** [7] G L Moore 2-9-4 G Parkin 4/1 FAV: 030041: 2 b c Fraam - Magic Maggie (Beveled) **64a**
Mid-div halfway, rdn over 3f out, prog/switched ins last & styd on well to lead nr fin, drvn out: well bckd: no bid: earlier in '99 scored at Folkestone (seller, rtd 71 at best, M Channon): eff at 7f, now suited by 1m, further may suit: acts on equitrack, fast & gd grnd: handles any trk, likes a sharp/undul one: enjoys sell grade.
192 **RIDGECREST 14** [5] R Ingram 2-8-12 S Drowne 5/1: 304242: 2 ch c Anshan - Lady Sabo (Prince Sabo) 1¼ **56a**
Led 1f & remained handy, drvn/led again ins last, hdd nr fin, no extra: op 7/2: handles both AWs: see 192, 150.
*192 **COME ON MURGY 14** [9] A Bailey 2-8-13 J Bramhill 8/1: 006013: 2 b f Weldnaas - Forest Song (Forzando) 2 **53a**
Prom, rdn/briefly outpcd halfway, rallied & ev ch ins last, no extra cl-home: op 5/1: stays 1m: acts on both AWs.
4517} **LORD HARLEY 64** [4] B R Millman 2-8-12 A Clark 20/1: 0004: Led over 5f out, hdd ins last & no extra: ½ **51$**
op 16/1, 2 month abs: unplcd earlier in '99 (rtd 32): stays 1m, handles equitrack: 7f/similar grade shld suit.
48 **GLENWHARGEN 44** [11] 2-8-7 J Fanning 5/1: 053045: Prom, onepace over 1f out: op 4/1, 6 wk abs. 1¾ **43a**
192 **WISHEDHADGONEHOME 14** [3] 2-8-7 (BL) S Whitworth 6/1: 050026: Dwelt, sn chsd ldrs, no impress ½ **42a**
ins last: op 4/1, first time blnks: fin well clr of rem: prob handles both AWs: see 192 (7f, fibresand).
4367} **QUEEN FOR A DAY 75** [10] 2-8-7 P M Quinn (5) 13/2: 342007: Led after 1f till over 5f out, sn btn: 11 10 **27a**
wk abs/AW bow: prev with C Wall, rnr-up earlier in '99 (rtd 66, nurs h'cap): stays 1m: acts on soft, handles firm: cost current connections 3,200gns, now with H J Collingridge.
88 **EXUDE 37** [2] 2-8-7 G Carter 20/1: 0658: Al towards rear: op 10/1: mod form. 3 **21a**
150 **CASTLEBRIDGE 23** [12] 2-8-12 M Tebbutt 20/1: 009: Wide/al rear: bckd at long odds, tchd 33/1. 1¼ **23a**
62 **BOMBELLINA 42** [1] 2-8-7 J Tate 7/1: 256040: Dwelt, sn prom, btn 3f out: 10th: abs, longer 1m trip. 1 **16a**
2348} **IVORYS GUEST 99** [8] 2-8-12 C Catlin (7) 33/1: -0000: Chsd ldrs 4f: 11th: 6 month abs/AW bow. 14 **0a**
-- **LANCRESS PRINCESS** [6] 2-8-9(2ow) T G McLaughlin 33/1: 0: Dwelt, sn well bhd: 12th: debut. dist **0a**
12 ran Time 1m 40.34 (4.14) (Mrs S M Redjep) G L Moore Woodingdean, E.Sussex.

237   2.45 HAPPY YEAR HCAP 3YO+ 0-100 (C)   1m4f aw   Going 34   +03 Fast   [85]
£6318   £1913   £934   £444   3 yo rec 5 lb

230   **WHITE PLAINS 2** [2]   K R Burke 6-9-8 (79)(t) D Sweeney 8/1: 054331: 6 b g Nordico - Flying Diva   84a
(Chief Singer) Held up in tch, prog to lead over 4f out, duelled with rnr-up ins last, styd on gamely to just prevail,
all out: best time of day: op 7/1, qck reapp: earlier in '99 scored here at Lingfield (stks, rtd 89a at best, subs
rtd 60 on turf, stks): '98 Southwell wnr (stks, rtd 93a at best): eff at 1m, suited by a sharp 10/12f: acts on
firm, gd & both AWs: handles any trk, loves Lingfield: wears a t-strap: eff weight carrier: tough & genuine.
219   **NIGHT CITY 7** [1]   K R Burke 8-9-7 (78) P Doe (3) 12/1: 511032: 8 b g Kris - Night Secret   shd 82a
(Nijinsky) Led, rdn/hdd over 4f out, rallied gamely for press to duel with wnr ins last, edged right/just
held: well clr rem: op 7/1: longer priced stablemate of wnr, shld win again this winter: see 92 (clmr).
200   **STEAMROLLER STANLY 12** [5]   K R Burke 6-8-13 (70)(VIS) S Whitworth 9/1: 366433: 6 b g Shirley   9 64a
Heights - Miss Demure (Shy Groom) Trkd ldrs till halfway, sn rdn/outpcd, kept on ins last to retake 3rd, no
threat: completed at 1-2-3 for connections: tried visor: jockey reported gelding would apprec return to 2m.
*151   **NOUKARI 23** [6]   P D Evans 6-9-10 (81) S Drowne 9/4: 131114: Chsd ldrs, outpcd 3f out: bckd, btr 151.   3 71a
135   **MAKARIM 28** [3]   3-8-10 (72) J Fanning 10/1: 610065: Trkd ldrs halfway, rdn/outpcd fnl 3f: tchd 12/1.   ¾ 61a
*200   **BODFARI QUARRY 12** [4]   3-9-9 (85)(t) M Hills 2/1 FAV: 100116: Chsd ldrs, rdn/btn 4f out: well   3 70a
backed tho' op 7/4: jockey reported filly appeared to be in season: well bckd: btr 200 (fibresand).
1298} **COPPER SHELL 99** [7]   5-8-12 (69) F Norton 25/1: 121207: Rdn after 4f, bhd fnl 4f: op 14/1, 8 mth   18 35a
abs: earlier in '99 scored thrice at Southwell (mdn h'cap & 2 amat h'caps) & subs at W'hampton (appr h'cap, rtd 69a,
no turf form): eff at 11/12f, tried 2m: eff in a t-strap: loves fibresand/Southwell: runs well for an appr/amat.
7 ran   Time 2m 32.93 (3.73)   (Nigel Shields)   K R Burke Newmarket.

238   3.15 SILKS&PLUS FOURS MDN 3YO+ (D)   1m2f aw   Going 34   -20 Slow
£2741   £770   £376

102   **BILLICHANG 35** [8]   P Howling 3-9-0 R Winston 25/1: 530301: 3 b c Chilibang - Swing O'The Kilt   53a
(Hotfoot) Led/dsptd lead, went on over 2f out, styd on well, rdn out: op 16/1: rnr-up twice earlier in '99 (rtd
58a & 55): unplcd in '98 (rtd 51a & 50): eff arnd 9/10f: acts on both AWs: likes a sharp trk: has tried a visor.
4258} **LADY OF THE NIGHT 85** [2]   Mrs L Stubbs 3-8-12 A Culhane 14/1: 042: 4 b f Night Shift - Joma   1¼ 50a
Kaanem (Double Form) Chsd ldrs, led over 5f out till 2f out, no extra nr line: 12 wk abs/AW bow: unplcd tho'
promise on 2 starts earlier in '99 for P Harris (rtd 62, mdn): stays 10f, handles equitrack & soft grnd.
97   **SING CHEONG 36** [5]   G C H Chung 3-9-0 A Clark 7/2: 000243: 3 b c Forest Wind - Lady Counsel (Law   3½ 47a
Society) Chsd ldrs, rdn halfway, kept on fnl 2f, not pace to chall: well bckd: stays a sharp 10f: see 97, 8 (7f/1m).
189   **PREDOMINANT 14** [3]   W J Haggas 3-9-0 M Hills 8/1: 04: Chsd ldrs, rdn/outpcd 4f out, kept on fnl   ¾ 46a
2f, no threat: prob likes longer 10f trip & handles equitrack.
4541} **PIPADOR 62** [10]   3-9-0 A Rawlinson 25/1: 000005: Rear, late gains, no threat: abs: unplcd   nk 45$
earlier in '99 (rtd 33 & 21a): rtd 59 in '98 (mdn, R Hannon): stays 10f & handles equitrack: has tried blnks.
1631} **CRESSET 99** [11]   3-9-0 M Tebbutt 7/1: 0006: Rear, nvr able to chall: 7 month abs/AW bow: clr   2½ 41a
of rem: unplcd on 3 starts earlier in '99 (rtd 61, mdn): longer 10f trip today for W Jarvis.
167   **SKY CITY 19** [9]   3-8-9 A McCarthy (3) 33/1: 000007: Rear, mod gains.   8 27a
225   **AMBUSHED 7** [12]   3-9-0 K Dalgleish (7) 9/1: 08: Led after 2f till over 5f out/fdd: op 6/1, lngr 10f trip.   ¾ 31a
1179} **HATHNI KHOUND 99** [4]   3-8-9 D Dineley 16/1: 030209: Trkd ldrs 7f: op 12/1: jumps fit.   1 25a
1392} **ILISSUS 99** [6]   3-9-0 W Ryan 9/4 FAV: 32U0: Held up, rdn/btn 4f out: 10th: hvly bckd, tchd 11/4: AW   ½ 29a
bow/7 month abs: plcd twice earlier in '99 (rtd 82, mdn, M P Tregoning): eff around 7f/1m, 10f could suit in time:
handles gd/soft & soft grnd & a gall/sharpish trk: now with P Mitchell.
229   **NOTIONAL 2** [1]   3-9-0 (tBL) S Drowne 7/1: 233000: Mid-div, rdn 3f out: 11th: op 11/2, blnks: qck reapp.   6 15a
173   **IRISH MELODY 18** [7]   3-8-9 T G McLaughlin 33/1: 000060: Al rear: 12th: longer 10f trip.   16 0a
12 ran   Time 2m 08.18 (5.38)   (Paul Howling Racing Syndicate)   P Howling Newmarket.

239   3.45 WHIPS & WOODS HCAP 3YO+ 0-80 (D)   7f aw rnd   Going 34   -02 Slow   [78]
£3892   £1178   £575   £273

208   **ELMHURST BOY 11** [1]   S Dow 3-10-0 (78)(vis) W Ryan 12/1: 310021: 3 b c Merdon Melody - Young Whip   84a
(Bold Owl) Held up in tch, prog/briefly no room 2f out, switched & styd on strongly ins last to lead nr fin, drvn out:
op 10/1, visor reapplied: earlier in '99 scored at Epsom (4 rnr mdn, rtd 80): plcd in '98 (rtd 83, nov): eff at 6f,
suited by 7f/1m: acts on any trk: acts on firm, hvy & equitrack: eff with/without visor or blnks: eff wght carrier.
3565} **COMEOUTOFTHEFOG 2** [2]   S Dow 4-8-7 (57) P Doe (3) 25/1: 610302: 4 b g Mujadil - Local Belle   1 60a
(Ballymore) Prom, briefly outpcd halfway, rdn/prog to lead over 1f out, hdd nr fin & no extra: op 16/1, 4 month
abs, stablemate of wnr: earlier in '99 won here at Lingfield (sell h'cap, rtd 58a, with A J McNae), plcd on turf
(rtd 44, h'caps): '98 wnr again at Lingfield (2, clmrs, 1 for D Ffrench Davis, rtd 69a & 56): eff at 7f/1m on
fast, firm & likes soft grnd: runs well fresh: likes to race with/force the pace.
*156   **APOLLO RED 21** [9]   G L Moore 10-9-8 (72) A Clark 14/1: 020613: 10 ch g Dominion - Woolpack   1¼ 72a
(Golden Fleece) Prom, led 3f out till over 1f out, no extra cl-home: op 8/1: see 156 (C/D, seller).
162   **SCISSOR RIDGE 21** [6]   J J Bridger 7-8-6 (56) G Bardwell 14/1: 441304: Rdn/towards rear, kept on   ¾ 55a
ins last for press, not pace to chall: op 12/1: see 29 (C/D).
220   **MALCHIK 7** [11]   3-7-10 (46)(bl) A McCarthy (2) 50/1: 000505: Rdn/bhd, late gains wide, nrst fin.   1¼ 42$
*121   **SWING ALONG 32** [5]   4-9-2 (66) M Tebbutt 8/1: 305316: Rdn/rear, late gains wide/no threat: op 5/1:   ½ 61a
now with R Guest: acts on gd, hvy, fibresand & prob handles equitrack: see 121 (fill h'cap, fibresand).
*210   **RESIST THE FORCE 11** [3]   M Hills 5/2 FAV: 140-17: Chsd ldrs, wknd over 1f out: hvly bckd.   1¾ 59a
210   **URSA MAJOR 11** [10]   5-8-12 (62)(bl) R Studholme (5) 11/1: 100048: Cl-up 5f: see 210.   nk 53a
162   **CANTINA 21** [8]   5-9-6 (70) G Carter 3/1: 045029: Led 4f, btn/eased fnl 1f: nicely bckd: btr 162 (C/D).   2½ 46a
180   **CARAMBO 16** [7]   4-9-0 (64) D Sweeney 25/1: 040000: Mid-div, btn 2f out: 10th: see 180 (fibresand).   2 46a
208   **CONSORT 11** [4]   6-9-8 (72) R Winston 7/1: 000030: Chsd ldrs halfway, rdn/btn 2f out & eased ins   6 45a
last: 11th: tchd 10/1: much closer to today's wnr in 208 (1m), something amiss today?
11 ran   Time 1m 25.35 (2.55)   (R E Anderson)   S Dow Epsom, Surrey.

LINGFIELD (Equitrack) SUNDAY JANUARY 2ND Lefthand, V Sharp Track

Official Going STANDARD. Stalls: Inside, Except 1m - Outside.

---

240 1.20 AULD LANG SYNE MDN 3YO (D) **1m2f aw Going 38 -22 Slow**
£2808 £864 £432 £216

4278} **BLUEBELL WOOD** 86 [5] G C Bravery 3-8-9 A Culhane 10/1: 0-1: 3 ch f Bluebird - Jungle Jezebel   71a
(Thatching) Chsd ldrs, hard on, styd on gamely to led nr line, all out: op 7/1: 3 month abs/AW bow:
unplcd on sole '99 start (mdn, rtd 62, A J McNae): apprec this step up to 10f, 12f+ cld suit: acts on equitrack
& on a sharp trk: runs well fresh: open to further improvement for new connections.
221 **BUGGY RIDE** 11 [3] Miss Gay Kelleway 3-9-0 S Whitworth 7/4 FAV: 0242-2: 3 b c Blues Traveller -   ½ 74a
Tambora (Darshaan) Cl-up, rdn to lead ins last, hard rdn & hdd nr line: well bckd: styd longer 10f trip well.
4570} **LAGO DI COMO** 62 [2] T J Naughton 3-9-0 P Doe (3) 12/1: 0000-3: 3 b c Piccolo - Farmer's Pet   1 73$
(Sharrood) Narrow lead till rdn & hdd well ins last, no extra: op 6/1: 2 month abs/AW bow: unplcd in '99 (rtd
63, mdn): stays 10f, acts on equitrack & a sharp trk: a return to h'cap company could suit.
204 **KUWAIT TROOPER** 12 [11] G A Butler 3-9-0 G Carter 12/1: 60-4: Dwelt, mid-div halfway, rdn & kept   3½ 68a
on for press fnl 2f, nrst fin: bckd at long odds, tchd 16/1: stays 10f, 12f+ suit on this evidence: apprec h'caps.
204 **BOX CAR** 15 [10] 3-9-0 F Norton 3/1: 0662-5: Chsd ldrs halfway, outpcd fnl 3f: op 6/1: see 204.   nk 67$
150 **ODYN DANCER** 27 [1] 3-8-9 G Baker 20/1: 0003-6: Twds rear, mod gains/no threat: see 150 (1m).   ½ 61a
125 **LE CAVALIER** 33 [12] 3-9-0 M Tebbutt 9/1: 0040-7: Mid-div at best: op 7/1: unplcd on turf in '99   ½ 65a
(rtd 67, subs tried blnks): longer 10f trip today.
3442} **AROB PETE** 99 [13] 3-9-0 T G McLaughlin 12/1: 0-8: Bhd halfway, mod prog: 5 mth abs/AW bow.   12 52a
204 **OPEN GROUND** 15 [8] 3-9-0 A McCarthy 20/1: 0063-9: Rear/wide, nvr factor: see 204 (C/D).   3 48a
171 **WEST END DANCER** 22 [7] 3-8-9 A Clark 11/1: 50-0: Dwelt, mid-div halfway, sn btn: 10th: op 8/1.   10 32a
-- **GRAND JURY** [2] 3-9-0 J Fanning 10/1: 0: Dwelt/al rear: 11th: op 8/1: debut, with E O'Neill.   1¾ 35a
204 **Beach Baby** 15 [9] 3-8-9 G Bardwell 40/1:   -- **Bryna** [6] 3-8-9 (VIS) N Callan (3) 25/1:
13 ran Time 2m 08.76 (5.96)   (The Iona Stud)   G C Bravery Newmarket, Suffolk

---

241 1.50 ESAPS CLAIMER 3YO (F) **1m aw rnd Going 38 -35 Slow**
£2194 £627 £313

192 **KIGEMA** 18 [1] C N Allen 3-8-8 L Newman (5) 9/4: 5506-1: 3 ch f Case Law - Grace de Bois (Tap On Wood)   52a
Sn trkd ldrs, briefly no room 2f out, chsd ldr fnl 1f & rdn to lead ins last, drvn out: op 7/4: '99 wnr at Brighton
(sell, rtd 66): eff at 6f, now stays a sharp 1m well: acts on equitrack & fast grnd: enjoys sell/claiming grade.
204 **MASTER JONES** 15 [6] Mrs L Stubbs 3-9-3 A Culhane 5/1: 0640-2: 3 b g Emperor Jones - Tight Spin   2¼ 55a
(High Top) Sn cl-up going well, led 2f out, rdn & hdd ins last & no extra: tchd 13/2: stays 1m: acts on equitrack
& soft grnd: shld find a similar contest, poss back at 7f: see 94 (7f).
236 **WISHEDHADGONEHOME** 4 [2] P D Evans 3-8-10 (vis) Joanna Badger (7) 2/1 FAV: 0026-3: 3 b f Archway -3   42a
Yavarro (Raga Navarro) Slowly away & bhd, kept on fnl 3f for press, no threat to front pair: well bckd: qck reapp.
204 **DR DUKE** 15 [7] Mrs N Macauley 3-9-3 (BL) Dean McKeown 10/1: 0555-4: Led 3f, wknd over 1f out: ½ 48$
op 8/1, blnks: place form in '99 (rtd 58, h'cap, R Hodges): eff at 5/7f, has tried 10f: handles firm & soft
grnd, prob handles equitrack: handles any trk: has tried a visor.
3579} **LUNAJAZ** 49 [4] 3-8-11 R Price 25/1: 000-5: Cl-up, led 5f out till 2f out: fdd: 4 month abs/AW bow: 1½ 39a
unplcd in '99 (rtd 40): longer 1m trip today.
192 **TALLYWHACKER** 18 [5] 3-8-6 G Bardwell 25/1: 00-6: Held up in tch, nvr factor: longer 1m trip.   5 24a
54 **SALLY GARDENS** 47 [3] 3-9-2 F Norton 6/1: 1500-7: Cl-up 6f: op 7/2, 7 wk abs: shorter priced   6 24a
stablemate of 6th: '99 wnr at W'hampton (fill sell, rtd 70a, M Channon), unplcd on turf (rtd 72, mdn): eff at 7f:
acts on fibresand, handles gd/soft grnd: handles a gall or sharp trk: enjoys sell grade.
7 ran Time 1m 42.07 (5.87)   (Green Square Racing)   C N Allen Newmarket, Suffolk

---

242 2.20 TESTERS HCAP 3YO 0-60 (F) **6f aw rnd Going 38 -27 Slow**   [67]
£2730 £840 £420 £210

207 **GREY FLYER** 15 [3] Mrs L Stubbs 3-9-2 (55) A Culhane 7/2: 0642-1: 3 gr g Factual - Faraway Grey   64a
(Absalom) Sn cl-up, led halfway, drvn out to hold on ins last: nicely bckd, op 5/1: '99 scorer at Musselburgh
(clmr, rtd 66 & 35a): eff at 5f/sharp 6f: acts on fast & equitrack: has run well fresh: likes a sharp trk.
153 **TOLDYA** 27 [8] E A Wheeler 3-8-11 (50) S Carson (5) 11/2: 0002-2: 3 b f Beveled - Run Amber Run   ½ 56a
(Run The Gantlet) Prom, rdn & ch over 1f out, kept on well for press: op 9/2: eff at 6f on e/track: encouraging.
*149 **MR GEORGE SMITH** 27 [9] G L Moore 3-9-7 (60) F Norton 5/4 FAV: 0031-3: 3 b c Prince Sabo - Nellie's   nk 65a
Gamble (Mummy's Game) Chsd ldrs, rdn & kept on ins last, not pace to chall: hvly bckd: eff at 6f, suited by 7f.
127 **MARITUN LAD** 35 [6] D Shaw 3-9-4 (57) N Callan (3) 16/1: 065-4: Chsd ldrs halfway, briefly no room   shd 62a
over 1f out, kept on ins last for press: op 8/1: unplcd from 3 starts in '99 (rtd 57a, no turf form):
eff at 6f & handles equitrack: encouraging h'cap bow.
228 **CACOPHONY** 6 [2] 3-9-2 (55) P Doe (3) 8/1: 3033-5: Dwelt/rdn rear, mod gains: op 5/1: qck reapp.   5 51a
155 **WHERES CHARLOTTE** 25 [10] 3-8-8 (47) P Fitzsimons (5) 10/1: 0300-6: Cl-up, fdd over 1f out: op 7/1.   6 32a
217 **XENOS** 12 [1] 3-8-10 (49) A McCarthy (3) 14/1: 0000-7: Led 2f, sn btn: unplcd in '99 (earlier with   ½ 32a
M R Channon, rtd 75, prob flattered, auct mdn): now with P Howling.
2905} **MINIMUS TIME** 99 [7] 3-8-3 (42) P M Quinn (5) 33/1: 0306-8: Dwelt/rear, nvr factor: 5 month abs/   ¾ 23a
AW bow: unplcd in '99 (rtd 50, sell): h'cap bow today for T Jones.
207 **EMMAS HOPE** 15 [4] 3-7-10 (35)(bl) Joanna Badger (7) 20/1: 0005-9: Chsd ldrs 3f: see 207 (clmr).   1¼ 13a
221 **CAPPUCINO LADY** 11 [5] 3-8-1 (40) G Bardwell 33/1: 3060-0: Dwelt/al bhd: 10th.   7 5a
10 ran Time 1m 14.3 (3.9)   (D M Smith)   Mrs L Stubbs Collingbourne Ducis, Wilts

---

243 2.50 FOOTING CLASS STKS 3YO+ 0-65 (E) **7f aw rnd Going 38 -16 Slow**
£2795 £860 £430 £215   3yo rec 18lb

166 **MISS DANGEROUS** 23 [4] M Quinn 5-9-6 (bl) F Norton 20/1: 0006-1: 5 b m Komaite - Khadine (Astec)   60a
Made all, rdn & clr 2f out, styd on gamely ins last, rdn out: bckd at long odds: '99 wnr here at Lingfield (fill
h'cap, rtd 60a), subs rnr-up on turf (rtd 42, h'cap): '98 wnr at W'hampton (2, sell & fills h'cap, rtd 67a),
Folkestone (clmr) & Warwick (h'cap, rtd 62): eff at 5/6f, loves to force the pace at 7f: acts on gd, soft & loves
both AWs: likes a sharp/undul trk, esp Lingfield: runs well fresh: eff in blnks: fine effort at today's weights.
180 **DAYS OF GRACE** 20 [9] L Montague Hall 5-9-8 Martin Dwyer 11/4: 3124-2: 5 gr m Wolfhound - Inshirah   2 59a

87

LINGFIELD (Equitrack)   SUNDAY JANUARY 2ND   Lefthand, V Sharp Track

(Caro) Handy halfway, rdn & kept on ins last, not pace to chall: well bckd, tchd 4/1: acts on both AWs, firm
& hvy grnd: remains in gd form: see 121 (h'cap).

212   **MUTAHADETH** 12 [11] D Shaw 6-9-9 (bl) J Fanning 20/1: 4040-3: 6 ch g Rudimentary - Music In My   3   54a
Life (Law Society) Towards rear/wide halfway, rdn & kept on fnl 2f, nrst fin: suited by 1m/Southwell: see 183.
212   **XSYNNA** 12 [8] T T Clement 4-9-9 M Tebbutt 12/1: 0435-4: Prom, outpcd 2f: op 8/1: see 212 (6f).   ¾   53a
*213   **MISS WORLD** 12 [10] 3-8-4 (t) L Newman (5) 3/1: 2321-5: Chsd ldrs, held over 1f out: see 213 (1m).   1¾   49a
3585} **SOUNDS LUCKY** 99 [2] 4-9-9 T G McLaughlin 14/1: 4500-6: Keen/chsd ldrs, not able to chall: op 10/1,   hd   49a
4 month abs: '99 wnr at W'hampton (2, sell & h'cap, rtd 58a) & Lingfield (h'cap, rtd 64): rtd 43 & 50a in '98: eff
at 5/6f on fast, gd/soft & fibresand, prob handles equitrack: likes a sharp/undul trk, esp W'hampton: best without
a visor: will be suited by a return to 6f & Wolverhampton.
*155   **PERLE DE SAGESSE** 25 [7] 3-8-6 A Daly 5/2 FAV: 2101-7: Chsd ldrs halfway, btn 2f out: see 155 (clmr).   1½   47a
147   **TRAWLING** 27 [1] 4-9-6 S Drowne 9/1: 3000-8: Chsd ldrs 5f: op 6/1: '99 wnr here at Lingfield   shd   43a
(mdn, B Hills, rtd 77a), unplcd on turf (rtd 62, h'cap): rnr-up both starts in '98 (mdn & auct mdn, rtd 77): eff
at 1m, has tried 12f, may suit in time: acts on fast, gd & equitrack: handles a sharp/gall trk: has run well fresh.
*159   **DARK MENACE** 25 [3] 8-9-11 (bl) D Kinsella (7) 12/1: 2301-9: Twds rear/nvr factor: op see 159 (sell).   3   42a
4319} **MUMMY NOSE BEST** 83 [6] 4-9-6 R Brisland (5) 50/1: 0000-0: Chsd ldrs 4f, sn btn: 10th: 12 wk abs.   8   25a
10 ran   Time 1m 26.59 (3.79)   (M Quinn)   M Quinn Sparsholt, Oxon

---

244   3.20 WELCOME TO Y2K HCAP 4YO+ 0-95 (C)   1m2f aw   Going 38   +08 Fast   [95]
£10676   £3285   £1642   £821   4yo rec 2lb

*237   **WHITE PLAINS** 4 [2] K R Burke 7-9-4 (85)(t) N Callan (3) 11/2: 4331-1: 7 b g Nordico - Flying   89a
Diva (Chief Singer) Towards rear, prog halfway & drvn to lead ins last, held on gamely, all out: fast time: op 6/1,
quick reapp: 6lb pen: '99 Lingfield wnr (2, stks & h'cap, rtd 89a), subs rtd 60 on turf: '98 Southwell wnr (stks,
rtd 93a at best): eff at 1m, suited by a sharp 10/12f: acts on fast, gd & loves both AWs: handles any trk, loves
a sharp one, wears a t-strap: eff weight carrier: tough & useful AW performer.
*160   **ANEMOS** 25 [11] M A Jarvis 5-8-8 (75) J Fanning 6/1: 6201-2: 5 ch g Be My Guest - Frendly Persuasion   hd   78a
(General Assembly) Sn prom, led going well over 2f out, hard rdn & hdd ins last, kept on well for press, just held:
5L clr rem, op 9/2: fine eff, will win more races: see 160 (C/D).
160   **PHILISTAR** 25 [8] K R Burke 7-8-3 (70) F Norton 16/1: 5265-3: 7 ch h Bairn - Philgwyn (Milford)   5   65a
Chsd ldrs, kept on onepace fnl 2f, no threat to front pair: tchd 20/1, longer priced stablemate of wnr: see 93 (1m).
*208   **SECRET SPRING** 15 [9] Mrs I Richards 8-9-9 (90) A Clark 3/1 FAV: 0211-4: Hmpd first 100yds &   shd   85a
dropped to rear, rdn & kept on fnl 3f, no threat to front pair: well bckd, op 4/1: no luck in running: see 208 (1m).
143   **FORTY FORTE** 29 [13] 4-8-2 (71) Joanna Badger (7) 20/1: 1320-5: Led/sn clr, hdd over 2f out & fdd: 1½   64a
op 16/1, stablemate of wnr: see 22 (C/D, appr h'cap).
230   **TIGHTROPE** 6 [6] 5-7-11 (64) C Cogan (3) 8/1: 2024-6: Dwelt/towards rear, mod prog: quick reapp.   8   48a
157   **DAUNTED** 25 [10] 4-8-7 (76)(bl) G Parkin 20/1: 6400-7: Chsd ldrs 6f: see 157 (C/D).   nk   59a
208   **HUGWITY** 15 [1] 8-9-4 (85) A Culhane 16/1: 2216-8: Rear, nvr factor: see 208 (1m).   1¾   66a
230   **ITALIAN SYMPHONY** 6 [12] 6-10-0 (95)(vis) S Drowne 12/1: 4415-9: Mid-div, btn 2f out: topweight.   nk   75a
172   **TALLULAH BELLE** 22 [4] 7-9-5 (86) T G McLaughlin 14/1: 6150-0: Al rear: 10th: btn 119 (fibresand).   1¼   64a
*161   **JUST WIZ** 25 [8] 4-9-1 (84)(bl) R Smith (7) 9/2: 3131-0: Chsd ldr 5f, sn btn: 13th: btr 161 (C/D).   0a
163   **Thomas Henry** 23 [3] 4-7-10 (65)(3oh) P M Quinn(5) 25/1: 237 **Makarim** 4 [5] 4-8-3 (72) P Doe(3) 25/1:
13 ran   Time 2m 05.84 (3.04)   (Nigel Shields)   K R Burke Newmarket, Suffolk

---

245   3.50 HANGOVER HCAP 4YO+ 0-85 (D)   1m4f aw   Going 38   +07 Fast   [81]
£4212   £1296   £648   £324   4yo rec 4lb

151   **SPACE RACE** 27 [8] C A Cyzer 6-9-9 (76) G Carter 5/1: 0202-1: 6 b g Rock Hopper - Melanoura (Imperial   82a
Fling) Cl-up going well 4f out, rdn/led over 1f out, rdn out: fast time: '99 wnr here at Lingfield (h'cap, rtd
78a), subs 2nd on turf (rtd 68, stks): rtd 83 in '98 (rnr-up, 4 rnr h'cap): eff at 1m/sharp 12f: acts on firm,
gd/soft & both AWs: handles any trk, likes Lingfield: has run well fresh: likes to race with/force the pace.
237   **NOUKARI** 4 [3] P D Evans 7-10-0 (81) Joanna Badger (7) 6/1: 1114-2: 7 b g Darshaan - Noufiyla (Top   2   82a
Ville) Mid-div/rdn halfway, kept on fnl 2f, no threat to wnr: op 4/1, quick reapp: topweight: see 237 (C/D).
237   **STEAMROLLER STANLY** 4 [1] K R Burke 7-9-3 (70)(vis) N Callan (3) 15/2: 6433-3: 7 b g Shirley Heights   1¾   69a
- Miss Demure (Shy Groom) Handy, led 4f out till over 1f out, onepace: tchd 10/1, quick reapp: see 237, 151.
220   **FAILED TO HIT** 11 [11] N P Littmoden 7-9-0 (67)(vis) J Tate 7/1: 1522-4: Chsd ldrs, kept on fnl 2f,   2   63a
not pace to chall: see 101 (C/D, clmr).
4443} **SEA DANZIG** 74 [6] 7-8-12 (65) R Brisland 5s 16/1: 1000-5: Rear, mod gains for press fnl 3f: op   2½   57a
12/1, 10 wk abs: '99 scorer at Epsom (h'cap, rtd 59), unplcd on sand (rtd 68a, h'cap): '98 wnr here at Lingfield
(2, rtd 74a), Goodwood & Folkestone (h'cap, rtd 69): eff at 1m/10f, stays a sharp 12f: acts on firm, soft & loves
equitrack/Lingfield: loves to force the pace: nicley h'capped & will apprec a return to 12f: acts on firm.
237   **NIGHT CITY** 4 [10] 9-9-8 (75) P Doe (3) 5/2 FAV: 1032-6: Led/sn clr, hdd 4f out & wknd: well bckd: 3½   62a
shorter priced stablemate of 3rd: quick reapp: see 92 (1m, clmr).
4270} **LORD EUROLINK** 87 [4] 6-9-9 (76) T G McLaughlin 16/1: 6045-7: Chsd ldrs, btn 3f out: jumps fit (rtd   15   47a
85h, nov): plcd on turf in '99 (rtd 79, appr h'cap): plcd sole '98 start for J Dunlop (h'cap, rtd 92): '97 Doncaster
wnr (mdn, rtd 90 at best): stays 10f: acts on fast & gd/soft grnd: handles any trk: AW bow today.
220   **HALF TIDE** 11 [9] 6-7-11 (50)(1ow)(8oh) Dale Gibson 7/2: 2133-8: Bhd 4f out: op 4/1: btr 220 (10f).   18   1a
90   **SHEER NATIVE** 40 [5] 4-9-1 (72) S Whitworth 14/1: 0013-9: Bhd halfway: op 8/1, 6 wk abs: btr 90, 50.   3   19a
9 ran   Time 2m 32.92 (3.72)   (R M Cyzer)   C A Cyzer Maplehurst, W Sussex

---

SOUTHWELL (Fibresand)   MONDAY JANUARY 3RD   Lefthand, Sharp, Oval Track

Official Going STANDARD. Stalls: Inside.

246   12.00 BEDS HCAP DIV 1 3YO+ 0-70 (E)   6f aw rnd   Going 49   -08 Slow   [70]
£3835   £1180   £590   £295   3 yo rec 16lb

218   **KEEN HANDS** 13 [6] Mrs N Macauley 4-9-12 (68)(vis) R Fitzpatrick (3) 6/1: 4024-1: 4 ch g Keen -   75a
Broken Vow (Local Suitor) Chsd ldrs, rdn to lead ins last, pushed out cl-home: '99 scorer at W'hampton (sell) &
here at Southwell (3, sells & h'cap, rtd 75a & 45): rtd 56a in '98: eff at 5/7f, suited by 6f: f/sand/Southwell
specialist: best in a visor: eff weight carrier: tough & can win again.

SOUTHWELL (Fibresand) MONDAY JANUARY 3RD Lefthand, Sharp, Oval Track

193	**SAND HAWK** 19 [10] D Shaw 5-8-12 (54)(bl) R Winston 4/1 FAV: 4512-2: 5 ch g Polar Falcon - Ghassanah (Pas de Seul) Rear, rdn & briefly no room 2f out, led 1f out, sn hdd & not pace of wnr: eff at 6f/1m.	1¾	56a
216	**BEST QUEST** 13 [13] K R Burke 5-9-4 (60)(t) N Callan (3) 12/1: 3200-3: 5 b h Salse - Quest For The Best (Rainbow Quest) Handy, ch 1f out, no extra cl home: acts on fast, gd & both AWs.	hd	61a
212	**SWINO** 13 [2] P D Evans 6-8-11 (53)(bl) S Drowne 6/1: 4002-4: Rdn in rear, late gains: blnks reapp.	3½	45a
87	**PETITE DANSEUSE** 42 [1] 6-7-12 (40)(2ow)(5oh) P Fessey 16/1: 4260-5: Led 5f, no extra: tchd 20/1, 6 wk abs: plcd form in '99 (rtd 38 & 29a): plcd form in '98 (rtd 58a & 57): '97 Leicester wnr (2 clmrs, rtd 66): eff at 5/7f on firm, soft & both AWs: handles any trk: has run well in a visor, disapp in blnks: nicely hcapped.	1	30a
226	**MISS BANANAS** 7 [4] 5-8-4 (46) T Williams 33/1: 0000-6: Trkd ldrs, btn fnl 2f: see 226.	¾	34a
232	**BARITONE** 7 [7] 6-8-2 (44)(vis) J Tate 40/1: 5000-7: Towards rear, mod gains: '99 Southwell wnr (h'cap, rtd 53a): plcd sev times in '98 (h'cap, rtd 50 & 64a): eff at 6/7f, stays 1m: acts on fast, gd & both AWs: best in a visor, not blnks: can force the pace: likes a sharp track.	½	30a
40	**BAPTISMAL ROCK** 51 [8] 6-8-11 (53) S Whitworth 15/2: 6300-8: Towards rear, nvr factor: 7 wk abs: completed hat-trick early in '99 at W'hampton, Lingfield & here at Southwell (h'caps, rtd 57a), subs plcd numerous times on turf (rtd 52, h'cap): plcd in '98 (rtd 36): eff at 5/6f on firm, soft & both AWs: loves a sharp trk.	2½	32a
232	**MARENGO** 7 [3] 6-9-2 (58) T G McLaughlin 6/1: 0103-9: Chsd ldrs 4f: btr 183 (C/D, made all).	1	35a
*226	**DONE AND DUSTED** 7 [12] 4-9-9 (65)(6ex) C Carver (3) 7/1: 0601-0: Mid-div at best: 10th: btr 226.	nk	41a
212	**CZAR WARS** 13 [5] 5-8-0 (42)(bl) J Bramhill 11/1: 5044-0: Al rear: broke a blood vessel: 13th: see 199.		0a
201	**Gunner Sam** 17 [9] 4-8-10 (52)(bl) Dean McKeown 25/1: 205 **French Grit** 16 [11] 8-8-6 (48) G Parkin 14/1:		
13 ran	Time 1m 16.7 (3.4) (Andy Peake) Mrs N Macauley Sproxton, Leics.		

---

247 12.30 CLASS CLAIMER DIV 1 4YO+ 0-60 (F) 7f aw rnd Going 49 -27 Slow
£1743 £498 £249

*195	**PIPPAS PRIDE** 17 [7] S R Bowring 5-9-3 R Winston 13/2: 0401-1: 5 ch g Pips Pride - Al Shany (Burslem) Chsd ldrs, rdn to lead dist, in command ins last, rdn out: jockey given a 2-day whip ban: '99 wnr here at Southwell (clmr) & Lingfield (h'cap, rtd 41, with M Fetherson Godley): eff arnd a sharp 7f/1m, has tried 10f: acts on both AWs: runs well fresh & enjoys claiming grade: in fine form.		63a
233	**GENIUS** 7 [11] D W Chapman 5-8-5 Lynsey Hanna (7) 8/1: 0040-2: 5 b g Lycius - Once In My Life (Lomond) Rdn in rear, kept on fnl 2f, no threat to wnr: eff at 7f, could find similar back at 1m: see 201.	3½	43a
134	**BEWARE** 33 [1] D Nicholls 5-8-13 F Norton 100/30: 0030-3: 5 br g Warning - Dancing Spirit (Ahonoora) Prom, ch 1f out, no extra: nicely bckd, tchd 5/1: see 30.	½	50a
232	**CHALUZ** 7 [10] N P Littmoden 6-8-12 (t) T G McLaughlin 7/2: 2255-4: Wide/prom, no extra ins last.	nk	48a
226	**AMARO** 7 [6] 4-8-9 G Carter 16/1: 4005-5: Chsd ldrs 6f: see 226 (6f).	3½	38a
63	**FAN TC GEM** 47 [2] 4-8-4 J Edmunds 33/1: 04/0-6: Held up, nvr on terms: 7 wk abs: unplcd on sole start in '99: rtd 48a in '98 (auct mdn): eff at 5f & handles fibresand.	½	32a
65	**SEVEN** 47 [5] 5-9-0 (bl) C Rutter 5/2 FAV: 2622-7: Chsd ldrs 5f: op 7/4: abs, blnks reapplied.	2½	37a
205	**ROYAL ORIGINE** 16 [3] 4-8-13 (tbl) P Doe 33/1: 6000-8: Led 6f, no extra: unplcd in '99 (rtd 59, M Quinn, mdn, prob flattered): plcd in mdns in '98, (M Channon): eff at 6f, tried 1m: handles fast grnd.	2	32a
195	**FOURTH TIME LUCKY** 17 [5] 4-8-6(1ow) G Parkin 50/1: 0060-9: Al rear: rnr-up in '99 (rtd 35a, h'cap): mod form previously: stays a sharp 1m & handles fibresand: best without blnks.	5	15a
3071}	**CORAL WATERS** 99 [4] 4-8-4 (BL) G Bardwell 33/1: 4300-0: Dwelt/al rear: 10th: jumps fit.	23	0a
425}	**MAID PLANS** 99 [8] 4-8-4 P M Quinn (5) 50/1: 6/05-0: Sn bhd: 11th: reapp, now with C N Kellett.	1¾	0a
11 ran	Time 1m 31.9 (5.3) (Roland M Wheatley) S R Bowring Edwinstowe, Notts.		

---

248 1.00 APPR MED AUCT MDN 4-6YO (F) 1m3f aw Going 49 -34 Slow
£2159 £617 £308 4 yo rec 3 lb

3970}	**MICE IDEAS** 99 [14] N P Littmoden 4-8-13 C Cogan (5) 4/1 CO FAV: 4054-1: 4 ch g Fayruz - Tender Encounter (Prince Tenderfoot) Chsd ldrs, led over 2f out, sn clr, pushed out cl-home: op 7/2: prev with S Mellor, 6 wk jumps abs (rtd 78h, last of 5, juv nov): unplcd in '99 (rtd 66 & 53a): rnr-up in '98 (juv auct mdn, rtd 74): eff arnd 1m, suited by 11f & has tried further: acts on fast, gd & f/sand: likes a sharp trk & runs well fresh.		47a
211	**TALECA SON** 13 [7] D Carroll 5-9-2 Joanna Badger (7) 8/1: 0434-2: 5 b g Conquering Hero - Lady Taleca (Exhibitioner) Held up racing keenly, prog to chall over 1f out, sn held: op 10/1: see 211, 144.	5	37a
2903}	**SEASON OF HOPE** 99 [12] D E Cantillon 4-8-8 Claire Bryan (5) 12/1: 0554-3: 4 ch f Komaite - Honour And Glory (Hotfoot) Chsd ldrs & hmpd after 1f, prog to lead 4f out, rdn & hdd 2f out & sn no extra: op 8/1, long jumps abs, rnr-up (juv nov, rtd 90h): unplcd in '99 (rtd 44a & 38): stays 9f, handles f/sand: tried visor/blnks.	3	28a
195	**PRETTY FLY GUY** 17 [5] J Parkes 4-8-13 R Fitzpatrick 40/1: 000-4: Chsd ldrs, onepace fnl 2f: bred to appreciate this longer 11f trip: ex-Irish, mod form.	½	32a
196	**WESTWOOD VIEW** 17 [8] 4-8-8 Paul Cleary (5) 20/1: 0004-5: Chsd ldrs 4f out, sn held: see 196 (C/D).	3½	22a
196	**SHOTLEY MARIE** 17 [4] 5-8-11 (b)) R Brisland (5) 40/1: 0056-6: Chsd ldrs 4f out, btn 2f out: see 196.	5	15a
167	**APPYABO** 24 [15] 5-9-2 R Studholme (3) 20/1: 6000-7: Led 7f, sn held.	¾	19a
224	**ANOTHER RAINBOW** 12 [13] 4-8-8 P Fredericks (7) 4/1 CO FAV: 6250-8: Dwelt/towards rear, mod prog.	8	5a
4300}	**DILETTO** 84 [2] 4-8-8 Melanie Worden (7) 15/2: 0306-9: Held up, nvr factor: op 6/1: 12 wk abs.	2	2a
--	**ROLLING HIGH** [9] 5-9-2 (t) C Carver (3) 33/1: 06/0: Prom, led 4f out, hdd/btn 2f out: 10th: jmps fit, long Flat absence, with D J G Murray Smith.	9	0a
3947}	**BUTTERSCOTCH** 99 [10] 4-8-8 R Cody Boutcher (5) 4/1 CO FAV: 0200-0: Al towards rear: 11th: op 7/2: jumps fit, plcd form (rtd 107h, juv nov): plcd form in '99 (rtd 61, h'cap): plcd in '98 (rtd 66, auct mdn): eff arnd 10f, tried 12f: handles firm & gd grnd. AW bow today.	3½	0a
194	**Lady Irene** 19 [3] 4-8-8 (BL) P Doe 20/1: -- **Kool Jules** [1] 4-8-8 S Carson (3) 20/1:		
101	**Estopped** 40 [11] 5-9-2 (BL) J Bosley (7) 50/1:		
14 ran	Time 2m 30.4 (9.1) (Mice Group plc) N P Littmoden Newmarket.		

---

249 1.30 CLASS CLAIMER DIV 2 4YO+ 0-60 (F) 7f aw rnd Going 49 -14 Slow
£1732 £495 £247

176	**DAVIS ROCK** 21 [6] W R Muir 6-8-12 Martin Dwyer 9/4 FAV: 5155-1: 6 ch m Rock City - Sunny Davis (Alydar) Rear, rdn 2f out & styd on strongly to lead ins last, going away: op 3/1: '99 scorer at Nottingham (h'cap, rtd 49 & 56a): '98 Lingfield (fill h'cap) & W'hampton wnr (sell, rtd 63 & 60): eff at 7f/1m on firm, soft & both AWs: eff weight carrier: handles any trk, likes a sharp one: enjoys sell/claim grade.		63a
134	**VICE PRESIDENTIAL** 33 [10] J G Given 5-9-1 Dean McKeown 7/1: 0010-2: 5 ch g Presidium - Steelock (Lochnager) Led & clr over 2f out, rdn & hdd ins last & no extra: op 6/1: see 32 (made virtually all, 6f).	3½	58a
177	**KINGCHIP BOY** 21 [4] M J Ryan 11-8-13 A Clark 7/1: 0000-3: 11 b g Petong - Silk St James (Pas de	2½	51a

89

SOUTHWELL (Fibresand)   MONDAY JANUARY 3RD   Lefthand, Sharp, Oval Track

Seul) Rdn mid-div, kept on for press fnl 2f, not pace to chall: '99 Southwell (3, h'caps & clmr) & W'hampton wnr (2, sell & clmr, rtd 64a): '98 wnr again at Southwell (2 h'caps, rtd 75a): eff at 7f, stays 9.4f, suited by 1m: acts on firm, gd/soft & eqtrk, fibresand/Southwell specialist: eff with/without a visor: eff weight carrier:

4361}	MOST RESPECTFUL 81 [2] N Tinkler 7-8-9 (t) Kim Tinkler 6/1: 6060-4: Chsd ldrs 6f: op 5/1, 12 wk abs: '99 wnr here at Southwell (appr sell h'cap, rtd 56a & 49): '98 wnr at Beverley (mdn, rtd 58) & here at Southwell (h'cap, AW bow, rtd 56a): eff at 5/6f, suited by a sharp 7f: acts on fast & fibresand: handles any trk, likes Southwell: wears a t-strap & runs well for an apprentice.		4	39a
201	ABOVE BOARD 17 [9] 5-8-13 S Righton 20/1: 0556-5: Bhd, late gains, no threat: see 201.		¾	42$
195	PRINCIPAL BOY 17 [3] 7-8-7 N Carlisle 15/2: 5304-6: Chsd ldrs halfway, held fnl 2f: see 195, 50.		1½	33a
201	TAPAUA 17 [8] 4-8-13 (bl) F Lynch 14/1: 0040-7: Trkd ldr, wknd over 1f out: op 12/1: see 201.		5	29a
199	TIME AND AGAIN 17 [7] 4-8-8(1ow) A Culhane 50/1: 0000-8: Wide/nvr factor: op 12/1: unplcd in '99 (rtd 38, h'cap, Mrs G S Rees): 3rd on 7 in '98 (auct mdn, rtd 51): tried up to 12f, now with D W Chapman.		2	20a
2406}	ANNANDALE 99 [1] 4-8-10 F Norton 16/1: 6005-9: Chsd ldrs 5f: 6 mth abs: now with D Nicholls.		½	21a
201	VOSBURGH 17 [5] 4-8-7 (bl) R Fitzpatrick (3) 12/1: 2340-P: Dwelt/al rear, p.u. 3f out.			0a
10 ran	Time 1m 31.00 (4.4) (Gordon B Cunningham) W R Muir Lambourn, Berks.			

---

250   2.05 BEDS HCAP DIV 2 3YO+ 0-70 (E)   6f aw rnd   Going 49 +04 Fast   [70]
£3815 £1174 £587 £293   3 yo rec 16lb

218	GARNOCK VALLEY 13 [4] A Berry 10-9-11 (67) G Carter 11/2: 1152-1: 10 b g Dowsing - Sunley Sinner (Try My Best) Rear, switched & strong run fnl 2f to lead well ins last, all out: tchd 7/1, gd time: prev with J Berry, '99 wnr at W'hampton, Lingfield (clmrs), Southwell (2, class stks & h'cap) & Newbury (h'cap, rtd 52 & 68a): '98 Musselburgh wnr (h'cap, rtd 57 & 57a): eff at 5/7f on fast & equitrack, loves soft/fibresand: eff with/without blnks: runs well fresh: handles any trk, loves Southwell: eff weight carrier: fine training start for A Berry.			76a
*232	FOREIGN EDITOR 7 [10] R A Fahey 4-9-2 (58)(6ex) P Hanagan (7) 1/1 FAV: 411-2D: 4 ch g Magic Ring - True Precision (Presidium) Went left after start & sn cl-up, rdn/led over 1f out, hdd line: disqual, rider given a 5-day careless riding ban: clr of rem, well bckd, 6lb pen: in fine form: see 232.	hd	67a
4331}	ITCH 83 [6] R Bastiman 5-7-12 (40)(2ow)(5oh) T Williams 20/1: 0000-2: 5 b h Puissance - Panienka (Dom Racine) Hmpd start & rear, styd on well fnl 2f, no threat to front pair: fin 3rd, plcd 2nd, 12 wk abs: unplcd in '99 (tried a visor): '97 Pontefract wnr (auct mdn, rtd 75): eff at 6f on gd/soft & fibresand.	6	38a
226	GRASSLANDIK 7 [8] A G Newcombe 4-8-10 (52) S Whitworth 8/1: 0502-3: Towards rear, kept on fnl 2f, never given a hard time, well h'capped & a likely type for similar this winter: see 226, 175.	1	48a
3599}	RUDE AWAKENING 99 [11] 6-8-4 (46) P Doe (3) 33/1: 5506-4: Trkd ldrs, led/hung left 2f out, sn hdd/ btn: 4 month abs: plcd form in '99 (rtd 49a & 47, h'caps): '98 Southwell wnr (h'cap, rtd 55a & 53): eff at 5/6f, stays 1m: acts on firm & gd/soft, likes f/sand: handles any trk, loves a sharp one: eff with/without a visor/blnks.	¾	40a
226	C HARRY 7 [13] 6-9-8 (64) P M Quinn (5) 10/1: 1303-5: Held up, nvr factor: op 8/1: see 130 (7f, sell).	3	49a
226	ERRO CODIGO 7 [3] 5-8-11 (53) J Tate 14/1: 0034-6: Prom 4f: tchd 16/1: see 180.	½	38a
148	TANCRED TIMES 28 [2] 5-8-0 (42) Kimberley Hart (5) 16/1: 5026-8: Led 3f, sn btn: see 87.	5	18a
218	ICE AGE 13 [1] 6-8-11 (53)(bl) T G McLaughlin 9/1: 0600-9: Cl-up 3f, sn btn: op 14/1: see 218.	¾	27a
199	SUE ME 17 [5] 8-8-4 (46)(bl) F Norton 16/1: 0006-0: Mid-div, btn 2f out: 10th: see 199 (sell).	3½	11a
218	SO WILLING 13 [7] 4-8-13 (55)(vis) F Lynch 33/1: 0000-0: Nvr on terms: 11th: see 218, 183.	½	18a
201	Palace Green 17 [9] 4-8-11 (53) A Culhane 40/1:3049} Sans Rivale 99 [12] 5-7-12 (40)(2ow)(12oh) P Fessey 50/1:		
13 ran	Time 1m 16.00 (2.7) (Robert Aird) A Berry Cockerham, Lancs.		

---

251   2.40 LINCS HCAP 4YO+ 0-90 (C)   1m aw rnd   Going 49 +04 Fast   [90]
£7117 £2190 £1095 £547

177	NOBLE CYRANO 21 [2] G Woodward 5-7-11 (58)(1ow) F Norton 11/2: 1002-1: 5 ch g Generous - Miss Bergerac (Bold Lad) Sn led, rdn/edged left over 1f out, in command ins last, rdn out: gd time: tchd 7/1: '99 scorer at Haydock (h'cap, rtd 59): plcd on '98 debut for G Wragg (mdn, rtd 70): eff at 1m: acts on fast, gd & fibresand: handles a sharp/gall trk: has run well fresh: can win again whilst in this form.		67a
216	ALMAZHAR 13 [16] J L Eyre 5-9-2 (78) T Williams 15/2: 2126-2: 5 b g Last Tycoon - Mosaique Bleue (Shirley Heights) Chsd ldrs wide halfway, rdn & kept on fnl 2f, not threat to wnr: most tough/prog: see 143 (7f).	3½	79a
224	DARE 12 [7] P D Evans 5-7-13 (61)(BL) Joanna Badger (7) 9/1: 1000-3: 5 b g Beveled - Run Amber Run (Run The Gantlet) Dwelt/rear, styd on fnl 2f to prom, nrst fin: op 8/1, blnks: see 83 (amat h'cap).	¾	61a
4447}	CIVIL LIBERTY 75 [14] D Sasse 7-8-5 (65)(t)(2ow) R Price 12/1: 1246-4: Sn rdn chasing ldrs, kept on onepace fnl 2f: op 10/1: '99 W'hampton scorer (h'cap, rtd 65a), plcd twice on turf, rtd 60): missed '98: '97 Nottingham wnr (G Lewis, h'cap, rtd 65): eff at 1m/10f: acts on fast, gd & fibresand: has run well fresh.	1	65a
216	WINDSFIELD 13 [10] 4-9-0 (76)(vis) R Winston 7/1: 4300-5: Towards rear, late gains, no threat: op 10/1.	½	73a
*177	FLITE OF LIFE 21 [5] 4-8-3 (65) Martin Dwyer 4/1 FAV: 0051-6: Chsd ldrs 6f: op 11/2: btr 177 (C/D).	¾	61a
--	STERLING HIGH 6 [6] 5-7-10 (58)(6oh) G Baker 7/1: 1105-7: Rear, mod prog, no threat: op 16/1: 12 wk abs: AW bow/Brit debut: ex-Irish, '99 wnr at Dundalk & Tramore (h'caps): '98 Roscommon wnr (h'cap): eff at 7f/9f on firm & gd/soft grnd: never won today: can improve for D Carroll.	3½	47a
232	CONSULTANT 7 [9] 4-7-10 (58)(2oh) A Polli (3) 33/1: 0000-8: Chsd ldrs 6f: see 232, 175.	¾	46a
4585}	ADELPHI BOY 62 [11] 4-10-0 (90) A Culhane 20/1: 5024-9: Wide/al towards rear: op 14/1: 2 mth abs, topweight: plcd sev times in '99 (rtd 73 & 92a, h'caps): '99 scorer twice here at Southwell (mdn & nurs) & subs at Lingfield (h'cap, rtd 91a & 80 at best): eff at 5f, seems suited by 7f/1m nowadays, has tried 10f: acts on fast, soft & both AWs: handles any trk, likes a sharp one.	nk	77a
4472}	REX IS OKAY 73 [15] 4-8-8 (70) Dale Gibson 12/1: 3330-0: Prom/wide 6f: 10th: op 10/1, 10 wk abs.	2½	52a
*176	STRAVSEA 21 [3] 5-7-10 (58)(9oh) P M Quinn (5) 20/1: 6001-0: Al twds rear: 11th: stiff task.	shd	40a
172	Still Waters 23 [4] 5-8-0 (62) P Fessey 16/1: 4564} Be Warned 65 [12] 9-9-2 (78)(bl) C Carver (3) 12/1:		
33	Crystal Lass 52 [1] 4-8-7 (69)(bl) J Edmunds 11/1: 197 Jibereen 17 [13] 8-9-0 (76) S Whitworth 12/1:		
180	Hibaat 21 [8] 4-7-10 (58)(3oh) G Bardwell 33/1:		
16 ran	Time 1m 43.00 (3.6) (Wetherby Racing Bureau) G Woodward Brierley, S.Yorks.		

---

252   3.15 DERBYSHIRE SELLER 4YO+ (G)   1m aw rnd   Going 49 -01 Slow
£2002 £572 £286

*197	RAMBO WALTZER 17 [12] D Nicholls 8-9-4 F Norton 6/4 FAV: 0141-1: 8 b g Rambo Dancer - Vindictive Lady (Foolish Pleasure) Prom, rdn/led over 3f out, hard rdn/asserted over 1f out, styd on strongly: well bckd: no bid, top-weight: '99 scorer at Catterick, Thirsk (h'caps, rtd 71) & thrice better at Southwell (2 clmrs & seller, rtd 75a at best): '98 W'hampton & Southwell wnr (2, h'caps, rtd 91a & 72): eff at 7f/9.5f on fast & soft, loves		68a

90

SOUTHWELL (Fibresand) MONDAY JANUARY 3RD Lefthand, Sharp, Oval Track

fibresand/Southwell: has run well fresh: tough & genuine 8yo who is hard to beat in sell/claiming grade here.
197 **APPROACHABLE 17** [1] Miss S J Wilton 5-8-12 T G McLaughlin 8/1: 6240-2: 5 b h Known Fact - Western *3* **55a**
Approach (Gone West) Held up, rdn/prog to chase wnr fnl 1f, kept on tho' al held: op 6/1: vis omitted, clr rem.
209 **MUSTANG 16** [6] J Pearce 7-8-12 (bl) G Bardwell 6/1: 4454-3: 7 ch g Thatching - Lassoo (Caerleon) *8* **43a**
Prom, rdn/chsd wnr 3f out, no extra fnl 1f: bckd at long odds, op 14/1: see 59 (h'cap, 7f).
227 **WAITING KNIGHT 7** [2] Mrs N Macauley 5-8-12 (vis) R Fitzpatrick (3) 12/1: 0200-4: Chsd ldrs going *2* **39a**
well halfway, kept on fnl 2f tho' no threat to ldrs: tchd 14/1: not given a hard time here: see 178.
50 **SHARP STEEL 49** [3] 5-8-12 C Rutter 6/1: 5002-5: Chsd ldrs 6f: op 5/1: 7 wk abs: see 50. *nk* **38a**
69 **NICE BALANCE 45** [11] 5-8-12 Joanna Badger (7) 50/1: 5050-6: Mid-div at best: jumps fit: unplcd *4* **30a**
in '99 (rtd 45 & 25a, tried blnks): mod hdle/bmpr form previously.
227 **AN LU ABU 7** [5] 4-8-12 (VIS) N Callan (3) 33/1: 0000-7: Prom 6f: visor: mod form. *¾* **29a**
197 **WITHOUT FRIENDS 17** [10] 6-8-12 A Clark 16/1: 4006-8: Dwelt/towards rear, mod gains: see 197. *1½* **26a**
231 **ADIRPOUR 7** [4] 6-8-12 Stephanie Hollinshea 20/1: 6030-9: Dwelt/nvr factor: see 178 (11f). *1½* **23a**
215 **PINE RIDGE LAD 13** [14] 10-8-12 (bl) Dean McKeown 25/1: 3050-0: Chsd ldrs 5f: 10th: '99 scorer *5* **13a**
at Southwell (h'cap, rtd 48a, rnr-up on turf, seller, rtd 50): '98 wnr at Southwell (seller, rtd 71a) & Redcar (amat
h'cap, rtd 60, J Eyre): eff btwn 7f/9.5f: acts on firm, soft & fibresand: eff with/without a vis, tried blnks.
138 **MR ROUGH 33** [15] 9-8-12 (vis) M Tebbutt 10/1: 0052-0: Held up, nvr factor: 12th: op 12/1: see 138. **0a**
199 **THATCHING LAD 17** [9] 7-8-12 T Williams 25/1: 0-0: Led, hdd 3f out, sn btn: 15th: longer 1m trip. **0a**
4129} **Awesome Venture 97** [13] 10-8-12 Martin Dwyer 33/1:3604} **Were Not Stoppin 99** [7] 5-8-12 S Whitworth 40/1:
215 **Pimpinella 13** [8] 4-8-7 (ebl) R Lappin 50/1:
15 ran Time 1m 43.3 (3.9) (W G Swiers) D Nicholls Sessay, N.Yorks.

253

3.45 HERTS HCAP 4YO+ 0-75 (E) 2m aw Going 49 -62 Slow **[75]**
£2795 £860 £430 £215 4 yo rec 7 lb

194 **ABOO HOM 19** [2] S Dow 6-8-2 (49)(t) P Doe (2) 13/2: /003-1: 6 b h Sadler's Wells - Maria Waleska **53a**
(Filiberto) Rear, prog/cl-up halfway, rdn/outpcd 4f out, styd on gamely for press to lead well ins last, drvn out:
op 6/1: mod recent jumps form: plcd on sand in '99 (rtd 58, h'cap, unplcd on turf, rtd 52, h'cap): 97/98 Haydock
hdles wnr (mdn, rtd 129h): eff at 2m on fibresand: eff in a t-strap.
4407} **FIFTEEN REDS 77** [7] D Shaw 5-7-10 (43)(vis)(5oh) A Polli (3) 33/1: 0000-2: 5 b g Jumbo Hirt - *1½* **45a**
Dominance (Dominion) Prom, rdn/led over 1f out, hung left & hdd ins last, prob just held when saddle slipped cl
home: 2 month jumps abs (rtd 77h): unplcd on the level in '99 (rtd 42a & 64): eff at 2m on fibresand in a visor.
37 **JAMAICAN FLIGHT 52** [9] Mrs S Lamyman 7-9-7 (68) A Culhane 7/2: 6505-3: 9 b h Sunshine Forever - *¾* **69a**
Kalamona (Hawaii) Prom, rdn/ch 3f out, kept on well tho' just held nr fin: op 9/4, jumps fit (rnr-up, h'cap, rtd
126h): '99 scorer at Pontefract (stks), Carlisle & Doncaster (h'caps, rtd 77): '98 W'hampton (h'cap) & Pontefract
wnr (stks, rtd 75 & 82a): eff at 14f/2m2f on firm, hvy & fibresand: likes to force the pace: handles any trk.
*194 **MAKNAAS 19** [3] T G Mills 4-7-12 (52) T Williams 5/2 FAV: 4531-4: Keen/led 3f out, led again *1½* **52a**
halfway till over 1f out, kept on ins last: op 7/2: clr rem: see 194.
4166} **DOC RYANS 95** [1] 6-10-0 (75) A Clark 100/30: 3260-5: Chsd ldrs, lost pl halfway & no impress ldrs *15* **64a**
after: topweight, jumps fit (Oct '99 Fakenham wnr, nov, rtd 112h): '99 scorer thrice here at Southwell (2 h'caps & a
clmr) & twice at W'hampton (clmrs, rtd 80a, plcd on turf, rtd 65): '98 Musselburgh wnr (2 h'caps, rtd 66 & 68a):
eff at 12f/2m on gd, soft, fibresand/Southwell & W'hampton specialist: eff in blnks: loves claimers: win more races.
*190 **ROYAL EXPRESSION 19** [8] 8-9-5 (66) N Callan (3) 5/1: 5201-6: Chsd ldrs 13f: op 4/1: btr 190. *5* **50a**
89 **ALMAMZAR 42** [5] 10-7-10 (43)(20oh) Kim Tinkler 50/1: 0005-7: Bhd halfway: 6 wk abs: see 89. *16* **15a**
182 **SUDDEN SPIN 21** [6] 10-7-10 (43)(2oh) P M Quinn (5) 10/1: 0/05-8: Handy halfway, btn 4f out. *nk* **15a**
211 **WELLCOME INN 13** [10] 6-7-12 (45)(t)(2ow)(22oh) Benedichte Halvorsen 33/1: 0500-9: Held up in *24* **0a**
tch, btn 5f out: see 211 (12f).
3471} **AGIOTAGE 99** [4] 4-9-5 (73) G Carter 25/1: 6040-0: Led after 3f till halfway, sn bhd: 5 mth abs/AW *dist* **0a**
bow: prev with H Cecil, now with S Williams.
10 ran Time 3m 43.7 (17.7) (Byerley Bloodstock) S Dow Epsom, Surrey.

WOLVERHAMPTON (Fibresand) TUESDAY JANUARY 4TH Lefthand, Sharp Track

Official Going STANDARD. Stalls: Inside, except 7f - Outside.

254

12.45 NEW YEAR AMAT HCAP DIV 1 4YO+ 0-75 (F) 1m100y aw rnd Going 49 -15 Slow **[53]**
£1949 £557 £278

220 **KINNINO 13** [8] G L Moore 6-9-3 (42)(7oh) Mr I Mongan 14/1: 5020-1: 6 b g Polish Precedent - On **44a**
Tiptoes (Shareef Dancer) Prom, led 2f out, styd on well ins last, rdn out: op 10/1: rnr-up on sand in '99 (rtd
43a & 45): unplcd in '98 (rtd 57 & 57a): eff arnd 1m: acts on both AWs, handles fast & gd grnd: best without
blnks: runs well for an amat, likes a sharp track: fine effort from 7lbs o/h.
220 **KAFIL 13** [10] J J Bridger 6-9-8 (47) Mrs S Bosley 5/1: 6560-2: 6 b g Housebuster - Alchaasibiyeh *1½* **47a**
(Seattle Slew) Prom wide halfway, chsd wnr ins last, kept on for press: op 4/1: acts on both AWs, handles
fast & gd/soft grnd: shown enough to win a similar contest: see 1 (equitrack).
251 **CONSULTANT 1** [9] C N Kellett 4-10-3 (56) Mrs C Williams 16/1: 000-03: 4 b g Man Of May - Avenita *1* **54a**
Lady (Free State) Prom, rdn & kept on onepace fnl 2f: op 12/1: qck reapp, unplcd at Southwell yesterday.
111 **DOBERMAN 39** [3] P D Evans 5-9-3 (42)(vis)(4oh) Miss E Folkes (5) 6/1: 6404-4: Led till 2f out, no *nk* **39a**
extra nr fin: 6L clr rem, jockey given a 1-day whip ban, op 4/1: rnr-up sev times in '99 (rtd 54 & 53a, with B
Meehan): 2nd twice in '98 (rtd 73 & 60a): eff arnd 1m, tried 10f: acts on fast & both AWs: has tried bl/visor.
177 **MOONLIGHT FLIT 22** [5] 5-9-5 (42)(2ow) Miss Diana Jones 8/1: 0050-5: Twds rear, late gains: vis omitted. *6* **32a**
2950} **DISTINCTIVE DREAM 99** [6] 6-11-7 (74) Miss Bridget Gatehou 8/1: 2140-6: Mid-div at best: 5 month *2½* **57a**
abs: '99 wnr at Haydock (class stks, first time vis, rtd 75, with Lady Herries): dual '98 rnr-up (h'cap, rtd 85):
'97 wnr at Windsor (3), Salisbury (claim h'cap), Southwell & Kempton (h'cap, rtd 89, K Ivory): eff at 6/7f: acts on
firm, gd/soft & fibresand: handles any trk, likes Windsor & Kempton: eff with blnks/visor: now with A Bailey.
197 **WARRIOR KING 18** [13] 6-9-4 (43)(1ow)(20oh) Mr S Dobson (0) 66/1: 0000-7: Chsd ldrs 6f: unplcd *½* **25a**
in '99 (rtd 38a & 31): '97 Musselburgh wnr (h'cap, rtd 53, J Banks): eff at 7/12f on firm & gd/soft: tried a visor.
3918} **MR CUBE 99** [12] 10-9-3 (42)(bl)(6oh) Mr W Jones (7) 8/1: 4542-8: Chsd ldrs, held over 2f out: op *¾* **23a**
10/1: 4 month abs: plcd sev times in '99 (rtd 39, h'cap): '97 Epsom wnr (h'cap): eff at 7f/1m on firm & gd/soft.
75} **BONANZA PEAK 99** [4] 7-10-1 (54)(VIS) Mr R Bailey (0) 20/1: 2300/9: Prom 4f: vis, now with D Burchell. *9* **22a**
4341} **MELOMANIA 83** [7] 8-9-3 (42)(2oh) Mr M A Hammond (1) 25/1: 0006-0: Sn bhd: 10th: abs/with T Clement. *5* **0a**

3532} **BIJA** 99 [1] 5-9-3 (42)(17oh) Miss Hayley Bryan (7) 66/1: 4604-0: Bhd halfway: 11th: 4 mth jmps abs. — 1¼ — 0a
172   **KARAKUL** 24 [2] 4-10-8 (61) Mr Nicky Tinkler 16/1: 0000-0: Sn bhd: 12th: op 12/1. — 7 — 5a
239   **SWING ALONG 6** [11] 5-10-13 (66) Mr V Coogan (5) 5/2 FAV: 5316-W: Unruly in stalls and withdrawn. — — 0a
13 ran   Time 1m 51.6 (5.4)   (A Moore)   G L Moore Woodingdean, E.Sussex.

---

255   1.15 NEW YEAR AMAT HCAP DIV 2 4YO+ 0-75 (F)   1m100y aw rnd Going 49 -18 Slow   [49]
£1939   £554   £277

*126   **TROJAN WOLF** 35 [1] P Howling 5-11-7 (70) Miss S Pocock (5) 2/1 FAV: 0511-1: 5 ch g Wolfhound - Trogan Lady (Irish River), pushed out to maintain advantage ins last, readily: nicely bckd: late '99 wnr at Southwell (2, h'caps, rtd 58 & 56a): rtd 76 in '98 (M Tompkins): eff at 1m/11f: loves to race with/force the pace: acts on firm, gd & equitrack, relishes fibresand: tried a t-strap: handles any trk, likes a sharp one. — 76a
227   **LILANITA** 8 [3] P D Evans 5-9-10 (45) Miss E Folkes (5) 5/1: 3203-2: 5 b m Anita's Prince - Jimlil (Nicholas Bill) Chsd wnr thr'out, ev ch over 1f out, kept on tho' al held: deserves similar: see 227, 45 (sell). — 1½ — 45a
58   **MUTABARI** 49 [11] Mrs S Lamyman 6-10-5 (54) Mr S Dobson (5) 10/1: 5600-3: 6 ch g Seeking The Gold - Cagey Exuberance (Exuberant) Chsd ldrs, kept on fnl 2f, not pace to chall: op 14/1: jumps fit (mod form): '99 wnr at Southwell, Lingfield (first time visor) & W'hampton (h'caps, rtd 64a & 50): eff at 7f, stays 12f: acts on fast, soft & likes both AWs: handles any trk: poss best in a visor, not won today: on a fair mark. — 2 — 50a
85   **MYTTONS MOMENT** 43 [2] A Bailey 4-10-1 (50)(bl) Miss Bridget Gatehou 5/1: 4633-4: Chsd ldrs, onepace fnl 2f: 6 wk abs, tchd 6/1: see 85. — 1¾ — 43a
58   **SHONTAINE** 49 [12] 7-9-3 (38) Mrs C Williams 20/1: 2000-5: Chsd ldrs, held over 1f out: 7 wk abs: '99 Ayr wnr (sell h'cap, rtd 45 & 43a): '98 wnr at Southwell (2, h'caps, rtd 66a): eff at 7f/1m on firm, gd/soft & both AWs: best without blnks: handles any track. — ¾ — 30a
4343} **DANZAS** 83 [10] 6-9-5 (40)(bl) Mr W Jones (7) 12/1: 4025-6: Towards rear, late gains, no threat: op 10/1, 12 wk abs: '99 Nottingham scorer (mdn h'cap, rtd 44 & 45a): eff at 1m/10f: likes firm/fast grnd, handles gd/soft & fibresand: handles any trk: eff with/without blnks. — 1¾ — 29a
210   **HEVER GOLF GLORY** 17 [8] 6-10-13 (62) Mr Stephen Harrison (7) 8/1: 4000-7: Chsd ldrs, btn 2f out: op 10/1: jockey reportedly given a 2-day ban for causing interference: see 119, 35. — ½ — 50a
189   **AZZAN** 20 [4] 4-10-11 (60)(t) Mrs H Keddy (5) 25/1: 4006-8: Towards rear thr'out: see 189 (mdn). — 4 — 40a
83   **BRANDONVILLE** 43 [7] 7-9-3 (38)(t)(2oh) Nicky Tinkler (2) 33/1: /000-9: Al rear: 6 wk abs. — shd — 18a
2530} **DREAM CARRIER** 99 [6] 12-9-9 (44)(6ow)(14oh) Mrs C Peacock (0) 50/1: 5506-0: Al bhd: 10th: abs. — 8 — 12a
*136   **WAIKIKI BEACH** 34 [9] 9-10-6 (55)(bl) Mrs J Moore 11/2: 3401-0: Eff halfway, btn/eased fnl 1f. — 18 — 0a
233   **QUEEN OF THE KEYS** 8 [5] 4-9-5 (39)(VIS)(1ow) Mr R Guest (0) 8/1: 0036-0: Bhd halfway: 12th: visor. — 12 — 0a
12 ran   Time 1m 51.9 (5.7)   (Max Pocock)   P Howling Newmarket.

---

256   1.45 CRACK OF NOON CLAIMER 4YO+ (F)   1m100y aw rnd Going 49 -02 Slow
£2268   £648   £324

230   **INTERNAL AFFAIR** 8 [5] T D Barron 5-8-13 Lynsey Hanna (7) 2/1: 4620-1: 5 b g Nicolas - Gdynia (Sir Ivor) Held up in tch, styd on well for press to lead ins last, rdn out: tchd 3/1: '99 W'hampton wnr (h'cap, rtd 67a): '98 wnr at W'hampton (auct mdn, rtd 79a): prev eff at 5f, now suited by 8.5f: acts on hvy, handles fast & loves fibresand/W'hampton: runs well for an apprentice. — 65a
176   **SHARP SHUFFLE** 22 [3] Miss S J Wilton 7-8-13 R Fitzpatrick (3) 9/1: 0110-2: 7 ch g Exactly Sharp - Style (Homing) Held up in tch, rdn to lead briefly 1f out, outpcd by wnr ins last: see 176, 138 (C/D, seller). — 2½ — 59a
193   **BLUSHING GRENADIER** 20 [2] S R Bowring 8-8-9 R Winston 7/1: 0340-3: 8 ch g Salt Dome - La Duse (Junius) Led till 1f out, no extra ins last: op 12/1: see 136, 38. — 2½ — 50a
195   **TAKHLID** 18 [1] D W Chapman 9-9-7 A Culhane 10/11 FAV: 3116-4: Prom, ev ch 1f out, rdn/fdd ins last: nicely bckd at odds on: twice below form now: see 142 (7f, clmr). — hd — 61a
7   **BUTRINTO** 57 [6] 6-9-3 T G McLaughlin 10/1: 0000-5: Chsd ldrs, rdn/btn 2f out & eased ins last: op 6/1, jmps fit (mod form): rnr-up in '99 (rtd 74a, h'cap), unplcd on turf (rtd 41, h'cap): '98 Newbury & Lingfield scorer (h'caps, rtd 75 & 75a): eff at 6f/1m on fast, gd & both AWs: best without blnks/visor. — 14 — 37a
208   **MAX** 17 [4] 5-9-3 (bl) R Brisland (5) 25/1: 2110-6: Rdn halfway & sn btn: op 16/1: thrice a wnr in Belgium in '99 (Ostend h'caps): eff around 1m: acts on firm & gd/soft grnd: eff in blnks: with J J Bridger. — 9 — 24a
6 ran   Time 1m 50.5 (4.3)   (Stephen Woodhall)   T D Barron Maunby, N.Yorks.

---

257   2.15 MORNING CALL HCAP 3YO 0-60 (F)   7f aw rnd Going 49 -24 Slow   [66]
£2299   £657   £328

155   **CROESO ADREF** 27 [2] S C Williams 3-8-4 (42) P M Quinn (5) 14/1: 0003-1: 3 ch f Most Welcome - Grugiar (Red Sunset) Led/dspted lead, styd on gamely ins last to hold on, all out: jockey given a 3-day whip ban: op 12/1, h'cap bow: plcd on final start in '99 (rtd 43a, clmr): eff at 7f, related to a mid-dist/staying wnr & 1m+ shld suit: acts on fibresand: likes to race with/force the pace: open to further improvement. — 47a
127   **LIONS DOMANE** 35 [8] P C Haslam 3-8-9 (47) M Tebbutt 20/1: 000-2: 3 b g Lion Cavern - Vilany (Never So Bold) Led/dspted lead till 2f out, styd on well for press ins last, just held nr fin: op 14/1, h'cap bow: mod form in '99 (rtd 48a): eff at 7f, shld stay 1m: acts on fibresand: could find similar. — ½ — 50a
179   **STAND BY** 22 [1] T D Easterby 3-9-4 (56) L Charnock 8/1: 005-3: 3 b f Missed Flight - Ma Rivale (Last Tycoon) Chsd ldrs, ev ch 1f out, kept on well, just held nr fin: h'cap bow: eff at 7f: acts on fibresand. — shd — 59a
188   **FOR HEAVENS SAKE** 20 [5] C W Thornton 3-9-7 (59) Dean McKeown 6/1: 0466-4: Sltly hmpd after 100y, styd on well, nrst fin: not btn far & a shade unlucky: eff at 7f on fibresand: see 188. — nk — 61a
188   **AISLE** 20 [11] 3-9-5 (57)(BL) R Fitzpatrick (3) 14/1: 1160-5: Prom, onepace fnl 1f: op 10/1, blnks. — ¾ — 58a
207   **UNFORTUNATE** 17 [10] 3-9-1 (53) N Carlisle 11/2: 0214-6: Chsd ldrs wide, held over 1f out: op 9/2. — 2 — 50a
181   **LADY SANDROVITCH** 22 [3] P Hanagan (7) 7/1: 5443-7: Chsd ldrs 5f: op 5/1: see 181 (6f). — 1¾ — 43a
155   **PONTIKONISI** 27 [6] 3-8-12 (50) P Doe (3) 11/1: 0545-8: Chsd ldrs 5f: op 8/1: blnks reapp. — 2½ — 39a
217   **NOWT FLASH** 14 [12] 3-9-2 (54) R Lappin 14/1: 0602-9: Held up, nvr factor: op 10/1: see 217 (sell, 5f). — 1 — 34a
241   **WISHEDHADGONEHOME** 2 [4] 3-9-2 (54)(vis) Joanna Badger (7) 6/1: 026-30: Slowly away/al rear: 10th. — 1 — 33a
128   **MERRYVALE MAN** 35 [9] 3-9-7 (59) R Winston 7/2 FAV: 5002-0: Al bhd: 11th: op 3/1: btr 128 (1m). — ¾ — 37a
118   **XANIA** 38 [7] 3-8-13 (51) J Fanning 12/1: 000-0: Prom 4f: 12th: op 8/1: h'cap bow. — 5 — 19a
12 ran   Time 1m 31.3 (5.1)   (Edgar Lloyd)   S C Williams Newmarket.

258	2.45 TOTE HCAP 3YO+ 0-85 (D)　　6f aw rnd　Going 49　+04 Fast	[84]
	£5291　　£1628　　£814　　£407	

*212 **BLUE KITE** 14 [9] N P Littmoden 5-9-2 (72) J Tate 3/1 FAV: 3261-1: 5 ch g Silver Kite - Gold And Blue 　**80a**
(Bluebird) Sn cl-up, rdn/led halfway, styd on strongly & forged clr ins last, rdn out: well bckd, tchd 6/1: '99 wnr
here at W'hampton & most recently at Southwell (h'caps, rtd 75a, rtd 65 on turf, stks): plcd in '98 (rtd 78 & 78a):
eff btwn 5/7f, suited by 6f: acts on fast, soft, fibresand, loves fibresand: likes sharp trks, esp W'hampton: best
without headgear: tough gelding, in great heart & runs well for J Tate.

129 **PIPS SONG** 35 [5] Dr J D Scargill 5-9-5 (75) F Norton 7/1: 0220-2: 5 ch g Pips Pride - Friendly Song 　2½　**77a**
(Song) Chsd ldrs, rdn & kept on ins last, no threat to wnr: op 5/1: likes W'hampton, shld win again: see 129.

216 **JUWWI** 14 [8] J M Bradley 6-9-13 (83) Claire Bryan (7) 8/1: 2155-3: 6 ch g Mujtahid - Nouvelle 　2　**80a**
Star (Luskin Star) Rdn in rear halfway, styd on well from over 1f out, nrst fin: op 6/1: beat today's rnr-up in 129.

129 **MALLIA** 35 [10] T D Barron 7-9-2 (72)(bl) L Charnock 9/1: 0460-4: Rdn/towards rear, styd on well 　¾　**67a**
fnl 2f, not pace to chall: op 7/1: lost unbtn record here at W'hampton: see 129.

3833 **BLUE STAR** 99 [2] 4-10-0 (84) R Thomas (7) 50/1: 3050-5: Towards rear, styd on fnl 2f under hands- 　1　**77+**
and-heels riding, no threat to ldrs: 4 month abs: longer priced stablemate of wnr: plcd twice on turf in '99 (rtd
71, h'cap): '98 juv scorer here at W'hampton (val stks, rtd 87a & 74): eff at 6f, stays a sharp 7f: handles firm &
gd/soft, likes fibresand/sharp trks: tenderly handled here, shld prove sharper next time & is one to keep an eye on.

162 **REDOUBTABLE** 27 [11] 9-9-2 (72) G Parkin 6/1: 3063-6: Chsd ldrs wide going well 2f out, sn onepace. 　¾　**63a**
223 **CHARGE** 13 [7] 4-8-9 (65)(t) J Stack 25/1: 3416-7: Cl-up 5f: op 14/1: see 95 (mdn, equitrack). 　½　**54a**
49 **KAYO** 50 [12] 5-9-12 (82) J Fanning 8/1: 1030-8: Prom, rdn/btn 2f out: op 6/1: 7 wk abs: see 49, 7. 　½　**69a**
223 **AURIGNY** 13 [6] 5-9-10 (80) P Doe (3) 10/1: 0055-9: Chsd ldrs, btn 2f out: see 191 (5f). 　3½　**58a**
191 **MUKARRAB** 20 [1] 6-9-9 (79) A Culhane 10/1: 5006-0: Led 3f, fdd: 10th: op 7/1: see 191. 　nk　**56a**
214 **POLLY MILLS** 14 [13] 4-9-5 (75)(vis) T G McLaughlin 16/1: 0020-0: Al twds rear: 11th: vis reapp. 　½　**50a**
218 **SANTANDRE** 14 [4] 4-9-0 (70) P M Quinn (5) 8/1: 0453-0: Al twds rear: 12th: tchd 9/1: see 143 (7f). 　1¾　**41a**
162 **DEMOCRACY** 27 [3] 4-9-5 (75)(bl) S Drowne 25/1: 2210-0: Dwelt/sn rdn & al rear: 13th: '99 wnr at 　4　**36a**
Bath (mdn, R Hannon, rtd 85): plcd on sole '98 start (mdn, rtd 78): eff at 5.5f/7f, stays 9f: acts on firm & gd:
eff in blnks/visor: best held up for a late run: prob handles any trk: now with P G Murphy.

13 ran　　Time 1m 14.5 (2.7)　　　　(T Clarke)　　　　N P Littmoden Newmarket.

259	3.15 SELLER 4-6YO (G)　　1m1f79y aw　Going 49　-01 Slow	
	£1939　　£554　　£277　　4yo rec 1lb	

178 **OVER THE MOON** 22 [4] Miss S J Wilton 6-8-10 (vis) T G McLaughlin 6/1: 4560-1: 6 ch m Beveled - 　**52a**
Beyond The Moon (Ballad Rock) Towards rear, prog halfway & hard rdn to lead ins last, forged clr, rdn out: no
bid: nicely bckd at long odds, op 12/1: visor reapplied: '99 scorer here at W'hampton (clmr, rtd 57a): won
thrice at W'hampton in '98 (3 clmrs, rtd 61a, N Littmoden): eff at 7f/9.5f: fibresand/W'hampton specialist:
enjoys claim/sell grade & was well suited by reapplication of headgear today.

176 **ABSOLUTE MAJORITY** 22 [12] P Howling 5-9-1 R Winston 7/1: 3040-2: 5 ch g Absalom - Shall We Run 3½　**50a**
(Hotfoot) Chsd ldrs, led 3f out, hard rdn/hdd ins last & no extra: op 4/1: well clr of rem: see 130.

141 **WESTMINSTER CITY** 31 [10] K O Cunningham Brown 4-9-0 (vis) L Charnock 10/1: 0500-3: 4 b h Alleged 11　**34a**
- Promenade Fan (Timeless Moment) Prom, chsd ldr 4f out, btn 2f out: tchd 12/1: unplcd in '99 (rtd 63 & 62a):
'98 Lingfield wnr (debut, rtd 79, C Brittain): eff at 6f: acts on gd, prob handles fast: best without a vis.

1476} **OUR JACK** 99 [6] C N Kellett 5-9-1 N Carlisle 20/1: 6-4: Dwelt/rear, styd on fnl 2f, nrst fin: op 16/1: 　3　**28a**
reapp: unplcd sole start in '99 (debut, rtd 35a).

252 **APPROACHABLE** 1 [1] 5-9-1 C Rutter 1/1 FAV: 240-25: Held up in tch, eff 4f out, hard rdn/btn 2f out: 　1　**26a**
hvly bckd, shorter priced stablemate of wnr: qck reapp, fin rnr-up at Southwell yesterday: see 45.

1625} **AMINGTON GIRL** 99 [8] S Drowne 5-8-10 (vis) 20/1: 4000-6: Chsd ldrs 7f: op 25/1: reapp: visor 　4　**13a**
reapplied: plcd form in '99 (rtd 41a, h'cap, unplcd on turf, rtd 39a, seller): '98 Nottingham wnr (clmr, rtd 50):
eff at 6f/1m on fast, soft & fibresand: handles a sharp or gall trk: eff in blnks/visor.

197 **RUNNING BEAR** 18 [2] 6-9-1 P Goode (5) 50/1: 0550-7: Led after 2f till after 3f out, sn btn: see 138. 　¾　**17a**
4496} **SARA MOON CLASSIC** 71 [11] 5-9-1 (bl) N Callan (3) 10/1: 0063-8: Al rear: op 8/1: jumps fit. 　1　**15a**
238 **PIPADOR** 6 [5] 4-9-0 A Rawlinson 9/1: 0005-9: Al rear: op 6/1, qck reapp: se 238 (10f). 　2½　**10a**
238 **AMBUSHED** 6 [7] 4-9-0 K Dalgleish (7) 14/1: 00-0: Led 2f, sn btn: 10th: op 9/1, qck reapp. 　4　**2a**
236} **GILDERSLEVE** 99 [3] 5-8-10 R Brisland (5) 20/1: 00/0-0: Prom 4f: 11th: reapp, now with G L Moore. 　4　**0a**
4566} **JUST A STROLL** 66 [9] 5-9-1 (VIS) R Price 33/1: 00/0-0: Al bhd: 12th: visor, 7 wk jumps absence. 　25　**0a**

12 ran　　Time 2m 02.9 (4.7)　　　　(John Pointon & Sons)　　　　Miss S J Wilton Wetley Rocks, Staffs.

260	3.45 RESOLUTION HCAP DIV 1 4YO+ 0-60 (F)　　1m4f aw　Going 49　-24 Slow	[60]
	£1939　　£554　　£277　　4yo rec 4lb	

194 **MANFUL** 20 [8] R Brotherton 8-7-13 (31)(bl) (3ow)(4oh) F Norton 5/2 FAV: 0300-1: 8 b g Efisio - 　**34a**
Mandrian (Mandamus) Chsd clr ldr, outpcd 4f out, rall & hung right appr fnl 1f, all out to lead cl-home: op 4/1,
jockey given 2 day ban for whip abuse: '99 Ayr wnr (h'cap, rtd 62 at best, Miss L Perratt): '98 wnr again at Ayr
(h'cap, rtd 64 & 49a): eff at 10/12f, tried 2m: acts on fast, both AWs, likes soft: wears blnks & is well h'capped.

177 **TIME ON MY HANDS** 22 [3] S R Bowring 4-9-7 (43)(t) Dean McKeown 20/1: 00P0-2: 4 b g Most 　¾　**45a**
Welcome - Zareeta (Free State) Tried to make all & sn clr, under press appr fnl 1f, worn down fnl strides: op 12/1,
blnks omitted: '99 Southwell wnr (clmr, rtd 57a, C Thornton): no turf form: eff at 1m/12f: acts on fibresand:
clrly suited forcing the pace on a sharp trk, with/without t-strap: shld be going one better soon.

*233 **THE BARGATE FOX** 8 [4] D J G Murray Smith 4-9-6 (56)(6ex) S Whitworth 3/1: 1041-3: 4 b g Magic 　½　**57a**
Ring - Hithermoor Lass (Red Alert) Bhd, wide prog to chase ldrs 3f out, kept on onepace dist: op 9/4: big
step up in trip, stays 12f, eff at 1m: remains in fine form: see 233.

312} **CASHAPLENTY** 99 [11] N P Littmoden 7-8-13 (45) T G McLaughlin 8/1: 62/6-4: Outpcd, prog 4f out, 　1½　**44a**
kept on, nvr troubled ldrs: recent jumps rnr, 98/99 wnr at Warwick, Uttoxeter & Doncaster (c.j. h'caps,
2m, gd & soft, rtd 105h): lightly rcd on the level, rnr-up in '98 (h'cap, rtd 43a): '97 wnr here at W'hampton
(mdn, rtd 50a): eff at 12f, will get further: acts on fibresand, sharp trks: open well fresh.

224 **INKWELL** 13 [2] 6-8-4 (36)(bl) A Mackay 5/1: 2204-5: Chsd ldrs, feeling pace 4f out, late hdwy: 　½　**34a**
drifter from 7/2: stays a sharp 12f, eff at 7f/1m, poss best at 10f: handles both AWs, likes gd & soft grnd.

3675} **COHIBA** 99 [12] 7-8-10 (42)(BL) N Callan (3) 11/1: /216-6: Cl-up 6f, styd on appr fnl 1f: jumps fit 　¾　**39a**
(plater), blnkd for 2nd AW run: '99 Nottingham wnr (sell h'cap, rtd 45 & 51$, B Curley): cost current connections
6,000gns: '98 reapp wnr at Brighton (h'cap, rtd 44): eff at 10f, 14f suits: acts on firm & gd/soft, prob fibresand.

WOLVERHAMPTON (Fibresand)   TUESDAY JANUARY 4TH   Lefthand, Sharp Track

126 **GOLDEN LYRIC 35** [9] 5-8-6 (38) C Rutter 8/1: 0300-7: Chsd ldrs, rdn halfway, fdd fnl 4f: tchd 12/1.   13 21a
70 **PREMIERE FOULEE 46** [6] 5-8-2 (34)(VIS) P Doe (3) 14/1: 0200-8: Handy till 4f out: op 10/1,   2 14a
visored, 7 wk abs: '99 sand rnr-up (h'cap, rtd 38a, clmr, rtd 57): modest jumper: ex-French, plcd in
2 '98 clmrs: eff at 12f, handles soft grnd & fibresand: with F Jordan.
215 **REPTON 14** [7] 5-9-0 (46) J Bosley (7) 12/1: 0600-9: Nvr in it.   3 22a
-- **TIMIDJAR** [10] 7-10-0 (60)(VIS) R Price 12/1: 5611/0: Sn struggling: 10th, jumps fit.   11 24a
174 **MR SPECULATOR 24** [1] 7-9-1 (47)(tbl) A Culhane 16/1: 00/3-0: Lost sev lengths start, al bhd: 11th.   dist 0a
11 ran   Time 2m 42.4 (8.8)   (Paul Stringer)   R Brotherton Elmley Castle, Worcs.

261   4.15 RESOLUTION HCAP DIV 2 4YO+ 0-60 (F)   1m4f aw   Going 49 -13 Slow   [58]
£1928   £551   £275   4yo rec 4lb

170 **DESERT SPA 24** [11] P J Makin 5-9-7 (51) A Clark 9/4 FAV: 3/02-1: 5 b g Sheikh Albadou - Healing   54a
Waters (Temperence Hill) Trkd ldrs, pulled out & rdn appr fnl 1f, ran on strongly to lead cl-home: tchd 7/2:
lightly rcd since '98 win here at W'hampton (h'cap, rtd 56a & 63, P Harris): eff over a sharp 12f: acts
on fibresand, handles fast & soft, likes W'hampton: has run well fresh, best without blnks.
170 **SOLE SINGER 24** [12] D Haydn Jones 4-9-2 (50)(BL) A Mackay 8/1: 0323-2: 4 b g Slip Anchor   nk 52a
- Singer On The Roof (Chief Singer) Wide early, rear, stdy prog fnl circuit, led ent fnl 2f, hard rdn & hdd nr
fin: op 6/1: another gd run in first time blnks, must surely find a race on fibresand soon: see 170 (C/D).
211 **OUR PEOPLE 14** [9] M Johnston 6-8-1 (31)(t) K Dalgleish (7) 20/1: 0550-3: 6 ch g Indian Ridge -   1¾ 31a
Fair And Wise (High Line) Bhd, ran on fnl 2f, nvr nrr: acts on firm, soft, fibresand, poss e/trk: see 102.
211 **EVEZIO RUFO 14** [1] N P Littmoden 8-8-10 (40)(vis) R Thomas (7) 10/1: 0455-4: Led till 5f out &   1¼ 38a
again briefly 2½f out, same pace: op 7/1: prob ran to mark: see 211.
231 **HILL FARM DANCER 8** [2] 9-8-0 (30) C Cogan (5) 7/1: 0403-5: Held up, chsd ldrs 4f out, no extra dist.   ¾ 27a
4602} **SEPTEMBER HARVEST 61** [7] 4-9-2 (50) A Culhane 20/1: 4000-6: Held up, imprvd halfway, same   1 46a
pace for press fnl 2f, nvr dngrs: op 14/1, jumps fit, AW bow: '99 Pontefract wnr (h'cap, rtd 60): stks plcd in '98
(rtd 89, B Meehan): eff at 1m, prob stays 12f: acts on firm & soft, handles fibresand, any trk: best without blnks.
211 **SOUHAITE 14** [5] 4-8-9 (43) Martin Dwyer 4/1: 1303-7: Cl-up, led 5f out till bef 2f out, fdd: bt wnr 68.   11 27a
*215 **MARKELLIS 14** [10] 4-8-4 (38) Joanna Badger (7) 9/2: 0041-8: Nvr a factor: see 215 (Southwell).   5 15a
4284} **TOTEM DANCER 87** [6] 7-9-10 (54) R Cody Boutcher (7) 10/1: 3200-9: Slow away, al bhd: op 8/1,   1¾ 29a
top-weight, 3 month abs: plcd in h'caps in '99 (rtd 74): '98 Chester wnr (amat h'cap, rtd 83 at best & 63a):
eff at 12/14f: acts on gd & soft, handles firm & fibresand, prob best without a visor: with J Eyre.
224 **FAMOUS 13** [3] 7-8-12 (42) R Brisland (5) 10/1: 4502-0: In tch till 5f out, op 7/1: btr 224 (10f).   4 11a
170 **SHANGHAI LIL 24** [4] 8-9-2 (46)(VIS) F Norton 25/1: 1000-0: Prom till halfway: 11th: '99 wnr   shd 15a
at Lingfield (2) & here at W'hampton (fnl h'caps, rtd 51a): '98 wnr again at Lingfield (ltd stks) & W'hampton
(2, clmr & h'cap, rtd 48a & 33): eff at 10/12f: handles fast, loves both AWs, sharp trks: tried a visor today.
4463} **HARVEY WHITE 75** [8] 8-8-7 (37) G Bardwell 12/1: 0006-0: Wide, handy for 6f: 12th, op 8/1.   5 0a
12 ran   Time 2m 41.0 (7.4)   (D M Ahier)   P J Makin Ogbourne Maisey, Wilts.

LINGFIELD (Equitrack)   WEDNESDAY JANUARY 5TH   Lefthand, V Sharp Track

Official Going   STANDARD. Stalls: 5f & 1m - Outside; Rem - Inside.

262   12.20 WARMER AMAT HCAP DIV 1 4YO+ 0-70 (F)   6f aw rnd   Going 44 -27 Slow   [44]
£1865   £533   £266

154 **ANOTHER NIGHTMARE 30** [4] D W Barker 8-10-0 (44) Mrs C Williams 6/4 FAV: 0403-1: 8 b m Treasure   49a
Kay - Carange (Known Fact) Broke well & clr after 1f, ran wide bend 2f out, strongly pressed/rdn ins last, styd
on gamely: nicely bckd: '99 wnr at W'hampton, Lingfield & Hamilton (2, h'caps, rtd 50 & 50a): plcd form in '98
(h'caps, rtd 41 & 40a): suited by 5/6f, stays 7f: acts on firm, soft & both AWs, handles any trk, likes W'hampton
& Hamilton: loves to force the pace: has run well fresh: best without blnks: reportedly to be retired.
235 **BRUTAL FANTASY 7** [2] P Howling 6-11-7 (65) Miss S Pocock (5) 100/30: 0025-2: 6 b g Distinctly   ½ 67a
North - Flash Donna (Well Decorated) Chsd wnr, rdn to chall ins last, kept on tho' al just held: op 5/2: see 205 (5f).
3751} **PRIORY GARDENS 99** [3] J M Bradley 6-9-10 (40) Miss Hayley Bryan (7 8/1: 4050-3: 6 b g Broken   3 35a
Hearted - Rosy O'Leary (Majetta) Rdn/chsd ldrs, kept on fnl 2f, not pace to chall: op 6/1: 4 month abs: '99
Leicester wnr (h'cap, rtd 45): '98 Goodwood & Carlisle wnr (h'caps, rtd 36): eff at 6/7f, stays a sharp 1m: acts
on firm, gd & equitrack: handles any trk: runs well for an amat/appr: encouraging AW bow.
4311} **FREDERICK JAMES 86** [6] H E Haynes 6-10-11 (55) Mr M Dobson (7) 7/1: 0300-4: Chsd wnr, rdn/no   nk 49a
extra ins last: op 5/1: reapp: '99 Nottingham wnr (h'cap, rtd 65 at best, plcd on sand, rtd 55a, stks): unplcd
sole '98 start: eff at 5/6f, tried 7f: acts on fast & hvy, handles both AWs: has run well fresh: handles any trk.
2663} **PRIVATE SEAL 99** [5] 5-9-3 (33)(t) (3oh) Ms D Goad (7) 33/1: 0000-5: Dwelt/rear, kept on fnl 2f, not   1¾ 23a
pace to chall: op 16/1: 6 mth abs: unplcd in '99 (rtd 51a & 38): '97 Brighton wnr (sell, rtd 71, G Moore), plcd
on sand, rtd 66a): eff at 5f, stays 7f, tried 10f: acts on firm & eqtrk: best without blnks/t-strap.
199 **ROWLANDSONS STUD 19** [9] 7-9-3 (33)(t) t Miss Leigh Hogben (3) 25/1: /000-6: Chsd ldrs, btn fnl 2f.   hd 22a
154 **SUPERLAO 30** [8] 8-9-3 (33)(2oh) Mr I Mongan 9/1: 0406-7: Wide/al towards rear: tchd 11/1.   ¾ 20a
4455} **ZELBECK 76** [7] 4-10-2 (46) Miss E Folkes (5) 14/1: 000-8: Dwelt/al rear: op 12/1: abs/AW bow.   5 24a
52 **LANDICAN LANE 50** [1] 4-9-13 (43) Mr T Radford (7) 40/1: 0030-9: Dwelt, rdn/mid-div, btn 1f out: abs.   3½ 23a
9 ran   Time 1m 14.65 (4.25)   (GM Engineering)   D W Barker Scorton, N.Yorks.

263   12.50 WARMER AMAT HCAP DIV 2 4YO+ 0-70 (F)   6f aw rnd   Going 44 -19 Slow   [34]
£1855   £530   £265

187 **DOLPHINELLE 21** [6] R Hannon 4-11-7 (55) Mr M Nakauchida (7) 7/2: 4654-1: 4 b c Dolphin Street -   61a
Mamie's Joy (Prince Tenderfoot) Sn cl-up, rdn/led over 2f out, held on gamely ins last, al out: op 3/1, visor
omitted: '99 scorer at Brighton (clm, rtd 75 & 61a): rtd 74 at best in '98: eff at 5/7f, suited by 6f: acts
on firm, soft & equitrack: handles any trk, likes a sharp/undul one: best without blnks/visor.
*225 **CORN DOLLY 14** [9] R F Johnson Houghton 4-11-1 (49) Miss E Johnson Houghton 9/2: 0041-2: 4 ch f   hd 54a
Thatching - Keepers Lock (Sunny's Halo) Chsd ldrs wide halfway, kept on well fnl 2f, just held: op 5/2: fine h'cap
bow, a likely type for instant, particularly with stronger handling: see 225 (mdn, 7f).
214 **NINEACRES 15** [7] J M Bradley 9-11-7 (55)(bl) Mr W Jones (7) 8/1: 4102-3: 9 b g Sayf El Arab -   1½ 56a
Mayor (Laxton) Handy, led halfway till over 2f out, wide on bend 2f out & sn no extra: op 9/2: see 214, 134 (fbsnd).

94

LINGFIELD (Equitrack)   WEDNESDAY JANUARY 5TH   Lefthand, V Sharp Track

154   **WHATTA MADAM** 30 [5] G L Moore 4-10-11 (45)(t) Mr I Mongan 9/4 FAV: 0064-4: Chsd ldrs, rdn/   3½   37a
outpcd halfway, no impress ldrs after: hvly bckd: btr 154 (C/D).
235   **DANCING JACK** 7 [8] 7-9-10 (30) Mr B Hitchcott (5) 8/1: 0006-5: Dwelt/wide & rear, mod gains: see 107.   6   11a
91   **CELTIC VENTURE** 43 [1] 5-11-3 (51) Ms D Goad (7) 12/1: 0000-6: Led 3f, sn btn: op 8/1: 6 wk abs: 2   27a
'99 reapp wnr at Brighton (clmr, rtd 60, mod form subs): missed '98: rnr-up in '97 (seller, rtd 62, M Channon):
eff at 5/6f: acts on firm grnd: likes to force the pace & runs well fresh: likes a sharp/undul track.
107   **RAMBOLD** 42 [2] 9-10-9 (43) Mrs S Bosley 33/1: 0000-7: Cl-up 3f: abs: rnr-up in '99 (fill h'cap):   shd   19a
'98 Chepstow wnr (fill h'cap) & Brighton (class stks, rtd 60): eff at 6f: acts on firm, gd & equitrack, any track.
109   **LADY BALLA CALM** 40 [4] 4-9-11 (25)(6ow) Miss R Illman (0) 50/1: /000-8: Trkd ldrs 4f, sn btn: abs.   nk   6a
4581}   **UNTOLD STORY** 65 [3] 5-10-4 (38) Mrs H Keddy (5) 33/1: 0000-9: Reared start, al bhd: 2 month   5   4a
abs: unplcd in '99 (no form): ex-Irish, rtd 81 in '97 (Gr 1, prob flattered, D Weld): AW bow for T Keddy.
9 ran   Time 1m 14.17 (3.77)   (Tommy Staunton)   R Hannon East Everleigh, Wilts.

---

264   1.20 HAPPY NEW YEAR MDN DIV 1 3YO+ (D)   1m aw rnd Going 44 -08 Slow
£2470   £760   £380   £190   3 yo rec 20lb

188   **THATS ALL FOLKS** 21 [6] P J Makin 3-8-6 A Clark 11/4: 0633-1: 3 b c Alhijaz - So It Goes (Free State)   77a
Chsd ldrs, rdn halfway, styd on gamely for press to lead ins last & forged clr cl-home: nicely bckd: rtd 73 &
73a in '99: eff at 1m, 10f+ may suit: acts on both AWs: likes a sharp trk: open to further improvement.
149   **ROYAL IVY** 30 [5] J Akehurst 3-8-1 F Norton 10/11 FAV: 4032-2: 3 ch f Mujtahid - Royal Climber   2   67a
(King's Lake) Chsd ldrs, rdn/chsd ldr 2f out, briefly led ins last, no extra cl-home: hvly bckd: prev with B Hills.
198   **DIRECT REACTION** 19 [3] Miss Gay Kelleway 3-8-6 N Callan (2) 8/1: 5053-3: 3 b g College Chapel -   nk   71a
Mary's Way (Night Shift) Led, rdn/hdd ins last, no extra cl-home: clr rem: op 4/1: see 198, 149.
220   **SUPERCHIEF** 14 [7] Miss B Sanders 5-9-12 (tvis) C Rutter 12/1: 3034-4: Prom, wknd 2f out: see 209.   8   55$
203   **MELLOW MISS** 18 [10] 4-9-7 (bl) S Drowne 14/1: 0440-5: Mid-div, nvr pace to chall: blnks reapp.   hd   49a
3007}   **ABU CAMP** 99 [1] 5-9-12 (t) S Carson (5) 33/1: 0060-6: Dwelt, nvr on terms: jumps fit (rtd 75h, nov):   8   42a
with M J Heaton Ellis in '99 (unplcd, rtd 46, h'cap): plcd in '98 (h'cap, rtd 63): eff at 7.6f on fast grnd: best
without a visor, wears a t-strap: now with C Cox.
164   **BEDOUIN QUEEN** 26 [4] 3-8-1 (bl) A Daly 16/1: 3005-7: Sn bhd: op 14/1: see 164 (7f).   5   27a
417}   **VEGAS** 99 [8] 4-9-7 T O'Neill (7) 33/1: 6650-8: Sn bhd: 11 month abs.   16   3a
4541}   **FASTESTBARBERALIVE** 69 [2] 5-9-12 A Eddery (5) 40/1: U-9: Dwelt/al rear: jumps fit (mod form):   11   0a
u.r. on sole start in '99 for J Bridger, now with M Madgwick.
--   **ROYAL PARTNERSHIP** [9] 4-9-12 Darren Williams (7) 10/1: 3000-P: Chsd ldrs halfway, wknd qckly/p.u.   0a
2f out: lame: op 7/1: 3 mth abs/AW bow & Brit debut: ex-Irish, plcd in '99 (7f mdn, fast, J Oxx): with K Burke.
10 ran   Time 1m 40.38 (4.18)   (Arron F A Banks)   P J Makin Ogbourne Maisey, Wilts.

---

265   1.50 HAPPY NEW YEAR MDN DIV 2 3YO+ (D)   1m aw rnd Going 44 -00 Slow
£2457   £756   £378   £189   3 yo rec 20lb

240   **BUGGY RIDE** 3 [4] Miss Gay Kelleway 3-8-6 N Callan (2) 6/5 FAV: 242-21: 3 b c Blues Traveller -   83a
- Tambora (Darshaan) Sn led, clr halfway, cruised home fnl 2f, unchall: val for 20L+: well bckd: qck reapp: plcd
form in '99 (rtd 74, mdn, R Charlton): eff at 1m, stays a sharp 10f: acts on fast & equitrack: handles any trk,
likes a sharp drive: relished the reappication of a visor and forcing tactics today, shld win again.
4506}   **ARMENIA** 72 [8] R Hannon 3-8-1 Martin Dwyer 100/30: 5403-2: 3 ch f Arazi - Atlantic Flyer (Storm   15   53a
Bird) Rdn mid-div, late gains, no ch with wnr: op 7/4: 10 wk abs/AW bow: plcd in '99 (rtd 77, fill mdn): eff
at 7f, 1m+ cld suit: handles hvy grnd.
225   **PIPE DREAM** 14 [7] P Burgoyne 4-9-12 P McCabe 16/1: 0000-3: 4 b g Khaya's Signet - Rather Warm   4   50$
(Tribal Chief) Chsd ldrs, rdn/chsd wnr 2f out, no impress: bckd at longs odds: op 25/1: see 225.
114   **TEMESIDE TINA** 40 [6] P D Evans 4-9-7 J P Spencer (5) 33/1: 0606-4: Rdn/rear, mod prog: 6 wk abs: 2   41a
unplcd in '99 (rtd 60, mdn, prob flattered): tried up to 9f prev, needs sellers.
3940}   **WHO GOES THERE** 99 [5] 4-9-7 P M Quinn (5) 20/1: 4250-5: Chsd ldrs till halfway: op 14/1: 4 mth   shd   41$
abs: rnr-up thrice in '99 (rtd 53 & 29a): rtd 41 at best in '98: eff at 7f/9f: handles firm & soft grnd, prob
handles any track: will apprec h'cap company.
109   **ABSOLUTE FANTASY** 40 [1] 4-9-7 (bl) S Carson (5) 15/2: 0004-6: Chsd wnr, btn 3f out: op 10/1, abs.   8   29a
225   **ROTHERHITHE** 14 [9] 4-9-12 F Norton 14/1: 0306-7: Bhd halfway: see 114.   2   30a
220   **ROOKIE** 14 [2] 4-9-12 (BL) A McCarthy (3) 50/1: 5020-8: Prom in chasing group, btn 3f out: blnks.   nk   29a
221   **BAHAMIAN PRINCE** 14 [3] 3-8-6 G Carter 9/1: 00-9: T.o. after 2f, longer 1m trip: see 221 (6f).   6   20a
9 ran   Time 1m 39.69 (3.49)   (Mr & Mrs Gary Pinchen)   Miss Gay Kelleway Lingfield, Surrey.

---

266   2.20 LINGFIELD HCAP 3YO 0-85   1m aw rnd Going 44 -15 Slow   [80]
£4056   £1248   £624   £312

221   **SHAMSAN** 14 [1] M Johnston 3-8-11 (63) J Fanning 2/1 JT FAV: 064-1: 3 ch c Night Shift - Awayil   68a
(Woodman) Dictated pace from start, styd on strongly when pressed from 2f out, in command cl-home, pushed out:
well bckd, first win: h'cap bow: rtd 66a & 60 in '99 (unplcd, mdns, earlier with B Hanbury): apprec this step
up to 1m, further could suit: acts on equitrack: eff forcing the pace: op to further improvement.
128   **JOELY GREEN** 36 [2] N P Littmoden 3-9-2 (68) T G McLaughlin 5/1: 0610-2: 3 b c Binary Star -   3½   67a
Comedy Lady (Comedy Star) Chsd wnr, rdn to chall 2f out, outpcd ins last: stays a sharp 1m: acts on both AWs.
4425}   **MUWAKALL** 78 [4] R W Armstrong 3-8-13 (65) A Clark 5/2: 0306-3: 3 b c Doyoun - Sabayik (Unfuwain)   2   60a
Trkd ldrs wide, rdn/outpcd over 2f out: well bckd: 11 wk abs/AW bow: unplcd in '99 (rtd 79, mdn): stays a
sharp 1m, tried 9f & a return to further shld suit: prob handles equitrack.
243   **MISS WORLD** 3 [3] C N Allen 3-9-7 (73)(t) L Newman (3) 2/1 JT FAV: 321-54: 3 b f Night Shift -   ½   67a
over 1m, no impress wnr after: nicely bckd: qck reapp: btr 213 (h'cap, fibresand).
4 ran   Time 1m 40.89 (4.69)   (A Al-Rostamani)   M Johnston Middleham, N Yorks.

---

267   2.50 RACEGOERS CLUB MDN 4YO+ (D)   1m4f aw Going 44 -11 Slow
£2795   £860   £430   £215   4 yo rec 4 lb

203   **FUSUL** 18 [7] G L Moore 4-8-13 G Parkin 11/4 FAV: 0004-1: 4 ch h Miswaki - Silent Turn (Silent Cal)   55a
Sn cl-up, led halfway & clr 4f out, styd well clr 2f out, pushed out & readily held on ins last: well bckd, tchd
5/1: unplcd in '99 (rtd 72 & 50a, B Hanbury): promise 2 '98 starts (mdns, rtd 72): eff at 10f, suited by this
step up to 12f: acts on equitrack: likes to race with/force the pace.

LINGFIELD (Equitrack)   WEDNESDAY JANUARY 5TH   Lefthand, V Sharp Track

209   **PEARL BUTTON** 18 [4] C A Cyzer 4-8-8 G Carter 20/1: 0000-2: 4 b f Seattle Dancer - Riflelina   3   43a
(Mill Reef) Rdn in mid-div halfway, prog/chsd clr wnr fnl 2f, closed to the line but al held: op 25/1: unplcd in
'99 (rtd 31a & 55): stays a sharp 12f & handles equitrack: a return to h'caps shld suit.

--   **BRILLIANCY** [12] Mrs A E Johnson 5-9-3 (t) A McCarthy (3) 25/1: 3: 5 b g Alleged - Crystal   2½   44a
Gazing (El Gran Senor) Wide/rear, rdn & kept on fnl 3f tho' al held ins last: jockey given a 6-day ban for excessive
use of whip: op 8/1, Flat debut: 8 month jumps abs (promise in M Rasen bmpr in 98/99, stays 13.5f & handles fast
grnd): prob stays a sharp 12f on the level & handles equitrack: wears a t-strap: fin well clr of rem today.

3187} **TUFAMORE** 99 [11] K R Burke 4-8-13 N Callan (3) 6/1: 3005-4: Trkd ldrs going well halfway, sn rdn   16   26a
& btn: tchd 15/2: 5 month abs: unplcd in '99 (rtd 53a & 51): stays 11.5f, handles gd & fibresand: has tried a vis.

238   **SKY CITY** 7 [5] 4-8-8 R Winston 33/1: 0000-5: Rear, mod prog: rnr-up in '98 (10f, rtd 65a, equitrack).   3½   16a

194   **MUSKETRY** 21 [15] 4-8-13 (bl) A Clark 33/1: 0000-6: Chsd wnr 5f out till 4f out, sn btn: see 194.   5   14a

189   **SPANKER** 21 [2] 4-8-8 (bl) J Fanning 9/2: 4230-7: Keen/led till halfway, sn btn: op 5/2: btr 144, 56.   4   0a

229   **TATTOO** 9 [13] 5-8-12 S Drowne 25/1: 0-8: Mid-div at best: longer 12f trip.   2   0a

992} **GO MAN** 99 [8] 6-9-3 S Whitworth 50/1: 6-9: Chsd ldrs 1m: 8 month absence.   2   0a

238   **PREDOMINANT** 7 [6] 4-8-13 M Tebbutt 4/1: 04-0: Sn rdn/bhd: 10th: nicely bckd, tchd 8/1: btr 238.   3½   0a

238   **LADY OF THE NIGHT** 7 [14] 4-8-12 J P Spencer 5/1: 042-0: Chsd ldrs 5f: 14th: op 5/2: btr 238 (10f).   0a

--   Mizog [3] 5-8-12 R Brisland (5) 33/1:   189 **Royal Mount** 21 [9] 4-8-13 C Catlin (7) 33/1:
--   Sohapara [10] 5-8-12 A Morris 66/1:

14 ran   Time 2m 35.8 (6.6)   (D Allen, B Prichard, W Russell)   G L Moore Woodingdean, E.Sussex.

---

268 3.20 BLIZZARD CLASS STKS 4YO+ 0-60 (F)   1m2f aw Going 44 + 02 Fast
£2383   £681   £340   4 yo rec 2 lb

220   **ADMIRALS PLACE** 14 [10] H J Collingridge 4-8-12 G Carter 3/1 JT FAV: 1205-1: 4 ch h Perugino -   64a
Royal Daughter (High Top) Trkd ldr halfway, rdn/led over 1f out, in command ins last & pushed out nr fin: best time
of day: well bckd, tchd 5/1: '99 wnr at Lingfield (mdn h'cap, rtd 59a) & Beverley (h'cap, rtd 65, R W Armstrong):
eff at 1m/10f, likes Lingfield: tough.

4481} **CLONOE** 74 [4] R Ingram 6-9-0 F Norton 25/1: 0060-2: 6 b g Syrtos - Anytime Anywhere (Daring March)   4   57$
Led, rdn/hdd over 1f out, sn held by wnr: jumps fit (no form): '99 wnr at Lingfield (h'cap, rtd 43a), subs scored
at Folkestone (h'cap, rtd 47): '98 wnr at Folkestone (appr h'cap) & Kempton (h'cap, rtd 53 & 47a): suited by 7f/10f
on firm, soft & both AWs: best without blnks: likes to front run on a sharp trk, loves Folkestone: cld find a h'cap.

209   **HIGH SHOT** 14 [3] 5-9-3 G L Moore 10-9-0 S Whitworth 7/1: /022-3: 10 b g Darshaan - Nollet (High Top)   1¼   55a
Trkd ldrs, kept on onepace fnl 2f: op 4/1: in gd form: see 209, 110 (C/D seller).

169   **MY BOLD BOYO** 26 [2] Jamie Poulton 5-9-0 (bl) J Fanning 20/1: 0000-4: Rear, rdn & kept on fnl 3f,   ½   54a
no threat to ldrs: blnks reapplied: unplcd in '99 (rtd 70): '98 Lingfield wnr (med auct mdn, rtd 74): eff at 7f/1m,
now stays a sharp 10f: acts on firm, hvy & equitrack: handles any track.

*220 **SAMMYS SHUFFLE** 14 [3] 5-9-3 (bl) N Carlisle 7/1: 3251-5: Chsd ldrs, onepace fnl 2f: op 6/1, fair run.   ¾   56a

224   **MAPLE** 14 [11] 4-8-12 P Doe (3) 7/1: 0063-6: Handy 3f out, sn btn: op 5/1: btr 224 (C/D).   ½   52a

210   **COUGHLANS GIFT** 18 [7] 4-8-12 P Dobbs (5) 3/1 JT FAV: 0125-7: Mid-div halfway/sn held: bckd: btr 210.   nk   51a

203   **FOREST DREAM** 18 [8] 5-8-11 T G McLaughlin 20/1: 2240-8: Prom 1m: op 12/1: see 43 (fibresand).   1   47a

210   **BRIMSTONE** 18 [9] 5-9-0 A Morris 25/1: 0006-9: Twds rear, no room 4f out/3f out & drpd rear, sn btn.   6   41a

*224 **MIGWAR** 14 [5] 7-9-3 (vis) D Sweeney 4/1: 0401-0: Al twds rear: 10th: nicely bckd: btr 224 (C/D).   5   37a

4492} Tsunami 74 [6] 4-8-9 Joanna Badger (7) 20/1:   4346} **Ihtimaam** 84 [12] 8-9-0 A Clark 33/1:
3860} Robber Red 99 [13] 4-8-12 S Drowne 33/1:

13 ran   Time 2m 06.95 (4.15)   (C G Donovan)   H J Collingridge Exning, Suffolk.

---

269 3.50 TRAVEL BY TRAIN HCAP 3YO 0-70 (E)   5f aw rnd Going 44 + 01 Fast   [74]
£2704   £832   £416   £208

*222 **CASTLE SEMPILL** 14 [5] R M H Cowell 3-9-7 (67)(vis) R Studholme (5) 5/2: 0431-1: 3 b c Presidium -   73a
La Suquet (Puissance) Chsd ldrs, rdn to chall over 1f out, styd on gamely to lead line, all out: gd time: hvly
bckd: '99 scorer at Newmarket (claim, J Fanshawe, rtd 74) & subs here at Lingfield (h'cap): eff at 5/7f, tried
1m: acts on firm, handles soft & loves equitrack: likes Lingfield: eff with/without a visor: tough & genuine.

*242 **GREY FLYER** 3 [6] Mrs L Stubbs 3-9-1 (61)(6ex) J P Spencer 9/4 FAV: 642-12: 3 gr g Factual -   shd   66a
Faraway Grey (Absalom) Cl-up, rdn/led over 1f out, hard rdn/hdd line: hvly bckd: eff at 5/6f: see 242 (6f).

62   **KIRSCH** 49 [3] C A Dwyer 3-9-6 (66)(VIS) F Norton 5/1: 4023-3: 3 ch f Wolfhound - Pondicherry   ¾   69a
(Sir Wimborne) Hmpd after 1f & drpd rear, rdn/switched over 1f out & styd on well ins last, nrst fin: op 6/1, abs:
shade unlucky in first time visor but lacked vital early pace to gain a positon today: should find compensation.

234   **ITSGOTTABDUN** 7 [2] K T Ivory 3-9-1 (61) C Catlin (7) 9/1: 0203-4: Chsd ldrs, onepace over 1f out.   1   62a

234   **WILLOW MAGIC** 7 [4] 3-9-2 (62) P Doe (3) 11/4: 6002-5: Led till over 1f out, btn/eased ins last: well   4   53a
bckd, tchd 3/1: ahd of today's 4th in 234 (C/D).

217   **APRILS COMAIT** 15 [7] 3-8-0 (45)(1ow) N Carlisle 16/1: 0003-6: Chsd ldrs 3f, an onepace: op 10/1.   2½   30a

234   **POLLYOLLY** 7 [1] 3-7-11 (43)(1ow)(2oh) G Bardwell 50/1: 0000-7: Sn rdn, cl-up 3f: mod form in '99.   2   22a

7 ran   Time 59.94 (2.14)   (Mrs J M Penney)   R M H Cowell Six Mile Bottom, Cambs.

WOLVERHAMPTON (Fibresand)   THURSDAY JANUARY 6TH   Lefthand, Sharp Track

Official Going   STANDARD. Stalls: Inside, except 7f/1m6f - Outside.

---

270 12.50 TALISMAN HCAP DIV 1 4YO+ 0-80 (D)   1m1f79y Going 24 -07 Slow   [79]
£3354   £1032   £516   £258   4 yo rec 1 lb

216   **AL MABROOK** 16 [8] K Mahdi 5-8-7 (58) S Drowne 20/1: 0500-1: 5 b h Rainbows For Life - Sky Lover   62a
(Ela Mana Mou): Prom, chsd ldr fnl 2f, styd on gamely for press to prevail cl-home: op 14/1: unplcd in '99
(rtd 65 & 60): late '98 wnr at Lingfield (mdn, rtd 70a, rtd 77 on turf, h'cap): eff at 6/7f prev, now stays a sharp
9f well: acts on fast & both AWs: likes a sharp trk: nicely h'capped, could win again.

227   **RIVER ENSIGN** 10 [3] W M Brisbourne 7-7-11 (48) Claire Bryan (7) 5/1: 0406-2: 7 br m River God -   hd   51a
Ensigns Kit (Saucy Kit): Led, rdn/duelled with wnr ins last, just hdd/no extra nr line: op 9/2: see 227.

2902} **GYPSY** 99 [6] M H Tompkins 4-9-2 (68) G Bardwell 6/1: 456W-3: 4 b g Distinctly North - Winscarlet   3½   64a
North (Garland Knight): Mid-div, rdn halfway, kept on final 2f for press, no threat to front pair: 6 mth abs,
AW bow: '99 Lingfield scorer (h'cap, rtd 72): '98 Yarmouth wnr (auct mdn, rtd 75 at best): eff at 9/10f, prob

stays 11f: acts on fast, gd/soft & fibresand: handles a sharp or gall trk: could find similar at 10f.

*229 HEATHYARDS JAKE 10 [4] R Hollinshead 4-8-11 (63)(6ex) Dean McKeown 4/1: 6221-4: Mid-div, kept   hd   58a
on fnl 2f, no threat to ldrs: op 3/1, clr rem: 6lb pen for 229 (1m, mdn).

3413} SHEER FACE 99 [9] 6-9-0 (65) Martin Dwyer 6/1: 3440-5: Mid-div, btn 2f out: op 9/2: 5 mth abs: 6   51a
plcd in '99 (h'cap, rtd 73, reapp): '98 Goodwood wnr (h'cap, rtd 77, also rtd 57a): acts on firm &
gd/soft grnd: likes a sharp/undul trk: best without eyehood & blnks: well h'capped.

2886} STATE APPROVAL 99 [7] 7-9-3 (68) Joanna Badger (7) 8/1: 6125-6: Chsd ldrs, rdn/held 3f out: op   6   45a
7/1, 6 mth abs: '99 wnr at Southwell (reapp) & W'hampton (clmrs, rtd 72a): '98 wnr again here at W'hampton (3
sells, one for P Eccles) & Southwell (3, sells/clmr, rtd 68a): eff at 9/13f: acts on fast, f/sand specialist:
runs well fresh: likes a sharp trk: well fresh: eff up with/forcing the pace: loves sell/clmrs.

*209 DAPHNES DOLL 19 [11] 5-8-2 (53) M Henry 3/1 FAV: 0041-7: Cl-up, wknd 2f out/eased finl 1f: op 7/2.   2   26a

4456} BOWCLIFFE 77 [2] 9-9-8 (73) R Winston 14/1: 0600-8: Held up, nvr a factor: op 12/1: 11 wk abs.   2   42a

143 POLAR ICE 33 [5] 4-9-12 (78) N Callan (3) 16/1: 3000-9: Wide/al rear, op 14/1.   11   31a

9 ran   Time 2m 01.1 (2.9)   (Hamad Al-Mutawa)   K Mahdi Newmarket, Suffolk.

---

271   1.20 TALISMAN HCAP DIV 2 4YO+ 0-80 (D)   1m1f79y Going 24 -00 Slow   [79]
£3334   £1026   £513   £256   4 yo rec 1 lb

*189 TROIS 22 [9] G Woodward 4-9-1 (67) T G McLaughlin 4/1: 4001-1: 4 b g Efisio - Drei (Lyphard):   72a
Chsd ldrs, rdn/prog to lead last, hung left ins last, styd on well, rdn out: h'cap bow: '99 scorer here at
W'hampton (mdn), mod form prev for L Cumani on turf (rtd 59, auct mdn): eff arnd 9f, 10f+ cld suit: acts on
fibresand & runs well fresh: likes W'hampton: open to further improvement.

176 WESTERN RAINBOW 24 [5] P D Evans 4-7-10 (48)(1oh) M Henry 4/1: 0022-2: 4 b g Rainbows For Life -   1   50a
Miss Galwegian (Sandford Lad): Mid-div, rdn/kept on final 2f, not pace of wnr: stays 9f, 10f+ could suit.

244 TIGHTROPE 4 [2] N P Littmoden 5-8-13 (64) G Carter 7/4 FAV: 024-63: 5 b g Alzao - Circus Act   1¾   63a
(Shirley Heights): Rear in tch, keen, rdn & kept on final 3f, not pace to chall: well bckd, qck reapp: see 172, 1.

147 DIM OFAN 31 [3] B Palling 4-8-8 (60) D Sweeney 14/1: 0046-4: Chsd ldrs, prog/led over 3f out, hdd   1¾   56a
over 1f out & no extra ins last: op 10/1: unplcd in '99 (rtd 72 & 61a): '98 Chepstow (auct mdn) & Nottingham
wnr (nov, rtd 87): stays a sharp 9.3f: acts on fast, fibresand & loves soft grnd: handles any trk: can force
the pace: well h'capped & can win similar with a drop back to 7f/1m.

131 AREISH 37 [1] 7-7-13 (50) A Polli (3) 6/1: 3020-5: Settled towards rear, rdn/outpcd over 2f out,   1½   43a
styd on inside last, no threat: op 5/1: return to 10f+ could suit on this evidence: see 67 (C/D).

2385} QUEDEX 99 [4] 4-9-2 (68) S Whitworth 12/1: 2114-6: Mid-div, rdn/outpcd 4f out: op 10/1: 6 mth   2½   56a
abs/AW bow: '99 Goodwood (h'cap) & Bath wnr (class stks, rtd 71 at best): unplcd in '98 (auct mdn, rtd 75): eff
at 10/11.6f, cld stay further: acts on firm & soft grnd, any trk: return to 10f+ will suit.

4603} ONE QUICK LION 63 [6] 4-9-3 (69) R Price 41/1: 065-7: Keen/cl-up, wknd over 1f out: op 6/1: 2 mth   2½   52a
abs: h'cap/AW bow: unplcd in '99 from 3 starts (rtd 72, 1m mdn): Ingr 9f trip today.

-- LAWNETT [8] 4-8-6 (58) Dean McKeown 14/1: 3351-8: Led 6f, sn btn: op 10/1: 3 mth jumps abs.   ½   40a

33 RIVERBLUE 55 [7] 4-9-11 (77) M Tebbutt 16/1: 0040-9: Rear/wide, nvr a factor: op 10/1: 8 wk abs.   3   53a

9 ran   Time 2m 00.5 (2.3)   (Mrs Jo Hardy)   G Woodward Brierley, Sth Yorks.

---

272   1.50 G MANNERING CLAIMER 4YO+ (F)   5f aw rnd Going 24 +06 Fast
£2310   £660   £330

214 NIFTY NORMAN 16 [10] D Nicholls 6-8-9 (bl) F Norton 8/1: 0665-1: 6 b g Rock City - Nifty Fifty   75a
(Runnett): Sn handy, led ins last & asserted nr fin, rdn out: gd time: '99 scorer at Southwell (2, rtd 73a) &
Chester (h'caps, rtd 69): '98 wnr again at Southwell (h'cap, rtd 58a): eff at 6f, suited by 5f, tried 7f: acts
on fast, loves gd/soft, hvy & both AW's: handles any trk, likes Southwell: eff with/without blnks: tough 6yo.

214 KRYSTAL MAX 16 [5] T G Mills 7-8-13 L Carter 2/1: 2420-2: 7 b g Classic Music - Lake Isle (Caerleon)   2   73a
Led, hdd inside last & not pace of wnr nr fin: op 11/8: back to form after 214: see 113 (equitrack).

258 POLLY MILLS 2 [7] P D Evans 4-8-12 (vis) J P Spencer 9/1: 020-03: 4 b f Lugana Beach - Danseuse   2   67a
Davis (Glow): Rdn/wide & towards rear, kept on final 2f for press, nrst fin: qck reapp: see 134 (6f).

*214 SAMWAR 16 [8] Mrs N Macauley 8-9-3 (vis) R Fitzpatrick (3) 7/4 FAV: 1501-4: Rdn/chsd leading pair   hd   71a
halfway, no impress over 1f out: tchd 2/1: ahead of todays 1st & 2nd in 214 (Southwell).

4133} CELTIC SEAL 99 [1] 4-7-12 S Righton 25/1: /400-5: Chsd ldrs, not pace to chall: 3 mth abs: unplcd   2½   45a
in '99 (rtd 57a & 32): late '98 scorer at Southwell (auct mdn, rtd 62a & 56): eff at 5f, tried 6f: acts on
fibresand, poss handles gd/soft: likes a sharp trk & has run well fresh.

*235 AA YOUKNOWNOTHING 8 [3] 4-9-3 (tvi) P Goode (5) 6/1: 3341-6: Chsd ldr 1f, outpcd halfway: see 235. nk   63a

214 AVONDALE GIRL 16 [9] 4-8-9(1ow) F Lynch 16/1: 6100-7: Nvr on terms: see 214.   nk   54$

199 SING FOR ME 20 [6] 5-8-6 Stephanie Hollinshea 66/1: 0000-8: Al towards rear: unplcd in '99 (rtd 39a   1½   47$
& 44): '98 wnr here at W'hampton (sell, rtd 50a, plcd on turf, rtd 53): eff at 5f, stays 7f: acts on gd, soft &
fibresand: has run well fresh: best without a visor: likes a sharp trk.

139 BLACKFOOT 36 [2] 4-8-3 J Edmunds (5) 51/1: 0200-9: Hmpd after 1f, sn bhd: s/mate of 5th: see 139 (C/D).   6   33a

132 DIVIDE AND RULE 36 [4] 6-8-3 M Henry 66/1: 0000-0: Sn outpcd/bhd: 10th: unplcd in '99 (rtd 39 &   3   26a
25a): plcd in '98 (clmr, rtd 34a): '96 Ripon wnr (auct mdn, rtd 66): eff at 5f, acts on fast & gd/soft grnd.

10 ran   Time 1m 01.1 (0.9)   (The Nifty Norman Partnership)   D Nicholls Sessay, Nth Yorks.

---

273   2.20 WAVERLEY MDN 3YO+ (D)   6f aw rnd Going 24 -13 Slow
£2847   £876   £438   £219   3 yo rec 16lb

95 SISAO 44 [13] Miss Gay Kelleway 4-9-10 (bl) N Callan (3) 6/4 FAV: 0632-1: 4 ch c College Chapel -   61a
Copt Hall Princess (Crowned Prince): Sn led, clr halfway, rdn/held on well ins last: nicely bckd, 6 wk abs: place
form in '99 (rtd 60a & 54): eff at 6f: acts on both AWs: likes a sharp trk & runs well fresh: eff in blnks:
likes to force the pace: open to further improvement in h'caps.

493} COLLEGE BLUE 99 [10] T G Mills 4-9-5 L Carter 5/1: 03/2-2: 4 b m College Chapel - Mitsubishi Centre   1¼   51a
(Thatching): Chsd wnr halfway, rdn & kept on ins last, nvr pace to chall: op 3/1, 11 mth abs: rnr-up on sole
'99 start (mdn, rtd 75a): rnr-up twice in '99 (rtd 82 & 77a): eff at 5/6f: handles both AWs & fast grnd: likes
a sharp/turning trk: eff with/without a visor: could find similar this winter.

4252} FOUND AT LAST 93 [5] G Woodward 4-9-10 T G McLaughlin 25/1: 5005-3: 4 b g Aragon - Girton   2   51a
(Balidar): Chsd ldrs, kept on fnl 1f, nvr pace to chall: 3 mth abs, AW bow: unplcd in '99 (rtd 66, mdn, Miss S
E Hall): unplcd sole '98 start (rtd 65, auct mdn): eff at 6f, has tried 1m, may yet suit: handles fibresand.

3777} CHOK DI 99 [7] Mrs M Reveley 4-9-10 C Teague 10/1: 5000-4: Held up racing keenly, rdn & kept on   1   49$
final 2f, no threat: op 6/1: 4 mth abs/AW bow: unplcd in '99 (rtd 45, mdn h'cap): unplcd in '98 (auct mdn,

rtd 56): eff at 6f: handles firm, fast & fibresand: a return to h'caps should suit.
-- **MILLER TIME** [4] 3-8-8 L Charnock 9/1: 5: Dwelt/rear, kept on final 2f, nrst fin: op 5/1, debut: *1¾* **45a**
clr rem: Timeless Times colt: could apprec 7f+ on this evidence, will know more next time for T D Easterby.
39 **JUST FOR YOU 54** [8] 4-9-10 S Drowne 9/2: 0-6: Prom, btn 2f out: op 4/1: 8 wk abs. *6* **34a**
3635} **RAJMATA 99** [12] 4-9-5 (vis) R Fitzpatrick (3) 10/1: 2500-7: Dwelt/al towards rear: op 8/1: 4 mth abs. *7* **16a**
95 **GOOD WHIT SON 44** [1] 4-9-10 A McCarthy (3) 33/1: 00-8: Al outpcd: 6 wk abs. *3½* **12a**
229 **ENVY 10** [6] 4-9-5 Dean McKeown 16/1: 0-9: Cl-up 3f: op 33/1. *2* **2a**
171 **ESPERE DOR 26** [2] 3-8-8 R Lappin 33/1: 0-0: Al outpcd rear: 10th. *1* **5a**
769} **BEST MUSIC METROFM 99** [9] 3-8-8 R Winston 9/1: 3-0: Dwelt, sn rdn/chsd ldrs, btn over 2f out: *8* **0a**
op 5/1, 9 mth abs/AW bow: prev with D Eddy, now with E J Alston.
11 ran Time 1m 15.0 (2.2) (Stable Investments Ltd) Miss Gay Kelleway Lingfield, Surrey.

274

2.50 RED GAUNTLET SELLER DIV 1 3YO+ (G) 7f aw Going 24 -20 Slow
£1527 £436 £218 3 yo rec 18lb

142 **ELITE HOPE 33** [3] N Tinkler 8-9-2 Dean McKeown 7/4: 3424-1: 8 ch m Moment Of Hope - Chervil **55a**
(Greenough): Cl-up, led halfway, always holding rival fnl 1f out, rdn out: op 5/4: no bid: '99 Southwell wnr
(2, h'cap & clmr, rtd 70a): '98 wnr at W'hampton (4, h'cap & clmrs, disq once, rtd 72a): eff at 6f, suited by 7f:
acts on fast, gd/soft, f/sand specialist: best without blnks: likes to force the pace: enjoys sell & claimers.
250 **C HARRY 3** [1] R Hollinshead 6-9-12 N Callan (3) 11/8 FAV: 303-52: 6 ch h Imperial Frontier - Desert *¾* **63a**
Gale (Taufan): Trkd ldrs, rdn/chsd wnr 2f out, kept on, not pace to chall: well bckd: clr rem: topweight: see 130.
225 **BALLYMORRIS BOY 15** [7] J Pearce 4-9-7 T G McLaughlin 5/1: 0534-3: 4 b c Dolphin Street - Solas Abu *5* **48$**
(Red Sunset): Chsd ldrs, rdn/outpcd by front pair final 2f: acts on firm, handles both AWs: h'caps should suit.
232 **LIVELY JACQ 10** [8] C N Allen 4-9-2 N Carlisle 8/1: 0466-4: Prom, btn 2f out: op 6/1: see 132 (6f). *hd* **42a**
232 **MIKES DOUBLE 10** [4] 6-9-7 (vis) R Fitzpatrick (3) 12/1: 5U60-5: Prom, outpcd halfway: op 16/1. *shd* **47$**
249 **TAPAUA 3** [5] 4-9-7 (bl) F Lynch 12/1: 040-06: Dwelt/held up in tch, rdn/btn 2f out & eased ins last. *4* **39a**
50 **HANDSOME BEAU 52** [2] 5-9-7 (bl) L Charnock 50/1: 6/00-7: Led 3f, sn btn: op 10/1, 7 wk abs: *nk* **38$**
lightly rcd/mod form in last 2 seasons: with A Bailey.
7 ran Time 1m 29.3 (3.1) (Elite Racing Club) N Tinkler Langton, Nth Yorks.

275

3.20 Q DURWARD HCAP 3YO 0-90 (C) 6f aw rnd Going 24 +02 Fast [92]
£6662 £2050 £1025 £512

202 **FEAST OF ROMANCE 20** [11] Miss Gay Kelleway 3-8-8 (72) S Whitworth 7/1: 0513-1: 3 b c Pursuit Of Love - **80a**
June Fayre (Sagaro): Rdn/chsd ldrs halfway, styd on gamely for press to lead inside last, rdn out: gd time: op 4/1:
'99 wnr at Southwell (auct mdn, rtd 77a, unplcd on turf, rtd 68): eff at 6f, 7f should suit: acts on fibresand:
likes a sharp trk: lightly raced & open to further improvement in similar contests.
*62 **BRANSTON PICKLE 50** [10] T J Etherington 3-9-2 (80) J Fanning 16/1: 4101-2: 3 ch c Piccolo - Indefinite *1½* **84a**
Article (Indian Ridge): Trkd ldrs, rdn/ch inside last, kept on well: abs, op 10/1: tough, win again: see 62 (clmr).
222 **SMOKIN BEAU 15** [7] J Cullinan 3-8-13 (77) D Sweeney 16/1: 3315-3: 3 b g Cigar - Beau Dada *¾* **79a**
(Pine Circle): Led, rdn/hdd inside last, no extra cl-home: op 12/1: pacey type, eff at 5/6f: see 222, 127.
*72 **ILLUSIVE 48** [4] H J Collingridge 3-8-7 (71)(bl) F Norton 11/4 FAV: 1021-4: Chsd ldrs, no room *½* **71a**
briefly over 1f out, swtchd & onepace inside last: abs, hvly bckd, morning gamble from 8/1: see 72 (5f).
*234 **DACCORD 8** [9] 3-9-2 (80)(6ex) S Carson (5) 5/1: 4311-5: Handy, ch over 1f out, no extra inside *2½* **73a**
last: op 7/2, 6lb pen for latest: acts on gd, soft & both AWs: return to 5f could suit: see 234 (5f, equitrack).
202 **OTIME 20** [2] 3-8-13 (77)(vis) Dean McKeown 14/1: 3014-6: Chsd ldrs, btn 2f out: op 10/1: see 165. *1½* **66a**
202 **SIRENE 20** [6] 3-7-10 (60)(bl) G Bardwell 8/1: 0102-7: Bmpd start & slowly away, sn rdn/wide, nvr *nk* **48a**
a factor: lost chance at start, prob worth another look: see 202, 88 (sell, 7f, made all).
4355} **LEEN 84** [3] 3-8-6 (70) A McCarthy (3) 25/1: 2140-8: Sn rdn/al towards rear: AW bow, 12 wk abs: '99 *2* **53a**
Bath wnr (fillies auct mdn, rtd 73): eff at 5/6f: acts on firm & gd/soft grnd: handles a turning or stiff/gall trk.
202 **JAMES STARK 20** [1] 3-9-7 (85)(VIS) G Carter 8/1: 5116-9: Towards rear, nvr a factor: tchd 10/1, visor. *6* **57a**
202 **CAUTIOUS JOE 20** [8] 3-8-12 (76) R Winston 14/1: 100-0: Sn outpcd: 10th: op 10/1: see 202. *8* **33a**
222 **TYCANDO 15** [5] 3-9-0 (78) N Callan (3) 7/2: 1022-0: Jinked start & slowly away, chsd ldrs halfway, *hd* **34a**
sn eased/btn: 11th: rider injured leaving stalls, unable to ride the gelding out: nicely bckd: this is best ignored.
11 ran Time 1m 14.1 (1.3) (K & W Racing Partnership) Miss Gay Kelleway Lingfield, Surrey.

276

3.50 RED GAUNTLET SELLER DIV 2 3YO+ (G) 7f aw rnd Going 24 -29 Slow
£1518 £433 £216 3 yo rec 18lb

*252 **RAMBO WALTZER 3** [8] D Nicholls 8-9-12 F Norton 1/4 FAV: 141-11: 8 b g Rambo Dancer - Vindictive Lady **62a**
(Foolish Pleasure): Chsd ldrs, led 3f out, rdn/asserted 2f out, in command when eased nr fin: value for 5L+:
hvly bckd at long odds on: qck reapp: recent Southwell wnr (sell): '99 scorer at Catterick, Thirsk (h'caps, rtd
71) & thrice at Southwell (2 clmrs & sell, rtd 75a at best): '98 W'hampton & Southwell wnr (2, h'caps, rtd 91a &
72): eff at 7f/9.5f on fast & soft, loves fibresand/Southwell & W'hampton: has run well fresh: 22 wins from 86.
229 **NADDER 10** [4] W M Brisbourne 5-9-7 (BL) T G McLaughlin 50/1: 0000-2: 5 ch g Lion Cavern - Nadia *3* **45$**
Nerina (Northern Dancer): Rdn/towards rear, kept on final 2f for press: first time blnks: eff at 7f on fibresand.
4578} **SCROOGE 66** [3] M H Tompkins 4-9-7 G Bardwell 25/1: 0050-3: 4 b g Tirol - Gay Appeal (Star Appeal): *1* **43a**
Dwelt/rear & sn rdn, kept on final 2f for press, no threat to wnr: jumps fit, mod form: unplcd in '99 (rtd 65,
flattered, mdn): mod form in '98: has tried a visor prev: eff at 7f, tried 10f: handles fibresand: AW bow today.
173 **NOBLE PATRIOT 26** [7] R Hollinshead 5-9-7 Dean McKeown 12/1: 0203-4: Chsd ldrs halfway, sn held. *½* **42$**
193 **RIVERDANCE 22** [2] 4-9-7 (vis) J P Spencer 9/1: 0006-5: Chsd ldrs 5f: op 6/1: visor reapp: see 139. *4* **34a**
226 **PURNADAS ROAD 10** [5] 5-9-2 (bl) J Bramhill 33/1: 0000-6: Led 4f, sn btn: see 226. *8* **18a**
199 **EMMAJOUN 20** [6] 5-9-2 (VIS) D Sweeney 9/1: 3625-7: Chsd ldrs 4f: op 5/1, visor: see 156, 32. *7* **8a**
195 **GINISKI PARK 20** [1] 4-9-2 R Fitzpatrick (3) 66/1: 00/0-8: In tch till halfway: mod form, tried blnks. *3* **2a**
8 ran Time 1m 29.9 (3.7) (W G Swiers) D Nicholls Sessay, Nth Yorks.

277

4.20 IVANHOE HCAP 4YO+ 0-65 (F) 1m6f166y Going 24 -44 Slow [65]
£2383 £681 £340 4 yo rec 6 lb

168 **HIGHLY PRIZED 27** [1] J S King 6-9-6 (57) S Drowne 4/1: 2543-1: 6 b g Shirley Heights - On The Tiles **63a**
(Thatch): Prom, led 4f out, duelled with rnr-up inside last, just prevailed on line, all-out: op 9/4: rnr-up in '99
(h'cap, rtd 70): '98 Salisbury wnr (h'cap, rtd 73): eff at 12/15f, tried 2m+: acts on firm, hvy & both AWs: handles

WOLVERHAMPTON (Fibresand)   THURSDAY JANUARY 6TH   Lefthand, Sharp Track

any trk: eff weight carrier: on a fair mark, can win again this winter.

*211   **COUNT DE MONEY 16** [3] S R Bowring 5-10-0 (65) R Fitzpatrick (3) 9/2: 5221-2: 5 b g Last Tycoon -   nk   70a
Menominee (Soviet Star): Held up, prog to chall ins last, just held: clr rem: op 9/4: stays 1m6.7f: progressive.

141   **CHILDRENS CHOICE 33** [11] J Pearce 9-8-4 (41) G Bardwell 11/4 FAV: 5026-3: 9 b m Taufan - Alice   5   40a
Brackloon (Melyno): Towards rear, rapid prog/chsd ldrs 4f out, kept on onepace after: nicely bckd: see 66.

194   **KAID 22** [5] N P Littmoden 5-8-0 (36)(VIS)(1ow) A Daly 4/1: 0005-4: Held up, mod gains: op 7/2, visor.   ¾   34a

260   **MR SPECULATOR 2** [8] 7-8-10 (47) S Whitworth 7/1: 0/3-05: Chsd ldrs, no extra over 1f out: qck   3½   40a
reapp: blinkers omitted: on a fair mark & a likely type for similar at 12f: see 174.

3341}   **RONQUISTA DOR 99** [2] 6-8-12 (49)(bl) S Carson (5) 8/1: 4253-6: Led halfway, hdd 4f out/sn btn: 5   35a
tchd 10/1: 5 mth abs: plcd sev times in '99 (rtd 51a & 50, h'cap): '98 scorer at Southwell (mdn h'cap) & Warwick
(sell h'cap) & here at W'hampton (h'cap, rtd 60a & 50): eff at 12f on firm, gd & fibresand: best in blnks.

190   **SCONCED 22** [9] 5-7-12 (35)(vis)(2ow)(6oh) L Charnock 10/1: 0533-7: Mid-div at best: see 190.   12   6a

4258}   **COPPER COOKIE 93** [12] 5-7-12 (35)(2ow)(12oh) P Fessey 66/1: 0006-8: Bhd 5f out: 2 mth jumps   18   0a
abs (no form): plcd in '99 (h'cap, rtd 30): plcd in '98 (rtd 30a): eff at 7f/12f: handles fibresand & gd/soft.

4564}   **CYMBAL MELODY 68** [4] 4-7-10 (35)(6oh) A Polli (3) 66/1: 0000-9: Sn bhd: jumps fit (rtd 65h, sell):   ¾   0a
only mod form on the level prev, with R Hollinshead.

--   **PETOSKIN** [10] 8-8-13 (50) T G McLaughlin 50/1: 3000/0: Bhd halfway: 10th: long abs.   29   0a

148}   **TEAM OF THREE 99** [11] 4-7-10 (39)(13oh) Joanna Badger (5) 66/1: 000/0: Led 1m, sn bhd: 11th: long abs. ½   0a
11 ran   Time 3m 19.7 (10.1)   (Mrs Marygold O'Kelly)   J S King Broad Hinton, Wilts.

SOUTHWELL (Fibresand)   FRIDAY JANUARY 7TH   Lefthand, Sharp, Oval Track

Official Going   STANDARD Stalls: Inside

278   12.40 HOOPLA MDN 3YO (D)   7f aw rnd Going 48 -32 Slow
£2847   £876   £438   £219

103   **INVER GOLD 44** [14] A G Newcombe 3-9-0 S Whitworth 5/1: 624-1: 3 ch c Arazi - Mary Martin (Be My   75a
Guest) Dwelt/towards rear, rdn/prog 3f out & led ins last, won going away, rdn out: 6 wk abs: rnr-up in '99 (rtd
77a, rtd 79 on turf, M Johnston): eff at 7f, stays 1m & a return to further will suit: acts on both AWs & gd/soft
grnd: runs well fresh: handles a sharp trk: op to further improvement, particularly when tackling further again.

118   **NIGHT AND DAY 41** [12] W Jarvis 3-8-9 M Tebbutt 6/1: 3-2: 3 ch f Anshan - Midnight Break (Night Shift)   1¾   66a
Handy, rdn/led over 1f out, hdd ins last & not pace of wnr: tchd 7/1, abs: eff at 7f on fibresand: win a race.

221   **LADYWELL BLAISE 16** [9] M L W Bell 3-8-9 C Carver (1) 5/1: 5-3: 3 b f Turtle Island - Duly Elected   2   62a
(Persian Bold): Prom, rdn/no extra ins last: op 4/1: styd longer 7f trip: acts on fibresand: see 221 (6f, debut).

1336}   **SILCA FANTASY 99** [13] P Howling 3-8-9 A McCarthy (3) 16/1: 0-4: Chsd ldrs, kept on fnl 2f, not   3   56a
pace to chall: op 14/1: AW bow, 6 month abs: unplcd sole start in '99 (rtd 56, M Channon): styd this longer 7f
trip & handles fibresand: some encouragement here for new connections.

264   **DIRECT REACTION 2** [7] 3-9-0 (VIS) P Fredericks (5) 3/1 FAV: 053-35: Led, rdn/hdd over 1f out & no   1¾   58a
extra: ran freely in 1st time visor: op 5/2: quick reapp: btr 264, 198.

198   **JUST THE JOB TOO 21** [6] 3-9-0 T Eaves (7) 33/1: 00-6: Prom, wknd fnl 2f: needs h'caps.   2   54a

4414}   **DONTBESOBOLD 81** [8] 3-9-0 J Stack 16/1: 0040-7: Rdn/towards rear, late gains, no threat: 12 wk   nk   53a
abs/AW bow: unplcd in '99 (rtd 75, auct mdn): stays a turning 6.7f, tried 1m: handles soft & prob fast grnd.

--   **PLANTAGEANT** [2] 3-9-0 R Price 9/1: 8: Dwelt/nvr factor: op 7/1: debut: with R Armstrong.   8   41a

4433}   **KINGS GINGER 80** [10] 3-9-0 D Dineley 16/1: 0305-9: Al towards rear: op 12/1: 11 wk abs/AW bow: 1¼   38a
prev with P R Chamings, now with D J Wintle.

221   **JUST MAC 16** [1] 3-9-0 A Culhane 4/1: 63-0: Chsd ldrs 5f: 10th: tchd 6/1: btr 221 (6f, equitrack).   hd   37a

171   **Blue Cavalier 27** [5] 3-9-0 F Norton 33/1:   4597} **Caprice 64** [4] 3-8-9 J Tate 25/1:

198   **Magical Jack 21** [3] 3-9-0 P Fessey 50/1:   --   **Tiger Princess** [11] 3-8-9 J Fanning 11/1:
14 ran   Time 1m 32.2 (5.6)   (M Patel)   A G Newcombe Huntshaw, Devon

279   1.10 CONKERS CLAIMER 4YO+ (F)   6f aw rnd Going 48 +08 Fast
£2121   £606   £303

197   **ROUGE 21** [5] J P Leigh 5-8-8 M Tebbutt 3/1: 1204-1: 5 gr m Rudimentary - Couleur de Rose   80a
(Kalaglow) Sn handy trav well, led over 2f out, rdn & readily pulled clr final 1f: op 2/1: good time: '99 wnr
at W'hampton (C/D, h'cap, 1st successive, rtd 71a, rtd 49 on turf): rtd 58a in '98 (mdn): eff at 6f/7f: likes to
race with/force the pace: likes a sharp track & loves fibresand: well suited by this return to 6f, can win again.

33   **ELTON LEDGER 56** [4] Mrs N Macauley 11-8-5 R Fitzpatrick (3) 12/1: 1406-2: 11 b g Cyrano de   5   65a
Bergerac - Princess Of Nashua (Crowned Prince) Trkd ldrs, rdn/outpcd over 2f out, kept on ins last tho' no ch with
wnr: op 8/1: 8 wk abs: '99 scorer here at Southwell (seller, C/D, rtd 66a): '98 wnr six times at Southwell in
'98 (rtd 72a & 58): stays 1m, suited by 6f: acts on gd & hvy, fibresand/Southwell specialist: eff in a visor: has
refused to enter stalls prev: suited by sell/clmg grade: tough 11yo, this is his time of year, keep him in mind.

*272   **NIFTY NORMAN 1** [8] D Nicholls 6-8-9 F Norton 9/4 FAV: 665-13: 6 b g Rock City - Nifty Fifty   hd   68a
(Runnett) Trkd ldrs, kept on for press fnl 2f, no ch with wnr: nicely bckd: won well at W'hampton yesterday.

175   **ALJAZ 27** [2] Miss Gay Kelleway 10-9-3 S Whitworth 6/1: 0223-4: Cl up, rdn/no extra fnl 2f: see 44.   5   65a

250   **ICE AGE 4** [3] 6-8-3 (bl) L Newman (5) 20/1: 600-05: Led, hdd & drifted right 2f out, sn held: qck reapp.   ½   49a

247   **BEWARE 4** [10] 5-8-7 J Fanning 10/1: 030-36: Mid-div, nvr pace to chall: op 7/1, stablemate of beat: btr 30.3   46a

256   **TAKHLID 3** [1] 9-9-7 A Culhane 3/1: 116-47: Cl-up 4f: qck reapp: tchd 4/1: btr 142 (7f).   ¾   58a

201   **OK JOHN 21** [9] 5-8-7 A Daly 20/1: 0303-8: Al outpcd: see 57 (5f, equitrack).   hd   44a

197   **MAJOR MORRIS 21** [6] 5-8-3 P M Quinn (5) 66/1: 00-9: Sn outpcd: no form.   3   32a

134   **ZOES NEWSBOX 37** [7] 6-7-12 P Fessey 40/1: 00-0: Chsd ldrs 3f: mod form.   1¾   23a
10 ran   Time 1m 15.8 (2.5)   (J M Greetham)   J P Leigh Willoughton, Lincs

280   1.40 FRENCH FILL HCAP 4YO+ 0-75 (E)   6f aw rnd Going 48 -20 Slow   [68]
£2769   £852   £426   £213

243   **DAYS OF GRACE 5** [2] L Montague Hall 5-9-7 (61) Martin Dwyer 9/4 FAV: 124-21: 5 gr m Wolfhound - Inshirah   66a
(Caro) Led, rdn/hdd over 2f out, rallied gamely for press to lead again ins last, rdn out/drifted right cl home:
nicely bckd: qck reapp: '99 wnr at Southwell & Wolverhampton (h'caps, rtd 62a & 56): eff at 5/7f on firm, hvy
& both AW's: handles any track, likes a sharp one: gd weight carrier: tough, can win more races.

*187   MUJAS MAGIC 23 [5] Mrs N Macauley 5-9-9 (63)(vis) R Fitzpatrick (3) 5/1: 3401-2: 5 b m Mujadil - Grave Error (Northern Treat) Dwelt & rdn/rear, rdn/not much room when prog 2f out, styd on ins last, nrst fin: op 3/1: remains in good heart, would apprec a return to 7f on this evidence: see 187.   **1   65a**

193   HAUNT THE ZOO 23 [9] J L Harris 5-9-0 (54) J Bramhill 5/2: 6110-3: 5 b m Komaite - Merryhill Maid (M Double M) Rdn/rear & wide, swtchd left/briefly no room over 1f out, styd on well, nrst fin: well bckd.   **nk   55a**

2851} ASHOVER AMBER 99 [8] T D Barron 4-10-0 (68) Lynsey Hanna (7) 3/1: 1313-4: Wide/chsd ldrs, prog *shd* to lead over 1f out, drifted left/hdd ins last & wknd cl home: op 4/1: 6 mth ags: '99 wnr here at Southwell (mdn, reapp, rtd 70a) & twice at Carlisle (h'cap & class stks, rtd 76): plcd in '98: eff over a stiff 5f/sharp 6f: acts on firm, gd/soft & fibresand: has run well fresh: likes to force the pace: spot on in similar back at 5f.   **shd   69a**

246   PETITE DANSEUSE 4 [7] 6-7-10 (36)(1oh) Claire Bryan (7) 10/1: 260-55: Led/dsptd lead 4f: op 8/1.   **2½   30a**

247   AMARO 4 [6] 4-8-2 (42) F Norton 9/1: 005-56: Chsd ldrs 4f: tchd 12/1: see 247, 226.   **nk   35a**

250   SANS RIVALE 4 [4] 5-7-10 (36)(8oh) Iona Wands (5) 50/1: 000-07: Chsd ldrs 4f: wide reapp: unplcd in '99 8 (rtd 36, h'cap, no sand form, J L Eyre): '98 Catterick wnr (ltd stks, rtd 56): eff over 5/6f on fast & good/soft grnd: likes a sharp trk & has run well fresh: well h'capped for D W Chapman.   **8   14a**

4568} WESTSIDE FLYER 69 [1] 4-8-3 (43) S Righton 33/1: 0000-8: Nvr on terms: abs: '99 Southwell wnr (class clmr, rtd 56a, A Kelleway, no turf form): rtd 74 & 44a in '98: eff at 6f on both AWs: has run well fresh.   **nk   20a**

63   LADY NAIRN 51 [3] 4-8-7 (47) P Fessey 50/1: 60/0-9: Prom 4f, sn btn: 7 wk abs, now with A Berry.   **3½   15a**

9 ran   Time 1m 17.4 (4.1)   (Steven & Michelle Bayless)   L Montague Hall Tadworth, Surrey

---

281   2.10 JACKS SELLER DIV 1 3YO (G)   7f aw rnd   Going 48   -29 Slow
£1500   £428   £214

4367} MODEM 84 [9] M H Tompkins 3-8-12 A Whelan 8/1: 000-1: 3 b g Midhish - Holy Water (Monseigneur) Trkd ldrs going well, prog/led & duelled with rnr-up over 1f out, asserted cl-home, drvn out: tchd 10/1: sold for 6,200 gns: 12 wk abs/AW bow: unplcd on turf from 3 starts in '99 (rtd 62): eff at 7f, tried 1m, shld suit in time: acts on fibresand & a sharp trk: runs well fresh: apprec drop to sell grade.   **59a**

217   PRICELESS SECOND 17 [4] J A Glover 3-8-12 R Winston 7/2: 0524-2: Led, rdn/hdd over 1f out, styd on gamely for press ins last, just held nr line: clr rem: jockey given a 2-day ban for misuse of whip: op 5/1: eff at 6/7f, tried 1m: can find similar: see 181.   **½   58a**

241   MASTER JONES 5 [6] Mrs L Stubbs 3-8-12 A Culhane 6/4 FAV: 640-23: 3 b g Emperor Jones - Tight Spin (High Top) Rdn/rear halfway, prog/chsd front pair over 1f out, no impress: well bckd, tchd 2/1: quick reapp: unplcd on both AWs & soft grnd: see 241, 194.   **5   48a**

88   FORTHECHOP 46 [8] Mrs H L Walton 3-8-12 S Righton 40/1: 6006-4: Cl-up 4f, fdd: 6 wk abs: unplcd in '99 (rtd 39a & 49): tried at up to 10f prev.   **4   40a**

86   COSMIC SONG 46 [2] 3-8-7 Dean McKeown 8/1: 005-5: Rdn/towards rear, nvr factor: op 9/2, 6 wk abs: unplcd in '99 (rtd 50 & 54a).   **1¼   32a**

234   FOXKEY 9 [3] 3-8-12 P Fredericks (5) 7/1: 1006-6: Cl-up 5f: op 4/1: '99 wnr at Catterick & here at Southwell (sells, E J Alston, rtd 71a, rnr-up on turf, rtd 61, subs with A J McNae): eff at 5f, return to that trip shld suit: acts on fibresand & soft grnd: best with blnks: handles a sharp/turning or gall trk: enjoys sell grade.   **3   31a**

150   INCH PINCHER 32 [1] 3-9-3 A McCarthy (3) 5/1: 0025-7: Prom 5f: op 3/1: btr 53.   **nk   35a**

192   BASIC INSTINCT 23 [5] 3-8-7 F Norton 16/1: 3500-8: Rdn mid-div, btn 2f out: op 12/1: see 192, 118.   **7   14a**

192   K ACE THE JOINT 23 [10] 3-8-12 Dale Gibson 33/1: 000-9: Cl-up 4f: mod form.   **2   15a**

2829} NEEDWOOD TRUMP 99 [7] 3-8-12 J Tate 33/1: 040-0: Prom 4f: 10th: 6 month abs.   **17   0a**

10 ran   Time 1m 32.00 (5.4)   (Www Raceworld.Co.UK)   M H Tompkins Newmarket, Suffolk

---

282   2.40 HOPSCOTCH HCAP 4YO+ 0-85 (D)   7f aw rnd   Going 48   -06 Slow   **[85]**
£3809   £1172   £586   £293

246   SAND HAWK 4 [8] D Shaw 5-7-11 (54)(VIS) F Norton 7/4 FAV: 512-21: 5 ch g Polar Falcon - Ghassanah (Pas de Seul) Travelled well bhd ldrs, rdn to lead over 1f out, asserted nr fin, rdn out: well bckd in 1st time vis: quick reapp: '99 scorer at W'hampton (mdn, rtd 54a, rnr-up on turf, rtd 47, h'cap): plcd in '98 (h'caps, rtd 51 & 50a): eff by 7f & stays 1m: acts on fast, gd/soft & loves fibresand: eff in blnks/visor: prob handles any trk, likes a sharp one: has run well fresh: sharpened up by headgear recently, shld win more races.   **61a**

251   ALMAZHAR 4 [1] J L Eyre 5-9-7 (78) T Williams 7/2: 126-22: 5 b g Last Tycoon - Mosaique Bleue (Shirley Heights) Wide/chsd ldrs, styd on for press, not pace of wnr: nicely bckd: quick reapp: tough: see 143.   **1   81a**

216   DAHLIDYA 17 [6] M J Polglase 5-8-5 (62) R Fitzpatrick (3) 10/1: 5310-3: 5 b m Midyan - Dahlawise (Caerleon) Rdn/rear, prog to chall 2f out, kept on onepace ins last: op 7/1: see 216, 180 (6f).   **½   64a**

216   TOPTON 17 [3] P Howling 6-10-0 (85)(bl) A McCarthy (3) 3/1: 0232-4: Cl-up, led over 2f out till over 1f out, no extra: nicely bckd: see 104 (equitrack).   **3   81a**

176   SEA YA MAITE 25 [5] 6-7-10 (53) G Bardwell 8/1: 1000-5: Towards rear, mod gains fnl 2f: op 10/1.   **½   48a**

251   REX IS OKAY 4 [2] 4-8-13 (70) Dale Gibson 12/1: 330-06: Led after 2f till 2f out, fdd: op 8/1: quick reapp, a/w bow: rnr-up numerous times in '99 (rtd 73a, h'cap): '98 wnr at Leicester & Doncaster (nurs h'caps, rtd 77): eff at 6f/1m: acts on firm & soft grnd, any trk: eff forcing the pace: eff with/without blnks.   **3½   58a**

--   IRON MAN [9] 8-8-3 (60) P Fessey 50/1: 0212/7: Towards rear/wide, nvr a factor: v long Brit abs: has reportedly been racing in Barbados: last rcd in Britain in '95, won at Lingfield (sell, rtd 59a, J White): eff at 7f/1m on fast & firm grnd, likes equitrack & a sharp trk, esp Lingfield: eff in blnks/visor: now with R Marvin.   **nk   47a**

249   ABOVE BOARD 4 [1] 5-7-10 (53)(21oh) Claire Bryan (7) 25/1: 556-58: Mid-div at best: bckd at long odds.   **½   39$**

212   LIFT THE OFFER 17 [10] 5-8-11 (68) A Culhane 25/1: 0000-9: Towards rear/wide, nvr factor: see 212.   **9   40a**

1237} AJNAD 99 [4] 6-9-3 (74) S Righton 25/1: 2630-0: Led 2f, btn 2f out & eased ins last: 8 month abs, op 14/1: '99 Lingfield scorer (mdn, rtd 74a, plcd on turf, rtd 57, h'cap): place form in '98 (rtd 64a & 59, h'caps): eff at 5/6f on fast, gd/soft & both AWs: has run well in blnks, also tried a vis: return to sprint trips shld suit.   **1   44a**

10 ran   Time 1m 30.4 (3.8)   (J C Fretwell)   D Shaw Averham, Notts

---

283   3.10 JACKS SELLER DIV 2 3YO (G)   7f aw rnd   Going 48   -42 Slow
£1500   £428   £214

236   COME ON MURGY 9 [6] A Bailey 3-8-12 J Bramhill 1/1 FAV: 6013-1: 3 b f Weldnaas - Forest Song (Forzando) Mid-div, prog/led over 1f out, rdn/in command ins last & eased nr fin: well bckd: no bid: '99 W'hampton scorer (sell, rtd 54a, unplcd on turf, rtd 53): eff at 7f, stays a sharp 1m: acts on both AWs: best without blnks: likes a sharp trk & has run well fresh: enjoys sell grade.   **55a**

217   SOUNDS CRAZY 17 [4] S R Bowring 3-8-7 (bl) G Bardwell 33/1: 0000-2: 3 b f Savahra Sound - Sugar Token (Record Token) Led, rdn/hdd 2f out & sn held by wnr: unplcd in '99 (rtd 57 & 40a): has tried blnks prev: prob stays a sharp 7f & handles fibresand.   **3½   41a**

SOUTHWELL (Fibresand)   FRIDAY JANUARY 7TH   Lefthand, Sharp, Oval Track

4345} **LADY CYRANO 86** [5] Mrs N Macauley 3-8-7 R Fitzpatrick (3) 14/1: 3000-3: 3 b f Cyrano de Bergerac - Hazy Kay (Treasure Kay) Dwelt/rear, kept on fnl 2f, nrst fin: op 12/1: 12 wk abs: plcd in '99 (rtd 58a, auct mdn, & 53, sell h'cap): eff at 6f, stays a sharp 7f & a return to 1m could suit on this evidence: handles fast grnd & fibresand: best without a visor: handles a sharp or stiff/gall trk. · · · · · · · · · · · · · · · ½ · · 40a

213   **BARRYS DOUBLE 17** [7] C W Fairhurst 3-8-12 J Fanning 6/1: 0040-4: Chsd ldrs, onepace fnl 2f. · · · nk · · 44a
242   **XENOS 5** [2] 3-8-12 R Winston 12/1: 000-05: Cl-up, wknd fnl 2f: quick reapp: longer 7f trip. · · · · · nk · · 42a
--   **ALL MINE** [9] 3-8-12 J Stack 14/1: 6: Al towards rear: op 5/1, debut: with B Mcmahon. · · · · · · · · 12 · · 25a
--   **GREAT CRAIC** [8] 3-8-7 A Mackay 8/1: 7: Chsd ldrs 5f: op 9/2, debut: with M Tompkins. · · · · · · · 3½ · · 13a
1412} **CHIEF JUSTICE 99** [3] T G McLaughlin 5/1: 0-8: Dwelt/al rear: op 3/1: 8 month abs/AW bow: unplcd sole start in '99 (6f mdn, rtd 34). · 5 · · 8a
8 ran   Time 1m 32.9 (6.3)   (K W Weale)   A Bailey Little Budworth, Cheshire

---

284

3.40 MARBLES HCAP 4YO+ 0-60 (F)   2m aw   Going 48 -91 Slow   [60]
£2373 £678 £339   4 yo rec 7 lb

68   **KENT 49** [9] P D Cundell 5-8-7 (39) Martin Dwyer 16/1: 0005-1: 5 b g Kylian - Precious Caroline (The Noble Player) Sn cl-up, rdn/duelled with rnr-up ins last, asserted/drifted right cl-home, rdn out: op 20/1: 7 wk abs: plcd in '99 (rtd 63, mdn, unplcd on sand, rtd 44a): apprec this step up to 2m: acts on fibresand & a sharp trk: best without blnks: runs well fresh: open to further improvement after this first success. · · · · · 45a
170   **MEILLEUR 27** [11] Lady Herries 6-9-10 (56) M Tebbutt 5/1: 5024-2: 6 b g Nordico - Lucy Limelight (Hot Spark) Mid-div, smooth prog to lead over 1f out, duelled with wnr & hdd ins last, no extra: see 68. · · 1¼ · · 60a
182   **PIPE MUSIC 25** [3] P C Haslam 5-10-0 (60)(bl) T Eaves (7) 8/1: 0236-3: 5 b g Mujadil - Sunset Cafe (Red Sunset) Handy, led over 5f out till over 4f out, kept on onepace fnl 2f: op 6/1: likes Southwell: see 124. · · 3½ · · 61a
*253   **ABOO HOM 4** [5] S Dow 6-9-9 (55)(6ex) W Ryan 6/4 FAV: 003-14: Held up in tch, rdn/kept on fnl 2f, not pace to chall: reportedly finished lame: hvly bckd, tchd 3/1: quick reapp: see 253 (C/D). · · · · · · · · · nk · · 56a
253   **ALMAMZAR 4** [2] 10-7-10 (28)(5oh) Kim Tinkler 40/1: 005-05: Chsd ldrs, onepace/held fnl 3f: see 89. · · 3½ · · 26a
196   **TOY STORY 21** [7] 4-8-10 (49) S Whitworth 10/1: 0602-6: Mid-div at best: op 6/1: btr 196 (11f). · · · 7 · · 40a
194   **MEDELAI 23** [8] 4-8-2 (41) A McCarthy (3) 4/1: 0502-7: Chsd ldrs, prog/led over 4f out, hdd over 1f out & sn no extra: op 3/1: btr 194. · 7 · · 25a
248   **SHOTLEY MARIE 4** [6] 5-7-11 (29)(bl)(1ow)(7oh) F Norton 40/1: 056-68: Al rear: quick reapp, mod form. 19 · · 0a
174   **FLORA DREAMBIRD 27** [10] 6-8-1 (33)(bl)(5ow)(7oh) S Righton 35/1: 5266-9: Keen/prom 13f: rnr-up in '99 (6 rnr sell, rtd 37, plcd on sand, rtd 26a): only mod recent runs form. · · · · · · · · · · · · · · 2½ · · 0a
--   **NIGELS CHOICE** [1] 8-8-10 (42) T Williams 40/1: 300/0: Led 11f, sn hung badly right & bhd: long abs: mod jumps form in 97/98: unplcd from 2 starts on the Level in '97 (rtd 48): plcd on sole '96 start (rtd 58, clmr): stays a sharp/undul 12f & handles firm grnd: AW bow today. · 22 · · 0a
190   **CRASH CALL LADY 23** [4] 4-7-10 (35)(1oh) G Bardwell 8/1: 5432-0: Rdn/chsd ldrs wide 5f out, sn btn: op 7/1, jumps fit (mod form): see 190, 89. · 1¾ · · 0a
11 ran   Time 3m 48.3 (22.3)   (P D Cundell)   P D Cundell Compton, Berks

---

LINGFIELD (Equitrack)   SATURDAY JANUARY 8TH   Lefthand, Very Sharp Track

Official Going   STANDARD Stalls: 5f - Outside; Rem - Inside.

285

1.20 AMAT RDRS HCAP 4YO+ 0-70 (F)   2m aw   Going 34 -16 Slow   [48]
£2278 £651 £325   4 yo rec 7 lb

253   **MAKNAAS 6** [6] T G Mills 4-9-11 (52) Miss Karen Jones (7) 2/1 FAV: 531-41: 4 ch c Wolfhound - White Wash (Final Straw) Sn clr ldr, drvn out to hold on: nicely bckd, quick reapp: late '99 scorer at W'hampton (h'cap, rtd 52a), plcd on turf prev for R Armstrong (mdn h'cap, rtd 49 & 44a): eff at 1m, suited by 2m: acts on soft & both AWs: loves to race up with/force the pace on sharp trks: has run well in blnks, prob best without. · · 56a
124   **ST LAWRENCE 39** [7] N Tinkler 6-9-8 (42) Mr Nicky Tinkler 12/1: 2060-2: 6 gr g With Approval - Mingan Isle (Lord Avie) Handy, chsd wnr over 4f out, rdn & no extra ins last: clr rem: plcd twice in '99 (amat h'cap, rtd 58 & 45a): lightly rcd in '98 (h'cap, rtd 70), rnr-up in '97 (mdn, rtd 79): stays 11.5f/2m on firm, both AWs. · · 2½ · · 43a
156   **CEDAR FLAG 31** [5] R J O'Sullivan 6-9-5 (38)(1ow) Miss S Pocock (0) 12/1: 060-3: 6 br g Jareer - Sasha Lea (Cawston's Clown) Chsd wnr, outpcd fnl 4f: up in trip on AW h'cap bow: sell h'caps shld suit: see 101. · · 12 · · 31a
167   **INDIGO BAY 29** [11] S Dow 4-10-11 (66)(VIS) Mr R Guest (5) 11/1: 0200-0: Chsd ldr, outpcd fnl 5f: visored: up in trip: see 52 (12f amat h'cap). · 4 · · 55a
2215} **MACHIAVELLI 99** [8] 6-11-7 (69)(bl) Mr A Quinn (7) 10/1: 00/6-5: Rear, prog 6f out, no extra fnl 3f: op 7/1: 9 wk jumps abs, earlier scored at Plumpton (nov chase, rtd 109c, eff at 2m2.5f on firm, handles gd/soft): well btn sole '98 Flat start (clmr, rtd 72$): rtd 69 at best in '98 (h'cap), prev term scored at Pontefract (mdn, rtd 89, H Cecil): eff at 10/12f: acts on fast, handles gd/soft: prob handles any trk. · · · 1 · · 57a
182   **DOUBLE RUSH 26** [3] 8-10-4 (52) Mrs H Keddy (5) 20/1: 3060-6: Rear, eff 7f out, sn wknd: placed in '99 (h'caps, rtd 42 at best): '98 wnr at Bath (sell, rtd 58 & 65a, T Mills): suited by 12/14f on firm, soft & e/track. 23 · · 24a
124   **LAKE DOMINION 39** [12] 11-9-3 (37)(bl)(13oh) Miss A Elsey 50/1: 0006-7: Prom, bhd 1m out: jmps fit. · · ½ · · 8a
--   **KEEN WATERS** [13] 6-9-3 (37)(bl)(1oh) Mr I Mongan 5/1: 4406/8: Prom, rdn/bhd fnl 6f: jumps rnr. · · · 10 · · 1a
4397} **BEAUMONT 84** [1] 10-10-7 (55) Mr S Callaghan (7) 9/1: 4400-9: Al in rear: jumps fit, new stable. · · · 1½ · · 18a
637} **SHEEP STEALER 99** [10] 12-9-8 (42)(5ow)(16oh) Mrs C Peacock (0) 50/1: 0/00-0: Al well in rear, 10th. 1½ · · 4a
3838} **MIDNIGHT WATCH 99** [2] 6-10-2 (50)(t) Miss A Wallace (7) 33/1: 0/00-0: Al in rear, 11th: jumps fit. · · 1½ · · 11a
194   **BEAUCHAMP MAGIC 24** [9] 5-10-13 (61)(24ow)(25oh) Mr J Shoulder (0) 11/1: 0016-0: Sn bhd, t.o. in 12th: impossible task under 31lbs o/w: much btr 141 (fibresand). · 6 · · 17a
231   **Katies Cracker 12** [4] 5-9-3 (37)(18oh) Mr M Nakauchida (5) 20/1:
2843} **Cochiti 99** [14] 6-9-3 (37)(t)(18oh) Mrs S Bosley (5) 7/1:
14 ran   Time 3m 28.0 (8.0)   (Travel Spot Ltd)   T G Mills Headley, Surrey

---

286

1.50 FRESHWATER CLAIMER 3YO (F)   1m2f aw   Going 34 -31 Slow
£2194 £627 £313

236   **GLENWHARGEN 10** [5] M Johnston 3-8-8 J Fanning 5/1: 3045-1: 3 b f Polar Falcon - La Veine (Diesis) Led 2f, remained with ldr, led again over 3f out, drvn out: op 7/2: up in trip, 1st win, claimed for £5,000: plcd twice in '99 (h'caps, rtd 65 & 54a): eff btwn 6f & 8.4f, styd this longer 10f trip well: acts on gd/soft & both AWs: handles a sharp or stiff/undul trk: has tried blnks, best without. · 56a

LINGFIELD (Equitrack)   SATURDAY JANUARY 8TH   Lefthand, Very Sharp Track

*236   **SHAMAN 10** [1] G L Moore 3-9-5 G Parkin 4/6 FAV: 0041-2: 3 b c Fraam - Magic Maggie (Beveled)   1¼   65a
Waited with, hdwy 5f out, sn lost place, ran on well for press fnl 2f, nvr nrr: nicely bckd, jockey received
a 5 day whip ban: eff btwn 7f & 10f: see 236.

4151) **WITTON WOOD 99** [4] M H Tompkins 3-8-9 A Whelan 7/1: -000-2: 3 b g Bluebird - Leyete Gulf (Slip   5   47a
Anchor) Prom, led 1m out to over 3f out, wknd: tchd 12/1, AW bow: unplcd in '99 (7f/1m mdns, rtd 56, blnks).

*241   **KIGEMA 6** [2] C N Allen 3-8-12 L Newman (5) 9/2: 506-14: Cl-up, rdn & wknd fnl 2f: quick reapp: 10   38a
up in trip, a return to 1m shld suit: btr 241.

236   **QUEEN FOR A DAY 10** [3] N Callan (3) 20/1: 2000-5: Bhd, prog 5f out, btn fnl 3f: see 236.   5   29a
5 ran   Time 2m 09.3 (6.5)   (Mark Johnston Racing Ltd)   M Johnston Middleham, N Yorks

---

287	**2.20 MANOR HOUSE FILLIES HCAP 3YO 0-65 7f aw rnd Going 34 -38 Slow** [70]
	£2756 £848 £424 £212

206   **LUCKY STAR 21** [5] D Marks 3-9-1 (57) D Dineley 14/1: 0666-1: 3 b f Emarati - Child Star (Bellypha)   62a
Cl-up, rdn to improve 2f out, led dist, drvn out: op 9/1: 1st win: failed to make the frame in '99 (rtd
62, nov stks): eff at 7f & acts on equitrack: showed improved form here on today's h'cap bow.

*257   **CROESO ADREF 4** [3] S C Williams 3-8-6 (48)(6ex) L Newman (5) 5/1: 003-12: 3 ch f Most Welcome -   ½   51a
Grugiar (Red Sunset) Handy, gd hdwy over 2f out, chall ldr dist, no extra cl-home: nicely bckd: in gd
form & not disgraced today under a pen: acts on both AWs: see 257.

228   **SUPREMELY DEVIOUS 12** [1] R M H Cowell 3-8-6 (48)(vis) Dale Gibson 12/1: 0626-3: 3 ch f Wolfhound   2   47a
- Clearly Devious (Machiavellian) Led, rdn/hdd over 1f out, wknd: op 10/1: see 155.

242   **TOLDYA 6** [6] E A Wheeler 3-8-10 (52)(BL) S Carson (5) 3/1 JT FAV: 002-24: Prom, hdwy to chall over   3   46a
3f out, wknd appr fnl 1f: quick reapp, tried in blnks: btr 242 (6f).

243   **PERLE DE SAGESSE 6** [8] 3-9-6 (62) A Daly 3/1 JT FAV: 101-05: Handy, rdn/wknd fnl 2f: qck reapp.   shd   56a

228   **BESCABY BLUE 12** [7] 3-9-4 (60) C Cogan (5) 6/1: 0602-6: Nvr a threat: btr 228 (6f, fibresand).   5   46a

112   **BROWNS DELIGHT 43** [9] 3-9-7 (63) W Ryan 8/1: 0020-7: Very keen, in tch, wknd fnl 4f: abs, op 6/1:   2   45a
rnr-up in 99 (h'cap/AW bow, rtd 62a, rtd 62 on turf): eff at 6f, 7f shld suit in time: handles equitrack.

192   **BLAZING PEBBLES 24** [2] 3-7-10 (38)(13oh) G Bardwell 50/1: 0000-8: Al bhd: mod form.   2½   16a

179   **DIAMOND GEORGIA 26** [4] 3-8-7 (49)(e) S Drowne 10/1: 660-9: Al bhd: unplcd in '99 (mdns, rtd 62).   shd   27a
9 ran   Time 1m 27.9 (5.1)   (D Marks)   D Marks Lambourn, Berks

---

288	**2.55 TRACKSIDE CLASS STKS 3YO+ 0-70 (E) 6f aw rnd Going 34 -04 Slow**
	£2704 £832 £416 £208 3 yo rec 16lb

262   **BRUTAL FANTASY 3** [4] P Howling 6-9-7 A McCarthy (3) 8/1: 025-21: 6 b g Distinctly North - Flash   70a
Donna (Well Decorated) Made all, strongly prsd 1f out, rdn out to hold on: op 9/2, quick reapp: '99 wnr at
Lingfield (h'cap, P Murphy), subs scored for current connections at Ascot (h'cap, rtd 72 at best): rtd 67a
& 79 at best in '98 (h'caps, J L Eyre): eff at 5/6f: acts on firm, gd/soft & both AWs: runs well fresh on
any trk, likes Lingfield: has tried blnks/visor, best without: tough, 8 wins from 51 starts.

*223   **MISTER TRICKY 3** [3] P Mitchell 5-9-11 W Ryan 10/11 FAV: 3111-2: 5 ch g Magic Ring - Splintering   1¾   67a
(Sharpo) Waited with, chall over 1f out, no extra ins last: nicely bckd, clr of rem: in gd form, win again sn.

*243   **MISS DANGEROUS 6** [6] M Quinn 5-9-6 (bl) F Norton 9/1: 006-13: 5 b m Komaite - Khadine (Astec)   5   53a
Cl-up, rdn & lost tch fnl 2f: quick reapp: btr 243 (7f, made all).

*207   **PARKSIDE PROSPECT 21** [1] T D McCarthy 3-8-6 J Fanning 7/1: 1231-4: Dsptd lead, rdn/wknd fnl 2f: 4   47a
tchd 10/1: prev with M Channon, now with T D McCarthy: apprec a return to claiming grade: btr 207 (made all).

223   **DIAMOND GEEZER 17** [2] 4-9-9 P Fitzsimons (5) 7/2: 2123-5: Sn rdn in tch, wknd fnl 3f: op 3/1: btr 113. 4   40a

205   **WILD THING 21** [5] 4-9-9 (bl) G Bardwell 25/1: 2003-F: Bhd, broke leg & fell over 1f out, sadly died.   0a
6 ran   Time 1m 12.7 (2.3)   (C Hammond)   P Howling Newmarket, Suffolk

---

289	**3.25 BROWN TROUT MDN 3YO 0-70 (D) 5f aw rnd Going 34 +14 Fast**
	£2691 £828 £414 £207

-127   **RED REVOLUTION 39** [2] T D Barron 3-9-0 N Callan (3) 5/4: -32-1: 3 ch c Explosive Red - Braided   80a
Way (Mining) Made all, clr 2f out, very easily: fast time: plcd on both '99 starts (mdns, rtd 72 & 70a):
dam a sprint wnr, sire high-class 1m/12f performer: eff at 5f, 6f will suit: acts on gd & both AWs: loves
to force the pace: easy wnr here in a fast time: potentially smart, keep on your side.

--   **LUSONG** [3] R Hannon 3-9-0 P Dobbs (5) 6/5 FAV: -2: 3 ch c Fayruz - Mildred Anne (Thatching)   7   65a
Chsd wnr, hdwy 2f out, kept on but no ch with easy wnr: nicely bckd on debut: debut: dam btn in an Irish bmpr.

153   **TEA FOR TEXAS 33** [1] H Morrison 3-8-9 C Rutter 14/1: 4-3: 3 ch f Weldnaas - Polly's Teahouse   2½   54a
(Shack) Dsptd lead, lost tch fnl 2f: quick reapp: op 7/1: a return to 6f shld suit: see 153.

3863) **STOP THE TRAFFIC 99** [4] C N Allen 3-8-10(1ow) R Morse 6/1: 0330-4: Handy, rdn & no extra fnl 2f: hd   55a
long abs, AW bow, op 3/1: plcd twice in '99 (mdn & nov stks, rtd 73 at best): eff at 5/5.7f, handles firm & gd.
4 ran   Time 58.8 (1.0)   (P D Savill)   T D Barron Maunby N Yorks

---

290	**4.00 MILLENNIUM HCAP 4YO+ 0-70 (E) 1m4f aw Going 34 -13 Slow** [65]
	£3607 £1110 £555 £277 4 yo rec 4 lb

211   **LOST SPIRIT 18** [11] P W Hiatt 4-8-4 (45) G Baker (7) 16/1: 0660-1: 4 b g Strolling Along -   49a
Shoag (Affirmed) Made all, styd on strongly, rdn out: tchd 40/1: '99 wnr at Southwell (clmr) & W'hampton
(h'cap, rtd 66a, plcd on turf, rtd 49): rnr-up in '99 (sell, rtd 55, B Hanbury): loves to force the pace
over 12f: acts on firm, gd/soft & both AWs, loves fibresand & a sharp trk: eff with/without blnks.

2890) **SLEAVE SILK 99** [6] J W Musson 5-8-11 (48) P McCabe 8/1: 1064-2: 5 b m Unfuwain - Shanira (Shirley   ¾   50a
Heights) Rear, hdwy to chall ins last, no extra cl-home: long abs: won thrice at Lingfield in '99 (h'caps,
rtd 50a): lightly rcd in '98: eff at 12f/2m: handles fibresand, equitrack/Lingfield: spot-on next time.

168   **HURGILL DANCER 29** [10] R J O'Sullivan 6-8-2 (39) T Williams 9/1: 0434-3: 6 b g Rambo Dancer -   nk   41a
Try Vickers (Fuzzbuster) Prom, drvn & hdwy 3f out, onepcd ins last: tchd 14/1: in gd form, on a fair mark.

*70   **HOMESTEAD 50** [1] R Hannon 6-9-5 (56) L Newman (5) 11/4 FAV: 0061-4: Rear, gd hdwy 2f out,   1¾   56a
styd on, nrst fin: nicely bckd: recently unplcd over jumps (2m nov, rtd 90h): see 70.

203   **BECKON 21** [5] 4-8-10 (51) T Ashley 5/1: 0013-5: Held up, gd hdwy 4f out, chall over 1f out,   ½   51a
wknd ins last, eased & lost 4th place cl-home: tchd 8/1: jockey received 4 day ban for not riding a fin: stays 10f.

3718) **LADY JO 99** [13] 4-9-7 (62) W Ryan 14/1: 6060-6: Rear, nvr a threat: op 8/1: long abs: '99 scorer   ½   61a
at Yarmouth & Lingfield (fill h'caps, rtd 67): showed promise in '98 (mdn, rtd 61): eff at 10f, this longer

LINGFIELD (Equitrack)   SATURDAY JANUARY 8TH   Lefthand, Very Sharp Track

12f trip could suit: acts on fast, gd & equitrack: handles a sharp/undul or gall trk.

209	**HAWKSBILL HENRY** 21 [7] 6-9-3 (54) A Clark 16/1: 3000-7: Sn rdn, late gains, no threat: up in trip.	½	52a
220	**BAAJIL** 17 [8] 5-9-8 (59) S Carson (5) 11/1: 0146-8: Prom, ev ch till wknd fnl 2f: op 6/1, up in trip.	6	49a
261	**FAMOUS** 4 [4] 7-8-5 (42) G Bardwell 20/1: 502-09: Al bhd: see 90.	1	31a
203	**CAERNARFON BAY** 21 [12] 5-9-5 (56) R Brisland (5) 12/1: 2620-0: Al bhd, fin 10th: btr 160 (10f).	hd	45a
209	**CONFRONTER** 21 [2] 11-9-4 (55) C Rutter 16/1: 0645-0: In tch, wknd fnl 4f: 11th: btr 161 (10f).	½	43a
227	**ROI DE DANSE** 12 [9] 5-8-9 (46) F Norton 7/1: 6312-0: Cl-up, ev ch until qckly lost tch fnl 2f: 12th:	2	31a

prob not stay this longer 12f trip, a return to 10f will suit: see 227.

203	**Mogin** 21 [14] 7-8-3 (40) Martin Dwyer 25/1: 3583}	**Divorce Action** 99 [3] 4-9-10 (65) A Daly 16/1:

14 ran   Time 2m 34.9 (5.7)   (Red Lion (Chipping Norton) Partnership)   P W Hiatt Hook Norton, Oxon

---

WOLVERHAMPTON (Fibresand)   SATURDAY JANUARY 8TH   Lefthand, Sharp Track

Official Going STANDARD. Stalls: Inside, except 7f - Outside.

291   7.00 MILLENNIUM HCAP 3YO+ 0-60 (F)   5f aw rnd   Going 49   +09 Fast   [57]
£2173   £621   £310   3 yo rec 15lb

214	**JACK TO A KING** 18 [11] J Balding 5-9-3 (46)(tbl) J Edmunds 9/1: 0506-1: 5 b g Nawwar - Rudda Flash (General David) Prom, led well ins last, edged left, rdn out: 1st win: bckd at long odds, tchd 14/1: best time of night: unplcd in '99 (rtd 36a): rtd 62 in '98: eff over a sharp 5f on fibresand: eff in blnks & t-strap.		52a
235	**WISHBONE ALLEY** 10 [10] M Dods 5-9-2 (45)(vis) A Clark 9/2: 0022-2: 5 b g Common Grounds - Dul Dul (Shadeed) Prom, sn rdn, ch ins last, kept on well for press: acts on fast, soft & both AWs: win at 6f: see 154.	½	48a
214	**SOUTHERN DOMINION** 18 [7] Miss J F Craze 8-9-12 (55)(bl) P Goode (5) 9/2: 2204-3: 8 ch g Dominion - Southern Sky (Comedy Star) Led, rdn/hdd well ins last & no extra: 12/2: v tough (has raced 101 times).	½	56a
232	**FEATHERSTONE LANE** 12 [9] Miss L C Siddall 9-9-1 (44) Dean McKeown 11/1: 0450-4: Dwelt, mid-div/ wide, kept on ins last, not pace to chall: on a fair mark & a W'hampton specialist: see 82.	2½	38a
116	**TINKERS SURPRISE** 42 [8] 6-9-0 (43)(bl) C Carver (3) 10/1: 5006-5: Wide, nvr pace to chall ldrs: abs.	1¼	34a
226	**WEETRAIN** 12 [6] 4-9-1 (44) J Fanning 33/1: 0300-6: Wide, nvr on terms: plcd form in '99 (rtd 48a, C/D sell h'cap & 51, clmr): ex-Irish, unplcd in 4 '98 starts (offic rtd 60): eff at 5/6f: handles hvy & fibresand.	1¼	32a
246	**GUNNER SAM** 5 [2] 4-9-9 (52) R Fitzpatrick 25/1: 065-07: Towards rear, nvr a factor: qck reapp.	hd	39a
235	**CARMARTHEN** 10 [12] 4-9-2 (45) Darren Williams (7) 8/1: 0444-8: Chsd ldrs 4f: op 6/1: btr 235 (eqtrk).	2½	25a
146	**SWEET MAGIC** 35 [5] 9-10-0 (57)(t) R Winston 20/1: 1056-9: Mid-div at best: see 146 (C/D).	½	35a
166	**LEGAL VENTURE** 29 [3] 4-9-9 (52) T G McLaughlin 16/1: 000U-0: Hmpd start, al rear: 10th: op 10/1: '99 W'hampton wnr (C/D seller, rtd 60a at best, unplcd on turf, rtd 48, h'cap): '98 Lingfield wnr (seller, rtd 66 & 68a at best, B J Meehan): eff at 5f on firm, gd & loves fibresand: eff in blnks, tried a visor: enjoys sell grade.	nk	29a
3944}	**ORIEL STAR** 99 [13] 4-10-0 (57) S Drowne 20/1: 0000-0: Chsd ldrs 3f: 11th: 4 month absence.	8	19a
4518}	**APPLES AND PEARS** 74 [1] 4-9-8 (51) G Bardwell 14/1: 4360-0: Nearly u.r. start, al rear: 12th: abs.	2½	6a
191	**FRILLY FRONT** 24 [4] 4-10-0 (57) N Callan (3) 5/2 FAV: 3410-P: Swerved badly left start & p.u. after 1f: dismounted: rider reportedly thought filly had gone lame, subs found to be sound: topweight: see 116 (C/D).		0a

13 ran   Time 1m 02.2 (2.0)   (J D & J R Evans)   J Balding Scrooby, Notts.

292   7.30 CELEBRATE 2000 CLAIMER 4YO+ (F)   1m1f79y   Going 49   -11 Slow
£2289   £654   £327   4 yo rec 1 lb

270	**RIVER ENSIGN** 2 [11] W M Brisbourne 7-8-3 Claire Bryan (7) 5/2 JT FAV: 406-21: 7 br m River God - Ensigns Kit (Saucy Kit) Prom, led over 3f out, styd well ins last, rdn out: qck reapp: '99 scorer here at W'hampton (clmr, rtd 33a) & Chepstow (h'cap, rtd 47): '98 Southwell & Nottingham wnr (h'caps, rtd 44a & 44): eff at 5/7f, seems best around 1m/10f nowadays: acts on gd, hvy & fibresand: acts on any trk, likes W'hampton: runs well fresh: likes to race with/force the pace: apprec this drop to claim grade.		51a
259	**WESTMINSTER CITY** 4 [3] K O Cunningham Brown 4-8-11 (vis) M Hills 14/1: 500-32: 4 b c Alleged - Promanade Fan (Timeless Moment) Chsd ldrs, chsd wnr ins last, kept on tho' not pace to chall: op 12/1: qck reapp: eff at 9.5f: acts on fast, gd & fibresand: prob flattered (offic rtd 42): see 259.	1	58$
233	**BORDER GLEN** 12 [7] D Haydn Jones 4-9-1 (bl) A Mackay 5/2 JT FAV: 4334-3: 4 b g Selkirk - Sulitelma (The Minstrel) Chsd wnr 3f out, rdn ins last: clr rem: nicely bckd: stays 9f, return to 1m shld suit: see 96.	3	56a
4295}	**MUTADARRA** 91 [5] G M McCourt 7-9-2 R Studholme (5) 6/1: 0000-4: Rear, styd on fnl 3f, no threat to ldrs & eased/held ins last: jockey reported he thought gelding had gone lame: op 4/1: 7 wk jumps abs (rtd 85h, nov): with W J Musson on the level in '99, scored at Sandown (h'cap, rtd 69 at best): rnr-up twice in '98 (rtd 55): suited by 10f on firm & gd, poss handles hvy: likes a stiff trk, handles any: AW bow today, shld do better.	7	45a
--	**RONS ROUND** [4] 6-8-4 C Rutter 6/1: 1422/5: Towards rear, kept on fnl 3f, no threat: op 5/1: 7 mth jumps absence (May '99 M Rasen wnr, mdn hdle, rtd 107h, best around 2m/2m1f on firm or soft/hvy): last rcd on the level in '98, won at Nottingham (sell h'cap, C Dwyer), Southwell & W'hampton (h'caps, M C Pipe, rtd 57 & 50a at best): eff at 9/11f: acts on gd/soft, loves fibresand, handles firm: handles any trk, likes a sharp one.	1¾	30a
231	**SIR WALTER** 12 [6] 7-8-2 (bl) J Fanning 20/1: 0600-6: Led 6f, sn held: rnr-up in '99 (h'cap, rtd 51a at best): ex-Irish, '98 Tramore wnr (eff around 1m/9f, prob stays a sharp 13f: handles both AWs & fast.	1¼	25a
50	**FRENCH GINGER** 54 [2] 9-7-11 Iona Wands (5) 33/1: 0000-7: Mid-div at best: 8 wk absence.	2	16a
333}	**UP IN FLAMES** 99 [10] 9-9-6 L Newman 25/1: 6/00-8: In tch 5f: long absence, now with R Simpson.	3	33a
2602}	**BOBS BUSTER** 99 [8] 4-8-5 F Norton 25/1: 3005-9: Al rear: 6 month absence.	5	9a
229	**MAJOR ATTRACTION** 12 [8] 5-8-6 S Drowne 25/1: 4340-0: Bhd 3f out: 10th: fin lame.	9	0a
131	**POLAR ECLIPSE** 39 [1] 7-8-2 C Cogan (5) 9/1: 4060-0: Prom 6f: 11th: op 6/1.	2½	0a

11 ran   Time 2m 03.8 (5.6)   (Crispandave Racing Associates)   W M Brisbourne Great Ness, Shropshire.

293   8.00 NEW YEAR BASH MDN 4YO+ (D)   7f aw rnd   Going 49   -05 Slow
£2626   £750   £375

229	**RAIN RAIN GO AWAY** 12 [6] D J S Cosgrove 4-9-0 C Rutter 12/1: 0433-1: 4 ch g Miswaki - Stormagain (Storm Cat) Held up, prog wide 2f out, rdn to lead well ins last: op 6/1: unplcd on turf in '99 (rtd 50, with E Dunlop), plcd on sand (rtd 54a): eff at 7f, stays 1m: acts on soft & both AWs: likes a sharp track.		61a
173	**WELCOME GIFT** 28 [5] W J Haggas 4-9-0 M Hills 5/4 FAV: 2-2: 4 b g Prince Sabo - Ausonia (Beldale Flutter) Prom, led 4f out, rdn/hdd nr fin, no extra: nicely bckd, tchd 11/8: eff at 7f on fibresand: see 173 (C/D).	¾	59a
229	**PUPPET PLAY** 4 [4] E J Alston 5-8-9 (bl) A Culhane 7/2: 6422-3: 5 ch m Broken Hearted - Fantoccini	3	48a

103

(Taufan) Chsd ldrs, kept on fnl 2f, not pace of front pair: clr rem: nicely bckd, tchd 4/1: eff at 7f/1m on both AWs.
187   **CITY REACH** 24 [2] P J Makin 4-9-0 D Sweeney 9/4: 6532-4: Dwelt/held up in tch, btn 2f out: op 7/4.   12   35a
276   **NADDER 2** [3] 5-9-0 (bl) T G McLaughlin 20/1: 000-25: Led 1f, btn 2f out/eased: qck reappb: btr 276.   6   26a
273   **JUST FOR YOU 2** [1] 4-9-0 S Drowne 25/1: 0-66: Led after 1f till 4f out, sn btn/eased: op 14/1, mod form.   0a
6 ran   Time 1m 30.0 (3.8)   (G G Grayson)   D J S Cosgrove Newmarket.

---

294   **8.30 MAGICAL NIGHT HCAP 3YO 0-85 (D)**   7f aw rnd   Going 49   -05 Slow   **[84]**
£3250   £1000   £500   £250

4044} **FOXS IDEA** 99 [5] D Haydn Jones 3-9-0 (70) S Drowne 16/1: 3340-1: 3 b f Magic Ring - Lindy Belle   77a
(Alleging) Held up in tch, prog/chsd ldrs 2f out, styd on gamely to lead line, all out: op 8/1: 4 month abs, AW
bow: plcd in '99 (rtd 72, auct mdn): apprec step up to 7f, 1m could suit: acts on fibresand, fast & gd grnd:
handles a sharp or stiff/undul trk: runs well fresh: lightly rcd, op to further improvement in similar events.
*188   **CHURCH FARM FLYER** 24 [1] C N Allen 3-8-4 (60) L Newman (5) 7/2: 6311-2: 3 b f College Chapel -   shd   66a
Young Isabel (Last Tycoon) Led, rdn/kept on well ins last, hdd line, just btn: op 3/1, clr of rem: see 188 (C/D).
266   **JOELY GREEN 3** [6] N P Littmoden 3-8-12 (68) T G McLaughlin 3/1 JT FAV: 610-23: 3 b c Binary   5   64a
Star - Comedy Lady (Comedy Star) Held up in tch, kept on fnl 2f, no threat to front pair: qck reapp: see 266, 41.
202   **TING 22** [4] P C Haslam 3-8-3 (59) Dale Gibson 3/1 JT FAV: 0055-4: Prom 6f: op 4/1: see 202 (5f).   1¼   52a
4477} **HEATHYARDS LAD** 78 [2] 3-9-7 (77) N Callan (3) 10/1: 4164-5: Rear/in tch, nvr land a blow: op 6/1:   5   60a
abs: '99 W'hampton scorer (mdn, rtd 73a, plcd on turf, rtd 80, prob flattered, auct mdn): eff at 8.5f: acts on
firm, soft & fibresand: handles a gall or sharp track.
188   **CROSBY DONJOHN 24** [7] 3-8-4 (60)(bl) F Norton 7/2: 5002-6: Chsd ldrs wide, btn/eased fnl 1f: op 5/2.   5   33a
118   **JOHN COMPANY 42** [3] 3-8-8 (64)(t) M Tebbutt 10/1: 4625-7: Keen/prom 5f: op 6/1: 6 wk absence: 8   25a
rnr-up in '99 (rtd 77, Newmarket Challenge Cup, P T Walwyn): prob stays a stiff/gall 7f & handles gd grnd.
7 ran   Time 1m 30.00 (3.8)   (J S Fox & Sons)   D Haydn Jones Efail Isaf, Rhondda C Taff.

---

295   **9.00 DON'T STOP SELLER 4-6YO (D)**   1m4f aw   Going 49   -47 Slow
£1512   £432   £216   4 yo rec 4 lb

227   **DREAM ON ME 12** [5] H J Manners 4-8-8 J Bosley (7) 7/2: 4350-1: 4 b f Prince Sabo - Helens   50a
Dreamgirl (Caerleon) Mid-div, rdn 4f out, prog wide fnl 2f & led ins last, in command cl-home, rdn out: tchd
9/2: no bid: '99 wnr at Lingfield (h'cap, rtd 82) & Leicester (seller, rtd 64, G L Moore): 98 Lingfield wnr
(sell, rtd 68a): eff at 7f/1m prev, stays 12f well: acts on firm, gd/soft & likes both AWs: enjoys sells.
248   **TALECA SON 5** [4] D Carroll 5-9-3 N Callan (3) 2/1 FAV: 434-22: 5 b g Conquering Hero - Lady   1½   52$
Taleca (Exhibitioner) Held up, rdn 5f out, prog wide over 1f out, rdn/hdd ins last, no extra: nicely bckd: see 211.
248   **ANOTHER RAINBOW 5** [6] Miss Gay Kelleway 4-8-8 S Drowne 4/1: 250-03: 4 br f Rainbows For Life -   nk   46a
Phylella (Persian Bold) Chsd ldrs, ch 1f out, kept on onepace: op 5/2: qck reapp: acts on firm, gd & fibresand.
261   **MARKELLIS 4** [7] D Carroll 4-9-4 R Fitzpatrick (3) 11/2: 041-04: Dwelt/bhd, styd on strongly fnl   3½   51$
2f, nrst fin: op 7/2, longer priced stablemate of rnr-up: qck reapp: gone close here with a level start: see 215.
254   **WARRIOR KING 4** [2] 6-9-3 A Culhane 14/1: 000-05: Prom, led halfway till over 1f out, sn held: op 12/1.   4   40$
178   **QUAKERESS 26** [10] 5-8-12 (et) D Williamson 7/2 33/1: 0000-6: Chsd ldrs halfway, btn 2f out: 1½   33$
unplcd in '99 (rtd 58, h'cap, subs tried blnks): missed '98, prev term plcd all 3 starts (mdn & nov auct, rtd 70): eff
at 5f: handles firm & fast grnd: officially rated 27, with J Berry.
233   **MY DARLING DODO 12** [9] 4-8-8 D Sweeney 10/1: 5600-7: Chsd ldr 5f out, btn 2f out: op 8/1: see 233.   2   30a
248   **DILETTO 5** [8] 4-8-08 R Winston 8/1: 306-08: Al bhd: tchd 9/1, qck reapp: plcd form in '99 (rtd 68,   2½   26a
h'cap, subs disapp in blnks): plcd form in '98 (rtd 70, nurs & 58a, auct mdn): eff around 1m/10f: acts on firm,
soft & fibresand: prob handles any trk: mdn, has shown enough prev to find a race.
252   **AN LU ABU 5** [3] 4-8-13 (vis) Dean McKeown 16/1: 000-09: Chsd ldrs 1m: reapp: longer 12f trip.   3   27a
3574} **GLORY OF LOVE** 99 [1] 5-9-3 Iona Wands (5) 20/1: 0650-0: Led till halfway, sn btn: 10th: unplaced   13   13a
in '99 (rtd 51, clmr, J Hetherton, tried a vis): unrcd in '98: AW bow tonight for K Ryan.
10 ran   Time 2m 45.1 (11.5)   (H J Manners)   H J Manners Highworth, Wilts.

---

296   **9.30 PRE-PURCHASE HCAP 4YO+ 0-85 (D)**   2m46y aw   Going 49   -19 Slow   **[82]**
£2730   £840   £420   £210   4 yo rec 7 lb

200   **BE GONE 22** [4] C A Dwyer 5-10-0 (82) G Bardwell 9/2: 5030-1: 5 ch g Be My Chief - Hence (Mr   87a
Prospector) Held up, prog halfway & chsd ldr 2f out, narrow lead ins last, kept on gamely, rdn out: plcd in '99 (rtd
84a, h'cap): no jumps form prev: earlier in '99 plcd on turf for H Cecil (rtd 99, stks, subs disapp in vis & blnks):
'98 Newcastle wnr (mdn, rtd 85): prev eff around 12f, styd this longer 2m trip well: acts on gd & both AWs, prob
handles firm: gd weight carrier: handles any trk: looks on a fair mark & can win again.
*182   **PRASLIN ISLAND 26** [8] A Kelleway 4-9-5 (80) J Tate 2/1 FAV: 2121-2: 4 ch c Be My Chief - Hence   ¾   83a
(Mr Prospector) Prom, led 5f out, hard rdn/duelled with wnr fnl 2f, just hdd ins last & held nr fin: clr rem, op 6/4.
253   **JAMAICAN FLIGHT 5** [5] Mrs S Lamyman 7-9-0 (68) A Culhane 7/2: 505-33: 7 b h Sunshine Forever -   5   66a
Kalamona (Hawaii) Led 11f, rdn/outpcd 3f out, kept on ins last but not pace of front pair: op 2/1, qck reapp.
141   **ALHESN 35** [2] C N Allen 5-9-1 (69) R Morse 6/1: 5015-4: Rdn/towards rear, rdn & kept on fnl 2f.   hd   67a
*174   **NOUFARI 28** [7] 9-9-10 (78) N Callan (3) 4/1: 0011-5: Bhd, mod gains: op 3/1: see 174 (sell).   4   72a
--   **TAM OSHANTER** [3] 6-7-10 (50)(3oh) Iona Wands (5) 12/1: 0200/6: Bhd halfway: jumps fit, June/July   22   28a
'99 wnr at Uttoxeter & Worcester (sell h'cap & nov, rtd 98h, eff around 2m4f on firm soft): last rcd on the level in
'97 (rnr up, mdn h'cap, rtd 52, C Thornton): stays a stiff 13f & handles gd grnd: with J G M O'Shea.
4609} **NEIGES ETERNELLES 64** [1] 5-9-6 (74) V Slattery 33/1: /055-7: Bhd halfway, t.o./virtually p.u.   dist   0a
ins last: 2 month abs, AW bow: unplcd in '99 for P Webber (rtd 65, stks): ex-French, '98 M-Laffitte wnr (10f).
7 ran   Time 3m 40.2 (11.0)   (Casino Racing Partnerhsip)   C A Dwyer Newmarket.

Official Going   STANDARD. Stalls: Inside.

297   **12.10 APPR HCAP DIV I 4YO+ 0-60 (F)**   **1m aw rnd   Going 69   -20 Slow**   [57]
£1641   £469   £234

255   **SHONTAINE** 6 [7] M Johnston 7-8-9 (38) K Dalgleish (7) 7/1: 000-51: 7 b g Pharly - Hinari Televideo   40a
(Caerleon) Chsd ldrs, rdn/led ins last, styd on well, rdn out: op 6/1, qck reapp: '99 Ayr wnr (sell h'cap, rtd 45
& 43a): '98 wnr here at Southwell (2, h'caps, rtd 66a): eff at 7f/1m on firm, gd/soft & both AWs: best without
blnks: handles any trk, likes Southwell: runs well for an apprentice: nicely h'capped, can win again.
243   **MUTAHADETH** 8 [4] D Shaw 6-10-0 (57)(bl) Joanna Badger (3) 7/2 JT FAV: 040-32: 6 ch g   1¼   55a
Rudimentary - Music In My Life (Law Society): Prom, rdn/led dist, hdd ins last, kept on: op 5/2: see 243, 183.
251   **STRAVSEA** 7 [6] R Hollinshead 5-9-6 (49) A Hawkins (5) 6/1: 001-03: 5 b m Handsome Sailor - La   1¼   44a
Stravaganza (Slip Anchor) Chsd ldrs, prog & ev ch ins last, kept on for press: op 9/2: see 176 (C/D).
58   **BUNTY** 55 [11] C A Dwyer 4-8-6 (35)(E) G Baker (5) 13/2: 0016-4: Wide/rear, prog to chase ldrs over   1¾   27a
1f out, held ins last: wore an eye-shield, 8 wk abs: '99 wnr at Epsom & Nottingham (h'caps, rtd 50), unplcd on
sand (rtd 39a, h'cap): suited by 1m, tried 10f: acts on firm, soft & f/sand: handles any trk: nicely h'capped.
189   **SWAMPY** 26 [2] 4-9-2 (45) Lynsey Hanna (3) 14/1: 6U20-5: Led over 1f out, no extra.   1½   34a
193   **IMBACKAGAIN** 26 [9] 5-8-7 (36) R Thomas (3) 33/1: 0000-6: Rear/wide, mod late gains: rnr-up in   ½   24a
'99 (rtd 59a, clmr): '98 wnr here at Southwell (h'cap, reapp, rtd 64a), subs plcd on turf (rtd 58, h'cap): eff at
6f, suited by 7/9f, tried 10f: acts on fibresand, fast & handles soft: has run well fresh: likes a sharp trk.
282   **ABOVE BOARD** 3 [1] 5-8-3 (32) P Mundy (6) 13/2: 56-507: Held up in tch, nvr factor: op 8/1, qck reapp.   ¾   19a
4270}   **BACHELORS PAD** 95 [5] 6-9-11 (54) Clare Roche (7) 7/2 JT FAV: 2520-8: Dwelt/rear, stumbled over   1   39a
2f out, late gains, no threat: AW bow: rnr-up twice in '99 (rtd 63, h'cap): plcd in '98 (rtd
76, class stks, W Jarvis): back in '96 won at Goodwood: eff at 7f/sharp 10f: acts on firm & gd/soft grnd: best
without blnks: prob handles any trk: nicely h'capped, shld prove sharper next time with stronger handling.
252   **WAITING KNIGHT** 7 [8] 5-9-9 (52)(vis) Sarah Robinson (7) 20/1: 200-49: Wide/mid-div, btn 2f out.   11   21a
43   **DESIRES GOLD** 58 [12] 5-8-6 (35) M Semple (5) 33/1: 000-0: Led 1f, struggling halfway: 10th: 8 wk   11   0a
abs: unplcd in '99 (lightly rcd, rtd 50, clmr): no form in '98: mdn, with M Brittain.
199   **ANCHOR VENTURE** 24 [3] 7-7-11 (26) D Kinsella (5) 50/1: /P00-0: Led after 1f till 5f out, sn btn: 11th.   1½   0a
247   **FAN TC GEM** 7 [10] 4-9-4 (47) D Hayden 16/1: 4/0-60: Chsd ldrs 5f: 12th: op 14/1: see 247 (7f).   hd   0a
12 ran   Time 1m 46.5 (7.1)   (Paul Dean)   M Johnston Middleham, N.Yorks.

298   **12.40 APPR HCAP DIV II 4YO+ 0-60 (F)**   **1m aw rnd   Going 69   -30 Slow**   [57]
£1638   £468   £234

252   **NICE BALANCE** 7 [8] M C Chapman 5-8-6 (35) Joanna Badger (3) 25/1: 050-61: 5 b g Shadeed - Fellwaati   40a
(Alydar) Sn prom wide, rdn/led over 1f out, styd on well ins last, rdn out: mod form over jumps prev: unplcd in
'99 on the level (rtd 45 & 25a, tried blnks): eff at 1m on fibresand: runs well for an appr: first success today.
247   **GENIUS** 7 [9] D W Chapman 5-9-9 (52) Lynsey Hanna (3) 7/1: 040-22: 5 b g Lycius - Once In My   1¼   53a
Life (Lomond) Chsd ldrs halfway, prog/ev ch fnl 1f, hung left/held nr fin: op 5/1: see 247, 201.
225   **FRANKLIN LAKES** 19 [3] M R Bosley 5-8-6 (35)(bl) G Baker (5) 16/1: 0500-3: 5 ch g Sanglamore -   1¾   33a
Eclipsing (Baillamont) Prom, led over 3f out, hdd over 1f out, no extra nr fin: eff at 7f/1m on firm, fast & fibresand.
251   **STERLING HIGH** 7 [10] D Carroll 5-9-9 (52) T Eaves (7) 2/1 FAV: 105-04: Wide/cl-up halfway, rdn/   nk   49a
outpcd 2f out, kept on ins last, not able to chall: op 3/1: clr of rem: see 251 (C/D).
4365}   **MEGA 88** [11] 4-9-5 (48) W Hutchinson 20/1: 0000-5: Dwelt/rear & wide, stdy gains fnl 4f, nrst fin: 5   35a
op 14/1: 7 wk jumps abs (rtd 75h, juv nov): unplcd on the level in '99 (rtd 63, fill mdn, subs tried a vis): unplcd
sole start in '98 (fill mdn, rtd 67): eye-catching late progress here on AW bow, shld prove sharper next time.
4301}   **FRENCH CONNECTION** 91 [4] 5-9-7 (50) Clare Roche (7) 4/1: 6505-6: Chsd ldrs, rdn/onepace fnl 3f: shd   37a
tchd 5/1: 3 month abs: AW bow: unplcd in '99 (rtd 62, h'cap): '98 Hamilton (auct mdn) & Haydock wnr (h'cap,
rtd 84 at best, J Berry): eff at 1m/9f, stays 10f: acts on fast & hvy grnd, best without blnks: has run well fresh:
likes a stiff/gall trk: well h'capped & shrewd connections will place to effect.
249   **KINGCHIP BOY** 7 [5] 11-9-11 (54) Gemma Jones (5) 100/30: 000-37: Cl-up halfway, btn 2f out: op 5/2.   ½   40a
227   **GADGE** 14 [2] 9-9-2 (45) D Kilcourse (7) 12/1: 3400-8: Led 4f, sn btn: op 8/1: see 83.   3   25a
73   **HOT POTATO** 52 [6] 4-8-8 (37) R Cody Boutcher 25/1: 0005-9: Rear, nvr a factor: 7 wk abs: unplcd   1½   14a
in '99 (rtd 47a & 27, tried visor): unplcd in '98 (C Smith, rtd 50): stays a sharp 6f & handles fibresand.
4166}   **BROUGHTON BELLE** 99 [7] 4-7-10 (25)(1oh) D Kinsella (5) 33/1: 0/00-0: All bhd: 10th: 3 month   hd   1a
abs/AW bow: lightly rcd & h'cap bow today, mod form at up to 12f previously.
380}   **Safe Sharp Jo** 99 [12] 5-8-10 (39) G Gibbons (7) 50/1:211   **Geegee Emmarr** 20 [1] 7-8-5 (34) P Hanagan 25/1:
12 ran   Time 1m 47.3 (7.9)   (R J Hayward)   M C Chapman Martket Rasen, Lincs.

299   **1.10 WICKLOW HCAP DIV I 4YO+ 0-70 (E)**   **7f aw rnd   Going 69   -00 Slow**   [68]
£2470   £760   £380   £190

177   **BOUND TO PLEASE** 28 [1] P J Makin 5-9-1 (55) A Clark 2/1 FAV: 5013-1: 5 b g Warrshan - Hong Kong   64a
Girl (Petong) Led, rdn clr over 1f out, rdn out strongly ins last & pushed out cl-home: tchd 9/2: '99 wnr here at
Southwell (h'cap), unplcd on turf (rtd 55): prev eff at 5/6f, now suited by a sharp 7f, has tried 1m: acts on
fibresand, handles fast: likes to force the pace: likes Southwell: has run well fresh: win again.
193   **ABERKEEN** 26 [7] M Dods 5-8-13 (53) A Culhane 9/2: 0603-2: 5 ch g Keen - Miss Aboyne (Lochnager)   3½   54a
Rear/wide, rcd keenly, kept on well for press fnl 2f, nrst fin: op 3/1: on a fair mark, cld find a race: see 193.
4541}   **TELECASTER** 74 [4] A McCarthy 4-8-0 (40)(BL) A McCarthy (3) 33/1: 000-3: 4 ch g Indian Ridge -   nk   40a
Monashee (Sovereign Dancer) Sn cl-up, ch 2f out, kept on onepace: first time blnks, 10 wk abs, h'cap bow:
unplcd/no form in '99: eff at 7f, tried further: acts on fibresand: first sign of form in headgear today.
280   **MUJAS MAGIC** 3 [6] Mrs N Macauley 5-9-9 (63)(vis) R Fitzpatrick (3) 7/2: 401-24: Chsd ldrs 3f out,   1¼   60a
rdn/sn held: quick reapp: op 4/1: see 280, 187.
4328}   **FANCY A FORTUNE** 90 [9] 6-8-8 (48)(bl) F Norton 16/1: 2620-5: Chsd leading trio, no impress over   4   37a
2f out: op 12/1: rnr-up 4 times in '99 (rtd 51, h'cap): '98 Thirsk (sell, first time blnks) & Beverley wnr (sell
h'cap, rtd 58): eff at 7f/1m, stays 9f: acts on firm & gd/soft grnd: likes an easy trk, loves Thirsk: eff with/
without blnks, has tried a visor: has run well fresh: likes to force the pace.
246   **SWINO** 7 [5] 6-8-13 (53)(bl) S Drowne 7/1: 002-46: Rdn/mid-div halfway, btn 2f out: btr 212 (6f).   nk   41a
255   **BRANDONVILLE** 6 [8] 7-7-10 (36)(t) Kim Tinkler 33/1: 000-07: Al towards rear: qck reapp: lightly   10   9a
rcd/no form in '99: '97 Ayr & Haydock wnr (h'caps, rtd 61): eff at 7f on fast & hvy grnd: likes a gall trk.
195   **ODDSANENDS** 24 [3] 4-10-0 (68) N Callan (3) 5/1: 6022-8: Cl-up 6f: now with T D Barron: btr 195.   1¼   38a

3976} **CHINABERRY 99** [2]　6-8-4 (44) G Bardwell 16/1: 2064-9: Dwelt/al rear: op 12/1: 4 month abs:　　**1¼　11a**
'99 wnr here at Southwell (h'cap, rtd 53a), subs rnr-up twice on turf (rtd 45, h'caps): rnr-up in '98 (rtd 60a),
no turf form: eff at 7f, suited by 1m: acts on firm, gd/soft & fibresand: handles a sharp or gall track.
9 ran　　Time 1m 31.4 (4.8)　　　(Mrs P J Makin)　　P J Makin Ogbourne Maisey, Wilts.

300　　**1.40 CLASSIFIED CLAIMER 3YO 0-60 (F)　6f aw rnd　Going 69　-21 Slow**
　　　　　　£2111　　£603　　£301

257　**NOWT FLASH 6** [8]　B S Rothwell 3-8-6 R Lappin 9/1: 602-01: 3 ch g Petardia - Mantlepiece (Common　　**60a**
Grounds) Chsd ldrs, rdn/led over 1f out, styd on strongly ins last, rdn out: op 6/1: qck reapp: rnr-up in '99 (rtd
55a, unplcd on turf, rtd 49): eff at 5/6f on fibresand: likes a sharp trk: best without blnks: enjoys sells/clmrs.
275　**SIRENE 4** [3]　M J Polglase 3-8-13 (bl) T G McLaughlin 4/1: 102-02: 3 ch f Mystiko - Breakaway (Song)　**3　60a**
Led after 2f, rdn/hdd 2f out, kept on ins last tho' al held: nicely bckd, tchd 5/1: qck reapp: eff at 6/7f: see 275.
165　**CALKO 31** [2]　T D Barron 3-8-11 (bl) N Callan (3) 5/2 FAV: 6315-3: 3 ch g Timeless Times -　　**3　52a**
Jeethgaya (Critque) Rdn/rear, switched 2f out & styd on well 2f out, nrst fin: tchd 7/2: worth a try at 7f now.
*283　**COME ON MURGY 3** [6]　A Bailey 3-8-3 J Bramhill 11/4: 013-14: Rdn mid-div halfway, kept on fnl　　**¾　43a**
2f tho' nvr pace to chall: quick reapp: eff at 6f, suited by 7f, stays 1m: see 283 (seller, 7f).
228　**SHOULDHAVEGONEHOME 14** [9]　3-8-1 (vis) Joanna Badger (7) 12/1: 0020-5: Chsd ldrs halfway,　**1¾　38a**
no extra over 1f out: op 10/1: visor reapplied: see 42.
213　**PAPAGENA 20** [1]　3-8-9 (bl) Dean McKeown 12/1: 0564-6: Chsd ldrs, btn over 1f out: see 213.　　**2　42a**
3491}　**TE ANAU 99** [10]　3-8-1 L Newman (5) 12/1: 0300-7: Mid-div at best: 5 month abs: with B J McMath　**1¼　31a**
in '99, plcd on sand (fill seller, rtd 64a, unplcd on turf, rtd 41): eff over 7f on fibresand: none with W Musson.
217　**LAMMOSKI 20** [7]　3-8-10 (vis) M Tebbutt 40/1: 0005-8: Led 2f, btn 2f out: see 217.　　　**5　30a**
217　**MOSAIC TIMES 20** [5]　3-8-2 A Mackay 25/1: 206-9: Al bhd: rnr-up in '99 (5f sell, rtd 55a).　　**4　14a**
241　**SALLY GARDENS 8** [11]　3-7-13 G Bardwell 16/1: 500-00: Al rear: 10th: op 14/1: see 241.　　　**5　0a**
202　**GEM OF WISDOM 24** [4]　3-8-6 (vis) F Norton 16/1: 6000-0: Bhd halfway: 11th: op 10/1: with A Berry.　**7　0a**
11 ran　　Time 1m 18.7 (5.4)　　　(David Scott)　　　B S Rothwell Musley Bank, N.Yorks.

301　　**2.10 WATERFORD MDN 4YO+ (D)　1m4f aw　Going 69　-03 Slow**
　　　　　　£2834　　£872　　£436　　£218　　4 yo rec 4 lb

4520}　**WOOD POUND 76** [14]　R Hollinshead 4-9-0 N Callan (3) 9/2: 5/20-1: 4 b c Woodman - Poundzig (Danzig)　**87a**
Chsd ldrs, prog/led over 4f out, styd on strongly ins last, rdn out: op 7/2: AW bow, 11 wk abs: rnr-up in '99
for Sir M Stoute (mdn, rtd 80): 5th or sole '98 start (rtd 79): eff at 10f, styd longer 12f trip well: acts on
fibresand & fast, sharp/gall trk: runs well fresh: open to further improvement in h'caps.
3077}　**ORO STREET 99** [6]　D G Bridgwater 4-9-0 A Culhane 11/8 FAV: 6404-2: 4 b g Dolphin Street - Love　**5　79a**
Unlimited (Dominion) Handy 4f out, rdn/onepace fnl 2f: hvly bckd: 5 month abs, AW bow: with G Chung in '99,
(unplcd, rtd 84 at best, mdn): styd this longer 12f trip, further could suit in time: acts on fibresand.
189　**DENS JOY 26** [11]　H J Collingridge 4-8-9 M Tebbutt 15/2: 35-3: 4 b f Archway - Bonvin (Taufan)　**4　68a**
Chsd ldrs 5f out, ch 2f out, sn no extra: op 6/1, clr rem: prob btn this longer 12f trip: handles fast & f/sand.
3548}　**INNES 99** [8]　Miss S E Hall 4-8-9 R Havlin 9/2: /630-4: Towards rear, prog halfway, rdn/no impress　**17　50a**
over 2f out: AW bow: jumps fit, earlier won at Hexham & Sedgefield (rtd 106h, eff arnd 2m1f on firm & gd/soft):
unplcd from 3 starts on the level in '99 (rtd 62, fill mdn): unplcd in '98 (sole start, rtd 62): may need further.
--　**SPOSA** [1]　4-8-9 S Yourston (7) 14/1: 5000-5: Rear, mod gains fnl 3f: 3 month abs/AW bow.　　**1¾　48a**
277　**KAID 4** [3]　5-9-4 T G McLaughlin 5/1: 005-46: Rear, mod prog: tchd 6/1, qck reapp: visor omitted.　**1　52$**
248　**WESTWOOD VIEW 7** [2]　4-8-9 A Clark 5/1: 004-57: Chsd ldrs 1m: longer 12f trip: see 196.　　**12　34$**
--　**THE NOBLEMAN** [12]　4-9-0 J Fanning 33/1: 0/8: Led halfway till 4f out, sn btn: AW bow/long abs.　**2½　35a**
251　**HIBAAT 7** [13]　4-9-0 R Fitzpatrick (3) 50/1: 500-09: Al towards rear: longer 12f trip.　　　**4　29a**
1062}　**SONICOS 99** [9]　4-9-0 R Winston 50/1: 0-0: Bhd halfway: 10th: 9 month abs/AW bow: jockey　**nk　28a**
referred to Portman Square under the totting-up procedure for whip bans.
87　**LAKE ARIA 49** [13]　7-8-13 (bl) J Edmunds 66/1: 0000-0: Led 6f: 12th: 7 wk abs, longer 12f trip.　　**0a**
267　**Tattoo 5** [5] S Drowne 33/1:　　　　4046} **Sherganzar 99** [7] 5-9-4 (bl) F Norton 12/1:
267　**Go Man 5** [4] 6-9-4 J P Spencer 50/1:　　229 **Little Lottie 14** [10] 4-8-9 R Lappin 50/1:
15 ran　　Time 2m 42.9 (8.6)　　　(Peter Wetzel)　　R Hollinshead Upper Longdon, Staffs.

302　　**2.40 CORK HCAP 4YO+ 0-90 (C)　1m3f aw　Going 69　+05 Fast**　　　　　**[85]**
　　　　　　£6532　　£2010　　£1005　　£502　　4 yo rec 3 lb

200　**QUINTRELL DOWNS 24** [8]　R M H Cowell 5-9-8 (79) M Hills 11/4 JT FAV: 1132-1: 5 b g Efisio -　**86a**
Nineteenth Of May (Homing) Sn handy, led over 3f out, rdn & in command ins last: fast time, op 9/4: '99 jumps
wnr at W'hampton (now h'cap, rtd 85h, eff at 2m on fast): earlier in '99 won at Southwell (2) & W'hampton (h'caps,
rtd 74a & 40): ex-Irish: eff at 11/12f on fast, handles gd/soft & loves fibresand/Southwell: tough & progressive.
245　**FAILED TO HIT 8** [6]　N P Littmoden 7-8-9 (66)(vis) J Tate 12/1: 522-42: 7 b g Warrshan - Missed　**1　71a**
Again (High Top) Led, rdn/hdd 4f out, rallied well for press ins last tho' al held by wnr: win again: see 101 (clmr).
1629}　**PUZZLEMENT 99** [1]　C E Brittain 6-9-4 (75) N Esler 7/1: 2645-3: 6 gr g Mystiko - Abuzz (Absalom)　**3　76a**
Trkd ldrs going well 3f out, switched/onepace fnl 2f: 8 month abs: rnr-up in '99 (rtd 74 & 76a, h'caps): '98
Beverley wnr (2, h'caps, rtd 73 & 66a): eff at 1m/12f, suited by 10f: acts on firm, soft & both AWs: handles
any trk, likes Lingfield & Beverley: best held up for a late run: well clr of rem here.
*170　**WESTERN COMMAND 30** [5]　Mrs N Macauley 4-8-7 (67) R Fitzpatrick (3) 5/1: 6221-4: Chsd ldrs 9f.　**6　59a**
4574}　**GREEN BOPPER 70** [4]　7-9-1 (72) T G McLaughlin 6/1: 3620-5: Held up in tch, rdn/switched wide 5f　**3½　59a**
out, held fnl 2f: nicely bckd, op 7/1, 10 wk abs: '99 Southwell (2, rtd 73a) & Haydock wnr (h'caps, rtd 70):
'98 wnr again at Southwell & W'hampton (2, h'caps, rtd 64a): eff at 1m, suited by 10/11f: acts on gd/soft & gd,
prob handles 1m fibresand: handles any trk, likes a sharp one: capable of more.
4122}　**FIORI 99** [10]　4-9-6 (80) M Tebbutt 11/4 JT FAV: 1550-6: Wide/mid-div, rdn/held fnl 2f: nicely bckd,　**8　58a**
tchd 5/1: jumps fit (rnr-up, juv nov, rtd 112h): '99 wnr at Hamilton (auct mdn), Beverley & York (h'caps, rtd 89):
plcd in '98 (rtd 89 & 72a): eff at 10/12f on fast, soft & fibresand, handles firm: handles any trk.
245　**NOUKARI 8** [11]　7-9-11 (82) J P Spencer 8/1: 114-27: Wide/chsd ldrs 9f: op 6/1: see 151 (eqtrk).　**1½　58a**
67　**KILLARNEY JAZZ 54** [3]　5-8-5 (62)(tbl) F Norton 20/1: 2044-8: Held up, wknd: see 67 (9f).　　**2　35a**
3987}　**WILCUMA 99** [7]　9-10-0 (85) A Clark 11/1: 50/0-9: Al bhd: topweight: 4 month abs/AW bow.　　**11　46a**
2021}　**DUTCH LAD 99** [9]　5-9-4 (75) G Bardwell 25/1: /050-0: Bhd halfway: 10th: 7 month abs/AW bow.　**dist　0a**
200　**DYNAMISM 24** [2]　5-9-4 (75) A Culhane 16/1: 0006-0: Sn bhd, t.o. & dismounted after line: 11th.　**4　0a**
11 ran　　Time 2m 28.3 (7.0)　　　(Mr & Mrs D A Gamble)　　R M H Cowell Six Mile Bottom, Cambs.

SOUTHWELL (Fibresand)　　MONDAY JANUARY 10TH　　Lefthand, Sharp, Oval Track

303　3.10 KERRY SELLER 3YO (G)　　1m aw rnd　Going 69　-21 Slow
£1909　£545　£272

31　**BOSS TWEED** 59 [9] G C Bravery 3-9-0 M Hills 7/4 FAV: 0650-1: 3 b g Persian Bold - Betty Kenwood (Dominion) Chsd ldrs wide going well halfway, led over 2f out & sn rdn clr, eased well ins last, cmftbly: val for 8L+, well bckd, sold for 5,600gns, 2 month abs: unplcd in '99 (rtd 59a & 57): apprec step up to 1m, stay further: acts on fibresand & a sharp trk: runs well fresh: apprec drop to sell grade.		66a
192　**IMARI** 26 [10] J G Given 3-8-9 A Culhane 7/1: 4640-2: 3 b f Rock City - Misty Goddess (Godswalk) Dwelt, chsd ldrs halfway, rdn & kept on fnl 2f, no ch with wnr: op 5/1: unplcd in '99 (rtd 70, nov fill stks): stays a sharp 1m & prob handles fibresand, fast & soft grnd: could find a similar contest.	6	53a
4151}　**BAYTOWN RHAPSODY** 99 [6] P S McEntee 3-8-9 S Drowne 7/1: 5500-3: 3 b f Emperor Jones - Sing A Rainbow (Rainbow Quest) Trkd ldr halfway, ch 2f out, sn held: 3 month abs/AW bow: rnr-up in '99 (debut, auct mdn, rtd 56): eff at 6f, this longer 1m trip shld suit in time: handles gd grnd & prob fibresand.	2	49a
198　**GENTLE ANNE** 24 [5] Ronald Thompson 3-8-9 A Clark 15/2: 0400-5: Chsd ldrs, held fnl 2f, 12 wk abs: plcd form in '99 (rtd 56, nurs h'cap), unplcd on sand (rtd 39a): handles fast & gd/soft, sharp/stiff track.	½	48a
4406}　**LITTLE CHRISTIAN** 84 [11] R Fitzpatrick (3) 3-9-0 C Rutter 16/1: 0400-5: Chsd ldrs, held fnl 2f: 12 wk abs: plcd form in '99 (rtd 56, nurs h'cap), unplcd on sand (rtd 39a): handles fast & gd/soft, sharp/stiff track.	5	43a
283　**XENOS** 3 [2] 3-9-0 A McCarthy (3) 12/1: 00-056: Chsd ldrs 5f: op 20/1: qck reapp: see 242.	3	37a
213　**NICIARA** 20 [7] 3-9-0 R Fitzpatrick (3) 8/1: 33P0-7: Al towards rear: op 5/1: see 128, 74.	1¾	34a
88　**SHEERNESS ESSITY** 49 [8] 3-9-0 (BL) F Lynch 8/1: 4100-8: Led 6f, sn btn: blnks, op 5/1: 7 wk abs.	6	25a
236　**CASTLEBRIDGE** 12 [1] 3-9-0 M Tebbutt 8/1: 000-9: Struggling halfway, bckd at long odds, op 33/1.	4	17a
204　**FOSTON FOX** 23 [3] 3-9-0 S Whitworth 16/1: 0604-0: Rear halfway: 10th: op 12/1: btr 204 (eqtrk, 10f).	11	0a
2829}　**LUCKY MELODY** 99 [4] 3-9-0 J Stack 33/1: 0330-0: Cl-up 4f: 11th: 6 month abs.	7	0a

11 ran　　Time 1m 46.6 (7.2)　　(G C Bravery)　　G C Bravery Newmarket, Suffolk

304　3.40 WICKLOW HCAP DIV II 4YO+ 0-70 (E)　　7f aw rnd　Going 69　-02 Slow　　[68]
£2470　£760　£380　£190

250　**ITCH** 7 [5] R Bastiman 5-7-12 (38)(2ow)(3oh) T Williams 3/1: 000-21: 5 b h Puissance - Panienka (Dom Racine) Chsd ldr halfway, led 2f out, styd on well & asserted ins last, rdn out: tchd 4/1: unplcd in '99 (tried a visor): back in '97 won at Pontefract (juv auct mdn, rtd 75): eff at 7f, now suited by 7f: acts on gd/soft & fibresand: handles a stiff/undul or sharp trk: open to further improvement in similar events.		43a
162　**MAI TAI 33** [8] D W Barker 5-9-1 (55)(vis) Kimberley Hart (5) 2/1 FAV: 4314-2: 5 b m Scenic - Oystons Propweekly (Swing Easy) Held up in tch, styd on fnl 2f for press, not pace of wnr: op 7/4: see 147 (1m).	2½	56a
249　**MOST RESPECTFUL 7** [3] N Tinkler 7-8-13 (53)(t) Kim Tinkler 12/1: 060-43: 7 ch g Respect - Active Movement (Music Boy) Chsd ldrs, keen early, kept on fnl 2f for press: see 249 (C/D, clmr).	3	48a
2036}　**THE BARNSLEY BELLE** 99 [9] G Woodward 7-7-12 (37)(1ow) P Fessey 20/1: 0656-4: Chsd ldrs, rdn 3f out, sn held: tchd 25/1, 7 month abs: '99 wnr here at Southwell (fill h'cap, rtd 41a, no turf form): plcd in '98 (appr fill h'cap, rtd 51a): eff at 7f/1m: acts on gd, loves fibresand/Southwell: on a fair mark.	3	27a
176　**SOLLYS PAL** 28 [2] 5-8-10 (50) A Clark 4/1: /004-5: Led, hdd 2f out & wknd: op 5/1: btr 176.	2	35a
212　**DEKELSMARY** 20 [6] 5-8-1 (41)(t) J Edmunds (5) 8/1: 0000-6: Dwelt, nvr on terms: op 6/1: see 212 (6f).	¾	25a
209　**SOUND THE TRUMPET** 23 [4] 8-8-6 (46)(t) G Baker (7) 8/1: 4130-7: Wide/nvr factor: op 6/1: btr 97 (eqtrk).	10	15a
4363}　**MELODIAN** 88 [7] 5-9-0 (54)(bl) G Bardwell 14/1: 0350-8: Sn bhd: op 10/1: 3 month abs: tough & progressive in '99, won h'caps at Beverley, Doncaster & Catterick (rtd 56): '98 Newcastle wnr (h'cap, rtd 44): eff forcing pace at 7f, stays 1m well: acts on gd/soft, suited by firm & gd, any trk: runs well for blnks: AW bow today.	27	0a

8 ran　　Time 1m 31.6 (5.0)　　(Robin Bastiman)　　R Bastiman Cowthorpe, N.Yorks.

WOLVERHAMPTON (Fibresand)　　TUESDAY JANUARY 11TH　　Lefthand, Sharp Track

Official Going　STANDARD. Stalls: Inside, Except 7f - Outside

305　1.10 NEWPORT APPR HCAP DIV 1 4YO+ 0-60 (G)　　1m1f79y aw　Going 56　-04 Slow　　[59]
£1466　£419　£209　4 yo rec 1 lb

271　**AREISH** 5 [4] J Balding 7-9-5 (50) P Dobbs (3) 9/2 JT FAV: 020-51: 7 b m Keen - Cool Combination (Indian King) Held up, prog to trk ldrs going well 4f out, rdn out: tchd 15/2, qck reapp: '99 W'hampton (sell) & Southwell wnr (fill h'cap, rtd 53a): '99 Southwell (h'cap, D Nicholls) & W'hampton wnr (sell h'cap, rtd 44a, M Pipe): eff at 1m/12f on fibresand, prob equitrack: loves a sharp trk: best without blnks: has run well fresh.		56a
203　**MYSTERIUM** 24 [11] N P Littmoden 6-9-2 (47) R Thomas (5) 5/1: 1240-2: 6 gr g Mystiko - Way To Go (Troy) Towards rear, smooth prog wide halfway, ev ch ins last, rdn/held nr fin: op 3/1: see 102, 67.	½	51a
126　**PERCHANCER** 42 [7] P C Haslam 4-9-3 (49) T Eaves (5) 7/1: 0006-3: 4 ch c Perugino - Irish Hope (Nishapour) Prom, led 4f out, hdd/no extra ins last: 6 wk abs: '99 Hddock wnr (appr mdn h'cap, rtd 55), rnr-up on sand (rtd 58a, h'cap): eff at 7/9.3f: acts on firm, gd/soft & both AWs: has run well in blnks, tried a visor.	2½	48a
100　**ERITHS CHILL WIND** 48 [13] G L Moore 4-9-0 (46)(BL) R Smith (3) 10/1: 1044-4: Keen/prom, onepace fnl 2f: blnks, op 6/1, 7 wk abs: 1st time blnks: acts on both AWs, firm & soft: a drop to 1m shld suit: see 100.	½	44a
261　**OUR PEOPLE** 7 [12] 6-8-0 (31)(t) K Dalgleish (7) 9/2 JT FAV: 550-35: Mid-div/not pace to chall: op 3/1.	¾	28a
4519}　**EMPIRE STATE** 75 [5] 5-8-13 (44) P Hanagan (5) 11/2: 4220-6: Chsd ldrs 1m: jumps fit, recent Catterick wnr (sell h'cap, rtd 82h), eff arnd 2m on gd/soft): dual '99 rnr-up (rtd 45, h'cap): '98 wnr at Carlisle & Catterick (h'caps, rtd 71): now suited by 10/11f: acts on firm & soft, any trk: best without blnks/visor.	¾	40a
211　**ALBERKINNIE** 21 [1] 5-7-10 (27) G Baker (5) 14/1: 4020-7: Prom 7f: tchd 16/1: see 211.	nk	22a
4522}　**SWIFT MAIDEN** 77 [2] 7-9-10 (55) S Carson (5) 16/1: 01/0-8: Led 5f, sn btn: op 16/1: 7 wk jumps abs (mod form): no form sole '99 start: '96 Newbury wnr (clmr, rtd 67): eff at 1m, stays 10f: handles firm, likes soft grnd: enjoys clmg grade: AW bow today.	9	36a
3446}　**PRIORS MOOR** 99 [10] 5-8-11 (42) J Bosley (5) 33/1: 0500-9: Mid-div/btn 3f out: abs, now with K Bell.	1¾	20a
3380}　**MISS TAKE** 99 [9] 4-10-0 (60) C Carver (5) 11/2: 0305-0: Sn bhd: 10th: op 10/1, abs: now with A Newcombe.	1	36a
254　**DOBERMAN** 7 [3] 5-8-7 (38) Joanna Badger (5) 8/1: 404-40: Strugg halfway: op 10/1: btr 254 (vis).	hd	13a
292　Up In Flames 3 [8] 9-8-7 (38) L Newman (3) 20/1:　　3788} Lochlass 99 [6] 6-7-12 (29)(bl) Claire Bryan (3) 50/1:		

13 ran　　Time 2m 03.8 (5.6)　　(Mrs J Coghlan-Everitt)　　J Balding Scrooby, Notts

---

306

1.40 NEWPORT APPR HCAP DIV 2 4YO+ 0-60 (G)   **1m1f79y aw Going 56 -09 Slow**   **[59]**
£1466   £419   £209   4 yo rec 1 lb

*227 **FRENCH SPICE** 15 [7] Sir Mark Prescott 4-9-0 (46) P Goode 4/6 FAV: 6061-1: 4 b f Cadeaux Genereux - **57a**
Hot Spice (Hotfoot) Chsd ldrs halfway, smooth prog to lead dist, pushed out: val for 3L+, bckd from 5/4: '99 wnr
here at W'hampton (h'cap, rtd 47a): eff at 1m/9.4f, 10f+ shld suit: likes fibresand/W'hampton: hat-trick beckons.
254 **CONSULTANT** 7 [1] C N Kellett 4-9-5 (51) C Carver 14/1: 00-032: 4 b g Man Of May - Avenita Lady   1 **55a**
(Free State) Led, rdn/hdd over 1f out, kept on ins last tho' al held: op 8/1: clr of rem: stays 9.4f: win soon.
178 **EMPERORS GOLD** 29 [10] M G Quinlan 5-8-13 (44) D McGann (5) 25/1: 0/00-3: 5 gr g Petong - Tarnside 6 **39a**
Rosal (Mummy's Game) Dwelt, sn mid-div, kept on fnl 3f, no threat to front pair: op 33/1: lightly rcd/no form
in '99: '98 Southwell wnr (sell, M J Polglase, rtd 72a, no turf form): eff around 1m/sharp 10f: acts on both AWs:
handles fast & gd/soft: best without a visor: has run well fresh: enjoys sell grade: looks nicely h'capped.
268 **CLONOE** 6 [3] R Ingram 6-8-5 (36) S Carson 5/1: 060-24: Pulled hard/hmpd early, chsd ldrs, held   ¾ **30a**
over 1f out: op 7/2: likes to dominate, unable to do so here: see 268 (equitrack).
270 **HEATHYARDS JAKE** 5 [9] 4-9-11 (57) Stephanie Hollinshead(7) 12/1: 221-45: Chsd ldrs 3f out, sn held.   2 **47a**
263 **UNTOLD STORY** 6 [8] 5-8-7 (38) L Newman (3) 33/1: 000-06: Mid-div at best: quick reapp: see 263.   3½ **21a**
220 **UTAH** 20 [5] 6-9-3 (48) P Dobbs (3) 20/1: 2000-7: Prom 6f: op 14/1: see 220.   1¼ **28a**
255 **LILANITA** 7 [2] 5-9-0 (45)(VIS) Joanna Badger (5) 13/2: 203-28: Cl-up 7f: vis, op 9/2: btr 255 (8.5f).   1¼ **22a**
229 **ALEANBH** 15 [11] 5-7-12 (29) P Hanagan (2) 0000-9: Al towards rear: tchd 33/1: see 229.   2 **2a**
216 **BLOOMING AMAZING** 21 [6] 6-9-9 (54) R Cody Boutcher (5) 9/1: 0530-0: Prom wide 6f: 10th: see 176.   1 **25a**
249 **Annandale** 8 [12] 4-8-9 (41) Iona Wands 33/1:   225 **Wild Nettle** 20 [4] 6-7-13 (30) Kristin Stubbs (7) 33/1:
12 ran   Time 2m 04.3 (6.1)   (J Morley)   Sir Mark Prescott Newmarket

---

307

2.10 YARMOUTH CLAIMER 4YO+ (F)   **1m4f aw Going 56 -33 Slow**
£2124   £607   £303   4 yo rec 4 lb

230 **JAVA SHRINE** 15 [3] D J Wintle 9-9-3 (bl) Joanna Badger (7) 8/1: 3260-1: 9 b g Java Gold - Ivory   **63a**
Idol (Alydar) Held up, rdn & outpcd 4f out, rallied to lead dist, kept on gamely, rdn out: op 6/1, slow time: '99
wnr at Lingfield (3, 1 for P Eccles & 2 for A Reid, rtd 75a): '98 Warwick & Lingfield wnr (sell h'caps, rtd 65 &
65a): suited by 10/12f on firm/fast, enjoys both AWs: likes a sharp trk: best in blnks, runs well fresh.
231 **BANNERET** 15 [6] Miss S J Wilton 7-9-1 (VIS) T G McLaughlin 14/1: 1534-2: 7 b g Imperial Falcon -   3 **56a**
Dashing Partner (Formidable) Slowly away & rdn, kept on fnl 2f, nrst fin: op 10/1, tried a visor: see 231.
277 **MR SPECULATOR** 5 [2] J L Spearing 7-8-9 S Whitworth 25/1: /3-053: 7 ch g Kefaah - Humanity   nk **49$**
(Ahonoora) Chsd ldrs, prog to lead over 2f out, sn rdn & hdd over 1f out, no extra: clr rem: see 174 (sell).
251 **BE WARNED** 8 [5] R Brotherton 9-9-7 (vis) C Carver (3) 15/8: 041-04: Held up, prog/rdn & chsd ldr 2f   6 **52a**
out, held over 1f out: well bckd, tchd 11/4: visor reapplied: '99 W'hampton scorer (clmr, rtd 85a at best, plcd on
turf, rtd 68, h'cap): '98 wnr at Southwell (2) & W'hampton (h'caps, rtd 81a & 66): eff btwn 7f/12f: acts on fast,
hvy & both AWs: handles any trk, likes W'hampton/Southwell: suited by a visor, tried blnks.
245 **NIGHT CITY** 9 [7] 9-9-7 N Callan (3) 11/8 FAV: 032-65: Led/dsp on slr, hard rdn/swished tail & lkd   21 **28a**
reluctant halfway, joined 6f out & rdn/btn 2f out, sn eased: mulish display, prefers Lingfield: see 92 (clmr, 1m).
4270} **METEOR STRIKE** 96 [1] 6-9-7 (t) M Tebbutt 10/1: 0300-6: Bhd 5f out: op 6/1: 3 month abs: rnr-   24 **1a**
up in '99 (rtd 70, class stks, 1st time blnks, Mrs A J Perrett): '98 Lingfield scorer (h'cap, rtd 83a): eff at 10/12f
on firm, fast & equitrack: reportedly suffered breathing probs prev, wore a t-strap today for D Nicholls.
172 **FEARSOME FACTOR** 31 [4] 5-9-7 J P Spencer 9/1: 3000-7: Dsptd lead halfway/wknd qckly fnl 2f: op 4/1.   2½ **0a**
7 ran   Time 2m 44.3 (10.7)   (Plough Twenty (Ashton Keynes))   D J Wintle Naunton, Glos

---

308

2.40 COWES MDN 4YO+ (D)   **1m100y a Going 56 +09 Fast**
£2795   £860   £430   £215

-- **SKIMMING** [7] B W Hills 4-9-0 M Hills 1/2 FAV: /660-1: 4 b c Nureyev - Skimble (Lyphard)   **77a**
Prom, led over 5f out, asserted ins last, eased cl-home: val for 5L+, hvly bckd, fast time, 3 month abs/AW bow:
ex-French, unplcd from 3 starts in '99: 2nd of 4 as a juv for A Fabre: eff at 8.5f, tried 12f, shld stay further:
acts on fibresand: well regarded & impress here in a fast time.
121 **SOVEREIGN ABBEY** 45 [5] Sir Mark Prescott 4-8-9 D Sweeney 7/1: /546-2: 4 b f Royal Academy - Elabella 3 **62$**
(Ela Mana Mou) Chsd ldrs, chsd wnr 2f out, kept on ins last tho' held & position accepted nr fin: clr rem, op 9/2,
6 wk abs: unplcd in '99 (mdn, rtd 50a): plcd in '98 (rtd 77 & 64a, mdns): eff at 7/8.5f: handles hvy & f/sand.
1920} **NAFITH** 99 [4] E L James 4-9-0 S Whitworth 14/1: 5000-3: 4 ch g Elmaamul - Wanisa (Topsider)   10 **52a**
Prom, outpcd by front pair fnl 3f: op 7/1: 6 wk jumps abs (rtd 94h, juv nov): unplcd in '99 for M P Tregoning
(rtd 76, mdn): rtd 72 in '98 (auct mdn): prob stays 1m, tried 10f: AW bow today, room for improvement.
229 **ANNADAWI** 15 [8] C N Kellett 5-9-0 N Carlisle 25/1: 0044-4: Chsd ldrs wide 4f out/sn held: see 173.   5 **42$**
276 **NOBLE PATRIOT** 5 [9] 5-9-0 Dean McKeown 33/1: 203-45: Mid-div at best: quick reapp: see 61 (sell).   1 **40a**
233 **DANESTAR** 15 [6] 5-8-9 (VIS) N Callan (3) 25/1: 5000-6: Rdn/prom halfway, sn btn: visor: see 233.   6 **26a**
229 **AUTUMN LEAVES** 15 [2] 4-8-9 C Cogan (5) 40/1: 0006-7: Keen/prom, btn 3f out: see 229.   ½ **25a**
238 **SING CHEONG** 13 [3] 4-9-0 (VIS) A Clark 11/2: 0243-8: Chsd ldrs 7f: op 4/1, visor: btr 238 (eqtrk).   1¼ **27a**
173 **MALAKAL** 31 [1] 4-9-0 J P Spencer 4200-9: Led 3f, btn 2f out: op 5/1.   9 **14a**
248 **KOOL JULES** 8 [10] 4-8-9 S Drowne 33/1: 00: Bhd 4f out: 10th: no form.   6 **0a**
10 ran   Time 1m 50.2 (4.0)   (K Abdulla)   B W Hills Lambourn, Berks

---

309

3.10 TOTE HCAP 3YO+ 0-90 (C)   **1m1f79y Going 56 +02 Fast**   **[75]**
£6857   £2110   £1055   £527   3 yo rec 22lb4 yo rec 1 lb

233 **HANNIBAL LAD** 15 [7] W M Brisbourne 4-9-0 (62) Martin Dwyer 11/1: 0042-1: 4 ch g Rock City -   **71a**
Appealing (Star Appeal) Chsd ldrs, styd on well for press to lead nr fin, drvn out: op 8/1, gd time: '99 wnr here
at W'hampton (for P Evans, sell, rtd 66a): '98 Southwell wnr (sell, rtd 67a & 69): eff at 7f, suited by 1m/9.3f:
acts on firm, loves fibresand/W'hampton: runs well fresh: can win again.
251 **DARE** 8 [2] P D Evans 5-9-0 (61)(bl) Joanna Badger (7) 13/2: 000-32: 5 b g Beveled - Run Amber Run   1 **67a**
(Run The Gantlet) Trkd ldrs, rdn/led over 2f out, hdd nr line, no extra: op 11/2: back to form in blnks last twice.
251 **WINDSHIFT** 8 [9] D Shaw 4-10-0 (76)(vis) R Winston 10/1: 300-53: 4 b g Forest Wind - Beautyofthepeace 3½ **75a**
(Exactly Sharp) Rdn/rear halfway, styd on well fnl 3f for press, nrst fin: stays 9.4f, loves 1m/Southwell: see 216.
143 **MY TESS** 38 [1] B A McMahon 4-9-8 (70) Dean McKeown (5) 60/1: 0614-4: Led, hdd 5f out, rdn/rallied to   1½ **66a**
lead over 2f out, sn hdd & no extra: op 5/1: stays 9.4f, best at 1m: see 78 (made all).

WOLVERHAMPTON (Fibresand) TUESDAY JANUARY 11TH Lefthand, Sharp Track

251 **CIVIL LIBERTY** 8 [8] 7-9-4 (65) (t) R Smith (5) 9/2: 246-45: Chsd ldrs 4f out, held fnl 2f: clr of rem. ½ 60a
230 **PARISIAN LADY** 15 [10] 5-8-9 (56) S Whitworth 14/1: 0106-6: Twds rear/nvr factor: see 152 (eqtrk, 1m). 7 40a
268 **MAPLE** 6 [1] 4-8-10 (58) A Clark 20/1: 063-67: Al towards rear: quick reapp: see 224 (equitrack). 2 38a
271 **TIGHTROPE** 5 [4] 5-9-3 (64) (VIS) L Newman (5) 6/1: 24-638: Chsd ldrs 4f out, sn held: vis: btr 271, 1. 4 36a
*251 **NOBLE CYRANO** 8 [6] 5-9-3 (64)(6ex) R Lappin 5/1: 002-19: Led/dsptd lead 7f, sn btn/eased ins last. 2 32a
*271 **TROIS** 5 [5] 4-9-11 (73)(6ex) T G McLaughlin 7/2 FAV: 001-10: Rdn in rear halfway, btn/eased 2f out: 18 14a
10th: reportedly finished lame: stable had fav & 3rd fav (fin last & 2nd last): see 271 (C/D).
10 ran Time 2m 03.3 (5.1) (John Pugh) W M Brisbourne Great Ness, Shropshire

---

310 3.40 VENTNOR SELLER 4YO+ (G) 7f aw Going 56 -25 Slow
£1895 £541 £270

177 **RA RA RASPUTIN** 29 [2] B A McMahon 5-9-2 L Newman (5) 5/1: 0300-1: 5 b g Petong - Ra Ra Girl 51a
(Shack) Chsd ldrs, rdn to lead dist & pulled clr, rdn out: bt in for 3,400gns: 2nd in '99 (h'cap, rtd 62a): '97
W'hampton wnr (val stks, rtd 83a): eff at 7f, stays 1m on fast, hvy & likes fibresand/W'hampton: best without blnks.
247 **CHALUZ** 8 [3] N P Littmoden 6-9-12 (tVIS) C Cogan (5) 3/1: 255-42: 6 b g Night Shift - Laluche 6 50a
(Alleged) Sn cl-up/wide, led halfway, rdn & hdd dist, sn held: op 4/1: ran to form in 1st time visor: see 75.
-- **NOBLE INVESTMENT** [4] J Neville 6-9-2 S Drowne 14/1: 0540/3: 6 b g Shirley Heights - Noble 2 36a
Destiny (Dancing Brave) Slowly away & rdn, kept on fnl 2f, no threat: op 10/1, jumps fit (no form).
274 **BALLYMORRIS BOY** 5 [5] J Pearce 4-8-11 F Norton 3/1: 534-34: Chsd ldrs, outpcd fnl 2f: op 2/1. 1¾ 28a
247 **MAID PLANS** 8 [7] 4-8-6 R Fitzpatrick (3) 40/1: /05-05: Nvr on terms: only mod form prev. ¾ 22a
252 **SHARP STEEL** 8 [1] 5-8-11 (VIS) C Rutter 6/4 FAV: 002-56: Led till halfway, sn rdn/btn: hvly bckd: 1 25a
disapp in 1st time visor: much better clearly expected: btr 50.
6 ran Time 1m 31.9 (5.7) (D J Allen) B A McMahon Hopwas, Staffs

---

311 4.10 SHANKLIN HCAP 3YO 0-70 (E) 1m100y a Going 56 -25 Slow [75]
£2664 £761 £380

213 **WILL IVESON** 21 [5] P C Haslam 3-8-6 (53) Dale Gibson 5/1: 5655-1: 3 b g Mukaddamah - Cherlinoa 59a
(Crystal Palace) Prom, led 2f out, held on well ins last, rdn out: op 4/1: unplcd in '99 (rtd 74 & 63a at best):
eff at 8.5f: acts on fibresand, prob handles firm & gd/soft: likes a sharp trk.
213 **COLOMBE DOR** 21 [3] P C Haslam 3-8-8 (55) M Tebbutt 5/1: 0006-2: 3 gr g Petong - Deep Divide ¾ 59a
(Nashwan) Chsd ldrs, rdn halfway, kept on well for press ins last, not rch s/mate: op 4/1: eff at 8.5f on f/sand.
257 **FOR HEAVENS SAKE** 7 [6] C W Thornton 3-8-12 (59) Dean McKeown 11/8 FAV: 466-43: 3 b c Rambo 1 61a
Dancer - Angel Fire (Nashwan) Chsd ldrs, prog/wide over 2f out & ev ch over 1f out, sn hung right & held:
nicely bckd, tchd 9/4: styd 8.5f: headgear may help: see 257, 188.
4406} **SPORTY MO** 85 [4] K R Burke 3-9-7 (68) N Callan (3) 9/2: 0501-4: Led, hdd 2f out, held/eased nr fin: 3½ 63a
op 7/2, 12 wk abs: '99 Southwell wnr (2, sells, rtd 71a): eff at 6f/1m: acts on fibresand & soft grnd.
3026} **SAMMIE DUROSE** 99 [7] 3-7-12 (43)(BL) (2ow) P Fessey 14/1: 000-5: Chsd ldrs, held fnl 1f: op 16/1, 4 32a
blnks: AW bow 5 month abs: '99 rap bow: rtd 49 at best in '99 (unplcd, tried at up to 7f).
286 **KIGEMA** 3 [2] 3-8-6 (53) L Newman (5) 11/2: 06-146: Chsd ldrs 5f, btn/eased fnl 1f: btr 246 (eqtrk). 15 18a
149 **SONBELLE** 36 [1] 3-9-7 (68) D Sweeney 10/1: 6064-7: Bhd halfway: op 7/1: btr 149 (equitrack, 7f). dist 0a
7 ran Time 1m 53.1 (6.9) (Lord Bolton) P C Haslam Middleham, N Yorks

---

LINGFIELD (Equitrack) WEDNESDAY JANUARY 12TH Lefthand, V Sharp Track

Official Going STANDARD. Stalls: 5f/1m - Outside; Rem - Inside.

312 12.50 COGNAC HCAP 3YO+ 0-75 (E) 5f aw rnd Going 27 +03 Fast [74]
£3412 £1050 £525 £262

291 **WISHBONE ALLEY** 4 [4] M Dods 5-7-13 (45) (vis) Dale Gibson 9/4 FAV: 022-21: 5 b g Common Grounds - 51a
Dul Dul (Shadeed) Chsd ldr halfway, rdn & chall dist, led nr fin, rdn out: gd time, qck reapp: '99 scorer at
Newcastle (h'cap, rtd 55), rnr-up on sand (rtd 45a, C/D): '98 Thirsk wnr (h'cap, rtd 64): eff at 5/6f: acts on
fast, soft & both AWs: handles firm & hvy: eff in blnks/visor, handles any trk: can win again.
191 **PALACEGATE JACK** 28 [5] A Berry 9-8-7 (53)(bl) D Allan (7) 7/1: 4052-2: 9 gr g Neshad - Pasadena ¾ 56a
Lady (Captain James) Sn led, jockey looking rnd 1f out, no pace to repel wnr cl home: prev with J Berry: see 191.
235 **TORRENT** 14 [7] D W Chapman 5-9-13 (73)(bl) Lynsey Hanna (7) 100/30: 2113-3: 5 ch g Prince Sabo - 2 71a
Maiden Pool (Sharpen Up) Chsd ldrs wide halfway, rdn/no impress ins last: op 11/4: see 205 (C/D).
*288 **BRUTAL FANTASY** 4 [8] P Howling 6-9-11 (71)(6ex) A McCarthy (3) 5/2: 25-214: Cl-up/wide, rdn & 1¼ 66a
outpcd fnl 2f: op 7/4, 6lb pen, qck reapp: not able to dominate as in 288 (6f, class stks).
291 **APPLES AND PEARS** 4 [1] 4-8-5 (51) A Whelan 8/1: 360-05: Dwelt/rdn & rear, mod prog: op 14/1, 2 41a
qck reapp: plcd sev times in '99 (rtd 55, h'cap, rtd 39a on sand, seller): rtd 69 at best in '98 (mdn): eff at 5f,
tried 6f: acts on gd grnd & fibresand: prob handles any trk: still a mdn but shown enough to win similar.
146 **KAYO GEE** 39 [3] 4-10-0 (74)(bl) Martin Dwyer 10/1: 0000-6: Rdn/rear, nvr factor: op 16/1: topweight: 2 59a
prev with A McNae, now with L Montague Hall: see 146.
291 **ORIEL STAR** 4 [6] 4-8-11 (57)(vis) Joanna Badger (7) 20/1: 000-07: Sn outpcd: qck reapp: vis reapp: 5 33a
'99 Windsor wnr (h'cap, rtd 67): '98 Ripon wnr (auct mdn, rtd 73 at best, first time blnks): eff at 5f, tried 6f:
acts on fast & soft grnd: loves a sharp trk: tried a visor, suited by blnks.
7 ran Time 58.99 (1.19) (Doug Graham) M Dods Piercebridge, Co Durham

---

313 1.25 CLASSIFIED STKS 3YO+ 0-60 (F) 6f aw rnd Going 27 -14 Slow
£2124 £607 £303 3 yo rec 16lb

246 **BEST QUEST** 9 [2] K R Burke 5-9-13 (t) N Callan (3) 7/4 FAV: 200-31: 5 b h Salse - Quest For The 70a
Best (Rainbow Quest) Cl-up, led halfway & rdn/clr 2f out, styd on well ins last, rdn out: plcd form in '99 (rtd 72a):
'98 Doncaster (clmr, rtd 65, J Gosden) & Lingfield wnr (h'cap, rtd 72a): eff at 6/7f, stays 1m on fast, gd & both
AWs: best without a visor: prob handles any trk, likes Lingfield: eff weight carrier.
263 **NINEACRES** 7 [11] J M Bradley 9-9-5 (bl) P Fitzsimons (5) 4/1: 102-32: 9 b g Sayf El Arab - Mayor 2½ 56a
(Laxton) Chsd ldrs halfway, rdn & kept on ins last, not pace to chall: op 7/2: see 214, 134 (fibresand).

130 **PALACEGATE TOUCH 43** [6] A Berry 10-9-7 (bl) P Bradley (5) 7/2: 6325-3: 10 gr g Petong - Dancing Chimes (London Bells) Chsd ldrs, briefly no room 2f out, kept on, not pace of wnr: op 3/1, abs: prev with J Berry. *shd* **58a**
138 **PAGEBOY 42** [3] P C Haslam 11-9-2 (vis) T Eaves (7) 12/1: 0066-4: Slowly away/towards rear, prog to chsd ldrs halfway, kept on ins last, no threat to wnr: op 7/1, abs: lost ch at the start, well h'capped 11yo. ¾ **51$**
154 **SPECKLED GEM 37** [4] 4-9-1 R Fitzpatrick (3) 100/1: 60/0-5: Led 3f, btn fnl 1f: no form from sole start in '99: rtd 55 & 50a at best in '98 (P Evans, tried visor & blnks): prob stays 6f & handles equitrack. 3½ **41$**
94 **FOX STAR 50** [1] 3-8-2 A Daly 20/1: 0600-6: Chsd ldrs, held fnl 2f: 7 wk abs: unplcd in '99 for R Hannon (rtd 67, auct fill mdn): eff at 5f, poss stays a sharp/undul 7f: prob handles firm & fast grnd. ½ **42a**
632} **BARR BEACON 99** [5] 4-9-2 L Carter 14/1: 2/50-7: Keen/prom 5f: op 12/1: 10 month abs: unplcd in '99 (rtd 51a, auct mdn): rnr-up in '98 (auct mdn, rtd 69a, rtd 56 on turf): eff at 5f on equitrack: tried blnks. ¾ **38a**
166 **MISTER RAIDER 33** [7] 8-9-3 (bl) S Carson (5) 25/1: 0500-8: Prom 3f, sn outpcd: see 139. *hd* **38a**
254 **MR CUBE 8** [13] 10-9-2 (bl) Claire Bryan (7) 25/1: 542-09: Dwelt/rdn & al twds rear: see 254 (1m). *nk* **36a**
205 **ELLWAY PRINCE 25** [8] 5-9-9 (vis) Dean McKeown 12/1: 0040-0: Cl-up wide 4f, fdd: 10th: op 10/1. ½ **41a**
263 **Dancing Jack 7** [14] 7-9-5 L Newman (5) 33/1: 247 **Royal Origine 9** [12] 4-9-7 (tbl) F Norton 25/1:
3411} **Courtney Gym 99** [9] 5-9-3 P McCabe 66/1: 265 **Rotherhithe 7** [10] 4-9-2 M Hills 20/1:
14 ran Time 1m 12.86 (2.46) (Nigel Shields) K R Burke Newmarket.

314

1.55 MALIBU MDN 4YO+ (D) 1m2f aw Going 27 -17 Slow
£2782 £856 £428 £214 4 yo rec 2 lb

189 **ROYAL FLAME 28** [5] J W Hills 4-8-9 (BL) M Hills 2/1: 2643-1: 4 b f Royal Academy - Samnaun (Stop The Music) Sn handy going well, led over 2f out & sn pulled clr, eased ins last, cmftbly: val for 12L+: op 9/4, first time blnks: rnr-up on turf in '99 (rtd 70, mdn, plcd on sand, rtd 55a): eff at 10f, tried 12f & shld suit: acts on both AWs & soft grnd: likes a sharp trk: imprvd by blnks today, can win again on this evidence. **68a**
210 **SPRINGTIME LADY 25** [6] S Dow 4-8-9 P Doe 7/4 FAV: 5220-2: 4 ch f Desert Dirham - Affaire de Coeur (Imperial Fling) Dwelt/rear, rdn & kept on fnl 2f to take poor 2nd: clr rem, op 2/1; longer 10f trip: see 152 (1m). *6* **58a**
255 **QUEEN OF THE KEYS 8** [2] S Dow 4-8-9 (vis) A Clark 16/1: 036-03: 4 b f Royal Academy - Piano Belle (Fappiano) Dwelt/rear, prog/chsd ldrs 3f out, sn held: op 10/1: best around 1m: see 233, 147 (h'cap, 1m). *5* **51$**
4283} **REACHFORYOURPOCKET 96** [9] M D I Usher 5-9-2 Martin Dwyer 33/1: 6660-4: Chsd ldrs, rdn/outpcd fnl 3f: 3 month abs/AW bow: unplcd for K Mahdi in '99 (rtd 64, debut, subs tried blnks & t-strap & suffered breathing problems): prev tried at up to 9f, may improve in sellers on sand. 2½ **52a**
3218} **MOUTON 99** [3] 4-8-9 L Newman (5) 11/2: 5322-5: Led after 3f, rdn/hdd over 2f out & sn btn: op 4/1: 5 month abs/AW bow: rnr-up in '99 (rtd 65, auct mdn, J W Hills): stays 9f, handles fast & gd: now with J J Bridger. 1¼ **45a**
267 **SKY CITY 7** [4] 4-8-9 A McCarthy (3) 25/1: 000-56: Chsd ldrs 7f: see 267. ¾ **44$**
4308} **WAR BABY 93** [1] 4-8-9 C Rutter 33/1: 0500-7: Led 3f, btn 3f out: abs/AW bow: unplcd in '99 (rtd 46). *hd* **44a**
1415} **DION DEE 99** [10] 4-8-9 F Norton 20/1: 00/0-8: Prom 7f: op 14/1: AW bow, now with Dr J R J Naylor. 1¾ **42a**
2164} **KUMON EILEEN 99** [7] 4-8-9 S Whitworth 33/1: 00-9: Chsd ldrs 6f: jumps fit, AW bow. *11* **30a**
1352} **COPYFORCE BOY 99** [11] 4-9-0 (t) S Carson (5) 33/1: 00/0-0: Wide/rear, bhd halfway: 10th: abs/AW bow. *13* **21a**
238 **ILISSUS 14** [8] 4-9-0 W Ryan 7/1: 32U0-0: Bhd halfway: 11th: op 5/2: see 238 (C/D). 2½ **17a**
11 ran Time 2m 07.24 (4.44) (Willy Coleman) J W Hills Upper Lambourn, Berks.

315

2.30 JAFFA HCAP 3YO 0-65 (F) 1m2f aw Going 27 -18 Slow **[72]**
£2310 £660 £330

188 **SPECIAL PROMISE 28** [2] P C Haslam 3-8-7 (51) Dean McKeown 8/1: 6005-1: 3 ch g Anjiz - Woodenitbenice (Nasty And Bold) Held up in tch, trkd ldrs when no room 3f out, styd on strongly ins last to lead nr line, rdn out: unplcd in '99 (rtd 61 & 55a): apprec step up to 10f, 12f+ cld suit: acts on equitrack: can win again. **62a**
4339} **KATHAKALI 92** [8] V Soane 3-9-2 (60) Martin Dwyer 25/1: 5400-2: 3 b c Dancing Dissident - She's A Dancer (Alzao) Rdn rear, chsd ldrs 4f out, led dist, just hdd nr line: clr of rem, AW bow, 3 month abs: unplcd in '99 (rtd 69, nov auct stks, subs tried a visor): apprec step up to 10f, 12f+ cld suit: acts on equitrack & fast: handles a sharp/gall trk: fine h'cap bow, likely type for compensation. *nk* **68a**
240 **BOX CAR 10** [1] G L Moore 3-9-1 (59) F Norton 7/1: 662-53: 3 b c Blues Traveller - Racey Naskra (Star de Naskra) Led, rdn/hdd over 1f out, no extra: op 5/1: stays a sharp 10f & handles equitrack: see 204 (C/D). *5* **60a**
158 **MAID TO LOVE 35** [6] G A Butler 3-9-2 (60) W Ryan 5/1: 0223-4: Prom, rdn/ev ch 2f out, no extra ins last: op 7/2: clr of rem but prob not quite stay longer 10f trip: see 158, 54 (1m). *3* **57a**
236 **RIDGECREST 14** [3] 3-8-13 (57) S Drowne 5/1: 4242-5: Cl-up, wknd fnl 2f: op 7/1: longer 10f trip. *12* **40a**
240 **ODYN DANCER 10** [10] 3-8-6 (50) G Baker (7) 12/1: 003-66: Wide/rear & bhd early, late gains, no threat to ldrs: op 7/1: longer 10f trip, apprec stronger handling: see 240, 150 (seller, 1m). *hd* **32a**
240 **LE CAVALIER 10** [5] 3-9-3 (61)(bl) R Morse 16/1: 040-07: Cl-up 7f: op 14/1: btr 240 (C/D). 2½ **39a**
4614} **CINEMA POINT 67** [7] 3-7-12 (42) A Mackay 25/1: 000-8: Rdn/rear early, chsd ldrs halfway, sn held: h'cap/AW bow: 10 wk abs: unplcd on turf in '99 (rtd 48, debut): longer 10f trip today. ¾ **19a**
158 **DONT WORRY BOUT ME 35** [12] 3-9-4 (62) A Clark 20/1: 3000-9: Rdn chasing ldrs halfway, sn held. *5* **32a**
240 **LAGO DI COMO 10** [11] 3-9-7 (65) N Callan (3) 6/1: 000-30: Keen/prom wide 6f: 10th: btr 240. *6* **26a**
241 **DR DUKE 10** [4] 3-8-3 (47) Dale Gibson 14/1: 555-40: Chsd ldrs 7f, wknd qckly: 11th: see 241 (1m). *2* **5a**
*266 **SHAMSAN 7** [9] 3-9-11 (69)(6ex) J Fanning 5/2 FAV: 064-10: Prom, rdn/wknd halfway & sn bhd: connections unable to offer explanation: see 266 (4 rnr h'cap, made all, 1m). *20* **5a**
12 ran Time 2m 07.25 (4.45) (R Young) P C Haslam Middleham, N.Yorks.

316

3.00 BASIL SELLER 4YO+ (G) 1m aw rnd Going 27 -10 Slow
£1951 £557 £278

239 **APOLLO RED 14** [3] G L Moore 11-9-5 A Clark 4/9 FAV: 0613-1: 11 ch g Dominion - Woolpack (Golden Fleece) Sn led, rdn 2f out, held on well ins last, rdn out: hvly bckd, no bid: '99 wnr here at Lingfield (sell, rtd 76a & 74): '98 Brighton wnr (h'cap, rtd 74 & 72a): stays 1m, suited by 6/7f: acts on firm, soft & equitrack: loves to force the pace on a sharp trk, esp Brighton/Lingfield: eff with/without blnks/visor: genuine 11yo. **65a**
276 **SCROOGE 6** [2] M H Tompkins 4-9-0 A Whelan 16/1: 050-32: 4 b g Tirol - Gay Appeal (Star Appeal) Dwelt, sn chsd ldrs, rdn/chsd wnr 2f out, kept on tho' not able to chall: op 10/1, qck reapp: eff at 7f/1m: handles both AWs: clr of rem here: see 276. ¾ **58$**
208 **SERGEANT IMP 25** [8] P Mitchell 5-9-0 M Tebbutt 16/1: 0600-3: 5 b g Mac's Imp - Genzyme Gene (Riboboy) Rear, rdn & kept on well fnl 1f, nrst fin: rnr-up in '99 (h'cap, rtd 47): '98 Brighton wnr (ltd stks, rtd 54, visored): eff over 6f/1m, tried further: eff with/without blnks/visor: handles fast, gd/soft & equitrack. *5* **48$**
154 **SURE TO DREAM 37** [7] R T Phillips 7-8-9 (bl) R Perham 20/1: 0000-4: Sn cl-up, wknd over 1f out: op 10/1: '99 Southwell wnr (h'cap, rtd 55a, no turf form): '98 Southwell wnr (h'cap, rtd 53a & 43): eff at 5f, *nk* **42a**

LINGFIELD (Equitrack) WEDNESDAY JANUARY 12TH Lefthand, V Sharp Track

suited by 6/7f: acts on both AWs & gd/soft grnd: has run well fresh: likes a sharp trk, esp Southwell.
187 **CHURCHILLS SHADOW 28** [4] 6-9-0 O Urbina 7/1: 2453-5: Chsd ldrs halfway, no extra over 1f out. ¾ **46a**
262 **PRIVATE SEAL 7** [1] 5-9-0 (t) A Daly 33/1: 000-56: Dwelt & rdn/rear, mod gains: see 262 (6f). 3 **40$**
163 **SHAMWARI SONG 33** [9] 5-9-0 J P Spencer 16/1: 0065-7: Prom 6f: op 10/1: see 163. 3½ **33a**
298 **GADGE 2** [10] 9-9-0 S Carson (5) 12/1: 400-08: Wide/led 1f, btn 2f out: op 8/1, qck reapp: see 83. *hd* **32a**
2127} **NICHOLAS MISTRESS 99** [6] 4-8-9 Joanna Badger (7) 25/1: 0000-9: Rear, hmpd aftr 2f, no impress: 2½ **22a**
op 14/1, 7 month abs: '99 wnr here at Lingfield (h'cap, rtd 49a, unplcd on turf, rtd 35): plcd in '98 (rtd 61, h'cap & rtd 47a, seller): eff at 6/7f: acts on fast, soft & both AWs: best without a visor: likes a sharp trk.
252 **MUSTANG 9** [11] 7-9-0 (bl) G Bardwell 12/1: 454-30: Chsd ldrs 4f: 10th: op 8/1: see 252, 59. 1½ **24a**
193 **ENTROPY 28** [12] 4-8-9 R Havlin 33/1: 0050-0: Sn bhd: 11th: op 16/1. 5 **9a**
11 ran Time 1m 39.13 (2.93) (A Moore) G L Moore Woodingdean, E Sussex

317 3.35 JERICHO HCAP 4YO+ 0-70 (E) 1m5f aw Going 27 +07 Fast [69]
£3461 £1065 £532 £266 4 yo rec 5 lb

151 **RAYIK 37** [6] G L Moore 5-9-5 (60) G Parkin 8/1: 0060-1: 5 br g Marju - Matila (Persian Bold) **70a**
Trkd ldr, led 2f out, forged clr ins last, rdn out: fast time: rnr-up in '99 (h'cap, rtd 81a): '98 Lingfield wnr (mdn, N Berry, rtd 76): eff at 10/12f, acts on both AWs: likes a sharp trk, esp Lingfield: on a fair mark.
*290 **LOST SPIRIT 4** [5] P W Hiatt 4-8-5 (51)(6ex) G Baker (7) 5/1: 660-12: 4 b g Strolling Along - Shoag 2½ **56a**
(Affirmed) Led, rdn/hdd 2f out, kept on well tho' held ins last: clr rem under 6lb pen: op 4/1, qck reapp: eff at 12/13f: front rnr in fine heart, should win more races: see 290 (12f).
3535} **BAISSE DARGENT 99** [1] D J S Cosgrove 4-8-6 (52) J Stack 10/1: 0600-3: 4 b g Common Grounds - 6 **48a**
Fabulous Pet (Somethingfabulous) Chsd ldrs halfway, rdn/held fnl 2f: op 7/1: 8 wk jumps abs, twice a wnr at Huntingdon this term (rtd 111h): unplcd on turf in '99 (rtd 66, h'cap): '98 Musselburgh wnr (auct mdn, rtd 79): eff at 1m, shld stay further: acts on fast & gd: best without blnks on a sharp trk: AW bow today.
141 **ANOTHER MONK 39** [9] R Ingram 9-8-8 (49) A Clark 5/2: 3320-4: Chsd ldrs 3f out, sn held: well 1¾ **43a**
bckd, op 7/2: prev with B Johnson, more expected here: see 141, 6.
245 **STEAMROLLER STANLY 10** [4] 7-10-0 (69)(vis) N Callan (3) 9/4 FAV: 433-35: Chsd ldrs 10f: well bckd. 7 **53a**
231 **KI CHI SAGA 16** [8] 8-7-12 (37)(bl)(2ow)(3oh) F Norton 14/1: 4020-6: Rear, nvr a factor: see 219, 115. 6 **14a**
245 **SEA DANZIG 10** [2] 7-9-8 (63) A Daly 10/1: 000-57: Held up, bhd 4f out: tchd 12/1: see 245. 1½ **36a**
163 **COLONEL NORTH 33** [7] 4-9-3 (63) M Hills 14/1: 6640-8: Bhd 5f out: op 10/1: see 90 (10f). 2½ **32a**
231 **SOME MIGHT SAY 16** [3] 5-8-3 (44)(BL) T Williams 12/1: 12-0-9: Chsd ldrs, struggling halfway: *dist* **0a**
op 10/1, blnks: mod form over jumps this winter: no form sole '99 Flat start: '98 wnr here at Lingfield (with M Johnston, mdn, rtd 68a), rnr-up on turf (rtd 70, h'cap): eff at 10f, stays 14f: acts on both AWs & fast grnd: handles a sharp/gall trk: has run well fresh & likes to force the pace: with N Hawke.
9 ran Time 2m 44.93 (2.63) (Lancing Racing Syndicate) G L Moore Woodingdean, E Sussex

WOLVERHAMPTON (Fibresand) THURSDAY JANUARY 13TH Lefthand, Sharp Track

Official Going STANDARD. Stalls: 7f - Outside; Rem - Inside.

318 1.40 PROBLEM SHARED HCAP 4YO+ 0-65 (F) 2m46y aw Going 24 -41 Slow [60]
£2320 £663 £331 4 yo rec 7 lb

284 **MEDELAI 6** [4] Mrs A E Johnson 4-8-2 (41) A McCarthy (3) 12/1: 502-01: 4 b f Marju - No Islands **45a**
(Lomond) Chsd ldrs, hdwy to lead 2f out, prsd dist, drvn out to hold on: quick reapp: unplcd on turf in '99 (h'caps, rtd 47 at best, J Bethell): '98 Nottingham wnr (sell, rtd 59): eff at 1m/10f, suited by 2m now: acts on gd, soft & fibresand: acts on a sharp or stiff/gall trk: tough.
261 **HARVEY WHITE 9** [5] J Pearce 8-8-5 (37)(VIS) G Bardwell 33/1: 006-02: 8 b g Petorius - Walkyria 1 **39a**
(Lord Gayle) Keen in tch, hdwy to lead over 4f out, hdd 2f out, ev ch until no extra well ins last: plcd on sand in '99 (h'caps, rtd 41a), unplcd on turf (h'caps, rtd 38 at best): plcd in '98, prev term won at Lingfield (h'cap, rtd 58 & 41a): eff at 12f/2m: acts on firm, gd & both AWs: sharpened up by visor today.
4592} **LADY RACHEL 71** [8] M W Easterby 5-9-0 (46) G Parkin 14/1: 0000-3: 5 gr m Priolo - Alpine Spring 1 **47a**
(Head For Heights) Mid-div, smooth hdwy 5f out, rdn & kept on onepcd ins last: op 10/1, abs: plcd twice in '99 (h'caps, rtd 59, with J L Eyre): '98 scorer at Pontefract & Carlisle (h'caps, rtd 69 at best): eff btwn 10f & 2m on firm, hvy & fibresand: runs well fresh: back to form here for new connections, win similar.
285 **BEAUCHAMP MAGIC 5** [9] M D I Usher 5-8-4 (36) G Baker (7) 14/1: 016-04: Bhd, styd on well fnl *nk* **37a**
4f, nvr nrr: quick reapp: fair eff: impossible task in 285, see 141.
261 **HILL FARM DANCER 9** [6] 9-7-12 (30) C Cogan (2) 14/1: 403-55: Settled rear, gd hdwy over 3f out, ½ **30a**
kept on, nrst fin: op 10/1: prob stays 2m: see 231 (sell).
*277 **HIGHLY PRIZED 7** [2] 6-10-3 (63)(6ex) S Drowne 3/1 FAV: 543-16: Led to over 4f out, rdn & 9 **56a**
wknd 2f out, eased: nicely bckd, quick reapp: poss too soon after 277 (14f).
190 **MUSALSE 29** [7] 5-9-3 (49) P Goode (5) 20/1: 6000-7: Rear, prog halfway, no extra fnl 4f: plcd twice 7 **36a**
in '99 (h'caps, rtd 54a & 36), subs rnr-up over hdles (2m6f nov, rtd 93h, firm): '98 wnr at Lingfield (rtd 52a), Redcar, Catterick & Warwick (h'caps, rtd 60): eff at 14f/2m on fast & both AWs: has tried visor, best without.
*260 **MANFUL 9** [12] 8-8-1 (33)(bl)(6ex) Dale Gibson 100/30: 300-18: Bhd, nvr a threat: best at 10/12f. 6 **15a**
66 **PAWSIBLE 57** [11] 4-8-6 (45) R Price 9/1: 3163-9: Chsd ldrs, rdn/lost tch fnl 4f: op 7/1: 8 wk abs. *nk* **27a**
231 **AMBIDEXTROUS 17** [3] 8-7-12 (30) J Bramhill 12/1: 2002-0: Handy, grad fdd from halfway: 10th. *nk* **12a**
284 **CRASH CALL LADY 6** [10] 4-7-12 (37)(2ow)(3oh) N Carlisle 14/1: 432-00: Al bhd, fin 11th: btr 190. 1½ **17a**
194 **MY LEGAL EAGLE 29** [1] 6-8-10 (42) Claire Bryan (7) 10/1: 3204-0: Cl-up, rdn & wknd qckly fnl 6f: 12th. 5 **17a**
12 ran Time 3m 39.8 (10.6) (Chasers IV) Mrs A E Johnson Newmarket

319 2.10 LITTLE ACORNS MDN 3YO (D) 1m1f79y Going 24 -40 Slow
£2795 £860 £430 £215

171 **YOURE SPECIAL 33** [3] P C Haslam 3-9-0 M Tebbutt 8/11 FAV: 5202-1: 3 b g Northern Flagship - **82a**
Pillow Mint (Stagedoor Johnny) Chsd ldrs, outpcd 6f out, ran on well appr fnl 1f, led ins last, pushed out, rdly: nicely bckd: rnr-up in '99 (auct mdn, rtd 81): eff at 1m, stays 9.4f well & mid-dists shld suit: acts on gd, gd/soft & fibresand: acts on a sharp trk: improving, shld win more AW races this term.
171 **ATALYA 33** [6] F Jordan 3-9-0 N Callan (3) 33/1: 060-2: 3 ch g Afzal - Sandy Looks (Music Boy) 1½ **75$**
Dwelt, keen & sn with ldrs, led over 3f out, hdd & not pace of wnr ins last: op 12/1, clr rem: unplcd on turf

in '99 (mdn, rtd 70): appr today's step up to 9.4f on fibresand: gd run & clr of rem today, can land similar.
264　**ROYAL IVY 8** [2]　J Akehurst 3-8-9 P Doe 7/2: 032-23: 3 ch f Mujtahid - Royal Climber (King's　　8　58a
Lake) Led till over 3f out, sn lost tch: op 2/1: up in trip: btr 264 (1m, equitrack).
3672}　**TORMENTOSO 99** [7]　M R Channon 3-9-0 S Drowne 11/2: -050-4: Prom, not pace of ldrs fnl 3f:　　4　57a
op 4/1, long abs/AW bow: unplcd on turf in '99 (7f/1m mdns, rtd 82 at best, fast & gd grnd).
4613}　**THE FINAL WORD 68** [9]　A Culhane 16/1: -5-5: Dwelt & well in rear, rdn & prog 3f out, eased　　3　47a
when btn ins last: AW bow: 5th on sole '99 start (1m auct mdn, hvy, rtd 62): lost all ch at start here.
265　**BAHAMIAN PRINCE 8** [4]　3-9-0 (VIS) M Hills 20/1: 00-06: Chsd ldrs, fdd fnl 2f: up in　　4　46$
trip/fibresand debut: tried a visor: see 221 (equitrack).
2420}　**UPPER BULLENS 99** [5]　3-9-0 A Mackay 16/1: 644-7: Al rear: op 10/1 on reapp: AW bow:　　2½　42a
rtd 66 at best from 3 unplcd '99 turf starts (nov stks, 7.5f, gd/soft grnd).
198　**ROYAL CZARINA 27** [8]　3-8-9 D Dineley 50/1: 0-8: Waited with, lost tch fnl 3f, eased: see 198.　　1½　34a
273　**BEST MUSIC METROFM 7** [1]　3-9-0 J Bramhill 50/1: 3-09: Prom, wknd 5f out, t.o.: no AW form.　　dist　0a
9 ran　　Time 2m 04.2 (6.0)　　(Les Buckley)　　P C Haslam Middleham, N Yorks

---

320　　2.40 SILVER LINING HCAP 3YO+ 0-100 (C)　　6f aw rnd　Going 24　+16 Fast　　[95]
£6695　　£2060　　£1030　　£515

4572}　**THE DOWNTOWN FOX 73** [7]　B A McMahon 5-8-9 (76)(vis) L Newman (5) 12/1: 0010-1: 5 br g Primo　　86a
Dominie - Sara Sprint (Formidable) Cl-up, smooth hdwy to lead ins last, rdn clr: v fast time: AW bow: '99 wnr
at York (class stks, rtd 81): '98 wnr at Leicester (h'cap, rtd 86), plcd thrice prev term (rtd 82): eff at 6/7f:
handles firm, likes gd, hvy & f/sand: runs well fresh on a gall or sharp trk: eff with/without blnks/visor.
+175　**CHERISH ME 33** [8]　J G Given 4-8-12 (79) A Culhane 5/1: 3011-2: 4 b f Polar Falcon - Princess　　3½　80a
Zepoli (Persepolis) Cl-up, ev ch until not pace of wnr ins last: op 3/1: not disgraced, shld wn again sn: see 175.
258　**JUWWI 9** [9]　J M Bradley 6-9-2 (83) Claire Bryan (7) 6/1: 155-33: 6 ch g Mujtahid - Nouvelle Star　　nk　84a
(Luskin Star) Sn outpcd, ran on strongly appr fnl 1f, nvr nrr: op 9/2: consistent, win similar sn: see 129.
223　**CLASSY CLEO 22** [6]　P D Evans 5-10-0 (95) Joanna Badger (7) 10/1: 2132-4: In tch, lost place over　　¾　95a
3f out, hmpd & switched over 1f out, ran on strongly, nvr nrr: unlucky in running here: v tough: see 64.
272　**KRYSTAL MAX 7** [12]　L Carter 16/1: 420-25: Chsd ldrs, ev ch until outpcd dist: qck reapp.　　nk　77a
*258　**BLUE KITE 9** [3]　5-8-11 (78)(6ex) T G McLaughlin 9/4 FAV: 261-16: Handy, rdn to improve 2f out,　　hd　77a
no extra fnl 1f: nicely bckd on hat-trick bid: shade disapp here, btr 258.
2081}　**RIFIFI 99** [10]　7-8-11 (78) A Clark 20/1: 0000-7: Nvr btr than mid-div: long abs: rnr-up on turf in '99　　1¾　73a
(h'cap, rtd 80): '98 wnr at Newbury, Sandown (rtd 80) & Lingfield (h'caps, rtd 79a): won 5 h'caps in '97: eff
at 5/6f, stays a sharp 7f: acts on firm, gd & equitrack: handles any trk, likes Lingfield.
223　**PRINCE PROSPECT 22** [4]　4-9-4 (85) J P Spencer 33/1: 6400-8: Handy, led 4f out, hdd 1f out, wknd.　　1½　76a
216　**DIL 23** [2]　5-9-10 (91) R Fitzpatrick 9/1: 0503-9: Led, hdd 4f out, fdn & fdd fnl 2f: btr 216.　　½　81a
129　**ROYAL CASCADE 44** [5]　6-8-13 (80)(bl.) S Righton 25/1: 0350-0: Slow start, nvr a threat, fin 10th:　　3½　61a
6 wk abs: lost all ch at start today: btr 33 (7f).
258　**MALLIA 9** [11]　7-8-5 (72)(bl) T Williams 11/1: 460-40: Chsd ldrs, no extra halfway: 11th: see 258.　　2　48a
223　**BOLD EFFORT 22** [13]　8-9-1 (92)(bl) M Hills 33/1: 4000-0: Prom, rdn & wknd qckly fnl 2f: 12th.　　shd　68a
12 ran　　Time 1m 13.3 (0.5)　　(Mrs J McMahon)　　B A McMahon Hopwas, Staffs

---

321　　3.10 MORE HASTE COND STKS 4YO+ (C)　　1m100y aw rnd　Going 24　+04 Fast
£5860　　£2167　　£1083　　£246

1145}　**WELVILLE 99** [2]　P J Makin 7-9-0 (t) A Clark 5/2: 1210-1: 7 b g Most Welcome - Miss Topville　　104a
(Top Ville) Keen & made all, chall 1f out, rdn out ins last: nicely bckd: gd time: long abs: v prog on sand in
'99, won at Lingfield (2) & here at W'hampton (h'caps, rtd 92): lightly rcd since '95 Goodwood wnr (mdn, rtd 92):
eff at 7/8.4f on gd/soft & both AWs: likes sharp trks & runs esp well fresh, with t-strap: loves to force the pace.
*230　**WEET A MINUTE 17** [3]　R Hollinshead 7-9-0 A Culhane 9/4 FAV: 2201-2: 7 ro h Nabeel Dancer -　　¾　102a
Ludovica (Bustino) Chsd wnr thr'out, ev ch till no extra ins last: nicely bckd tho' op 6/4: tough & useful.
230　**KING PRIAM 17** [1]　M J Polglase 5-9-0 (bl) T G McLaughlin 7/2: 1152-3: 5 b g Priolo - Barinia　　1　100a
(Corvaro) Prom, lost pl halfway, ran on strongly ins last, nvr nrr: gd run, eff at 1m, will apprec return to 9f+.
49　**WEETMANS WEIGH 59** [5]　R Hollinshead 7-9-0 N Callan (3) 4/1: 4222-4: Rdn/rear, nvr a danger:　　5　92a
op 3/1, 8 wk abs: stable-mate of rnr-up: 10 of his 12 wins have come at 6/7f: see 49.
244　**ITALIAN SYMPHONY 11** [4]　6-9-6 (vis) J P Spencer 16/1: 415-05: Prom, wknd fnl 2f: op 10/1:　　10　85a
stiff task at the weights here: btr 216 (7f h'cap).
5 ran　　Time 1m 47.9 (1.7)　　(T G Warner)　　P J Makin Ogbourne Maisey, Wilts

---

322　　3.45 PENNY WISE SELLER 4YO+ (G)　　1m100y aw rnd　Going 24　-24 Slow
£1981　　£566　　£283

292　**WESTMINSTER CITY 5** [2]　K O Cunningham Brown 4-9-0 (vis) M Hills 11/4: 00-321: 4 b c Alleged -　　54a
Promanade Fan (Timeless Moment) Cl-up, gd hdwy to lead dist, pushed out, rdly: nicely bckd, qck reapp, bt by D
Elsworth for 6,200gns: unplcd in '99 (rtd 63 & 62a): '98 scorer at Lingfield (debut, rtd 79, C Brittain): eff
at 6/8.4f, has tried 2m: acts on gd & fibresand, handles fast grnd: eff with/without visor: prob on a fair mark.
*238　**BILLICHANG 15** [9]　P Howling 4-9-5 T Williams 8/1: 0301-2: 4 b c Chilibang - Swing O'The Kilt　　1¾　54a
(Hotfoot) Led till 6f out, drvn to lead again 5f out, hdd appr fnl 1f & not pace of wnr: will apprec return to 10f.
176　**ETISALAT 31** [10]　J Pearce 5-9-5 A Polli (3) 12/1: 0010-3: 5 b g Lahib - Sweet Repose (High Top)　　¾　53$
Waited with, smooth prog halfway, ev ch until no extra ins last: op 10/1: see 100 (10f h'cap, equitrack).
259　**APPROACHABLE 9** [12]　Miss S J Wilton 5-9-0 T G McLaughlin 4/1: 40-254: Settled rear, gd hdwy　　1　46a
5f out, ev ch when twice tried to bite Guest Envoy 2f out, onepcd over 1f out: see 45.
292　**BOBS BUSTER 5** [5]　4-9-0 A Culhane 20/1: 005-05: Chsd ldrs, lost place & no room 4f out, late　　4　40a
gains: quick reapp: plcd once on turf in '99 (auct mdn, rtd 57 at best): stays 1m & handles soft & hvy grnd.
295　**DILETTO 5** [11]　4-8-9 S Drowne 20/1: 06-006: Nvr better than mid-div: quick reapp: see 295.　　1½　32a
256　**SHARP SHUFFLE 9** [1]　7-9-5 R Fitzpatrick 3/1 FAV: 110-27: Bhd, rdn/eff 6f out, no danger:　　3　37a
nicely bckd: much better expected here: btr 256 (C/D, clmr).
4213}　**GUEST ENVOY 99** [7]　5-8-9 L Newman (5) 14/1: 4050-8: With ldr, ev ch when nearly bitten by　　1¾　24a
Approachable 2f out, wknd qckly fnl 1f: reapp: '99 scorer here at W'hampton (h'cap, rtd 62a at best):
'98 wnr at Hamilton (h'cap, rtd 47): eff at 6f/8.5f: acts on gd, soft & fibresand.
252　**MR ROUGH 10** [6]　9-9-0 (vis) M Tebbutt 10/1: 052-09: Nvr a threat: btr 138.　　9　15a
3912}　**AFTER EIGHT 99** [4]　5-9-0 R Price 33/1: 0600-0: Chsd ldrs, led briefly 6f out, wknd halfway, fin 10th:　　hd　15a
unplcd in '99 (rtd 50a & 44): '98 Lingfield wnr (sell, rtd 68a & 56): best up with/forcing the pace over 6f,

stays a sharp 7f: acts on fast grnd & equitrack: eff in blnks.
3323} **COURT HOUSE 99** [8] 6-9-0 Claire Bryan (7) 50/1: 0-65-0: Sn rdn in rear, fin 11th: unplcd in 2 '99 starts (stks, rtd 31, B Johnson): rtd 41 for M Chapman in '98, prev term won at Pontefract (sell, rtd 64 at best, B McMahon): eff at 6f/1m on firm & gd: now with R J Price. *7* **5a**
272 **DIVIDE AND RULE 7** [3] 6-9-0 J P Spencer 50/1: 000-00: Mid-div, lost tch 5f out, t.o., 12th: qck reapp. *24* **0a**
12 ran Time 1m 50.3 (4.1) (A J Richards) K O Cunningham Brown Stockbridge, Hants

323 **4.15 FRIEND IN NEED HCAP 4YO+ 0-75 (E) 7f aw Going 24 -26 Slow [73]**
£2873 £884 £442 £221

*282 **SAND HAWK 6** [7] D Shaw 5-9-1 (60)(vis)(6ex) A Clark 11/8 FAV: 12-211: 5 ch g Polar Falcon - Ghassanah (Pas de Seul) Dwelt, rdn & plenty to do 2f out, ran on strongly appr fnl 1f, drvn out to lead fnl strides: qck reapp: recent Southwell wnr (h'cap): '99 wnr at W'hampton (mdn, rtd 54a & 47): plcd in '98 (h'caps, rtd 51 & 50a): eff at 6/7f, stays 1m: acts on fast & gd/soft, loves f/sand & any trk: eff in blnks/visor: runs well fresh. **67a**
216 **RONS PET 23** [12] K R Burke 5-9-11 (70)(tvi) N Callan (3) 7/1: 0260-2: 5 ch g Ron's Victory - Penny Mint (Mummy's Game) Prom, led over 1f out, rdn/hdd fnl strides: op 9/2: clr rem: win again sn: see 33. *hd* **75a**
293 **PUPPET PLAY 5** [9] E J Alston 5-8-5 (50) S Drowne 12/1: 422-33: 5 ch m Broken Hearted - Fantoccini (Taufan) Led, hdd 4f out, led again over 2f out, hdd dist & no extra: quick reapp: worth another try at 1m now. *3½* **49a**
216 **GIFT OF GOLD 23** [6] A Bailey 5-9-0 (59) A Mackay 8/1: 3040-4: In tch, chall 3f out, no extra fnl 2f. *¾* **57a**
274 **C HARRY 7** [1] 6-9-6 (65) J P Spencer 8/1: 03-525: Waited with, lost place halfway, late gains ins last: quick reapp: will apprec a return to sell grade: see 130. *hd* **63a**
250 **SO WILLING 10** [4] 4-8-10 (55)(vis) F Lynch 25/1: 000-06: Cl-up, ev ch until wknd ins last, eased eased: will apprec a return to 6f: see 183. *¾* **52a**
255 **DANZAS 9** [11] 6-7-10 (41)(bl)(1oh) J Bramhill 10/1: 025-67: Dwelt & bhd, late gains, nvr a threat. *nk* **38a**
226 **FACILE TIGRE 17** [8] 5-8-8 (53) P Doe 16/1: 4466-8: In tch, brief eff 2f out, sn btn: see 146 (5f). *¾* **49a**
3766} **MUJKARI 99** [3] 4-7-10 (41)(vis) G Bardwell 20/1: 2160-9: Dwelt, al bhd: reapp: '99 scorer at Brighton (mdn h'cap, rtd 42, also rtd 47a): unplcd for R Hannon in '98 (rtd 58): eff over a sharp 7f: acts on firm grnd: eff in a visor, has tried blnks: handles a sharp/undul trk. *2½* **32a**
262 **PRIORY GARDENS 8** [5] 6-7-10 (41)(1oh) Claire Bryan (7) 6/1: 050-30: Nvr btr than mid-div, fin 10th. *¾* **31a**
273 **FOUND AT LAST 7** [2] 4-8-8 (53) T G McLaughlin 8/1: 005-30: Cl-up, led 4f out till 2f out, wknd qckly, eased when btn: 11th: quick reapp: a drop back to 6f shld suit: see 273 (mdn). *1½* **40a**
4472} **STORM CRY 83** [10] 5-9-9 (68) C Carver (3) 20/1: 6100-0: In tch, lost tch fnl 2f, fin 12th: seasonal/ AW bow: '99 wnr at Lingfield (h'cap, rtd 77 at best): '98 Bath wnr (mdn auct, rtd 83, D Chappell): eff at 7f/ 1m on firm & soft, prob any trk: likes to force the pace & eff in a t-strap (not worn today). *1¾* **52a**
12 ran Time 1m 29.7 (3.5) (J C Fretwell) D Shaw Averham, Notts

SOUTHWELL (Fibresand) FRIDAY JANUARY 14TH Lefthand, Sharp, Oval Track

Official Going STANDARD. Stalls: Inside.

324 **12.20 AMAT HCAP DIV 1 4YO+ 0-65 (G) 1m3f aw Going 57 -09 Slow [35]**
£1568 £448 £224 4 yo rec 3 lb

4458} **SWAGGER 85** [4] Sir Mark Prescott 4-10-4 (42) Mr I Mongan 5/4 FAV: 3416-1: 4 ch g Generous - Widows Walk (Habitat) Prom, led ent str, sn clr, cmftbly: 12 wk abs, hvly bckd: '99 wnr here at Southwell (amat h'cap, rtd 45a, plcd on turf, mdn h'cap, rtd 43): eff at 11f/14f, stays a stiff 2m1f: acts on firm, likes fibresand, goes on any trk, likes Southwell: best up with/forcing the pace: runs well fresh. **52a**
131 **CLARINCH CLAYMORE 45** [1] J M Jefferson 4-10-10 (48) Mr T Best (5) 5/1: 1420-2: 4 b g Sabrehill - Salu (Ardross) Narrow lead, hard prsd halfway & hdd over 3f out, outpcd by wnr: 6 wk abs: better effort with forcing tactics: acts on fast, soft grnd & fibresand, any trk: see 131. *3½* **51a**
285 **ST LAWRENCE 6** [8] N Tinkler 6-10-7 (42) Mr Nicky Tinkler (7) 6/1: 060-23: 6 gr g With Approval - Mingan Isle (Lord Avie) Wide in tch, prog to chase ldrs 4f out, same pace: back in trip, op 4/1, qk reapp. *1½* **44a**
255 **MYTTONS MOMENT 10** [5] A Bailey 4-10-12 (50)(bl) Miss Bridget Gatehouse (5) 10/1: 633-44: Struggled to go pace, went past btn horses in the straight: jop 8/1: jumps rnr since 255, see 85. *9* **43a**
259 **ABSOLUTE MAJORITY 10** [10] 5-11-1 (50) Miss S Pocock (5) 14/1: 040-25: Wide, nvr nr to chall: op 10/1. *1* **42a**
261 **EVEZIO RUFO 10** [2] 8-10-5 (40) Mr O Gunter (7) 8/1: 455-46: Prsd lead till halfway, fdd 3f out: tchd 10/1. *9* **24a**
224 **EI EI 23** [6] 5-10-0 (35) Mr A Quinn (7) 40/1: 0000-7: Chsd ldrs 1m: drop back in trip?: see 224. *6* **14a**
37 **PALAIS 63** [12] 5-11-7 (56) Mrs M Morris (3) 16/1: 5000-8: Al towards rear: top-weight, 7 wk jmps abs (unplcd, 100/1, flattered 4th, rtd 94h): early '99 wnr here at Southwell (mdn, rtd 66a & 58): with Sir M Stoute in '98 (mdn/h'cap, rtd 78): eff at 11f, tried 2m: acts on fibresand, prob fast: tried vis, prob best up with the pace. *3½* **32a**
4525} **MODEST HOPE 79** [13] 13-9-3 (24)(3oh) Mr S Dobson (3) 33/1: 0000-9: V slow away, al bhd: 6 wk jumps absence, long standing mdn (stays 2m2f on gd & firm): '99 rnr-up on the level (sell h'cap, rtd 28a): '98 wnr at Brighton (sell h'cap, rtd 32): eff at 10/12f, stays 14f: acts on any grnd, both AWs, without visor. *¾* **0a**
248 **SEASON OF HOPE 11** [11] 4-9-9 (33) Miss Hayley Bryan (7) 20/1: 554-30: V wide rear, sn btn: 10th. *2* **6a**
70 **Grooms Gold 56** [7] 8-10-9 (44) Mrs L Pearce 14/1: 4127} **Amsara 99** [9] 4-10-1 (39) Miss A Deniel 33/1:
138 **Winleah 44** [14] 4-9-3 (27)(7oh) Miss C Hannaford (2) 33/1:
252 **Were Not Stoppin 11** [3] 5-9-9 (24)(6ow) Miss R Bastiman (0) 50/1:
14 ran Time 2m 30.6 (7.3) (G Moore) Sir Mark Prescott Newmarket.

325 **12.50 AMAT HCAP DIV 2 4YO+ 0-65 (G) 1m3f aw Going 57 -48 Slow [44]**
£1568 £448 £224 4 yo rec 3 lb

126 **JAMORIN DANCER 45** [13] D Nicholls 5-10-2 (46) Mr I Mongan 3/1 FAV: 3500-1: 5 b g Charmer - Geryea (Desert Wine) Wide, rear, stdy prog after 4f to lead 3f out, rdn out: 6 wk abs: plcd in '99 for W Jarvis (h'cap, rtd 53): plater over hdles for M Banks in 98/99: '98 Lingfield wnr (med auct mdn, rtd 80, M Jarvis): eff at 9f/11f, tried 12f: acts on fast, soft grnd & fibresand, sharp or gall trks: can force the pace & runs well fresh. **49a**
254 **SWING ALONG 10** [11] R Guest 5-11-7 (65) Mr V Coogan (5) 5/1: 316-W2: 5 ch m Alhijaz - So It Goes (Free State) Waited with, kept on well fnl 4f, not get to wnr: op 3/1: held up to get the trip, clrly stays 11f. *1½* **66a**
190 **IRSAL 30** [2] D W Chapman 6-9-3 (33)(11oh) Miss A Deniel 16/1: 0050-3: 6 ch g Nashwan - Amwag (El Gran Senor) Cl-up, led over 4f out till 3f out, onepace: '99 turf rnr-up (clmr, rtd 59): '97 Salisbury wnr (h'cap, rtd 78): 98/99 wnr over timber at Worcester (h'cap, 2m, fast & gd/soft, blnkd, rtd 132h, M Pipe): eff *3½* **31$**

around 12f: acts on fast & gd/soft, handles fibresand, any trk: fair effort 11lbs o/h.
177 **SHABAASH 32** [7] P Howling 4-9-7 (40) Miss S Pocock (5) 7/1: 0530-4: Prsd ldrs till 3f out: stays 11f? *5* **33a**
233 **KIRISNIPPA 18** [8] 5-10-4 (48) Mr T Best (5) 16/1: 0060-5: Nvr better than mid-div: vis omitted, *2½* **39a**
op 12/1: plcd on turf last term (mdn, rtd 67 at best): eff at 6f, tried 11f: prob handles fast, without blnks or visor.
83 **PARK ROYAL 53** [5] 5-9-3 (33) Mr R Lucey Butler (7) 20/1: 0/00-6: In tch till 3f out: recent jumps rnr. *1* **23a**
4127} **BLOWING AWAY 99** [1] 6-9-10 (40) Mrs L Pearce 13/2: 0/00-7: Nvr dngrs: 15 wk abs: stewards *1¾* **28a**
inquired into ride & noted explanation that the mare was slowly away, styd on past btn horses & ndd the run.
252 **AWESOME VENTURE 11** [4] 10-9-5 (35) Mrs M Morris (2) 25/1: 005-08: Prom till 4f out. *½* **22a**
255 **DREAM CARRIER 10** [6] 12-9-7 (37)(4ow)(7oh) Mrs C Peacock (0) 25/1: 506-09: Al bhd: stiff task. *4* **20a**
252 **PINE RIDGE LAD 11** [9] 10-9-13 (43)(bl) Mrs C Williams 14/1: 050-00: Early ldr, lost pl 4f out, lame: 10th. *1¼* **25a**
3521} **DANCE TO THE BEAT 99** [3] 5-10-1 (45)(bl) Mrs S Bosley 12/1: 6540-0: Led 2f-4½f out, wknd qckly: 12th. *3½* **0a**
295 **Warrior King 6** [12] 6-9-3 (33)(10oh) Mr S Dobson (3) 8/1:
298 **Safe Sharp Jo 4** [10] 5-10-13 (39)(18ow) Mr L Heath (0) 40/1:
13 ran Time 2m 32.8 (11.5) (Miss Karen Shine) D Nicholls Sessay, N.Yorks.

326

1.20 PRIMROSE HCAP DIV 1 4YO+ 0-70 (E) 1m aw rnd Going 57 -19 Slow [70]
£3874 £1192 £596 £298

271 **DIM OFAN 8** [10] B Palling 4-9-4 (60) D Sweeney 8/1: 046-41: 4 gr f Petong - Wilsonic (Damister) **66a**
Wide in tch, switched & prog over 2f out, led bef dist, rdn out: op 6/1: unplcd in '99 (rtd 72 & 61a): '98
Chepstow (auct mdn) & Nottingham wnr (nov, rtd 87): eff at 1m, stays a sharp 9.3f: acts on fast, fibresand,
likes soft: goes on any trk, can force the pace: nicely h'capped.
176 **KASS ALHAWA 32** [6] D W Chapman 7-8-12 (54) A Culhane 5/1: 4310-2: 7 b g Shirley Heights - Silver *1¾* **55a**
Braid (Miswaki) In tch, prog 2½f out, kept on for press: op 4/1: back to form: see 38.
282 **SEA YA MAITE 7** [3] S R Bowring 6-8-11 (53) R Winston 7/2 FAV: 000-53: 6 b g Komaite - Marina Plata *¾* **52a**
(Julio Mariner) Led till ent str, kept on: qck reapp, tchd 5/1: eff at 6f/1m, prob best at 7f now: see 33.
255 **MUTABARI 10** [5] Mrs S Lamyman 6-8-12 (54) J Fanning 7/1: 600-34: Cl-up, ch appr fnl 1f, same pace. *nk* **52a**
2472} **DANAKIL 99** [2] 5-9-13 (69) N Callan(3) 7/1: 0036-5: Bhd ldrs, chall ent str, onepace: top-weight, reapp: *1* **65a**
'99 W'hampton wnr (mdn, rtd 77a & 64, J Banks): missed '98, plcd both juv starts in '97 in France for A Fabre:
eff at 1m/9.5f: acts on fast grnd & f/sand, handles gd & soft, sharp tracks suit: can go well fresh.
-- **SACREMENTUM** [9] 5-9-6 (62) S Drowne 5/1: 0064-6: With ldrs till halfway, btn & hmpd bef dist: *nk* **57a**
3 mth abs, Brit/AW bow: '98 Leopardstown wnr (h'cap): eff at 6/7f on fast grnd & gd/soft: drop back in trip?
193 **ABLE MILLENIUM 30** [4] 4-8-13 (55) R Price 7/1: 3330-7: Cl-up, fdd fnl 2f: see 133 (W'hampton mdn). *shd* **50a**
117} **SATWA BOULEVARD 99** [8] 5-8-10 (50)(2ow) P McCabe 33/1: 0320/8: Waited with, some prog 3f out, *2½* **42a**
nvr in it: abs: back in 98/99 rnr-up over timber for C Mann (2m, firm, rtd 92h): modest mdn when last
seen on the level 2 yrs ago for M Channon (incl blnkd): now with P Burgoyne.
100 **ABLE PETE 51** [7] 4-7-11 (39) M Baird 25/1: 0000-9: Wide, al bhd: 7 wk abs. *6* **19a**
210 **RAYWARE BOY 27** [11] 4-9-5 (61)(bl) L Newton 14/1: 0000-0: Trkd ldrs wide for 5f: 10th. *3* **35a**
3912} **TIERRA DEL FUEGO 99** [1] 6-7-10 (38)(15oh) G Bardwell 40/1: 5000-0: Outpcd: 11th, 4 month abs. *5* **2a**
11 ran Time 1m 45.5 (6.1) (Mrs J E Morton) B Palling Cowbridge, Vale Of Glamorgan.

327

1.50 DAISY CLAIMER 4YO+ (F) 2m aw Going 57 -81 Slow
£2145 £613 £306 4 yo rec 7 lb

296 **NOUFARI 6** [13] R Hollinshead 9-9-8 J P Spencer 1/1 FAV: 011-51: 9 b g Kahyasi - Noufiyla (Top Ville) **72a**
Patiently rdn, styd on from 5f out, led bef dist, ran on well: nicely bckd, slow time, qck reapp: '99 wnr at
Nottingham, Thirsk (rtd 76) & W'hampton (clmr, rtd 83a at best): '98 wnr here at Southwell (2), W'hampton (2) &
Newcastle (h'caps, rtd 81a & 71): eff at 14f/2m, stays 2½m: acts on firm & gd/soft, loves fibresand, any track.
317 **STEAMROLLER STANLY 2** [11] K R Burke 7-9-8 N Callan (3) 9/4: 33-352: 7 b g Shirley Heights - Miss *1½* **69a**
Demure (Shy Groom) Made most till ent fnl 2f, kept on: clr rem, qck reapp: vis omitted & back to form.
174 **CHAHAYA TIMOR 34** [7] Miss S J Wilton 8-9-2 T G McLaughlin 16/1: 64/4-3: 8 b g Slip Anchor - Roxy *7* **57a**
Hart (High Top) Prom, ev ch appr fnl 3f, styd on same pace: op 8/1: shld get lngr 2m trip: see 174.
*124 **GRAND CRU 45** [9] J Cullinan 9-9-0 (e) Barry Smith (7) 6/1: 0341-4: Well in rear, went past btn horses *2½* **53a**
4f out, nvr a factor: clr rem, 6 wk abs, tried eye-shield: see 124 (1m6f here).
3566} **COLORFUL AMBITION 99** [6] 10-8-8 F Lynch 50/1: R/06-5: V slow to stride & nvr got in it: 5 month *14* **37a**
abs: lightly rcd & little form since '95 wins at Newcastle (ltd stks) & Redcar (amat h'cap, rtd 74): 96/97 h'cap
hdle wnr at Kelso & Hexham (2m6.5f, rtd 118h, Mrs A Swinbank): eff at 9/11f, stays 12f: acts on any grnd/trk.
4270} **CAPITALIST 99** [10] 4-8-7 Dean McKeown 50/1: 0000-6: Nvr troubled ldrs: recent jumps rnr (plater): *1¾* **42a**
no worthwhile form (incl blnkd/vis) since plcd in '98 (nurs h'cap, rtd 72): unproven beyond 1m on fast & gd/soft.
-- **MALWINA** [4] 4-8-4 J Fanning 14/1: P: Handy till 5f out: op 10/1, Brit bow, ex-German, wnr *1* **38a**
up to 10f in native land: bght by current connections for 1,000gns: with M Quinlan.
284 **FLORA DREAMBIRD 7** [8] 6-8-5 (bl) G Baker (7) 33/1: 266-07: Lost tch 5f out: qck reapp: see 284. *12* **23a**
196 **DEVILS NIGHT 28** [3] 5-8-8 J Bosley (7) 50/1: /000-8: Mid-div till wknd appr fnl 4f: no worthwhile form. *24* **8a**
301 **HIBAAT 4** [1] 4-8-9 Joanna Badger (7) 50/1: 00-009: Sn struggling: 10th: qck reapp, see 251. *6* **11a**
248 **PRETTY FLY GUY 11** [5] 4-8-9 R Fitzpatrick (3) 50/1: 000-40: Nvr a factor: 11th: see 248. *18* **0a**
256 **Butrinto 10** [2] 6-9-0 (vis) R Price 20/1: -- **Forest Echo** [12] 6-9-0 R Studholme (5) 50/1:
13 ran Time 3m 48.1 (22.1) (Ed Weetman) R Hollinshead Upper Longdon, Staffs.

328

2.20 COWSLIP MDN 3YO (D) 1m aw rnd Going 57 -10 Slow
£2847 £876 £438

-- **NATIONAL DANCE** [12] J G Given 3-9-0 S Ritchie (7) 10/1: 45-1: 3 b g Deploy - Fairy Flax (Dancing **65a**
Brave) V slow away & detached, relentess prog after halfway, rdn & edged left dist, got up towards fin: op 6/1, 6
wk abs, Brit/AW bow: glimmer of promise in 2 French starts at up to 9f late in '99 (J Hammond): eff at 1m,
sure to get further: acts on fibresand: goes well fresh: remarkable win, lkd to have no chance at halfway.
4431} **JUMP 87** [11] J A Osborne 3-9-0 S Drowne 5/4 FAV: -05-2: 3 b c Trempolino - Professional Dance *½* **63a**
(Nijinsky) Trkd ldr, led 2½f out, rdn & hung left below dist, hdd nr fin: 12 wk abs, AW bow, well bckd: 5th
of 18 fnl of 2 '99 starts for D Marks (med auct mdn, rtd 66): half-brother to sev wnrs: eff at 1m, bred for
further: acts on fibresand: first runner for J Osborne & shld recoup losses soon.
4404} **LOUS WISH 88** [2] M J Polglase 3-9-0 (BL) T G McLaughlin 25/1: 0600-3: 3 b c Thatching - Shamaka *nk* **62a**
(Kris) Rear, gd prog to chall 2f out till dist, no extra: 3 month abs, revitalised by blnks: unplcd & sometimes
highly tried juv, best run when 6th in a nurs h'cap (rtd S2): eff at 1m on fibresand, drop back to 6/7f may suit.
278 **DONTBESOBOLD 7** [7] B S Rothwell 3-9-0 J Stack 14/1: 040-04: Led/dsptd lead till 2f out, onepace *1½* **59a**

ins last: qck reapp: prob stays 1m, handles soft grnd & fibresand, prob fast: see 278.
303 **NICIARA 4** [3] 3-9-0 (BL) R Fitzpatrick (3) 50/1: 3P0-05: Led/dsptd lead till 2½f out, no extra: *1¼* **57$**
qck reapp, blnkd: surely flattered: see 74 (seller).
4446} **SECRETARIO 86** [1] 3-8-9 Dean McKeown 33/1: 00-6: Outpcd, late hdwy: 12 wk abs, AW bow: unplcd *3* **46a**
in 2 fillies mdns last term (rtd 64): promises to handle this surface & do better: with C Thornton.
171 **CUIGIU 34** [8] 3-9-0 J P Spencer 14/1: 2540-7: Prom till wknd str: rnr-up in native Ireland in *5* **42a**
'99 on gd grnd, rtd higher AW bow 118.
77 **MANTILLA 55** [6] 3-8-9 A Culhane 2/1: 534-8: Al bhd: well bckd & more expected tho' big step up *1* **35a**
in trip & reportedly resented the kickback: see 77 (AW bow, 5f).
4582} **BLAIR 73** [13] 3-9-0 F Lynch 50/1: 0-9: Wide, nvr in it: AW bow, 10 wk abs: unplcd sole '99 start. *10* **25a**
273 **MILLER TIME 8** [5] 3-9-0 R Winston 12/1: 50: Sn outpcd: 10th, see 273. *¾* **24a**
4358} **XATIVA 92** [4] 3-8-9 A Daly 12/1: 500-0: Chsd ldrs till 3f out: 11th, 3 month abs, AW bow: prob *nk* **18a**
flattered on debut last term (fill mdn, rtd 70): half-sister to sev wnrs: with M Channon.
3933} **Sounds Special 99** [9] 3-8-9 D Sweeney 16/1: 4498} **Dennis Bergkamp 81** [10] 3-9-0 N Callan (3) 50/1:
13 ran Time 1m 44.8 (5.4) (Michael Payton) J G Given Willoughton, Lincs.

329

2.50 PRIMROSE HCAP DIV 2 4YO+ 0-70 (E) 1m aw rnd Going 57 +02 Fast [68]
£3854 £1186 £593 £296

203 **THE STAGER 27** [6] J R Jenkins 8-9-4 (58)(t) S Whitworth 6/1: 0602-1: 8 b g Danehill - Wedgewood **68a**
Blue (Sir Ivor) Chsd ldrs, outpcd ent str, hdwy 2f out, led below dist, held on well: fair time: '99 wnr here at
Southwell (h'cap, rtd 60a & 36): '98 wnr again here at Southwell (h'cap, rtd 55a): eff at 7f/1m, stays a sharp
10f: acts on firm, gd, both AWs, loves Southwell: best without blnks/visor: wears a t-strap.
297 **BACHELORS PAD 4** [8] D Nicholls 6-9-0 (54) M Tebbutt 6/1: 520-02: 6 b g Pursuit Of Love - Note Book *¾* **62a**
(Mummy's Pet) In tch, wide, rdn & ran on to press wnr ins last, al held: drifter from 4/1, qck reapp: reportedly
a tricky ride who does not respond to vigorous riding: acts on firm & gd/soft & fibresand: see 297.
*247 **PIPPAS PRIDE 11** [5] S R Bowring 5-9-0 (54)(6ex) R Winston 7/2 FAV: 401-13: 5 ch g Pips Pride - *2½* **57a**
Al Shany (Burslem) Led till hdd & no extra fnl 1f: tchd 9/2: remains in fine form: see 247.
175 **MYSTIC RIDGE 34** [7] B J Curley 6-9-6 (60) J P Spencer 9/1: 3100-4: Prsd ldr till no extra appr *3* **57a**
fnl 1f: op 5/1: acts on firm, gd grnd, handles fibresand: see 96.
297 **MUTAHADETH 4** [10] 6-9-3 (57)(bl) Joanna Badger (7) 6/1: 40-325: Wide, rear, styd on ent str, *4* **46a**
sn onepace: qck reapp: rcd v wide: in front of this rnr-up 297, see 183.
*297 **SHONTAINE 4** [4] 7-7-12 (38) K Dalgleish (7) 11/2: 00-516: Nvr better than mid-div: drifter from 4/1. *3½* **21a**
298 **GENIUS 4** [2] 5-8-12 (52) Lynsey Hanna (7) 12/1: 40-227: Nvr a factor: op 8/1, qck reapp: see 201. *6* **25a**
2472} **NAKED OAT 99** [3] 5-9-10 (64) J Bosley (7) 16/1: 0600-8: Al in rear: op 12/1 on reapp, top-weight: *4* **29a**
'99 wnr at W'hampton (mdn, rtd 65a) & Warwick (appr h'cap, rtd 60): plcd in '98 (mdn, rtd 68a): eff at
1m/9.3f on fast grnd & fibresand: sharper at W'hampton next time?: with B Smart.
227 **RED WOLF 18** [9] 4-8-8 (48) Dean McKeown 50/1: 6000-9: Wide, in tch till lost pl ent str: *½* **12a**
glimmer of ability on debut last term (soft grnd mdn, rtd 64): with J Given.
2813} **GIRLIE SET 99** [1] 5-9-8 (62) L Newton 11/1: 1110-0: Dwelt, prog to chase ldrs 3f out, sn wknd: last: *16* **6a**
tchd 14/1, 7 wk jumps abs: '99 wnr at Musselburgh, Lingfield (2) & Yarmouth (h'caps, rtd 74 & 50a, Sir M Prescott):
missed '98: eff forcing the pace at 1m/9f, stays 11f: acts on firm, gd/soft, prob both AWs: likes sharp/undul trks.
10 ran Time 1m 43.8 (4.4) (J B Wilcox) J R Jenkins Royston, Herts.

330

3.20 BLUEBELL SELLER 3YO (G) 7f aw rnd Going 57 -20 Slow
£1918 £548 £274

300 **CALKO 4** [6] T D Barron 3-9-4 (bl) J P Spencer 6/4 FAV: 315-31: 3 ch g Timeless Times - Jeethgaya **66a**
(Critique) Prom, wide, rdn after halfway, kept on strongly despite hanging left to lead ent fnl 1f, going away:
well bckd from 9/4, bt in for 4,100gns, qck reapp: late '99 wnr here at Southwell (sell, rtd 61a, mdn, rtd 69):
eff at 6f, relished step up to 7f: acts on fibresand, fast & gd grnd: prob imprvd since blnkd: best on sharp trks.
4360} **AMELIA JESS 92** [10] B S Rothwell 3-8-7 R Lappin 33/1: 0000-2: 3 ch f Mac's Imp - Vieux Carre *3½* **48a**
(Pas de Seul) Outpcd till ran on appr fnl 2f, onepace ins last: op 16/1 on reapp/AW bow: down the field in
4 '99 runs, tried a t-strap: apprec step up to 7f on fibresand.
281 **PRICELESS SECOND 7** [8] J A Glover 3-8-12 N Callan (3) 5/2: 524-23: 3 b g Lugana Beach - Early *nk* **52a**
Gales (Precocious) Tried to make all & clr 2½f out, under press, onepcd & hdd below dist: tchd 7/2, qck reapp.
300 **COME ON MURGY 4** [3] A Bailey 3-8-13 D Hayden (7) 6/1: 13-144: Mid-div, eff appr fnl 2f, styd *¾* **51a**
on without threatening: op 4/1, clr rem, qck reapp: shade btr 283 (C/D).
281 **FORTHECHOP 7** [12] 3-8-12 S Righton 25/1: 006-45: Cl-up till fdd appr fnl 1f: stiff task, qk reapp, *4* **42a**
283 **LADY CYRANO 7** [4] 3-8-7 R Fitzpatrick (3) 14/1: 000-36: Nvr better than mid-div: qck reapp, btr 283. *6* **27a**
3612} **PICCATA 99** [7] 3-8-12 S Drowne 14/1: 00-7: Handy till wknd 2f out: op 10/1 on reapp/AW bow: *1¼* **30a**
well btn in 2 '99 starts: sprint bred, with M Channon.
283 **ALL MINE 7** [1] 3-8-12 J Bramhill 33/1: 68: Dwelt, nvr a factor: qck reapp. *1½* **27a**
155 **QUICKTIME 37** [13] 3-8-7 J Stack 10/1: 0040-9: Well plcd 4f: 4th of 19 in '99 (clmr, rtd 52, soft). *1* **20a**
283 **SOUNDS CRAZY 7** [5] 3-8-7 (bl) Dean McKeown 16/1: 000-20: Prsd ldr till 3f out, sn wknd: 10th. *1¾* **17a**
287 **Blazing Pebbles 6** [11] 3-8-7 L Newman (5) 33/1: 4345} **Dixie Flyer 93** [2] 3-8-7 R Winston 33/1:
303 **Little Christian 4** [9] 3-8-12 C Rutter 25/1:
13 ran Time 1m 32.0 (5.4) (T Calver) T D Barron Maunby, N.Yorks.

331

3.50 SPEEDWELL BLUE HCAP 3YO 0-65 (F) 6f aw rnd Going 57 +05 Fast [70]
£2331 £666 £333

4414} **OSCAR PEPPER 88** [7] T D Barron 3-8-11 (53) J P Spencer 9/2: 5000-1: 3 b g Brunswick - Princess Baga **65a**
(Conquistador Cielo) In tch, eff ent str, ran on strongly to lead bef fnl 1f, sn clr, cmftbly: well bckd, best time
of day, first win on AW bow: well btn all 5 turf starts last term (auct mdn, rtd 64): US bred, related to 3 wnrs:
eff at 6f, tried 1m & shld stay: acts on fibresand, runs well fresh: expect a qck follow up & improvement.
257 **AISLE 10** [2] S R Bowring 3-9-1 (57)(bl) L Newman (5) 5/1: 160-52: 3 b c Arazi - Chancel (Al Nasr) *4* **59a**
Led, hung right ent str, hdd & outpcd bef fnl 1f: op 4/1: back to form since blnkd: see 128.
257 **STAND BY 10** [6] T D Easterby 3-9-0 (56) R Winston 9/2: 005-33: 3 b f Missed Flight - Ma Rivale *1¾* **54a**
(Last Tycoon) Prom, rdn 2f out, unable to qckn: return to 7f shld suit: see 257.
179 **FOXY BROWN 32** [12] Miss I Foustok 3-9-7 (63) M Henry 14/1: 2023-4: Unruly start, handy till no *1½* **55a**
extra appr fnl 1f: op 8/1, jt top-weight, longer trip: btr 179.
257 **UNFORTUNATE 10** [1] 3-8-11 (53) N Carlisle 12/1: 214-65: Dwelt, sn rdn, in tch, same pacem fnl 2f. *nk* **44a**

SOUTHWELL (Fibresand) FRIDAY JANUARY 14TH Lefthand, Sharp, Oval Track

4605} **COULD BE EXPENSIVE** 70 [4] 3-8-5 (47)(BL) A Whelan 10/1: 000-6: Dwelt, nvr better than mid-div: 2   32a
blnkd, 10 wk abs, AW bow, op 8/1: well btn in 3 '99 starts: with M Tompkins.
179   **DIAMOND RACHAEL** 32 [8] 3-9-7 (63)(vis) R Fitzpatrick (3) 16/1: 034-7: Trkd ldrs, wknd 2f out: op 10/1. 1¼   44a
*300   **NOWT FLASH** 4 [11] 3-9-4 (60)(6ex) R Lappin 4/1 FAV: 02-018: Prom till lost pl appr fnl 2f: op 3/1,   ¾   39a
nicely bckd: came too soon under a penalty for 300.
128   **PADDYWACK** 45 [10] 3-8-0 (42)(bl) P Fessey 20/1: 1060-9: Outpcd - 6 wk abs: '99 Redcar wnr (nurs   5   11a
h'cap, rtd 59): eff at 6f on gd/soft grnd, handles firm: wears blnks: with D Chapman.
300   **LAMMOSKI** 4 [3] 3-8-2 (44) Joanna Badger (7) 50/1: 005-00: Speed till halfway: 10th, qck reapp. 1¾   10a
145   **CLOPTON GREEN** 41 [9] 3-8-6 (48) N Callan (1) 12/1: 306-0: Bhd ldrs till appr fnl 2f: 11th,   ¾   12a
6 wk abs, h'cap bow, t-strap omitted: see 46.
3423} Miss Sincere 99 [5] 3-8-11 (53)(VIS) J Bramhill 33/1: 4279} Mister Gill 98 [13] 3-9-0 (56)(t) Dean McKeown 20/1:
13 ran   Time 1m 16.4 (3.1)   (Ian Armitage)   T D Barron Maunby, N.Yorks.

LINGFIELD (Equitrack) SATURDAY JANUARY 15TH Lefthand, V Sharp Track

Official Going   STANDARD. Stalls: 1m - Outside; Rem - Inside.

332

12.50 STUBBS AMAT HCAP 4YO+ 0-80 (F)   **1m4f aw**   **Going 26**   **-11 Slow**   [57]
£2124   £607   £303   4yo rec 4lb

290   **HAWKSBILL HENRY** 7 [2] Mrs A J Perrett 6-9-6 (49) Mr B Hitchcock(5) 9/1: 000-01: 6 ch g Known Fact -   56a
Novel Approach (Codex) Chsd ldrs, rdn & led over 2f out, styd on gamely ins last, rdn out: nicely bckd: rnr-up
thrice in '99 (stks, rtd 61a & 50): '98 Lingfield wnr (h'cap, rtd 56a & 49): eff at 9/10f, now stays 12f: acts
on fast & gd, loves equitrack/Lingfield: has run well fresh: best without visor/blnks: runs well for an amateur.
*219   **FAHS** 24 [4] N Hamilton 8-11-7 (78) Mr G Rothwell (5) 9/1: 6031-2: 8 b g Riverman - Tanwi   1¼   82a
(Vision) Held up rear, smooth prog to chase ldrs 3f out, chsd wnr 2f out, held in last: clr rem, well bckd.
4467} **HARIK** 85 [6] G L Moore 6-11-1 (72) Mr A Quinn (7) 16/1: 2200-3: 6 ch g Persian Bold - Yaqut   7   66a
(Northern Dancer) Wide in rear, kept on fnl 3f, no threat to front pair: op 12/1: jumps fit (plcd, nov h'cap, rtd
80c): '99 Lingfield wnr (h'cap, rtd 74a, no form on turf): '98 Lingfield wnr (2, mdn & amat h'cap, rtd 75a & 44):
eff at 12f/2m, Lingfield/Equitrack specialist: has run well fresh: suited by forcing tactics: spot on next time.
*255   **TROJAN WOLF** 11 [1] P Howling 5-11-6 (77) Miss S Pocock (5) 5/2: 511-14: Led 9f, sn held: op 6/4.   7   61a
285   **INDIGO BAY** 7 [5] 4-10-3 (64)(vis) Mr R Guest (5) 50/1: 200-45: Twds rear/late gains, nvr a threat. 2½   44a
203   **ARDENT** 28 [11] 6-9-7 (50)(hd) Miss L Sheen (3) 14/1: 2206-6: Prom, led over 3f out, hdd/wknd 2f out. 1¼   28a
285   **MIDNIGHT WATCH** 7 [10] 6-9-3 (46)(t)(6oh) Miss A Wallace (7) 50/1: /00-07: Handy halfway, btn 3f   7   14a
out: recent mod hdles form (tried a visor): unplcd on the level in '99 (rtd 43): plcd back in '97 for H Cecil
(h'cap, rtd 75): eff at 1m, tried 13.5f: handles fast & gd grnd.
52   **ROMAN REEL** 60 [7] 9-9-7 (50) Mrs J Moore 16/1: 0040-8: Sn towards rear & no impress: unplcd in   3   14a
'99 (rtd 53a & 44 at best): '98 wnr here at Lingfield (2, amat h'caps, rtd 61a) & Brighton (appr h'cap, rtd 60):
eff at 1m/10f, stays 12f well: acts on firm & equitrack: Brighton/Lingfield specialist.
262   **LANDICAN LANE** 9 [4] 4-9-3 (50)(14oh) Mr H Radford (6) 66/1: 030-09: Wide/sn bhd.   9   4a
268   **FOREST DREAM** 10 [3] 5-9-12 (55) M Allen (7) 20/1: 240-00: Prom 1m: 10th: see 43 (fibresand).   8   0a
244   **DAUNTED** 13 [8] 4-10-11 (72)(bl) Mr I Mongan 8/1: 400-00: Bhd halfway: 11th: stablemate of 3rd. dist   0a
11 ran   Time 2m 33.63 (4.43)   (Miss G Harwood)   Mrs A J Perrett Pulborough, W.Sussex.

333

1.20 HARRINGTON CLAIMER 4YO+ (F)   **1m2f aw**   **Going 26**   **+09 Fast**
£2289   £654   £327   4yo rec 2lb

244   **HUGWITY** 13 [4] G C Bravery 8-8-9 M Hills 10/11 FAV: 216-01: 8 ch g Cadeaux Genereux - Nuit d'Ete   80a
(Super Concorde) Handy, led going well 3f out, in command dist, rdn out: fast time, well bckd: '99 wnr here at
Lingfield (h'cap, rtd 86a): '98 wnr at Yarmouth (5), Southwell (clmr) & Lingfield (h'cap, rtd 80 & 86a): eff
at 7f/1m, stays 10f well: acts on fast grnd & both AWs: handles any trk, loves Lingfield: tough & genuine 8yo.
307   **NIGHT CITY** 4 [3] K R Burke 9-9-5 N Callan (3) 2/1: 32-652: 9 b g Kris - Night Secret (Nijinsky)   5   82a
Led 7f, rdn/held over 1f out: op 5/4, clr of rem, qck reapp: back to form after 307: see 92 (1m).
245   **LORD EUROLINK** 13 [7] C A Dwyer 6-9-3 (VIS) T G McLaughlin 7/1: 045-03: 6 b h Danehill - Lady   5   73$
Eurolink (Kala Shikari) Chsd ldrs halfway, rdn/no impress 2f out: first time visor: see 245.
252   **WITHOUT FRIENDS** 12 [1] Mrs N Macauley 6-8-6(1ow) A Clark 33/1: 006-04: Wide/twds rear, mod gains.   6   53$
239   **MALCHIK** 17 [6] 4-8-5 R Winston 25/1: 050-05: Chsd ldrs 1m: see 159 (7f).   4   48$
159   **WILD RICE** 38 [5] 8-8-5 A Morris 14/1: 0/40-6: Chsd ldrs, tchd 16/1: mod '99 form: unplcd sole   ½   45$
'98 start (rtd 52a), last won back in '95: suited by sharp 7f/10f with blnks/visor: acts on firm, fast & equitrack.
--   **MAUERSCHWALBE** [9] 5-7-12 G Bardwell 25/1: /430-7: Sn drvn in rear, nvr factor: abs, AW/Brit bow: 3   34a
ex-German mare, a 12f wnr in '98: with J J Bridger.
224   **PRINCESS MO** 24 [8] 4-8-2 A Polli (3) 33/1: 0005-8: Bhd halfway: see 224.   10   29a
256   **MAX 11** [2] 5-9-3 A Daly 33/1: 110-69: Chsd ldrs 5f: see 256.   nk   41a
9 ran   Time 2m 04.5 (1.7)   (Sawyer Whately Partnership)   G C Bravery Newmarket.

334

1.50 NORCAL LOUISIANA MDN 3YO (D)   **6f aw rnd**   **Going 26**   **-38 Slow**
£2782   £856   £428   £214

278   **LADYWELL BLAISE** 8 [1] M L W Bell 3-8-9 C Carver (2) 9/4: 5-31: 3 b f Turtle Island - Duly Elected   69a
(Persian Bold) Dwelt/rdn in rear, prog to chase ldrs 2f out, led ins last, rdn out: nicely bckd, slow time: eff
at 6f, stays a sharp 7f & a return to that trip shld suit: acts on both AWs: likes a sharp trk.
289   **LUSONG** 7 [5] R Hannon 3-9-0 P Dobbs (5) 11/10 FAV: -22: 3 ch c Fayruz - Mildred Anne (Thatching) 3½   63a
Led 2f, remained handy, rdn & kept on onepace in last: hvly bckd, tchd 13/8: stays a sharp 7f: see 289 (5f).
287   **TOLDYA** 7 [6] E A Wheeler 3-8-9 (bl) S Carson (5) 8/1: 02-243: 3 b f Beveled - Run Amber Run   ¾   56$
(Run The Gantlet) Sn cl-up/wide, led after 2f & clr halfway, 4L ahd & rdn when stumbled & lost momentum over
1f out, hdd & no extra ins last: op 6/1: wld prob have fin 2nd: h'caps cld suit best: see 287, 242.
269   **ITSGOTTABDUN** 10 [10] K T Ivory 3-9-0 C Catlin (7) 12/1: 203-44: Rdn/rear, late gains, no threat   1   59$
to ldrs: op 10/1: stays a sharp 6f, 7f+ cld suit: see 234 (h'cap).
198   **CUPIDS DART** 29 [8] 3-9-0 R Winston 10/1: 3036-5: Rdn/twds rear, mod gains: op 8/1: see 80 (sell). nk   58$
278   **JUST MAC** 8 [2] 3-9-0 (BL) A Culhane 4/1: 63-06: Prom 4f: op 4/1: blnks: btr 221.   3   51a
4408} **TABBETINNA BLUE** 89 [4] 3-8-9 Martin Dwyer 16/1: 0-7: Struggling halfway: op 14/1: AW bow, 3   6   35a

116

LINGFIELD (Equitrack)   SATURDAY JANUARY 15TH   Lefthand, V Sharp Track

month abs: unplcd sole start in '99 (auct mdn, rtd 43).
4457} **VIKING PRINCE 86** [3] 3-9-0 O Urbina 25/1: 0000-8: Sn bhd: 12 wk abs: mod form prev for M Quinn. *dist* **0a**
8 ran   Time 1m 14.21 (3.81)   (Lady G Parker)   M L W Bell Newmarket.

---

335   2.25 P WARD CLASS STKS 4YO+ 0-70 (E)   **1m2f aw   Going 26 -05 Slow**
£2563   £732   £366   4yo rec 2lb

317   **SEA DANZIG 3** [5] J J Bridger 7-9-2 A Daly 7/1: 00-501: 7 ch g Roi Danzig - Tosara (Main Reef)   **66a**
Made virtually all, pulled clr ins last: op 6/1, qck reapp: '99 scorer at Epsom (h'cap, rtd 59), unplcd on sand
(rtd 68a, h'cap): '98 Lingfield (2, rtd 74a), Goodwood & Folkestone wnr (h'caps, rtd 69): suited by 1m/10f, stays
12f: acts on firm, soft & loves equitrack: loves a sharp trk, esp Lingfield: best when allowed to dominate.
224   **BARBASON 24** [3] G L Moore 8-9-2 P Dobbs (5) 5/4 FAV: 3130-2: 8 ch g Polish Precedent - Barada   6 **56a**
(Damascus) Keen/trkd ldrs, smooth prog to chall 2f out, rdn/held over 1f out: see 163 (C/D, stks).
322   **BILLICHANG 2** [4] P Howling 4-9-2 R Winston 9/1: 301-23: 4 b c Chilibang - Swing O'The Kilt   ½ **57$**
(Hotfoot) Led early remained prom, rdn/ch 3f out, sn held: op 7/1, qck reapp: see 322, 238 (C/D, mdn).
290   **BECKON 1** [1] B R Johnson 4-8-13 A Clark 13/2: 013-54: Trkd ldrs, eff 2f out, sn held: see 111 (sell).   2½ **49a**
270   **GYPSY 9** [2] M Hills 13/8: 56W-35: Rear, eff 4f out, sn struggling & btn/eased fnl 2f: hvly bckd: 10 **39a**
jockey reported gelding resented kick-back: btr 270 (9f, fibresand).
5 ran   Time 2m 05.85 (3.05)   (P Cook)   J J Bridger Liphook, Hants.

---

336   3.00 ECLIPSE SUITE HCAP 4YO+ 0-80 (D)   **1m aw rnd   Going 26 -02 Slow**   [77]
£3926   £1208   £604   £302

3450} **CANADIAN APPROVAL 99** [4] P W Harris 4-9-9 (72) J Fanning 11/2: 0440-1: 4 ch f With Approval -   **77a**
Atasteforlace (Laomedonte) Handy, pulled clr with rnr-up 2f out, held on gamely, all out: op 7/1, 5 month abs/AW
bow: plcd in '99 (val h'cap, rtd 78): '98 Lingfield wnr (med auct mdn, rtd 78): eff arnd 1m on firm, gd & e/track:
prob handles any trk, likes a sharp/undul one: runs well fresh: open to further improvement.
239   **URSA MAJOR 17** [1] C N Allen 6-8-11 (60) R Morse 7/1: 0040-2: 6 b g Warning - Double Entendre   nk **65a**
(Dominion) Led, pulled clr with wnr 2f out, just hdd ins last & no extra: tchd 9/1: loves to force the pace.
239   **SCISSOR RIDGE 17** [12] J J Bridger 8-8-6 (55) G Bardwell 8/1: 1304-3: 8ch g Indian Ridge - Golden   1¼ **57a**
Scissors (Kalaglow) Rdn/wide & towards rear, kept on fnl 2f for press: op 6/1: stays a sharp 1m, suited by 7f.
223   **KILMEENA LAD 24** [8] E A Wheeler 4-10-0 (77) S Carson (5) 10/1: 1004-4: Chsd ldrs 3f out, sn held.   1½ **76a**
239   **COMEOUTOFTHEFOG 17** [6] 5-8-11 (60) P Doe 5/1 FAV: 0302-5: Chsd ldrs, held over 1f out: op 3/1.   ½ **58a**
270   **SHEER FACE 9** [11] 6-8-13 (62) Martin Dwyer 11/2: 440-56: Rdn/mid-div, nvr pace to chall: op 4/1.   1 **58a**
3721} **CAVERSFIELD 99** [2] 5-8-7 (56) S Drowne 25/1: 3000-7: Dwelt/rdn & bhd, mod gains fnl 2f, no   2½ **47a**
threat: jumps fit (plcd 79h, nov): with R Hannon in '99 (plcd numerous times, rtd 59, h'cap): plcd sev times in
'98 (rtd 73 & 59a): '97 wnr at Windsor & Leicester (h'caps, rtd 80): eff at 7f/1m: acts on firm, soft & handles
equitrack: best without visor/blnks: has run well fresh: handles any trk: with Miss E C Lavelle.
268   **ROBBER RED 10** [7] 4-7-13 (48) C Rutter 33/1: 060-08: Chsd ldrs 6f, rnr-up in '99 (h'cap, rtd 64):   5 **29a**
'98 Lingfield wnr (clmr, rtd 83, B Meehan), plcd sev times: eff at 5/6f, stays a sharp 1m well: acts on firm &
gd/soft: handles a sharp/undul or gd trk: eff forcing the pace: best without blnks: has tried a t-strap.
2763} **BOLD HUNTER 99** [5] 6-7-12 (47) Dale Gibson 33/1: /000-9: Al towards rear: 10 wk jumps abs, Aug   nk **27a**
'99 Stratford wnr (mdn hdle, rtd 96h): with Mrs P N Dutfield in '99, unplcd on the level (rtd 31): plcd in '98
(rtd 68 at best): ex-Irish, '97 Sligo wnr (mdn): eff over 7f/8.5f on gd & fast grnd: eff with/without blnks.
243   **TRAWLING 13** [3] 4-8-6 (55) W Ryan 16/1: 000-00: Chsd ldr 2f, sn strugg: 10th: op 12/1: see 243.   ½ **34a**
316   **CHURCHILLS SHADOW 3** [9] 6-7-13 (48) L Newman 33/1: 453-50: Al rear: 11th: qck reapp.   1¾ **24a**
239   **CONSORT 17** [10] 7-9-7 (70) R Winston 11/2: 0030-0: Dwelt/sn bhd: 12th: tchd 13/2: btr 208 (C/D).   shd **46a**
12 ran   Time 1m 38.42 (2.22)   (Ayton, Cordero, Rodway & Harris)   P W Harris Ringshall, Bucks.

---

337   3.35 LADBROKE HCAP 4YO+ (B)   **7f aw rnd   Going 26 -03 Slow**   [90]
£10725   £3300   £1650   £825

143   **NAUTICAL WARNING 42** [16] B R Johnson 5-9-1 (77)(t) M Hills 10/1: 1412-1: 5 b g Warning - Night   **85a**
At Sea (Night Shift) Handy/wide, rdn to lead dist, styd on strongly, rdn out: tchd 14/1, 6 wk abs: '99 wnr here
at Lingfield (4, 3 AW, rtd 80a & 1 on turf, rtd 56, h'caps): '98 wnr again at Lingfield (h'cap, rtd 62a & 54, J
Noseda): suited by 7f/1m on firm, hvy & f/sand, plcd/Lingfield specialist: eff in a t-strap: runs well
fresh: likes to race with/force the pace: tough & progressive, produced a fine effort from a tricky high draw.
282   **TOPTON 8** [10] P Howling 6-9-8 (84)(bl) R Winston 14/1: 232-42: 6 b g Royal Academy - Circo (High   1½ **87a**
Top) Sn chsd ldrs, briefly no room 2f out, styd on for press ins last, not pace of wnr: op 10/1: win again: see 104.
227   **RAINBOW RAIN 19** [2] S Dow 6-7-10 (58) P Doe 20/1: 2305-3: 6 b g Capote - Grana (Miswaki)   hd **60a**
Sn handy, rdn/ch over 1f out, kept on for press: can win again on this evidence: see 227, 28.
258   **REDOUBTABLE 11** [5] D W Chapman 9-8-8 (70) A Culhane 13/2: 063-64: Chsd ldrs, rdn & kept on   hd **71a**
ins last, not pace to chall: see 162 (C/D).
223   **BLAKESET 24** [4] 5-9-6 (82)(bl) A Clark 12/1: 0120-5: Towards rear, switched & kept on fnl 2f, nrst   nk **82a**
at fin: op 10/1: loves to dominate, unable to do so & ran well in circumstances: see 180, 106 (C/D, made all).
244   **FORTY FORTE 3** [8] 4-8-8 (70) N Callan (3) 12/1: 320-56: Rdn to go handy, led over 3f out, hard   nk **69a**
rdn/hdd over 1f out & sn no extra: tchd 14/1: stays a sharp 10f well, loves to dominate at 7f/1m: see 22.
244   **SECRET SPRING 13** [14] 8-10-0 (90) O Urbina 12/1: 211-47: Chsd ldrs halfway, keeping on when no room ¾ **88a**
ins last: poss placed with a clear run: eff at 7f, win again back at 1m/10f: see 208 (1m, stks).
169   **SONG OF SKYE 36** [6] 6-8-12 (74) C Rutter 14/1: 3022-8: Rdn/towards rear, kept on fnl 2f, no threat.   nk **71a**
*162   **SALTY JACK 38** [3] 6-9-3 (79) J Fanning 4/1: 0201-9: Chsd ldrs halfway, sn held: btr 162 (C/D).   6 **67a**
*246   **KEEN HANDS 12** [11] 4-8-12 (74)(vis) R Fitzpatrick (3) 20/1: 024-10: Al rear: see 246 (6f, fbrsnd).   dht **62a**
*263   **DOLPHINELLE 10** [15] 4-7-13 (59)(2ow) Martin Dwyer 20/1: 654-10: Al towards rear: see 263 (6f).   ½ **48a**
288   **MISTER TRICKY 7** [12] 5-8-8 (70) W Ryan 7/2 FAV: 111-20: Towards rear & hmpd after 1f, eff/no   1¾ **54a**
room over 2f out, position soon accepted & eased: 12th: well bckd, tchd 5/1: nvr able to gain a crucial handy
position, this probably best performance: see 288, 223.
258   **Democracy 11** [14] 4-8-8 (70)(bl) S Drowne 33/1:   97   **Roisin Splendour 53** [9] 5-8-4 (66) L Newman(5) 25/1:
239   **Cantina 17** [7] 6-8-8 (70) S Carson (5) 14/1:
15 ran   Time 1m 24.84 (2.04)   (The Twenty Five Club)   B R Johnson Epsom, Surrey.

117

Official Going STANDARD. Stalls: Inside.

---

338   **12.30 APP MDN HCAP DIV 1 4YO+ 0-60 (F)**   **1m4f aw** **Going 50** **-34 Slow**   [61]
        £1806   £516   £258   4 yo rec 4 lb

84   **MORGANS ORCHARD** 56 [7] A G Newcombe 4-10-0 (57) P Fredericks 3/1 CO FAV: 053-1: 4 ch g Forest   **65a**
Wind - Regina St Cyr (Doulab) Keen & prom, smooth prog to chall over 3f out, led 2f out, al just holding rival ins
last, rdn out: 8 wk abs, op 4/1: no form form 2 turf starts in '99, plcd on sand (rtd 61a, mdn): eff at 12f, shld
stay further: acts on fibresand: runs well fresh & likes a sharp trk: gd weight carrier.

271   **WESTERN RAINBOW** 11 [5] P D Evans 4-9-8 (51) Joanna Badger (3) 3/1 CO FAV: 022-22: 4 b g   ½ **57a**
Rainbows For Life - Miss Galwegian (Sandford Lad) Held up in tch, prog to chase ldrs 3f out, rdn to chall over 1f
out, kept on well ins last, just held: op 5/2: styd longer 12f well: clr rem & can find similar: see 271.

85   **NEPTUNE** 56 [2] K C Comerford 4-8-6 (35) C Cogan 20/1: 0540-3: 4 b g Dolphin Street - Seal Indigo   7 **31a**
(Glenstal) Chsd ldrs, kept on fnl 3f, no threat to front pair: 8 wk abs: unplcd in '99 for W J Haggas (rtd 59,
mdn): prob stays a sharp 12f & handles fibresand, gd & gd/soft grnd.

298   **HOT POTATO** 7 [6] J S Wainwright 4-8-8 (37) R Cody Boutcher (3) 25/1: 005-04: Handy, led 4f out,   1½ **31a**
rdn/hdd 2f out & sn held: see 298 (1m).

295   **TALECA SON** 9 [4] 5-8-4 (29) G Baker (5) 3/1 CO FAV: 34-225: Cl-up wide over 3f out, sn rdn/wknd.   1¼ **21a**

178   **SOUNDS COOL** 35 [10] 4-8-0 (29) L Newman 20/1: 0000-6: Chsd ldrs 10f: op 14/1: rnr-up in '99   7 **11a**
(seller, rtd 48): plcd in '98 (AW seller, rtd 52a, mod turf form prev): eff around 1m/10f: handles fast, hvy &
fibresand: handles a sharp or gall trk: best without blnks.

308   **NOBLE PATRIOT** 6 [1] 5-8-11 (36) A Hawkins (5) 14/1: 03-457: Held up, eff 4f out, sn held: op 9/1.   ½ **17a**

238   **CRESSET** 19 [3] 4-9-11 (54) J Bosley (3) 10/1: 0006-8: Strugg halfway: op 7/1: h'cap bow: see 238.   ½ **34a**

295   **QUAKERESS** 9 [9] 5-7-10 (26)(et)(1oh) K Dalgleish (5) 20/1: 000-69: Led 1m: see 295.   15 **0a**

215   **BARANN** 27 [8] 4-7-10 (27)(2oh) Claire Bryan 25/1: 0000-0: Al bhd: 10th: mod form.   7 **0a**

10 ran   Time 2m 44.5 (10.1)   (After Hours Partnership)   A G Newcombe Huntshaw, Devon.

---

339   **1.0 APP MDN HCAP DIV 2 4YO+ 0-60 (F)**   **1m4f aw** **Going 50** **-41 Slow**   [57]
        £1806   £516   £258   4 yo rec 4 lb

3528} **ALNAJASHEE** 99 [4] M R Bosley 4-9-12 (55)(t) G Baker (5) 6/1: 2556-1: 4 b g Generous - Tahdid   **62a**
(Mtoto) Handy, led halfway, pushed clr fnl 2f, easily: AW bow, 5 month abs: prev with P T Walwyn, rnr-up on turf
in '99 (mdn, rtd 77): rtd 72 in '98: eff at 12f, has tried 2m: acts on fibresand, handles firm: likes a sharp
trk & runs well fresh: eff in a t-strap: plenty in hand here, can win again.

215   **BROUGHTONS LURE** 27 [9] W J Musson 6-8-9 (34) L Newman 5/6 FAV: 0052-2: 6 ch m Archway - Vaal   8 **33a**
Salmon (Salmon Leap) Held up in tch wide, rdn to chall over 2f out, kept on, no ch with wnr: hvly bckd: see 215.

4154} **TELLION** 99 [8] J R Jenkins 6-9-9 (48)(vis) P Fredericks 12/1: 0/00-3: 6 b g Mystiko - Salchow   shd **47a**
(Niniski) Chsd ldrs wide 3f out, rdn/hung left 2f out & sn held: clr rem, AW bow, op 14/1: jumps fit, Nov '99
Kempton wnr (nov h'cap, rtd 86): unplcd in '99 (rtd 32, h'cap): plcd in '98 (rtd 65): eff at 12f on fast & gd/soft.

298   **MEGA 7** [5] M H Tompkins 4-9-5 (48) W Hutchinson(3) 5/1: 000-54: Chsd ldrs 3f out/sn held: see 298 (1m) 12 **34a**

285   **COCHITI** 9 [6] 6-7-10 (23)(t)(2oh) Joanna Badger (3) 20/1: 560-05: Prom 9f: unplcd in '99 (rtd 27):   1¼ **5a**
plcd over hdles in 98/99 (rtd 75h, nov & sellers): only mod form on the level in '98.

306   **UNTOLD STORY** 6 [1] 5-8-7 (32) C Cogan 33/1: 00-066: Pulled hard tracking ldrs, rdn/wknd 3f out.   1¼ **14a**

4300} **LADY IONA** 98 [7] 4-8-3 (32) P Fitzsimons 16/1: 6005-7: Handy 4f out, sn wknd: 7 wk jumps abs, (no   2 **11a**
form): rnr-up in '99 (seller, rtd 51): mod form prev: stays 1m & handles gd/soft grnd: AW bow today.

254   **BIJA** 13 [2] 5-8-0 (25) Claire Bryan 16/1: 604-08: Struggling halfway: op 12/1: longer 12f trip.   3 **0a**

--   **FLEETING FOOTSTEPS** [3] 8-8-5 (30) R Smith 33/1: 0000/9: Led till halfway, sn bhd: long abs.   dist **0a**

9 ran   Time 2m 45.3 (10.9)   (Mrs Jean M O'Connor)   M R Bosley Kingston Lisle, Oxon.

---

340   **1.30 FAIR ISLE HCAP DIV 1 4YO+ 0-65 (F)**   **1m aw rnd** **Going 50** **-00 Slow**   [56]
        £1970   £563   £281

*329 **THE STAGER** 3 [3] J R Jenkins 8-10-2 (64)(t)(6ex) S Whitworth 5/2 FAV: 602-11: 8 b g Danehill -   **71a**
Wedgewood Blue (Sir Ivor) Chsd ldrs, smooth prog to lead 2f out, sn in command, rdn clr ins last, easily: hvly
bckd, tchd 3/1: 6lb pen, qck reapp: recent Southwell wnr (C/D h'cap): '99 wnr again here at Southwell (h'cap,
rtd 60a & 36): '98 wnr again at Southwell (h'cap, rtd 55a): eff at 7f/1m, stays a sharp 10f: acts on firm, gd,
equitrack, fibresand/Southwell specialist: best without blnks/visor: gd weight carrier: wears a t-stap: win again.

--   **PREPOSITION** [11] M A Peill 4-8-8 (40)(2ow) F Lynch 50/1: 4000/2: 4 b g Then Again - Little   10 **40a**
Emmeline (Emarati) Prom, ch 2f out, sn outpcd by easy wnr: 7 wk jumps abs (no form): missed '99 on the level:
unplcd in '98 (rtd 50, debut, Mrs J R Ramsden): AW bow today.

--   **DANGERMAN** [1] M W Easterby 5-8-4 (38)(t) Dale Gibson 8/1: 0501/3: 5 ch g Pips Pride - Two   3 **30a**
Magpies (Doulab) Rdn chasing ldrs, kept on fnl 2f, no ch with wnr: op 6/1: jumps fit (rtd 98c, nov): missed '99,
'98 Nottingham wnr (h'cap, rtd 44): eff at 10f: acts on gd & gd grnd: likes a gall trk & has run well fresh.

297   **SWAMPY** 7 [12] R F Marvin 4-8-11 (45) S Righton 14/1: U20-54: Chsd ldrs 6f: now with R Marvin.   ¾ **36a**

304   **MAI TAI** 7 [5] 5-9-7 (55)(vis) Kimberley Hart (5) 11/4: 314-25: Chsd ldrs 6f: nicely bckd: btr 304.   ½ **45a**

3611} **SARTEANO** 99 [13] 6-7-10 (30)(6oh) A Polli (3) 50/1: 00/0-6: Rdn/rear, mod gains: 5 month abs/   ½ **19a**
AW bow: no form in '99 on turf: mod form when last rcd prev in '96.

299   **FANCY A FORTUNE** 7 [6] 6-9-0 (48)(bl) Clare Roche (5) 10/1: 620-57: Led 5f: op 8/1: see 299 (7f).   1 **35a**

302   **KILLARNEY JAZZ** 7 [2] 5-10-0 (62)(tbl) S Carson (5) 12/1: 044-08: Led/dsptd lead 6f, fdd: see 67.   shd **49a**

298   **STERLING HIGH** 7 [10] 5-9-4 (58)(t) R Fitzpatrick (3) 7/1: 05-049: Al twds rear: op 5/1: btr 298.   hd **38a**

249   **PRINCIPAL BOY** 14 [9] 7-8-3 (43) N Carlisle 10/1: 304-60: Mid-div, wide 3f out, sn held: 10th: see 50.   1 **21a**

152   **Dorothy Allen** 42 [8] 4-7-13 (33) Joanna Badger (7) 25/1:

297   **Anchor Venture** 7 [4] 7-7-10 (40)(4oh) D Kinsella (7) 50/1:

12 ran   Time 1m 43.4 (4.0)   (J B Wilcox)   J R Jenkins Royston, Herts.

---

341   **2.00 CLASSIFIED CLAIMER 4YO+ 0-60 (F)**   **7f aw rnd** **Going 50** **-09 Slow**
        £2160   £617   £308

*249 **DAVIS ROCK** 14 [9] W R Muir 6-8-12 Martin Dwyer 9/4 FAV: 155-11: 6 ch m Rock City - Sunny Davis   **63a**
(Alydar) Mid-div, rdn/prog halfway, styd on well to lead ins last, rdn out: op 11/4: recent wnr here at Southwell
(clmr): '99 Nottingham wnr (h'cap, rtd 49 & 56a): '98 Lingfield (fill h'cap) & W'hampton wnr (sell, rtd 67a & 60):

SOUTHWELL (Fibresand)   MONDAY JANUARY 17TH   Lefthand, Sharp, Oval Track

eff at 7f/1m on firm, soft & both AWs: gd weight carrier: handles any trk, loves Southwell: enjoys sell/claim grade.
298   **FRENCH CONNECTION** 7 [1] D Nicholls 5-8-1 (bl) Iona Wands (5) 8/1: 505-62: 5 b g Tirol - Heaven   1¼   48a
Liegh Grey (Grey Desire) Led, rdn/hdd 2f out, kept on well for press ins last, just held nr fin: op 13/2: clmd
for £3,000: acts on fast, hvy & fibresand: a likely type for similar: see 298.
256   **BLUSHING GRENADIER** 13 [4] S R Bowring 8-8-1 C Cogan (5) 4/1: 340-33: 8 ch g Salt Dome - La Duse shd   48a
(Junius) Handy, rdn/led 2f out, hdd ins last & no extra cl-home: tchd 5/1: see 136, 38.
*310   **RA RA RASPUTIN** 6 [10] R A McMahon 5-8-7 L Newman (5) 11/2: 300-14: Chsd ldrs, not pace to chall.   2½   49a
310   **CHALUZ** 6 [3] 6-8-5 (t) D Sweeney (5): 55-425: Prom 5f: op 3/1: visor omitted: see 310, 75.   3   41a
700}   **SOUNDS SOLO** 99 [2] 4-8-3 (evis) Clare Roche (7) 14/1: 1/50-6: Dwelt, sn chsd ldrs, btn 2f out: op   1   37a
8/1: 10 month abs: longer priced stablemate of rnr-up: unplcd in '99 (rtd 38a, S R Bowring, C/D, seller): '98
Southwell wnr (sell, rtd 62a): eff at 7f on fibresand: likes to force the pace in a vis: has run well fresh.
297   **FAN TC GEM** 7 [11] 4-7-12 S Righton 33/1: /0-607: Mid-div at best: see 247.   1¼   29a
313   **MR CUBE** 3 [6] 10-8-1 (bl) Claire Bryan (7) 20/1: 42-008: Al towards rear: qck reapp: see 254.   3½   25a
212   **MY TYSON** 27 [8] 5-9-1 J Fanning 25/1: 0/60-9: Chsd ldrs 5f: see 183.   2   35a
156   **CLADANTOM** 40 [7] 4-8-6 A Culhane 25/1: 0006-0: Al rear: 10th: 6 wk abs: see 156.   5   16a
4253}   **MY BROADSTAIRS JOY** 99 [5] 4-8-1 T Williams 40/1: 06/0-0: Al rear: 11th: 2 month jumps abs, (mod   1½   8a
form, tried blnks): unplcd on the level in '99 for J J O'Neill: mod form prev: AW bow today for D Shaw.
11 ran   Time 1m 30.7 (4.1)   (Gordon B Cunningham)   W R Muir Lambourn, Berks.

---

342   2.30 ISLE OF MULL HCAP 4YO+ 0-80 (D)   6f aw rnd   Going 50   +08 Fast   [78]
£4173 £1284 £642 £321

4436}   **RAFTERS MUSIC** 90 [4] D Nicholls 5-7-12 (48) Clare Roche (7) 9/1: 0460-1: 5 b g Thatching - Princess   58a
Dixieland (Dixieland Band) Led/dsptd lead till asserted ins last, rdn out: fast time, op 7/1, AW bow/3 month abs:
'99 Epsom wnr (clmr, Mrs A J Perratt, rtd 59): unplcd in '98 (rtd 55, mdns): stable by 6f, tried further: acts
on firm, hvy & f/sand: eff with/without blnks, wears a t-strap: likes a sharp trk, runs well fresh: can win again.
3770}   **BEDEVILLED** 99 [5] T D Barron 5-9-3 (67) C Lowther 7/1: 6010-2: Prom, led over 2f out till 1f out,   5   68a
sn held by wnr: tchd 8/1: 5 month abs: '99 Beverley wnr (mdn, rtd 71, no
sand form): eff at 5/6f on fast & soft, handles fibresand: can force the pace: handles a sharp/stiff trk.
232   **SHARP HAT** 21 [9] D W Chapman 6-8-8 (58) A Culhane 14/1: 1300-3: 6 b g Shavian - Madam Trilby   ¾   57a
(Grundy) Held up in tch, prog wide over 2f out, kept on ins last, no threat to wnr: op 12/1: see 246, 91.
282   **DAHLIDYA** 10 [2] M J Polglase 5-8-12 (62) R Fitzpatrick (3) 9/2: 310-34: Dwelt/nvr mount chall: btr 180.   ½   59a
*191   **YABINT EL SHAM** 33 [1] 4-9-0 (64) L Newman (5) 8/1: 0001-5: Led/dsptd lead 4f: op 5/1: see 191 (5f).   ½   59a
*250   **GARNOCK VALLEY** 14 [8] 5-10-9-10 (74) P Bradley (5) 11/4 FAV: 152-16: Rear, nvr factor: nicely bckd.   3½   60a
280   **HAUNT THE ZOO** 10 [3] 5-8-4 (54) J Bramhill 100/30: 110-37: Chsd ldrs 4f: btr 280, 148 (C/D).   hd   39a
282   **AJNAD** 10 [7] 6-9-8 (72) S Righton 14/1: 630-08: Al towards rear: op 12/1: see 282.   2   52a
--   **MANORBIER** [6] 0-9-6 (70) F Lynch 20/1: 1250/9: Chsd ldrs wide, btn 2f out: op 14/1, AW bow, long   4   40a
abs: missed '99: 98 Chepstow wnr (juv auct mdn, D Arbuthnot, rtd 83 at best): eff at 5f: acts on fast & gd grnd.
9 ran   Time 1m 15.8 (2.5)   (Miss N F Thesigner)   D Nicholls Sessay, N.Yorks.

---

343   3.00 ANGLESEY HCAP 4YO+ 0-80 (D)   1m3f aw   Going 50   -06 Slow   [79]
£4134 £1272 £636 £318   4yo rec 3lb

2177}   **CHALCEDONY** 99 [9] T D Barron 4-8-12 (66) C Lowther 8/1: 1350-1: 4 ch g Highest Honor - Sweet   73a
Holland (Alydar) Chsd ldrs, rdn/led over 2f out, styd on well ins last, pushed out cl-home: op 10/1: 7 mth abs:
'99 Lingfield & Southwell wnr (h'caps, rtd 66a & 62): plcd in '98 (nurs, rtd 56a & 58): eff at 10/11f, stays 14f:
acts on both AWs & firm: best without blnks: likes a sharp trk & forcing tactics: runs well fresh.
*301   **WOOD POUND** 7 [8] R Hollinshead 4-10-3 (85)(6ex) N Callan (3) 7/2: /20-12: 4 b c Woodman -   ¾   90a
Poundzig (Danzig) Towards rear, smooth prog wide to chall fnl 3f, edged right/rdn & no extra cl-home: tchd
4/1, clr of rem: h'cap bow: 6lb pen for latest, can find more races: see 301 (12f, mdn).
302   **FAILED TO HIT** 7 [7] N P Littmoden 7-9-1 (66)(vis) C Cogan (5) 7/2: 22-423: 7 b g Warrshan - Missed   5   64a
Again (High Top) Led, rdn/hdd over 2f out, kept on onepace: op 3/1: clr rem: see 101 (clmr).
251   **JIBEREEN** 14 [3] P Howling 8-9-8 (73) S Whitworth 25/1: 200-04: Chsd ldrs 9f: see 197 (1m).   6   62a
302   **WESTERN COMMAND** 7 [5] 4-9-1 (69)(vis) R Fitzpatrick (3) 13/2: 221-45: Rear/in tch, mod gains: op 5/1.   2   55a
4615}   **MY DESPERADO** 72 [4] 7-9-2 (67) F Lynch 14/1: 5/00-6: Towards rear, btn 3f out: jumps fit (unplcd,   5   46a
rd 95h): unplcd in '99 (rtd 66, h'cap): '98 Thirsk (mdn, rtd 74), Pontefract (h'cap) & Redcar wnr (class stks,
with L Lloyd James), subs Catterick hdles wnr (mares nov, rtd 102h): eff at 10/12f on fast & gd/soft: AW bow.
151   **ROBELLITA** 42 [1] 6-9-2 (67) J Stack 3/1 FAV: 1126-7: Chsd ldrs, btn 3f out: nicely bckd, 6 wk abs.   ½   45a
270   **STATE APPROVAL** 11 [6] 7-9-0 (65) L Newman (5) 12/1: 125-68: Bhd halfway: op 10/1: see 270.   11   31a
--   **SOPHOMORE** [2] 6-9-10 (75) S Righton 25/1: 0446/9: Prom 1m: 10 month jumps abs (mod form,   dist   0a
A Murphy): last rcd on the level in '97 (unplcd, rtd 89 for B Hills): mdn wnr on sole juv start in '96 (rtd 86):
eff at 7f, bred to apprec mid-dists: acts on gd grnd & a gall trk: AW bow today for J Harris.
9 ran   Time 2m 27.5 (6.2)   (J Baggott)   T D Barron Maunby, N.Yorks.

---

344   3.30 LUNDY SELLER 4-6YO (G)   1m4f aw   Going 50   -23 Slow
£1901 £543 £271   4 yo rec 4 lb

324   **ABSOLUTE MAJORITY** 3 [5] P Howling 5-9-3 T Williams 7/2: 40-251: 5 ch g Absalom - Shall We Run   55a
(Hotfoot) Prom, led 2f out, held on well, drvn out: op 3/1, sold for 6,000gns, qck reapp: '99 W'hampton wnr (mdn,
rtd 66a, B Curley): eff at 9/12f on fibresand, prob handles equitrack: likes a sharp trk: apprec sell grade.
307   **METEOR STRIKE** 6 [1] D Nicholls 6-9-3 (t) M Tebbutt 6/1: 300-62: 6 ch g Lomond - Meteoric (High   ½   53a
Line) Led, rdn/hdd 2f out, styd on well ins last, just held nr fin: acts on firm, fast & both AWs: see 307.
*231   **COLONEL CUSTER** 21 [3] J Pearce 5-9-8 G Bardwell 13/8 FAV: 5001-3: 5 ch g Komatie - Mohican (Great   12   46a
Nephew) Prom, rdn/chsd ldr 4f out, btn 2f out: well bckd: btr 231.
292   **RONS ROUND** 9 [2] J M Bradley 6-9-3 Claire Bryan (7) 6/1: 422/54: Chsd ldrs 4f out, btn over 2f out.   4   37a
295   **MARKELLIS** 9 [4] 4-9-4 R Fitzpatrick (3) 13/2: 41-045: Chsd ldrs 9f: op 5/1: flattered 295.   ¾   41$
252   **ADIRPOUR** 14 [7] 6-9-3 Stephanie Hollinshea 25/1: 030-06: Chsd ldrs halfway: btn 3f out: see 178.   nk   35$
259   **OUR JACK** 13 [10] 5-9-3 N Carlisle 20/1: 6-47: Bhd halfway: reportedly p.u feelingly: longer 12f trip.   12   23a
3777}   **PRECIOUS YEARS** 99 [6] 5-9-3 J Fanning 40/1: 0/00-8: Bhd halfway: no form, longer 12f trip.   ½   22a
698}   **RIBBLE PRINCESS** 99 [8] 5-8-12 Iona Wands (5) 16/1: 30/0-9: Al rear: 10 month abs/AW bow: 13½   13a
unplcd sole start in '99 (rtd 19): plcd in '98 (rtd 72, mdn): stays 1m, handles gd grnd.
284   **SHOTLEY MARIE** 10 [9] 5-8-12 (bl) Martin Dwyer 33/1: 56-60P: Dwelt/bhd, rdn/chsd ldrs 7f out, sn   0a
struggling & bhd/p.u. lame 3f out: only mod form previously.

SOUTHWELL (Fibresand)   MONDAY JANUARY 17TH   Lefthand, Sharp, Oval Track

10 ran   Time 2m 42.3 (8.0)   (Richard Berenson)   P Howling Newmarket.

345
4.0 FAIR ISLE HCAP DIV 2 4YO+ 0-65 (F)   1m aw   Going 50 -03 Slow   [62]
£1970 £563 £281

326 **SEA YA MAITE** 3 [6] S R Bowring 6-9-4 (52) N Callan (3) 4/1: 00-531: 6 b g Komatie - Marina Plata   59a
(Julio Mariner) Prom, prog to lead over 1f out, sn rdn clr, held on well ins last, rdn out: op 9/2, qck reapp:
'99 Southwell scorer (h'cap, rtd 64a & 30): '98 wnr here at Southwell (h'cap, rtd 68a & 48): eff at 6f, suited by
7f/1m: acts on fast, gd/soft, loves fibresand/Southwell: has run well fresh: best without blnks: well h'capped.
233 **GODMERSHAM PARK** 21 [8] P S Felgate 8-8-13 (47) Dean McKeown 8/1: 0305-2: 8 b g Warrshan -   3 48a
Brown Velvet (Mansingh) Prom, rdn/led over 2f out, sn hdd, kept on for press: op 6/1: well h'capped: see 45.
305 **DOBERMAN** 6 [2] P D Evans 5-8-5 (39)(bl) D Sweeney 20/1: 04-403: 5 b g Dilum - Switch Blade   1½ 37a
(Robellino) Chsd ldrs halfway, kept on for press fnl 2f, no threat to wnr: op 14/1: see 254.
*298 **NICE BALANCE** 7 [5] M C Chapman 5-8-1 (35) Joanna Badger (7) 8/1: 50-614: Mid-div, nvr pace   1¼ 30a
to chall: op 5/1: see 298 (C/D, appr h'cap).
297 **STRAVSEA** 7 [12] 5-9-1 (49) P M Quinn (5) 10/1: 01-035: Mid-div, nvr able to chall: op 7/1: see 176.   nk 43a
329 **SHONTAINE** 3 [7] 7-8-3 (37) J Fanning 11/2: 0-5166: Towards rear, mod gains: qck reapp: see 297.   ¾ 30a
298 **KINGCHIP BOY** 7 [1] 11-9-4 (52) P McCabe 6/1: 00-307: Led 6f, hung right/fdd: btr 249 (clmr).   ¾ 44a
*256 **INTERNAL AFFAIR** 13 [3] 5-10-0 (62) Lynsey Hanna (7) 7/2 FAV: 620-18: Dwelt/nvr factor: btr 256 (clmr).   nk 53a
3934} **OSWALD** 99 [4] 4-8-4 (38) T Williams 20/1: 000-9: Mid-div, btn 2f out: 4 month abs/AW bow: h'cap   13 9a
debut: rtd 44 at best in '99 (unplcd, tried only at 5f).
133 **KIDNAPPED** 47 [11] 4-8-10 (43)(1ow) T G McLaughlin 40/1: 0000-0: Bhd halfway: 10th: 7 wk abs: 19 0a
unplcd in '99 (rtd 70, mdn, prob flattered): mod form prev for Mrs A L M King.
277 **Team Of Three** 11 [10] 4-7-10 (30)(4oh) A Polli (3) 40/1:
4208} **Cool Prospect** 99 [9] 5-9-10 (58)(VIS) Iona Wands (5) 25/1:
12 ran   Time 1m 43.6 (4.2)   (S R Bowring)   S R Bowring Edwinstowe, Notts.

WOLVERHAMPTON (Fibresand)   TUESDAY JANUARY 18TH   Lefthand, Sharp Track

Official Going STANDARD. Stalls: Inside, except 7f - Outside.

346
1.20 HAMMERSMITH APPR HCAP 3YO 0-60 (G)   7f aw rnd   Going 64 -25 Slow   [62]
£1904 £544 £272

328 **LOUS WISH** 4 [5] M J Polglase 3-9-6 (54)(bl) R Fitzpatrick 3/1: 600-31: 3 b g Thatching - Shamaka   62a
(Kris) Chsd ldrs halfway, hard rdn/duelled with rnr-up ins last, just prevailed on line, all out: op 4/1: qck reapp:
unplcd in '99 (rtd 62, nurs h'cap), subs gelded: eff at 7f, stays a sharp 1m: acts on fibresand & a sharp trk: eff
in blnks: reportedly wants to come late.
303 **BAYTOWN RHAPSODY** 8 [1] P S McEntee 3-9-1 (49) L Newman (5) 16/1: 500-32: 3 b f Emperor Jones - shd   56a
Sing A Rainbow (Rainbow Quest) Sn cl-up, rdn/led 3f out, duelled with wnr ins last, just held: well clr rem:
op 12/1: eff at 6/7f: acts on gd & fibresand: deserves to find similar: see 303 (seller).
287 **SUPREMELY DEVIOUS** 10 [2] R M H Cowell 3-8-13 (47)(vis) R Studholme (3) 10/1: 626-33: 3 ch f   8 42a
Wolfhound - Clearly Devious (Machiavellian) Led/dsptd lead 4f out, wknd fnl 1f: op 9/1: see 155 (clmr, eqtrk).
330 **COME ON MURGY** 4 [10] A Bailey 3-9-7 (55) D Kilcourse (7) 10/1: 3-1444: Dwelt/rear, mod gains   nk 49a
for press: op 7/1, qck reapp: both wins in selling grade: see 330, 283 (seller).
331 **PADDYWACK** 4 [7] 3-8-8 (42)(bl) Lynsey Hanna (7) 14/1: 060-05: Prom 6f: qck reapp: see 331 (6f).   2 32a
257 **LIONS DOMANE** 14 [3] 3-9-0 (48) P Goode (3) 13/8 FAV: 000-26: Dwelt, sn rcd prom, wknd qckly 2f   5 28a
out: hvly bckd, tchd 2/1: more expected after latest: see 257 (C/D).
234 **POWER AND DEMAND** 20 [6] 3-9-0 (48) N Callan (3) 20/1: 0604-7: Chsd ldrs 4f: op 12/1: see 234 (5f).   3½ 21a
3239} **BERKELEY DIDO** 99 [8] 3-9-6 (54)(BL) J Mackay (7) 6/1: 0306-8: Dwelt, rdn/chsd ldrs halfway, soon   8 15a
held: op 4/1, blnks: AW bow, 5 month abs: unplcd in '99 (rtd 62, 4 rnr nov auct stks).
4044} **INDIANA SPRINGS** 99 [4] 3-9-2 (50) C Cogan (5) 16/1: 000-9: Sn strugg: hcap bow, AW bow/abs.   8 0a
3941} **RATHCLOGHEENDANCER** 99 [5] 3-8-12 (46) Iona Wands (5) 25/1: 0460-0: Prom 3f: 10th: 4 month   2½ 0a
abs: unplcd in '99 (rtd 58 & 29a, subs tried blnks): has tried up to 1m prev, prob handles gd & soft grnd.
10 ran   Time 1m 32.4 (6.2)   (Ian Puddle)   M J Polglase Southwell, Notts.

347
1.50 WESTMINSTER CLAIMER 4YO+ (F)   1m4f aw   Going 64 -44 Slow
£2257 £645 £322   4 yo rec 4 lb

307 **BANNERET** 7 [4] Miss S J Wilton 7-9-1 (vis) T G McLaughlin 2/1: 534-21: 7 b g Imperial Falcon -   54a
Dashing Partner (Formidable) Chsd ldrs & rdn from halfway, led 1f out, forged clr ins last & in command nr fin:
'99 scorer at Southwell (class clmr) & here at W'hampton (C/D h'cap, rtd 66a, no turf form): '98 W'hampton
wnr (2, seller & auct mdn) G Woodward, rtd 71a) & Southwell (seller): suited by 10/12f: handles fast, fibresand/
Southwell & W'hampton specialist: eff in a visor, has tried blnks: loves sell/claim grade.
248 **APPYABO** 15 [5] M Quinn 5-8-7 S Drowne 50/1: 000-02: 5 ch g Never So Bold - Cardinal Palace   5 37$
(Royal Palace) Prom, rdn 5f out, kept on for press fnl 2f, not pace of wnr: plcd in '99 (auct mdn, rtd 45a, rtd 27
on turf): plcd form in '98 (rtd 72a, rtd 45a, & rtd 52 on turf, tried visor): stays 10f, has tried 2m: handles fast
grnd & both AWs: offic rtd 23, treat rating with caution.
4444} **XYLEM** 90 [6] J Pearce 9-8-9 R Price 33/1: 2000-3: 9 ch g Woodman - Careful (Tampa Trouble)   nk 38a
Rdn/towards rear, prog to chase ldrs 2f out, kept on tho' not pace to chall: 3 month abs: plcd form in '99 (rtd
43, h'cap, unplcd on sand, rtd 34a, h'cap): with J Gosden in '98, (unplcd, rtd 67): '97 Newcastle wnr (amat h'cap,
rtd 73, L Cumani): eff at 10f/12f, poss stays sharp 13f: acts on firm, soft & handles both AWs: best without a vis.
307 **MR SPECULATOR** 7 [1] J L Spearing 7-8-11 (bl) S Whitworth 8/1: 3-0534: Led, rdn/hdd 1f out & no   ¾ 39a
extra: op 6/1: also bhd today's wnr in 307 (C/D).
295 **ANOTHER RAINBOW** 10 [3] 4-8-2 Martin Dwyer 9/1: 50-035: Chsd ldrs, outpcd fnl 3f: see 295, 167.   3½ 29a
*307 **JAVA SHRINE** 7 [8] 9-9-3 (bl) Joanna Badger (7) 4/5 FAV: 260-16: Held up in tch, prog wide/chsd   2½ 36a
ldrs 3f out, sn rdn/wknd: hvly bckd: disapp effort, ahd of today's 4th & wnr latest: same terms prev: see 307.
3782} **KINGS CAY** 99 [9] 9-8-5 (vis) J P Fessey 50/1: 0000-7: Chsd ldrs 1m: 8 wk jumps abs (rtd 67h, nov):   5 17a
unplcd on the level in '99 (rtd 38, h'cap): plcd form in '98 (rtd 61, first time visor): back in '96 scored at Ripon,
Carlise & Hamilton (rtd 60): eff over 11/12f, stays 14f well: acts on firm, AW bow today.
-- **SPARKLING DOVE** [7] 7-8-6 (BL) N Carlisle 50/1: 8: Sn bhd: blnks: jumps fit, Flat/AW bow.   26 0a

120

WOLVERHAMPTON (Fibresand) TUESDAY JANUARY 18TH Lefthand, Sharp Track

8 ran   Time 2m 46.5 (12.9)   (John Pointon & Sons)   Miss S J Wilton Wetley Rocks, Staffs.

---

348 2.20 TOWER HCAP STKS 4YO+ 0-75 (E)   2m46y aw Going 64 -31 Slow   **[69]**
£2601   £743   £371   4 yo rec 7 lb

296 ALHESN 10 [8] C N Allen 5-9-12 (67) R Morse 9/2: 015-41: 5 b g Woodman - Deceit Princess   **72a**
(Vice Regent) Off the pace, imprvd fnl circuit to lead 3½f out, kept on well: op 7/2: '99 wnr at W'hampton
(2, mdn h'cap & h'cap, rtd 45), Lingfield & here at W'hampton (2, h'caps, rtd 71a at best): eff at 14f/2m: acts
on firm, fast, both AWs, likes sharp trks, esp W'hampton & Yarmouth: best without visor: gd weight carrier.

284 PIPE MUSIC 11 [2] P C Haslam 5-9-5 (60)(vis) T Eaves (7) 9/2: 236-32: 5 b g Mujadil - Sunset   3 **61a**
Cafe (Red Sunset) Cl-up, led 6f out till bef 3f out, kept on: op 7/2: vis reapplied: both wins at Southwell.

284 MEILLEUR 11 [3] Lady Herries 6-9-5 (60) M Tebbutt 11/4 FAV: 024-23: 6 b g Nordico - Lucy Limelight   1 **60a**
(Hot Spark) Rear, prog to trk front pair 4f out, rdn 2f out, kept on same pace: nicely bckd from 7/2: ran
v similar race at the weights to 284 (in front on this rnr-up): see 68.

296 JAMAICAN FLIGHT 10 [5] J Balding 7-9-12 (67) A Culhane 4/1: 05-334: Well plcd, led 6f till   3½ **63a**
6f out, no extra appr str: drifter from 11/4: well clr rem: see 253.

141 TIME CAN TELL 45 [7] N Callan (3) 20/1: 6450-5: In tch till 5f out: jumps fit, see 66.   29 **25a**
253 FIFTEEN REDS 15 [9] 5-8-3 (44)(vis) T Williams 4/1: 000-26: Dwelt, went prom after 5f till 5f out.   1 **18a**
285 KATIES CRACKER 10 [1] 5-7-10 (37)(18oh) P M Quinn (5) 50/1: 000-07: Led 6f, btn 6f out: stiff task.   18 **0a**
298 GEEGEE EMMARR 8 [4] 7-7-10 (37)(3oh) S Yorston (4) 66/1: 000-08: Saddle slipped, handy, lost   18 **0a**
tch after 1m: stiffish task: failed to make the frame last term (amat h'cap, rtd 32a, ladies h'cap, rtd 35,
S Gollings): plcd fnl '98 start (h'cap, rtd 42): unproven beyond 7f, acts on soft grnd: with Mark Polglase.

978} MISCHIEF 99 [6] 4-8-7 (55) C Rutter 12/1: 5303-9: Al bhd: abs: plcd fnl of just 4 '99 starts   14 **0a**
(h'cap, rtd 66, P Cole): unrcd juv: poss stays 12f on hvy grnd, without blnks: with M Quinn.
9 ran   Time 3m 44.6 (15.4)   (J T B Racing)   C N Allen Newmarket.

---

349 2.50 ALBERT HCAP 4YO+ 0-85 (D)   1m1f79y Going 64 -07 Slow   **[69]**
£3789   £1166   £583   £291   4 yo rec 1 lb

*305 AREISH 7 [3] J Balding 7-8-7 (48) J Edmunds 11/4 FAV: 20-511: 7 b m Keen - Cool Combination   **54a**
(Indian King) Bhd ldrs, rdn to lead dist, held on well: bckd from 10/3, qk reapp: earlier won here at W'hampton
(appr h'cap): '99 wnr again at W'hampton (sell) & Southwell (fill h'cap, rtd 53a): '98 Southwell (h'cap, D Nicholls)
& W'hampton wnr (sell h'cap, rtd 44a, M Pipe): eff at 1m/12f on firm & gd grnd, prob equitrack, sharp trks, without blnks.

309 DARE 7 [6] P D Evans 5-9-6 (61)(bl) Joanna Badger (7) 3/1: 00-322: 5 b g Beveled - Run Amber   ½ **65a**
Run (Run The Gantlet) Well plcd, chall ent str, edged left under press, held towards fin: nicely bckd from 7/2:
last Friday won over timber at Warwick (2m now h'cap on soft grnd, rtd 70h): in a rich vein of form: see 83.

23 ULTRA CALM 68 [2] P C Haslam 4-9-3 (59) P Goode (5) 10/1: 6500-3: 4 ch g Doubletour - Shyonn   ½ **62a**
(Shy Groom) Tried to make all, hdd dist, styd on for press: op 8/1, 10 wk abs: '99 wnr here at W'hampton
(2, class stks & clmr, rtd 64a) & Ripon (h'cap, rtd 65 at best): unplcd in '98: eff at 1m/10f: acts on fast,
soft & fibresand: suited by sharp trks, esp W'hampton: eff up with/forcing the pace, maybe wnts: spot on soon.

260 THE BARGATE FOX 14 [9] D J G Murray Smith 4-9-0 (56) S Whitworth 7/2: 041-34: Wide, bhd, imprvd   2½ **54a**
over 3f out, rdn to chase ldrs 2f out, unable to chall: fair run back in trip, worth another try at 12f: see 233.

*309 HANNIBAL LAD 7 [4] 4-9-12 (68)(6ex) Martin Dwyer 5/1: 042-15: Cl-up, rdn & onepace ent fnl 2f: 1¼ **63a**
op 4/1, qk reapp & pen: btr 309 (C/D, beat this rnr-up).

268 MIGWAR 13 [7] 7-9-2 (57)(vis) C Cogan (5) 10/1: 401-06: Dwelt, nvr in it: best at 11/12f at Southwell.   3 **46a**
258 SANTANDRE 14 [8] 4-10-0 (70) P M Quinn (5) 12/1: 453-07: Held up wide, nvr plcd to chall: see 143.   2 **55a**
4410} JADE TIGER 92 [5] 4-9-6 (62) N Callan (3) 20/1: 0460-8: In tch till 3f out: AW bow: jumps fit, best run   3 **41a**
when a last flight faller (juv nov, prob stays 2m1f, gd/soft, rtd 937): '99 Leicester wnr (nurs, rtd 75 in a
h'cap): juv rnr-up for B Meehan (nurs, rtd 79): eff at 1m, stays 10f: acts on firm & gd grnd, any trk, without blnks.

271 RIVERBLUE 12 [1] 4-10-0 (70) M Tebbutt 20/1: 040-09: Prom till 4f out: '99 rnr-up (h'cap, rtd 92,   ½ **48a**
M Channon) & '98 wnr at Catterick (mdn) & Thirsk (nurs, rtd 90, Mrs Ramsden): eff at 7f/1m on fast & gd/soft grnd,
without visor, any trk: yet to take to sand: with D Wintle.
9 ran   Time 2m 04.8 (6.6)   (Mrs J Coghlan Everitt)   J Balding Scrooby, Notts.

---

350 3.20 VAUXHALL SELLER 3YO (G)   1m100y aw rnd Going 64 -34 Slow   **[69]**
£1850   £528   £264

303 CASTLEBRIDGE 8 [7] D Morris 3-8-11 (VIS) M Tebbutt 20/1: 000-01: 3 b g Batshoof - Super Sisters   **65a**
(Call Report) Well plcd, led 2f out, ran on strgly: sold for 6,100gns & reportedly joins M Pipe: bckd at big odds
but no form prev, unrcd on turf: eff over a sharp 1m on fibresand, didn't stay further: woken up by visor & positive ride.

158 WILEMMGEO 41 [8] P C Haslam 3-8-6 Dale Gibson 11/10 FAV: 3010-2: 3 b f Emarati - Floral Spark   2 **54a**
(Forzando) Prom, went after wnr 3f out, styd on without threatening: nicely bckd from 11/8, clr rem, 6 wk
abs: back to form after trying equitrack: likes W'hampton: see 80.

*286 GLENWHARGEN 10 [3] Julian Poulton 3-8-11 A Daly 3/1: 045-13: 3 b f Polar Falcon - La Veine (Diesis)   6 **50a**
Held up, imprvd over 3f out, onepace dist: op 2/1: clmd by current connections after 286 (10f equitrack).

192 CARDINAL FAIR 34 [1] B P J Baugh 3-8-6 R Lappin 12/1: 05-4: Chsd ldrs till outpcd 2f out: lngr trip.   2½ **38a**
257 WISHEDHADGONEHOME 14 [5] 3-8-6 (vis) Joanna Badger (7) 8/1: 26-305: Bmpd after 1f, al bhd.   1¼ **37a**
286 WITTON WOOD 10 [6] 3-8-11 A Whelan 9/1: 000-36: Led till 4f out, fdd: see 286 (equitrack).   7 **31a**
303 SHEERNESS ESSITY 8 [4] 3-8-7(1ow) F Lynch 14/1: 100-07: Hmpd & stumbled after 1f, al bhd: 6 **18a**
op 7/1, forget this, blnks omitted: '99 wnr here at W'hampton (fill seller, rtd 61a & 66, M Channon):
eff forcing the pace around 1m: acts on soft grnd & fibresand, sharp or gall trks: with M Dods.

283 CHIEF JUSTICE 11 [2] 3-8-11 T G McLaughlin 20/1: 0-08: Al towards rear: mkt drifter, no form.   2½ **17a**
8 ran   Time 1m 54.5 (8.3)   (D P Barrie)   D Morris Newmarket.

---

351 3.50 CHELSEA HCAP DIV I 3YO+ 0-60 (F)   6f aw rnd Going 64 +02 Fast   **[59]**
£1928   £551   £275

82 PRESS AHEAD 59 [1] B A McMahon 5-9-5 (50) L Newman (5) 7/1: 6020-1: 5 b g Precocious - By Line   **57a**
(High Line) Bhd ldrs, led ent str, shade rdly: tchd 9/1, 8 wk abs: fair time: lightly rcd, '99 rnr-up (h'cap,
rtd 51): '98 wnr here at W'hampton (C/D auct mdn, rtd 66a & 50): eff over a sharp 5/6f on gd/soft grnd
& fibresand, likes W'hampton: best up with the pace: likely to improve again & win more on this surface.

243 XSYNNA 16 [8] T T Clement 4-10-0 (59) M Tebbutt 3/1 FAV: 435-42: 4 b g Cyrano de Bergerac - Rose   1½ **60a**

121

Ciel (Red Sunset) In tch, wide, prog 2f out, rdn to chase wnr bef dist, al held: gamble from 7/1, jt top-weight, ran well back at 6f, acts on firm, gd/soft grnd, both AWs: caught an unexposed sort: see 212.
291 **TINKERS SURPRISE 10** [11] J Balding 6-8-9 (40)(bl) C Carver (2) 8/1: 006-53: 6 b g Cyrano de Bergerac - Lils Fairy (Fairy King) Bhd, keen, gd prog 2f out, rdn dist, kept on same pace: stays 6f, best at 5f. 2 **36a**
313 **PAGEBOY 6** [10] P C Haslam 11-8-8 (39)(vis) T Eaves (7) 6/1: 066-44: Dwelt/bhd till ran on in the str. 1 **33a**
232 **DAYNABEE 22** [3] 5-9-1 (46) P Doe 6/1: 4252-5: Led till 2½f out, no extra bef dist: drifter from 4/1. 1½ **36a**
246 **FRENCH GRIT 15** [2] 8-9-2 (47)(VIS) Iona Wands (5) 10/1: 025-06: Chsd ldrs till ent fnl 2f: visored. ½ **35a**
*199 **CANTGETYOURBREATH 32** [13] 4-9-9 (54)(bl) J Bosley (7) 7/1: 0051-7: Slow away, nvr on terms: best in sellers, see 199. 1½ **38a**
250 **TANCRED TIMES 15** [7] 5-8-10 (41) Kimberley Hart (5) 12/1: 026-08: Cl-up, led bef fnl 2f till appr dist. 1¼ **22a**
246 **MISS BANANAS 15** [6] 5-8-10 (41) D Meah (7) 20/1: 000-69: Handy till 2f out: op 14/1, see 226. ¾ **20a**
243 **SOUNDS LUCKY 16** [5] 4-10-0 (59) T G McLaughlin 12/1: 500-60: Nvr going pace: 10th, op 10/1. ¾ **36a**
323 **SO WILLING 5** [4] 4-9-4 (49)(vis) F Lynch 5/1: 00-060: Chsd ldrs 3f: 11th: best at Southwell?, see 183. 6 **15a**
250 **PALACE GREEN 15** [9] 4-9-3 (48) A Culhane 20/1: 000-00: Mid-div till 3f out: last: '99 Southwell wnr (h'cap, rtd 70a): '98 wnr again at Southwell (2 sells for M Channon, rtd 77a & 70): eff at 5/6f: acts on fast grnd, fibresand/Southwell specialist, handles hvy: can go well fresh, up with/forcing the pace. 2 **9a**
12 ran Time 1m 16.5 (3.7) (R L Bedding) B A McMahon Hopwas, Staffs.

352

4.20 CHELSEA HCAP DIV II 3YO+ 0-60 (F) 6f aw rnd Going 64 +04 Fast [59]
£1928 £551 £275

299 **TELECASTER 8** [8] C R Egerton 4-8-9 (40)(bl) D Sweeney 9/4 FAV: 000-31: 4 ch g Indian Ridge - Monashee (Sovereign Dancer) Sn led, pld a long way clr ent str, easing down: bckd from 3/1, best time of day, first win: unplcd in 3 '99 starts: eff at 7f, revelation back at 6f, has the pace for 5f: acts on fibresand, sharp trk: clrly much imprvd since blnkd with forcing tactics: qck follow-up likely. **57a**
193 **INVIRAMENTAL 34** [12] D Haydn Jones 4-9-1 (46)(bl) A Mackay 8/1: 0504-2: 4 b c Pursuit Of Love - Corn Futures (Nomination) Struggled to go pace till gd wide prog appr fnl 2f, kept on but wnr had long gone: caught a tartar back in trip: handles fibresand & is likely to score off this lowly mark: see 193. 5 **50a**
233 **CAREQUICK 22** [13] A Bailey 4-8-9 (40) J Fanning 12/1: 0053-3: 4 ch f Risk Me - Miss Serlby (Runnett) Chsd ldrs, feeling pace appr str, late hdwy: clrly unsuited by drop back to 6f, needs further. 1¾ **40a**
226 **TROJAN HERO 22** [9] K C Comerford 9-9-12 (57) C Cogan (5) 10/1: 2100-4: Prom, eff 2f out, onepce. nk **56a**
121 **HOT LEGS 52** [5] 4-8-8 (39) L Newman (5) 25/1: 6000-5: Al around same place: 7 wk abs, no form. 3 **31a**
262 **FREDERICK JAMES 13** [3] 6-9-8 (53) R Cody Boutcher (7) 5/1: 300-46: Nvr able to chall: see 262. ¾ **43a**
166 **YOUNG IBNR 39** [6] 5-9-1 (46) L Newton 6/1: /533-7: Early ldr, fdd ent str: 6 wk abs, stablemate 5th. ¾ **34a**
2154} **VILLAGE NATIVE 99** [4] 7-10-0 (59)(bl) N Callan (3) 16/1: 0261-8: Chsd ldrs, btn 2f out & eased dist: op 12/1, top-weight, reapp: landed fnl '99 start at Salisbury (clmr, rtd 70 & 65a): '98 wnr here at W'hampton (h'cap, rtd 61a), Sandown & Bath (clmrs, rtd 66): eff at 5/6f, gets 1m well on turf: acts on firm, soft, equitrack, likes fibresand/W'hampton: eff in visor, best in blnks: now a 7yo, sharper next time. 1½ **43a**
291 **LEGAL VENTURE 10** [10] 4-9-2 (47)(vis) T G McLaughlin 20/1: 00U-09: Nvr troubled ldrs: see 291. 2 **26a**
288 **MISS DANGEROUS 10** [1] 5-9-4 (49)(bl) S Drowne 9/2: 06-130: Handy 3f: 10th, tchd 11/1, see 243. 1 **26a**
304 **DEKELSMARY 8** [11] 5-8-10 (41)(t) J Edmunds 8/1: 000-60: Nvr a factor: 11th, see 212. 1 **16a**
235 **Snap Cracker 20** [2] 4-9-6 (51) A Culhane 20/1: 262 **Zelbeck 13** [7] 4-8-10 (41) P McCabe 20/1:
13 ran Time 1m 16.4 (3.6) (Casting Partners) C R Egerton Chaddleworth, Berks.

LINGFIELD (Equitrack) WEDNESDAY JANUARY 19TH Lefthand, V Sharp Track

Official Going STANDARD. Stalls: 5f & 1m - Outside; Rem - Inside.

353

1.10 CHAMPAGNE MDN 4YO+ (D) 1m aw rnd Going 26 +01 Fast
£2808 £864 £432 £216

4593} **MULLAGHMORE 77** [4] M Kettle 4-9-0 (bl) N Callan (3) 7/1: 3604-1: 4 b g Petardia - Comfrey Glen (Glenstal) Chsd ldrs halfway, smooth prog to lead over 1f out, styd on strongly, rdn out: gd time: op 6/1: 11 wk abs, AW bow: plcd form in '99 (rtd 67, h'cap): mod form in '98: eff at 1m & improved on equitrack, acts on fast & gd: handles a gall or sharp trk: eff in blnks, has worn a t-strap: runs well fresh: open to improvement. **68a**
314 **SPRINGTIME LADY 7** [2] S Dow 4-8-9 P Doe 7/2 JT FAV: 220-22: 4 ch f Desert Dirham - Affaire de Coeur (Imperial Fling) Chsd ldrs, rdn & kept on fnl 2f, not pace of wnr: apprec return to 1m: see 314, 96 (h'cap). 2 **58a**
265 **PIPE DREAM 14** [3] P Burgoyne 4-9-0 P McCabe 25/1: 000-33: 4 b g King's Signet - Rather Warm (Tribal Chief) Prom, led halfway, rdn/hdd over 1f out & no extra: clr rem: eff at 1m on equitrack, mod form prev. 1½ **60$**
271 **ONE QUICK LION 13** [6] R W Armstrong 4-9-0 M Hills 7/2 JT FAV: 065-04: Mid-div, rdn/prog to chase ldrs 2f out, held over 1f out: nicely bckd, tchd 5/1: see 271 (h'cap, fibresand). 6 **51a**
4552} **SYLVA LEGEND 82** [7] 4-9-0 N Esler (7) 4/1: 3364-5: Mid-div at best: op 7/2: AW bow, 12 wk abs: plcd sev times in '99 (rtd 89, reapp, mdn): rtd 81 at best in '98: eff at 1m, prob suited by 10/12f: handles firm & soft, likes a sharp/easy trk: has run well in a visor: worth another try in similar over further. 1¾ **48a**
314 **REACHFORYOURPOCKET 7** [1] 5-9-0 G Baker (7) 33/1: 660-46: Nvr on terms: see 314 (10f). 2½ **43a**
4314} **OUDALMUTEENA 99** [9] 5-9-0 (VIS) Martin Dwyer 14/1: 5600-7: Dwelt, sn chsd ldrs, wknd 2f out: op 10/1: jumps fit (rtd 102h, nov hdle): rnr-up in '99 (h'cap, rtd 67 & 42a at best): plcd fnl of 2 '98 starts (rtd 73, mdn, A Stewart): eff around 9/10f: handles fast, gd/soft & equitrack: tried a visor today: handles any trk. ¾ **42a**
273 **COLLEGE BLUE 13** [10] 4-8-9 L Carter 5/1: 3/2-28: Led 5f: op 7/2: jockey given a 6-day ban for irresponsible riding: longer 1m trip, a return to shorter will suit: btr 273 (6f, fibresand). 2 **33a**
2954} **MUDDY WATER 99** [8] 4-8-9 D Dineley 25/1: 6462-9: Al towards rear: 6 month absence. 5 **23a**
314 **MOUTON 7** [12] 4-8-9 L Newman (5) 9/1: 322-50: Prom 6f: 10th: btr 314. ½ **22a**
314 **Sky City 7** [11] 4-8-9 T Williams 33/1: 111 **Micky Dee 54** [5] 4-9-0 (t) Joanna Badger (7) 66/1:
12 ran Time 1m 38.22 (2.02) (Greenacres) M Kettle Blewbury, Oxon.

354

1.40 TRADE SHOWS CLAIMER 4YO+ (F) 6f aw rnd Going 26 -12 Slow
£2009 £574 £287

320 **KRYSTAL MAX 6** [1] T G Mills 7-8-9 L Carter 4/11 FAV: 20-251: 7 b g Classic Music - Lake Isle (Caerleon) Sn led/clr after 2f, rdn & held on well ins last: hvly bckd at odds on: qck reapp: '99 wnr here at Lingfield (3) & also W'hampton (clmrs, rtd 79a): '98 Lingfield (2) & Southwell wnr (h'caps, rtd 80a): eff **70a**

LINGFIELD (Equitrack) WEDNESDAY JANUARY 19TH Lefthand, V Sharp Track

at 5/6f on fast, poss gd/soft, AW/sharp trk specialist: can force the pace effectively: tough, loves claimers.
313 **NINEACRES** 7 [5] J M Bradley 9-8-5 (bl) Claire Bryan (7) 5/2: 02-322: 9 b g Sayf El Arab - Mayor   1¾ 58a
(Laxton) Rdn/towards rear, styd on to chase wnr fnl 2f, al held: op 7/4: clr rem, ran to best: see 313.
276 **EMMAJOUN** 13 [4] W G M Turner 5-8-0 T Williams 14/1: 625-03: 5 b m Emarati - Parijoun (Manado)   6 42a
Chsd wnr/rdn halfway, wknd over 1f out: op 12/1: visor omitted: sell h'caps suit better: see 156, 32.
313 **SPECKLED GEM** 7 [2] J R Best 4-7-12 Joanna Badger (7) 20/1: 0/0-54: Al outpcd: see 313.   1 38a
262 **SUPERLAO** 14 [3] 8-7-12 G Baker (7) 33/1: 406-05: Al outpcd rear: plcd in '99 (clmr, rtd 35, unplcd   3½ 29a
on sand, rtd 30a, C/D seller): rtd 40a at best in '98 (tried visor): '97 wnr here at Lingfield (h'cap, rtd 42): eff
at 5/6f: acts on fast & gd/soft, prob handles equitrack: likes a sharp/undul trk
5 ran   Time 1m 12.65 (2.25)   (Shipman Racing Ltd)   T G Mills Headley, Surrey.

---

355 | 2.10 DELLAFERA HCAP STKS 3YO 0-60 (F)   1m aw rnd   Going 26   -22 Slow   [63]
£2236   £639   £319

*303 **BOSS TWEED** 9 [3] Ronald Thompson 3-9-9 (58) (6ex) A Clark 9/4 FAV: 650-11: 3 b g Persian Bold -   67a
Betty Kenwood (Dominion) Rdn bhd early, hdwy 3f out, led ins last, rdn out: nicely bckd tho' op 6/4: 6lb pen for
recent Southwell success (seller, easily, with G C Bravery): unplcd in '99 (rtd 59a & 57): eff at 1m, shld stay
further: acts on both AWs & a sharp trk: has run well fresh: gd weight carrier: looks one to follow on sand.
4461} **LEGENDAIRE** 90 [5] C A Dwyer 3-9-6 (55) M Hills 7/2: 4000-2: 3 gr c Fly Till Dawn - Iolani (Alzao)   1¼ 57a
Sn led/dsptd lead trav well, rdn/hdd ins last & no extra cl-home: op 5/2: 3 month abs/AW bow: rnr-up in
'99 (4 rnr nov stks, rtd 70): stays a sharp 1m: handles equitrack & prob gd grnd: win similar back at 7f?
287 **CROESO ADREF** 11 [2] S C Williams 3-9-1 (50) G Faulkner (3) 11/4: 03-123: 3 ch f Most Welcome -   3½ 45a
Grugiar (Red Sunset) Led/dsptd lead, wknd over 1f out: nicely bckd, op 4/1: clr rem: stays sharp 1m, suited by 7f.
153 **DAMASQUINER** 44 [6] T E Powell 3-8-10 (45) R Lappin 50/1: 0066-4: Keen/held up, rdn/held 2f out: 6 31a
6 wk abs: unplcd in '99 (rtd 65, mdn): prev tried at up to 6f.
287 **DIAMOND GEORGIA** 11 [8] 3-8-9 (44) (VIS) S Drowne 20/1: 660-05: Trkd ldrs 6f: visor: longer 1m trip.   2 26a
294 **TING** 11 [4] 3-9-7 (56) P Goode (5) 7/2: 055-46: Nvr factor: op 4/1: btr 294, 202 (5f, fibresand).   2½ 33a
241 **LUNAJAZ** 17 [7] 3-8-7 (42) R Price 25/1: 000-57: Trkd ldrs 5f: btr 241 (C/D, clmr).   ½ 18a
303 **LUCKY MELODY** 9 [1] J Stack 33/1: 330-08: Chsd ldrs 5f: unplcd in '99 (rtd 51a, seller).   7 10a
8 ran   Time 1m 40.04 (3.84)   (B Bruce)   Ronald Thompson Stainforth, S.Yorks.

---

356 | 2.40 TOTE EXACTA HCAP 4YO+ 0-100 (C)   1m4f aw   Going 26   +05 Fast   [97]
£6742   £2090   £1045   £522   4 yo rec 4 lb

*302 **QUINTRELL DOWNS** 9 [2] R M H Cowell 4-9-2 (85) (6ex) R Studholme (5) 7/2: 132-11: 5 b g Efisio -   92a
Nineteenth Of May (Homing) Sn prom, led over 4f out, styd on well & asserted ins last, rdn out: gd time: op 3/1:
6lb pen for recent Southwell success (h'cap): '99 jumps wnr at W'hampton (nov h'cap, rtd 85h, eff at 2m on fast):
earlier in '99 won at Southwell (2) & W'hampton (h'caps, rtd 74a & 40): ex-Irish: eff at 11f/12f on fast, handles
gd/soft & loves both AWs, esp Southwell: tough/useful & progressive AW performer, keep on the right side.
*317 **RAYIK** 7 [5] G L Moore 5-9-1 (66) (6ex) P Doe 4/1: 060-12: 5 b g Marju - Matila (Persian Bold)   4 67a
Led, rdn/hdd 4f out, held ins last: op 7/2: 6lb pen for latest: running well: see 317 (13f).
302 **PUZZLEMENT** 9 [7] C E Brittain 6-8-6 (75) L Newman (5) 5/1: 645-33: 6 gr g Mystiko - Abuzz (Absalom)   ¾ 75a
Chsd ldrs 3f out, sn effort & no impress ins last: tchd 7/1: spot on back at 9/10f? see 302.
3521} **RANDOM KINDNESS** 99 [6] R Rowe 7-9-2 (85) A Clark 14/1: 2000-4: Held up, mod prog, no threat: 4 79a
op 16/1: 12 wk jumps absence (rtd 59h, mdn hdle): rnr-up twice in '99 (rtd 72, h'cap & 86a, R Ingram): '98 Nov
at Lingfield (2, stks rtd 89a) & Brighton (ltd stks, rtd 76): eff at 11f/2m on firm, gd & both AW's, any trk.
302 **NOUKARI** 9 [1] 7-8-13 (82) Joanna Badger (7) 10/1: 14-205: Held up, rdn/held 3f out: op 8/1: see 151.   1 75a
*245 **SPACE RACE** 17 [4] 6-8-11 (80) M Hills 3/1 FAV: 202-16: Held up in tch, btn 3f out: hvly bckd: btr 245.   7 63a
157 **CHINA CASTLE** 42 [3] 7-10-0 (97) M Tebbutt 9/2: 0254-7: Al rear: 17f: abs, topweight: see 157, 27.   3½ 75a
7 ran   Time 2m 31.67 (2.47)   (Mr & Mrs D A Gamble)   R M H Cowell Six Mile Bottom, Cambs.

---

357 | 3.10 BILSTON SELLLER 3YO 0-70 (G)   5f aw rnd   Going 26   -38 Slow
£1800   £514   £257

242 **MINIMUS TIME** 17 [4] T M Jones 3-8-7 (BL) R Price 20/1: 306-01: 3 ch f Timeless Times - Glenfield   57a
Greta (Gabitat) Broke well & clr lead halfway, rdn/styd on strongly ins last, rdn out: no bid: unplcd in '99 (rtd
50): eff at 5f on equitrack: set alight by forcing tactics in first time blnks on drop to selling grade.
228 **DIAMOND PROMISE** 23 [3] P D Evans 3-8-13 S Drowne 4/6 FAV: 1235-2: 3 b f Fayruz - Cupid Miss   3½ 52a
(Anita's Prince) Chsd wnr, rdn 2f out, kept on for press, nvr a threat: hvly bckd: acts on both AWs, gd & soft grnd.
281 **MASTER JONES** 12 [6] Mrs L Stubbs 3-8-12 A Culhane 9/4: 40-233: 3 b g Emperor Jones - Tight Spin   hd 50a
(High Top) Chsd ldrs, rdn/briefly chsd wnr ins last, al held: nicely bckd, clr rem: big drop in trip, see 281.
331 **MISS SINCERE** 5 [2] B S Rothwell 3-8-7 (vis) J Bramhill 15/2: 450-04: Al bhd: tchd 10/1: qck reapp: 8 33a
unplcd in '99 (rtd 57, auct mdn): worn a visor last 2 starts.
242 **CAPPUCINO LADY** 17 [1] A Daly 25/1: 060-05: Dwelt/al outpcd: rtd 59 at best in '99 (flattered).   2 28a
234 **SKI FREE** 21 [5] 3-8-7 (t) A Clark 16/1: 3605-6: Sn outpcd: tchd 20/1: t-strap: rtd 55 & 20a in '99   6 17a
(unplcd for R Guest): now with J L Harris.
6 ran   Time 1m 01.01 (3.21)   (Mervyn J Evans)   T M Jones Albury, Surrey.

---

358 | 3.40 COMET HCAP 4YO+ 0-70 (E)   6f aw rnd   Going 26   -06 Slow   [70]
£2626   £750   £375

250 **RUDE AWAKENING** 16 [3] C W Fairhurst 6-8-2 (44) P Doe 9/1: 506-41: 6 b g Rudimentary - Final Call   59a
(Town Crier) Made all & clr halfway, rdn/styd on strongly, unchall: op 10/1: plcd form in '99 (rtd 49a & 47,
h'caps): '98 Southwell wnr (h'cap, rtd 55a & 53): eff at 5/6f, stays 1m: acts on firm, gd/soft & fibresand,
enjoys equitrack: best forcing the pace: qk follow-up?
*280 **DAYS OF GRACE** 12 [6] L Montague Hall 5-9-8 (64) Martin Dwyer 7/2 CO FAV: 24-212: 5 gr m Wolfhound   -8 64a
Inshirah (Caro) Chsd ldrs halfway, kept on for press ins last, no ch with wnr: nicely bckd: caught a tartar.
*312 **WISHBONE ALLEY** 7 [4] M Dods 5-8-11 (53) (vis) (66ex) A Clark 7/2 CO FAV: 22-213: 5 b g Common   nk 52a
Grounds - Dul Dul (Shadeed) Chsd wnr 4f out, rdn/held over 1f out: well bckd: al gd form: see 312 (5f).
246 **BARITONE** 16 [7] S E Kettlewell 6-7-10 (38) (vis) P Fessey 16/1: 000-04: Trkd ldrs, rdn/outpcd   2½ 30a
halfway, kept on ins last, no threat: see 246 (fibresand).
2351} **JONATHANS GIRL** 99 [10] 5-7-11 (39) G Bardwell 50/1: 6000-5: Rdn/rear, late gains/no threat: 7 mth   ½ 29a

LINGFIELD (Equitrack)   WEDNESDAY JANUARY 19TH   Lefthand, V Sharp Track

abs: rnr-up in '99 (C/D mdn, rtd 44a, rtd 30 on turf, h'cap): stays a sharp 6f, tried 10f: handles equitrack.

272	**POLLY MILLS 13** [5] 4-10-0 (70)(bl) Joanna Badger (7) 8/1: 20-036: Rdn/bhd, mod prog: see 134.	1¼	57a
3855}	**CHAKRA 99** [2] 6-7-13 (41) T Williams 25/1: 3040-7: Sn handy, wknd over 1f out: 4 month abs:	1¼	25a

rnr-up in '99 (h'cap, rtd 45): '98 wnr at Warwick (2, h'caps, rtd 54): eff at 5f on firm & gd grnd: handles any trk, likes Warwick: best held up for a late run: sharper next time back at 5f.

312	**BRUTAL FANTASY 7** [9] 6-10-0 (70) M Hills 7/2 CO FAV: 5-2148: Prom wide 3f: nicely bckd: btr 288.	¾	52a
323	**PRIORY GARDENS 6** [1] 6-7-11 (39) Claire Bryan (7) 12/1: 50-309: Slowly away, nvr factor: op 10/1.	hd	20a
4604}	**DAY STAR 76** [12] 4-9-11 (67) M Tebbutt 10/1: 4010-0: Chsd ldrs wide 4f: 10th: op 8/1, abs: AW	2½	41a

bow: '99 Redcar wnr (h'cap, rtd 69): eff over a gall 6f, 7f+ may yet suit: acts on fast: likes force the pace.

4391} **Sotonian 95** [8] 7-9-11 (67) P M Quinn (5) 12/1:   218 **Young Bigwig 29** [11] 6-9-12 (68) A Culhane 14/1:
12 ran   Time 1m 12.31 (1.91)   (William Hill)   C W Fairhurst Middleham, N.Yorks.

WOLVERHAMPTON (Fibresand)   THURSDAY JANUARY 20TH   Lefthand, Sharp Track

Official Going   STANDARD. Stalls: 7f/1m6f Upwards - Outside, Rem - Inside.

---

359   1.30 WILSON FILLIES HCAP 4YO+ 0-65 (F)   1m1f79y aw   Going 45 -04 Slow   [65]
£2299   £657   £328   4 yo rec 1 lb

*306   **FRENCH SPICE 9** [6] Sir Mark Prescott 4-8-8 (46) D Sweeney 4/9 FAV: 061-11: 4 b f Cadeaux Genereux -   58a
Hot Spice (Hotfoot): Chsd ldrs, swtchd halfway & smooth prog to chall 2f out, led over 1f out & sn clr, easily: value for 8L+: nicely bckd at odds-on: completed a hat-trick after 2 wins here at W'hampton (h'caps): eff at 1m/9.4f, 10f+ shld suit: loves fibresand/W'hampton: plenty in hand here & is one to follow.

2959} **SURE QUEST 99** [4] D W P Arbuthnot 5-8-12 (49) S Whitworth 25/1: 0000-2: 5 b m Sure Blade - Eagle's   5   49a
Quest (Legal Eagle): Held up in tch, kept on final 2f for pressure, no threat to wnr: AW bow/6 mth abs: unplcd in '99 (rtd 55, h'cap): '98 Folkestone wnr (mdn h'cap, rtd 61): eff at 10/11f on gd & firm, handles fibresand: likes a sharp/undul trk: best without a visor: took to the sand well, could find similar at 10f+.

4017} **CHAMBOLLE MUSIGNY 99** [8] M J Polglase 4-8-6 (44) Dean McKeown 50/1: 4500-3: 4 b f Majestic Light   1¼   41a
- Bridalup (Sharpen Up): Keen/cl up, led 3f out, rdn/hdd over 1f out & no extra: 4 mth abs/AW bow: unplcd in '99 (rtd 55, P Cole, tried blnks): eff arnd 9f, has tried 12f: handles fibresand & probably fast grnd.

325	**SWING ALONG 6** [5] R Guest 5-10-0 (65) A Rawlinson 8/1: 16-W24: Pulled hard rear, mod late gains.	¾	61a
178	**JATO DANCER 38** [7] 5-7-10 (33)(11oh) P M Quinn (5) 66/1: 0000-5: Led 6f, fdd: unplcd in '99 (rtd 24	2	25a

& 19a): '98 Windsor wnr (clmr, J R Arnold, rtd 59 & 50a): eff at 7/8.3f on fast, gd & equitrack: likes a sharp trk.

*314   **ROYAL FLAME 8** [2] 4-9-6 (58)(bl) (6ex) M Hills 5/2: 643-16: Trkd ldrs halfway, wknd 2f out & eased/   7   39a
btn fnl 1f: tchd 3/1: 6lb pen: disapp, connections reported filly was nvr travelling: btr 314 (mdn, 1st time blnks).

--   **MURRON WALLACE** [3] 6-8-7 (44) S Drowne 50/1: 2110/7: Swtchd wide/bhd 4f out: long abs/AW bow16   1a
7 ran   Time 2m 02.8 (4.6)   (J Morley)   Sir Mark Prescott Newmarket

---

360   2.00 GLADSTONE CLAIMER 4YO+ (F)   1m1f79y aw   Going 45 +01 Fast
£2236   £639   £319   4 yo rec 1 lb

329   **BACHELORS PAD 6** [10] D Nicholls 6-9-0 M Tebbutt 6/4 FAV: 20-021: 6 b g Pursuit Of Love - Note Book   62a
(Mummy's Pet): Rear/wide, stdy prog fnl 3f, led line, all-out: hvly bckd, clmd by J Pointon for £8,000, qck reapp: rnr-up twice in '99 (rtd 63, h'cap): plcd in '98 (rtd 76, class stks, W Jarvis): '96 Goodwood wnr: eff at 7/10f: acts on firm, gd/soft & fibresand: best without blnks: prob handles fibresand: likes a sharp one.

267   **TUFAMORE 15** [8] K R Burke 4-9-1 (vis) N Callan (3) 16/1: 005-42: 4 ch g Mt Livermore - Tufa   shd   63$
(Warning): Sn prom, led over 2f out, hard rdn/strongly prsd inside last, just held line: eff at 9f/11.5f: vis reapp.

*292   **RIVER ENSIGN 12** [1] W M Brisbourne 7-8-5 Claire Bryan (7) 7/1: 06-213: 7 br m River God - Ensigns Kit   2   48a
(Saucy Kit): Led 7f, no extra wel inside last: op 5/1: tough performer, can win more races: see 292 (C/D).

307   **FEARSOME FACTOR 9** [6] B J Curley 5-9-4 J P Spencer 3/1: 000-04: Mid-div, rdn/chsd ldrs 3f out,   4   53a
held over 1f out: nicely bckd, tchd 5/1: acts on soft, hvy & fibresand: clr of rem here.

344   **ADIRPOUR 3** [9] 6-8-8 Stephanie Hollinshea 33/1: 30-065: Towards rear, nvr a factor: qck reapp.   11   27a

102   **BADRINATH 57** [7] 6-8-8 P M Quinn (5) 25/1: 0350-6: Mid-div, btn 3f out: 8 wk abs: place form in   2   23a
'99 (rtd 60, class stks): '98 Lingfield (mdn, rtd 50a), Newmarket & Redcar wnr (appr & sell h'cap, rtd 54 at best): eff at 1m/10f, stays 11.4f: acts on fast, gd & equitrk: has run well fresh.

327   **MALWINA 6** [11] 4-8-8 J Fanning 33/1: P7: Prom 5f: qck reapp: see 327.   1¼   21a

*259   **OVER THE MOON 16** [2] 6-8-7 (vis) T G McLaughlin 7/1: 560-18: Pulled hard rear, nvr a factor: op 5/1.   6   10a

143   **LOCOMOTION 47** [4] 4-8-9 P Doe 9/2: 2000-9: Keen/prom, wknd 2f out & eased inside last: 7 wk abs: 9   0a
'99 Southwell scorer (auct mdn, rtd 74a, W Haggas, plcd on turf, rtd 80, mdn): eff at 6f, suited by a sharp 1m: acts on firm, gd & fibresand: handles a stiff/gall or sharp trk: lngr 9f trip today.

292   **MUTADARRA 12** [5] 7-9-4 R Studholme (5) 7/1: 000-40: Towards rear, nvr a factor: 10th: see 292.   1   6a

674}   **KHALED 99** [3] 5-9-8 Clare Roche (7) 16/1: 1/2-50: Mid-div, struggling 3f out: 11th: op 10/1: lngr   1¼   7a
priced stablemate of wnr: 10 mth abs: unplcd in '99 for K Mahdi (rtd 76a & 43): '98 Warwick scorer (mdn, rtd 77): eff over a turning 1m on fast grnd: has run well fresh.
11 ran   Time 2m 02.3 (4.1)   (N Honeyman)   D Nicholls Sessay, Nth Yorks.

---

361   2.30 MACMILLAN HCAP 3YO (D)   5f aw rnd   Going 45 -01 Slow   [85]
£3711   £1142   £571   £285

269   **KIRSCH 15** [3] C A Dwyer 3-8-9 (66)(vis) M Hills 11/4: 023-31: 3 ch f Wolfhound - Pondicherry   71a
(Sir Wimborne): Rdn in rear, styd on strongly under handes & heels riding fnl 2f to overhaul ldr nr fin, pushed out: op 4/1: '99 Lingfield scorer (clmr, rtd 68 & 70a): eff at 5/6f, could stay further: acts on firm, gd & both AWs: handles any trk, likes a sharp/undul one: eff in a visor: fine ride by M Hills.

275   **SMOKIN BEAU 14** [1] J Cullinan 3-9-7 (78) D Sweeney 6/5 FAV: 315-32: 3 b g Cigar - Beau Dada   ½   80a
(Pine Circle): Sn led & clr 2f out, rdn/hdd wel inside last & no extra: clr rem: hvly bckd: see 275, 127.

4212} **PIPS STAR 99** [2] D W P Arbuthnot 3-8-7 (64) R Price 8/1: 3001-3: 3 b f Pips Pride - Kentucky Starlet   4   56a
(Cox's Ridge): Chsd ldr, rdn/outpcd halfway: 4 mth abs: '99 wnr on final start here at W'hampton (C/D, sell, rtd 68a, earlier plcd on turf, rtd 77, auct mdn): eff at 5f on fast & fibresand: likes a sharp trk: enjoys sells.

*228   **MISS SKICAP 24** [4] Miss S J Wilton 3-9-1 (72) T G McLaughlin 4/1: 421-4: Al outpcd: prev with T D Barron.   4   54a

228   **WELCHS DREAM 24** [5] 3-8-13 (70) P Bradley(5) 5/1: 4424-5: Chsd ldr/btn 2f out: op 7/2, now with A Berry 5   43a
5 ran   Time 1m 02.5 (2.3)   (Cedar Lodge Syndicate)   C A Dwyer Newmarket

362 | **3.00 DISRAELI MDN 3YO (D) 7f aw rnd Going 45 -19 Slow**
£2795 £860 £430 £215

46	**BULAWAYO** 66 [8] B A McMahon 3-9-0 S Righton 33/1: 06-1: 3 b c Prince Sabo - Ra Ra Girl (Shack):	72a

Led/dsptd lead, asserted ins last, pushed out: 2 mth abs: unplcd in '99 (rtd 49 & 47a): apprec step up to 7f, cld stay further: acts on fibresand: likes to force the pace: handles a sharp trk & runs well fresh.

278 **NIGHT AND DAY** 13 [6] W Jarvis 3-8-9 M Tebbutt 4/6 FAV: 3-22: 3 ch f Anshan - Midnight Break 1¾ 63a
(Night Shift): Keen/dsptd lead with wnr, ev ch over 1f out, hard rdn/no extra inside last: hvly bckd: see 278, 118.

-- **LADY OF BILSTON** [3] D R C Elsworth 3-8-9 S Drowne 11/1: 3: 3 b f Bin Ajwaad - Takeshi (Cadeaux 2½ 58a
Genereux): Mid-div, rdn/styd on steadily final 3f, nrst fin: op 5/1: IR 7,000gns purchase, dam styd 1m: eff at 7f, 1m+ shld suit: acts on fibresand: encouraging intro, could find similar when stepped up to 1m.

278 **SILCA FANTASY** 13 [10] P Howling 3-8-9 T Williams 12/1: 0-44: Chsd leading pair, rdn/flashed tail 2 54a
& wknd over 1f out: op 8/1: see 278.

289 **TEA FOR TEXAS** 12 [1] 3-8-9 C Rutter 7/1: 4-35: Chdrs ldrs, btn 3f out: see 289, 153 (5/6f). 1½ 51a

-- **FINERY** [2] 3-9-0 Martin Dwyer 16/1: 6: Dwelt, mid-div halfway, nvr a factor: op 10/1: Baratbea nk 55a
gelding, cost 36,000gns: half-brother to a German 10f wnr: dam a German 6/7f wnr: with W Jarvis.

-- **SUAVE PERFORMER** [9] 3-9-0 T G McLaughlin 20/1: 7: Dwelt/towards rear & wide, nvr a factor: op 2½ 50a
16/1, debut: dam a modest 7f/12f wnr: apprec 1m+ in time for S C Williams.

-- **PERCHINO** [4] 3-9-0 O Urbina 5/1: 8: Mid-div at best: mkt drifter, op 5/2: debut. 2½ 45a

328 **MILLER TIME** 6 [11] 3-9-0 J Fanning 33/1: 509: Towards rear/wide, nvr a factor: btr 273 (6f, debut). 4 37a

-- **SWIFT DISPERSAL** [7] 3-8-9 G Faulkner (3) 16/1: 0: Slowly away/al bhd: 10th: op 10/1, debut. 1 30a

198 **Subadar Major** 34 [5] 3-9-0 Angela Hartley (7) 50/1: 127 **Mr Stickywicket** 51 [12] 3-9-0 S Whitworth 33/1:
12 ran Time 1m 30.7 (4.5) (D J Allen) B A McMahon Hopwas, Staffs.

---

363 | **3.30 THATCHER SELLER 4YO+ (G) 1m6f166y Going 45 -52 Slow**
£1941 £554 £277 4 yo rec 6 lb

277 **CHILDRENS CHOICE** 14 [4] J Pearce 9-8-12 (vis) G Bardwell 2/1: 026-31: 9 b m Taufan - Alice Brackloon 49a
(Melyno): Wide/bhd, prog halfway, outpcd 5f out, styd on well fnl 2f to lead ins last, rdn out: no bid, slow time: in '99 won at Brighton (sell h'cap) & Redcar (sell, rtd 46 & 40a): '98 Newmarket wnr (fill h'cap, first time visor, rtd 55 at best): eff at 12f/2m on firm, soft & f/sand, handles any trk: eff with/without a visor.

231 **SWAN HUNTER** 24 [3] D J Cosgrove 7-9-3 N Callan (3) 7/4 FAV: 0025-2: 7 b h Sharrood - Cache 4 51a
(Bustino): Chsd ldrs halfway, rdn/prog to lead 2f out, hdd inside last & no extra: op 11/8: see 174 (C/D).

327 **CHAHAYA TIMOR** 6 [7] Miss S J Wilton 8-9-3 T G McLaughlin 2/1: 4/4-33: 8 b g Slip Anchor - Roxy 3½ 48a
Hart (High Top): Led 9f out, rdn/hdd 2f out & no extra: clr rem: nicely bckd: also bhd fraction rnr-up in 174 (C/D).

347 **KINGS CAY** 2 [5] T H Caldwell 9-9-3 (vis) Rebecca Bolton (7) 50/1: 000-04: Chsd ldrs, btn 5f out. 20 33$

277 **CYMBAL MELODY** 14 [9] 4-8-6 P M Quinn (5) 50/1: 000-05: Rear, nvr a factor: see 277. 22 12a

325 **SAFE SHARP JO** 6 [8] 5-9-3 G Gibbons (7) 50/1: /0-006: Chsd ldrs, bhd 5f out: lngr 14.8f trip: no 4 13a
form in '99: unplcd in '98 (rtd 60, auct mdn, M Jarvis): with W Clay.

-- **LUTINE BELL** [1] 5-9-3 J P Spencer 12/1: 000/7: Bhd, nvr a factor: op 8/1: 12 wk jumps abs (no 1½ 12a
form): missed '99 on the level: no form from 3 starts in '98: 11m bow today, owner trained.

1203 **DOBAANDI SECRET** 99 [2] 4-8-11 S Drowne 50/1: 0/00-8: Led 5f, sn btn: jumps fit (rtd 60h, nov hdle): ¾ 11a
9 mth Flat abs: rtd 49 in '99 (mdn): with P Evans & N Littmoden in '98 (no form, unplcd).

348 **GEEGEE EMMARR** 2 [6] 7-8-12 Dean McKeown 25/1: 00-009: Keen/prom till halfway: qck reapp: hd 6a
unplcd in '99 (rtd 35 & 32a, h'caps): plcd final '98 start (h'cap, rtd 42, S Gollings): eff at 7f, stays a stiff/ gall 10f: handles firm, soft & fibresand: with M J Polglase.
9 ran Time 3m 24.00 (14.4) (Mr & Mrs S Fernandes) J Pearce Newmarket

---

364 | **4.00 LLOYD GEORGE HCAP 4YO+ 0-80 (D) 7f aw rnd Going 45 +04 Fast** **[80]**
£3848 £1184 £592 £296

250 **FOREIGN EDITOR** 17 [2] R A Fahey 4-8-13 (65) P Hanagan (7) 2/1 FAV: 11-2D1: 4 ch g Magic Ring - True 80a
Precision (Presidium): Made all, readily pulled clr over 1f out, easily: fast time: well bckd: value for 8L+:
'99 wnr twice here at W'hampton (h'caps, rtd 69a, earlier unplcd on turf, rtd 54): plcd in '98 (mdn, rtd 67): eff at 6/7f on gd/soft & loves fibresand/W'hampton: runs well on an appr: very progressive, win again.

258 **BLUE STAR** 16 [3] N P Littmoden 4-10-0 (80) L Newman (5) 5/1: 050-52: 4 b g Whittingham - Gold And 3½ 84a
Blue (Bluebird): Trkd ldrs halfway, rdn & kept on final 2f, no ch with wnr: op 4/1: caught a tartar: see 258 (6f).

323 **RONS PET** 7 [4] K R Burke 5-9-4 (70)(tbl) N Callan (3) 11/4: 260-23: 5 ch g Ron's Victory - Penny ¾ 73a
Mint (Mummy's Game): Sn cl-up, rdn/onepace final 2f: well bckd, tchd 7/2: see 323, 33.

323 **C HARRY** 7 [7] R Hollinshead 6-8-12 (64) P M Quinn 15 16/1: 3-5254: Towards rear, mod gains. 3½ 60a

309 **MY TESS** 9 [6] 4-9-4 (70) Dean McKeown 13/2: 614-45: Chsd ldrs, outpcd/hung left 2f out: see 309, 78. ½ 65a

342 **DAHLIDYA** 3 [8] 5-8-10 (62) R Fitzpatrick (3) 7/1: 10-346: Mid-div, nvr on terms: qck reapp: see 180 (6f). 3 51a

4615] **INDIAN WARRIOR** 75 [10] 4-8-10 (62) S Whitworth 20/1: 0010-7: Slowly away & rear, mod prog: 11 2½ 46a
wk abs: AW bow: '99 Lingfield wnr (sell, J Noseda, rtd 59): '98 Warwick wnr (auct mdn, made all, rtd 92): eff at 6/7f, tried 1m: best without a visor: acts on firm & gd grnd: likes a sharp/undul trk & has run well fresh: likes to race up with/force the pace & enjoys sell grade: sharper next time.

258 **KAYO** 16 [1] 5-10-0 (80) J Fanning 8/1: 030-08: Chsd ldrs 4f: see 49, 7. 2½ 59a

270 **POLAR ICE** 14 [9] 4-9-7 (73) J Stack 33/1: 000-09: Slowly away/al rear: '99 wnr twice here at 14 31a
W'hampton (C/D mdn & h'cap, Sir M Prescott, rtd 84a, rnr-up on turf, rtd 77, h'cap): plcd in '98 (rtd 81, mdn): eff at 6/7f, tried 1m: acts on fast, hvy & loves fibresand/W'hampton: with D J S Cosgrove.

293 **NADDER** 12 [5] 5-7-10 (48)(bl)(10oh) G Bardwell 40/1: 00-250: Prom, hmpd after 2f & sn bhd: 10th. 2 0a
10 ran Time 1m 29.1 (2.9) (Pride Of Yorkshire Racing Club) R A Fahey Butterwick, Nth Yorks.

SOUTHWELL (Fibresand)   FRIDAY JANUARY 21ST   Lefthand, Sharp, Oval Track

Official Going   STANDARD Stalls: Inside

365

1.10 SHARK HCAP 3YO 0-70 (E)   6f aw   Going 60 -02 Slow   [75]
£2782   £856   £428   £214

*331   **OSCAR PEPPER 7** [3]   T D Barron 3-8-12 (59)(6ex) J P Spencer 8/15 FAV: 000-11: 3 b g Brunswick - Princess   **71a**
Baja (Conquistador Cielo) Rdn in mid-div, styd on strongly fnl 2f & led ins last, pushed out: well bckd: recent
wnr here at Southwell (h'cap, 1st success): well btn all turf starts in '99 (auct mdn, rtd 64): eff at 6f, tried
1m, shld stay on this evidence: acts on f/sand & Southwell: has run well fresh: can win again, poss at 7f+.
331   **AISLE 7** [2]   S R Bowring 3-8-9 (56)(bl) Dean McKeown 6/1: 60-522: 3 b c Arazi - Chancel (Al Nasr)   2   **59a**
Led, rdn over 1f out, hdd ins last & no extra cl-home: could find similar: also bhd today's wnr in 331 (C/D).
294   **JOHN COMPANY 13** [7]   R M Beckett 3-8-11 (58)(tVIS) M Tebbutt 33/1: 625-03: 3 ch c Indian Ridge -   2½   **54a**
Good Policy (Thatching) Trkd ldrs, rdn/outpcd 2f out, kept on ins last, not pace to chall: 1st time visor: handles
gd & fibresand: eff at 6f, interesting for similar at 7f: see 294 (7f).
--   **TROPICAL KING** [4]   D Carroll 3-9-3 (64) J Fanning 20/1: 0400-4: Trkd ldrs, rdn/ch over 1f out, no extra   ½   **58a**
ins last: op 12/1: AW bow/3 month abs: ex-Irish, unplcd in '99 (mdns): eff at 6f & handles fibresand.
311   **SPORTY MO 10** [5]   N Callan (3) 8/1: 501-45: Trkd ldrs, rdn/btn over 1f out: op 5/1: btr 311.   ½   **60a**
287   **BESCABY BLUE 13** [6]   3-8-11 (58) S Carson (5) 25/1: 602-66: Al outpcd: btr 287, 228.   2   **45a**
294   **CROSBY DONJOHN 13** [1]   3-8-13 (60)(bl) S Drowne 25/1: 002-67: Al outpcd rear: btr 188 (7f).   1   **45a**
*217   **SERGEANT SLIPPER 31** [9]   3-9-1 (62)(vis) R Fitzpatrick (3) 16/1: 4011-8: Dwelt/al rear: op 10/1: btr 217 (5f).¾   **45a**
2254}   **BEWILDERED 99** [8]   3-9-1 (62) A Culhane 25/1: 064-9: Al bhd: AW bow/7 month abs: unplcd for   17   **14a**
G Lewis in '99 (rtd 62): h'cap bow today for D W Chapman.
9 ran   Time 1m 17.00 (3.7)   (Ian Armitage)   T D Barron Maunby, N Yorks

366

1.40 HALIBUT APPR CLAIMER 4YO+ (F)   1m aw rnd   Going 60 -01 Slow
£2005   £573   £286

329   **PIPPAS PRIDE 7** [5]   S R Bowring 5-9-2 S Finnamore (3) 5/2: 01-131: 5 ch g Pips Pride - Al Shany (Burslem)   **65a**
Chsd ldr over 2f out, led over 1f out, styd on well, rdn out: nicely bckd: recent scorer here at Southwell (clmr):
'99 wnr at Southwell (clmr) & Lingfield (h'cap, rtd 41a, M Fetherston Godley): eff arnd a sharp 7f/1m, tried 10f:
acts on both AWs, loves Southwell: runs well fresh: enjoys claiming grade: in good heart & can win more races.
*276   **RAMBO WALTZER 15** [3]   D Nicholls 8-8-13 Iona Wands 2/5 FAV: 41-112: 8 b g Rambo Dancer - Vindictive 4   **54a**
Lady (Foolish Pleasure) Led, hdd over 1f out, held ins last: heavily bckd: clr rem: see 276 (7f).
297   **IMBACKAGAIN 11** [4]   N P Littmoden 5-8-10 C Cogan (3) 33/1: 000-63: 5 b g Mujadil - Ballinclogher   8   **39$**
(Creative Plan) Rdn/rear, mod gains whole 3f out, sn held: apprec a return to h'caps: see 297.
306   **HEATHYARDS JAKE 10** [1]   R Hollinshead 4-8-13 Stephanie Hollinshead (7) 14/1: 21-454: Rear/mod prog. 7   **31a**
322   **BOBS BUSTER 8** [2]   4-8-10 S Carson 50/1: 05-055: Cl-up 4f, sn btn: see 322.   4   **20a**
--   **CICATRIX** [6]   6-8-7 R Cody Boutcher (5) 100/1: 6: Chsd ldrs 4f: bckwd, jumps fit (no form).   7   **6a**
6 ran   Time 1m 44.3 (4.9)   (Roland M Wheatley)   S R Bowring Edwinstowe, Notts

367

2.15 OYSTER MED AUCT MDN 4-6YO (F)   7f aw rnd   Going 60 -09 Slow
£2215   £633   £316

293   **CITY REACH 13** [8]   P J Makin 4-9-0 (VIS) D Sweeney 4/1: 532-41: 4 b g Petong - Azola (Alzao)   **61a**
Chsd ldrs racing keenly, led over 1f out & styd on well ins last, drvn out: op 3/1, 1st time vis: plcd in '99
(rtd 57a & 75): rtd 77 when rnr-up on sole '98 start: tried 1m: acts on both AWs & hvy grnd:
handles a sharp/undul or gall trk: sharpened up by headgear today: open to further improvement.
293   **WELCOME GIFT 13** [3]   W J Haggas 4-9-0 M Hills 8/15 FAV: 2-22: 4 b g Prince Sabo - Ausonia   1¼   **59a**
(Beldale Flutter) Led after 1f, rdn/hdd over 1f out & no extra: well bckd: clr rem: ahead of today's wnr in 293.
225   **WOOLLY WINSOME 30** [9]   B Smart 4-9-0 J Bosley (7) 11/1: 0065-3: 4 br g Lugana Beach - Gay Mind   8   **47a**
(Gay Meadow) Led 1f, remained prom, wknd 2f out: see 225 (equitrack).
2768}   **AHOUOD 99** [5]   K Mahdi 4-8-9 C Lowther 10/1: 0036-4: Rdn/towards rear, mod gains for press: op   2½   **37a**
6/1, 6 month abs: unplcd in '99 (rtd 73, mdn, prob flattered, R Armstrong): rtd 63 on sole '98 start: has tried
up to 10f prev: rate more highly when tackling 1m+ & could prove interesting in h'cap company.
173   **MARIANA 41** [10]   5-8-9 (BL) T G McLaughlin 100/1: 0000-5: Chsd ldrs 4f: blnks/abs: unplcd in   3½   **30a**
'99 (rtd 43a & 26): placed '98 (rtd 50a & 44, R Whitaker): stays 1m, handles fast, soft & equitrack: tried a visor.
4252}   **FAS 99** [2]   4-9-0 (bl) K Sked 100/1: 0000-6: Dwelt/ rear, nvr factor: abs: unplcd in '99 (blnkd).   shd   **35a**
341   **FAN TC GEM 4** [4]   4-8-9 J Edmunds 50/1: 0-6007: Towards rear, nvr on terms: quick reapp: see 247.   ¾   **29a**
50   **FANNY PARNELL 67** [6]   4-8-9 T Williams 100/1: 0-8: Keen/prom 5f: 2 month abs, no form.   1¼   **26a**
4405}   **SARPEDON 95** [7]   4-9-0 R Fitzpatrick (3) 66/1: 0000-9: Chsd ldrs 4f: 10 wk jumps abs.   8   **19a**
196   **KINGS CHAMBERS 35** [1]   4-9-0 (bl) S Righton 100/1: 0/00-0: Unruly stalls, prom 3f: 10th: no form.   4   **11a**
10 ran   Time 1m 31.4 (4.8)   (T W Wellard Partnership)   P J Makin Ogbourne Maisey, Wilts

368

2.45 BLUE MARLIN HCAP 4YO+ 0-70 (E)   7f aw   Going 60 +10 Fast   [63]
£2899   £892   £446   £223

299   **ABERKEEN 11** [10]   M Dods 5-9-4 (53) A Culhane 4/1: 603-21: 5 ch g Keen - Miss Aboyne (Lochnager)   **62a**
Wide in rear, rdn & prog fnl 2f to lead ins last, styd on well, drvn out: best time of day: '99 Doncaster wnr
(appr h'cap, rtd 61 & 55a): plcd in '98 (h'cap, rtd 62): eff at 6/7f, tried 10f: acts on firm, gd/soft & f/sand:
handles a sharp or stiff/gall trk: over a fair mark & can win again.
326   **MUTABARI 7** [8]   Mrs S Lamyman 6-9-4 (53) J Fanning 10/1: 00-342: 6 ch g Seeking The Gold - Cagey   2   **57a**
Exuberance (Exuberant) Trkd ldrs, rdn to lead over 1f out, hdd ins last & no extra: could find similar: see 255.
*304   **ITCH 11** [11]   R Bastiman 5-8-8 (43)(6ex) T Williams 100/30: 00-213: 5 b h Puissance - Panienka (Dom   1   **45a**
Racine) Chsd ldrs, rdn/ch over 1f out, kept on onepace: 6lb pen for latest: nicely bckd: see 304 (C/D).
*323   **SAND HAWK 8** [4]   D Shaw 5-10-1 (64)(vis)(6ex) N Callan (3) 9/4 FAV: 2-2114: Chsd ldrs/onepace fnl 2f.   ¾   **65a**
--   **BROUGHTON MAGIC** [2]   5-8-1 (35)(1ow) L Newton 20/1: 0500/5: Towards rear, rdn & kept on fnl 2f, nrst   6   **28a**
fin: op 14/1, long abs: missed '99: unplcd in '98 (rtd 42 & 41a): eff at 7f, tried 9f & further cld suit: handles
fibresand: encouraging reapp, should prove sharper next time in similar.
279   **BEWARE 14** [1]   5-9-4 (53) F Norton 20/1: 30-366: Led 5f, fdd: forcing tactics to no avail: op 14/1: see 30.¾   **44a**
306   **BLOOMING AMAZING 10** [12]   6-9-5 (54) C Lowther 20/1: 530-07: Mid-div/wide, nvr factor: see 176 (1m).hd   **44a**
291   **GUNNER SAM 13** [6]   4-8-13 (48) R Fitzpatrick (3) 33/1: 65-008: Mid-div, nvr factor: see 201, 130 (C/D, sell)2½   **33a**

SOUTHWELL (Fibresand)   FRIDAY JANUARY 21ST   Lefthand, Sharp, Oval Track

304	**MOST RESPECTFUL 11** [7] 7-9-2 (51)(t) Kim Tinkler 12/1: 60-439: Keen/chsd ldrs 4f: btr 304, 249.	2	32a
316	**SHAMWARI SONG 9** [5] 5-8-5 (40)(t) D Sweeney 50/1: 065-00: Dwelt/al rear: 10th: see 163.	1	19a
4615}	**KUWAIT THUNDER 76** [3] 4-9-8 (57)(vis) M Hills 12/1: 0000-0: Cl-up 4f, fdd: 11th: 11 wk abs: AW bow:	1¾	33a

op 10/1: visor reapplied, plcd on reapp in '99 (h'cap, K Mahdi, rtd 79): plcd twice as a juv in '98 (rtd 80): eff at
6/7f, tried 1m: handles firm & gd/soft grnd, sharp or stiff/gall trk: now with J L Eyre.

282	**LIFT THE OFFER 14** [9] 5-9-13 (62) J Stack 40/1: 000-00: Wide/al rear: 12th: see 212 (6f).	4	30a

12 ran   Time 1m 30.1 (3.5)   (N A Riddell)   M Dods Piercebridge, Co Durham

---

369   3.20 LOBSTER SELLER 4YO+ (G)   1m3f aw   Going 60   -24 Slow
£1909   £545   £272   4 yo rec 3 lb

344	**METEOR STRIKE 4** [7] J Nicholls 6-9-2 (t) F Norton 4/9 FAV: 00-621: 6 ch g Lomond - Meteoric		62a

(High Line) Led after 5f, rdn 3f out, held on for press ins last: no bid, well bckd: rnr-up in '99 (rtd 70, stks, 1st
time blnks, Mrs A J Perrett): '98 Lingfield scorer (h'cap, rtd 83a): eff at 10/12f on firm, fast & both AWs: eff in
a t-strap, has reportedly suffered breathing probs: apprec forcing tactics & drop to sell grade.

253	**WELLCOME INN 18** [2] G Woodward 6-9-2 (t) C Lowther 14/1: 500-02: 6 ch g Most Welcome - Mimining	¾	60$

(Tower Walk) Held up in tch, prog/chsd wnr 4f out, rdn to chall fnl 2f, al just held: well clr rem: op 20/1: offic
rtd 27, treat rating with caution: see 211 (C/D h'cap).

215	**RAED 31** [3] J Pearce 7-9-2 R Price 5/1: 0060-3: 7 b g Nashwan - Awayed (Sir Ivor)	17	42a

Chsd ldrs, btn 3f out: op 3/1: '99 Windsor wnr (appr h'cap, rtd 62 & 65a): '98 wnr here at Southwell (2 h'caps,
rtd 77a & 69, Mrs Swinbank): eff btwn 9/11f on firm, gd/soft & loves fibresand/Southwell: likes a sharp trk.

324	**GROOMS GOLD 7** [4] J Pearce 8-9-2 (bl) G Bardwell 12/1: 330-04: Chsd ldrs, hmpd when btn 3f out:	5	35a

op 7/1: place form in '99 (rtd 52a, unplcd on turf, rtd 40, h'caps): plcd in '98 (rtd 57a, P Harris): back in '95 won
at Redcar (h'cap): eff at 1m/10f, stays 12f & has tried 2m: acts on fast, gd/soft & both AWs: best without blnks.

4262}	**CHICAGO BEAR 99** [6] 4-8-13 (tbl) N Callan (3) 20/1: 1000-5: Rdn to chase wnr 6f out, btn 4f out:	15	19a

jumps fit (mod form): '99 scorer at Sandown (clmr, P Cole, rtd 67, 1st time blnks): rtd 67 in '98: stays a stiff
10f, has tried 11f+: acts on gd grnd, suited by forcing tactics: has tried a vis: eff in clmg grade: AW bow today.

267	**MUSKETRY 16** [1] 4-8-13 (bl) Dean McKeown 16/1: 000-66: Led 3f, sn btn: op 20/1: see 194.	11	7a
324	**MODEST HOPE 7** [5] 13-9-2 A Culhane 50/1: 000-07: Sn struggling, btn/eased fnl 3f: see 324.	13	0a

7 ran   Time 2m 30.5 (9.2)   (James E Greaves)   D Nicholls Sessay, N Yorks

---

370   3.50 OCTOPUS HCAP 4YO+ 0-70 (E)   1m4f aw   Going 60   -06 Slow   [70]
£2899   £892   £446   £223   4 yo rec 4 lb

*324	**SWAGGER 7** [13] Sir Mark Prescott 4-8-3 (49) (1ow) (6ex) D Sweeney 4/6 FAV: 416-11: 4 ch g Generous -		60a

Widows Walk (Habitat) Chsd ldrs, led 4f out, rdn clr over 2f out, styd on well fnl 1f, eased nr line: hvly bckd:
recent Southwell wnr (amat h'cap): '99 Southwell wnr (appr h'cap, rtd 45a & 43): eff at 11/12f, stays 2m1f on
firm, likes fibresand/Southwell, handles any trk: best forcing the pace: has run well fresh & for an amateur.

285	**CEDAR FLAG 13** [8] R J O'Sullivan 6-7-10 (38) P M Quinn (5) 50/1: 060-32: 6 br g Jareer - Sasha Lea	2½	42a

(Cawston's Clown) Prom, rdn/chsd wnr fnl 2f, kept on tho' al held: effective at 12f, tried 2m, may yet suit: prob
handles both AWs: lightly raced & could find similar on this evidence.

277	**COUNT DE MONEY 19** [9] S R Bowring 5-9-10 (70) S Finnamore (7) 8/1: 221-23: 5 b g Last	1¾	72a

Tycoon - Menominee (Soviet Star) Chsd ldrs, rdn/kept on fnl 3f, no threat: tchd 12/1: see 277, 211 (C/D).

338	**WESTERN RAINBOW 4** [4] P D Evans 4-8-5 (51)(BL) N Callan (0) 11/1: 22-224: Prom, kept on onepace	1¼	51a

fnl 2f, no threat to wnr: qck reapp, tried blnks: mdn, can find a race: see 338.

261	**SOLE SINGER 17** [14] A 4-8-7 (53) A Mackay 12/1: 323-25: Prom halfway, chsd wnr 3f out/fdd fnl 2f.	1½	51a
*248	**MICE IDEAS 18** [6] 4-8-8 (54) T G McLaughlin 16/1: 054-16: Chsd ldrs halfway, btn 3f out: op 10/1.	1¼	50a
343	**WESTERN COMMAND 4** [5] 4-9-9 (69) R Fitzpatrick (3) 16/1: 21-457: Chsd ldrs 10f: op 12/1: btr 170.	2	62a
*325	**JAMORIN DANCER 7** [7] 5-8-10 (52) (6ex) Clare Roche (7) 16/1: 500-18: Nvr able to chall: op 10/1.	4	39a
260	**CASHAPLENTY 17** [1] 7-8-1 (43)(t) A Daly 25/1: 2/6-49: Bhd 4f out: see 260.	6	21a
317	**LOST SPIRIT 9** [11] 4-8-1 (47) G Baker (7) 12/1: 60-120: Led 5f out, sn hdd/btn: 10th: btr 317 (eqtrk).	6	16a
260	**TIME ON MY HANDS 17** [2] 4-7-12 (44)(t) Dale Gibson 25/1: Led 7f, sn btn: 14th: btr 260.		0a
4447}	**Topaz 93** [3] 5-7-10 (38)(12oh) G Bardwell 100/1:		
344	**Markellis 4** [10] 4-7-10 (42)(5oh) R Brisland (4) 50/1:		
271	**Quedex 15** [12] 4-9-6 (66) S Whitworth 33/1:		

14 ran   Time 2m 42.2 (7.9)   (G Moore - Osborne House)   Sir Mark Prescott Newmarket

---

LINGFIELD (Equitrack)   SATURDAY JANUARY 22ND   Lefthand, Very Sharp Track

Official Going   STANDARD. Stalls: 5f & 1m - Outside; Rem - Inside.

---

371   1.20 CRUSADER HCAP DIV 3YO+ 0-60 (F)   5f aw rnd   Going 26   -20 Slow   [60]
£1865   £533   £266   3 yo rec 15lb

291	**SOUTHERN DOMINION 14** [2] Miss J F Craze 8-9-10 (56)(bl) P Goode (5) 11/4 FAV: 204-31: 8 ch g		64a

Dominion - Southern Sky (Comedy Star) Made all, styd on well ins last, rdn out: nicely bckd: '99 rnr-up (h'cap,
rtd 54 & 56a): '98 Musselburgh wnr (2 h'caps, rtd 63): dual sand rnr-up (rtd 57a): eff at 5/6f on firm, soft &
both AWs: suited by blnks, tried a visor: often sharp trks, esp Musselburgh: v tough (102nd career start today).

358	**WISHBONE ALLEY 3** [3] M Dods 5-9-4 (50)(vis) A Clark 7/2: 2-2132: 5 b g Common Grounds - Dul Dul	2	52a

(Shadeed) Chsd wnr, not pace to chall ins last: op 5/2, quick reapp: in gd form, win again sn: see 312.

358	**BARITONE 3** [7] S E Kettlewell 6-8-6 (38)(vis) L Newman (5) 12/1: 00-043: 6 b g Midyan - Zinzi (Song)	½	38a

Outpcd early, styd on strongly appr fnl 1f, ran on well, nrst fin: quick reapp: eff at 5f but best at 6/7f.

166	**JUST DISSIDENT 43** [9] R M Whitaker 8-9-9 (55) P Doe 9/1: 4445-4: Rcd wide & settled rear, rdn to	hd	54a

improve 2f out, styd on well ins last, nvr nrr: op 7/1, 6 wk abs: will apprec a return to 6/7f now: see 91.

154	**CHEMCAST 47** [6] 7-9-0 (46)(bl) S Drowne 8/1: 0100-5: Prom, rdn/not pace of ldrs fnl 2f: 7 wk abs.	¾	44a
279	**OK JOHN 15** [4] 5-9-5 (51)(bl) A Daly 9/1: 303-06: Al outpcd: needs 6f: see 154.	4	40a
3886}	**CALANDRELLA 99** [8] 7-7-12 (30)(2ow)(4oh) P Fessey 16/1: 1500-7: Prom, rdn & lost place halfway:	½	18a

op 10/1: '99 scorer at Musselburgh (clmr, P Harris, rtd 43): plcd once in '98 for G B Balding (clmr, rtd 45
& 30a): eff at 5/6f: acts on gd & hvy grnd, sharp trks.

175	**CATCHTHEBATCH 42** [1] 4-10-0 (60) S Carson (5) 6/1: 0300-8: Dwelt, rdn to improve over 2f out,	½	47a

wknd/eased ins last: tchd 10/1, 6 wk abs: '99 scorer here at Lingfield (med auct mdn, rtd 72a), plcd on turf
(h'cap, rtd 56): rtd 48 & 59a in '98 (mdns): eff forcing the pace at 6f: acts on fast grnd & equitrack.

LINGFIELD (Equitrack) SATURDAY JANUARY 22ND Lefthand, Very Sharp Track

4471} **KALAR 92** [5] 11-8-5 (37)(bl) Lynsey Hanna (7) 20/1: 1000-9: Cl-up, wknd qckly fnl 1f: '99 wnr at
Ripon (sell h'cap, rtd 43): rtd 35a & 30 in '98 (h'cap), '97 wnr at W'hampton & Lingfield (clmrs, rtd 75a & 57
at best): best dominating at 5f, stays 6f: acts on soft, likes gd, firm & both AWs: eff in blnks, on a fair mark.   **1 21a**
9 ran   Time 1m 00.1 (2.3)   (Mrs Angela Wilson)   Miss J F Craze Elvington, N Yorks

---

372

1.50 CRUSADER HCAP DIV II 3YO+ 0-60 (F)   5f aw   Going 26 -35 Slow   [60]
£1855   £530   £265   3 yo rec 15lb

175 **RING OF LOVE** 42 [3] J L Eyre 4-9-10 (56) M Hills 13/2: 5045-1: 4 b f Magic Ring - Fine Honey   **61a**
(Drone) Waited wth, outpcd halfway, rall & styd on well over 1f out, drvn out to lead fnl strides: tchd 10/1:
6 wk abs: '99 scorer at Musselburgh (2, h'caps, rtd 70): '98 Chester wnr (mdn, rtd 76): stays a sharp 6f,
all 3 wins at 5f: acts on firm, soft & both AWs: handles any trk, likes a sharp one: has tried visor, best without.
*166 **BOLDLY CLIFF** 43 [1] E C Denderland 6-9-8 (54)(bl) L Newman (5) 5/1: 5401-2: 6 b h Never So   **¾ 56a**
Bold - Miami Beach (Miami Springs) Cl-up, led over 3f out, rdn & went clr over 1f out, drvn & hdd cl-home:
op 7/2, 6 wk abs: Belgian raider, prev trained by A Hermans: speedy sort: see 166.
*358 **RUDE AWAKENING** 3 [2] C W Fairhurst 6-9-4 (50)(6ex) P Doe 5/4 FAV: 06-413: 6 b g Rudimentary -   **nk 51a**
Final Call (Town Crier) Cl-up, ev ch till no extra fnl 50y: nicely bckd tho' op 4/5, qck reapp: pen for 358 (6f).
337 **DOLPHINELLE** 7 [5] R Hannon 4-9-12 (58) P Dobbs (5) 10/1: 54-104: Sn outpcd, ran on well for   **1¼ 56a**
press over 1f out, nrst fin: op 8/1, quick reapp: top weight: best at 6f: see 263.
*291 **JACK TO A KING** 14 [6] 5-9-4 (50)(tbl) J Edmunds 11/2: 506-15: Handy, lost place halfway,   **nk 47a**
rallied & styd on ins last: op 4/1: shade btr 291 (fibresand).
358 **CHAKRA** 3 [7] 6-8-9 (41) T Williams 16/1: 040-06: Al outpcd: quick reapp: tchd 14/1: see 358.   **7 24a**
279 **ZOES NEWSBOX** 15 [8] 6-7-12 (28)(2ow) P Fessey 40/1: 00-07: Al bhd: h'cap bow: mod form.   **nk 12a**
263 **LADY BALLA CALM** 17 [4] 4-7-10 (28)(3oh) G Bardwell 66/1: 000-08: Nvr a threat: poor performer.   **hd 10a**
166 **BOWCLIFFE GRANGE** 43 [9] 8-8-10 (42) Lynsey Hanna (7) 20/1: 2000-9: Led, hdd over 3f out,   **5 15a**
wknd qckly appr fnl 1f: 6 wk abs: sharper next time: see 57.
9 ran   Time 1m 00.84 (3.04)   (Dab Hand Racing)   J L Eyre Sutton Bank, N Yorks

---

373

2.20 CHIEFTAIN MED AUCT MDN 3YO (E)   1m aw rnd Going 26 -06 Slow
£2743   £844   £422   £211

315 **KATHAKALI** 10 [7] V Soane 3-9-0 Martin Dwyer 5/4 FAV: 400-21: 3 b c Dancing Dissident - She's A   **74a**
Dancer (Alzao) Cl-up, hdwy to lead dist, rdn clr ins last: well bckd: unplcd in '99 (rtd 69, nov auct, tried
visor): eff at 1m/10f, further cld suit: acts on fast & equitrack, sharp or gall trk: can win h'caps.
334 **CUPIDS DART** 7 [4] P Howling 3-9-0 T Williams 16/1: 036-52: 3 ch g Pursuit Of Love - Tisza (Kris)   **4 64a**
Led, rdn & hdd over 1f out, not pace of wnr: quick reapp: handles firm grnd & both AWs: see 80 (sell).
-- **MONSIEUR RICK** [2] Miss Gay Kelleway 3-9-0 P Fredericks (5) 10/1: 3: 3 b c Sillery - Movieland   **¾ 63a**
(Nureyev) Cl-up, rdn & not pace of wnr over 1f out: op 7/2, clr rem: debut, half brother to a 10f wnr in
France: dam a 1m juv wnr: stays 1m, further could suit: handles equitrack: promising intro, shld improve.
3849} **PEDRO PETE** 99 [6] M R Channon 3-9-0 A Daly 6/1: 00-4: Settled rear, rdn to improve 2f out,   **5 55a**
wknd over 1f out: op 5/1 on AW bow: unplcd in 2 '99 turf starts (mdns, rtd 68).
-- **SHARP RISK** [3] 3-9-0 T G McLaughlin 16/1: 5: Dwelt, sn with ldrs, rdn/wknd over 1f out: **2 51a**
op 10/1 on debut: half brother to 10f wnr Beneventus: wth P Howling, better for race.
328 **JUMP** 8 [5] 3-9-0 S Drowne 9/4: -05-26: Prom, rdn & wknd fnl 2f: nicely bckd: disapp effort but   **1¾ 47a**
reportedly struck into during race, forget this: see 328.
334 **ITSGOTTABDUN** 7 [8] 3-9-0 C Catlin (7) 14/1: 03-447: Held up, hdwy to chall halfway, wknd qckly   **2 43a**
fnl 2f: op 10/1, quick reapp: poss not suited by step up to 1m: see 334.
240 **BRYNA** 20 [1] 3-8-9 (vis) J Fanning 66/1: 08: Al bhd, t.o.: no form.   **dist 0a**
8 ran   Time 1m 38.8 (2.6)   (M B N Clements)   V Soane East Garston, Berks

---

374

2.50 SILKS SUITE HCAP 4YO+ 0-100 (C)   1m2f aw Going 26 +06 Fast   [93]
£6467   £1990   £995   £497   4 yo rec 2 lb

336 **URSA MAJOR** 7 [7] C N Allen 6-7-11 (62) Martin Dwyer 15/2: 040-21: 6 b g Warning - Double   **67a**
Entendre (Dominion) Made all, styd on strongly, rdn out: op 6/1, qck reapp, best time of day: '99 wnr at York
(h'cap, rtd 64): '98 wnr at Southwell (2 clmrs, A Kelleway) & Lingfield (with current connections, h'caps, rtd
90a): eff at 6f, suited by 7/10f on firm, soft, loves both AWs: handles any trk, loves Lingfield/Southwell.
157 **PUNISHMENT** 45 [3] K O Cunningham Brown 9-9-2 (81)(t) M Hills 8/1: 0306-2: 9 b h Midyan -   **2½ 81a**
In The Shade (Bustino) Rear, hdwy 5f out, rdn & styd on fnl 2f, no extra well ins last: 6 wk abs: well h'capped.
244 **ANEMOS** 20 [1] M A Jarvis 5-8-13 (78) J Fanning 4/1 JF: 201-23: 5 ch g Be My Guest - Frendly   **¾ 77a**
Persuasion (General Assembly) Cl-up, no extra ins last: well clr rem: consistent: see 160.
*244 **WHITE PLAINS** 20 [2] K R Burke 7-9-10 (89)(t) N Callan (3) 7/2: 331-14: Prom, lost tch wth ldrs   **8 76a**
fnl 2f: op 3/1: top-weight: better here in 244.
335 **BARBASON** 7 [6] 8-7-12 (63) P Doe 10/1: 130-25: Held up, nvr a threat: op 6/1, qck reapp: see 163.   **nk 50a**
353 **SYLVA LEGEND** 3 [4] 4-8-1 (68) F Norton 10/1: 364-56: Handy, wknd qckly fnl 2f: qck reapp: see 353.   **9 42a**
*335 **SEA DANZIG** 7 [5] 7-8-0 (64)(1ow) A Daly 5/1: 0-5017: Rdn/rear, lost tch halfway: op 4/1, qck   **6 31a**
reapp: best when allowed to dominate: much btr 335 (C/D, stks).
7 ran   Time 2m 04.81 (2.01)   (Newmarket Connections Ltd)   C N Allen Newmarket

---

375

3.20 TRACKSIDE CLUB CLAIMER 4YO+ (F)   1m2f aw Going 26 -23 Slow
£2170   £620   £310   4 yo rec 2 lb

*333 **HUGWITY** 7 [9] G C Bravery 8-8-13 M Hills 8/11 FAV: 16-011: 8 ch g Cadeaux Genereux - Nuit   **83a**
d'Ete (Super Concorde) Chsd ldrs, hdwy to lead over 3f out, sn clr, easily: val 7/8L: nicely bckd, qck reapp:
earlier won here at Lingfield (clmr): '99 scorer again at Lingfield (h'cap, rtd 86a), prev term won at Yarmouth
(h'cap), Southwell (clmr) & Lingfield (h'cap, rtd 80 & 86a): eff on fast grnd & both AWs:
handles any trk, loves Lingfield: tough & genuine, can complete hat-trick.
333 **NIGHT CITY** 7 [10] K R Burke 9-9-3 Joanna Badger (7) 11/4: 2-6522: 9 b g Kris - Night Secret   **3½ 74a**
(Nijinsky) Led, hdd 3f out, not pace of wnr fnl 2f: op 9/4: loves to dominate: again bhnd this wnr in 333.
268 **HIGH SHOT** 17 [7] G L Moore 10-8-3 J Fanning 8/1: 022-33: 10 b g Darshaan - Nollet (High Top)   **3 55a**
Mid-div, rdn to improve 2f out, not pace of wnr over 1f out: op 7/1: gd run & not disgraced at
these weights: return to h'cap company shld suit: see 110.

LINGFIELD (Equitrack)   SATURDAY JANUARY 22ND   Lefthand, Very Sharp Track

4276}	**SEA SPOUSE** 99 [3] M Blanshard 9-8-5 Dale Gibson 25/1: 0600-4: Held up, late gains fnl 2f: plcd in '99 (sell & clmr, rtd 56a, flattered): '98 wnr at Southwell (h'cap) & Lingfield (2, class stks, rtd 68a at best, also rtd 38): eff at 7f/9.4f, has tried further: acts on gd, soft, both AWs & a sharp/undul trk.	5	49$
333	**MALCHIK** 7 [6] 4-8-5 R Brisland (5) 33/1: 505-55: Cl-up, lost tch over 2f out, quick reapp: stiff task.	1	49$
310	**BALLYMORRIS BOY** 11 [4] 4-8-8(1ow) T G McLaughlin 25/1: 34-346: Nvr a threat: up in trip: see 274.	7	42a
--	**LADY QUINTA** [2] 4-8-4 L Newman (5) 16/1: 1000-7: Al in rear: 8 wk abs: Belgian raider, AW bow: wnr in native country in Oct '99 (11f, soft grnd).	6	29a
332	**MIDNIGHT WATCH** 7 [11] 6-8-3 (t) A Daly 50/1: 00-008: Waited with, rdn/wknd halfway: qck reapp.	2	22a
314	**QUEEN OF THE KEYS** 10 [5] 4-8-2 (vis) P Doe 20/1: 36-039: Dwelt, al rear: flattered 314.	hd	23a
209	**JUBILEE SCHOLAR** 35 [12] 7-8-3 (bl) F Norton 25/1: 050P-0: Al bhd, t.o., 10th: plcd twice in '99 (amat h'cap & stks, rtd 58a): '98 scorer at Lingfield (2, h'caps, rtd 54a & 32): eff at 1m/10f, stays a sharp 12f: acts on fast & both AWs, handles gd/soft: tried a visor, best blnkd: can go well fresh, likes Lingfield.	17	0a
--	**KENTISH ROCK** [1] 5-8-9 S Carson (5) 66/1: 0: Lost tch halfway, t.o., 11th: poor bmpr/hdles form.	28	0a
11 ran	Time 2m 07.66 (4.86) (Sawyer Whatley Partnership) G C Bravery Newmarket		

---

376   3.50 DUDLEY CONDITION STKS 3YO+ (C)   6f aw rnd   Going 26 -01 Slow
£5890   £2178   £1089   £495   3 yo rec 16lb

320	**PRINCE PROSPECT** 9 [4] Mrs L Stubbs 4-9-4 J P Spencer 12/1: 400-01: 4 b g Lycius - Princess Dechtra (Bellypha) Cl-up, hdwy to lead 2f out, rdn clr dist, styd on strongly, drvn out: '99 Sandown wnr (h'cap, rtd 81 & 91a), prev term scored at Lingfield (mdn, rtd 82a & 87, J Noseda): eff at 5/6f on firm, gd/soft & e/track: handles any trk, likes Lingfield: has tried a visor, best without: loves to force the pace: career best effort.		85a
320	**CLASSY CLEO** 9 [5] P D Evans 5-8-13 Joanna Badger (7) 8/15 FAV: 132-42: 5 b m Mujadil - Sybaris (Crowned Prince) Cl-up, hdwy to chall over 1f out, kept on but not pace of wnr ins last: nicely bckd at odds-on: tough & consistent, but better expected at the weights today: see 64 (h'cap).	1	77a
358	**BRUTAL FANTASY** 3 [1] P Howling 6-9-6 A Clark 16/1: -21403: 6 b g Distinctly North - Flash Donna (Well Decorated) Led, hdd over 2f out, rdn & not pace of wnr ins last: quick reapp, clr rem: see 288.	1½	80$
320	**BOLD EFFORT** 9 [2] K O Cunningham Brown 8-9-4 (bl) M Hills 5/1: 000-04: Rdn/rear, no threat to ldrs fnl 2f: backed at long odds (tchd 12/1): see 223.	5	68a
275	**TYCANDO** 16 [3] 3-8-2 (vis) F Norton 6/1: 022-05: Dwelt, rear, rdn/wknd 2f out: visored: see 275.	5	58a
5 ran	Time 1m 12.07 (1.67) (Maurice Parker) Mrs L Stubbs Collingbourne Ducis, Wilts		

---

377   4.20 FILLIES HCAP 4YO+ 0-70 (E)   1m4f aw   Going 26 -21 Slow   [61]
£2664   £761   £380   4 yo rec 4 lb

4590}	**SPINNING STAR** 80 [5] C F Wall 4-10-0 (65) M Tebbutt 7/1: 3540-1: 4 ch f Arazi - Queen Midas (Glint Of Gold) Led 2f, rem prom & led again over 3f out, sn clr, eased ins last: val 4/5L, 1st win, nicely bckd, top weight, AW bow: plcd once on turf in '99 (fill mdn, rtd 68): eff at 12f, has tried 2m: acts on equitrack, handles fast & gd/soft grnd: eff weight carrier & runs v well fresh: fine AW bow, win more races.		71a
305	**ALBERKINNIE** 11 [4] J L Harris 5-7-10 (29)(2oh) G Baker (7) 16/1: 020-02: 5 b m Ron's Victory - Trojan Desert (Troy) Held up, rdn/chsd wnr fnl 2f, no dngr fnl 1f: tchd 25/1, clr rem: handles fast, gd/soft & equitrack.	2	27a
305	**ERITHS CHILL WIND** 11 [3] G L Moore 4-8-13 (48)(bl) F Norton 9/1: 044-43: 4 b f Be My Chief - William's Bird (Master Willie) Settled rear, hdwy over 4f out, rdn/not pace of ldrs fnl 2f: op 5/1: up in trip.	4	40a
290	**MOGIN** 14 [10] L Montague Hall 7-8-8 (41) Martin Dwyer 40/1: 400-04: Dwelt, sn with ldrs, led after 2f, hdd over 3f out, wknd: rnr-up in '99 (fill h'cap, reapp, rtd 46a, subs tried blnks): early '98 scorer here at Lingfield (2, h'caps, rtd 46a, T Naughton): eff at 1m, stays 10f well: acts on fast grnd & both AWs: likes Lingfield: has run well fresh & best held up for a late chall.	3½	28a
335	**BECKON** 7 [9] 4-9-3 (54) A Clark 4/1: 13-545: Waited with, rdn/no extra fnl 3f: nicely bckd, qck reapp.	nk	40a
264	**MELLOW MISS** 17 [8] 4-9-0 (51) S Drowne 12/1: 440-56: Rear, rdn/hdwy 4f out, no extra over 2f out.	nk	37a
314	**KUMON EILEEN** 10 [2] 4-8-3 (40) P Doe 33/1: 00-07: Held up, nvr a threat: h'cap bow: modest.	8	14a
290	**SLEAVE SILK** 14 [7] 5-9-6 (53) P McCabe 13/8 FAV: 064-28: Mid-div, lost tch fnl 2f, eased: nicely bckd: capable of much better: see 290 (C/D).	hd	27a
285	**KEEN WATERS** 14 [1] 6-8-4 (37) A Daly 20/1: 406/09: Nvr a factor: 98/99 jumps wnr at N Abbot (nov chase, rtd 86c, eff arnd 2m1f on firm & gd/soft, M Pipe), prev term won at M Rasen (2, mdn & nov h'cap): '97 Flat scorer at Brighton (sell h'cap, 9f, J Arnold): eff at 12f, likes firm/fast grnd & a sharp/undul trk.	2	8a
261	**TOTEM DANCER** 18 [11] 7-9-7 (54)(vis) M Hills 9/1: 200-00: Dwelt, al bhd, t.o. in 10th: see 261.	dist	0a
267	**PEARL BUTTON** 17 [6] 4-8-8 (45) N Callan (3) 9/1: 00-20: Al well bhd, t.o. in 11th: op 5/1.	dist	0a
11 ran	Time 2m 34.86 (5.66) (S Fustok) C F Wall Newmarket		

WOLVERHAMPTON (Fibresand)   SATURDAY JANUARY 22ND   Lefthand, Sharp Track

Official Going STANDARD. Stalls: Inside.

378   7.00 MIDLANDS MDN 4YO+ (D)   1m1f79y aw   Going 48 +05 Fast
£2613   £746   £373   4 yo rec 1 lb

308	**SOVEREIGN ABBEY** 11 [7] Sir Mark Prescott 4-8-8 D Sweeney 1/5 FAV: 546-21: 4 b g Royal Academy - Elabella (Ela Mana Mou) Chsd ldrs halfway, led over 1f out, sn rdn/clr, hung left 1f out when in command: hvly bckd at long odds on: best time of night: unplcd in '99 (mdn, rtd 50a): plcd in '98 (rtd 77 & 64a, mdns): eff at 7f/9.4f: handles hvy grnd & fibresand: likes a sharp track: reportedly heads for the sales.		57a
308	**NAFITH** 11 [1] E L James 4-8-13 S Whitworth 9/1: 000-32: 4 ch g Elmaamul - Wanisa (Topsider) Prom, led over 2f out, hdd over 1f out, kept on tho' al held by wnr: op 5/1: acts on fibresand, eff at 1m/9.4f.	6	52a
102	**SALORY** 59 [3] Miss Jacqueline S Doyle 4-8-13 (t) T G McLaughlin 66/1: 0000-3: 4 b c Salse - Mory Kante (Icecapade) Sn led, rdn/hdd over 2f out & sn held: 2 month abs: unplcd in '99 (rtd 69, mdn): rtd 58 on 2nd of 2 juv starts in '98: juve h'caps will suit.	3½	45$
308	**ANNADAWI** 11 [5] C N Kellett 5-9-0 N Carlisle 50/1: 044-44: Dwelt/rear, mod prog: see 173.	4	37$
338	**NOBLE PATRIOT** 5 [10] 5-9-0 Dean McKeown 33/1: 3-4505: Nvr on terms: qck reapp: see 61 (seller, 7f).	7	26a
2869}	**SAMEEAH** 99 [2] 4-8-8 Dale Gibson 14/1: 50-2: Keen/led early, btn 3f out: op 10/1: 6 month abs/ AW bow: last of 5 on sole start in '99 (mdn, rtd 47).	12	3a
--	**DORANFIELD LADY** [6] 5-8-9 A Mackay 100/1: 7: Chsd ldrs 5f: Flat debut, jumps fit (no form, bmpr).	5	0a
--	**CASTRATO** [4] 4-8-13 R Studholme (5) 25/1: 8: Sn bhd: op 14/1, debut: with G McCourt.	14	0a

-- **CRACK ON CHERYL** [3] 6-8-9 A Culhane 100/1: 9: Dwelt/al bhd: Flat debut, jumps fit. ½ **0a**
4566} **WILCOY WARRIER 84** [8] 4-8-13 R Fitzpatrick (3) 100/1: 0-0: Chsd ldrs 4f: 10th: 12 wk absence. *dist* **0a**
10 ran Time 2m 02.2 (4.0) (G S Shropshire) Sir Mark Prescott Newmarket.

379 **7.30 STAFFS CLAIMER 3YO+ (F) 5f aw rnd Going 48 -10 Slow**
£2103 £601 £300 3 yo rec 15lb

214 **OFF HIRE 32** [10] C Smith 4-9-6 (vis) G Faulkner (3) 14/1: 0003-1: 4 b g Clantime - Lady Pennington **57a**
(Blue Cashmere) Led/dsptd lead thr'out, asserted ins last, rdn out: op 12/1: rnr-up in '99 (rtd 58, stks, plcd on sand, rtd 57a, clmr): '98 Musselburgh wnr (sell nurs, rtd 42, plcd on sand, rtd 63a, nurs): eff at 5f, stays 6f, tried further: acts on gd/soft, soft & fibresand: likes a sharp/turning trk: eff with/without a visor.
279 **NIFTY NORMAN 15** [2] D Nicholls 6-9-10 (bl) F Norton 13/8 FAV: 65-132: 6 b g Rock City - Nifty *1½* **57a**
Fifty (Runnett) Dwelt, stly hmpd after 2f, styd on well for press ins last, not reach wnr: bckd, rtd higher 272.
352 **LEGAL VENTURE 4** [6] N P Littmoden 4-9-6 (bl) T G McLaughlin 20/1: 0U-003: 4 ch g Case Law - *nk* **52a**
We Two (Glenstal) Chsd ldrs/sn rdn, kept on for press fnl 1f: qck reapp: return to sell grade wld suit: see 291.
352 **HOT LEGS 4** [9] B A McMahon 4-8-11 (BL) Dean McKeown 20/1: 000-54: Chsd ldrs wide, outpcd over *¾* **41$**
2f out, kept on for press ins last: op 16/1, blnks: qck reapp: eff at 5f, handles fibresand: mod form prev.
352 **YOUNG IBNR 4** [5] 5-9-10 L Newton 6/1: 533-05: Led/dsptd lead till ins last, fdd cl-home: op 10/1. *½* **52$**
351 **TINKERS SURPRISE 4** [3] 6-9-4 (bl) C Carver (3) 7/1: 06-536: Chsd ldrs, held/sltly hmpd ins last: *1* **44$**
jockey given a 2-day ban for careless riding: qck reapp: see 116 (h'cap).
272 **CELTIC SEAL 16** [8] 4-8-11 J Edmunds 14/1: 400-57: Dwelt/nvr on terms: op 12/1: see 272. *nk* **36a**
272 **AVONDALE GIRL 16** [1] 4-9-7 F Lynch 16/1: 100-08: Trkd ldr, rdn/briefly led over 1f out, fdd ins last. *½* **44a**
272 **SAMWAR 16** [4] 8-9-12 (vis) R Fitzpatrick (3) 9/4: 501-49: Dwelt, nvr on terms: nicely bckd: btr 214. *1½* **36a**
156 **ARAB GOLD 45** [7] 5-9-2 (VIS) R Studholme (5) 50/1: 5000-0: Al outpcd rear: 10th: 6 wk abs: unplcd *¾* **34$**
in '99 (rtd 43a & 31, tried up to 10f): tried a visor: no form for Miss S E Hall in '98.
10 ran Time 1m 03.1 (2.9) (John Martin-Hoyes) C Smith Temple Bruer, Lincs.

380 **8.00 CHESHIRE HCAP 4YO+ 0-85 (D) 2m46y aw Going 48 -36 Slow [80]**
£2769 £852 £426 £213 4 yo rec 7 lb

302 **WILCUMA 12** [3] P J Makin 9-10-0 (80) A Clark 20/1: 0/0-01: 9 b g Most Welcome - Miss Topville **85a**
(Top Ville) Held up in tch, smooth prog to lead 3f out, rdn out to hold on ins last: unplcd on sole '99 start (rtd 78, h'cap): lightly rcd in '98 (rtd 90, rtd h'cap): back in '96 won at York (val h'cap) & Newbury (rtd h'cap, rtd 105): eff at 9/10f, stays 2m on firm, soft & fibresand: eff with/without blnks: handles any trk: win again.
302 **FIORI 12** [5] P C Haslam 4-9-5 (78) M Tebbutt 13/2: 550-62: 4 b g Anshan - Fen Princess (Trojan *1½* **81a**
Fen) Cl-up halfway, chsd wnr 2f out, kept on for press, not able to chall: op 5/1: eff at 10/12f, stays 2m well.
296 **PRASLIN ISLAND 14** [4] A Kelleway 4-9-10 (83) P Fredericks (5) 2/1: 121-23: 4 ch c Be My Chief - *3½* **83a**
Hence (Mr Prospector) Cl-up, led halfway, rdn/hdd 3f out & sn held: op 6/4: see 182 (14f).
327 **STEAMROLLER STANLY 8** [6] D W Chapman 7-9-3 (69) A Culhane 7/1: 3-3524: Rear, eff 5f out, rdn/ *5* **64a**
held over 2f out: op 9/2: prev with K R Burke: see 151 (equitrack).
244 **MAKARIM 20** [1] 4-8-5 (64) R Fitzpatrick (3) 33/1: 065-05: Held up in tch, btn 2f out: op 16/1: see 135. *2* **57a**
633} **DARGO 99** [2] 6-8-8 (60) S Drowne 6/5 FAV: 2/13-6: Led till halfway, sn btn: hvly bckd, op 11/8: *11* **45a**
7 month jumps abs (June '99 Worcester wnr, mdn hdle, rtd 100h, eff at 2½m/3m on fast & gd/soft): '99 wnr on the level here at W'hampton (C/D h'cap, rtd 62a): plcd sev times in '98 (rtd 57 & 44a, C Thornton): eff at 11f, suited by 2m: acts on gd, soft & fibresand: likes to force the pace & has run well fresh: more expected tonight.
6 ran Time 3m 42.8 (13.6) (T G Warner) P J Makin Ogbourne Maisey, Wilts.

381 **8.30 DERBYS HCAP 4YO+ 0-85 (D) 1m100y aw Going 48 -05 Slow [77]**
£3136 £965 £482 £241

309 **WINDSHIFT 11** [1] D Shaw 4-9-11 (74)(vis) N Callan (3) 7/2 FAV: 00-531: 4 b g Forest Wind - **80a**
Beautyofthepeace (Exactly Sharp) Rear/wide, rdn/prog fnl 3f & led ins last, styd on well, rdn out: well bckd, op 11/2: '99 wnr at Southwell (2, h'caps, rtd 79a) & Warwick (h'cap, rtd 83): '98 wnr again at Southwell (nurs h'cap, rtd 58a & 57): eff at 7f, suited by 1m, stays 9.4f, tried further: acts on gd/soft, soft & loves fibresand: likes a sharp/turning trk, esp Southwell: best in a visor: tough & genuine shld win more races.
349 **HANNIBAL LAD 4** [10] W M Brisbourne 4-9-4 (67) Martin Dwyer 8/1: 42-152: 4 ch g Rock City - *½* **71a**
Appealing (Star Appeal) Rear, prog halfway, rdn & kept on ins last, just btn: qck reapp: see 309 (9.4f).
290 **ROI DE DANSE 14** [4] M Quinn 5-7-13 (46)(2ow) F Norton 6/1: 312-03: 5 ch g Komaite - Princess *2½* **47a**
Lucy (Local Suitor) Led, hard rdn fnl 2f & hdd ins last, no extra: op 5/1: loves to dominate: see 227, 203.
326 **SACREMENTUM 8** [8] J A Osborne 5-8-11 (60) S Drowne 7/1: 064-64: Chsd ldrs, onepace fnl 2f: *1½* **56a**
clr rem: op 5/1: stays a sharp 8.5f: acts on fibresand, fast & gd/soft grnd: see 326.
337 **DEMOCRACY 7** [7] 4-9-2 (65)(bl) C Carver (3) 20/1: 10-005: Rear, mod prog halfway, held fnl 1f. *7* **50a**
320 **ROYAL CASCADE 9** [3] 6-10-0 (77) P Mundy (7) 14/1: 350-06: Bhd, mod late gains: op 10/1: see 33 (7f). *¾* **61a**
360 **RIVER ENSIGN 2** [9] 7-8-1 (50) Claire Bryan (7) 11/2: 6-2137: Prom 6f: op 4/1, qck reapp: btr 360. *6* **25a**
306 **CONSULTANT 11** [5] 4-8-5 (54) T Williams 4/1: 0-0328: Chsd ldrs 5f: op 3/1: btr 306 (led). *1¾* **26a**
251 **FLITE OF LIFE 19** [6] 4-9-2 (65) Martin Dwyer 11/2: 051-69: Dwelt, eff halfway, sn held: btr 177. *3* **31a**
323 **STORM CRY 9** [2] 5-9-0 (63) V Slattery 25/1: 100-00: Mid-div, wknd qckly 4f out, t.o.: 10th: see 323. *21* **0a**
10 ran Time 1m 50.7 (4.5) (G E Griffiths) D Shaw Averham, Notts.

382 **9.00 WORCS SELLER 3YO (G) 1m1f79y aw Going 48 -43 Slow**
£1505 £430 £215

350 **WILEMMGEO 4** [3] P C Haslam 3-8-13 (VIS) P Goode (5) 4/11 FAV: 010-21: 3 b f Emarati - Floral **54a**
Spark (Forzando) Trkd ldr going well 6f out, led over 4f out & sn clr, eased down ins last, cmftbly: val for 6L+: slow time: hvly bckd at long odds on in first time visor: bght in for 4,800gns: qck reapp: '99 scorer here at W'hampton (seller, rtd 55a, earlier plcd on turf, rtd 62, seller): eff at 1m/9.4f: acts on firm, gd/soft & loves fibresand/W'hampton: eff with/without a visor: handles a stiff/undul or sharp trk: relishes sell grade.
311 **SAMMIE DUROSE 11** [1] R A Fahey 3-8-12 P Fessey 11/4: 000-52: 3 b g Forest Wind - La Calera *3* **41a**
(Corvaro) Led 1f, rdn/chsd wnr 4f out, kept on tho' al held: well clr rem: see 311.
330 **DIXIE FLYER 8** [2] E J Alston 3-8-7 (BL) A Culhane 14/1: 000-03: 3 b f Blues Traveller - African *25* **0a**
Cousin (Kampala) Keen/led after 1f, hdd 4f out & sn btn: op 10/1, first time blnks: unplcd in '99 (rtd 45 & 40a).
350 **CHIEF JUSTICE 4** [4] N P Littmoden 3-8-12 T G McLaughlin 14/1: 0-004: Sn outpcd: op 12/1, qck reapp. *5* **0a**

WOLVERHAMPTON (Fibresand)   SATURDAY JANUARY 22ND   Lefthand, Sharp Track

150	**BLAZING ROCK 47** [5] 3-8-12 (E) A McCarthy (2) 33/1: 00-5: Sn bhd: 7 wk abs: eyeshield, no form.		15	0a
5 ran	Time 2m 06.8 (8.6) (M J Cunningham) P C Haslam Middleham, N.Yorks.			

---

383   9.30 SHROPS HCAP 4YO+ 0-70 (E)   **1m1f79y aw Going 48 -01 Slow**   [67]
£2619   £748   £374   4 yo rec 1 lb

305	**MYSTERIUM 11** [4] N P Littmoden 6-8-10 (49) T G McLaughlin 100/30 FAV: 240-21: 6 gr g Mystiko - Way To Go (Troy) Rear, rdn/prog made 4f out, strong run for press ins last to lead nr line, all out: jockey given a 2-day ban for excessive use of the whip: '99 wnr at Yarmouth (h'cap, rtd 44) & W'hampton (C/D h'cap, rtd 53a): unplcd in 98 (tried vis): eff at 9.4f/11.5f on fast, gd & loves fibresand/W'hampton: enjoys exaggerated waiting tactics.		53a
3949)	**OCEAN LINE 99** [8] G M McCourt 5-7-10 (36)(1oh) R Studholme (5) 20/1: 4130-2: 5 b g Kefaah - Tropic Sea (Sure Blade) Prom, rdn/led ins last, hdd nr line: op 14/1, 4 month abs: '99 wnr at Windsor (sell h'cap, first success) & Brighton (clmr, rtd 47, unplcd on sand, rtd 20a): eff btwn 1m/11.5f: acts on fast, gd & fibresand: likes to race with/force the pace: likes a sharp trk: on a fair mark & can find compensation in similar.	nk	38a
345	**SHONTAINE 5** [3] M Johnston 7-8-3 (42) K Dalgleish (7) 14/1: -51663: 7 b g Pharly - Hinari Televideo (Caerleon) Chsd ldr, led 4f out, rdn/hdd ins last, kept on for press: op 10/1, qck reapp: eff at 7f/1m, stays 9.4f.	1¼	42a
255	**HEVER GOLF GLORY 18** [2] C N Kellett 6-9-6 (59) N Carlisle 16/1: 000-04: Keen/rear, styd on well fnl 1f, nrst fin: op 12/1: '99 scorer here at W'hampton (2, h'cap & amat h'cap, rtd 78a, unplcd on turf, rtd 49, h'cap): rtd 83a & 73 in '98 (with T J Naughton & N P Littmoden): eff around 1m, stays a gall 9f: acts on firm & soft, unplcd on sand: prob handles equitrack: eff held up or forcing the pace: on a fair mark at present.	2½	54a
323	**GIFT OF GOLD 9** [7] 5-9-4 (57) A Mackay (5) 40-45: Held up, prog/2f out, sn held: op 6/1: jockey reported gelding finished lame: see 216.	nk	51a
326	**DANAKIL 8** [9] 5-10-0 (67) N Callan (3) 6/1: 036-56: Held up, prog/ch 2f out, sn no extra: see 326.	½	60a
3765)	**CHARTER FLIGHT 99** [6] 4-9-11 (65) Dean McKeown 4/1: /301-7: Keen/rear, chsd ldrs/hmpd over 3f out & held after: nicely bckd, op 6/1: '99 scorer here at W'hampton (h'cap, rtd 65a, unplcd on turf, rtd 42): rtd 56 & 61a from 2 '98 starts (auct mdns): eff at 8.5f: acts on fibresand & runs well fresh.	shd	58a
349	**ULTRA CALM 4** [1] 4-9-5 (59) P Goode (5) 4/1: 500-38: Held up, eff 3f out, held/eased ins last: op 7/2.	4	44a
349	**THE BARGATE FOX 4** [5] 4-9-2 (56) S Whitworth 4/1: 41-349: Rear, eff 3f out, nvr able: op 5/1, qck reapp.	¾	40a
310	**NOBLE INVESTMENT 11** [10] 6-8-8 (47) S Drowne 16/1: 540/30: Led 5f, sn btn: 10th: op 12/1.	12	13a
10 ran	Time 2m 02.8 (4.6) (Alcester Associates) N P Littmoden Newmarket.		

SOUTHWELL (Fibresand)   MONDAY JANUARY 24TH   Lefthand, Sharp, Oval Track

Official Going   STANDARD. Stalls: Inside.

---

384   1.15 GOLD FILL HCAP 4YO+ 0-70 (E)   **1m aw   Going 53 -07 Slow**   [68]
£2769   £852   £426   £213

345	**STRAVSEA 7** [11] R Hollinshead 5-8-8 (48) P M Quinn (5) 13/2: 1-0351: 5 b m Handsome Sailor - La Stravaganza (Slip Anchor) Rear/in tch, stdy prog from halfway & rdn to lead well ins last, pushed out cl home: op 5/1: '99 wnr twice here at Southwell (fill mdn h'cap & h'cap, rtd 50a, unplcd on turf, rtd 36, h'cap): plcd in '98 (rtd 53a, auct mdn, also rtd 44): eff at 7f, suited by 1m: acts on gd/soft, fibresand/Southwell specialist.		55a
78	**BOBBYDAZZLE 65** [6] Dr J D Scargill 9-9-2 (56)(ebl) F Norton 9/1: 0003-2: 5 ch m Rock Hopper - Billie Blue (Ballad Rock) Prom, led after 2f, rdn/clr 2f out, hdd well ins last & no extra: abs, op 4/1, clr rem.	1¾	59a
159	**OARE KITE 47** [8] P S Felgate 5-7-13 (39) Dale Gibson 14/1: 0366-3: 5 b m Beldale - Portvasco (Sharpo) Chsd ldrs, rdn & kept on fnl 2f, not pace to chall: 7 wk abs: op 8/1: '99 Leicester wnr (seller, G L Moore, rtd 50, unplcd on sand, rtd 43a): '98 wnr again at Leicester (appr mdn, rtd 68): eff over a stiff/gall 7f, stays 1m well: acts on firm, soft & fibresand: prob handles any trk, likes Leicester: eff in blnks/visor, not worn today.	4	34a
340	**MAI TAI 7** [9] D W Barker 5-9-1 (55)(vis) Kimberley Hart (5) 13/1: 14-254: Chsd ldr 3f out, onepace: clr rem.	¾	49a
304	**THE BARNSLEY BELLE 14** [10] 7-7-13 (39)(3ow)(4oh) P Fessey 10/1: 656-45: Led 2f, cl-up wide 5f, fdd.	9	20a
239	**CARAMBO 26** [5] 5-9-6 (60) C Lowther 14/1: 0000-6: Held up in tch, nvr a threat: op 12/1: see 180.	nk	40a
326	**SATWA BOULEVARD 10** [7] 5-8-8 (47)(1ow) P McCabe 5/1: 320/07: Mid-div, rdn halfway, no progress: well bckd, tchd 10/1: more expected here? see 326.	6	19a
305	**MISS TAKE 13** [4] 4-9-1 (55) S Whitworth 20/1: 305-08: Dwelt, struggling halfway: '99 W'hampton wnr (h'cap, P D Evans, rtd 64a, plcd on turf, 45, h'cap): '98 wnr thrice at W'hampton (2 sellers & nov stks, rtd 69a & 59): eff at 7f/9.5f: acts on gd & gd/soft grnd, both AWs: loves fibresand/W'hampton: best in a visor.	¾	25a
4352)	**ITSANOTHERGIRL 99** [1] 4-9-13 (67) T Lucas 10/1: 2035-9: Prom 6f: tchd 16/1: jumps fit (rtd 92h, juv nov): plcd twice in '99 on the level (rtd 71, h'cap): '98 Catterick wnr (nurs, rtd 74): eff at 9/10f: acts on firm & hvy grnd: handles a sharp or gall/stiff trk: AW bow today.	1	35a
297	**BUNTY 14** [2] 4-7-10 (36)(3oh) G Baker (7) 13/2: 016-40: AI rear: 10th: op 5/1: btr 297.	2½	0a
*326	**DIM OFAN 10** [3] 4-9-11 (65) D Sweeney 2/2 FAV: 46-410: Rear, switched wide for eff halfway, btn over 2f out: 11th: well bckd: disapp, more expected after latest: see 326 (C/D).	11	11a
11 ran	Time 1m 44.2 (4.8) (E Bennion) R Hollinshead Upper Longdon, Staffs.		

---

385   1.45 SCARLET CLASS CLAIMER 3YO 0-65 (F)   **1m aw rnd   Going 53 -45 Slow**
£2052   £586   £293

*330	**CALKO 10** [2] T D Barron 3-8-11 (bl) C Lowther 5/2: 15-311: 3 ch g Timeless Times - Jeethgaya (Critique) Trkd ldr, led 3f out, styd on well & in command ins last, pushed out: slow time: op 2/1: recent wnr here at Southwell (seller): late '99 wnr again here at Southwell (seller, rtd 61a & 69 on turf): eff at 7f, relished step up to 1m: handles fast & gd, loves fibresand/Southwell: best in blnks: loves sell/claim grade.		66a
315	**MAID TO LOVE 12** [3] G A Butler 3-9-0 (t) L Newman (5) 5/1: 223-42: 3 ch f Petardia - Lomond Heights (Lomond) Chsd ldrs, rdn/chsd wnr over 2f out, kept on fnl 1f, not pace to chall: wore a t-strap, gd run.	1½	65a
36	**FRENCH MASTER 73** [1] P C Haslam 3-8-7 (BL) T Eaves (7) 14/1: 3364-3: 3 b g Petardia - Reasonably French (Reasonable) Sn led, rdn/hdd 3f out, no extra ins last: op 12/1, abs, clr rem: plcd form in '99 (rtd 68, clmr): eff at 7f/1m: handles firm, fast & fibresand: handles any trk: eff in blnks or a visor.	3	52a
*355	**BOSS TWEED 5** [4] Ronald Thompson 3-8-12 A Clark 6/4 FAV: 50-114: Held up in tch, rdn halfway, nvr a threat to ldrs: nicely bckd tho' op 5/4: qck reapp: btr 355, 303.	6	48a
303	**IMARI 14** [5] 3-7-10 G Bardwell 7/2: 640-25: Prom, rdn/no extra over 2f out: jockey reported filly was hanging left down the straight during the final 2f: btr 303.	¾	31a
128	**PEPPERCORN 55** [6] 3-8-0 G Baker (7) 40/1: 5000-6: Rear/wide halfway, nvr a factor: 8 wk abs:	½	34a

unplcd in '99 (rtd 44a & 44): dam a 1m wnr, shld apprec this trip in time.

330 **LITTLE CHRISTIAN 10** [8] 3-8-1 C Rutter 33/1: 00-507: Bhd halfway: see 303.	2½	30a
4570} **EURO DANDY 84** [7] 3-8-7 F Norton 25/1: 0000-8: Led 1f, hung right after 3f & sn bhd: AW bow/12 wk abs: unplcd in '99 (rtd 48): with D Nicholls.	20	6a

8 ran   Time 1m 45.6 (6.2)   (T Calver)   T D Barron Maunby, N.Yorks.

---

386   2.15 TOTE EXACTA HCAP DIV 1 4YO+ 0-80 (D)   6f aw   Going 53   +06 Fast   [80]
£4706   £1448   £724   £362

*352 **TELECASTER 6** [2] C R Egerton 4-7-10 (48)(6ex) P M Quinn (5) 8/11 FAV: 00-311: 4 ch g Indian Ridge - Monashee (Sovereign Dancer) Sn led, rdn over 2f out, asserted ins last, pushed out: blnks omitted: hvly bckd: gd time: qck reapp under a 6lb pen after recent easy W'hampton success (first win, h'cap): unplcd in 3 '99 starts: eff at 6f, stays 7f on fibresand & a sharp trk: much improved by forcing tactics: eff with/without blnks.		63a
*313 **BEST QUEST 12** [9] K R Burke 5-9-0 (66)(t) N Callan (3) 8/1: 00-312: 5 b h Salse - Quest For The Best (Rainbow Quest) Prom, wide halfway, rdn to chall 2f out, no extra ins last: op 6/1: see 313 (stks, eqtrk).	3½	70a
*279 **ROUGE 17** [6] J P Leigh 5-9-13 (79) S Finnamore (7) 5/1: 204-13: 5 gr m Rudimentary - Couleur de Rose (Kalaglow) Trkd ldrs, eff 2f out, rdn/no extra ins last: see 279 (C/D, clmr).	1¾	79a
342 **SHARP HAT 7** [8] D W Chapman 6-8-6 (58) A Culhane 11/1: 300-34: Towards rear/in tch, wide, late gains for press, no threat: op 9/1: still on a fair mark, could win again: see 91 (5f, equitrack).	shd	58a
320 **MALLIA 11** [1] 7-9-3 (69)(bl) Lynsey Hanna (7) 20/1: 60-405: Rear/wide, mod prog for press: see 129.	3½	60a
146 **RUSSIAN ROMEO 51** [7] 5-9-3 (69)(bl) Dean McKeown 14/1: 3030-6: Dwelt, al towards rear: 7 wk abs.	2½	53a
2205} **BERNARDO BELLOTTO 99** [4] 5-8-5 (57) Clare Roche (7) 20/1: 0110-7: Chsd ldrs halfway, sn btn/eased fnl 1f: stewards inquired into run, noted trainers explanation that the gelding had lost his action: op 12/1, 7 mth abs: '99 wnr at Redcar (seller, first time blnks) & Musselburgh (clmr, rtd 60): rtd 64 in '98 (M Bell): eff at 6/7f on firm, soft & fibresand, any trk: eff with/without blnks & enjoys well/claim grade: AW bow today, sharper next time.	shd	41a
342 **AJNAD 7** [3] 6-9-6 (72) S Righton 40/1: 30-008: Cl-up 4f: see 282.	1½	52a
279 **ICE AGE 17** [5] 6-7-13 (51)(bl) P Fessey 25/1: 00-059: Cl-up wide 4f, sn btn: see 218.	6	20a

9 ran   Time 1m 16.1 (2.8)   (Casting Partners)   C R Egerton Chaddleworth, Berks.

---

387   2.45 JADE JEWEL MDN 4YO+ (D)   1m4f aw   Going 53   -25 Slow
£2613   £746   £373   4 yo rec 4 lb

301 **ORO STREET 14** [3] D G Bridgwater 4-8-12 A Culhane 1/3 FAV: 404-21: 4 b g Dolphin Street - Love Unlimited (Dominion) Led after 2f & al trav well, maintained narrow advantage thr'out fnl 2f with rider motionless, cheekily: val for 6L+: hvly bckd at long odds on: with G Chung in '99 (unplcd, rtd 84 at best): eff at 12f, further could suit in time: acts on fibresand & a sharp trk: any amount in hand here, op to further improvement.		70a
338 **CRESSET 7** [8] W Jarvis 4-8-12 (BL) M Tebbutt 16/1: 006-02: 4 ch c Arazi - Mixed Applause (Nijinsky) Mid-div, prog wide/cl-up 3f out, rdn to chall fnl 2f, al lkd held & positon accepted cl-home: op 14/1, first time blnks: clr rem: stays a sharp 12f & handles fibresand: imprvd for headgear today & return to h'caps shld suit.	¾	61a
4080} **KUSTOM KIT KEVIN 99** [1] S R Bowring 4-8-12 N Callan (3) 50/1: 60-3: 4 b g Local Suitor - Sweet Revival (Claude Monet) Prom, rdn/outpcd fnl 3f: 4 month abs/AW bow: unplcd from 2 turf starts in '99 (rtd 38).	13	47a
338 **TALECA SON 7** [10] D Carroll 5-9-2 (t) R Fitzpatrick (3) 16/1: 4-2254: Rear, rdn & mod prog fnl 4f.	7	37$
301 **THE NOBLEMAN 14** [7] 4-8-12 J Fanning 50/1: 0/05: Led 2f, cl-up 1m: mod form.	1½	35a
4546} **MELVELLA 87** [5] 4-8-7 G Baker 5/1: 6300-6: Mid-div at best: 12 wk abs: plcd in '99 for M Bell (stks, rtd 51a, unplcd on turf, rtd 74, flattered): tried 14.7f prev, now with J L Harris.	4	24a
359 **CHAMBOLLE MUSIGNY 4** [4] 4-8-7 Dean McKeown 10/1: 500-37: In tch 1m: qk reapp: btr 359 (9.4f).	2½	20a
4351} **BEHARI 99** [9] 6-9-2 P M Quinn (5) 40/1: 0-8: Bhd halfway: jumps fit (mod form): no form sole '99 start.	3½	20a
-- **ANUGRAHA** [6] 7-9-2 A Clark 40/1: 9: Rear/wide halfway, nvr factor: Flat debut, 6 wk jmps abs (mod form).	¾	19a
308 **AUTUMN LEAVES 13** [2] 4-8-7 C Cogan (5) 50/1: 006-00: Al bhd: 10th: longer 12f trip, mod form.	5	7a

10 ran   Time 2m 43.6 (9.3)   (Led Astray Again Partnership)   D G Bridgwater Lambourn, Berks.

---

388   3.15 TOTE EXACTA HCAP DIV 2 4YO+ 0-80 (D)   6f aw rnd   Going 53   +01 Fast   [78]
£4706   £1448   £724   £362

337 **REDOUBTABLE 9** [7] D W Chapman 9-9-6 (70) A Culhane 7/1: 63-641: 9 b h Grey Dawn II - Seattle Rockette (Seattle Slew) Sn chsd ldrs wide, rdn to lead dist, edged left ins last & rdn out to hold: nicely bckd: '99 Thirsk wnr (h'cap, rtd 81 & 74a): '98 Lingfield, Ayr & Newcastle wnr (h'cap, rtd 79 & 78a): suited by 6/7f, stays a sharp 1m on firm, soft & both AWs: handles any trk, likes a sharp one: best without blnks: tough 9yo.		80a
*342 **RAFTERS MUSIC 7** [3] D Nicholls 5-8-4 (54)(6ex) Clare Roche (7) 11/8 FAV: 460-12: 5 b g Thatching - Princess Dixieland (Dixieland Band) Mid-div, briefly outpcd 2f out, kept on for press ins last, nrst fin: hvly bckd: 6lb pen for latest: can win again, particularly with stronger handling: see 342.	½	61a
358 **DAYS OF GRACE 5** [8] L Montague Hall 5-9-0 (64) C Rutter 5/1: 4-2123: 5 gr m Wolfhound - Inshirah (Caro) Held up in tch wide, eff 2f out, kept on tho' nvr pace to chall: op 9/2: qck reapp: see 358, 280.	2	66a
337 **KEEN HANDS 9** [4] Mrs N Macauley 4-9-10 (74)(vis) R Fitzpatrick (3) 12/1: 24-104: Twds rear/mod prog.	½	74a
249 **VICE PRESIDENTIAL 21** [5] 5-9-8 (58) Dean McKeown 10/1: 010-25: Led, clr fwy, rdn/hdd over 1f out & fdd: op 14/1: pacey type, could win again in claiming/selling grade: see 32 (clmr, C/D).	½	56a
282 **REX IS OKAY 17** [6] 4-9-3 (67)(bl) S Finnamore (7) 16/1: 30-066: Prom 4f: op 14/1: see 282.	½	63a
183 **GENERAL KLAIRE 42** [1] 5-9-7 (71) A Clark 6/1: 5653-7: Al rear: abs, now with R A Fahey: btr 129 (C/D).	9	50a
246 **MARENGO 21** [2] 6-8-6 (56) G Bardwell 16/1: 103-08: Chsd ldrs 3f: op 14/1: btr 183 (C/D, made all).	1¼	32a

8 ran   Time 1m 16.4 (3.1)   (David W Chapman)   D W Chapman Stillington, N.Yorks.

---

389   3.45 SILVER ICE SELLER 3YO+ (G)   6f aw rnd   Going 53   -29 Slow
£2002   £572   £286   3 yo rec 16lb

279 **ELTON LEDGER 17** [3] Mrs N Macauley 11-9-7 (vis) R Fitzpatrick (3) 100/30 FAV: 406-21: 11 b g Cyrano de Bergerac - Princess Of Nashua (Crowned Prince) Chsd lds, prog to lead dist, held on well ins last, rdn out: no bid, well bckd: '99 Southwell wnr (sell, rtd 66a): '98 Southwell wnr (6, rtd 72a & 58): stays 1m, suited by 6f: acts on gd & hvy, fibresand/Southwell specialist: eff in a visor: well suited by selling/claiming grade.		65a
254 **DISTINCTIVE DREAM 20** [12] A Bailey 6-9-7 D Hayden (7) 8/1: 140-62: 6 b g Distinctly North - Green Side (Green Dancer) Dwelt/rear & wide, prog over 2f out, styd on well, nrst fin: op 6/1: can find similar: see 254.	½	62a
341 **SOUNDS SOLO 7** [1] D Nicholls 4-9-7 (cvis) Clare Roche (7) 16/1: /50-63: 4 b g Savahra Sound - Sola Mia (Tolomeo) Chsd ldrs, kept on fnl 2f, not pace to chall: op 14/1: eff at 6f, suited by 7f: see 341.	¾	60a

SOUTHWELL (Fibresand) MONDAY JANUARY 24TH Lefthand, Sharp, Oval Track

341 **BLUSHING GRENADIER 7** [11] S R Bowring 8-9-7 S Finnamore(7) 4/1: 40-334: Wide/mid-div, no dngr. 1¼ **57$**
352 **TROJAN HERO 6** [4] 9-9-12 T G McLaughlin 6/1: 100-45: Rear, late gains, nrst fin: op 5/1: see 201. ¾ **60a**
61 **FLYING HIGH 68** [8] 5-9-7 J Fanning 33/1: 0000-6: Rear/rdn, mod gains for press: 10 wk abs: ¾ **53$**
unplcd/no form in '99 (tried blnks): no form in '98 for F Murphy: prob stays a sharp 6f & handles fibresand.
313 **ROYAL ORIGINE 12** [5] 4-9-7 (tbl) P Doe 33/1: 00-007: Led, rdn/hdd over 1f out & fdd ins last: eff ½ **51$**
at 6f & handles fast & fibresand: see 247.
297 **ABOVE BOARD 14** [9] 5-9-7 (bl) S Righton 20/1: 6-5008: Chsd ldrs, wknd fnl 1f: see 201 (C/D). ¾ **49$**
761} **TRUMPET BLUES 99** [14] 4-9-7 M Tebbutt 11/2: 02/6-9: Wide/mid-div, btn over 1f out: nicely bckd ¾ **47a**
tho' op 4/1: 10 month abs/AW bow: rcd just once for J L Dunlop in '99 (unplcd, mdn, rtd 69): rnr-up in '98 (mdn, rtd 77): eff at 6f, tried 7f, may yet suit: handles soft grnd: now with D Nicholls.
351 **CANTGETYOURBREATH 6** [10] 4-9-12 (bl) J Bosley (7) 10/1: 051-00: Towards rear, nvr factor: 10th. *shd* **52a**
226 **Ready To Rock 28** [13] 4-9-7 A Clark 16/1: 291 **Weetrain 16** [2] 4-9-2 F Norton 16/1:
273 **Envy 18** [7] 4-9-2 Dean McKeown 33/1: 262 **Rowlandsons Stud 19** [6] 7-9-7 (t) N Callan (3) 33/1:
14 ran Time 1m 18.2 (4.9) (Mrs N Macauley) Mrs N Macauley Sproxton, Leics.

390 **4.15 BLUE VELVET HCAP 4YO+ 0-70 (E) 1m3f aw Going 53 -17 Slow [69]**
£2977 £916 £458 £229 4 yo rec 3 lb

325 **KIRISNIPPA 10** [4] Derrick Morris 5-8-1 (42) P Doe 20/1: 060-51: 5 b g Beveled - Kiri Te (Liboi) **52a**
Trkd ldrs going well halfway, led 2f out, styd on strongly, rdn out: bckd at long odds: plcd on turf in '99 (rtd 67, mdn): prev eff at 6f, suited by 11f, shld stay further: acts on fibresand, prob handles fast grnd: likes a sharp trk: best without blnks/visor: decisive success today, can follow up.
97 **LOVE DIAMONDS 62** [1] N P Littmoden 4-9-11 (69) T G McLaughlin 25/1: 3000-2: 4 b g Royal Academy - 6 **71a**
Baby Diamonds (Habitat) Rear, prog to chase ldrs halfway, rdn & kept on fnl 2f, no ch with wnr: 2 month abs: '99 Lingfield wnr (h'cap, M Johnston, rtd 77a & 51): '98 wnr at Lingfield (nurs h'cap, rtd 64a & 58): eff at 1m, stays a sharp 11f: acts on gd, soft & both AWs: best without blnks: prob handles any trk, loves a sharp one.
345 **NICE BALANCE 7** [8] M C Chapman 5-7-12 (39) Joanna Badger (7) 14/1: 0-6143: 5 b g Shadeed - *nk* **40a**
Fellwaati (Alydar) Mid-div, prog/chsd ldrs wide 3f out, kept on onepace: op 12/1: stays 11f: see 298 (1m).
*339 **ALNAJASHEE 7** [7] M R Bosley 4-8-11 (55)(t) G Baker (7) 5/4 FAV: 556-14: Chsd ldrs, smooth prog 2½ **52a**
to chall over 2f out, sn rdn/onepace: hvly bckd, op 7/4: btr 339 (12f, appr h'cap).
326 **ABLE PETE 10** [6] 4-7-10 (40)(7oh) M Baird 25/1: 000-05: Led 5f out, hdd 2f out, no extra: unplcd in ½ **36a**
'99 for D J S Cosgrove (rtd 33a & 30): unplcd in '98 for J L Dunlop (rtd 68, auct mdn): prob stays a sharp 11f & handles fibresand: finished well clr of rem today.
306 **EMPERORS GOLD 13** [2] 5-8-1 (42) A Mackay 13/2: /00-36: Chsd ldrs, btn 3f out: btr 306 (9.4f). *12* **25a**
284 **NIGELS CHOICE 17** [9] 8-7-12 (39)(2ow)(4oh) P Fessey 66/1: 300/07: Mid-div at best: see 284. *4* **16a**
301 **DENS JOY 14** [12] 4-9-4 (62) M Tebbutt 5/1: 35-38: Mid-div, btn 3f out: h'cap bow: btr 301 (12f) *3* **35a**
340 **DANGERMAN 7** [13] 5-7-11 (38)(t) Dale Gibson 13/2: 501/39: Rear, eff 4f out, no prog: nicely bckd. *4* **5a**
343 **STATE APPROVAL 7** [5] 7-9-10 (65) N Callan (3) 20/1: 25-600: Cl-up 1m: 10th: see 270. *1* **31a**
131 **RIVER CAPTAIN 55** [10] 7-9-0 (55)(t) C Lowther 20/1: 6500-0: Dwelt/rear & wide, prog/chsd ldrs *8* **12a**
wide 4f out, sn rdn/held: 11th: 8 wk abs: '99 Southwell wnr (h'cap, rtd 62a & 26): '98 Southwell wnr (2, h'cap & class stks, rtd 62a): eff over 11/13f: has run well fresh: likes both AWs, Southwell/fibresand specialist.
3093} **ACCYSTAN 99** [3] 5-10-0 (69) J Weaver 20/1: /010-0: Led 6f, sn btn: 12th: topweight: 6 mth abs: *4* **20a**
'99 Southwell wnr (sell, rtd 68a & 32): Nov '98 jumps wnr at Catterick (juv nov, rtd 83h, eff at 2m on fast & gd): '98 W'hampton (clmr) & Southwell wnr (h'cap, P Haslam, rtd 68a & 67): eff at 10/12f on fibresand, gd & gd/soft.
279 **MAJOR MORRIS 17** [11] 5-7-10 (37)(t) P M Quinn (5) 50/1: 00-00: Bhd halfway: 13th: longer 11f trip. *4* **0a**
13 ran Time 2m 29.00 (7.7) (Michael Appleby) Derrick Morris Lambourn, Berks.

WOLVERHAMPTON (Fibresand) TUESDAY JANAURY 25TH Lefthand, Sharp Track

Official Going STANDARD. Stalls: 7f - Outside; Rem - Inside.

391 **1.30 HANSOM SELLER DIV 1 4YO+ (G) 7f aw rnd Going 49 -01 Slow**
£1547 £442 £221

351 **DAYNABEE 7** [5] A J McNae 5-8-7 T G McLaughlin 5/1: 252-51: 5 b m Common Grounds - Don't Wary **55a**
(Lomond) Trkd ldrs, rdn/led over 2f out, styd on well ins last, rdn out: op 4/1: bght in for 6,200gns: plcd sev times in '99 (rtd 47 & 44a, h'caps): '98 Windsor wnr (h'cap, rtd 56, plcd on sand, rtd 45a): eff at 5f, suited by 6/7f: acts on firm, soft & both AWs: likes a sharp trk, handles any: apprec drop to sell grade, deserved this.
364 **C HARRY 5** [3] R Hollinshead 6-9-3 P M Quinn (5) 1/2 FAV: -52542: 6 ch h Imperial Frontier - Desert 3½ **57a**
Gale (Taufan) Mid-div, rdn/prog to chase wnr 2f out, kept on tho' al held: well bckd: clr rem: qck reapp: see 130.
316 **GADGE 13** [8] A Bailey 9-8-12 C McCavish (7) 11/1: 00-003: 9 br g Nomination - Queenstyle (Moorestyle) 5 **42a**
Rdn/towards rear, late gains, no threat: op 9/1: see 83 (h'cap).
354 **EMMAJOUN 6** [4] W G M Turner 5-8-7 T Williams 14/1: 25-034: Led/dsptd lead 5f, fdd: qck reapp. *6* **26a**
316 **NICHOLAS MISTRESS 13** [9] 4-8-7 Joanna Badger (7) 16/1: 000-05: Slowly away/rear, mod gains. *nk* **27a**
327 **BUTRINTO 11** [2] 6-8-12 (bl) R Price 9/1: 00-506: Led/dsptd lead till over 3f out, sn btn: op 6/1. *6* **23a**
162 **SHADY DEAL 48** [7] 4-8-12 A Clark 14/1: 0000-7: Mid-div, btn halfway: op 12/1: abs: plcd in '99 2½ **18a**
(rtd 57a & 68, h'caps): rtd 79 in '98 (nov stks, flattered): eff at 6f/7f, tried further: handles equitrack & gd/soft.
132 **NEEDWOOD MINSTREL 55** [10] 4-8-12 S Whitworth 33/1: 0600-8: Al rear, 8 wk abs: unplcd in '99 1½ **15a**
(rtd 52, stks): rtd 66 in '98: eff at 6f, handles fast & soft grnd: handles a sharp or stiff/undul track.
280 **LADY NAIRN 18** [1] 4-8-7 (t) P Fessey 50/1: 0/0-09: Bhd 3f out: lightly rcd/no form in '99: rtd 1½ **7a**
59 in '98 (nov stks, J J Quinn): with A Berry.
313 **COURTNEY GYM 13** [6] 5-8-12 (bl) P McCabe 40/1: 000-00: Al rear: 10th. 4 **4a**
10 ran Time 1m 29.60 (3.4) (T L Beecroft) A J McNae Compton, Berks.

392 **2.00 BROUGHAM HCAP 3YO 0-75 (E) 1m1f79y aw Going 48 -05 Slow [81]**
£2689 £768 £384

*315 **SPECIAL PROMISE 13** [1] P C Haslam 3-8-5 (58) Dean McKeown 8/11 FAV: 005-11: 3 ch g Anjiz - **69a**
Woodenitbenice (Nasty And Bold) Held up in tch, hdwy to lead over 1f out & rdn clr ins last: nicely bckd: recent Lingfield wnr (h'cap, first success): unplcd in '99 (rtd 61 & 55a): eff at 9.4f/10f, 12f+ could suit: acts on both AWs & likes a sharp trk: much improved for step up in trip recently & shld land a quick hat-trick.

300 **PAPAGENA 15** [5] C W Thornton 3-7-13 (51)(bl)(1ow) F Norton 14/1: 564-62: 3 b f Robellino - Morning Crown (Chief's Crown) Prom, rdn/briefly led over 1f out, sn outpcd by wnr: op 10/1: styd longer 9.4f trip: handles firm, gd/soft & fibresand: eff in blnks: see 213. *5* **52a**
213 **PURE BRIEF 35** [6] D J G Murray Smith 3-7-13 (52) P Doe 20/1: 0000-3: 3 b g Brief Truce - Epure (Bellypha) Dwelt/held up in tch, kept on fnl 2f, nvr pace to chall: also bhd today's rnr-up in 213 (1m). *3* **46a**
294 **HEATHYARDS LAD 17** [3] R Hollinshead 3-9-6 (73) P M Quinn (5) 13/2: 164-54: Keen/prom, wknd fnk 2f. *2½* **62a**
213 **TOWER OF SONG 35** [4] 3-9-2 (69) A Culhane 9/2: 1420-5: Prom, led 6f out, hdd/wknd qckly 1f out. *4* **50a**
4130} **STORM PRINCE 99** [2] 3-9-7 (74) J Weaver 9/2: 4412-6: Led 3f, btn over 1f out: op 8/1: 4 mth abs: '99 Leicester scorer (sell nurs h'cap, rtd 70, subs rnr-up on turf, rtd 71a, nov auct stks): eff at 1m, further could suit in time: acts on firm grnd & fibresand: handles a sharp or stiff/undul trk: has worn a t-strap. *1¼* **52a**
278 **KINGS GINGER 18** [7] 3-8-9 (62) D Dineley 33/1: 305-07: Rdn/rear, btn 3f out: plcd twice in 99 (rtd 74, auct mdn, P R Chamings): stays 1m, further could suit: handles fast & gd grnd & a sharp/undul or fair trk. *7* **29a**
7 ran Time 2m 03.2 (5.0) (R Young) P C Haslam Middleham, N.Yorks.

393

2.30 DOG CART CLAIMER 4YO+ (F) 1m100y aw Going 48 -05 Slow
£2177 £622 £311

345 **INTERNAL AFFAIR 8** [11] T D Barron 5-9-1 Lynsey Hanna (7) 5/4 FAV: 20-101: 5 b g Nicholas - Gdynia (Sir Ivor) Mid-div, stdy prog fnl 3f to lead 1f out, styd on well, rdn out: well bckd: earlier scored here at W'hampton (C/D, clmr): '99 W'hampton wnr (h'cap, rtd 67a, rnr-up on turf, rtd 58): '98 W'hampton scorer (auct mdn, rtd 79a): suited by 8.5f on soft/hvy, handles fast, fibresand/W'hampton specialist: enjoys claiming grade. **65a**
313 **ELLWAY PRINCE 13** [4] Mrs N Macauley 5-8-9 Dean McKeown 16/1: 040-02: 5 b g Prince Sabo - Star Arrangement (Star Appeal) Mid-div, prog to chall over 1f out, kept on for press, not pace of wnr: op 12/1: styd longer 8.5f trip with visor omitted: apprec drop to claim grade, could find similar: see 166 (5f). *1¾* **55a**
335 **BILLICHANG 10** [5] P Howling 4-8-13 T Williams 13/2: 01-233: 4 b c Chilibang - Swing O'The Kilt (Hotfoot) Trkd ldr, rdn/led over 2f out, hdd over 1f out & no extra: op 5/1: see 238 (mdn). *3½* **52a**
322 **APPROACHABLE 12** [9] Miss S J Wilton 5-8-9 T G McLaughlin 8/1: 0-2544: In tch, onepace fnl 2f: clr rem. *¾* **47a**
264 **ROYAL PARTNERSHIP 20** [3] 4-9-1 Darren Williams (7) 20/1: 000-P5: Chsd ldrs, held fnl 2f: op 12/1. *6* **44a**
323 **DANZAS 12** [2] 6-8-7 (bl) Claire Bryan (7) 12/1: 25-606: Mid-div halfway, nvr threat: op 25/1: see 255. *1½* **33a**
-- **STICKS AND STONES** [1] 8-8-9 A Mackay 25/1: 0445/7: Chsd ldrs 5f: AW bow: last rcd in Britain in '96 (rtd 76, h'cap, Mrs J Cecil): back in '94 won at Lingfield (mdn): eff around 1m: acts on fast & gd/soft. *4* **27a**
323 **MUJKARI 12** [7] 4-8-7 (vis) P Fitzsimons (5) 40/1: 160-08: Bhd halfway: see 323. *1¾* **22a**
60} **BALLYCROY RIVER 99** [12] 4-8-11 S Righton 33/1: 0003/9: Al rear: jumps fit (rtd 63h, juv nov): missed '99: plcd in '98 (rtd 53a, C/D seller, also rtd 49): stays 8.5f & handles fibresand: has tried blnks. *nk* **25a**
360 **FEARSOME FACTOR 5** [10] 5-9-5 (bl) J P Spencer 11/4: 00-040: Led, rdn/hdd over 2f out & sn btn: 10th: op 9/4, qck reapp: blnks reapplied: see 360, 172. *hd* **32a**
244 **THOMAS HENRY 23** [6] 4-8-9 A Clark 7/1: 416-00: Sn bhd: 11th: op 6/1: see 110 (10f, equitrack). *17* **0a**
181} **SAN GLAMORE MELODY 99** [8] 6-8-11 F Norton 33/1: 5002/0: Sn bhd: long abs: missed '99: rnr-up twice in '98 (rtd 47, h'cap, plcd on sand, rtd 46a, h'cap): eff at 9f/14f: handles firm, gd & fibresand: mdn. *11* **0a**
12 ran Time 1m 50.7 (4.5) (Stephen Woodall) T D Barron Maunby, N.Yorks.

394

3.00 D.A.D. HCAP 3YO+ 0-95 (C) 5f aw rnd Going 48 +12 Fast [94]
£6630 £2040 £1020 £510 3 yo rec 15lb

320 **DIL 12** [4] Mrs N Macauley 5-9-9 (89) R Fitzpatrick (3) 6/1: 503-01: 5 b g Primo Dominie - Swellegant (Midyan) Prom, led over 1f out, drifted right/held on gamely ins last, all out: op 9/2, fast time: '99 scorer at Southwell (h'cap) & W'hampton (h'cap, rtd 96a, unplcd on turf, rtd 82): '98 Doncaster wnr (2, auct mdn & h'cap, rtd 83, B Hanbury) & also Leicester (h'cap, current connections): best at 5/6f, stays a sharp 7f: acts on firm, gd/soft & fibresand: handles any trk, likes a sharp one & racing up with/force the pace: tough & useful AW performer. **93a**
342 **YABINT EL SHAM 8** [5] B A McMahon 4-7-12 (64) L Newman (2) 9/2: 001-52: 4 b f Sizzling Melody - Dalby Dancer (Bustiki) Chsd ldrs, rdn to chall ins last, styd on well/just held: apprec return to 5f: see 191 (C/D). *nk* **67a**
376 **CLASSY CLEO 3** [10] P D Evans 5-10-0 (94) Joanna Badger (7) 9/2: 32-423: 5 b m Mujadil - Sybaris (Crowned Prince) Mid-div, kept on for press from over 1f out, not able to chall: qck reapp, op 6/1, ultra tough. *¾* **95a**
258 **MUKARRAB 21** [8] D W Chapman 6-8-10 (76) A Culhane 7/1: 006-04: Mid-div/wide, kept on well ins last, not able to chall: op 9/1: signs of a return to form here, on a fair mark & loves Lingfield (last 6 wins there). *½* **75a**
358 **SOTONIAN 6** [9] 7-8-1 (67) P M Quinn (5) 14/1: 620-05: Rear/wide, late gains under a kind ride, nrst fin: qck reapp: '99 scorer at W'hampton, Lingfield (2), Warwick & Catterick (h'caps, rtd 68 & 64a at best): '98 W'hampton wnr (h'cap, rtd 45a & 50): stays 6f, all wins over a sharp/turning 5f: acts on fast, gd/soft & both AWs: best without blnks: slipping to a handy mark & should be winning again soon in similar events. *¾* **64a**
320 **BLUE KITE 12** [1] 5-8-13 (79) D Sweeney 11/2: 61-166: Slowly away & rdn/rear, late gains: op 7/2. *shd* **76a**
342 **BEDEVILLED 8** [7] 5-8-1 (67) F Norton 4/1 FAV: 010-27: Dwelt, sn chsd ldrs, no extra fnl 1f: see 342. *shd* **63a**
223 **ZIGGYS DANCER 34** [11] 9-8-4 (70) J Fanning 10/1: 4000-8: Towards rear/wide, nvr on terms: op 8/1. *¾* **64a**
3033} **JACKIES BABY 99** [2] 4-9-0 (80) M Tebbutt 10/1: 2310-9: Led till over 1f out, btn/eased ins last: op 16/1, 6 month abs: '99 Bath wnr (h'cap, rtd 86, unplcd on sand, rtd 63a): '98 Southwell (2, mdn & nurs, rtd 84a) & Folkestone wnr (nurs, rtd 84): loves to force the pace at 5f: acts on firm, gd/soft & fibresand: handles any trk. *3* **67a**
3578} **SOAKED 99** [3] 7-9-4 (84) G Parkin 16/1: 5604-0: Prom, btn over 1f out & eased ins last: 10th: op 14/1: 5 month abs, longer priced stablemate of 4th: '99 Lingfield scorer (h'cap, rtd 87a, unplcd on turf, rtd 56, h'cap): prolific '98 wnr, scored at Musselburgh (2), Hamilton (amat h'cap), Southwell (3, h'caps) & Lingfield (2, h'caps, rtd 83a & 65): eff at 5/6f on fast, gd/soft & both AWs: eff with/without blnks: handles any trk. *5* **62a**
-- **LISAS PRINCESS** [6] 7-7-10 (62)(29oh) G Bardwell 66/1: 00/6-0: Sn bhd: 11th: stiff task. *3* **33a**
11 ran Time 1m 02.0 (1.8) (Mrs N Macauley) Mrs N Macauley Sproxton, Leics.

395

3.30 SULKY MDN 3YO (D) 1m1f79y aw Going 49 -23 Slow
£2782 £428 £214

4432} **SOLLER BAY 98** [10] K R Burke 3-9-0 N Callan (3) 5/4 FAV: 2-1: 3 b g Contract Law - Bichette (Lidhame) Sn chsd ldrs, smooth prog to lead over 1f out, duelled with rnr-up ins last & rdn/asserted cl-home: op 1/2: AW bow, 3 month abs: rnr-up on sole start in '99 (auct mdn, rtd 76): apprec step up to 9.4f, further could suit: acts on fibresand & gd grnd: runs well fresh: handles a sharp/undul trk: op to further improvement. **64a**
315 **LE CAVALIER 13** [7] C N Allen 3-9-0 R Morse 12/1: 40-002: 3 b c Mister Baileys - Secret Deed (Shadeed) Led, hdd/hung right over 1f out, styd on well for press ins last, just held nr fin: op 9/1: blnks omitted: eff at 9.4f, shld stay further: acts on fibresand: return to h'caps could suit: see 240. *½* **62a**
328 **DONTBESOBOLD 11** [9] B S Rothwell 3-9-0 J Stack 5/2: 40-043: 3 b g River Falls - Jarmar Moon *1½* **59a**

WOLVERHAMPTON (Fibresand) TUESDAY JANAURY 25TH Lefthand, Sharp Track

(Unfuwain) In tch, eff to chall 2f out, held over 1f out: clr of rem: op 6/1: styd longer 9.4f trip: see 328.
```
--    ROOM TO ROOM MAGIC  [2]  B Palling 3-8-9 D Sweeney 14/1: 4: Chsd ldrs halfway, outpcd fnl 3f: op    6   45a
```
8/1, debut: Casteddu filly, with B Palling.
```
4460} ALBERGO 96  [8]  3-9-0 Dale Gibson 20/1: 00-5: Rdn/chsd ldrs, outpcd fnl 3f: op 12/1: 3 month abs/    1½  47a
```
AW bow: unplcd from 2 '99 starts (rtd 45): sire a high-class 12f performer: h'caps/10f+ shld now suit.
```
319   TORMENTOSO 12  [4]  3-9-0 A Daly 5/1: 050-46: Chsd ldrs 7f: op 7/2: btr 319 (C/D).                    3   41a
319   THE FINAL WORD 12  [1]  3-8-9 A Culhane 10/1: 5-57: Rear/in tch, eff/no prog 3f out: btr 319 (C/D).  2½  31a
328   DENNIS BERGKAMP 11  [3]  3-9-0 P M Quinn (5) 20/1: 300-08: Chsd ldrs wide halfway, sn btn: op 14/1.  27  0a
240   AROB PETE 23  [6]  3-9-0 T G McLaughlin 20/1: 0-09: Sn bhd: op 12/1: mod form.                        20  0a
9 ran       Time 2m 04.9 (6.7)        (Mrs Melba Bryce)        K R Burke Newmarket.
```

396 4.0 HANSOM SELLER DIV 2 4YO+ (G) 7f aw rnd Going 48 -23 Slow
£1536 £439 £219

```
341   RA RA RASPUTIN 8  [7]  B A McMahon 5-9-3 L Newman (5) 5/1: 00-141: 5 b g Petong - Ra Ra Girl         54a
```
(Shack) Chsd ldrs, rdn/prog to lead over 1f out, styd on well, rdn out: tchd 6/1, bght in for 3,000gns: earlier
scored nap at W'hampton (C/D seller): rnr-up in '99 (h'cap, rtd 62a): eff at 7f, stays 1m: acts on fast, hvy &
fibresand/W'hampton: best without blnks: loves sell grade.
```
274   MIKES DOUBLE 19  [3]  Mrs N Macauley 6-8-12 (vis) R Fitzpatrick (3) 12/1: U60-52: 6 br g Cyrano de  2   46a
```
Bergerac - Glass Minnow (Alzao) Rear/wide, styd on well for press fnl 2f, nrst fin: win a sell h'cap.
```
322   GUEST ENVOY 12  [1]  C N Allen 5-8-7 J Bosley (7) 25/1: 050-03: 5 b m Paris House - Peace Mission    2   37a
```
(Dunbeath) Led/dsptd lead till went on 3f out, rdn/hdd over 1f out & no extra: see 322.
```
306   UTAH 14  [6]  G L Moore 6-8-12 (bl) P Dobbs 25/1: 000-04: Towards rear, late gains: blnks reapp.     ¾   41a
345   DOBERMAN 8  [9]  5-8-12 (bl) D Sweeney 16/1: 4-4035: Dwelt, held up in tch wide, mod prog for press. ½   40a
341   MR CUBE 8  [5]  10-8-12 (bl) Claire Bryan (7) 33/1: 2-0006: Held up in tch, nvr a threat: see 254.   6   31a
353   COLLEGE BLUE 6  [2]  4-8-7 L Carter 11/2: -2207: Led/dsptd lead 4f, sn btn: op 9/4: btr 273 (6f, mdn). 2½  21a
*274  ELITE HOPE 19  [4]  8-8-12 Dean McKeown 1/2 FAV: 424-18: Chsd ldrs, rdn/ch 3f out, wknd over 1f out: ½  25a
```
hvly bckd: reportedly fin distressed: see 274 (C/D, seller).
```
378   NOBLE PATRIOT 3  [8]  5-8-12 (bl) N Callan (3) 33/1: -45059: Chsd ldrs wide 5f: qck reapp: see 61.   1½  22a
9 ran       Time 1m 31.2 (5.0)        (D J Allen)        B A McMahon Hopwas, Staffs.
```

397 4.30 PHAETON HCAP 3YO 0-65 (F) 6f aw rnd Going 48 -07 Slow [69]
£2205 £630 £315

```
346   BAYTOWN RHAPSODY 7  [6]  P S McEntee 3-8-6 (47) L Newman (5) 4/6 FAV: 00-321: 3 b f Emperor Jones -  58a
```
Sing A Rainbow (Rainbow Quest) Trkd ldrs, led 1f out, asserted ins last, rdn out: first success: hvly bckd: plcd
form in '99 (auct mdn, rtd 56 & seller, rtd 49a): eff at 6/7f on fibresand & gd grnd: likes a sharp trk.
```
289   STOP THE TRAFFIC 17  [7]  C N Allen 3-9-3 (58) R Morse 10/1: 330-42: 3 b f College Chapel - Miss    1¼  64a
```
Bagatelle (Mummy's Pet) Led after 1f, rdn/hdd over 2f out, kept on for press, not pace of wnr: op 8/1: handles
firm, gd & fibresand: lightly raced and could find similar: see 289 (mdn).
```
242   MARITUN LAD 23  [2]  D Shaw 3-9-3 (58)(VIS) N Callan (3) 4/1: 065-43: 3 b g Presidium - Girl Next    shd  64a
```
Door (Local Suitor) Cl-up, led over 2f out till over 1f out, no extra: op 7/2, visor: handles both AWs: str rem.
```
242   CACOPHONY 23  [5]  S Dow 3-8-13 (54) P Doe 10/1: 033-54: Towards rear, mod gains: op 8/1: see 228.   5   51a
288   PARKSIDE PROSPECT 17  [4]  3-9-7 (62) J Fanning 4/1: 231-45: Led 1f, btn 2f out: op 6/1: btr 207 (eqtrk). 1  57a
331   COULD BE EXPENSIVE 11  [8]  3-8-3 (44) A Whelan 12/1: 000-66: Sn outpcd: op 8/1: see 331.             6   28a
300   SHOULDHAVEGONEHOME 15  [3]  3-8-13 (54)(bl) J P Spencer 11/2: 020-57: Slowly away & al bhd:           7   25a
```
op 8/1: blnks reapp: see 42 (seller, 5f).
```
328   XATIVA 11  [1]  3-8-13 (54) A Culhane 20/1: 500-08: Al outpcd rear: see 328 (1m, mdn).               3   18a
8 ran       Time 1m 16.1 (3.3)        (Mrs B A McEntee)        P S McEntee Newmarket.
```

LINGFIELD (Equitrack) WEDNESDAY JANUARY 26TH Lefthand, V Sharp Track

Official Going STANDARD. Stalls: Inside, except 5f/1m - Outside.

398 1.50 MACKEREL CLAIMER 4YO+ (F) 7f aw rnd Going 40 -01 Slow
£2331 £666 £333

```
386   ROUGE 2  [9]  J P Leigh 5-9-2 S Finnamore (7) 5/2 FAV: 04-131: 5 gr m Rudimentary - Couleur de Rose 80a
```
(Kalaglow): Sn cl-up, rdn/led over 1f out, styd on strongly inside last, rdn out: hvly bckd: clmd by N Shields
for £12,000: qck reapp: recent Southwell wnr (clmr): '99 W'hampton wnr (h'cap, first success, rtd 71a, rtd
49 on turf): stays 1m, suited by a sharp 6/7f & loves both AWs & claiming grade: likely to join K R Burke.
```
*316  APOLLO RED 14  [7]  G L Moore 11-8-13 A Clark 7/2: 613-12: 11 ch g Dominion - Woolpack (Golden      2   72a
```
Fleece): Led, rdn/hdd over 1f out, kept on for press: op 5/2: v tough 11yo: see 316 (sell).
```
364   RONS PET 6  [6]  K R Burke 5-9-3 (tvis) N Callan (3) 4/1: 60-233: 5 ch g Ron's Victory - Penny Mint  nk  75a
```
(Mummy's Game): Sn rdn chsg ldrs, kept on final 2f, not pace to chall: acts on firm, soft & both AWs: visor reapp.
```
313   PALACEGATE TOUCH 14  [5]  A Berry 10-8-7 (bl) P Bradley (5) 8/1: 325-34: Cl-up 4f, no extra final 2f. 2½  60a
316   SCROOGE 14  [4]  4-8-3 A Whelan 9/1: 50-325: Rear/rdn, late gains: clsr to today's rnr-up in 316 (1m). 2  52$
375   MALCHIK 4  [3]  4-8-7 R Brisland 50/1: 05-556: Chsd ldrs, btn 2f out: qck reapp: see 159.            hd  55$
336   COMEOUTOFTHEFOG 11  [8]  5-8-9 P Doe 7/1: 302-57: Rear/rdn, nvr a factor: see 239.                  1¾  54a
375   BALLYMORRIS BOY 4  [10]  4-8-3 (BL) G Bardwell 25/1: 4-3468:  Wide/rear, nvr a factor: blnks, qck reapp. 3  42$
313   MISTER RAIDER 14  [1]  8-8-5 (bl) S Carson (5) 50/1: 500-09: Hmpd after 1f, rear/wide halfway, nvr factor. 8  32a
136   FLASHFEET 56  [2]  10-8-3 G Baker (7) 100/1: 0000-0: 10th: 8 wk abs: unplcd in '99 (rtd               2   26a
```
34a, no turf form): only mod form in '98: back in '95 scored at W'hampton (9f h'cap, rtd 55a, K Bishop).
```
10 ran       Time 1m 25.66 (2.86)        (J M Greetham)        J P Leigh Willoughton, Lincs.
```

135

LINGFIELD (Equitrack)   WEDNESDAY JANUARY 26TH   Lefthand, V Sharp Track

---

399
2.20 BARRY DENNIS MDN 3YO+ (D)   6f aw rnd   Going 40 -11 Slow
£2730   £840   £420   £210   3 yo rec 16lb

278   **DIRECT REACTION** 19 [2] Miss Gay Kelleway 3-8-8 (vis) N Callan (3) 15/8 FAV: 53-351: 3 b g College   **70a**
Chapel - Mary's Way (Night Shift): Broke well & sn clr lead, in command over 1f out, rdn out, unchall: hvly bckd:
rnr-up in '99 (mdn, rtd 77a, rtd 81 on turf, stks): eff at 6f, stays a sharp 1m well: acts on equitrack, handles
gd & fibresand: eff in a vis, tried blnks: likes a sharp trk & front running tactics: win again in h'cap company.
265   **ABSOLUTE FANTASY** 21 [3] E A Wheeler 4-9-5 (bl) S Carson (5) 7/1: 004-62: 4 b f Beveled - Sharp   6 **47a**
Venita (Sharp Edge): Sn rdn chsg wnr, kept on tho' nvr any threat: hvly bckd: h'caps could suit best: see 109 (1m).
280   **AMARO** 19 [5] J Wharton 4-9-5 F Norton 12/1: 05-563: 4 b f Emarati - Redcross Miss (Tower Walk):   4 **37a**
Chsd ldrs, sn rdn, kept on final 2f, no threat: op 14/1: needs h'cap coy: see 226.
--   **DEADLY SERIOUS** [7] D R C Elsworth 4-9-10 J Stack 5/2: 4: Dwelt, rdn/rear, mod gains halfway: shd **42a**
well bckd, tchd 7/2: debut: Emarati colt, unrcd prev for G Lewis: know more next time for D Elsworth.
353   **MOUTON** 7 [6] 4-9-5 A Clark 16/1: 22-505: Sn rdn/al outpcd: op 14/1: see 314 (10f).   5 **28a**
273   **RAJMATA** 20 [8] 4-9-5 (vis) A Clark 14/1: 500-06: Sn struggling rear: op 10/1: rnr-up thrice in '99   1¼ **25a**
(rtd 66a, h'cap, rtd 81 on fibresand): eff at 5f, stays 6f: handles fast & fibresand: eff with/without a vis.
353   **MICKY DEE** 7 [1] 4-9-10 (t) Joanna Badger (7) 100/1: /00-07: Chsd ldrs 4f: no form.   1¾ **26§**
269   **WILLOW MAGIC** 21 [4] 3-8-3 P Doe 3/1: 002-58: Sn rdn/bhd: nicely bckd: btr 234 (5f, h'cap).   1½ **17a**
8 ran   Time 1m 13.43 (3.03)   (A P Griffin)   Miss Gay Kelleway Lingfield, Surrey.

400
2.50 TOTE EXACTA HCAP 4YO+ 0-80 (D)   1m2f aw   Going 40 -04 Slow   [70]
£5239   £1612   £806   £403   4 yo rec 2 lb

337   **FORTY FORTE** 11 [6] K R Burke 4-9-11 (69) N Callan (3) 5/1: 20-561: 4 b g Pursuit Of Love - Cominna   **74a**
(Dominion): Made all, hard rdn 4f out, clr over 2f out, held on well inside last, rdn out: nicely bckd: '99 wnr
at Nottingham (sell, M Channon), Beverley (h'cap, rtd 78) & Lingfield (C/D h'cap, rtd 71a): eff at 7f/sharp 10f:
acts on firm, hvy & both AWs: loves Lingfield: handles any trk: loves Lingfield: tough, win again.
*268   **ADMIRALS PLACE** 21 [3] H J Collingridge 4-9-7 (65) M Hills 3/1 FAV: 205-12: 4 ch c Perugino - Royal   1½ **67a**
Daughter (High Top): Rdn in mid-div halfway, kept on for press final 2f, nvr a threat to wnr: hvly bckd.
316   **SERGEANT IMP** 14 [11] P Mitchell 5-7-10 (38)(1oh) P M Quinn (5) 25/1: 600-33: 5 b g Mac's Imp -   hd **39a**
Genzyme Gene (Riboboy): Rear, stdy prog for press final 4f, no threat to wnr: op 14/1: well clr of rem: eff over
6f/1m, stays a sharp 10f: see 316 (sell).
381   **ROI DE DANSE** 4 [5] M Quinn 5-8-4 (46) F Norton 6/1: 12-034: Chsd wnr, rdn/btn 2f out: qck reapp.   8 **38a**
*353   **MULLAGHMORE** 7 [9] 4-9-5 (63)(bl) A Clark 13/2: 604-15: Chsd ldrs 1m: see 353 (1m, mdn).   2½ **51a**
290   **LADY JO** 18 [7] 4-9-2 (60) P Doe 5/1: 060-66: Bhd after 1f, mod gains final 4f: tchd 8/1: see 290.   6 **39a**
349   **MIGWAR** 8 [2] 7-9-1 (57)(vis) C Cogan (5) 20/1: 01-067: Towards rear, nvr a factor: btr 224 (C/D).   1½ **34a**
268   **SAMMYS SHUFFLE** 21 [4] 5-9-1 (57)(bl) O Urbina 8/1: 251-58: Mid-div at best, eased/btn final 1f.   2½ **30a**
290   **BAAJIL** 18 [8] 5-9-1 (57) S Carson (5) 14/1: 146-09: Rdn mid-div/wide halfway, sn held: op 10/1: btr 3.   3½ **25a**
270   **DAPHNES DOLL** 20 [1] 5-8-11 (53) M Henry 14/1: 041-00: Struggling halfway: 10th: op 14/1: trainer   ½ **20a**
reported mare had breathing problems after the race: see 209 (C/D).
333   **LORD EUROLINK** 11 [10] 6-10-0 (70)(vis) T G McLaughlin 14/1: 45-030: Chsd ldrs wide, btn 4f out: 11th.   ¾ **36a**
11 ran   Time 2m 07.18 (4.38)   (Nigel Shields)   K R Burke Newmarket, Suffolk.

401
3.20 BARRYS BISMARCK HCAP 3YO 0-85 (D)   1m aw rnd   Going 40 +06 Fast   [83]
£3757   £1156   £578   £289

*265   **BUGGY RIDE** 21 [2] Miss Gay Kelleway 3-9-6 (75)(vis) N Callan (3) 11/8 FAV: 42-211: 3 b c Blues   **87a**
Traveller - Tambora (Darshaan): Made all, rdn/clr over 2f out, in command final 1f, rdn out: hvly bckd: fast
time: earlier scored here at Lingfield (mdn, C/D): plcd form in '99 (rtd 74, mdn, R Charlton): eff at 1m, stays
a sharp 10f: acts on fast, loves equitrack/Lingfield, prob handles any trk: loves to dominate in a vis: win again.
*311   **WILL IVESON** 15 [1] P C Haslam 3-8-3 (58)(VIS) Dale Gibson 5/1: 655-12: 3 b g Mukaddamah - Cherlinoa 7 **58a**
(Crystal Palace): Chsd wnr, rdn over 1f out, held over 1f out: wknr: op 7/2, first time visor: acts on
both AWs, prob handles firm & gd/soft: clr of rem trying a visor but caught a tartar here: see 311.
294   **CHURCH FARM FLYER** 18 [3] C N Allen 3-8-8 (60) K Newman (5) 4/1: 311-23: 3 b f College Chapel -   8 **53a**
Young Isabel (Last Tycoon): Chsd ldrs, rdn/outpcd final 3f: tchd 9/2: btr 294, 188.
294   **JOELY GREEN** 18 [4] N P Littmoden 3-8-13 (68) T G McLaughlin 10/1: 10-234: Rdn/rear, btn 4f out.   1 **54a**
*125   **BOLD EWAR** 57 [5] 3-9-7 (76)(bl) M Hills 7/2: 0041-5: Rdn/bhd & swtchd near 1f out: 8 wk abs: 6 **53a**
disapp, soon struggling here: btr 125 (made most, fibresand, h'cap).
5 ran   Time 1m 38.92 (2.72)   (Mr & Mrs Gary Pinchen)   Miss Gay Kelleway Lingfield, Surrey.

402
3.50 SALMON SELLER 4YO+ (G)   2m aw   Going 40 -15 Slow
£1859   £531   £265

317   **ANOTHER MONK** 14 [5] R Ingram 9-9-4 (VIS) A Clark 7/4 FAV: 320-41: 9 b g Supreme Leader - Royal   **47a**
Demon (Tarboosh): Chsd ldrs, trkd ldr 5f out, rdn/led 1f out, drvn out to assert inside last: hvly bckd: no bid:
first time visor: place form in '99 (rtd 52a & 44, h'caps, B R Johnson): missed '98: '97 Lingfield wnr (2, h'cap
& amat h'cap, rtd 52a, current trainer): eff at 12f/2m on both AWs, likes a sharp trk: runs
well fresh: revitalised by hdgr & drop to sell grade today.
2957}   **COASTGUARDS HERO** 99 [10] L A Dace 7-9-4 T G McLaughlin 50/1: 6606-2: 7 ch g Chilibang - Aldwick   3 **43$**
Colonnade (Kind Of Hush): Led, hard rdn 3f out & hdd 1f out, held inside last: clr rem: 7 wk jumps abs (rtd 47h,
sell hdle): unplcd on the level in '99 for B A Pearce (rtd 17a): '98 wnr at Lingfield (3, h'cap & sell h'cap,
M Usher & h'cap, rtd 39a): eff at 13f/2m: acts on fast grnd, both AWs & likes a sharp trk: enjoys sell grade.
318   **HARVEY WHITE** 13 [2] J Pearce 8-9-4 (BL) G Bardwell 7/2: 06-023: 8 b g Petorius - Walkyria   10 **33a**
(Lord Gayle): Trkd wnr, rdn/lost place 5f out, no impress after: op 5/1, first time blnks: clr of rem: see 318.
338   **QUAKERESS** 9 [3] John Berry 5-8-13 (te) D Williamson (7) 66/1: 00-604: Rear, mod prog halfway/sn held.   7 **21a**
327   **FLORA DREAMBIRD** 12 [1] 6-8-13 (tbl) J Bosley (7) 33/1: 66-005: Prom 10f: see 284.   3½ **18a**
--   **AL RABEH** [8] 8-9-4 G A Parkin 8/1: 3-6: Rdn/bhd halfway, mod gains: jumps fit (no form): ex-   1 **22a**
Belgium performer, plcd at up to 13f in '99: with G L Moore.
363   **SWAN HUNTER** 6 [7] 7-9-4 (BL) N Adams 3-13 A Daly 11/4: 025-27: Mid-div/wide, btn 3f out: 1st time blnks.   5 **17a**
333   **MAUERSCHWALBE** 11 [9] 5-8-13 A Daly 20/1: 430-08: Struggling halfway: see 333 (10f).   20 **0a**

LINGFIELD (Equitrack) WEDNESDAY JANUARY 26TH Lefthand, V Sharp Track

317 KI CHI SAGA 14 [6] 8-9-4 (bl) P McCabe 14/1: 020-69: Rear/wide, bhd 5f out: tchd 20/1: see 219. 6 0a
547} GHOST PATH 99 [4] 5-8-13 P M Quinn (5) 50/1: 02/5-0: Sn bhd: 10th: 3 mth jumps abs (no form): 16 0a
only mod form prev on the level, including for C Brittain.
10 ran   Time 3m 28.73 (8.73)   (D G Wheatley)   R Ingram Epsom, Surrey.

403	4.20 AUSTRALIA DAY HCAP 3YO+ 0-75 (E) 5f aw rnd Going 40 -01 Slow		[73]
	£2769 £852 £426 £213		

291 FRILLY FRONT 18 [6] T D Barron 4-8-12 (57) C Lowther 6/1: 410-P1: 4 ch f Aragon - So So (Then 62a
Again): Trkd ldrs, rdn to chall final 2f, styd on gamely to prevail nr line, all-out: tchd 7/1: '99 W'hampton
scorer (h'cap, rtd 58a, plcd sev times on turf, rtd 61, h'cap): '98 debut wnr at Musselburgh (med auct mdn, subs
rtd 83 at best): eff at 5f, stays 6f well: acts on fast, soft & both AWs: handles any trk, loves a sharp one:
has run well fresh: best without blnks: should win more races.
272 AA YOUKNOWNOTHING 20 [1] Miss J F Craze 4-9-8 (67)(tvis) S Finnamore (7) 9/2: 341-62: 4 b g hd 71a
Superpower - Bad Payer (Tanfirion): Led, hard rdn/duelled with rivals ins last, just hdd nr line: op 7/2: see 235.
386 BEST QUEST 2 [7] K R Burke 5-9-7 (66)(t) N Callan (3) 4/1 FAV: 0-3123: 5 b h Salse - Quest For shd 70a
The Best (Rainbow Quest): Sn trkd ldrs wide, rdn to chall over 1f out, styd on well for press, just held: well
bckd, tchd 5/1: qck reapp: eff at 5/7f, stays 1m: win more races: see 313 (stks, 6f).
4518} BRAMBLE BEAR 92 [5] M Blanshard 6-8-7 (52) D Sweeney 6/1: 5653-4: Dwelt & rdn/rear, kept on final 3 49a
2f, not pace to chall: nicely bckd, tchd 7/1: 3 mth abs: place form in '99 (rtd 62, h'cap): '98 Lingfield wnr
(h'cap, rtd 73): eff at 5f on firm & soft, handles equitrack: nicely h'capped & posted a encouraging AW bow here.
312 PALACEGATE JACK 14 [3] 9-8-11 (56)(bl) Christina Christians 5/1: 052-25: Cl-up, wknd over 1f out. nk 52a
312 TORRENT 14 [8] 5-10-0 (73)(bl) Lynsey Hanna (7) 6/1: 113-36: Chsd ldrs wide/held 1f out: see 205 (C/D). 1¼ 66a
258 CHARGE 22 [9] 4-9-3 (62)(t) J Stack 11/2: 416-07: Wide/rear, nvr on terms: bckd, op 8/1: see 95 (6f). 1¾ 51a
279 ALJAZ 19 [2] 10-9-7 (66) S Whitworth 12/1: 223-48: Al towards rear: op 10/1: see 44. nk 54a
8 ran   Time 59.85 (2.05)   (M Dalby)   T D Barron Maunby, Nth Yorks.

WOLVERHAMPTON (Fibresand) THURSDAY JANUARY 27th Lefthand, Sharp Track

Official Going STANDARD. Stalls: Inside.

404	1.10 AMAT HCAP DIV 1 4YO+ 0-65 (G) 1m1f79y aw Going 62 -15 Slow		[44]
	£1636 £467 £233 4 yo rec 1 lb		

359 SWING ALONG 7 [6] R Guest 5-11-7 (65) Mr V Coogan (5) 11/2: 6-W241: 5 ch m Alhijaz - So It Goes 71a
(Free State): Trkd ldrs, rdn/led 1f out, styd on well ins last, rdn out: op 4/1: '99 W'hampton scorer (fill h'cap,
rtd 68a & 70): rnr-up in '98 (rtd 91, mdn): eff at 7/9.4f, stays a sharp 11f: acts on gd, hvy & f/sand: handles
a sharp or stiff/gall trk, likes W'hampton: has run well fresh, gd mount for an amateur.
324 EI EI 13 [5] G L Moore 5-9-3 (33)(2oh) Mr I Mongan 10/1: 000-02: 5 b g North Briton - Branitska 2 34a
(Mummy's Pet): Held up in tch, rdn/prog wide over 3f out, styd on inside last, not able to chall: eff at 7f,
now suited by 9.4f, could stay further: acts on fast, hvy & fibresand: nicely h'capped: see 224.
383 SHONTAINE 5 [8] M Johnston 7-9-12 (42) Mrs C Williams 11/2: 516633: 7 b g Pharly - Hinari Televideo 3½ 36a
(Caerleon): Chsd ldrs wide halfway, rdn & kept on onepace final 2f: op 4/1, qck reapp: see 383, 297 (Southwell).
393 DANZAS 2 [10] J M Bradley 6-9-8 (38)(bl) Miss Hayley Bryan (7) 12/1: 5-6064: Mid-div, cl-up wide hd 31a
halfway, led over 2f out, hdd 1f out & no extra: op 6/1: qck reapp: see 255 (1m).
338 SOUNDS COOL 10 [1] 4-9-3 (34)(5oh) Mrs M Morris (3) 33/1: 000-65: Led/dsptd lead 7f, sn no extra. 3 21a
254 KAFIL 23 [7] 6-10-3 (47) Mrs S Bosley 4/1 FAV: 560-26: Held up in tch, swtchd wide/efft 4f out, sn held. 2½ 29a
359 JATO DANCER 7 [4] 5-9-5 (35)(2ow)(13oh) Miss A Knobbs (0) 40/1: 000-57: Rear halfway, no impress. ¾ 16a
306 LILANITA 16 [9] 5-10-3 (47) Miss E Folkes (5) 7/1: 03-208: Prom 5f: op 5/1: btr 45 (sell, 1m). ½ 27a
215 WHATSITSNAME 37 [3] 4-9-9 (40) Miss Diana Jones 16/1: /050-9: Mid-div, btn 3f out: mod form. hd 19a
325 WARRIOR KING 13 [2] 6-9-4 (34)(1ow)(11oh) Mr S Dobson (0) 33/1: 0-0500: Chsd ldrs 5f: 10th. 6 4a
-- RISKY LOVER [13] 7-9-3 (33)(8oh) Mr P Collington (3) 66/1: 5000/0: Bhd/wide halfway: 11th: 1 1a
jumps fit (mod form): missed '99 on the level, no prev form.
316 MUSTANG 15 [12] 7-9-11 (41)(bl) Mrs L Pearce 10/1: 54-300: V slowly away & al bhd: 12th: blindfold hd 8a
reportedly became caught in the blinkers, this best forgotten:: see 58 (7f).
329 GENIUS 13 [11] 5-10-9 (53) Miss R Clark 8/1: 0-2200: Hmpd in rear after 2f, btn halfway: 13th: op 10/1. ½ 19a
13 ran   Time 2m 05.4 (7.2)   (A B Coogan)   R Guest Newmarket

405	1.40 AMAT HCAP DIV 2 4YO+ 0-65 (G) 1m1f79y aw Going 62 -05 Slow		[43]
	£1627 £465 £232 4 yo rec 1 lb		

322 ETISALAT 14 [6] J Pearce 5-10-6 (49) Mrs L Pearce 13/2: 010-31: 5 b g Lahib - Sweet Repose (High 58a
Top): Bhd, rapid prog to lead dist, well in command ins last, rdn out: op 5/1: '99 Yarmouth (sell h'cap) &
Lingfield wnr (h'cap, rtd 53 & 47a): unplcd in '98 (R Armstrong, rtd 61): eff at 1m/10f on fast, gd & both AWs:
likes a sharp/fair trk: plenty in hand here, can win again whilst in this form.
305 PERCHANCER 16 [8] P C Haslam 4-10-4 (48) Miss A Armitage (5) 5/1: 006-32: 4 ch g Perugino - Irish 5 48a
Hope (Nishapour): Cl-up halfway, rdn/led 2f out, sn hdd & no ch with wnr: op 3/1: find similar: see 305 (C/D).
*254 KINNINO 23 [5] G L Moore 6-10-1 (44) Mr I Mongan 5/2 FAV: 020-13: 6 b g Polish Precedent - On Tiptoes 2½ 39a
(Shareef Dancer): Rdn/chsd ldrs over 3f out, kept on onepace, no threat: op 3/1: stays 9.4f: see 254 (1m).
340 PREPOSITION 10 [4] M A Peill 4-9-10 (40) Mr Nicky Tinkler (7) 13/2: 000/24: Keen, led after 2f till 1¾ 32a
2f out, no extra: op 5/1: clr rem: see 340.
383 HEVER GOLF GLORY 5 [1] 6-11-2 (59) Mr T Best (5) 5/1: 00-045: Chsd ldrs halfway, held over 2f out. 7 40a
260 PREMIERE FOULEE 23 [2] 5-9-3 (32)(3oh) Mr F Windsor Clive (4) 16/1: 200-06: Chsd ldrs 7f: vis omitted. 1½ 10a
305 UP IN FLAMES 16 [12] 9-9-4 (33) Miss V Vollaro (5) 20/1: 00-007: Wide/rear halfway, no impress: 1¼ 8a
unplcd in '99 (rtd 30a, h'cap, tried blnks, S Bowring): '98 Southwell scorer (h'cap, rtd 53a), subs plcd on turf
(rtd 51, h'cap): eff at 1m/10f on firm, gd/soft & fibresand: poss handles hvy: best without hdgr: with R Simpson.
156 SCOTLAND BAY 50 [7] 5-9-13 (42) Mr R Lucey Butler (7 33/1: 0000-8: Al towards rear: jumps fit 1 15a
(no form): rnr-up in '99 (rtd 47a, clmr, unplcd on turf, rtd 41, h'cap): '98 Lingfield wnr (h'cap, rtd 64a at best,
R Hannon) & Folkestone (sell, rtd 63): suited by 7f/1m: acts on gd/soft & both AWs: likes a sharp trk.
254 MELOMANIA 23 [13] 8-9-11 (40) Mr M A Hammond (7) 33/1: 006-09: Rear/wide halfway, sn btn: '99 1¼ 10a
Lingfield wnr (amat h'cap, rtd 46a, P Howling, unplcd/no form on turf): eff at 1m on equitrack: has run well fresh.

349 **DARE 9** [11] 5-11-7 (64)(bl) Miss E Folkes (5) 11/2: 0-3220: Cl-up halfway, rdn/wknd final 2f: qck reapp, fin 4th over timber at Southwell yesterday: has been busy recenly: see 349, 83. *1* **32a**
4496} **MOUNTAIN MAGIC 94** [10] 5-9-13 (42)(bl) Mr A Jones (5) 33/1: 0030-0: Led 2f, btn halfway: jumps fit (mod form, h'cap): plcd twice in '99 on the level (D J S Ffrench Davis, incl first time blnks, rtd 46, rtd 20a on sand): '98 reapp wnr at Newbury (fillies h'cap, rtd 61): eff at 7f/1m: acts on fast & firm: with A G Juckes. **0a**
-- **Missed The Boat** [9] 10-9-3 (32)(8oh) Mr D Ross (0) 50/1:339 **Bija 10** [3] 5-9-3 (32)(7oh) Mr W Jones (7) 40/1:
13 ran Time 2m 04.5 (6.3) (Mrs E M Clarke) J Pearce Newmarket

406

2.10 BRITISH COLUMBIA CLAIMER 4YO+ (F) 6f aw rnd Going 62 +13 Fast
£2124 £607 £303

183 **ASTRAC 45** [4] A J McNae 9-9-10 J Weaver 2/1 FAV: 0335-1: 9 b g Nordico - Shirleen (Daring Display): Led/dsptd, clr 2f out, readily & eased nr fin: value for 8L+, best time of day, 6 wk abs: '99 Catterick scorer (appr stks, rtd 87), plcd on sand (rtd 85a, h'cap): '98 wnr at Ayr (h'cap) & Hamilton (stks, rtd 103): eff at 5/7f, suited by 6f: acts on gd/soft, hvy & both AWs, handles fast: handles any trk: gd weight carrier. **85a**
279 **TAKHLID 20** [7] D W Chapman 9-9-10 A Culhane 11/2: 16-402: 9 b h Nureyev - Savonnerie (Irish River): Mid-div, rdn/kept on final 2f, no ch with wnr: op 4/1: can win again in this grade: see 142 (7f). *5* **69a**
389 **BLUSHING GRENADIER 3** [9] S R Bowring 8-8-10 (bl) S Finnamore (6) 12/1: 0-3343: 8 ch g Salt Dome - La Duse (Junius): Led/dsptd lead 4f, outpcd final 2f: op 10/1: qck reapp: return to h'caps will suit: see 38. *½* **53a**
291 **FEATHERSTONE LANE 19** [10] Miss L C Siddall 9-8-6 Dean McKeown 20/1: 450-44: Rear/wide, mod prog. *2* **44a**
386 **MALLIA 3** [2] 7-9-4 (bl) C Lowther 9/4: 0-4055: Well bhd early, mod gains: nicely bckd, qck reapp. *hd* **55a**
354 **NINEACRES 8** [3] 9-8-6 (bl) Claire Bryan (7) 5/1: 2-3226: Prom 5f, fdd: op 4/1: btr 354, 134 (C/D). *hd* **42a**
3194} **WOODCUT 99** [1] 4-8-4 P M Quinn (5) 66/1: 0000-7: Wide/rear, nvr a factor: 6 mth abs: mod form. *½* **38$**
272 **SING FOR ME 21** [6] 5-8-5 Stephanie Hollinshead (6) 50/1: 000-08: Al rear: see 272. *9* **23a**
54} **TANGERINE FLYER 99** [8] 5-8-8 Joanna Badger (7) 33/1: 0000/9: Chsd ldrs 3f, sn btn: long abs: missed '99: '98 Lingfield wnr (2, h'cap & clmr, rtd 81a, J Berry, unplcd on turf subs for P D Evans, rtd 56, h'cap): eff at 5f, stays sharp 6f: acts on both AWs & gd grnd: likes to force the pace: has run well fresh. *1½* **22a**
3959} **MANOLO 99** [5] 7-8-10 F Norton 11/2: 5350-0: Rdn chsg ldrs 4f, sn btn: 4 mth abs: unplcd sole Brit start in '99 (h'cap, rtd 47), plcd in France (1m, soft): '98 wnr at Lingfield (2, h'caps, rtd 71a, D Loder): eff at 5/6f on both AWs, loves Lingfield: eff in blnks/visor, not worn today. *5* **15a**
10 ran Time 1m 15.6 (2.8) (Clive Titcomb) A J McNae Compton, Berks.

407

2.40 MANITOBA HCAP 4YO+ 0-80 (D) 1m4f aw Going 62 -03 Slow [76]
£3867 £1190 £595 £297 4 yo rec 4 lb

-- **APOLLO BAY** [4] P Mitchell 4-9-1 (67)(bl) J Fanning 16/1: 0303-1: 4 b c Farma Way - Ottomwa (Strawberry Road): Trkd ldr, led over 2f out, styd on well ins last, rdn out: op 12/1: 4 mth abs, Brit/AW bow: first success: ex-Irish, plcd in a Listowel mdn on final start in '99 (1m, D Weld): eff at 1m, apprec this step up to 12f, cld stay further: acts on fibresand, gd/soft & soft: runs well fresh & likes a sharp trk: eff in blnks. **70a**
343 **FAILED TO HIT 10** [6] N P Littmoden 7-9-6 (68)(vis) J Weaver 3/1 FAV: 2-4232: 7 b g Warrshan - Missed Again (High Top): Led, rdn/hdd over 2f out, kept on well for press inside last, not pace of wnr: nicely bckd. *1¾* **68a**
370 **WESTERN COMMAND 6** [7] Mrs N Macauley 4-9-1 (67) R Fitzpatrick (3) 7/1: 1-4503: 4 b g Saddlers' Hall - Western Friend (Gone West): Chsd ldrs, onepace/held final 2f: op 5/1, qck reapp: see 170 (C/D). *3½* **62a**
335 **GYPSY 12** [11] M H Tompkins 4-8-13 (65) A Mackay 12/1: 6W-354: Rdn/chsd ldrs wide halfway, sn onepace/held: op 7/1: poss stays this sharp 12f trip, best arnd 9/10f: see 270. *1½* **58a**
471} **LYSANDROS 99** [5] 6-10-0 (76) J P Spencer 9/2: 2321-5: Towards rear, mod prog: op 5/1, 7 wk jumps abs (plcd, rtd 96h, nov): '99 W'hampton wnr (C/D h'cap, rtd 76a): ex-French, plcd form in '98: eff at 12f, stays 2m: acts on fibresand & a sharp trk: topweight today. *nk* **68a**
66 **SILVER GYRE 71** [10] 4-7-12 (49)(1ow) C Rutter 25/1: 4006-6: Rear, mod late gains: 10 wk abs: '99 Bath wnr (mdn h'cap, rtd 60): rtd 76 in '98 (fillies mdn, Mrs J Ramsden): eff at 12f, suited by 2m/2m1f: acts on firm & soft grnd: likes a sharp/turning trk: interesting for similar when stepped up in trip. *4* **36a**
307 **BE WARNED 16** [3] 9-9-3 (65)(vis) F Norton 8/1: 41-047: Towards rear, no prog: op 5/1, kind ride. *2* **48a**
4307} **ROMAN CANDLE 99** [2] 4-9-4 (70) M Tebbutt 100/30: 1150-8: Chsd ldrs 10f out: op 3/1, abs/AW bow. *2½* **49a**
167 **ESHTIAAL 48** [8] 6-8-12 (60)(bl) G Parkin 9/1: 3324-9: Chsd ldrs 1m, btn/eased final 2f: 7 wk abs. *15* **23a**
332 **FOREST DREAM 12** [1] 5-8-0 (48)(t) P Doe 16/1: 40-000: Chsd ldrs, btn 4f out: 10th: t-strap. *dist* **0a**
1362} **TEN PAST SIX 99** [9] 8-8-12 (60) A Culhane 33/1: 0/50-0: T.o. halfway: 11th: 9 mth abs. *28* **0a**
11 ran Time 2m 41.5 (7.9) (The Chint Racing Club) P Mitchell Epsom, Surrey.

408

3.10 ALBERTA SELL HCAP DIV 1 4YO+ 0-60 (G) 1m4f aw Going 62 -17 Slow [51]
£1545 £441 £220 4 yo rec 4 lb

344 **COLONEL CUSTER 10** [10] J Pearce 5-9-11 (48)(VIS) G Bardwell 2/1 FAV: 001-31: 5 ch g Komaite - Mohican (Great Nephew): Trkd ldrs, led over 5f out & rdn clr3f out, styd on well, rdn out: well bckd, sold for 5,200gns, first time visor: '99 Southwell (h'cap) & W'hampton wnr (sell, rtd 62a & 51): plcd in '98 (rtd 66a, C Thornton): suited by 11/12f & fibresand, has disapp on equitrack: enjoys sell grade & woken up by first time visor here. **54a**
318 **HILL FARM DANCER 14** [12] W M Brisbourne 9-8-6 (29) C Cogan (5) 7/2: 03-552: 9 ch m Gunner B - Loadplan Lass (Nicholas Bill): Dwelt/rear, rdn & kept on well final 4f, nrst fin: tchd 9/2: see 318, 231 (C/D). *4* **29a**
338 **NEPTUNE 10** [2] K C Comerford 4-8-8 (35) T G McLaughlin 9/1: 540-33: 4 b g Dolphin Street - Seal Indigo (Glenstal): Chsd ldrs, rdn/chsd wnr 4f out, held final 2f: clr of rem: see 338. *1½* **33a**
333 **WITHOUT FRIENDS 12** [8] Mrs N Macauley 6-8-12 (35) A Clark 10/1: 06-044: Held up, nvr a factor. *14* **18a**
231 **NORTH ARDAR 31** [6] 10-8-13 (36) F Norton 10/1: 0246-5: Twds rear, prog wide halfway, held fnl 3f. *2½* **15a**
2750} **PARDAN 99** [7] 6-8-11 (34) D Sweeney 9/1: 0100-6: Prom, rdn/btn 4f out: op 6/1, jumps fit (Nov '99 plcd, nov h'cap, rtd 73h): '99 Nottingham scorer (sell h'cap, rtd 39): plcd thrice in '98 (sell h'cap, rtd 42 & 40a): eff at 14f/2m: acts on gd & gd/soft grnd: best without blnks. *8* **4a**
260 **COHIBA 23** [1] 7-9-1 (38)(bl) N Callan (3) 8/1: 216-67: Mid-div at best: op 5/1: see 260. *5* **1a**
23 **SASEEDO 77** [3] 10-9-10 (47)(bl) A Daly 33/1: 0600-8: Towards rear, nvr a factor: 11 wk abs: blnks reapplied: '99 Lingfield scorer (sell, rtd 54a, subs plcd on turf, rtd 50, h'cap): rtd 66a & 52 in '98 (unplcd, L Dace): eff between 1m/12f on firm, gd/soft & both AWs: handles any trk. *6* **1a**
370 **TIME ON MY HANDS 6** [4] 4-9-3 (44)(t) Dean McKeown 10/1: P0-209: Led 7f, sn btn: btr 260 (C/D). *15* **0a**
344 **RONS ROUND 10** [5] 6-10-0 (51) A Culhane 14/1: 22/540: Al rear: 10th: op 10/1: see 344, 292. *9* **0a**
332 **Roman Reel 12** [9] 9-9-6 (43)(BL) R Brisland (5) 12/1: 353 **Sky City 8** [11] 4-8-5 (32) A McCarthy (3) 20/1:
12 ran Time 2m 43.1 (9.5) (D Leech) J Pearce Newmarket

409 3.40 QUEBEC MDN 3YO+ (D) 1m100y aw Going 62 -07 Slow
£2808 £864 £432 £216 3 yo rec 20lb

3852} **CRIMSON GLORY 99** [3] G C Bravery 4-9-7 M Hills 6/4 FAV: 3540-1: 4 ch f Lycius - Crimson Conquest **71a**
(Diesis): Sn handy, led 2f out, held on gamely inside last, all-out: hvly bckd, tchd 9/4: 5 mth abs/AW bow:
rnr-up in '99 for C E Brittain (rtd 73, h'cap): rtd 79 in '98 (fillies mdn): eff arnd 1m, has tried further: acts
on firm, fast & fibresand: likes a sharp/undul trk: runs well fresh: open to further improvement.

328 **MANTILLA 13** [8] R Hollinshead 3-8-1 P M Quinn (5) 5/1: 534-02: 3 b f Son-Pardo - Well Tried nk **70a**
(Thatching): Rear, rdn/prog wide over 3f out, styd on well inside last, just held: op 4/1: stays 8.5f: win soon.

-- **STRETFORD LASS** [2] J Noseda 3-8-1 P Doe 7/4: 3: 3 b f Woodman - Ladanum (Green Dancer): 2 **66a**
Led, rdn/hdd 2f out, no extra inside last: hvly bckd: debut: $22,000 purchase, dam a French 12f wnr: eff at
1m, further could suit in time: acts on fibresand: encouraging debut, can find similar on sand this winter.

362 **FINERY 7** [5] W Jarvis 3-8-6 Martin Dwyer 10/1: 64: Trkd ldrs, rdn/no extra over 1f out: tchd 12/1, 1¾ **68a**
clr of rem: stays 8.5f & handles fibresand: going the right way after debut.

4256} **TAKE ACTION 99** [6] 3-8-6 N Callan (1) 33/1: 5000-5: Chsd ldrs wide over 3f out, sn held: 4 mth 5 **58$**
abs: unplcd in '99, auct mdn): has tried up to 10f: AW bow today.

3516} **POLIZIANO 99** [1] 4-9-12 A Culhane 5/1: 2/33-6: Bhd, mod gains under a kind ride: 5 mth abs/AW 8 **46a**
bow: plcd on both starts in '99 for H Cecil (mdns, rtd 79): eff arnd 1m: handles fast & hvy grnd & a stiff/undul
trk: not given a hard time, will know more next time for W W Haigh.

362 **SUBADAR MAJOR 7** [10] 3-8-6 Angela Hartley (7) 66/1: 0-07: Al towards rear: no form. 17 **21a**
367 **WOOLLY WINSOME 6** [7] 4-9-12 J Bosley (7) 16/1: 065-38: Nvr a factor: qck reapp: see 225 (7f). 2½ **16a**
4226} **ANNELIINA 99** [11] 4-9-7 R Morse 20/1: 0250-9: Chsd ldrs, wknd qckly final 3f: 4 mth abs, AW bow: nk **10a**
rnr-up in '99 (rtd 63, mdn): rtd 81 in '98 (unplcd, stks): eff at 6f & a drop to that trip should suit: handles fast.
310 **MAID PLANS 16** [4] 4-9-7 R Fitzpatrick (3) 66/1: 05-050: Al rear: 10th: mod form. 18 **0a**
10 ran Time 1m 52.1 (5.9) (G C Bravery) G C Bravery Newmarket

410 4.10 ALBERTA SELL HCAP DIV 2 4YO+ 0-60 (G) 1m4f aw Going 62 -29 Slow [51]
£1545 £441 £220 4 yo rec 4 lb

387 **CRESSET 3** [3] W Jarvis 4-9-13 (54)(bl) M Tebbutt 7/2: 06-021: 4 ch c Arazi - Mixed Applause **61a**
(Nijinsky): Mid-div, prog wide halfway, led over 3f out, held on well last, rdn out: sold to D Chapman for
7400gns: bckd from 6/1, qck reapp: unplcd in '99 (rtd 61 & 44a): eff over a sharp 12f: acts on fibresand:
galvanised by blnks last twice: gd weight carrier: suited by this drop to sell grade.

347 **XYLEM 9** [7] J Pearce 9-8-13 (36) R Price 10/1: 000-32: 9 ch g Woodman - Careful (Tampa Trouble): 1½ **40a**
Rear halfway, rdn/prog wide final 3f, styd on well, nrst fin: op 8/1: on a fair mark, find similar: see 347 (C/D).

305 **OUR PEOPLE 16** [12] M Johnston 6-8-8 (31)(t) K Dalgleish (7) 6/4 FAV: 50-353: 6 ch g Indian Ridge - 4 **29a**
Fair And Wise (High Line): Held up, prog wide/dsptd lead over 3f out, held over 1f out: hvly bckd: see 261, 102.

318 **AMBIDEXTROUS 14** [6] E J Alston 8-8-5 (28) F Norton 10/1: 002-04: Chsd ldrs halfway, nvr pace to chall. 1¼ **23a**
2569} **VICTORY STAR 99** [9] 5-9-4 (44)(bl) J P Spencer 10/1: 6000-5: Cl-up halfway, btn over 2f out: op 8/1, nk **38a**
jumps frt (mod recent form in first time visor): Sept '99 Hereford wnr (sell hdle, rtd 89h, blnks): unplcd on the
level in '99 (rtd 43, Lady Herries): AW bow today, with M C Pipe.

347 **MR SPECULATOR 9** [2] 7-9-5 (42)(bl) J Weaver 10/1: -05346: Led, hdd after 2f, led again over 5f ¾ **35a**
out, headed over 3f out & sn no extra: also bhd todays rnr-up in 347.

325 **SHABAASH 13** [5] 4-8-10 (37) T Williams 16/1: 530-47: Chsd ldrs 9f: op 12/1: see 325, 111 (10f, eqtrk). 9 **20a**
370 **JAMORIN DANCER 6** [11] 5-9-11 (48) A Culhane 6/1: 00-108: Cl-up 4f out, sn rdn/wknd: op 3/1. 1 **30a**
*178 **BOBONA 45** [4] 4-8-5 (32) G Baker (7) 8/1: 3401-9: Al towards rear: abs: see 178 (11f, clmr). 1 **13a**
292 **MAJOR ATTRACTION 19** [8] 5-8-11 (34) P Doe 12/1: 340-00: Bhd 4f out: 10th: op 10/1: plcd in 6 **6a**
'99 (rtd 35a, sell): mod form prev for M Mullineaux): stays 11f & handles fibresand.

333 **WILD RICE 12** [10] 8-9-3 (40)(bl) A Morris 25/1: /40-60: Led after 2f, hdd over 5f out/wknd: 11th. 25 **0a**
4540} **MIRAGGIO 91** [1] 4-9-1 (42) A Clark 25/1: 4440-0: Struggling halfway: 12th: 3 mth abs: plcd in '99 dist **0a**
(rtd 45, sell, also rtd 30a, H Morrison): eff at 10/12f, prob stays 2m1f: handles firm & gd: best without blnks.
12 ran Time 2m 44.5 (10.9) (Rams Racing Club) W Jarvis Newmarket

411 4.40 ONTARIO HCAP 4YO+ 0-70 (E) 1m100y aw Going 62 -13 Slow [59]
£2802 £800 £400

360 **TUFAMORE 7** [4] K R Burke 4-9-1 (46)(vis) N Callan (3) 15/8 FAV: 05-421: 4 ch g Mt Livermore - Tufa **51a**
(Warning): Chsd ldrs halfway, rdn final 2f, led inside last, styd on well, rdn out: well bckd: 1st win: plcd in
'99 (rtd 53a & 51): eff at 1m/9.3f, stays 11.5f: acts on gd & fibresand: eff in a vis: likes a sharp trk.

336 **SCISSOR RIDGE 12** [7] J J Bridger 8-9-10 (55) A Daly 12/1: 304-32: 8 ch g Indian Ridge - Golden 1 **57a**
Scissors (Kalaglow): Cl-up, led over 5f out, rdn/hdd inside last, no extra cl-home: op 8/1: topweight: see 29.

345 **GODMERSHAM PARK 10** [5] P S Felgate 8-9-2 (47) Dean McKeown 5/1: 305-23: 8 b g Warrshan - Brown 3½ **42a**
Velvet (Mansingh): Dwelt & rear, prog/chsd ldrs wide 3f out, sn onepace: op 4/1: likes to front run: see 345, 45.

323 **PUPPET PLAY 14** [9] E J Alston 5-9-4 (49) J P Spencer 9/2: 22-334: Trkd ldrs, ch 3f out, sn held: op 7/2. 5 **34a**
-368 **MUTABARI 6** [2] 6-9-8 (53) J Fanning 3/1: 0-3425: Mid-div, btn 2f out: nicely bckd: btr 368 (7f). 3 **32a**
304 **SOUND THE TRUMPET 17** [8] 8-8-13 (44)(t) G Baker (7) 10/1: 130-06: Held up in tch, btn 3f out. 2 **19a**
381 **CONSULTANT 5** [3] 4-9-9 (54) T G McLaughlin 8/1: -03207: Led 3f, btn 2f out: op 6/1: qck reapp. 1¾ **26a**
4394} **PAARL ROCK 99** [10] 5-9-2 (47)(VIS) J Bramhill 33/1: 3000-8: Held up in tch, btn 3f out: visor, 3 month nk **18a**
abs: unplcd in '99 (rtd 48, no sand form): rtd 54a & 51 in '98 (K Wingrove): has tried blnks.

396 **DOBERMAN 2** [6] 5-8-7 (38)(vis) D Sweeney 12/1: -40359: Rdn/rear, nvr a factor: qck reapp: btr 396. 1¾ **6a**
4548} **MY DILEMMA 90** [1] 4-8-4 (35) M Baird 25/1: 0060-0: Al rear: 10th: op 14/1, 8 wk jumps abs (rnr-up, 17 **0a**
4 rnr juv nov, rtd 90h): unplcd in '99 (rtd 48, no sand form): rtd 54a & 51 in '98 (K Wingrove): has tried blnks.
10 ran Time 1m 52.6 (6.4) (D G & D J Robinson) K R Burke Newmarket

SOUTHWELL (Fibresand)   FRIDAY JANUARY 28TH   Lefthand, Sharp, Oval Track

Official Going   STANDARD.   Stalls: Inside.

---

412   **1.10 B'TON AMAT HCAP DIV 1 4YO+ 0-60 (G)**   **1m4f aw   Going 76   -49 Slow**   **[26]**
   £1568   £448   £224   4 yo rec 4 lb

324   **ST LAWRENCE** 14 [10] N Tinkler 6-11-1 (41) Mr Nicky Tinkler (7) 9/4 FAV: 60-231: 6 gr g With   **47a**
Approval - Mingan Isle (Lord Avie) Chsd ldrs, hdwy to lead over 3f out, styd on strongly, drvn out: first win
on 27th starts: plcd twice in '99 (amat h'cap, rtd 58 & 45a): lightly rcd in '98 (h'cap, rtd 70): eff btwn
11.5f & 2m on firm grnd & both AWs: likes a sharp trk & runs well for an amateur.
327   **GRAND CRU** 14 [4] J Cullinan 9-11-10 (50)(vis) Miss L Vollaro (5) 4/1: 341-42: 9 ch g Kabour -   ½ **55a**
Hydrangea (Warpath) Rear, rdn to impr 3f out, chall dist, no extra cl-home: clr rem: top-weight, likes Southwell.
340   **SARTEANO** 11 [7] D Shaw 4-11-9 (24) Mrs S Bosley 12/1: 0/0-63: 6 ch m Anshan - Daisy Girl (Main   8 **21a**
Reef) Cl-up, rdn & not pace of ldrs fnl 2f: first time in the frame: prob stays 12f on fibresand: see 340.
3947} **GOLD BLADE** 99 [3] J Pearce 11-11-5 (45) Mrs L Pearce 4/1: 1125-4: Mid-div, hdwy 5f out, btn fnl 2f: 5 **36a**
long abs: '99 Lingfield & Pontefract wnr (amat/ladies h'cap, rtd 48): lightly rcd in '98, plcd in '97 (h'caps,
rtd 62 & 57a): eff at 1m, best at 10/13f: acts on firm, soft, both AWs & any trk: runs well fresh & for Mrs L Pearce.
224   **HIGHFIELDER** 37 [1] 4-11-0 (44) Mrs S Moore (5) 16/1: 0306-5: Led, hdd over 3f out, not pace of ldrs.   8 **27a**
324   **AMSARA** 14 [11] 4-10-3 (33) Mr S Dobson (5) 12/1: 000-06: Prom, rdn & btn over 2f out: op 8/1:   10 **6a**
'99 Pontefract scorer (seller, rtd 59, M Channon), subs rnr-up on sand for current connections (h'cap, rtd
43a): eff over a sharp or stiff/undul 12f: acts on gd/soft & fibresand.
325   **DREAM CARRIER** 14 [2] 12-10-4 (30) Mrs C Peacock (5) 33/1: 06-007: In tch, lost pl 6f out,   14 **0a**
wknd fnl 3f: unplcd in '99 (rtd 51a): back in '97 won here at Southwell (amat h'cap, rtd 51): all wins at 7f,
stays 1m: acts on firm & gd/soft, loves fibresand/Southwell: best forcing the pace.
--   **TABORITE** [5] 6-10-1 (27) Miss C Hannaford (5) 25/1: 0500/8: Al in rear: long abs: modest form.   4 **0a**
--   **LAMBRINI LAD** [8] 5-10-12 (38) Mr F Giuliani (7) 33/1: 0603/9: Al bhd, t.o.: 8 wk hdle abs,   3 **0a**
modest form this term: rnr-up 4 times for A Bailey in 98/99 (juv novs, rtd 105h), stays 2m1f/2½m on gd & gd/
soft: plcd on the Flat in '98 (seller, rtd 60 at best): stays 1m & handles gd grnd.
--   **HOTSPUR STREET** [6] 8-10-12 (38)(bl) Miss S Samworth 20/1: 0606/0: Sn struggling, t.o. in   15 **0a**
10th: jumps fit, plcd twice this term (h'cap hdles, rtd 79h at best), stays 2m/2½m on gd & gd/soft): hdles
wnr back in 97/98 (amat seller, rtd 85h): modest form when last seen on the Flat back in '96.
1393} **NON VINTAGE** 99 [12] 9-11-7 (47) Mrs F Needham 20/1: 06/0-0: Dwelt, al well bhd, t.o. in 11th: 6 **0a**
well btn sole '99 Flat start (stks, rtd 44$), subs plcd over fences (h'cap, rtd 94c, stays 2m/2m5f on fast & soft):
h'cap chase wnr in 98/99 (h'cap, rtd 104c): unplcd on the Flat in '98: stays 2m+ on any grnd, with/without blnks.
11 ran   Time 2m 49.3 (15.0)   (Mrs C M Tinkler)   N Tinkler Langton, N.Yorks.

---

413   **1.40 B'TON AMAT HCAP DIV 2 4YO+ 0-60 (G)**   **1m4f aw   Going 76   -48 Slow**   **[20]**
   £1599   £445   £222   4 yo rec 4 lb

*370   **SWAGGER** 7 [1] Sir Mark Prescott 4-12-5 (57)(5ex) Mr I Mongan 1/2 FAV: 16-111: 4 ch g Generous -   **63a**
Widows Walk (Habitat) Made all, strongly pressed 2f out, styd on strongly, drvn out: qck reapp, well bckd, top
weight: hat-trick completed after scoring twice here at Southwell (amat h'cap & h'cap): '99 wnr again at
Southwell (amat h'cap, rtd 45 & 43): eff at 11/12f, stays 2m1f on firm, loves fibresand/Southwell but handles
any trk: loves to force the pace & runs well fresh, goes well for an amat: fine run under a welter burden.
369   **WELLCOME INN** 7 [6] G Woodward 6-10-3 (23)(t) Miss H Garrett (7) 8/1: 00-022: 6 ch g Most   1 **26a**
Welcome - Mimining (Tower Walk) Settled rear, gd hdwy over 2f out, chall over 1f out, no extra cl-home: op
6/1: gd run, acts on firm, gd/soft & fibresand: see 369 (flattered), 211.
324   **CLARINCH CLAYMORE** 14 [10] J M Jefferson 4-11-10 (48) Mr T Best (5) 4/1: 420-23: 4 b g Sabrehill -   ¾ **50a**
Salu (Ardross) Cl-up, ev ch till no extra ins last: clr rem: consistent form: see 324.
170   **DR EDGAR** 48 [5] J L Eyre 8-12-0 (48)(vis) Miss Diana Jones 33/1: 22/0-4: Mid-div, hdwy 2f out,   6 **42a**
no extra appr fnl 1f: 7 wk abs: lightly rcd: see 170.
324   **EVEZIO RUFO** 14 [4] 8-11-4 (38) Mr O Gunter (7) 25/1: 55-465: Dsptd lead, hdd 6f out, btn fnl 2f: op 16/1.¾   31a
70   **NUBILE** 70 [11] 6-10-11 (31)(bl) Mrs A Deniel 33/1: 0160-6: Dwelt, nvr with ldrs: jumps fit, back   20 **4a**
in June '99 plcd in a mdn hdle (rtd 90h, stays 2m1.5f on firm): '99 Flat scorer at Southwell (fill h'cap, rtd 34a):
back in '97 won at Windsor (seller, rtd 50, B Hills): eff around 11/12f on firm, gd & fibresand: eff in blnks.
369   **MODEST HOPE** 7 [9] 13-10-0 (20) Mrs M Morris (3) 100/1: 00-007: Rear, nvr a threat: see 324.   2½ **0a**
325   **PARK ROYAL** 14 [8] 5-10-7 (27) Mr R Lucey Butler (7) 50/1: /00-68: Al in rear: see 325.   hd **0a**
325   **IRSAL** 14 [2] 6-10-9 (29) Miss R Clark 25/1: 050-39: Prom, wknd over 3f out, t.o.: btr 325.   ¾ **0a**
325   **BLOWING AWAY** 14 [3] 6-11-6 (40) Mrs L Pearce 20/1: /00-00: Al bhd, fin lame in 10th: see 325.   9 **0a**
259   **AMBUSHED** 24 [7] 4-10-6 (30) Mrs C Williams 20/1: 00-00: Handy, lost tch halfway, t.o. in 11th.   24 **0a**
11 ran   Time 2m 49.2 (14.9)   (G Moore - Osborne House)   Sir Mark Prescott Newmarket.

---

414   **2.15 ANNESLEY CLASS STKS 4YO+ 0-60 (F)**   **6f aw rnd   Going 76   +06 Fast**
   £2268   £648   £324

247   **SEVEN** 25 [9] Miss S J Wilton 5-8-11 (bl) T G McLaughlin 8/1: 622-01: 5 ch g Weldnass - Polly's   **62a**
Teahouse (Shack) Dwelt, rapid hdwy to chall 4f out, led 2f out, ran on well, drvn out: op 5/1, best time of
day: '99 wnr here at Southwell (clmr, B Smart, rtd 68a, plcd on turf, rtd 59, h'cap): '98 rnr-up at Lingfield
(auct mdn, rtd 67): eff at 6/7f: acts on gd/soft, likes fibresand/Southwell: best in blnks & handles any trk.
386   **SHARP HAT** 4 [5] D W Chapman 6-9-0 A Culhane 100/30 FAV: 00-342: 6 b g Shavian - Madam Trilby   2 **59a**
(Grundy) Cl-up, hdwy to chall 2f out, no extra ins last: nicely bckd, qck reapp: consistent form: see 91.
2013} **REGAL SONG** 99 [2] T J Etherington 4-8-11 J Fanning 16/1: 0431-3: 4 b g Anita's Prince - Song   3 **49a**
Beam (Song) Rear, hdwy for press 2f out, styd on, nrst fin: reapp: '99 scorer at Hamilton (auct mdn, rtd 63):
plcd fnl 2 '98 starts (nurs, rtd 65): eff at 5/6f on fast & fibresand, suited by gd/soft: wears blnks: gd reapp.
384   **CARAMBO** 4 [4] T D Barron 5-8-8 (bl) N Callan 5/1: 000-64: Chsd ldrs, rdn & no extra fnl 2f: qk reapp. ½ **45a**
372   **DOLPHINELLE** 6 [8] 4-9-0 L Newman (5) 8/1: 4-1045: Prom, drvn 2f out & sn btn: qck reapp: op 5/1. 3½ **43a**
351   **XSYNNA** 10 [1] 4-8-11 M Tebbutt 7/2: 35-426: Prom, drvn & grad lost tch fnl 3f: op 9/4: btr 351. 1¼ **38a**
371   **JUST DISSIDENT** 6 [7] 8-8-11 P Doe 12/1: 445-47: Handy, wknd fnl 2f: see 371. ½ **37a**
381   **SACREMENTUM** 6 [3] 5-8-11 (bl) J P Spencer 9/1: 64-648: Dwelt, nvr a dngr: drop in trip: op 5/1. 2½ **31a**
388   **VICE PRESIDENTIAL** 4 [6] 5-9-0 Dean McKeown 10/1: 10-259: V keen to post, led, hdd 2f out &   2 **29a**
wknd qckly: lost ch in preliminaries today: see 32 (clmr, made all).
9 ran   Time 1m 17.6 (4.3)   (John Pointon & Sons)   Miss S J Wilton Wetley Rocks, Staffs.

---

415   **2.45 DANETHORPE MDN 3YO (D)**   1m aw rnd   Going 76   -25 Slow
£2847   £876   £438   £219

265   **ARMENIA 23** [8] R Hannon 3-9-0 R Smith (5) 3/1 FAV: 403-21: 3 ch f Arazi - Atlantic Flyer (Storm Bird)   **72a**
Settled in tch, hdwy 4f out, led over 2f out, sn clr, cmftbly: plcd form in '99 (rtd 77, fill mdn): eff at 7f, stays
1m well, further could suit: handles hvy, acts on fibresand & a sharp trk: easy wnr today, shld win again.

--   **AIR MAIL** [5] J M P Eustace 3-9-0 P McCabe 4/1: 2: 3 b f Night Shift - Wizardry (Shirley Heights)   5   **64a**
Dwelt, rcd wide & gd hdwy to lead 5f out, hdd 2f out & not pace of wnr: op 3/1, clr rem: half-brother to 3 wnrs,
incl a 7f scorer: stays 1m on fibresand: gd debut & will know more next time, shld improve & win a modest race.

328   **NICIARA 14** [6] M C Chapman 3-9-0 R Fitzpatrick (3) 6/1: P0-053: 3 b g Soviet Lad - Verusa (Petorius)   12   **47a**
Cl-up, rdn & no extra fnl 2f: blnks omitted today: low grade h'caps shld suit: see 328.

362   **SILCA FANTASY 8** [3] P Howling 3-9-0 T Williams 7/2: 0-444: Sn rdn in tch, wknd fnl 2f: needs h'caps.   5   **36a**

--   **LYDIAS LOOK** [4] 3-8-9 J Fanning 25/1: 5: Cl-up, drvn/btn fnl 2f: Distant View filly, with T Etherington.   3   **31a**

--   **WHITLEYGRANGE GIRL** [7] 3-8-9 A Culhane 33/1: 6: Chsd ldrs, wknd fnl 3f: debut: Rudimentary filly.   7   **21a**

346   **INDIANA SPRINGS 10** [1] 3-9-0 T G McLaughlin 50/1: 000-07: Led, hdd 5f out, sn lost tch: mod form.   11   **12a**

--   **AL KING SLAYER** [9] 3-9-0 J Stack 4/1: 8: V slow to start, eff 5f out, well btn fnl 3f: debut: op 2/1:   4   **6a**
brother to useful 7/9f wnr King Slayer: with B Smart: lost ch at start today.

8 ran   Time 1m 47.5 (8.1)   (Barouche Stud Ltd)   R Hannon East Evereigh, Wilts.

---

416   **3.20 CARLTON-ON-TRENT HCAP 3YO 0-85 (D)**   7f aw rnd   Going 76   00 Slow   [86]
£4251   £1308   £654   £327

125   **SIGN OF THE TIGER 59** [9] P C Haslam 3-7-13 (57) Dale Gibson 8/1: 0043-1: 3 b g Beveled - Me Spede   **63a**
(Valiyar) Sn rdn in tch, gd hdwy over 2f out, led dist, drvn out to hold on: 8 wk wks: first win: plcd once in
'99 (nurs, rtd 57a): eff at 7f/1m: acts on fibresand: runs well fresh on a sharp trk: improving.

*346   **LOUS WISH 10** [11] M J Polglase 3-8-2 (60)(bl) Martin Dwyer 5/1: 00-312: 3 b g Thatching - Shamaka   nk   **65a**
(Kris) Held up, smooth hdwy over 2f out, ev ch dist, styd on, just held: in fine form, win again soon: see 346.

*294   **FOXS IDEA 20** [10] D Haydn Jones 3-9-4 (76) L Newman (5) 8/1: 340-13: 3 b f Magic Ring - Lindy   2½   **77a**
Belle (Alleging) Cl-up, hdwy to lead over 1f out, hdd & no extra dist: op 6/1, clr rem: in gd form: see 294.

213   **MYTTONS AGAIN 38** [5] A Bailey 3-8-12 (70) J Weaver (2) 10/1: 4260-4: Rdn/rear, styd on late, nvr   8   **59a**
nrr: will apprec a return to 1m: see 158 (nursery).

365   **AISLE 7** [1] 3-8-2 (60)(bl) P Doe 5/1: 0-5225: Led, hdd over 1f & wknd: better here in 365 (6f h'cap).   2½   **45a**

*275   **FEAST OF ROMANCE 22** [2] 3-9-7 (79) S Whitworth 2/1 FAV: 513-16: Prom, fdd appr fnl 1f: nicely   2½   **60a**
bckd, top-weight: poss not stay this longer 7f trip: much btr 275 (6f).

275   **OTIME 22** [8] 3-9-4 (76)(vis) Dean McKeown 20/1: 014-67: Cl-up, lost tch fnl 2f: btr 165 (6f, e'track).   hd   **57a**

213   **HEATHYARDS MATE 38** [7] 3-9-2 (74) P M Quinn 8/1: 1143-8: Al outpcd: best at 1m: see 128.   ¾   **54a**

365   **SPORTY MO 7** [3] 3-8-9 (67) Darren Williams (7) 14/1: 01-459: Prom, lost tch fnl 2f: qck reapp.   2½   **43a**

4583}   **AGUA CABALLO 87** [6] 3-8-6 (64) P Fessey 25/1: 0656-0: Al bhd, 10th: AW bow: '99 wnr at   13   **24a**
Carlisle & Beverley (auct mdn & clmr, rtd 81 at best): v eff over a stiff/undul 5f: acts on firm & fast grnd.

275   **LEEN 22** [4] 3-8-8 (66) F Norton 16/1: 140-00: Al bhd, t.o. in 11th: see 275.   6   **16a**

11 ran   Time 1m 31.9 (5.3)   (Middleham Park Racing)   P C Haslam Middleham, N.Yorks.

---

417   **3.55 FACKLEY SELLER 3YO (G)**   7f aw rnd   Going 76   -45 Slow
£1842   £526   £263

330   **PRICELESS SECOND 14** [6] J A Glover 3-8-12 N Callan 9/4: 24-231: 3 b g Lugana Beach - Early   **58a**
Gales (Precocious) Chsd ldrs, hdwy to lead 4f out, styd on well, btn out: first win, no bid: unplcd on turf in
'99 (rtd 54, P Calver): eff at 6/7f, tried 1m: acts on fibresand, with/without blnks: enjoys sell grade.

365   **BESCABY BLUE 7** [4] J Wharton 3-8-13 (BL) S Carson (5) 85/40 FAV: 02-662: 3 b f Blues Traveller -   3   **52a**
Nurse Tyra (Dr Blum) Cl-up, edged left & no extra appr fnl 1f: qck reapp: fair effort in blnks dropped to seller.

330   **AMELIA JESS 14** [2] B S Rothwell 3-8-7 R Lappin 7/2: 000-23: 3 ch f Mac's Imp - Vieux Carre   1¾   **43a**
(Pas de Seul) Led, hdd 5f out, ev ch till no extra over 1f out: fin ahd of today's wnr in 330 (C/D).

330   **PICCATA 14** [8] M R Channon 3-8-12 A Culhane 20/1: 00-04: Dwelt, late gains fnl 2f: op 12/1.   1½   **45$**

179   **DIAMOND VANESSA 46** [1] 3-8-7 N Carlisle 14/1: 000-5: Outpcd, mod gains: 6 wk wks: mod prev form.   nk   **40a**

330   **ALL MINE 14** [5] 3-8-12 (t) J Stack 33/1: 606: Cl-up, rdn & no extra fnl 2f: modest form.   2½   **41a**

4607}   **NORTHERN TRIO 84** [3] 3-8-12 R Fitzpatrick (3) 8/1: 000-7: Al outpcd: reapp/AW bow: rtd 51   5   **33a**
on '99 debut (unplcd, 6f mdn, gd grnd).

350   **CARDINAL FAIR 10** [7] 3-8-7 (BL) G Parkin 16/1: 05-48: Dwelt, al bhd: first time blnks.   ¾   **27a**

8 ran   Time 1m 35.1 (8.5)   (Vic Atherton)   J A Glover Carburton, Notts.

---

418   **4.25 NEWARK HCAP 4YO+ 0-65 (F)**   1m aw rnd   Going 76   -10 Slow   [64]
£2520   £720   £360

390   **NICE BALANCE 4** [11] M C Chapman 5-8-3 (39) Joanna Badger (7) 16/1: -61431: 5 b g Shadeed -   **46a**
Fellwaati (Alydar) Fly-jumped start, rcd wide & rapid hdwy to lead 6f out, edged right fnl 2f, drvn out to hold on:
earlier won here at Southwell (appr h'cap): unplcd on the level in '99 (rtd 45 & 25a, tried blnks), subs modest
form over jumps: suited fnl jm, poss stays 11f: goes well on fibresand & for an appr: in good form.

393   **ELLWAY PRINCE 3** [6] Mrs N Macauley 5-9-0 (50) Dean McKeown 20/1: 40-022: 5 b g Price Sabo -   2   **52a**
Star Arrangement (Star Appeal) Ran loose bef start, near, rdn on strongly for press fnl 2f: nvr nrr: qck
reapp: fine eff considering pre-race exertions & shld win again soon: see 393.

340   **STERLING HIGH 11** [13] D Carroll 5-9-1 (51)(t) R Fitzpatrick (3) 10/1: 5-0403: 5 b g Mujadil -   shd   **53a**
Verusa (Petorius) Cl-up, chall 2f out, no extra fnl 2f: eff on firm, gd/soft & fibresand: see 251.

*340   **THE STAGER 11** [5] J R Jenkins 8-10-6 (70)(t)(6ex) S Whitworth 2/1 FAV: 02-114: Rdn/rear,   1¾   **69a**
hdwy fnl 2f, nrst fin: nicely bckd: loves this 6/7f: see 340.

*345   **SEA YA MAITE 11** [15] 6-9-9 (59)(6ex) S Finnamore (7) 5/1: 0-5315: Trkd ldr, hdwy to lead over   3½   **52a**
2f out, hdd over 1f out & wknd: nicely bckd: bad draw: 6lb pen for 345.

329   **MUTAHADETH 14** [2] 6-9-8 (58)(bl) J Fanning 10/1: 0-3256: Chsd ldrs, rdn/onepcd appr fnl 1f.   1¾   **48a**

298   **FRANKLIN LAKES 18** [12] 5-7-12 (34)(tbl) G Baker (7) 33/1: 500-37: Prom, rdn & no extra fnl 2f.   1½   **21a**

377   **MELLOW MISS 6** [10] 4-8-11 (47) F Norton 20/1: 40-568: Dwelt, al well held: see 152 (equitrack).   ¾   **35a**

345   **KINGCHIP BOY 11** [9] 11-9-0 (50)(vis) P McCabe 20/1: 0-3009: Led, hdd/fdd over 2f out: op 12/1.   ¾   **35a**

336   **ROBBER RED 13** [3] 4-8-7 (43) C Rutter 33/1: 60-000: Al in rear, fin 10th: see 336.   9   **14a**

SOUTHWELL (Fibresand)   FRIDAY JANUARY 28TH   Lefthand, Sharp, Oval Track

4447} **BROUGHTONS MILL 99** [14] 5-8-8 (44) L Newton 14/1: 5003-0: Sn struggling in rear, fin 11th: 4   8a
op 12/1: plcd on fnl '99 start (h'cap, rtd 40, also rtd 47a): eff at 10f & handles gd/soft grnd.
*411   **TUFAMORE 1** [4] 4-8-10 (46)(vis)(6ex) N Callan 9/2: 5-4210: Cl-up, rdn & wknd qckly fnl 3f: 14   0a
12th: op 7/2: W'hampton wnr just 24hrs ago, this prob came too soon: see 411.
433}   **Brandon Magic 99** [7] 7-9-12 (62) Clare Roche 7/1: 25/1:
96   **Captain Logan 66** [1] 5-9-0 (50)(tBL) P Fredericks (5) 25/1:
14 ran   Time 1m 46.3 (6.9)   (R J Hayward)   M C Chapman Market Rasen, Lincs.

LINGFIELD (Equitrack)   SATURDAY JANUARY 29TH   Lefthand, V Sharp Track

Official Going STANDARD. Stalls: Inside, except 1m (Outside).

419   1.25 PELLEW APPR HCAP 3YO 0-60 (G)   1m aw rnd   Going 34 -24 Slow   [65]
£1802   £515   £257

401   **WILL IVESON 3** [4] P C Haslam 3-9-7 (58)(vis) S Finnamore 4/6 FAV: 55-121: 3 b g Mukaddamah -   65a
Cherlinoa (Crystal Palace) Made all, duelled with rnr-up fnl 1f, narrowly prevailed, rdn out: hvly bckd, qck
reapp: earlier scored at W'hampton (h'cap, first win): unplcd in '99 (rtd 74 & 63a at best): eff around 1m on
both AWs, prob handles firm & gd/soft grnd: likes a sharp trk: eff forcing the pace: runs well for an appr.
236   **LORD HARLEY 31** [5] B R Millman 3-9-1 (52) Cheryl Nosworthy (7) 6/1: 0004-2: 3 b c Formidable -   shd   58a
Nanny Doon (Dominion) Prom, rdn/duelled with wnr fnl 1f, just held: tchd 13/2: h'cap debut: could find similar.
4414}   **CHILLI 99** [6] C E Brittain 3-9-3 (54) N Esler (5) 10/1: 0040-3: 3 br g Most Welcome - So Saucy   3½   53a
(Teenoso) Chsd ldrs, rdn/onepace over 1f out, tchd 14/1: 9 month abs/AW bow: unplcd in '99 (rtd 56, nov stks):
stays a sharp 1m, bred to apprec mid-dists this term: handles equitrack.
278   **JUST THE JOB TOO 22** [8] P C Haslam 3-9-1 (52) R Smith 7/1: 00-64: Mid-div, chsd ldrs 2f out,   ¾   50a
held ins last: op 6/1: prob stays an easy 1m & handles equitrack: h'cap bow today: see 278, 198.
4454}   **OFFENBURG 99** [2] 3-8-5 (42) J Bosley (3) 50/1: 5000-5: Rdn/hbd, kept on well fnl 3f, nrst fin: 3 mth   ½   39a
abs/AW bow: h'cap debut: unplcd in '99 (rtd 61, mdn): has tried blnks prev: apprec 10f+ on this evidence.
315   **ODYN DANCER 17** [3] 3-8-8 (45) G Baker (5) 12/1: 03-666: Mid-div, btn fnl 2f: op 10/1: see 315, 150.   1½   39a
150   **BLAYNEY DANCER 54** [1] 3-8-3 (40) D Kinsella (5) 33/1: 060-7: Rdn/bhd, nvr on terms: h'cap bow/abs.   1¼   31a
346   **BERKELEY DIDO 11** [9] 3-9-0 (51)(VIS) J Mackay (5) 10/1: 306-08: Prom wide 6f: op 8/1, visor.   13   16a
4600}   **FINCH 86** [7] 3-8-12 (49) C Haddon (7) 10/1: 000-9: Rear halfway, nvr factor: op 6/1: h'cap/AW   nk   13a
bow: unplcd in '99 (rtd 45, tried at 6/7f): with R Charlton.
9 ran   Time 1m 40.85 (4.65)   (Lord Bolton)   P C Haslam Middleham, N.Yorks.

420   2.00 BLACKWOOD STKS 3YO (C)   1m2f aw   Going 34 -23 Slow
£6217   £2299   £1149   £522

*373   **KATHAKALI 7** [2] V Soane 3-8-13 Martin Dwyer 100/30: 00-211: 3 b c Dancing Dissident - She's A   77a
Dancer (Alzao) Led 1f, remained handy & rdn/led again 1f out, styd on well, rdn out: op 9/4: recent wnr here at
Lingfield (auct mdn): unplcd in '99 (rtd 69, nov auct, tried visor): eff at 1m/10f, could stay further: acts on
fast, loves equitrack/Lingfield: handles a sharp or gall trk: in gd heart, can win more races.
*264   **THATS ALL FOLKS 24** [4] P J Makin 3-9-1 A Clark 9/1: 633-12: 3 b c Alhijaz - So It Goes (Free   ½   77a
State) Rear, rdn & outpcd 4f out, styd on strongly ins last: op 4/1, not btn far: stays a sharp 10f.
*204   **DOUBLE BANGER 42** [3] M Johnston 3-9-1 J Fanning 8/13 FAV: 341-3: 3 b c Ela Mana Mou - Penny   ½   76a
Banger (Pennine Walk) Led/dsptd lead after 1f till 1f out, kept on tho' held ins last: hvly bckd, clr rem: abs.
*328   **NATIONAL DANCE 15** [1] J G Given 3-9-1 S Ritchie (7) 9/1: 45-14: Chsd ldrs, held fnl 2f: op 5/1.   8   67a
401   **JOELY GREEN 3** [5] 3-9-1 (vis) T G McLaughlin 25/1: 0-2345: Chsd ldrs, led halfway till 3f out, rdn/btn   8   58a
2f out: op 14/1: qck reapp: btr 266, 41 (7f/1m).
5 ran   Time 2m 08.47 (5.67)   (M B N Clements)   V Soane East Garston, Berks.

421   2.30 TRACKSIDE MDN 3YO+ (D)   7f aw rnd   Going 34 -11 Slow
£2808   £864   £432   £216   3 yo rec 18lb

319   **ROYAL IVY 5** [5] J Akehurst 3-8-0 F Norton 7/2: 32-231: 3 ch f Mujtahid - Royal Climber (King's Lake)   69a
Chsd ldrs, prog to lead 1f out, styd on well, rdn out: op 9/4: plcd form in '99 (h'caps, rtd 70 & 74a, B W Hills):
eff at 7f/1m, loved stat further: acts on firm, soft & equitrack: handles any trk, likes a sharp one: deserved this.
264   **SUPERCHIEF 24** [8] Miss B Sanders 5-9-9 (tbl) C Rutter 25/1: 034-42: 5 b g Precocious - Rome Express   2   69$
(Siberian Express) Cl-up, rdn/briefly led over 1f out, not pace of wnr ins last: blnks reapplied: offic rated 39.
373   **CUPIDS DART 7** [4] P Howling 3-8-5 T Williams 8/1: 36-523: 3 ch g Pursuit Of Love - Tisza (Kris)   2½   64a
Led/dsptd lead till went on over 2f out, hdd over 1f out & no extra ins last: op 6/1: see 373, 80 (seller).
4498}   **YOU DA MAN 96** [2] R Hannon 3-8-5 L Newman (5) 1/2 FAV: 0600-4: Led/dsptd lead 5f, rdn/btn over   1¼   61a
1f out: hvly bckd: AW bow/3 month abs: unplcd in '99 (rtd 66): prob stays 7f, tried 1m: handles equitrack.
352   **INVIRAMENTAL 11** [9] 4-9-9 (bl) A Mackay 14/1: 504-25: Dwelt, chsd ldrs halfway/held fnl 2f: op 10/1.   ½   60$
173   **JAZZNIC 49** [7] 4-9-4 A Clark 10/1: 22-5/6: Prom 4f: op 7/1: 7 wk abs: see 173.   6   46a
4184}   **FRENCH FANCY 99** [1] 3-8-0 Martin Dwyer 33/1: 0504-7: Dwelt/rdn & rear, no prog: 4 month abs/AW   12   28a
bow: plcd in '99 (rtd 61, seller, C Dwyer): eff at 6f, tried 7f: handles fast & soft grnd: handles a gall or sharp/
undul trk: has tried a visor: now with B A Pearce.
--   **MILLENNIUM DREAM** [6] 3-8-6(1ow) N Callan 25/1: 8: Dwelt & al bhd: op 14/1, debut: with T Naughton.¾   33a
--   **MISTER HAVANA** [3] 3-8-5 S Carson (5) 33/1: 9: Slowly away & bhd halfway: debut, with E A Wheeler.   ½   31a
9 ran   Time 1m 25.97 (3.17)   (The Goldmine Partnership)   J Akehurst Epsom, Surrey.

422   3.05 JERVIS HCAP 4YO+ 0-95 (C)   1m4f aw   Going 34 -02 Slow   [93]
£6890   £2120   £1060   £530   4 yo rec 4 lb

356   **RAYIK 10** [1] G L Moore 5-8-2 (67) P Doe 7/2 FAV: 60-121: 5 br g Marju - Matila (Persian Bold)   72a
Handy, led after 4f, rdn/duelled with rnr-up over 2f out, narrowly asserted ins last, all out: op 3/1: recent wnr
here at Lingfield (h'cap): '99 rnr-up (h'cap, rtd 81a): '98 Lingfield wnr (mdn, N Berry, rtd 76): eff at 10/13f
on both AWs, loves Lingfield/equitrack: eff forcing the pace: tough/genuine gelding, in great heart.
*375   **HUGWITY 7** [5] G C Bravery 8-9-3 (82) M Hills 5/1: 6-0112: 8 ch g Cadeaux Genereux - Nuit d'Ete   ½   85a

142

LINGFIELD (Equitrack) SATURDAY JANUARY 29TH Lefthand, V Sharp Track

(Super Concorde) Chsd ldrs, cl-up/duelled with wnr over 2f out, rdn/just held nr fin: stays a sharp 12f well: tough.
356 **PUZZLEMENT** 10 [6] C E Brittain 6-8-10 (75) N Esler (7) 8/1: 45-333: 6 gr g Mystiko - Abuzz (Absalom) *nk* **77a**
Chsd ldrs halfway, ch 2f out, rdn/held nr fin: op 5/1: stays 12f, just best at 9/10f?: clr rem: see 356, 302.
356 **NOUKARI** 10 [8] P D Evans 7-9-1 (80) Joanna Badger (7) 16/1: 4-2054: Dwelt & rear/wide, mod gains. 15 **66a**
343 **WOOD POUND** 12 [3] 4-9-4 (87) J Weaver 9/2: 20-125: In tch, rdn/btn 3f out: nicely bckd: btr 343 (fbrsnd). 3½ **68a**
375 **NIGHT CITY** 7 [2] 9-8-13 (78) Darren Williams (7) 12/1: -65226: Keen/handy, rdn/btn 4f out: op 7/1. 5 **52a**
4359} **HIBERNATE** 99 [4] 6-8-12 (77) N Callan 9/2: 0240-7: Led 1m, btn 4f out, nicely bckd, stablemate of 6th: 7 **41a**
abs: '99 Lingfield wnr (mdn, rtd 65a), subs progressive on turf, won at Musselburgh, Carlisle & Brighton (h'caps,
rtd 87): eff at 10/12f on firm, soft & equitrack: handles any trk: gd weight carrier who loves to force the pace
374 **WHITE PLAINS** 7 [7] 7-9-10 (89)(t) D Sweeney 5/1: 31-148: Chsd ldrs, btn 3f out: topweight: btr 244 (10f). 3 **49a**
8 ran Time 2m 33.51 (4.31) (Lancing Racing Syndicate) G L Moore Woodingdean, E Sussex

---

423	3.40 ARENA LEISURE HCAP 3YO+ 0-100 (C) 7f aw rnd Going 34 +01 Fast	[93]
	£7020 £2160 £1080 £540	

*364 **FOREIGN EDITOR** 9 [2] R A Fahey 4-8-8 (73) P Hanagan (7) 3/1 FAV: 1-2D4: 4 ch g Magic Ring - **78a**
True Precision (Presidium) Made all, drvn/held on gamely ins last, rdn out: fast time, tchd 9/2: recent wnr at
W'hampton (h'cap): '99 wnr at W'hampton (2, h'caps, rtd 69a & 54): plcd in '98 (rtd 67): eff forcing the pace
at 6/7f on gd/soft, loves both AWs, esp W'hampton: runs well for an appr: progressive
337 **SALTY JACK** 14 [5] V Soane 6-9-0 (79) Martin Dwyer 5/1: 201-02: 6 b h Salt Dome - Play The Queen hd **82a**
(King Of Clubs) Mid-div/rdn, kept on well ins last, just held: win more races: see 162 (C/D).
337 **SONG OF SKYE** 14 [6] T J Naughton 6-8-9 (74) F Norton 14/1: 022-03: 6 b m Warning - Song Of Hope ¾ **76a**
(Chief Singer) Rdn mid-div, kept on well fnl 1f, just hld: on a fair mark for similar: see 169, 78.
364 **BLUE STAR** 9 [7] N P Littmoden 4-9-2 (81)(vis) L Newman (5) 9/1: 50-524: Chsd ldrs, rdn/kept on hd **82a**
well ins last, not pace to chall: visor reapplied: acts on both AWs, handles firm & gd/soft: bhd this wnr in 364.
320 **JUWWI** 16 [9] 6-9-4 (83) S Carson (5) 12/1: 55-335: Outpcd/bhd, wide/styd on well fnl 2f, nrst fin. ¾ **83a**
337 **TOPTON** 14 [3] 6-9-6 (85)(bl) M Hills 7/2: 32-426: Rdn chasing ldrs, nvr pace to chall: well bckd. shd **85a**
337 **SECRET SPRING** 14 [8] 8-9-11 (90) O Urbina 7/1: 11-407: Mid-div/rdn, late gains wide, no threat. nk **89a**
320 **RIFIFI** 16 [10] 7-8-10 (75) A Clark 14/1: 000-08: Chsd ldrs wide trav well, rdn/chall over 1f out, 1¾ **71a**
no extra ins last: op 10/1: eyecatching effort, stays 7f, could prove spot on back at 6f in similar: see 320.
394 **CLASSY CLEO** 4 [4] 5-10-0 (93) P McCabe 9/1: 2-4239: Trkd ldrs, rdn/wknd fnl 1f & eased nr fin: op 6/1. nk **88a**
321 **ITALIAN SYMPHONY** 16 [1] 6-10-0 (93)(vis) Joanna Badger (7) 16/1: 15-050: Slowly away/al rear: 10th. ½ **87a**
364 **KAYO** 9 [11] 5-8-13 (78) J Fanning 14/1: 30-000: In tch wide, rdn/btn fnl 2f: 11th: op 12/1: see 49. 5 **62a**
11 ran Time 1m 25.8 (2.28) (Pride Of Yorkshire Racing Club) R A Fahey Butterwick, N.Yorks.

424	4.15 COLLINGWOOD HCAP 4YO+ 0-75 (E) 2m aw Going 34 +00 Fast	[70]
	£2651 £757 £378 4 yo rec 7 lb	

332 **HARIK** 14 [8] G L Moore 6-10-0 (70) R Brisland (5) 4/1: 200-31: 6 ch g Persian Bold - Yaqut (Northern **79a**
Dancer) Chsd ldrs, led 5f out, rdn/clr 3f out, in command fnl 1f, rdn out: plcd over jumps this term (nov h'cap,
rtd 80c): '99 Lingfield wnr (h'cap, rtd 74a, no turf form): '98 Lingfield wnr (2, mdn & amat h'cap, rtd 75a & 44):
eff at 12f, suited by return to 2m: Lingfield/Equitrack specialist: has run well fresh: suited by forcing tactics.
317 **BAISSE DARGENT** 17 [4] D J S Cosgrove 4-8-1 (50) C Rutter 10/1: 600-32: 4 b g Common Grounds - 6 **52a**
Fabulous Pet (Somethingfabulous) Prom, rdn/outpcd by wnr 4f out, held after: op 14/1: styd longer 2m trip.
*348 **ALHESN** 11 [6] C N Allen 5-10-0 (70) R Morse 6/1: 15-413: 5 b g Woodman - Deceit Princess (Vice nk **71a**
Regent) Chsd ldrs wide halfway, rdn/kept on fnl 3f, no threat to wnr: tchd 7/1: see 348 (fibresand, W'hampton).
370 **CEDAR FLAG** 8 [1] R J O'Sullivan 4-6-13 (41) P M Quinn (5) 11/1: 60-324: Chsd ldrs, outpcd fnl 4f: op 8/1. 4 **38a**
*285 **MAKNAAS** 21 [2] 4-8-4 (53) A Clark 3/1: 31-415: Led 11f, sn held: well bckd: ahd of 4th in 285. ½ **49a**
*168 **NATURAL EIGHT** 50 [7] 6-8-9 (51) O Urbina 11/4 FAV: 3261-6: Held up, eff 5f out, rdn/btn 3f out: 10 **39a**
well bckd, tchd 3/1: 7 wk abs: stays 2m, prob best at 13f: see 168 (13f).
318 **HIGHLY PRIZED** 16 [5] 6-9-6 (62) N Callan 10/1: 43-167: Handy 12f: op 8/1: btr 277 (fibresand). 5 **45a**
6 **PADAUK** 82 [3] 6-9-0 (56)(bl) F Norton 25/1: 5060-8: Bhd halfway: 12 wk abs: '99 Lingfield wnr dist **0a**
(this race, rtd 57a at best, unplcd on turf, rtd 39, h'cap): plcd form in '98 (h'caps, rtd 59 & 48): eff at 14f/2m
on fast, gd/soft & equitrack: eff with/without blnks: best held up for a late run.
8 ran Time 3m 25.38 (5.38) (The Best Beech Partnership) G L Moore Woodingdean, E.Sussex.

SOUTHWELL (Fibresand) MONDAY JANUARY 31ST Lefthand, Sharp, Oval Track

Official Going STANDARD. Stalls: Inside.

425	1.50 ARMAGH HCAP 4YO+ 0-70 (E) 6f aw rnd Going 80 -02 Slow	[66]
	£3188 £981 £490 £245	

388 **RAFTERS MUSIC** 7 [9] D Nicholls 5-9-6 (58) Clare Roche (7) 11/4: 60-121: 5 b g Thatching - Princess **68a**
Dixieland (Dixieland Band) Mid-div/wide, prog & hung left 1f out, sn hld, pushed out: jockey given a 1 day careless
riding ban: earlier won here at Southwell (h'cap): '99 Epsom wnr (clmr, Mrs A Perratt, rtd 59): suited by 6f,
tried further: acts on firm, hvy & f/sand: likes a sharp/undul trk: eff with/without blnks, has worn a t-strap.
*386 **TELECASTER** 7 [6] C R Egerton 4-9-5 (57)(bl)(6ex) P M Quinn (5) 6/4 FAV: 0-3112: 4 ch g Indian 1¾ **61a**
Ridge - Monashee (Sovereign Dancer) Led, rdn/hdd ins last, held/eased nr line: hvly bckd under a 6lb pen.
403 **BEST QUEST** 5 [2] K R Burke 5-10-0 (66)(t) N Callan 4/1: -31233: 5 b h Salse - Quest For The Best ½ **68a**
(Rainbow Quest) Trkd ldrs, rdn/just held when hmpd ins last, kept on: qck reapp: see 403, 313 (stks).
371 **BARITONE** 9 [5] S E Kettlewell 4-8-0 (38)(vis) J Tate 6/1: 0-0434: Chsd ldrs, kept on onepace fnl 2 **35a**
2f: won this race last term over a 9lb higher mark: see 371, 246 (C/D).
367 **SARPEDON** 10 [4] 4-7-10 (34)(4oh) Joanna Badger (7) 50/1: 000-05: Dwelt/rear, kept on fnl 2f, nrst ½ **29a**
fin: only mod form over jumps & on the level perm: 7f+ & sell h'cap company shld suit on this evidence.
358 **YOUNG BIGWIG** 12 [7] 6-9-13 (65) A Culhane 33/1: 000-06: Chsd ldrs, held fnl 2f: '99 Wolverhampton 2½ **53a**
W'hampton (2) & Redcar (h'caps, rtd 69 & 70a at best): '98 wnr at Thirsk (h'cap) & Hamilton (amat h'cap, rtd
76): eff on firm, soft & f/sand: handles any trk, likes W'hampton: best without blnks.
273 **CHOK DI** 25 [3] 4-8-7 (44)(1ow) C Teague 14/1: 000-47: Trkd ldr, wknd 2f out, btn/eased fnl 1f. 2½ **26a**
379 **AVONDALE GIRL** 9 [11] 4-9-3 (55) J Fanning 33/1: 00-008: Rear/wide, eff 2f out, sn held: see 214. 1¾ **33a**
312 **APPLES AND PEARS** 19 [8] 4-8-9 (47) A Whelan 20/1: 60-059: Al rear: see 312. 2½ **18a**

143

SOUTHWELL (Fibresand)   MONDAY JANUARY 31ST   Lefthand, Sharp, Oval Track

2531} **GLASTONBURY 99** [10] 4-8-10 (48) F Norton 50/1: 0000-0: Rdn/bhd, nvr factor: 10th: 7 mth abs: *18* **0a**
'99 Lingfield wnr (sell, P Howling, rtd 62a & 50): '98 wnr at Lingfield (sell, M Channon, rtd 60a & 67): eff at
7f, prob stays 1m: acts on soft/hvy & equitrack: likes a sharp trk & forcing the pace: enjoys sell grade.
3136} **SWEET AS A NUT 99** [1] 4-9-13 (65) R Fitzpatrick (3) 16/1: 0250-0: Hmpd after 1f & drpd rear, no   *18* **0a**
impress after: 11th: op 20/1: 6 month abs: rnr-up twice in '99 (rtd 65, clmr, C Dwyer, unplcd on sand, rtd 57a,
h'cap): '98 wnr at Beverley, Hamilton & Doncaster (rtd 86 at best): eff at 5f/sharp 6f on firm & soft, any trk.
11 ran   Time 1m 18.2 (4.9)   (Miss N F Thesiger)   D Nicholls Sessay, N.Yorks.

426   2.20 DOWN CLAIMER 3YO (F)   6f aw rnd   Going 80   -12 Slow
£2091   £597   £298

179   **CHRISTOPHERSSISTER 49** [11] T J Etherington 3-8-2 J Fanning 13/2: 4520-1: 3 br f Timeless Times -   **65a**
Petite Elite (Anfield) Chsd ldrs wide, rdn/led 2f out, clr ins last, rdn out: op 11/2, abs: prev with N Bycroft,
rnr-up in '99 (rtd 64a & 69): eff at 5/6f, may stay further: acts on fibresand, handles firm grnd: handles a
gall/sharp trk: runs well fresh: open to further improvement.
4404} **RISKY GEM 99** [12] J Pearce 3-8-11 A Polli (3) 11/1: 0600-2: 3 ch c Risk Me - Dark Kristal (Gorytus)   *2* **66a**
Rear wide, kept on for press fnl 3f, no threat to wnr: op 8/1, 3 month abs: '99 W'hampton wnr (h'cap, rtd 67a
& 66, with R Hannon): eff at 5/7f: acts on fibresand, firm & fast grnd: handles a sharp/gall track.
217   **BILLYS BLUNDER 41** [1] P D Evans 3-8-0 F Norton 33/1: 00-3: 3 b f Hamas - Open Date (Thatching)   *1½* **51+**
Mid-div, squeezed out/dropped towards rear after 1f, staying on when hmpd 1f out, kept on well ins last: 6 wk abs:
only mod form prev: eff at 6f, 7f+ cld suit: handles fibresand: unlucky in running, interesting in h'caps.
*417   **PRICELESS SECOND 3** [6] J A Glover 3-8-6(3ow) N Callan 9/4 FAV: 4-2314: Led 4f, no extra.   *1½* **53a**
1354   **NORTHERN TIMES 99** [10] 3-8-7 G Parkin 16/1: 0-5: Dwelt/rear, kept on fnl 2f, nrst fin: op 12/1: AW   *3½* **45a**
bow/9 month abs: unplcd sole start in '99 (rtd 61, mdn): will apprec 7f+ on this evidence & know more next time.
257   **LADY SANDROVITCH 27** [8] 3-8-0 P Hanagan (5) 8/1: 443-06: Mid-div at best: op 6/1: see 181 (sell). *nk* **37a**
331   **NOWT FLASH 17** [9] 3-8-11 R Lappin 4/1: 2-0107: Chsd ldrs, held over 1f out: op 7/2: btr 300 (C/D). *½* **46a**
269   **APRILS COMAIT 26** [2] 3-7-12 N Carlisle 12/1: 003-68: Chsd ldrs wide/held fnl 2f: op 10/1: see 217 (5f). nk **32a**
331   **LAMMOSKI 17** [7] 3-8-5 (tBL) Joanna Badger (7) 50/1: 05-009: Cl-up 4f: jockey given a 1-day ban for   *4* **29a**
careless riding: tried blnks: see 217.
4517} **PAPE DIOUF 97** [4] 3-8-7 J Stack 9/2: 2550-0: Trkd ldr for 4f, sn btn: 10th: op 7/2: 3 month abs: rnr- *3* **24a**
up in '99 twice for K McAuliffe (rtd 64a, seller & 63, h'cap): eff at 5f, return to that trip could suit: acts on firm,
fast & fibresand: has run well in blnks, not worn today: now with B Smart.
330   **Blazing Pebbles 17** [3] 3-8-0 (BL) P M Quinn (5) 66/1: 127   **Jenny West 62** [5] 3-7-12(2ow) P Fessey 66/1:
12 ran   Time 1m 18.8 (5.5)   (Mike Smallman)   T J Etherington Norton, N.Yorks.

427   2.50 FERMANAGH MED AUCT MDN 3-5YO (F)   7f aw rnd   Going 80   -01 Slow
£2278   £651   £325   3 yo rec 18lb

3774} **BOND DIAMOND 99** [7] B Smart 3-8-6 J Stack 7/1: 0054-1: 3 gr g Prince Sabo - Alsiba (Northfields)   **67a**
Chsd ldrs wide, prog/led over 1f out & sn rdn clr, won readily: val for 8L+: op 5/1: AW bow/5 month abs:
unplcd in '99 (rtd 67, mdn): eff at 7f, tried 1m & shld stay further: acts on fibresand & a sharp trk: runs well
fresh: plenty in hand here, well regarded by connections & can score again under a challenge.
367   **FANNY PARNELL 10** [8] J G FitzGerald 4-9-5 T Williams 66/1: 0-02: 4 b f Local Suitor - Heart Broken   *6* **54a**
(Bustino) Rear/wide, kept on for press fnl 2f, no threat to wnr: only mod form prev: eff at 7f on fibresand.
362   **NIGHT AND DAY 11** [1] W Jarvis 3-8-1 F Norton 4/5 FAV: 3-223: 3 ch f Anshan - Midnight Break   *1½* **51a**
(Night Shift) Cl-up, led over 4f out, rdn/hdd over 1f out & sn btn: hvly bckd: clr of rem: btr 362, 278.
2186} **THREEFORTYCASH 99** [6] Andrew Turnell 3-8-6 A Culhane 40/1: 00-4: Rdn/rear, mod gains: AW bow,   *5* **46a**
7 month abs: unplcd in '99 (rtd 50): tried at up to 5f prev.
397   **STOP THE TRAFFIC 6** [2] 3-8-1 Martin Dwyer 13/8: 30-425: Led, hdd 4f out, rdn/btn 2f out: op 9/4.   *½* **40a**
308   **KOOL JULES 20** [4] 4-9-5 G Faulkner (3) 66/1: 006: Chsd ldrs 4f: mod form.   *14* **19a**
887}   **SILVER PRINCE 99** [3] 5-9-10 M Tebbutt 16/1: 000-7: Mid-div/btn 3f out: 10 month abs: *23* **0a**
unplcd in '99 (rtd 33): AW bow today for D Nicholls.
4369} **SABICA 99** [5] 3-8-2(1ow) J Fanning 20/1: 00-8: Bhd halfway: op 10/1, AW bow.   *9* **0a**
8 ran   Time 1m 32.3 (5.7)   (R C Bond)   B Smart Lambourn, Berks.

428   3.20 ANTRIM HCAP 4YO+ 0-70 (E)   2m aw   Going 80   +02 Fast   [66]
£3526   £1085   £542   £271   4 yo rec 7 lb

*51   **BUSTLING RIO 77** [4] P C Haslam 4-9-2 (61) P Goode (5) 9/4 FAV: 3421-1: 4 b g Up And At 'Em - Une   **68a**
Venitienne (Green Dancer) Rear, prog to lead 3f out, held on v gamely, all-out: best time of day, 11 wk abs: '99
Southwell (2, rtd 61a) & Pontefract wnr (h'caps, rtd 61): eff at 11/12f, suited by 2m: acts on gd, loves f/sand &
Southwell: runs well fresh: handles a sharp or stiff trk: progressive 4yo stayer, can complete a hat-trick.
*284   **KENT 24** [6] P D Cundell 5-8-7 (45) Martin Dwyer 9/2: 005-12: 5 b g Kylian - Precious Caroline   *hd* **51a**
(The Noble Player) Chsd ldrs halfway, briefly short of room 2f out, ev ch ins last, just held: clr of rem: see 284.
318   **ALMAMZAR 24** [10] Don Enrico Incisa 10-7-11 (35)(1ow)(12oh) Kim Tinkler 50/1: 05-054: Chsd ldrs 13f.   *7* **26a**
Nurse (On Your Mark) Rear, prog fnl 4f & chsd front pair 2f out, held ins last: clr rem: see 141, 126.
284   **MARKELLIS 10** [7] 4-7-10 (41)(6oh) Joanna Badger (7) 33/1: -04505: Mid-div, held fnl 3f: see 215 (12f).   *1¾* **30a**
4578} **I CANT REMEMBER 91** [9] 6-9-2 (54) S Finnamore (7) 20/1: 5100-6: Cl-up 14f: 3 month abs: '99   *1½* **42a**
wnr at Nottingham (sell, M Pipe), Pontefract & Ripon (h'caps, rtd 65): '98 Chester wnr (clmr, P Evans, rtd 62 & 51a):
suited by 12/14f nowadays: acts on firm, soft & equitrack: handles any trk, likes Nottingham: best without a visor.
318   **LADY RACHEL 18** [8] 5-8-8 (46) G Parkin 4/1: 000-37: Cl-up, rdn/wknd fnl 3f: op 3/1: btr 318.   *7* **27a**
318   **BEAUCHAMP MAGIC 18** [5] 5-7-12 (36) G Baker (7) 8/1: 16-048: Towards rear, no impress: see 141.   *nk* **17a**
343   **ROBELLITA 14** [11] 6-9-13 (65) J Bosley (7) 6/1: 126-09: Al rear: op 5/1: see 81 (12f).   *11* **38a**
390   **STATE APPROVAL 7** [5] 7-9-8 (60) N Callan 33/1: 5-6000: Rdn/hdd 3f out, btn/eased fnl 1f: 10th.   *nk* **33a**
324   **PALAIS 17** [1] 5-8-13 (51) R Fitzpatrick (3) 20/1: 000-00: Chsd ldrs, struggling halfway: see 324.   *dist* **0a**
11 ran   Time 3m 48.4 (12.4)   (Rio Stainless Engineering Ltd/R Tutton)   P C Haslam Middleham, N.Yorks.

SOUTHWELL (Fibresand)   MONDAY JANUARY 31ST   Lefthand, Sharp, Oval Track

429
3.50 TYRONE SELL HCAP 3YO 0-60 (G)   1m aw rnd   Going 80 -31 Slow   [66]
£1909   £545   £272

417   **AMELIA JESS** 3 [3] B S Rothwell 3-8-8 (46)(t) Joanna Badger (7) 6/1: 00-231: 3 ch f Mac's Imp - **51a**
Vieux Carre (Pas de Seul) Chsd ldrs, rdn/prog to lead over 1f out, styd on well, rdn out: no bid, first success:
unplcd in '99 (rtd 47): eff at 7f, apprec step up to 1m: acts on fibresand & a sharp trk: eff in a t-strap.
315   **CINEMA POINT** 19 [5] M H Tompkins 3-8-0 (38) A Whelan 8/1: 000-02: 3 b g Doyoun - Airport (Warpath)2½ **38a**
Rear, rdn & kept on for press fnl 2f, nrst fin: op 10/1: eff at 1m, tried 10f, shld suit in time: handles fibresand.
385   **FRENCH MASTER** 7 [4] P C Haslam 3-9-5 (57)(bl) P Goode (5) 5/1: 364-33: 3 b g Petardia - Reasonably 2 **53a**
French (Reasonable) Rdn/rear halfway, styd on under hands-and-heels fnl 2f, nrst fin: op 4/1: see 385 (C/D).
330   **FORTHECHOP** 17 [7] Mrs H L Walton 3-8-3 (41) S Righton 14/1: 06-454: Chsd ldrs, led over 2f out, 1 **35a**
rdn/hdd over 1f out & no extra: tchd 16/1: stays a sharp 1m & handles fibresand: see 281 (seller).
257   **MERRYVALE MAN** 27 [11] 3-9-7 (59) A Culhane 3/1 FAV: 002-05: Chsd ldrs halfway, drvn/held fnl 2f. nk **52a**
315   **DR DUKE** 19 [9] 3-8-5 (43)(bl) Dean McKeown 10/1: 55-406: Chsd ldrs wide 6f: blnks reapplied. ½ **36a**
319   **BAHAMIAN PRINCE** 18 [8] 3-8-0 (38)(BL) M Henry 11/2: 00-067: Chsd ldrs 6f: tried blnks, op 7/2. 1½ **27a**
385   **PEPPERCORN** 7 [1] 3-8-2 (40) G Baker (7) 33/1: 000-68: Rear/wide, nvr factor: see 385. 5 **19a**
300   **TE ANAU** 21 [12] 3-8-11 (49) J P Spencer 9/1: 300-09: Towards rear/wide, nvr factor: see 300 (6f). 2½ **23a**
355   **DIAMOND GEORGIA** 12 [6] 3-8-2 (40)(vis) F Norton 20/1: 60-050: Rdn/al twds rear: 10th: see 355, 287. 1¼ **11a**
382   **SAMMIE DUROSE** 9 [2] 3-8-8 (44)(VIS) P Fessey 12/1: 00-520: Led 6f: 11th: visor: btr 382. 3½ **8a**
330   **SOUNDS CRAZY** 17 [10] 3-8-3 (41)(bl) G Bardwell 25/1: 00-200: Prom 4f, bhd/virtually p.u. fnl 2f: 12th. dist **0a**
12 ran   Time 1m 48.3 (8.9)   (Michael Saunders)   B S Rothwell Musley Bank, N.Yorks.

430
4.20 LONDONDERRY FILLIES HCAP 4YO+ 0-75 (E)   1m aw rnd   Going 80 -14 Slow   [72]
£2769   £852   £426   £213

*384   **STRAVSEA** 7 [3] R Hollinshead 5-8-10 (54)(6ex) P M Quinn (5) 5/2: -03511: 5 b m Handsome Sailor - **60a**
La Stravaganza (Slip Anchor) Dwelt, prog to lead ins last, styd on gamely, drvn out: well bckd: recent wnr
at Southwell (fill h'cap): '99 Southwell wnr (2, h'caps, rtd 50a & 36): plcd in '98 (rtd 58a & 44): eff at 7f,
suited by 1m: acts on gd/soft, fibresand/Southwell specialist: runs well for an apprentice.
364   **MY TESS** 11 [6] B A McMahon 4-9-10 (68) L Newman (5) 7/4 FAV: 14-452: 4 br f Lugana Beach - hd **73a**
Barachois Princess (Barachois) Led, rdn/hdd 1f out, rallied well for press ins last, just held: clr of rem:
jockey given a 3-day whip ban: well bckd, op 9/4: loves to dominate & can win again: see 309.
2845] **JESSINCA** 99 [4] Derrick Morris 4-8-2 (46) F Norton 20/1: 0/40-3: 4 b f Minshaanshu Amad - Noble Soul 7 **40a**
(Sayf El Arab) Chsd ldrs, rdn/held fnl 2f: op 12/1: 6 mth abs: unplcd in '99 (rtd 45a & 25, h'caps, R T Phillips):
unplcd in '98 (rtd 46a & 57, A P Jones): stays 1m, tried further: handles fibrfesand.
299   **MUJAS MAGIC** 21 [1] Mrs N Macauley 5-9-5 (63)(vis) R Fitzpatrick (3) 11/2: 01-244: Chsd ldrs 6f: op 4/1. ¾ **56a**
384   **OARE KITE** 7 [5] 5-7-11 (41)(1ow)(2oh) Dale Gibson (7) 7/1: 366-35: Cl-up 6f: see 384. 5 **24a**
384   **DIM OFAN** 7 [7] 4-9-7 (65)(BL) D Sweeney 15/2: 6-4106: Cl-up 6f: op 5/1, blnks: btr 326 (C/D). 4 **40a**
387   **CHAMBOLLE MUSIGNY** 7 [2] 4-7-12 (42) P Fessey 14/1: 00-307: Twds rear, rdn/strugg halfway: op 10/1. ½ **16a**
7 ran   Time 1m 46.9 (7.5)   (E Bennion)   R Hollinshead Upper Longdon, Staffs.

WOLVERHAMPTON (Fibresand)   TUESDAY FEBRUARY 1ST   Lefthand, Sharp Track

Official Going   STANDARD. Stalls: Inside

431
1.25 AMAT RDRS HCAP DIV I 4YO+ 0-70 (G)   1m100y aw rnd   Going 46 -36 Slow   [37]
£1551   £443   £221

375   **MIDNIGHT WATCH** 10 [1] A G Newcombe 6-9-10 (33)(3oh) Miss C Hannaford (5) 33/1: 0-0001: 6 b g Capote - **39a**
Midnight Air (Green Dancer) Chsd ldrs, led going well over 2f out & sn rdn clr, rdly: mod form in '99 (with P
Winkworth, tried a t-strap & visor, rtd 43): plcd back in '97 to H Cecil (h'cap, rtd 75): eff at 8.5f on f/sand,
handles fast & gd grnd, best 10f/2m: likes a sharp trk: runs well for an amat: revitalised by new connections.
404   **MUSTANG** 5 [11] J Pearce 7-10-4 (41)(bl) Mrs L Pearce 7/1: 4-3002: 7 ch g Thatching - Lassoo 4 **41a**
(Caerleon) Rear/wide, prog halfway, kept on fnl 2f for press, nvr pace of wnr: bckd, op 14/1: see 59 (Lingfield).
411   **DOBERMAN** 5 [9] P D Evans 5-10-1 (38)(bl) Miss E Folkes 16/1: 403503: 5 br g Dilum - Switch 1¾ **35a**
Blade (Robellino) Led, rdn/hdd over 2f out, kept on for press: op 12/1: quick reapp: blnks reapp: see 254 (C/D).
405   **KINNINO** 5 [8] G L Moore 6-10-7 (44) Mr I Mongan 5-2 FAV: 20-134: Mid-div/wide, prog halfway/ nk **40a**
briefly led over 2f out, sn onepace: op 2/1, quick reapp: clr of rem: see 405, 254 (C/D).
4499] **MR SPEAKER** 99 [5] 7-10-11 (48) Miss H Welsby 55 14/1: 0130-5: Chsd ldrs halfway, no extra fnl 2f: 6 **35a**
3 month abs: '99 Brighton scorer (ladies amat h'cap, rtd 62 at best): '98 Beverley wnr (h'cap, rtd 61, plcd on sand,
rtd 40a, h'cap): eff at 7f/9f on fast & gd/soft grnd: handles a stiff or sharp/undul trk: runs well for an amat.
418   **SEA YA MAITE** 4 [3] 6-11-7 (58) Mrs M Morris (3) 7/1: -53156: Chsd ldrs halfway, held fnl 2f: qck reapp. shd **45a**
368   **KUWAIT THUNDER** 11 [7] 4-11-0 (51) Miss Diana Jones 20/1: 000-07: Rear/wide halfway, mod prog. 4 **30a**
255   **WAIKIKI BEACH** 28 [2] 9-11-3 (54)(bl) Mrs J Moore 12/1: 401-08: Al rear: op 8/1, stablemate of 4th. ½ **32a**
*404   **SWING ALONG** 5 [8] 5-12-5 (70)(5ex) Mr V Coogan (5) 3/1: -W2419: Al rear: op 5/2: btr 404 (9.4f). 4 **40a**
4548] **TROIS ELLES** 95 [4] 4-10-0 (37) Mr T Best (5) 12/1: 0003-0: Mid-div, btn 4f out: 10th: op 7/1, 3 mth 16 **0a**
abs: '99 Lingfield wnr (appr h'cap, rtd 37a & 49): eff arnd 7/9f, tried further: acts on firm, gd/soft & equitrack.
306   **CLONOE** 21 [10] 6-10-5 (42) Miss L McIntosh (7) 9/1: 60-240: Cl-up 6f, eased/btn fnl 1f: 11th: op 7/1. 8 **0a**
11 ran   Time 1m 53.2 (7.0)   (M B Clemence)   A G Newcombe Huntshaw, Devon

432
1.55 AMAT RDRD HCAP DIV II 4YO+ 0-70 (G)   1m100y a   Going 46 -43 Slow   [38]
£1542   £440   £220

405   **PERCHANCER** 5 [11] P C Haslam 4-10-10 (48) Miss A Armitage (5) 3/1: 06-321: 4 ch g Perugino - Irish **60a**
Hope (Nishapour) Mid-div/wide, smooth prog halfway & led over 2f out, sn in command, easily: op 5/2: quick
reapp: '99 Thirsk wnr (appr mdn h'cap, rtd 55), rnr-up on sand (rtd 58a, h'cap): eff at 7f/9.3f on firm, gd/soft &
both AWs: has run well in blnks, tried a vis: handles any trk, likes a sharp one: runs well for an amateur.
*405   **ETISALAT** 5 [2] J Pearce 5-11-2 (54)(5ex) Mrs L Pearce 6/4 FAV: 10-312: 5 b g Lahib - Sweet Repose 8 **56a**
(High Top) Rear/in tch, prog/chsd wnr fnl 2f, al held: op 2/1, qck reapp: beat today's wnr cmftbly in 405 (9.4f).

145

340 **KILLARNEY JAZZ** 15 [1] G C H Chung 5-11-6 (58)(bl) Mr Paul J Morris (5) 16/1: 44-003: 5 b g Alhijaz - *shd*   **60a**
Killarney Belle (Irish Castle) Mid-div, rdn/kept on fnl 2f, no threat to wnr: op 10/1: loves Southwell: see 67.
404 **EI EI 5** [7] G L Moore 5-9-10 (34)(BL)(3oh) Mr I Mongan 4/1: 00-024: Chsd ldrs, hard rdn/onepace   4   **28a**
fnl 2f: tried blnks, op 5/2: slightly disapp after latest, a return to further shld suit: btr 404 (9.4f).
324 **WERE NOT STOPPIN 18** [5] 5-9-11 (35)(1ow)(15oh) Miss R Bastiman (0) 66/1: 00-005: Chsd ldrs 4f.   3½   **22a**
383 **DANAKIL 10** [3] 5-12-0 (66) Mr L Phillips (5) 11/1: 36-566: Towards rear, mod prog: op 5/1: see 326.   2½   **48a**
340 **FANCY A FORTUNE 15** [10] 6-11-2 (44)(bl)(10ow) Mr G Gibson (0) 20/1: 20-507: Led/dsptd lead, v wide 2½   **31a**
on bend after 1f, went on over 3f out, hdd over 2f out & wknd qckly: op 12/1: needs stronger handling: see 299.
363 **SAFE SHARP JO 12** [9] 5-10-11 (49)(15ow)(27oh) Mr L Heath (0) 66/1: 0-0068: Al rear: see 363 (14f).   4   **18a**
218 **SAN MICHEL 42** [8] 8-10-3 (41) Mrs J M Hill (7) 20/1: 6305-9: Mid-div, btn halfway: abs, vis omitted.   1   **8a**
404 **LILANITA 5** [4] 5-10-9 (47)(BL) Miss E Folkes (3) 12/1: 3-2000: Led/dsptd lead 5f: 10th: blnks: btr 45.   6   **5a**
195 **BICTON PARK 46** [6] 6-9-10 (34)(9oh) Mr T Best (3) 66/1: 0000-0: Dwelt, al bhd: 11th: abs: rnr-up   10   **0a**
in '99 (sell, rtd 40a, rtd 43 on turf): rtd 43a & 22 in '98 (unplcd): eff over a sharp 7f & handles fibresand.
11 ran   Time 1m 53.8 (7.6)   (N P Green)   P C Haslam Middleham, N Yorks

---

433   **2.25 CLAIMING STKS 4YO+ (F)**   **1m1f79y Going 46 -03 Slow**
£2061   £589   £294

*360 **BACHELORS PAD 12** [11] Miss S J Wilton 6-8-13 M Tebbutt 9/4: 0-0211: 6 b g Pursuit Of Love - Note   **65a**
Book (Mummy's Pet) Rear/wide, prog to chase ldrs 3f out, styd on gamely to lead nr line, all out: op 7/4: prev won
here at W'hampton (clmr, with D Nicholls): rnr-up twice in '99 (rtd 63, h'cap): plcd in '98 (rtd 76, stks, W Jarvis):
eff at 7/10f on firm, gd/soft & f/sand: best without blnks: prob handles any trk, likes W'hampton: can win again.
382} **TYLERS TOAST 99** [7] S Dow 4-8-9 P Doe 16/1: 6640-2: 4 ch g Grand Lodge - Catawba (Mill Reef)   *shd*   **60a**
Mid-div, smooth prog to chall fnl 4f, rdn/ld over 1f out, hdd line: op 8/1: 5 month abs: prev with W Jarvis,
unplcd in '99 (rtd 80$, mdn): rtd 78 in '98 (stks): eff at 9.4f, tried further: acts on f/sand & a sharp trk.
393 **BILLICHANG 7** [8] P Howling 4-8-9 T Williams 6/1: 1-2333: 4 b c Chilibang - Swing O The Kilt   1¼   **57a**
(Hotfoot) Trkd ldrs, rdn/led over 4f out, hdd over 1f out & no extra cl-home: op 5/1: see 238 (mdn).
*393 **INTERNAL AFFAIR 7** [10] T D Barron 5-9-1 Lynsey Hanna (7) 11/8 FAV: 0-1014: Dwelt, towards rear,   ½   **62a**
prog/chsd ldrs 4f out, onepace: well bckd, op 7/4: stys 9.4f, suited by 8.5f: ahd of today's 3rd in 393 (8.5f).
360 **MALWINA 12** [12] 4-8-2 J Fanning 50/1: 10-005: Rear, prog/chsd ldrs 3f out, kept on onepace for   1¼   **46a**
press ins last: well clr of rem: only mod form prev: eff at 9.4f on fibresand: see 372 (2m).
268 **TSUNAMI 27** [6] 4-8-0 Joanna Badger (7) 14/1: 464-06: Prom 5f: op 10/1: unplcd in '99 (rtd 74,   9   **30a**
mdn, D Elsworth, prob flattered): rtd 76 in '98 (fill mdn): eff around 7f, tried 10f: handles fast & hvy grnd.
366 **HEATHYARDS JAKE 11** [4] 4-8-5 P M Quinn (5) 12/1: 1-4547: Bolted to post, mid-div at best: op 7/1.   4   **27a**
360 **ADIRPOUR 12** [3] 6-8-9 Stephanie Hollinshead(7) 50/1: 0-0658: Keen/chsd ldrs 5f: see 178.   hd   **30a**
366 **IMBACKAGAIN 11** [2] 5-8-5 C Cogan (5) 16/1: 00-639: Bhd halfway: op 12/1: see 366, 297.   1   **24a**
387 **TALECA SON 8** [5] 5-8-5 R Fitzpatrick (2) 33/1: -22540: Led/dsptd lead 6f, sn btn: 10th: see 211 (12f).   6   **15a**
404 **SOUNDS COOL 5** [1] 4-8-1 G Bardwell 20/1: 00-650: Led 4f, sn btn: 11th: abs: see 338.   3   **5a**
240$} **FLICKER 99** [9] 5-7-12 Iona Wands 50/1: 0-0: Bhd 6f out: 12th: jumps fit (mod form): unplcd   8   **0a**
in 2 '99 starts on the level: plcd in '98 (rtd 46, h'cap, Lord Huntingdon, visor): prob stays 10f & handles soft grnd.
12 ran   Time 2m 02.8 (4.6)   (John Pointon & Sons)   Miss S J Wilton Wetley rocks, Staffs

---

434   **3.00 BEST BETS MDN 3YO+ (D)**   **6f aw rnd Going 46 -32 Slow**
£2730   £840   £420   £210   3 yo rec 15lb

367 **WELCOME GIFT 11** [5] W J Haggas 4-9-12 J P Spencer 1/1 FAV: 2-221: 4 b g Prince Sabo - Ausonia   **68a**
(Beldale Flutter) Cl-up, rdn/led ins last, sn in command, rdn out: hvly bckd, op 7/4: rnr-up all 3 starts prev:
apprec this drop to 6f, stys a sharp 7f: acts on fibresand & a sharp trk: gd weight carrier.
365 **TROPICAL KING 11** [2] D Carroll 3-8-11 R Fitzpatrick (3) 15/8: 400-42: 3 b g Up And At 'Em -   4   **58a**
Princess Gay (Fairy King) Cl-up, led over 3f out, rdn/hdd ins last & sn held: op 6/4: see 365 (h'cap).
--   **FINE MELODY 1** [1] B W Hills 3-8-7(1ow) M Hills 4/1: 3: 3 b f Green Desert - Sit Alkul (Mr Prospector)   1¼   **51a**
Dwelt, sn chsd ldrs racing keenly, rdn/eff 2f out, sn held: op 7/4, debut: well bred filly: eff at 6f & handles
fibresand: market told story today but will improve when learning restraint.
362 **SUAVE PERFORMER 12** [6] S C Williams 3-8-11 G Faulkner (3) 25/1: 04: Sn outpcd: see 362 (7f).   4   **45a**
379 **HOT LEGS 10** [4] 4-9-7 (bl) L Newman (5) 25/1: 00-545: Led 3f, sn btn: see 379 (clmr).   ½   **38a**
238} **LUCKY RASCAL 99** [3] 4-9-12 F Norton 14/1: 4000-6: Chsd ldrs 2f, sn btn/eased fnl 1f: 7 month abs: 12   **20a**
plcd for B Hanbury in '99 (rtd 62, unplcd on sand, rtd 38a, subs tried blnks): rtd 72 in '98: stays 1m & handles gd.
6 ran   Time 1m 17.5 (4.7)   (M H Wilson)   W J Haggas Newmarket

---

435   **3.35 ITV TEXT HCAP 3YO+ 0-95 (C)**   **6f aw rnd Going 46 +04 Fast**   **[93]**
£6890   £2120   £1060   £530   3 yo rec 15lb

423 **BLUE STAR 3** [7] N P Littmoden 4-9-2 (81)(vis) C Cogan (5) 7/1: 0-5241: 4 b g Whittingham - Gold And   **88a**
Blue (Bluebird) Rdn rear, switched wide/prog to lead dist, styd on strongly, rdn out: gd time, op 5/1: qck reapp:
plcd twice on turf in '99 (rtd 71, h'cap): '98 W'hampton wnr (val stks, rtd 87a & 74): eff at 6/7f: handles
firm, gd/soft & equitrack, likes W'hampton: eff with/without a visor: potentially useful AW performer.
*388 **REDOUBTABLE 8** [3] D W Chapman 9-8-11 (76)(6ex) A Culhane 6/1: 3-6412: 9 b h Grey Dawn II - Seattle 1¼   **80a**
Rockette (Seattle Slew) Chsd ldrs, rdn/ch over 1f out, kept on well: op 5/1: 6lb pen: see 388 (Southwell).
423 **JUWWI 3** [1] J M Bradley 6-9-4 (83) Claire Bryan (7) 7/1: 5-3353: 6 ch g Mujtahid - Nouvelle Star   hd   **86a**
(Luskin Star) Dwelt/bhd, styd on well fnl 2f for press, nrst fin: tchd 9/1, quick reapp: see 129.
216 **FIRST MAITE 42** [11] S R Bowring 7-9-10 (89)(bl) N Callan (4) 11/1: 1540-4: Chsd ldrs/ch 1f out, kept on: abs.¾   **90a**
129 **TOM TUN 63** [9] 5-8-11 (76) T Williams 9/1: 0026-5: Cl-up, led over 2f out till over 1f out/no extra: abs.   1   **75a**
349 **SANTANDRE 14** [8] 4-8-3 (68) P M Quinn (5) 14/1: 53-006: Chsd ldrs, switched wide/mod late gains.   2   **62a**
423 **CLASSY CLEO 3** [4] 5-10-0 (93) Joanna Badger (7) 13/2: -42307: Nvr able to chall: qck reapp: see 64.   hd   **86a**
+394 **DIL 7** [5] 5-10-2 (95)(6ex) R Fitzpatrick (3) 12/1: 03-018: Led 3f, fdd: op 10/1: see 394 (5f).   1   **86a**
394 **BLUE KITE 7** [13] 5-9-0 (79) J Tate 7/1: 1-1669: Cl-up wide,led 3f out till over 2f out, sn held: tchd   1¾   **66a**
8/1, stablemate of wnr: ahead of today's wnr in 258 (C/D).
275 **BRANSTON PICKLE 26** [2] 3-8-3 (83) J Fanning 10/1: 101-20: Cl-up, rdn/wknd fnl 2f: 10th: op 8/1.   9   **54a**
+320 **THE DOWNTOWN FOX 19** [6] 5-9-5 (84)(vis) L Newman (5) 3/1 FAV: 010-10: Dwelt, al bhd: 11th: 5   **46a**
nicely bckd, tchd 4/1: reportedly resented kick-back: btr 320 (C/D, rcd prom).
376 **Bold Effort 10** [12] 8-9-4 (83)(bl) J M Hills 16/1:   458$} **Goes A Treat 91** [10] 4-8-8 (73) G Carter 33/1:
13 ran   Time 1m 15.3 (2.5)   (T Clarke)   N P Littmoden Newmarket, Suffolk

WOLVERHAMPTON (Fibresand) TUESDAY FEBRUARY 1ST Lefthand, Sharp Track

436
4.05 BET DIRECT SKY TEXT SELLER 4YO+ (G)   6f aw rnd Going 46 -21 Slow
£1941   £554   £277

364 **DAHLIDYA** 12 [6] M J Polglase 5-9-0 R Fitzpatrick (3) 7/2: 0-3461: 5 b m Midyan - Dahlawise (Caerleon) **57a**
Towards rear, switched inner & rdn/prog 2f to lead well ins last, rdn out: op 5/2: no bid: '99 Southwell wnr
(h'cap, rtd 59a, mod turf form): '98 W'hampton & Southwell wnr (h'caps, rtd 52a): eff at 5f, stays 7f well, suited
by 6f: acts on gd/soft & equitrack, fibresand specialist: best without blnks: apprec this drop to sell grade.

406 **FEATHERSTONE LANE** 5 [9] Miss L C Siddall 9-8-13 Dean McKeown 16/1: 50-442: 9 b g Siberian Express ½ **53$**
- Try Gloria (Try My Best) Rdn mid-div/wide, styd on strongly fnl 2f, just held: op 14/1, qck reapp: offic rtd 43.

389 **TROJAN HERO** 8 [12] K C Comerford 9-9-5 N Callan 6/1: 00-453: 9 ch g Raise A Man - Helleness hd **58$**
(Northfields) Cl-up, rdn/ch ins last, kept on well, just held cl-home: tchd 8/1: see 201.

351 **SOUNDS LUCKY** 14 [5] N P Littmoden 4-8-13 C Carver (3) 16/1: 00-604: Cl-up, led 3f out till well ½ **50a**
ins last, no extra cl-home: op 14/1: see 243.

*351 **PRESS AHEAD** 14 [10] S A E Newman (5) 100/30: 020-15: Led 1f, cl-up till no extra ins last: op 5/2. ¾ **54a**

323 **FACILE TIGRE** 19 [11] 5-8-13 P Doe 10/1: 466-06: Chsd ldrs wide, held over 1f out: see 146 (5f). 3 **41a**

406 **MANOLO** 5 [4] 7-8-13 (bl) F Norton 8/1: 350-07: Chsd ldrs, rdn/outpcd halfway: qck reapp: see 406. nk **40a**

1223} **LITTLE IBNR** 99 [2] 9-8-13 (vis) J P Spencer 16/1: 4636-8: Towards rear/wide, nvr any impress: 9 mth 1 **38a**
abs: plcd numerous times in '99 (rtd 58a, clmr): plcd in '98 (rtd 46a, clmr): '97 wnr here at W'hampton (2, sells,
rtd 68a): eff btwn 5/7f on fast, soft, equitrack, fibresand/W'hampton & sell specialist: often blnkd/visored.

132 **THATS LIFE** 62 [8] 5-8-13 J Weaver 9/4 FAV: 1003-9: Led after 1f, hdd 3f out, wknd qckly: op 5/2, abs. 3 **31a**

389 **ROYAL ORIGINE** 8 [1] 4-8-13 (tbl) A Culhane 16/1: 0-0000: Al outpcd rear: 10th: see 389, 247. 9 **15a**

4019} **BEVERLEY MONKEY** 99 [3] 4-8-8 T Williams 25/1: U055-0: Al outpcd rear: 11th: 5 month abs: plcd 5 **1a**
in '99 for J Berry (sell, rtd 46, no sand form): '98 wnr at Newcastle, Hamilton & Lingfield (clmrs, rtd 79, also rtd
48a): eff at 6/7f on firm & gd, handles soft: eff in blnks: prob handles any trk: now with J Bradley.

11 ran   Time 1m 16.8 (4.0)   (The Lovatt Partnership)   M J Polglase Southwell, Notts

437
4.40 BET DIRECT HCAP 4YO+ 0-70 (E)   1m4f aw Going 46 -20 Slow [70]
£2651   £757   £378   4 yo rec 3 lb

413 **EVEZIO RUFO** 4 [4] N P Littmoden 8-7-10 (38)(bl) P M Quinn (5) 10/1: 5-4651: 8 b g Blakeney - **48a**
Empress Corina (Free State) Cl-up, led 4f out, clr 2f out, rdn out: op 6/1, qck reapp, blnks reapplied: '99 wnr
at W'hampton (2, sell & h'cap, rtd 47a & 34): '98 Lingfield, Southwell & W'hampton wnr (h'caps, rtd 61a & 55): eff
at 11/14.8f on fast, hvy & equitrack, fibresand/W'hampton specialist: eff in a visor/blnks: can win again.

*410 **CRESSET** 5 [8] W Jarvis 4-8-7 (52)(bl) (6ex) A Culhane 9/2: 6-0212: 4 ch c Arazi - Mixed Applause 5 **57a**
(Nijinsky) Held up, prog fnl 4f, chsd wnr over 1f out, nvr pace to chal: op 7/2, clr of rem: 6lb pen for 410.

407 **WESTERN COMMAND** 5 [9] Mrs N Macauley 4-9-6 (65) R Fitzpatrick (3) 8/1: -45033: 4 b g Saddlers' Hall 9 **60a**
- Western Fervent (Gone West) Prom, led after 2f till hdd over 4f out, sn held: op 6/1, quick reapp: see 170 (C/D).

*378 **SOVEREIGN ABBEY** 10 [1] Sir Mark Prescott 4-8-11 (56) D Sweeney 11/10 FAV: 46-214: Chsd ldrs 5 **44a**
halfway going well, chsd wnr 3f out, sn rdn/held & wknd ins last: hvly bckd: not stay longer 12f trip: see 378.

271 **LAWNETT** 26 [5] 4-8-10 (55) Dean McKeown 12/1: 351-05: Rear, mod prog: op 8/1: rcnt jumps wnr ¾ **42a**
(cj sell h'cap, rtd 93h), eff at 2m on gd grnd: ex-Irish, '99 wnr on the level at Dundalk (4 rnr 9f h'cap): eff at
9f on fast grnd: eff forcing the pace: now with M Todhunter.

4443} **ZAHA** 99 [3] 5-9-8 (64) A Polli (3) 12/1: 1050-6: Held up, rdn 5f out, sn btn: op 16/1, 3 month abs: 1½ **49a**
'99 Southwell wnr (auct mdn, rtd 66a) & Yarmouth (class stks, rtd 60): rtd 58 in '98 (R Armstrong): eff at 10/11f
on gd, hvy & both AWs, prob handles firm: has run well in a vis, tho' best without blnks/vis: has run well fresh.

*347 **BANNERET** 14 [7] 7-9-0 (56)(vis) M Tebbutt 8/1: 34-217: Prom 7f: op 11/2: see 347. 18 **21a**

-- **SHY PADDY** 6 [6] 8-7-10 (38)(20h) G Bardwell 33/1: 0422/8: Led 2f, sn bhd: long abs: last rcd in 12 **0a**
'97, rnr-up twice (rtd 36a): '94 W'hampton wnr (mdn, rtd 60): eff at 10f/14f: acts on fibresand, best without blnks.

237 **COPPER SHELL** 34 [2] 6-9-11 (67)(t) J P Spencer 25/1: 1200-9: Bhd halfway: see 237. 27 **0a**

9 ran   Time 2m 41.5 (7.9)   (O A Gunter)   N P Littmoden Newmarket

LINGFIELD (Equitrack) WEDNESDAY FEBRUARY 2ND Lefthand, Very Sharp Track

Official Going STANDARD. Stalls Inside, Except 5f - Outside.

438
1.30 MDN HCAP DIV I 4YO+ 0-65 (F)   7f aw rnd Going 17 -29 Slow [60]
£1907   £545   £272

353 **REACHFORYOURPOCKET** 14 [4] M D I Usher 5-8-8 (40) Martin Dwyer 14/1: 60-461: 5 b g Royal Academy **45a**
- Gemaasheh (Habitat) Chsd ldrs, led 2f out, rdn out: op 8/1, first win: unplcd for K Mahdi in '99 (rtd 64, blnks
& t-strap, suffered breathing probs so had a soft palate op): apprec drop back to 7f on equitrack: on a gd mark.

58 **FRANKLIN D** 78 [5] J R Jenkins 4-8-13 (45) J Weaver 3/1 FAV: 0003-2: 4 ch g Democratic - English 1½ **46a**
Mint (Jalmood) Led till 2f out, kept on: op 2/1 after 11 wk abs: lightly raced & cld win similar: see 58.

396 **UTAH** 8 [9] G L Moore 6-8-11 (43)(bl) P Dobbs 14/1: 00-043: 6 b g High Estate - Easy Romance shd **44a**
(Northern Jove) Outpcd till fnl 1½f flourish, too late: op 8/1: handles both AWs, return to 1m shld suit.

308 **SING CHEONG** 22 [10] G C H Chung 4-9-2 (48) C Carver (3) 8/1: 243-04: Prom, eff turning from home, 1¾ **46a**
unable to qckn: tchd 10/1: apprec return to equitrack: see 8.

352 **CAREQUICK** 15 [2] 4-8-7 (39) J Fanning 4/1: 053-35: Front rank, chall 3f out till 2f out, onepace: 1 **35a**
tchd 5/1: back up in trip on equitrack now, better on fibresand prev: see 352, 197.

353 **PIPE DREAM** 14 [12] 4-9-10 (56) P McCabe 4/1: 00-336: Wide, rear, chase ldrs appr fnl 2f, sn no extra. 2½ **47a**

358 **JONATHANS GIRL** 14 [6] 5-8-3 (35) L Newman (5) 14/1: 000-57: Bhd ldrs till lost pl 2f out: Ingr trip. 5 **16a**

298 **BROUGHTON BELLE** 23 [8] 4-7-10 (28)(8oh) P M Quinn (5) 50/1: /00-08: Al struggling: see 298. 2½ **4a**

367 **MARIANA** 12 [1] 5-7-12 (30)(bl) G Bardwell 33/1: 000-59: Al towards rear: see 367. nk **5a**

267 **LADY OF THE NIGHT** 28 [13] 4-9-1 (47)(t) A Culhane 10/1: 042-00: Nvr in it: 10th: op 8/1, t-strap. 1¾ **20a**

313 **Rotherhithe** 21 [3] 4-8-8 (40) F Norton 16/1:   352 **Zelbeck** 15 [7] 4-8-3 (35)(VIS) Joanna Badger (7) 25/1:

12 ran   Time 1m 26.02 (3.22)   (Bryan Fry)   M D I Usher Kingston Lisle, Oxon

---

439 | **2.00 MDN HCAP DIV II 4YO+ 0-65 (F)**   7f aw rnd   Going 17 -21 Slow   [55]
£1907   £545   £272

421 **SUPERCHIEF** 4 [12] Miss B Sanders 5-8-12 (39)(tbl) M Hills 11/10 FAV: 34-421: 5 b g Precocious - Rome Express (Siberian Express) Held up, prog to lead halfway, held on well for press: hvly bckd: plcd in late '99 (mdn, rtd 67a): rtd 53 at best in '98 (h'cap, tried visor, J Banks): eff at 7f, stays 10f: acts on equitrack, sharp trk: eff in a visor, best in blnks & t-strap: improved of late & looks well h'capped.		50a
557} **BEGUILE** 99 [10] R Ingram 6-9-3 (44) P M Quinn (5) 10/1: /460-2: 6 b g Most Welcome - Captivate (Mansingh) Rear, gd prog ent fnl 2f, kept on well to press wnr nr fin: op 14/1 on reapp, clr rem: unplcd in '99 for B Johnson: plcd prev term (h'caps, rtd 49a): eff at 7f, suited by 1m: acts on equitrack: goes well fresh.	½	52a
304 **SOLLYS PAL** 23 [11] P J Makin 5-9-6 (47) A Clark 6/1: 004-53: 5 gr g Petong - Petriece (Mummy's Pet) Rear, gd prog going well halfway, asked for eff appr fnl 1f, put head to one side & flashed tail, sn btn: op 5/1, clr rem: worth a try in headgear: handles both AWs: see 176.	5	45a
391 **SHADY DEAL** 8 [5] M D I Usher 4-9-10 (51) Martin Dwyer 20/1: 000-04: Prom, rdn & onepace fnl 2f.	10	34a
405 **PREPOSITION** 6 [8] 4-9-0 (41) G Parkin 8/1: 00/245: Handy till wknd ent fnl 3f: op 5/1, e/track bow.	2½	19a
399 **AMARO** 7 [4] 4-8-12 (39) F Norton 15/2: 5-5636: Cl-up till halfway: quick reapp, see 226.	½	16a
371 **OK JOHN** 11 [9] 5-9-8 (49)(bl) A Daly 10/1: 03-067: Wide, al towards rear: up in trip, see 57.	1¾	22a
375 **QUEEN OF THE KEYS** 11 [6] 4-8-12 (39)(vis) P Doe 11/1: 6-0308: Very slow away, nvr in it: op 8/1.	shd	14a
399 **MOUTON** 7 [1] 4-9-4 (45) A Daly 25/1: 2-5059: Set pace till halfway, wknd qckly: qck reapp, see 314.	9	0a
273 **GOOD WHIT SON** 27 [2] 4-8-8 (35) A McCarthy (3) 20/1: 00-00: Trkd ldrs 3f: 10th, tchd 33/1, no form.	5	0a
372 **Lady Balla Calm** 11 [7] 4-7-10 (23) G Bardwell 66/1: 3422} **Blazing Billy** 99 [3] 5-8-6 (33) Dale Gibson 33/1:		

12 ran   Time 1m 25.45 (2.65)   (Copy Xpress Ltd)   Miss B Sanders Epsom, Surrey

---

440 | **2.30 0800 211 222 CLAIMER 3YO+ (F)**   5f aw rnd   Going 17 -26 Slow
£2009   £574   £287   3 yo rec 14lb

4604} **SEREN TEG** 90 [1] R M Flower 4-9-8 (BL) A Clark 13/2: 0000-1: 4 ch f Timeless Times - Hill Of Far (Brigadier Gerard) Chsd ldr, rdn to lead ins last, pshd out nr fin: tchd 8/1, 3 month abs: thrice rnr-up in '99 (h'caps, rtd 79a & 76): prev term won at W'hampton (auct mdn) & here at Lingfield (clmr, rtd 76a): eff over a sharp 5/6f on fast & gd grnd, both AWs: likes Lingfield: revitalised by blnks.		61a
403 **ALJAZ** 7 [7] Miss Gay Kelleway 10-9-13 P Fredericks (5) 11/2: 23-402: 10 b g Al Nasr - Santa Linda (Sir Ivor) Wide, in tch, ld disp, ran on towards fin, not btn far: quick reapp, 6 wins on firesand.	¾	63a
379 **NIFTY NORMAN** 11 [5] D Nicholls 6-9-9 (bl) F Norton 10/11 FAV: 5-1323: 6 b g Rock City - Nifty Fifty (Runnett) Rear, imprvd after halfway, rdn to chase wnr below dist, held towards fin: well bckd: a shade below par here: acts on both AWs but prob best on fibresand: 5L in front of this 2nd in 279 (Southwell).	nk	58a
379 **LEGAL VENTURE** 11 [3] N P Littmoden 4-9-3 (bl) T G McLaughlin 25/1: U-0034: Tried to make all, clr appr fnl 1f, onepace & hdd ins last: op 7/2 & a bold attempt tho' surely flattered: acts on both AWs: see 291.	½	51a
372 **CHAKRA** 11 [6] 6-9-3 J Weaver 25/1: 40-065: Nvr going pace to chall: v stiff task, see 358.	3½	63$
291 **SWEET MAGIC** 25 [4] 9-9-5 (t) J Fanning 12/1: 056-06: Chsd ldrs till 2f out: op 8/1: see 146.	3	36a
399 **MICKY DEE** 7 [2] 4-9-1 (t) Joanna Badger (7) 100/1: 00-007: Al struggling: impossible task, no form.	3	23$

7 ran   Time 59.95 (2.15)   (K & D Computers Ltd)   R M Flower Jevington, E Sussex

---

441 | **3.00 BEST BETS HCAP 4YO+ 0-85 (D)**   1m4f aw   Going 17 -07 Slow   [82]
£3768   £1159   £579   £289   4 yo rec 3 lb

*267 **FUSUL** 28 [4] G L Moore 4-7-10 (53)(2oh) P Doe 9/2: 004-11: 4 ch c Miswaki - Silent Turn (Silent Cal) Trkd ldrs, led 3f out, sn rdn clr, cmftbly: tchd 6/1: earlier won here at Lingfield (mdn): unplcd in '99 (rtd 72 & 50a, B Hanbury): promise both '98 starts (mdns, rtd 72): eff at 10f, a revelation since stepped up to 12f: acts on equitrack: best set up with/forcing the pace on a sharp trk: shld make it 3 on the bounce v soon.		63a
370 **LOST SPIRIT** 12 [2] P W Hiatt 4-7-11 (54) G Baker (7) 8/1: 0-1202: 4 b g Strolling Along - Shoag (Affirmed) Led till 3f out, no ch with wnr: caught an imprvg, unexposed sort & ran to best: see 290 (C/D).	8	56a
*332 **HAWKSBILL HENRY** 18 [3] Mrs A J Perrett 4-7-13 (53) G Bardwell 8/1: 00-013: 6 ch g Known Fact - Novel Approach (Codex) Prom, eff 4f out, onepace: op 4/1: ran to best & pulled clr of rem: see 332 (C/D).	¾	54a
268 **MY BOLD BOYO** 28 [7] Jamie Poulton 5-8-2 (56)(bl) J Fanning 14/1: 000-44: Nr nr ldrs: see 268.	10	47a
332 **FAHS** 18 [5] 8-9-12 (80) J Bosley (7) 9/2: 031-25: Held up, eff 4f out, fdd: op 7/2, clrly not his form.	8	63a
*369 **METEOR STRIKE** 12 [1] 6-8-6 (60)(tbl) F Norton 9/1: 0-6216: Chsd ldrs till lost place 4f out: op 5/1: blnks reapplied on return to h'cap company: much btr 369 (fibresand stble).	7	36a
400 **SAMMYS SHUFFLE** 7 [6] 5-8-6 (57)(bl) (3ow) O Urbina 11/1: 51-507: Al bhd: op 8/1, quick reapp.	shd	36a
407 **FAILED TO HIT** 6 [8] 7-8-13 (67)(vis) J Tate 5/2 FAV: -42328: Bhd ldrs till halfway, sn btn: well bckd from 7/2: another quick reapp, possibly in need of a rest: see 101.	7	38a

8 ran   Time 2m 32.06 (2.86)   (Dave Allen, Barry Pritchard, Wayne Russell)   G L Moore Woodingdean, E Sussex

---

442 | **3.30 TOTE TRIFECTA HCAP 4YO+ 0-95 (C)**   1m2f aw   Going 17 +07 Fast   [94]
£6792   £2090   £1045   £522   4 yo rec 1 lb

*157 **ZANAY** 56 [1] Miss Jacqueline S Doyle 4-10-0 (95) T G McLaughlin 11/4: 1041-1: 4 b c Forzando - Nineteenth Of May (Homing) Cl-up, led appr fnl 3f, sn clr, not extended: nicely bckd tho' op 9/4, gd time, 8 wk abs: '99 wnr at Nottingham (mdn, rtd 86) & here at Lingfield (stks, rtd 93a): dual '98 rnr-up for R Phillips (mdn, rtd 81): eff at 1m, suited by 10f: acts on gd, soft, both AWs, loves equitrack, any trk: v useful & progressive colt, easily conceded 11lbs + today: shld be followed, incl when turf season starts.		107a
*374 **URSA MAJOR** 11 [4] C N Allen 6-8-1 (67) Martin Dwyer 5/2 FAV: 40-212: 6 b g Warning - Double Entendre (Dominion) Led, collared appr fnl 3f & sn outpcd: nicely bckd: met a fast imprvg colt, prob ran to best.	9	69a
374 **PUNISHMENT** 11 [3] K O Cunningham Brown 9-9-2 (82)(t) M Hills 6/1: 306-23: 9 b h Midyan - In The Shade (Bustino) In tch, niggled before halfway, onepace fnl 4f: got closer to this rnr-up in 374.	6	77a
374 **ANEMOS** 11 [2] M A Jarvis 5-8-12 (78) J Fanning 3/1: 01-234: Chsd ldrs, fdd appr fnl 3f: bckd: btr 374.	4	68a
244 **JUST WIZ** 31 [5] 4-9-3 (84)(bl) R Smith (5) 10/1: 131-05: Al bhd: much btr 161 (C/D).	6	68a
2104} **BANK ON HIM** 99 [7] 5-8-9 (75) G Parkin 9/1: 0404-6: Struggling from halfway, fin lame: reapp, tchd 12/1: 6th sole hdles start back in July: '99 wnr here at Lingfield (2, h'caps, rtd 78a): '98 W'hampton wnr (mdn h'cap, rtd 62a & 44): eff at 1m, suited by 10f: acts on both AWs, likes sharp trks: with G L Moore.	shd	59a

6 ran   Time 2m 03.78 (0.98)   (Sanford Racing)   Miss Jacqueline S Doyle Upper Lambourn, Berks

LINGFIELD (Equitrack)   WEDNESDAY FEBRUARY 2ND   Lefthand, Very Sharp Track

---

443

4.00 TEXT P368 SELLLER 3YO (G)   **6f aw rnd   Going 17 -56 Slow**
£1817   £519   £259

*120 **JANICELAND** 67 [1] S E Kettlewell 3-8-12 J Tate 8/11 FAV: 2541-1: 3 b f Foxhound - Rebecca's Girl   **55a**
(Nashamaa) Went on halfway & held on well, drvn out: well bckd, slow time, 10 wk abs, no bid: '99 W'hampton wnr
(sell, rtd 66a, fill auct mdn, rtd 75): eff at 5/6f: acts on fast, gd & both AWs: likes sharp trks & sellers.
357 **MASTER JONES** 14 [2] Mrs L Stubbs 3-8-12 A Culhane 4/1: 0-2332: 3 b g Emperor Jones - Tight Spin   ½ **53a**
(High Top) Trkd ldrs, ev ch going well ent str, rdn ins last, found zero: eff at 5/6f, stays 1m: try headgear now?
4597} **COLEY** 90 [3] L Montague Hall 3-8-12 (BL) Martin Dwyer 4/1: 0100-3: 3 ch f Pursuit Of Love - Cole   ¾ **51a**
Slaw (Absalom) Led for 3f, onepace below dist: nicely bckd, tchd 11/2, blnkd for reapp/AW bow: '99 wnr here at
Lingfield (turf clmr, ddht, rtd 56, H Candy, bght for £4,000): eff at 6f on soft & equitrack: runs well fresh.
421 **FRENCH FANCY** 4 [4] B A Pearce 3-8-7 (BL) O Urbina 25/1: 504-04: Chsd ldrs wide, feeling pace   hd **46a**
ent fnl 2f & hard rdn, no impress till ran on nr fin: quick reapp, blnkd: difficult task on offic ratings,
ran to best: handles fast, soft grnd & equitrack: worth another try at 7f in this grade: see 421.
397 **SHOULDHAVEGONEHOME** 8 [5] 3-8-12 T G McLaughlin 10/1: 20-505: Sn struggling: op 14/1, see 42.   3½ **42a**
-- **KATIE KING** [6] 3-8-7 L Newton 20/1: 6: Sn out the back: op 10/1 on debut: 2,000 gns River   12 **7a**
Falls filly, stoutly bred on dam's side: with W Musson.
6 ran   Time 1m 14.77 (4.37)   (Cable Media Consultancy Ltd)   S E Kettlewell Middleham, N Yorks

---

444

4.30 TEXT P372 HCAP STKS 3YO 0-85 (D)   **6f aw rnd   Going 17 -22 Slow**   **[92]**
£3785   £1164   £582   £291

275 **ILLUSIVE** 27 [2] H J Collingridge 3-8-7 (71) (bl) F Norton 11/4: 021-41: 3 b c Night Shift - Mirage (Red   **79a**
Sunset) Trkd ldrs, qcknd to lead appr fnl 1f, hard rdn, just held on: bckd from 3/1: '99 wnr here at Lingfield
(W Jarvis) & Southwell (nurseries, rtd 71a & 49): eff at 5/6f: handles gd/sft, likes both AWs, sharp trks: best blnkd.
*269 **CASTLE SEMPILL** 28 [3] R M H Cowell 3-8-6 (70) (vis) P M Quinn 2/1 FAV: 431-12: 3 b c Presidium   hd **76a**
- La Suquet (Puissance) Held up in tch, switched ent fnl 2f & rdn to chall below dist, ran on, just failed:
hvly bckd from 5/2: continues to improve, this was a competitive little sprint: see 269.
275 **DACCORD** 27 [1] E A Wheeler 3-9-7 (85) S Carson (5) 7/1: 311-53: 3 ch g Beveled - National Time   1¾ **87a**
(Lord Avie) Led, under press & hdd appr fnl 1f, onepace nr fin: gd run giving plenty of weight away tho'
again shaped like a return to 5f would suit: see 234 (5f, here).
*399 **DIRECT REACTION** 7 [4] Miss Gay Kelleway 3-8-11 (75) (vis) (6ex) N Callan 13/2: 3-3514: Prsd ldr   2½ **71a**
till outpcd appr fnl 1f: quick reapp, return to h'caps after facile win in a C/D mdn in 399 (made all).
*361 **KIRSCH** 13 [5] 3-8-7 (70) (vis) (1ow) M Hills 10/3: 23-315: Held up, eff 2f out, no impress: 2½ **61a**
nicely bckd: clrly not her form: see 361, 269 (much closer to this rnr-up over 5f here).
5 ran   Time 1m 12.76 (2.36)   (J B Com)   H J Collingridge Exning, Suffolk

---

WOLVERHAMPTON (Fibresand)   THURSDAY FEBRUARY 3RD   Lefthand, Sharp Track

Official Going   STANDARD. Stalls: 7f - Outside; Rem - Inside.

445

1.50 BET DIRECT HCAP 3YO+ 0-60 (F)   **5f aw rnd   Going 48 -02 Slow**   **[60]**
£2268   £648   £324   3 yo rec 14lb

425 **BARITONE** 3 [13] S E Kettlewell 6-8-6 (38) (vis) J Tate 7/1: -04341: 6 b g Midyan - Zinzi (Song):   **45a**
Rear/wide, prog to lead ins last, styd on strongly, rdn out: quick reapp: '99 Southwell wnr (h'cap, rtd 53a): place
form in '98 (h'cap, rtd 50 & 64a): eff at 5/6f, stays 1m: acts on fast, gd & loves both AWs: best in a visor.
372 **JACK TO A KING** 12 [8] J Balding 5-9-4 (50) (tbl) J Edmunds 4/1 JT FAV: 06-152: 5 b g Nawwar - Rudda 1¾ **52a**
Flash (General David): Mid-div, effort/no room 1f out, styd on strongly inside last, wnr had flown: unlucky,
may have won this with a clr run: can find compensation: see 291 (C/D).
*372 **RING OF LOVE** 12 [11] J L Eyre 4-10-0 (60) M Hills 4/1 JT FAV: 045-13: 4 b f Magic Ring - Fine Honey   nk **61a**
(Drone): Rdn mid-div/wide, prog to chall final 1f, kept on: mkt drifter, op 7/4: at 9d heart: see 372 (equitrack).
440 **SWEET MAGIC** 1 [3] L R Lloyd James 9-9-7 (53) (t) P Goode (5) 14/1: 56-064: Towards rear, swtchd/ 1 **52a**
kept on inside last: unplcd yesterday in 440 (clmr, equitrack).
246 **BAPTISMAL ROCK** 31 [12] 6-9-4 (50) S Whitworth 10/1: 300-05: Rear/wide, late gains, nrst fin: op 6/1. 1 **47a**
379 **YOUNG IBNR** 12 [7] 5-9-0 (46) L Newman (5) 8/1: 33-056: Chsd ldrs 4f: op 10/1: see 166, 116 (C/D). 1 **41a**
386 **ICE AGE** 10 [2] 6-9-5 (51) (bl) L Newton 25/1: 0-0507: Chsd ldrs 4f: on a fair mark, likes Southwell. hd **45a**
425 **CHOK DI** 3 [9] 4-8-12 (44) C Teague 16/1: 00-408: Prom 4f: op 14/1, qck reapp: see 273. ½ **36a**
372 **BOWCLIFFE GRANGE** 12 [1] 8-9-2 (50) A Culhane 14/1: 000-09: Led till inside last, fdd: op 12/1. shd **31a**
440 **LEGAL VENTURE** 1 [6] 4-9-1 (47) (bl) T G McLaughlin 10/1: -00340: Dwelt, al rear: 10th, qck reapp. 1¾ **36a**
371 **WISHBONE ALLEY** 12 [5] 5-9-5 (51) (vis) A Clark 5/1: -21320: Rear, swtchd inner halfway/sn btn: 12th. 0a
371 **Kalar** 12 [4] 11-8-1 (33) (bl) Kimberley Hart 33/1:   4563} **Brief Call** 96 [10] 8-8-8 (54) D Sweeney 33/1:
13 ran   Time 1m 02.7 (2.5)   (Hollinbridge Racing)   S E Kettlewell Middleham, Nth Yorks.

446

2.20 BET DIRECT MDN 4YO+ (D)   **1m1f79y aw Going 48 -24 Slow**
£2730   £840   £420   £210

378 **NAFITH** 12 [7] E L James 4-9-0 S Whitworth 9/2: 00-321: 4 ch g Elmaamul - Wanisa (Topsider):   **52a**
Held up in tch, rdn/prog to lead over 2f out, held on well inside last, rdn out: op 4/1: rtd 94h over timber this
term (juv nov): unplcd on the level in '99 for M P Tregoning (rtd 76, mdn): unplcd in '98 (rtd 72): eff at 1m/9.4f,
tried further: acts on fibresand & a sharp trk: open to further improvement in h'caps.
367 **AHOUOD** 13 [1] K Mahdi 4-8-9 C Lowther 16/1: 036-42: 4 b f Merdon Melody - Balidilemma (Balidar): 1¾ **44a**
Led, lost pl near 2f out, rallied fnl 2f, not rch wnr: stays 9.4f, 10f+ shld suit: acts on fibresand & a sharp trk.
4371} **HAPPY LADY** 99 [6] B W Hills 4-8-9 M Hills 6/5 FAV: 3055-3: 4 b f Cadeaux Genereux - Siwaayib   2½ **39a**
(Green Desert): Handy, led 5f out till over 2f out, kept on tho' held inside last: hvly bckd: 4 mth abs/AW bow:
plcd in '99 (rtd 73, mdn): rtd 56 in '98 (mdn): stays a stiff/undul 1m: handles gd & fibresand: fin clr of rem.
339 **UNTOLD STORY** 17 [2] T Keddy 5-9-0 V Slattery 66/1: 0-0664: Prom, led 7f out till 5f out, sn btn. 10 **29$**
412 **HIGHFIELDER** 6 [8] 4-9-0 (vis) Pat Eddery 20/1: 306-55: In tch, eff 3f out/sn btn: vis reapp. 12 **11a**
1892} **UNCLE OBERON** 99 [3] 4-9-0 P Clarke (7) 12/1: 0/50-6: Keen/cl up 5f: op 8/1: AW bow/6 mth abs: 4 **5a**

149

prev with G Butler, unplcd in '99 (rtd 68, auct mdn): rtd 58 in '98: lngr 9f trip today for C Dwyer.

4220} **PURSUIVANT 99** [5] 6-9-0 R Fitzpatrick (3) 3/1: 2300-7: Held up in tch, rdn/btn 3f out: op 5/2, jumps   5   **0a**
fit (mod form): rnr-up twice in '99 (rtd 64a & 62): eff arnd 1m/9f: acts on firm, soft & f/sand: tried blnks.

4435} **BITTER SWEET 99** [4] 4-8-9 A Mackay 6/1: 0020-8: Rear, hmpd/nearly u.r. over 3f out, position sn   ½   **0a**
accepted/eased: op 4/1: jumps fit (mod form): AW bow, now with J Spearing: this prob best forgotten.

8 ran   Time 2m 05.00 (6.8)   (Nicholas Cowan)   E L James East Garston, Berks.

---

447   **2.50 BEST BETS HCAP 4YO+ 0-80 (D)**   **1m1f79y aw Going 48 -04 Slow**   [70]
£3750   £1154   £577   £288

*349   **AREISH 16** [2] J Balding 7-8-12 (54) J Edmunds 5/2 FAV: 0-5111: 7 b m Keen - Cool Combination   **58a**
(Indian King) Chsd ldrs, outpcd 3f out, strong run to lead line, all-out: op 6/4: recent W'hampton wnr (2, h'caps):
'99 wnr at W'hampton (sell) & Southwell (fill h'cap, rtd 53a): '98 Southwell (D Nicholls) & W'hampton wnr (h'caps,
rtd 44a, M Pipe): eff at 1m/12f, suited by 9f: handles equitrack, f/sand & W'hampton specialist: best without blnks.

400   **ROI DE DANSE 8** [4] M Quinn 5-8-4 (46) F Norton 7/2: 2-0342: 5 ch g Komaite - Princess Lucy   hd   **49a**
(Local Suitor): Keen/led, rdn final 2f, hdd line: tchd 4/1: game front rnr, can win again: see 227, 203.

381   **HANNIBAL LAD 12** [8] W M Brisbourne 4-10-0 (70) T G McLaughlin 3/1: 2-1523: 4 ch g Rock City -   nk   **72a**
Appealing (Star Appeal): Held up in tch, rdn/prog to chall over 1f out, styd on well, just held: op 4/1.

270   **BOWCLIFFE 28** [1] E J Alston 9-9-12 (68) J P Spencer 20/1: 600-04: Dwelt, in tch, prog to chall   nk   **69a**
dist, just held cl-home: clr rem, op 12/1: recent jumps rnr (plcd, nov h'cap, rtd 78h): '99 Musselburgh wnr (class
stks, rtd 67): '98 W'hampton & Doncaster wnr (h'caps, rtd 77a & 68): eff at 1m/9f, stays 10f: acts on firm, gd/
soft & fibresand, handles soft: has run well fresh: best without blnks.

418   **STERLING HIGH 6** [6] 5-8-7 (49)(t) R Fitzpatrick (3) 3/1: -04035: Cl-up h'way, outpcd 2f out: tchd 4/1.   5   **40a**
390   **ACCYSTAN 10** [5] 5-9-13 (69) J Weaver 33/1: 010-06: Prom 6f: see 390.   9   **47a**
352   **VILLAGE NATIVE 16** [7] 7-9-1 (57)(bl) M Hills 14/1: 260-17: Held up in tch, btn 2f out/sn eased: op 10/1. 12   **17a**

7 ran   Time 2m 03.1 (4.9)   (Mrs J Coghlan-Everitt)   J Balding Scrooby, Notts.

---

448   **3.20 ITV CONDITIONS STKS 3YO+ (C)**   **1m100y aw Going 48 +06 Fast**
£5887   £2233   £1116   £507   3 yo rec 19lb

321   **KING PRIAM 21** [5] M J Polglase 5-9-6 (bl) R Fitzpatrick (3) 7/2: 152-31: 5 b g Priolo - Barinia (Corvaro)   **101a**
Held up in tch, hard rdn/prog to chall & narrow lead inside last, styd on gamely, all-out: fast time: op 3/1:
'99 wnr at W'hampton (2, h'caps), Southwell (2, h'caps, rtd 98a), Leicester (class stks), Haydock & York (h'caps, rtd 80):
'98 Newmarket wnr (clmr, rtd 70, M Pipe): eff at 1m/10f, stays 12f: acts on firm & gd, relishes soft/fibresand:
handles any trk, loves W'hampton: best in blnks: tough & useful AW performer.

321   **WEET A MINUTE 21** [4] R Hollinshead 7-9-6 A Culhane 9/4: 201-22: 7 ro g Nabeel Dancer - Ludovica   nk   **100a**
(Bustino): Chsd ldrs, rdn to chall dist, styd on well, just held: tough & useful, bt this wnr in 230 (C/D).

251   **ADELPHI BOY 31** [1] M C Chapman 4-9-6 R Studholme (5) 20/1: 024-03: 4 ch g Ballad Rock - Toda   1¼   **97$**
(Absalom): Handy, led over 2f out, rdn/edged right & hdd inside last, held cl-home: offic rtd 87: see 251.

*308   **SKIMMING 23** [6] B W Hills 4-9-10 M Hills 5/4 FAV: 660-14: Led, hdd over 2f out, no extra inside   3½   **94a**
last: hvly bckd: reportedly broke a blood vessel: highly tried after 308 (C/D, mdn).

423   **ITALIAN SYMPHONY 5** [3] 6-9-12 (vis) Joanna Badger (7) 33/1: 5-0505: Held up in tch, held final 2f.   2   **92a**
356   **CHINA CASTLE 15** [2] 7-9-10 P Goode (5) 20/1: 254-06: Rdn/rear, al outpcd: op 15/1, 25/1.   hd   **89a**
4204} **PANTAR 99** [7] 5-9-6 Martin Dwyer 7/1: 0330-7: Cl-up, rdn/held 2f out: op 5/1: 4 mth abs/AW bow: hd   **84a**
plcd form in '99 (rtd 102, h'cap): '98 Goodwood wnr (val h'cap, rtd 102 at best): eff at 1m/10f: acts on firm
& gd/soft grnd: handles any trk: useful at best.

7 ran   Time 1m 49.8 (3.6)   (Ian Puddle)   M J Polglase Southwell, Notts.

---

449   **3.50 TEXT P372 SELL STKS 4YO+ (G)**   **7f aw rnd Going 48 -11 Slow**
£1932   £552   £276

389   **DISTINCTIVE DREAM 10** [7] A Bailey 6-8-12 J Weaver 2/1 FAV: 40-621: 6 b g Distinctly North - Green   **62a**
Side (Green Dancer): Handy travelling well, led over 2f out, rdn/asserted inside last, styd on well: nicely bckd:
no bid: '99 Haydock wnr (classified stks, first time vis, rtd 75, Lady Herries): dual '98 rnr-up (h'cap, rtd 85): eff
at 6/7f on firm, gd/soft & fibresand: handles any trk, likes Windsor & Kempton: eff with/without blnks or visor.

75   **NITE OWLER 76** [12] J Balding 6-8-12 J Edmunds 7/1: 2100-2: 6 b g Saddlers' Hall - Lorne Lady   3   **55a**
(Local Suitor): Mid-div/wide, rdn to chall 2f out, kept on tho' held inside last: op 5/1: abs: see 75.

396   **MIKES DOUBLE 9** [3] Mrs N Macauley 6-8-12 (vis) R Havlin 14/1: 60-523: 6 br g Cyrano de   1½   **52$**
Bergerac - Glass Minnow (Alzao): Rear/wide & rdn, styd on well final 2f, no threat: op 10/1: see 396, 142.

436   **LITTLE IBNR 2** [9] P D Evans 4-8-12 (vis) J P Spencer 12/1: 636-04: Dwelt, held up in tch wide,   1¾   **49$**
smooth prog/trkd ldrs 2f out, sn onepcd/held: op 14/1, qck reapp: see 436 (6f).

*391   **DAYNABEE 9** [8] 5-8-13 T G McLaughlin 7/2: 52-515: Chsd ldrs, held final 1f: op 2/1: see 391 (C/D).   ¾   **49a**
391   **C HARRY 9** [11] 6-9-4 Pat Eddery 3/1: 525426: Held up wide, effort 2f out, no impress: see 130.   ½   **53a**
360   **LOCOMOTION 14** [2] 4-8-12 P Doe 10/1: 000-07: Dwelt/towards rear, mod gains: op 6/1: see 360.   4   **39a**
391   **GADGE 9** [6] 9-8-12 C McCavish (7) 20/1: 0-0038: Led 1f, btn 3f out: lngr prcd stablemate of rnr.   ½   **38$**
396   **NOBLE PATRIOT 9** [4] 5-8-12 Dean McKeown 33/1: 450509: Handy, led after 1f till over 2f out, wknd.   1   **36$**
389   **CANTGETYOURBREATH 10** [5] 4-9-4 (bl) J Bosley (7) 20/1: 51-000: Strugg halfway: 10th: op 14/1.   10   **27a**
379   **Arab Gold 12** [10] 5-8-12 (vis) R Studholme (5) 50/1: 409   **Maid Plans 7** [1] 4-8-7 D Meah (3) 66/1:
12 ran   Time 1m 30.3 (4.1)   (A Thomson)   A Bailey Little Budworth, Cheshire.

---

450   **4.20 TEXT P372 HCAP 3YO 0-70 (E)**   **7f aw rnd Going 48 -15 Slow**   [74]
£2613   £746   £373

*416   **SIGN OF THE TIGER 6** [3] P C Haslam 3-9-3 (63)(6ex) P Goode (5) 2/1: 043-11: 3 b g Beveled - Me Spede   **74a**
(Valiyar): Handy, led 3f out, rdn/in command final 1f, eased nr line: value for 4L, nicely bckd, 6lb pen/qck reapp:
recent Southwell wnr (h'cap, first win): plcd once in '99 (rtd 57a): eff at 7f, stays 1m well: acts on fibresand
& a sharp trk: has run well fresh: progressive 3yo, can win again.

419   **LORD HARLEY 5** [6] B R Millman 3-8-6 (52) A Clark 8/1: 004-22: 3 b c Formidable - Nanny Doon   2½   **55a**
(Dominion): Chsd ldrs, rdn/chsd wnr final 2f, kept on tho' al held: op 5/1: qck reapp: handles both AWs.

*287   **LUCKY STAR 26** [4] D Marks 3-9-1 (61) D Dineley 16/1: 666-13: 3 b f Emarati - Child Star (Bellypha):   3½   **57a**
Led 4f, held final 2f: op 8/1: acts on equitrack, prob handles fibresand: see 287 (fillies h'cap).

*334   **LADYWELL BLAISE 19** [7] M L W Bell 3-9-7 (67) C Carver (3) 4/1: 5-314: In tch wide, rdn/btn 2f out.   2½   **58a**

WOLVERHAMPTON (Fibresand) THURSDAY FEBRUARY 3RD Lefthand, Sharp Track

4474} TURNED OUT WELL 99 [1] 3-7-13 (45) Dale Gibson 25/1: 000-5: Rear/in tch, outpcd final 3f: op   **2 32a**
16/1, lngr prcd stablemate of wnr: 3 mth abs: unplcd in '99 from 3 starts (rtd 41): AW/h'cap bow today.
416   **LOUS WISH 6** [2] 3-9-5 (65)(bl) Pat Eddery 6/4 FAV: 0-3126: Chsd ldrs, rdn/btn 3f out: well bckd.   **1¾ 49a**
346   **COME ON MURGY 16** [5] 3-8-5 (51) J Bramhill 12/1: -14447: Strugg halfway: op 10/1: see 300, 283 (sell).   **3 29a**
7 ran   Time 1m 30.6 (4.4)   (Middleham Park Racing)   P C Haslam Middleham, Nth Yorks.

SOUTHWELL (Fibresand) FRIDAY FEBRUARY 4TH Lefthand, Sharp, Oval Track

Official Going   STANDARD. Stalls: Inside.

451   1.40 BET DIRECT HCAP 3YO 0-70 (E)   1m aw rnd   Going 81 - 13 Slow   [72]
£2821   £868   £434   £217

*392   **SPECIAL PROMISE 10** [6] P C Haslam 3-9-6 (64)(6ex) P Goode (5) 2/5 FAV: 05-111: 3 ch g Anjiz -   **75a**
Woodenitbenice (Nasty And Bold) Handy/trav well, led over 2f out, pushed out fnl 1f, readily: val for 5L+: recent
Lingfield & Wolverhampton wnr (h'caps): unplaced in '99 (rtd 61 & 55a); eff at 1m/10f, 12f+ cld suit: acts on
both AWs & likes a sharp track: progressive 3yo.
415   **NICIARA 7** [5] M C Chapman 3-8-4 (48)(bl) R Fitzpatrick(1) 7/1: 0-0532: 3 b g Soviet Lad - Verusa (Petorius) 3   **49a**
Dwelt, cl-up after 2f/rdn, kept on for press fnl 2f, al held: op 5/1: blnks reapp: eff at 7f/1m on fibresand.
*281   **MODEM 28** [2] D Shaw 3-8-12 (56)(VIS) N Callan 5/1: 000-13: 3 b g Midhish - Holy Water (Monseigneur) 1¾   **54a**
Handy, rdn & outpcd 3f out, kept on ins last, no threat: tried a visor: stays 1m: see 281 (sell, 7f, with D Shaw).
188   **DUN DISTINCTLY 51** [3] P C Haslam 3-8-4 (48) Dale Gibson 12/1: 0000-5: Led 6f, sn btn: op 20/1:   **3½ 39a**
7 wk abs, longer priced stablemate of wnr: longer 1m trip today: see 188.
198   **JONLOZ 49** [1] 3-7-13 (43) P Fessey 25/1: 0040-5: Cl up 4f, sn btn: abs: btr 128 (6f).   **15 11a**
5 ran   Time 1m 46.90 (7.5)   (R Young)   P C Haslam Middleham, N Yorks

452   2.10 BET DIRECT APPR CLAIMER 4YO+ (F)   1m aw rnd   Going 81 - 35 Slow
£2002   £572   £286

383   **NOBLE INVESTMENT 13** [10] J Neville 6-8-4 Paul Cleary 25/1: 40/301: 6 b g Shirley Heights -   **50a**
Noble Destiny (Dancing Brave) Mid-div/wide, rdn & hung left ins last & led nr fin, rdn out: 1st win: mod form over
jumps: ex German wnr, mod Brit Flat form: eff at 1m on fibresand: likes a sharp trk: runs well for an appr.
631}   **CELESTIAL KEY 99** [11] M Johnston 10-8-4 K Dalgleish (5) 1/1: 0/03-2: 10 br g Star de Naskra -   **¾ 48a**
Casa Key (Cormorant) Handy halfway, led over 2f out, strongly prsd ins last & hdd/no extra nr fin: op 3/1, 10 mth
abs: plcd in Germany in '99 (stks, unplcd in Britain, rtd 90, unplcd on soft, rtd 75a): eff at 7/9f on firm, soft & fibresand: best without a t-strap: handles any trk.
244   **PHILISTAR 33** [3] K R Burke 7-8-13 P Hanagan 5/4 FAV: 265-33: 7 ch h Bairn - Philgwyn (Milford)   **shd 57a**
Chsd ldrs, rdn & keeping on when briefly no room 1f out, styd on well nr line: well bckd: poss a shade unlucky,
wld have gone close here with a clr run: acts on firm, gd/soft & both AWs: see 93 (equitrack).
404   **GENIUS 8** [2] D W Chapman 5-8-1 Lynsey Hanna 6/1: -22004: Towards rear, rdn & styd on well fnl   **hd 44a**
2f & briefly no room ins last, kept on nr fin: op 9/2: shade unlucky in running, back to form here: see 298, 201.
418   **FRANKLIN LAKES 7** [9] 5-8-1 (tbl) G Baker (3) 20/1: 00-305: Chsd ldr, led over 2f out, hdd/fdd in last.   **3½ 37$**
368   **BLOOMING AMAZING 14** [8] 6-8-13 D Hayden 10/1: 30-006: Twds rear, eff 3f out/sn held: see 176.   **nk 48$**
389   **SOUNDS SOLO 11** [4] 4-8-7 (cvi) Clare Roche 4/1: 50-637: Led 6f, fdd: see 389, 341 (6/7f).   **2 38a**
433   **IMBACKAGAIN 3** [12] 5-8-7 L Paddock (5) 25/1: 0-6308: Wide/prom 6f: quick reapp: see 297.   **5 28$**
425   **SARPEDON 4** [7] 4-8-7 Joanna Badger 20/1: 00-059: chsd ldrs 5f, sn btn: quick reapp: see 425 (6f).   **½ 27$**
398   **FLASHFEET 9** [6] 10-8-1 D Allan (6) 50/1: 000-00: Al rear: 10th: see 398.   **hd 20a**
404   **Jato Dancer 8** [5] 5-8-8 Stephanie Hollinshead (7) 50/1: 368   **Shamwari Song 14** [1] 5-8-7 J Bosley 40/1:
12 ran   Time 1m 48.7 (9.3)   (Mrs P K Chick)   J Neville Coedkernew, Monmouths

453   2.40 BEST BETS MED AUCT MDN 3-4YO (E)   1m aw rnd   Going 81 - 07 Slow
£2651   £757   £378   3 yo rec 19lb

4426}   **EPERNAY 99** [10] J R Fanshawe 4-9-7 O Urbina 2/1 FAV: 25-1: 4 b f Lion Cavern - Decant (Rousillon)   **72+**
Led after 2f, rdly pulled clr fnl 2f & eased nr fin: val for 12L+: op 7/4: AW bow, 4 month abs: rnr-up on debut
in '99 (auct mdn, rtd 76): eff at 1m, mid-dists cld suit: acts on fibresand & soft grnd & a sharp/turning trk:
runs well fresh: eff forcing the pace: plenty in hand, open to further improvement.
387   **KUSTOM KEVIN 11** [9] S R Bowring 4-9-7 S Finnamore (7) 16/1: 60-32: 4 b g Local Suitor -   **9 61a**
Sweet Revival (Claude Monet) Chsd wnr, chsd wnr fnl 2f, kept on tho' al held: op 25/1: caught a tartar, see 387.
198   **CANNY HILL 49** [3] D Moffatt 3-8-9(2ow) C Lowther 4/1: 064-3: 3 ch g Bold Arrangement - Jersey   **nk 62a**
Maid (On Your Mark) Rdn/rear halfway, rdn & kept on well fnl 2f, no threat: 7 wk abs: h'caps/10f+ may suit.
373   **MONSIEUR RICK 13** [6] Miss Gay Kelleway 3-8-7 N Callan 5/2: 34: Led 2f, btn 2f out: op 3/1:   **2½ 55a**
395   **ROOM TO ROOM MAGIC 10** [7] 3-8-2 L Newman (5) 20/1: 45: Cl-up early, rdn/btn 2f out: see 395.   **nk 49a**
--   **ROOFTOP** [4] 4-9-12 Dean McKeown 14/1: 5200-6: Dwelt, sn chsd ldrs, rdn/hung right & btn 3f out: **5 44a**
op 16/1: jumps fit (no form): ex-Irish, plcd in '99 at Cork (h'cap): stays 7f, handles fast: AW bow today.
328   **BLAIR 21** [5] 3-8-7 J Tate 50/1: 0-07: Chsd ldrs til halfway: see 328.   **10 29a**
430   **CHAMBOLLE MUSIGNY 4** [11] 4-9-7 (bl) T G McLaughlin 33/1: 0-3008: Wide, chsd ldrs 4f: qck reapp.   **15 2a**
4557}   **ICICLE QUEEN 97** [8] 3-8-2 T Williams 50/1: 00-9: Wide/sn bhd: 3 month abs/AW bow: no form   **28 0a**
on turf in 2 starts in '99 (S Williams): now with A G Newcombe.
9 ran   Time 1m 46.4 (7.0)   (Mrs E Fanshawe)   J R Fanshawe Newmarket

454   3.10 TEXT P368 HCAP 4YO+ 0-80 (D)   6f aw rnd   Going 81 +03 Fast   [74]
£4270   £1314   £657   £328

388   **KEEN HANDS 11** [10] Mrs N Macauley 4-10-0 (74)(vis) R Fitzpatrick (3) 8/1: 4-1041: 4 ch g Keen -   **79a**
Broken Vow (Local Suitor) Handy, rdn/led & hung left ins last, styd on gamely, drvn out: op 10/1: earlier scored
here at Southwell (C/D h'cap): '99 scorer at W'hampton (sell) & here at Southwell (3, sells & h'cap, rtd 75a & 45):
rtd 56a in '98: eff at 5/7f, suited by 6f: handles fibresand/Southwell specialist: best in a vis, gd weight carrier: tough.
4297}   **PLEADING 99** [7] M A Buckley 7-8-13 (59) Martin Dwyer 20/1: 1000-2: 7 b g Never So Bold - Ask Mama   **1 61a**
(Mummy's Pet) Rdn/rear & wide, styd on well fnl 2f for press, nrst fin: 4 month abs: '99 wnr at Chepstow

SOUTHWELL (Fibresand)   FRIDAY FEBRUARY 4TH   Lefthand, Sharp, Oval Track

(h'cap, 1st time blnks, W Musson, rtd 69): '98 Pontefract wnr (h'cap, rtd 69): eff at 6/7f on fast, hvy & f/sand:
has run well fresh: handles any trk, likes a stiff one: eff with/without blnks: can find compensation.

425	**BEST QUEST 4** [4] K R Burke 5-9-6 (66)(t) N Callan 3/1: 312333: 5 b h Salsa - Quest For The Best (Rainbow Quest) Prom, led over 1f out till ins last, no extra: op 4/1: quick reapp: see 403.	shd	68a
414	**SHARP HAT 7** [9] D W Chapman 6-8-11 (57) A Culhane 5/1: 0-3424: Handy, rdn/chs 2f out, held when hmpd/checked ins last, no impress after: see 91 (5f).	1½	56a
250	**GRASSLANDIK 32** [8] 4-8-7 (53) S Whitworth 10/1: 502-35: Rdn/rear, mod gains: op 8/1: see 226.	4	42a
*425	**RAFTERS MUSIC 4** [2] 5-9-4 (64)(6ex) Clare Roche (7) 9/4 FAV: 0-1216: Dwelt, chsd ldrs, btn 2f out: quick reapp under a pen: ahead of today's 3rd in 425 (C/D).	1½	49a
386	**AJNAD 11** [6] 6-9-9 (69) S Righton 50/1: 0-0007: Mid-div, btn 2f out: see 282.	2	39a
*273	**SISAO 29** [3] 4-9-1 (61)(bl) P Fredericks (5) 11/1: 632-18: Dwelt, al twds rear: op 8/1: see 273 (mdn).	1	39a
372	**RUDE AWAKENING 13** [1] 6-8-11 (57) P Doe 8/1: 6-4139: Led, hdd over 1f out & wknd qckly: see 358.	2½	28a
386	**RUSSIAN ROMEO 11** [5] 5-9-9 (69)(bl) L Newman (5) 25/1: 030-60: Drvn mid-div, btn halfway: 10th.	15	12a

10 ran   Time 1m 18.00 (4.7)   (Andy Peake)   Mrs N Macauley Sproxton, Leics

---

455   3.40 TEXT P372 SELLER 4YO+ (G)   1m3f aw   Going 81   +02 Fast
£1892   £540   £270   4 yo rec 2 lb

393	**ROYAL PARTNERSHIP 10** [12] K R Burke 4-8-12 Darren Williams (7) 11/1: 00-P51: 4 b g Royal Academy - Go Honey Go (General Assembly) Trkd ldrs going well, swtchd stnds side fnl 2f, styd on gamely to lead cl home, just prevailed: bt in for 6200gns: ex-Irish, plcd in '99 (7f mdn, fast, J Oxx): apprec this step up to 11f, may stay further: acts on fibresand and a sharp trk: runs well for an appr: apprec drop to selling grade.		49a
393	**APPROACHABLE 10** [10] Miss S J Wilton 5-9-0 M Tebbutt 4/1: -25442: 5 b h Known Fact - Western Approach (Gone West) Handy, led halfway, rdn/hdd ins last, just held: op 7/2: eff btwn 7/11f: see 45 (1m).	hd	48a
400	**MIGWAR 9** [9] N P Littmoden 7-9-5 T G McLaughlin 5/1: 1-0603: 7 b g Unfuwain - Pick Of The Pops (High Top) Dwelt, prog/trkd ldrs going well h'way, kept on well fnl 2f, just held nr fin: clr rem: nicely bckd.	nk	52a
260	**GOLDEN LYRIC 31** [6] J Pearce 5-9-0 J Weaver 12/1: 300-04: Cl up 9f: op 10/1: see 60.	10	36$
3604}	**SHAMOKIN 99** [7] 8-9-0 C Lowther 14/1: 6060-5: Rear, mod gains: 5 mth abs: plcd in '99 (h'cap, 42a, rtd 51 on turf): plcd in '98 (rtd 26a): eff arnd 7f/1m on fast, gd/soft & fibresand: tried a visor.	6	27a
428	**MARKELLIS 4** [2] 4-9-3 Iona Wands (5) 12/1: 045056: Rear/rdn, nvr factor: op 14/1: see 215.	nk	31a
408	**NORTH ARDAR 8** [13] 10-9-0 F Norton 6/1: 246-57: Dwelt, twds rear/wide, nvr factor: see 176.	7	16a
--	**OUTPLACEMENT** [8] 5-9-0 S Finnamore (7) 50/1: 65/8: Sn bhnd: jumps fit (no form): mod '98 Flat form.	½	15a
324	**SEASON OF HOPE 21** [1] 4-8-7 Claire Bryan (7) 16/1: 54-309: Led 6f, sn btn: btr 248 (C/D).	nk	10a
4509}	**PUIWEE 99** [11] 5-8-9 (bl) J Bramhill 66/1: 5000-0: Prom 6f: 10th: 3 mth abs: unplcd in 99 (rtd 38a & 33): plcd in '98 (rtd 45): eff arnd 7f/1m: handles fast, gd/soft and prob fibresand.	15	0a
68	**Royal Dolphin 77** [4] 4-8-12 (t) L Newton 50/1:		
114	**Wilomeno 70** [5] 4-8-7 P Goode (4) 66/1:		

178 **Sea God 53** [3] 9-9-0 Joanna Badger (7) 50/1:

13 ran   Time 2m 31.6 (10.3)   (Tendorra)   K R Burke Newmarket

---

456   4.10 TEXT PAGE HCAP 4YO+ 0-75 (E)   1m4f   Going 81   -05 Slow   [70]
£2795   £860   £430   £215   4 yo rec 3 lb

437	**CRESSET 3** [1] D W Chapman 4-8-7 (52)(bl)(6ex) A Culhane 100/30: -02121: 4 ch c Arazi - Mixed Applause (Nijinsky) Rear & rdn halfway, swtchd wide over 3f out, prog to lead dist, drvn clr: nicely bckd, qck reapp: recent W'hampton scorer (sell h'cap, W Jarvis): unplcd in '99 (rtd 61 & 44a): eff at 12f, stay further: acts on fibresand and a sharp trk: has improved for blnks: shld win again, particularly when tackling further.		63a
343	**JIBEREEN 18** [6] P Howling 8-10-0 (70) S Whitworth 20/1: 00-042: 8 b g Lugana Beach - Fashion Lover (Shiny Tenth) Rear, drvn/chall over 2f out, held 1f out: topweight: op 14/1: prob stays 11f: see 197 (1m).	7	70a
*390	**KIRISNIPPA 11** [5] Derrick Morris 5-8-6 (48)(6ex) P Doe 9/2: 60-513: 5 b g Beveled - Kiri Te (Liboi) Chsd ldrs, led over 4f out, rdn/hdd over 1f out, sn held: 6lb pen for latest: see 390 (11f).	4	44a
4264}	**FATEHALKHAIR 99** [4] B Ellison 8-9-7 (63) F Norton 13/2: 4130-4: Chsd ldr, rdn/held 3f out: 10 wk jmps abs (rtd 120h, Gr 2 hdle): '99 Flat wnr at Redcar, Catterick (2) & Thirsk (hcaps, rtd 64, rnr up on sand, rtd 46a, h'cap): plcd in '98 (rtd 38): eff at 12/13f: acts on firm, soft & fibresand: handles any trk, likes Catterick.	7	49a
*338	**MORGANS ORCHARD 18** [3] 4-9-3 (62) P Fredericks (5) 6/4 FAV: 053-15: Rdn chsng ldrs 3f out/sn held.	hd	48a
437	**WESTERN COMMAND 3** [2] 4-9-6 (65)(bl) R Fitzpatrick (3) 6/1: 450336: Led 1m: qck reapp: btr 170.	13	37a

6 ran   Time 2m 44.6 (10.3)   (Michael Hill)   D W Chapman Stillington, N Yorks

---

LINGFIELD (Equitrack)   SATURDAY FEBRUARY 5TH   Lefthand, V Sharp Track

Official Going   STANDARD. Stalls: Inside, except 1m - Outside.

457   12.50 BET DIRECT MDN 3YO+ (D)   1m4f aw   Going 35   -04 Slow
£2808   £864   £432   £216   3 yo rec 24lb4 yo rec 3 lb

315	**DONT WORRY BOUT ME 24** [11] T G Mills 3-8-5 (VIS)(2ow) A Clark 11/2: 000-01: 3 b g Brief Truce - Coggle (Kind Of Hush) Al handy, led 4f out, held on gamely ins last, rdn out: op 4/1, first time visor: plcd 3 times in '99 (mdns, rtd 84 & 63a): apprec this step up to 12f, could stay further: acts on equitrack, handles fast & gd grnd: likes a sharp trk: galvanized by headgear, can win again.		61a
--	**ESTUARY 10** [10] Mrs A E Johnson 5-9-13 A McCarthy (3) 4/1: 2: 5 ch g Riverman - Ocean Ballad (Grundy) Sn handy, ev ch 2f out, chall under hands-and-heels riding ins last, just held: op 7/1 on Flat debut: 3 month jumps abs (unplcd, bmpr): eff at 12f, 14f+ looks sure to suit: acts on equitrack: clr of rem today.	hd	58a
353	**SPRINGTIME LADY 17** [6] S Dow 4-9-5 P Doe 11/8 FAV: 20-223: 4 ch f Desert Dirham - Affaire de Coeur (Imperial Fling) Chsd ldrs halfway, eff over 3f out, sn held: op 4/6: longer 12f trip: btr 152, 96 (1m).	9	43a
2799}	**RUSHED 99** [1] G P Enright 5-9-13 A Daly 25/1: 2000-4: Led 1m, sn held: jumps fit (mod form): rnr-up in '99 (h'cap, rtd 36a): plcd in '98 (rtd 44a, mdn, no turf form for M Stoute): stays 12f & handles equitrack.	9	38a
348	**MISCHIEF 18** [2] 4-9-10 (bl) F Norton 14/1: 303-05: Chsd ldrs 5f out, sn held: see 348.	hd	37a
419	**OFFENBURG 7** [12] 3-8-3 Martin Dwyer 14/1: 000-56: Dwelt, chsd ldrs 7f: op 20/1: see 419 (1m).	7	27a
314	**DION DEE 24** [3] 4-9-10 S Drowne 20/1: 0/0-07: Prom, stuggling 5f out: see 314 (10f).	1¾	20a
387	**MELVELLA 12** [4] 4-9-5 Dean McKeown 11/2: 300-68: Mid-div, rdn/struggling halfway: op 4/1: see 387.	1	19a
204	**KAHYASI MOLL 49** [9] 3-7-12 P M Quinn (5) 25/1: 5006-9: Al towards rear: 7 wk abs: see 204 (10f).	1¾	17a
240	**WEST END DANCER 34** [8] 3-7-12 (BL) G Bardwell 12/1: 50-00: Rdn/strugg after 3f: 10th: blnks.	18	0a

--   **TRUE ROMANCE** [5] 4-9-10 J P Spencer 10/1: 0/0: Bhd halfway: 11th: op 8/1: long abs.   9   **0a**
11 ran   Time 2m 33.83 (4.63)   (Thorpe Vernon)   T G Mills Headley, Surrey.

---

458   1.20 BETS SELL HCAP DIV 1 4YO+ 0-60 (G)   1m5f aw   Going 35 -02 Slow   [56]
£1526   £436   £218   4 yo rec 4 lb

347   **APPYABO** 18 [10] M Quinn 5-8-0 (28) F Norton 10/1: 00-021: 5 ch g Never So Bold - Cardinal Palace   **32a**
(Royal Palace) Sn handy, rdn/chsd ldr over 1f out, led ins last, styd on well, rdn out: no bid, op 12/1: plcd in
'99 (auct mdn, rtd 45a, rtd 27 on turf): plcd in '98 (rtd 72a, h'cap, also rtd 52 on turf, tried a visor): eff at
10/13f, tried 2m: handles fast grnd & both AWs: likes a sharp trk: appreciates sell grade.
369   **GROOMS GOLD** 15 [3] J Pearce 8-8-2 (30) A Polli (3) 8/1: 30-042: 8 ch g Groom Dancer - Gortynia   nk   **34a**
(My Swallow) Prom, rdn/led 5f out till ins last, kept on well, just held: op 6/1: eff at 1m/sharp 13f: see 369.
410   **OUR PEOPLE** 9 [12] M Johnston 6-8-2 (30)(t) K Dalgleish (7) 3/1 JT FAV: 0-3533: 6 ch g Indian   3½   **29a**
Ridge - Fair And Wise (High Line) Rear, rdn & prog halfway, kept on ins last, no threat: nicely bckd: see 261.
*402   **ANOTHER MONK** 10 [4] R Ingram 9-9-4 (46)(vis) J P Spencer 3/1 JT FAV: 20-414: Chsd ldrs/held fnl 2f.   7   **35a**
377   **ALBERKINNIE** 14 [1] 5-7-12 (26) G Baker (7) 13/2: 20-025: Twds rear, eff 4f out, held fnl 2f: see 377.   2   **12a**
410   **SHABAASH** 9 [9] 4-8-2 (34) A McCarthy (3) 20/1: 30-406: Handy/wide 9f: op 14/1: see 111 (10f).   5   **13a**
402   **KI CHI SAGA** 10 [5] 8-8-2 (30)(bl) D R McCabe 8/1: 20-607: Rear/wide, nvr on terms: tchd 10/1.   6   **0a**
2793}   **MARCIANO** 99 [6] 4-8-8 (40) S Whitworth 25/1: 0000-8: Rdn/wide & rear, no ch halfway: 11 wk jmps   4   **4a**
abs (rtd 73h, claim nov hdle, first time blnks): unplcd in '99 (rtd 53 & 37a, C W Thornton): mod form in '98.
402   **COASTGUARDS HERO** 10 [8] 7-8-11 (38) T G McLaughlin 15/2: 606-29: Led 1m, sn btn: btr 402 (2m).   2   **0a**
405   **BIJA** 9 [11] 5-7-10 (24)(5oh) Claire Bryan (7) 40/1: 4-0000: Rdn/rear, bhd 4f out: 10th: plcd in '99   6   **0a**
(rtd 26, sell h'cap, rtd 40a on sand, mdn): prob stays 1m & handles firm grnd.
10 ran   Time 2m 47.11 (4.81)   (M Quinn)   M Quinn Sparsholt, Oxon.

---

459   1.50 CLASSIFIED CLAIMER 3YO 0-60 (F)   7f aw   Going 35 -23 Slow
£2289   £654   £327

355   **DAMASQUINER** 17 [6] T E Powell 3-8-6 R Lappin 50/1: 066-41: 3 b f Casteddu - Hymn Book (Darshaan)   **58a**
Chsd ldrs, prog to lead over 1f out, in command ins last, rdn out: surprise success, unplcd all prev starts, rtd 65
in '99 (mdn): eff at 7f, tried 1m, shld suit in time: acts on equitrack & sharp trk: apprec drop to claim grade.
365   **JOHN COMPANY** 15 [1] R M Beckett 3-8-9 (tvi) M Tebbutt 11/2: 25-032: 3 ch c Indian Ridge - Good   2   **57a**
Policy (Thatching) Dwelt, cl-up after 2f, briefly led over 1f out, not pace of wnr in last: op 7/1: eff at 6/7f:
handles gd & both AWs: shown enough to win similar this winter: see 365 (fibresand).
*397   **BAYTOWN RHAPSODY** 11 [7] P S McEntee 3-8-10 L Newman (5) 5/2 JT FAV: 0-3213: 3 b f Emperor   2½   **53a**
Jones - Sing A Rainbow (Rainbow Quest) Chsd ldrs wide, onepace fnl 2f: nicely bckd: acts on both AWs & gd grnd.
287   **PERLE DE SAGESSE** 28 [3] Julian Poulton 3-8-12 A Daly 5/2 JT FAV: 01-054: Handy, rdn/outpcd fnl 3f.   1¾   **52a**
281   **INCH PINCHER** 29 [9] 3-8-5 (BL) T Williams 9/1: 025-05: Led, rdn over 2f out & hdd over 1f out, fdd: 1   **43a**
op 6/1, showed pace in first time blnks: return to sell grade shld suit: see 53 (C/D).
355   **CROESO ADREF** 17 [8] P M Quinn (5) 100/30: 3-1236: In tch halfway, wide 4f out & btn 2f out.   1¼   **39a**
355   **LUNAJAZ** 17 [5] 3-8-7 R Price 9/1: 00-507: Al outpcd towards rear: clmd for £6,000 by A Kelleway.   12   **24a**
4381}   **PHANTOM STAR** 99 [8] 3-8-1 A McCarthy (3) 25/1: 0505-8: Chsd ldrs/rdn halfway, sn outpcd: 2½   **13a**
4 month abs/AW bow: unplcd in '99 (N Tinkler, rtd 52, seller, first time visor): stays a sharp 7f & handles gd.
357   **CAPPUCINO LADY** 17 [4] 3-8-0 G Bardwell 50/1: 60-059: Sn well bhd: see 357 (seller).   29   **0a**
9 ran   Time 1m 26.83 (4.03)   (Miss P I Westbrook)   T E Powell Reigate, Surrey.

---

460   2.20 BETS SELL HCAP DIV 2 4YO+ 0-60 (G)   1m5f aw   Going 35 -18 Slow   [54]
£1517   £433   £216   4 yo rec 4 lb

--   **NEGATIVE EQUITY** [10] D G Bridgwater 8-8-4 (30)(bl) S Righton 10/1: 0025/1: 8 ch g Be My Chief -   **35a**
Rather Romantic (Verbatim) Cl-up, led after 2f & in command fnl 1f, styd on well, rdn out: op 8/1: no bid:
jumps fit, mod recent form, rtd 90h back in 97/98 for A Turnell: last rcd on Flat back in '95, rnr-up twice (rtd
45, h'cap, K Burke): eff at 10/12f on equitrack, fast & gd: likes a sharp trk: eff in blnks/vis: likes sell grade.
4412}   **CLOUD INSPECTOR** 99 [8] M Johnston 9-8-4 (30) J Fanning 6/1: 0005-2: 9 b g Persian Bold - Timbale   2   **31a**
d'Argent (Petingo) Chsd ldrs, rdn & kept on fnl 3f, not pace to chall: op 5/1: 4 mth abs: unplcd in '99 (tried a
visor, rtd 52, h'cap): rtd 82 at best in '98 (h'cap): '97 Goodwood scorer (h'cap), also won in Switzerland (rtd 86
at best): eff at 13f, suited by 2m/2m4f: acts on firm, gd & equitrack: handles any trk: well h'capped 9yo.
410   **XYLEM** 9 [3] J Pearce 9-8-12 (38)(vis) R Price 9/2: 00-323: 9 ch g Woodman - Careful (Tampa   shd   **39a**
Trouble) Rdn/rear & wide, prog/chsd ldrs 5f out, kept on for press, no ch to chall: op 5/2: visor reapp.
377   **MOGIN** 14 [6] L Montague Hall 7-8-4 (30) Martin Dwyer 5/1: 00-044: Chsd ldrs, trkd wnr 5f out,   1¾   **29a**
rdn/no extra ins last: op 7/1: stays a sharp 13f, could prove interesting in similar back at 10f: see 377.
209   **FUERO REAL** 49 [1] 5-8-12 (38) O Urbina 11/4 FAV: 2240-5: Chsd ldrs, rdn/kept on fnl 3f, nvr pace   2   **34a**
to chall: well bckd, tchd 5/1: 7 wk abs: handles fast & equitrack: see 209.
316   **PRIVATE SEAL** 24 [9] 5-8-4 (30)(t) A Daly 20/1: 00-566: Bhd, rdn/mod gains: see 262 (6f).   2   **23a**
174   **CREME DE CASSIS** 56 [12] 4-8-9 (39) A Clark 14/1: 0035-7: Chsd ldrs 1m: op 10/1, 8 wk abs: plcd   11   **20a**
in '99 (rtd 39, h'cap): rtd 65 & 9a in '98: stays a gall 14f: handles fast grnd.
203   **RAWI** 49 [7] 7-9-3 (43) Pat Eddery 15/2: 5030-8: Drpd rear after 4f, no impress after: op 5/1: abs.   8   **15a**
3822}   **JELLYBEEN** 99 [4] 5-9-5 (54) N Callan 14/1: 6350-9: Rear/rdn, nvr factor: op 12/1: 5 month abs.   ½   **25a**
363   **LUTINE BELL** 16 [5] 5-8-2 (28) M Baird 25/1: 000/00: Sn bhd: 10th: see 363.   16   **0a**
338   **Barann** 19 [2] 4-7-10 (26)(6oh) P Doe 33/1:   --   **Ferns Memory** [11] 5-7-10 (22)(1oh) G Bardwell 33/1:
12 ran   Time 2m 49.18 (6.88)   (D E McDowell)   D G Bridgwater Lambourn, Berks.

---

461   2.55 40+ RECRUITMENT HCAP 3YO 0-70 (E)   1m2f aw   Going 35 -08 Slow   [74]
£2926   £836   £418

*240   **BLUEBELL WOOD** 34 [3] G C Bravery 3-9-7 (67) M Hills 8/13 FAV: 0-11: 3 ch f Bluebird - Jungle   **74a**
Jezebel (Thatching) Made all, rdn fnl 2f, in command ins last, rdn out: well bckd at odds on: h'cap bow:
earlier scored here at Lingfield (C/D mdn): rtd 62 on sole '99 start (unplcd, mdn, A J McNae): eff at 10f,
12f+ could suit: likes equitrack/Lingfield: has run well fresh: eff forcing the pace: can rate more highly.
311   **COLOMBE DOR** 25 [2] P C Haslam 3-8-12 (58) P Goode (5) 6/4: 006-22: 3 gr g Petong - Deep Divide   2½   **59a**
(Nashwan) Trkd wnr, eff/briefly outpcd & lkd reluctant over 1f out, no impress ins last: eff at 8.5f/sharp 10f:
acts on both AWs & headgear may help: see 311, 213.

LINGFIELD (Equitrack) SATURDAY FEBRUARY 5TH Lefthand, V Sharp Track

419 **BLAYNEY DANCER 7** [1] Jamie Poulton 3-7-10 (42)(6oh) D Kinsella (7) 9/1: 060-03: 3 b c Contract   **3** **39$**
Law - Lady Poly (Dunbeath) Cl-up, rdn/outpcd over 3f out: tchd 12/1: stiffish task/longer 10f trip: plcd
in '99 (rtd 89): dam a hdles wnr, could apprec mid-dists: h'cap bow today.
3 ran   Time 2m 07.37 (4.57)   (The Iona Stud)   G C Bravery Newmarket.

---

462   **3.30 TEXT P368 HCAP 4YO+ 0-90 (C)** **7f aw rnd Going 35 -02 Slow**   **[83]**
         £6630   £2040   £1020   £510

336 **KILMEENA LAD 21** [9] E A Wheeler 4-9-7 (76) S Carson (5) 16/1: 004-41: 4 b g Minshaanshu Amad -   **84a**
Kilmeena Glen (Beveled) Prom, rdn/led over 1f out, styd on strongly ins last, rdn out: op 12/1: '99 scorer
at Newmarket & Lingfield (h'caps, rtd 75 & 81a): '98 Newbury scorer (mdn, rtd 85): eff at 6f/sharp 7f, stays
a sharp 1m: acts on firm, hvy & loves equitrack: handles any trk, likes Lingfield: op to further improvement.
435 **JUWWI 4** [4] J M Bradley 6-10-0 (83) Claire Bryan (7) 9/1: -33532: 6 ch g Mujtahid - Nouvelle Star   **2** **85a**
(Luskin Star) Dwelt, sn rdn/well bhd, styd on well from halfway to take 2nd ins last, no threat: qck reapp: see 129.
*423 **FOREIGN EDITOR 7** [2] R A Fahey 4-9-7 (76) P Hanagan (7) 9/4: -2D113: 4 ch g Magic Ring - True   **¾** **77a**
Precision (Presidium) Led after 1f till over 1f out, no extra fnl 1f: well bckd: see 423 (C/D, made all).
*337 **NAUTICAL WARNING 21** [10] B R Johnson 5-10-0 (83)(t) M Hills 7/4 FAV: 412-14: Rdn/in tch   **1** **82a**
wide halfway, kept on for press fnl 2f, not able to chall: topweight: remains in gd heart: see 337 (C/D).
454 **BEST QUEST 1** [11] 5-8-13 (68)(t) N Callan 12/1: 123335: Chsd ldrs 5f: 3rd yesterday at Southwell.   **2** **63a**
398 **APOLLO RED 10** [8] 11-9-1 (70) A Clark 25/1: 13-126: In tch wide, nvr plcd to chall: see 316 (sell).   **1½** **62a**
337 **RAINBOW RAIN 21** [7] 6-8-3 (58) P Doe 10/1: 305-37: Towards rear/wide, nvr on terms: op 6/1.   **1½** **47a**
423 **RIFIFI 7** [1] 7-9-3 (72) J Weaver 7/1: 00-008: Trkd ldrs, short of room 2f out, sn btn: btr 423, 320.   **2½** **56a**
3767} **JAMES DEE 99** [5] 4-9-7 (76) S Drowne 25/1: 4401-9: Prom 5f: op 14/1, 5 month abs: '99 wnr at   **½** **59a**
Brighton (clmr) & W'hampton (h'cap, rtd 77a & 69 at best): rnr-up in '98 (auct mdn, rtd 74, also rtd 56a): eff at
6f, suited by a sharp 7f, stays 1m: acts on firm, hvy & soft & fibresand: has run well fresh: handles any trk.
*376 **PRINCE PROSPECT 14** [6] 4-9-11 (80) J P Spencer 16/1: 00-010: Slowly away & bhd/wide thr'out: 10th.   **1** **61a**
376 **BRUTAL FANTASY 14** [3] 6-9-0 (69) A McCarthy (3) 20/1: 214030: Led 1f, struggling halfway: 11th.   **5** **40a**
11 ran   Time 1m 25.37 (2.57)   (Mrs J A Cleary)   E A Wheeler Whitchurch-On-Thames, Oxon.

---

463   **4.05 TEXT P372 HCAP 3YO+ 0-85 (D)** **1m aw rnd Going 35 +07 Fast**   **[85]**
         £3838   £1181   £590   £295   3 yo rec 19lb

423 **TOPTON 7** [2] P Howling 6-10-0 (85)(bl) A Clark 5/1: 2-4261: 6 b g Royal Academy - Circo (High Top)   **93a**
Chsd ldrs, led 3f out, styd on strongly, rdn out: gd time: '99 wnr at Lingfield (h'cap, rtd 86a), Doncaster (2)
& Yarmouth (h'caps, rtd 80): '98 Doncaster (rtd 72), Southwell & Lingfield wnr (h'cap, rtd 75a): eff at 7f/1m:
acts on firm, gd/soft & both AWs: loves Lingfield & Doncaster: gd weight carier: suited by blnks/visor: tough.
*409 **CRIMSON GLORY 9** [6] G C Bravery 4-9-9 (94) M Hills 7/1: 540-12: 4 ch f Lycius - Crimson Conquest   **5** **70a**
(Diesis) Rdn/bhd, stdy prog halfway to take 2nd ins last, no threat to wnr: op 5/1: acts on both AWs, firm & fast.
2930} **PACIFIC ALLIANCE 99** [5] P S McEntee 4-8-8 (65) Dean McKeown 16/1: 0014-3: 4 b g Fayruz - La   **1** **63a**
Gravotte (Habitat) Rear/wide, kept on fnl 4f, no threat to wnr: 7 month abs: '99 Lingfield (auct mdn) & Sandown
(h'cap, rtd 68a & 65, with R Armstrong): rtd 73 in '98: eff at 1m, tried 10f, shld suit in time: acts on fast,
gd & equitrack: eff in blnks, not worn today: handles any trk: likes to force the pace: sharper for this.
411 **SCISSOR RIDGE 9** [9] J J Bridger 8-8-0 (57) G Bardwell 15/2: 04-324: Rear/rdn & wide, late gains: op 4/1.   **½** **54a**
*239 **ELMHURST BOY 38** [3] 4-9-11 (82)(vis) Pat Eddery 2/1 FAV: 0021-5: Chsd ldrs 7f: well bckd.   **nk** **78a**
*400 **FORTY FORTE 10** [1] 4-9-1 (72) N Callan 11/4: 0-5616: Led after 1f till over 3f out, sn held: op 9/4.   **1½** **65a**
227 **GHAAZI 40** [8] 4-8-1 (58)(bl) Martin Dwyer 16/1: 4314-7: Chsd ldrs, held 3f out: op 12/1, 6 wk abs.   **4** **43a**
411 **SOUND THE TRUMPET 9** [7] 8-7-10 (53)(tvi)(11oh) G Baker (7) 25/1: 30-068: In tch 5f: vis reapp.   **nk** **37a**
398 **MALCHIK 10** [4] 4-7-10 (53)(11oh) R Brisland (3) 50/1: 5-5569: Led 1f, struggling fnl 3f: see 159.   **½** **36a**
9 ran   Time 1m 38.47 (2.27)   (Liam Sheridan)   P Howling Newmarket.

WOLVERHAMPTON (Fibresand) SATURDAY FEBRUARY 5TH Lefthand, Sharp Track

Official Going   STANDARD Stalls: 1m6f - Outside; Rem - Inside.

464   **7.00 BET DIRECT HCAP 4YO+ 0-60 (F)** **1m4f aw Going 53 -22 Slow**   **[60]**
         £2425   £693   £346   4 yo rec 3 lb

*261 **DESERT SPA 32** [3] P J Makin 5-9-9 (55) A Clark 11/4 FAV: /02-11: 5 b g Sheikh Albadou - Healing   **60a**
Waters (Temperence Hill) Chsd ldrs, gd hdwy to lead 2f out, edged right ins last, drvn out: op 7/4: jockey
received a two day whip ban: earlier won here at W'hampton (h'cap): '98 wnr again at W'hampton (h'cap, rtd 56a
& 63, P Harris): best over a sharp 12f on fibresand, handles fast & soft: loves W'hampton: best without blnks.
4525} **IRISH CREAM 99** [10] Andrew Reid 4-8-9 (44) M Henry 16/1: 0003-2: 4 b f Petong - Another Baileys   **hd** **48a**
(Deploy) Mid-div, gd hdwy appr fnl 1f, chall when carried right ins last, just held: clr rem: '99 wnr at Southwell
(3, sells & clmr, rtd 73a), plcd on turf (rtd 46): '98 wnr at Hamilton (auct mdn, rtd 74) & Southwell (clmr, rtd 79a):
stays 12f on gd/soft, hvy & equitrack, fibresand/Southwell specialist: eff with/without a visor: win sn at Southwell.
383 **OCEAN LINE 14** [5] G M McCourt 5-8-5 (37) L Newman (5) 11/2: 130-23: 5 b g Kefaah - Tropic Sea   **3½** **36a**
(Sure Blade) Handy, rdn to imprv over 3f out, kept on but not pace of ldrs: stays 12f: see 383 (9.4f).
290 **HURGILL DANCER 28** [4] R J O'Sullivan 6-8-8 (40) P M Quinn (5) 10/1: 434-34: V keen & cl-up,   **hd** **39a**
rdn & no extra appr fnl 1f: op 8/1: see 100.
441 **LOST SPIRIT 3** [1] 4-9-5 (54) G Baker (7) 6/1: -12025: Led, hdd 2f out, wknd qckly ins last: qck reapp.   **5** **46a**
348 **MEILLEUR 18** [8] 6-10-0 (60) M Tebbutt 5/1: 24-236: Bhd, rdn to improve 4f out, wknd appr fnl   **5** **45a**
1f: will apprec a return to further, top-weight: see 348 (2m).
370 **MICE IDEAS 15** [12] 4-9-1 (50) T G McLaughlin 12/1: 54-167: Rear, imprvd halfway, btn fnl 2f: btr 248.   **5** **28a**
405 **PREMIERE FOULEE 9** [7] 5-7-13 (29)(2ow) P Fessey 20/1: 00-068: Al bhd: see 260.   **1** **7a**
305 **EMPIRE STATE 25** [9] 5-8-10 (42) A Culhane 9/1: 220-69: Nvr a threat: op 7/1: see 305 (9.4f).   **3** **14a**
277 **RONQUISTA DOR 30** [6] 6-9-3 (49)(bl) S Drowne 9/2: 253-60: Al rear: t.o. in 10th: op 8/1: btr 277 (14f). **15** **6a**
2438} **EPWORTH 99** [2] 6-8-7 (39) F Norton 33/1: 0530-0: Rdn in tch, wknd qckly halfway, t.o. in 11th: **5** **0a**
reapp: plcd twice in '99 (AW mdn & mdn h'cap, rtd 49a & 35): rtd 49 & 24a at best in '98 (tried visor):
eff around 10f, stays 12f: handles fast, soft & fibresand: has tried blnks/visor, best without.
11 ran   Time 2m 42.6 (9.0)   (D M Ahier)   P J Makin Ogbourne Maisey, Wilts

465 7.30 B FAIRWEATHER CLAIMER 4YO+ (F)   6f aw rnd   Going 53 -07 Slow
£2135   £610   £305

406 **MALLIA** 9 [3] T D Barron 7-8-13 C Lowther 4/1: -40551: 7 b g Statoblest - Pronetta (Mr Prospector) **69a**
Led for 1f, again halfway, strongly prsd over 1f out, drvn out to hold on: op 5/2: '99 wnr here at W'hampton
(2, clmr & h'cap, rtd 76a) & Haydock (h'cap, rtd 76): 'quick reapp: gd run at the weights on fav trk, win sn: see 436.

406 **TAKHLID** 9 [8] D W Chapman 9-9-3 A Culhane 3/1 FAV: 6-4022: 9 b h Nureyev - Savonnerie (Irish River) ¾ **70a**
Chsd ldr, hdwy to chall 2f out, styd on, no extra cl-home: op 9/4: loves claiming grade, 7f & Wolverhampton.

449 **LITTLE IBNR** 2 [7] P D Evans 9-8-1 (vis) J Tate 16/1: 36-043: 9 b g Formidable - Zalatia (Music Boy) nk **53a**
Cl-up, outpcd 2f out, drvn/styd on well fnl 1f: quick reapp: gd run at the weights on fav trk, win sn: see 436.

394 **ZIGGYS DANCER** 11 [2] E J Alston 9-9-3 J P Spencer 9/2: 000-04: Waited with, rdn to improve 1¼ **65a**
appr fnl 1f, no extra ins last: op 7/2: see 223.

*414 **SEVEN** 8 [5] 5-9-3 (bl) T G McLaughlin 9/2: 22-015: Cl-up, rdn/no extra over 1f out: gd run. 1¼ **62a**

379 **SAMWAR** 14 [4] 8-8-13 (vis) R Fitzpatrick (3) 6/1: 01-406: Prom, lost tch over 1f out: suited by 5f. 3 **51a**

436 **TROJAN HERO** 4 [1] 9-8-7 N Callan 8/1: 0-4537: Led after 1f, hdd halfway, rdn/fdd fnl 1f: qck reapp. 1 **42a**

378 **DORANFIELD LADY** 14 [6] 5-8-0 A Mackay 66/1: 08: Dwelt, al bhd: mod form. 9 **17a**
8 ran   Time 1m 16.4 (3.6)   (H T Duddin)   T D Barron Maunby, N Yorks

466 8.00 G BASNETT FILLIES HCAP 4YO+ 0-70 (E)   6f aw rnd   Going 53 -07 Slow   [70]
£3493   £1075   £537   £268

388 **DAYS OF GRACE** 12 [9] L Montague Hall 5-9-8 (64) Martin Dwyer 9/4 FAV: -21231: 5 gr m Wolfhound - **67a**
Inshirah (Caro) Led, hdd halfway, rdn/chall over 1f out, styd on strongly to lead well ins last, drvn out: earlier
won at Southwell (fill h'cap): '99 wnr at Southwell & W'hampton (h'caps, rtd 62a & 56): eff at 5/7f: acts on
firm, hvy & both AWs: handles any trk, likes W'hampton/Southwell: gd weight carrier: very tough/consistent.

3549} **MOY** 99 [11] W M Brisbourne 5-8-2 (44)(bl) A McCarthy (3) 25/1: 0000-2: 5 ch m Beveled - Exceptional hd **46a**
Beauty (Sallust) Cl-up, hdwy to lead halfway, hdd 2f out, styd on well, just held: reapp: plcd once in
'99 (h'cap, rtd 48a), subs mod form on turf: rnr-up in '98 (h'cap): eff at 6/7f: acts on
gd/soft & fibresand: gd reapp, could break mdn tag sn if running to this form again.

-394 **YABINT EL SHAM** 11 [6] B A McMahon 4-9-13 (69) L Newman (5) 4/1: 01-523: 4 b f Sizzling Melody - ½ **70a**
Dalby Dancer (Bustiki) Rcd keen in tch, led 2f out, hdd ins last, no extra: consistent: stays 6f, poss best at 5f.

3767} **PRIDEWAY** 99 [7] W M Brisbourne 4-10-0 (70) T G McLaughlin 20/1: 0200-4: Outpcd, ran on well fnl 1½ **67a**
2f, nvr nrr: top weight, poss best: new stable & stable-mate of rnr-up: '99 reapp wnr here at W'hampton (h'cap,
rtd 75a, A Bailey), rnr-up twice on turf (h'cap & sell, rtd 70): plcd in '98 (rtd 71): eff at 6f, suited
by 7f/1m: acts on fast, suited by gd/soft, soft & fibresand: without blnks: keep in mind at 7f+.

358 **POLLY MILLS** 17 [1] 4-9-10 (66)(vis) N Callan (5) 9/1: 0-0365: Prom, lost place 2f out, late gains: op 7/1. shd **63a**

246 **DONE AND DUSTED** 33 [10] 4-9-8 (64) F Norton 13/2: 601-06: Chsd ldrs, outpcd 2f out, late hdwy. ½ **60a**

*25 **AUBRIETA** 26 [2] 4-9-0 (56)(bl) A Mackay 11/2: 0601-7: Mid-div at best: abs: btr 25 (equitrack, mdn). 2 **47a**

280 **PETITE DANSEUSE** 29 [8] 6-7-10 (38)(5oh) Iona Wands (5) 16/1: 60-558: Nvr a danger: see 246. 1½ **26a**

3387} **SPRINGS NOBLEQUEST** 99 [3] 4-8-12 (54) J P Spencer 20/1: 0030-9: Prom, lost tch fnl 2f: plcd 3 **34a**
twice for T D Easterby in '99 (h'cap, rtd 56 at best): '98 wnr at Carlisle (mdn, rtd 77): eff btwn 5f & 7f:
acts on firm & gd/soft grnd: likes Carlisle: now with E J Alston.

381 **RIVER ENSIGN** 14 [5] 7-8-7 (49) P M Quinn (5) 11/1: -21300: Al bhd, 10th: needs further: see 292 (9.4f). 2½ **23a**

1172} **MEGS PEARL** 99 [12] 4-8-4 (46)(vis) J Tate 33/1: -21300: Dwelt, al bhd, fin 11th: new stable: ½ **19a**
unplcd in 3 '99 starts for P D Evans (fill mdns, rtd 58, tried visor): now with W M Brisbourne.

394 **LISAS PRINCESS** 11 [13] 7-7-10 (38)(5oh) Joanna Badger (7) 20/1: 0-6-00: Handy, btn halfway, 12th. 3½ **3a**
12 ran   Time 1m 16.4 (3.6)   (Stephen & Michelle Bayless)   L Montague Hall Tadworth, Surrey

467 8.30 0800 211222 MDN 3YO (D)   1m1f79y aw   Going 53 -05 Slow
£2613   £746   £373

4473} **FAIR LADY** 99 [1] B W Hills 3-8-9 M Hills 7/4 FAV: 026-1: 3 b f Machiavellian - Just Cause **76a**
(Law Society) Made all, prsd & bmpd over 1f out, rdn out to hold on: nicely bckd tho' op 11/10 on
seasonal/AW bow: showed promise when rnr-up in '99 (fill mdn, rtd 80): eff at 1m, stays 9.4f well:
acts on firm, fresh & runs well fresh on a sharp trk: strip fitter for this, win again.

421 **YOU DA MAN** 7 [4] R Hannon 3-9-0 L Newman 100/30: 600-42: 3 b c Alzao - Fabled Lifestyle ½ **78a**
(King's Lake) Cl-up, hdwy to chall when hung badly left over 1f out, styd on stongly but al held: nicely
bckd, quick reapp: styd this longer 9.4f trip well: handles equitrack & fibresand: see 421.

409 **MANTILLA** 9 [2] R Hollinshead 3-8-9 P M Quinn 3/1: 34-023: 3 b f Son Pardo - Well Tried 1½ **70a**
(Thatching) Cl-up, lost place 2f out, rdn/no extra fnl 1f: stays 9.4f: h'cap company may now suit: see 409.

362 **LADY OF BILSTON** 16 [3] D R C Elsworth 3-8-9 S Drowne 100/30: 34: V keen in tch, wknd qckly 15 **54a**
fnl 3f: op 2/1: poss not stay this longer 9.4f trip: better on debut in 362 (7f).

236 **LANCRESS PRINCESS** 38 [5] 3-8-9 C Lowther 66/1: 0-5: Dwelt, al well bhd: no form sole '99 start. dist **0a**
5 ran   Time 2m 03.7 (5.5)   (Maktoum Al Maktoum)   B W Hills Lambourn, Berks

468 9.00 BEST BETS SELL STKS 4-6YO (G)   1m6f166y   Going 53 -62 Slow
£1470   £420   £210   4 yo rec 5 lb

402 **QUAKERESS** 10 [7] John Berry 5-8-13 (et) J P Spencer 25/1: 0-6041: 5 b m Brief Truce - Deer Emily **31a**
(Alzao) Bhd, gd hdwy 4f out, led going well over 1f out, easily: 1st win: sold for 2,300 gns to S Murphy:
unplcd in '99 (rtd 58, h'cap, tried blnks): plcd all 3 '97 starts (mdn & nov auct, rtd 70): apprec this
step up to 14.7f: handles firm, fast & fibresand: excellent effort at today's weights (offic rtd only 16!).

408 **NEPTUNE** 9 [6] K C Comerford 4-8-13 T G McLaughlin 11/8 FAV: 40-332: 4 b g Dolphin Street - Seal 2½ **30a**
Indigo (Glenstal) Cl-up, led over 3f out, hdd dist, not pace of wnr: nicely bckd: stays 14.7f: see 338.

3769} **HILL STORM** 99 [1] K McAuliffe 4-8-13 C Lowther 9/2: /640-3: 4 b g Mukaddamah - Brockley Hill Lass 7 **23a**
(Alzao) V keen in tch, hdwy to lead over 4f out, hdd 3f out, wknd fnl 2f: unplcd in 3 '99 starts
(rtd 56a at best, mdn, tried visor): rtd 60 in '98: poss stays 12f & handles fibresand.

348 **KATIES CRACKER** 18 [4] M Quinn 5-8-13 F Norton 3/1: 00-004: Led to 5f out, outpcd, late gains. shd **18a**

339 **COCHITI** 19 [3] 6-8-13 (t) Joanna Badger (7) 16/1: 60-055: In tch, wknd fnl 5f, t.o.: see 339. 16 **6a**

1645} **BE VALIANT** 99 [9] S Drowne 7/1: /440-6: Cl-up, led briefly 5f out, sn lost tch: op 7/2: shd **11a**

155

reapp: twice 4th in '99 for Mrs N Macauley (clmrs, rtd 45a at best): '98 wnr at Ripon (sell, rtd 61 at best, J Fanshawe): eff over 10f on fast, gd & fibresand: has tried visor, best without: now with C L Popham.

363	**CYMBAL MELODY 16** [8] 4-8-8 P M Quinn (5) 25/1: 0-057: Al bhd, t.o.: see 277.		20	0a
301	**SONICOS 26** [5] 4-8-13 R Cody Boutcher (7) 25/1: 0-08: Al rear: see 301.		2	0a
4520}	**BIN ALMOOJID 99** [2] 4-8-13 (BL) V Slattery 33/1: 0/0-9: Keen cl-up, bhd, hdles rnr. *dist*			0a
9 ran	Time 3m 26.6 (17.0) (John Berry) John Berry Newmarket			

---

469   **9.30 TEXT P368 HCAP 4YO+ 0-70 (E)**   **1m1f79y aw**   Going 53   +12 Fast   [70]
£2790   £797   £398

*359   **FRENCH SPICE 16** [2] Sir Mark Prescott 4-9-1 (57) D Sweeney 11/10 FAV: 61-111: 4 b f Cadeaux   **72a**
Genereux - Hot Spice (Hotfoot) Chsd ldrs going well, smooth hdwy to lead 3f out, pshd clr: fast time: 4 timer completed after 3 wins earlier here at W'hampton (h'caps): unplcd/mod form early in '99 (rtd 41, mdn): eff at 1m/9.4f, 10f+ shld suit in time: loves fibresand/W'hampton: tough & progressive, can extend winning sequence.

*383   **MYSTERIUM 14** [3] N P Littmoden 6-8-10 (52) T G McLaughlin 5/1: 40-212: 6 gr g Mystiko - Way To Go   7   **55a**
(Troy) Prom, chased wnr fnl 2f, styd on but no ch with wnr: clr rem: met a prog here, win again sn: see 383.

447   **BOWCLIFFE 2** [7] E J Alston 9-9-12 (68) J P Spencer 6/1: 00-043: 9 b g Petoski - Gwiffina (Welsh   7   **61a**
Saint) Waited with, gd hdwy over 2f out, kept on but not ch with ldrs: quick reapp: too sn after 447?.

349   **JADE TIGER 18** [11] F Jordan 4-9-1 (57) N Callan 20/1: 460-04: Rear, prog halfway, no extra fnl 2f.   1¾   **48a**

349   **RIVERBLUE 18** [10] 4-9-7 (63) M Tebbutt 16/1: 40-005: Rear, btn when short of room fnl 2f: see 349.   ½   **53a**

418   **ELLWAY PRINCE 8** [9] 5-8-10 (52) Dean McKeown 8/1: 0-0226: Bhd, eff 3f out, held fnl 2f: btr 418 (1m).   5   **35a**

344   **RIBBLE PRINCESS 19** [1] 5-9-1 (57)(VIS) S Drowne 33/1: 0/0-07: Led, hdd over 3f out, rdn &   ½   **39a**
wknd sn after: 1st time visor: see 344 (sell).

*270   **AL MABROOK 30** [5] 5-9-5 (61) Iona Wands (5) 12/1: 500-18: Handy, lost tch fnl 2f: op 8/1:   2   **40a**
disapp first run for A R Ryan, much better for K Mahdi in 270.

329   **NAKED OAT 22** [13] 5-9-4 (60) J Bosley (7) 12/1: 600-09: Prom, fdd fnl 3f: see 329.   1½   **36a**

3407}   **MONO LADY 99** [4] 7-9-12 (68)(bl) A Mackay 12/1: 5420-0: Al bhd, fin 10th: '99 wnr at Chester   6   **36a**
(h'cap, rtd 72 at best): '98 wnr at Leicester (h'cap, rtd 73), prev term won 4 times (h'caps, rtd 72a & 70): eff at 10/12.5f: acts on firm, gd/soft & both AWs: runs well fresh on any trk, with/without blnks.

3675}   **SUMMER BOUNTY 99** [6] 4-10-0 (70) A Culhane 12/1: 3602-0: Keen in tch, wknd qckly fnl 2f,   7   **30a**
fin 11th, top-weight: 10 wk jumps abs (unplcd, rtd 94h, juv nov): '99 Flat wnr at Lingfield (mdn, rtd 78a, with B Hills), plcd on turf (h'cap, rtd 80): eff at 7f/10f: acts on fast, gd & equitrack: has tried blnks, best without.

359   **Murron Wallace 16** [8] 6-7-10 (38)(1oh) J Bramhill 50/4:   **No No Nora** [12] 5-7-12 (40) P Fessey 66/1:
13 ran   Time 2m 02.1 (3.9)   (J Morley)   Sir Mark Prescott Newmarket

---

Official Going   STANDARD. Stalls: Inside.

470   **1.30 BET DIRECT AMAT HCAP 4YO+ 0-80 (F)**   **2m aw**   Going 67   -104 Slow   [46]
£2299   £657   £328   4 yo rec 6 lb

922}   **THROWER 99** [8] S A Brookshaw 9-10-4 (50) Mrs S Owen (5) 13/2: 4/11-1: 9 b g Thowra - Atlantic   shd   **56a**
Line (Capricorn Line) Trkd ldrs wide halfway, rdn/ev ch when hmpd 1f out, switched & styd on well ins last, just held: fin 2nd, plcd 1st: slow time: 10 month abs: '99 wnr of both starts, at Leicester (h'cap) & Nottingham (amat h'cap, rtd 51): 97/98 wnr over timber at Bangor & thrice at Haydock (rtd 128h): eff at 10/12f, stays a sharp 2m well: acts on firm, soft & fibresand: eff forcing the pace: runs well fresh: handles any trk: tough & genuine.

*412   **ST LAWRENCE 10** [11] B S Rothwell 6-9-10 (42) Mr Nicky Tinkler (5) 8/1: -2311D: 6 gr g With   **47a**
Approval - Mingan Isle (Lord Avie) Held up in tch wide, prog/led over 5f out, rdn/hung left ins last, just held: fin first, disqual & plcd 2nd: jockey given a 2-day ban for careless riding: op 5/1, prev with N Tinkler: in fine form.

412   **GRAND CRU 10** [10] J Cullinan 9-10-4 (50)(vis) Miss L Vollaro (5) 9/2: 41-423: 9 ch g Kabour -   1½   **53a**
Hydrangea (Warpath) Held up in tch, trkd ldrs halfway, ev ch fnl 2f, onepace: also bhd today's 2nd in 412.

348   **JAMAICAN FLIGHT 20** [4] Mrs S Lamyman 7-11-6 (66) Mr S Dobson (5) 4/1 FAV: 5-3344: Led/dsptd   ½   **68a**
lead till rdn/outpcd fnl 2f, kept on for press, not pace to chall: op 5/1, suited by setting stronger pace.

182   **URGENT SWIFT 56** [5] 7-11-2 (62) Mrs J Powell (7) 12/1: 0523-5: Chsd ldrs ch fnl 3f out, sn held: abs.   3½   **60a**

380   **STEAMROLLER STANLY 16** [7] 6-11-7 (67) Miss R Clark 9/1: -35246: Trkd ldrs halfway, outpcd fnl 3f.   2   **63a**

348   **PIPE MUSIC 20** [3] 5-11-0 (60)(bl) Miss A Armitage (5) 9/2: 36-327: Led/dsptd lead 6f, rdn/btn 4f out.   6   **50a**

413   **CLARINCH CLAYMORE 10** [1] 4-9-12 (50) Mr T Best (5) 7/1: 20-238: Chsd ldrs 14f: see 324, 131 (11f).   shd   **40a**

620}   **SPECIALIZE 99** [7] 8-9-6 (38)(bl)(3ow)(5oh) Miss K Warnett (0) 25/1: 40/3-9: Prom, btn 3f out: 1¼   **27a**
jumps fit (mod recent form, June '99 wnr at Uttoxeter, rtd 124c, h'cap, eff at 2m/3m on firm & hvy, blnks/visor): plcd in '99 on the level (rtd 27a, mdn h'cap): rnr-up in '98 (rtd 31a): stays a sharp 12f: handles fibresand.

2588}   **NOSEY NATIVE 99** [9] 7-9-5 (37) Mrs L Pearce 20/1: 3000-0: Struggling fnl 5f: 10th: 7 month abs: 15   **15a**
plcd in '99 (rtd 34a, amat h'cap, rtd 42 on turf): '98 wnr at Ripon & Catterick (h'caps, rtd 47 & 50a at best): eff at 14f/2m, suited by 12f: acts on fast, gd/soft & fibresand, handles equitrack: best without a vis: handles any trk.

37   **CASTLE SECRET 87** [2] 14-10-3 (35)(14ow) Mr R Bailey (0) 50/1: 0/00-0: Sn bhd: 11th: 12 wk abs.   *dist*   **0a**
11 ran   Time 3m 53.3 (27.3)   (C M & S J Owen)   S A Brookshaw Uffington, Shropshire.

---

471   **2.0 TEXT P372 HCAP DIV 1 4YO+ 0-60 (F)**   **7f aw rnd**   Going 67   -12 Slow   [60]
£1939   £554   £277

368   **ITCH 17** [4] R Bastiman 5-8-11 (43) T Williams 5/2 FAV: 0-2131: 5 b h Puissance - Panienka (Dom   **50a**
Racine) Prom, led over 2f out, sn in command, styd on strongly, rdn out: op 7/2: recent wnr here at Southwell (C/D h'cap): unplcd in '99 (tried a visor): eff at 6f, suited by a sharp 7f, may stay further: acts on gd/soft, likes fibresand: handles a stiff/undul or sharp trk, likes Southwell: in great heart, can win again.

438   **UTAH 5** [10] G L Moore 6-8-8 (40)(bl) Martin Dwyer 7/1: 0-0432: 6 b g High Estate - Easy Romance   3   **41a**
(Northern Jove) Rdn/bhd & wide, styd on well fnl 2f, nrst fin: 1m mdn h'caps will suit: see 438, 220.

*367   **CITY REACH 7** [7] P J Makin 4-10-0 (60)(vis) D Sweeney 6/1: 32-413: 4 b g Petong - Alzada (Alzao)   3½   **54a**
Towards rear, prog wide/cl-up 3f out, rdn/onepcd fnl 2f: op 9/2: return to h'caps after C/D mdn win in 367.

411   **GODMERSHAM PARK 11** [9] P S Felgate 8-9-1 (47) Dean McKeown 7/1: 05-234: Led 5f, fdd: see 45.   1   **39a**

431   **SEA YA MAITE 6** [3] 6-9-12 (58) S Finnamore (7) 7/1: 531565: Mid-div, eff 3f out/no impress: op 11/2.   1¾   **47a**

3307}   **OCHOS RIOS 99** [2] 9-8-5 (37) A Culhane 20/1: 0000-6: Rear, rdn/late gains, no threat: 6 month abs: 3   **20a**

plcd in '99 (rtd 46, clmr): '98 wnr at Beverley & Thirsk (hcaps, rtd 50): eff at 7f/1m on fast & soft: AW bow today.

r418	**MUTAHADETH** 10 [6]	6-9-11 (57)(bl) J Fanning 10/1: -32567: Mid-div at best: best at 1m, btr 183.		6	31a
218	**GOLD EDGE** 48 [11]	6-7-13 (31) P Fessey 33/1: 0500-8: Chsd ldrs 5f: 7 wk abs: see 148 (6f).		4	0a
341	**FRENCH CONNECTION** 21 [5]	5-9-2 (48) T G McLaughlin 8/1: 05-629: Rdn/al bhd: op 6/1, with B Leavy.	shd		14a
*396	**RA RA RASPUTIN** 13 [8]	5-9-4 (50) N Carlisle 8/1: 0-1410: Sn rdn/bhd: 10th: op 6/1, now with B Baugh.		3	10a
340	**SWAMPY** 21 [1]	4-8-10 (42) S Righton 16/1: 20-540: Cl-up 4f, wknd qckly: 11th: op 14/1: see 340, 189.		17	0a

11 ran   Time 1m 32.1 (5.5)   (Robin Bastiman)   R Bastiman Cowthorpe, N.Yorks.

---

472   2.30 0800 211222 MDN 3YO+ (E)   6f aw rnd Going 67 -21 Slow
£2769   £426   £213   3 yo rec 15lb

--	**CASTLEBAR** [5]	Miss Gay Kelleway 3-8-9 N Callan 11/2: 1: 3 b g Formidable - Nineteenth Of May (Homing) Sn prom, led 2f out, rdn/prsd over 1f out, asserted ins last, rdn out: op 7/2, debut: IR 20,000gns yearling: related to useful AW mid-dist performer Quintrell Downs, half-brother to smart/progressive 10f AW wnr Zanay: eff at 6f, 7f+ shld suit: acts on fibresand & a sharp trk: runs well fresh: open to improvement.			66a
389	**ABOVE BOARD** 14 [7]	R F Marvin 5-9-10 (bl) T G McLaughlin 20/1: -50002: 5 b g Night Shift - Bundled Up (Sharpen Up) Chsd ldrs halfway, rdn & kept on fnl 2f, not able to chall: offic rtd 36, treat rating with caution.	1½		59$
--	**NITE OWL MATE** [8]	G Woodward 3-8-9 C Lowther 100/30: 3: 3 b c Komaite - Nite Owl Dancer (Robellino) Dwelt/towards rear, prog wide to chall fnl 2f, rdn/no extra ins last: nicely bckd, op 7/2: dam a 5f wnr: eff at 6f on fibresand: fr clr of rem: could improve.	shd		59a
34	**KIND EMPEROR** 87 [6]	M J Polglase 3-8-9 Dean McKeown 11/4: 0203-4: Led 4f/sn btn: abs, op 7/4.		7	46a
417	**ALL MINE** 10 [4]	3-8-9 (etBL) J Stack 25/1: 6065: Chsd ldrs 4f: blnks: see 417 (seller).		6	35a
399	**ABSOLUTE FANTASY** 12 [2]	4-9-5 (bl) S Carson (5) 9/1: 04-620: Struggling halfway: btr 399 (eq'track).		2	25a
2693}	**ELTARS** 99 [1]	3-8-9 S Righton 10/1: 0-7: Al towards rear: op 7/1, 7 month abs: AW bow: unplcd sole start in '99 (P T Walwyn, rtd 45): cost current connections 5,000gns: with R F Marvin.		12	13a
4539}	**MOUNT PARK** 99 [9]	3-8-4 A Culhane 5/2 FAV: 0253-8: Sn rdn/al outpcd: nicely bckd: 3 month abs: AW bow: plcd for H S Howe in '99 (rtd 70, mdn & h'cap): eff at 5/6f on fast & gd/soft: handles a sharp/gall trk.	1		1a
389	**READY TO ROCK** 14 [3]	4-9-10 A Clark 33/1: 030-09: Cl-up 3f: see 199 (seller).	½		3a

9 ran   Time 1m 18.6 (5.3)   (Mr & Mrs Gary Pinchen)   Miss Gay Kelleway Lingfield, Surrey.

---

473   3.00 BEST BETS HCAP 3YO+ 0-75 (E)   1m aw rnd Going 67 -06 Slow   [68]
£2782   £856   £428   £214   3 yo rec 19lb

*366	**PIPPAS PRIDE** 17 [8]	S R Bowring 5-9-5 (59) S Finnamore (7) 5/1: 1-1311: 5 ch g Pips Pride - Al Shany (Burslem) Chsd ldrs, prog to lead over 1f out, styd on strongly ins last, rdn out: op 9/2: earlier won twice here at Southwell (clmr & appr clmr): '99 winner again here at Southwell (clmr), Lingfield (h'cap, rtd 41a, M Fetherston Godley, no turf form): eff around a sharp 7f/1m: acts on both AWs, loves Southwell: runs well fresh: tough.			65a
*75	**OUT OF SIGHT** 80 [6]	B A McMahon 6-10-0 (68) Dean McKeown 4/1: 0001-2: 6 ch g Salse - Starr Danias (Sensitive Prince) Chsd ldr, rdn/led over 2f out, hdd over 1f out, onepace: abs, topweight, stays 1m.	1¼		70a
4459}	**PIPS BRAVE** 99 [5]	M J Polglase 4-8-11 (51)(bl) R Lappin 20/1: 0000-3: 4 b g Be My Chief - Pipistrelle (Shareef Dancer) Rear/rdn & chall fnl 2f, nrst fin: clr rem: 4 month abs: '99 wnr here at Southwell (mdn) & Warwick (h'cap, rtd 61a & 55): rtd 72 on turf in '98 (mdn, subs rtd 49a on AW): eff at 1m/ sharp 10.5f, tried further: acts on fast grnd & fibresand: eff in blnks: likes a sharp trk: sharper over 9/10f.	1¾		50a
383	**CHARTER FLIGHT** 16 [4]	A G Newcombe 4-9-11 (65) S Whitworth 10/1: 301-04: Chsd ldr, outpcd halfway.	6		55a
*418	**NICE BALANCE** 10 [1]	5-8-4 (44) Joanna Badger 15/2: 614315: Rear/rdn halfway, no impress: op 13/2.	1		32a
*430	**STRAVSEA** 7 [2]	5-9-5 (59)(6ex) P M Quinn (5) 7/1: 035116: Rear/wide, mod prog: btr 430 (fill h'cap).	nk		46a
*427	**BOND DIAMOND** 7 [3]	3-8-10 (69)(6ex) J Stack 11/4 FAV: 054-17: Cl-up 6f: well bckd: btr 427 (7f, mdn).	6		47a
309	**NOBLE CYRANO** 27 [9]	5-9-13 (67) F Norton 6/1: 02-108: Led 6f, sn btn: reportedly lame: see 251.	2		41a
282	**IRON MAN** 31 [7]	8-9-1 (55) S Righton 40/1: 212/09: Chsd ldrs, wknd qckly 3f out: see 282.	dist		0a

9 ran   Time 1m 44.8 (5.8)   (Roland M Wheatley)   S R Bowring Edwinstowe, Notts.

---

474   3.30 TEXT P368 HCAP 4YO+ 0-70 (E)   1m3f aw Going 67 -16 Slow   [70]
£2782   £856   £428   £214   4 yo rec 2 lb

456	**KIRISNIPPA** 3 [1]	Derrick Morris 5-8-9 (51) P Doe 6/1: 0-5131: 5 b g Beveled - KiriTe (Liboi) Held up in tch, rdn fnl 3f, styd on well for press to lead ins last, rdn out: op 5/1: qck reapp: recent wnr here at Southwell (C/D h'cap, first success): plcd on turf in '99 (rtd 67, mdn): suited by 11f, shld stay further: handles fast grnd, loves fibresand/Southwell: best without blnks/visor: in gd heart, can win again.			54a
302	**GREEN BOPPER** 28 [6]	G Woodward 7-10-0 (70) C Lowther 5/2 FAV: 620-52: 7 b g Green Dancer - Wayage (Mr Prospector) Trkd ldr, prog/led 4f out, rdn/hdd ins last & no extra cl-home: well bckd: topweight.	½		71a
359	**SURE QUEST** 18 [10]	D W P Arbuthnot 5-8-7 (49) S Whitworth 3/1: 000-23: 5 b g Sure Blade - Eagle's Quest (Legal Eagle) Wide/mid-div, rdn to chall fnl 2f, no extra ins last: tchd 7/2: well clr of rem: see 359.	1¾		48a
384	**MISS TAKE** 14 [4]	A G Newcombe 4-8-6 (50) T Williams 20/1: 05-004: Cl-up 6f: op 14/1: see 384 (1m).	8		40a
336	**SHEER FACE** 23 [8]	6-9-3 (59) Martin Dwyer 12/1: 40-565: Towards rear, rdn/held 3f out: op 10/1.	8		40a
390	**RIVER CAPTAIN** 14 [9]	7-8-8 (50)(t) N Callan 12/1: 500-06: Towards rear, eff wide 3f out, sn btn.	10		20a
378	**ANNADAWI** 16 [7]	5-9-12 (40)(BL)(2ow)(5oh) N Carlisle 16/1: 44-447: Held up in tch, btn 3f out: blnks.	6		1a
404	**WARRIOR KING** 11 [3]	6-7-10 (38)(vis)(15oh) A Polli (3) 66/1: -05008: Led 7f: visor reapp: see 254.	12		0a
390	**LOVE DIAMONDS** 14 [5]	4-9-11 (69) T G McLaughlin 13/2: 000-29: Rear, eff/btn 2f out: op 5/1: btr 390.	10		6a
309	**CIVIL LIBERTY** 27 [2]	7-9-8 (64)(t) R Price 10/1: 46-45P: Pulled up 3f out, broke leg, sadly died.			0a

10 ran   Time 2m 30.4 (9.1)   (Michael Appleby)   Derrick Morris Lambourn, Berks.

---

475   4.00 TEXT P372 SELLER 3YO+ (G)   6f aw rnd Going 67 +07 Fast
£1867   £533   £266   3 yo rec 15lb

*436	**DAHLIDYA** 6 [2]	M J Polglase 5-9-8 P Doe 1/1 FAV: -34611: 5 b m Midyan - Dahlawise (Caerleon) Dwelt, sn chsd ldrs, rdn/led 2f out & styd on strongly ins last, rdn out: well bckd: gd time: no bid: qck reapp: recent W'hampton wnr (seller): '99 Southwell wnr (h'cap, rtd 59a, mod turf form): '98 W'hampton & Southwell wnr (h'caps, rtd 52a): suited by 6f, eff btwn 5f/7f: acts on gd/soft & equitrack: fibresand specialist: best without blnks: likes to come with a late rattle & relishes sell grade.			67a
*389	**ELTON LEDGER** 14 [1]	Mrs N Macauley 11-9-13 (vis) R Fitzpatrick (3) 3/1: 06-212: 11 b g Cyrano de Bergerac - Princess Of Nashua (Crowned Prince) Taken down early, led till over 2f out, rdn/onepace: op 7/4.	2		66a
406	**BLUSHING GRENADIER** 11 [3]	S R Bowring 8-9-9 S Finnamore (7) 11/4: -33433: 8 ch g Salt Dome -		5	53a

SOUTHWELL (Fibresand)   MONDAY FEBRUARY 7TH   Lefthand, Sharp, Oval Track

La Duse (Junius) Cl-up, rdn/wknd fnl 2f: op 5/2: see 38.
406   **SING FOR ME 11** [4] R Hollinshead 5-9-4 Stephanie Hollinshea 50/1: 00-004: Handy, wide/briefly   6   37a
led over 2f out, sn held: see 272.
434   **HOT LEGS 6** [5] 4-9-4 Dean McKeown 11/1: 0-5455: Rdn/outpcd fnl 3f: qck reapp, op 14/1: see 379.   hd   36a
5 ran   Time 1m 16.9 (3.6)   (The Lovatt Partnership)   M J Polglase Southwell, Notts.

476	4.30 TEXT P372 HCAP DIV 2 4YO+ 0-60 (F) 7f aw rnd Going 67 -02 Slow	[60]
	£1939 £554 £277	

329   **MYSTIC RIDGE 24** [11] B J Curley 6-9-12 (58) J P Spencer 5/2: 100-41: 6 ch g Mystiko - Vallauris   65a
(Faustus) Prom, led 2f out & clr 1f out, held on well ins last, rdn out: well bckd, tchd 7/2: '99 wnr of
h'caps at Brighton, Leopardstown, Galway & Lingfield (rtd 75 & 17a at best): plcd in '98 (h'cap, rtd 55): suited
by 7f/1m, stays 12f: acts on firm, gd & fibresand: eff with/without blnks: handles any trk, enjoys a sharp/turning
one: best dominating & a gd weight carrier: shld win more races on this evidence.
+368   **ABERKEEN 17** [1] M Dods 5-9-13 (59) A Culhane 9/4 FAV: 03-212: 5 ch g Keen - Miss Aboyne   ¾   64a
(Lochnager) Rear, no room/switched 4f out, styd on well for press fnl 2f, nrst fin: nicely bckd: clr of rem, in form.
411   **MUTABARI 11** [9] Mrs S Lamyman 6-9-9 (55)(vis) J Fanning 5/1: -34253: 6 ch g Seeking The Gold -   9   47a
Cagey Exuberance (Exuberant) Prom, rdn/outpcd fnl 2f: tchd 7/1: visor reapplied: see 255.
389   **FLYING HIGH 14** [8] B Ellison 5-8-3 (35) F Norton 33/1: 000-64: Rear, late gains/nrst fin: see 389.   shd   27a
351   **PAGEBOY 20** [7] 11-8-8 (39)(vis) P Goode (4) 7/1: 66-445: Rear, rdn/mod gains: see 313, 138.   5   22a
87   **STRATS QUEST 77** [4] 6-8-10 (42)(vis) S Whitworth 9/1: 0045-6: Chsd ldrs, held fnl 2f: op 6/1, abs: 4   16a
'99 Southwell scorer (sell h'cap, rtd 47a, rnr-up on turf, rtd 51, fillies h'cap): plcd in '98 (h'cap, rtd 60, also
rated 38a): eff at 6f/sharp 7f, tried 1m: handles fast, suited by soft & fibresand: eff in a visor: enjoys sell grade.
3815} **LAA JADEED 99** [5] 5-8-9 (41) R Price 16/1: 0530-7: Chsd ldrs 5f: op 12/1: 5 month abs: '99   2   11a
Southwell wnr (appr auct mdn, rtd 46a, mod form subs incl on turf, rtd 42, h'cap): rtd 53 & 56a at best in '98
(J Glover): eff forcing the pace at 11f, tried further: acts on fibresand & soft grnd: has run well fresh.
368   **MOST RESPECTFUL 17** [6] 7-9-2 (48)(t) Kim Tinkler 16/1: 0-4308: Mid-div at best: see 249.   1½   15a
225   **HUNAN SCHOLAR 47** [10] 5-8-12 (44) D R McCabe 20/1: 0500-9: Towards rear/wide, no prog: abs: 2½   6a
ex-Irish, unplcd prev: may improve.
4232} **TAKER CHANCE 99** [2] 4-9-2 (48) N Callan 20/1: 1040-0: Mid-div, btn 3f out: 10th: jmps fit (rtd 92h).   9   0a
406   **WOODCUT 11** [3] 4-7-11 (29) P M Quinn 25/1: 000-00: Led 5f, sn btn: 11th: see 406.   2½   0a
11 ran   Time 1m 31.4 (4.8)   (P Byrne)   B J Curley Newmarket.

WOLVERHAMPTON (Fibresand)   TUESDAY FEBRUARY 8TH   Lefthand, Sharp Track

Official Going   STANDARD. Stalls: 7f - Outside; Rem - Inside.

477	1.40 CLASSIFIED STKS 4YO+ 0-60 (F) 1m100y aw rnd Going 43 +10 Fast
	£2341 £669 £334

+469   **FRENCH SPICE 3** [7] Sir Mark Prescott 4-9-1 D Sweeney 2/7 FAV: 1-1111: 4 b f Cadeaux Genereux -   72a
Hot Spice (Hotfoot) In tch going well, smooth hdwy 4f out, led 2f out, pushed out, cmftbly: nicely bckd, fast
time, qck reapp: 5 timer completed after 4 wins here at W'hampton (h'caps): unplcd/mod form early in '99 (rtd 41,
mdn): eff at 1m/9.4f, further shld suit: loves fibresand/W'hampton: tough & progressive, win more races.
3860} **ONE DINAR 99** [13] K Mahdi 5-8-12 A Culhane 12/1: 4610-2: 5 b h Generous - Lypharitissima   1   64a
(Lightning) Dwelt, imprvd halfway, chsd wnr fnl 2f, styd on well but al held: op 8/1 on reapp, clr rem: '99 wnr
at Lingfield (mdn, rtd 75): eff at 7f/8.5f, has tried 10f: acts on firm, gd & f/sand, any trk: fine reapp.
381   **DEMOCRACY 17** [5] P G Murphy 4-8-12 (bl) S Drowne 25/1: 0-0053: 4 ch g Common Grounds -   9   50a
Inonder (Belfort) Waited with, prog halfway, no extra fnl 2f: btr 263 (6f amat h'cap).
384   **BOBBYDAZZLE 15** [12] Dr J D Scargill 5-8-9 (ebl) F Norton 10/1: 003-24: Chsd ldrs, led halfway,   ½   46a
hdd 2f out & not pace of ldrs: op 8/1: btr 384.
374   **BARBASON 17** [4] 8-8-12 I Mongan (7) 12/1: 30-255: Bhd, rdn to improve over 3f out, kept on but   3   44a
no ch with ldrs: op 7/1: will appreciate a return to soft on equitrack: see 360.
*293   **RAIN RAIN GO AWAY 31** [1] 4-9-0 C Rutter 12/1: 433-16: Bhd, nvr a threat: much btr 293 (7f mdn).   1¾   43a
428   **STATE APPROVAL 8** [10] 7-8-12 N Callan 33/1: -60007: Mid-div at best: needs further: see 270.   nk   41a
432   **KILLARNEY JAZZ 7** [2] 5-8-12 (bl) C Carver (2) 14/1: 4-0038: In tch when stumbled after 2f &   1¼   39a
lost place, no threat after: qck reapp: ignore this: see 432.
405   **HEVER GOLF GLORY 12** [11] 6-8-12 (BL) N Carlisle 25/1: 0-0459: Led 4f, lost tch fnl 2f: blnks.   2   36a
126   **REGAL SPLENDOUR 70** [8] 8-8-12 Dean McKeown 33/1: 2660-0: Cl-up, fdd fnl 3f, fin 10th: 10 wk   1¾   33a
abs: rnr-up at Newmarket in '99 (amat h'cap, rtd 35, also rtd 48a): back in '97 won at Lingfield (amat h'cap, rtd
64a, R O'Sullivan): suited by 7f/1m: acts on firm & fast & both AWs.
383   **ULTRA CALM 17** [9] 4-8-12 (vis) P Goode (5) 10/1: 00-300: Handy, lost tch fnl 3f: 12th: btr 349 (9.4f).   0a
360   **Mutadarra 19** [6] 7-8-12 R Studholme (5) 33/1:   4387} **Gablesea 99** [3] 6-8-12 J Bosley (7) 33/1:
13 ran   Time 1m 49.0 (2.8)   (J Morley)   Sir Mark Prescott Newmarket

---

478	2.10 0800 211222 MDN 4YO+ (D) 7f aw rnd Going 43 -21 Slow
	£2588 £739 £369

--   **CHAMELEON** [8] M L W Bell 4-8-9 M Hills 6/1: 0/1: 4 b f Green Desert - Old Domesday Book   78+
(High Top) Waited with, smooth hdwy to lead dist, rdn clr: reapp/AW bow, drifted from 3/1: missed '99, well btn
sole '98 start (mdn, rtd 43): full sister to smart sprinter Owington, dam a 10f wnr: eff over 7f, 1m will suit:
acts on f/sand: runs v well fresh on a sharp trk: excellent reapp, can win more AW races.
3934} **PALAWAN 99** [4] I A Balding 4-9-0 A Nicholls 3/1: 4 FAV: 5220-2: 4 br g Polar Falcon - Krameria   7   71a
(Kris) Led, hdd over 1f out, flashed tail & no extra ins last: clr rem: reapp/AW bow: rnr-up 3 times in '99
(mdns, rtd 75 at best): half brother to a 1m wnr: eff btwn 5f & 7f: acts on gd & fast, handles fibresand.
399   **DEADLY SERIOUS 13** [2] D R C Elsworth 4-9-0 J Stack 7/1: 43: 4 ch c Emarati - Bentinck Hotel   5   63$
(Red God) Prom, hdwy over 3f out, wknd appr fnl 1f: op 5/1: up in trip: see 399 (6f, equitrack).
4426} **WELODY 99** [5] K Mahdi 4-9-0 A Culhane 4/1: /540-4: Sn outpcd, nvr with ldrs: gambled from   1¼   61a
16/1: rtd 71 at best from 3 '99 starts (7f mdn): shld do better in time over 1m+.
3228} **TEYAAR 99** [1] 4-9-0 (BL) N Callan 4/1: 2003-5: Keen in tch, wknd fnl 3f: op 3/1, blnkd on reapp/   nk   61a
AW bow: plcd twice in '99 (mdns, rtd 85 at best): stays 7f, handles firm & soft: needs to settle better.

678} **KUWAIT FLAVOUR 99** [7] 4-9-0 C Lowther 6/1: 4/3-6: Al outpcd on reapp: plcd on sole '99 start   3   56a
(6f mdn, rtd 69), rtd 64 when 4th sole '98 start: shld apprec 1m+ in time.
446   **UNCLE OBERON 5** [3] 4-9-0 J P Spencer 25/1: /50-67: Al bhd: quick reapp: see 446.   6   47a
--   **LASTOFTHECASH** [6] 4-9-0 T G McLaughlin 20/1: 8: Dwelt, al last: debut, with N P Littmoden.   ½   46a
8 ran   Time 1m 30.7 (4.5)   (Lordship Stud)   M L W Bell Newmarket

---

479
2.40 TOTE HCAP 3YO 0-75 (E)   **6f aw rnd**   **Going 43**   **-07 Slow**   [77]
£5135   £1580   £790   £395

444   **CASTLE SEMPILL 6** [7] R M H Cowell 3-9-7 (70)(vis) R Studholme (5) 2/1 FAV: 31-121: 3 b c Presidium   78a
- La Suquet (Puissance) Cl-up, hdwy to lead over 2f out, pushed out, cmftbly: qck reapp: recent Lingfield wnr
(h'cap): '99 wnr at Newmarket (sell, rtd 74, J Fanshawe) & Lingfield (h'cap): eff at 5/7f, has tried 1m: acts
on firm, soft & fibresand, loves equitrack/Lingfield: eff with/without a visor: tough, genuine & in fine form.
427   **STOP THE TRAFFIC 8** [4] C N Allen 3-8-12 (61) R Morse 6/1: 0-4252: 3 b f College Chapel - Miss   1¼   64a
Bagatelle (Mummy's Pet) Led, hdd over 2f out, not pace of wnr ins last: shown enough to win a race: see 397.
450   **LOUS WISH 5** [1] M J Polglase 3-9-2 (65)(bl) R Fitzpatrick (3) 7/1: -31263: 3 b g Thatching -   1¼   65a
Shamaka (Kris) Sn rdn in rear, gd hdwy fnl 2f, styd on, nrst fin: quick reapp: needs 7f+: see 346.
426   **RISKY GEM 8** [6] J Pearce 3-9-3 (66) A Polli (3) 7/1: 600-24: Sn outpcd, mod late gains: 5   56a
jockey reportedly received a 4 day whip ban: better on reapp in 426 (clmr).
416   **AISLE 11** [3] 3-8-11 (60) S Finnamore (7) 9/2: -52255: Nvr a threat: btr 365.   nk   50a
373   **ITSGOTTABDUN 17** [2] 3-8-9 (58)(VIS) C Catlin (7) 16/1: 3-4406: In tch, wknd over 2f out: visor.   2   42a
*426   **CHRISTOPHERSSISTER 8** [8] 3-9-5 (68)(6ex) A Nicholls (3) 7/1: 520-17: Prom 3f, sn btn: op 5/1:   5   42a
prev with T J Etherington, better expected on today's debut for D Nicholls: see 448 (C/D).
361   **MISS SKICAP 19** [5] 3-9-5 (68) I Mongan (7) 8/1: 421-48: Handy, btn fnl 3f: op 5/1: btr 228 (clmr).   shd   42a
8 ran   Time 1m 15.8 (3.0)   (Mrs J M Penney)   R M H Cowell Six Mile Bottom, Cambs

---

480
3.10 BEST BETS COND STKS 3YO+ (C)   **1m1f79y aw**   **Going 43**   **-05 Slow**
£6107   £2167   £1083   £492

448   **ADELPHI BOY 5** [3] M C Chapman 4-9-8 R Studholme (5) 9/1: 24-031: 4 ch g Ballad Rock - Toda   102a
(Absalom) V keen, chsd ldrs, gd hdwy 2f out, styd on well to lead ins last, drvn out: op 6/1, qck reapp: plcd sev
times in '99 (h'caps, rtd 73 & 92a): '98 wnr at Southwell (2, mdn & nurs) & Lingfield (h'cap, rtd 91a & 80): suited
by 7/9.4f, has tried 10f: acts on fast, soft & both AWs: handles any trk, likes a sharp one: tough & useful.
448   **WEET A MINUTE 5** [2] R Hollinshead 7-9-8 A Culhane 8/11 FAV: 01-222: 7 ro h Nobeel Dancer -   ¾   100a
Ludovica (Bustino) Cl-up, hdwy to lead 3f out, rdn/hdd ins last, no extra: ahead of today's wnr in 448 (8.5f).
*448   **KING PRIAM 5** [1] M J Polglase 5-10-0 (bl) R Fitzpatrick (3) 11/4: 52-313: 5 b g Priolo - Barinia   3½   100a
(Corvaro) Prom, rdn/not pace of ldrs appr fnl 1f: not disgraced under top-weight: beat today's front 2 in 448.
422   **HUGWITY 10** [4] G C Bravery 5-9-8 M Hills 9/2: -01124: Led, hdd 3f out, rdn & no extra fnl 2f: shd   94$
op 3/1: stiff task at the weights here (offic only 83): will apprec a return to 10f+: see 375 (clmr).
4 ran   Time 2m 02.8 (4.6)   (Barry Brown)   M C Chapman Market Rasen, Lincs

---

481
3.40 TEXT P368 SELLER 3YO (G)   **1m1f79y aw**   **Going 43**   **-43 Slow**
£1822   £520   £260

*350   **CASTLEBRIDGE 21** [4] M C Pipe 3-9-3 (vis) J P Spencer 1/1 FAV: 00-011: 3 b g Batshoof - Super   71a
Sisters (Call Report) Chsd ldrs, smooth hdwy to lead halfway, went clr on bit 2f out, easily: well bckd, new stable:
bt in for 10,200gns: earlier won for D Morris here at W'hampton (sell, 1st time visor): mod form prev: eff at 1m/
9.4f, further shld suit: rejuvenated by visor recently: can win more races for new connections.
*382   **WILEMMGEO 17** [6] P C Haslam 3-8-12 (vis) P Goode (5) 3/1: 10-212: 3 b f Emarati - Floral Spark   4   54a
(Forzando) Bhd, hdwy over 3f out, styd on, not pace of easy wnr: clr rem: consistent plater: see 382 (C/D).
303   **XENOS 29** [1] P Howling 3-8-12 T Williams 20/1: 0-0563: 3 b g Owington - Little Change (Grundy)   6   44a
Handy, rdn & no extra fnl 2f: longer 9.4f trip: see 424 (6f, equitrack).
429   **DR DUKE 8** [3] Mrs N Macauley 3-8-12 (bl) Dean McKeown 20/1: 5-4064: In tch, rcd wide 3f out,   2½   40a
sn rdn & no threat after: see 241 (1m clmr, equitrack).
*429   **AMELIA JESS 8** [5] 3-8-12 (t) Joanna Badger (7) 7/2: 0-2315: Led 2f, rdn/wknd 2f out: btr 429.   2   36a
281   **COSMIC SONG 32** [2] 3-8-7 A Culhane 8/1: 005-56: Led 7f out to halfway, hmpd 3f out, wknd, t.o.   26   0a
6 ran   Time 2m 06.3 (8.1)   (David S Lewis)   M C Pipe Nicholashayne, Devon

---

482
4.10 TEXT P372 HCAP 4YO+ 0-65 (F)   **2m46y aw**   **Going 43**   **-44 Slow**   [65]
£2352   £672   £336   4 yo rec 6 lb

424   **MAKNAAS 10** [5] T G Mills 4-8-10 (53) A Clark 9/2: 1-4151: 4 ch c Wolfhound - White Wash (Final   66a
Straw) Led & sn clr, pressed 3f out, rdn & went clr again appr fnl 1f: earlier won at Lingfield (amat h'cap): '99
W'hampton wnr (h'cap, rtd 52a), plcd on turf for R Armstrong (mdn h'cap, rtd 49): eff at 1m, suited by 2m: acts on
soft & both AWs: loves to race up with/force the pace on sharp trks: eff with/without blinkers: remains in fine form.
428   **MY LEGAL EAGLE 8** [8] R J Price 6-8-3 (40) P Doe 10/1: 04-032: 6 b g Law Society - Majestic Nurse   7   45a
(On Your Mark) Waited with, chsd ldr 6f out, no extra for press fnl 2f: clr rem: see 428.
253   **ROYAL EXPRESSION 36** [4] G M Moore 8-8-12 N Callan 7/1: 201-63: 8 b g Sylvan Express -   5   63a
Edwins' Princess (Owen Dudley) Handy, rdn/btn appr fnl 2f: new stable, prev with F Jordan: see 190 (C/D).
407   **SILVER GYRE 12** [1] D J Wintle 4-8-5 (48) C Rutter 7/1: 006-64: Mid-div, nvr with ldrs: see 407.   4   45a
*428   **BUSTLING RIO 8** [2] 4-9-10 (67)(6ex) P Goode (5) 4/5 FAV: 421-15: Waited with, gd hdwy 5f out,   8   58a
wknd fnl 3f: well bckd: disapp run, has shown best form at Southwell: see 428.
2816} **HETRA HEIGHTS 99** [9] 5-8-1 (37)(1ow) L Newton 33/1: 2-05-08: Bhd, eff 5f out, nvr with ldrs: reapp: ½   28a
unplcd in '99, subs had a wind operation: '98 rnr-up (h'cap, rtd 51): eff at 12f on fast: sharper next time.
*318   **MEDELAI 26** [10] 4-8-1 (44) A McCarthy (3) 6/1: 02-017: Rear, hdwy 5f out, styd on: btr 318 (C/D).   6   29a
285   **MACHIAVELLI 31** [11] 6-10-0 (65)(bl) I Mongan (7) 12/1: 0/6-58: Cl-up, btn fnl 5f: see 285 (equitrack).   3   47a
277   **SCONCED 33** [3] 5-7-12 (35)(vis)(2ow)(10oh) P Fessey 20/1: 533-09: In tch, wknd fnl 4f: stiff task.   6   12a
413   **NUBILE 11** [7] 6-7-10 (33)(bl)(5oh) P M Quinn (5) 25/1: 160-60: Al bhd, fin 10th: see 413.   4   6a
10 ran   Time 3m 43.4 (14.2)   (Travel Spot Ltd)   T G Mills Headley, Surrey

LINGFIELD (Equitrack)   WEDNESDAY FEBRUARY 9TH   Lefthand, V Sharp Track

Official Going   STANDARD. Stalls: 5f - Outside, Rem - Inside

483

2.10 BET MED AUCT MDN 4-6YO (F)   **1m5f aw**   **Going 25**   **-05 Slow**
£2205   £630   £315   4 yo rec 4 lb

370 **WESTERN RAINBOW** 19 [4] P D Evans 4-9-0 J P Spencer 8/11 FAV: 2-2241: 4 b g Rainbows For Life - Miss Galwegian (Sandford Lad) Handy halfway, smooth prog to lead 2f out, al in command after, easily: val for 8L+: hvly bckd: blnks omitted: rtd 34 on turf in '99 (H Akbary, h'cap): eff at 12/13f: acts on both AWs & likes a sharp trk: has run well in blnks: can rate more highly, poss when tackling further.   **58a**

219 **COCO GIRL** 49 [5] Mrs A E Johnson 4-8-9 P Doe 9/1: 4604-2: 4 ch f Mystiko - Cantico (Green Dancer) Handy, led 5f out, rdn/hdd 2f out, kept on for press: flattered by margin of defeat: op 7/1, 7 wk abs: eff at 13f & handles equitrack: clr of rem here: see 219 (C/D, h'cap).   **1¾ 41a**

284 **TOY STORY** 33 [8] Miss Gay Kelleway 4-9-0 (VIS) N Callan 100/30: 602-63: 4 b g Fijar Tango - Grundygold (Grundy) Prom, rdn 4f out, sn btn: nicely bckd in 1st time visor: btr 196 (11f, fibresand).   **6 37a**

265 **ROOKIE** 35 [2] Mrs A E Johnson 4-9-0 A McCarthy (3) 13/2: 020-04: Keen/led 1m, sn btn: blnks omitted: rnr-up thrice in '99 (rtd 58a, 4 rnr mdn & 68, auct mdn, C Cyzer): eff at 1m/10f, handles fast & eqtrk.   **7 27a**

1614} **BALLA DAIRE** 99 [1] 5-9-4 (bl) A Clark 25/1: 4/00-5: Cl-up 3f, rdn/btn 5f out: jumps fit (rtd 71h, sell): rtd 39a at best in '99 (h'cap): rtd 56 in '98 (M Bell, mdn): no improvement in blnks.   **2½ 23a**

402 **FLORA DREAMBIRD** 14 [7] 6-8-13 (bl) J Bosley 33/1: 6-0056: Keen/chsd ldrs 5f: see 284.   **1¾ 16a**

3914} **HAMERKOP** 99 [3] 5-8-13 (e) D Williamson 7/1: 5605-7: Slowly away/al bhd: jumps fit (plcd, sell hdle, rtd 59h): rtd 44 at best in '99 on the level (clmr): stays 1m & handles gd grnd: has tried blnks.   **2½ 12a**

196 **ELENII** 54 [6] 4-8-9 (BL) P M Quinn 50/1: 0500-8: Sn bhd: blnks: jumps fit.   *dist* **0a**

8 ran   Time 2m 46.21 (3.91)   (J D Duggan)   P D Evans Leighton, Powys

484

2.40 CLASSIFIED CLAIMER 4YO+ 0-60 (F)   **6f aw rnd**   **Going 25**   **-03 Slow**
£2081   £594   £297

396 **COLLEGE BLUE** 15 [2] G L Moore 4-8-2 F Norton 6/1: 2-2001: 4 b f College Chapel - Mitsubishi Centre (Thatching) Trkd ldr, led 2f out, styd on strongly fnl 1f, rdn out: op 5/1: prev with T G Mills, rnr-up on sole '99 start (rtd 75a, mdn): rcd twice in '98 (rtd 82 & 77a): eff at 5/6f: acts on both AWs & fast grnd: likes a sharp/turning trk: eff with/without a visor: 1st success today, apprec drop to clmg grade.   **58a**

398 **PALACEGATE TOUCH** 14 [9] A Berry 10-8-7 (bl) P Bradley (5) 7/2: 25-342: 10 gr g Petong - Dancing Chimes (London Bells) Sltly hmpd after 1f, mid-div, styd on fnl 2f for press, no ch with wnr: tchd 9/2: no luck in running from tricky high draw: loves to force the pace & this genuine 10yo could find similar: see 92, 61.   **6 52a**

414 **CARAMBO** 12 [1] T D Barron 5-8-8 (bl) N Callan 9/2: 00-643: 5 b m Rambo Dancer - Light The Way (Nicholas Bill) Led, rdn/hdd 2f out, wknd ins last: op 3/1: acts on fast, gd/soft & both AWs: see 180 (fbrsnd).   **1 51a**

414 **DOLPHINELLE** 12 [5] R Hannon 4-8-13 R Winston 3/1 FAV: -10454: Twds rear, rdn/late gains: op 5/2.   **½ 54a**

341 **CHALUZ** 23 [4] 6-8-5 (vis) J Tate 8/1: 5-4255: Chsd ldrs, onepace fnl 2f: op 10/1: see 310, 75.   **1½ 42a**

472 **READY TO ROCK** 2 [7] 4-8-1 (bl) P M Quinn (5) 16/1: 30-006: Chsd ldrs halfway/sn btn: qck reapp.   **½ 36a**

358 **PRIORY GARDENS** 21 [3] 6-8-5 A Daly 40/1: 0-3007: Sn rdn/outpcd: see 262.   **2 35$**

354 **SUPERLAO** 21 [8] 8-7-12 (bl) G Baker 66/1: 06-058: Wide/rear, nvr factor: blnks reapp: see 354.   **2½ 21a**

440 **CHAKRA** 7 [6] 6-8-5 A Clark 20/1: 0-0659: Chsd ldrs 4f: op 12/1: see 358.   **½ 26a**

436 **FACILE TIGRE** 8 [11] 5-8-5 P Doe 12/1: 66-060: Twds rear/wide, nvr factor: 10th: op 7/1: see 146 (5f).   **½ 24a**

125} **ADORABLE** 99 [10] 4-8-0 P Fessey 66/1: 000/0: Al outpcd: 11th: long abs/no form: with T D McCarthy.   **14 0a**

11 ran   Time 1m 12.1 (1.7)   (Danny Bloor)   G L Moore Woodingdean, E Sussex

485

3.10 BEST BETS HCAP 4YO+ 0-95 (C)   **1m aw rnd**   **Going 25**   **+10 Fast**   **[91]**
£6435   £1980   £990   £495

423 **SALTY JACK** 11 [2] V Soane 6-9-4 (81) Martin Dwyer 3/1: 01-021: 6 b h Salt Dome - Play The Queen (King Of Clubs) Trkd ldrs, rdn/led ins last, held on gamely nr fin, drvn out: well bckd, op 4/1: gd time: rnr-up twice on turf in '99 (rtd 89, val h'cap), subs scored here at Lingfield (h'cap, rtd 81a): '98 wnr at Doncaster, Folkestone (ltd stks), Epsom & Newmarket (h'caps, rtd 89 & 75a at best): suited by 7f, stays a sharp 1m well: acts on firm, hvy & equitrack: handles any trk, likes Lingfield: has run well fresh: gd weight carrier: tough & genuine.   **86a**

398 **RONS PET** 14 [1] K R Burke 5-8-9 (72)(tbl) N Callan 10/1: 0-2332: 5 ch g Ron's Victory - Penny Mint (Mummy's Game) Led, rdn 2f out, hdd ins last, kept on well nr fin, just held: op 6/1: blnks reapplied.   **nk 76a**

*463 **TOPTON** 4 [7] P Howling 6-10-0 (91)(bl) (6ex) A Clark 4/1: -42613: 6 b g Royal Academy - Circo (High Top) Rdn/cl-up, ev ch over 1f out, onepace: 6lb pen for recent win: op 3/1: see 463 (C/D).   **1½ 92a**

463 **ELMHURST BOY** 4 [4] S Dow 4-9-5 (82)(vis) W Ryan 8/1: 021-54: Held up in tch, prog/trkd ldrs 2f out, onepace ins last: op 6/1, quick reapp: also bhd today's 3rd winner: see 239 (7f).   **shd 83a**

423 **SECRET SPRING** 11 [6] 8-9-12 (89) O Urbina 11/4 FAV: 1-4005: Held up in tch, rdn/outpcd fnl 3f.   **4 82a**

423 **SONG OF SKYE** 11 [5] 6-8-11 (74) F Norton 13/2: 22-036: Held up, rdn/outpcd fnl 3f, eased fnl 1f.   **¾ 66a**

448 **ITALIAN SYMPHONY** 6 [3] 6-10-0 (91)(vis) J P Spencer 14/1: -05057: Chsd ldrs, btn 2f out: op 8/1.   **1¾ 80a**

7 ran   Time 1m 37.37 (1.17)   (Salts Of The Earth)   V Soane East Garston, Berks

486

3.40 TERRY MAHER HCAP 4YO+ 0-80 (D)   **1m4f aw**   **Going 25**   **-01 Slow**   **[80]**
£3803   £1170   £585   £292   4 yo rec 3 lb

441 **HAWKSBILL HENRY** 7 [7] Mrs A J Perrett 6-8-1 (53) G Bardwell 12/1: 0-0131: 6 ch g Known Fact - Novel Approach (Codex) Made all, styd on strongly fnl 1f, rdn out: earlier won here at Lingfield (amat h'cap): rnr-up thrice in '99 (stks, rtd 61a & 50): '98 wnr here at Lingfield (h'cap, rtd 56a & 49): eff at 9/12f: acts on fast, gd grnd & loves equitrack/Lingfield: has run well fresh: best without blnks/visor: eff forcing the pace: in gd heart.   **62a**

356 **SPACE RACE** 21 [3] C A Cyzer 6-10-0 (80) G Carter 11/2: 02-162: 6 b g Rock Hopper - Melanoura (Imperial Fling) Prom, trkd wnr 3f out, chall 2f out, sn rdn/no impress: op 9/2: top weight: see 245 (C/D).   **5 82a**

*441 **FUSUL** 7 [6] G L Moore 4-8-2 (57)(6ex) P Doe 8/11 FAV: 04-113: 4 ch c Miswaki - Silent Turn (Silent Cal) Cl-up halfway till 3f out, sn rdn/outpcd by front pair: hvly bckd: 6lb pen for 441.   **2½ 55a**

422 **NOUKARI** 11 [1] P D Evans 7-9-12 (78) J P Spencer 8/1: -20544: Held up in tch/outpcd fnl 3f: btr 151.   **hd 75a**

400 **SERGEANT IMP** 14 [5] 5-7-10 (48)(10oh) P M Quinn 15/1: 00-335: Rear/rdn halfway, eff 3f out/sn held.   **4 39a**

1755} **PASSIONS PLAYTHING** 99 [2] 4-9-6 (75) Martin Dwyer 12/1: 044-6: Chsd wnr 1m, sn btn/eased fnl 2f: op 10/1, 8 month abs: AW/h'cap bow: promise from 3 starts at 1m in '99 (rtd 44, mdn): bred to apprec mid-dists: stays a sharp 1m & handles gd grnd.   **12 53a**

LINGFIELD (Equitrack)   WEDNESDAY FEBRUARY 9TH   Lefthand, V Sharp Track

290   **CONFRONTER 32** [4] 11-8-1 (53) F Norton 20/1: 645-07: Twds rear, btn 4f out/sn eased: see 161 (10f).   6   22a
7 ran   Time 2m 32.35 (3.15)   (Miss G Harwood)   Mrs A J Perrett Pulborough, W Sussex

487

4.10 NAC RE SELLER 3YO (G)   5f aw rnd   Going 25 -13 Slow
£1825   £521   £260

426   **PAPE DIOUF 9** [1] B Smart 3-8-12 (bl) J Stack 9/2: 550-01: 3 b g Prince Sabo - Born To Dance   56a
(Dancing Brave) Made all, styd on well when prsd over 1f out, rdn out: no bid: tchd 11/2: blnks reapplied: rnr-
up in '99 twice for K McAuliffe (rtd 64a, sell & 63, h'cap): eff at 5f: acts on firm, fast & both AWs: galvanised
by reapplication of blnks & return to sell grade & appeared well suited by forcing tactics.
346   **POWER AND DEMAND 22** [2] D Shaw 3-8-12 (BL) F Norton 10/1: 604-02: 3 b g Formidable - Mazurkanova   2½   49a
(Song) Trkd ldrs halfway, rdn/chsd wnr over 1f out, rdn/held ins last: tchd 12/1, gd run in 1st time blnks.
331   **CLOPTON GREEN 26** [6] J W Payne 3-8-12 (BL) N Callan 14/1: 306-03: 3 b g Presidium - Silkstone   2   44a
Lady (Puissance) Chsd ldrs, rdn/onepace fnl 2f: op 10/1, 1st time blnks: eff at 5f on equitrack: see 46 (fbrsnd).
*357   **MINIMUS TIME 21** [5] T M Jones 3-9-0 (bl) A Clark 3/1 FAV: 06-014: Chsd wnr halfway, btn over 1f   2½   39a
out: nicely bckd, op 5/1: see 357 (C/D, made all).
443   **MASTER JONES 7** [3] 3-8-12 (BL) A Culhane 4/1: -23325: Prom, outpcd fnl 2f: blnks: op 7/2.   ½   35a
445   **BRIEF CALL 6** [7] 3-8-7 D Sweeney 9/1: 035-06: Wide/towards rear, nvr factor: op 7/1, quick reapp: 2   25a
plcd in '99 (rtd 71, fill stks & 54a, sell): eff at 5f, tried 6f: handles firm & fibresand: best without a visor.
*443   **JANICELAND 7** [8] 3-9-0 (VIS) J Tate 7/2: 541-17: Slowly away & well bhd, no impress after: well   1   30a
bckd tho' op 2/1: lost ch at start in 1st time visor, best forgotten: see 443 (6f).
--   **ADDICKS ADDICTS** [4] 3-8-12 Martin Dwyer 25/1: 8: Sn outpcd: debut, with J Best.   2½   21a
8 ran   Time 59.7 (1.9)   (Willie McKay)   B Smart Lambourn, Berks

488

4.40 TEXT P368 HCAP 3YO 0-75 (E)   7f aw rnd   Going 25 -32 Slow   [79]
£2782   £856   £428   £214

444   **DIRECT REACTION 7** [5] Miss Gay Kelleway 3-9-4 (69) (vis) D Holland 11/1: -35141: 3 b g College   77a
Chapel - Mary's Way (Night Shift) Led/dsptd lead thr'out, all out to hold on nr line: jockey given a 2-day whip
ban, op 8/1: earlier scored here at Lingfield (mdn): rnr-up in '99 (rtd 77a & 81): eff at 6/7f, stays 1m well:
acts on equitrack, handles gd & f/sand: suited by a visor, tried blnks: loves Lingfield & front running tactics.
355   **LEGENDAIRE 21** [10] C A Dwyer 3-8-7 (58) M Hills 11/4: 000-22: 3 gr c Fly Till Dawn - Iolani   nk   64a
(Alzao) Midway/wide halfway, sustained run fnl 2f for press, just held: well bckd, tchd 7/2: see 355.
416   **SPORTY MO 12** [7] K R Burke 3-8-13 (64)(VIS) N Callan 14/1: 1-4503: 3 b g Namaqualand - Miss   1¼   67a
Fortunate (Taufan) Trkd ldrs, rdn/outpcd over 2f out, kept on ins last, no threat: 1st time visor, op 12/1: acts
on both AWs & soft: back to form with headgear applied: see 311.
*450   **SIGN OF THE TIGER 6** [3] P C Haslam 3-9-4 (69)(6ex) P Goode (5) 7/4 FAV: 43-114: Led/dsptd   1   70a
lead till rdn & no extra well ins last: hvly bckd: 6lb pen for latest: acts on both AWs: see 450 (fibresand).
443   **FRENCH FANCY 7** [9] 3-7-10 (47)(bl) (1oh) D Kinsella (7) 25/1: 04-045: Mid-div, rdn/outpcd halfway,   ½   47a
kept on fnl 2f for press, nvr pace to chall: stays 7f, 1m & similar company could suit: see 443 (6f, sell).
397   **CACOPHONY 15** [6] 3-7-13 (50) P Doe 25/1: 33-546: Dwelt/rear, mod late gains: op 10/1: see 228, 94   ¾   49a
416   **AGUA CABALLO 12** [11] 3-8-8 (59) P Fessey 25/1: 656-07: Towards rear, nvr on terms: see 416.   2½   53a
4616}   **SAFARADNO 95** [4] 3-9-7 (72) C Cogan (5) 7/1: 1220-8: Rear, nvr factor: tchd 10/1, 3 month abs: 1   64a
'99 scorer at Yarmouth (sell, R Hannon) & Lingfield (nurs h'cap, current connections, rtd 75 at best): eff at 7f,
stays a stiff 1m well: acts on firm & soft, any trk: proved tough last time, AW bow today, will know more next time.
*421   **ROYAL IVY 11** [8] 3-9-6 (71) F Norton 6/1: 2-2319: Chsd ldrs, outpcd 3f out: op 5/1: see 421 (mdn).   1   61a
4381}   **COLLEGE ROCK 99** [1] 3-8-10 (61) A McCarthy (3) 33/1: 0033-0: Prom 2f: AW bow: 10th: 4 mnth   2   47a
abs/AW bow: plcd sev times in '99 (rtd 63, sell, S C Williams): eff over a sharp/undul 6/7f: has run well in a vis.
1921}   **CHILWORTH 99** [2] 3-9-6 (71) A Clark 33/1: 064-0: Prom 3f, sn btn: 11th: h'cap/AW bow, 8 month   11   41a
abs: unplcd in '99 (rtd 71, auct mdn): stays 7f & handles gd grnd: with T M Jones.
11 ran   Time 1m 26.8 (4.0)   (A P Griffin)   Miss Gay Kelleway Lingfield, Surrey

WOLVERHAMPTON (Fibresand)   THURSDAY FEBRUARY 10TH   Lefthand, Sharp Track

Official Going   STANDARD Stalls: Inside, Except 7f - Outside

489

2.00 AMAT RDRS HCAP 4YO+ 0-70 (G)   1m4f aw   Going 25 -17 Slow   [49]
£1995   £570   £285   4 yo rec 3 lb

+477   **FRENCH SPICE 2** [9] Sir Mark Prescott 4-10-10 (62)(5ex) Mrs C Williams 8/13 FAV: -11111: 4 b f Cadeaux   76a
Genereux - Hot Spice (Hotfoot) Held up, smooth prog 4f out, cled over 1f out, pushed out, cmftbly: well bkcd at
odds-on, qk reapp: completed a sixth consecutive win here at W'hampton (4 h'caps & a class stks): unplcd/mod form
on turf in '99 (rtd 41, mdn): eff at 1m/9.4f, suited by step up to 12f: loves fibresand/W'hampton: gd weight
carrier: v tough & progressive, typically well trained & placed by Sir Mark Prescott.
*470   **ST LAWRENCE 3** [12] B S Rothwell 6-9-7 (42) Mr Nicky Tinkler (5) 8/1: 2311D2: 6 gr g With Approval   2½   49a
- Mingan Isle (Lord Avie) Chsd ldrs, led over 3f out, rdn/hdd over 1f out & not pace of wnr: qk reapp: jockey
given a 3-day ban for careless riding: well clr of rem & continues in fine form: op 11/2: see 470, 412.
*437   **EVEZIO RUFO 9** [1] N P Littmoden 8-9-6 (41)(bl) (5ex) Mr O Gunter (7) 8/1: -46513: 8 b g Blakeney -   12   35a
Empress Corina (Free State) Led/clr halfway, hdd 3f out & no extra: op 5/1, 5lb pen for latest: see 437 (C/D).
--   **ICHI BEAU** [11] F Murphy 6-9-5 (40) Mr K Hogan (7) 25/1: 0003-4: Held up in tch wide, kept on fnl   hd   33a
3f, no threat to ldrs: jumps fit (rtd 71h, sell h'cap): ex-Irish, plcd in '99 (h'cap): Sept '99 Dundalk scorer
(bmpr): eff at 10f, shld stay further: acts on soft grnd: AW bow today: shld apprec further.
--   **WESLEYS LAD** [8] 6-10-3 (49)(3ow) Mr R Bailey (6) 25/1: 6305/5: Held up, mod late gains: 6 wk   5   38a
jumps abs, 98/99 Stratford scorer (h'cap hdle, rtd 128h): last rcd on the Level in '98 (rtd 38, appr h'cap).
460   **RAWI 5** [6] 7-9-8 (43) Mr M Sheridan (7) 50/1: 030-06: Chsd ldr, btn 5f out: see 110.   6   20a
405   **DARE 14** [7] 5-11-5 (64) (vis) Miss E Folkes 14/1: -32207: Mid-div, nvr factor: op 12/1: see 349.   1   40a
470   **STEAMROLLER STANLY 3** [5] 7-11-4 (67) Miss R Clark 25/1: 352468: Mid-div at best: quick reapp.   nk   42a
*408   **COLONEL CUSTER 14** [2] 5-10-6 (55)(vis) Mr A Evans 16/1: 01-319: No danger: changed stable.   12   17a
413   **DR EDGAR 13** [3] 8-9-11 (46) (vis) Miss Diana Jones 14/1: 2/0-40: Al rear: 10th: op 16/1: see 170.   13   0a
431   **Swing Along 9** [4] 5-11-7 (70) Mr V Coogan (5) 20/1: 3137} **Lunar Lord 99** [10] 4-9-3 (41) Mrs S Moore (5) 50/1:
12 ran   Time 2m 38.6 (5.0)   (J Money)   Sir Mark Prescott Newmarket, Suffolk

---

490   2.30 0800 211 222 MDN 4YO+ (D)   1m1f79y aw   Going 25   -01 Slow
     £2743   £844   £422   £211

433   **TYLERS TOAST** 9 [5]   S Dow   4-9-0 P Doe   4/6 FAV: 640-21: 4 ch g Grand Lodge - Catawba (Mill Reef)   **63a**
Chsd ldrs, led going well over 3f out, sn in command, styd on strongly his last, rdn out: nicely bckd: unplcd
in '99 (rtd 80$, mdn, W Jarvis): rtd 78 in '98: eff at 9.4f, further may suit: acts on fibresand & a sharp trk.
446   **AHOUOD** 7 [4]   K Mahdi   4-8-9 C Lowther   7/2: 36-422: 4 b f Merdon Melody - Balidilemma (Balidar)   10   **43a**
Chsd ldr, led 5f out till over 3f out, sn no ch with wnr: op 5/2: clr of rem: h'caps may suit best: see 446.
393   **SAN GLAMORE MELODY** 16 [4]   R Ingram   6-9-0 J P Spencer   50/1: 002/03: 6 b g Sanglamore -   10   **34a**
Lypharitissima (Lightning) Held up rear, rdn & mod gains for press fnl 2f: mdn after 23: see 393.
446   **BITTER SWEET** 7 [2]   J L Spearing   4-8-9 A Mackay   9/2: 020-04: Rear/rdn halfway, no threat: see 446.   2   **25a**
474   **ANNADAWI** 3 [6]   5-9-0 (tbl) N Carlisle   20/1: 4-4405: Trkd ldrs 6f: quick reapp: see 173.   4   **22a**
338   **HOT POTATO** 24 [1]   4-9-0 R Cody Boutcher   (7)   25/1: 05-046: Led 4f, fdd: see 298.   5   **12a**
4090}   **WEE JIMMY** 99 [3]   4-9-0 S Righton   25/1: 0/00-7: Struggling wide halfway: jumps fit (rtd 50h):   7   **1a**
unplcd both turf starts in '99: rtd 67 in '98 (mdn, debut): AW bow today.
7 ran   Time 2m 00.6 (2.4)   (Byerley Bloodstock)   S Dow Epsom, Surrey

---

491   3.00 BEST BETS HCAP 3YO+ 0-85 (D)   5f aw rnd   Going 25   +01 Fast   [80]
     £3848   £1184   £592   £296   3 yo rec 14lb

4610}   **EASTERN TRUMPETER** 97 [9]   J M Bradley   4-8-9 (61)   Claire Bryan (7)   10/1: 3305-1: 4 b c First Trump -   **68a**
Oriental Air (Taufan) Trkd ldrs, led 1f out, styd on well ins last, rdn out: op 14/1: 3 mth abs: '99 scorer at
Folkestone (clmr) & Ayr (h'caps, rtd 70 & 63a at best): '98 rnr-up (sell, rtd 64, G Lewis): all 3 wins at 5f,
stays a sharp 6f: acts on fast, loves soft & fibresand: handles any trk: runs well fresh: tough/genuine colt.
465   **SAMWAR** 5 [7]   Mrs N Macauley   8-9-5 (71)(vis)   R Fitzpatrick (3)   20/1: 1-4062: 8 b g Warning - Samaza   1¼   **73a**
(Arctic Tern) Forced wide in mid-div after 1f, styd on well fnl 2f for press, not pace of wnr: qck reapp: see 214.
435   **BLUE KITE** 9 [3]   N P Littmoden   5-9-13 (79)   J Tate   15/2: -16603: 5 ch g Silver Kite - Gold And   1   **79a**
Blue (Bluebird) Rdn/rear, prog wide halfway, styd on well ins last, nrst fin: op 6/1: prob just best at 6f.
394   **JACKIES BABY** 16 [10]   W G M Turner   4-9-11 (77)   A Daly   8/1: 310-04: Led 4f, no extra: op 10/1.   ½   **75a**
403   **TORRENT** 15 [5]   5-9-6 (72)   Lynsey Hanna (7)   14/1: 13-365: Mid-div, nvr pace to chall: see 205.   nk   **69a**
445   **RING OF LOVE** 7 [8]   4-8-8 (60)   T Williams   13/2: 45-136: Checked after 1f & switched right chasing   ¾   **55a**
ldrs, rdn/not pace to chall over 1f out: op 5/1: see 445, 372 (equitrack).
3944}   **JAWHARI** 99 [2]   6-8-11 (63)   F Norton (7)   0600-7: Cl-up 4f, no extra: op 11/4: 5 month abs/AW   ½   **56a**
bow: '99 reapp scorer at Catterick (h'cap, gamble, rtd 68, subs unplcd & tried blnks): '98 rnr-up (stks, rtd 64):
eff at 5f, stays 1m well: acts on firm & gd/soft grnd: runs well fresh: likes a sharp/undul trk.
394   **SOAKED** 16 [11]   7-10-0 (80)   A Culhane   25/1: 604-08: Chsd ldr, wknd over 1f out: jockey given   4   **63a**
a 4-day ban for careless riding: see 394.
466   **YABINT EL SHAM** 5 [4]   4-9-3 (69)   Dean McKeown   4/1 FAV: 1-5239: Rdn/chasing ldrs when checked   shd   **52a**
& lost place halfway, no impress after: op 3/1: quick reapp: this is prob best forgotten: see 466, 191 (C/D).
361   **SMOKIN BEAU** 21 [6]   3-9-0 (80)   S Dweeney   7/1: 15-320: Chsd ldrs, checked halfway/sn held: 10th.   1¼   **60a**
394   **SOTONIAN** 16 [1]   7-8-12 (64)   P M Quinn (5)   11/2: 20-050: Rear/wide, no impress: 11th: op 4/1: see 394.   1   **42a**
11 ran   Time 1m 01.4 (1.2)   (R G G Racing)   J M Bradley Sedbury, Glos

---

492   3.30 TEXT SELL HCAP DIV 1 4YO+ 0-60 (G)   2m46y aw   Going 25   -56 Slow   [50]
     £1527   £436   £218   4 yo rec 6 lb

3306}   **THE COTTONWOOL KID** 99 [7]   Mrs Merrita Jones   8-7-12 (20)(bl) (2ow)(5oh)   P Fessey   20/1: 0000-1: 8   **29a**
b g Blakeney - Relatively Smart (Great Nephew) Held up in tch, smooth prog/trkd ldrs 4f out, led 2f out & sn clr,
easily: val for 15L+: 1st win, bought in for 3,400 gns: 4 mth jmps abs, prev with Mrs A M Naughton (mod form):
no form on the Level in '99 (rtd 23a): eff at 2m on fibresand: eff in blnks, tried a vis: runs well fresh: has
reportedly had a wind problem operated upon since latest start and clearly enjoys selling grade.
410   **BOBONA** 14 [4]   M D I Usher   4-8-2 (30)   G Baker (7)   7/1: 401-02: 4 b c Interrex - Puella Bona   12   **28a**
(Handsome Sailor) Held up, prog/chsd ldrs 4f out, rdn/briefly led over 2f out, sn held: op 5/1: longer 2m trip.
*363   **CHILDRENS CHOICE** 21 [10]   J Pearce   9-9-10 (46)(vis)   G Bardwell 11/4: 26-313: 9 b m Taufan - Alice   2   **42a**
Brackloon (Melyno) Rear/rdn early, chsd ldrs halfway, rdn/led over 3f out till over 2f out, sn held: top-weight:
jockey given a 2-day ban for careless riding: op 2/1, clr of rem: see 363 (14.8f).
460   **CLOUD INSPECTOR** 5 [9]   M Johnston   9-8-8 (30)   J Fanning   2/1 FAV: 005-24: Prom wide, rdn/btn over 2f   7   **19a**
out: quick reapp: op 7/4: see 460 (equitrack).
4438}   **ROLE MODEL** 99 [5]   4-8-8 (36)   Dean McKeown   6/1: 0062-5: Handy, led over 4f out till over 3f out,   8   **17a**
wknd: op 9/1, jumps fit (rtd 56h, nov): rnr-up in '99 (rtd 37, sell h'cap): stays a gall 14f on fast & gd.
468   **CYMBAL MELODY** 5 [8]   4-7-10 (24)(5oh)   P M Quinn (5)   50/1: 0-0506: Rear, mod prog: quick reapp.   19   **0a**
402   **GHOST PATH** 15 [2]   5-7-12 (20)   P Doe   33/1: 2/5-07: Bhd halfway: see 402.   2   **0a**
190   **DANKA** 57 [1]   6-8-12 (34)(vis)   T G McLaughlin 8/1: 4005-8: Led 12f, btn/eased fnl 2f: abs, vis reapp.   6   **0a**
412   **AMSARA** 13 [6]   4-8-1 (28)   D Mernagh (4)   8/1: 00-069: Chsd ldrs 1m: op 5/1: see 412 (12f).   25   **0a**
259   **JUST A STROLL** 37 [4]   5-8-3 (25)   J Lowe   33/1: 0/0-00: Prom till halfway: 10th: lightly rcd/no   dist   **0a**
form last 2 seasons: rnr-up in '97 as a juv (debut).
10 ran   Time 3m 42.3 (13.1)   (Mrs S E Cooper)   Mrs Merrita Jones Lambourn, Berks

---

493   4.0 TEXT P368 MDN 3YO (D)   7f aw rnd   Going 25   -38 Slow
     £2730   £840   £420   £210

--   **WASEEM** [6]   M Johnston   3-9-0 D Holland   4/11 FAV: 1: 3 ch c Polar Falcon - Astolat (Rusticaro)   **68a**
Chsd ldrs halfway, led over 2f out, rdn/pulled clr fnl 1f despite wandering, cmftbly: hvly bckd at odds-on: debut:
52,000 gns purchase, half brother to a 7f/1m wnr: eff at 7f, 1m+ shld suit: acts on fibresand & a sharp trk: runs
well fresh: plenty in hand here despite running green & can rate more highly.
426   **BILLYS BLUNDER** 10 [7]   P D Evans   3-8-10 (t)   (1ow)   J P Spencer   7/1: 00-32: 3 b f Hamas - Open Date   5   **52a**
(Thatching) Chsd ldrs, rdn/chall 3f out, no extra fnl 2f: op 4/1: prob stays a sharp 7f: see 426 (6f).
--   **ARCTIC HIGH** [1]   M S Saunders   3-8-9 R Price   14/1: 3: 3 b f Polar Falcon - Oublier L'Ennui (Bellman)   3   **45a**
Chsd ldrs halfway, rdn/outpcd over 2f out, kept on ins last for press: op 8/1, debut: half sister to a 6f wnr.
2285}   **CAROLS CHOICE** 99 [2]   D Haydn Jones   3-8-9 A Mackay   4/1: 0536-4: Led, rdn/hdd over 2f out & sn no   nk   **44a**
extra: op 4/1, AW bow/8 month abs: plcd in '99 (auct mdn, rtd 70): eff at 5f on gd grnd: longer 7f trip today.

WOLVERHAMPTON (Fibresand) THURSDAY FEBRUARY 10TH Lefthand, Sharp Track

3499} **SEDONA 99** [4] 3-9-0 C Lowther 40/1: 00-5: Dwelt, in tch wide halfway, outpcd fnl 2f: abs/AW bow. 1¾ **46a**
-- **FOLK DANCE** [5] 3-8-9 G Baker (7) 20/1: 6: Dwelt, al rear: op 14/1, debut. 11 **25a**
415 **WHITLEYGRANGE GIRL 13** [8] 3-8-9 A Culhane 33/1: 67: Chsd ldr, stly hmpd 3f out when struggling. 2½ **20a**
7 ran Time 1m 30.6 (4.4) (A Al-Rostamani) M Johnston Middleham, N Yorks

494 **4.30 TEXT SELL HCAP DIV 2 4YO+ 0-60 (G) 2m46y aw Going 25 -67 Slow [40]**
£1527 £436 £218 4 yo rec 6 lb

*468 **QUAKERESS 5** [9] John Berry 5-8-10 (22)(6ex) F Norton 3/1: -60411: 5 b m Brief Truce - Deer Emily (Alzao) Held up, smooth prog to trk ldrs 4f out, rdn to chall fnl 1f, hard rdn to prevail nr line: op 7/4: bought in for 5,000 gns: 6lb pen for recent win here at W'hampton (sell, John Berry, 1st success): unplcd in '99 (rtd 58, h'cap, tried blnks): eff at 14.7f/2m: handles firm, fast & likes fibresand/W'hampton: enjoys sell grade. **27a**
458 **GROOMS GOLD 5** [5] J Pearce 8-9-4 (30) A Polli (3) 5/1: 0-0422: 8 ch g Groom Dancer - Gortynia (My Swallow) Held up, prog halfway & led 2f out, rdn/strongly prsd ins last, hdd nr line: op 3/1: quick reapp: eff at 1m, suited by 11f/sharp 2m, can find similar: see 369. *hd* **34a**
408 **HILL FARM DANCER 14** [7] W M Brisbourne 9-9-4 (30) C Cogan (5) 5/2 FAV: 3-5523: 9 ch m Gunner B - Loadplan Lass (Nicholas Bill) Towards rear, rdn/prog wide 4f out & ch 2f out, held ins last: op 3/1: see 318. 2 **32a**
194 **TALIB 57** [3] P W Hiatt 6-8-8 (20)(t) Joanna Badger (7) 33/1: 0600-4: Led/dsptd lead after 4f till 2f out, no extra over 1f out: 8 wk abs: rtd 60 in '99 (flattered, rtd h'cap): '98 Windsor wnr (clmr, rtd 62 at best, Mrs Cecil): eff around 12f, prob stays a sharp 2m: handles firm, gd & fibresand. 3½ **19a**
428 **BEAUCHAMP MAGIC 10** [4] 5-9-10 (36) G Baker (7) 5/1: 6-0405: Chsd ldrs 5f out, onepace: see 141. 3½ **32a**
412 **SARTEANO 13** [2] 6-8-8 (20) N Callan 9/2: /0-636: Led/dsptd lead till 5f out, btn 2f out: see 412 (12f). 2½ **14a**
455 **MARKELLIS 6** [8] 4-9-3 (35) R Fitzpatrick (3) 10/1: 450567: Held up, eff 4f out, sn held: op 7/1. 6 **23a**
3824} **NOTATION 99** [1] 6-8-5 (17) A Culhane 20/1: 0000-8: Dwelt/al rear: 5 mth abs: unplcd in '99 (rtd 23a, h'cap): place form in '98 (rtd 55a & 31): '97 wnr at Southwell (2, h'caps, rtd 52a): eff at 14f, stays 2m well: acts on fibresand & gd/soft grnd, likes Southwell. 18 **0a**
404 **RISKY LOVER 14** [6] 7-8-13 (25) N Carlisle 40/1: 000/09: Bhd halfway: see 404. *dist* **0a**
9 ran Time 3m 44.1 (14.9) (Ms Gerardine P O'Reilly) John Berry Elmley Castle, Worcs

495 **5.0 TEXT P372 HCAP 3YO 0-85 (D) 1m100y aw rnd Going 25 -39 Slow [86]**
£3906 £1202 £601 £300

*451 **SPECIAL PROMISE 6** [2] P C Haslam 3-9-1 (73)(6ex) P Goode (5) 1/1 FAV: 5-1111: 3 ch g Anjiz - Woodenitbenice (Nasty And Bold) Mid-div/rdn halfway, switched right & prog over 1f out, styd on to lead nr line, going away: hvly bckd, 6lb pen: completed a 4 timer after wins at Lingfield, W'hampton & Southwell (h'caps): unplcd in '99 (rtd 61 & 55a): eff at 1m/10f, 12f shld suit: acts on both AWs & likes a sharp trk: progressive. **79a**
4274} **NOBLE PASAO 99** [7] Andrew Turnell 3-8-12 (70) C Lowther 12/1: 0010-2: 3 b g Alzao - Belle Passe (Be My Guest) Led, rdn fnl 1f, wknd cl-home & hdd nr line: op 14/1: AW bow/4 month abs: '99 Musselburgh scorer (nurs h'cap, rtd 73): eff around 1m/8.5f on gd & fibresand: best without blnks: shld win again. ½ **73a**
416 **FOXS IDEA 13** [1] D Haydn Jones 3-9-4 (76) S Finnamore (7) 8/1: 40-133: 3 b f Magic Ring - Lindy Belle (Alleging) Prom, rdn/no extra fnl 1f: op 6/1, clr rem: stays a sharp 8.5f, poss just best at 7f: see 416. 1¼ **76a**
392 **TOWER OF SONG 16** [3] D W Chapman 3-8-9 (67) A Culhane 14/1: 420-54: Prom, no extra over 1f out. 4 **59a**
4380} **COMMON PLACE 99** [5] 3-9-7 (79) A Clark 5/1: 0100-5: Held up, eff 2f out, not pace to chall: op 4/1: AW bow/4 month abs: topweight: '99 Goodwood scorer (nurs h'cap, rtd 81): eff at 7f, 1m+ may suit: acts on gd. *hd* **70a**
451 **MODEM 6** [9] 3-8-0 (58)(vis) F Norton 14/1: 00-136: Dwelt, rdn/mid-div halfway, no impress: qck reapp. 1¼ **46a**
392 **HEATHYARDS LAD 16** [8] 3-8-11 (69) P M Quinn (5) 5/1: 64-547: Mid-div/btn 2f out: op 12/1: see 294. 3 **51a**
392 **STORM PRINCE 16** [6] 3-8-13 (71) Joanna Badger (7) 14/1: 412-68: Al rear: op 12/1: see 392. *nk* **52a**
365 **BEWILDERED 20** [10] 3-7-10 (54) Iona Wands (5) 33/1: 064-09: Prom 5f, sn btn: see 365 (6f). 5 **25a**
9 ran Time 1m 51.6 (5.4) (R Young) P C Haslam Middleham, N Yorks

SOUTHWELL (Fibresand) FRIDAY FEBRUARY 11TH Lefthand, Sharp, Oval Track

Official Going STANDARD. Stalls: Inside.

496 **1.40 BET DIRECT HCAP DIV 1 3YO+ 0-65 (F) 1m aw rnd Going 63 -06 Slow [63]**
£2339 £668 £334 3 yo rec 19lb

*432 **PERCHANCER 10** [5] P C Haslam 4-9-5 (54)(6ex) P Goode (5) 9/4: 6-3211: 4 ch g Perugino - Irish Hope (Nishapour) Mid-div, prog/chsd ldrs over 2f out, led ins last, styd on well, rdn out: tchd 5/2: 6lb pen for recent W'hampton success (amat riders h'cap): '99 Thirsk wnr (appr mdn h'cap, rtd 55), plcd on sand (rtd 58a, h'cap): eff at 7f/9.3f on firm, gd/soft & both AWs: has run well in blnks, tried a visor: likes a sharp trk: in fine form. **60a**
471 **SEA YA MAITE 4** [9] S R Bowring 6-9-9 (58) S Finnamore (7) 9/1: 315652: 6 b g Komaite - Marina Plata (Julio Mariner) Chsd ldrs wide, led over 2f out, hdd ins last, kept on: clr rem, qk reapp, loves Southwell. ¾ **63a**
437 **SOVEREIGN ABBEY 10** [12] Sir Mark Prescott 4-9-7 (56) D Sweeney 7/4 FAV: 6-2143: 4 b g Royal Academy - Elabella (Ela Mana Mou) Chsd ldrs, rdn/ch 2f out, held over 1f out: hvly bckd: back at 1m, see 437. 6 **52a**
83 **CLEAR NIGHT 81** [11] J J Sheehan 4-9-3 (52) D R McCabe 14/1: 6002-4: Led after 2f, rdn/hdd over 2f out & sn no extra: op 10/1, 12 wk abs: drop back to 7f may suit: see 83 (C/D). 1¼ **45a**
407 **BE WARNED 15** [13] 9-10-0 (63)(vis) F Norton 20/1: 1-0405: Dwelt/rear, late gains: wants further. ¾ **55a**
*452 **NOBLE INVESTMENT 7** [2] 6-8-5 (40) Paul Cleary (7) 9/1: 0/3016: Chsd ldrs 6f: op 7/1: btr 452 (clmr). 1¼ **29a**
410 **MAJOR ATTRACTION 15** [8] 5-7-10 (31)(3oh) P M Quinn (5) 50/1: 40-007: Led 2f, struggling fnl 3f. 12 **2a**
230} **WINSTON 99** [3] 7-8-3 (35)(3ow) R Lappin 40/1: 30/6-8: Chsd ldrs 5f: long abs: unplcd sole start in '99 (rtd 32a, h'cap): plcd form in '98 (rtd 42, h'cap): '96 Nottingham & Newcastle wnr (h'caps, rtd 73): eff at 1m, tried 10f: acts on firm & gd/soft: eff with/without blnks: handles any track. 2 **5a**
4166} **HETRA HAWK 99** [10] 4-8-7 (42) L Newton 33/1: 0/00-9: Dwelt/al towards rear: 4 month abs: unplcd in '99 (rtd 34a, lightly rcd): rtd 42 on both '98 starts (mdns): h'cap bow today. 1 **7a**
2192} **PLEASURE TRICK 99** [4] 9-8-11 (46) Kim Tinkler 25/1: 0500-0: Al rear: 10th: 8 month abs: with current connections & N Tinkler in '99 (unplcd, rtd 53a & 53 at best): '98 wnr here at Southwell (h'cap, rtd 60a): eff at 7f/1m on firm, gd & loves fibresand/Southwell: eff with/without blnks, has tried a vis: handles any trk. 2½ **6a**
431 **MR SPEAKER 10** [1] 7-8-13 (48) A Clark 50/1: 130-50: Al bhd: 12th: op 7/1: see 431. **0a**
215 **Wry Ardour 52** [6] 4-7-12 (33)(2ow)(7oh) P Fessey 10/1: 409 **Woolly Winsome 15** [7] 4-8-11 (46)(bl) J Stack 20/1:
13 ran Time 1m 44.9 (5.5) (N P Green) P C Haslam Middleham, N.Yorks

497   2.10 BET DIRECT HCAP DIV 2 3YO+ 0-65 (F)   1m aw rnd   Going 63 -02 Slow   [63]
£2326   £664   £332   3 yo rec 19lb

368   **BROUGHTON MAGIC 21** [4] W J Musson 5-7-13 (33)(1ow) F Norton 7/1: 500/51: 5 ch g Archway - Magic   45a
Green (Magic Mirror) Prom, led over 2f out, readily pulled clr ins last, pushed out: val for 8L+, op 8/1, first
win: missed '99: unplcd in '98 (rtd 42 & 41a): eff at 7f/1m on fibresand: at the right end of the h'cap.
469   **ELLWAY PRINCE 6** [12] Mrs N Macauley 5-9-3 (52) Dean McKeown 8/1: -02262: 5 b g Prince Sabo -   4 52a
Star Arrangement (Star Appeal) Chsd ldrs, prog/chall 2f out, kept on: op 6/1, clr rem: qck reapp, tough: see 393.
*431   **MIDNIGHT WATCH 10** [11] A G Newcombe 6-8-1 (36)(6ex) P Fessey 100/30 FAV: -00013: 6 b g Capote - 5 26a
Midnight Air (Green Dancer) Towards rear, eff wide halfway, mod gains for press: 6lb pen: op 9/4: see 431.
471   **GODMERSHAM PARK 4** [1] P S Felgate 8-8-12 (47) S Finnamore (7) 7/1: 5-2344: Led 6f: qck reapp.   ¾ 36a
418   **KINGCHIP BOY 14** [10] 11-8-11 (46)(vis) P McCabe 14/1: -30005: Chsd ldrs wide 6f: see 249.   ¾ 34a
473   **NICE BALANCE 4** [6] 5-8-9 (44) Joanna Badger (7) 8/1: 143156: Reared start/dwelt, mid-div at best.   ½ 31a
367   **FAS 21** [8] 4-8-3 (34)(bl) A G Newcombe 40/1: 000-67: Wide/rear, mod gains: see 367.   ½ 26a
452   **BLOOMING AMAZING 7** [9] 6-9-1 (50)(BL) C Lowther 14/1: 0-0068: Mid-div, eff 3f out/no impress: blnks. ¾ 26a
*341   **DAVIS ROCK 25** [7] 6-9-13 (62) Martin Dwyer 9/2: 55-119: Mid-div, eff 3f out/sn held: see 341 (7f, clmr).   3 32a
418   **BRANDON MAGIC 14** [5] 7-9-6 (55) Clare Roche 12/1: /01-00: Mid-div at best: 10th: op 8/1:   7 14a
lightly rcd in '99, scored here at Southwell (C/D appr clmr, rtd 64a): missed '98: plcd with I Balding in '97 (rtd
84, h'cap): eff at 1m, prev suited by 10/14f: acts on gd/st & fibresand, handles firm.
408   **Time On My Hands 15** [3] 4-8-7 (42)(tbl) N Callan 20/1:   126   **Domino Flyer 73** [2] 7-9-7 (56) R Lappin 25/1:
12 ran   Time 1m 44.7 (5.2)   (Broughton Thermal Insulation)   W J Musson Newmarket.

498   2.40 BET DIRECT CLAIMER 4YO+ (F)   1m4f aw   Going 63 -27 Slow
£2289   £654   £327   4 yo rec 3 lb

370   **COUNT DE MONEY 21** [5] S R Bowring 5-9-2 S Finnamore (7) 4/6 FAV: 21-231: 5 b g Last Tycoon -   68a
Menominee (Soviet Star) Chsd ldrs, prog/led over 4f out, rdn/forged clr over 2f out, unchal: well bckd at odds on:
clmd by J Poynton for £8,000, will join S J Wilton: '99 scorer 5 times here at Southwell (2 h'caps, 2 clmrs &
class stks) & W'hampton (clmr, rtd 68a, also rtd 35): '98 Southwell wnr (amat h'cap, rtd 54a): eff at 11f/14f:
handles firm & fast, fibresand/Southwell specialist: tough/genuine & relished this drop to claiming grade.
447   **ACCYSTAN 8** [6] M D Hammond 5-9-0 J Weaver 9/1: 10-062: 5 ch g Efisio - Amia (Nijinsky)   6 57a
Chsd ldrs halfway, kept on for press fnl 2f, no threat to wnr: clr rem: signs of a return to form here: see 390.
413   **WELLCOME INN 14** [2] G Woodward 6-8-10 (t) C Lowther 10/1: 0-0223: 6 ch g Most Welcome -   7 43$
Mimining (Tower Walk) Mid-div halfway, prog/joined wnr 3f out, sn rdn/outpcd: op 20/1: see 413, 211 (C/D).
433   **ADIRPOUR 10** [8] R Hollinshead 6-8-10 Stephanie Hollinshea 50/1: -06504: Chsd ldrs halfway, sn held.   nk 42$
437   **BANNERET 10** [9] 7-9-4 (vis) T G McLaughlin 11/1: 4-2105: Mid-div, nvr a factor: op 8/1: see 347.   3 46a
196   **TANTISPER 56** [10] 4-8-5 (VIS) G Bardwell 50/1: 00/5-6: Drvn mid-div, btn 4f out: visor, changed stable.   10 25a
422   **NIGHT CITY 13** [1] 9-9-6 N Callan 7/2: 652267: Led 1m, sn btn: nicely bckd: topweight: see 92 (1m).   1 36a
452   **SARPEDON 7** [4] 4-8-3 (BL) Joanna Badger (7) 50/1: 0-0508: Prom 1m: blnks: see 425 (6f).   2½ 24a
413   **MODEST HOPE 14** [3] 13-8-4 (vis) Sarah Thomas (6) 100/1: 0-0009: Al rear: see 324.   9 6a
4509}   **ILEWIN JANINE 99** [7] 9-8-3 P M Quinn 15/1: 6-0: Dwelt, sn t.o.: 10th: AW bow, jumps fit   15 0a
(mod form): unplcd on sole Flat start in '99 (P Evans, rtd 49): 97/98 Uttoxeter hurdles wnr (sell h'cap, rtd 87h).
10 ran   Time 2m 45.1 (10.8)   (Roland M Wheatley)   S R Bowring Edwinstowe, Notts.

499   3.10 BEST BETS HCAP 3YO+ 0-75 (E)   6f aw rnd   Going 63 +08 Fast   [74]
£2821   £868   £434   £217   3 yo rec 15lb

4610}   **DAAWE 98** [12] D Nicholls 9-9-10 (70)(bl) Clare Roche (7) 10/1: 6060-1: 9 b h Danzig - Capo Di   86a
Monte (Final Straw) Made all, in command fnl 2f & eased nr fin, unchal: val for 7l+: fast time: op 5/1, 3 mth
abs: '99 scorer at Pontefract & Newcastle (h'caps, earlier with J Glover, rtd 71 & 68a at best): '98 wnr at Thirsk
& Doncaster (ltd stks, rtd 81 & 75a): best at 5/6f, stays 1m: acts on firm, hvy & fibresand: handles any trk: eff
with/without a visor, has tried blnks: runs alwys fresh & loves to dominate: can win again on this evidence.
414   **REGAL SONG 14** [13] T J Etherington 4-8-9 (55) J Fanning 6/1: 431-32: 4 b g Anita's Prince -   4 57a
Song Beam (Song) Chsd ldrs, kept on fnl 2f for press, no ch with wnr: gd run: see 414 (C/D).
454   **PLEADING 7** [5] M A Buckley 7-8-13 (59) Martin Dwyer 11/4 FAV: 000-23: 7 b g Never So Bold -   ¾ 59a
Ask Mama (Mummy's Pet) Dwelt/towards rear, rdn & kept on fnl 2f, nvr a threat: more expected after 454 (C/D).
342   **GARNOCK VALLEY 25** [8] A Berry 10-10-0 (74) G Carter 11/2: 52-164: Rear/wide, late gains for press.   ½ 72a
454   **AJNAD 7** [11] 6-9-5 (65) S Righton 33/1: -00005: Mid-div, rdn/held 2f out: see 282.   hd 62a
4586}   **BATALEUR 99** [10] 7-7-10 (42)(7oh) P M Quinn (5) 20/1: 0021-6: Chsd ldrs 4f: 3 month abs: '99   nk 38a
wnr on fnl start at Catterick (clmr, rtd 51): '98 Newcastle wnr (h'cap rtd 50, no sand form): eff at 5/6f on firm &
gd, loves eff/hvy: eff with/without blnks: handles any track.
430   **MUJAS MAGIC 11** [5] 5-9-3 (63)(vis) R Fitzpatrick (3) 7/1: 1-2447: Mid-div at best: op 6/1: see 187 (7f).   1 57a
440   **ALJAZ 9** [4] 10-9-4 (64) S Whitworth 6/1: 3-4028: Towards rear, no impress: see 44.   2½ 51a
466   **PETITE DANSEUSE 6** [9] 6-7-10 (42)(9oh) Joanna Badger (7) 33/1: 0-5509: Chsd ldrs 4f: qck reapp.   2½ 50a
454   **SISAO 7** [7] 4-8-13 (59)(bl) N Callan 12/1: 32-100: Chsd ldrs 4f: 10th: op 10/1: see 273 (mdn).   2½ 32a
445   **Ice Age 8** [6] 6-8-2 (47)(bl)(1ow) L Newton 20/1:   280   **Sans Rivale 35** [1] 5-7-10 (42)(14oh) Iona Wands (5) 50/1:
425   **Sweet As A Nut 11** [2] 4-9-5 (65) J P Spencer 33/1:
13 ran   Time 1m 16.6 (3.3)   (Mrs Andrea M Mallinson)   D Nicholls Sessay, N.Yorks.

500   3.40 TEXT P368 MDN STKS 3YO+ (D)   1m aw rnd   Going 63 -12 Slow
£2743   £844   £422   £211   3 yo rec 19lb

--   **KARA SEA** [7] D J G Murray Smith 3-8-1 P Doe 13/2: 1: 3 ch f River Special - Arctic Interlude   63a
(Woodman) Prom, rdn/led over 2f out, in command fnl 1f & styd on well, pushed out: op 10/1, debut: half-brother
to a French 7f 2yo wnr: eff at 1m, further shld suit: acts on fibresand & a sharp trk: runs well fresh.
453   **KUSTOM KIT KEVIN 7** [4] S R Bowring 4-9-11 S Finnamore (7) 14/1: 60-322: 4 b g Local Suitor -   5 57$
Sweet Revival (Claude Monet) Held up in tch, kept on for press fnl 2f, not pace of wnr: op 10/1: eff at 1m,
tried 12f: acts on fibresand: h'caps shld suit: see 453, 387.
4453}   **DANCING MARY 99** [3] B Smart 3-8-1 F Norton 4/1: 5550-3: 3 gr f Sri Pekan - Fontenoy (Lyphard's   ½ 51a
Wish) Prom, rdn/briefly led over 2f out, sn no extra: tchd 6/1, 4 month abs: AW bow: unplcd in 4 mdn starts
in '99 (rtd 72): stays 1m, mid-dists shld suit: handles fibresand & gd/soft grnd: clr rem, apprec h'cap company.

SOUTHWELL (Fibresand)　　FRIDAY FEBRUARY 11TH　　Lefthand, Sharp, Oval Track

451　**NICIARA 7** [5] M C Chapman 3-8-6 (bl) Joanna Badger (7) 9/1: -05324: Dwelt, sn rdn/chsd ldrs 6f.　　10　**41a**
427　**THREEFORTYCASH 11** [2] 3-8-6 A Culhane 20/1: 00-45: Cl-up 6f: op 14/1: see 427.　　4　**33a**
4340}　**SEVEN O SEVEN 99** [1] 7-9-11 S Whitworth 40/1: 4400-6: Led 6f, sn btn/eased: 4 mth abs: plcd　　16　**9a**
in '99 (mdn, rtd 61a, rtd 33 on turf): mod form over hdles prev: stays a sharp 12f, tried further: handles equitrack.
86　**ROYAL CAVALIER 81** [6] 3-8-6 P M Quinn (5) 4/5 FAV: 3422-7: Reared badly start & slowly away/bhd,　　29　**0a**
nvr on terms after & eased fnl 2f: hvly bckd: abs: gelding reportedly hit his head on the stalls, this best forgiven.
7 ran　　Time 1m 45.4 (6.0)　　(D Murray Smith)　　D J G Murray Smith Gumley, Leics.

501

4.10 TEXT P372 SELLER 3YO+ (G)　　7f aw rnd　Going 63　-07 Slow
　£1909　£545　£272　　3 yo rec 17lb

388　**GENERAL KLAIRE 18** [1] R A Fahey 5-9-3 R Winston 4/6 FAV: 653-01: 5 b m Presidium - Klairover　　**58a**
(Smackover) Chsd ldrs, rdn to chall fnl 2f, asserted cl-home: rdn out: bckd at odds on: bght in for 5,000gns: '99
wnr here at Southwell (fill h'cap, rtd 77a, B A McMahon, plcd on turf, rtd 52 at btr, h'cap): '98 W'hampton wnr
(auct mdn, rtd 67a, unplcd on turf, rtd 65): eff at 6f/1m, suited by 7f on gd, soft & loves fibresand/Southwell.
396　**GUEST ENVOY 17** [7] C N Allen 5-9-3 J Bosley (7) 11/1: 50-032: 5 b m Paris House - Peace Mission　　2　**53$**
(Dunbeath) Prom, led over 3f out, rdn/hdd well ins last & no extra: op 12/1: would apprec sell h'caps.
449　**LOCOMOTION 8** [8] S Dow 4-9-8 P Doe 9/1: 00-003: 4 ch g Seattle Dancer - Pipe Opener (Prince　　4　**50a**
Sabo) Cl-up halfway, rdn/ch 3f out, no extra over 1f out: op 7/1: clr of rem: see 360 (clmr).
452　**FRANKLIN LAKES 7** [5] M R Bosley 5-9-8 (tbl) G Baker (7) 14/1: 0-3054: In tch, outpcd fnl 2f: op 20/1.　　7　**39$**
438　**MARIANA 9** [6] 5-9-3 (bl) T G McLaughlin 40/1: 00-505: Chsd ldrs, outpcd fnl 3f: see 367 (mdn).　　2½　**29a**
452　**SOUNDS SOLO 7** [2] 4-9-8 (cvi) Clare Roche (7) 8/1: 0-6306: Led 4f, fdd: btr 389 (6f).　　1½　**31a**
2465}　**ROTOSTAR 99** [4] 4-9-3 S Whitworth 20/1: /006-7: Struggling halfway: 7 month abs: unplcd in '99　　27　**0a**
(rtd 40, mdn h'cap, P D Evans): rtd 65 (mdn) & 31a at best in '98: stays a gall 6f & handles fast grnd.
316　**SURE TO DREAM 30** [3] 7-9-3 (bl) R Perham 9/1: 000-4P: P.u. after 2f, sadly died.　　**0a**
8 ran　　Time 1m 31.5 (4.9)　　(Tommy Staunton)　　R A Fahey Butterwick, N.Yorks.

502

4.40 RACING CHANNEL HCAP 4YO+ 0-70 (E)　　2m aw　Going 63　-73 Slow　　[60]
　£2821　£868　£434　£217　　4 yo rec 6 lb

428　**KENT 11** [7] P D Cundell 5-8-13 (45) Martin Dwyer 13/8 FAV: 05-121: 5 b g Kylian - Precious Caroline　　**52a**
(The Noble Player) Trkd ldrs halfway, led over 2f out, styd on well/edged right ins last, forged clr: hvly bckd,
tchd 15/8: earlier scored here at Southwell (C/D h'cap, first win): plcd in '99 (rtd 63, mdn, unplcd on sand,
rtd 44a): suited by a sharp 2m, shld stay further: loves fibresand/Southwell: best without blnks: runs well fresh.
*456　**CRESSET 7** [5] D W Chapman 4-9-12 (64)(5ex) A Culhane 5/1: 021212: 4 ch c Arazi - Mixed Applause　　7　**64a**
(Nijinsky) Held up in tch, prog/chsd ldrs 4f out, rdn/ev ch 2f out, no extra ins last: op 4/1, 5lb pen for latest:
prob styd the longer 2m trip, appears tough/progressive and should win more races: see 456 (12f).
424　**CEDAR FLAG 13** [9] R J O'Sullivan 6-8-9 (41) P M Quinn (5) 7/1: 0-3243: 6 br g Jareer - Sasha Lea　　2½　**38a**
(Cawston's Clown) Mid-div, prog/led over 5f out, hdd over 2f out, no extra: op 9/1: clr rem: see 370 (12f).
428　**ALMAMZAR 11** [10] Don Enrico Incisa 10-7-10 (28)(5oh) Kim Tinkler 40/1: 5-0544: Hndy, outpcd fnl 3f.　　7　**18a**
428　**I CANT REMEMBER 11** [3] 6-9-8 (54) S Finnamore (7) 25/1: 100-65: Cl-up, led 9f out till 5f out, fdd.　　11　**36a**
390　**ALNAJASHEE 18** [8] 4-10-0 (66)(t) G Baker (7) 14/1: 56-146: Cl-up 13f: op 10/1: btr 339 (12f).　　hd　**48a**
470　**GRAND CRU 4** [6] 9-9-4 (50)(vis) D Sweeney (7) 1-4237: Rear/in tch, chsd ldrs halfway, btn 4f out.　　7　**25a**
339　**BROUGHTONS LURE 25** [2] 6-8-2 (34) L Newton (7): 052-28: Chsd ldrs, strugg 4f out: btr 339, 215 (12f).　nk　**9a**
3305}　**COLERIDGE 99** [4] 12-9-0 (46)(bl) A Clark 20/1: 2600-9: Al rear: 6 month abs: '99 wnr here at　　25　**2a**
Southwell (h'cap, C/D, rtd 53a, rnr-up on turf, rtd 34, h'cap): '98 Lingfield wnr (h'cap, rtd 55a at best, rnr-up on
turf, rtd 40): eff at 2m: acts on fast, soft & both AWs: prob handles any trk, likes a sharp one: best blnkd.
--　**ONEFOURSEVEN** [1] 7-10-0 (60) T Williams 14/1: 2404/0: Strugg fnl 5f: 10th: long abs: missed '99:　　3½　**13a**
rnr-up twice in '98 (h'caps, rtd 69 & 65a): '97 wnr at Doncaster, Thirsk & W'hampton (h'caps, rtd 76 & 65a at best):
eff around 14f/2m2f: acts on fast, reportedly best on soft & fibresand: best without blnks: likes to force the pace.
455　**SEA GOD 7** [11] 9-7-10 (28)(3oh) Joanna Badger (7) 50/1: /00-00: Led 7f, sn bhd: 11th: no form　　dist　**0a**
sole '99 start: last won on the level in '96 at Southwell (h'cap, rtd 47a): eff at 1m/12f on fibresand & fast grnd.
11 ran　　Time 3m 47.8 (21.8)　　(P D Cundell)　　P D Cundell Compton, Berks.

LINGFIELD (Equitrack)　　SATURDAY FEBRUARY 12TH　　Lefthand, V Sharp Track

Official Going　STANDARD. Stalls: Inside, except 5f & 1m - Outside.

503

1.25 DIRECT APPR HCAP DIV 1 4YO+ 0-70 (F)　　7f aw rnd　Going 11　-13 Slow　　[68]
　£1809　£517　£258

462　**APOLLO RED 7** [4] G L Moore 11-10-0 (68) I Mongan (3) 6/1: 3-1261: 11 ch g Dominion - Woolpack　　**77a**
(Golden Fleece) Made all, clr halfway, styd on strongly fnl 2f, rdn out: op 9/2: earlier scored here at Lingfield
(seller): '99 wnr here at Lingfield (seller, rtd 76a, plcd on turf, rtd 57, clmr): '98 Brighton wnr (h'cap, rtd
74 & 72a): stays 1m well, suited by 6/7f: acts on firm, soft & equitrack: loves to force the pace on a sharp trk,
esp Brighton/Lingfield: eff with/without blnks/visor: gd weight carrier: tough/genuine 11yo.
*438　**REACHFORYOURPOCKET 10** [7] M D I Usher 5-8-4 (44) G Baker (5) 11/2: 0-4612: 5 b g Royal Academy　3　**47a**
- Gemaasheh (Habitat) Trkd ldrs, rdn/chsd wnr 2f out, kept on: op 4/1: in gd heart: see 438 (C/D, mdn h'cap).
466　**DONE AND DUSTED 7** [10] R Brotherton 4-9-9 (63) S Finnamore (3) 10/1: 01-063: 4 ch f Up And At　1¾　**63a**
'Em - Florentink (The Minstrel) Chsd wnr, rdn/outpcd over 2f out: just best at 6f: see 226 (6f, fibresand).
439　**BEGUILE 10** [11] R Ingram 6-8-9 (48) P M Quinn 100/30 FAV: 460-24: Towards rear/wide, chsd ldrs　nk　**47a**
halfway, sn rdn/held: tchd 4/1: see 439 (C/D).
263　**CORN DOLLY 38** [8] 4-8-11 (51) S Carson 7/2: 041-25: Chsd ldrs 5f: tchd 4/1: see 263, 225.　　½　**49a**
364　**INDIAN WARRIOR 23** [7] 4-9-4 (58) P Shea (5) 9/1: 010-06: Mid-div halfway, sn outpcd: see 364 (fbrsnd).　nk　**55a**
396　**MR CUBE 18** [3] 10-7-10 (36)(bl)(2oh) Claire Bryan (5) 40/1: -00067: Chsd ldrs, outpcd fnl 3f: see 254.　3　**27a**
425　**GLASTONBURY 12** [6] 4-8-2 (42) D Mernagh 25/1: 000-08: Towards rear, nvr on terms: see 425.　　3½　**26a**
436　**BEVERLEY MONKEY 11** [2] 4-7-10 (36)(2oh) R Brisland 33/1: 055-09: Sn outpcd: see 436 (seller, 6f).　3½　**13a**
466　**LISAS PRINCESS 7** [9] 7-7-10 (36)(3oh) Joanna Badger (5) 50/1: /6-000: Outpcd halfway, sn bhd.　　3　**7a**
10 ran　　Time 1m 24.46 (1.66)　　(A Moore)　　G L Moore Woodingdean, E.Sussex.

LINGFIELD (Equitrack) SATURDAY FEBRUARY 12TH Lefthand, V Sharp Track

---

504 1.55 DIRECT APPR HCAP DIV 2 4YO+ 0-70 (F) 7f aw rnd Going 11 -19 Slow [68]
£1806 £516 £258

*439 **SUPERCHIEF** 10 [1] Miss B Sanders 5-8-4 (44)(tbl) S Carson 2/1 FAV: 4-4211: 5 b g Precocious - Rome **52a**
Express (Siberian Express) Chsd ldr, rdn/led over 2f out, in command fnl 1f, rdn out: op 6/5: recent wnr here
at Lingfield (h'cap, C/D): plcd in late '99 (mdn, rtd 67a): rtd 53 at best in '98 (h'cap, tried visor, J Banks):
best at 7f, stays 10f: acts on equitrack & a sharp trk: eff in a vis, suited by blnks/t-strap: hat-trick on the cards.
462 **RAINBOW RAIN** 7 [3] S Dow 6-9-4 (58) P Dobbs 3/1: 05-302: 6 b g Capote - Grana (Miswaki) 3 **60a**
Rdn/chsd ldrs halfway, kept on ins last, no threat: op 5/1: back to form, can win similar: see 227, 28 (C/D).
352 **MISS DANGEROUS** 25 [2] M Quinn 5-8-9 (49)(bl) R Studholme 8/1: 6-1303: 5 b m Komaite - Khadine ½ **50a**
(Astec) Led 5f, no extra fnl 1f: tchd 10/1: loves to front run: see 243 (C/D, class stks, made all).
4118} **BREAD WINNER** 99 [4] I A Balding 4-9-2 (56) Michael Doyle (7) 9/1: 4405-4: Chsd ldrs, rdn/outpcd 1¼ **54a**
halfway, kept on fnl 1f, no threat: op 6/1: AW bow: plcd numerous times in '99 (rtd 61, h'cap): rtd 70 on first
of 2 starts in '98 (mdn): rtd at 6f/9.8f, tried further: handles fast & gd/soft, any trk: has run well in blnks.
*449 **DISTINCTIVE DREAM** 9 [7] 6-9-11 (65) D Hayden (5) 8/1: 0-6215: Dwelt, prog/chsd ldrs wide h'way, 1 **61a**
sn rdn/onepace: op 6/1: acts on firm, gd/soft & both AWs: see 449 (seller, fibresand).
404 **DANZAS** 16 [5] 6-7-10 (36)(bl) Claire Bryan (3) 16/1: -60646: Chsd ldrs halfway, sn outpcd: op 14/1. 1¼ **29a**
114 **MAGIQUE ETOILE** 78 [8] 4-9-1 (55) L Newman 20/1: 0332-7: Chsd ldrs 4f: op 14/1, abs: see 114, 25. 2 **44a**
463 **MALCHIK** 7 [9] 4-8-2 (42) R Brisland 20/1: -55608: Towards rear, sn struggling: see 159. ½ **30a**
393 **MUJKARI** 18 [6] 4-7-11 (37)(vis) D Mernagh 33/1: 60-009: Mid-div, btn 3f out: see 323. 6 **16a**
57 **CLARA BLUE** 88 [10] 4-7-11 (37) P M Quinn 33/1: 0000-0: Dwelt, al outpcd: 10th: abs: unplcd 17 **0a**
in '99 (rtd 50, h'cap): '98 Folkestone wnr (auct mdn, rtd 71): eff at 5f on fast & gd/soft: likes to force the pace.
10 ran Time 1m 24.89 (2.09) (Copy Xpress) Miss B Sanders Epsom, Surrey.

---

505 2.30 BEST BETS SELLER 4YO+ (G) 1m aw rnd Going 11 -37 Slow

375 **HIGH SHOT** 21 [10] G L Moore 10-8-13 (t) S Whitworth 4/1: 22-331: 10 b g Darshaan - Nollet (High **49a**
Top) Trkd ldrs wide halfway, rdn/styd on well to lead ins last, drvn out: no bid: op 2/1: wore a t-strap: rnr-up
in '99 (rtd 58a, C/D h'cap): '98 rnr-up for R Rowe (h'cap, rtd 71): ex-French, back in '95 won at Evry: eff at
1m/10f on firm, soft & equitrack: has reportedly choked prev: appreciated return to sell grade.
452 **SHAMWARI SONG** 8 [4] Mrs L C Jewell 5-8-13 N Callan 33/1: 5-0002: 5 b g Sizzling Melody - Spark Out 2 **44$**
(Sparkler) Prom, led 2f out, rdn/hdd ins last & no extra: see 163.
398 **BALLYMORRIS BOY** 17 [1] J Pearce 4-8-13 J Weaver 20/1: -34603: 4 b c Dolphin Street - Solas Abu ½ **43$**
(Red Sunset) Led 6f, sn rdn/kept on onepace: blnks omitted after latest: eff at 6f, stays a sharp 1m: see 274.
431 **CLONOE** 11 [8] R Ingram 6-8-13 P Doe 7/2: 0-2404: Trkd ldrs halfway, onepace: tchd 5/1: see 268 (10f). 1¼ **40a**
375 **LADY QUINTA** 21 [5] 4-9-0 (bl) L Newman 25/1: 000-05: Chsd ldrs, outpcd fnl 3f: blnks reapplied. hd **40a**
393 **THOMAS HENRY** 18 [8] 4-9-5 T O'Neill (7) 8/1: 16-006: Rdn/towards rear halfway, mod gains: op 5/1. ½ **44a**
227 **TITAN** 47 [9] 5-8-13 T Williams 50/1: 0060-7: Cl-up for 6f: 7 wk abs: see 92. 1¼ **35a**
471 **UTAH** 5 [2] 6-8-13 (bl) I Mongan (3) 11/4 FAV: -04328: Rdn/bhd & wide, no impress: tchd 100/30, ½ **34a**
shorter price stablemate of wnr: qck reapp: see 438, 220.
408 **SASEEDO** 16 [7] 10-8-13 (b) G Bardwell 33/1: 600-09: Dwelt/al bhd: see 408. 3 **28a**
421 **JAZZNIC** 14 [3] 4-8-8 A Clark 13/2: 2/5-60: Cl-up, btn 3f out & eased ins last: 10th: see 173 (7f). 9 **10a**
10 ran Time 1m 40.06 (3.86) (The Tuesday Syndicate) G L Moore Woodingdean, E.Sussex.

---

506 3.00 0800 211222 HCAP 3YO+ 0-90 (C) 5f aw rnd Going 11 -03 Slow [82]
£6922 £2130 £1065 £532 3 yo rec 14lb

*403 **FRILLY FRONT** 17 [2] T D Barron 4-8-6 (60) N Callan 6/1: 10-P11: 4 ch f Aragon - So So (Then Again) **69a**
Rdn/trkd ldr, led over 2f out, styd on strongly ins last, rdn out: op 5/1: recent Lingfield scorer (h'cap): '99
W'hampton scorer (h'cap, rtd 58a, plcd sev times on turf, rtd 61, h'cap): '98 debut Musselburgh wnr (med auct mdn,
subs rtd 83): eff at 5f, stays 6f on fast, soft & both AWs: likes Lingfield: has run well fresh: tried blnks.
4288} **BATCHWORTH BELLE** 99 [7] E A Wheeler 5-10-0 (82) S Carson (5) 7/2 FAV: 0032-2: 5 b m Interrex - 2 **85a**
Treasurebound (Beldale Flutter) Held up in tch wide, prog/chsd ldrs fnl 2f, kept on tho' al held: tchd 4/1: '99
wnr here at Lingfield (C/D, reapp, h'cap) & Newmarket (h'cap, rtd 96 & 82a): '98 Brighton & Epsom wnr (h'caps, rtd
88): stays 7f, suited by 5f on firm, gd/soft & equitrack: runs well fresh: best without blnks: gd reapp.
394 **MUKARRAB** 18 [8] D W Chapman 6-9-7 (75) A Culhane 5/1: 06-043: 6 b g Dayjur - Mahassin (Biscay) 1¾ **74a**
Chsd ldrs wide halfway, kept on fnl 2f, nvr a threat: tchd 11/2: in gd form, spot on here when returned to 6f.
*440 **SEREN TEG** 10 [1] R M Flower 4-9-4 (69)(bl) A Clark 14/1: 000-14: Sn outpcd/rear, styd on inner fnl 2f. ¾ **66a**
280 **ASHOVER AMBER** 36 [10] 4-9-0 (68) C Lowther 8/1: 313-45: Rear/wide, mod late gains: op 6/1: longer hd **64a**
priced stablemate of wnr, tricky high draw today, don't discount for similar: see 280 (6f).
462 **BRUTAL FANTASY** 7 [4] 6-8-13 (67) T Williams 16/1: 140306: Rdn/chsd ldrs, outpcd fnl 2f: op 10/1. 2½ **56a**
403 **AA YOUKNOWNOTHING** 17 [5] 4-9-1 (69)(tvi) S Finnamore (7) 8/1: 41-627: Prom wide 2f/sn outpcd. ¾ **56a**
258 **AURIGNY** 39 [6] 5-9-0 (71) P Doe 14/1: 055-08: Dwelt/rear, eff wide 2f out/no prog: see 191 (fbrsnd). hd **63a**
491 **JACKIES BABY** 2 [9] 4-9-9 (77) A Daly 8/1: 10-049: Cl-up wide 2f, sn struggling: tchd 10/1, qck reapp. 1 **61a**
372 **BOLDLY CLIFF** 21 [3] 6-8-2 (56)(bl) L Newman (4) 6/1: 401-20: Led 3f, wknd qckly fnl 1f: btr 372, 116. 1 **38a**
10 ran Time 58.48 (0.68) (M Dalby) T D Barron Maunby, N.Yorks.

---

507 3.35 DEMPSTER'S DIARY MDN 3YO+ (D) 5f aw rnd Going 11 -00 Slow
£2704 £832 £416 £208 3 yo rec 14lb

77 **LICENCE TO THRILL** 84 [4] D W P Arbuthnot 3-8-5 R Price 1/1 FAV: 025-1: 3 ch f Wolfhound - Crime Of **74a**
Passion (Dragonara Palace) Gd speed to lead after 1f, readily pulled clr under hand-and-heels riding fnl 1f: hvly
bckd, 12 wk abs: rnr-up in '99 (rtd 77a, mdn, rtd 38 on sole turf start): dam a Group winning juv, half-sister to
sev wnrs: eff at 5f, stays 6f well: acts on equitrack & a sharp trk: runs well fresh: shld win again.
334 **TOLDYA** 28 [8] E A Wheeler 3-8-5 (bl) S Carson (5) 11/4: 2-2432: 3 b f Beveled - Run Amber Run 7 **58a**
(Run The Gantlet) Cl-up halfway, rdn/outpcd over 1f out: op 2/1: h'caps shld suit best: see 334 (6f), 287 & 242.
449 **ARAB GOLD** 9 [5] M Quinn 5-9-10 R Studholme (5) 100/1: 00-003: 5 b g Presidium - Parklands Belle 2½ **56$**
(Stanford) Rdn/outpcd halfway, sn outpcd over fnl 2f, no threat: offic rtd 24, treat rating with caution: see 379.
438 **JONATHANS GIRL** 10 [2] J J Bridger 5-9-5 G Bardwell 25/1: 00-504: Rdn/rear, mod prog: see 358. shd **51$**
421 **CUPIDS DART** 14 [6] 3-8-10 T Williams 4/1: 6-5235: Cl-up early, outpcd halfway: op 7/2: btr 421 (7f). ¾ **54a**

166

LINGFIELD (Equitrack) SATURDAY FEBRUARY 12TH Lefthand, V Sharp Track

440	**MICKY DEE 10** [1] 4-9-10 (t) Joanna Badger (7) 66/1: 0-0006: Sn outpcd/struggling: see 440.	2	49$
439	**SHADY DEAL 10** [3] 4-9-10 Martin Dwyer 16/1: 00-047: Dwelt/rdn & rear, nvr factor: see 391.	nk	48$
426	**BLAZING PEBBLES 12** [7] 3-8-5 L Newman (5) 50/1: 0-0008: Sn outpcd: mod form.	6	32$
8 ran	Time 58.34 (0.54) (Christopher Wright) D W P Arbuthnot Lambourn, Berks.		

508

4.10 TEXT P368 HCAP 4YO+ 0-100 (C)   1m4f aw   Going 11   +02 Fast   [95]
£8268   £2544   £1272   £636   4 yo rec 3 lb

442	**URSA MAJOR 10** [2] C N Allen 6-8-0 (67) Martin Dwyer 10/1: 0-2121: 6 b g Warning - Double Entendre (Dominion) Made all, readily pulled clr over 2f out, eased down ins last, unchall: val for 8L+: gd time: op 6/1: earlier scored here at Lingfield (h'cap); '99 wnr at York (h'cap, rtd 64): '98 wnr at Southwell (2 clmrs, A Kelleway) & Lingfield (current connections, h'cap, rtd 90a): prev eff at 6f/7f, now seems suited by a sharp 10f/12f: acts on firm, soft & fibresand, loves equitrack/Lingfield: best dominating: looks well h'capped, shld win more races.		78a
*343	**CHALCEDONY 26** [1] T D Barron 4-8-1 (71) J Tate 7/1: 350-12: 4 ch g Highest Honor - Sweet Holland (Alydar) Trkd wnr 4f out, outpcd fnl 3f: op 9/2, clr of rem: shld win again: see 343 (fibresand).	4	73a
*296	**BE GONE 35** [4] C A Dwyer 5-9-5 (86) G Bardwell 10/1: 030-13: 5 ch g Be My Chief - Hence (Mr Prospector) Dwelt/towards rear & sn rdn, kept on for press fnl 4f, nvr a threat: op 7/1: needs further: see 296 (2m).	6	79a
*422	**RAYIK 14** [9] G L Moore 5-8-3 (70) P Doe 7/2: 0-1214: Cl-up 4f, sn rdn/held: tchd 4/1: see 422 (C/D).	¾	62a
+27	**ALBERICH 93** [3] 5-10-0 (95) D Holland 2/1 FAV: 0311-5: In tch halfway, btn 3f out: hvly bckd, tchd 3/1: 3 month abs, topweight: btr 27 (C/D stks).	8	78a
448	**CHINA CASTLE 9** [8] 7-9-9 (90) P Goode (5) 10/1: 54-066: Bhd, mod prog: op 6/1: see 157, 27.	8	64a
356	**RANDOM KINDNESS 24** [5] 7-9-1 (82) A Clark 10/1: 000-47: Rdn/bhd, btn 4f out: op 8/1: see 356.	1½	54a
422	**HIBERNATE 14** [6] 6-8-8 (75)(VIS) N Callan 10/1: 240-08: Cl-up 6f, sn rdn/btn: vis, op 6/1: see 422.	nk	46a
464	**LOST SPIRIT 7** [7] 4-7-10 (66)(12oh) G Baker (7) 33/1: 120259: Prom 1m: stiff task: btr 441 (C/D, led).	1¾	35a
9 ran	Time 2m 30.25 (1.05) (Newmarket Connectons Ltd) C N Allen Newmarket, Suffolk.		

509

4.40 JACK & GILL HCAP 3YO 0-85 (D)   1m2f aw   Going 11   -49 Slow   [82]
£4114   £1266   £633   £316

*461	**BLUEBELL WOOD 7** [1] G C Bravery 3-9-5 (73) A Culhane 9/4: 0-111: 3 ch f Bluebird - Jungle Jezebel (Thatching) Cl-up, rdn/hmpd & lost pl 5f out, rallied/chsd ldr over 2f out, styd on gamely for press ins last to lead nr line, all out: slow time: op 7/4: completed a hat-trick after a mdn & h'cap success prev (C/D): rtd 62 on sole '99 start (unplcd, mdn, A J McNae): eff at 10f, 12f+ shld suit: loves equitrack/Lingfield: has run well here: eff forcing the pace: tough, genuine & improving filly.		82a
171	**SERVICE STAR 63** [3] M A Jarvis 3-9-7 (75)(bl) N Callan 9/1: 2013-2: 3 b c Namaqualand - Shenley Lass (Prince Tenderfoot) Handy, led 4f out & clr over 2f out, hard rdn/drifted left ins last & hdd nr line: op 6/1, 2 month abs: well clr of rem: stays a sharp 10f: acts on both AWs: see 86 (1m, fibresand).	nk	83a
*395	**SOLLER BAY 18** [2] K R Burke 3-9-4 (72) D McGann (7) 6/1: 2-13: 3 b g Contract Law - Bichette (Lidhame) Keen, led/dsptd lead 7f, sn btn: btr 395 (fibresand).	13	66a
*415	**ARMENIA 15** [4] R Hannon 3-9-1 (69) P Fitzsimons (5) 15/2: 03-214: Cl-up wide, btn 4f out: op 6/1.	½	62a
420	**THATS ALL FOLKS 14** [5] 3-9-5 (73) A Clark 11/8 FAV: 33-125: Led/dsptd lead wide 7f: hvly bckd.	3½	61a
5 ran	Time 2m 08.75 (5.95) (The Iona Stud) G C Bravery Newmarket.		

SOUTHWELL (Fibresand) MONDAY FEBRUARY 14TH Lefthand, Sharp, Oval Track

Official Going   STANDARD. Stalls: Inside.

510

2.10 BET CLASSIFIED STKS 4YO+ 0-65 (E)   1m4f aw   Going 59   -14 Slow
£2588   £739   £369

*489	**FRENCH SPICE 4** [5] Sir Mark Prescott 4-9-4 D Sweeney 1/5 FAV: 111111: 4 b f Cadeaux Genereux - Hot Spice (Hotfoot) Trkd ldrs, cruised into lead 2f out, canter: well bckd, qck reapp, any amount in hand: landed a 7-timer, prev 6 at W'hampton (h'caps & class stks): eff btwn 8.5/12f, loves f/sand & W'hampton: hds to stud.		82a
456	**WESTERN COMMAND 10** [2] Mrs N Macauley 4-8-13 R Fitzpatrick (3) 8/1: 503362: 4 b g Saddlers' Hall - Western Friend (Gone West) Prom, eff 5f out, styd on, no ch with facile wnr: caught a tartar, ran to best.	4	64a
4085}	**CANNY CHIFTANE 99** [3] J I A Charlton 4-8-11 M Tebbutt 14/1: 6310-3: 4 b g Be My Chief - Prudence (Grundy) Led till 2½f out, no extra: op 10/1, hdles fit (stays 2m on gd/soft, rtd 91h): '99 W'hampton wnr (h'cap, rtd 62a & 60, M Jarvis): eff at 12f on fibresand: best up with/forcing the pace.	7	55a
407	**GYPSY 18** [4] M H Tompkins 4-8-11 (BL) S Finnamore (7) 14/1: W-3544: Well plcd, chall appr fnl 2f, fdd: op 8/1, blnkd: drop back in trip now required: see 407, 270.	2	53a
498	**SARPEDON 3** [1] 4-8-11 (bl) Joanna Badger (7) 100/1: -05005: Chsd ldrs till 4f out: flattered.	6	47$
5 ran	Time 2m 43.1 (8.8) (J Morley) Sir Mark Prescott Newmarket.		

511

2.40 0800 211 222 CLAIMER 4YO+ (F)   7f aw rnd   Going 59   +03 Fast
£2081   £594   £297

4219}	**BANDBOX 99** [3] M Salaman 5-9-3 D Dineley 14/1: 0300-1: 5 ch g Imperial Frontier - Dublah (Private Account) Rear, ran on for press appr fnl 2f, led towards fin: op 8/1, gd time: wng reapp/AW bow: '99 Leicester wnr (class stks, rtd 67): dual '98 rnr-up (h'cap, rtd 74): prev term won again at Leicester (mdn auct, rtd 81, S Mellor): eff at 5/7f on firm, gd/soft grnd & f/sand: eff with/without vis/blnks, tried a t-strap: goes well fresh.		68a
501	**GUEST ENVOY 3** [5] C N Allen 5-8-2 L Newman (4) 8/1: 0-0322: 5 b m Paris House - Peace Mission (Dunbeath) Chsd ldrs, gd hdwy to lead turning for home, sn rdn, worn down fnl 100y: qck reapp: another gd effort at unfavourable weights: in sound form: see 322.	½	51$
381	**ROYAL CASCADE 23** [4] B A McMahon 6-8-13 (bl) P Mundy (7) 9/4: 50-063: 6 b g River Falls - Relative Stranger (Cragador) In tch, feeling pace halfway, rallied for press appr fnl 1f, nrst fin: blnks reapplied back in trip: fav'd by weights on official ratings: will apprec being reunited with a stronger jockey: see 33.	nk	61a
449	**DAYNABEE 11** [7] Miss S J Wilton 5-8-6 P M Quinn (5) 6/1: 2-5154: Prom, rdn appr fnl 2f, no impress.	1¼	51a
465	**TAKHLID 9** [8] 9-9-3 A Culhane 1/1 FAV: -40225: Keen, well plcd, ev ch appr fnl 2f, fdd under press dist: hvly bckd: clrly better expected, poss best at W'hampton now: see 142.	½	61a
474	**WARRIOR KING 7** [1] 6-8-1 (vis) A Polli (3) 66/1: 050006: Sn struggling to go pace: qck reapp.	16	20a

SOUTHWELL (Fibresand)   MONDAY FEBRUARY 14TH   Lefthand, Sharp, Oval Track

327 **HIBAAT 31** [2] 4-9-3 Joanna Badger (7) 66/1: 0-0007: Al bhd: no ch at these weights, see 180.   *1* **34$**
--   **PROPERTY MAN** [6] 8-8-3 (VIS) A Nicholls (3) 40/1: 3000/3: Pulled hard & led till 2½f out, wknd: *3½* **14a**
visored, jumps fit, nr 3 yr Flat abs: been abroad, '95 Ostend wnr (5f, firm): '94 Southwell rnr-up (5f clmr).
8 ran   Time 1m 30.5 (3.9)   (M Salaman, R Brookes, G Else)   M Salaman Baydon, Wilts.

---

512   3.10 BEST BETS HCAP 4YO+ 0-85 (D)   **1m3f aw Going 59 -07 Slow**   **[70]**
   £4056   £1248   £624   £312   4 yo rec 2 lb

447 **HANNIBAL LAD 11** [5] W M Brisbourne 4-9-12 (70) T G McLaughlin 6/1: -15231: 4 ch g Rock City -   **75a**
Appealing (Star Appeal) Held up, gd wide hdwy appr str to lead dist, rdn out: earlier won at W'hampton (h'cap):
'99 wnr again at W'hampton (seller for P Evans, rtd 66a): '98 wnr here at Southwell (sell, rtd 67a & 69): eff
at 1m/9.3f, suited by step up to 11f: acts on firm, loves fibresand, sharp trks: goes well fresh: tough & versatile.
477 **STATE APPROVAL 6** [7] D Shaw 7-8-10 (52) N Callan 25/1: 600002: 7 b g Pharly - Tabeeba (Diesis)   *1¼* **54a**
Tried to make all, hdd dist, styd on: qck reapp & back to form returned to 11f from the front: see 270.
474 **GREEN BOPPER 7** [1] G Woodward 7-10-0 (70) P Goode (5) 10/3: 20-523: 7 b g Green Dancer -   *nk* **71a**
Wayage (Mr Prospector) Bhd ldrs, late gains: qck reapp: won this race off 11lb lower in '99.
508 **CHALCEDONY 2** [3] T D Barron 4-9-13 (71) C Lowther 9/4 FAV: 50-124: Sn rear, rdn & ran on 2f   *hd* **72a**
out, no extra cl-home: nicely bckd, ran Saturday: in-form: see 343 (C/D).
4615} **KENNET 99** [6] 5-9-11 (67) Martin Dwyer 8/1: 6310-5: Chsd ldrs, fdd appr fnl 1f: tchd 10/1 on   *3* **64a**
reapp: '99 wnr at Lingfield (mdn, rtd 72a), Windsor & Brighton (class stks, rtd 72): '98 rnr-up (auct mdn,
rtd 73): eff at 10/12f: goes on any grnd, likes sharp trks: can runs well fresh.
*474 **KIRISNIPPA 7** [2] 5-9-1 (57)(6ex) P Doe 33/2: -51316: Prom, ch appr fnl 2f, btn bef dist: shade   *½* **53a**
below best reappearing qckly with a penalty for 474 (beat this 3rd).
456 **JIBEREEN 10** [4] 8-10-0 (70) S Whitworth 6/1: 0-0427: Cl-up, wknd 2f out: op 9/2: btr 456 (12f).   *8* **56a**
7 ran   Time 2m 28.6 (7.3)   (John Pugh)   W M Brisbourne Great Ness, Shropshire.

---

513   3.40 TEXT FILLIES HCAP 4YO+ 0-70 (E)   **1m aw rnd Going 59 -02 Slow**   **[70]**
   £2756   £848   £424   £212

430 **JESSINCA 14** [9] Derrick Morris 4-8-2 (44) F Norton 12/1: /40-31: 4 b f Minshaanshu Amad - Noble   **52a**
Soul (Syaf El Arab) Chsd ldrs, eff 3f out, kept on to lead dist, pushed out: first win: unplcd in '99 (h'caps,
rtd 45a & 25, R Phillips): eff at 1m, tried further: goes on fibresand/sharp trks: improved for new connections.
430 **MY TESS 14** [1] B A McMahon 4-10-0 (70) L Newman (5) 5/2 FAV: 4-4522: 4 br f Lugana Beach -   *¾* **75a**
Barachois Princess (Barachois) Tried to make all, under press & hdd ent fnl 1f, rallied but held: op 3/1, clr of
rem: holding her form well tho' had this wnr 7L in arrears in 430 (C/D).
473 **STRAVSEA 7** [7] R Hollinshead 5-9-1 (57) P M Quinn (5) 5/1: 351163: 5 b m Handsome Sailor - La   *6* **52a**
Stravaganza (Slip Anchor) Dwelt, stdy late hdwy to go 3rd appr fnl 1f, nvr nr front pair: op 4/1, qck reapp.
430 **OARE KITE 14** [10] P S Felgate 5-7-11 (39)(bl)(1ow)(2oh) Dale Gibson 14/1: 66-354: Chsd ldrs 6f.   *1¾* **31a**
251 **CRYSTAL LASS 42** [4] 4-9-10 (66)(bl) P Dobbs (5) 5/1: 404-05: Dwelt, nvr better than mid-div: 6 wk   *4* **50a**
abs, op 4/1: '99 wnr here at Southwell (fill mdn h'cap, rtd 74a): plcd in '98 (auct mdn, rtd 62a, nurs, rtd 62):
eff at 7f, suited by 1m now: acts on fast & fibresand & prob best without blnks: can carry big weights.
384 **BUNTY 21** [5] 4-7-10 (38)(7oh) A Polli (3) 14/1: 16-406: Front rank till fdd appr fnl 2f: stiffish task.   *¾* **21a**
--   **CAPTIVATING** [2] 5-7-10 (38)(7oh) G Baker (7) 50/1: 0030/7: Handy till 3f out: stablemate of 6th,   *6* **11a**
stiff task: missed '99, plcd prev term for Mrs S Lamyman (h'cap, rtd 48): stays 10f on fast grnd, without visor.
339 **MEGA 28** [6] 4-8-0 (42)(BL) A Whelan (5) 14/1: 00-548: Bhd from halfway: blnkd, op 11/1: see 298.   *4* **9a**
463 **CRIMSON GLORY 9** [3] 4-10-0 (70) A Culhane (7) 2: 40-129: Al bhd: see 409 (W'hampton mdn).   *4* **31a**
--   **TOTAL TROPIX** [8] 5-7-12 (40)(VIS) P Doe 50/1: 0044/0: Sn struggling: 10th, visored: hdles fit, 2nd   *12* **0a**
in Oct '99 (2m nov on gd/soft, rtd 80h): no worthwhile Flat form 2 yrs ago for B Meehan: with Mrs Bradburne.
10 ran   Time 1m 44.3 (4.9)   (The Lambourn Racing Club)   Derrick Morris Lambourn, Berks.

---

514   4.10 TEXT FILLIES SELLER 3YO (G)   **1m aw rnd Going 59 -45 Slow**
   £1842   £526   £263

481 **WILEMMGEO 6** [1] P C Haslam 3-9-4 (vis) P Goode (5) 5/4 FAV: 0-2121: 3 b f Emarati - Floral Spark   **55a**
(Forzando) Prom, led 3f out, pushed 3L clr 2f out, rdn out: well bckd, slow time, sold for 4,400gns, qck reapp:
earlier won at W'hampton (seller): '99 wnr again at W'hampton (seller, rtd 55a & 62): eff at 1m/9.4f: acts
on firm, gd/soft grnd, loves fibresand, esp W'hampton: eff with/without visor, goes on any trk, likes sharp ones.
330 **LADY CYRANO 31** [4] Mrs N Macauley 3-8-12 R Fitzpatrick (3) 16/1: 00-362: 3 b f Cyrano de Bergerac -   *1¼* **46$**
Hazy Kay (Treasure Kay) Rear, hdwy 2f out, chsd wnr ins last, no extra cl-home: stays a sharp 1m: see 283.
48   **RITA MACKINTOSH 91** [5] R Brotherton 3-8-12 F Norton 11/1: 4030-3: 3 b f Port Lucaya - Silver   *nk* **45a**
Stream (Silver Hawk) Chsd ldrs, feeling pace 3f out, late rally: op 8/1, 3 month abs: plcd last term (fill sell in
1st time vis, rtd 49a & sell, rtd 51, M Tompkins): eff at 7f/8.4f: handles gd grnd & fibresand, with/without visor.
481 **AMELIA JESS 6** [2] B S Rothwell 3-9-4 (t) Joanna Badger (7) 5/1: -23154: Led till 3f out, onepace dist.   *1* **49a**
459 **PERLE DE SAGESSE 9** [7] 3-9-4 A Daly 4/1: 0-0545: Chsd ldrs, shkn up & carr head high 2f out,   *2½* **44a**
sn btn: back up in trip, beat over 7f at Lingfield: see 459.
350 **WISHEDHADGONEHOME 27** [3] 3-8-12 (vis) T G McLaughlin 10/1: 6-3056: Nvr in it after slow start.   *4* **30a**
319 **ROYAL CZARINA 32** [6] 3-8-12 D Dineley 16/1: 0-07: Prsd lead 3f, eased fnl 2f: no form.   *¾* **29a**
7 ran   Time 1m 47.9 (8.5)   (M J Cunningham)   P C Haslam Middleham, N.Yorks.

---

515   4.40 TEXT HCAP 3YO 0-60 (F)   **6f aw rnd Going 59 -11 Slow**   **[63]**
   £2205   £630   £315

459 **BAYTOWN RHAPSODY 9** [4] P S McEntee 3-9-6 (55) J Weaver 11/4 FAV: -32131: 3 b f Emperor Jones -   **62a**
Sing A Rainbow (Rainbow Quest) Prom, eff 3f out, ran on strgly ins last, led line: earlier won at W'hampton
(h'cap): plcd in '99 (auct mdn, rtd 56 & sell, rtd 49a): eff at 6/7f: acts on gd grnd, likes fibresand & sharp trks.
346 **PADDYWACK 27** [1] D W Chapman 3-8-1 (36)(bl) Dale Gibson 13/2: 60-052: 3 b g Bigstone - Millie's   *shd* **42a**
Return (Ballad Rock) Tried to make all & clr after 3f, worn down fnl stride: acts on gd/soft & f/sand, handles firm.
488 **FRENCH FANCY 5** [7] B A Pearce 3-8-11 (46)(bl) O Urbina 10/1: 4-0453: 3 gr f Paris House -   *3½* **43a**
Clipping (Kris) Not go early pace, wide hdwy over 2f out, nvr nr ldrs: op 8/1, qck reapp: needs further.
362 **MILLER TIME 25** [3] T D Easterby 3-8-12 (47) R Winston 9/2: 5004: Struggled to go pace, late hdwy.   *3* **35a**
443 **COLEY 12** [2] 3-9-2 (51)(bl) Martin Dwyer 15/2: 100-35: Dsptd lead early, rdn & losing pl when   *4* **29a**
bmpd rival appr fnl 2f: fibresand bow: much btr 443 (1st time blnks).

168

SOUTHWELL (Fibresand)   MONDAY FEBRUARY 14TH   Lefthand, Sharp, Oval Track

426 **NOWT FLASH** 14 [6] 3-9-7 (56) D Mernagh (5) 11/2: -01006: In tch, improving on inner when badly 2 28a
hmpd & nrly b.d. 2½f out, no extra: op 7/1: forget this: see 300.
357 **DIAMOND PROMISE** 26 [8] 3-9-6 (55) Joanna Badger (7) 5/1: 235-27: Chsd ldrs till appr fnl 2f: op 11/4. 1½ 23a
357 **SKI FREE** 26 [5] 3-8-0 (35) S Righton 33/1: 605-68: Al bhd: tchd 50/1, see 357. 1¾ 0a
8 ran   Time 1m 17.5 (4.2)   (Mrs B A McEntee)   P S McEntee Newmarket.

WOLVERHAMPTON (Fibresand)   TUESDAY FEBRUARY 15TH   Lefthand, Sharp Track

Official Going   STANDARD. Stalls: Inside.

516   2.10 BET DIRECT HCAP 4YO+ 0-75 (E)   1m1f79y aw   Going 16   -01 Slow   [69]
£2689   £768   £384

*490 **TYLERS TOAST** 5 [1] S Dow 4-9-7 (62)(6ex) P Doe 7/4 FAV: 40-211: 4 ch g Grand Lodge - Catawba 68a
(Mill Reef) Trkd ldrs, al trav well, led over 1f out, styd on well ins last, pushed out: nicely bckd, op 2/1: qck
reapp: earlier scored here at W'hampton (mdn): unplcd in '99 (rtd 80S, mdn, W Jarvis): rtd 78 in '98: eff at
9.4f, 10f+ cld suit: loves W'hampton/fibresand: gd weight carrier: open to further improvement.
447 **ROI DE DANSE** 12 [3] M Quinn 5-8-5 (46) F Norton 3/1: -03422: 5 ch g Komaite - Princess Lucy (Local 1 48a
Suitor) Keen/led till over 1f out, kept on for press: tchd 7/2: consistent: see 447, 227 & 203.
*446 **NAFITH** 12 [8] E L James 4-8-10 (51) S Whitworth 11/2: 0-3213: 4 ch g Elmaamul - Wanisa (Topsider) ½ 52a
Held up in tch, rdn/briefly no room 2f out, styd on ins last, not pace to chall: op 4/1: see 446 (C/D, mdn).
390 **EMPERORS GOLD** 22 [7] M G Quinlan 5-7-11 (38) G Baker (7) 11/1: 00-364: In tch, eff wide 2f out/sn held.3½ 32a
418 **TUFAMORE** 18 [2] 4-9-2 (57)(vis) N Callan 5/1: -42105: Keen/prom, fdd fnl 2f: see 418, 411. nk 50a
469 **SUMMER BOUNTY** 10 [4] 4-9-10 (65) A Culhane 25/1: 602-06: Rear/in tch, outpcd fnl 3f: see 469. 3½ 51a
469 **NAKED OAT** 10 [9] 5-9-1 (56) J Bosley (7) 20/1: 00-007: Prom 7f: op 12/1: see 329. 1¼ 39a
3728} **CHAMPAGNE GB** 99 [6] 4-9-7 (62) M Henry 25/1: 0410-8: Chsd ldrs 6f, sn btn: op 16/1, 6 month 3 39a
abs: '99 Leicester scorer (clmr, first success, rtd 66, R Charlton): eff at 10f, tried 12f, could suit in time: acts
on gd grnd & runs well fresh: enjoys claim grade: AW bow today for A Reid.
471 **FRENCH CONNECTION** 8 [5] 5-8-8 (48)(bl)(1ow) T G McLaughlin 12/1: 5-6209: Rear, rdn/bhd 3f out. 20 0a
9 ran   Time 1m 59.8 (1.6)   (Byerley Bloodstock)   S Dow Epsom, Surrey.

517   2.40 0800 211 222 CLAIMER 4YO+ (F)   1m1f79y aw   Going 16   +07 Fast
£2072   £592   £296

366 **RAMBO WALTZER** 25 [6] D Nicholls 8-8-11 F Norton 2/1: 1-1121: 8 b g Rambo Dancer - Vindictive Lady 66a
(Foolish Pleasure) Trkd ldrs, led 4f out, clr dist, rdn out: fast time, op 5/4, clmd for £6,000: earlier won
at Southwell (2, sell): '99 Catterick, Thirsk (h'caps, rtd 71) & Southwell wnr (3, 2 clmrs & sell, rtd 75a): '98
W'hampton & Southwell wnr (2, h'caps, rtd 91a & 72): eff at 7/9.4f on fast & soft, loves fibresand: run well fresh.
*433 **BACHELORS PAD** 14 [7] Miss S J Wilton 4-9-3 M Tebbutt 7/2: -02112: 6 b g Pursuit Of Love - 2½ 65a
Note Book (Mummy's Pet) Towards rear/in tch, rdn 5f out, styd on wide fnl 3f, not pace to chall: clr of rem.
433 **BILLICHANG** 14 [4] P Howling 4-8-11 (BL) T Williams 9/2: -23333: 4 b c Chilibang - Swing O'The Kilt 7 48a
(Hotfoot) Chsd wnr 4f out, rdn/held fnl 1f: first time blnks, no improvement: h'caps could suit best: see 238 (mdn).
466 **RIVER ENSIGN** 10 [5] W M Brisbourne 7-8-6 Claire Bryan (7) 10/1: 213004: Led after 1f till 4f out, fdd. 3½ 36a
431 **MUSTANG** 14 [1] 7-8-9 (vis) A Polli (3) 14/1: -30025: Led 1f, prom fd: tchd 20/1: visor reapp: see 59. 1 37a
477 **ULTRA CALM** 7 [3] 4-9-4 P Goode (5) 8/1: 0-3006: Mid-div, eff wide 4f out/no impress: op 6/1: btr 349. nk 45a
458 **SHABAASH** 10 [2] 4-8-8(1ow) D Holland 25/1: 0-4067: Chsd ldrs/sn rdn & strugg: btr 111 (eqtrck). 10 20a
452 **JATO DANCER** 11 [8] 5-8-0 P M Quinn (5) 50/1: 0-5008: Al rear: see 359. 2½ 7a
452 **FLASHFEET** 11 [9] 10-8-3 G Baker 66/1: 00-009: Sn bhd: see 398. 1½ 7a
9 ran   Time 1m 59.00 (0.8)   (W G Swiers)   D Nicholls Sessay, N.Yorks.

518   3.10 BEST BETS HCAP 3YO+ 0-70 (E)   5f aw rnd   Going 16   -08 Slow   [69]
£2808   £864   £432   £216   3 yo rec 14lb

491 **JAWHARI** 5 [2] D Nicholls 6-9-8 (63) F Norton 6/1: 600-01: 6 b g Lahib - Lady Of The Land (Wollow) 69a
Cl-up, led halfway, held on well ins last, drvn out: qck reapp: '99 Catterick wnr (h'cap, reapp, rtd 68): '98
rnr-up (stks, rtd 64): eff arnd 5f, stays 6f: acts on firm, gd/soft & f/sand: runs well fresh, has tried blnks.
491 **SAMWAR** 5 [4] Mrs N Macauley 8-10-0 (69)(vis) R Fitzpatrick (3) 5/1: -40622: 8 b g Warning - Samaza ¾ 72a
(Arctic Tern) Trkd ldrs, rdn/ev ch fnl 1f, kept on well: op 7/2, qck reapp: ahd of today's wnr in 491: see 214.
465 **ZIGGYS DANCER** 10 [3] E J Alston 9-9-10 (65) J P Spencer 6/1: 00-043: 9 b h Ziggy's Boy - My Shy ½ 66a
Dancer (Northjet) Chsd ldrs/sn rdn well fnl 1f, just held/no room cl-home: op 10/1: win soon: see 223.
*379 **OFF HIRE** 24 [7] C Smith 4-9-0 (55)(vis) G Faulkner (3) 7/1: 003-14: Led till halfway, outpcd fnl 1f. 1¼ 53a
491 **RING OF LOVE** 5 [5] 4-9-5 (60) R Cody Boutcher (7) 6/1: 5-1365: Chsd ldrs halfway, outpcd fnl 1f. shd 58a
388 **REX IS OKAY** 22 [1] 4-9-9 (64)(bl) S Finnamore (7) 14/1: 0-0666: Rdn/outpcd rear, mod gains: op 1½ 58a
10/1: acts on firm, soft & fibresand: return to 6f+ shld suit: slipping to a favourable mark: see 282 (7th).
445 **JACK TO A KING** 12 [6] 5-8-11 (52)(tbl) J Edmunds 3/1 FAV: 6-1527: Chsd ldrs, rdn/outpcd when ½ 44a
bmpd over 1f out, no impress after: op 4/1: btr 445, 291.
475 **SING FOR ME** 8 [9] 5-7-10 (37)(2oh) P M Quinn (5) 25/1: 0-0048: Al outpcd: see 272 (clmr). nk 28a
445 **SWEET MAGIC** 12 [8] 9-8-10 (51)(t) P Goode (7) 13/2: 6-0649: Chsd ldrs wide halfway/sn btn: op 5/1. ½ 40a
4303} **BODFARI TIMES** 99 [11] 4-9-0 (55) S Drowne 66/1: 0/00-0: Sn outpcd/wide: 10th: mod form in '99 (rtd 3½ 35a
33a & 40): rtd 83 in early '98 (flattered, mdn, A Bailey): eff at 5f & handles firm grnd.
352 **SNAP CRACKER** 28 [10] 4-8-5 (46) A Culhane 20/1: 000-00: Sn rdn/outpcd: 11th: op 12/1: see 235. 1 24a
11 ran   Time 1m 01.4 (1.2)   (Geoffrey Thompson)   D Nicholls Sessay, N.Yorks.

519   3.40 TEXT P368 MDN 4YO+ (D)   1m4f aw   Going 16   -45 Slow
£2613   £746   £373   4 yo rec 3 lb

1443} **HIGH POLICY** 99 [2] D J G Murray Smith 4-8-11 J P Spencer 5/4 FAV: 0/63-1: 4 ch g Machiavellian - 70a
Road To The Top (Shirley Heights) Trkd ldrs, smooth prog to lead 2f out, in command fnl 1f, pushed out: nicely
bckd, 9 month abs/AW bow: plcd on turf in '99 (rtd 86, mdn, Sir M Stoute): eff arnd a sharp/turning 12f, 14f+
shld suit: acts on fibresand & runs well fresh: open to further improvement in h'cap company.

-- **EUROLINK APACHE** [8] D R C Elsworth 5-9-0 L Branch (7) 6/1: 2/2: 5 b g Be My Chief - Eurolink Dancer (Petoski) Rear, stdy prog fnl 3f, kept on well ins last, nrst fin: jumps fit (mod form): missed '99 on the level: rnr-up sole Flat start in '98 (rtd 83, mdn): stays 12f, 14f+ looks sure to suit: acts on fast grnd & f/sand: handles a sharp trk: tenderly handled by inexperienced rider on AW bow: one to keep a close eye on. 4 **61+**
483 **TOY STORY 6** [9] Miss Gay Kelleway 4-8-11 (vis) D Holland 8/1: 02-633: 4 b g Fijar Tango - Grundygold (Grundy) Trkd ldr, led over 4f out, hdd 2f out & sn outpcd: op 6/1: qck reapp: jockey given a 4-day ban for careless riding: treat rating with caution, offic rtd 39: see 483, 196. *2½* **57$**
2213} **DRYING GRASS MOON 99** [1] J R Fanshawe 4-8-6 O Urbina 11/4: 46-4: Held up in tch, nvr pace to chall: op 5/4: 8 month abs/AW bow: unplcd tho' promise 2 '99 starts (rtd 69, mdn): stays 10f, this longer 12f trip shld suit: prob handles gd grnd & fibresand: well clr of rem today. *¾* **51a**
457 **MISCHIEF 10** [7] 4-8-11 F Norton 16/1: 03-055: Dwelt/rear, nvr factor: op 12/1: see 348 (h'cap). *9* **46$**
1903} **THE FOSSICK 99** [5] 4-8-11 P Hanagan (7) 12/1: 5-6: Led 1m, sn btn: op 33/1: 8 mth abs. *15* **30a**
457 **TRUE ROMANCE 10** [4] 4-8-11 P Clarke (7) 50/1: 0/07: Chsd ldrs till 5f out: no form. *9* **20a**
-- **LITTLE FINTLOCH** [6] 7-8-9 P McCabe 66/1: 8: Al rear: Flat debut, 3 month jumps absence. *27* **0a**
8 ran Time 2m 39.7 (6.1) (D Murray Smith) D J G Murray Smith Gumley, Leics.

520 4.10 TEXT P372 HCAP DIV 1 4YO+ 0-60 (F) 1m4f aw Going 16 -45 Slow [55]
£1722 £492 £246 4 yo rec 3 lb

494 **HILL FARM DANCER 5** [7] W M Brisbourne 9-8-3 (30) C Cogan (5) 3/1: -55231: 9 ch m Gunner B - Loadplan Lass (Nicholas Bill) Rear, prog 5f out, styd on well to lead well ins last, rdn out: jockey given a 1-day whip ban: qck reapp: '99 Southwell wnr (appr sell, rtd 54a & 30): '98 Musselburgh wnr (fill h'cap, rtd 59): eff at 12f, stays 2m: acts on firm, gd/soft & both AWs: handles any trk, likes W'hampton: runs well for an apprentice. **34a**
464 **OCEAN LINE 10** [6] G M McCourt 5-8-10 (37) A Nicholls (3) 9/4 FAV: 30-232: 5 b g Kefaah - Tropic Sea (Sure Blade) Led/dsptd lead till rdn/hdd ins last & no extra: clr rem: can find compensation: see 464, 383. *1¾* **38a**
458 **ALBERKINNIE 10** [3] J L Harris 5-7-12 (25) P M Quinn (5) 11/2: 0-0253: 5 b m Ron's Victory - Trojan Desert (Troy) Keen/prom, rdn/outpcd 3f out & sn held: op 4/1: see 377, 211. *10* **15a**
431 **KUWAIT THUNDER 14** [10] J L Eyre 4-9-1 (45) J P Spencer 16/1: 00-004: Held up, eff 3f out/sn held. *nk* **34a**
160 **FLUSH 69** [5] 5-9-4 (45) T G McLaughlin 5/1: /000-5: Prom, fdd fnl 2f: op 7/2: jumps fit, recent Ludlow wnr (sell hdle, rtd 88h, R Peacock, eff over 2m on gd/soft & hvy): no form in '99: '98 Flat wnr for J Hills at Leicester (clmr, rtd 74 at best): eff at 1m on firm & hvy, any trk: with Miss S Wilton. *1* **33a**
446 **UNTOLD STORY 12** [1] 5-7-13 (26) A Polli (3) 16/1: -06646: Rear, mod gains: op 10/1: see 263. *nk* **13a**
460 **XYLEM 10** [4] 9-8-11 (38)(vis) R Price 11/2: 0-3237: Al towards rear: btr 460, 347 (C/D). *1¾* **23a**
494 **NOTATION 5** [9] 6-7-10 (23)(bl)(6oh) Claire Bryan (7) 40/1: 000-08: Keen, led/dsptd lead till 3f out, sn btn: qck reapp: blnks reapp: see 494. *4* **2a**
405 **UP IN FLAMES 19** [2] 9-8-2 (29)(t) F Norton 20/1: 0-0009: Held up, outpcd/btn 3f out: changed stable. *3* **4a**
469 **JADE TIGER 10** [8] 4-9-10 (54) N Callan 14/1: 60-040: Keen, chsd ldrs 1m: 10th: op 10/1: topweight. *7* **19a**
10 ran Time 2m 39.7 (6.1) (M E Hughes) W M Brisbourne Great Ness, Shropshire.

521 4.40 TEXT P372 HCAP 4YO+ 0-75 (E) 1m100y a Going 16 -16 Slow [67]
£2639 £754 £377

433 **INTERNAL AFFAIR 14** [5] T D Barron 5-9-9 (62) Lynsey Hanna (7) 8/1: -10141: 5 b g Nicholas - Gdynia (Sir Ivor) In tch, rdn fnl 2f, switched ins last & styd on well to lead line: earlier won here at W'hampton (2, clmrs): '99 W'hampton wnr (h'cap, rtd 67a & 58): '98 W'hampton scorer (auct mdn, rtd 79a): suited by 8.5f, stays 9.4f: acts on soft/hvy, handles fast, fibresand/W'hampton specialist: enjoys claim grade. **66a**
476 **ABERKEEN 8** [4] M Dods 5-9-6 (59) A Culhane 8/11 FAV: 3-2122: 5 ch g Keen - Miss Aboyne (Lochnager) Held up, rdn to chall over 1f out, squeezed thr' gap to lead ins last, hdd line: hvly bckd, op 11/10: eff at 6f, suited by 7f/sharp 8.5f: remains in gd heart: see 368. *shd* **62a**
432 **DANAKIL 14** [2] K R Burke 5-9-11 (64) N Callan 10/1: 6-5663: 5 b g Warning - Danilova (Lyphard) Chsd ldr, rdn/led over 1f out, hdd ins last & just held nr fin: op 8/1: imprvd racing close to the pace: see 326. *¾* **66a**
435 **SANTANDRE 14** [7] R Hollinshead 4-9-13 (66) P M Quinn (5) 12/1: 3-0064: Led, hdd over 1f out, no extra cl-home: op 8/1: eff at 6f/sharp 8.5f: looks on a fair mark & could find similar: see 143 (7f). *nk* **67a**
*473 **PIPPAS PRIDE 8** [3] 5-9-12 (65)(6ex) S Finnamore (7) 5/1: -13115: Prom/keen, wknd fnl 1f: op 7/2. *4* **58a**
469 **BOWCLIFFE 10** [6] 9-10-0 (67) J P Spencer 7/1: 0-0436: Held up in tch, rdn/outpcd fnl 2f: op 11/2. *1¼* **57a**
477 **DEMOCRACY 7** [1] 4-9-7 (60)(bl) S Drowne 16/1: -00537: Dwelt/al rear: op 14/1: see 258 (6f). *6* **41a**
438 **PIPE DREAM 13** [8] 4-9-0 (53) P McCabe 16/1: 0-3368: Keen/prom 7f, eased/btn fnl 1f: flattered 353. *3* **28a**
8 ran Time 1m 48.9 (2.7) (Stephen Woodall) T D Barron Maunby, N.Yorks.

522 5.10 TEXT P372 HCAP DIV 2 4YO+ 0-60 (F) 1m4f aw Going 16 -44 Slow [51]
£1712 £489 £244 4 yo rec 3 lb

458 **OUR PEOPLE 10** [9] M Johnston 6-8-7 (30)(t) K Dalgleish (7) 5/1: -35331: 6 ch g Indian Ridge - Fair And Wise (High Line) Prom, led/dsptd lead halfway till went on 3f out, styd on well ins last, rdn out: op 4/1: unplcd in '99 (rtd 38a & 52, h'caps): '98 Carlisle & Redcar wnr (h'caps, rtd 63): eff at 1m/sharp 13f, acts on firm, soft & both AWs: handles any trk: best without blnks/visor, eff in a t-strap: nicely h'capped at present. **36a**
482 **MY LEGAL EAGLE 7** [8] R J Price 6-9-1 (38) P Doe 6/4 FAV: 4-0322: 6 b g Law Society - Majestic Nurse (On Your Mark) Prom, led 5f out till over 3f out, rdn & kept on fnl 2f, not pace of wnr: op 3/1: see 141, 126. *3* **39a**
215 **GENUINE JOHN 56** [3] J Parkes 7-8-13 (36) R Fitzpatrick (3) 6/1: 0063-3: 7 b g High Estate - Fiscal Folly (Foolish Pleasure) Mid-div, rdn 5f out, kept on fnl 2f, no threat to wnr: op 4/1, jumps fit (rtd 73h). *1* **36a**
*455 **ROYAL PARTNERSHIP 11** [6] K R Burke 4-9-10 (50) Darren Williams (7) 4/1: 0-P514: Keen/prom, chsd ldr going well 2f out, fdd fnl 1f: op 11/4: did not appear to get home over longer 12f trip: see 455 (11f, sell). *5* **43a**
336 **BOLD HUNTER 31** [1] 6-9-5 (42) S Whitworth 20/1: 000-05: Rear, eff 3f out, no impress: op 14/1. *5* **28a**
492 **BOBONA 5** [4] 4-8-4 (30) G Baker (7) 8/1: 01-026: Strugg halfway: op 4/1, qck reapp: btr 492, 178. *9* **6a**
3559} **BASHER JACK 99** [2] 4-9-7 (47)(t) J Bosley (7) 8/1: 4164-7: Al rear: tchd 10/1, 6 month abs: '99 wnr here at W'hampton (appr mdn h'cap, rtd 48a & 45): rtd 67 on sole start in '98 (mdn): eff at 12f, tried further: acts on fibresand, handles soft grnd: runs well for an apprentice. *4* **17a**
-- **REINHARDT** [5] 7-8-3 (26)(t) Joaana Badger (7) 50/1: 0605/8: Mid-div, struggling halfway: jumps fit (mod form, blnks): missed '99 on the level: unplcd in '98 (rtd 49 & 15a): '97 wnr at Beverley (appr mdn, rtd 40, D Nicholls): eff at 5f/10f on firm & gd/soft grnd: best without blnks: with L R Lloyd James. *½* **0a**
449 **MAID PLANS 12** [7] 4-7-10 (22) A Polli (3) 50/1: -05009: Keen/led till halfway, sn btn: mod form. *dist* **0a**
9 ran Time 2m 40.8 (7.2) (Mark Johnston Racing Ltd) M Johnston Middleham, N.Yorks.

LINGFIELD (Equitrack)   WEDNESDAY FEBRUARY 16TH   Lefthand, V Sharp Track

Official Going   STANDARD. Stalls: Inside, Except 5f - Outside

---

523   **2.10 BET DIRECT MDN 3YO (D)**   **1m2f aw   Going 34   -14 Slow**
£2782   £856   £428   £214

453   **MONSIEUR RICK 12** [3] Miss Gay Kelleway 3-9-0 D Holland 6/1: 341: 3 b c Sillery - Movieland   **78a**
(Nureyev) Trkd ldrs/hmpd after 1f, led over 3f out & sn rdn clr, eased nr fin, cmftbly: val for 14L+: op 5/1:
apprec this step up to 10f, may stay further: acts on equitrack & a sharp trk: clrly going the right way, win again.
467   **YOU DA MAN 11** [7] R Hannon 3-9-0 Pat Eddery 2/1: 00-422: 3 b c Alzao - Fabled Lifestyle (King's Lake) 11   **60a**
Led, hung badly left/hdd over 3f out, continued to hang left & not run on fnl 1f: well bckd: longer 10f trip.
3988} **VANISHING DANCER 99** [5] K R Burke 3-9-0 D Hayes (7) 50/1: 00-3: 3 ch g Llandaff - Vanishing Prairie   ½   **59a**
(Alysheba) Chsd ldrs, outpcd 3f out: abs, AW bow: unplcd in '99 (rtd 59, auct mdn): bred to apprec mid-dists.
287   **BROWNS DELIGHT 39** [1] S Dow 3-8-9 P Doe 20/1: 020-04: Chsd ldrs halfway, btn 3f out: see 287 (7f).   ½   **53a**
4159} **SPANISH STAR 99** [6] 3-9-0 M Tebbutt 7/4 FAV: 43-5: In tch wide halfway, sn rdn/no impress: well   hd   **57a**
bckd: 5 month abs/AW bow: promise both starts in '99 (rtd 77, mdn): stays a stiff/gall 1m & handles gd/soft
& soft grnd, mid-dists could suit this term: shld apprec h'caps.
453   **ROOM TO ROOM MAGIC 12** [2] 3-8-9 D Sweeney 20/1: 456: Prom till 5f out: longer 10f trip.   3½   **47a**
500   **DANCING MARY 5** [9] 3-8-9 J Stack 9/1: 550-37: Strugg halfway: op 5/1, qck reappr: btr 500 (1m).   12   **34a**
--   **MEDOOZA** [8] 3-8-9 A Culhane 10/1: 8: Sn rdn/bhd: op 6/1, debut: with G Bravery.   28   **4a**
8 ran   Time 2m 07.63 (4.83)   (The Dan Abbott Racing Partnership Two)   Miss Gay Kelleway Lingfield, Surrey

---

524   **2.40 0800 211 222 CLAIMER 4YO+ (F)**   **1m5f aw   Going 34   +01 Fast**
£2052   £586   £293   4 yo rec 4 lb

332   **INDIGO BAY 32** [4] S Dow 4-8-7 (vis) P Doe 4/1: 00-451: 4 b g Royal Academy - Cape Heights (Shirley   **65a**
Heights) Trkd ldr after 4f, led 3f out, forged clr fnl 2f: gd time: '99 Brighton (sell h'cap) & Lingfield wnr
(h'cap, rtd 72): rtd 71 in '98 for A Stewart: eff at 11/13f, tried further: acts on firm, fast & equitrack:
eff with/without blnks/visor: likes a sharp/undul trk: eff up with/forcing the pace: apprec drop to clmg grade.
498   **NIGHT CITY 5** [5] K R Burke 9-9-7 N Callan 11/4 FAV: 522602: 9 b g Kris - Night Secret (Nijinsky)   9   **65a**
Led, rdn/hdd over 3f out, no impress fnl 2f: well bckd, tchd 7/2: quick reapp: see 92 (1m).
*458   **APPYABO 11** [2] M Quinn 5-8-9 F Norton 7/1: 0-0213: 5 ch g Never So Bold - Cardinal Palace (Royal   19   **33a**
Palace) Prom, lost place after 5f, mod late gains, no impress front pair: tchd 9/1: see 458 (C/D, sell h'cap).
*460   **NEGATIVE EQUITY 11** [1] D G Bridgwater 8-8-5 (bl) S Righton 5/1: 025/14: Rdn/bhd, mod gains.   ¾   **28a**
408   **PARDAN 20** [7] 6-8-9 D Sweeney 20/1: 100-65: In tch wide 5f, sn btn: see 408.   6   **23a**
468   **KATIES CRACKER 11** [6] 5-8-0 Martin Dwyer 12/1: 0-0046: Strugg halfway, op 8/1, stablemate of 3rd.   3   **10a**
115   **TWOFORTEN 82** [3] 5-8-11 (bl) A Nicholls (3) 14/1: 3305-7: Trkd ldrs halfway, btn 5f out: op 10/1, abs: 5   **14a**
blnks reapplied: plcd sev times in '99 (rtd 41, h'cap): plcd in '98, (rtd 46, appr h'cap): eff arnd 10/12f, has tried
2m: acts on firm & good, prob handles equitrack: likes a sharp/undul trk: eff with/without blnks, has tried a visor.
482   **MACHIAVELLI 8** [9] 6-9-3 (bl) J Mongan (7) 11/2: /6-508: Dwelt, in tch wide after 1f, btn 6f out: op 7/2.   7   **10a**
8 ran   Time 2m 46.62 (4.32)   (Byerley Bloodstock)   S Dow Epsom, Surrey

---

525   **3.10 BEST BETS HCAP 4YO+ 0-80 (D)**   **7f aw rnd   Going 33   -01 Slow**   **[78]**
£4192   £1290   £645   £322

435   **REDOUBTABLE 15** [1] D W Chapman 9-9-13 (77) A Culhane 4/1: -64121: 9 b h Grey Dawn II - Seattle   **84a**
Rockette (Seattle Slew) Trkd ldrs, squeezed thro' gap ins last to lead, drvn out: nicely bckd: earlier scored at
Southwell (h'cap): '99 Thirsk wnr (h'cap, rtd 81 & 74a): '98 Lingfield, Ayr & Newcastle wnr (h'caps, rtd 79 & 78a):
suited by 6/7f, stays a sharp 1m: acts on firm, soft & loves both AWs: handles any trk, likes a sharp one: best
without blnks: gd weight carrier: tough & genuine 9yo, a credit to connections.
-485   **RONS PET 7** [2] K R Burke 5-9-8 (72)(tbl) N Callan 4/1: -23322: 5 ch g Ron's Victory - Penny Mint   1¼   **76a**
(Mummy's Game) Dwelt & rdn to go handy after 1f, hard rdn/led over 1f out, hdd ins last, kept on: nicely bckd.
454   **RUDE AWAKENING 12** [4] C W Fairhurst 6-8-6 (56) P Doe 14/1: -41303: 6 b g Rudimentary - Final   2   **56a**
Call (Town Crier) Led, rdn/hdd over 1f out, no extra ins last: op 10/1: stays 1m, suited by 5/6f: see 358 (6f).
491   **BLUE KITE 6** [9] N P Littmoden 5-10-0 (78) J Tate 9/1: 166034: Held up in tch wide, kept on for press   ¾   **77a**
fnl 2f, no threat: op 6/1: qck reappr: ran his usual game race but had a high draw here: see 258 (6f, fibresand).
466   **AUBRIETA 11** [6] 4-8-4 (54)(bl) A Mackay 9/1: 601-05: Held up in tch, kept on fnl 2f/not pace to chall.   shd   **53a**
503   **INDIAN WARRIOR 4** [7] 4-8-8 (58) Pat Eddery 7/2 FAV: 10-066: Held up, eff over 1f out/no impress: bckd. 1¼   **54a**
466   **POLLY MILLS 11** [3] 4-9-1 (65)(bl) T G McLaughlin 11/1: -03657: Chsd ldrs, held fnl 2f: blnks reapp.   4   **53a**
4298} **ACID TEST 99** [5] 5-9-1 (65) R Fitzpatrick (3) 8/1: 0400-8: Chsd ldrs 4f: op 6/1, abs: '99 Lingfield   1   **51a**
(2, rtd 66a), Catterick & Chester wnr (h'caps, rtd 78): '98 Lingfield wnr (2, rtd 60a & 70, W Muir): eff at 6/7f,
stays a sharp 1m: acts on firm, soft & equitrack: has run well fresh: loves to force the pace: likes Lingfield.
506   **BRUTAL FANTASY 4** [8] 6-9-3 (67) T Williams 16/1: 403069: Chsd ldrs 4f: op 12/1, quick reapp.   5   **43a**
9 ran   Time 1m 25.16 (2.36)   (David W Chapman)   D W Chapman Stillington, N Yorks

---

526   **3.40 NAC RE HCAP 3YO 0-70 (E)**   **5f aw rnd   Going 34   +01 Fast**   **[77]**
£2730   £840   £420   £210

507   **TOLDYA 4** [2] E A Wheeler 3-8-6 (55)(bl) S Carson (5) 9/2: -24321: 3 b f Beveled - Run Amber Run   **62a**
(Run The Gantlet) Dwelt, rdn/rapid prog to lead over 3f out, clr 2f out, held on well ins last, rdn out: gd time:
op 4/1, quick reappr: unplcd on turf in '99 (rtd 51, rnr-up on sand, rtd 50a, mdn): eff forcing the pace at 5f,
stays 6f well: acts on equitrack & a sharp trk: eff in blnks: could win in similar grade again.
361   **PIPS STAR 27** [1] D W P Arbuthnot 3-8-13 (62) R Price 7/1: 001-32: 3 b f Pips Pride - Kentucky   1¼   **64a**
Starlet (Cox's Ridge) Led till 3f out, outpcd, kept on ins last: acts on fast & both AWs: enjoys sell grade.
487   **CLOPTON GREEN 7** [6] J W Payne 3-7-10 (45)(bl) P M Quinn (5) 9/1: 06-033: 3 b g Presidium -   1   **45a**
Silkstone Lady (Blakeney) Chsd ldrs, kept on fnl 2f for press, not pace to chall: op 6/1: see 487 (sell, C/D).
515   **PADDYWACK 2** [7] D W Chapman 3-7-10 (45)(bl)(9oh) Claire Bryan (7) 9/1: 0-0524: Chsd ldrs,   1   **43a**
outpcd halfway: quick reapp: acts on both AWs, firm & gd/soft grnd: see 515 (led, 6f, fibresand).
487   **POWER AND DEMAND 7** [8] 3-7-10 (45)(bl) F Norton 13/2: 04-025: Sn rdn, nvr on terms: op 5/1.   ½   **41a**
444   **KIRSCH 14** [5] 3-9-7 (70)(vis) P Clarke (7) 9/1: 3-3156: Rear/wide, outpcd: op 7/1: btr 361 (fbrsnd).   2½   **59a**
397   **PARKSIDE PROSPECT 22** [3] 3-8-9 (58) G Hannon (7) 6/1: 31-457: Sn outpcd: op 9/2: btr 207 (6f, clmr). 2½   **40a**
269   **GREY FLYER 42** [4] 3-9-0 (63) A Culhane 4/1 FAV: 42-128: Sn outpcd/bhd: nicely bckd, tchd 5/1:   5   **36a**

171

LINGFIELD (Equitrack)   WEDNESDAY FEBRUARY 16TH   Lefthand, V Sharp Track

6 wk abs: disapp eff, capable of better: see 269, 242.
8 ran   Time 59.46 (1.66)   (Benham Racing)   E A Wheeler Whitchurch On Thames, Oxon

527	4.10 TEXT P368 SELLLER 3YO (G) 6f aw rnd Going 34 -25 Slow	
	£1867 £533 £266	

479   **ITSGOTTABDUN** 8 [3]   K T Ivory 3-8-11 (bl) C Catlin (7)   9/2: -44061: 3 b g Foxhound - Lady Ingrid **60a**
(Taufan) Chsd ldrs, wide & stdy run from 2f out to lead ins last, rdn out: bought in for 3,800 gns: slow time: blnks
reapplied: rnr-up on turf in '99 (sell, rtd 62, rtd 57a on sand): eff at 5f, suited by 6f, has tried 1m: acts on
equitrack, handles soft grnd: likes a sharp trk: eff in blnks, has tried a visor: apprec drop to sell grade.
362   **TEA FOR TEXAS** 27 [1]   H Morrison 3-8-6 C Rutter 5/2: 4-352: 3 ch f Weldnaas - Polly's Teahouse   2 **49a**
(Shack) Chsd ldrs halfway, rdn/briefly led ins last, kept on: well bckd: eff at 6f on eqtrk: apprec drop to sells.
487   **MASTER JONES** 7 [6]   Mrs L Stubbs 3-8-11 G Hannon (7)   7/1: 233253: 3 b g Emperor Jones - Tight Spin 1¾ **50a**
(High Top) Chsd ldrs, kept on onepace fnl 2f: op 5/1: blnks omitted after latest: see 443, 281 & 94.
*487   **PAPE DIOUF** 7 [7]   B Smart 3-9-4 (bl) J Stack 15/8 FAV: 50-014: Rdn/sn led, hdd over 1f out & no   ¾ **55a**
extra ins last: hvly bckd tho' op 11/8: had to work hard to gain lead from high draw: see 487 (5f, low draw).
459   **INCH PINCHER** 11 [2]   3-9-4 (bl) T Williams 8/1: 25-055: Cl-up, led over 1f out, hdd ins last & no extra.   ½ **53$**
443   **SHOULDHAVEGONEHOME** 14 [8]   3-8-13 (bl) T G McLaughlin 16/1: 0-5056: Wide/in tch, outpcd fnl 1f: ½ **46a**
op 8/1, blnks reapplied: btr 42 (5f, fibresand).
--   **CHARTWELL** [5]   3-8-11 R Price 20/1: 7: V slowly away & al bhd: op 12/1, debut: with T Jones.   8 **29a**
443   **KATIE KING** 14 [4]   3-8-6 L Newton 25/1: 68: Sn outpcd: no form.   5 **15a**
8 ran   Time 1m 13.96 (3.56)   (Stephen Williams)   K T Ivory Radlett, Herts

528	4.40 TEXT P372 FILLIES HCAP 4YO+ 0-75 (E) 1m4f aw Going 34 -06 Slow	[67]
	£2691 £828 £414 £207 4 yo rec 3 lb	

377   **SLEAVE SILK** 25 [3]   W J Musson 5-8-10 (49) L Newton 4/1: 64-201: 5 b m Unfuwain - Shanira (Shirley   **51a**
Heights) In tch, prog to lead over 1f out, held on, pushed out: op 2/1: '99 Lingfield wnr (3, h'caps, rtd 50a &
39): eff at 12f/sharp 2m: handles fibresand, equitrack/Lingfield specialist: good ride by L Newton.
469   **MONO LADY** 11 [5]   D Haydn Jones 7-9-12 (65) (bl) A Mackay 11/2: 420-02: 7 b m Polish Patriot -   nk **66a**
Phylella (Persian Bold) Held up in tch, smooth prog & ev ch fnl 1f, kept on well for press, just held: op 5/1.
309   **PARISIAN LADY** 36 [4]   A G Newcombe 5-9-1 (54) S Whitworth 9/1: 106-63: 5 b m Paris House - Mia Gigi 3½ **50a**
(Hard Fought) Trkd ldrs, briefly no room over 1f out, rdn/onepace ins last: op 7/1: prob styd longer 12f trip.
4546}   **ORDAINED** 99 [2]   Miss Gay Kelleway 7-7-11 (36) P Doe 8/1: 0000-4: Cl-up, led over 5f out till 1f out,   1¾ **30a**
no extra: op 12/1, 4 month abs: unplcd in '99 for E J Alston (rtd 55, h'cap): plcd twice in '98 (h'caps, rtd 61):
eff at 10/12f on firm & gd grnd, likes a stiff/gall trk: well h'capped if recapturing form for new connections.
*377   **SPINNING STAR** 25 [1]   A 4-10-0 (70) M Cotton (7)   8/11 FAV: 540-15: Led till over 5f out, remained cl-up   2 **61a**
till wknd fnl 1f: hvly bckd at odds-on: trainer reported filly was difficult to settle & ran freely early on: btr 377 (C/D).
5 ran   Time 2m 33.99 (4.79)   (Broughton Bloodstock)   W J Musson Newmarket, Suffolk

WOLVERHAMPTON (Fibresand)   THURSDAY FEBRUARY 17TH   Lefthand, Sharp Track

Official Going   STANDARD. Stalls: Inside, Except 7f - Outside

529	2.00 FILLIES HCAP 4YO+ 0-70 (E) 1m1f79y aw Going 17 -03 Slow	[59]
	£2743 £844 £422 £211	

517   **RIVER ENSIGN** 2 [7]   W M Brisbourne 7-9-2 (47) Claire Bryan (7)   5/1: 130041: 7 br m River God -   **51a**
Ensigns Kit (Saucy Kit) Made all, held on well ins last, rdn out: qck reapp: earlier won here at W'hampton (clmr):
'98 W'hampton (clmr, rtd 53a) & Chepstow wnr (h'cap, rtd 47): '97 Southwell & Nottingham wnr (h'caps, rtd 44a & 44):
eff at 5/7f, best arnd 1m/10f: acts on gd, hvy & f/sand: likes W'hampton: runs fresh: best dominating.
*447   **AREISH** 14 [8]   J Balding 7-9-10 (55) J Edmunds 4/9 FAV: -51112: 7 b m Keen - Cool Combination   1¼ **56a**
(Indian King) Held up in tch, prog to chase wnr fnl 2f, kept on ins last, no pace to chall: well bckd at odds-on.
4328}   **TYCOON TINA** 99 [3]   W M Brisbourne 6-7-11 (28) P M Quinn (5)   20/1: 0600-3: 6 b m Tina's Pet - Royal 3½ **22a**
Tycoon (Tycoon II) Rear, late gains wide for press, nrst fin: op 12/1, longer precd stablemate of wnr: 10 wk
jumps abs (rtd 56h, nov clmr): rnr-up in '99 (rtd 35, clmr, no sand form): '98 wnr at Hamilton & Beverley (h'caps,
rtd 57 & 47a): best without blnks.
474   **MISS TAKE** 10 [4]   A G Newcombe 4-9-5 (50) T Williams 12/1: 5-0044: Cl-up, no extra fnl 2f: op 10/1.   ½ **43a**
494   **SARTEANO** 7 [1]   6-7-10 (27)(7oh) Joanna Badger (7)   20/1: 0-6365: Trkd ldrs, rdn/outpcd from halfway.   1¼ **17a**
--   **SHARWAY LADY** [5]   5-9-1 (46) F Lynch 11/1: 0660/6: Al bhd: op 6/1: jumps fit, Col '99 wnr at   9 **23a**
Bangor (cj nov h'cap, rtd 89h, eff arnd 2m1f on firm & soft): missed '99, '98 Southwell wnr (sell, B A McMahon,
rtd 54a & 43): eff over 1m, tried 12f: acts on fibresand: eff in blnks & enjoys sells.
469   **RIBBLE PRINCESS** 12 [6]   5-9-7 (52) (vis) S Drowne 33/1: /0-007: Trkd ldrs halfway, btn 3f out: see 469.   13 **10a**
7 ran   Time 2m 00.1 (1.9)   (Crispandave Racing Associates)   W M Brisbourne Great Ness, Shropshire

530	2.30 0800 211 222 CLAIMER 4YO+ (F) 1m4f aw Going 17 -27 Slow	
	£2062 £589 £294 4 yo rec 3 lb	

441   **FAILED TO HIT** 15 [1]   N P Littmoden 7-9-3 (vis) J Tate 4/5 FAV: 423201: 7 b g Warrshan - Missed Again   **61a**
(High Top) Made all, styd on well fnl 2f, rdn out: nicely bckd: '99 W'hampton (h'cap) & Lingfield wnr (clmr, rtd
74a): '98 wnr at Lingfield (3, h'caps & ltd stks) & W'hampton (3, clmr & h'caps, rtd 68a): eff at 1m, suited by
12f, tried further: handles fast grnd, AW/sharp trk specialist: eff in blnks/visor: loves to force the pace.
502   **I CANT REMEMBER** 6 [4]   S R Bowring 6-8-11 S Finnamore (7)   8/1: 00-652: 6 gr g Petong - Glenfield   1¾ **51a**
Portion (Mummy's Pet) Chsd ldrs, outpcd 5f out, kept on fnl 2f, no threat to wnr: quick reapp: acts
on firm, soft & gd with AWS: return to h'cap company could best wnr: see 428.
455   **APPROACHABLE** 13 [6]   Miss S J Wilton 5-8-13 M Tebbutt 8/1: 254423: 5 b h Known Fact - Western   4 **47a**
Approach (Gone West) Chsd ldrs, cl-up 4f out/ev ch, rdn/no extra fnl 2f: return to 10/11f could suit: see 455, 45.
512   **JIBEREEN** 3 [7]   P Howling 8-9-7 S Whitworth 7/2: -04204: Held up in tch, eff 5f out, no impress: qck   5 **48a**
reapp: stays a sharp 12f, prob best around 7f/1m: see 197 (1m).
400   **LORD EUROLINK** 22 [3]   6-8-11 (E) J Weaver 6/1: 5-0305: Sn bhd: tried eyeshield, op 9/2: recent   *dist*   **0a**

172

WOLVERHAMPTON (Fibresand) THURSDAY FEBRUARY 17TH Lefthand, Sharp Track

jumps rnr (unplcd, rtd 74h): btr 333 (10f, equitrack).

4258} **TEEPLOY GIRL 99** [2] 5-8-0 A Daly 66/1: 00/0-6: Cl-up 5f, sn struggling: jumps fit (no form): no '99   5   0a
Flat form for J P Smith: plcd back in '97 here at W'hampton (sell, rtd 51a, N P Littmoden): stays 6f on f/sand.

--   **GLADIATORIAL** [5] 8-8-7 T Williams 33/1: 1/7: Sn bhd: jumps fit (mod form): ex-Irish, won sole   7   0a
prev Flat start in '97 at Downpatrick (13f mdn, fast): AW bow today for Miss S E Baxter.
7 ran   Time 2m 38.9 (5.3)   (Trojan Racing)   N P Littmoden Newmarket

---

531 3.05 BEST BETS MDN 3YO+ (D) 7f aw rnd Going 17 -32 Slow
£2704   £832   £416   £208   3 yo rec 17lb

478   **PALAWAN 9** [4] I A Balding 4-9-10 A Nicholls (3) 1/4 FAV: 220-21: 4 br g Polar Falcon - Krameria (Kris)   71a
Sn led, rdly pulled clr over 2f out, easily: val for 7L+, hvly bckd: rnr-up thrice in '99 (mdns, rtd 75): eff
btwn 5/7f, 6f may suit best: acts on fast, gd & f/sand: handles a stiff/undul or sharp trk: eff forcing the pace.

--   **OCEAN SONG** [2] S R Bowring 3-8-2 Dale Gibson 20/1: 2: 3 b f Savahra Sound - Marina Plata (Julio   3½   52a
Mariner) Dwelt/rdn & bhd, kept on fnl 2f for press, no threat to wnr: op 8/1, debut: half sister to 4 wnrs on
fibresand incl tough/useful h'capper First Maite: 1m+ could suit on this evidence, prob handles fibresand.

389   **TRUMPET BLUES 24** [5] D Nicholls 4-9-10 O Pears 5/1: 2/6-03: 4 br g Dayjur - Iosifa (Top Ville)   3   51a
Prom, rdn/no extra fnl 2f: op 3/1: see 389 (6f, sell).

490   **ANNADAWI 7** [1] C N Kellett 5-9-10 (VIS) N Carlisle 14/1: -44054: Towards rear, nvr on terms: visor.   5   41$
465   **DORANFIELD LADY 12** [6] 5-9-5 A Mackay 50/1: 005: Al bhd: see 378.   4   28a
478   **LASTOFTHECASH 9** [3] 4-9-10 T G McLaughlin 25/1: 06: Sn outpcd: no form.   4   25a
6 ran   Time 1m 29.6 (3.4)   (Robert Hitchins)   I A Balding Kingsclere, Hants

---

532 3.35 TEXT P368 HCAP 3YO+ 0-100 (C) 6f aw rnd Going 17 +04 Fast   [97]
£6727   £2070   £1035   £517   3 yo rec 15lb

*499   **DAAWE 6** [2] D Nicholls 9-8-7 (76)(bl)(6ex) Clare Roche (7) 11/4 FAV: 060-11: 9 b h Danzig - Capo Di   82a
Monte (Final Straw) Led after 1f, edged left/pushed out to hold fnl 1f: fast time, nicely bckd, jockey given a
1-day careless riding ban: recent Southwell wnr (h'cap): '99 scorer at Pontefract & Newcastle (h'caps, rtd 71 &
68a): '98 Thirsk & Doncaster wnr (ltd stks, rtd 81 & 75a): best at 5/6f, stays 1m: acts on firm, hvy & f/sand:
handles any trk: eff with/without a visor/blnks: runs well fresh & loves to dominate: tough 9yo, in great heart.

462   **JUWWI 12** [12] J M Bradley 6-9-1 (84) Claire Bryan (7) 9/1: 335322: 6 ch g Mujtahid - Nouvelle Star   ¾   87a
(Luskin Star) Rdn/towards rear, styd on well fnl 2f, nrst fin: ran his usual game race: see 129.

+406   **ASTRAC 21** [8] A J McNae 9-9-0 (83) J Weaver 9/1: 335-13: 9 b g Nordico - Shirleen (Daring Display)   hd   85a
Led 1f, remained cl-up, kept on well for press fnl 1f: tchd 10/1: encouraging return to h'caps: see 406 (C/D clmr).

258   **PIPS SONG 44** [7] Dr J D Scargill 5-8-8 (77) F Norton 13/2: 220-24: Chsd ldrs, rdn & kept on well   shd   79a
fnl 1f, just held when eased cl-home: op 5/1, 6 wk abs: see 258, 129.

*435   **BLUE STAR 16** [9] 4-9-2 (85)(vis) C Cogan (5) 13/2: -52415: Rear/wide, styd on well fnl 1f, nrst fin.   ½   85a
*465   **MALLIA 12** [11] 7-8-0 (69) T Williams 14/1: 405516: Prom, onepace fnl 1f: op 16/1: see 465 (clmr).   nk   68a
*454   **KEEN HANDS 13** [1] 4-8-10 (79)(vis) R Fitzpatrick (3) 12/1: -10417: Chsd ldrs, rdn/held fnl 1f: op 10/1.   ½   76a
462   **BEST QUEST 12** [3] 5-7-13 (68)(f) Joanna Badger (7) 20/1: 233358: Mid-div, nvr pace to chall: see 403.   ½   63a
435   **CLASSY CLEO 16** [6] 5-9-10 (93) J P Spencer 16/1: 423009: Prom, outpcd halfway: op 14/1: see 64.   nk   87a
435   **FIRST MAITE 16** [13] 7-9-5 (88)(bl) R Winston 8/1: 540-40: Chsd ldrs wide 5f: 10th: tchd 10/1.   nk   81a
435   **THE DOWNTOWN FOX 16** [10] 5-9-1 (84)(vis) L Newman (5) 8/1: 10-100: Rear/wide, no impress: 12th.   0a
*475   **Dahlidya 10** [4] 5-7-12 (67)(6ex) P Doe 16/1:   435 **Bold Effort 16** [5] 8-8-8 (77) A Culhane 33/1:
13 ran   Time 1m 13.6 (0.8)   (Mrs Andrea M Mallinson)   D Nicholls Sessay, N Yorks

---

533 4.10 TEXT P372 SELLER 3YO+ (G) 5f aw rnd Going 17 -21 Slow
£1913   £546   £273   3 yo rec 14lb

342   **MANORBIER 31** [11] K A Ryan 4-9-7 F Lynch 5/1: 250/01: 4 ch g Shalford - La Pirouette (Kennedy Road)   59a
Mid-div, strong run fnl 1f for press to lead nr line: op 10/1, bt in for 5,000gns: missed '99: '98 Chepstow wnr
(juv auct mdn, D R Arbuthnot, rtd 83): eff at 5f, 6f shld suit on fast, gd & fibresand: apprec drop to sellers.

72   **LISA B 90** [3] D L Williams 3-8-2 (bl) G Baker (7) 12/1: 0000-2: 3 b f Case Law - Nishiki (Brogan)   nk   53a
Handy, briefly led well ins last, hdd nr line: tchd 16/1, 3 month abs: '99 Southwell & W'hampton wnr (sells,
rtd 70a & 59, with J Glover): eff at 6f, tried 7f: acts on f/sand & a sharp trk: best blnkd, has tried visor.

403   **PALACEGATE JACK 22** [8] A Berry 9-9-7 (bl) D Allan (7) 6/1: 52-253: 9 gr g Neshad - Pasadena   ¾   56a
Lady (Captain James) Led after 1f, rdn over 1f out, hdd well ins last & no extra: op 5/1: see 312, 191.

436   **SOUNDS LUCKY 16** [4] N P Littmoden 4-9-7 C Carver (3) 7/1: 0-6044: Chsd ldrs, kept on well fnl 1f.   ½   54a
379   **TINKERS SURPRISE 26** [7] 6-9-7 (bl) J Edmunds 20/1: 6-5365: Towards rear, mod gains: see 116.   1   52$
440   **NIFTY NORMAN 15** [5] 6-9-12 (bl) F Norton 1/1 FAV: -13236: Rdn/chsd ldrs, btn 1f out: hvly bckd.   1¼   54a
475   **BLUSHING GRENADIER 16** [6] 8-9-7 (bl) S Finnamore (7) 12/1: 333437: Towards rear, nvr on terms.   hd   44a
445   **YOUNG IBNR 14** [1] 5-9-7 L Newman (5) 9/1: 3-0568: Led 1f, prom 4f: op 14/1: see 166, 116.   1   46$
518   **SWEET MAGIC 2** [2] 9-9-7 (tVl) P Goode (5) 6/1: -06409: Dwelt, mid-div halfway, btn 1f out: visor.   nk   45a
465   **LITTLE IBNR 12** [10] 9-9-7 (vis) J P Spencer 10/1: 6-0430: Al rear/wide: 10th: op 8/1: btr 465 (6f).   2   40a
499   **ICE AGE 6** [9] 6-9-7 (bl) T G McLaughlin 20/1: 050000: Mid-div/wide, hung right 2f out/sn btn: 11th.   ¾   38a
11 ran   Time 1m 02.1 (1.9)   (Uncle Jacks Pub)   K A Ryan Hambleton, N Yorks

---

534 4.45 TEXT P372 HCAP 3YO 0-80 (D) 7f aw rnd Going 17 -20 Slow   [86]
£3789   £1166   £583   £291

488   **SAFARANDO 8** [3] N P Littmoden 3-9-0 (72) T G McLaughlin 15/2: 220-01: 3 b c Turtle Island - Hertford   80a
Castle (Reference Point) Prom, led over 2f out, styd on well ins last, rdn out: op 6/1: '99 scorer at Yarmouth
(sell, R Hannon) & Lingfield (nurs h'cap, current connections, rtd 75 at best): eff at 7f, stays a stiff 1m well: acts
on firm, soft & fibresand: handles any trk: likes to race with/force the pace: tough & genuine, win more races.

*365   **OSCAR PEPPER 27** [2] T D Barron 3-8-10 (68) C Lowther 5/4 FAV: 00-112: 3 b g Brunswick - Princess   2½   70a
Baja (Conquistador Cielo) Sn hmpd after 1f, held up in trk, rdn 3f out & prog to chase wnr fnl 1f, kept on tho'
al held: jockey given a 2-day ban for misuse of whip: hvly bckd: eff at 6/7f: see 365 (6f).

4279} **KINSMAN 99** [5] I A Balding 3-8-10 (68) A Nicholls (3) 7/1: 6215-3: 3 b g Distant Relative - Besito   1½   67a
(Wassl) Trkd ldrs, chsd wnr 2f out, held fnl 1f: op 6/1, abs: '99 Brighton scorer (nurs h'cap, 1st success,
rtd 70 & 62a): eff at 6/7f on fast & soft grnd, handles fibresand: handles a sharp trk: eff in blnks/visor.

*362   **BULAWAYO 28** [4] B A McMahon 3-9-0 (72) S Righton 6/1: 06-14: Trkd ldrs, rdn/held 1f out: op 8/1.   1¾   68a

173

WOLVERHAMPTON (Fibresand)   THURSDAY FEBRUARY 17TH   Lefthand, Sharp Track

416	**FEAST OF ROMANCE 20** [7] 3-9-7 (79) S Whitworth 5/1: 13-165: Held up in tch, outpcd fnl 2f: btr 275 (6f).	¾	**74a**
401	**CHURCH FARM FLYER 22** [8] 3-8-7 (65) L Newman (5) 8/1: 11-236: Held up in tch, eff 3f out, sn held.	hd	**59a**
493	**BILLYS BLUNDER 7** [6] 3-7-10 (54)(t)(2oh) Joanna Badger (7) 16/1: 00-327: Held up in tch, btn 3f out.	8	**36a**
376	**TYCANDO 26** [1] 3-9-4 (76) D Sweeney 10/1: 22-058: Led 5f, sn btn/eased fnl 1f: op 9/1: vis omitted.	½	**57a**

8 ran   Time 1m 28.8 (2.6)   (Paul J Dixon)   N P Littmoden Newmarket

SOUTHWELL (Fibresand)   FRIDAY FEBRUARY 18TH   Lefthand, Sharp, Oval Track

Official Going   STANDARD. Stalls: Inside

535   1.10 TEXT HCAP DIV 1 4YO+ 0-60 (F)   2m aw   Going 46   -82 Slow   [52]
£1907   £545   £272   4 yo rec 6 lb

455	**OUTPLACEMENT 14** [6] S R Bowring 5-8-1 (25) Dale Gibson 50/1: 65/01: 5 b g Mountain Cat - Coolernearthelake (Hail The Pirates) Led/dsptd lead, asserted over 2f out, styd on well, rdn out: mod form on the level & over jumps prev: apprec this step up to 2m & forcing tactics: acts on fibresand & a sharp trk.		**30a**
482	**SILVER GYRE 10** [7] D J Wintle 4-9-4 (48) S Finnamore (7) 6/1: 06-642: 4 b f Silver Hawk - Kraemer (Lyphard) Mid-div/wide, rdn from halfway, styd on well fnl 2f for press: op 8/1: acts on firm, soft & fibresand.	3	**49a**
470	**SPECIALIZE 11** [8] K R Burke 8-8-9 (33)(bl) D Sweeney 13/2: 0/3-03: 8 b g Faustus - Scholastika (Alpenkonig) Held up in tch, smooth prog/trkd ldrs 4f out, rdn/kept on onepace fnl 2f: stays 2m: see 470.	hd	**34a**
*470	**THROWER 11** [3] S A Brookshaw 9-10-4 (56)(6ex) Joanna Badger (7) 6/4 FAV: /11-14: Chsd ldrs, rdn/ev ch over 2f out, no extra ins last: nicely bckd: see 470 (C/D).	2½	**55a**
464	**MICE IDEAS 13** [2] 4-9-4 (48) T G McLaughlin 8/1: 4-1605: Held up in tch, chsd ldrs 3f out, sn held.	17	**34a**
190	**DALWHINNIE 65** [4] 7-8-6 (30)(bl) S Ritchie (5) 20/1: 5004-6: Held up in tch, btn 4f out: 2 mth abs.	17	**13a**
502	**GRAND CRU 7** [9] 9-9-12 (50)(vis) Barry Smith (7) 9/2: -42307: Led/dsptd lead after 3f till 4f out, fdd.	3½	**23a**
494	**TALIB 8** [5] 6-7-10 (20)(t) G Baker (7) 20/1: 600-48: Struggling 4f out: op 16/1: btr 494 (W'hampton).	13	**0a**
412	**TABORITE 21** [1] 6-7-12 (22) P Fessey 33/1: 500/09: Al rear: no form.	30	**0a**

9 ran   Time 3m 46.4 (20.4)   (The Royal George Racing Partnership)   S R Bowring Edwinstowe, Notts

536   1.40 LITTLEWOODS HCAP DIV 1 3YO 0-60 (F)   1m3f aw   Going 46   -25 Slow   [65]
£2251   £643   £321

4445}	**XELLANCE 99** [4] M Johnston 3-7-12 (35) K Dalgleish (7) 6/1: 000-1: 3 b g Be My Guest - Excellent Alibi (Exceller) Chsd ldrs, rdn/prog to lead over 1f out, styd on well, rdn out: unplcd in '99 (rtd 43, auct mdn, tried up to 7f): apprec this step up to 11f, 12f+ shld suit: acts on fibresand & a sharp trk: runs well fresh: open to further improvement: well rdn by up & coming appr K Dalgleish.		**42a**
451	**DUN DISTINCTLY 14** [8] P C Haslam 3-8-8 (45) P Goode (5) 4/1: 000-42: 3 b g Distinctly North - Dunbally (Dunphy) In tch, rdn 3f out, styd on well fnl 2f, nvr pace to chall: op 8/1: stays 11f on fibresand.	2½	**48a**
429	**MERRYVALE MAN 18** [7] J G Given 3-9-7 (58) A Culhane 13/2: 02-053: 3 b c Rudimentary - Salu (Ardross) Led/dsptd lead, went on 2f out till hdd dist & no extra ins last: op 5/1: stays 11f: see 128.	hd	**60a**
392	**PAPAGENA 24** [9] C W Thornton 3-9-2 (53)(bl) F Norton 5/1: 64-624: Held up in tch wide, smooth prog to chall 3f out, rdn/held fnl 2f: op 9/2: see 392 (9f).	4	**49a**
450	**TURNED OUT WELL 15** [6] 3-8-3 (40) Dale Gibson 7/2 FAV: 000-55: Chsd ldrs, rdn/outpcd over 3f out: shorter priced stablemate of rnr-up: mid-dist bred, 12f+ shld suit in time: see 450 (7f).	1¼	**34a**
395	**DONTBESOBOLD 24** [2] 3-9-7 (58) J Stack 6/1: 0-0436: Led/dsptd lead, wknd qckly 2f out: op 9/2.	18	**32a**
392	**PURE BRIEF 24** [1] 3-8-12 (49) P Doe 10/1: 000-37: Held up in tch, btn 3f out: see 392, 213 (1m/9f).	6	**14a**
419	**FINCH 20** [5] 3-8-7 (44) S Drowne 16/1: 000-08: Al bhd: longer 11f trip.	4	**3a**
481	**DR DUKE 10** [3] 3-8-5 (42)(E) Dean McKeown 20/1: -40649: Mid-div/wide halfway, sn rdn/struggling: tried an eye-shield, longer 11f trip: btr 241 (1m, equitrack).	24	**0a**

9 ran   Time 2m 29.1 (7.8)   (T T Bloodstocks)   M Johnston Middleham, N Yorks

537   2.10 LITTLEWOODS HCAP DIV 2 3YO 0-60 (F)   1m3f aw   Going 46   -33 Slow   [65]
£2251   £643   £321

4339}	**CHIEF OF JUSTICE 99** [8] D Shaw 3-9-7 (58) J P Spencer 7/2 JT FAV: 000-1: 3 b c Be My Chief - Clare Court (Glint Of Gold) Led/dsptd lead 9f, led again over 1f out, hard rdn to hold on ins last, all out: jockey given a 2-day whip ban, tchd 9/2, 4 month abs/h'cap bow: unplcd on turf in '99 (rtd 61, mdn, tried up to 7f): apprec this step up to 11f, 12f - could suit: acts on fibresand & a sharp trk: runs well fresh.		**65a**
419	**ODYN DANCER 20** [6] M D I Usher 3-8-5 (42) G Baker (7) 5/1: 3-6662: 3 b f Minshaanshu Amad - Themeda (Sure Blade) Trkd ldrs wide, styd on well ins last, just held: op 7/2: stays 11f, acts on both AWs.	hd	**48a**
429	**FRENCH MASTER 18** [7] P C Haslam 3-9-7 (58)(bl) P Goode (5) 4/1: 64-333: 3 b g Petardia - Reasonably French (Reasonable) Led/dsptd lead after 2f, rdn clr over 2f out, hdd over 1f out & no extra ins last: op 3/1: prob styd longer 11f trip, 9/10f could prove ideal: see 429, 385 (clmr).	4	**58a**
303	**GENTLE ANNE 39** [5] Ronald Thompson 3-8-10 (47) A Clark 7/2 FAV: 345-44: Held up in tch, rdn/kept on for press wide fnl 2f, no threat to ldrs: tchd 4/1: longer 11f trip shld suit in time: see 36 (1m, sell).	1	**46a**
415	**INDIANA SPRINGS 21** [4] 3-8-1 (38)(VIS) J Tate 20/1: 00-005: Chsd ldrs 4f out, rdn/held fnl 2f: visor.	2	**34a**
500	**NICIARA 7** [1] 3-8-12 (49)(bl) R Fitzpatrick (3) 7/1: 053246: Rdn chasing ldrs halfway, held fnl 2f.	2½	**41a**
48	**GILFOOT BREEZE 95** [9] 3-7-12 (35) G Bardwell 25/1: 0060-7: Prom, btn over 3f out: 3 month abs: unplcd in '99 (rtd 61, nov auct stks, no form on sand): longer 11f trip today.	6	**18a**
429	**SAMMIE DUROSE 18** [3] 3-8-7 (44) R Winston 12/1: 0-5208: Rear in tch, btn 3f out: op 16/1: btr 382 (9f).	3½	**22a**
481	**XENOS 10** [2] 3-8-8 (45) T Williams 20/1: -05639: Prom, rdn/btn 3f out: longer 11f trip: btr 481, 242.	2	**20a**

9 ran   Time 2m 30.0 (8.7)   (J C Fretwell)   D Shaw Averham, Notts

538   2.40 0800 211 222 CLAIMER 4YO+ (F)   6f aw rnd   Going 46   +01 Fast
£2320   £663   £331

532	**DAHLIDYA 1** [8] M J Polglase 5-8-10 P Doe 7/2 FAV: 461101: 5 b m Midyan - Dahlawise (Caerleon) Dwelt, prog over 2f out & led ins last, styd on strongly, rdn out: op 3/1, qck reapp: earlier scored at W'hampton & here at Southwell (sells): '99 Southwell wnr (h'cap, rtd 59a): '98 W'hampton & Southwell wnr (h'caps, rtd 52a): suited by 6f, eff btwn 5/7f on gd/soft & equitrack, f/sand specialist: best without blnks: loves sell/claimers.		**65a**

174

SOUTHWELL (Fibresand) FRIDAY FEBRUARY 18TH Lefthand, Sharp, Oval Track

475 **ELTON LEDGER 11** [5] Mrs N Macauley 11-8-6 (vis) R Fitzpatrick (3) 4/1: 6-2122: 11 b g Cyrano de Bergerac - Princess Of Nashua (Crowned Prince) Chsd ldrs, rdn/ch fnl 2f, kept on tho' not pace of wnr: op 5/2. *1* **58a**
511 **TAKHLID 4** [2] D W Chapman 9-9-3 A Culhane 13/2: 402253: 9 b h Nureyev - Savonnerie (Irish River) Held up in tch, styd on fnl 2f for press, not pace to chall: op 5/1, quick reapp: see 465, 142 (7f). *nk* **68a**
465 **SEVEN 13** [6] Miss S J Wilton 5-9-0 (bl) T G McLaughlin 9/2: 2-0154: Handy, rdn/led over 1f out, hung left & hdd ins last, no extra: op 6/1: treat rating with caution: see 414 (C/D). *nk* **64$**
454 **RUSSIAN ROMEO 14** [7] 5-8-11 (bl) Dean McKeown 14/1: 30-605: Sn prom/wide, wknd over 1f out. *1¾* **57a**
533 **LITTLE IBNR 1** [3] 9-8-1 (vis) J Tate 16/1: -04306: Held up, nvr pace to chall: unplcd yesterday. *4* **37a**
-- **GREEN PURSUIT** [4] 4-9-3 J P Spencer 4/1: 3106-7: Cl-up, rdn/fdd fnl 2f: op 5/1, AW/Brit debut: ex-Irish, '99 Cork wnr (mdn): eff at 6f on fast grnd: AW bow for J Osborne. *3* **46a**
414 **VICE PRESIDENTIAL 21** [1] 5-8-11 S Ritchie (7) 9/1: 0-2508: Led, rdn/hdd over 1f out: fdd: btr 32. *1¼* **37a**
8 ran Time 1m 16.0 (2.7) (The Lovatt Partnership) M J Polglase Southwell, Notts

539 3.15 BEST BETS HCAP 3YO+ 0-100 (C) 7f aw Going 46 -01 Slow [98]
£6532 £2010 £1005 £502

473 **OUT OF SIGHT 11** [2] B A McMahon 6-7-12 (68) L Newman (5) 6/4 FAV: 001-21: 6 ch g Salse - Star Danias (Sensitive Prince) Trkd ldrs, led over 1f out, pushed out to maintain advantage ins last: well bckd: '99 wnr here at Southwell (h'cap, rtd 67a, rtd 72 on turf, h'cap): rtd 75 in '98: '97 York wnr (h'cap, rtd 80): eff at 7f/1m: acts on firm, gd & fibresand, handles hvy: handles any trk, likes Southwell: gd weight carrier: can win again. **75a**
368 **SAND HAWK 28** [7] D Shaw 5-7-10 (66)(vis)(2oh) F Norton 5/1: -21142: 5 ch g Polar Falcon - Ghassanah (Pas de Seul) Chsd ldrs, kept on well fnl 1f, always just held by wnr: remains in gd heart: see 323. *nk* **71a**
504 **DISTINCTIVE DREAM 6** [3] A Bailey 6-7-10 (66)(1oh) C McCavish (7) 20/1: -62153: 6 b g Distinctly North - Green Side (Green Dancer) Cl-up, led over 3f out till over 1f out, no extra: qck reapp: see 504, 449. *3½* **64a**
*480 **ADELPHI BOY 10** [9] M C Chapman 4-10-0 (98)(6ex) R Studholme (5) 16/1: 4-0314: Chsd ldrs wide 6f. *½* **95a**
532 **KEEN HANDS 1** [6] 4-8-9 (79)(vis) R Fitzpatrick (3) 8/1: 104105: Chsd ldrs 5f: op 6/1: unplcd yesterday. *¾* **75a**
321 **WEETMANS WEIGH 36** [1] 7-9-13 (97) A Hawkins (7) 12/1: 222-46: Rear/in tch, nvr pace to chall: op 8/1. *½* **92a**
485 **ITALIAN SYMPHONY 9** [8] 6-9-6 (90)(vis) Joanna Badger (7) 10/1: 050507: Twds rear/wide, nvr factor. *1* **83a**
532 **FIRST MAITE 1** [5] 7-9-4 (88) S Finnamore (7) 9/2: 40-408: Led 4f, fdd: unplcd yesterday: see 35. *1¼* **78a**
8 ran Time 1m 29.9 (3.3) (D J Allen) B A McMahon Hopwas, Staffs

540 3.45 TEXT P368 HCAP 3YO 0-70 (E) 1m aw rnd Going 46 -37 Slow [74]
£4095 £1260 £630 £315

*385 **CALKO 25** [2] T D Barron 3-9-2 (62)(bl) C Lowther 2/1: 5-3111: 3 ch g Timeless Times - Jeethgaya (Critique) Chsd ldr, led dist, pushed out: nicely bckd: earlier won here at Southwell (2, clmr & sell): late '99 Southwell wnr (sell, rtd 61a & 69): eff at 7f/1m: handles fast & gd, fibresand/Southwell specialist: best in blnks: tough. **68a**
420 **NATIONAL DANCE 20** [1] J G Given 3-9-7 (67) Dean McKeown 6/5 FAV: 45-142: 3 b g Deploy - Fairy Flax (Dancing Brave) Held up, rdn/styd on well fnl 2f, not pace to chall wnr: well bckd: see 420, 328 (C/D, mdn). *1¼* **69a**
392 **KINGS GINGER 24** [7] D J Wintle 3-8-10 (56) S Righton 40/1: 05-003: 3 ch g King's Signet - Cosset (Comedy Star) Rear/wide, kept on fnl 2f for press, no threat: handles fast, gd & fibresand: see 392. *1¼* **55a**
495 **MODEM 8** [3] D Shaw 3-8-10 (56)(BL) L Newman (5) 12/1: 0-1364: Dwelt, rdn/prog to lead after 1f, hdd over 1f out & no extra: op 10/1, tried blnks: stays 1m but a return to 7f could suit: see 451, 281 (sell, 7f). *2½* **50a**
514 **AMELIA JESS 4** [5] 3-8-8 (54)(t) Joanna Badger (7) 14/1: 231545: Led 1f, prom 6f: op 8/1: qck reapp. *½* **47a**
479 **LOUS WISH 10** [6] 3-9-5 (65)(bl) R Fitzpatrick (3) 9/2: 312636: Prom 6f: op 3/1: btr 346 (7f). *8* **46a**
427 **SABICA 18** [4] 3-8-3 (49) F Norton 40/1: 00-07: In tch/rdn halfway, sn btn: hcap bow, longer 1m trip. *10* **15a**
7 ran Time 1m 46.0 (6.6) (T Calver) T D Barron Maunby, N Yorks

541 4.20 TEXT P372 SELLER 3YO (G) 7f aw rnd Going 46 -24 Slow
£1842 £526 £263

426 **NORTHERN TIMES 18** [4] T D Easterby 3-8-11 R Winston 5/4 FAV: 0-51: 3 ch g Cahill Road - Northern Nation (Northrop) Handy, rdn/led over 2f out, sn in command, pushed out nr fin: well bckd: sold for 5,500 gns: 1st win: rtd 61 on sole turf start in '99: apprec this step up to 7f, 1m+ shld suit: acts on fibresand & a enjoys sell grade. **59a**
488 **CACOPHONY 9** [3] S Dow 3-8-11 P Doe 2/1: 3-5462: 3 b g Son Pardo - Ansellady (Absalom) Cl-up, hard rdn 2f out, onepace/sn held: nicley bckd, op 5/2: see 207, 94. *4* **51a**
426 **PRICELESS SECOND 18** [1] J A Glover 3-9-3 R Fitzpatrick (3) 9/4: -23143: 3 b g Lugana Beach - Early Gales (Precocious) Led 5f, sn rdn/held: nicley bckd tho' op 11/8: see 417 (C/D). *1¾* **54a**
451 **JONLOZ 14** [2] G Woodward 3-8-11 P Fessey 33/1: 040-54: Bhd halfway: op 10/1: btr 128. *21* **18a**
4 ran Time 1m 31.5 (4.9) (Times Of Wigan) T D Easterby Great Habton, N Yorks

542 4.50 TEXT HCAP DIV 2 4YO+ 0-60 (F) 2m aw Going 46 -62 Slow [52]
£1907 £545 £272 4 yo rec 6 lb

489 **ST LAWRENCE 8** [3] B S Rothwell 6-9-4 (42) D Mernagh (5) 6/4 FAV: 311D21: 6 gr g With Approval - Mingan Isle (Lord Avie) Trkd ldrs, led going well over 2f out, styd on strongly, rdn clr: nicley bckd: earlier won here at Southwell (2, amat h'caps, disq once): plcd form in '99 (rtd 58 & 45a): eff btwn 11.5f & 2m on firm grnd & both AWs, loves Southwell: runs well for an amateur: in great heart & cld win again. **49a**
393 **FEARSOME FACTOR 24** [1] B J Curley 5-10-0 (52) J P Spencer 10/1: 0-0402: 5 b g Allleged - Spark Of Success (Topsider) In tch, smooth prog wide to chall 3f out, onepcd fnl 2f: topweight, blnks omitted: stays 2m. *6* **52a**
*492 **THE COTTONWOOL KID 8** [8] Mrs Merrita Jones 8-7-11 (21)(bl)(6ex) P Fessey 2/1: 000-13: 8 b g Blakeney - Relatively Smart (Great Nephew) Chsd ldrs, efft over 2f out, sn onepace: btr 492 (Wolverhampton). *6* **15a**
135 **TORY BOY 79** [5] Ian Williams 5-9-9 (47) R Fitzpatrick (3) 7/1: 6043-4: Trkd ldrs, onepace fnl 2f: abs. *1¼* **40a**
141 **BLACK ICE BOY 76** [6] 9-8-7 (31)(vis) Dean McKeown 20/1: 010P-5: Led 14f, no extra: abs: see 141. *1½* **23a**
492 **CLOUD INSPECTOR 8** [9] 9-8-6 (30) J Fanning 9/1: 05-246: Chsd ldrs 14f: op 7/1: btr 460 (eqtrk, 13f). *7* **15a**
502 **ALMAMZAR 7** [4] 10-7-13 (23) Kim Tinkler 10/1: -05447: Bhd 4f out: op 25/1: see 89. *dist* **0a**
393 **BALLYCROY RIVER 24** [7] 4-9-1 (45) S Righton 40/1: 003/08: Prom 11f, sn strugg: jumps fit: see 393. *2* **0a**
520 **NOTATION 3** [2] 6-7-10 (20)(bl)(3oh) Claire Bryan (7) 40/1: 00-009: Dwelt, sn bhd: qck reapp: see 494. *¾* **0a**
9 ran Time 3m 43.3 (17.3) (Northern Cladding Ltd) B S Rothwell Musley Bank, N Yorks

Official Going   STANDARD Stalls: 1m - Outside; Rem - Inside.

543	**1.50 BET DIRECT APPR HCAP 3YO+ 0-70 (F)** 6f aw rnd Going 35 -17 Slow	**[69]**
	£2268 £648 £324 3 yo rec 15lb	

525   **RUDE AWAKENING** 3 [6] C W Fairhurst 6-9-1 (56) P Goode 4/1: 413031: 6 b g Rudimentary - Final Call **62a**
(Town Crier) Made all, strongly prsd & rdn over 1f out, drvn out to hold on, op 3/1, quick reapp: earlier
won here at Lingfield (h'cap): plcd form in '99 (rtd 49a & 47, h'caps): prev term scored at Southwell (h'cap,
rtd 55a & 53): stays 1m, suited by 5/6f: acts on firm, gd/soft & fibresand: likes equitrack & Lingfield:
best forcing the pace around a sharp trk: eff with/without visor/blnks: in gd form.
403   **CHARGE** 24 [3] K R Burke 4-9-4 (59)(t) Darren Williams (3) 12/1: 16-002: 4 gr g Petong - Madam   hd **64a**
Petoski (Petoski) Chsd ldrs, hdwy to chall dist, styd on, just held: gd eff for new connections: see 95 (mdn).
462   **RIFIFI** 14 [2] R Ingram 7-10-0 (69) P Fredericks 7/2 FAV: 0-0003: 7 ch g Aragon - Bundled Up   1¾ **70a**
(Sharpen Up) Prom, hdwy 2f out, no extra ins last: nicely bckd, top weight: on a fair mark, win similar: see 320..
454   **SHARP HAT** 15 [10] D W Chapman 6-9-4 (59) Lynsey Hanna (5) 10/1: -34244: Front rank, lost place   ½ **59a**
2f out, late gains for press ins last: see 454.
*445   **BARITONE** 16 [14] 6-8-3 (44)(vis) R Cody Boutcher (3) 12/1: 043415: Rcd wide & outpcd, styd on   ¾ **42a**
strongly ins last, nvr nrr: not disgraced from a poor draw: see 445 (5f).
403   **BRAMBLE BEAR** 24 [1] 6-8-10 (51) R Brisland 8/1: 653-46: Hmpd & lost grnd after 1f, prog halfway,   hd **49a**
no extra ins last: ignore this run: see 403.
507   **SHADY DEAL** 7 [8] 4-8-2 (43) G Baker (5) 33/1: 0-0407: Handy, rdn/btn over 1f out: qck reapp, mdn.   shd **41a**
484   **READY TO ROCK** 10 [11] 4-7-13 (40)(bl) C Cogan (3) 33/1: 0-0068: Prom, held fnl 2f: see 199 (sell).   1½ **34a**
525   **POLLY MILLS** 3 [9] 4-9-10 (65)(vis) Joanna Badger (5) 20/1: 036509: Mid-div at best: qck reapp.   hd **59a**
447   **VILLAGE NATIVE** 16 [5] 7-8-11 (52)(bl) P M Quinn 33/1: 61-000: Mid-div, lost tch halfway, fin 10th.   2 **41a**
484   **CARAMBO** 10 [4] 5-8-11 (52)(bl) S Finnamore (3) 14/1: 0-6430: Hmpd after 1f, al bhd: 11th: btr 484.   nk **40a**
507   **ARAB GOLD** 7 [7] 5-7-10 (37)(1oh) D Kinsella (5) 16/1: 0-0030: In tch, lost action & bhd after   hd **25a**
halfway, fin 12th: quick reapp, mdn: see 507 (mdn).
*484   **COLLEGE BLUE** 10 [13] 4-9-5 (60) I Mongan (3) 6/1: -20010: Al bhd, fin 13th: much btr 484 (clmr).   1¼ **44a**
371   **CATCHTHEBATCH** 28 [12] 4-9-0 (55) S Carson 25/1: 300-00: Blindfold not removed until stalls opened   1½ **35a**
& lost many lengths, al well bhd, fin last: forget this: see 371.
14 ran   Time 1m 13.52 (3.12)   (William Hill)   C W Fairhurst Middleham, N Yorks

---

544	**2.25 0800 211222 MDN 3YO+ (D)** 1m aw rnd Going 35 -11 Slow	
	£2743 £844 £422 £211 3 yo rec 19lb	

409   **STRETFORD LASS** 23 [9] J Noseda 3-8-3(1ow) G Hind 6/5: 31: 3 b f Woodman - Ladanum (Green Dancer) **67a**
Cl-up, hdwy to lead over 3f out, carried head high but styd on strongly ins last, rdn out: nicely bckd: dam a
French 12f wnr: eff arnd 1m, further shld suit: acts on both AWs & a sharp trk: could follow up in a h'cap.
385   **MAID TO LOVE** 26 [5] T D Barron 3-8-2 P Doe 11/10 FAV: 23-422: 3 ch f Petardia - Lomond Heights   2½ **61a**
(Lomond) Sn rdn in rch, gd hdwy over 3f out, styd on fnl 2f but al held by wnr: well clr rem: new stable, gd run.
373   **SHARP RISK** 28 [6] P Howling 3-8-7 R Winston 12/1: 53: 3 ch c Risk Me - Dara Dee (Dara Monarch)   8 **52a**
Chsd ldrs, outpcd halfway, h'cap company will suit in time: see 373.
446   **HIGHFIELDER** 16 [8] J S Moore 4-9-12 (bl) T O'Neill (7) 33/1: 06-554: Led, hdd over 3f out,   4 **45$**
drvn & wknd fnl 2f: stiff task: needs sell h'caps: see 101.
56   **LAUTREC** 95 [7] 4-9-12 R Studholme (5) 25/1: 3360-5: Trkd ldrs, lost tch after halfway: recently t.o.   8 **33a**
over hdles: plcd twice for R J R Williams in '99 (mdn h'caps, rtd 61): stays 10/12f, acts on firm/fast grnd.
4387   **RED APOLLO** 9 [2] 4-9-12 T G McLaughlin 25/1: 0000-6: Chsd ldrs, stly hmpd after 2f, no extra   1¼ **31a**
halfway: reapp: rnr-up in '99 (clmr, 1st time blnks, rtd 65a, also rtd 63): eff at 6/7f: acts on fibresand.
238   **IRISH MELODY** 52 [1] 4-9-7 (t) M Pattinson (7) 66/1: 0060-7: Al outpcd: 8 wk abs: mod form.   5 **19$**
--   **DANGEROUS LADY** [4] 3-8-2 Joanna Badger (7) 33/1: 8: Dwelt, al outpcd: J R Best newcomer.   1¾ **16a**
306   **WILD NETTLE** 39 [10] 6-9-7 (BL) P Dobbs (5) 100/1: 460-09: Handy, lost tch halfway, t.o.: blnks.   11 **1a**
9 ran   Time 1m 39.88 (3.68)   (John G Sikura)   J Noseda Newmarket, Suffolk

---

545	**2.55 BEST BETS CLAIMER 3YO (F)** 1m2f aw Going 35 -30 Slow	
	£2205 £630 £315	

488   **SPORTY MO** 1 [1] K R Burke 3-9-3 (vis) D Sweeney 2/1: -45031: 3 b g Namaqualand - Miss Fortunate **75a**
(Taufan) Keen in tch, led after 3f, clr over 2f, styd on well, rdn out: op 5/4, up in trip: '99 wnr at Southwell
(2 sells, rtd 71a): eff at 6f/1m, apprec this step up to 10f: acts on soft & both AWs: eff in a visor.
409   **FINERY** 23 [8] W Jarvis 3-9-1 Martin Dwyer 7/2: 642: 3 ch g Barathea - Micky's Pleasure (Foolish   4 **66a**
Pleasure) Chsd clr ldr, hdwy to chall 3f out, rdn & no extra fnl 2f: stays 1m/10f, handles both AWs: see 409.
509   **ARMENIA** 7 [5] R Hannon 3-8-4 P Fitzsimons (5) 6/4 FAV: 3-2143: 3 ch f Arazi - Atlantic Flyer (Storm   2 **51a**
Bird) Prom, lost place 4f out, no threat aftr: nicely bckd, quick reapp: much btr 415 (1m mdn, fibresand).
488   **COLLEGE ROCK** 10 [3] Mrs A E Johnson 3-8-5 A McCarthy (3) 11/1: 033-04: Led, hdd after 3f, sn   2½ **48a**
last, mod late gains for press: up in trip: see 488.
459   **PHANTOM STAR** 14 [2] 3-8-1 P Doe 33/1: 505-05: Chsd ldrs, outpcd 5f out, no dngr after: up in trip.   3 **39a**
457   **OFFENBURG** 14 [4] 3-8-1 (VIS) F Norton 14/1: 00-566: Bhd, hdwy over 3f out, wknd qckly fnl 2f: visor.   2 **36a**
6 ran   Time 2m 09.36 (6.56)   (Maurice Charge)   K R Burke Newmarket, Suffolk

---

546	**3.30 TEXT P368 HCAP 3YO+ 0-90 (C)** 1m2f aw Going 35 +06 Fast	**[88]**
	£6727 £2070 £1035 £517 3 yo rec 22lb	

3436}   **JUST IN TIME** 99 [4] T G Mills 5-10-0 (88) A Clark 9/4 FAV: 0060-1: 5 b g Night Shift - Future Past **97a**
(Super Concorde) Chsd clr ldr, drvn/styd on well 2f out, led ins last, rdn clr: best time of day, top weight:
seasonal/AW bow: plcd twice in '99, incl in the val Duke Of Edinburgh h'cap at Royal Ascot (rtd 92): '98 wnr
at Goodwood (mdn auct, rtd 89): eff at 10f, stays 12f: acts on firm, fast & equitrack: runs well fresh on
any trk, likes Goodwood: eff weight carrier: tough/useful, may return here for the Winter Derby next month.
463   **FORTY FORTE** 14 [2] K R Burke 4-8-11 (71) P Doe 7/2: -56162: 4 b g Pursuit Of Love - Cominna   5 **73a**
(Dominion) Set v fast pace, sn clr, rdn over 2f out, hdd dist, wknd: prob went off too fast here: see 400.
422   **WHITE PLAINS** 21 [1] K R Burke 7-9-13 (87)(t) D Sweeney 11/2: 1-1403: 7 b g Nordico - Flying   1¼ **87a**
Diva (Chief Singer) In tch, hdwy over 4f out, kept on but not pace of wnr: op 9/2, clr rem: see 244.

LINGFIELD (Equitrack)   SATURDAY FEBRUARY 19TH   Lefthand, Very Sharp Track

480   **HUGWITY** 11 [7] G C Bravery 8-9-9 (83) S Drowne 4/1: 011244: Chsd ldrs, drvn & btn fnl 3f: 10   71a
poss flattered in claimers these days: flattered 480 (9.4f stks, fibresand).
442   **JUST WIZ** 17 [3] 4-9-5 (79)(vis) P Dobbs (5) 7/1: 31-055: Cl-up, rdn/btn 4f out: much btr 161 (C/D).   1¾   65a
292   **BORDER GLEN** 42 [5] 4-7-13 (59)(bl) A Mackay 12/1: 334-36: Bhd, lost tch halfway, t.o.: prev   dist   15a
with D Haydn Jones, now with J J Bridger: btr 292.
6 ran   Time 2m 05.73 (2.93)   (Mrs Pauline Merrick)   T G Mills Headley, Surrey

547   4.00 SKY TEXT CLASSIFIED STKS 3YO+ 0-60 (F)   7f aw rnd   Going 35 -01 Slow
£2331   £666   £333   3 yo rec 17lb

477   **RAIN RAIN GO AWAY** 11 [2] D J S Cosgrove 4-9-8 C Rutter 9/1: 33-161: 4 ch g Miswaki - Stormagain   69a
(Storm Cat) Made all, prsd 3f out, drvn clr appr fnl 1f: earlier won at W'hampton (mdn): unplcd on turf
for E Dunlop in '99 (rtd 50), plcd on sand (rtd 54a): suited by 7f, stays 1m: acts on soft & both AWs:
loves to force the pace & likes a sharp trk: tough & in fine form.
504   **RAINBOW RAIN** 7 [4] S Dow 6-9-6 P Doe 2/1 FAV: 5-3022: 6 b g Capote - Grana (Miswaki)   5   58a
Cl-up, chall 3f out, rdn/no extra appr fnl 1f: nicely bckd, quick reapp: in gd form: see 504 (appr h'cap).
4042}   **BONDS GULLY** 99 [5] R W Armstrong 4-9-6 R Price 9/1: 4000-3: 4 b c Pips Pride - Classic Ring   1½   55a
(Auction Ring) Outpcd early, drvn/styd on well fnl 2f, nrst fin: 5 mnth abs: stays 7f (mdns, rtd 76,
tried blnks): gd AW bow, keep in mind when returning to 1m.
484   **DOLPHINELLE** 10 [12] R Hannon 4-9-8 L Newman (5) 8/1: 104544: Outpcd, rdn & prog over 1f   1½   54a
out, styd on, nrst fin: clr rem: see 263.
504   **MISS DANGEROUS** 7 [11] 5-9-5 (bl) F Norton 10/1: -13035: Prom, rdn & no extra fnl 2f: quick   6   42a
reapp: needs to dominate: btr 243 (class stks, made all).
*459   **DAMASQUINER** 14 [11] 3-8-2 N Carlisle 9/1: 66-416: In tch, brief eff 3f out, sn btn: btr 459 (clmr).   1½   39a
484   **PALACEGATE TOUCH** 10 [3] 10-9-6 (bl) P Bradley (5) 11/2: 5-3427: Cl-up, hmpd/lost place after 2f,   3   35a
al struggling after: op 9/2: forget this: see 484.
243   **DARK MENACE** 48 [1] 8-9-8 (bl) D Kinsella (7) 14/1: 301-08: Handy when collided with rail &   5   30a
lost grnd after 2f, fdd fnl 3f: 7 wk abs: ignore this run: see 159 (sell).
505   **TITAN** 7 [6] 5-9-6 T Williams 33/1: 060-09: Prom, lost tch halfway: quick reapp: see 92.   nk   28a
4436}   **MASTER MAC** 99 [9] 5-9-6 S Whitworth 40/1: 0000-0: Dwelt, al rear: 10th: new stable: unplcd in '99   1   26a
(h'caps, rtd 70 at best, N Hamilton): unplcd in '98 for M Jarvis J Akehurst (rtd 74), '98 wnr at Goodwood
(auct mdn) & Lingfield (nurs, rtd 85): eff at 6/7f on firm, gd/soft & a sharp/undul trk: now with R O'Sullivan.
10 ran   Time 1m 25.33 (2.53)   (G G Grayson)   D J S Cosgrove Newmarket

548   4.35 TEXT P372 HCAP 4YO+ 0-85 (D)   2m aw   Going 35 +01 Fast   [78]
£3768   £1159   £579   £289   4 yo rec 6 lb

*424   **HARIK** 21 [4] G L Moore 6-10-0 (78) I Mongan (7) 15/8 FAV: 00-311: 6 ch g Persian Bold - Yaqut   82a
(Northern Dancer) Mid-div, hdwy to lead halfway, clr 3f out, styd on strongly, rdn out: nicely bckd: gd time:
top weight: earlier won at Lingfield (h'cap), plcd over jumps prev (nov h'cap, rtd 80c): '99 Lingfield
wnr (h'cap, rtd 74a, no turf form): '98 Lingfield wnr (2, mdn & amat h'cap, rtd 75a & 44): eff at 12f, suited
by 2m: Lingfield/equitrack specialist: runs well fresh, up with/forcing the pace: gd weight carrier: v tough.
424   **BAISSE ARGENT** 21 [2] C N Allen 5-9-6 (70) R Morse 3/1: 5-4132: 5 b g Woodman - Deceit Princess (Vice Regent)   3   71a
Prom, led briefly 1m out, outpcd 5f out, styd on fnl 2f, no ch with wnr: consistent: also bhd this wnr in 424.
424   **BAISSE DARGENT** 21 [5] D J S Cosgrove 4-7-10 (52)(2oh) P Doe 7/1: 00-323: 4 b g Common Grounds -   1   52a
Fabulous Pet (Somethingfabulous) Cl-up, chall halfway, drvn & no extra fnl 3f: beat today's rnr-up in 424.
3341}   **WILD COLONIAL BOY** 99 [7] G P Enright 5-7-10 (46)(4oh) M Henry 33/1: /000-4: Al bhd, late gains   4   42a
fnl 2f: AW bow: unplcd in 3 '99 starts (h'caps, rtd 38): plcd sev times for R Hannon in '98 (h'caps, rtd
60): eff at 10/13f, poss stays 2m: acts on gd & fast, handles equitrack: has prev tried blnks.
486   **NOUKARI** 10 [6] 7-9-12 (76) Joanna Badger 6/1: 205445: Handy, drvn & btn fnl 4f: recent jumps   1¼   71a
wnr at Catterick (2m h'cap hdle, gd/soft, rtd 115h): btr 151.
*528   **SLEAVE SILK** 3 [3] 5-8-5 (55)(6ex) L Newton 7/2: 4-2016: Al rear, t.o.: up in trip: btr 528 (12f).   22   35a
1751}   **STOPWATCH** 99 [1] 5-8-2 (52) F Norton 33/1: 6000-7: Led, hdd halfway, wknd qckly, t.o.:   3½   29a
big step up in trip: recently p.u. over hdles, 98/99 wnr at Plumpton (juv nov h'cap, rtd 107h, eff at
2m1f on gd): unplcd/mod form on the Flat in '99: ex-Irish, '98 Cork wnr (mdn, 1m, soft, T Stack).
7 ran   Time 3m 25.49 (5.49)   (The Best Beech Partnership)   G L Moore Woodingdean, E Sussex

WOLVERHAMPTON (Fibresand)   SATURDAY FEBRUARY 19TH   Lefthand, Sharp Track

Official Going   STANDARD. Stalls: Inside.

549   7.00 BET DIRECT MDN 3YO (D)   6f aw rnd   Going 21 -12 Slow
£2834   £872   £436   £218

331   **DIAMOND RACHAEL** 36 [3] Mrs N Macauley 3-8-9 (vis) R Fitzpatrick (3) 16/1: 034-01: 3 b f Shalford -   63a
Brown Foam (Horage) Towards rear, rdn & prog wide fnl 2f, styd on strongly for press to lead line: op 12/1: no
turf form in '99, plcd on sand (rtd 63a, mdn): eff at 6f, 7f+ shld suit: acts on f/sand & a sharp trk: eff in a visor.
493   **CAROLS CHOICE** 9 [7] D Haydn Jones 3-8-9 S Drowne 20/1: 536-42: 3 ch f Emarati - Lucky Song (Lucky   hd   62a
Wednesday) Led/dsptd lead, narrowly asserted well ins last, rdn & hdd nr line: op 12/1: eff at 5/6f: acts on
fibresand & gd grnd: can find a race & h'caps may suit best: see 493 (7f).
472   **NITE OWL MATE** 12 [10] G Woodward 3-9-0 C Lowther 4/1: 33: 3 b c Komaite - Nite Owl Dancer   ½   65a
(Robellino) Keen/prom, led over 2f out till well ins last, no extra: op 5/1: see 472.
4408}   **RISKY REEF** 99 [5] I A Balding 3-9-0 A Nicholls (3) 7/2: 52-4: Rdn/rear, styd on well fnl 2f, nrst fin: 1½   61a
op 9/4, 4 month abs/AW bow: rnr-up on 2nd of 2 turf starts in '99 (rtd 80, auct mdn): eff at 6f, mid-dist bred:
handles fibresand & gd grnd: one to note in similar or h'caps over further.
434   **TROPICAL KING** 18 [8] 3-9-0 J Fanning 8/1: 00-425: Led/dsptd lead after 1f till 2f out, no extra.   1¼   58a
334   **LUSONG** 35 [9] 3-9-0 J Weaver 3/1 FAV: -226: Prom wide 5f/eased fnl 1f: op 7/2: btr 334, 289 (eqtrk).   2½   51a
3658}   **HOXTON SQUARE** 99 [4] 3-8-9 T G McLaughlin 11/2: 0223-7: Nvr pace to chall: rnr-up twice in '99   7   33a
(rtd 73a & 73, auct mdns): eff at 5f, bred to apprec 6/7f: acts on fast grnd & fibresand: likes a sharp track.
281   **BASIC INSTINCT** 43 [1] 3-8-9 S Finnamore (6) 25/1: 500-08: Dwelt/nvr factor: abs: see 192 (sell).   1   31a
273   **ESPERE DOR** 44 [11] 3-9-0 R Lappin 50/1: 0-09: Dwelt/al rear: 6 wk abs, mod form.   nk   35a

177

WOLVERHAMPTON (Fibresand)   SATURDAY FEBRUARY 19TH   Lefthand, Sharp Track

3804} **CAPE COAST 99** [6] 3-9-0 J P Spencer 11/2: 26-0: Sn outpcd: 10th: op 7/2, 5 month abs: AW bow: nk **34a**
rnr-up on first of 2 starts in '99 (auct mdn, rtd 77, D Marks): eff at 6f, dam a 10f wnr: acts on fast grnd: now
with J Osborne: reportedly needs further & now qual for h'caps.
278   **CAPRICE 43** [2] 3-8-9 G Faulkner (5) 50/1: 0-00: Dwelt/al outpcd: 11th: 6 wk abs: mod form.   nk **28a**
11 ran   Time 1m 14.8 (2.0)   (Diamond Racing Ltd)   Mrs N Macauley Sproxton, Leics.

---

550 | 7.30 CLASSIFIED CLAIMER 3YO+ 0-60 (F)   1m100y aw Going 21 -24 Slow
£2166   £619   £309   3 yo rec 19lb

431   **DOBERMAN 18** [11] P D Evans 5-9-4 (bl) S Drowne 25/1: 035031: 5 br g Dilum - Switch Blade   **49a**
(Robellino) Made all, styd on well fnl 1f, drvn out: rcnt jmps rnr (mod form): rnr-up sev times in '99 (rtd 54 &
53a, B Meehan): plcd twice in '98 (rtd 73 & 60a): eff around 1m/10f: acts on fast & both AWs: eff in blnks,
tried a visor: suited by front-running tactics on a sharp track: apprec return to claim grade.
322   **SHARP SHUFFLE 37** [3] Ian Williams 7-9-10 A Nicholls (3) 5/1: 10-202: 7 ch g Exactly Sharp - Style   nk **54a**
(Homing) Rear, prog 3f out, hard rdn/chall ins last, just held: op 4/1: prev with Miss S J Wilton: see 138 (sell).
516   **TUFAMORE 4** [4] K R Burke 4-10-0 (BL) D Hayes (7) 7/1: 421053: 4 ch g Mt Livermore - Tufa (Warning) 3½   **51a**
Chsd ldrs, outpcd over 3f out, kept on: op 9/2, blnks: qck reapp: see 411 (C/D h'cap, visor).
517   **BILLICHANG 4** [7] P Howling 4-9-8 T Williams 100/30 FAV: 233334: Chsd wnr 3f out, held fnl 1f: bckd. 2   **41a**
484   **CHALUZ 10** [9] 6-9-4 (t) J Tate 15/2: -42555: Mid-div, nvr pace to chall: see 75 (7f). nk   **36a**
511   **DAYNABEE 5** [5] 5-9-5 T G McLaughlin 8/1: -51546: Chsd ldrs 7f: op 11/2, qck reapp: btr 391 (7f, sell). 1¼   **34a**
449   **MIKES DOUBLE 16** [1] 6-9-4 (vis) R Fitzpatrick (3) 10/1: 0-5237: Mid-div at best: tchd 12/1: see 449 (7f). 3   **27a**
218   **TAYOVULLIN 60** [6] 6-9-1 Iona Wands (5) 6/1: 1230-8: Prom 6f: op 4/1, 2 month abs: '99 scorer at 2   **20a**
W'hampton (fill h'cap, rtd 55a, H Morrison, plcd on turf, rtd 46, h'cap): '98 Nemarket wnr (appr h'cap), plcd sev
times (rtd 53 & 53a): suited by 7f, stays 1m: acts on firm, gd/soft & fibresand, any trk: best without a visor.
391   **NICHOLAS MISTRESS 25** [2] 4-9-1 Joanna Badger (7) 25/1: 00-059: Mid-div, btn 3f out: see 316. hd   **19a**
505   **BALLYMORRIS BOY 7** [13] 4-9-4 J Weaver 20/1: 346030: Al rear: see 505, 274 & 156. ½   **21a**
471   **RA RA RASPUTIN 12** [12] 5-9-8 A Eddery (5) 8/1: -14100: Al rear: 11th: op 6/1: btr 396 (7f, sell). 3½   **18a**
322 Diletto 37 [8] 4-9-1 J P Spencer 25/1:   484 **Priory Gardens 10** [10] 6-9-4 A Daly 25/1:
13 ran   Time 1m 50.1 (3.9)   (P D Evans)   P D Evans Leighton, Powys.

---

551 | 8.00 S J DIXON HCAP 3YO+ 0-85 (D)   1m100y aw Going 21 +06 Fast   [85]
£3477 £1070 £535 £267 3 yo rec 19lb

3993} **GRALMANO 99** [2] K A Ryan 5-10-0 (85) F Lynch 5/1: 1120-1: 5 b g Scenic - Llangollen (Caerleon)   **90a**
Led/dsptd lead till went on over 3f out, drifted right for press ins last, held on gamely: gd time, op 9/2, 5 month
abs: '99 scorer at Redcar (class stks) & Pontefract (h'cap, rtd 72 & 92a, earlier with N Littmoden): '98 Lingfield
wnr (stks, rtd 99a & 82): best arnd 1m, stays 11f: acts on both AWs, firm & gd/soft grnd: handles any trk, likes
W'hampton: runs well fresh: eff with/without blnks/visor: gd weight carrier: loves to force the pace: tough.
119   **ARC 84** [6] G M Moore 6-8-7 (64) C Lowther 7/1: 1024-2: 6 b g Archway - Columbian Sand (Salmon hd   **68a**
Leap) In tch, prog to chase wnr 2f out, styd on well ins last, just held: clr of rem: op 4/1, 10 wk jumps abs
(mod form): prev with F Jordan: can find similar, see 38 (C/D).
448   **PANTAR 16** [1] I A Balding 5-10-0 (85)(BL) J A Nicholls (3) 4/1: 330-03: 5 b g Shirley Heights - Spring 10   **74a**
Daffodil (Pharly) Held up, rdn/outpcd 3f out, held after: first time blnks, no improvement: see 448 (C/D).
244   **TALLULAH BELLE 48** [5] N P Littmoden 7-9-13 (84) T G McLaughlin 6/1: 150-04: Chsd ldrs 7f: abs. 2   **69a**
521   **DANAKIL 4** [4] 5-8-7 (64)(VIS) D Sweeney 5/2 FAV: -56635: Chsd ldrs, btn 3f out: visor, op 3/1. 1½   **46a**
*481   **CASTLEBRIDGE 11** [7] 3-7-10 (72)(vis)(3oh)* P Doe 11/4: 0-0116: Led/dsptd lead 5f: op 2/1: see 481 (sell). 4   **46a**
6 ran   Time 1m 47.5 (1.3)   (Coleorton Moor Racing)   K A Ryan Hambleton, N.Yorks.

---

552 | 8.30 BEST BETS HCAP 4YO+ 0-70 (E)   2m46y aw Going 21 -27 Slow   [70]
£2626 £750 £375 4 yo rec 6 lb

482   **ROYAL EXPRESSION 11** [6] G M Moore 8-9-4 (60) J Weaver 5/1: 01-631: 8 b g Sylvan Express - Edwins'   **67a**
Princess (Owen Dudley) Trkd ldr, led 5f out, clr over 1f out, eased nr fin: op 6/1: '99 scorer here at W'hampton
(rtd 64a, F Jordan) & Nottingham (h'cap, rtd 71 at best): missed '98: eff at 12f, suited by 2m: acts on firm,
gd/soft & fibresand: best without a visor: handles a sharp/gall trk: win more races.
522   **MY LEGAL EAGLE 4** [5] R J Price 6-7-12 (40) P Doe 6/1: -03222: 6 b g Law Society - Majestic Nurse 3½   **42a**
(On Your Mark) Rear/in tch, prog to chall over 2f out, sn outpcd by wnr: op 5/1, qck reapp: see 141, 126.
4211} **MAJESTIC 99** [3] Ian Williams 5-9-12 (68)(tbl) R Fitzpatrick (3) 11/2: /516-3: 5 b g Belmez - Noble 1   **69a**
Lily (Vaguely Noble) Led 11f, rdn/outpcd & held 3f out: 11 wk jumps abs, completed hat-trick of nov hdle wins in
Oct/Nov '99 at Plumpton & Cheltenham (2, rtd 130h, eff at 2m5f on fast & gd): '99 W'hampton wnr (mdn, rtd 69a &
66: eff at 12/14f, 2m+ shld suit: acts on firm, soft & f/sand: prob handles any trk: eff in blnks & t-strap.
*413   **SWAGGER 22** [4] Sir Mark Prescott 4-9-1 (63) D Sweeney 10/11 FAV: 6-1114: Held up in tch, eff 3f ½   **63a**
out, sn held: well bckd at odds on: disapp eff at longer 2m trip: see 413 (12f).
324   **MYTTONS MOMENT 36** [1] 4-7-12 (46)(bl) Iona Wands (5) 10/1: 33-445: Chsd ldrs, rdn/btn 3f out. 1½   **45a**
1170} **JAZZ TRACK 99** [2] 6-9-9 (65)(bl) F Lynch 33/1: 10-0:6: Rear, btn 4f out: points fit (mod form): 23   **47a**
no form sole start '99 for M C Pipe (h'cap): unplcd sole '98 start (h'cap): rtd 124h over timber in 97/98: '97
Catterick wnr (h'cap, rtd 82, P Chapple Hyam): eff at 2m on firm & soft: eff in blnks: AW bow tonight for M Peill.
4231} **HAPPY DAYS 99** [7] 5-8-0 (42) P M Quinn (5) 20/1: 1000-7: Al bhd: AW bow, jumps fit (mod form, 8   **16a**
vis): '99 Ripon scorer (h'cap, rtd 45): eff at 2m on fast, handles hvy: best without blnks.
7 ran   Time 3m 37.00 (7.8)   (Mrs A Roddis)   G M Moore Middleham, N.Yorks.

---

553 | 9.00 TEXT P368 SELLER 4-6YO (G)   1m1f79y aw Going 21 -06 Slow
£1732 £495 £247

517   **BACHELORS PAD 4** [10] Miss S J Wilton 6-9-5 M Tebbutt 1/1 FAV: 021121: 6 b g Pursuit Of Love -   **58a**
Note Book (Mummy's Pet) Chsd ldrs, rdn & prog wide fnl 2f & styd on well ins last to lead nr fin, rdn out: nicely
bckd, bt in for 4,800gns, qck reapp: earlier won here at W'hampton (2, clmrs, one for D Nicholls): rnr-up twice
in '99 (rtd 63, h'cap): plcd in '98 (rtd 76, stks, W Jarvis): eff at 7/10f on firm, gd/soft & fibresand: best
without blnks: handles any trk, likes W'hampton: loves sell/claiming grade.
455   **GOLDEN LYRIC 15** [3] J Pearce 5-8-13 J Weaver 14/1: 00-007: 5 ch g Lycius - Adjala (Northfields) ¾   **50$**
Led, hard rdn/hdd well ins last & no extra: op 16/1: offic rtd 33, treat rating with caution: see 60 (C/D, h'cap).
498   **WELLCOME INN 8** [1] G Woodward 6-8-13 (t) C Lowther 8/1: -02233: 6 ch g Most Welcome - 1   **48$**

WOLVERHAMPTON (Fibresand) SATURDAY FEBRUARY 19TH Lefthand, Sharp Track

Mimining (Tower Walk) Prom wide, onepace fnl 1f: op 10/1: eff at 9/12f: see 413, 211.

447	STERLING HIGH 16 [12] D Carroll 5-8-13 (t) J P Spencer 3/1: 040354: Mid-div, onepace fnl 2f: bckd.		3½	41a
516	EMPERORS GOLD 4 [6] 5-8-13 G Baker (7) 16/1: 0-3645: Prom, no extra fnl 2f: tchd 20/1, qck reapp.		½	40$
496	MAJOR ATTRACTION 8 [9] 5-8-13 (VIS) R Fitzpatrick (3) 33/1: 0-0006: Prom 4f, sn held: tried visor.		3	34$
455	ROYAL DOLPHIN 15 [4] 4-8-13 (BL) Dean McKeown 40/1: 000-07: Prom 7f: blnks: unplcd in '99		4	26a
(rtd 43 & 24a): only mod form previously.				
433	HEATHYARDS JAKE 18 [11] 4-9-5 P M Quinn (5) 14/1: -45408: Nvr on terms: op 10/1: btr 229 (mdn).		shd	32a
--	PELIGRO [5] 5-8-13 F Lynch 25/1: 9: Al bhd: Flat debut, jumps fit (mod bmpr form).		19	0a
468	BE VALIANT 14 [13] 6-8-13 S Drowne 20/1: 440-60: Prom wide 3f: 10th: op 12/1: see 468.		6	0a
530	TEEPLOY GIRL 2 [7] 5-8-8 A Daly 50/1: 0/0-60: Sn bhd: 11th: qck reapp: see 530.		dist	0a
--	GILWILL [2] 5-8-13 T Williams 33/1: B: Bhd/brght down 3f out: debut: with J Bradley.			0a
496	NOBLE INVESTMENT 8 [8] 6-8-13 Paul Cleary (7) 10/1: /3016F: Prom, wkng when stumbled/fell 3f out.			0a
13 ran	Time 2m 0.7 (2.5)	(John Pointon & Sons)	Miss S J Wilton Wetley Rocks, Staffs.	

---

554 9.30 TEXT P372 HCAP 4YO+ 0-65 (E) 1m4f aw Going 21 -20 Slow [64]
£2373 £678 £339 4 yo rec 3 lb

489	ICHI BEAU 9 [5] F Murphy 6-8-4 (40) A Daly 7/1: 003-41: 6 b g Convinced - May As Well (Kemal)			46a
Keen, led after 4f, styd on well fnl 2f, rdn out: rtd 71h over timber this winter (sell h'cap): ex-Irish, picd				
in '99 (h'cap): Sept '99 Dundalk scorer (bmpr): eff at 10/12f on fibresand & soft grnd: likes a sharp trk.				
*483	WESTERN RAINBOW 10 [2] P D Evans 4-9-0 (53) J P Spencer 13/8 FAV: -22412: 4 b g Rainbows For		nk	58a
Life - Miss Galwegian (Sandford Lad) Chsd ldrs, rdn to chall over 2f out, hung left fnl 1f, styd on well cl-home,				
just held: well clr of rem: see 483 (13f, auct mdn, equitrack).				
*522	OUR PEOPLE 4 [8] M Johnston 6-7-11 (33)(t) (6ex) K Dalgleish (7) 7/4: 353313: 6 ch g Indian Ridge -		8	29a
Fair And Wise (High Line) Held up in tch, eff/onepace fnl 2f: 6lb pen for recent C/D success: see 522.				
167	NERONIAN 71 [1] Miss D A McHale 6-7-10 (32)(2oh) C Cogan (5) 33/1: 6056-4: Led 4f, btn 2f out:		8	19a
10 wk abs: rnr-up in '99 for K R Burke (first time visor, clmr, rtd 65, unplcd on sand, rtd 43a, seller): back in				
'97 won at Beverley (ltd stks, rtd 72, B W Hills): eff at 1m/10f: acts on fast & gd: has tried blnks prev.				
--	YATTARNA [4] 4-9-6 (59) J Weaver 14/1: 601005: Sn bhd: op 8/1: 6 month abs: AW/Brit bow: ex-		13	32a
Irish, '99 winr at Wexford (h'cap, K Prendergast): eff at 13f on fast, tried leather: has tried blnks.				
529	SHARWAY LADY 2 [6] 5-8-10 (46)(bl) F Lynch 20/1: 660/66: Keen/chsd ldr, btn/eased 2f out: qck reapp.		¾	18a
432	SAFE SHARP JO 18 [7] 5-7-10 (32)(10oh) P M Quinn (5) 40/1: -00607: Keen/al bhd: jmps fit (mod form).		¾	3a
469	AL MABROOK 14 [9] 5-9-10 (60) S Drowne 40/1: 00-108: Bhd 4f out, eased 2f out: op 6/1: btr 270 (9f).		1¼	29a
8 ran	Time 2m 38.5 (4.9)	(Mrs Fiona Butterly)	F Murphy West Witton, N.Yorks.	

SOUTHWELL (Fibresand) MONDAY FEBRUARY 21ST Lefthand, Sharp, Oval Track

Official Going STANDARD. Stalls: Inside.

555 1.50 BET DIRECT MDN HCAP 3YO 0-60 (F) 1m aw rnd Going 34 -37 Slow [63]
£2362 £675 £337

419	JUST THE JOB TOO 23 [5] P C Haslam 3-9-3 (52) P Goode (5) 4/1 FAV: 00-641: 3 b g Prince Of Birds -			56a
Bold Encounter (Persian Bold) Chsd ldrs, rdn to lead ins last, styd on well, rdn out: op 5/2: mod form in '99:				
eff arnd an easy 1m, may stay further: acts on fibresand, prob handles equitrack: likes a sharp track.				
2514}	THE SHEIKH 99 [13] M L W Bell 3-9-7 (56) C Carver (3) 9/2: 000-2: 3 b g Sri Pekan - Arabian Dream		¾	58a
(Royal Academy) Chsd ldrs wide, rdn/kept on well fnl 1f: op 3/1: 8 month abs: AW/h'cap bow: unplcd in '99				
(rtd 61, no auct stks): apprec this step up to 1m: acts on fibresand: gd run from awkward high draw, win soon.				
429	FORTHECHOP 21 [6] Mrs H L Walton 3-8-8 (40) S Righton 14/1: 6-4543: 3 b g Minshaanshu Amad -		nk	41a
Cousin Jenny (Midyan) Cl-up, led over 4f out, rdn/hdd ins last & no extra: see 429, 281 (seller).				
397	COULD BE EXPENSIVE 27 [7] M H Tompkins 3-8-5 (40)(bl) A Whelan 12/1: 00-664: Chsd ldrs, kept on		2½	36a
fnl 2f, not able to chall: styd longer 1m trip: handles fibresand: blnks reapplied today: see 331 (6f).				
150	VICKY VETTORI 77 [9] 3-7-10 (31)(5oh) M Baird 66/1: 0600-5: Led 4f, fdd fnl 2f: 11 wk abs: unplcd		2	23a
in '99 (rtd 24a, seller): prob stays an easy 1m & handles fibresand: h'cap bow today.				
86	ST GEORGES BOY 91 [12] 3-7-11 (32)(VIS)(1ow)(2oh) J Bramhill 50/1: 000-6: Dwelt, rdn/towards		nk	23a
rear halfway, kept on for press fnl 2f, nrst fin: 3 month abs: h'cap bow: imprvd for visor today, mod form prev.				
417	CARDINAL FAIR 24 [14] 3-8-8 (43) R Lappin 33/1: 05-407: Wide/mid-div, mod late prog: blnks omitted.	shd	34a
355	LUCKY MELODY 33 [10] 3-8-3 (38)(VIS) Joanna Badger (7) 50/1: 30-008: Keen/chsd ldrs 6f: see 355.		2	25a
3561}	TIMELESS CHICK 99 [8] 3-9-6 (55) M Henry 25/1: 6660-9: Prom 3f, sn struggling: 6 month abs/		3½	35a
h'cap bow: unplcd in '99 (rtd 47a & 52, tried blnks): longer 1m trip.				
537	NICIARA 3 [4] 3-9-0 (49)(VIS) D Mernagh (3) 13/2: 532460: Twds rear, nvr factor: 10th: vis, qck reapp.		½	28a
355	TING 33 [3] 3-9-5 (54) Dale Gibson 7/1: 55-460: Mid-div at best: 11th: op 6/1, stablemate of wnr.		nk	32a
514	LADY CYRANO 7 [11] 3-8-6 (41)(BL) R Fitzpatrick (3) 5/1: 0-3620: Wide/al twds rear: 12th: blnks.		3½	12a
514	RITA MACKINTOSH 7 [2] 3-8-13 (48) F Norton 10/1: 030-30: Dwelt/al bhd: 13th: op 8/1: btr 514.		3½	12a
493	SEDONA 11 [3] 3-9-1 (50) C Lowther 25/1: 00-5U: Swerved/u.r. start: h'cap bow, longer 1m trip.			0a
14 ran	Time 1m 45.1 (5.7)	(A Stancliffe & J Trevillion)	P C Haslam Middleham, N.Yorks.	

---

556 2.20 0800 CLAIMER 4YO+ (F) 1m4f aw Going 34 -09 Slow
£2081 £594 £297 4 yo rec 3 lb

498	ADIRPOUR 10 [6] R Hollinshead 6-8-8 Stephanie Hollinshead(7) 25/1: 065041: 6 gr g Nishapour - Adira			54a
(Ballad Rock) Held up wide, smooth prog to lead 4f out, clr 2f out, held on well ins last, rdn out: '99 scorer at				
Leicester (seller) & Newcastle (clmr, rtd 66 & 45a): rnr-up in '98 (rtd 48a, N Chance): eff at 6f, both prev wins				
at 7f, now stays an easy 12f: acts on fast, soft & fibresand: enjoys sell/claiming grade.				
*498	COUNT DE MONEY 10 [5] Miss S J Wilton 5-9-0 T G McLaughlin (3) 4/6 FAV: 1-2312: 5 b g Last Tycoon -		nk	60a
Menominee (Soviet Star) In tch, cl-up wide 4f out, outpcd 2f out, kept on ins last, al just held: bt this wnr in 498.				
301	SPOSA 42 [1] M J Polglase 4-9-0 R Fitzpatrick (3) 9/1: 31-53: 4 b f St Jovite - Barelyabride (Blushing		2	60a
Groom) In tch, eff/switched 4f out, kept on fnl 2f, not pace to chall: op 6/1, 6 wk abs: ran under the name of				
Generate in 301: ex-Irish, '99 winr at Tramore (mdn): eff at 12f on fast & fibresand: fin clr of rem here.				
530	I CANT REMEMBER 4 [7] S R Bowring 6-8-10 S Finnamore 7/2: 0-6524: Led 1m, btn fnl 2f: op 5/1.		11	41a
510	SARPEDON 7 [3] 4-8-7 (bl) Joanna Badger (7) 50/1: 050055: Held up in tch, outpcd fnl 3f: see 425.		3	37$

179

SOUTHWELL (Fibresand)   MONDAY FEBRUARY 21ST   Lefthand, Sharp, Oval Track

4403} **ICE PACK** 99 [4] 4-8-6 Kim Tinkler 10/1: 0220-6: Cl-up 1m: op 8/1: 4 month abs: rnr-up thrice in '99   **7 26a**
(rtd 61, J Hills, auct mdn, unplcd on turf, rtd 41, h'cap): stays a sharp 12f & handles fibresand: with N Tinkler.
1808} **FLIGHT FOR FREEDOM** 99 [8] 5-7-13 D Kinsella (7) 20/1: 00/0-7: Prom, struggling 4f out: jumps   **10 5a**
fit (mod form): unplcd in '99, acts on fast/firm): rnr-up in '98 (rtd 56, class stks): 97/98 hdles wnr
at Perth (2m juv nov, rtd 85h at best, acts on fast/firm): stays 10f & acts on gd: with D W P Arbuthnot.
--   **MYSTIC GEM** [2] 4-8-7 Martin Dwyer 50/1: 8: Cl-up 4f, struggling halfway & virtually p.u. over   *dist* **0a**
2f out: Flat debut, jumps fit (no form, bmpr): with J S Wainwright.
8 ran   Time 2m 39.5 (5.2)   (R Hollinshead)   R Hollinshead Upper Longdon, Staffs.

557	2.50 BEST BETS FILLIES HCAP 3YO+ 0-75 (E) 6f aw rnd Going 34 +02 Fast	[73]
	£3461 £1065 £532 £266 3 yo rec 15lb	

511   **GUEST ENVOY** 7 [8] C N Allen 5-7-12 (43) P M Quinn (5) 9/2: -03221: 5 b m Paris House - Peace   **49a**
Mission (Dunbeath) Wide/chsd ldrs, rdn to lead over 1f out, styd on well, rdn out: best time of day: '99 W'hmpton
scorer (h'cap, rtd 62a at best): '98 Hamilton wnr (h'cap, rtd 47): eff at 6f/8.5f: acts on gd, soft & loves f/sand:
handles any trk, likes a sharp one: best without a visor: in good heart, could win again.
499   **MUJAS MAGIC** 10 [2] Mrs N Macauley 5-9-2 (61)(vis) R Fitzpatrick (3) 7/1: -24402: 5 b m Mujadil -   **1¼ 63a**
Grave Error (Northern Treat) Held up in tch, rdn & kept on well fnl 2f, not pace of wnr: see 280, 187 (7f).
*466   **DAYS OF GRACE** 16 [6] L Montague Hall 5-8-6 (67) Martin Dwyer 100/30 FAV: 212313: 5 gr m Wolfhound   **2½ 62a**
- Inshirah (Caro) Cl-up, rdn/no extra fnl 1f: op 5/2: see 466.
466   **PRIDEWAY** 16 [5] W M Brisbourne 4-9-10 (69) T G McLaughlin 11/2: 200-44: Chsd ldrs, not able to chall.   **¾ 62a**
*538   **DAHLIDYA** 3 [1] 5-9-10 (69)(6ex) P Doe 5/1: 611015: Chsd ldrs, prog/led over 2f out, hdd over 1f   **3½ 53a**
out & sn held: op 4/1, qck reapp: 6lb pen for latest: loves sell/claim grade: see 538.
466   **MOY** 16 [7] 5-8-1 (46)(bl) A McCarthy (3) 11/2: 000-26: Led/dsptd lead 4f, fdd: op 4/1: btr 466.   **3 23a**
3886} **E B PEARL** 99 [4] 4-8-0 (45) A Nicholls (3) 25/1: 0000-7: Nvr on terms: 5 month abs: '99 scorer at   **1¾ 18a**
Southwell (mdn clmr, rtd 47a) & Redcar (sell h'cap, rtd 51): eff at 5/6f on firm, fast & f/sand: best without blnks.
4547} **NESYRED** 99 [9] 4-10-0 (73) P McCabe 16/1: 610-8: Led/dsptd lead 3f: tchd 16/1, 4 month abs: AW   **5 37a**
/h'cap bow: '99 Folkestone scorer (auct mdn, rtd 75, Mrs D Haine): eff at 6f, tried 7f: acts on gd: with M J Ryan.
8 ran   Time 1m 15.2 (1.9)   (Shadowfaxracing.Com)   C N Allen Newmarket.

558	3.20 TEXT P368 MDN 3YO+ (D) 6f aw rnd Going 34 -04 Slow	
	£2795 £860 £430 £215 3 yo rec 15lb	

478   **TEYAAR** 13 [5] D Shaw 4-9-10 N Callan 5/1: 003-51: 4 b g Polar Falcon - Music In My Life (Law Society)   **69a**
Led/dsptd lead, went on over 3f out, in command fnl 1f, pushed out: op 7/2: plcd twice in '99 (rtd 85, mdns):
eff at 6/7f on f/sand, handles firm & soft: gd weight carrier: tried blnks, best without: op to improvement.
472   **ABOVE BOARD** 14 [4] R F Marvin 5-9-10 (bl) T G McLaughlin 8/1: 500022: 5 b g Night Shift - Bundled   **4 59$**
Up (Sharpen Up) Prom, rdn/kept on fnl 2f, no threat to wnr: tchd 10/1: see 472, 201.
478   **DEADLY SERIOUS** 13 [6] D R C Elsworth 4-9-10 J Stack 5/1: 433: 4 ch c Emarati - Bentinck Hotel   **1¼ 56a**
(Red God) Led/dsptd lead 3f, rdn/outpcd over 1f out: op 6/1: h'cap company shld now suit: see 478, 399.
415   **LYDIAS LOOK** 24 [1] T J Etherington 3-8-4 J Fanning 25/1: 54: Prom, no extra fnl 1f: see 415 (1m).   **1¾ 47a**
--   **PORT OF CALL** 19 [2] 3-8-9 P McCabe 40/1: 5: Dwelt, bhd/wide, late gains fnl 2f, nrst fin: Flat   **1¾ 48a**
debut, 11 month bmpr abs (mod form): looks sure to apprec 7f+: stablemate of rnr-up.
2771} **SOBA JONES** 99 [8] 3-8-9 R Winston 3/1 FAV: 3-6: Rdn/wide mid-div, eff over 2f out, wk on btn: mkt   **¾ 46a**
drifter, op 6/4: 7 mth abs/AW bow: unplcd sole '99 start (rtd 72, mdn): sire a high-class 1m/10f performer.
334   **JUST MAC** 37 [11] 3-8-9 G Hannon (7) 6/1: 63-067: Trkd ldrs wide 4f: op 4/1, blnks omitted.   **hd 45a**
362   **MR STICKYWICKET** 32 [2] 3-8-9 S Whitworth 50/1: 0-08: Al towards rear: mod form.   **9 29a**
472   **ELTARS** 14 [10] 3-8-9 S Righton 33/1: 0-09: Wide/al bhd: stablemate of rnr-up.   **3 22a**
4172} **COLONEL SAM** 99 [9] 4-9-10 S Finnamore (7) 9/2: 20000-0: Prom wide 4f: 10th: op 5/1: 5 mth abs: **2 17a**
with J Glover in '99, rnr-up (rtd 54, h'cap, unplcd on sand, rtd 58a, h'cap): rtd 79 on debut in '98: eff at 5f/
sharp 6f, has tried 1m: handles firm, gd & fibresand: has run well in blnks: now with S R Bowring.
507   **MICKY DEE** 3 [3] 4-9-10 (t) Dean McKeown 50/1: -00060: Dwelt, chsd ldrs 4f: 11th: mod form.   **3 10a**
11 ran   Time 1m 15.6 (2.3)   (Justin R Aaron)   D Shaw Averham, Notts.

559	3.50 TEXT P372 SELLER 3YO+ (G) 6f aw rnd Going 34 +01 Fast	
	£1892 £540 £270 3 yo rec 15lb	

368   **BEWARE** 31 [7] D Nicholls 5-9-7 (BL) O Pears 11/2: 0-3661: 5 br g Warning - Dancing Spirit (Ahonoora)   **55a**
Led early, styd on strongly fnl 1f, rdn out: no bid: galvanized by first time blnks: rnr-up in '99 (rtd 76 &
51): plcd in '98 (rtd 77): '97 Newbury wnr (h'cap, rtd 84, R Armstrong): eff at 5/7f: acts on fast, soft &
fibresand: handles any trk: has run well fresh: eff forcing the pace in sell grade.
538   **ELTON LEDGER** 3 [3] Mrs N Macauley 11-9-12 (vis) R Fitzpatrick (3) 5/4 FAV: -21222: 11 b g Cyrano   **2 54a**
de Bergerac - Princess Of Nashua (Crowned Prince) Chsd ldrs, rdn/fnl 3f, kept on, not pace to chall: qck reapp.
388   **MARENGO** 28 [1] M J Polglase 6-9-12 A Nicholls (3) 7/2: 03-003: 6 b g Never So Bold - Born To Dance   **1¾ 50a**
(Dancing Brave) Led early, sn chasing wnr, rdn/hung left & held over 1f out: op 9/2: loves to dominate: see 183.
518   **SING FOR ME** 6 [5] R Hollinshead 5-9-2 Stephanie Hollinshead(7) 14/1: -00404: Nvr on terms: op 16/1.   **4 30a**
487   **JANICELAND** 12 [6] 3-8-6 J Tate 4/1: 41-105: Slowly away, chsd ldrs 4f: op 11/4: see 487, 443.   **4 25a**
436   **MANOLO** 20 [4] 7-9-7 Clare Roche (7) 16/1: 50-006: In tch, outpcd fnl 2f: stablemate of wnr.   **4 15a**
3073} **PEACE PACT** 99 [2] 4-9-2 (bl) I Mongan (7) 50/1: 0000-7: Dwelt, sn outpcd: jumps fit: no form.   **18 0a**
7 ran   Time 1m 15.3 (2.0)   (A A Bloodstock Ltd)   D Nicholls Sessay, N.Yorks.

560	4.20 TEXT P372 HCAP DIV 1 4YO+ 0-65 (F) 1m3f aw Going 34 -11 Slow	[63]
	£1960 £560 £280 4 yo rec 2 lb	

510   **WESTERN COMMAND** 7 [7] Mrs N Macauley 4-9-13 (62) R Fitzpatrick (3) 11/2: 033621: 4 b g Saddlers   **67a**
Hall - Western Friend (Gone West) Mid-div, prog to lead 2f out, held on well in last, rdn out: op 4/1: '99 wnr
at Southwell (2, h'caps, rtd 76a, Sir M Prescott) & W'hampton (h'cap): suited by 11/12f, stays 14f: acts on
eqtrk, fibresand/Southwell specialist: best without blnks/visor: gd weight carrier: tough, win more races.
413   **IRSAL** 26 [6] D W Chapman 6-7-10 (30)(bl) (1oh) Claire Bryan (7) 16/1: 50-302: 6 ch g Nashwan -   **1 32a**
Amwag (El Gran Senor) Led 9f, rdn & kept on well fnl 2f: blnks reapplied, gd run: see 325 (C/D).
512   **STATE APPROVAL** 7 [5] D Shaw 7-9-3 (50) N Callan 7/2 FAV: 000023: 7 b g Pharly - Tabeeba (Diesis)   **3 49a**
Chsd ldr, rdn/outpcd over 3f out, styd on well fnl 1f, no threat to wnr: see 512, 270.

SOUTHWELL (Fibresand) MONDAY FEBRUARY 21ST Lefthand, Sharp, Oval Track

2713} **THE LAMBTON WORM 99** [13] N Bycroft 6-8-3 (36) J Fanning 25/1: 0556-4: Held up in tch, kept on   1¼ **33a**
for press fnl 2f, no threat: jumps fit (rtd 69h, sell hdle): unplcd in '99 on the level (rtd 23a & 39, h'caps): back
in '96 scored at Ayr (rtd 85 at best, mdn, Denys Smith): eff at 6f, tried 1m: acts on firm & hvy: has tried a visor.
513   **STRAVSEA 7** [10] 5-9-10 (57) P M Quinn (5) 12/1: 511635: Held up, mod gains: op 7/1: see 430 (1m).   1¾ **52a**
473   **PIPS BRAVE 14** [6] 4-9-2 (51)(bl) R Lappin 9/2: 000-36: Trkd ldrs, wknd fnl 2f: btr 473 (1m).   5 **39a**
500   **SEVEN O SEVEN 10** [1] 7-8-10 (43) S Whitworth 25/1: 400-67: Mid-div at best: see 500 (1m).   6 **22a**
490   **HOT POTATO 11** [8] 4-7-10 (30)(4oh) D Mernagh (0) 25/1: 5-0468: Chsd ldrs 1m: see 298 (1m).   2 **7a**
390   **ABLE PETE 28** [4] 4-7-12 (33) M Baird 8/1: 00-059: Mid-div, btn 3f out: op 7/2: see 390.   1¼ **7a**
512   **KIRISNIPPA 7** [11] 5-9-8 (55) I Mongan (7) 11/2: 513160: Chsd ldrs 1m, sn btn: 10th: nicely bckd.   4 **23a**
4603} **On Porpoise 99** [2] 4-8-11 (46) C Lowther 14/1:   327 **Pretty Fly Guy 38** [3] 4-7-11 (31)(1ow)(8oh) J Bramhill 33/1:
3932} **Rosies All The Way 99** [12] 4-8-8 (43) Dean McKeown 20/1:
13 ran   Time 2m 26.3 (5.0)   (Andy Peake)   Mrs N Macauley Sproxton, Leics.

561	4.50 TEXT P372 HCAP DIV 2 4YO+ 0-65 (F) 1m3f aw Going 34 -24 Slow	[61]
	£1949 £557 £278 4 yo rec 2 lb	

433   **MALWINA 20** [10] M G Quinlan 4-8-9 (44) J Fanning 5/1 CO FAV: 0-0051: 4 ch f Greinton - Micky's   **46a**
Pleasure (Foolish Pleasure) Rear, prog fnl 3f, styd on well for press to lead nr line: tchd 6/1: ex-German, wnr up
to 10f in native land: cost current connections 1,000gns: eff at 11f, stay further: acts on fibresand & a sharp trk.
522   **GENUINE JOHN 6** [3] J Parkes 7-8-3 (36) R Fitzpatrick (5) 6/1: 063-32: 7 b g High Estate - Fiscal   ½ **36a**
Folly (Foolish Pleasure) Led, rdn fnl 2f, hdd nr line: qck reapp: on a fair mark, can find similar: see 215, 131.
387   **THE NOBLEMAN 28** [5] T J Etherington 4-7-13 (32)(3ow)(8oh) F Norton 12/1: 0/053: 4 b g Quiet   3½ **29a**
American - Furajet (The Minstrel) Held up, briefly no room 4f out, kept on fnl 2f, not pace to chall: h'cap bow,
eff at 11f on fibresand: only mod form previously.
542   **NOTATION 3** [6] D W Chapman 6-7-10 (29)(bl)(16oh) Claire Bryan (7) 50/1: 0-0004: Mid-div, prog/ch   1¼ **22a**
2f out, onepace: eff at 11/14f, stays 2m well: see 494.
497   **NICE BALANCE 10** [2] 5-8-10 (43) Joanna Badger (7) 11/1: 431565: Rear, mod gains: op 8/1: see 418 (1m).3   **32a**
529   **TYCOON TINA 4** [12] 6-7-10 (29)(1oh) J Bramhill 6/1: 600-36: Chsd ldrs 9f: qck reapp.   ½ **17a**
498   **ACCYSTAN 10** [9] 5-9-12 (59) J Weaver 5/1 CO FAV: 0-0627: Chsd ldrs, rdn/ch 2f out, sn no extra.   nk **46a**
516   **NAKED OAT 6** [4] 5-9-9 (56) J Bosley (7) 16/1: 0-0008: Cl-up 9f: op 14/1: qck reapp: see 329 (1m).   6 **34a**
517   **FLASHFEET 6** [11] 10-7-10 (29)(1oh) G Baker 33/1: 0-0009: Held up in tch, btn 3f out: qck reapp.   3 **3a**
500   **KUSTOM KIT KEVIN 10** [8] 4-9-4 (53) S Finnamore (7) 5/1 CO FAV: 0-3220: Prom till 5f out, sn btn: 2½ **23a**
10th: nicely bckd: more expected after 500, 453 (1m, mdns).
474   **River Captain 14** [7] 7-8-12 (45)(tBL) C Lowther 12/1: -- **Ancient Almu** [1] 4-9-5 (54) J P Spencer 14/1:
452   **Imbackagain 17** [13] 5-8-0 (33) Dale Gibson 16/1:
13 ran   Time 2m 27.7 (6.4)   (D Donovan)   M G Quinlan Newmarket.

WOLVERHAMPTON (Fibresand) TUESDAY FEBRUARY 22ND Lefthand, Sharp Track

Official Going   STANDARD. Stalls: 7f - Inside, rem - Outside.

562	1.40 APPR HCAP 4YO+ 0-80 (C) 1m4f aw Going 29 -03 Slow	[76]
	£2149 £614 £307 4 yo rec 3 lb	

489   **EVEZIO RUFO 12** [4] N P Littmoden 8-7-12 (46)(bl) K Dalgleish (5) 8/1: 465131: 8 b g Blakeney -   **52a**
Empress Corina (Free State) Cl-up, led after 4f, held on well, rdn out: op 11/2: earlier won at W'hampton (h'cap):
'99 W'hampton wnr (2, sell & h'cap, rtd 47a & 34): '98 Lingfield, Southwell & W'hampton wnr (h'caps, rtd 61a & 55):
eff at 11/14.8f on fast, hvy & equitrack, loves fibresand/W'hampton: eff in visor/blnks: loves to force the pace.
456   **MORGANS ORCHARD 18** [2] A G Newcombe 4-8-9 (60) G Baker 8/1: 53-152: 4 ch g Forest Wind -   ½ **64a**
Regina St Cyr (Doulab) Led/dsptd lead 4f, remained cl-up, chased wnr fnl 2f, styd on well: op 6/1: clr rem.
422   **PUZZLEMENT 24** [3] C E Brittain 6-9-13 (75) R Esler 5/1: 5-3333: 6 gr g Mystiko - Abuzz (Absalom)   15 **63a**
Cl-up, rdn/no extra fnl 3f: op 4/1: return to 9/10f shld suit: see 422, 303.
*510   **FRENCH SPICE 8** [6] Sir Mark Prescott 4-10-1 (80)(6ex) M Worrell (5) 4/7 FAV: 111114: In tch wide,   5 **61a**
chsd ldr halfway, rdn/btn 3f out: nicely bckd at odds on: began winning run off a mark of 40: see 510.
552   **MYTTONS MOMENT 3** [5] 4-7-10 (47)(bl)(1oh) C McCavish (7) 14/1: 3-4455: Cl-up 6f: qck reapp.   3½ **23a**
474   **LOVE DIAMONDS 15** [1] 4-9-4 (69) L Paddock (7) 20/1: 00-206: Held up in tch, rdn/btn 4f out.   28 **21a**
6 ran   Time 2m 37.4 (3.8)   (O A Gunter)   N P Littmoden Newmarket.

563	2.10 HCAP DIV I 3YO+ 0-60 (F) 5f aw Going 29 -05 Slow	[59]
	£1855 £530 £265 3 yo rec 14lb	

533   **SOUNDS LUCKY 5** [3] N P Littmoden 4-9-6 (55)(vis) C Carver (3) 7/2 JT FAV: -60441: 4 b g Savahra   **58a**
Sound - Sweet And Lucky (Lucky Wednesday) Trkd ldrs, prog to lead over 1f out, hung right ins last, pushed out:
op 3/1: qck reapp, visor reapplied: '99 W'hampton (2, sell & h'cap, rtd 58a) & Lingfield wnr (h'cap, rtd 64):
eff at 5/6f on fast, gd/soft & prob handles equitrack, fibresand/W'hampton specialist: loves with/without a visor.
518   **OFF HIRE 7** [1] C Smith 4-9-10 (55)(vis) G Faulkner (3) 11/2: 03-142: 4 b g Clantime - Lady   2 **56a**
Pennington (Blue Cashmere) Cl-up, led over 1f out, hdd over 1f out & no exttra: loves claimers: see 379.
*526   **TOLDYA 6** [5] E A Wheeler 3-9-2 (61)(bl)(6ex) S Carson (5) 4/1: 243213: 3 b f Beveled - Run Amber   1½ **58a**
Run (Run The Gantlet) Bmpd start, chsd ldrs, kept on fnl 1f, not pace to chall: op 7/2, qck reapp: acts on both AWs.
3777} **BEVELED HAWTHORN 99** [7] D Nicholls 5-8-1 (32) F Norton 7/2 JT FAV: 0/61-4: Held up in tch, eff/   1¼ **26a**
onepace fnl 2f: AW bow, 6 month abs: '99 Thirsk wnr (mdn h'cap, made all, rtd 31): eff at 5f on firm grnd.
445   **KALAR 19** [6] 11-7-12 (29)(bl) Iona Wands (5) 16/1: 00-005: Led 1f, cl-up 4f: op 12/1: see 371.   1¼ **20a**
533   **TINKERS SURPRISE 5** [8] 6-8-9 (40)(bl) J Edmunds (7) 14/1: -53656: Slowly away & al bhd: lost cl start.   ¾ **29a**
371   **CALANDRELLA 31** [2] 7-7-10 (27)(1oh) G Sparkes (4) 25/1: 500-07: Cl-up, outpcd fnl 2f: see 371.   nk **15a**
4604} **MAMMAS F C 99** [4] 4-9-7 (52) Claire Bryan (7) 10/1: 4020-8: Dwelt, al onepace: op 9/1, 4 mth   1¼ **37a**
abs: '99 scorer at Folkestone, Bath (clmrs) & Ripon (h'cap, rtd 60): '98 Southwell (auct mdn), Musselburgh &
Haydock wnr (clmrs, rtd 63 & 65a, J Berry): eff at 5f, suited by 6/7f: acts on firm, soft & f/sand: tough.
8 ran   Time 1m 01.9 (1.7)   (Paul J Dixon)   N P Littmoden Newmarket.

564   **2.40 HCAP DIV II 3YO+ 0-60 (F)**   **5f aw rnd**   **Going 29** **-03 Slow**   [60]
£1855   £530   £265   3 yo rec 14lb

406 **NINEACRES 26** [1] J M Bradley 9-9-7 (53)(bl) Claire Bryan (7) 13/2: -32261: 9 b g Sayf El Arab -   **58a**
Mayor (Laxton) Made all, rdn fnl 2f, styd on well ins last & al holding rival: '99 scorer here at W'hampton (clmr,
rtd 59a, plcd on turf, rtd 42, h'cap): missed '98: eff at 5/6f, stays a gall 7f: acts on firm, fast & likes both
AWs: eff in blnks/vis: handles any trk, likes W'hampton: eff forcing the pace: has run well fresh: tough.
518 **JACK TO A KING 7** [7] J Balding 5-9-6 (52)(tbl) J Edmunds 4/1: -15202: 5 b g Nawwar - Rudda Flash   ¾ **54a**
(General David) Trkd ldrs, rdn/chall fnl 1f, kept on well tho' al just held: op 7/2: see 445, 291 (C/D).
543 **BARITONE 3** [6] S E Kettlewell 4-8-12 (44)(vis) J Tate 7/2: 434153: 6 b g Midyan - Zinzi (Song)   2 **41a**
Chsd wnr 3f, rdn/onepace over 1f out: op 9/2: qck reapp: see 445 (C/D).
503 **GLASTONBURY 10** [5] D Shaw 4-8-5 (37) F Norton 20/1: 00-004: Chsd ldrs, outpcd over 1f out: op 12/1. 1 **32a**
471 **GOLD EDGE 15** [2] 6-7-10 (28)(BL)(1oh) G Sparkes (4) 20/1: 500-05: Sn rdn, nvr on terms: tried blnks. nk **22a**
484 **CHAKRA 13** [3] 6-8-4 (36) P Fitzsimons (5) 10/1: -06506: Chsd ldrs 3f: tchd 12/1, stablemate of wnr. 2½ **23a**
*518 **JAWHARI 7** [8] 6-10-6 (66)(6ex) A Nicholls (3) 7/4 FAV: 00-017: Held up in tch wide, eff 2f out, sn nk **52a**
held: well bckd, topweight: ahd of today's rnr-up 518 (C/D).
7 ran   Time 1m 01.8 (1.6)   (J M Bradley)   J M Bradley Sedbury, Glos.

565   **3.10 BEST BETS MDN 3YO+ (D)**   **1m4f aw**   **Going 29** **-21 Slow**
£2782   £856   £428   £214   3 yo rec 24lb4 yo rec 3 lb

523 **SPANISH STAR 6** [8] W Jarvis 3-8-3 Martin Dwyer 2/1: 43-51: 3 b g Hernando - Desert Girl (Green   **63a**
Desert) Trkd ldrs, imprvd to lead dist, styd on gamely, all out: qck reapp: promise both turf starts in '99 (rtd
77, mdn): apprec step up to 12f: acts on f/sand, gd/soft & soft: handles a sharp/gall trk: open to improvement.
395 **LE CAVALIER 28** [2] C N Allen 3-8-3 L Newman (5) 9/2: 0-0022: 3 b g Mister Baileys - Secret Deed nk **62a**
(Shadeed) Led/dsptd lead, hdd dist, styd on gamely, just held: eff at 12f, stays 14f well: see 395, 240.
457 **DION DEE 17** [1] Dr J R J Naylor 4-9-5 S Drowne 33/1: /0-003: 4 ch f Anshan - Jade Mistress (Damister) 10 **46$**
Cl-up 9f, sn outpcd by front leaders: unplcd/mod form previously.
519 **EUROLINK APACHE 7** [4] D R C Elsworth 5-9-13 L Branch (7) 6/4 FAV: 2/24: Held up in tch, outpcd 1¾ **49a**
4f out & no impress after: reportedly broke a blood vessel: well bckd: see 519 (C/D).
-- **STICIBOOTS** [7] 3-8-3 J Tate 9/1: 5: Held up in tch, outpcd fnl 4f: op 7/1, debut, with N Littmoden. nk **48a**
536 **DONTBESOBOLD 4** [5] 3-8-3 D Mernagh (3) 6/1: -04366: Pulled hard & led after 3f, hdd over 4f out ½ **47a**
& wknd over 2f out: op 9/2, qck reapp: not settle over longer 12f trip: h'caps & 1m/9f shld suit: see 395, 328.
457 **MELVALIA 17** [3] 4-9-5 R Fitzpatrick (3) 20/1: 00-607: Sn struggling: op 14/1: see 387. 23 **17a**
395 **THE FINAL WORD 28** [6] 3-7-12 P M Quinn (5) 20/1: 5-508: Al rear: btn 4f out: see 319 (9f). 4 **11a**
8 ran   Time 2m 39.6 (6.0)   (Miss V R Jarvis)   W Jarvis Newmarket.

566   **3.40 TEXT P368 HCAP 3YO 0-80 (D)**   **1m100y aw rnd**   **Going 29** **-19 Slow**   [85]
£3789   £1166   £583   £291

*534 **SAFARANDO 5** [4] N P Littmoden 3-9-5 (76)(6ex) T G McLaughlin 2/1 FAV: 20-011: 3 b c Turtle Island -   **87a**
Hertford Castle (Reference Point) Made all, clr 2f out, eased nr fin: val for 7L+, qck reapp: recent W'hampton
wnr (h'cap): '99 Yarmouth (sell, R Hannon) & Lingfield wnr (nurs h'cap, rtd 75): eff at 7/8.5f, further cld suit:
acts on firm, soft & f/sand, handles any trk: loves to force the pace: tough, genuine & progressive.
495 **TOWER OF SONG 12** [5] D W Chapman 3-8-8 (65) Claire Bryan (7) 7/1: 20-542: 3 ch g Perugino -   5 **66a**
New Rochelle (Lafontaine) Chsd ldrs, rdn/chsd wnr 2f out, kept on tho' al held: op 6/1: see 36 (seller).
419 **CHILLI 24** [2] C E Brittain 3-7-11 (54) A Nicholls (2) 11/2: 040-33: 3 br g Most Welcome - So Saucy   1 **53a**
(Teenoso) Held up in tch, outpcd 4f out, rdn/keeping on when no room over 1f out, styd on well, no threat:
handles both AWs: looks sure to relish mid-dists & one to note over further: see 419 (equitrack).
416 **HEATHYARDS MATE 25** [7] R Hollinshead 3-9-1 (72) P M Quinn (5) 8/1: 143-04: Held up in tch,   2 **67a**
eff over 2f out, no impress: op 6/1: see 128 (Southwell).
488 **AGUA CABALLO 13** [1] 3-7-12 (54)(1ow) P Fessey 16/1: 56-005: Chsd ldrs, held fnl 2f: longer 1m trip. 1½ **47a**
495 **NOBLE PASAO 12** [8] 3-9-2 (73) C Lowther 3/1: 010-26: Chsd wnr 3f out, rdn/btn 2f out: op 5/2. 1¾ **62a**
540 **LOUS WISH 4** [3] 3-8-8 (65)(bl) R Winston 10/1: 126367: Held up, eff 3f out/sn btn: op 6/1: btr 346 (7f). 7 **44a**
4477} **STAFFORD PRINCE 99** [3] 3-7-10 (53)(1oh) Joanna Badger (7) 40/1: 0600-8: Sn rdn/bhd: AW bow, 10 **17a**
4 months abs: unplcd in '99 (rtd 58, auct mdn, subs tried visor): bred to apprec 1m+ for J G M O'Shea.
3863} **DANAKIM 99** [6] 3-9-7 (78) J Fanning 12/1: 2040-9: Chsd wnr 5f, btn 2f out: op 8/1, 6 month abs shd **42a**
AW bow: rnr-up for R Hannon in '99 (rtd 82, mdn): eff at 5/6f, not stay longer 1m trip today: handles firm
& fast grnd: now with J R Weymes, will apprec a drop in trip.
9 ran   Time 1m 50.3 (4.1)   (Paul J Dixon)   N P Littmoden Newmarket.

567   **4.10 TEXT P372 SELLER 3YO+ (G)**   **7f aw rnd**   **Going 29** **-28 Slow**
£1922   £549   £274

398 **COMEOUTOFTHEFOG 27** [8] S Dow 5-9-8 P Doe 100/30: 02-501: 5 b g Mujadil - Local Belle (Ballymore)   **51a**
Trkd ldrs halfway, briefly no room 2f out, rdn to lead ins last, held on well, rdn out: op 9/4, sold for 4,000gns:
'99 Lingfield wnr (sell h'cap, rtd 58a & 44, A J McNae): '98 Lingfield wnr (2, clmrs, 1 for D Ffrench Davis, rtd
69a & 56): eff at 7f/1m on firm, fast & loves both AWs: likes a sharp trk, esp Lingfield: runs well fresh.
550 **DILETTO 3** [4] E J Alston 4-9-3 L Swift (7) 33/1: -00602: 4 b f Mujadil - Avidal Park (Horage)   ½ **44a**
Towards rear, styd on strongly ins last, nrst fin: qck reapp: eff at 7f, return to 1m+ shld suit: see 295.
550 **DAYNABEE 3** [7] Miss S J Wilton 5-9-4 I Mongan (7) 7/1: 515463: 5 b m Common Grounds - Don't Wary 1 **47a**
(Lomond) Cl-up, led 5f out, rdn fnl 2f & hdd ins last, no extra: op 5/1, qck reapp: see 391 (C/D).
315 **RIDGECREST 41** [9] R Ingram 3-8-5 S Drowne 5/1: 242-54: Held up in tch wide, outpcd over 3f out, 2 **26a**
kept on ins last, no threat: op 7/2: 6 wk abs: a return to 1m+ will suit on this evidence: see 236, 150.
501 **LOCOMOTION 11** [11] J Weaver 4-9-8 (0035): Chsd ldr halfway, hit over 1f out/fdd: stablemate of wnr.nk **42a**
449 **NITE OWLER 19** [2] 6-9-8 J Edmunds 9/4 FAV: 100-26: Chsd ldrs halfway, outpcd fnl 3f: op 4/1: see 75. ¾ **41a**
449 **NOBLE PATRIOT 19** [10] 5-9-8 N Callan 25/1: 505007: Chsd ldrs wide halfway, sn held: see 61 (C/D). ¾ **40a**
475 **HOT LEGS 15** [6] 4-9-3 (bl) L Newman (5) 12/1: -54558: Chsd ldrs 5f: op 8/1: see 379 (5f). 10 **20a**
351 **FRENCH GRIT 35** [1] 8-9-8 (vis) Iona Wands (5) 14/1: 25-069: Prom 5f: op 10/1: see 166. hd **24a**
519 **TRUE ROMANCE 7** [12] 4-9-8 P Clarke (7) 33/1: 0/000: Dwelt/al outpcd: 10th: no form. hd **23a**
276 **PURNADAS ROAD 47** [5] 5-9-3 Dean McKeown 33/1: 000-60: Led 2f: 11th: abs: with Dr J R Naylor. 8 **6a**

WOLVERHAMPTON (Fibresand)   TUESDAY FEBRUARY 22ND   Lefthand, Sharp Track

11 ran   Time 1m 30.2 (4.0)   (Raging Rhinos)   S Dow Epsom, Surrey.

| **568** | 4.40 HCAP DIV I 4YO+ 0-60 (F)   1m1f79y Going 29 -01 Slow | | [60] |
| | £1928   £551   £275 | | |

469   **RIVERBLUE** 17 [11] D J Wintle 4-10-0 (60) M Tebbutt 6/1: 0-0051: 4 b c Bluebird - La Riveraine   66a
(Riverman) In tch, prog to trk ldrs over 2f out, led dist & hung left ins last, styd on well, rdn out: op 8/1:
'99 rnr-up (h'cap, rtd 92, M Channon): '98 wnr at Catterick (mdn) & Thirsk (nurs, rtd 90, Mrs Ramsden): eff at
7f, suited by 1m/9.4f: acts on fast, gd/soft & fibresand: best without a visor on any trk: gd weight carrier.
504   **BREAD WINNER** 10 [12] I A Balding 4-9-8 (54)(VIS) Michael Doyle 9/1: 405-42: 4 b g Reprimand -   1½ 56a
Khubza (Green Desert) Cl-up, rdn to lead dist, sn hdd & no extra: 1st time visor: handles fast, gd/soft & both AWs.
383   **THE BARGATE FOX** 31 [9] D J G Murray Smith 4-9-9 (55) J P Spencer 9/1: 1-3403: 4 b g Magic Ring -   1 55a
Hithermoor Lass (Red Alert) Towards rear, stdy prog from halfway, kept on onepace fnl 1f: op 7/1: see 233 (8.5f).
474   **SURE QUEST** 15 [6] D W P Arbuthnot 5-9-3 (49) S Whitworth 11/2: 00-234: Chsd ldrs, not able to chall.   1½ 46a
516   **ROI DE DANSE** 7 [8] 5-9-0 (46) R Studholme (5) 11/4 FAV: 034225: Led after 1f till over 1f out, fdd.   ¾ 42a
432   **ETISALAT** 21 [4] A Polli (3) 5/1: 0-3126: Keen/chsd ldrs, rdn/fdd over 1f out: op 4/1.   3½ 47a
504   **DANZAS** 10 [10] 4-8-1 (33)(bl) Claire Bryan (7) 16/1: 606467: Trkd ldrs, wknd fnl 2f: see 255.   4 14a
418   **BROUGHTONS MILL** 25 [5] 5-8-7 (39) L Newton 8/1: 003-08: Chsd ldrs, lost pl after 2f, no impress.   4 12a
4541} **TRY PARIS** 99 [2] 4-8-12 (44)(vis) N Callan 33/1: 0060-9: Mid-div, btn/eased 2f out: 4 month abs: 1¾ 14a
unplcd for Mrs L C Jewell in '99 (rtd 43 & 42a): mod form prev: now with J H Collingridge.
340   **ANCHOR VENTURE** 36 [13] 7-7-10 (28)(8oh) Iona Wands (5) 50/1: 00-000: Al towards rear/wide: 6 0a
10th: unplcd in '99 (rtd 31a, h'cap): '98 rnr-up at Lingfield (amat h'cap, rtd 59a, S Woods): '97 Pontefract wnr
(seller, rtd 50): eff around 1m/10f, ideal further: acts on gd grnd & equitrack: has run well fresh.
537} **WEET AND SEE** 99 [1] 6-9-6 (52) P M Quinn (5) 10/1: 0/00-0: Led 1f, sn bhd: 13th: on 8/1: 5 mth jmps   0a
abs, July/Sept '99 wnr N Abbot (2) & Worcester (h'caps, rtd 99h, eff arnd 2m on firm & soft): no form on the
level in '99: back in '97 scored here at W'hampton (h'cap, rtd 67a, R Hollinshead): eff at 7f/1m on fibresand.
85   **Ciel De Reve** 92 [3] 6-8-13 (45)(VIS) T G McLaughlin 33/1: 476   **Taker Chance** 15 [7] 4-8-10 (42) R Lappin 33/1:
13 ran   Time .2m 01.00 (2.8)   (Mrs Joan L Egan)   D J Wintle Naunton, Glos.

| **569** | 5.10 HCAP DIV II 4YO+ 0-60 (F)   1m1f79y aw Going 29 +08 Fast | | [60] |
| | £1918   £548   £274 | | |

170   **SILVERTOWN** 73 [3] B J Curley 5-9-9 (55) J P Spencer 6/1: 0020-1: 5 b g Danehill - Docklands   65a
(Theatrical) Cl-up, led 6f out, clr fnl 2f, wandered & swished tail ins last, eased nr fin: val for 7L+, fast
time, op 3/1, 10 wk abs: '99 Epsom & York wnr (h'caps, rtd 56): plcd in '98 (h'cap, rtd 61): suited by 9/10f,
stays 11.5f: acts on firm, gd/soft & fibresand: loves to force the pace: runs well fresh.
477   **GABLESEA** 14 [6] B P J Baugh 6-9-0 (46) J Bosley (7) 33/1: 000-02: 6 b g Beveled - Me Spede   5 46a
(Valiyar) Chsd ldrs, outpcd/lost pl halfway, styd on press fnl 2f, no ch with wnr: plcd sev times in '99 (rtd 60,
h'cap, no sand form): '98 Chepstow & Haydock wnr (h'caps, rtd 55 & 55a): eff at 7f/8.5f on firm, gd/soft & f/sand.
404   **SHONTAINE** 26 [2] M Johnston 7-8-9 (41) K Dalgleish (7) 10/1: 166333: 7 b g Pharly - Hinari   7 31a
Televideo (Caerleon) Chsd ldrs, rdn/held fnl 2f: op 8/1: see 383, 297 (Southwell).
469   **MYSTERIUN** 17 [13] N P Littmoden 6-9-7 (53) T G McLaughlin 5/2 FAV: 0-2124: Towards rear, eff wide   4 35a
over 4f out, held fnl 2f: op 3/1: see 383 (C/D).
4449} **IMPULSIVE AIR** 99 [1] 8-9-0 (46) D Holland 7/1: 0405-5: Led 3f, wknd fnl 2f: tchd 9/1: '99 Hamilton   1½ 25a
scorer (h'cap, rtd 52 at best, E Weymes): '98 wnr at Ripon & Carlisle (h'caps, rtd 68): eff at 1m/9f, stays 10f
well: acts on firm & gd/soft grnd: handles any trk, likes a stiff finish: AW bow & nicely h'capped for J Weymes.
497   **KINGCHIP BOY** 11 [11] 11-8-11 (43) P McCabe 20/1: 300056: Held up, eff wide 4f out, no impress.   1¼ 19a
476   **LAA JADEED** 15 [12] 5-8-6 (38) R Price (7) 20/1: 530-07: Held up, eff 5f out, sn struggling: see 476.   1¾ 11a
553   **STERLING HIGH** 3 [10] 5-9-5 (51)(fl) R Winston 12/1: 403548: Held up, nvr factor: op 10/1, qck reapp.   3 18a
326   **KASS ALHAWA** 39 [5] 7-9-9 (55) D Mernagh (3) 8/1: 310-29: Prom 6f: op 6/1: btr 326, 38 (8.5f).   4 14a
*496 **PERCHANCER** 11 [7] 4-9-12 (58) P Goode (5) 7/2: -32110: Dwelt, al towards rear, 10th: op 5/2.   ¾ 16a
520   **Untold Story** 7 [9] 5-7-10 (28)(bl)(2oh) A Polli (3) 25/1:   529 **Miss Take** 5 [4] 4-8-13 (45)(bl) S Whitworth 14/1:
248   **Rolling High** 50 [8] 5-7-12 (30)(t)(2ow)(10oh) P Doe 40/1:
13 ran   Time 2m 0.2 (2.0)   (Mrs B J Curley)   B J Curley Newmarket.

LINGFIELD (Equitrack)   WEDNESDAY FEBRUARY 23RD   Lefthand, Very Sharp Track

Official Going   STANDARD Stalls: Inside, Except 5f/1m - Outside

| **570** | 2.10 SEA OF HEAT MDN 3YO+ (D)   7f aw rnd Going 29 -25 Slow | | |
| | £2704   £832   £416   £208   3 yo rec 17lb | | |

434   **FINE MELODY** 22 [4] B W Hills 3-8-4 P Doe 2/1 FAV: 31: 3 b f Green Desert - Sit Alkul (Mr Prospector)   65a
Led after 1f, clr 2f out, rdn over 1f out, rdn out to hold on: op 11/10: apprec this step up to 7f & positive
ride: acts on both AWs & a sharp trk: likes to force the pace: clearly going the right way.
3913} **THE GIRLS FILLY** 99 [5] Miss B Sanders 3-8-4 S Carson (5) 11/4: 3400-2: 3 b f Emperor Jones -   1½ 62a
Sioux City (Simply Great) Rdn/rear, prog to chase wnr over 1f out, styd on well fnl 1f, nrst fin: nicely bckd:
5 month abs/AW bow: unplcd in '99 for J H M Gosden (rtd 67, fill mdn, debut): eff at 7f, looks sure to relish
1m+: acts on equitrack: fin clr of rem & is a likely type for similar over further.
438   **FRANKLIN D** 21 [2] J R Jenkins 4-9-12 J Weaver 7/2: 003-23: 4 ch g Democratic - English Mint (Jalmood) 6 54$
Led 1f, chsd wnr till over 1f out, no extra: nicely bckd, tchd 5/1: return to h'cap company shld suit: see 58 (C/D).
544   **RED APOLLO** 4 [6] P Howling 4-9-12 T G McLaughlin 20/1: 000-64: Mid-div, strugg halfway: qck reapp.   11 38a
493   **WHITLEYGRANGE GIRL** 13 [3] 3-8-4 Martin Dwyer 33/1: 605: Rdn/chsd ldrs 4f: mod form.   ¾ 32a
4569} **BOOMSHADOW** 99 [1] 3-8-9 R Cody Boutcher (7) 50/1: 00-6: Slowly away/al bhd: 4 month abs/AW   1¼ 34a
bow: unplcd from 2 yr '99 starts (rtd 58, auct mdn): half brother to a 3yo 1m wnr: h'caps will suit.
460   **FERNS MEMORY** 18 [8] 5-9-7 (BL) A Daly 100/1: 000/07: Dwelt/al bhd: tried blnks, no form.   nk 28$
488   **CHILWORTH** 14 [7] 3-8-9 A Clark 8/1: 064-08: Sn bhd: tchd 10/1: see 488.   12 15a
8 ran   Time 1m 26.58 (3.78)   (Maktoum Al Maktoum)   B W Hills Lambourn, Berks

571   2.40 STIEBEL ELTRON CLAIMER 4YO+ (E)   7f aw rnd   Going 29   -15 Slow
£2601   £743   £371

*503   **APOLLO RED 11** [2] G L Moore 11-8-6 A Clark 4/7 FAV: -12611: 11 ch g Dominion - Woolpack (Golden **62a**
Fleece) Led, rdn/hdd over 2f out, switched & rallied gamely ins last for press to lead nr line, all out: well bckd:
earlier scored twice here at Lingfield (sell & appr h'cap): '99 wnr here at Lingfield (sell, rtd 76a, plcd on turf,
rtd 57, clmr): '98 Brighton wnr (h'cap, rtd 74 & 72a): stays 1m well, suited by 6/7f: acts on firm, soft & is an
equitrack/Lingfield specialist: loves to force the pace: eff with/without blnks/vis: gd weight carrier: tough/genuine.

532   **BEST QUEST 6** [3] K R Burke 5-8-13 (t) N Callan 11/8: 333502: 4 b h Salse - Quest For The Best   nk **68a**
(Rainbow Quest) Cl-up, rdn/led over 2f out, hard rdn in last & just hdd nr line: bckd, consistent.

389   **ROWLANDSONS STUD 30** [1] K C Comerford 7-8-2 (t) S Righton 50/1: 00-603: 7 br g Distinctly North - 10 **37$**
Be My Million (Taufan) Dwelt/outpcd, nvr on terms: rtd 40a in '99 (unplcd): '98 Lingfield wnr (C/D appr sell
h'cap, rtd 51a, no turf form): eff at 5/7f on equitrack, handles firm & fast grnd, best without blnks.

375   **KENTISH ROCK 32** [4] D C O'Brien 5-8-4 (BL)(1ow) G Carter 100/1: 04: Cl-up 3f: blnks: no form.   18 **12a**
4 ran   Time 1m 25.9 (3.1)   (A Moore)   G L Moore Woodingdean, E Sussex

572   3.10 SPACE AIR HCAP 4YO+ 0-95 (C)   1m4f aw   Going 29   +01 Fast   [87]
£6500   £2000   £1000   £500   4 yo rec 3 lb

*508   **URSA MAJOR 11** [3] C N Allen 6-9-5 (78) Martin Dwyer 3/1 FAV: -21211: 6 b g Warning - Double   **85a**
Entendre (Dominion) Prom, led 4f out, styd on strongly, rdn out: well bckd: gd time: earlier
scored twice here at Lingfield (h'caps): '99 wnr at York (h'cap, rtd 64): '98 wnr at Southwell (2 clmrs, A Kelleway)
& Lingfield (current connections, h'cap, rtd 90a): prev eff at 6/7f, now seems suited by a sharp 10/12f on sand:
acts on firm, soft & fibresand, equitrack/Lingfield specialist: loves to dominate: tough & progressive on the a/w.

486   **SPACE RACE 14** [6] C A Cyzer 6-9-7 (80) G Carter 13/2: 2-1622: 6 b g Rock Hopper - Melanoura   4 **81a**
(Imperial Fling) Rdn/dropped to rear after 4f, prog/chsd ldrs 3f out, onepace/held fnl 2f: op 8/1: see 245 (C/D).

546   **WHITE PLAINS 4** [7] K R Burke 7-10-0 (87)(t) D Sweeney 9/2: -14033: 7 b g Nordico - Flying Diva   shd **88a**
(Chief Singer) Chsd ldrs halfway, rdn/onepace fnl 3f: op 6/1, quick reapp: topweight: see 244 (10f).

546   **FORTY FORTE 4** [2] K R Burke 4-8-10 (72) N Callan 10/1: 561624: Led, hdd 4f out, sn btn: needs 10f.   3 **69a**

442   **PUNISHMENT 21** [8] 9-9-7 (80)(t) M Hills 5/1: 06-235: Twds rear, eff halfway, held 3f out: see 157 (10f).   4 **71a**

*530   **FAILED TO HIT 6** [1] 7-9-1 (74)(vis)(6ex) J Tate 16/1: 232016: Sn rdn chasing ldrs, btn 4f out: op 8/1.   2 **62a**

*486   **HAWKSBILL HENRY 14** [4] 6-8-2 (61) F Norton 9/1: -01317: Chsd ldrs 1m: op 6/1: btr 486 (C/D).   10 **38a**

528   **MONO LADY 7** [5] 7-8-6 (65)(bl) S Drowne 13/2: 20-028: Sn rdn/bhd: tchd 8/1: btr 528 (C/D).   9 **32a**
8 ran   Time 2m 32.53 (3.33)   (Newmarket Connections Ltd)   C N Allen Newmarket, Suffolk

573   3.40 GLEN DIMPLEX HCAP 3YO+ 0-75 (E)   5f aw rnd   Going 29   -00 Slow   [71]
£2769   £852   £426   £213   3 yo rec 14lb

543   **READY TO ROCK 4** [1] J S Moore 4-7-11 (40)(bl) P M Quinn (5) 16/1: -00601: 4 b g Up And At 'Em -   **50a**
Rocklands Rosie (Muscatite) Sn led, rdn/clr over 1f out, in command ins last, rdn up: op 14/1, quick reapp: 1st
success: plcd in '99 (rtd 41a, sell): ex-Irish: apprec drop to 5f, stays 6f: acts on both AWs: eff in blnks &
clearly well suited by forcing tactics on a sharp trk.

543   **CHARGE 4** [2] K R Burke 4-9-2 (59)(t) N Callan 7/4 FAV: 6-0022: 4 gr g Petong - Madam Petoski   3 **60a**
(Petoski) Cl-up, rdn/outpcd over 1f out: well bckd: quick reapp: eff at 5f, just best at 6f?: open 5/1, 95 (mdn, 6f).

518   **RING OF LOVE 8** [5] J L Eyre 4-9-3 (60) R Cody Boutcher (7) 11/2: -13653: 4 b f Magic Ring - Fine   nk **60a**
Honey (Drone) Rdn/rear, kept on fnl 2f for press, no threat: op 9/2: see 372 (C/D).

445   **WISHBONE ALLEY 20** [6] M Dods 5-8-8 (51)(vis) A Clark 8/1: 213204: Trkd ldrs wide, outpcd fnl 2f.   1¼ **48a**

491   **TORRENT 13** [4] 5-10-0 (71)(bl) Lynsey Hanna (7) 11/2: 3-3655: Cl-up, rdn/btn over 1f out: reportedly   nk **67a**
broke a blood vessel: blnks reapplied: see 205 (C/D).

526   **PIPS STAR 7** [3] 3-8-5 (62) D Kinsella 7/1: 01-326: In tch, outpcd fnl 2f: btr 526 (C/D).   2½ **51a**
6 ran   Time 59.25 (1.45)   (J P FitzGerald)   J S Moore East Garston, Berks

574   4.10 ECA SELLER 3YO+ (G)   1m aw rnd   Going 29   -00 Slow
£1901   £543   £271   3 yo rec 19lb

505   **CLONOE 11** [4] R Ingram 6-9-8 J Weaver 6/1: -24041: 6 b g Syrtos - Anytime Anywhere (Daring March)   **52a**
Made all & rdly pulled clr from 3f out, rdn out ins last, unchall: no bid: tchd 10/1: '99 wnr here at Lingfield
& Folkestone (h'caps, rtd 43a & 47): '98 Folkestone wnr (appr h'cap) & Kempton (h'cap, rtd 53 & 47a): best forcing
pace at 7f/10f on firm, soft & both AWs, loves Lingfield & Folkestone: best without blnks: eff in sell grade.

504   **MALCHIK 11** [1] P Howling 4-9-8 F Norton 33/1: 556002: 4 ch c Absalom - Very Good (Noalto)   13 **38a**
Chsd ldrs, rdn/kept on to take 2nd ins last, no threat: one win in 43 starts: see 159.

530   **LORD EUROLINK 6** [11] C A Dwyer 6-9-8 (tvi) T G McLaughlin 14/1: -03053: 6 b g Danehill - Lady   1 **36a**
Eurolink (Kala Shikari) Rdn/chasing wnr wide halfway, sn outpcd: on 8/1, quick reapp: see 530, 333 & 245 (12f).

*505   **HIGH SHOT 11** [3] G L Moore 10-9-13 (t) S Whitworth 5/1: 2-3314: Mid-div, mod gains: top-weight.   2½ **36a**

489   **SWING ALONG 13** [6] 5-9-8 S Carson (5) 4/1 FAV: 241005: Rear, rdn halfway, mod gains: op 3/1.   1¼ **28a**

1283   **FORT KNOX 99** [10] 9-9-8 (bl) O Urbina 25/1: /000-6: Mid-div at best: 6 wk jumps abs (plcd, rtd 85h,   2½ **23a**
h'cap): lightly rcd/no form in '99 on the Level (rtd 29, h'cap, R M Flower): rnr-up in '98 (h,cap rtd 37): '96 wnr
here at Lingfield (2, rtd 66a): suited by 7f/1m, stays 9f: acts on firm, gd & both AWs: eff with/without blnks.

515   **FRENCH FANCY 8** [8] 3-7-12 (bl) D Kinsella (7) 8/1: -04537: Prom 5f: op 10/1: see 488, 443 (6/7f).   1¼ **15a**

375   **SEA SPOUSE 32** [2] 9-9-8 Dale Gibson 12/1: 600-48: Rdn/al towards rear: op 8/1: see 375.   1 **18a**

505   **SHAMWARI SONG 11** [9] 5-9-8 N Callan 12/1: -00029: Wide/twds rear, nvr factor: op 8/1: see 505.   5 **8a**

452   **CELESTIAL KEY 19** [7] 10-9-8 K Dalgleish 9/2: /03-20: Sn rdn/al rear: 10th: op 3/1: btr 452 (fbrsnd).   2½ **3a**

501   **MARIANA 12** [5] 5-9-3 (vis) J Stack 66/1: 0-5050: Sn bhd: 11th: visor reapp: see 367 (auct mdn).   14 **0a**
11 ran   Time 1m 38.47 (2.27)   (P McKernan)   R Ingram Epsom, Surrey

LINGFIELD (Equitrack)   WEDNESDAY FEBRUARY 23RD   Lefthand, Very Sharp Track

575	4.40 LEES HCAP 3YO+ 0-85 (D) 1m2f aw Going 29 -08 Slow				[75]
	£3715	£1143	£571	£285 3 yo rec 22lb4 yo rec 1 lb	

441   **SAMMYS SHUFFLE** 21 [4] Jamie Poulton 5-8-8 (55)(bl) O Urbina 8/1: 1-5001: 5 b h Touch Of Grey - **60a**
Cabinet Shuffle (Thatching) Sn handy, al travelling well, went on 2f out, styd on well ins last, drvn out: op 6/1:
'99 scorer here at Lingfield (C/D h'cap, rtd 59a, plcd on turf, rtd 37, h'cap): '98 Brighton (2, h'caps, rtd 48) &
Lingfield wnr (h'cap, rtd 44a): eff at 10/12f on firm & equitrack: best in blnks.

400   **ADMIRALS PLACE** 28 [2] H J Collingridge 4-9-3 (65) G Carter 6/5 FAV: 05-122: 4 ch c Perugino - Royal 2½   **65a**
Daughter (High Top) Held up in tch, rdn/outpcd 4f out, kept on for press to take 2nd ins last, al held: hvly
bkcd, tchd 6/4: consistent colt, can win again: see 268 (C/D).

525   **RONS PET** 7 [1] K R Burke 5-10-0 (75)(tbl) N Callan 4/1: 233223: 5 ch g Ron's Victory - Penny Mint   ½   **74a**
(Mummy's Game) Led, rdn/hdd 2f out & no extra: op 7/2: topweight: stays sharp 10f, prob best at 7f/1m: see 398.

374   **SEA DANZIG** 32 [3] J J Bridger 7-9-3 (64) A Daly 11/2: -50104: Dwelt, rdn to join ldr after 2f, strugg   7   **53a**
4f out: op 4/1: loves to dominate, unable to do so here: btr 335 (C/D, stks).

418   **THE STAGER** 26 [5] J S Whitworth 5/1: 2-1145: Held up, btn 4f out: op 7/2: btr 340 (1m).   1¾   **61a**
5 ran   Time 2m 06.47 (3.67)   (Mrs G M Temmerman)   Jamie Poulton Telscombe, E Sussex

---

WOLVERHAMPTON (Fibresand)   THURSDAY FEBRUARY 24TH   Lefthand, Sharp Track

Official Going   STANDARD Stalls: Inside, Except 7f - Outside

576	1.25 BET DIRECT HCAP DIV 1 4YO+ 0-60 (F) 2m46y aw Going 14 -48 Slow			[60]
	£1928	£551	£275 4 yo rec 6 lb	

482   **HETRA HEIGHTS** 16 [10] W J Musson 5-8-5 (37) L Newton 16/1: 005-61: 5 b m Cox's Ridge - Top Hope   **45a**
(High Top) Chsd ldrs halfway, led 5f out, rdn/hdd over 2f out, rallied gamely for press ins last to lead again nr
fin, rdn out: op 8/1: unplcd in '99, subs had a wind operation: '98 rnr-up (h'cap, rtd 51): eff at 12f, now
stays a sharp 2m well: acts on fast & fibresand: likes a sharp trk: game performance, could win again.

554   **OUR PEOPLE** 5 [7] M Johnston 6-8-1 (33)(t)(6ex) K Dalgleish (7) 8/1: 533132: 6 ch g Indian Ridge -   ¾   **39a**
Fair And Wise (High Line) Chsd ldrs, led over 2f out, tired ins last & hdd nr fin: op 6/1: clr of rem, qck reapp.

*542   **ST LAWRENCE** 6 [5] B S Rothwell 6-9-7 (53)(6ex) D Mernagh 3) 4/5 FAV: 11D213: 6 gr g With Approval 22   **43a**
- Mingan Isle (Lord Avie) In tch, pushed along & prog to lead halfway, eased & hdd 7f out, no extra over 2f out &
eased ins last: jockey given a 14 day ban for riding a finish a circuit early: nicely bckd, qck reapp: see 542.

492   **CHILDRENS CHOICE** 14 [3] J Pearce 9-8-12 (44)(vis) J P Spencer 10/1: 6-3134: Towards rear, prog/chsd   3   **31a**
ldrs wide 4f out, kept on fnl 2f: op 7/1: see 363 (14.7f, sell).

470   **PIPE MUSIC** 17 [9] 5-10-0 (60)(bl) P Goode(5) 8/1: 6-3205: In tch, btn 3f out: jmps fit (mod form).   hd   **47a**

535   **TALIB** 1 [1] 6-7-10 (28)(t)(10oh) Joanna Badger (7) 50/1: 00-406: Chsd ldrs, btn 4f out: quick reapp.   3   **12a**

524   **PARDAN** 8 [4] P Doe 20/1: 00-657: Led 1f/cl-up, btn 3f out: see 408.   hd   **15a**

477   **MUTADARRA** 16 [8] 7-9-6 (52) R Studholme (5) 33/1: 0-4008: Held up, eff 4f out, sn held: btr 292 (9f).   2   **34a**

3888}   **KEEPSAKE** 99 [2] 6-7-10 (28)(bl)(3oh) G Baker (7) 12/1: 4400-9: Dwelt, al rear: op 8/1: jumps fit,   16   **0a**
Dec '99 rnr-up (h'cap, rtd 64h): plcd thrice in '99 (h'caps, rtd 27a): '97 Salisbury wnr (h'cap, rtd 52):
eff at 12f, stays a sharp 2m well: acts on both AWs, firm & gd grnd: handles soft: best without blnks/vis.

524   **NEGATIVE EQUITY** 8 [6] 8-8-8 (40)(bl) S Righton 10/1: 25/140: Led after 1f till halfway, led again   5   **5a**
over 7f out till 5f out, sn btn: 10th: op 7/1: btr 460 (equitrack, 13f).

124   **TURGENEV** 86 [11] 11-8-2 (34) P Fessey 50/1: 0000-0: Sn t.o.: 11th: 12 wk abs: no form in '99   dist   **0a**
(rtd 27, stks): '98 Sandown wnr (h'cap, rtd 69): eff at 12/14f: acts on fast, prefers gd & soft: likes a gall trk.
11 ran   Time 3m 39.3 (10.1)   (K L West)   W J Musson Newmarket

577	1.55 BET DIRECT HCAP DIV 2 4YO+ 0-60 (F) 2m46y aw Going 14 -63 Slow			[58]
	£1928	£551	£275 4 yo rec 6 lb	

542   **FEARSOME FACTOR** 6 [7] B J Curley 5-9-8 (52) J P Spencer 5/4 FAV: -04021: 5 b g Alleged - Spark Of   **57a**
Success (Topsider), Rear, smooth prog wide fnl 4f, rdn/led & drifted left 1f out, styd on well, rdn out: well bckd,
qck reapp: no form in '99: ex-Irish, '98 Leopardstown wnr (mdn, 10f): prev suited by 9/10f, now stays a sharp 2m
well: acts on fibresand, soft & hvy grnd: seems best held up for a late run: can win more races.

520   **XYLEM** 9 [9] J Pearce 9-8-8 (38)(vis) R Price 10/1: -32302: 9 ch g Woodman - Careful (Tampa Trouble)   2½   **39a**
Held up in tch, rdn/prog 4f out, ev ch over 1f out, not pace of wnr: op 8/1: eff at 10/12f, now stays a sharp 2m.

*494   **QUAKERESS** 14 [8] R Brotherton 5-7-12 (27)(1ow) F Norton 6/1: 604113: 5 b m Brief Truce - Deer Emily   ¾   **28a**
(Alzao) Rear/in tch, prog fnl 4f, briefly no room 3f out, kept on well, nrst fin: op 4/1: prev with John Berry.

494   **BEAUCHAMP MAGIC** 14 [3] M D I Usher 5-8-3 (33) G Baker (7) 10/1: -04054: Led 15f, no extra.   1¾   **32a**

1127}   **PEN FRIEND** 99 [5] 6-9-10 (54) Martin Dwyer 7/1: /2-0-5: Chsd ldrs, rdn/held over 2f out: op 9/2,   ½   **52a**
10 month abs: AW bow: unplcd sole start in '99 (rtd 45, h'cap): rnr-up in '98 (rtd 54, h'cap): '97 scorer at
Beverley & Thirsk (h'caps, rtd 53 at best): eff at 2m on gd & fast grnd.

535   **SILVER GYRE** 6 [6] 4-8-6 (42)(BL) N Callan 9/2: 6-6426: Trkd ldrs wide, ch 4f out, onepace: blnks.   nk   **40a**

2676}   **GOLDENGIRLMICHELLE** 99 [1] 5-7-10 (26)(6oh) K Dalgleish (7) 25/1: /004-7: Handy, fdd over 2f out: 6   **18a**
4 month jumps abs: rtd 40 at best in '99 (clmr): 98/99 hdles wnr at Musselburgh (juv mdn): tried blnks & a t-strap.

502   **COLERIDGE** 13 [10] 12-8-12 (42)(bl) D R McCabe 33/1: 600-08: Rear, nvr factor: see 502.   2½   **32a**

502   **ONEFOURSEVEN** 13 [2] 7-9-8 (52) I Mongan (7) 33/1: 404/09: Handy 12f: op 14/1: see 502.   3½   **39a**

437   **SHY PADDY** 23 [4] 8-8-4 (34) P Doe 33/1: 422/00: Held up in tch, rdn/btn 3f out: see 437 (12f).   ¾   **20a**
10 ran   Time 3m 41.6 (12.4)   (M M Woods)   B J Curley Newmarket, Suffolk

578	2.25 DRAYTON MDN 4YO+ (D) 1m1f79y aw Going 14 -19 Slow			
	£2730	£840	£420	£210

--   **GENERATE** [1] M J Polglase 4-8-9 L Newton 9/1: 5000-1: 4 b f Generous - Ivorine (Blushing Groom)   **64a**
Handy, led over 3f out, held on well ins last, rdn out: op 5/1: AW/Brit bow, 5 month abs: ex-French mdn, rnr-
up over 9f at Dieppe in '99: eff over 9.4f, could stay further: acts on fibresand & a sharp trk: runs well fresh.

478   **WELODY** 16 [5] K Mahdi 4-9-0 (BL) D Shakallis 7/2: 540-42: 4 ch g Weldnaas - The Boozy News   1¾   **66a**
(L'Emigrant) Held up in tch pulling hard, prog/chsd wnr fnl 2f, edged left/no extra ins last: op 9/2: not

settle in blnks: eff at 9.4f on fibresand: a likely type for similar when learning restraint: see 478.
490 **SAN GLAMORE MELODY 14** [2] R Ingram 6-9-0 J P Spencer 25/1: 02/033: 6 b g Sanglamore - Lypharitissima (Lightning) Towards rear, eff 3f out, kept on onepace for press: see 393. 3½ **59$**
-- **DARK VICTOR** [7] D Shaw 4-9-0 N Callan 5/1: 4: Chsd ldrs 7f: Flat debut, jumps fit (plcd in a bmpr). 5 **49a**
-- **SAGAPONACK** [3] 4-9-0 Dean McKeown 5/1: 5: Slowly away, eff wide halfway, sn held: op 3/1, debut. 3½ **42a**
446 **HAPPY LADY 21** [8] 4-8-9 M Hills 11/8 FAV: 055-36: Led 6f, btn fnl 2f: well bckd: see 446. 9 **24a**
409 **ANNELIINA 28** [6] 4-8-9 (t) Martin Dwyer 20/1: 250-07: Chsd ldrs 6f: see 409. 10 **9a**
378 **CASTRATO 33** [4] 4-9-0 R Studholme (5) 40/1: 08: Prom, btn 4f out: no form. 10 **0a**
8 ran Time 2m 01.3 (3.1) (L & K Racing) M J Polglase Southwell, Notts

579

3.00 0800 211 222 HCAP 3YO+ 0-100 (C) 5f aw Going 14 +10 Fast [92]
£6597 £2030 £1015 £507 3 yo rec 14lb

*532 **DAAWE 7** [2] D Nicholls 9-9-8 (86)(bl)(6ex) Clare Roche (7) 5/1 FAV: 60-111: 9 b h Danzig - Capo Di Monte (Final Straw) Handy, went on halfway, rdly pulled clr over 1f out, pushed out: val for 5L+, fast time, op 4/1: earlier won at Southwell & here at W'hampton (h'caps): '99 scorer at Pontefract & Newcastle (h'caps, rtd 71 & 68a): '98 Thirsk & Doncaster wnr (ltd stks, rtd 81 & 75a): suited by 5/6f, stays 1m on firm, hvy & f/sand: handles any trk, loves a sharp one: eff with/without visor/blnks: has run well fresh: loves to force the pace. **98a**
435 **TOM TUN 23** [7] Miss J F Craze 5-8-11 (75) K Darley 7/1: 026-52: 5 b g Bold Arrangement - B Grade (Lucky Wednesday) Towards rear/wide, kept on fnl 2f for press, no ch with wnr: see 129, 47. 4 **76a**
539 **FIRST MAITE 6** [9] S R Bowring 7-9-10 (88)(bl) J P Spencer 16/1: 0-4003: 7 b g Komaite - Marina Plata (Julio Mariner) Towards rear/wide, styd on fnl 2f for press, nrst fin: op 10/1: quick reapp: blnks reapp. ½ **87a**
*491 **EASTERN TRUMPETER 14** [10] J M Bradley 4-8-2 (66) Claire Bryan (7) 6/1: 305-14: Chsd wnr 2f out/sn btn. ¾ **63a**
525 **BLUE KITE 8** [4] 5-9-1 (79) A Culhane 9/1: 660345: Towards rear, mod gains: op 6/1: see 258 (6f). nk **75a**
191 **MANGUS 71** [11] 6-9-1 (79) M Hills 12/1: 2014-6: Prom wide 3f, sn onepace: op 10/1: 10 wk abs. ½ **73a**
491 **YABINT EL SHAM 14** [6] 4-8-6 (70) L Newman (5) 15/2: -52307: Chsd ldrs, outpcd from halfway. ¾ **62a**
532 **JUWWI 7** [5] 6-9-6 (84) Darren Williams (7) 10/1: 353228: Bhd, staying on when no room fnl 1f. shd **76a**
435 **DIL 23** [3] 5-10-0 (92) R Fitzpatrick (3) 6/1: 3-0109: Prom 3f, sn outpcd: btr 394 (C/D). hd **83a**
506 **JACKIES BABY 12** [1] 4-8-12 (76) A Daly 9/1: 0-0400: Led till halfway, sn btn: 10th: op 6/1: btr 491. 1½ **64a**
*506 **FRILLY FRONT 12** [8] 4-8-4 (68) N Callan 6/1: 0-P110: Mid-div, btn fnl 2f: 11th: op 9/2: btr 506. 7 **44a**
11 ran Time 1m 00.4 (0.2) (Mrs Andrea M Mallinson) D Nicholls Sessay, N Yorks

580

3.35 BEST BETS HCAP 3YO+ 0-100 (C) 1m100y aw Going 14 +08 Fast [99]
£6695 £2060 £1030 £515 3 yo rec 19lb

-477 **ONE DINAR 16** [3] K Mahdi 5-7-10 (67)(3oh) Dale Gibson 3/1 FAV: 610-21: 5 b h Generous - Lypharitissima (Lightning) Held up in tch, rdn/chsd clr ldr 2f out: styd on well for press to lead nr fin: nicely bckd: fast time: '99 Lingfield wnr (mdn, rtd 75): eff at 7f/8.5f, further may suit: acts on firm, gd & fibresand: handles any trk. **76a**
4011} **FLOATING CHARGE 99** [2] J R Fanshawe 6-8-8 (77)(2ow) M Hills 5/1: 4361-2: 6 b g Sharpo - Poyle Fizz (Damister) Led, pulled clr over 2f out, hdd & no extra well ins last: clr of rem: op 4/1: 5 month abs: '99 wnr at Windsor & Kempton (h'caps, rtd 77): '98 Redcar wnr (class stks, rtd 67): suited by 1m/9f: acts on firm, hvy & f/sand: handles any trk: has run well fresh: best without blnks/visor: eff forcing the pace: encouraging AW bow. 1 **85a**
*521 **INTERNAL AFFAIR 9** [4] T D Barron 5-7-11 (68)(6ex) P M Quinn (5) 15/2: 101413: 5 b g Nicholas - Gdynia (Sir Ivor) Towards rear, rdn & kept on fnl 2f, no threat front pair: op 6/1: see 521 (C/D). 8 **62a**
539 **WEETMANS WEIGH 6** [11] R Hollinshead 7-9-12 (97) J P Spencer 20/1: 22-464: Towards rear, mod gains. 5 **81a**
337 **BLAKESET 40** [1] 5-8-11 (82)(bl) A Clark 9/1: 120-55: Chsd ldr 4f out, wknd fnl 2f: 6 wk abs, op 6/1. nk **65a**
*381 **WINDSHIFT 33** [8] 4-8-7 (78)(BL) R Winston 13/2: 0-5316: Rdn/bhd halfway, no threat: blnks: btr 381. 2 **57a**
*539 **OUT OF SIGHT 6** [7] 6-8-6 (77)(6ex) L Newman (5) 7/1: 01-217: Chsd ldrs 4f out, sn held: qck reapp. 1½ **53a**
511 **ROYAL CASCADE 10** [9] 6-8-4 (75)(bl) P Mundy (7) 25/1: 0-0638: Mid-div at best: see 511, 33 (7f). 1½ **48a**
4395} **TARAWAN 99** [5] 4-9-2 (87)(vis) K Darley 10/1: 1210-9: Al towards rear: op 7/1: jumps fit (rtd 78h, unplcd, juv nov): '99 wnr at Newcastle (mdn) & Sandown (h'cap, rtd 89, plcd sev times): eff at 1m, stays sharp 10f well: acts on firm & hvy grnd, any trk: tried blnks, best in a visor: AW bow today. 13 **41a**
2019} **LATALOMNE 99** [6] 6-9-7 (92) J Fanning 16/1: 2100-0: Prom wide 5f: 10th: op 10/1: 8 month abs/AW bow: '99 Thirsk wnr (h'cap, rtd 96): rtd 94 in '98 (E Dunlop): eff at 1m on firm & gd/soft: likes to force the pace. 4 **38a**
*336 **CANADIAN APPROVAL 40** [10] 4-8-5 (76) N Callan 15/2: 440-10: Prom wide 5f: 11th: op 6/1, abs. 1¾ **19a**
11 ran Time 1m 46.7 (0.5) (Mrs T L Lund) K Mahdi Newmarket

581

4.10 TEXT P368 SELLER 4YO+ (G) 1m4f aw Going 14 -52 Slow
£1895 £541 £270 4 yo rec 3 lb

3666} **ARTIC COURIER 99** [6] D J S Cosgrove 9-9-5 C Rutter 9/2: 2030-1: 9 gr g Siberian Express - La Reine de France (Queens Hussar) Mid-div, rdn/prog to take narrow lead over 1f out, drvn out to assert nr fin: op 5/2: no bid: 6 month abs: plcd numerous times in '99 (rtd 57a, stks & 52, h'cap): back in '96 scored at Epsom & Kempton (h'caps, awarded race, rtd 83): eff at 12/14f, tried further: acts on firm, soft & both AWs: handles any trk, likes a sharp/undul one: best without blnks: gd weight carrier: runs well fresh: apprec drop to sells. **46a**
393 **STICKS AND STONES 30** [9] J A Gilbert 8-9-5 A Mackay 7/2: 445/02: 8 b g Waajib - Majacourt (Malacate) Handy, led after 3f, rdn/hdd over 1f out & no extra: op 11/2: stays 12f, acts on fast, gd/soft & fibresand. 1½ **44a**
498 **BANNERET 13** [1] Miss S J Wilton 7-9-10 (vis) I Mongan (7) 3/1 FAV: -21053: 7 b g Imperial Falcon - Dashing Partner (Formidable) Handy, rdn/outpcd over 3f out, kept on fnl 1f: op 2/1: see 347 (C/D, clmr). 1 **48a**
*520 **HILL FARM DANCER 9** [3] W M Brisbourne 9-9-5 D Hayden (7) 4/1: 552314: Held up, prog/chsd ldrs 3f out, sn onepace: see 520 (C/D, h'cap). 1 **42$**
410 **AMBIDEXTROUS 28** [5] 8-9-5 L Swift (7) 14/1: 02-045: Held up in tch wide, nvr pace to chall: jmps fit. 1½ **40$**
-- **SOCIALIST** [4] 4-9-2 J P Spencer 9/2: 6: Held up in tch, rdn/btn 2f out & eased fnl 1f: op 6/4, debut: IR 30,000gns yearling: dam unrcd half sister to an American wnr: with J A Osborne. 13 **26a**
517 **JATO DANCER 9** [7] 5-9-0 A Culhane 25/1: -50007: Led 3f, cl-up till 3f out: see 359 (9f). 5 **14a**
468 **COCHITI 19** [2] 6-9-0 (tbl) Joanna Badger (7) 33/1: 0-0558: Mid-div, btn 4f out: jumps fit (no form). 1 **13a**
52 **PREMIER LEAGUE 99** [8] 10-9-5 R Price 16/1: 0450-9: Sn bhd: op 10/1: 3 month abs: unplcd in '99 (rtd 45a & 37 at best, h'caps): '98 Windsor wnr (2, h'caps, rtd 52, rnr-up on sand, rtd 46a, clmr): eff at 11/12f on fast, soft & equitrack: likes to dominate on a sharp trk, handles any: prev with K O Cunningham Brown, now M Salaman. 9 **8a**
9 ran Time 2m 41.5 (7.9) (D J S Cosgrove) D J S Cosgrove Newmarket, Suffolk

WOLVERHAMPTON (Fibresand)   THURSDAY FEBRUARY 24TH   Lefthand, Sharp Track

582   4.40 TEXT P372 HCAP DIV 1 3YO+ 0-65 (F)   7f aw rnd   Going 14 -36 Slow   [65]
£1949   £557   £278   3 yo rec 17lb

496   **SEA YA MAITE** 13 [12] S R Bowring 6-9-9 (60) N Callan 7/2: 156521: 6 b g Komaite - Marina Plata   **67a**
(Julio Mariner) Trkd ldrs wide, rdn/led 2f out, styd on strongly, rdn out: op 3/1: earlier scored at Southwell
(h'cap): '99 Southwell scorer again (h'cap, rtd 64a & 30): '98 Southwell wnr (h'cap, rtd 68a & 47): eff at 6f,
suited by 7f/1m: acts on fast, gd/soft, loves fibresand: has run well fresh: best without blnks: gd weight carrier.

414   **SACREMENTUM** 27 [7] J A Osborne 5-9-5 (56) S Carson (5) 8/1: 4-6402: 5 b g Night Shift - Tanturn Ergo 3   **57a**
(Tanfirion) Held up in tch, rdn & kept on well fnl 1f, not pace of wnr: op 5/1: see 381, 326.

351   **SO WILLING** 37 [11] M Dods 4-8-12 (49)(BL) A Culhane 14/1: 0-0603: 4 gr g Keen - Sweet Whisper   ½   **49a**
(Petong) Dwelt, chsd ldrs wide halfway, kept on fnl 2f, op 8/1, imprvd run in blnks: eff at 6/7f.

*471   **ITCH** 17 [9] R Bastiman 5-8-13 (50) Dean McKeown 13/8 FAV: -21314: Trkd ldrs, ch 2f out/sn held: bckd.   1½   **47a**

345   **COOL PROSPECT** 38 [2] 5-8-13 (50) K Darley 12/1: 000-05: Rdn/bhd, kept on well fnl 2f, nrst fin: 1¾   **44a**
op 16/1: '99 Redcar wnr (h'cap, rtd 50, unplcd on sand, rtd 65a, h'cap): rnr-up thrice in '98 (rtd 67a, blnks & 65,
h'caps): eff at 6f, stays 1m: acts on firm, gd/soft & fibresand: prob handles any trk: eff with/without blnks.

568   **DANZAS** 2 [8] 6-7-10 (33)(bl) Claire Bryan (7) 12/1: 064606: Handy, led 3f out till 2f out, fdd: op 20/1.   shd   **27a**

550   **NICHOLAS MISTRESS** 5 [6] 4-8-1 (38)(vis) Joanna Badger (7) 25/1: 0-0507: Towards rear, mod gains.   2½   **27a**

557   **MOY** 3 [5] 5-8-9 (46)(bl) A McCarthy (3) 12/1: 00-268: Prom 5f, op 10/1, quick reapp: btr 466 (6f).   nk   **34a**

3381}   **INDIAN SWINGER** 99 [1] 4-9-13 (64) R Winston 12/1: 3305-9: Al towards rear: op 8/1: 6 month abs: 9   **39a**
prev with J M P Eustace, rnr-up in '99 (rtd 68a, h'cap): '98 Southwell wnr (nurs h'cap, rtd 70a), rtd 69 on turf
(mdn): eff at 6f/sharp 7f: acts on fibresand & a sharp trk: now with P Howling.

4261}   **TECHNICIAN** 99 [4] 5-9-1 (52)(bl) J P Spencer 7/1: 2030-0: Led 4f, fdd: 10th: plcd numerous times   3   **21a**
in '99 (rtd 67 & 54a, h'caps): plcd numerous times in '98 (rtd 54a, M Jarvis, also rtd 63): eff around 6f/1m: acts
on firm, soft & fibresand: eff in blnks/visor: handles any trk: remarkably still a mdn.

4449} **Dancing Lawyer** 99 [10] 9-8-6 (43) J Fanning 14/1:   435 **Goes A Treat** 23 [3] 4-10-0 (65) G Carter 25/1:
12 ran   Time 1m 29.7 (3.5)   (S R Bowring)   S R Bowring Edwinstowe, Notts

583   5.10 TEXT P372 HCAP DIV 2 3YO+ 0-65 (F)   7f aw rnd   Going 14 -29 Slow   [65]
£1939   £554   £277   3 yo rec 17lb

503   **DONE AND DUSTED** 12 [8] R Brotherton 4-9-11 (62) F Norton 2/1 FAV: 1-0631: 4 ch f Up And At 'Em -   **68a**
Florentink (The Minstrel) Prom, duelled with rnr-up fnl 2f, took narrow lead ins last, styd on gamely, all out: well
bckd, tchd 7/2: '99 Lingfield (rtd 69a), Windsor (rtd 72) & W'hampton (h'caps): '98 Southwell (sell, J Berry) &
Lingfield wnr (clmr, rtd 65a & 57): eff at 6/7f on both AWs & firm: likes a sharp trk, esp W'hampton & Lingfield.

496   **CLEAR NIGHT** 13 [4] J J Sheehan 4-8-13 (50) D R McCabe 10/1: 002-42: 4 b c Night Shift - Clarista   hd   **55a**
(Riva Ridge) Led, hard rdn/hdd ins last & just held: eff at 7f/1m: had the rest well covered & deserves similar.

471   **MUTAHADETH** 17 [10] D Shaw 6-9-4 (55)(bl) A Nichalls 8/1: 325603: 6 ch g Rudimentary - Music In   3½   **53a**
My Life (Law Society) Held up in tch wide, kept on fnl 2f for press, no threat: eff at 7f, prob best at 1m: see 183.

518   **REX IS OKAY** 9 [5] S R Bowring 4-9-3 (64)(bl) S Finnamore (7) 7/1: -06664: Prom, onepace fnl 2f.   1   **60a**

550   **MIKES DOUBLE** 5 [3] 6-8-7 (44)(vis) R Fitzpatrick (3) 10/1: -52305: Towards rear, switched & prog   1½   **37a**
wide 4f out, onepace/held fnl 1f: quick reapp: see 142.

438   **CAREQUICK** 22 [7] 4-8-0 (37) A Nichalls (3) 7/1: 53-356: Chsd ldrs 5f: op 11/2: see 438, 233 & 197.   shd   **30a**

521   **DEMOCRACY** 9 [11] 4-9-7 (58)(bl) S Drowne 16/1: 005307: Dwelt, eff halfway, no impress: op 14/1.   nk   **50a**

341   **MY TYSON** 38 [12] 5-8-13 (50) K Darley 3/1: /60-08: Dwelt, mid-div halfway, btn 2f out: see 183.   5   **32a**

*497   **BROUGHTON MAGIC** 13 [2] 5-8-6 (43) L Newton (7) 00/519: Sn rdn/nvr on terms: op 13/8: btr 497 (1m).   1   **23a**

476   **FLYING HIGH** 17 [1] 5-7-12 (33)(2ow) P Fessey 12/1: 00-640: Held up, eff/btn 3f out: 10th: see 389 (6f).   3   **9a**

4362} **Three Leaders** 99 [9] 4-8-10 (47) A Culhane 14/1:   543 **Village Native** 5 [6] 7-9-1 (52)(bl) A Clark 25/1:
12 ran   Time 1m 29.2 (3.0)   (Paul Stringer)   R Brotherton Elmley Castle, Worcs

SOUTHWELL (Fibresand)   FRIDAY FEBRUARY 25TH   Lefthand, Sharp, Oval Track

Official Going STANDARD. Stalls: Inside.

584   1.50 APPR MDN HCAP DIV 1 4YO+ 0-60 (F)   1m aw rnd   Going 45 -28 Slow   [57]
£1806   £516   £258

561   **KUSTOM KIT KEVIN** 4 [10] S R Bowring 4-9-10 (53) J Bosley 6/1: -32201: 4 b g Local Suitor - Sweet   **57a**
Rival (Claude Monet) Rdn towards rear & wide, prog to lead dist, styd on well, rdn out: qck reapp: op 4/1:
unplcd in '99 (rtd 38): eff at 1m, has tried 12f: acts on fibresand & a sharp track.

2942}   **KOCAL** 99 [11] D W Barker 4-9-2 (45) P Rody Boutcher 33/1: 0000-2: 4 b g Warrshan - Jeethgaya   2½   **43a**
(Critique) Towards rear/wide, kept on fnl 2f for press, not pace of wnr: 7 month abs/AW bow: unplcd in '99
(rtd 53, auct mdn): eff at 1m, mid-dists could suit: handles fibresand.

561   **THE NOBLEMAN** 4 [5] T J Etherington 4-7-11 (26) P Hangan 9/4 FAV: 0/0533: 4 b g Quiet American -   ¾   **23a**
Furajet (The Minstrel) Chsd ldrs, prog/ch over 1f out, onepace: op 7/4, qck reapp: ahead of this wnr in 561 (11f).

553   **ROYAL DOLPHIN** 6 [3] B A McMahon 4-7-12 (27)(bl) (2ow)(3oh) P Mundy 33/1: 00-004: Keen/cl-up, nk   **23a**
led after 3f till over 1f out, no extra: qck reapp: eff around 1m on fibresand: now wears blnks.

497   **FAS** 14 [6] 4-8-3 (32)(bl) K Dalgleish (3) 25/1: 00-605: Led 3f, no extra fnl 1f: eff at 1m on fbrsnd.   2½   **23a**

567   **DILETTO** 3 [2] 4-8-8 (37) L Swift (7) 11/4: 006026: Trkd ldrs, lost pl halfway, mod gains: qck reapp.   1½   **25a**

432   **WERE NOT STOPPIN** 24 [1] 5-7-10 (25)(5oh) Joanna Badger 16/1: 0-0057: Towards rear, nvr factor.   5   **32a**

196   **MOLLYTIME** 70 [9] 4-7-10 (25)(8oh) Clare Roche (3) 33/1: 0500-8: Nvr on terms: abs: mod form.   hd   **2a**

505   **UTAH** 13 [4] 6-9-0 (43)(bl) G Baker (3) 6/1: 043209: Cl-up fnl 6f, wknd: op 6/1: btr 474, 438 (7f).   nk   **19a**

411   **PAARL ROCK** 29 [12] 5-8-13 (42) A Hawkins (5) 20/1: 000-00: Struggling halfway: 10th: see 411.   2   **14a**

--   **ROYAL SIX** [8] 7-9-7 (50) L Paddock (7) 9/1: 600-0: Slowly away, nvr on terms wide: 11th: op 8/1:   nk   **21a**
h'cap/AW bow: 5 month abs: British debut, ex-Irish, unplcd from 3 starts on the Level in '99: with N P Littmoden.

469   **NO NO NORA** 20 [7] 5-8-1 (30) G Sparkes 33/1: 600/00: Sn well bhd: unplcd in '99 (rtd 59,   22   **0a**
auct mdn, flattered, S C Williams, subs tried blnks): with A Newcombe.
12 ran   Time 1m 45.2 (5.8)   (Charterhouse Holdings Plc)   S R Bowring Edwinstowe, Notts.

SOUTHWELL (Fibresand)   FRIDAY FEBRUARY 25TH   Lefthand, Sharp, Oval Track

585
2.20 APPR MDN HCAP DIV 2 4YO+ 0-60 (F)   1m aw rnd   Going 70 -25 Slow   [56]
£1806   £516   £258

413   **AMBUSHED 28** [7] M Johnston 4-7-11 (25)(BL) K Dalgleish (3) 16/1: 00-001: 4 b g Indian Ridge -   **34a**
Surprise Move (Simply Great) Prom, led over 1f out, styd on strongly & rdn clr: galvanized by first time blnks:
only mod form up at to 12f prev: eff at 1m on fibresand: acts on a sharp trk: plenty in hand here, can win again.
439   **PREPOSITION 23** [3] M A Peill 4-8-10 (38) J Bosley 6/1: 0/2452: 4 b g Then Again - Little Emmeline   7 **38a**
(Emarati) Handy, ev ch over 1f out, sn outpcd by wnr: see 340.
583   **FLYING HIGH 1** [10] B Ellison 5-8-5 (33) P Hanagan 7/1: 0-6403: 5 b g Fayruz - Shayista (Tap   1½ **30a**
On Wood) Held up, rdn & kept on fnl 2f, no threat: unplcd over 7f yesterday: see 389 (6f, seller).
433   **SOUNDS COOL 24** [12] S R Bowring 4-7-10 (24)(1oh) Joanna Badger 12/1: 0-6504: Led 6f, no extra.   nk **20a**
490   **AHOUOD 15** [6] 4-9-1 (43) R Cody Boutcher 7/4 FAV: 6-4225: Chsd ldrs, no extra fnl 1f: btr 490, 446.   2 **35a**
501   **FRANKLIN LAKES 14** [8] 5-8-4 (32)(tbl) G Baker (3) 7/1: -30546: Chsd ldrs, led 2f out till over 1f out, fdd.   ½ **23a**
339   **TELLION 39** [5] 6-9-6 (48)(vis) P Shea (5) 7/1: /00-57: Dwelt, nvr on terms: btr 339 (12f).   5 **29a**
455   **PUIWEE 21** [4] 5-7-10 (24)(bl) (1ooh) C McCavish (7) 50/1: 000-08: Dwelt, nvr a factor: see 455.   1 **3a**
438   **BROUGHTON BELLE 23** [11] 4-7-10 (24)(4oh) D Kinsella (5) 33/1: 00-009: Prom 4f: see 298.   9 **0a**
427   **KOOL JULES 25** [1] 4-8-1 (29)(BL) N Esler (3) 20/1: 0060: Dwelt, nvr factor: 10th: blnks, h'cap bow.   1 **0a**
542   **Ballycroy River 7** [2] 4-9-3 (45) P Mundy (7) 25/1:   3380} **State Wind 99** [9] 4-9-10 (52)(bl) D Hayden 12/1:
12 ran   Time 1m 45.00 (5.6)   (Mark Johnston Racing Ltd)   M Johnston Middleham, N.Yorks.

586
2.50 BET DIRECT CLAIMER 3YO (E)   1m3f aw   Going 45 -24 Slow
£2613   £746   £373

536   **MERRYVALE MAN 7** [2] J G Given 3-8-8 N Callan 5/2: 2-0531: 3 b c Rudimentary - Salu (Ardross)   **70a**
Chsd ldrs, no room over 2f out, rdn to lead over 1f out, in command fnl 1f & eased down nr fin: val for 8L+: plcd
on turf & sand in '99 (rtd 73 & 60a): eff at 11f, 12f+ shld suit: acts on fibresand & gd/soft: likes a sharp trk.
566   **HEATHYARDS MATE 3** [6] R Hollinshead 3-8-8 P M Quinn (5) 2/1 FAV: 43-042: 3 b g Timeless Times -   6 **61a**
Quenlyn (Welsh Pageant) In tch, prog wide to lead 3f out, hdd dist & sn held: qck reapp: not stay 11f?.
566   **TOWER OF SONG 3** [1] D W Chapman 3-8-8 A Culhane 11/4: 0-5423: 3 ch g Perugino - New Rochelle   2½ **57a**
(Lafontaine) Held up in tch, rdn/onepace & held fnl 2f: qck reapp: ahd of today's rnr-up in 566 (8.5f).
537   **GILFOOT BREEZE 7** [4] J Norton 3-8-5 (BL) O Pears 50/1: 060-04: Held up, eff 3f out/sn held: blnks.   5 **47$**
537   **GENTLE ANNE 7** [7] 4-8-1 (29)(BL) K Dalgleish (7) 12/1: 45-445: Cl-up, rdn/btn over 2f out: see 537, 36.   10 **31a**
461   **COLOMBE DOR 20** [3] 3-8-11 (BL) Dean McKeown 11/2: 06-226: Keen/handy, led 5f out till over 3f   8 **33a**
out, sn btn: not settle her in first time blnks: see 461, 311.
1784} **PERPETUAL PRIDE 99** [5] 3-8-4 R Fitzpatrick (3) 50/1: 00-7: Led 6f, btn 4f out: 9 month abs: no   28 **0a**
form from 2 starts in '99 for E J Alston (rtd 28 & 59a, tried at up to 6f): now with Mrs N Macauley.
7 ran   Time 2m 28.9 (7.6)   (Arthur Symons Key)   J G Given Willoughton, Lincs.

587
3.20 BEST BEST HCAP 3YO+ 0-80 (D)   6f aw rnd   Going 45 -01 Slow   [80]
£4309   £1326   £331   3 yo rec 15lb

425   **TELECASTER 25** [7] C R Egerton 4-8-7 (59)(bl) D Sweeney 5/1: -31121: 4 ch g Indian Ridge - Monashee   **65a**
(Sovereign Dancer) Led/dsptd lead, went on to dist, just prevailed, all out: earlier won at W'hampton & Southwell
(h'caps): unplcd in '99: eff at 6/7f: loves fibresand & front running: eff with/without blnks: tough & genuine.
462   **JAMES DEE 20** [15] A P Jarvis 4-9-9 (75) W Ryan 3/1: 401-02: 4 b g Shalford - Glendale Joy   shd **80a**
(Glenstal) Chsd ldrs, rdn to chall 1f out, duelled with wnr ins last, just held: can find similar: see 462.
539   **SAND HAWK 7** [6] D Shaw 5-8-12 (64)(vis) F Norton 11/2: 211423: 5 ch g Polar Falcon - Ghassanah   1¼ **66a**
(Pas de Seul) Rdn/rear, styd on well fnl 2f, nrst fin: tchd 7/1: remains in gd heart, spot on back at 7f.
539   **DISTINCTIVE DREAM 7** [1] A Bailey 6-8-11 (63) J Weaver 16/1: 621534: Held up, nvr able to chall.   shd **65a**
538   **RUSSIAN ROMEO 7** [10] C R Egerton 5-8-13 (65)(bl) R Winston 33/1: 0-6055: Wide/chsd ldrs, not able to chall.   ½ **65a**
+579 **DAAWE 1** [2] 9-10-6 (86)(bl) (6ex) Clare Roche (7) 2/1 FAV: 0-1116: Dsptd lead, led over 4f out till over   ¾ **84a**
1f out, fdd ins last: op 4/5: qck reapp, won over 5f at Wolverhampton yesterday: see 579.
559   **MARENGO 4** [14] 6-8-2 (54) S Yourston(7) 33/1: 3-0037: Dwelt, nvr on terms: qck reapp: see 183 (made all)1¾ **48a**
454   **RAFTERS MUSIC 21** [8] 5-8-12 (64) O Pears 7/1: -12168: Chsd ldrs 4f: op 11/2: stablemate of 6th.   1 **56a**
3502} **FOIST 99** [5] 8-8-8 (60) T Lucas 20/1: 0050-9: Al outpcd: unplcd in '99 (rtd 53, h'cap): '98 wnr at Hamilton nk **51a**
(h'cap) & Warwick (stks, rtd 63 at best): suited by 6/7f, stays 1m: acts on firm, loves soft & fibresand: handles
any trk, likes Hamilton: has run well fresh: likes to race with/force the pace.
557   **NESYRED 4** [9] 4-9-7 (73) P McCabe 50/1: 610-00: Nvr a factor: 10th: qck reapp.   2½ **57a**
476   **Mutabari 18** [3] 6-8-1 (53)(vis) P Doe 25/1:   --   **Queen Sarabi** [13] 5-8-4 (56) A Nicholls (3) 25/1:
4233} **Sharp Edge Boy 99** [4] 4-7-11 (49) J Bramhill 33/1:
13 ran   Time 1m 16.0 (2.7)   (Casting Partners)   C R Egerton Chaddleworth, Berks

588
3.50 TEXT FILLIES HCAP 3YO+ 0-70 (E)   7f aw rnd   Going 45 +01 Fast   [70]
£3558   £1095   £547   £273   3 yo rec 17lb

513   **MY TESS 11** [2] B A McMahon 4-10-0 (70) L Newman (5) 6/4 FAV: -45221: 4 br f Lugana Beach - Barachois   **75a**
Princess (Barachois) Made all, styd on well/asserted ins last, rdn out: nicely bckd: best time of day: '99 scorer at
Nottingham (fill mdn, rtd 74) & Wolverhampton (fillies h'cap, rtd 70a): rtd 81 in '98 (plcd, mdn): eff forcing the
pace at 7f/8.5f, stays 10f: acts on gd/sft, soft & fibresand, prob hvy: handles any trk, likes a sharp one.
513   **OARE KITE 11** [8] P S Felgate 5-7-11 (39)(bl) (1ow)(2oh) Dale Gibson 14/1: 6-3542: 5 b m Batshoof -   1½ **39a**
Portvasco (Sharpo) Handy, ev ch 2f out, sn onepace/held: op 12/1: could find similar: see 384.
*501 **GENERAL KLAIRE 14** [5] R A Fahey 5-9-11 (67) R Winston 6/1: 53-013: 5 b m Presidium - Klairover   1¾ **64a**
(Smackover) Held up, rdn/kept on fnl 2f, no threat: op 9/2: see 501 (C/D, seller).
*557 **GUEST ENVOY 4** [7] C N Allen 5-8-7 (49)(6ex) J Bosley (7) 4/1: 032214: Held up wide, nvr threat: see 557.   3 **40a**
*513 **JESSINCA 11** [3] 4-8-8 (50)(6ex) F Norton 13/2: 40-315: Chsd ldrs, held fnl 2f: op 4/1: btr 513 (1m).   2½ **36a**
466   **SPRINGS NOBLEQUEST 20** [6] 4-8-7 (49) S Drowne 20/1: 030-06: Held up, nvr on terms: see 466.   ½ **34a**
557   **MUJAS MAGIC 4** [4] 5-9-5 (61)(vis) R Fitzpatrick (3) 11/2: 244007: Rdn/chsd ldrs 4f: qck reapp: op 4/1.   1½ **43a**
4335} **VICTOIRE 99** [1] 4-9-8 (64) J Stack 33/1: 0400-8: Bhd halfway: Aw bow/5 mth abs: unplcd in '99   12 **28a**
(rtd 59, debut, tried upto 10f): only 2nd start in a h'cap today for H Akbary.
8 ran   Time 1m 29.7 (3.1)   (J D Graham)   B A McMahon Hopwas, Staffs

SOUTHWELL (Fibresand) FRIDAY FEBRUARY 25TH Lefthand, Sharp, Oval Track

---

589 **4.25 TEXT P372 SELLER 3YO (G)** 7f aw rnd Going 45 -25 Slow
£1825 £521 £260

515 **NOWT FLASH 11** [5] B S Rothwell 3-9-4 J P Spencer 3/1 FAV: 010061: 3 ch c Petardia - Mantlepiece **63a**
(Common Grounds) Held up in tch, no room/swtchd over 1f out, styd on well under hands & heels riding to lead well
ins last: no bid: earlier scored here at Southwell (clmr): rnr-up in '99 (rtd 55a, unplcd on turf, rtd 49): eff at 6/7f
& loves fibresand/Southwell: best without blnks: enjoys sell/clmg grade.
4315} **DULZIE 99** [2] A P Jarvis 3-8-6 W Ryan 7/2: 60-2: 3 b f Safawan - Dulzura (Daring March) ¾ **49a**
Held up in tch, prog to lead 2f out, rdn/hdd well ins last & no extra: clr rem: op 3/1: 5 mth abs/AW bow: unplcd
in '99 (rtd 72, debut): eff at 7f on fibresand: can find similar on this evidence.
331 **UNFORTUNATE 42** [7] Miss J F Craze 3-8-13 V Halliday 7/2: 14-653: 3 ch f Komaite - Honour And 7 **46a**
Glory (Hotfoot) Prom wide, rdn/outpcd over 1f out: op 9/2: 6 wk abs: see 181 (6f).
459 **CROESO ADREF 20** [1] S C Williams 3-8-13 G Faulkner (3) 11/2: -12364: Led 5f, fdd: op 9/2. 2½ **41a**
450 **COME ON MURGY 22** [6] 3-8-13 (bl) D Kilcourse (7) 11/2: 144405: Keen/prom, rdn/btn over 1f out. ½ **40a**
527 **MASTER JONES 9** [3] 3-8-11 G Hannon (7) 6/1: 332536: Trkd ldr, btn over 1f out: op 9/2: see 443, 281. 5 **28a**
6 ran Time 1m 31.5 (4.9) (B Valentine) B S Rothwell Musley Bank, N Yorks

---

590 **5.00 RACING CHANNEL HCAP 4YO+ 0-70 (E)** 1m4f aw Going 45 -08 Slow **[67]**
£2782 £856 £428 £214 4 yo rec 3 lb

470 **URGENT SWIFT 18** [5] A P Jarvis 7-9-7 (60) W Ryan 5/2: 523-51: 7 ch g Beveled - Good Natured **65a**
(Troy) Held up in tch, prog wide over 3f out, stdy run fnl 2f to lead ins last, rdn out: nicely bckd, op 7/2: '99
scorer at Salisbury & Haydock (h'caps, rtd 78, plcd on sand, rtd 56a): unplcd in '98 (rtd 54, h'cap): eff at 12/14f
on fibresand, firm & gd, handles gd/soft: handles any trk: best without blnks: on a fair mark, could win again.
560 **ABLE PETE 4** [7] A G Newcombe 4-7-10 (38)(5oh) Joanna Badger (7) 25/1: 0-0502: 4 b c Formidable - 1¼ **40a**
An Empress (Affirmed) Handy, led 7f out, rdn fnl 2f, hdd/no extra ins last: nicely bckd: qck reapp: eff at 11/12f on fibresand.
*344 **ABSOLUTE MAJORITY 39** [2] H S Howe 5-8-12 (51) S Whitworth 12/1: 0-2513: 5 ch g Absalom - ½ **52a**
Shall We Run (Hotfoot) Chsd ldrs, ch 2f out, kept on onepace: op 8/1: see 344 (C/D, sell, P Howling).
*562 **EVEZIO RUFO 3** [1] N P Littmoden 8-8-7 (46) K Dalgleish (7) 9/4 FAV: 651314: Chsd ldrs, rdn/ 1 **46a**
lost place 4f out, kept on again fnl 2f, no threat: nicely bckd: qck reapp under a pen: not able to dominate today.
4455} **PARABLE 99** [9] 4-10-0 (70) F Lynch 33/1: 656-5: Trkd ldrs, fdd fnl 2f: h'cap/AW bow, 4 mth abs: 8 **60a**
unplcd from 3 starts for L Cumani in '99 (rtd 74, tried up to 10f): ran well for a long way, drop in trip shld suit.
*560 **WESTERN COMMAND 4** [4] 4-9-12 (68)(6ex) R Fitzpatrick (3) 9/2: 336216: Mid-div, btn 2f out: qck reapp. 7 **48a**
464 **IRISH CREAM 20** [3] 4-8-7 (49) M Henry 5/1: 0063-7: Mid-div, efft/held over 2f out: btr 464 (W'hmpton). 1¾ **27a**
502 **BROUGHTONS LURE 14** [8] 6-7-10 (35)(3oh) P M Quinn (5) 16/1: 52-208: Al bhnd: op 12/1: btr 339. nk **12a**
693} **APPROVED QUALITY 99** [6] 7-8-1 (40) A Nicholls (3) 16/1: 5/20-9: Led 5f, sn bhnd: op 12/1: reapp: *dist* **0a**
rnr-up in '99 (rtd 41a, C/D h'cap, F Murphy): ex-Irish mdn prev: stays a sharp 12f & handles fibresand.
9 ran Time 2m 40.6 (6.3) (A P Jarvis) A P Jarvis Aston Upthorpe, Oxon

---

LINGFIELD (Equitrack) SATURDAY FEBRUARY 26TH Lefthand, V Sharp Track

Official Going STANDARD. Stalls: 1m - Outside, Rem - Inside.

---

591 **1.50 BET DIRECT MED AUCT MDN 3YO (F)** 1m aw rnd Going 34 -04 Slow
£2247 £642 £321

4333} **BONAGUIL 99** [4] C F Wall 3-9-0 R Mullen 1/1 FAV: 04-1: 3 b g Septieme Ciel - Chateaubrook (Alleged) **77a**
Trkd ldrs going well halfway, rdn to lead ins last, in command nr fin, pushed out: well bckd, op 6/4: 5 month
abs/AW bow: unplcd both '99 starts on turf (rtd 77, mdn): subs gelded: apprec step up to 1m, further
shld suit: acts on equitrack & a sharp trk: runs well fresh: open to further improvement.
1868} **STORMY RAINBOW 99** [6] W Soane 3-9-0 Martin Dwyer 8/1: 0-2: 3 b c Red Rainbow - Stormy Heights 3 **70a**
(Golden Heights) Handy, rdn/led 2f out, hdd ins last & no extra: op 16/1: 9 month abs/AW bow: unplcd
sole turf start in '99 for R Simpson (rtd 49, stks): styd longer 1m trip, further could suit: handles equitrack.
2497} **CELEBES 99** [2] I A Balding 3-9-0 K Darley 7/2: 564-3: 3 b g Weldnaas - Shift Over (Night Shift) 3½ **63a**
Chsd ldrs halfway, rdn/onepace over 2f out: op 5/2, AW bow, 8 month abs: unplcd in '99 (rtd 79, auct mdn):
eff at 6f, 1m+ shld suit: acts on firm & soft: handles a gall or sharp/undul trk.
488 **LEGENDAIRE 17** [1] C A Dwyer 3-9-0 M Hills 2/1: 00-224: Led 6f, no extra: op 6/4: see 488, 355. ½ **62a**
26 **NO REGRETS 99** [5] 3-9-0 F Norton 20/1: 4600-5: Held up, rdn/btn 4f out: op 10/1, 3 month abs. 14 **41a**
421 **MILLENNIUM DREAM 28** [3] 3-9-0 J Weaver 40/1: 06: Dwelt/bhd, no ch halfway: mod form. 5 **31a**
6 ran Time 1m 39.23 (3.03) (Mrs R M S Neave) C F Wall Newmarket.

---

592 **2.20 J CHEEVER HCAP 3YO 0-80 (D)** 6f aw rnd Going 34 -09 Slow **[84]**
£3750 £1154 £577 £288

*444 **ILLUSIVE 24** [4] M Wigham 3-9-5 (75)(bl) F Norton 15/8 FAV: 21-411: 3 b c Night Shift - Mirage **82a**
(Red Sunset) Trkd ldrs wide halfway, rdn to lead 2f out, styd on well ins last, rdn out: tchd 9/4: prev with H J
Collingridge, earlier scored here at Lingfield (C/D h'cap): '99 wnr here at Lingfield (W Jarvis, C/D) & Southwell
(nurs h'caps, rtd 71a & 49 at best): eff at 5/6f: handles gd/soft, likes both AWs, esp Lingfield: best blnkd.
416 **OTIME 29** [6] Mrs N Macauley 3-9-4 (74)(vis) Dean McKeown 9/1: 14-602: 3 b g Mujadil - Kick 1¼ **77a**
The Habit (Habitat) Cl-up wide, kept on fnl 2f for press, not pace of wnr: op 7/1: see 165 (C/D, made all).
*479 **CASTLE SEMPILL 18** [1] R M H Cowell 3-9-7 (77)(vis) R Studholme (5) 2/1: 1-1213: 3 b c Presidium - 2 **75a**
La Suquet (Puissance) Keen, saddle slipped after 1f, rdn/trkd ldrs till outpcd fnl 2f: nicely bckd: see 479.
*527 **ITSGOTTABDUN 10** [2] K T Ivory 3-8-4 (60)(bl) C Catlin (3) 10/1: 440614: Led 1f, btn 2f out: btr 527 (slr). 4 **48a**
526 **GREY FLYER 10** [3] 3-8-7 (63) G Hannon (7) 7/1: 2-1205: Led after 1f till 2f out, fdd: op 11/2: btr 269. nk **50a**
450 **LADYWELL BLAISE 23** [5] 3-8-11 (67) C Carver (7) 5/1: 5-3146: Dwelt, nvr factor: btr 334 (C/D, mdn). nk **53a**
6 ran Time 1m 12.96 (2.56) (Danny Bloor) M Wigham Newmarket.

LINGFIELD (Equitrack) SATURDAY FEBRUARY 26TH Lefthand, V Sharp Track

593 **2.55 DERBY TRIAL COND STKS 3YO+ (B) 1m2f aw Going 34 +12 Fast**
£9309 £3531 £1765 £802 3 yo rec 22lb

*442 **ZANAY 24** [8] Miss Jacqueline S Doyle 4-9-12 T G McLaughlin 1/3 FAV: 041-11: 4 b c Forzando - Nineteenth Of May (Homing) Dwelt, wide & rdn/towards rear early, prog to lead over 2f out & forged clr ins last, rdn out: fast time: well bckd at long odds on: earlier scored here at Lingfield (C/D h'cap): '99 Nottingham wnr (mdn, rtd 86) & here at Lingfield (stks, C/D, rtd 93a): dual '99 rnr-up for R Phillips (mdn, rtd 81): eff at 1m, suited by 10f: acts on gd, soft & fibresand, equitrack/Lingfield specialist: gd weight carrier: useful & tough AW performer. **100a**
551 **TALLULAH BELLE 7** [1] N P Littmoden 7-9-5 J Tate 16/1: 50-042: 7 b m Crowning Honors - Fine A Leau (Youth) Chsd ldrs, kept on for press fnl 3f, not pace of wnr: op 12/1: gd run: see 119 (h'cap, fibresand). *5* **82a**
546 **HUGWITY 7** [4] G C Bravery 8-9-8 M Hills 20/1: 112443: 8 ch g Cadeaux Genereux - Nuit d'Ete (Super Concorde) Chsd ldr, rdn/led over 4f out till over 2f out, no extra: op 12/1: tough 8yo: see 375 (C/D, claimer). *nk* **84a**
*523 **MONSIEUR RICK 10** [6] Miss Gay Kelleway 3-8-3 F Norton 12/1: 3414: Chsd ldrs, held fnl 3f: op 8/1. *3½* **82a**
4602} **PHILATELIC LADY 99** [2] 4-9-3 S Carson 20/1: 0421-5: Rdn/towards rear, nvr factor: 4 month abs: '99 wnr at Lingfield & Windsor (h'caps, rtd 80): late '98 wnr at Lingfield (AW mdn, rtd 75a), prev rtd 75 on turf: eff over a sharp/undul 1m/10f, stays 11.8f well: acts on gd, soft & equitrack: runs well fresh: wants h'caps. *1½* **72a**
2153} **MODUS OPERANDI 99** [7] 4-9-10 N Callan 15/2: 0415-6: Cl-up, rdn/btn 3f out: op 6/1: 8 month abs/AW bow: '99 scorer at Redcar for H R A Cecil (mdn, rtd 91 at best): eff at 10f: acts on firm & a gall trk. *2½* **75a**
485 **TOPTON 17** [3] 6-9-8 (bl) R Winston 6/1: 426137: Led, rdn/hdd over 4f out, sn btn: btr 463 (1m). *1¼* **71a**
556 **SPOSA 5** [5] 4-9-3 S Yourston 100/1: 31-538: Sn bhd: qck reapp: highly tried: see 556, 301 (12f). *4* **60a**
8 ran Time 2m 04.97 (2.17) (Sandford Racing) Miss Jacqueline S Doyle Upper Lambourn, Berks.

594 **3.25 LODESTONE HCAP DIV 1 3YO+ 0-75 (E) 1m aw rnd Going 34 -03 Slow [75]**
£2276 £650 £325 3 yo rec 19lb

3619} **TEOFILIO 99** [4] A J McNae 6-9-1 (62)(bl) J Weaver 9/4 FAV: 3260-1: 6 ch h Night Shift - Rivoltade (Sir Ivor) Held up in tch, smooth prog wide halfway to lead 2f out, al holding rivals after, drvn out: 6 month abs: '99 wnr at Lingfield (C/D stks, rtd 65a), subs scored at Sandown & Newmarket (h'caps, rtd 77 at best): rtd 65 in '98: eff at 7f/1m on firm, gd & equitrack, handles any trk: best in blnks & runs well fresh: proved tough/progressive last term & looks nicely h'capped on sand, win another h'cap. **67a**
463 **SCISSOR RIDGE 21** [8] J J Bridger 8-8-9 (56) C Carver (3) 12/1: 4-3242: 8 ch g Indian Ridge - Golden Scissors (Kalaglow) Chsd ldrs wide, rdn from halfway, kept on fnl 2f, no threat to wnr: op 9/1: see 336, 29. *1¼* **57a**
2470} **MELLORS 99** [7] John Berry 7-9-1 (62) V Slattery 20/1: 5140-3: 7 b g Common Grounds - Simply Beautiful (Simply Great) Chsd ldrs, kept on fnl 2f for press, not pace to chall: op 12/1, 8 month abs: twice a wnr in '99 at Brighton (h'caps, rtd 61 at best, M J Heaton Ellis, unplcd on sand, rtd 49a, h'cap): '98 wnr at Brighton (2, h'caps, rtd 54) & Lingfield (2, h'caps, rtd 65a): eff at 1m/sharp 10f: acts on firm, gd & equitrack: handles any trk, loves Brighton & Lingfield: has run well fresh: best without a visor: likes to force the pace. *shd* **63a**
*547 **RAIN RAIN GO AWAY 7** [10] D J S Cosgrove 4-9-5 (66) C Rutter 7/2: 3-1614: Prom wide, outpcd fnl 2f. *½* **66a**
575 **RONS PET 3** [9] 5-10-0 (75)(tbl) N Callan 9/2: 332235: Handy, no extra fnl 2f: qck reapp: see 398, 33. *1½* **72a**
525 **INDIAN WARRIOR 10** [2] 4-8-8 (55) Pat Eddery 5/1: 0-0666: Twds rear, nvr factor: op 3/1: see 364. *3* **46a**
147 **ANNIE APPLE 82** [3] 4-8-4 (51) P Doe 25/1: 2300-7: Led 6f, fdd: 12 wk abs: '99 scorer here at Lingfield (C/D seller, rtd 59a, R Hannon), subs plcd sev times for G Lewis & current connections (rtd 54 at best, h'cap): '98 Folkestone wnr (sell, rtd 59): eff at 6f/1m on firm, soft & equitrack, any trk: best without a vis. *1¼* **39a**
463 **SOUND THE TRUMPET 21** [5] 8-7-10 (43)(t)(1oh) J Mackay (7) 16/1: 0-0608: Dwelt, wide/nvr on terms. *5* **21a**
2730} **REGENT 99** [1] 5-8-0 (47) A Nicholls (3) 25/1: 6400-9: Dwelt, nvr a factor: jumps fit. *4* **17a**
547 **TITAN 7** [6] 5-7-10 (43)(9oh) R Brisland (3) 50/1: 60-000: Prom 5f: 10th: see 92. *½* **12a**
10 ran Time 1m 39.16 (2.96) (L R Gotch) A J McNae Compton, Berks.

595 **3.55 BEST BETS CLAIMER 3YO (F) 1m aw rnd Going 34 -17 Slow**
£2032 £580 £290

*545 **SPORTY MO 7** [6] K R Burke 3-9-1 (vis) N Callan 4/7 FAV: 450311: 3 b g Namaqualand - Miss Fortunate (Taufan) Led after 2f & readily pulled clr from 3f out, rdn out ins last, unchall: hvly bckd at odds on: recent Lingfield wnr (clmr): '99 wnr at Southwell (2 sells, rtd 71a, unplcd on turf, rtd 69, sell): eff at 6/7f, now suited by 1m/sharp 10f: acts on soft & fibresand, loves equitrack/Lingfield: suited by a vis: enjoys sell/claimers. **81a**
311 **KIGEMA 46** [3] C N Allen 3-7-12 J Mackay (7) 11/2: 6-1462: 3 ch f Case Law - Grace de Bois (Tap On Wood) Towards rear, rdn & kept on fnl 3f, no threat: op 9/2, 6 wk abs: see 241 (C/D). *5* **52a**
547 **DAMASQUINER 7** [5] T E Powell 3-8-6 R Lappin 100/30: 6-4163: 3 b f Casteddu - Hymn Book (Darshaan) Pulled hard/chsd ldrs, chsd wnr over 2f out till over 1f out, al held: op 4/1: see 459 (7f). *3* **54a**
537 **XENOS 8** [4] P Howling 3-8-2 (BL)(1ow) R Mullen 20/1: 056304: Chsd ldrs, outpcd from halfway: blnks. *4* **42a**
589 **MASTER JONES 1** [2] 3-8-9 Kristin Stubbs (7) 20/1: 325365: Al towards rear: op 12/1: unplcd yesterday. *2* **45a**
527 **CHARTWELL 10** [7] 3-8-6(1ow) R Price 25/1: 06: Led 2f, btn 2f out: longer 1m trip. *14* **21a**
6 ran Time 1m 40.3 (4.1) (Maurice Charge) K R Burke Newmarket.

596 **4.30 LODESTONE HCAP DIV 2 3YO+ 0-75 (E) 1m aw rnd Going 34 -03 Slow [71]**
£2276 £650 £325 3 yo rec 19lb

*504 **SUPERCHIEF 14** [4] Miss B Sanders 5-8-8 (51)(tbl) S Carson (5) 4/1: -42111: 5 b g Precocious - Rome Express (Siberian Express) Sn trkd ldr, rdn to lead 1f out, styd on well, rdn out: nicely bckd: completed a hat-trick here at Lingfield after 2 earlier h'cap wins (incl a mdn h'cap): plcd in late '99 (mdn, rtd 67a): rtd 53 at best in '98 (h'cap, tried visor, J Banks): eff at 7f/1m, stays 10f: loves equitrack/Lingfield: eff in a visor, suited by t-strap & blnks: still ahead of the h'capper, could win again on this evidence. **58a**
546 **BORDER GLEN 7** [8] J J Bridger 4-9-0 (57)(bl) J Weaver 12/1: 34-362: 4 b g Selkirk - Sulitelma (The Minstrel) Led, rdn/hdd 1f out, no extra ins last: op 16/1, clr of rem: see 546, 96 (C/D). *2* **59a**
431 **TROIS ELLES 25** [6] R C Spicer 4-7-11 (40)(1ow)(5oh) A Mackay 33/1: 003-03: 4 b g Elmaamul - Ca Ira (Dancing Dissident) Rear, rdn & kept on fnl 3f, took 3rd ins last, no threat: see 431. *7* **31a**
463 **PACIFIC ALLIANCE 21** [5] M Wigham 4-9-8 (65) Dean McKeown 7/4 FAV: 014-34: Rdn/chsd ldrs, outpcd over 3f out: nicely bckd: prev with P S McEntee: step up to 10f could suit on this evidence. *¾* **55a**
497 **ELLWAY PRINCE 15** [1] 5-8-9 (52) A Clark 6/1: 022625: Broke well, stdd to rear, rdn/mod gains fnl 3f. *1¼* **39a**
525 **ACID TEST 10** [9] 5-9-5 (62) R Fitzpatrick (3) 16/1: 400-06: Held up wide, nvr on terms: op 12/1. *3* **43a**
582 **SACREMENTUM 2** [2] 5-8-13 (56) S Drowne 10/1: -64027: Chsd ldrs till outpcd halfway: qck reapp. *1¾* **34a**

LINGFIELD (Equitrack) SATURDAY FEBRUARY 26TH Lefthand, V Sharp Track

239 **RESIST THE FORCE** 59 [3] 10-9-10 (67) M Hills 3/1: 0/10-8: Sltly hmpd start, chsd ldrs 6f: op 4/1, **3½ 38a**
2 month abs: topweight: btr 210 (C/D).
431 **KINNINO** 25 [7] 6-8-0 (43)(bl) P Doe 14/1: 0-1349: Mid-div/wide, btn 3f out: op 10/1: blnks reapp. **2 10a**
9 ran   Time 1m 39.13 (2.93)   (Copy Xpress Ltd)   Miss B Sanders Epsom, Surrey.

597	5.00 AWESOME POWER HCAP 3YO 0-70 (E) 1m2f aw Going 34 -12 Slow	[75]
	£2563 £732 £366	

373 **PEDRO PETE** 35 [4] M R Channon 3-8-12 (59) A Daly 11/2: 00-41: 3 ch g Fraam - Stride Home (Absalom) **69a**
Trkd ldr all trav well, went on 4f out & rdn/pulled clr fnl 1f: op 10/1: h'cap debut: unplcd in 2 turf '99 starts
(mdn, rtd 68): apprec step up to 10f, 12f+ may suit: acts on equitrack & a sharp trk: clearly going the right way.
566 **CHILLI** 4 [5] C E Brittain 3-8-7 (54) A Nicholls (3) 11/2: 40-332: 3 br g Most Welcome - So Saucy **7 54a**
(Teenoso) Chsd ldrs wide, rdn/chsd wnr 1f out: clr rem: qck reapp: prob styd longer 10f trip
& handles both AWs: caught a tartar here but has shown enough to find similar: see 566, 419.
*544 **STRETFORD LASS** 7 [6] J Noseda 3-9-7 (68) G Hind 2/1: 313: 3 b f Woodman - Ladanum (Green Dancer)8 **58a**
Dwelt & rdn to lead after 1f, not settle, hdd 4f out & sn btn: nicely bckd: needs to learn restraint: see 544 (1m).
523 **BROWNS DELIGHT** 10 [1] S Dow 3-8-10 (57)(VIS) P Doe 14/1: 20-044: Held up, btn 3f out: op 10/1, vis. **1½ 44a**
*536 **XELLANCE** 8 [3] 3-7-10 (43)(10h) K Dalgleish (7) 6/4 FAV: 000-15: Rdn/rear after 3f, nvr on terms: eff **4 24a**
well bckd: connections unable to offer explanation: btr 536 (11f, fibresand).
461 **BLAYNEY DANCER** 21 [2] 3-7-10 (43)(7oh) D Kinsella (7) 14/1: 60-036: Held up, btn 3f out: see 461 (C/D). nk **23a**
6 ran   Time 2m 07.39 (4.59)   (Peter Taplin)   M R Channon West Isley, Berks.

SOUTHWELL (Fibresand) MONDAY FEBRUARY 28TH Lefthand, Sharp, Oval Track

Official Going STANDARD. Stalls: Inside.

598	1.40 BET DIRECT AMAT HCAP DIV 1 4YO+ 0-75 (G) 7f aw rnd Going 37 -20 Slow	[54]
	£1526 £436 £218	

587 **DISTINCTIVE DREAM** 3 [9] A Bailey 6-10-9 (63) Miss Bridget Gatehouse (5) 9/2 FAV: 215341: 6 b g **67a**
Distinctly North - Green Side (Green Dancer): Cl-up, led 3f out, styd on strongly, rdn out: nicely bckd, qck
reapp: earlier won at W'hampton (sell): '99 wnr at Haydock (class stks, visor, rtd 75, Lady Herries): '98
rnr-up (h'cap, rtd 85): eff at 6/7f on firm, gd/soft, fibresand & any trk: eff with/without blnks or visor.
*511 **BANDBOX** 14 [7] M Salaman 5-10-11 (65) Mr Ben Salaman (7) 5/1: 300-12: 5 ch g Imperial Frontier - **1¾ 65a**
Dublah (Private Account): Mid-div, swtchd wide & gd prog 2f out, styd on strongly: shld win again: see 511.
574 **SWING ALONG** 5 [3] R Guest 5-11-0 (68) Mr V Coogan (5) 14/1: 410053: 5 ch m Alhijaz - So It Goes **1½ 65a**
(Free State): Settled rear, rdn to impr over 2f out, styd on well inside last, nvr nrr: op 10/1: qck
reapp: gd effort over an inadequate trip: best over further at W'hampton: see 404 (9.4f).
583 **MUTAHADETH** 4 [8] D Shaw 6-10-1 (55)(bl) Mrs C Williams 8/1: 256034: Rcd wide cl-up, hdwy to **¾ 50a**
chall over 1f out, no extra inside last: clr rem: qck reapp: see 583.
332 **TROJAN WOLF** 44 [11] 5-11-7 (75) Miss S Pocock (5) 6/1: 11-145: Led to halfway, wknd final 2f: **6 61a**
6 wk abs: top-weight: needs further: btr 255 (8.5f).
538 **TAKHLID** 10 [2] 9-11-2 (70) Miss R Clark 6/1: 022536: Chsd ldrs, lost tch final 2f: op 9/2: btr 538. **1¾ 53a**
432 **SAN MICHEL** 27 [10] 8-9-4 (44)(1ow)(5oh) Miss Diana Jones 16/1: 305-07: Rcd wide in tch, btn fnl 2f. **5 19a**
431 **WAIKIKI BEACH** 27 [6] 9-9-12 (52)(bl) Mrs J Moore 20/1: 01-008: Held up, eff 2f out, no extra dist. **¾ 26a**
2103} **SARUM** 99 [4] 14-9-4 (44)(e)(10w)(24oh) Mr T Waters (7) 33/1: 0000-9: Prom, rdn/lost tch over **½ 17a**
3f out: reapp: unplcd in '99 (sell, rtd 35a at best): last won back in '96 at Lingfield (amat h'cap,
rtd 53a, C Wildman): eff at 6f/1m on gd, fast & both AWs: now 14yo.
558 **ABOVE BOARD** 7 [1] 5-9-6 (46)(bl) Mrs M Morris (5) 8/1: 000220: Al bhd, 10th: op 4/1: btr 558 (6f mdn).½ **18a**
432 **LILANITA** 27 [5] 5-9-4 (44) Miss E Folkes (5) 16/1: -20000: Cl-up, lost tch fnl 3f, 11th: btr 45 (1m sell). **4 10a**
11 ran   Time 1m 30.6 (4.0)   (A Thomson)   A Bailey Little Budworth, Cheshire.

599	2.10 BET DIRECT AMAT HCAP DIV 2 4YO+ 0-75 (G) 7f aw rnd Going 37 -23 Slow	[50]
	£1526 £436 £218	

*531 **PALAWAN** 11 [6] I A Balding 4-11-7 (71) Mr J Gee (7) 7/2: 20-211: 4 br g Polar Falcon - Krameria **76a**
(Kris): Made all, styd on strongly final 2f, drvn out: op 5/2, top weight: earlier won at W'hampton (mdn):
thrice rnr-up in '99 (mdns, rtd 75): eff at 5f, stays 7f well: acts on fast, gd & likes fibresand: handles a
stiff/undul or sharp trk: bold front running effort under top weight today, could complete hat-trick.
582 **ITCH** 4 [8] R Bastiman 5-10-0 (50) Miss R Bastiman (5) 5/2 FAV: 213142: 5 b h Puissance - Panienka **1 52a**
(Dom Racine): Rcd wide in mid-div, gd hdwy over 3f out, chsd wnr appr final 1f, hung left & no extra well
inside last: nicely bckd, clr rem: consistent & a fine eff here having to race wide thro'out: see 471.
343 **SOPHOMORE** 42 [1] J L Harris 6-11-6 (70) Mrs Annette Harris (7) 25/1: 446/03: 6 b g Sanglamore - **3½ 66a**
Livry (Lyphard): Cl-up, hdwy to chall ldrs 2f out, onepcd final 1f: drop in trip: 4th over hdles (2m
sell h'cap, soft grnd, rtd 66h) since 343 (11f).
587 **MUTABARI** 3 [4] Mrs S Lamyman 6-10-3 (53) Mr S Dobson (5) 11/2: 425304: In tch, swtchd wide 3f **3 44a**
out, rdn & kept on onepcd over 1f out: see 255.
299 **ODDSANENDS** 49 [7] 4-11-0 (64) Miss M Keuthen (5) 12/1: 022-05: Prom, hdwy to chall over 2f out, **2 51a**
edged left & btn over 1f out: see 195 (clmr).
4436} **GRAND VIEW** 99 [9] 4-11-2 (66) Mr L Richardson (7) 11/2: 0300-6: Handy, rdn & lost tch over 2f out: **3 48a**
op 3/1 on reapp, new stable: AW bow: '99 scorer for R Hannon at Salisbury (h'cap, rtd 71 at best): unplcd in 3
'98 mdns: eff at 5/6f, further shld suit: acts on firm & soft, stiff/gall trks: sharper next time for D Nicholls.
*550 **DOBERMAN** 9 [5] 5-9-9 (45)(bl) Miss E Folkes (5) 9/1: 350317: Al bhd: op 6/1: btr 550 (8.5f clmr). **1¾ 24a**
325 **AWESOME VENTURE** 45 [10] 10-9-3 (39)(8oh) Mr J Roe (4) 40/1: 05-008: Prom 5f: jumps fit. **2 15a**
496 **PLEASURE TRICK** 17 [3] 9-9-0 (42)(17ow) Mrs R Howell (0) 40/1: 500-09: Dwelt, al well bhd: 17lbs o/w. **8 24a**
2507} **PANSY** 99 [2] 4-10-5 (55) Miss E Gordon 25/1: 6406-0: Al well bhd, t.o. in 10th: seasonal/AW bow: **8 9a**
new stable: 4th at Brighton in '99 (mdn h'cap, rtd 55, H Morrison, subs tried visor): stays 7f, handles fast grnd.
10 ran   Time 1m 30.8 (4.2)   (Robert Hitchins)   I A Balding Kingsclere, Hants.

SOUTHWELL (Fibresand)   MONDAY FEBRUARY 28TH   Lefthand, Sharp, Oval Track

600

2.40 0800 211 222 CLAIMER 4YO+ (F)   1m aw rnd   Going 37   -03 Slow
£2179   £622   £311

360   **OVER THE MOON 39** [1] Miss S J Wilton 6-8-1 (vis) P M Quinn (5) 16/1: 60-101: 6 ch m Beveled - Beyond **58a**
The Moon (Ballad Rock): In tch, hdwy 2f out, chall dist, drvn out to lead cl-home: op 12/1: clmd by M Polglase
for £5,000: earlier won at W'hampton (sell): '99 W'hampton wnr (clmr, rtd 57a): won again at W'hampton in '98
(3 clmrs, rtd 61a, N Littmoden): eff at 7f/9.5f, loves fibresand/W'hampton: suited by a visor & claim/sell grade.

3731} **SAGUARO 99** [11] K A Morgan 6-8-8 L Newman (5) 9/2 CO FAV: 0000-2: 6 b g Green Desert - Badawi   ¾ **63a**
(Diesis): Keen & prom, hdwy to lead over 3f out, styd on for press, hdd cl-home: reapp: '99 scorer at
Southwell & W'hampton (h'caps, rtd 79a), subs well btn on turf & fibresand: unplcd in '98 for J Gosden
(tried visor): eff at 7/9.3f on soft grnd & fibresand: gd weight carrier & can go well fresh: win sn.

4342} **WILTON 99** [10] J Hetherton 5-8-10 (t) (2ow) M Tebbutt 25/1: 0-003: 5 ch g Sharpo - Poyle Amber   1¾ **61a**
(Sharrood): Rcd wide mid-div, gd hdwy over 2f out, ev ch until no extra final 1f: op 14/1 on reapp:
well btn in 2 '99 starts (rtd 44a): '98 wnr at Pontefract, Redcar (h'caps, rtd 70) & Lingfield (AW h'cap,
rtd 79a at best): eff at 7f/9.3f: acts on gd/soft, hvy & both AWs: eff weight carrier: gd run on reapp.

521   **PIPPAS PRIDE 13** [12] S R Bowring 5-9-2 S Finnamore (7) 9/2 CO FAV: 131154: Cl-up, gd hdwy   1 **65a**
over 2f out, rdn/btn inside last: see 473.

580   **INTERNAL AFFAIR 4** [4] 5-9-2 Lynsey Hanna (7) 11/2: 014135: Rear, hdwy & rcd v wide turning for   nk **65a**
home, styd on, nvr nrr: qck reapp: all 5 wins at W'hampton: see 521 (h'cap).

452   **PHILISTAR 24** [10] 7-8-6 J Tate 9/2 CO FAV: 65-336: Prom, rdn to impr 2f out, no extra inside last: 1 **53a**
prev with K R Burke, now with N P Littmoden: see 452.

574   **CELESTIAL KEY 5** [9] 10-8-4 K Dalgleish (7) 16/1: 03-207: Led early, remnd cl-up until wknd over   1 **49a**
1f out: op 10/1, qck reapp: see 452.

410   **WILD RICE 32** [5] 8-8-2 (bl) A McCarthy (3) 50/1: 40-608: Al bhd, mod gains: see 333 (10f).   ½ **46$**

496   **BE WARNED 17** [2] 9-9-0 (vis) F Norton 10/1: -04059: Dwelt, al rear: btr 307 (12f).   1¼ **55a**

567   **LOCOMOTION 6** [15] 4-8-2 P Doe 16/1: -00350: Keen/prom, wknd qckly final 1f: 10th: qck reapp.   nk **43a**

522   **ROYAL PARTNERSHIP 13** [7] 4-8-12 Darren Williams (7) 12/1: -P5140: Waited with, rcd wide over 2f   ½ **52$**
out, btn final 2f: 11th: op 7/1: see 455 (11f).

297   **WAITING KNIGHT 49** [13] 5-8-6 (vis) R Fitzpatrick (3) 33/1: 00-400: Led 5f out till 3f out, wknd, 14th: abs.   **0a**

582   Indian Swinger 4 [14] 4-8-6 R Winston 20/1:   569   Kingchip Boy 6 [8] 11-8-6 D R McCabe 20/1:

511   Hibaat 14 [3] 4-9-2 Joanna Badger (7) 66/1:

15 ran   Time 1m 42.6 (3.2)   (John Pointon & Sons)   Miss S J Wilton Wetley Rocks, Staffs.

601

3.10 BEST BETS HCAP 3YO+ 0-85 (D)   1m aw rnd   Going 37   -07 Slow   **[80]**
£4153   £1278   £639   £319   3 yo rec 19lb

497   **DAVIS ROCK 17** [6] W R Muir 6-8-8 (60) Martin Dwyer (5) 5-1101: 6 ch m Rock City - Sunny Davis   **68a**
(Alydar): Chsd ldrs, chall over 1f out, led well ins last, drvn out: op 6/1: earlier won here at Southwell
(2 clmrs): '99 Nottingham wnr (h'cap, rtd 49 & 56a), '98 wnr at Lingfield (fillies h'cap) & W'hampton (sell,
rtd 67a & 60): eff at 7f/1m on gd, stays 9f: acts on fast & both AWs, any trk, esp Southwell: eff weight carrier: in fine form.

4574} **RUTLAND CHANTRY 99** [8] S Gollings 6-9-4 (70) A Culhane 16/1: 0000-2: 6 b g Dixieland Band -   1 **75a**
Christchurch (So Blessed): Settled rear, smooth hdwy 4f out, styd on to lead over 1f out, rdn & hdd well ins
last: clr rem on reapp: '99 wnr at Beverley (h'cap, rtd 78 at best): '98 Newbury wnr (h'cap, rtd 75, Lord
Huntingdon): eff at 10f, stays 12f: acts on gd/soft, hvy & fibresand: handles fast: likes stiff/gall trks
& runs well fresh up with/forcing the pace: gd reapp over an inadequate trip, spot-on next time at 10f.

401   **BOLD EWAR 33** [1] C E Brittain 3-8-4 (75)(bl) A Nicholls (3) 9/1: 041-53: 3 ch c Persian Bold -   5 **72a**
Hot Curry (Sharpen Up): Led 1f, hdd over 1f out, rdn & btn inside last: op 7/1: see 125.

261   **SEPTEMBER HARVEST 55** [3] Mrs S Lamyman 4-7-10 (48)(3oh) K Dalgleish (7) 10/1: 000-64: Sn rdn   1¾ **42a**
& well outpcd, styd on strongly final 2f, nvr nrr: 8 wk abs & will apprec a return to 10f+: see 261.

*453   **EPERNAY 24** [7] 4-9-6 (72) O Urbina 7/4 FAV: 25-15: Chsd ldrs, ev ch until lost action & wknd final   3½ **61a**
2f: h'cap bow: btr 453 (auct mdn).

251   **STILL WATERS 56** [2] 5-8-5 (57) D Sweeney 16/1: 000-06: Rear, prog/hmpd 3f out, no extra: 8 wk abs.   8 **35a**

4266} **WUXI VENTURE 99** [9] 5-9-13 (79) O Pears 11/4: 5064-7: Trkd ldrs, outpcd halfway, brief effort 2f   1¾ **54a**
out, btn over 1f out: op 9/4 on reapp for new stable: 4th at best in '99 (h'caps, rtd 82 at best, S Woods):
'98 wnr at Ripon (mdn), Haydock & Hamilton (h'caps, rtd 93): eff at 1m, stays 10.4f: acts on fast, likes gd/soft
& hvy grnd: best without blnks/visors: likes to come late off a strong pace: sharper next time for D Nicholls.

4395} **SILKEN DALLIANCE 99** [4] 5-10-0 (80) N Chalmers (7) 10/1: 5000-8: Prom, rdn & lost tch final 3f: ½ **54a**
rnr-up in '99 (rtd h'cap, rtd 85): prog in '98 for Lord Huntingdon, won at Southwell (AW auct mdn, rtd 75a),
Kempton, Ascot & Newmarket (h'caps, rtd 85): eff at 1m on fast, likes gd, gd/soft & fibresand: sharper next time.

566   **DANAKIM 6** [5] 3-8-7 (78) J Fanning 25/1: 040-09: Led early, lost tch halfway, t.o: qck reapp.   21 **32a**

9 ran   Time 1m 42.9 (3.5)   (Gordon B Cunningham)   W R Muir Lambourn, Berks.

602

3.40 TEXT P372 SELL HCAP DIV 1 3YO+ 0-60 (G)   6f aw rnd   Going 37   -20 Slow   **[59]**
£1534   £438   £219

533   **BLUSHING GRENADIER 11** [4] S R Bowring 8-9-5 (50)(bl) S Finnamore (7) 7/1: 343301: 8 ch g Salt   **54a**
Dome - La Duse (Junius): Trkd ldr, hdwy to lead dist, styd on well, rdn out: op 10/1, no bid: '99 wnr at Redcar
& Carlisle (clmrs, rtd 67 & 55a): '98 wnr at W'hampton (sell, rtd 55a), Warwick (clmr, M Fetherston Godley), Haydock
& Newcastle (h'cap, rtd 63): eff at 5/8.5f, all wins at 6f: acts on fast, both AWs & in blnks/visor: tough.

559   **SING FOR ME 7** [6] R Hollinshead 5-8-3 (34) Stephanie Hollinshead (1) 20/1: 004042: 5 b m Songlines -   1 **35a**
Running For You (Pampabird): Dwelt, hdwy to chall ldr 2f out, drvn/no extra well ins last: qck reapp: see 272.

2921} **KOMASEPH 99** [8] R F Marvin 8-8-4 (35)(bl) D R McCabe 16/1: 0050-3: 8 b g Komaite - Starkist   nk **35a**
(So Blessed): Handy, swtchd wide & styd on 2f out, nvr nrr: reapp: unplcd in '99 (rtd 39a & 26, tried visor/blnks):
'99 Southwell wnr (2, stks & h'cap, rtd 58a): eff at 6f, stays 7f: likes fibresand/Southwell: can run well fresh.

550   **CHALUZ 9** [9] N P Littmoden 6-9-0 (45)(t) T G McLaughlin 6/1: 425554: Outpcd, late hdwy: btr 75 (7f).   1½ **41a**

476   **STRATS QUEST 21** [3] 6-8-7 (38)(vis) S Whitworth 4/1: 045-65: Prom, rdn & btn over 1f out: see 476.   nk **33a**

557   **E B PEARL 7** [7] 4-9-0 (45) Martin Dwyer 20/1: 000-06: Dwelt, hdwy to go prom over 2f out, no   1 **37a**
extra over 1f out: qck reapp: see 557.

*585   **AMBUSHED 3** [2] 4-7-10 (27)(bl) (2oh) K Dalgleish (7) 3/1 FAV: 0-0017: Slow start, sn with ldrs, hmpd   ¾ **17a**
& no extra over 1f out: nicely bckd, qck reapp: unsuited by drop back to 6f, much btr 585 (1m appr mdn h'cap).

154   **REAL TING 84** [11] 4-7-13 (30)(vis) Joanna Badger (7) 12/1: /005-8: Al rear, mod late gains: long abs.   1½ **16a**

192

559 **MANOLO 7** [10] 7-9-9 (54)(bl) F Norton 16/1: 0-0069: Dwelt, rcd wide, rdn/btn over 1f out: qck reapp.   2 35a
3744} **LORD BERGERAC 99** [1] 4-10-0 (59)(bl) J Weaver 16/1: 4600-0: Led, rdn/hdd 2f out, sn no extra: *shd* 40a
fin 10th: top-weight: jockey reportedly unable to ride a finish due to a slipped saddle: plcd once in '99
(clmr, rtd 60a, also rtd 49): eff at 6f, handles soft & fibresand: can go well fresh.
484 **FACILE TIGRE 19** [5] 5-8-12 (43) P Doe 10/1: 6-0600: Prom, lost tch final 2f, fin 11th: see 146 (5f).   1 21a
3194} **SQUIRE CORRIE 99** [12] 8-9-6 (51) A Culhane 20/1: 0000-0: Rcd wide mid-div, wknd halfway, eased,   *dist* 0a
12th: '99 Lingfield wnr (h'cap, rtd 60a & 52): rnr-up in '98 (h'cap, rtd 66 & 68a): won 6 times in '97 (h'caps,
rtd 85 & 74a): eff at 6f, best at 5f: acts on firm, soft & both AWs: eff with/without blnks: back on a wng mark.
12 ran   Time 1m 16.7 (3.4)   (S R Bowring)   S R Bowring Edwinstowe, Notts.

603
4.15 TEXT P368 MDN 3YO+ (D) 1m4f aw Going 37 -20 Slow
£2782 £856 £428 £214 3yo rec 24lb 4yo rec 3lb

-- **SHAREEF** [4] P F I Cole 3-8-3 D Sweeney 4/5 FAV: 1: 3 b c Shareef Dancer - Bustling Nelly   76a
(Bustino): Dwelt, sn with ldrs, led over 1f out, pushed clr ins last: nicely bckd: 100,000gns purchase, half-
brother to useful mid-dist performer Busy Flight: eff at 12f, further cld suit: acts on f/sand & runs well fresh.
565 **LE CAVALIER 6** [7] C N Allen 3-8-3 L Newman (5) 7/2: -00222: 3 b c Mister Baileys - Secret Deed   8 62a
(Shadeed): Led, jnd 3f out, hdd over 1f out, no ch with wnr: qck reapp: consistent: see 565.
-- **MI ODDS** [6] Mrs N Macauley 4-9-10 R Fitzpatrick (3) 20/1: 3: 4 b g Sure Blade - Vado Via (Ardross)   11 49a
Handy when ran v wide after 3f, late hdwy fnl 3f: dam a 12f & hdles wnr: ran v green here, should improve.
523 **YOU DA MAN 12** [2] R Hannon 3-8-3 (BL) Martin Dwyer 3/1: 0-4224: Prom, rdn & gradually wknd 5f   3 45a
out, well btn when hung right for press final 2f: up in trip, first time blnks: looks a tricky ride: see 523.
550 **BALLYMORRIS BOY 9** [5] 4-9-10 J Weaver 33/1: 460305: Chsd ldrs, lost tch halfway: see 505.   ¾ 44$
519 **MISCHIEF 13** [3] 4-9-10 (bl) F Norton 25/1: 3-0556: Prom, wknd halfway, t.o: see 348.   5 37a
2026} **AN SMEARDUBH 99** [1] 4-9-5 P McCabe 25/1: 0000-7: Bhd, ran v wide after 3f, lost tch halfway, t.o: *dist* 0a
no promise on today's AW bow: modest turf form in '99.
7 ran   Time 2m 41.1 (6.8)   (H R H Prince Fahd Salman)   P F I Cole Whatcombe, Oxon.

604
4.50 TEXT P372 SELL HCAP DIV 2 3YO+ 0-60 (G) 6f aw rnd Going 37 -11 Slow [58]
£1526 £436 £218

499 **PETITE DANSEUSE 17** [7] D W Chapman 6-8-3 (33) Claire Bryan (7) 10/1: -55001: 6 b m Aragon - Let Her   37a
Dance (Sovereign Dancer): Cl-up, hdwy to chall over 1f out, drvn out to lead cl-home: no bid: tchd 14/1:
plcd in '99 (rtd 38 & 29a), back in '97 won at Leicester (2, clmrs, rtd 66): eff at 5/7f on firm, soft & both AWs:
handles any trk: had prev run well in a visor, not blnks: on a fair mark.
538 **LITTLE IBNR 10** [1] P D Evans 9-9-4 (48)(vis) S Drowne 16/1: 043062: 9 b g Formidable - Zalatia   ½ 50a
(Music Boy): Prom, gd hdwy 2f out, styd on strongly, just held: gd run, see 166.
4372} **BODFARI ANNA 99** [4] J L Eyre 4-8-13 (43)(vis) A Culhane 16/1: 0000-3: 4 br f Casteddu - Lowrianna   2 40a
(Cyrano de Bergerac): Dwelt, rear, gd hdwy 3f out, rdn/btn dist: '99 Haydock wnr (sell h'cap, rtd 50): '98
Nottingham wnr (sell h'cap, rtd 66, M Easterby): eff at 6f, stays 7f on firm, soft & fibresand: eff in blnks/visor.
538 **VICE PRESIDENTIAL 10** [2] J G Given 5-9-10 (54) Dean McKeown 9/2: -25004: Led, drvn over 1f out,   ½ 50a
hdd & wknd well inside last: top weight: btr 32 (clmr).
567 **DAYNABEE 6** [9] 5-9-1 (45) I Mongan (7) 5/1: 154635: Cl-up, rdn/btn 2f out: qck reapp: btr 567 (7f).   1¼ 37a
587 **MARENGO 3** [5] 6-9-10 (54) S Finnamore (7) 100/30 FAV: -00306: Prom, rdn/no extra over 1f out: *shd* 46a
qck reapp: see 183 (made all).
449 **GADGE 25** [10] 9-8-7 (37) D Kilcourse (7) 14/1: -00307: Rear, modest late gains: see 391.   1 26a
4068} **PATRINIA 99** [6] 4-8-6 (36) D R McCabe 33/1: 0000-8: Held up, nvr a threat: reapp: well btn in '99.   6 15a
476 **WOODCUT 21** [3] 4-7-10 (26)(1oh) P M Quinn (5) 16/1: 00-009: Chsd ldrs, lost tch final 2f: mod form.   1¾ 1a
550 **TAYOVULLIN 9** [8] 6-9-7 (51)(BL) Iona Wands 10/1: 230-00: Al bhd, fin 10th: blnkd.   4 17a
-- **CHRISTENSEN** [11] 4-9-5 (49) A Nicholls (3) 4/1: 4632-0: Sn rdn in rear, nvr a dngr: 11th: reapp,   14 0a
British bow: place form in native Ireland prev (5.5/7f h'caps, gd & soft, E Lynam): now with D Nicholls.
11 ran   Time 1m 16.2 (2.9)   (David W Chapman)   D W Chapman Stillington, Nth Yorks.

605
5.20 TEXT P372 HCAP 3YO+ 0-85 (D) 1m3f aw Going 37 +08 Fast [85]
£4114 £1266 £633 £316 4 yo rec 2 lb

*512 **HANNIBAL LAD 14** [7] W M Brisbourne 4-9-1 (74) T G McLaughlin 7/1: 152311: 4 ch g Rock City -   80a
Appealing (Star Appeal): Rear, rcd wide & gd hdwy 3f out, rdn to chall dist, drvn out to lead cl-home: gd time:
earlier won at W'hampton & here at Southwell (h'caps): '98 wnr again at W'hampton (sell, P Evans, rtd 66a): '98
Southwell wnr (sell, rtd 67a & 69): eff at 1m/11f on firm, loves f/sand & sharp trks: runs well fresh: tough.
508 **CHINA CASTLE 16** [9] P C Haslam 7-10-0 (85) P Goode (5) 6/4 FAV: 4-0662: 7 b g Sayf El Arab -   *nk* 90a
Honey Plum (Kind Of Hush): Settled rear, gd hdwy over 2f out, led dist, styd on well, hdd cl-home: well bckd,
top weight: well h'capped on '99 AW form & should score again: see 27.
560 **STATE APPROVAL 7** [3] D Shaw 7-7-10 (53) Claire Bryan (7) 15/2: 000233: 7 b g Pharly - Tabeeba   1¾ 55a
(Diesis): Cl-up, led over 1f out, no extra inside last: qck reapp: see 512.
512 **GREEN BOPPER 14** [8] G Woodward 7-9-0 (71) J Weaver 7/1: 0-5234: Prom, hdwy to chall over 1f out,   1¾ 70a
no extra final 1f: op 5/1: won this race last year off a 6lb lower mark: see 302.
453 **ROOFTOP 24** [5] 4-8-1 (60) P Doe 33/1: 200-65: Waited with, hdwy & short of room over 1f out,   1½ 57a
swtchd inside & onepcd inside last: see 453.
512 **KENNET 14** [4] 5-8-9 (66) Martin Dwyer 6/1: 310-56: Cl-up, eff over 2f out, wknd over 1f out: see 512.   *shd* 63a
374 **SYLVA LEGEND 37** [6] 4-8-4 (63) A Nicholls (3) 20/1: 64-567: Prom, rdn/wknd final 2f.   1½ 57a
590 **WESTERN COMMAND 3** [1] 4-8-7 (66)(6ex) R Fitzpatrick (3) 8/1: 362168: Trkd ldrs, lost tch final   5 52a
3f: qck reapp: well in class here: btr 560 (low-grade h'cap).
37 **SWIFT 99** [2] 6-9-4 (75) I Mongan (7) 16/1: 0500-9: Handy, wknd qckly halfway, t.o: abs.   29 31a
9 ran   Time 2m 24.5 (3.2)   (John Pugh)   W M Brisbourne Great Ness, Shropshire.

CAGNES-SUR-MER   WEDNESDAY FEBRUARY 23RD

Official Going   STANDARD

606 | **3.10 PRIX DU TRAYAS 3YO   1m2f   Standard**
£4803   £1921   £1441

-- **SHEER TENBY** R W Armstrong 3-8-11 J Windrif : -401: 3 b c Tenby - Take My Pledge (Ahonoora) **71a**
In tch, gd hdwy over 3f out, styd on to lead over 1f out, drvn out: recently 4th & unplaced in similar contests over this C/D: eff at 10f, further could suit: eff on an AW surface

4494} **FIELD MASTER 17** S Dow 3-8-11 M Sautjeau : 440-32: 3 ch c Foxhound - Bold Avril (Persian Bold) ½ **69a**
Mid-div, prog 3f out, styd on well fnl 2f, not reach wnr: 17 days ago 3rd in a similar race here (ahd of today's wnr): with A Stewart in '99, 4th at best (6/7f mdns/nursery, rtd 76 at best): eff at 10f on AW.

266 **MUWAKALL 10** R W Armstrong 3-8-11 R Price : 06-353: 3 b c Doyoun - Sabayik (Unfuwain) 2½ **65a**
Dwelt, sn rdn to go prom, styd on but not pace of ldrs fnl 2f: stablemate of wnr & completed a 1-2-3 for the Brit raiders: 5th over C/D just 10 days ago: eff at 1m/10f: see 266.

12 ran   Time 2m 06.07   (R J Arculli)   R W Armstrong Newmarket

WOLVERHAMPTON (Fibresand)   TUESDAY FEBRUARY 29TH   Lefthand, Sharp Track

Official Going   STANDARD. Stalls: Inside.

607 | **1.40 AMAT HCAP DIV 1 4YO+ 0-60 (G)   1m4f aw   Going 18 -22 Slow**   [36]
£1456   £416   £208   4 yo rec 3 lb

562 **MORGANS ORCHARD 7** [3] A G Newcombe 4-11-7 (60) Miss C Hannaford (5) 100/30: 3-1521: 4 ch g Forest **65a**
Wind - Regina St Cyr (Doulab) Prom, led over 2f out, edged left dist, styd on well: plcd on sand in '99 (rtd 61a, mdn): eff at 12f, cld stay further: likes f/sand & a sharp trk: has run well fresh: gd weight carrier: win again.

576 **OUR PEOPLE 5** [4] M Johnston 6-9-13 (35)(t) Mrs C Williams 11/4 FAV: 331322: 6 ch g Indian Ridge - ¾ **39a**
Fair And Wise (High Line) Cl-up, led halfway till over 2f out, kept on: clr of rem, op 2/1, qck reapp: see 576.

136 **AMAZING FACT 90** [10] J M Bradley 5-9-8 (30) Miss Hayley Bryan (7 33/1: 0000-3: 5 b g Known Fact - 9 **24a**
Itsamazing (The Minstrel) Bhd, styd on well wide fnl 3f, no threat to front pair: 12 wk jumps abs (no form): no form in '99 on the level (rtd 35a & 21): plcd on reapp in '98 (rtd 72, mdn, Lady Herries): 14f+ shld suit.

520 **KUWAIT THUNDER 14** [7] J L Eyre 4-10-1 (40) Miss Diana Jones 7/1: 0-0044: Chsd ldrs halfway, sn held: 2½ **30a**
590 **EVEZIO RUFO 4** [9] 8-10-10 (46)(bl) Mr O Gunter (7) 7/2: 513145: Handy, led after 4f till 6f out, fdd. 2½ **32a**
520 **JADE TIGER 14** [6] 4-10-12 (51) Mr F Windsor Clive(5) 16/1: 0-0406: Chsd ldrs 5f out, btn over 2f out. 4 **31a**
464 **HURGILL DANCER 24** [2] 6-10-4 (40) Mr T Best (5) 8/1: 34-347: Mid-div, eff 4f out, sn held: op 10/1. 5 **13a**
-- **CHARLIE BIGTIME** [12] 10-9-10 (32)(bl) Miss E J Jones 20/1: 6563/8: Slowly away, al bhd: 7 **0a**
8 wk jumps abs (mod form): last rcd on the level in '97 (plcd, rtd 38, sell h'cap): '95 Leicester & W'hampton wnr (h'cap, B McMath): eff at 1m/12f, stays 15f: acts on fast & fibresand, any trk: eff with/without blnks.
492 **AMSARA 19** [11] 4-9-3 (28)(BL) (4oh) Miss A Deniel 33/1: 0-0609: Al rear: blnks: see 412. nk **0a**
558} **AMONG ISLANDS 99** [1] 9-9-10 (32) Mr F Giuliani (7) 33/1: 50/6-0: Al bhd: 10th: 10 month jumps abs 1½ **0a**
(mod form, tried blnks): mover in '99 (G Charles Jones): 97/98 Ludlow hdles wnr (sell, rtd 82h, R Lee).
489 **COLONEL CUSTER 19** [5] 5-11-3 (53)(vis) Mr A Evans 6/1: 1-3100: Led 4f: 11th: see 408 (sell). 8 **4a**
363 **KINGS CAY 40** [8] 9-9-13 (35)(vis)(10ow)(13oh) Mr B Wharfe(0) 33/1: 00-040: Bhd 4f out: 12th: abs. 2½ **0a**
12 ran   Time 2m 38.4 (4.8)   (After Hours Partnership)   A G Newcombe Huntshaw, Devon.

608 | **2.10 AMAT HCAP DIV 2 4YO+ 0-60 (G)   1m4f aw   Going 18 -45 Slow**   [32]
£1456   £416   £208   4 yo rec 3 lb

590 **ABLE PETE 4** [4] A G Newcombe 4-9-12 (33) Miss C Hannaford (5) 11/4 FAV: -05021: 4 b c Formidable **38a**
- An Empress (Affirmed) Made all, rdn/clr 2f out, held on well ins last, rdn out: qck reapp: first success: unplcd in '99 for D J S Cosgrove (rtd 33a & 30): unplcd in '98 for J L Dunlop (rtd 68, auct mdn): eff at 11f/12f on f/sand: likes a sharp trk: runs well for an amat & likes to force the pace.

260 **INKWELL 56** [3] G L Moore 6-10-0 (32)(bl) Mr A Quinn (7) 7/1: 204-52: 6 b g Relief Pitcher - Fragrant ¾ **35a**
Hackette (Simply Great) In tch, prog to chase wnr dist, kept on well: op 5/1, jumps fit (mod form): nicely h'capped.

520 **ALBERKINNIE 14** [9] J L Harris 5-9-4 (22) Miss E Folkes (4) 12/1: -02533: 5 b g Ron's Victory - Trojan 4 **19a**
Desert (Troy) Trkd wnr halfway, rdn/no extra over 1f out: op 10/1: handles both AWs, fast & gd/soft: eff arnd 12f.

553 **WELLCOME INN 10** [2] G Woodward 6-10-5 (37)(t) Miss H Garrett (7) 11/2: 022334: Held up in tch, 3½ **29a**
prog/chsd ldrs 4f out, sn onepace: see 553, 369 & 211.

535 **THROWER 11** [12] 9-11-7 (53) Mrs S Owen (5) 3/1: 11-145: Towards rear, mod gains, nvr pace to 2½ **41a**
threaten ldrs: op 7/4: needs a return to further: see 470 (2m).

524 **APPYDAO 13** [7] 5-9-13 (31) Mr S Dobson (5) 8/1: -02136: Prom 1m: btr 524, 458 (equitrack). ¾ **18a**
305 **PRIORS MOOR 49** [11] 5-10-5 (37) Mr D Crosse (7) 25/1: 500-07: Mid-div, btn 5f out: 7 wk abs: 17 **6a**
plcd form in '99 (rtd 48a, h'cap, R W Armstrong): '98 Yarmouth wnr (mdn h'cap, rtd 55): rtd 60 & 45a in '97: eff over 1m, stays a sharp 10f well: acts on fast & equitrack: best without blnks.
-- **HAYA YA KEFAAH** [1] 8-11-2 (47)(1ow) Mr G Wigley (0) 20/1: 0640/8: Dwelt/al bhd: long abs: 8 **8a**
missed '99: unplcd in '98 (rtd 54, h'cap, tried blnks): back in 1m96 scored at Doncaster (2) & Haydock (h'cap, rtd 65): eff at 12f: handles fast, likes gd/soft & fibresand: has run well fresh.
544 **LAUTREC 10** [8] 4-10-10 (45)(BL) Mr M Nakauchida (5) 10/1: 360-59: Prom 9f: blnks: see 544. 7 **0a**
561 **NOTATION 8** [5] 6-9-3 (21)(bl)(8oh) Miss A Deniel 12/1: -00040: Mid-div, btn 4f out: 10th: op 10/1. 5 **0a**
3509} Brynkir 99 [6] 6-11-3 (49)(BL) Miss E J Jones 11/1: 561 **Ancient Almu 8** [10] 4-11-5 (54)(BL) Mr C Bonner 14/1:
12 ran   Time 2m 41.2 (7.6)   (Alex Gorrie)   A G Newcombe Huntshaw, Devon.

609 | **2.40 O800 211222 HCAP DIV 1 3YO+ 0-70 (E)   5f aw rnd   Going 18 +04 Fast**   [67]
£2213   £632   £316   3 yo rec 14lb

564 **JACK TO A KING 7** [1] J Balding 5-8-12 (32)(bl) J Edmunds 11/2: 152021: 5 b g Nawwar - Rudda **59a**
Flash (General David) Cl-up, went on halfway, styd on well ins last, rdn out: earlier scored here at W'hampton (h'cap): unplcd in '99 (rtd 36a): rtd 62 in '98: eff over a sharp 5f on fibresand, handles equitrack: eff in

blnks & with/without a t-strap: eff held up or forcing the pace: likes W'hampton.

506	**ASHOVER AMBER 17** [2] T D Barron 4-10-0 (67) C Lowther 13/8 FAV: 13-452: 4 b f Green Dancer - Zafaaf (Kris) Led till halfway, rdn & kept on well ins last, not pace of wnr: hvly bckd, op 2/1: find similar.	1¼	71a
518	**ZIGGYS DANCER 14** [3] E J Alston 9-10-0 (67) D Holland 7/2: 0-0433: 9 b h Ziggy's Boy - My Shy Dancer (Northjet) Handy, rdn/outpcd fnl 2f: tchd 9/2: see 518, 223 (6f).	1¼	68a
*533	**MANORBIER 12** [6] K A Ryan 4-9-7 (60) F Lynch 8/1: 50/014: Chsd ldrs wide, nvr pace to chall.	nk	60a
436	**PRESS AHEAD 28** [5] 5-9-3 (56)(bl) L Newman (5) 7/1: 20-155: Chsd ldrs, outpcd halfway: see 351 (6f).	2½	49a
*563	**SOUNDS LUCKY 7** [7] 4-9-4 (57)(vis) (6ex) C Carver (3) 13/2: 604416: Chsd ldrs wide 3f: op 5/1.	3	43a
533	**LISA B 12** [8] 3-7-13 (52)(bl) G Baker (7) 10/1: 000-27: In tch wide 3f: op 7/1: btr 533 (C/D, sell).	nk	37a
414	**JUST DISSIDENT 32** [4] 8-9-1 (54) Dean McKeown 14/1: 45-408: Rdn/cl-up 3f: op 12/1: see 371, 91.	1¾	35a
8 ran	Time 1m 00.9 (0.7) (J D & J R Evans) J Balding Scrooby, Notts.		

---

610 3.10 BEST BETS MDN 3YO (D) 1m1f79y Going 18 -05 Slow
£2795 £860 £430 £215

4364}	**FAVORISIO 99** [3] Miss J A Camacho 3-9-0 K Darley 14/1: 00-1: 3 br g Efisio - Dixie Favor (Dixieland Band) Keen/prom, led dist, styd on well ins, rdn out: AW bow/5 month abs: unplcd from 2 turf starts at 6f in '99 (rtd 64, mdn): apprec step up to 9f, 10f+ cld suit: acts on fibresand & a sharp trk: runs well fresh.		82a
493	**ARCTIC HIGH 19** [8] M S Saunders 3-8-9 R Price 14/1: 32: 3 b f Polar Falconm - Oublier L'Ennui (Bellman) Handy, led over 2f out, sn ran v wide into str & hdd, kept on for press fnl 1f: op 12/1: would have gone v close here without steering problems: styd longer 9.4f trip & acts on fibresand: clrly going the right way.	3½	70a
1043}	**COWBOYS AND ANGELS 99** [7] W G M Turner 3-9-0 A Daly 11/1: 320-3: 3 b g Bin Ajwaad - Halimah (Be My Guest) Led 7f, no extra fnl 1f: 10 month abs/AW bow: plcd twice in '99 (rtd 79, auct mdn, debut): eff at 5f, prob styd this longer 9.4f trip: handles fibresand, fast & hvy: could find similar back at 7f/1m.	3	69a
319	**ATALYA 47** [11] F Jordan 3-9-0 N Callan 9/4 JT FAV: 060-24: Chsd ldrs, not pace to chall: op 6/4, abs.	2	65a
4414}	**CITY FLYER 99** [2] 3-9-0 F Lynch 5/1: 4504-5: Mid-div, nvr pace to chall: op 8/1, 5 month abs/AW bow: unplcd in '99 (rtd 75, mdn): tried up to 1m prev, mid-dists shld suit: handles fast grnd & fibresand.	1¾	62a
4452}	**TUFTY HOPPER 99** [1] 3-9-0 R Winston 14/1: 0-6: Rear, mod gains: op 12/1: 4 mth abs, with P Howling.	5	52a
--	**LOVE IN VAIN** [4] 3-8-9 M Fenton 9/4 JT FAV: 7: Dwelt, mid-div, btn 3f out: op 5/2, debut, with M Bell.	13	28a
4514}	**PIX ME UP 99** [10] 3-8-9 A Culhane 7/1: 0320-8: Rear, nvr factor: op 5/1: 4 month abs/AW bow.	nk	27a
555	**ST GEORGES BOY 8** [5] 3-9-0 (vis) J Bramhill 33/1: 000-69: Mid-div, btn 4f out: see 555 (mdn h'cap).	¾	31a
--	**THE WALRUS** [6] 3-9-0 T G McLaughlin 8/1: 0: Dwelt, mid-div, btn 4f out: 10th: with N Littmoden.	shd	31a
493	**FOLK DANCE 19** [9] 3-8-9 Darren Williams (7) 33/1: 60: Sn bhd: 11th: longer 9.4f trip.	22	0a
11 ran	Time 2m 00.4 (2.2) (Elite Racing Club) Miss J A Camacho Norton, N.Yorks.		

---

611 3.40 TEXT P372 HCAP 4YO+ 0-85 (D) 1m1f79y Going 18 -01 Slow
£5343 £1644 £822 £411 [83]

529	**AREISH 12** [2] J Balding 7-8-0 (55) C Rutter 5/2 FAV: 511121: 7 b m Keen - Cool Combination (Indian King) In tch, styd on well for press to lead well ins last, rdn out: bckd from 9/2: earlier won here at W'hampton (3, h'caps): '99 W'hampton (sell) & Southwell wnr (fill h'cap, rtd 53a): '98 Southwell (D Nicholls) & W'hampton wnr (h'caps, rtd 44a, M Pipe): eff at 1m/12f, suited by 9f: handles equitrack, fibresand/W'hampton specialist.		60a
551	**PANTAR 10** [1] A Balding 3-9-0 (83)(bl) K Darley 7/1: 30-032: 5 b g Shirley Heights - Spring Daffodil (Pharly) Handy, rdn to lead ins last, sn hdd & no extra cl-i-ome: topweight: acts of f/sand, firm & gd/soft grnd.	1	87a
309	**TROIS 49** [6] J G Given 4-9-2 (71) T G McLaughlin 7/1: 01-103: 4 b g Efisio - Drei (Lyphard) Rear, prog 4f out, sitly hmpd 3f out, kept on for press ins last, not pace to chall: abs: prev with G Woodward.	1¼	72a
551	**ARC 10** [10] G M Moore 6-9-0 (69) C Lowther 9/2: 024-24: Held up towards rear, prog to lead 2f out, hdd ins last & no extra: tchd 11/2: stays an abs at 8.5f here: see 551, 38 (8.5f).	1½	67a
*568	**RIVERBLUE 7** [9] 4-8-11 (66)(6ex) M Tebbutt 5/1: -00515: Rear, late gains fnl 2f: see 568 (C/D).	nk	63a
*529	**RIVER ENSIGN 12** [11] 7-7-10 (51)(1oh) Claire Bryan (7) 7/1: 300416: Led 7f: ahd of this wnr in 529.	2½	43a
473	**CHARTER FLIGHT 22** [5] 4-8-8 (63) S Whitworth 12/1: 01-047: Prom, fdd fnl 2f/eased in last: op 10/1.	3½	48a
169	**GULF SHAADI 81** [8] 8-9-6 (75) D Holland 12/1: 6000-8: Mid-div, btn 3f out: op 10/1, abs: see 169.	7	49a
489	**DARE 19** [7] 5-8-7 (62)(bl) Joanna Badger (7) 10/1: 322009: Chsd ldrs 7f: tchd 12/1: see 349, 83.	¾	35a
364	**POLAR ICE 40** [3] 4-8-13 (68) N Callan 9/1: 00-000: Chsd ldrs 5f: tchd 20/1: abs: broke blood vessel.	11	25a
516	**Summer Bounty 14** [4] 4-8-6 (60)(1ow) A Culhane 20/1: 309 **Tightrope 49** [12] 5-8-7 (62) M Fenton 12/1:		
12 ran	Time 2m 00.00 (1.8) (Mrs J Coghlan-Everitt) J Balding Scrooby, Notts.		

---

612 4.10 TEXT P368 SELLER 3YO+ (G) 1m100y aw rnd Going 18 -20 Slow
£1922 £549 £274 3 yo rec 19lb

574	**LORD EUROLINK 6** [9] C A Dwyer 6-9-7 (tvi) D Holland 9/2: 030531: 6 b g Danehill - Lady Eurolink (Kala Shikari) Led after 1f, rdn clr over 1f out, styd on well, rdn out: no bid: op 3/1: qck reapp: plcd on turf in '99 (rtd 79, appr h'cap): plcd sole '98 start for J Dunlop (h'cap, rtd 92): '97 Doncaster wnr (mdn, rtd 90 at best): eff at 1m/10f: acts on fast, gd/soft & fibresand, handles equitrack: eff in a t-strap/vis: enjoys sell grade.		52a
553	**GOLDEN LYRIC 10** [7] J Pearce 5-9-7 J Weaver 4/1: 0-0422: 5 ch g Lycius - Adjala (Northfields) Led 1f, chsd wnr after, held over 1f out: eff at 1m/9f, winning form at 11f: see 60 (h'cap).	4	42a
584	**ROYAL DOLPHIN 4** [4] B A McMahon 4-9-7 (bl) L Newman (5) 20/1: 0-0043: 4 b c Dolphin Street - Diamond Lake (King's Lake) Chsd ldrs, kept on fnl 2f, not pace to chall: qck reapp: see 584, 553.	1¼	39$
474	**SHEER FACE 22** [3] W R Muir 6-9-7 (bl) Martin Dwyer 3/1: 0-5654: Held up, outpcd fnl 4f: op 2/1.	1½	36a
*567	**COMEOUTOFTHEFOG 7** [6] 5-9-13 T G McLaughlin 2/1 FAV: 2-5015: Chsd ldrs 6f: op 7/4, new stable.	4	34a
432	**EI EI 28** [8] 5-9-7 i Mongan (7) 12/1: 0-0246: Chsd ldrs, outpcd fnl 3f: op 10/1: see 404 (amat h'cap).	2½	23a
1054}	**MULLAGH HILL LAD 99** [2] 7-9-7 L Paddock (7) 25/1: 0500-7: Dwelt/al rear: 10 month abs: unplcd in '99 (rtd 32a): rnr-up in '98 (rtd 61a, h'cap): eff at 5/6f on fm, gd/soft & fibresand: best without blnks/vis.	2	19a
550	**RA RA RASPUTIN 10** [5] 5-9-13 N Carlisle 11/1: 141008: Al bhd: op 8/1: btr 396 (7f).	12	7a
570	**RED APOLLO 6** [1] 4-9-7 (bl) R Winston 25/1: 00-649: Dwelt/al rear: see 544.	1	0a
9 ran	Time 1m 49.4 (3.2) (Roalco Ltd) C A Dwyer Newmarket.		

WOLVERHAMPTON (Fibresand)　　TUESDAY FEBRUARY 29TH　　Lefthand, Sharp Track

613　　4.40 TEXT P372 HCAP 3YO 0-80 (D)　　1m100y a　Going 18　-16 Slow　　　　　　[86]
　　　　　£3809　　£1172　　£586　　　£293

450　**LORD HARLEY 26** [7]　B R Millman 3-7-13 (56)(1ow) F Norton 5/1: 04-221: 3 b c Formidable - Nanny Doon　　**62a**
(Dominion) Held up in tch, prog/chsd ldr 3f out, styd on well for press to lead well ins last, drvn out: first win:
unplcd in '99 (rtd 32 & 51a): eff at 7f/8.5f: acts on both AWs & a sharp trk: tough/consistent: deserved this.
*566　**SAFARANDO 7** [3]　N P Littmoden 3-9-13 (86)(6ex) T G McLaughlin 6/4 FAV: 0-0112: 3 b c Turtle　　1　**87a**
Island - Hertford Castle (Reference Point) Led, rdn/clr dist, hdd well ins last, no extra: well bckd: see 566 (C/D).
534　**CHURCH FARM FLYER 12** [8]　C N Allen 3-8-4 (62) L Newman 5} 8/1: 1-2363: 3 b f College Chapel -　　1　**62a**
Young Isabel (Last Tycoon) Held in tch wide, outpcd 3f out, styd on well fnl 1f, not able to chall: op 12/1: clr rem.
540　**KINGS GINGER 11** [2]　D J Wintle 3-7-12 (56) Joanna Badger (7) 10/1: 5-0034: Rear/in tch, outpcd fnl 3f.　　7　**45a**
555　**THE SHEIKH 8** [6]　3-7-12 (56) J Mackay (7) 11/2: 000-25: Chsd ldrs 6f: op 9/2: btr 55 (Southwell).　　2½　**40a**
*118　**THE PROSECUTOR 94** [4]　3-9-1 (73) K Darley 9/2: 0301-6: Sn chsd ldrs, btn 3f out: op 7/1, abs.　　5　**47a**
*540　**CALKO 11** [5]　3-8-9 (67)(bl) C Lowther 9/2: -31117: Held up, rdn halfway, sn btn: op 7/2: btr 540.　　3　**37a**
4591}　**JUMBOS FLYER 99** [1]　3-8-6 (63)(1ow) A Culhane 25/1: 500-8: Keen/chsd ldr, btn 3f out: AW/h'cap　　14　**13a**
bow: 4 month abs: unplcd in '99 (rtd 77, flattered, debut): with J L Eyre.
8 ran　　　Time 1m 49.1 (2.9)　　　　　(H Gooding)　　　　B R Millman Kentisbeare, Devon.

614　　5.10 0800 211222 HCAP DIV 2 3YO 0-70 (E)　　5f aw　Going 18　+02 Fast　　　　　[67]
　　　　　£2213　　£632　　£316　　　3 yo rec 14lb

563　**OFF HIRE 7** [8]　C Smith 4-9-1 (54)(vis) G Faulkner (3) 4/1: 3-1421: 4 b g Clantime - Lady Pennington　　**59a**
(Blue Cashmere) Made all, held on gamely ins last, all out: op 2/1: earlier won here at W'hampton (clmr): rnr-up
in '99 (rtd 58 & 57a): '98 Musselburgh wnr (sell nurs, rtd 42), plcd on sand (rtd 63a, nurs): suited by 5f, stays
6f: acts on gd/soft, soft & loves fibresand/W'hampton: eff with/without visor, likes to force the pace.
394　**BEDEVILLED 35** [5]　T D Barron 5-10-0 (67) C Lowther 11/10 FAV: 10-202: 5 ch g Beveled - Putout　　nk　**71a**
(Dowsing) Chsd wnr, led to chall fnl 1f, just held: nicely bckd, op 6/4: topweight: win similar: see 342 (6f).
4087}　**SUPREME ANGEL 99** [7]　M P Muggeridge 5-9-6 (59)(bl) T G McLaughlin 6/1: 0000-3: 5 b m Beveled -　　1¾　**59a**
Blue Angel (Lord Gayle) Dwelt, chsd ldrs halfway, nvr pace to chall: op 5/1, 5 month abs: AW bow: unplcd
in '99 (rtd 63, tumbled down h'cap): '98 Kempton wnr (h'cap, rtd 88): eff at 5/6f on firm, soft & fibresand:
best form without blnks tho' ran well in them today: resumes on an attractive mark, shld win this term.
3766}　**GRAND ESTATE 99** [1]　D W Chapman 5-9-3 (56) A Culhane 12/1: 0405-4: Chsd ldrs 4f: 6 month abs:　　3½　**47a**
'99 scorer twice at Hamilton (class stks & h'cap, rtd 66, rnr-up on sand, rtd 57a, clmr): plcd in '98 (T Easterby, rtd
81): eff at 6f on firm, soft & fibresand, any trk, likes Hamilton: best without blnks: has run well fresh.
582　**MOY 5** [6]　5-8-7 (46)(bl) A McCarthy (3) 10/1: 0-2605: Dwelt, nvr factor: op 8/1, qck reapp: btr 486.　　½　**35a**
499　**ALJAZ 18** [3]　10-9-9 (62) P Fredericks (5) 6/1: -40206: Chsd ldrs, btn 1f out: op 9/2: see 440, 44.　　5　**42a**
4090}　**TRUMP STREET 99** [4]　4-9-0 (53) S Carson (5) 16/1: 0030-7: Sn outpcd: 5 month abs/AW bow:　　3½　**24a**
plcd in '99 (rtd 59, auct mdn, N A Graham): rtd 89 at best in '98 (mdn, rnr-up): stays a sharp 7f, tried further:
handles firm & gd grnd: will appreciate a return to 7f: now with S G Knight.
564　**GLASTONBURY 7** [2]　4-7-13 (37)(BL)(1ow) F Norton 7/1: 0-0048: Sn outpcd: blnks: needs further.　　7　**0a**
8 ran　　　Time 1m 01.00 (0.8)　　　　(John Martin-Hoyes)　　　C Smith Temple Bruer, Lincs.

LINGFIELD (Equitrack)　　WEDNESDAY MARCH 1ST　　Lefthand, Very Sharp Track

Official Going　STANDARD. Stalls: 5f/1m - Outside; Rem - Inside.

615　　2.10 BET DIRECT MDN 3YO+ (D)　　1m aw rnd　Going 38　-05 Slow
　　　　　£2717　　£836　　£418　　　£209　　3 yo rec 18lb

3755}　**F ZERO 99** [3]　C F Wall 3-8-8 R Mullen 1/1 FAV: 020-1: 3 b g Bin Ajwaad - Saluti Tutti (Trojan Fen)　　**68a**
Dwelt, settled rear, hdwy to chall over 2f out, drvn out to lead well ins last: nicely bckd on seasonal/AW bow:
rnr-up on 2nd of 3 '99 starts at Ayr (med auct mdn, rtd 79): eff at 7f/1m, even further could suit: acts on
fast grnd & equitrack: runs more freely on a sharp or gall trk: could rate more highly & win again.
507　**CUPIDS DART 18** [1]　P Howling 3-8-8 R Winston 4/1: -52352: 3 ch g Pursuit Of Love - Tisza (Kris)　　½　**66a**
Cl-up, hdwy to lead 4f out, strongly prsd over 1f out, hdd well inside last: clr rem: eff at 7/8.5f: see 373.
570　**THE GIRLS FILLY 7** [4]　Miss B Sanders 3-8-3 S Carson (5) 13/8: 400-23: 3 b f Emperor Jones - Sioux　　4　**54a**
City (Simply Great) Cl-up, hdwy ch until no extra for press appr final 1f: nicely bckd, qck reapp: btr 570 (7f).
314　**COPYFORCE BOY 49** [2]　Miss B Sanders 4-9-12 (t) I Mongan (7) 50/1: 0/0-04: Led, hdd halfway,　　15　**28a**
sn lost tch: 7 wk abs: stiff task, modest prev form: sell h'caps needed.
4 ran　　　Time 1m 39.64 (3.44)　　　　(S Fustok)　　　C F Wall Newmarket.

616　　2.40 0800 211 222 CLAIMER 4YO+ (F)　　7f aw rnd　Going 38　-14 Slow
　　　　　£2150　　£614　　£307

210　**UNCHAIN MY HEART 74** [4]　B J Meehan 4-8-10 (bl) M Tebbutt 5/1: 0130-1: 4 b f Pursuit Of Love -　　**61a**
Addicted To Love (Touching Wood) Led 5f out, clr appr fnl 1f, tired ins last, all-out & just lasted: op 3/1, 10 wk abs:
late '99 wnr here at Lingfield (mdn), plcd on turf (h'caps, rtd 70): plcd in '98 (auct mdn, rtd 70): eff at 7f/1m,
stays a sharp 10f on firm, soft & equitrack, any trk: likes Lingfield: wears blnks, runs well fresh, forcing the pace.
571　**BEST QUEST 7** [6]　K R Burke 5-9-3 (t) N Callan 5/4 FAV: 335022: 5 b h Salse - Quest For The Best　　¾　**66a**
(Rainbow Quest) Keen in tch, short of room & lost 4/5L after 2f, rdn to impr 3f out, styd on strongly inside
last, just held: well bckd, qck reapp: unfortunate, deserves compensation: v consistent: see 403.
574　**SHAMWARI SONG 7** [10]　Mrs L C Jewell 5-8-5 R Mullen 20/1: 000203: 5 b g Sizzling Melody - Spark　　nk　**53$**
out (Sparkler) Sn rdn in rear, hdwy over 2f out, styd on, nvr nrr: qck reapp: return to 1m shld suit: see 505.
3484}　**FULHAM 99** [9]　M J Haynes 4-8-1 (BL) F Norton 40/1: 0000-4: Sn detached last, ran on strongly for　　½　**48$**
press final 2f, flying at finish: seasonal/AW bow: unplcd in 4 '99 starts (mdns, rtd 53), subs rnr-up over hdles
(2m juv nov, gd grnd, rtd 88h): eff at 7f, 1m+ shld suit: acts on equitrack: galvanised by first time blnks today.
4131}　**RED VENUS 1** [1]　4-8-8 (bl) (2ow) D Holland 11/2: 0654-5: Led, hdd 5f out, sn reluctant to pace　　nk　**54a**
& lost tch, ran on strongly for press inside last: '99 scorer at Southwell (2, sell for J Berry & h'cap, rtd 60a):
eff at 5/7f, further could suit: acts on both AWs & soft grnd, with/without blnks: best with forcing tactics.

309	**MAPLE 50** [5] 4-8-1 (VIS) P Doe 13/2: 63-606: Fly jmpd start, sn prom, rdn/no extra final 2f: abs, visor.	½	46a
567	**FRENCH GRIT 8** [2] 8-8-3 Iona Wands (5) 16/1: 5-0607: Keen cl-jup, lost grnd over 3f out, btn fnl 2f.	1	46$
547	**DARK MENACE 11** [7] 8-8-5 (bl) S Carson (5) 7/1: 01-008: Prom, hdwy to chall 3f out, wknd 2f out.	6	38a

8 ran   Time 1m 26.48 (3.68)   (Mascalls Stud)   B J Meehan Upper Lambourn, Berks.

---

617   3.10 BEST BETS HCAP 3YO 0-75 (E)   7f aw   Going 38 -20 Slow   [81]
£3477   £1070   £535   £267

*488   **DIRECT REACTION 21** [8] Miss Gay Kelleway 3-9-6 (73)(vis) D Holland 11/4 FAV: 351411: 3 b g College **79a**
Chapel - Mary's Way (Night Shift): Led early, cl-up, chall 2f out, led dist, drvn out to hold on: earlier won
here at Lingfield (2, mdn & h'cap): '99 rnr-up (rtd 77a & 81): eff at 6/7f, stays 1m: handles aw & fibresand,
loves equitrack/Lingfield: suited by a visor, has tried blnks: eff forcing the pace: genuine & improving.

3379} **FIRST VENTURE 99** [1] C N Allen 3-9-7 (74) R Morse 8/1: 2235-2: 3 b c Formidable - Diamond Wedding ½ **78a**
(Diamond Shoal): Led after 1f, hdd appr final 1f, styd on, just held: clr rem on reapp: plcd 3 times in '99
(mdn & nurseries, rtd 75a), also rtd 66, subs tried blnks): eff at 6/7f, handles both AWs: gd run, win soon.

315   **SHAMSAN 49** [4] M Johnston 3-9-1 (68) J Fanning 100/30: 64-103: 3 ch c Night Shift - Awayil 5 **64a**
(Woodman): Trkd ldrs, outpcd halfway, styd on late, no dngr: 7 wk abs: nicely bckd: may apprec a return to 1m.

574   **FRENCH FANCY 7** [6] B A Pearce 3-7-10 (49)(bl) (4oh) P M Quinn (5) 16/1: 045304: Dwelt, late gains. 1 **43a**

473   **BOND DIAMOND 23** [7] 3-9-3 (70) J Stack 9/2: 54-105: Unruly in paddock, chsd ldrs, no extra fnl 2f. ½ **63a**

105   **DRAGON STAR 98** [5] 3-8-3 (56) Nicola Cole (7) 16/1: 3665-6: Nvr a factor: long abs, op 10/1: see 105. 1¾ **46a**

526   **PARKSIDE PROSPECT 14** [3] 3-8-1 (54) P Doe 9/1: 1-4507: Cl-up, rdn/lost tch fnl 2f: op 6/1: btr 207. 10 **29a**

4197} **BEBE DE CHAM 99** [2] 3-9-6 (73) R Cody Boutcher (7) 10/1: 6100-8: Prom to halfway, sn well bhd: 12 **33a**
reapp: '99 scorer at Thirsk (2, fillies nov & nursery, rtd 76, subs tried blnks): eff at 5/7f on firm & gd/soft):
likes to run up with/force the pace, esp at Thirsk: only 2nd AW start: with J Eyre.

8 ran   Time 1m 26.87 (4.07)   (A P Griffin)   Miss Gay Kelleway Lingfield, Surrey.

---

618   3.40 TEXT P368 HCAP DIV 1 3YO+ 0-65 (F)   1m2f aw   Going 38 00 Slow   [64]
£2002   £572   £286   3 yo rec 21lb

*569   **SILVERTOWN 8** [13] B J Curley 5-9-11 (61)(6ex) J P Spencer 5/4 FAV: 020-11: 5 b g Danehill - Docklands **73+**
(Theatrical) Settled in tch, gd hdwy halfway, chall on bit 2f out, toyed with rnr-up, pshd to assert nr fin, v cheeky:
hvly bckd, edgy in prelims: earlier won at W'hampton (h'cap, fast time): '99 scorer at Epsom & York (h'caps,
rtd 56), place form prev term (h'cap, rtd 61): suited by 9/10f, stays 11.5f: acts on firm, gd/soft & both AWs:
likes to race up with/force the pace & runs well fresh: fast improving on sand, win more races.

575   **SEA DANZIG 7** [8] J J Bridger 7-10-0 (64)(BL) D Holland 8/1: 501042: 7 ch g Roi Danzig - Tosara hd **67a**
(Main Reef): Sn led, jnd by wnr 2f out, styd on well but v flattered to finish within a hd of wnr: op 6/1, 1st time blnks:
clr rem: qck reapp, 1st time blnks: brave effort trying to make all & back to form in blinkers: see 335 (stks).

4499} **PROSPECTORS COVE 99** [3] J Pearce 7-9-12 (62) J Weaver 13/2: 1000-3: 7 b g Dowsing - Pearl Cove 6 **57a**
(Town And Country): Handy, ev ch until no extra over 1f out: reapp: '99 scorer at Newmarket & Yarmouth
(h'caps, rtd 77 & 65a): '98 wnr at Brighton (rtd 63) & here at Lingfield (h'caps, rtd 62a): eff at 1m/10f,
stays 2m: acts on firm, gd/soft & both AWs: runs well fresh on any trk: best without visor: spot-on next time.

486   **SERGEANT IMP 21** [2] P Mitchell 5-8-2 (38) R Mullen 7/1: 0-3354: Cl-up early, lost tch after 3f, 1 **31a**
styd on well final 3f, nvr nrr: blnkrd, back in trip: see 400, 316.

553   **EMPERORS GOLD 11** [12] 5-7-11 (33) G Baker (7) 16/1: -36455: Chsd ldrs, rdn & btn appr final 1f. nk **26a**

528   **ORDAINED 14** [7] 7-7-11 (33) K Dalgleish (7) 10/1: 000-46: Rdn/rear, hdwy halfway, no threat to ldrs. 3½ **21a**

582   **COOL PROSPECT 6** [6] 5-9-0 (50) F Lynch 16/1: 00-057: Nvr better than mid-div: up in trip, op 10/1. 1¾ **35a**

574   **MALCHIK 7** [11] 4-8-2 (38) F Norton 16/1: 560028: Cl-up, rdn/lost tch fnl 3f: qck reapp: btr 574 (sell). 1¼ **21a**

486   **CONFRONTER 21** [14] 11-8-13 (49) P Doe 16/1: 45-009: Bhd, rdn to impr halfway, btn fnl 3f: see 161. ½ **31a**

384   **SATWA BOULEVARD 37** [1] 5-8-8 (44) D R McCabe 20/1: 20/000: Led early, lost tch halfway, fin 10th. ½ **25a**

441   **MY BOLD BOYO 28** [10] 5-9-4 (54)(bl) O Urbina 12/1: 00-440: In tch, hdwy to chall halfway, wknd 3 **30a**
qckly final 3f, eased, fin 11th: op 8/1: see 268 (class stks).

375   Jubilee Scholar 39 [9] 7-8-7 (43)(bl) C Rutter 20/1:   404   Whatsitsname 34 [4] 4-7-13 (35) Iona Wands (5) 25/1:

13 ran   Time 2m 06.64 (3.84)   (Mrs B J Curley)   B J Curley Newmarket.

---

619   4.10 TEXT P372 SELLER 3YO (G)   5f aw rnd   Going 38 -22 Slow
£1817   £519   £259

527   **PAPE DIOUF 14** [14] B Smart 3-9-2 (bl) J Bosley (7) 2/1 FAV: 0-0141: 3 b g Prince Sabo - Born To Dance **58a**
(Dancing Brave): Cl-up, rdn to impr over 2f out, led well ins last, rdn out: bght in for 3,800 gns: earlier won
here at Lingfield (sell): rnr-up twice in '99 for K McAuliffe (sell, rtd 64a, h'cap rtd 63): eff at 5f, poss stays
6f on firm, fast & both AWs, likes Lingfield: eff with blnks & racing up with/forcing the pace: best in sellers.

592   **ITSGOTTABDUN 4** [1] K T Ivory 3-9-2 (bl) C Catlin (7) 4/1: 406142: 3 b g Foxhound - Lady Ingrid ¾ **55a**
(Taufan) Rear, ran on for press ins last, never cl-home: nicely bckd, qck reapp: beat today's wnr in 527 (6f).

526   **CLOPTON GREEN 14** [6] J W Payne 3-8-11 (bl) N Callan (7) 6-0333: 3 b g Presidium - Silkstone hd **49$**
Lady (Puissance): Led early, led again 2f out, clr dist, wknd/hdd well inside last: see 526.

526   **POWER AND DEMAND 14** [3] D Shaw 3-8-11 (bl) L Newman (5) 7/1: 4-0254: Prom, no extra fnl 1f. shd **49a**

559   **JANICELAND 9** [2] 3-8-11 M Fenton 4/1: 1-1055: Dwelt & bhd, styd on, nvr got in it: nicely bckd. nk **48a**

487   **MINIMUS TIME 21** [7] 3-8-11 (bl) R Price 8/1: 6-0146: Led 4f out, hdd 2f out, wknd final 1f: btr 357. 1½ **44a**

6 ran   Time 1m 00.82 (3.02)   (Willie McKay)   B Smart Lambourn, Berks.

---

620   4.45 TEXT P368 HCAP DIV 2 3YO+ 0-65 (F)   1m2f aw   Going 38 -06 Slow   [64]
£1991   £569   £284   3 yo rec 21lb

400   **MULLAGHMORE 35** [1] M Kettle 4-9-13 (63)(bl) N Callan 5/1: 04-151: 4 b g Petardia - Comfrey Glen **71a**
(Glenstal) Trkd ldrs, smooth hdwy to lead 4f out, clr dist, rdn out: nicely bckd: earlier won here at
Lingfield (mdn): plcd in '99 (h'cap, rtd 67): imprvd on equitrack, handles fast & gd grnd:
acts on a gall or sharp trk & eff in blnks, has worn a t-strap: runs well fresh: progressive, shld win again.

547   **BONDS GULLY 14** [8] R W Armstrong 4-9-8 (58) R Price 9/2: 000-32: 4 b c Pips Pride - Classic Ring 5 **58a**
(Auction Ring): Cl-up, chsg wnr 2f out, kept on but no threat: up in trip, poss stays 10f: see 547 (7f stks).

360   **BADRINATH 41** [3] H J Collingridge 6-8-2 (38) P Doe 6/1: 350-63: 6 b g Imperial Frontier - Badedra 1¼ **36a**
(King's Lake): Mid-div, smooth hdwy 3f out, rdn & no extra appr final 1f: bckd from 10/1, 6 wk abs: see 360 (clmr).

505   **SASEEDO 18** [9] J J Bridger 10-8-1 (37)(bl) G Bardwell 33/1: 00-004: Sn remote last, well in rear 1½ **32a**

197

LINGFIELD (Equitrack)   WEDNESDAY MARCH 1ST   Lefthand, Very Sharp Track

until ran on strongly for press final 3f, nvr nrr: see 408.

*575	**SAMMYS SHUFFLE** 7 [14] 5-9-11 (61)(bl)(6ex) O Urbina 6/1: -50015: Rcd wide in tch, rdn & no extra final 2f: qck reapp, op 4/1: poor draw here, worth ignoring: see 575.	3½	51a
574	**SEA SPOUSE** 7 [2] 9-8-8 (44) Dale Gibson 33/1: 00-406: Led early, sn lost place, btn fnl 3f: qck reapp.	2½	30a
583	**MY TYSON** 6 [5] 5-9-0 (50) F Lynch 33/1: 60-007: Led briefly halfway, lost tch fnl 2f: qck reapp.	1½	33a
496	**MR SPEAKER** 19 [4] 7-8-7 (43) R Mullen 14/1: 30-508: Bhd, gd hdwy over 3f out, wknd for press fnl 2f.	1½	23a
265	**WHO GOES THERE** 56 [6] 4-7-11 (33) P M Quinn (5) 16/1: 250-59: Al bhd: 8 wk abs: see 265.	3	8a
517	**SHABAASH** 15 [12] 4-7-12 (34)(2ow)(4oh) F Norton 40/1: -40600: Sn in rear, lost tch halfway, fin 10th.	hd	9a
*574	**CLONOE** 7 [7] 6-8-8 (44)(6ex) A Clark 11/4 FAV: 240410: Sn led, hdd halfway, rdn & wknd qckly final 3f, fin 13th: well bckd, qck reapp: best when allowed to dominate: much btr 574 (1m sell).		0a
408	**Without Friends** 34 [13] 6-7-11 (33)(vis) A Polli (3) 25/1: ₺47 **Master Mac** 11 [10] 5-8-13 (49) S Whitworth 20/1:		

13 ran   Time 2m 07.18 (4.38)   (Greenacres)   M Kettle Blewbury, Oxon.

---

621   5.15 TEXT P372 HCAP 4YO+ 0-75 (E)   1m4f aw   Going 38   +06 Fast   [74]
£3461   £1065   £532   £266   4 yo rec 2 lb

508	**RAYIK** 18 [6] G L Moore 5-9-10 (70) I Mongan (7) 7/4 FAV: -12141: 5 br g Marju - Matila (Persian Bold) Keen cl-up, rdn to chall over 2f out, led dist, rdn clr: nicely bckd from 5/2, best time of day: top-weight: prev won here at Lingfield (2 h'caps): '99 rnr-up (h'cap, rtd 81a), '98 wnr again at Lingfield (mdn, N Berry, rtd 78a): eff at 10/13f on both AWs, loves Lingfield/equitrack & racing up with/forcing the pace: tough/genuine, in fine form.		77a
520	**OCEAN LINE** 15 [1] G M McCourt 5-7-10 (42)(2oh) D Kinsella (7) 4/1: 0-2322: 5 b g Kefaah - Tropic Sea (Sure Blade): Prom, hdwy to lead 5f out, rdn/hdd over 1f out, not pace of wnr: consistent: handles both AWs.	5	42a
572	**HAWKSBILL HENRY** 7 [4] Mrs A J Perrett 6-9-1 (61) A Clark 6/1: 013103: 6 ch g Known Fact - Novel Approach (Codex) Led, hdd 5f out, rdn & btn appr final 2f: qck reapp, op 9/2: see 486 (made all).	¾	60a
528	**PARISIAN LADY** 14 [3] A G Newcombe 5-8-6 (52) S Whitworth 11/1: 06-634: Held up, rdn to impr halfway, late gains, nvr nrr: op 7/1: former sprinter, tried 12f last twice: see 528, 152.	1½	48a
407	**ROMAN CANDLE** 34 [2] 4-9-6 (68) N Callan 5/2: 150-05: Keen, with ldr, chall on bit 4f out, drvn & wknd qckly final 2f: possibly still needed this tho' hvly bckd: '99 wnr at Windsor & Ripon (h'caps, rtd 74): eff at 12f, poss worth a try at 10f on this surface: acts on firm, gd, sharp or gall trk: sharper next time.	3	60a
505	**THOMAS HENRY** 18 [2] 4-8-2 (50) F Norton 16/1: 6-0066: Handy, rdn & no extra final 2f: op 10/1.	¾	41a

6 ran   Time 2m 33.08 (3.88)   (Lancing Racing Syndicate)   G L Moore Woodingdean, East Sussex.

WOLVERHAMPTON (Fibresand)   THURSDAY MARCH 2ND   Lefthand, Sharp Track

Official Going   STANDARD. Stalls: Inside, except 7f - Outside.

622   2.20 BET DIRECT HCAP 3YO+ 0-70 (E)   6f aw rnd   Going 33   +05 Fast   [70]
£2912   £896   £448   £224

*587	**TELECASTER** 6 [9] C R Egerton 4-9-9 (65)(bl)(6ex) D Sweeney 6/4 FAV: 311211: 4 ch g Indian Ridge - Monashee (Sovereign Dancer): Cl-up, led over 3f out, rdn clr 2f out, decisively: best time of day: qck reapp: earlier won here at W'hampton & twice at Southwell (h'caps): unplcd in '99: all wins at 6f, stays 7f: loves fibresand & front running: eff with/without blnks: lightly rcd, proving tough & most progressive.		74a
557	**DAYS OF GRACE** 10 [6] L Montague Hall 5-9-11 (67) Martin Dwyer 9/2: 123132: 5 gr m Wolfhound - Inshirah (Caro): Led 1f, rdn halfway, kept on for press appr final 1f, no impress on wnr: see 440.	2½	68a
454	**GRASSLANDIK** 27 [11] A G Newcombe 4-8-10 (52) L Newman (5) 5/1: 02-353: 4 b c Ardkinglass - Sophisticated Baby (Bairn) Chsd ldrs, onepace over 1f out: bckd from 8/1: sole win in sell grade: stays 6f.	1	50a
506	**SEREN TEG** 19 [5] R M Flower 4-9-11 (67)(bl) A Clark 8/1: 00-144: Bhd, kept on over 1f out, no dngr: best in clmrs: see 440 (first time blnks).	¾	64a
*559	**BEWARE** 10 [2] 5-8-13 (55)(bl)(6ex) O Pears 5/1: -36615: Prom, wknd over 1f out: btr 559 (seller).	1¼	48a
588	**SPRINGS NOBLEQUEST** 6 [7] 4-8-7 (49) P M Quinn (5) 33/1: 30-066: Led after 1f till 4f out, wknd.	½	40a
4172}	**MOOCHA CHA MAN** 99 [10] 4-9-6 (62) P Mundy (7) 20/1: 1240-7: In tch, wknd 2f out: op 10/1: reapp, in '99 won at Pontefract (clmr, first time blnks, rtd 73 at best): '98 scorer at W'hampton (auct mdn, rtd 69a): suited by 5f, stays 6f on fast, hvy & fibresand: prob handles any trk & has won in first time blnks.	nk	52a
587	**SHARP EDGE BOY** 6 [3] 4-8-7 (49) S Drowne 33/1: 000-08: Nvr a factor: reapp: in '99 won at Hamilton & Haydock (h'caps, rtd 75 in '98: eff at 6/7f on fast, likes gd/soft & hvy: handles any trk: tried a visor, best without: slipped back to a handy mark.	nk	39a
564	**GOLD EDGE** 9 [1] 4-9-2 (38)(bl)(11oh) G Sparkes (4) 33/1: 00-059: Bhd, slightly hmpd 4f out, no dngr.	1½	24a
563	**MAMMAS F C** 9 [8] 4-8-10 (52) Claire Bryan (7) 14/1: 020-00: No dngr: see 563.	½	37a
445	**BAPTISMAL ROCK** 28 [4] 6-8-5 (47) S Whitworth 9/2: 00-050: In tch, btn after halfway: see 246.	¾	30a

11 ran   Time 1m 14.5 (1.7)   (Casting Partners B)   C R Egerton Chaddleworth, Berks.

---

623   2.50 0800 CLASSIFIED STKS 3YO+ 0-70 (E)   7f aw rnd   Going 33   -01 Slow
£2588   £739   £369   3 yo rec 16lb

521	**SANTANDRE** 16 [3] R Hollinshead 4-9-7 P M Quinn (5) 7/2 CO FAV: -00641: 4 ch g Democratic - Smartie Lee (Dominion): Made most, kept on well for press over 1f out, just held on: gamble from 8/1: in '99 won at W'hampton (h'cap, rtd 73a), plcd on turf (rtd 60): '98 Thirsk scorer (nursery h'cap, rtd 78 & 64a): eff at 5f, suited by 6/7f: acts on firm, soft, likes fibresand & W'hampton (sharp trks): genuine gelding.		69a
*517	**RAMBO WALTZER** 16 [1] Miss S J Wilton 8-10-1 I Mongan (7) 9/1: -11212: 8 b g Rambo Dancer - Vindictive Lady (Foolish Pleasure): Led 1f, cl-up, kept on for press final 1f, just held: op 7/1: prev with D Nicholls & this most tough (23 career victories) & game fibresand specialist continues to run well.	hd	76a
594	**RAIN RAIN GO AWAY** 5 [7] D J S Cosgrove 4-9-7 C Rutter 7/2 CO FAV: -16143: 4 ch g Miswaki - Stormagain (Storm Cat): Handy, kept on for press over 1f out, just held in a 3-way photo: clr of rem & ran to best: qck reapp in gd form, see 547 (made all, equitrack).	nk	71a
4297}	**DOUBLE ACTION** 99 [8] T D Easterby 6-9-7 R Winston 7/1: 2006-4: Chsd ldrs, rdn & outpcd over 1f out: reapp, op 4/1: plcd on 3 of 14 '99 starts (rtd 77 at best): plcd twice in '98 (rtd 99): '97 wnr at Ripon & York (val h'cap, rtd 104), also rnr-up in Ayr Gold Cup: eff at 5f, suited by 6f & stays 7f: acts on fast grnd, likes hvy: has tried blnks: better than this at his best.	6	57a
549	**RISKY REEF** 12 [5] 3-8-11(6ow) Martin Dwyer 9/2: 52-45: Prom, rdn & btn 2f out: see 549.	hd	63a
4372}	**INTRICATE WEB** 99 [4] 4-9-7 S Drowne 7/1: 6301-6: Nvr a factor: reapp: in '99 won final & only	5	49a

198

start at Redcar (h'cap, rtd 68): unplcd in Irish mdns for D Weld (blnks) prev: eff at 7f on fast & soft grnd.

557　**PRIDEWAY 10** [6]　4-9-4 T G McLaughlin　7/2 CO FAV: 00-447: Al bhd: much btr 466.　　　1¾　42a

*500　**KARA SEA 20** [2]　3-8-4 P Doe　5/1: 18: Al bhd: op 3/1: btr expected after 500 (mdn).　　2½　39a

8 ran　　　Time 1m 28.6 (2.4)　　　(Geoff Lloyd)　　　R Hollinshead Upper Longdon, Staffs.

624　　3.20 BEST BETS MDN 3YO+ (D)　　5f aw rnd　Going 33　-11 Slow
　　　£2704　　£832　　£416　　£208　　3 yo　rec 13lb

397　**MARITUN LAD 37** [6]　D Shaw 3-8-11 (BL)　N Callan　4/5 FAV: 65-431: 3 b g Presidium - Girl Next Door　62a
(Local Suitor): Handy, hdwy to chall halfway, led appr final 1f, pushed out, cmftbly: nicely bckd in first
time blnks: consistent form prev this term (tried visor): unplcd in 3 '99 starts (rtd 57a, no turf form):
eff at 6f, apprec step back to 5f & blnks, has tried a visor.

549　**TROPICAL KING 12** [2]　D Carroll 3-8-11 J Fanning　4/1: 0-4252: 3 b g Up And At 'Em - Princess Gay　1¾　55a
(Fairy King): Led, hdd over 1f out, kept on, not pace of wnr: op 2/1: eff at 5/6f on fibresand: see 365 (h'cap).

543　**ARAB GOLD 12** [7]　M Quinn 5-9-10 R Studholme (5)　25/1: -00303: 5 b g Presidium - Parklands Belle　1　53$
(Stanford): Rdn/rear, hdwy for press appr final 1f, styd on, nvr nrr: gd run, will apprec h'caps over 6f + .

357　**MISS SINCERE 43** [1]　B S Rothwell 3-8-6 M Fenton　33/1: 50-044: Dwelt, hdwy 2f out, btn 1f out.　1¼　43$

434　**SUAVE PERFORMER 30** [8]　3-8-11 G Faulkner (3)　25/1: 045: Wide, held up, kept on under minimal　2½　46+
press fnl 2f, nvr plcd to chall: reportedly 'lost his action' but showed plenty of promise here & one to be
interested in if reappearing in a h'cap over further (mid-dist breeding): see 323.

558　**SOBA JONES 10** [4]　3-8-11 R Winston　11/2: 3-66: Chsd ldrs, wknd appr fnl 1f: mkt drifter: see 558.　nk　40a

323　**FOUND AT LAST 49** [5]　4-9-10 T G McLaughlin　7/2: 05-307: Trkd ldr, rdn/wknd final 2f: nicely　1¼　36a
bckd (tchd 10/1): 7 wk abs: prev with G Woodward, now with J Balding: see 323.

389　**WEETRAIN 38** [3]　4-9-5 Dean McKeown　14/1: 00-608: Handy, lost tch appr final 1f: stiff task.　nk　30a

8 ran　　　Time 1m 02.4 (2.2)　　　(M G Vines)　　　D Shaw Averham, Notts.

625　　3.50 TEXT P368 HCAP 3YO 0-85 (D)　　1m1f79y aw　Going 33　-03 Slow　　　[89]
　　　£3828　　£1178　　£589　　£294

509　**SERVICE STAR 19** [2]　M A Jarvis 3-9-5 (80)(bl)　N Callan　9/2: 013-21: 3 b c Namaqualand - Shenley Lass　89a
(Prince Tenderfoot): Trkd ldrs, hdwy to lead 2f out, pushed clr, cmftbly: op 3/1: late '99 scorer at Southwell
(auct mdn, rtd 85a), rnr-up twice prev on turf (rtd 77, auct mdn): eff at 1m, stays 10f well: acts on firm &
both AWs: handles a stiff/gall or sharp trk: has improved recently in headgear: comfortable wnr, follow up.

613　**CHURCH FARM FLYER 2** [4]　C N Allen 3-8-11 (62) J Mackay (7)　100/30: -23632: 3 b f College Chapel -　6　62a
Young Isabel (Last Tycoon): Waited with, hdwy when hung left over 1f out, styd on but no threat to ldr:
ran 48 hrs ago: possibly stays 9.4f: see 188.

500　**ROYAL CAVALIER 20** [3]　R Hollinshead 3-9-3 (78) P M Quinn (5)　14/1: 422-03: 3 b g Prince Of Birds　2　75a
- Gold Belt (Bellypha): Handy, chsg ldrs when hmpd by rnr-up over 1f out, no dngr after: unfortunate not to fin closer.

*509　**BLUEBELL WOOD 19** [5]　G C Bravery 3-9-7 (82) A Culhane (3)　3/1: 0-1114: Keen, led to 2f out, no extra　nk　79a
when hmpd appr final 1f: not disgraced on 4-timer bid here: completed an equitrack hat-trick in 509.

3957}　**RUNNING TIMES 99** [7]　3-8-7 (68) R Winston　8/1: 4400-5: Chsd ldrs, rdn/no extra final 2f:　¾　64a
reapp: plcd on '99 debut (nov stks, rtd 72 +): this 9.4f trip should suit in time: sharper next time.

495　**COMMON PLACE 21** [1]　3-9-4 (79) R Mullen　7/4 FAV: 100-56: Dwelt, bhd, hdwy when short of room　hd　75a
over 1f out, eased when btn: op 7/2: unlucky in running, forget this: see 495.

4274}　**RHODAMINE 99** [6]　3-8-9 (70) Dean McKeown　8/1: 0354-7: Keen in mid-div, lost tch final 2f: reapp,　11　52a
AW bow: '99 scorer at Newcastle (auct mdn, rtd 73): eff at 6f, stays 1m: acts on gd & a stiff trk.

7 ran　　　Time 2m 01.6 (3.4)　　　(N S Yong)　　　M A Jarvis Newmarket.

626　　4.20 TEXT P372 SELLER 4YO+ (G)　　1m4f aw　Going 33　-15 Slow
　　　£1941　　£554　　£277　　4 yo　rec 2 lb

*581　**ARTIC COURIER 7** [9]　D J S Cosgrove 9-9-5 C Rutter　7/1: 030-11: 9 gr g Siberian Express - La Reine　51a
de France (Queens Hussar) Mid-div, smooth prog after 1m, slight lead bef dist, hung left, drvn out, narrowly: op 3/1,
no bid, qck reapp: recent wnr here at W'hampton (C/D sell): plcd sev times in '99 (h'cap, rtd 57a, stks, rtd 52):
back in '96 won at Epsom & Kempton (h'caps, awdd race, rtd 83): eff at 12/14f, tried further: acts on firm,
soft, both AWs: goes on any trk, likes plenty/undul ones: best without blnks: gd weight carrier, runs well fresh.

530　**APPROACHABLE 14** [5]　Miss S J Wilton 5-9-0 M Tebbutt　5/1: 544232: 5 b h Known Fact - Western　¾　44a
Approach (Gone West) Nvr far away, led 2½f out till bef fnl 1f, kept on: tchd 6/1, clr rem: acts again, see 45.

581　**HILL FARM DANCER 7** [2]　W M Brisbourne 9-9-0 C Cogan (5)　11/2: 523143: 9 ch m Gunner B -　6　34a
Loadplan Lass (Nicholas Bill) Held up, prog to chase ldrs 3f out, no extra bef final 1f: op 7/2, qck reapp.

550　**BILLICHANG 12** [6]　P Howling 4-9-3 R Winston　8/1: 333344: Well plcd till onepace appr final 2f:　5　31a
prob unsuited by step up to 12f: see 433, 238.

*556　**ADIRPOUR 10** [1]　6-9-5 Stephanie Hollinshead (7)　16/1: 650415: Pulled hard, al mid-div: op 10/1:　10　16a

--　　**SPRING ANCHOR 8** [8]　5-9-0 D Sweeney　7/1: 3212/6: Led till 5f out, gradually wknd: op 4/1,　2½　7a
9 wk jump abs (poor form): last seen on the Flat in '98, plcd sev times before wng at Lingfield (turf auct mdn,
rtd 86 at best, mdn, rtd 80a, Pcole): eff at 12f/14f: acts on firm, soft grnd & fibresand: with P Dalton.

553　**MAJOR ATTRACTION 12** [7]　5-9-0 (BL) R Fitzpatrick (3)　40/1: -00067: Cl-up, led 5f out till　¾　6a
2½f out, lost place: stiff task & now blnkd.

340}　**QUIET ARCH 99** [11]　7-9-0 L Newman (5)　14/1: 0/40-8: Nvr in it: jumps fit, plcd in a clmr 15 days　6　0a
ago (2m, hvy, rtd 80h): lightly rcd last year, '98 wnr at Lingfield (2, ltd stks & h'cap, rtd 74a) & Brighton
(clmr, rtd 67, W Muir): eff at 10/12f on firm & gd/soft grnd, Lingfield/equitrack specialist: best without visor.

--　　**MOUNT VERNON 3** [3]　4-8-12 (t)　J P Spencer (5)　7/4 FAV: 9: Al bhd: bckd from 5/2 on Flat/Brit bow:　9　0a
Irish raider, 6th of 9 in a hvy grnd bmprs 3 wks ago: with T Stack.

3657}　**DAYS OF THUNDER 99** [4]　12-9-0 C Carver (3)　33/1: 44/0-0: Mid-div till 5f out: 10th, stiff task, jumps rnr.　13　0a

2072}　**LEADING SPIRIT 99** [10]　8-9-0 J Weaver　7/1: -0RR-R: Ref to race: tchd 16/1, new stable, one to avoid.　0a

11 ran　　　Time 2m 39.4 (5.8)　　　(D J S Cosgrove)　　　D J S Cosgrove Newmarket, Suffolk.

WOLVERHAMPTON (Fibresand)   THURSDAY MARCH 2ND   Lefthand, Sharp Track

627
4.50 TEXT P372 HCAP 4YO+ 0-80 (D)   2m46y aw Going 33 -11 Slow   [78]
£3750   £1154   £577   £288   4 yo rec 5 lb

*482   **MAKNAAS 23** [6] T G Mills 4-8-6 (61) A Clark 7/4 FAV: -41511: 4 ch c Wolfhound - White-Wash (Final   **68a**
Straw) Made all, pushed out: earlier won at Lingfield (amat h'cap) & here at W'hampton (C/D h'cap): 98/99 wnr
again here at W'hampton (h'cap, rtd 52a), plcd on turf for R Armstrong (mdn h'cap, rtd 49): suited by 2m now:
acts on soft, both AWs, loves W'hampton, sharp trks: best forcing the pace: eff with/without blnks: imprvg on sand.
*552   **ROYAL EXPRESSION 12** [4] G M Moore 8-9-1 (65) J Weaver 4/1: 1-6312: 8 b g Sylvan Express - Edwins' 3 **68a**
Princess (Owen Dudley): Well plcd, tried to go with wnr appr final 2f, no impress: caught a tartar but was clr
of rem & prob improved again in defeat: see 552 (C/D).
548   **ALHESN 12** [2] C N Allen 5-9-6 (70) R Morse 7/2: -41323: 5 b g Woodman - Deceit Princess (Vice Regent) 8 **65a**
Bhd, rems after 1m, styd on thro' btn horses, nvr a factor: mulish display back on fibresand: see 548, 348.
4397} **GENEROUS WAYS 99** [3] E J Alston 5-8-10 (60) S Drowne 14/1: 3550-4: Bhd ldrs till wknd 3f out: 2 **53a**
reapp/AW bow: '99 Ascot wnr (h'cap, rtd 65): '98 wnr at Redcar for E Dunlop (h'cap, rtd 72): eff at
14f/2m: acts on fast grnd, any trk, without blnks: with E Alston.
*607   **MORGANS ORCHARD 2** [7] 4-8-11 (66)(6ex) S Whitworth 5/2: -15215: Well plcd till 3f out: op 7/2: 1¼ **58a**
too soon over longer trip with a penalty after 607 (amat h'cap, Tuesday)?
1571} **YES KEEMO SABEE 99** [5] 5-9-2 (66) L Newton 16/1: 0210-6: Nvr in it: op 10/1 on reapp: '99 dist **0a**
wnr at Thirsk (h'cap, rtd 71): with B McMahon in '98 when Southwell rnr-up (h'cap, rtd 59a): eff at
2m/2m2f on gd/soft, soft grnd & fibresand: with D Shaw.
508   **RANDOM KINDNESS 19** [1] 7-10-0 (78) I Mongan (7) 9/1: 00-407: In tch till halfway: top-weight. 16 **0a**
7 ran   Time 3m 36.4 (7.2)   (Travel Spot Ltd)   T G Mills Headley, Surrey.

LINGFIELD (Equitrack)   SATURDAY MARCH 4TH   Lefthand, V Sharp Track

Official Going   STANDARD. Stalls: Inside, Except 5f - Outside.

628
1.40 TEXT P372 HCAP DIV 1 3YO+ 0-60 (F)   6f aw rnd Going 18 -20 Slow   [58]
£1897   £542   £271

564   **CHAKRA 11** [2] J M Bradley 6-8-2 (32) Claire Bryan (7) 14/1: 065061: 6 gr g Mystiko - Maracuja   **37a**
(Riverman) Trkd ldrs, rdn to lead well ins last, rdn out: op 10/1: rnr-up in '99 (h'cap, rtd 45): '98 wnr at Warwick
(2, h'caps, rtd 54): eff at 5/6f on firm, gd & equitrack: handles any trk, likes a sharp/turning one, best held up.
525   **AUBRIETA 17** [1] D Haydn Jones 4-9-8 (52)(bl) P Doe 5/2 FAV: 01-052: 4 b f Dayjur - Fennel ½ **54a**
(Slew O'Gold) Rdn/chsd ldrs, stly hmpd over 1f out, kept on in last: nicely bckd, tchd 7/2: see 25 (C/D, mdn).
543   **SHADY DEAL 14** [4] M D I Usher 4-8-10 (40) G Baker (7) 12/1: -04003: 4 b g No Big Deal - Taskalady ½ **40a**
(Touching Wood) Led, hdd well ins last, & no extra: op 10/1: see 391.
499   **SISAO 22** [8] Miss Gay Kelleway 4-9-12 (56)(bl) P Fredericks (5) 9/1: 2-1004: Wide, rdn/chsd ldrs 2½ **49a**
halfway, not pace to chall: op 6/1: see 273.
547   **MISS DANGEROUS 14** [7] 5-9-4 (48) F Norton 8/1: 130355: Prom 5f: op 6/1: see 243 (stks, 7f). nk **40a**
564   **BARITONE 11** [5] 6-8-13 (43)(vis) J Fortune 3/1: 341536: Sn outpcd wide: tchd 4/1: see 445 (5f, f/sand). 1½ **31a**
543   **COLLEGE BLUE 14** [3] 4-10-0 (58) I Mongan (5) 9/2: 200107: Sn outpcd: op 7/2: btr 484 (C/D, clmr). 4 **36a**
472   **ABSOLUTE FANTASY 26** [6] 4-9-0 (44)(bl) S Carson (5) 12/1: 4-6268: Al outpcd: op 10/1: see 399, 109. ¾ **20a**
8 ran   Time 1m 12.65 (2.25)   (Clifton Hunt)   J M Bradley Sedbury, Glos

629
2.10 BET DIRECT MDN 3YO+ (D)   1m2f aw Going 18 -25 Slow
£2769   £852   £426   £213   3 yo rec 21lb

603   **YOU DA MAN 5** [1] R Hannon 3-8-5 P Fitzsimons (5) 11/2: -42241: 3 b c Alzao - Fabled Lifestyle   **75a**
(King's Lake) Held up in tch, stdy prog fnl 3f to lead well ins last, rdn out: op 5/2: quick reapp: unplcd in '99
(rtd 66): eff over a sharp 10f, further may suit in time: acts on equitrack & a sharp trk: best without blnks.
4602} **DONATUS 99** [2] S Dow 4-9-12 P Doe 13/8 FAV: 0260-2: 4 b c Royal Academy - La Dame Du Lac ¾ **71a**
(Round Table) Handy, rdn/narrow lead dist, hdd well ins last & no extra: nicely bckd: jumps fit (rnr-up thrice
this term, rtd 115h, juv rtg): rnr-up twice in '99 (rtd 73, h'cap): mdn plcd in Ireland in '98: eff arnd 1m/sharp
10f: acts on firm, soft & equitrack: handles a sharp/undul or stiff trk: prob best held up for a late run.
--   **ACHILLES WINGS 10** K R Burke 4-9-12 J Weaver 6/1: 3: 4 b c Irish River - Shirley Valentine ¾ **70a**
(Shirley Heights) Sn handy, led halfway till over 1f out, onepace: op 3/1: debut: eff at 10f on equitrack.
545   **FINERY 14** [3] W Jarvis 3-8-5 Martin Dwyer 7/2: 6424: Chsd ldrs halfway, held fnl 2f: op 5/2: see 545. 3 **66a**
597   **BLAYNEY DANCER 7** [4] 3-8-7(2ow) O Urbina 33/1: 0-0365: Held up in tch, btn 3f out: see 461. 8 **59$**
--   **GIRARE 7** [4] 4-9-12 I Mongan (5) 8/1: 50-6: Struggling 4f out: op 5/1: AW bow, 6 month abs: 10 **46a**
ex-French, unplcd from 2 starts in '99: with G L Moore.
591   **NO REGRETS 7** [9] 3-8-5 F Norton 16/1: 600-57: Led 5f, sn btn: op 12/1: unplcd in '99 (rtd 69, mdn). 4 **40a**
4314} **WESTBROOK 99** [8] 4-9-12 (VIS) N Carlisle 33/1: 0500-8: Al bhd: AW bow, visor: 4 mth jmps abs. 5 **33a**
--   **CANCUN CARIBE** [6] 3-8-5 J Tate 12/1: 9: Chsd ldrs till halfway: tchd 14/1, debut: with K McAuliffe. 3 **29a**
--   **PORTHILLY BUOY** [11] 5-9-12 S Carson (5) 50/1: 0500/0: Bhd halfway: 10th: 4 mth jmps abs. dist **0a**
10 ran   Time 2m 07.05 (4.25)   (Buddy Hackett)   R Hannon East Everleigh, Wilts

630
2.45 0800 211 222 STKS 3YO+ (C)   7f aw rnd Going 18 -13 Slow
£6061   £2298   £1149   £522   3 yo rec 16lb

3827} **MAGIC RAINBOW 99** [8] M L W Bell 5-9-4 M Fenton 2/1: 2030-1: 5 b g Magic Ring - Blues Indigo   **90a**
(Music Boy) Chsd ldrs halfway, smooth prog to lead 1f out, styd on well, rdn out: abs: '99 wnr here at Lingfield
(rtd 94a) & Kempton (h'caps, rtd 88): '98 Southwell & Newmarket (h'caps, rtd 86a & 84): eff at 5/6f, stays 7f:
acts on firm, gd/soft & both AWs: goes well fresh: eff up with/forcing the pace: handles any trk, likes Lingfield.
462   **PRINCE PROSPECT 28** [7] Mrs L Stubbs 4-9-10 J P Spencer 33/1: 0-0102: 4 b g Lycius - Princess 1¼ **92a**
Dechtra (Bellypha) Prom, rdn/outpcd fnl 1f, kept on onepace: eff at 5/6f, stays a sharp 7f: see 376 (6f).
+485   **SALTY JACK 24** [4] V Soane 4-9-4 Martin Dwyer 13/8 FAV: 1-0213: 6 b h Salt Dome - Play The Queen ¾ **85a**
(King Of Clubs) Rdn/bhd halfway, styd on strongly wide from over 1f out, nrst fin: op 7/2: see 485 (1m).
108   **RISK FREE 99** [3] N P Littmoden 3-8-2 J Tate 14/1: 2002-4: Prom, rdn/outpcd 2f out, kept on well shd **85a**

200

ins last: op 10/1, 3 month abs: see 108 (C/D).
485 **ELMHURST BOY 24** [5] 4-9-8 (vis) W Ryan 13/2: 21-545: Rear, rdn/late gains wide, nrst fin: op 8/1. ½ **88$**
596 **BORDER GLEN 7** [1] 4-9-4 (vis) J Weaver 14/1: 4-3626: Led 6f, fdd: tchd 16/1: see 546, 292 & 96. ½ **83$**
4517} **KAMARAZI 20** [2] 3-8-6 M Sautjeau 20/1: -00-07: Al outpcd rear: op 10/1: recent French rnr, back 2½ **82$**
in Jan scored at Cagnes Sur Mer (1m, fibresand): unplcd in '99 for P F I Cole (rtd 54, tried blnks): with S Dow.
3467} **SAFRANINE 99** [6] 3-7-13 Dale Gibson 9/1: 0120-8: Struggling halfway: op 6/1: 7 month abs: *27* **35a**
'99 Redcar scorer (fill mdn, rtd 96 at best, unplcd on sand, rtd 41a): eff over a gall 6f on firm & fast grnd.
8 ran Time 1m 24.98 (2.18) (P T Fenwick) M L W Bell Newmarket

631

3.15 BEST BETS HCAP 3YO+ 0-80 (D) 5f aw rnd Going 18 -04 Slow [80]
£3768 £1159 £579 £289 3 yo rec 13lb

579 **FRILLY FRONT 9** [1] T D Barron 4-9-2 (68) C Lowther 5/2 FAV: -P1101: 4 ch f Aragon - So So (Then **79a**
Again) Sn led, drew clr over 1f out, styd on strongly, rdn out: earlier won twice here at Lingfield (C/D h'caps):
'99 W'hampton scorer (h'cap, rtd 58a & 61, h'cap): '98 debut Musselburgh wnr (auct mdn, subs rtd 83): stays 6f,
suited by 5f on fast, soft & both AWs, loves Lingfield: has run well fresh: best without blnks: can win again.
*573 **READY TO ROCK 10** [5] J S Moore 4-7-10 (48)(bl) P M Quinn (5) 6/1: 006012: 4 b g Up And At 'Em - *4* **49a**
Rocklands Rosie (Muscatite) Rdn chasing ldrs halfway, kept on, no threat: op 5/1: see 573 (C/D, made all).
1641} **NORTHERN SVENGALI 99** [4] T D Barron 4-9-12 (78) J Fortune 6/1: 0444-3: 4 b g Distinctly North - *1½* **76a**
Trilby's Dream (Mansooj) In tch, rdn/outpcd over 2f out, kept on ins last, no threat: op 5/1: 9 month abs:
plcd in '99 (rtd 79, h'cap): '98 wnr at Catterick (2, mdn & nurs, rtd 84, plcd on sand, rtd 80a, h'cap): eff at 5/6f:
handles any trk, loves a sharp/turning one: acts on firm, hvy & both AWs: stablemate of wnr, win more races.
506 **AA YOUKNOWNOTHING 21** [3] Miss J F Craze 4-9-3 (69)(tvi) S Finnamore (7) 11/2: 1-6204: Cl-up 3f. *hd* **66a**
543 **CATCHTHEBATCH 14** [7] 4-8-3 (55)(BL) S Carson (5) 16/1: 00-005: Chsd ldrs, held fnl 2f: blnks. *shd* **52a**
543 **BRAMBLE BEAR 14** [6] 6-7-12 (49)(1ow) Dale Gibson 5/1: 53-466: Rear/wide, nvr on terms: op 7/2. *nk* **46a**
4006} **AMARANTH 99** [2] 4-10-0 (80)(t) Dean McKeown 9/2: 0016-7: Rdn/towards rear, al outpcd: op 7/1, *nk* **75a**
6 month abs: topweight: '99 wnr at Newcastle & Newmarket (h'caps, rtd 83): '98 juv wnr at Redcar (auct mdn, rtd
76): eff at 5/6f on firm or soft, up with/forcing the pace, likes a stiff/gall trk: suited by a t-strap: AW bow.
7 ran Time 58.91 (1.11) (M Dalby) T D Barron Maunby, N Yorks

632

3.50 TEXT P368 HCAP 3YO+ 0-95 (C) 1m2f aw Going 18 -00 Slow [88]
£8385 £2580 £1290 £645

611 **TIGHTROPE 4** [2] N P Littmoden 5-8-2 (62) F Norton 16/1: -63001: 5 b g Alzao - Circus Act (Shirley **70a**
Heights) Chsd ldrs, led over 2f out, sn clr, styd on well ins last, rdn out: op 14/1: quick reapp: '99 wnr at
Yarmouth (sell, gamble, rtd 56, Sir M Prescott), rnr-up on sand for current connections (rtd 61a, C/D): eff at
1m/10f: acts on fast, gd/soft & both AWs: handles any trk: has run well fresh: best without a visor.
442 **ANEMOS 31** [10] M A Jarvis 5-9-2 (76) J Fanning 5/1: 1-2342: 5 ch g Be My Guest - Frendly Persuasion *5* **77a**
(General Assembly) Chsd ldrs halfway, rdn/chsd wnr fnl 1f, nvr pace to chall: see 160 (C/D).
620 **SAMMYS SHUFFLE 3** [1] Jamie Poulton 5-7-13 (59)(bl) N Carlisle 16/1: 500153: 5 b h Touch Of Grey ½ **59a**
- Cabinet Shuffle (Thatching) Sltly hmpd/lost place after 1f, chsd ldrs halfway, kept on fnl 2f, no threat: op 12/1.
572 **FORTY FORTE 10** [7] K R Burke 4-8-12 (72) N Callan 8/1: 616244: Led 1m, no extra fnl 1f: op 7/1. ¾ **71a**
485 **SECRET SPRING 24** [8] 8-10-0 (88) O Urbina 15/2: -40055: Mid-div, no threat: op 6/1: see 208 (1m). 2½ **83a**
594 **SCISSOR RIDGE 7** [3] 8-7-11 (57) G Bardwell 14/1: -32426: Mid-div, btn over 2f out: op 12/1: see 336. *3* **48a**
593 **TALLULAH BELLE 7** [5] 7-9-8 (82) J Tate 9/2 FAV: 0-0427: Towards rear, nvr factor: stablemate of wnr. 1¾ **71a**
593 **HUGWITY 7** [13] 8-9-9 (83) A Culhane 10/1: 124438: Twds rear/wide, nvr factor: op 6/1: see 375 (clmr). *3* **68a**
568 **ROI DE DANSE 11** [6] 5-7-10 (56)(10oh) G Baker (7) 33/1: 342259: Chsd ldrs 7f: see 227. *6* **32a**
600 **PHILISTAR 5** [9] 7-8-5 (65)(bl) P M Quinn (5) 16/1: 5-3360: Al rear: 10th: op 10/1, stablemate of wnr. ½ **40a**
486 **FUSUL 24** [4] 4-8-3 (63) P Doe 6/1: 4-1130: Struggling halfway: 11th: btr 441 (12f). 1¾ **36a**
4013} **Arawak Prince 99** [12] 4-9-9 (83)(BL) W Ryan 25/1: 336 **Consort 49** [11] 7-8-6 (66)(t) R Winston 12/1:
13 ran Time 2m 04.62 (1.82) (Wilwyn Racing) N P Littmoden Newmarket

633

4.20 TEXT P372 HCAP 3YO+ 0-100 (C) 1m4f aw Going 18 +04 Fast [98]
£10286 £3165 £1582 £791

605 **CHINA CASTLE 5** [6] P C Haslam 7-9-1 (85) P Goode (5) 11/2: -06621: 7 b g Sayf El Arab - Honey **91a**
Plum (Kind Of Hush) In tch, prog wide over 3f out, led ins last, styd on well, drvn out: op 4/1, gd time, qck reapp:
'99 Southwell (4), W'hampton (3) & Hamilton wnr (h'caps, rtd 52 & 107a): '98 Southwell (ltd stks) & W'hampton wnr
(h'caps, rtd 87a): suited by 11/12f on firm & equitrack, fibresand/sharp trk specialist: on a handy mark.
*621 **RAYIK 3** [5] G L Moore 5-8-6 (76)(6ex) I Mongan (2) 6/1: 121412: 5 br g Marju - Matila (Persian Bold) *1* **79a**
Handy, rdn/led 4f out till ins last, kept on well: clr of rem, quick reapp under a 6lb pen: in gd heart: see 621.
572 **WHITE PLAINS 10** [3] K R Burke 7-9-3 (87)(tE) N Callan 10/1: 140333: 7 b g Nordico - Flying Diva *5* **83a**
(Chief Singer) Handy, rdn/chsd ldr 4f out till over 2f out, sn held: op 8/1: tried an eye-shield: see 244 (10f).
593 **MODUS OPERANDI 7** [8] K R Burke 4-8-10 (80) J Fortune 8/1: 415-64: Cl-up 10f: see 593 (10f). 1½ **74a**
572 **SPACE RACE 10** [9] 6-8-10 (80) A Clark 12/1: -16225: Held up in tch, nvr on terms: sadly died after race. 3½ **69a**
*572 **URSA MAJOR 10** [1] 6-9-1 (85) Martin Dwyer 2/1 FAV: 212116: Led 1m, sn btn: well bckd: see 572 (C/D). 3½ **69a**
512 **CHALCEDONY 19** [2] 4-7-13 (69) P M Quinn (5) 6/1: 0-1247: Struggling halfway: btr 508, 343. 3½ **48a**
3865} **MARDANI 99** [4] 5-10-0 (98) J Fanning 6/1: 2020-8: Wide/towards rear, nvr on terms: op 5/1: 5 mth *5* **70a**
abs: '99 Beverley & York wnr (h'caps, rtd 100 at best): ex-Irish, '98 wnr at Dundalk (mdn) & Leopardstown (stks):
eff at 12/14f, tried 2m: acts on firm & gd grnd: likes to dominate: gd weight carrier: AW bow today.
2685} **TAMING 99** [7] 4-9-4 (88)(t) A McGlone 12/1: 53/1-9: Bhd halfway: op 8/1: t-strap: jumps fit (fell, *18* **40a**
rtd 104?): '99 wnr on sole start, at Kempton (mdn, rtd 92, H Cecil): plcd in '98 (rtd 84, mdn): eff at 12f,
shld stay further: goes well fresh on fast grnd & an easy trk: AW bow today for D G Bridgwater.
9 ran Time 2m 30.85 (1.65) (J M Davis & Middleham Park Racing I) P C Haslam Middleham, N Yorks

634

4.50 TEXT P372 HCAP DIV 2 3YO+ 0-60 (F) 6f aw rnd Going 18 -21 Slow [58]
£1897 £542 £271 3 yo rec 14lb

624 **ARAB GOLD 2** [6] M Quinn 5-8-6 (36) Martin Dwyer 5/1: 003031: 5 b g Presidium - Parklands Belle **40a**
(Stanford) Chsd ldrs, hard rdn ins last to lead line, all out: op 10/1, quick reapp: unplcd in '99 (rtd 43a & 31,
tried at 10f): no form for Miss S Hall in '98: eff at 6f on equitrack: best without a visor: 1st success today.
573 **WISHBONE ALLEY 10** [8] M Dods 5-9-6 (50)(vis) A Clark 5/1: 132042: 5 b g Common Grounds - Dul Dul *shd* **53a**

LINGFIELD (Equitrack)   SATURDAY MARCH 4TH   Lefthand, V Sharp Track

(Shadeed) Handy, rdn/led ins last, just hdd line: op 6/1: see 312 (5f).

547	**DOLPHINELLE 14** [2] R Hannon 4-9-10 (54) P Dobbs (5) 2/1 FAV: 045443: 4 b c Dolphin Street - Mamie's Joy (Prince Tenderfoot) Outpcd twds rear, kept on fnl 2f under hands & heels riding, nrst fin: well bckd: see 263.	1	55a
*564	**NINEACRES 11** [3] J M Bradley 9-9-12 (56)(bl) Claire Bryan (7) 3/1: 322614: Led 5f, no extra: op 9/4.	hd	56a
436	**FEATHERSTONE LANE 32** [7] 9-9-1 (45) N Callan 11/1: 0-4425: Chsd ldrs wide, nvr pace to chall: op 8/1.	¾	43a
571	**ROWLANDSONS STUD 10** [4] 7-8-0 (30)(t) A McCarthy (3) 20/1: 0-6036: Chsd ldrs, held over 1f out.	½	26a
602	**FACILE TIGRE 5** [1] 5-8-13 (43) P Doe 11/1: -06007: Rear, nvr on terms: op 7/1, qck reapp: btr 146.	½	37a
3491	**MAGIC BABE 99** [5] 3-8-11 (55) O Urbina 20/1: 0000-8: Al twds rear: 7 mth abs: AW bow: unplcd	¾	47a

in '99 for D Elsworth (rtd 64, mdn): eff at 6f, tried 7f: handles gd grnd & a sharp/undul trk: now with J Poulton.

8 ran   Time 1m 12.72 (2.32)   (W Trezise)   M Quinn Sparsholt, Oxon

WOLVERHAMPTON (Fibresand)   SATURDAY MARCH 4TH   Lefthand, Sharp Track

Official Going   STANDARD. Stalls: 7f - Outside, Rem - Inside.

635   7.00 BRINDLEY MDN HCAP 3YO+ 0-60 (F)   7f aw rnd   Going 29 -14 Slow   [55]
£2341 £669 £334

503	**BEGUILE 21** [1] R Ingram 6-9-7 (48) J P Spencer 2/1 FAV: 60-241: 6 b g Most Welcome - Captivate		52a
(Mansingh) Prom, led over 1f out, styd on well, all out: nicely bckd: unplcd in '99 for B Johnson: plcd prev term (h'caps, rtd 49a): eff at 7f/1m: acts on both AWs & has run well fresh: likes a sharp track.			
411	**PUPPET PLAY 37** [11] E J Alston 5-9-6 (47) S Drowne 5/1: 2-3342: 5 ch m Broken Hearted - Fantoccini	nk	50a
(Taufan) Prom, hard rdn/chall ins last, just held: shown enough to win similar: see 293, 133.			
614	**MOY 4** [2] W M Brisbourne 5-9-3 (44)(bl) J Weaver 6/1: -26053: 5 ch m Beveled - Exceptional	1	45a
Beauty (Sallust) Led 6f, kept on onepace: tchd 8/1, qck reapp: see 466.			
2766	**MANIKATO 99** [12] R M Beckett 6-8-10 (37) M Tebbutt 16/1: 0600-4: Held up in tch, eff 3f out, hung	3½	32a
left/held fnl 1f: op 12/1: 8 month abs: unplcd in '99 (rtd 36a & 34, D Cosgrove & T T Clement): plcd in '98 (mdn, rtd 57a): eff at 7f/1m, poss stays 12f: acts on fast & gd/soft grnd, prob handles both AWs: prob best without a vis.			
4593	**KESTRAL 99** [3] 4-9-0 (41) R Winston 20/1: 0000-5: Chsd ldrs, held fnl 2f: 4 month abs: unplcd in	½	35a
'99 (rtd 55, h'cap, no sand form): unplcd in '98 (rtd 62): eff at 6f/7f: handles fast grnd & a sharp or stiff trk.			
585	**STATE WIND 8** [6] 4-9-3 (44)(vis) F Norton 16/1: 600-06: Hmpd start/bhd, mod gains: plcd form in	nk	38a
'99 (rtd 54a, C/D h'cap, unplcd on turf, rtd 37, N P Littmoden): rtd 56 & 55a at best in '98: eff at 7f, has tried 9f: acts on fibresand: has run well in blnks/visor: now with D Shaw.			
4581	**LV GIRL 99** [9] 4-9-10 (51) L Newman (5) 12/1: 0040-7: Twds rear, mod gains: 6 wk jmps abs, op 8/1.	nk	44a
558	**COLONEL SAM 12** [4] 4-9-6 (47)(bl) S Finnamore (7) 12/1: 000-08: Sltly hmpd start, prom 5f: tchd 14/1.	6	31a
529	**RIBBLE PRINCESS 16** [8] 5-9-3 (44)(vis) A Culhane 25/1: 0-0009: Mid-div at best: see 469, 344.	½	27a
578	**ANNELIINA 9** [5] 4-9-4 (45) R Morse 16/1: 50-000: Hmpd start, al bhd: 10m abs: op 12/1: see 409.	hd	28a
476	**HUNAN SCHOLAR 26** [7] 5-9-0 (41) P McCabe 4/1: 500-00: Chsd ldrs, btn 2f out: 11th: bckd, op 8/1.	¾	23a
582	**TECHNICIAN 9** [10] 5-9-9 (50) L Swift (7) 10/1: 030-00: Al bhd: 12th: op 8/1: see 582 (C/D).	½	31a

12 ran   Time 1m 29.2 (3.0)   (D G Wheatley)   R Ingram Epsom, Surrey.

636   7.30 CLASSIFIED STKS 3YO 0-60 (E)   1m100y aw rnd   Going 29 00 Slow
£2236 £639 £319

450	**LUCKY STAR 30** [3] D Marks 3-8-11 J Fortune 6/1: 66-131: 3 b f Emarati - Child Star (Bellypha)		62a
Led, held on well ins last, rdn out: op 5/1: earlier scored at Lingfield (fill h'cap): unplcd in '99 (rtd 62, nov stks): eff at 7f/8.5f: acts on both AWs: likes a sharp trk: eff forcing the pace: in gd form.			
311	**FOR HEAVENS SAKE 53** [4] C W Thornton 3-8-12 Dean McKeown 6/1: 66-432: 3 b c Rambo Dancer -	¾	61a
Angel Fire (Nashwan) Chsd wnr, hard rdn/kept on fnl 1f, al held: op 5/1, 8 wk abs: see 311, 257.			
555	**CARDINAL FAIR 12** [9] B P J Baugh 3-8-9 R Lappin 33/1: 5-4003: 3 b f Namaqualand - Irish Affaire	4	51$
(Fairy King) Rear, kept on fnl 2f, no threat: stays 8.5f & handles fibresand: mod form prev, has tried blnks.			
*597	**PEDRO PETE 7** [8] M R Channon 3-9-0 A Daly 4/6 FAV: 00-414: Prom, rdn/outpcd over 2f out, kept on	1¾	53a
ins last: well bckd at odds on: btr 597 (10f, equitrack).			
567	**RIDGECREST 11** [2] 3-8-12 S Drowne 12/1: 42-545: Chsd ldrs, held fnl 3f: op 10/1: see 236, 150 (sell).	1½	49a
3928	**CHILI PEPPER 99** [6] 3-8-9 R Fitzpatrick (3) 25/1: 4450-6: Held up in tch wide, btn 2f out: op 14/1.	5	39a
6 month abs: AW bow: rnr-up in '99 (debut, rtd 63, seller): eff at 5f, handles fast & gd/soft grnd: tried blnks.			
*541	**NORTHERN TIMES 15** [7] 3-9-0 S Finnamore (7) 7/1: 0-517: Dwelt/al rear: now with R Brotherton.	1	42a
4425	**ROMANECH 99** [1] 3-8-12 (VIS) F Norton 25/1: 0500-8: Al bhd: visor: AW bow: 4 mth abs: unplcd in	3	35a
'99 (rtd 61, auct mdn): eff at 6f & handles gd/soft grnd.			
4389	**PTAH 99** [5] 3-8-12 A Culhane 25/1: 5000-9: Bhd halfway: op 14/1, 5 month abs: AW bow: unplcd	16	15a
in '99 (rtd 69, debut, auct mdn): with J L Eyre.			

9 ran   Time 1m 48.7 (2.5)   (D Marks)   D Marks Lambourn, Berks.

637   8.00 0800 211222 HCAP 3YO+ 0-75 (E)   1m1f79y aw   Going 29 +05 Fast   [67]
£2834 £872 £436 £218

*516	**TYLERS TOAST 18** [4] S Dow 4-10-0 (67) P Doe 7/2: 0-2111: 4 ch g Grand Lodge - Catawba (Mill		72a
Reef) Chsd ldrs, prog to lead over 2f out, rdn & edged left 1f out, styd on well, rdn out: gd time: earlier won here at W'hampton (2, mdn & h'cap): unplcd in '99 (rtd 80$, mdn, W Jarvis): rtd 78 in '98: eff at 9.4f, 10f+ shld suit: fibresand/W'hampton specialist: gd weight carrier: shld win more races.			
568	**BREAD WINNER 11** [3] I A Balding 4-9-3 (56)(vis) K Darley 11/4 FAV: 05-422: 4 b g Reprimand - Khubza	¾	59a
(Green Desert) Prom, led over 4f out till over 2f out, ev ch ins last, no extra: nicely bckd, op 7/2: see 568, 504.			
611	**DARE 4** [6] P D Evans 5-9-9 (62)(bl) S Drowne 10/1: 220003: 5 b g Beveled - Run Amber Run (Run	nk	64a
The Gantlet) Rear, styd on well fnl 2f, nrst fin: qck reapp: signs of a return to form here: see 83 (visor).			
569	**GABLESEA 11** [8] B P J Baugh 6-9-4 (46) J Bosley (7) 5/1: 00-024: Hmpd/lost pl after 3f, mod late gains.	3	43a
569	**LAA JADEED 11** [9] 5-7-10 (35) Joanna Badger (7) 20/1: 30-005: Chsd ldrs 7f: see 476 (7f).	1½	29a
553	**HEATHYARDS JAKE 14** [5] 4-8-12 (51) P M Quinn 25/1: 454006: Rear, mod prog: see 229 (8.5f, mdn).	2	42a
569	**MYSTERIUM 11** [12] 6-8-13 (50) C Cogan (5) 4/1: -21247: Wide/nvr factor: op 5/1: btr 469.	shd	43a
611	**RIVER ENSIGN 4** [2] 7-8-11 (50) Claire Bryan (7) 9/1: 004168: Led 5f, sn btn: op 7/1, qck reapp.	6	32a
--	**TURN TO STONE** [10] 6-7-10 (35)(3oh) K Dalgleish (7) 20/1: 0/00-9: Bhd halfway: 7 wk jumps abs	1½	14a
(mod form): last rcd in Britain in '98 (unplcd, rtd 36, h'cap, J Neville): has tried a visor prev: AW bow tonight.			

WOLVERHAMPTON (Fibresand) SATURDAY MARCH 4TH Lefthand, Sharp Track

400	**BAAJIL 38** [7] 5-9-1 (54) J Fortune 16/1: 46-000: Held up, btn 3f out: 10th: op 14/1: btr 3 (eqtrk).	11	18a
430	**DIM OFAN 33** [11] 4-9-11 (64) D Sweeney 14/1: -41060: Mid-div, bhd 3f out: 11th: op 12/1: btr 326.	8	18a

11 ran   Time 2m 00.4 (2.2)   (Byerley Bloodstock)   S Dow Epsom, Surrey.

---

638   8.30 S.J. DIXON HCAP 3YO 0-70 (E)   6f aw rnd Going 29 -01 Slow   [74]
£2717   £836   £418   £209

526	**PADDYWACK 17** [7] D W Chapman 3-7-10 (42)(bl) Claire Bryan (7) 11/4: -05241: 3 b g Bigstone - Millie's Return (Ballad Rock) Led after 1f, clr dist, eased nr fin: nicely bckd tho' op 9/4: '99 Redcar wnr (nurs h'cap, rtd 59): eff at 6f on firm, gd/soft & both AWs: suited by forcing tactics: win more races.	49a
*549	**DIAMOND RACHAEL 14** [2] Mrs N Macauley 3-9-4 (64)(vis) R Fitzpatrick (3) 11/4: 34-012: 3 b f Shalford - Brown Foam (Horage) Chsd ldrs, kept on fnl 1f, no threat: met an imprvd rival here: see 549 (C/D clmr). ¾ 65a
*515	**BAYTOWN RHAPSODY 19** [6] P S McEntee 3-9-2 (62) J Weaver 15/8 FAV: 321313: 3 b f Emperor Jones - Sing A Rainbow (Rainbow Quest) Led 1f, chsd wnr 5f, sn held: see 515. -3 57a
534	**BILLYS BLUNDER 16** [3] P D Evans 3-8-6 (52)(t) S Drowne 11/1: 0-3204: Chsd ldrs, outpcd fnl 2f: op 8/1. 5 36a
31	**RAINWORTH LADY 99** [1] 3-8-3 (49) Martin Dwyer 25/1: 0400-5: Sn rdn, bhd halfway: unplcd in '99 (rtd 66, 4 rnr mdn, flattered). 2½ 27a
4476}	**SHAW VENTURE 99** [4] 3-9-7 (67) D Sweeney 25/1: 6060-6: Chsd ldrs 3f: 5 month abs/AW bow: '99 Windsor scorer (auct mdn, rtd 81, subs disapp in blnks): eff at 5f: acts on fast grnd & enjoys a sharp trk. 5 35a
416	**MYTTONS AGAIN 36** [5] 3-9-7 (67) J Fortune 8/1: 260-47: Sn outpcd: btr 416, 158. 2½ 31a

7 ran   Time 1m 14.6 (1.8)   (J B Wilcox)   D W Chapman Stillington, N.Yorks.

---

639   9.00 BEST BETS SELLER 4YO+ (G)   5f aw rnd Going 29 -05 Slow
£1877   £536   £268

533	**YOUNG IBNR 16** [9] B A McMahon 5-8-11 L Newman (5) 14/1: -05601: 5 b g Imperial Frontier - Zalatia (Music Boy) Made all, styd on well fnl 1f, drvn out: op 8/1, no bid: plcd in '99 (rtd 49a, C/D h'cap): rnr-up twice in '98 (clmr, P Evans, rtd 68a & 67): eff at 5f, tried 6f: acts on firm, soft & fibresand: best without blnks/visor. 49a
445	**LEGAL VENTURE 30** [2] Julian Poulton 4-8-11 (bl) A Daly 10/1: 003402: 4 ch g Case Law - We Two (Glenstal) Chsd wnr, kept on for press, not able to chall: op 8/1: prev with N Littmoden: see 440, 291. ½ 47a
533	**NIFTY NORMAN 16** [4] D Nicholls 6-9-3 (61) O Pears 5/2: 132363: 6 b g Rock City - Nifty Fifty (Runnett) Prom, onepace over 1f out, op 2/1: see 440, 272 (C/D clmr). ¾ 51a
563	**TINKERS SURPRISE 11** [7] J Balding 6-8-11 (bl) C Carver (2) 10/1: 536564: Dwelt, mod late gains. 2 40a
425	**AVONDALE GIRL 33** [5] 4-8-6 F Lynch 11/2: 0-0005: Chsd ldrs 3f: op 12/1: see 214. shd 35a
406	**TANGERINE FLYER 37** [1] 5-8-11 S Drowne 25/1: 000/06: Al outpcd: see 406. 3 32a
--	**ARJAN** [3] 5-8-6 A Culhane 8/1: 0000/7: Chsd ldrs 3f: long abs/AW bow: missed last term: '98 Catterick scorer (h'cap, J Berry, rtd 85 at best): eff forcing the pace over a sharp/turning 5f: acts on gd, enjoys gd/soft & soft grnd: likes Catterick: pacey type, may prove sharper next time for J L Eyre. nk 26a
379	**CELTIC SEAL 42** [6] 4-8-6 (BL) J Edmunds 12/1: 00-508: Sn outpcd: op 10/1, blnks, abs: see 272 (C/D). ½ 25a
2784}	**SAMMAL 99** [8] 4-8-11 (BL) J Fortune 2/1 FAV: 6043-9: Sn rdn, al outpcd: hvly bckd, blnks: 8 month abs: AW bow: plcd in '99 (rtd 56, sell h'cap): '98 Carlisle wnr (mdn, rtd 87 at best): eff at 5f, tried 6f: acts on firm & gd/soft grnd: likes to force the pace on a stiff/gall trk, best without a visor. 2½ 25a

9 ran   Time 1m 01.9 (1.7)   (Roy Penton)   B A McMahon Hopwas, Staffs.

---

640   9.30 PAUL BOOKER HCAP 3YO 0-75 (E)   1m4f aw Going 29 -09 Slow   [76]
£2613   £746   £373

*537	**CHIEF OF JUSTICE 15** [3] D Shaw 3-9-1 (63) J P Spencer 7/4: 000-11: 3 b c Be My Chief - Clare Court (Glint Of Gold) Handy, led 4f out & clr dist, styd on strongly, readily: op 5/2: recent Southwell wnr (h'cap): unplcd on turf in '99 (rtd 61, mdn): eff at 11/12f on fibresand & a sharp trk: has run well fresh: win again. 72a
*586	**MERRYVALE MAN 8** [2] J G Given 3-9-7 (69) R Winston 7/2: -05312: 3 b c Rudimentary - Salu (Ardross) Held up, rdn & kept on fnl 2f, no threat to wnr: op 3/1: this longer 12f trip will suit: see 586 (11f, clmr). 6 69a
*565	**SPANISH STAR 11** [1] W Jarvis 3-9-5 (67) Martin Dwyer 4/1 FAV: 43-513: 3 b g Hernando - Desert Girl (Green Desert) Held up in tch, eff 3f out, sn rdn/held: op 5/4: h'cap debut: see 565 (C/D mdn). 5 60a
537	**INDIANA SPRINGS 15** [4] N P Littmoden 3-7-10 (44)(vis)(9oh) P M Quinn (5) 16/1: 0-0054: Bhd 5f out. 7 28a
586	**TOWER OF SONG 8** [5] 3-9-4 (66) A Culhane 10/1: -54235: Led 1m, sn btn: op 5/1: see 36 (1m, seller). 6 42a

5 ran   Time 2m 38.2 (4.6)   (J C Fretwell)   D Shaw Averham, Notts.

SOUTHWELL (Fibresand)   MONDAY MARCH 6TH Lefthand, Sharp, Oval Track

Official Going STANDARD: Stalls: Inside.

---

641   1.40 P372 HCAP DIV I 3YO+ 0-65 (F)   1m4f aw Going 40 -05 Slow   [65]
£1960   £560   £280   3 yo rec 23lb4 yo rec 2 lb

*554	**ICHI BEAU 16** [4] F Murphy 6-8-12 (47) A Daly 6/1: 03-411: 6 b g Convinced - May As Well (Kemai) Made all, rdn fnl 2f, styd on well, rdn out: op 4/1: recent W'hampton wnr (h'cap): rtd 71h over timber this winter: ex-Irish, plcd in '99 (h'cap): eff at 10/12f on fibresand & soft: likes to force the pace: improving. 53a
227	**TEMPRAMENTAL 70** [2] S R Bowring 4-8-3 (40) Dale Gibson 20/1: 5530-2: 4 ch f Midhish - Musical Horn (Music Boy) Trkd wnr, rdn/rn fnl 2f, kept on, held in last: abs: prev with D Haydn Jones: styd longer 12f trip. 2½ 42a
611	**RIVERBLUE 6** [9] D J Wintle 4-10-0 (65) M Tebbutt 7/1: 005153: 4 b c Bluebird - La Riveraine (Riverman) Held up in tch, eff over 2f out, sn onepace: op 5/1, qck reappr: styd longer 12f trip: see 568 (9.3f). 1¾ 65a
*590	**URGENT SWIFT 10** [8] A P Jarvis 7-9-10 (63) W Ryan 11/4 FAV: 23-514: 7 b h, eff wide 4f out/sn held. ½ 62a
590	**ABSOLUTE MAJORITY 10** [7] 5-9-2 (51) S Whitworth 12/1: -25135: Mid-div/keen, btn 2f out: see 344. 2 47a
560	**THE LAMBTON WORM 14** [10] 6-7-13 (34) Martin Dwyer 12/1: 556-46: Mid-div, btn 2f out: op 10/1. 3 26a
4438}	**BEST PORT 99** [5] 4-7-12 (35)(2ow)(13oh) N Carlisle 40/1: 6006-7: Chsd ldrs 9f: 5 mth abs: unplcd in '99 (rtd 42 & 5a): no form for M Jarvis in '98. ½ 26$
318	**MANFUL 53** [1] 8-7-12 (32)(vis) F Norton 12/1: 00-108: Rear/in tch, btn 4f out: op 8/1, 8 wk abs. 5 17a
605	**ROOFTOP 7** [3] 4-9-9 (60) R Cochrane 4/1: 00-659: Chsd ldrs 10f: op 9/2: see 453 (1m). 6 35a
215	**AJDAR 76** [6] 9-8-2 (37) K Dalgleish (7) 50/1: 0000-0: Held up, bhd 5f out: 10th: 11 wk abs: unplcd. 4 6a

203

SOUTHWELL (Fibresand)   MONDAY MARCH 6TH   Lefthand, Sharp, Oval Track

in '99 (rtd 43a & 21): '98 Southwell wnr (C/D h'cap, rtd 57a at best, plcd on turf, rtd 47): eff at 11/12f on fibresand,
firm & gd/soft grnd: likes Southwell.
10 ran   Time 2m 39.7 (5.4)   (Mrs Fiona Butterly)   F Murphy West Witton, N.Yorks.

642   2.10 P372 HCAP DIV II 3YO+ 0-65 (F)   1m4f aw   Going 40 -13 Slow   [65]
£1949   £557   £278   3 yo rec 23lb4 yo rec 2 lb

561	ACCYSTAN 14 [4] M D Hammond 5-9-1 (50) J Weaver 9/2: -06201: 5 ch g Efisio - Amia (Nijinsky) Chsd ldrs, led over 2f out, styd on strongly ins last, pushed out cl-home: '99 wnr here at Southwell (seller, rtd 68a, unplcd on turf, rtd 32): Nov '98 Catterick jumps wnr (rtd 83h): '98 W'hampton (clmr) & Southwell wnr (h'cap, P Haslam, rtd 68a & 67): eff at 10/12f on fibresand, gd & gd/soft: likes Southwell: on a fair mark, can win again.				56a
*561	MALWINA 14 [4] M G Quinlan 4-8-7 (44) J Fanning 2/1 FAV: -00512: 4 ch f Greinton - Micky's Pleasure (Foolish Pleasure) Held up in tch, prog & rdn/chsd wnr over 1f out, kept on onepace: op 6/4: eff at 11/12f.	1¾	46a
605	WESTERN COMMAND 7 [2] Mrs N Macauley 4-10-0 (65) R Fitzpatrick (3) 11/1: 621603: 4 b g Saddlers' Hall - Western Friend (Gone West) Chsd ldrs, led over 4f out till over 2f out, sn onepace: op 8/1: see 560 (11f).	2½	63a
601	SEPTEMBER HARVEST 7 [6] Mrs S Lamyman 4-8-8 (45) R Mullen 10/1: 00-644: Twds rear, rdn halfway, mod gains fnl 3f: op 12/1: see 261.	4	37a
522	BOBONA 20 [10] 4-7-10 (33) (7oh) G Baker (7) 16/1: 1-0265: Rdn/rear, eff wide/ch over 2f out, no extra.	9	15a
605	STATE APPROVAL 7 [3] 7-9-4 (53) Claire Bryan (7) 9/4: 002336: Led 1m, sn btn: op 11/4: see 512, 270.	3	31a
584	MOLLYTIME 10 [5] 4-7-11 (34) (10w) (17oh) J Bramhill 66/1: 500-07: Handy, btn 3f out: see 584 (1m).	7	2a
496	WINSTON 24 [7] 7-7-11 (32) K Dalgleish (7) 33/1: 0/6-08: Held up in tch, rdn/btn 3f out: see 496 (1m).	14	0a
470	NOSEY NATIVE 28 [1] 7-8-2 (37) A Polli (3) 33/1: 000-09: Rdn/rear, nvr factor: see 470 (2m).	7	0a
483}	PICKENS 99 [8] 8-9-11 (60) Kim Tinkler 25/1: 6014-0: Keen/cl-up 7f, sn btn: 10th: 13 month abs:	3	0a

'99 scorer here at Southwell (seller, rtd 64a): '98 wnr here at Southwell (4, sell/h'caps, rtd 71a): '97 Redcar wnr
(clmr, rtd 62): eff at 11/12f, stays 14f: acts on firm & gd/soft, fibresand specialist & relishes sell grade.
10 ran   Time 2m 40.6 (6.3)   (G Heap)   M D Hammond Coverham, N.Yorks.

643   2.40 0800 211222 MDN 3YO+ (D)   1m4f aw   Going 40 +02 Fast
£2886   £888   £444   £222   3 yo rec 23lb4 yo rec 2 lb

578	SAGAPONACK 11 [10] J R Fanshawe 4-9-10 R Cochrane 11/1: 51: 4 b g Broad Brush - Sharp Dance (Dancing Czar) Trkd ldrs, smooth prog to lead 3f out & sn clr, in command fnl 1f, eased nr fin: gd time: relished step up to 12f, further could suit: acts on fibresand & a sharp trk: gd weight carrier: op to further improvement.				74a
603	LE CAVALIER 7 [11] C N Allen 3-8-3 L Newman (5) 7/2: 002222: 3 b g Mister Baileys - Secret Deed (Shadeed) Led 9f, rdn/held fnl 2f & position accepted nr fin: clr rem: op 9/4: caught a tartar: see 565, 240.	11	62a
523	DANCING MARY 19 [7] B Smart 3-7-12 F Norton 20/1: 50-303: 3 gr f Sri Pekan - Fontenoy (Lyphard's Wish) Towards rear, rdn halfway, mod gains fnl 2f, no threat: longer 12f trip, needs h'caps: see 520.	6	48a
610	TUFTY HOPPER 6 [2] P Howling 3-8-3 R Winston 25/1: 0-64: Rdn/bhd, late gains, nrst fin: qck reapp: unplcd sole '99 start (rtd 70, mdn): 14f + & h'cap company shld suit on this evidence.	1¼	51a
565	STICIBOOTS 13 [12] 3-8-3 A Daly 20/1: 55: Mid-div, outpcd 4f out, see 565.	1¼	49a
2193}	THE FLYER 99 [8] 3-8-4 (1ow) D Sweeney 4/7 FAV: 6-6: Dwelt, rdn to chase ldrs after 1f, rdn/btn 3f out: hvly bckd at odds on: 8 month abs/AW bow: unplcd sole '99 start (rtd 74, auct mdn): shld apprec mid-dists.	shd	50a
603	MI ODDS 7 [4] 4-9-10 R Fitzpatrick (3) 16/1: 37: Chsd ldrs, keen, btn 4f out: op 14/1: btr 603 (debut).	5	42a
578	DARK VICTOR 11 [6] 4-9-10 N Callan 25/1: 48: Mid-div, btn 3f out: btr 578 (9f).	6	33a
565	DION DEE 13 [9] 4-9-5 S Drowne 14/1: 0-0099: Cl-up 9f: op 14/1: flattest 565.	5	21a
519	THE FOSSICK 20 [1] 4-9-10 P Hanagan (7) 33/1: 5-60: Dwelt, al bhd: 10th: mod form.	30	0a

4039} High Beauty 99 [5] 3-7-12 M Baird 25/1:   3090} Grey Bird 99 [3] 3-7-12 P Fessey 33/1:
12 ran   Time 2m 38.9 (4.6)   (Joseph Allen)   J R Fanshawe Newmarket.

644   3.10 BEST BETS HCAP 4YO+ 0-60 (F)   2m aw   Going 40 -66 Slow   [60]
£2394   £684   £342   4 yo rec 5 lb

*576	HETRA HEIGHTS 11 [16] W J Musson 5-8-12 (44) L Newton 9/1: 05-611: 5 b m Cox's Ridge - Top Hope (High Top) Settled towards rear, prog/chsd ldrs wide halfway, smooth prog to lead over 1f out, shkn up to assert ins last, pushed out cl-home: op 7/1: recent W'hampton (h'cap): unplcd in '99 (rtd 29, subs had a wind op): '98 rnr-up (h'cap, rtd 51): eff at 12f, now suited by a sharp 2m: acts on fast & fibresand: in fine form.				50a
593	SPOSA 13 [13] M J Polglase 4-9-0 R Fitzpatrick (3) 11/1: 1-5302: 4 b f St Jovite - Barelyabride (Blushing Groom) Handy halfway, rdn/led over 2f out till over 1f out, held by wnr ins last: clr rem, stays 2m.	2½	62a
576	ST LAWRENCE 11 [6] B S Rothwell 6-9-4 (50) M Fenton 4/1: 1D2133: 6 gr g With Approval - Mingan Isle (Lord Avie) Mid-div, rdn/outpcd 5f out, kept on fnl 2f, no threat to front rapr: op 5/2: tough, see 576.	6	46a
577	QUAKERESS 11 [11] R Brotherton 5-7-10 (28) F Norton 12/1: 041134: Towards rear, mod late gains.	4	20a
348	TIME CAN TELL 48 [2] 6-8-11 (43) P Doe 33/1: 450-55: Mid-div, outpcd fnl 4f: 7 wk abs: see 66.	1	34a
*502	KENT 24 [1] 5-9-7 (53) Martin Dwyer 11/4 FAV: 5-1216: Trkd ldrs, btn 4f out: btr 502 (C/D).	8	36a
577	ONEFOURSEVEN 11 [8] 7-8-13 (45) I Mongan (5) 33/1: 04/007: Handy, hard rdn halfway, btn 3f out.	3	25a
--	PRIMATICCIO 10 [5] 5-9-5 (51)(VIS) N Callan 25/1: 16615/8: Handy, led over 6f out till over 2f out, wknd qckly: tried a visor: 9 month jumps abs (4th in a Cork mdn hdle, 2m1f): missed '99 on the level: '99 wnr at Folkestone & here at Southwell (h'caps, rtd 55a & 52, Sir M Prescott): eff around 14/15f: acts on fast & fibresand & likes a sharp/undul trk: likes to race with/force the pace: has run well fresh: suited by blnks.	2½	29a
607	OUR PEOPLE 6 [5] 6-8-7 (39)(t) K Dalgleish (7) 11/2: 313229: Trkd ldrs halfway, btn 2f out: op 8/1.	1¾	15a
527	COLERIDGE 11 [15] 12-8-3 (35)(bl) A Nicholls (3) 33/1: 00-000: Rear, nvr factor: 10th: see 502.	1	10a
*535	OUTPLACEMENT 17 [3] 5-7-12 (30) Dale Gibson 10/1: 65/010: Led 10f, sn bhd: 12th: btr 535 (C/D).		0a

494 Grooms Gold 25 [14] 8-8-0 (32)(VIS) A Polli 14/1: 599 Mutabari 7 [7] 6-9-4 (50) J Fortune 16/1:
-- Kippanour [4] 8-8-8 (40)(bl) Claire Bryan (7) 33/1:
14 ran   Time 3m 43.0 (17.0)   (K L West)   W J Musson Newmarket.

645   3.40 TEXT P368 HCAP 3YO+ 0-80 (D)   6f aw rnd   Going 40 +08 Fast   [78]
£4348   £1338   £669   £334   3 yo rec 14lb

579	BLUE KITE 11 [10] N P Littmoden 5-10-0 (78) J Weaver 14/1: 603451: 5 ch g Silver Kite - Gold And Blue (Bluebird) Chsd ldrs wide, rdn/led & edged left over 1f out, styd on strongly, rdn out: fast time: op 12/1: earlier scored at W'hampton (h'cap): '99 wnr at W'hampton & Southwell h'caps, rtd 75a & 65): plcd in '98 (rtd 78 & 78a): suited by 6f, stays 7f on fast & soft, loves fibresand: vest without headgear: gd weight carrier: tough.				85a

204

SOUTHWELL (Fibresand) MONDAY MARCH 6TH Lefthand, Sharp, Oval Track

587 **JAMES DEE** 10 [2] A P Jarvis 4-10-0 (78) W Ryan 4/1 JT FAV: 01-022: 4 b g Shalford - Glendale Joy 1½ 80a
(Glenstal) Chsd ldrs, rdn to chall & ev ch fnl 1f, not pace of wnr: op 5/1, top-weight: can find similar.
462 **FOREIGN EDITOR** 30 [5] R A Fahey 4-9-12 (76) P Hanagan (7) 4/1 JT FAV: 2D1133: 4 ch g Magic shd 78a
Ring - True Precision (Presidium) Chsd ldrs, rdn/ch over 1f out, kept on onepace: see 423 (made all, 7f, a/w).
532 **MALLIA** 18 [11] T D Barron 7-9-4 (68) C Lowther 16/1: 055164: Bhd/wide, late gains, nrst fin: op 14/1. 3 63a
*622 **TELECASTER** 4 [13] 4-9-5 (69)(bl) (6ex) D Sweeney 5/1: 112115: Led/dsptd lead till over 1f out, 2½ 57a
no extra: op 3/1, qck reapp & a 6lb pen: not disgraced from a tricky high draw: been in fine form: see 622.
4413} **CAUTION** 99 [7] 6-9-3 (67) J Fortune 16/1: 2305-6: Rdn/towards rear, eff/hung left over 1f out, no ½ 53a
threat: 5 month abs: rnr-up twice in '99 (rtd 70, h'cap): landed fnl '98 start at Redcar (stks, rtd 68): eff at 5/7.5f
on fast & hvy grnd: best without blnks: can start v slowly: AW bow today.
*558 **TEYAAR** 14 [6] 4-9-6 (70) N Callan 11/1: 03-517: Mid-div/wide, btn 2f out: op 14/1: see 558 (C/D, mdn). 1½ 52a
539 **KEEN HANDS** 17 [15] 4-10-0 (78)(vis) R Fitzpatrick (3) 16/1: 041058: Mid-div/wide, btn 2f out: see 454. hd 59a
557 **DAHLIDYA** 14 [8] 5-8-12 (62) P Doe 16/1: 110159: Dwelt/towards rear, mod gains: btr 538 (C/D clmr). nk 42a
2882} **EURO VENTURE** 99 [14] 5-9-7 (71) F Norton 8/1: 1203-0: Mid-div/wide, btn 2f out: 10th: 8 month nk 50a
abs: '99 wnr here at Southwell (C/D h'cap, rtd 73a), subs scored at Thirsk & Carlisle (h'caps, rtd 79 at best):
'98 W'hampton wnr (mdn, rtd 78a & 59): eff at 6/7f on fast, soft & fibresand: loves to front run & handles any trk.
491 **SOTONIAN** 25 [1] 7-8-13 (63) A Nicholls (3) 20/1: 0-0500: Chsd ldrs, led over 3f out till over 2f out, btn/eased 0a
fnl 1f: 15th: slipping to a handy mark & all wins at 5f: see 394 (5f).
3959} **Arpeggio** 99 [4] 5-9-11 (75) O Pears 16/1: 587 **Nesyred** 10 [3] 4-9-1 (65) P McCabe 33/1:
614 **Grand Estate** 6 [16] 5-8-6 (56) Claire Bryan (7) 20/1: -- **Bodfari Pride** [9] 5-9-9 (73) Clare Roche (7) 16/1:
425 **Young Bigwig** 35 [12] 6-8-12 (62) A Culhane 20/1:
16 ran Time 1m 15.2 (1.9) (T Clarke) N P Littmoden Newmarket.

646

4.10 TEXT P372 SELLER 4YO+ (G) 1m aw rnd Going 40 -21 Slow
£1934 £552 £276

612 **GOLDEN LYRIC** 6 [14] J Pearce 5-8-12 J Weaver 13/2: -04221: 5 ch g Lycius - Adjala (Northfields) 48a
Sn prom wide, rdn/led 2f out, held on well ins last, drvn out: no bid: qck reapp: '99 Southwell wnr (mdn h'cap,
rtd 43a): plcd in '98 (h'caps, rtd 36a & 44, G Wragg): eff at 1m/12f: acts on firm, loves fibresand/Southwell.
600 **WAITING KNIGHT** 7 [13] Mrs N Macauley 5-8-12 (vis) R Fitzpatrick (3) 25/1: 0-4002: 5 b h St Jovite - nk 47a
Phydilla (Lyphard) Chsd ldrs wide, rdn to chall fnl 2f, styd on well, just held: could find similar: see 178.
598 **SWING ALONG** 7 [3] R Guest 5-8-13 R Cochrane 10/11 FAV: 100533: 5 ch m Alhijaz - So It Goes ¾ 47a
(Free State) Trkd ldrs, smooth prog/ev ch fnl 2f, sn rdn/onepace: nicely bckd: see 598, 404 (9f, W'hampton).
585 **PREPOSITION** 10 [4] M A Peill 4-8-12 J Bosley (7) 8/1: /24524: Led 6f, onepace: eff around 1m on 3 40a
fibresand: sell h'caps shld suit: see 585, 340.
600 **INDIAN SWINGER** 7 [6] 4-8-12 R Winston 14/1: 05-005: Dwelt, mod late gains for press: op 12/1. 3½ 33a
556 **SARPEDON** 14 [16] 4-8-12 (bl) Joanna Badger 50/1: 500556: Wide/mid-div, btn 2f out: recent jmps rnr. ¾ 32$
-- **BENTICO** [8] 11-8-12 (vis) Sarah Robinson (7) 33/1: 3046/7: Towards rear, mod gains: stablemate 3 26a
of rnr-up: long abs, missed '99: plcd in '98 (rtd 58, C/D h'cap): '97 Southwell wnr (clmr, C/D, rtd 72a): eff arnd
7f/9f, stays 12f: acts on fast & good for AWs: eff with/without a visor.
585 **FLYING HIGH** 10 [2] 5-8-12 J Fanning 20/1: -64038: Chds ldrs 4f: btr 585, 476. 6 17a
455 **NORTH ARDAR** 31 [11] 10-8-12 F Norton 20/1: 46-509: Dwelt/al bhd: see 178. 1 15a
600 **KINGCHIP BOY** 7 [7] 11-8-12 (bl) K Parkin (7) 16/1: 005600: Cl-up 6f: 10th: op 12/1: see 249. ¾ 14a
452 **GENIUS** 31 [1] 5-8-12 P Doe 10/1: 220040: Mid-div, btn 3f out: 15th: op 8/1: now with A G Jukes. 0a
4451} **Ghutah** 99 [5] 6-8-12 (bl) S Whitworth 50/1: 600 **Wild Rice** 7 [15] 8-8-12 (bl) S Finnamore (7) 14/1:
3631} **Samiyah** 99 [9] 4-8-8(1ow) A Culhane 25/1: 367 **Kings Chambers** 45 [12] 4-8-12 (bl) S Righton 50/1:
604 **Patrinia** 7 [10] 4-8-8(1ow) P McCabe 25/1:
16 ran Time 1m 44.3 (4.9) (Saracen Racing) J Pearce Newmarket.

647

4.40 HCAP DIV I 3YO+ 0-70 (D) 1m aw rnd Going 40 -14 Slow [68]
£2522 £776 £388 £194 3 yo rec 18lb

600 **INTERNAL AFFAIR** 7 [9] T D Barron 5-9-10 (64) Lynsey Hanna (7) 11/1: 141351: 5 b g Nicholas - 67a
Gdynia (Sir Ivor) Towards rear, stdy run wide fnl 2f & led nr fin, rdn out: op 8/1: earlier won thrice at W'hampton
(2 clmrs & a h'cap): '99 W'hampton scorer (auct mdn, rtd 79a): suited by
1m/8.5f, stays 9.5f: acts on soft/hvy, handles fast, fibresand/W'hampton specialist: seems best held up for a late run.
69 **ERUPT** 99 [6] M Brittain 7-7-12 (38) G Bardwell 14/1: 0006-2: 7 b g Beveled - Sparklingsovereign ½ 39a
(Sparkler) Mid-div, rdn/prog 3f out & led 1f out, hard rdn/hdd nr line: nicely bckd, tchd 20/1: 4 month abs:
acts on fast, soft & fibresand: can find similar: see 60.
530 **JIBEREEN** 18 [11] P Howling 8-10-0 (68) R Winston 16/1: 042043: 8 b g Lugana Beach - Fashion Lover 1¼ 66a
(Shiny Tenth) Rdn/prom wide, ev ch fnl 2f, edged left/just held nr fin: op 14/1: topweight: fine run: see 530.
598 **MUTAHADETH** 7 [5] D Shaw 6-9-0 (54)(bl) N Callan 6/1: 560344: Chsd ldrs, rdn/prog to lead 2f out, ¾ 51a
edged left & extra 1f out: see 183.
584 **KOCAL** 10 [4] 4-8-5 (45) Kimberley Hart (5) 14/1: 000-25: Led 6f, onepace: see 584 (C/D mdn h'cap). 5 32a
588 **GENERAL KLAIRE** 10 [14] 5-9-12 (66) P Hanagan (7) 8/1: 3-0136: Mid-div/wide, held fnl 2f: op 6/1. nk 52a
599 **PLEASURE TRICK** 7 [11] 9-8-2 (42) Kim Tinkler 33/1: 00-007: Bhd, late gains, nrst fin: see 496. ½ 27a
*584 **KUSTOM KIT KEVIN** 10 [7] 4-9-5 (59) S Finnamore (7) 13/2: 322018: Chsd ldrs 6f: btr 584 (mdn h'cap). 6 35a
76 **SEVEN SPRINGS** 99 [1] 4-8-0 (40) P M Quinn (5) 20/1: 0000-9: Reared start, nvr factor: 4 month abs: ¾ 15a
unplcd in '99 (rtd 63 & 61, h'caps): '98 W'hampton wnr (auct mdn, rtd 72a, 66 on turf): eff over 6f, stays a sharp 7f:
acts on fibresand, prob handles soft: likes a sharp trk & eff forcing the pace.
583 **BROUGHTON MAGIC** 11 [5] 5-8-3 (43) L Newton 13/2: 0/5100: Handy, ch 2f out, wknd: 10th: op 5/1. hd 17a
599 **ITCH** 7 [8] 5-8-10 (50) Joanna Badger 14/1: 131420: Bhd, sn rdn & no impress: 12th: op 7/2: 0a
connections reported that the horse resented the kick-back: btr 599, 471 (7f).
561 **Flashfeet** 14 [3] 10-7-10 (36)(12oh) G Baker (7) 50/1: *600 **Over The Moon** 7 [12] 6-9-3 (57)(BL) (6ex) P Doe 12/1:
596 **Ellway Prince** 9 [13] 5-8-11 (51) Dean McKeown 12/1:601 **Still Waters** 7 [10] 5-9-3 (57) J Fortune 12/1:
15 ran Time 1m 43.7 (4.3) (Stephen Woodall) T D Barron Maunby, N.Yorks.

648

5.10 HCAP DIV II 3YO+ 0-70 (D) 1m aw rnd Going 40 -05 Slow [68]
£2509 £772 £386 £193 3 yo rec 18lb

497 **GODMERSHAM PARK** 24 [12] P S Felgate 8-8-5 (45) Dean McKeown 7/1: -23441: 8 b g Warrshan - Brown 50a
Velvet (Mansingh) Prom, rdn/chsd ldr halfway, hung left over 1f out, styd on to lead nr line, drvn out: tchd 8/1:
rnr-up in '99 (rtd 71a, h'cap), tried blnks: '98 wnr thrice here at Southwell (h'caps) & once at W'hampton (h'cap,

SOUTHWELL (Fibresand)   MONDAY MARCH 6TH   Lefthand, Sharp, Oval Track

rtd 78a & 57): eff at 7f/1m on fast & gd, loves fibresand/Southwell: best without vis/blnks: nicely h'capped.
583   **CLEAR NIGHT 11** [3] J J Sheehan 4-8-13 (53)(t) P McCabe 100/30 FAV: 02-422: 4 b c Night Shift -   ¾ 57a
Clarista (Riva Ridge) Led after 1f & clr over 2f out, hard rdn/hdd his last: op 3/1, clr rem: deserves similar.
561   **NICE BALANCE 14** [14] M C Chapman 5-8-0 (40) Joanna Badger (7) 15/2: 315653: 5 b g Shadeed -   5 34a
Fellwaati (Alydar) Chsd ldrs, held fnl 2f: see 418 (C/D).
4560}   **INDIUM 99** [11] W J Musson 6-9-12 (66) P Shea (7) 11/2: 4100-4: Towards rear, mod gains: op 7/1,   6 51a
4 month abs: '99 scorer at Ascot (val h'cap, rtd 81): '98 Newmarket scorer (subs disqual) & Newbury (h'caps, rtd
79 & 38a): best at 1m, prob stays 10f: acts on fast & hvy, handles any trk, likes a stiff/gall one: gd weight carrier.
516   **CHAMPAGNE GB 20** [7] 4-9-3 (57) M Henry 25/1: 410-05: Outpcd halfway, mod late gains: see 516 (9f). 1½ 39a
583   **THREE LEADERS 11** [6] 4-8-5 (42)(3ow) S Drowne 12/1: 505-06: Mid-div at best: op 8/1: '99 scorer   5 17a
at Beverley (h'cap, rtd 60, D Nicholls, unplcd on sand, rtd 22a, h'cap): rtd 52 in '98 (mdn): eff at 5/6f, stays a
sharp 7f: acts on fast & soft grnd: handles a stiff/gall or sharp trk: best without blnks: now with E J Alston.
560   **PIPS BRAVE 14** [9] 4-8-11 (51)(bl) R Lappin 5/1: 00-367: Chsd ldr 4f, sn btn: op 4/1: btr 473 (C/D).   nk 22a
473   **IRON MAN 28** [5] 8-8-8 (48) P Fessey 33/1: 12/008: Rdn/al towards rear: see 282.   2½ 14a
4232}   **WATERFRONT 99** [13] 4-8-7 (47) A Daly 20/1: 0000-9: Held up, btn 3f out: 5 month abs: AW bow: 1½ 10a
rnr-up in '99 (rtd 74, mdn, P W Chapple Hyam): rtd 87 on sole '98 start (mdn): eff around 7f on fast grnd.
851}   **LOGANLEA 99** [4] 4-8-6 (46) S Whitworth 50/1: /000-0: Prom 5f: 10th: jumps fit, with M J Polglase.   7 0a
4513}   **TIME TEMPTRESS 99** [2] 4-9-6 (60) J Weaver 11/2: 0506-0: Sn bhd: 11th: nicely bckd: 4 month abs.   4 4a
588   **VICTOIRE 10** [1] 4-9-4 (58) J Stack 25/1: 400-00: Led 1f, sn struggling: 12th: see 588 (7f).   7 0a
4592}   **PILOTS HARBOUR 99** [10] 4-9-1 (55) A Culhane 20/1: 0000-0: Dwelt/al rear: 13th: op 12/1, AW bow.   3 0a
13 ran   Time 1m 43.00 (3.6)   (P S Felgate)   P S Felgate Grimston, Leics.

LINGFIELD (Equitrack)   WEDNESDAY MARCH 8TH   Lefthand, V Sharp Track

Official Going   STANDARD. Stalls: 5f - Outside, Rem- Inside.

649   2.10 BET DIRECT APPR HCAP 4YO+ 0-70 (F)   2m   Going 25 -02 Slow   [60]
£2173   £621   £310   4 yo rec 5 lb

*627   **MAKNAAS 6** [6] T G Mills 4-10-2 (67)(6ex) P Shea (4) 5/4 FAV: 415111: 4 ch c Wolfhound - White Wash   78a
(Final Straw): Led after 2f & sn clr, styd on strongly fnl 4f, easily: val for 15L+: earlier won here at Lingfield
& W'hampton (2, h'caps): '99 wnr again at W'hampton (h'cap, rtd 52a), plcd on turf (rtd 49, R Armstrong): suited
by front running at 2m: acts on soft, relishes both AWs & a sharp trk: eff with/without blnks: gd weight carrier.
603   **MISCHIEF 9** [9] M Quinn 4-8-2 (39)(VIS) J Mackay (4) 25/1: -05562: 4 ch g Generous - Knight's   11 39a
Baroness (Rainbow Quest): Slowly away, prog/chsd wnr halfway, al held: first time visor: see 348.
577   **BEAUCHAMP MAGIC 13** [8] M D I Usher 5-7-13 (31) G Baker (4) 4/1: 040543: 5 b g Northern Park -   3½ 28a
Beauchamp Buzz (High Top): Chsd ldrs halfway, no impress: op 5/1: see 141.
548   **WILD COLONIAL BOY 18** [3] G P Enright 5-8-10 (42) D McGann (4) 12/1: 000-44: Chsd ldrs 4f out,   4 35a
sn no impress: tchd 14/1: see 548 (C/D).
219   **BIGWIG 77** [5] 7-8-12 (44)(bl) J Bosley 12/1: 1145-5: In tch halfway, btn 3f out: op 8/1, jumps fit.   14 26a
483   **FLORA DREAMBIRD 28** [7] 6-7-10 (28)(13oh) D Kinsella (4) 66/1: -00566: Bhd halfway: jumps fit.   5 5a
301   **KAID 58** [10] 5-8-3 (35) Michael Doyle (6) 10/1: 05-467: Looked reluctant & al bhd: op 7/1: recent   1¾ 10a
jumps rnr-up (rtd 90, nov h'cap): see 277, 194.
483   **COCO GIRL 28** [4] 4-8-5 (42) G Sparkes (4) 12/1: 604-28: In tch 11f: op 8/1: btr 483 (13f, mdn).   21 2a
4074}   **ZOLA 99** [1] 4-8-9 (46) K Dalgleish (4) 9/1: 2210-9: Led 2f, sn chsd wnr till 6f out, sn btn: op 14/1, 5 mth 1½ 5a
abs: '99 wnr at Yarmouth (clmr, first success) & Lingfield (C/D h'cap, rtd 48a & 52): unplcd in '98 (rtd 54): eff
at 11f, should by 2m: acts on firm, fast & equitrack, handles gd/soft & fibresand.
644   **PRIMATICCIO 2** [2] 5-9-5 (51)(vis) M Worrell (4) 16/1: 615/00: In tch halfway, sn btn: 10th: op 12/1.   1½ 9a
10 ran   Time 3m 24.32 (4.32)   (Travel Spot Ltd)   T G Mills Headley, Surrey, Epsom.

650   2.40 0800 211 222 CLAIMER STKS 4YO+ (F)   1m4f aw   Going 25 -23 Slow
£2101   £600   £300   4 yo rec 2 lb

524   **NIGHT CITY 21** [1] K R Burke 9-9-7 N Callan 5/2: 226021: 9 b g Kris - Night Secret (Nijinsky):   66a
Made all, rdn clr 2f out, eased down nr line: val for 10L: '99 scorer at Hamilton, York (clmrs), Brighton (h'cap,
rtd 74) & here at Lingfield (clmr, rtd 82a): '98 Lingfield (4, AW clmrs & h'cap & turf h'cap), Hamilton (2), Thirsk,
Catterick, Brighton & York (h'cap/clmrs, rtd 80 & 86a): eff at 1m/13f on any grnd/trk, loves Lingfield.
626   **BILLICHANG 6** [2] P Howling 4-8-11 R Winston 11/1: 333442: 4 b c Chilibang - Swing O' The Kilt   8 47a
(Hotfoot): Chsd wnr, rdn/ch 4f out, sn outpcd: qck reapp: see 517, 238 (10f).
572   **FAILED TO HIT 14** [8] N P Littmoden 7-9-3 (vis) J Tate 7/4 FAV: 320163: 7 b g Warrshan - Missed Again 1¾ 49a
(High Top): Rdn/chsd ldrs 4f out, sn held: well bckd: likes to dominate, unable to do so here: see 530 (fbrsnd).
464   **RONQUISTA DOR 32** [7] G A Ham 6-9-1 S Drowne 25/1: 53-604: Mid-div, mod late gains: see 277 (fbsnd).1¾ 45a
608   **APPYABO 8** [14] 5-8-10 F Norton 33/1: 021365: Mid-div halfway, mod late prog: see 458 (sell h'cap, 13f). shd 40$
612   **El El 8** [12] 5-8-1 Mongan (5) 33/1: -02466: Rdn/chsd ldrs 4f out, no impress: see 404, 224 (9/10f).   1 38$
618   **MALCHIK 7** [5] 4-8-9 P Fessey 33/1: 600207: Chsd ldrs, outpcd from 5f out: see 159 (7f, sell).   hd 39a
621   **THOMAS HENRY 7** [3] 4-8-7 J Bosley (7) 10/1: -00668: Chsd ldrs halfway, btn 3f out: btr 110 (10f, sell).   ½ 36a
457   **RUSHED 32** [6] 5-9-7 A Nicholls (3) 50/1: 000-49: Rear, nvr a factor: see 457.   12 34a
620   **SASEEDO 7** [10] 10-8-5 (bl) G Bardwell 20/1: 0-0040: Slowly away, al rear: 10th: op 12/1: btr 620.   2½ 14a
618   **Ordained 7** [4] 7-8-6 K Dalgleish (7) 20/1:   620 **Shabaash 7** [9] 4-8-8(1ow) D Holland 50/1:
618   **Emperors Gold 7** [13] 5-8-9 G Baker (7) 25/1:   489 **Rawi 27** [11] 7-8-9 (bl) D Sweeney 25/1:
14 ran   Time 2m 35.00 (5.8)   (Nigel Shields)   K R Burke Newmarket, Suffolk.

651   3.10 BEST BETS MDN 3YO+ (D)   7f aw rnd   Going 25 -27 Slow
£2808   £864   £432   £216   3 yo rec 16lb

415   **AIR MAIL 40** [6] J M P Eustace 3-8-7 J Tate 3/1: 21: 3 b g Night Shift - Wizardry (Shirley Heights):   75a
Led, rdn clr 2f out, styd on strongly his last, rdn out: 6 wk abs: apprec drop to 7f, stays a sharp 1m: acts on
equitrack & fibresand: sure to impr: clearly progressing well.
3986}   **WOODWIND DOWN 99** [3] M R Channon 3-8-2 P Fessey 8/1: 00-2: 3 b g Piccolo - Bint El Oumara   3½ 62a
(Al Nasr): Rear/in tch, kept on final 2f, no threat to wnr: tchd 10/1, 6 mth abs/AW bow: unplcd in '99 (rtd
59, debut): stays 7f, 1m+ should suit: handles equitrack, clr of rem here, could impr & find similar.

615   **CUPIDS DART** 7 [7] P Howling 3-8-7 R Winston 4/1: 523523: 3 ch g Pursuit Of Love - Tisza (Kris):   6   58a
Rdn/chsd wnr over 2f out, sn edged right & no extra: nicely bckd, tchd 9/2: btr 615.

4457} **TRAJAN** 99 [5] A P Jarvis 3-8-7 D Holland 10/11 FAV: 5655-4: Held up in tch wide, rdn/effort over   shd   58a
2f out, sn held: hvly bckd: 5 mth abs/AW bow: rnr-up twice in '99 (rtd 87 at best, Gr 2 Gimcrack Stks): eff
at 6f, 7f+ could suit: handles firm, & gd grnd, sharp/undul or stiff/gall trk: h'cap company could suit.

4414} **KATY IVORY** 99 [2] 3-8-2 C Catlin (7) 14/1: 0200-5: Keen/chsd wnr 2f, sn btn: op 10/1, 5 mth abs: 10   38a
AW bow: rnr-up in '99 for P W Harris (h'cap, rtd 70): stays a stiff/undul 1m & handles gd/soft: now with K T Ivory.

1492} **WHITE WATERS** 99 [1] 4-9-9 S Whitworth 50/1: 450-6: Chsd wnr after 2f till over 2f out, wknd/eased   shd   43a
fnl 1f: 4 mth jumps abs (mod form): AW bow: unplcd on turf for C Dwyer in '99 (rtd 55): with Mrs P Townsley.

610   **FOLK DANCE** 8 [4] 3-8-2 G Baker (7) 100/1: 607: Sn outpcd: mod form.   5   28a
7 ran   Time 1m 26.46 (3.66)   (Gary Coull)   J M P Eustace Newmarket

---

652   3.40 TEXT P368 HCAP 3YO 0-85 (D)   5f aw rnd   Going 25   +02 Fast   [90]
£4056   £1248   £624   £312

*507   **LICENCE TO THRILL** 25 [4] D W P Arbuthnot 3-8-8 (70) R Price 11/10 FAV: 025-11: 3 ch f Wolfhound -   78a
Crime Of Passion (Dragonara Palace): Made all, asserted 2f out, styd on strongly under hands & heels fnl 1f: fast
time, hvly bckd: earlier scored here at Lingfield (mdn): rnr-up in '99 (rtd 77a, mdn): eff at 5f, stays 6f well:
acts on equitrack: likes to force the pace on a sharp trk, likes Lingfield: has run well fresh: fine h'cap bow.

*592   **ILLUSIVE** 11 [2] M Wigham 3-9-5 (81)(bl) F Norton 5/2: 1-4112: 3 b c Night Shift - Mirage (Red   1½   83a
Sunset): Rdn/outpcd early, styd on well for press final 2f, nrst fin: bckd: eff at 5f, suited by 6f, can win again.

3963} **LOST IN HOOK** 99 [5] A P Jarvis 3-9-7 (83) D Holland 4/1: 6452-3: 3 b f Dancing Dissident - Rathbawn   1¼   81a
Realm (Doulab): Cl-up, rdn/outpcd & no extra from 2f out: op 7/2, 6 mth abs: AW bow, top weight: '99 debut
wnr at Ripon (fillies auct mdn, rtd 92): eff at 5f, tried 6f: acts on firm, gd & equitrack: has run well fresh.

4529} **JUDIAM** 99 [6] C A Dwyer 3-8-12 (94) L Newman (5) 14/1: 3021-4: Trkd ldrs, outpcd over 2f out: op   2½   65a
8/1, 4 mth abs: AW bow: '99 wnr on final start at Yarmouth (nursery h'cap, rtd 71): eff at 5f, tried 6f, should suit
in time: acts on fast, enjoys gd/soft & soft grnd: handles a sharp or stiff/gall trk.

619   **CLOPTON GREEN** 7 [3] 3-7-10 (58)(bl) (13oh) G Baker (7) 20/1: -03335: Chsd ldrs, nvr pace to chall.   ½   47a

4539} **PERUVIAN JADE** 99 [1] 3-8-12 (74) D Sweeney 8/1: 1044-6: Dwelt, sn outpcd & bhd: op 5/1: 4 mth   2½   56a
abs: '99 wnr at Goodwood & Leicester (h'caps, rtd 82 & 74a): eff at 6f, shld stay further: acts on fast, gd/soft
& fibresand, any trk: has run well fresh: leave this bhnd over further.
6 ran   Time 58.96 (1.16)   (Christopher Wright)   D W P Arbuthnot Lambourn, Berks.

---

653   4.10 TEXT P372 SELLER 3YO+ (G)   6f aw rnd   Going 25   -16 Slow
£1850   £528   £264   3 yo rec 14lb

599   **GRAND VIEW** 3 [5] D Nicholls 4-9-7 F Norton 11/8 FAV: 300-61: 4 ch g Grand Lodge - Hemline   63a
(Sharpo): Led 1f & remnd cl-up till went on again over 2f out, in command final 1f, rdn out: bght in for 5,400gns:
well bckd tho' op evens: '99 scorer for R Hannon at Salisbury (h'cap, rtd 71 at best): unplcd in 3 '98 mdns: eff
at 5/6f, further could suit: acts on firm, soft & equitrack, sharp or stiff/gall trk: apprec drop to sell grade.

634   **FEATHERSTONE LANE** 4 [2] Miss L C Siddall 9-9-7 N Callan 8/1: -44252: 9 b g Siberian Express - Try   3½   53a
Gloria (Try My Best): Rear/wide, rdn & kept on final 2f, no threat: tchd 10/1, qck reapp: W'hampton specialist.

616   **MAPLE** 7 [5] S Dow 4-9-7 (vis) P Doe 5/1: 3-6063: 4 ch g Soviet Lad - Little Red Rose (Precocious):   1¾   49a
Trkd ldrs, effort 2f out, sn onepace: see 224, 106.

*634   **ARAB GOLD** 4 [6] A M Quinn 5-9-12 Martin Dwyer 8/1: 030314: Rdn chsg ldrs, outpcd: op 6/1, qck reapp.   5   45a

628   **COLLEGE BLUE** 4 [1] 4-9-7 (BL) W Ryan 2/1: 001005: Rdn to lead after 1f, hdd over 2f out, sn btn: 1¾   36a
nicely bckd in first time blnks, tchd 5/2: qck reapp: thrice below 484 (C/D, clmr).

558   **MICKY DEE** 16 [4] 4-9-7 (t) Joanna Badger (7) 50/1: 000606: Sn outpcd: mod form.   4   26a
6 ran   Time 1m 12.85 (2.45)   (V Greaves)   D Nicholls Sessay, Nth Yorks.

---

654   4.40 TEXT P372 HCAP 3YO 0-60 (F)   7f aw rnd   Going 25   -43 Slow   [67]
£2808   £864   £432   £216

*638   **PADDYWACK** 4 [2] D W Chapman 3-8-9 (48)(bl) (6ex) Claire Bryan (7) 13/8 FAV: 052411: 3 b g Bigstone -   55a
Millie's Return (Ballad Rock): Led/dsptd lead, put out ins last & tired nr fin, just held on: hvly bckd, qck
reapp: recent W'hampton wnr (h'cap): '99 Redcar wnr (h'cap, rtd 59): eff at 6/7f on firm, gd/soft & both AWs:
suited by blnks & forcing tactics: runs well for an apprentice: in great form.

595   **KIGEMA** 11 [4] C N Allen 3-8-12 (51) R Morse 9/1: -14622: 3 ch f Case Law - Grace de Bois (Tap On   hd   57a
Wood): Led 2f, remnd cl-up, rdn/not pace of wnr over 1f out, rallied well for press nr fin, just held: see 241 (1m).

619   **ITSGOTTABDUN** 7 [1] K T Ivory 3-9-7 (60)(bl) C Catlin 9/1: 061423: 3 b g Foxhound - Lady Ingrid   3½   59a
(Taufan): Towards rear, rdn & kept on final 3f, no threat to front pair: op 7/1: eff at 5/7f: see 527 (6f, sell).

589   **DULZIE** 12 [6] A P Jarvis 3-9-0 (53) D Holland 7/1: 60-24: Chsd ldrs 5f: op 6/1: se 589 (sell).   ¾   51a

595   **DAMASQUINER** 11 [10] 3-9-3 (56) R Lappin 12/1: -41635: Chsd ldrs wide, nvr on terms: op 8/1:   nk   53a
not disgrcd from a poor high draw, prob worth another chance: see 459 (C/D clmr).

515   **COLEY** 23 [3] 3-8-12 (51)(bl) Martin Dwyer 10/1: 00-356: Prom, outpcd 2f out: op 8/1: btr 443 (6f).   ¾   47a

527   **TEA FOR TEXAS** 21 [5] 3-8-12 (51) C Rutter 12/1: 4-3527: Nvr on terms: op 8/1: btr 527, 289 (5/6f).   ½   46a

597   **BROWNS DELIGHT** 11 [9] 3-9-2 (55)(vis) P Doe 20/1: 0-0448: Slowly away, al towards rear: op 12/1.   5   40a

4616} **BIG ISSUE** 99 [8] 3-9-7 (60) J Bosley (7) 4/1: 0010-9: Sn rdn/bhd: bckd, op 12/1: h'cap/AW bow: 4   37a
4 mth abs: '99 Bath scorer (sell, rtd 61): eff at 5/7f, gd+ should suit: acts on gd/soft grnd & enjoys sell grade.

555   **VICKY VETTORI** 16 [7] 3-7-10 (35)(9oh) M Baird 66/1: 600-50: Chsd ldrs 2f, sn bhd: 10th: see 555.   8   0a
10 ran   Time 1m 27.54 (4.74)   (J B Wilcox)   D W Chapman Stillington, N Yorks.

NAD AL SHEBA THURSDAY MARCH 2ND Lefthand, Flat, Fair Track

Official Going DIRT - FAST

655 **5.15 LISTED MAKTOUM CHALLENGE 4YO+** 1m2faw Dirt
£34972 £11647 £5824

4098} **DUBAI MILLENNIUM 99** Saeed bin Suroor 4-8-11 L Dettori : 0111-1: 4 b c Seeking The Gold - Colorado **128a**
Dancer (Shareef Dancer) Prom, led on bit 2f out & sn qcknd clr, impressive: reapp, broke trk record: '99 wnr at
Doncaster (stks), Goodwood (List), M Laffitte (Gr 2), Deauville & Ascot (Gr 1's, rtd 128), met sole defeat when
tried 12f in Epsom Derby: '98 Yarmouth mdn wnr: eff at 1m/10f: acts on firm, soft & dirt: runs well fresh on
any trk: can force the pace: top-class colt, still improving: will be hard to bt in the Dubai World Cup.
186 **LEAR SPEAR 81** D R C Elsworth 5-8-11 N Pollard : 0103-2: 5 b h Lear Fan - Golden Gorse (His 4½ **118a**
Majesty) Hld up, prog to chse wnr 2f out, nvr any impress: cght a tartar, 12 wk abs: '99 wnr at Epsom (Gr 3), R
Ascot (Gr 2) & Goodwood (Gr 3, rtd 119): '98 wnr at Sandown (mdn) & Newmarket (Cambridgeshire h'cap, rtd 104):
eff at 1m/10f: acts on firm, gd/sft grnd & dirt: runs well fresh, any trk: high class, lks as good as ever.
-- **COMEONMOM** Godolphin 4-8-11 D O'Donohoe : 3:4 b c Jolie's Halo - Single Blade (Hatchet Man) 3½ **113a**
6 ran Time 1m 59.6 (Godolphin) Saeed bin Suroor UAE

KRANJI SATURDAY MARCH 4TH -

Official Going GOOD

656 **12.20 SINGAPORE PLATE 3YO+** 1m2f Good
£166667 £59028 £29861

4049} **TIMAHS 99** Saeed bin Suroor 4-9-0 L Dettori : 2310-1: 4 b c Mtoto - Shomoose (Habitat) **112**
In tch, smooth prog to lead bef dist, rdn out: reapp: '99 Doncaster wnr (stks, rtd 105): '98 wnr at Newmarket
(mdn, rtd 101, D Loder): eff at 12f, handles soft, eff at 10f on firm & gd, handles soft, any trk: runs v well fresh: smart.
3792} **GRAF PHILIPP 99** A Schutz 5-9-0 J Saimee : 3/1-2: 5 b h Acatenango - Grey Pearl (Magic Mirror) 3¼ **107**
-- **IRON HORSE** Singapore 8-9-0 M de Montfort : 3: 8 b g Zephyr Zip - Spyglass (Sir Sian) ½ **106**
4419} **NIGHT STYLE 99** E A L Dunlop 3-8-8 G Carter : 2011-6: Never figured from high draw: beaten arnd 82
10L into 6th: '99 wnr at Ripon (mdn), Leicester (stks) & San Siro (Gr 1): eff at 7f/1m, shld get 10f: acts on
firm/fast grnd, any trk: useful, shld leave this behind.
14 ran Time 2m 02.7 (Godolphin) Saeed bin Suroor UAE

657 **1.40 SINGAPORE INTENATIONAL CUP 3YO+** 1m2f Firm
£666667 £236111 £119444

709} **OUZO 99** M Thwaites 7-7-7 J Saimee 7/1: 12-111: 7 b g Oregon - Halloween (War Hawk II) **123**
*186 **JIM AND TONIC 83** F Doumen 6-7-7 G Mosse 7/5 FAV: 6201-2: 6 ch g Double Bed - Jimka nk **121**
(Jim French) -:
3991} **CARRY THE FLAG 99** M C Kent 5-7-7 M J Kinane 10/1: 421-13: 5 b h Tenby - Tamassos (Dance ¾ **120**
in Time) -:
4544} **MONSAJEM 99** E A L Dunlop 5-7-7 J Reid 22/1: 3313-7: Nvr a factor from high draw: btn arnd 7L into **111**
6th on reapp: '99 wnr at Epsom (1st time visor), Newbury & Ascot (val h'caps, rtd 111): '98 Yarmouth wnr (2, stks
& h'cap): eff at 10/12f: acts on firm grnd, likes gd & soft, any trk: can run well fresh, with/without visor.
4399} **SHOWBOAT 99** 6-7-7 M Hills 74/1: 4610-0: Finished 11th from wide draw: '99 wnr at Newmarket (rtd **104**
h'cap), R Ascot (Hunt Cup, by 6L), & Newbury (stks, rtd 109 & 115$): '97 Salisbury wnr (stks, rtd 93): eff at
1m/9f on firm/fast, acts on soft: best coming late off a fast pace: can run well fresh.
185 **SEA WAVE 83** 5-7-7 L Dettori : /343-0: Clipped heels early, made most till appr str: 13th: 3rd & 4th **103**
in Gr 2's in '99 (rtd 118): prev term won at Lingfield (mdn), Leicester (stks) & York (Gr 2, rtd 123): eff at 12f
on firm and gd/sft grnd: can run well frsh, any trk: high class at best, but that was nrly 2 years ago.
14 ran Time 2m 03.4 (Eres Tu No 2) M Thwaites Singapore

WOLVERHAMPTON (Fibresand) SATURDAY MARCH 11TH Lefthand, Sharp Track

Official Going STANDARD.

658 **1.40 INTERCLASS MDN DIV 1 3YO+ (D)** 1m100y aw Going 27 -41 Slow
£2418 £744 £372 £186 3 yo rec 18lb

578 **WELODY 16** [4] K Mahdi 4-9-12 (bl) J Reid 4/1: 40-421: 4 ch g Weldnaas - The Boozy News (L'Emigrant) **73a**
Dictated pace, strongly pressed from over 1f out, held on well ins last, drvn out: rtd 72 at best from 3 '99 starts
(mdn): eff at 8.5f/9.3f, further may suit: acts on fibresand & a sharp trk: suited by blnks: gd weight carrier:
improved today for forcing tactics & could win in h'cap company.
3931} **MARJU GUEST 99** [6] M R Channon 3-8-3 P Fessey 11/2: 044-2: 3 b f Marju - Dance Ahead (Shareef 1¼ **65a**
Dancer) Held up, prog/chsd wnr 3f out, rdn/chall ins last, held cl-home: 6 month abs/AW bow: unplcd in '99
(rtd 82, fill mdn): styd lngr 8.5f trip, further could suit: handles fm & fibresand & a sharp trk.
610 **ARCTIC HIGH 11** [9] M S Saunders 3-8-3 G Carter 7/2 JT FAV: 323: 3 b f Polar Falcon - Oublier L'Ennui 1½ **62a**
(Bellman) Mid-div, rdn/kept on fnl 2f, not pace to chall: eff at 8.5f, return to 9.4f+ in h'caps shld suit.
625 **ROYAL CAVALIER 9** [7] R Hollinshead 3-8-8 P M Quinn (5) 7/2 JT FAV: 22-034: Towards rear, rdn/ shd **67a**
styd on fnl 2f, nrst fin: op 11/4: needs a return to 9f+: btr 625 (9f, h'cap).
-- **JAVELIN** [3] 4-9-12 R Fitzpatrick (3) 12/1: /400-5: Chsd ldrs 7f: op 10/1: British debut/AW bow: 6 **58a**
ex-French gelding, unplcd in France in '99 (tried up to 10.5f): stays 1m & handles soft: with I Williams.
-- **PRUDENT** [2] 3-8-3 R Ffrench 9/2: 6: Rdn/al towards rear: op 7/2, debut: Caerleon filly, sister to 5 **43a**
a winning miler: with J R Fanshawe, shld know more next time.
643 **STICIBOOTS 5** [1] 3-8-8 J Tate 25/1: 557: Prom 6f: qck reapp: see 565 (12f). 4 **40a**
1921} **SWIFTUR 99** [8] 3-8-4(1ow) D Sweeney 14/1: 0-8: Mid-div, btn 4f out: op 12/1, 9 month abs/AW bow: 10 **21a**

WOLVERHAMPTON (Fibresand)   SATURDAY MARCH 11TH   Lefthand, Sharp Track

unplcd sole start in '99 (7f mdn, rtd 39): bred to apprec mid-dists, with P F I Cole.
-- **TAYAR** [5] 4-9-12 (t) J P Spencer 25/1: 9: Dwelt/wide, bhd halfway: debut, with H Akbary.   *dist* **0a**
9 ran   Time 1m 52.00 (5.8)   (Prospect Etates Ltd)   K Mahdi Newmarket.

659	2.10 DET DIRECT SELLER 3YO (G) 5f aw rnd Going 27 +05 Fast
	£1842 £526 £263

624   **TROPICAL KING** 9 [9] D Carroll 3-8-12 J P Spencer 9/2: -42521: 3 b g Up And At 'Em - Princess   **63a**
Gay (Fairy King) Mid-div, rdn/prog to lead ins last, styd on well, rdn out: best time of day: op 7/2: unplcd in
'99 in native Ireland (mdns): eff at 5f, stays 6f: acts on fibresand & a sharp trk: apprec drop to selling grade.
573   **PIPS STAR** 17 [1] D W P Arbuthnot 3-8-7 R Price 10/11 FAV: 1-3262: 3 b f Pips Pride - Kentucky   1¾ **52a**
Starlet (Cox's Ridge) Led after 1f, rdn/hdd ins last & not pace of wnr: well bckd: drop to selling grade.
619   **POWER AND DEMAND** 10 [2] D Shaw 3-8-12 (bl) N Callan 12/1: -02543: 3 b g Formidable -   1 **55$**
Mazurkanova (Song) Chsd ldrs, kept on onepace fnl 2f: op 8/1: acts on both AWs, sell h'caps could suit.
638   **BILLYS BLUNDER** 7 [6] P D Evans 3-8-7 (vis) S Drowne 9/1: -32044: Led wide 1f, outpcd over 1f out: 2½ **43a**
op 7/1: visor reapplied, t-strap omitted: btr 493, 426 (6/7f).
426   **APRILS COMAIT** 40 [5] 3-8-7 V Halliday 25/1: 03-605: Mid-div at best: 6 wk abs: see 217.   3 **36a**
281   **K ACE THE JOINT** 64 [3] 3-8-12 S Finnamore (5) 50/1: 000-06: Al outpcd: 2 month abs, mod form.   hd **40$**
589   **UNFORTUNATE** 15 [7] 3-8-7 N Carlisle 10/1: 4-6537: Dwelt/al rear: tchd 12/1: see 181 (6f, seller).   1½ **31a**
624   **MISS SINCERE** 9 [8] 3-8-7 Joanna Badger (7) 20/1: 0-0448: Al outpcd: op 12/1: see 357.   1½ **29a**
3063} **BLACKPOOL MAMMAS** 99 [4] 3-8-13 Claire Bryan (5) 9/1: 5224-9: Sn bhd: mkt drifter, op 5/1: 7 month 2 **30a**
abs: prev with J Berry, '99 wnr at Musselburgh (debut, auct mdn), Newcastle & Chepstow (clmrs, rnr-up on sand, rtd
82 & 72a at best): eff at 5f, suited by 6f, could stay further: acts on firm, gd & fibresand: handles any trk:
has run well fresh: enjoys claiming grade: with J M Bradley.
9 ran   Time 1m 01.3 (1.1)   (Mrs Annie Hughes)   D Carroll Southwell, Notts.

660	2.40 TOTE SCOOP6 HCAP 3YO+ 0-105 (B) 6f aw Going 27 -05 Slow	[105]
	£11232 £3456 £1728 £864 3 yo rec 14lb	

532   **BLUE STAR** 23 [1] N P Littmoden 4-8-8 (85)(vis) J Tate 9/1: 524151: 4 b g Whittingham - Gold And Blue   **92a**
(Bluebird) Trkd ldrs halfway, prog/led 2f out, styd on well, drvn out: op 7/1: earlier scored here at W'hampton
(h'cap, C/D): plcd twice on turf in '99 (rtd 71, h'cap): '98 W'hampton wnr (val stks, rtd 87a & 74): eff at 6/7f:
handles firm, gd/soft & equitrack, fibresand/W'hampton specialist: eff with/without a visor: useful AW performer.
579   **FIRST MAITE** 16 [2] S R Bowring 7-8-10 (87)(bl) J Weaver 9/2: -40032: 7 b g Komaite - Marina Plata   ¾ **91a**
(Julio Mariner) Trkd ldrs, hdd 2f out, hard rdn & styd on well ins last, just held nr fin: tchd 6/1: tough: see 35 (7f).
587   **DAAWE** 15 [13] D Nicholls 9-9-5 (96)(bl) Clare Roche (7) 15/2: -11163: 9 b h Danzig - Capo Di Monte   1 **98a**
(Final Straw) Sn cl-up, ev ch 1f out, kept on well: useful AW performer, handles in gd heart: see 579 (7f).
2067} **LONE PIPER** 99 [5] C E Brittain 5-9-6 (97) P Robinson 25/1: /020-4: Chsd ldrs, rdn/ch over 1f out,   shd **99a**
kept on well for press: 9 month abs: AW bow: lightly rcd in '99 (rtd 101, stks): '98 Newmarket wnr (stks) & also
York (rtd h'cap, rtd 103): eff at 6/7f: acts on fast, gd & fibresand, prob not soft: acts on any trk: useful reapp.
4198} **KING OF PERU** 99 [11] 7-8-7 (84)(vis) C Cogan (5) 20/1: 0022-5: Handy, no extra fnl 1f: stablemate   ½ **84a**
of wnr: 5 months abs: '99 Brighton wnr (h'cap, plcd numerous times, rtd 71, h'cap & unplcd on sand, rtd 81a,
h'cap): plcd in '98 (rtd 94a & 77, h'caps): eff at 5/6f, stays 7f: acts on firm, gd/soft & fibresand, prob handles
soft: handles any trk, enjoys a sharp/undul one: eff with/without blnks/visor: often placed.
579   **JUWWI** 16 [7] 6-8-7 (84) Claire Bryan (5) 8/1: 532206: Dwelt/rear, kept on fnl 2f, nvr nrr: see 129.   ½ **82a**
4620} **CRETAN GIFT** 99 [12] 9-10-0 (105)(vis) T G McLaughlin 7/1: 4030-7: Mid-div, not pace of chall: op   1¼ **100a**
12/1: 4 month abs: '99 wnr at Ascot (rtd h'cap) & Yarmouth (stks, rtd 103 at best): '98 Newmarket wnr at W'hampton
(h'cap, rtd 104a), subs 4th at Royal Ascot (Gr2, rtd 115): eff at 5f, suited by 6f, stays 7f: acts on firm, soft/
hvy & fibresand: eff with/without blnks/visor on any trk: has run well fresh: v useful gelding, stablemate of wnr.
579   **DIL** 16 [10] D Nicholls 5-9-0 (91) R Fitzpatrick (3) 16/1: -01008: Chsd ldrs 4f: op 12/1: btr 394 (5f).   1 **84a**
*630   **MAGIC RAINBOW** 7 [8] 5-9-2 (93) M Fenton 7/2 FAV: 030-19: Trkd ldrs halfway, eff/held over 1f out.   1¼ **83a**
4610} **DOUBLE OSCAR** 99 [4] 7-9-2 (93)(bl) A Nicholls (3) 20/1: 4000-0: Nvr on terms: 10th: 4 month abs.   hd **82a**
*645   **BLUE KITE** 5 [9] 5-8-8 (84)(1ow)(6ex) D Holland 7/1: 034510: Mid-div, nvr on terms: 11th.   ½ **72a**
3992} **REFERENDUM** 99 [6] 6-8-11 (88) O Pears 14/1: 6000-0: Al rear: 12th: op 12/1, 6 month absence.   4 **65a**
4486} **NIGHT FLIGHT** 99 [3] 6-8-9 (86) R Winston 8/1: 0006-0: Trkd ldrs, wknd qckly fnl 2f: 13th: 5 mth abs.   nk **62a**
13 ran   Time 1m 14.7 (1.3)   (T Clarke)   N P Littmoden Newmarket.

661	3.15 INTERCLASS MDN DIV 2 3YO+ (D) 1m100y aw Going 27 -34 Slow
	£2418 £744 £372 £186 3 yo rec 18lb

--   **ULUNDI** [3] Lady Herries 5-9-12 P Doe 4/1: 1: 5 b g Rainbow Quest - Flit (Lyphard)   **65a**
Chsd ldrs, chsd ldr over 2f out & led over 1f out, edged left/styd on well, rdn out: op 9/2: Flat debut, 6 wk jmps
abs, earlier this term scored at N Abbot (2, bmprs), Fontwell (nov) & Cheltenham (nov h'cap, rtd 110h, eff arnd
2m/2m2f on gd & gd/soft, handles firm): eff at 8.5f, stay further: acts on fibresand & a sharp trk: runs well fresh.
565   **DONTBESOBOLD** 18 [1] B S Rothwell 3-8-8 M Fenton 7/1: 043662: 3 b g River Falls - Jarmar Moon   2½ **59a**
(Unfuwain) Chsd ldrs, rdn/kept on fnl 2f, not pace of wnr: clr of rem: shld apprec h'cap company: see 565, 328.
--   **HARVEY LEADER** [8] J R Fanshawe 5-9-12 O Urbina 6/1: 3: 5 b g Prince Sabo - Mrs Leader (Mr   5 **49a**
Leader) Held up, prog/led over 3f out, hdd over 1f out & no extra: op 7/2, Flat debut: jumps fit (unplcd
fav in a Huntingdon bmpr & p.u. sole start over timber, wore a t-strap).
629   **ACHILLES WINGS** 7 [4] K R Burke 4-9-12 J Weaver 9/4 FAV: 34: Chsd ldrs, onepace fnl 2f: op 6/4.   nk **48a**
610   **ATALYA** 11 [7] 3-8-8 N Callan 4/1: 60-245: Chsd ldr, btn 2f out: btr 610, 319 (9.4f).   7 **37a**
415   **SILCA FANTASY** 43 [6] 3-8-3 R Ffrench 9/1: 0-4446: Led 5f, sn btn: 6 wk abs: btr 278 (7f).   3½ **25a**
3755} **TONDYNE** 99 [5] 3-8-8 R Winston 25/1: 00-7: Al rear: AW bow, 6 month abs: unplcd on 2 '99   6 **21a**
turf starts (tried up to 7f, rtd 45): with T D Easterby.
--   **PENALTA** [2] 4-9-12 Dean McKeown 33/1: 8: Al rear: debut, with M Wigham.   hd **20a**
8 ran   Time 1m 51.4 (5.2)   (D Heath)   Lady Herries Angmering, W.Sussex.

WOLVERHAMPTON (Fibresand)

662

3.50 HANDYMAN COND STKS 3YO+ (C)   1m1f79y   Going 27   -23 Slow
£6061   £2299   £1149   £522   3 yo rec 20lb

611   **PANTAR 11** [7] I A Balding 5-9-7 (bl) K Darley 5/2: 0-0321: 5 b g Shirley Heights - Spring Daffodil   **92a**
(Pharly) Held up in tch, prog 3f out, hard rdn to chase ldr over 1f out, styd on gamely to lead nr line, all out:
op 2/1: plcd form in '99 (rtd 102, h'cap): '98 Goodwood wnr (val h'cap, rtd 102 at best): eff at 1m/10f: acts on
firm, gd/soft & fibresand: handles any trk: eff with/without blnks: gd weight carrier, benefited from a strong ride.
480   **WEET A MINUTE 32** [6] R Hollinshead 7-9-7 A Culhane 11/8 FAV: 1-2222: 7 ro h Nabeel Dancer -   nk **91a**
Ludovica (Bustino) Trkd ldr halfway, went on over 1f out, kept on well for press, just hdd nr line: op 4/5:
proving consistent but frustrating to follow this term, ahd of today's wnr in 448 (8.5f).
4536} **CLARANET 99** [4] K Mahdi 3-7-11(1ow) Dale Gibson 7/1: 34-3: 3 ch f Arazi - Carmita (Caerleon)   3 **81a**
Prom, led over 5f out till over 1f out, sn held: 5 month abs/AW bow: lightly rcd in'99 (rtd 79, debut, mdn):
eff at 1m/9.4f, further could suit: handles gd/soft & fibresand: now qual for h'caps, can find a race.
4560} **STOPPES BROW 99** [5] G L Moore 8-9-7 I Mongan (5) 20/1: 3100-4: Chsd ldrs, outpcd fnl 2f: 4 mth   ¾ **84$**
abs: '99 wnr at Lingfield (2, AW h'caps, rtd 79a), Kemptcn & Epsom (h'caps, rtd 82): '98 Goodwood wnr (h'cap,
rtd 73 & 70a): eff at 7f/1m: acts on firm, soft & both AWs, loves equitrack/Lingfield: suited by
blnks/visor: likes sharp trks: tough, 12 wins from 81 starts & a return to h'caps shld suit.
633   **WHITE PLAINS 7** [2] 7-9-13 (t) N Callan 10/1: 403335: Chsd ldrs 6f: op 7/1: topweight: btr 244 (eqtrk).   4 **82a**
4602} **SPRING PURSUIT 99** [3] 4-9-7 P Doe 8/1: 1162-6: In tch 6f: op 10/1: AW bow, 4 month abs: 6 **67a**
rattled off a 4-timer on turf in '99 at Brighton, York, Windsor & Lingfield (h'caps, rtd 78): '98 Warwick wnr (nov
auct, rtd 86, R Charlton): eff at 9/10f on gd, soft & any trk: best without blnks: gd weight carrier: do better.
266   **MISS WORLD 66** [1] 3-7-10 (t) G Bardwell 20/1: 21-547: Led 4f, btn 3f out: 2 mth abs: btr 213.   12 **44a**
7 ran   Time 2m 02.9 (4.7)   (Robert Hitchins)   I A Balding Kingsclere, Hants.

663

4.25 LINCOLN TRIAL HCAP 4YO+ 0-105 (B)   1m100y aw   Going 27   -20 Slow   [101]
£32500   £10000   £5000   £2500

4456} **THE PRINCE 99** [4] Ian Williams 6-9-3 (90)(t) J Weaver 14/1: 1303-1: 6 b g Machiavellian - Mohican   **97a**
Girl (Dancing Brave) Slowly away & settled near, prog wide from halfway & rdn/chsd ldr over 2f out, styd on
gamely ins last to lead nr line, all out: op 12/1: 5 month abs, AW bow: prev with R M H Cowell, '99 scorer at
Lingfield (class stks) & Hamilton (h'cap, rtd 93): missed '98: eff at 7.5f/8.5f: acts on firm, gd & fibresand:
handles any trk & runs v well fresh: eff with/without a visor, suited by a t-strap: well suited by waiting tactics.
3872} **RIVER TIMES 99** [5] T D Easterby 4-9-6 (93)(bl) R Winston 12/1: 5150-2: 4 b c Runaway - Miss   shd **99a**
Riverton (Fred Astaire) Led, rdn/clr over 3f out, hard rdn ins last & hdd line: op 9/1: 6 month abs: AW
bow: '99 wnr at Beverley (stks) & Newmarket (val h'cap, rtd 96, first time blnks): '98 Haydock wnr (auct
mdn, rtd 88 at best): suited by 1m, tried 10f: acts on firm, gd & fibresand: handles any trk: best up with/
forcing the pace: suited by blnks: entered in the Lincoln h'cap & shld give a gd account on this evidence.
4560} **JOHN FERNELEY 99** [12] P F I Cole 5-9-3 (90) J Fortune 6/1: 4133-3: 5 b g Polar Falcon - I'll Try   hd **95a**
(Try My Best) Chsd ldrs, rdn over 2f out, styd on strongly ins last, just held: op 9/2: magic: '99 York
wnr (rtd h'cap, rtd 92 at best): '98 Folkestone wnr (appr mdn), Thirsk (ltd stks) & Sandown (h'cap, rtd 84):
eff at 7f/8.5f on fast, hvy & fibresand: handles any trk & runs well fresh with/without blnks: tough/progressive.
*551   **GRALMANO 21** [7] K A Ryan 5-9-3 (90) F Lynch 100/30 FAV: 120-14: Held up in tch, outpcd 4f out,   1¾ **92a**
switched wide & styd on well fnl 2f, nvr pace to chall: nicely bckd, tchd 9/2: gd run, loves to dominate: see 551.
912} **INVADER 99** [8] 4-9-3 (90) P Robinson 16/1: 4/45-5: Chsd ldrs, outpcd 2f out: 11 mth abs, AW bow.   nk **91a**
480   **KING PRIAM 32** [3] 5-9-12 (99)(bl) D Holland 10/1: 2-3136: Towards rear, rdn halfway, no impress.   2½ **95a**
4204} **THE WHISTLING TEAL 99** [1] 4-9-2 (89) M Tebbutt 4/1: 2320-7: Twds rear, mod gains: op 6/1, 5 mth abs.   1¼ **82a**
580   **WEETMANS WEIGH 16** [11] 7-9-7 (94) J P Spencer 12/1: 2-4648: Al twds rear: op 10/1: see 321, 49.   2½ **82a**
3995} **DEBBIES WARNING 99** [2] 4-9-13 (100)(t) J Reid 5/1: 0530-9: Prom 6f: op 10/1, 6 month abs.   2½ **83a**
4395} **NOMORE MR NICEGUY 99** [10] 6-9-10 (97) J Murtagh 12/1: 5200-0: Prom 6f: 10th: tchd 14/1, reapp.   3½ **73a**
593   **TOPTON 14** [9] 6-9-6 (93)(bl) K Darley 14/1: 261300: Mid-div, btn 2f out: 11th: op 12/1: btr 463.   hd **68a**
4337} **NOUF 99** [6] 4-9-3 (90) N Callan 25/1: 104-0: Al rear, eased fnl 1f: 12th: 5 month abs/AW bow.   14 **44a**
4401} **ROCK FALCON 99** [13] 7-9-6 (93)(bl) R Cochrane 15/2: 0003-0: In tch, btn/eased fnl 1f: 13th: reapp.   3 **41a**
13 ran   Time 1m 50.2 (4.0)   (Patrick Kelly)   Ian Williams Alvechurch, Worcs.

664

5.00 0800 211222 HCAP 4YO+ 0-85 (D)   2m46y aw   Going 27   -50 Slow   [85]
£3828   £1178   £589   £294   4 yo rec 5 lb

*649   **MAKNAAS 3** [7] T G Mills 4-8-7 (69)(2ow) S Finnamore (5) 2/1 FAV: 151111: 4 ch c Wolfhound - White   **80a**
Wash (Final Straw) Made all, clr 3f out, eased ins last, unchall: val 10L+: qk reapp: earlier won at Lingfield
(2, amat & appr h'caps) & W'hampton (2, C/D h'caps): '98 wnr again here at W'hampton (h'caps, rtd 52a), plcd on
turf for R Armstrong (td 49): suited by 2m on soft, AW/sharp trk specialist: eff with/without blnks: v progressive.
*548   **HARIK 21** [4] G L Moore 6-9-10 (81) I Mongan (5) 6/1: 0-3112: 6 ch g Persian Bold - Yaqut (Northern   6 **81a**
Dancer) Held up, rdn/prog to chase wnr over 1f out, no impress: handles equitrack & fibresand: see 548.
627   **ROYAL EXPRESSION 9** [3] G M Moore 8-8-9 (65)(1ow) J Weaver 11/2: -63123: 8 b g Sylvan Express -   3½ **63a**
Edwins Princess (Owen Dudley) Rear, well bhd halfway, mod late gains fnl 2f: btr 552 (C/D).
644   **SPOSA 5** [5] M J Polglase 4-7-12 (60) P Doe 6/1: -53024: Chsd wnr, btn 2f out: op 9/2, qck reapp.   ¾ **56a**
*380   **WILCUMA 49** [6] 9-9-13 (84) A Clark 11/2: /0-015: In tch, struggling 4f out: 7 wk abs: btr 380 (C/D).   18 **67a**
554   **WESTERN RAINBOW 21** [1] 4-7-12 (60)(VIS) Dale Gibson 7/1: 224126: Chsd ldrs, struggling 5f out: ½ **42a**
op 6/1, visor: recent jumps rnr (plcd, nov, rtd 102h): see 483 (13f, equitrack).
508   **BE GONE 28** [2] 5-10-0 (85) G Bardwell 4/1: 30-137: Rear, rdn halfway & bhd 4f out, eased over   dist **0a**
1f out: op 6/1: topweight: not his form here: btr 296 (C/D).
7 ran   Time 3m 41.6 (12.4)   (Travel Spot Ltd)   T G Mills Headley, Surrey.

SAINT CLOUD SATURDAY MARCH 11TH Lefthand, Galloping Track

Official Going HOLDING

665 2.15 GR 3 PRIX EXBURY 4YO+ 1m2f Holding
£21134 £8453 £4227

1543} **RUSSIAN HOPE 99** H A Pantall 5-8-9 G Toupel 33/10: 012-11: 5 ch h Rock Hopper - Dievotchka (Dancing   **115**
Brave) Chsd ldrs going well, smooth hdwy to lead over 2f out, drvn clr appr fnl 1f: campaigned over staying
trips last term & clearly apprec this step back to 10f: acts well on on hvy grnd: v smart.
4532} **AMILYNX 99** A Fabre 4-9-6 C Soumillon 54/10: 2311-2: 4 gr c Linamix - Amen (Alydar)   6 **117**
-- **DOUBLE HEART** Mlle V Dissaux 4-8-9 S Guillot 101/10: 1331-3: 4 b c Akarad - Slanderous Facts   3 **101**
(Slip Anchor) -:
4354} **AMALIA 99** P W Harris 4-8-6 Pat Eddery 347/10: 1410-0: Al in rear, t.o. in last: '99 wnr at Redcar   **0**
(mdn), Chester & Doncaster (h'caps, rtd 97): eff arnd 1m on fast & dirt, handles hvy:
eff on a sharp or gall trk: can force the pace or come from bhd: can leave this bhd back on a sound surface.
11 ran Time 2m 15.3 (Barod Edouard de Rothschild) H A Pantall France

NAD AL SHEBA SUNDAY MARCH 12TH Lefthand, Flat, Fair Track

Official Going FAST

666 5.00 AL FUTTAIM TROPHY 4YO+ 7f110y aw Dirt
£5824 £2912 £1747

2709} **BLUE SNAKE 99** Saeed bin Suroor 4-8-7 L Dettori : 0/21-1: 4 br c Gone West - Dabaweyaa (Shareef   **113a**
Dancer) Won by 1¼L: '99 scorer at Doncaster (mdn, rtd 97): eff arnd 1m in '99 (rtd 72a, clmr, C N Allen):
186 **RUNNING STAG 91** P Mitchell 6-8-9 W Ryan : 1422-2: 6 b h Cozzene - Fruhlingstag (Orsini)   1¼ **112a**
Trkd ldr, hdwy 2f out, dsptd lead dist, rdn & no extra cl-home: 3 month abs: not disgraced over a trip shorter
than ideal: tough & v smart globe-trotting entire: see 55.
-- **JILA** Dubai 5-8-7 R Hills : 3: 5 ch h Kris - Enaya (Caeleon) -:   shd **109a**
5 ran Time 1m 29.0 (Mohammed Obaida) Saeed bin Suroor Newmarket

SOUTHWELL (Fibresand) TUESDAY MARCH 14TH Lefthand, Sharp, Oval Track

Official Going STANDARD Stalls: 5f - Outside, Rem - Inside

667 1.45 CLASSIFIED STKS 3YO+ 0-60 (F) 7f aw rnd Going 10 -59 Slow
£2278 £651 £325 3 yo rec 16lb

599 **ODDSANENDS 15** [2] T D Barron 4-9-7 C Lowther 7/2 FAV: 22-051: 4 b g Alhijaz - Jans Contessa (Rabdan)   **64a**
Made all, rdn/clr over 1f out, in command nr fin, pushed out: tchd 9/2: rnr-up in '99 (rtd 72a, clmr, C N Allen):
'98 Ascot wnr (nurs h'cap, rtd 77), also plcd on sand, (rtd 83a): eff at 6f, stays 1m: suited by front running
tactics at 7f: acts on firm, fast grnd & fibresand: likes a sharp trk, handles eqny.
646 **INDIAN SWINGER 8** [4] P Howling 4-9-7 K Darley 12/1: 5-0052: 4 ch c Up And At 'Em - Seanee Squaw   3 **57$**
(Indian Ridge) Dwelt/towards rear wide, rdn to chase wnr over 1f out, kept on tho' al held: gd run, tchd 14/1.
616 **RED VENUS 13** [9] Miss Gay Kelleway 4-9-4 (bl) D Holland 10/1: 654-53: 4 ch f Perugino -   shd **54a**
Reflection Time (Fayruz) Chsd ldrs, kept on onepace fnl 2f: op 9/1: see 616 (equitrack).
634 **NINEACRES 10** [5] J M Bradley 9-9-9 (bl) W Jones (7) 10/1: 226144: Trkd wnr, wknd over 1f out: 1¾ **56a**
op 8/1: stays 7f, just best at 5/6f: see 564 (5f).
449 **C HARRY 40** [11] 6-9-7 P M Quinn 5/1 254065: Towards rear/wide, rdn/mod gains fnl 2f: abs.   hd **53a**
*578 **GENERATE 19** [8] 4-9-6 L Newton (3) 20/1: 000-16: Prom early, outpcd halfway, late gains: btr 578 (9.4f).   1½ **49a**
4510} **PEPPIATT 99** [7] 6-9-7 A Culhane 10/1: 6050-7: Towards rear, hard rdn over 2f out, no impress: 4 **42a**
tchd 16/1, 5 month abs: AW bow: '99 Ayr wnr (h'cap, rtd 73): '98 Goodwood scorer (h'cap, rtd 77 at best,
D Nicholls): eff at 6/7f on firm, likes soft grnd: handles any trk: best held up for a late run.
616 **SHAMWARI SONG 13** [6] 5-9-7 R Mullen 20/1: 002038: Nvr on terms: see 616, 163.   nk **41a**
567 **NITE OWLER 21** [10] 6-9-7 G Duffield 6/1: 00-269: Chsd ldrs 5f: see 75.   3 **35a**
499 **REGAL SONG 32** [1] 4-9-7 J Fanning 5/1: 31-320: Held up, eff 2f out, sn btn: 10th: btr 499, 414.   2½ **30a**
-- **WILLYEVER** [3] 6-9-7 (VIS) R Fitzpatrick (3) 6/1: 6100-0: Dwelt, nvr in it: 11th: op 4/1, vis, AW bow: 3 **24a**
Irish raider, 10 wk jmps abs: '99 scorer at Galway (5 rnr stks): '98 Tralee wnr (h'cap): eff at 7f/1m on gd & hvy.
11 ran Time 1m 31.4 (4.8) (Harrowgate Bloodstock Ltd) T D Barron Maunby, N Yorks

668 2.15 0800 211 222 CLAIMER 4YO+ 0-60 (F) 1m6f aw Going 10 -65 Slow
£2124 £607 £303 4 yo rec 4 lb

590 **IRISH CREAM 18** [8] Andrew Reid 4-8-3 (vis) M Henry 11/2: 03-201: 4 b f Petong - Another Baileys   **45a**
(Deploy) Led/dsptd lead till went on 4f out ,clr over 1f out, rdn on well, rdn out: op 9/2: '99 wnr here at Southwell
(3, sells & clmr, rtd 73a & 46): '98 Hamilton scorer (auct mdn, rtd 74) & Southwell (clmr, rtd 79a): eff at
12/14f: acts on gd/soft, hvy & equitrack, fibresand/Southwell specialist: suited by reapp of visor, eff without.
577 **PEN FRIEND 19** [6] W J Haggas 6-9-2 G Faulkner (3) 6/4 FAV: 2/0-52: 6 b g Robellino - Nibbs Point   1¾ **51a**
(Sure Blade) Towards rear/wide, prog/rdn & chsd front pair 3f out, kept on: tchd 5/2: stewards enquired into
running, jockey reported gldg wld not face kick back: acts on gd, fast & fibresand: eff at 14f, spot on at 2m.
577 **XYLEM 19** [12] J Pearce 9-8-10 (vis) J Weaver 6/1: 323023: 9 ch g Woodman - Careful (Tampa Trouble)   4 **39a**
Held up, prog/went on over 6f out, rdn/hdd 4f out & no extra fnl 2f: op 9/2: see 577, 347 (12f, clmr).
524 **KATIES CRACKER 27** [5] M Quinn 5-8-3 C Rutter 16/1: -00464: Chsd ldrs, btn 4f out: see 168.   12 **19a**
494 **MARKELLIS 33** [7] 4-8-0 Joanna Badger (7) 12/1: 505605: Towards rear, mod gains: recent jmps rnr.   4 **14a**
607 **AMAZING FACT 14** [11] 5-8-8 R Ffrench (3) 12/1: 000-36: Nvr on terms: op 8/1: see 607 (12f).   6 **9a**
3657} **BREAK THE RULES 99** [3] 8-8-10 R Fitzpatrick (3) 14/1: 34/0-7: Chsd ldrs, btn 4f out: op 12/1, 8 wk   1¼ **9a**
jumps abs (rnr-up 4 times this winter, rtd 93h, sell hdle): unplcd sole Flat start in '99 (rtd 38): '98 Chester wnr

211

(h'cap, D Nicholls, rtd 73, unplcd on sand, rtd 59a): suited by 10f, stays 12f: acts on firm & hvy: loves Chester.

498	**TANTISPER** 32 [2] 4-8-4 G Duffield 25/1: 0/5-68: Held up, eff halfway, sn btn: see 498, 196 (11f).	13 0a
646	**GHUTAH** 8 [9] 6-8-7 (bl) (1ow) S Whitworth 25/1: 400-09: Prom 9f: unplcd in '99 (rtd 59, subs	10 0a

tried blnks): ex-French, promise over 6f as a juv, well btn since then in 3 starts in the UAE: longer trip here.

556	**ICE PACK** 22 [1] 4-8-3 Kim Tinkler 12/1: 220-60: Al bhd: 10th: op 8/1: see 556 (12f).	8 0a
519	**TOY STORY** 28 [13] 4-9-0 (bl) D Holland 8/1: 2-6330: Led 2f, wknd 5f out, eased: 13th: recent jmps	0a

rnr (rtd 51h, 1st time blnks, mdn hdle): stiff task: see 519, 196 (11f).

4108} **MIDDAY COWBOY** 99 [14] 7-8-4 (bl) Iona Wands (5) 33/1: 0000-0: Led after 2f, hdd/btn 7f out: 14th:
6 month abs: unplcd/no form in '99 (rtd 37, mdn): mod form over timber prev: AW bow today.

4128} **Portite Sophie** 99 [15] 9-8-1 G Bardwell 14/1:   576 **Turgenev** 19 [4] 11-8-8 Dean McKeown 25/1:
14 ran   Time 3m 10.3 (10.5)   (A S Reid)   Andrew Reid Mill Hill, Greater London

---

669   2.50 BEST BETS HCAP 3YO+ 0-80 (D)   1m aw rnd Going 10 -60 Slow   [76]
£3828   £1178   £589   £294   3 yo rec 18lb

575	**THE STAGER** 20 [7] J R Jenkins 8-9-8 (70)(tvi) S Whitworth 8/1: -11451: 8 b g Danehill - Wedgewood	76a

Blue (Sir Ivor): Prom, led 2f out, rdn & held on well: op 6/1: earlier scored here at Southwell (2 h'caps):
'99 wnr again here at Southwell (h'cap, rtd 60a & 36): '98 wnr again at Southwell (h'cap, rtd 55a): eff at
7f/1m, stays a sharp 10f: acts on firm, gd & equitrack, fibresand/Southwell specialist: best without blnks/
visor: gd weight carrier: best in a t-strap: shd win more races.

*580	**ONE DINAR** 19 [2] K Mahdi 5-9-12 (74) J Reid 11/10 FAV: 10-212: 5 b h Generous - Lypharitissima	½ 78a

(Lightning) Mid-div, rdn to chase wnr over 1f out, styd on well, not able to chall: op 2/1: return to 8.5f + will
suit: clr of rem here & can win again: see 580.

598	**TROJAN WOLF** 15 [8] P Howling 5-9-11 (73) D Holland 7/1: 1-1453: 5 ch g Wolfhound - Trojan Lady	6 68a

(Irish River) Led 2f, hdd & kept on fnl 2f: op 5/1: see 255 (amat h'cap).

647	**MUTAHADETH** 8 [9] D Shaw 6-8-5 (53)(bl) J Fanning 12/1: 603444: Chsd ldrs, onepace over 2f out.	1½ 45a
601	**RUTLAND CHANTRY** 15 [5] 6-9-11 (73) A Culhane 6/1: 000-25: Rear/in tch wide, eff 3f out, sn held.	nk 64a
*601	**DAVIS ROCK** 15 [1] 6-9-3 (65) R Cochrane 12/1: -11016: Held up, btn 3f out: op 9/2: btr 601 (C/D).	9 43a
601	**SILKEN DALLIANCE** 15 [10] 5-10-0 (76) K Darley 10/1: 000-07: Cl-up 6f: op 8/1: see 601 (C/D).	2 50a
601	**WUXI VENTURE** 15 [4] 5-10-0 (76) O Pears 8/1: 064-08: Trkd ldrs 6f: op 7/1: see 601 (C/D).	4 42a
600	**WILTON** 15 [6] 5-9-4 (66)(t) M Tebbutt 12/1: /00-39: Al bhd: tchd 14/1: btr 600 (C/D).	6 23a
--	**CASTLE FRIEND** [3] 5-8-3 (51) A Nicholls (3) 25/1: 3263/0: Bhd halfway: 10th: long abs: missed	8 0a

'99: plcd thrice on turf in '98 (h'cap, rtd 57): eff around 9/11f: handles fast & hvy, prob any trk: AW bow today.
10 ran   Time 1m 44.0 (5.6)   (J B Wilcox)   J R Jenkins Royston, Herts

---

670   3.25 TEXT P372 SELLER DIV 1 3-6YO (G)   1m3f aw Going 10 -85 Slow
£1509   £431   £215   3 yo rec 22lb4 yo rec 1 lb

535	**MICE IDEAS** 25 [1] N P Littmoden 4-9-9 C Cogan (5) 9/4: -16051: 4 ch g Fayruz - Tender Encounter	50a

(Prince Tenderfoot) Led till halfway, again over 2f out, in command fnl 1f: op 4/1: bght in for 3000gns: prev won
here at Southwell (C/D, appr auct mdn): earlier sh S Mellor (12/1: op rtd 66 & 53a):
rnr-up in '98 (rtd 74, auct mdn): suited by 11f, tried further: acts on gd, fast & likes fibresand/Southwell.

4129}	**LOYAL TOAST** 99 [6] N Tinkler 3-9-10 Kim Tinkler 16/1: 0000-2: 5 b g Lyphard - Lisieux (Steady	5 42$

Growth) Prom, rdn/chsd wnr over 1f out, sn held: op 14/1, 6 month abs: unplcd in '99 (rtd 59, L Cumani, h'cap)
'98 Goodwood wnr (h'cap, rtd 77): eff over a sharp/undul 10f on firm & fast grnd: has worn a t-strap.

385	**BOSS TWEED** 50 [4] Ronald Thompson 3-8-6 (t) K Dalgleish (7) 7/4 FAV: 0-1143: 3 b g Persian Bold -	¾ 45a

Betty Kenwood (Dominion) Held up, rdn & kept on fnl 2f, no threat: op 5/4, 7 wk abs: wore a t-strap: see 355.

626	**ADIRPOUR** 12 [7] R Hollinshead 6-10-0 Stephanie Hollinshea 12/1: 504154: Chsd ldr 5f out, btn fnl 2f.	5 37a
584	**WERE NOT STOPPIN** 18 [5] 5-9-10 H Bastiman 25/1: -00505: Cl-up, led over 5f out till over 2f out, fdd.	shd 33$
544	**DANGEROUS LADY** 24 [3] 3-7-11 Joanna Badger (7) 20/1: 06: Dwelt, bhd 5f out: longer 11f trip.	14 13a
326	**TIERRA DEL FUEGO** 70 [9] 6-9-5 M Tebbutt 25/1: 000-07: Held up, bhd 4f out: 2 month abs, no form.	nk 11a
259	**PIPADOR** 70 [2] 4-9-9 R Cochrane 12/1: 005-08: Bhd halfway: op 10/1, 10 wk abs: see 238.	10 5a
640	**TOWER OF SONG** 10 [8] 3-8-6 G Parkin 5/2: 542359: Held up/keen, bhd 5f out: op 2/1: btr 586, 566.	7 0a

9 ran   Time 2m 31.8 (10.5)   (Mice Group Plc)   N P Littmoden Newmarket, Suffolk

---

671   4.05 TEXT P368 HCAP 3YO+ 0-85 (D)   1m4f aw Going 10 -57 Slow   [76]
£4173   £1284   £642   £321   3 yo rec 23lb4 yo rec 2 lb

590	**PARABLE** 18 [8] D W Barker 4-9-2 (66) F Lynch 10/1: 656-51: 4 b c Midyan - Top Table (Shirley	70a

Heights) Held up, prog to chall fnl 2f, narrowly led ins last, styd on gamely, all out: unplcd in 3 starts for
L Cumani in '99 (rtd 74, tried up to 10f): eff over a sharp 12f, could stay further: acts on fibresand.

605	**GREEN BOPPER** 15 [10] G Woodward 7-9-8 (70) C Lowther 11/2: -52342: 7 b g Green Dancer - Wayage	hd 73a

(Mr Prospector) Chsd ldr after 4f, led over 5f out & rdn clr 3f out, hdd ins last, just held: win soon: see 302 (11f).

*605	**HANNIBAL LAD** 15 [1] W M Brisbourne 4-10-0 (78) T G McLaughlin 3/1: 523113: 4 ch g Rock City -	¾ 80a

Appealing (Star Appeal) Held up in tch, rdn/styd on well fnl 2f: op 5/2: clr rem, topweight: stays 12f: see 605.

*553	**BACHELORS PAD** 24 [1] Miss S J Wilton 6-9-2 (64) M Tebbutt 6/1: 211214: Trkd ldrs, held 2f out.	5 59a
560	**KIRISNIPPA** 22 [9] 5-8-5 (53) P Doe 11/1: 131605: Held up, eff 3f out, sn held: tchd 14/1: btr 474.	hd 47a
*642	**ACCYSTAN** 8 [5] 5-8-8 (56)(6ex) J Weaver 2/1 FAV: 062016: Held up, eff 3f out, no impress: op 5/2.	2½ 46a
605	**SWIFT** 15 [3] 6-9-7 (69) S Whitworth 14/1: 500-07: Chsd ldr 4f out, btn 2f out & eased fnl 1f: op 12/1:	10 48a

'99 wnr here at Southwell (2 h'caps, rtd 80a), Nottingham, Warwick & York (h'caps, rtd 70): '98 wnr at Wincanton
over timber (nov, rtd 80h): eff at 10/12f, stays 14f: acts on fast, hvy & both AWs: handles any trk: tough.

642	**STATE APPROVAL** 8 [6] 7-8-5 (53) L Newman (5) 6/1: 023368: Led 6f, btn 2f out: see 512, 270.	2½ 28a
642	**PICKENS** 8 [7] 8-8-12 (60) Kim Tinkler 20/1: 014-09: Al bhd: see 642.	4 29a
627	**YES KEEMO SABEE** 12 [2] 5-9-0 (62) L Newton 14/1: 210-60: 10th: op 12/1: see 627 (2m).	24 4a

10 ran   Time 2m 42.3 (8.0)   (Triple G Da Racing Syndicate)   D W Barker Scorton, N Yorks

---

672   4.40 TEXT P372 SELLER DIV 2 3-6YO (G)   1m3f aw Going 10 -65 Slow
£1500   £428   £214   3 yo rec 22lb4 yo rec 1 lb

647	**OVER THE MOON** 8 [6] M J Polglase 6-9-9 T G McLaughlin 15/2: -10101: 6 ch m Beveled - Beyond The	58a

Moon (Ballad Rock) Chsd ldr 4f out, rdn & styd on gamely ins last to lead nr line, all out: no bid: earlier
scored at W'hampton (sell) & here at Southwell (clmr, Miss S J Wilton): '99 W'hampton wnr (clmr, rtd 57a): won

SOUTHWELL (Fibresand) TUESDAY MARCH 14TH Lefthand, Sharp, Oval Track

again at W'hampton in '98 (3 clmrs, rtd 61a, N Littmoden): eff at 7f, suited by 1m/9.3f, now stays a sharp 11f well: loves fibresand & a sharp trk: eff with/without a visor & loves clmg/sell grade.

600 **ROYAL PARTNERSHIP 15** [8] K R Burke 4-9-13 Darren Williams (7) 11/2: P51402: 4 b g Royal Academy - Go Honey Go (General Assembly) Led 7f out, rdn/edged right ins last & hdd nr line: op 4/1, well clr of rem. *nk* **62$**

646 **SWING ALONG 8** [9] R Guest 5-9-9 R Cochrane 6/4 FAV: 005333: 5 ch m Alhijaz - So It Goes (Free State) Held up, rdn & kept on fnl 3f, no threat to front pair: op 5/4: clr of rem: btr 404 (amat h'cap, W'hampton). *5* **50a**

626 **APPROACHABLE 12** [5] Miss S J Wilton 5-9-10 M Tebbutt 5/2: 442324: Chsd ldrs 1m: op 3/1: see 455. *18* **31a**

641 **THE LAMBTON WORM 8** [1] 6-9-10 J Fanning 14/1: 56-465: Prom 1m: op 12/1: see 560. *2* **28a**

531 **DORANFIELD LADY 26** [4] 5-9-5 R Lappin 25/1: 0056: Led 4f, sn btn: longer 11f trip. *17* **4a**

586 **GILFOOT BREEZE 18** [2] 3-8-3 (bl)(1ow) O Pears 14/1: 60-047: Al bhd: op 10/1: flattered 586 (C/D). *15* **0a**

648 **PILOTS HARBOUR 8** [3] 4-9-9 (bl) A Culhane 10/1: 000-08: Prom 6f: op 8/1: unplcd in '99 (rtd 70, J L Dunlop, h'cap): '98 wnr at Beverley (mdn) & Newmarket (nurs, rtd 87): eff at 1m on fast & gd/soft grnd: likes a stiff trk & can force the pace: best without blnks: with D Chapman. *3½* **0a**

648 **WATERFRONT 8** [7] 4-9-9 H Bastiman 20/1: 000-09: Keen/prom, btn 5f out: see 648 (1m)., *22* **0a**

9 ran Time 2m 29.6 (8.3) (The Lovatt Partnership) M J Polglase Southwell, Notts

673 **5.15 TEXT P372 HCAP DIV 1 3YO+ 0-70 (E) 5f aw str Going 10 +06 Fast [70]**
£2296 £656 £328 3 yo rec 13lb Raced across track, winner alone on stands rail

71 **LORD HIGH ADMIRAL 99** [12] C G Cox 12-8-8 (50)(vis) S Drowne 10/1: 3004-1: 12 b g Bering - Baltic Sea (Danzig) Chsd ldr stands rail, went on halfway & styd on well, rdn out: 4 month abs: '99 Doncaster wnr (clmr, rtd 70): rnr-up 3 times in '98 (rtd 78 at best): best dominating over 5f, stays 6f well: acts on firm, soft & fibresand: eff with/without a visor: runs well fresh: handles any trk: tough 12yo, looks nicely hcapped. **57a**

631 **READY TO ROCK 10** [5] J S Moore 4-8-6 (48)(bl) P M Quinn (5) 7/1: 060122: 4 b g Up And At 'Em - Rocklands Rosie (Muscatite) Led in centre till halfway, rdn & kept on fnl 1f, not pace of wnr: op 6/1, see 573. *1¾* **49a**

609 **ASHOVER AMBER 14** [1] T D Barron 4-10-0 (70) C Lowther 11/4 FAV: 3-4523: 4 b f Green Desert - Zafaaf (Kris) Dwelt, towards rear centre, rdn & kept on fnl 2f, not pace to chall: top-weight: see 280. *2½* **64a**

472 **KIND EMPEROR 36** [4] M J Polglase 3-9-1 (70) Dean McKeown 8/1: 203-44: Chsd ldrs, onepace fnl 2f. *nk* **63a**

602 **E B PEARL 15** [2] 4-7-12 (40) J Bramhill 20/1: 00-065: Twds rear, late gains, no threat: clr rem. *shd* **33a**

205 **FAUTE DE MIEUX 87** [10] 5-9-8 (64)(BL) S Carson (5) 9/1: 0000-6: Prom 3f: op 12/1: blnks, abs. *5* **48a**

4331} **TREASURE TOUCH 99** [3] 6-9-3 (59) O Pears 9/1: 4020-7: Nvr on terms: op 8/1, 5 month abs: rnr-up in '99 (rtd 60, class stks): '97 wnr at Southwell, Nottingham (2), Newmarket & Thirsk (rtd 71a & 89 at best): eff at 5f, suited by 6f: acts on firm, gd/soft & fibresand: handles any trk: well h'capped, with D Nicholls. *1½* **40a**

*614 **OFF HIRE 14** [7] 4-9-2 (58)(vis) G Faulkner (3) 5/1: -14218: Hampered start, nvr on terms: op 7/2. *½* **37a**

3869} **KOSEVO 99** [6] 6-8-11 (53)(vis) N Callan 9/1: 6000-9: Al outpcd: op 7/1: '99 Haydock wnr (h'cap): '98 wnr here at Southwell (2, sell & h'cap, 1st for A Kelleway, rtd 51a): eff btwn 5f/7f on firm, gd/soft & both AWs: likes to race with/force the pace: eff with visor/blnks: tough/consistent & shld leave this bhd soon. *½* **30a**

635 **COLONEL SAM 10** [8] 4-8-1 (43)(tbl) Dale Gibson 14/1: 00-000: Hmpd start/al rear: 10th: op 12/1. *1* **18a**

563 **KALAR 21** [9] 11-7-10 (38)(bl)(12oh) K Dalgleish (7) 25/1: 0-0050: In tch till halfway: 11th: see 371. *½* **11a**

563 **BEVELED HAWTHORN 21** [11] 5-7-10 (38)(7oh) Iona Wands (5) 10/1: /61-40: Prom 3f: 12th, op 8/1. *9* **0a**

12 ran Time 58.00 (0.2) (Elite Racing Club) C G Cox Lyneham, wilts

674 **5.45 TEXT P372 HCAP DIV 2 3YO+ 0-70 (E) 5f aw str Going 10 -06 Slow [68]**
£2296 £656 £328 3 yo rec 13lb Raced across track, no advantage

614 **SUPREME ANGEL 14** [9] M P Muggeridge 5-9-5 (59)(bl) T G McLaughlin 6/1: 000-31: 5 b m Beveled - Blue Angel (Lord Gayle) Chsd ldrs, rdn to chall/hung left over 1f out, led well ins last, drvn out: op 4/1: unplcd in '99 (rtd 63): '98 Kempton wnr (h'cap, rtd 88): eff at 5/6f on firm, soft & fibresand: eff with/without blnks. **65a**

*609 **JACK TO A KING 14** [2] J Balding 5-9-3 (57)(bl) J Edmunds 7/2 FAV: 520212: 5 b g Nawwar - Rudda Flash (General David) Led, rdn/hdd well ins last & no extra: tough sort, remains in gd heart: see 609. *½* **60a**

587 **QUEEN SARABI 18** [4] D Nicholls 5-8-10 (50) A Nicholls (3) 9/1: 404-03: 5 b m Mujtahid - Sharp Slipper (Sharpo) Chsd ldrs, rdn/hung left & swished tail over 1f out, no extra ins last: op 6/1: ex-Irish, back in '98 scored at Tipperary (mdn): eff at 5f: acts on fibresand, gd/soft & hvy grnd. *2½* **46a**

653 **ARAB GOLD 6** [5] M Quinn 5-8-0 (40) C Rutter 8/1: 303144: Prom, onepace fnl 2f: op 6/1, quick reapp: acts on both AWs: see 634 (6f, equitrack). *1* **34a**

622 **MAMMAS F C 12** [1] 4-8-6 (46) R Ffrench 12/1: 20-005: Rdn/towards rear, nvr pace to chall: op 10/1. *½* **38a**

*602 **BLUSHING GRENADIER 15** [3] 8-9-0 (54)(bl) S Finnamore (7) 5/1: 433016: Sn outpcd, mod late gains. *½* **44a**

559 **ELTON LEDGER 22** [7] 11-9-7 (61)(vis) R Fitzpatrick (3) 8/1: 212227: Dwelt/twds rear, late prog: op 5/1. *nk* **50a**

2633} **CHILLIAN 99** [10] 4-7-10 (36)(2oh) G Bardwell 33/1: /000-8: Chsd ldrs 3f: 8 month abs: AW bow: no form in '99: unplcd in '98 (rtd 54, debut): with M Brittain. *1* **23a**

2102} **PRESENT CHANCE 99** [11] 6-9-10 (64)(bl) L Newton 11/2: 1534-9: Al outpcd: op 8/1, 9 month abs: '99 scorer here at Southwell (C/D, h'cap, 1st time blnks, rtd 65a, plcd on turf, rtd 73 at best, h'cap): '98 Goodwood wnr (stks, rtd 82 at best, B McMahon): eff at 5f/7f, stays 1m: acts on fm, soft & fibresand: eff with/without blnks. *1½* **48a**

639 **SAMMAL 10** [6] 4-8-13 (53) D Holland 10/1: 043-00: Chsd ldr 3f, btn/eased 1f out: 10th: op 8/1. *2* **32a**

558 **Mr Stickywicket 22** [8] 3-7-12 (51)(2ow)(21oh) S Righton 33/1:

602 **Squire Corrie 15** [12] 8-8-7 (47)(bl) G Parkin 20/1:

12 ran Time 58.6 (0.8) (Least Moved Partners) M P Muggeridge Eastbury, Berks

WOLVERHAMPTON (Fibresand) THURSDAY MARCH 16TH Lefthand, Sharp Track

Official Going STANDARD. Stalls: Inside, Except 7f - Outside.

675 **1.50 AMAT HCAP DIV 1 4YO+ 0-60 (G) 1m100y aw rnd Going 51 -41 Slow [36]**
£1572 £449 £224

588 **JESSINCA 20** [2] Derrick Morris 4-10-12 (48) Mr T Doyle 8/1: 0-3151: 4 b f Minshaanshu Amad - Noble Soul (Sayf El Arab) Chsd ldrs, briefly outpcd 2f out, styd on well ins last to lead nr fin, rdn out: tchd 10/1: earlier scored at Southwell (fill h'cap, 1st win): unplcd in '99 (rtd 45a & 25, R Phillips): eff arnd 1m, further cld suit: acts on fibresand & a sharp trk: open to further improvement. **53a**

637 **BREAD WINNER 12** [6] I A Balding 4-11-7 (57)(vis) Mr J Gee (5) 3/1 FAV: 5-4222: 4 b g Reprimand - Khubza (Green Desert) Held up, rdn/styd on wide fnl 2f, not reach wnr: tchd 100/30: see 568, 504. *1* **59a**

650   **MALCHIK 8** [8] P Howling 4-10-2 (38) Miss S Pocock (5) 16/1: 002003: 4 ch g Absalom - Very Good   nk   **39a**
(Noalto) Towards rear, styd on well fnl 3f for press, nrst fin: see 159 (7f, sell).
550   **SHARP SHUFFLE 26** [1] Ian Williams 7-11-4 (54) Mr D Dennis (5) 8/1: 0-2024: Handy, chsd ldr over 1f   nk   **54a**
briefly led ins last, no extra cl-home: op 7/1: see 138 (C/D, sell).
618   **COOL PROSPECT 15** [5] 5-10-10 (46) Miss E Ramsden (5) 8/1: 0-0505: Prom, rdn/ch over 1f out, no extra.   ½   **45a**
637   **GABLESEA 12** [12] 6-10-10 (46) Miss S M Potts (2) 6/1: 0-0246: Twds rear/wide, late gains, nrst fin.   nk   **44a**
621   **OCEAN LINE 15** [4] 5-10-4 (40) Mr T Best (5) 9/2: -23227: Led after 1f till over 1f out, fdd ins last.   ¾   **37a**
599   **DOBERMAN 17** [7] 5-10-7 (43) (bl) Miss E Folkes (5) 12/1: 503108: Led 1f, btn 1f out: see 550 (clmr).   2½   **35a**
412   **DREAM CARRIER 48** [11] 12-9-6 (25) (3ow) Mrs C Peacock (0) 33/1: 6-0009: Al rear: abs: see 412.   ¾   **19a**
569   **MISS TAKE 23** [9] 4-10-6 (42) Miss C Hannaford (5) 11/1: 004400: Al bhd: 10th: op 14/1: see 384.   7   **22a**
3815} **Cheerful Groom 99** [3] 9-9-11 (33) Mr P Aspell (7) 20/1: 517 **Mustang 30** [10] 7-10-5 (41) (vis) Mrs L Pearce 12/1:
12 ran   Time 1m 54.00 (7.8)   (The Lambourn Racing Club)   Derrick Morris Lambourn, Berks

676   2.20 AMAT HCAP DIV 2 4YO+ 0-60 (G)   **1m100y aw rnd   Going 51   -31 Slow**   [33]
£1572   £449   £224

620   **MY TYSON 15** [8] K A Ryan 5-10-11 (44) Miss E Ramsden (5) 14/1: 0-0001: 5 b g Don't Forget Me -   **50a**
Shuckran Habibi (Thatching) Chsd ldrs, rdn/prog to lead ins last, styd on well, pushed out cl-home: op 12/1:
unplcd in '99 (rtd 41a): unplcd in '98 (rtd 54 & 45a, h'caps, K Mahdi): '97 Lingfield wnr (mdn, rtd 68a, rtd 66 on
turf): suited by 1m nowadays: acts on both AWs & poss handles fast: likes a sharp trk & runs well for an amateur.
497   **MIDNIGHT WATCH 34** [6] A G Newcombe 6-10-7 (40) Miss C Hannaford (5) 7/2 JT FAV: 000132: 6 b g   1¾   **42a**
Capote - Midnight Air (Green Dancer) Led, edged right & hdd ins last, no extra: op 3/1: remains in gd heart.
554   **NERONIAN 26** [10] Miss D A McHale 6-9-11 (30) Miss L Johnston (7) 14/1: 056-43: 6 ch g Mujtahid -   1¾   **29a**
Nimieza (Nijinsky) Chsd ldrs, rdn to chall fnl 2f, onepace: op 12/1: acts on fast, gd & firebsand: see 554.
*648   **GODMERSHAM PARK 10** [5] P S Felgate 8-11-3 (50) (5ex) Mr P Collington (7) 7/2 JT FAV: 234414: Chsd   2   **45a**
ldr, outpcd over 3f out, kept on again fnl 1f: clr rem: see 648 (Southwell).
581   **JATO DANCER 21** [1] 5-9-13 (22) (10ow) Miss A Knobbs (2) 20/1: 500005: Mid-div, btn 3f out: see 359.   8   **15a**
569   **KASS ALHAWA 23** [3] 7-11-7 (54) Miss R Clark 11/2: 10-206: Rear/hmpd after 2f, nvr factor: see 38.   4   **29a**
404   **KAFIL 49** [4] 6-10-13 (46) Mr T Best (5) 5/1: 60-267: Chsd ldrs 6f: 7 wk abs: btr 254, 1.   shd   **21a**
612   **RA RA RASPUTIN 16** [7] 5-10-12 (45) Miss S M Potts (4) 7/1: 410008: Al bhd: op 12/1: see 471, 396.   4   **12a**
4574} **BRIDAL WHITE 99** [9] 4-10-10 (43) Mr P Close (5) 25/1: 0000-9: Prom 5f: 3 month jmps abs (unplcd,   3   **4a**
rtd 71h): unplcd in '99 (rtd 66 & 24a): plcd twice in '98 (rtd 72, K Wingrove): keeps 6/7f, handles fast & soft.
635   **STATE WIND 12** [11] 4-10-8 (41) (vis) Mrs C Williams 8/1: 00-060: Bhd halfway: 10th: see 635.   1   **0a**
582   **NICHOLAS MISTRESS 21** [2] 4-10-0 (33) Miss E Folkes (5) 20/1: -05000: Sn bhd: 11th: see 316.   ½   **0a**
4225} **BELLAS GATE BOY 99** [12] 8-11-1 (48) Mrs L Pearce 8/1: 6110-0: Al rear: 12th: keeps fig: '99   2½   **1a**
wnr at Warwick & W'hampton (h'caps, rtd 53 & 47a): '98 Lingfield wnr (lady riders h'cap, rtd 54): eff at 7f/8.5f,
stays 12f: acts on firm, soft & fibresand: handles any trk, likes Lingfield: goes well for an amateur.
12 ran   Time 1m 53.2 (7.0)   (Mrs Candice Reilly)   K A Ryan Hambleton, N Yorks

677   2.55 0800 211 222 CLAIMER 3YO+ (F)   **7f aw rnd   Going 51   -06 Slow**
£2415   £690   £345   3 yo rec 15lb

580   **BLAKESET 21** [4] T G Mills 5-9-11 (bl) L Carter 15/8 FAV: 20-551: 5 ch h Midyan - Penset (Red   **84a**
Sunset) Made all, rdn/clr over 2f out, eased nr fin, rdly: val for 8L+: '99 Lingfield scorer (h'cap, rtd 82a at best),
earlier rnr-up on turf for R Hannon, (rtd 85, stks): plcd in '98 (rtd 88, h'cap): eff at 7/7.5f: acts on firm, gd &
both AWs: eff in blnks, tried a t-strap: gd weight carrier: loves to force the pace on a sharp trk.
580   **ROYAL CASCADE 21** [1] B A McMahon 6-9-7 (bl) T Quinn 5/1: -06302: 6 b g River Falls - Relative   5   **68a**
Stranger (Cragador) Rdn/towards rear, kept on fnl 2f, no impress: op 4/1: see 511, 33.
645   **DAHLIDYA 10** [6] M J Polglase 5-9-4 P Doe 12/1: 101503: 5 b m Midyan - Dahlawise (Caerleon)   6   **56a**
Dwelt, kept on fnl 2f, no threat: op 10/1: btr 538 (6f).
604   **DAYNABEE 17** [0] Miss S J Wilton 5-8-13 I Mongan (5) 14/1: 546354: Chsd wnr, btn over 1f out.   1¼   **48$**
594   **RONS PET 19** [2] 5-9-13 (tbl) N Callan 3/1: 322355: Prom 4f: op 5/1: btr 398, 33.   nk   **61a**
598   **TAKHLID 17** [8] 9-9-9 A Culhane 7/1: 225366: Nvr a factor: op 6/1: btr 142 (C/D).   nk   **56a**
667   **C HARRY 2** [3] 6-9-5 P M Quinn 10/1: 542657: Chsd ldrs 5f: op 12/1: qck reapp: likes sells.   nk   **51a**
4586} **FIRE DOME 99** [9] 8-9-13 Alex Greaves 11/2: 1004-8: Wide/chsd ldrs 5f: 5 month abs: '99 wnr at   6   **50a**
Sandown & Redcar (clmrs, rtd 83, rtd 106 in Gr 2 company, prob flattered): '98 Thirsk (stks) & Sandown wnr (List,
rtd 107): stays 7f, suited by 5/6f: acts on firm & fibresand, enjoys gd & hvy: handles any trk, likes Sandown:
best without blnks & well suited by clmg grade nowadays: 8yo who can be placed to effect.
612   **COMEOUTOFTHEFOG 16** [5] 5-9-3 L Newman 12/1: -50159: Al outpcd rear: op 10/1: btr 567 (sell).   6   **31a**
553   **GILWILL 27** [7] 5-9-4 A Daly 50/1: B0: Bhd halfway: 10th: no form.   8   **20a**
10 ran   Time 1m 30.2 (4.0)   (Epsom Downs Racing Club)   T G Mills Headley, Surrey, Epsom

678   3.30 BEST BETS HCAP 3YO+ 0-85 (D)   **5f aw   Going 51   +05 Fast**   [76]
£3750   £1154   £577   £288   3 yo rec 12lb

579   **EASTERN TRUMPETER 21** [6] J M Bradley 4-9-4 (66) J Weaver 3/1: 05-141: 4 b c First Trump - Oriental   **72a**
Air (Taufan) Chsd ldrs, led 1f out, in command fnl 1f, pushed out: best time of day: earlier won at W'hampton
(h'cap): '99 scorer at Folkestone (clmr) & Ayr (5f, rtd 70 & 63a): '98 rnr-up (rtd 64, sell, G Lewis): stays
a sharp 6f, all wins at 5f: acts on fast, loves soft & f/sand: handles sharp trk, loves W'hampton: tough & genuine.
645   **TELECASTER 10** [1] C R Egerton 4-9-10 (72) (bl) D Sweeney 5/2 FAV: 121152: 4 ch g Indian Ridge -   1   **74a**
Monashee (Sovereign Dancer) Led, rdn/hdd 1f out & not pace of wnr: tchd 3/1: ran to best: see 622 (C/D).
64   **PURE COINCIDENCE 99** [7] K R Burke 5-9-13 (75) N Callan 8/1: 3600-3: 5 b g Lugana Beach - Esilam   ½   **75a**
(Frimley Park) Chsd ldrs, rdn/nvr able to chall: op 7/1: 4 month abs: '99 Carlisle scorer (h'cap, rtd 83 at best,
unplcd on sand, rtd 62a): plcd in '98 (rtd 80, unplcd on sand, rtd 65a, G Lewis): eff at 6f, all wins at 5f: acts
on firm, soft & fibresand: handles any trk: has run well in blnks tho' best without: can win more races this term.
129   **DOUBLE O 99** [5] W Jarvis 6-9-11 (73) (bl) T Quinn 11/2: 0030-4: Outpcd wide halfway, mod prog: abs.   2½   **66a**
614   **BEDEVILLED 16** [8] 5-9-8 (70) C Lowther 9/2: 0-2025: Chsd ldr, fdd fnl 1f: see 342.   shd   **63a**
518   **SAMWAR 30** [3] 8-9-11 (73) (vis) R Fitzpatrick (3) 5/1: 406226: Al outpcd: op 9/2: see 214 (clmr).   1   **64a**
4610} **WHIZZ KID 99** [2] 6-7-10 (44) (7oh) Claire Bryan (5) 8/1: 0100-7: Sn outpcd: op 14/1, 4 month abs: 8   **20a**
'99 scorer at Ripon, Redcar, Chepstow, Ayr & Newcastle (h'caps, rtd 82 at best, unplcd on sand, rtd 43a): missed
'98: stays 6f, suited by 5f: acts on firm & both AWs, enjoys gd/soft & soft grnd: handles any trk.
491   **SOAKED 35** [4] 7-10-0 (76) A Culhane 14/1: 04-008: Nvr on terms: op 16/1: topweight: see 394.   2½   **45a**
8 ran   Time 1m 02.5 (2.3)   (R G G Racing)   J M Bradley Sedbury, Glos

WOLVERHAMPTON (Fibresand)   THURSDAY MARCH 16TH   Lefthand, Sharp Track

679
4.10 ITV TEXT CLASSIFIED STKS 3YO+ (E)   1m4f aw   Going 51   -25 Slow
£2538   £725   £362   3 yo rec 22lb 4 yo rec 2 lb

556   **COUNT DE MONEY 24** [3] Miss S J Wilton 5-9-12 (t) I Mongan (5) 7/1: -23121: 5 b g Last Tycoon - **76a**
Menominee (Soviet Star) Held up, prog to lead halfway, rdn clr 2f out, pushed out: earlier won at Southwell (clmr,
S Bowring): '99 Southwell (5, in gd/soft/clmrs/class stks) & W'hampton wnr (clmr, rtd 68a & 35): '98 Southwell wnr
(amat h'cap, rtd 54a): eff at 11/14f on firm & fast, fibresand/Southwell & W'hampton specialist: eff in a t-strap.
618   **SEA DANZIG 15** [2] J J Bridger 7-9-10 (bl) D Holland 5/1: 010422: 7 ch g Roi Danzig - Tosara   3½ **68a**
(Main Reef) Led/dsptd lead till over 2f out, onepace/held over 2f out: acts on both AWs: best dominating.
548   **NOUKARI 26** [6] P D Evans 7-9-8 Joanna Badger (7) 9/2: 054453: 7 b g Darshaan - Noufiyla (Top Ville)   2 **63a**
Held up, eff over 2f out, sn held: plcd over timber 3 days ago: see 151 (equitrack).
4295} **SUPERSONIC 99** [1] R F Johnson Houghton 4-9-3 M Hills 5/2: 2520-4: Led/dsptd lead till over 7f out,   4 **54a**
btn fnl 2f: op 3/1, 5 month abs: AW bow: rnr-up thrice in '99 (rtd 75, h'cap): no form sole start in '98 (mdn):
eff at 10f, return to that trip shld suit: acts on fast & gd/soft grnd, any trk: still a mdn but can find a race.
*407   **APOLLO BAY 49** [5] 4-9-8 J Fanning 9/4 FAV: 303-15: Bhd 2f out, eased: lame, abs: see 407 (blnks).   *dist* **0a**
2858} **SHAMEL 99** [4] 4-9-6 J P Spencer 5/1: 3134-6: Rear, bhd 5f out: 8 month abs: AW bow: '99   24 **0a**
Yarmouth scorer (h'cap, rtd 73, J Dunlop): rtd 70 in '98 (mdn): eff at 12f, suited by 14f, tried 2m: acts on firm
& gd grnd: gd weight carrier, now with D Shaw.
6 ran   Time 2m 42.7 (9.1)   (John Pointon & Sons)   Miss S J Wilton Wetley Rocks, Staffs

680
4.40 TEXT P372 SELLER 3YO+ (G)   6f aw rnd Going 51   +01 Fast
£1913   £546   £273   3 yo rec 13lb

609   **MANORBIER 16** [6] K A Ryan 4-9-12 F Lynch 5/2 FAV: 0/0141: 4 ch g Shalford - La Pirouette (Kennedy   **64a**
Road) Chsd ldr over 2f out, rdn/led over 1f out & sn in command, rdn out: op 7/2: bought in for 7,800 gns:
earlier scored here at W'hampton (sell): missed '99: '98 Chepstow wnr (juv auct mdn, D Arbuthnott, rtd 83):
eff at 5/6f: acts on fast, gd & fibresand: likes W'hampton & sell grade.
604   **MARENGO 17** [9] M J Polglase 6-9-12 T G McLaughlin 12/1: 003062: 6 b g Never So Bold - Born To   4 **52a**
Dance (Dancing Brave) Mid-div, rdn & kept on fnl 2f for press, no chit with wnr: op 183 (3m made all).
47   **PALO BLANCO 99** [11] Andrew Reid 9-9-2 M Henry 16/1: 06/0-3: 9 b m Precocious - Linpac Mapleleaf   1½ **38a**
(Dominion) Held up, kept on fnl 2f for press, no threat: 4 mth abs: no form sole '99 start: plcd sev times in '98
(rtd 65a & 61 , G Moore & M Ryan): '97 Sandown scorer (clmr, rtd 70): handles AW: eff at 5/7f on firm, gd/soft & both AWs.
639   **NIFTY NORMAN 12** [5] D Nicholls 6-9-12 (bl) Alex Greaves 9/2: 323634: Led after 1f, hdd over 1f   nk **47a**
out & no extra: also bhd this wnr in 533, a return to 5f shld suit: see 440, 272 (5f).
547   **PALACEGATE TOUCH 26** [7] 10-9-7 (bl) P Bradley (5) 13/2: -34205: Mid-div, nvr on terms: op 5/1.   ¾ **40a**
3116} **NOW IS THE HOUR 99** [1] 4-9-7 A Nicholls (3) 20/1: 0060-6: Prom 5f: 8 mth abs: mod form.   3 **33a**
634   **ROWLANDSONS STUD 14** [13] 7-9-7 (t) A McCarthy (3) 16/1: -60367: Prom 4f: see 571 (equitrack).   shd **33$**
583   **MIKES DOUBLE 21** [12] 6-9-7 (vis) R Fitzpatrick (3) 14/1: 523058: Al outpcd: op 12/1: btr 142 (7f).   ½ **31a**
635   **MOY 12** [3] 5-9-2 (bl) J Weaver 4/1: 260539: Chsd ldrs 4f, op 5/1: btr 466 (C/D h'cap).   2½ **19a**
609   **PRESS AHEAD 16** [2] 5-9-12 T Quinn 9/1: 0-1550: Mid-div, outpcd fnl 2f: 10th: btr 351 (C/D hcap).   nk **28a**
604   **LITTLE IBNR 17** [4] 5-9-7 (vis) S Drowne 8/1: 430620: Al rear: 11th: see 465, 436.   ½ **21a**
507   **JONATHANS GIRL 33** [10] 5-9-2 D Holland 14/1: 0-5040: Led 1f, btn 2f out: 12th: op 12/1: see 358.   1 **14a**
--   **JOKEL** [8] 5-9-2 Claire Bryan (5) 20/1: 0: Dwelt, sn bhd: 13th: debut, with J Bradley.   22 **0a**
13 ran   Time 1m 15.8 (3.0)   (Uncle Jacks Pub)   K A Ryan Hambleton, N Yorks

681
5.15 DON ALLEN HCAP 3YO+ 0-85 (D)   1m1f79y aw Going 51   -01 Slow   [78]
£3926   £1208   £604   £302   3 yo rec 19lb

551   **DANAKIL 26** [8] K R Burke 5-9-0 (64) N Callan 7/1: 566351: 5 b g Warning - Danilova (Lyphard)   **69a**
Chsd ldrs, rdn to lead ins last, rdn out: visor omitted: '99 W'hampton wnr (mdn, rtd 77a & 64, J Banks): missed
'98: eff at 1m/9.5f on fast & f/sand, handles gd & soft: likes a sharp trk, esp W'hampton: has run well fresh.
611   **ARC 16** [1] G M Moore 6-9-4 (68) J Weaver 4/1: 24-242: 6 b g Archway - Columbian Sand (Salmon Leap)   1 **70a**
Held up in tch, prog/rdn to lead over 1f out, hdd/no extra ins last: op 5/1: see 611, 551 & 38.
*611   **AREISH 16** [9] J Balding 7-8-9 (59) J Edmunds 5/2 FAV: 111213: 7 b m Keen - Cool Combination (Indian   2 **57a**
King) Held up in tch, rdn to chase ldrs wide fnl 2f, kept on, not able to chall: op 2/1: see 611 (C/D).
*672   **OVER THE MOON 2** [3] M J Polglase 6-8-11 (61)(6ex) T G McLaughlin 7/1: 101014: Rear, rdn 3f out, sn   2 **55a**
onepace/held: quick reapp: see 672 (11f).
637   **DARE 12** [5] 5-8-13 (63)(vis) S Drowne 4/1: 200035: Led over 4f out till over 1f out, no extra: vis reapp.   nk **56a**
623   **RAMBO WALTZER 14** [2] 8-9-6 (70) I Mongan (5) 9/2: 112126: Trkd ldr, led 6f out till over 4f out, sn held.   ½ **62a**
611   **SUMMER BOUNTY 16** [7] 4-8-5 (55) P M Quinn (5) 10/1: 2-0607: Dwelt, chsd ldrs 7f: see 469.   7 **36a**
4522} **DIAMOND FLAME 99** [6] 6-10-0 (78) W R Swinburn 6/1: 4020-8: Chsd ldrs, rdn/btn 3f out: tchd 7/1, 2 **55a**
5 month abs, topweight: rnr-up in '99 (rtd 61, class stks, unplcd on sand, rtd 78a, h'cap): '98 wnr at Lingfield
(mdn) & W'hampton (stks, rtd 93a & 84): eff at 9.4f/10f: acts on both AWs, handles soft grnd: handles any trk.
3860} **CEDAR WELLS 99** [4] 4-9-11 (61) Claire Bryan (5) 14/1: 2200-9: Led 3f, btn 3f out: op 12/1: 6 mth   12 **20a**
abs: rnr-up twice in '99 (rtd 71, clmr, G Lewis): late '98 Lingfield (nurs h'cap, rtd 59a, unplcd on turf, rtd
78, prob flattered): eff around 7f/1m: acts on firm, gd & equitrack: likes a sharp/undul trk: with J M Bradley.
9 ran   Time 2m 03.1 (4.9)   (The Danakillists)   K R Burke Newmarket

SOUTHWELL (Fibresand)   FRIDAY MARCH 17TH   Lefthand, Sharp, Oval Track

Official Going STANDARD. Stalls: Inside.

682
1.40 AMAT HCAP DIV 1 3YO+ 0-70 (F)   1m4f aw Going 43   -14 Slow   [70]
£1799   £514   £257   4 yo rec 2 lb

502   **CEDAR FLAG 35** [6] R J O'Sullivan 6-7-12 (40) P M Quinn 9/4: -32431: 6 br g Jareer - Sasha Lea   **49a**
(Cawston's Clown) In tch, smooth prog to lead 3f out, sn in command, pushed out, easily: val for 8L+, 1st win:
unplcd in '99 (rtd 47a): eff arnd 12f, stays 2m: acts on f/sand, handles equitrack: could win again.
4590} **WINSOME GEORGE 99** [9] C W Fairhurst 5-8-5 (47) R Cody Bouthcer (2) 20/1: 0000-2: 5 b g Marju -   6 **47a**

215

June Moon (Sadler's Wells) Mid-div, rdn to chase front pair over 3f out, kept on to take 2nd ins last, no ch with wnr: op 14/1: unplcd in '99 (rtd 66, h'cap): '98 Beverley & Redcar wnr (h'caps, rtd 82): eff at 11/14f on fast & gd, handles fibresand: handles any trk & suited by a visor: creditable AW bow, on a fair mark.
641 **MANFUL 11** [4] R Brotherton 8-7-10 (38)(bl)(6oh) J Mackay (5) 16/1: 0-1003: 8 b g Efisio - Mandrian (Mandamus) Chsd ldrs, rdn/lost place over 3f out, kept on fnl 2f to take 3rd, no threat: blnks reapp: see 260. 3½ 33a
*608 **ABLE PETE 17** [7] A G Newcombe 4-7-10 (40)(1oh) Joanna Badger (5) 2/1 FAV: 050214: Cl-up, led over 5f out till over 3f out, sn btn: well clr of rem: btr 608 (amat h'cap, made all). 1 33a
637 **TURN TO STONE 13** [3] 6-7-10 (38)(bl)(8oh) K Dalgleish (5) 25/1: /00-05: Chsd ldrs 1m: see 637 (9f). 22 6a
508 **LOST SPIRIT 34** [5] 4-8-8 (52) Darren Williams (3) 13/2: 202506: Led 7f, sn strugg: btr 441 (eqtrk). nk 19a
-- **PEKAY** [1] 7-10-0 (70) J Bosley (5) 6/1: 4312/7: Al bhd: op 7/1, 10 month jumps abs (plcd, rtd 102h, h'cap, M C Pipe): '98 Salisbury wnr (h'cap, rtd 75 at best): eff btwn 9/12f, could stay further: acts on fast & soft grnd: gd weight carrier who wears blnks, eff without: AW bow today for B Smart. 12 24a
4434} **BRATBY 99** [2] 4-8-3 (47) Joanna Badger (5) 25/1: 4000-8: Sn bhd: 5 month abs: '99 wnr at Lingfield (appr h'cap, made all, rtd 49a, M Bell): eff over a sharp 1m on equitrack: runs well fresh: with M C Chapman. 30 0a
502 **ALNAJASHEE 35** [8] 4-9-6 (64)(t) G Baker (5) 11/1: 6-1469: Struggling halfway, virtually p.u. str: op 8/1: not his form: btr 339 (12f, mdn h'cap, C/D). dist 0a
9 ran Time 2m 41.1 (6.8) (R O S Racing) R J O'Sullivan Epsom, Surrey

683 2.10 AMAT HCAP DIV 2 3YO+ 0-70 (F) 1m4f aw Going 43 -37 Slow [70]
£1795 £513 £256 4 yo rec 2 lb

607 **EVEZIO RUFO 17** [6] N P Littmoden 8-8-8 (50)(vis) S Finnamore (3) 6/1: 131451: 8 b g Blakeney - Empress Corina (Free State) Chsd ldrs, styd on gamely for press to lead nr line, all out: earlier won at W'hampton (2, h'caps): '99 W'hampton wnr (2, sell & h'cap, rtd 47a & 34): '98 Lingfield, Southwell & W'hampton wnr (h'caps, rtd 61a & 56): eff at 11/14.8f on fast, hvy & equitrack, f/sand specialist: eff in vis/blnks & for an appr. 56a
641 **TEMPRAMENTAL 11** [7] S R Bowring 4-7-11 (40)(1ow) C Cogan 11/4: 530-22: 4 ch f Midhish - Musical Hom (Music Boy) Led, rdn/clr over 3f out, hard rdn/hdd nr line: clr rem: deserves similar: see 641, 136. nk 46a
*641 **ICHI BEAU 11** [1] F Murphy 6-8-11 (53)(6ex) P Goode 6/4 FAV: 3-4113: 6 b g Convinced - May As Well (Kemal) Cl-up, rdn 3f out, hung left/no extra & hit rail over 1f out: clr rem: op 7/4, 6lb pen: btr 641 (C/D). 6 49a
600 **HIBAAT 18** [4] M C Chapman 4-7-10 (40)(11oh) Joanna Badger (5) 50/1: 000004: Well bhd, mod gains. 15 20a
608 **INKWELL 17** [9] 6-8-4 (46)(bl)(8ow)(11oh) I Mongan (0) 15/2: 04-525: Held up in tch, eff halfway, rdn/btn 3f out: op 5/1: see 260, 224. 3 22a
369 **RAED 56** [5] 7-7-12 (40) L Newman 14/1: 060-36: Cl-up, strugg 4f out: abs, op 10/1: with A McNae. 4 10a
637 **LAA JADEED 13** [8] 5-7-10 (38)(6oh) S Yourston (6) 20/1: 0-0057: Prom 6f, sn btn: see 476. nk 7a
2607} **FERNY FACTORS 99** [3] 4-8-5 (49) K Dalgleish (5) 14/1: 1100-8: Sn bhd: 8 month abs: '99 Beverley wnr (2, sell & h'cap, rtd 57): '98 wnr again at Beverley (sell, 1st time blnks, rtd 60): eff at 10f, stays a slow run 12f: acts on gd & gd/soft, loves Beverley: eff with/without blnks, tried a visor: enjoys sell grade. dist 0a
8 ran Time 2m 43.90 (9.6) (O A Gunter) N P Littmoden Newmarket

684 2.40 CLASS CLAIMER DIV 1 3YO+ 0-60 (F) 1m aw rnd Going 43 -11 Slow
£1722 £492 £246 3 yo rec 17lb

*612 **LORD EUROLINK 17** [8] C A Dwyer 6-9-8 (tvi) D Holland 5/2 FAV: 305311: 6 b g Danehill - Lady Eurolink (Kala Shikari) Made most, rdn clr over 1f out, pushed out ins last: val for 10L+: recent W'hampton wnr (sell): plcd on turf in '99 (rtd 79, appr h'cap): plcd sole '98 start for J Dunlop (h'cap, rtd 92): eff at 1m/10f on fast, gd/soft & fibresand, handles equitrack: eff in a t-strap: likes to force the pace & enjoys sell/claiming grade. 64a
541 **CACOPHONY 28** [3] S Dow 3-8-0 (VIS) P Doe 4/1: -54622: 3 b g Son Pardo - Ansellady (Absalom) Prom, hard rdn 2f out, sn held: op 6/1: tried a visor: see 94 (mdn). 8 47a
550 **TUFAMORE 27** [6] K R Burke 4-9-10 (bl) D Hayes (7) 11/2: 210533: 4 ch g Mt Livermore - Tufa (Warning) Prom, rdn & outpcd fnl 2f: op 3/1: see 550, 411 (h'cap). 1 52a
646 **BENTICO 11** [4] Mrs N Macauley 11-9-3 (vis) R Fitzpatrick (3) 14/1: 046/04: Handy, onepace fnl 2f: op 12/1: jockey given a 3-day ban for careless riding: see 646 (reapp after long abs). nk 44a
647 **PLEASURE TRICK 11** [10] 9-9-6 Kim Tinkler 20/1: 0-0005: Handy wide halfway, sn outpcd: see 496. nk 46$
637 **HEATHYARDS JAKE 13** [1] 4-9-5 P M Quinn (5) 6/1: 540066: Bhd, efft wide 3f out, sn held: btr 229. 1¾ 42a
555 **FORTHECHOP 25** [5] 3-8-3 S Righton 10/1: -45437: Prom, strugg 3f out: tchd 12/1: see 429 (sell). 12 25a
647 **ERUPT 11** [9] 7-9-7 G Bardwell 11/2: 006-28: Rear/sn rdn, no impress: btr 647 (C/D h'cap). 2 22a
585 **SOUNDS COOL 21** [7] 4-9-4 S Finnamore (7) 25/1: -65049: Sn bhd: see 338 (mdn h'cap). 2¾ 16a
502 **SEA GOD 35** [2] 9-9-3 Joanna Badger (7) 50/1: 00-000: Sn bhd: 10th: recent jmps rnr: see 502. ½ 14a
10 ran Time 1m 43.7 (4.3) (Roalco Limited) C A Dwyer Newmarket

685 3.10 BEST BETS MDN 3YO+ (D) 6f aw rnd Going 43 -05 Slow
£2847 £876 £438 £219 3 yo rec 13lb

2377} **LORD YASMIN 99** [12] J Noseda 3-8-11 J Weaver 12/1: 02-1: 3 b c Lahib - Adieu Cherie (Bustino) Trkd ldrs, rdn to lead dist, pushed out cl-home: 9 month abs/AW bow, op 7/1: rnr-up on 2nd start in '99 (sell, rtd 67): eff at 6f, 7f+ shld suit: acts on gd grnd & f/sand: likes a sharp trk & runs well fresh. 77a
4369} **WELSH VALLEY 99** [11] M L W Bell 3-8-6 M Fenton 3/1: 02-2: 3 b f Irish River - Sweet Snow (Lyphard) Led, rdn & hdd dist, styd on well for press tho' al just held: clr of rem, 5 month abs/AW bow: rnr-up on 2nd of 2 '99 starts (fill mdn, rtd 72): eff at 6f, 7f+ looks sure to suit: acts on fast & f/sand: now qual for h'caps. ½ 69a
598 **ABOVE BOARD 18** [7] R F Marvin 5-9-10 (bl) T G McLaughlin 14/1: 002203: 5 b g Night Shift - Bundled Up (Sharpen Up) Cl-up, drvn/no extra fnl 2f: offic rtd 50, treat rating with caution: see 558, 201 (C/D, sell). 8 54a
4309} **STROMSHOLM 99** [5] J R Fanshawe 4-9-10 R Cochrane 11/8 FAV: 02-4: Mid-div, rdn/nvr able to chall: well bckd: AW bow/5 month abs: rnr-up on 2nd of 2 '99 starts (mdn, rtd 76): stays 1m & a return to 7f+ will surely suit: acts on gd grnd: now qual for h'caps & shld leave this bhd over further. 3 47a
643 **DARK VICTOR 11** [4] 4-9-10 N Callan 33/1: 405: Dwelt, chsd ldrs halfway, sn onepcd: big drop in trip. hd 46a
558 **PORT OF CALL 25** [10] 5-9-10 P McCabe 25/1: 56: Rear, eff wide halfway, mod late gains: see 558. 1½ 43a
4106} **TAKE MANHATTAN 99** [3] 3-8-11 S Drowne 10/1: 0-7: Dwelt, rear, mod prog: reapp/AW bow, 6 month abs, op 6/1: unplcd in '99 (rtd 64, mdn, sole start): 7f+ shld suit: with M R Channon. 2½ 36a
77 **POP THE CORK 99** [9] 3-8-11 Dean McKeown 40/1: 0-8: Dwelt, chsd ldrs 6f: 4 month abs. ½ 34a
334 **TABBETINNA BLUE 62** [1] 3-8-6 A McGlone 20/1: 0-09: Prom 4f, sn strugg: 2 mth abs, op 25/1. 3½ 20a
3541} **MAJOR BART 99** [14] 3-8-11 P Hanagan(7) 40/1: 00-0: Al rear: 10th, AW bow: now with R Fahey. hd 24a
1714} **Sunleys Picc 99** [6] 3-8-6 P Fessey 12/1:
4390} **Mcquillan 99** [2] 3-8-11 D Sweeney 50/1:
362 **Swift Dispersal 57** [13] 3-8-6 J Tate 40/1:
-- **Peng** [8] 3-8-11 (t) D Holland 16/1:

14 ran   Time 1m 16.2 (2.9)   (L P Calvente)   J Noseda Newmarket, Suffolk

---

686   **3.40 CLASS CLAIMER DIV 2 3YO+ 0-60 (F)**   **1m aw rnd** **Going 43** **-20 Slow**
   £1722   £492   £246   3 yo rec 17lb

600 **BE WARNED 18** [7] R Brotherton 9-9-9 (vis) F Norton 9/4 JT FAV: 040501: 9 b g Warning - Sagar   **63a**
(Habitat) Chsd ldrs, led over 2f out, sn in command & eased nr fin, rdly: val for 6L +, well bckd: '99 W'hampton
scorer (clmr, rtd 85a & 68): '98 wnr at Southwell (2) & W'hampton (h'caps, rtd 81a & 66): eff btwn 7/12f on fast,
hvy & both AWs: handles any trk, likes W'hampton/Southwell: suited by a visor, tried blnks: enjoys claming grade.

667 **INDIAN SWINGER 3** [4] P Howling 4-9-6 K Darley 9/4 JT FAV: -00522: 4 ch c Up And At 'Em -   2½ **52a**
Seanee Squaw (Indian Ridge) Chsd ldrs, kept on fnl 2f for press, no ch with wnr fnl 1f: well bckd: see 582.

612 **ROYAL DOLPHIN 17** [9] B A McMahon 4-9-5 (tbl) T Quinn 20/1: -00433: 4 b c Dolphin Street -   shd **51$**
Diamond Lake (King's Lake) Prom, hard rdn 2f out, kept on onepace: h'cap company could well suit.

598 **WAIKIKI BEACH 18** [3] G L Moore 9-9-4 I Mongan (5) 10/1: 1-0004: Dwelt, nvr on terms: op 7/1.   4 **42a**

602 **CHALUZ 18** [8] 6-9-3 (t) T G McLaughlin 7/1: 255545: Led 6f, fdd: op 5/1: see 75.   3 **35a**

654 **KIGEMA 9** [6] 3-8-0 J Mackay (7) 9/2: 146226: Trkd ldrs 6f: op 3/1: btr 241 (equitrack).   2½ **30a**

561 **NAKED OAT 25** [2] 5-9-8 J Bosley (7) 16/1: -00007: Chsd ldrs, sn rdn & btn 3f out: see 329 (C/D).   2 **31a**

4020} **MR MAJICA 99** [1] 6-9-3 (bl) M Pattinson (7) 14/1: 4000-8: Rear, eff 2f out, no impress: 6 month abs: hd **25a**
plcd in '99 (rtd 58, h'cap): '98 Salisbury wnr (clmr, rtd 79, B Meehan): eff arnd 1m on firm & hvy grnd, handles
any trk: eff with/without blnks: well h'capped & shld prove sharper next time.

560 **SEVEN O SEVEN 25** [5] 7-9-5 S Whitworth 33/1: 00-609: Al rear: see 500 (mdn).   11 **11a**

9 ran   Time 1m 44.4 (5.0)   (Paul Stringer)   R Brotherton Elmley Castle, Worcs

---

687   **4.10 TEXT P368 HCAP 3YO+ 0-95 (C)**   **7f aw rnd** **Going 43** **+06 Fast**   **[93]**
   £10871   £3345   £1672   £836   3 yo rec 15lb

*623 **SANTANDRE 15** [8] R Hollinshead 4-8-0 (65) P M Quinn (5) 16/1: 006411: 4 ch g Democratic - Smartie   **70a**
Lee (Dominion) Led/dsptd lead thr'out, went on dist, styd on gamely, drvn out: fast time: recent W'hampton wnr
(stks): '99 W'hampton wnr (h'cap, rtd 73a), plcd on turf (rtd 60): '98 Thirsk scorer (nurs h'cap, rtd 78 & 64a):
eff at 5f, suited by 6/7f: acts on firm, soft, likes fibresand & sharp trks: tough & genuine.

*660 **BLUE STAR 6** [7] N P Littmoden 4-9-12 (91) (vis) (6ex) J Tate 14/1: 241512: 4 b g Whittingham - Gold   ½ **94a**
And Blue (Bluebird) Chsd ldrs, rdn to chall fnl 2f, kept on well: op 10/1, qck reapp under a pen: see 660 (6f).

580 **OUT OF SIGHT 22** [5] B A McMahon 6-8-9 (74) T Quinn 9/2: 1-2103: 6 ch g Salse - Starr Danias   ¾ **76a**
(Sensitive Prince) Chsd ldrs, rdn to chall over 1f out, onepace/just held fnl fin: apprec return to 7f: see 539.

660 **FIRST MAITE 6** [14] S R Bowring 7-9-8 (87) J Weaver 15/2: 400324: Chsd ldrs wide halfway, rdn &   ¾ **88a**
kept on fnl 2f, not able to chall: quick reapp: blnks omitted: tough & consistent: see 35 (C/D).

587 **SAND HAWK 21** [4] 5-8-5 (70) (vis) F Norton 13/2: 114235: Mid-div, rdn/prog 2f out, no extra ins last.   ¾ **70a**

669 **DAVIS ROCK 3** [10] 6-8-0 (65) R Brisland (5) 14/1: 110166: Rear, late gains, no threat: quick reapp.   6 **56a**

598 **BANDBOX 18** [1] 5-8-1 (66) G Bardwell 16/1: 00-127: Rdn/rear, switched wide & mod gains: see 511.   ½ **56a**

669 **WUXI VENTURE 3** [9] 5-8-11 (76) A Nicholls (3) 20/1: 64-008: Chsd ldrs 5f: quick reapp: see 601.   1 **64a**

4395} **PEARTREE HOUSE 99** [15] 6-9-3 (82) O Pears 14/1: 4000-9: Mid-div wide halfway, held over 2f out: 1¼ **67a**
5 month abs: rnr-up in '99 (h'cap, rtd 89, with W Muir): '98 wnr at Lingfield (ltd stks, rtd 94): eff at 7.5f/1m:
acts on firm & gd/soft: handles a sharp/undul or stiff trk: bld prove sharper for a visor: lks well h'capped for D Nicholls.

532 **ASTRAC 29** [13] 9-9-4 (83) T G McLaughlin 20/1: 35-130: Chsd ldrs 5f: 10th: see 406 (6f, clmr).   ¾ **67a**

580 **FLOATING CHARGE 22** [6] 6-9-5 (84) M Hills 9/4 FAV: 361-2U: Stumbled & u.r. leaving stalls: nicely   **0a**
bckd, op 7/2: unfortunate mishap, his best forgotten: see 580.

4448} **Jo Mell 99** [2] 7-9-9 (88) J Fortune 20/1:   4363} **Mantles Pride 99** [12] 5-9-3 (82) (bl) K Darley 20/1:
663 **Rock Falcon 6** [16] 7-10-0 (93) (bl) R Cochrane 33/1:   4511} **Hyde Park 99** [3] 6-8-3 (68) Clare Roche (7) 33/1:
15 ran   Time 1m 29.2 (2.6)   (Geoff Lloyd)   R Hollinshead Upper Longdon, Staffs

---

688   **4.40 TEXT P372 SELLER 3YO (G)**   **7f aw rnd** **Going 43** **-36 Slow**
   £1892   £540   £270

638 **BAYTOWN RHAPSODY 13** [6] P S McEntee 3-8-13 J Weaver 4/5 FAV: 213131: 3 b f Emperor Jones -   **57a**
Sing A Rainbow (Rainbow Quest) Keen, trkd ldr halfway, rdn/led over 1f out, drvn out nr fin: well bckd: sold
for 6000gns: earlier won twice at Wolverhampton (h'caps): plcd in '99 (rtd 56 & 49a): eff at 6/7f on gd grnd,
likes fibresand & sharp tracks: tough & genuine filly who appreciated this drop to selling grade.

541 **PRICELESS SECOND 28** [4] J A Glover 3-9-4 (VIS) S Finnamore (7) 5/1: 231432: 3 b g Lugana   1¼ **58a**
Beach - Early Gales (Precocious) Prom, led halfway till dist, kept on well ins last: gd run in a 1st time visor.

610 **LOVE IN VAIN 17** [8] M A L Hoad-Robson 3-8-7 M Fenton 3/1: 03: 3 b f Lahib - Little America (Belmez)   5 **37a**
Chsd ldrs, rdn/onepace & held fnl 2f: dropped in trip & into selling grade.

549 **BASIC INSTINCT 27** [7] R Brotherton 3-8-7 S Drowne 20/1: 00-004: Prom 5f: see 192.   5 **27a**

636 **ROMANECH 13** [9] 3-8-12 (BL) F Norton 12/1: 500-05: Bhd, drvn/no impress: blnks: see 636.   nk **31a**

555 **LADY CYRANO 25** [5] 3-8-7 R Fitzpatrick (3) 9/1: -36206: Kicked at start, dwelt/nvr factor.   1½ **23a**

4159} **PORTRACK JUNCTION 99** [2] 3-8-12 (BL) Dean McKeown 10/1: 0005-7: Led, hdd/wknd qckly fnl 2f: 2 **24a**
blnks: 6 mth abs/AW bow: unplcd in '99 (rtd 47, tried upto 1m).

555 **LUCKY MELODY 25** [3] 3-8-12 A Culhane 20/1: 0-0008: Bhd 3f out: mod form.   18 **0a**

8 ran   Time 1m 32.1 (5.5)   (Mrs B A McEntee)   P S McEntee Newmarket

---

689   **5.10 TEXT P372 HCAP 3YO+ 0-85 (D)**   **6f aw rnd** **Going 43** **-12 Slow**   **[89]**
   £5408   £1664   £832   £416

613 **THE PROSECUTOR 17** [4] B A McMahon 3-8-12 (73) K Darley 9/2: 301-61: 3 b c Contract Law - Elsocko   **79a**
(Swing Easy) Held up in tch, rdn to chall over 1f out, led nr fin & pushed out: '99 W'hampton wnr (mdn, rtd 74a
& 66): eff at 5f, suited by 6f, has tried further: acts on fibresand & gd/soft grnd, prob handles fast: handles
a sharp or stiff/gall trk: apprec return to 6f, win again.

534 **OSCAR PEPPER 29** [5] T D Barron 3-8-9 (70) J Fortune 1/1 FAV: 0-1122: 3 b g Brunswick - Princess   ½ **73a**
Baja (Conquistador Cielo) Led, rdn over 1f out, hdd nr fin & no extra: clr of rem: hvly bckd: see 365 (C/D).

638 **DIAMOND RACHAEL 13** [3] Mrs N Macauley 3-8-4 (65) (vis) R Fitzpatrick (2) 13/2: 4-0123: 3 b f Shalford   5 **59a**
- Brown Foam (Horage) Held up, rdn/chsd ldr 2f out, sn held: op 4/1: see 549 (mdn).

4575} **FRAMPANT 99** [7] M Quinn 3-8-7 (68) F Norton 20/1: 4402-4: Cl-up, btn 2f out: 5 month abs: '99   5 **53a**
Windsor wnr (fill auct mdn, rtd 72 at best): eff at 5/6f: acts on gd/soft grnd: handles a sharp/gall trk: AW bow.

SOUTHWELL (Fibresand) FRIDAY MARCH 17TH Lefthand, Sharp, Oval Track

592 **CASTLE SEMPILL 20** [1] 3-9-2 (77)(vis) M Hills 100/30: -12135: Chsd ldrs, stly hmpd after 1f, sn outpcd. 6 51a
674 **MR STICKYWICKET 3** [2] 3-7-12 (59)(2ow)(29oh) S Righton 66/1: 0-0006: Chsd ldrs/btn 2f out: no form. 4 23a
4269} **ZIETZIG 99** [6] 3-9-7 (82) N Callan 9/1: 1420-7: Cl-up, wknd qckly fnl 2f: 5 month abs, op 7/1: AW 3½ 37a
bow under topweight: '99 York wnr (sell, rtd 84 at best): eff at 6f: acts on firm & fast grnd & a stiff/gall trk.
7 ran Time 1m 16.6 (3.3) (Whiston Management Ltd) B A McMahon Hopwas, Staffs

LINGFIELD (Equitrack) SATURDAY MARCH 18TH Lefthand, V Sharp Track

Official Going STANDARD: Stalls: Inside.

690 **3.55 LISTED WINTER DERBY STKS 3YO+ (A) 1m2f Standard Inapplicable**
£31900 £12100 £6050 £2750 3 yo rec 20lb

+593 **ZANAY 21** [4] Miss Jacqueline S Doyle 4-9-7 T G McLaughlin 5/4 FAV: 41-111: 4 b c Forzando - 107a
Nineteenth Of May (Homing) Broke well & led 1f, sn lost pl/rdn, switched wide halfway & rdn/prog to lead over 1f out,
styd on strongly, rdn out: hvly bckd: earlier scored twice here at Lingfield (C/D h'cap & stks): '99 Nottingham
wnr (mdn, rtd 86) & here at Lingfield (stks, C/D, rtd 93a): dual '98 rnr-up for R Phillips (mdn, rtd 81): eff at
1m, suited by 10f: acts on gd, soft & fibresand, equitrack/Lingfield specialist: v useful & progressive.
-- **ALJAARIF** [13] M Hofer 6-9-7 G Bocskai 25/1: 11-152: 6 ch h Rainbow Quest - Jasoorah (Sadler's 1¾ 103a
Wells) Towards rear/wide, smooth prog to trk ldrs over 2f out, rdn & onepace ins last: German raider: earlier
this term scored at Dortmund (9f, h'cap, AW): won 5 times in '99: eff btwn 9f/12.5f on gd, soft & equitrack.
-- **WIDAR** [3] Andreas Lowe 6-9-7 P A Johnson 20/1: -32123: 6 b h Soviet Star - Waseela (Ahonoora) ½ 102a
Trkd ldrs, switched & rdn over 1f out, held fnl 1f: German raider, earlier this year scored at Neuss (9.5f h'cap,
AW): twice a wnr in '99: eff at 7f/9.5f: acts on gd grnd & equitrack: useful entire.
*546 **JUST IN TIME 28** [11] T G Mills 5-9-7 T Quinn 3/1: 060-14: Chsd ldrs wide halfway, rdn 4f out & 2 99a
no impress over 1f out: well bckd, op 7/2: gd run: see 546 (C/D h'cap).
663 **INVADER 7** [6] 4-9-7 P Robinson 10/1: /45-55: Chsd ldrs, rdn & kept on onepace fnl 2f: bckd at shd 99a
long odds, op 12/1: clr of rem: unplcd from 2 starts in '99 (rtd 102, Gr 3): mdn promise in '98 (rtd 83$ at best):
eff at 9f on fast & equitrack: lightly rcd & has plenty of ability, must win a mdn.
*401 **BUGGY RIDE 52** [1] 3-8-1 (vis) F Norton 20/1: 2-21106: Led after 1f, hdd over 1f out/fdd: recently 8 88a
unplcd in Dubai: see 401 (1m).
632 **HUGWITY 14** [7] 8-9-7 M Hills 33/1: 244307: Held up in tch, btn 3f out: see 375 (C/D clmr). 2 85a
*206 **STAYIN ALIVE 91** [12] 3-8-1 (t) G Carter 20/1: 441-08: Chsd ldrs, btn 2f out/eased fnl 1f: recently 3 81a
unplcd in Dubai: see 206 (7f, stks).
*625 **SERVICE STAR 16** [5] 3-8-1 (bl) J Fanning 20/1: 13-219: Chsd ldrs 7f: btr 625 (fibresand, 9f, h'cap). 3 77a
-- **ROYMILLON** [9] 6-9-10 A Helfenbein 25/1: 1-1410: Sn bhd: 10th: German raider. 1½ 78a
2582} **Boldly Goes 99** [10] 4-9-7 Dean McKeown 33/1: 633 **Ursa Major 14** [8] 6-9-7 R Morse 25/1:
662 **White Plains 7** [14] 7-9-7 (et) N Callan 20/1: 462 **Nautical Warning 42** [2] 5-9-7 (t) J Weaver 16/1:
14 ran Time 2m 05.03 (2.23) (Sandford Racing) Miss Jacqueline S Doyle Upper Lambourn, Berks.

691 **5.00 0800 211222 HCAP 3YO+ 0-65 (F) 6f aw rnd Standard Inapplicable** [63]
£2331 £666 £333 3 yo rec 13lb

573 **CHARGE 24** [8] K R Burke 4-9-13 (62)(t) N Callan 4/1: ·00221: 4 gr g Petong - Madam Petoski 77a
(Petoski) Made all & sn clr, pushed out nr fin, unchall: well bckd, tchd 13/2: '99 Lingfield scorer (C/D mdn, rtd
70 on turf, plcd): eff at 5f, suited by 6f: acts on fast, gd & equitrack: handles a gall or sharp trk, likes
Lingfield & has run well fresh: gd weight carrier: eff in a t-strap: a revelation with forcing tactics today.
631 **BRAMBLE BEAR 14** [2] M Blanshard 6-8-12 (47) D Sweeney 9/2: 3-4662: 6 b m Beveled - Supreme Rose 7 47a
(Frimley Park) Dwelt/rdn towards rear, mod gains fnl 2f, no threat: bckd, tchd 11/2: stays 6f, suited by 5f: see 403.
*653 **GRAND VIEW 10** [9] D Nicholls 4-10-0 (63) A Nicholls (3) 2/1 FAV: 00-613: 4 ch g Grand Lodge - ½ 61a
Hemline (Sharpo) Prom wide, rdn/outpcd from halfway, kept on fnl 1f, no threat: hvly bckd: see 653 (sell).
614 **ALJAZ 18** [7] Miss Gay Kelleway 10-9-10 (59) S Whitworth 20/1: 402064: Chsd wnr, no impress fnl 2f. 1½ 53a
674 **MAMMAS F C 4** [5] 4-8-11 (46) Claire Bryan (5) 16/1: 0-0055: Chsd ldrs, nvr on terms: qck reapp. 2 35a
596 **ACID TEST 21** [11] 5-9-9 (58) R Fitzpatrick (3) 12/1: 00-066: Rdn/wide & towards rear, mod gains. nk 46a
634 **DOLPHINELLE 14** [10] 4-9-5 (54) R Smith (5) 6/1: 454437: Rdn/towards rear & wide, mod prog. nk 41a
558 **DEADLY SERIOUS 26** [12] 4-9-7 (50) J Stack 12/1: 4338: Mid-div/wide, nvr factor: op 10/1: hcap bow. nk 42a
594 **ANNIE APPLE 21** [6] 4-8-13 (48) P Doe 25/1: 300-09: Sn outpcd: see 594 (1m). ½ 32a
616 **FRENCH GRIT 17** [3] 8-8-5 (40) J Fanning 16/1: -06000: Chsd ldrs, outpcd halfway: 10th: see 166. 1½ 20a
628 **Shady Deal 14** [13] 4-8-6 (41) G Baker 7/14/1: 4372} **Emma Lyne 99** [4] 4-8-12 (47) T G McLaughlin 33/1:
12 ran Time 1m 11.87 (1.47) (D Lacey, N Buckham) K R Burke Newmarket.

SOUTHWELL (Fibresand) MONDAY MARCH 20TH Lefthand, Sharp, Oval Track

Official Going STANDARD: Stalls: Inside, except 5f - Outside.

692 **2.15 APPR FILLIES HCAP 4YO+ 0-65 (F) 1m aw rnd Going 52 -07 Slow** [56]
£2145 £613 £306

3940} **MY ALIBI 99** [13] K R Burke 4-10-0 (56) P Bradley 10/1: 0056-1: 4 b f Sheikh Albadou - Fellwaati 60a
(Alydar) Trkd ldrs trav well, prog to lead over 1f out, drvn out to just hld on: top-weight: op 6/1, 6 month abs/AW
bow: prev unplcd in '99 (rtd 57, h'cap): unplcd sole '98 start (rtd 66, mdn): eff at 1m, tried 10f:
acts on gd & soft: runs well fresh: gd weight carrier: open to further improvement for new connections.
608 **ALBERKINNIE 20** [12] J L Harris 5-7-10 (24)(2oh) G Baker (5) 14/1: 025332: 5 b m Ron's Victory - shd 27a
Trojan Desert (Troy) Towards rear/wide, rdn & styd on well fnl 2f, just held: op 11/1: eff around 1m/12f, mdn.
667 **RED VENUS 6** [5] Miss Gay Kelleway 4-10-0 (56)(bl) I Mongan 10/1: 54-533: 4 ch f Perugino - 1½ 56a
Reflection Time (Fayruz) Chsd ldrs wide, kept on onepace for press fnl 2f: op 8/1: clr rem: eff arnd 7f/1m.
588 **OARE KITE 24** [3] P S Felgate 5-8-12 (40)(bl) Clare Roche (5) 8/1: -35424: Led, rdn/edged right 6 31a
2f out, hdd over 1f out & fdd: both wins at Leicester: see 384.
683 **TEMPRAMENTAL 3** [7] 4-8-12 (40) S Finnamore 3/1 FAV: 30-225: Hndy, outpcd fnl 2f: qck reapp, op 7/2. hd 30a

4118} **WATER LOUP 99** [1] 4-9-4 (46) A Beech 12/1: 4000-6: Bhd, late gains, no threat: op 10/1, 6 month   3   30a
abs/AW bow: plcd in '99 (rtd 63, fill mdn): rtd 61 in '98 (auct mdn): stays 1m, tried 10f: handles firm & gd grnd.

560   **STRAVSEA 28** [10] 5-9-13 (55) A Hawkins (5) 8/1: 116357: Rear, eff 2f out, no impress: see 430 (C/D).   ¾   38a

635   **PUPPET PLAY 16** [6] 5-9-7 (49) L Swift (7) 12/1: -33428: Cl-up 6f: op 10/1: btr 635, 323 (7f).   3   26a

384   **MAI TAI 56** [8] 5-9-12 (54) (vis) R Cody Boutcher (3) 12/1: 4-2549: Dwelt, mid-div, eff over 2f out, sn   nk   30a
held: op 10/1: 8 wk abs: btr 147 (equitrack).

*675   **JESSINCA 4** [2] 4-9-12 (54) (bex) K Dalgleish (5) 6/1: -31510: Chsd ldrs 6f: op 5/1, 6lb pen, qck reapp.   nk   29a

642   **Mollytime 14** [9] 4-7-10 (24)(BL) (7oh) Claire Bryan 25/1: 635   **Lv Girl 16** [4] 4-9-6 (48) R Smith 14/1:
4362} **Belle Of Hearts 99** [11] 4-8-11 (39) Jonjo Fowle 50/1:
13 ran   Time 1m 44.1 (4.7)   (LFS Associates Ltd)   K R Burke Newmarket.

---

693   2.45 0800 211 222 CLAIMER 3YO+ (F)   7f aw rnd   Going 52   +03 Fast
£2310   £660   £330   3 yo rec 15lb

681   **RAMBO WALTZER 4** [5] Miss S J Wilton 8-9-8 I Mongan (5) 10/11 FAV: 121261: 8 b g Rambo Dancer -   65a
Vindictive Lady (Foolish Pleasure) Prom, led over 2f out & sn rdn clr, eased down nr fin, unchall: val for 10L+:
best time of day: hvly bckd: qck reapp: earlier scored here at S'wampton (C/D seller) & twice at W'hampton (sell
& clmr, D Nicholls): '99 scorer at Catterick, Thirsk (h'caps, rtd 71) & thrice here at Southwell (2 clmrs & seller,
rtd 75 at best): '98 W'hampton & Southwell wnr (2, h'caps, rtd 91a & 72): eff at 7f/9.5f on fast & soft, loves
fibresand/Southwell: has run well fresh: tough/genuine 8yo, relishes sell/claim grade.

646   **WAITING KNIGHT 14** [2] Mrs N Macauley 5-9-3 (vis) R Fitzpatrick (3) 16/1: -40022: 5 b h St Jovite -   9   45a
Phydilla (Lyphard) Chsd ldrs, rdn & kept on fnl 2f, no threat to wnr: op 14/1: sole win at 1m: see 178.

130   **LEOFRIC 99** [6] M J Polglase 5-9-7 (bl) L Newton 25/1: 0040-3: 5 b g Alhijaz - Wandering Stranger   ½   48$
(Petong) Led, rdn/hdd over 2f out & sn held: 4 month abs: '99 scorer at Southwell (C/D clmr, rtd 53a) & also
Sandown (appr h'cap, rtd 47): rtd 54 in '98: best up with/forcing the pace at 7f/1m, poss stays 10f: acts on
fibresand, fast & gd grnd: eff with/without blnks, has tried a visor: fin well clr of rem today.

602   **SING FOR ME 21** [4] R Hollinshead 5-8-12 Stephanie Hollinshead (6) 25/1: 040424: Sn outpcd.   19   10a

598   **SAN MICHEL 21** [1] 8-9-3 R Cody Boutcher (7) 40/1: 05-005: Rdn/chsd ldrs 4f, sn btn: see 148 (6f).   2½   10a

--   **SPRING BEACON** [7] 5-9-0 R Morse 40/1: 0440/6: Struggling halfway: long abs: missed '99:   1½   4a
rnr-up twice in '98 (rtd 51a, clmr & 42, h'cap): eff around 7f/9.4f: handles fibresand, gd & soft grnd.

616   **BEST QUEST 19** [3] 5-9-10 (t) N Callan 5/4: 350227: Chsd ldrs, eff wide over 2f out, sn eased   dist   0a
& virtually p.u. fnl 1f: bckd: reportedly struck into himself during race: top-weight: btr 616, 403 & 313.
7 ran   Time 1m 30.00 (3.4)   (John Pointon & Sons)   Miss S J Wilton Wetley Rocks, Staffs.

---

694   3.15 BEST BETS MDN 3YO+ (D)   1m aw rnd   Going 52   -02 Slow
£2821   £868   £434   £217   3 yo rec 17lb

4495} **ATLANTIC RHAPSODY 99** [2] M Johnston 3-9-0 (BL) D Holland 8/13 FAV: 2232-1: 3 b c Machiavellian -   91a
First Waltz (Green Dancer) Made all, rdn clr over 2f out, in command fnl 1f & eased nr fin: first time blnks: well
bckd at odds-on: 5 month abs/AW bow: plcd all 4 starts in '99 (rtd 91, mdn): eff at 1m, further could suit:
acts on firm & soft, any trk: runs well fresh: useful, enjoyed front-running in blnks today.

591   **STORMY RAINBOW 23** [3] V Soane 3-9-0 Martin Dwyer 4/1: 0-22: 3 b c Red Rainbow - Stormy Heights   14   63a
(Golden Heights) Handy, rdn/outpcd by wnr 3f out, just held 2nd for press ins last: op 7/2: see 591.

4432} **PRINCE OMID 99** [5] J R Fanshawe 3-9-0 R Cochrane 9/2: 05-3: 3 b c Shualiaan - Matilda The Hun   nk   62+
(Young Bob) Chsd ldrs halfway, kept on fnl 2f under very minimal press, nvr plcd to chall: jockey banned for
5 days for injudicious ride: 5 month abs/AW bow: ran with promise on 2 unplcd '99 starts (rtd 74): bred to
apprec 10f+: sure to do better with a more positive ride over further now he qualifies for h'caps: keep in mind.

531   **OCEAN SONG 32** [1] S R Bowring 3-8-9 Dale Gibson 14/1: 24: Chsd ldrs 4f: op 10/1: see 531 (7f).   4   49a

555   **NICIARA 28** [8] 3-9-0 (bl) C Lowther 40/1: 324605: Sn outpcd: blnks reapp: see 451 (h'cap).   9   41a

--   **MJOLNIR** [7] 3-9-0 (t) A Rawlinson 50/1: 6: Chsd ldrs halfway, sn btn: debut, with T T Clement.   5   31a

4543} **NINETEENNINETYNINE 99** [6] 3-9-0 (VIS) R Fitzpatrick (3) 25/1: 506-7: Chsd ldrs 6f: visor: 5 mth   shd   31a
abs/AW bow: unplcd from 3 starts in '99 for R Armstrong (rtd 75): now with Mrs N Macauley, h'cap company shld suit.

--   **CHANCY DEAL** [4] 3-8-9 A Culhane 50/1: 8: Dwelt/al bhd: debut, with Miss M E Rowland.   13   6a
8 ran   Time 1m 43.7 (4.3)   (Atlantic Racing Ltd)   M Johnston Middleham, N.Yorks.

---

695   3.45 TEXT P368 HCAP 4YO+ 0-100 (C)   1m4f aw   Going 54   -06 Slow   [100]
£6467   £1990   £995   £497   4 yo rec 2 lb

671   **GREEN BOPPER 6** [5] G Woodward 7-7-12 (70) F Norton 7/2: 523421: 7 b g Green Dancer - Wayage (Mr   74a
Prospector) Held up in tch, rdn over 2f out, strong chall ins last, styd on gamely to narrowly prevail, all out: op
3/1: qck reapp: '99 Southwell (2, rtd 73a) & Haydock wnr (h'caps, rtd 70): h'cap wnr in '98 at Southwell &
W'hampton (2, rtd 64a): eff at 1m, now suited by 10/12f: acts on gd & soft, fibresand specialist: tough.

4619} **MURGHEM 99** [2] M Johnston 5-10-0 (100) D Holland 100/30 FAV: 0320-2: 5 b h Common Grounds -   shd   103a
Fabulous Pet (Somethingfabulous) Handy, led 4f out till 3f out, styd on strongly for press ins last, just held:
op 7/2: 5 month abs/AW bow: topweight: '99 Sandown scorer for B Hanbury (h'cap, rtd 100 at best): '98 scorer at
Kempton (mdn, rtd 105 at best): eff at 12f, suited by 14f & stays 2m well: acts on firm, soft & fibresand: likes
to race with/force the pace on any trk: has run well fresh: best without blnks: tough & useful, fine reappearance.

*671   **PARABLE 6** [7] D W Barker 4-7-12 (72)(6ex) R Ffrench 5/1: 56-513: 4 b g Midyan - Top Table (Shirley   shd   75a
Heights) Handy, led 3f out, rdn over 1f out & narrowly hdd ins last, styd on, just held: just ahd of this wnr in 671.

650   **FAILED TO HIT 12** [3] N P Littmoden 7-7-10 (68) (vis) (3oh) P M Quinn (5) 14/1: 201634: Led, rdn/hdd   1¼   69a
4f out, styd on well & ch fnl 1f, held nr fin: op 12/1: see 530 (clmr).

671   **HANNIBAL LAD 6** [1] 4-8-4 (78) Martin Dwyer 3/1: 231135: Rear/in tch, rdn halfway, nvr pace to chall.   3½   74a

671   **SWIFT 6** [4] 6-7-11 (69) Dale Gibson 20/1: 00-006: Held up in tch, outpcd fnl 3f: qck reapp: see 671.   2½   61a

4122} **TURTLE VALLEY 99** [6] 4-9-7 (95) P Doe 11/2: 6040-7: Held up in tch, rdn/outpcd 3f out: Flat reapp,   4   81a
jumps fit (rtd 107h when plcd in a juv nov hdle): rattled off a hat-trick in '99 on the level, at York (stks), Newbury
& Salisbury (h'caps, rtd 103 at best, Gr 3): rtd 82 in '98 (rnr-up): eff at 12/14f, tried 2m, could yet suit: acts
on gd, relishes gd/soft & hvy grnd, prob handles equitrack: handles any trk, likes a stiff/gall one: very useful.
7 ran   Time 2m 41.5 (7.2)   (Wetherby Racing Bureau 35)   G Woodward Brierly, S.Yorks.

SOUTHWELL (Fibresand)   MONDAY MARCH 20TH   Lefthand, Sharp, Oval Track

696   4.15 TEXT P372 SELLER 3YO (G)   5f aw str   Going 54 -24 Slow
£1817   £519   £259

*659   **TROPICAL KING** 9 [7] D Carroll 3-9-4 J P Spencer 8/11 FAV: 425211: 3 b g Up And At'Em - Princess   **56a**
Gay (Fairy King) Chsd ldrs, rdn from halfway, switched 1f out & styd on gamely for strong press to lead nr line,
all out: hvly bckd, bght in for 8,200gns: recent W'hampton wnr (seller): unplcd in '99 in native Ireland (mdns):
suited by 5f, stays 6f: acts on fibresand & a sharp trk: relishing selling grade at present.
652   **CLOPTON GREEN** 12 [5] J W Payne 3-8-12 (bl) N Callan 8/1: 033352: 3 b g Presidium - Silkstone   nk   **49a**
Lady (Puissance) Handy, rdn/led over 1f out, hdd well ins last & no extra: op 6/1: eff at 5f on both AWs.
659   **APRILS COMAIT** 9 [1] Miss J F Craze 3-8-7 V Halliday 25/1: 3-6053: 3 br f Komaite - Sweet Caroline   hd   **43a**
(Squill) Went left start, sn handy, drvn & ch 1f out, just held nr fin: see 217 (C/D).
659   **PIPS STAR** 9 [2] D W P Arbuthnot 3-8-13 R Price 2/1: -32624: Handy, no extra fnl 1f: claimed by   ¾   **48a**
D W Barker for £5000: also bhd this wnr in 659.
426   **LAMMOSKI** 49 [3] 3-8-12 (bl) A Culhane 50/1: 5-0005: Led, rdn/hdd over 1f out & no extra: 7 wk abs.   2   **43$**
1999   **SHARP SMOKE** 99 [4] 3-8-7 Kimberley Hart (5) 20/1: 4-6: Cl-up 3f: 9 month abs/AW bow: unplcd   14   **16a**
sole '99 start (rtd 45, nov med auct stks): with D W Barker.
--   **THE DIDDLER** [6] L Newton 25/1: 0: Sn bhd: debut: Presidium gelding, with M J Polglase.   3   **15a**
7 ran   Time 1m 01.7 (3.9)   (Mrs Annie Hughes)   D Carroll Southwell, Notts.

697   4.45 TEXT P372 HCAP DIV 1 3YO+ 0-75 (E)   6f aw rnd   Going 54 -06 Slow   [73]
£2408   £688   £344   3 yo rec 13lb

677   **DAHLIDYA** 4 [2] M J Polglase 5-9-1 (60) P Doe 7/1: 015031: 5 b m Midyan - Dahlawise (Caerleon)   **66a**
Dwelt & rdn/rear, prog over 2f out & led over 1f out, styd on well ins last & rdn out: qck reapp: earlier scored
at W'hampton (seller) & twice here at Southwell (seller & clmr): '99 Southwell wnr (h'cap, rtd 59a): '98 W'hampton
& Southwell wnr (h'caps, rtd 52a): suited by 6f, eff btwn 5/7f on gd/soft & equitrack, fibresand specialist: best
without blnkrs: loves to come late off a fast pace: tough & genuine mare.
587   **RUSSIAN ROMEO** 24 [4] B A McMahon 5-9-5 (64)(bl) R Winston 5/2 FAV: -60552: 5 b g Soviet Lad -   1½   **65a**
Aotearoa (Flash Of Steel) Handy, smooth prog to lead over 1f out, hard rdn/hdd over 1f out/no extra: well bckd.
351   **TANCRED TIMES** 62 [9] D W Barker 5-7-10 (41)(2oh) Kimberley Hart (2) 20/1: 26-003: 5 ch m Clantime   nk   **41a**
- Mischievous Miss (Niniski) Cl-up, rdn/ch 2f out, sn onepace: 3 month abs, op 14/1: see 87 (C/D).
588   **GUEST ENVOY** 24 [3] C N Allen 5-8-4 (49) L Newman (5) 11/2: 322144: Chsd ldrs, not pace to chall.   ¾   **47a**
4298}   **SEALED BY FATE** 99 [8] 5-8-7 (51)(vis)(1ow) D Holland 12/1: 0000-5: Chsd ldrs wide, onepace fnl   hd   **49a**
2f: op 9/1: 5 month abs: '99 Carlisle scorer (h'cap, rtd 62, first success): plcd sev times in '98 (h'caps, rtd
55 & 53a): suited by a stiff 5f, stays 7f: acts on firm, soft & fibresand: suited by blnks/visor.
602   **KOMASEPH** 21 [5] 8-7-10 (41)(bl)(6oh) P M Quinn (5) 10/1: 050-36: Trkd ldrs, no extra fnl 2f: op 14/1.   4   **28a**
645   **GRAND ESTATE** 14 [7] 5-8-7 (52) A Culhane 11/2: 05-407: Led 2f, btn 2f out: op 7/1: see 614.   2   **34a**
427   **FANNY PARNELL** 49 [6] 4-8-8 (53) C Lowther 14/1: 0-028: Led after 2f, sn hdd, btn 2f out: op 10/1, abs.   7   **22a**
604   **BODFARI ANNA** 21 [10] 4-7-12 (43)(vis) A Mackay 9/1: 000-39: Dwelt/wide & al rear: btn 604.   5   **3a**
678   **SAMWAR** 4 [1] 8-10-0 (73)(vis) R Fitzpatrick (3) 10/1: 062260: Chsd ldrs 3f: 10f: op 7/1, qck reapp.   3   **26a**
10 ran   Time 1m 16.9 (3.6)   (The Lovatt Partnership)   M J Polglase Southwell, Notts.

698   5.15 TEXT P372 HCAP DIV 2 3YO+ 0-75 (E)   6f aw rnd   Going 54 -06 Slow   [73]
£2408   £688   £344   3 yo rec 13lb

3767}   **CARRIE POOTER** 99 [4] T D Barron 4-9-10 (69) C Lowther 6/1: 0245-1: 4 b f Tragic Role - Ginny Binny   **75a**
(Ahonoora) Cl-up, wide on bend over 1f out, styd on well, rdn out: op 9/2, 7 month abs: '99 scorer
at Southwell & Hamilton (h'caps, rtd 72a & 72 at best): '98 Redcar wnr (fill auct mdn, rtd 69): eff at 6/7f, stays
1m: acts on fast, hvy & fibresand: handles any trk: eff with/without blnks: runs well fresh: gd weight carrier.
680   **MARENGO** 4 [3] M J Polglase 6-8-8 (52)(1ow) D Holland 9/4 FAV: 030622: 6 b g Never So Bold - Born To   ½   **56a**
Dance (Dancing Brave) Handy, led over 2f out, rdn/hung left over 1f out, sn hdd, kept on for press: nicely bckd.
674   **ELTON LEDGER** 6 [5] Mrs N Macauley 11-9-2 (61)(vis) R Fitzpatrick 9/1: 122203: 11 b g Cyrano de   3   **57a**
Bergerac - Princess Of Nashua (Crowned Prince) Chsd ldrs, kept on fnl 2f, not pace to chall: see 389 (C/D, sell).
*604   **PETITE DANSEUSE** 21 [9] D W Chapman 6-7-10 (41)(3oh) Claire Bryan (5) 11/2: 550014: Towards rear, 1½   **33a**
kept on onepace fnl 2f, no threat: see 604 (C/D).
3283}   **ROBBIES DREAM** 99 [6] 4-8-5 (50) Dale Gibson 8/1: /000-5: Rdn/bhd halfway, kept on fnl 2f, nrst   1¼   **39a**
fin: op 14/1, 7 month abs/AW bow: lightly rcd/unplcd for D Morris in '99 (rtd 51, stks): unplcd in '98 (rtd 75,
75, mdn): a return to 7f+ shld suit in similar company: now with R M H Cowell.
622   **SPRINGS NOBLEQUEST** 18 [2] 4-7-13 (44) F Norton 9/1: 0-0666: Dwelt, led after 1f till 2f out, fdd.   2   **28a**
673   **KOSEVO** 6 [1] 6-8-8 (53)(vis) N Callan 25/1: 000-07: Cl-up 4f: see 673.   2½   **30a**
601   **DANAKIM** 21 [7] 3-8-10 (68) T Williams 25/1: 40-008: Chsd ldrs 4f: see 566.   1¼   **42a**
4134}   **TANCRED ARMS** 99 [8] 4-8-2 (47) Kimberley Hart (5) 20/1: 0000-9: Al rear: 6 month abs: '99   hd   **20a**
Catterick scorer (h'cap, made most, rtd 69, plcd on sand, rtd 45a, auct mdn): rnr-up thrice in '98 (rtd 67): suited
by 6f, tried 1m: acts on gd & soft grnd: handles any trk: likes a sharp/turning one, best without a visor.
9 ran   Time 1m 16.9 (3.6)   (Stephen Woodall)   T D Barron Maunby, N.Yorks.

DONCASTER   THURSDAY MARCH 23RD   Lefthand, Flat, Galloping Track

Official Going   GOOD TO FIRM. STALLS: Str Course - Stds Side, Rnd Course - Inside, Except Rnd 1m - Outside

699   1.30 FURNITURE APPR HCAP 4YO+ 0-80 (F)   1m4f   Good/Firm 24 +04 Fast   [80]
£3016   £928   £464   £232   4 yo rec 2 lb

4577}   **RAKEEB** 99 [2] M W Easterby 5-8-8 (60)(bl) P Goode (3) 10/1: 003D-1: 5 ch g Irish River - Ice House   **71**
(Northfields) Chsd ldrs, rdn to lead 3f out, in command over 1f out, pushed out cl-home, readily: op 8/1: fit, 2
mth jumps abs (unplcd, rtd 96h): rtd 75 in '99: '98 wnr at Ayr (mdn) & Haydock (h'cap, rtd 90, A Stewart): eff
at 10/12f on fast & gd/soft: likes a gall trk: best without blnkrs: runs well fresh: well h'capped, qk follow up?
3636}   **DOUBLE BLADE** 99 [6] Mrs M Reveley 5-8-7 (59) R Fitzpatrick 5/2 FAV: /040-2: 5 b g Kris - Sesame   4   **61**
(Derrylin) Mid-div, rdn/prog to chase wnr fnl 2f, kept on tho' al held: well bckd, padd pick: 4 month jumps

220

abs (won 4 novs, thrice at Sedgefield & also Wetherby, rtd 123h, eff around 2m/2m1f on firm & gd): unplcd on the Level in '99 (rtd 62, h'cap): plcd in '98 (h'cap, rtd 82, M Johnston): eff at 12/14f on fast & gd/soft: best without blnks: well h'capped now & in gd form over hdles, shld win an early season h'cap.
690 **HUGWITY 5** [7] G C Bravery 8-9-4 (70) A Nicholls 10/1: 443003: 8 ch g Cadeaux Genereux - Nuit d'Ete (Super Concorde) Mid-div, rdn & kept on fnl 3f, held ins last: tchd 12/1, bandaged front: quick reapp: eff btwn 7/10f, stays 12f: Lingfield specialist: see 375 (AW clmr). *2* **69**
641 **URGENT SWIFT 17** [21] A P Jarvis 7-9-1 (67) A Beech (5) 7/1: 3-5144: Held up, rdn/kept on fnl 4f. *½* **65**
556 **I CANT REMEMBER 31** [23] 6-8-8 (60) J Bosley (5) 20/1: -65245: Chsd ldrs, onepace fnl 2f: see 530. *3* **54**
37 **LANCER 99** [17] 8-8-13 (65)(vis) D Watson (7) 16/1: 0420-6: Towards rear, switched & stdy prog fnl 3f, no threat to ldrs: tchd 20/1, fit after 4 month abs: '99 Folkestone wnr (amat stks, rtd 74, unplcd on sand, rtd 37a): '98 wnr at Leicester, Folkestone & York (h'caps, rtd 75 & 45a at best): eff at 12f, stays 14f well: acts on firm & hvy, any trk: suited by a vis, runs well for an amat: gd weight carrier: tough & genuine, shld win this term. *1¼* **57**
3862} **BATSWING 99** [3] 5-9-2 (68) P Hanagan (5) 14/1: 0406-7: Rear, late gains fnl 3f, no threat: op 10/1: 6 month jumps abs (rtd 95h, unplcd, h'cap): plcd on the Level in '99 (rtd 75, h'cap, B R Millman): 98/99 Taunton hdles wnr (mdn, rtd 104h, 2m3.5f, soft): back in '97 scored at Lingfield on the Level (mdn, M Meade, rtd 94 at best): stays 12f: handles fast, likes gd/soft & hvy: eff with/without blnks: well h'capped now for B Ellison. *1¼* **58**
52 **PROTOCOL 99** [5] 6-8-0 (52)(t) Kimberley Hart (3) 10/1: 2510-8: Towards rear, nvr factor: 4 mth abs: '99 Nottingham scorer (amat stks, rtd 63, unplcd on sand, rtd 51a, h'cap): '98 Doncaster & Leicester wnr (h'caps, 84 & 61a): eff at 10/14f: acts on firm & gd, relishes soft/hvy grnd, handles both AWs: best in a t-strap, tried a vis. *3* **38**
4509} **FIELD OF VISION 99** [20] 10-8-1 (53) S Carson (1) 33/1: 5/40-9: Mid-div, btn 2f out: 3 mth jumps abs (rtd 73h, unplcd, h'cap): lightly rcd/unplcd in '99 on the Level (rtd 50, clmr): '98 Hamilton & Beverley wnr (h'caps, rtd 72, rnr-up on sand, rtd 67a at best): suited by 12/13f on firm, gd/soft & both AWs: handles any trk. *1¼* **37**
27 **CASHMERE LADY 99** [1] 8-8-4 (56) B Sooful (5) 20/1: 0065-0: Rear, late gains, no threat: ndd this, 7 wk jumps abs (unplcd, rtd 84h, mdn hdle): '99 Haydock scorer (amat h'cap, rtd 62): '98 wnr at Southwell & Thirsk (h'caps, rtd 92a & 76): eff at 1m/10f, stays 12f: acts on fast, hvy grnd & fibresand: on a fair mark. *nk* **39**
508 **HIBERNATE 40** [13] 6-10-0 (80) D McGann (7) 20/1: 40-000: Led 3f, btn 2f out: 11th: abs, vis omitted. *nk* **62**
437 **ZAHA 51** [19] 5-8-5 (57) R Lake (7) 33/1: 050-60: Dwelt, nvr on terms: 12th: stablemate of 6th, abs. *nk* **38**
*524 **INDIGO BAY 36** [4] 4-8-11 (65)(vis) Joanna Badger (5) 12/1: 0-4510: Chsd ldrs 9f: 13th: now with P Evans. *1¼* **44**
513 **BUNTY 38** [24] 4-7-10 (50)(2oh) G Baker (7) 50/1: 6-4060: Led after 3f till over 3f out, sn btn: 18th. **0**
608 **Haya Ya Kefaah 23** [18] 8-7-12 (50) P Bradley (1) 33/1:
581 **Ambidextrous 28** [8] 8-8-1 (53)(5ow)(6oh) L Swift (0) 25/1:
3584} **Mukhlles 99** [16] 7-7-12 (50) Gemma Jones (0) 25/1:
377 **Totem Dancer 61** [10] 7-8-8 (60)(vis) R Cody Boutcher (5) 20/1:
699} **Prince Nicholas 99** [22] 5-8-5 (57) C Cogan (3) 12/1: 568 **Try Paris 30** [11] 4-7-10 (50)(6oh) K Dalgleish (7) 50/1:
486 **Passions Plaything 43** [12] 4-9-2 (70) R Brisland (3) 25/1:
683 **Ferny Factors 6** [14] 4-8-1 (55) Jonjo Fowle (5) 25/1:
4163} **Rainbow Raver 99** [15] 4-7-10 (50)(6oh) D Kinsella (7) 50/1:683 **Hibaat 6** [9] 4-7-10 (50) C Catlin (5) 33/1:
24 ran Time 2m 32.19 (2.39) (Lady Manton) M W Easterby Sheriff Hutton, N Yorks

700

2.05 BROCKLESBY COND STKS 2YO (D) 5f Good/Firm 24 -23 Slow
£5694 £1752 £876 £438 Raced centre - stands side, no advantage

-- **NEARLY A FOOL** [13] B A McMahon 2-8-11 K Darley 10/1: 1: 2 b g Komaite - Greenway Lady (Prince Daniel) Rdn chasing ldrs, styd on well to lead ins last, drvn out: op 9/1, fit: Mar first foal, dam a sell hdle wnr: eff at 5f, 6f shld suit: acts on fast grnd & a gall trk: runs well fresh: fine debut, could improve. **91**
-- **SHOESHINE BOY** [11] B J Meehan 2-8-11 Pat Eddery 8/1: 2: 2 b g Prince Sabo - Susie Sunshine (Waajib) Led, rdn over 1f out, hdd ins last & no extra cl-home under press: op 7/1, just sharper for this: Feb foal, 8,500gns purchase: half brother to a 3yo minor 7f wnr: dam an Irish 9f 2yo wnr: handles fast grnd: win a race. *1½* **85**
-- **MILLYS LASS** [5] M R Channon 2-8-6 S Drowne 10/1: 3: 2 b f Mind Games - Millie's Lady (Common Grounds) Mid-div, rdn/kept on fnl 2f for press, not pace to chall: op 8/1, lkd fit, small: Mar foal, 30,000 gns purchase: dam unrcd, sire a high-class/precocious 2yo: eff at 5f, 6f shld suit: handles fast: encouraging debut. *¾* **78**
-- **VISCOUNT BANKES** [8] W G M Turner 2-8-11 A Daly 10/1: 4: Cl-up, rdn/briefly outpcd halfway, kept on well fnl 1f: op 6/1: Clantime colt, Feb foal, cost 9,000 gns: half brother to a 6f wnr: eff at 5f, 6f - shld suit: handles fast grnd: tall, scopey colt who really got the hang of things close home: improve. *1¼* **80**
-- **SIR FRANCIS** [2] 2-8-11 W R Swinburn 2/1 FAV: 5: Sn handy, ch 2f out, rdn/no extra fnl 1f: well bckd tho' op evens: lkd well: Commond Grounds colt, Mar foal, cost 36,000 gns: half brother to 2 juv 5f scorers: sire a high-class 2yo/miler: well regarded & just sharper for this, will know more next time for J Noseda. *½* **78**
-- **MAGIC BOX** [1] 2-8-11 W Ryan 13/2: 6: Mid-div, rdn/no impress fnl 2f: lkd well tho' just sharper for this: Magic Ring colt, Apr foal, 50,000 gns purchase: dam an unrcd half sister to sev wnrs, sire a speed influence. *nk* **77**
-- **QUIZZICAL LADY** [9] 2-8-6 F Norton 13/2: 7: Slowly away & lost 8L, rdn/kept on fnl 2f, no threat to ldrs: gamble from 12/1: Mind Games filly, Feb foal, 22,000 gns purchase: half sister to 3 juv scorers btwn 5f/7f: dam a juv Irish wnr: lost ch at start here, made eye-catching late hdwy & will surely leave this behind. *¾* **70+**
-- **BOLD MCLAUGHLAN** [6] 2-8-11 A Culhane 25/1: 8: Rdn/towards rear, kept on unders hands & heels riding fnl 2f, no threat: op 16/1, fit: Mind Games colt, Apr foal, 26,000 gns purchase: half brother to 3 sprint wnrs: dam a wng sprinter: not given a hard time on intro & could be placed to effect in small Northern contests. *¾* **73**
-- **MIDNIGHT VENTURE** [14] 2-8-11 G Hannon (7) 33/1: 9: Dwelt, chsd ldrs, sn outpcd: early to post. *nk* **72**
-- **DENSIM BLUE** [12] 2-8-11 G Bardwell 20/1: 0: Rdn/prom, fdd fnl 2f: 10th: strong, scopey, ndd this. *1¾* **68**
-- **IMPISH LAD** [7] 2-8-11 M Fenton 20/1: 0: Chsd ldrs, struggling halfway: 11th: op 14/1, ndd this. *hd* **67**
-- **GOLDEN DRAGONFLY** [3] 2-8-11 O Pears 25/1: 0: Outpcd rear thr'out: 12th, ndd race: with D Nicholls. *1¾* **63**
-- **HOBO** [4] 2-8-11 F Lynch 20/1: 0: Sn outpcd/well bhd: 13th: op 16/1, ndd race, with D W Barker. *15* **35**
13 ran Time 1m 0.55 (2.35) (Nearly A Fool Partnership) B A McMahon Hopwas, Staffs

701

2.35 TOTE HCAP 3YO 0-85 (D) 1m2f60y Good/Firm 24 -03 Slow **[86]**
£4485 £1380 £690 £345

4616} **KAIPOI 99** [6] R Hollinshead 3-8-9 (67) A Culhane 16/1: 1000-1: 3 ch c Elmaamul - Salanka (Persian Heights) Rear, rdn/stdy prog fnl 3f, hard rdn ins last to lead line: op 14/1, 4 month abs: '99 Chester scorer (mdn, rtd 72): well suited by step up to 10f, 12f will suit: acts on fast & hvy grnd: handles a sharp/gall trk: runs well fresh: light framed/unfurnished colt, op to further improvement, particularly when tackling further. **75**
4462} **POMPEII 99** [2] P F I Cole 3-9-3 (75) J Fortune 8/1 CO FAV: 620-2: 3 b c Salse - Before Dawn (Raise A Cup) Chsd ldrs, rdn to lead over 1f out, just hdd line: lkd well, 5 month abs: h'cap bow: plcd on middle of 3 '99 starts (rtd 79, earlier with P W Chapple Hyam): suited by step up to 10f, shld stay further: acts on fast & soft grnd & likes a stiff/gall trk: attractive colt, a likely type for similar. *shd* **81**

DONCASTER THURSDAY MARCH 23RD Lefthand, Flat, Galloping Track

4139} **ROYAL MINSTREL 99** [4] M H Tompkins 3-9-7 (79) S Sanders 10/1: 664-3: 3 ch c Be My Guest - Shanntabariya (Shernazar) Mid-div, rdn/kept on well fnl 3f, not pace to chall & carried head high: op 14/1: lengthy, padd pick: 6 month abs/h'cap bow: unplcd in '99 (rtd 84, mdn): styd longer 10f trip, 12f shld suit: handles fast & gd grnd: worth a try in blnks. **1½ 83**
4601} **SUNDAY RAIN 99** [5] P F I Cole 3-8-10 (68) D Sweeney 14/1: 0440-4: Chsd ldrs, rdn/ch 2f out, kept on onepace: longer priced stablemate of rnr-up: 5 month abs, just sharper for this: plcd in '99 (rtd 71, h'cap): eff arnd 1m/10f, stay further: acts on fast & hvy, easy/gall trk: eff with/without blnks. *1* **71**
4550} **JATHAAB 99** [15] 3-9-7 (79) Pat Eddery 8/1 CO FAV: 4103-5: Keen, trkd ldr, rdn/led 2f out, sn hdd & no extra ins last: 5 month abs, just sharper for this: '99 Haydock scorer (mdn, rtd 84): styd longer 10f trip, 12f+ could suit: handles fast & soft grnd: sturdy colt, will be plcd to eff. *nk* **81**
4380} **DIVINE PROSPECT 99** [7] 3-9-2 (74) W Ryan 10/1: 1506-6: Towards rear, eff 3f out, kept on tho' no threat: 5 month abs: clr rem: '99 Newmarket scorer (nurs, rtd 77): eff arnd 7f/1m, stays 10f on fm & sft. *3* **72**
4477} **ENTITY 99** [11] 3-9-0 (72) C Lowther 12/1: 5440-7: Rear, eff 3f out, no impress: op 14/1, 5 mth abs. *7* **60**
*514 **WILEMMGEO 38** [16] 3-8-2 (60) Joanna Badger (7) 20/1: -21218: Led/sn clr, drifted right/fdd fnl 2f. *1* **47**
625 **RHODAMINE 21** [3] 3-8-11 (69) Dean McKeown 16/1: 354-09: Mid-div, eff 3f out/sn held: still ndd this. *2½* **52**
4614} **GOLDEN ROD 99** [10] 3-8-13 (71) M Roberts 14/1: 400-0: Chsd ldrs, rdn/btn 3f out: 10th: 5 mth abs. *1* **53**
*319 **YOURE SPECIAL 70** [1] 3-9-5 (77) M Tebbutt 8/1 CO FAV: 202-10: Rear, no impress: 11th: abs. *½* **58**
625 **RUNNING TIMES 21** [12] 3-8-10 (68) K Darley 12/1: 400-50: Al rear: 12th: tchd 14/1: see 625. *3* **45**
*615 **F ZERO 22** [17] 3-9-4 (76) R Mullen 11/1: 020-10: Al rear: 13th: btr 615 (1m, equitrack). *1½* **51**
4569} **HAITHEM 99** [14] 3-9-2 (74) J Fanning 8/1 CO FAV: 420-0: Chsd ldrs, keen, btn 4f out: 14th: 5 mth abs. *hd* **48**
4059} **Wintzig 99** [13] 3-8-13 (71) M Fenton 11/1: 610 **City Flyer 23** [9] 3-8-4 (62) G Carter 12/1:
629 **No Regrets 19** [8] 3-8-7 (65) Martin Dwyer 33/1:
17 ran Time 2m 09.22 (2.82) (J D Graham) R Hollinshead Upper Longdon, Staffs

702

3.10 TOTE EXACTA HCAP 3YO+ 0-105 (B) 5f Good/Firm 24 +13 Fast [101]
£18362 £5650 £2825 £1412 3 yo rec 12lb Raced centre to stands side.

4486} **PERRYSTON VIEW 99** [5] J A Glover 8-9-11 (98)(bl) K Darley 10/1: 0401-1: 8 b h Primo Dominie - Eastern Ember (Indian King) Made most, forged ahead/drifted right 2f out, styd on strongly, rdn out: gd time, lkd superb after 5 month abs, prev with P Calver: '99 scorer at Newmarket (reapp, h'cap) & here at Doncaster (rtd h'cap, rtd 99): '98 Ripon wnr (rtd h'cap, rtd 93): eff at 5/6f on firm & soft, any trk, loves Newmarket & Doncaster: suited by blnks/vis & front running tactics: gd weight carrier, runs well fresh: v tough/useful, worth a try in Listed grade. **108**
4469} **SHEER VIKING 99** [10] B W Hills 4-9-3 (90) M Hills 4/1 FAV: 0000-2: 4 b g Danehill - Schlefalora (Mas Media) Dwelt, rdn/chsd ldrs halfway, chsd wnr fnl 1f, kept on well tho' al held: hvly bckd & a morning gamble from 12/1: fit & lkd well on reapp: rnr-up on reapp in '99 (rtd 107, stks, subs disapp & tried blnks): '98 wnr at Newmarket (mdn) & Doncaster (Gr2, rtd 107, C/D): eff at 5f, stays a sharp 6f: acts on fast & gd/soft, any trk: runs well fresh: well h'capped & gelded since last term, tardy start proved costly but can find compensation. *1½* **95**
506 **BATCHWORTH BELLE 40** [8] E A Wheeler 5-9-6 (93) S Carson (5) 11/1: 032-23: 5 b m Interrex - Treasurebound (Beldale Flutter) Chsd ldrs, rdn/kept on onepace fnl 1f: abs: tough mare, win more races. *3½* **89**
4177} **DAMALIS 99** [13] E J Alston 4-9-2 (89) R Hughes 25/1: 6440-4: Handy, rdn/kept on onepace fnl 2f: 6 mth abs, sharper for this: '99 Sandown scorer (rtd h'cap, rtd 96): '98 wnr at Chester (fill mdn) & Ripon (stks, rtd 98): all 3 wins at 5f, tried 6f: acts on firm, likes soft, any trk: nicely h'capped, keep in mind for similar. *¾* **83+**
129 **IVORYS JOY 99** [12] 5-8-9 (82) G Duffield 20/1: 0010-5: Chsd ldrs, rdn/kept on for press: 4 mth abs. *hd* **75**
4486} **HENRY HALL 99** [20] 4-9-5 (92) Kim Tinkler 16/1: 0200-6: Chsd ldrs, rdn/switched 2f out, held ins last: ndd this after 5 mth abs: rnr-up 4 times in '99 (rtd 100, h'cap): '98 Beverley scorer (nov), Thirsk (clmr) & Doncaster (C/D stks, rtd 98): tried 6f, suited by 5f: acts on firm & soft, any trk, loves a stiff one: on a fair mark. *1* **83**
2390} **GUINEA HUNTER 99** [7] 4-10-0 (101) J Fortune 25/1: 3D03-7: Chsd ldrs, outpcd fnl 2f: sharper for this after 9 month abs: topweight: '99 Haydock scorer (stks, rtd 103): '98 Carlisle wnr (rtd 92 at best, mdn): suited by 6f: acts on firm & gd/soft grnd, any trk: spot on next time over 6f in similar company. *nk* **91**
4538} **AMBITIOUS 99** [4] 5-8-5 (78) A Nicholls (3) 20/1: 1120-8: Towards rear, rdn/mod gains: 5 mth abs: progressive in '99, scored at Southwell (fill h'cap, rtd 65a, J Fanshawe), Sandown (2, h'cap & clmr), Redcar (class stks) & York (h'cap, rtd 79): eff at 6f, suited by 5f: acts on firm & fibresand, prob fibresand, likes gd/soft: eff with/without blnks/visor: handles any trk, likes Sandown: runs well for an apprentice: fitter for this on soft. *½* **66**
660 **NIGHT FLIGHT 12** [2] 6-9-5 (92) R Winston 14/1: 006-09: Towards rear, mod prog: lkd superb. *hd* **79**
2390} **THREAT 99** [21] 4-9-11 (98) G Faulkner (3) 25/1: 0402-0: Dwelt, towards rear, switched left/mod gains fnl 2f: 10th: prev with J H M Gosden, now with S C Williams, lightly rcd gldg, not given a hard time here. *hd* **84**
4356} **ALMATY 99** [18] 7-9-13 (100) R Brisland (5) 14/1: 4603-0: Cl-up 4f: 11th: op 12/1, abs, needed this. *hd* **85**
4391} **CARTMEL PARK 99** [9] 4-8-7 (80) O Pears 25/1: 5001-0: Cl-up 4f, 12th: 5 mth abs, on toes. *¾* **63**
4413} **LAGO DI VARANO 99** [11] 8-8-8 (81)(vis) W Ryan 20/1: 0064-0: Twds rear, no impress: 13th: 5 mth abs. *¾* **62**
3990} **PIPS MAGIC 99** [14] 4-8-12 (85) A Culhane 25/1: 0000-0: Al rear: 14th: slipping down weights. *hd* **65**
3408} **FURTHER OUTLOOK 99** [17] 6-9-12 (99) S Sanders 14/1: 1060-0: Prom 3f, fdd: 15th: 7 mth abs. *hd* **78**
4486} **CAUDA EQUINA 99** [19] 6-8-8 (81) S Drowne 14/1: 0300-0: Al rear: 16th: op 12/1, 5 month abs. *½* **58**
4572} **RIBERAC 99** [3] 4-8-7 (80) J Fanning 20/1: 0360-0: Towards rear, nvr factor: 17th: 5 month abs. *1* **55**
660 **DOUBLE OSCAR 12** [16] 7-8-1 (74)(bl) F Norton 10/1: 000-00: Al bhd: 18th: op 8/1. *nk* **48**
631 **AMARANTH 19** [1] 4-8-7 (80)(t) Dean McKeown 16/1: 016-00: Mid-div, btn 2f out: 19th: see 631. *½* **52**
4486} **ELLENS LAD 99** [15] 6-9-8 (95) Pat Eddery 10/1: 1412-0: Al bhd: 20th: 5 month abs. *¾* **65**
20 ran Time 58.72 (0.52) (Mrs Janis Macpherson) J A Glover Carburton, Notts

703

3.40 LISTED DONCASTER MILE 4YO+ (A) 1m rnd Good/Firm 24 -07 Slow
£14605 £4494 £2247 £1123

2512} **HASTY WORDS 99** [1] B W Hills 4-8-7 M Hills 5/1: 3/06-1: 4 b f Polish Patriot - Park Elect (Ahonoora) Keen/trkd ldrs, no room trav well 2f out, switched & rdn to lead ins last, shade cosily: op 6/1: 9 month abs: lightly rcd/unplcd in '99 (rtd 107, Gr2): '98 Sandown wnr (fill mdn), also Gr 2 plcd (rtd 107): eff at 7f/1m on firm & gd: runs well fresh: likes a stiff/gall trk: useful, lightly rcd filly, op to improvement. **104**
4559} **SWALLOW FLIGHT 99** [6] G Wragg 4-8-12 M Roberts 5/2 FAV: 5124-2: 4 b c Bluebird - Mirage (Red Sunset) Cl-up, led over 2f out, rdn/hdd ins last & not pace of wnr cl-home: well bckd: just ndd this after 5 mth abs: '99 scorer at York (h'cap) & Doncaster (C/D stks, rtd 106 at best): plcd in '98: eff at 1m/10.4f on firm, gd/soft & any trk: gd weight carrier who can force the pace: tough/v useful colt, good reappearance. *¾* **107**
3868} **DESERT KNIGHT 99** [7] J Noseda 4-8-12 W R Swinburn 4/1: 12-3: 4 b c Green Desert - Green Leaf (Alydar) Trkd ldrs, rdn/ev ch over 1f out, not pace of wnr: op 7/2, 7 month abs: won 1st of just 2 starts in '99 (debut, mdn, rtd 100 at best): eff around 1m on firm & fast grnd: likes a stiff/gall trk: strong, lengthy colt who was bandaged in front but is thriving physically, should be placed to win again. *½* **106**

4559} **BOMB ALASKA** 99 [2] G B Balding 5-9-1 J F Egan 3/1: 1221-4: Trkd ldrs, rdn/kept on fnl 2f, not   nk   108
pace to chall: nicely bckd tho' op 9/4: looks superb after 5 month abs: tough/prog in '99, scored at Doncaster,
Newbury & Goodwood (h'caps) & on fnl start at Newmarket (listed, rtd 106): '98 Newbury wnr (mdn, rtd 77): eff at
1m/10f on firm & gd, relishes soft/hvy grnd: handles any trk: tough & progressive, will appreciate a stronger pace.

662   **WEET A MINUTE** 12 [3] 7-8-12 A Culhane 12/1: -22225: Led, rdn/kept on fnl 2f, not pace to chall.   ½   104$

663   **DEBBIES WARNING** 12 [5] 4-8-12 (t) Demetris Shakallis 14/1: 530-06: Held up, eff 3f out, no   4   93
impress: fit: '99 Kempton scorer (mdn, rtd 87, also rtd 111, Gr3, flattered): eff at 1m on firm & soft grnd, any trk.

4049} **DANCING KRIS** 99 [8] 7-8-12 J Weaver 25/1: 2310-7: Held up in tch, eff 3f out, sn btn: jumps fit   18   69
(mod form): '99 scorer at Longchamp & Deauville (h'cap, rtd 101): eff at 1m/10f on gd & v/soft: likes a gall trk.

--   **PRINCE DU SOLEIL** [4] 4-8-12 S Sanders 20/1: 1422-8: In tch, outpcd fnl 4f: ndd this, 3 mth abs.   3   63
8 ran   Time 1m 38.59 (2.49)   (W J Gredley)   B W Hills Lambourn, Berks

---

704   **4.10 BADSWORTH MDN 3YO (D)**   **1m str**   Good/Firm 24   -09 Slow
     £4270   £1314   £657   £328   Raced stands side

4601} **KOOKABURRA** 99 [5] B J Meehan 3-9-0 Pat Eddery 9/2: 3324-1: 3 b c Zafonic - Annoconnor (Nureyev)   99
Dictated pace, rdn/prsd 2f out, styd on strongly & pushed out to assert ins last: lkd fit & well after 5 month abs:
plcd sev times in '99 (rtd 92, nurs h'cap): eff at 1m, may stay further: acts on firm & gd/soft, handles soft grnd:
handles any trk: runs well fresh: given a fine tactical ride by Pat Eddery.

4400} **CLOG DANCE** 99 [7] B W Hills 3-8-9 M Hills 4/7 FAV: 32-2: 3 b f Pursuit Of Love - Discomatic   1½   91
(Roberto) Trkd wnr, rdn to chall fnl 2f, outpcd ins last: well clr of rem: hvly bckd tho' op 4/1: 5 month abs:
rnr-up on 2nd of 2 starts in '99 (Gr2 Rockfel, rtd 107): eff at 7f/1m, 10f could suit: acts on fast & gd/soft grnd:
shown more than enough to win a race & winner has a tactical advantage (dictated from front) today.

662   **CLARANET** 12 [4] K Mahdi 3-8-9 Demetris Shakallis 12/1: 34-33: 3 ch f Arazi - Carmita (Caerleon)   7   77
Held up in tch, rdn/outpcd by front pair fnl 2f: op 16/1: some promise & mid-dists h'caps shld suit.

3451} **GOLDEN LEGEND** 99 [2] G Wragg 3-9-0 M Roberts 16/1: 00-4: Keen/trkd ldrs, outpcd over 2f out: nk   81$
op 12/1, ndd this after 7 month abs: unplcd both '99 starts (rtd 62): not given hard time on h'cap qualifier.

4526} **WAVERLEY ROAD** 99 [6] 3-9-0 W Ryan 33/1: 4-5: Held up in tch, outpcd over 2f out: ndd this after   2½   76
5 month abs: unplcd sole '99 start (rtd 77, mdn, promise): bred to apprec mid-dists this term for A Jarvis.

--   **STRATEGIC DANCER** [3] 3-9-0 J Fortune 10/1: 6: Held up in tch, rdn/outpcd fnl 3f: op 6/1,   hd   75
debut: mid-dist bred colt, 10f+ will suit in time: with P Cole.

--   **STRAWMAN** [1] 3-9-0 J Weaver 25/1: 7: Held up, outpcd fnl 2f: debut, half brother to 2 high-class   2½   70
mid-dist performers: apprec 10f+ in time, longer priced stablemate of rnr-up.
7 ran   Time 1m 39.12 (2.62)   (Mrs Susan Roy)   B J Meehan Upper Lambourn, Berks

---

705   **4.40 LADY RIDERS HCAP 4YO+ 0-75 (F)**   **1m2f60y**   Good/Firm 24   -34 Slow   [54]
     £2509   £717   £358

170   **ACEBO LYONS** 99 [4] A P Jarvis 5-10-2 (56) Mrs J Powell (6) 16/1: 0400-1: 5 b m Waajib - Etage (Ile   60
de Bourbon) Rear, switched & strong run fnl 3f to lead ins last, rdn out: bckd at long odds, tchd 25/1: 3 mth abs:
rnr-up in '99 (rtd 57, h'cap, unplcd on sand, rtd 20a): '98 Haydock wnr (stks, rtd 70): eff at 10/12f on fast &
gd/soft: best without a visor: runs well fresh & likes a gall trk.

679   **NOUKARI** 7 [6] P D Evans 7-11-2 (70) Miss E Folkes (5) 7/1: 544532: 7 b g Darshaan - Noufiyla   nk   72
(Top Ville) Mid-div, rdn & styd on well fnl 2f: op 6/1: v tough performer: see 151 (12f, AW).

160   **PRODIGAL SON** 99 [5] Mrs V C Ward 5-11-4 (72) Miss E Ramsden 5/1 FAV: 2620-3: 5 b g Waajib -   ¾   73
Nouveau Lady (Taufan) Chsd ldrs, kept on fnl 2f, not pace of front pair: op 6/1: 3 month abs: see 119.

49   **FINAL DIVIDEND** 99 [12] J M P Eustace 4-11-6 (74) Miss Joanna Rees (7) 20/1: 6100-4: Rear, styd on   ½   74
well fnl 2f, nrst fin: 6 wk jumps abs (unplcd, rtd 75h, nov): '99 Salisbury & Beverley wnr (h'caps, rtd 76): plcd in
'98 (rtd 76): eff at 7f/1m, stays gall 10f well: acts on firm & soft grnd: likes a stiff/gall trk: good reapp.

650   **THOMAS HENRY** 15 [1] 4-10-3 (57) Mrs S Moore (5) 20/1: 006605: Handy, led 3f out till ins last, no   nk   56
extra: acts on equitrack, firm & fast: both wins at Lingfield (equitrack): see 110 (AW sell).

4437} **TAJAR** 99 [8] 8-9-3 (43) Mrs H Keddy (5) 7/1: 6030-6: Mid-div, kept on fnl 3f, not pace to chall: tchd   3   38
14/1, just sharper for this: 5 mth abs: '99 Windsor scorer (h'cap, rtd 53): '98 wnr at Pontefract (ladies h'cap)
& Warwick (class stks, rtd 50): eff at 10/12f on firm & soft, best without blnkrs: goes well fresh & handles any trk.

681   **OVER THE MOON** 7 [15] 6-9-5 (45) Marchioness Blandfor 14/1: 010147: Keen to post, mid-div & rear   1¾   38
till ins last: acts on any grnd, best at Ascot on fast & gd/soft (rtd 52): likes a gall trk: best at best.

608   **THROWER** 23 [10] 9-9-13 (53) Mrs S Owen (5) 11/1: 1-1458: Al mid-div: op 8/1: see 470 (AW, 2m).   3   42

607   **KUWAIT THUNDER** 23 [3] 4-9-6 (46) Miss Diana Jones 12/1: -00449: Chsd ldrs 1m: see 368 (7f).   ½   34

3775} **DESERT FIGHTER** 99 [20] 9-10-10 (64) Miss L Hay (7) 10/1: 1114-0: Towards rear, nvr factor: op   nk   51
9/1, 7 month abs, sharper for this: rattled off claimer 4 timer in '99 at Thirsk, Haydock, Hamilton & Catterick:
plcd in '98 (h'caps, rtd 71): eff at 10/12f on gd & firm, handles soft, any trk: tough 9yo, relishes clmg grade.

569   **PERCHANCER** 30 [19] 4-9-12 (52) Miss A Armitage (5) 12/1: 321100: Chsd ldrs, btn 2f out: 11th.   2½   35

2080} **BEGORRAT** 99 [9] 6-10-6 (60)(vis) Mrs C Williams 25/1: 0200-0: Chsd ldrs 7f: 12th: jumps fit (mod   1   42
form): rnr-up in '99 (h'cap, rtd 63): '98/'99 Ayr hdles wnr (nov, rtd 104h): '98 Flat wnr at Ayr (h'cap, rtd 68): eff
at 10/11f on fast & soft/hvy: eff with/without blnks, wore a visor today: loves Ayr.

599   **SOPHOMORE** 24 [2] 6-11-7 (75) Mrs Annette Harris 25/1: 46/030: Led 7f: 13th: see 590, 343.   shd   57

669   **TROJAN WOLF** 9 [11] 5-10-8 (62) Miss S Pocock (5) 8/1: -14530: In tch 6f: 19th: op 6/1: btr 255 (AW).   0

412   **GOLD BLADE** 55 [16] 11-9-7 (47) Mrs L Pearce 9/1: 125-40: Dwelt, al bhd: 20th: 8 wk abs: see 412.   0

2177} **Eastern Rainbow** 99 [14] 4-9-4 (44) Mrs S Bosley 25/1:

4441} **Mr Perry** 99 [13] 4-10-3 (57) Mrs A Hammond (7) 14/1:

2011} **Mansa Musa** 99 [7] 5-11-2 (70) Ms T Dzieciolwska (5) 16/1:

642   **September Harvest** 17 [17] 4-9-10 (50) Mrs M Morris (3) 16/1:

136   **Bodfari Signet** 99 [18] 4-10-0 (54) Miss S M Potts (5) 33/1:
20 ran   Time 2m 12.41 (6.01)   (Terence P Lyons II)   A P Jarvis Aston Upthorpe, Oxon

WOLVERHAMPTON (Fibresand)   THURSDAY MARCH 23RD   Lefthand, Sharp Track

Official Going STANDARD. Stalls: 7f - Outside; Rem - Inside.

706 2.15 BET DIRECT HCAP 3YO 0-60 (F)   6f aw rnd Going 42 -15 Slow   [67]
£2194   £627   £313

636 **CHILI PEPPER** 19 [4] A Smith 3-9-0 (53) C Carver (3) 14/1: 450-61: 3 gr f Chillibang - Game Germaine   58a
(Mummy's Game) Trkd ldr, hdwy to chall ins last, drvn to lead cl-home: op 10/1, 1st win: '99 rnr-up (debut, rtd 63,
seller): eff at 5/6f, tried 8.5f: handles fast, gd/soft & fibresand: acts on any trk: tried blnks, best without.

*654 **PADDYWACK** 15 [2] D W Chapman 3-9-2 (55)(bl) Claire Bryan (5) 1/1 FAV: 524112: 3 b g Bigstone -   ¾ 57a
Millie's Return (Ballad Rock) Led, 3L clr & jockey looking round 2f out, drvn ins last, hdd cl-home: nicely
bckd on hat-trick bid & ran well: back in trip, shows enough pace to even cope with a drop to 5f: see 654 (e/trk).

555 **SEDONA** 31 [1] Andrew Turnell 3-8-11 (50) P Fessey 40/1: 00-5U3: 3 b g Namaqualand - Talahari (Roi   1½ 48a
Danzig) Dwelt, sn prom, drvn/not pace of ldrs fnl 1f: first sign of form: eff at 6f on fibresand: see 555, 493.

589 **COME ON MURGY** 27 [6] A Bailey 3-8-9 (48)(bl) J Bramhill 12/1: 444054: Prom, drvn/btn appr fnl   1½ 42a
1f: drop in trip: suited by 7f & both wins have come in sell grade: see 283.

2705} **WILLRACK TIMES** 99 [7] R Cochrane 9/1: 3004-5: Cl-up, drvn/wknd fnl 2f: 8 month abs,   1¼ 51a
plcd in '99 (nov fill stks, rtd 68): eff 5f & handles fast & gd/soft grnd: sharper next time.

*696 **TROPICAL KING** 3 [3] 3-9-13 (66)(6ex) J P Spencer 2/1: 252116: Cl-up, wknd qckly appr fnl 2f: 3½ 49a
qck reapp, top-weight: below par on hat-trick bid over longer 6f trip: too sn with penalty after 696, 659 (5f, sells).

495 **BEWILDERED** 42 [5] 3-8-9 (48) G Parkin 40/1: 64-007: Sn well outpcd: 6 wk abs: see 365.   9 13a

7 ran   Time 1m 16.2 (3.4)   (Mrs R Auchterlounie)   A Smith Beverley, E.Yorks.

707 2.45 CLASSIFIED STKS 3YO+ 0-60 (F)   1m100y aw rnd Going 42 -21 Slow
£2278   £651   £325   3 yo rec 17lb

2098} **THE IMPOSTER** 99 [8] Miss S J Wilton 5-9-8 I Mongan (5) 10/1: /142-1: 5 ch g Imp Society - Phoenix   63a
Dancer (Gorytus) Sn led, pushed clr over 2f out, styd on strongly, rdn out: reapp after 9 month abs: '99
scorer here at W'hampton (seller, rtd 60a, D Murray Smith): plcd in '98 (mdn & h'cap, rtd 68a at best): suited
by 8.5f, stays 9.3f: acts on fast, likes fibresand/W'hampton: runs v well fresh.

*686 **BE WARNED** 6 [9] R Brotherton 9-9-0 (vis) J P Spencer 2/1 FAV: 405012: 9 b g Warning - Sagar   2 61a
(Habitat) Wide/settled in tch, smooth hdwy over 2f out, drvn & no extra ins last: nicely bckd, qck reapp: gd run
having to race wide throughout: remains in fine form, can win again soon: see 686 (clmr).

675 **BREAD WINNER** 7 [2] I A Balding 4-9-8 (vis) R Cochrane 11/4: -42223: 4 b g Reprimand - Khubza   2 55a
(Green Desert) Settled mid-div, gd hdwy over 3f out, drvn/btn fnl 1f: nicely bckd, clr rem: consistent, see 568.

477 **BOBBYDAZZLE** 44 [6] Dr J D Scargill 5-9-5 (ebl) J Lowe 9/2: 03-244: Rear, mod late hdwy: 6 wk abs.   5 44a

4576} **MERCHANT PRINCE** 99 [7] 4-9-8 C Carver (3) 50/1: 0000-5: Sn well bhd, mod late gains: reapp/AW   8 35a
bow: failed to make the frame in 5 '99 starts (mdn & h'caps, rtd 57 at best).

686 **ROYAL DOLPHIN** 6 [3] 4-9-8 (tbl) S Righton 14/1: 004336: Prom, wknd halfway: qck reapp.   nk 34a

4535} **KINGFISHERS BONNET** 99 [10] 4-9-5 P Fitzsimons (5) 25/1: 2624-7: Chsd ldrs, fdd appr fnl 2f: 1¾ 28a
reapp after 9 month abs: rnr-up thrice in '99 (h'caps & seller, rtd 52 at best, well btn on AW bow): eff at
1m/10f, has tried 12f: acts on fast & gd/soft, handles hvy grnd: with S Knight.

4313} **ELBA MAGIC** 94 [4] 5-9-5 D R McCabe 10/1: 2100-8: Led early, with ldrs till wknd qckly fnl 2f: 1¼ 26a
op 8/1 on reapp: '99 scorer at Beverley (h'caps, rtd 62, C A Dwyer): '98 scorer at Yarmouth (amat h'cap),
Southwell & Ripon (h'caps, rtd 67 & 64a): eff at 1m/10f: acts on firm, soft & fibresand, handles any trk:
can go well fresh, can carry big weights: now with Mrs N Macauley, should be fitter next time.

583 **VILLAGE NATIVE** 28 [1] T G McLaughlin 25/1: -00009: Chsd ldrs, lost tch fnl 4f: see 352.   2 25a

549 **ESPERE DOR** 33 [5] 3-8-6(1ow) R Lappin 100/1: 0-000: Al bhd: fin 10th: no form.   20 0a

10 ran   Time 1m 51.6 (5.4)   (John Pointon & Sons)   Miss S J Wilton Wetley Rock, Staffs.

708 3.20 BEST BETS MED AUCT MDN 3YO (F)   1m100y aw rnd Going 42 -07 Slow
£2278   £651   £325

3128} **PETIT MARQUIS** 99 [1] J R Fanshawe 3-9-0 R Cochrane 1/2 FAV: 2-1: 3 b c Lost World - Ephemeride   91a
(Al Nasr) Held up, smooth hdwy over 3f out, styd on strongly & drvn out to lead cl-home: reapp/AW bow: promise
sole '99 start, at Leicester (med auct mdn, rtd 87): half-brother to a French 10/11f wnr: eff at 6f/8.5f, 10f
shld suit: acts on fast & fibresand: runs well fresh on a sharp or gall trk: looks useful, win more races.

4306} **SIR FERBET** 99 [5] B W Hills 3-9-0 A Eddery (5) 2/1: 43-2: 3 b c Mujadil - Mirabiliary (Crow)   nk 90a
Cl-up, hdwy to lead 5f out, drvn, no extra & hdd cl-home: reapp/AW bow: 15L clr rem: plcd on 2nd of
2 '99 starts (mdn, rtd 89): eff at 6f, stays 8.5f v well: acts on gd grnd & fibresand: useful, mdn a formality.

610 **COWBOYS AND ANGELS** 23 [3] W G M Turner 3-9-0 P Fitzsimons (5) 11/2: 320-33: 3 b c Bin Ajwaad -   15 70a
Halimah (Be My Guest) Led, hdd 5f out, ev ch till wknd over 2f out: tchd 7/1, met a pair of useful rivals: see 610.

629 **CANCUN CARIBE** 19 [4] K McAuliffe 3-9-0 J Tate 66/1: 04: Handy, lost tch halfway: see 629.   1 68a

636 **CARDINAL FAIR** 19 [2] 3-8-9 R Lappin 40/1: -40035: Al last: v stiff task: see 636.   16 43a

5 ran   Time 1m 50.4 (4.2)   (Miss A Church)   J R Fanshawe Newmarket.

709 3.50 TEXT P368 HCAP 3YO 0-75 (E)   1m1f79y aw Going 42 -21 Slow   [80]
£2782   £856   £428   £214

*610 **FAVORISIO** 23 [3] Miss J A Camacho 3-9-7 (73) J P Spencer 13/8 FAV: 00-11: 3 br g Efisio - Dixie Favor   86a
(Dixieland Band) Prom, shkn up to impr 3f out, led on bit over 1f out, v easily: nicely bckd, val 6L+: earlier
won here at W'hampton (mdn): unplcd in 2 '99 turf starts at 6f (mdns, rtd 64): v eff over a sharp 9.4f on
fibresand, further shld suit: runs well fresh, likes W'hampton: clrly ahd of the H'capper, quick follow-up likely.

617 **SHAMSAN** 22 [8] M Johnston 3-9-0 (66) R Ffrench 6/1: 4-1032: 3 ch c Night Shift - Awayil (Woodman)   2 66a
Led, rdn/hdd appr fnl 1f, drvn & styd on but no ch with easy wnr: stays 1m/9.4f: handles both AWs: see 266.

536 **PAPAGENA** 34 [7] C W Thornton 3-8-0 (52)(bl) P Doe 5/1: 4-6243: 3 b f Robellino - Morning Crown   1½ 49a
(Chief's Crown) Trkd ldrs, rdn & no extra fnl 1f: tchd 7/1: back in trip: see 392.

591 **CELEBES** 26 [9] I A Balding 3-9-3 (69) R Cochrane 6/1: 564-34: Handy, rdn/btn over 1f out: up in trip.   ¾ 64a

662 **MISS WORLD** 12 [1] 3-9-3 (69)(t) L Newman (5) 10/1: 1-5405: Sn well bhd, late hdwy: btr 213 (1m).   2½ 60a

4570} **FISHER ISLAND** 99 [2] 3-8-2 (54) P M Quinn (5) 10/1: 3450-6: Nvr a threat: reapp/AW bow: plcd   1¼ 42a
once in '99 (nurs, rtd 59): eff at 7f, stays 1m: acts on gd & soft grnd.

4495} **PINCHANINCH** 99 [5] 3-8-11 (63)(BL) C Rutter 16/1: 500-7: Dwelt, sn handy, lost tch fnl 3f: 2 48a

WOLVERHAMPTON (Fibresand)   THURSDAY MARCH 23RD   Lefthand, Sharp Track

reapp: AW/h'cap bow, first time blnks: unplcd at long odds in 3 '99 turf mdns (rtd 73): with J Portman.
566	**NOBLE PASAO** 30 [6] 3-9-7 (73) P Fessey 11/1: 10-268: Prom, fdd fnl 3f: btr 495 (led).	nk	57a
555	**TIMELESS CHICK** 31 [4] 3-7-13 (51) M Henry 33/1: 660-09: Al rear: see 555.	4	28a
9 ran	Time 2m 04.2 (6.0) (Elite Racing Club) Miss J A Camacho Norton, N.Yorks.		

---

710   4.20 TEXT P372 SELLER 4YO+ (G)   1m4f aw   Going 42 -28 Slow
£1859   £531   £265   4 yo rec 2 lb

568   **SURE QUEST** 30 [9] D W P Arbuthnot 5-8-8 S Whitworth 15/8 FAV: 0-2341: 5 b m Sure Blade - Eagle's   **50a**
Quest (Legal Eagle) Trkd ldrs, hdwy to lead over 2f out, pushed clr, cosily: nicely bckd, bght in for 3,800gns:
unplcd in '99 (h'cap, rtd 55), prev term scored at Folkestone (mdn h'cap, rtd 61): eff at 10/12f: acts on
gd, firm & fibresand: likes a sharp/undul trk: has tried visor, best without: suited by selling grade now.

672   **APPROACHABLE** 9 [5] Miss S J Wilton 5-8-13 I Mongan (5) 6/1: 423242: 5 b h Known Fact - Western   4   46a
Approach (Gone West) Held up, rdn/hdwy 2f out, kept on but no dngr: consistent: eff at 7f/12f: see 626, 45.

675   **MALCHIK 7** [4] P Howling 4-8-11 R Cochrane 25/1: 020033: 4 ch c Absalom - Very Good (Noalto)   ¾   45a
Chsd ldrs, lost pl halfway, rallied & styd on well fnl 2f, no dngr: fair run at the weights, stays 12f: see 159.

*626   **ARTIC COURIER** 21 [7] D J S Cosgrove 9-9-5 C Rutter 7/2: 30-114: Held up, rdn to improve 3f out,   1   49a
no extra fnl 2f: clr rem: hat-trick bid: shade better over C/D in 626 (in front of this 2nd).

607   **COLONEL CUSTER** 23 [1] 5-9-5 (BL) J P Spencer 11/2: -31005: Led, hdd over 2f out, wknd qckly: 10   37a
first time blnks: thrice below 408 (sell h'cap, different connections).

650   **BILLICHANG** 15 [8] 4-9-3 T Williams 8/1: 334426: Wide/trkd ldr, wknd over 2f out: better at 1m/10f?   1¼   35a

670   **ADIRPOUR** 9 [2] 6-9-5 Stephanie Hollinshead (7) 33/1: 041547: Rcd wide, nvr a threat: see 556.   ¾   34a

3602}   **COL WOODY** 99 [3] 4-8-11 D Kinsella (7) 16/1: 3206-8: Handy, lost tch 5f out, t.o.: reapp, new   23   3a
stable: plcd sev times in '99 (h'caps & clmrs, rtd 71), tried visor, A P Jarvis), subs rnr-up on hdles bow for
G McCourt (juv clmr, rtd 79h, stays 2m on fast): eff at 10/12f on fast & gd/soft: now with J P Portman.

347   **SPARKLING DOVE** 65 [10] 7-8-8 N Carlisle 12/1: 09: Al bhd: tchd 33/1: jumps fit, recent   8   0a
wnr at Chepstow (sell h'cap hdle, rtd 64h, eff at 2m on hvy, blnkd): modest Flat/hdles form previously.

468   **HILL STORM** 47 [6] 4-8-11 (t) T G McLaughlin 25/1: 640-30: Handy, al bhd halfway, t.o.: abs.   16   0a
10 ran   Time 2m 41.9 (8.5)   (Miss P E Decker)   D W P Arbuthnot Upper Lambourn, Berks.

---

711   4.50 TEXT P372 HCAP 3YO+ 0-70 (E)   7f aw rnd   Going 42 +08 Fast   [70]
£2842   £812   £406   3 yo rec 15lb

4510}   **VICTORIOUS** 99 [1] B A McMahon 4-9-2 (58) R Cochrane 10/1: 0050-1: 4 ch c Formidable - Careful   65a
Dancer (Gorytus) Led early, rmnd cl-up, led again over 3f out, strongly pressed ins last, all out to hold on:
best time of day: reapp/AW bow: '99 scorer at Haydock (h'cap, rtd 66): promise in '98 (mdn, rtd 67): suited
by 7f, has tried 1m: acts on gd, gd/soft gnrd & fibresand, any trk: runs esp well fresh: rate higher/win again.

*8   **ROYAL ARTIST** 99 [6] W J Haggas 4-9-12 (68) J P Spencer 7/4 FAV: 4231-2: 4 b g Royal Academy -   hd   74a
Council Rock (General Assembly) Waited with, hdwy over 2f out, styd on strongly for press in last, just failed:
bckd from 3/1, long abs: jockey received a 3 day whip ban: eff on fast, gd/soft & both AWs: win again soon.

4317}   **ROLLER** 99 [11] J G Given 4-9-5 (61) T G McLaughlin 16/1: 0005-3: 4 b g Bluebird - Tight Spin   4   60a
(High Top) Sn well outpcd, rdn & ran on strongly fnl 2f, no threat to ldrs: reapp/AW bow: '99 scorer at
Warwick (mdn, rtd 78 at best, H Candy, first time blnks): eff at 7f, return to 1m will suit, has tried 12f:
acts on soft, handles fast, prob fibresand: prob best in blnks & on a sharp/turning trk: now with J G Given.

675   **COOL PROSPECT** 7 [10] K A Ryan 5-8-4 (46) Iona Wands (5) 7/1: -05054: Waited with, rdn to impr   8   32a
over 3f out, btn appr fnl 1f: qck reapp: see 582.

*583   **DONE AND DUSTED** 28 [7] 4-9-11 (67) N Callan 4/1: -06315: Nvr better than mid-div: btr 583 (C/D).   2   49a

698   **PETITE DANSEUSE** 3 [8] 6-7-10 (38) Claire Bryan 8/1: 500146: Nvr a threat: qck reapp: btr 604.   3   15a

538   **SEVEN 34** [3] 5-9-5 (61)(bl) I Mongan (5) 7/1: -01547: Chsd ldrs, wknd fnl 2f: recent 6th on   2   34a
hdles bow (2m nov, soft, rtd 87h): see 414 (6f ltd stks).

602   **STRATS QUEST** 24 [2] 6-7-10 (38)(vis)(2oh) P Fessey 16/1: 45-658: Al outpcd: see 476.   1½   8a

582   **SO WILLING** 28 [5] 4-8-6 (48)(bl) Dale Gibson 8/1: -06039: Prom, rdn/lost tch over 3f out: btr 582.   1¼   15a

680   **MOY 7** [4] 5-8-2 (44)(bl) A McCarthy (3) 16/1: 605300: Prom, wknd qckly over 3f out: 10th: qck reapp.   2   9a

647   **SEVEN SPRINGS** 17 [12] 4-7-10 (38)(2oh) P M Quinn (5) 14/1: 000-00: Sn led, hdd 3f out, sn btn: 11th.   2   0a

614   **TRUMP STREET** 23 [9] 4-8-6 (48) Jonjo Fowle (7) 14/1: 030-00: Al well bhd, fin last: bckd from 33/1.   6   0a
12 ran   Time 1m 28.6 (2.4)   (Tommy Staunton)   B A McMahon Hopwas, Staffs.

DONCASTER   FRIDAY MARCH 24TH   Lefthand, Galloping Track

Official Going   GOOD (watered - bordering on GOOD/SOFT). Stalls: Str - Stands Side; Rnd - Ins; Rnd 1m - Outside.

---

712   1.30 BAWTRY MDN SELLER 2YO (F)   5f   Good 60 -54 Slow
£2769   £852   £426   £213

--   **NINE TO FIVE** [8] W G M Turner 2-8-9 A Daly 3/1 FAV: 1: 2 b f Imp Society - Queen And Country   72
(Town And Country) Made all, hard prsd fnl 2f, kept on gamely for press: fit, nicely bckd for debut win, bt in for
7,000 gns, jock rec 1-day whip ban: Apr first foal: dam plcd at 5f: eff at 5f when fresh on gd grnd.

--   **UHOOMAGOO** [3] R A Fahey 2-9-0 R Winston 4/1: 2: 2 b c Namaqualand - Point Of Law (Law Society) shd   76
Prom, eff to chall 2f out, hard rdn & kept on ins last, just held: clr of rem, jock rec 7-day whip ban: gamble
from 16/1: Mar foal, cost 1,200 gns: half-brother to a 7f wnr: eff at 5f on gd grnd: shld win a seller.

--   **MOLLY IRWIN** [4] J S Moore 2-8-9 J F Egan 10/1: 3: 2 b f General Monash - Bunny Run (Dowsing)   8   53
Chsd ldrs, rdn & btn 2f out: lack scope, just better for race: Feb foal, bred for sprint trips.

--   **MANX GYPSY** [5] K W Hogg 2-8-9 R Lappin 7/1: 4: In tch, outpcd halfway: ndd race: Apr foal: 1½   49
half-sister to wnrs over 5/7f: sprint bred.

--   **REGAL MISTRESS** [1] 2-8-9 J P Spencer 4/1: 5: Slow away & al bhd: Mar foal, cost 2,000gns: 3½   40
half-sister to a 5f juv scorer: dam styd 10f: with D Shaw.

--   **HARRY JUNIOR** [6] 2-9-0 K Darley 4/1: 6: Al bhd: well grown, edgy.   7   25

--   **NEVER FEAR** [2] 2-8-9 J Fortune 11/1: 7: Chsd ldrs till wknd halfway: op 8/1, small.   5   8
7 ran   Time 1m 03.93 (5.73)   (Paul Thorman)   W G M Turner Corton Denham, Somerset.

---

713   **2.05 MALTBY MDN 3YO (D)**   **1m2f60y**   **Good 60**   **+07 Fast**
£4075   £1254   £627   £313

4523} **TANTALUS 99** [1] B W Hills 3-9-0 M Hills 11/10 FAV: 2-1: 3 ch c Unfuwain - Water Quest (Rainbow   **93**
Quest) Cl-up, hdwy to lead well over 1f out, styd on fnl 1f, rdn out, flashed tail: well bckd, best time of day:
rtd 95+ when rnr-up in a mdn on sole '99 start: eff at 7f, enjoyed this step up to 10.3f & 12f looks sure to suit:
acts on gd, gd/soft & on a gall trk: runs well fresh: signs of temperament but looks v useful & is lightly raced.

4379} **RIVER BANN 99** [3] P F I Cole 3-9-0 J Fortune 2/1: 2-2: 3 ch c Irish River - Spiritual Star (Soviet   2½ **88**
Star) Cl-up, led 3f out, rdn & hdd well over 1f out, not pace of wnr but clr of rem: well bckd, ndd race, reapp,
gd bodied: promising rnr-up in some '99 start: cost 120,000 gns: dam 1m juv wnr: eff at 1m,
apprec step up 10.3f & acts on gd grnd & a gall trk: useful, only twice raced & a mdn looks there for the taking.

3672} **FULL AHEAD 99** [7] M H Tompkins 3-9-0 S Sanders 16/1: 45-3: 3 b c Slip Anchor - Foulard (Sadler's   4 **81$**
Wells) Set pace till over 3f out, onepace for press fnl 2f: op 10/1, ndd race on reapp: promise on both unplcd
'99 starts (rtd 95$ at best): eff at 10.3f, bred to stay further: handles firm & gd: win on a minor track.

4229} **HINT OF MAGIC 99** [6] J G Portman 3-9-0 S Drowne 25/1: 52-4: In tch, rdn & no impress 2f out: 1½ **79**
swtg on reapp: rtd 78 when rnr-up on 2nd of only 2 '99 starts: dam 7f wnr: stays 10f, not bred for further:
acts on gd & gd/soft: shld apprec h'cap company now.

4524} **INCA STAR 99** [4] 3-9-0 J Fanning 9/1: 3-5: Waited with, brief effort over 3f out, no impress: 13 **62**
op 6/1, ndd race: rtd 85+ when plcd on sole juv start: dam 9f scorer: eff at 1m, bred to relish mid-dists this
term: acts on gd/soft grnd: shld do better.

4263} **PETEURESQUE 99** [5] J Fox 3-9-0 C Lowther 12/1: 25-6: Chsd ldrs, wknd halfway: quite fit for reapp.   6 **54**

694 **NICIARA** 4 [2] 3-9-0 R Studholme (5) 100/1: 246057: Al bhd.   10 **40**

7 ran   Time 2m 11.91 (5.51)   (K Abdulla)   B W Hills Lambourn, Berks.

---

714   **2.35 ONE-IN-A-HUNDRED HCAP 4YO+ 0-90 (C)**   **2m2f**   **Good 60**   **+00 Fast**   **[86]**
£7085   £2180   £1090   £545   4 yo rec 6 lb

664 **ROYAL EXPRESSION 13** [4] G M Moore 8-8-12 (70) J Weaver 14/1: 631231: 8 b g Sylvan Express - Edwins'   **73**
Princess (Owen Dudley) Led 5f out, kept on gamely for press fnl 1f, drvn out: fit from AW, earlier won at
W'hampton (h'cap, rtd 68a): '99 wnr again at W'hampton (h'cap, rtd 64a, with F Jordan) & Nottingham (h'cap, rtd 71):
eff at 12f, stays 2m2f on firm, gd/soft & fibresand: best without a visor on any trk: tough (8 wins from 45).

668 **PEN FRIEND 10** [6] W J Haggas 6-7-10 (54)(1oh) P M Quinn (5) 8/1: /0-522: 6 b g Robellino - Nibbs   shd **57**
Point (Sure Blade) Chsd ldrs, hdwy to chall over 1f out, hard drvn ins last, just failed to get up: jock rec
a 6-day whip ban: fit from AW & enjoyed this step up to 2m2f: in gd form, see 668, 577.

470 **JAMAICAN FLIGHT 46** [1] Mrs S Lamyman 7-9-3 (75) J Fortune 14/1: -33443: 7 b h Sunshine Forever - 1¼ **77**
Kalamona (Hawaii) Set pace till 5f out, kept on same pace for press over 2f out: not btn far & clr of rem:
recent unplcd jumps tmr: tough & game, thorough stayer, likes Pontefract: see 470.

1960} **DISTANT STORM 99** [9] B J Llewellyn 7-7-10 (54)(bl)(1oh) Claire Bryan (5) 10/1: 0222-4: In tch,   4 **52**
eff over 3f out, onepace: fit from hdlg, earlier won at Wincanton & Chepstow (h'caps, rtd 115h, stays 2m6f on
any grnd & trk, best in blnks): rnr-up on 3 of 4 '99 Flat starts (rtd 57): won 4 times over hdles in 97/98: last
won on the Flat back in '95, at Brighton: stays 2m2f well on any grnd & track: best in blnks now: tough.

4231} **OLD HUSH WING 99** [8] 7-7-11 (55) A Nicholls (3) 7/1: 2110-5: Sn bhd, effort 3f out, onepace: v fit,   2½ **51**
last rcd over hdles 8 wks ago, won at Sedgefield (h'cap, rtd 123h at best, stays 2m6f on fast & hvy): won
again at Sedgefield over timber in 98/99: '99 Flat scorer at Newcastle & Pontefract (h'caps, rtd 53): needs
at least 2m now, extreme trip will suit: acts on fast, hvy & fibresand: has run well fresh on occasions.

3880} **STAR RAGE 99** [13] 10-10-0 (86) J Fanning 12/1: 1131-6: Waited with, rdn over 3f out, no impress: ½ **81**
ndd race: last rcd over jumps 4 month ago, plcd at Cheltenham (val h'cap hdle, rtd 137h, eff at 2m, prob stays
3m & loves gd & firm): plcd over fences in 98/99 (rtd 109c, with D Elsworth), also tried blnks & rtd 149h prev:
incredibly tough & progressive on the Flat in '99, won at Lingfield (h'cap, rtd 84a), Beverley (2), Redcar &
Goodwood (h'caps, rtd 86): '98 wnr at W'hampton (h'cap, rtd 81a): best around 2m on firm, gd/soft & both AWs:
can carry big weights on any trk: amazingly tough 10yo (19 wins from 82 Flat starts), a credit to his trainer.

4259} **WEET FOR ME 99** [10] 4-8-12 (76) A Culhane (2) 0: 4402-7: In tch, eff over 3f out, onepace: doing   3 **68**
well physically, reapp: sole win in '99, at Haydock (mdn, 10.5f, rtd 82): rtd 85 prev term: eff at 10.5f,
stays 2m on firm, hvy grnd & likes gall trks: much sharper for this.

482 **BUSTLING RIO 45** [11] 4-8-0 (64) Dale Gibson 14/1: 21-158: Nvr a factor: best 428 (Southwell).   1 **55**

4590} **DANEGOLD 99** [12] 8-8-5 (63) P Fessey 9/4 FAV: 0000-9: Waited with, brief effort 4f out, sn   5 **49**
btn: well bckd: fit from hdlg, recent fast finishing nk rnr-up in Gr 3 County H'cap Hdle at Cheltenham (2m, rtd
130h), in 98/99 won hdles at Cartmel, Fontwell & Bangor (rtd 142h, acts on firm & gd/soft): busy on the Flat in
'99, won at Doncaster (this v h'cap) & Ascot (h'cap, rtd 72 at best): '98 wnr at Catterick, Yarmouth, Goodwood &
again at Ascot (h'caps, rtd 69): eff at 12f, best at 2m+ on fast & soft grnd, with/without a visor: handles any
trk: loves to come late off a fast pace through horses & has slipped back to a handy mark.

649 **MISCHIEF 16** [3] 4-7-10 (60)(vis) J Mackay (7) 33/1: 055620: In tch, wknd 3f out: see 649 (a/w).   5 **41**

4054} **MAZZELMO 99** [7] 7-8-5 (63)(VIS) Pat Eddery 11/1: 5301-0: Al bhd: 11th, not enjoy first time visor?   25 **24**

664 **SPOSA 13** [5] 4-7-10 (60) M Henry 11/1: 530240: In tch, wknd 5f out.   15 **7**

12 ran   Time 4m 03.38 (10.88)   (Mrs A Roddis)   G M Moore Middleham, N.Yorks.

---

715   **3.10 SPRING MILE HCAP 4YO+ (B)**   **1m str**   **Good 60**   **-19 Slow**   **[88]**
£14560   £4480   £2240   £1120   Field raced centre-stands side (stands side poss favoured)

4456} **KATY NOWAITEE 99** [4] P W Harris 4-9-10 (84) A Beech (5) 7/1: 1512-1: 4 b f Komaite - Cold   **94+**
Blow (Posse) Prom centre, hdwy to lead over 2f out, hung badly right over 1f out but styd on strongly, pushed
out, cmftbly on reapp: well bckd, ballotted out of Lincoln (well bckd): progressive in late '99, won at Newmarket
(mdn) & Redcar (h'cap, rtd 86): eff over a str/rnd 1m on firm & gd/soft: likes a gall trk & runs v well fresh:
most progressive, lightly raced & v useful filly, can rate more highly (came from low draw to stands rail to win this).

663 **TOPTON 13** [17] P Howling 6-9-0 (74)(bl) R Winston 20/1: 613002: 6 b g Royal Academy - Circo   2½ **76**
(High Top) Chsd ldrs stands side, effort 2f out, kept on well ins last: fine run & likes this trk: v tough, see 463.

-- **ROBZELDA** [8] K A Ryan 4-9-1 (75)(bl) F Lynch 33/1: /313-3: 4 b g Robellino - Zelda (Sharpen   1 **75**
Up) Chsd ldrs centre, styd on well over 1f out, not pace of front 2: reapp: Irish import, in '99 won at
Leopardstown (appr mdn): eff at 6f, stays 1m well, could get further: acts on gd & gd/soft: fine run.

4585} **TAFFS WELL 99** [22] B Ellison 7-8-13 (73) F Norton 14/1: 0606-4: Waited with stands side, hdwy   ¾ **73+**
& not clr run 2f out, switched over 1f out, styd on well ins last under hands-and-heels: fit for reapp: in

'99 scored at Musselburgh, Chester, Haydock & Newcastle (h'caps, rtd 83 at best): rtd 75 when rnr-up for Mrs J Ramsden in '98: eff at 7f, suited by 1m now on a gall trk, handles any: likes gd & gd/firm, handles hvy: tough & genuine, back on a winning mark & would have gone closer with a clear run here, keep in mind.
4176} **TUMBLEWEED QUARTET 99** [6] 4-9-5 (79)(t) M Tebbutt 20/1: 0000-5: Chsd ldrs centre, effort to chase wnr over 1f out, kept on same pace: fit for reapp: unplcd in '99 (tried blnks, 10f, rtd 92 at best): '98 scorer at Newbury (stks, rtd 110 when plcd in a Gr 2): eff at 7f/1m on fast & hvy grnd: has run well fresh: promising reapp from wrong side of the course, has tumbled down the weights & could prove interesting. *nk* **77+**
137 **TONY TIE 99** [13] 4-9-0 (74) A Culhane 20/1: 0210-6: In tch, effort over 2f out, kept on same pace ins last: ndd race on reapp: sole win in '99, here at Doncaster (lady riders h'cap, rtd 74): '98 wnr at Salisbury (stks) & Chester (nurs, rtd 89, with W G M Turner): eff at 5/7f, stays 1m well on firm, likes gd/soft & hvy: handles any trk & has run well fresh: much sharper for this encouraging comeback. *½* **71**
687 **MANTLES PRIDE 7** [23] 5-9-8 (82)(bl) K Darley 20/1: 130-07: In tch stands side, wknd over 1f out: in '99 scored at Carlisle, Redcar & Haydock (h'caps, rtd 84): rtd 86 when plcd in '98: last 3 wins at 7f, stays 1m on firm & soft: handles any trk & wears blnks/visor: has run well fresh: enjoy a return to 7f. *5* **70**
669 **ONE DINAR 10** [24] 5-8-9 (69)(5ex) Dale Gibson 9/1: 0-2128: Bhd stands side, nvr a factor: see 669. *3* **52**
583 **REX IS OKAY 29** [20] 4-8-10 (70)(bl) Dean McKeown 25/1: 066649: Sn clr ldr stands side, hdd over 2f out, wknd: free to post & in race: both wins at 7f, see 583. *nk* **52**
663 **WEETMANS WEIGH 13** [9] 7-9-4 (78) N Callan 25/1: -46400: Chsd ldrs, wknd over 1f out: 10th. *nk* **60**
618 **PROSPECTORS COVE 23** [7] 7-8-12 (72) J Weaver 16/1: 000-30: Bhd far side, some late gains, nvr dngrs: 11th: will do better: see 618. *2½* **50**
4174} **GREAT NEWS 99** [19] 5-9-9 (83) M Hills 11/1: 0130-0: In tch stands side, btn halfway: 12th, ndd race on reapp, now with W Haggas. *½* **60**
662 **SPRING PURSUIT 13** [11] 4-9-4 (78) P Doe 25/1: 162-60: Al bhd stands side: 15th. *5* **47**
4357} **KALA SUNRISE 99** [15] 7-9-3 (77) R Fitzpatrick (3) 20/1: 4240-0: In tch centre, wknd 2f out: 14th. *shd* **46**
4475} **PENTAGON LAD 99** [16] 4-8-7 (67) R Lappin 25/1: 4000-0: In tch stands side, btn 2f out: 15th. *3½* **30**
4579} **SCENE 99** [14] 5-9-2 (76) G Duffield 16/1: 0041-0: Nvr a factor in centre: 16th: better than this. *½* **38**
4266} **TOM DOUGAL 99** [3] 5-9-6 (80) J F Egan 16/1: 5000-0: Chsd ldrs far side, btn halfway: 17th, reapp. *1½* **39**
648 **INDIUM 18** [18] 6-9-5 (79) Pat Eddery 8/1: 100-40: Al bhd: 18th. *3½* **31**
4560} **WILD SKY 99** [1] 6-9-7 (81)(t) S Drowne 11/1: 0000-0: In tch far side, wknd 2f out: 19th, reapp. *1* **31**
4357} **Parkside 99** [2] 4-9-5 (79) Martin Dwyer 33/1:
3386} **Indian Plume 99** [10] 4-9-4 (78) J Fortune 25/1:
687 **Wuxi Venture 7** [5] 5-9-5 (79) A Nicholls (3) 20/1:
4562} **Route Sixty Six 99** [12] 4-9-1 (75) I Mongan (5) 33/1:
23 ran Time 1m 42.8 (6.3) (The Stable Maites) P W Harris Ringshall, Bucks.

716 3.40 TOWN MOOR HCAP 3YO+ 0-90 (C) 6f Good 60 -15 Slow [88]
£7735 £2380 £1190 £595 3 yo rec 13lb Field raced stands side - centre

*680 **MANORBIER 8** [10] K A Ryan 4-8-5 (65)(6ex) F Lynch 25/1: /01411: 4 ch g Shalford - La Pirouette (Kennedy Road) Chsd ldrs, styd on strongly over 1f out, rdn clr ins last: recently won 2 sellers at W'hampton (fibresand, rtd 64a): missed '99, '98 Chepstow wnr (juv auct mdn, with D Arbuthnott, rtd 83): suited by 6f now on fast, gd & fibresand: in fine heart & fast improving. **79**
4572} **CADEAUX CHER 99** [3] B W Hills 6-9-2 (76) R Cochrane 8/1: 0040-2: 6 ch g Cadeaux Genereux - Home Truth (Known Fact) Waited with, gd hdwy 2f out, styd on ins last, not pace of wnr: tumbled down the weights & unplcd in '99 (rtd 88 at best): v progressive in '98, won at Doncaster, Leicester (class stks), Ripon & Doncaster (val h'caps, rtd 96): suited by 5.5/6f on firm & gd grnd: runs well fresh & likes Doncaster: best without blnks: v well h'capped on best form & this was most encouraging. *4* **81**
579 **TOM TUN 29** [12] Miss J F Craze 5-9-6 (80) K Darley 5/1 FAV: 26-523: 5 b g Bold Arrangement - B Grade (Lucky Wednesday) Cl-up, eff to chall 2f out, onepace for press: well bckd: in gd form & likes Doncaster. *1½* **81**
4491} **BARRINGER 99** [16] M R Channon 3-9-3 (90) S Drowne 25/1: 1000-4: Chsd ldrs stands side, kept on same pace for press over 1f out: reapp: in '99 won at Hamilton (nov stks), Nottingham & Windsor (stks): eff at 5f, stays 6f on fast & hvy grnd: handles any trk: useful, gd reapp. *2* **86**
4172} **FRANCPORT 99** [19] 4-8-12 (72) G Carter 33/1: 0200-5: Bhd, styd on strongly appr fnl 1f, nrst fin: burly, has thrived physically, reapp: in '99 scored at Beverley (mdn, rtd 75 at best): brother to useful sprinter Pips Pride: eff at 5f, stays 6f & further may suit: acts on firm, gd/soft & on a stiff trk: caught the eye here, strip fitter for this & one to keep an eye on. *1* **67+**
3992} **CRYHAVOC 99** [18] 6-10-0 (88) Alex Greaves 16/1: 5650-6: In tch, kept on same pace over 1f out: reapp, top-weight: in fine form in '99, won at Yarmouth, Goodwood (appr), Windsor, Catterick & Beverley (h'caps, rtd 89 at best): unplcd for J Arnold in '98 (tried blnks): winning form btwn 5/7f on any trk: acts on firm, gd/soft: typically tough & genuine D Nicholls sprinter. *nk* **81**
3992} **ZUHAIR 99** [20] 7-9-12 (86) F Norton 20/1: 1000-7: Bhd, kept on nicely over 1f out, nrst fin: ndd race on reapp: much improved by D Nicholls in '99, won at Lingfield, Goodwood (2) & York (h'caps, rtd 88 at best): rtd 75 when rnr-up for D McCain in '98: '97 W'hampton wnr (rtd 93 & 80a): eff over 5/6f & likes fast/firm, handles gd/soft & fibresand: best without blnks on any trk, likes Goodwood: gd reapp, much sharper for this. *shd* **79**
4610} **INDIAN SPARK 99** [13] 6-9-4 (78) A Culhane 20/1: 0000-8: Led 1f, cl-up till wknd over 1f out: ndd race on reapp: in '99 scored at York (rtd h'cap, rtd 91 at best): '98 scorer at Thirsk & Doncaster (2, h'caps, rtd 89): eff at 5/6f on firm & soft grnd: gd weight carrier who likes a gall trk, esp Doncaster: v well h'capped. *nk* **70**
4448} **UNSHAKEN 99** [17] 6-9-1 (75) J Fortune 20/1: 4300-9: Nvr a factor: reapp: in '99 scored at Hamilton (2) & Newcastle (h'caps, rtd 81 at best): '98 scorer at Carlisle & Hamilton (stks, rtd 68): 6f specialist, acts on firm & hvy grnd & likes a stiff/uphill fin, esp Hamilton: back on last winning mark. *½* **66**
1982} **JAY AND A 99** [15] 5-9-5 (79) J P Spencer 20/1: 0505-0: In tch, no impress over 1f out: 10th, fit. *1¾* **66**
660 **DAAWE 13** [14] 9-8-9 (69)(bl) Clare Roche (7) 11/2: 111630: Dwelt, led after 1f, hdd over 1f out, wknd & edged left fnl 1f: 11th, nicely bckd, padd pick: rtd much higher on AW in 660. *nk* **55**
4562} **MISTER RAMBO 99** [2] 5-9-5 (79) Pat Eddery 6/1: 0540-0: In tch, btn 2f out: 12th. *2* **60**
4439} **IVORY DAWN 99** [22] 6-8-10 (70) C Carver (3) 20/1: 3000-0: In tch, wknd 2f out: 13th, reapp. *½* **50**
3789} **SULU 99** [11] 4-9-1 (75) G Parkin 33/1: 6233-0: Dwelt, al bhd on reapp: 14th, jumps rnr, chngd stable. *2½* **49**
631 **NORTHERN SVENGALI 20** [21] 4-9-5 (79) C Lowther 14/1: 444-30: In tch, wknd 2f out: 15th. *1¼* **49**
532 **Classy Cleo 36** [8] 5-9-12 (86) J F Egan 20/1:
4510} **Johayro 99** [6] 7-8-5 (65) Dawn Rankin (6) 33/1:
660 **Referendum 13** [4] 6-10-0 (88) O Pears 20/1:
2216} **Lucky Cove 99** [5] 4-8-4 (64) Kim Tinkler 50/1:
645 **Caution 18** [1] 6-8-8 (1ow)(67) S Sanders 20/1:
543 **Rififi 34** [7] 7-8-13 (73) J Weaver 20/1:
4207} **Card Games 99** [9] 3-9-1 (88) T Lucas 16/1:
22 ran Time 1m 15.3 (4.5) (Uncle Jacks Pub) K A Ryan Hambleton, N.Yorks.

717   4.10 MEXBOROUGH MDN 3YO (D)   7f str Good 60 -27 Slow
     £4231   £1302   £651   £325

4265} **RUSHMORE 99** [5] P F I Cole 3-9-0 J Fortune 7/4 FAV: 3-1: 3 ch c Mt Livermore - Crafty Nan (Crafty   **82**
Prospector) Cl-up, hdwy to lead 2f out, pushed clr ins last, v cmftbly: bckd, fit: rtd 76 sole '99 start: brother to
a smart 7f wnr: apprec this step up to 7f, 1m sure to suit: runs well fresh: looks v useful: win again.

4493} **MANA DARGENT 99** [8] M Johnston 3-9-0 J Fanning 9/2: 633-2: 3 b c Ela Mana Mou - Petite D Argent 2½ **68**
(Noalto) Cl-up, eff to chase wnr appr fnl 1f, no impress: just better for race on reapp: plcd on 2 of 3 juv
starts (rtd 83): eff at 6/7f on gd & hvy grnd: shld win a race on a minor track.

4183} **ANDYS ELECTIVE 99** [4] J R Jenkins 3-9-0 Pat Eddery 16/1: 054-3: 3 b c Democratic - English Mint 1¼ **65$**
(Jalmood) Set pace till halfway, kept on same pace fnl 2f: op 16/1, just better for race, clr of rem on reapp:
rtd 70 when unplcd on 3 juv starts: eff at 7f on gd grnd: some promise here.

4083} **ZABIONIC 99** [7] B A McMahon 3-9-0 K Darley 4/1: 600-4: Waited with, eff over 3f out, sn onepace: 5 **56**
strong, burly: unplcd as a juv (rtd 74): eff at 7f on gd grnd: shld stay at least 1m.

--   **SARAH MADELINE** [9] 3-8-9 C Lowther 50/1: 5: Waited with, rdn & btn 2f out: debut: Pelder filly. 1¾ **48**

4409} **PILLAGER 99** [3] 3-9-0 J Stack 33/1: 0-6: Al bhd. 1 **51**

4474} **STAFFORD KING 99** [6] 3-9-0 A Culhane 100/1: 00-7: No dngr: ndd race. hd **51**

3189} **WETHAAB 99** [2] 3-9-0 M Hills 4/1: 0-8: Prom, led halfway, hdd 2f out, wknd: op 5/2. 1½ **49**

--   **CRYFIELD** [1] 3-9-0 Kim Tinkler 33/1: 9: In tch, btn over 3f out: debut. 11 **31**

9 ran   Time 1m 29.33 (6.13)   (J S Gutkin)   P F I Cole Whatcombe, Oxon.

WOLVERHAMPTON (Fibresand)   SATURDAY MARCH 25TH   Lefthand, Sharp Track

Official Going STANDARD. Stalls: 7f - Outside, Rem - Inside.

718   7.00 BET DIRECT HCAP 3YO+ 0-75 (E)   1m100y aw rnd Going 44 -01 Slow   [73]
     £2786   £796   £398

*684 **LORD EUROLINK 8** [6] C A Dwyer 6-9-3 (62)(tvi) R Ffrench 100/30: 053111: 6 b g Danehill - Lady   **68a**
Eurolink (Kala Shikari) Sn led, styd on well fnl 1f, rdn out: op 2/1: recent wnr at W'hampton (seller) & Southwell
(clmr): plcd on turf in '99 (rtd 79, appr h'cap): plcd sole '98 start for J Dunlop (h'cap, rtd 92): eff forcing pace
at 1m/10f on fast, gd/soft & fibresand, handles equitrack: eff in a t-strap/vis: handles any trk, likes W'hampton.

594 **MELLORS 28** [2] John Berry 7-9-4 (63) V Slattery 8/1: 140-32: 7 b g Common Grounds - Simply 2 **63a**
Beautiful (Simply Great) Chsd ldrs, rdn & kept on to chase wnr fnl 1f, al held: op 6/1: acts on frm, gd & both AWs.

*676 **MY TYSON 9** [4] K A Ryan 5-8-5 (49)(1ow) F Lynch 7/1: -00013: 5 b g Don't Forget Me - Shuckran 1½ **47a**
Habibi (Thatching) Rear, rdn/kept on fnl 2f, nvr threat: op 5/1: see 676 (amat h'cap).

681 **ARC 9** [1] G M Moore 6-9-11 (70) J Weaver 5/2 FAV: 4-2424: Led 1f, chsd wnr, btn 1f out: op 9/2. ½ **66a**

*647 **INTERNAL AFFAIR 19** [3] Lynsey Hanna (7) 4/1: 413515: In tch, outpcd fnl 2f: op 3/1, btr 647. ¾ **63a**

*681 **DANAKIL 9** [5] 5-9-9 (68) N Callan 9/2: 663516: Al rear: op 6/1: btr 681 (9.4f). 6 **54a**

6 ran   Time 1m 50.00 (3.8)   (Roalco Ltd)   C A Dwyer Newmarket.

719   7.30 0800 211 222 CLAIMER 4YO+ (F)   6f aw rnd Going 44 -03 Slow
     £2236   £639   £319

645 **MALLIA 19** [5] T D Barron 7-9-5 C Lowther 2/1 FAV: 551641: 7 b g Statoblest - Pronetta (Mr Prospector)   **69a**
Rdn/rear, prog wide fnl 2f to lead ins last, hung left/rdn out: op 5/2: earlier won here at W'hampton (C/D clmr):
'99 wnr here at W'hampton (2, clmr & h'cap, rtd 76a) & Haydock (h'cap, rtd 76): '98 wnr at Southwell, W'hampton &
Ripon (h'caps, rtd 78a & 71): eff at 5f, suited by 6f: acts on firm, hvy & fibresand, any trk, loves W'hampton:
eff with/without blnks or visor: relishes claiming grade.

697 **RUSSIAN ROMEO 5** [4] B A McMahon 5-9-1 (bl) R Winston 9/4: 605522: 5 b g Soviet Lady - Aotearoa nk **64a**
(Flash Of Steel) Chsd ldr, led over 2f out, rdn/hdd ins last, kept on well, just held: op 7/4: qck reapp: see 40.

680 **PALO BLANCO 9** [1] Andrew Reid 9-8-4 M Henry 12/1: 6/0-33: 9 b m Precocious - Linpac Mapleleaf 1¾ **50a**
(Dominion) Prom, rdn/onepace fnl 2f: op 10/1: see 680 (C/D, seller).

677 **RONS PET 9** [2] K R Burke 5-9-5 (t) D Hayes (7) 7/2: 223554: Rdn/rear, nvr factor: op 3/1: needs 7f+. 3 **59a**

604 **VICE PRESIDENTIAL 26** [6] 5-8-9 Dean McKeown 12/1: 250045: Led 4f, fdd: op 10/1: btr 32. 3 **43a**

697 **SAMWAR 5** [3] 8-9-1 (vis) R Fitzpatrick (3) 8/1: 622606: Chsd ldrs, fdd 1f out: qck reapp: btr 214 (5f). 1½ **46a**

6 ran   Time 1m 15.6 (2.8)   (H T Duddin)   T D Barron Maunby, N.Yorks.

720   8.00 BEST BETS MDN 3YO+ (D)   1m1f79y aw Going 44 -03 Slow
     £2758   £788   £394   3 yo rec 19lb

658 **ROYAL CAVALIER 14** [6] R Hollinshead 3-8-7 P M Quinn (5) 7/4: 2-0341: 3 b g Prince Of Birds - Gold   **83a**
Belt (Bellypha) Led after 2f, rdn/styd on well fnl 1f: well bckd, op 3/1: rnr-up in '99 on turf & sand (rtd 87 & 70a):
eff at 1m, suited by 9.4f, further could suit: acts on fibresand, gd/soft & hvy grnd: handles a sharp/gall trk.

198 **SEA SQUIRT 98** [7] M Johnston 3-8-7 J Fanning 13/8 FAV: 622-2: 3 b g Fourstars Allstar - Polynesian 2¼ **77a**
Goddess (Salmon Leap) Chsd wnr, rdn/ch over 1f out, onepace: clr rem: well bckd: abs: styd longer 9.4f trip.

658 **MARJU GUEST 14** [2] M R Channon 3-8-2 P Fessey 100/30: 044-23: 3 b f Marju - Dance Ahead (Shareef 6 **63a**
Dancer) Prom, rdn/ch 2f out, sn outpcd: op 5/2: ahd of today's wnr in 658 (8.5f).

658 **JAVELIN 14** [8] Ian Williams 4-9-12 R Fitzpatrick (3) 14/1: 400-54: Dwelt, rdn rear, mod prog: op 7/1. 6 **59a**

707 **ESPERE DOR 2** [4] 3-8-7 R Ffrench 100/1: 0-0005: Bhd halfway, mod form, longer 9.4f trip. 17 **34a**

4299} **EMERALD IMP 99** [3] 3-8-2 R Price 20/1: 04-6: Led 2f, btn 4f out: op 14/1, AW bow: 6 month 4 **21a**
abs: rtd 68 on 2nd of 2 starts in '99 (mdn): poss stays a gall 7f & handles hvy grnd.

--   **MEPHITIS** [1] 6-9-12 (t) Sophie Mitchell 50/1: 424/7: Sn bhd: jumps fit (mod form): last rcd 7 **12a**
on the level in native France in '97 (plcd) eff arnd 7f/1m on gd & hvy grnd: AW bow tonight for R Ford.

7 ran   Time 2m 02.6 (4.4)   (The Three R's)   R Hollinshead Upper Longdon, Staffs

WOLVERHAMPTON (Fibresand) SATURDAY MARCH 25TH Lefthand, Sharp Track

721 8.30 TEXT P368 HCAP 3YO+ 0-85 (D) **7f aw rnd** **Going 44** **+05 Fast** [82]
£3770 £1160 £580 £290 3 yo rec 15lb

623 **RAIN RAIN GO AWAY** 23 [3] · D J S Cosgrove 4-8-12 (66) R Ffrench 7/2: 161431: 4 ch g Miswaki - **73a**
Stormagain (Storm Cat) Handy, rdn/led over 1f out, styd on gamely, all out: best time of night: op 3/1: earlier
scored here at W'hampton (C/D mdn) & Lingfield (stks): unplcd on turf for E Dunlop in '99 (rtd 50), plcd on sand
(rtd 54a): suited by 7f, stays 1m: acts on soft, likes both AWs, loves W'hampton: likes to force the pace.
630 **RISK FREE** 21 [6] · N P Littmoden 3-8-13 (82) T G McLaughlin 8/1: 002-42: 3 ch g Risk Me - Princess *shd* **88a**
Lily (Blakeney) Prom, rdn/ch when edged left fnl 1f, just held: op 7/1: see 108.
*588 **MY TESS** 29 [5] · B A McMahon 4-9-6 (74) K Darley 5/2 FAV: 452213: 4 br f Lugana Beach - Barachois 3 **73a**
Princess (Barachois) Led, rdn/hdd over 1f out, held/eased nr line: nicely bckd: see 588 (made all).
*525 **REDOUBTABLE** 38 [7] · D W Chapman 9-10-0 (82) A Culhane 6/1: 641214: Chsd ldrs, held over 1f out. 1¾ **77a**
645 **KEEN HANDS** 19 [9] · 4-9-8 (76)(vis) R Fitzpatrick (3) 14/1: 410505: Prom 6f: op 10/1: btr 454 (6f) 2½ **64a**
669 **MUTAHADETH** 11 [2] · 6-7-12 (52)(bl) F Norton 10/1: 034446: Al outpcd: see 583, 183 4 **30a**
*598 **DISTINCTIVE DREAM** 26 [4] · 6-8-13 (67) J Weaver 3/1: 153417: Chsd ldrs wide, btn 2f out: op 4/1. ½ **43a**
2217} **PERUVIAN STAR** 99 [1] · 4-9-5 (73) D Sweeney 25/1: /000-8: Sn bhd: 9 month abs: unplcd in '99 (rtd 8 **34a**
66 & 59a, N P Littmoden): '98 W'hampton wnr (mdn, rtd 84a): eff at 6/7f, acts on fibresand & has run well fresh.
8 ran Time 1m 28.9 (2.7) (G G Grayson) D J S Cosgrove Newmarket

722 9.00 TEXT P372 SELLER 2YO (G) **5f aw rnd** **Going 44** **-72 Slow**
£1844 £527 £263

712 **MOLLY IRWIN** 1 [2] · J S Moore 2-8-6 F Norton 8/1: 31: 2 b f General Monash - Bunny Run (Dowsing) **62a**
Led bef halfway & clr 2f out, styd on well, rdn out: bght in for 5,000gns: op 6/1: qck reapp: fin 3rd in a
Doncaster seller yesterday: eff at 5f & lost: handles gd: likes a sharp trk: going the right way.
-- **DUSTY DEMOCRAT** [3] · W G M Turner 2-8-11 A Daly 5/1: 2: 2 b c Democratic - Le Saule d'Or (Sonnen 2 **61a**
Gold) Dwelt, kept on fnl 2f, nvr pace of wnr: May foal, cost 650gns: dam a 1m juv wnr: handles fibresnd.
-- **DECEIVES THE EYE** [1] · J G Given 2-8-11 Dean McKeown 12/1: 3: 2 b c Dancing Spree - Lycius Touch 1¾ **57a**
(Lycius) Dwelt/rdn towards rear, late gains, no threat: tchd 20/1: Feb foal, cost 800gns: dam a 5f juv wnr:
sire a high-class sprinter: eff over a sharp 5f, 6f+ shld suit in time: handles fibresand.
-- **ELEANOR J** [6] · K R Burke 2-8-6 N Callan 7/1: 4: Chsd ldrs, held over 1f out: op 6/1: Imp Society 1¼ **49a**
filly, Mar foal, cost 3,800gns: could improve in time.
-- **BLAKESHALL JOE** [4] · 2-8-11 S Drowne 13/8 FAV: 5: Chsd ldrs 4f: nicely bckd: Fraam colt, Mar 3½ **45a**
foal: sire smart 7f/1m performer: dam a winning hdler: with M R Channon.
-- **RAISAS GOLD** [7] · 2-8-6 M Fenton 11/2: 6: In tch 3f: op 4/1: Goldmark filly, Feb foal, cost 3,800 gns: hd **39a**
half-sister to a 6f juv wnr: sire high-class French 2yo 1m performer: with B Rothwell.
-- **BAYRAMI** [5] · 2-8-6 J Tate 7/1: 7: Led 1f, btn/eased fnl 1f: op 5/1, with S E Kettlewell. 10 **20a**
7 ran Time 1m 06.00 (5.8) (Alljays Racing) J S Moore East Garston, Berks

723 9.30 TEXT P372 HCAP 3YO+ 0-65 (F) **1m4f** **Going 44** **-25 Slow** [65]
£2299 £657 £328 3 yo rec 22lb4 yo rec 2 lb

*683 **EVEZIO RUFO** 8 [7] · N P Littmoden 8-9-3 (54)(bl) C Cogan (5) 7/2 FAV: 314511: 8 b g Blakeney - **61a**
Empres Corina (Free State) Held up in tch, prog to lead 1f out, styd on strongly ins last, rdn out: op 5/2:
scored twice here at W'hampton (h'caps) & most recently at Southwell (amat h'cap): '99 W'hampton wnr (2, seller &
h'cap, rtd 47a & 34): '98 Lingfield, Southwell & W'hampton wnr (h'caps, rtd 61a & 56): eff at 11/14.8f, suited by
12f: acts on fast, hvy & equitrack, fibresand specialist: suited by vis/blnks: loves a sharp trk & runs well for an appr.
681 **SUMMER BOUNTY** 9 [8] · F Jordan 4-8-10 (49) P M Quinn (5) 10/1: -06002: 4 b g Lugana Beach - 4 **49a**
Tender Moment (Caerleon) Slowly away, prog halfway & led over 1f out, hdd 1f out & no extra: stays a sharp
12f well: acts on fast, gd & both AWs: see 469.
695 **FAILED TO HIT** 5 [10] · N P Littmoden 7-10-0 (65)(vis) J Tate 4/1: 016343: 7 b g Warrshan - Missed 2 **62a**
Again (High Top) Chsd ldrs, led 5f out, hdd over 1f out & no extra: op 9/2, qck reapp: see 530 (clmr, made all).
642 **WESTERN COMMAND** 19 [6] · Mrs N Macauley 4-9-10 (63) R Fitzpatrick (3) 4/1: 216034: Chsd ldrs 10f. 5 **53a**
699 **AMBIDEXTROUS** 2 [5] · 8-7-10 (33)(7oh) J Bramhill 10/1: -04505: Mid-div, rdn/lost pl halfway, mod 7 **13a**
late gains: qck reapp: see 231 (C/D, seller).
683 **LAA JADEED** 8 [3] · 5-7-10 (33)(3oh) Joanna Badger (7) 16/1: -00506: Mid-div, strugg 4f out: see 476. 23 **0a**
682 **LOST SPIRIT** 8 [4] · 4-8-11 (50) G Baker 7/1: 025067: Led 5f: op 10/1: btr 290 (equitrack). 1½ **2a**
683 **ICHI BEAU** 8 [9] · 6-9-2 (53) A Daly 9/2: -41138: Led 7f out till 5f out, sn btn: btr 683, 641. 5 **0a**
566 **STAFFORD PRINCE** 32 [11] · 3-7-10 (55)(10oh) A McCarthy (3) 50/1: 600-09: Sn bhd: lngr 12f trip. *dist* **0a**
1722} **YOUNG BUTT** 99 [2] · 7-7-10 (33)(1oh) M Henry 33/1: 000-P: Sn bhd, t.o./p.u. & dismounted 1f out, **0a**
lame: 7 month abs, AW bow: unplcd in '99 (rtd 38, clmr, B Pearce): lightly rcd & no form since '96 Goodwood
wnr (h'cap, rtd 64, J Fitch Heyes): eff at 7f/1m, stays a stiff 10f: acts on fast, gd/soft & fibresand.
10 ran Time 2m 41.9 (8.3) (O A Gunter) N P Littmoden Newmarket

KEMPTON SATURDAY MARCH 25TH Righthand, Flat, Fair Track

Official Going GOOD. Stalls: Str - Stands Side; Rem - Inside.

724 2.15 EBF 24 HOUR BETTING MDN 2YO (D) **5f str** **Good 48** **-40 Slow**
£4173 £1284 £642 £321

-- **Y TO KMAN** [1] · R Hannon 2-9-0 J Weaver 7/2: 1: 2 b c Mujadil - Hazar (Thatching) **80**
With ldr, went on over 1f out, kept on well, hands-and-heels: Feb foal, cost 15,500gns: dam 7/9f scorer: eff
at 5f, 6f will suit: nice walk fresh on gd: pleasing debut.
-- **FACTUAL LAD** [2] · B R Millman 2-9-0 G Carter 7/2: 2: 2 b c So Factual - Surprise Surprise 1¼ **75**
(Robellino) Set pace till over 1f out, not pace of wnr under hands-and-heels riding: nicely bckd on debut:
Apr foal, cost 8,000gns: half-brother to a 5f scorer: eff at 5f, 6f in time: sharper for this.
-- **COLOUR SERGEANT** [3] · M L W Bell 2-9-0 M Fenton 15/8 FAV: 3: 2 ch c Candy Stripes - Princess 2 **70**
Afleet (Afleet) Chsd ldrs, rdn & onepace over 1f out: well bckd, padd pick: Jan first foal, cost 45,000$: fair debut.

229

-- **IMPERIAL DANCER** [4] M R Channon 2-9-0 S Drowne 3/1: 4: In tch on outside, btn 2f out: 5   58
op 2/1: Apr foal, cost 40,000gns: half-brother to a 1m/10f scorer: dam styd mid-dists: improve in time?
-- **BOHEMIAN SPIRIT** [5] 2-9-0 P Doe 20/1: 5: Free to post, chsd ldrs till btn well over 1f out: 3½   48
Feb foal, cost IR 5,500gns: half-brother to a 10f wnr: with P Murphy.
5 ran   Time 1m 02.69 (4.39)   (The Cayman A Team)   R Hannon East Everleigh, Wilts.

725   2.50 BET BLUESQ.COM HCAP 3YO+ 0-95 (C)   7f jub   Good 48   +14 Fast   [95]
        £14430   £4440   £2220   £1110   3 yo rec 15lb

4560} **PREMIER BARON** 99 [2] P S McEntee 5-8-13 (80) G Carter 16/1: 6220-1: 5 b g Primo Dominie - Anna   84
Karietta (Precocious) Dwelt, held up, stdy hdwy over 2f out to get up cl-home, drvn out, narrowly: reapp,
best time of day: in '99 trained by P Mitchell, won at Sandown (h'cap, rtd 88 & 68a at best): in '98 rtd
83 for T Clement): suited 7f, prob stays 1m: acts on fast, soft, fibresand & any trk: runs well fresh.
4560} **PULAU TIOMAN** 99 [13] M A Jarvis 4-10-0 (95) M Tebbutt 12/1: 1500-2: 4 b c Robellino - Ella Mon   shd   98
Amour (Ela Mana Mou) Chsd ldrs, gd hdwy to chall over 1f out, led ins last till collared last strides: reapp:
in '99 scored at Haydock (rtd h'cap) & Sandown (stks, rtd 100): '98 Nottingham wnr (mdn, rtd 88): stays 9f,
suited by 7f: acts on firm, gd & any trk: runs well fresh: tough & useful, fine reapp under topweight.
4580} **ADJUTANT** 99 [9] B J Meehan 5-9-11 (92) R Ffrench 11/1: 2313-3: 5 b g Batshoof - Indian Love Song   ½   94
(Be My Guest) Hld up, gd hdwy & short of room over 1f out, styd on strongly ins last, not btn far: op 8/1: in
'99 won at Leicester (stks, rtd 94): '98 scorer at Goodwood (h'cap, awdd race) & Haydock (h'cap, rtd 92): all
wins at 7f, stays 1m on firm, soft & on any trk, likes Haydock: runs well fresh: useful, should win again.
3767} **PRESENT LAUGHTER** 99 [6] P F I Cole 4-9-4 (85) L Newman (5) 14/1: 2500-4: Cl-up, gd hdwy to lead   ½   87
2f out, rdn & collared ins last, only btn 1L on reapp: in '99 won on reapp at Warwick (mdn, rtd 88 at best):
eff at 5f, stays 7f on gd & soft grnd: runs well fresh on a gall or sharp trk: looks best when fresh.
4488} **EASTER OGIL** 99 [11] 5-9-1 (82) Michael Doyle 25/1: 5000-5: In tch, hdwy over 1f out, kept on   shd   83
ins last, nvr dngrs: reapp: won 1 of 16 '99 starts, at Bath (h'cap, rtd 85): '98 scorer at Beverley (mdn) &
Sandown (stks, rtd 83): eff at 5.5/7f on firm & soft: runs well fresh in a visor: gd reapp, apprec a stiffer trk.
*594 **TEOFILIO** 28 [1] P Doe 7/1 FAV: 260-16: Dwelt, waited with, eff well over   3½   69
1f out, no extra ins last: well bckd, rtd lower on equitrack despite winning in 594 (1m).
687 **PEARTREE HOUSE** 8 [15] 6-9-3 (84) Alex Greaves 8/1: 000-07: Cl-up, ev ch over 1f out, no extra   1   77
ins last: trainer does well with these well h'capped older horses from other yards: see 687.
*663 **THE PRINCE** 14 [1] 6-9-9 (90)(t) J Weaver 8/1: 303-18: Dwelt, waited with, eff over 2f out, onepace.   2½   79
143 **TEMERAIRE** 99 [12] 5-9-2 (83) C Rutter 12/1: 0510-9: Waited with, nvr dngrs: abs, see 143, 104.   5   63
104 **VOLONTIERS** 99 [4] 5-8-12 (79) M Fenton 12/1: 0025-0: With ldr till wknd 2f out: 10th, 3 month abs.   1¼   57
*677 **BLAKESET** 9 [16] 5-8-7 (74)(bl) C Lowther 9/1: 0-5510: Led till 2f out, wknd: 11th: now with T D Barron.   ½   51
4572} **BRAVE EDGE** 99 [10] 9-9-10 (91) R Smith (5) 20/1: 0440-0: Al bhd: 12th, reapp: plcd thrice in   2   64
'99 (rtd 100): '98 Newbury wnr (rtd h'cap, rtd 101): rtd 109 at best in '97: stays at 6f on firm or hvy
grnd: gd weight carrier who handles any trk: has run well fresh: slipping back down the weights.
3990} **ELLENS ACADEMY** 99 [7] 5-8-12 (79) S Drowne 11/1: 1000-0: Slow start, nvr a factor: 13th, reapp.   ¾   50
4319} **SEA MARK** 99 [3] 4-9-3 (84) A Clark 10/1: 02/1-0: In tch till wknd over 2f out: 15th: reapp.   0
4562} **Analytical** 99 [5] 4-8-8 (75) S Whitworth 25/1:   4560} **Wealthy Star** 99 [14] 5-9-10 (91)(t) W Ryan 25/1:
4395} **Petrus** 99 [8] 4-9-6 (87) A Nicholls 16/1:
17 ran   Time 1m 26.49 (2.39)   (Miss T J FitzGerald)   P S McEntee Newmarket.

726   3.20 BLUE SQUARE HCAP 4YO+ 0-85 (D)   1m6f92y   Good 48   -08 Slow   [84]
        £7085   £2180   £1090   £545   4 yo rec 4 lb

4519} **FINAL SETTLEMENT** 99 [7] J R Jenkins 5-8-5 (61) L Newman (5) 8/1: 0433-1: 5 b g Soviet Lad - Tender   65
Time (Tender King) In tch, hdwy over 2f out, styd on well ins last to get up last strides: last rcd over hdles 7
wks ago, won at Kempton (nov hdle, rtd 113h, 2m, gd): plcd on 2 of 4 '99 Flat starts (rtd 63): '98 wnr at Windsor
& Lingfield (h'caps, rtd 64): apprec step up to 14.4f: acts on firm, soft & any trk: runs well fresh: improving.
4259} **SALFORD FLYER** 99 [10] D R C Elsworth 4-9-2 (76) J Stack 9/2 FAV: 4225-2: 4 b g Pharly - Edge Of   hd   79
Darkness (Vaigly Great) Waited with, hdwy to lead over 1f out, kept on till collared cl-home, just btn: fit from
hdlg, recently won at Wincanton (mdn hdle, also plcd sev times, rtd 122h, 2m, gd & soft): in '99 trained by G Wragg,
won at Haydock (clmr), Yarmouth (h'cap) & Salisbury (class stks, rtd 78 at best): suited by 14.4f, shld stay 2m:
acts on firm, gd/soft & on a gall or sharp trk: in gd form, prob done running late as possible.
424 **NATURAL EIGHT** 56 [8] Jamie Poulton 6-7-10 (52)(2oh) M Henry 10/1: 261-63: 6 b g In The Wings -   1½   53
Fenny Rough (Home Guard) Hld up, hdwy 4f out, kept on same pace for press over 1f out: 8 wk abs & a fine run.
89 **LEGAL LUNCH** 99 [4] P W Harris 5-8-11 (67)(vis) M Fenton 6/1: 5233-4: In tch, gd hdwy to lead on   ½   67
bit over 2f out, hdd over 1f out, no extra: 4 month abs, finds less than expected off the bit (1 win in 26 starts).
664 **WILCUMA** 14 [1] 9-10-0 (84) A Clark 16/1: 0-0155: Waited with, eff over 2f out, kept on same pace: ¾   83
gd run under a big weight & clr of rem: see 380.
4467} **TAUFAN BOY** 99 [2] 7-8-2 (58)(vis) A Nicholls (3) 20/1: 6045-6: Prom, rdn over 4f out, no impress   5   51
fnl 2f: fit from hdlg, unplcd (rtd 111h at best), 98/99 wnr at Ascot (2, nov h'caps) & Newbury (h'cap, rtd 128h,
stays 2m6f & likes soft grnd): unplcd on the Flat in '99 (rtd 60): '98 Haydock wnr (h'cap, rtd 65): eff at 10f,
stays 14f on firm, hvy & fibresand: eff with/without blnks/a visor.
649 **WILD COLONIAL BOY** 17 [13] 5-7-10 (52)(13oh) A McCarthy (3) 33/1: 00-447: Prom, eff & sltly short   11   31
of room over 4f out, wknd over 2f out: see 649 (AW), 548.
901} **TARXIEN** 99 [6] 6-9-13 (83) J Weaver 15/2: 4/40-8: Cl-up, rdn over 5f out, btn over 3f out: 1½   60
fit from hdlg, recently plcd (novs, rtd 120h, stays 2m4f): unplcd on both '99 starts (rtd 85 at best): '98
wnr at Haydock, Newbury & Goodwood (h'caps, rtd 89, with K Burke): eff at 14f/2m on fast, soft & any trk.
3040} **MALIAN** 99 [12] 4-8-1 (61) R Mullen 20/1: 0550-9: Al bhd on reapp: unplcd in '99 (rtd 65, 2m2f).   1¾   36
682 **PEKAY** 8 [3] 7-8-9 (65)(bl) J Bosley (7) 33/1: 312/00: Led 6f out, hdd over 2f out, wknd: 10th.   4   35
627 **GENEROUS WAYS** 23 [5] 5-8-4 (60) S Drowne 10/1: 550-40: Al bhd: 11th: see 627.   8   20
3643} **DIABLO DANCER** 99 [1] 4-8-12 (72) G Carter 13/2: 0000-0: Bhd, rdn 4f out, sn btn: 12th, jumps rnr.   1½   30
3925} **CITY STANDARD** 99 [14] 4-9-0 (74) P Doe 20/1: 3300-0: Cl-up, wknd over 3f out: 13th: changed stable.   ½   31
4618} **GROSVENOR FLYER** 99 [9] 4-8-13 (73) A McGlone 10/1: 3220-0: Led till 6f out: 14th, jumps rnr.   3½   26
14 ran   Time 3m 10.95 (8.15)   (T H Ounsley)   J R Jenkins Royston, Herts.

---

727 | **3.55 INTERACTIVE CLASSIFIED STKS 3YO 0-80 (D   1m1f   Good 48   -20 Slow**
£5512   £1696   £848   £424   3 yo rec 19lb Slow run race

625 **COMMON PLACE 23** [5] C F Wall 3-8-11 R Mullen 6/1: 00-561: 3 b g Common Grounds - One Wild Oat   88
(Shereef Dancer) Waited with, gd hdwy to lead 2f out, kept on ins last, rdn out: fit from AW (rtd 75a): '99
Goodwood wnr (nurs h'cap, rtd 81): eff at 7f, apprec this step up to 9f: acts on gd grnd & likes an easy track.

4136} **ROSHANI 99** [4] M R Channon 3-8-8 S Drowne 4/1: 530-2: 3 b f Kris - Maratona (Be My Guest)   2   80
Keen, prom, eff to chase wnr fnl 1f, no impress: nicely bckd on reapp: plcd on 2nd of 3 juv starts (rtd 80):
eff at 7f, apprec this step up to 9f & acts on gd grnd: shld win a race on this form.

4480} **TRAVELLING LITE 99** [3] B R Millman 3-8-11 G Carter 11/4 FAV: 1260-3: 3 b c Blues Traveller - Lute   ½   82
And Lyre (The Noble Player) With ldr, rdn & onepace over 1f out: in '99 scored at Lingfield (nurs h'cap, rtd
84 at best): eff at 7f, stays 9f: acts on gd grnd & on any track.

4432} **ATAVUS 99** [1] W R Muir 3-8-11 R Brisland (5) 9/2: 531-4: Keen in tch, eff to chall over 1f out, no   ½   81
extra ins last: drifter from 2/1 on reapp: in '99 won last of 3 starts, at Lingfield (auct mdn, rtd 84):
eff at 7f, stays 9f on gd grnd, poss soft: sharper for this.

4380} **SEEKING UTOPIA 99** [2] B R Millman 3-8-8 L Newman (5) 9/2: 1205-5: Prom, eff over 2f out, sn no impress: reapp: 2   75
consistent in '99, won at Musselburgh (auct mdn, rtd 80 at best): eff at 7f/1m on firm, gd grnd & on any trk.

4140} **PIPS WAY 99** [6] 3-8-8 Darren Williams (7) 8/1: 0040-6: Keen, handy, brief eff well over 1f out,   ½   74
sn btn: op 6/1: best effort in '99 when debut wnr at Ripon (mdn, rtd 84): eff at 6f/1m on fast & gd/soft grnd:
prob handles any trk & has tried a visor to no avail: runs well fresh.

4494} **SARENA PRIDE 99** [7] 3-8-8 P Doe 10/1: 5120-7: Led till 2f out, no extra: in '99 scored at Windsor   2   71
(auct mdn) & Warwick (nurs h'cap, rtd 78): eff at 6f, shld stay further: acts on gd & soft grnd, handles firm
& a sharp track: will do better back around 6/7f.

7 ran   Time 1m 56.12 (6.12)   (Induna Racing Partners Two)   C F Wall Newmarket.

---

728 | **4.30 B S ON OPEN HCAP 3YO+ 0-100 (C)   6f str   Good 48   -06 Slow**   [97]
£10822   £3330   £1665   £832   3 yo rec 13lb 2 Groups - no apparent advantage.

4144} **PASSION FOR LIFE 99** [17] J Akehurst 7-9-0 (83) P Doe 5/1 FAV: 2061-1: 7 br g Charmer - Party Game   88
(Red Alert) Early to post, made all far side, drvn out ins last: won reapp & fnl start in '99, at Kempton &
Salisbury (h'caps, rtd 84): in '98 rtd 79 for W Jarvis: suited by 6f & acts on fast, likes gd & soft: best up
with/forcing the pace & runs well fresh on any trk, loves Kempton: has tried blnks: tough & useful.

*599 **PALAWAN 26** [3] I A Balding 4-8-2 (71) A Nicholls (3) 9/1: 0-2112: 4 br g Polar Falcon - Krameria   1   73
(Kris) Set pace this side group, kept on well ins last, btn by far side rnr: op 7/1: continues in fine heart.

2067} **AL MUALLIM 99** [14] J W Payne 6-10-0 (97) A McGlone 20/1: 5020-3: 6 b g Theatrical - Gerri N Jo Go   1¼   99+
(Top Command) Waited with far side, hdwy & not clr run appr fnl 1f till ins last, fin well, prob unlucky: rnr-up
on 1 of 4 '99 starts (rtd 100): plcd on 3 of 4 '98 starts (vai h'caps, rtd 99): '97 Lingfield & Newmarket wnr: eff
at 6/7f on any trk: acts on firm & gd/soft: useful, v encouraging reapp under 10-0, win a nice prize this term.

4610} **LIVELY LADY 99** [18] J R Jenkins 4-8-12 (81)(vis) S Whitworth 10/1: 2501-4: Cl-up far side, eff/chsd   nk   80
wnr over 1f out, kept on same pace: reapp: in '99 won at Nottingham (reapp), Kempton & Doncaster (h'caps, rtd
82): '98 Folkestone wnr (juv seller): eff at 5/6f on fast, likes gd & hvy, handles fibresand: wears a visor
& has run well fresh: tough & still improving.

4401} **MARSAD 99** [9] 6-9-9 (92) R Perham 12/1: 4330-5: Dwelt, bhd stands side, kept on fnl 1f: reapp: hd   90
stablemate of wnr: in '99 won on reapp at Doncaster (h'cap, rtd 94 at best): '98 Kempton scorer (reapp, h'cap):
suited by 6f on any trk: acts on fast, likes gd/soft & hvy: runs esp well fresh: useful & tough.

660 **MAGIC RAINBOW 14** [12] 5-9-4 (87) M Fenton 12/1: 30-106: Chsd wnr far side till over 1f out, no extra.   1   82

4093} **EMERGING MARKET 99** [5] 8-9-7 (90) G Carter 14/1: 4366-7: Early to post, waited with stands side,   ¾   83
eff & not clr run 2f out, kept on late: reapp: plcd once in '99 (rtd '93 at best): rnr-up in '98 (rtd 98) & '97
(rtd 100): '96 Wokingham wnr at Royal Ascot (rtd 101): poss stays 1m, best coming late in a big field at 6f:
handles soft grnd, likes gd or firm: expensive to follow (last win 4 yrs ago) but slipping down the weights.

4093} **ROYAL RESULT 99** [11] 7-9-9 (92) Alex Greaves 14/1: 0130-8: Cl-up stands side, onepace over 1f out: hd   84
reapp: in fine '99 form, won at York & Goodwood (val h'cap), also head 3rd in Ayr Gold Cup (rtd 95 at best):
'98 wnr again at York & Ayr (val h'cap, rtd 82): suited by big fields/strong pace at 6f, has won at 1m: acts
on firm, soft grnd & on any trk, likes York & Ayr: has tried blnks: useful & tough, sharper for this.

2265} **RETURN OF AMIN 99** [10] 6-9-7 (90) R Brisland (5) 16/1: 5500-9: Switched to race far side, waited   hd   81
with, some late gains: reapp: in '99 trained by J Bethell (unplcd, rtd 98 at best, tried blnks): '98 wnr at
Pontefract (h'cap, rtd 97): '97 York scorer (val h'cap): winning form over 6/7f & handles fast grnd, loves
gd/soft & soft, handles fibresand & any trk: useful, on a fair mark now & should be plcd to land a soft grnd h'cap.

532 **PIPS SONG 37** [16] 5-8-6 (75) J Lowe 14/1: 20-240: In tch far side, wknd over 1f out: 10th: see 532.   shd   66
660 **JUWWI 14** [15] 6-6-8 (77) Claire Bryan (5) 12/1: 322060: Slow away, nvr a factor far side: 11th, see 129.   nk   67
674 **PRESENT CHANCE 11** [6] 6-8-1 (70)(bl) L Newton 33/1: 534-00: Bhd stands side, wknd over 1f out: 12th. ¾   58
2085} **SUNLEY SENSE 99** [7] 4-9-6 (89) S Drowne 25/1: 0600-0: Handy stands side, wknd over 1f out: 13th.   1½   73
3992} **TWICE AS SHARP 99** [2] 8-9-5 (88) L Newman (5) 12/1: 4060-0: Cl-up stands side, wknd over 1f out: 14th.   1   69
4120} **ALWAYS ALIGHT 99** [1] 6-9-7 (90) A Clark 14/1: 0363-0: Early to post, al bhd stands side: 15th.   shd   71
687 Astrac 8 [13] 9-9-1 (84) I Mongan 25/1:   660 Lone Piper 14 [4] 5-10-0 (97) M Tebbutt 12/1:
4469} Muqtarb 99 [8] 4-9-7 (90) P Shea (7) 40/1:
18 ran   Time 1m 14.33 (3.27)   (Canisbay Bloodstock Ltd)   J Akehurst Epsom, Surrey.

---

729 | **5.00 BLUESQ.COM MDN 3YO+ (D)   6f str   Good 48   -19 Slow**
£4251   £1308   £654   £327   3 yo rec 13lb

2513} **TAMBOURINAIRE 99** [2] B J Meehan 3-8-11 M Tebbutt 13/2: 330-1: 3 gr g Kendor - Rotina (Crystal   87
Glitters) Early to post, prom, led over 1f out, styd on well ins last, pushed out: plcd on first 2 of 3 '99
starts (rtd 83): brother to a 9f wnr: eff at 6f, 7f/1m shld suit: acts on gd/firm, gd/soft & on a sharp '99
gall trk: runs well fresh: looks to have improved since being gelding during the winter, could go in space.

3541} **PORT ST CHARLES 99** [4] N A Callaghan 3-8-11 W Ryan 4/1: 33-2: 3 b c Night Shift - Safe Haven   2   80
(Blakeney) Keen with ldr, eff over 1f out, not pace of wnr: reapp: plcd on both '99 starts (mdns, rtd 80):
half-brother to a smart sprinter: eff at 5/6f on gd & gd/firm: showed enough to win a race, right of rem here.

4599} **BUDELLI 99** [1] M R Channon 3-8-11 S Drowne 15/2: 5-3: 3 b c Elbio - Eves Temptation (Glenstal)   4   71
Waited with, kept on nicely under a kind ride over 1f out, nrst fin: rtd 70 when unplcd sole '99 start:
shld stay further than 6f on this evidence & will rate more highly with a more positive ride.

KEMPTON SATURDAY MARCH 25TH Righthand, Flat, Fair Track

4072} **BOND BOY 99** [7] B Smart 3-8-11 J Stack 5/4 FAV: 4362-4: Led till over 1f out, no extra appr fnl 1f: well bckd: plcd twice from 4 '99 starts (rtd 91): eff at 5/6f on firm & soft grnd & on an sharp trk: shld do better. ½ **68**
4007} **ALPHA ROSE 99** [11] 3-8-6 M Fenton 12/1: 6-5: Slow away, bhd, some late gains: unplcd on sole '99 start for R J R Williams (rtd 68): half-sister to wnrs over 7f/10f: now with M Bell, shld do better. ¾ **61**
685 **SUNLEYS PICC 8** [8] 3-8-6 R Mullen 25/1: 6-06: Bhd, modest late gains: rtd 58 when unplcd sole '99 start: dam 6/7f wnr: stablemate of 3rd. *hd* **61**
-- **CRAFTY PICK** [9] 3-8-6 C Rutter 12/1: 7: Prom, wknd over 1f out: half brother to a mid-dist wnr. *6* **49**
-- **ADRIANA** [6] 3-8-6 A Nicholls (3) 10/1: 8: Unruly stalls, dwelt, in tch till btn over 2f out: Tragic Role filly. *6* **37**
-- **PIETA** [3] 3-8-6 G Carter 12/1: 9: Prom, wknd 2f out: half sister to a 6f juv wnr. ¾ **35**
4599} **GROVE LODGE 99** [12] 3-8-11 S Whitworth 33/1: 000-0: Al bhd: 10th. ¾ **38**
1024} **CEDAR LIGHT 99** [5] 3-8-11 P Doe 33/1: 0-0: Prom, wknd qckly over 2f out: 11th. *2* **34**
4431} **ON THE TRAIL 99** [10] 3-8-11 A Clark 14/1: 06-0: Keen, in tch till wknd over 2f out: fin last. *2½* **29**
12 ran Time 1m 15.15 (4.05) (Abbott Racing Ltd) B J Meehan Upper Lambourn, Berks.

DONCASTER SATURDAY MARCH 25TH Lefthand, Flat, Galloping Track

Official Going GOOD. Stalls: Str Course - Stands Side; Round Course - Inside, Except 1m Round - Outside.

730 **1.55 PA MDN AUCT 2YO (E) 5f Good 57 -27 Slow**
£3705 £1140 £570 £285 Field raced stands side (high numbers favoured)

-- **DIVINE WIND** [12] B A McMahon 2-8-2 G Duffield 5/1: -1: 2 ch f Clantime - Breezy Day (Day Is Done) Trkd ldrs, imprvd to lead ent fnl 1f, kept on strongly, drvn out: 10,000gns Mar foal: half sister to 6f wnr Positive Air: dam sprint wnr: eff at 5f on gd & runs well fresh: handles a gall trk: scopey, shld win again. **72**
-- **SQUIRREL NUTKIN** [11] M L W Bell 2-8-7 A Beech (5) 15/2: -2: 2 br c Bluebird - Saltoki (Ballad Rock) Dwelt, prog halfway, switched & styd on strongly 1f, just btn in a close fin: op 4/1: Mar foal, cost 12,000 gns: related to 5f juv wnr Don't Be Koi: dam a 5f/1m wnr in France, sire a top class sprinter: eff at 5f on gd grnd, handles a gall trk: most pleasing debut from this small, stocky colt: shld soon go one better. *nk* **76+**
-- **KACHINA DOLL** [10] M R Channon 2-8-2 P Fessey 7/1: -3: 2 br f Mujadil - Betelgeuse (Kalaglow) Chsd ldrs, chall fnl 1f, kept on & just btn in a close fin: 4L clr 4th: Apr foal, cost 11,500gns: half sister to a 2yo wnr abroad: eff at 5f, bred to apprec 6/7f: handles a gall trk: small, sharp filly who shld win similar. *hd* **71**
-- **SLIPPER ROSE** [1] R Hollinshead 2-7-13 P M Quinn (5) 33/1: -4: Rear, styd on stdly fnl 2f, nvr plcd to chall: ndd this & a v promising run from a poor low draw: Mar foal, half sister to a couple of wnrs, incl 6f scorer Solo Spirit: dam won over 5f, sire a useful miler: strong filly, sharper next time & shld not be missed. *4* **56+**
-- **FENWICKS PRIDE** [8] 2-8-7 J F Egan 12/1: -5: In tch, pushed halfway, kept on fnl 1f: tchd 20/1, just better for debut: Mar foal, cost 10,000gns: 1st foal, dam unrcd: sire a useful juv scorer: strong gelding. *2½* **57**
-- **JUSTALORD** [13] 2-8-4 A Daly 7/1: -6: Broke well & set pace till ent fnl 1f, fdd: cost 1,700gns, Apr foal: dam a 5f juv wnr: sire a useful sprinter: with W Turner, bred to be speedy & sure to learn from this. *hd* **54**
-- **KANDYMAL** [9] 2-8-1 P Hanagan (7) 16/1: -7: Mid-div, late hdwy, nvr dngrs under a kind ride. ¾ **48**
-- **BRIEF STAR** [16] 2-7-13 G Bardwell 33/1: -8: Gd speed 4f, fdd: attractive filly. ¾ **43**
-- **EASTERN RED** [6] 2-8-1(1ow) J Fanning 12/1: -9: Prom 3½f, grad wknd: ndd this debut: poor draw. ¾ **42**
-- **BANNINGHAM BLIZ** [3] 2-7-13 T Williams 33/1: -0: Nvr a factor in 10th from a poor low draw. *1¼* **36**
-- **DENNIS EL MENACE** [5] 2-8-11 Martin Dwyer 12/1: -0: Ran green & al towards rear: fin 11th, poor low draw: attractive, scopey colt who ndd this: must be given another chance. ½ **47**
-- **YOUNG ALEX** [7] 2-8-5 N Callan 25/1: -0: Slowly away, al towards rear: fin 12th, poor low draw. *nk* **40**
-- **TROJAN PRINCE** [2] 2-8-9 M Hills 4/1 FAV: -0: Mid-div, eff halfway, nvr nr ldrs under a kind ride: fin 13th, well bckd: 16,000gns purchase, Apr foal, dam a wnr in the USA: sire a smart miler: scopey colt, had a poor low draw today: clrly shown something at home & must be given another chance. ½ **43**
-- **Lion Song** [4] 2-8-4 O Pears 33/1: -- **Euro Import** [14] 2-8-6 F Norton 25/1:
-- **Akatib** [17] 2-8-2 Kim Tinkler 33/1: -- **Century Star** [15] 2-8-6 J Tate 20/1:
17 ran Time 1m 02.41 (4.21) (Mrs J McMahon) B A McMahon Hopwas, Staffs

731 **2.25 POLYPIPE MDN 3YO (D) 6f Good 57 -23 Slow**
£4309 £1326 £663 £331 Field raced stands side (high numbers best)

-- **LOOK HERE NOW** [8] B A McMahon 3-9-0 K Darley 20/1: -1: 3 gr c Arkdinglass - Where's Carol (Anfield) Dwelt, recovered & rcd in tch, switched & ran on strongly to lead ins fnl 1f, drvn out: op 14/1, just better for debut: half brother to 6/7f wnr Now Look Here: eff at 6f on gd grnd, 7f will suit: handles a gall trk, runs well fresh: strong colt, shld improve further & win again: stable are off to a flyer this Flat season. **83**
673 **KIND EMPEROR 11** [9] M J Polglase 3-9-0 Dean McKeown 20/1: 03-442: 3 br g Emperior Jones - Kind Lady (Kind Of Hush) Tried to make all, collared over 1f out, rallied fnl 1f & not btn far: op 14/1, swtg: fit from the AW, has shown enough to win a small event: see 34 (sand). *1* **79**
4378} **CAMBERLEY 99** [12] P F I Cole 3-9-0 J Fortune 5/6 FAV: 62-3: 3 b c Sri Pekan - NSX (Roi Danzig) Hmpd start, recovered to chase ldrs, led dist till ins last, no extra: hvly bckd from 7/4 on reapp: trained by Miss G Kelleway in '99, rnr-up at Newmarket (stks, rtd 85): eff at 6/7f, acts on gd grnd: athletic colt. *1* **76**
4310} **IN THE ARENA 99** [4] B W Hills 3-9-0 M Hills 9/1: 00-4: Held up, late prog under a kind ride, nvr plcd to chall on reapp: drifted from 5/1: failed to figure in 2 6f mdns in '99: handles gd grnd: eff at 6f, crying out for 7f: now qual for h'caps, v eye-catching effort today: one to keep a close eye on. *1½* **72+**
3319} **SUMTHINELSE 99** [7] 3-9-0 T G McLaughlin 6/1: 3340-5: Prom till onepcd fnl 1f: plcd on a couple of '99 starts, plcd here at Doncaster (nov, rtd 81): half brother to sev wnrs, dam a 6f 2yo scorer: eff at 5f on gd & fast grnd, 7f+ shld now suit: sharper next time. *3½* **62**
4607} **ALMASHROUK 99** [6] 3-9-0 Demetris Shakallis 12/1: 040-6: Prom, ev ch 2f out, onepcd under a kind ride: op 8/1: lightly rcd in '99, 4th at Newmarket (mdn, rtd 83): half brother to useful 1m wnr Kuwait Dawn: eff at 6f on gd/soft grnd, ran as tho' 7f+ will suit today: with K Mahdi & capable of better. *2* **56**
549 **NITE OWL MATE 35** [10] 3-9-0 R Cochrane 14/1: -337: Chsd ldrs, onepcd fnl 2f: see 549 (AW). *1¼* **52**
3690} **SCAFELL 99** [11] 3-9-0 R Fitzpatrick (3) 25/1: 3250-8: Swerved start, chsd ldrs till halfway, sn btn. *nk* **51**
685 **TAKE MANHATTAN 8** [13] 3-9-0 P Fessey 40/1: 0-09: Nvr a factor: see 685 (AW). *nk* **50**
696 **LAMMOSKI 5** [1] 3-9-0 Joanna Badger(7) 100/1: -00050: Al outpcd, fin 10th: quick reapp. *hd* **50**
4599} **PACIFIC PLACE 99** [5] 3-9-0 F Norton 66/1: 00-0: In tch 3f, sn btn: fin 11th: ndd this. *2½* **43**
-- **Bokay** [3] 3-8-9 Pat Eddery 14/1: -- **Nicolai** [2] 3-9-0 A Beech (5) 20/1:
13 ran Time 1m 15.65 (4.85) (S L Edwards) B A McMahon Hopwas, Staffs

DONCASTER SATURDAY MARCH 25TH Lefthand, Flat, Galloping Track

732 **3.00 DONCASTER COND STKS 4YO+ (B) 1m4f Good 57 +15 Fast**
£10335 £3180 £1590 £795 4yo rec 2lb

4617} **LARGESSE 99** [8] John Berry 6-9-2 J F Egan 6/1: 3405-1: 6 b h Cadeaux Genereux - Vilanika (Top Ville) In tch, gd hdwy to lead 2f out, clr fnl 1f, pushed out: lkd well, best time of day: 3rd in a nov hdle 6 wks ago (2m soft, rtd 95h, O Sherwood): in '99 won this v race here at Doncaster, subs rnr-up at York (Gr 2, rtd 114): '98 Nottingham (reapp), York (h'cap) & Ayr wnr (List, rtd 112): '97 Haydock scorer (2, h'caps): eff at 10/14f: handles fast, loves gd & soft: handles any trk, likes Doncaster: gd weight carrier, runs well fresh: smart. **110**
695 **MURGHEM 5** [3] M Johnston 5-8-12 J Fanning 4/1: 320-22: 5 b h Common Grounds - Fabulous Pet (Somethingfabulous) Chsd ldrs, impvd to lead over 3f out till hdd 2f out, kept on but not pace of wnr: qck reapp, clr rem: eff at 12f, suited by 14f/2m & a return to further will suit: see 695 (AW). *5* **96**
2738} **RAIN IN SPAIN 99** [1] J Noseda 4-8-10 W R Swinburn 5/1: 113-3: 4 b c Unfuwain - Marie Isabella (Young Generation) Trkd ldrs going well, smooth hdwy & ev ch 2f out, sn rdn & onepace: op 7/2, just better for reapp: '99 wnr at Kempton (mdn, debut) & Windsor (stks), subs plcd at Newmarket (stks, rtd 106): eff at 12f on gd & firm grnd: handles a sharp trk, runs well fresh: scopey colt, spot on next time. *6* **87**
4617} **SALMON LADDER 99** [4] P F I Cole 8-8-12 J Fortune 5/1: 0133-4: Chsd ldr, ev ch 2f out, sn outpcd: lkd fit & well for reapp: '99 wnr at Goodwood & Chester (rtd h'cap, rtd 104), also 2nd in this race: '99 Hamilton & Bath wnr (stks, rtd 104): '97 Windsor wnr (stks, rtd 110): eff at 9/13f, stays 14f well: acts on firm & soft: gd weight carrier who can run well fresh: has tried blnks, best without: tough & useful entire, capable of better. *1¾* **85**
3945} **LOOP THE LOUP 99** [6] 4-8-10 A Culhane 15/2: 2122-5: Rear, some late hdwy, nvr nr ldrs: bckd from 14/1: disapp fav on sole hdle outing 10 wks ago (rtd 86h, with M Hammond): trained by J Dunlop in '99, tough & consistent, won at Lingfield (mdn auct), Salisbury & York (h'caps), also plcd sev times (rtd 99): eff at 12/15f, 2m shld suit: acts on firm, hvy grnd & on any trk: now with Mrs Reveley & capable of much better. *5* **77**
3102} **CHRISTIANSTED 99** [9] 5-8-12 R Cochrane 33/1: 4152-6: Waited with, eff 4f out, no impress fnl 2f: ndd this reapp: '99 Ripon (reapp) & Nottingham wnr (h'cap, rtd 75): 98/99 hdles wnr at Catterick, Doncaster & Musselburgh (juv nov h'cap, rtd 120h, eff at 2m/2½m on gd & fast): eff at 12/14f, stays 2m: acts on fast & soft grnd: gd weight carrier: little chance at today's weights, needs h'caps. *4* **71**
672} **TURAATH 99** [2] 4-8-10 M Hills 7/2 FAV: 43/1-7: Set pace till hdd over 3f out, fdd: lkd fit & well for reapp, bckd from 9/2: once rcd in '99, won here at Doncaster (mdn, rtd 97+): brother to a 9/15f wnr, cost 200,000gns: eff at 10f, 12f shld suit: acts on gd & soft grnd, can run well fresh: scopey colt, had problems. *5* **63**
663 **NOUF 14** [7] 4-8-5 F Norton 66/1: 104-08: Chsd ldrs till halfway, wknd: not stay this longer 12f trip. *½* **57**
-- **SACHO** [10] 7-8-12 Dean McKeown 16/1: 2246/9: Al bhd, nvr a factor on comeback. *2* **59**
*658 **WELODY 14** [5] 4-8-10 (bl) K Darley 100/1: 0-4210: Chsd ldrs till halfway, sn btn, t.o.: highly tried. *dist* **0**
10 ran Time 2m 34.89 (5.09) (Mrs Rosemary Moszkowicz) John Berry Newmarket

733 **3.40 WORTHINGTON LINCOLN HCAP 4YO+ (B) 1m str Good 57 +00 Fast [108]**
£43761 £13465 £6732 £3366 Stalls 1-13 raced far side, rem centre (no apparent advantage)

663 **JOHN FERNELEY 14** [1] P F I Cole 5-8-10 (90) J Fortune 7/1 JT FAV: 133-31: 5 b g Polar Falcon - I'll Try (Try My Best) In tch far side, imprvd to lead 1½f out, styd on well ins last, drvn out: well bckd, lkd superb: '99 York wnr (rtd h'cap, rtd 92): '98 Folkestone (appr mdn), Thirsk (ltd stks) & Sandown wnr (h'cap, rtd 84): eff at 7f/1m on fast, hvy grnd & fibresand: handles any trk, runs well fresh: has tried blnks, prob better without: tough & progressive gldg who shld prove a real force in the top 1m h'caps this year. **99**
663 **KING PRIAM 14** [2] M J Polglase 5-8-9 (89)(bl)(5ex) R Fitzpatrick (3) 25/1: -31362: 5 b g Priolo - Barinia (Corvaro) Held up far side, hdwy under press 2f out, fin strongly fnl 1f, not quite reach wnr: fit from the AW: fine effort, must hold sound claims in the Newbury Spring Cup: see 448 (fibresand). *¾* **96**
4580} **RIGHT WING 99** [21] J L Dunlop 6-9-10 (104)(vis) Pat Eddery 9/1: 0301-3: 6 b h In The Wings - Nekhbet (Artaius) Badly hmpd & nearly u.r. start, gd hdwy 2f out, fin v strongly up the centre of the crse, only btn 1L: lkd superb, top weight: '99 wnr here at Doncaster (reapp, this race, rtd 107) & Nottingham (stks): '98 wnr again at Doncaster (rtd h'cap, rtd 102): '97 Ascot & Ayr wnr (stks, rtd 95, with W Hern): suited by a stiff/gall 1m, loves Doncaster: handles any grnd, runs well fresh: best in a visor: most unlucky today, lost about 4L at the start & only btn 1L: reopposes today's 2nd in the Newbury Spring Cup & must hold strong claims. *nk* **110**
*662 **PANTAR 14** [8] I A Balding 5-9-0 (94)(bl)(5ex) K Darley 16/1: -03214: In tch far side, switched 2f out, kept on fnl 1f: lkd v well: often runs well in these big field h'caps: fit from the AW, see 662 (9.5f). *2* **96**
4094} **CULZEAN 99** [16] 4-8-5 (85) P Fitzsimons (5) 40/1: 5303-5: Set gd pace in centre, hdd 1½f out, fdd: reapp: plcd sev times in '99 (h'cap, rtd 88): '98 Leicester wnr (mdn, debut, rtd 87): eff at 10f, prob suited by this drop back to 1m: handles fast & soft: fairly h'capped & one to keep in mind in a less competitive h'cap. *½* **86**
4401} **ESPADA 99** [3] 4-8-5 (85) G Duffield 25/1: 2150-6: Chsd ldrs far side, onepcd fnl 1f: reapp: '99 wnr at Thirsk (class stks) & Ayr (h'cap, rtd 88): '98 Ripon wnr (mdn auct, rtd 82): eff at 1m, wng form at 7f: acts on fast & gd/soft grnd: spot on next time, esp back at 7f. *¾* **84**
216 **INDIAN BLAZE 95** [19] 6-8-6 (86) P Goode (5) 33/1: 1034-7: In tch in centre, imprvd 2f out, edged left & onepcd ins last: lkd fit & well after 3 month abs: see 143 (AW). *nk* **84**
580 **LATALOMNE 30** [24] 6-8-12 (92) J Fanning 25/1: 100-08: In tch centre, onepcd fnl 1½f: won a Catterick nov hdle (rtd 120h, 2m gd grnd) since 580: fine effort today, Thirsk Hunt Cup wnr in '99. *hd* **90**
4174} **WAHJ 99** [13] 5-8-10 (90) F Lynch 20/1: 3040-9: Chsd ldrs far side & rcd keenly, onepcd fnl 2f: lightly rcd in '99, plcd at Haydock (List, rtd 100): '98 wnr at Windsor (mdn, debut) & Chepstow (stks, rtd 109+): half brother to high class miler Desert King: eff at 7f/1m, acts on gd & fast grnd: handles a sharp or undul trk, can run well fresh: can set the pace: prev trained by M Stoute, now with C Dwyer: fairly h'capped on old form. *2* **84**
-- **MUCHEA** [7] 6-9-6 (100) M Roberts 12/1: /000-0: Hmpd start, nvr reach ldrs on far side: fin 10th, ndd this: thrice rcd & unplcd in Hong Kong in '99: '98 wnr at The Curragh & Newmarket (Gr 3, rtd 113): '96 Catterick, Newmarket (stks) & German wnr (Gr 2): eff at 6f, best at 7f, does stay 1m: acts on firm & hvy grnd, handles any trk: can run well fresh: smart colt who is slipping down the h'cap: little luck in running here. *nk* **93**
663 **THE WHISTLING TEAL 14** [18] 4-8-5 (84)(1ow) A Culhane 7/1 JT FAV: 320-00: Rear in centre, eff halfway, nvr nr ldrs: fin 11th, bckd from 11/1: '99 wnr at Windsor & W'hampton (h'caps, rtd 88a & 86): eff at 1m, stays 10f: acts on firm, hvy & f/sand: handles a sharp or gall trk, runs well fresh. *hd* **78**
4560} **NIMELLO 99** [14] 4-8-8 (88)(BL) D Sweeney 33/1: /520-0: Chsd ldrs centre, grad fdd fnl 1f: lkd well for reapp, fin 12th, blnkd 1st time: lightly rcd in '99, rnr-up at Ayr (stks, rtd 93): '98 Newmarket wnr (mdn, sole start, rtd 100): eff at 1m on firm & hvy: lightly rcd stable-mate of today's wnr: sharper next time. *2* **77**
663 **RIVER TIMES 14** [4] 4-8-13 (93)(bl) R Winston 12/1: 150-20: Led far side, hdd 2f out, fdd into 13th. *1½* **79**
4101} **NAVIASKY 99** [20] 5-8-4 (84) Martin Dwyer 16/1: 1016-0: Swerved right start, rcd keenly in rear, imprvd 2f out, sn no impress: fin 14th: '99 wnr at Goodwood (2) & Leicester (h'caps, rtd 84): '98 Carlisle wnr (h'cap, rtd 67, with Mrs J Ramsden): '97 Thirsk wnr (mdn auct, rtd 70): eff at 7/10f, acts on firm & gd/soft *¾* **68**

grnd, handles any trk, likes Goodwood: capable of much better.

4560} **HORNBEAM** 99 [9] 6-8-9 (88)(t)(1ow) S Sanders 20/1: 0505-0: Rcd keenly in rear on far side, 2½ 68
btn over 1f out: fin 15th.

663 **NOMORE MR NICEGUY** 14 [22] 6-8-7 (87) J F Egan 33/1: 200-00: In tch 5f centre, fdd into 16th. shd 66

*690 **ZANAY** 7 [10] 4-8-10 (90)(5ex) T G McLaughlin 14/1: 1-1110: In tch 4f far side, sn outpcd: fin 17th: nk 68
much better on equitrack in 690 (10f, 7 days ago).

630 **SALTY JACK** 21 [5] 6-8-11 (91)(5ex) R Cochrane 25/1: -02130: Chsd ldrs far side, eff when badly 1¼ 66
hmpd over 1f out, sn btn & eased: fin 18th: usually comes late, lost all chnc when hmpd here: see 630, 485 (AW).

4560} **TAYSEER** 99 [6] 6-8-6 (86) F Norton 8/1: 5111-0: Chsd ldrs far side, rdn & btn 2f out, eased: fin shd 61
19th, drifted from 5/1 tho' big ante-post gamble: ended '99 with wins at Brighton (clmr, with W Muir), Ayr &
Newmarket (val h'cap, rtd 87): '98 Southwell wnr (clmr, rtd 86a): '97 York wnr (val h'cap, rtd 99+, with E Dunlop):
eff at 6f, suited by 1m: acts on firm, soft & f/sand, handles any trk: can run well fresh: remains h'capped.

4485} **Kuwait Dawn** 99 [23] 4-8-10 (90) Dale Gibson 25/1:

687 **Rock Falcon** 8 [12] 7-8-13 (93)(bl) Dean McKeown 25/1:

3471} **Tammam** 99 [15] 4-8-11 (91) J P Spencer 25/1: 4560} **Silk St John** 99 [17] 6-8-10 (90) P McCabe 25/1:

3454} **Compton Arrow** 99 [11] 4-9-3 (97) M Hills 33/1:

24 ran Time 1m 41.12 (4.62) (Richard Green (Fine Paintings)) P F I Cole Whatcombe, Oxon

---

734 4.15 LISTED CAMMIDGE TROPHY 3YO+ (A) 6f Good 57 -04 Slow
£17410 £5357 £2678 £1339 3yo rec 13lb Field raced centre to stands side

4620} **ANDREYEV** 99 [4] R Hannon 6-9-2 J Fortune 9/1: 2440-1: 6 ch g Presidium - Missish (Mummy's Pet) 109
Chsd ldrs, imprvd to lead dist, styd on strongly fnl 1f, drvn out: op 7/1, reapp: failed to score in '99, rnr-up
twice, incl a Gr 3 in France (rtd 109), also 4th in this very race: '98 Kempton (reapp, stks), Newcastle (List) &
Deauville (Gr 3), also 3rd in Gr 2 Cork & Orrery at R Ascot (rtd 117): '97 Newmarket List wnr: eff at 6/7f on fast
grnd, suited by gd or hvy: handles any trk: eff with/without blnks, runs well fresh: smart sprinter who was back
to best here (has reportedly been gelded & had a wind operation since last year).

4547} **NOW LOOK HERE** 99 [5] B A McMahon 4-9-2 R Winston 16/1: 3033-2: 4 b g Reprimand - Where's Carol 1¼ 106$
(Anfield) Prom, hmpd & lost place after 2f, gd hdwy over 1f out, ev ch ins last, no extra cl-home: lkd well for
reapp, bckd at long odds: '99 Haydock wnr (mdn, reapp), subs plcd sev times (rtd 95 at best): eff at 6/7f, handles
firm, prob best on gd & hvy: likes a gall trk, runs well fresh: fine run in this much better company, prob unlucky.

660 **CRETAN GIFT** 14 [13] N P Littmoden 9-9-2 (vis) T G McLaughlin 9/1: 030-03: 9 ch g Cadeaux Genereux 1¼ 102
- Caro's Niece (Caro) Chsd ldrs, rdn 2f out, styd on under press fnl 1f, nrst fin: 5th in this race last year, rnr-up
in '98: 9yo who retains plenty of ability & has not finished winning: see 660 (AW).

687 **FIRST MAITE** 8 [14] S R Bowring 7-9-2 (bl) N Callan 14/1: 003244: Chsd ldrs, ev ch 2f out, onepcd nk 101
fnl 1f: fit from the AW: likes soft grnd: see 660.

4100} **HALMAHERA** 99 [12] 5-9-5 K Darley 4/1 FAV: 2406-5: Chsd ldrs till outpcd halfway, kept on again fnl ½ 103
1f: well bckd, just better for reapp: '99 Newcastle wnr (List), rnr-up on 5 starts (rtd 110 at best): failed to
win in '98 (rtd 106), prev term scored at Chepstow (mdn auct), Goodwood (h'cap), Ayr (List) & Ascot (Gr 3, rtd 113):
eff at 6f, on firm & hvy: handles a sharp/undul or gall trk: can run well fresh: tough & v useful sprinter.

4396} **LOTS OF MAGIC** 99 [1] 4-9-7 M Hills 7/1: 4140-6: Front rank till fdd ins fnl 1f: swtg & ndd this reapp: 1¼ 101+
'99 wnr at Lingfield (nov) & R Ascot (Gr 3 Jersey, rtd 118): '98 Epsom (mdn auct, rtd 95): eff at 6f, suited by
7f: handles any trk, acts on firm/str one: handles gd/soft, enjoys fast grnd: can run well fresh: smart, loves
to dominate: has thrived physically since last term, spot on next time at 7f on fast ground.

4620} **NIGRASINE** 99 [3] 6-9-2 (bl) A Culhane 16/1: 0400-7: Chsd ldrs till outpcd 2f out, no ch after: just nk 95
better for reapp: '99 wnr at Thirsk & Yarmouth (stks, rtd 112): '98 Haydock scorer (List, rtd 107): '97 Redcar
(mdn auct) & Pontefract wnr (stks, rtd 107): best at 6/7f, has tried 1m: acts on firm & gd/soft grnd: likes to
run-up with or force the pace, handles any trk: suited by blnks or a visor: tough & smart entire.

3992} **EASTERN PURPLE** 99 [8] 5-9-7 F Lynch 14/1: 3000-8: Held up, short of room halfway, no impress fnl 1 97
2f: ndd this reapp, little luck in running today: '99 wnr at The Curragh (Gr 3, rtd 113): '98 Haydock wnr (rtd
h'cap, rtd 108, with R Fahey), also 3rd in the Stewards Cup: '97 Newcastle scorer: eff at 6f: handles firm, likes
gd & gd/soft grnd: handles any trk: eff with/without blnks, has tried a visor: smart colt, will rate more highly.

3992} **BON AMI** 99 [7] 4-9-2 Pat Eddery 16/1: 4220-9: Set pace 5f, sn btn: bckd at long odds, just better nk 91
for reapp: trained by J Berry in '99.

4541} **TOUCH OF FAIRY** 99 [15] 4-9-2 Demetris Shakallis 50/1: 2-0: In tch 4f stands side: fin 10th. hd 91$

4469} **BOOMERANG BLADE** 99 [6] 4-8-11 W R Swinburn 20/1: 5200-0: Prom till lost place halfway, no ch 2½ 79
after: fin 11th, little luck in running.

99 **AWAKE** 99 [10] 3-8-3 J Fanning 12/1: 112D-0: Prsd ldrs 4½f, fdd into 12th: stiff task: long abs. hd 84

3896} **TEDBURROW** 99 [11] 8-9-7 J F Egan 9/2: 1110-0: Prom till short of room & lost place halfway, 8 65
position sn excepted, eased: fin last, reportedly lkd dull in coat: '99 wnr here at Doncaster (reapp, this race),
Chester (2, incl List) & Leopardstown (Gr 3, rtd 115): '98 wnr at Newmarket, Chester (List) & Leopardstown (Gr 3,
rtd 112): '97 Haydock, York, Ascot (h'caps) & Chester wnr (List): eff at 5/6f on firm & soft grnd: handles any
trk, loves Chester: gd weight carrier who runs well fresh: v tough & smart gelding, this is not his form.

13 ran Time 1m 14.50 (3.70) (J Palmer-Brown) R Hannon East Everleigh, Wilts

---

735 4.45 MITSUBISHI COND STKS 3YO (C) 1m str Good 57 -05 Slow
£7052 £2170 £1085 £542 Field raced towards centre

4614} **SUMMONER** 99 [9] R Charlton 3-8-11 S Sanders 9/2: 61-1: 3 b c Inchinor - Sumoto (Mtoto) 112+
Trkd ldrs going well, smooth hdwy to lead dist, qcknd well clr, impress: padd pick, op 3/1, val for 6L+: '99 wnr
here at Doncaster (mdn auct, rtd 97+): half brother to high class 10f wnr Compton Admiral: dam a 6/7f 2yo wnr:
eff at 1m, 10f will suit: acts on gd & hvy, runs well fresh: most impressive today & potentially high class:
may take in the Thirsk Classic Trial on the way to the Italian 2,000 Guineas, keep on your side.

4468} **ZYZ** 99 [6] B W Hills 3-8-13 M Hills 9/4 FAV: -213-2: 3 b c Unfuwain - Girette (General Assembly) 3 104
Set pace till collared by wnr dist, kept on but no ch with impress rival: well bckd, just better for reapp: '99
Leicester wnr (mdn), subs plcd at Newbury (Gr 3, rtd 103): eff at 1m, bred for mid-dist: acts on firm & gd/soft,
handles a gall trk: tough front rnr who met an above average rival today: will come into his own over mid-dists.

4136} **NICOBAR** 99 [1] A Balding 3-8-13 K Darley 11/2: 1525-3: 3 b c Indian Ridge - Duchess Of Alba 1¾ 100
(Belmez) Chsd ldrs, eff 2f out, onepcd ins last: op 8/1, lkd well tho' just better for reapp: '99 Haydock wnr
(mdn), subs not disgraced in much better company (rtd 100): eff at 7f/1m, handles firm, prob best on gd or gd/
soft grnd: can set the pace: useful, raced too freely for own gd today.

4613} **BLUSIENKA** 99 [10] G A Butler 3-8-6 A Beech (5) 4/1: -1-4: Rdn in rear, styd on well fnl 1f, nrst fin: ¾ 91+
won sole '99 start, here at Doncaster (mdn auct, rtd 85): sire a high class mid-dist wnr: eff at 1m, crying out

for mid-dists: acts on gd & hvy grnd, runs well fresh: one to keep a close eye on over 10/12f next time.

4427} **ABDERIAN 99** [3] 3-8-13 W R Swinburn 8/1: 142-5: Chsd ldrs till onepcd fnl 2f under a kind ride: 2½   93
'99 Ripon wnr (mdn, debut), subs rnr-up at Yarmouth (nov, rtd 100): cost IR 150,000gns & half brother to a 7f
juv wnr: eff at 7f, 1m + shld suit: acts on gd/firm & gd/soft grnd, can run well fresh: sure to improve.

4411} **FIRST TRUTH 99** [5] 3-8-13 G Duffield 33/1: 0215-6: Chsd ldrs 6f, fdd: better for this reapp: '99 wnr   2½   88
at Pontefract (mdn, rtd 88), subs tried in List company: half brother to a 7f wnr: eff at 1m, shld stay further
this term: acts on gd/soft grnd, handles a gall or stiff/undul trk.

3266} **ROYAL EAGLE 99** [7] 3-8-11 J Fortune 9/1: 2412-7: Prom, rdn halfway, grad fdd: ndd this.   ¾   84

4285} **KING O THE MANA 99** [4] 3-8-11 M Roberts 10/1: 1216-8: Al towards rear on reapp: better for race.   ½   83

3919} **EYELETS ECHO 99** [8] 3-8-11 R Cochrane 100/1: 6-9: Al rear, fin last on reapp: highly tried.   3   77

9 ran   Time 1m 41.47 (4.97)   (Michael Pescod)   R Charlton Beckhampton, wilts

---

736   5.15 MARCH HCAP 3YO 0-85 (D)   7f str   Good 57   -08 Slow   [90]
     £4524   £1392   £696   £348   Field raced centre to far side

613   **SAFARANDO 25** [2] N P Littmoden 3-9-1 (77) T G McLaughlin 11/2: -01121: 3 b c Turtle Island - Hertford   90+
Castle (Reference Point) Prom far side, went on halfway, clr fnl 2f, easily: fit from the AW, earlier scored at
W'hampton (2, h'cap, rtd 86a): '99 wnr at Yarmouth (sell, rtd 100): cost IR 150,000gns & Lingfield (nurs h'cap, rtd 75): eff
at 7f/1m, shld stay further: acts on firm, soft & f/sand: handles any trk: tough, fast improving colt.

617   **FIRST VENTURE 24** [16] C N Allen 3-8-10 (72) R Morse 14/1: 235-22: 3 b c Formidable - Diamond   5   74
Wedding (Diamond Shoal) Led till halfway, sn outpcd by easy wnr: met a well h'cap rival here: see 617 (AW).

4588} **LOVES DESIGN 99** [4] J Noseda 3-8-13 (75) W R Swinburn 12/1: 0631-3: 3 b g Pursuit Of Love -   1   75
Cephista (Shirley Heights) Prom, eff 2f out, sn onepcd: reapp: lightly rcd in '99, won at Musselburgh (mdn auct),
1st time visor, rtd 75): eff at 7f, bred to apprec further: acts on fast & soft grnd: visor omitted today.

488   **SIGN OF THE TIGER 45** [3] P C Haslam 3-8-8 (70) P Goode (5) 10/1: 3-1144: Chsd ldrs far side, onepcd 2½   65
fnl 2f: 6 wk abs: see 450 (AW).

--   **KEBABS** [21] J P Spencer 20/1: 4160-5: Waited wth centre, imprvd halfway, no impress   1½   75
fnl 1f on reapp: ex-Irish, won at The Curragh in '99: eff at 6f on gd grnd, prob stays 7f: fair effort from
an unfavourable draw & one to keep in mind: with J Osbourne.

4376} **STORMVILLE 99** [19] R Cochrane 12/1: 6355-6: Mid-div, late prog, nvr nr ldrs on reapp: 1   66
lightly rcd in '99, plcd at Beverley (nov auct), rtd 90$ when 5th at Newmarket (val event): half brother to an
11f wnr, sire a high class 6/7f performer: eff at 6/7f on gd grnd: with M Brittain.

534   **KINSMAN 37** [12] M Roberts 12/1: 215-37: Chsd ldrs far side, onepcd fnl 2f: see 534 (AW).   hd   58

4376} **DISTINCTLY EAST 99** [3] 3-8-13 (75) G Duffield 25/1: 6020-8: Mid-div, some late prog, nvr dngrs: 5   55
reapp: '99 Ripon wnr (mdn, debut), subs rnr-up at Yarmouth (stks): half brother to a wnr abroad, dam a
9f scorer: eff at 5/6f on fast & soft grnd: handles a sharp trk, can run well fresh: with M Tompkins.

4302} **GOLDEN MIRACLE 99** [7] 3-9-7 (83) J Fanning 20/1: 1315-9: Prom far side, wknd 2f out: '99 wnr at   1½   60
Hamilton (2, nurs, rtd 84): eff at 7/8f, shld stay 7f: acts on firm & gd/soft grnd, likes Hamilton.

617   **BEBE DE CHAM 24** [15] 3-8-11 (73) R Cody Boutcher (7) 25/1: 100-00: Chsd ldrs centre, wknd fnl 2f.   hd   50

4480} **LORDOFENCHANTMENT 99** [5] 3-8-1 (63) Joanna Badger(7) 33/1: 1566-0: Outpcd far side, nvr a factor: ½   39
fin 11th: '99 Ripon wnr (sell, 1st time visor, rtd 77): eff at 6f, tried 7f: acts on fast grnd & on a sharp trk.

3058} **ANTHEMION 99** [14] 3-8-8 (70) Dean McKeown 25/1: 0300-0: Rcd keenly mid-div, no impress fnl 2f.   nk   45

4528} **SHRIVAR 99** [12] 3-8-10 (72) P Fessey 20/1: 605-0: Al towards rear, fin 13th.   1½   44

4480} **OCEAN RAIN 99** [18] 3-9-4 (80) K Darley 20/1: 2105-0: Rear in centre, eff halfway, sn btn: fin 14th.   hd   52

4491} **CHARMING LOTTE 99** [8] 3-9-0 (76)(vis) Kim Tinkler 20/1: 0315-0: Chsd ldrs till wknd 3f out: fin 15th.   1   46

534   **BULAWAYO 37** [10] 3-8-8 (70) R Winston 12/1: 06-140: In tch till halfway: fin 17th: see 362 (AW).   0

4616} **SLICK WILLIE 99** [1] 3-9-0 (76)(bl) Pat Eddery 7/2 FAV: 2232-0: Chsd ldrs 3f far side, sn fdd: fin 19th,   0
bckd from 6/1 on reapp: '99 Beverley wnr (mdn auct, blnkd 1st time), also plcd on numerous occasions (rtd 77 at
best): eff at 5/7f on fast & hvy, handles a stiff or sharp trk: best in blnks: with T Easterby & better expected.

638   **Myttons Again 21** [11] 3-8-13 (75) J Fortune 20/1:   3311} **Sunrise 99** [20] 3-7-13 (61) Martin Dwyer 33/1:

4498} **Pretending 99** [17] 3-7-12 (60) K Dalgleish (7) 33/1:   46   **Marshall St Cyr 99** [13] 3-8-13 (75) J F Egan 25/1:

21 ran   Time 1m 27.76 (4.56)   (Paul J Dixon)   N P Littmoden Newmarket

---

Official Going   STANDARD. Stalls: Inside, except 5f - Outside.

737   2.15 BET DIRECT HCAP 4YO+ 0-60 (F)   2m aw   Going 40   -68 Slow   [60]
     £2394   £684   £342   4 yo rec 5 lb

644   **TIME CAN TELL 21** [14] A G Juckes 6-8-8 (40) R Fitzpatrick (3) 12/1: 50-551: 6 ch g Sylvan Express -   48a
Stellaris (Star Appeal) Trkd ldrs, led 3f out, asserted ins last, rdn out: '99 W'hampton wnr (h'cap, rtd 62a): '98
Lingfield wnr (clmr, J Payne, rtd 66a & 51): eff at 13f/2m on both AWs, fast & gd/soft: eff with/without blnks.

428   **LADY RACHEL 56** [16] M W Easterby 5-8-13 (45)(BL) G Parkin 10/1: 00-302: 5 gr m Priolo - Alpine   5   47a
Spring (Head For Heights) Rdn in rear, prog & fdn fnl 2f, no extra ins last: op 6/1, clr of rem: 8 wk abs, back
to form in first time blnks: well hcapped for a similar contest: see 318.

1039} **IMAD 99** [10] K C Comerford 10-9-3 (49)(t) M Fenton 33/1: 0/01-3: 10 b g Al Nasr - Blue Grass Field   6   45a
(Top Ville) Mid-div, prog to lead over 5f out, rdn & hdd 3f out, grad fdd: 12 wk jumps abs (mod form): '99 wnr at
Pontefract on 2nd of only 2 starts (h'cap, rtd 47): 98/99 jumps wnr at Folkestone (h'cap hdle, rtd 106h & 106c):
rnr-up in '98 (h'cap, rtd 51a): eff at 2m/2m5.5f on any grnd, handles f/sand: best in a t-strap: thorough stayer.

644   **KENT 21** [12] P D Cundell 5-9-5 (51) D Holland 13/8 FAV: -12164: Chsd ldrs, prog to trk ldrs over 2f   1¼   46a
out, rdn & held over 1f out: hvly bckd, tchd 9/4: btr 502 (C/D).

644   **QUAKERESS 21** [9] 5-7-10 (28)(2oh) J Mackay (7) 6/1: 411345: Chsd ldrs 5f out, held fnl 3f: op 9/2.   ¾   22a

253   **SUDDEN SPIN 84** [3] 10-8-4 (36) J Fanning 16/1: /05-06: Rear, prog/chsd ldrs halfway, btn 4f out: 14   19a
op 10/1, jumps fit (plcd, rtd 80h, sell h'cap): see 182.

3636} **MR MORIARTY 99** [6] 9-7-12 (30)(t) Dale Gibson 12/1: 15/0-7: Led halfway, hdd 5f out, sn btn: 13   3a
tchd 14/1: jumps fit (mod form): unplcd sole start on the level in '99 (h'cap, rtd 17): '98 Newmarket wnr
(ladies amat h'cap, rtd 85): eff at 12f, prob stays a sharp 2m: acts on firm, gd/soft & both AWs.

1960} **CHARMING ADMIRAL 99** [15] 7-9-0 (46)(bl) G Duffield 16/1: 3345-8: Trkd ldrs halfway, rdn/wknd   1¾   17a
fnl 3f: 10 month abs: rnr-up in '99 (rtd 49 & 39a): 98/99 Carlisle wnr over fences (nov, rtd 98c, blnkd):
plcd on the level in '98 (appr h'cap, rtd 55a): eff at 14f: acts on fast, soft & fibresand.

552 **JAZZ TRACK** 37 [7] 6-10-0 (60)(t) F Lynch 33/1: 0/0-69: Al towards rear: see 552.   14   **20a**
2406} **BISHOPSTONE POND** 99 [5] 4-7-10 (33)(3oh) M Henry 14/1: 0050-0: Bhd halfway: 10th: jmps fit.   hd   **0a**
644 **GROOMS GOLD** 21 [8] 8-7-11 (29)(vis) G Bardwell 12/1: 042200: Bhd halfway: 11th: op 14/1: btr 494.   hd   **0a**
2446} **ACTION JACKSON** 99 [2] 8-8-1 (33)(t) J Tate 9/1: 4604-0: Led 1m: 12th: op 14/1, reapp, new stable.   1¾   **0a**
3970} **SHARAF** 99 [11] 7-9-0 (46) R Brisland (5) 16/1: 3045-P: Bhd halfway, t.o./p.u. over 3f out: reportedly   **0a**
broke a blood vessel: op 14/1, 6 month abs.
649 **Primaticcio** 19 [4] 5-9-5 (51)(vis) W Ryan 20/1:   699 **Hibaat** 4 [1] 4-7-10 (33)(4oh) Joanna Badger (7) 66/1:
668 **Markellis** 13 [13] 4-7-10 (33)(3oh) Hayley Turner (6) 25/1: P
16 ran   Time 3m 43.2 (17.2)   (A C W Price)   A G Juckes Abberley, Worcs.

738	2.45 CLASSIFIED STKS 3YO+ 0-70 (E) 6f aw rnd Going 40 -02 Slow
	£2716 £776 £388 3 yo rec 13lb

645 **TEYAAR** 21 [3] D Shaw 4-9-8 I Mongan (5) 5/1: 3-5101: 4 b g Polar Falcon - Music In My Life (Law   **70a**
Society) Made all, held on gamely fnl 2f, all out: op 7/2: earlier scored at Southwell (mdn): plcd in '99 (rtd
85, mdn): eff at 6/7f, handles firm & soft, likes f/sand & Southwell: gd weight carrier: best without blnks.
3462} **ROCK ISLAND LINE** 99 [4] G Woodward 6-9-6 D Holland 5/1: 1010-2: 6 b g New Express - Gail's   hd   **67a**
Crystal (Crofter) Trkd ldr, rdn to chall fnl 2f, kept on well ins last, just held: '99 Southwell wnr (3, sell/
clmr/h'cap, rtd 67a): '98 wnr again at Southwell (2, clmrs, rtd 61a & 60, J Berry): eff at 6/7f, stays 1m
well: acts on firm, soft, fibresand/Southwell specialist: runs well fresh.
721 **DISTINCTIVE DREAM** 2 [2] A Bailey 6-9-10 J Weaver 6/1: 534103: 6 b g Distinctly North - Green   1¼   **67a**
Side (Green Dancer) Handy, rdn/onepace fnl 2f: tchd 8/1: qck reapp: see 598 (C/D, amat h'cap).
673 **ASHOVER AMBER** 13 [5] T D Barron 4-9-3 C Lowther 8/11 FAV: -45234: Handy, hard rdn/onepace fnl   ¾   **58a**
2f: hvly bckd at odds on: btr 596, 280 (C/D).
698 **ELTON LEDGER** 7 [1] 11-9-8 (vis) R Fitzpatrick (3) 12/1: 222005: In tch, kept on fnl 2f, not pace to chall.   1   **59a**
5 ran   Time 1m 15.8 (2.5)   (Justin R Aaron)   D Shaw Averham, Notts.

739	3.15 BEST BETS FILLIES HCAP 3YO+ 0-80 (D) 7f aw Going 40 +03 Fast	**[68]**
	£3789 £1166 £583 £291 3 yo rec 15lb	

697 **GUEST ENVOY** 7 [6] C N Allen 5-8-9 (49) L Newman (5) 7/1: 221441: 5 b m Paris House - Peace Mission   **54a**
(Dunbeath) In tch, prog wide to lead over 1f out, styd on well ins last, rdn out: best time of day: earlier won
here at Southwell (fill h'cap): '99 W'hampton wnr (h'cap, rtd 62a at best): '98 Hamilton wnr (h'cap, rtd 47):
eff at 6f/8.5f: acts on gd, soft & loves fibresand: handles any trk, likes a sharp one: best without a visor.
*692 **MY ALIBI** 7 [2] K R Burke 4-9-2 (56) F Norton 6/4 FAV: 056-12: 4 b f Sheikh Albadou - Fellwaati (Alydar)   1   **58a**
Keen, led after 1f, rdn & hdd over 1f out, kept on: nicely bckd: eff at 7f/1m: see 602 (1m).
*697 **DAHLIDYA** 7 [3] M J Polglase 5-9-11 (65)(6ex) D Holland 4/1: 150313: 5 b m Midyan - Dahlawise   ½   **66a**
(Caerleon) Held up in tch, eff wide over 2f out, kept on onepace: op 7/2, 6lb pen: stays 7f, suited by 6f.
647 **GENERAL KLAIRE** 21 [4] R A Fahey 5-9-10 (64) R Winston 4/1: -01364: Handy 5f: see 501 (C/D, seller).   4   **57a**
588 **MUJAS MAGIC** 31 [7] 5-9-8 (62)(vis) R Fitzpatrick (3) 9/1: 440205: Chsd ldrs, rdn/fdd fnl 2f.   3   **49a**
4511} **CHASETOWN CAILIN** 99 [5] 5-7-10 (36) Kim Tinkler 25/1: 0030-6: Led 1f, clup 5f: op 16/1, 5 mth abs: 1¾   **20a**
rnr-up in '99 (h'cap, rtd 43, D E Incisa): eff at 1m/10.7f on fast & gd/soft grnd: now with N Tinkler.
342 **HAUNT THE ZOO** 70 [1] 5-8-13 (53) J Bramhill 11: 10-307: Cl-up 4f, btn/eased fnl 2f: op 8/1, abs.   13   **17a**
7 ran   Time 1m 29.2 (2.6)   (Shadowfaxracing.com)   C N Allen Newmarket.

740	3.45 TEXT P368 MDN 3YO+ (D) 5f aw str Going 40 -24 Slow
	£2743 £844 £422 £211 3 yo rec 12lb

558 **LYDIAS LOOK** 35 [3] T J Etherington 3-8-7 J Fanning 40/1: 541: 3 b f Distant View - Mrs Croesus   **54a**
(Key To The Mint) Chsd ldrs, rdn halfway, styd on well to lead ins last, rdn out: only mod form prev from 2 starts
at 6f/1m: apprec depth by 5f, 6f+ could suit in future: acts on fibresand & a sharp track.
--   **UNITED PASSION** [4] D Shaw 3-8-7 J P Spencer 20/1: 2: 3 b f Emarati - Miriam (Forzando)   1¼   **50a**
Handy, rdn 2f out, kept on for press: tchd 25/1, debut: dam a 5f juv wnr: eff over a sharp 5f on fibresand.
685 **ABOVE BOARD** 10 [6] R F Marvin 3-8-7 (bl) A McCarthy (3) 16/1: 022033: 5 b g Night Shift - Bundled   nk   **54a**
Up (Sharpen Up) Handy, led after 2f, rdn/hdd ins last, no extra: eff at 5/6f, h'caps shld suit: see 685, 201.
1951} **IM SOPHIE** 99 [5] T D Barron 3-8-7 C Lowther 9/1: 2-4: Led 2f, outpcd over 2f out, kept on for press   nk   **48a**
ins last: op 4/1: 10 mth abs: AW bow: rnr-up sole '99 start (fill auct mdn, rtd 75): eff at 5f on gd & fbrsnd.
4302} **GARTH POOL** 99 [8] 3-8-12 K Darley 11/2: 5250-5: Handy, ch over 1f out, no extra ins last: op 4/1,   ½   **51a**
6 month abs: rnr-up in '99 (rtd 74, h'cap, first time blnks, J Berry): eff at 5f on fast, handles firm, gd/soft &
fibresand: AW bow today for A Berry: reapplication of headgear could suit.
1569} **DISTINCTLY BLU** 99 [8] 3-8-7 F Lynch 16/1: 00-6: Dwelt, nvr pace to chall: op 10/1, 10 mth abs/AW bow. nk   **45a**
685 **WELSH VALLEY** 10 [7] 3-8-7 M Fenton 4/5 FAV: 02-27: Hndy, outpcd fnl 2f: hvly bckd: btr 685 (6f).   ¾   **43a**
685 **POP THE CORK** 10 [2] 3-8-12 Dean McKeown 25/1: 0-08: Held up in tch, outpcd halfway.   3   **41a**
8 ran   Time 1m 01.00 (3.2)   (Callers & Clerks)   T J Etherington Norton, N.Yorks.

741	4.15 TEXT P372 SELLER 3YO (G) 7f aw rnd Going 40 -13 Slow
	£1859 £531 £265

586 **HEATHYARDS MATE** 31 [5] R Hollinshead 3-9-2 P M Quinn (5) 6/4 FAV: 3-0421: 3 b g Timeless Times -   **67a**
Quenlyn (Welsh Pageant) Held up in tch, prog wide over 2f out, led over 1f out & sn in command, pushed out:
nicely bght in for 7,000gns: '99 scorer twice here at Southwell (auct mdn & nurs h'cap, rtd 76a, plcd on
turf, rtd 72, auct mdn): eff at 7f/8.5f, tried further: acts on fast, gd, any trk, fibresand/Southwell specialist.
688 **PRICELESS SECOND** 10 [1] A Glover 3-9-2 (vis) B Sooful (7) 5/1: 314322: 3 b g Lugana Beach -   2   **61a**
Early Gales (Precocious) Led, rdn/hdd over 1f out, kept on onepace: op 9/2: can win similar: see 417 (C/D).
706 **COME ON MURGY** 4 [3] A Bailey 3-8-11 J Bramhill 8/1: 440543: 3 b f Weldnaas - Forest Song (Forzando) 4   **48a**
Chsd ldrs, outpcd over 2f out: op 10/1, qck reapp: see 300, 283 (C/D).
670 **TOWER OF SONG** 13 [6] D W Chapman 3-9-2 A Culhane 7/2: 423504: Chsd ldrs 5f: op 5/2: btr 36 (1m). 8   **41a**
328 **CUIGIU** 73 [7] 3-8-12 (BL) J P Spencer 9/2: 540-05: In tch 5f: op 4/1, blnks, abs: new stable.   4   **29a**
--   **ARTHURS QUAY** [2] 3-8-12 S Clancy 7/1: 6: Chsd ldrs 3f, sn btn: op 4/1: related to 7f wnrs.   8   **17a**
--   **THE OMALLEY** [4] 3-8-7 Sophie Mitchell 25/1: 7: Sn bhd: debut, with R Ford.   21   **0a**
7 ran   Time 1m 30.3 (3.7)   (L A Morgan)   R Hollinshead Upper Longdon, Staffs.

SOUTHWELL (Fibresand)   MONDAY MARCH 27TH   Lefthand, Sharp, Oval Track

---

742   4.45 TEXT P372 HCAP 3YO+ 0-70 (E)   1m3f aw   Going 40   -29 Slow   [66]
£2842   £812   £406   3 yo rec 11lb 4 yo rec 1 lb

646   **PREPOSITION 21** [7] M A Peill 4-7-13 (37)(1ow) F Norton 25/1: 245241: 4 b g Then Again - Little   43a
Emmeline (Emarati) Handy, led halfway, hdd 2f out, rallied gamely ins last, led nr line, all out: missed '99, no
jumps form: unplcd in '98 (rtd 50, Mrs J Ramsden): eff at 1m, suited by this step up to 11f: acts on fibresand.
*670   **MICE IDEAS 13** [6] N P Littmoden 4-8-7 (46) C Cogan (5) 7/2: 160512: 4 ch g Fayruz - Tender Encounter shd   50a
(Prince Tenderfoot) Chsd ldrs, prog to lead 2f out, hard rdn ins last, hdd line: op 5/2: see 670 (C/D, seller).
671   **ACCYSTAN 13** [5] M D Hammond 5-9-3 (55) J Weaver 9/4 FAV: 620163: 5 ch g Efisio - Amia (Nijinsky)   2½   55a
Prom, ch 2f out, sn onepace: op 3/1: clr of rem: see 642.
692   **STRAVSEA 7** [2] R Hollinshead 5-9-3 (55) P M Quinn (5) 16/1: 163504: Rear, mod prog: btr 430 (1m).   9   45a
671   **STATE APPROVAL 13** [8] 7-8-12 (50) I Mongan (3) 8/1: 233605: Chsd ldrs 1m: btr 512, 270.   1   39a
723   **WESTERN COMMAND 2** [4] 4-9-10 (63) R Fitzpatrick (3) 9/2: 160346: Chsd ldrs, btn 4f out: op 6/1.   9   42a
670   **LOYAL TOAST 13** [9] 5-7-13 (37) Kim Tinkler 7/1: 000-27: Al bhd: btr 670.   3   12a
560   **IRSAL 35** [3] 6-7-10 (34)(bl)(4oh) K Dalgleish (7) 12/1: 0-3028: Led, wk halfway, sn btn: op 16/1.   1½   7a
4393}   **FILIAL 99** [1] 7-9-5 (57) G Duffield 25/1: 0035-9: Bhd halfway: op 14/1, 7 wk jumps abs (no form):   10   19a
plcd in '99 on the level (rtd 50, clmr): '98 Southwell (clmr, rtd 69a), Ripon (h'cap) & Redcar wnr (clmr, rtd 75 at
best): eff at 11/13f on fast & hvy grnd, both AWs: handles any track.
9 ran   Time 2m 28.9 (7.6)   (Ms V B Foster)   M A Peill Malton, N.Yorks.

WINDSOR   MONDAY MARCH 27TH   Sharp, Fig 8 Track

Official Going   GOOD TO FIRM. Stalls: Inside.   Round Course rail re-alignment rendered pace figures unreliable.

---

743   2.00 NEW TURF SEASON MDN 2YO (D)   5f   Good/Firm   Inapplicable
£2717   £836   £418   £209

--   **STREGONE** [2] B J Meehan 2-9-0 Pat Eddery 10/3: 1: 2 b g Namaqualand - Sabonis (The Minstrel)   79
Cl-up, rdn to lead 2f out, pushed out: op 5/2: 9,000gns Mar foal, half-brother to 2 juv wnrs, notably sprinter Hoh
Discovery: dam 6f juv wnr, sire a miler: eff over a sharp 5f, shld get 6f: acts on fast grnd, goes well fresh.
--   **MAMORE GAP** [1] R Hannon 2-9-0 Dane O'Neill 4/1: 2: 2 b c General Monash - Ravensdale Rose   1   74
(Henbit) Went left out of stalls, chsd ldrs, eff to chall appr fnl 1f, not pace of wnr towards fin: 22,000gns Mar
foal, half-brother to a wnr abroad: eff over a sharp 5f on fast grnd: shld improve/find an early season mdn.
--   **SPEEDY GEE** [4] M R Channon 2-9-0 P Robinson 8/13 FAV: 3: 2 b c Petardia - Champagne Girl   2½   67
(Robellino) Slow away & lost at least 5L, grad recov'd, nvr on extra: wk bckd: IR£55,000
Feb foal, sister to Gr 3 wng juv Halmahera: dam 5f juv wnr, sire a sprinter: rate more highly next time.
--   **STORMING FOLEY** [3] W G M Turner 2-9-0 A Daly 16/1: 4: Led till after halfway, sn outpcd: shd   67
op 8/1: Makbul Apr foal: dam unrcd.
4 ran   Time 1m 02.0 (3.2)   (A Rovai)   B J Meehan Upper Lambourn, Berks.

---

744   2.30 BURFORD HCAP 3YO 0-75 (E)   1m67y rnd   Good/Firm   Inapplicable   [82]
£2968   £848   £424

4414}   **SIGN OF HOPE 99** [12] I A Balding 3-9-2 (70) K Fallon 11/2 FAV: 4003-1: 3 ch g Selkirk - Rainbow's   83
End (My Swallow) Towards rear, imprvd appr fnl 2f, kept on strgly under hands-and-heels to lead ins last, ridden
nicely bckd tho' op 9/2 on reapp: 1st win, plcd fnl '99 start (nurs, 1st time vis, rtd 80 at best): eff at 1m,
bred for further: acts on fast & gd grnd & any trk: goes well fresh, with/without visor: could go in again.
*629   **YOU DA MAN 23** [18] R Hannon 3-9-2 (70) R Hughes 15/2: 422412: 3 b c Alzao - Fabled Lifestyle   1¾   78
(King's Lake) Prom in chasing pack, pushed along & gd hdwy to lead dist, sn hdd & outpcd by wnr: tchd 10/1:
back at 1m, stays 10f: acts on fast & gd grnd & equitrack: in good form: see 629.
*595   **SPORTY MO 30** [13] K R Burke 3-9-2 (70)(bl) N Callan 11/1: 503113: 3 b g Namaqualand - Miss   2   74
Fortunate (Taufan) Led, 5L clr halfway, rdn appr fnl 1f, hdd dist, no extra: op 8/1: fit from fruitful AW campaign:
bold attempt up in grade after wng 2 clmrs: acts on fast, soft & fibresand, loves equitrack: effective in blnks/vis.
4433}   **SECOND PAIGE 99** [10] N A Graham 3-8-6 (60) P Robinson 33/1: -000-4: Handy in the pack, effort   1¾   60
2f out, styd on without threatening: reapp/h'cap bow: unplcd in '99 (aual mdn, rtd 71): stays 1m on fast grnd.
4139}   **BORDER RUN 99** [9] 3-9-0 (68) W R Swinburn 10/1: -056-5: Held up, late prog under hands-and-heels: 1¼   65
op 8/1 on reapp/h'cap bow: highly tried in '99 (mdns, rtd 73): handles fast grnd, step up to 10f will suit.
2998}   **ESTABLISHMENT 99** [4] 3-9-4 (72) L Dettori 16/1: -600-6: Bhd, pushed along & not clr run 2f   nk   68
out till ent fnl 1f, ran on, nrst fin: op 12/1 on reapp/h'cap bow: ran in above-average mdns last term (rtd
88 at best): middle-distance bred, expect improvement over further in time.
4460}   **SPIRIT OF LIGHT 99** [16] 3-9-2 (70) M Tebbutt 10/1: 0205-7: Bhd, some late hdwy but nvr plcd to   1½   63
chall: trainer received £1,500, jockey banned for 10 days & horse for 40 days under 'non-triers' rule: rnr-up
2nd of 4 '99 starts (mdn, rtd 73): eff at 1m on fast & hvy grnd: will do better with a more positive ride.
4498}   **FRENCH HORN 99** [6] 3-8-12 (66) P McCabe 10/1: 0651-8: Pulled hard out the back, modest prog &   ¾   57+
hmpd appr fnl 1f, nvr on terms under a kind ride: won fnl '99 start, at Leicester (nurs, rtd 66): eff at 7f,
further suit (half-brother to a winning hdler): acts on soft grnd, poss firm, stiff trk: much sharper next time.
651   **WOODWIND DOWN 19** [2] 3-8-11 (65) T Quinn 12/1: 00-29: Prom in the pack till no extra ent fnl 2f.   shd   56
4305}   **STRICTLY SPEAKING 99** [7] 3-8-13 (67) J Fortune 10/1: 6345-0: Nvr troubled ldrs: 10th on reapp.   1¼   55
658   **ARCTIC HIGH 16** [15] 3-8-8 (62) R Price 25/1: 3230: Rcd in 2nd, fdd appr fnl 2f: 11th, turf/h'cap bow.   shd   50
615   **THE GIRLS FILLY 26** [11] 3-8-9 (62)(1ow) S Sanders 20/1: 00-230: Handy till effort & btn appr   2   46
fnl 2f, eased dist: 12th, nicely bckd from 33/1, AW fit: best at 7/f: see 570.
4606}   **TWEED 99** [14] 3-8-0 (52) Pat Eddery 6/1: 050-0: Nvr recovered from v slow start: 13th, op 9/2, h'cap bow.½   49
4476}   Sweet Haven 99 [8] 3-8-6 (60) S Drowne 40/1:   4476} Groesfaen Lad 99 [3] 3-9-7 (75) G Faulkner (3) 25/1:
4597} Unimpeachable 99 [5] 3-8-10 (64) Claire Bryan (5) 25/1:   4494} Muffin Man 99 [1] 3-8-12 (66) J Reid 16/1:
17 ran   Time 1m 42.6 (0.3)   (George Strawbridge)   I A Balding Kingsclere, Hants.

237

745 3.00 BOURNE END FILLIES MDN 3YO (D)   1m67y rnd   Good/Firm   Inapplicable
£2782   £856   £428   £214

4556} **VERBOSE 99** [6] J H M Gosden 3-8-11 L Dettori 6/4 FAV: 5-1: 3 b f Storm Bird - Avemia (Alydar)   **92**
Sn led, rdn to assert ins last, shade cosily: well bckd tho' op 4/5 on reapp: 5th in a Newmarket mdn sole '99 start
(rtd 90): eff forcing the pace at 1m, shld stay further (dam 9f wnr): runs well fresh on fast & soft: useful.

2621} **TWEED MILL 99** [2] I A Balding 3-8-11 K Fallon 5/2: 3-2: 3 b f Selkirk - Island Mill (Mill Reef)   2   **85**
Went left start but sn recovered, imprvd to press wnr appr fnl 1f, held fnl 100y: well bckd from 4/1 on reapp:
3rd sole '99 start (fill mdn here, rtd 74): eff at 8.3f on fast grnd: lightly raced & shld win a mdn.

3802} **ALLEGRESSE 99** [1] J L Dunlop 3-8-11 Pat Eddery 6/1: 36-3: 3 b f Alzao - Millie Musique (Miller's   2½   **80$**
Mate) Chsd ldrs, feeling pace 3f out, rallied appr fnl 1f but unable to chall: debut rnr-up last term (fill
mdn, rtd 78): eff at 7f/1m, mid-dists & h'caps should see improvement: handles fast & good grnd.

4473} **NABADHAAT 99** [7] E A L Dunlop 3-8-11 R Hills 5/1: 40-4: Early ldr, cl-up, no extra appr fnl   ½   **79$**
1f: bckd tho' big drifter from 7/4: pleasing 4th on debut last term (fill mdn, rtd 84): bred to apprec 1m+.

--   **ANASTASIA VENTURE** [8] 3-8-11 N Callan 16/1: 5: Chsd ldrs, rdn & same pace fnl 2f: op 12/1 on   1   **77**
debut: Lion Cavern half-sister to sev wnrs, notably decent stayer Pearl Venture, dam 10f wnr: promising.

5   **BETTINA BLUE 99** [4] 3-8-11 J F Egan 66/1: 5065-6: Al bhd: best effort on debut last term   12   **53**
(5f mdn on soft grnd, rtd 69): longer trip & stiff task today: with R Ingram.

240   **BEACH BABY 85** [5] 3-8-11 A Nicholls (3) 100/1: 00-07: In tch till after halfway: turf bow, 12 wk abs.   4   **45$**

4431} **LITTLE TARA 99** [3] 3-8-11 P Dobbs (5) 66/1: 00-8: Nvr in it: highly tried, no worthwhile form.   hd   **45**
8 ran   Time 1m 43.1 (0.8)   (K Abdulla)   J H M Gosden Manton, Wilts.

746 3.30 TOTE TOTALBET.COM HCAP 3YO+ 0-80 (D)   6f   Good/Firm   Inapplicable   [77]
£7280   £2240   £1120   £560   3 yo rec 13lb

728   **JUWWI 2** [10] J M Bradley 6-10-0 (77) Darren Williams (7) 13/2: 220601: 6 ch g Mujtahid - Nouvelle   **84**
Star (Luskin Star) Slow away & bhd till kept on strongly appr fnl 2f, led bef dist, shkn up, shade readily: qk reapp,
defied top-weight: '99 wnr at N Abbot (2 bmprs), Carlisle, Chepstow (rtd 79) & Southwell (h'caps, rtd 85a): '98 wnr at W'hampton (sell)
& Lingfield (h'cap, rtd 80a & 70): eff at 5/6f, stays 7f on firm, hvy, both AWs: gd weight carrier: v tough.

622   **DAYS OF GRACE 25** [15] L Montague Hall 5-8-8 (54) Martin Dwyer 3/1 FAV: 231322: 5 gr m Wolfhound - 1   **56**
Inshirah (Caro) Led till appr fnl 1f, kept on under press, btn 1L: well bckd: v tough, on a fair turf mark.

4472} **RED DELIRIUM 99** [4] I A Balding 4-9-3 (66) K Fallon 8/1: 5000-2: 4 b g Robellino - Made Of Pearl   dht   **68+**
(Nureyev) Stdd start & bhd, nowhere to go 2f out till 1f out & struck by rival's whip, ran on, too late: op 6/1:
failed to make the frame last term for R Hannon & tried a visor (h'caps, rtd 71): juv wnr at Goodwood (mdn, rtd 96
at best): eff at 6f, return to 7f suit: acts on firm & gd/soft: v well h'capped now & shld go close next time.

4553} **SUSANS PRIDE 99** [14] B J Meehan 4-9-12 (75) Pat Eddery 13/2: 6511-4: Bhd ldrs, not much room   ¾   **75**
appr fnl 1f, styd on, not pace to chall: gd comeback: '99 wnr at Nottingham (med auct mdn), Doncaster & Brighton
(clmrs, rtd 75): return to 7f/1m looks sure to suit: acts on firm & soft, any trk: win another claimer.

622   **GRASSLANDIK 25** [8] A 4-8-7 (56) S Whitworth 14/1: 2-3535: Keen, rear, bhd horses een fnl 2f, ran on   1   **53**
ins last, unable to chall: AW fit: not much luck in running, prob handles fast grnd, acts on fibresand & gd: see 175.

3714} **MILADY LILLIE 99** [1] C Catlin (7) 20/1: 3603-6: Wide, cl-up & ev ch till no extra   nk   **54**
bef dist: ran well enough from tricky draw 1: '99 Brighton wnr (class stks, rtd 63 & 53a): unplcd juv (rtd 62):
eff at 6f, suited by 7f, tried 8.5f: acts on firm/good grnd, sharp/without t-strap: sharp trks suit: without t-strap.

*674   **SUPREME ANGEL 13** [12] 5-8-13 (62)(bl) T G McLaughlin 6/1: 00-317: Prom, drifted left under press   nk   **57**
appr fnl 1f, onepace: up in trip, fit from a win on the AW: see 674.

4298} **ROGUE SPIRIT 99** [6] 4-9-10 (73) W R Swinburn 13/2: 0305-8: Well plcd, ch 2f out, no extra &   1½   **63**
not much room below dist: op 11/2 on reapp: '99 Folkestone wnr (mdn, rtd 78 at best): eff at 5/6f, tried
7f: acts on firm & gd/soft grnd, prob any trk: with P Harris.

2400} **AMBER BROWN 99** [9] 4-8-9 (58) A Daly 25/1: 6050-9: Front rank, edged left, fdd appr fnl 1f: ½   **47**
reapp, stablemate 6th: failed to make the frame last term (mdn, rtd 69, fill h'cap, rtd 60): unraced juvenile.

4604} **CONTRARY MARY 99** [7] 5-8-10 (59) S Sanders 12/1: 0345-0: Prom till 2f out, eased ins last: 10th.   4   **38**

2240} **ANSTAND 99** [5] 5-9-3 (66) R Price 14/1: 0500-0: Wide & ev ch till btn bef dist, eased: 11th.   6   **30**

*635   **BEGUILE 23** [3] 6-8-2 (51)(t)P Doe 20/1: 0-2410: Wide, nvr on terms: 12th, AW fit, t-strap reapplied.   nk   **14**

439   **MOUTON 54** [2] 4-8-6 (55) A Nicholls (3) 40/1: -50500: Held up, hmpd 2f out, nvr dngrs: 13th, 8 wk abs.   3½   **10**

691   **MAMMAS F C 9** [11] 4-8-8 (57) Claire Bryan (5) 12/1: -0055F: Mid-div & shkn up when fell 2 out: see 563.   **0**
14 ran   Time 1m 13.4 (3.1)   (J M Bradley)   J M Bradley Sedbury, Glos.

747 4.00 DOWNLEY CLASS STKS 3YO+ 0-80 (D)   1m2f   Good/Firm   Inapplicable
£3770   £1160   £580   £290   3 yo rec 20lb

*661   **ULUNDI 16** [4] Lady Herries 5-9-8 P Doe 5/1: 11: 5 b g Rainbow Quest - Flit (Lyphard)   **90**
Hld up, imprvd going well 3f out, led bef dist, going away, readily: tchd 6/1: earlier won at W'hampton (mdn):
prev won at N Abbot (2 bmprs), Fontwell (nov) & Cheltenham (nov h'cap hdle, rtd 110h, 2m2f, firm & gd/soft): eff
stays 10f well, 12f will suit: acts on fast & fibresand: runs well fresh: progressive & useful, shld win again.

4308} **AEGEAN DREAM 99** [2] R Hannon 4-9-3 R Hughes 4/1 JT FAV: 5105-2: 4 b f Royal Academy - L'Ideale   3½   **78**
(Alysheba) Prom, led briefly 2f out, styd on but no ch with wnr: nicely bckd tho' op 3/1 on reapp: '99 wnr at
Epsom (mdn, rtd 79): rnr-up 4 times over 10f, best at 1m: acts on firm/fast & sharp/undul trks: fitter back at 1m.

593   **PHILATELIC LADY 30** [7] M J Haynes 4-9-3 S Carson (5) 4/1 JT FAV: 421-53: 4 ch f Pips Pride -   ½   **77**
Gold Stamp (Golden Act) Held up, rdn to impr 3f out, onepace bef dist: AW fit: acts on fast, soft & equitrack.

4130} **FAIT LE JOJO 99** [1] S P C Woods 3-8-0 R Ffrench 8/1: -313-4: Early ldr & again 3f out, sn hdd,   hd   **80**
rdn & flashed tail 2f out, onepace: op 5/1 on turf bow, reapp: '99 W'hampton wnr (mdn, rtd 83a): eff at 1m,
prob stays 10f on fast & fibresand: best up with/forcing the pace on a sharp track.

1775} **CHIEF CASHIER 99** [5] 5-9-6 A Nicholls (3) 5/1: 2148-5: Pld hard, trkd ldrs, shkn up/unable to qckn   1¾   **78**
fnl 2f: reapp: '99 Epsom wnr (val h'cap, rtd 83): earlier tried hdles (rtd 101h): '98 wnr again at Epsom (2,
h'caps, rtd 78): eff at 10f, stays a sharp 12.5f: acts on firm, likes soft & Epsom.

1109} **RANEEN NASHWAN 99** [3] 4-9-6 L Dettori 5/1: 1/40-6: In tch, outpcd 3f out: op 7/2 on reapp: 1   **77**
lightly rcd last term (rtd h'cap, rtd 79): won last of 4 juv starts, at Musselburgh (mdn, rtd 83 at best): eff
over a sharp 1m, bred for mid-dists: acts on soft grnd: with M Channon.

3284} **DIRECT DEAL 99** [6] 4-9-6 (t)J Reid 12/1: 0413-9: Sn led, hdd 3f out, fdd: reapp: '99 Bath   3½   **72**
wnr (mdn, rtd 85, E Dunlop): promise sole '98 start (mdn, rtd 80): eff at 10f, tried further: acts on
firm & gd/soft grnd: eff forcing the pace on a sharp trk: now with G McCourt.

WINDSOR   MONDAY MARCH 27TH   Sharp, Fig 8 Track

4509} **SUEZ TORNADO 99** [8] 7-9-6 K Fallon 20/1: 1650-8: Nvr in it: stiff task, 7 wk jumps abs (well btn)   13 54
'99 wnr at Ayr (h'cap) & Newmarket (clmr, rtd 61, E Alston): eff at 1m/12f on firm & hvy grnd, stiff/gall trks.
8 ran   Time 2m 04.5 (u0.2)   (D Heath)   Lady Herries Angmering, W.Sussex.

748	**4.30 SID PAYNTER HCAP 3YO+ 0-70 (E) 1m3f135y Good/Firm Inapplicable**			[68]
	£3010 £860 £430 3 yo rec 22lb4 yo rec 2 lb			

*167 **ZORRO 99** [2] Jamie Poulton 6-8-12 (52) O Urbina 15/2: 4/51-1: 6 gr g Touch Of Grey - Snow Huntress   55
(Shirley Heights) Bhd ldrs, went on 2f out, drifted left under press, held on well: abs: '99 wnr at Lingfield
(AW h'cap, rtd 57a & 51): rnr-up thrice in '98 (h'cap, rtd 51a, R Flower): '97 Yarmouth wnr (appr h'cap, rtd 67):
eff at 10f/13f: acts on firm/fast grnd & equitrack, any trk, likes sharp ones: goes well fresh: in gd form.
*322 **WESTMINSTER CITY 74** [6] D R C Elsworth 4-8-11 (53) N Pollard 8/1: 0-3212: 4 b c Alleged -   ½ 54
Promanade Fan (Timeless Moment) Mid-div, prog for press appr fnl 1f, styd on, held towards fin: tchd 10/1, 11 wk
abs: fine run for new connections: acts on fast, gd grnd & firesand: eff at 1m/11.5f, tried 2m: see 322.
4540} **FEE MAIL 99** [3] I A Balding 4-9-9 (65) K Fallon 11/4 FAV: 0021-3: 4 b f Danehill - Wizardry   shd 66
(Shirley Heights) In tch, prog to press wnr appr fnl 1f, hard rdn, switched & onepace till kept on cl-home: well
bckd from 9/2, clr of rem on reapp: landed fnl '99 start here at Windsor (C/D h'cap, rtd 65): plcd 2nd of 2 '98
starts (fill mdn, rtd 71): suited by 11.5f nowadays, may stay further: acts on fast & gd/soft grnd, sharp trks.
675 **OCEAN LINE 11** [13] G M McCourt 5-8-3 (43) A Beech 5/1: 232204: Held up, gd wide hdwy &   3 40
ch ent fnl 2f, no extra late: AW fit: consistent & likes claiming/selling grade: see 383.
3804} **LADY SANTANA 99** [14] 3-8-5 (67) J F Egan 12/1: 000-5: In rear, nudged along & ran on into 5th   1½ 62
ins last, nvr nrr: reapp/h'cap bow: unplcd in 3 '99 sprints: bred for mid-dists & looks capable of better.
621 **HAWKSBILL HENRY 26** [4] 6-8-6 (46) D Sweeney 8/1: 131036: Early ldr, again 4f out till 2f out, onepace.1¾ 39
290 **FAMOUS 79** [20] 7-8-8 (48) A Daly 33/1: 02-007: Bhd, some hdwy 3f out, nvr nr to chall: 6 wk jmps abs.   nk 40
620 **BONDS GULLY 26** [18] 4-9-3 (59) R Price 13/2: 00-328: Cl-up, shkn up 2f out, onepace when hmpd   shd 51
bef dist: op 9/2, AW fit: longer trip for this sprint-bred colt: see 620, 547.
3263} **TITUS BRAMBLE 99** [16] 3-7-12 (60) R Ffrench 25/1: 0600-9: Al same place: reapp: unplcd & tried   2 49
blnks once in '99 (mdn, rtd 74): with B Millman.
618 **SATWA BOULEVARD 26** [11] 5-7-11 (37) A Mackay 25/1: 0/0000: Al towards rear: 10th, see 326.   nk 25
681 **DIAMOND FLAME 11** [15] 6-9-5 (59) W R Swinburn 10/1: 020-00: Led after 2f till 4f out, grad wknd: 11th. 1¾ 45
643 **DION DEE 21** [12] 4-8-4 (45)(1ow) S Drowne 25/1: -00300: Keen, chsd ldrs till 3f out: 12th, see 565.   hd 32
290 **CAERNARFON BAY 79** [9] 5-8-7 (47) A Nicholls(3) 25/1: 620-00: Nvr trbld ldrs: 13th, jmps fit, new stable. 1¼ 31
603 **AN SMEARDUBH 28** [17] 4-8-7 (49) P McCabe 33/1: 000-00: Al bhd: 14th, no worthwhile form.   shd 33
4307} **DIZZY TILLY 99** [19] 6-8-10 (50) P Doe 10/1: 6230-0: Chsd ldrs, rdn & btn 3f out: 16th, op 8/1.   0
on reapp, jumps fit (no form): '99 wnr here at Windsor (C/D fill h'cap, rtd 53): '97 wnr again here at Windsor
(2, ltd stks & h'cap, rtd 66, T Naughton): eff at 10f/12f on firm & gd/soft grnd, prob soft, handles fibresand.
706} **Red Bordeaux 99** [7] 5-9-6 (60) S Sanders 16/1:   332 **Landican Lane 72** [5] 4-8-4 (43)(bl)(3ow) L Newton 40/1:
3421} **Sewards Folly 99** [8] 4-9-0 (56) R Hughes 33/1:   253 **Agiotage 84** [1] 4-10-0 (70) G Faulkner (3) 33/1:
--   **Fairfield Bay** [10] 4-8-0 (42) J Lowe 40/1:
20 ran   Time 2m 26.6 (0.8)   (Mrs G M Temmerman)   Jamie Poulton Telscombe, E.Sussex.

WOLVERHAMPTON (Fibresand)   TUESDAY MARCH 28TH   Lefthand, Sharp Track

Official Going   STANDARD Stalls: Inside, Except 7f - Outside

749	**2.10 BET247.CO.UK HCAP 3YO+ 0-65 (F) 1m1f79y aw Going 43 -02 Slow**			[60]
	£2331 £666 £333 3 yo rec 19lb			

608 **WELLCOME INN 28** [12] G Woodward 6-8-3 (35)(t) L Newton 7/1: 223341: 6 ch g Most Welcome - Mimining 40a
(Tower Walk) Mid-div, rdn/chsd ldrs over 2f out, styd on well ins last to lead nr line, all out: op 6/1: rnr-up in
'99 (rtd 42, clmr): '97 Beverley wnr (stks): eff arnd 9/12f: acts on firm, gd/soft & fibresand: best in a t-strap.
676 **MIDNIGHT WATCH 12** [7] A G Newcombe 6-8-10 (42) G Sparkes (7) 5/1: 001322: 6 b c Capote - Midnight nk 46a
Air (Green Dancer) Trkd ldrs, led over 4f out, rdn/hdd nr line, just btn: op 6/1: eff at 1m/9.4f: see 676, 431.
568 **ETISALAT 35** [3] J Pearce 5-9-11 (57) J Weaver 6/1: -31263: 5 b g Lahib - Sweet Repose (High Top)   2 57a
Rear, prog wide & rdn to chall 2f out, edged left/no extra ins last: op 5/1: see 405 (C/D, amat h'cap).
647 **FLASHFEET 22** [9] P D Purdy 10-7-10 (28)(5oh) G Baker 100/1: 000004: Prom, onepace fnl 3f.   3 22a
681 **AREISH 12** [11] 7-9-13 (59) P Dobbs (5) 5/2 FAV: 112135: Held up in tch, eff 3f out/sn held: btr 611. 1¾ 50a
635 **MANIKATO 24** [4] 6-8-3 (35) A McCarthy (3) 14/1: 600-46: Held up in tch, outpcd fnl 3f: op 12/1. 1½ 23a
676 **GODMERSHAM PARK 12** [10] 8-9-3 (49) R Hughes 8/1: 344147: Led 5f, fdd: btr 648 (Southwell, 1m).   ¾ 36a
692 **JESSINCA 8** [1] 4-9-5 (51) S Carson (5) 9/1: 315108: Chsd ldrs 5f: op 6/1: btr 675 (8.5f).   6 29a
676 **NERONIAN 12** [5] 6-7-11 (29) P M Quinn (5) 6/1: 56-439: Bhd 4f out: btr 676, 554.   8 0a
635 **KESTRAL 24** [2] 4-8-6 (38) G Bardwell 16/1: 000-50: Keen/rear, al struggling: 10th: see 635 (7f).   9 0a
--   **ARM AND A LEG** [6] 5-9-4 (50) V Slattery 33/1: 2000/0: Struggling halfway, 11th: jumps fit (fell):   3 0a
last rcd on the Level in '98, rnr-up on sand (rtd 53a, sell, unplcd on turf, rtd 49, clmr, C A Dwyer): '97 Yarmouth wnr
(sell, rtd 64): eff at 7f/9f, stays sharp 12f: acts on fast, gd/soft & handles fibresand: best without visor.
11 ran   Time 2m 04.4 (4.2)   (Burntwood Sports Ltd)   G Woodward Brierley, S Yorks

750	**2.40 APPRENTICE CLAIMER 3YO+ (F) 1m100y aw Going 43 -22 Slow**		
	£2299 £657 £328 3 yo rec 17lb		

*693 **RAMBO WALTZER 8** [3] Miss S J Wilton 8-9-11 l Mongan (5) 6/4 FAV: 212611: 8 b g Rambo Dancer -   68a
Vindictive Lady (Foolish Pleasure) Led/dsptd lead, went on 3f out & rdn/pulled clr fnl 1f, eased nr fin: rdly:
earlier scored twice here at W'hampton (sell & clmr), & Southwell (2, sell & clmr, one for D Nicholls): '99 scorer
at Catterick, Thirsk (h'caps, rtd 71) & Southwell (3, 2 clmrs & a sell, rtd 75 at best): '98 W'hampton & Southwell
wnr (2, h'caps, rtd 91a & 72): eff at 7f/9.5f on fast & soft, fibresand/sharp trk specialist: most tough & genuine.
684 **BENTICO 11** [9] Mrs N Macauley 11-9-5 (vis) R Fitzpatrick 25/1: 46/042: 11 b g Nordico - Bentinck   6 50a
Hotel (Red God) Rear, rdn halfway, kept on fnl 3f to take 2nd ins last, no threat: signs of a return to form: see 646.
546 **JUST WIZ 38** [5] R Hannon 4-9-13 (bl) R Smith (5) 3/1: 1-0553: 4 b g Efisio - Jade Pet (Petong)   shd 58a
Handy, rdn/ch fnl 2f, wknd ins last: op 2/1: btr 161 (10f, h'cap, equitrack).
580 **CANADIAN APPROVAL 33** [6] I A Wood 4-9-9 S Carson (3) 7/2: 40-104: Keen/led after 1f, hdd 3f out & 2½ 49a
sn held: op 5/2: btr 336 (1m, equitrack).

684   **HEATHYARDS JAKE 11** [1] 4-9-7 P M Quinn (3) 25/1: 400665: Rear, mod late prog: btr 229 (mdn).   3   41a
--   **BLUE STYLE** [7] 4-9-9 G Faulkner 14/1: 00-6: Handy, btn 3f out: AW bow, 6 month abs: Brit debut: 5   33a
mod form in France/Ireland prev (tried blnks, 7.5f mdn, D Weld): with J Poulton.
675   **CHEERFUL GROOM 12** [8] 9-9-5 A McCarthy 25/1: 000-07: Handy, btn 3f out, eased fnl 1f: unplcd in   shd   29a
'99 (rtd 40 & 36a): '98 wnr here at W'hampton (3, h'caps, rtd 61a, unplcd on turf, rtd 28, h'cap): stays 9f, suited
by 8.5f: acts on fast, fibresand/W'hampton specialist: runs well for an amat & likes to come with a late run.
463   **GHAAZI 52** [2] 4-9-10 P Fredericks (3) 12/1: 314-08: In tch, btn 3f out: op 8/1, abs: btr 227, 109.   3   28a
553   **NOBLE INVESTMENT 38** [4] 6-9-7 Jonjo Fowle 25/1: 3016F9: Rear, bhd 5f out: reportedly fin lame.   1¾   22a
9 ran   Time 1m 51.7 (5.5)   (John Pointon & Sons)   Miss S J Wilton Wetley Rocks, Staffs

---

751	**3.15 FILLIES HCAP 3YO+ (E)** 5f aw rnd Going 43 -19 Slow	**[69]**
	£2688 £768 £384 3 yo rec 12lb	

673   **E B PEARL 14** [2] N Bycroft 4-7-13 (38)(2ow) Martin Dwyer 3/1: 0-0651: 4 ch f Timeless Times - Petite   43a
Elite (Anfield) Cl-up, hard rdn fnl 2f, styd on well for press to narrowly prevail, all out: tchd 4/1: '99 wnr at
Southwell (mdn clmr, rtd 47a) & Redcar (sell h'cap, rtd 51): eff at 5/6f on firm, fast & fibresand: best without blnks.
518   **SNAP CRACKER 42** [3] D W Chapman 4-8-1 (42) K Dalgleish (7) 20/1: 00-002: 4 b f Inchinor - Valkyrie   nk   44a
(Bold Lad) Just led, rdn 2f out, hdd nr line: op 14/1, 6 wk abs: acts on fast & fibresand, enjoys gd & hvy.
567   **HOT LEGS 35** [4] B A McMahon 4-7-10 (37)(2oh) P M Quinn (5) 7/1: 545503: 4 b f Sizzling Melody -   2½   32a
Ra Ra Girl (Shack) In tch, outpcd before halfway, styd on fnl 2f for press, no threat: mdn, see 379 (clmr).
4279}   **BELIEVING 99** [6] R Hannon 3-9-7 (74) R Hughes 11/4: 4150-4: Chsd ldrs, outpcd fnl 2f: op 7/4, 6   5   60a
mth abs: '99 Brighton wnr (auct fill mdn, rtd 81, unplcd on sand, rtd 51a): eff over a sharp 5f, stays 6f on firm.
3665}   **ANTONIAS DOUBLE 99** [5] 5-10-0 (69) P Bradley (5) 5/4 FAV: 2210-5: Dwelt, chsd ldrs wide, btn   2   50a
over 1f out: op 4/5: 7 mth abs: '99 h'cap wnr at Redcar, Salisbury & Newcastle (rtd 78, rnr-up on sand, rtd 68a,
C/D): '98 Newcastle wnr (mdn, rtd 64): best forcing pace at 5f on firm, gd & both AWs, any trk: has run well fresh.
5 ran   Time 1m 03.3 (3.1)   (T Umpleby)   N Bycroft Norton, N Yorks

---

752	**3.50 MILLION MDN 3YO+ (D)** 1m4f aw Going 43 -45 Slow	
	£2730 £840 £420 £210 3 yo rec 22lb 4 yo rec 2 lb	

--   **MASSEY** [2] J Pearce 4-9-11 G Bardwell 7/1: 1: 4 br c Machiavellian - Massaraat (Nureyev)   65a
Keen, held up in tch, prog wide to chall fnl 2f, kept on gamely to lead line, all out: gamble from 25/1 on debut:
eff over 12f, connections feel a drop in trip shld suit on turf: acts on fibresand & a sharp trk: runs well fresh.
643   **LE CAVALIER 22** [8] C N Allen 3-8-5 L Newman (5) 9/4: 022222: 3 b g Mister Baileys - Secret Deed   shd   64a
(Shadeed) Led, rdn/strongly prsd fnl 2f, edged right nr fin, hdd line: clr rem, op 11/4, deserves a win.
4526}   **BARCELONA 99** [6] J Noseda 3-8-7(2ow) J Weaver 7/4 FAV: 003-3: 3 b c Barathea - Pipitina (Bustino)   8   57a
In tch wide, prog/chsd ldrs 3f out, sn held: op 4/6, clr of rem: 5 month abs/AW bow: plcd on fnl '99 start (mdn,
rtd 80): stays 1m, not stay 12f?: acts on gd/soft: return to shorter trips & h'caps wld help.
4435}   **PAPERWEIGHT 99** [1] Miss K M George 4-9-6 N Callan 11/2: 5230-4: Prom, fdd fnl 2f, op 7/2:   5   43a
jumps fit (no form): AW bow: rnr-up twice in '99 for L Cumani, (mdn, debut, rtd 85, prob flattered): eff at 10f on fm & hvy.
643   **MI ODDS 22** [4] 4-9-11 R Fitzpatrick (3) 33/1: 305: Handy, fdd fnl 3f: see 603.   1¼   46a
1989}   **HORTON DANCER 99** [5] 3-8-5 Martin Dwyer 10/1: 4-6: Prom 1m: op 7/1: 9 month abs/AW bow: 2½   42a
unplcd sole '99 start (med auct mdn, rtd 68): mid-dists shld suit this term.
584   **UTAH 32** [7] 6-9-11 J Mongan (5) 20/1: 432007: Wide/al twds rear: now with A G Juckes: btr 438 (7f).   11   30a
668   **TOY STORY 14** [3] 4-9-11 S Sanders 33/1: -63308: Bhd halfway: see 668, 519.   dist   0a
73   **HONEY HOUSE 99** [9] 4-9-6 (t) P Mundy (7) 40/1: 00-9: T.o. halfway: mod form, longer 12f trip.   13   0a
9 ran   Time 2m 44.2 (10.6)   (Jeff Pearce)   J Pearce Newmarket, Suffolk

---

753	**4.20 BIG MATCH STATS SELL 3YO+ (G)** 5f aw rnd Going 43 +05 Fast	
	£1897 £542 £271 3 yo rec 12lb	

61   **PRIDE OF BRIXTON 99** [6] Andrew Reid 7-9-7 M Henry 7/1: 0000-1: 7 b g Dominion - Caviar Blini (What   69a
A Guest) Sn cl-up & went on halfway, in command over 1f out/rdn clr, easily nr line: bought in for 6,200 gns: op
6/1, 4 mth abs: rnr-up twice in '99 (clmr, rtd 73a & 25, h'cap): '98 wnr at W'hampton (5, sell & h'cap for C
Thornton & 2 h'caps for P Evans, rtd 74a), earlier won at Carlisle (ltd stks, rtd 61): eff at 5/6f on fast & soft,
fibresand/W'hampton specialist: runs well fresh: best without a visor: with another seller.
533   **PALACEGATE JACK 40** [4] A Berry 9-9-7 (bl) R Hughes 3/1 JT FAV: 2-2532: 9 gr g Neshad - Pasadena   5   54a
Lady (Captain James) Led till halfway, sn outpcd by easy wnr: op 9/4: 6 wk abs: game 9yo: see 312, 191 (C/D).
719   **SAMWAR 3** [3] Mrs N Macauley 5-9-12 (vis) R Fitzpatrick (3) 3/1 JT FAV: 226063: 8 b g Warning -   1¼   58a
Samaza (Arctic Tern) Rdn/towards rear, late gains, nvr a threat: quick reapp, op 2/1: btr 214 (clmr, Southwell).
*639   **YOUNG IBNR 24** [9] B A McMahon 5-9-12 L Newman (5) 5/1: 056014: Chsd ldrs, outpcd fnl 2f: see 639.   ½   56$
693   **SING FOR ME 8** [1] 5-9-2 Stephanie Hollinshea 16/1: 404245: Rear, mod prog: op 12/1: see 272.   shd   46$
680   **NOW IS THE HOUR 12** [7] 4-9-7 (BL) A Nicholls (3) 25/1: 00-66: Chsd ldrs wide 3f, sn outpcd: blnks.   ¾   49$
639   **LEGAL VENTURE 24** [8] 4-9-7 (bl) P Fitzsimons (5) 7/2: 034027: Bmpd start, chsd ldrs 3f: bckd, tchd 5/1.   2   44a
697   **GRAND ESTATE 8** [2] 5-9-7 S Sanders 8/1: 5-4008: Chsd ldrs 4f: op 6/1: btr 614.   shd   44a
1241}   **BRIANS SONG 99** [5] 5-9-7 J Bosley (7) 20/1: /000-9: Sn bhd: reapp, mod form.   15   17a
9 ran   Time 1m 02.1 (1.9)   (A S Reid)   Andrew Reid Mill Hill, Greater London

---

754	**4.55 Y. O'HALLORAN HCAP 3YO+ 0-60 (F)** 7f aw rnd Going 43 -04 Slow	**[59]**
	£2383 £681 £340 3 yo rec 15lb	

38   **ADOBE 99** [9] W M Brisbourne 5-9-2 (47) T G McLaughlin 12/1: 3000-1: 5 b g Green Desert - Shamshir   55a
(Kris) Handy, led going well 1f out, styd on well, rdn out: op 16/1: 5 month abs: '99 wnr at Bath (mdn h'cap)
& Nottingham (h'cap, rtd 55, plcd on sand, rtd 49a): plater f Gosden in '98: eff at 1m on firm, gd &
fibresand, handles soft & any trk: eff with/without a t-strap: runs well fresh.
653   **FEATHERSTONE LANE 20** [12] Miss L C Siddall 9-8-13 (44) N Callan 12/1: 442522: 9 b g Siberian   1½   48a
Express - Try Gloria (Try My Best) Held up in tch, prog/rdn to chall 1f out, no extra: stays sharp 7f, best at 5/6f.
691   **DOLPHINELLE 10** [8] R Hannon 4-9-8 (53) R Hughes 6/1: 544303: 4 b c Dolphin Street - Mamie's Joy   2   53a
(Prince Tenderfoot) Held up in tch, rdn & kept on fnl 2f, no threat: op 8/1: acts on firm, soft & both AWs: see 263.
570   **FRANKLIN D 34** [4] J R Jenkins 4-9-0 (45) D Sweeney 9/1: 03-234: Handy, led over 3f out till 1f out,   nk   44a
no extra: op 8/1: clr of rem: acts on both AWs: see 58 (equitrack).
697   **BODFARI ANNA 8** [5] 4-8-12 (43)(bl) R Cody Boutcher (7) 7/1: 00-305: Rear, rdn halfway, mod prog: 6   33a

WOLVERHAMPTON (Fibresand)   TUESDAY MARCH 28TH   Lefthand, Sharp Track

op 14/1: blnks reapplied: see 604 (6f, sell h'cap).

692	**OARE KITE** 8 [6] 5-8-9 (40)(bl) A Nicholls (3) 7/1: 354246: Hndy, outpcd/no room 3f out, held after.	nk	29a
667	**NITE OWLER** 14 [10] 6-9-6 (51) C Rutter 16/1: 0-2607: Cl-up halfway, wknd 2f out: see 75.	½	39a
4479}	**NORTHGATE** 99 [3] 4-9-1 (46)(bl) G Bardwell 25/1: 5200-8: Dwelt/bhd, nvr factor: 5 month abs: AW	1	32a
	bow: rnr-up in '99 (rtd 49, mdn h'cap): no form prev: eff at 7f/1m: acts on fast, prob handles firm: eff in blnks.		
667	**NINEACRES** 14 [7] 9-9-11 (56)(bl) W Jones (7) 9/1: 261449: Chsd ldrs 4f: op 7/1: btr 564 (5f).	1¾	39a
620	**CLONOE** 27 [1] 6-9-6 (51) J Weaver 11/2: 404100: Led 4f, sn btn: 10th: op 7/2: btr 574 (sell, made all).	4	26a
675	**SHARP SHUFFLE** 12 [11] 7-9-9 (54) R Fitzpatrick (3) 7/2 FAV: -20240: Smart/al bhd: 11th: op 5/2.	1	27a
449	**CANTGETYOURBREATH** 54 [2] 4-9-3 (48)(bl) J Bosley (7) 25/1: 1-0000: Strugg halfway: 12th: 8 wk abs.	5	11a
12 ran	Time 1m 29.5 (3.3) (P R Kirk) W M Brisbourne Great Ness, Shropshire		

NEWCASTLE   TUESDAY MARCH 28TH   Lefthand, Galloping, Stiff Track

Official Going Str - GOOD (Good/Soft places); Rnd - GOOD/SOFT (Good places). Stalls: Str & 2m - Stands; 10f - Far.

---

755   2.20 EBF MDN 2YO (D)   5f   Soft 99   -49 Slow
£3419   £1052   £526   £262

--	**BLUE FOREST** [9] J Noseda 2-9-0 W R Swinburn 4/1: 1: 2 b c Charwood Forest - Vian (Far Out East)		84
	Prom, styd on well for press over 1f out to get up ins last, drvn out: op 2/1 on debut: Apr foal, cost 38,000gns:		
	half-brother to sev wnrs: eff at 5f, 6f will suit: runs well fresh on soft: responded well to pressure today.		
--	**CHARLIE PARKES** [4] A Berry 2-9-0 K Darley 9/4 JT FAV: 2: 2 ch c Pursuit Of Love - Lucky Parkes	½	82
	(Full Extent), rdn & hdd ins last, not btn far: op 6/4: Mar first foal: dam smart/prolific 5f scorer:		
	eff at 5f, 6f shld suit in time: handles soft grnd & a stiff trk: clr of rem here & the type to win races.		
--	**THORNTOUN DIVA** [3] J S Goldie 2-8-9 Dean McKeown 14/1: 3: 2 ch f Wolfhound - Al Guswa	5	69+
	(Shernazar) Slow away, bhd, ran green & outpcd 2f out, styd on well fnl 2f, nrst fin: op 8/1: Mar foal, cost		
	17,500gns: half-sister to a 7f juv scorer: dam 1m/10f wnr: bred to relish 6/7f+: rate much higher next time.		
--	**RAGAMUFFIN** [7] T D Easterby 2-9-0 R Winston 9/4 JT FAV: 4: Sn hndy, eff ch over 1f out, no	hd	71
	extra ins last under hands-and-heels riding: nicely bckd on debut: Mar foal, cost 10,000gns: half-brother		
	to 2 wnrs: dam multiple 5f scorer: speedily bred & showed some promise for the future here.		
--	**DISPOL LAIRD** [8] 2-9-0 G Duffield 16/1: 5: Slow away, sn in tch, outpcd 2f out, kept on ins	nk	71$
	last: Apr foal, cost 6,200gns: brother to a multiple 5f scorer: sprint bred, got the hang of things late, improve.		
--	**HOPGROVE** [2] 2-8-9 T Williams 14/1: 6: Chsd ldrs, wknd well over 1f out: Feb foal, cost 2,000gns:	5	56
	half-sister to 7f juv scorer: So Factual filly, with M Brittain.		
--	**OREGON FLIGHT** [6] 2-8-9 O Pears 33/1: 7: Slow away, al bhd: May foal, cheaply bght: sprint bred.	6	44
--	**CHEMICALATTRACTION** [1] 2-9-0 F Lynch 14/1: 8: Swerved left start & al bhd on debut.	3	43
712	**MANX GYPSY** 4 [5] 2-8-9 R Lappin 25/1: 49: Keen, prom, ev ch 2f out, sn wknd: see 712.	1	36
9 ran	Time 1m 05.59 (7.39) (Hesmonds Stud) J Noseda Newmarket.		

---

756   2.50 INTER-BET.COM SELLER 3YO+ (G)   6f   Soft 99   -43 Slow
£1862   £532   £266   3 yo rec 3lb

4481}	**PATSY CULSYTH** 99 [13] Don Enrico Incisa 5-8-13 Kim Tinkler 33/1: 0000-1: 5 b m Tragic Role -		45
	Regal Salute (Dara Monarch) Handy, kept on over 1f out to lead just ins fnl 1f, drvn out: no bid, op 14/1, reapp:		
	best effort in '99 when rnr-up on reapp (fill h'cap, rtd 52): '98 Ayr sell h'cap wnr for N Tinkler (rtd 49): eff		
	at 5f, stays by 6/7f on fast, likes soft grnd: eff with/without a visor: possibly best fresh now.		
698	**TANCRED ARMS** 8 [12] D W Barker 4-9-3 F Lynch 7/1: 000-02: 4 b f Clantime - Mischievous Miss	nk	48
	(Niniski) Chsd ldrs, eff 2f out, no extra well ins last, op 5/1: apprec drop to sell company: see 698.		
2550}	**BIRCHWOOD SUN** 99 [1] M Dods 10-9-8 (vis) A Culhane 12/1: 0003-3: 10 b g Bluebird - Shapely Test	1	51
	(Elocutionist) Sn bhd, eff 2f out, ev ch just ins last, only btn 1L: op 6/1 on reapp, well clr of rem: in '99		
	scored early on at Pontefract (seller, rtd 60 at best): '98 wnr at Carlisle (2, h'cap & seller), Redcar (seller)		
	& Newcastle (clmr, rtd 63): eff at 6/7f on any grnd, loves soft/hvy: best in blnks/visor: loves to come late on		
	an uphill fin (esp Carlisle/Pontefract) in sell/claim grade, keep in mind when J Weaver is booked.		
3543}	**HENRY THE HAWK** 99 [7] M Dods 9-9-4 P Goode 10/1: 5204-4: In tch, eff over 2f out, btn over	5	37
	1f out: reapp, stablemate of 3rd: rnr-up twice in '99 (rtd 44): '98 scored at Hamilton (h'cap, rtd 46 & 41a):		
	'97 wnr again at Hamilton: eff with/without vis: likes Hamilton.		
697	**TANCRED TIMES** 8 [3] 5-8-13 Kimberley Hart (5) 9/2: 6-0035: Led 2f, led over 2f out till ins last.	¾	30
3655}	**COLLEGE DEAN** 99 [11] 4-9-4 O Pears 50/1: 0000-6: Bhd, modest late gains: in '99 trained by J J	8	19
	O'Neill, rtd 61 at best, tried a visor: '98 wnr at Hamilton (nurs h'cap, rtd 76): eff over a stiff 6f on gd & soft.		
680	**PALACEGATE TOUCH** 12 [8] 10-9-8 (bl) K Darley 4/1 FAV: 342057: In tch, btn halfway: see 547, 484.	5	13
2989}	**BEYOND THE CLOUDS** 99 [6] 4-9-4 (vis) R Winston 10/1: 3065-8: Led after 2f till over 2f out, no extra.	2½	4
4588}	**THE REPUBLICAN** 99 [2] 3-8-5 T Williams 50/1: 00-9: Slow away, al bhd: reapp.	1¾	0
3678}	**FROSTED AIRE** 99 [10] 4-9-4 G Duffield 7/1: 000P-0: In tch, btn halfway: 10th, reapp.	3½	0
145	**DIMMING OF THE DAY** 99 [4] 3-8-4 (bl) Dean McKeown 7/1: 2133-0: Bhd after 3f: 11th, now	2½	0
	with J J O'Neill, 4 month absence.		
2944}	**CARLISLE BAY** 99 [9] 6-9-4 (BL) J F Egan 16/1: 6/00-0: Al bhd: last, blnks.	18	0
12 ran	Time 1m 19.82 (8.52) (Don Enrico Incisa) Don Enrico Incisa Coverham, N.Yorks.		

---

757   3.25 INTER-BET.COM HCAP 3YO+ 0-95 (C)   1m2f32y   Soft   Inapplicable   [94]
£6857   £2110   £1055   £527   3 yo rec 20lb

4032}	**MILLIGAN** 99 [5] D Nicholls 5-8-9 (75) Pat Eddery 6/1: /000-1: 5 b g Exit To Nowhere - Madigan Mill		86+
	(Mill Reef) Cl-up, strong run to lead 2f out, qcknd clr, readily, eased ins last: val 6L, nicely bckd: recent		
	ready wnr of a nov hdle at Catterick (2m, gd, rtd 115h+, with Miss V Williams): unplcd over inadequate sprint		
	trips on 3 '99 Flat starts & subs well h'capped here: plcd in Listed company in France in '98 (10f): relished		
	this return to 10f: sure to suit: acts on gd, soft & a gall trk: type to run up a quick sequence.		
4363}	**CHIEF MONARCH** 99 [6] R A Fahey 6-8-4 (70) R Winston 9/1: 0/00-2: 6 b g Be My Chief - American	2½	72
	Beauty (Mill Reef) Dwelt, held up, gd hdwy to chall 2f out, kept on for press fnl 1f, not pace of easy wnr: fit		
	from a successful hdles campaign, won at Catterick (mdn) & Musselburgh (2, nov & h'cap hdles, rtd 113h, 2m		
	gd & hvy): well btn both Flat starts in '99, rtd 83 in '98: stays 10f on fast, soft & any trk: on a handy mark.		
4135}	**IPLEDGEALLEGIANCE** 99 [9] E A L Dunlop 4-9-13 (93) J Reid 7/1: 3105-3: 4 b g Alleged - Yafill	shd	95

(Nureyev) Prom, eff to chall 2f out, kept on ins last, not btn far: clr of rem on reapp: in fine '99 form, won at Pontefract (mdn), Sandown & Newbury (h'caps, rtd 94 at best): all 3 wins at 10f, tried 12f: acts on firm, soft grnd & on any trk, likes a stiff one: tough & useful, likes to come late & looks to have retained all his ability.
4499} **CAPTAINS LOG 99** [13] M L W Bell 5-8-6 (72) M Fenton 11/2 FAV: 0660-4: Waited with, eff to chall 2f out, sn no extra: reapp: rnr-up once in '99 (rtd 80 at best): '98 wnr at Warwick (mdn) & Newcastle (h'cap, rtd 82): eff over 10/12f on firm & gd/soft grnd: handles any trk & has run well fresh. 4 **69**
4359} **AL AZHAR 99** [12] 6-10-0 (94) F Lynch 40/1: 5430-5: Held up, kept on nicely fnl 2f, nvr dngrs: reapp: in '99 trained by I Balding, plcd twice (rtd '96): missed '98, '97 wnr at Doncaster (h'cap, rtd 96): eff at 1m, stays 12f well on fast, soft & on any trk, likes Doncaster: encouraging reapp under a big weight for new stable & shld win again with a slight drop in the ratings. 2½ **88**
4484} **CELESTIAL WELCOME 99** [14] 5-9-5 (85) A Culhane 6/1: 6006-6: Waited with, effort 2f out, no dngr: reapp: '99 wnr at Newcastle (reapp) & Haydock (2, h'caps incl val Old Newton Cup, rtd 91): '98 wnr at Hamilton (rtd mdn), Carlisle, Newcastle & Redcar (h'caps): eff at 1m, stays 12f well on firm, hvy & on any trk, likes a gall one, esp Newcastle/Haydock: has run well fresh under big weights: tough, back on her last winning mark. ¾ **77**
73 **EL SALIDA 99** [3] 4-8-9 (75) J Carroll 16/1: 4344-7: Waited with, eff over 2f out, onepcd: recent jmp rnr. ¾ **66**
380 **FIORI 66** [4] 4-9-4 (84) M Tebbutt 10/1: 50-628: Hld up rear, hdwy over 2f out, sn short of room, kept on, not given hard time: abs & an encouraging run: back on a winning mark, win again, prob over further. ½ **75+**
695 **PARABLE 8** [7] 4-8-2 (68) R Ffrench 16/1: 6-5139: In tch, eff over 2f out, no impress: btr 671 (12f). ½ **58**
4475} **DISPOL ROCK 99** [2] 4-8-8 (74) K Darley 20/1: 2160-0: In tch, btn 2f out: 10th, reapp. 1½ **62**
4510} **COLWAY RITZ 99** [10] 6-8-9 (75) T Williams 33/1: 6500-0: Led over 2f out, sn hdd & wknd: reapp. 2½ **59**
4317} **SPREE VISION 99** [16] 4-7-12 (64) Dale Gibson 16/1: 6000-0: Handy, wknd 2f out: 12th, chngd stable. ¾ **47**
611 **TROIS 28** [8] 4-8-5 (71) G Duffield 12/1: 1-1030: Cl-up, rdn & btn over 2f out: 13th: btr 611 (fibresand). nk **54**
4562} **SALIGO 99** [1] 5-8-9 (75) Kim Tinkler 50/1: 3000-0: Led till over 2f out, wknd qckly: 15th: reapp. **0**
-- **Elvis Reigns** [15] 4-9-5 (85) L Dettori 20/1: 124 **Il Principe 99** [17] 6-9-0 (80) J F Egan 25/1:
4335} **Atlantic Charter 99** [18] 4-8-4 (70) Dean McKeown 20/1:
632 **Tightrope 24** [11] 5-7-12 (64)(2ow)(4oh) F Norton 14/1:
18 ran Time 2m 17.7 (11.2) (G H Leatham) D Nicholls Sessay, N.Yorks.

758 4.00 INTERBET HCAP 3YO+ 0-85 (D) 5f Soft 99 +11 Fast [83]
£3835 £1180 £590 £295 3 yo rec 12lb Two Groups, 4 on far side probably favoured

678 **BEDEVILLED 12** [3] T D Barron 5-8-12 (67) Lynsey Hanna (7) 12/1: -20251: 5 ch g Beveled - Putout (Dowsing) Made virtually all far side, qcknd clr 1f out, styd on well, drvn out: best time of day: fit from the AW, rnr-up twice (rtd 71a): '99 Beverley wnr (mdn, rtd 71): eff at 5/6f on fast & soft grnd, handles fibresand: best up with/forcing the pace on any trk: made most of fav'able low draw today. **73**
4413} **MUNGO PARK 99** [9] M Dods 6-9-2 (71) A Culhane 7/2 FAV: 5200-2: 6 b g Selkirk - River Dove (Riverman) Mid-div stands side, imprvd over 1f out, fin well but no ch with wnr: nicely bckd, reapp: '99 Thirsk wnr (class stks), also plcd sev times (h'caps, rtd 84 at best): '98 wnr here at Newcastle (2), Beverley & Nottingham (h'caps, rtd 80, with Mrs J Ramsden): '97 Carlisle & Newcastle wnr (h'cap): stays 6f, best held up for a late run over 5f: acts on any grnd & on any trk, loves Newcastle: has tried blnks: spot on next time & h'capped to win races. 2 **72**
677 **FIRE DOME 12** [13] D Nicholls 8-10-0 (83) Alex Greaves 12/1: 004-03: 8 ch g Salt Dome - Penny Habit (Habitat) In tch stands side, fin strongly fnl 1f despite hanging left, not given a hard ride: top-weight: likes Sandown, plenty to like about this effort & spot on next time: see 677 (AW). 1¾ **82**
533 **SWEET MAGIC 40** [4] L R Lloyd James 9-8-6 (60)(t)(1ow) K Darley 50/1: 064004: Dsptd lead far side, kept on fnl 1f but not pace of ldrs: 6 wk abs: best up with/forcing the pace, handles any trk: see 146. shd **58**
4391} **BLESSINGINDISGUISE 99** [1] 7-9-8 (77)(bl) T Lucas 14/1: 0010-5: Dwelt far side, sn recovered & prom, ev ch dist, no extra ins last: drifted from 9/1, reapp: '99 wnr here at Newcastle (h'cap, rtd 79): '98 wnr at York & Ascot (val rtd h'cap, rtd 101): '97 wnr at Redcar, Haydock, Ayr & again at Ascot (val h'cap, rtd 98): stays 6f, all wins at 5f: acts on firm, gd/soft grnd & on gall trks, likes Ascot: best in blnks, can run well fresh: likes to force the pace: still nicely h'capped & spot on next time. ½ **73**
702 **LAGO DI VARANO 5** [12] 8-9-12 (81)(vis) Dean McKeown 9/1: 064-06: Mid-div stands side, kept on under press fnl 1f, nvr nr ldrs: qck reapp: '99 wnr at York & Sandown (h'caps, rtd 87): '98 Ripon wnr (h'cap, rtd 93), also plcd in the Ayr Gold Cup: '97 wnr here at Newcastle (h'cap): eff at 6f, all wins at 5f: acts on firm & soft grnd, handles any trk: wears blnks/visor, loves to force the pace: v tough & game gelding. 2½ **72**
4006} **SIR SANDROVITCH 99** [2] 4-9-2 (71) P Hanagan (7) 16/1: 4600-7: Slowly away far side, recovered to chase ldrs, no impress fnl 2f: reapp: '99 Musselburgh wnr (mdn), subs fast finishing 2nd at Sandown (h'cap, rtd 78): v eff at 5f, has tried 6f: handles a sharp or gall trk: must have fast or firm grnd: needs to be held up for a late chall: on a winning mark when the grnd turns in his favour. 1½ **59**
4610} **GORETSKI 99** [15] 7-9-6 (75) J Carroll 20/1: 0020-8: Prom stands side, led that group halfway, wknd. nk **62**
564 **JAWHARI 35** [10] 6-8-9 (64) F Norton 8/1: 0-0109: Prom 4f stands side: see 518 (AW). 2 **47**
4612} **ELVINGTON BOY 99** [11] 3-8-7 (74) O Pears 25/1: 2100-0: Led stands side 3f, drifted left & fdd: 10th. 2 **53**
4450} **MARY JANE 99** [5] 5-8-6 (61) Kim Tinkler 20/1: 5215-0: In tch 3f in centre: op 14/1, 11th: new stable. ¾ **38**
47 **MALADERIE 99** [7] 6-8-5 (60) F Lynch 20/1: 0000-0: Al bhd stands side, fin 12th: s/mate of 2nd. 2½ **32**
2400} **WATERFORD SPIRIT 99** [8] 4-9-6 (75) C Lowther 16/1: 1040-0: Al bhd stands side, fin 13th: op 10/1. 1¼ **45**
3600} **POP SHOP 99** [6] 3-9-4 (85) R Cochrane 16/1: 1662-0: Bhd fnl 3f on stands side: fin 14th. 1½ **52**
4610} **PANDJOJOE 99** [14] 4-8-7 (62) R Winston 6/1: 0000-0: Dwelt, al bhd stands side; fin last. 8 **13**
15 ran Time 1m 02.59 (4.39) (Mrs J Hazell) T D Barron Maunby, N.Yorks.

759 4.30 INTER-BET.COM MDN 3YO+ (D) 7f str Soft 99 -12 Slow
£3848 £1184 £592 £296 3 yo rec 15lb 2 Groups (far side favoured)

4390} **DANCING BAY 99** [5] Miss J A Camacho 3-8-11 R Cochrane 25/1: 50-1: 3 b g Suave Dancer - Kabayil (Dancing Brave) Trkd ldrs far side, imprvd to lead ent fnl 1f, rdn clr: some promise on 2 juv starts (rtd 72 at best): dam 10f wnr, sire a top-class 12f performer: eff at 7f, bred to apprec mid-dists: acts on soft grnd & on a gall trk, runs well fresh: open to further improvement as he steps up in trip. **88**
4136} **CABRIAC 99** [6] J L Dunlop 3-8-11 Pat Eddery 4/6 FAV: 20-2: 3 br c Machiavellian - Chief Bee (Chief's Crown) Prom far side, led that group halfway & overall ldr over 1f out, hdd ins last & not pace to repel wnr: hvly bckd, reapp: twice rcd in '99, rnr-up at Newmarket on debut (mdn, rtd 95): 70,000gns purchase, dam a 9/14f wnr: eff at 7f, bred to apprec 1m/10f+: acts on soft, rtd higher on firm grnd: has shown enough to win a mdn. 3 **83**
-- **PENNYS PRIDE** [8] Mrs M Reveley 5-9-7 A Culhane 16/1: 3: 5 b m Pips Pride - Mursuma (Rarity) Dwelt far side, sn recovered & in tch, chall over 1f out, not qckn ins fnl 1f: Flat debut: fit from the jumps, dual NH Flat race wnr (eff at 2m on gd & soft): half-sister to smart NH performers Direct Route, Joe Mac & Penny A Day: fine effort over this inadequate 7f trip, one to keep in mind over mid-dists: shld win a mdn. 3½ **73+**

4277} **MOON SOLITAIRE 99** [10] E A L Dunlop 3-8-11 J Reid 10/1: 6-4: Prom far side, ev ch dist, fdd ins last: 1   76
tchd 14/1, reapp: 6th in a Lingfield mdn (rtd 75) on sole juv start: 12,000gns brother to a 6f wnr: half-
brother to a 12f wnr: shld apprec 1m+ this term: fitter next time.

--   **TOUGH TIMES** [14] 3-8-11 R Winston 66/1: 5: Chsd ldr stands side, imprvd to lead over 2f out till   4   70
hdd ent fnl 1f, fdd: first home on unfav'able far side on racecourse bow: IR 9,000gns purchase: bred to apprec
mid-dists: ran well from an unfav'able draw today, sure to learn from this.

1264} **FLYING CARPET 99** [1] 3-8-6 K Darley 33/1: 0-6: Dwelt & rear far side, late prog, nvr nr ldrs: unplcd   2½   61
at York (nov, 5f) on sole juv start: dam a sprinter, sire a top-class miler: showed some promise here.

2156} **NORTHERN ECHO 99** [9] 3-8-11 Dale Gibson 100/1: 0-7: Chsd ldrs far side, wknd fnl 2f.   1¼   64

--   **NIGHT SIGHT** [15] 3-8-11 M Roberts 7/1: 8: Al bhd stands side, nvr dngrs: op 5/1: poor high draw.   8   50

1435} **HAPPY HOOLIGAN 99** [3] 3-8-11 D Holland 7/1: 2-9: Prom far side, lost pl halfway, no ch after.   3   45

4258} **ADULATION 99** [2] 6-9-12 Dean McKeown 16/1: 4005-0: In tch till halfway on far side: fin 10th,   ¾   44
recent jumps rnr, new stable.

--   **GRAND BAHAMIAN** [4] 3-8-11 L Dettori 9/1: 0: Slowly away, al bhd on far side: fin 11th, op 5/1.   ¾   43

--   **PRECISION** [16] 5-9-12 J F Egan 200/1: 0/0: Clr ldr stands side, hdd over 2f out, wknd: fin 13th.   0

556   **Mystic Gem 36** [13] 4-9-12 C Lowther 50/1:   4455} **Grub Street 99** [11] 4-9-12 T Williams 100/1:
3428} **Dunkeld Champ 99** [7] 3-8-11 G Duffield 100/1:   --   **Newryman** [12] 5-9-12 G Arnolda (7) 500/1:
16 ran   Time 1m 31.84 (7.74)   (Elite Racing Club)   Miss J A Camacho Norton, N.Yorks.

---

760   5.05 INTERBET HCAP 4YO+ 0-70 (E)   2m   Soft   Inapplicable   [70]
       £2853   £878   £439   £219   4 yo rec 5 lb

3270} **SWIFTWAY 99** [11] K W Hogg 6-8-2 (44) J Bramhill 4/1: U/34-1: 6 ch g Anshan - Solemn Occasion   49+
(Secreto) Chsd ldrs, lost pl ent str, short of room & switched 2f out, styd on strongly to lead cl-home, won going
away: well bckd: recent jumps rnr, Sept '99 wnr at M Rasen (h'cap hdle, rtd 118h, eff at 2½m/3m on fast & soft):
in '99 plcd here at Newcastle (h'cap, rtd 49): Musselburgh & Carlisle hdle wnr in 98/99: '98 Flat wnr at Beverley
(h'cap, rtd 51): stays 2m on firm & soft: likes a gall trk, esp Newcastle: fairly h'capped & can follow up.

4587} **CINDER HILLS 99** [7] M W Easterby 5-9-4 (60) T Lucas 9/1: 0/00-2: 5 ch m Deploy - Dame Du Moulin   ¾   62
(Shiny Tenth) Led 1f, remained prom & regained lead 4f out, kept on well fnl 1f but not pace of repel wnr cl-
home: won a h'cap hdle here at Newcastle 7 wks ago (rtd 95h, eff at 2½m on gd & hvy): unplcd on both '99 Flat
starts: '98 wnr at Ripon (2, h'caps, rtd 70): eff at 10/12f, stays a stiff 2m: acts on fast & hvy, handles
f/sand: likes to run-up with/force the pace on a sharpish or gall trk: fairly h'capped & shld go one better.

644   **ONEFOURSEVEN 22** [9] D Shaw 7-7-13 (40) (1ow) F Norton 20/1: 4/0003: 7 b g Jumbo Hirt -   1½   41
Dominance (Dominion) Held up, hdwy to ch ldrs 2f out, kept on under press ins last: fit from AW, well h'capped.

4329} **SPARTAN ROYALE 99** [5] P Monteith 6-9-11 (67) P Hanagan (7) 10/1: 0342-4: Rear, smooth hdwy to   shd   67
chall 2f out, no extra ins fnl 1f: tchd 14/1: recent jumps rnr, earlier this winter won here at Newcastle (mdn)
& Ayr (h'cap hdle, rtd 111h, eff at 2m on gd/soft & hvy): failed to win on the Flat in '99, tho' rnr-up 4 times
(10/13f h'caps, rtd 69 at best): '98 Carlisle wnr (mdn h'cap, rtd 59): eff at 13f, stays 2m1f: acts on fast,
loves gd & soft: handles a stiff/gall track: travelled like a wnr, found less than expected under press.

4231} **LEDGENDRY LINE 99** [15] 7-9-4 (60) A Culhane 11/2: 2240-5: Held up, imprvg when hmpd 3f out,   1½   59
short of room again 2f out, styd on but ch had gone: op 7/1: last rcd over jumps 8 wks ago, won at Kelso &
Sedgefield (nov chases, rtd 115c, stays 3m1f on firm & hvy): plcd sev times on the Flat in '99 (h'caps, rtd 62):
back in 97/98 won at Kelso & Newcastle (nov hdles, rtd 128h): '97 Flat wnr at Ayr (mdn h'cap, rtd 75): eff at
12f, stays 2m+: acts on firm & hvy: fairly h'capped now, no luck in running today: one to keep in mind.

--   **CASTLETOWN COUNT** [13] 8-7-10 (38) (2oh) P Fessey 25/1: 0240/6: In tch, onepce fnl 2f: fit from   1   36
the jumps, earlier won at Catterick (h'cap chase, rtd 102c, eff at 2½m on gd & soft): 98/99 Catterick wnr (nov
h'cap): missed '99 on the Flat, unplcd on sole start prev term: back in '96 rnr-up in a seller (rtd 55):
'94 Redcar wnr (sell, rtd 58): eff at 10f, prob stays 2m: acts on firm & soft: with M Easterby.

4447} **STORMLESS 99** [3] 9-8-3 (42) (3ow) O Pears 66/1: 000-7: Rear, kept on fnl 2f, nrst fin: jmps fit.   4   40

4085} **GIVE AN INCH 99** [1] 5-9-13 (69) T Williams 6/1: 1410-8: Imprvd from rear to chase ldrs 4f out,   ½   63
wknd dist: drifter from 7/2, top-weight, reapp.

542   **ALMAMZAR 39** [4] 10-7-10 (38) (t) (18oh) Kim Tinkler 100/1: 054409: Rear, mod late hdwy, nvr dngrs.   1   31

552   **HAPPY DAYS 38** [8] 5-7-10 (38) (1oh) Iona Wands (5) 20/1: 000-00: Chsd ldrs 13f, fdd: fin 10th.   11   21

4054} **PLEASANT MOUNT 99** [12] 4-9-2 (63) K Darley 2/1 FAV: 1112-0: In tch, ev ch ent str, wknd 2f out: 3   43
hvly bckd from 9/2, fin 11th on reapp: in fine form at the end of '99, won at Beverley (mdn h'cap), Thirsk &
Redcar (h'caps, rtd 63): eff at 14f/2m on firm & hvy grnd: handles any trk: capable of much better.

542   **BLACK ICE BOY 39** [2] 9-8-4 (44) (vis) (2ow) Dean McKeown 16/1: 10P-50: Made most till 4f out, fdd.   1½   24

1571} **Highfield Fizz 99** [6] 8-8-3 (45) G Duffield 20/1:   318 **Musalse 75** [10] 5-7-12 (40) Dale Gibson 16/1:
--   **Inclination** [14] 6-7-13 (40) (1ow) R Ffrench 66/1:
15 ran   Time 3m 47.05 (21.55)   (Anthony White)   K W Hogg Isle Of Man.

SANDOWN   TUESDAY MARCH 28TH   Righthand, Galloping Track, Stiff Uphill Finish

Official Going   5f - GOOD/FIRM; 1m - GOOD (GOOD/FIRM back straight). Stalls: 5f - Far Side; 1m - Inside.

---

761   4.10 SUMMIT HCAP 3YO 0-90 (C)   1m rnd   Good   Inapplicable   [93]
       £7150   £2200   £1100   £550

*591   **BONAGUIL 31** [1] C F Wall 3-8-13 (78) R Mullen 2/1 JT FAV: 04-11: 3 b g Septieme Ciel - Chateaubrook   85
(Alleged) Rear, shkn up ent fnl 3f, ran on to lead dist despite rider dropping whip, shade cosy: well bckd: earlier
impressive wnr at Lingfield (AW bow, mdn auct, rtd 77a): unpld both '99 starts (mdn, rtd 77), bids gelded: imprvd
since stepped up to 1m, shld get 10f: acts on gd grnd & equitrack, sharp or stiff trk: runs well fresh.

4474} **SAHARA SPIRIT 99** [3] E A L Dunlop 3-8-11 (76) G Carter 8/1: 340-2: 3 b g College Chapel - Desert   1¾   78
Palace (Green Desert) Pulled hard bhd ldrs, shkn up to lead 2f out till 1f out, kept on for press: op 5/1 on
reapp/h'cap bow: plcd on debut last term (mdn auct, rtd 83): eff at 6/7f, stays 1m: acts on gd & soft.

636   **PEDRO PETE 24** [5] M R Channon 3-8-5 (70) A Daly 8/1: 0-4143: 3 ch g Fraam - Stride Home   1½   69
(Absalom) Led till 2f out, onepace for pressure: op 5/1: fair run back on turf, return to 10f shld suit: see 597.

3664} **NOBLE PURSUIT 99** [2] T G Mills 3-9-7 (86) A Clark 2/1 FAV: 412-4: Pld hard, in tch, pshd along   1¾   81
appr fnl 2f, no impress on ldrs: hvly bckd, possibly just held it: '99 wnr at Salisbury (auct mdn, rtd 87 at best):
eff at 7f, shld get at least 1m: acts on fast & gd grnd, prob any trk: sharper next time.

206   **INSIGHTFUL 99** [4] 3-9-1 (80) Dane O'Neill 4/1: 5312-5: Cl-up till 2f out, onepace & sn short of room: 4   67

SANDOWN

TUESDAY MARCH 28TH   Righthand, Galloping Track, Stiff Uphill Finish

op 11/4, 15 wk abs: back up in trip: btr 108 (made all over a sharp 7f on equitrack).
5 ran   Time 1m 46.57 (7.57)   (Mrs R M S Neave)   C F Wall Newmarket.

---

762   **4.45 STAR & GARTER FILLIES MDN 2YO (D)**   5f   **Good/Firm Slow**
        £3428   £1055   £527   £263

--   **MILLENNIUM MAGIC** [5] J G Portman 2-8-11 A Beech (5) 20/1: 1: 2 b f Magic Ring - Country Spirit   **90**
(Sayf El Arab) Cl-up, led halfway, edged left & right under press fnl 1½f but kept on well: op 12/1, slow time:
1,200gns Apr foal, dam unrcd: sire a precocious juv: eff over a stiff 5f on fast grnd: runs well fresh.
--   **CELTIC ISLAND** [1] W G M Turner 2-8-11 A Daly 9/1: 2: 2 b f Celtic Swing - Chief Island (Be My   1¼   **86**
Chief) Struggled to go pace till kept on strongly fnl 1f, too late: op 5/2: Jan first foal, dam half-sister to sev wnrs,
sire outstanding 2yo, won French Derby at 3: gd run considering inadequate trip, handles fast grnd.
--   **SERVICEABLE** [2] J M P Eustace 2-8-11 J Tate 4/1: 3: 2 ch f Pursuit Of Love - Absaloute Service   2   **80**
(Absalom) Chsd ldrs, onepace ent fnl 1f: op 3/1: Jan foal, half-sister to 3 wnrs, dam 5f juv wnr, sire 6f/1m wnr.
--   **QUANTUM LADY** [6] B R Millman 2-8-11 P Robinson 5/2 JT FAV: 4: Led till halfway, no extra bef dist: 4   **70**
well bckd: 6,000gns Mujadil Mar foal, dam 6/7f wnr, sire a fast 2yo: surely shown something at home: sharper trk?
--   **NIGHT FALL** [7] 2-8-11 Dane O'Neill 5/2 JT FAV: 5: Slow away, al bhd: well bckd tho' op 7/4:   8   **50**
IR 46,000gns Night Shift Mar foal: dam multiple wnr in France from the age of 3: sire a speed influence.
--   **KWAHERI** [3] 2-8-11 S Whitworth 14/1: W: Refused to enter stalls: IR 21,000gns Efisio Apr foal,   **0**
half-sister to 7 wnrs up to mid-dists, dam 10/12f wnr: sire 6f/1m wnr: with Mrs P Dutfield.
6 ran   Time 1m 02.82 (3.22)   (Madhatter Racing)   J G Portman Compton, Berks.

---

763   **5.20 M. HEATON-ELLIS HCAP 3YO+ 0-80 (D)**   5f   **Good/Firm Fair**   [78]
        £4309   £1326   £663   £331   3 yo rec 12lb   Rcd centre/far side - high no's (far side) favoured

4298} **FEARBY CROSS** 99 [15] W J Musson 4-9-6 (70) G Carter 16/1: 0006-1: 4 b g Unblest - Two Magpies   76
(Doulab) Bhd ldrs, rdn appr fnl 1f, strong run to lead towards fin, flashed tail: narrowly on reapp: one decent
effort for J Bethell last term (h'cap, rtd 83), tumbled down the h'cap: '98 Ayr wnr (auct mdn, rtd 90): eff over
a stiff 5f, 6f suits, tried 7f: acts on fast & soft grnd, without blnks: runs well fresh: well h'capped.
630   **PRINCE PROSPECT** 24 [11] Mrs L Stubbs 4-9-13 (77) J P Spencer 12/1: -01022: 4 b g Lycius -   nk   82
Princess Dechtra (Bellypha) Front rank, rdn to lead appr fnl 1f, ran on but hdd fnl 50y: just btn, op 10/1,
top-weight, AW fit: remains in fine form, eff btwn 5f & 7f: likes Sandown: see 376 (equitrack).
47   **KHALIK** 99 [10] Miss Gay Kelleway 6-9-0 (64)(t) P Robinson 20/1: 0000-3: 6 b g Lear Fan - Silver   1¼   65
Dollar (Shirley Heights) Cl-up, eff appr fnl 1f, kept on but unable to chall: gd run, reapp: won 1st 2 in '99 at
Salisbury & Lingfield (h'caps, rtd 64): eff at 5/7f on fast & gd/soft, any trk: tried blnks, wears a t-strap.
*673   **LORD HIGH ADMIRAL** 14 [12] C G Cox 12-8-5 (55)(vis) S Drowne 11/2 JT FAV: 004-14: Led till 1½f   shd   56
out, onepace: well bckd, op 9/2: a bold attempt to land the race named in honour of his late trainer: see 763.
660   **KING OF PERU** 17 [8] 7-9-7 (71)(vis) C Cogan (5) 12/1: 022-55: Well plcd, rdn 2f out, no impression.   1½   68
691   **BRAMBLE BEAR** 10 [13] 6-8-2 (52) N Pollard 8/1: -46626: Towards rear, some late hdwy but nvr dngrs.   ½   48
697   **SEALED BY FATE** 8 [14] 5-8-4 (54)(t) P Doe 7/1: 000-57: Rear, hdwy 2f out, onepace dist: AW fit.   1½   46
4010} **AT LARGE** 99 [16] 6-9-6 (70) L Newton 10/1: 4200-8: Restrained & bhd till styd on appr fnl 1f: tchd 12/1, 1¼   59
stablemate wnr: '99 run-up here at Sandown (h'cap, rtd 74, first time blnks, J Toller): '97 Nottingham wnr (h'cap,
rtd 80, J Fanshawe): eff at 5/7f on firm & soft, likes stiff trks: best without blnks: looks well h'capped.
*678   **EASTERN TRUMPETER** 12 [4] 4-8-13 (63) K Fallon 11/2 JT FAV: 5-1419: Rcd in centre, nvr any ch   1   49
with far side: nicely bckd from 7/1 on turf return: unfavourably drawn, probably best ignored: likes soft grnd.
691   **SHADY DEAL** 10 [7] 4-8-1 (51) G Baker (7) 33/1: 400300: Towards centre, al around same pl: 10th,   ½   36
turf return: unsuitd by drop back to 5f & could do with stronger handling: see 391.
525   **BRUTAL FANTASY** 41 [9] 6-9-2 (66) J Fortune 20/1: 030600: Prom till fdd ent fnl 2f: 11th, 6 wk abs.   ½   49
288   **DIAMOND GEEZER** 80 [1] 4-8-13 (63) Dane O'Neill 14/1: 123-50: Centre, nvr on terms with far side: 12th. nk   45
678   **WHIZZ KID** 12 [2] 6-8-9 (59) A Beech (5) 25/1: 100-00: Nvr in it centre: 13th, AW fit, see 678.   ½   40
4494} **Cd Flyer** 99 [5] 3-9-3 (79) T Quinn 20/1:   4227} **Half Tone** 99 [6] 8-7-10 (46)(bl)(1oh) J Mackay(7) 25/1:
622   **Seren Teg** 26 [3] 4-8-7 (57)(bl) A Clark 16/1:
16 ran   Time 1m 01.36 (1.76)   (Mrs Rita Brown)   W J Musson Newmarket.

NAD AL SHEBA (Dubai)

SATURDAY MARCH 25TH   Lefthand, Flat, Fair Track

Official Going   TURF - GOOD; Dirt - FAST.

---

764   **2.00 LISTED GODOLPHIN MILE 4YO+**   1m rnd   Dirt
        £91463   £30488   £15244   £7622

3434} **CONFLICT** 99 [10] N Robb 4-8-9 T Durcan : 16-111: 4 b c Warning - La Dama Bonita (El Gran Senor)   **109a**
Prom, gd hdwy to lead over 1f out, collared ins last but rallied v gamely to get up again cl-home: recently won
twice here in Dubai: in '99 trained by C Brittain, won at Haydock (h'cap, rtd 100): '99 Leicester wnr (stks):
best up with/forcing the pace over 1m/10.5f on gd/soft & dirt: v useful, game & improving.
4485} **IFTITAH** 99 [11] Saeed bin Suroor 4-8-9 D O'Donohoe : 1/5-32: 4 ch c Gone West - Mur Taasha   shd   **108a**
(Riverman) With ldr, styd on well to lead ins fnl 1f, hard rdn & collared cl-home, just btn: rtd 88 sole '99
start: '98 wnr at Newmarket (stks, rtd 102): eff at 7f/1m on firm & dirt: runs well fresh: lightly rcd, useful.
184   **MUHTATHIR** 99 [9] Saeed bin Suroor 5-9-6 L Dettori : 5414-3: 5 ch h Elmaamul - Majmu (Al Nasr)   nk   **118a**
Led after 1f till over 1f out, kept on well for press ins last, just held in a 3-way photo: top-weight: in '99
won at San Siro (Gr 1, rtd 118 at best): '98 wnr at Doncaster, Newbury (Gr 3), Goodwood (Gr 2) & rnr-up in French
2,000 Guineas (rtd 120): best up with/forcing the pace over 7f/1m on firm, dirt & poss hvy: tough & high-class.
2599} **SIEGE** 99 [13] Saeed bin Suroor 4-8-10 S Guillot : 2-1518: Bhd, some late gains: in '99 trained by   3½   **98a**
Sir M Stoute, won at Kempton (mdn), subs rnr-up in 2 val h'caps (rtd 106): eff over 1m/10.3f on gd/firm, poss dirt.
*666   **BLUE SNAKE** 13 [3] 4-8-9 J Carroll : 1-1519: Led 1f, btn 2f out: fin 9th: see 666.   2   **93a**
4320} **LATE NIGHT OUT** 99 [2] 5-8-9 K Fallon : 4524-0: Sn outpcd eff over 3f out, no impress: 10th.   4½   **85a**
4248} **SLIP STREAM** 99 [6] 4-8-10 (VIS) J D Bailey : 55-540: Al bhd: 11th: visor.   2   **80a**
--   **THUNDER SKY** [6] 4-8-9 P Robinson : 5540/0: Bhd from halfway: 12th, 2 year abs.   2   **75a**
13 ran   Time 1m 36.4   (Sheikh Marwan Al Maktoum)   N Robb Dubai

765
2.35 UAE DERBY 3YO   1m1f rnd   Dirt
£182927 £60976 £30488 £15244

-- **CHINA VISIT** [2] Saeed bin Suroor 3-9-0 R Hills : 1-1: 3 b c Red Ransom - Furajet (The Minstrel) **120a**
Cl-up, styd on to lead over 1f out, drvn clr fnl 1f, readily: reapp: won sole '99 start by 8L at Deauville (with D Loder): stays 9f well, 10f will act: acts on dirt: lightly raced & potentially high-class, looks sure to win Group races & connections believe he will make his presence felt in the 2,000 Guineas or Kentucky Derby (10f).

4025} **BACHIR 99** [1] Saeed bin Suroor 3-9-0 S Guillot : 133-12: 3 b c Desert Style - Morning Welcome 4¼ **112a**
(Be My Guest) Led after 2f till over 1f out, not pace of wng stable-mate: recent wnr here in Dubai: useful juv, won at Chepstow (mdn auct) & broke juv course record at Goodwood (Gr2, with J Godsden, subs rtd 108 when plcd in a Gr 1): eff at 6/7f, stays 9f: acts on firm, v soft & dirt, any trk: retains all his ability.

-- **CURULE 99** [16] K McLaughlin 3-9-0 E Ahern : -4133: 3 br c Go For Gin - Reservation (Cryptoclearance) nk **111a**
Sn bhd, kept on well over 1f out, nrst fin.

4137} **CRIMPLENE 99** [13] C E Brittain 3-8-11 P Robinson : 3013-6: Prom, btn 2f out: fin 6th: in '99 won 3½ **101a**
at Redcar (auct mdn) & Salisbury (stks), also 2½L 3rd in Gr1 Cheveley Park (rtd 106): eff at 6f, 7f/1m shld suit (dam styd mid-dists): useful, would enjoy listed company back in Britain.

9 **COMPTON BOLTER 99** [3] 3-9-0 D Holland : 123-48: Chsd ldrs, rdn & onepace fnl 2f: fin 8th: in 1 **102a**
'99 scored at Chepstow (auct mdn) & plcd in a Gr 2 (rtd 107 at best): eff over 7f/1m on firm, best run on hvy: handles any trk & has run well fresh: v useful.

4611} **SHOUF AL BADOU 99** [15] 3-9-0 N Pollard : 4111-0: Nvr a factor: reapp, fin 12th: won fnl 3 as a juv, 6 **92a**
at W'hampton (2, mdn & stks, rtd 97a) & Doncaster (stks, rtd 97): eff at 7f/1m on fast, hvy & fibresand: acts on a gall or sharp trk: useful & progressive, will find easier opportunities.

656 **NIGHT STYLE 21** [12] 3-9-0 J Reid : 011-60: Chsd ldrs, till btn 2f out: fin 13th, see 656. 6 **82a**

4482} **TRINCULO 99** [7] 3-9-0 O Peslier : 1354-0: Al bhd: 15th, reapp, longer trip. 11½ **67a**

4558} **PARADISE GARDEN 99** [10] 3-9-0 K Fallon : 1224-0: Prom, wknd over 3f out: reapp, turf form prev. 2 **63a**
16 ran   Time 1m 49.5   (Godolphin)   Saeed bin Suroor Dubai

766
3.35 LISTED DUBAI GOLDEN SHAHEEN 4YO+   6f   Dirt
£365854 £121951 £60976 £30488

17 **BIG JAG** [10] T Pinfield 7-9-0 A Solis : 133-21: 7 br g Kleven - In Hopes (Affirmed) **121a**
Chsd ldrs, led 2f out, rdn clr on far side: 3L 3rd in Gr1 Breeders Cup Sprint last term (rtd 114a): eff at 6f on dirt: v speedy & top class sprinter.

4246} **BERTOLINI 99** [12] Saeed bin Suroor 4-9-0 (vis) S Guillot : 3320-2: 4 b c Danzig - Aquilegia 4 **112a**
(Alydar) In tch, hdwy 2f out, kept on for press ins last on stands side, no impress on wnr: in '99 won at Newmarket (Listed Free h'cap, with J Gosden), also placed in Gr 1 July Stks, & Sprint Cup at Haydock (rtd 122 at best): '98 wnr at Newmarket (Gr 3): eff at 6/7f on firm, soft grnd, handles dirt: likes a gall trk: eff with/without a visor, disapp sole start in blnks: has run well fresh: v tough & high-class.

-- **BET ME BEST** [16] W Elliott Walden 4-9-0 (BL) J D Bailey : 602-43: 4 ch c Barberstown - Tough shd **112a**
Wendy (Tough Assignment) Chsd ldrs, eff over 2f out, no extra stands side ins last: tried blnks, useful.

16 **LEND A HAND 99** [7] Saeed bin Suroor 5-9-0 L Dettori : 0124-6: Nvr went pace in 6th: in '99 5 **100a**
scored at Dubai (Listed, by 6L) & Newbury (Gr 3, rtd 120), also narrowly btn 4th in Breeders Cup Mile: with M Johnston in '98, rnr-up in 2,000 Guineas at Newmarket: eff at 7.3f/1m on firm, gd/soft & dirt: runs well fresh: high-class & tough, will find this behind him.

4100} **BOLD EDGE 99** [2] 5-9-0 Dane O'Neill : 2041-0: Prom, ev ch over 2f out, no extra ins last: reapp, fin 11 **80a**
13th: in '99 won at Newmarket (List, reapp) & Ascot (2, Gr 2's, Cork & Orrery & Diadam, rtd 120): '98 wnr at Leicester, Newbury & Newmarket: stays 7f, best when able to dominate at 6f: handles any grnd & likes a stiff trk, esp Newmarket or Ascot: has run well fresh: high-class on turf, expect much better.
14 ran   Time 1m 08.1   (Julius H Zolezzi)   T Pinfield Santa Anita, California

767
4.10 GR 3 DUBAI SHEEMA TURF CLASSIC 4YO+   1m4f   Good
£731707 £243902 £212951 £60976   4 yo rec 2 lb

4247} **FANTASTIC LIGHT 99** [16] Sir Michael Stoute 4-8-9 K Fallon : 3110-1: 4 b c Rahy - Jood (Nijinsky) **124**
Waited with, gd hdwy over 2f out, led appr fnl 1f, rdn clr: reapp: in fine '99 form, wng at Sandown (Gr 3, reapp), York (Gr 2 Great Voltigeur) & Newbury (Listed, rtd 125): '98 wnr at Sandown (2): eff at 10/12f on fast, soft & any trk: has run well fresh: tough, high-class & progressive: now to be trained by Saeed bin Suroor, win more Gr races.

2326} **CAITANO 99** [8] A Schutz 6-8-11 (bl) A Starke : 311-02: 6 b h Niniski - Eversince (Foolish Pleasure) 3 **118**
Held up, gd hdwy over 2f out, styd on ins last, nrst fin: won twice in native Germany in '99, incl a Gr 2 (rtd 119): stays 12f well on fast & soft grnd: wears blnks: high-class, this was promising reappearance.

123 **HIGH RISE 99** [1] Saeed bin Suroor 5-8-11 L Dettori : 263-13: 5 b h High Estate - High Tern (High 2 **116**
Line) Chsd ldrs, eff over 2f out, chall over 1f out till no extra well ins last: far from disgraced, but subs found to have injured an ankle: high-class, now to be trained in America.

3817} **RHAGAAS 99** [5] Saeed bin Suroor 4-8-9 (vis) R Hughes : 3323-4: Waited with, gd hdwy over 2f out, 2 **113**
staying on at the fin: plcd in Gr company in '99 (rtd 114): '99 Nottingham mdn wnr (rtd 104, with D Loder): eff at 12f, stays 14f on firm & soft: has run well in blnks & a visor: v useful, but hard to win with.

2495} **SAGAMIX 99** [4] 5-8-11 J D Bailey : 11/449: Waited with, mod late gains: rtd 119 when 4th in a Gr 1 10 **103**
on 2nd of only 2 '99 starts: in '98 won at St Cloud & Longchamp (3, notably Gr1 Arc, rtd 127, with A Fabre): eff at 12f on gd, likes soft & hvy: runs well fresh: top-class at best.

3996} **PEGNITZ 99** [2] 5-8-11 B Doyle : 2053-0: Led till over 2f out, wknd: 12th on reapp. 5¼ **98**

4596} **YAVANAS PACE 99** [6] 8-8-11 R Hughes : 1206-0: Prom, wknd over 2f out: 15th, reapp, better than this. 5 **93**
16 ran   Time 2m 27.7   (Maktoum Al Maktoum)   Sir Michael Stoute Newmarket

768
4.45 GR 3 DUBAI DUTY FREE 4YO+   1m1f   Good
£731707 £243902 £121951 £60976

2691} **RHYTHM BAND 99** [3] Saeed bin Suroor 4-9-0 T Durcan : /1-321: 4 gr c Cozzene - Golden Wave Band **115**
(Dixieland Band) Held up, hdwy & not clr run over 1f out, styd on strongly ins last to get up cl-home: in '99 scored at Doncaster (stks, sole race): juv wnr in the USA: eff at 1m/9f, further shld suit: acts on firm, gd & dirt: runs well fresh: v useful, improving & has a turn of foot, win more Gr races.

1091} **EASAAR 99** [2] Saeed bin Suroor 4-9-0 R Hills : 1/0-12: 4 b c Machiavellian - Matila (Persian Bold) ¾ **113**

NAD AL SHEBA (Dubai) SATURDAY MARCH 25TH Lefthand, Flat, Fair Track

Cl-up, hard rdn to lead dist, kept on till collared by stable-mate cl-home: recent wnr here in Dubai: rtd 103 when 10th in the 2,000 Guineas sole '99 start: juv wnr at Newmarket (mdn): eff at 7f/9f on gd grnd & dirt: runs well fresh: v useful & improving.

2322} **KINGSALSA 99** [4] A Fabre 4-9-0 O Peslier : 135-13: 4 br c Kingmambo - Caretta (Caro) *1* **111**
Held up, kept on well fnl 2f, nvr dangerous: '99 wnr at Longchamp & plcd in French 2,000 Guineas (rtd 116): eff at 7f/9f, further shld suit: acts on gd, soft & dirt: v useful French raider.

186 **KABOOL 99** [1] Saeed bin Suroor 5-9-0 L Dettori : 2334-4: Waited with, eff 2f out, kept on same pace: plcd in Gr1/2 company in '99 (rtd 122 at best): '98 wnr in France (2, Gr 3 & Gr 2): eff over 9/10f on gd/firm & hvy: tough & smart, should rate higher. *½* **110**

657 **SHOWBOAT 21** [9] 6-9-0 N Pollard : 610-06: Handy, hdwy to lead over 1f out, sn hdd & no extra: fin 6th: will enjoy a return to Listed company: see 657. *1½* **107**

3795} **FLY TO THE STARS 99** [8] 6-9-0 J D Bailey : /100-7: Led till over 1f out, no extra: won reapp in '99 at Newbury (Gr1 Lockinge, rtd 122, made all): in '98 won at Deauville & Longchamp (Gr2): loves to dominate & all wins at 1m, stays 10f on firm, loves soft: runs well fresh on any trk: high-class at best. *2½* **102**

657 **MONSAJEM 21** [11] 5-9-0 J Reid : 313-69: Nvr a factor: fin 9th: see 657. *7* **92**

2018} **GOLDEN SILCA 99** [6] 4-8-11 R Quinn : 2022-0: Waited with, brief eff over 2f out, sn no impress: fin 10th: rnr-up in 3 of 4 '99 starts, incl Gr 1 Irish 1,000 Guineas & Coronation Stakes (rtd 115): v tough juv, won at Newbury (4, incl Gr 2) & in Germany: eff at 5/6f, stays 1m on firm & hvy, likes Newbury: runs well fresh: v tough & smart, should put this firmly bhd her. *½* **88**

11 ran Time 1m 48.6 (Sheikh Rashid Bin Mohammed) Saeed bin Suroor Dubai

769 — 5.30 GR 1 DUBAI WORLD CUP 4YO+ 1m2f Dirt
£2195122 £731707 £365854 £182927

*655 **DUBAI MILLENNIUM 23** [11] Saeed bin Suroor 4-9-0 L Dettori : 111-11: 4 b c Seeking The Gold - Colorado Dancer (Shareef Dancer) Led after 1f, made rest, pushed well clr appr fnl 1f, most impressive: earlier won here in Dubai (Listed): v progressive/high-class in '99, won at Doncaster (stks), Goodwood (Listed), M-Laffitte (Gr 2), Deauville & Ascot (Gr 1, rtd 128), met sole defeat over 12f in Epsom Derby: '98 Yarmouth mdn wnr: v eff over 1m/10f, handles firm, likes soft & dirt: runs well fresh on any trk: can force the pace: most progressive & out of the very highest draw, will reportedly have a global campaign in the top 1m/10f races & prove v hard to beat. **134a**

1733} **BEHRENS 99** [5] H J Bond 6-9-0 (bl) J Chevez : 20-312: 6 br h Pleasant Colony - Hot Novel (Mari's Book) Chsd ldrs, hdwy 4f out, outpcd by wnr fnl 2f: well clr of rem: recently won a Gr1 in native USA: in '99 won a Gr 2: stays 10f well on dirt: top class US raider who had all the field bar the wnr well covered. *6* **124a**

3701} **PUBLIC PURSE 99** [10] R J Frankel 6-9-0 C Naktanis : 312-13: 6 b h Private Account - Prodigious (Pharly) In tch, hdwy over 2f out, kept on to take 3rd well ins last: smart for A Fabre last term. *5½* **116a**

-- **PUERTO MADERO** [6] R Mandella 6-9-0 L Pincay Jr : 34-634: Bhd, kept on fnl 2f, nrst fin. *hd* **116a**

-- **ECTON PARK** [4] 4-9-0 C McCarron : 10-335: Bhd, kept on late, nvr dangerous. *3* **111a**

-- **WORLD CLEEK** [13] 5-9-0 K Kato : 111-66: Slow away, nvr a factor. *1½* **109a**

666 **RUNNING STAG 13** [12] 6-9-0 S Sellers : 422-27: Cl-up, wknd fnl 2f: best in Gr 2 class: see 666. *2* **105a**

123 **INDIGENOUS 99** [2] 7-9-0 B Marcus : 024-08: In tch, btn over 2f out: capable of better. *½* **104a**

655 **LEAR SPEAR 23** [9] 5-9-0 N Pollard : 103-29: Al bhd: closer to this wnr in 655 & can rate higher. *¾* **103a**

1399} **WORLDLY MANNER 99** [3] 4-9-0 (vis) J D Bailey : 00-2D0: Trkd ldr till 4f out, wknd: fin last. **88a**

13 ran Time 1m 59.5 (Godolphin) Saeed bin Suroor Dubai

THE CURRAGH SUNDAY MARCH 26TH Righthand, Galloping Track

Official Going SOFT

770 — 3.30 LISTED LOUGHBROWN STAKES 3YO 7f rnd Soft
£16250 £4750 £750

4533} **MONASHEE MOUNTAIN 99** A P O'Brien 3-9-7 M J Kinane 1/3 FAV: 11-1: 3 b c Danzig - Prospectors Delite (Mr Prospector) Waited with, gd hdwy over 1f out to lead well ins last, shade cosily: won both juv starts, at Leopardstown (List & Gr 3, rtd 105): eff at 7f, looks sure to stay 1m: acts on gd/soft & soft: runs well fresh on a gall trk: looks potentially high class & can win in Gr company. **115**

4029} **JAMMAAL 99** D K Weld 3-9-0 P J Smullen 13/2: 413-2: 3 b c Robellino - Navajo Love Song (Dancing Brave) Set pace, kept on well fnl 1f till collared cl-home: clr of rem on reapp: juv wnr at Leopardstown (mdn), subs 1L 3rd in Gr 1 National Stks: eff at 7f, relish a return to 1m & further shld suit: acts on soft: win races. *½* **104**

-- **COIS CUAIN** J M Oxx 3-8-11 N G McCullagh 7/1: 01-3: 3 b f Night Shift - Pitmarie (Pitskelly) Waited with, some late gains, nvr dangerous: Curragh mdn wnr as a juv (6f, soft). *7* **86**

6 ran Time 1m 34.5 (Michael Tabor) A P O'Brien Ballydoyle, Co Tipperary

LINGFIELD (Equitrack) WEDNESDAY MARCH 29TH Lefthand, V Sharp Track

Official Going STANDARD. Stalls: 5f - Outside, Rem - Inside.

771 — 2.00 BET247.CO.UK MDN 3YO+ (D) 1m2f aw Going 33 -12 Slow
£2717 £836 £418 £209 3 yo rec 20lb

606 **FIELD MASTER 35** [2] S Dow 3-8-6(1ow) S Sanders 2/1 CO FAV: -03221: 3 ch c Foxhound - Bold Avril (Persian Bold): Made all, clr over 2f out, unchall/easily: value for 16L+: nicely bckd: recent rnr-up twice at Cagnes Sur Mer, including on this surface (10f, stks): with A Stewart in '99 (unplcd, rtd 76, h'cap): eff arnd a sharp 10f, could stay further: acts on equitrack & a sharp track. **75a**

616 **FULHAM 28** [3] M J Haynes 4-9-11 (bl) F Norton 16/1: 000-42: 4 ch c Safawan - Sister Sal (Bairn) Chsd wnr halfway, held final 2f: tchd 25/1, prob flattered: this longer 10f trip should suit in h'caps: see 616. *8* **56$**

457 **ESTUARY 53** [6] Mrs A E Johnson 5-9-11 A McCarthy (3) 2/1 CO FAV: 23: 5 ch g Riverman - Ocean Ballad (Grundy) Keen/prom, struggling over 2f out: hvly bckd, op 4/1: 8 wk abs: see 457 (12f, debut). *9* **46a**

-- **BONIFACIO** [5] P F I Cole 4-9-11 K Fallon 2/1 CO FAV: 3-4: Pulled v hard/held up, chsd ldrs 5f out, btn 3f out: 10 mth abs/AW bow: ominous mkt drifter, op 1/2: ex-French, plcd sole '99 start (mdn, 11f, Longchamp). *½* **45a**

LINGFIELD (Equitrack)   WEDNESDAY MARCH 29TH   Lefthand, V Sharp Track

4516} **DESTINATION 99** [4] 3-8-5 G Carter 25/1: 0-5: Chsd wnr 4f, rdn/outpcd halfway: 5 mth abs/AW bow: *hd*   **45a**
unplcd sole '99 start (rtd 54, mdn): bred to apprec mid-dists for C Cyzer.

26   **FOOLS PARADISE 99** [1] 3-8-5 G Bardwell 50/1: 0-6: T.o. halfway: 5 mth abs, stablemate of 5th.   *dist*   **0a**
6 ran   Time 2m 07.3 (4.5)   (Zero 3 Racing)   S Dow Epsom, Surrey.

772

2.30 CLASSIFIED STKS 3YO+ 0-70 (E)   **1m4f aw**   **Going 33**   **-19 Slow**
£2716   £776   £388   3 yo rec 22lb 4 yo rec 2 lb

679   **SEA DANZIG 13** [3] J J Bridger 7-9-11 J Weaver 2/1: 104221: 7 ch g Roi Danzig - Tosara (Main Reef)   **71a**
Led till halfway, rdn/lost tch with front pair 4f out, styd on strgly for press from 2f out & drifted left/drvn to lead
well ins last: op 5/4: blnks omitted: earlier scored here at Lingfield (C/D stks): '99 wnr at Epsom (h'cap, rtd 59,
unplcd on sand, rtd 68a): '98 Lingfield (2, rtd 74a), Goodwood & Folkestone wnr (h'caps, rtd 69): suited by 1m/10f,
stays 12f: acts on firm, soft & fibresand, loves eqtrk/Lingfield: best without blnks: gd weight carrier.

4308} **PULAU PINANG 99** [4] G A Butler 4-9-4 D Holland 8/11 FAV: 310-2: 4 ch f Dolphin Street - Inner Pearl   1¼   **64a**
(Gulf Pearl) Handy, led halfway, rdn/hdd 4f out, rallied to lead again 2f out, hdd well inside last & no extra: bckd
from evens: AW bow/6 mth abs: '99 Lingfield turf wnr (auct mdn, rtd 71): eff arnd a sharp 11/12f on firm & eqtrk.

4527} **SIGNS AND WONDERS 99** [2] C A Cyzer 6-9-6 K Fallon 9/2: 6420-3: 6 b m Danehill - Front Line   2½   **60a**
Romance (Caerleon) Trkd ldrs, led 4f out, rdn/hdd 2f out, no extra when slightly hmpd inside last: 5 mth abs:
rnr-up in '99 (rtd 58, h'cap): '98 reapp wnr here at Lingfield (C/D fillies h'cap, rtd 70a, flattered on turf,
rtd 77, stks): eff btwn 7f/10f, stays a sharp 12f: acts on firm, gd/soft & equitrack, any trk: has run well fresh.

650   **ORDAINED 21** [1] Miss Gay Kelleway 7-9-6 S Sanders 50/1: 0-4604: Sn bhd: highly tried: see 528.   *dist*   **0a**
4 ran   Time 2m 35.46 (6.26)   (P Cook)   J J Bridger Liphook, Hants.

773

3.00 BET247 FILLIES HCAP 3YO 0-70 (E)   **7f aw rnd**   **Going 33**   **-26 Slow**   **[75]**
£2702   £772   £386

*570   **FINE MELODY 35** [2] B W Hills 3-9-4 (65) J Reid 1/1 FAV: 311: 3 b f Green Desert - Sit Alkui (Mr   **73a**
Prospector) Keen, made all/hung right thro'out, clr/in command over 1f out, rdn out: nicely bckd tho' op 1/2:
h'cap debut: earlier scored here at Lingfield (C/D mdn): likes to dominate at 7f, 1m could yet suit: acts on both
AWs & a sharp trk, yet to run on turf: probably best suited by strong handling.

617   **FRENCH FANCY 28** [1] B A Pearce 3-7-11 (44)(bl) P M Quinn 9/1: 453042: 3 gr f Paris House -   6   **43a**
Clipping (Kris) Chsd wnr after 3f, kept on tho' al held: eff at 6/7f, handles both AWs, fast & soft: see 421.

689   **FRAMPANT 12** [3] M Quinn 3-9-4 (65) T Quinn 8/1: 402-43: 3 ch f Fraam - Potent (Posen)   2   **60a**
Chsd ldrs, outpcd halfway, brief rally wide 2f out, sn held: lngr 7f trip could suit in time: see 689 (6f, fbrsnd).

397   **XATIVA 64** [4] J A Osborne 3-8-1 (48) F Norton 25/1: 00-004: Chsd wnr 3f/sn held: abs, new trainer.   *shd*   **43a**

4353} **ANNIJAZ 99** [6] A Beech 3-9-7 (68) A Beech 5/1: 4232-5: Wide/rear, nvr a factor: op 9/2, 6 mth abs: AW &   1¼   **60a**
h'cap bow: rnr-up twice in '99 (A P Jarvis, rtd 70, fillies auct mdn): eff arnd 6/7f, handles firm & gd grnd.

654   **DAMASQUINER 21** [5] 3-8-7 (54) A Nicholls (3) 5/1: 416356: Chsd ldrs, outpcd halfway, btr 459 (clmr).   2½   **41a**
6 ran   Time 1m 26.94 (4.14)   (Maktoum Al Maktoum)   B W Hills Lambourn, Berks.

774

3.30 MARSHALLS HCAP 3YO+ 0-85 (D)   **5f aw rnd**   **Going 33**   **-17 Slow**   **[78]**
£3705   £1140   £570   £285   3 yo rec 12lb

532   **BOLD EFFORT 41** [4] K O Cunningham Brown 8-9-6 (70)(bl) S Sanders 12/1: -04001: 8 b g Bold   **81a**
Arrangement - Malham Tarn (Riverman) Trkd ldrs wide, al travelling well, shkn up inside last & readily led/pulled
clr nr fin: value for 4L+: tchd 14/1, 6 wk abs: back to form, connections reported gelding had been suffering
from a lung infection: blnks reapplied: '99 scorer here at Lingfield (h'cap, rtd 97a), unplcd on turf subs
(rtd 83, h'cap): '98 wnr at Sandown & Kempton (h'caps, rtd 96 & 87a): eff at 5/6f, stays 1m: acts on firm,
gd/soft & both AWs, any trk: suited by blnks: runs well fresh: well h'capped, could strike again soon.

4033} **AIRA FORCE 99** [1] J Noseda 3-9-5 (81) J Weaver 11/2: 3310-2: 3 ch g Dehere - Cinnamon Splendor   2½   **81a**
(Trempolino): Led, rdn/hdd inside last & sn held by wnr: op 5/2, 6 mths abs/AW bow: '99 Haydock wnr (mdn,
rtd 84): eff forcing the pace at 5f on fast & equitrack, any trk: encouraging h'cap bow, win more races.

645   **SOTONIAN 23** [3] P S Felgate 7-8-10 (60) A Nicholls (3) 9/1: -05003: 7 br g Statoblest - Visage   1   **58a**
(Vision): Trkd ldrs, effort/onepace over 1f out: op 7/1: has slipped to a winning mark: see 394 (fibresand).

673   **READY TO ROCK 15** [7] J S Moore 4-8-1 (51)(bl) P M Quinn 5/1: 601224: Chsd ldrs wide, nvr   nk   **48a**
able to chall: well bckd, op 4/1: btr 573 (C/D, made all).

579   **MANGUS 34** [6] 6-10-0 (78) J Reid 7/1: 014-65: Chsd ldr till over 1f out, fdd: op 5/1: btr 146 (fbrsnd).   ½   **73a**

*631   **FRILLY FRONT 25** [5] 4-10-0 (78) C Lowther 7/4 FAV: P11016: Reared start & slowly away, al held: 2½   **66a**
well bckd: lost any chance at the start, this is best forgiven: btr 631 (C/D).

312   **KAYO GEE 77** [2] 4-9-6 (70)(bl) Martin Dwyer 14/1: 000-67: Reluctant to face kick-back & sn well bhd.   12   **35a**
7 ran   Time 1m 0.31 (2.51)   (J A Richards)   K O Cunningham Brown Stockbridge, Hants.

775

4.00 PLAY THE POOLS SELLER 3YO+ (G)   **1m2f aw**   **Going 33**   **-19 Slow**
£1886   £539   £269   3 yo rec 20lb

710   **BILLICHANG 6** [9] P Howling 4-9-13 K Fallon 9/4 JT FAV: 344261: 4 b c Chilibang - Swing O'The Kilt   **47a**
(Hotfoot) Made all, rdn/prsd 2f out, forged clr inside last: nicely bckd: bght in for 3,400 gns: qck reapp:
'99 Lingfield scorer (C/D, mdn, earlier rnr-up, rtd 58a): unplcd in '98 (rtd 51a & 50): eff forcing pace at 10f,
stays sharp 12f: acts on both AWs, likes a sharp trk: best without blnks/vis: appreciated drop to sell grade.

620   **BADRINATH 28** [1] H J Collingridge 6-9-9 J Reid 9/4 JT FAV: 50-632: 6 b g Imperial Frontier - Badedra   3   **38a**
(King's Lake) Trkd wnr, rdn to chall over 1f out, no extra inside last: well bckd: see 360.

710   **MALCHIK 6** [4] P Howling 4-9-9 F Norton 9/1: 200333: 4 ch c Absalom - Very Good (Noalto)   4   **32a**
Handy, outpcd 3f out, held after: drifter from 9/2, qck reapp: see 710, 159.

458   **KI CHI SAGA 53** [7] P Burgoyne 8-9-9 (bl) T Quinn 8/1: 0-6004: Chsd ldrs, outpcd 3f out: tchd 12/1, abs.   5   **25a**

460   **MOGIN 53** [2] 7-9-4 Martin Dwyer 15/2: 0-0445: Mid-div, nvr on terms: jumps fit (rtd 71h, clmg hdle).   3½   **15a**

524   **TWOFORTEN 42** [6] 5-9-9 (bl) A Nicholls (3) 16/1: 305-06: Chsd ldrs 1m: op 14/1, abs: see 524.   ½   **19a**

4434} **GAELIC FORAY 99** [8] 4-9-4 N Pollard 50/1: 0-7: Cl-up 7f, fdd: 5 mth abs, AW bow: no form.   2½   **10a**

650   **SASEEDO 21** [3] 10-9-9 (bl) G Bardwell 14/1: -00408: V slowly away, t.o. till mod late prog.   ½   **14a**

683   **INKWELL 12** [10] 6-9-9 (bl) I Mongan (5) 8/1: 4-5259: Slowly away, chsd ldrs halfway, btn 3f out: op 6/1.   3½   **9a**

--   **MISS SCARLETT** [5] 7-9-4 D Griffiths 50/1: 0: T.o. halfway: 10th: Flat debut, 8 wk jmps abs, no form.   *dist*   **0a**
10 ran   Time 2m 08.02 (5.22)   (Paul Howling Racing Syndicate)   P Howling Newmarket, Suffolk.

LINGFIELD (Equitrack) WEDNESDAY MARCH 29TH Lefthand, V Sharp Track

776 4.30 WIN #2 MILLION HCAP 3YO+ 0-60 (F) 1m aw rnd Going 33 +13 Fast [60]
£2362 £675 £337 3 yo rec 17lb

647 **ELLWAY PRINCE 23** [9] M Wigham 5-9-2 (48) F Norton 12/1: 262501: 5 b g Prince Sabo - Star Arrangement 64a
(Star Appeal) Cl-up, led after 2f, rdn clr over 1f out, styd on strongly inside last: tchd 20/1, fast time: right
back to form, connections reported gelding had been cured of a bad back: rnr-up in '99 (h'cap, rtd 67a, unplcd on
turf, rtd 45, Mrs N Macauley): '98 Lingfield wnr (mdn, rtd 72a): eff at 6f, now suited by a sharp 1m: acts on
firm, gd & both AWs, any trk, likes Lingfield: likes to force the pace: eff with/without vis, not blnks: well h'capped.
632 **ROI DE DANSE 25** [7] M Quinn 5-9-0 (46) T Quinn 15/2: 422502: 5 ch g Komaite - Princess Lucy 10 46a
(Local Suitor) Chsd ldrs, rdn/chsd wnr 2f out, al held: see 227, 203 (made al, 10f).
4527} **THATCHAM 25** [1] R W Armstrong 4-9-4 (50) R Price 8/1: 4000-3: 4 ch g Thatching - Calaloo Sioux nk 49a
(Our Native) Led 2f, lost place/bhd halfway, rdn/kept on final 2f: tchd 10/1: reapp: unplcd in '99 (rtd 60 & 21a).
632 **SCISSOR RIDGE 25** [10] J J Bridger 8-9-11 (57) J Weaver 13/2: 324264: Wide/chsd ldrs, nvr on terms. ½ 55a
*596 **SUPERCHIEF 32** [12] 5-9-12 (58)(tbl) S Carson (5) 7/2: 421115: Wide/handy, fdd final 2f: op 3/1. 1¾ 53a
*616 **UNCHAIN MY HEART 28** [8] 4-10-0 (60)(bl) D Glennon (7) 10/1: 130-16: Cl-up 6f: btr 616 (7f, clmr). 3 49a
692 **RED VENUS 9** [11] 4-9-8 (54)(bl) D Holland 7/1: 4-5337: Wide/mid-div, no ch final 3f: btr 692, 616. 1¾ 40a
400 **DAPHNES DOLL 63** [2] 5-9-5 (51) A Nicholls (3) 16/1: 41-008: Bhd halfway: tchd 20/1, 2 mth abs. 1 35a
4579} **CALEDONIAN EXPRESS 99** [6] 5-9-7 (53) R Mullen 50/1: 0/60-9: Sn bhd: jumps fit (Feb Fakenham 10 22a
wnr, sell h'cap, rtd 67h): no form in '99: rtd 69 in '98 (plcd, h'cap, J Dunlop): stays 9.6f, handles firm & soft.
4521} **BONNIE DUNDEE 99** [5] 4-9-0 (46) D Kinsella (7) 16/1: 6160-0: Sn bhd: 10th: op 14/1, 5 mth abs: 2 11a
AW draw: '99 Salisbury wnr (clmr, M Kettle, rtd 62, subs awarded a Nottingham sell h'cap): rtd 64 in '98 (clmr): eff
at 7f/1m on firm & gd/soft, any trk, likes a stiff/gall one: suited by blnks/t-strap, tried a vis: has run well fresh.
686 **INDIAN SWINGER 12** [4] 4-9-6 (52) K Fallon 3/1 FAV: 005220: Sn bhd: 11th: well bckd: btr 686 (fbrsnd). 14 0a
336 **CHURCHILLS SHADOW 74** [3] 6-8-13 (45) O Urbina 20/1: 53-500: Chsd ldrs, bandages unravelled at *dist* 0a
lost action after 3f, t.o: 12th: op 14/1, 11 wk abs: best forgotten: see 187.
12 ran Time 1m 37.83 (1.63) (Stephen Roots) M Wigham Newmarket, Suffolk.

CATTERICK WEDNESDAY MARCH 29TH Lefthand, Undulating, Very Tight Track

Official Going GOOD (GOOD/FIRM places). Stalls: Inside.

777 2.20 SPRINGTIME CLASSIFIED STKS 3YO 0-60 (F) 5f Good/Firm 30 -36 Slow
£2254 £644 £322

4589} **BENNOCHY 99** [7] A Berry 3-8-11 O Pears 16/1: 6000-1: 3 ch g Factual - Agreloui (Tower Walk): 58
In tch, short of room dist till ins last, led in fnl well to lead cl-home: styd on: mod '99 form (rtd 65$): half-brother
to sev wnrs, incl a 5f juv scorer: eff over a sharp 5f, will stay 6f: acts on fast grnd, runs well fresh.
4612} **COLLEGE MAID 99** [5] J S Goldie 3-8-8 F Lynch 7/2: 0056-2: 3 b f College Chapel - Maid Of Mourne nk 53
(Fairy King): Prom, led ins fnl 1f, not pace to repel wnr cl-home: reapp: '99 Musselburgh wnr (mdn auct), also
plcd sev times (rtd 74): eff at 5/6f: acts on firm, gd/soft, handles hvy: handles a sharp or gall trk.
696 **APRILS COMAIT 9** [6] Miss J F Craze 3-8-8 V Halliday 20/1: -60533: 3 br f Komaite - Sweet Caroline ¾ 50
(Squill): Dwelt, recovered to chase ldrs, styd on under press fnl 1f: btn arnd 1L, fit from the AW: see 696.
4514} **LIZZIE SIMMONDS 99** [4] N Tinkler 3-8-8 (t) Pat Eddery 8/1: 0300-4: Tried to make all, collared ins nk 49
last, no extra: reapp: plcd in '99 (mdn, rtd 73), little other form: eff at 5/6f on fast & gd/soft: wears a t-strap.
3893} **LAYAN 99** [8] 3-8-8 J Edmunds 14/1: 4006-5: Prom, chall dist, no extra cl-home: reapp, btn under 2L: ½ 48
trained by J Berry in '99, rnr-up at Redcar (mdn auct, rtd 70): eff at 5f on fast & gd/soft: now with J Balding.
*624 **MARITUN LAD 27** [10] J P Spencer 3-9-0 (bl) 2/1 FAV: 5-4316: In tch, onepcd ins fnl 1f: well bckd. ¾ 51
4616} **BLUE LINE LADY 99** [3] 3-8-8 R Winston 9/2: 6000-7: Rdn & rear, styd on fnl 1f, nrst fin: nicely bckd. ¾ 42
365 **SERGEANT SLIPPER 68** [9] 3-8-11 (vis) G Faulkner (3) 14/1: 011-08: Stumbled leaving stalls, nvr 1¾ 40
dngr: mkt drifter, 10 wk abs: see 217 (AW).
*631 **PAPE DIOUF 28** [1] 3-9-3 (bl) J F Egan 4/1: -01419: Prom 3½f: btr 619 (sand). 2 40
731 **LAMMOSKI 4** [2] 3-8-11 Joanna Badger (7) 33/1: 000500: Al bhd, fin last: qck reapp. hd 34
10 ran Time 1m 00.6 (3.3) (Mrs Norma Peebles) A Berry Cockerham, Lancs.

---

778 2.50 FORCETT SELLER 3YO+ (G) 7f rnd Good/Firm 30 -27 Slow
£1960 £560 £280

584 **DILETTO 33** [5] E J Alston 4-9-1 L Swift (7) 8/1: 060261: 4 b f Mujadil - Avidal Park (Horage): 38
Trkd ldrs, imprvd to lead dist, held on well fnl 1f, drvn out: no bid: fit from the AW, rnr-up once: place form
in '99 (h'caps, rtd 68): eff at 7f, stays 1m/10f: acts on firm, soft grnd & fibresand: probably handles any trk,
has tried blnks: eff in sell company, first win today.
3781} **SHAANXI ROMANCE 99** [13] J Semple 5-9-12 (vis) R Winston 3/1 FAV: 1400-2: 5 b g Darshaan - Easy ¾ 47
Romance (Northern Jove): Pushed in rear, imprvd 2f out, short of room dist till ins last, fin well but too late:
top wtght: '99 wnr at Carlisle (class stks, rtd 60): '98 W'hampton wnr (mdn, rtd 73a & 79, with M Bell): eff
at 7f/1m, has tried 10f: acts on firm, soft & f/sand: eff with/without a visor, runs well fresh: can front run
or come from bhd: gd effort from a poor high draw here, no luck in running: should win a selling h'cap.
476 **PAGEBOY 51** [3] P C Haslam 11-9-6 (vis) P Goode (5) 9/1: 6-4453: 11 b g Tina's Pet - Edwins' Princess nk 40
(Owen Dudley): Mid-div, imprvd to chall dist, no extra cl-home: btn arnd 1L, 7 wk abs: see 313, 138 (AW).
187 **MYBOTYE 99** [12] A B Mulholland 7-9-6 (t) Pat Eddery 20/1: 0000-4: Rcd keenly in rear, imprvd 2f 1¼ 37
out, no extra ins last: long abs: lightly rcd & modest '99 form: plcd in '98 (h'cap, rtd 59): '97 Chepstow &
Catterick wnr (subs disq, h'caps, rtd 61, with R Bastiman): eff at 7f, has tried 1m/10f: acts on fast & soft,
handles fibresand: can run well fresh: wears a t-strap: poor high draw today, well h'capped, fitter next time.
676 **STATE WIND 13** [1] 4-9-6 (vis) J P Spencer 25/1: 0-0605: Chsd ldr, led halfway, hdd dist, no extra. ½ 36
433 **TSUNAMI 57** [6] 4-9-1 J F Egan 4/1: 64-066: Rear, imprvd 2f out, nrst fin: btn under 3L, 8 wk abs. hd 34
646 **SARPEDON 23** [8] 4-9-6 R Studholme (5) 14/1: 005567: Prom, ev ch dist, gradually fdd: bckd at 1¾ 33
long odds: plcd in a sell h'cap hdle since 646.
684 **PLEASURE TRICK 12** [2] 9-9-6 (vis) Kim Tinkler 12/1: -00058: Rear, some hdwy 2f out, sn no impress. 1 31
2604} **CYRAN PARK 99** [15] 4-9-6 T Williams 25/1: 0060-9: Dwelt, imprvg when short of room dist, sn btn & hd 31
eased: no hdles form this winter: lightly rcd & modest plating class form in '99: some '98 promise (mdn auct,

rtd 74): handles fast grnd: prev with W Jarvis, now with W Storey: poor high draw here.

3578} **YOUNG BEN 99** [4] 8-9-6 R Cody Boutcher (7) 25/1: 0000-0: Led 3f, wknd dist: fin 10th, reapp. | 1¼ | 28
604 **GADGE 30** [14] 9-9-6 J Carroll 10/1: 003000: In tch 5f, fdd into 11th: poor high draw. | ½ | 27
639 **TANGERINE FLYER 25** [7] 5-9-6 Joanna Badger (7) 25/1: 00/060: Rcd keenly & trkd ldrs, eased | 4 | 19
when btn final 2f: fin 12th, saddle reportedly slipped.
33 **MARJAANA 99** [9] 7-9-1 G Faulkner (3) 8/1: /000-0: Trkd ldrs, sn btn & fin last: bckd from 16/1, abs. | 7 | 0
13 ran   Time 1m 27.0 (4.0)   (Liam & Tony Ferguson)   E J Alston Longton, Lancs.

---

779   3.20 WHORLTON HCAP 4YO+ 0-80 (D)   1m5f175y   Good/Firm 30   -04 Slow   [74]
£4309   £1326   £663   £331   4yo rec 4lb

705 **NOUKARI 6** [8] P D Evans 11-9-10 (70) J F Egan 7/1: 445321: 7 b g Darshaan - Noufiyla (Top Ville): | | 74
Mid-div, rdn to impr 2f out, kept on gamely to lead on line, all-out: tchd 9/1, qck reapp: fit from the AW, plcd
on a couple of starts: '99 wnr at Lingfield (4), Chester (clmr), Newmarket (h'caps) & Pontefract (stks, rtd 74 & 82a):
99/00 dual wnr over hdles (rtd 104h, eff at 2m on gd & firm): '98 Southwell (h'caps, rtd 63 & 63a):
eff at 10/15f on firm, soft & on both AWs: handles any trk, loves Lingfield: ultra tough, genuine & consistent.
4095} **MOONLIGHT MONTY 99** [9] B Ellison 4-8-3 (53) D Mernagh (3) 8/1: /50-2D: 4 ch c Elmaamul - Lovers *shd* | | 56
Light (Grundy): Trkd ldrs, imprvd to lead 2½f out, edged left fnl 1f, collared cl-home, rallied & just btn in a
thrilling fin: subs disq & plcd 3rd, rider given a 2 day careless riding ban: lightly rcd in '99 (with J Dunlop),
place form prev (mdn auct, rtd 72): stays a sharp 14f on fast & firm grnd: can run well fresh: win a race.
699 **PRINCE NICHOLAS 6** [7] K W Hogg 5-8-11 (57) J Bramhill 16/1: /11-02: 5 ch g Midyan - Its My Turn | hd | 60
(Palm Track): In tch, chall 2f out, ev ch when hmpd ins last, recovered to lead briefly, caught nr line: just
btn in a thrilling fin, fin 3rd, subs plcd 2nd, 5L clr rem: dual '99 wnr, at Doncaster & Hamilton (h'caps, rtd
55): eff at 10/14f on fast & hvy, handles a tight or stiff/gall trk: can run well fresh: probably unlucky.
*699 **RAKEEB 6** [15] M W Easterby 5-9-0 (60)(bl) P Goode (5) 13/8 FAV: 03D-14: Prom, ev ch dist, fdd | 5 | 55
cl-home: hvly bckd, qck reapp: not disgraced from a poor high draw: rtd higher 699 (12f).
3287} **DESERT RECRUIT 99** [13] 4-7-10 (46) Clare Roche (7) 9/1: 0514-5: Rcd keenly & led till 2f out, kept | nk | 40+
on onepcd fnl 1f: tchd 14/1: trained by I Semple to win at Hamilton (appr h'cap, rtd 47) in '99: eff at 11f,
prob stays 14f: acts on fast grnd: now with D Nicholls & will be plcd to effect with a more experienced pilot.
437 **LAWNETT 6** [6] J P Spencer 20/1: 51-056: Waited with, prog over 3f out, no impress final | 1½ | 50
1f: plcd in a nov hdle here at Catterick (2m, gd) since 437.
4458} **SALVAGE 99** [14] 5-8-5 (51) F Lynch 33/1: 4610-7: Rear, late hdwy, nvr nr ldrs: reapp: '99 Catterick | ¾ | 42
wnr (h'cap, rtd 53): Apr '99 jumps wnr at Carlisle (nov hdle, eff at 2m, rtd 94h): eff at 2m on soft grnd, has
tried a t-strap over hdles: poor high draw today, will apprec a return to further & fitter next time.
456 **FATEHALKHAIR 54** [11] 8-9-3 (63) R Winston 10/1: 130-48: In tch, ev ch 2f out, fdd: 8 wk abs. | 1¾ | 52
4478} **ONCE MORE FOR LUCK 99** [10] 9-9-10 (70) C Teague 15/2: 3304-9: Rear, mod late gains, nvr dngrs: | ½ | 58
mkt drifter: recent jumps rnr, won at Wetherby & Sedgefield (h'cap hdls, rtd 131h, eff at 2m/2m5f on firm & hvy):
lightly rcd on the Flat in '99, plcd in a couple of h'caps (rtd 77): 98/99 hdles wnr at Leicester & Wetherby: '98
Flat wnr at York, Musselburgh (h'caps) & here at Catterick (appr clmr, rtd 76): eff at 10/14f, best at 12f: acts
on firm, soft grnd & fibresand: best held up for a late run: back on a wng mark.
182 **FLETCHER 99** [4] 6-9-5 (65) C Rutter 25/1: 3000-0: Chsd ldrs till outpcd 4f out, no ch after: fin 10th. | 1 | 51
3950} **TIME LOSS 99** [5] 5-8-12 (58) R Cody Boutcher 33/1: 2000-0: Prom, ev ch 2f out, fdd into 11th. | 3½ | 39
4275} **FLOWER OCANNIE 99** [3] 5-10-0 (78) T Lucas 20/1: 4200-0: Rear, rdn & btn 2f out: fin 12th, reapp. | 2 | 52
576 **PIPE MUSIC 34** [12] 5-7-11 (43)(bl) Dale Gibson 8/1: -32050: Mid-div till btn after 1m: fin last. | | 0
--   **Cadillac Jukebox** [1] 5-9-6 (65) P Hanagan (7) 33/1: 3880} **Bergamo 99** [2] 4-9-10 (74) T Williams 25/1:
15 ran   Time 3m 00.2 (4.8)   (J E Abbey)   P D Evans Leighton, Powys.

---

780   3.50 GODS SOLUTION HCAP 3YO+ 0-80 (D)   7f rnd   Good/Firm 30   +10 Fast   [79]
£4332   £1333   £666   £333   3yo rec 15lb

746 **SUSANS PRIDE 2** [2] B J Meehan 4-9-10 (75) Pat Eddery 9/4: 511-41: 4 b g Pips Pride - Piney Pass | | 80
(Persian Bold): Trkd ldrs, effort to lead ins fnl 1f, ran on strongly, rdn out: well bckd, best time of day, qck
reapp: '99 wnr at Nottingham (mdn auct), Doncaster & Brighton (clmrs, rtd 79): eff at 6f, best at 7f, stays 1m:
acts on firm & soft grnd & on any trk: in gd form & could win again.
645 **FOREIGN EDITOR 23** [4] R A Fahey 4-8-10 (61) P Hanagan(7) 2/1 FAV: D11332: 4 ch g Magic Ring - | ½ | 65
True Precision (Presidium): Tried to make all, collared ins last, just btn in a cl fin: well bckd, 3L clr 3rd: likes
to force the pace, a sound effort: acts on fast, gd/soft & on both AWs: loves a sharp 7f: see 423.
691 **ACID TEST 11** [3] M A Buckley 5-9-3 (68) R Fitzpatrick (5) 8/1: 0-0663: 5 ch g Sharpo - Clunk Click | 3 | 66
(Star Appeal): Chsd ldrs, styd on under press final 1f: usually likes to dominate: see 525 (AW).
716 **NORTHERN SVENGALI 5** [8] T D Barron 4-10-0 (79) J P Spencer 20/1: 44-304: In tch, keeping on when | 1¼ | 74
hmpd dist, onepcd after: qck reapp, top weight: fine run in the circumstances, likes it here at Catterick:
stays a sharp 7f: stable in excellent form, should sn gain compensation: see 533.
635 **TECHNICIAN 25** [10] 5-8-7 (58)(bl) M Fenton 20/1: 30-005: Early ldr, remnd prom & ch 2f out, fdd | ½ | 52
inside last: not disgraced from a tricky draw: see 582 (sand).
35 **ONLY FOR GOLD 99** [16] 5-8-6 (57) J Carroll 20/1: 2336-6: Chsd ldrs, rdn & ev ch 2f out, sn onepcd: | ¾ | 49
long abs: plcd numerous times in '99 (h'caps, rtd 67): 4th of 29 on best '98 run (val h'cap, rtd 77), prev term
won at Chester & Beverley (stks, rtd 90): eff at 7f/1m on fast & soft grnd: handles any trk, can force the pace:
can run well fresh: has tried a visor, better without: poor high draw today.
3052} **YAROB 99** [13] 7-9-13 (78) Alex Greaves 20/1: 0505-7: Held up, keeping on when hmpd 1f out, nvr nr | nk | 69+
to chall: reapp: '99 Doncaster wnr (h'cap, rtd 84): rnr-up in '98 (h'cap, rtd 83a, with D Loder): eff at 10/11f on gd,
firm & f/sand: ran well from a poor high draw over a trip short of best: fairly h'capped & one to keep in mind.
4568} **RETALIATOR 99** [5] 4-9-4 (69) J F Egan 33/1: 0000-8: Prom, ch 2f out, fdd: reapp: '99 Chester wnr (2, | 3 | 54
clmr & h'cap, rtd 78): '98 Leicester wnr (nurs, rtd 72): eff at 6/7f on firm & soft: handles a gall trk, loves a sharp
one, esp Chester: best up with the pace, has tried a visor: well h'capped & one to keep in mind at Chester.
617 **BOND DIAMOND 28** [15] 3-8-2 (68) Dale Gibson 20/1: 4-1059: Dwelt, in tch, rdn & btn 2f out. | 1¼ | 50
4447} **KHABAR 99** [14] 7-8-0 (51) T Williams 20/1: 0200-0: Nvr a factor in 10th: reapp: plcd numerous | hd | 33
times in '98 (h'caps, rtd 56 at best): missed '99: eff at 1m/10f on firm & soft grnd: remains a mdn.
645 **ARPEGGIO 23** [9] 5-9-8 (73) O Pears 14/1: 000-00: Nvr a factor in 11th: lightly rcd in '99, reapp wnr | nk | 54
at Thirsk (mdn, rtd 84): eff at 6/7f on fast & soft grnd: handles a gall trk, can run well fresh.
97 **INCHALONG 99** [1] 5-8-13 (64)(vis) D Mernagh(3) 10/1: 0206-0: Dwelt, al rear: fin 12th, long abs. | 1½ | 42
645 **EURO VENTURE 23** [11] 5-9-11 (76) Ioan Wands(5) 10/1: 203-00: Prom 3f, sn wknd & fin 15th. | | 0
1122} **Isle Of Sodor 99** [7] 4-8-4 (55) J Bramhill 25/1:   341 **Cladantom 72** [6] 4-8-7 (58) F Lynch 50/1:
4075} **Indian Dance 99** [12] 4-8-5 (56)(t) Joanna Badger (7) 100/1:

CATTERICK WEDNESDAY MARCH 29TH Lefthand, Undulating, Very Tight Track

16 ran   Time 1m 24.4 (1.4)   (Mrs Susan Roy)   B J Meehan Upper Lambourn, Berks.

781	4.20 TOYTOP MDN 3YO+ (D) 6f rnd Good/Firm 30 -16 Slow
	£2702 £772 £386 3yo rec 13lb

4172} **PISCES LAD 99** [8] T D Barron 4-9-10 J P Spencer 8/1: 4000-1: 4 b g Cyrano de Bergerac - Tarnside **58**
Rosal (Mummy's Game): Made all, rdn final 2f, held on gamely inside last, all-out: op 7/1: 6 mth abs, prev with
S Dow: rnr-up on sand in '99 (mdn auct, rtd 59a & 56): plcd in '98 (rtd 79, nursery h'cap): eff at 5/6f on firm,
gd/soft & equitrack: likes to force the pace on a sharp/turning trk: runs well fresh.
698   **DANAKIM 9** [5] J R Weymes 3-8-11 (BL) T Williams 4/1: 0-0002: 3 b g Emarati - Kangra Valley hd **57**
(Indian Ridge): Keen/trkd wnr, rdn to chall final 1f, just held: first time blnks, imprvd effort: see 566 (AW).
624   **FOUND AT LAST 27** [1] J Balding 4-9-10 P Goode (5) 20/1: 5-3003: 4 b g Aragon - Girton (Balidar): ¾ **54**
Towards rear, kept on final 2f, not pace of front pair: eff at 6f: handles fibresand & fast grnd: see 273 (AW).
4445} **NODS NEPHEW 99** [6] Miss J A Camacho 3-8-11 J Carroll 6/1: 00-4: Rear, prog 2f out, no room & nk **53**
swtchd inside last, kept on nr fin: 5 mth abs: shade unlucky, may have been plcd with a clr run: unplcd both
'99 starts (rtd 61, debut): should improve now h'capped.
2124} **FOXDALE 99** [2] 3-8-6 C Rutter 7/1: 0-5: Chsd ldrs, onepace fnl 2f: reapp: rtd 60 sole '99 start (mdn). 2 **42**
3863} **HOUT BAY 99** [3] 3-8-11 O Pears 10/1: 6440-6: Towards rear, nvr on terms: op 8/1: 7 mth abs: 1¾ **42**
best in '99 when 4th in a mdn (rtd 74): eff at 5/6f on gd grnd: h'cap company should suit best.
4600} **MAGIC SISTER 99** [7] 3-8-6 M Fenton 13/8 FAV: 66-7: Dwelt, chsd ldrs till over 1f out: well bckd: ¾ **34**
5 mth abs: unplcd both '99 starts (rtd 68): now qual for h'caps for M Bell.
4430} **ITS ANOTHER GIFT 99** [4] 3-8-6 Pat Eddery 5/1: 2300-8: Prom 5f: 5 mth abs: rnr-up in '99 (rtd 73, ¾ **31**
fillies auct mdn): eff over a sharp 5f on fast & gd grnd: prev with J Berry, now with A Berry.
8 ran   Time 1m 13.1 (2.8)   (Mr J Falvey & Mr G Williamson)   T D Barron Maunby, Nth Yorks.

782	4.50 YARM HCAP 3YO 0-75 (E) 1m4f Good/Firm 30 -06 Slow [82]
	£2814 £804 £402

640   **MERRYVALE MAN 25** [1] J G Given 3-8-11 (65) P Goode (5) 10/1: 053121: 3 b c Rudimentary - Salu **69**
(Ardross): Chsd ldrs after halfway, rdn/led over 1f out, styd on well inside last, all-out: op 8/1: earlier won
at Southwell (clmr, 1st win, rtd 70a): plcd on turf & sand in '99 (rtd 73 & 60a): eff at 11/12f, cld stay further:
acts on fast, gd/soft & fibresand: likes a sharp/turning trk: op to further improvement.
701   **SUNDAY RAIN 6** [4] P F I Cole 3-9-0 (68) J Carroll 9/4 JT FAV: 440-42: 3 b c Summer Squall - Oxava nk **71**
(Antheus): Prom, rdn/chall final 2f, kept on inside last, just held: nicely bckd, qck reapp: styd lngr 12f trip.
*640   **CHIEF OF JUSTICE 25** [9] J P Spencer 9/4 JT FAV: 00-113: 3 b c Be My Chief - nk **69**
Clare Court (Glint Of Gold): Led after 2f, rdn/hdd over 1f out, kept on well: hvly bckd: acts on fast grnd &
fibresand: clr of rem: ahead of this wnr in 640 (AW).
4059} **BOLLIN NELLIE 99** [2] T D Easterby 3-8-9 (63) R Winston 4/1: 4354-4: Chsd ldrs 3f out, held over 1f 9 **51**
out: tchd 5/1, 6 mth abs: plcd final start in '99 (rtd 63, h'cap): stays 1m, apprec mid-dists, handles fm & gd.
643   **DANCING MARY 23** [5] 3-8-11 (65) J Bosley (7) 25/1: 0-3035: Mid-div halfway, outpcd final 2f: see 500. ¾ **51**
536   **DUN DISTINCTLY 40** [12] 3-7-10 (50) Dale Gibson 7/1: 00-426: Mid-div/hmpd halfway, btn 3f out: abs. 5 **28**
4358} **TUMBLEWEED WIZARD 99** [7] 3-9-0 (68) Pat Eddery 7/1: 000-7: Led 2f, btn 4f out: op 5/1, 6 mth abs: 1 **44**
h'cap bow: unplcd from 3 '99 starts (rtd 72, tried up to 1m): a drop in trip may suit.
429   **DIAMOND GEORGIA 58** [6] 3-7-10 (50)(oh) D Mernagh(1) 50/1: 0-0508: Keen/held up, efft/btn 2f out. 2 **23**
4389} **DARVAN 99** [11] 3-8-0 (54)(t) C Rutter 33/1: 5060-9: Struggling 3f out: op 12/1, 5 mth abs: rtd 74 24 **0**
at best in '99 (mdn, debut): prob stays 7f & handles firm grnd: has tried a t-strap, mid dists could suit.
4263} **MERRY 99** [8] 3-7-10 (50)(t)(20oh) Kim Tinkler 100/1: 000-0: Bhd fnl 4f: 10th: 6 mth abs/h'cap bow. 7 **0**
10 ran   Time 2m 35.6 (4.4)   (Arthur Symons Key)   J G Given Willoughton, Lincs.

NOTTINGHAM WEDNESDAY MARCH 29TH Lefthand, Galloping Track

Official Going   GOOD (GOOD/FIRM Places). Stalls 5f, 6f & 1m6f - Stands Side; Rem - Inside.
Realignment of round course rendered pace figures unreliable

783	2.10 WELCOME BACK SELLER 3YO (G) 1m54y rnd Good Inapplicable
	£1939 £554 £277

3319} **LAGO DI LEVICO 99** [2] A P Jarvis 3-8-12 W Ryan 13/2: -0-1: 3 ch g Pelder - Langton Herring **60**
(Nearly A Hand): Slow away, prom by halfway, led bef 2f out, rdn & went badly right dist, all-out: op 4/1 on reapp,
bt in for 3,400gns: well btn sole '99 start: apprec step up to 1m, shld get 14f: acts on gd grnd & a gall trk.
103   **BONDI BAY 99** [10] J J O'Neill 3-8-7 Dean McKeown 4/1: 0035-2: 3 b f Catrail - Sodium's Niece shd **55**
(Northfields): Dwelt, imprvd dmnr aft 4f, chall fnl 2f, just failed: op 33/1, over 4 month abs, new stable: styd this
longer 1m trip: acts on gd grnd & fibresand & has shown enough to win in a seller.
207   **PRINCESS VICTORIA 99** [5] N A Callaghan 3-8-11 L Dettori 13/8 FAV: 1026-3: 3 b f Deploy - Scierpan 3 **53**
(Sharpen Up) Led till 2½f out, no extra 1f out: op 11/10, 15 wk abs: back up in trip: see 165 (AW, 6f).
643   **HIGH BEAUTY 23** [11] M J Ryan 3-8-7 P McCabe 10/1: 000-04: Held up, chsd ldrs 4f out till ent fnl 2f. 5 **39**
541   **JONLOZ 40** [1] 3-8-12 L Newton 33/1: 40-545: Prom, feeling pace after 4f, no threat: 6 wk abs, see 128. 1¾ **41**
3595} **ROYAL PASTIMES 99** [8] R Lappin 14/1: 6500-6: Nvr a factor: reapp: modest, bred for mid-dists. 2½ **31**
3573} **MARTIN 99** [6] J Fortune 8/1: 0004-7: Keen, cl-up till wknd over 3f out: tchd 12/1 on reapp: 1 **34**
glimmer of promise fnl '99 start (6f seller on fast grnd, rtd 55): with M Wane.
507   **BLAZING PEBBLES 46** [4] 3-8-7 R Ffrench 50/1: -00008: Chsd ldrs till 3f out: 7 wk abs, no form. 11 **11**
4367} **COURT FLIRT 99** [7] 3-8-7 J Fanning 12/1: 0-9: Held up, brief eff halfway: reapp, unplcd sole '99 start. 3 **5**
688   **BASIC INSTINCT 12** [3] 3-8-7 G Duffield 16/1: 0-0040: Handy till wknd qckly appr fnl 3f: 10th, see 192. 15 **0**
10 ran   Time 1m 48.8   (A P Jarvis)   A P Jarvis Aston Upthorpe, Oxon

784

2.40 1-IN-A 100 MDN 3YO+ (D)   1m54y rnd   **Good**   Inapplicable
£3835   £1180   £590   £295   3yo rec 17lb

4263} **AUCHONVILLERS 99** [8] B A McMahon 3-8-9 K Darley 6/1: 6-1: 3 b g Deploy - Forbearance (Bairn)   83
Cl-up, led ent str, rdn to assert ins last: op 4/1 on reapp: fair 6th in an auct mdn sole '99 start (rtd 76): eff at
1m, bred for mid-dists: acts on gd grnd & a gall trk: goes well fresh up with the pace: improve again over further.

4455} **SLOANE 99** [10] M L W Bell 4-9-12 J Fortune 5/1: 4620-2: 4 ch c Machiavellian - Gussy Marlowe   2   78
(Final Straw) Trkd ldrs, rdn to press wnr appr fnl 1f, outpcd fnl 100y: gd reapp & well clr rem: '99 rnr-up for G
Wragg (mdn, rtd 80): eff at 1m, shld stay 10f: acts on firm & gd grnd, gall trks: shld find a maiden.

--   **EXPLODE** [3] R Charlton 3-8-9 R Hughes 13/8 FAV: 3: 3 b c Zafonic - Didicoy (Danzig)   9   62
Keen, well plcd, eff appr fnl 2f, sn outpcd by front pair & position accepted: nicely bckd on debut: half-
brother to several wnrs, notably smart 1m performer Didina: shld know more next time.

661   **ACHILLES WINGS 18** [12] K R Burke 4-9-12 S Whitworth 20/1: 344: Bhd, weaved thro' btn horses fnl   1   60
2f, nvr a threat: turf bow, AW fit: not given hard time back in trip, 10f + h'caps will suit.

4455} **COMMANDER 99** [1] 4-9-12 N Callan 20/1: -05-5: Chsd ldrs, no extra appr fnl 2f: reapp: 5th of   ½   59
18 fnl of 2 '99 starts for H Cecil (mdn, rtd 71): now with M Kettle.

--   **TALIBAN** [14] 4-9-12 M Roberts 7/1: 6: Keen bhd, passes btn horses fnl 2f: op 4/1 on debut: 6   49
Bigstone half-brother to Aoife (6f AW wnr) & Samaka Hara (1m wnr): with G Wragg.

685   **PORT OF CALL 12** [2] 5-9-12 P McCabe 33/1: 567: Rear, not clr run & switched ent str, nvr a factor.   1   47

3083} **TYRA 99** [6] A Daly 14/1: -2-8: Led 4f, btn 2½f out: op 7/1, 5 wks ago fell on hdles bow: 1   40
rnr-up sole '99 start for H Cecil (mdn, rtd 70): eff at 1m on firm grnd: now with D Burchell.

--   **COURT CHAMPAGNE** [11] 4-9-7 P Doe 66/1: 00/9: Nvr troubled ldrs: 2 year abs, no form.   nk   39

4542} **HAMBLEDEN 99** [9] 3-8-9 R Robinson 11/2: 00-0: Mid-div thr'out: 10th, op 4/1 on reapp: some   2   40+
promise in a Newmarket mdn fnl '99 start (rtd 70): tenderly handled h'cap qualifying run: with M Jarvis.

2921} **NOBLE CHARGER 99** [13] 5-9-12 D R McCabe 50/1: 0000-0: Very slow away, nvr got in it: 11th,   1   38
stablemate of 7th, reapp: no worthwhile form, has tried blnks & a visor: with R Marvin.

565   **THE FINAL WORD 36** [15] 3-8-4 Dean McKeown 33/1: 5-5000: Stdd start, al bhd: 12th, AW fit, nds sells.   1½   30
--   **Ryka** [5] 5-9-12 J Tate 50/1:   --   **Tenacious Melody** [4] 4-9-12 T G McLaughlin 50/1:
--   **All Bleevable** [7] 3-8-9 G Duffield 50/1:

15 ran   Time 1m 47.2   (Major W R Paton Smith)   B A McMahon Hopwas, Staffs

785

3.10 SPONSORSHIP HCAP 3YO 0-70 (E)   6f   **Good**   Inapplicable   [77]
£3062   £875   £437   Stalls 1,2 & 3 raced far side, finished 1st, 3rd & 12th.

661   **TONDYNE 18** [1] T D Easterby 3-7-10 (45)(10h) P Fessey 25/1: 00-01: 3 b g Owington - Anodyne   55
(Dominion) Trkd ldrs far side, led appr fnl 1f, rdn out: tchd 40/1: 1st win/form on h'cap bow, referred to P Square
under instruction H19 (imprvd performances): apprec drop back to gall 6f on gd grnd: well plcd by connections.

706   **PADDYWACK 6** [6] D W Chapman 3-8-6 (55)(bl) G Parkin 4/1: 241122: 3 b g Bigstone - Millie's   3   57
Return (Ballad Rock) Led stands side thr'out & came clr of that group appr fnl 1f, not pace of wnr far side:
op 3/1, quick reapp: in terrific form, likely to go in again soon: see 654 (equitrack).

549   **LUSONG 39** [3] R Hannon 3-8-13 (62) Dane O'Neill 8/1: -2263: 3 ch c Fayruz - Mildred Anne   2½   58
(Thatching) Cl-up far side, led 2½f till before dist, onepace: 6 wk abs: turf/h'cap bow: eff at 6f, drop
back to 5f might suit this speedy sort: acts on gd grnd & equitrack.

4310} **MISTER CLINTON 99** [7] K T Ivory 3-7-13 (47)(10w) A Daly 66/1: 000-4: Hmpd & bhd, stands side,   2½   38
ran on for press fnl 2f, nvr nr to chall: reapp/h'cap bow: well btn all 3 '99 starts (mdn, rtd 55).

222   **WATERGRASSHILL 98** [10] 3-8-8 (57) R Ffrench 7/1: 0254-5: Chsd ldrs stands side, onepace fnl 2f.   1¾   42

654   **ITSGOTTABDUN 21** [13] 3-8-11 (60)(bl) G Duffield 9/1: 614236: Al around same place stands side.   3½   37

417   **NORTHERN TRIO 61** [5] 3-8-3 (52) J Fanning 66/1: 000-07: Prom stands side till 2f out: 9 wk abs.   1¾   24

479   **AISLE 50** [4] 3-8-12 (61) N Callan 14/1: 522558: In tch stands side till 2f out, sn edged left: 7 wk abs.   hd   32

549   **CAROLS CHOICE 39** [16] 3-9-2 (65) S Drowne 9/1: 36-429: Nvr troubled ldrs stands side: not given   1¾   32
a hard time after 6 wk abs: h'cap bow: see 549, 493.

592   **OTIME 32** [14] 3-9-5 (68)(vis) Dean McKeown 11/1: 4-6020: Well plcd stands side, outpcd 2f out: 10th.   nk   34

4302} **ALJAZIR 99** [15] 3-8-10 (59) R Hughes 9/1: 0054-0: Al towards rear stands side: 11th, reapp: promise   1   22
more than once in '99 (mdn, debut, rtd 70, nurs, rtd 58): eff at 6f, handles soft & hvy grnd, without blnks.

549   **CAPE COAST 39** [2] 3-9-7 (70)(BL) L Dettori 11/1: 26-00: Led far side till after halfway, bhd: 12th, op 7/1.   1½   42

706   **WILLKOR TIMES 6** [11] 3-8-11 (60) K Darley 7/1: 004-50: Nvr better than mid-div stands side: 13th.   2½   13

479   **CHRISTOPHERSSISTER 50** [9] 3-9-4 (67) M Tebbutt 14/1: 20-100: Al bhd stands side: 15th, 7 wk abs.   0

2905} **Arcadian Chief 99** [12] 3-7-10 (45)(10h) C Catlin(6) 50/1:

4210} **Fantasy Adventurer 99** [8] 3-9-6 (69) A Culhane 20/1:

16 ran   Time 1m 14.2 (3.4)   (Dr M Gelfand)   T D Easterby Great Habton, N Yorks

786

3.40 TOTE TRIFECTA HCAP 3YO+ 0-85 (D)   1m2f   **Good**   Inapplicable   [85]
£7410   £2280   £1140   £570

632   **FORTY FORTE 25** [6] K R Burke 4-9-0 (71) N Callan 11/2: 162441: 4 b g Pursuit Of Love - Cominna   76
(Dominion) Made ev yard, 3L clr bef dist, hard rdn ins last, just lasted: prev won at Lingfield (h'cap, rtd 74a): '99
wnr here at Nottingham (sell, M Channon), Beverley (rtd 78) & Lingfield (h'caps, rtd 71a): eff at 7/10f: acts on
firm, hvy grnd & both AWs: likes equitrack, Lingfield & Nottingham: loves to dominate: tough.

715   **SPRING PURSUIT 5** [10] R J Price 4-9-7 (78) P Doe 12/1: 62-602: 4 b g Rudimentary - Pursuit Of   hd   82
Truth (Irish River) Rear, shaken up & wide into str, ran on strongly under press fnl 2f, just failed: wnr in
another 10 yards, tchd 16/1, quick reapp: apprec return to 10f & prob imprvd in defeat: see 662.

4429} **MANTUSIS 99** [7] P W Harris 5-9-4 (83) W R Swinburn 9/2: 4001-3: 5 ch g Pursuit Of Love - Mana   1¼   85
(Windwurf) Mid-div, prog 3f out, rdn 2f out, kept on, unable to chall: gd reapp/rtd' returned with a cut fetlock:
won fnl '99 start at Yarmouth (h'cap, rtd 85): '98 rnr-up (h'cap, rtd 94): '97 Haydock wnr (mdn, rtd 87): eff
at 7/10f, poss stays 11.8f: acts on firm & hvy, former prob suits: goes on any trk: suited by a furious gallop.

4530} **PINCHINCHA 99** [5] D Morris 6-9-4 (75) J Tate 10/1: 2023-4: Towards rear, gd prog to chase wnr 2f   ½   76
out, fnd no extra & onepace ins last: rnr-up sev times in '99 (h'caps, rtd 78): last win in '97 at Folkestone, Doncaster
(ltd stks) & Pontefract (h'caps, rtd 85): suited by 10f on firm & gd/soft, any trk, without visor: well h'capped.

705   **THOMAS HENRY 6** [4] 4-8-0 (57) A Daly 7/1: 066055: In tch, shkn up halfway, sn briefly short of   1½   56
room, styd on for press ins last: op 5/1, quick reapp: shaped like a return to 12f would suit: see 705, 110.

632   **ANEMOS 25** [11] 5-9-0 (71) P Robinson 4/1 FAV: -23426: Rcd in 2nd, eff 3f out, unable to qckn: see 160.   1½   68

NOTTINGHAM WEDNESDAY MARCH 29TH Lefthand, Galloping Track

4574} **YOUNG UN 99** [9] 5-8-8 (65) P McCabe 11/1: 0251-7: Bhd, mod hdwy 3f out, nvr dangerous: reapp, op 8/1: '99 wnr at Newcastle, here at Nottingham & Redcar (h'caps, rtd 65): eff at 9/10f: acts on firm & gd/soft grnd, likes stiff/gall trks: best without blnks & t-strap: shld be much sharper for this. — 3 57

4603} **HINDI 99** [12] 4-8-9 (66) G Duffield 25/1: 0456-8: Chsd ldrs, rdn & no impress 3f out: reapp, op 16/1, h'cap bow: promise middle of 5 '99 starts (1m mdn on firm, rtd 70): front-runner last term: with N Graham. — 2 55

473 **NOBLE CYRANO 51** [2] 5-8-2 (58)(1ow) J Fanning 25/1: 2-1009: Keen towards rear, imprvd ent str, fdd 2f out: 7 wk abs, new stable, longer trip, usually forces the pace: see 251 (1m, fibresand). — 1 47

4574} **SANDABAR 99** [3] 7-8-5 (60)(t) (2ow) A Culhane 12/1: 1004-0: Nvr a factor: 10th, op 8/1 on reapp: '99 wnr at Ripon (h'cap, rtd 63): 98/99 scorer 4 times over hdles (rtd 124h at best), loves fast grnd, stays 2m1f: eff at 1m/10f on gd grnd, loves firm: goes on any trk & wears a t-strap. — 3 46

611 **CHARTER FLIGHT 29** [1] 4-8-1 (58) L Newman (3) 10/1: 1-0400: Keen, in tch till 3f out: 11th, tchd 14/1. — hd 42

3159} **THE EXHIBITION FOX 99** [8] 4-9-9 (80) K Darley 12/1: 4100-0: Slow away, chsd ldrs till ent str: 12th: reapp: '99 York wnr (mdn, rtd 85, last both h'cap starts): eff at 1m, tried 10f: acts on gd grnd. — 15 49

12 ran   Time 2m 10.4   (Nigel Shields)   K R Burke Newmarket, Suffolk

---

787   4.10 CENTENARY CLUB HCAP 4YO+ 0-70 (E)   6f   Good   Inapplicable   [67]
£3255 £930 £465   Raced in 2 groups, far side probably held sway

3576} **BUNDY 99** [10] M Dods 4-9-3 (56) A Clark 14/1: 4000-1: 4 b g Ezzoud - Sanctuary Cove (Habitat) Led far side, began hanging right & hard rdn/hard prsd dist, just prevailed in a v tight finish: op 10/1 on reapp: 3rd in this race in '99 (h'cap, rtd 71): '98 wnr at Newcastle (sell) & Warwick (h'cap, rtd 73): eff at 6f, tried 1m: acts on fast & hvy grnd, sharp or gall trks: goes well fresh, well h'capped. — 62

645 **JAMES DEE 23** [1] A P Jarvis 4-9-8 (61) W Ryan 7/2 FAV: 1-0222: 4 b g Shalford - Glendale Joy (Glenstal) Cl-up far side, strong chall appr fnl 1f, just failed: AW fit: ran to turf best, see 462. — shd 65

35 **ABBAJABBA 99** [17] C W Fairhurst 4-9-9 (62) J Fanning 25/1: 6660-3: 4 b g Barrys Gamble - Bo' Babbity (Strong Gale) Front rank stands side, rdn appr fnl 1f, styd on, nvr reached far side ldrs: unpicd last term (mdn, rtd 67): juv rnr-up (rtd 82 in a nursery): eff at 5/6f, tried 7f: acts on gd & gd/soft grnd: maiden. — ¾ 64

130 **ENCOUNTER 99** [8] J Hetherton 4-8-12 (51) K Darley 20/1: 0000-4: Chsd ldrs far side, styd on for press but not pace to chall: op 16/1, 4 month abs: landed a 24hr brace in '99 at Ayr (sell) & Hamilton (h'cap, rtd 58): flattered in '98 for C Brittain (mdn, rtd 77S): eff at 6/7f, tried 1m: acts on fast grnd, stiff/gall trks. — 2 47

499 **BATALEUR 47** [4] 7-8-13 (52) R Lappin 14/1: 021-65: Cl-up far side, ev ch appr fnl 2f no extra fnl 100y. — nk 47

711 **SEVEN SPRINGS 6** [2] 4-8-7 (45)(1ow) L Dettori 16/1: 00-006: In tch far side, styd on fnl 2f without threatening: tchd 25/1, quick reapp: jockey fined for coming out of wrong stall (shld have been 3): see 647. — ½ 39

543 **SHARP HAT 39** [20] 6-9-7 (60) A Culhane 7/1: 342447: Dsptd lead stands side till ent fnl 2f, no extra: op 8/1 after 6 wk abs: shld be spot on for this: see 91. — 1½ 49

628 **AUBRIETA 25** [12] 4-8-11 (50)(bl) S Drowne 10/1: 1-0528: Went to race far side, al same place. — 2 33

*628 **CHAKRA 25** [3] 6-8-1 (40) R Ffrench 12/1: 650619: Chsd ldrs far sidr till 2f out: tchd 16/1: see 628. — 1¾ 19

550 **PRIORY GARDENS 39** [6] 6-8-1 (40) A Daly 20/1: 300000: Chsd ldrs far side, outpcd 2f out: 10th. — 1 16

648 **THREE LEADERS 23** [18] 4-8-12 (51) Dane O'Neill 20/1: 05-060: In tch stands side till 2f out: 11th. — nk 26

660 **DIL 18** [5] 5-9-10 (63) P McCabe 15/2: 010000: Slow away, sn cl-up, fdd fnl 2f: 12th, op 6/1, see 394. — nk 38

-- **LANDING CRAFT** [7] 6-9-7 (60) T G McLaughlin 20/1: 0434-0: Dwelt, nvr in it far side: 13th on reapp/Brit bow, op 14/1: ex-Irish, plcd last term, back in '98 won at Fairyhouse (7f h'cap on gd/soft grnd): stays 9f, acts on fast & gd/soft grnd: with D Carroll. — ¾ 33

4077} **RUM LAD 99** [19] 6-9-10 (63) J Fortune 10/1: 4500-0: Chsd ldrs stands side till 2f out: 16th, op 8/1 on reapp: won back-to-back races at Pontefract in '99 (h'cap & class stks, rtd 69 & 52a): '98 W'hampton wnr (h'cap, rtd 69a & 66): eff at 5/6f, stays 7f: acts on firm, hvy grnd & fibresand, likes Pontefract. — 0

531 **TRUMPET BLUES 41** [16] 4-9-2 (55) M Tebbutt 12/1: /6-030: Led stands side for 3f, wknd qckly: op 7/1. — 0

4496} **D W Mccee 99** [13] 4-8-13 (52) G Duffield 33/1:   635 **Hunan Scholar 25** [14] 5-8-5 (44) D R McCabe 33/1:
673 **Colonel Sam 15** [11] 4-8-11 (50)(tbl) N Callan 25/1:   4384} **Time To Fly 99** [15] 7-8-5 (44)(bl) D Sweeney 20/1:
1790} **King Uno 99** [9] 6-9-7 (60) R Hughes 20/1:

20 ran   Time 1m 13.8 (3)   (A J Henderson)   M Dods Piercebridge, Co Durham

---

788   4.40 COME RACING HCAP 4YO+ 0-70 (E)   1m6f   Good   Inapplicable   [64]
£3132 £895 £447   4 yo rec 4 lb

285 **DOUBLE RUSH 81** [15] T Keddy 8-8-0 (36)(t) J Tate 20/1: 060-61: 8 b g Doulab - Stanza Dancer (Stanford) Mid-div, clsd ent str, led bef dist, styd on strgly: jumps fit: plcd in '99 (h'cap, rtd 42): '98 Bath wnr (sell, rtd 58 & 65a, T Mills): eff at 12f/14f on firm, soft & equitrack, any trk: imprvd for t-strap. — 44

552 **MY LEGAL EAGLE 39** [11] R J Price 6-9-3 (53) P Fitzsimons (5) 12/1: 032222: 6 b g Law Society - Majestic Nurse (On Your Mark) Waited with, smooth hdwy 4f out to chall 2f out, sn rdn, same pace ins last: op 10/1, 6 wk abs: consistent, deserves a change of luck, possibly back at 12f: see 141, 126. — 2 57

-- **MENTAL PRESSURE** [8] Mrs M Reveley 7-8-9 (45) A Culhane 6/1: 0000/3: 7 ch g Polar Falcon - Hysterical (High Top) Dwelt, imprvd after 1m, rdn to chall 2f out, unable to qckin under press ins last: clr rem, tchd 8/1 after 2 year abs: last worthwhile form when plcd 6 of 7 '96 starts in h'caps, rtd 84): eff arnd 12/14f on firm & gd grnd: prob goes on any trk: should shed maiden tag off this mark. — nk 48

699 **I CANT REMEMBER 6** [14] S R Bowring 6-9-10 (60) P Dobbs (5) 8/1: 652454: Mid-div, boxed in 4f out, rdn 2f out, onepace: tchd 12/1: not much luck in running, capable of better: see 428. — 6 56

4458} **VERSATILITY 99** [9] 7-9-0 (50) G Duffield 20/1: 0160-5: Mid-div, switched for eff appr fnl 3f, no impress on ldrs: '99 Warwick wnr (h'cap, rtd 53, G McCourt): prev won over timber at Ludlow (nov sell, 2m, soft): lightly rcd on the Flat before that: eff at 14.5f, tried 2m: acts on soft grnd, sharp trks. — ½ 45

4370} **CUPBOARD LOVER 99** [7] 4-9-10 (64) S Drowne 20/1: 3010-6: Trkd ldrs, outpcd appr fnl 2f: reapp, top-weight: '99 wnr at Hamilton & here at Nottingham (h'caps, rtd 64): unplcd juv (tried blnks): eff at 12f, suited by 14f: acts on fast & gd grnd, stiff/gall trks: fitter next time: with D Haydn Jones. — 1½ 57

699 **PROTOCOL 6** [2] 6-9-2 (52)(t) J Fortune 9/1: 510-07: Shuffled back towards rear aft 2f, wide effort turning for home, kept on same pace: op 7/1, quick reapp: handles fast, best on soft grnd: see 699. — 1 44

3426} **FAITH AGAIN 99** [12] 4-8-5 (45) L Newton 20/1: 2534-8: Nvr better than mid-div: won 3 hdles in late '99 at Bangor, Taunton & Ludlow (juv novs, 2m1f, fast & gd grnd, rtd 114h): rnr-up for C Wall in '99 (clmr, 2m 1m/9f: acts on firm & gd grnd: with A Streeter. — ¾ 36

4397} **MURCHAN TYNE 99** [6] 7-9-8 (58) K Darley 8/1: 5150-9: Held up, gd prog to lead 2½f out, hdd & wknd qckly before dist: reapp: '99 Ripon wnr (h'cap, rtd 60, E Alston): '98 Leicester scorer (fill h'cap, rtd 63): eff at 12f, suited by 2m1f: acts on firm, hvy grnd, any trk: with B McMahon. — hd 49

*668 **IRISH CREAM 15** [10] 4-8-0 (40)(vis) M Henry 10/1: 3-2010: Cl-up, led turning for home till before 2f out, sn wknd: 10th: op 8/1, fit from an AW win, see 668. — nk 30

252

NOTTINGHAM   WEDNESDAY MARCH 29TH   Lefthand, Galloping Track

526} **SHERIFF 99** [5] 9-9-5 (55) M Hills 16/1: 4-24-0: Nvr a factor: 11th on reapp: '99 rnr-up (h'cap, rtd   3½   42
77a): prev won over hdles at N Abbot (stays 3m, firm & gd/soft): 97/98 wnr at Worcester & Southwell (rtd 118h):
'98 hat-trick scorer on the Flat at Lingfield (h'cap, rtd 76a & 55): eff at 2m: handles fast grnd but is an
equitrack/Lingfield specialist: goes well fresh & can carry big weights: with J Hills.
380   **PRASLIN ISLAND 67** [3] 4-9-6 (60) W R Swinburn 7/2 FAV: 21-230: Led for 1m, btn 3f out: 12th,   1¾   46
10 wk abs, new stable, gone from A Kelleway to P Harris: see 182.
190   **CLASSIC REFERENDUM 99** [4] 6-9-7 (57) L Dettori 4/1: 0000-0: Trkd ldrs, lost place ent str: 15th, op 2/1.   0
2752} Silent Valley 99 [13] 6-7-10 (32)(2oh) J Lowe 40/1:   4255} **Urgent Reply 99** [16] 7-8-4 (40)(t) P Fessey 16/1:
15 ran   Time 3m 08.3   (The Barneby Partnership)   T Keddy Alfrick, Worcs

---

LEICESTER   THURSDAY MARCH 30TH   Righthand, Stiff, Galloping Track

Official Going   GOOD.

789	2.10 BESCABY MDN 3YO (D) 1m str Good 45 -09 Slow
	£4004 £1232 £616 £308

3588} **MAN OMYSTERY 99** [13] J Noseda 3-9-0 W R Swinburn 14/1: 0-1: 3 b c Diesis - Eurostorm (Storm Bird)   90
In tch, keen, styd on to lead over 2f out, rdn out ins last: reapp: rtd 74 when unplcd on sole '99 start: dam
7f juv wnr: stays a stiff 1m well on gd grnd & runs well fresh: open to plenty of further improvement.
3755} **EVEREST 99** [3] P F I Cole 3-9-0 J Fortune 6/4 FAV: 2-2: 3 ch c Indian Ridge - Reine d'Beaute   1¼   87
(Caerleon) Waited with, hdwy over 2f out, kept on ins, btn just over 1L: bckd tho' op 8/1: rnr-up in a
Haydock mdn sole juv start (rtd 89): dam 1m/9f scorer: stays 1m on firm & gd, gall trk: should win similar.
4569} **STAR DYNASTY 99** [15] E A L Dunlop 3-9-0 J Reid 13/2: 4-3: 3 b c Bering - Siwaayib (Green Desert)   nk   87
Led over 5f, rdn & kept on same pace for press despite edging left appr fnl 1f: clr of rem on reapp, jockey
received a 1 day careless riding ban: rtd 80 when 4th on sole '99 start: half-brother to a useful stayer: dam
6f juv wnr: stays 1m, further sure to suit: acts on gd & gd/soft: shld win a race, probs over further.
4358} **KNIGHTS EMPEROR 99** [12] J Noseda 3-9-0 J Weaver 7/1: 0-4: Handy, keen, rdn & sltly outpcd over   4   81+
2f out, short of room over 1f out, kept on nicely ins last: stablemate of wnr: rtd 78 sole juv start: half-
brother to a speedy sprinter, dam 6f scorer: speedily bred but stays 1m & further cld suit: improve, win a race.
--   **AMJAD** [11] 3-9-0 L Dettori 12/1: 5: Dwelt & hmpd start, bhd till effort over 2f out, onepace: nk   78
half-brother to wnrs over 7f/12f: dam useful 6f juv scorer: encouraging debut run, learn plenty from this.
--   **KRISPIN** [10] 3-9-0 D Holland 14/1: 6: Waited with, went right start, bhd, eff 2f out, sn wknd: 1   76
debut: half-brother to wnrs over 5f/12f: encouraging first run, shld relish further.
4543} **THUNDERING SURF 99** [5] 3-9-0 S Whitworth 20/1: 5-7: Slow away, bhd, kept on late, nrst fin: 1   74
rtd 81 when unplcd sole juv start: dam 10f wnr: shaped promisingly here, worth a try over further.
3658} **GRUINART 99** [6] 3-9-0 C Rutter 50/1: 0-8: Chsd ldrs, rdn & not clr run 2f out, sn no impress: reapp.   1½   71
4495} **SAN DIMAS 99** [4] 3-9-0 M Hills 66/1: 00-9: Waited with, effort over 3f out, sn no impress: had 3 runs.   ¾   69
4523} **GIVE NOTICE 99** [9] 3-9-0 Pat Eddery 16/1: 60-0: Cl-up till wknd 2f out, eased: 10th, had 3 runs.   ½   68
717   **PILLAGER 6** [2] 3-9-0 J Stack 66/1: 0-60: Al bhd: 11th.   1   66
4606} **THE ROBSTER 99** [8] 3-9-0 K Fallon 15/2: 00-0: In tch, eff over 2f out, wkng & hmpd over 1f out: 12th.   2¼   61
3055} Swinging Trio 99 [1] 3-9-0 (t) A Clark 50/1:   --   Love Bitten [17] 3-9-0 J Fanning 20/1:
4493} Expedient 99 [14] 3-9-0 G Carter 33/1:   610   St Georges Bay 30 [16] 3-9-0 J Bramhill 66/1:
16 ran   Time 1m 38.7 (4.3)   (Ecurie Pharos)   J Noseda Newmarket.

790	2.40 BILLESDON SELLER 3YO+ (G) 7f str Good 45 -31 Slow
	£2033 £581 £290 3 yo rec 15lb

2408} **DANDY REGENT 99** [11] J L Harris 6-9-7 D Holland 10/1: 4450-1: 6 b g Green Desert - Tahilla   54
(Mooresty1e) Led over 4f, kept on well for press ins last to get up again cl-home: no bid, reapp, rnr-up once
in '99 (rtd 50): in '98 won at Brighton (h'cap, rtd 74 & 60a): eff at 6f, suited by 7f/1m on firm, hvy or
equitrack: handles any trk & runs well fresh in sell grade.
628   **ABSOLUTE FANTASY 26** [15] E A Wheeler 4-9-2 (bl) S Carson (5) 33/1: -62602: 4 b f Beveled - Sharp   nk   48
Venita (Sharp Edge) Handy, effort to lead over 2f out, hard rdn & collared cl-home, just btn: jockey received
a 4 day whip ban: enjoyed ride to suit: suited by a seller & handles equitrack & gd: see 399, 109.
756   **BIRCHWOOD SUN 2** [16] M Dods 10-9-7 (vis) J Weaver 5/1 FAV: 003-33: 10 b g Bluebird - Shapely   ½   52
Test (Elocutionist): In tch, rdn over 1f out, kept on ins last, not btn far: loves a stiff fin & J Weaver on board.
2150} **LEONIE SAMUAL 99** [3] R J Hodges 5-9-2 S Drowne 50/1: 00-4: Keen, waited with, effort 2f out,   1¼   45
kept on same pace appr fnl 1f: reapp, well btn both '99 starts: stays 7f on gd grnd: sell h'caps will suit.
497   **BLOOMING AMAZING 48** [9] 6-9-7 T G McLaughlin 11/2: -00605: In tch, rdn & sltly outpcd over 1f   nk   49
out, late gains: 7 wk abs: likes Beverley & a shade further: blnks discarded, see 497, 176.
4553} **HALMANERROR 99** [10] 3-9-0 T Quinn 11/2: 0000-6: Waited with, some late gains: reapp: '99   nk   48
scored twice at Chepstow (h'caps, rtd 66): '98 wnr at Brighton (clmr) & Salisbury (h'cap, rtd 58 & 53a): eff at
6f/1m, 7f ideal: acts on firm, hvy & fibresand: likes Chepstow: sharper for this & interesting in a sell h'cap.
667   **SHAMWARI SONG 16** [7] P F Egan 25/1: 020307: In tch, effort 2f out, onepaced.   1½   45
3765} **TAMASHAN 99** [19] 4-9-7 Dane O'Neill 50/1: 0600-8: In tch, wknd over 1f out: modest '99 form.   1   43
353   **OUDALMUTEENA 71** [18] 5-9-7 Martin Dwyer 13/2: 600-09: Al bhd: abs, no visor, mdn.   nk   42
--   **CASTLE BEAU** [4] 5-9-7 R Havlin 50/1: 0/0: Slow away & al bhd: 10th.   shd   42
711   **STRATS QUEST 7** [12] 6-9-2 S Whitworth 14/1: 5-6500: In tch till wknd well over 1f out: 11th.   2½   32
381   **FLITE OF LIFE 68** [13] 4-9-12 P Doe 8/1: 51-600: Dwelt, al bhd, fin last: 10 wk abs, btr 177.   0
585   Puiwee 34 [1] 5-9-2 J Bramhill 50/1:   594   Sound The Trumpet 33 [5] 8-9-12 (t) A Mackay 33/1:
578   Castrato 35 [8] 4-9-7 R Studholme 50/1:   4607} Newdowd Trident 99 [17] 3-8-1 J Tate 14/1:
246   Czar Wars 87 [14] 5-9-7 (bl) D Sweeney 25/1:   710   Sparkling Dove 7 [2] 7-9-2 (bl) R Price 25/1:
18 ran   Time 1m 27.3 (5.3)   (J L Harris)   J L Harris Eastwell, Leics.

791	3.10 SIRRUS HCAP 4YO+ 0-70 (E) 1m3f183y Good 45 +08 Fast	[70]
	£2856 £816 £408 4 yo rec 2 lb	

562   **PUZZLEMENT 37** [14] C E Brittain 6-10-0 (70) N Esler (7) 6/1: -33331: 6 gr g Mystiko - Abuzz   76
(Absalom) Slow away, waited with, gd hdwy to lead 3f out, kept on well, shade cosily: best time of day: fit
from sev plcd AW runs (rtd 77a): rnr-up in '99 (rtd 74 & 76a): '98 Beverley wnr (2, h'caps, rtd 73): eff over

10/12f on firm, soft & both AWs: handles any trk, likes Lingfield & Beverley: best held up: tough & in form.

4370} **RARE GENIUS 99** [15] P W Harris 4-9-6 (64) W R Swinburn 3/1 FAV: 3052-2: 4 ch g Beau Genius - Aunt Nola (Olden Times) Cl-up, ev ch well over 1f out, not pace of wnr ins last: plcd on 2 of 7 '99 starts (rtd 65): eff at 10/14f on gd/firm, gd & on a stiff or sharpish trk: shown enough to pinch a h'cap. — 1¼ 66

642 **NOSEY NATIVE 24** [4] J Pearce 7-8-0 (42) G Bardwell 25/1: 00-003: 7 b g Cyrao de Bergerac - Native Flair (Be My Native) Dwelt, waited with, hard rdn over 2f out, kept on late, no dngr: slipped down the weights. — 2 42

4336} **GOLDEN ACE 99** [9] R C Spicer 7-7-11 (39)(tbl)(1ow)(2oh) A Mackay 9/1: 0050-4: Waited with, eff over 3f out, onepace fnl 2f: won 1 of 10 '99 starts, Folkestone (appr h'cap, rtd 42): rtd 56 in '98: suited by 12f, stays 14f: acts on fast, likes gd & hvy grnd & any trk: wears a t-strap & blnks: encouraging reapp. — ¾ 37

3950} **SMART SPIRIT 99** [13] 6-8-5 (47) A Culhane 100/30: 1440-5: Led 4f, led over 4f out till 3f out, no extra fnl 2f: last rcd over hdles 2 months ago, won at Sedgefield & Wetherby (h'caps, rtd 115h, 2m1f, firm & soft): '99 Flat wnr at Nottingham (h'cap, rtd 49): 98/99 nov hdle wnr at Perth & Sedgefield: eff at 10/11f on firm & soft. — 7 36

2032} **MAY KING MAYHEM 99** [2] 7-8-0 (42) S Righton 10/1: 0116-6: Waited with, nvr a factor: last rcd back in June '99, scored at Leicester (appr h'cap) & Newmarket (lady amat h'cap, rtd 43): '98 scorer at Haydock & Pontefract (appr h'cap, rtd 43): all win at 12f, stays 15f: acts on fast, gd/soft & loves fibresand: likes a gall trk: best in blnks, tried a visor: runs well for an amat/appr & will do better when blnks are reapplied. — 4 25

522 **BASHER JACK 44** [1] 4-7-10 (40)(t)(2oh) J Mackay (7) 25/1: 164-07: In tch, wknd over 2f out: see 522. — ½ 22

1366} **MULTI FRANCHISE 99** [10] 7-7-10 (38)(2oh) Joanna Badger (7) 40/1: 6/00-8: In tch till wknd 2f out. — 3½ 15

3521} **KHUCHN 99** [6] 4-9-4 (62) G Carter 16/1: 0010-9: Led 1m out till 4f out, wknd: now with M Brittain. — shd 39

1442 **CROMER PIER 99** [8] 5-7-10 (38)(12oh) G Baker 50/1: 0000-0: Al bhd, 10th, jumps rnr. — hd 15

2454} **ARTHURS KINGDOM 99** [5] 4-9-5 (63) W Ryan 7/1: 3006-0: Nvr a factor: 11th: reapp. — ½ 39

-- **Ruby Estate** [3] 9-7-10 (38)(1oh) C Halliwell (7) 33/1: 2382} **Grey Buttons 99** [11] 5-7-11 (39) M Henry 33/1:

13 ran   Time 2m 32.7 (4.4)   (Mrs C Brittain)   C E Brittain Newmarket.

---

792 **3.40 TOTE PLACEPOT HCAP 3YO 0-90 (C)**   7f str Good 45 -08 Slow   [97]
£7124   £2192   £1096   £548

4601} **I PROMISE YOU 99** [4] C E Brittain 3-8-1 (70) A Nicholls (3) 8/1: 4035-1: 3 b g Shareef Dancer - Abuzz (Absalom) Prom, styd on to lead over 2f out, edged left under press ins last, just held on, drvn out: jockey rec a 6 day careless riding ban: plcd on 1 of 6 '99 start (rtd 70): threat to 1m/12f wnr Puzzlement: eff at 7f, stays 1m on gd & fast, reportedly not soft: acts on a stiff trk & runs well fresh: shade fortunate to keep this. — 72

4355} **PROUD CHIEF 99** [1] A P Jarvis 3-8-7 (76) W Ryan 5/1: 0000-2: 3 ch c Be My Chief - Fleur de Foret (Green Forest) Cl-up, kept on for press despite hanging right over 1f out, just held: reapp: won 1 of 6 '99 starts, at Goodwood (mdn, rtd 85): eff at 6/7f on gd/firm, gd & on any trk: runs well fresh: gd reapp. — nk 77

3593} **LOVE LANE 99** [2] M Johnston 3-8-11 (80) J Fanning 11/2: 3010-3: 3 b g Mujtahid - Ibda (Mtoto) Cl-up, eff for press & only ½L down when badly hmpd & snatched up ins last, not recover: value for a narrow defeat, reapp: won 1 of 6 juv starts when making all at Beverley (nurs h'caps, rtd 80): dam 7f juv wnr: eff at 6/7.5f on firm & gd: has run well fresh from the front: tried vis/blnks: shld win a race this term. — 3 81

4491} **INDIAN SUN 99** [8] J L Dunlop 3-8-12 (81) Pat Eddery 6/1: 0610-4: In tch, keen, rdn & onepace over 1f out: won 1 of 4 juv starts, at Lingfield (mdn, rtd 84): eff at 6f, prob stays 7f & acts on soft, handles fm. — ½ 75

*689 **THE PROSECUTOR 13** [3] 3-8-3 (70)(2ow) L Newman (5) 9/2: 01-615: Sn rdn, handy, outpcd 2f out, some late gains: shld stay 7f: see 689 (fibresand). — 1½ 63

2745} **DIGITAL IMAGE 99** [6] 3-9-7 (90) Dane O'Neill 12/1: 1060-6: Cl-up, wknd well over 1f out: reapp. — 6 71

4355} **HUNTING TIGER 99** [5] 3-9-5 (88) J Reid 11/4 FAV: 0152-7: Led over 4f, wknd 2f out: reapp: as a juv won at Haydock (made all, mdn, rtd 90): dam 7f Gr 3 wnr: eff at 6/7f on firm, gd grnd & on a gall trk: can force the pace: genuine, better than this. — 3½ 63

7 ran   Time 1m 25.7 (3.7)   (Mrs C Brittain)   C E Brittain Newmarket.

---

793 **4.10 GEORGE VANN HCAP 4YO+ 0-80 (D)**   1m2f Good 45 +00 Fast   [79]
£4043   £1244   £622   £311

4317} **TOTAL DELIGHT 99** [2] Lady Herries 4-9-9 (74)(t) T Quinn 4/1 FAV: /320-1: 4 b g Mtoto - Shesadelight (Shirley Heights) Chsd ldr till went on over 1f out, kept on, rdn out: nicely bckd on reapp: plcd in '99 (rtd 77): eff at 10f, further shld suit: acts on gd/firm & gd/soft: runs well fresh & may have improved for a t-stap. — 80

4262} **BATTLE WARNING 99** [9] M D Hammond 5-8-4 (55) J Fanning 14/1: 0500-2: 5 b g Warning - Royal Ballet (Sadler's Wells) Prom, eff over 2f out, kept on for press ins last, no impress: unplcd for H Candy in '99 (rtd 60): imprvd for new connections (prev with H Candy) & stays 10f on gd grnd, worth a try over further. — 2½ 57

575 **ADMIRALS PLACE** [7] H J Collingridge 4-8-13 (64) G Carter 13/2: 5-1223: 4 ch c Perugino - Royal Daughter (High Top) Keen, waited with, hdwy & sltly short of room over 1f out, kept on ins last: gd run. — 1¼ 63

4264} **FREEDOM QUEST 99** [16] B S Rothwell 5-8-11 (62) M Roberts 14/1: 2410-4: In tch, rdn & edged left over 1f out, onepace: jockey received a 1 day careless riding ban: proved tough in '99, won at Beverley & Musselburgh (h'caps, also plcd sev times, rtd 64): rtd 76 in '98: eff at 1m, stays 12f on firm, gd/soft & fibresand: best without a visor on any trk: sharper from this encouraging come-back run. — nk 61

4232} **POLRUAN 99** [8] 4-8-8 (59) S Drowne 25/1: 5004-5: Led till over 1f out, no extra ins last: in '99 trained by Lady Herries (unplcd, rtd 64): '98 Warwick wnr (mdn, rtd 79, with B Millman): eff at 7f, prob stays 10f on gd & soft grnd & on any trk: slipped right down the ratings & spot on next time. — 1¼ 56

*705 **ACEBO LYONS 99** [13] 5-8-11 (62)(6ex) W Ryan 9/2: 400-16: Waited with, eff over 2f out, hmpd over 1f out, not given hard time: see 705. — ½ 58

4530} **LADY ROCKSTAR 99** [4] 5-9-10 (75) P McCabe 16/1: 0405-7: Waited with, brief eff over 2f out, no extra over 1f out: in '99 scored at Newbury (h'cap, rtd 83): in tremendous '98 form, won 8 races in 32 days, at Ayr, Folkestone, Haydock, Yarmouth, Nottingham, Windsor (2, incl a ltd stks) & Folkestone (h'caps, rtd 88): wng form at 1m/10f on firm, soft & any trk: tried blnks, better without: best with waiting tactics & can carry big weights: thoroughly tough & genuine, gradually slipping back to a fair mark. — 1 69

4370} **KILCREGGAN 99** [1] 6-8-9 (60) A Culhane 13/2: 4610-8: Nvr a factor: reapp. — 1 53

4262} **PRINCE DARKHAN 99** [15] 4-8-12 (63) W R Swinburn 12/1: 0450-9: Waited with, btn 3f out: reapp. — ½ 55

-- **ALCOVE** [12] 9-8-9 (60) S Carson (5) 40/1: 3000/0: Keen, cl-up, wknd over 3f out: 10th, jump rnr. — 3½ 47

594 **INDIAN WARRIOR 33** [11] 4-8-11 (62) Pat Eddery 10/1: -06660: Al bhd: 11th: see 364 (7f, AW). — 4 43

4116} **DARLING COREY 99** [5] 4-9-7 (72) J Reid 8/1: 624-0: Al bhd: fin last, now with E Dunlop. — 3 49

12 ran   Time 2m 07.00 (4.5)   (D Heath)   Lady Herries Angmering, W Sussex

LEICESTER   THURSDAY MARCH 30TH   Righthand, Stiff, Galloping Track

794   **4.40 KEYTHORPE FILLIES MDN 3YO (D)   7f str   Good 45   -25 Slow**
£3965   £1220   £610   £305

4433} **CINNAMON COURT** 99 [5] J R Arnold 3-8-11 Martin Dwyer 40/1: 00-1: 3 b f College Chapel - Henrietta   **76**
Street (Royal Academy) Cl-up, led over 1f out, kept on ins last, rdn out: unplcd both juv starts: dam
1m scorer: clearly runs well fresh over a stiff 7f on gd grnd: lightly raced.
4480} **NIGHT EMPRESS** 99 [3] J R Fanshawe 3-8-11 O Urbina 4/1: 4230-2: 3 br f Emperor Jones - Night Trader ½   **75**
(Melyno) Chsd ldrs, eff to chall over 1f out, kept on ins last, just btn: plcd on 2 of 4 juv starts (rtd 84): eff
at 6/7f on gd & soft grnd & on a stiff 7f or easy trk: shown enough to win similar.
4616} **EVERGREEN** 99 [10] R Hannon 3-8-11 Dane O'Neill 14/1: 0030-3: 3 ch f Lammtarra - Nettle (Kris) ½   **74**
Chsd ldrs, eff to chall over 1f out, only btn 1L: plcd on 2 of 6 juv starts (rtd 85 at best): dam styd 12f:
eff at 7f/8.5f on gd & gd/soft grnd & on any trk: has ability, but may need headgear.
4506} **GOLDEN LOCKET** 99 [14] M Kettle 3-8-11 W Ryan 33/1: 500-4: Sn bhd, eff 2f out, kept on onepace   2   **70**
over 1f out: trained by A Foster in '99, unplcd on 3 starts (rtd 79): eff at 7f on gd grnd, poss handles hvy.
--   **SAVANNAH QUEEN** [13] 3-8-11 R Mullen 12/1: 5: Waited with, rdn 2f out, some late gains: half ½   **69**
sister to a 1m/10f h'cap wnr: looks sure to apprec a step up to 1m & will learn plenty from sellers.
694   **OCEAN SONG** 10 [7] 3-8-11 J F Egan 25/1: 246: Waited with, rdn & outpcd halfway, kept on late: 1¼   **67+**
pleasing h'cap qualifying run & could prove interesting in h'caps: stays 7f on gd, should appreciate further.
3379} **ANYHOW** 99 [8] 3-8-11 M Henry 33/1: 3-7: Keen, handy, rdn & onepace fnl 2f: rtd 65a when plcd ¾   **65**
sole '99 start: eff at 7f on gd & fibresand.
4092} **SADAKA** 99 [2] 3-8-11 R Hills 14/1: 30-8: In tch till wknd 2f out: reapp.   1   **63**
--   **SAVE THE PLANET** [12] 3-8-11 T G McLaughlin 50/1: 9: Sn bhd, some late gains: bred to apprec 1m+.1¾   **59**
--   **PASADENA** [4] 3-8-11 C Rutter 33/1: 0: Dwelt, al bhd: 10th: Emarati filly.   nk   **59**
2513} **TORROS STRAITS** 99 [6] 3-8-11 W R Swinburn 8/13 FAV: 4-0: Keen, led till over 1f out, wkng & eased hd   **58**
ins last: fin 11th, hvly bckd & reportedly lost action: reapp: rtd 83 when 4th on sole juv start: eff at 7f,
bred to stay further: handles firm grnd.
4263} **Presidents Lady** 99 [9] 3-8-11 S Drowne 50/1:   731   **Bokay** 5 [1] 3-8-11 Pat Eddery 16/1:
--   **Scratch The Dove** [11] 3-8-11 R Price 66/1:
14 ran   Time 1m 27.1 (5.1)   (Prof C D Green)   J R Arnold Upper Lambourn, Berks

---

MUSSELBURGH   THURSDAY MARCH 30TH   Righthand, Sharp Track

Official Going   GOOD. Stalls: Inside, except 5f & 2m - Stands Side.

795   **2.20 TIT SELL HCAP 3YO+ 0-60 (F)   1m1f   Good/Soft 67   +06 Fast   [60]**
£2492   £712   £356   3yo rec 19lb

45   **ACE OF TRUMPS** 99 [7] J Hetherton 4-9-4 (50)(t) M Fenton 16/1: 3500-1: 4 ch g First Trump - Elle   **55**
Reef (Shareef Dancer) Made all, ran on strongly fnl 1f, rdn out: no bid, op 12/1, best time of day, long abs:
'99 wnr at Nottingham (sell h'cap) & Warwick (clmr, trained by W Haggas, rtd 70): '98 Newmarket wnr (sell, rtd
66): eff at 7/10f on firm & soft: wears a t-strap, eff with/without blnks or a visor: runs well fresh in sellers.
600   **CELESTIAL KEY** 31 [13] M Johnston 10-10-0 (60) J Carroll 14/1: 3-2002: 10 b g Star de Naskra - ¾   **62**
Casa Key (Cormorant) Nvr far away, chsd wnr fnl 2f, kept on & not btn far: op 10/1, long ab: fit from the AW.
635   **RIBBLE PRINCESS** 26 [10] K A Ryan 5-8-6 (38) F Lynch 14/1: -00003: 5 b m Selkirk - Ricochet Romance ½   **39**
(Shadeed) Mid-div, rdn to improve 3f out, kept on under press & nrst fin: tchd 20/1, btn just over 1L: visor
omitted on return to turf: eff at 1m/9f on gd & gd/soft grnd: ran to best here, see 344 (AW).
4444} **CAMAIR CRUSADER** 99 [11] W McKeown 6-8-2 (34) G Duffield 16/1: 0000-4: Outpcd, imprvd halfway, 2½   **31**
ran on fnl 1f & nrst fin: recent jumps rnr, in Feb rnr-up at Newcastle (cj sell h'cap hdle, rtd 68h, eff at 2m on
gd/soft & soft): plcd in '99 (rtd 60): eff at 9f, a return to 10f+ will suit: handles gd/soft & fast grnd.
3892} **COSMIC CASE** 99 [16] 5-8-7 (39)(vis) A McGlone 7/2 FAV: 5000-5: Rdn in rear, imprvd 3f out, sn ½   **35**
onepace: recent jumps rnr, Feb wnr at Catterick (nov h'cap hdle, rtd 81h, eff at 2m on gd, wears a visor): mod
Flat form in '99, prev term scored here at Musselburgh (h'cap, rtd 65): eff at 1m on fast & gd/soft: eff in a vis.
4251} **DENTON LADY** 99 [8] 3-7-10 (47)(1oh) P Fessey 20/1: 0450-6: Prom till fdd fnl 2f: reapp: 4th of 15   3   **37**
in an Ayr sell in '99 (rtd 59, blnkd 1st time): eff at 1m on soft grnd: with W Kemp.
45   **BAYARD LADY** 99 [12] 4-8-8 (40) V Halliday 14/1: 0550-7: In tch, rdn & btn over 2f out: op 10/1.   nk   **29**
582   **DANCING LAWYER** 35 [6] 9-8-7 (39) F Norton 12/1: 100-08: Prom, grad fdd from halfway.   1½   **25**
4301} **GO THUNDER** 99 [4] 6-8-11 (43)(t) K Sked 33/1: /000-9: Mid-div & rcd wide, imprvd 3f out, sn btn.   hd   **29**
4366} **JAMMIE DODGER** 99 [5] 4-8-12 (44) Dean McKeown 12/1: 0540-0: Imprvd from rear 3f out, sn btn   1   **28**
& fin 10th: op 8/1, reapp.
672   **ROYAL PARTNERSHIP** 16 [2] 4-9-11 (57) N Callan 7/1: 514020: Trkd ldrs, ev ch 3f out, wknd qckly: ½   **40**
fin 11th, rcd to keenly today: flattered 672 (AW, 11f).
445   **CHOK DI** 56 [15] 4-8-9 (38)(3ow) C Teague 16/1: 0-4000: Dwelt, nvr a factor, fin 12th: 8 wk abs.   4   **16**
569   **IMPULSIVE AIR** 37 [9] 8-9-0 (46) C Lowther 13/2: 405-50: Dwelt, imprvd to chase ldrs halfway, wknd.   4   **13**
4459} **PETURA** 99 [3] 4-9-2 (48)(VIS) K Darley 9/1: /000-0: Al bhd, fin last: op 6/1, 1st time visor.   0
4592} **Done Well** 99 [1] 8-8-8 (40) O Pears 50/1:   584   **Fas** 34 [14] 4-7-11 (29)(bl) K Dalgleish (7) 20/1:
16 ran   Time 1m 56.2 (5.5)   (C D Barber Lomax)   J Hetherton Malton, N Yorks

796   **2.50 KING OF SHOW MDN AUCT 2YO (F)   5f   Good/Soft 67   -03 Slow**
£2646   £756   £378

--   **NIFTY ALICE** [2] A Berry 2-8-0 F Norton 6/4 FAV: -1: 2 ch f First Trump - Nifty Fifty (Runnett)   **75**
Made all, pushed clr fnl 1f, rdn out: fair juv time: 4,500gns Apr foal: half sister to sev wnrs, incl juv scorer
Nifty Major: dam a multiple 6f wnr, sire a top class juv: eff over a sharp 5f, may stay 6f: acts on gd/soft grnd,
runs well fresh: speedy filly who can set the pace: shld win again.
--   **DAM ELHANAH** [4] R A Fahey 2-7-12 P Hanagan(5) 9/2: -2: 2 b f Mind Games - Kimberley Park ¾   **69**
(Try My Best) Chsd ldrs till outpcd over 1f out, rallied strongly dispite drifting left ins last, not rch wnr: tchd
6/1, 7L clr 3rd, ran v green: cheaply bgt Apr foal: half sister to a juv wnr abroad: dam scored over 7f, sire a
high class 2yo: eff over a sharp 5f, 6f will suit: handles gd/soft grnd: sure to learn from this & win similar.
730   **BRIEF STAR** 5 [3] M Brittain 2-7-12 D Mernagh (3) 10/3: -03: 2 b f Brief Truce - Millionetta (Danehill)   7   **49**

Chsd wnr till wknd over 1f out: tchd 9/2, qck reapp: Apr foal, half sister to a 10f wnr: dam scored over 6f in Ireland, sire a top class 1m/10f performer: likely to apprec 6f given time: shld improve.

-- **PHARAOH HATSHEPSUT** [6] J S Goldie 2-8-0 P Fessey 16/1: -4: Outpcd, styd on fnl 1f, nrst fin: *hd* **51**
op 10/1: 4,000gns purchase: May foal, half sister to a couple of wnrs, incl juv scorer College Maid: dam a 6f 2yo wnr, sire a smart mid-dist wnr: 6f+ looks likely to suit: got the hang of things too late today.

-- **DANCING PENNEY** [1] 2-7-12 Iona Wands (5) 8/1: -5: Slowly away & outpcd, late prog but nvr *nk* **48**
dngrs: op 5/1: cheaply bt Feb foal: dam unrcd, sire a juv wnr: with K Ryan.

-- **MISS PROGRESSIVE** [5] 2-8-2 Kim Tinkler 11/2: -6: Chsd ldrs till wknd fnl 1½f: cost 6,000gns: *nk* **51**
Feb foal, half sister to sev wnrs, incl a List scorer abroad: sire a useful miler: with N Tinkler.

6 ran Time 1m 01.0 (3.5) (Mrs Norma Peebles) A Berry Cockerham, Lancs

797

3.20 LATVIAN HCAP 4YO+ 0-75 (E) 2m Good/Soft 67 -08 Slow [66]
£3526 £1085 £542 £271 4yo rec 5lb

3511} **BATOUTOFTHEBLUE 99** [6] W W Haigh 7-8-4 (42) F Lynch 5/1: 4443-1: 7 br g Batshoof - Action **46**
Belle (Auction Ring) Waited with, imprvd 3f out, ev ch dist, forged ahead cl-home, drvn out: recent jumps rnr, plcd sev times this winter in nov/h'cap company (eff at 2m/3m on firm & soft, rtd 102h): '99 wnr here at Musselburgh (h'cap, this race, rtd 48): '98 Pontefract wnr (h'cap, rtd 43 & 67a, with J Hetherton): eff at 14f, suited by 2m: acts on fast, soft & f/sand: can run well fresh: has tried blnks: likes Musselburgh.

3695} **INDIANA PRINCESS 99** [11] Mrs M Reveley 7-9-13 (65) T Eaves(7) 7/1: 3133-2: 7 b m Warrshan - Lovely *hd* **68**
Greek Lady (Ela Mana Mou) Chsd ldrs till outpcd 6f out, rallied to lead dist, caught cl-home: rnr-up in a h'cap hdle in Oct '99 (rtd 126h): in gd form on the Flat in '99, won here at Musselburgh (2) & Redcar (h'caps, rtd 69): 98/99 hdles wnr at Perth & Ludlow (h'caps, rtd 110h): '98 Pontefract wnr (2, h'caps, rtd 58): eff at 14f/2m on firm & soft: handles any trk, likes Pontefract & Musselburgh: gd weight carrier, runs well fresh: spot on next time.

-- **STELLISSIMA** [2] Lindsay Woods 5-8-7 (45)(t) P Robinson 12/1: /100-3: 5 ch m Persian Bold - *3* **45**
Ruffling Point (Gorytus) Led till dist, no extra ins last: tchd 14/1: Irish raider, 6th in a h'cap hdle at D Royal 2 wks ago: '99 Flat wnr at D Royal (14f mdn): eff at 14f/2m, acts on gd/soft grnd: wears a t-strap.

3978} **RIGADOON 99** [10] M W Easterby 4-8-13 (56)(bl) G Parkin 5/1: 3161-4: Prom, ev ch 3f out till fdd ins *½* **55**
last: tried hdles this winter, Nov '99 wnr at Wetherby (juv nov hdle, rtd 114h, eff at 2m on gd in blnks): '99 Flat wnr at Carlisle, Nottingham & Catterick (h'caps, rtd 57): eff at 2m on gd & fast: suited by blnks.

4590} **NORTHERN MOTTO 99** [4] 7-9-1 (53) A McGlone 8/1: 2440-5: Waited with, imprvd 3f out, no impress *½* **51**
fnl 1f: op 5/1: twice rcd over hdles this winter (rtd 93h, 3m nov h'cap): '99 wnr here at Musselburgh & Chester (h'caps, rtd 57): '98 Musselburgh (2) & Chester wnr (h'caps, rtd 60): '97 Doncaster & W'hampton wnr (h'caps, rtd 54 & 59a): eff at 12f, best arnd 2m: acts on firm, soft & f/sand: best on a sharp trk, loves Musselburgh & Chester.

627 **ALHESN 28** [3] 5-8-7 (45) K Darley 9/2 FAV: 413236: In tch, came wide into str, onepcd fnl 2f: *2½* **40**
fit from the AW: see 627, 348.

644 **ST LAWRENCE 24** [5] 6-8-4 (42) M Fenton 11/2: D21337: Chsd ldrs till grad fdd fnl 2f: in gd AW form. *1* **36**

-- **ASPEN GEM** [9] 6-7-10 (34)(t)(8oh) K Dalgleish (7) 50/1: 4530-8: In tch, came wide into str, ch over *3* **25**
2f out, sn rdn & btn: Irish raider, longer priced stable-mate of 3rd.

1076} **SLASHER JACK 99** [7] 9-9-8 (60) O Pears 12/1: 01/2-9: Chsd ldrs, fdd fnl 3f: tchd 16/1, new stable. *9* **41**

3782} **BREYDON 99** [1] 7-7-10 (34)(6oh) P Hanagan(2) 50/1: 6500-0: Chsd ldrs, rdn & btn 4f out: fin 10th. *1½* **13**

668 **MIDDAY COWBOY 16** [8] 7-7-10 (34)(19oh) Iona Wands (5) 200/1: 000-00: al bhd, t.o. in last: stiff task. *16* **0**

11 ran Time 3m 34.6 (12.1) (Mrs I Gibson) W W Haigh Melsonby, N Yorks

798

3.50 CHIQUITA HCAP 3YO+ 0-70 (E) 5f Good/Soft 67 -03 Slow [67]
£2847 £876 £438 £219

3610} **BOW PEEP 99** [9] M W Easterby 5-8-7 (46)(bl) G Parkin 12/1: 0000-1: 5 br m Shalford - Gale Force **56**
Seven (Strong Gale) Prom, went on dist, styd on well fnl 1f, rdly: tchd 16/1, reapp: reportedly wrong & little form in '99, subs tumbled down the h'cap: '98 wnr at Ripon (h'cap) & Nottingham (class stks, rtd 68): eff at 5/6f on fast & gd/soft: eff with/without blnks, runs well fresh: v well h'capped now & could follow up.

631 **AA YOUKNOWNOTHING 26** [3] Miss J F Craze 4-9-9 (62)(tvi) P Goode (5) 11/2 FAV: -62042: 4 b g *1¾* **65**
Superpower - Bad Payer (Tanfirion) Set pace till hdd dist, kept on but not pace of wnr: fit from the AW.

445 **BOWCLIFFE GRANGE 56** [5] D W Chapman 8-8-0 (39) Kimberley Hart (5) 9/1: 00-003: 8 b g Dominion *2½* **35**
Royale - Cala Vadella (Mummy's Pet) Dwelt, recovered to chase ldrs, edged right fnl 1f, kept on: 8 wk abs: rider reportedly cautioned for careless riding: usually a front rnr, missed the break today: see 57 (AW).

716 **JOHAYRO 6** [6] J S Goldie 7-9-12 (65) A McGlone 7/1: 000-04: In tch, outpcd halfway, keeping on *hd* **61+**
nicely when hmpd ins last: op 5/1, qck reapp, top weight: '99 wnr here at Musselburgh (2), Ayr & Thirsk (broke trk record, h'caps, rtd 75): '98 wnr at Ayr (h'cap, rtd 70): wng form over 5/7f, likes firm, acts on soft: eff with/without blnks or a visor: likes Ayr & Musselburgh: tough, back on a winning mark & spot on next time.

71 **SWYNFORD DREAM 99** [8] 7-9-7 (60) P Robinson 6/1: 0600-5: Prom, wkng when sltly hmpd & switched *¾* **53**
ins fnl 1f: long abs: '99 wnr here at Musselburgh (this race, reapp, rtd 65, with T Etherington): in '98 with current trainer & won at Catterick (h'cap, rtd 58 & 55a): best dominating over 5f on gd or firm grnd, handles gd/soft: can run well fresh on any trk, likes Musselburgh: h'capped to win.

3133} **JACKERIN 99** [7] 5-8-13 (52)(bl) M Fenton 14/1: 0500-6: Held up, imprvd halfway, no impress fnl 1f: *1¼* **41**
failed to win in '99 (rtd 53 at best, h'cap): '98 Ayr wnr (h'cap, rtd 67): '97 Doncaster wnr (2, incl sell, rtd 80): tried 7f, best at 5f: acts on fast & soft, likes a gall trk, esp Doncaster: has tried a visor, best in blnks.

4234} **UNMASKED 99** [4] 4-7-13 (38) N Carlisle 25/1: 40/0-7: Rear, keeping on when switched ins fnl 1f, nrst *1* **24**
fin: reapp, unplcd on sole '99 start (1m mdn): trained by J Berry in '98: h'cap debut & a modicum of promise here.

4120} **BEST KEPT SECRET 99** [10] 9-7-10 (35)(19oh) K Dalgleish(7) 100/1: 0000-8: Nvr a factor on reapp. *2½* **14**

4267} **AMERICAN COUSIN 99** [2] 5-9-6 (59) Alex Greaves 6/1: 5240-9: In tch till halfway: reapp. *nk* **37**

291 **CARMARTHEN 82** [12] 4-8-13 (52) N Callan 12/1: 444-00: Chsd ldrs till rdn & wknd 2f out: 10th, abs. *1¾* **25**

3783} **XANADU 99** [1] 4-9-3 (56) C Lowther 10/1: 0103-0: Chsd ldr, wkng when hmpd ins lfnl 1f: op 7/1, 11th. *1* **26**

673 **BEVELED HAWTHORN 16** [11] 5-7-10 (35)(3oh) Clare Roche (7) 9/1: 61-40W: Broke out of stalls & **0**
withdrawn not under orders: see 563 (AW).

12 ran Time 1m 01.0 (3.5) (Mrs Anne Jarvis) M W Easterby Sheriff Hutton, N Yorks

799

4.20 CLASSIFIED STKS 3YO 0-60 (F) 1m4f Good/Soft 67 -12 Slow
£2576 £736 £368

240 **KUWAIT TROOPER 88** [8] G A Butler 3-8-12 K Darley 3/1: 60-41: 3 br c Cozzene - Super Fan (Lear Fan) **66**
Held up, imprvd to lead ent fnl 1f, pulled clr, cmftbly: 12 wk abs: turf debut: apprec this step up to 12f, 14f will suit: handles equitrack, likes gd/soft grnd & a sharp trk: runs well fresh.

MUSSELBURGH   THURSDAY MARCH 30TH   Righthand, Sharp Track

3913} **ESTABELLA** 99 [6] S P C Woods 3-8-9 G Duffield 9/1: 0005-2: 3 ch f Mujtahid - Lady In Green   5   55
(Shareef Dancer) Chsd ldrs, imprvd to lead over 2f out, hdd ent fnl 1f & outpcd by wnr: 11L clr 3rd, reapp: lightly
rcd in '99, 5th in a nurs h'cap (rtd 55): half sister to a 6f juv wnr: stays a sharp 12f & acts on gd/soft grnd.
4575} **TYCOONS LAST** 99 [3] W M Brisbourne 3-8-9 F Norton 5/1: 4000-3: 3 b f Nalchik - Royal Tycoon   11   40
(Tycoon II) Waited with, outpcd 3f out, some late hdwy but nvr dngrs: reapp: in '99 4th at Bath (fill mdn, rtd 73$):
half sister to a 1m/10f scorer: dam scored over timber: big step up in trip today & shld stay.
86   **UNICORN STAR** 99 [5] J S Wainwright 3-8-12 J Carroll 9/1: 040-4: Rear, eff 3f out, nvr nr ldrs: 3½   38
long abs: rtd 61 in '99 (4th, mdn auct): eff at 6f on gd grnd, shld apprec mid-dists: seems modest.
303   **FOSTON FOX** 80 [1] 3-8-9 F Lynch 33/1: 064-05: Rear, some hdwy 3f out, sn btn: 12 wk abs.   3½   30
752   **LE CAVALIER** 2 [4] 3-8-12 R Morse 4/1: 222226: Led till over 2f out, wknd qckly: too sn after 752?   11   18
4536} **DAME FONTEYN** 99 [7] 3-8-9 M Fenton 10/1: 000-P: Chsd ldr, wknd over 2f out, lost action & p.u.   0
523   **VANISHING DANCER** 43 [2] 3-8-12 N Callan 5/2 FAV: 00-3W: Withdrawn not under starters orders: 0
6 wk abs: see 523 (10f, AW).
8 ran   Time 2m 40.1 (9.5)   (Sheikh Khaled Duaij Al Sabah)   G A Butler Blewbury, Oxon

800	4.50 SEATTLE ART MDN HCAP 3YO 0-70 (E) 1m rnd Good/Soft 67 -00 Slow	[74]
	£2925 £900 £450 £225	

4306} **SMOOTH SAND** 99 [4] M A Jarvis 3-9-7 (67) P Robinson 9/4 FAV: -040-1: 3 b c Desert Secret -   74
Baby Smooth (Apalachee) Chsd ldrs, rdn to lead dist, kept on well, drvn out: bckd from 9/2, fast time: thrice rcd
in '99, 4th at Nottingham (mdn, rtd 72): half brother to sev wnrs in the States, dam a multiple scorer in the US:
apprec this step up to 1m, acts on gd & gd/soft: handles a sharp trk, runs well fresh: open to further improvement.
4425} **RED CANYON** 99 [6] M L W Bell 3-9-1 (61) M Fenton 6/1: 6000-2: 3 b g Zieten - Bayazida (Bustino)   nk   67
Chsd ldr, chall over 1f out, kept on well & only just btn: reapp: some promise in mdns in '99 (rtd 66 at best):
half brother to a high-class staying h'capper: eff at 1m on gd/soft: runs well fresh.
481   **COSMIC SONG** 51 [5] R M Whitaker 3-7-13 (45) D Mernagh (3) 50/1: 05-563: 3 b f Cosmonaut - Hotaria   1¼   48
(Sizzling Melody) Chsd ldrs, kept on under press ins fnl 1f, not btn far: 7 wk abs: eff at 1m on gd/soft: see 281.
4495} **RICH VEIN** 99 [10] S P C Woods 3-8-9 (65) N Callan 11/2: 500-4: In tch, styd on under press fnl 1f: 1   66
drifted from 3/1, reapp: thrice rcd in '99, 5th in a mdn on debut (rtd 71), disapp after: half brother to a 12f
wnr: dam scored over 1m/10f: likely to apprec 10f+ & spot on next time in same company.
4514} **PUPS PRIDE** 99 [14] 3-8-7 (53) R Winston 11/2: 0600-5: Chsd ldrs till outpcd over 1f out, rallied cl   ¾   52
home: well bckd from 10/1, reapp: little mdn/nurs form in '99: half brother to a couple of juv wnrs, dam a 6f
2yo scorer: off near an easy 1m on gd/soft grnd, 10f may suit: clrly thought capable of better.
636   **FOR HEAVENS SAKE** 26 [1] 3-9-0 (60) Dean McKeown 12/1: 6-4326: Led till over 1f out, fdd: see 636.   ½   58
3595} **WELCOME BACK** 99 [8] 3-8-1 (47) Iona Wands (5) 20/1: 0006-7: Mid-div, onepcd fnl 2f: reapp.   1   43
4327} **CLASSIC LORD** 99 [12] 3-8-13 (59) J Carroll 8/1: 5500-8: Rear, eff 3f out, keeping on when short   hd   55
of room ins fnl 1f, eased: reapp: some promise here: with M Johnston.
515   **MILLER TIME** 45 [2] 3-7-12 (44)(BL) P Fessey 8/1: 50049: In tch, rdn 2f out, sn outpcd: op 5/1, blnks.   nk   39
3810} **HONG KONG** 99 [7] 3-8-1 (47)(tbl) F Norton 10/1: 0002-0: Dwelt, imprvd 2f out, no room ent fnl   2   38
1f, nvr dngrs in 10th: mkt drifter, reapp.
4151} **CONCINO** 99 [13] 3-7-11 (42)(1ow) Dale Gibson 12/1: 000-0: Al towards rear, fin 11th: reapp.   3   28
4302} **Floating Ember** 99 [11] 3-7-13 (45) M Baird 33/1:   3308} **Four Men** 99 [3] 3-8-3 (49) O Pears 33/1:
4409} **Ellpeedee** 99 [9] 3-8-8 (54) Kim Tinkler 25/1:
14 ran   Time 1m 42.9 (5.4)   (Mrs B Sadowska)   M A Jarvis Newmarket

SOUTHWELL   FRIDAY MARCH 31ST   Lefthand, Sharp, Oval Track

Official Going   AW: STANDARD   TURF: GOOD (GOOD/SOFT places).

801	2.10 WWW.BET247 MED AUCT MDN 2YO (F) 5f aw str Standard Inapplicable	
	£2205 £630 £315	

--   **MAMMAS TONIGHT** [3] A Berry 2-9-0 G Carter 100/30 JT FAV: 1: 2 ch c Timeless Times - Miss   82a
Merlin (Manacle) Dwelt, sn handy, rdn/led halfway, drifted lead/forged clr ins last: op 2/1: Mar foal, cost
5,200 gns: brother to a 5f wnr, dam a 6f juv wnr: eff at 5f, 6f+ suit: acts on fibresand: runs well fresh.
--   **DIM SUMS** [1] T D Barron 2-9-0 C Lowther 100/30 JT FAV: 2: 2 b g Repriced - Regal Baby   3½   71a
(Northern Baby) Chsd ldrs, rdn/kept on fnl 1f, not pace of wnr: well bckd, tchd 9/2: half brother to a wng
US juv: dam unrcd, sire smart 5f/1m US performer: handles fibresand: encouraging intro.
--   **SMALL FRY** [5] T D Easterby 2-8-9 K Darley 11/2: 3: 2 b f Tagula - Alaroos (Persian Bold)   2   61a
Dwelt, rdn/kept on fnl 2f, nvr on terms: Apr foal, 6,200 IR gns purchase: half sister to useful juvenile
Arawak Cay: dam unrcd, sire top class 6f juv: sure to improve for this & relish 6f.
--   **COUNTESS BANKES** [4] W G M Turner A Daly 5/1: 4: Sn rdn/outpcd, nvr a factor: op 7/1:   2½   54a
Son Pardo filly, Jan foal, cost 800 gns: half sister to a juv 6f wnr: dam a 5f juv wnr.
--   **FIRE PRINCESS** [7] 2-8-9 G Duffield 7/2: 5: Cl-up 5f: op 6/4: Emarati filly, Apr foal, cost 2,800gns: 2   49a
half sister to juv wng sprinters, dam a 5f/1m US wnr: will suit in time: with J Wharton.
--   **WATERPARK** [2] 2-8-9 C Teague 16/1: 6: Keen/led till halfway, fdd: op 14/1: Namaqualand filly,   5   40a
Jan first foal, cost 4,500 gns: dam a 7f 3yo wnr: 6f+ will suit in time: with M Dods.
--   **PREMIER LASS** [6] 2-8-9 M Fenton 16/1: 7: Al bhd: op 14/1: Distinctly North filly, Apr first foal,   3   33a
cost 1,000IR gns: dam a lightly rcd mdn: sire a high-class 2yo: with B Rothwell.
7 ran   Time 1m 01.50 (3.7)   (K J Brown)   A Berry Cockerham, Lancs

802	2.40 WWW.BET247.CO.UK HCP 3YO+ 0-65 (F) 6f rnd Good Inapplicable	[64]
	£2436 £696 £348 3 yo rec 13lb	

754   **NINEACRES** 3 [2] J M Bradley 9-8-7 (43)(bl) S Drowne 9/2: 614401: 9 b g Sayf El Arab - Mayor   54
(Laxton) Made all, rdn/clr over 1f out, styd on strongly ins last, pushed out nr fin: bckd: quick reapp: earlier
scored at W'hampton (AW h'cap, rtd 58a): '99 scorer at W'hampton (clmr, rtd 59a, plcd on turf, rtd 42, h'cap): eff
at 5/6f, stays a gall 7f: acts on firm, gd & bkes both AWs, loves W'hampton: eff in blnks/visor: likes to force
the pace: has run well fresh: looks on a fair turf mark, could win again.
1922} **BALI STAR** 99 [9] M J Weeden 5-9-0 (50) N Callan 33/1: 000-2: 5 b g Alnasr Alwasheek - Baligay   5   50
(Balidar) Mid-div/wide, sltly hmpd over 1f out, kept on well ins last, no ch with wnr: tchd 50/1: 10 mth abs/

h'cap bow: unplcd from 3 starts in '99 (rtd 51, mdn): eff over a sharp 6f, return to 7f could suit: handles gd grnd.

					nk	59
667   **PEPPIATT** 17 [11] N Bycroft 6-9-10 (60) K Darley 10/1: 050-03: 6 ch g Efisio - Fleur Du Val (Valiyar)
Dwelt/rear, rdn & kept on fnl 2f, no threat: op 8/1: on a good mark & enjoys soft grnd: see 667.

4471}   **GRACE 99** [1] J M Bradley 6-9-0 (50) P Fitzsimons (5) 7/1: 0402-4: Trkd ldrs, onepace fnl 2f: nk   48
longer priced stablemate of wnr: plcd sev times in '99 (rtd 55, rnr-up, h'cap): '98 Chepstow
wnr (mdn h'cap, rtd 60): eff at 5f/7f: acts on firm & soft, any trk: has run in blnks: 1 win in 37 starts.

674   **SAMMAL** 17 [7] 4-9-3 (53) V Venkaya 25/1: 43-005: Chsd ldrs, kept on onepace fnl 2f: see 639.   1   49

312   **ORIEL STAR** 79 [10] 4-9-1 (51)(bl) J F Egan 25/1: 00-006: Held up wide, onepace fnl 2f: abs, blnks reapp.   nk   46

738   **ELTON LEDGER** 4 [6] 11-8-12 (48)(vis) R Fitzpatrick (3) 16/1: 220357: Chsd ldrs, held over 1f out.   shd   43

753   **GRAND ESTATE** 3 [14] 5-9-10 (64) A Culhane 16/1: -40008: Rear, prog/no room over 1f out, kept on   1¼   56+
ins last: op 12/1, qk reapp, top-weight: no luck in running, worth another ch, enjoys a stiff 6f, esp Hamilton.

2081}   **PREMIUM PRINCESS 99** [12] 5-9-11 (61) J Fortune 10/1: 0140-9: Mid-div at best: op 8/1, 10 mth abs: ¾   51
'99 Newcastle wnr (h'cap, rtd 60): eff at 5f/7f: acts on firm & soft, any trk: suited by fast/firm.

698   **KOSEVO** 11 [5] 6-9-6 (56)(vis) I Mongan (5) 10/1: 00-000: Cl-up 4f: 10th: bckd, op 12/1: btr 673.   ¾   44

634   **WISHBONE ALLEY** 27 [4] 5-9-3 (53)(vis) A Clark 7/2 FAV: 320420: Cl-up 4f, fdd: 12th: well bckd.   ½   0

4581} Alconleigh 99 [13] 5-8-7 (43) F Norton 14/1:   3375} Meranti 99 [3] 7-8-4 (40) R Ffrench 16/1:

351   Miss Bananas 73 [8] 5-8-6 (42) C Carver (3) 20/1:

14 ran   Time 1m 15.10   (J M Bradley)   J M Bradley Sedbury, Glos

---

803   3.10 PLAY THE POOLS HCAP 3YO+ 0-70 (E)   7f rnd   Good   Inapplicable   [68]
         £2996   £856   £428   3 yo rec 15lb

521   **ABERKEEN** 45 [8] M Dods 5-9-5 (59) A Culhane 5/1: -21221: 5 ch g Keen - Miss Aboyne (Lochnager)   67
Towards rear, prog to lead over 1f out, styd on well ins last, drvn out: 6 wk abs: earlier scored at Southwell
(AW h'cap, rtd 62a): '99 Doncaster wnr (appr h'cap, rtd 61 & 55a): plcd in '99 (rtd 62, h'cap): eff at 6f, stays
sharp 8.4f, suited by 7f: acts on firm, gd/soft & fibresand: handles any trk: runs fresh: tough/genuine gldg.

304   **MELODIAN** 81 [11] M Brittain 5-9-0 (54)(bl) D Mernagh 25/1: 350-02: 5 b h Grey Desire - Mere   1¾   58
Melody (Dunphy) Chsd ldrs, rdn to briefly lead over 1f out, kept on ins last: abs, clr rem & still improving.

446   **PURSUIVANT** 57 [10] M D Hammond 6-9-2 (56) R Fitzpatrick (3) 16/1: 300-03: 6 b g Pursuit Of Love -   6   51
Collapse (Busted) Chsd ldrs, onepace fnl 2f: abs: return to 1m+ could suit: maiden, see 446 (AW mdn).

478   **UNCLE OBERON** 52 [16] C A Dwyer 4-8-12 (52) P Clarke (7) 25/1: 50-604: Keen/rear & wide, kept on   1   45
well fnl 2f, nrst at fin: 8 wk abs: only mod form prev but eye-catching late hdwy today: 1m h'caps could suit.

711   **SO WILLING** 8 [3] 4-9-6 (60)(bl) J Weaver 25/1: 060305: Rear, rdn/mod gains fnl 2f: see 582, 183   2   49

596   **SACREMENTUM** 34 [15] 5-9-2 (56) S Carson (5) 20/1: 640206: Dwelt/rear, mod gains fnl 2f: op 12/1.   ½   44

4518}   **BOWLERS BOY 99** [2] 7-8-10 (50) J Fortune 12/1: 0035-7: Chsd ldrs, held over 1f out: op 14/1: plcd   hd   37
in '99 (1st time blnks, rtd 49, h'cap): '98 Pontefract wnr (2, h'caps) & Redcar (stks, rtd 76): suited by 5/6f: acts
on fast, loves gd/soft & hvy, prob handles fibresand & any trk, likes Pontefract: well h'capped & sharper at 5/6f.

622   **SHARP EDGE BOY** 29 [4] 4-9-8 (62) S Sanders 16/1: 00-008: Trkd ldrs, eff/no room 2f out, sn held.   nk   48

721   **MUTAHADETH** 6 [12] 6-8-4 (44)(bl) J Fanning 25/1: 344469: Wide/mid-div, no impress: see 183.   1½   27

4394}   **MAMMAS BOY** 55 [5] 5-8-9 (49) P Bradley (5) 16/1: 6400-0: Dwelt, nvr factor: 10th: op 14/1:   2½   27
6 month abs: '99 wnr at Thirsk (sell) & Musselburgh (clmr, rtd 62): '98 Doncaster wnr (mdn h'cap) & Sandown
(clmr, rtd 72): eff at 5f/7f: acts on firm & hvy, any trk: best without blnks: enjoys sell/clmg grade.

-780   **FOREIGN EDITOR** 2 [1] 4-9-7 (61) P Hanagan (7) 11/10 FAV: 113320: Led till over 2f out, fdd: 1   37
hvly bckd, tchd 7/4: quick reapp: poss too sn after gd turf return in 780: see 423 (AW).

711   **SEVEN** 8 [13] 5-9-6 (60)(bl) I Mongan (5) 20/1: 015400: Hndy, led over 2f out till over 1f out, fdd: 11th.   2½   31

*667   **ODDSANENDS** 17 [9] 4-9-11 (65) C Lowther 8/1: 2-0510: Cl-up, wkng/hmpd over 2f out, eased: 16th: op 8/1.   0

569   Sterling High 38 [6] 5-8-12 (52)(t) R Winston 25/1:   681 Cedar Wells 15 [7] 4-9-3 (57) R Ffrench 33/1:

4096} Night Adventure 99 [14] 4-9-3 (57) S Drowne 33/1:

16 ran   Time 1m 28.50   (N A Riddell)   M Dods Piercebridge, Co Durham

---

804   3.40 WIN £2 MILLION MDN 3YO (D)   7f rnd   Good   Inapplicable
         £2899   £892   £446   £223

4222}   **RAYYAAN 99** [13] N A Graham 3-9-0 R Hills 2/1 FAV: 5422-1: 3 ch c Cadeaux Genereux - Anam (Persian   84
Bold) Chsd ldrs, prog/rdn to lead over 1f out, held on well ins last, pushed out cl-home: 6 mth abs: rnr-up twice
in '99 (mdns, rtd 86, P Walwyn): eff at 6/7f, shld stay 1m: acts on gd & soft: likes a sharp trk & runs well fresh.

4292}   **SUTTON COMMON 99** [5] K A Ryan 3-9-0 F Lynch 7/1: 04-2: 3 b c Common Grounds - Fadaki Hawaki   1¼   79
(Vice Regent) Mid-div, rdn & kept on well fnl 2f, not reach wnr: tchd 20/1 early: 6 month abs: rtd 73 on 2nd of 2
'99 starts (mdn): eff at 7f, return to 1m+ shld suit: acts on gd grnd: now qual for h'caps, going the right way.

736   **FIRST VENTURE** 6 [11] C N Allen 3-9-0 (bl) R Morse 5/1: 35-223: 3 b c Formidable - Diamond Wedding   3   73
(Diamond Shoal) Led/sn clr, rdn/hdd over 1f out & no extra: op 4/1: quick reapp: blnks reapplied: return
to h'caps shld suit: acts on both AWs & gd grnd: often placed: see 736, 617.

--   **WINGED ANGEL** [3] Miss J A Camacho 3-9-0 A Culhane 20/1: 4: Bhd halfway, switched over 2f out   3½   66
& styd on well ins last, nrst fin: debut: looks sure to apprec 1m+ on this evidence, encouraging intro.

4614}   **BILLY BATHWICK 99** [9] 3-9-0 J Stack 5/1: 0406-5: Chsd ldrs, held fnl 2f: 5 month abs: plcd in '99   ¾   65
(rtd 71, nurs h'cap): stays a sharp 7f, tried 1m: handles firm & soft, likes a sharp trk: return to h'caps shld suit.

4457}   **MACHUDI 99** [8] 3-8-9 K Darley 10/1: 0-6: Cl-up fnl 5f: op 6/1, 5 month abs: unplcd sole '99 start   1¼   57
(rtd 52, mdn): longer 7f trip today for B A McMahon.

3486}   **DOM MIGUEL 99** [1] 3-9-0 N Pollard 10/1: 05-7: Mid-div, btn 2f out: op 7/1, 7 month abs: unplcd   5   52
both '99 starts (rtd 67, mdn): dam a French 9f wnr: 1m+ & h'caps shld suit.

685   **MCQUILLAN** 14 [7] 3-9-0 D Sweeney 66/1: 00-08: Bhd, nvr on terms.   1½   49

--   **WAY OUT WEST** [4] 3-8-9 Dean McKeown 25/1: 9: Al bhd: debut, with C Thornton.   1¼   41

694   **MJOLNIR** 11 [2] 3-9-0 (t) J A Rawlinson 66/1: 60: Mid-div, btn 2f out: 10th: mod form.   7   35

4523}   **BURGUNDIAN RED 99** [10] 3-9-0 J Carroll 7/1: 504-0: Dwelt, mid-div/wide halfway, rdn/btn 2f out: 1¾   32
11th: op 4/1, 5 month abs: prev with R W Armstrong, now with A Berry.

11 ran   Time 1m 29.20   (Hamdan Al Maktoum)   N A Graham Newmarket, Suffolk

---

805   4.10 BIG MATCH STATS HCAP 4YO+ (D)   1m4f   Good   Inapplicable   [75]
         £3692   £1136   £568   £284   4 yo rec 2 lb

3743}   **ACHILLES SKY 99** [1] K R Burke 4-9-8 (71) J Weaver 11/4: /016-1: 4 b c Hadeer - Diva Madonna (Chief   75
Singer) Hld up in tch, swtchd/smooth prog fnl 2f to lead over 1f out, in command fnl 1f, pushed out, readily: op
9/4: 7 mth abs: '99 Nottingham mdn h'cap wnr (rtd 74): rtd 83 in '98 (mdn): eff at 10f/sharp 12f, could get

further: acts on gd: handles a gall or sharp trk: runs well fresh: has broken a blood vessel previously.
714 **JAMAICAN FLIGHT 7** [3] Mrs S Lamyman 7-10-0 (75) J Fortune 5/2: 334432: 7 b h Sunshine Forever - 1¼ 75
Kalamona (Hawaii) Soon led, rdn fnl 4f, hdd over 1f out, kept on tho' al held by wnr: tchd 100/30: needs further.
682 **WINSOME GEORGE 14** [4] C W Fairhurst 5-8-1 (47)(1ow) N Pollard 7/2: 000-23: 5 b g Marju - June Moon hd 47
(Sadler's Hall), rdn/onepace fnl 2f: op 3/1: resumes on turf well h'capped: see 682 (AW).
*779 **NOUKARI 2** [2] P D Evans 7-10-1 (76)(6ex) J F Egan 9/4 FAV: 453214: Handy, onepace fnl 2f: op 7/4. 2 72
4 ran   Time 2m 40.30   (Achilles International)   K R Burke Newmarket, Suffolk

---

806   4.40 BEST BET ONLINE SELLER 3YO (G)   1m2f   Good Inapplicable
£1968   £562   £281

537 **FRENCH MASTER 42** [3] P C Haslam 3-8-11 (vis) P Goode (5) 9/4 FAV: 4-3331: 3 b g Petardia - Reasonably 57
French (Reasonable) Dwelt, rear/in tch, stdy prog wide fnl 5f, rdn/narrow lead fnl 1f, asserted nr fin, rdn out:
nicely bckd, op 11/4, first win: bought in for 3400 gns: 6 wk abs: plcd in '99 (rtd 68, clmr): eff at 10f, stays
sharp 11f: acts on firm, gd & fibresand, any track: runs well fresh: apprec drop to sell grade.
545 **COLLEGE ROCK 41** [8] Mrs A E Johnson 3-8-11 N Doe 4/1: 33-042: 3 ch c Rock Hopper - Sea Aura (Roi 1 55
Soleil) Handy, led over 1f out till ins last, kept on: 10d 7/1: abs: now stays a sharp 10f, handles firm & soft.
610 **THE WALRUS 31** [5] N P Littmoden 3-8-11 M Fenton 20/1: 03: 3 b g Sri Pekan - Cathy Garcia (Be My 2½ 51
Guest) Chsd ldrs, kept on fnl 2f, not pace to chall: stays sharp 10f and handles gd ground.
709 **TIMELESS CHICK 8** [2] Andrew Reid 3-8-6 (VIS) M Henry 20/1: 60-004: Led/dsptd lead till over 1f 1¾ 44
out, no extra ins last: op 16/1, tried a vis, clr rem: prob styd longer 10f trip: see 555 (mdn h'cap, 1m).
-- **CHEZ BONITO** [13] 3-8-6 Pat Eddery 9/2: 5: Trkd ldrs, rdn/no impress fnl 2f: op 3/1, debut. 5 37
36 **RED KING 99** [11] 3-8-11 G Carter 16/1: 0000-6: Mid-div, btn 2f out: 5 mth abs: op 14/1: unplcd at 2 39
upto 1m in '99 (rtd 57, J Berry): now with A Berry.
3525} **ISLA 99** [12] 3-8-6 O Pears 20/1: 0-7: Mid-div/wide, btn 2f out: reapp: no form sole '99 start at 6f. ½ 33
240 **OPEN GROUND 89** [4] 3-8-11 K Darley 14/1: 063-08: Rdn/mid-div halfway, sn btn: abs: btr 204 (AW). 5 31
741 **TOWER OF SAND 6** [6] 3-9-2 A Culhane 8/1: 235049: Hld up, no impress: op 6/1, qk reapp: btr 36 (1m). 1¾ 34
417 **DIAMOND VANESSA 63** [1] 3-8-6 J F Egan 12/1: 000-50: Handy 7f: 10th, op 14/1, abs, longer 10f trip. 1¼ 22
36 **SEASAME PARK 99** [9] 3-8-11 (BL) J Fortune 9/1: 4020-0: Led 1m, fdd: op 7/1, blnks: 5 mth abs; '99 8 18
Wolverhampton winner (7f, sell, rtd 61a, unplcd on turf, rtd 51): eff at 7f on fibresand.
545 **Phantom Star 41** [10] 3-8-11 A McCarthy 33/1: 25/1:   688 **Portrack Junction 14** [7] 3-8-11 (bl) Kim Tinkler 20/1:
13 ran   Time 2m 13.00   (Middleham Park Racing XIX)   P C Haslam Middleham, N Yorks

---

807   5.10 FILLIES HCAP 3YO 0-70 (E)   1m2f   Good Inapplicable   [74]
£2842   £812   £406

4338} **FANTASTIC FANTASY 99** [1] J L Dunlop 3-9-7 (67) Pat Eddery 13/8 FAV: 300-1: 3 b f Lahib - Gay Fantasy 73
(Troy) Trkd ldrs, rdn to lead over 2f out, styd on well ins last, rdn out: well bckd: 6 month abs/h'cap bow: rtd
80 at best in '99 (fill mdn): apprec step up to 10f, 12f + could suit: acts on gd & a sharp trk: runs well fresh.
4414} **DOUBLE RED 99** [7] M L W Bell 3-9-4 (62) M Fenton 9/4: 0022-2: 3 b f Thatching - Local Custom 1½ 64
(Be My Native) Handy, rdn & kept on fnl 2f, not pace of wnr: op 5/4: 5 month abs: rnr-up fnl 2 starts in '99 (rtd
65, h'cap): eff at 1m/10f on gd & soft: handles a sharp/stiff or gall trk: shown enough to find similar.
589 **CROESO ADREF 35** [6] S C Williams 3-8-0 (46) P M Quinn 25/1: 123643: 3 ch f Most Welcome - 2 45
Grugiar (Red Sunset) Led 3f, remained handy, onepace over 1f out: op 16/1: stays 10f on both AWs & gd grnd.
625 **CHURCH FARM FLYER 29** [2] C N Allen 3-8-12 (58) L Newman (5) 14/1: 236324: Rear, styd on fnl 2f, hd 56
no threat: op 8/1: prob stays a sharp 10f: acts on both AWs & handles gd grnd: see 188 (7f, AW).
701 **WILEMMGEO 8** [8] 3-8-13 (59) Joanna Badger (7) 12/1: 212105: Handy, onepace fnl 2f: op 10/1. ½ 56
328 **SECRETARIO 77** [3] 3-8-8 (54) Dean McKeown 12/3: 00-66: Handy 1m: h'cap bow: abs: Ingr 10f trip. 5 44
4059} **BITTY MARY 99** [2] 3-8-9 (55) F Lynch 14/1: 0050-7: Al bhd: op 16/1, 6 month abs: unplcd in '99 nk 44
(rtd 58, auct mdn): longer 10f trip today.
3939} **ALABAMA WURLEY 99** [5] 3-9-5 (65) J Fortune 10/1: 2103-8: Keen/hmpd after 1f, prog to lead after 1¾ 52
3f, hdd over 2f out & wknd: op 7/1, 7 month abs: '99 Newmarket scorer (sell, rtd 65, rnr-up on sand, rtd 69a): eff
at 7f, stays 1m: acts on firm, soft & fibresand: handles any trk: enjoys soft grnd.
8 ran   Time 2m 15.10   (Windflower Overseas Holding Inc)   J L Dunlop Arundel, W Sussex

---

Official Going   GOOD (GOOD/SOFT in places).

808   2.10 WINNER ALRIGHT MDN 3YO+ (D)   5f   Good/Soft 72 +00 Fast
£3295   £1014   £507   £253   3 yo rec 11lb

2553} **SARTORIAL 99** [2] P J Makin 4-9-8 S Sanders 9/2: /232-1: 4 b g Elbio - Madam Slaney (Prince 99
Tenderfoot) Sn cl-up, went on 2f out, pushed out to assert inside last, cmftbly: plcd all 3 '99 starts
(rtd 89 & 78a): eff at 6f, enjoyed this drop back to 5f & acts on firm, gd/soft, fibresand & any trk:
runs well fresh: v speedy & useful, should win again in this form.
-- **ANNETTE VALLON** [6] P W Harris 3-8-8 Pat Eddery 7/2: 2: 3 b f Efisio - Christine Daae (Sadler's 3½ 85+
Wells) Dwelt, in tch, effort to chase wnr over 1f out, outpcd ins last: bckd tho' op 9/4, debut: half sister to
smart sprinter To The Roof & useful miler Risque Lady: eff at 5f, 6f will suit: improve plenty for this fine debut.
- **SAN SALVADOR** [1] J Noseda 3-8-11 L Dettori 6/1: 3: 3 b c Dayjur - Sheer Gold (Cutlass): 2½ 85+
Sn outpcd, late hdwy under a kind ride: cost 42,000 gns: dam 10f wnr: sure to learn plenty from this
educational debut & 6f+ will suit: type to go on, rate higher & win races.
734 **TOUCH OF FAIRY 7** [5] K Mahdi 4-9-8 K Fallon 2/1 FAV: 2-04: Sn rdn bhd, effort over 1f out, no hd 85
dngr: rtd 73 when rnr-up in a mdn sole juv start: brother to a couple of wng sprinters: sure to apprec a
return to 6f & handles gd grnd: tried a visor.
729 **BOND BOY 7** [7] 3-8-11 J Stack 7/1: 362-45: Handy, rdn & btn over 1f out: needs headgear: see 729. hd 84
4250} **GREY COSSACK 99** [8] 3-8-11 (VIS) D Mernagh (3) 4/6: Slow away & bmpd just after start, sn 5 72
handy till wknd well over 1f out: rtd 74 sole 4th on sole juv start: bred to apprec 7f+: tried a visor.
716 **LUCKY COVE 8** [10] 4-9-8 Kim Tinkler 50/1: 003-07: In tch, edged left for press 2f out, no dngr: 1¾ 68$
plcd twice in '99 (rtd 70 & 54a): eff at 5f on fast, gd/soft & fibresand.
-- **NEEDWOOD TRICKSTER** [4] 3-8-11 (t) P Robinson 50/1: 8: Slow away & al bhd: cost 25,000 gns. 3 61

687} **CAROLES DOVE 99** [11] 4-9-3 N Carlisle 100/1: -0-9: Al bhd: reapp. *shd* **56**
4580} **RATHLEA 99** [3] 6-9-8 P M Quinn (5) 100/1: 000-0: Al bhd: 10th, reapp, modest. *4* **49**
4457} **PRIME RECREATION 99** [9] 3-8-11 Dale Gibson 20/1: 003-0: Dwelt, sn recovered to lead till 2f out, wknd: fin last, reapp. *1½* **47**
11 ran Time 1m 02.4 (3.6) (Mrs Greta Saffaty Marchant) P J Makin Ogbourne Maisey, Wilts.

809

3.15 ESTUARY HCAP 4YO+ 0-90 (C) 1m4f Good/Soft 72 +03 Fast [87]
£6565 £2020 £1010 £505 4 yo rec 1 lb

4079} **INIGO JONES 99** [2] P W Harris 4-10-0 (88) W R Swinburn 8/1: 2133-1: 4 b g Alzao - Kindjal (Kris): Handy, hdwy to lead 5f out, pushed clr over 3f out, kept on, drvn out: op 6/1, gd time on reapp: in '99 won at Nottingham (mdn), plcd on all other 6 starts (rtd 90 at best): eff at 12/14f on firm, gd/soft grnd & on any trk: runs well fresh under big weights: v useful & tough, the front two fin 12L clr of rem here. **95**
370 **QUEDEX 71** [3] E L James 4-8-8 (68) S Whitworth 50/1: 14-602: 4 b c Deploy - Alwal (Pharly): In tch, eff to chase wnr over 3f out, kept on, wnr had first run: well clr of rem, abs: '99 scorer at Goodwood (h'cap) & Bath (class stks, rtd 71): eff at 10/12f, 14f will suit: acts on firm, soft & any trk: progressive. *¾* **73**
4264} **MASTER BEVELED 99** [8] P D Evans 10-8-8 (67)(bl) J F Egan 10/1: 06/0-3: 10 b g Beveled - Miss Anniversary (Tachypous): Waited with, rdn over 4f out, kept on for press fnl 2, no dngr: op 7/1: v smart hdler, plcd num times this winter (rtd 158h): well btn sole Flat start last term: 98/99 hdle wnr at Haydock (Gr 2, rtd 162h, best at 2m, stays 2m4f on fast, likes gd & hvy): Flat wnr in '98 at Ayr (amat h'cap, rtd 73): stays 12f on firm, hvy & equitrack: handles any trk & has tried blnks/visor. *12* **60**
4397} **HILL FARM BLUES 99** [4] Miss S E Baxter 7-9-5 (78) L Newman (5) 16/1: 0400-4: Slow away, bhd, eff 3f out, no dngr: in '99 trained by W Brisbourne, won twice here at Haydock (h'caps, rtd 82 at best): '98 scorer at Nottingham (h'cap, rtd 54): eff at 12f, suited by 14f/2m & handles firm, likes gd, soft grnd, Nottingham & Haydock: has run well fresh: much fitter for this over further next time. *1½* **70**
3528} **ENFILADE 99** [6] 4-9-1 (75)(t) J Reid 12/1: 1444-5: In tch, rdn over 3f out, onepace: reapp, op 9/1: clr rem: '99 wnr at Chester & Haydock (h'caps, rtd 80 at best): wng form over 12f/14f on firm, gd/soft & any trk. *hd* **67**
4546} **KATHRYNS PET 99** [9] 7-9-0 (73) A Culhane 7/2 FAV: 0041-6: Waited with, eff over 3f out, sn held: nicely bckd: fit from hdling, earlier won at Kelso (h'cap hdle, rtd 125h, 2m, firm & gd/soft): won first & last '99 Flat starts, at Catterick & Newmarket (h'caps, rtd 72): '98 Flat wnr again at Catterick: eff at 12f/2m on fast & soft. *5* **59**
*695 **GREEN BOPPER 12** [1] 7-8-9 (68) A Beech (5) 5/1: 234217: In tch, btn well over 3f out: btr 695 (a/w). *hd* **54**
4619} **EVANDER 99** [7] 5-9-11 (84) J Fortune 9/2: 0524-8: Chsd ldrs till wknd over 2f out: nicely bckd on reapp: rnr-up on 1 of 5 '99 starts (rtd 85): '99 Goodwood scorer (mdn, rtd 89): eff over 10/12f on firm & hvy. *4* **65**
699 **HIBERNATE 9** [10] 6-9-5 (78) D McGann (7) 25/1: 0-0009: Keen, led after 1f till over 5f out, wknd. *11* **47**
-- **ALS ALIBI** [5] 7-8-11 (70) Pat Eddery 25/1: 1061/0: Led 1f, wknd over 3f out: 10th, 2 yr abs. *¾* **38**
3945} **HUNTERS TWEED 99** [11] 4-8-12 (72) K Fallon 7/1: 1505-0: Al bhd: fin last on reapp. *3* **36**
11 ran Time 2m 36.1 (8.3) (Mrs P W Harris) P W Harris Ringshall, Bucks.

810

4.15 TOTALBET.COM HCAP 3YO 0-100 (C) 1m30y rnd Good/Soft 72 -07 Slow [101]
£7052 £2170 £1085 £542

*736 **SAFARANDO 7** [6] N P Littmoden 3-9-2 (89) T G McLaughlin 9/2 JT FAV: 011211: 3 b c Turtle Island - Hertford Castle (Reference Point) Prom, went on 3f out, clr over 1f out, won eased down: val 5L: earlier won at W'hampton (2, h'caps, rtd 87a) & Doncaster (h'cap): '99 scorer at Yarmouth (sell, with R Hannon) & Lingfield (nursery h'cap, rtd 75): eff over 7f/1m, should stay further: acts on firm, soft grnd & fibresand: handles any trk: tough, most progressive & v useful colt, in terrific form & a hat-trick looks on the cards. **101**
4274} **VINTAGE PREMIUM 99** [4] R A Fahey 3-8-11 (84) R Winston 25/1: 2210-2: 3 b c Forzando - Julia Domna (Dominion) In tch, rdn over 2f out, kept on over 1f out, no threat to easy wnr: reapp: lightly rcd juv, won at Beverley (mdn auct, rtd 89 at best): half-brother to a useful 7f/1m wnr: stays 1m well, further should suit: acts on gd/firm, gd/soft & on any trk: has run well fresh: lightly raced, looks sure to improve for this gd reapp. *2* **88**
2879} **BUYING A DREAM 99** [3] Andrew Turnell 3-8-4 (77) K Darley 33/1: 0124-3: 3 ch g Prince Of Birds - Cartagena Lady (Prince Rupert) Keen in tch, eff over 2f out, sn onepace: reapp: lightly rcd juv, won at Thirsk (med auct mdn, rtd 79): eff at 7f/1m on gd/firm & gd/soft, any trk: pleasing comeback, should strip fitter for this. *1½* **78**
735 **FIRST TRUTH 7** [8] A Bailey 3-9-3 (90) M Roberts 25/1: 215-64: Chsd ldrs, rdn 2f out, onepace. *½* **91**
4389} **DILSAA 99** [7] 3-8-6 (79) Pat Eddery 10/1: 5525-5: Bhd, effort over 2f out, sn no impress: rnr-up on 1 of 4 juv starts (mdn, rtd 82): eff at 7f, should stay 1m+: acts on gd & soft grnd & on a gall trk. *2* **77**
495 **HEATHYARDS LAD 51** [10] 3-7-10 (69)(8oh) P M Quinn (5) 50/1: 4-5406: Led after 1f till 3f out, no extra over 1f out: 7 wk abs. *1* **65**
*694 **ATLANTIC RHAPSODY 12** [1] 3-9-1 (88)(bl) D Holland 9/2 JT FAV: 232-17: Slow away & bhd, brief effort over 2f out, no dngr: better expected after 694 (fibresand, first time blnks). *hd* **84**
3361} **SPIN A YARN 99** [2] 3-8-13 (86) J Reid 13/2: 4441-8: Waited with, rdn & no impress final 2f: reapp: won last of 5 juv starts, at Newbury (nursery h'cap, rtd 86): half-brother to a 10.5f wnr: stays 7.3f, further should suit: acts on firm/fast grnd & on a gall trk. *1½* **80**
4601} **MENTIGA 99** [5] 3-8-12 (85) P Robinson 16/1: 0213-9: Led 1f, chsd ldrs till wknd over 2f out: reapp: won 1 of 8 juv starts, at Newbury (nursery h'cap, rtd 85 at best): stays 7.3f well & likes soft or hvy. *¾* **78**
4607} **MAC BE LUCKY 99** [9] 3-8-2 (75) G Duffield 14/1: 320-0: Al bhd: 10th, reapp. *nk* **68**
4543} **AL TOWD 99** [11] 3-9-7 (94) R Hills 5/1: 3123-0: Waited with, rdn & btn over 2f out: 11th: top weight: reapp: won 1 of 4 juv starts, at Newcastle (mdn), plcd all 3 other starts (rtd 96 at best): eff at 7f/1m on firm, gd/soft grnd & on a gall trk: should be capable of better. *shd* **87**
4591} **MAKASSEB 99** [13] 3-8-13 (86) T Quinn 14/1: 3225-0: Prom till wknd 3f out: 12th. *3* **75**
4550} **TRUE OBSESSION 99** [12] 3-8-3 (76) D Sweeney 11/1: 3600-0: Keen in tch, btn over 3f out: fin last. *17* **35**
13 ran Time 1m 46.92 (6.42) (Paul J Dixon) N P Littmoden Newmarket, Suffolk.

811

5.20 LEVY BOARD FILLIES HCAP 3YO+ 0-75 (D) 7f30y Good/Soft 72 -13 Slow [73]
£2912 £832 £416 3 yo rec 14lb

*739 **GUEST ENVOY 5** [11] C N Allen 5-7-11 (42)(6ex) P M Quinn (5) 12/1: 214411: 5 b m Paris House - Peace Mission (Dunbeath) Hld up, eff over 3f out, led dist, rdn out: qck reapp under a pen having recently scored at Southwell (fill h'cap, rtd 54a), earlier won again at Southwell: '99 W'hampton wnr (h'cap, rtd 62a): '98 Hamilton h'cap wnr: wng form over 6f/8.5f on gd, soft & fibresand: handles any trk & best without a visor: on a fair mark. **50**
721 **MY TESS 7** [16] B A McMahon 4-9-2 (61) K Darley 6/1: 522132: 4 br f Lugana Beach - Barachois Princess (Barachois): Led till dist, outpcd by wnr: in gd form: see 588 (fibresand, made all). *2½* **64**
4232} **DORISSIO 99** [2] I A Balding 4-9-5 (64) K Fallon 7/2 FAV: 0011-3: 4 b f Efisio - Floralia (Auction *1½* **65**

Ring) Dwelt, sn in tch, not clr run over 2f out, swtchd right & kept on ins last, no dngr: nicely bckd on reapp: won fnl 2 '99 starts, at Bath (sell h'cap, first win) & Pontefract (h'cap, rtd 63): eff at 7f, sure to apprec a return to 1m: acts on firm & gd/soft grnd & on a stiff/undul trk: sharper next time over further.

754	**BODFARI ANNA** 4 [6] J L Eyre 4-8-2 (46)(vis)(1ow) J F Egan 25/1: 0-3054: In tch, effort 2f out, swished tail & no extra inside last: qck reapp: see 754.			¾	46
4576}	**FEATHERTIME** 99 [13] 4-8-9 (54) G Duffield 20/1: 6514-5: Chsd ldrs till wknd over 1f out: reapp: sole '99 win, at Newcastle (clmg h'cap, rtd 53): stays 8.3f & likes gd/soft, handles firm & a gall trk.			5	46
585	**AHOUOD** 36 [5] 4-8-5 (50) R Cody Boutcher (5) 20/1: -42256: In tch, rdn over 2f out, no impress.			1¼	40
610	**PIX ME UP** 32 [7] 3-8-8 (67) F Lynch 25/1: 320-07: Bhd, rdn & short of room over 2f out, no dngr: plcd twice in '99 (mdns, rtd 80): eff at 6/7f, 1m should suit: acts on firm/fast & on a gall or sharp trk.			¾	56
780	**ISLE OF SODOR** 3 [1] 4-8-10 (55) J Bramhill 50/1: 000-08: Bhd, nvr a factor.			nk	43
384	**ITSANOTHERGIRL** 68 [10] 4-9-8 (67) T Lucas 25/1: 035-09: Bhd, nvr a threat: unplcd over hdles.			2	52
780	**INCHALONG** 3 [9] 5-9-5 (64)(vis) D Mernagh (3) 14/1: 206-00: Handy till wknd well over 1f out.			shd	49
739	**GENERAL KLAIRE** 5 [4] 5-8-4 (49) P Hanagan (7) 10/1: 013640: Chsd ldrs till wknd over 2f out: 11th, qck reapp: btr 501 (sell, fibresand).			2	31
4063}	**CARINTHIA** 99 [14] 5-9-5 (64) S Sanders 4/1: /000-0: Chsd ldrs till wknd 2f out: 12th, well bckd on reapp: unplcd all 3 '99 starts (rtd 68 at best): '98 Salisbury scorer (h'cap, rtd 72): eff at 6f/1m on firm, gd/soft grnd & on any trk: has run well fresh.			5	38
3583}	**ROUGE ETOILE** 99 [12] 4-10-0 (73) J Carroll 33/1: 0000-0: Al bhd: 13th: in '99 trained by A McNae, unplcd (rtd 63): '98 Folkestone wnr (auct mdn, rtd 78): eff at 6f on soft grnd.			11	29
3807}	**CAJOLE** 99 [8] 4-8-13 (58) J Reid 9/1: 0002-0: In tch, btn over 4f out: 14th, op 7/1.			½	13
3890}	**DESERT SAFARI** 99 [3] 3-9-1 (74) L Swift (7) 20/1: 4041-0: Keen, handy till wknd over 2f out: 15th.			hd	29
2136}	**GUEST OF HONOUR** 99 [15] 4-8-13 (58) D Holland 10/1: 0205-0: Al bhd: fin last, reapp.			4	6
16 ran	Time 1m 33.11 (6.01) (Shadowfaxracing.Com) C N Allen Newmarket.				

Official Going SOFT (HEAVY places). Stalls: Inside.

812 | 2.20 WARWICK AUCT MDN 2YO (E) 5f rnd Soft Inapplicable
£2949 £842 £211 £211 Field raced centre to stands side in straight

700	**SHOESHINE BOY** 11 [9] B J Meehan 2-8-8 Pat Eddery 5/4 FAV: 21: 2 b g Prince Sabo - Susie Sunshine (Waajib): Sn handy, rdn/led over 1f out, styd on well for press ins last, rdn out: hvly bckd: half-brother to a minor 7f wnr, dam 9f 2yo wnr: eff at 5f, 6f shld suit: acts on firm & gd/soft, sharp or gall trk: in fine form.			85
--	**FRANICA** [5] A Bailey 2-8-0 A Mackay 20/1: 2: 2 b f Inzar - Comfrey Glen (Glenstal) Towards rear/outpcd, styd on well fnl 2f under hands-and-heels riding, not reach wnr: op 10/1: Mar foal, 2,200 gns purchase: half-sister to 3 wnrs, dam styd 1m: eff at 5f, 6f suit: acts on soft: improve & win a race.			¾	74
700	**MIDNIGHT VENTURE** 11 [4] Mrs L Stubbs 2-8-8 A Culhane 10/1: 03: 2 b c Night Shift - Front Line Romance (Caerleon): Handy, rdn/led halfway, hdd over 1f out, kept on well for press ins last: op 8/1, left debut bhd: Feb foal, cost 9,000gns: dam 7f juv wnr: eff at 5f, 6f will suit: going the right way, shld win a race.			½	81
--	**FIAMMA ROYALE** [2] Mrs P N Dutfield 2-8-3 L Newman (5) 14/1: 4: Chsd ldrs, kept on fnl 2f for press, not pace of wnr: op 10/1: Fumo Di Londra filly, Apr foal: half-sister to a smart 6f wnr: dam 2m winner: eff at 5f, 6f+ shld suit: acts on soft grnd: open to plenty of improvement.		dht	76
--	**WANNA SHOUT** [6] 2-7-13 A Nicholls (3) 14/1: 5: Dwelt, sn chsd ldrs, ch over 1f out, no extra ins last: op 12/1: Missed Flight filly, Feb foal: 6,000gns 2yo: sire a high-class 7f 1m performer: with R Dickin.			2	68
--	**SAWBO LAD** [7] 2-8-4 F Norton 20/1: 6: Rdn/outpcd early, rdn & kept on well fnl 2f, nrst at fin: Namaqualand colt, Jan foal, cost 1,200gns: dam unrcd, sire useful 2yo/miler: apprec 6f+: improve for this intro.			½	72
730	**KACHINA DOLL** 9 [14] 2-8-4 P Fessey 7/2: -37: Chsd ldrs, rdn/outpcd 2f out, kept on again ins last, no threat: op 5/2: looks sure to relish 6f+: see 730 (gd).			nk	71
--	**JOHN FOLEY** [10] 2-8-6 P Fitzsimons (5) 12/1: 8: Chsd ldrs, outpcd over 2f out: op 10/1: Petardia colt, Apr foal, cost 5,000gns: half-brother to 3 wnrs abroad: sire a smart 2yo: with W G M Turner.			3	67
--	**PRINCE GRIGORI** [3] 2-8-11 J F Egan 25/1: 9: Rdn halfway towards rear, no impress: Prince Of Birds colt, Mar foal, cost IR £15,000: half-brother to a 1m Irish juv wnr: dam a 5f Irish juv wnr: with E J Alston.			5	64
--	**SIZE DOESNT MATTER** [13] 2-8-5 R Mullen 16/1: 0: Rdn/outpcd, no impress: 10th: op 20/1: Greensmith colt, Mar foal, cost 3,000gns: dam a 5f juv wnr: sire a smart miler: with J R Best.			2	54
--	**IF BY CHANCE** [12] 2-8-7 (1ow) T Quinn 12/1: 0: Prom 4f: 11th: op 10/1, with D Arbuthnot.			¾	55
730	**LION SONG** 9 [8] 2-8-4 O Pears 50/1: -00: Keen/led 3f, btn/eased over 1f out: 12th.			nk	51
--	**ACORN CATCHER** [11] 2-8-0 M Henry 14/1: 0: Chsd ldrs, btn 2f out: 13th: op 10/1, with B Palling.			8	35
13 ran	Time 1m 04.50 (Oneoneone Racing) B J Meehan Upper Lambourn, Berks.				

813 | 2.50 KINGSBURY CLASSIFIED STKS 3YO 0-65 (E) 6f168y rnd Soft Inapplicable
£2930 £837 £418 Raced centre to stands side in straight

659	**BLACKPOOL MAMMAS** 23 [4] J M Bradley 3-8-9 R Ffrench 8/1: 224-01: 3 b f Merdon Melody - Woodland Steps (Bold Owl): Chsd ldr, led over 4f out, rdn/clr ins last, styd on strongly, rdn out: tchd 10/1: with J Berry in '99, scored at Musselburgh (debut, auct mdn), Newcastle & Chepstow (clmrs, rnr-up on sand, rtd 82 & 72a at best): eff at 5f, now stays sharp 6.8f well: acts on firm, soft & fibresand: handles any trk: has run well fresh.			69
4524}	**DISTANT GUEST** 99 [6] G G Margarson 3-8-12 P Robinson 5/1: 000-2: 3 b c Distant Relative - Teacher's Game (Mummy's Game): Dwelt, rdn/chsd ldrs halfway, kept on fnl 2f for press, not pace of wnr: op 9/2: 5 month abs: unplcd in '99 (rtd 76, mdn): eff over a sharp 7f, return to 1m+ shld suit: handles soft: apprec h'caps.		4	65
2300}	**ISLAND THYMES** 99 [3] R Dickin 3-8-12 J Reid 9/2: 406-3: 3 br g Alhijaz - Harmonious Sound (Auction Ring): Chsd ldrs, rdn/no extra fnl 1f: 9 month abs: op 6/1: prev with B J Meehan, unplcd in '99 (rtd 75, mdn, debut): eff at 6f, 7f shld suit: handles gd/soft & soft grnd.		3	61
592	**LADYWELL BLAISE** 27 [7] M L W Bell 3-8-12 M Fenton 3/1 FAV: -31464: Chsd ldrs 5f: op 7/4, turf bow.		1¾	59
570	**CHILWORTH** 40 [8] 3-8-12 R Price 11/1: 64-005: Prom, btn 2f out: op 12/1, 6 wk abs: see 488.		6	51
558	**JUST MAC** 42 [1] 3-8-12 G Hannon (7) 10/1: 3-0606: Chsd ldrs, btn 2f out: op 6/1, 6 wk abs: see 221 (6f).		5	44
744	**WOODWIND DOWN** 7 [5] 3-8-9 T Quinn 100/30: -00-207: Well bhd halfway: op 5/2: btr 651 (AW).		29	11
4383}	**LA BIRBA** 99 [9] 3-8-9 Pat Eddery 10/1: 0004-8: Led 2f: reapp, unplcd '99 (rtd 56 & 44a, tried blnks).		3½	6
8 ran	Time 1m 32.40 (D J & L & Mrs C Gardiner) J M Bradley Sedbury, Glos.			

---

814   **3.20 WARWICK RHT.NET FILLIES MDN 3YO (D)   1m2f110y Soft Inapplicable**
£3545   £1091   £545   £272 Raced towards centre in straight.

4561} **BEDARA** 99 [8] B W Hills 3-8-11 M Hills 11/10 FAV: 02-1: 3 b f Barathea - Cutting Reef (Kris)   83
Chsd ldrs, rdn over 3f out, prog to lead ins last, rdn to assert: well bckd tho' op 4/7: 5 month abs: rnr-up
in '99 (Listed, rtd 95): eff at 1m/10.5f, further shld suit: acts on soft: runs well fresh: useful.
--   **SIONED LYN** [5] D Burchell 3-8-11 R Price 50/1: 2: 3 b f Perpendicular - Lady Spider (Ring Bidder)   2   80
Dwelt, held up in tch, prog/rdn to lead over 3f out, hdd ins last & no extra: debut: eff over a sharp 10.5f,
could stay further: acts on soft grnd: very encouraging introduction.
3671} **DOODLE BUG** 99 [9] T R Watson 3-8-11 V Slattery 25/1: 30-3: 3 b f Missed Flight - Kasierlinde   nk 79$
(Frontal) Rear, rdn/outpcd 4f out, kept on well fnl 2f, nrst fin: clr of rem: 7 month abs: plcd in '99 (rtd 81,
debut, auct mdn): stays a sharp 10.5f, 12f shld suit: handles fast & soft, any trk: should win a race.
4555} **REEMATNA** 99 [6] M A Jarvis 3-8-11 P Robinson 3/1: 0-4: Held up in tch, rcd keenly, rdn/btn over   8   70
1f out: well bckd, tchd 5/1: 5 month abs: unplcd sole '99 start (fill mdn, rtd 87): shld stay 10f & do better.
3998} **SHAM SHARIF** 99 [3] 3-8-11 Pat Eddery 9/1: 00-5: Led 7f, btn 2f out: op 6/1, 6 month abs: unplcd   1¾ 68
both '99 starts (mdn, 7f mdns): bred to apprec mid-dists.
--   **FAY** [4] 3-8-11 J Fortune 9/2: 6: Chsd ldr, btn 2f out: op 3/1, debut: half-sister to 7f/10.5f wnr   ½   67
Starry Night: mid-dists shld suit: with P Cole.
4597} **RIDGEWOOD BAY** 99 [1] 3-8-11 P Dobbs (5) 66/1: 0000-7: Chsd ldrs 6f: 5 month abs, mod '99 form. *dist* 0
--   **THEATRO DANIELLI** [7] 3-8-11 (t) W R Swinburn 16/1: 5-8: Struggling 4f out: op 12/1: Brit   21 0
debut, ex-Irish, last of 5 sole '99 start for K Prendergast, now with R Fahey.
8 ran   Time 2m 32.50   (John Poynton)   B W Hills Lambourn, Berks.

---

815   **3.50 TOTE HCAP 3YO+ 0-80 (D)   1m4f56y Soft Inapplicable**   [79]
£7117   £2190   £1095   £547   3 yo rec 21lb4 yo rec 1 lb Raced centre fnl 2f

699   **LANCER** 11 [9] J Pearce 8-8-12 (63)(vis) T Quinn 5/1: 420-61: 8 ch g Diesis - Last Bird (Sea Bird II)   67
Held up in tch, stdy prog/trkd ldrs 3f out, led over 1f out, styd on well, rdn out: op 7/2: '99 Folkestone wnr (amat
stks, rtd 74, unplcd on sand, rtd 37a): '98 wnr at Leicester, Folkestone & York (h'caps, rtd 75 & 45a at best): best
at 12f, stays 14f well: acts on firm & hvy, any trk: suited by a visor: gd weight carrier: tough.
726   **LEGAL LUNCH** 9 [3] P W Harris 5-9-2 (67)(vis) W R Swinburn 100/30 FAV: 233-42: 5 b g Alleged -   1   69
Dinner Surprise (Lyphard) Sn handy, led going well over 3f out, rdn/hdd over 1f out & no extra: clr of rem, bckd.
714   **MISCHIEF** 10 [12] M Quinn 4-8-5 (57)(vis) F Norton 20/1: 556203: 4 ch g Generous - Knight's Baroness   5   54
(Rainbow Quest) Towards rear, rdn/prog fnl 3f, not pace to chall front pair: eff around 12f on soft/hvy grnd.
641   **RIVERBLUE** 28 [13] D J Wintle 4-10-0 (80) J F Egan 12/1: 051534: Held up, prog/chsd ldrs halfway,   1¾ 75
held over 1f out: op 8/1, topweight, longer trip & softer grnd: see 641, 568 (9f).
3444} **LEMON BRIDGE** 99 [6] 5-9-12 (77) Martin Dwyer 6/1: /220-5: Rear/in tch, eff 3f out, sn held: Flat   20 57
reapp, 2 month jumps abs (plcd, rtd 105h, mdn hdle): rnr-up twice in '99 on the level (rtd 81, h'cap): '98
Goodwood wnr (med auct mdn, rtd 78, J Hills): eff at 10/12f on any grnd & trk: eff forcing the pace.
*387   **ORO STREET** 70 [10] 4-9-8 (74) A Culhane 5/1: 04-216: Handy, wknd 3f out: op 4/1, jumps fit (Feb   1¼ 53
Warwick wnr, juv nov, rtd 118h): see 387 (12f, AW, mdn).
726   **GROSVENOR FLYER** 9 [4] 4-9-5 (71) Pat Eddery 10/1: 220-07: Handy, led 7f out, hdd/wknd 3f out: 6   44
op 8/1: unplcd over jumps this winter (rtd 105h, juv nov): rnr-up thrice in '99 (rtd 80, auct mdn, P W Chapple
Hyam, subs tried blnks): eff around 10f/14.6f, tried 2m+: handles firm & soft, any trk: mdn, now with T McCarthy.
604} **KIND SIR** 99 [2] 4-9-7 (73) J Reid 10/1: 5/14-8: Mid-div, btn 3f out: op 7/1, jumps fit (rnr-up twice,   3   43
rtd 92h, juv nov): '99 wnr on the level for B W Hills at Lingfield (AW mdn, rtd 76a): rtd 71 in '98: eff at 10, 12f+
could suit: acts on equitrack & poss gd/soft: has run well fresh & likes to force the pace: now with R Dickin.
4597} **BOLDER ALEXANDER** 99 [1] 3-7-11 (69)(1ow)(17oh) A Nicholls (0) 40/1: 0300-9: Led 3f, btn 3f out: 11 31
5 month abs: '99 Brighton scorer (first time blnks, seller, P Cole, rtd 64), subs with G L Moore (rtd 39a): eff
over a sharp 7f, mid-dists could suit: acts on firm & gd & likes a sharp/undul trk: best in blnks: with F Jordan.
4484} **LITTLE AMIN** 99 [11] 4-9-11 (77) J Weaver 8/1: 4160-0: Led after 3f, hdd 7f out, sn btn: 10th: 10 31
5 month abs: '99 reapp Newcastle wnr (mdn, J Bethell), subs scored for current connections at Haydock (h'cap,
rtd 80): plcd in '98 (rtd 79+, mdn): eff over a gall 12f: suited by gd/soft & soft grnd: likes to force the pace.
10 ran   Time 2m 58.20   (Chris Marsh)   J Pearce Newmarket.

---

816   **4.20 LEEK WOOTTON CLAIMER 3YO+ (F)   6f168y rnd Soft Inapplicable**
£2520   £720   £360   3 yo rec 14lb Raced towards centre in straight

790   **STRATS QUEST** 4 [5] D W P Arbuthnot 6-8-9 T Quinn 10/1: -65001: 6 b m Nicholas - Eagle's Quest   54
(Legal Eagle) Held up in tch, prog halfway & led ins last, sn in command, eased nr fin: op 8/1: qck reapp: '99
Southwell wnr (sell h'cap, rtd 47a, rnr-up on turf, rtd 51, fill h'cap): plcd in '98 (h'cap, rtd 60, also rtd 38a):
eff at 6f/sharp 7f: handles fast & fibresand, loves soft: eff with/without a vis: enjoys sellers/claimers.
4472} **AGENT MULDER** 99 [3] P D Cundell 6-10-0 (bl) D Holland 100/30 FAV: 1000-2: 6 b g Kylian - Precious 3½ 67
Caroline (The Noble Player) Held up in tch, prog to lead over 1f out, rdn/hdd ins last & no ch with wnr: op 11/4,
5 month abs: blnks reapplied: '99 h'cap wnr at Nottingham & Salisbury (rtd 79): '98 wnr at Nottingham (2, clmr
& class stks, rtd 62): stays 1m, suited by 6f: handles gd, hvy & Nottingham: eff with/without blnks.
719   **RUSSIAN ROMEO** 9 [12] B A McMahon 5-9-10 (bl) K Darley 6/1: 055223: 5 b g Soviet Lad - Aotearoa 1¾ 61
(Flash Of Steel) Chsd ldrs halfway, kept on onepace fnl 2f: nicely bckd, tchd 7/1: acts on fast, soft & fibresand.
787   **PRIORY GARDENS** 5 [6] J M Bradley 6-9-2 R Ffrench 20/1: 000004: Led 5f, fdd: qck reapp: see 262. 3½ 48
693   **LEOFRIC** 14 [14] 5-9-4 (bl) L Newton 20/1: 040-35: Held up, nvr pace to chall: clr rem: see 693. 1¼ 48
2159} **LYNTON LAD** 99 [9] 8-9-6 L Swift (7) 7/1: 0125-6: Chsd ldrs, outpcd over 2f out: op 6/1, 10 month 12 36
abs: '99 Ayr wnr (h'cap, rtd 67), unplcd on sand (rtd 42a): eff at 1m on fast & soft: eff with/without blnks.
728   **ASTRAC** 9 [2] 9-10-0 J Weaver 7/2: -13007: Chsd ldrs, wknd over 1f out: op 5/2: btr 406 (AW).   nk 43
--   **ALRIGHT POPS** [13] 4-8-9 S Righton 66/1: 6000/8: Prom 5f: 5 month jumps abs (mod form).   9   14
4604} **MONTENDRE** 99 [8] 13-9-0 J Reid 10/1: 4030-9: Al rear: 5 month abs: '99 Kempton wnr (clmr, rtd 64 ½   18
at best): '98 Nottingham & Haydock wnr (clmrs, rtd 77 at best): eff at 5/6f, stays 7f on firm, suited by gd & soft.
501   **SOUNDS SOLO** 52 [7] 4-9-0 O Pears 33/1: -63060: Keen/prom, btn 2f out: 10th: 7 wk abs.   hd 17
583   **DEMOCRACY** 39 [1] 4-10-0 (bl) S Drowne 8/1: 053000: Al bhd: 12th: see 258.   0
680   **Mikes Double** 18 [10] 6-9-2 (vis) R Fitzpatrick (3) 20/1:654 **Vicky Vettori** 26 [11] 3-7-11 M Baird 66/1:
13 ran   Time 1m 31.40   (Jack Blumenow)   D W P Arbuthnot Upper Lambourn, Berks.

MONDAY APRIL 3RD **Lefthand, Sharp, Turning Track**

817

4.50 LEAMINGTON HCAP 3YO+ 0-80 (D) **7f146y rnd** **Soft** **Inapplicable** [78]
£4303 £1324 £662 £331 3 yo rec 15lb Raced centre in straight.

716 **MISTER RAMBO 10** [8] B J Meehan 5-10-0 (78) R Hughes 7/1: 540-01: 5 b g Rambo Dancer - Ozra 83
(Red Alert) Chsd ldrs, rdn fnl 2f, styd on well ins last to lead nr fin, rdn out: op 5/1: '99 Ascot scorer (ladies
h'cap, rtd 88 at best): '98 wnr in Germany (List, rtd 90): eff at 6f, suited by 7f/7.5f: acts on fast & soft grnd:
runs well fresh: handles any trk: best without blnks: gd weight carrier: back on a handy mark.
711 **TRUMP STREET 11** [14] S G Knight 4-7-12 (46)(2ow) F Norton 20/1: 30-002: 4 b f First Trump - Pepeke 1¾ 50
(Mummy's Pet) Led 2f & remained cl-up, rdn/led again over 1f out, hdd nr line: acts on firm & soft grnd: see 614.
4297} **AMBER FORT 99** [11] J M Bradley 7-9-8 (72)(bl) J Fortune 5/1: 2000-3: 7 gr g Indian Ridge - hd 73
Lammastide (Martinmas) Held up in tch, kept on fnl 2f, not pace of wnr: op 6/1, reapp: plcd sev times in '99
(rtd 78, h'cap): '98 wnr at Goodwood (appr h'cap) & Kempton (h'cap, rtd 91 at best, D Elsworth): all 5 wins at
at 7f, stays 1m: acts on firm, soft & equitrack: likes Goodwood: eff in a blnks/visor: h'capped to win.
611 **GULF SHAADI 34** [10] Miss Gay Kelleway 8-9-9 (73) S Sanders 6/1: 000-04: Rdn/towards rear, styd 2 71
on well for press fnl 2f, nrst fin: nicely bckd, tchd 14/1: see 169.
594 **TITAN 37** [16] 5-7-10 (46)(2oh) R Brisland (4) 25/1: 0-0005: Chsd ldrs, fdd fnl 1f: rnr-up in '99 (rtd 52, 2 41
h'cap, S Dow): plcd in '98 (rtd 69): '97 Goodwood wnr (nurs, rtd 80): eff at 7f/1m on firm & soft grnd.
738 **DISTINCTIVE DREAM 7** [2] 6-9-8 (72) D Kilcourse (7) 10/1: 341036: Dwelt, led after 2f, hdd over 1f out, fdd.3¼ 62
*718 **LORD EUROLINK 9** [6] 6-9-6 (70)(tvi) D Holland 7/2 JT FAV: 531117: Rear, late gains under hands- 1 59
and-heels riding, no threat: not knocked about on return to turf, return to 1m+ & forcing tactics may suit.
4472} **COMPRADORE 99** [13] 5-8-12 (62) D Sweeney 12/1: 5030-8: Held up, eff 2f out, sn held: op 10/1: nk 50
5 month abs: plcd sev times in '99 (rtd 71, h'cap): '98 Folkestone wnr (stks,rtd 72): eff at 5f, suited by 6f/1m:
acts on firm & hvy grnd, any trk: on a handy mark when returning to form.
4615} **CAD ORO 99** [1] 7-9-2 (66) A Nicholls (3) 6/1: 0200-9: Held up, eff over 2f out, no impress: 5 mth abs: 1½ 52
'99 Kempton scorer (h'cap, rtd 71): '98 Nottingham wnr (h'cap, rtd 65): eff at 7f/1m: acts on fast & gd, relishes
gd/soft & hvy grnd: handles any trk: likes Nottingham: has run well fresh.
4196} **SAMARA SONG 99** [7] 7-9-0 (64) R Fitzpatrick (3) 20/1: 0000-0: Held up, rdn/btn 2f out: 10th: reapp. nk 49
4585} **MISTER MAL 99** [4] 4-9-13 (77) K Darley 7/2 JT FAV: 0313-0: Dwelt, sn handy, rdn/wkng when hmpd 17 43
over 1f out: 10th: op 3/1, 5 month abs: '99 wnr at Catterick (mdn), Leicester & Redcar (h'caps, rtd 77 & 75a
at best): all 3 wins at 7f, stays 1m on firm & fibresand, loves gd/soft & soft: likes a galloping one: tough.
2988} **LIONESS 99** [5] 4-9-8 (72) W Jones (7) 33/1: 4430-0: Slowly away, al bhd: 12th: 8 month absence. dist 0
623 **INTRICATE WEB 32** [9] 4-9-4 (68) J F Egan 8/1: 301-60: Mid-div, drvn/btn 4f out, sn eased: 13th. 0
13 ran Time 1m 48.20 (Abbott Racing Ltd) B J Meehan Upper Lambourn, Berks.

SATURDAY APRIL 1ST **Righthand, Undulating Track**

Official Going GOOD TO YIELDING

818

2.30 ESSO EBF CHALLENGE RACE 3YO **1m1f100y** **Good/Yielding**
£5520 £1280 £560

-- **GRAND FINALE** [2] D K Weld 3-9-0 P J Smullen 9/1: 3-1: 3 b c Sadler's Wells - Final Figure 101
(Super Concorde) In tch, rdn to improve 3f out, rdn to lead appr fnl 1f, sn hdd, rall well for press to get up line:
op 6/1: fin 3rd in a Leopardstown mdn sole '99 start: eff at 9.5f on gd/yldg, further could suit: tough/useful.
-- **APOLLO VICTORIA** [1] A P O'Brien 3-9-7 M J Kinane 1/5 FAV: 1-2: 3 b c Sadler's Wells - Dame shd 107
Solitaire (Halo) Cl-up, led over 3f out, hdd appr fnl 1f, led again fnl 1f, sn hdd fnl stride: well bckd at long
odds-on: landed a 7f Leopardstown mdn on sole '99 start (front 2 10L clr rest): eff at 7f/9.5f, acts on gd/yldg
& soft grnd: highly rated by connections, poss just better for run.
-- **THREE CLOUDS** [7] J M Oxx 3-9-0 J P Murtagh 7/1: 3: 3 b c Rainbow Quest - Three Tails (Blakeney) 2½ 95
Prom, hdwy cl-up, no extra ins last: op 4/1, 6L clr rem: half-brother to a useful mid-dist performer: fine debut.
10 ran Time 2m 10.4 (Moyglare Stud Farm) D K Weld Curragh, Co Kildare

SUNDAY APRIL 2ND **Righthand, Galloping Track**

Official Going HOLDING

819

2.20 GR 2 PRIX D'HARCOURT 4YO+ **1m2f** **Holding**
£28818 £11527 £5764

2322} **INDIAN DANEHILL 99** [2] A Fabre 4-8-11 O Peslier 7/10 FAV: 1632-1: 4 b c Danehill - Danse Indienne 119
(Green Dancer) Keen in tch, hdwy to lead appr fnl 1f, pushed out, cmftbly: val 2/3L: '99 scorer on reapp at
Longchamp (Gr 3), subs plcd twice in Gr 1 company (rtd 116): eff at 1m/10f: loves soft/hvy grnd: v smart.
2983} **CHELSEA MANOR 99** [3] P Bary 4-8-11 T Thulliez 53/10: 1124-2: 4 b c Grand Lodge - Docklands 1 115
(Theatrical) Waited with, gd hdwy over 1f out, styd on but always held by cmftble wnr: gd run, eff at 10f on hvy.
1406} **BARBOLA 99** [1] J de Roualle 5-8-11 G Mosse 28/10: -123-3: 5 ch h Diesis - Barboukh (Night Shift) 1 113
Cl-up, hdwy when short of room & lost grnd over 1f out, styd on well ins last, shade unlucky.
5 ran Time 2m 13.9 (Baron Edouard de Rothschild) A Fabre France

MAISONS-LAFFITTE TUESDAY APRIL 4TH Left & Righthand, Sharpish Track

Official Going HEAVY

820 **3.15 LISTED PRIX COR DE CHASSE 3YO+ 5f110y Heavy**
£13449 £4612 £3458 3 yo rec 11lb

1735} **DANANEYEV 99** C Laffon Parias 4-9-5 D Boeuf : 3-1: 4 br c Goldneyev - Danagroom (Groom Dancer) **109**
Hmpd on sev occasions, would reportedly have won by much further with a clr run: eff at 5.5f on hvy: v useful.
734 **HALMAHERA 10** I A Balding 5-9-9 O Peslier : 406-52: 5 b g Petardia - Champagne Girl (Robellino) ½ **108**
Trkd ldrs till went on ins fnl 3f, edged right ins last & hdd fnl 50y: another sound run by this v tough & useful sprinter, looks set for another successful campaign: see 734.
4021} **TERROIR 99** France 5-9-5 C Soumillon : 5112-3: 5 b h Fairy King - Terracotta Hut (Habitat) 1½ **100**
4246} **ANTINNAZ 99** T Stack 4-9-6 W J O'Connor : 1535-9: Nvr a threat, btn arnd 9L into 9th: reportedly **82**
unsuited by the 'gluey' grnd conds: '99 scorer at Haydock (Listed), subs an excellent 5th in the Gr 1 Prix de L'Abbaye (rtd 112): eff at 5/6f: acts on gd & hvy grnd & a galloping trk: smart sprinter at best.
11 ran Time 1m 09.2 (Wertheimer Brothers) C Laffon Parias France

RIPON WEDNESDAY APRIL 5TH Righthand, Sharpish Track

Official Going SOFT. Stalls: Straight Course - Stands Side, Round Course - Inside

821 **2.15 EBF SPA WELTER MDN 2YO (D) 5f Soft 90 -24 Slow**
£3523 £1084 £542 £271 Field raced in 2 Groups - First two clear on far side

-- **ROMANTIC MYTH** [10] T D Easterby 2-8-9 K Darley 3/1: 1: 2 b f Mind Games - My First Romance **87**
(Danehill) Handy far side, led halfway, styd on strongly, pushed out, cosily: nicely bckd tho' op 7/4: lkd fit & well: Jan foal, 16,000 gns purchase, half sister to a 5f juv wnr: sire high-class sprinter: eff at 5f, 6f shld suit in time: acts on soft & runs well fresh: open to improvement.
700 **SIR FRANCIS 13** [13] J Noseda 2-9-0 W R Swinburn 2/1 FAV: 52: 2 b c Common Grounds - Red Note 1½ **86**
(Rusticaro) Handy far side, rdn/chsd wnr fnl 2f, kept on well for press: handles fast & soft: clr rem, win sn.
-- **BOUNCING BOWDLER** [2] M Johnston 2-9-0 D Holland 14/1: 3: 2 b c Mujadil - Prima Volta (Primo 3½ **79**
Dominie) Sn led stands side, rdn/kept on ins last, no impress front pair far side: op 8/1: needed this: Feb 1st foal, 12,000gns purchase: dam a 6f juv wnr, sire a speedy 2yo: eff at 5f, 6f shld suit: handles soft: win a race soon.
-- **TARAS EMPEROR** [4] J J Quinn 2-9-0 A Culhane 9/1: 4: Chsd ldrs stands side, kept on for press ¾ **78**
fnl 2f: op 5/1: Common Grounds gldg, Apr foal, cost 29,000 IR gns: brother to a 1m wnrs: dam 9/10f 3yo wnr: 6f+ looks sure to suit in time: handles soft grnd: leggy, scopey gelding, improve for this.
700 **QUIZZICAL LADY 13** [5] 2-8-9 F Norton 7/1: 05: Unruly in stalls, prom stands side, no impress over ½ **72**
1f out: op 5/1, fit: also bhd today's rnr-up in 700.
-- **BALL GAMES** [15] 2-9-0 G Duffield 14/1: 6: Led far side till halfway, held over 1f out: op 25/1, ndd 1 **75**
this: Mind Games colt, Apr foal, 9,800 gns 2nd foal: dam a minor 12/13f wnr: sire a high-class 2yo: with D Moffatt.
-- **WHARFEDALE LADY** [14] 2-8-9 J Fortune 16/1: 7: Rdn far side, kept on fnl 2f, no threat to ldrs: 1¼ **67**
Charmer filly, Apr foal: half sister to a minor 6f juv wnr: v burly, strong filly who can improve for W T Kemp.
-- **MON SECRET** [6] 2-9-0 R Lappin 33/1: 8: Rdn halfway stands side, no impress fnl 2f: fit: 1½ **69**
General Monash Mar first foal, cost 6,800 IR gns: dam a minor 1m/9f 3yo wnr: stay further in time for J L Eyre.
-- **ORANGE TREE LAD** [8] 2-9-0 G Carter 16/1: 9: Dwelt, in tch stands side, held fnl 2f: op 10/1, ndd ¾ **68**
this: Tragic Role gldg, Feb foal, 3,600 gns purchase: half brother to a multiple Italian wnr, dam a mdn.
700 **GOLDEN DRAGONFLY 13** [3] 2-9-0 O Pears 50/1: 00: Prom stands side 3f: 10th: well bhd today's rnr-up 3 **62**
prev: Eagle Eyed colt, Apr foal, cost 15,000 gns: dam a multiple Belgian: with D Nicholls.
-- **WINDCHILL** [1] 2-8-9 J Carroll 33/1: 0: Al rear stands side: 11th: Handsome Sailor filly, Apr foal. 3½ **50**
-- **SIENA STAR** [12] 2-9-0 T Quinn 16/1: 0: Chsd ldrs far side 3f: 12th: op 20/1, stablemate of 8th. ¾ **54**
-- **PEEJAY HOBBS** [11] 2-9-0 T Lucas 33/1: 0: Bhd halfway far side: 13th: ndd this. ¾ **53**
-- **POPPYS CHOICE** [7] 2-8-9 G Parkin 33/1: 0: Dwelt, bhd stands side, nvr factor: 14th. ½ **47**
-- **MR PERTEMPS** [9] 2-9-0 G Faulkner (3) 12/1: 0: Sn bhd far side: 15th: op 10/1. 4 **44**
15 ran Time 1m 03.5 (5.7) (T G Holdcroft) T D Easterby Great Habton, N Yorks

822 **2.50 MARKINGTON SELL HCAP 4YO+ 0-60 (F) 1m4f60y Soft 90 -08 Slow [59]**
£2310 £660 £330 4 yo rec 1 lb

699 **HAYA YA KEFAAH 13** [18] N M Babbage 8-9-2 (47) J Fortune 10/1: 40/001: 8 b g Kefaah - Hayat **51**
(Sadler's Wells) Held up in tch, rdn/prog fnl 4f & led ins last, styd on well, drvn out: no bid: op 8/1: lkd well: missed '99, unplcd in '98 (rtd 54, h'cap, tried blnks): back in '96 scored at Doncaster (2) & Haydock (h'cap, rtd 65): suited by 12f: handles fast, likes soft & fibresand: has run well fresh: well h'apped & apprec drop to sell grade.
4447} **SKYERS A KITE 99** [20] Ronald Thompson 5-8-12 (43) R Cochrane 13/2: 0130-2: 5 b m Deploy - Milady *nk* **46**
Jade (Drumalis) Towards rear, prog fnl 4f, styd on well ins last, just held: jumps fit (plcd, rtd 70h, sell): '99 Beverley scorer (h'cap, rtd 45, unplcd on sand, rtd 18a): '98 Beverley & Catterick wnr (sell h'cap, rtd 50 at best): eff at 10/12f, tried further: acts on firm & gd, loves soft grnd: handles any trk, likes Beverley: can win similar.
795 **CAMAIR CRUSADER 6** [10] W McKeown 6-8-3 (34) G Duffield 12/1: 000-43: 6 br g Jolly Jake - Sigrid's ¾ **36**
Dream (Triple Bend) Mid-div, prog to lead over 3f out, rdn/hdd ins last, kept on for press: op 8/1: quick reapp: eff at 9/12f: handles fast & soft grnd: see 795.
3053} **WAFIR 99** [15] D Nicholls 8-9-11 (56) O Pears 7/1: 5256-4: Mid-div, rdn & kept on fnl 3f, not pace to 1 **57**
chall: op 6/1, jumps fit (rnr-up, rtd 90h, mdn hdle): '99 Redcar wnr (clmr, rtd 66): '98 Newcastle wnr (class stks, rtd 83, P Calver): eff at 10/12f on fast & hvy, any trk: clr of rem here & remains on a fair mark.
4017} **MISS ARCH 99** [4] 4-8-4 (36) R Mullen 14/1: 3200-5: Dwelt/towards rear, rdn & kept on fnl 3f, no 7 **30**
threat ldrs: v burly, op 16/1: 5 month jumps abs (unplcd, rtd 86h): plcd twice in '99 (rtd 38, sell h'cap): eff around 10f, may stay further: handles fast, poss soft.
215 **A DAY ON THE DUB 99** [14] 7-9-5 (50) J Weaver 13/2: 1125-6: Dwelt/rear, prog wide 4f out, held 1½ **42**
fnl 2f: op 5/1, jumps fit (Jan Catterick wnr, nov h'cap chase, rtd 99c): see 215 (AW).
*742 **PREPOSITION 9** [1] 4-8-11 (43)(6ex) K Hodgson 8/1: 452417: Chsd ldrs, ch 3f out, fdd: lkd well. ½ **34**
710 **ADIRPOUR 13** [13] 6-8-8 (39) Stephanie Hollinshead (6) 20/1: 415408: Mid-div, eff 4f out, no impress. 3 **27**
668 **XYLEM 22** [9] 9-7-13 (30)(vis) G Bardwell 6/1 FAV: 230239: Rear, rdn/mod gains: op 5/1: btr 577 (AW). 2 **16**
3465} **NIGHTGLADE 99** [19] 4-8-6 (38) D Mernagh (3) 20/1: 0650-0: Mid-div, eff over 3f out, held fnl 2f: 10th: 1 **23**

plcd in '99 (rtd 42, h'cap): eff at 10/12f, tried 2m: handles fast & gd/sft grnd.
742 **LOYAL TOAST 9** [2] 5-8-6 (37) Kim Tinkler 12/1: 00-200: Rear, mod gains: 11th, burly: op 16/1. *shd* **22**
748 **SATWA BOULEVARD 9** [11] 5-8-6 (37) D R McCabe 25/1: /00000: Mid-div, no impress fnl 4f: 12th. *1* **21**
497 **TIME ON MY HANDS 54** [17] 4-8-4 (34)(t)(2ow) J F Egan 33/1: -20000: Led after 3f till over 3f out, wknd qckly: 13th: 8 wk abs: see 260 (AW). *½* **19**
742 **IRSAL 9** [6] 6-8-4 (35)(bl) Kimberley Hart (5) 20/1: -30200: Led 3f, cl-up 9f: 14th: see 560, 325 (AW). *5* **13**
-- **Green Power** [3] 6-9-3 (48) R Havlin 20/1:
668 **Amazing Fact 22** [5] 5-7-10 (27) Claire Bryan (5) 25/1:
795 **Jammie Dodger 6** [7] 4-8-12 (44) Dean McKeown 20/1:
4519} **Whistling Jack 99** [8] 4-10-0 (60)(tbl) W R Swinburn 20/1:
18 ran Time 2m 45.6 (12.1) (Alan G Craddock) N M Babbage Brockhampton, Glos

823

3.20 GALPHAY CLASSIFIED STKS 3YO 0-90 (C) 1m1f Soft 90 -16 Slow
£6331 £1948 £974 £487

4047} **GOING GLOBAL 99** [2] S P C Woods 3-8-12 J Reid 10/11 FAV: 31-1: 3 ch c Bob Back - Ukraine Girl (Targowice) Held up in tch, rdn/briefly outpcd over 3f out, styd on well fnl 2f to lead ins last, rdn out: hvly bckd: still ndd this: '99 Goodwood wnr (mdn, rtd 90 at best): eff at 1m/9f, looks sure to relish 10f+: acts on fast & soft, likes a sharp/undul trk: runs well fresh: useful, open to further improvement when tackling further. **96**
3891} **COOL INVESTMENT 99** [3] M Johnston 3-8-12 J Fanning 7/1: 1-2: 3 b c Prince Of Birds - Superb Investment (Hatim) Settled rear/in tch, prog/narrow lead 2f out, rdn & hdd ins last, kept on: 7 mth abs, op 6/1, ndd this & has thrived physically: won sole juv start at Musselburgh (auct mdn, rtd 78): styd longer 9f trip, further shld suit: acts on fast & soft grnd, sharp trk: tall, lengthy colt, shld win more races. *½* **94**
3753} **COTE SOLEIL 99** [4] M L W Bell 3-8-12 M Fenton 8/1: 6404-3: 3 ch c Inchinor - Sunshine Coast (Posse) Chsd ldr, rdn/ch over 2f out, no extra ins last: op 6/1, fit after 7 mth abs: '99 debut scorer for M Channon at Nottingham (mdn, subs rtd 94 at best in Listed cpmpany): eff at 5f, stays 1m: handles firm & soft ground. *2* **90**
4611} **CLEVER GIRL 99** [1] T D Easterby 3-8-9 K Darley 5/2: 1215-4: Led, rdn/hdd 2f out, no extra ins last: nicely bckd, op 7/2: 5 mth abs: tough/prog in '99, scoring at Pontefract (auct mdn) & twice at Ayr (nurs h'caps, rtd 89): eff at 6f/1m, may get further: acts on fast & soft, likes a stiff/gall trk, esp Ayr: runs well fresh. *3* **82**
4164} **CHAPEL ROYALE 99** [5] 3-8-12 O Pears 11/1: -001-5: Held up in tch, rcd keenly, rdn/outpcd fnl 3f: sharper for this after abs: '99 Newcastle scorer (auct mdn, A Turnell): eff at 7f on soft grnd. *6* **76**
5 ran Time 1m 59.50 (9.5) (Dwayne Woods) S P C Woods Newmarket, Suffolk

824

3.50 FOUNTAINS HCAP STKS 3YO+ 0-95 (C) 6f Soft 90 +03 Fast [93]
£6818 £2098 £1049 £524 3 yo rec 12lb Two groups, far side favoured

716 **FRANCPORT 12** [19] A Berry 4-8-5 (70) G Carter 5/1: 200-51: 4 b c Efisio - Elkie Brooks (Relkino) Chsd ldrs far side, hdwy to lead over 1f out, hdd ins last, rallied gamely for press to get up again cl home: gd time: well bckd: '99 Beverely wnr (mdn, rtd 75): eff at 5f, stays 6f on firm & soft, any trk: game, in gd form. **77**
*716 **MANORBIER 12** [16] K A Ryan 4-8-12 (77) F Lynch 9/2 FAV: 014112: 4 ch g Shalford - La Pirouette (Kennedy Road) Held up in tch far side, styd on to lead ins last, collared cl home, just btn: clr rem: hvly bckd: acts on fast, soft & fibresand: tough/progressive, ahead of this wnr in 716. *shd* **83**
721 **REDOUBTABLE 11** [10] D W Chapman 9-9-0 (79) A Culhane 14/1: 412143: 9 b h Grey Dawn II - Seattle Rockette (Seattle Slew) Twds rear far side, rdn/kept on fnl 2f, no threat to front pair: tchd 16/1: see 525 (7f, AW). *4* **77**
*719 **MALLIA 11** [15] T D Barron 7-8-4 (69) R Ffrench 7/1: 516414: Held up in tch far side, kept on fnl 2f, not pace of front pair: op 8/1: likes soft grnd: see 719 (W'hampton clmr). *nk* **66**
*746 **JUWWI 9** [14] 6-9-3 (82)(6ex) Darren Williams (7) 8/1: 206015: Held up far side, prog/cl-up over 1f out, no extra ins last: 6lb pen, perennial late fin who poss got to lead too early today: see 746. *1* **77**
716 **CAUTION 12** [18] 6-8-1 (66) D Mernagh (3) 20/1: 05-606: Sn rdn chasing ldrs far side, kept on fnl 2f. *2½* **56**
716 **SULU 12** [17] 4-8-5 (70) T Lucas 33/1: 233-07: Rear far side, styd on fnl 2f, nrst fin: plcd sev times in '99 (rtd 80, mdn, I A Balding): rtd 70 sole '98 start (auct mdn): eff at 5f/7f on firm & gd/soft, sharp/gall trk. *½* **59**
4486} **FIRST MUSICAL 99** [11] 4-9-13 (92) K Darley 10/1: 0004-8: Rdn to lead far side halfway, hdd over 1f out, fdd: ndd this: 5 month abs, rnr-up in '99 (rtd 105, val h'cap, reapp): '98 juv wnr at Pontefract (2, mdn & stks), Ayr (nov auct) & Windsor (fill stks, rtd 100): eff over 5/6f on firm & soft, any trk: has run well fresh. *2½* **76**
715 **REX IS OKAY 12** [3] 4-8-4 (69)(bl) Dale Gibson 14/1: 666409: Sn rdn/led stands side, no ch far side fnl 2f: op 12/1, 1st home on unfav stands side: appreciated return to 6f, both wins at 7f: see 715, 282. *nk* **52**
690 **BOLDLY GOES 18** [4] 4-9-8 (87) P Goode (3) 33/1: /63-00: Chsd ldrs stands side, held fnl 2f: 10th: unplcd from 2 '99 starts (rtd 91, stks): '98 wnr at Pontefract, W'hampton (rtd 86a), Thirsk (stks) & Ripon (listed, rtd 104): eff at 6/7f: acts on firm, hvy & fibresand: has run well fresh. *shd* **70**
728 **RETURN OF AMIN 11** [1] 6-9-9 (88) Martin Dwyer 12/1: 500-00: Held up stands side, no impress: 11th. *1½* **68**
728 **PRESENT CHANCE 11** [12] 6-8-3 (68) L Newton 20/1: 34-000: Prom far side 4f: 12th: see 674 (AW). *¾* **47**
716 **CRYHAVOC 12** [5] 6-9-7 (86) O Pears 11/1: 650-60: Rear stands side, no threat: 13th: see 716. *1½* **62**
746 **ROGUE SPIRIT 9** [6] 4-8-8 (73)(BL) J Fortune 14/1: 305-00: In tch stands side 4f: 14th: blnks. *3* **43**
716 **Card Games 12** [7] 3-8-7 (84) G Parkin 33/1:
4298} **Bollin Rita 99** [9] 4-8-7 (72) J Carroll 20/1:
702 **Riberac 13** [2] 4-8-12 (77) J Fanning 25/1:
2166} **Sir Jack 99** [13] 4-9-1 (80) Clare Roche (7) 33/1:
733 **Rock Falcon 11** [8] 7-9-13 (92)(bl) R Cochrane 16/1:
19 ran Time 1m 15.2 (5.2) (R A Popely) A Berry Cockerham, Lancs

825

4.25 JO BATE IS 50 HCAP 3YO+ 0-70 (E) 1m4f60y Soft 90 -12 Slow [69]
£2814 £866 £433 £216 4 yo rec 1 lb

699 **CASHMERE LADY 13** [7] J L Eyre 8-8-13 (54) D Holland 12/1: 065-01: 8 b m Hubbly Bubbly - Choir (High Top) Settled towards rear, pushed along before halfway, prog fnl 4f & rdn to lead ins last, styd on for press to lead ins last: padd pick, op 8/1: unplcd over jumps this winter (rtd 84h): '99 Haydock scorer (amat h'cap, rtd 62): '98 wnr at Southwell & Thirsk (rtd 92a & 76): eff at 1m/12f on fast, hvy & fibresand: well h'capped. **61**
779 **PRINCE NICHOLAS 7** [2] K W Hogg 5-9-2 (57) J Bramhill 5/2 FAV: 11-022: 5 ch g Midyan - Its My Turn (Palm Track) Held up in tch, prog to lead over 2f out, drvn/hdd ins last & no extra: hvly bckd, swtg: see 779. *1½* **61**
4459} **OTAHUNA 99** [6] M D Hammond 4-9-4 (60) T Quinn 10/1: 1600-3: 4 b g Selkirk - Stara (Star Appeal) Mid-div, chsd ldrs fnl 3f, kept on well under hands & heels riding, not pace to chall: op 8/1: jumps fit (no form): '99 scorer at Nottingham (class stks, rtd 65, R Hollinshead): rnr-up in '99 (rtd 81): eff at 10f, stays 12f well, could get further: acts on fast & soft, any trk: encouraging Flat reapp, not knocked about, can find similar. *3* **60**
633 **CHALCEDONY 32** [4] T D Barron 4-9-2 (58) C Lowther 9/1: -12404: Chsd ldrs, chall 3f out, onepace: tchd 10/1, clr rem: acts on both AWs, firm & soft: see 343 (AW). *2* **55**
791 **GOLDEN ACE 6** [3] 7-7-11 (37)(tbl)(1ow) A Mackay 9/2: 050-45: Mid-div, rdn/chall over 2f out, onepace. *6* **27**

4571} **ARCHIE BABE 99** [12] 4-9-11 (67) A Culhane 9/1: 2531-6: Chsd ldrs, outpcd fnl 3f: ndd this & not given a hard time: '99 h'cap scorer at Pontefract & twice at Redcar (rtd 70): '98 Thirsk wnr (auct mdn, rtd 75): suited by 10/12f on firm & soft, any trk, likes Redcar: tough/genuine last term, leave this bhd in similar events. *6* **48**
53} **MELS BABY 99** [11] 7-9-0 (55) R Cody Boutcher (7) 50/1: 000P/7: Rear, eff 4f out, no impress: lngr priced stablemate of wnr, long abs: missed '99: unplcd '98 (rtd 53a & 47, h'caps): '97 Beverley wnr (h'cap, rtd 73, also rtd 44a): eff at 9/10f, 12f may yet suit: acts on firm, soft & prob fibresand, any trk: best without a visor. *hd* **36**
699 **INDIGO BAY 13** [13] 4-9-7 (63)(vis) Dean McKeown 25/1: -45108: Towards rear, eff 4f out, sn held: prev with P D Evans, now with R Bastiman: see 524 (AW clmr). *6* **36**
4366} **NOWELL HOUSE 99** [5] 4-9-12 (68) G Parkin 13/2: 1211-9: Led, tried to run out after 2f, rcd keenly, hdd over 3f out & fdd: '99 wnr of h'caps at Beverley, Pontefract & Redcar (rtd 66): plcd in '98 (rtd 72, mdn): eff at 10/12f on fast & soft, any trk: has run well fresh: better than this. *2* **38**
4584} **RED ROSES 99** [9] 4-8-5 (47) Kim Tinkler 20/1: 0036-0: Towards rear, eff 4f out, no impress: 10th: plcd in '99 (rtd 48, h'cap, D E Incisa, earlier flattered with L Cumani): mod form '98: eff at 1m/11f on fast & soft. *3* **13**
705 **Eastern Rainbow 13** [10] 4-7-12 (40)(2ow)(3oh) F Norton 25/1 3465} **Manzoni 99** [1] 4-8-12 (54) T Lucas 14/1:
12 ran Time 2m 46.00 (12.5) (Mrs Sybil Howe) J L Eyre Sutton Bank, N Yorks

826

4.55 GRANTLEY MDN 3YO+ (D) 1m rnd Soft 90 +04 Fast
£3588 £1104 £552 £276 3 yo rec 15lb

4419} **MOON EMPEROR 99** [13] H Akbary 3-8-12 J Stack 2/1 FAV: 3545-1: 3 b c Emperor Jones - Sir Hollow (Sir Ivor) Chsd ldrs, switched & rdn/prog to lead over 1f out, styd on strongly, rdn out: well bckd: 6 month abs: gd time: plcd in '99 (rtd 82, debut, auct mdn, subs rtd 100 when 5th in an Italian Gr 1, poss flattered): eff over 1m on fast & soft grnd, sharp/gall trk: runs well fresh: strong, gd bodied colt, open to improvement. **88**
4083} **AUTUMN RAIN 99** [2] E A L Dunlop 3-8-12 J Reid 9/4: 55-2: 3 br c Dynaformer - Edda (Ogygian) Chsd ldrs, led over 2f out, rdn/hdd over 1f out, no extra ins last: lkd fit & well, 6 month abs: nicely bckd: rtd 77 at best in '99 (mdn): apprec step up to 1m: handles firm & soft, sharp/gall trk: clr of rem, win a race. *1¾* **84**
-- **DIANEME** [10] T D Easterby 3-8-7 J Carroll 20/1: 3: 3 b f Primo Dominie - Aunt Jemima (Busted) Towards rear, stdy prog fnl 4f under hands & heels riding, no threat to front pair: op 10/1, pleasing intro: half sister to 2 minor wnrs: 1m+ shld suit in time, prob handles soft: not knocked about & can rate more highly. *7* **68**
-- **SPEED VENTURE** [7] S P C Woods 3-8-12 G Duffield 10/1: 4: Mid-div, rdn & kept on fnl 3f, kind ride: op 8/1, lkd fit & well on debut: Owington gldg: improve plenty for this. *shd* **73+**
759 **HAPPY HOOLIGAN 8** [5] 3-8-12 D Holland 10/1: 2-05: Chsd ldrs, onepace/held fnl 2f: op 8/1: promise sole '99 start (rtd 78, auct mdn): bred to apprec 1m+: acts on gd grnd: h'cap company shld now suit. *¾* **72**
759 **TOUGH TIMES 8** [16] 3-8-12 K Darley 10/1: 56: Chsd ldr, rdn/ch 3f out, sn held: op 8/1: see 759 (7f). *1½* **70**
3374} **MONDURU 99** [8] 3-8-12 Martin Dwyer 20/1: 0-7: Mid-div, hard rdn/no impress fnl 2f: lkd well tho' still sharper for this: 8 month abs: unplcd sole '99 start (rtd 57): shld apprec this longer 1m trip in time. *1½* **68**
-- **TATE VENTURE** [1] 3-8-12 N Callan 10/1: 8: Keen/chsd ldrs, no impress fnl 2f: op 6/1, stablemate of 6th: ndd this: Deploy gldg, full brother to mid-dist/staying h'capper Deploy Venture, further shld suit in time. *2* **65**
3138} **THIEVES WELCOME 99** [14] 3-8-7 J Fanning 20/1: -63-9: Towards rear, mod late gains under hands & heels riding fnl 3f: ndd this, 7 month abs: plcd in '99 (rtd 64, mdn, also rtd 36a): eff at 6f on firm grnd, bred to apprec 1m+: kind ride, will do better in low grade Northern h'caps. *1¾* **58+**
759 **PRECISION 8** [12] 5-9-13 J F Egan 100/1: 0/00: Led, rcd freely & sn clr, hdd over 2f out, fdd: 10th. *5* **56**
4569} **KINGS VIEW 99** [3] 3-8-12 G Carter 12/1: 50-0: Al rear: 11th: op 10/1, stablemate of rnr-up: 5 mth abs. *½* **55**
3076} **It Can Be Done 99** [11] 3-8-12 Dean McKeown 33/1: 685 **Peng 19** [6] 3-8-12 (t) T Williams 33/1:
-- **Brigmour** [9] 4-9-8 Carolyn Bales (7) 100/1: -- **Pinmoor Hill** [4] 4-9-13 O Pears 33/1:
-- **Quigleys Point** [15] 4-9-13 R Lappin 100/1:
16 ran Time 1m 44.4 (6.9) (David Metcalf) H Akbary Newmarket, Suffolk

827

5.25 SAWLEY HCAP 3YO 0-70 (E) 1m2f Soft 90 -15 Slow [77]
£2980 £917 £458 £229

670 **BOSS TWEED 22** [3] Ronald Thompson 3-8-10 (59) R Cochrane 20/1: -11431: 3 b g Persian Bold - Betty Kenwood (Dominion) Mid-div, prog fnl 3f & rdn/led 1f out, styd on strongly to pull clr nr fin: earlier scored at Southwell (sell, G Bravery) & Lingfield (AW h'cap, current connections, rtd 68a): unplcd in '99 (rtd 59a & 57): eff at 1m/10f, stays 11f: acts on both AWs & soft grnd: likes a sharp trk: has run well fresh: gd weight carrier. **67**
4570} **BLUE HAWAII 99** [7] S R Bowring 3-8-5 (54) J F Egan 20/1: 6000-2: 3 ch c Up And At 'Em - Astral Way (Hotfoot) Held up towards rear, rdn/stdy prog fnl 3f, not pace of wnr: 5 month abs, ndd this, prev with B Rothwell, plcd in '99 (rtd 75, mdn): relished step up to 10f, stay further: handles gd & soft, gall/sharp trk: fine reapp. *3½* **56**
4550} **SELTON HILL 99** [4] N A Callaghan 3-8-12 (61) A Beech (5) 12/1: 5644-3: 3 b g Bin Ajwaad - Ivory Gull (Storm Bird) Chsd ldrs, rdn & kept on for press fnl 2f, not pace of wnr: tchd 14/1, 5 month abs: unplcd in '99 (rtd 68, mdn): styd longer 10f trip well: handles fast & soft grnd. *1* **62**
624 **SUAVE PERFORMER 34** [14] S C Williams 3-8-2 (51) R Ffrench 10/1: 0454: Chsd ldrs, rdn/led over 1f out, sn hdd & no extra nr fin: tchd 12/1, h'cap bow: relished longer 10f trip, acts on soft: going the right way. *nk* **51**
3988} **MANSTAR 99** [16] 3-8-11 (60) N Kennedy 25/1: 3450-5: Chsd ldrs, kept on onepace fnl 2f: ndd this, 7 mth abs: plcd in '99 (rtd 70, mdn): eff at 7f, this longer 10f trip shld suit: prob handles gd/soft & soft grnd. *2½* **57**
4229} **DEBS SON 99** [21] 3-8-13 (62) G Duffield 20/1: 454-6: Mid-div, rdn/kept on fnl 3f, not pace to chall: 6 mth abs, h'cap bow: unplcd in '99 (rtd 72, nov auct stks): prob stays 10f, 12f+ shld suit: handles soft grnd. *hd* **59**
4445} **PATACAKE PATACAKE 99** [20] 3-9-5 (68) D Holland 10/1: 644-7: Rear, not clr run 4f out till over 1f out, styd on strongly under hands & heels riding ins last, nrst fin: op 6/1, 6 month abs: h'cap bow: unplcd in '99 (rtd 75): eff at 10f, 12f suit: handles soft & gd/soft: no luck in running here, eye-catching, keep in mind. *hd* **64+**
701 **RHODAMINE 13** [10] 3-9-4 (67) Dean McKeown 20/1: 54-008: Towards rear, mod gains for press fnl 3f. *¾* **62**
636 **PTAH 32** [19] 3-8-3 (52) R Lappin 25/1: 000-09: Rear halfway, switched & stdy late gains for press. *½* **46**
4570} **HIGH CAPACITY 99** [22] 3-7-12 (47) P Fessey 20/1: 0000-0: Mid-div, no impress: 10th: 5 month abs: unplcd in '99 (rtd 62, auct mdn, subs tried blnks): could apprec mid-dists this term for T D Easterby. *1¾* **39**
*419 **WILL IVESON 67** [24] 3-9-1 (64) P Goode (3) 8/1: 5-1210: Mid-div at best: 11th, abs, lngr trip. *1½* **55**
*555 **JUST THE JOB TOO 44** [2] 3-8-6 (55) J Mackay (7) 16/1: 0-6410: Mid-div, btn 2f out: 12th: 6 wk abs. *½* **45**
3677} **SEND IT TO PENNY 99** [12] 3-8-1 (49)(1ow) J Fanning 14/1: 0504-0: Led 2f, fdd fnl 2f: 13th: 7 mth abs. *hd* **40**
4278} **FIFE AND DRUM 99** [18] 3-8-13 (62) J Reid 14/1: 000-0: Mid-div, fdd fnl 3f under a quiet ride: 14th: op 12/1, 6 month abs/h'cap bow: bred to apprec mid-dists, shld leave this bhd in time. *5* **47**
701 **ENTITY 13** [13] 3-9-7 (70) C Lowther 10/1: 440-00: Led after 2f till over 1f out, fdd: 15th: op 12/1. *½* **54**
744 **BORDER RUN 9** [9] 3-9-5 (68) W R Swinburn 4/1 FAV: 056-50: Mid-div, rdn 3f out, no prog: 16th: bckd. *½* **51**
4601} **COSMIC BUZZ 99** [5] 3-9-5 (68) J Fortune 14/1: 5500-0: Chsd ldrs halfway, fdd fnl 3f: 17th: 5 mth abs. *½* **50**
4570} **Loblite Leader 99** [11] 3-8-11 (60) J Weaver 25/1: 4514} **Paddy Mul 99** [17] 3-7-10 (45)(t)(3oh) J Bramhill 33/1:

RIPON   WEDNESDAY APRIL 5TH   Righthand, Sharpish Track

4274} **Castanea Sativa 99** [23] 3-8-13 (62) K Darley 10/1:
4498} **Best Ever 99** [1] 3-8-10 (59) T Lucas 25/1:
4575} **Loden Blue 99** [6] 3-7-10 (45)(1oh) A Polli (3) 50/1:
25 ran   Time 2m 13.8 (10.5)   (B Bruce)

4498} **Sorrento King 99** [25] 3-8-4 (53) G Parkin 20/1:
3491} **Mountrath Rock 99** [15] 3-8-11 (60) Kim Tinkler 20/1:
4570} **Proper Gent 99** [8] 3-7-10 (45)(5oh) G Bardwell 33/1:
Ronald Thompson Stainforth, S Yorks

LEICESTER   THURSDAY APRIL 6TH   Righthand, Stiff, Galloping Track

Official Going   GOOD TO SOFT. Stalls: Stands Side.

828
2.15 KNIGHTON MED AUCT MDN 2YO (F)   5f   Good/Soft 76   -18 Slow
£2464   £704   £352 Raced centre - stands side

700   **MILLYS LASS** 14 [3] M R Channon 2-8-9 T Quinn 5/4 FAV: 31: 2 b f Mind Games - Millie's Lady (Common   76
Grounds): Chsd ldrs, rdn/led over 1f out, in command/pushed clr inside last: well bckd: confirmed promise of
debut: eff at 5f, 6f should suit: likes a stiff/gall trk: going the right way.
743   **STORMING FOLEY** 10 [8] W G M Turner 2-9-0 A Daly 13/2: 42: 2 ch c Makbul - Cute Dancer   3½   70
(Remainder Man) Led to halfway, ch over 1f out, kept on well: op 5/1: eff at 5f on gd/soft: win a race.
--   **GALY BAY** [2] D Morris 2-8-9 R Cochrane 9/2: 3: 2 b f Bin Ajwaad - Sylhall (Sharpo):   hd   64
Dwelt/rdn early, kept on final 2f for press, not pace to chall: op 8/1: Feb 1st foal, dam unrcd tho' halfway sister
to 6 wnrs: sure to apprec 6f in time, handles gd/soft grnd: encouraging.
724   **BOHEMIAN SPIRIT** 12 [7] P G Murphy 2-9-0 S Drowne 20/1: 54: Chsd ldrs, onepace final 2f: see 724.   ¾   67
--   **IZZET MUZZY** [6] 2-9-0 N Carlisle 20/1: 5: Prom, rdn/wknd final 2f: Piccolo colt, Mar foal, cost   1¾   63
7,500 gns: dam a juv wnr abroad: half-brother to a 3yo 1m wnr abroad: with C N Kellett.
--   **RUNNING FOR ME** [5] 2-8-9 G Gibbons (7) 33/1: 6: Handy, led halfway, hdd/fdd over 1f out: Eagle   4   48
Eyed filly, Feb foal, cost 4,000 gns: dam a 5f wnr: dam a 1m wnr abroad: with R Hollinshead.
--   **PASO DOBLE** [1] 2-9-0 P Robinson 5/1: In tch till halfway: Dancing Spree colt, Jan foal, cost   ¾   51
11,000 gns: dam unrcd: sire a high class sprinter: with B Millman.
730   **CENTURY STAR** 12 [4] 2-9-0 J Tate 50/1: -08: Dwelt, rdn/sn handy, btn 2f out: mod form.   4   41
8 ran   Time 1m 03.00 (4.7)   (Ken Lock Racing Ltd)   M R Channon West Isley, Berks.

829
2.45 LODDINGTON COND STKS 3YO (C)   6f   Good/Soft 76   +10 Fast
£6345   £2406   £1203   £547 Raced towards centre

2510} **SIR NICHOLAS 99** [9] J Noseda 3-9-0 L Dettori 8/11 FAV: 123-1: 3 b c Cadeaux Genereux - Final Shot   110
(Dalsaan) Trckd ldr halfway, rdn to lead inside last, styd on well, rdn out, shade cosy: fast time: hvly bckd:
'99 debut wnr at Doncaster (mdn), subs rnr-up at Royal Ascot (Gr 3, rtd 112): eff over a stiff/gall 6f: acts on
firm & gd/soft: runs well fresh on a gall trk: smart sprinter, prob best coming late, can win again.
4286} **WATCHING 99** [6] R Hannon 3-9-0 R Hughes 7/2: 5423-2: 3 ch c Indian Ridge - Sweeping (Indian King):nk   107
Led, rdn over 1f out & hdd inside last, kept on well: rest well covered: 6 mth abs: '99 Chester wnr (mdn), subs
plcd in Gr company (rtd 100): eff at 5/6f on firm & soft, any trk: tough/consistent & very useful colt.
3437} **DAY JOURNEY 99** [8] E A L Dunlop 3-9-6 J Reid 15/2: 0114-3: 3 b c Dayjur - Dayflower (Majestic Light): 3½   104
Chsd ldrs, rdn 2f out, kept on onepace: op 6/1, 8 mth abs: '99 wnr at Newmarket (novs stks) & Haydock (conds
stks, rtd 100): eff over a stiff/gall 6f: acts on firm & gd grnd, gall trk: useful, sharper for this.
4542} **PAX 99** [1] J W Payne 3-9-0 R Cochrane 11/1: 1-4: Twds rear, kept on under hands & heels riding fnl   4   88+
2f, no threat: op 8/1, 5 mth abs: '99 sole start wnr at Newmarket (rtd 96, mdn): eff at 6f, looks sure to relish
7f + (dam a 10f wnr): acts on gd/soft grnd: has run well fresh: useful colt, one to note when tackling further.
731   **KIND EMPEROR** 12 [10] 3-8-10 R Fitzpatrick (3) 33/1: 3-4425: Chsd ldr, btn 2f out: see 34 (mdn, AW).   3½   75
--   **SORBETT** [7] 3-9-2 G Sparkes (7) 25/1: 1-6: Dwelt, nvr on terms: 5 mth abs: '99 sole start wnr in   1   81
Milan (7.5f, soft): a return to 7f + shld suit.
4235} **IYAVAYA 99** [4] 3-8-13 T Quinn 25/1: 4055-7: Held up, btn 2f out: 6 mth abs: '99 wnr at   1¾   72
Warwick (fill mdn) & Chepstow (fill stks, rtd 88): eff at 5f on fast & soft: has run well fresh.
3885} **HAIKAL 99** [3] 3-8-10 R Hills 33/1: 0-8: Al outpcd rear: 7 mth abs.   1¼   66
--   **MOONLIGHT SONG** [2] 3-8-5 M Roberts 25/1: 140-9: Bhd halfway: 5 mth abs.   9   45
9 ran   Time 1m 13.8 (4.0)   (Lucayan Stud)   J Noseda Newmarket, Suffolk.

830
3.20 BURTON OVERY SELLER 3YO (G)   6f   Good/Soft 76   -06 Slow
£1991   £569   £284 Raced stands side

--   **PEGGYS ROSE** [3] P D Evans 3-8-9 J F Egan 10/1: 1: 3 b f Shalford - Afrique Noir (Gallic League):   68
Chsd ldrs, rdn/led over 1f out & rdn out: bght in for 8,000 gns: may stay further: acts on a stiff/gall trk & runs well fresh.
736   **MYTTONS AGAIN** 12 [6] A Bailey 3-9-5 (bl) J Weaver 11/4 FAV: 0-4002: 3 b g Rambo Dancer - Sigh   4   68
(Highland Melody): Prom, rdn/chsd wnr inside last, al held: blnks reapplied: eff at 6/7f, stays 1m: see 158.
783   **PRINCESS VICTORIA** 8 [8] N A Callaghan 3-9-0 J Mackay (7) 3/1: 026-33: 3 b f Deploy - Scierpan   2   58
(Sharpen Up): CI-up, led halfway till over 1f out, no extra: op 5/1, 9 mth abs: eff at 6/7f, handles gd, gd/soft & eqtrk: see 783, 165.
741   **CUIGIU** 10 [7] D Carroll 3-9-0 J P Spencer 5/1: 40-054: Led 2f, btn 1f out: op 7/2, blnks omitted.   2½   51
717   **CRYFIELD** 13 [4] 3-9-0 Pat Eddery 14/1: 05: Held up, rdn/no room 2f out, sn held: op 12/1: mod form.   ¾   49
659   **UNFORTUNATE** 26 [5] 3-9-0 V Halliday 10/1: -65306: Dwelt, rdn halfway, sn held: op 12/1: see 181.   ¾   47
4406} **JENSENS TALE 99** [1] 3-9-0 D Sweeney 11/1: 6500-7: Sn rdn bhd ldrs, held final 2f: broke blood   3½   38
vessel (op 25/1): 6 mth abs: rnr-up in '99 (rtd 66, sell): eff at 6f/7f, handles firm & gd/soft: best without a vis.
785   **NORTHERN TRIO** 8 [2] 3-9-0 J Fanning 9/1: 00-008: In tch 3f: mod from.   hd   37
--   **SUNRISE GIRL** [9] 3-8-9 N Pollard 16/1: 9: Dwelt, sn struggling: op 14/1, debut: with A Hobbs.   16   0
9 ran   Time 1m 14.7 (4.9)   (Global Racing Club)   P D Evans Pandy, Gwent.

831
3.55 A GADSBY FILLIES HCAP 4YO+ 0-80 (D)   1m str   Good/Soft 76   -20 Slow   [80]
£3945   £1214   £607   £303 Raced centre - stands side

715   **SCENE 13** [7] J A Glover 5-9-10 (76) T G McLaughlin 9/4 FAV: 041-01: 5 b m Scenic - Avebury Ring   80
(Auction Ring): Held up in tch, rdn to lead 2f out, forged clr/drifted left inside last, eased nr fin: val for 4L +:
op 7/4: '99 h'cap wnr at Ascot, Epsom & Nottingham (rtd 80): '98 Thirsk & Haydock wnr (fillies h'caps, rtd 77):

267

eff at 1m/10f on firm, suited by gd & soft: likes a gall trk: best without a visor: gd weight carrier: tough.
732 **NOUF 12** [1] K Mahdi 4-10-0 (80) L Dettori 5/1: 04-002: 4 b f Efisio - Miss Witch (High Line): *2* **79**
Led 3f, remnd handy, kept on onepace for press inside last: op 6/1: '99 Doncaster wnr (debut, mdn, rtd 94): eff at 7f/1m, tried 12f: handles gd/soft & soft grnd, stiff/gall trk: has run well fresh: good comeback.
4441} **NATALIE JAY 99** [6] M R Channon 4-8-13 (65) M Roberts 5/2: 0525-3: 4 b f Ballacashtal - Falls Of Lora *2½* **59**
(Scottish Rifle): Handy, led over 4f out, hdd 2f out & no extra: nicely bckd: 6 mth abs: '99 Salisbury wnr (h'cap, rtd 69) & rnr-up on sand (rtd 68a, h'cap): plcd in '98 (rtd 77): eff at 1m/sharp 10f on gd, hvy & equitrack, any trk.
699 **BUNTY 14** [4] Mrs S Lamyman 4-7-10 (48) J Mackay (7) 7/1: -40604: Keen/prom 6f: see 297 (AW). *5* **32**
811 **ISLE OF SODOR 5** [3] 4-8-3 (55) J Bramhill 11/1: 00-005: Dwelt/held up, rdn/btn 2f out & eased: qck *23* **6**
reapp: unplcd in '99 (rtd 55 & 32a): '98 Leicester wnr (nursery, rtd 66): eff at 6f, stays 7f: acts on fast & gd/soft.
4439} **TALARIA 99** [2] 4-9-6 (72) G Faulkner (3) 7/1: 4000-6: Keen/cl-up, btn 3f out: 6 mth abs, prev with *4* **15**
G Wragg, '99 Newmarket wnr (mdn, rtd 86): rtd 87 in '98 (stks): eff at 6f on firm, handles gd/soft: likes a stiff/gall trk: wng form in a t-strap, not worn today for S C Williams.
6 ran Time 1m 42.10 (7.7) (Paul J Dixon) J A Glover Carburton, Notts.

832

4.30 LANGHAM MDN 3-4YO (D) 1m3f183y Good/Soft 76 -37 Slow
£3926 £1208 £504 £302 3 yo rec 21lb4 yo rec 1 lb

701 **POMPEII 14** [1] P F I Cole 3-8-7(1ow) J Fortune 4/5 FAV: 620-21: 3 b c Salse - Before Dawn (Raise A Cup): **80**
Made all, readily pulled clr final 2f, in command when eased well inside last: value for 10L+: hvly bckd: plcd in '99 (rtd 79, earlier with P W Chapple Hyam): eff at 10f, styd lngr 12f trip well, could get further: acts on fast & soft grnd & likes a stiff/gall trk: plenty in hand here.
4584} **SELIANA 99** [4] G Wragg 4-9-7 M Roberts 9/2: 0/3-2: 4 b f Unfuwain - Anafi (Slip Anchor): *4* **63**
Chsd wnr, rdn/ch 2f out, sn held: 5 mth abs: plcd in '99 (rtd 74, mdn, sole start): unplcd sole '98 start: eff at 12f on soft grnd, prob handles gd/soft: lightly rcd filly, now qual for h'caps.
4597} **DURLSTON BAY 99** [5] R Ingram 3-8-6 A Daly 100/1: 0-3: 3 b c Welsh Captain - Nelliellamay (Super *½* **67**
Splash): Sn handy, rdn/outpcd 4f out, kept on for press inside last: 5 mth abs: no form sole start '99 (sell).
643 **TUFTY HOPPER 31** [7] P Howling 3-8-6 Pat Eddery 33/1: 0-644: Chsd ldrs, outpcd 4f out, kept on *2½* **63**
inside last under hands & heels riding: h'cap company & 12f+ should now suit: see 643.
4076} **MURJAN 99** [8] 3-8-6 G Carter 7/1: 434-5: Keen/prom, btn 2f out: op 9/2: 6 mth abs: plcd in '99 *1¾* **61**
for M Johnston (rtd 80, auct mdn): eff arnd 1m/9f on firm & gd & a stiff/gall trk.
3508} **NAILER 99** [6] 4-9-12 W Ryan 100/1: 00-6: Dwelt/held up, effort 4f out, sn held: 7 mth abs: mod form. *4* **55**
4066} **SINGLE CURRENCY 99** [9] 4-9-12 D Griffiths 9/1: 3-7: Al bhd: op 6/1, 6 mth abs: lngr priced *28* **25**
stablemate of wnr: plcd sole '99 start (mdn, rtd 79): eff at 10.5f, could get further: handles soft grnd.
4158} **HOWABOYS QUEST 99** [2] 3-8-8(2ow) J P Spencer 50/1: 440-8: Held up, nvr a factor: 6 mth abs. *1* **26**
-- **SIBELIUS** [3] 3-8-6 L Dettori 6/1: 9: Held up, struggling 3f out: injured in stalls. *dist* **0**
9 ran Time 2m 41.8 (13.5) (Highclere Thor'bred Racing Ltd) P F I Cole Whatcombe, Oxon.

833

5.00 DE MONTFORT MDN 3YO+ (D) 1m2f Going 76 -42 Slow
£4062 £1250 £625 £312 3 yo rec 19lb

-- **GARGALHADA FINAL** [6] J Noseda 3-8-7 L Dettori 4/7 FAV: 1: 3 b c Sabrehill - Secret Waters (Pharly) **94+**
Handy, trkd wnr 4f out, cruised up to lead over 1f out, al holding rivals, easily: value for 7L+: hvly bckd at on debut: 23,000 gns purchase, dam a middle dist styr: eff at 10f, 12f+ should suit: acts on gd/soft grnd & a stiff/gall trk: runs well fresh: well regarded, looks useful & one to follow.
4528} **ST EXPEDIT 99** [8] G Wragg 3-8-7 D Holland 4/1: 3-2: 3 b c Sadler's Wells - Miss Rinjani (Shirley *1½* **84**
Heights): Led after 2f till over 1f out, sn held by wnr: flattered by margin of defeat: op 7/2: plcd in '99 (rtd 91, mdn): styd lngr 10f trip well, further could suit: acts on gd/soft grnd: caught a tartar here, can find similar.
4153} **BAY VIEW 99** [7] K Mahdi 5-9-7 J Reid 20/1: 0/2-3: 5 b m Slip Anchor - Carmita (Caerleon): *3½* **74$**
Held up, rdn/outpcd 4f out, kept on well final 1f, no threat: op 16/1: 6 mth abs: rnr-up sole '99 start (mdn, rtd 74): eff at 10f, looks sure to relish 12f+: handles gd/soft & soft: shld relish mid-dist/staying h'caps.
4614} **FAYRWAY RHYTHM 99** [15] M A Jarvis 3-8-7 P Robinson 8/1: 2244-4: Chsd ldrs, rdn/onepace final 2f: *1¾* **77**
op 6/1: 5 mth abs: rnr-up twice in '99 (rtd 85, mdn): eff at 7f/1m: handles gd & hvy grnd.
-- **BID FOR FAME** [14] 3-8-7 A Clark 12/1: 5: Held up, prog 4f out, sn onepace: op 8/1: debut: *1½* **75**
130,000 gns purchase, Quest For Fame colt, mid-dist bred: with T G Mills.
708 **COWBOYS AND ANGELS 14** [2] 3-8-7 A Daly 66/1: 20-336: Led 1f, cl-up till fdd final 2f: lngr 10f trip. *nk* **74$**
759 **PENNYS PRIDE 9** [9] 5-9-7 A Culhane 20/1: 37: Held up, efft 5f out, btn final 2f: op 14/1: lngr 10f trip. *½* **68**
-- **ICE CRYSTAL** [12] 3-8-7 C Rutter 20/1: 8: Held up, nvr able to chall: op 12/1, debut: Slip Anchor *3* **69**
colt, mid-dist bred, should improve in time for H Candy.
784 **RYKA 8** [1] 5-9-12 J Tate 100/1: 09: Dwelt/al rear: lngr 10f trip, no form. *1½* **67$**
4124} **PRINCE SLAYER 99** [10] 4-9-12 J Stack 12/1: 2352-0: Prom 1m: 10th: op 8/1: 6 mth abs. *shd* **67**
694 **CHANCY DEAL 17** [11] 3-8-2 J Fanning 100/1: 00: Led early, btn 3f out: 15th: no form. **0**
704 **Strategic Dancer 14** [4] 3-8-7 J Fortune 25/1: 720 **Javelin 12** [3] 4-9-12 R Fitzpatrick (3) 66/1:
3322} **Night Omen 99** [5] 3-8-7 G Faulkner (2) 66/1: 4014} **Smarts Megan 99** [13] 4-9-7 A Nicholls (3) 100/1:
15 ran Time 2m 14.3 (11.8) (Goncalo Borges Torrealba) J Noseda Newmarket, Suffolk.

834

5.30 KIBWORTH HCAP 3YO+ 0-85 (D) 7f Good/Soft 76 -03 Slow [84]
£4160 £1280 £540 £320 3 yo rec 14lb

4481} **SECOND WIND 99** [3] C A Dwyer 5-9-0 (70) D Holland 11/1: 6304-1: 5 ch g Kris - Rimosa's Pet (Petingo) **81**
Made all, rdn/clr over 1f out & styd on strongly inside last: op 8/1: 6 mth abs: '99 wnr at Brighton (clmr, Miss G Kelleway) & Epsom (current connections, h'cap, rtd 74): rnr-up for P Cole in '98 (rtd 85): eff at 5/6f, best forcing pace at 7f, tried 1m: acts on firm & soft, any trk: runs well fresh: eff with/without a t-strap.
725 **TEMERAIRE 12** [11] D J S Cosgrove 5-9-12 (82) J F Egan 11/1: 510-02: 5 b h Dayjur - Key Dancer *4* **83**
(Nijinsky): Chsd wnr final 2f, kept on but al held: op 8/1: prob handles gd/soft, prefers firm, gd & equitrack.
499 **PLEADING 55** [8] M A Buckley 7-8-11 (67) Martin Dwyer 8/1: 00-233: 7 b g Never So Bold - Ask Mama *3½* **61**
(Mummy's Pet): Dwelt, held up towards rear, kept on final 2f, no threat: op 10/1, 8 wk abs: in good form.
+725 **PREMIER BARON 12** [1] P S McEntee 5-9-13 (83) G Carter 5/2 FAV: 220-14: Held up, effort/no room *½* **76**
2f out, kept on onepace inside last, no threat: well bckd: shade unlucky in running, but no threat to wnr.
736 **KEBABS 12** [7] 3-8-12 (82) J P Spencer 11/1: 160-55: Chsd ldrs 5f: see 736. *½* **74**
531 **ANNADAWI 49** [9] 5-7-10 (52)(20oh) K Dalgleish (7) 66/1: 440546: Mid-div at best: abs, vis omitted. *1½* **41$**
4562} **BINTANG TIMOR 99** [4] 6-9-0 (70) L Newton 14/1: 0013-7: Dwelt, rdn halfway, no impress: op 12/1, *1¾* **56**
5 mth abs: '99 scorer at Newmarket (appr h'cap) & Yarmouth (h'cap, rtd 73 at best): '98 Leicester wnr (h'cap,

LEICESTER THURSDAY APRIL 6TH Righthand, Stiff, Galloping Track

rtd 72): eff at 6f, suited by a stiff/gall 7f on firm & soft grnd: best held up for a late run.
685 **STROMSHOLM 20** [5] 4-9-2 (72) R Cochrane 9/1: 02-48: Keen/chsd ldrs, fdd final 2f: h'cap bow. *1* **56**
+780 **SUSANS PRIDE 8** [6] 4-9-11 (81)(6ex) Pat Eddery 4/1: 11-419: Chsd ldrs 5f: op 7/2: btr 780. *3* **59**
644 **MUTABARI 31** [2] 6-7-10 (52)(vis)(8oh) D Glennon (6) 40/1: 530400: Prom 5f: 10th: recent jmps rnr. *1¾* **27**
383 **GIFT OF GOLD 75** [10] 5-9-11 (81) A Mackay 11/1: 40-450: Chsd ldrs 5f: 11th: abs: see 383, 216 (AW). *5* **46**
4510} **SMART PREDATOR 99** [12] 4-9-6 (76) J Fortune 10/1: 1006-0: Trkd ldrs, btn/eased final 1f: 12th: *3½* **34**
op 6/1, 5 mth abs: '99 York wnr (mdn, rtd 84): eff at 7f/1m on firm & soft grnd, likes a gall or stiff/undul trk.
12 ran Time 1m 27.5 (5.5) (John Purcell) C A Dwyer Newmarket, Suffolk.

LINGFIELD FRIDAY APRIL 7TH Lefthand, Sharp, Undulating Track

Official Going GOOD/SOFT (GOOD places), AW - STANDARD. Stalls: Turf Crse - Stands Side, AW - Inside.

835 1.50 GOLF APPR HCAP 3YO+ 0-70 (E) 1m5f aw Standard Inapplicable [65]
£2842 £812 £406 3 yo rec 22lb4 yo rec 2 lb

458 **ANOTHER MONK 62** [4] R Ingram 9-8-4 (41) L Newman (3) 10/1: 0-4141: 9 b g Supreme Leader - Royal **48a**
Demon (Tarboosh) Handy & led halfway, styd on well to assert ins last, pushed out cl-home: op 8/1: jumps fit (mod form): earlier scored here at Lingfield (sell): plcd form in '99 (rtd 52 & 44, h'caps, B Johnson): eff at 12f/2m on both AWs, loves Lingfield: runs well fresh: eff with/without a visor: eff up with/forcing the pace.
632 **FUSUL 34** [11] G L Moore 4-9-8 (61) I Mongan (6) 8/1: -11302: 4 ch c Miswaki - Silent Turn (Silent *1½* **65a**
Cal) Chsd leading pair & clr of rem halfway, chsd wnr over 3f out, kept on but held fnl 1f: clr of rem, op 12/1: eff at 10/13f: back to form here & should win more races on sand: see 441 (12f).
737 **QUAKERESS 11** [2] R Brotherton 5-7-10 (33)(7oh) J Mackay (7) 20/1: 113453: 5 b m Brief Truce - Deer *7* **27a**
Emily (Alzao) Rear, eff 5f out, kept on fnl 3f, no impress on front pair: clr rem: see 577, 494 (fibresand).
775 **KI CHI SAGA 9** [6] P Burgoyne 8-7-10 (33)(bl)(8oh) G Baker (7) 12/1: -60044: Rear, mod prog: op 8/1. *5* **20a**
*723 **EVEZIO RUFO 13** [7] 8-9-9 (60)(vis) C Cogan (6) 5/1: 145115: Bhd halfway, mod late prog: op 3/1. *¾* **46a**
4374} **KING FLYER 99** [13] 4-9-2 (55)(t) A Beech (3) 4/1 FAV: 2320-6: Nvr on terms with ldrs: op 5/1, 6 *1¾* **39a**
mth abs: '99 Newmarket scorer (clmr, rtd 70 & 59a): rtd 78 for B Hanbury in '98: eff at 10/14f on equitrack, firm & gd grnd: handles any trk, likes a stiff/gall one: eff with/without a t-strap.
650 **APPYABO 30** [10] 5-7-10 (33)(3oh) G Oliver (1) 16/1: 213657: Mid-div, nvr any impress: op 12/1. *5* **10a**
4256} **ESTABLISHED 99** [5] 3-7-10 (55)(6oh) D Glennon (7) 33/1: 0000-8: Struggling halfway: 6 month abs: *1½* **30a**
unplcd in '99 (rtd 49, h'cap, earlier with H Candy): longer 13f trip/AW bow today.
723 **LOST SPIRIT 13** [9] 4-8-7 (46) Joanna Badger (5) 20/1: 250609: Led till 6f out, sn wknd: btr 290 (12f). *1¾* **19a**
723 **SUMMER BOUNTY 13** [3] 4-8-11 (50) A Nicholls 11/2: 060020: Twds rear, rdn/strugg halfway: 10th. *½* **22a**
314 **WAR BABY 86** [8] 4-7-11 (36) D Kinsella (7) 33/1: 500-00: Struggling after 4f: 11th: 3 month abs. *1* **7a**
*682 **CEDAR FLAG 21** [12] 6-8-10 (47) S Carson 5/1: 324310: Chsd ldrs halfway, btn 2f out: op 3/1. 12th. *1* **17a**
4525} **ZINCALO 99** [1] 4-9-12 (65) A Polli (3) 7/1: 4600-0: Chsd ldrs halfway, btn 5f out: 13th, 5 mth abs, top- *7* **25a**
weight: rnr-up twice in '99 (rtd 85, mdn, flattered), subs disapp in a visor: eff arnd 14f, handles fast & gd/soft.
13 ran Time 2m 44.32 (2.02) (D G Wheatley) R Ingram Epsom, Surrey.

836 2.20 BIDBOROUGH CLAIMER 2YO (F) 5f Good/Soft 87 -29 Slow
£2226 £636 £318

*712 **NINE TO FIVE 14** [1] W G M Turner 2-8-5 A Daly 4/9 FAV: 11: 2 b f Imp Society - Queen And Country **73**
(Town And Country) Broke well & sn switched to lead stands rail, in command fnl 1f, pushed out: well bckd: debut Doncaster wnr (sell, made all): eff forcing pace at 5f on gd & gd/soft: handles a sharp/gall trk: enjoys sellers.
*722 **MOLLY IRWIN 13** [4] J S Moore 2-8-5 L Newman(5) 6/1: 312: 2 b f General Monash - Bunny Run *2* **64**
(Dowsing) Chsd wnr, rdn 2f out, kept tho' al held: acts on fibresand, gd & gd/soft: bhd this wnr in 712.
-- **DRIPPING IN GOLD** [3] J J Bridger 2-8-5 A Nicholls (3) 10/1: 3: 2 ch f Alhijaz - Fanny's Choice *2* **59**
(Fairy King) Chsd ldrs, rdn halfway, nvr pace to chall: op 8/1: Apr foal, 17,000gns 2yo: dam a 6f 2yo wnr.
722 **DECEIVES THE EYE 13** [5] J G Given 2-8-4 (BL) Dean McKeown 8/1: 34: Dwelt, rdn/chsd ldrs halfway, *3½* **50**
sn held: tried blnks, also bhd today's rnr-up in 722 (AW).
-- **CEDAR BILL** [2] 2-9-4 R Miles (7) 10/1: 5: Dwelt & sn outpcd: So Factual colt, Feb foal, 9,500gns *5* **54**
2yo: dam related to a winner abroad, sire a top-class sprinter: with R J O'Sullivan.
5 ran Time 1m 02.61 (5.81) (Paul Thorman) W G M Turner Corton Denham, Somerset.

837 2.55 BARHAM MED AUCT MDN 3YO (F) 6f Good/Soft 87 +05 Fast
£2492 £712 £356 Raced stands side, high no's favoured

-- **LOCHARATI** [5] J M P Eustace 3-9-0 J Tate 14/1: 1: 3 ch c Emarati - Lochspring (Precocious) **89**
Led/dsptd lead till went on over 1f out, styd on strongly ins last, rdn out: best time of day: op 10/1, debut: looks bred for speed, dam a half-sister to top-class sprinter Lochsong: eff over sharp 6f on gd/soft grnd: runs well fresh: fine run from an unfav low draw: possesses plent of speed, open to further improvement & will win again.
3804} **DIVERS PEARL 99** [10] J R Fanshawe 3-8-9 R Cochrane 11/4 FAV: 63-2: 3 b f Prince Sabo - Seek The *1¾* **78**
Pearl (Rainbow Quest) Chsd ldrs halfway, rdn/chsd wnr over 1f out, kept on tho' al held: well bckd, tchd 3/1: 7 month abs: plcd in '99 (auct mdn, rtd 87): eff at 6f, 7f+ cld suit: handles firm & gd/soft grnd.
206 **TATTENHAM STAR 99** [12] M J Haynes 3-9-0 S Drowne 33/1: 6350-3: 3 b c Mistertopogigo - Candane *3* **76$**
(Danehill) Held up, no room when eff over 2f out till dist, styd on well under hands-&-heels riding ins last, nrst fin: 4 month abs: handles equitrack, gd & gd/soft grnd: offic rtd 68, poss unlucky today & shld win h'caps.
731 **SUMTHINELSE 13** [14] N P Littmoden 3-9-0 C Cogan (5) 14/1: 340-54: Prom, kept on onepace fnl 1f: *nk* **75**
op 8/1: handles fast & gd/soft grnd: see 731.
-- **CAREW CASTLE** [2] 3-9-0 S Whitworth 33/1: 5: Dwelt, switched to stands rail after start, chsd ldrs *1¾* **71**
halfway, onepcd dist: debut: 15,000gns purchase: not disgraced from poor low draw: improve for D Arbuthnot.
729 **BUDELLI 13** [8] 3-9-0 T Quinn 7/1: 5-36: Held up, kept on fnl 2f, no threat to ldrs: op 10/1: not given *½* **69**
a hard time, 7f+ & h'cap company shld now suit: see 729.
4260} **DANCEMMA 99** [15] 3-8-9 Dane O'Neill 9/1: 2602-7: Cl-up, fdd fnl 2f: op 4/1, 6 month abs: rnr-up *¾* **62**
twice in '99 (rtd 79, mdn): eff at 5/6f on gd & soft grnd: return to h'caps shld suit.
334 **VIKING PRINCE 83** [13] 3-9-0 R Mullen 33/1: 000-08: Held up, rdn/btn 2f out: 12 wk abs: see 334 (AW). *hd* **66$**
789 **GRUINART 8** [6] 3-9-0 C Rutter 33/1: 0-09: Mid-div, rdn 2f out, no impress: dropped in trip. *nk* **65**
3442} **PROTECTOR 99** [18] 3-9-0 M Hills 16/1: 50-0: Rear, rdn/switched 2f out, mod gains: 10th: op 10/1, *nk* **64**

LINGFIELD FRIDAY APRIL 7TH Lefthand, Sharp, Undulating Track

8 month abs: rtd 77 on first of 2 '99 starts (mdn): step up to 7f+ & h'cap company shld now suit.
4600} **COMPTON BANKER 99** [16] 3-9-0 Pat Eddery 5/1: 605-0: Rear halfway, rdn/no impress: 11th: op 1½ 60
3/1: 5 month abs: unplcd in '99 (rtd 84, Gr 2).
4445} **HILLTOP WARNING 99** [17] 3-9-0 J Reid 4/1: 223-0: Trkd ldrs, hung left/btn 2f out: 15th: op 7/2, nk 0
6 month abs: plcd all 3 '99 starts (rtd 88, mdn): eff at 6f on firm & soft grnd.
--   **DESERT NORTH** [3] 3-9-0 S Sanders 7/1: 0: Prom 4f centre: 16th, bckd from 33/1 on debut: poor draw. ¾ 0
--   Mobo Baco [1] 3-9-0 J Weaver 33/1:   2447} Distant Flame 99 [9] 3-8-9 D Holland 16/1:
--   Hand Chime [7] 3-9-0 K W Marks 33/1:   729 Pieta 13 [11] 3-8-9 G Carter 33/1:
2889} Walnut Wonder 99 [4] 3-8-9 A Daly 50/1:
18 ran   Time 1m 13.73 (4.93)   (J C Smith)   J M P Eustace Newmarket.

838 3.30 LEISURE CLASS STKS 3YO+ 0-70 (E)   7f str Good/Soft 87 +02 Fast
£3022 £930 £465 £232   3 yo rec 14lb Raced stands side, high no's favoured

4439} **I CRIED FOR YOU 99** [9] J G Given 5-9-7 Dean McKeown 9/1: 0000-1: 5 b g Statoblest - Fall Of The 74
Hammer (Auction Ring) In tch, smooth prog to lead dist, styd on well, rdn out: reapp: '99 wnr at Nottingham (class
stks) & Windsor (h'cap, rtd 76): eff at 6/7f on firm & soft, prob handles any trk: tried blnks/visor, runs well fresh.
687   **BLUE STAR 21** [6] N P Littmoden 4-9-11 (vis) J Tate 7/4 FAV: 415122: 4 b g Whittingham - Gold And ¾ 77
Blue (Bluebird) Prom, rdn/briefly led 2f out, kept on well for press ins last, al just held: hvly bckd: see 660 (AW).
4186} **TICKLISH 99** [11] W J Haggas 4-9-4 M Hills 7/2: 1025-3: 4 b f Cadeaux Genereux - Exit Laughing (Shaab) 3½ 64
Trkd ldrs halfway, briefly no room 3f out, kept on fnl 2f, not pace to chall: op 9/4, reapp: '99 Warwick wnr
(h'cap, rtd 72): '98 Ripon & Brighton wnr (h'caps, rtd 73): eff at 6/7f on gd & soft: handles a sharp/gall trk.
4518} **SHUDDER 99** [10] R J Hodges 5-9-7 J Weaver 16/1: 0000-4: Keen in tch, rdn & kept on fnl 2f, no nk 66
threat: op 14/1, reapp: '99 Haydock wnr (clmr, W Haggas, rtd 81, first time visor): '97 Goodwood wnr (auct mdn,
rtd 101): eff at 6/7f on fast & gd, prob any trk: enjoys claim grade: sharper next time with headgear reapplied.
721   **PERUVIAN STAR 13** [13] 4-9-7 D Holland 25/1: 000-05: Cl-up 6f: see 721.   4 59
3923} **AEGEAN FLAME 99** [3] 4-9-4 S Drowne 20/1: 0000-6: Towards rear, eff 3f out, no impress: reapp: 1¼ 53
unplcd in '99 (rtd 83, rtd h'cap, with B Meehan): '98 Ripon (fill mdn) & Newbury wnr (stks, rtd 90): eff at 5f,
6f+ cld suit: acts on gd & hvy, handles fast: can front run, handles any trk: poor low draw today.
716   **IVORY DAWN 14** [14] 6-9-4 M Roberts 6/1: 000-07: Towards rear halfway, mod gains under a kind ride ¾ 52+
fnl 2f: op 4/1: '99 Brighton & here at Lingfield wnr (h'caps, rtd 77): '98 Brighton & again here at Lingfield
wnr (h'caps, rtd 74): 6f specialist, stays a sharp 7f: acts on firm & gd/soft, likes sharp/undul trks.
687   **BANDBOX 21** [2] 5-9-9 L Newman 5/2 (2) 1/2: 0-1208: Prom 5f: op 10/1, poor draw: btr 598, 511 (AW). 1½ 54
3285} **ROYAL TARRAGON 99** [8] 4-9-4 R Cody Boutcher (7) 66/1: 0000-9: Held up, eff centre 3f out, no 3 44$
impress: 8 month abs: prev with J Arnold, unplcd in '99 (rtd 24a & 11): rtd 48 at best in '98: tried visor & blnks.
4439} **DELTA SOLEIL 99** [12] 8-9-7 R Cochrane 14/1: 0000-0: Chsd ldrs 5f: 10th: op 10/1, 6 month abs. 1 45
673   **FAUTE DE MIEUX 24** [1] 5-9-7 S Carson (5) 16/1: 000-60: Led 5f: 12th: op 14/1: blnks omitted. 0
3879} My Petal 99 [7] 4-9-4 Dane O'Neill 12/1:   405 Scotland Bay 71 [5] 3-9-0 J F Egan 33/1:
111   End Of Story 99 [15] 4-9-7 R Mullen 50/1:   168 Maylan 99 [4] 5-9-4 P McCabe 66/1:
15 ran   Time 1m 26.36 (5.96)   (One Stop Partnership)   J G Given Willoughton, Lincs.

839 4.05 KBA MDN DIV 1 3YO (D)   7f str Good/Soft 87 -08 Slow
£2713 £835 £417 £208 Raced stands side, high no's favoured.

1867} **DIAMOND LOOK 99** [14] E A L Dunlop 3-9-0 J Reid 8/11 FAV: 2-1: 3 b c Dayjur - Pedestal (High Line) 84
Trkd ldrs/keen early, shkn up to lead 2f out, asserted well ins last, drvn out: hvly bckd: rnr-up in '99 (mdn, rtd
83): eff at 6/7f, related to wnrs at 1m/10f: acts on gd/soft & a sharp/gall trk: runs well fresh.
4599} **WIND CHIME 99** [9] C E Brittain 3-9-0 P Robinson 8/1: 24-2: 3 ch c Arazi - Shamisen (Diesis) 1 80
Prom, rdn to chall over 1f out, just held by wnr well ins last: 5 month abs: rnr-up on debut in '99 (rtd 77, mdn):
eff at 6/7f, cld stay further: handles firm & gd/soft grnd & a sharp trk: now qual for h'caps.
--   **DESAMO** [2] J Noseda 3-9-0 Pat Eddery 7/1: 3: 3 br c Chief's Crown - Green Heights (Miswaki) 1¾ 77
Trkd ldrs towards centre, rdn to chall 2f out, kept on ins last, not pace of front pair: op 5/1: $70,000 purchase:
eff at 7f, 1m+ cld suit: handles gd/soft grnd: pleasing intro from a tricky low draw.
2995} **BALI BATIK 99** [5] G Wragg 3-9-0 D Holland 20/1: 0-4: Held up in tch, switched left 2f out & styd on ¾ 76+
well under hands-&-heels riding ins last, nrst fin: op 12/1, reapp: unplcd sole '99 start (rtd 51, mdn): stays
a sharp 7f, 1m+ looks sure to suit: handles gd/soft grnd: encouraging reapp, rate more highly over 1m+.
3851} **SHADOW PRINCE 99** [1] S Drowne 16/1: 6-5: Chsd ldrs, onepace over 1f out: 7 month abs: hd 75
unplcd sole '99 start (mdn, rtd 66): bred to apprec 1m+ for R Charlton: poor low draw today.
731   **ALMASHROUK 13** [4] 3-9-0 J Fortune 20/1: 040-66: Led 5f, onepace: poor draw: see 731 (6f). 1¾ 72
4607} **ANTIGONEL 99** [3] 3-8-9 Dane O'Neill 33/1: 00-7: Dwelt, sn prom, rdn/fdd over 1f out: 5 month abs: 4 60
rtd 67 at best in '99 (fill mdn): poor low draw here, now quals for h'caps for R Hannon.
4542} **SHOWING 99** [8] R Cochrane 66/1: 00-8: Keen traking ldrs, wknd 2f out, sn held & eased ins ¾ 64
last: 5 month abs, not given a hard time on reapp, now quals for h'caps.
--   **WILLOUGHBYS BOY** [6] 3-9-0 W Ryan 16/1: 9: Prom 5f: op 10/1, debut: with B Hanbury. 2½ 59
4164} **HOME FORCE 99** [7] 3-9-0 R Mullen 33/1: 40-0: Rdn/towards rear, nvr factor: 6 month absence. ½ 58
--   **LUCKYS SON** [10] 3-9-0 T Quinn 9/1: 0: Mid-div, wknd qckly over 1f out: 16th: debut, with J Dunlop. 0
3986} Eurolink Mayfly 99 [11] 3-8-9 G Carter 33/1:   -- Captain Boycott [13] 3-9-0 J F Egan 50/1:
4506} Maiysha 99 [12] 3-8-9 S Sanders 33/1:   -- Lite A Candle [15] 3-8-9 N Pollard 50/1:
591   Millennium Dream 41 [16] 3-9-0 F Norton 66/1:
16 ran   Time 1m 27.04 (6.64)   (Jaber Abdullah)   E A L Dunlop Newmarket.

840 4.40 KBA MDN DIV 2 3YO (D)   7f str Good/Soft 87 -15 Slow
£2697 £830 £415 £207 Raced stands side, high no's favoured

759   **GRAND BAHAMIAN 10** [9] J Noseda 3-9-0 J Weaver 20/1: 01: 3 gr c Distant View - Flora Scent 83
(Fluorescent Light) Made all, styd on well ins last, rdn out: eff at 7f on gd/soft grnd: likes to force the
pace on a sharp trk: clearly going the right way, can win more races.
4306} **LEEROY 99** [5] R Hannon 3-9-0 Dane O'Neill 5/1: 3224-2: 3 b c Dancing Dissident - Birdhill (Petorius) 1½ 78
Trkd ldrs, rdn & kept on ins last, not pace to chall: reapp, op 6/1: rnr-up twice in '99 (rtd 86, 4 rnr mdn):
eff at 6/7f on fast & soft grnd, likes a sharp/undul trk: has shown enough to win at this stage.
3632} **BREAK THE GLASS 99** [16] E A L Dunlop 3-9-0 J Reid 25/1: 44-3: 3 b g Dynaformer - Greek Wedding 1 76
(Blushing Groom) Rear, eff/no room over 2f out, kept on well ins last, nrst fin: 7 month abs: unplcd both '99
starts (rtd 69): eff at 7f, a return to 1m+ in h'cap company will suit: spot on next time.
270

--   **JUMBO JET** [3]   G A Butler 3-9-0 D Holland 5/1: 4: Rear, rdn/switched & kept on fnl 2f: debut: nk   75
dam a 7f wnr: eff at 7f on gd/soft grnd: encouraging intro from a tricky low draw.
--   **SALIENT POINT** [11] 3-8-9 N Callan 12/1: 5: Chsd ldrs, onepace fnl 2f: debut, IR 32,000gns   2   66
purchase: half-sister to a 1m wnr: with S P C Woods.
--   **PEKANESE** [8] 3-9-0 A McCarthy (3) 16/1: 6: Trkd ldrs, held over 1f out: debut: IR 26,000gns   nk   70
purchase related to a couple of winning juvs: sire a smart 2yo: with A C Stewart.
704   **GOLDEN LEGEND 15** [2] 3-9-0 M Roberts 7/1: 00-47: Prom 5f: poor low draw: btr 704 (1m).   hd   69
--   **TARSHEEH** [12] 3-8-9 Pat Eddery 4/1 FAV: 8: Rear, mod gains fnl 2f: debut, op 2/1: Mr Prospector   3   58
filly, half-sister to v smart 7/9f performer Haami: will know more next time for J L Dunlop.
729   **GROVE LODGE 13** [13] 3-9-0 S Whitworth 33/1: 000-09: Cl-up 5f: off rtd 45.   shd   63$
3802} **DILETIA 99** [6] 3-8-9 G Duffield 33/1: 60-0: Rdn/towards rear, no threat: 10th: 7 month absence.   hd   57
--   **INDIANA JONES** [1] 3-9-0 J Fortune 5/1: 0: Al rear: 15th: debut, with P Cole: poor low draw.   0
--   **WOODLAND RIVER** [10] 3-9-0 R Cochrane 9/2: 0: Al rear: 16th: debut, with J Fanshawe.   0
735   Eyelets Echo 13 [7] 3-9-0 S Sanders 14/1:   789   Love Bitten 8 [4] 3-9-0 J Fanning 25/1:
--   Loup Cervier [15] 3-9-0 P Doe 20/1:   729   Crafty Pick 13 [14] 3-8-9 P Dobbs (5) 12/1:
16 ran   Time 1m 27.52 (7.12)   (Lucayan Stud)   J Noseda Newmarket.

841	5.10 BUCKS BAR SELL HCAP 3YO 0-60 (G) 7f str Good/Soft 87 -29 Slow	[67]
	£1926 £550 £275 Raced stands side, high no's favoured	

636   **NORTHERN TIMES 34** [8] R Brotherton 3-9-5 (58) J P Spencer 12/1: 0-5101: 3 ch g Cahill Road -   60
Northern Nation (Northrop) Rear, hard rdn over 2f out, styd on gamely for press ins last to lead nr line, all out:
bt in for 5,000gns: earlier scored at Southwell (sell, rtd 59a, T Easterby): rtd 61 on sole turf start in '99:
eff at 7f/sharp 1m: acts on fibresand & gd/soft grnd: likes a sharp trk: relishes sell grade.
685   **TABBETINNA BLUE 21** [10] J W Payne 3-7-10 (35) G Baker (7) 20/1: 0-002: 3 b f Interrex - True Is   hd   36
Blue (Gabitat) Led, going best 2f out, shkn up ins last & hdd nr line: eff at 7f on gd/soft grnd: mod form prev.
4353} **MISS SPRINGFIELD 99** [7] D Morris 3-8-0 (39) J Tate 25/1: 000-3: 3 b f Environment Friend - Esilam   1   38
(Frimley Park) Prom, rdn & kept on onepace fnl 2f: 6 month abs, h'cap bow: no form in '99: eff at 7f on gd/soft.
773   **FRENCH FANCY 9** [11] B A Pearce 3-8-7 (46)(bl) Pat Eddery 5/1: 530424: Trkd ldrs, onepace fnl 2f.   ½   44
4600} **DOVES DOMINION 99** [5] 3-9-5 (58) T Quinn 6/1: 000-5: Rear, rdn 2f out, kept on, not pace to chall: ½   55
op 4/1, reapp, h'cap bow: unplcd all 3 starts at 6f in '99 (rtd 64): prob stays a sharp 7f & handles gd/soft grnd.
785   **ITSGOTTABDUN 9** [9] 3-9-7 (60)(bl) C Catlin (7) 7/1: 142366: Cl-up, wknd fnl 1f: see 654, 527 (sell).   1½   54
80   **CYBER BABE 99** [13] 3-9-7 (60) M Henry 25/1: 0000-7: Rear, mod gains fnl 2f: 5 month abs: rnr-   hd   53
up twice in '99 (rtd 58, M Tompkins): eff at 6/7f, prob stays 1m: handles firm & gd grnd: has run well in a vis.
745   **BEACH BABY 11** [4] 3-7-13 (38) A Nicholls (1) 20/1: 00-008: Prom, fdd fnl 2f: h'cap bow: mod form.   ¾   30
654   **COLEY 30** [12] 3-8-12 (51) Martin Dwyer 9/1: 0-3569: Cl-up 5f: see 443 (6f, AW).   1¼   40
80   **IRISH DANCER 99** [2] 3-8-10 (49) R Cochrane 4/2 FAV: 6004-0: Dwelt, trkd ldrs 5f: 10th: 5 month   ¾   37
abs: unplcd in '99 (rtd 67, auct mdn): poor low draw today.
736   **SUNRISE 13** [1] 3-9-4 (57) J Reid 9/1: 003-00: Struggling halfway: 13th: poor low draw: plcd in '99   0
(rtd 70, fill mdn): eff at 6f on gd grnd.
4369} Lyrical Legacy 99 [3] 3-8-10 (49) G Duffield 16/1:   595   Master Jones 41 [6] 3-9-7 (60) G Hannon (7) 25/1:
13 ran   Time 1m 28.51 (8.11)   (Ms Gerardine P O'Reilly)   R Brotherton Elmleigh Castle, Worcs.

842	5.40 SHEFFIELD PARK HCAP 4YO+ 0-70 (E) 1m2f aw Standard Inapplicable	[69]
	£2870 £820 £410	

+776 **ELLWAY PRINCE 9** [3] M Wigham 5-8-13 (54)(6ex) Dean McKeown 6/4 FAV: 625011: 5 b g Prince Sabo -   64a
Star Arrangement (Star Appeal) Rear, smooth prog fnl 4f, led dist & sn clr, eased nr line: val for 5L+: 6lb
pen for recent Lingfield win (h'cap): rnr-up in '99 (h'cap, rtd 67a, Mrs N Macauley): '98 Lingfield wnr (mdn, rtd
72a): eff at 6f, suited by 1m/10f now: acts on firm, gd & both AWs: eff with/without vis, tried blnks: hat-trick?
411   **CONSULTANT 71** [4] C N Kellett 4-8-11 (52) R Cochrane 14/1: 032002: 4 b g Man Of May - Avenita Lady   1   55a
(Free State): Led, clr over 2f out, rdn/hdd over 1f out & sn held: clr of rem: abs: suited by 1m/10f on both AWs.
477   **HEVER GOLF GLORY 59** [5] C N Kellett 6-8-12 (53) N Carlisle 25/1: -04503: 6 b g Efisio - Zaius   4   50a
(Artaius) Rear, rdn, kept on fnl 2f, nrst fin: longer priced stablemate of rnr-up: 8 wk abs: blnks omitted: acts
on firm, soft & both AWs, loves W'hampton: see 383.
790   **SHAMWARI SONG 8** [1] Mrs L C Jewell 5-8-3 (43)(1ow) J F Egan 33/1: 203004: Prom, onepace 2f out.   1¾   39a
209   **ROGER ROSS 99** [12] 5-8-12 (53) S Drowne 12/1: 0100-5: Wide/chsd ldrs, btn 2f out: 4 month abs.   4   42a
746   **BEGUILE 11** [1] 6-8-9 (50)(t) A Nicholls (3) 10/1: -24106: Prom 1m: clr rem: 4 month h'cap).   1½   37a
632   **SAMMYS SHUFFLE 34** [13] 5-9-4 (59)(bl) O Urbina 12/1: 001537: Wide/chsd ldrs 7f: btr 575 (C/D).   7   36a
*775 **BILLICHANG 9** [7] 4-8-8 (49)(6ex) D Holland 6/1: 442618: Prom, strugg 3f out: btr 775 (C/D, sell).   hd   25a
715   **PROSPECTORS COVE 14** [10] 7-9-7 (62) J Weaver 4/1: 00-309: Wide/rear, nvr factor: see 618 (C/D).   4   32a
4475} **KEZ 99** [2] 4-9-13 (68) N Callan 16/1: 1000-0: Mid-div, btn 3f out: 10th: 6 month abs: AW bow: 1   36a
'99 Brighton scorer (auct mdn, long odds on, rtd 78): eff at 10/12f on firm & gd, any trk.
637   Baajil 34 [14] 5-8-10 (51) G Carter 25/1: 557}**Ertlon 99** [6] 10-8-13 (54) P Robinson 20/1:
3762} April Ace 99 [11] 4-9-2 (57) T Quinn 14/1:
13 ran   Time 2m 06.87 (4.07)   (Stephen Roots)   M Wigham Newmarket.

HAMILTON   SATURDAY APRIL 8TH   Righthand, Undulating Track, Stiff Uphill Finish

Official Going   GOOD (GOOD/SOFT places). Stalls: 1m/9f - Inside; Rem - Stands Side.

843	1.10 LE BISTRO NOV STKS 2YO (D) 5f Good 55 -56 Slow	
	£3558 £1095 £547 £273 Stands side pair behind from halfway	

--   **TIME N TIME AGAIN 75** [5] E J Alston 2-8-12 A Culhane 20/1: 1: 2 b g Timeless Times - Primum Tempus   89
(Primo Dominie): Prom far side, rdn/hung badly left to stands side over 1f out, styd on well for press, led line:
3rd foal, half-brother to 2 juv wnrs: dam a mod sprinter: eff at 5f, 6f+ : suit in time: acts on gd grnd & a stiff/
undul trk: runs well fresh: would have won this if keeping a str line, can rate more highly.
730   **SQUIRREL NUTKIN 14** [9] M L W Bell 2-8-12 M Fenton 2/1: -22: 2 b c Bluebird - Saltoki (Ballad Rock): shd   88
Prom far side, rdn/led inside last, hdd line: hvly bckd: can sn go one better: see 730.
*801 **MAMMAS TONIGHT 8** [6] A Berry 2-9-0 J Fortune 9/1: 13: 2 ch c Timeless Times - Miss Merlin (Manacle):1   87

Led far side, rdn/hdd inside last, just held cl-home: op 7/1: acts on gd grnd & fibresand: see 801 (AW auct mdn).
*700 **NEARLY A FOOL 16** [10] B A McMahon 2-9-5 K Darley 6/4 FAV: 14: Cl-up far side, rdn halfway, kept on inside last, not pace to chall: well bckd, op 2/1: not disgraced under top-weight: acts on fast & gd grnd. *1* **89**
-- **CO DOT UK** [8] 2-8-12 F Lynch 20/1: 5: Rear far side, kept on final 2f, no threat: op 25/1: Distant Relative gelding, May foal, cost 6,500 gns: dam a 7f 2yo wnr, sire top class at 1m: 6f+ should suit in time. *3½* **73+**
-- **CARTMEL PRINCE** [7] 2-8-12 Darren Moffatt 50/1: 6: Dwelt/rear far side, kept on final 2f, no threat: May foal, cheaply bought: half-brother to dual 5f 2yo wnr/sprint h'capper Cartmel Park: sire US 1m/11f performer, 6f+ should suit in time for D Moffatt. *shd* **73**
-- **THORNTOUN DANCER** [4] 2-8-7 J Fanning 50/1: 7: Bhd halfway far side: Unfuwain filly, Mar foal, dam unrcd: sire top class 12f performer: looks sure to apprec 7f+ in time for J S Goldie. *4* **58**
755 **OREGON FLIGHT 11** [3] 2-8-7 O Pears 100/1: 08: Prom 3f far side, fdd: see 755. *5* **49**
700 **VISCOUNT BANKES 16** [2] 2-8-12 A Daly 4/1: 49: Bhd final 2f stands side: no ch with far side, this best forgotten: much clsr to todays 4th in 700. *1¼* **51**
755 **THORNTOUN DIVA 11** [1] 2-8-7 Dean McKeown 14/1: 30: Bhd halfway stands side: 10th: forget this. *¾* **44**
10 ran Time 1m 02.7 (4.6) (Springs Equestrian Ltd) E J Alston Longton, Lancs.

844 1.40 CLYDESDALE BANK HCAP 3YO+ 0-85 (D) 6f Good 55 +05 Fast [85]
£6032 £1856 £928 £464 3 yo rec 12lb Far side (high nos) held a big advantage

787 **ABBAJABBA 10** [6] C W Fairhurst 4-8-6 (63) J Fanning 10/1: 660-31: 4 b g Barrys Gamble - Bo' Babbity (Strong Gale): Held up in tch far side, smooth prog to lead over 1f out, styd on strongly inside last, pushed out: gd time, 1st win: unplcd in '99 (rtd 67): juv rnr-up (rtd 82 in a nursery): eff at 5/6f, tried 7f: acts on gd & gd/soft, any trk: looks nicely h'capped and should make a quick follow-up. **76**
716 **UNSHAKEN 15** [8] E J Alston 6-9-2 (73) F Norton 8/1: 300-02: 6 b g Environment Friend - Reel Foyle (Irish River): Twds rear far side, rdn/styd on final 2f, not pace of wnr: op 7/1: gd run at fav trk: see 716. *4* **74**
667 **REGAL SONG 25** [12] T J Etherington 4-8-7 (63)(bl)(1ow) D Holland 25/1: 1-3203: 4 b g Anita's Prince - Song Beam (Song): Rear far side, switched & kept on fnl 2f, no threat: jock given 3-day irresponsible riding ban. *1* **62**
1589} **MAGIC MILL 99** [13] J S Goldie 7-8-10 (67) A Culhane 25/1: /040-4: Hmpd/dropped rear after 1f, prog when hmpd dist, styd on strongly ins last, nrst fin: op 16/1, reapp: lightly rcd in '99 (rtd 70, h'cap): '98 Newcastle wnr (h'cap, rtd 86, J Eyre): eff at 6f, suited by 7f/1m, stays 10f: acts on fast, gd & equitrack, loves soft/hvy: eye-catching effort: no luck in running, looks well h'capped & is one to note over 7f+. *nk* **65+**
4331} **NAISSANT 99** [11] 7-7-13 (56) P Fessey 9/1: 5000-5: Chsd ldrs far side, onepace final 2f: op 12/1: 6 mth abs: '99 wnr here at Hamilton (appr h'cap) & Carlisle (class stks, rtd 67 at best): '98 wnr again at Hamilton (2, h'caps, rtd 65, M Wane): eff btwn 5/7f on firm & hvy, any trk, loves Hamilton: on handy mark & sharper for this. *3½* **45**
763 **KING OF PERU 11** [16] 7-8-13 (70)(vis) C Cogan (5) 9/1: 22-556: Chsd ldrs 2f out, sn no extra: see 660. *4* **49**
4448} **GET STUCK IN 99** [7] 4-10-0 (85) C Lowther 25/1: 0140-7: Led far side till over 1f out, fdd: '99 wnr at Hamilton (C/D, class stks), Ripon & York (h'caps, rtd 87): rnr-up 7 times in '98 (rtd 94$ at best): eff at 5/6f on fast & soft, any trk: best without blnks: eff held up or forcing the pace: tough & progressive last term. *5* **55**
758 **MARY JANE 11** [15] 5-8-3 (60) Kim Tinkler 33/1: 215-08: In tch far side, held final 2f: '99 h'cap wnr at W'hampton (2, rtd 70a), Chepstow & Leicester (rtd 63, R Cowell): '98 wnr again at W'hampton & Southwell (2, clmrs, rtd 66a & 56): stays 6f, suited by 5f: acts on firm, gd & both AWs, any trk, likes W'hampton: with N Tinkler. *1¾* **26**
622 **MOOCHA CHA MAN 37** [14] 4-9-1 (72)(bl) K Darley 10/1: 240-09: Chsd ldrs far side, rdn/badly hmpd over 1f out & position accepted: tchd 14/1: best forgotten, clsr with a clr run: blnks reapplied: see 622 (AW). *shd* **38**
2376} **JAYPEECEE 99** [9] 4-8-7 (64) R Lappin 50/1: 1000-0: Nvr a factor far side: 10th: 9 mth abs: '99 debut wnr at Beverley (mdn, rtd 72, subs disapp): eff at 5f, 6f+ could suit: acts on gd/stiff trk: has run well fresh. *½* **28**
798 **XANADU 9** [10] 4-7-12 (55) Dale Gibson 33/1: 103-00: In tch far side 4f: 11th: '99 wnr here at Hamilton (C/D sell) & Carlisle (h'cap, rtd 56): eff at 6f on firm grnd: likes a stiff trk. *hd* **18**
824 **MANORBIER 3** [4] 4-9-6 (77) F Lynch 5/1: 141120: Rdn/led stands side halfway, no impress with far side: 12th: qck reapp: proved badly drawn, forget this: see 824, 716. *1½* **36**
728 **PALAWAN 14** [2] 4-9-3 (74) J Fortune 9/2: -21120: Stands side, no ch halfway: 17th: best forgotten. **0**
660 **BLUE KITE 28** [18] 5-8-2 (59) J Tate 7/2 FAV: 345100: Handy far side, wkng/badly hmpd over 1f out, eased: 18th: hvly bckd: more expected on return to turf, looks on a handy turf mark: see 645 (AW). **0**
4121} **Shatin Beauty 99** [17] 3-7-11 (66) K Dalgleish (7) 33/1: 47 **Demolition Jo 99** [1] 5-9-3 (74)(vis) N Callan 20/1:
746 **Grasslandik 12** [5] 4-7-12 (55) T Williams 16/1: 4391} **Miss Fit 99** [3] 4-9-5 (76) G Duffield 50/1:
18 ran Time 1m 12.8 (3.0) (North Cheshire Trading & Storage Ltd) C W Fairhurst Middleham, Nth Yorks.

845 2.10 CLYDESBANK HCAP 4YO+ 0-85 (D) 1m5f Good 55 -00 Slow [85]
£10676 £3285 £1642 £821 4 yo rec 2 lb

1106} **EXALTED 99** [3] T A K Cuthbert 7-8-3 (60) Dale Gibson 20/1: 0/40-1: 7 b g High Estate - Heavenward (Conquistador Cielo): Mid-div, styd on well for press fnl 2f to lead ins last, drvn out: jumps fit, Jan '00 Ayr wnr (h'cap, rtd 114h, eff at 2½m on fast & hvy): plcd in '99 on the level (rtd 59, h'cap): juv wnr at Thirsk: eff at 10.5/13f, tried 2m: acts on fast & gd/soft grnd, any trk. **65**
4393} **MR FORTYWINKS 99** [14] J L Eyre 6-8-3 (60) J Tate 10/1: 0300-2: 6 ch g Fool's Holme - Dream On (Absalom): Chsd ldr, led over 4f out, rdn/hdd ins last, kept on well for press: 6 mth abs: '99 h'cap wnr here at Hamilton, Ripon (lady riders) & Carlisle (rtd 70): '98 wnr at W'hampton, Southwell & Nottingham (h'caps, rtd 63 & 71a): eff up with/forcing the pace at 11/13f on firm, hvy & fibresand: handles any trk, likes Hamilton. *1½* **62**
726 **WILCUMA 14** [4] P J Makin 9-9-12 (83) A Clark 7/1: -01553: 9 b g Most Welcome - Miss Topville (Top Ville): Rear, prog/chsd ldrs 5f out, chall over 1f out, kept on well: seems best at 13f/2m nowadays: see 380. *¾* **84**
825 **PRINCE NICHOLAS 3** [6] K W Hogg 5-8-4 (61) J Bramhill 9/2 FAV: 1-0224: Held up, prog/chall 2f out, no extra inside last: op 3/1: qck reapp: see 825, 779. *¾* **61**
627 **MORGANS ORCHARD 37** [8] 4-8-1 (60) G Duffield 8/1: 152155: Chsd ldrs 4f out, rdn/chall 2f out, held inside last: eff at 12/13f on fibresand & gd grnd: see 607 (AW, amat h'cap). *hd* **59**
4351} **ROMAN KING 99** [5] 5-10-0 (85) T Quinn 12/1: 541-6: Chsd ldrs halfway, rdn/no extra final 2f: op 14/1, 6 mth abs: '99 scorer at Haydock (mdn, rtd 85, J Gosden): eff at 12f, could get further: acts on gd & hvy grnd. *3* **80**
1954} **EMBRYONIC 99** [1] 8-8-9 (66) Dean McKeown 50/1: 5/60-7: Rear, rdn/stdy prog final 2f, nrst fin: 10 mth abs: lightly rcd in '99 (rtd 65, h'cap): rtd 73 in '98 (h'cap): '97 wnr at Doncaster & Newcastle (h'caps, rtd 79): eff at 14f, 2m suits: acts on fast & hvy, any trk: looks nicely h'capped, not given a hard time, one too note at 2m. *¾* **60+**
779 **BERGAMO 10** [11] 4-8-11 (70)(bl) F Norton 10/1: 435-08: Held up in tch, effort/no impress final 3f: blnks reapp: '99 Beverley & Yarmouth wnr (h'cap, with J Noseda, rtd 81 at best): '98 Bath wnr (mdn, rtd 86): eff at 12/14f, tried 2m, may yet suit: acts on firm & gd, fair/stiff trk: suited by blnks/vis: now with B Ellison. *1¾* **62**
4293} **HOME COUNTIES 99** [2] 11-7-12 (55)(t) N Carlisle 10/1: 5232-9: Rear, rdn/mod gains: jumps fit (rtd 106h, h'cap): plcd 3 times in '99 (rtd 54, h'cap): eff at 14f, stays 2m2f well: handles any grnd/trk: eff in a t-strap. *5* **40**

757   **SPREE VISION** 11 [10] 4-8-1 (60) A Daly 14/1: 000-00: Towards rear, effort/no impress final 3f: 10th.   *shd*   45
757   **IL PRINCIPE** 11 [13] 6-9-9 (80) M Fenton 20/1: 124-00: Al rear: 11th: see 89 (AW).   ½   64
2624} **OCTANE** 99 [9] 4-8-1 (60) A McCarthy (3) 50/1: 0500-0: Held up, btn 3f out: 12th: reapp, new trainer.   7   34
4546} **LADY COLDUNELL** 99 [7] 4-8-1 (60)(BL) J Fanning 5/1: 2505-0: Chsd ldrs 10f: 13th: blnks, jmps fit.   2½   30
809   **HIBERNATE** 7 [12] 6-9-4 (75) N Callan 12/1: -00000: Led 9f, fdd, bhd/eased final 1f: 14th: op 8/1.   ½   44
14 ran   Time 2m 52.6 (7.1)   (Railway Lochmaben)   T A K Cuthbert Little Corby, Cumbria.

---

846   **2.40 ANNUAL MEMBERS HCAP 3YO+ 0-75 (E)**   **1m1f36y   Good 55   -06 Slow**   **[74]**
£4543   £1048   £1048   £349   3 yo rec 17lb

705   **PERCHANCER** 16 [10] P C Haslam 4-8-5 (51) J Mackay (7) 12/1: 211001: 4 ch g Perugino - Irish Hope   57
(Nishapour): Mid-div, prog to lead over 1f out, styd on well ins last, rdn out: earlier scored at W'hampton (amat
h'cap) & Southwell (h'cap, rtd 62a): '99 Thirsk wnr (appr mdn h'cap, rtd 55 & 58a): eff at 7/9.3f on firm, gd/soft
& both AWs, any trk: eff with/without blnks, tried a visor: runs well for an apprentice.
715   **TONY TIE** 15 [15] J S Goldie 4-10-0 (74) A Culhane 5/1: 210-62: 4 b g Ardkinglass - Queen Of The Quorn   1¾   76
(Governor General): Held up, rdn/kept on final 3f, not pace to chall: op 4/1: stays 9f well: see 715.
4389} **DISTINCTLY WELL** 99 [7] P D Evans 3-8-4 (67) Joanna Badger (5) 33/1: 0W00-2: 3 b g Distinctly North - *dht*   69
Brandywell (Skyliner): Towards rear, rdn & kept on fnl 3f, not pace to chall: clr rem: reapp: '99 Chester wnr
(nurs, rtd 82): eff at 7f, stays 9f on firm, soft & fibresand, any trk: tried a vis: gd reapp, h'capped to win.
803   **PURSUIVANT** 8 [12] M D Hammond 6-8-8 (54) R Fitzpatrick (3) 12/1: 00-034: Chsd ldr 3f out, sn held.   8   44
*786 **FORTY FORTE** 10 [18] 4-10-0 (74) N Callan 3/1 FAV: 624415: Led/clr halfway, rdn/hdd over 1f out &   2½   59
sn held: well bckd, op 7/2: front rnr who found this stiff uphill fin against him: see 786.
718   **MY TYSON** 14 [8] 5-7-12 (44) F Norton 7/1: 000136: Mid-div, rdn/held final 2f: jockey given a five   2   25
day ban for irresponsible riding: see 676 (AW).
705   **MR PERRY** 16 [4] 4-8-7 (53) D Holland 10/1: 500-07: Chsd ldrs halfway, no extra final 2f: op 8/1:   1   32
'99 W'hampton wnr (mdn h'cap, rtd 70a & 80, J S Moore): eff arnd 1m, tried further: acts on fibresand, handles
hvy: has run well fresh & likes a sharp trk: now with M D Hammond.
4301} **AMRON** 16 [16] 13-8-4 (50) O Pears 12/1: 0000-8: Rear, effort/hmpd 3f out, mod gains under hands   *hd*   28
&-heels riding final 2f: 6 mth abs, prev with J Berry, '99 h'cap wnr at Redcar & Ayr (rtd 56): '98 Redcar wnr (h'cap,
rtd 50): formerly a sprinter, now suited by 1m/10f: acts on any going/trk: game 13yo, mother first.
4444} **OCEAN DRIVE** 99 [6] 4-8-2 (48) Dale Gibson 16/1: 0030-9: Al towards rear: 6 mth abs: '99 Hamilton   1   24
wnr (appr h'cap, rtd 62, first win): plcd in '98 (rtd 75, mdn): eff at 12/13f on fast & gd grnd, stiff trk.
749   **MIDNIGHT WATCH** 11 [3] 6-7-10 (42) G Sparkes (7) 14/1: 013220: Mid-div, btn 2f out: 10th: btr 749.   *shd*   18
1863} **WESTERN GENERAL** 99 [17] 9-9-0 (60) K Darley 20/1: 0/42-0: Towards rear, hmpd 3f out, no impress: 2½   31
11th: 2 mth jumps abs (rtd 93h, h'cap): rnr-up in '99 (C/D sell, rtd 48): '98/99 Newcastle jumps wnr (sell h'cap,
rtd 84): '96 Hamilton wnr (h'cap, rtd 72): eff at 1m/10f on firm & soft: has run well fresh: best without blnks.
453   **CANNY HILL** 64 [13] 3-8-5 (68) Darren Moffatt 20/1: 064-30: Chsd ldrs, fdd final 3f: 12th: 2 mth abs.   2½   34
*795 **ACE OF TRUMPS** 9 [1] 4-8-9 (55)(t) N Kennedy 10/1: 500-10: In tch, rdn/btn 4f out: 16th.   0
4447} Navan Project 99 [9] 6-7-13 (44)(1ow) A Daly 16/1:   2332} **Philmist** 99 [2] 8-8-1 (47)(bl) J Bramhill 33/1:
517   Ultra Calm 53 [11] 4-9-0 (60)(t) P Goode (3) 16/1:   4578} **Jona Holley** 99 [15] 7-8-5 (51)(bl) G Duffield 12/1:
757   **Tightrope** 11 [14] 5-8-11 (57) M Fenton 14/1:
18 ran   Time 1m 59.7 (5.6)   (N P Green)   P C Haslam Middleham, Nth Yorks.

---

847   **3.05 CALCUTTA CLASSIFIED STKS 3YO+ 0-65 (E)**   **1m65y   Good 55   -14 Slow**
£2847   £876   £438   £219   3 yo rec 15lb

669   **WILTON** 25 [3] J Hetherton 5-9-7 G Duffield 9/1: 00-301: 5 ch g Sharpo - Poyle Amber (Sharrood):   68
In tch, styd on well to lead well ins last, drvn out: well btn in 2 '99 starts (rtd 44a): '98 wnr at Pontefract,
Redcar (rtd 70) & Lingfield (h'caps, rtd 79a): eff at 7f, suited by 1m/9.3f on gd, hvy & both AWs, any trk.
4295} **BOLD AMUSEMENT** 99 [9] W S Cunningham 10-9-7 D Holland 10/1: 2250-2: 10 ch g Never So Bold -   ½   66
Hysterical (High Top): Trkd ldrs, chall fnl 3f, styd on well ins last: reapp: '99 Newcastle wnr (2, h'caps, rtd
67): '98 scorer at Redcar (h'cap, rtd 60): stays 12f, suited by 10f on firm & gd/soft: eff with/without blnks.
811   **DORISSIO** 7 [7] I A Balding 4-9-4 K Darley 1/2 FAV: 011-33: 4 b f Efisio - Floralia (Auction Ring):   *hd*   62
Chsd ldrs, prog/led over 2f out, rdn/hdd wide inside last & just held cl-home: hvly bckd: see 811.
661   **DONTBESOBOLD** 28 [8] B S Rothwell 3-8-6 M Fenton 16/1: 436624: Held up in tch, prog/chsd ldrs fnl   1¼   62
3f, kept on, not pace to chall: eff arnd 1m/9f: handles fast, soft & fibresand: see 278 (AW mdn).
715   **PENTAGON LAD** 15 [4] A Culhane 4-9-7 5/1: 000-05: Chsd ldrs 3f out, onepace: op 9/2: '99 h'cap   1¼   59
wnr at Carlisle, Thirsk, Ripon & Chester (rtd 75): eff at 1m, stays sharp 10.3f well: acts on fm & gd/soft, any trk.
3253} **FLOORSOTHEFOREST** 99 [10] 4-9-7 C Lowther 14/1: 2014-6: In tch, prog to chall 3f out, no extra   3½   52
over 1f out: op 12/1: 8 mth abs: '99 Hamilton scorer (h'cap, rtd 65, 1st win): eff at 9f on fast, poss handles soft.
756   **COLLEGE DEAN** 11 [2] 4-9-7 O Pears 100/1: 000-67: Held up in tch, effort/held final 2f: see 756.   1½   49$
827   **MANSTAR** 3 [5] 3-8-6 N Kennedy 14/1: 450-58: Held up, rdn/btn 2f out: op 12/1: qck reapp: btr 827.   3½   42
787   **KING UNO** 10 [6] 6-9-7 L Swift (7) 33/1: 500-09: Al rear: unplcd in '99 (rtd 61a & 63, h'caps): '98 wnr   ½   41
at Nottingham, Pontefract & Leicester (h'caps, with Mrs J Ramsden, rtd 68): eff at 6/7f, stays 1m: acts on fast
& soft: loves a stiff/gall trk, esp Pontefract: eff in a vis, tried blnks: nicely h'capped for sprint h'caps.
--   **NIZAAL** [1] 9-9-7 Dale Gibson 50/1: 0604/0: Mid-div, rdn/btn 2f out: 10th: jumps fit (mod form,   11   25
nov chase): last rcd on the level in '96 (unplcd): '94 wnr at Lingfield (7f h'cap): with T A K Cuthbert.
--   **SARMATIAN** [1] 9-9-7 (t) K Sked 66/1: 5030/0: Led tlst over 2f out, wknd qckly: 11th: 6 mth jmps   5   15
abs (rtd 74h at best, h'cap): last rcd on the level in '97 for M D Hammond (plcd, rtd 71): '96 wnr at Ayr (h'cap,
rtd 73): eff at 1m/10f on fast & hvy: best without blnks: gd weight carrier: with D Nolan.
11 ran   Time 1m 49.5 (5.7)   (George A Moore)   J Hetherton Malton, Nth Yorks.

---

848   **3.35 IF I WIN MDN STKS 3YO+ (D)**   **1m3f   Good 55   -47 Slow**
£2821   £868   £434   £217   3 yo rec 20lb

4453} **HIDDEN BRAVE** 99 [11] M Johnston 3-8-6 D Holland 4/7 FAV: 2-1: 3 b c Bin Ajwaad - Fire Lily   78
(Unfuwain): Made all, styd on well to assert ins last, rdn out: hvly bckd, reapp: rnr-up on sole '99 start (mdn,
rtd 92): apprec step up to 11f, 12f+ will suit: acts on gd & gd/soft: op to further improvement.
--   **DEEP WATER** [10] M D Hammond 6-9-12 T Quinn 2/1: 5253/2: 6 b g Diesis - Water Course (Irish   2½   72
River): Chsd ldrs, rdn 4f out, prsd wnr final 2f, held inside last: long Flat abs, jumps fit, Feb '00 Haydock wnr
(hdle, rtd 140h): last rcd on the level in '97 (rtd 72, plcd, h'cap): eff arnd 11/12f: acts on gd & soft grnd.
806   **THE WALRUS** 8 [8] N P Littmoden 3-8-6 M Fenton 50/1: 033: 3 b g Sri Pekan - Cathy Garcia (Be My Guest)   1¼   70$
Handy, rdn/chall 2f out, no extra inside last: styd this lngr 11f trip: acts on gd grnd: going the right way.
273

HAMILTON   SATURDAY APRIL 8TH   Righthand, Undulating Track, Stiff Uphill Finish

3548} **LADY BENSON 99** [2] W M Brisbourne 7-9-7 (t) A McCarthy (3) 100/1: 0000-4: In tch, onepace/held final 3f: 4 mth jumps abs (no form): rnr-up twice in '99 (h'caps, rtd 39): eff arnd 9f/10f on fast & gd/soft grnd.   **2** **62$**

809} **LASTMAN 99** [5] 5-9-12 Dean McKeown 10/1: 34/5-5: Slowly away/rear, mod gains final 2f: jumps fit, Feb '00 Musselburgh wnr (nov, rtd 104h): rtd 75 on sole start in '99 (mdn, D Nicholson): rtd 63 in '98 (mdn, British bow): eff at 10f, could stay further: acts on soft grnd: with J J O'Neill.   **hd** **66$**

--   **ROBERT THE BRUCE** [9] 5-9-12 C Lowther 50/1: 00/6: Rear, rdn/mod gains: 6 wk jumps abs (plcd thrice, rtd 101h, nov hdle): mod form on the Flat from 2 starts in '97.   **½** **65**

626   **MAJOR ATTRACTION 37** [1] 5-9-12 N Callan 100/1: 000607: Mid-div, rdn/btn 3f out: new stable.   **1** **64$**

--   **ALFAHAD** [3] 7-9-12 R Cody Boutcher (7) 200/1: 00/8: Mid-div, btn 2f out: long abs, no form.   **1** **63**

--   **WELDUNFRANK** [6] 7-9-12 J Tate 100/1: 9: Bhd 3f out: Flat debut, mod hdles form in 97/98.   **8** **54**

2012} **ROYAL CANARY 99** [7] 3-8-6 Dale Gibson 100/1: 0205-0: Al bhd: 10th: 10 mth abs: rnr-up in '99 (sell, rtd 61): eff over a sharp 5f, much lngr trip today: handles firm grnd.   **dist** **0**

10 ran   Time 2m 30.1 (11.3)   (Salem Suhail)   M Johnston Middleham, Nth Yorks.

WINDSOR   MONDAY APRIL 10TH   Sharp Figure 8 Track

Official Going   GOOD. Stalls: Inside. Round Course rail re-alignment rendered pace figures unreliable.

849 | 2.00 BANTRY AUCT MDN 2YO (E)   5f str   Good   Inapplicable
£2926   £836   £418

--   **THREEZEDZZ** [5] J G Portman 2-8-8 T Quinn 8/1: 1: 2 ch c Emarati - Exotic Forest (Dominion) Chsd ldr, rdn to lead over 1f out, drvn out: tchd 14/1: May foal, cost 4,600 gns: dam a wnr at 1m: eff at 5f, 6f shld suit: acts on gd grnd & runs well fresh on a sharp trk: fine debut, open to improvement.   **78**

--   **BARON CROCODILE** [10] A Berry 2-8-11 S Sanders 6/1: 2: 2 b c Puissance - Glow Again (The Brainstan) Prom till went on over 2f out, hdd over 1f out, not pace of wnr ins last: drifted from 7/4: Apr foal, cost 8,500 gns: half brother to a 5f juv wnr: dam 5/6f 2yo wnr: eff at 5f on gd: has shown enough to win a mdn.   **1** **77**

724   **FACTUAL LAD 16** [2] B R Millman 2-8-8 P Robinson 7/4 FAV: 23: 2 b c So Factual - Surprise Surprise (Robellino) Broke well & sn led, hdd halfway, no extra for press ins last: well bckd: another solid run, win similar.   **½** **73**

--   **GAME MAGIC** [14] R Hannon 2-9-0 P Dobbs (5) 100/30: 4: In tch, hdwy to chal 2f out, drvn & no extra appr fnl 1f: nicely bckd: 14,000 gns May foal, half brother to a juv 5f wnr: stays 5f on gd, shld improve.   **2** **74**

--   **DIAMOND MILLENNIUM** [15] 2-8-0 Joanna Badger (7) 33/1: 5: Mid-div, lost place over 2f out, kept on appr fnl 1f: cheaply bought Apr foal, dam a mdn: with P D Evans, 6f shld suit in time.   **2** **55**

--   **KALUKI** [7] 2-8-8 Martin Dwyer 33/1: 6: Handy, rdn & kept on at onepce fnl 2f: 6,500 gns First Trump foal, dam modest: 6f shld suit: with W R Muir.   **½** **62**

--   **DIAMOND MAX** [8] 2-8-8 J F Egan 33/1: 7: Dwelt, rdn to improve halfway, sn btn: Nicolotte Mar foal, half brother to 3 juv wnrs: shld learn from this, improve.   **2½** **56**

--   **INZACURE** [13] 2-8-8 G Hind 20/1: 8: Sn well bhd, late gains under hands & heels fnl 2f: Mar foal, dam a juv wnr: not given a hard time on debut today: with R M Beckett.   **shd** **56**

--   **LADY EBERSPACHER** [9] 2-8-6 S Whitworth 16/1: 9: Chsd ldrs, fdd fnl 2f: Royal Abjar half sister to sev wnrs, incl a 5f juv wnr: with Mrs P M Dutfield.   **1¼** **51**

--   **SOONA** [12] 2-8-8 W Ryan 9/1: 0: Mid-div at best, fin 10th: op 5/1: 12,000 gns Apr foal: dam 5f 3yo scorer: with A P Jarvis.   **1¼** **48**

--   **EASTER ISLAND** [3] 2-8-3 P Doe 33/1: 0: Very slow start, al outpcd, fin 11th: stoutly bred Turtle Island 1st foal: dam 9/11f scorer: imprve when sent over further.   **¾** **43**

--   **Naughty Knight** [4] 2-8-5 S Drowne 50/1:   --   **Sea Ray** [11] 2-8-5 A Daly 50/1:

--   **Benjamin** [1] 2-8-11 J Fortune 33/1:   --   **Quercus** [6] 2-8-8 A Clark 33/1:

15 ran   Time 1m 02.2 (3.4)   (Steve Evans)   J G Portman Compton, Berks

850 | 2.30 KENMARE MDN 3YO (D)   1m2f   Good   Inapplicable
£3055   £940   £470   £235

4348} **COVER UP 99** [2] Sir Michael Stoute 3-9-0 W R Swinburn 7/1: 32-1: 3 b g Machiavellian - Sought Out (Rainbow Quest) Trkd ldrs, rdn & switched wide over 1f out, styd on well to lead ins last, flashed tail for press, drvn out: op 4/1: plcd on both '99 starts (mdn & stks, rtd 88): eff at 1m/10f, 12f shld suit: acts on gd, poss handles hvy: runs well fresh on a sharp/turning trk: useful, can improve further.   **91**

4312} **SHAMAH 99** [15] R Hannon 3-8-9 R Hills 11/8 FAV: 22-2: 3 ch f Unfuwain - Shurooq (Affirmed) Veered right after start, sn chasing ldrs, hdwy to lead over 1f out, edged right dist, hdd well ins last: well bckd: rnr-up on both '99 starts (fill mdn, rtd 96): eff at 7f/10f on firm & gd/soft: gd reapp, mdn a formality.   **½** **85**

4605} **BUCKMINSTER 99** [13] J H M Gosden 3-9-0 L Dettori 9/4: 4-3: 3 br c Silver Hawk - Buckarina (Buckaroo) Slow start, rapid hdwy to lead after 2f, hdd over 1f out, kept on onepace under hands & heels ins last: nicely bckd: win on sole '99 start (7f mdn, hvy, rtd 83): stays 10f & acts on gd: should find a base.   **3** **85**

4333} **ARISTOCRAT 99** [4] R Hannon 3-9-0 R Hughes 8/1: 03-4: Led early, remained cl-up until chall ldrs 3f out, carried head high & no extra when slightly hmpd appr fnl 1f: well clr rem: rnr-up on 2nd of 2 '99 starts (mdn, rtd 79): eff at 7f, imprvd for step up to 10f: acts on gd & gd/soft: should improve.   **¾** **84**

46   **SKYE BLUE 99** [12] 3-9-0 S Drowne 20/1: 50-5: Mid-div, rdn & styd on stdly fnl 2f, no ch with ldrs: 5th sole '99 turf start (6f mdn, rtd 57): now h'capped & shld do better in that sphere.   **8** **72**

4613} **GUARD DUTY 99** [8] 3-9-0 A Daly 6/1: -33-6: Cl-up, lost place halfway, onepcd after: tchd 8/1 on reapp: plcd on both '99 starts (mdns, rtd 84): eff at 1m, mid-dists shld suit: acts on gd/soft & hvy grnd.   **½** **71**

4495} **FIRECREST 99** [1] 3-8-9 T Quinn 12/1: 00-7: Rear, switched wide & late hdwy under hands & heels, not given a hard time: op 8/1: well down the field in 2 mdns in '99 (7f/1m, rtd 58): stoutly bred & type to do much better over 12f+: now qual for h'caps & one to keep an eye on in that sphere.   **2½** **62+**

1391} **DIAMOND KISS 99** [7] 3-8-9 S Whitworth 33/1: 0-8: Waited on, outpcd 4f out, mod late gains: well btn sole '99 start (6f mdn, rtd 43): with Mrs P N Dutfield.   **2½** **58**

789   **SWINGING TRIO 11** [6] 3-9-0 L Carter 33/1: 0-09: Bhd, nvr a factor: up in trip.   **nk** **63**

--   **FIRST OFFICER** [3] 3-9-0 O Urbina 12/1: 0: Dwelt, held up, mod late hdwy, fin 10th: op 8/1: Lear Fan colt, dam a mid-dist scorer: learn from this & imprve: with J F Fanshawe.   **2** **60**

4333} **WOODBASTWICK CHARM 99** [11] 3-9-0 R Price 50/1: 0-0: Nvr a threat, fin 11th: t.o. sole '99 start.   **nk** **59**

4462} **SHARVIE 99** [16] 3-9-0 G Bardwell 33/1: 0-0: Hmpd start, keen & sn prom, wknd qckly fnl 3f: fin 12th.   **5** **52**

704   **WAVERLEY ROAD 18** [10] 3-9-0 W Ryan 14/1: 4-50: Al bhd, fin 13th: btr 704.   **1** **50**

3518} **Blues Whisperer 99** [9] 3-9-0 P Robinson 40/1:   773 **Annijaz 12** [5] 3-8-9 Martin Dwyer 16/1:

--	**Nautical Light** [14] 3-8-9 V Slattery 33/1:		

16 ran   Time 2m 06.3 (1.6)   (Lord Weinstock)   Sir Michael Stoute Newmarket

---

851   3.00 R REED CLASS STKS 3YO+ 0-90 (C)   1m67y rnd   Good   Inapplicable
£6386   £1965   £982   £491   3 yo rec 15lb

4512} **SECRET AGENT** 99 [5] Sir Michael Stoute 3-8-5 W Ryan 7/2 CO FAV: 12-1: 3 b c Machiavellian - Secret **97**
Obsession (Secretariat) Settled rear, gd hdwy 2f out, styd on to lead ins last, drvn out: '99 debut scorer at
Warwick (mdn, rtd 89), subs turned over at odds-on at Redcar (nov stks): half brother to wnrs up to 10f: eff at
7f/8.3f, further shld suit: acts on gd, soft & a sharp/turning trk: runs well fresh: useful, improve over further.

-- **WELSH WIND** [3] R Ingram 4-9-3 J F Egan 16/1: 3000-2: 4 b g Tenby - Bavaria (Top Ville) nk **93**
Waited with, rdn to improve halfway, styd on well to chall ins last, just failed: ex-Irish, reapp: '99 scorer at
Leopardstown (10f mdn, fast grnd, D Hanley), subs plaayin in soft grnd h'caps: eff at 1m/10f on fast & gd
grnd: clearly goes well fresh: useful, reapp for new stable, shld be plcd to effect.

4339} **FERZAO** 99 [4] Mrs A J Perrett 3-8-5 T Quinn 9/2: 01-3: 3 b c Alzao - Fe de Lance (Diesis) 1½ **93**
Pulled hard & sn led, drvn/hdd ins last, sn btn: nicely bckd: won 2nd of 2 '99 starts, at Leicester (mdn,
rtd 91): eff at 7/8.3f, further will suit: acts on gd, gd/soft & a sharp or stiff/gall track: useful reapp.

4488} **KUSTER** 99 [6] L M Cumani 4-9-3 L Dettori 7/2 CO FAV: /120-4: Cl-up, rdn to chall appr fnl 1f, ¾ **88**
wknd: nicely bckd: '99 debut scorer at Epsom (mdn, rdn 91 at best): eff at 1m/10f: acts on gd & gd/soft
grnd: runs well fresh: shld apprec a return to 10f.

4277} **FRONTIER** 99 [2] 3-8-5 Dane O'Neill 7/2 CO FAV: -421-5: Prom, rdn/no extra over 1f out: op 11/4: ½ **90**
consistent in '99, won at Lingfield (mdn, rtd 92): eff at 7f, stays 8.3f on firm, soft & any trk: useful reapp.

4204} **REGAL PHILOSOPHER** 99 [1] 4-9-3 R Hills 11/2: 0420-6: Held up, rdn to impr 2f out, no extra for ¾ **85**
press ins last: op 4/1: wnr of first 2 '99 starts, at Bath (med auct mdn) & Newcastle (h'cap, impressive, rtd 93),
subs not disgraced in smart h'cap company: eff over a gall 1m, stays 10f: acts on any grnd & runs well fresh.

4273} **NIGHT OF GLASS** 99 [7] 7-9-3 (vis) C Rutter 6/1: 0354-7: Keen, chsd ldrs to 2f out, sn btn: 1¾ **82**
op 5/1, reapp: '99 scorer at Beverley (rtd h'cap, rtd 94 at best, J L Eyre): subs well btn on hdles bow: prog
in '98, won at Catterick, Thirsk (2), Carlisle, Beverley & Musselburgh (h'caps, rtd 90): v eff at 7/8.5f on firm
& hvy, any trk: eff in blnks/visor: tough & v useful at best, sharper next time for new connections.

7 ran   Time 1m 43.9 (1.6)   (Cheveley Park Stud)   Sir Michael Stoute Newmarket.

---

852   3.30 TOTE EXACTA HCAP 3YO 0-80 (D)   6f str   Good   Inapplicable   [85]
£7410   £2280   £1140   £570

689 **CASTLE SEMPILL** 24 [5] R M H Cowell 3-9-2 (73) L Dettori 10/1: 121351: 3 b c Presidium - La Suquet **76**
(Puissance) In tch, rdn to impr over 2f out, led appr fnl 1f, strongly press ins last, all out to hold on: op 8/1:
earlier won at Lingfield & W'hampton (h'caps, rtd 78a): '99 scorer at Newmarket (seller, rtd 74, J Fanshawe) &
Lingfield (h'cap): eff at 5/7f on firm, soft & fibresand, loves equitrack/Lingfield: eff with/without a visor.2

785 **WATERGRASSHILL** 12 [6] N A Callaghan 3-7-12 (55) J Mackay (7) 12/1: 254-52: 3 b f Terimon - shd **57**
Party Game (Red Alert) Dwelt, well bhd till styd on well for press 2f out, chall ldr ins last, drvn out, just
failed: tchd 16/1: gd run, eff at 6/7f on gd & equitrack: shld win a race: see 158, 105.

4494} **LAKELAND PADDY** 99 [3] M Blanshard 3-9-2 (73) D Sweeney 25/1: 4256-3: 3 b c Lake Coniston - 1½ **71**
Inshad (Indian King) Rcd wide cl-up, rdn & styd on appr fnl 1f, nrst fin: reapp: rnr-up in '99 (mdn, rtd 81 at
best): eff at 5/6f: handles firm & gd, poss not hvy: gd reapp, spot on next time.

785 **LUSONG** 12 [4] R Hannon 3-8-5 (62) Dane O'Neill 16/1: -22634: Wide in tch, rdn to impr 2f out, nk **59**
styd on, nvr nrr: consistent: see 785.

727 **SARENA PRIDE** 16 [12] 3-9-5 (76) P Doe 20/1: 120-05: Mid-div till styd on well for press over 1f out, nk **73**
nvr nrr: clr reen: drop in trip: see 727 (9f stks).

763 **CD FLYER** 13 [19] 3-9-6 (77) T Quinn 10/1: 105-06: Held up, drvn & styd on fnl 2f, no threat: '99 3 **67**
scorer at Thirsk (nov stks, rtd 83) & Newmarket (h'cap): eff at 6f, 7f suit: acts on fast, likes gd/soft & any trk.

4431} **ALAWAR** 99 [21] 3-9-1 (72)(t) R Hughes 16/1: -030-7: Bhd, hdwy & switched wide over 2f out, 1 **59**
short of room & switched again dist, kept on but no threat to ldrs: h'cap bow: plcd on 2nd of 2 '99 starts
(mdn, rtd 76): eff at 6f on firm: no luck in running here, keep in mind for similar.

4462} **JACK DAWSON** 99 [14] 3-8-7 (64) G Hall 33/1: 000-8: Sn well bhd till switched wide & hdwy over 1½ **47**
2f out, no extra ins last: unplcd in 3 '99 starts for J Noseda (7f/1m, rtd 75): now with John Berry.

736 **LOVES DESIGN** 16 [17] 3-9-4 (75)(vis) W R Swinburn 7/2 FAV: 631-39: Led, hdd over 1f out, nk **--**
wknd qckly: hvly bckd: better expected after a gd reapp in 736 (7f).

*813 **BLACKPOOL MAMMAS** 7 [11] 3-8-11 (68)(6ex) R Ffrench 16/1: 24-010: Cl-up, drvn/fdd ins last, ¾ **49**
fin 10th: qck reapp: 6lb pen for scoring on soft grnd in 813 (class stks, 7f).

4106} **SWING CITY** 99 [7] 3-8-5 (62) N Pollard 25/1: -400-0: Bhd, nvr a threat, fin 11th: h'cap bow: shd **43**
4th of three of 3 '99 starts (auct mdn, rtd 70): half-sister to wnrs at 1m/10f: eff at 6f on gd.

804 **FIRST VENTURE** 10 [15] 3-9-2 (73)(bl) R Morse 10/1: 5-2230: Trkd ldrs, lost tch over 1f out, fin 12th. ½ **53**

736 **MARSHALL ST CYR** 16 [10] 3-8-13 (70) J F Egan 33/1: 025-00: Handy, rdn/btn fnl 2f, fin 13th. 1 **47**

736 **KINSMAN** 16 [1] 3-8-10 (67)(bl) J Fortune 16/1: 15-300: Wide in mid-div, drvn/btn 2f out, fin 14th. 1¾ **40**

4367} **PERFECT MOMENT** 99 [20] 3-8-0 (57) Martin Dwyer 20/1: 1000-0: Al bhd, fin 15th: new stable. 2 **25**

2712} **BAJAN BELLE** 99 [13] 3-9-7 (78) R Hills 14/1: -31-0: Dwelt, al rear: 16th: top-weight, h'cap bow. shd **46**

*651 **AIR MAIL** 33 [9] 3-9-6 (77) J Tate 14/1: 210: Cl-up, wknd qckly fnl 2f: 17th: btr 651 (7f, equitrack). 1¾ **41**

3985} **DANZIGEUSE** 99 [18] 3-8-7 (64) S Drowne 10/1: -500-0: Well plcd, fdd fnl 2f, fin 18th: h'cap bow. 1 **25**

72 **Great White** 99 [2] 3-8-9 (66) L Newman 25/1:

4612} **Lady Noor** 16 [16] 3-8-13 (70) Kathleen McDermott (7) 25/1:

729 **On The Trail** 16 [8] 3-8-4 (60)(1ow) A Clark 33/1:

21 ran   Time 1m 13.9 (3.6)   (Mrs J M Penney)   R M H Cowell Six Mile Bottom, Cambs.

---

853   4.00 FILLIES HCAP 3YO+ 0-80 (D)   1m3f135y   Good   Inapplicable   [77]
£3926   £1208   £604   £302   3 yo rec 21lb4 yo rec 1 lb

*710 **SURE QUEST** 18 [5] D W P Arbuthnot 5-8-0 (49) Martin Dwyer 11/2: -23411: 5 b m Sure Blade - Eagle's **52**
Quest (Legal Eagle) Waited with, gd hdwy over 3f out, hdwy to lead dist, drvn out: op 4/1: recent wnr on the AW
at W'hampton (seller, rtd 50a): unplcd in '99 (h'cap, rtd 55), prev term scored at Folkestone (mdn h'cap, rtd 61):
eff at 10/12f on gd, firm & fibresand, loves equitrack/Lingfield: has tried visor, best without: in fine form.

4551} **ROYAL PATRON** 99 [8] J L Dunlop 4-9-6 (70) T Quinn 7/2 JT FAV: 5562-2: 4 ch f Royal Academy - 1 **71**
Indian Queen (Electric) Trkd ldrs, rdn to chall over 1f out, no extra ins last: '99 scorer at Lingfield (mdn, rtd 74):
eff at 11f/2m on gd & gd/soft: gd reapp over an inadequate trip: shld win again when returning to further.

747   **AEGEAN DREAM 14** [4] R Hannon 4-10-0 (78) R Hughes 7/2 JT FAV: 105-23: 4 b f Royal Academy -   nk   79
L'Ideale (Alysheba) Settled rear, gd hdwy & switched over 2f out, chall over 1f out, drvn & btn ins last: nicely
bckd, top-weight: remains in gd heart, eff at 1m/11.6f: see 747.

4090} **STREET WALKER 99** [6] S Mellor 4-8-4 (54) A Clark 20/1: 4253-4: Rear, short of room 3f out, styd   3   50
on strongly for press fnl 2f, nvr nrr: op 14/1: recently unplcd over hdles (2m mdn, rtd 61h, tried blnks):
rnr-up twice in '99 (stks & clmr, rtd 59 at best): eff at 1m/11.6f on gd: shade unlucky, win a sell h'cap.

4546} **SIFAT 99** [7] 5-8-6 (55) (vis) S Whitworth 14/1: 5040-5: Keen clp-up, led over 3f out, wknd/hdd ins   nk   51
last: 8 wk jumps abs, plcd in late '99 (2m nov, gd/soft, rtd 97h): unplcd in '99 for N A Graham (h'caps, rtd 63,
blnkd): '98 Pontefract wnr (mdn, M Tregoning, rtd 74, visor): eff over 1m, styd 10f on fast & soft: with J Jenkins.

4520} **I TINA 99** [11] 4-9-5 (69) A Daly 9/1: 2364-6: Keen & chsd ldrs, rdn/ wknd fnl 2f: rnr-up on   5   58
'99 debut (mdn, rtd 72): eff at 11.6f: handles firm & gd/soft grnd.

4148} **RUBY LASER 99** [3] 4-7-11 (47) G Bardwell 20/1: 0403-7: Trkd ldrs, outpcd halfway, drvn/wknd fnl 3f: 1¼   34
plcd final '99 start for R Johnson Houghton (h'cap, rtd 68 at best): prob stays 12/14f on fast & soft: with E James.

4546} **JOLI SADDLERS 99** [9] 4-8-2 (52) C Rutter 25/1: 5600-8: Handy, btn fnl 2f: unplcd in '99 (rtd 74).   ½   38

748   **DIZZY TILLY 14** [1] 6-7-11 (46) (1ow) (2oh) A McCarthy (0) 7/1: 230-09: Led, hdd halfway, lost tch fnl 3f.   2½   28

3931} **SILVER QUEEN 99** [2] 3-8-5 (75) P Robinson 12/1: 5440-0: Cl-up, eff 3f out, wknd qckly: 10th.   11   45

4598} **DEAR PRUDENCE 99** [10] 4-7-12 (48) (2ow) (5oh) N Carlisle 20/1: -000-0: V keen, hdwy to lead   5   11
over 5f out, hdd over 3f out & qckly lost tch: fin 11th.

11 ran   Time 2m 27.9 (2.1)   (Miss P E Decker)   D W P Arbuthnot Upper Lambourn, Berks.

---

854   **4.30 BALTIMORE HCAP 3YO+ 0-75 (E)**   **1m67y rnd   Good   Inapplicable**   **[72]**
        £3237   £925   £462   3 yo rec 15lb

4522} **POLISH SPIRIT 99** [14] B R Millman 5-9-1 (59) T Quinn 9/2: 0003-1: 5 b g Emarati - Gentle Star   68
(Comedy Star) Trkd ldrs, hdwy to chall over 2f out, led appr fnl 1f, styd on strongly & rdn clr ins last, readily:
nicely bckd, crse rec time: '99 wnr here at Windsor (h'cap, rtd 63): '98 wnr at Warwick (mdn, rtd 65): eff around
1m: acts on fast, gd/soft, poss soft: likes a sharp trk, esp Windsor: runs v well fresh & loves to come late.

1914} **LEGAL SET 99** [17] K R Burke 4-9-10 (68) Darren Williams (7) 14/1: 0300-2: 4 gr c Second Set -   2½   70
Tiffany's Case (Thatching) Keen, waited with, smooth hdwy 3f out, rdn to chall over 1f out, no extra ins last:
reapp/new stable: top-weight: plcd once in '99 (h'cap bow, rtd 70, C A Horgan): eff at 1m, 10f shld suit:
handles firm & gd grnd: gd reapp, spot on next time for new connections.

--   **RED CAFE** [16] P D Evans 4-8-8 (52) J F Egan 8/1: 4003/3: 4 ch f Perugino - Test Case (Busted)   1½   51
Handy, rdn to impr 2f out, kept on but not pace of ldrs appr fnl 1f: op 14/1 after 2 yr abs: missed '99, plcd on
fnl '98 start (seller, rtd 63 at best): eff at 6f/1m: handles fast & gd/soft grnd: good reapp.

707   **BREAD WINNER 18** [15] I A Balding 4-8-12 (56) (vis) R Hughes 7/2 FAV: 422234: Prom, rdn/hdwy   2   52
over 2f out, no extra ins last: well bckd: turf reapp, consistent from on the AW prev: see 707, 568.

4313} **PATSY STONE 99** [4] 4-9-3 (61) L Dettori 9/1: 0100-5: Settled rear, improving when hmpd/lost   hd   57
grnd over 2f out, styd on well, nvr nrr: op 6/1, reapp: '99 scorer at Yarmouth (mdn h'cap, rtd 64, W J Musson):
plcd 4 times in '98 for current connectons (rtd 64 at best): eff at 6f/1m on firm & soft: gd reapp.

793   **POLRUAN 11** [13] 4-9-0 (58) S Drowne 12/1: 004-56: Set fast pace & sn clr, wknd/hdd over 1f out.   ½   53

516   **NAFITH 55** [9] 4-8-13 (57) S Whitworth 12/1: -32137: Rdn/rear, drvn & hdwy over 2f out, no   2½   48
(threat to ldrs: 8 wk abs: see 446 (9.4f, fibresand, mdn).

3441} **THE SHADOW 99** [10] 4-9-2 (60) R Price 14/1: 0615-8: Bhd, nvr a dngr: '99 wnr at W'hampton   3½   45
h'cap, rtd 67a, rtd 65 on turf): rtd 72 when unplcd in '98: eff at 9.3f on gd/soft, fibresand & a sharp track.

3939} **MANXWOOD 99** [8] 3-8-5 (64) C Rutter 33/1: 0460-9: Settled bhd, brief hdwy 3f out, sn btn: 1½   46
unplcd in mdns in '99 (rtd 67 at 68a).

4152} **LOUGH SWILLY 99** [5] 4-9-2 (60) Martin Dwyer 20/1: 0000-0: Slow start, bhd till hdwy over 2f out,   nk   42
wknd appr fnl 1f, fin 10th: unplcd for B W Hills in '99 (h'caps, rtd 83 at best): useful in '98, won at Nottingham
(nov auct) & Goodwood (auct stks, rtd 99): eff at 6/7f, 1m shld suit: acts on fast grnd & any trk: with V Soane.

2176} **HIGHLY PLEASED 99** [12] 5-9-2 (60) D R McCabe 25/1: 0006-0: Waited with, prog when short of   hd   42
room over 2f out, sn btn: 11th.

1971} **CABARET QUEST 99** [18] 4-9-4 (62) W Jones (7) 14/1: 0136-0: Held up, nvr a threat: 12th: new stable.   1½   41

3544} **ARZILLO 99** [11] 4-8-11 (55) J Fortune 14/1: 0030-0: Chsd ldr, drvn/wknd ovr 2f out, 13th: new stable.   1   32

3833} **EIGHT 99** [6] 4-9-10 (68) Dane O'Neill 25/1: 3300-0: Handy, lost tch fnl 3f, fin 14th.   2   42

308   **MALAKAL 90** [13] 4-9-7 (65) J P Spencer 8/1: 200-00: Cl-up, fdd appr fnl 3f: 15th: see 56.   2½   35

4152} **Goodenough Mover 99** [2] 4-8-6 (50) N Pollard 33/1: 632   **Consort 37** [1] 7-9-7 (65) T G McLaughlin 20/1:

803   **Night Adventure 10** [3] 4-8-7 (51) R Ffrench 33/1:

18 ran   Time 1m 41.3 (u1.0) Course Record Time   (Mrs Izabel Palmer)   B R Millman Kentisbeare, Devon.

Official Going   Turf Crse - GOOD/SOFT;   AW - STANDARD.

855   **1.45 LIVINGSTONE APPR HCAP 4YO+ 0-70 (G)**   **1m3f   Good/Soft   Inapplicable**   **[68]**
        £1883   £538   £269

671   **BACHELORS PAD 27** [13] Miss S J Wilton 6-9-0 (54) I Mongan (3) 13/2: 112141: 6 b g Pursuit Of Love -   60
Note Book (Mummy's Pet) Chsd ldrs, prog to lead dist, styd on well, drvn out: op 11/2: earlier won at W'hampton
(3, 2 clmrs (1 for D Nicholls) & sell, rtd 65a): rnr-up twice in '99 (rtd 63, h'cap): plcd in '98 (rtd 76, stks,
W Jarvis): eff at 7/11f on firm, gd/soft & f/sand: likes a sharp trk, handles any: loves sell/claim grade.

*196   **PLURALIST 99** [10] W Jarvis 4-10-0 (68) D McGaffin (3) 6/1: 5621-2: 4 b c Mujadil - Encore Une   1½   71
Fois (Shirley Heights) Chsd ldrs, prog to lead halfway, rdn/hdd over 1f out, kept on for press: 4 month abs: acts
on firm, gd/soft & fibresand: gd return to h'caps: see 196 (AW auct mdn).

742   **MICE IDEAS 14** [9] N P Littmoden 4-8-6 (46) C Cogan 4/1 FAV: 605123: 4 ch g Fayruz - Tender   3½   44
Encounter (Prince Sabo) Mid-div, prog to briefly lead halfway, onepace fnl 2f: acts on fast, gd/soft & f/sand.

561   **GENUINE JOHN 49** [5] J Parkes 7-8-0 (40) Jonjo Fowle (3) 10/1: 63-324: Towards rear, late gains   3   34
fnl 2f, no threat: 6 wk jumps abs (unplcd, rtd 62h): see 215, 131.

3837} **TUI 99** [7] 5-7-10 (36) (3oh) Claire Bryan (3) 16/1: 6000-5: Chsd ldrs, onepace/held fnl 3: op 10/1,   3   26
jumps fit (no recent form): unplcd on the level in '99 (rtd 38), '99 wnr over hdles at Sedgefield & Worcester (rtd
97h): '98 h'cap wnr at Beverley & Newmarket (rtd 55 at best): eff at 10/12f on fast & gd/soft & a stiff trk.

779   **ONCE MORE FOR LUCK 12** [1] 9-9-13 (67) T Eaves (5) 7/1: 304-06: Rear, kept on fnl 3f, nrst fin.   1¼   55

710 **COLONEL CUSTER 18** [2] 5-8-2 (42) R Cody Boutcher (2) 16/1: 310057: Rear, rdn/mod gains wide fnl 3f. *2* **27**
428 **PALAIS 70** [6] 5-7-10 (36)(vis) P M Quinn 25/1: 00-008: Rear, eff 3f out, no impress: jmps fit, vis reapp. *½* **20**
4459} **FANDANGO DREAM 99** [8] 4-8-3 (43) G Baker (5) 25/1: 0000-9: Mid-div, rdn/held fnl 3f: 6 month abs: unplcd in '99 (rtd 76, flattered, mdn), subs disapp in blnks/visor. *½* **26**
489 **STEAMROLLER STANLY 60** [12] 7-9-3 (57)(bl) R Studholme 16/1: 524600: Chsd ldr, rdn/outpcd fnl 5f: 10th, 2 month abs: jockey given a 2-day careless riding ban: blnks reapplied: see 380, 151. *1* **39**
822 **IRSAL 5** [16] 6-7-10 (36)(bl)(6oh) Kimberley Hart 25/1: 302000: Led till 6f out, sn fdd: 13th: qck reapp. **0**
784 **PORT OF CALL 12** [4] 5-8-10 (50) S Finnamore (3) 9/1: 5600: Rear, rdn/brief eff wide 3f out, sn btn: 16th. **0**
795 **Dancing Lawyer 11** [11] 9-7-10 (36) K Dalgleish (5) 20/1: 3137} **La Cinecitta 99** [3] 4-7-13 (39) D Mernagh 33/1:
648 **Champagne Gb 35** [14] 4-9-8 (62) A Beech (3) 16/1: -- **Da Boss** [15] 5-9-6 (60) R Brisland 16/1:
16 ran Time 2m 28.20 (John Pointon & Sons) Miss S J Wilton Wetley Rocks, Staffs.

856

2.15 VASCO DA GAMA SELLER 2YO (G) 5f aw Standard Inapplicable
£1831 £523 £261 Raced centre - stands side.

801 **COUNTESS BANKES 10** [3] W G M Turner 2-8-6 G Duffield 2/1 JT FAV: 41: 2 b f Son Pardo - Lowrianna (Cyrano de Bergerac) Chsd ldrs, rdn fnl 2f, styd on well ins last to lead nr fin, rdn out: no bid, op 5/2: eff at 5f, 6f+ will suit in time: acts on fibresand & a sharp trk: apprec drop to sell grade. **61a**
-- **SAND BANKES** [7] W G M Turner 2-8-11 S Finnamore (5) 10/1: 2: 2 ch c Efisio - Isabella Sharp (Sharpo) Sn rdn in tch, kept on well under hands-&-heels riding ins last, just held: longer priced stablemate of wnr: 5,000gns Jan foal: dam a 5f juv wnr, related to high-class mid-dist performer Saumarez: sire a tough 6f/1m performer: eff at 5f, shld stay further: acts on fibresand: can win in this grade. *nk* **65a**
-- **COZZIE** [1] J G Given 2-8-6 V Halliday 9/1: 3: 2 ch f Cosmonaut - Royal Deed (Shadee) Prom centre, ev ch fnl 1f, kept on, just held: op 6/1: Feb foal, 1,000gns purchase: dam a minor 2yo wnr: eff at 5f on fibresand, runs well fresh: sharper next time. *nk* **59a**
-- **ROYLE FAMILY** [5] A Berry 2-8-11 P Bradley (5) 5/1: 4: Led after 1f, rdn/hung left 2f out & hdd, no extra when sltly hmpd ins last: op 3/1: Mar first foal: dam a mdn, sire often produces sprinters. *1* **62a**
-- **BOBANVI** [4] 2-8-6 K Darley 20/1: 5: Handy, rdn halfway, no extra/sltly hmpd over 1f out: Timeless Times filly, Mar foal, cost 5,000gns: half-sister to a 9f juv Irish wnr: dam juv wnr at 6f/m: with J S Wainwright. *2½* **50a**
722 **ELEANOR J 16** [6] 2-8-6 Dean McKeown 10/1: 46: Led 1f, no extra over 1f out: op 8/1: see 722. *½* **48a**
-- **LASTOFTHEWHALLEYS** [2] 2-8-6 F Lynch 20/1: 7: Went left from start, al outpcd: op 14/1: Noble Patriarch filly, Apr foal, cost only 600gns: dam plcd as a juv, sire a smart performer at up to 10f: shld apprec further. *5* **39a**
712 **REGAL MISTRESS 17** [9] 2-8-6 T Williams 20/1: 58: Chsd ldrs 4f: op 14/1: AW bow: see 712. *¾* **37a**
836 **MOLLY IRWIN 3** [8] 2-8-11 Pat Eddery 2/1 JT FAV: 3129: Cl-up, rdn/btn 2f out: bckd, op 5/2: qck reapp: trainer reported filly unsuited by surface tho' handled it well in 722 (W'hampton). *3½* **33a**
9 ran Time 1m 2.60 (4.8) (T Lightbowne) W G M Turner Corton Denham, Somerset.

857

2.45 MARCO POLO HCAP 3YO 0-80 (D) 7f rnd Good/Soft Inapplicable [85]
£4121 £1268 £634 £317

3567} **CELEBRATION TOWN 99** [15] D Morris 3-8-10 (67) R Cochrane 20/1: 505-1: 3 b g Case Law - Battle Queen (Kind Of Hush) Keen in rear, prog to lead ins last, styd on well, drvn out: reapp: unplcd in '99 for J J O'Neill (rtd 73, debut): apprec step up to 7f, 1m+ shld suit: acts on gd/soft & a sharp trk: runs well fresh. **73**
761 **SAHARA SPIRIT 13** [2] E A L Dunlop 3-9-5 (76) G Carter 6/4 FAV: 340-22: 3 b g College Chapel - Desert Palace (Green Desert) Handy, rdn/led over 1f out, hdd ins last, not pace of wnr: well bckd, tchd 11/4. *1¼* **78**
810 **HEATHYARDS LAD 9** [11] R Hollinshead 3-8-5 (62) P M Quinn (5) 14/1: -54063: 3 b c Petardia - Maiden's Dance (Hotfoot) Chsd ldrs, no room 2f out, switched & styd on well fnl 1f: relish a return to 1m+. *¾* **63**
744 **GROESFAEN LAD 14** [12] B Palling 3-9-1 (72) G Faulkner (3) 25/1: 000-04: Led, rdn/hdd over 1f out, no extra: op 16/1: rnr-up thrice in '99 (rtd 83): eff at 5/7f on firm & gd/soft: best without blnks. *1¾* **70**
4140} **PINHEIROS DREAM 99** [1] 3-9-1 (72) Pat Eddery 7/1: 0300-5: Chsd ldrs, kept on fnl 2f, not pace to chall: 7 mth abs: unplcd in '99 (rtd 81, flattered): eff arnd 7f, 1m+ could suit: prob handles firm & gd/soft. *shd* **70**
709 **CELEBES 18** [16] 3-9-3 (74) F Lynch 14/1: 64-346: Trkd ldr, no extra over 1f out: op 12/1: see 591 (mdn). *2* **68**
717 **MANA DARGENT 17** [6] 3-9-7 (78) D Holland 3/1: 633-27: Towards rear, rdn/late gains fnl 2f, no threat: nicely bckd, tchd 4/1: needs 1m+ & similar company on this evidence: see 717. *nk* **71**
709 **NOBLE PASAO 18** [3] 3-8-13 (70) C Lowther 14/1: 0-2608: Chsd ldrs, fdd over 1f out: tchd 16/1. *1¼* **60**
792 **THE PROSECUTOR 11** [7] 3-8-11 (68) K Darley 8/1: 1-6159: Mid-div, no impress fnl 2f: see 689 (AW, 6f). *1¼* **55**
624 **SOBA JONES 39** [4] 3-7-12 (55) P Fessey 11/1: 3-660: Mid-div, held fnl 2f: 10th: op 10/1, h'cap bow. *2* **38**
794 **Ocean Song 11** [10] 3-8-12 (69) G Duffield 14/1: 4493} **Moose Malloy 99** [13] 3-7-10 (53) M Baird 16/1:
785 **Fantasy Adventurer 12** [14] 3-8-8 (65) A Culhane 33/1:
741 **Priceless Second 14** [5] 3-7-13 (56)(vis) B Sooful (7) 20/1:
4480} **Marvel 99** [8] 3-8-13 (70) Kim Tinkler 20/1: 4257} **Dorothea Sharp 99** [9] 3-7-11 (53)(1ow) Dale Gibson 20/1:
16 ran Time 1m 29.90 (Meadowcrest Ltd) D Morris Newmarket.

858

3.15 COOK MED AUCT MDN 3YO (F) 1m2f Good/Soft Inapplicable
£2404 £687 £343

4380} **KINGS MILL 99** [7] N A Graham 3-9-0 D Holland 13/2: 0223-1: 3 b c Doyoun - Adarika (King's Lake) Keen, mid-div, prog fnl 3f & led ins last, styd on well, rdn out: op 9/2, 6 month abs: plcd fnl 3 starts in '99 (h'cap, rtd 83): eff at 1m, well suited by this step up to 10f, could get further: acts on gd & soft grnd: handles a sharp or stiff/gall track: runs well fresh: open to further improvement. **94**
4561} **MOSELLE 99** [1] W J Haggas 3-8-9 M Hills 2/1: 3-2: 3 b f Mtoto - Miquette (Fabulous Dancer) Chsd ldrs, prog/rdn to briefly lead 2f out, hdd/not pace of wnr ins last: nicely bckd: promise sole '99 start (plcd, rtd 93, List): styd longer 10f trip, 12f+ cld suit: acts on gd/soft & soft grnd, handles a stiff/sharp trk. *1¼* **86**
4495} **MACHRIE BAY 99** [3] J L Dunlop 3-9-0 Pat Eddery 6/5 FAV: 003-3: 3 b c Emarati - Fleeting Rainbow (Rainbow Quest) Chsd ldr, rdn to chall fnl 2f, not much room when onepace ins last: well clr rem: hvly bckd: plcd fnl '99 start (rtd 90, mdn): styd longer 10f trip: acts on gd/soft & soft, sharp/gall trk: h'caps shld suit. *3* **87**
694 **PRINCE OMID 21** [5] J R Fanshawe 3-9-0 R Cochrane 9/1: 05-34: Led, rdn fnl 3f & hdd 2f out, fdd: change of tactics over this longer 10f trip, eye-catching in 694: h'cap company will suit best. *9* **77$**
4119} **MISTER WEBB 99** [8] 3-9-0 J Stack 20/1: 64-5: Held up, prog wide/chsd ldrs halfway, rdn/btn 3f out: op 14/1, 7 month abs: unplcd both '99 starts (rtd 67, auct mdn): mid-dists/h'cap company shld suit. *9* **67**
4524} **BOLD BAHAMIAN 99** [2] 3-9-0 K Darley 11/1: 540-6: Dwelt, rear, rdn/mod gains fnl 4f: op 6/1: 5 month abs: unplcd in '99 (rtd 75, mdn): this longer 10f trip may suit in h'cap company. *1¾* **65**
752 **HORTON DANCER 13** [11] 3-9-0 D Mernagh (3) 66/1: 4-67: Mid-div, no impress over 3f out: see 752. *4* **59**

640 **INDIANA SPRINGS** 37 [10] 3-9-0 (vis) M Fenton 66/1: -00548: Twds rear, strugg halfway: mod form. 1½ 57$
395 **ALBERGO** 76 [12] 3-9-0 Dale Gibson 66/1: 00-59: Prom 5f, sn struggling: 11 wk abs: see 395. 5 50
713 **NICIARA** 17 [9] 3-9-0 P Goode 66/1: 460500: Al bhd: 10th: btr 451 (AW h'cap, 1m, blnks). 4 44
784 **All Bleevable** 12 [4] 3-9-0 G Duffield 100/1: -- **Shuffle** [6] 3-9-0 R Fitzpatrick (3) 40/1:
12 ran   Time 2m 12.90   (First Millennium Racing)   N A Graham Newmarket.

---

859 3.45 WALTER FILLIES HCAP 3YO+ 0-65 (F) 1m2f Good/Soft Inapplicable [64]
£2415 £690 £345 3 yo rec 19lb

637 **RIVER ENSIGN** 37 [3] W M Brisbourne 7-8-10 (46) P M Quinn (5) 12/1: 041601: 7 br m River God - 51
Ensigns Kit (Saucy Kit) Chsd ldr halfway, rdn/led 1f out, held on well ins last, rdn out: op 10/1: earlier scored
at W'hampton (2, clmr & fill h'cap, rtd 51a): '98 W'hampton wnr (clmr, rtd 53a) & Chepstow wnr (h'cap, rtd 47): eff
at 5/7f, now suited by 1m/10f on gd, hvy & fibresand: likes a sharp trk: runs well fresh & likes to force the pace.
3940} **CASSANDRA** 99 [2] M Brittain 4-9-0 (50) K Darley 14/1: 0500-2: 4 b f Catrail - Circo (High Top) ½ 53
Mid-div, rdn/prog to chall fnl 3f, kept on well: op 10/1, 7 mth abs: unplcd '99 (rtd 66, mdn): eff at 10f on gd/sft.
692 **TEMPRAMENTAL** 21 [13] S R Bowring 4-8-9 (45) Dale Gibson 13/2: 0-2253: 4 ch f Midhish - Musical Horn ¾ 47
(Music Boy) Led, rdn fnl 2f & hdd 1f out, no extra cl-home: op 8/1: eff around 10/12f on firm, gd/soft & both AWs.
672 **SWING ALONG** 27 [1] R Guest 5-9-9 (59) R Cochrane 7/2: 053334: Rear, prog fnl 3f, onepace ins last. ¾ 60
795 **RIBBLE PRINCESS** 11 [10] F Lynch 5/1: 000035: Rear, eff 3f out, held 1f out: see 795 (9f). 3 37
67 **CASHIKI** 99 [5] 4-8-10 (46) G Duffield 25/1: 0000-6: Chsd ldrs, rdn/forced wide over 2f out, sn held: 1½ 41
5 mth abs: plcd twice in '99 (rtd 66, h'cap): '98 wnr at Lingfield (seller), Chepstow (clmr) & Pontefract (nurs, rtd
73): winning form at 6f, stays 10f well: acts on firm & gd/soft, prob any trk: looks nicely h'capped.
692 **WATER LOUP** 21 [12] 4-8-10 (46) R Brisland (5) 9/1: 000-67: Rear, mod gains: op 7/1: see 692. 5 34
390 **DENS JOY** 77 [6] 4-9-9 (59) D Hayes (7) 20/1: 35-308: Chsd ldrs halfway, rdn/btn over 2f out: 11 wk shd 47
abs: prev wth H Collinridge, now wth Miss D A McHale: see 301 (12f, mdn).
791 **SMART SPIRIT** 11 [8] 6-8-8 (44) A Culhane 3/1 FAV: 440-59: Chsd ldrs halfway, btn 2f out: op 9/4. ¾ 31
676 **BRIDAL WHITE** 25 [14] 4-8-4 (40) G Carter 20/1: 000-00: Al rear: 10th: see 676 (1m). 5 20
969} **First Legacy** 99 [11] 4-8-4 (40) D Mernagh (3) 33/1: 707 **Elba Magic** 18 [7] 5-9-10 (60)(VIS) R Fitzpatrick (3) 12/1:
930} **Eclectic** 99 [9] 4-8-6 (42) M Fenton 25/1: 748 **Sewards Folly** 14 [4] 4-8-13 (49) Claire Bryan (5) 14/1:
14 ran   Time 2m 14.70   (Crispandave Racing Associates)   W M Brisbourne Great Ness, Shropshire.

---

860 4.15 COLUMBUS HCAP 4YO+ 0-65 (F) 2m Good/Soft Inapplicbale [60]
£2446 £699 £349 4 yo rec 4 lb

4458} **LE KHOUMF** 99 [6] J Neville 9-9-4 (50) Dean McKeown 25/1: 50/5-1: 9 ch g Son Of Silver - Bentry (Ben 57
Trovato) Rear, prog & no room 4f out, switched & prog to lead 1f out, styd on strongly, rdn clr nr fin: 5 month
jumps abs (rnr-up, h'cap, rtd 115h): unplcd sole '99 start (rtd 44, h'cap): back in 96/97 won at Taunton over
timber (h'cap, rtd 124h): eff at 2m/2m2f on fast & gd/soft grnd, handles hvy, any trk: runs well fresh, looks
a thorough stayer & gall trk/further could suit, can win more races.
*788 **DOUBLE RUSH** 12 [7] T Keddy 8-8-10 (42)(t) G Carter 9/1: 60-612: 8 b g Doulab - Stanza Dancer 3 44
(Stanford) Held up in tch, prog fnl 4f & rdn to chall over 1f out, no pace of wnr ins last: op 7/1: eff at 12f/2m.
788 **VERSATILITY** 12 [12] Dr J R J Naylor 7-9-1 (47) M Hills 11/1: 160-53: 7 b m Teenoso - Gay Criselle 1½ 48
(Decoy Boy) Chsd ldr, led 7f out, rdn/hdd 1f out, no extra: clr rem: eff at 14f/2m on gd/sft & soft: bhd rnr-up in 788.
737 **IMAD** 14 [2] K C Comerford 10-9-0 (46)(t) M Fenton 12/1: /01-34: Held up, chsd ldrs 3f out, onepace. 5 42
737 **LADY RACHEL** 14 [13] 5-8-13 (45)(bl) G Parkin 15/2: 0-3025: Chsd ldrs, no extra fnl 2f: see 737, 318. ¾ 40
714 **OLD HUSH WING** 17 [10] 7-9-8 (54) A Culhane 9/2: 110-56: Chsd ldrs, onepace fnl 2f: op 11/2. shd 49
3970} **CINDESTI** 99 [8] 4-9-6 (56) K Darley 3/1 FAV: 0011-7: Mid-div, eff 3f out, no impress: bckd, op 4/1: 1 50
jumps fit, Feb '00 Doncaster wnr (juv nov, rtd 119h): '99 winr at W'hampton (2, h'cap & class stks, rtd 67a & 71):
mod form in '98 for L Cumani: eff at 12f, stays 14.7f: likes fibresand/W'hampton.
535 **GRAND CRU** 52 [14] 9-8-5 (37)(BL) R Brisland (5) 20/1: 423008: Rear, eff 3f out, sn held: blnks, abs. nk 30
699 **TOTEM DANCER** 18 [16] 7-9-11 (57) D Holland 20/1: 0-0009: Mid-div, chsd ldrs 3f out, sn held. 1½ 49
682 **MANFUL** 24 [1] 8-9-3 (49)(bl) F Norton 20/1: -10030: Rear, eff 5f out, no impress: 10th: btr 620 (12f). 4 37
788 **I CANT REMEMBER** 12 [11] 6-9-11 (57) G Duffield 10/1: 524540: Prom 11f: 12th: op 8/1: see 428. 0
788 **PRASLIN ISLAND** 12 [3] 4-9-5 (55)(bl) J Fanning 5/1: 1-2300: Led 9f, sn btn: 13th: blnks reapp. 0
760 **Highfield Fizz** 13 [4] 8-8-11 (43) R Cochrane 20/1: -- **Aztec Flyer** [9] 7-9-4 (50) T Eaves (7) 20/1:
410 **Miraggio** 74 [5] 4-8-6 (42) Dale Gibson 33/1: -- **Count Tony** [15] 6-10-0 (60) Claire Bryan (5) 25/1:
16 ran   Time 3m 41.90   (George Moore)   J Neville Coedkernew, Monmouthshire.

Official Going HEAVY.

---

861 2.30 GR 3 PRIX EDMOND BLANC 4YO+ 1m Holding
£21134 £7685 £3842

3795} **DANSILI** 99 [1] A Fabre 4-9-2 O Peslier 6/10 FAV: 4133-1: 4 b c Danehill - Hasili (Kahyasi) 120
Chsd ldr, hdwy to lead 1f out, pushed clr: in '99 won at Chantilly & Deauville (Gr 3), also fine rnr-up to Sendawar
in French 2000 Guineas (rtd 122): v eff at 1m on gd & hvy grnd: high-class, mild wnr of more Gr 2/3 races.
1987} **IRIDANOS** 99 C Laffon Parias 4-8-12 D Boeuf 510/10: 402-32: 4 b c Sabrehill - Loxandra (Last Tycoon) 2 109
Waited wth, eff over 1f out, not got to wnr: rtd 107 when plcd in Gr 3 company in '99: stays 1m on soft & hvy.
3208} **BARTEX** 99 T Clout 4-8-12 T Gillet 34/10: 14-113: 6 b g Groom Dancer - Belisonde (Gay Mecene) ¾ 107
Prom, rdn & onepace over 1f out: Longchamp stks wnr in '99: eff over 7f/8.5f on gd & hvy grnd.
6 ran   Time 1m 54.0   (K Abdulla)   A Fabre France

CURRAGH   SUNDAY APRIL 9TH   Righthand, Galloping Track

Official Going   YIELDING

862   4.00 GR 3 GLADNESS STKS 3YO+   7f   Yielding
£22750   £6650   £3150   £1050   3 yo rec 14lb

4025) **GIANTS CAUSEWAY 99** [4] A P O'Brien 3-9-0 M J Kinane 8/11 FAV: -111-1: 3 ch c Storm Cat - Mariah's   **120**
Storm (Rahy) Prom, gd hdwy to lead 1f out, styd on, rdn out: reapp: won all 3 juv starts, at Naas, Curragh (Gr
3) & Longchamp (Gr 1 Prix Salamandre, rtd 118): eff at 7f, 1m will suit: acts on gd/soft & soft, unrcd on fast:
runs well fresh: high-class & unbtn, fine run against elders today & looks primed for a big run in the 2000 Guineas.
4320) **TARRY FLYNN 99** [3] D K Weld 6-9-10 (bl) P Shanahan 12/1: 041-52: 6 br g Kenmare - Danzig Lass   ¾ **114**
(Danzig) Cl up, eff over 1f out, kept on for press ins last, not btn far: '99 scorer at Leopardstown (2), Curragh
(h'caps) & Cork (Gr 3, rtd 109): eff at 6/7f on fast & soft: wears blnks: tough, useful & progressive.
4415) **NAMID 99** [6] J Oxx 4-9-7 J P Murtagh 13/2: 1/23-3: 4 b h Indian Ridge - Dawnsio (Tate Gallery)   1 **109**
In tch, hdwy 2f out, kept on ins last, not btn far: only twice rcd in '99 (rtd 107): eff at 7f on gd/soft & hvy.
15   **WRAY 99** L Browne 8-9-7 S Craine 14/1: 2142-4: Hld up, eff over 2f out, kept on same pace: reapp.   1 **108**
*15   **ONE WON ONE 99** [9] 6-9-7 K J Manning 12/1: 3621-5: Cl up, led 2f out till 1f out, no extra.   ½ **107**
11 ran   Time 1m 30.1   (Mrs John Magnier)   A P O'Brien Ireland

863   5.30 EBF APRIL FILLIES RACE 3YO+   1m   Yielding
£9660   £2240   £980   3 yo rec 15lb

*14   **CHIANG MAI 99** A P O'Brien 3-9-0 M J Kinane 8/11 FAV: -11-1: 3 b f Sadler's Wells - Eljazzi   **103**
(Artaius) Made all, kept on for press over 1f out, just held on: reapp: in '99 won at Navan (mdn) & Leopardstown
(List, rtd 106): eff at 1m/9f: acts on gd/soft & soft grnd: unbeaten & useful filly.
4204) **SHES OUR MARE 99** A J Martin 7-9-7 J A Heffernan 4/1: 5011-2: 7 b m Commanche Run - Miss   shd **94**
Polymer (Doulab) Hld up, eff over 2f out, slightly hmpd ins last & kept on, just failed: shade unlucky: plcd in
2 val h'cap hdls 3 months ago (rtd 141h, 2m/2m2f, fm & soft): won 5 hdls in 98/99, including Gr 3 Swinton at
Haydock: on the Flat in '99 won at Navan, Curragh (h'caps) & Newmarket (val Cambridgeshire H'cap, rtd 88): eff
at 1m/12f on fast & soft, any trk: often wears a t-strap: v tough, genuine & still on the upgrade, credit to trainer.
--   **THREE WISHES** J Oxx 3-8-6 S W Kelly 5/1: 56-3: 3 b f Sadler's Wells - Valley Of Hope (Riverman)   hd **94**
Prom, eff to chall over 1f out, drifted right ins last, only just btn: shade unlucky: stays 1m on gd/soft.
8 ran   Time 1m 51.9   (Mrs David Nagle)   A P O'Brien Ireland

LONGCHAMP   SUNDAY APRIL 9TH   Righthand, Stiff, Galloping Track

Official Going   VERY SOFT

864   2.20 GR 2 PRIX NOAILLES 3YO   1m3f   V Soft
£28818   £11527   £5764   £2882

--   **KUTUB** [8] F Head 3-9-2 D Bonilla 6/1: 1-1: 3 b c In The Wings - Minnie Habit (Habitat)   **118**
Hld up, gd hdwy to lead ins last, pushed clr: won sole juv start: stays 11f well on v soft: win more Gr races.
4236) **LORD FLASHEART 99** [9] A de Royer Dupre 3-9-2 G Mosse 38/10: 21D1-2: 3 b c Blush Rambler - Miss   2 **114**
Henderson Co (Silver Hawk) Chsd ldrs, hdwy to chall over 1f out, led briefly ins last, no extra cl home: '99 wnr at
Longchamp (Gr 3, rtd 109) & won 4 times in the provinces: stays 11f on soft & hvy: v smart & tough, still improving.
4322) **CIRO 99** [3] A P O'Brien 3-9-2 W R Swinburn 3/1: 211-3: 3 ch c Woodman - Gioconda (Nijinsky)   1½ **112**
Led till ins fnl 1f, no extra: in '99 won at Galway (mdn) & subs awarded the Gr 1 Grand Criterium at Longchamp
(rtd 112): eff at 1m, stays 11f on v soft grnd: smart, from a powerful stable.
4594) **PETROSELLI 99** Mme C Head 3-9-2 J Fortune 106/10: 332-24: In tch, eff over 1f out, onepace: 2 **110**
rtd 110 when rnr-up in a Gr 1 last term: stays 11f on hvy grnd & has run well in blnks.
4558) **MONTE CARLO 99** [4] 3-9-2 Dane O'Neill 142/10: 3311-8: Cl up, short of room 2f out, sn btn: **99**
reapp, jockey rec a 4-day ban for careless riding: in 99 won at Epsom (mdn) & Newmarket (Listed, 10f, rtd 103):
eff at 10f, 12f+ shld suit this term: acts on firm & soft, any trk: genuine & useful, apprec Listed/Gr 3 class.
9 ran   Time 2m 20.6   (Hamdan Al Maktoum)   F Head France

SOUTHWELL (Fibresand)   TUESDAY APRIL 11TH   Lefthand, Sharp, Oval Track

Official Going   STANDARD. Stalls: 5f/1m - Outside, Rem - Inside

865   2.30 SHADOWFAX FILLIES AUCT MDN 2YO (F)   5f aw str Going 45 -15 Slow
£2299   £657   £328   Raced centre - stands side

--   **TICCATOO** [1] R Hollinshead 2-8-2 P M Quinn (5) 25/1: 1: 2 br f Dolphin Street - Accountancy Jewel   **75a**
(Pennine Walk) Bmpd start, sn in tch centre, styd on well under hands & heels to lead line: Feb foal, cost IR
4,000gns: dam a 7f juv wnr, sire top class 6/7f performer: eff at 5f on f/sand & a sharp trk: runs well fresh.
--   **BEVERLEY MACCA** [12] A Berry 2-8-4 G Carter 4/7 FAV: 2: 2 ch f Piccolo - Kangra Valley (Indian   hd **76a**
Ridge) Sn prom, rdn/led over 1f out, hung left ins last & hdd line: well bckd at odds-on: Jan foal, cost 8,000
gns: dam a 5f juv wnr, sire a high-class sprinter: eff at 5f, 6f could suit: acts on fibresand & a sharp trk.
--   **REGAL AIR** [11] B I Case 2-8-4 S Drowne 25/1: 3: 2 b f Distinctly North - Dignified Air (Wolver   3½ **67a**
Hollow) Led, drifted left/hdd over 1f out, sn held: Feb foal, cost 8,000 gns: half sister to a 7f wnr, subs a 7f
3yo List scorer: dam 6f wnr, sire a high-class juv: 6f+ cld suit in time, some promise on intro here.
--   **SHINNER** [6] T D Easterby 2-8-0 P Fessey 10/1: 4: Prom, no extra over 1f out: op 8/1: Charnwood   1¾ **59a**
Forest filly, Feb foal, cost 2,400gns: dam a 10f wnr, sire high-class 7f/1m performer: need further in time.
--   **SHARP SECRET** [9] 2-8-7 J Fanning 8/1: 5: Rdn chasing ldrs, outpcd fnl 2f: op 6/1: College Chapel   ½ **64a**
filly, Mar foal, cost 10,000 gns: dam related to a Gr 3 wnr: sire a high-class 6/7f wnr: with M Johnston.
--   **APRIL LEE** [7] 2-8-2 (E) F Norton 20/1: 6: Chsd ldrs 3f, fdd: op 14/1, wore eye-shield: Apr foal,   3½ **50a**
cost 4,500gns: dam multiple sprint wnr, incl as a juv: with K McAuliffe.

796   **MISS PROGRESSIVE** 12 [3] 2-8-2 Kim Tinkler 20/1: -67: Went left start, prom 3f , sn btn: see 796.   1¼   47a
--   **KEEP DREAMING** [10] 2-8-2 N Pollard 6/1: 8: Dwelt, sn rdn, no impress: tchd 7/1: Mistertopogigo,   1¾   43a
Apr foal: 5,200gns purchase: dam 7f juv wnr, half sister to 3 juv wnrs at 7f: will apprec 6f for S Gollings.
722   **RAISAS GOLD** 17 [5] 2-8-0 Joanna Badger (7) 25/1: 69: In tch 3f: see 722.   hd   40a
--   **FESTINO** [4] 2-8-4 R Ffrench 14/1: 0: Prom centre 3f, 10th: Lake Coniston filly, cost 4,000gns: 2½   37a
Apr foal, dam 10/12f Irish wnr, sire top class sprinter: apprec further in time for N P Littmoden.
--   **DISGLAIR** [8] 2-8-0 Dale Gibson 25/1: 0: Al outpcd rear: 11th: with C W Thornton.   4   23a
11 ran   Time 1m 0.8 (3.0)   (John L Marriott)   R Hollinshead Upper Longdon, Staffs

---

866   3.00 STRIDER CLAIMER 4YO+ (F)   1m3f aw   Going 45 -17 Slow
£2310   £660   £330

647   **JIBEREEN** 36 [5] P Howling 8-9-1 R Mullen 7/2: 420431: 8 b g Lugana Beach - Fashion Lover (Shiny   59a
Tenth) Chsd ldrs, hard rdn over 3f out, styd on gamely ins last to lead nr fin, drvn out: op 9/4: '99 wnr here at
Southwell (clmr, rtd 84a), turf rnr-up (h'cap, rtd 77a & 56): '98 wnr at Southwell (amat h'cap, rtd 77a & 56): eff at 7f/
1m, now stays sharp 11f: acts on gd, soft & fibresand, any trk: likes Southwell: apprec drop to clmg grade.
710   **APPROACHABLE** 19 [9] Miss S J Wilton 5-8-11 I Mongan (5) 7/1: 232422: 5 b h Known Fact - Western   1¼   52$
Approach (Gone West) In tch, rdn & kept on wide fnl 3f, nrst fin: op 8/1: see 710, 45 (sell).
795   **ROYAL PARTNERSHIP** 12 [1] K R Burke 4-8-11 Darren Williams (7) 5/1: 140203: 4 b g Royal Academy -   ¾   51a
Go Honey Go (General Assembly) Chsd ldr, prog to lead 2f out, hdd in last, no extra: best held up till last moment.
750   **CANADIAN APPROVAL** 14 [2] I A Wood 4-9-0 Dean McKeown 10/1: 0-1044: Keen/led & clr after 3f,   ½   53a
hdd 2f out, no extra: op 8/1: stays sharp 11f, handles both AWs, firm & gd: best arnd 1m: see 336 (1m, eqtrk).
642   **MALWINA** 36 [8] 4-8-10 J P Spencer 13/2: 005125: Rear, rdn/mod gains wide fnl 3f: op 8/1: see 642.   2½   45a
671   **PICKENS** 28 [4] 8-8-7 Kim Tinkler 20/1: 14-006: Chsd ldr 3f, btn 2f out: see 642.   5   35a
707   **BE WARNED** 19 [3] 9-9-1 (vis) F Norton 2/1 FAV: 050127: Held up, eff 4f out/sn held: bckd: btr 686 (1m).   ¾   42a
2569} **POLISH PILOT** 99 [7] 5-9-1 R Hughes 25/1: /000-8: Held up, eff 3f out, no impress: 4 month jumps   1   41a
abs, AW bow: Nov '99 jmps wnr (rtd 103h), no Flat form: unplcd '98 (rtd 66 & 50a): stays 9f on fast, without blnks.
4351} **MENTEITH** 99 [6] 4-8-11 J Fanning 50/1: 00-9: Prom 6f: 6 month abs, AW bow: unplcd both '99 starts   12   24a
(rtd 66, mdn, prob flattered): with B Baugh.
9 ran   Time 2m 28.1 (6.8)   (Liam Sheridan)   P Howling Newmarket, Suffolk

---

867   3.30 ELROND HCAP 3YO+ 0-60 (F)   7f aw rnd   Going 45 -12 Slow   [59]
£2425   £693   £346   3 yo rec 14lb

692   **MAI TAI** 22 [11] D W Barker 5-9-7 (52)(vis) A Beech (5) 14/1: -25401: 5 b m Scenic - Oystons Propweekly   57a
(Swing Easy) Chsd ldrs halfway, prog to lead ins last, styd on well, rdn out: '99 scorer at Southwell (auct mdn),
Redcar (rtd 55), & Lingfield (h'caps, rtd 57a): plcd in '98 (rtd 58a, Mrs Dutfield): eff at 6f, suited by sharp
7f/1m: acts on fm, gd/sft & both AWs: tried blnks, eff with/without a visor, likes Southwell.
*811   **GUEST ENVOY** 10 [8] C N Allen 5-9-7 (52) L Newman (5) 3/1 FAV: 144112: 5 b m Paris House - Peace   ¾   55a
Mission (Dunbeath) Chsd ldrs, rdn/prog wide to lead 2f out, hdd ins last, kept on: well bckd: abs 811 (gd/soft).
802   **GRAND ESTATE** 11 [3] D W Chapman 5-9-0 (45) S Sanders 8/1: 400003: 5 b g Prince Sabo - Ultimate   1   46a
Dream (Kafu) Rdn, towards rear halfway, styd on well for press fnl 2f: eff at 6f, stays sharp 7f well: see 802, 614.
803   **MUTAHADETH** 11 [7] D Shaw 6-9-5 (50)(bl) J Fanning 12/1: 444604: Rear/wide, kept on fnl 2f, nrst fin.   ¾   50a
677   **C HARRY** 26 [5] 6-9-9 (54) J P Spencer 12/1: 426505: Mid-div, onepace fnl 2f: op 8/1: see 130 (sell).   2½   49a
616   **DARK MENACE** 41 [2] 8-9-0 (45)(bl) D Kinsella (7) 16/1: 1-0006: Rear, eff wide 3f out, kept on: abs.   1   38a
386   **BERNARDO BELLOTTO** 78 [16] 5-9-10 (55) O Pears 20/1: 110-07: Chsd ldrs wide, kept on fnl 2f,   nk   47a
nvr a threat: abs: not disgraced here from a tricky draw, shld prove sharper for this in similar: see 386.
647   **ITCH** 36 [10] 5-9-8 (53) H Bastiman 12/1: 314208: Hmpd after 1f, nvr on terms: see 599, 471 (C/D).   ¾   44a
*754   **ADOBE** 14 [12] 5-9-10 (55) T G McLaughlin 11/2: 000-19: Prom 6f: op 6/1: see 754 (W'hampton).   ¾   45a
587   **FOIST** 46 [13] 8-9-11 (56) T Lucas 8/1: 050-00: Prom wide 6f: 10th: op 10/1: abs: see 587 (6f).   ¾   45a
816   **SOUNDS SOLO** 8 [6] 4-9-4 (49)(vis) F Norton 25/1: 630600: Led/dsptd lead 5f, fdd: 13th: see 389, 341.   0a
3448} **YORKIE TOO** 99 [15] 4-9-3 (48)(VIS) O Urbina 25/1: 0400-0: Led/dsptd lead 5f, sn btn: 15th, reapp, AW   0a
bow, 1st time visor: unplcd in '99 (rtd 61, clmr, 1st time blnks): tried up to 10f prev.
776   Red Venus 13 [4] 4-9-0 (55)(bl) I Mongan (5) 12/1:   25   **Neela** 99 [1] 4-9-8 (53) Dane O'Neill 14/1:
2039} Desert Invader 99 [14] 9-8-12 (43) G Parkin 25/1:   504   Magique Etoile 99 [9] 4-9-5 (50)(vis) R Hughes 20/1:
16 ran   Time 1m 30.6 (4.0)   (L H Gilmurray & T J Docherty)   D W Barker Scorton, N Yorks

---

868   4.00 MORDOR HCAP 3YO+ 0-85 (D)   1m6f aw   Going 45 -16 Slow   [83]
£3770   £1160   £580   £290   3 yo rec 23lb4yo rec 3 lb

*679   **COUNT DE MONEY** 26 [4] Miss S J Wilton 5-9-3 (72)(t) I Mongan (5) 6/1: 231211: 5 b g Last Tycoon -   77a
Menominee (Soviet Star) Chsd ldrs, rdn to lead over 3f out, clr 2f out, held on well ins last: op 9/2: earlier won
here at Southwell (clmr, S Bowring) & W'hampton (class stks): '99 Southwell (5, h'cap/clmr/class stks) & W'hampton
wnr (clmr, rtd 68a & 35): '98 Southwell wnr (h'cap, rtd 54a): eff at 11/14f on firm & fast, fibresand/Southwell &
W'hampton specialist: eff in a t-strap: tough & progressive gelding, win more races
502   **CRESSET** 60 [5] D W Chapman 4-8-5 (63)(bl) S Sanders 5/1: 212122: 4 ch g Arazi - Mixed Applause   1½   65a
(Nijinsky) Held up in tch, rdn/chsd ldr 3f out, styd on well for press ins last, not pace to chall: op 3/1, 2 mth abs:
eff at 12/14f, stays 2m & worth another try at that trip: see 502, 456.
805   **WINSOME GEORGE** 11 [6] C W Fairhurst 5-7-10 (51)(4oh) N Kennedy 12/1: 00-233: 5 b g Marju - June   3½   48a
Moon (Sadler's Wells) Held up in tch, rdn halfway, kept on fnl 3f press, nvr threat: op 14/1: see 682 (12f).
*643   **SAGAPONACK** 36 [1] J R Fanshawe 4-9-10 (82) O Urbina 5/4 FAV: 514: Chsd ldrs, smooth prog to lead   3   75a
5f out, hdd 3f out & sn no extra: hvly bckd, op 7/4, topweight: not stay longer 14f trip: see 643 (mdn, 12f).
788   **CUPBOARD LOVER** 13 [8] 4-8-3 (60)(1ow) S Drowne 7/1: 010-65: Rear, eff 4f out, no impress: op 5/1.   ¾   53a
723   **FAILED TO HIT** 17 [7] 7-8-10 (65)(vis) P M Quinn (5) 10/1: 163436: Led 9f: op 7/1: see 530 (12f).   1   56a
2299} **THAMES DANCER** 99 [2] 4-8-8 (65)(1ow) Dane O'Neill 10/1: 6623-7: Held up, nvr a threat: op 8/1, 10   3   53a
month abs: plcd twice in '99 (rtd 71 & 62a, h'caps): rtd 77 in '98 (debut): eff at 12f & handles gd/soft & a gall trk.
726   **CITY STANDARD** 17 [3] 4-8-12 (70) J P Spencer 33/1: 300-08: Cl-up, fdd fnl 4f: AW bow: plcd in   dist   0a
'99 for Sir M Stoute (mdn, rtd 73): eff over a stiff/undul 12f: prob handles gd/soft & fast: best without a visor.
8 ran   Time 3m 08.4 (8.6)   (John Pointon)   Miss S J Wilton Wetley Rocks, Staffs

SOUTHWELL (Fibresand) TUESDAY APRIL 11TH Lefthand, Sharp, Oval Track

---

869	4.30 SARUMAN SELLER 3YO+ (G) 1m aw rnd Going 45 -04 Slow
	£1925 £550 £275 3 yo rec 15lb

477 **KILLARNEY JAZZ 63** [5] G C H Chung 5-9-7 (vis) Dane O'Neill 13/2: -00301: 5 b g Alhijaz - Killarney **59a**
Belle (Irish Castle) Chsd ldrs, went on over 4f out & sn clr, styd on strongly, eased nr fin, cmftbly: val for 10L+, op
11/2, bt in for 3,000gns, vis reapp: plcd in '99 (h'caps & clmr), rtd 63a): prev with N Littmoden, won 3 here at
Southwell in '98 (mdn h'cap/clmrs, 1st 2 for J Wharton, rtd 75a): eff at 7f/1m, handles gd/soft, fibresand/Southwell
specialist: runs well fresh: eff with/without blnks or vis, tried a t-strap: apprec drop to sell grade.

693 **WAITING KNIGHT 22** [7] Mrs N Macauley 5-9-7 (vis) R Fitzpatrick (3) 8/1: 400222: 5 b h St Jovite - 6 **44a**
Phydilla (Lyphard) Chsd ldrs, rdn halfway, kept on fnl 2f, no ch with wnr: op 10/1: caught a tartar here: see 178.

822 **ADIRPOUR 6** [2] R Hollinshead 6-9-11 Stephanie Hollinshead (7) 33/1: 154003: 6 gr g Nishapour - 3 **42$**
Adira (Ballad Rock) Towards rear, kept on fnl 2f, nrst fin: quick reapp: see 556 (12f, clmr).

497 **DOMINO FLYER 60** [11] Mrs A Duffield 7-9-7 S Sanders 14/1: 450-04: Rdn chasing ldrs, onepace fnl 3f: ½ **37a**
tchd 16/1, 2 month abs: rnr-up in '99 (clmr, rtd 60a, unplcd on turf, rtd 58, clmr): '98 Southwell wnr (h'cap, rtd
63a): eff at 7f/10f on gd, gd/soft & fibresand, prob handles fast: handles any trk, likes Southwell.

778 **SHAANXI ROMANCE 13** [15] 5-9-7 (vis) R Hughes 2/1 FAV: 400-25: Chsd ldrs halfway, rdn/held fnl ½ **36a**
2f & eased in last: claimed by M Polglase for £5,000: jockey explained that he eased down gelding when he
became tired as he has a history of leg trouble: hvly bckd: unlucky on turf in 778.

-- **STANDIFORD GIRL** [1] 3-8-1 C Cogan (5) 20/1: 6: Dwelt, rdn/towards rear, mod gains fnl 2f: debut. 3½ **24a**
776 **INDIAN SWINGER 13** [13] 4-9-7 R Mullen 4/1: 052207: Slowly away, mod late gains: bckd, op 6/1. 1 **27a**
778 **TSUNAMI 13** [16] 4-9-2 G Carter 16/1: 4-0668: Dwelt, nvr on terms: btr 433. 1 **20a**
686 **MR MAJICA 25** [12] 6-9-7 (bl) T G McLaughlin 16/1: 000-09: Held up, nvr factor: see 686 (C/D). ½ **24a**
469 **MURRON WALLACE 66** [10] 6-9-2 S Drowne 25/1: 10/000: Held up, al bhd: 10th: 2 mth abs: missed shd **19a**
'98 & '99: '97 Hamilton (mdn h'cap) & Bath wnr (sell h'cap, rtd 49): eff at 7f/1m on fast & gd, stiff/undul trk.
472 **MOUNT PARK 64** [8] 3-8-1 N Pollard 12/1: 253-00: Led 3f, btn 3f out: 12th: op 10/1, abs: see 472 (6f). **0a**
783 **BONDI BAY 13** [14] 3-8-1 R Ffrench 11/2: 035-20: Held up, eff/btn 3f out: 14th: btr 783, 41. **0a**
433 Taleca Son 70 [9] 5-9-7 J P Spencer 25/1: 111 The Wild Widow 99 [3] 6-9-2 (bl) I Mongan (5) 14/1:
-- Picassos Heritage [6] 4-9-7 F Norton 25/1: 995} Milad 99 [4] 5-9-7 L Newman (5) 33/1:
16 ran Time 1m 43.3 (3.9) (G C H Chung) G C H Chung Newmarket, Suffolk

---

870	5.00 WARLORD HCAP 3YO 0-70 (E) 5f aw str Going 45 +05 Fast	[73]
	£2884 £824 £412 Raced centre/stand side	

777 **SERGEANT SLIPPER 13** [10] C Smith 3-9-1 (60)(vis) L Newman (5) 10/1: 11-001: 3 ch g Never So Bold - **67a**
Pretty Scarce (Handsome Sailor) Dwelt, trkd ldrs 2f out, rdn to lead ins last, drvn out: best time of day: '99
sell wnr at W'hampton & Southwell, rnr-up on turf (rtd 60a & 48): tried 6f, suited by 5f: acts on f/sand & gd
grnd: eff in a visor: likes a sharp trk, esp Southwell: likes to come with a late run.

785 **PADDYWACK 13** [9] D W Chapman 3-8-13 (58)(bl) S Sanders 4/1 FAV: 411222: 3 b g Bigstone - Millie's 1¾ **59a**
Return (Ballad Rock) Al handy, led over 1f out, hdd ins last, not pace of wnr: op 3/1: eff at 5/7f: see 654 (7f).

785 **CAROLS CHOICE 13** [13] D Haydn Jones 3-9-4 (63)(BL) S Drowne 9/1: 6-4203: 3 ch f Emarati - Lucky 1¼ **61a**
Song (Lucky Wednesday) Led 3f, kept on well for press in last: gd run in 1st time blnks: see 549, 493.

777 **MARITUN LAD 13** [4] D Shaw 3-9-2 (61)(bl) J P Spencer 5/1: -41414: Cl-up, onepace over 1f out. 1 **57a**
659 **BILLYS BLUNDER 31** [7] 3-8-1 (46)(tvi) Joanna Badger (7) 14/1: 320445: Chsd ldrs, outpcd over 2f 2 **37a**
out, kept on ins last: return to 6f shld suit: see 493, 426.
689 **DIAMOND RACHAEL 25** [8] 3-9-6 (65) R Fitzpatrick (3) 8/1: -01236: Prom 3f: vis omitted: btr 549 (6f, vis). nk **55a**
689 **MR STICKYWICKET 25** [12] 3-7-10 (41)(VIS)(11oh) S Righton 33/1: -00067: Rear/rdn, mod gains: vis. nk **30a**
4508} **DUNKELLIN HOUSE 99** [2] 3-9-1 (60) R Hughes 14/1: 000-09: Cl-up 3f: h'cap/AW bow, 6 month abs: ½ **47a**
unplcd all 3 '99 starts (rtd 65, debut): not given a hard time once held, shld prove sharper for this.
*740 **LYDIAS LOOK 15** [3] 3-9-4 (63) J Fanning 10/1: 5419: Chsd ldrs 3f, sn outpcd: op 9/1: see 740 (mdn). ½ **48a**
4082} **HOT ICE 99** [11] 3-8-8 (53) A Beech 10/1: 0310-0: Al outpcd: 10th: op 8/1, 7 mth abs: AW bow: 1 **36a**
'99 Musselburgh scorer (nurs h'cap, H Morrison, rtd 56): eff forcing the pace over a sharp 5f on fast grnd.
4514} **Roman Emperor 99** [6] 3-8-4 (49) T Lucas 25/1: 4347} Alustar 99 [1] 3-9-7 (66) G Parkin 14/1: P
12 ran Time 59.8 (2.0) (C Smith) C Smith Temple Bruer, Lincs

PONTEFRACT TUESDAY APRIL 11TH Lefthand, Undulating Track, Stiff Uphill Finish

Official Going GOOD TO SOFT. Stalls: 2m1f - Centre; Rem - Inside.

871	2.15 PONTEFRACT APP HCAP 3YO+ 0-70 (F) 1m2f Soft 120 -04 Slow	[70]
	£2205 £630 £315	

4593} **SMARTER CHARTER 99** [7] Mrs L Stubbs 7-8-8 (50) Kristin Stubbs (7) 33/1: 2463-1: 7 br g Master Willie - **55**
Irene's Charter (Persian Bold) Sn rdn in tch, hdwy to chall 2f out, led well ins last, going away: reapp: '99
wnr at Musselburgh (h'cap, rtd 57): '98 wnr at Beverley & Kempton (h'caps, rtd 63): eff at 7.5f/10f: acts on
any grnd & trk, likes Beverley: best coming late off a strong pace: tough 7yo, h'capped to win again.

4125} **STITCH IN TIME 99** [16] G C Bravery 4-7-13 (41) G Baker (3) 20/1: 0000-2: 4 ch g Inchinor - Late 1¼ **43**
Matinee (Red Sunset): Chsd ldrs, rdn/hdwy over 2f out, led inside last, sn hdd & no extra cl-home: reapp:
failed to make the frame in '99 (mdns & h'caps, rtd 65 at best): eff at 10f on soft grnd: acts on a stiff/undul trk.

510 **GYPSY 57** [6] M H Tompkins 4-9-12 (68) P Shea (3) 20/1: -35443: 4 b g Distinctly North - Winscarlet 1 **68**
North (Garland Knight): Trkd ldrs, hdwy to lead over 1f out, hdd/no extra inside last: 8 wk abs, blnks omitted.

822 **A DAY ON THE DUB 6** [13] D Eddy 7-8-8 (50) P Hanagan 14/1: 125-64: Held up, rdn/hdwy over 3f 1¾ **47**
out, kept on but no ch with ldrs: quick reapp: best in sell h'caps/claimers: see 822 (sell h'cap).

779 **DESERT RECRUIT 13** [1] 4-8-2 (44) Clare Roche 11/2: 514-55: Slow start, drvn up to lead shd **41**
after 1f, hdd over 1f out, wknd: lost ch with low start & needs to dominate thro'out: see 779.

669 **RUTLAND CHANTRY 28** [11] 6-10-0 (70) M Jackay 7/1: 4/1 FAV: 00-256: Mid-div, gd hdwy over 1f 2½ **63**
out, drvn/wknd inside last: turf return: top weight: clr rem: btr 601 (1m AW h'cap).

699 **BATSWING 19** [2] 5-9-10 (66) K Dalgleish (3) 11/1: 406-07: Dwelt, late gains, nrst fin: suited by 12f. 5 **52**
521 **BOWCLIFFE 56** [14] J Swift (5) 14/1: -04368: In tch, prog 3f out, wknd final 2f: 3 **39**
8 wk abs & probably best suited by 1m: see 447.

281

PONTEFRACT   TUESDAY APRIL 11TH   Lefthand, Undulating Track, Stiff Uphill Finish

825   **CHALCEDONY** 6 [5] 4-9-2 (58) Lynsey Hanna 12/1: 124049: Cl-up, wknd qckly appr fnl 2f: qck reapp.   1¼   38
791   **KHUCHN** 12 [12] 4-9-4 (60) R Farmer (5) 25/1: 010-00: Nvr a threat, fin 10th: '99 scorer for   3½   35
R Armstrong at Nottingham (classified stks, first win, rtd 68 at best): eff at 10f, has tried 12f: acts on good.
705   **DESERT FIGHTER** 19 [9] 9-9-7 (63) T Eaves (5) 12/1: 114-00: Chsd ldrs, fdd final 2f: 11th: see 705.   ¾   37
775   **BADRINATH** 13 [4] 6-9-2 (58) J Bosley 16/1: 0-6320: Prom, drvn/wknd qckly fnl 2f: 12th: see 775 (sell).   hd   32
3053} **WHAT A FUSS** 99 [15] 7-8-4 (46) D Glennon (5) 10/1: 1/00-0: Chsd ldrs till lost tch final 3f, fin 16th: 0
mkt drifter from 6/1: late '99 hdles scorer at M Rasen & Hexham (h'caps, rtd 108h, 2m/2m2.5f on gd, gd/soft &
any trk): well btn both '99 Flat starts, back in '97 won at W'hampton (reapp, mdn h'cap) & Yarmouth (h'cap, rtd
61, B Hanbury): eff between 9.5f & 11.5f on fast, soft & fibresand: likes sharp trks & racing up with the pace.
795   **BAYARD LADY** 12 [10] 4-7-10 (38) G Sparkes (1) 33/1: 550-00: Led early, lost tch final 2f, fin 17th.   0
37   **Santa Lucia** 99 [8] 4-9-7 (63) W Hutchinson 25/1:
795   **Cosmic Case** 12 [19] 5-8-2 (44)(vis)(6ow) Dawn Rankin (0) 20/1:
705   **September Harvest** 19 [18] 4-8-6 (48)(VIS) Sarah Thomas (7) 25/1:
3682} **Big Chief** 99 [17] 4-7-13 (40)(t)(1ow) R Lake (0) 33/1:
18 ran   Time 2m 20.5 (12.4)   (O J Williams)   Mrs L Stubbs Newmarket.

872   2.45 BENTLEY SELLER 3YO+ (F)   6f rnd   Soft 120   -33 Slow
£2394   £684   £342   3 yo rec 12lb

802   **MISS BANANAS** 11 [2] C N Kellett 5-9-2 D Meah (7) 33/1: 0-6001: 5 b m Risk Me - Astrid Gilberto   49
(Runnett): Trkd ldr, hdwy to lead appr fnl 1f, styd on strongly when prsd inside last, drvn out: slow time,
no bid: '99 scorer at Leicester (amat h'cap, rtd 41, rtd 57a on AW): '98 Lingfield wnr (h'cap, rtd 63a):
eff racing up with the pace at 5/6f, has tried 7f: acts on gd, soft & both AWs, sharp or stiff/undul trk.
756   **TANCRED ARMS** 14 [15] D W Barker 4-9-2 A Culhane 6/1: 00-022: 4 b f Clantime - Mischievous Miss   ¾   47
(Niniski): Rcd wide in mid-div, stay'd on strongly beside dropping left ins last, just held: in gd form in sells.
698   **MARENGO** 22 [13] M J Polglase 6-9-12 K Darley 11/2: 306223: 6 b g Never So Bold - Born To Dance   nk   57
(Dancing Brave): Chsd ldrs racing wide, hdwy to chall 2f out, onepcd inside last: consistent: see 698.
790   **BIRCHWOOD SUN** 12 [18] M Dods 10-9-7 (vis) J Weaver 9/1 FAV: 03-334: Held up, ran on well for   2   48
press over 1f out, nvr nrr: consistent plater: see 790, 756.
75   **OAKWELL ACE** 99 [5] 4-9-2 B Sooful (7) 14/1: 0030-5: Rear, styd on late, nvr nrr: long abs: '99   ½   42
wnr at Warwick (clmr, rtd 59, subs tried visor): eff at 7f/1m: suited by soft grnd & a sharp or gall trk.
674   **BLUSHING GRENADIER** 28 [6] 8-9-12 (bl) S Finnamore (5) 6/1: 330166: Led, hdd appr fnl 1f, wknd.   4   44
*790 **DANDY REGENT** 12 [12] 6-9-12 D Holland 9/1: 450-17: Trkd ldrs, wknd over 1f out: btr 790 (7f, gd).   hd   44
778   **STATE WIND** 13 [4] 4-9-7 (vis) L Newton 20/1: -06058: Handy, lost place 3f out, no dngr: see 635.   ¾   38
4361} **SYCAMORE LODGE** 99 [1] 9-9-7 Clare Roche (7) 12/1: 5000-9: Chsd ldrs, drvn & fdd appr final 1f: ½   37
reapp: won 3 times at Catterick in '99 (clmr, sell & appr h'cap, rtd 68): dual '98 rnr-up (rtd 54): eff at
6/7f on firm or soft grnd: runs well fresh & best with hold up tactics: keep in mind for Catterick.
751   **HOT LEGS** 14 [9] 4-9-2 (bl) G Duffield 40/1: 455030: Rcd wide in mid-div, wknd qckly final 2f, fin 10th.   hd   32
4589} **SCHATZI** 99 [10] 3-8-4 J Bramhill 20/1: 5005-0: Prom, lost tch 2f out, fin 11th: thrice rnr-up in   6   20
'99 (sells & clmrs, rtd 68 at best): eff at 5/6f on fast & soft grnd.
3568} **VENTURE CAPITALIST** 99 [17] 11-9-7 R Cochrane 8/1: 1450-0: Dwelt, al bhd, virtually p.u. fnl 2f, 16th: 0
reapp: '99 scorer at Catterick (clmr, rtd 69 at best), subs banned under the non-triers Rule (on 88th career
start!!): '98 Doncaster wnr (stks, rtd 91): plcd in '97 (rtd 103), prev term won a Gr 3 at York (rtd 117):
eff at 5f, suited by 6f, just stays 7f: acts on firm & gd/soft, not softer: eff with/without blnks: v tough.
201   **Cairn Dhu** 99 [7] 6-9-7 Kimberley Hart (5) 50/1:   682   **Bratby** 25 [8] 4-9-7 R Studholme (5) 50/1:
3691} **Get A Life** 99 [3] 7-9-2 C Lowther 50/1:   756   **Frosted Aire** 14 [14] 4-9-7 P Robinson 20/1:
16 ran   Time 1m 23.3 (9.2)   (W Meah)   C N Kellett Smisby, Derbys.

873   3.15 BEAST FAIR MED AUCT MDN 3YO (E)   1m2f   Soft 120   -05 Slow
£2899   £892   £446   £223

--   **INFORAPENNY** [1] R A Fahey 3-8-9 R Winston 12/1: 40-1: 3 b g Deploy - Morina (Lyphard):   83
Cl-up, rdn/outpcd appr final 2f, rallied & styd on strongly for press to lead well inside last, drvn out: op 8/1
on reapp/Brit bow: rcd twice in native Ireland in '99 for K Prendergast: apprec this step up to 10f, 12f sure to
suit: acts on soft grnd & a stiff/undul trk: goes v well fresh: type to continue to improve over further.
4473} **CABALLE** 99 [5] S P C Woods 3-8-9 L Dettori 5/6 FAV: 2-2: 3 ch f Opening Verse - Attirance   ½   80
(Crowned Prince): Trkd ldrs, rdn/led 3f out, styd on, hdd cl-home: well bckd on reapp: rnr-up on sole '99
start, at Doncaster (fill mdn, rtd 87): eff over a stiff or gall 1m/10f on soft grnd: should win a mdn.
3946} **MINGLING** 99 [3] M H Tompkins 3-9-0 G Duffield 8/1: 450-3: 3 b c Wolfhound - One The Tide (Slip   1½   81
Anchor): Mid-div, outpcd 2f out, styd on inside last: bckd from 14/1 on reapp: failed to make the frame in '99
(7f mdns, rtd 84): styd this lngr 10f trip well, 12f shld suit: handles firm & soft: should win a race.
713   **HINT OF MAGIC** 18 [9] J G Portman 3-9-0 T Quinn 4/1: 52-44: Prom, rdn to chall over 3f out,   1½   79
drvn & fdd inside last: well clr rem: op 7/1: acts on gd grnd: see 713.
--   **ADAWAR** [4] 3-9-0 W R Swinburn 10/1: 5: Waited with, effort & ran v green over 2f out, no threat: 6   72
Perugino colt, mid-dist bred: ran v green here & sure to impr for the experience: with Sir M Stoute.
783   **JONLOZ** 13 [7] 3-9-0 L Newton 100/1: 0-5456: Al bhd: v stiff task.   14   58$
--   **LANNTANSA** [8] 3-9-0 J Reid 12/1: 7: Al well in rear: op 6/1 on debut: Dolphin Street   nk   58
half-brother to 10f wnrs in Europe: should improve for the run: with E Dunlop.
4086} **DEE DIAMOND** 99 [6] 3-8-9 C Lowther 66/1: -40-8: Led, rdn/hdd over 3f out, wknd qckly, fin last: 1¾   51
up in trip: 4th on 1st of 2 '99 starts (7f fillies mdn, rtd 71, gd grnd).
8 ran   Time 2m 20.6 (12.5)   (Colin McEvoy)   R A Fahey Butterwick, Nth Yorks.

874   3.45 CLASSIFIED STKS 3YO+ 0-90 (C)   1m2f   Soft 120   -10 Slow
£6792   £2090   £1045   £522   3 yo rec 19lb

690   **JUST IN TIME** 24 [7] T G Mills 5-9-12 A Clark 9/2: 60-141: 5 b g Night Shift - Future Past (Super   92
Concorde): Made all, ran on well when prsd inside last, drvn out: a/w wnr at Lingfield (h'cap, rtd 99a at
best): plcd twice in '99, incl a val h'cap at Royal Ascot (rtd 92): '98 wnr at Goodwood (mdn auct, rtd 89):
eff at 10f, stays 12f on firm, soft & equitrack: runs well fresh on any trk: likes Goodwood: tough & useful.
2487} **SEEK** 99 [3] L M Cumani 4-9-8 L Dettori 11/8 FAV: 21-2: 4 br c Rainbow Quest - Souk (Ahonoora):   ¾   86
Waited with, rdn/hdwy 3f out, styd on to chall inside last, just held: nicely bckd on reapp: wnr on 2nd of
2 '99 starts, here at Pontefract (mdn, rtd 82): half-brother to 2 middle dist wnrs: eff at 10/12f, further
should suit: acts on gd/soft & soft, handles firm grnd: gd reapp & will be suited by a return to 12f.

282

PONTEFRACT   TUESDAY APRIL 11TH   Lefthand, Undulating Track, Stiff Uphill Finish

*747   ULUNDI 15 [5] Lady Herries 5-10-0 P Doe 6/1: 113: 5 b g Rainbow Quest - Flit (Lyphard):   ½   91
Rear, hdwy to chall 2f out, no extra well ins last: op 4/1, gd run, top-weight: acts on fast, soft & firesand.
2909} BAWSIAN 99 [1] J L Eyre 5-9-8 D Holland 8/1: 304B-4: Settled rear, hdwy for press 2f out, styd on,   shd   85
nrst fin: clr rem: plcd twice in '99 (h'caps, rtd 92a & 88): '98 wnr at W'hampton (2 h'caps, rtd 96a), Doncaster
& York (h'caps): '97 Redcar wnr (rtd 74): eff at 10/12 on fast, soft, firesand & any trk: on a fair mark.
572   PUNISHMENT 48 [4] 9-9-8 (t) J Reid 16/1: 6-2355: Prom, rdn & fdd final 2f: 7 wk abs, stiffish task.   7   75
4374} ZILARATOR 99 [2] 4-9-8 J F Egan 6/1: 0355-6: Chsd ldrs till lost tch fnl 3f: '99 scorer at Leicester   1¾   73
(mdn, rtd 89 at best): eff at 13/15f on gd & hvy, stiff trk: inadequate trip here, sharper next time over further.
4272} BELLA BELLISIMO 99 [6] 3-8-0 D Mernagh (3) 10/1: 5535-7: Al in rear, t.o. final 2f: tchd 14/1:   18   52
'99 wnr at York (debut, mdn, rtd 88): eff at 6f/1m on gd grnd & runs well fresh: has tried blnks.
7 ran   Time 2m 21.1 (13.0)   (Mrs Pauline Merrick)   T G Mills Headley, Surrey.

875   4.15 TOTE HCAP 3YO+ 0-85 (D)   1m rnd   Soft 120   +04 Fast   [83]
£7442   £2290   £1145   £572   3 yo rec 14lb

780   YAROB 13 [9] D Nicholls 7-9-8 (77) Clare Roche (7) 20/1: 505-01: 7 ch g Unfuwain - Azyaa (Kris)   84
Sn led, made rest, styd on well, hands & heels: gd time: '99 Doncaster wnr (h'cap, rtd 84): rnr-up for D Loder
in '98 (h'cap, rtd 83a): eff at 1m/11f on firm, soft, fibresand & any trk, likes a stiff/gall one: best forcing the pace.
4101} PRINCE BABAR 99 [11] R A Fahey 9-9-9 (78) K Darley 20/1: 0000-2: 9 b g Fairy King - Bell Toll   1½   82
(High Line): Settled rear, gd hdwy over 2f out, hung left & styd on appr final 1f, not get to wnr: unplcd in '99
for J Banks (h'caps, rtd 83): rnr-up over jumps in 98/99 (rtd 99h, nov, eff at 2m on gd & gd/soft): '98 Newmarket
wnr (h'cap, rtd 97): eff at 7f/1m on firm, soft & any trk: best without vis: v well h'capped, encouraging.
733   THE WHISTLING TEAL 17 [20] J G Smyth Osbourne 4-10-0 (83) J F Egan 9/2 JT FAV: 20-003: 4 b c   1¼   85
Rudimentary - Lonely Shore (Blakeney) In tch, gd hdwy over 2f out, onepace over 1f out: bckd, gd effort.
715   INDIUM 18 [16] W J Musson 6-9-9 (78) P Shea (7) 20/1: 00-404: Waited with, kept on late, no dngr.   1   78
757   CHIEF MONARCH 14 [13] 6-9-3 (72) R Winston 13/2: /00-25: Dwelt, bhd, hdwy when slightly hmpd   ½   71
& switched 3f out, styd on strongly, nvr nrr: crying out for a return to 10f & shld win at that trip: see 757.
757   ATLANTIC CHARTER 14 [5] 4-8-12 (67) L Dettori 14/1: 010-06: Rear, styd on for press final 2f,   2½   62
nrst fin: '99 Redcar wnr (h'cap, rtd 75 at best): suited by 10f, further should suit: acts on firm &
fast grnd, stiff/gall trk: needs a return to 10f+.
715   KALA SUNRISE 18 [4] 7-9-7 (76) M Fenton 11/1: 240-07: Mid-div till outpcd halfway, late gains: '99 wnr   ¾   70
at Leicester (h'cap, rtd 86): rtd 81 in '98: eff at 7f/1m on firm & gd/soft, stiff/gall trk: slipped down weights.
715   WUXI VENTURE 18 [8] 5-9-8 (77) D Holland 16/1: -00008: Waited with, modest late gains, no threat: 3   66
on a handy mark now & trainer D Nicholls is the man to exploit it: see 601.
715   GREAT NEWS 18 [7] 5-10-0 (83) T Quinn 14/1: 130-09: Prom, fdd final 2f: joint top weight: '99   2   69
wnr at Ascot & Windsor (val h'cap & rtd h'cap, rtd 86): '98 Lingfield wnr (h'cap, rtd 75), plcd 5 other
starts: eff at 7f/8.3f: acts on any grnd/trk: runs well fresh: possibly just needed this.
4615} DONNAS DOUBLE 99 [19] 5-8-12 (67) J Weaver 20/1: 0110-0: Nvr a threat, fin 10th: reapp.   1½   51
7   EASTERN CHAMP 99 [12] 4-9-4 (73)(t) G Duffield 20/1: 2020-0: Waited with, gd hdwy over 2f out,   nk   57
wknd quickly appr final 1f, fin 11th: long abs.
3847} REDSWAN 99 [10] 5-9-4 (73)(t) G Faulkner (3) 25/1: 5401-0: Mid-div, drvn/outpcd ovr 2f out: 12th.   1½   55
623   DOUBLE ACTION 40 [1] 6-8-12 (67) J Carroll 16/1: 006-40: V keen & chsd ldrs, btn qckly 3f out: 13th.   1   47
4204} NOMINATOR LAD 99 [17] 6-9-0 (67) J Fortune 11/1: 00000-: Cl-up, rdn/lost tch final 2f, fin 14th.   ¾   50
715   TOPTON 18 [3] 6-9-7 (76)(bl) Pat Eddery 9/2 JT FAV: 130020: Dwelt, nvr a factor: 17th, btr 715.   0
3459} Royal Arrow Fr 99 [18] 4-9-13 (82) A Culhane 33/1:   4178} Its Magic 99 [6] 4-9-4 (73)(bl) W Ryan 14/1:
4401} Young Precedent 99 [15] 6-9-12 (81) W R Swinburn 16}445} Boanerges 99 [2] 3-8-12 (81) J Reid 20/1:
19 ran   Time 1m 51.1 (9.3)   (Lucayan Stud)   D Nicholls Sessay, Nth Yorks.

876   4.45 WWW.PONTEFRACT HCAP 4YO+ 0-75 (E)   2m1f22y   Soft 120   -01 Slow   [73]
£3029   £932   £466   £233   4 yo rec 5 lb

737   CHARMING ADMIRAL 15 [10] Mrs A Duffield 7-8-3 (48)(bl) G Duffield 14/1: 345-01: 7 b g Shareef Dancer -   52
Lilac Charm (Bustino): Handy, rdn to impr halfway, styd on well to lead inside last, drvn clr: first Flat win:
rnr-up in '99 (h'caps, rtd 49 & 39a): 98/99 Carlisle wnr over fences (nov, rtd 98c, blnks): plcd on the Flat in
'98 (appr h'cap, rtd 55a): eff at 14f, stays 2m5.5f: acts on fast, soft & fibresand: thorough stayer.
788   PROTOCOL 13 [16] Mrs S Lamyman 6-8-3 (48)(t) J F Egan 8/1: 10-002: 6 b g Taufan - Ukraine's   2   50
Affair (The Minstrel): Trkd ldrs till went on halfway, hdd 4f out, drvn to lead again over 2f out, hdd
& no extra inside last: bckd from 14/1: styd this lngr 2m1f trip well & loves soft grnd: see 788, 699.
3661} HAYAAIN 99 [5] K C Bailey 7-9-6 (65) J Reid 8/1: 0/03-3: 7 b h Shirley Heights - Littlefield   ½   66
(Bay Express) Always mid-div till styd on for press fnl 2f: jumps fit, late '99 scorer at Huntingdon (h'cap hdle,
rtd 127h, eff at 2m/2½m on gd & fast): plcd on 2nd of 2 '99 Flat starts (h'cap, rtd 66): last won on the Flat
back in '96, at Bath (mdn): eff at 2m & even further should suit: acts on fast & soft grnd: likes a stiff trk.
135   LITTLE BRAVE 99 [11] J M P Eustace 5-9-0 (59) J Tate 10/1: 0024-4: In tch, hdwy 1m out, ev ch   ½   59
until wknd over 1f out: long abs, sharper for this: see 135, 51.
714   MAZZELMO 18 [14] 7-9-4 (63) J Fortune 16/1: 301-05: Bhd, gd hdwy 6f out, drvn & no extra appr   1¾   61
final 1f: clr rem: visor omitted: '99 wnr at Chepstow & Chester (h'caps, rtd 62), also won over hdles at Kelso
(2m2f, rtd 101h, firm, soft & any trk): '98 wnr at W'hampton (clmr, rtd 61a) & again at Chester (h'cap, rtd 63):
suited by 2m/2m2f on any grnd or trk, likes Chester: has tried blnks/visor, best without: likes to force the pace.
*714   ROYAL EXPRESSION 18 [6] 8-10-0 (73) J Weaver 9/1: 312316: Cl-up, hdwy to lead 4f out, hdd &   10   63
wknd appr final 2f: better on gd grnd in 714 (2m2f).
4590} BOLD CARDOWAN 99 [12] 4-7-13 (49) R Brisland (5) 7/1: 1460-7: Waited with, gd hdwy halfway, ev ch   3   36
till wknd qckly over 2f out: op 11/2 on reapp: '99 wnr at Lingfield (h'cap, rtd 51, first win): eff over a
sharp/undul 2m: handles fast, suited by soft/hvy: ran well for a long way here & should be spot-on next time.
760   HAPPY DAYS 14 [3] 5-7-10 (41)(7oh) J Bramhill 50/1: 00-008: Handy, rdn/prog halfway, btn fnl 3f.   16   15
760   GIVE AN INCH 14 [2] 5-9-7 (66) T Williams 5/1 FAV: 410-09: Rear, chsg ldrs halfway, wknd qckly   8   34
final 3f: '99 wnr at Pontefract & Ayr (h'caps, rtd 71): '99 Redcar scorer (mdn sell) & Ayr (2, h'caps,
rtd 64): suited by 2m/2m2f: acts on gd/soft & hvy: handles any trk, likes Ayr.
737   JAZZ TRACK 15 [8] 6-8-5 (50)(tbl) D Mernagh (3) 33/1: /0-600: Dwelt, nvr a threat: 10th: see 552.   3   16
760   BLACK ICE BOY 14 [4] 9-7-11 (42)(vis) K Dalgleish (5) 16/1: 0P-500: Dwelt, sn chsg ldrs, wknd   1¾   7
qckly final 4f: best when able to dominate, likes soft grnd & Pontefract: see 141.
412   NON VINTAGE 74 [15] 9-7-10 (41)(6oh) D Glennon (5) 66/1: 6/0-00: Al bhd, t.o. in 12th: jumps fit.   9   0
797   NORTHERN MOTTO 12 [7] 7-8-8 (53) A McGlone 14/1: 440-50: Nvr a threat: t.o. in 13th: btr 797.   4   7
*664   MAKNAAS 31 [13] 4-9-2 (66) A Clark 11/2: 511110: Led, to halfway, wknd 4f out & virtually   dist   0

283

PONTEFRACT   TUESDAY APRIL 11TH   Lefthand, Undulating Track, Stiff Uphill Finish

p.u. str: 14th: nicely bckd & much better expected on turf return here: completed an AW 4-timer in 664.
-- **HUNT HILL** [1] 5-8-13 (58) L Dettori 8/1: 1130/0: Waited with, rear halfway, t.o. final 4f, **11** **0**
fin last: reportedly suffering from a breathing problem: 8 wk jumps abs, earlier won at Newcastle (h'cap,
rtd 107h, eff at 2m/3m on gd/soft & hvy): 2 yr Flat abs, '98 wnr at Southwell, Brighton & Leicester (h'caps,
rtd 67, Sir M Prescott): eff at 1m/10f on gd, fast & fibresand: runs well fresh on a sharp or gall/undul trk.
15 ran   Time 4m 01.2 (20.9)   (The Old Spice Girls)   Mrs A Duffield Constable Burton, Nth Yorks.

877 5.15 SPRING FILLIES MDN 3YO (D)   6f rnd   Soft 120 -15 Slow
£3542   £1090   £545   £272

685 **SWIFT DISPERSAL** 25 [10] S C Williams 3-8-11 G Faulkner (3) 66/1: 001: 3 gr f Shareef Dancer - Minsden's **75**
Image (Dancer's Image) Chdrs ldrs, hdwy to lead dist, strongly prsd ins last, held on all-out for a surprise victory:
showed little on 2 prev runs on the AW: apprec 6f on soft: lightly raced.
4591} **KANAKA CREEK** 99 [1] A Berry 3-8-11 J Carroll 12/1: 3235-2: 3 ch f Thunder Gulch - Book Collector *hd* **74**
(Irish River): Prom, rdn & styd on strongly inside last, just failed: reapp: clr rem: plcd 4 times in '99 (mdns
& h'cap, rtd 76 at best, J Berry): eff at 6f/1m: acts on fast & hvy grnd, any trk: worth a try in headgear.
4260} **POLAR LADY** 99 [7] J R Fanshawe 3-8-11 R Cochrane 4/1: 6-3: 3 ch f Polar Falcon - Soluce (Junius): **3** **67**
Keen with ldrs, hdwy to lead when hung left over 1f out, hdd inside last, sn btn: nicely bckd on reapp: shwd
promise when 6th sole '99 run (fill mdn, rtd 66): half-sister to a useful sprinter & a wng miler: better for race.
3986} **MADAME GENEREUX** 99 [5] N A Graham 3-8-11 L Dettori 14/1: 0-4: Mid-div, short of room 3f out, **3** **61**
modest late gains: well btn on sole '99 start (6f mdn, firm grnd): half-sister to a useful 7f juv: apprec further.
-- **JODEEKA** [11] 3-8-11 G Duffield 25/1: 5: Veered right start, rear till ran on strongly inside last, **¾** **60**
nvr nrr: half-sister to wng 6/7f AW performers Blue Kite & Blue Star: with J A Glover, sure to impr for the run.
4294} **BETHESDA** 99 [4] 3-8-11 T Quinn 1/1 FAV: 265-6: Cl-up, wknd qckly over 1f out: hvly bckd on **½** **59**
reapp: rnr-up on '99 debut (fillies mdn), subs ddhtd for 6th in the Gr 1 Cheveley Park (rtd 96): suited
by 6f on gd & gd/soft: disapp run today but possibly not handle testing conditions.
759 **FLYING CARPET** 14 [6] 3-8-11 K Darley 20/1: 0-67: Dwelt, modest late gains: see 759 (7f). **3** **53**
794 **SAVANNAH QUEEN** 12 [2] 3-8-11 M Fenton 14/1: 58: Led, hdd appr final 1f, wknd quickly: op 10/1. **2½** **48**
4081} **CUPIDS CHARM** 99 [8] 3-8-11 J Fortune 9/1: 4-9: Al in rear: 4th on sole '99 start (fillies mdn, **1¾** **45**
rtd 76, P Chapple Hyam): stays 6f on firm: now with R Guest.
2595} **PERUGINO PEARL** 99 [3] 3-8-11 D Mernagh (3) 66/1: -00-0: Prom, wknd fnl 2f: 10th: mod form. **6** **35**
-- **DAYLILY** [9] 3-8-11 Pat Eddery 10/1: 0: Dwelt, al rear, fin last: op 7/1: Pips Pride filly: **7** **25**
cost 30,000gnd: should learn plenty for the run: with T D Easterby.
11 ran   Time 1m 22.2 (8.1)   (Mrs Marion E Southcott)   S C Williams Newmarket

LINGFIELD (Equitrack)   WEDNESDAY APRIL 12TH   Lefthand, V Sharp Track

Official Going   STANDARD. Stalls: Inside, Except 5f - Outside

878 2.00 EBF TANDRIDGE MDN 2YO (D)   5f aw rnd   Going 21 -31 Slow
£3201   £985   £492   £246

730 **JUSTALORD** 18 [4] W G M Turner 2-9-0 A Daly 3/1: -61: 2 b g King's Signet - Just Lady (Emarati) **71a**
Broke well & sn clr in lead, held on well under hands & heels riding ins last: op 5/2: Apr foal, dam a 5f juv wnr,
sire a useful sprinter: eff over a sharp 5f on equitrack: likes to force the pace.
743 **MAMORE GAP** 16 [3] R Hannon 2-9-0 Dane O'Neill 30/100 FAV: 22: 2 b c General Monash - *nk* **70a**
Ravensdale Rose (Henbit) Sn chsd ldr, kept on well ins last, post came to sn: bckd: acts on fast & equitrack.
812 **SIZE DOESN'T MATTER** 9 [1] J R Best 2-9-0 S Sanders 20/1: 03: 2 b c Greensmith - Singing Rock **12** **47a**
(Ballad Rock) Sn bhd, nvr nr front 2: see 812 (turf).
3 ran   Time 1m 00.4 (2.6)   (Mrs M S Teversham)   W G M Turner Corton Denham, Somerset

879 2.30 MARSHALLS HCAP 3YO+ 0-75 (E)   7f aw rnd   Going 21 +05 Fast   [70]
£2758   £788   £394   3 yo rec 14lb

*721 **RAIN RAIN GO AWAY** 18 [1] D J S Cosgrove 4-10-0 (70) R Ffrench 15/8 FAV: 614311: 4 ch g Miswaki - **76a**
Stormagain (Storm Cat) Led after 1f, rdn & clr dist, styd on under hands & heels riding, eased nr line: well bckd,
gd time: earlier scored at W'hampton (2, mdn & h'cap) & here at Lingfield (stks): unplcd in '99 (rtd 50 & 54a, E
Dunlop): suited by 7f, stays 1m on soft, likes both AWs: likes to race with/force the pace: gd weight carrier.
4219} **ITHADTOBEYOU** 99 [4] G L Moore 5-8-7 (49) D Holland 13/2: 3600-2: 5 b h Prince Sabo - Secret **2** **49a**
Valentine (Wollow) Led 1f, remained handy, kept on fnl 2f tho' al held by wnr: clr rem, reapp: plcd in '99 (rtd
59 & 49a): '98 Lingfield wnr (mdn, debut, rtd 86a, P Cole): eff at 5/7f on fast & both AWs: eff with/without blnks.
776 **UNCHAIN MY HEART** 14 [8] R J Meehan 4-9-2 (58)(bl) J R McCabe 12/1: 30-163: 4 b f Pursuit Of Love - *6* **49a**
Addicted To Love (Touching Wood) Chsd ldrs wide, outpcd fnl 2f: op 7/1: see 616 (C/D, clmr, made most).
754 **DOLPHINELLE** 15 [2] R Hannon 4-8-11 (53) Dane O'Neill 9/2: 443034: Sn bhd, rdn/mod late gains. *nk* **43a**
776 **ROI DE DANSE** 14 [6] 5-8-5 (47) F Norton 13/2: 225025: Rdn/chsd ldrs, outpcd over 2f out: op 4/1. **¾** **36a**
106 **ELEGANT DANCE** 99 [3] 6-8-7 (49) A Clark 20/1: 0000-6: Dwelt, sn struggling rear: reapp, op 14/1: **12** **20a**
plcd in '99 (rtd 66 & 43a, h'cap): '98 Salisbury wnr (fill h'cap, rtd 66): eff at 6f, stays 1m: acts on gd & fast.
630 **BORDER GLEN** 39 [5] 4-9-6 (62)(bl) J Weaver 5/1: -36267: Sn outpcd/switched wide, no impress: btr 596. **6** **24a**
750 **GHAAZI** 15 [7] 4-8-12 (54)(bl) I Mongan (5) 11/1: 14-008: Sn rdn/struggling halfway: blnks reapp. **6** **7a**
8 ran   Time 1m 23.89 (1.09)   (G G Grayson)   D J S Cosgrove Newmarket, Suffolk

880 3.00 P HALL MEMORIAL HCAP 3YO+ 0-75 (E)   1m2f aw   Going 21 -14 Slow   [72]
£2730   £780   £390   3 yo rec 19lb

*420 **KATHAKALI** 74 [2] V Soane 3-8-10 (73) Martin Dwyer 11/2: 0-2111: 3 b c Dancing Dissident - She's **77a**
A Dancer (Alzao) Sn rdn, chsd ldrs, styd on gamely for press fnl 2f to lead ins last, rdn out: op 4/1, 10 wk abs:
earlier scored here at Lingfield (auct mdn & C/D h'cap): unplcd '99 (rtd 69, nov auct, fred stks): eff at
1m/10f, further could suit: acts on fast, equitrack/Lingfield specialist: handles a sharp/gall trk: runs well fresh.
776 **THATCHAM** 14 [7] R W Armstrong 4-8-6 (50) G Hall 13/2: 000-32: 4 ch g Thatching - Calaloo Sioux **1** **52a**
(Our Native) Cl-up, led over 3f out, rdn over 1f out & hdd ins last, no extra: styd longer 10f trip, acts on eqtrk.

LINGFIELD (Equitrack)   WEDNESDAY APRIL 12TH   Lefthand, V Sharp Track

618   **SERGEANT IMP** 42 [1] P Mitchell 5-7-10 (40)(3oh) M Henry 12/1: -33543: 5 b g Mac's Imp - Genzyme   1   41$
Gene (Riboboy) Rdn/rear, prog 5f out, kept on onepace fnl 2f: clr rem: op 8/1: 6 wk abs: see 400, 316 (sell).
596   **PACIFIC ALLIANCE** 46 [5] M Wigham 4-9-5 (63)(bl) Dean McKeown 100/30: 14-344: Keen, led 7f out,   7   54a
wknd qckly fnl 1f: well bckd tho' op 5/2, 6 wk abs: blnks reapplied & possibly raced too freely: see 463.
*620   **MULLAGHMORE** 42 [6] 4-10-0 (72)(bl) D Holland 5/2 FAV: 4-1515: Chsd ldrs, btn 3f out: op 3/1,   4   57a
jockey reported gldg hung left thr'out: 6 wk abs, top weight: btr 620 (C/D).
842   **SAMMYS SHUFFLE** 5 [4] 5-9-1 (59)(bl) O Urbina 9/1: 015306: Bhd 4f out, no impress: quick reapp.   2½   40a
*772   **SEA DANZIG** 14 [3] 7-9-12 (70)(bl) J Weaver 8/1: 042217: Rear/wide, btn 4f out: op 5/1: stewards   1¾   49a
enquired into running, jockey reported gldg taken wide to avoid kick back: blnks reapp today: btr 772 (4 rnr stks).
771   **FULHAM** 14 [8] 4-8-6 (50)(bl) F Norton 20/1: 00-428: Bhd halfway: op 12/1: flattered 771 (C/D, mdn).   3½   24a
8 ran   Time 2m 06.27 (3.47)   (M B N Clements)   V Soane East Garston, Berks

881	3.30 N. KENT-LEMON HCAP 3YO+ 0-80 (D) 6f aw rnd Going 21 + 04 Fast [80]
	£3802 £1170 £585 £292 3 yo rec 12lb

337   **MISTER TRICKY** 88 [2] P Mitchell 5-9-4 (70) J F Egan 3/1 JT FAV: 11-201: 5 ch g Magic Ring - Splintering   79a
(Sharpo) Trkd ldrs, rdn to lead dist, styd on strongly, pushed out: gd time, 3 month abs: '99 Windsor, Goodwood
(h'cap), Brighton (class stks, rtd 66) & Lingfield wnr (4, incl 1 turf, rtd 73a): '98 wnr here at Lingfield (2
h'caps, rtd 66a): stays 1m, suited by 6/7f: acts on firm, gd/soft & loves eqtrack/Lingfield: handles any trk:
runs well fresh: tough & genuine gelding who should win more races this time.
763   **DIAMOND GEEZER** 15 [5] R Hannon 4-9-1 (67) Dane O'Neill 11/2: 23-502: 4 br c Tenby - Unaria (Prince   2½   68a
Tenderfoot) Rdn/outpcd 2f out, kept on ins last, al held: see 113 (C/D).
802   **WISHBONE ALLEY** 12 [7] M Dods 5-8-0 (52)(vis) C Rutter 10/1: 204203: 5 b g Common Grounds - Dul   1   51a
Dul (Shadeed) Cl-up wide, onepace/held over 1f out: op 8/1: see 312 (5f).
719   **PALO BLANCO** 18 [8] Andrew Reid 9-7-10 (48) M Henry 14/1: /0-334: Cl-up wide, onepace fnl 2f.   1   45a
*691   **CHARGE** 25 [1] 4-9-11 (77)(t) Darren Williams (7) 100/30: 002215: Led, hdd over 1f out, fdd: bckd.   1¼   71a
785   **OTIME** 14 [4] 3-8-11 (75)(vis) Dean McKeown 16/1: -60206: Sn rdn/towards rear, nvr factor: op 10/1.   6   58a
611   **POLAR ICE** 43 [9] 4-8-10 (62) D Young (7) 16/1: 0-0007: Reluctant to race, sn t.o., mod late gains: 1   43a
op 10/1, 6 wk abs: prev with D J S Cosgrove, now with N P Littmoden: see 611, 364.
628   **MISS DANGEROUS** 39 [6] 9-7-10 (48)(bl) (2oh) J Mackay (7) 16/1: 303558: Al outpcd: op 12/1:   1¼   26a
blnks reapplied: see 243 (7f, made all, stks).
*774   **BOLD EFFORT** 14 [3] 8-10-0 (80)(bl) S Sanders 3/1 JT FAV: 040019: In tch wide 3f: bckd: btr 774.   30   0a
9 ran   Time 1m 11.44 (1.04)   (The Magicians)   P Mitchell Epsom, Surrey

882	4.00 SPONSORSHIP SELLER 3YO (G) 1m2f aw Going 21 -23 Slow
	£1834 £524 £262

286   **SHAMAN** 95 [2] G L Moore 3-9-4 I Mongan (5) 8/11 FAV: 041-21: 3 b g Fraam - Magic Maggie (Beveled)   66a
Trkd ldr halfway, rdn/led 3f out & sn in command, pushed out: hvly bckd, no bid, reapp: '99 scorer at Folkestone
(rtd 71, M Channon) & here at Lingfield (sells, rtd 66a): eff at 1m/above 10f on fast & gd, likes equitrack/
Lingfield, handles any trk: enjoys sell grade & runs well fresh.
545   **ARMENIA** 53 [4] R Hannon 3-8-13 Dane O'Neill 11/4: -21432: 3 ch f Arazi - Atlantic Flyer (Storm Bird)   6   51a
Trkd ldrs, rdn/chsd wnr over 1f out, al held: op 2/1: claimed for £5,000: abs: stays a sharp 10f: see 415 (1m).
688   **LOVE IN VAIN** 26 [1] M L W Bell 3-8-7 M Fenton 9/2: 033: 3 b f Lahib - Little America (Belmez)   3   41a
Led 1f & remained handy, onepace fnl out: op 6/1: longer 10f trip, mod form prev.
807   **CROESO ADREF** 12 [3] S C Williams 3-8-13 G Faulkner (3) 7/1: 236434: Led after 1f till 3f out, sn btn.   1¾   45a
4 ran   Time 2m 07.23 (4.43)   (Mrs S M Redjep)   G L Moore Woodingdean, E Sussex

883	4.30 WATCH THE TRIAL MDN 3YO+ (D) 5f aw rnd Going 21 -08 Slow
	£2743 £844 £422 £211 3 yo rec 11lb

505   **JAZZNIC** 60 [1] W G M Turner 4-9-4 A Daly 20/1: /5-601: 4 b f Alhijaz - Irenic (Mummy's Pet)   59a
Made all, rdn & clr over 1f out, held on gamely ins last, all out: 2 month abs: mod '99 form (P Makin): rnr-up
twice in '98 (rtd 66a & 66): eff forcing pace at 5f, stays 7f: acts on equitrack, handles soft: runs well fresh.
731   **SCAFELL** 18 [1] C Smith 3-8-12 R Fitzpatrick (3) 5/4 FAV: 250-02: 3 b c Puissance - One Half Silver   nk   63a
(Plugged Nickle) Chsd wnr, rdn/outpcd 2f out, kept on well ins last, just held: hvly bckd: AW bow: plcd
4 times in '99 (rtd 79, mdn): eff at 5/6f on firm, gd & equitrack: prob handles any trk.
4430} **CORBLETS** 99 [6] S Dow 3-8-7 P Doe 2/1: 4250-3: 3 b f Timeless Times - Dear Glenda (Gold Song)   1   56a
Chsd ldrs, eff wide over 1f out, not pace to chall: 6 month abs, AW bow: rnr-up in '99 (rtd 79, mdn): eff at
5f, tried 6f, could yet suit: handles fast grnd & equitrack.
4600} **STEVAL** 99 [5] R Guest 3-8-7 Martin Dwyer 20/1: 000-4: In tch, outpcd fnl 2f: 5 month abs, AW   5   47a
bow: rtd 57 at best in '99 (debut, mdn): sire a 6f/1m performer, could apprec further.
729   **ALPHA ROSE** 18 [4] 3-8-7 M Fenton 7/2: 6-55: Sn outpcd rear: AW bow, op 2/1: btr 729.   nk   46a
5 ran   Time 59.23 (1.43)   (O J Stokes)   W G M Turner Corton Denham, Somerset

WARWICK   WEDNESDAY APRIL 12TH   Lefthand, Sharp, Turning Track

Official Going   HEAVY. Stalls: Inside.

884	2.20 NATTRASS GILES MDN 3YO (D) 7f164y Heavy Inapplicable
	£3948 £1215 £607 £303

4460} **MY RETREAT** 99 [14] B W Hills 3-9-0 M Hills 5/1: 52-1: 3 b c Hermitage - My Jessica Ann (Native Rythm)   80
Chsd ldrs till went on briefly over 1f out, rallied well to regain lead ins last, rdn out: in '99 trained by L Cumani
& rnr-up at Brighton (mdn auct, rtd 84): half brother to wnrs in the States, dam a dual wnr: eff at 7.5f, will
stay 1m: handles firm, acts on gd/soft & hvy grnd: handles a sharp/turning trk, runs well fresh: improving colt.
3262} **CRISS CROSS** 99 [17] R Hannon 3-9-0 R Hughes 8/1: 6-2: 3 b c Lahib - La Belle Katherine (Lyphard)   1   78
Trkd ldrs, went on over 1f out, rdn & collared ins last: bckd from 14/1, reapp: IR 15,000 gns purchase:
eff at 7.5f on hvy grnd, runs well fresh: sound run, can find similar.
4515} **UP THE KYBER** 99 [19] R F Johnson Houghton 3-9-0 J Reid 33/1: 00-3: 3 b c Missed Flight - Najariya   2   75

(Northfields) In tch, kept on under press fnl 1f, not pace of front 2: unplcd both juv starts, no luck in running on debut (rtd 62+): eff at 7.5f, 1m/10f suit: handles hvy: qual for h'caps, interesting in that sphere over 1m+.

1894} **GIMCO 99** [20] G C H Chung 3-9-0 R Cochrane 14/1: 5-4: Rear, imprvd halfway, styd on under press fnl 1f: reapp: trained by A Kelleway & 5th at Sandown (mdn, rtd 79+) on sole juv start: appreciate 1m/10f+.   3   70

804   **BILLY BATHWICK 12** [13] 3-9-0 Pat Eddery 4/1: 406-55: Led 3f, again 2f out till dist, fdd: prob not stay 7.5f in these testing conditions: see 804.   4   64

4523} **COCO LOCO 99** [12] 3-8-9 R Price 100/1: 0-6: Prom, rdn & btn over 1f out: reapp: unplcd in a Yarmouth mdn on sole '99 start: interesting 7f/1m performer: with J Pearce.   ½   58

--   **DICKIE DEADEYE** [4] 3-9-0 S Drowne 20/1: 7: Rear, styd on fnl 1f, nvr plcd to chall: debut, op 14/1: related to useful mid-dist h'capper Star Precision & wng hdler Brave Tornado: caught the eye, improve.   ½   62

4613} **KELTECH GOLD 99** [5] 3-9-0 D Sweeney 40/1: -50-8: Prom till hmpd & lost pl halfway, no ch after: 5th in a mdn auct on debut in '99 (rtd 69): cost IR 14,000gns: not much luck in running here, now qual for h'caps.   1   61

4614} **LAHAAY 99** [18] 3-9-0 R Hills 10/1: 05-9: Trkd ldrs 6½f, fdd: reapp.   1½   59

3486} **POLAR CHALLENGE 99** [7] 3-9-0 W R Swinburn 9/4 FAV: -54-0: In tch 5f, fdd into 10th: well bckd tho' op 7/4, reapp: twice eff 2yo, caught the eye when 4th at Chester (mdn, rtd 79+): half brother to a 6/7f wng 2yo: dam mid-dist bred: handles fast & gd/soft, 1m+ will suit: should do better on faster grnd.   10   43

4462} **TAXMERE 99** [15] 3-8-9 J Fanning 66/1: 60-0: Nvr a factor in 11th.   1¼   36

--   **SILVER AURIOLE** [1] 3-8-9 N Pollard 33/1: 0: Al towards rear, fin 12th on debut.   ¾   35

729   **ADRIANA 18** [3] 3-8-9 P Robinson 25/1: 00: Chsd ldrs, led 4f out till over 2f out, wknd into 13th.   2   32

4582} **HYPERSONIC 99** [16] 3-9-0 M Roberts 15/2: 5423-0: Prom till halfway: fin 14th, op 5/1, reapp.   ¾   35

794   Scratch The Dove 13 [8] 3-8-9 N Carlisle 66/1:   --   Erebos [6] 3-9-0 G Duffield 33/1:

4332} Hadath 99 [2] 3-9-0 J Carroll 16/1:   797} Joebertedy 99 [11] 3-9-0 T Williams 66/1:

804   Machudi 12 [9] 3-8-9 K Darley 33/1:

19 ran   Time 1m 44.3   (Ms A Soltesova)   B W Hills Lambourn, Berks

---

885   **2.50 INDEX EVOLUTION HCAP 3YO+ 0-80 (D)**   **1m6f135y Heavy Inapplicable**   [76]
£4102   £1262   £631   £315   4 yo rec 3 lb

860   **GRAND CRU 2** [6] J Cullinan 9-7-10 (44)(bl) (7oh) P M Quinn (5) 33/1: 230001: 9 ch g Kabour - Hydrangea (Warpath) Held up, stdy hdwy to lead over 4f out, qcknd well clr, held on well cl-home: qck reapp: '99 wnr at Southwell (amat class, rtd 68a): unplcd in '98, prev term won at Newbury (h'cap, rtd 66) & again at Southwell (2, clmr for Mrs Reveley & sell for R Craggs, rtd 66a): eff btwn 12f & 2m, acts on gd/soft, hvy grnd & f/sand: likes a sharp trk & has worn blnks last 2 starts: enterprisingly rdn by P Quinn today.   49

788   **MY LEGAL EAGLE 14** [7] R J Price 6-8-7 (55) P Fitzsimons (5) 7/1: 322222: 6 b g Law Society - Majestic Nurse (On Your Mark) Held up, stdy prog to chase wnr over 2f out, ran on well & just btn: clr rem.   ½   59

--   **SHAMPOOED** [12] R Dickin 6-8-2 (50) G Duffield 13/2: 5120/3: 6 b m Law Society - White Cap's (Shirley Heights) Mid-div, hdwy & came stands side home str, no impress on front 2 fnl 1f: recent jumps rnr, this winter won here at Warwick (h'cap hdles, rtd 87h, eff at 2m on firm & soft): missed '99 on the Flat, prev term won at Thurles (stks) & rnr-up at Bath (h'cap, rtd 59): eff at 11f, stays 2m: acts on firm & soft grnd.   12   43

4317} **SEGAVIEW 99** [3] Mrs P Sly 4-9-1 (66) J Fanning 16/1: 1006-4: Prom till outpcd fnl 2f: reapp: '98 York wnr (mdn auct, rtd 80+), caught the eye sev times prev: eff at 12f, shld stay 14f: handles firm, best on gd & soft grnd: handles a gall trk: on a handy mark now.   3   56

726   **DIABLO DANCER 18** [9] 4-9-5 (70) G Hind 20/1: 000-05: Chsd ldrs till went on after 6f, hdd 4f out, grad fdd: op 14/1: rnr-up in a mdn hdle at Ludlow (rtd 99h, eff at 2m on gd/soft) in Feb '00: in early '99 rnr-up at Salisbury (h'cap, rtd 92): '98 wnr at Nottingham (mdn auct) & Lingfield (nov, rtd 91): eff at 10/11.5f, acts on firm & soft grnd: handles a sharp or gall trk, can run well fresh: has tumbled down the weights.   hd   60

1016} **GET THE POINT 99** [1] 6-8-5 (53) D Mernagh (3) 15/2: /0/3-6: Chsd ldrs till wknd fnl 2f: clr of rem: recent jumps rnr, won this winter at Leicester & Doncaster (h'cap hdles, rtd 120h, eff at 2m on gd & hvy): plcd in a Nottingham h'cap (rtd 55) on sole Flat start in '99: 98/99 wnr at Towcester ('97 rnr-up twice in h'caps (rtd 75 for R Hollinshead): eff at 14f, handles fast & soft: should be capable of better.   nk   43

779   **FLETCHER 14** [4] 6-8-12 (60) R Hughes 12/1: 000-07: Nvr a factor: see 182 (sand).   17   36

809   **QUEDEX 11** [13] 4-9-7 (72) S Whitworth 5/1 FAV: 4-6028: Mid-div, wkng when hmpd 3f out: op 7/2: better expected after 809 (12f, gd/soft).   ¾   47

4618} **TRAMLINE 99** [8] 7-9-0 (62) Dale Gibson 16/1: 2000-9: Nvr nr ldrs on reapp: '99 wnr at Sandown (2) & Doncaster (h'caps, rtd 71): '97 Newmarket wnr (ltd stks, rtd 84): eff at 14f/2m, acts on firm & soft grnd: likes a stiff/gall trk, esp Sandown: tough & genuine, capable of much better & back on a wng mark now.   4   33

3718} **RENAISSANCE LADY 99** [2] 4-7-11 (48) A McCarthy (1) 25/1: P200-0: Al rear, fin 10th: jumps fit.   6   13

815   **MISCHIEF 9** [11] 4-8-6 (57)(vis) J Carroll 14/1: 562030: Dwelt, al rear, t.o. in 11th: btr 815.   11   12

805   **JAMAICAN FLIGHT 12** [14] 7-10-0 (76)(VIS) W R Swinburn 8/1: 344320: Led after 1f till 7f out, fdd: fin 12th, top weight: tried a visor, much better without in 805 (12f).   3½   28

714   **WEET FOR ME 19** [5] 4-9-11 (76) A Culhane 7/1: 402-00: Mid-div till btn leaving back str: fin 13th.   4   24

790   **SPARKLING DOVE 13** [10] 7-7-12 (46)(bl) (2ow)(26oh) N Carlisle 50/1: 0000: Early ldr, wknd qckly 4f out: fin last, v stiff task.   10   0

14 ran   Time 3m 27.7   (Turf 2000 Limited)   J Cullinan Quainton, Bucks

---

886   **3.20 EBF MDN FILL 2YO (D)**   **5f rnd Heavy Inapplicable**
£3125   £961   £480   £240

762   **SERVICEABLE 15** [1] J M P Eustace 2-8-11 J Tate 8/1: 31: 2 ch f Pursuit Of Love - Absaloute Service (Absalom) Chsd ldrs, styd far side ent str, went on halfway, ran on strongly, drvn out: half sister to 3 wnrs, notably 6f 2yo wnr Ring Cycle: dam a 5f 2yo scorer: eff over a sharp 5f on hvy grnd, handles fast: acts on a sharp or gall trk: imprvg filly who put her prev experience to gd use today.   82

812   **FRANICA 9** [10] A Bailey 2-8-11 A Mackay 3/1: 22: 2 b f Inzar - Comfrey Glen (Glenstal) Chsd ldrs, came stands side home str, drifted left & kept on fnl 1f, not quite reach wnr: knocking on the door, shld find a similar event: acts on soft & hvy: see 812.   1¾   77

--   **OPEN WARFARE** [5] M Quinn 2-8-11 J Carroll 25/1: 3: 2 br f General Monash - Pipe Opener (Prince Sabo) Outpcd & detached ent home str, ran on strongly far side fnl 1½f, nrst fin: IR 3,800gns Mar foal: half sister to a couple of wnrs, incl an Irish 2yo wnr: sire a useful juv wnr: made up an enormous amount of late grnd, already looks in need of 6f: acts on hvy grnd: eye-catching eff & one to keep in mind.   1¾   73+

--   **EXTRA GUEST** [7] M R Channon 2-8-11 T Quinn 8/1: 4: Chsd ldrs, drifted right & fdd fnl 1f: mkt drifter: Feb foal, cost 19,000gns: half sister to 5f 2yo scorer Patriot: dam a 5f wng juv.   1   71

812   **WANNA SHOUT 9** [4] 2-8-11 J Reid 14/1: 55: Front rank, ev ch dist, sn no extra: see 812.   3½   64

--   **OH SO DUSTY** [2] 2-8-11 Pat Eddery 11/4 FAV: 6: Led till halfway, fdd fnl 1½f: well bckd tho' op   2½   59

7/4: Feb foal, half sister to a mod performer: dam a 5/6f wng juv, sire a v smart sprinter: shld do better.
-- **BLUE LADY** [6] 2-8-11 T G McLaughlin 25/1: 7: Nvr nr ldrs on debut: 6,000 gns Jan foal: 1st foal, dam won over 11f: sire a v smart 6/7f performer: likely to apprec 6f given time: with N Littmoden. *1* **57**
-- **ANTONIAS DILEMMA** [8] 2-8-11 K Darley 8/1: 8: Slowly away, recovered to chase ldrs 3½f, grad fdd: Feb foal, cost 8,000gns: half sister to a 5f wng juv: dam won over 5f as a 2yo, sire a high-class juv. *1¾* **53**
-- **ASTER FIELDS** [3] 2-8-11 J P Spencer 8/1: 9: Front rank, led briefly halfway, wknd over 1f out. *6* **41**
-- **MARGARITA** [9] 2-8-11 Dale Gibson 9/1: 0: Swerved right start, al bhd, fin last: bckd from 20/1. *9* **23**
10 ran Time 1m 4.4 (Major M G Wyatt) J M P Eustace Newmarket

887 3.50 BUSINESSPARTNERS HCAP 3YO 0-65 (F) 6f168y Heavy Inapplicable [72]
£2499 £714 £357

4151} **BALFOUR 99** [1] C E Brittain 3-8-13 (57) L Dettori 8/1: -600-1: 3 b c Green Desert - Badawi (Diesis) Chsd ldrs, hdwy 2f out to lead ins last, drvn out: reapp, first win on h'cap bow: unplcd on 3 juv starts (rtd 70$): dam useful miler: stays 7f & likes hvy grnd: handles an easy trk & runs well fresh: lightly raced. **62**
785 **ALJAZIR 14** [6] E J Alston 3-8-13 (57) L Swift (7) 16/1: 054-02: 3 b g Alhijaz - Duxyana (Cyrano de Bergerac) Prom, hdwy to lead over 1f out, stumbled path, hdd ins last, just btn under hands & heels riding: stays 7f: shade unlucky here, shown enough to win a race: see 785. *hd* **61**
4212} **DIAMOND OLIVIA 99** [11] John Berry 3-8-9 (53) O Pears 20/1: 3640-3: 3 b f Beveled - Queen Of The Quorn (Governor General) Slow away, bhd till hdwy over 2f out, edged right & switched left ins last, kept on, not btn far: plcd on debut as a juv for W Turner (rtd 67a): eff at 5f, stays 7f on fibresand & hvy. *½* **56**
4539} **AN JOLIEN 99** [4] M J Ryan 3-9-2 (60) P McCabe 20/1: 0050-4: In tch, eff 2f out, onepace: reapp: unplcd on 4 juv starts (rtd 67 at best): eff at 6/7f on firm & hvy grnd: has run poorly in blnks. *2* **60**
785 **AISLE 14** [9] 3-9-2 (60)(bl) S Finnamore (5) 16/1: 225505: Prom, led halfway till over 1f out, no extra. *½* **59**
731 **TAKE MANHATTAN 18** [17] 3-9-1 (59) T Quinn 12/1: 0-006: Chsd ldrs, well over 1f out: lngr trip. *5* **51**
813 **ISLAND THYMES 9** [12] 3-9-0 (58) J Reid 7/1 FAV: 406-37: Led till halfway, wknd: btr 813. *6* **41**
4454} **GLEN VALE WALK 99** [5] 3-9-4 (62) G Duffield 20/1: 003-8: Al bhd: reapp: plcd on last of 3 juv starts (sell, rtd 66): stays 8.3f on gd/soft: dam styd 12f. *3* **40**
4498} **TERM OF ENDEARMENT 99** [13] 3-8-11 (55) R Price 20/1: 0060-9: Al bhd: won 2nd of 10 juv starts, at Bath (auct mdn, rtd 81): eff at 5.8f on gd grnd. *nk* **33**
4408} **BERKELEY HALL 99** [20] 3-9-0 (58) K Darley 8/1: -003-0: In tch, wknd halfway: 10th. *hd* **35**
813 **DISTANT GUEST 9** [18] 3-9-7 (65) P Robinson 10/1: 000-20: In tch till wknd over 2f out: 11th. *1* **41**
3160} **SEA EMPEROR 99** [16] 3-9-0 (58) A Mackay 20/1: -000-0: Al bhd: 12th: reapp. *1¼* **32**
112 **PHOEBUS 99** [10] 3-9-6 (64) R Brisland (5) 14/1: 0415-0: In tch, wknd over 2f out: 13th, op 10/1. *2* **35**
4182} **BOTTELINO JOE 99** [8] 3-9-5 (63) M Roberts 10/1: 0045-0: Dwelt, al bhd: 14th, reapp. *1¼* **32**
2775} **WONDERLAND 99** [2] 3-9-0 (58) C Lowther 12/1: -656-0: Handy till btn halfway: 15th: reapp. *2* **24**
*706 **CHILI PEPPER 20** [19] 3-8-9 (53)(bl) C Carver (3) 8/1: 50-610: Handy, wknd 3f out: 16th, btr 706 (a/w). *shd* **19**
773 **Xativa 14** [14] 3-8-11 (55) J P Spencer 20/1: 24 **Lea Valley Express 99** [15] 3-8-10 (54)(vis) S Whitworth 25/1:
479 **Risky Gem 64** [7] 3-9-1 (59) G Bardwell 12/1:
19 ran Time 1m 30.2 (Sheikh Marwan Al Maktoum) C E Brittain Newmarket

888 4.20 LUCENT CLASSIFIED STKS 3YO 0-75 (D) 6f rnd Heavy Inapplicable
£4084 £1256 £628 £314

4508} **FOOTPRINTS 99** [7] M Johnston 3-8-8 J Fanning 4/1: 021-1: 3 b f College Chapel - Near Miracle (Be My Guest) Led, hard rdn & collared just ins last, rallied gamely to get up again nr line: won last of 3 juv starts, at Redcar (med auct mdn, rtd 75): eff at 5/6f on fast, likes hvy grnd, any trk: runs well fresh: genuine. **76**
4612} **CHORUS 99** [6] B R Millman 3-8-8 P Robinson 10/1: 2544-2: 3 b f Bandmaster - Name That Tune (Fayruz) Handy, eff over 1f out, led ins last, collared again nr fin: reapp: rnr-up twice as a juv (rtd 71 at best): eff at 5/6f on firm, hvy grnd & on any trk: shown enough to win a race. *hd* **76**
3629} **KEEP TAPPING 99** [5] J A Osborne 3-8-11 J P Spencer 20/1: 0000-3: 3 b c Mac's Imp - Mystery Bid (Auction Ring) In tch, eff over 1f out, kept on ins last, not btn far: as a juv trained by A Jarvis, won one of 11 starts at Sandown (mdn, rtd 84): dam mid-dist mdn: eff at 5/6f on gd/firm, hvy & on any trk: sharper for this. *½* **78**
652 **PERUVIAN JADE 35** [1] N P Littmoden 3-8-8 T G McLaughlin 20/1: 044-64: In tch, hdwy to chall just ins fnl 1f, no extra: acts on fast, hvy & fibresand: see 652. *shd* **74**
811 **DESERT SAFARI 11** [4] 3-8-8 L Swift (7) 20/1: 041-05: Slow away, waited with, kept on nicely over 1f out, hands & heels riding: won once as a juv, at Musselburgh (fills med auct mdn, rtd 74): eff at 5f, stays 6f on fast, hvy & prob fibresand: won last term when wearing blnks, much closer next time when refitted. *1¼* **72**
4491} **RAILROADER 99** [8] 3-8-11 S Drowne 20/1: 0340-6: Handy, rdn & edged left over 1f out, onepace: fin 3rd on 2 of 6 juv starts (rtd 78): stays 6f on gd & hvy grnd & on a stiff trk. *¾* **73**
+179 **DANCING EMPRESS 99** [15] 3-8-8 Lindsey Rutty (7) 20/1: 3021-7: Front rank 1f, sn well bhd, styd on nicely on stands side fnl 2f with jockey adjusting goggles twice: abs & Stewards noted this was jockey's first public ride: acts on firm, hvy & fibresand: plenty of encouragement here, interesting with an experienced pilot. *1¼* **68+**
4089} **MELLOW JAZZ 99** [11] 3-8-8 L Dettori 9/4 FAV: 1-8: Waited with, hdwy & not clr run over 1f out, onepace: won sole juv start, at Nottingham (mdn, rtd 75): eff at 6f, 7f sure to suit: handles gd, hvy & when fresh. *¾* **66**
491 **SMOKIN BEAU 62** [13] 3-8-11 D Sweeney 20/1: 5-3209: Waited with, eff & slightly short of room over 1f out, no danger: btr 361 (5f, fibresand). *2* **65**
4491} **GRANDMA ULLA 99** [16] 3-8-8 S Whitworth 25/1: 1000-0: Slow away, al bhd: 10th: won one of 5 juv starts, at Kempton (med auct mdn, rtd 82): likes to front run over 6f on gd/firm grnd. *2½* **57**
3861} **BORN TO RULE 99** [2] 3-8-11 L Newman (5) 25/1: -044-0: With ldrs till wknd well over 1f out: 11th. *shd* **60**
*472 **CASTLEBAR 65** [3] 3-9-0 T Quinn 20/1: 10: Cl-up till wknd 2f out: 12th: 2 month abs, btr 472 (a/w). *3* **57**
4355} **SANTIBURI GIRL 99** [9] 3-8-8 R Mullen 10/1: 5400-0: With ldrs, wkng when sltly short of room over 1f out: 13th, bckd from 20/1: reapp. *4* **43**
4612} **INDIAN MUSIC 99** [14] 3-8-11 G Carter 12/1: 4001-0: Al bhd: reapp, 14th. *3½* **39**
4431} **DOUBLE GUN 99** [12] 3-8-11 R Hughes 10/1: 043-0: Cl-up, wknd 2f out: 15th, reportedly lost action. *3½* **32**
15 ran Time 1m 21.5 (Mrs Joan Keaney) M Johnston Middleham, N Yorks

889 4.50 INDEX HCAP DIV 1 3YO+ 0-60 (F) 1m2f110y Heavy Inapplicable [60]
£2478 £708 £354 3 yo rec 19lb

707 **KINGFISHERS BONNET 20** [19] S G Knight 4-8-10 (42) L Newman (5) 12/1: 624-01: 4 b f Hamas - Mainmast (Bustino) Waited with, gd hdwy over 2f out to lead ins fnl 1f, kept on, drvn out: 1st win on 21st start: rnr-up 3 times in '99 (rtd 52): stays 10.5f well on fast, likes hvy grnd. **47**

WARWICK WEDNESDAY APRIL 12TH Lefthand, Sharp, Turning Track

-- **ROCK SCENE** [6] A Streeter 8-8-7 (39) P Dobbs (3) 33/1: 1000/2: 8 b g Scenic - Rockeater (Roan Rocket) Waited with, gd hdwy to lead over 1f out, hdd & no extra ins last: clr of rem on 1st start for 2 seasons: back in '98 won at Warwck (mdn h'cap, rtd 48): stays 11f on gd & hvy grnd: fine comeback. *3* **40**
835 **LOST SPIRIT 5** [20] P W Hiatt 4-8-9 (41) Joanna Badger (7) 25/1: 506003: 4 b g Strolling Along - Shoag (Affirmed) Keen, led 6f out till over 1f out, no extra: quick reapp, btr 290 (equitrack). *5* **36**
803 **SACREMENTUM 12** [8] J A Osborne 5-9-8 (54) Pat Eddery 11/1: 402064: In tch, outpcd over 4f out, eff over 2f out, onepace: big step up in trip: see 582 (7f). *1½* **47**
4522} **VANBOROUGH LAD 99** [13] 11-8-6 (38) G Duffield 8/1: 0046-5: In tch, no impress fnl 2f: busy in '99, won at Bath (reapp) & Haydock (amat h'caps, rtd 50): '98 wnr at Windsor (h'cap): suited by 10f, stays 11.5f on firm, hvy & on any trk, likes Bath: has run well fresh: tough 11yo, on a handy mark & runs well for an amateur. *2* **29**
790 **OUDALMUTEENA 13** [1] 5-9-7 (53) R Cochrane 16/1: 00-006: In tch, rdn & btn 2f out: frustrating mdn. *2½* **41**
1326} **DANCING DERVISH 99** [12] 5-9-6 (52)(vis) W Hutchinson (6) 33/1: 0/00-7: Al bhd: well btn both '99 starts: '98 Brighton wnr (with I Balding, h'cap, rtd 64): styd 9.5f on firm, soft & on any trk: eff in blnks/visor. *nk* **39**
705 **TAJAR 20** [7] 8-8-11 (43) S Whitworth 9/1: 030-68: Chsd ldrs, hdwy over 3f out & sn ev ch, wknd appr fnl 1f: slipped down the weights & could do better on a sounder surface: see 705. *3½* **26**
699 **ZAHA 20** [11] 5-9-9 (55) R Price 5/1 FAV: 50-609: Slow away, sn in tch, eff over 3f out, wknd 2f out. *14* **22**
859 **BRIDAL WHITE 2** [10] 4-8-8 (40) G Carter 20/1: 00-000: Al bhd: 10th: quick reapp: see 676. *8* **0**
846 **ACE OF TRUMPS 4** [5] 4-9-9 (55)(t) N Kennedy 10/1: 00-100: Led till over 6f out, wknd 3f out: 11th. *2* **12**
4522} **COUNT FREDERICK 99** [17] 4-9-1 (47) L Dettori 11/2: 0220-0: Al bhd, t.o. last: plcd sev times in '99 (rtd 47): stays 10f on fast, soft grnd & on any trk. **0**
784 **Court Champagne 14** [15] 4-8-12 (44) P Fitzsimons(5) 33/1:
803 **Sterling High 12** [4] 5-9-2 (48)(t) R Winston 25/1:
496 **Woolly Winsome 61** [14] 4-9-0 (46) T Quinn 20/1:
3530} **Druridge Bay 99** [3] 4-8-12 (44) S Righton 20/1:
750 **Just Wiz 15** [2] 4-10-0 (60)(bl) R Hughes 16/1:
651 **White Waters 35** [9] 4-9-5 (51) D Griffiths 33/1:
18 ran Time 2m 28.4 (P J Wightman) S G Knight West Hatch, Somerset

890

5.20 INDEX HCAP DIV 2 3YO+ 0-60 (F) 1m2f110y Heavy Inapplicable [60]
£2467 £705 £352 3 yo rec 19lb

675 **GABLESEA 27** [3] B P J Baugh 6-9-0 (46) A Culhane 16/1: -02461: 6 b g Beveled - Me Spede (Valiyar) Hmpd start & held up, prog & no room over 2f out, led ins last, rdn out: plcd sev times in '99 (rtd 60, h'cap): '98 Chepstow & Haydock wnr (h'caps, rtd 55 & 55a): eff at 7f/1m, now stays a sharp 10.5f: acts on firm, hvy & fibresand: looks nicely h'capped, can win again. **53**
648 **PIPS BRAVE 37** [15] M J Polglase 4-8-12 (44)(bl) R Lappin 12/1: 0-3602: 4 b g Be My Chief - Pipistrelle (Shareef Dancer) Held up, rdn & kept on well fnl 2f, not pace of wnr: acts on fast, hvy & f/sand. *1¼* **49**
4579} **DINAR 99** [2] R Brotherton 5-8-9 (41) Claire Bryan (5) 14/1: 1200-3: 5 b h Dixieland Band - Bold Jessie (Never So Bold) Keen, prom, led halfway till ins last, no extra nr fin: 5 month abs: prev with P Bowen, '99 Kempton scorer (h'cap, rtd 46): eff at 12f, tried 2m: acts on firm & hvy: likes a sharp/easy trk. *3* **42**
4574} **KATIE KOMAITE 99** [11] Mrs G S Rees 7-8-7 (39)(vis) A Mackay 16/1: 0010-4: Dwelt, towards rear, rdn & kept on well fnl 2f, not pace to chall: op 12/1: 5 month abs: '99 Newcastle scorer (h'cap, rtd 43 at best): '98 Pontefract wnr (h'cap, rtd 45 at best): eff at 1m/10f on firm, likes gd/soft & soft grnd, handles any trk, likes a stiff/gall one: best in a visor, tho' is eff without: best held up for late run. *hd* **39**
3970} **LEGENDARY LOVER 99** [12] 6-9-7 (53) S Whitworth 12/1: 6066-5: Held up, rdn & kept on fnl 2f, no threat: 12 wk jumps abs, Nov '99 Fontwell wnr (mdn hdle, rtd 100h, subs tried visor): rnr-up in '99 (rtd 67, h'cap, also rtd 42a): eff at 10f/11.4f on fast & hvy grnd. *hd* **53**
238 **HATHNI KHOUND 99** [7] 4-9-4 (50) G Duffield 20/1: 0200-6: Held up, not pace to chall: jumps fit (mod form): plcd twice in '99 (rtd 51, h'cap, no sand form): eff arnd 10f on gd/soft & soft: still a mdn. *1½* **48**
1205} **GINNER MORRIS 99** [14] 5-8-13 (45) R Winston 16/1: 0045-7: Chsd ldrs, wknd fnl 1f: jumps fit (rtd 96h, nov, current connections): prev with C Booth, unplcd in '99 (rtd 46 & 26a, h'caps): place form in '98 (rtd 50 & 46a): eff arnd 1m/10f: handles equitrack, gd/soft & hvy: handles a sharp/gall trk: mdn, with J Hetherton. *shd* **43**
3444} **PAS DE PROBLEME 99** [10] 4-9-13 (59) Dale Gibson 25/1: 6050-8: Prom, rdn & wknd over 1f out: top weight, reapp: unplcd in '99 (rtd 70, h'cap): '98 rnr-up (stks, debut, rtd 79+): stays 9f on gd & fast grnd. *2* **54**
2407} **I RECALL 99** [16] 9-8-10 (42)(tvi) L Newman (5) 20/1: /200-9: Dwelt, nvr on terms: jumps fit. *4* **33**
4579} **BRIERY MEC 99** [13] 5-8-11 (43) G Bardwell 10/1: 0233-0: Held up, rdn halfway, no impress: 10th, abs. *3* **31**
4522} **JUNIKAY 99** [1] 6-9-9 (55) K Darley 13/2: 5044-0: Held up, rdn/no impress 3f out: 11th, reapp. *5* **37**
4578} **HAROLDON 99** [19] 11-8-8 (40) P Fitzsimons (5) 25/1: 3305-0: Dwelt, al rear: 12th: 5 month abs. *hd* **21**
4156} **HOH GEM 99** [4] 4-8-8 (40) G Carter 20/1: 0000-0: Led 5f, btn 2f out: 16th, 7 month abs. **0**
*618 **SILVERTOWN 42** [8] 5-9-9 (55) J P Spencer 3/1 FAV: 20-110: Chsd ldrs, btn 3f out, eased over 2f out: bckd tho' op 5/2, 6 wk abs: jockey reported gldg clipped rivals heels & nvr trav after: nicely h'capped. **0**
2309} **Delta Georgia 99** [5] 4-9-1 (47) D Griffiths 25/1:
699 **Ferny Factors 20** [9] 4-9-9 (55) R Cochrane 14/1:
810} **City Pursuit 99** [18] 4-9-10 (56) T Quinn 20/1:
3364} **Burning 99** [20] 8-9-5 (51) T G McLaughlin 20/1:
255 **Azzan 99** [17] 4-9-9 (55)(t) J Reid 33/1:
19 ran Time 2m 29.2 (Messrs Chrimes, Winn & Wilson) B P J Baugh Audley, Staffs

BRIGHTON THURSDAY APRIL 13TH Lefthand, Very Sharp, Undulating Track

Official Going GOOD/SOFT (GOOD places). Stalls: Inside, except 10f & 12f - Outside.

891

2.00 GO RACING FREE MDN 2YO (D) 5f59y rnd Good/Soft 78 -20 Slow
£3181 £978 £489 £244

821 **SIR FRANCIS 8** [6] J Noseda 2-9-0 W R Swinburn 4/5 FAV: 521: 2 b c Common Grounds - Red Note (Rusticaro): Front rank, went on halfway, held on well cl-home, drvn out: hvly bckd: 36,000gns half-brother to a couple of 2yo wnrs: eff at 5.3f, will stay 6f: acts on fast & soft, can run up with/force the pace: in form. **86**
-- **BRAM STOKER** [4] R Hannon 2-9-0 Dane O'Neill 9/1: 2: 2 ch c General Monash - Taniokey (Grundy): Dwelt, imprvd from rear 2f out, styd on well fnl 1f, just failed: op 7/1: 30,000gns Feb foal: half-brother to sev wnrs, incl prolific mid-dist scorer Harlequin Walk: dam won over 1m in Ireland: eff at 5f, already needs 6f: acts on gd/soft grnd & handles a sharp/undul trk: will sn go one better. *¾* **84**
-- **BLAKESHALL BOY** [1] M R Channon 2-9-0 T Quinn 6/1: 3: 2 b c Piccolo - Giggleswick Girl (Full Extent): Chsd ldrs, rdn & onepcd fnl 1f: ran green: Mar foal, dam a 6f wng juv: handles gd/soft: fair debut. *2½* **78**
-- **REPEAT PERFORMANCE** [5] W G M Turner 2-9-0 A Daly 4/1: 4: Set pace till halfway, no extra fnl 1f: *½* **76**

tchd 11/2: 34,000gns Apr foal: dam a wng styr: sire an influence for speed, but plenty of stamina on dams side.
-- **BLUEBEL** [7] 2-8-9 J F Egan 25/1: 5: Chsd ldrs 3f, fdd: ran green, ndd race: Jan foal, cost 3,000 gns: half-sister to a 2yo wnr abroad: sire a high class sprinter: early 2yo who prob needs sell grade. 9 **53**
-- **A B MY BOY** [2] 2-9-0 S Carson (5) 33/1: 6: Outpcd, nvr a factor: May foal, half-brother to a couple of fair wnrs, incl juv scorer Two Left Feet: dam won over 10f as a juv: with E Wheeler. 7 **44**
-- **HURLINGHAM STAR** [3] 2-9-0 Pat Eddery 14/1: 7: Slowly away, al bhd, t.o. in last: op 10/1: Apr foal, cost 17,000gns: sire a smart 2yo: with P Mitchell. 17 **14**
7 ran Time 1m 05.2 (5.2) (L P Calvente) J Noseda Newmarket.

892

2.30 CUMING PENTAR HCAP 3YO 0-70 (E) 1m2f Good/Soft 78 -17 Slow [77]
£3174 £976 £488 £244

*800 **SMOOTH SAND 14** [1] M A Jarvis 3-9-7 (70) P Robinson 9/2 JT FAV: 040-11: 3 b c Desert Secret - Baby Smooth (Apalachee): Prom, went on 2f out, kept on gamely fnl 1f, drvn out: bckd from 6/1, jnt top-weight: recent reapp wnr at Musselburgh (mdn h'cap): dam a multiple scorer in the States: eff at 1m, stays a sharp 10f: acts on gd & gd/soft, likes a sharp trk: runs v well fresh, a gd weight carrier: imprvg colt who cld complete hat-trick. **77**
103 **RATIFIED 99** [20] H Candy 3-7-12 (46)(1ow) C Rutter 25/1: 0000-2: 3 b g Not In Doubt - Festival Of Magic (Clever Trick): Waited with, gd hdwy to chall over 1f out, kept on & not btn far: 5L clr 3rd, reapp: unplcd in mdn company in '99: half-brother to a juv wnr in the USA: dam scored over 1m: apprec this step up to 10f, acts on gd/soft grnd: runs well fresh & handles a sharp/undul trk: open to further improvement. ¾ **52**
597 **CHILLI 47** [17] C E Brittain 3-8-5 (54) G Hall 16/1: 0-3323: 3 br g Most Welcome - So Saucy (Teenoso): Prom, rdn & onepcd final 1½f: 7 wk abs: see 597 (AW). 5 **52**
744 **ESTABLISHMENT 17** [9] C A Cyzer 3-9-7 (70) L Dettori 9/2 JT FAV: 600-64: Rear, imprvd 3f out, styd on under press but not pace to chall: bckd from 6/1: jnt top weight: stays an easy 10f, middle dist bred. 1 **67**
*783 **LAGO DI LEVICO 15** [14] 3-8-13 (62) W Ryan 11/1: 0-15: Rear, prog to chase ldrs 2f out, no impress fnl 1f: tchd 20/1: prob not quite get home over this lngr 10f trip: see 783 (1m sell, reapp, gd grnd). 1½ **57**
806 **COLLEGE ROCK 13** [5] 3-8-8 (57)(vis) P Doe 25/1: 3-0426: Front rank, led 4f out till 2f out, fdd. 2½ **48**
744 **SECOND PAIGE 17** [6] 3-8-9 (58) R Cochrane 13/2: 000-47: Chsd ldrs, onepcd fnl 2f: bt 4th in 744. 1 **48**
744 **SPIRIT OF LIGHT 17** [10] 3-9-7 (70) T Quinn 7/1: 205-08: Mid-div, effort 3f out, no impress fnl 1½f: prob not stay this lngr 10f trip: eye-catching reapp in 744 (1m, fast grnd). 2 **57**
4516} **TWOS BETTER 99** [15] 3-9-1 (64) I Mongan (5) 16/1: 000-9: Nvr better than mid-div on reapp: some promise in 7f/1m juv mdns last year: dam a mid-dist wnr: bred to apprec mid-dists & shld be capable of better. 2½ **47**
3531} **BLESS 99** [2] 3-8-6 (54)(1ow) Pat Eddery 25/1: 0006-0: Led till 5f out, wknd 3f out: fin 10th, reapp: on debut in '99 4th at Folkestone (mdn auct, rtd 69): dam a hdles wnr: prob handles hvy grnd, has tried blnks. ¾ **37**
4461} **LENNY THE LION 99** [16] 3-8-8 (57) R Hughes 11/1: 0065-0: Dwelt, recovered to chase ldrs, wknd 2f out: fin 11th, reapp: caught the eye styg on over 7f here at Brighton (h'cap) on fnl '99 start (rtd 55): half-brother to a 12f wnr, dam won over 2m+: handles gd/soft & prev rcd as tho' this 10f trip would suit: with R Hannon. 6 **31**
373 **JUMP 82** [12] 3-8-13 (62) J P Spencer 10/1: 05-260: Rear, effort 3f out, sn btn: fin 12th, 12 wk abs, op 7/1: stable has yet to send out a wnr: see 328 (1m, AW). 1 **35**
709 **MISS WORLD 21** [7] 3-8-13 (62)(t) L Newman (5) 25/1: -54050: Rear, nvr nr ldrs: fin 13th: see 213. 2½ **32**
744 **THE GIRLS FILLY 17** [8] 3-8-9 (58) N Pollard 20/1: 0-2300: Prom, led 5f out till 4f out, sn wknd & eased: fin 16th: see 615, 570 (AW). **0**
4558} **Anns Mill 99** [13] 3-8-11 (60) J F Egan 33/1: 744 **Unimpeachable 17** [3] 3-8-13 (62) Claire Bryan(5) 33/1:
2516} **Brokenborough 99** [4] 3-9-0 (63) D Sweeney 33/1: 782 **Diamond Georgia 15** [11] 3-7-10 (45) R Brisland(5) 33/1:
2638} **Sober As A Judge 99** [18] 3-7-10 (45)(2oh) G Bardwell 50/1:3939} **Gavel 99** [19] 3-9-3 (66) S Sanders 20/1:
20 ran Time 2m 07.3 (9.5) (Mrs B Sadowska) M A Jarvis Newmarket.

893

3.00 GO RACING FREE CLAIMER 4YO+ (F) 1m3f196y Good/Soft 78 -04 Slow
£2228 £636 £318 4 yo rec 1 lb

750 **BLUE STYLE 16** [10] Jamie Poulton 4-8-11 O Urbina 25/1: 00-61: 4 ch g Bluebird - Style For Life (Law Society): Rear, imprvd after 1m, strong run to lead dist, sprinted clr, easily: clmd by Philip Mitchell for £7,000: mod French/Irish form in '99 (tried blnks): apprec step up to 12f, acts on gd/soft & on a sharp/undul trk. **66**
650 **EI EI 36** [16] G L Moore 5-8-4 J F Egan 33/1: 024662: 5 b g North Briton - Branitska (Mummy's Pet): Rear, gd hdwy to lead over 2f out till hdd dist, sn outpcd by facile wnr: appeared not to get home over 12f here. 11 **44**
581 **SOCIALIST 49** [12] J A Osborne 4-8-7 Pat Eddery 11/1: 63: 4 b g Hermitage - Social Missy (Raised Socially): Rear, prog to chall 3f out, sn outpcd: op 8/1, 7L clr rem, 7 wk abs: prob handles gd/soft grnd. 5 **42**
*650 **NIGHT CITY 36** [4] K R Burke 9-9-4 D Sweeney 2/1 FAV: 260214: Sn in clr lead, hdd over 2f out, wknd qckly: possibly reserves best for N Callan: front rnr, see 650 (AW). 7 **45**
267 **BRILLIANCY 99** [7] 5-8-4 (t) P Doe 10/1: 35: Prom till wknd 3f out, eased fnl 1f: abs: see 267. 3½ **27**
775 **TWOFORTEN 15** [2] 5-8-8 D Holland 33/1: 05-066: Well bhd, some late hdwy tho' nvr dngr: clr rem. nk **30**
784 **TYRA 15** [3] 4-8-3(1ow) R Price 12/1: 2-07: Rear, imprvd to chase ldrs 3f out, sn btn: tchd 16/1. 12 **14**
264 **VEGAS 99** [15] 4-8-2 A Daly 33/1: 650-08: Rcd keenly in tch, btn 4f out: long abs: caught the eye styg on in 5th at Lingfield in '99 (mdn auct, rtd 51+): eff at 1m on equitrack: with J S Moore. 4 **9**
791 **GREY BUTTONS 14** [14] 5-8-5 (t) J Tate 12/1: /00-09: Slowly away, al bhd: no form. nk **10**
4336} **GRIEF 99** [8] 7-9-8 N Pollard 33/1: 4013-0: Chsd ldrs till wknd 3f out, t.o. in 10th: well bckd from 4/1: 99/00 hdle wnr at Plumpton & Folkestone (2, h'caps, rtd 114h, eff at 2m2f on any grnd, wears blnks): '99 Flat wnr here at Brighton (clmr, rtd 65): back in '97 won at Epsom (h'cap, rtd 93): eff at 10/12f on firm & soft grnd, likes a sharp/undul trk: prev with D Elsworth, now with Miss A Newton-Smith: capable of much better. 6 **21**
2230} **LA CHATELAINE 99** [11] 6-7-13 R Brisland(5) 66/1: 0563-0: Chsd ldr 7f, wknd, t.o. in 11th: jmps fit. ½ **0**
302 **DUTCH LAD 94** [1] 5-8-10 (BL) S Sanders 5/1: 050-00: Rcd keenly & prom, wknd 4f out, t.o. in 12th: op 11/4, first time blnks: jump rnr last month. 19 **0**
723 **Young Butt 19** [5] 7-8-10 T G McLaughlin 40/1: 4179} **Sapphire Son 99** [13] 8-8-8 S Righton 66/1:
14 ran Time 2m 38.0 (9.8) (Come Tacing Ltd) Jamie Poulton Telscombe, East Sussex.

894

3.30 BURGESS CLASSIFIED STKS 3YO 0-70 (E) 1m rnd Good/Soft 78 -16 Slow
£2681 £766 £383

744 **SPORTY MO 17** [7] K R Burke 3-9-6 (vis) D Sweeney 11/2: 031131: 3 b g Namaqualand - Miss Fortunate (Taufan): Rcd keenly in tch, imprvd to lead ent final 1f, ran on well, rdn out: earlier won at Lingfield (2, clmrs): '99 Southwell scorer (2, sells, rtd 71a & 69): eff at 7f/1m: acts on fast, soft grnd & fibresand, loves equitrack: eff in blnks/visor: suited by sell/clmg grade: tough, well plcd to win here. **77**
4557} **INCHINNAN 99** [3] C Weedon 3-8-13 J Tate 6/1: 2552-2: 3 b f Inchinor - Westering (Auction Ring): ¾ **68**

Trkd ldrs, went on 3f out till hdd ent fnl 1f, kept on, not pace of wnr: reapp: in '99 trained by D Morris, rnr-up 3 times (incl h'cap, rtd 73): eff at 1m on firm & soft: handles a sharp or gall trk, runs well fresh: gd reapp.
4453} **EASTWOOD DRIFTER 99** [9] W R Muir 3-9-2 Martin Dwyer 25/1: 600-3: 3 ch c Woodman - Mandarina (El Gran Senor): Slowly away, no impress till ran on strongly final 1f, nrst fin: reapp: lightly rcd in mdn company in '99 (rtd 60): dam a 7f wng 2yo: eff at 1m, needs 10f judged on this: handles gd/soft: sharper over further. *1½* **68+**
4539} **NUTMEG 99** [4] M H Tompkins 3-8-13 S Sanders 10/1: 0045-4: Rear, effort halfway, kept on final 1f despite wandering: reapp: 4th at Lingfield in '99 (mdn, rtd 83$): half-sister to an 11f wnr: eff at 7f on gd grnd, seems to stay an easy 1m: fitter next time. *3* **59**
736 **SHRIVAR 19** [8] 3-9-2 T Quinn 10/1: 605-05: Trkd ldrs, rdn & btn final 1f: 5th at Yarmouth (mdn, rtd 84) in '99: dam a 2m wnr: handles gd/soft grnd: with M Channon. *½* **61**
717 **ANDYS ELECTIVE 20** [10] 3-9-2 K Fallon 10/1: 054-36: Led till 3f out, grad wknd: btr 717 (7f). *½* **60**
4376} **RAPID DEPLOYMENT 99** [6] 3-9-2 S Drowne 10/1: 5030-7: Nvr nr ldrs on reapp. *4* **52**
*493 **WASEEM 63** [11] 3-9-4 D Holland 5/2 FAV: -18: Prom till lost place halfway, no ch after: hvly bckd, 9 wk abs: reportedly unsuited by this trk: see 493 (AW, debut). *2* **50**
4461} **DOCTOR DENNIS 99** [1] 3-9-2 (bl) Pat Eddery 10/1: 6002-9: Rcd keenly & prom 5f, wknd on reapp. *3½* **41**
4305} **BLOODY MARY 99** [2] 3-8-13 R Hughes 6/1: 0234-0: Stdd start, brief effort 2f out, sn eased & fin last: reapp: reportedly sweated up, off the bridle thro'out & unco-ordinated in the latter stages: with R Hannon. *hd* **38**
10 ran Time 1m 39.5 (7.5) (Maurice Charge) K R Burke Newmarket.

895 **4.00 TOTE CREDIT HCAP 3YO+ 0-90 (C) 1m rnd Good/Soft 78 +09 Fast [90]**
£6922 £2130 £1065 £532 3yo rec 15lb

104 **SILCA BLANKA 99** [5] A G Newcombe 8-8-13 (75) L Dettori 7/1: 0000-1: 8 b h Law Society - Reality (Known Fact): Trkd ldrs, eff to lead dist, ran on strongly, rdn out: best time of day, reapp: '99 wnr at Lingfield (AW h'cap, rtd 89a) & Epsom (h'cap, rtd 90): '98 Warwick wnr (stks, rtd 86): eff at 7f/1m on firm & soft grnd, also equitrack: loves a sharp trk & is an Epsom specialist (3 wins there): can run well fresh: well h'capped. **83**
596 **RESIST THE FORCE 47** [11] R Rowe 10-9-2 (78) Pat Eddery 16/1: /10-02: 10 br g Shadeed - Countess Tully (Hotfoot): Rcd keenly in rear, prog when short of room 2f out, fin well to take 2nd cl-home, not quite rch wnr: 7 wk abs: acts on fast, gd/soft & equitrack: usually runs up with or forces the pace: sharp trk specialist. *2* **81**
699 **HUGWITY 21** [2] G C Bravery 8-8-8 (70) M Hills 9/1: 430033: 8 ch g Cadeaux Genereux - Nuit d'Ete (Super Concorde): Led after 2f till hdd dist, no extra: op 7/1: gd run, win anaother claimer: see 699 (12f). *1* **71**
725 **VOLONTIERS 19** [3] P W Harris 5-9-1 (77) W R Swinburn 11/1: 025-04: Rcd keenly in rear, hdwy when short of room over 2f out till dist, kept on cl-home but ch had gone: slipping down the weights & little luck in running here: change of tactics today, usually dominates: one to keep in mind, see 7 (AW h'cap). *¾* **76+**
725 **WEALTHY STAR 19** [13] 5-9-12 (88)(t) J Reid 14/1: 000-05: Trkd ldrs, ev ch 2f out, edged left & fdd ins last: top weight: lightly rcd in '99, 4th at Yarmouth (stks, rtd 94) on debut: '98 Nottingham wnr (mdn, rtd 90): eff at 1m on gd/soft grnd: handles a gall trk, can run well fresh: wears a t-strap: lightly rcd. *1½* **84**
715 **TUMBLEWEED QUARTET 20** [9] 4-9-3 (79)(t) R Hughes 5/1 FAV: 000-56: Held up, short of room over 2f out, onepcd final 1f: nicely bckd: better expected after promising reapp (poor draw) in 715. *1¼* **72**
817 **GULF SHAADI 10** [1] 8-8-11 (73) S Sanders 8/1: 00-047: In tch, short of room over 1f out, no ch after: forget this: see 817, 169. *shd* **66**
842 **PROSPECTORS COVE 6** [12] 7-8-10 (72) J Weaver 10/1: 0-3008: Dwelt, short of room halfway & swtchd outside 2f out, no prog final 1f: qck reapp: see 618 (10f, AW). *2½* **60**
161 **PAGAN KING 99** [15] 4-8-12 (74) S Whitworth 14/1: D156-9: Mid-div, effort 2f out, btn dist: long abs: '99 Brighton wnr (h'cap, rtd 75): '98 wnr again at Brighton (mdn auct, rtd 89): stays 1m, best at 7f: acts on fast & firm, enjoys soft grnd: handles any trk, likes Brighton: capable of better in a less competitive h'cap. *6* **50**
705 **MANSA MUSA 21** [7] 5-8-8 (70) T Quinn 8/1: 640-00: Chsd ldrs, badly hmpd over 2f out, no ch after: fin 10th, forget this: '99 Brighton wnr (class stks, rtd 75): rnr-up twice in '98 (h'caps, rtd 73): eff at 1m/10f, has tried 12f: acts on firm & gd/soft, handles hvy: handles any trk, likes to race up with/force the pace. *¾* **44**
*476 **MYSTIC RIDGE 66** [10] 6-8-11 (73) J P Spencer 8/1: 00-410: Front rank till wknd over 1f out, eased: fin 11th, 9 wk abs: not enjoy gd/soft? see 476 (7f, AW). *3½* **40**
4429} **HORMUZ 99** [4] 4-9-6 (82) S Drowne 25/1: 1050-0: Prom 6f, fdd into 12th, reapp. *10* **29**
715 **ROUTE SIXTY SIX 20** [14] 4-8-11 (73)(BL) Dane O'Neill 12/1: 200-00: Rcd keenly & early ldr, wknd 2f out, fin last: op 9/1, tried in blnks. *¾* **18**
13 ran Time 1m 37.5 (5.5) (Duckhaven Stud) A G Newcombe Huntshaw, Devon.

896 **4.30 DONATELLO LADY RIDERS HCAP 3YO+ 0-70 (F) 7f rnd Good/Soft 78 -28 Slow [43]**
£2256 £644 £322

582 **DANZAS 49** [10] J M Bradley 6-9-11 (40)(bl) Mrs S Moore(5) 20/1: 646061: 6 b g Polish Precedent - Dancing Rocks (Green Dancer): Trkd ldrs, hdwy to lead over 2f out, qcknd clr, held on cl-home: op 14/1, 7 wk abs: '99 wnr at Nottingham (mdn h'cap, rtd 44 & 45a): eff at 7f/10f, acts on firm & gd/soft, also fibresand: handles any trk, eff with/without blnks: runs well fresh: gd mount for an amateur. **47**
871 **STITCH IN TIME 2** [2] G C Bravery 4-9-12 (41) Mrs S Bosley 5/1 JT FAV: 000-22: 4 ch g Inchinor - Late Matinee (Red Sunset): Chsd ldrs, imprvd to chase wnr over 1f out, ran on well cl-home & just failed: nicely bckd, qck reapp: eff at 7/10f on gd/soft & soft grnd: deserves to go one better, see 871. *nk* **47**
418 **MELLOW MISS 76** [16] R M Flower 4-10-9 (52) Miss E J Jones 33/1: 0-5603: 4 b f Danehill - Like The Sun (Woodman): Bhd, imprvd 2f out, ran on strongly fnl 1f, nrst fin: 11 wk abs: eff at 7f, a return to 1m will suit: handles gd/soft & equitrack: reportedly in foal, see 152. *2½* **53**
816 **PRIORY GARDENS 10** [3] J M Bradley 6-9-8 (37) Miss Hayley Bryan(7) 14/1: 000044: Prom till onepcd fnl 2f: shorter priced stablemate of wnr: slipping down h'cap: see 262 (AW). *1½* **35**
3751} **FLYING PENNANT 99** [4] 7-9-13 (42)(bl) Miss S Samworth 16/1: 0350-5: Rear, imprvd 2f out, onepcd ins fnl 1f: reapp, stablemate of 1st & 4th: plcd over hdles in 99/00 (h'cap, rtd 71h, tried blnks): plcd in '99 (h'cap, rtd 43): '98 Chepstow wnr (h'cap, rtd 56): '96 Salisbury scorer (clmr, awdd race, rtd 69, with R Hannon): eff at 7f/1m on firm & gd/soft: handles any trk, can run well fresh: usually wears blnks/visor: well h'capped. *3* **34**
787 **JAMES DEE 15** [18] 4-11-7 (64) Mrs J Powell (5) 11/2: -02226: Prom & rcd wide, ev ch 2f out, wknd & drifted left final 1f: see 787, 645 (6f, AW). *¾* **54**
698 **ROBBIES DREAM 24** [6] 4-10-4 (47) Miss C Cooper (5) 8/1: 000-57: Trkd ldrs till wknd over 1f out. *1* **35**
*816 **STRATS QUEST 10** [13] 6-10-11 (54)(6ex) Miss J Allison 12/1: 650018: Rear, rcd wide, bhd 2f out, late hdwy but nvr dngr: given plenty to do here: btr 816 (professionally rdn). *1¼* **39**
680 **ROWLANDSONS STUD 28** [1] 7-9-9 (38)(t) Miss A Elsey 40/1: 603609: Set pace 5f, fdd: see 571. *2* **19**
4311} **TOP BANANA 99** [14] 9-11-4 (61) Mrs C Dunwoody (7) 16/1: 0620-0: Chsd ldrs 5f, fdd into 10th: reapp: 2nd twice in '99 (h'caps, rtd 63): caught eye in '98, plcd at Doncaster (h'cap, rtd 83, reapp): last won *3* **36**

BRIGHTON THURSDAY APRIL 13TH Lefthand, Very Sharp, Undulating Track

in '96, at Newmarket (rtd 95): eff at 5/6f: acts on firm & soft: incredibly well h'capped but winless for 4 years.
4186} **ONES ENOUGH 99** [17] 4-11-0 (57) Mrs A Perrett 5/1 JT FAV: 0000-0: Hmpd start, some late prog, nvr dngrs in 11th: reapp, lost all ch at the start here: modest '99 form (incl in blnks), subs tumbled down the h'cap: '98 Folkestone (mdn auct) & Lingfield wnr (stks, rtd 85): eff at 5f, has tried 6/7f: acts on fast & hvy grnd, likes to run-up with/force the pace: has tried an eye-hood (only has one eye): well h'capped now. *2* **28**
4604} **DENBRAE 99** [8] 8-10-8 (51) Mrs L Pearce 7/1: D300-0: Rcd keenly in rear, nvr dngr in 17th: reapp. **0**
-- **Corsecan** [5] 5-9-9 (38) Miss A Wallace(7) 50/1: 3801} **Pericles 99** [11] 6-10-4 (47)(bl) Mrs C Williams 14/1:
817 **Titan 10** [9] 5-10-1 (44) Miss E Folkes (5) 20/1: 746 **Mouton 17** [12] 4-10-6 (49) Miss R Illman (5) 66/1:
691 **Emma Lyne 26** [7] 4-10-2 (45) Miss Joanna Rees (7) 25/1:
803 **Uncle Oberon 13** [15] 4-10-7 (50) Miss Michelle Saunders(7) 25/1:
18 ran Time 1m 27.2 (7.4) (Martyn James) J M Bradley Sedbury, Gloucs.

897 5.00 BACK GROUP HCAP 3YO+ 0-75 (E) 5f59y rnd Good/Soft 78 -01 Slow [75]
£2702 £772 £386 3yo rec 11lb

4311} **MISS HIT 99** [6] G A Butler 5-9-3 (64) L Dettori 6/1: 4000-1: 5 b m Efisio - Jennies' Gem (Sayf El Arab): Waited with, gd hdwy to lead dist, qcknd clr, eased cl-home & nearly caught napping: nicely bckd, reapp: in '99 trained by Miss G Kelleway to win at Lingfield (AW h'cap, rtd 75a) & by D Elsworth at Salisbury (h'cap, rtd 72): '98 Newmarket & W'hampton wnr (h'caps, rtd 71a & 67): eff at 5/6f on firm & gd/soft, acts on both AWs: handles any trk, runs well fresh: gd weight carrier who is on a handy mark: could win again. **73**
4610} **FORGOTTEN TIMES 99** [4] K T Ivory 6-9-3 (64) C Catlin (7) 12/1: 0060-2: 6 ch m Nabeel Dancer - Etoile d'Amore (The Minstrel): Chsd ldrs on ins, no room 1½f out till ins fnl 1f, ran on late but the line came too sn: '99 wnr at Goodwood (2), Folkestone, Brighton, Salisbury & Windsor (h'caps, rtd 66): '98 Lingfield wnr (AW h'cap, rtd 71a & 51): '97 Lingfield wnr (2, mdn & h'cap): stays 7f, best at 5f on firm, relishes soft & hvy, also equitrack: likes a sharp one: best in blnks/visor, not worn today: v unlucky, deserves compensation. *nk* **70+**
*802 **NINEACRES 13** [2] J M Bradley 9-8-7 (54)(bl) S Drowne 13/2: 144013: 9 b g Sayf El Arab - Mayor (Laxton): Tried to make all, hdd dist, no extra cl-home: op 7/2: see 802 (6f, raised 11lb for that win). *1¾* **55**
844 **KING OF PERU 5** [11] N P Littmoden 7-9-9 (70)(vis) D Holland 13/2: 2-5564: Rcd keenly rear, effort 2f out, drifted left & kept on final 1f: tchd 10/1, qck reapp: see 660 (AW). *2* **65**
4471} **TINAS ROYALE 99** [5] 4-8-3 (50) G Bardwell 10/1: 2400-5: Dwelt, well bhd till styd on well final 1f, short of room ins last, nvr nrr: op 7/1: trained by H Candy in '99, 2nd at Ripon (mdn, rtd 66): eff at 5/6f on gd & soft: often races up with the pace, change of tactics today: now with J Pearce & one to keep a cl eye on. *2½* **38+**
787 **CHAKRA 15** [9] 6-7-10 (43)(5oh) Claire Bryan (5) 20/1: 506106: Rcd keenly rear, onepcd when carried left final 1f: lngr priced stablemate of 3rd: see 628 (AW). *hd* **31**
763 **BRAMBLE BEAR 16** [10] 6-8-4 (51) D Sweeney 7/1: 466267: Chsd ldrs, ev ch 2f out, fdd: op 12/1. *hd* **39**
678 **DOUBLE O 28** [3] 6-9-9 (70)(bl) T Quinn 11/4 FAV: 030-48: Front rank 3f, eased when btn final 1f: hvly bckd from 9/2: much better expected after 678, see 91 (AW). *1¼* **54**
3926} **QUITE HAPPY 99** [12] 5-8-8 (55) S Sanders 20/1: 1400-9: Chsd ldrs, ch 2f out, gradually fdd: reapp: '99 Catterick wnr (clmr, rtd 64): '98 Folkestone scorer (fillies h'cap, rtd 74): eff at 5f on firm & soft grnd: has tried blnks/visor, seems better without: v well h'capped nowadays, both wins at 5f. *1* **36**
4529} **QUEENSMEAD 99** [7] 3-8-6 (64) J F Egan 20/1: 2625-0: Chsd ldrs, wkng when short of room fnl 1f. *3½* **35**
2197} **KNOCKEMBACK NELLIE 99** [8] 4-9-4 (65) N Pollard 20/1: 5005-0: Chsd ldrs till halfway, sn lost place. *4* **24**
3760} **THAT MAN AGAIN 99** [1] 8-10-0 (75)(bl) G Faulkner (3) 12/1: 6660-0: Slowly away, al well bhd, fin last: op 8/1, top weight, reapp. *5* **19**
12 ran Time 1m 04.2 (4.2) (D R Windebank) G A Butler Blewbury, Oxon.

MUSSELBURGH THURSDAY APRIL 13TH Righthand, Sharp Track

Official Going GOOD/SOFT. Stalls: Inside, except 5f & 2m - Stands Side.

898 2.20 RACING CHANNEL AUCT MDN 2YO (F) 5f str Good/Soft 79 +03 Fast
£2702 £772 £386

-- **RED MILLENNIUM** [9] A Berry 2-8-0 F Norton 9/1: 1: 2 b f Tagula - Lovely Me (Vision) Chsd ldrs, hdwy for press to lead ins last, kept on, drvn out: gd juv time: Feb foal, cost 2,000 gns: modest dam: eff at 5f, 6f shld suit: runs well fresh on gd/soft grnd: pleasing debut. **72**
821 **BOUNCING BOWDLER 8** [1] M Johnston 2-8-11 J Fanning 4/5 FAV: 32: 2 b c Mujadil - Prima Volta (Primo Dominie) Set pace, rdn & collared ins fnl 1f, not pace of wnr: well bckd: speedy, shown enough to win. *1¼* **79**
730 **FENWICKS PRIDE 19** [7] B S Rothwell 2-8-11 M Fenton 12/1: -53: 2 b g Imperial Frontier - Stunt Girl (Thatching) Cl-up, ev ch appr fnl 1f, onepace for press ins last: imprvd for reapp & handles soft grnd: see 730. *1½* **76**
796 **DAM ELHANAH 14** [4] R A Fahey 2-8-0 P Hanagan (7) 6/1: -24: In tch, rdn & slightly outpcd 2f out, kept on same pace final 1f: looks in need of 6f: rtd higher 796. *½* **63**
-- **OLYS DREAM** [13] 2-8-4 Dean McKeown 33/1: 5: Chsd ldrs, onepace over 1f out on debut: Mar foal, cost 8,000 gns: full sister to a 1m juv scorer: dam 9f wnr: bred to apprec 6f+ in time: some promise here. *hd* **66**
-- **ELAINES REBECCA** [5] 2-8-0 T Williams 100/1: 6: Slow away & outpcd, rdn 2f out, kept on over 1f out: cheaply bt Apr foal: half-sister to a 5f juv wnr: green here, looks sure to improve for the experience. *1* **60**
-- **DULCIFICATION** [2] 2-8-7 J Fortune 33/1: 7: In tch, rdn & btn over 1f out: Feb foal, cost 5,000 gns: dam 1m scorer: apprec 6f in time, with J Weymes. *1½* **63**
-- **DISPOL CHIEFTAN** [8] 2-8-11 K Darley 16/1: 8: In tch, btn over 1f out: Mar foal, cost 10,000 gns: half-brother to a 5f scorer: sprint bred, with S Kettlewell. *shd* **67**
-- **SEA STORM** [10] 2-8-9 G Duffield 50/1: 9: Wide & nvr a factor: Mar foal, cost IR£7,000: half-brother to a 1m scorer: Dolphin Street gelding. *2½* **59**
-- **PERCY VERANCE** [3] 2-8-7 R Winston 50/1: 0: Dwelt, hung right & al bhd: 10th. *1¼* **54**
812 **MIDNIGHT VENTURE 10** [12] 2-8-9 A Culhane 8/1: 030: In tch, btn 2f out: 11th, btr 812. *¾* **54**
796 **PHARAOH HATSHEPSUT 14** [11] 2-8-2 P Fessey 50/1: -40: Dwelt, al bhd: 12th, see 796. *1½* **43**
-- **NETTLES** [6] 2-8-5 J Carroll 50/1: 0: Slow away, al bhd: fin last on debut. *6* **34**
13 ran Time 1m 01.3 (3.8) (The Red Shirt Brigade) A Berry Cockerham, Lancs.

899 2.50 7 TIL 11 TEXT HCAP 3YO+ 0-75 (E) 1m rnd Good/Soft 79 +07 Fast [68]
£3201 £985 £492 £246 3 yo rec 15lb

718 **ARC** 19 [4] G M Moore 6-9-6 (60) K Darley 3/1 JT FAV: -24241: 6 b g Archway - Columbian Sand 65
(Salmon Leap) Chsd ldrs, hdwy over 1f out to lead inside last, rdn out: nicely bckd, best time of day: rnr-up
on a/w this winter (rtd 70a): with F Jordan in '99, won at W'hampton (mdn h'cap, rtd 67a) & Carlisle (stks, rtd
64): eff at 1m/10f on firm, gd/soft & fibresand: handles any trk: proving tough.

846 **MR PERRY** 5 [1] M D Hammond 4-8-13 (53) J Fortune 15/2: 00-002: 4 br g Perugino - Elegant Tune 2 54
(Alysheba): Trkd ldr, led over 1f out till inside last, not pace of wnr: qck reapp: better run, see 846.

*846 **PERCHANCER** 5 [6] P C Haslam 4-9-3 (57)(6ex) P Goode (3) 3/1 JT FAV: 110013: 4 ch g Perugino - Irish ½ 57
Hope (Nishapour): Keen, prom, eff to chall over 1f out, onepace ins last: well bckd under pen, apprec return to 9f.

4394} **LUNCH PARTY** 99 [3] A Berry 8-9-5 (59) J Carroll 4/1: 0060-4: Set pace, travelling well till hdd appr 2 56+
fnl 1f, no extra: reapp: in '99 won at Catterick (class stks) & Thirsk (h'cap, rtd 67): '98 wnr at Musselburgh
& Catterick (2, h'caps, rtd 67): 7f sharp trk specialist, stays 1m: acts on firm & soft grnd & loves to front
run, especially at Catterick or Musselburgh: game, back on a winning mark & of interest next time at 7f.

754 **NORTHGATE** 16 [2] 4-8-6 (46)(bl) D Mernagh (3) 14/1: 200-05: In tch, rdn 2f out, no impress 1f out. 1¾ 40

803 **SO WILLING** 13 [8] 4-9-2 (56) A Culhane 14/1: 603056: Waited with, brief effort over 2f out, no dngr. ¾ 48

795 **DENTON LADY** 14 [5] 3-7-10 (51)(7oh) K Dalgleish (7) 50/1: 450-67: Ran wide in tch, btn over 3f out. ½ 42

641 **ROOFTOP** 38 [7] 4-9-10 (64) J Fanning 7/1: 0-6508: Hmpd after 1f, keen cl-up, wknd over 2f out: see 453. 3 50
8 ran Time 1m 43.3 (5.8) (Mrs A Roddis) G M Moore Middleham, Nth Yorks.

900 3.20 SPORTS CLASS STKS 3YO+ 0-75 (D) 7f30y rnd Good/Soft 79 -12 Slow
£4075 £1254 £627 £313 3 yo rec 14lb

715 **INDIAN PLUME** 20 [1] C W Thornton 4-9-7 J Fortune 5/1: 400-01: 4 b c Efisio - Boo Hoo (Mummy's Pet): 81
Made all, qcknd well over 1f out, rdn out: op 3/1: plcd on 1st of only 4 '99 starts (rtd 85): '98 Pontefract wnr
(mdn, rtd 86): eff at 7f/1m on fast, gd/soft & gall or sharp trk: back to best today with forcing tactics.

715 **ROBZELDA** 20 [2] K A Ryan 4-9-7 (bl) F Lynch 1/1 FAV: 313-32: 4 b g Robellino - Zelda (Sharpen Up): 1½ 77
Chsd ldrs, effort to chase wnr over 1f out, hung slightly right inside last, onepace: nicely bckd & rdn, gd run.

4476} **DISPOL JAZZ** 99 [5] S E Kettlewell 3-8-5(1ow) K Darley 5/1: 2410-3: 3 ch f Alhijaz - Foxtrot Pie 6 65
(Shernazar) In tch, eff for press over 2f out, sn btn: reapp: in '99 scored at Thirsk (sell), Carlisle (nov auct)
& Catterick (all nursery h'cap, rtd 74): wng form over 6/7f on fast & soft grnd, any trk: sharper for this.

4582} **GDANSK** 99 [4] A Berry 3-8-7 J Carroll 20/1: -055-4: Prom, wknd well over 1f out: unplcd juv. 3 62

4582} **LADY OF WINDSOR** 99 [6] 3-8-4 (vis) G Duffield 8/1: 0404-5: Chsd wnr till over 2f out, no extra: plcd 5 51
sev times as a juv (rtd 74): eff at 6/7f on fast, soft & on any trk: tried blnks, has run well in a visor.

4557} **INDY CARR** 99 [3] 3-8-4 Dale Gibson 15/2: 1-6: Slow away, in tch till btn over 2f out: won sole 3 47
juv start, at Newmarket (sell, with H Collingridge, rtd 78): eff at 1m (dam 12f wnr) & further should suit:
acts on soft & a stiff trk in sell grade: has run well fresh.
6 ran Time 1m 31.4 (6.5) (Guy Reed) C W Thornton Coverham, Nth Yorks.

901 3.50 FILLIES MDN HCAP 3YO+ 0-70 (E) 5f str Good/Soft 79 -13 Slow [49]
£2756 £848 £424 £212 3 yo rec 11lb

740 **DISTINCTLY BLU** 17 [6] K A Ryan 3-9-11 (57) F Lynch 11/2: 00-61: 3 b f Distinctly North - Stifen 61
(Burslem): Prom, hdwy to lead over 1f out, drvn out to hold on ins last: modest form prev: dam 5f juv wnr:
eff at 5f on gd/soft grnd in modest grade.

711 **MOY** 21 [3] W M Brisbourne 5-8-7 (28)(bl) J Fanning 14/1: 053002: 5 ch m Beveled - Exceptional Beauty ½ 30
(Sallust): In tch, effort to chall dist, kept on, not btn far: op 10/1: mdn after 35: see 466.

781 **ITS ANOTHER GIFT** 15 [1] A Berry 3-10-0 (60)(BL) J Carroll 5/1: 300-03: 3 b f Primo Dominie - 3 56
Margaret's Gift (Beveled) Led till over 1f out, no extra: tried blnks: big weight for a 3yo: acts on fast & gd/soft.

659 **MISS SINCERE** 33 [9] B S Rothwell 3-9-5 (51) M Fenton 20/1: -04404: In tch, btn over 2f out: see 357. ½ 46

777 **LIZZIE SIMMONDS** 15 [4] 3-9-10 (56)(t) K Darley 9/2 FAV: 300-45: Dwelt, sn in tch, btn 2f out. 2 47

777 **LAYAN** 15 [5] 3-9-10 (56) S Finnamore (5) 11/2: 006-56: Prom till wknd well over 1f out: see 777. ¾ 45

4450} **DUBAI NURSE** 99 [2] 6-9-4 (39) Dean McKeown 14/1: 2-00-7: With ldrs till wknd over 1f out: poor 2½ 23
form in 2 starts last term: rtd 43 when rnr-up 4 times in '98: eff at 5f on gd & soft grnd.

798 **UNMASKED** 14 [8] 4-8-13 (34) N Carlisle 6/1: 0/0-08: Chsd ldrs, rdn & btn over 2f out: bckd, btr 798. hd 17

604 **CHRISTENSEN** 45 [5] 4-10-0 (49) F Norton 8/1: 632-09: Al bhd: abs: see 674. 1¼ 29

777 **APRILS COMAIT** 15 [7] 3-9-6 (52) V Halliday 7/1: 605330: Dwelt, al bhd: fin 10th: see 777, 696. nk 31
10 ran Time 1m 02.1 (4.6) (The Gloria Darley Racing Partnership) K A Ryan Hambleton, Nth Yorks.

902 4.20 RACING CHANNEL MDN 3YO+ (D) 1m1f Good/Soft 79 -21 Slow
£2758 £788 £394 3 yo rec 17lb

4570} **ARIZONA LADY** 99 [2] I Semple 3-8-2 G Duffield 40/1: 3040-1: 3 ch f Lion Cavern - Unfuwaanah 70
(Unfuwain) Chsd ldrs, rdn & outpcd over 2f out, rallied over 1f out to lead ins last, drvn out: surprise reapp
scorer: some promise as a juv (rtd 62): eff at 7f, apprec step up to 9f: acts on firm, gd/soft & when fresh.

4526} **HIGH TOPPER** 99 [1] M Johnston 3-8-7 J Fanning 6/1: 0-2: 3 b c Wolfhound - Blushing ½ 74
Barada (Blushing Groom) Chsd ldrs, eff over 2f out, onepace: reapp: rtd 69 when unplcd sole juv start:
half-brother to a useful mdn-dist/styr: eff on gd/soft grnd: should be placed to advantage.

789 **EVEREST** 8 [8] P F I Cole 3-8-7 J Fortune 4/9 FAV: 2-23: 3 ch c Indian Ridge - Reine de'Beaute shd 74
(Caerleon): Led, rdn, hung right & hdd ins last, no extra: bckd, clr of rem: rtd higher prev: needs headgear?

736 **STORMVILLE** 19 [4] M Brittain 3-8-7 D Mernagh (3) 9/2: 355-64: Prom, btn 2f out: Ingr trip, see 736. 11 58

3189} **LUCKY JUDGE** 99 [3] 3-8-7 F Lynch 20/1: 0-5: Al bhd: rtd 63 sole juv start: dam 11f wnr. shd 58

833 **RYKA** 7 [5] 5-9-10 P Fessey 100/1: 006: Al bhd. 4 52

4360} **ROBIN HOOD** 99 [7] 3-8-7 C Lowther 50/1: 0-7: Keen with ldrs till wknd 2f out: Komaite colt. nk 51

-- **GENERAL DOMINION** [6] 3-8-7 J Carroll 14/1: 8: Slow away, sn in tch till wknd 2f out: with D Smith. ¾ 49
8 ran Time 1m 59.7 (9) (Ian Crawford) I Semple Carluke, Sth Lanarks.

MUSSELBURGH THURSDAY APRIL 13TH Righthand, Sharp Track

903 | 4.50 PRIZEWINNERS HCAP 4YO+ 0-70 (E) 1m6f Good/Soft 79 -38 Slow [69]
£3526 £1085 £542 £271 4 yo rec 3 lb

4095} **HASTA LA VISTA** 99 [4] M W Easterby 10-8-2 (43)(vis) T Lucas 10/1: 4220-1: 10 b g Superlative - Falcon **48**
Berry (Bustino) Made all, kept on for press over 1f out, drvn out: reapp: rnr-up twice in '99 (rtd 45): '98
wnr at Musselburgh, Catterick & Beverley (h'caps, rtd 60): eff at 12f, suited by 14f/2m now on firm, soft or
fibresand: likes Catterick & Musselburgh & eff in blnks/visor: runs well fresh: v tough 10yo, on a gd mark.
699 **FIELD OF VISION** 21 [10] Mrs A Duffield 10-8-10 (51) G Duffield 12/1: /40-02: 10 b g Vision - Bold 1¾ **53**
Meadows (Persian Bold) Prom, eff over 2f out, kept on for press fnl 1f: another veteran returning to form, stays 14f.
779 **SALVAGE** 15 [11] W W Haigh 5-8-6 (47) F Lynch 13/8 FAV: 610-03: 5 b g Kahyasi - Storm Weaver 1½ **47**
(Storm Bird) Hld up, eff over 2f out, kept on ins last, nvr dngr: hvly bckd: should win again at 2m: see 779.
793 **FREEDOM QUEST** 14 [7] B S Rothwell 5-9-7 (62) M Fenton 6/1: 410-44: In tch, rdn 3f out, onepace ¾ **61**
over 1f out: stays 14f: see 793.
626 **HILL FARM DANCER** 42 [12] 9-7-10 (37)(9oh) Iona Wands (5) 11/1: 231435: Waited with, effort over 2f 2½ **34**
out, no impress: all wins arnd 12f, mostly on fibresand: see 626.
797 **INDIANA PRINCESS** 14 [5] 7-10-0 (69) T Eaves (7) 11/2: 133-26: In tch, btn 2f out: btr 797 (2m). 1½ **64**
779 **PIPE MUSIC** 15 [6] 5-7-11 (38)(bl) Dale Gibson 12/1: 320507: Prom till btn 2f out: see 348 (fibresand). shd **33**
797 **BREYDON** 14 [3] 7-7-10 (37)(9oh) P Hanagan (2) 50/1: 500-08: Waited with, hung right over 3f out, 6 **26**
sn btn: hdle rnr earlier: back in Aug '99 won at Perth (sell h'cap, rtd 84h, 2m, fast & soft): 98/99 wnr again
at Perth (h'cap): in '99 rtd 44 at best: '98 Hamilton wnr (sell h'cap, rtd 44): stays 2m on fast & hvy.
845 **EMBRYONIC** 5 [8] 8-9-11 (66) Dean McKeown 11/1: /60-09: In tch, wknd over 2f out: see 845. ½ **54**
795 **DONE WELL** 14 [9] 8-7-10 (37)(7oh) J Bramhill 66/1: 0/0-00: Al bhd: 10th: p.u. in 2 hdles earlier: 15 **11**
well btn sole '99 Flat start: hdles wnr back in 96/97 (rtd 120h): rtd 98 on the Flat way back
in '95: eff at 7f on firm & gd/soft.
4412} **FISHERMANS COVE** 99 [1] 5-9-8 (63) K Darley 8/1: 4020-0: Al bhd: last: in '99 trained by L Lungo, dist **0**
rnr-up (rtd 65): stays 2m1f on gd/soft.
11 ran   Time 3m 13.0 (16.5)   (Mr K Hodgson & Mrs J Hodgson)   M W Easterby Sheriff Hutton, Nth Yorks.

THIRSK FRIDAY APRIL 14TH Lefthand, Flat, Oval Track

Official Going SOFT (HEAVY places). Stalls: Rnd Crse - Inside; Str Crse - Stands' Side.

904 | 2.20 FEATHERS NOV FILLIES STKS 2YO (D) 5f str Soft 105 -37 Slow
£4049 £1246 £623 £311

-- **REEDS RAINS** [1] T D Easterby 2-8-8 J Carroll 7/2: -1: 2 b f Mind Games - Me Spede (Valiyar) **81**
Dwelt, gd hdwy to lead ins fnl 1f, drifted left, won going away: nicely bckd, ran green: 5,800gns May foal: half
sister to a couple of 7f wnrs: eff at 5f, 6f will suit: acts on soft & runs well fresh: athletic, well regarded filly.
*828 **MILLYS LASS** 8 [4] M R Channon 2-8-10 W Supple 7/4: -312: 2 b f Mind Games - Millie's Lady 2½ **76**
(Common Grounds) Trkd ldrs, led 2f out till ins last, not pace to repel wnr: well bckd: acts on fast & soft grnd.
-- **STILMEMAITE** [2] N Bycroft 2-8-8 J Bramhill 33/1: -3: 2 b f Komaite - Stilvella (Camden Town) 1 **71**
Chsd ldrs, hdwy & ev ch dist, sn onepcd: just better for debut: Jan foal, half sister to a 5f winning juv.
*730 **DIVINE WIND** 20 [5] B A McMahon 2-8-12 G Duffield 11/8 FAV: -14: Led/dsptd lead, onepcd fnl 1½f: 2 **70**
well bckd, top-weight: reportedly unsuited by today's soft grnd: see 730 (gd, debut).
730 **EASTERN RED** 20 [3] 2-8-8 F Lynch 16/1: -05: Led till 2f out: 3,400gns first foal: dam a multiple juv wnr. 7 **48**
5 ran   Time 1m 04.1 (7.1)   (Ron George)   T D Easterby Great Habton, N Yorks.

905 | 2.50 HAMBLETON CLASS STKS 3YO+ 0-80 (D) 5f str Soft 105 +03 Fast
£4127 £1270 £635 £317 3yo rec 11lb Field raced stands side

702 **AMBITIOUS** 22 [9] K T Ivory 5-9-1 C Catlin (7) 7/1: 120-01: 5 b m Ardkinglass - AAyodhya (Astronef) **85**
Trkd ldrs, smooth hdwy to lead dist, pushed clr fnl 1f: lkd well, fair time: '99 wnr at Southwell (fill h'cap, rtd 65a,
with J Fanshawe), Sandown (2, h'cap & clmr), Redcar (class stks) & York (h'cap, rtd 79): eff at 6f, suited by 5f:
acts on firm & f/sand, soon over this trip: handles any trk: runs well for an appr: progressive.
702 **CAUDA EQUINA** 22 [7] M R Channon 6-9-4 P Fessey 15/2: 300-02: 6 gr g Statoblest - Sea Fret (Habat) 2½ **80+**
Held up, no room 2f out till ins last, fin fast fnl 1f but wnr had flown: '99 wnr at Bath (2) & Lingfield (class
stks), also plcd sev times (rtd 84): '98 Bath (2, clmr & h'cap) & Salisbury wnr (h'cap, rtd 80): '96 wnr again at
Bath (2) & Ripon (h'caps): eff at 5/6f on fast & soft grnd: handles any trk, a real Bath specialist: tough
gelding who was most eye-catching today, one to keep in mind, especially back at beloved Bath.
4391} **GAY BREEZE** 99 [11] P S Felgate 7-9-4 S Finnamore (5) 11/2: 2445-3: 7 b g Dominion - Judy's Dowry 1 **77**
(Dragonara Palace) Prom, ev ch dist, not qckn ins last: op 9/2, better for reapp: trained by D Nicholls in '99,
plcd sev times (h'caps, rtd 81): '98 Nottingham, Doncaster & Haydock wnr (h'caps, rtd 80, current trainer): '97
wnr at Leicester & Yarmouth (h'caps): wng form at 5/6f on firm & soft: runs well fresh: fitter next time.
716 **INDIAN SPARK** 21 [2] J S Goldie 4-9-4 A Culhane 5/1 FAV: 000-04: Chsd ldrs, rdn & onepcd final 1f: shd **77**
lkd superb tho' still better for race: v well h'capped now & spot-on next time: see 716.
702 **CARTMEL PARK** 22 [3] 4-9-4 O Pears 8/1: 100-05: Led till dist, no extra: still better for race: '99 ½ **76**
Sandown (1st time visor) & Catterick wnr (h'caps, rtd 80): '98 Musselburgh & Newcastle wnr (nov, rtd 84): eff at
5f on firm & soft, handles any trk: eff with/without a visor: has thrived physically since last term.
758 **LAGO DI VARANO** 17 [1] 8-9-4 (vis) Dean McKeown 8/1: 64-066: Outpcd, late hdwy, nvr in race. ¾ **73**
702 **AMARANTH** 22 [8] 4-9-4 (t) J Carroll 10/1: 16-007: Nvr better than mid-div: lkd fit: see 631 (AW). 1¼ **69**
532 **THE DOWNTOWN FOX** 57 [5] 5-9-4 (bl) G Duffield 15/2: 0-1008: Outpcd, nvr nr to chall: lkd well ¾ **66**
after 8 wk abs: needs 6/7f: see 320 (AW, 6f).
758 **POP SHOP** 17 [10] 3-8-7 R Cochrane 14/1: 662-09: Front rank 3f, fdd: lkd well: '99 Nottingham wnr 1¾ **61**
(mdn auct, rtd 80): eff at 5f on gd & firm grnd, handles gd/soft & a gd/soft trk: with J Payne.
824 **SIR JACK** 9 [6] 4-9-4 T Hamilton (7) 33/1: 000-00: Slowly away, nvr nr to chall: failed to feature in 1½ **57**
'99, 7th at Leicester (stks, rtd 84): '98 Newcastle wnr (mdn, rtd 87, with D Loder): eff at 6f on gd grnd, has
tried blnks: slipping down the weights now, with D Nicholls & capable of much better.
435 **BRANSTON PICKLE** 73 [4] 3-8-7 J Fanning 9/1: 01-200: Rear, eff halfway, sn btn & fin last: abs. 3 **48**
11 ran   Time 1m 02.1 (5.1)   (Dean Ivory)   K T Ivory Radlett, Herts.

293

THIRSK   FRIDAY APRIL 14TH   Lefthand, Flat, Oval Track

906
3.20 CRAB AND LOBSTER MDN 3YO (D)   1m4f   Soft 105   -26 Slow
£4445   £1270   £635

701   **ROYAL MINSTREL 22** [3] M H Tompkins 3-9-0 G Duffield 13/8: 664-31: 3 ch c Be My Guest - Shanntabariya   **85**
(Shernazar) Prom, went on over 3f out till 2f out, led again dist, kept on well, drvn out: lkd magnificent: unplcd
in '99 (rtd 84, mdn): eff at 10f, stays 12f well: battled on well today.
713   **RIVER BANN 21** [2] P F I Cole 3-9-0 G Hall 8/11 FAV: 2-22: 3 ch c Irish River - Spiritual Star (Soviet   1¾   **82**
Star) Prom till hmpd on bend after 2f, imprvd to lead 2f out till dist, hard drvn & no extra cl home: well bckd:
lkd all over the wnr 2f out, not appce this soft grnd? stays 12f: see 713 (10f gd grnd).
720   **SEA SQUIRT 20** [1] M Johnston 3-9-0 K Dalgleish (7) 7/1: 622-23: 3 b g Fourstars Allstar - Polynesian   1¾   **80**
Goddess (Salmon Leap) Led till 3f out, rallied ins fnl 1f: lkd well: stays 12f on soft grnd: see 720 (AW).
3 ran   Time 2m 45.6 (15.8)   (Mrs Debbie Sakal)   M H Tompkins Newmarket

907
3.50 CARPENTERS ARMS HCAP 3YO+ 0-65 (F)   1m rnd   Soft 105   +04 Fast   **[65]**
£3614   £1112   £556   £278

*43   **INCH PERFECT 99** [6] R A Fahey 5-10-0 (65) R Cochrane 10/3 FAV: 1131-1: 5 b g Inchinor - Scarlet Veil   **73**
(Tyrnavos) Trkd ldrs, prog to lead 1½f out, held on gamely cl-home, all-out: well bckd, best time of day, top
weight, padd pick: '99 wnr at Southwell (reapp, sell, rtd 56a), Redcar (sell h'cap, with J Hetherton), Pontefract,
Newcastle, Bath & W'hampton (h'caps, rtd 63 & 63a): eff at 1m, stays 12f: acts on firm, soft grnd & fibresand:
handles any trk, runs v well fresh: gd weight carrier: tough & v progressive gelding.
711   **ROLLER 22** [14] J G Given 4-9-10 (61) T G McLaughlin 4/1: 005-32: 4 b g Bluebird - Tight Spin (High   nk   **68**
Top) Mid-div, prog 3f out, styd on strongly fnl 1f, just failed: apprec return to 1m & gd run from unfav draw.
803   **MELODIAN 14** [10] M Brittain 5-9-5 (56)(bl) D Mernagh (3) 12/1: 50-023: 5 b h Grey Desire - Mere Melody 3   **58**
(Dunphy) In tch, kept on under press final 2f: op 8/1, lkd well: acts on firm & soft, ran to v best here.
4334} **ZECHARIAH 99** [7] J L Eyre 4-8-13 (50) R Cody Boutcher (7) 25/1: 6005-4: Led halfway till over 1f out,   1¾   **48**
no extra: lkd fit for reapp: '99 reapp wnr at W'hampton (sell, rtd 69a), subs rnr-up at Beverley (clmr, rtd 65):
eff at 7f/1m on fast grnd & fibresand: can run well fresh: apprec sell/clmrs.
677   **TAKHLID 29** [17] 5-9-11 (62) A Culhane 16/1: 253665: Mid-div, styd on fnl 1f, nrst fin: not disgraced.   1   **58**
718   **INTERNAL AFFAIR 20** [13] 5-8-12 (49) Lynsey Hanna (7) 7/1: 135156: Rear, imprvd 2f out, ran on   nk   **44**
fnl 1f & nrst fin: nicely bckd, poor high draw, clr of rem: best held up for a late run, see 647 (sand).
685   **DARK VICTOR 28** [16] 4-8-13 (50) N Callan 25/1: 4057: Slowly away, kept on nicely final 2f, not pace   6   **35**
to chall on h'cap/turf debut: poor high draw: tried a variety of trips: will do better over 10/12f: see 685.
568   **TAKER CHANCE 52** [3] 4-8-13 (50) G Duffield 16/1: 40-008: Chsd ldrs till wknd final 1f: 7 wk abs: hd   **35**
'99 Beverley wnr (clmr, rtd 56): trained by W Haggas as a juv: eff at 7.5f on gd & fast grnd: can run well
fresh & has tried a visor, seems better without: with J Hetherton.
*867   **MAI TAI 3** [4] 5-8-11 (48)(vis)(6ex) A Beech(5) 6/1: 254019: Prom 6f, fdd: op 4/1: too sn after 867?   ½   **32**
790   **BLOOMING AMAZING 15** [2] 6-9-11 (62) C Lowther 20/1: 006050: Rear, late hdwy, nvr dngrs in 10th.   ½   **45**
787   **LANDING CRAFT 16** [8] 6-9-6 (57) R Fitzpatrick (3) 20/1: 434-00: Slowly away, nvr dngrs in 11th.   ¾   **35**
4511} **CYBERTECHNOLOGY 99** [9] 6-9-13 (64) A Clark 20/1: 5000-0: Nvr better than mid-div, fin 12th: reapp   5   **35**
& ndd this: '99 Doncaster wnr (h'cap, rtd 74): '98 Redcar (h'cap, rtd 82, with Mrs J Cecil): '97 Newmarket wnr
(h'cap, rtd 84, with B Hills): eff at 7f/1m, does stay 12f: acts on fast & gd/soft grnd, handles a stiff or gd
trk: has tried blnks/visor, best without: back on a wng mark & fitter next time.
2542} **REQUESTOR 99** [1] 5-9-11 (62) W Supple 10/1: 0663-0: Mid-div, rdn & btn over 2f out: fin 13th, reapp.   ¾   **31**
687   **HYDE PARK 28** [18] 6-9-9 (60) T Hamilton(7) 16/1: 340-00: Led till halfway, wknd & eased consid,   0
fin last: went off too fast in order to overcome poor high draw: failed to win in '99, plcd numerous times (rtd
72a & 63, h'caps): '98 wnr at Brighton, Pontefract & Chester (h'caps, rtd 72): '96 Lingfield wnr (mdn, rtd 76 &
75): suited by a sharp 7f/1m, acts on firm, gd/soft & on both AWs: can carry big weights & likes to force the
pace: prev trained by Sir M Prescott, now with D Nicholls: v well h'capped, this is best forgotten.
4162} **Gymcrak Flyer 99** [5] 9-9-2 (53) J Fanning 20/1:   831 **Bunty 8** [11] 4-8-11 (48) J Mackay (7) 16/1:
2142} **Kafi 99** [12] 4-9-11 (62) L Newton 33/1:
17 ran   Time 1m 43.5 (8.1)   (Tommy Staunton)   R A Fahey Butterwick, Nth Yorks.

908
4.20 NAGS HEAD HCAP 3YO+ 0-70 (E)   7f rnd   Soft 105   -12 Slow   **[70]**
£3932   £1210   £605   £302

*711   **VICTORIOUS 22** [6] R A Fahey 4-9-2 (58) R Cochrane 7/2 FAV: 050-11: 4 ch c Formidable - Careful Dancer   **61**
(Gorytus) Trkd ldrs, prog to lead over 2f out, hdd briefly ins last, battled on most gamely, all-out: recent
W'hampton wnr (AW h'cap, with B McMahon, rtd 65a): '99 Haydock wnr (h'cap, rtd 66): suited by 7f, has tried 1m:
acts on gd, soft & f/sand, handles any trk: runs v well fresh: tough & v game colt who is in great form.
676   **KASS ALHAWA 29** [2] D W Chapman 4-9-11 (67) A Culhane 12/1: 0-2062: 7 b g Shirley Heights - Silver   shd   **69**
Braid (Miswaki) In tch, chall strongly fnl 1f & led briefly ins last, just btn in a most thrilling fin: acts on firm,
soft & on both AWs: deserves similar & loves Beverley: see 38 (AW).
3959} **DAY BOY 99** [4] Denys Smith 4-9-13 (69) A Beech (5) 9/1: 0430-3: 4 b g Prince Sabo - Lady Day   2   **67**
(Lightning) Rear, imprvd halfway, styd on fnl 1f but not rch front 2: top weight, just better for reapp: well btn
in a juv hov hdle in Dec '99: plcd at Musselburgh in '99 (h'cap, rtd 71): '98 Ayr wnr (debut, mdn auct, rtd 84):
eff at 6/7f on fast & soft grnd: spot-on next time.
802   **PEPPIATT 14** [16] N Bycroft 6-9-4 (60) J Fanning 9/1: 50-034: Rear, imprvd 2f out, ran on fnl 1f &   nk   **57**
nrst fin: gd run from a poor high draw: eff at 6/7f on firm, likes soft grnd: see 802, 667.
4362} **BOLLIN ROBERTA 99** [9] 4-9-4 (60) G Duffield 12/1: 0100-5: In tch, onepcd fnl 1f: just better for   2   **53**
reapp: '99 Musselburgh wnr (mdn auct, rtd 68): 71 in '98: eff at 6/7.5f, acts on gd & hard, handles soft grnd.
4368} **OLLIES CHUCKLE 99** [13] 5-8-11 (53) J P Spencer 16/1: 3000-6: Mid-div, imprvd 2f out, ev ch dist,   2   **42**
sn no extra: ndd this reapp, poor high draw: '99 Redcar wnr (appr mdn h'cap, rtd 58): plcd in '98 (mdn auct, rtd
65 & 68a): eff at 7/10f on fast & gd/soft grnd, also fibresand: can run well fresh.
803   **SHARP EDGE BOY 14** [14] 4-9-4 (60) W Supple 11/1: 0-0007: Rear, kept on final 2f, nrst fin: op   1¾   **46**
8/1, poor high draw: see 622 (sand).
719   **RONS PET 20** [7] 5-9-6 (62) C Lowther 10/1: 235548: Rear, kept on final 2f, nvr nrr: lkd fit: 1   **46**
prev with K Burke, now with P D Barron: see 575 (AW).
758   **MALADERIE 14** [10] 6-9-2 (58) F Lynch 20/1: 000-09: Early ldr, remnd prom till wknd final 2f: still   1¾   **39**
ndd race: '99 Bath wnr (h'cap), also plcd many times (rtd 72): trained mostly by M Channon in '98, won at
Windsor, Haydock & York (h'caps, rtd 74): '96 Windsor wnr: eff at 5/6f, just stays a sharp 7f: acts on firm

294

& gd/soft grnd, handles any trk: best in a visor: well h'capped & a return to 6f will suit.
803 **ODDSANENDS 14** [11] 4-9-6 (62) Lynsey Hanna (7) 14/1: -05100: Prom, rcd wide, wknd final 2f: 10th. *2½* **39**
798 **JOHAYRO 15** [8] 7-9-7 (63) Dawn Rankin (7) 10/1: 00-040: Prom, ran wide into str, btn over 1f out. *1¼* **37**
738 **ROCK ISLAND LINE 18** [12] 6-9-0 (56) L Newton 13/2: 010-20: Mid-div, effort 2f out, btn dist: 12th. *3½* **24**
867 **BERNARDO BELLOTTO 3** [5] 5-8-13 (55)(bl) O Pears 8/1: 10-000: Prom on inside, led halfway till over 2f out, fdd into 13th: qck reapp. *3* **17**
76 **GOLDEN BIFF 99** [1] 4-9-4 (60) J Carroll 16/1: 0106-0: Prom, led after 1f till halfway, wknd: fin 14th, reapp: '99 Catterick wnr (mdn auct, rtd 77): plcd in '98 (rtd 76): eff at 6/7f: handles fast & fibresand, likes soft grnd: has tried blnks/visor: with I Semple. *1* **20**
802 **KOSEVO 14** [15] 6-8-11 (53)(vis) N Callan 20/1: 0-0000: Chsd ldrs, wknd fnl 3f, fin last: poor draw. *6* **3**
15 ran Time 1m 31.1 (8.2) (Tommy Staunton) R A Fahey Butterwick, Nth Yorks.

909

4.50 WHITE SWAN MED AUCT MDN 3-4YO (E) 6f str Soft 105 -21 Slow
£3822 £1176 £588 £294 Stalls 1-8 raced far side

4556} **EXORCET 99** [4] I A Balding 3-8-7 G Duffield 10/1: 00-1: 3 b f Selkirk - Stack Rock (Ballad Rock) **80**
Led far side, overall ldr halfway, clr final 2f, cmftbly: unplcd in a couple of juv mdns in '99: 18,000gns purchase, dam a sprinter: eff forcing the pace at 6f, 7f suit: runs well fresh on soft: open to further improvement.
4607} **MI AMIGO 99** [13] L M Cumani 3-8-12 J P Spencer 7/1: 0-2: 3 b f Primo Dominie - Third Movement *3½* **76**
(Music Boy) In tch stands side, led that group dist, kept on well, no ch with wnr: op 5/1: unplcd in a Doncaster mdn on sole juv start: cost IR 36,000gns: brother to a wng sprinter abroad: eff at 6f on soft: win a race.
829 **KIND EMPEROR 8** [12] M J Polglase 3-8-12 Dean McKeown 6/1: -44253: 3 br g Emperor Jones - Kind *3½* **68**
Lady (Kind Of Hush) Dsptd lead stands side, drifted left fnl 2f & onepcd: mdn after 19: see 731.
5 **BRANSTON FIZZ 99** [10] M Johnston 3-8-7 J Fanning 4/1: 223-4: Prom stands side, onepcd final 1f: *¾* **60**
nicely bckd tho' op 5/2, reapp: see 5 (AW).
740 **IM SOPHIE 18** [21] 3-8-7 L Newton 14/1: 2-45: Dwelt, recovered to lead stands group till dist, fdd. *2* **55**
800 **ELLPEEDEE 15** [16] 3-8-12 (t) Kim Tinkler 50/1: 000-06: Prom stands side, onepcd final 2f: plcd at *nk* **59$**
Nottingham in '99 (mdn, rtd 74): eff at 5f on fast grnd, wears a t-strap: with N Tinkler, offic rtd just 48.
759 **NORTHERN ECHO 17** [20] 3-8-12 Dale Gibson 33/1: 0-07: In tch stands side, no ch with ldrs: ndd *1¾* **55**
this: unplcd in 2 mdns prev: shwd a modicum of promise here & now qual for h'caps: with M Dods.
4158} **TRICCOLO 99** [11] 3-8-12 M Roberts 5/2 FAV: 55-8: Slowly away stands side, hdwy to chse ldrs *hd* **55+**
halfway, wknd fnl 1f: nicely bckd, reapp, lkd in need of race: 5th in 2 mdns in '99 (rtd 77+ at best): 70,000 gns half-brother to a wnr abroad: handles fast & soft grnd: attractive colt who is now qual for h'caps.
804 **WINGED ANGEL 14** [19] 3-8-12 A Culhane 10/1: 49: Rear stands side, kept on final 2f, nvr plcd to *1½* **51**
chall: prob unsuited by this drop back to 6f: caught the eye, tho' needs one more run to qual for h'caps.
3933} **TWO JACKS 99** [17] 3-8-12 P Goode (3) 50/1: 00-0: Dwelt, nvr dngrs on stands side: fin 10th, reapp. *shd* **51**
-- **SEAHORSE BOY** [18] 3-8-12 W Supple 33/1: -0: Nvr better than mid-div stands side: fin 11th, debut. *2½* **45**
3613} **OZAWA 99** [15] 3-8-12 R Cochrane 25/1: 0-0: Nvr better than mid-div stands side: fin 12th, ndd this. *nk* **44**
-- **RUDETSKI** [14] 3-8-12 C Teague 33/1: -0: Al towards rear stands side, fin 13th: debut, lkd well. *hd* **44**
4018} **SECRET RENDEZVOUS 99** [5] 3-8-7 F Norton 16/1: 0600-0: Chsd wnr far side, wknd fnl 2f: new stable. *hd* **39**
877 **Daylily 3** [8] 3-8-7 G Parkin 33/1:
3942} **Paradise 99** [3] 3-8-12 C Lowther 33/1:
731 **Nicolai 20** [9] 3-8-12 M Fenton 25/1:
830 **Cryfield 8** [6] 3-8-12 O Pears 50/1:
-- **Needwood Tribesman** [7] 3-8-12 J Carroll 20/1:
-- **Aiwin** [1] 3-8-12 O Urbina 16/1:
1996} **Shes Magic 99** [2] 3-8-7 D Mernagh (3) 50/1:
21 ran Time 1m 17.1 (7.6) (J C Smith) I A Balding Kingsclere, Hants.

910

5.20 LEVY BOARD FILLIES HCAP 3YO+ 0-75 (E) 6f str Soft 105 -08 Slow [74]
£3900 £1200 £600 £300 3yo rec 12lb Stalls 1-12 raced far side (prob favoured)

746 **AMBER BROWN 18** [4] K T Ivory 4-8-9 (55) G Duffield 16/1: 050-01: 4 b f Thowra - High Velocity **61**
(Frimley Park) Chsd ldrs far side, styd on strongly to lead fnl 100y, won going away: first win: bckd at long odds: unplcd in '99 (rtd 69 at best): eff at 6f on soft grnd: open to further improvement.
*798 **BOW PEEP 15** [10] M W Easterby 5-8-9 (55)(bl) G Parkin 8/1: 000-12: 5 br m Shalford - Gale Force *1* **57**
Seven (Strong Gale) Set pace far side, clr 2f out, overhauled cl-home: op 5/1: gd run: acts on fast & soft.
872 **TANCRED ARMS 3** [3] D W Barker 4-8-8 (54) Kimberley Hart(5) 8/1: 0-0223: 4 b f Clantime - Mischievous *nk* **55**
Miss (Niniski) Held up far side, swtchd centre & styd on nicely fnl 1½f, not quite rch ldrs: qk reapp, bckd.
802 **GRACE 14** [17] J M Bradley 6-8-4 (50) P Fitzsimons (5) 10/1: 402-44: In tch stands side, ran on *¾* **48+**
strongly fnl 1f, nrst fin: first home on stands side: gd effort in the circumstances, see 802.
763 **WHIZZ KID 17** [9] 6-8-12 (58) Claire Bryan (5) 20/1: 00-005: Chsd ldrs far side, onepcd final 1f: *3* **49**
lngr priced stablemate of 4th: a return to 5f will now suit: see 678 (sand).
*698 **CARRIE POOTER 25** [7] 4-9-10 (70)(bl) C Lowther 6/1 FAV: 245-16: Chsd ldr far side, wknd final 1f: *shd* **61**
lkd well: 3rd in this race last year off a 1lb lower mark: see 698 (sand).
639 **AVONDALE GIRL 41** [1] 4-9-10 (70) F Lynch 33/1: -00057: Chsd ldrs far side, no impress fnl 1f: abs. *nk* **60**
824 **CAUTION 9** [14] 6-9-6 (66) D Mernagh (3) 12/1: 5-6068: Prom stands side, led that group 2f out till *½* **55**
inside last, fdd: 2nd home on what was probably unfav stands side: see 645 (fibresand).
*756 **PATSY CULSYTH 17** [18] 5-8-4 (50) Kim Tinkler 16/1: 000-19: Rear stands side, kept on final 2f, *1¾* **35**
nvr dngr: lkd well: rnr-up in this race last year: see 756 (sell).
811 **ROUGE ETOILE 13** [20] 4-9-7 (67) L Swift (7) 33/1: 000-00: Bhd stands side, styd on final 2f, nvr *½* **51**
nrr in 10th: lkd fit & well: see 811.
802 **PREMIUM PRINCESS 14** [2] 5-9-0 (60) J P Spencer 14/1: 140-00: In tch far side, btn dist: fin 11th. *1¼* **41**
4604} **SUGAR CUBE TREAT 99** [13] 4-8-12 (58) J Bramhill 12/1: 0010-0: Rear stands side, some late hdwy, *½* **38**
nvr dngrs in 12th: reapp: '99 Ayr wnr (h'cap, rtd 57): plcd in '98 (nursery h'cap, rtd 66): eff at 6/7f: acts on fast, likes gd/soft & soft grnd: handles a sharp or stiff/gall trk, runs well fresh: with M Mullineaux.
4005} **ON TILL MORNING 99** [11] 4-9-6 (66) A Clark 20/1: 1100-0: Chsd ldrs far side, btn over 1f out: fin *1* **43**
13th, reapp: trained by P Calver to win at Pontefract (class stks) & Ayr (h'cap, rtd 70): '98 Musselburgh wnr (mdn auct, rtd 68): eff at 6/7f on gd & firm, handles gd/soft grnd & any trk: now with M Dods.
751 **SNAP CRACKER 17** [12] 4-9-2 (62) A Culhane 25/1: 0-0020: Chsd ldrs 3f far side, fdd: fin 14th. *1* **36**
4303} **MISS GRAPETTE 99** [8] 4-8-3 (49) G Carter 25/1: 6000-0: Bhd final 3f on far side: 15th, new stable. *1* **20**
674 **QUEEN SARABI 31** [24] 5-8-10 (56) O Pears 8/1: 04-030: Led stands side till halfway, wknd: fin 17th. **0**
4572} **ANGEL HILL 99** [16] 5-9-7 (67) P Hanagan (7) 12/1: 4000-0: Al bhd stands side, fin 18th: reapp. **0**
824 **Bollin Rita 9** [5] 4-9-12 (72) J Carroll 16/1:
4303} **Record Time 99** [15] 4-9-1 (61) W Supple 16/1:
40 **Piggy Bank 99** [23] 4-9-0 (60) G Hall 20/1:
4077} **Highly Fancied 99** [6] 4-8-2 (48) Dale Gibson 33/1:
4389} **Tangerine 99** [22] 3-9-0 (72) T Lucas 16/1:
746 **Milady Lillie 18** [19] 4-8-11 (57) C Catlin (7) 16/1:

THIRSK
FRIDAY APRIL 14TH   **Lefthand, Flat, Oval Track**

23 ran   Time 1m 16.3 (6.8)   (K T Ivory)   K T Ivory Radlett, Herts.

NEWBURY
FRIDAY APRIL 14TH   **Lefthand, Flat, Galloping Track**

Official Going   SOFT. Stalls: Rnd - Outside; Str - Stands Side, except 3.10 - centre.

---

911   2.10 EBF BECKHAMPTON NOV STKS 2YO (D)   5f34y   Soft 100   -27 Slow
£5005   £1540   £770   £385

--   **INSPECTOR GENERAL** [5] P F I Cole 2-8-12 J Fortune 6/1: 1: 2 b c Dilum - New Generation (Young   84
Generation) Dwelt, sn prom, rdn 2f out, kept on to lead appr fnl 1f, drvn clr: op 3/1: Apr foal, cost 13,000gns:
half brother to wnrs over 6f/12f: dam 1m wnr: eff at 5f, further will suit: acts on soft & when fresh: improve.
*724   **Y TO KMAN** 20 [2] R Hannon 2-9-5 L Newman (5) 9/4: 12: 2 b c Mujadil - Hazar (Thatching)   1½   87
Led till over 1f out, kept on same pace over 1f out: well bckd, clr rem, top-weight: prob handles soft.
--   **BARAKANA** [3] B J Meehan 2-8-12 Pat Eddery 2/1 FAV: 3: 2 b c Barathea - Safkana (Doyoun)   7   66
Sn rdn, outpcd over 2f out, kept on late: bckd tho' op 6/4: Jan foal, cost IR 42,000gns: dam 1m wnr: apprec 6f.
--   **HAMATARA** [4] I A Balding 2-8-12 K Fallon 5/1: 4: Dwelt, sn handy, wknd 2f out: op 3/1: Mar foal.   hd   65
--   **HARD TO CATCH** [1] 2-8-12 T Quinn 10/1: 5: Fly jumped start, wknd 2f out: op 6/1: May foal,   3½   58
cost IR 28,000gns: half brother to wnrs over 5f/1m: dam 6f wnr: Namaqualand colt.
5 ran   Time 1m 06.8 (6.5)   (The Blenheim Partnership)   P F I Cole Whatcombe, Oxon

---

912   2.40 DUBAI DUTY FREE RTD HCAP 3YO 0-100 (B)   1m rnd   Soft 100   -35 Slow   [105]
£9092   £3448   £1724   £783

810   **VINTAGE PREMIUM** 13 [4] R A Fahey 3-8-9 (86) R Winston 4/1: 210-21: 3 b c Forzando - Julia Domna   95
(Dominion) Made all, rdn clr over 1f out, drifted right inside last, eased cl-home: value 5/6L: juv scorer at
Beverley (mdn auct, rtd 89): half-brother to a 1m scorer: stays 1m well, further should suit: acts on gd/firm,
clearly likes soft & a gall trk: has run well fresh: useful, fine start to the season.
4487} **SAILING** 99 [9] P F I Cole 3-9-2 (93) J Fortune 7/1: 1105-2: 3 ch f Arazi - Up Anchor (Slip Anchor)   4   95
Chsd ldrs, effort 2f out, kept on same pace: reapp: won 2 of 5 juv starts, at Goodwood (fillies mdn) & Sandown
(stks, rtd 100): dam 1m wnr: stays 1m, could get further: acts on fast, soft grnd & on any trk: has run well
fresh: useful filly, should prove fit for this encouraging reapp.
4582} **CHEMS TRUCE** 99 [3] W R Muir 3-8-13 (90) Martin Dwyer 10/1: 521-3: 3 b c Brief Truce - In The   nk   91
Rigging (Topsider). Keen, prom, rdn & slightly outpcd over 2f out, kept on again ins last: reapp: won last of
3 juv starts, at Catterick (auct mdn, rtd 86): half-brother to a mid-dist wnr, dam miler: stays 1m, further
looks sure to suit: acts on fast, soft & has run well fresh: useful, lightly rcd & should win again soon & further.
4601} **IMPERIAL ROCKET** 99 [2] R Hannon 3-9-1 (92) Dane O'Neill 6/1: 0011-4: 3 ch f Rock City, eff over 2f   2½   89
out, wknd appr final 1f: reapp: progressive juv, won final 2 of 4 starts, at Leicester (mdn) & Windsor
(nursery h'cap, rtd 91): eff at 1m on gd/soft grnd & on any trk: useful, sharper for this.
4468} **ASAAL** 99 [1] R Hills 3-9-1 (98) R Hills 8/1: 3110-5: Waited with, gd hdwy to chase wnr over 2f out till   2   92
over 1f out, fdd: won 2 of 4 juv starts, at Pontefract (mdn) & Salisbury (stks, rtd 101): eff at 6f, bred
to stay 7/8f: acts on fast & soft & has run well fresh: useful at best, sharper back at 6/7f.
3980} **SCOTTISH SPICE** 99 [6] K Fallon 7/2 FAV: 6411-6: Waited with, effort 3f out, sn   4   77
rdn & btn: hvly bckd on reapp: won fnl 2 as a juv, at Folkestone (fillies mdn) & Newbury (nursery h'cap, rtd
93): eff at 7f (should stay further, dam 1f wnr): acts on firm, gd grnd & on any trk: progressive & useful
last term, should prove a different proposition on a sounder surface.
4487} **ROO** 99 [5] 3-9-4 (95) L Dettori 8/1: 1420-7: Al bhd on reapp: won 2 of 10 juv starts, at Bath (debut,   4   79
mdn auct) & Haydock (nov fillies, rtd 94): eff at 5/6f on firm, soft & any trk: tried a t-strap & has run well fresh.
4460} **WURZEL** 99 [7] 3-8-8 (85) R Hughes 13/2: 031-8: Chsd wnr till over 2f out, wknd: reapp: lngr trip.   3½   65
8 ran   Time 1m 46.63 (10.83)   (J C Parsons)   R A Fahey Butterwick, Nth Yorks.

---

913   3.10 GR 3 FRED DARLING STKS 3YO (A)   7f str   Soft 100   -28 Slow
£21000   £8050   £4025   £1925

4487} **IFTIRAAS** 99 [9] J L Dunlop 3-9-0 Pat Eddery 7/1: 2142-1: 3 b f Distant Relative - Ideal Home (Home   111
Guard) Hld up, hdwy over 2f out, styd on for press to lead dist, rdn clr, shade cosily on reapp: juv wnr at Lingfield
(med auct mdn, rtd 94) & just scrbd off in Listed (rtd 104): eff arnd 7.3f (sprint bred, but 1m should suit on this evidence):
handles firm, likes soft & hvy & runs well fresh on any trk: much improved, win another Gr race in these conditions.
4290} **GLEN ROSIE** 99 [6] B W Hills 3-9-0 D Holland 25/1: 3663-2: 3 ch f Mujtahid - Silver Echo (Caerleon)   4   104
Chsd ldrs, outpcd 3f out, flashed tail when keeping on dist, kept on: reapp: won 1st of 5 juv starts,
at Newbury (fillies mdn, rtd 94 at best): eff at 7f & handles firm, much imprvd on soft today: progressed
through the season with a nice race over further.
765   **CRIMPLENE** 20 [7] C E Brittain 3-9-0 L Dettori 9/2: 013-63: 3 ch f Lion Cavern - Crimson Conquest   ¾   103
(Diesis) Waited with, hdwy over 2f out, kept on same pace final 2f: reportedly in season: acts on firm, soft & dirt.
4400} **LAHAN** 99 [1] J H M Gosden 3-9-0 R Hills 9/4 FAV: 11-4: Cl-up, gd hdwy to lead trav well 2f out,   ½   102
rdn & hdd dist, fdd: well bckd: won both juv starts, at Redcar (fillies mdn) & Newmarket (Gr 2 Rockfel, rtd 109,
flashed tail): dam 1m wnr: eff at 7f, 1m at least shld suit: smart form on fast grnd, poss not handle this
testing surface: runs well fresh on gall trks: v useful & scopey, different proposition on a sounder surface.
4490} **OUT OF REACH** 99 [4] 3-9-0 M Hills 9/2: 1-5: Keen in tch, rdn & btn appr 2f out: reapp: won sole   10   87
juv start, at Newbury (mdn, rtd 86): half-sister to a 1m wnr: dam 1m scorer: eff at 6f, bred to apprec
7f/1m: acts on hvy grnd & has run well fresh on a gall trk: stiff task here, could improve in lesser grade.
856} **YAZMIN** 99 [5] 3-9-0 T Quinn 25/1: 2134-6: Set pace till over 3f out, wknd: juv scorer at Windsor   7   77
(fill mdn, rtd 88 at best): eff at 6f, should stay at least 7f: acts on firm/fast grnd & a sharp/undul trk:
stablemate of wnr, will apprec h'cap company.
4137} **SERAPHINA** 99 [3] 3-9-0 K Darley 14/1: 0204-7: Chsd ldr till went on over 3f out till over 2f out,   1½   75
wknd: reapp: won first of 8 juv starts, at Doncaster (stks), subs nk rnr-up in a Gr 2 (rtd 106): speedily bred
& v eff at 6f, should stay 7f: likes gd & soft, gall trk: has run well fresh: tough & useful.
4400} **TOTAL LOVE** 99 [2] 3-9-0 J Reid 6/1: 0233-8: Handy till wknd over 3f out: won 1 of 9 juv starts,   10   60
at Leicester (mdn), subs plcd in Listed/Gr 2 company (rtd 106): stays 1m on fast, gd/soft & on a gall trk.
4294} **OUT OF AFRICA** 99 [8] 3-9-0 R Hughes 10/1: 2111-9: Al bhd: reapp: in '99 trained by B Hills &   25   30
landed final 3 starts, at Doncaster, Newmarket (nursery h'caps) & York (Listed, rtd 96): cost current connections

200,000 gns: eff at 6/7f on firm, soft & on any trk: v tough, useful last term, better than this.
9 ran   Time 1m 33.24 (8.94)   (Kuwait Racing Syndicate II)   J L Dunlop Arundel, West Sussex.

---

914   3.40 SPY RATED HCAP 4YO+ 0-110 (B)   5f34y   Soft 100   +20 Fast   [117]
£9108   £3454   £1727   £785

4469} **MONKSTON POINT** 99 [9] D W P Arbuthnot 4-8-6 (95)(vis) J Reid 12/1: 0200-1: 4 b g Fayruz - Doon Belle   **101**
(Ardoon) In tch stands rail, rdn & kept on Press to chall appr final 1f, drvn out to get on top cl-home:
fast time: reapp: rnr-up once in '99 (rtd h'cap, first time visor, rtd 97): useful juv, won at Bath (2) & Ayr
(Listed, rtd 105): all 4 wins at 5f, stays 6f: acts on fast, relishes soft grnd & a gall trk: best in a visor
now: has slipped right down the weights, v useful at best & relishes these conditions.

2965} **LORD KINTYRE** 99 [10] B R Millman 5-8-6 (95) Cheryl Nosworthy (7) 40/1: 0/50-2: 5 b g Makbul -   nk   **100**
Highland Rowena (Royben) Waited with, gd hdwy stands rail over 2f out, led appr fnl 1f, rdn & collared cl-home,
just btn on reapp: has reportedly broken blood vessels & unplcd both '99 starts (rtd 68): plcd sev times in '98
(rtd 109 when 3rd in Gr 2 Kings Stand): '97 wnr at Windsor & Newbury (val Super Sprint, rtd 112): prob beat at
5f, stays 6f: acts on firm, hvy & on any trk: runs well fresh: gelded since last term & has slipped to fav mark.

734   **NOW LOOK HERE** 20 [8] B A McMahon 4-8-13 (102) T Quinn 11/2 CO FAV: 033-23: 4 b g Reprimand -   hd   **106**
Where's Carol (Anfield) Prom, effort to chall over 1f out, kept on ins last, just btn in a 3-way photo: confirmed
improved form of 734 (6f): often placed & worth a try in headgear.

*808   **SARTORIAL** 13 [7] P J Makin 4-8-6 (95) S Sanders 11/2 CO FAV: 232-14: Led over 2f out till appr   2½   **94**
final 1f, no extra: not disgraced, see 808 (mdn).

734   **CRETAN GIFT** 20 [6] 9-8-10 (99)(vis) L Dettori 13/2: 30-035: Sn bhd, effort over 1f out, nvr dngr: 1¾   **94**
tough 9yo, wants 6f: see 734.

734   **FIRST MAITE** 20 [5] 7-8-13 (102)(bl) K Fallon 11/2 CO FAV: 032446: Sn rdn & nvr a factor: do better.   2   **93**

4531} **REPERTORY** 99 [3] P Price 12/1: 2543-7: Led till over 2f out, wknd over 1f out: reapp: hd   **97**
plcd 3 times in '99, incl a Gr 3 (rtd 106): '98 wnr at the Curragh (Listed h'cap) & Epsom (h'cap, rtd 106): v eff
at 5f on firm or hvy, handles any trk: has run well fresh: v speedy & useful, loves to force the pace.

4620} **SUPERIOR PREMIUM** 99 [4] 6-9-7 (110) R Winston 9/1: Chsd ldrs, rdn & btn well over 1f out: 2½   **95**
top weight: in '99 won in Sweden (Listed), Ascot & Newbury (h'caps, rtd 114 at best): '98 wnr at Chester (rtd
h'cap), Haydock & Goodwood (val Stewards Cup H'cap, rtd 107): eff at 5f, prob best at 6f: acts on firm, hvy &
any trk: has run well fresh & can carry big weights: tough & v smart sprinter at best (9 wins from 37 starts).

4620} **YORKIES BOY** 99 [2] 5-8-13 (102) J Fortune 7/1: 0000-9: In tch, btn halfway: in '99 trained by   1½   **84**
B McMahon, plcd twice (incl Gr 3, rtd 110): '98 Newmarket wnr (2, Listed & Gr 3, rtd 114): stays 6f, all 3 wins
at 5f & handles fast, likes gd/soft: has run well fresh prev: v smart at best, has slipped down the weights.

*734   **ANDREYEV** 20 [1] 6-9-5 (108) R Hughes 11/2 CO FAV: 440-10: Dwelt, sn in tch, wknd well over 1f   2   **86**
out: best over 6/7f & better than this: see 734 (wng reapp).
10 ran   Time 1m 04.4 (4.1)   (Derrick C Broomfield)   D W P Arbuthnot Upper Lambourn, Berks.

---

915   4.10 BRIDGET FILLIES MDN 3YO (D)   7f str   Soft 100   -20 Slow
£5330   £1640   £820   £410

--   **TANZILLA** [12] C E Brittain 3-8-11 L Dettori 11/2: 1: 3 b f Warning - Tanz (Sadler's Wells):   **93**
Led 1f, cl up till went on again over 2f out, kept on well ins last, idle out: wng debut: sister to a smart 10f wnr:
eff at 7f, 1m + sure to suit: runs well fresh on soft & a gall trk: v useful debut, sure to win in better grade.

--   **VELVET LADY** [2] P F I Cole 3-8-11 J Fortune 7/4 FAV: 2: 3 b f Nashwan - Velvet Moon (Shaadi):   nk   **92**
Keen, prom, effort to chall over 1f out, kept on for press ins last, just held: debut: dam smart 6/10f wnr:
eff at 7f, 1m/10f sure to suit: acts on soft & runs well fresh: useful/promising debut, sure to win races.

--   **POETIC** [13] H R A Cecil 3-8-11 T Quinn 7/2: 3: 3 b f Nureyev - Draw Straws (Key To The Mint)   3   **88+**
Keen, handy, kept on nicely fnl 2f, no dngr under hands & heels: op 2/1: bred to relish 1m & handles soft
grnd: sure to leave this form/promising intro & one to keep an eye on.

--   **EUROLINK ARTEMIS** [11] J L Dunlop 3-8-11 Pat Eddery 16/1: 4: Dwelt, sn in tch, rdn over 2f   2½   **84**
out, some late gains under a kind ride: half-sister to wnrs over 7f/9f: dam 10f scorer: sure to relish
a step up to 1m+: handles soft grnd: a mdn should prove a formality & the type to progress from here.

--   **TWIN LOGIC** [9] 3-8-11 J Reid 11/1: 5: In tch, rdn over 2f out, onepace: Diesis filly: improve.   nk   **83**

--   **HAZY HEIGHTS** [6] 3-8-11 D R McCabe 33/1: 6: Chsd ldrs, rdn & slightly outpcd over 2f out,   5   **75**
onepace: debut: dam 6f scorer: Shirley Heights filly: should apprec a step up to 1m+: with B Meehan.

--   **LET ALONE** [5] 3-8-11 M Hills 12/1: 7: Sn bhd, some late gains: full sister to a 7f scorer: dam   1¼   **73+**
1m/9f wnr: Warning filly: with B Hills, sure to relish 1m & improve considerably for this.

--   **EFFERVESCENT** [7] 3-8-11 K Fallon 14/1: 8: In tch till wknd 2f out: dam 6f scorer: Efisio filly.   ½   **72**

--   **POLAR DIAMOND** [8] 3-8-11 D Griffiths 50/1: 9: Al bhd: debut.   shd   **72**

--   **RASMALAI** [4] 3-8-11 Dane O'Neill 16/1: 0: Al bhd: 10th, debut.   ¾   **71**

--   **ICON** [10] 3-8-11 K Darley 14/1: 0: Al bhd: 11th, debut.   1¼   **69**

--   **PRIM N PROPER** [14] 3-8-11 R Hughes 20/1: 0: Led after 1f till over 2f out, wknd: 12th.   nk   **68**

--   **NUNKIE GIRL** [1] 3-8-11 P Dobbs (5) 33/1: 0: In tch till wknd over 2f out: 13th, debut.   hd   **68**

--   **KOSMIC LADY** [3] 3-8-11 S Buckley 33/1: 0: Al bhd: fnl 1, last, debut.   1½   **65**
14 ran   Time 1m 32.72 (8.42)   (Abdullah Saeed Bel Hab)   C E Brittain Newmarket.

---

916   4.40 PETER SMITH MDN 3YO (D)   1m3f   Soft 100   -117 Slow
£5200   £1600   £800   £400

3964} **MILLENARY** 99 [3] J L Dunlop 3-9-0 Pat Eddery 4/1: -35-1: 3 b c Rainbow Quest - Ballerina (Dancing   **89**
Brave) Chsd ldrs, eff 2f out, styd on to lead cl home, rdn out: nicely bckd: plcd in '99 (rtd 89): eff at 1m,
stays 11f well & further could suit: acts on firm & soft, gall trk: runs well fresh: useful.

--   **TOTAL CARE** [6] H R A Cecil 3-9-0 W Ryan 9/2: 2: 3 br c Cearleon - Totality (Dancing Brave)   hd   **88+**
Hld up, hdwy to lead over 1f out, hdd ins last but kept on, just held: op 3/1: dam 14f wnr: eff at 11f, 12f+
sure to suit: acts on soft grnd & runs well fresh: looks sure to improve & win races, esp over further.

--   **BOX BUILDER** [2] M R Channon 3-9-0 S Drowne 50/1: 3: 3 ch c Fraam - Ena Olley (Le Moss)   nk   **88**
Led over 4f out till over 1f out, rallied to lead again ins last, hdd cl home, just btn in a 3-way photo: clr
rem: stays 11f on soft grnd: fine debut, can win a mdn.

4606} **ANDROMEDES** 99 [4] H R A Cecil 3-9-0 T Quinn A/6 FAV: 3 4: Chsd ldrs, eff 2f out, sn btn: 7   **81**
well bckd, stablemate of lesser fancied wnr: rtd 86+ when plcd on sole '99 start: eff at 7f, bred to stay mid-dists:
acts on hvy grnd: should be capable of better.

3706} **RAINBOW SPIRIT** 99 [1] 3-9-0 K Darley 33/1: 0-5: Led till over 4f out, wknd: well btn sole juv start: ½   **80**

297

half brother to wnrs over 6f/11f: with A Jarvis.

--   **MAZAARR** [5] 3-9-0 L Dettori 13/2: 6: Sn bhd: cost 100,000 gns: Woodman colt.   12   68
6 ran   Time   (L Neil Jones)   J L Dunlop Arundel, W Sussex

---

917   5.10 LEVY BOARD HCAP 4YO+ 0-100 (C)   2m   Soft 100 -44 Slow   **[100]**
     £6955   £2140   £1070   £535   4 yo rec 4 lb

--   **BRAVE TORNADO** [10] G B Balding 9-7-10 (68)(3oh) R Brisland (5) 100/30 FAV: 1154/1: 9 ch g Dominion   75
- Accuracy (Gunner B) Prom, hdwy to lead 3f out, edged left 2f out & ins last but styd on, rdn out: nicely bckd: rtd
139h in a recent 3m hdle, in 98/99 wnr at Ascot & Cheltenham (h'caps, rtd 148h, gd & hvy): last rcd on the Flat
back in '98 (rtd 66): last won in '94: stays 2m well & relishes soft & hvy grnd & a gall trk.

1980} **BRIDIES PRIDE 99** [5] G A Ham 9-7-10 (68) G Bardwell 20/1: 3200-2: 9 b g Alleging - Miss Monte Carlo   3   72
(Reform) Led till 3f out, kept on gamley for press over 1f out: clr of rem on reapp: last rcd over hdles 10
wks ago, p.u. on sole start: plcd on first 2 of 4 '99 Flat starts (rtd 67): '98 wnr at Ascot (h'cap, rtd 69):
eff at 2m/2m2f on firm, soft grnd & likes a gall trk: runs well fresh: tough & genuine front rnr.

4329} **KATTEGAT 99** [4] J A B Old 4-9-2 (92) J Reid 6/1: /231-3: 4 b g Slip Anchor - Kirsten (Kris)   13   87
Chsd ldr till over 4f out, onepace: fit from hdling, earlier rnr-up twice (rtd 122h, 2m, gd grnd): in '99 won
on the Flat at Ayr (h'cap, rtd 94): '98 wnr at Nottingham (rtd 81): prob stays 14f on gd & loves soft grnd:
handles any trk & has run well fresh: probably apprec a return to 14f.

732   **MURGHEM 20** [3] M Johnston 5-10-0 (100) D Holland 7/1: 20-224: Chsd ldrs till over 2f out: topweight.   ¾   94
4618} **FANTASY HILL 99** [2] 4-9-1 (91) Pat Eddery 7/2: 1302-5: In tch, brief eff over 3f out, sn wknd: reapp: 10   78
in '99 scored at Nottingham (h'cap, rtd 92 at best): stays 2m on fast, hvy & a gall trk: has run well fresh.

1170} **PRAIRIE FALCON 99** [1] 6-9-2 (88) M Hills 10/1: 0/24-6: Waited with, no impress final 3f: reapp: 4   72
rcd only twice in '99, hd rnr-up in Queens Prize & 4½L 4th in Chester Cup (rtd 91): '98 wnr at Haydock & Goodwood
(amat h'caps, rtd 85): stays 2m2.7f on firm & gd grnd & on any trk: gd weight carrier who has run well fresh:
expect a much bigger run next time on a sounder surface, poss in the Queens Prize at Kempton.

845   **IL PRINCIPE 6** [7] 6-8-8 (80) K Fallon 8/1: 24-007: Keen bhd, rdn & btn 3f out: '99 4 time h'cap wnr.   nk   64
4584} **HISTORIC 99** [9] 4-8-6 (82) J F Egan 5/1: 422-8: Bhd, btn over 3f out: rnr-up on 2 of 3 '99   5   62
starts (mdns, rtd 83): eff at 12f, bred to stay further: acts on hvy grnd & on any trk.

3277} **TREASURE CHEST 99** [6] 5-8-1 (73)(vis) Martin Dwyer 25/1: 5250-9: Bhd, btn over 4f out: jumps fit.   *dist*   0
9 ran   Time 3m 49.11 (23.11)   (Miss B Swire)   G B Balding Fyfield, Hants.

Official Going   STANDARD. Stalls: Inside.

---

918   7.00 EQUESTRIAN HCAP 4YO+ 0-65 (F)   2m46y aw   Going 21 -37 Slow   **[60]**
     £2338   £668   £334   4 yo rec 4 lb

760   **PLEASANT MOUNT 18** [1] Miss J A Camacho 4-9-13 (63) K Darley 9/4 FAV: 112-01: 4 b g First Trump -   70a
Alo Ez (Alzao) Mid-div, prog to lead 4f out, pshd out: bckd two op 13/8, slow time: '99 wnr at Beverley, Thirsk &
Redcar (h'caps, rtd 63): eff at 14f/2m on firm, hvy grnd & fibresand, any trk: gd AW bow, progressive.

835   **QUAKERESS 8** [4] R Brotherton 5-7-10 (28)(2oh) J Mackay (7) 9/2: 134532: 5 b m Brief Truce - Deer   2   31a
Emily (Alzao) Waited with, imprvd 4f out, kept on without threatening wnr: op 8/1: ran to best back up in trip.

*737   **TIME CAN TELL 19** [3] A G Juckes 6-9-1 (47) N Callan 7/2: 0-5513: 6 ch g Sylvan Express - Stellaris   ¾   49a
(Star Appeal) Held up, hdwy fnl 2f, unable to chall: op 9/2: ran to best: see 737.

742   **WESTERN COMMAND 19** [5] Mrs N Macauley 4-9-11 (61) R Fitzpatrick (3) 14/1: 603464: Keen, prom,   ½   62a
ch 3f out, onepcd dist: op 10/1: better run up in trip, prob stays 2m, see 560 (11f).

822   **XYLEM 10** [8] 9-8-5 (37)(vis) G Bardwell 10/1: 302305: Settled bhd, nvr nr ldrs: see 577, 347.   6   33a
788   **IRISH CREAM 17** [9] 4-8-8 (44)(vis) M Henry 10/1: -20106: Sn led, hdd 4f out & no extra: longer trip.   2½   38a
788   **MURCHAN TYNE 17** [2] 7-9-9 (55) S Sanders 8/1: 150-07: Held up, brief eff 5f out, btn 4f out: AW bow.   9   42a
6   **RED RAJA 159** [7] 7-9-4 (50) J Fortune 10/1: 4560-8: Early ldr, wknd qckly 5f out: tried fences over the   1   36a
winter: '99 wnr at Lingfield (2 AW h'cap, rtd 55a & turf h'cap, rtd 61 at best): former 118h rtd hdler (2m, fast
& soft): eff at 2m on firm, soft grnd & equitrack, likes Lingfield: with P Mitchell.

554   **SAFE SHARP JO 56** [6] 5-7-12 (30)(2ow)(8oh) J Bosley (0) 50/1: 006009: Chsd ldrs 12f out: new stable.   *dist*   0a
9 ran   Time 3m 38.6 (9.4)   (Shangri-La Racing Club)   Miss J A Camacho Norton, N.Yorks.

---

919   7.30 DRESSAGE CLAIMER 3YO+ (F)   5f aw rnd   Going 21 -09 Slow
     £2240   £640   £320   3 yo rec 11lb

*753   **PRIDE OF BRIXTON 18** [1] Andrew Reid 7-9-6 M Henry 11/10 FAV: 000-11: 7 b g Dominion - Caviar Blini   65a
(What A Guest) Sn led, made rest, rdn out: well bckd: recent W'hampton wnr (seller): dual '99 rnr-up (clmr,
rtd 73a): '98 wnr again here at W'hampton (4, sell & h'cap for C Thornton & 2 h'caps for P Evans, rtd 74a),
earlier won at Carlisle (ltd stks, rtd 61): eff at 5/6f, tried 7f: acts on fast & soft, fibresand/W'hampton
specialist: goes on any trk: runs well fresh, without visor: suited by plating class.

753   **SAMWAR 18** [4] Mrs N Macauley 8-9-4 (vis) R Fitzpatrick (3) 9/2: 260632: 8 b g Warning - Samaza   1¾   57a
(Arctic Tern) Struggled to go pace till kept on well fnl 1½f, nvr nrr: op 7/2: capable of better: see 214.

753   **PALACEGATE JACK 18** [2] A Berry 9-9-6 (bl) K Darley 9/2: -25323: 9 gr g Neshad - Pasadena Lady   ½   58a
(Captain James) Early ldr, cl-up till outpcd appr fnl 1f: stiff task at the weights, clrly in gd heart: see 191.

753   **YOUNG IBNR 18** [3] B A McMahon 5-9-2 P Mundy (7) 6/1: 560144: Prom till appr fnl 1f: stiff task.   4   44a
87   **RED SYMPHONY 145** [5] 4-9-5 I Mongan (5) 6/1: 0030-5: Nvr troubled ldrs: 5 mth abs, tchd 9/1: plcd   1   44a
twice last year (clmr, rtd 58, h'cap, rtd 54): '98 wnr here at W'hampton (sell, rtd 60a) & Musselburgh (2, sell, J
Berry, nurs, rtd 70): eff at 5f on gd, hvy grnd & with/forcing the pace on a sharp trk.

830   **SUNRISE GIRL 9** [6] 3-8-0 A McCarthy (3) 50/1: 06: Sn btn: AW bow, no form.   3½   26a
6 ran   Time 1m 01.7 (1.5)   (A S Reid)   Andrew Reid Mill Hill, London NW7.

920   8.00 FIBRESAND MDN 3YO+ (D)   1m100y aw rnd   Going 21   +09 Fast
£2828   £808   £404   3 yo   rec 15lb

708   **SIR FERBET** 23 [7] B W Hills 3-8-9 J Weaver 1/2 FAV: 43-21: 3 b c Mujadil - Mirabiliary (Crow)   **90a**
Easily made ev yd: well bckd to land the odds, gd time: plcd 2nd of 2 '99 starts (mdn, rtd 89): eff at
6f, suited by 1m now & may get further: acts on gd grnd & fibresand, sharp tks.

4390} **BAILEYS PRIZE** 182 [8] M Johnston 3-8-9 J Fanning 5/1: 45-2: 3 ch c Mister Baileys - Mar Mar   10   **69a**
(Forever Casting) Rcd in 2nd thr'out, nvr any impress on wnr: tchd 7/1, AW bow: promise both '99 starts (auct
mdn, rtd 74): well bred colt, shld get 1m this term: will find easier mdns.

709   **FISHER ISLAND** 23 [9] R Hollinshead 3-8-4 P M Quinn (5) 25/1: 450-63: 3 b f Sir Pekan - Liberty   7   **50a**
Song (Last Tycoon) Dwelt, bhd, went past btn horses in the straight: see 709.

3961} **SALVA** 211 [10] P J Makin 4-9-5 S Sanders 7/1: -30-4: Prom till 4f out: AW bow, reapp: plcd   1¾   **49a**
first of 2 '99 starts (mdn, rtd 75): eff at 1m on gd grnd.

--   **READING RHONDA** [6] 4-9-5 J Weaver 5/1: 5/5: In tch till 4f out: 2 yr abs since 5th of   1½   **46a**
7 on juv debut for I Balding (rtd 68): now with P Mitchell.

4605} **CHARLEM** 162 [4] 3-8-4 F Norton 66/1: 00-6: Nvr troubled ldrs: reapp/AW bow, modest form.   ¾   **44a**

--   **BELINDA** [3] 3-8-4 J Bosley (6) 66/1: 7: Sn struggling: belated debut for this Mizoram filly.   nk   **44a**

--   **EVIYRN** [1] 4-9-10 S Whitworth 25/1: 04-8: Chsd ldrs 4f: 7 wk hdles abs, Flat bow in   2   **45a**
this country: ex-Irish, 4th of 17 fnl of 2 '99 starts (1m5f mdn on gd/soft grnd).

--   **CEINWEN** [5] 5-9-5 S Drowne 50/1: 9: Nvr on terms: half-sister to useful h'capper Concer Un.   dist   **0a**

378   **WILCOY WARRIER** 84 [2] 4-9-10 R Fitzpatrick (3) 50/1: 0-0P: Sn t.o., dismounted & p.u. 5f out, lame.   **0a**
10 ran   Time 1m 47.2 (1.0)   (International Plywood)   B W Hills Lambourn, Berks.

921   8.40 J CHALK HCAP 3YO+ 0-85 (D)   1m100y aw rnd   Going 21   +01 Fast   [78]
£3887   £1196   £598   £299   3 yo   rec 15lb

721   **RISK FREE** 21 [9] N P Littmoden 3-9-6 (85) T G McLaughlin 9/2: 02-421: 3 ch g Risk Me - Princess   **90a**
Lily (Blakeney) Nvr far away, led ent fnl 2f, held on well despite drifting left: '99 wnr at Southwell (auct
mdn, rtd 91a & 87): formerly eff at 5f, suited by this step up to 8.5f: goes on both AWs, tho' prefers fibresand: best
up with the pace: improving, may head for an overseas Listed contest.

867   **ADOBE** 4 [12] W M Brisbourne 5-8-5 (55) A McCarthy (3) 12/1: 00-102: 5 b g Green Desert -   ½   **58a**
Shamshir (Kris) Rear, imprvd halfway & kept on well beside dnst: not btn far: op 8/1, qck reapp: back to form.

*278   **INVER GOLD** 99 [10] A G Newcombe 3-8-9 (74) S Whitworth 10/1: 624-13: 3 ch c Arazi - Mary Martin   ¾   **75a**
(Be My Guest) Mid-div, eff 3f out, ran on appr fnl 1f, nvr nrr: tchd 14/1, 14 wk abs: h'cap bow, type to win again.

817   **LORD EUROLINK** 12 [7] C A Dwyer 6-9-3 (67) (tvi) D Holland 7/2: 311104: Early ldr, cl-up, onepcd dnst.   nk   **68a**

715   **ONE DINAR** 22 [4] 5-10-0 (78) J Fortune 11/4 FAV: -21205: Held up, wide prog 3f out, same pace fnl 1f.   hd   **79a**

711   **DONE AND DUSTED** 23 [11] 4-9-3 (67) F Norton 14/1: 063156: Prom, no extra fnl 1f: op 10/1, btr 583.   3½   **62a**

717   **ZABIONIC** 22 [5] 3-8-5 (69)(1ow) K Darley 12/1: 600-47: Al same place: tchd 10/1: see717.   2   **61a**

*707   **THE IMPOSTER** 23 [8] 5-8-13 (63) I Mongan (5) 8/1: 142-18: Led after 2f till ent fnl 2f, fdd: op 6/1.   ¾   **53a**

4470} **LIGHT PROGRAMME** 176 [1] 6-9-9 (73) S Drowne 25/1: 1/00-9: Nvr troubled ldrs: over 3 month   hd   **63a**
hdle abs, AW bow: lightly rcd & no form since won 2nd of 2 '97 starts for H Cecil at Newmarket (mdn, rtd 86):
eff over a stiff 10f on fast & gd/sft grnd: with J G Smyth Osbourne.

705   **TROJAN WOLF** 23 [3] 5-9-7 (71) R Winston 14/1: 145300: Al towards rear: 10th: see 255.   8   **48a**

677   **ROYAL CASCADE** 30 [7] 6-9-4 (68)(bl) P Mundy (7) 25/1: 063020: Sn bhd: 11th: much better 677.   3½   **39a**

*669   **THE STAGER** 32 [6] 8-9-12 (76)(tvi) S Sanders 9/1: 114510: Hmpd 1f & bhd: 12th, best ignored.   6   **37a**
12 ran   Time 1m 47.9 (1.7)   (Mrs P J Sheen)   N P Littmoden Newmarket.

922   9.25 PUISSANCE SELLER 3YO+ (G)   1m1f79y aw   Going 21   -09 Slow
£1913   £546   £273   3 yo   rec 17lb

775   **MALCHIK** 17 [2] P Howling 4-9-9 R Winston 10/1: 003331: 4 ch c Absalom - Very Good (Noalto)   **55a**
Readily made all: tchd 14/1: plcd sev times in '99 (h'caps, rtd 49a): '98 wnr at Leicester (sell nurs, rtd 55):
eff at 9.5f, stays 12f: acts on gd grnd, both AWs, prob prefers fibresand: best without blnks: goes on any track.

869   **THE WILD WIDOW** 4 [5] Miss S J Wilton 6-9-4 (bl) I Mongan (5) 5/1: 000-02: 6 gr m Saddlers'   5   **40a**
Hall - No Cards (No Mercy) Prsd wnr, outpcd 2f out: op 8/1, qck reapp: '99 wnr here at W'hampton (sell,
H Collingridge, rtd 59a) & Warwick (sell in first time blnks, rtd 52): plcd prev term for J Eustace (h'cap,
rtd 69): eff at 1m/11f on gd, soft & fibresand: best on sharp/turning trks & in sellers, with/without blnks.

806   **SEASAME PARK** 15 [9] B Palling 3-8-1 M Henry 10/1: 020-03: 3 b f Elmaamul - Holyrood Park   6   **30a**
(Sharrood) Prom, no extra appr fnl 2f: op 7/1: back up in trip: see 806.

750   **BENTICO** 18 [13] Mrs N Macauley 11-9-9 (vis) R Fitzpatrick (3) 11/2: 6/0424: Al around same place.   shd   **35a**

646   **GENIUS** 40 [8] 5-9-9 J Fortune 7/1: 200405: Sn outpcd, went past btn horses in str: tchd 9/1, 6 wk abs.   3½   **29a**

749   **FLASHFEET** 18 [4] 10-9-9 G Baker (7) 33/1: 000046: Held up, eff 5f out, btn 3f out: see 398.   5   **21a**

750   **HEATHYARDS JAKE** 18 [1] 4-10-0 P M Quinn (5) 16/1: 006657: Nvr a factor: stiff task, see 229 (mdn).   ½   **25a**

--   **ESPERTO** [3] 7-9-9 G Bardwell 12/1: 3322/8: In tch till 4f out: tchd 20/1, 2 yr abs since plcd all   10   **5a**
3 '98 starts (sell, rtd 54): '97 Nottingham wnr (10f seller, rtd 53): eff at 10f, stays 12f on firm & soft,
handles fibresand: runs well fresh, any track: with J Pearce.

841   **SUNRISE** 8 [11] 3-8-1 Martin Dwyer 12/1: 03-009: Chsd ldrs till halfway: AW bow.   nk   **0a**

759   **MYSTIC GEM** 18 [7] 4-9-9 S Whitworth 50/1: 000: Nvr in it: 10th, modest.   21   **0a**

846   **TIGHTROPE** 7 [12] 5-10-0 M Fenton 2/1 FAV: 001000: Dwelt, closed bef halfway, lost pl 4f out &   **0a**
eased fnl 2f: op 6/4: last, op 6/4, qck reapp: finished distressed, see 632 (Lingfield).

--   **Flying Green** [6] 7-9-9 (bl) J Bosley (7) 20/1:   --   **Sable Cloak** [10] 5-9-4 O Pears 50/1:
13 ran   Time 2m 01.0 (2.8)   (I G Mirzolan)   P Howling Newmarket.

923   9.50 HORSE O'YEAR HCAP 3YO+ 0-70 (E)   6f aw rnd   Going 21   -04 Slow   [70]
£2870   £820   £410

*738   **TEYAAR** 19 [1] D Shaw 4-9-11 (67) I Mongan (5) 15/2: -51011: 4 b g Polar Falcon - Music In My Life   **72a**
(Law Society) Sn led, under press appr fnl 1f, held on grimly: earlier won at Southwell (2, mdn & class
stks): plcd in '99 (mdn, rtd 85): eff at 6f, stays 7f: goes on firm & soft grnd, likes fibresand: gd weight
carrier, best without blnks: improving & genuine front-runner.

754   **FEATHERSTONE LANE** 18 [5] Miss L C Siddall 9-8-5 (47) N Callan 14/1: 425222: 9 b g Siberian   nk   **51a**

Express -Try Gloria (Try My Best) Struggled early on, imprvd appr fnl 2f, ev ch below dist, held nr fin: op 10/1: in gd form but is proving hard to win with nowadays: see 82.
739 **DAHLIDYA 19** [7] M J Polglase 5-9-9 (65) P Doe 7/1: 503133: 5 b m Midyan - Dahlawise (Caerleon) *1½* **65a**
Dwelt & out the back till ran on ent fnl 2f, finished strongly: tchd 9/1: holding form v well: see 697.
787 **AUBRIETA 17** [11] D Haydn Jones 4-8-12 (54)(bl) S Drowne 15/2: -05204: Chsd ldrs, onepace dist. *hd* **54a**
844 **MOOCHA CHA MAN 7** [3] 4-9-3 (59)(bl) K Darley 9/2: 40-005: Prom, hard rdn 2f out, unable to qckn. *nk* **58a**
763 **SEALED BY FATE 18** [6] 5-8-8 (50)(vis) D Holland 12/1: 00-506: Struggled to go pace: vis reapplied. *3* **42a**
844 **GRASSLANDIK 7** [10] 4-8-9 (51) S Whitworth 10/1: 353507: Dwelt, chsd ldrs after 3f till bef dist. *nk* **42a**
98 **THE FUGATIVE 150** [9] 7-9-0 (56) J Fortune 3/1 FAV: 35D0-8: Early pace, lost position after 2f: *1½* **43a**
bckd after 5 mnth abs: '99 wnr at Epsom (h'cap, rtd 90 & 54a): '98 wnr at Folkestone (stks), Lingfield & again at Epsom (h'cap, rtd 73): eff forcing it over a sharp/undul 6f, stays 7f: acts on fast, soft & equitrack, likes Epsom.
4573} **SUPERFRILLS 166** [12] 7-7-13 (41) F Norton 33/1: 0006-9: Al bhd: reapp: '99 rnr-up (h'cap, rtd 49): *2* **23a**
'98 wnr at Hamilton (2) & Newcastle (h'cap, rtd 49 & 43a): eff at 5f, stays 6f on fast, soft grnd & fibresand.
4056} **POLAR MIST 206** [8] 5-9-9 (65)(tbl) Dean McKeown 20/1: 2000-0: Early ldr, btn 2f out: 10th: op 14/1 *½* **46a**
on reapp: '99 wnr at Folkestone (stks, rtd 72) & here at W'hampton (3, sell, clmr & h'cap, rtd 67a): '98 wnr again at W'hampton (mdn, rtd 78a, Sir M Prescott): eff at 6f, suited by 5f on gd/soft & hvy grnd, fibresand/W'hampton specialist: eff in blnks/visor & a t-strap, can run well fresh up with/forcing the pace: with Mrs Macauley.
465 **TROJAN HERO 70** [2] 9-8-12 (54) A McCarthy (3) 20/1: -45300: In tch 4f: 11th, 10 wk abs, op 14/1. *1½* **31a**
754 **FRANKLIN D 18** [13] 4-8-3 (45) J Fanning 10/1: 3-2340: Well plcd till 2f out: 12th: btr 570, 438 (7f). *hd* **22a**
838 **PERUVIAN STAR 8** [4] 4-9-9 (65) T G McLaughlin 16/1: 00-050: Sn struggling: 13th, see 721. *1½* **38a**
13 ran Time 1m 14.3 (1.5) (Justin R Aaron) D Shaw Averham, Notts.

THIRSK SATURDAY APRIL 15TH Lefthand, Flat, Oval Track

Official Going GOOD/SOFT. Stalls: Rnd Crse - Inside; Str Crse - Stands Side.

924 — 2.05 ALLERTON CLASSIFIED STKS 3YO 0-70 (E) 1m4f Soft 98 -10 Slow
£3614 £1112 £556 £278

4414} **SUDDEN FLIGHT 180** [3] E A L Dunlop 3-8-11 J Reid 10/3: 0130-1: 3 b c In The Wings - Ma Petite Cherie **79**
(Caro): Trkd ldrs, imprvd to lead 2f out, rdn clr fnl 1f despite edging left: just better for reapp: '99 Yarmouth wnr (nursery h'cap), subs plcd at Nottingham (unlucky, rtd 70): apprec todays step up to 12f & likes soft grnd: runs well fresh, handles a gall trk: can continue to improve as he steps up in trip.
782 **SUNDAY RAIN 17** [6] P F I Cole 3-8-11 (bl) D Sweeney 2/1 FAV: 40-422: 3 b c Summer Squall - Oxava *6* **70**
(Antheus): Chsd ldr, went on after 5f, hdd 2f out, kept on but not pace of wnr: well bckd, lkd well, 8L clr 3rd.
701 **RUNNING TIMES 23** [5] T D Easterby 3-8-11 K Darley 9/1: 00-503: 3 b c Brocco - Concert Peace (Hold *8* **58**
Your Peace): Dwelt, ran in snatches bhd, styd on fnl 1f: tchd 12/1: shapes like a thor' stayer, blnks may suit.
827 **RHODAMINE 10** [2] J L Eyre 3-8-11 Dean McKeown 9/1: 4-0004: Rear, nvr a factor: op 13/2: longer *1* **57**
12f trip: again bhd today's 3rd in 625 (AW).
701 **WINTZIG 23** [7] 3-8-8 M Fenton 7/1: 561-05: Hdwy from rear 4f out, btn 2f out: '99 Pontefract wnr *¾* **53**
(nursery h'cap, rtd 72): half-sister to a 5/6f wnr juv: eff at 1m, not stay 12f here? acts on gd/soft grnd.
827 **PATACAKE PATACAKE 10** [1] 3-8-8 J Fanning 9/2: 644-06: Chsd ldr, wknd over 2f out: drifted from *¾* **52**
3/1: attractive filly, longer 12f trip: worth another ch after eye-catching reapp in 827 (10f h'cap).
3957} **DESRAYA 211** [4] 3-8-11 F Lynch 25/1: 4000-7: Set pace 4f, wknd leaving back-str, t.o: reapp: *dist* **0**
4th in a Ripon mdn in '99 (rtd 73): handles gd/soft grnd: with K Ryan.
7 ran Time 2m 42.8 (13.0) (Maktoum Al Maktoum) E A L Dunlop Newmarket.

925 — 2.35 LISTED THIRSK CLASSIC TRIAL 3YO (A) 1m rnd Soft 98 +11 Fast
£14558 £5522 £2761 £1255

4025} **RACE LEADER 210** [2] B W Hills 3-8-11 J Reid 9/4: -132-1: 3 b c Gone West - Dubian (High Line): **113**
Trkd ldrs, prog to chall 2f out, went on over 1f out, styd on strongly, rdn out: nicely bckd tho' drifted from 6/4, lkd well on reapp, best time of day: '99 Newmarket wnr (mdn, debut), subs 2L 2nd to Giants Causeway at Longchamp (Gr 1, rtd 112): half-brother to 1,000 Guineas wnr Sayyedati, dam plcd in the Oaks: eff at 1m, acts on firm & soft, any trk: runs well fresh: smart, likely to step up in class in the 2,000 Guineas next time.
4285} **FRENCH FELLOW 189** [3] T D Easterby 3-9-0 K Darley 6/5 FAV: 1211-2: 3 b c Suave Dancer - *¾* **114+**
Mademoiselle Chloe (Night Shift): Trkd ldrs till went on 2½f out, collared dist, kept on & not btn far: hvly bckd from 5/2, lkd in need of this reapp, 4L clr 3rd: most progressive in '99, won at Ayr (mdn auct), Redcar, York, Doncaster (h'caps) & Ascot (List, rtd 105): eff at 1m, 10f will suit: acts on firm & soft & on a stiff/gall trk: has progressed well from 2 to 3 & this was a smart eff conceding this wnr 3lbs, much fitter next time.
4419} **WHYOME 181** [6] M L W Bell 3-8-11 M Fenton 13/2: 3122-3: 3 b c Owington - Al Corniche (Bluebird): *4* **104**
Set pace till 2½f out, outpcd by front 2: just better for reapp: '99 wnr at Nottingham (nov) & Pontefract (stks), subs awdd 2nd in Italy (Gr 1, rtd 105 at best): eff at 1m, cld stay further: acts on fast & soft grnd, can run well fresh: handles a stiff/undul trk & likes to force the pace: fitter over further next time.
735 **KING O THE MANA 21** [1] R Hannon 3-8-11 J Carroll 8/1: 216-04: In tch till outpcd halfway, some *3½* **98**
late hdwy but no ch with ldrs: tchd 12/1: '98 wnr at Warwick (mdn auct) & Newcastle (nursery h'cap, rtd 99): half-brother to a 14f wnr: eff at 1m, 10f+ shld suit this term: acts on fast & soft: apprec further.
4468} **SIR NINJA 176** [4] 3-8-11 G Carter 10/1: 0210-5: Chsd ldrs till btn 2f out: ndd this reapp: '99 wnr at *9* **83**
Thirsk (mdn auct) & Ascot (stks, rtd 100), subs tried Gr company: eff at 7f, shld stay 1m: acts on firm & hvy grnd, handles any trk: strong colt who has thrived physically from 2 to 3.
736 **BEBE DE CHAM 21** [5] 3-8-6 R Cody Boutcher 100/1: 00-006: Al outpcd, t.o. in last: highly tried. *24* **48**
6 ran Time 1m 42.4 (7.0) (Mohamed Obaida) B W Hills Lambourn, Berks.

926 — 3.10 THOMAS LORD HCAP 3YO+ 0-90 (C) 5f Soft 98 +02 Fast [90]
£8011 £2465 £1232 £616 3yo rec 11lb Stalls 1-14 raced far side

824 **JUWWI 10** [17] J M Bradley 6-9-6 (82) Darren Williams (7) 11/1: 060151: 6 ch g Mujtahid - Nouvelle Star **94**
(Luskin Star): Held up stands side, swtchd centre dist, strong run to lead ins fnl 1f, sprinted clr: fair time, op 8/1, lkd superb: earlier won at Windsor (h'cap): '99 wnr at Carlisle, Chepstow & Southwell (h'caps, rtd 85a & 79): '98 wnr at W'hampton (sell) & Lingfield (h'cap, rtd 80a & 70): all wins at 5/6f, stays 7f: acts on firm & hvy & on both AWs: gd weight carrier who is best held up for a late run: well rdn & may make a qck reapp under a penalty.

THIRSK SATURDAY APRIL 15TH Lefthand, Flat, Oval Track

702 **NIGHT FLIGHT 23** [21] R A Fahey 6-10-0 (90) R Winston 10/1: 06-002: 6 gr g Night Shift - Ancestry (Persepolis): Front rank stands side, ev ch ent fnl 1f, outpcd by ready wnr: top weight: '99 York, Haydock & Ascot wnr (val h'cap, rtd 105): '98 Newcastle wnr (h'cap): '97 Pontefract wnr (h'cap, reapp, rtd 82, with J J O'Neill): eff at 5/6f on firm & soft, prob handles f/sand: gd weight carrier, can run well fresh: on a wng mark. 3½ 93

4267} **BRECONGILL LAD 192** [19] D Nicholls 8-8-12 (74) A Nicholls (3) 16/1: 2133-3: 8 b g Clantime - Chikala (Pitskelly): Prom stands side, led dist till ins last, not pace to repel wnr: just better for reapp: most progressive in '99, won at Catterick, Pontefract, Yarmouth & Goodwood (h'cap), also plcd sev times (rtd 75): dual rnr-up in '98 (h'caps, rtd 68, with M Hammond): '96 Beverley wnr (h'cap, rtd 69, with Miss S Hall): eff at 5/6f on firm & soft grnd: handles any trk, runs well fresh: eff with/without blnks: tough, spot-on next time. ¾ 75

609 **ZIGGYS DANCER 46** [8] E J Alston 9-9-2 (78) L Swift (7) 20/1: -04334: Front rank far side, led that group dist, kept on: lkd superb after 7 wk abs: first home on far side: well h'capped nowadays & loves Chester. ½ 78

844 **MISS FIT 7** [5] 4-8-13 (75) A Mackay 33/1: 003-05: Mid-div far side, fin fast but too late: '99 Chester wnr (h'cap, rtd 83): '98 Southwell (fill mdn, debut), Carlisle & Redcar wnr (novs, rtd 91): eff at 5/6f on firm, soft & f/sand: handles any trk, runs well fresh: back on a wng mark, hinted at a return to form & likes Chester. *nk* 74+

702 **IVORYS JOY 23** [24] 5-9-4 (80) C Catlin (7) 13/2: 010-56: Chsd ldrs stands side, onepcd final 1f: lkd well: rnr-up in this race off a 14lbs lower mark last term: tough, likes soft grnd: see 64 (AW). *hd* 79

4429} **CUSIN 179** [20] 4-8-12 (74) O Pears 20/1: 0100-7: Rear stands side, fin v well under hands-&-heels riding fnl 1f, nrst fin: reapp: trained by J Fanshawe to win at Salisbury in '99 (h'cap, rtd 79): dual rnr-up in '98 (nov, rtd 85, with Mrs J Cecil): eff at 6f, better over 1m: acts on firm grnd, handles soft: can run well fresh & a gd weight carrier: spot-on next time & one to keep a close eye on, esp over further: with D Nicholls. ½ 72+

728 **SUNLEY SENSE 21** [12] 4-9-10 (86) P Fessey 25/1: 600-08: Trkd ldrs far side, ev ch dist, no extra: failed to win in '99, 6th at Haydock (List h'cap, rtd 92): '98 wnr at Sandown & Newbury (h'caps, rtd 95): eff at 5f, shld stay 6f: acts on fast, likes soft & any trk: best up with the pace. ¾ 81

4391} **PIERPOINT 182** [2] 5-8-8 (70) T Hamilton (7) 20/1: 1000-9: Prom far side, onepcd final 1f: lkd well tho' just better for reapp, lngr prcd stablemate of 3rd: '99 wnr at Southwell (AW), Redcar & Pontefract (h'caps, rtd 67a & 73): plcd in '98 (rtd 73, with R Fahey): '97 Hamilton wnr (clmr & nursery, rtd 82): eff at 5/6f, prob stays 1m: acts on firm, gd/soft grnd & fibresand: all wins came when blnkd in '99, left off today, has tried a visor: gd weight carrier, handles any trk: best up with the pace: go closer when headgear re-applied. *nk* 64

758 **GORETSKI 18** [18] 7-8-12 (74) J Carroll 16/1: 020-00: Led 3f stands side, fdd into 10th: mkt drifter: '99 wnr at Hamilton, Pontefract & Beverley (h'caps, rtd 78): '98 wnr at Southwell (2, rtd 79a), Pontefract (stks) & Beverley (h'cap, rtd 76): '97 wnr at Southwell (2), Hamilton, Bath, Catterick & Beverley (h'caps, rtd 81): stays 6f, best at 5f on fast, gd/soft grnd & fibresand: likes Beverley: tough sprinter who is capable of better. *hd* 68

758 **BLESSINGINDISGUISE 18** [15] 7-9-0 (76)(bl) T Lucas 20/1: 010-50: Swerved leaving stalls, imprvd halfway stands side, bmpd dist, sn eased: fin 11th, not given a hard ride: capable of better, forget this. ¾ 67

4538} **MOUSEHOLE 170** [16] 8-8-13 (75) M Fenton 33/1: 6060-0: Nvr a factor on stands side, fin 12th. 1½ 62

780 **EURO VENTURE 17** [14] 5-8-12 (74) F Norton 25/1: 03-000: Front rank far side, ev ch dist, wknd qckly: fin 13th, stablemate of 3rd: see 645 (sand). *nk* 60

702 **HENRY HALL 23** [23] 4-10-0 (90) J Reid 5/1 FAV: 200-60: Trkd ldrs stands side, wknd over 1f out: jnt top weight, fin 14th, bckd from 8/1: better expected, v edgy in the paddock & this is prob best forgiven. *nk* 75

+758 **BEDEVILLED 18** [6] 5-8-13 (75) Lynsey Hanna (7) 10/1: 202510: Chsd ldrs far side, wknd over 1f out. *hd* 60

639 **Arjan 42** [22] 5-8-11 (73) R Cody Boutcher (7) 25/1:
2873} **Storyteller 267** [9] 6-9-10 (86) Dale Gibson 33/1:
716 **Zuhair 22** [13] 7-9-8 (84) Clare Roche(7) 25/1:
3678} **Venika Vitesse 229** [1] 4-8-9 (71) L Newton 20/1:
4620} **Saphire 161** [10] 4-9-6 (82) A Culhane 33/1:
4612} **Uncle Exact 162** [4] 3-8-8 (81) Iona Wands (5) 25/1:
758 **Waterford Spirit 18** [7] 4-8-12 (74) C Lowther 20/1:
3943} **Nifty Major 212** [3] 3-8-10 (83) G Carter 16/1:
3943} **Coco De Mer 212** [11] 3-9-2 (89) P Hanagan (7) 33/1:

24 ran Time 1m 01.8 (4.8) (J M Bradley) J M Bradley Sedbury, Gloucs.

927 **3.45 M FOSTER COND STKS 3YO+ (C) 6f str Soft 98 +02 Fast**
£6539 £2480 £1240 £563 Raced stands side

4620} **PIPALONG 161** [3] T D Easterby 4-9-2 K Darley 10/11 FAV: 0521-1: 4 b f Pips Pride - Limpopo (Green Desert): Trkd ldrs, swtchd dist, gd prog to lead on bit ins fnl 1f, pushed clr, easily: fair time, well bckd, just better for reapp: '99 wnr at Ripon (val h'cap) & Doncaster (List), also 5th in the Ayr Gold Cup (rtd 107): '98 wnr at Ripon (debut), York (nov fill) & Redcar (val 2yo Trophy, rtd 105): prob stays 7f, best at 5/6f on firm, likes gd & hvy: runs v well fresh: genuine & v useful: hds for the Gr 3 Duke of York Stks in fine heart. 112

3846} **HOT TIN ROOF 219** [1] T D Easterby 4-8-12 R Winston 7/1: 1230-2: 4 b f Thatching - No Reservations (Commanche Run) Prom, led over 1f out till ins last, easily outpcd by wnr: op 11/2, better for reapp: longer priced stablemate of wnr: '99 wnr at Newcastle (with J Banks, fill mdn), subs plcd in List company (rtd 103): eff at 6/7f on firm & soft, prob prefers the former: handles any trk: lightly raced, spot-on next time. 3½ 98

734 **EASTERN PURPLE 21** [2] K A Ryan 5-9-7 F Lynch 4/1: 000-03: 5 b h Petorius - Broadway Rosie (Absalom) Rcd keenly in lead, hdd over 1f out, no extra: 9L clr rem: not disgrcd conceding weight all-round: see 734. ¾ 105

3997} **ROSSELLI 209** [6] A Berry 4-9-0 (t) J Carroll 4/1: 0050-4: Prom, wknd over 1f out: swtg & ndd this reapp: rtd 105 in '99 when 5th at Leopardstown (Gr 3): smart juv, won at Newcastle, Beverley (stks) & R Ascot (Gr 3, rtd 110): stays 6f, v eff at 5f on fast, likes soft: runs well fresh, handles any trk: wears a t-strap. *9* 76

-- **BLUE ACE** [4] 7-9-0 A Culhane 150/1: 0-5: Prom till outpcd final 2f: recent jumps rnr, plcd at Taunton (mdn hdle, rtd 100h, eff at 2m on soft): reportedly won on the Flat in native NZ (1m/10f on soft & firm): highly tried over a trip well short of best: attractive gelding who should do much better when stepped up in trip. *4* 66

4170} **SPEEDY JAMES 198** [5] 4-9-0 O Pears 16/1: /360-6: In tch, wknd over 2f out: ndd this reapp: lightly rcd in '99, plcd at Newmarket (stks, with J Berry, rtd 103, reapp): '98 Newcastle (mdn) & Newmarket wnr (stks, rtd 103), also plcd in Gr company: eff at 5f on firm & gd/soft: has tried a visor: can run well fresh. *7* 50

6 ran Time 1m 15.3 (5.8) (T H Bennett) T D Easterby Great Habton, Nth Yorks.

928 **4.15 KNAYTON CLAIMER 2YO (E) 5f str Soft 98 -38 Slow**
£3266 £1005 £502 £251 Raced stands side

712 **UHOOMAGOO 22** [8] D Nicholls 2-9-1 O Pears 4/1: -21: 2 b c Namaqualand - Point Of Law (Law Society): Chsd ldrs till went on over 1f out, kept on strongly, rdn out: prev trained by R Fahey & cost current connections £6,000: half-brother to a 7f wnr: eff at 5f on gd & soft grnd, handles a gall trk: eff in sell/clmg grade. 76

821 **ORANGE TREE LAD 10** [14] A Berry 2-9-3 G Carter 9/2: -02: 2 b g Tragic Role - Adorable Cherub (Halo) Dwelt, prog after 2f, chall fnl 1f, just btn in a cl fin: better in claiming grade on soft: win similar. ¾ 75

801 **WATERPARK 15** [7] M Dods 2-8-4 Dale Gibson 33/1: -63: 2 b f Namaqualand - Willisa (Polar Falcon): Nvr far away, ev ch inside final 1f, no extra cl-home: eff at 5f on soft grnd: see 801 (AW, debut). 1¾ 58

849 **DIAMOND MAX 5** [3] P D Evans 2-8-13 W Supple 3/1 FAV: -04: Trkd ldrs, ev ch ent fnl 1f, no extra *hd* 67

cl-home: nicely bckd, 4L clr rem, qck reapp: better expected on this drop into clmg grade: eff at 5f on soft.
-- **CHORUS GIRL** [11] 2-8-8 T Lucas 25/1: -5: Outpcd, styd on final 1f, nrst fin: May foal, sire a decent sprinter: should apprec 6f given time: small filly who is sure to learn from this. *4* **52+**
821 **POPPYS CHOICE 10** [15] 2-8-8 J Fanning 25/1: -06: Slowly away, styg on steadily final 1½f under hands-&-heels riding: stablemate of 5th: cheaply bought Jan foal: half-sister to last season's juv Honesty Fair: dam a wng sprinter, sire high class over 1m: eye-catching effort today, sure to improve. *hd* **52+**
821 **WINDCHILL 10** [10] 2-8-2 D Mernagh (3) 16/1: -07: Outpcd till styd on final 1f, nvr nr ldrs: drifted from 8/1: Apr foal, sire a high class sprinter: already looks in need of 6f: see 821. *hd* **46**
-- **PETIT TOR** [1] 2-8-4 R Winston 33/1: -8: Outpcd, some late hdwy, nvr dngrs: lkd fit for debut: cheaply bought May foal: first foal from an unrcd mare: sire a useful juv: with J Norton. *nk* **47**
812 **JOHN FOLEY 12** [16] 2-8-13 A Daly 6/1: -09: Led till 2f out, fdd: tchd 9/1: benefit from faster grnd? *¾* **54**
801 **PREMIER LASS 15** [9] 2-7-13 Joanna Badger (7) 33/1: -00: Gd speed to 3f, fdd into 10th: see 801. *hd* **40**
-- **CITRUS** [12] 2-8-4 Dean McKeown 12/1: -0: Chsd ldrs till wknd 2 out: op 8/1, fin 11th, debut: 10,000gns Jan foal: half-sister to a 6f 2yo wnr in Ireland: sire smart over 1m/10f in Ireland: with P Haslam. *shd* **45**
-- **LUVLY TIMES** [6] 2-8-13 G Parkin 25/1: -0: Dwelt, al outpcd on debut: 12th, stablemate of 5th & 6th. *3* **46**
796 **DANCING PENNEY 16** [4] 2-8-6 F Lynch 8/1: -50: Speedy 3f, fdd into 13th, eased: see 796. *1* **36**
856 **Lastofthewhalleys 5** [13] 2-8-6 J Carroll 33/1: -- **Beacon Of Light** [5] 2-8-9 P Goode (3) 20/1:
15 ran Time 1m 03.8 (6.8) (The David Nicholls Racing Club) D Nicholls Sessay, Nth Yorks.

929 **4.45 BYLAND RTD MDN DIV 1 3YO+ 0-65 (F) 7f rnd Soft 98 -29 Slow**
£2567 £790 £395 £197 3yo rec 14lb

4570} **STARLIGHT 166** [6] E A L Dunlop 3-8-7 G Carter 13/8 FAV: 0545-1: 3 br f King's Signet - Petinata (Petong): Trkd ldrs, hdwy to chall over 1f out, led cl-home, drvn out, flashed tail: well bckd, reapp: 4th in a nursery in '99 (rtd 68): eff at 7f on soft grnd, handles a gall trk: runs well fresh. **65**
780 **TECHNICIAN 17** [4] E J Alston 5-9-10 (bl) L Swift (7) 6/1: 0-0052: 5 ch g Archway - How It Works (Commanche Run): Tried to make all, clr 2f out, worn down cl-home: 5L clr 3rd: mdn after 44 starts. *¾* **66$**
4159} **ONE DOMINO 199** [1] M Dods 3-8-10 A Culhane 12/1: 3406-3: 3 ch g Efisio - Dom One (Dominion): Chsd ldrs, rdn & onepcd final 1½f: tchd 16/1, lkd fit for reapp: trained by J Berry in '99, plcd at Ayr (mdn, rtd 72): eff at 7f on soft grnd, probably needs 1m+ now: stocky gelding. *5* **56**
3930} **COMEX FLYER 213** [3] D Nicholls 3-8-10 A Nicholls (3) 10/1: 0646-4: Rear, prog halfway, swtchd outside & onepace final 1f: just better for reapp: 4th in a Newcastle mdn in '99 (rtd 74, with J Berry). *1¾* **53**
4583} **CLEAR MOON 165** [7] 3-8-10 N Kennedy 10/1: 0063-5: Imprvd from rear to chase ldrs 2f out, sn no impress: mkt drifter, ndd this reapp: plcd on fnl '99 start (nursery h'cap, rtd 59): eff at 6f on gd/soft & soft. *5* **45**
1510} **GOOD EVANS ABOVE 327** [2] 3-8-7 Joanna Badger(7) 11/1: 4040-6: Dwelt, imprvd to chase ldrs halfway, sn btn on reapp: bckd at long odds. *3* **37**
729 **SUNLEYS PICC 21** [9] 3-8-7 W Supple 5/1: 6-067: Mid-div, wide into str, sn btn: see 729. *11* **19**
4508} **RED SONNY 172** [5] 3-8-10 J Carroll 15/2: 5000-8: Chsd ldr till wknd 3f out, t.o: not stay 7f. *13* **0**
3268} **NOVELTY 248** [8] 5-9-7 V Halliday 66/1: 0/00-9: Al outpcd, t.o. in last: no form. *16* **0**
9 ran Time 1m 31.8 (8.9) (Mrs Mollie Cooper Webster) E A L Dunlop Newmarket.

930 **5.20 BYLAND RTD MDN DIV 2 3YO+ 0-65 (F) 7f rnd Soft 98 -36 Slow**
£2567 £790 £395 £197 3yo rec 14lb

4251} **ALPATHAR 193** [1] M Dods 3-8-7 T Williams 4/1: 4025-1: 3 ch f Simply Great - Royal Language (Conquistador Cielo): Trkd ldrs, short of room 2f out, qckndto lead dist, kept on, drvn out: lkd fit & well for reapp, rider reportedly given a 2-day careless riding ban: rnr-up in '99 (Newcastle mdn auct, rtd 70): eff at 7f on soft, 1m shld suit: runs well fresh, handles a gall trk: bit reportedly slipped thro' fillies mouth here. **55**
830 **CUIGIU 9** [7] D Carroll 3-8-10 F Lynch 14/1: 0-0542: 3 b c Persian Bold - Homosassa (Burslem): Set pace till collared dist, kept on but not pace of wnr: front rnr, eff at 7f on soft grnd: see 830, 741. *1* **55**
781 **MAGIC SISTER 17** [5] M L W Bell 3-8-7 M Fenton 10/3: 66-03: 3 ch f Cadeaux Genereux - Gunner's Belle (Gunner B) Keen rear, styd on under press fnl 1½f: 5L clr rem: eff at 7f on soft, 1m+ & h'caps suit. *nk* **51**
781 **HOUT BAY 17** [3] S E Kettlewell 3-8-10 O Pears 6/1: 440-64: Rcd keenly rear, no impress final 2f. *5* **46**
872 **GET A LIFE 4** [4] 7-9-7 R Lappin 50/1: 000-05: Slowly away, imprvg when hmpd halfway, no ch after: qck reapp: modest prev form in '99 over 7/10f, incl in blnks: rnr-up in '98 (appr h'cap, rtd 29): eff at 1m, stays 12f, acts on gd & gd/soft grnd: offic rtd just 25, treat this rating with caution. *nk* **42$**
3580} **CLEAR CRYSTAL 233** [2] 3-8-7 J Reid 11/4 FAV: 560-6: Prom, chsd ldr till wknd 2f out: lkd well on reapp, padd pick, eased once ch had gone: some promise in mdns in '99 (rtd 75 at best): half-sister to a 5f juv wnr: athletic filly who appeared not to stay 7f here or handle this soft grnd: with R Cowell & capable of better. *½* **41**
4514} **KUUIPO 172** [9] 3-8-7 J Carroll 6/1: 0600-7: Slowly away, nvr a factor: op 10/1 on reapp: plcd at York in '99 (nursery h'cap, rtd 65): eff at 5f on fast grnd, wears a t-strap. *4* **34**
848 **ROYAL CANARY 7** [8] 3-8-10 C Lowther 50/1: 205-08: Chsd ldr 4f, fdd: see 848. *13* **15**
3174} **MOTHER CORRIGAN 253** [6] 4-9-7 D Mernagh (3) 12/1: 0046-9: Chsd ldrs 5f, wknd into last: needed this reapp: trained by L Cumani in '99, 4th at Warwick (mdn, rtd 69): eff at 7f on fast grnd, has tried blnks tho' not today: now with M Brittain & worth another ch on faster grnd. *2½* **8**
9 ran Time 1m 32.3 (9.4) (Harry Whitton) M Dods Piercebridge, Co Durham.

931 **5.50 LEVY BOARD FILLIES HCAP 3YO+ 0-80 (D) 1m rnd Soft 98 -08 Slow** **[79]**
£4517 £1390 £695 £347 3yo rec 15lb

811 **ITSANOTHERGIRL 14** [5] M W Easterby 4-9-0 (65) T Lucas 16/1: 35-001: 4 b f Reprimand - Tasmim (Be My Guest): Held up, imprvd 2f out, styd on well to lead cl-home, drvn out: padd pick: some promise over hdles this winter (rtd 93h, eff at 2m on gd grnd, tried blnks): plcd in '99 (h'caps, rtd 71): '98 Catterick wnr (nursery, rtd 74): eff at 1m, stays 10f: acts on firm & hvy, handles a sharp or stiff/gall trk: on a fair mark. **70**
4451} **FALLS OMONESS 178** [7] E J Alston 6-7-10 (47)(2oh) J Bramhill 11/1: 3050-2: 6 b m River Falls - Sevens Are Wild (Petorius): Held up, gd hdwy to lead 2f out & sn qcknd clr, collared cl-home: op 14/1, reapp: '99 wnr here at Thirsk (sell h'cap, rtd 53): '98 wnr again at Thirsk & Hamilton (h'caps, rtd 57): '97 Ayr wnr (clmr, rtd 62, with K Burke): eff at 1m/9f, stays 10f on firm & hvy, handles any trk, loves Thirsk: eff with/without blnks: enjoys sells & needs to be held up for as late a run as poss, hit the front too soon today. *½* **50**
811 **FEATHERTIME 14** [4] Mrs G S Rees 4-8-3 (54) A Mackay 8/1: 514-53: 4 b f Puissance - Midnight Owl (Ardross): Mid-div, kept on under press final 1f, no ch with front 2: 5L clr rem: see 811 (reapp). *3½* **51**
811 **MY TESS 14** [15] B A McMahon 4-8-12 (63) Dean McKeown 13/2: 221324: Led till 2f out, no extra. *5* **51**
794 **EVERGREEN 16** [8] 3-8-10 (76) L Newman(5) 12/1: 030-35: In tch, onepcd fnl 2f: bred to apprec 10f+. *¾* **62**

THIRSK   SATURDAY APRIL 15TH   Lefthand, Flat, Oval Track

854   **RED CAFE 5** [11] 4-8-1 (52) Joanna Badger(7) 12/1: 003/36: Chsd ldrs, rdn & no impress final 2f.   ¾ 36
*831   **SCENE 9** [9] 5-10-0 (79) G Hall 8/1: 41-017: Rear, imprvd 2f out, nvr nr to chall: lkd well, top-weight.   1 61
*859   **RIVER ENSIGN 5** [13] 7-8-1 (52)(6ex) Claire Bryan(5) 12/1: 416018: Chsd ldrs till fdd final 2f: 2½ 30
      lkd well: qck reapp & pen for 859 (10f).
4598}   **CELTIC FLING 163** [14] 4-9-12 (77) P Doe 5/2 FAV: 21-9: Prom till wknd final 2f: lkd fit for reapp & hvly   3 50
      bckd: twice rcd in '99, won at Windsor (mdn by 5L, rtd 82+): half-sister to high class mid-dist performer Celtic
      Swing: eff at 1m on gd/soft grnd, can run well fresh: rcd too freely today.
2881}   **ZAGALETA 267** [1] 3-8-10 (76) C Lowther 11/1: 322-0: Chsd ldrs, wkng when hmpd 3f out: fin 10th,   1¼ 47
      reapp: plcd on all 3 juv starts (mdns, rtd 81): half-sister to a useful 7f/1m wng juv: eff at 6f on gd & firm,
      7f+ shld suit: scopey filly who was swtg & boiled over in the preliminaries: worth another ch on faster grnd.
3575}   **SUNSET LADY 233** [3] 4-8-9 (60) P Goode (3) 25/1: 2504-0: Al bhd, fin 11th: jumps left, new stable.   1¼ 29
757   **SALIGO 18** [12] 5-9-7 (72) Kim Tinkler 33/1: 000-00: Al towards rear, fin 12th.   ¾ 40
831   **NATALIE JAY 9** [10] 4-8-13 (64) J Reid 8/1: 525-30: Chsd ldrs till wknd final 2f, fin 14th: btr 831.   0
709   **Papagena 23** [6] 3-7-10 (62)(bl)(6oh) M Palmer(7) 33/1: 604   **Tayovullin 47** [16] 6-7-10 (47) Iona Wands(5) 33/1:
2698}   **Lady Lazarus 275** [2] 4-7-12 (49)(2ow)(6oh) Dale Gibson 33/1:
16 ran   Time 1m 43.9 (8.5)   (Miss V Foster)   M W Easterby Sheriff Hutton, Nth Yorks.

WINDSOR   MONDAY ARPIL 17TH   Sharp, Fig 8 Track

Official Going   HEAVY. Stalls: Inside.

932   2.10 ROYAL BONUS QUALIFIER MDN 2YO (D)   5f str   Heavy   Inapplicable
£3477   £1070   £535   £267

--   **SECRET INDEX** [12] Mrs P N Dutfield 2-8-9 L Newman (5) 25/1: 1: 2 b f Nicolotte - Deerussa (Jareer)   86
      Sn bhd, sustained run fnl 2f to get up well ins last, going away: cheaply bght Mar foal: dam unrcd: eff at
      5f, further looks sure to suit: runs well fresh & handled this hvy grnd well: fine debut.
724   **IMPERIAL DANCER 23** [3] M R Channon 2-9-0 T Quinn 7/2: 42: 2 b c Primo Dominie - Gorgeous Dancer   ¾ 89
      (Nordico) Cl-up, led 2f out, sn clr till rdn & collared well ins last, not btn far & clr of rem: op 2/1: improved
      for debut: handles hvy & further will suit: shld win a race: see 724
--   **ROMANTIC POET** [11] B R Millman 2-9-0 P Robinson 9/2: 3: 2 b g Cyrano de Bererac - Lady Quinta   5 80
      (Gallic League) Chsd ldrs, rdn & no impress over 1f out, hands-and-heels: Feb foal: dam 5f juv scorer:
      speedily bred & sharper for this encouraging debut.
--   **TIMES SQUARE** [10] G C H Chung 2-9-0 R Cochrane 16/1: 4: Led to halfway, drifted left & onepace   ½ 79
      over 1f out under pressure, hands-and-heels riding: Mar foal, cost 3,300gns: dam 7f scorer: bred to apprec 6/7f.
--   **FIENNES** [1] 2-9-0 M Fenton 11/4 FAV: 5: With ldrs till wknd appr fnl 1f: nicely bckd on   3½ 73
      debut: Feb first foal, cost IR £49,000: dam US scorer: Dayjur colt, bred for speed.
--   **FOREST MOON** [5] 2-8-9 Dane O'Neill 20/1: 6: Prom, led over 2f out, sn hdd & wknd: op 12/1:   3 63
      May foal, cost 10,000gns: half-sister to a French scorer: bred to apprec 6f+ in time: with P Evans.
--   **LONDON EYE** [6] 2-8-9 J Reid 25/1: 7: Slow away, nvr a factor: Apr first foal, cost only   6 51
      800gns: modest dam: bred for speed.
--   **SPIRIT OF TEXAS** [2] 2-9-0 K Fallon 8/1: 8: Sn bhd, no dngr: op 5/1: Apr foal, cost IR £18,000:   hd 56
      half-brother to sev wnrs: dam styd 7f: bred to apprec 6/7f in time: with K McAuliffe.
--   **CEDAR JENEVA** [4] 2-8-9 P Doe 25/1: 9: In tch till wknd well over 2f out: debut.   11 29
--   **WATTNO ELJOHN** [8] 2-9-0 R Hughes 16/1: 0: Handy, wknd halfway, 10th, debut.   6 22
--   **DANCE WITH ME** [9] 2-9-0 Pat Eddery 8/1: 0: Al bhd: 11th, op 5/1, debut.   11 0
--   **KINGS CREST** [7] 2-9-0 G Faulkner (3) 14/1: 0: Slow away & al bhd: fin last on debut.   14 0
12 ran   Time 1m 04.2 (5.4)   (Index Storage Systems Ltd)   Mrs P N Dutfield Axmouth, Devon.

933   2.40 FORT WILLIAM HCAP 3YO 0-85 (D)   1m67y rnd   Heavy   Inapplicable   [90]
£4355   £1340   £670   £335

509   **SOLLER BAY 65** [10] K R Burke 3-8-10 (72) N Callan 12/1: 2-131: 3 b g Contract Law - Bichette   80
      (Lidhame) Prom, kept on to lead dist, drvn out, gamely: 2 month abs, earlier won at W'hampton (mdn, rtd 66a) & 76
      when rnr-up sole '99 turf start: eff at 8.3/9.3f on fibresand, hvy & a sharp trk: runs well fresh: game & improving.
4600}   **PIPSSALIO 165** [7] Jamie Poulton 3-7-12 (60) M Henry 12/1: 000-2: 3 b c Pips Pride - Tesalia   ½ 67
      (Finissimo) Dwelt, sn well bhd, styd on strongly well over 1f out, nrst fin, would have won in two more strides:
      modest on 3 juv sprint starts: enjoyed this step up to 8.3f, further will suit: acts well on hvy: win a race.
4616}   **OMNIHEAT 163** [5] M J Ryan 3-8-10 (72) P McCabe 8/1: 0461-3: 3 b f Ezzoud - Lady Bequick (Sharpen   1¼ 77
      Up) Waited with, hdwy on bit to lead 2f out till dist, no extra: reapp: won last of 7 juv starts, at Doncaster
      (nurs h'cap, rtd 71): half-sister to wnrs up to 10f: stays 8.3f, further shld suit: handles firm, has won on
      hvy & handles any trk: improving, fitter next time.
717   **STAFFORD KING 24** [15] J G M O'Shea 3-7-11 (59)(7oh) R Brisland (4) 33/1: 00-04: Dwelt, sn   3 60
      bhd, late gains: stays 8.4f on hvy: promise here.
810   **MENTIGA 16** [16] 3-9-7 (83) G Carter 3/1 FAV: 213-05: Led after 1f till 2f out, no extra: nicely bckd.   ½ 83
3706}   **GOOD FRIDAY 229** [13] 3-8-7 (69) L Newman (5) 16/1: 6530-6: Sn bhd, modest late gains: plcd once   5 61
      as a juv (auct mdn, rtd 68): eff at 7f (dam winning stayer/hdler) & shld stay further: acts on gd grnd.
3968}   **TADREEJ 212** [4] 3-9-1 (77) L Dettori 9/1: 032-7: In tch, wknd 2f out: op 6/1 on reapp: plcd   2½ 65
      on 2 of 3 juv starts (rtd 79 & 68a): stays 8.5f & handles firm & fibresand.
3856}   **FLYING RUN 220** [11] 3-8-0 (62) Martin Dwyer 20/1: 4500-8: In tch, wknd over 3f out: unplcd juv   8 38
      (rtd 68): dam 10f wnr & bred to stay 1m.
4185}   **ATYLAN BOY 199** [9] 3-8-10 (72) Pat Eddery 12/1: 0650-9: Led 1f, chsd ldr till wknd over 2f out: 2 45
      unplcd on 4 juv starts (rtd 78 at best, 7.5f, gd & soft grnd).
4462}   **EASTERN SPICE 179** [3] 3-9-1 (77) J Reid 12/1: 2035-0: In tch, wknd over 3f out: 10th, reapp.   3½ 45
3281}   **GRACE AND POWER 250** [2] 3-9-7 (83) T Quinn 13/2: 242-0: In tch till wknd well over 2f out: 11th.   hd 51
4461}   **Hard Days Night 179** [8] 3-7-11 (59)(1ow)(7oh) Dale Gibson 33/1:
613   **Kings Ginger 48** [14] 3-8-5 (67) Joanna Badger (7) 33/1:
4048}   **Cedar Prince 208** [6] 3-9-5 (81) M Fenton 16/1:
242   **Mr George Smith 106** [1] 3-7-13 (61)(3ow)(4oh) C Rutter 12/1:
15 ran   Time 1m 50.6 (8.3)   (Mrs Melba Bryce)   K R Burke Newmarket.

WINDSOR

MONDAY ARPIL 17TH   Sharp, Fig 8 Track

---

934 **3.10 INVERARY FILLIES MDN 3YO (D)   1m67y rnd   Heavy   Inapplicable**
£4459   £1372   £686   £343

704   **CLARANET 25** [9] K Mahdi 3-8-11 L Dettori 9/4: 34-331: 3 ch f Arazi - Carmita (Caerleon)   75
Led after 1f till 5f out, sn led again & rdn out to assert ins last: well bckd, deserved win after sev plcd efforts:
rtd 79 & 99: eff at 1m/9.4f on fibresand, enjoyed this hvy: handles a gall or easy trk: going the right way.
4536} **ORIGINAL SPIN 172** [14] J L Dunlop 3-8-11 T Quinn 11/10 FAV: 42-2: 3 b f Machiavellian - Not Before   2   72
Time (Polish Precedent) Cl-up, hdwy to chall 2f out, not pace of wnr ins last under hands-and-heels riding: bckd
tho' op 4/6, reapp: rtd 83 when rnr-up on 2nd of only 2 '99 starts: stays 8.4f, further suit, on gd/soft & hvy.
3173} **LULLABY 255** [3] J R Fanshawe 3-8-11 R Cochrane 14/1: -0-3: 3 b f Unfuwain - Heart's Harmony   ½   71
(Blushing Groom) Waited with, eff over 2f out, kept on same pace under hand-and-heels: reapp: well btn sole juv
start: half-sister to a 10f scorer: eff at 8.4f, 10f looks sure to suit: handles hvy grnd: open to improvement.
794   **PASADENA 18** [2] H Morrison 3-8-11 R Hughes 25/1: 04: Dwelt, bhd, eff over 2f out, sn drifted left   1¾   68
& no impress: handles hvy & stays 8.4f: see 794.
--   **MOST STYLISH** [10] 3-8-11 S Sanders 33/1: 5: In tch, eff over 3f out, onepace: Most Welcome filly.   2½   64
--   **ARIALA** [12] 3-8-11 N Callan 20/1: 6: Dwelt, sn in tch, btn 3f out: half-sister to a 12f scorer: nk   63
dam won at up to 10f: Arazi filly, sure to apprec further for K Burke.
4614} **FANFARE 163** [13] K Fallon 13/2: 50-7: Sn in tch, rdn & wknd over 2f out: rtd 70 on first   4   57
of 2 unplcd juv starts: half-sister to a 7f/1m wnr: with G Butler.
523   **MEDOOZA 61** [6] 3-8-11 M Hills 50/1: 08: Al bhd: 2 month abs: see 523.   9   41
806   **ISLA 17** [16] 3-8-11 V Slattery 50/1: 0-09: Led after 3f till 4f out, no extra: modest form.   1½   39
841   **FRENCH FANCY 10** [4] 3-8-11 (bl) Martin Dwyer 33/1: 304240: Handy till wknd over 3f out: see 773.   3   35
794   Save The Planet 18 [1] 3-8-11 S Ritchie (7) 25/1:   794 Presidents Lady 18 [5] 3-8-11 S Drowne 33/1:
658   Swiftur 37 [15] 3-8-11 D Sweeney 20/1:   -- Napper Blossom [8] 3-8-11 L Newman (5) 33/1:
14 ran   Time 1m 54.2 (11.9)   (Greenfield Stud)   K Mahdi Newmarket.

---

935 **3.40 MALLAIG CLASSIFIED STKS 3YO+ 0-90 (C)   6f str   Heavy Inapplicable**
£6500   £2000   £1000   £500   3yo rec 11lb   Field slit in 2 Groups

728   **ALWAYS ALIGHT 23** [7] K R Burke 6-9-0 K Fallon 6/1 FAV: 363-01: 6 ch g Never So bold - Fire Sprite   92
(Mummy's Game) Held up far side, imprvd 2f out, strong run to lead ins fnl 1f, drvn out: failed to win in '99, plcd
at Doncaster (reapp, List, rtd 98): '98 wnr at Ayr (2, class stks, & notably Ayr Gold Cup h'cap) & Doncaster
(h'cap, rtd 98): '97 Newbury & Goodwood wnr (h'caps, rtd 81): stays 7f, all win at 6f: handles fast, enjoys soft
& hvy grnd: handles any trk: has tried blnks & a visor, better without: can run well fresh, useful gelding.
733   **HORNBEAM 23** [2] J R Jenkins 6-9-0 W R Swinburn 10/1: 505-02: 6 b h Rich Charlie - Thinkluckybelucky   hd   91
(Maystreak) Held up far side, prog dist, ev ch ins last, just btn in a cl fin: failed to win in '99, 4th at York
(val h'cap, rtd 95): best eff on reapp in '98, won at Doncaster (List, rtd 107): '97 wnr at Newbury (mdn): eff
at 6f/1m: handles firm, likes gd/soft & hvy: runs well fresh: well h'capped but hard to win with.
725   **BRAVE EDGE 23** [14] R Hannon 9-9-0 Pat Eddery 8/1: 440-03: 9 b g Beveled - Daring Ditty (Daring   1¾   88
March) Chsd ldrs stands side, carr left fnl 2f, kept on: best of group of 4 who rcd on stands side: on fair mark.
*76   **CARLTON 149** [12] D R C Elsworth 6-9-3 N Pollard 16/1: 1121-4: Prom, went on stands side over   nk   90$
1f out, edged left & kept on: abs: fine run at today's weights, offic rtd 73: progressive on sand earlier.
716   **BARRINGER 24** [5] 3-8-3 S Drowne 13/2: 000-45: Prom far side, led over 2f out till ins last, held   ¾   85
when no room cl-home: op 4/1: likes soft & hvy: see 716.
734   **BOOMERANG BLADE 23** [13] 4-8-11 J Stack 12/1: 200-06: Prom stands side, onepcd fnl 1f: rnr-up at   shd   82
Hamilton in '99 (stks, rtd 94): '98 Folkestone (mdn, nurs rec) & Doncaster wnr (val St Leger stks, rtd 103): eff at
6/7f, has tried 1m/10f: acts on firm & gd/soft, runs well fresh: handles any trk: fairly h'capped now.
64   **DANIELLES LAD 152** [1] 4-9-0 D Sweeney 14/1: 2500-7: Overall ldr far side till 2f out, grad fdd: long   1¼   83
abs: rnr-up twice in '99 (h'caps, rtd 91): '98 Goodwood wnr (nurs h'cap, rtd 88): eff
at 5/6f on fast & hvy grnd: handles any trk: sharper next time.
*728   **PASSION FOR LIFE 23** [9] 7-9-5 P Doe 7/1: 061-18: Led stands side group till dist, no extra: ¾   86
824   **RETURN OF AMIN 12** [3] 6-9-0 Martin Dwyer 10/1: 00-009: Held up far side, improving when short   3   75
of room 2f out, sn btn: likes soft, worth another look when stable returns to form: see 728.
4219} **HILL MAGIC 198** [8] 5-9-0 M Fenton 16/1: 0005-0: Chsd ldrs far side, fdd over 1f out: fin 10th, reapp: 4   67
trained by D Elsworth to win at Kempton in '99 (stks, reapp, rtd 107): '98 Lingfield wnr (h'cap, rtd 95): '97
Bath mdn wnr: suited by 6f, has tried 1m: acts on firm & gd/soft, runs v well fresh: useful, now with L Cottrell.
829   **PAX 11** [11] 3-8-6 R Cochrane 7/1: 1-40: Dwelt, recovered to chase ldrs far side, btn 2f out: 11th.   3   64
808   **TOUCH OF FAIRY 16** [6] 4-9-0 L Dettori 10/1: 2-040: Chsd ldrs 4f far side, wknd into 12th: see 808.   1¾   59
3805} **MIDHISH TWO 223** [4] 4-9-0 R Mullen 20/1: 0606-0: In tch 4f far side: fin 13th, reapp.   1½   57
--   **CHOTO MATE** [15] 4-9-0 R Hughes 10/1: 0046/W: Broke out of stalls & withdrawn bef start: comeback.   0
14 ran   Time 1m 17.7 (7.4)   (R W & Mrs J A Allen)   K R Burke Newmarket.

---

936 **4.10 GLENCOE MDN 3YO (D)   1m2f   Heavy Inapplicable**
£4043   £1244   £622   £311

4141} **MASTER GEORGE 201** [7] I A Balding 3-9-0 Martin Dwyer 15/8 FAV: 2-1: 3 b g Mtoto - Topwinder (Topsider)   80
Rear, prog halfway, kept on under press to lead ins fnl 1f, drvn out: bckd from 5/2, reapp: rnr-up on sole '99
start (mdn, rtd 81): 25,000gns half-brother to a 7f 2yo wnr: sire a top-class mid-dist performer: apprec this step
up to 10f, shld stay 12f: acts on soft & hvy, runs well fresh: handles a sharp or gall trk: shld win again.
771   **DESTINATION 19** [10] C A Cyzer 3-9-0 G Carter 33/1: 0-52: 3 ch g Deploy - Veuve (Tirol)   ½   79
Rcd keenly in tch, outpcd ent str, rallied well fnl 2f & just btn in a close fin: now qual for h'caps & a step up
to 12f is sure to suit: handles hvy grnd: shown enough to win a race: see 771 (AW).
3998} **STORM WIZARD 211** [8] M R Channon 3-9-0 S Drowne 20/1: 0-3: 3 b g Catrail - Society Ball (Law   1½   77
Society) Prom, ev ch ent str, onepcd ins last: reapp: unplcd in a Newbury mdn on sole juv start: eff over
an easy 10f on hvy grnd, 12f will suit: runs well fresh: sharper next time.
--   **STALLONE** [3] J Noseda 3-9-0 M Hills 6/1: -4: Rear, imprvd to lead 2f out, hdd ins last, no extra: 2   74
op 4/1, debut: eff at 10f on hvy grnd, handles a sharp trk: Brief Truce gelding, sure to learn from this.
3998} **JEUNE PREMIER 211** [9] 3-9-0 Pat Eddery 10/1: 0-5: Dsptd lead till 4f out, wkng when short of room   3   70
ins fnl 1f: clr rem, reapp: unplcd in a Newbury mdn on sole juv start: with B Meehan.
1490} **CEDAR LORD 331** [11] 3-9-0 R Miles (7) 33/1: 0-6: Nvr nr to chall on reapp: last of 12 at Lingfield   8   60
(nov auct) on sole '99 start: cheaply bght half-brother to a mid-dist wnr: with R O'Sullivan.

304

WINDSOR   MONDAY ARPIL 17TH   Sharp, Fig 8 Track

-- **BORDERLINE** [2] 3-9-0 T Quinn 9/2: -7: Mid-div, imprvd to chase ldrs 4f out, btn 2f out on debut: drifter from 6/4: first foal, dam styd 12f: with H Cecil, stable reportedly suffering from some coughing.	shd	60
4605} **JUDICIOUS** 164 [5] 3-9-0 M Roberts 14/1: 00-8: Front rank, led 4f out till 2f out, eased consid when btn: well btn on a couple of juv starts (rtd 74): 180,000gns purchase: with G Wragg & now qual for h'caps.	nk	59
-- **ORLANDO SUNRISE** [4] 3-8-9 Dane O'Neill 9/1: -9: Mid-div till btn 2f out: tchd 20/1 on debut.	5	47
832 **DURLSTON BAY** 11 [6] 3-9-0 J P Spencer 10/1: 0-30: Dsptd lead 6f, wknd into 10th: see 832.	2½	49
833 **STRATEGIC DANCER** 11 [1] 3-9-0 D Griffiths 9/1: -600: Well bhd from halfway, t.o. in last.	23	24

11 ran   Time 2m 22.3 (17.6)   (David R Watson)   I A Balding Kingsclere, Hants.

937   4.40 TOBERMORY HCAP 3YO 0-70 (E)   1m3f135y   Heavy   Inapplicable   [77]
£3066   £876   £438

4338} **SAMSAAM** 188 [5] J L Dunlop 3-9-3 (66) R Hills 5/1: -000-1: 3 b c Sadler's Wells - Azyaa (Kris) Mid-div, prog 2f out, kept on well to lead cl-home, rdn out: op 7/2, reapp: promise in 7f/1m mdns in '99 (rtd 74 at best): related to 7/10f wnr Yarob: sire a top-class mid-dist performer: apprec this step up to 12f, will get further: acts on hvy grnd, runs well fresh: type to improve further as he steps up in trip.		74
315 **BOX CAR** 96 [11] G L Moore 3-8-13 (62) I Mongan (5) 12/1: 62-532: 3 b c Blues Traveller - Racey Naskra (Star de Naskra) Prom, went on 2f out & sn clr, overhauled cl-home: 3 month abs: stays an easy 11.6f, acts on hvy grnd & equitrack: runs well fresh: deserves similar, see 204 (AW mdn).	1¼	67
846 **DISTINCTLY WELL** 9 [14] P D Evans 3-9-7 (70) Dane O'Neill 8/1: W00-23: 3 b g Distinctly North - Brandywell (Skyliner) Rear, hdwy 2f out, not qckn ins last: top-weight: stays 11.6f on fm, hvy & fibresand.	2	72
4141} **FLIQUET BAY** 201 [9] Mrs A J Perrett 3-8-11 (60) M Roberts 16/1: 600-4: Led 1m, eased considerably when short of room ins 1f: reapp: rtd 73 in a Salisbury mdn auct on debut in '99: half-brother to a 10f wnr: ran well for a long way in these testing conditions: not given a hard time & shld win similar.	3	58
835 **ESTABLISHED** 10 [18] 3-9-7 (45) R Brisland (5) 4/1: 000-05: Mid-div, eff 2f out, not pace to chall.	3	39
744 **STRICTLY SPEAKING** 21 [8] 3-9-1 (64)(BL) J Fortune 14/1: 345-06: Prom, ev ch 2f out, sn no extra: tried in blnks: plcd at Kempton in '99 (mdn, rtd 79): half-brother to numerous wnr, incl smart miler Hawksley Hill: eff at 1m on hvy grnd, poss not stay 11.6f in these testing conditions: with P Cole.	½	57
4038} **BARROW** 209 [16] 3-9-7 (70) Pat Eddery 7/1: 034-7: Rdn in rear, late hdwy, nvr nr to chall: op 7/1, stablemate of wnr: thrice rcd in '99, plcd at Nottingham (mdn, rtd 74): eff at 1m, bred to apprec mid-dists: handles fast grnd: fitter next time & sure to benefit from faster grnd.	6	55
*782 **MERRYVALE MAN** 19 [3] 3-9-5 (68) T Quinn 10/1: 531218: Prom, led 3f out till 2f out, fdd: tchd 14/1.	4	48
4132} **THE FROG QUEEN** 202 [7] 3-9-1 (64) J Reid 16/1: 3001-9: Chsd ldrs 9f, fdd on reapp: '99 Southwell wnr (sell, rtd 69a): eff at 7f on fast & f/sand, handles a sharp trk: a return to 7f/1m & sell company shld suit.	nk	43
799 **VANISHING DANCER** 18 [15] 3-8-11 (60)(VIS) N Callan 8/1: 00-3W0: Prom 1m, fdd: 10th, 1st time visor.	2½	36
*841 **NORTHERN TIMES** 10 [20] 3-8-12 (61) J P Spencer 16/1: -51010: Nvr nr to chall, fin 11th: btr 841.	4	32
*799 **KUWAIT TROOPER** 18 [10] 3-9-2 (65) L Dettori 7/2 FAV: 60-410: Chsd ldrs 1m, fdd 2f out: fin 12th.	8	26
748 **TITUS BRAMBLE** 21 [2] 3-8-7 (56) K Fallon 10/1: 600-00: Mid-div till btn 3f out: fin 17th, op 7/1.		0

4114} **Cedar Chief** 203 [12] 3-7-10 (45)(5oh) R Miles(7) 33/1: 629   **Blayney Dancer** 44 [13] 3-7-10 (45)(5oh) M Henry 25/1:
858 **Albergo** 7 [6] 3-8-1 (50) Dale Gibson 33/1:   709 **Pinchaninch** 25 [1] 3-8-13 (62)(bl) R Studholme (5) 25/1:
839 **Maiysha** 10 [17] 3-8-6 (55) S Sanders 33/1:   827 **Border Run** 12 [4] 3-9-2 (65)(BL) D R McCabe 14/1:

19 ran   Time 2m 46.2 (20.4)   (Hamdan Al Maktoum)   J L Dunlop Arundel, W.Sussex.

PONTEFRACT   MONDAY APRIL 17TH   Lefthand, Undulating Track, Stiff Uphill Finish

Official Going   HEAVY. Stalls: 2m5f - Centre; Rem - Inside.

938   2.20 MED AUCT FILLIES MDN 2YO (E)   5f rnd   Heavy 186   -20 Slow
£3146   £968   £484   £242

762 **CELTIC ISLAND** 20 [1] W G M Turner 2-8-11 A Daly 13/8 FAV: 21: 2 b f Celtic Swing - Chief Island (Be My Chief) Made all, rdn out ins last: well bckd: Jan first foal, dam half-sister to sev wnrs, one outstanding 2yo, won French Derby: eff at 5f, bred for 6f+: handles fast, acts on hvy & on a stiff/undul trk: scopey filly.		88
-- **ERRACHT** [9] P C Haslam 2-8-11 P Goode (3) 25/1: 2: 2 gr f Emarati - Port Na Blath (On Your Mark) Wide, cl-up, ch appr fnl 1f, held towards fnl & flashed tail: better for debut: 1,200gns Mar foal, half-sister to 5f juv wnr Flood's Fancy, dam 6f wnr: eff over a stiff/undul 5f on hvy: will know more next time.	1½	84
886 **EXTRA GUEST** 5 [7] M R Channon 2-8-11 J P Fessey 9/2: 43: 2 b f Fraam - Gibaltarik (Jareer) Front rank, ch ent fnl 2f, onepace ins last: small, fit filly, handles hvy grnd: sharper trk may suit next time.	2	79
-- **HIT THE TRAIL** [3] D Carroll 2-8-11 J F Egan 25/1: 4: Rear, some prog 2f out, nvr nr ldrs: lkd well: 2,600gns Mar foal: dam 5f wnr, sire a sprinter: ran green, shld learn from this.	3½	72
-- **BEREZINA** [2] 2-8-11 K Darley 5/1: 5: Dwelt, chsd ldrs, ch ent fnl 2f, fdd: drifter from 9/4, better for race: 13,000gns Brief Truce Feb first foal, dam modest, sire got 10f: leggy, scopey filly with T Easterby.	2½	67
-- **DANCE QUEEN** [4] 2-8-11 G Duffield 33/1: 6: Chsd ldrs till hmpd/snatched up over 2f out, no threat: Puissance Mar foal, sire a sprinter: leggy, close coupled filly.	1	65
-- **FAYZ SLIPPER** [5] 2-8-11 R Winston 20/1: 7: V slow away, wide prog to chase ldrs 2f out, sn btn: op 12/1, stablemate 5th: IR 5,000gns Fayruz Mar foal, half-sister to 5f juv wnr Double J, sire a sprinter.	4	57
-- **TUPGILL FLIGHT** [6] 2-8-11 O Pears 33/1: 8: In tch till outpcd 2f out: 3,500gns Be My Chief Feb first foal: dam 12f wnr, sire a top-class 1m juv: needs further & time.	4	48
-- **WANNABE BOLD** [8] 2-8-11 Dean McKeown 33/1: 9: Bhd from halfway: ndd this reapp: IR 4,000gns Persian Bold Apr foal: sire a miler: scopey filly, with P Haslam.	2	45

9 ran   Time 1m 11.6 (10.3)   (Bill Brown)   W G M Turner Corton Denham, Somerset.

939   2.50 FRIENDLY SELLER 3YO (F)   1m4f   Heavy 186   -32 Slow
£2247   £642   £321

806 **OPEN GROUND** 17 [1] P Howling 3-8-12 K Darley 14/1: 63-001: 3 ch g Common Grounds - Poplina (Roberto) Trckd ldrs, shkn up to lead 2f out, styd on strongly: lkd well, bght in for 5,800gns: first worthwhile form: clrly apprec step up to a stiff/undul 12f on hvy grnd: staying type, could win more sellers.		55
799 **DAME FONTEYN** 18 [7] M L W Bell 3-8-7 J Mackay (7) 4/1: 000-P2: 3 b f Suave Dancer - Her Honour (Teenoso) Mid-div, prog to chall 2f out, not pace of wnr fnl 1f: clr rem: btn all 3 '99 starts: stays 12f on hvy.	4	47
53 **CROSS DALL** 153 [2] Lady Herries 3-8-7 (e) J F Egan 5/1 FAV: 0003-3: 3 b f Blues Traveller - Faapette	11	40

(Runnett) Pld hard, sn led, hdd 2f out & sn btn: well bckd, wore eye-shield (prev tried a visor), reapp, on toes in paddock: prev trained by R Ingram, big step up in trip: similar tactics back at 10f may pay off: see 53.
858 **NICIARA 7** [5] M C Chapman 3-8-12 A Culhane 16/1: 605004: Towards rear, nvr able to chall: 7 40
qck reapp, op 10/1: stiff task, longer trip: see 451.
782 **DUN DISTINCTLY 19** [4] 3-8-12 (VIS) P Goode(3) 7/2: 0-4265: Early ldr, lost pl 4f out: vis, padd pck, op 6/1. 1¾ 39
873 **JONLOZ 6** [6] 3-8-12 L Newton 10/1: -54566: Al bhd: hard fit, qck reapp, longer trip, flattered latest. 26 21
784 **THE FINAL WORD 19** [3] 3-8-7 P M Quinn (5) 9/2: -50007: Chsd ldrs till 4f out, t.o.: moderate. 12 7
4260} **FLIGHT OF DREAMS 195** [9] 3-8-7 W Supple 12/1: 000-8: In tch 1m: rider given 1 day whip ban. 17 0
783 **ROYAL PASTIMES 19** [8] 3-8-7 R Lappin 20/1: 500-69: Al bhd: longer trip, stiffish task. 6 0
9 ran Time 3m 00.2 (26.1) (S J Hammond) P Howling Newmarket.

940

3.20 TOTE MARATHON HCAP 4YO+ 0-70 (E) 2m5f122y Heavy 186 -68 Slow [63]
£3737 £1150 £575 £287 4 yo rec 6 lb

860 **IMAD 7** [3] K C Comerford 10-8-11 (46)(t) T G McLaughlin 6/1 CO FAV: 01-341: 10 b g Al Nasr - 50
Blue Grass Field (Top Ville) Rear, imprvd halfway, chall 2f out, drvn to assert fnl 100y despite drifting right: won here at Pontefract in '99 (h'cap, this race, rtd 47): 98/99 Folkestone jumps wnr (h'cap hdle, rtd 106h & 106c): eff at 2m/2m5.5f, goes on any grnd, likes gd/soft & hvy: wears a t-strap: out-&-out stayer, likes Pontefract.
*876 **CHARMING ADMIRAL 6** [11] Mrs A Duffield 7-9-4 (53)(bl)(5ex) G Duffield 6/1 CO FAV: 45-012: 7 b g ½ 56
Shareef Dancer - Lilac Charm (Bustino) Mid-div, prog & strong chall fnl 2f, hung right dist, held cl-home: clr rem, qck reapp, padd pick: 1½L 2nd to this same horse in this race in '99 (rtd 49): acts on fast & hvy grnd.
876 **PROTOCOL 6** [17] Mrs S Lamyman 6-8-13 (48)(t) J F Egan 7/1: 0-0023: 6 b g Taufan - Ukraine's 11 45
Affair (The Minstrel) Well plcd, led 5f out, und press 2f out, sn hdd, no extra: op 5/1, qck reapp: stamina appeared to give out over this marathon 2m5.5f trip tho' a gd run nevertheless: see 876 (2L bhd this rnr-up).
482 **MEDELAI 69** [15] Mrs A E Johnson 4-7-11 (38)(1ow)(5oh) A McCarthy (0) 10/1: 2-0104: Mid-div, 1¾ 34
trkd ldrs 5f out, chall bef fnl 2f, fdd appr fnl 1f: 10 wk abs, clr rem: see 318 (2m).
644 **KIPPANOUR 42** [6] 8-8-0 (35)(bl) Claire Bryan (5) 100/1: 045/05: Nvr a factor: fit despite 6 wk abs: 14 23
lightly rcd since '95 wnr in native Ireland at Clonmel (10f h'cap), also won over hdles: acts on gd & firm, now blnkd.
876 **LITTLE BRAVE 6** [13] 5-9-10 (59) J Tate 8/1: 024-46: In tch, eff after 12f, btn 4f out, eased fnl 2f: 16 37
lkd well, op 11/2: top-weight in this grnd & poss came too soon after 876, see 51.
826 **PINMOOR HILL 12** [4] 4-8-5 (46) O Pears 25/1: 00/07: Prom till 5f out: shown little so far 1¾ 23
but ndd this race & is now in the capable hands of D Nicholls.
876 **BLACK ICE BOY 6** [1] 9-8-7 (42)(vis) D Mernagh (3) 6/1 CO FAV: P-5008: Led till 5f out, wknd: 17 8
qck reapp, capable of better: won this race 2 yrs ago: see 141.
649 **FLORA DREAMBIRD 40** [10] 6-7-10 (31)(bl)(11oh) D Kinsella (7) 66/1: 005669: In tch till 6f out: 11 0
stiff task, unplcd over hdles since 649 & blnks reapplied, see 284.
*644 **HETRA HEIGHTS 42** [8] 5-8-3 (38) L Newton 13/2: 5-6110: Al towards rear: 10th, 6 wk abs: see 644. 2½ 0
868 **CRESSET 6** [7] 4-9-5 (60)(bl) A Culhane 10/1: 121220: Nvr a factor: qck reapp: prev consistent on AW. 0
607 **Amsara 48** [14] 4-7-10 (37)(12oh) G Baker(7) 100/1: 760 **Almamzar 20** [5] 10-7-10 (31)(t)(11oh) Kim Tinkler 25/1:
458 **Marciano 72** [2] 4-7-13 (40)(3ow)(7oh) A Mackay 50/1: 726 **Malian 23** [12] 4-9-4 (59) K Darley 16/1:
860 **Highfield Fizz 7** [9] 8-8-8 (43) T Williams 25/1: P 737 **Hibaat 21** [16] 4-8-2 (43) A Nicholls (3) 66/1: P
17 ran Time 5m 34.3 (54.5) (Alan Brackley) K C Comerford Brill, Bucks.

941

3.50 TOTE PLACEPOT HCAP 3YO+ 0-90 (C) 6f rnd Heavy 186 -01 Slow [87]
£7572 £2330 £1165 £582 3 yo rec 11lb 2 groups till 2f out, low no's (far side) favoured

728 **PIPS SONG 23** [8] Dr J D Scargill 5-9-1 (74) J Lowe 10/1: 0-2401: 5 ch g Pips Pride - Friendly Song 86
(Song) Swerved right start, grad recovered, led bef fnl 1f, rdn clr, readily: tchd 12/1, rider given 1 day whip ban: '99 W'hampton & Leicester wnr (h'caps, rtd 78a & 77): '98 W'hampton wnr (auct mdn, rtd 77a & 73): eff at 6f on firm, loves f/sand, gd/soft & hvy: handles any trk, likes W'hampton: runs well fresh: strong gldg, quick follow-up?
824 **REDOUBTABLE 12** [11] D W Chapman 9-9-5 (78) A Culhane 12/1: 121432: 9 b h Grey Dawn II - Seattle 5 81
Rockette (Seattle Slew) Slow away, imprvd after halfway, got to within 1½L of wnr 200y from home, no extra: lkd well: ultra-consistent, acts on any grnd, including both AWs: see 525.
816 **AGENT MULDER 14** [4] P D Cundell 6-8-12 (71)(bl) J Carroll 8/1: 000-23: 6 b g Kylian - Precious ½ 73
Caroline (The Noble Player) Prom, eff appr fnl 1f, kept on but not pace to chall: gd run back in trip, see 816 (7f).
*926 **JUWWI 2** [9] J M Bradley 6-10-1 (88)(6ex) Darren Williams (7) 6/1 FAV: 601514: Settled in last, kept 3½ 84
on fnl 1f, nvr nrr: lks superb, qck turnout after winning on Saturday: v tough: see 926.
817 **MISTER MAL 14** [2] 4-9-4 (77) G Duffield 10/1: 313-05: Keen, cl-up, led 2½f out till bef dist, fdd: ¾ 71
op 14/1, lkd well: back in trip, all 3 wins at 7f: see 817.
763 **AT LARGE 20** [16] 6-8-9 (68) L Newton 8/1: 200-06: Wide & outpcd, kept on appr fnl 1f, nvr nrr: ½ 61+
op 6/1: ndd this & not given a hard time: poor high draw, keep in mind: see 763.
780 **NORTHERN SVENGALI 19** [3] 4-9-4 (77) J F Egan 16/1: 4-3047: Al mid-div: back in trip, see 780, 631. 4 62
4362} **SQUARE DANCER 186** [13] 4-8-12 (71) T Williams 33/1: 0100-8: Rcd wide & was nvr really on terms 2½ 51
with those drawn low: reapp: '99 wnr at Carlisle (auct mdn) & Brighton (stks, rtd 75): unplcd for Mrs J Ramsden in '98 (rtd 71): eff at 7f, both wins at 6f: acts on firm & soft grnd, any trk: with M Dods.
725 **BLAKESET 23** [6] 5-9-0 (73) C Lowther 33/1: -55109: Prom till 2f out: big, strong entire, stablemate ½ 52
of 7th: blnks omitted over a shorter trip: see 677 (7f AW).
725 **EASTER OGIL 23** [12] 5-9-9 (82)(vis) K Darley 13/2: 000-50: Nvr nr ldrs: 10th, op 10/1, lkd well, vis reapp. 1¼ 59
645 **BODFARI PRIDE 42** [15] 5-9-0 (73) Clare Roche (7) 33/1: 500/00: Front rank till appr fnl 2f: 11th, 3½ 44
6 wk abs: missed '99, prev term won at Redcar (auct mdn) & Chester (h'cap, rtd 86 at best, A Bailey): eff at 6/7.5f on fast & hvy grnd: goes on a tight or gall trk, likes Chester: now with D Nicholls.
716 **REFERENDUM 24** [10] 6-9-10 (83)(BL) O Pears 33/1: 00-000: Chsd ldrs till wknd 2f out: 12th, blnkd, nk 53
stablemate of 11th: 4th in a val rtd h'cap last year (rtd 94): last won as a juv in '96 at Goodwood (mdn), Gr 1 plcd (rtd 111, G Lewis): eff at 6/7f, tried 1m: acts on firm & gd/soft grnd & can go well fresh/force the pace.
824 **CRYHAVOC 12** [18] 6-9-10 (83) A Nicholls (3) 7/1: 50-600: In tch wide for 4f: 15th, stablemate 0
11th: lkd well & this is worth forgetting from the widest of draws: well h'capped, see 716.
824 **CARD GAMES 12** [7] 3-8-10 (80) T Lucas 33/1: 20-000: Led till appr fnl 2f, sn lost pl: 17th: '99 wnr 0
at Salisbury (nov auct stks) & Pontefract (nurs, rtd 86, I Balding): eff at 6f, stays 7f: acts on firm & hvy grnd, has run well in a visor: loves to force the pace: stiff task against elders at this stage: with M Easterby.
-- **Sharp Gossip** [5] 4-8-13 (72) S Whitworth 20/1: 4362} **Shirley Not 186** [17] 4-8-8 (67) D Mernagh (3) 25/1:
831 **Talaria 11** [14] 4-8-8 (67) J Tate 33/1:
17 ran Time 1m 25.3 (11.2) (P J Edwards) Dr J D Scargill Newmarket.

PONTEFRACT   MONDAY APRIL 17TH   Lefthand, Undulating Track, Stiff Uphill Finish

942	4.20 EXACTA CLASSIFIED STKS 3YO+ 0-60 (F) 1m rnd Heavy 186 +01 Fast
	£2467 £705 £352 3 yo rec 14lb

*854 **POLISH SPIRIT** 7 [13] B R Millman 5-9-10 K Darley 5/4 FAV: 003-11: 5 b g Emarati - Gentle Star   72
(Comedy Star) Prom, led halfway & stdly drew clr: hvly bckd, best time of day, lkd superb, qck reapp: recent
Windsor wnr (h'cap, crse record): '99 wnr again at Windsor (h'cap, rtd 63): '98 Warwick wnr (mdn, rtd 65): eff
arnd 1m, stays 10f: acts on fast, hvy grnd, any trk, likes Windsor: runs v well fresh: cld complete hat-trick.
*899 **ARC** 4 [3] G M Moore 6-9-10 J Weaver 5/1: 242412: 6 b g Archway - Columbian Sand (Salmon Leap)   8 60
Trkd ldrs, eff to chase wnr 2f out, sn outpcd & not persevered with: op 7/2, qck reapp: met an in-form rival,
but remains in grand form: acts on firm, fibresand & prob hvy grnd: see 899.
834 **ANNADAWI** 11 [7] C N Kellett 5-9-8 G Baker (7) 66/1: 405463: 5 b g Sadler's Wells - Prayers'n   1¼ 56$
Promises (Foolish Pleasure) Held up, prog halfway, rdn 2f out, kept on for 3rd but no ch with ldrs: swtg: v
stiff task at the weights & looks flattered yet again despite being 10L clr of rest: see 834, 173.
4548} **HIGH SUN** 171 [4] S Gollings 4-9-8 A Nicholls (3) 7/1: 0411-4: Waited with, wide prog 3f out, rdn 2f   10 44
out, sn no extra, eased fnl 1f: op 5/1, has thrived from 3 to 4: '99 Leicester (clmr), Doncaster & Newmarket
wnr (appr h'caps, rtd 61): rtd 73 in '98 (auct mdn): eff at 7f/1m, tried 12f: acts on fast & soft grnd, likes
stiff/gall trks: best without blnks & goes well here at apprentice: spot on next time.
4511} **RYMERS RASCAL** 174 [2] 8-9-8 W Supple 8/1: 0500-5: Mid-div, imprvd 3f out, fdd 2f out: ndd this   2 41
reapp: '99 Chester wnr (h'cap, rtd 68): '98 Redcar wnr (h'cap, rtd 63): stays 1m, best at 7f: acts on firm,
hvy grnd, any trk: tough: with E Alston.
846 **JONA HOLLEY** 9 [9] 7-9-8 (bl) C Lowther 10/1: 614-06: Rear, eff 3f out, nvr able to chall: stiff   shd 41
task: '99 Ayr wnr (sell, rtd 54): '97 wnr at Folkestone & Southwell (h'caps, rtd 52 & 53a, G L Moore): eff
btwn 1m & 10f: acts on fibresand & fast, suited by gd & soft grnd, any trk: eff with/without blnks, not visor.
793 **INDIAN WARRIOR** 18 [10] 4-9-8 P Shea (7) 16/1: 066607: Nvr in it under a quiet ride: lkd well.   1½ 39
872 **OAKWELL ACE** 6 [1] 4-9-5 B Sooful (7) 25/1: 030-58: Al same place: qck reapp, stiff task, see 872.   shd 36
638 **RAINWORTH LADY** 44 [5] 3-8-5 R Fitzpatrick (3) 50/1: 400-59: Nvr on terms: 6 wk abs, fit, lengthy filly.   4 32
612 **RED APOLLO** 48 [16] 4-9-8 (VIS) L Newton 66/1: 0-6400: U.r./loose bef start, al bhd: 10th, vis, new stable.   3 32
808 **Rathlea** 16 [14] 6-9-8 P M Quinn (5) 100/1:   705 **Bodfari Signet** 25 [11] 4-9-8 G Parkin 33/1:
686 **Naked Oat** 31 [12] 5-9-8 J Bosley (7) 25/1:   3415} **Knaves Ash** 244 [6] 9-9-8 Dean McKeown 33/1:
--   **Tiheros Glenn** [8] 4-9-8 V Halliday 66/1:
15 ran   Time 1m 56.6 (14.8)   (Mrs Izabel Palmer)   B R Millman Kentisbeare, Devon.

943	4.50 PUNTERS CHOICE HCAP 4YO+ 0-75 (E) 1m2f Heavy 186 -34 Slow	[74]
	£4199 £1292 £646 £323	

*847 **WILTON** 9 [3] J Hetherton 5-9-7 (67)(t) G Duffield 11/2: 0-3011: 5 ch g Sharpo - Poyle Amber   68
(Sharrood) In tch, prog 3f out, wide into str & styd on dourly to lead dist: lkd well, tchd 13/2: prev wnr at
Hamilton (class stks): btn both '99 starts, '98 wnr here at Pontefract, Redcar (rtd 70) & Lingfield (h'caps, rtd
79a): eff at 1m/10f on gd, hvy & both AWs, any trk, likes Pontefract: eff with/without t-strap: improve further.
4447} **NOIRIE** 180 [10] M Brittain 6-7-10 (42)(10oh) D Mernagh (3) 25/1: 0300-2: 6 bb g Warning -   1¼ 41
Callipoli (Green Dancer) Front rank, narrow lead 2f out, hdd ent fnl 1f, styd on: reapp: plcd in '99 (h'cap, rtd
35): '98 wnr here at Pontefract (appr h'cap, rtd 44 at best): eff at 10f on fast grnd, likes soft/hvy, without
blnks/visor: goes well here at Pontefract, had a stiff task 10lbs o/h.
726 **PEKAY** 23 [6] B Smart 7-9-0 (60) J Weaver 10/1: 12/003: 7 b g Puissance - K Sera (Lord Gayle)   1¼ 58
Dsptd lead, led 5f out till 2f out, styd on: op 8/1: pulled clr rem, back in trip: well h'capped: see 682.
4475} **SHARP SPICE** 178 [8] D J Coakley 4-9-2 (62) J F Egan 10/1: 4334-4: Mid-div, prog to chall appr   10 53
fnl 2f, sn no extra: rcd in yr, ndd this: '99 Goodwood wnr (mdn h'cap, rtd 64 at best): rcd thrice in '98 for
Lord Huntingdon (rtd 62): eff at 10f on gd & hvy grnd, handles fast: best held up: attractive filly.
825 **ARCHIE BABE** 12 [17] 4-9-7 (67) W Supple 7/1: 531-65: Mid-div, prog to press ldrs appr fnl   nk 58
2f, wknd dist: fit: had plenty of use made of him: handles soft: see 825.
706} **NORTHERN ACCORD** 385 [4] 6-7-13 (45)(BL) T Williams 25/1: 14/0-6: Prom, eff 3f out, no impress: 5 32
blnkd & ndd this reapp: tried fences this winter, ran just once last term: '98 wnr at Hamilton (mdn h'cap) &
Beverley (h'cap, rtd 45, Mrs J Ramsden): eff at 1m/12f on fast & gd/soft grnd: fitter next time on faster grnd.
779 **LAWNETT** 19 [1] 4-9-10 (56) Dean McKeown 10/1: 1-0567: Nvr better than mid-div: op 8/1, small & fit.   6 38
825 **NOWELL HOUSE** 12 [5] 4-9-6 (66) G Parkin 4/1 FAV: 211-08: Nvr on terms with ldrs: hvly bckd   1¼ 47
from 6/1: clearly better expected, yet to come to hand: see 825.
869 **TALECA SON** 1 [1] 5-7-10 (42)(VIS)(15oh) G Bayer (7) 50/1: 254009: Mid-div, no ch from 3f out: visor.   4 20
4346} **COURAGE UNDER FIRE** 187 [14] 5-8-5 (51) R Price 12/1: 2/45-0: Chsd ldrs till 4f out: 10th, just better   nk 29
for race: 6 wk jumps abs (unplcd over hdles): ran just twice last term (h'cap, rtd 50): '98 wnr at Southwell
(h'cap, rtd 51a & 54): eff at 10f, sole wnr at 12f: acts on fast, soft grnd & fibresand: strong, lengthy.
4587} **SHAFFISHAYES** 167 [19] 8-9-6 (66) A Culhane 10/1: 4455-0: Nvr a factor: 11th: not given a hard   ¾ 43
time & lkd in need of this: '99 Ripon wnr (h'cap, rtd 71): '98 wnr at Thirsk & Nottingham (stks, rtd 68): eff at
10f, suited by 12f, stays 14f: acts on fast, soft grnd, handles fibresand, any trk: with Mrs M Reveley.
757 **TROIS** 20 [15] 4-9-6 (66) T G McLaughlin 14/1: -10300: Al towards rear: 14th, see 271.   0
4372} **Anniversary Day** 185 [13] 4-8-1 (47) P Fessey 20/1:   825 **Red Roses** 12 [16] 4-7-10 (42)(2oh) Kim Tinkler 20/1:
889 **Sterling High** 5 [11] 5-8-2 (48)(tbl) J Fanning 33/1:   580 **Windshift** 53 [9] 4-9-10 (70)(vis) R Winston 16/1:
791 **Ruby Estate** 18 [12] 9-7-10 (42)(9oh) C Halliwell (7) 33/1: 200 **Legal Issue** 122 [18] 8-9-6 (66) R Lappin 16/1:
18 ran   Time 2m 30.1 (22)   (George A Moore)   J Hetherton Malton, N.Yorks.

SAINT CLOUD   WEDNESDAY APRIL 12TH   Lefthand, Galloping Track

Official Going   VERY SOFT

944	2.35 GR 3 PRIX PENELOPE 3YO 1m2f110y V Soft
	£21134 £7685 £3842

--   **VOLVORETA** [6] C Lerner 3-9-0 T Thulliez 4/5 FAV: 11-1: 3 ch f Suave Dancer - Robertiya (Don   118$
Roberto) In tch, smooth hdwy 2f out, rdn to lead appr fnl 1f, pushed clr ins last: reapp: unbtn in '99, incl a
Gr 3 at Deauville: eff arnd 10f on soft, further shld suit: runs well fresh & a gall trk: tough & smart filly.

SAINT CLOUD   WEDNESDAY APRIL 12TH   Lefthand, Galloping Track

-- **REVE DOSCAR** [4] Mme M Bollack Badel 3-9-0 A Badel 143/10: 2-22: 3 gr f Highest Honor -   6   108
Numidie (Baillamont) Waited with, gd hdwy 2f out, styd on but not pace of cmftble wnr.
-- **SADLERS FLAG** [3] Mme C Head 3-9-0 O Doleuze 52/10: 2-13: 3 b f Sadler's Wells - Animatrice   2½   104
(Alleged) Led, hdd appr fnl 1f, sn not pace of front 2.
6 ran   Time 2m 21.9   (Mme M S Vidal)   C Lerner France

MAISONS LAFFITTE   FRIDAY APRIL 14TH   Left & Righthand, Sharpish Track

Official Going   SOFT

945   1.55 LISTED PRIX DJEBEL 3YO   7f   Soft
       £13449   £4612   £3458

-- **DANGER OVER** [5] P Bary 3-9-2 T Thulliez 11/10 FAV: 1: 3 b c Warning - Danilova (Lyphard)   108
Chsd ldrs till went on appr fnl 1f, styd on well, pushed out: eff at 7f, 1m will suit: acts on soft grnd
& a sharpish trk: smart & imprvng colt, heads for the French 2,000 Guineas.
-- **ONLYMAN** [2] Mme C Head 3-9-2 O Doleuze 3/1: 2: 3 ch c Woodman - Only Seule (Lyphard)   3   102
Dsptd lead till drvn & not pace of wnr over 1f out: stays 7f on soft: useful.
-- **CAZOULIAS** [6] Mme N Rossio 3-9-2 D Bonilla 173/10: 3: 3 b g Rasi Brasak - Cazouls (Gairloch)   ½   101
Led, hdd over 1f out, sn btn: stays 7f on soft.
6 ran   Time 1m 25.7   (K Abdulla)   P Bary France

946   2.25 LISTED PRIX IMPRUDENCE 3YO   7f   Soft
       £13449   £4612   £3458

-- **PEONY** [6] D Sepulchre 3-9-0 C Asmussen 7/1: 1: 3 ch f Lion Cavern - Persiandale (Persian Bold)   109
Settled rear, gd hdwy over 1f out, styd on strongly for press to lead fnl strides: eff at 7f, 1m shld suit:
acts on soft grnd: v useful filly who now tackles the French 1,000 Guineas.
4245} **LADY VETTORI 194** [7] F Rohaut 3-9-0 O Peslier 11/10 FAV: 1113-2: 3 b f Vettori - Lady Golconda   shd   108
(Kendor) Rear, smooth hdwy over 2f out, rdn to lead dist, styd on well, hdd fnl strides: v prog in '99, won
1st 5 starts (incl a Listed & Gr 3), subs 3rd in a Gr 1 at Longchamp (rtd 108): eff at 7f/1m on gd & hvy
grnd: v tough & useful filly: will reportedly wear blnks if taking her chance in the 1,000 Guineas.
-- **BLUEMAMBA** [8] P Bary 3-9-0 S Guillot 23/10: 3: 3 b f Kingmambo - Black Penny (Private Account)   snk   107
Trkd ldr, rdn to chall ins last, styd on, just held: eff at 7f on soft: useful.
8 ran   Time 1m 26.92   (Mme J Moore)   D Sepulchre France

LEOPARDSTOWN   SUNDAY APRIL 16TH   Lefthand, Galloping Track

Official Going   SOFT

947   3.00 LISTED 2,000 GUINEAS TRIAL 3YO   1m   Soft
       £16250   £4750   £2250   £750

2045} **BACH 304** [4] A P O'Brien 3-8-13 M J Kinane 11/10: -11-1: 3 b c Caerleon - Producer (Nashua)   109
Made all, hard prsd ent fnl 1f, styd on strongly, drvn out: reapp: '99 scorer at Gowran Park (mdn) & notably
Royal Ascot (Listed Chesham stks, rtd 104): half brother to a high-class 6/10f wnr: eff at 7f/1m, mid-dists
will suit in time: acts on fast, soft & a stiff/gall trk: progressive & unbeaten colt, can land a Gr race.
-- **LEGAL JOUSTING** [1] D K Weld 3-8-10 P J Smullen 1/1 FAV: 2-12: 3 b c Indian Ridge - In   hd   105
Anticipation (Sadler's Wells) Cl-up, prog 3f out, styd on well to chall dist, just held: recent Curragh wnr (mdn):
rnr-up to a smart rival on sole '99 juv start: eff at 7f/1m, runs well fresh on soft: useful colt, can win similar.
-- **RIVER SOUNDS** [2] J G Murphy 3-8-10 J P Spencer 50/1: 51-053: 3 b c Shalford - Classical Flair   1½   101
(Riverman) Dwelt, bhd, rdn/hdwy over 2f out, styd on, nvr nrr: much imprvd here: stays 1m on soft grnd.
4606} **GOLOVIN 163** [3] M J Grassick 3-8-10 E Ahern 8/1: 1-4: Trkd ldr, drvn & no extra appr fnl 1f: reapp: 4½   94
won sole '99 start, at Doncaster (mdn, rtd 90): eff at 7f, mid-dists shld suit: runs well fresh on hvy grnd.
4 ran   Time 1m 49.5   (Satish K Sanan)   A P O'Brien Ballydoyle, Co Tipperary

948   3.30 LISTED 1,000 GUINEAS TRIAL 3YO   7f   Soft
       £16250   £4750   £2250   £750

4482} **AMETHYST 176** [5] A P O'Brien 3-8-10 M J Kinane 11/8 FAV: 1243-1: 3 b f Sadler's Wells - Zummerudd   110
(Habitat) Chsd ldrs going well, led 2f out, rdn clr, eased cl-home, easily: reapp: '99 Naas wnr (debut, mdn),
subs not disgraced in Listed/Gr company (rtd 106): eff at 6/7f, 1m will suit: acts on gd, soft & runs v well
fresh: prog & smart filly with a useful turn of foot: heads for the 1,000 Guineas with a leading chance.
4561} **ARETHA 169** [3] J S Bolger 3-8-10 K J Manning 4/1: 3135-2: 3 ch f Indian Ridge - Smaoineamh   5   98
(Tap On Wood) Waited with, switched & hdwy over 1f out, kept on but no ch with easy wnr: '99 scorer at Naas
(mdn), subs plcd in Listed company at Newbury (rtd 100): eff at 6f/7.3f on yldg/soft & soft, handles hvy grnd.
4533} **MARGAY 174** [6] M J Grassick 3-8-10 E Ahern 8/1: 3153-3: 3 b f Marju - Almarai (Vaguely Noble)   shd   98
Cl-up, chall ldr 2f out, rdn/not pace of wnr ins last: op 5/1 on reapp: '99 wnr at Galway (fill mdn, 7f, soft).
-- **BELLS ARE RINGING** [4] A P O'Brien 3-8-10 C O'Donoghue 12/1: 616-4: Mid-div, rdn & no extra   2   94
appr fnl 1f: stable-mate of wnr: '99 wnr at Tipperary (7f mdn, soft/hvy grnd), subs down the field in Listed
company: open to improvement & sure to be placed to effect by connections.
8 ran   Time 1m 36.9   (Mrs John Magnier & John T L Jones)   A P O'Brien Ballydoyle, Co Tipperary

---

949   5.00 LISTED BALLYSAX STAKES 3YO   1m2f   Soft
£16250   £4750   £2250   £750

*818   **GRAND FINALE 15** [4]   D K Weld 3-8-12 P J Smullen 2/1: 3-11: 3 b c Sadler's Wells - Final Figure   110
(Super Concorde) Chsd ldr, styd on to lead dist, drvn out: recent scorer at Gowran Park (stks): eff at 9.5/10f,
further shld suit: acts on gd/yldg & soft grnd: tough & useful.

4029} **SINNDAR 210** [1]   J Oxx 3-9-5 (t) J P Murtagh 5/2: -11-2: 3 b c Grand Lodge - Sinntara (Lashkari)   hd 116
Led, strongly prsd 2f out, hdd dist, rallied well, just held: clr rem: '99 wnr at The Curragh (2, incl Gr 1
National stks, rtd 107): eff at 1m/10f & loves soft grnd: wears a t-strap: tough & v useful.

--   **LAMMAS** [2]   D K Weld 3-8-12 P Shanahan 20/1: 3-13: 3 b c Lammtarra - Overcall (Bustino)   15 89
Chsd ldrs, rdn & wknd qckly fnl 2f: stablemate of wnr: recent Cork scorer (9f mdn, yldg/soft).

2656} **SHAKESPEARE 280** [5]   A P O'Brien 3-8-12 M J Kinane 6/4 FAV: 1-4: Cl-up, rdn/wknd qckly over 2f   15 79
out, eased to a walk fnl 1f: drifted from 1/1 & reportedly returned distressed: landed sole '99 start, at The
Curragh (mdn, rtd 90): eff at 7f, 10f shld suit: acts on fast grnd & runs well fresh: better expected.

4 ran   Time 2m 19.7   (Moyglare Stud Farm)   D K Weld Curragh, Co Kildare

---

NEWMARKET (ROWLEY)

Official Going   GOOD. Stalls: Far Side.

950   1.35 GR 3 GREENHAM STKS 3YO (A)   7f str   Good 44   -09 Slow
£18000   £6900   £3450   £1650

4322} **BARATHEA GUEST 191** [5]   G G Margarson 3-9-0 P Robinson 13/2: 111D-1: 3 b c Barathea - Western   115
Heights (Shirley Heights) Waited with, rdn halfway, styd on well for press over 1f out to get up on line, all-out:
reapp, jockey received a 1-day whip ban: progressive juv, won at Yarmouth (mdn), Salisbury (stks), Deauville
(Listed) & disq from 1st at Longchamp (Gr 1, rtd 113, 3 rnrs): half-brother to a 1m/10f wnr: eff at 7f, a
return to 1m is sure to suit: likes gd & v soft, stiff trk: runs well fresh: v smart, genuine & still improving:
bunched finish in this race but he will relish the extra furlong in the 2000 Guineas.

4398} **DISTANT MUSIC 185** [6]   B W Hills 3-9-0 M Hills 8/13 FAV: 111-2: 3 b c Distant View - Musicanti   hd 113
(Nijinsky) Dwelt, held up, hdwy & slightly short of room over 1f out, styd on well to lead ins last, hard rdn &
collared cl-home, just btn on reapp: hvly bckd: unbtn juv, won at Doncaster (2, mdn & Gr 2) & Newmarket (Gr 1
Dewhurst, by 1L, rtd 122 at best): dam 14.5f wnr: eff at 7f, 1m looks sure to suit: acts on gd & gd/firm & runs
well fresh on a gall trk: reportedly finished 'slightly lame' after this race: top-class last term & has a fine
turn of foot, different proposition in the 2000 Guineas.

4419} **WINNING VENTURE 184** [1]   S P C Woods 3-9-0 W R Swinburn 25/1: 322D-3: 3 b c Owington - Push   nk 112
A Button (Bold Lady) Waited with, hdwy over 2f out, led dist till ins last, kept on, just btn in a 3-way photo: fine
reapp: tough/useful juv, won at Kempton (stks) & plcd all other starts, incl in Listed & an Italian Gr 1 (rtd 105):
eff over 7f/1m on firm, soft & any trk: runs well fresh: smart & tough, clearly improved through the winter.

4483} **SCARTEEN FOX 178** [7]   D R C Elsworth 3-9-0 T Quinn 13/2: 3110-4: Chsd ldrs, effort to chall appr   ¾ 110
fnl 1f, no extra well ins last: reapp: won middle 2 of 4 juv starts, at Newbury (mdn) & Newmarket (List, rtd
110): dam 7f wnr: eff at 7f on firm & gd, below best sole start on soft: smart, should win a Gr race this term.

3983} **MA YORAM 213** [3]   3-9-0 L Dettori 25/1: -123-5: Keen cl-up, ev ch appr final 1f, sn btn: reapp: 1½ 107
thrice rcd juv, debut wnr at Kempton (mdn), subs plcd in a couple of Gr 2 6f contests (rtd 105): eff at 5/6f,
stays 7f: acts on firm & gd grnd: useful & lightly raced, interesting back at 6f in Listed company.

*810   **SAFARANDO 17** [2]   3-9-0 T G McLaughlin 14/1: 112116: Chsd ldr, hdwy to lead halfway till dist, wknd: nk 106
another fine run on massive step up from h'cap company: see 810 (1m).

4482} **SEVEN NO TRUMPS 178** [4]   3-9-0 J Weaver 20/1: 0322-7: Led till halfway, wknd over 1f out: reapp: 3½ 99
rcd 10 times as a juv, won at Nottingham (mdn auct mdn), Newcastle (now stks), also plcd sev times incl in List (rtd
106): eff forcing the pace over 5/6f on firm, soft & on any trk: enjoy a return to sprint trips in List company.

7 ran   Time 1m 26.88 (3.68)   (John Guest)   G G Margarson Newmarket.

---

951   2.05 ALPHAMERIC MDN 3YO (D)   1m4f   Good 44   -50 Slow
£4836   £1488   £744   £372

4611} **WELLBEING 165** [2]   H R A Cecil 3-9-0 T Quinn 7/2: 3-1: 3 b c Sadler's Wells - Charming Life (Sir   99+
Tristram) Cl-up, led 4f out, styd on well, pushed out, shade cosily: op 9/4: rtd 76 sole juv start: half brother
to a smart 10/12f scorer: dam 7f wnr: relished step up to 12f & further looks sure to suit: acts on gd & a gall
trk: runs well fresh: potentially smart & open to any amount of improvement, should develop into a Listed/Gr wnr.

4493} **SOLITARY 178** [3]   B W Hills 3-9-0 J Reid 8/1: 4-2: 3 b c Sanglamore - Set Fair (Alleged)   ¾ 97+
Handy, eff to chase wnr over 3f out, ran green & styd on fnl 1f, not btn far: well clr of rem on reapp: rtd 80 when
4th sole juv start: half-brother to 7f/12f wnr Valentine Girl: dam 10f wnr: relished this step up to 12f, further
shld suit: acts on gd, prob hvy & on a gall trk: v useful, sure to improve for this & the type to win races.

833   **BID FOR FAME 12** [1]   T G Mills 3-9-0 A Clark 11/1: 53: 3 b c Quest For Fame - Shroud (Vaguely   7 86
Noble) Waited with in tch, eff over 3f out, onepace final 2f: stays 12f on gd: should win a minor trk mdn, see 833.

4139} **CAPA 203** [7]   B W Hills 3-9-0 M Hills 11/8 FAV: 22-4: Waited with, rdn & outpcd well over 2f out, late   ¾ 85
gains: hvly bckd: reapp, stablemate of rnr-up: rnr-up both juv starts (mdns, rtd 92): dam 12f wnr: stays 12f
& further will suit on this evidence: acts on gd & fast: looks sure to win a race with a stiffer test of stamina.

4569} **MORNING LOVER 169** [6]   3-9-0 N Callan 33/1: 0-5: Chsd ldrs, rdn & btn 2f out: reapp: rtd 63 sole juv   ½ 84
start: dam 7f scorer: bred for mid-dists this term: showed some promise here & will relish a minor trk mdn.

--   **MAC HALL** [8]   3-9-0 L Dettori 16/1: 3-6: Waited with, brief effort 4f out, wknd over 2f out: 4 78
plcd in Italy sole juv start (7f, soft): dam mid-dist bred, with M Quinlan.

2824} **CHÂTER FLAIR 272** [5]   3-9-0 K Darley 50/1: -00-7: Led till 4f out, wknd 3f out: rtd 66 when unplcd   4 72
as a juv: dam mid-dist wnr & minor trk mid-dist h'caps will suit.

--   **WILD RIVER** [4]   3-9-0 K Fallon 8/1: 8: Slow away, sn handy till wknd 4f out: Sadler's Wells   22 40
colt, should stay mid-dists: with M Johnston.

8 ran   Time 2m 40.03 (11.23)   (Eoxrs Of The Late Lord Howard de Walden)   H R A Cecil Newmarket.

952	2.35 LISTED ABERNANT STKS 3YO+ (A) 6f str Good 44 +02 Fast

£13711   £5200   £2600   £1182

914   **CRETAN GIFT 4** [1] N P Littmoden 9-9-3 (vis) T G McLaughlin 14/1: 0-0351: 9 ch g Cadeaux Genereux -   **111**
Caro's Niece (Caro) Waited with, gd hdwy over 1f out, styd on well to lead ins last, rdn clr: gd time, qck reapp:
'99 scorer at Ascot (rtd h'cap) & Yarmouth (stks, rtd 103), also rnr-up in this race for 2nd successive year: '98
wnr at W'hampton (h'cap, rtd 104a), rtd 115 when 4th at Royal Ascot (Gr 2): eff at 5f & 7f, suited by 6f on firm,
soft/hvy & fibresand: eff with/without blnks/visor on any trk, has run well fresh: admirably tough & smart 9yo.
4396} **WARNINGFORD 185** [9] J R Fanshawe 6-9-9 W R Swinburn 8/1: 2206-2: 6 b h Warning - Barford Lady 1½ **113**
(Stanford) Waited with, hdwy & slightly short of room over 1f out, kept on nicely ins last on reapp: in '99 won
at Warwick (stks), Leicester (Gr 3) & Haydock (List, rtd 114): '98 wnr at Yarmouth & Goodwood (h'caps, rtd 105):
eff at 6f, all 5 wins at 7f, stays 1m: acts on fast, loves gd/soft & hvy, any trk: eff with/without a visor & runs
well fresh: smart, genuine & tough, spot-on next time at 7f & a repeat bid in the Gr 3 at Leicester looks ideal.
4100} **GORSE 205** [4] H Candy 5-9-9 T Quinn 6/1: 1125-3: 5 b h Sharpo - Pervenche (Latest Model)   ½ **112**
Led 3f, led again 2f out, rdn & collared ins last, only btn 2L: in '99 scored at Hamburg & Leopardstown (Gr 3s, rtd
115): '98 scorer at Salisbury (mdn), Newmarket (stks) & Doncaster (Listed, rtd 108): all 5 wins at 6f & handles fm
grnd, loves gd & soft & a stiff trk: v tough & smart, as good as ever & should win another Group race this term.
4246} **ARKADIAN HERO 198** [3] L M Cumani 5-9-7 L Dettori 6/1: 1130-4: Cl-up, hdwy trav well over 1f out, sn nk **109**
rdn, hung right ins last & onepcd: reapp: in '99 scored at Newbury & Newmarket (List), also fine 2L 3rd in Gr
1 Sprint Cup at Haydock (rtd 119): in '98 rtd 118: stays 7f, all wins at 6f & likes firm & gd, prob handles soft:
acts on any trk: high-class sprinter at best & should prove much sharper for this.
3334} **TEAPOT ROW 249** [6] 5-9-3 Pat Eddery 10/1: 2412-5: Missed break & lost arnd 6/7L, bhd, styd on 1½ **103+**
strongly fnl 2f, nrst fin: reapp: '99 scorer at Newbury (stks), also rnr-up in a Gr 3 (rtd 108): failed to win
in '98 (rtd 112): smart juv: eff at 6f, sure to relish a return to 7f/1m & does stay 10f: likes gd & firm, handles
soft & a stiff trk: v smart at best & very promising here, one to follow next time over further in stks/Listed.
4377} **DEEP SPACE 186** [7] 5-9-3 J Reid 11/1: 0120-6: In tch, hdwy well over 1f out, kept on same pace: nk **101**
op 8/1: in fine '99 form, won at Lingfield (h'cap), Royal Ascot (val Wokingham h'cap) & Nottingham (stks,
rtd 108 at best): '98 scorer at Sandown & Newmarket (h'caps, rtd 85): suited by 6/7f on any trk: handles
gd/soft, likes firm/fast: tough & v useful gelding with a turn of foot, sharper for this encouraging reapp.
734   **TEDBURROW 24** [5] 8-9-9 J F Egan 11/1: 110-07: Handy, effort well over 1f out, no extra: better run. ¾ **105**
820   **HALMAHERA 14** [11] 5-9-7 K Fallon 4/1 FAV: 06-528: Waited with, effort well over 1f out, no impress. 1½ **99**
914   **SUPERIOR PREMIUM 4** [2] 6-9-7 R Winston 10/1: 110-09: Led 3f out till 2f out, no extra ins last. 1 **96**
914   **ANDREYEV 4** [8] 6-9-7 R Hughes 12/1: 40-100: Waited with, rdn & no response well over 1f out: 2 **90**
10th: qck reapp, twice below winning reapp in 734.
734   **BON AMI 24** [12] 4-9-3 K Darley 25/1: 220-00: Al bhd: 11th. hd **85**
927   **BLUE ACE 3** [10] 7-9-3 R Cochrane 200/1: 0-50: In tch, btn after halfway: last, qck reapp, see 927. 11 **55**
12 ran   Time 1m 13.3 (2.5)   (T Clarke)   N P Littmoden Newmarket.

953	3.10 GR 3 NELL GWYN STKS 3YO (A) 7f str Good 44 +10 Fast

£20300   £7700   £3850   £1750

4312} **PETRUSHKA 190** [4] Sir Michael Stoute 3-8-9 K Fallon 7/2 FAV: 1-1: 3 ch f Unfuwain - Ballet Shoes   **116+**
(Ela-Mana-Mou) Dwelt, waited with, gd hdwy over 2f out, led over 1f out, powered clr, most readily: well bckd,
fast time on reapp: won sole juv start at Leicester (back-end mdn, rtd 100+): eff at 7f, sure to relish 1m &
further could suit: acts on gd, gd/soft & runs well fresh on a stiff trk: lightly raced & displayed a fine
turn of foot here, top-class & exciting filly who must take all the beating in the 1,000 Guineas.
4137} **SEAZUN 203** [5] M R Channon 3-8-9 L Dettori 7/1: 6121-2: 3 b f Zieten - Sunset Cafe (Red Sunset): 4 **109**
Chsd ldrs, eff & slightly short of room over 2f out, styd on over 1f out to chase wnr ins last, no impress: op
5/1: reapp: juv scorer at Brighton (mdn) & Newmarket (Gr 1 Cheveley Park, rtd 113): half-sister to a 1m/2m
wnr: dam 12f scorer: eff at 6/7f, looks sure to apprec 1m & further could suit: acts on firm, gd & on any
trk: smart filly, encouraging reapp behind a v high class sort, can rate more highly & should win more Gr races.
4400} **AUNTY ROSE 185** [12] J L Dunlop 3-8-9 Pat Eddery 6/1: 130-3: 3 b f Caerleon - Come On Rosi (Valiyar) 1½ **102**
Waited with, rdn & slightly short of room over 2f out, kept on for press appr fnl 1f: rcd thrice as a juv, won at
Newmarket (fill mdn, debut) & plcd in a Gr 3 (rtd 101): from a talented but temperamental family: eff at 7f/1m,
further cld suit: acts on gd/firm & gd & has run well fresh: v useful, encouraging reapp, win races over further.
2970} **ALHUFOOF 266** [7] M P Tregoning 3-8-9 R Hills 14/1: 31-4: Chsd ldr, chall over 1f out, no extra ½ **101**
inside last: reapp: won 2nd of only 2 juv starts, at Goodwood (fillies mdn, made all, rtd 94): eff at
6/7f on firm & gd grnd & handles any trk: useful, would enjoy a drop into Listed company.
4136} **CROESO CARIAD 203** [2] 3-8-9 T Quinn 16/1: 52-01: 5: Waited with, effort over 2f out, onepace: ½ **100**
reapp: as a juv scored at Chepstow (mdn auct) & San Siro (Listed), also just tchd off in a Gr 3 at Goodwood
(rtd 99): stays 7.5f, 1m should suit: acts on fast & gd grnd: would enjoy a drop to Listed/stks company.
4482} **HALLAND PARK GIRL 178** [9] 3-8-9 R Hughes 10/1: 2111-6: Set pace till over 1f out, no extra: reapp: 2½ **95**
in tremendous juv form, won at Lingfield (nov auct), Ascot (nursery h'cap), Salisbury, Curragh (stks) &
Doncaster (Listed, rtd 106 at best): suited by 6f on firm or soft grnd & on any trk: has run well fresh:
tough & v useful at 6f last term & should gain further success over that trip shortly.
4506} **DECISION MAID 176** [1] 3-8-9 J Reid 14/1: 51-7: In tch, rdn over 2f out, wkng & hung right inside ½ **94**
last: reapp: won 2nd of only 2 juv starts, at Lingfield (fillies mdn, rtd 87): eff at 7f, 1m+ should suit
(dam 9f scorer): acts on gd & hvy grnd: find easier opportunities.
4400} **PRINCESS ELLEN 185** [11] 3-8-9 J Fortune 10/1: 1105-8: Cl-up, rdn & btn 2f out: reapp: won first 1 **92**
of 2 juv starts, at Ascot (mdn) & Newmarket (Listed, rtd 102, with P Chapple Hyam): eff at 7f, should stay
further: acts on fast grnd & has run well fresh on a gall trk.
4137} **JEMIMA 203** [8] 3-8-12 K Darley 20/1: 1105-9: Keen, handy, wknd over 1f out: reapp: juv scorer at shd **95**
York (fillies mdn), Ripon (nov) & York (Gr 2 Lowther, by a nk, rtd 107): eff at 5/6f, should stay 7f:
acts on firm, gd/soft & on any trk: tough & smart last term at shorter trips.
3989} **MISTY MISS 213** [10] 3-8-9 J F Egan 33/1: 1103-0: V keen, in tch, hdwy appr 2f out, wknd fnl 1f: 10th: ½ **91**
reapp: juv scorer at Bath (sell), W'hampton (val stks, rtd 100a) & Goodwood (Gr 3 Molecomb, at 33/1, rtd 100):
eff at 5/6f on firm, gd & handles any trk & runs well fresh: interesting back at 6f in lesser grade.
4487} **BEDAZZLING 178** [13] 3-8-9 P Robinson 10/1: 3120-0: In tch, wknd 2f out: 11th, reapp. 2½ **86**
4561} **SILVER COLOURS 171** [3] 3-8-9 W R Swinburn 12/1: 61-0: In tch till wknd over 2f out: 12th, reapp, 2 **82**
4476} **BANDANNA 179** [6] 3-8-9 R Cochrane 50/1: 2350-0: Dwelt, al bhd on reapp: 13th, lngr trip. shd **82**
13 ran   Time 1m 25.6 (2.4)   (Highclere Thor'bred Racing Ltd)   Sir Michael Stoute Newmarket.

NEWMARKET (ROWLEY) TUESDAY APRIL 18TH Righthand, Stiff, Galloping Track

954

3.40 WILLIAM HILL HCAP 3YO 0-95 (C) 7f str Good 44 -15 Slow [99]
£8021 £2468 £1234 £617

*804 **RAYYAAN 18** [5] N A Graham 3-8-9 (80) R Cochrane 14/1: 422-11: 3 ch c Cadeaux Genereux - Anam (Persian Bold) Waited with, imprvd 2f out, strong run to lead ins fnl 1f, drvn out: recent Southwell wnr (mdn): dual rnr-up in '99 (mdns, rtd 86, with P Walwyn): eff at 6/7f, will stay 1m: acts on gd & soft grnd & on a sharp or gall trk: runs well fresh: progressive colt, in fine form. **90**
731 **CAMBERLEY 24** [10] P F I Cole 3-8-11 (82) J Fortune 8/1: 62-32: 3 b c Sri Pekan - NSX (Roi Danzig): Rear, gd hdwy to lead dist, worn down dying strides: bckd from 11/1, just btn in a thrilling fin: win at 1m? *shd* **91**
*839 **DIAMOND LOOK 11** [4] E A L Dunlop 3-8-11 (82) J Reid 5/1 FAV: 2-13: 3 b c Dayjur - Pedestal (High Line): Chsd ldrs, ev ch 1f out, kept on final 1f & not btn far: well bckd: acts on gd & gd/soft: lightly rcd. *1¼* **88**
3664} **QUEENS BENCH 232** [13] B Hanbury 3-9-2 (87)(t) Pat Eddery 12/1: 3311-4: Chsd ldrs, ev ch 1f out, no extra cl-home: '99 Beverley (fill mdn) & Epsom wnr (nurs h'cap, rtd 88): half-sister to a sprint wnr, dam won over 7/1m: eff at 7f on fast & gd/soft, 1m will suit: runs well fresh: wears a t-strap: spot-on next time. *2* **89**
736 **OCEAN RAIN 24** [12] 3-8-6 (77)(VIS) M Fenton 33/1: 105-05: Made most till dist, no extra: gd run in first time visor: '99 Haydock wnr (mdn auct, rtd 81 at best): eff at 6f on fast & gd/soft grnd, handles a gall trk: probably stays a stiff 7f, a drop back to 6f should suit: eff in a visor. *½* **78$**
792 **PROUD CHIEF 19** [18] 3-8-7 (78) K Darley 12/1: 000-26: Chds ldrs, ev ch dist, not qckn cl-home. *½* **78**
4476} **BABY BARRY 179** [20] 3-8-13 (84) S Sanders 25/1: 4012-7: Mid-div, imprvd over 1f out, no impress ins last: reapp: '99 Redcar wnr (mdn auct), subs 2nd at Doncaster (val stks, rtd 84): eff at 5/6f on firm, soft & f/sand: handles any trk, eff in blnks/visor, not today: can force the pace: may benefit from a drop back in trip. *½* **83**
888 **PERUVIAN JADE 6** [19] 3-8-3 (74) N Pollard 20/1: 44-648: Held up, no impress fnl 1f: qck reapp. *2½* **68**
4041} **BROMPTON BARRAGE 210** [21] 3-8-4 (75) P Fitzsimons (5) 33/1: 0640-9: Prom, ev ch dist, fdd: reapp: 4th at Kempton (mdn auct, rtd 81) in '99: half-brother to sev juv wnrs: handles soft grnd, 7f should suit. *shd* **69**
*792 **I PROMISE YOU 19** [17] 3-8-2 (73) A Nicholls (3) 14/1: 035-10: Nvr nr ldrs, fin 10th: btr 792. *nk* **66**
*794 **CINNAMON COURT 19** [6] 3-8-7 (78) Martin Dwyer 25/1: 00-10: Rear, nvr nr ldrs: fin 11th, btr 794. *nk* **70**
4140} **ALPHILDA 203** [14] 3-8-11 (82) M Hills 12/1: 2220-0: Hdwy from rear 2f out, sn btn: fin 12th: '99 Ayr wnr (nurs h'cap), rnr-up 4 times (rtd 85 at best): eff at 6f on fast & gd/soft grnd, 7f+ shld suit: handles a stiff/gall or sharp trk: with B Hills & capable of better. *½* **73**
4547} **RULE OF THUMB 172** [3] 3-8-13 (84) J F Egan 12/1: 16-0: Nvr troubled ldrs, fin 13th: reapp: twice rcd juv, won at Pontefract (mdn auct, rtd 82, debut): half-brother to a sprint wnr: dam scored over 5f: eff at 6f on gd grnd, runs well fresh: with G L Moore. *1¼* **72**
54 **DATURA 154** [9] 3-7-13 (70) J Mackay(7) 20/1: 2400-0: Outpcd, nvr featured in 14th: reapp, new stable. *1¼* **55**
792 **DIGITAL IMAGE 19** [8] 3-9-2 (87) R Hughes 25/1: 060-60: Nvr a factor in 15th: see 792. *nk* **71**
4445} **ABUZAID 181** [16] 3-9-2 (87) R Hills 7/1: 501-0: Hdwy from rear 2f out, btn dist: fin 16th, reapp. *¾* **69**
*840 **GRAND BAHAMIAN 11** [7] 3-9-0 (85) L Dettori 12/1: 010: Al outpcd, fin 19th: much btr 840. **0**
4427} **Aretino 182** [15] 3-9-7 (92) W R Swinburn 20/1: 4507} **Lord Pacal 176** [11] 3-9-7 (92) R Ffrench 25/1:
4364} **Royal Insult 187** [1] 3-9-0 (85) N Callan 20/1: 4130} **Joey Tribbiani 203** [2] 3-8-0 (71) G Bardwell 40/1:
21 ran Time 1m 27.33 (4.13) (Hamdan Al Maktoum) N A Graham Newmarket.

955

4.15 BTSME STKS 3YO (C) 7f str Good 44 -04 Slow
£6948 £2635 £1317 £599

4333} **MISRAAH 189** [6] Sir Michael Stoute 3-9-1 R Hills 8/11 FAV: 41-1: 3 ch c Lure - Dwell (Habitat): Held up, smooth hdwy to lead dist, eased cl-home & nearly caught: hvly bckd, reapp: twice rcd juv, Leicester mdn wnr (rtd 99+): 160,000gns half-brother to wnrs abroad, dam & sire milers: eff at 7f, 1m will suit: acts on gd & gd/soft grnd, runs well fresh: handles a stiff/gall trk: highly regarded colt who ran green today & reportedly ndd this: open to plenty more improvement, 3rd fav for the 2,000 Guineas. **108+**
4600} **FREE RIDER 166** [13] I A Balding 3-9-1 R Cochrane 6/1: 221-2: 3 b c Inchinor - Forever Roses (Forzando): Tried to make all, collared dist, rallied well & only just btn: reapp: '99 Windsor wnr (mdn, rtd 97+): eff at 7f, 1m will suit: acts on gd & hvy grnd, runs well fresh: handles any trk: useful, win again. *shd* **106**
4344} **SELKING 188** [2] K R Burke 3-8-11 N Callan 33/1: 3402-3: 3 ch c Selkirk - Stay That Way (Be My Guest): Rcd keenly & front rank, ev ch fnl 1f, no extra cl-home: reapp: '99 Carlisle wnr (mdn auct, rtd 88), subs rnr-up on the AW (rtd 93a): clearly stays 7f, rcd v keenly here & may benefit from a drop back to sprinting: acts on fast grnd & fibresand, probably handles soft: will be plcd to win races by v capable trainer. *2½* **97**
3558} **MOUNT ABU 240** [9] J H M Gosden 3-9-1 J Fortune 11/1: 1526-4: Trkd ldrs, ev ch 2f out, kept on fnl 1f: reapp: trained by P Chapple-Hyam in '99, won at Newbury (mdn), subs rnr-up in Gr 3 company in France (rtd 105): stays 7f on fast & gd/soft grnd: handles a gall trk: can rate more highly. *shd* **101**
3958} **SHABLAM 214** [10] 3-9-4 K Fallon 16/1: 31-5: Rdn in rear, imprvd 2f out, styd on strongly final 1f, nrst fin: reapp: twice rcd in '99, won at Ayr (stks, rtd 94): $100,000 purchase: eff at 7f, sure to relish 1m+: acts on firm & gd/soft grnd: longer priced stablemate of wnr, eye-catching effort over an inadequate 7f today: one to keep a close eye on when stepped up to 1m+. *hd* **104+**
4468} **ACROBATIC 179** [12] 3-9-1 W R Swinburn 20/1: 16-6: Hdwy from rear over 1f out, nrst fin: mkt drifter, reapp: twice rcd juv, Newbury mdn wnr on debut (rtd 87), subs 6th in Gr company: half-brother to a wng sprinter, dam a 6/7f wnr: eff at 6f, will stay 7f+: acts on firm grnd & can run well fresh: sharper for this useful reapp. *1* **99**
4466} **CEDAR MASTER 179** [3] 3-8-11 P Doe 33/1: 3024-7: Prom till outpcd after halfway, rallied ins last. *¾* **93**
*826 **MOON EMPEROR 13** [1] 3-9-1 J Stack 33/1: 545-18: Nvr a factor: see 826 (1m mdn, soft grnd). *nk* **96**
4175} **MERRY MERLIN 200** [5] 3-9-1 T Quinn 20/1: 15-9: Rcd keenly in bhd ldrs, btn dist: reapp. *1¼* **93**
2478} **AREYDHA 287** [4] 3-8-10 L Dettori 16/1: 100-0: Prom till fdd final 1½f: fin 10th, reapp. *shd* **88**
2447} **STEALTHY TIMES 290** [8] 3-8-6 Dean McKeown 50/1: 1-0: Prom 5f, fdd: fin 11th. *1¾* **80**
4376} **LOVE YOU TOO 186** [11] 3-8-6 J Reid 33/1: 4540-0: Chsd ldrs 5f, fdd into 12th: new stable. *½* **79**
735 **ABDERIAN 24** [7] 3-9-1 Pat Eddery 16/1: 142-50: Trkd ldrs 5f, wknd: fin last: see 735 (1m). *½* **87**
13 ran Time 1m 26.60 (3.40) (Hamdan Al Maktoum) Sir Michael Stoute Newmarket.

956

4.45 STETCHWORTH MDN 3YO (D) 6f str Good 44 +02 Fast
£5070 £1560 £780 £390

4112} **MAY CONTESSA 204** [2] D R C Elsworth 3-8-9 N Pollard 12/1: 35-1: 3 b f Bahri - Copper Creek (Habitat): Held up, gd hdwy 2f out, led ins fnl 1f, ran on strongly, rdn out: gd time: twice rcd in '99, plcd at Goodwood (fill mdn, rtd 80, debut): IR 135,000gns half-sister to smart sprinter Tipsy Creek: dam a 6f wnr: eff at 6f, 7f will suit: acts on gd, disapp on gd/soft: handles a sharp or gall trk, runs well fresh: can rate higher. **94**

NEWMARKET (ROWLEY) TUESDAY APRIL 18TH Righthand, Stiff, Galloping Track

808 **SAN SALVADOR 17** [3] J Noseda 3-9-0 L Dettori 11/4 FAV: -32: 3 b c Dayjur - Sheer Gold (Cutlass): 1½ 92
Trkd ldrs, imprvd to lead dist, not pace to repel wnr cl-home: well bckd tho' op 2/1: stays 6f, win soon.
-- **CORNER HOUSE** [8] A C Stewart 3-8-9 J Reid 12/1: -3: 3 gr f Lion Cavern - Snowing (Icecapade): 1¼ 83+
Rear, imprvd over 1f out, fin well, nvr nrr: op 8/1, debut: half-sister to useful 1m wnr Bomb Alaska: eff at 6f, will relish 7f/1m: handles a gall trk: sharper for this & one to keep in mind over 7f+ next time.
839 **ALMASHROUK 11** [5] K Mahdi 3-9-0 J Fortune 16/1: 40-664: Set pace till dist, no extra: see 839, 731. 1¾ 82$
-- **VILLA VIA** [11] 3-8-9 R Ffrench 33/1: -5: Chsd ldrs, wandered 2f out, fdd final 1f: debut: 15,000 gns half-sister to sev wnrs arnd 1m: with J Toller & sharper next time. 3½ 67
-- **MAGIC EAGLE** [7] 3-9-0 J F Egan 50/1: -6: Chsd ldrs, drifted left & fdd final 1½f: debut: dam a wng middle dist performer, sire a smart sprinter: with G L Moore. 1¾ 66
2069} **SUSSEX LAD 305** [9] 3-9-0 R Hughes 11/1: 60-7: Trkd ldrs, ev ch dist, wknd & eased: tchd 14/1, reapp: twice rcd juv, highly tried on final start (rtd 80): half-brother to sev wnrs, sire a high class juv: with R Hannon & clearly thought capable of something, now h'capped & may do better. nk 65
-- **SHARP LIFE** [6] 3-9-0 T Quinn 11/2: -8: Chsd ldrs till halfway: drifted from 3/1, debut: dam related to top class middle dist wnr Royal Anthem: with H Cecil & should do better. 2½ 58
3179} **ALASAN 256** [1] 3-9-0 K Fallon 7/2: 3-9: Dwelt, nvr a factor on reapp: well bckd: trained by L Cumani & plcd here at Newmarket (mdn, rtd 80+) on sole '99 start: dam a 1m/9f wnr in France: eff at 7f on gd grnd, will apprec 1m+: now with Sir M Stoute & should do better back over 7f+. 2½ 51
-- **SMILE ITS SHOWTIME** [10] 3-9-0 J Weaver 50/1: -0: Dwelt, al outpcd, fin 10th on debut. 7 31
-- **PRINCE NICO** [4] 3-9-0 R Cochrane 50/1: -0: Mid-div till btn 2f out: fin last, debut. 1¾ 26
11 ran Time 1m 13.35 (2.55) (Dgh Partnership) D R C Elsworth Whitsbury, Hants.

957 5.20 MUSEUM MDN 3YO (D) 1m2f str Good 44 -31 Slow
£5252 £1616 £808 £404

-- **BIEN ENTENDU** [8] H R A Cecil 3-9-0 T Quinn 2/1 FAV: 1: 3 b c Hernando - Entente Cordiale (Affirmed): 98+
Trkd ldrs till went on 2f out, sprinted clr, readily: hvly bckd, racecourse debut: 130,000gns purchase: middle dist bred, eff at 10f, 12f will suit: acts on gd grnd & on a gall trk: highly regarded colt who is reportedly a 'big baby': open to any amount of improvement, to the fore of Derby betting with this most promising debut.
4339} **AIR DEFENCE 189** [11] B W Hills 3-9-0 M Hills 11/2: 2-2: 3 br c Warning - Cruising Height (Shirley Heights): In tch, rdn & ev ch dist, kept on final 1f but not pace of impress wnr: op 3/1: rnr-up in a Leicester mdn (rtd 86+) on sole juv start: half-brother to smart middle dist/styrs High And Low & Corradini: eff at 10f on gd & gd/soft grnd, 12f will suit: runs well fresh: caught a tartar today, looks nailed on for similar. 3 92
4606} **ZAFONICS SONG 165** [7] Sir Michael Stoute 3-9-0 K Fallon 11/2: 4-3: 3 br c Zafonic - Savoureuse Lady (Caerleon): Chsd ldrs, outpcd by front 2 final 1f: nicely bckd tho' op 3/1: 4th in a Doncaster mdn (rtd 85+) on sole '99 start: half-brother to a 1m wnr abroad, dam a smart scorer: eff at 10f, 12f will suit: handles gd & hvy grnd: sure to learn from this & will win at least a mdn. 3 87
4339} **EJTITHAAB 189** [16] R W Armstrong 3-9-0 R Hills 25/1: 6-4: Rear, imprvd to chase ldrs 4f out, fdd ins last: 6th at Leicester (mdn, rtd 67, P Walwyn) sole '99 start: dam smart mid-dist performer: shld apprec 10f. 1½ 84
-- **CARNBREA DANCER** [3] 3-8-9 J F Egan 50/1: 5: Rear, styd on fnl 1½f, nvr nrr on debut: dam won over 12f/2m: sire a top class mid-dist performer: mid-dist bred filly who caught the eye staying on nicely. 2½ 76+
4076} **ACCEPTING 207** [12] 3-9-0 L Dettori 11/1: 02-6: Nvr a factor: op 8/1, reapp: rnr-up on fnl of 2 '99 starts (rtd 89): brother to a high class mid-dist wnr: eff at 9f on firm, bred for mid-dists: fitter next time. ¾ 79
833 **ST EXPEDIT 12** [5] 3-9-0 Pat Eddery 11/1: 3-27: Rcd keenly & prom, drifted right & fdd final 1½f: tchd 14/1: better expected after 833. shd 79
4452} **TROILUS 180** [6] 3-9-0 J Fortune 33/1: 50-8: Led 3f, remnd prom till wknd over 1f out. 1¾ 75
4171} **PENTAGONAL 201** [14] 3-9-0 W R Swinburn 12/1: 0-9: In tch, wknd fnl 1½f, btn when hmpd cl home. shd 75
4556} **FOREST FRIENDLY 171** [10] 3-8-9 R Cochrane 16/1: 4-0: Hdwy from rear 3f out, btn dist: fin 10th. ½ 69
544 **SHARP RISK 59** [4] 3-9-0 R Winston 66/1: 530: Rcd keenly & trkd ldrs, led after 3f till hdd 2f out, wkng when hmpd cl-home: fin 11th, 8 wk abs. ½ 73
-- **TARBOUSH** [13] 3-9-0 W Ryan 12/1: 0: Hdwy from rear 3f out, btn fnl 2f: 12th, stablemate of wnr. shd 73
-- **TAKWIN** [9] 3-9-0 (t) J Weaver 50/1: 0: Al in rear, fin 13th: debut, t-strap. 8 61
-- **PHANTOM RAIN** [1] 3-8-9 J Reid 16/1: 0: Dwelt, al bhnd: fin 14th on debut: stablemate of 2nd. 1 55
3581} **MONKEY BUSINESS 236** [2] 3-8-9 R Ffrench 50/1: 34-0: Rcd keenly & in tch 1m, wknd into 15th: reapp. 3½ 50
4526} **AFTER THE BLUE 174** [15] 3-9-0 W Supple 33/1: 6-0: Al in rear, fin last on reapp. 6 46
16 ran Time 2m 09.62 (7.52) (Niarchos Family) H R A Cecil Newmarket

FOLKESTONE TUESDAY APRIL 18TH Righthand, Sharpish, Undulating Track

Official Going SOFT (GOOD/SOFT In Places). Stalls: Str Crse - Stands Side; Rnd Crse - Outside.
After 1st race fields stayed far side, which appears to have a significant advantage when ground is soft.

958 1.45 LEVY BOARD APPR HCAP 3YO+ 0-60 (G) 6f Soft 110 -33 Slow [60]
£1879 £537 £268 3 yo rec 11lb

353 **MUDDY WATER 90** [13] D Marks 4-9-6 (52) R Naylor (5) 16/1: 462-01: 4 b f Salse - Rainbow Fleet (Nomination) Outpcd far side till ran on appr fnl 2f, led dist, ran on well: 1st win, dual '98 rnr-up (mdn, rtd 56a, h'cap, rtd 53), unrcd juv: eff at 6/7f, tried 9f: acts on fast, soft grnd & fibresand, suited by sharp trks. 57
872 **MARENGO 7** [3] M J Polglase 6-9-5 (51) Hayley Turner (8) 10/1: 062232: 6 b g Never So Bold - Born To Dance (Dancing Brave) Off the pace far side till ran on strongly ent fnl 2f, styd on but al held by wnr: op 8/1, clr rem, quick reapp: holding his form well, fine run from a poor low draw: see 183. 1 52
790 **LEONIE SAMUAL 19** [8] R J Hodges 5-8-10 (42) P Shea 10/1: 00-43: 5 b m Safawan - Hy Wilma (Jalmood) Bhd far side, kept on fnl 2f, nvr nrr: tchd 14/1 on h'cap bow: handles soft, return to 7f will suit. 4 35
4439} **TOBLERSONG 181** [16] Mrs L Stubbs 5-9-7 (53)(t) Kristin Stubbs (3) 10/1: 0050-4: Prom far side, onepace appr fnl 1f: tchd 20/1 on reapp: thrice rnr-up in '99 for C Dwyer (h'caps, rtd 64): last won in '97 at Epsom & Yarmouth (mdn & stks, rtd 97, R Akehurst): eff at 6/7.5f, tried further: acts on firm & gd/soft grnd, without visor, best in a t-strap now: goes on any trk, likes sharp ones & is v well h'capped. 1½ 43
*872 **MISS BANANAS 7** [12] 5-9-1 (47)(7ex) D Meah 12/1: -60015: Front rank far side, led appr fnl 2f, till 1f out, fdd: op 8/1, quick reapp with a penalty: btr 872. 1¼ 34
910 **GRACE 4** [7] 6-9-4 (50) C Catlin 13/2: 02-446: Chsd ldrs till lost pl halfway, styd on fnl 1f despite drifing to stands isde, nvr nrr: not disgraced from a poor low draw, worth another chance after 910. ½ 36

897   **NINEACRES** 5 [10] 9-9-8 (54)(bl) K Dalgleish 4/1 FAV: 440137: Led till 2½f out, grad wknd: op 3/1,   1½   37
quick reapp, stablemate 6th, faster grnd suits: see 802.
790   **ABSOLUTE FANTASY** 19 [9] 4-8-13 (45)(bl) D Kinsella (3) 12/1: 626028: Nvr troubled ldrs: btr 790.   1   25
802   **BALI STAR** 18 [15] 5-9-4 (50) R Thomas 6/1: 000-29: In tch far side till appr fnl 1f: op 4/1: see 802.   1½   27
763   **HALF TONE** 21 [6] 8-8-11 (43)(bl) M Worrell 16/1: 050-00: Nvr going pace: 10th: '99 Lingfield wnr   1½   17
(h'cap, rtd 64a & 57): '98 wnr at Sandown & Bath (h'caps, rtd 64 & 66a): eff at 5/6f, tried further: acts on firm,
hvy grnd, both AWs: can run well fresh & is best in blnks: likes Sandown & coming late off a furious pace.
746   **CONTRARY MARY** 22 [1] 5-9-11 (57) D Glennon 10/1: 345-00: Al bhd stands side: 12th, op 8/1, top-   0
weight: '99 wnr here at Folkestone (class stks, rtd 67): '98 wnr at Lingfield (turf h'cap) & Pontefract (clmr, subs
disq, rtd 74 & 59a): eff at 6/7f on firm & soft, likes sharp trks, handles easy: can force the pace: poor draw.
816   Montendre 15 [4] 13-9-4 (50) G Sparkes 16/1:   3855} **Rocklands Lane** 222 [11] 4-8-12 (44) D Watson 25/1:
628   **Sisao** 45 [2] 4-9-6 (52)(bl) Michael Doyle (5) 16/1:
14 ran   Time 1m 19.6 (8.6)   (R J F Brothers)   D Marks Lambourn, Berks

---

959   **2.15 CHATHAM CLAIMER 3YO (F)**   **5f**   **Soft 110   -22 Slow**
          £2268   £648   £324

3579}   **BREEZY LOUISE** 236 [6] R J Hodges 3-8-4 (BL) S Drowne 10/1: 6250-1: 3 br f Dilum - Louise Moillon   69
(Mansingh) Prom, led appr fnl 1f, shaken up, readily: op 6/1, wng reapp in 1st time blnks: '99 Windsor
wnr (sell, rtd 66, AW nurs rnr-up, rtd 63a): stays 6f, best at 5f: acts on fast, soft grnd & fibresand, sharp
trks suit: best up with the pace, with/without blnks: runs well fresh.
3472}   **ARGENT FACILE** 242 [5] D J S Cosgrove 3-9-7 (t) S Carson (5) 4/1: 0410-2: 3 b c Midhish - Rosinish   1¾   81
(Lomond) Chsd ldrs, rdn 2f out, styd on for 2nd but no ch with wnr: op 5/1 on reapp: '99 Leicester wnr
(nurs, rtd 85): eff at 5f, worth a try at 6f: acts on fast, soft grnd, with/without t-strap, not blnks.
830   **PRINCESS VICTORIA** 12 [4] N A Callaghan 3-8-0 P M Quinn (5) 7/2: 26-333: 3 b f Deploy - Scierpan   ¾   58
(Sharpen Up) Struggled to go pace, prog appr fnl 1f, kept on without threatening: clr of rem but found this
drop back to a sharp 5f an inadequate test: acts on gd, soft grnd & equitrack: see 830, 165.
619   **MINIMUS TIME** 48 [7] T M Jones 3-7-11 (bl) N Carlisle 10/1: -01464: Led till appr fnl 1f, fdd: 7 wk abs.   5   45$
652   **JUDIAM** 41 [1] 3-8-12 L Newman (5) 6/4 FAV: 021-45: In tch till no extra appr fnl 1f: 6 wk abs, btr 652.   2½   55
777   **PAPE DIOUF** 20 [3] 3-8-7 (bl) G Hind 8/1: 014106: Al bhd: tchd 10/1, see 619 (equitrack sell).   4   42
813   **JUST MAC** 15 [2] 3-8-11 J P Spencer 16/1: -06067: Sn struggling: op 10/1, back in trip, see 221.   2½   41
7 ran   Time 1m 05.0 (6.6)   (R J Hodges)   R J Hodges Charlton Adam, Somerset

---

960   **2.45 GILLINGHAM CLASS STKS 3YO+ 0-70 (E)**   **5f**   **Soft 110   +06 Fast**
          £2817   £805   £402   3 yo rec 10lb

838   **FAUTE DE MIEUX** 11 [7] E A Wheeler 5-9-3 S Carson (5) 9/4 FAV: 00-601: 5 ch g Beveled - Supereme   77
Rose (Frimley Park) Grabbed far rail & easily made all: well bckd from 7/2, gd time, val 8L+: '99 Windsor
wnr (stks, rtd 77 in a h'cap, D Morris): dual '98 rnr-up (mdns, rtd 71, A Jones): eff at 5/6f, tried 7f: acts on
firm, hvy grnd, any trk, likes sharp ones: suited forcing the pace.
4216}   **CORNDAVON** 199 [5] M L W Bell 4-9-0 C Carver (5) 9/2: 3000-2: 4 b f Sheikh Albadou - Ferber's   5   68
Follies (Saratoga Six) Chsd ldrs, nvr any impress: op 7/2, clr rem, reapp: '99 Warwick wnr (mdn, rtd 76, M F
Godley): plcd in '98 (nurs, rtd 77): eff at 5/6f, tried 7f: acts on firm & gd grnd, handles soft, any trk.
838   **SHUDDER** 11 [6] R J Hodges 5-9-3 O Urbina 7/2: 000-43: 5 b g Distant Relative - Oublier L'Ennui   6   59
(Bellman) Handy far side, same pace fnl 2f: nicely bckd tho' op 5/2: unsuited by drop back to 5f on soft grnd?
746   **SUPREME ANGEL** 22 [4] M P Muggeridge 5-9-3 (bl) D Griffiths 8/1: 0-3104: Nvr trbled ldrs: tchd 10/1.   ½   58
852   **MARSHALL ST CYR** 8 [3] 3-8-7 R Mullen 12/1: 25-005: Bhd after 2f: back in trip: '99 rnr-up   8   42
(auct mdn, rtd 76): eff at 5f on gd/soft grnd: with P Evans.
852   **GREAT WHITE** 8 [1] 3-8-7 L Newman (5) 20/1: 000-06: Dwelt, nvr on terms: plcd on debut last   6   30
term (mdn, rtd 79): eff at 5f, tried 6f, bred for 7f/1m: handles fast grnd: with R Hannon.
897   **DOUBLE O** 5 [2] 6-9-3 (bl) D McGaffin (7) 4/1: 30-407: Nvr dangerous: quick reapp, see 91.   4   22
7 ran   Time 1m 03.6 (5.2)   (Dagfell Properties Ltd)   E A Wheeler Whitchurch On Thames, Oxon

---

961   **3.20 PRIVY COUNCILLOR MDN DIV 1 3YO+ (D)**   **7f str**   **Soft 110   -07 Slow**
          £2646   £756   £378   3 yo rec 13lb

4333}   **TAP** 189 [8] J A R Toller 3-8-10 S Whitworth 9/4 FAV: 2-1: 3 b c Emarati - Pubby (Doctor Wall)   87+
Grabbed far rail, made ev yard & won v easily: drifted from 11/10 on reapp: 10L rnr-up to 2,000 Guineas
fancy Misraah sole '99 start (mdn, rtd 80): eff at 7f, bred to apprec mid-dists: acts on soft grnd, sharp/undul
trk: clrly effective forcing the pace & runs well fresh: looks decent, likely to rate higher.
415   **AL KING SLAYER** 81 [10] T P McGovern 3-8-10 I Mongan (5) 25/1: 02: 3 b c Batshoof - Top   7   75
Sovereign (High Top) Slow away, sn racing in 2nd, rdn 2f out, hung right & easily outpcd by wnr: turf debut,
12 wk abs, new stable: prob handles soft grnd & a return to 1m shld suit.
4312}   **SALZGITTER** 190 [3] H Candy 3-8-5 C Rutter 3/1: 5-3: 3 b f Salse - Anna Of Brunswick (Rainbow Quest)   6   60
Bhd, shkn up 3f out, styd on thro' btn horses: op 2/1, clr rem: 7L 5th to current 1,000 Guineas fav Petrushka
sole '99 start (fill mdn, rtd 82): bred for 1m+, handles gd/sft: poor draw today, sharper over further next time.
1479}   **BAHRAIN** 332 [9] J W Hills 4-9-9 M Henry 14/1: 0/50-4: Al around same place: op 10/1: promise   9   51
1st of 2 '99 starts for A Jarvis (mdn, rtd 80): well btn side '98 start for Sir M Prescott: needs h'caps.
4603}   **FARRIERS GAMBLE** 166 [13] 4-9-4 D Sweeney 50/1: 0-5: Ran in snatches, outpcd fnl 2f: no form.   2   42
4505}   **THE JAM SAHEB** 176 [2] 3-8-10 O Urbina 16/1: 00-6: Nvr troubled ldrs: no form, new stable.   2   43
840   **INDIANA JONES** 11 [4] 3-8-10 M Tebbutt 10/1: 07: Nvr a factor: one more run for h'cap mark.   hd   43
829   **HAIKAL** 12 [12] 3-8-10 G Duffield 4/1: 0-08: Chsd ldrs till 3f out, eased before dist: op 10/1, h'caps next.   1½   41
4072}   **BALIDARE** 207 [11] 3-8-5 S Drowne 50/1: 00-9: Bhd from halfway: reapp, no form.   16   16
784   **TALIBAN** 20 [5] 4-9-9 M Roberts 6/1: 60: Al bhd: 10th: see 784.   25   0
920   **Ceinwen** 3 [1] 5-9-4 Claire Bryan (5) 50/1:   1731} **Larimar Bay** 320 [7] 4-9-9 R Mullen 50/1:
4310} **Final Kiss** 190 [6] 3-8-10 A Whelan 50/1:
13 ran   Time 1m 32.4 (8.2)   (Philip Wroughton)   J A R Toller Newmarket

---

962   3.55 PRIVY COUNCILLOR MDN DIV 2 3YO+ (D)   7f str   Soft 110   -23 Slow
£2632   £752   £376   3 yo rec 13lb

759   **MOON SOLITAIRE 21** [8] E A L Dunlop 3-8-10 G Carter 4/7 FAV: 6-41: 3 b c Night Shift - Gay   87
Fantastic (Ela Mana Mou) Prom, pushed along 2f out, styd on ins last to lead towards fin, shade readily:
hvly bckd from 9/4: promise both prev starts, incl sole juv run (mdn, rtd 75): brother to a 6f wnr, half-brother
to a 12f wnr: eff at 7f, shapes like further is going to suit: goes on soft grnd, shrp/undul trk: improving.
3942} **GLORY QUEST 215** [1] Miss Gay Kelleway 3-8-10 M Tebbutt 7/2: -33-2: 3 b c Quest For Fame - Sonseri   1   84
(Prince Tenderfoot) Cl-up, led 2f out, under press before dist, hdd & no extra well ins last: clr rem, big drifter
from 1/1 on reapp: 3rd both '99 starts (mdn auct, rtd 93): half-brother to a 7f wnr, dam a sprinter, sire won
Derby: eff at 6/7f on firm & soft grnd: gd effort from a poor low draw, shld find similar.
4603} **SPELLBINDER 166** [5] G B Balding 4-9-4 S Drowne 14/1: 0-3: 4 b f Magical Wonder - Shamanka   5   69
(Shernazar) Off the pace, kept on unders hands & heels fnl 2f, nvr on terms: reapp: well btn sole '99 start
(mdn, rtd 57): dam 10f wnr: type to do better over further in h'caps.
837   **MOBO BACO 11** [12] R J Hodges 3-8-10 O Urbina 14/1: 04: Held up, chsd ldrs halfway till ent fnl 2f.   1¼   72
884   **BILLY BATHWICK 6** [3] 3-8-10 (BL) G Hind 7/1: 06-555: Led after 3f till 2f out, fdd: tchd 14/1, blnkd.   hd   72
--   **SLIEVE BLOOM** [11] J A Carter 16/1: 6: Slow away, prog & in tch after 3f, no extra 2f out: ¾   71
Dancing Dissident newcomer with T Mills.
837   **DISTANT FLAME 11** [4] 3-8-5 G Duffield 20/1: 0-07: Chsd ldrs till 2f out: poor draw, no form.   11   50
--   **CROSS LUGANA** [9] 4-9-4 R Mullen 50/1: 0/8: At bhd: 2 year abs, no form.   22   25
4504} **REKEN 176** [2] 4-9-9 P McCabe 100/1: 0000-9: In tch till halfway: stiff task, reapp, no form up to 10f   10   20
--   **MAX THE MAN** [7] 3-8-10 Claire Bryan (5) 33/1: 0: Nvr dngrs: 10th, debut: Bold Arrangement colt.   ½   19
748   **FAIRFIELD BAY 22** [10] 4-9-9 (BL) D R McCabe 50/1: 000/00: Led 3f, sn lost place: 11th, blinkered.   1   18
841   **BEACH BABY 11** [6] 3-8-5 R Brisland (5) 66/1: 0-0000: Sn struggling: 12th, no form.   7   0
12 ran   Time 1m 33.5 (9.3)   (Maktoum Al Maktoum)   E A L Dunlop Newmarket

---

963   4.25 GRAVESEND HCAP 4YO+ 0-70 (E)   1m7f92y   Soft 110   -68 Slow   [61]
£3115   £890   £445   4 yo rec 3 lb

860   **VERSATILITY 8** [15] Dr J R J Naylor 7-9-0 (47) G Duffield 5/1: 60-531: 7 b m Teenoso - Gay Criselle   54
(Decoy Boy) Cl-up, led 5f out, grad drew clr, easing down: slow time: '99 Warwick wnr (h'cap, rtd 53, G McCourt):
prev won over hdles at Ludlow (nov sell, 2m, soft): eff at 14f/2m: acts on gd/soft & soft grnd, likes sharp trks.
788   **SHERIFF 20** [7] J W Hills 9-9-3 (50) M Henry 20/1: /24-02: 9 b g Midyan - Daisy Warwick (Ribot)   12   51
Bhd, imprvd after 1m & took rnr-up spot appr fnl 1f, nvr nr wnr: prob ran to best, handles soft grnd: see 788.
726   **NATURAL EIGHT 24** [1] Jamie Poulton 6-9-6 (53) O Urbina 5/1: 61-633: 6 b g In The Wings - Fenny   2½   52
Rough (Home Guard) Well in rear till styd on fnl 3f, nvr in it: op 7/2: gave ldrs too much rope: see 424, 168.
*885   **GRAND CRU 6** [12] J Cullinan 9-8-10 (43)(bl)(6ex) P M Quinn (5) 4/1 FAV: 300014: Held up, late   5   39
hdwy thro' btn horses, nvr on terms: quick reapp with a penalty, see 885.
--   **WASSL STREET** [9] 8-9-1 (48) L Newman (5) 16/1: 000-75: Chsd ldrs, no extra fnl 4f: hdles fit,   8   39
dual wnr in 96/97 (stays 3m2f, fast & hvy, rtd 102h at best): no form in 3 Flat starts nearly 5 years ago.
4407} **MISTER PQ 183** [13] 4-8-10 (46) A Daly 12/1: 0540-6: In tch till 4f out: reapp: '99 Brighton wnr   4   34
(h'cap, rtd 52): rtd 65 in '98 (nov auct): eff at 12f on gd/soft grnd: with J G Smyth-Osbourne.
737   **KENT 22** [11] 5-8-12 (45) D Harrison 8/1: 121647: Handy till appr str: turf reapp: see 502.   1   32
825   **GOLDEN ACE 13** [2] 7-8-3 (36) (tbl) A Mackay 12/1: 50-458: Chsd ldrs till 4f out: best at 12f, see 791.   8   18
--   **ZAFARELLI** [16] 6-9-1 (48)(vis) S Whitworth 50/1: 5160/9: Nvr troubled ldrs: hdles fit, 98/99 wnr at   5   27
Folkestone & Plumpton (h'caps, rtd 97h, 2m1f, soft & hvy grnd, blnks): nr 3 year Flat abs, '97 wnr here at
Folkestone (h'cap, rtd 60): eff at 2m on firm & gd/soft grnd: with J Jenkins.
4403} **JOLI FLYERS 183** [6] 6-8-11 (44) S Drowne 11/1: 0520-0: Led till 5f out, sn btn: 10th, op 20/1,   3   21
14 wk hdles abs (plcd in 2m/2m1f novs, soft grnd, rtd 108h): '99 rnr-up (appr h'cap, rtd 46, V Soane): '98
Kempton wnr (h'cap, rtd 49): eff up with/forcing the pace at 12/14f, poss stays 2m: acts on gd/soft & soft.
788   **CLASSIC REFERENDUM 20** [4] 6-9-5 (52) J P Spencer 8/1: 000-00: Nvr in it: 13th, op 6/1: no form in   0
this country, ex-Irish, '99 wnr at Leopardstown (mdn) & Wexford (h'cap): eff at 13/14f on fast & gd/soft grnd.
748   **Red Bordeaux 22** [8] 5-9-7 (54) A Clark 33/1:   848   **Major Attraction 10** [3] 5-8-7 (40)(bl) A McCarthy(3) 50/1:
893   **Grey Buttons 5** [14] 5-8-6 (39) J Tate 50/1:   748   **Agiotage 22** [5] 4-9-10 (60) G Faulkner (3) 25/1:
853   **Dear Prudence 8** [10] 4-8-7 (43) A Beech (5) 25/1:
16 ran   Time 3m 44.8 (27.6)   (Magno-Pulse Ltd)   Dr J R J Naylor Shrewton, Wilts

---

964   4.55 DARTFORD FILLIES MDN 3YO+ (D)   1m4f   Soft 110   -67 Slow
£2758   £788   £394   3 yo rec 20lb4 yo rec 1 lb

4536} **SKIMRA 173** [7] R Guest 3-8-4 G Duffield 9/4: 26-1: 3 b f Hernando - Skuld (Kris)   78
Well plcd, led 2½f out, hard rdn to repel rnr-up in last: nicely bckd tho' op 6/4, slow time, reapp: rnr-up
1st of 2 juv starts (rtd 77 at best): clrly apprec step up to 12f on soft grnd & looks a genuine sort.
4473} **BUSY LIZZIE 179** [6] J L Dunlop 3-8-4 G Carter 15/2: 00-2: 3 b f Sadler's Wells - Impatiente   hd   77
(Vaguely Noble) Held up, prog 4f out, went after wnr 2f out, styd on, just failed: op 10/1, well clr of rem on
reapp: unplcd both '99 starts: sister to useful, late-maturing stayer Eminence Grise: eff at 12f, shapes like
further will suit: acts on soft grnd & runs well fresh: shld find similar.
832   **SELIANA 12** [5] G Wragg 4-9-9 M Roberts 7/4 FAV: 0/3-23: 4 b f Unfuwain - Anafi (Slip Anchor)   20   62
Early ldr, again ent fnl 5f till before fnl 2f, fdd: op 5/2: drop back to 10f may suit now: see 832.
4453} **AWTAAN 180** [2] M P Tregoning 3-8-4 R Perham (5) 33: 43-4: Stumbled leaving stalls but led after 1f   29   42
till appr fnl 4f, sn btn: drifted from 11/10 on reapp: promise both '99 starts (fill mdn, rtd 91): eff at 1m,
bred for further (sister to a 12f wnr): handles gd/soft grnd.
814   **FAY 15** [3] 3-8-4 D Sweeney 14/1: 65: Chsd ldrs till 4f out: up in trip: see 814.   23   27
204   **SHARAVAWN 122** [1] 3-8-4 Joanna Badger(7) 50/1: 0000-6: Al bhd: reapp, new stable, no form, incl blnkd.3½   25
848   **LADY BENSON 10** [4] 7-9-10 (t) A McCarthy (3) 50/1: 000-47: Nvr in it: flattered 848.   2   24
7 ran   Time 2m 52.7 (21.2)   (Miss K Rausing)   R Guest Newmarket

314

FOLKESTONE   TUESDAY APRIL 18TH   Righthand, Sharpish, Undulating Track

965   5.30 BILSINGTON HCAP 4YO+ 0-70 (E)   1m1f149y   Soft 110   -60 Slow   [69]
£3395   £970   £485

793   **ADMIRALS PLACE 19** [14]   H J Collingridge 4-9-9 (64) G Carter 11/4 FAV: -12231: 4 ch c Perugino - Royal   **68**
Daughter (High Top) Trkd ldrs, ran on to lead dist, narrowly but snugly: tchd 5/1, slow time: earlier won at
Lingfield (AW class stks, rtd 67a at best): '99 wnr at Lingfield (mdn h'cap, rtd 59a) & Beverley (h'cap, rtd 65,
R Armstrong): eff at 1m/10f, tried 12f: acts on gd, soft grnd & both AWs: goes on any trk, likes sharp ones.

786   **HINDI 20** [15]   N A Graham 4-9-8 (63) G Duffield 12/1: 456-02: 4 b g Indian Ridge - Tootsiepop   hd   **65**
(Robellino) Chsd ldrs, drvn to chall appr fnl 1f, styd on but being held: op 25/1: gd run, eff at 9.5f on soft.

931   **RIVER ENSIGN 3** [2]   W M Brisbourne 7-8-11 (52)(6ex) P M Quinn (5) 4/1: 160103: 7 b rm River God -   1   **52**
Ensigns Kit (Saucy Kit) Sn led, under press 2f out, hdd dist, onepace: tchd 7/1, clr rem, quick reapp with a
penalty: back to form back up in trip: see 859.

855   **PLURALIST 8** [13]   W Jarvis 4-9-13 (68) M Tebbutt 6/1: 621-24: Chsd ldrs, outpcd appr fnl 1f: op 4/1,   5   **61**
top-weight: prefers faster grnd & prob further nowadays: see 196.

618   **MY BOLD BOYO 48** [9]   5-9-5 (60) O Urbina 16/1: 0-4405: Prom, btn appr fnl 2, eased: 7 wk abs: see 268. 9   **43**

596   **TROIS ELLES 52** [7]   4-8-4 (45) A Mackay 12/1: 03-036: Held up, prog 4f out, btn 3f out: 7 wk abs.   2   **25**

710   **COL WOODY 26** [10]   4-9-5 (60)(bl) R Studholme (5) 25/1: 206-07: Nvr a factor: recent blnkd jumps rnr.   ¾   **39**

816   **LEOFRIC 15** [3]   5-8-4 (45)(bl) R Fitzgerald (4) 12/1: 40-358: Handy till 3f out: not get 9.5f on soft?   6   **17**

748   **DIAMOND FLAME 22** [5]   6-9-0 (55) M Roberts 8/1: 20-009: Wide, nvr better than mid-div: see 681.   4   **28**

3584}   **DR MARTENS 236** [1]   6-8-10 (51) L Newton 20/1: 0006-0: In tch, not much room 5f out, sn btn: ¾   **17**
10th on reapp: no worthwhile form since '98 Windsor wnr (mdn, rtd 85, L Cumani): eff at 1m on fast grnd.

893   **GRIEF 5** [12]   7-9-10 (65)(bl) D Sweeney 10/1: 013-00: Chsd ldrs till halfway: 11th, qck reapp, blnkd.   nk   **30**

3950}   **SWING BAR 215** [4]   7-8-7 (48) Claire Bryan (5) 12/1: 4100-0: Al bhd: 12th, reapp: '99 Beverley wnr   4   **8**
(appr mdn h'cap, rtd 51), Worcester hdles wnr (2m sell h'cap on fast, rtd 76h): eff at 1m/10f on gd & fast grnd.

817   **LIONESS 15** [6]   4-9-13 (68) S Drowne 25/1: 430-00: Nvr in it: 13th, stablemate 12th: plcd   18   **13**
for J Fanshawe last term (auct mdn, rtd 76 at best): eff at 1m/9f on gd & firm grnd.

187   **THE THIRD CURATE 125** [11]   5-8-10 (51) J P Spencer 10/1: 0000-0: Early ldr, lost place 5f out: last.   2   **0**

14 ran   Time 2m 44.4 (16.4)   (C G Donovan)   H J Collingridge Exning, Suffolk

NEWMARKET (ROWLEY)   WEDNESDAY APRIL 19TH   Righthand, Stiff, Galloping Track

Official Going   GOOD/SOFT. Stalls: Far Side.

966   2.05 HEIDSIECK RTD HCAP 4YO+ 0-105 (B)   7f str   Good/Soft 61   +08 Fast   [107]
£10138   £3845   £1922   £874

725   **PRESENT LAUGHTER 25** [12]   P F I Cole 4-8-6 (85) L Newman (5) 14/1: 500-41: 4 b c Cadeaux Genereux -   **89**
Ever Genial (Brigadier Gerard) Al cl-up, led just ins fnl 1f, styd on well, rdn out: '99 wnr at Warwick (mdn, reapp,
rtd 88): eff at 5f, suited by 7f now on gd, soft & on any trk: runs well fresh: useful, in gd form.

733   **MUCHEA 25** [18]   M R Channon 6-9-7 (100) T Quinn 12/1: 000-02: 6 ch h Shalford - Bargouzine (Hotfoot)   ½   **103**
Handy, hdwy over 1f out, kept on ins fnl 1f, just failed: wl h'capped on best form (former Gr 3 wnr): see 733.

734   **NIGRASINE 25** [20]   J L Eyre 6-9-7 (100)(bl) J Fortune 33/1: 400-03: 6 b h Mon Tresor - Early Gales   ½   **102**
(Precocious) Set pace, rdn & collared just ins fnl 1f, kept on, only btn 1L: fine run, tough, rtd 112 in '99.

4620}   **CARIBBEAN MONARCH 165** [10]   Sir Michael Stoute 5-8-13 (92) K Fallon 10/1: /040-4: Waited with,   shd   **94+**
short of room over 2f out, kept on well over 1f out, nrst fin: reapp: rtd 84 when 4th on 2nd of only 4 '99 starts:
'98 wnr at Newmarket (mdn) & Windsor (h'cap, rtd 95): eff at 6f/1m on fast, soft grnd & has run well fresh on
any trk: must go close next time with a more positive ride.

895   **WEALTHY STAR 6** [2]   5-8-9 (88)(t) J Reid 16/1: 00-055: Cl-up centre, kept on same pace fnl 2f.   ½   **89**

208   **CHEWIT 123** [17]   8-8-4 (83)(3oh) R Fitzgerald (3) 33/1: 0035-6: Dwelt, sn in tch, kept on appr fnl   ½   **83**
1f, nvr dngrs: 4 mth abs: on a winning mark, sharper for this & should be placed to advantage: see 137.

733   **TAMMAM 25** [16]   4-8-10 (89) J P Spencer 50/1: 534-07: Waited with, eff over 1f out, kept on same pace   1¼   **87**
ins last: now with Mrs L Stubbs: rcd 4 times in '99, won at Chester (mdn, rtd 95): eff at 7f, crying out for
further & stays 10.3f on firm, prob handles soft: acts on any trk: tried blnks: will relish a return to further.

4395}   **PERSIANO 186** [8]   5-8-13 (92) D Harrison 16/1: 3050-8: Waited with, effort 2f out, onepace: plcd   ½   **89**
twice last trm (rtd 101 at best, h'cap): '98 wnr at Warwick, Salisbury & Doncaster (h'caps, rtd 100): all 3 wins
at 7f, stays 1m on firm, gd/soft: acts on any trk: has run poorly in a visor: useful at best.

834   **PREMIER BARON 13** [5]   5-8-4 (83) G Carter 14/1: 20-149: Rear, kept on nicely fnl 2f, nvr nrr: encouraging. ½   **79**

834   **TEMERAIRE 13** [6]   5-8-4 (83) J F Egan 11/1: 10-020: In tch, rdn over 2f out, no impress: 10th,   1¼   **77**
nicely bckd: rnr-up in this race last term off a 5lb higher mark & better expected: btn 834.

4395}   **MAYARO BAY 186** [13]   4-9-3 (96) R Hughes 12/1: 4632-0: Waited with, rdn over 2f out, no impress: 11th on   nk   **89**
reapp: '99 scorer at Goodwood (h'cap, rtd 98), also plcd sev times: '98 wnr at Warwick (mdn, rtd 84): eff
over 7f/1m on firm, gd/soft & on any trk: has run well fresh: tough & consistent, has a turn of foot.

728   **MARSAD 25** [3]   6-8-13 (92) P Doe 14/1: 330-50: Waited with, brief effort 2f out, sn btn: 12th.   hd   **84**

733   **SALTY JACK 25** [7]   6-8-7 (86) Martin Dwyer 16/1: 021300: Hld up, rdn 2f out, no impress: see 733.   ½   **77**

4423}   **ARCTIC CHAR 184** [21]   4-9-5 (98) Pat Eddery 20/1: 3052-0: Handy, rdn & wknd 2f out: reapp: won   nk   **88**
1st 2 in '99, at Leicester (fillies mdn) & Kempton (fillies stks), subs rnr-up in Listed company (rtd 104 at best):
eff over 6/7f on fast, soft & on a stiff or easy trk: has run well fresh: v useful at best.

725   **ADJUTANT 25** [11]   5-9-0 (93) T G McLaughlin 13/2 FAV: 313-30: Handy, rdn & wknd well over 1f out: ½   **82**
now with N Littmoden, morning gamble & better expected after 725 (all wins at 7f).

728   **AL MUALLIM 25** [15]   6-9-4 (97) A McGlone 14/1: 020-30: Bhd, rdn over 2f out, sn btn: 16th, much   3½   **80**
better than this, especially on a sounder surface: see 728.

733   **Kuwait Dawn 25** [19] 4-8-7 (86) R Hills 33/1:   728   **Magic Rainbow 25** [1] 5-8-7 (86) M Fenton 20/1:
4401}   **Tayif 186** [4] 4-9-4 (97)(t) R Cochrane 16/1:   4377}   **Undeterred 187** [9] 4-9-3 (96) R Mullen 33/1:
728   **Lone Piper 25** [14] 5-9-2 (95) L Dettori 20/1:
21 ran   Time 1m 26.92 (3.72)   (Penelope, Viscountess Portman)   P F I Cole Whatcombe, Oxon.

315

NEWMARKET (ROWLEY) WEDNESDAY APRIL 19TH Righthand, Stiff, Galloping Track

967 **2.35 GR 3 EARL OF SEFTON STKS 4YO+ (A) 1m1f str Good/Soft 61 -02 Slow**
£20300 £7700 £3850 £1750

4375} **INDIAN LODGE 187** [9] Mrs A J Perrett 4-8-10 M J Kinane 10/1: 0211-1: 4 b c Grand Lodge - Repetitious **116**
(Northfields) Led 1f, cl-up, led over 2f out, sprinted clr appr fnl 1f, readily: reapp: progressive late in '99, won at Newbury, Yarmouth & Newmarket (2, Listed, rtd 112): rtd 94 in '98: v eff over 1m/9f, shld get further: acts on gd & gd/soft, handles firm & likes a stiff trk, esp Newmarket: runs well fresh: smart, progressive & genuine colt with a turn of foot, should win more Group races in this form.
1869} **FAIRY GODMOTHER 314** [10] R Charlton 4-8-7 R Hughes 12/1: 11-2: 4 b f Fairy King - Highbrow *2½* **108+**
(Shirley Heights) Prom, rdn 2f out, kept on well over 1f out: op 8/1 on reapp: won both '99 starts, at Newbury (mdn & List, rtd 106+): eff at 9f, will apprec a return to 10f & further could suit: acts on gd/soft & a gall trk: runs well fresh: v useful & progressive, will relish a faster pace/stiffer test & can land a nice prize.
4544} **MUJAHID 173** [5] J L Dunlop 4-8-10 R Hills 8/1: 5042-3: 4 b c Danzig - Elrafa Ah (Storm Cat) *nk* **111**
Waited with, hdwy well over 1f out, kept on ins last, no dngr: plcd twice in '99 incl when 1½L 3rd in Newmarket 2000 Guineas (rtd 114): champion 2yo, won at Salisbury & Newmarket (2, stks & Gr 1 Dewhurst, rtd 123): eff over 1m/9f on firm, gd/soft & on a stiff trk: has run well fresh: below best in blnks: remains smart, rate higher.
703 **BOMB ALASKA 27** [2] G B Balding 5-8-10 J F Egan 7/1: 221-44: Prom, rdn 2f out, onepaced: op 5/1: *1* **110**
can rate higher in a more strongly run race: see 703.
2322} **BRANCASTER 297** [11] 4-8-10 K Fallon 11/1: 2400-5: Waited with, rdn 2f out, kept on for press fnl 1f: *½* **108**
rnr-up on reapp in '99, in Gr 3 Craven, subs fine 2½L 4th in Newmarket 2000 Guineas (rtd 112, with P Chapple Hyam): juv scorer at Haydock (mdn) & Newbury (Gr 3): suited by 1m/9f on firm, handles gd/soft: has run well fresh & run poorly in a visor: now with Sir M Stoute who excels with smart older horses.
*703 **HASTY WORDS 27** [8] 4-8-7 M Hills 12/1: /06-16: Keen in tch, rdn & slightly outpcd over 2f out, *shd* **106**
kept on ins last: acts on firm & gd/soft: stays 9f & should apprec a stronger run race: see 703 (List).
4399} **SHIVA 186** [4] 5-9-1 T Quinn 11/10 FAV: 1102-7: Handy, rdn & btn over 1f out: hvly bckd on reapp: *½* **113**
won first 2 in '99, here at Newmarket (Gr 3, this race) & Curragh (Gr 1, beat Daylami, rtd 121): '98 scorer at Kempton (fill mdn): eff at 8.5/10.5f on gd/firm & gd grnd: has run well fresh on a gall trk: top-class filly at best, should put this bhd her on a sounder surface.
4354} **DIAMOND WHITE 188** [6] 5-8-12 G Hall 25/1: 2110-8: Led after 1f till over 2f out, no extra: in fine *shd* **110**
'99 form, won at Goodwood (List), Longchamp (Gr 2, rtd 113) & plcd num times: '98 wnr at Folkestone (fill h'cap, with G Bravery), Nottingham & Doncaster: eff at 1m, suited by 9/10f on firm & fibresand, likes hvy: tough & smart.
733 **KING PRIAM 25** [7] 5-8-10 (bl) T G McLaughlin 50/1: 313629: Waited with, rdn 3f out, sn btn: *3½* **103$**
v stiff task, much better off back in h'caps as in 733 (rnr-up in Lincoln).
2016} **DESARU 308** [12] 4-8-10 W R Swinburn 25/1: 3/00-0: Sn bhd, btn over 2f out: rcd only twice in '99, *5* **95**
arnd 5L 9th in Newmarket 2000 Guineas (rtd 106): '98 wnr at Doncaster (stks, rtd 106): eff at 7f/1m & reportedly likes gd or firm grnd, handles gd/soft: v useful at best.
4270} **SERGEANT YORK 195** [1] 4-8-10 A Clark 100/1: 0300-0: Waited with, eff over 4f out, wknd 2f out: 11th. *3* **91$**
11 ran Time 1m 54.9 (5.7) (S Cohen & Sir Eric Parker) Mrs A J Perrett Pulborough, W Sussex

968 **3.10 SCOTS EQUITABLE HCAP 4YO+ 0-95 (C) 1m4f Good/Soft 61 +05 Fast [95]**
£7553 £2324 £1162 £581 4 yo rec 1 lb

-- **MOWELGA** [10] Lady Herries 6-9-12 (93) Pat Eddery 20/1: 3110/1: 6 ch g Most Welcome - Galactic Miss **99**
(Damister) Waited with, gd hdwy over 2f out to lead over 1f out, styd on strongly, rdn out: gd time: missed '99, prev term scored at Doncaster, Pontefract & Newbury (class stks, rtd 98): suited by 12f, further shld suit: acts on fast, gd/soft, likes a gall one: runs v well fresh: v useful & has a turn of foot, gd training performance.
4397} **ALHAWA 186** [12] K R Burke 7-8-12 (79) J Weaver 25/1: 1006-2: 7 ch g Mt Livermore - Petrava (Imposing) *½* **84+**
Slow away, hld up, hdwy & not clr run over 2f out, styd on well fnl 1f, just failed: in fine '99 form, scored a 4-timer at Doncaster & Newmarket (3, h'caps, rtd 83, with N Littmoden): hdles rnr-up prev term (rtd 91h): rtd 73 in '98: eff at 12f, suited by arnd 2m now: acts on firm, gd/soft, handles hvy & any trk, loves a gall one, esp Newmarket: best without blnks: fine return over an inadequate trip & should be wng again over further shortly.
4308} **GENTLEMAN VENTURE 191** [15] J Akehurst 4-8-8 (76) T Quinn 10/1: 0000-3: 4 b g Polar Falcon - Our *2* **78+**
Shirley (Shirley Heights) Cl-up, rdn over 1f out, kept on, hands-&-heels riding: in '99 trained by S Woods, won at Redcar (mdn) & plcd in h'caps (rtd 84): stays 12f on firm, soft grnd & likes a gall trk: sharper for this encouraging reapp & h'capped to win for new connections.
4271} **LITTLE PIPPIN 195** [16] G B Balding 4-9-3 (85) S Drowne 20/1: 1140-4: Waited with, eff 2f out, kept *shd* **87**
on for press ins last, reapp: '99 scorer at Salisbury (fill h'cap) & Kempton (h'cap, rtd 86): eff at 12f/13f & handles fast, suited by gd or soft: likes a gall one: runs well fresh, without a t-strap: gd return.
4317} **AFTERJACKO 191** [7] 4-9-1 (83) N Pollard 8/1 FAV: 0153-5: Prom, led over 2f out till over 1f out, *½* **84**
onepace for press: gamble from 14/1 on reapp: in '99 scored at Bath (mdn, rtd 83): stays 12f on firm, gd/soft & on a stiff trk: lightly raced.
*815 **LANCER 16** [21] 8-7-13 (66)(vis) R Ffrench 11/1: 20-616: Hld up, kept on nicely over 1f out, too late. *shd* **67**
4470} **CLARENDON 180** [4] 4-8-9 (77) R Cochrane 14/1: 1300-7: Prom, rdn 2f out, onepace: in '99 scored at *hd* **78**
Chepstow & Ascot (h'caps, rtd 77): wng form at 10f, stays 12f: acts on gd/firm, gd & on a stiff trk: tried blnks.
2598} **BANBURY 284** [9] 6-9-13 (94)(t) J P Spencer 14/1: 3222-8: Dwelt, waited with, effort 2f out, sn no *1¾* **92**
impress on reapp: in fine '99 form, scored at Lingfield (3, clmr, appr h'cap & class stks, rtd 83a), subs plcd sev times on turf (rtd 95): rtd 78 when lightly raced for M Johnston in '98: eff at 12/14f on fast, hvy & equitrack: eff in an eye-hood: v tough & consistent, useful.
4271} **GALLERY GOD 195** [18] 4-9-2 (84) M Roberts 16/1: 0316-9: Keen, waited with, rdn & short of room over *nk* **81**
1f out, no dngr on reapp: in '99 scored at Newcastle (class stks, rtd 86, made all, first win): eff at 12f on firm, handles hvy & any trk: likes to force the pace: sharper for this.
4465} **ANGELS VENTURE 181** [6] 4-9-0 (82) L Dettori 12/1: 0321-0: Hld up, wknd 2f out: chngd stable. *2½* **76**
3529} **WILLIAMSHAKESPEARE 240** [13] 4-8-12 (80) M Hills 14/1: 2232-0: Nvr a factor: 11th, better than this. *nk* **73**
4374} **TEMPLE WAY 187** [8] 4-8-7 (75) J Fortune 16/1: 5420-0: Cl-up, wknd 2f out on reapp: 12th. *1½* **66**
2271} **NAUTICAL STAR 297** [5] 5-9-13 (94) R Hills 14/1: 2202-0: Led till over 2f out, wknd: 13th, reapp. *hd* **84**
809 **ALS ALIBI 18** [3] 7-8-0 (67) Martin Dwyer 50/1: 061/00: Handy till wknd 2f out: 14th. *½* **56**
3981} **WHO CARES WINS 214** [14] 4-8-12 (80) P Robinson 25/1: 3120-0: Hld up, eff 2f out, wknd: 15th. *shd* **68**
815 **LEGAL LUNCH 16** [20] 5-8-1 (68)(vis) G Carter 12/1: 33-420: Hld up, not clr run over 2f out, wknd: 16th. *2½* **53**
4284} **Wait For The Will 193** [19] 4-8-11 (79) I Mongan (5) 25/1:
2266} **Bay Of Islands 298** [17] 8-9-13 (94) R Hughes 25/1:
508 **Alberich 67** [1] 5-10-0 (95) K Fallon 12/1: 1980} **Wave Of Optimism 309** [2] 5-8-9 (76) G Bardwell 33/1:
833 **Bay View 13** [11] 5-8-3 (70) J F Egan 14/1:

21 ran Time 2m 35.48 (6.68) (L G Lazarus) Lady Herries Angmering, West Sussex.

969 **3.45 LISTED EUROPEAN FREE HCAP 3YO (A) 7f str Good/Soft 61 +00 Fast [117]**
£17400 £6600 £3300 £1500

4468} **CAPE TOWN 180** [1] R Hannon 3-9-2 (105) R Hughes 100/30: 12-1: 3 gr c Desert Style - Rossaldene (Mummy's Pet) Cl-up, hdwy to lead over 1f out, rdn clr ins last, cmftbly: bckd tho' op 9/4: twice rcd juv, won at Lingfield (mdn) & rnr-up in a Gr 3 (rtd 103): eff at 7.3f, 1m shld suit despite being sprint bred: acts on gd/soft & soft & runs well fresh on any trk: smart colt with a turn of foot, should win a Gr race on this form. **110**

4427} **CATCHY WORD 183** [9] E A L Dunlop 3-9-2 (105) G Carter 10/1: 1361-2: 3 ch c Cadeaux Genereux - Lora's Guest (Be My Guest) Set pace till over 1f out, rdn & not pace of wnr ins last: reapp: won 1st & last of 4 juv starts, at Haydock (mdn) & Yarmouth (stks, rtd 106): eff at 7f, should stay 1m (half-brother to a smart miler): acts on firm & gd/soft: runs well fresh: v useful colt, type to land a nice prize abroad. *3½* **103**

3799} **EUROLINK RAINDANCE 227** [6] J L Dunlop 3-9-6 (109) L Dettori 9/1: 1125-3: 3 b f Alzao - Eurolink Mischief (Be My Chief) Hld up, hdwy for press over 1f out, kept on ins last: reapp: in '99 won at Chepstow (nov stks) & Salisbury (fill stks), also rnr-up in Listed (rtd 105): eff at 7f, dam useful at up to 13f & 1m+ sure to suit: acts on firm, gd/soft & on a stiff trk: v useful filly, interesting in similar grade over further next time. *nk* **106+**

3437} **FULL FLOW 245** [5] B W Hills 3-9-1 (104) M Hills 9/1: 120-4: Waited with, eff over 1f out, edged right & kept on same pace ins last: thrice rcd juv, won on debut at Newcastle (mdn), subs rnr-up in Listed (rtd 102): eff at 6/7f (half-brother to a smart 7f juv wnr): has run well fresh on firm &gd/soft: useful. *1¼* **99**

4607} **ROYAL HIGHLANDER 166** [7] 3-9-1 (104) R Hills 2/1 FAV: 1-5: Cl-up, rdn & no extra appr final 1f: hvly bckd: won sole juv start for A Foster, at Doncaster (backend mdn, rtd 99+): eff at 6f, 7f should suit (half-brother to a 6f/12f scorer): handles hvy grnd & has run well fresh on a gall trk: better expected. *¾* **97**

3983} **TROUBLE MOUNTAIN 214** [3] 3-9-7 (110) J Reid 12/1: 1132-6: In tch, rdn & wknd over 1f out: reapp, stablemate of 4th: won first 2 juv starts, at Haydock & Doncaster (stks, subs rnr-up in Gr 2 Mill Reef, rtd 110): eff at 6/7f on firm grnd: has run well fresh on a gall trk: may do better on a sounder surface, smart at best. *1¼* **101**

765 **TRINCULO 25** [2] 3-9-5 (108) T G McLaughlin 10/1: 354-07: Keen bhd, rdn & wknd 2f out: well bckd: juv scorer at Leicester (med auct mdn), subs rnr-up in a val stks (rtd 107 at best): eff at 6f, should stay further (dam 1m scorer): acts on fast & gd/soft & on a stiff trk. *1¾* **95**

3794} **HUNTING LION 229** [8] 3-9-5 (108) S Drowne 25/1: 4123-8: Waited with, rdn & btn 2f out: juv wnr at Bath (mdn), subs rnr-up in a Gr 2 (rtd 99+): eff at 6f, should stay further: half-brother to wnrs over 5/13f: acts on firm/fast grnd & has run well fresh on any trk: v useful at best. *shd* **95**

8 ran Time 1m 27.5 (4.3) (S A Six) R Hannon East Everleigh, Wilts.

970 **4.15 BARTLOW FILL MDN 2YO (D) 5f str Good/Soft 61 -41 Slow**
£4810 £1480 £740 £370

-- **ICE MAIDEN** [6] M R Channon 2-8-11 T Quinn 4/1: -1: 2 b f Polar Falcon - Affair Of State (Tate Gallery): Made all, kept on strongly fnl 1f under hands-&-heels riding: 15,500gns Feb foal: half-sister to sev wnrs, incl 5f juv scorer Stately Princess: dam a sprint wng juv, sire top class over 1m: eff forcing the pace over a stiff 5f, 6f will suit: acts on gd/soft grnd, runs well fresh: sure to rate more highly & win more races. **85**

-- **PASHMEENA** [5] R Hannon 2-8-11 R Hughes 7/1: -2: 2 b f Barathea - Auriga (Belmez): Prsd wnr till outpcd over 1f out, rallied well & not btn far under hands & heels: clr rem, op 4/1: Feb foal, cost IR 68,000gns: first foal: eff over a stiff 5f, 6f will suit: acts on gd/soft: looks sure to win races. *nk* **84+**

886 **OPEN WARFARE 7** [10] M Quinn 2-8-11 J Fortune 10/1: -33: 2 br f General Monash - Pipe Opener (Prince Sabo): Prom, ev ch 1f out, sn outpcd by front 2: op 7/1: has shwn enough to find a race, poss over 6f. *3½* **75**

-- **BABY BUNTING** [9] M L W Bell 2-8-11 M Fenton 3/1 FAV: -4: Trkd ldrs, swtchd dist, kept on fnl 1f: nicely bckd tho' op 9/4: 32,000gns Apr foal: half-sister to numerous wnrs, incl sprint h'capper Emerging Market & useful sprinters Son Pardo & Atraf: dam 1m wnr, sire high class from 5-7f: sprint bred, sure to learn from this. *hd* **75**

-- **CARRABAN** [7] 2-8-11 D R McCabe 12/1: -5: Chsd ldrs, short of room dist, not qckn ins last: Feb foal, related to sev wnrs, incl 5f 2yo scorer Natalia Bay, also smart jmpr Paddy's Return: shld apprec 6f. *1* **72**

886 **BLUE LADY 7** [1] 2-8-11 T G McLaughlin 33/1: -06: Prom, onepcd fnl 1f: see 886 (bhd this 3rd). *nk* **71**

856 **COZZIE 9** [2] 2-8-11 V Halliday 25/1: -37: Dwelt, recovered to chase ldrs, wknd fnl 1f: see 856 (AW). *½* **70**

-- **MISE EN SCENE** [3] 2-8-11 Pat Eddery 6/1: -8: Dwelt, nvr a factor on debut: Feb foal, cost 6,200gns: first foal, dam a sprint wnr: sire a v useful sprinter: with P Howling & will find easier races. *3* **61**

-- **DELPHYLLIA** [4] 2-8-11 P Robinson 12/1: -9: Al outpcd on debut: cheaply bought Feb foal: first foal, dam styd 7f as a 2yo: sire a high class juv: with G Margarson. *1½* **57**

-- **PELLI** [8] 2-8-11 A Clark 33/1: -0: Slowly away & al well bhd, fin last: cost 3,700gns: Apr foal, half-sister to sev wnrs, incl 6f/1m performer Mr Majica: sire a top class mid-dist performer: apprec 6/7f+. *17* **27**

10 ran Time 1m 03.31 (5.11) (Stephen Crown & Brook Land) M R Channon West Isley, Berks.

971 **4.45 G BARLING FILLIES MDN 3YO (D) 7f str Good/Soft 61 -20 Slow**
£5278 £1624 £812 £406

4260} **ALSHAKR 197** [2] B Hanbury 3-8-11 R Hills 6/1: 64-1: 3 b f Bahri - Give Thanks (Relko): Trkd ldr, smooth prog to lead dist, ran on strongly, rdn out: well bckd on reapp: trained by P Walwyn in '99, 4th at Nottingham (mdn, rtd 76): half-sister to 12f wnr Saffaanh, dam won the Irish Oaks: eff at 7f, 1m+ will suit: acts on gd/soft & soft, runs well fresh: can win in better company, esp when stepped up in trip. **101**

-- **MISS DORDOGNE** [8] G Wragg 3-8-11 Pat Eddery 20/1: -2: 3 br f Brief Truce - Miss Bergerac (Bold Lad) Dwelt, imprvd 1½f out, fin strongly but too late: eye-catching debut: half-sister to wnrs over 7f/1m: eff at 7f, 1m will suit: acts on gd/soft grnd & on a gall trk, runs well fresh: nailed on to win soon. *1¼* **97+**

4555} **ARABESQUE 172** [11] H R A Cecil 3-8-11 T Quinn 2/1 FAV: 32-3: 3 b f Zafonic - Prophecy (Warning): Nvr far away, ev ch 1f out, not qckn cl-home: hvly bckd on reapp: twice rcd juv, rnr-up here at Newmarket (fill mdn, rtd 93+): sister to useful sprint juv Threat, dam a high-class wng sprinter as a 2yo: eff at 7f on gd/soft & soft, crying out for 1m: can run well fresh: reportedly held in some regard, holds a 1,000 Guineas entry. *1¾* **93**

-- **LAST RESORT** [18] B W Hills 3-8-11 M Hills 10/1: -4: Prom, went on 2f out till hdd dist, no extra on debut: half-sister to juv wnr Head A Whisper: dam won over 6/7f: eff at 7f, 1m will suit: acts on gd/soft grnd, handles a stiff/gall trk: sure to benefit from this v encouraging debut. *nk* **92**

4555} **SECRET DESTINY 172** [12] 3-8-11 J Fortune 9/1: -033-5: Waited with, short of room 2f out, ran on nicely but ch had gone: op 6/1, reapp: trained by A Foster in '99, plcd here at Newmarket (fill mdn, rtd 92+): $100,000 purchase, dam a 10f wnr in the States: eff at 7f, must try 1m now: acts on gd/soft & soft grnd: now with J Gosden, did not get the best of runs here & spot-on next time. *1* **90**

4556} **MISS KIRSTY 172** [9] 3-8-11 L Dettori 8/1: 3-6: Rear, drifted right when imprvg over 1f out, nvr nr *shd* **90**

ldrs: reapp: plcd here at Newmarket (fills mdn, rtd 92) on sole juv start: IR 33,000gns purchase: dam a Gr 1 10f wnr in the USA: eff at 7f, 1m will suit: acts on soft grnd: fitter next time over 1m.

-- **MISS RIVIERA GOLF** [13] 3-8-11 W Ryan 25/1: -7: Rear, kept on nicely final 1f, nvr plcd to chall: stablemate of rnr-up, racecourse bow: half-sister to a middle dist wnr, dam scored over 10f: bred to apprec 1m/10f+: eye-catching debut & one to keep in mind, esp over 1m+. *1½* **87+**

3671} **POWERLINE 233** [3] 3-8-11 R Hughes 20/1: -06-8: Set pace 5f, gradually fdd: twice rcd juv, 6th at Chepstow (fill mdn, rtd 72): sire a top class miler: bred to apprec 7f/1m, with R Hannon. *½* **86$**

-- **SEEKING SUCCESS** [16] 3-8-11 K Fallon 10/1: -9: Rear, rdn to impr when short of room 2f out, nvr nr ldrs: op 7/1, debut: with Sir M Stoute & sure to improve. *1½* **83**

4446} **AKHIRA 182** [1] 3-8-11 W R Swinburn 16/1: 45-0: Trkd ldrs 6f, fdd into 10th: op 10/1. *1½* **80**

-- **SIPSI FAWR** [15] 3-8-11 M Fenton 33/1: -0: Chsd ldrs 5½f, wknd: fin 11th, debut. *¾* **78**

1930} **SILVER ARROW 312** [7] 3-8-11 J Reid 20/1: 4-0: Prom, wkng when short of room ins fnl 1f: 12th. *1½* **75**

4315} **BEADING 191** [5] 3-8-11 M Henry 50/1: 0-0: Rcd keenly rear, btn 2f out: fin 13th. *¾* **73**

4040} **Rose Of Hymus 211** [10] 3-8-11 R Ffrench 40/1: -- **Baileys On Line** [4] 3-8-11 M Roberts 33/1:

4605} **Hounds Of Love 166** [6] 3-8-11 R Cochrane 50/1: -- **Peaches** [17] 3-8-11 G Carter 33/1:

4257} **Wrotham Arms 197** [14] 3-8-11 J Lowe 50/1:

18 ran Time 1m 28.85 (5.65) (Hamdan Al Maktoum) B Hanbury Newmarket.

972

5.20 WOOD DITTON STKS 3YO (D) 1m str Good/Soft 61 -11 Slow
£6175 £1900 £950 £475

-- **FANAAR** [19] J Noseda 3-9-0 J Weaver 7/1: -1: 3 ch c Unfuwain - Catalonda (African Sky): Waited with, swtchd & gd hdwy over 1f out, led ent fnl 1f, ran on strongly, readily: 45,000gns purchase, related to sev 1m/10f wnrs: eff at 1m, bred to apprec 10f+: acts on gd/soft & on a gall trk, runs well fresh: reportedly held in some regard, holds a Derby entry: sure to rate more highly & win more races, esp over further. **102+**

-- **CHAMPION LODGE** [3] J A R Toller 3-9-0 S Whitworth 25/1: -2: 3 b c Sri Pekan - Legit (Runnett): Prom, went on over 1f out, collared ins last & not pace to repel wnr: sire a useful sprinter: eff at 1m on gd/soft grnd, handles a stiff/gall trk: fine debut, probably caught a tartar today: can win a mdn. *2* **97**

-- **MEDICEAN** [7] Sir Michael Stoute 3-9-0 K Fallon 6/1: -3: 3 ch c Machiavellian - Mystic Goddess (Storm Bird): Waited with, imprvd 2f out, kept on fnl 1f under a kind ride: op 4/1: sire a top class miler: eff at 1m, 10f may well suit: handles gd/soft grnd: open to plenty of improvement & sure to repay this kind debut. *½* **96+**

-- **TRAHERN** [5] J H M Gosden 3-9-0 L Dettori 8/1: -4: Rear, imprvg when hmpd over 1f out, styd on well & nrst fin: brother to a 1m wnr in France: eff at 1m on gd/soft grnd: little luck in running today, plenty to like about this effort & one to keep a close eye on. *2* **92+**

-- **INGLENOOK** [8] 3-9-0 G Carter 14/1: -5: Trkd ldrs, ev ch 1f out, no extra cl-home: 120,000 gns purchase: dam a middle dist wnr, sire a top class sprinter: with J Dunlop & sure to learn from this. *½* **91**

-- **BORDER SUBJECT** [18] 3-9-0 Pat Eddery 5/2 FAV: -6: Prom till no impress final 1f: hvly bckd from 4/1: sire a top class miler: shld apprec 1m & clearly been shwg something at home: with R Charlton. *1½* **88**

-- **BLUE STREAK** [13] 3-9-0 F Lynch 50/1: -7: Dwelt, effort 2f out, no impress till late hdwy: lngr prcd stablemate of 3rd: related to a smart miler in the States: with Sir M Stoute & may benefit from 10f. *¾* **86$**

-- **YERTLE** [17] 3-9-0 R Ffrench 33/1: -8: Led till dist, no extra: stablemate of rnr-up: sire a v smart miler: likely to apprec 10f: with J Toller. *nk* **85$**

-- **SHATHER** [14] 3-9-0 R Hills 25/1: -9: Rear, effort 2f out, hmpd 1f out, nvr nr ldrs: with J Hills. *1* **83**

-- **POLLSTER** [1] 3-9-0 W R Swinburn 25/1: -0: Rear, eff when hmpd dist, no ch after: s/mate of 3rd. *¾* **81**

-- **BOLD GUEST** [21] 3-9-0 M Henry 50/1: -0: Trkd ldrs till wknd over 1f out: fin 11th. *½* **80**

-- **LADY LUCHA** [9] 3-8-9 M Hills 16/1: -0: Chsd ldrs 6f, fdd into 12th: with B Hills. *hd* **75**

-- **LAST SYMPHONY** [16] 3-9-0 P Robinson 33/1: -0: Rcd keenly in rear, imprvg when badly hmpd dist, no ch after: fin 13th: forget this. *hd* **80**

-- **JAHMHOOR** [2] 3-9-0 J Reid 50/1: -0: Rear, effort when hmpd over 1f out, nvr a factor in 14th. *½* **79**

-- **BALDAQUIN** [12] 3-9-0 J Fortune 25/1: -0: V slowly away, al bhd: fin 15th, lost all ch start. *shd* **79**

-- **VALDERO** [6] 3-9-0 Martin Dwyer 33/1: -0: Al towards rear, fin 16th. *1* **77**

-- **ANGIOLINI** [11] 3-9-0 T Quinn 8/1: -0: Chsd ldrs 6f, wknd qckly: fin 20th. **0**

-- **Encore Du Cristal** [10] 3-8-9 G Hall 20/1: -- **Amritsar** [15] 3-9-0 R Hughes 16/1:

-- **Polmara** [20] 3-8-9 R Cochrane 33/1: -- **Work Of Fiction** [4] 3-9-0 M Roberts 33/1:

21 ran Time 1m 42.23 (5.73) (Saleh Al Homeizi) J Noseda Newmarket.

BEVERLEY WEDNESDAY APRIL 19TH Righthand, Oval Track with Stiff Uphill Finish

Official Going HEAVY (SOFT in places). Stalls: Inside.

973

2.15 CRAIG SIMMS SELLER 3YO+ (G) 1m100y rnd Heavy 130 -22 Slow
£2184 £624 £312 3 yo rec 14lb

670 **WERE NOT STOPPIN 36** [10] R Bastiman 5-9-5 H Bastiman 10/1: 005051: 5 b g Mystiko - Power Take Off (Aragon) Handy in the pack, ran on under press final 2½f to lead below dist, drfited left, all-out: tchd 25/1, no bid: first worthwhile form: eff over a stiff 8.5f, tried 11f: acts on hvy grnd. **38**

-- **KIERCHEM** [11] C Grant 9-9-5 O Pears 50/1: 0030/2: 9 b g Mazaad - Smashing Gale (Lord Gayle) Mid-div, prog for press 2f out, ch inside last, held nr fin: op 20/1, 4 yr Flat abs: better known as a hdler, 98/99 Sedgefield wnr (c.j. h'cap, 2m, gd/soft, suited by fast, rtd 102h): won on the Flat way back in '93 on debut: eff at 8.5f, stays a sharp 12f: goes on gd grnd, hvy & fibresand: runs well fresh. *½* **37**

965 **LEOFRIC 1** [14] M J Polglase 5-9-11 (bl) L Newton 8/1: 0-3503: 5 b g Alhijaz - Wandering Stranger (Petong) Bhd, hdwy & briefly short of room appr final 1f, ran on strongly, not btn far: ran much better than yesterday, clearly apprec drop into a seller: acts on fast, soft/hvy grnd & fibresand: see 693. *nk* **42**

3049} **COLLEGE PRINCESS 263** [17] E J O'Neill 6-9-0 M Tebbutt 14/1: 0540-4: Prom in the pack, effort 2f out, styd on but not pace of ldrs: reapp: unplcd in '99 (h'cap, rtd 42, S Williams): plcd in '98 (h'cap, rtd 49): '97 Redcar wnr (sell h'cap, rtd 49): eff at 5f, stays 8.5f: acts on fast, gd grnd & fibresand, handles hvy. *2½* **28**

893 **BRILLIANCY 6** [2] 5-9-5 (t) A McCarthy (3) 12/1: 355: Held up, late hdwy, nvr on terms: op 8/1, qk reapp. *½* **32**

822 **TIME ON MY HANDS 14** [16] 4-9-11 (bl) Dean McKeown 25/1: 200006: Sn pulled himself into a long lead, tired 2f out, hdd below dist: raced too freely with blnks reapplied: see 260. *1½* **36**

560 **HOT POTATO 58** [8] 4-9-5 R Winston 20/1: -04607: Rear, not much rm 2f out, nvr nr to chall: 8 wk abs. *½* **29**

668 **GHUTAH 36** [6] 6-9-5 K Dalgleish (7) 12/1: 00-008: Nvr a factor: see 668. *3* **25**

778   PLEASURE TRICK 21 [15] 9-9-5 Kim Tinkler 14/1: 000509: Al towards rear: op 10/1: see 496.   1½   23
826   BRIGMOUR 14 [12] 4-9-0 Carolyn Bales (7) 50/1: 00: Led chsg pack till lost pl 2f out, 10th, no form.   shd   18
850   ANNIJAZ 9 [3] 3-8-0 W Supple 9/4 FAV: 32-500: Held up, imprvd 4f out, sn rdn, btn: 11th, nicely   8   8
bckd tho' op 11/8: fav'd by weights on offic. ratings but form has been on much faster grnd than this: see 773.
569   SHONTAINE 57 [9] 7-9-11 Kristin Stubbs (7) 8/1: 663330: Nvr dngrs: 13th, 8 wk abs, new stable, see 383.   0
790   TAMASHAN 20 [1] 4-9-5 O Urbina 7/1: 600-00: Nvr a factor: 15th, no form.   0
871   BAYARD LADY 8 [4] 4-9-0 (t) K Darley 8/1: 50-000: Prom in the pack till wknd qckly 3f out: 0
t-strap reapplied: made the frame once last term (sell h'cap, rtd 42 at best): '98 Hamilton wnr (mdn,
rtd 66, D Moffatt): sole win at 5f, poss stays 12f: handles firm & hvy grnd: with L Lloyd James.
2302} Allrighthen 296 [5] 4-9-5 R Lappin 25/1:   --   Stamford Hill [7] 5-9-5 G Parkin 50/1:
16 ran   Time 1m 56.7 (12.9)   (I B Barker)   R Bastiman Cowthorpe, Nth Yorks.

974   2.45 COMERACING MDN AUCT 2YO (E)   5f   Heavy 130 -44 Slow
£3062   £875   £437

--   MEDIA MOGUL [5] T D Barron 2-8-6 C Lowther 7/1: 1: 2 b g First Trump - White Heat (Last Tycoon)   85
Chsd ldrs, effort appr final 1f, kept on to lead cl-home, pshd out: op 10/1, slow time: 4,000 gns Apr foal, sire
a sprinter: acts on hvy grnd & a stiff trk: runs well fresh: already gelded.
--   UP TEMPO [4] T D Easterby 2-8-9 K Darley 13/8 FAV: 2: 2 b c Flying Spur - Musical Essence (Song)   ½   86
Tried to make all, worn down well ins last: nicely bckd, clr of rem: IR£12,000 half-brother to 3 wnrs abroad,
dam moderate, sire top class 2yo/miler in Australia: eff forcing the pace at 5f on hvy grnd: should find similar.
730   SLIPPER ROSE 25 [6] R Hollinshead 2-7-12 P M Quinn (5) 11/4: -43: 2 ch f Democratic - Brown Taw   6   63
(Whistlefield) Fly jmpd start, chsd ldrs, same pace fnl 2f: drifted from 6/4: rtd higher on gd grnd debut.
--   TIME MAITE [2] M W Easterby 2-8-3 G Parkin 25/1: 4: Slow away, prog to chase front pair 2f out,   1   66
sn no extra: drifted from 12/1: 2,400 gns Komaite half-brother to a wng sprinter, dam a 5f juv wnr: gelded.
700   IMPISH LAD 27 [3] W Supple 7/1: 05: In tch till 2f out: op 4/1: 950gns Imp Society Mar foal,   2   62
dam well-related, sire useful dirt performer in the States.
--   TENERIFE FLYER [11] 2-7-12 Dale Gibson 25/1: 6: Nvr going pace, op 12/1: 9,000 gns Rock City   3   51
May first foal, dam once rcd, sire a sprinter: with J Norton.
856   REGAL MISTRESS 9 [9] 2-7-12 T Williams 33/1: 507: In tch, fdd 2f out: market drifter, see 712.   2½   46
821   PEEJAY HOBBS 14 [7] 2-8-4(1ow) T Lucas 10/1: 08: Slow away, al bhd: op 8/1, stablemate 4th: 5   42
700 gns Alhijaz Feb foal: half-brother to 2 wnrs abroad, sire a miler.
--   SOMETHINGABOUTMARY [1] 2-8-1 D Mernagh (3) 7/1: 9: Al bhd: tchd 10/1: 5,500 gns Fayruz Feb   6   29
foal, sister to useful 1m wng juv Deadline Time & half-brother to a 12f wnr, dam a stayer, sire a sprinter.
730   EURO IMPORT 25 [10] 2-8-6 A Nicholls (3) 16/1: -00: Keen, cl-up, eff no extra when hmpd 2f out: 10th, 1¼   32
op 9/1: 8,200 gns Imp Society Feb 1st foal, dam half-sister to useful chaser Cumbrian Challenge: with D Nicholls.
10 ran   Time 1m 10.0 (8.7)   (Mrs J Hazell)   T D Barron Maunby, Nth Yorks.

975   3.20 SANDERSON HCAP STKS 3YO+ 0-85 (D)   1m2f   Heavy 130 00 Slow   [83]
£3961   £1219   £609   £304   3 yo rec 17lb

4574} RINGSIDE JACK 170 [9] C W Fairhurst 4-8-9 (64) J Fanning 12/1: 3050-1: 4 b g Batshoof - Celestine   71
(Skyliner) Nvr far away, rdn to lead appr final 1f, readily: rnr-up in '99 (h'cap, rtd 82): juv wnr at Redcar
(mdn, nurs plcd, rtd 82): eff at 1m/10f: acts on fast, likes hvy, any trk: runs well fresh: well h'capped.
667   GENERATE 36 [1] M J Polglase 4-8-2 (56)(1ow) L Newton 8/1: 00-162D: 4 b f Generous - Ivorine   4   58
(Blushing Groom) Led, under press when hdd appr final 1f, hung right below dist, onepace, fin 2nd, plcd 3rd:
bckd from 14/1: probably ran to best, eff at 9.5f/10f: acts on hvy grnd & fibresand: see 578.
793   LADY ROCKSTAR 20 [8] M J Ryan 5-9-5 (74) P McCabe 11/2: 405-02: 5 b m Rock Hopper - Silk St   nk   74
James (Pas de Seul) Rear, gd hdwy ent fnl 2f, rdn & about to go 2nd when hmpd/snatched up ins last: fin 3rd,
plcd 2nd: tchd 7/1: wld not have troubled the wnr tho' this was a nursery to form: acts on firm & hvy, see 793.
4301} MINDANAO 191 [4] Miss J A Camacho 4-9-13 (82) K Darley 2/1 FAV: 2121-4: Held up, prog 3f out, sn   1¼   80
rdn, nvr able to chall: hvly bckd from 3/1 on reapp: '99 wnr at Newcastle, here at Ripon & Ayr (h'caps,
rtd 83): eff at 9/10f: acts on firm & hvy grnd, any trk: needed last year's reapp, go closer next time.
871   KHUCHN 8 [11] 4-8-5 (60) D Mernagh (3) 25/1: 10-005: Al same place: see 871.   ¾   57
871   RUTLAND CHANTRY 8 [2] 6-9-1 (70) S Sanders 6/1: 0-2566: Cl-up, chall 2f out, wknd dist: op 9/2.   1½   65
757   EL SALIDA 22 [10] 4-9-4 (73) J Carroll 10/1: 344-07: Mid-div thro'out: faster grnd suits?: see 73.   3½   64
875   WUXI VENTURE 8 [7] 5-9-8 (77) A Nicholls (3) 7/1: 000008: Nvr in it: op 4/1: back up in trip.   ½   67
786   SANDABAR 21 [3] 7-8-6 (0)(t)(1ow) A Culhane 20/1: 004-09: In tch tll 3f out: faster grnd suits.   6   45
845   OCTANE 11 [12] 4-7-11 (52)(1ow)(2oh) A McCarthy (0) 50/1: 500-00: Dwelt, al bhd: 10th: with   1½   34
H Cecil when fav for 1st 2 last term (flattered when rtd 80 on debut): yet to find a trip, tried blnks & t-strap.
825   MELS BABY 14 [6] 7-7-10 (51)(4oh) P M Quinn (5) 33/1: 00P/00: Nvr dngrs: 11th: see 825.   5   28
757   FIORI 22 [5] 4-10-0 (83) M Tebbutt 7/1: 0-6200: Chsd ldrs, lost pl 3f out: 12th, op 5/1, something amiss?   3   57
12 ran   Time 2m 15.3 (13)   (M G J Partnership)   C W Fairhurst Middleham, Nth Yorks.

976   3.55 WELCOME TO SALLY HCAP 3YO 0-75 (E)   7f100y rnd   Heavy 130 -07 Slow   [79]
£3224   £992   £496   £248

781   NODS NEPHEW 21 [10] Miss J A Camacho 3-8-8 (59) J Carroll 7/2 FAV: 00-41: 3 b g Efisio - Nordan Raider   64
(Domynsky) Made all, rdn out inside last: nicely bckd, winning h'cap bow: unplcd both '99 starts (rtd 61):
apprec step up to a stiff 7.5f on hvy grnd with forcing tactics: lightly raced.
857   HEATHYARDS LAD 9 [4] R Hollinshead 3-8-11 (62) P M Quinn (5) 5/1: 540632: 3 b c Petardia - Maiden's   2   63
Dance (Hotfoot) In tch, went after wnr 2f out, no extra nr fin: bckd from 10/1: acts on firm, hvy & fibresand.
826   HAPPY HOOLIGAN 14 [12] M Johnston 3-9-7 (72) J Fanning 8/1: 2-053: 3 b c Ezzoud - Continual   ¾   72
(Damascus) Mid-div, styd on under press final 2f, nvr nrr: tchd 10/1, top weight on h'cap bow: goes
on gd & hvy grnd, shld find similar in the north over 10f in the near future: see 826.
4040} CARELESS 211 [13] T D Easterby 3-8-6 (57) R Winston 7/1: 400-4: Towards rear, kept on steadily fnl   nk   56
2f, nvr on terms: drifter from 9/2 on reapp/h'cap bow: 4th on debut last term for J Banks (auct mdn,
rtd 66): handles fast & hvy grnd: stoutly bred, should improve over mid-dists.
736   LORDOFENCHANTMENT 25 [11] 3-8-9 (60) Kim Tinkler 14/1: 566-05: Prom, effort 3f out, unable to   1   57
qckn: prob handles hvy grnd, acts on fast: see 736.
827   JUST THE JOB TOO 14 [15] 3-8-1 (52) J Mackay (7) 9/1: -64106: In tch, chsd ldrs 3f out, sn onepace.   3   44
*589   NOWT FLASH 54 [1] 3-8-9 (60) W Supple 14/1: 100617: Nvr nr to chall: op 7/1, 8 wk abs: see 589.   nk   51
744   SWEET HAVEN 23 [14] 3-8-5 (56) A Nicholls (3) 33/1: 600-08: Nvr a factor: '99 wnr here at   9   33
319

BEVERLEY WEDNESDAY APRIL 19TH Righthand, Oval Track with Stiff Uphill Finish

Beverley (auct mdn, rtd 77, M H Ellis): unproven beyond 5f on fast grnd: with C Cox.
827 **ENTITY 14** [7] 3-9-2 (67) C Lowther 8/1: 40-009: Nvr trbld ldrs: promise more than once last term ½ 43
(nursery, rtd 71): eff at 6f, bred for further, handles firm & gd/soft grnd: capable of better: with T Barron.
811 **PIX ME UP 18** [6] 3-9-0 (65) A Culhane 14/1: 20-000: Al towards rear: 10th, form is on fast grnd. 1½ 39
1587} **BLUEGRASS MOUNTAIN 327** [3] 3-9-5 (70) K Darley 12/1: -360-0: In tch till 3f out: 13th, op 5/1 on 0
reapp/h'cap bow, stablemate of 4th: plcd on debut last term (5f mdn on gd/sft, rtd 74): brother to a useful miler.
780 **BOND DIAMOND 21** [8] 3-8-12 (63) J Stack 9/1: -10500: Dwelt, brief effort halfway: 16th: see 427 (fibresand). 0
870 **Mr Stickywicket 8** [16] 3-7-10 (47)(vis)(17oh) S Righton 33/1:
3884} Old Feathers 219 [5] 3-9-3 (68) S Sanders 14/1:
4250} Rum Lass 197 [9] 3-8-11 (62) G Duffield 25/1: 806 **Tower Of Song 19** [2] 3-8-6 (57)(BL) G Parkin 25/1:
16 ran   Time 1m 41.1 (10.3)   (Brian Nordan)   Miss J A Camacho Norton, Nth Yorks.

| 977 | 4.25 LECONFIELD CLASS STKS 3YO+ 0-90 (C) | 7f100y rnd | Heavy 130 | + 05 Fast |
| | £6435   £1980   £900   £495   3 yo rec 13lb | | | |

687 **JO MELL 33** [1] T D Easterby 7-9-5 K Darley 5/1: 150-01: 7 b g Efisio - Militia Girl (Rarity) 90
Made just about all, repelled a strong chall ent final 2f & just held off fast finishing rnr-up: op 7/1, best time of day:
'99 Newcastle wnr (class stks, rtd 91, rtd h'cap, rtd 99): '98 wnr at Ascot (val h'cap, rtd 109), Listed rnr-up:
5 time wnr in '97 (rtd 107): stays 1m, suited by 7f/7.5f: acts on firm, likes soft & hvy nowadays: acts on any
trk, likes Ascot: best up with/forcing the pace: well treated back in h'caps, smart at best & very game.
*708 **PETIT MARQUIS 27** [3] J R Fanshawe 3-8-8 O Urbina 3/1: 2-12: 3 b c Lost World - Ephemeride hd 90
(Al Nasr) Rear, swtchd for effort 2f out, no impress on ldrs till strong burst towards fin, post came too sn: op 4/1:
imprvd again in defeat tho' clearly unsuited by drop back to 7.5f: acts on fast, hvy grnd & fibresand: smart.
823 **COTE SOLEIL 14** [2] M L W Bell 3-8-3 A Beech (5) 5/2 FAV: 404-33: 3 ch c Inchinor - Sunshine Coast ¾ 85
(Posse) Prom, strong chall 2f out till ent fnl 1f, onepace nr fin: bckd tho' op 7/4: clr rem, goes on firm & hvy.
851 **NIGHT OF GLASS 9** [6] N Tinkler 7-9-2 Kim Tinkler 4/1: 354-04: Held up, prog & ch 2f out, kept 3 80
on same pace: nicely bckd tho' op 5/2, visor omitted: see 851.
1385} **SECRETS OUT 337** [7] 4-9-2 A Culhane 20/1: /100-5: Pld hard bhd ldrs, outpcd appr fnl 1f: op 12/1, 4 74
tchd 33/1 on reapp: jmps fit (stays 2m1f): '99 reapp wnr at Windsor (mdn, rtd 88, Sir M Stoute): rnr-up all 4 juv
starts (mdn, rtd 89): eff at 1m/10f: acts on firm & gd grnd & likes to force the pace: sharper next time on faster grnd.
824 **BOLDLY GOES 14** [5] 4-9-2 Dean McKeown 8/1: 63-006: Chsd ldrs, wknd ent final 2f: tchd 11/1. shd 74
733 **NOMORE MR NICEGUY 25** [4] 6-9-2 W Supple 8/1: 00-007: Keen, nvr troubled ldrs, eased final 1f: 15 54
'99 wnr at Chester (rtd h'cap, rtd 89 & 99a, plus coods rnr-up, rtd 93): '98 Chester (h'cap, rtd 90), W'hampton &
Lingfield wnr (h'cap & stks, rtd 99a): eff at 6f/1m: acts on gd/soft but suited by firm, gd, both AWs: can
run well fresh, any trk, likes sharp ones, especially Chester: with E Alston.
7 ran   Time 1m 40.2 (9.4)   (C H Newton Jnr Ltd)   T D Easterby Great Habton, Nth Yorks.

| 978 | 4.55 BAY FILLIES HCAP 3YO 0-70 (E) | 1m4f | Heavy 130 | -32 Slow | [69] |
| | £2852   £815   £407 | | | | |

799 **ESTABELLA 20** [10] S P C Woods 3-9-0 (55) G Duffield 3/1: 005-21: 3 ch f Mujtahid - Lady In Green 64
(Shareef Dancer) Dictated stdy pace, cmftbly drew clr final 1½f: nicely bckd, well rdn, 1st win: 5th last term
(nurs, rtd 55): imprvd since stepped up to 12f, shld get further: acts on gd/soft & hvy grnd & suited forcing it.
4557} **WINDMILL LANE 172** [7] B S Rothwell 3-9-5 (60) W Supple 20/1: 5505-2: 3 b f Saddlers' Hall - Alpi Dora 8 60
(Valiyar) Chsd wnr, effort appr final 2f, outstyd: op 12/1 on reapp: unplcd over 7f/1m last term (nov stks,
rtd 70, A Jarvis): prob gets 12f, handles firm & hvy grnd.
807 **DOUBLE RED 19** [11] M L W Bell 3-9-7 (62) A Beech (5) 2/1 FAV: 022-23: 3 b f Thatching - Local Custom 5 57
(Be My Native) Well plcd, shkn up 4f out, same pace: bckd, clr rem, top weight: stays 12f?: see 807 (10f, gd).
827 **CASTANEA SATIVA 14** [9] T D Easterby 3-9-4 (59) K Darley 5/1: 420-04: Al mid-div: lngr trip: 6 48
'99 rnr-up (mdn, rtd 63): unproven beyond 7f tho' is bred to stay mid-dists: handles hvy grnd.
799 **TYCOONS LAST 20** [5] 3-8-12 (53) S Sanders 12/1: 000-35: Held up, prog & in tch after 6f, onepace 1 41
final 4f: tchd 16/1, stoutly bred, longer trip may suit: got closer to this winner in 799 (gd/sft).
827 **HIGH CAPACITY 14** [6] 3-8-3 (44) P Fessey 10/1: 00-006: Nvr a factor: stablemate 4th, longer trip. 3½ 28
782 **DANCING MARY 21** [12] 3-9-5 (60) J Bosley (7) 10/1: -30357: Nvr dngrs: tchd 14/1: see 500. shd 44
783 **HIGH BEAUTY 21** [2] 3-8-6 (47) P McCabe 20/1: 00-048: Handy tll 4f out: back up in trip, see 783. 12 18
3262} **LE PIN 252** [3] 3-9-5 (60) Paul Cleary (7) 8/1: 5000-9: Al towards rear: tchd 14/1: big step up in trip 7 24
on reapp/h'cap bow (auct mdn, rtd 70): half-sister to smart miler Handsome Ridge.
537 **ODYN DANCER 61** [8] 3-8-13 (52) G Baker (7) 14/1: -66620: Nvr on terms: 10th: op 8/1, 9 wk abs. 5 14
827 **Mountrath Rock 14** [1] 3-9-3 (58) Dean McKeown 40/1: 4194} **Desert Charm 200** [4] 3-8-1 (42) J Fanning 50/1:
12 ran   Time 2m 50.8 (19.5)   (Ben Allen & Mrs Catherine Hine)   S P C Woods Newmarket, Suffolk.

NEWMARKET (ROWLEY) THURSDAY APRIL 20TH Righthand, Stiff, Galloping Track

Official Going   GOOD/SOFT, SOFT after 4.15 (Rain Throughout Afternoon). STALLS: Far Side.

| 979 | 2.05 HORSESMOUTH.CO.UK HCAP 3YO 0-95 (C) | 1m2f str | Good/Soft | Fair | [99] |
| | £7631   £2348   £1174   £587 | | | | |

*858 **KINGS MILL 10** [7] N A Graham 3-9-1 (86)(5ex) R Cochrane 11/2 JT FAV: 223-11: 3 b c Doyoun - Adarika 94
(King's Lake) Waited with, hdwy & bmpd over 2f out, styd on well over 1f out to lead cl-home, rdn out:
recently won at Southwell (med auct mdn): plcd fnl 3 '99 starts (rtd 83): improved this term on step-up
to 10f, shld stay further: acts on gd & soft, any trk: runs well fresh: useful, in fine form & improving.
601 **BOLD EWAR 52** [14] C E Brittain 3-8-4 (75)(bl) G Duffield 20/1: 41-532: 3 ch c Persian Bold - ½ 81
Hot Curry (Sharpen Up) Al cl-up, went on over 2f out, kept on for press ins last till collared cl-home, not
btn far: 7 wk abs: enjoyed step up to 10f & acts on gd/soft & fibresand, any trk: game, see 125.
4561} **DOLLAR BIRD 173** [4] J L Dunlop 3-9-1 (86) T Quinn 10/1: 610-3: 3 b f Kris - High Spirited (Shirley 1¼ 90
Heights) Prom, eff over 1f out, kept on same pace for press: reapp: won 2nd of only 3 juv starts, at
Nottingham (fills mdn, rtd 902): dam stayer: at 1m/10f, 12f+ looks sure to suit: acts on gd & gd/soft
& on a gall trk: type to progress with racing & win similar over further.
4433} **CRACOW 184** [8] J W Hills 3-8-12 (83) M Hills 14/1: 052-4: Waited with, hdwy & not clr run over 2f nk 87+
out, switched over 1f out & kept on nicely ins last, nrst fin: op 10/1, clr of rem on reapp: rtd 84 when rnr-up

on last of 3 juv starts: apprec step up to 10f, further will suit: acts on gd & gd/soft, any trk: caught the eye.

4452} **ARANYI 182** [10] 3-8-13 (84) Pat Eddery 8/1: 644-5: Waited with, eff & not clr run over 2f out, 4 82
kept on same pace over 1f out: op 6/1, stablemate of 3rd, reapp: rtd 92 at best when 4th on 2 of only
3 juv starts: stays 10f, further could suit: acts on gd & gd/soft: sharper for this, expect improvement.

4512} **OSOOD 177** [11] 3-9-5 (90) L Dettori 8/1: 161-6: Waited with, rdn & outpcd over 3f out, kept on ½ 87+
over 1f out, nrst fin: reapp: won 2 of only 4 juv starts, at Salisbury (debut, mdn) & Redcar (nov stks, rtd 92):
eff at 7f/10f, looks sure to relish 12f+ (dam 11/14f wnr): acts on gd/soft, soft & a stiff trk: has run well
fresh with/forcing the pace: will much closer next time over further.

4494} **CRYSTAL FLITE 180** [6] 3-8-1 (72) Martin Dwyer 20/1: 5063-7: Dwelt, waited with, eff over 1f out, 1 68
onepace: reapp: plcd on last of 5 juv starts (nurs h'cap, rtd 77 at best): eff at 7f, prob stays 10f on gd & hvy.

4338} **CONSTANT 191** [5] 3-8-4 (75) N Pollard 14/1: -005-8: Waited with, rdn over 2f out, no impress: 1¼ 69
reapp: rtd 78 when 5th on 3 of only 3 juv starts: eff at 1m, bred to relish mid-dists this term: handles gd/soft.

4376} **ECSTASY 188** [1] 3-8-7 (78) G Hind 20/1: 4030-9: Keen, waited with, brief eff over 3f out, wknd nk 71
2f out: reapp: in '99 trained by P Walwyn, scored at Warwick (auct mdn, rtd 81 at best): stays 7f, further shld
suit (dam 10f scorer): acts on fast, gd/soft & on any trk.

4380} **BOLD STATE 188** [2] 3-8-2 (73) A Whelan 33/1: 2100-0: Waited with, rdn & sltly hmpd over 2f out, hd 66
no impress: 10th, reapp, longer trip.

4380} **EL CURIOSO 188** [9] 3-9-7 (92) W R Swinburn 12/1: 5014-0: Chsd ldrs, till wknd over 1f out: 11th. 2 83
826 **AUTUMN RAIN 15** [12] 3-8-13 (84) J Reid 9/1: 55-20: Waited with, wknd over 2f out: 12th, bckd. nk 75
*720 **ROYAL CAVALIER 26** [3] 3-8-11 (82) P M Quinn (5) 25/1: -03410: Cl-up till wknd over 2f out: 13th. 10 63
4526} **SCOTTY GUEST 176** [13] 3-8-9 (80) P Robinson 11/2: 01-0: Led till over 2f out, wknd: fin 14th, 10 51
reportedly choked: won 2nd of only 2 juv starts, at Yarmouth (mdn, made all, rtd 92): eff at 1m (half
brother to a 10f wnr): acts on gd/soft & a gall trk.
14 ran   Time 2m 08.93 (6.83)   (First Millennium Racing)   N A Graham Newmarket

---

980	**2.35 LISTED FEILDEN STKS 3YO (A) 1m1f str Good/Soft Fair**
	£13780 £5227 £2613 £1188

4379} **PAWN BROKER 188** [8] D R C Elsworth 3-8-11 M J Kinane 14/1: 61-1: 3 ch c Selkirk - Dime Bag 110
(High Line) Keen, waited with, rdn well over 2f out, styd on well over 1f out to get up ins last, rdn out: reapp:
won 2nd of only 2 juv starts, at Newmarket (back-end mdn, rtd 91+): half brother to a 7f wnr: dam stayer: eff at
1m/9f, further suit: acts on gd, gd/soft: runs well fresh: progressive & smart, bags of scope for further improvement.

4466} **ISLAND SOUND 181** [7] D R C Elsworth N Pollard 7/2: 411-2: 3 b g Turtle Island - Ballet ¾ 108
(Sharrood) Set pace till over 2f out, rallied gamely ins last, kept on, narrowly btn by lesser fancied stablemate:
hvly bckd on reapp: won fnl 2 of 3 juv starts, at Salisbury (mdn) & Newbury (stks, rtd 105): eff at 1m/9f, 10f+
will suit (half brother to a hdles wnr): likes gd/soft & soft & handles a stiff/undul trk: useful & genuine.

3857} **THREE POINTS 223** [1] J L Dunlop 3-8-11 Pat Eddery 10/1: -113-3: 3 b c Bering - Trazl (Zalzal) ½ 107
Chsd ldr till went on over 2f out, kept on for press ins last till collared cl-home: clr of rem on reapp: won
1st 2 of only 3 juv starts, at Kempton (mdn) & Nottingham (nov stks, rtd 103 at best): eff at 1m/9f, bred to stay
further: acts on firm/fast & on a stiff or easy trk: has run well fresh: useful, shld be placed to advantage.

4452} **WESTERN SUMMER 182** [2] H R A Cecil 3-8-11 T Quinn 6/4 FAV: 1-4: Handy, rdn over 3f out, btn 5 100
over 1f out: hvly bckd on reapp: won sole juv start at Nottingham (mdn, rtd 93+): eff at 8.3f (dam 1m
juv wnr): acts on gd/soft & has run well fresh: clearly been showing plenty at home for powerful stable.

4102} **CHINATOWN 207** [3] 3-8-11 K Fallon 5/1: 314-5: In tch, rdn over 3f out, wknd well over 1f out: 1¼ 98
nicely bckd on reapp: in '99 trained by P Chapple Hyam, won 2nd of only 3 juv starts, at Newcastle (mdn),
subs 4th in a Gr 2 (rtd 106): stays 1m, could get further: acts on gd & soft grnd & on a stiff trk.

4453} **ALVA GLEN 182** [6] 3-8-11 W R Swinburn 12/1: 421-6: In tch, rdn & wknd 2f out: reapp: won last of 1 96
3 juv starts, at Nottingham (back-end mdn, rtd 96): eff at 8.3f, bred to stay further: acts on gd/soft &
soft, handles fast & a gall trk: useful, would appreciate stakes company.

3724} **SHADY POINT 231** [5] 3-8-7(1ow) L Dettori 25/1: -03-7: Waited with, rdn over 3f out, sn btn: 22 62
-- **PRIESTLAW** [4] 3-8-11 J Reid 33/1: 13-8: Sn bhd: reapp. shd 66
8 ran   Time 1m 55.14 (5.94)   (Raymond Tooth)   D R C Elsworth Whitsbury, Hants

---

981	**3.10 GR 3 CRAVEN STKS 3YO (A) 1m str Good/Soft Fair**
	£20300 £7700 £3850 £1750

4468} **UMISTIM 181** [1] R Hannon 3-8-9 R Hughes 8/1: 1151-1: 3 ch c Inchinor - Simply Sooty (Absalom) 116
Chsd ldr, rdn & sltly outpcd 2f out, rallied appr fnl 1f to get up again ins last, styd on well, drvn out: reapp:
tough juv, won at Windsor (stks) & Newbury (2, mdn & Gr 3 Horris Hill, working out well, rtd 112): stays 1m
well & handles firm grnd, likes gd/soft: enjoys racing up with/forcing the pace on any trk: smart, progressive
& genuine colt, would enjoy an easy surface in the 2000 Guineas.

4398} **KINGS BEST 187** [5] Sir Michael Stoute 3-8-9 K Fallon 7/2: 115-2: 3 b c Kingmambo - Allegretta ¾ 115
(Lombard) Keen, cl-up, went on & qcknd over 2f out, hard drvn & drifted left ins last, collared cl-home: bckd
on reapp: v promising juv, won at Newmarket (mdn) & York (Listed), subs too keen in Dewhurst (rtd 112 at best):
half brother to Arc wnr Urban Sea: dam 1m/9f wnr: eff at 7f/1m on fast & gd/soft, further shld suit: runs well
fresh: v smart but threw away wng chance by hanging here: win Gr races if hanging/keeness is kept in check.

4483} **EKRAAR 180** [2] M P Tregoning 3-8-9 (bl) R Hills 4/1: 2143-3: 3 b c Red Ransom - Sacahuista (Raja 2 112
Baba) Prom, rdn & outpcd over 1f out, kept on again appr fnl 1f: reapp: in '99 scored at Goodwood (Gr 3) &
1½L 3rd in Gr 1 Racing Post Trophy (1st time blnks, rtd 114): eff at 1m, crying out for a step up to 10f+:
acts on firm, soft & on any trk: runs well in blnks: smart, looks sure to rate higher & win Gr races over further.

3866} **ROSSINI 223** [3] A P O'Brien 3-8-12 M J Kinane 7/4 FAV: W112-4: Keen, waited with, eff over 2f out, 1½ 113
rdn & onepace over 1f out, eased cl-home: hvly bckd on reapp under top weight: high-class juv, won at
The Curragh (2, incl in Gr 3) & M-Laffitte (Gr 2, rtd 117 at best): eff at 5/7f, prob stays 1m: acts on firm,
soft/hvy grnd & on any trk: has run well fresh & can force the pace: v smart, not disgraced today.

4378} **ADILABAD 188** [6] 3-8-9 W R Swinburn 9/1: 11-5: Led till over 2f out, onepace: reapp: won both nk 109
juv starts, at Sandown (nov stks) & Newmarket (stks, rtd 96): eff at 7f/1m, could get further (dam
useful 9f scorer): acts on gd & gd/soft, stiff trks: lightly raced & v useful, better off in Listed grade.

3830} **SHAMROCK CITY 225** [4] 3-8-9 Pat Eddery 10/1: -421-6: Waited with, rdn & outpcd 3f out: reapp: 21 79
won last of 3 juv starts, at Doncaster (mdn, rtd 101): stays 1m well (dam 10.5f wnr): acts on gd/firm & a gall trk.
6 ran   Time 1m 41.11 (4.61)   (Mrs S Joint)   R Hannon East Everleigh, Wilts

982	3.45 H & K HCAP 3YO 0-95 (C) 6f Good/Soft Slow	[102]
	£7748 £2384 £1192 £596	

4265} **STRAHAN** 197 [12] J H M Gosden 3-8-13 (87) L Dettori 8/1: -321-1: 3 b c Catrail - Soreze (Gallic **92**
League) Waited with, hdwy 2f out, styd on well ins last to get up cl-home, rdn out reapp: won last of 3 juv
starts, at York (mdn, rtd 86): eff at 6f, 7f looks sure to suit: acts on fast, gd/soft grnd & on a gall trk:
runs well fresh: useful & progressive, type to rate higher & go in again.

77   **KATHOLOGY** 152 [4] D R C Elsworth 3-8-10 (84) N Pollard 12/1: 2223-2: 3 b c College Chapel - Wicken   nk   **88**
Wonder (Distant Relative) Set pace, rdn over 1f out, kept on well till collared last strides: landed each-way
gamble after a long abs: deserves a race: see 46.

4207} **NOTHING DAUNTED** 201 [15] E A L Dunlop 3-9-5 (93) J Reid 7/1: 2132-3: 3 ch c Selkirk - Khubza   nk   **96+**
(Green Desert) Held up, hdwy & switched over 1f out, kept on nicely under kind ride, just held, nrst fin: reapp:
juv scorer at Goodwood (mdn), also plcd sev times (rtd '97): eff at 6f, stays 1m & crying out for a return to
further: acts on fast, gd/soft grnd & on any trk: runs well fresh: v useful, caught the eye here (Stewards
enquired into run - jockey reported he did not get the run of the race) & one to be with over further next time.

729   **PORT ST CHARLES** 26 [16] N A Callaghan 3-8-4 (78) W Ryan 11/1: 33-24: In tch, eff over 2f out,   ½   **80**
kept on for press ins last, not btn far: progressive, deserves a race: acts on gd/firm & gd/soft.

4214} **CHIQUITA** 201 [6] 3-8-6 (80) R Ffrench 14/1: 3211-5: Waited with, sltly hmpd appr 2 out, kept   2   **78+**
on nicely over 1f out, nrst fin on reapp: in '99 trained by W Haggas, won fnl 2, at W'hampton (AW nurs, rtd
80a) & Sandown (nurs, rtd 80): eff at 6f, looks sure to apprec a step up to 7f: acts on firm, hvy & fibresand,
any trk: progressive, v encouraging here & interesting over further next time.

4491} **BLUE VELVET** 180 [2] 3-8-12 (86) G Duffield 12/1: 1024-6: Keen, waited with, gd hdwy to chall over   ½   **83**
1f out, no extra ins last: reapp: in '99 scored at Southwell (fills auct mdn, rtd 80a) & Newmarket (nurs
h'cap, rtd 86 at best): eff at 5/6f on firm, gd & both AWs, handles hvy & any trk: tough, fitter for this.

4480} **EASTWAYS** 180 [13] 3-9-5 (93) D Holland 12/1: 2132-7: Handy, rdn over 2f out, onepace over 1f out: shd   **89**
reapp: tough juv, nvr out of the frame & scored at Beverley (stks, rtd '93): eff at 5/7f, could get further:
acts on fast, soft grnd & on any trk: has run well fresh: sharper for this & will relish a return to 7f+.

852   **LOVES DESIGN** 10 [14] 3-8-1 (75) (vis) P Robinson 20/1: 31-308: Hld up, eff over 1f out, no impress.   ½   **69**

4547} **DONT SURRENDER** 174 [11] 3-9-3 (91) Pat Eddery 6/1 FAV: 2211-9: Cl-up, wknd well over 1f out: hd   **84**
reapp, well bckd: won fnl 2 in '99, at Lingfield (auct mdn) & Newmarket (stks, rtd 100): eff at 6f on fast,
gd/soft & on any trk: tough & useful last term, sharper for this.

4207} **LAS RAMBLAS** 201 [10] 3-8-11 (85) J Fortune 33/1: 3100-0: Slow away, bhd, some late gains: 10th   ½   **76**
on reapp: juv scorer at Newmarket (mdn, rtd 89 at best): eff at 6f on firm/fast grnd & a stiff trk: do better.

4355} **BRANDON ROCK** 189 [9] 3-8-2 (76) Martin Dwyer 20/1: 0100-0: In tch, rdn & btn over 2f out, 11th.   3   **59**

837   **SUMTHINELSE** 13 [8] 3-8-2 (76) (VIS) J Tate 33/1: 40-540: In tch, wknd 2f out: 12th.   ¾   **57**

834   **KEBABS** 14 [3] 3-8-6 (80) S Carson 5/1: 60-550: Chsd ldr till wknd over 1f out: 14th, see 834.   nk   **60**

792   **HUNTING TIGER** 21 [5] 3-8-13 (87) T Quinn 20/1: 152-00: Al bhd, 14th: see 792.   1¾   **62**

652   **ILLUSIVE** 43 [18] 3-7-11 (71) (bl) C Rutter 10/1: -41120: In tch, wknd 2f out: 15th, btr 652 (aw).   5   **34**

690   **STAYIN ALIVE** 33 [19] 3-8-12 (86) (t) K Fallon 10/1: 41-000: In tch, wknd over 3f out: 16th.   nk   **48**

275   James Stark 105 [7] 3-8-9 (83) G Carter 25/1:   840   **Golden Legend** 13 [17] 3-8-0 (74) P Doe 20/1:
4466} **Launfal** 181 [1] 3-9-7 (95) R Hughes 20/1:
19 ran   Time 1m 16.01 (5.21)   (Sheikh Mohammed)   J H M Gosden Manton, Wilts

983	4.15 ALEX SCOTT MDN 3YO (D) 7f str Good/Soft Slow
	£5382 £1656 £828 £414	

--   **SHIBBOLETH** [13] H R A Cecil 3-8-11 T Quinn 5/1: 1: 3 b c Danzig - Razyana (His Majesty)   **103+**
Chsd ldrs, hdwy to lead over 2f out, powered clr over 1f out, v readily: op 5/2 on debut: full brother to a
2000 Guineas 3rd: dam styd 10f: eff at 7f, sure to relish 1m: acts on gd/soft grnd & runs well fresh on a
stiff trk: most impressive debut, looks potentially high-class & comes right into the 2000 Guineas frame.

4265} **MATERIAL WITNESS** 197 [16] W R Muir 3-8-11 Martin Dwyer 10/1: -32-2: 3 b c Barathea - Dial Dream   5   **90**
(Gay Mecene) Slow away, waited with, hdwy over 2f out, hard rdn & kept on over 1f out on reapp: nicely bckd:
plcd both juv starts (mdns, rtd 85): eff at 6/7f, 1m shld suit: acts on fast, gd/soft: win a mdn.

4171} **PEACEFUL PROMISE** 203 [7] E A L Dunlop 3-8-11 J Reid 20/1: 0-3: 3 b c Cadeaux Genereux - Island   ¾   **88**
Wedding (Blushing Groom) Handy, chall 2f out, no extra ins last: reapp rtd 73 sole unplcd juv start: brother
to a 1m/10f wnr: dam 7f/1m scorer: eff at 7f, sure to relish a step up to 1m: handles gd/soft: must win a mdn.

4440} **DANDILUM** 183 [4] V Soane 3-8-11 G Hind 25/1: 3022-4: Waited with, rdn over 2f out, kept on fnl   2   **85**
1f, no danger: plcd on 4 of 5 juv starts (rtd 89): eff at 6/7f, could get further: acts on fast & gd/soft.

3733} **BLUE MOUNTAIN** 231 [14] 3-8-11 L Dettori 20/1: -235-5: In tch, eff to chall over 2f out, no extra   hd   **84**
appr fnl 1f: plcd on 2 of 3 juv starts (mdns, rtd 89): eff at 5/6f, stays 7f on firm & gd/soft & on any trk.

4542} **HAMLYN** 174 [1] 3-8-11 M J Kinane 14/1: 50-6: Waited with, eff over 2f out, wknd fnl 1f: unplcd   nk   **83**
on 2 juv starts (rtd 76): stays 7f on gd/soft, bred to get further.

--   **PARAGON OF VIRTUE** [11] 3-8-11 K Fallon 13/8 FAV: 7: Slow away, bhd, eff 2f out, sn no impress: ¾   **82**
hvly bckd on debut: half brother to wnrs at up to 12f: dam smart Park Hill stks scorer: should do better.

840   **JUMBO JET** 13 [6] 3-8-11 (t) J Fortune 20/1: 48: Waited with, rdn 2f out, no danger: see 840.   1¾   **79**

--   **ELGHANI** [15] 3-8-11 R Hills 33/1: 9: In tch, wknd over 2f out on debut: dam 6f juv scorer: ½   **78**
bred to apprec 7f/1m: with R Armstrong.

4542} **GOLDEN RETRIEVER** 174 [2] 3-8-11 N Pollard 33/1: 0-0: Al bhd: 10th, reapp.   2   **75**

789   **KNIGHTS EMPEROR** 21 [3] 3-8-11 J Weaver 25/1: 0-40: Al bhd, 11th, apprec 1m+.   1   **74**

4493} **FREDDY FLINTSTONE** 180 [9] 3-8-11 R Hughes 33/1: 05-0: Led over 4f, wknd 2f out: 12th.   hd   **74**

--   **ORIENT EXPRESS** [10] 3-8-11 D R McCabe 33/1: 0: Handy till wknd over 2f out: 13th, dam 7f wnr.   hd   **74**

--   **APACHE POINT** [12] 3-8-11 W Ryan 16/1: 0: Keen, cl-up till wknd over 2f out: 14th, stable-mate   ¾   **72**
of wnr: dam useful over 6/11f: bred for 1m+.

789   **Krispin** 21 [5] 3-8-11 D Holland 50/1:   --   **Precious Love** [8] 3-8-11 M Hills 20/1:
--   **Under The Sand** [18] 3-8-11 P Robinson 33/1:   840   **Woodland River** 13 [17] 3-8-11 R Cochrane 25/1:
18 ran   Time 1m 28.84 (5.64)   (K Abdulla)   H R A Cecil Newmarket

984 4.45 EBF KIRKWOOD MDN 2YO (D)   5f   Soft Inapplicable
£4914   £1512   £756   £378

-- **CERTAIN JUSTICE** [7] P F I Cole 2-8-11 J Fortune 11/10 FAV: 1: 2 gr c Lit de Justice - Pure **96+**
Misk (Rainbow Quest) With ldrs till went on over 1f out, styd on strongly, shade cosily: hvly bckd on debut:
Mar foal, cost 36,000 gns: half brother to wnrs over 7f/10f: speed to win at 5f, sure to stay further in
time: runs well fresh on soft grnd: type to progress with racing & score plenty more times.
-- **DOMINUS** [8] R Hannon 2-8-11 R Hughes 10/1: 2: 2 b c Primo Dominie - Howlin' (Alleged) 1¼ **91**
Led halfway till over 1f out, not pace of wnr ins last: debut: Apr foal, cost IR 33,000: dam won in France:
eff at 5f, 6f will suit: handles soft grnd: gd debut, shld be winning on a minor trk sn.
-- **BARKING MAD** [5] M L W Bell 2-8-11 M Fenton 8/1: 3: 2 b c Dayjur - Avian Assembly (General 2 **87+**
Assembly) Slow away & sn bhd, styd on strongly over 1f out, nrst fin: op 5/1 on debut: Jan foal, cost $32,000:
dam smart at up to 9f: eff at 5f, will relish a step up to 6f: acts on soft grnd: learn plenty from this
promising debut, will rate much more highly & one to note next time.
700 **MAGIC BOX 28** [1] A P Jarvis 2-8-11 L Dettori 15/2: 64: Led till halfway, btn over 1f out. 1¼ **82**
-- **BANJO BAY** [10] 2-8-11 G Duffield 14/1: 5: With ldrs, wknd fnl 1f: debut: Apr 3rd foal, 2½ **76**
cost 27,000 gns: bred to apprec 6f/7f later on & showed some promise here.
-- **HOMELIFE** [6] 2-8-11 W Ryan 25/1: 6: Al bhd on debut: Mar foal, cost 13,000 gns: half brother 5 **64**
to a 7f scorer: bred to need 6f+ & time.
-- **SOLDIER ON** [3] 2-8-11 T Quinn 9/1: 7: In tch, wknd & faulted over 1f out: Apr foal, cost 3½ **56**
17,500 gns: half brother to a 7f scorer: dam 9f wnr: will apprec 6f+ later on.
-- **WALDOR** [4] 2-8-11 D Harrison 25/1: 8: Dwelt, al bhd. ¾ **54**
-- **MEDIA BUYER** [9] 2-8-11 Pat Eddery 9/1: 9: Al outpcd: debut. shd **54**
-- **ULTIMAJUR** [2] 2-8-11 D Holland 14/1: 0: In tch, btn over 2f out: last: reportedly lost a shoe. 7 **40**
10 ran   Time 1m 03.8 (4.88)   (The Blenheim Partnership)   P F I Cole Whatcombe, Oxon

985 5.20 THETFORD CONDITIONS STKS 2YO (C)   5f   Soft Inapplicable
£5712   £2112   £1056   £480

*812 **SHOESHINE BOY 17** [5] B J Meehan 2-9-2 Pat Eddery 7/2: 211: 2 b g Prince Sabo - Susie Sunshine **94**
(Waajib) Made all, kept on for press over 1f out despite edging left, rdn out: nicely bckd: earlier scored
at Warwick (auct mdn): half brother to a 7f wnr, dam 9f scorer: eff at 5f, 6f will suit in time: acts
on fast, soft & on any trk: useful & held in some regard.
-- **EMMS** [2] P F I Cole 2-8-9 J Fortune 2/1 FAV: 2: 2 gr c Fastness - Carnation (Carwhite) 1¼ **84+**
Dwelt, sn in tch, eff over 3f out, kept on nicely ins last under hands & heels riding: hvly bckd on debut: Apr
foal: half brother to a 1m scorer: sure to relish 6f in time: handles soft: pleasing debut, improve & win races.
843 **NEARLY A FOOL 12** [1] B A McMahon 2-9-4 G Duffield 9/1: 143: 2 b g Komaite - Greenway Lady (Prince ¾ **90**
Daniel) Chsd wnr, eff over 1f out, no extra fnl 1f: consistent, handles gd/firm & soft.
891 **BLAKESHALL BOY 7** [4] M R Channon 2-8-12 T Quinn 9/2: 34: In tch, wkng when hung left over 1f out. 6 **70**
-- **KOMPLIMENT** [3] 2-8-9 K Fallon 4/1: 5: Dwelt, al bhd: nicely bckd: Apr foal, cost 16,000 gns: 1¾ **62**
half brother to a 1m wnr: with A Bailey.
5 ran   Time 1m 03.12 (4.92)   (Oneoneone Racing)   B J Meehan Upper Lambourn, Berks

Official Going   HEAVY after 2nd Race (Heavy Rain).

986 1.30 CHEADLE CLASSIFIED STKS 3YO+ 0-85 (C)   1m2f120y Heavy Slow
£8437   £2596   £1298   £649   3yo rec 19lb   Field came stands side in staight.

757 **CELESTIAL WELCOME 25** [1] Mrs M Reveley 5-9-4 A Culhane 9/4 FAV: 006-61: 5 b m Most Welcome - **83**
Choral Sundown (Night Shift) Slow away & niggled thr'out, hdwy to lead over 1f out, drvn to assert ins last,
gamely: nicely bckd: '99 scorer at Newcastle (reapp) & Haydock (2, h'caps, incl val Old Newton Cup, rtd 91):
'98 wnr at Hamilton, Carlisle, Newcastle & Redcar: eff at 1m, stays 12f on firm, likes hvy grnd & any trk, esp
a gall one such as Newcastle/Haydock: has run well fresh under big weights: v tough & genuine mare.
786 **MANTUSIS 24** [3] P W Harris 5-9-9 Pat Eddery 9/2: 001-32: 5 ch g Pursuit Of Love - Mana (Windwurf) 1 **88**
Hld up, hdwy over 2f out, chall ins last, kept on for press, only btn 1L: acts on firm & hvy: knocking on door.
733 **CULZEAN 28** [4] R Hannon 4-9-7 R Hughes 5/2: 303-53: 4 b g Machiavellian - Eileen Jenny (Kris) 4 **81**
Prom, led over 3f out till over 1f out, slightly squeezed & no extra ins last: bckd: handles hvy grnd.
1728} **RAPIER 324** [6] M D Hammond 6-9-7 T Quinn 11/1: /010-4: Handy, onepace fnl 2f: won 2nd of 3 hd **81**
'99 starts, at Ayr (h'cap, rtd 84): in 98/99 won at Ayr (nov hdle, rtd 100h, 2m): '98 Flat wnr at York (h'cap,
rtd 90): eff at 1m/10f on firm, soft & on any trk: has run well fresh: gd reapp, has broken blood vessels.
4271} **FREDORA 198** [7] 5-9-4 Dale Gibson 12/1: 0200-5: Keen, handy, ev ch over 2f out, wknd well over 4 **73**
1f out: reapp: '99 scorer at Salisbury (class stks, rtd 87 at best): '98 wnr at Kempton (2, mdn & h'cap,
rtd 91): eff at 7f, stays 10.2f on firm & gd, handles gd/soft & any trk: will do better on a sounder surface.
3984} **MAKE WAY 217** [2] 4-9-7 J F Egan 9/1: D436-6: Held up, eff well over 2f out, sn wknd: reapp, op 2½ **73**
7/1: '99 wnr at Windsor (mdn, rtd 86 at best): eff at 1m/10f on firm, gd/soft & any trk: has run well in blnks.
884 **HADATH 10** [5] 3-8-2 G Duffield 40/1: 425-07: Led till over 3f out, sn btn: in '99 rnr-up at dist **0**
Salisbury (nov stks, rtd 91): eff at 7f on firm, soft & a gall trk.
7 ran   Time 2m 28.14 (18.14)   (The Welcome Alliance)   Mrs M Reveley Lingdale, N Yorks

987 2.00 GR 3 JOHN PORTER STKS 4YO+ (A)   1m4f   Heavy Fair
£21000   £8050   £4025   £1925   4yo rec 1lb   Field came stands side in str

767 **YAVANAS PACE 28** [11] M Johnston 8-9-1 D Holland 7/1: 206-01: 8 ch g Accordion - Lady In Pace **114**
(Burslem) Set pace, rdn & hdd over 3f out, rallied gamely for hard driving to lead again over 1f out, kept on,
all out, gamely: op 5/1: '99 scorer at Leicester, Goodwood (List) & Epsom (Gr 3, rtd 115): '98 wnr at Ayr,
Sandown (h'cap), Galway (List) & Doncaster (November H'cap, rtd 113): eff at 12/14f on firm, likes soft & hvy,

any trk: runs well fresh: smart, v tough & most genuine entire, credit to his trainer.

2479} **CAPRI 291** [8] H R A Cecil 5-9-3 T Quinn 11/2: -010-2: 5 ch h Generous - Island Jamboree (Explodent)　hd　115
Cl-up, led on bit over 3f out, rdn & hdd over 1f out, rallied cl-home for press, just held: jockey received
a one day whip ban, top-weight: won 2nd of only 3 '99 starts, at Chantilly (Gr 2, rtd 116): '98 wnr at Newmarket
(2, mdn & stks) & Ascot (Gr 3, rtd 116): suited by 12f, just stays 2m: handles firm, likes gd/soft & hvy: runs
well fresh on any trk: v smart, win another Gr race in similar conditions.

4608} **LIFE IS LIFE 169** [2] M A Jarvis 4-8-8 P Robinson 8/1: 3102-3: 4 b f Monsonnien - Le Vie Immobile　2　104
(Alleged) Keen in rear, hdwy over 2f out, kept on same pace: reapp: lightly rcd in '99, won at Kempton (mdn, rtd
100 at best): ex-French: eff at 12f, stays 14.6f & a return to that trip will suit: enjoys hvy grnd: v useful.

2046} **BIENNALE 310** [1] Sir Michael Stoute 4-8-11 R Hughes 10/1: 2/13-4: Prom, eff over 2f out, onepace:　4　102
drifted from 5/1 on reapp: only twice rcd in '99, won at Hamilton (mdn) & 3rd in a val h'cap at R Ascot (rtd
97): rtd 96 when rnr-up in mdns in '98: stays 12f well on fast & gd/soft, poss just handles hvy: has run
well fresh on a stiff trk: encouraging reapp, sharper on a sounder surface next time.

4608} **RAISE A PRINCE 169** [9] 7-8-12 (t) N Callan 16/1: 3033-5: Slow away, sn in tch, rdn & no impress　4　97
fnl 2f: reapp: '99 scorer at Nottingham (stks) & plcd sev times (rtd 108 at best): '98 scorer at Ayr, Newmarket
& Ascot (h'caps, rtd 102): eff at 12f/2m & handles firm & both A/Ws, loves soft: eff with/without a visor &
wears a t-strap: tough & useful, sharper for this.

-- **ORCHESTRA STALL** [6] 8-8-12 Pat Eddery 14/1: 0121/6: Waited with, eff well over 3f out, no impress:　1½　95
comeback: missed '99 & '98, in '97 won at Ascot, The Curragh & Longchamp (all Gr 3s, rtd 121): v eff at 14f/2m
& handles firm, likes gd/soft & handles hvy: enjoys a gall trk: high-class stayer at best, much sharper for this.

3817} **ASHGAR 228** [4] 4-8-11 G Duffield 33/1: 1340-7: In tch, rdn & btn over 2f out.　2½　92

4617} **MAYLANE 168** [5] 6-8-12 M Roberts 7/1: 3511-8: Slow away & lost 8L, eff over 3f out, sn btn: reapp:　hd　92
in '99 won fnl 2, at Haydock & Doncaster (List, rtd 108): unplcd both '98 starts for S Bin Suroor: Gr 3 wnr in '97
(rtd 117): eff at 12f on firm & hvy: best without blnks: v smart but is temperamental (often loses ch at start).

+732 **LARGESSE 28** [10] 6-8-12 J F Egan 10/3 FAV: 405-19: In tch, rdn & btn 3f out: enjoys the mud,　4　87
something amiss?: much btr 732.

-- **TAUFANS MELODY** [3] 9-8-12 K Darley 14/1: 5114/0: With ldrs, wknd 3f out: op 10/1, comeback.　½　86

4489} **LIGHTNING ARROW 182** [7] 4-8-11 W Supple 14/1: 0430-0: Al bhd: fin last on reapp.　nk　85

11 ran　　Time 2m 45.86 (18.06)　　(Mrs Joan Keaney)　　M Johnston Middleham, N Yorks

---

988   2.30 LISTED FIELD MARSHAL STKS 3YO (A)   5f str   Heavy Fair
　　　£16445　£5060　£2530　£1265

-829 **WATCHING 16** [1] R Hannon 3-8-11 R Hughes 5/1 CO FAV: 423-21: 3 ch c Indian Ridge - Sweeping　　115
(Indian King) Switched from far side to lead over on stands rail, pushed clr over 1f out, impressive: '99 scorer
at Chester (mdn), subs plcd in Gr company (rtd 100): stays 6f, much improved dominating over 5f here: acts on fm,
relishes hvy & handles any trk: tough colt, smart eff from the front & can win a Gr race under these conditions.

4197} **PIPADASH 203** [13] T D Easterby 3-8-6 K Darley 5/1 CO FAV: 3150-2: 3 b f Pips Pride - Petite Maxine　5　99
(Sharpo) Cl-up, rdn well over 1f out, kept on but not pace of impress wnr: nicely bckd, reapp: juv scorer at
Haydock (auct mdn), Pontefract & Ascot (stks, rtd 96): all wins at 5f, stays 6f: acts on fast & hvy grnd, likes
a gall trk: eff with/without blnks: game & useful, gd comeback, shld be plcd to effect.

4286} **TARAS GIRL 196** [12] J J Quinn 3-8-6 A Culhane 14/1: 0020-3: 3 b f Fayruz - Florissa (Persepolis)　2½　95
Sn in tch, rdn 2f out, kept on over 1f out: juv scorer at Beverley (2, auct mdn & stks), subs rnr-up in List
company (rtd 100): eff at 5f, races like 6f will suit: acts on fast, likes soft & hvy, stiff trk: has run well
fresh when forcing the pace: useful, spot on next time over slightly further.

734 **AWAKE 28** [11] M Johnston 3-8-11 D Holland 13/2: 12D-04: In tch, hdwy & slightly short of room　3½　93
over 1f out, onepace: as a juv scored at Epsom (mdn) & Newbury (nurs h'cap, rtd 98 at best): suited by 6f
& handles fast, enjoys hvy grnd & any trk: has run well fresh: should do better.

4073} **SUSIES FLYER 211** [9] 3-8-6 J Carroll 20/1: W115-5: Sn rdn in tch, no impress over 1f out: reapp:　3　82
as a juv won at Lingfield (mdn) & Newbury (nurs h'cap, rtd 89): eff at 5f & likes firm/fast grnd, prob handles soft.

913 **SERAPHINA 8** [10] 3-8-6 G Duffield 5/1 CO FAV: 204-06: Cl-up trav well, wknd qckly over 2f out.　½　81

4482} **LABRETT 182** [8] 3-8-11 (bl) D R McCabe 33/1: 5000-7: Nvr a factor on reapp: in '99 scored at Redcar　1¾　83
& Chester (nov stks, rtd 98 at best): eff at 5/6f on fast, gd/soft grnd & on any trk: wears blnks.

3694} **PUNCTUATE 235** [5] 3-8-11 J F Egan 7/1: 11-8: Sn rdn & nvr a factor: won both juv starts, at Sandown　½　82
& Ripon (stks, rtd 100): eff at 6f on fast & gd grnd & on any trk: do better on a sound surface.

2396} **BRAVE BURT 295** [7] 3-8-11 J Weaver 16/1: 1130-9: Chsd ldrs, wknd over 2f out: in '99 trained by　¾　80
J Berry, won 1st 2, at Carlisle (mdn) & Bath (stks), plcd at R Ascot (stkd, rtd 91): eff at 5f, shld stay
6f: has run well fresh on firm & gd grnd: useful at best, this was his first run on testing grnd.

4137} **KALINDI 207** [2] 3-8-6 T Quinn 14/1: 5200-0: In tch, btn halfway, 10th, reapp.　3½　69

4482 **KELSO MAGIC 182** [6] 3-8-6 Pat Eddery 8/1: 0546-0: Bhnd fnl 3f: 11th, reapp.　hd　69

2561} **BOLEYN CASTLE 288** [4] 3-8-11 A Clark 20/1: 165-0: Handy till wknd halfway: 12th, reapp, softer grnd.　1¾　71

3256} **GALLOWAY BOY 258** [3] 3-8-11 W Supple 14/1: 1040-0: In tch till wknd over 2f out: reapp.　1¾　68

13 ran　　Time 1m 07.34 (8.54)　　(Mrs Dare Wigan)　　R Hannon East Everleigh, Wilts

---

989   3.05 WELCOME BREAK MDN AUCT 2YO (E)   5f str   Heavy Slow
　　　£2975　£850　£425

-- **SULTAN GAMAL** [7] B A McMahon 2-8-3 P Robinson 14/1: -1: 2 b c Mind Games - Jobiska (Dunbeath)　84+
Slowly away & badly outpcd, virtually t.o. over 1f out, amazing late run to lead nr line: 6,200gns Mar foal:
half brother to a couple of wnrs, sire a high-class juv: eff at 5f, sure to relish 6f+: acts on a gall trk &
revels in testing conditions: runs well fresh: big sort, looks sure to improve & rate higher.

886 **FRANICA 10** [5] A Bailey 2-7-12 A Mackay 9/2: -222: 2 b f Inzar - Comfrey Glen (Glenstal)　nk　77
Prom, went on 2f out till caught entering strides: another sound run, deserves a change of luck: see 886, 812.

-- **FANTASY BELIEVER** [14] J J Quinn 2-8-6 A Culhane 20/1: -3: 2 b g Sure Blade - Delicious (Dominion)　1¾　82
Prsd ldrs, ev ch 2f out, not qckn in fnl 1f: Apr foal, cost 8,000gns: eff at 5f on hvy, sure to learn from this.

843 **SQUIRREL NUTKIN 14** [4] M L W Bell 2-8-6 M Fenton 9/2: -224: Prom, onepcd fnl 1f: op 3/1, 8L　1　80
clr rem: handles hvy, better on gd grnd in 843 & 730.

-- **ELSIE PLUNKETT** [6] 2-7-12 C Rutter 10/1: -5: Prsd ldrs till wknd over 1f out: op 16/1: 6,500gns　8　57
Feb foal: sire a high-class 2yo wnr: with R Hannon, ran well for a long way & worth another ch on better grnd.

755 **RAGAMUFFIN 25** [8] 2-8-6 K Darley 7/2 FAV: -46: Led, drifted left, hdd over 1f out & sn fdd:　3½　59
hvly bckd from 5/1: better expected after 755.

-- **HUMES LAW** [2] 2-8-3 O Pears 14/1: -7: Chsd ldrs & sn rdn, no impress fnl 2f: 4,000gns purchase:　shd　56
May foal, related to a 6f juv wnr: with A Berry & shld do better on faster grnd.

-- **TOMAMIE** [13] 2-7-12 Dale Gibson 33/1: -8: Al outpcd, nvr dangerous: cheaply bought Apr foal: 1¼ 48
dam a 6f 2yo wnr: sire a high-class sprint wnr: with J Norton.

-- **NAKWA** [11] 2-8-8 W Supple 10/1: -9: Nvr nr ldrs, well bhd on debut: IR 15,000gns purchase: Mar 9 42
foal, half brother to 5f 2yo wnr Fairy Gem: sire a useful miler: with E Alston & worth another ch on better grnd.

-- **ONLY ONE LEGEND** [3] 2-8-8 J Carroll 16/1: -0: Dwelt, nvr a factor: longer riced stable-mate of 6th. 1 40

-- **MISS BRIEF** [10] 2-8-3(2ow) J F Egan 20/1: -0: Prsd ldrs 3f, wknd, t.o. in 11th. 9 19

-- **LA FOSCARINA** [9] 2-8-2(4ow) D R McCabe 14/1: -0: Al outpcd, t.o. in 12th. nk 17

-- **PRINCESS OF GARDA** [1] 2-8-3 G Duffield 33/1: -U: Swerved left leaving stalls, sn u.r. 0

13 ran   Time 1m 08.27 (9.77)   (G S D Imports Ltd)   B A McMahon Hopswas, Staffs

---

990	3.35 SPONSORSHIP RTD HCAP 3YO 0-100 (C) 1m2f120y Heavy Slow	[104]

£6613 £2035 £1017 £508   Runners came to the centre in the home straight

4483} **HOLDING COURT** 182 [7] M A Jarvis 3-9-7 (97) P Robinson 15/8 FAV: 6210-1: 3 b c Hernando - Indian 108
Love Song (Be My Guest) Made all, clr fnl 2f, drvn out: well bckd on reapp, top weight: trained by B Meehan to
win here at Haydock in '99 (stks, rtd 97), unplcd in Gr 1 Racing Post Trophy on fnl start: half brother to
high-class 6/7f performer Tomba: eff at 10.5f, will stay 12f: acts on gd & hvy grnd, handles a gall trk, likes
Haydock: runs well fresh & likes to set the pace: gd weight carrier: holds a Derby entry, clearly useful.

810   **FIRST TRUTH** 21 [4] A Bailey 3-8-13 (89) G Duffield 8/1: 15-642: 3 b c Rudimentary - Pursuit Of Truth 3½ 94
(Irish river) Chsd wnr thr'out, no impress fnl 2f: well clr of rem: stays a stiff 10f on gd/soft & hvy: fine run.

4528} **PRINCE AMONG MEN** 178 [3] M C Pipe 3-8-7 (83)(1oh) M Roberts 8/1: 3336-3: 3 b c Robellino - 19 69
Forelino (Trempolino) Chsd ldrs till outpcd ent str, no ch with front 2: reapp: trained mainly in Ireland in
'99, plcd in mdns & h'caps: eff at 6/7f, much longer 10f trip today: acts on gd & soft grnd: capable of better.

4561} **MISBEHAVE** 20 [2] M L W Bell 3-9-3 (93) M Fenton 8/1: 010-04: Sn well bhd, nvr nr ldrs: unplcd in 1¼ 77
a List event in Italy 3 wks ago: '99 wnr at Warwick (mdn auct), Windsor (stks) & Newmarket (nurs h'cap): eff
at 1m, shld stay 10f: acts on firm, soft & f/sand: handles any trk: can set the pace: capable of much better.

4215} **UNAWARE** 203 [6] Pat Eddery 4/1: 4104-5: In tch till btn ent str, eased, t.o.: reapp: '99 22 56
Chepstow wnr (mdn, rtd 92+): half brother to smart stayer Brimming: dam & sire high-class mid-dist performers:
eff at 1m, bred for mid-dists: acts on gd & fast grnd, handles a gall trk: capable of better on a sound surface.

*709   **FAVORISIO** 30 [1] 3-8-7 (83)(1oh) K Darley 5/1: 00-116: Chsd ldrs till ent str, sn well bhd, t.o. 2½ 45

4348} **ASTON MARA** 192 [5] D Holland 3-8-10 (86) D Holland 16/1: -154-7: Prsd ldrs till wknd qckly 4f out, t.o. fnl 3f: 3 45
reapp: lightly rcd in '99, debut wnr at Newcastle (mdn, rtd 89), subs tried List company: dam a 1m/14f wnr:
eff at 7f, bred for mid-dists: acts on fast grnd, has disapp twice on hvy: can run well fresh on a gall trk.

7 ran   Time 2m 31.41 (21.41)   (J R Good)   M A Jarvis Newmarket

---

991	4.05 TOTE HCAP 4YO+ 0-100 (C) 1m4f Heavy Fair	[99]

£7442 £2290 £1145 £572   4yo rec 1lb   Runners stayed far side home straight

786   **SPRING PURSUIT** 24 [5] R J Price 4-8-8 (80) P Fitzsimons (5) 11/1: 2-6021: 4 b g Rudimentary - 88
Pursuit Of Truth (Irish River) Trkd ldrs, smooth hdwy to lead 2f out, sn clr, readily: '99 wnr at Brighton, York,
Windsor & Lingfield (h'caps, rtd 78): '98 Warwick wnr (nov auct, rtd 86, with R Charlton): eff at 10f, stays 12f:
acts on gd, relishes hvy: has tried blnks, seems best without: gd weight carrier: v progressive in testing grnd.

4619} **LORD LAMB** 168 [3] Mrs M Reveley 8-9-5 (90) K Darley 8/1: /323-2: 8 gr g Dunbeath - Caroline Lamb 6 92
(Hotfoot) Waited with, imprvd 3f out, styd on fnl 1f but no ch with wnr: hdle wnr at Doncaster & here at Haydock
this winter (h'cap, rtd 144h, eff at 2m/2½m on any grnd/trk): lightly rcd on the Flat in '99, plcd on all 3
starts, incl cl 3rd in the November H'cap (rtd 92): '98 4yo hdles wnr at Newcastle (2) & Wetherby (nov): '98 Flat
wnr at Haydock (h'cap, rtd 81): eff at 12f, stays 2m well on firm & hvy, likes a gall trk: deserves a val prize.

4619} **CARLYS QUEST** 168 [2] J Neville 6-8-11 (82)(tvi) T Quinn 8/1: 3302-3: 6 ch g Primo Dominie - Tuppy 4 80
(Sharpen Up) Chsd ldrs, ev ch 2f out, onepace fnl 1f: 10L clr rem, reapp: failed to win in '99, plcd sev times,
notably when hdd 2nd in the November H'cap (rtd 84): '98 wnr at Newmarket & Warwick (h'caps): eff at 10/12f on
fm & hvy: handles a sharp or gall trk, wears blnks or visor & t-strap: best held up for a late run: win again.

*809   **INIGO JONES** 21 [16] P W Harris 4-9-8 (94) Pat Eddery 7/2 FAV: 133-14: Front rank, led briefly 10 82
after 2f, again 5f out till 2f out, fdd: well bckd: nvr bettr fin past these testing conditions: see 809 (C/D).

809   **HILL FARM BLUES** 21 [11] 7-8-5 (76) G Gibbons (7) 14/1: 400-45: Dwelt, hdwy 3f out, no impress 11 53
fnl 2f: ideally suited by 14f/2m: see 809 (C/D).

4103} **LIGNE GAGNANTE** 209 [7] 4-9-4 (90) J F Egan 9/1: 3532-6: In tch till outpcd fnl 3f: reapp: '99 wnr 1½ 65
at Ayr (rtd mdn), Goodwood & Newcastle (h'caps), subs plcd sev times (rtd 90 at best): eff at 9/13f: acts on
fast & soft grnd, handles a sharp/undul or gall trk: can run well fresh: progressive last term, fitter next time.

4359} **COULTHARD** 191 [10] 7-9-1 (86) M Fenton 12/1: 1000-7: Mid-div, outpcd fnl 2f: recent jumps rnr, 6 55
in Jan '00 rnr-up at Cheltenham (h'cap hdle, rtd 128h, eff at 2m on gd/soft & hvy): '99 wnr here at Haydock
(h'cap, rtd 92, reapp): this race, 1lb lower mark, scored (h'cap, rtd 92, reapp): 98/99 Towcester & Warwick hdles wnr (h'caps): '98 Windsor
wnr (mdn, rtd 89): eff at 10/12f, acts on firm, likes soft grnd: acts on any trk: on a fair mark.

845   **WILCUMA** 16 [6] 9-8-13 (84) A Clark 14/1: 015538: Nvr a factor: see 845. 2½ 50

1302} **THREE GREEN LEAVES** 344 [1] 4-9-11 (97) J Fanning 20/1: 4/04-9: Prom till lost place 3f out, no 2½ 60
ch after: twice rcd in '99, 4th at Newbury (List, rtd 98): '98 wnr at Beverley (2), Newcastle, Cork & Pontefract
(List, rtd 99): eff at 10f, 12f shld suit: acts on firm & soft: can force the pace & run well fresh.

815   **LITTLE AMIN** 19 [13] 4-8-3 (75) Martin Dwyer 25/1: 160-00: Chsd ldrs till lost place ent str, fin 10th. 5 33

4204} **DEE PEE TEE CEE** 203 [14] 6-9-1 (86) T Lucas 6/1: 6100-0: Early ldr, rem prom till wknd 3f out, 15 29
t.o. in 11th: recent jumps rnr.

845   **HIBERNATE** 14 [4] 6-7-13 (70) Joanna Badger 50/1: 000000: Led after 2f till 5f out, wknd nk 12
qckly, t.o.: fin 12th, saddle reportedly slipped: see 422 (AW).

805   **NOUKARI** 22 [8] 7-8-3 (74) D R McCabe 20/1: 532140: Chsd ldrs till wknd ent str, t.o. in 13th: 1½ 14
h'cap hdle wnr at Ludlow (2m, gd) since 805.

732   **LOOP THE LOUP** 28 [15] 4-9-12 (98) A Culhane 16/1: 122-50: In tch till btn over 3f out, t.o. in 14th. 17 23

4545} **RUM POINTER** 176 [9] 4-9-8 (94) J Carroll 14/1: 5100-0: Al bhd, t.o. in last: reapp. 6 13

15 ran   Time 2m 49.66 (21.86)   (E G Bevan)   R J Price Ullingswick, Hereford

---

992	4.40 BADGEHOLDERS MDN 3YO (D) 7f130y rnd Heavy Slow	

£4043 £1244 £622 £311   Runners stayed far side home straight

3662} **MR COSPECTOR** 236 [1] T H Caldwell 3-9-0 O Urbina 33/1: 5400-1: 3 b c Cosmonaut - L'Ancressaan 74
(Dalsaan) Chsd ldrs, styd on well to lead ins fnl 1f, drvn out: reapp: 4th at Pontefract in '99 (mdn auct, rtd 71):
dam won at 6f as a 2yo: eff at 7f, handles fast grnd, clrly revels in hvy: handles a gall trk, runs well fresh.

884   **CRISS CROSS** 10 [9]   R Hannon 3-9-0 R Hughes   4/9 FAV: 6-22: 3 b c Lahib - La Belle Katherine   1½   71
(Lyphard) Trkd ldrs, imprvd to lead over 2f out & qcknd clr, worn down cl-home: hvly bckd, 5L clr rem: see 884.

--   **WELCOME ABOARD** [3]   J G Given 3-8-9 Dean McKeown   10/1: -3: 3 ch f Be My Guest - Loreef (Main   5   58
Reef) Trkd ldrs, rdn halfway, not pace to chall: mkt drifter, debut: half sister to a 6/10f wnr: will apprec 1m+.

--   **MORNINGS MINION** [2]   R Charlton 3-9-0 R Perham   8/1: -4: Chsd ldrs till outpcd fnl 2f: op 6/1:   5   55
8,000gns half brother to 1m wnr Dom Shadeed: dam a 1m/10f wnr: with R Charlton & shld benefit from faster grnd.

877   **MADAME GENEREUX** 11 [4]   3-8-9 G Duffield   8/1: 0-45: Chsd ldrs till outpcd over 2f out: prob needs   9   38
1m+ & faster grnd: now qual for h'caps, see 877.

3755} **INVISIBLE FORCE** 231 [6]   3-9-0 J Fanning   20/1: -40-6: Led till over 2f out, wknd qckly, t.o. in last: 18   23
trained by B Rothwell in '99 & fin last on both starts (rtd 71): half brother to a 5f juv wnr: with M Johnston.

6 ran   Time 1m 42.38 (15.28)   (R Cabrera-Vargas)   T H Caldwell Appleton, Cheshire

---

KEMPTON   SATURDAY APRIL 22ND   Righthand, Flat, Fair Track

Official Going   SOFT (HEAVY in places). Stalls: Str Crse - Stands Side; 1m2f - Outside; rem - Inside.

993
2.05 EBF SOVEREIGN 0% TAX MDN 2YO (D)   **5f str**   **Soft 128**   **-61 Slow**
£3575   £1100   £550   £275

--   **SHUSH** [5]   C E Brittain 2-9-0 L Dettori   7/2 FAV: 1: 2 b c Shambo - Abuzz (Absalom)   84
In tch, eff 2f out, sn slightly outpaced, styd on well to lead ins last, going away: op 9/4: Apr foal,
half-brother to sev wnrs, notably smart juv World Premier, dam winning 5f juv, sire mid-dist performer: eff
at 5f but is going to apprec much further in time: acts on soft/hvy grnd & runs well fresh: well regarded.

--   **PRINCES STREET** [4]   R Hannon 2-9-0 Dane O'Neill   4/1: 2: 2 b c Sri Pekan - Abbey Strand (Shadeed)   2   78
Prom, led ent fnl 2f, hdd & no extra ins last: op 5/2: Apr foal, half-brother to a 7f wnr & stayer Temple Way,
dam wng miler, sire a top-class juv: eff at 5f, will get 6f in time: handles soft/hvy grnd & shld find similar.

--   **THE TRADER** [6]   M Blanshard 2-9-0 D Sweeney   12/1: 3: 2 ch c Selkirk - Snowing (Tate Gallery)   3½   71
Mid-div, switched to impr 2f out, sn onepcd: 23,000gns Apr foal, dam 5f wnr: poss handles soft/hvy, apprec 6f.

812   **IF BY CHANCE** 19 [9]   D W P Arbuthnot 2-9-0 J Reid   12/1: 04: Chsd ldrs till fdd appr fnl 1f: 5,000gns   1½   68
Risk Me Mar foal, half-brother to a wng juv sprinter, dam 5f winning juvenile.

--   **MY FRIEND JACK** [2]   2-9-0 K Fallon   9/2: 5: Led till ent fnl 2f, sn btn: 5,000gns Petong Feb   shd   68
foal, dam unrcd, sire a sprinter: clr of rem, with J Akehurst.

--   **ZHITOMIR** [3]   2-9-0 W Ryan   10/1: 6: V slow away & detached, nvr got in it: 22,000gns Lion Cavern   5   58
Feb first foal, dam well related mdn, sire 6/7f performer: shld do better in time: with S Dow.

--   **THOMAS SMYTHE** [8]   2-9-0 G Carter   7/1: 7: V slow away, nvr in it: gamble from 14/1: IR 10,000gns   9   42
College Chapel Feb foal, half-brother to a 3yo wnr abroad: dam a mdn, sire 6/7f wnr: with N Littmoden.

--   **JACKS BIRTHDAY** [1]   2-9-0 S Sanders   20/1: 8: Handy till 2f out: op 14/1: 2,500gns Mukaddamah   2½   37
Feb foal, dam unrcd, sire a miler: with R O'Sullivan.

--   **THATS ALL JAZZ** [7]   2-8-9 T G McLaughlin   33/1: 9: Veered right start, al rear: 800gns Prince Sabo   9   17
Mar first foal, dam modest, sire a sprinter: with T Clement.

9 ran   Time 1m 07.74 (9.44)   (Mrs C E Brittain)   C E Brittain Newmarket

994
2.40 SOVEREIGN 0% TAX HCAP 3YO 0-85 (D)   **6f str**   **Soft 128**   **-40 Slow**   [92]
£5414   £1666   £833   £416   2 groups, far side (high no's) had a significant advantage

4490} **DUKE OF MODENA** 182 [13]   G B Balding 3-9-1 (79) S Carson (5)   10/1: -603-1: 3 ch g Salse - Palace   87
Street (Secreto) Cl-up far side, rdn to lead appr fnl 1f, kept on well: reapp/h'cap bow: plcd fnl '99 start (mdn,
rtd 75), gelded since: half-brother to wng miler Cad Oro: eff at 6f, 7f+ will suit: goes well fresh on soft/hvy.

888   **SMOKIN BEAU** 10 [10]   J Cullinan 3-8-9 (73) J Fortune   12/1: -32002: 3 b c Cigar - Beau Dada (Pine   1½   77
Circle) Narrow lead far side till appr fnl 1f, kept on: tchd 20/1: gd run, acts on both AWs, gd/soft & sft/hvy.

852   **LAKELAND PADDY** 12 [6]   M Blanshard 3-8-9 (73) D Sweeney   14/1: 256-33: 3 b c Lake Coniston - Inshad   ¾   75+
(Indian King) Cl-up stands side, led that group 2f out, ran on: remarkable run, nrly 10L clr of next home on
his unfav'd side: goes on firm & soft/hvy grnd, deserves to shed mdn tag: see 852.

852   **CD FLYER** 12 [14]   M R Channon 3-8-11 (75) S Drowne   11/2: 05-064: Prom far side, under press appr   1½   74
fnl 1f, sn btn: acts on fast & gd/soft, handles soft/hvy: see 852.

2282} **CAIR PARAVEL** 300 [11]   3-9-7 (85) L Newman   9/1: 11-5: Bhd ldrs far side, unable to qckn appr   hd   84
fnl 1f: reapp/h'cap bow: won both '99 starts at Leicester (med auct mdn) & Doncaster (stks, match, rtd 89):
eff forcing the pace at 5/6f on fast & gd/soft grnd, poss sft/hvy: not disgraced under top-weight in this grnd.

792   **INDIAN SUN** 23 [8]   3-9-2 (80) K Fallon   7/2 FAV: 610-46: Outpcd far side, late hdwy, nvr a threat,   hd   78
well bckd: return to 7f may suit: see 792.

4164} **INFOTEC** 206 [15]   3-8-10 (74) J Stack   20/1: 022-7: Prom far side till 1½f out: op 14/1, reapp/h'cap   1¼   69
bow: rnr-up fnl 2 of 3 '99 starts (mdn, rtd 76): eff at 7f, bred for 1m+: acts on gd/soft & soft: with H Akbary.

852   **WATERGRASSHILL** 12 [6]   3-7-10 (60) (20h) J Mackay (7)   8/1: 54-528: Led stands side till 2f out,   6   43
sn btn: no ch from poo low draw: beat this 3rd & 4th last time in 852 (gd), see 105.

852   **ALAWAR** 12 [4]   3-8-7 (70)(1ow)(t) J Reid   16/1: 030-09: In tch 4f stands side: poor draw: see 852.   5   43

4542} **MAGELTA** 176 [3]   3-9-1 (79) Dane O'Neill   14/1: -043-0: Prom stands side 3f: 10th, stablemate of   10   32
5th, reapp/h'cap bow: plcd fnl '99 start (mdn, rtd 85 at best): eff at 6f on gd & gd/soft grnd.

888   **GRANDMA ULLA** 10 [7]   3-8-5 (69) S Sanders   33/1: 000-00: Sn struggling stands side: 11th: see 888.   ½   21

*852   **CASTLE SEMPILL** 12 [1]   3-8-13 (77) M Hills   10/1: 213510: Prom stands side till halfway: 13th, ignore.   0

4038} Best Bond 214 [5] 3-8-4 (68) D Young (5)   25/1:   3747} **Night Shifter** 232 [9] 3-8-6 (70) R Mullen 20/1:
14 ran   Time 1m 20.17 (10.07)   (Miss B Swire)   G B Balding Fyfield, Hants.

995
3.15 LISTED MASAKA STKS 3YO (A)   **1m jub**   **Soft 128**   **+05 Fast**
£14950   £4600   £2300   £1150

4487} **LADY UPSTAGE** 182 [2]   B W Hills 3-8-8 M Hills   11/2: 3014-1: 3 b f Alzao - She's The Tops (Shernazar)   103
Trkd ldrs, rdn to lead appr fnl 1f, ran on, drvn out: nicely bckd from 7/1, gd time: '99 Brighton wnr (mdn,
List 4th, rtd 98): eff at 1m, stay further: handles gd/soft/hvy, handles fast: goes well fresh: useful.

*915   **TANZILIR** 8 [1]   C E Brittain 3-8-8 L Dettori   5/4 FAV: 12: 3 b f Warning - Tanz (Sadler's Wells)   1   100
In tch, outpcd turning for home, gd hdwy under press appr fnl 1f, styd on but held by wnr: hvly bckd from
7/4: imprvd in defeat up in grade after debut win: eff at 1m, 10f+ is going to suit: acts on soft/hvy grnd: useful.

735 **BLUSIENKA 28** [5] G A Butler 3-8-8 N Pollard 5/1: -1-43: 3 b f Blues Traveller - Pudgy Poppet ¾ **99**
(Danehill) Chsd ldrs, feeling pace 2f out, rallied ins last: op 7/2: gd run, further improvement likely over 10f+.
4201} **SOLAIA 186** [7] P F I Cole 3-8-8 J Fortune 9/1: 1555-4: Cl-up, led 3f out till ent fnl 2f, onepace: *nk* **98**
op 6/1: '99 debut wnr at Newmarket (fill mdn, Gr 3 5th of 6, rtd 100): eff at 7f/1m, bred for further: acts on firm & soft/hvy grnd: finished clr of rem & this was a useful effort.
4136} **TEODORA 207** [4] 3-8-8 W Ryan 12/1: 1453-5: Keen, bhd ldrs, fdd fnl 2f: tchd 16/1 on reapp: *9* **83**
Windsor debut wnr last term (fill mdn), plcd in a val sales race (rtd 97): eff at 6/7f on firm & gd grnd: with S Dow.
4373} **AL GHABRAA 190** [3] 3-8-8 R Hills 14/1: 1-6: Keen in lead, hdd 3f out, sn btn: ruined any chance by *6* **74**
pulling: won sole '99 start at Redcar (med auct mdn, rtd 90): eff at 1m on fast grnd: can run well fresh, gall track.
4201} **FAIRY GEM 203** [6] 3-8-8 Dane O'Neill 10/1: 6460-7: Went it alone on ins rail & had no ch from 2f out: *3* **70**
op 6/1 on reapp: '99 debut wnr at Salisbury (fill stks, rtd 88, later 6th in a fill Gr 1, rtd 104$): eff at 5f, stays 7f: acts on firm & gd grnd: can leave this bhd on a faster surface: with R Hannon.
7 ran Time 1m 48.65 (9.85) (Mrs E Roberts) B W Hills Lambourn, Berks.

996

3.45 LISTED EASTER STKS 3YO (A) 1m jub Soft 128 -04 Slow
£15145 £4660 £2330 £1165

4102} **KINGSCLERE 209** [1] I A Balding 3-8-8 K Fallon 3/1 JT FAV: 4323-1: 3 b c Fairy King - Spurned **111**
(Robellino) Led, shkn up 2f out, drvn out ins last: drifter from 7/4, reapp: won first 2 in '99, at Newbury & York (stks, Gr 2 3rd, rtd 106): half-brother to smart miler Hidden Meadow: eff at 7f/1m, shld get further (will be aimed at the Derby): acts on fast, suited by gd/soft & hvy, any trk: goes well fresh, up with/forcing the pace: smart.
950 **SAFARANDO 4** [7] N P Littmoden 3-8-8 T G McLaughlin 9/2: 121162: 3 b c Turtle Island - Hertford *2½* **106**
Castle (Reference Point) Held up, prog 2f out, went 2nd bef dist, nvr any impress on wnr: well bckd, qck reapp, fair 6th in the Greenham on Tuesday & is clrly a much improved colt: acts on any grnd & fibresand: see 810.
735 **ZYZ 28** [4] B W Hills 3-8-8 M Hills 3/1 JT FAV: 213-23: 3 b c Unfuwain - Girette (General Assembly) *1* **104**
Well plcd, lost pl 2f out, rallied towards fin: well bckd: was reportedly struck into & a good run in the circumstances: acts on firm & soft/hvy grnd, needs 10f+ now: useful: see 735.
1978} **LINCOLN DANCER 312** [6] M A Jarvis 3-8-8 M Tebbutt 6/1: 1310-4: Chsd ldrs, rdn to go 2nd appr *1½* **102**
fnl 1f, no extra & eased towards fin: tchd 8/1 on reapp: '99 wnr at Warwick (mdn, debut) & York (stks, rtd 104, G Lewis): eff at 6f, shld get at least 7f: acts on gd/soft, prob sft/hvy grnd: useful at best.
4411} **BOGUS DREAMS 187** [5] 3-8-8 W R Swinburn 4/1: 113-5: Trkd wnr, rdn/btn 2f out: tchd 13/2: '99 *5* **94**
Thirsk (auct mdn) & Ascot wnr (stks, rtd 99): eff at 7f/1m on firm & soft: reportedly W Swinburn's last ride.
-- **JAMADYAN** [2] 3-8-8 J Stack 33/1: 1-6: Stumbled start, sn struggling, t.o.: op 16/1, returned *dist* **69**
lame on Brit bow: won sole '99 start in Italy (1m on gd grnd): with H Akbary.
6 ran Time 1mm 47.35 (10.55) (M Tabor) I A Balding Kingsclere, Hants.

997

4.15 QUEEN'S PRIZE HCAP 4YO+ 0-100 (C) 2m Soft 128 -04 Slow [95]
£10871 £3345 £1672 £836 4 yo rec 4 lb

1895} **CAPTAIN MILLER 316** [6] N J Henderson 4-7-10 (67) J Mackay (7) 16/1: 0210-1: 4 b g Batshoof - **76**
Miller's Gait (Mill Reef) Nvr far away, switched to lead going well appr fnl 1f, drifted left, shkn up, readily: op 20/1, jumps fit, won at Folkestone, Leicester & Huntingdon (juv novs, 2m1f, gd/soft, hvy grnd, rtd 126h): '99 wnr at Leicester (h'cap), Hamilton (class stks) & Ripon (clmr, rtd 71, M Channon): '98 Lingfield wnr (mdn auct, rtd 69): prev eff at 1m, relished step up to 2m (half-brother to smart stayer Bold Gait): acts on firm grnd, suited by soft/hvy: goes on any trk & runs well fresh, up with/forcing the pace: unexposed, progressive stayer.
*917 **BRAVE TORNADO 8** [8] G B Balding 9-8-9 (76) R Brisland (5) 11/4 FAV: 154/12: 9 ch g Dominion - *4* **80**
Accuracy (Gunner B) Cl-up, led 2½f out till bef dist, not pace of wnr: hvly bckd: lost nothing in defeat, loves soft.
4176} **BANGALORE 204** [9] Mrs A J Perrett 4-8-10 (81) K Fallon 5/1: 0336-3: 4 ch c Sanglamore - Ajuga *1½* **84**
(The Minstrel) Towards rear, imprvd appr fnl 2f, rdn bef fnl 1f, same pace: nicely bckd: hdles fit, won at Fontwell (juv nov) & Uttoxeter (nov, 10th in the Gr 1 Triumph inbtwn, 2m/2½m, firm & gd, handles hvy, rtd 134h): '99 reapp wnr at Pontefract (auct mdn, h'cap rnr-up, rtd 86, B Hills): eff at 10f/12f, stays 2m: goes on any grnd.
917 **BRIDIES PRIDE 8** [3] G A Ham 9-8-5 (72) G Bardwell 9/1: 200-24: Led till 2½f out, onepace fnl 1f. *1½* **74**
1349} **SERENUS 342** [2] 7-8-7 (74) N Pollard 10/1: 4/10-5: Chsd ldrs, squeezed for room turning for home & *1½* **75**
lost pl: shorter-priced stablemate of wnr, chase fit, scored at Newbury & Kempton (Gr 2 nov, 2m/2m4f, firm & soft, rtd 140c), former v useful hdler: '99 wnr here at Kempton (h'cap, rtd 75), lightly rcd on the Flat since '96: eff at 12f, this 2m trip is going to suit: acts on firm/fast, sharp or gall trk: worth another chance.
*726 **FINAL SETTLEMENT 28** [5] 5-7-12 (65) L Newman (0) 10/1: 433-16: Mid-div, prog & ev ch turning for *hd* **62**
home, fdd 2f out: tchd 12/1: further step up in trip: see 726 (1m6f here).
695 **TURTLE VALLEY 33** [4] 4-9-10 (95) P Doe 16/1: 040-07: Nvr a factor: remains unproven beyond 14f. *4* **93**
140 **SEREN HILL 144** [1] 4-9-0 (85) L Dettori 9/2: 3130-8: Held up, eff to chase ldrs 4f out, btn over 2f out, *5* **79**
eased: tchd 11/2 on reapp: '99 Haydock wnr (h'cap, rtd 89): '98 Redcar wnr (nurs, rtd 76): eff at 12/14f, stays a gall 2m: acts on fast & hvy, prob firm: likes gall trks & can run well fresh: with G Butler.
917 **PRAIRIE FALCON 8** [10] 6-9-6 (87) M Hills 14/1: /24-69: Held up, brief eff 3f out, eased: nds faster grnd. *5* **77**
845 **ROMAN KING 14** [7] 5-9-2 (83) J Fortune 12/1: 541-60: Nvr troubled ldrs: 10th, longer trip, see 845. *hd* **73**
10 ran Time 3m 45.37 (21.17) (W H Ponsonby) N J Henderson Lambourn, Berks.

998

4.50 SOVEREIGN CLASS STKS 3YO 0-90 (C) 1m2f Soft 128 +01 Fast
£6613 £2035 £1017 £508

4114} **SADDLERS QUEST 208** [3] G A Butler 3-8-12 L Dettori 15/8 FAV: 1-1: 3 b g Saddlers' Hall - Seren Quest **102**
(Rainbow Quest) Waited with, imprvd to lead ent fnl 2f, rdn clr dist, readily in the end: gd time, well bckd on reapp: unbtn, won sole '99 start at Bath (mdn, rtd 87+): half-brother to 14f wnr Siren Hill: eff at 10f, 12f is going to suit: acts on gd/soft & soft/hvy grnd: runs v well fresh: useful & progressive, shld win again.
4558} **KEW GARDENS 175** [2] Mrs A J Perrett 3-8-12 K Fallon 10/3: 0416-2: 3 ch c Arazi - Hatton Gardens *5* **94**
(Auction Ring) Prom, led ent fnl 3f till bef dist, sn outpcd by wnr: op 9/4 on reapp: '99 Pontefract wnr (mdn, rtd 86, List 6th, rtd 92$): eff at 1m/10f on gd/soft & prob soft/hvy grnd.
4263} **MISS LORILAW 199** [4] J W Hills 3-8-9 M Hills 5/1: 1-3: 3 b f Homme de Loi - Miss Lorika (Bikala) *1½* **89**
In tch, prog & ch 2f out, sn no extra: op 4/1 on reapp: won sole '99 start at York (med auct mdn, rtd 87): eff at 1m, bred to get 10f (Oaks entry): acts on gd/soft grnd & a gall trk: can run well fresh.
3560} **BLUE SUGAR 241** [1] J R Fanshawe 3-8-12 R Cochrane 4/1: 1-4: Held up, going well 3f out, sn pushed *10* **77**
along & btn, eased dist: op 3/1 on reapp: landed sole '99 start at Lingfield (med auct mdn, rtd 89): eff at 7.5f, shld stay further: acts on gd grnd & can run well fresh: prob worth another chance on faster grnd.
2193} **BREATHLESS DREAMS 303** [6] 3-8-12 J Fortune 12/1: 21-5: Led till 2½f out, wknd qckly: op 7/1 *19* **57**

on reapp: landed fnl of 2 '99 starts at Salisbury (auct mdn, rtd 88, M Bell): eff at 7f on firm grnd, handles soft, stiff/gall trk: reportedly hung in the closing stages & is better than this: with S Kettlewell.
5 ran   Time 2m 15.04 (12.74)   (The Fairy Story Partnership)   G A Butler Blewbury, Oxon.

999	**5.25 SOVEREIGN NO TAX HCAP 3YO 0-85 (D)** 1m1f **Soft 128 -12 Slow**	[92]
	£4621 £1422 £711 £355	

*727   **COMMON PLACE** 28 [4] C F Wall 3-9-7 (85) R Mullen 11/2: 0-5611: 3 b g Common Grounds - One Wild **90**
Oat (Shareef Dancer) Mid-div, prog 2f out, kept on gamely under press to wear down ldr nr fin: op 4/1: earlier won here at Kempton (C/D class stks): '99 Goodwood wnr (nurs h'cap, rtd 81): imprvd since stepped up to 9f: acts on gd & soft/hvy grnd, likes easy trks, esp Kempton: useful, in fine form.
892   **SPIRIT OF LIGHT** 9 [2] M R Channon 3-8-3 (67) S Drowne 9/2: 05-002: 3 b g Unblest - Light Thatch   *hd* **71**
(Thatch) Prom, led appr fnl 2f, under press this, held: well bckd, clr rem: gd run, eff at 1m/9f.
744   **FRENCH HORN** 26 [8] M J Ryan 3-8-2 (66) G Carter 7/4 FAV: 651-03: 3 b g Fraam - Runcina (Runnett)   4 **64**
Waited with, hdwy to chase ldrs 2f out, onepace ins last: hvly bckd from 5/2: eff at 9f, acts on soft: see 744.
4516}   **TOP HAND** 179 [1] B W Hills 3-8-11 (75) M Hills 7/1: 61-4: Chsd ldrs, wide into str & lost pl, rallied   3½ **68**
fnl 1f: reapp/h'cap bow: landed fnl of 2 '99 starts, at Bath (auct mdn, rtd 81): eff at 1m, shaped like further would suit here tho' sire a sprinter: acts on gd/soft grnd.
744   **YOU DA MAN** 26 [5] Dane O'Neill 13/2: 224125: Mid-div, prog 2f out, sn rdn, wknd: tchd 9/1.   4 **60**
813   **CHILWORTH** 19 [7] 3-7-11 (60) (BL) (1ow) A Nicholls (0) 33/1: 4-0056: Led till 2½f out, wknd: blinkered.   5 **42**
4373}   **TUMBLEWEED TOR** 190 [6] M J Tebbutt 20/1: 643-8: Al bhd: op 12/1 on reapp/h'cap   2½ **63**
bow: highly tried first 2 '99 starts (stks, rtd 89): half-brother to a winning sprinter: with B Meehan.
*771   **FIELD MASTER** 24 [3] 3-8-11 (75) S Sanders 14/1: 032218: Prom till 4f out, wknd qckly: see 771.   *dist* **0**
8 ran   Time 2m 02.57 (12.57)   (Induna Racing Partners Two)   C F Wall Newmarket.

Official Going   HEAVY (SOFT Places).   No stalls in use

1000	**2.00 SUNRISE FILLIES MED AUCT MDN 2YO (E)** 5f rnd **Heavy Inapplicable**	
	£2917 £833 £416 Flag start	

821   **QUIZZICAL LADY** 19 [2] M Quinn 2-8-11 Dane O'Neill 11/4: 051: 2 b f Mind Games - Salacious (Sallust)   **81**
Cl-up, rdn/led over 1f out, rdn clr ins last & eased nr fin: eff at 5f, shld get further: acts on hvy grnd, prob handles fast: likes a sharp/turning trk: reveled in these testing conditions, could win again.
865   **BEVERLEY MACCA** 13 [1] A Berry 2-8-11 J Carroll 2/1 FAV: 22: 2 ch f Piccolo - Kangra Valley   9 **70**
(Indian Ridge) Led 3f, rdn/no extra ins last: nicely bckd, op 5/2: turf bow: see 865 (AW).
--   **INNIT** [4] M R Channon 2-8-11 S Drowne 9/4: 3: 2 b f Distinctly North - Tidal Reach (Kris)   2½ **65**
Sltly hmpd start, sn rdn in tch, no impress over 1f out: op 13/8: Apr foal, cost IR 12,500gns: dam a 1m juv wnr, sire a high-class 2yo: shld apprec 6f+ in time: al struggling after hmpd at start, will know more next time.
--   **DISTANT DAWN** [3] B R Millman 2-8-11 M Fenton 4/1: 4: Dwelt, nvr on terms: op 5/2: Petong filly,   3 **59**
Apr foal, cost 5,000gns: dam 1m 2yo wnr, sire a high-class sprinter: worth another ch on faster grnd.
4 ran   Time 1m 06.20   (Mr & Mrs Gary Pinchen)   M Quinn Sparsholt, Oxon

1001	**2.30 AMADEUS MEDIUM RARE MDN 2YO (D)** 5f rnd **Heavy Inapplicable**	
	£3096 £952 £476 £238 Flag Start	

932   **IMPERIAL DANCER** 7 [2] M R Channon 2-9-0 S Drowne 15/8: 421: 2 b c Primo Dominie - Gorgeous Dancer **84**
(Nordico) Made virtually all, hdd briefly ins last, kept on gamely, rdn out: tchd 5/2: eff at 5f, will stay 6f+ (related to mid-dists performers): acts on hvy grnd & a sharp/turning trk: clrly going the right way.
849   **BARON CROCODILE** 14 [3] A Berry 2-9-0 J Carroll 7/4 FAV: 22: 2 b c Puissance - Glow Again (The   1¼ **80**
Brianstan) Handy, led briefly ins fnl 1f, no extra well ins last: 6L clr of rem: handles gd & hvy grnd.
849   **FACTUAL LAD** 14 [4] B R Millman 2-9-0 M Fenton 7/2: 233: 2 b c So Factual - Surprise Surprise   6 **72**
(Robellino) Cl-up, hung right 2f out & sn held: op 5/2: btr 849, 724 (gd).
--   **JOINT INSTRUCTION** [1] M R Channon 2-9-0 M Tebbutt 15/2: 4: Chsd ldrs, rdn/no impress fnl 2f: shd **72**
op 5/1: Forzando colt, Feb foal, cost 7,000gns: dam a 2m wnr, sire styd 9f: appreciate further in time.
4 ran   Time 1m 04.50   (Imperial Racing)   M R Channon West Isley, Berks

1002	**3.00 APRIL HCAP 3YO 0-70 (E)** 1m2f110y **Heavy Inapplicable**	[76]
	£2993 £855 £427 Flag Start	

551   **CASTLEBRIDGE** 65 [11] M C Pipe 3-9-7 (69) (vis) J Carroll 7/1: -01161: 3 b g Batshoof - Super Sisters   **75**
(Call Report) Made all, rdn/clr over 1f out, held on well ins last, rdn out: op 6/1, 2 month abs: earlier scored at W'hampton (2, sells, 1 for D Morris, rtd 71a): mod form prev: eff at 1m/10.5f on hvy grnd & f/sand: suited by a visor: likes sharp/turning trks & can force the pace: gd weight carrier: runs well fresh.
933   **STAFFORD KING** 7 [1] J G M O'Shea 3-8-4 (52) R Brisland (5) 7/1: 00-042: 3 b c Nicolotte - Opening   1¼ **56**
Day (Day Is Done) Rear, prog to trk ldrs 2f out, kept on ins last, not rch wnr: stays 10f on hvy: cld win similar.
784   **HAMBLEDEN** 26 [2] M A Jarvis 3-9-3 (65) M Tebbutt 7/1: 00-03: 3 b g Vettori - Dalu (Dancing Brave)   2½ **66**
In tch, rdn/chsd wnr 2f out, onepace fnl 1f: h'cap bow, op 6/1: stays 10.5f on hvy grnd, 12f shld suit.
847   **DONTBESOBOLD** 16 [3] B S Rothwell 3-9-1 (63) M Fenton 9/1: 366244: Dwelt/towards rear, prog/chsd   nk **64**
ldrs 3f out, no extra ins last: op 10/1: clr of rem: eff around 1m/10.5f: handles fast, hvy & fibresand.
894   **SHRIVAR** 11 [10] 3-9-4 (66) S Drowne 9/1: 05-055: Chsd ldrs, btn 2f out: op 7/1: longer 10.5f trip.   7 **60**
937   **STRICTLY SPEAKING** 7 [7] 3-7-11 (60) (BL) J Sweeney 7/1: 45-066: Cl-up 1m, btn over 2f out: see 937.   1¼ **57**
744   **TWEED** 28 [5] D Harrison 3-9-1 (63) M Fenton 9/1: 050-07: In tch, btn halfway, btn 3f out: op 11/2: bred   3 **53**
to apprec longer trip, less testing ground will probably suit.
892   **UNIMPEACHABLE** 11 [9] 3-8-9 (57) Claire Bryan (5) 8/1: 15-008: Dwelt, nvr a factor: op 6/1: '99   1 **46**
Nottingham wnr for P Cole (sell, rtd 66): eff at 7/8.3f on gd/soft & hvy grnd & a gall trk: enjoys sell grade.
709   **SHAMSAN** 32 [6] 3-9-5 (67) J Fanning 7/2 FAV: -10329: Chsd ldrs, wknd 2f out: op 9/2: btr 709 (AW).   8 **48**
4059}   **CALICO** 214 [8] 3-9-6 (68) Dane O'Neill 10/1: 0550-0: In tch halfway, rdn/btn 3f out: 10th: op   dist **0**
8/1, 7 month abs: unplcd in '99 (rtd 71, mdn): tried up to 1m prev, mid-dists could suit this term.

720 **ESPERE DOR 30** [4] 3-7-10 (44)(10oh) A Polli(3) 50/1: -00050: Al rear: longer 10.5f trip: mod form. *6* **0**
11 ran Time 2m 30.90 (David S Lewis) M C Pipe Nicholashayne, Devon

1003

3.30 INISFREE HCAP 4YO+ 0-80 (D) 1m2f110y Heavy Inapplicable [69]
£4066 £1251 £625 £312 Flag Start

890 **PAS DE PROBLEME 12** [1] M Blanshard 4-9-1 (56) Dale Gibson 7/1: 050-01: 4 ch g Ela Mana Mou - Torriglia (Nijinsky) Held up in tch, prog halfway, rdn/led over 1f out, gamely held rnr-up fnl 1f, all out: unplcd in '99 (rtd 70, h'cap): '98 rnr-up (stks, debut, rtd 79): eff at 9/10.5f on fast & hvy grnd: 1st win today. **64**
942 **ANNADAWI 7** [5] C N Kellett 5-7-10 (37)(2oh) G Baker (7) 9/2: 054632: 5 b g Sadler's Wells - Prayers 'n Promises (Foolish Pleasure) Held up, smooth prog to chall ins last, kept on despite hanging in bhnd wnr: clr rem: maiden, eff around 1m/10.5f on hvy grnd: mod form on sand previously. *nk* **44**
943 **NOIRIE 7** [2] M Brittain 6-7-10 (37)(5oh) P M Quinn (5) 5/2 FAV: 300-23: 6 br g Warning - Callipoli (Green Dancer) Handy, rdn/led halfway, hdd over 1f out & no extra ins last: op 4/1, well clr rem: see 943. *6* **38**
854 **POLRUAN 14** [7] S G Knight 4-9-1 (56)(t) S Drowne 7/1: 04-564: Chsd ldrs 3f out, sn held: t-strap. *12* **47**
889 **LOST SPIRIT 12** [8] 4-7-10 (37) Joanna Badger (7) 5/1: 060035: Led 1f, btn 2f out: op 4/1: btr 889. *11* **19**
2298} **ZORBA 301** [3] 6-9-3 (58)(bl) R Brisland (5) 13/2: /000-6: Prom, btn 4f out: op 16/1, jumps fit (rnr-up, sell, rtd 71h): no form in '99: '98 wnr at Hamilton & Southwell (clmrs, rtd 53a & 62 at best, J Hetherton): eff arnd 9/11f on firm, hvy & fibresand, any trk: likes to force the pace: best without blnks/vis: gd weight carrier. *14* **28**
817 **SAMARA SONG 21** [6] 7-9-6 (61) J Weaver 12/1: 000-07: Led after 1f till 5f out, sn btn: op 8/1: '99 Salisbury & York wnr (h'caps, rtd 73): '98 Sandown wnr (rtd 63, h'cap): eff at 7f/1m on firm & gd/soft, any trk: tough & genuine h'capper at best, interesting back at 7f/1m on faster ground. *1¼* **30**
73 **HIDDEN ENEMY 157** [9] 4-9-10 (65) A Hawkins (7) 12/1: 046-8: Dwelt/al rear & btn 4f out: op 8/1, 5 month abs/h'cap bow: rtd 71 in '99 (tried up to 1m): bred to apprec mid-dists this term. *2½* **32**
854 **CABARET QUEST 14** [4] 4-9-5 (60) Claire Bryan (5) 12/1: 136-09: Struggling halfway: op 8/1: '99 Leicester wnr (clmr, R Hannon, rtd 73 at best): rtd 67 in '98 (auct mdn): eff at 1m on fast: likes a stiff/gall trk. *8* **21**
9 ran Time 2m 30.70 (Captain Francis Burne) M Blanshard Upper Lambourn, Berks

1004

4.05 WEST MIDLANDS COND STKS 4YO+ (C) 6f168y rnd Heavy Inapplicable
£5927 £2248 £1124 £511 Flag Start

703 **DESERT KNIGHT 32** [5] J Noseda 4-8-12 J Weaver 7/2: 12-31: 4 b h Green Desert - Green Leaf (Alydar) Dwelt, held up, prog to lead dist, styd on well, drvn out: won 1st of just 2 '99 starts, at Pontefract (debut, mdn, rtd 100 at best): eff arnd 7f/1m on firm & hvy: handles a stiff or sharp/turning trk: smart entire. **108**
966 **MUCHEA 5** [6] M R Channon 6-8-8 S Drowne 8/11 FAV: 00-022: 6 ch h Shalford - Bargouzine (Hotfoot) Handy halfway, rdn to chall & hung left ins last, held nr fin: clr rem: well bckd, quick reapp: see 966, 733. *1¾* **100**
935 **BRAVE EDGE 7** [3] R Hannon 9-8-8 Dane O'Neill 7/1: 40-033: 9 b g Beveled - Daring Ditty (Daring March) Chsd ldr, led over 2f out, hdd over 1f out & sn held: op 6/1: better in h'caps: see 725 (h'cap). *6* **91$**
952 **BON AMI 6** [8] A Berry 4-8-8 J Carroll 8/1: 20-004: Held up, rcd keenly, no impress fnl 1f: op 6/1, qck reapp: rnr-up thrice in '99 for J Berry (rtd 101, rtd h'cap): '98 wnr at Leicester (auct mdn), Newcastle (nurs h'cap) & Ripon (stks, rtd 99): wng form at 5/6f, stays a sharp 7f: acts on firm & hvy, any trk: has run well fresh. *½* **90**
790 **HALMANERROR 25** [7] 10-8-8 D Harrison 33/1: 000-65: Held up, held fnl 2f: treat rating cautiously. *1½* **88$**
935 **BOOMERANG BLADE 7** [9] 4-8-3 J Stack 12/1: 00-066: Chsd ldrs 5f: op 8/1: see 935 (6f). *½* **82**
352 **FREDERICK JAMES 97** [4] 6-8-8 M Fenton 50/1: 00-467: Led 5f, sn held: 3 month abs: see 262 (AW). *½* **86$**
952 **BLUE ACE 6** [2] 7-8-8 J Fanning 50/1: 0-508: Prom 3f: quick reapp: see 927. *nk* **85$**
970} **BALLET MASTER 367** [1] 4-8-8 T Lucas 10/1: 1/4-9: Bhd halfway: op 8/1, 3 month jumps abs (rtd 95h, juv nov, current connections): unplcd sole '99 start on the level for H Cecil (rtd 90, stks): '98 Yarmouth wnr (mdn, rtd 100): eff at 7f, bred to apprec further: acts on soft & has run well fresh: with M W Easterby. *19* **65**
9 ran Time 1m 28.80 (Sheikh Khaled Duaij Al Sabah) J Noseda Newmarket

1005

4.35 CHANDLER HCAP 3YO+ 0-70 (E) 5f rnd Heavy Inapplicable [68]
£2993 £855 £427 3 yo rec 10lb Ragged Flag Start, low numbers worst affected

910 **WHIZZ KID 10** [19] J M Bradley 6-9-2 (56) Claire Bryan (5) 6/1: 0-0051: 6 b m Puissance - Panienka (Dom Racine) Sn handy & smooth prog to lead over 1f out, pushed clr ins last, cmftbly: val for 5L+: op 7/1: '99 scorer at Ripon, Redcar, Chepstow, Ayr & Newcastle (h'caps, rtd 62): missed '98: stays 6f, suited by 5f: acts on firm & both AWs, likes gd/soft & hvy: handles any trk: ragged start enabled her to overcome poor high draw. **66**
787 **SEVEN SPRINGS 26** [11] R Hollinshead 4-8-3 (43) P M Quinn (5) 20/1: 0-0062: 4 b c Unblest - Zaydeen (Sassafras) Held up in tch, switched & kept on fnl 2f, no impress on wnr: acts on fibresand & hvy grnd. *3½* **43**
798 **AA YOUKNOWNOTHING 25** [10] Miss J F Craze 4-9-11 (65)(tvi) S Finnamore (5) 6/1: 620423: 4 b g Superpower - Bad Payer (Tanfirion) Quickly away & led till dist & sn held: op 7/1: see 235 (AW). *2½* **60**
787 **BATALEUR 26** [17] G Woodward 7-8-11 (51) R Lappin 11/1: 21-654: In tch, kept on fnl 2f, no threat: fair run from a poor high draw, loves soft & hvy grnd: see 787, 499. *¾* **45**
798 **JACKERIN 25** [9] 5-8-9 (49)(bl) M Fenton 16/1: 500-65: Chsd ldrs, no extra fnl 1f: see 798. *nk* **42**
4615} **DIAMOND DECORUM 170** [13] 4-10-0 (68) Dane O'Neill 14/1: 0000-6: Chsd ldrs, onepace fnl 2f: op 10/1, 6 month abs, top-weight: '99 Lingfield wnr (h'cap, rtd 81 & 66a): '98 Thirsk wnr (auct mdn, rtd 76): eff at 5/6f, stays 7f: acts on fast & gd grnd, handles soft/hvy: handles any trk: spot on next time. *hd* **60**
958 **MISS BANANAS 6** [16] 5-8-11 (51) D Meah (7) 16/1: 600157: Dwelt, late gains, no threat: qck reapp. *1½* **40**
299 **SWINO 105** [20] 6-9-2 (56)(vis) S Drowne 14/1: 02-468: Mid-div, nvr on terms: 3 mth abs, vis reapp. *¾* **44**
896 **STRATS QUEST 11** [5] 6-8-12 (52) J Weaver 10/1: 500109: Slowly away, rear, mod gains: see 816 (7f, clmr) *1¼* **37**
881 **MISS DANGEROUS 12** [18] 5-8-0 (40) A McCarthy(3) 16/1: 035500: Mid-div at best: 10th: blnks omitted. *½* **24**
214 **ROSES TREASURE 125** [2] 4-8-3 (43)(vis) Joanna Badger (7) 25/1: 0000-0: Slowly away, nvr on terms: 11th, 4 mth abs, vis reapp: rnr-up in '99 (rtd 66, h'cap): '98 Doncaster wnr (auct mdn, rtd 82): eff at 5f, tried 6f: acts on fast & hvy: best without blnks/visor: goes on any trk & has run well fresh: well h'capped. *½* **26**
499 **GARNOCK VALLEY 73** [1] 10-8-12 (52) J Carroll 9/1: 2-1640: Slowly away, nvr on terms: 13th: 10 wk abs. **0**
4610} **POLLY GOLIGHTLY 171** [6] 7-9-11 (65)(bl) Dale Gibson 10/1: 0044-0: Slowly away, nvr factor: 15th, 6 month abs: '99 Chester wnr (h'cap, rtd 71 at best): '98 wnr at Chester & York (h'caps, rtd 73): stays 7f, all wins at 5f: acts on firm, likes gd/soft & hvy: suited by blnks/visor: likes to force the pace on any trk, loves Chester & is slipping to a handy mark: hmpd at the start today & this is best forgotten. **0**
*960 **FAUTE DE MIEUX 6** [8] 5-10-3 (71)(6ex) S Carson (5) 7/2 FAV: 0-6010: Slowly away & nvr factor: 16th: op 5/2, quick reapp: lost chance at start, best forgiven, see 960 (stks). **0**
923 **POLAR MIST 9** [14] 5-9-4 (58)(tbl) A Clark 16/1: 000-00: Strugg halfway: 20th: op 10/1: fin lame. **0**
824 **Sulu 19** [7] 4-9-13 (67) T Lucas 11/1: 802 **Sammal 24** [15] 4-8-11 (51) D Harrison 20/1:

82   **Distant King 156** [4] 7-7-10 (36)(1oh) G Arnolda(7) 40/1870   **Roman Emperor 13** [12] 3-7-13 (49) A Mackay 40/1:
958   **Rocklands Lane 6** [3] 4-8-4 (44) M Henry 25/1:
20 ran   Time 1m 03.30   (B Paling)   J M Bradley Sedbury, Glos

---

NEWCASTLE   MONDAY APRIL 24TH   Lefthand, Stiff, Galloping Track

Official Going   SOFT. Stalls: Str Crse - Stands Side; Rnd Crse - Inside.

1006   2.15 EBF & GNER NOV STKS 2YO (D)   5f str   Heavy 144   -12 Slow
£3406   £1048   £524   £262

821   **TARAS EMPEROR 19** [5] J J Quinn 2-8-12 A Culhane 9/2: 41: 2 b g Common Grounds - Strike It Rich   86
(Rheingold) Bmpd start, prom, led appr fnl 1f, drvn out: IR 29,000gns Apr foal, brother to a 1m wnr, dam 10f
wnr: eff at 5f, further will suit: goes on soft/hvy grnd, stiff/gall trk: leggy, scopey, improving gelding.

843   **THORNTOUN DIVA 16** [9] J S Goldie 2-8-7 Dean McKeown 25/1: 302: 2 ch f Wolfhound - Al Guswa   1½   77
(Shernazar) Trkd ldrs, keen, shkn up 2f out, styd on for 2nd but not pace of wnr: left prev efforts well bhd
(badly drawn latest): eff at 5f but is crying out for 6f: acts on hvy grnd & can find a northern mdn: see 755.

843   **MAMMAS TONIGHT 16** [6] A Berry 2-9-0 O Pears 6/1: 133: 2 ch c Timeless Times - Miss Merlin   1¾   80
(Manacle) Bhd ldrs, going well but nowhere to go 1½f out till switched ins last, ran on but the race was over:
unlucky not to have gone close: acts on gd, hvy grnd & fibresand, deserves compensation: see 801.

812   **PRINCE GRIGORI 21** [10] E J Alston 2-8-12 F Norton 33/1: 04: Led till bef dist, no extra: left   2½   73
debut bhd with more positive tactics on this hvy grnd: see 812.

904   **STILMEMAITE 10** [1] 2-8-7 J Bramhill 12/1: -35: In tch, shkn up & styd on ins last, nvr pace to chall.   ½   67

*743   **STREGONE 28** [7] 2-9-5 G Duffield 9/2: 16: Front rank, chall bef dist, fdd: fast grnd debut wnr in 743.   1¾   75

--   **SIGN THE TRUCE** [8] 2-8-12 R Winston 16/1: 7: Nvr a factor: debut: 16,500gns Brief Truce   2   64
Apr foal, dam mid-dist/hdles wnr, sire 1m/10f performer: needs more time/further: with T Easterby.

812   **KACHINA DOLL 21** [3] 2-8-7 P Fessey 10/1: -308: Bhd from halfway: btr 730 (gd).   4   51

--   **CUMBRIAN HARMONY** [2] 2-8-7 K Darley 7/1: 9: Slow away, nvr in it: stablemate 7th, debut, op 5/1:   ¾   50
IR 5,500gns Distinctly North Apr foal, half-sister to a winning 5f juv: dam 7f wnr: sire a sprinter.

*891   **SIR FRANCIS 11** [4] 2-9-5 (VIS) L Dettori 5/2 FAV: 5210: Veered right out of stalls, chsd ldrs till   21   42
halfway, eased, t.o.: 10th, well bcd, visored: 1st try on hvy, surely something amiss, see 891, 821 (bt this wnr).

10 ran   Time 1m 06.0 (7.8)   (Tara Leisure)   J J Quinn Settrington, N.Yorks.

1007   2.50 JOURNAL HOMEMAKER HCAP 3YO+ 0-75 (E)   1m rnd   Heavy 144   -20 Slow   [73]
£3094   £952   £476   £228   3 yo rec 14lb

907   **ROLLER 10** [9] J G Given 4-9-6 (66) K Darley 5/2 FAV: 05-321: 4 b g Bluebird - Tight Spin (High Top)   77
Mid-div, gd prog to lead 2f out, styd on strongly to draw clr ent fnl 1f: nicely bckd: '99 Warwick wnr (mdn,
rtd 78 at best, H Candy, first time blnks): eff at 7f, suited by 1m, tried 12f: likes soft/hvy grnd, handles
fast & prob fibresand: acts well without blnks, any trk, likes turning ones: improving, qk reapp under a pen?

*931   **ITSANOTHERGIRL 9** [8] M W Easterby 4-9-11 (70) P Dobbs (5) 11/1: 5-0012: 4 b f Reprimand - Tasmim   8   70
(Be My Guest) Bhd till kept on strongly fnl 2f, nvr nrr: caught a tartar, in gd form: see 931.

907   **LANDING CRAFT 10** [6] D Carroll 8-9-0 (54) K Dalgleigh(7) 9/1: 34-003: 6 ch g Zilzal - Dockage   ½   53
(Riverman) In tch, prog to chall appr fnl 2f, sn outpcd by wnr & no extra ins last: op 6/1: acts on fast & hvy.

871   **A DAY ON THE DUB 13** [14] D Eddy 7-8-3 (48) G Duffield 12/1: 25-644: Rear till kept on up the   2½   43
straight, nvr on terms: appeared unsuited by drop back to 1m: see 215.

169   **STYLE DANCER 136** [11] 6-9-3 (62) C Lowther 20/1: 0330-5: Towards rear, prog to go 3rd appr fnl   2   54
1f, sn onepace: over 4 month abs, vis left off, clr rem: suited by faster grnd, L Dettori & 6/7f: see 79.

816   **LYNTON LAD 21** [2] 8-9-6 (65) L Swift (7) 25/1: 125-66: Early ldr, prom till 2f out: see 816.   10   43

942   **HIGH SUN 7** [5] 4-9-1 (60) D Holland 6/1: 411-47: Nvr better than mid-div: op 8/1, not given a hard   4   32
time once ldrs had got away: see 942.

899   **ROOFTOP 11** [7] 4-9-0 (59)(BL) P Goode (3) 33/1: -65008: Al same place: blnkd: see 453.   1¾   29

4615]   **TIPPERARY SUNSET 170** [19] 6-9-4 (63) N Callan 20/1: 0025-9: Dwelt, nvr on terms: reapp: ¾   32
'99 Beverley wnr (h'cap, rtd 66, J J Quinn): '98 Hamilton wnr (h'cap, rtd 60): eff at 7.5f/10f on firm &
soft grnd, any trk: best held up: has run well fresh: now with D Shaw.

907   **TAKHLID 10** [15] 9-9-1 (60) A Culhane 16/1: 536650: Chsd ldrs till 3f out: 10th: see 142.   1   28

875   **CHIEF MONARCH 13** [12] 6-9-13 (72) R Winston 6/1: 00-250: Nvr troubled ldrs: 11th, top-weight.   nk   39

921   **ONE DINAR 9** [17] 5-9-8 (67) L Dettori 8/1: 212050: Al towards rear: faster grnd or fibresand suits.   0   0

908   **OLLIES CHUCKLE 10** [13] 5-8-7 (52) F Norton 12/1: 000-60: Nvr in it: 16th, see 908.   0   0

756   **BEYOND THE CLOUDS 27** [10] 4-8-6 (51)(vis) J Bramhill 33/1: 065-00: Sn led, hdd 2f out & lost pl: 18th: 0
plcd last term (h'cap, rtd 54), unrcd juv: unproven beyond 6f on fast grnd: now visored: likes to force the pace.

3957] **Gargoyle Girl 220** [16] 3-7-13 (58) P Fessey 33/1:   69   **Oriole 157** [20] 7-8-6 (51) Kim Tinkler 25/1:
907   **Cybertechnology 10** [18] 6-9-3 (62) F Lynch 25/1:   846   **Amron 16** [11] 13-8-3 (48) O Pears 14/1:
975   **Khuchn 5** [3] 4-8-11 (56) D Mernagh (3) 20/1:
19 ran   Time 1m 52.1 (13.1)   (Mrs Jo Hardy)   J G Given Willoughton, Lincs.

1008   3.20 SUNDAY SUN HCAP 3YO+ 0-80 (D)   5f   Heavy 144   -02 Slow   [80]
£4160   £1280   £640   £320   3 yo rec 10lb   False start led to 6 withdrawals

905   **INDIAN SPARK 10** [1] J S Goldie 6-9-12 (78) A Culhane 13/8 FAV: 00-041: 6 ch g Indian Ridge - Annes   89
Gift (Ballymoss) Nvr far away far side, led after halfway, kept on strongly under press: hvly bckd from 3/1:
'99 York wnr (rtd h'cap, rtd 91): '98 wnr at Thirsk & Doncaster (2f, h'caps, rtd 89): eff at 5/6f: acts on
firm & hvy grnd, likes galloping trks: gd weight carrier: well h'capped: qck follow up likely.

*923   **TEYAAR 9** [19] D Shaw 4-9-8 (74) N Callan 16/1: 510112: 4 b g Polar Falcon - Music In My Life   3   79
(Law Society) Led stands side, styd on well but al playing second fiddle to wnr on far side: fine run back in
trip on turf: goes on firm, hvy grnd & fibresand: return to 6f looks sure to suit: see 923.

941   **SHIRLEY NOT 7** [2] S Gollings 4-9-1 (67) G Duffield 20/1: 000-03: 4 gr g Paris House - Hollia   1½   69
(Touch Boy) Chsd ldrs far side, went after wnr appr fnl 1f, nvr any impress: qck reapp: dual '99 rnr-up (h'caps,
rtd 72): '98 wnr at Southwell (sell, J Berry, rtd 60a) & Chester (nurs, rtd 77), tried Listed: eff at 5f, tried
further: acts on fast, gd/soft, fibresand, prob hvy: goes well fresh, sharp trks suit.

844   **UNSHAKEN 16** [17] E J Alston 6-9-8 (74) F Norton 11/1: 00-024: Slow away stands side, imprvd under   1¼   73

press 2f out, no extra dist: well clr of next on stands side: back on a fair mark now & best at 6f.
758 **PANDJOJOE 27** [5] 4-8-8 (60) R Winston 16/1: 000-05: Slow away far side, late gains, nvr a threat: *1½* **56**
op 12/1: landed a hat-trick first 3 in '99 here at Newcastle, Windsor (h'caps) & Haydock (appr h'cap, rtd 78): unplcd juv: eff at 6f, worth a try at 7f: acts on fast & gd grnd, poss handles hvy: goes on sharp or gall trks & can run well fresh: gd weight carrier who is now v well h'capped: with R Fahey.
680 **NIFTY NORMAN 39** [4] 6-8-10 (62) O Pears 16/1: 236346: Led far side till halfway, fdd dist: 6 wk abs. *2½* **53**
4391} **WILLIAMS WELL 191** [3] 6-9-0 (66)(bl) P Goode (3) 16/1: 5004-7: Prom far side till 2f out: tchd 20/1 *5* **47**
on reapp: '99 wnr at Carlisle & Catterick (h'caps, rtd 70 at best): back in '97 won at Catterick & Musselburgh (h'caps, rtd 60): eff at 6f, all wins at 5f: acts on firm & soft grnd, likes Catterick: wears blinkers.
910 **ANGEL HILL 10** [7] 5-8-12 (64) B McHugh(7) 14/1: 000-08: Dwelt, nvr troubled ldrs far side: *3½* **38**
stablemate of 5th: '99 wnr here at Newcastle (4 rnr h'cap in first time blnks, rtd 76): back in '97 won again here at Newcastle (mdn, debut, rtd, T Barron): eff at 5f, 6f suits now: acts on firm & soft grnd, gall trks, likes Newcastle: eff with/without blnks (not worn today): well h'capped back at 6f.
758 **SIR SANDROVITCH 27** [12] 4-9-3 (69) Dean McKeown 20/1: 600-09: In tch stands side for 3f: see 758. *½* **42**
844 **MARY JANE 16** [10] 5-8-6 (58) Kim Tinkler 20/1: 15-000: Nvr dngrs stands side: 10th, faster grnd suits. *20* **11**
716 **TOM TUN 31** [16] 5-10-0 (80) K Darley 9/1: 6-5230: Prom stands side for 2½f: 11th, op 7/1. *2½* **30**
763 **EASTERN TRUMPETER 27** [15] 4-8-10 (62) L Dettori 7/1: -14100: Al bhd stands side: 12th: see 678, *2½* **9**
844 **REGAL SONG 16** [6] 4-8-11 (63)(bl) D Holland 6/1: -3203W: Withdrawn, completed crse after false start. **0**
926 **Goretski 9** [11] 7-9-7 (73) F Lynch 16/1: 803 **Bowlers Boy 24** [8] 7-7-11 (49) P Fessey 14/1: W
3869} **Legs Be Frendly 227** [13] 5-8-13 (65) T Hamilton(7) 33/1: W
926 **Bedevilled 9** [18] 5-9-8 (74) Lynsey Hanna (7) 16/1: W
4160} **Bodfari Komaite 208** [9] 4-8-9 (61) P Dobbs (5) 16/1: W 926 **Waterford Spirit 9** [14] 4-9-6 (72) C Lowther 25/1: W
19 ran Time 1m 05.5 (7.3) (Frank Brady) J S Goldie Uplawmoor, E.Renfrews.

1009

3.50 CHRONICLE MDN 3YO+ (D) 1m4f93y Heavy 144 -31 Slow
£3802 £1170 £585 £292 3 yo rec 20lb4 yo rec 1 lb

-- **ALMOST FREE** [7] M Johnston 3-8-6 D Holland 5/1: 1: 3 b c Darshaan - Light Fresh Air (Rahy) **91**
Cl-up, led 3f out, rdn 2f out (flashed tail), pshd out towards fin: op 4/1 on debut: had colic last year: dam a well-related French bred: eff at 12f, looks a thorough stayer: goes on hvy grnd, gall trk: runs well fresh.
858 **MACHRIE BAY 14** [5] J L Dunlop 3-8-6 K Darley 11/8 FAV: 003-32: 3 b c Emarati - Fleeting Rainbow *6* **85**
(Rainbow Quest) Bhd ldrs, hdwy to chall 3f out, outstyd by wnr ins last: nicely bckd, clr rem: stays 12f on hvy.
4014} **MAJESTIC BAY 217** [1] P W Harris 4-9-11 G Duffield 11/4: 2423-3: 4 b g Unfuwain - That'll Be The *13* **75**
Day (Thatching) Chsd ldrs, eff appr fnl 3f, no impress: reapp: dual '99 rnr-up (mdn, rtd 90): eff at 10f, stays 12f on firm & gd, prob hvy: should prove sharper next time.
4524} **FRATERNITY 180** [6] W Jarvis 3-8-6 L Dettori 10/3: 02-4: Led till 3f out, sn btn: reapp: rnr-up fnl *3½* **72**
'99 start (mdn, rtd 88): eff at 1m on gd/sft, shld stay further (half-brother to smart mid-div filly Catchascatchcan).
-- **DARK SHADOWS** [2] 5-9-12 J Bramhill 10/1: 5: Al bhd: Flat bow, bmpr fit (stays 13.5f on *15* **60**
firm grnd): related to wnrs on the Flat: with W Storey.
873 **LANNTANSA 13** [4] 3-8-6 R Winston 14/1: 06: In tch till 5f out: longer trip, not bred for 12f: see 873. *4* **57**
4444} **ROYAL REPRIMAND 187** [3] 5-9-12 Dean McKeown 50/1: 4545-7: Mid-div till after halfway: reapp: *30* **33**
plcd last year (h'cap, rtd 36 & 55$): flattered in '98: poss stays 9f on fast grnd, handles gd/soft, tried a visor.
7 ran Time 2m 59.7 (21.8) (Maktoum Al Maktoum) M Johnston Middleham, N.Yorks.

1010

4.25 JOURNAL FILLIES MDN 3YO+ (D) 1m rnd Heavy 144 -81 Slow
£3835 £1180 £590 £295 3 yo rec 14lb

727 **ROSHANI 30** [3] M R Channon 3-8-6 L Dettori 13/8 FAV: 530-21: 3 b g Kris - Maratona (Be My Guest) **74**
Settled bhd leading duo, pulled out to chall ent fnl 2f, rdn to get on top towards fin: hvly bckd, slow time: plcd 2nd of 3 juv starts (rtd 80): eff at 1m/9f: acts on gd & hvy grnd, sharp or gall trks: has started the season well.
833 **PENNYS PRIDE 18** [4] Mrs M Reveley 5-9-6 A Culhane 8/1: 302: 5 b m Pips Pride - Mursuma (Rarity) *nk* **73**
Held up, prog to lead dist till fnl 50y: clr rem, suited by drop back to 1m: acts on soft/hvy: see 759.
4555} **SUCH FLAIR 177** [2] J Noseda 3-8-6 D Holland 5/2: 0-3: 3 b f Kingmambo - Lady Fairfax (Sharrood) *5* **65**
Prsd ldr, ev ch 3f out till onepace dist: nicely bckd, reapp: 9th sole '99 start (fill mdn, rtd 79): cost $100,000.
4381} **SUMMER SONG 192** [1] E A L Dunlop 3-8-6 K Darley 2/1: 1-4: Set slow pace till 1f out, wknd: well *2½* **61**
bckd from 3/1: landed the meaningless Newmarket Challenge Cup sole '99 start (rtd 79): prob eff at 7f on gd grnd.
4 ran Time 1m 57.0 (18) (Sheikh Ahmed Al Maktoum) M R Channon West Isley, Berks.

1011

5.00 CHRONICLE HCAP 3YO+ 0-85 (D) 7f str Heavy 144 +02 Fast [83]
£4078 £1255 £627 £313 Field raced in 2 groups, two on stands side clear

907 **MELODIAN 10** [16] M Brittain 5-8-1 (56)(bl) D Mernagh (3) 12/1: 0-0231: 5 b h Grey Desire - Mere **63**
Melody (Dunphy) Made all stands side, kept on well, pushed out: tchd 16/1, best time of day: '99 wnr at Beverley, Doncaster & Catterick (h'caps, rtd 56): '98 wnr here at Newcastle (h'cap, rtd 44): eff forcing the pace at 7f, stays 1m: acts on firm & hvy grnd, any trk, likes gall ones, esp Newcastle: runs well in blnks: tough.
817 **AMBER FORT 21** [20] J M Bradley 7-9-3 (72)(bl) K Darley 11/1: 000-32: 7 gr g Indian Ridge - *3* **73**
Lammastide (Martinmas) Chsd ldrs stands side, went after wnr ent fnl 2f, no extra towards fin: clr rem: apprec drop back to 7f: acts on firm, hvy grnd & equitrack & has started the season in good form.
*838 **I CRIED FOR YOU 17** [14] J G Given 5-9-4 (73) Dean McKeown 9/1: 000-13: 5 b g Statoblest - Fall *5* **66**
Of The Hammer (Auction Ring) Mid-div far side, smooth prog to lead that group ent fnl 2f, sn rdn, same pace: tchd 11/1: stiff 7f on hvy grnd prob stretches stamina: worth another chance at a sharper trk/6f: see 838.
875 **DOUBLE ACTION 13** [2] T D Easterby 6-8-9 (64) P Goode (3) 14/1: 06-404: Held up far side, kept *nk* **57**
on strongly appr fnl 1f & almost grabbed 3rd: hard to win with now but undoubtedly well h'capped & likes soft.
875 **DONNAS DOUBLE 13** [4] 5-8-10 (65) P Fessey 20/1: 110-05: Prom far side & chall ldr that side 2f out, *1¾* **56**
sn onepace: '99 wnr at Catterick & Redcar (h'caps, rtd 67): '98 wnr at Musselburgh & again Hamilton (mdn h'cap & h'cap, rtd 57): eff at 7f/8.5f, stays 12f on firm, soft, any trk, likes Hamilton: slowly coming to hand.
3244} **SUPREME SALUTATION 259** [19] 4-9-10 (79) C Lowther 14/1: 2121-6: Sn prom stands side, eff 2f *¾* **69**
out, fdd: '99 wnr at Catterick & Thirsk (h'caps, rtd 80): unrd juv: eff at 7f/1m on fast & gd/soft grnd, any trk.
834 **SUSANS PRIDE 18** [9] 4-9-11 (80) G Duffield 16/1: 1-4107: Cl-up far side, wknd ent fnl 2f: handles hvy? *1½* **68**
908 **PEPPIATT 10** [13] 6-8-5 (60) F Norton 14/1: 0-0348: Far side, prog to press ldrs 2f out, sn wknd: 10th. *3* **44**
1288} **TONIC 347** [12] 4-9-13 (82) D Holland 16/1: /100-9: Outpcd far side, styd on late thr' btn horses: *½* **65**
top-weight, reapp: '99 reapp wnr at Ripon (mdn, rtd 88): plcd both juv starts (mdn, rtd 86): eff at 1m, worth a try at 10f: acts on gd & hvy grnd: can run well fresh but this was an inadequate trip: will do better.

NEWCASTLE MONDAY APRIL 24TH Lefthand, Stiff, Galloping Track

162 **NOBALINO 138** [6] 6-8-7 (62)(vis) V Halliday 33/1: 3135-0: Struggling far side till kept on fnl 2f: 10th, over 4 month abs, new stable: see 59. *hd* **45**
910 **ON TILL MORNING 10** [18] 4-8-10 (65) F Lynch 33/1: 100-00: Chsd ldrs stands side till 2f out: 11th. *hd* **47**
941 **REDOUBTABLE 7** [5] 9-9-9 (78) A Culhane 9/2 FAV: 214320: In tch till 2f out: 12th, bckd from 7/1. *hd* **60**
844 **MAGIC MILL 16** [11] 7-8-12 (67) N Callan 6/1: 040-40: Chsd ldrs far side till 2f out: 13th, eye-catching 844. *6* **41**
4585} **PERSIAN FAYRE 174** [8] 8-8-6 (61) O Pears 20/1: 0000-0: Led far side till appr fnl 2f, sn btn: 14th, reapp: '99 hat-trick wnr at Redcar (sell), Carlisle (clmr) & Ayr (h'cap, rtd 79): '98 wnr at Haydock (stks, rtd 76): eff at 7f, stays 1m: acts on firm & gd/soft grnd, likes stiff/gall trks/forcing the pace: fitter on a sounder surface. *¾* **34**
*908 **VICTORIOUS 10** [3] 4-8-7 (62) R Winston 5/1: 50-110: Prom far side till halfway: 18th, tough race in 908. **0**
831 **NOUF 18** [10] 4-9-9 (78) L Dettori 8/1: 4-0020: Nvr in it far side: 19th, tchd 11/1: see 831. **0**
824 **Present Chance 19** [17] 6-8-10 (65) L Newton 33/1: 931 **Saligo 9** [1] 5-8-13 (68) Kim Tinkler 33/1:
834 **Smart Predator 18** [7] 4-9-5 (74) P Dobbs(5) 25/1: 817 **Intricate Web 21** [15] 4-8-13 (68) L Swift (7) 33/1:
20 ran Time 1m 34.1 (10) (Mel Brittain) M Brittain Warthill, N.Yorks.

KEMPTON MONDAY APRIL 24TH Righthand, Flat, Fair Track

Official Going SOFT. Stalls: Straight - Stands Side: 10f - Outside; Rem - Inside.

1012

2.00 EXHIBITIONS MDN DIV I 3YO+ (D) 7f rnd Soft 113 -30 Slow
£3932 £1210 £605 £302 3 yo rec 13lb Field came stands side straight

-- **WILDFLOWER** [5] R Charlton 3-8-6 S Sanders 14/1: 1: 3 b f Namaqualand - Faijour (Fairy King) **73**
Sltly hmpd start, held up, rdn 3f out, styd on well to lead appr fnl 1f, rdn out: eff at 7f, 1m sure to suit: runs well fresh on soft grnd: v pleasing debut, learn from this & shld rate higher.
840 **PEKANESE 17** [10] A C Stewart 3-8-11 M Roberts 10/1: 62: 3 b c Sri Pekan - Tottle (Main Reef) *¾* **76+**
In tch, hdwy to chall over 2f out, kept on nicely under hands & heels riding: eff at 7f, 1m looks sure to suit: acts on soft grnd: likely wnr with a more positive ride & looks sure to win his mdn sn.
826 **MONDURU 19** [12] W R Muir 3-8-11 Martin Dwyer 25/1: 0-03: 3 b c Lion Cavern - Bint Albadou (Green Desert) Chsd ldrs, hdwy to lead 2f out till over 1f out, onepace: eff at 7f on soft: win a minor trk mdn. *1½* **73**
4606} **FINISHED ARTICLE 171** [7] D R C Elsworth 3-8-11 N Pollard 10/1: 50-4: Hmpd start, bhd, eff over 2f out, kept on same pace over 1f out: op 7/1: reapp: rtd 74 when showed promise on debut as a juv: brother to an Irish Derby rnr-up: dam 1m/10f wnr: sure to rate more highly & relish 1m/10f h'caps. *1* **72+**
3664} **INNKEEPER 238** [6] 3-8-11 P Robinson 25/1: 2400-5: Set pace till 2f out, no extra on reapp: in '99 trained by Sir M Stoute, rnr-up on 1 of 6 juv starts (mdn, rtd 82): stays 6f on firm & gd: now with Miss G Kelleway. *3½* **67**
3385} **FLIGHT SEQUENCE 252** [3] 4-9-5 D Wallace (7) 14/1: 2424-6: Chsd ldrs, hdwy & sltly short of room over 1f out, kept on nicely late under v tender handling: op 8/1 on reapp: jockey rec a 5 day ban, trainer a £750 fine & horse a 30 day ban for 'schooling in public': rnr-up on 2 of 4 juv '99 starts (rtd 82): eff at 1m on firm, gd & on any trk: interesting in h'caps, over further & with a more experienced jockey. *nk* **62+**
-- **DANCE WEST** [11] 3-8-11 T Quinn 3/1 JT FAV: 7: Chsd ldrs, wknd well over 1f out: bckd, with H Cecil. *1½* **64**
840 **LEEROY 17** [2] 3-8-11 R Hughes 4/1: 224-28: In tch, eff & switched well over 1f out, sn wknd: bckd. *1½* **61**
4528} **FAIR IMPRESSION 180** [1] 3-8-6 J Reid 3/1 JT FAV: 02-9: Chsd ldrs, eff & sltly short of room over 1f out, no extra: op 9/4: rtd 86 when rnr-up on 2nd of only 2 juv starts: stays 7f on gd/soft, further suit. *hd* **56**
838 **ROYAL TARRAGON 17** [9] 4-9-5 R Cody Boutcher (7) 66/1: 000-00: In tch, wknd 3f out: 10th. *shd* **56**
-- **Roisterer** [8] 4-9-10 R Perham 25/1: 4217} **Hoh Hoh Seven 205** [4] 4-9-10 Pat Eddery 33/1:
12 ran Time 1m 34.1 (10) (Anglia Bloodstock Syndicate 1998) R Charlton Beckhampton, Wilts

1013

2.35 SALISBURY'S HCAP 3YO+ 0-95 (C) 5f str Soft 113 +09 Fast [95]
£7377 £2270 £1135 £567 3 yo rec 10lb High No's (far side) favoured

728 **LIVELY LADY 30** [7] J R Jenkins 4-9-0 (81)(vis) Pat Eddery 5/1 FAV: 501-41: 4 b f Beveled - In The Papers (Aragon) Switched to race far side, in tch, hdwy & short of room 2f out, styd on well to lead dist, rdn clr ins last: nicely bckd, gd time: '99 scorer at Nottingham (reapp), Kempton & Doncaster (h'caps, rtd 82): '98 Folkestone wnr (juv sell): eff over 5/6f on fast, loves gd & hvy, handles fibresand & any trk: likes Kempton, wears a visor & has run well fresh: tough, useful & improving, well ridden. **88**
2935} **PARADISE LANE 274** [10] B R Millman 4-9-2 (83) Cheryl Nosworthy (7) 20/1: 0000-2: 4 ch g Alnasr Alwasheek - La Belle Vie (Indian King) Set pace till dist, onepace: reapp: early season '99 wnr at Nottingham (mdn) & Chester (h'cap, rtd 90): loves to dominate over 5f, just stays 6f: acts on firm & soft & on a sharp or gall trk: fine reapp, h'capped to win now & v interesting with a low draw in the 5f h'cap at Chester next month. *3* **83**
4486} **THE PUZZLER 184** [4] B W Hills 9-9-2 (83) M Hills 16/1: 0050-3: 9 br g Sharpo - Enigma (Ahonoora) Waited with, switched right after 1f, staying on when hmpd ins last, kept on: reapp: '99 scorer at Sandown (h'cap, rtd 89): rtd 99 in '98: eff over 5/6f, stays 7f: acts on fast, loves gd & hvy: acts on any trk: has run well fresh: best without blnks: no luck in running today, much closer next time on a stiffer trk with cut in the grnd. *½* **83+**
935 **DANIELLES LAD 7** [5] B Palling 4-9-7 (88) A Beech (5) 20/1: 500-04: Bhd & rcd centre 1f bef switching far side, hdwy over 1f out, kept on ins last: gd run: see 935. *hd* **87**
702 **ELLENS LAD 32** [8] 6-10-0 (95) P Shea (7) 25/1: 412-05: Sn bhd, rdn 2f out, late gains, no danger: top weight: in fine late '99 form, won at Newbury, Haydock & Newmarket (h'caps, rtd 95): '98 Newmarket wnr (h'cap, rtd 86, with E Alston): stays 6f, all wins at 5f: acts on firm, soft & on any trk, likes a stiff one, esp Newmarket: best without blnks: useful & tough, sharper for this. *¾* **92**
716 **DAAWE 31** [15] 9-8-1 (68)(bl) Clare Roche (7) 7/1: 116306: Cl-up, rdn & wknd fnl 1f: tough 9yo. *shd* **65**
4093} **MIDNIGHT ESCAPE 212** [9] 7-9-6 (87) S Sanders 14/1: 0040-7: Sn bhd, rdn over 2f out, late gains, no danger: reapp: fin 4L 4th in Portland H'cap in '99 (rtd 99 at best): '98 Kempton wnr (List, rtd 115): all 5 wins at 5f, stays 5.6f on firm & soft: handles any trk & has run well fresh: gradually slipping to a fav mark. *nk* **83**
678 **PURE COINCIDENCE 39** [12] 5-9-0 (81) Darren Williams(7) 7/1: 600-38: Handy, rdn & btn appr fnl 1f. *2½* **72**
926 **IVORYS JOY 9** [13] 5-8-12 (79) C Carver (3) 9/1: 10-569: In tch, no impress over 1f out: do better. *1¾* **66**
926 **MOUSEHOLE 9** [6] 8-8-7 (74) M Roberts 25/1: 060-00: Slow away, al bhd, 10th: '99 wnr at Nottingham (2, h'cap & stks) & Windsor (2, h'caps, rtd 76): '98 wnr at Carlisle & Bath (stks, rtd 73): eff at 6f, best at 5f on gd or firm: handles any trk & carry big weights: sure to do better on a firmer surface. *1½* **58**
897 **THAT MAN AGAIN 11** [11] 8-8-8 (75)(bl) N Pollard 33/1: 660-00: Handy, btn 2f out: 11th. *3* **53**
4413} **SPEED ON 189** [3] 7-9-1 (82) C Rutter 10/1: 0660-0: Sn bhd & rcd centre 1f before switching to far side, no impress: 12th, reapp: '99 scorer at Newbury (rtd h'cap, reapp) & Chepstow (h'cap, rtd 90): '98 scorer at Bath (reapp, stks, 94): all wins at 5f: acts on firm & soft & on any trk, likes a stiff/undul *2½* **55**

one: runs esp well fresh: tried a visor, best without: capable of more.

897	**FORGOTTEN TIMES 11** [1] 6-8-1 (69) C Catlin (7) 10/1: 060-20: Sn rdn in tch, btn 2f out: 13th, btr 897.	6	29
4547}	**SAILING SHOES 178** [2] 4-9-6 (87) R Hughes 16/1: 0050-0: In tch, btn 2f out: 14th.	3	42
702	**BATCHWORTH BELLE 32** [14] 5-9-12 (93) S Carson (5) 10/1: 32-23R: Refused to race: see 702.		0

15 ran   Time 1m 03.52 (5.22)   (Mrs Jean Powell)   J R Jenkins Royston, Herts

---

1014   3.05 LISTED MAGNOLIA STKS 4YO+ (A)   1m2f   Soft 113   -01 Slow
£15015   £4620   £2310   £1159   Field came stands side in straight

733	**RIGHT WING 30** [6] J L Dunlop 6-8-11 (vis) Pat Eddery 7/2 FAV: 301-31: 6 b h In The Wings - Nekhbet (Artaius) Held up, gd hdwy over 1f out to lead ins last, rdn out: unlucky when 1L 3rd in Lincoln H'cap on reapp: '98 wnr at Doncaster (reapp, Lincoln h'cap, rtd 107) & Nottingham (stks): '98 scorer again at Doncaster (rtd h'cap): all 5 prev wins at 1m, clearly stays an easy 10f well: handles any grnd, likes gd, soft & Doncaster: runs well fresh in a visor: v tough & smart, loves to come late & in the form of his life.		112
4354}	**SWEET SORROW 193** [7] C F Wall 5-8-6 S Sanders 12/1: 3445-2: 5 b m Lahib - So Long Boys (Beldale Flutter) Chsd ldr, went on appr 2f out, rdn & collared ins last, kept on but not pace of wnr: reapp, clr of rem: in '99 won at Ayr (mdn) & Goodwood (class stks), subs improved to be plcd in Listed company (rtd 105): wng form over 10/12f & acts on firm, soft & on any trk: has run well fresh: tough & v useful, deserves another nice prize.	½	105
4544}	**ZAAJER 178** [2] E A L Dunlop 4-9-0 R Hills 4/1: 0604-3: 4 ch g Silver Hawk - Crown Quest (Chief's Crown) Cl-up, ev ch 2f out, onepace over 1f out: nicely bckd on reapp: in '99 won on reapp at York (List, rtd 111): '98 Ascot scorer (stks, rtd 105+): styd 10.4f well & enjoys gd/soft & soft: runs well fresh: smart, gd reapp.	3½	108
768	**MONSAJEM 30** [3] E A L Dunlop 5-8-11 J Reid 4/1: 13-604: In tch, rdn 2f out, onepcd over 1f out: nicely bckd: can rate higher, see 657.	¾	104
3867}	**AZOUZ PASHA 227** [8] 4-9-0 T Quinn 9/2: 4121-5: Chsd ldrs, rdn & btn well over 1f out: op 3/1: prog in '99, won at Lingfield (mdn), Goodwood (val h'cap) & Doncaster (List, rtd 114, 1st time visor): eff at 10f, stays 12f well on firm/fast grnd & on any trk: has run well fresh in a visor: lightly raced & smart, better on fast.	2	105
916}	**CAPE GRACE 373** [1] 4-8-6 R Hughes 15/2: 6/44-6: Keen, waited with, rdn & btn 2f out: reapp: only twice rcd in '99, 4th in List (rtd 98): '98 debut Ascot wnr (fill mdn, rtd 103 at best): stays 10f on fast & gd.	5	90
732	**TURAATH 30** [4] 4-8-11 W Supple 25/1: 3/1-07: Led till over 2f out, no extra over 1f out: see 732.	5	88
3556}	**ANNAPURNA 246** [5] 4-8-6 M Roberts 20/1: /220-8: Bhd, eff over 3f out, sn btn: rnr-up on 1st 2 of 3 '99 starts (h'cap, rtd 94): juv scorer at Kempton (fill stks, rtd 97): stays 10f on gd & gd/firm, any trk.	3½	79

8 ran   Time 2m 13.71 (11.41)   (The Earl Cadogan)   J L Dunlop Arundel, W Sussex

---

1015   3.40 CORAL ROSEBERY HCAP 4YO+ 0-105 (B)   1m rnd   Soft 113   -01 Slow   [103]
£22100   £6800   £3400   £1700   Field came stands side in straight

-725	**PULAU TIOMAN 30** [10] M A Jarvis 4-9-8 (97) P Robinson 9/1: 500-21: 4 b c Robellino - Ella Mon Amour (Ela Mana Mou) Handy, hdwy over 1f out, qcknd to lead ins last, drvn out to hold on: well bckd: '99 scorer at Haydock (rtd h'cap) & Sandown (stks, rtd 100): '98 Nottingham scorer (mdn, rtd 88): suited by 7f/1m, stays 9f: acts on firm, soft & any trk: runs well fresh: tough & v useful, at the top of his form.		103
733	**ESPADA 30** [8] M H Tompkins 4-8-10 (85) S Sanders 20/1: 150-62: 4 b c Mukaddamah - Folk Song (The Minstrel) Waited with, hdwy 2f out, switched left & styd on well ins last, just held: prev with P Calver: acts on fast & soft grnd & deserves a nice prize whilst in this form: useful, 733.	nk	90
733	**PANTAR 30** [4] I A Balding 5-9-4 (93) (bl) K Fallon 6/1 FAV: 032143: 5 b g Shirley Heights - Spring Daffodil (Pharly) Held up, gd hdwy well over 1f out to chase wnr ins last, no extra cl-home: gamble from 10/1: gd run: acts on firm, soft & fibresand: often runs well in big field h'caps, but only 2 wins from 28.	1½	96
875	**PRINCE BABAR 13** [13] R A Fahey 9-8-5 (80) M Roberts 10/1: 000-24: In tch, eff over 2f out, kept on same pace over 1f out: on a handy mark: see 875.	¾	82
*834	**SECOND WIND 18** [17] 5-8-3 (78) A Beech (5) 14/1: 304-15: Led, rdn till collared ins last, no extra: well clr of rem & another fine run: stays 1m, prob just best at 7f: see 834.	¾	79
4456}	**DANGEROUS FORTUNE 186** [12] 4-8-6 (81) R Hills 25/1: 3215-6: In tch, rdn & no impress fnl 2f: '99 wnr at Redcar (mdn, rtd 83): eff at 7f/8.3f on firm, gd/soft & fibresand: handles any trk: sharper for this.	6	73
4560}	**SMOOTH SAILING 177** [20] 5-8-10 (85) J F Egan 14/1: 0020-7: In tch, eff to chall 2f out, sn wknd: last raced over hdles 10 wks ago: earlier won at Leicester (nov hdle, rtd 98h, 2m, soft): rnr-up twice in '99 on the Flat (rtd 90): '98 Leicester wnr (h'cap, rtd 88): stays 1m on fast, soft & enjoys stiff trks, handles any.	nk	76
*817	**MISTER RAMBO 21** [19] 5-8-6 (81) T Quinn 12/1: 40-018: Chsd ldr, rdn & btn 2f out: btr 817 (7.5f).	1	70
*875	**YAROB 13** [15] 7-8-7 (82) W Supple 12/1: 05-019: Cl-up, wknd well over 1f out: btr 875 (made all).	nk	70
733	**SILK ST JOHN 30** [6] 6-8-13 (88) P McCabe 14/1: 300-00: Waited with, mod late gains: 10th: '99 scorer at Sandown, & Newbury (h'caps, rtd 97), also rtd 106$ when plcd in List company: '98 wnr at Chepstow (ltd stks), Haydock (val h'cap, subs disq), Windsor (2) & Newbury (rtd 97): suited by 1m, stays 11f: acts on firm, hvy & fibresand, any trk: v tough, genuine & useful, loves to come late & well h'capped when returning form.	2½	73
3987}	**TACTFUL REMARK 219** [9] 4-10-0 (103) Martin Dwyer 33/1: 4103-0: In tch, wknd 2f out: 11th: in '99 trained by J Gosden, scored at Kempton (h'cap, reapp) & Newbury (h'cap, rtd 95): eff over 9/10f on firm/fast grnd: has run well fresh on a gall trk: now with J Osborne (yet to open his account).	2	85
733	**INDIAN BLAZE 30** [14] 6-8-10 (85) N Pollard 9/1: 034-00: Bhd, eff 2f out, no extra: btr 733 (gd).	¾	66
2931}	**LOVERS LEAP 274** [7] 4-8-6 (81) C Rutter 20/1: 3120-0: Bhd after 3f: 13th: reapp: in '99 scored at Newbury (mdn, rtd 82): eff at 7f, stays 1m: acts on firm, gd/soft & on a gall trk.	4	56
967	**KING PRIAM 5** [3] 5-9-3 (92) (bl) T G McLaughlin 9/1: 136200: Sn rdn & al bhd, 14th: better than this.	¾	66
690	**INVADER 37** [18] 4-9-1 (90) N Esler (7) 45-550: In tch, wknd 3f out: 15th, not handle soft?	1½	62
1260}	**Surprise Encounter 349** [5] 4-8-8 (83) J Reid 14/1:	3984} Crystal Creek 219 [2] 4-8-11 (86) J Fortune 25/1:	
966	**Mayaro Bay 5** [1] 4-9-7 (96) R Hughes 12/1:	703 Prince Du Soleil 32 [16] 4-9-1 (90) Pat Eddery 20/1:	
4560}	**Calcutta 177** [11] 4-9-10 (99) M Hills 20/1:		

20 ran   Time 1m 45.92 (9.12)   H R H Sultan Ahmad Shah)   M A Jarvis Newmarket

---

1016   4.10 KICKON.COM COND STKS 3YO+ (C)   6f   Soft 113   +07 Fast
£6235   £2365   £1182   £537   3 yo rec 11lb

+914	**MONKSTON POINT 10** [4] D W P Arbuthnot 4-9-1 (vis) T Quinn 9/2 CO FAV: 200-11: 4 b g Fayruz - Doon Belle (Ardoon) Trkd ldr till went on after 2f, rdn clr fnl 1f: gd time: reapp scorer at Newbury (h'cap): rnr-up once in '99 (1st time visor, rtd 97): useful juv scorer, rtd 97, rtd 105: eff at 5/6f & handles fast, relishes soft & a gall or easy trk: best in a visor: back to very useful best on favoured soft grnd.		104
4197}	**PRESENTATION 205** [1] R Hannon 3-8-2 J F Egan 10/1: 0633-2: 3 b f Mujadil - Beechwood (Blushing Groom) In tch wide till joined main group after 2f, eff to chase wnr over 2f out, onepace: clr of rem on reapp:	3	97

333

won on debut in '99, at Windsor (fill mdn), subs 5½L 4th in a Gr2: eff at 5/6f on firm/fast & soft: handles a stiff or easy trk & runs well fresh: v useful.
3870} **DESERT FURY 226** [8] B Hanbury 3-8-7 A Beech (5) 9/2 CO FAV: 13-3: 3 b c Warning - Number One Spot 4 **94**
(Reference Point) Sn in tch, rdn & onepace well over 1f out: reapp, nicely bckd: only twice rcd juv, won at Chester (mdn, rtd 103): eff at 5/6f, looks sure to apprec 7f: has run well fresh on firm: fitter for this on a sounder surface.
829 **DAY JOURNEY 18** [2] E A L Dunlop 3-8-12 J Reid 11/2: 114-34: Chsd ldrs, rdn & btn over 1f out. *1* **97**
914 **YORKIES BOY 10** [6] 5-9-1 J Fortune 12/1: 000-05: Led 2f, chsd wnr over 2f out till wknd over 1f out. *1½* **87**
4377} **HARMONIC WAY 192** [7] 5-9-1 R Hughes 9/2 CO FAV: 2200-6: Waited with, brief eff 2f out, sn btn & eased ins last: in '99 scored at Goodwood (val Stewards Cup h'cap) & plcd in sev other val h'caps (rtd 103): no wins in '98: v eff at 6f, stays 7f: likes firm, acts on soft & any trk: tough & useful, expect better. *½* **86**
966 **AL MUALLIM 5** [3] 6-9-1 K Fallon 9/2 CO FAV: 20-307: Sn rdn & nvr a factor: twice below pleasing reapp in 728 (may do better on a sounder surface). *7* **72**
4093} **BLACKHEATH 212** [5] 4-9-4 S Whitworth 12/1: 0330-8: In tch, btn halfway: reapp, reportedly not handle this grnd: '99 wnr at Lingfield (mdn), rtd 97 at best: suited by 6f on firm or gd grnd, handles gd/soft. *13* **49**
8 ran Time 1m 17.45 (6.35) (Derrick C Broomfield) D W P Arbuthnot Upper Lambourn, Berks

1017 **4.45 DAFFODIL MDN 3YO (D)** **1m3f30y Soft 113 -36 Slow**
£4387 £1350 £675 £337 Field came stands side in straight

4453} **JOLLY SHARP 186** [13] H R A Cecil 3-9-0 T Quinn 4/1 FAV: 4-1: 3 ch c Diesis - Milly Ha Ha (Dancing Brave) Cl-up, led over 2f out, styd on ins last, shade cosily: bckd tho' op 5/2 on reapp: 4th on sole juv start (rtd 86): dam useful mid-dist performer & relished this step up to 11f, further shld suit: acts on soft: useful. **95**
4555} **BANCO SUIVI 177** [6] B W Hills 3-8-9 M Hills 9/2: 5-2: 3 b f Nashwan - Pay The Bank (High Top) Keen in tch, hdwy to chall over 2f out, kept on ins last, only btn 1L: bckd tho' op 3/1 on reapp: 5th sole juv start (rtd 91+): dam 1m wng juv: relished this step up to 11f & handles soft: maiden shld prove a formality. *¾* **88**
4515} **MBELE 181** [14] W R Muir 3-9-0 Martin Dwyer 6/1: 2-3: 3 b c Mtoto - Majestic Image (Niniski) Held up, rdn & outpcd over 2f out, hdwy & short of room appr fnl 1f, styd on well ins last, nrst fin: nicely bckd on reapp: rnr-up in a mdn sole juv start (rtd 89): enjoyed this step up to 11f & further is sure to suit (dam 14f/2m scorer): acts on soft grnd: useful, can rate more highly & looks one to follow over further. *2½* **91+**
4171} **BANIYAR 207** [11] Sir Michael Stoute 3-9-0 K Fallon 9/1: 0-4: In tch, eff & badly hmpd 3f out (lost around 5/6L), hdwy over 1f out, sn onepace under a kind ride: reapp: unplcd sole juv start (rtd 70): half brother to wnrs over 10f/2m: stays 11f on soft grnd: looks sure to rate more highly & win races. *1½* **89**
-- **WAFFIGG** [7] 3-9-0 P Robinson 7/1: 5: Handy, outpcd over 2f out, onepace under a kind ride: half brother to French Derby wnr Celtic Swing & looks sure to come on for this encouraging debut . *3½* **85**
-- **FILM SCRIPT** [5] 3-8-9 R Hughes 8/1: 6: Waited with, eff over 3f out, sn no impress: mid-dist bred. *3* **76**
833 **ICE CRYSTAL 18** [8] 3-9-0 C Rutter 40/1: 07: In tch, wknd 2f out: see 833. *1¾* **78**
4606} **CLOTH OF GOLD 171** [10] 3-9-0 P Doe 50/1: 0-8: Sn bhd, no danger: well btn sole juv start: bred to apprec 1m/10f. *1* **77**
4473} **LAFLEUR 185** [9] 3-8-9 M Roberts 20/1: 0-9: Nvr a factor on reapp. *nk* **71**
4613} **PRINCE ELMAR 170** [12] 3-9-0 J Reid 50/1: 30-0: In tch, wknd 3f out, 10th. *1½* **74**
-- **MANIATIS** [3] 3-9-0 J Fortune 7/1: 0: Led over 3f out till over 2f out, wknd: 11th, op 4/1. *1¾* **71**
643 **The Flyer 49** [1] 3-9-0 N Pollard 50/1: 704 **Strawman 32** [2] 3-9-0 R Hills 50/1:
936 **Jeune Premier 7** [4] 3-9-0 Pat Eddery 20/1:
14 ran Time 2m 33.87 (16.47) (Cliveden Stud) H R A Cecil Newmarket

1018 **5.20 EXHIBITIONS MDN DIV II 3YO+ (D)** **7f rnd Soft 113 -19 Slow**
£3913 £1204 £602 £301 3 yo rec 13lb Field came stands side in straight

-- **BIG FUTURE** [6] Mrs A J Perrett 3-8-11 Pat Eddery 4/1: 1: 3 b c Bigstone - Star Of The Future (El Gran Senor) Slow away, waited with, hdwy over 2f out, styd on to lead dist, pushed out: nicely bckd on debut: half brother to a 7f scorer: stays 7f well, 1m sure to suit: runs well fresh on soft: open to improvement. **77**
2854} **SARENA SPECIAL 276** [11] R J O'Sullivan 3-8-11 S Sanders 16/1: 2426-2: 3 b c Lucky Guest - Lariston Gale (Pas de Seul) Chsd ldr till went on over 1f out, hdd dist, hung right & no extra: reapp: rnr-up twice as a juv (mdns, rtd 81): eff over 6/7f on fast, soft grnd & on any trk: has ability, worth a try in headgear. *1¼* **74**
708 **CANCUN CARIBE 32** [3] K McAuliffe 3-8-11 J F Egan 50/1: 043: 3 ch g Port Lucaya - Miss Tuko (Good Times) In tch, lost place over 2f out, kept on well fnl 1f, nrst fin: eff at 7f, further looks sure to suit: handles soft grnd, encouraging h'cap qualifying run. *½* **73+**
4116} **CATAMARAN 210** [7] Lady Herries 5-9-10 P Doe 16/1: 30-4: Led till over 1f out, no extra: in '99 trained by J Gosden, plcd in a mdn (rtd 75): eff at 7f, prob stays 10f & that trip shld suit: handles soft. *1¾* **70**
4339} **LUCKY SWEEP 195** [10] 3-8-11 R Hughes 11/2: 64-5: Waited with, rdn & onepace fnl 2f: clr of rem on reapp: some promise when 4th on 2nd of 2 juv starts (rtd 71): eff at 7f, bred to apprec 1m+ in h'caps. *½* **69**
4505} **SHAHED 182** [9] 3-8-11 R Hills 4/1: 443-6: Chsd ldrs till wknd 2f out: plcd on last of 3 juv starts (mdn, rtd 77): eff at 7f, bred to stay 1m+ (dam mid-dist wnr): handles fast & hvy grnd. *9* **56**
839 **SHADOW PRINCE 17** [2] 3-8-11 Steven Harrison (7) 10/1: 6-57: Keen in tch, btn over 3f out. *1¾* **53**
-- **ASTRONAUT** [1] 3-8-11 M Hills 10/1: 8: Slow away, no danger: half brother to a 7f scorer. *6* **44**
-- **TALBIYA** [4] 3-8-6 K Fallon 7/2 FAV: 9: In tch, wknd 2f out: op 7/4: Mujtahid filly: with Sir M Stoute. *hd* **38**
-- **QUIET READING** [5] 3-8-11 A Morris 33/1: 0: Sn rdn & al bhd: last: with C Cyzer. *3* **39**
10 ran Time 1m 33.33 (9.23) (K Abdulla) Mrs A J Perrett Pulborough, W Sussex

NOTTINGHAM MONDAY APRIL 24TH Lefthand, Galloping Track

Official Going HEAVY; Back Str - SOFT. Stalls: 5f - Far Side; 1m6f - Stands Side; Rem - Inside.

1019 **2.10 COME RACING SELLER 2YO (G)** **5f str Heavy Inapplicable**
£1926 £550 £275

928 **DIAMOND MAX 9** [1] P D Evans 2-8-11 J P Spencer 3/1 JT FAV: -041: 2 b c Nicolotte - Kawther (Tap On Wood) Broke well & made all, clr fnl 1f, drvn out: bt in for 11,200gns: half-brother to sev 2yo wnrs: eff at 5f on soft & hvy grnd: handles a gall trk, can force the pace: suited by this drop to sell company. **66**
898 **ELAINES REBECCA 11** [3] W T Kemp 2-8-6 L Newman (5) 13/2: -62: 2 ch f Missed Flight - Pretty Scarce (Handsome Sailor) Prom, kept on fnl 1f but not pace of wnr: eff at 5f, 6f will suit: acts on hvy grnd. *3* **55**

911 **HARD TO CATCH 10** [4] M R Channon 2-8-11 R Cochrane 3/1 JT FAV: -53: 2 b c Namaqualand - Brook's Dilemma (Known Fact) Nvr far away, not qckn ins fnl 1f: op 5/1, clmd for £5,000: eff at 5f on hvy grnd. *nk* **59**
856 **BOBANVI 14** [10] J S Wainwright 2-8-6 R Mullen 8/1: -54: Slowly away, outpcd till late hdwy, nrst fin: first debut, made up a lot of late grnd: already looks in need of 6f+: see 856 (AW seller). *2½* **49**
849 **NAUGHTY KNIGHT 14** [5] 2-8-11 A Nicholls (3) 25/1: -05: Chsd ldrs, onepace fnl 2f: cheaply bght Apr foal: first foal, dam unrcd but related to a couple of wnrs: sire a smart sprinter: with G Balding. *¾* **52**
*856 **COUNTESS BANKES 14** [7] 2-8-11 (VIS) A Daly 11/2: -416: Front rank till wknd dist: turf debut, rcd keenly in first time visor: see 856 (sand). *¾* **50**
-- **PERTEMPS GILL** [9] 2-8-6 G Hind 33/1: -7: Dwelt, rdn in rear, nvr nr ldrs on debut: cheaply bght Apr foal: half-sister to sev wnrs, dam won over 1m: sire a useful 1m h'capper: with A D Smith. *3* **39**
-- **ORCHARD RAIDER** [8] 2-8-11 G Bardwell 9/1: -8: Chsd ldrs 3f, fdd: debut: 12,000gns purchase: Mar foal, sire a decent juv: with C Dwyer & shld do btr, poss on faster grnd. *3½* **38**
928 **LUVLY TIMES 9** [2] 2-8-11 G Parkin 20/1: -09: Al outpcd: see 928. *¾* **36**
-- **EVERMOORE** [6] 2-8-6 R Fitzpatrick(3) 14/1: -0: Dwelt, eff 2f out, sn btn & fin last. *7* **17**
10 ran Time 1m 06.7 (Diamond Racing Ltd) P D Evans Pandy, Gwent.

1020

2.40 BLACKBROOK.CO.UK MDN 2YO (D) 5f str Heavy Inapplicable
£2842 £812 £406

-- **DAYGLOW DANCER** [5] M R Channon 2-9-0 G Hall 2/1 FAV: -1: 2 b c Fraam - Fading (Pharly) Dsptd lead till halfway, imprvd to lead 1f out, ran on strongly, rdn out: Mar foal, dam unrcd: sire a smart miler: eff at 5f, will stay 6f: acts on hvy grnd: can run well fresh & force the pace: sure to race more highly. **77**
-- **SILKEN TOUCH** [4] N A Callaghan 2-8-9 R Cochrane 9/4: -2: 2 b f Pivotal - Prima Silk (Primo Dominie) Led/dsptd lead, went on halfway, collared ent fnl 1f, kept on but not pace of wnr: op 6/4, 12L clr 3rd: Mar foal, dam a 5/7f wnr, incl as a juv: sire a smart sprinter: eff at 5f on hvy: not given a hard time. *1¾* **67**
-- **MAYSBOYO** [1] B P J Baugh 2-9-0 G Hind 14/1: -3: 2 b g Makbul - Maysimp (Mac's Imp) Dwelt, rdn thr'out & no ch with front 2: ran green: first foal: Apr foal, sire a decent juv: sure to learn from this. *12* **52**
-- **CUMBRIAN CASPER** [3] T D Easterby 2-9-0 G Parkin 10/3: -4: Swerved start, recovered to chase ldrs 3f, fdd into last: 22,000gns Mar foal: dam a 10f wnr in Ireland: ran well for a long way. *18* **22**
-- **EXELLENT ADVENTURE** [2] 2-9-0 J P Spencer 11/2: -W: Refused to ent stalls & withdrawn: June foal, sire won over mid-dists: with P D Evans. **0**
5 ran Time 1m 08.3 (Surrey Laminators Ltd) M R Channon West Isley, Berks.

1021

3.10 LIZ REID MED AUCT MDN 3YO (F) 5f str Heavy Inapplicable
£2352 £672 £336

2471} **HELEN ALBADOU 294** [8] J M P Eustace 3-8-9 J Tate 3/1 FAV: 3-1: 3 b f Sheikh Albadou - Sister Troy (Far North) Prom, led briefly halfway, rallied gamely to regain lead cl-up, drvn out: plcd in a Windsor mdn on sole juv start (rtd 77): 15,000gns sister to a wnr in the USA: dam & sire both sprinters: eff at 5f on fast & hvy grnd, runs well fresh: handles a sharp & gall trk: shld rate more highly. **71**
837 **BUDELLI 17** [10] M R Channon 3-9-0 A Daly 8/1: 5-362: 3 b c Elbio - Eves Temptation (Glenstal) Chsd ldrs, imprvd to lead dist, collared dying strides: eff at 5f, return to 6f will suit: acts on gd & hvy grnd. *hd* **75**
808 **NEEDWOOD TRICKSTER 23** [5] B C Morgan 3-9-0 (t) G Hind 50/1: -03: 3 gr g Fayrux - Istaraka (Darshaan) Slowly away, hdwy to chall halfway, not pace of front 2 ins last: eff at 5f on hvy grnd, shld stay further: wears a t-strap: has lost ch at the start on both races to date. *2* **71**
781 **DANAKIM 26** [9] J R Weymes 3-9-0 (bl) L Newman (5) 6/1: -00024: Led till halfway, not qckn fnl 1f: op 9/2: imprvd effort, eff at 5f on hvy: see 781 (first time blnks). *1½* **68**
837 **CAREW CASTLE 17** [3] 3-9-0 R Cochrane 11/2: -55: Chsd ldrs till outpcd fnl 1f: see 837 (gd/soft, 6f). *3½* **62**
4607} **STAR PRINCESS 171** [11] 3-8-9 A Nicholls (3) 7/2: 0324-6: Prom till wknd over 1f out: reapp: lightly rcd in '99, rnr-up at Newbury (mdn, rtd 79): half-sister to sev wnrs, incl sprinter Prince Belfort: eff at 6f on fast & hvy grnd: capable of much better. *2½* **52**
740 **UNITED PASSION 28** [2] 3-8-9 J P Spencer 10/1: -27: Dwelt, imprvd to chall after halfway, wknd fnl 1f: tchd 16/1: ran better than finishing position suggest, prob unsuited by this hvy grnd: see 740 (sand). *3½* **46**
909 **NICOLAI 10** [4] 3-9-0 R Mullen 50/1: -008: Al outpcd: with M Bell & no form to date. *½* **50**
781 **FOXDALE 26** [6] 3-8-9 D Griffiths 16/1: 0-59: Front rank 3f, wknd: mkt drifter: see 781. *¾* **43**
4181} **ONLYONEUNITED 206** [7] 3-8-9 O Urbina 5/1: 052-0: Front rank 3f, fdd into 10th: reapp: '99 rnr-up at Lingfield on fnl start (mdn, rtd 75): eff at 5f on soft grnd, will stay 6f+: with M Blanshard. *3½* **37**
4089} **RAPIDASH 212** [1] 3-9-0 (vis) R Fitzpatrick (3) 50/1: 00-0: In tch till halfway, sn left bhd: no form. *4* **34**
11 ran Time 1m 06.2 (J C Smith) J M P Eustace Newmarket.

1022

3.45 LADYSAN HCAP 3YO 0-65 (F) 1m2f Heavy 172 -02 Slow [71]
£2562 £732 £366

892 **RATIFIED 11** [10] H Candy 3-8-8 (51) G Bardwell 9/4 FAV: 000-21: 3 b g Not In Doubt - Festival Of Magic (Clever Trick) Held up, improving when slipped ent str, recovered to lead dist, styd on well, drvn out: bckd from 4/1: unplcd in mdns in '99: eff over a sharp or stiff 10f on gd/soft & hvy: can run well fresh. **55**
827 **SELTON HILL 19** [15] N A Callaghan 3-9-4 (61) J Mackay (7) 7/2: 644-32: 3 b g Bin Ajwaad - Ivory Gull (Storm Bird) Prom, kept on under press fnl 1f, not btn far: 4L clr 3rd: acts on fast & hvy grnd: see 827. *1¾* **63**
892 **CHILLI 11** [6] C E Brittain 3-8-10 (53) A Nicholls (3) 7/1: -33233: 3 br g Most Welcome - So Saucy (Teenoso) Dwelt, rapid prog to lead after 3f & sn clr, hdd dist, fdd: consistent, acts on gd/soft, hvy & both AWs. *4* **50**
3189} **LATE ARRIVAL 262** [5] D Morris 3-9-1 (58) R Cochrane 11/2: 040-4: Mid-div, short of room 3f out, no impress fnl 2f: op 8/1, reapp: lightly rcd in '99, trained by J J O'Neill & 4th at Ayr (mdn, rtd 57): half-brother to wnrs btwn 5f & 12f: worth another chance on faster grnd. *4* **50**
790 **NEEDWOOD TRIDENT 25** [12] 3-8-4 (46)(1ow) G Hind 50/1: 00-05: Rear, came wide & styd on fnl 2f nrst fin: unplcd on both '99 starts (mdns): half-sister to a winning stayer, dam 12f wnr: in need of 12f+. *1¾* **37**
4274} **WADENHOE 200** [13] 3-9-6 (63) A Daly 16/1: 0000-6: Held up, eff 3f out, nvr nr ldrs: op 10/1, reapp: '99 Ayr wnr (mdn, rtd 82): eff at 7f on gd & gd/soft grnd: handles a stiff/gall trk, can force the pace. *1¾* **51**
789 **SAN DIMAS 25** [3] 3-9-7 (64) R Fitzpatrick (3) 25/1: 00-07: Prom till outpcd fnl 2f: see 789. *3* **48**
4059} **EVER REVIE 214** [9] 3-8-13 (56) G Parkin 14/1: 0100-8: Rcd keenly & prom, wknd 3f out: op 10/1, reapp: '99 Beverley wnr (sell, rtd 68, bl 1st time): eff at 7.5f, shld stay further: acts on gd/soft & blnks. *¾* **39**
4514} **STORMSWELL 181** [14] 3-9-0 (57) P Hanagan(7) 14/1: 0060-9: Nvr btr than mid-div on reapp. *1¾* **38**
789 **EXPEDIENT 25** [11] 3-8-8 (51) G Carter 9/1: 00-00: Al outpcd, fin 10th. *8* **22**
745 **LITTLE TARA 28** [8] 3-7-10 (39)(1oh) J Lowe 40/1: 00-00: Nvr a factor in 11th: see 745. *¾* **9**

892	**MISS WORLD** 11 [2] 3-9-0 (57)(t) L Newman (5) 16/1: 540500: Front rank 7f, wknd qckly, t.o. in 12th.				*21*	2
684	**CACOPHONY** 38 [1] 3-8-5 (48) C Cogan (5) 12/1: 546220: Rcd keenly & led 3f, sn wknd & virtually				*dist*	0

p.u.: reportedly lost a shoe & fin sore: prev trained by S Dow, now with S Bowring: see 684, 541 (sand).
13 ran   Time 2m 19.7 (17.4)   (Mrs David Blackburn)   H Candy Wantage, Oxon.

1023   4.20 EASTER MONDAY HCAP 4YO+ 0-70 (E)   1m6f   Heavy 172   +02 Fast   [66]
             £3157   £902   £451   4yo rec 2lb

885   **MY LEGAL EAGLE** 12 [12] R J Price 6-9-5 (57) P Fitzsimons (5) 4/1 FAV: 222221: 6 b g Law Society -   62
Majestic Nurse (On Your Mark). Waited with, smooth hdwy to lead dist, kept on fnl 1f, drvn out: best time of
day: deserved win, rnr-up on prev 5 starts: '99 Salisbury wnr (appr h'cap, rtd 54): '98 Thirsk wnr (mdn h'cap,
with J Hills, rtd 51 & 48a): eff at 10/12f, stays 2m well: acts on fast, hvy grnd & on both AWs: eff
with/without blnks, handles any trk: best held up for a late run, well rdn by P Fitzsimons today.

791   **NOSEY NATIVE** 25 [6] J Pearce 9-7-8-3 (41) G Bardwell 16/1: 0-0032: 7 b g Cyrano de Bergerac - Native   ¾   45
Flair (Be My Native) Rear, came wide into str, prog to chall 2f out, no extra cl home, just btn: acts on
fast, hvy grnd & fibresand: well h'capped now: see 791, 470.

860   **DOUBLE RUSH** 14 [5] T Keddy 8-8-6 (44)(t) G Carter 13/2: 0-6123: 8 b g Doulab - Stanza Dancer   2½   45
(Stanford) Mid-div, prog 3f out, not pace of front 2 ins last: op 5/1: eff btwn 12f & 2m on firm, hvy & equitrack.

835   **ZINCALO** 17 [1] C E Brittain 4-9-6 (60)(t) A Nicholls (3) 25/1: 600-04: In tch, eff 2f out, onepcd ins   1½   59
fnl 1f: back to form, handles fast & hvy grnd: see 835.

4127} **SPA LANE** 209 [10] 7-8-1 (37)(2ow) R Mullen 16/1: 0000-5: Prom, onepcd fnl 1f: reapp: '99 wnr   shd   38
at Southwell & Pontefract (h'caps, rtd 38a & 48 at best), also plcd sev times: '98 wnr at Beverley (h'cap, rtd 52):
'96 W'hampton wnr (2, stks, rtd 57a): eff btwn 12f & 2m2f on firm, hvy & f/sand: encouraging reapp, on fair mark.

4412} **EVENING SCENT** 189 [13] 4-8-7 (47) N Carlisle 16/1: 0130-6: Mid-div, prog to chall 3f out, no impress   nk   45
fnl 2f: recent jumps rnr (rtd 76h in jʋv nov hdles): '99 Catterick wnr (sell, rtd 60): stays a sharp 2m, acts
on fast & soft grnd: can run well fresh: shld benefit from a return to soft grade.

860   **LADY RACHEL** 14 [17] G Parkin 15/2: -30257: Rear, imprvd 2f out, no impress fnl 1f.   ¾   39

788   **SILENT VALLEY** 26 [8] 6-7-10 (34)(7oh) J Mackay(7) 66/1: /00-08: Rear, kept on under press fnl 2f,   hd   31
nvr nr ldrs: likely rcd & modest '99 form: dual 97/98 hdles wnr (rtd 91h): last won on the Flat in '97, at
Nottingham (mdn auct, rtd 58): eff at 10f, stays a sharp 2m over timber: acts on gd & firm grnd & on both AWs:
eff in blnks/visor, can run well fresh: well h'capped nowadays.

464   **MEILLEUR** 79 [15] 6-9-7 (59) R Cochrane 16/1: 4-2369: Rear, eff 3f out, no impress fnl 2f: 11 wk abs.   ½   55

876   **BOLD CARDOWAN** 13 [4] 4-8-6 (46) G Hall 5/1: 460-00: Front rank, chall 3f out, led briefly dist, fdd: hd   42
fin 10th: seemed not to get home in these testing conditions, but does stay 2m: capable of better, see 876.

4618} **NEEDWOOD SPIRIT** 170 [11] 5-9-10 (62) J Tate 12/1: 0345-0: Front rank, led 3f out till over 1f out,   6   52
wknd into 11th: tried hdles this winter, 4th at Uttoxeter (nov, rtd 102h): '99 Folkestone wnr (h'cap, rtd 66):
plcd sev times: '98 Catterick scorer (class stks, rtd 71): eff at 14/15.4f on gd/soft & hvy grnd, prob handles
fast: has tried a visor, best without: sharper next time.

822   **SKYERS A KITE** 19 [16] 5-8-6 (44) J Lowe 9/1: 130-20: Rcd keenly in rear, eff 3f out, eased when   11   22
btn fnl 2f: fin 12th: unproven beyond 12f: see 822 (12f sell h'cap).

853   **DIZZY TILLY** 14 [9] 6-8-7 (44)(1ow) J D Smith 16/1: 30-000: Nvr better than mid-div: fin 13th.   ¾   22

853   **STREET WALKER** 14 [3] 4-9-0 (54) A Daly 12/1: 253-40: Front rank, led after 6f till 3f out, wknd qkly.   0

3822} **Jane Ann** 229 [14] 4-8-6 (46) W Ryan 12/1:   866   **Menteith** 13 [2] 4-8-4 (42)(2ow) G Hind 66/1:
16 ran   Time 3m 22.1 (23.8)   (E G Bevan)   R J Price Ullingswick, H'fords.

1024   4.50 FINN HCAP 3YO 0-60 (F)   1m54y rnd   Heavy 172   -36 Slow   [67]
             £2593   £741   £370

4151} **BOLD RAIDER** 208 [16] I A Balding 3-9-7 (60) A Nicholls (3) 8/1: 000-1: 3 b g Rudimentary - Spanish   64
Heart (King Of Spain) Rear, imprvd 2f out, strong run to lead dying strides, drvn out: reapp, top-weight: some
jʋv promise (mdn, rtd 70), often slowly away: half-brother to a 7f winning 2yo, dam scored over 7/9f: eff at 1m,
10f well soft: acts on hvy grnd & on a gall trk, runs well fresh: open to further improvement.

4260} **MIDNIGHT ALLURE** 202 [4] C F Wall 3-9-5 (58) R Mullen 6/1: 500-2: 3 b f Aragon - Executive Lady   nk   60
(Night Shift) Prom, styd on well under press fnl 2f, not btn far: reapp: thrice rcd juv (debut, mdn, rtd 62):
half-sister to sprint wnr Midnight Escape: eff over a stiff 1m, may stay 10f: acts on hvy & runs well fresh.

839   **ANTIGONEL** 17 [3] R Hannon 3-9-4 (57) R Smith (5) 9/1: 00-03: 3 b f Fairy King - Euromill (Shirley   shd   58
Heights) Waited with, prog 2f out, styd on strongly cl-home & just btn in a tight fin: eff over a stiff 1m on hvy.

887   **DIAMOND OLIVIA** 12 [15] John Berry 3-9-2 (55) G Hall 3/1 FAV: 640-34: Rear, gd prog to lead just   ½   56
ins last with jockey looking rnd, sn rdn, drifted left & hdd: stays 1m: do better with a stronger ride.

3736} **DOUBLE FAULT** 235 [5] 3-9-2 (55) G Faulkner (3) 16/1: 2040-5: Led 3f out, again 2f out till ins   1¼   53
last, no extra: reapp: rnr-up in '99 (rtd 65): half-sister to a 7f 2yo wnr: handles fast & hvy, stays a stiff 1m.

887   **TAKE MANHATTAN** 12 [8] 3-9-4 (57) A Daly 14/1: 0-0066: Mid-div, styd on under press fnl 1f, nrst fin.   1   53

800   **PUPS PRIDE** 25 [13] 3-8-12 (51) R Cochrane 4/1: 600-57: Trkd ldrs, onepcd fnl 1f: see 800.   ½   46

840   **GROVE LODGE** 17 [6] 3-9-0 (53) L Newman(5) 11/1: 00-008: Prom, led over 3f out till 2f out, no extra: 1¾   45
tchd 20/1: modest form to date, dam a 12f wnr: with S Woodman & better expected today.

46   **PRESTO** 161 [9] 3-9-7 (60) J P Spencer 10/1: 000-9: Mid-div, no impress fnl 2f: jt top-weight: 2½   48
lightly rcd juv, cost 12,500gns: with W Haggas.

847   **MANSTAR** 16 [1] 3-9-4 (57) N Kennedy 8/1: 50-500: Front rank 5f, fdd into 10th: see 827 (10f).   3½   45

706   **SEDONA** 32 [7] 3-8-11 (50) P Fitzsimons(5) 20/1: 0-5U30: Prsd ldrs 5f, sn fdd: fin 11th: see 706.   2   28

827   **SEND IT TO PENNY** 19 [12] 3-8-8 (47) G Parkin 12/1: 504-00: Chsd ldrs till wknd 3f out: fin 12th: 2½   21
in '99 4th at Ripon (seller, rtd 54): eff at 6f, shld stay further: handles fast grnd, with M W Easterby.

171   **GYMCRAK FIREBIRD** 135 [18] 3-9-2 (55) G Hind 20/1: 0246-0: Nvr a factor in 13th: see 171 (AW).   nk   28

4256} **PORTIA LADY** 202 [14] 3-8-12 (51) W Ryan 9/1: 4020-0: Nvr dngrs, fin 14th: op 14/1, reapp, shorter   1¼   21
priced stablemate of 5th: in '99 rnr-up at Beverley (sell nurs, rtd 54): eff at 7.5f on gd & gd/soft: usually
blnkd, not today: capable of better on a sounder surface.

500   **Threefortycash** 73 [11] 3-8-12 (51) J Tate 25/1:   806   **Diamond Vanessa** 24 [10] 3-8-7 (46)(t) R Fitzpatrick(3) 25/1:
16 ran   Time 1m 56.1 (16.7)   (The Farleigh Court Racing Partnership)   I A Balding Kingsclere, Hants.

LONGCHAMP SUNDAY APRIL 23RD Righthand, Galloping Track

Official Going HEAVY

1025
2.05 GR 3 PRIX DE FONTAINEBLEAU 3YO 1m Heavy
£21134 £7685 £3842 £2305

-- **BERINES SON** [5] A Fabre 3-9-0 C Soumillon 7/2: 2-11: 3 b c Irish River - Berine (Bering) **114**
Hmpd start, settled rear, smooth hdwy 2f out, led ins last, drvn out: eff at 1m on hvy: v useful.

-- **PREMIER PAS** [7] Mme C Head 3-9-0 O Doleuze 29/10 FAV: 113-2: 3 b c Sillery - Passionee (Woodman) 1 **111**
Trkd ldrs, styd on strongly ins last to take 2nd nr fin: eff at 1m on hvy, further shld suit: win similar.

-- **SLIPSTREAM KING** [2] A Fabre 3-9-0 S Guillot 64/10: -13: 3 gr c Linamix - Slipstream Queen nk **110**
(Conquistador Cielo) Hmpd start, sn prom, ev ch till no extra well ins last: stablemate of wnr: stays 1m on hvy.

4594} **CRYSTAL DASS** 175 [6] T Clout 3-9-0 (bl) T Gillet 87/10: 242-14: Led, hdd ins last, onepace. ¾ **109**
4594} **ROYAL KINGDOM** 175 [3] 3-9-0 M J Kinane 43/10: 1115-5: Chsd ldrs, rdn to improve 2f out, kept on ½ **108**
onepace for press: Irish raider, reportedly disliked this v hvy grnd: '99 scorer at The Curragh (2, incl List)
& notably Ascot (Gr 2, rtd 110): eff at 7f/1m, mid-dists will suit: acts on fast & hvy grnd: v smart at best.
8 ran Time 1m 52.8 (Baron E de Rothschild) A Fabre France

1026
3.10 GR 2 PRIX GREFFULHE 3YO 1m2f110y Heavy
£28818 £11527 £5764

-- **RHENIUM** [3] J C Rouget 3-9-2 T Jarnet 138/10: 411-11: 3 ch c Rainbows For Life - Miss Mulaz 2 **114**
(Luthier) Mid-div, drvn/hdwy over 1f out, ev ch till no extra ins last, fin 2nd, awarded race: eff arnd 10f on hvy.

-- **BOUTRON** [2] P Costes 3-9-2 A Junk 91/10: 20-332: 3 b c Exit To Nowhere - Vindelonde (No Lute) 1½ **111**
Hmpd start, keen/prom, hdwy when badly hmpd over 1f out, styd on ins last, fin 3rd, placed 2nd.

4483} **ARISTOTLE** 183 [6] A P O'Brien 3-9-2 M J Kinane 5/2: 11-1D: 3 b c Sadler's Wells - Flamenco Wave **117**
(Desert Wine) Led to 1m out, led again 4f out, drvn & veered left twice during fnl 2f, styd on well, drvn out:
fin 1st, disqual & plcd 3rd: landed both '99 juv starts, at Galway (mdn) & Doncaster (Gr 1 Racing Post Trophy,
rtd 117): eff at 1m/10f, 12f shld suit: runs well fresh on gd & hvy grnd: v smart & shld find compenstaion sn.
7 ran Time 2m 30.0 (R Bousquet) J C Rouget France

1027
3.40 GR 3 PRIX DE LA GROTTE 3YO FILLIES 1m Heavy
£21134 £7685 £3842

4245} **LADY OF CHAD** 203 [3] R Gibson 3-9-0 G Mosse 13/10 FAV: -11-1: 3 b f Last Tycoon - Sahara Breeze **114**
(Ela Mana Mou) Chsd ldr, went on 2f out, drvn out to hold on ins last: reapp: '99 wnr at Longchamp (2, incl
Gr 1, rtd 114): v eff over a stiff 1m, further shld suit: acts on gd & hvy: v smart, win more Group races.

-- **TEXALINA** [2] J de Roualle 3-9-0 O Peslier 6/4: 111-12: 3 b f Kaldoun - Texan Beauty (Vayrann) nk **113**
Prom, hdwy to chall ins last, styd on, just held: clr rem: recent Listed wnr: eff at 1m on hvy: win a Gr race.

-- **GOLD ROUND** [6] Mme C Head 3-9-0 O Doleuze 67/10: 2121-3: 3 b f Caerleon - Born Gold (Blushing 4 **107**
Groom) Waited with, styd on for press appr fnl 1f, nvr nrr.
6 ran Time 1m 51.5 (J D Martin) R Gibson France

EPSOM WEDNESDAY APRIL 26TH Lefthand, Very Sharp, Undulating Track

Official Going HEAVY. Stalls Inside, Except 6f - Outside. Fields came stands side in straight in all races.

1028
2.05 VICTOR CHANDLER HCAP 3YO+ 0-95 (C) 6f rnd Heavy 145 +13 Fast [91]
£7052 £2170 £1085 £542 3 yo rec 11lb

*844 **ABBAJABBA** 18 [5] C W Fairhurst 4-8-11 (74) J Fanning 5/1: 60-311: 4 b g Barrys Gamble - Bo' Babbity 80
(Strong Gale) Well plcd, shaken up to chall appr fnl 1f, rdn to get on top towards fin: well bckd, gd time:
recent Hamilton wnr (h'cap, first win): unplcd in '99 (rtd 67): juv rnr-up (nurs, rtd 82): eff at 6f, tried
7f: likes gd & hvy grnd, any trk: in terrific form, on a fair mark & shld land a quick hat-trick.

935 **CARLTON** 9 [4] D R C Elsworth 6-8-10 (73) N Pollard 7/2 FAV: 121-42: 6 ch g Thatching - Hooray 1 76
Lady (Ahonoora) Mid-field, prog appr fnl 2f, rdn to lead before dist, sn hard prsd, hdd & no extra fnl 50y: bckd.

3847} **FULL SPATE** 230 [1] J M Bradley 5-8-1 (64) P Fitzsimons (4) 25/1: 0000-3: 5 ch h Unfuwain - Double 1 65
River (Irish River) Trkd ldrs, chall 2f out, same pace below dist: fine reapp: '99 Thirsk wnr (h'cap, sole win,
rtd 79): '98 debut rnr-up (rtd 80, R Charlton): eff at 6f, 7f suits, stays 1m: acts on fast & hvy grnd, any
trk: has slipped to an attractive mark, should go very close next time.

923 **THE FUGATIVE** 11 [2] P Mitchell 7-9-13 (90) M Tebbutt 7/1: 5D0-04: Set strong pace, hdd ent fnl 2f, 1 89
rdn & onepace dist: acts on fast & equitrack, likes soft, hvy & Epsom: won this race last year off 18lb lower mark.

4010} **COLD CLIMATE** 219 [3] 5-7-12 (60) (1ow) F Norton 20/1: 1300-5: Off the pace till kept on well shd 60
fnl 2f, nvr nrr: sharper for reapp: '99 Newmarket wnr (h'cap, rtd 61 at best): with R Charlton in '98
(mdn, rtd 80): eff at 6f, suited by 6f, tried 7f: acts on firm, soft, prob hvy, any trk: with Bob Jones.

630 **ELMHURST BOY** 53 [2] P Doe 25/1: 1-5456: Detached till kept on strongly under hands ¾ 74+
& heels fnl 2f, nvr on terms: 8 wk abs, turf return: spot on next time at 7f+ with headgear reapplied: see 239.

838 **TICKLISH** 19 [8] 4-8-5 (68) J F Egan 10/1: 025-37: Chsd ldrs, eff 2f out, drifted left, unable to qckn. 1¾ 62
895 **RESIST THE FORCE** 13 [9] 10-9-3 (80) Pat Eddery 10/1: 10-028: Al in mid-div: faster grnd/7f+ suits. 1¼ 71
905 **CAUDA EQUINA** 12 [11] 6-9-3 (80) T Quinn 8/1: 00-029: In tch, fdd 2f out: tchd 10/1: Bath specialist. 6 61
3708} **SELHURSTPARK FLYER** 238 [10] 9-9-3 (80) P Roberts 16/1: 0000-0: Cl-up till wknd 2f out: 10th, ½ 60
tchd 20/1 on reapp: failed to make the frame last term (Listed, rtd 91): '98 wnr here at Epsom (val h'cap)
& R Ascot (Wokingham h'cap, tchd 16): best up with/forcing the pace at 6f, stays a sharp 7f: acts on firm &
soft & can go well fresh, any trk, likes Ascot/Epsom: tried vis: can carry big weights: well h'capped 9yo.

4355} **RUSSIAN FOX** 195 [15] 3-9-4 (92) R Hughes 14/1: 3201-0: Front rank till turning for home, eased: 1 70
11th on reapp, reportedly hung left & jockey unable to ride out: progrsesive juv, won at Lingfield (2, mdn & nurs)
& Newmarket (nurs, rtd 93): eff at 5/6f on firm, soft grnd, any trk, forcing the pace: apprec a return to own age grp.

838 **BLUE STAR** 19 [13] 4-8-12 (75) J Tate 7/1: 151220: Chsd ldrs for 3f: better than this, 1st try on hvy. 1¼ 50
524} **Just For You Jane** 432 [12] 4-8-0 (63) R Mullen 50/1:
3467} **Charlottevalentina** 250 [14] 3-8-9 (83) Joanna Badger (7) 50/1:

14 ran Time 1m 15.74 (7.94) (North Cheshire Trading & Storage Ltd) C W Fairhurst Middleham, N Yorks

1029 **2.35 BLUE RIBAND COND STKS 3YO (B) 1m2f Heavy 145 -23 Slow**
£12480 £4614 £2307 £1048

3988} **ETERNAL SPRING 221** [4] E A L Dunlop 3-8-12 K Fallon 2/1 FAV: 2132-1: 3 b c Persian Bold - Emerald Waters (King's Lake) Made all, found extra for hands & heels when prsd 2f out, shade cmftbly: hvly bckd on reapp: '99 Beverley wnr (mdn), prev 4L rnr-up to Distant Music on debut (rtd 100): eff at 10f, likely to stay 12f: acts on fast & hvy grnd, prob any trk: best forcing the pace, runs well fresh: useful, improving colt. **102**
4411} **MODISH 191** [3] M H Tompkins 3-8-12 S Sanders 9/2: 0114-2: 3 b c Tenby - Moorfield Daisy (Waajib) Bhd wnr, pulled out to chall appr fnl 2f, rdn dist & no extra: nicely bckd, clr rem on reapp: '99 wnr at Beverley (nov auct) & Ayr (nov stks, beat this wnr 1½L, rtd 95): eff at 1m/10f: acts on gd & hvy grnd, runs well fresh, prob any trk: useful colt, type for a Listed race abroad. *3* **97**
4558} **GALLEON BEACH 179** [5] J W Hills 3-8-12 R Hills 100/30: 3132-3: 3 b c Shirley Heights - Music In My Life (Law Society) Cl-up, outpcd turning for home, late gains to take a moderate 3rd: reapp: '99 Hamilton wnr (mdn), Listed rnr-up (rtd 99): eff at 10f, shapes like a thorough stayer: acts on firm & hvy grnd, stiff/gall trks: stable yet to hit top gear, shld leave this behind over 12f on a stiffer trk. *8* **87**
4332} **BLUE GOLD 197** [1] R Hannon 3-8-12 J Reid 7/2: 5133-4: Held up, prog to chall appr fnl 2f, btn before dist: op 5/2 on reapp: '99 Sandown wnr (mdn, rtd 92 at best): eff at 7f/1m, bred for 10f+: acts on fast & gd/soft grnd, stiff/gall trks: shld do better next time, prob on faster grnd. *nk* **86**
955 **CEDAR MASTER 8** [2] 3-8-10 T Quinn 12/1: 024-05: Al bhd, no ch from 3f out & sn eased: nibbled from 16/1: '99 Chepstow wnr (auct mdn, rtd 87), cl-up 3rd in val Newbury sprint (rtd 104, 1st time blnks): eff at 5/6f, stays 7f, not bred for 10f: acts on firm & gd/soft grnd, prob best in blnks (not worn yet this term). *18* **66**
5 ran Time 2m 20.81 (17.01) (Paul & Jenny Green) E A L Dunlop Newmarket, Suffolk

1030 **3.10 GREAT MET HCAP 3YO+ 0-95 (C) 1m4f Heavy 145 -20 Slow [92]**
£10773 £3315 £1657 £828 4 yo rec 1 lb

874 **ZILARATOR 15** [5] W J Haggas 4-9-6 (85) T Quinn 7/1: 355-61: 4 b g Zilzal - Allegedly (Sir Ivor) Slow to stride, stdy prog after halfway to lead before 2f out, pshd out: nicely bckd tho' op 6/1: '99 Leicester scorer (mdn, rtd 89 at best), unrcd juv: eff at 12f/15f: acts on gd, loves hvy grnd, goes on any trk: improving. **91**
*893 **BLUE STYLE 13** [12] P Mitchell 4-7-11 (62)(t)(1ow)(2oh) F Norton 8/1: 00-612: 4 ch g Bluebird - Style For Life (Law Society) Midfield, gd prog over 3f out till run blocked by ldrs bef dist, clr ins last, ran on, too late: poss unlucky on 1st start for new connections: acts on gd/soft & hvy grnd, wore a t-strap: progressive. *1¼* **65**
4619} **MONTECRISTO 172** [1] R Guest 7-9-10 (88) N Pollard 3/1 FAV: 1100-3: 7 br g Warning - Sutosky (Great Nephew) Waited with, prog 3f out, ch bef fnl 1f, no extra under press ins last: hvly bckd, reapp, clr rem: '99 wnr at Newbury (stks) & Hamilton (h'cap, also unlucky rnr-up in this race, rtd 93): '98 wnr at W'hampton (h'cap, rtd 76a), Warwick & Brighton & Epsom (h'caps, rtd 90): eff at 12f, stays 14f: acts on firm, suited by gd/soft, hvy, both AWs: likes Epsom: gd weight carrier, runs well fresh & best coming late. *shd* **91**
-- **LIGHTNING STAR** [2] T P McGovern 5-8-13 (77) A Nicholls (3) 12/1: 0036/4: Rear, styd on up the str, nvr pace to chall: hdles fit, earlier won at Chepstow & Folkestone (sells, 2m/2½m, firm & hvy, rtd 101h, with/without blnks): 2 year Flat abs, ex-Irish, '97 Galway wnr (mdn): eff at 10f, 12f shld suit, goes on gd/soft & soft. *5* **73**
4359} **FAIR WARNING 195** [10] 4-9-13 (92) R Hills 7/1: 0412-5: Held up, gd prog to chall appr fnl 2f, sn rdn, no extra & not persevered with: op 6/1, top-weight, reapp: '99 wnr at Yarmouth (mdn) & York (class stks, rtd 93): plcd in '98 (rtd 87): eff at 1m/12f: acts on firm & gd/soft grnd, any trk: sharper next time on faster grnd. *3* **83**
714 **SPOSA 33** [3] 4-7-10 (61)(4oh) Hayley Turner (6) 50/1: 302406: Pld hard, rcd in 2nd till ent str, fdd. *6* **44**
3763} **KINNESCASH 235** [4] 7-9-4 (82) K Fallon 11/2: 0001-7: Chsd ldrs till wknd 3f out: op 9/2: hdles fit, unplcd, stable out of form: 98/99 wnr at Huntingdon & Aintree (2, h'caps, 2m/2m2f, handles hvy, loves firm, rtd 136h): '99 wnr here at Epsom (2, incl this h'cap, rtd 83): '97 Leicester & Windsor wnr (h'caps, rtd 65): eff at 12f/13f on firm & hvy grnd, prob fibresand, likes Epsom: with P Bowen. *9* **56**
965 **GRIEF 8** [7] 7-8-1 (65)(bl) Martin Dwyer 33/1: 13-008: Well plcd till wknd 3f out: see 893. *1¼* **38**
880 **SEA DANZIG 14** [13] 7-7-10 (60)(bl)(3oh) R Brisland (5) 25/1: 422109: Sn pulled himself into clr lead, tired entering str, hdd & btn 2½f out: far too keen on turf return: see 772. *11* **22**
4085} **BALSOX 214** [9] 4-9-0 (79) P Doe 25/1: 6540-0: Al bhd, btn 4f out: 10th, 4 month jumps abs, 11L rnr-up over 2m2f (rtd 99h): '99 reapp wnr at Nottingham (mdn, rtd 90 at best, J Dunlop): promising 4th in '98 (mdn, rtd 78): eff at 1m on soft/hvy grnd, tried 14f: tried blnks/visor, better without: with S Dow. *dist* **0**
748 **WESTMINSTER CITY 30** [6] 4-7-10 (61)(8oh) J Mackay (7) 13/2: -3212U: U.r. start: bckd despite 8lbs o/h. **0**
11 ran Time 2m 54.6 (19.8) (Wentworth Racing (Pty) Ltd) W J Haggas Newmarket, Suffolk

1031 **3.45 CITY & SUBURBAN HCAP 4YO+ 0-105 (B) 1m2f Heavy 145 -13 Slow [102]**
£14690 £4520 £2260 £1130

4359} **NIGHT VENTURE 195** [13] B W Hills 4-8-9 (83) R Hills 20/1: 0506-1: 4 b c Dynaformer - Charming Ballerina (Caerleon) Rear, switched left & hdwy over 1f out, squeezed thro' to lead cl home, drvn out: reapp: '99 wnr at Ripon (mdn) & Newcastle (h'cap, rtd 90): eff at 10f, 12f shld suit: acts on firm & hvy grnd: handles a sharp/undul or gall trk: can force the pace or come from bhd: runs esp well fresh: tough & on a fair mark. **89**
757 **CAPTAINS LOG 29** [1] M L W Bell 5-7-12 (72) J Mackay (7) 10/1: 660-42: 5 b g Slip Anchor - Cradle Of Love (Roberto) Chsd clr ldr, chall appr fnl 1f, styd on, but not pace of wnr cl home: tchd 16/1: acts on any grnd. *1* **76**
846 **FORTY FORTE 18** [15] K R Burke 4-8-0 (74) P Doe 16/1: 244153: 4 b g Pursuit Of Love - Cominna (Dominion) Sn clr ldr, drvn & caught well ins last: another bold front running effort: v tough: see 786. *2½* **74**
665 **AMALIA 46** [5] P W Harris 4-9-10 (98) A Beech(5) 25/1: 410-04: Held up, gd hdwy 3f out, drvn & styd on onepace appr fnl 1f: 7 wk abs: handles hvy, likes a sound surface: see 665. *½* **97**
4546} **APRIL STOCK 180** [4] 5-7-13 (73) N Pollard 10/1: 0410-5: Sn well bhd, styd on well for press fnl 3f, nvr nrr: reapp: '99 scorer at Folkestone (fill mdn, Miss G Kelleway) & Windsor (stks, rtd 72): plcd sev times in '98: eff at 12f, stays 2m on gd & hvy: acts on any trk, with/without t-strap: spot on over further next time. *½* **71+**
1728} **PRINCE OF MY HEART 328** [8] 7-8-12 (86) T Quinn 12/1: 00/6-6: Prom, hdwy to trk ldrs over 2f out, drvn/no extra fnl 1f: nicely bckd, reapp: 6th sole '99 start for D Haydn Jones (h'cap, rtd 81): prev 4th over hdles (rtd 95h, nov, Mrs M Jones): plcd in '98 (rtd 95, h'cap, tried visor), '97 Newbury wnr (h'cap, rtd 109, B Hills): eff at 9/10f, stays a sharp 12f on firm & gd/soft, handles hvy & any trk: well h'capped now for H Cecil. *nk* **84**
3666} **SUPPLY AND DEMAND 240** [20] 6-8-9 (83) J Fortune 10/1: 0606-7: Held up, plenty to do over 3f out, switched & styd on fnl 2f, no extra ins last: op 8/1, clr rem: plcd once in '99 (h'cap, rtd 92, G L Moore): '98 Goodwood (h'cap, rtd 102, 1st time blnks): 97/98 hdles wnr at Newbury & Lingfield (rtd 117h): eff at 10f on fast & gd/soft, likes sharp/undul trks, with/without blnks: v well h'capped, spot on next time for J Gosden. *1¼* **79+**

EPSOM
WEDNESDAY APRIL 26TH   Lefthand, Very Sharp, Undulating Track

931	**SCENE** 11 [7] 5-8-4 (78) D Harrison 16/1: 1-0108: Chsd ldrs, rdn/wknd fnl 2f: twice below 831 (1m).	10	62
786	**PINCHINCHA** 28 [6] 6-8-1 (75) (vis) J Tate 16/1: 023-49: Cl-up, wknd qckly fnl 2f: btr 786 (gd).	1½	57
747	**CHIEF CASHIER** 30 [11] 5-8-5 (79) S Drowne 15/2: 148-50: Chsd ldr, drvn/btn fnl 3f, 10th: well bckd.	5	54
4173}	**SMART SQUALL** 208 [21] 5-9-10 (98) G Carter 40/1: 32/0-0: Dwelt, rear, t.o. halfway, late gains for press, no ch with ldrs: top weight: hdles plcd 7 wks ago (nov, rtd 85h, 2m3f, gd/soft): well btn in a List race sole '99 start (rtd 74, D Oakley): highly tried in '98, rnr-up in a German Gr 2 (rtd 105, Lord Huntingdon), prev term won at Chepstow (mdn), Ascot (nurs) & Toulouse (List, rtd 100): eff at 12/14f on gd & hvy: with E Stanners.	7	65
4488}	**KOMISTAR** 186 [12] 5-9-0 (88) M Roberts 16/1: 0610-0: Chsd ldrs to halfway, sn bhd, fin 12th: '99 Doncaster & Newbury wnr (h'caps, rtd 89): rnr-up in '98 (stks, rtd 94): eff at 1m/10f, has tried 12f: acts on firm & gd/soft, reportedly unsuited by this hvy grnd (rnr-up once prev on hvy): likes to force the pace.	5	48
757	**IPLEDGEALLEGIANCE** 29 [19] 4-9-7 (95) J Reid 9/1: 105-30: Held up, nvr a factor, fin 13th: lame.	3½	50
3915}	**FIRST FANTASY** 224 [10] 4-8-9 (83) R Cochrane 12/1: 1411-0: In tch, wknd qckly 3f out, t.o. in 17th: '99 Warwick, Yarmouth (2) & Folkestone wnr (h'caps, rtd 82): eff arnd 10f on firm & gd/soft: likes Yarmouth.		0
*793	**TOTAL DELIGHT** 27 [16] 4-8-8 (82)(t) Pat Eddery 7/1 FAV: 320-10: Al bhd, t.o. fnl 3f, fin 19th: well bckd & reportedly unsuited by these v testing conditions: much btr 793 (reapp, mdn).		0
662	**Stoppes Brow** 46 [17] 8-8-6 (80)(bl) N Callan 25/1: 314 **Ilissus** 105 [22] 4-8-1 (75) R Mullen 33/1:		
--	**Marching Orders** 2 [4] 4-9-0 (88) S Sanders 25/1: 580 **Tarawan** 62 [9] 4-8-13 (87) (vis) K Fallon 14/1:		
55	**Calidat Seventeen** 162 [3] 4-8-3 (77) L Newman 25/1: 16/1:		
20 ran	Time 2m 19.81 (16.01) (Maktoum Al Maktoum) B W Hills Lambourn, Berks		

1032   4.15 SPRING MDN 3YO+ (D)   1m114y rnd   Heavy 145   -41 Slow
£4270 £1314 £657 £328   3 yo rec 14lb

745	**TWEED MILL** 30 [1] I A Balding 3-8-4 M Roberts 5/2 FAV: 3-21: 3 b f Selkirk - Island Mill (Mill Reef) Prom, hdwy to lead 3f out, rdn & drew sight away from rivals fnl 2f: nicely bckd: 3rd sole '99 start (fill mdn, rtd 74): eff arnd 8.5f, further shld suit: acts on fast, clrly relished these v testing conditions: improving.		82+
962	**GLORY QUEST** 8 [4] Miss Gay Kelleway 3-8-9 K Darley 3/1: -33-22: 3 b c Quest For Fame - Sonseri (Prince Tenderfoot) Waited with, rdn & kept on fnl 3f, took 2nd ins last but no ch with wnr: nicely bckd tho' op 2/1: stays 1m & will prob apprec a more gall trk: see 962.	9	76
915	**RASMALAI** 12 [3] R Hannon 3-8-4 Dane O'Neill 20/1: 03: 3 b f Sadler's Wells - Raymouna (High Top) Led, hdd 3f out, kept on but sn well outpcd by wnr: imprvd for debut: poss stays 8.5f on hvy.	½	70
936	**STORM WIZARD** 9 [2] M R Channon 3-8-9 S Drowne 9/1: 0-34: Handy, rdn to improve 2f out, sn onepace: worth another try over further: see 936 (reapp, 10f).	1	73
4495}	**GRENADIER** 184 [5] 3-8-9 Martin Dwyer 9/1: 4-5: Keen cl-up, rdn & ran green over 2f out, sn btn: op 6/1 on reapp: 4th sole '99 start (mdn, rtd 78): shld apprec mid-dists: better for race, shld improve.	¾	72
26	**SPIRIT OF TENBY** 167 [6] 3-8-9 P Doe 9/1: 5005-6: Waited with, nvr a factor: 6 month abs: plcd on '99 debut (auct mdn, rtd 80 at best): stays 7f, further shld suit: handles firm.	3	67$
909	**KIND EMPEROR** 12 [8] 3-8-9 T G McLaughlin 20/1: 442537: Prom, rdn, short of room & wknd fnl 2f.	11	55
--	**FLITWICK** [10] 3-8-9 T Quinn 3/1: 8: Bhd, drvn & lost tch over 2f out, t.o.: well bckd on debut: Warning half brother to 1,000 Guineas wnr Wince: disapp debut, poss not handle this hvy grnd: with H Cecil.	8	45
--	**YAFA** 7 [4-9-10] R Cochrane 25/1: 9: Keen/prom, wknd qckly fnl 3f: Elmaamul gldg, with N Graham.	nk	46
4114}	**CARNAGE** 212 [9] 3-8-9 R Havlin 50/1: 000-0: Al last, t.o. in 10th: unplcd in 3 '99 mdns (rtd 65).	4	39
10 ran	Time 1m 57.9 (15.89) (D H Back) I A Balding Kingsclere, Hants		

1033   4.50 BANSTEAD CLASSIFIED STKS 3YO+ 0-70 (E)   1m114y rnd   Heavy 145   -67 Slow
£4309 £1326 £663 £331   3 yo rec 14lb

894	**INCHINNAN** 13 [11] C Weedon 3-8-4 J Tate 4/1 JT FAV: 552-21: 3 b f Inchinor - Westering (Auction Ring) Cl-up, hdwy to chall appr fnl 1f, led well ins last, drvn out: deserved 1st win: in '99 rnr-up 3 times for D Morris (incl h'cap, rtd 73): eff at 1m on firm & hvy: handles a sharp or gall trk & goes well fresh: tough.		69
895	**MANSA MUSA** 13 [4] M R Channon 5-9-8 T Quinn 4/1 JT FAV: 40-002: 5 b g Hamas - Marton Maid (Silly Season) Set stdy pace, drvn over 1f out, hdd & hung left ins last, no extra: gd run: see 895.	1¼	70
--	**SOVEREIGNS COURT** [9] L G Cottrell 7-9-8 A Clark 10/1: 1020/3: 7 ch g Statoblest - Clare Celeste (Coquelin) Keen/rear, rdn/hdwy 2f out, chall ldrs dist, sn no extra: bckd from 16/1 on reapp: missed '99, plcd in '98 (3 h'caps, rtd 77 at best): '97 wnr at Nottingham (2, h'caps, rtd 74): eff at 1m, suited by 10f on fast, likes gd/soft & hvy grnd: handles a gall trk, likes Nottingham: clrly runs well fresh: fine reapp, win similar.	1	68
*830	**PEGGYS ROSE** 20 [5] P D Evans 3-8-6 J F Egan 10/1: 14: Waited with, rdn & styd on fnl 2f, nvr nrr: gd run up in trip, stays 8.5f & further shld suit: see 830 (sell, debut).	½	65
100	**MISSILE TOE** 154 [1] 7-9-8 D McGaffin (7) 25/1: 0000-5: Pulled hard in rear, plenty to do ent str, styd on, nvr nrr: clr rem: 5 month abs: '99 wnr at Newmarket (h'cap, rtd 46): plcd in '98 (rtd 55$): eff at 1m/10f on fast, hvy & fibresand: handles any trk: treat rating with caution (offic only 43).	1¼	65$
834	**STROMSHOLM** 20 [6] 4-9-8 R Cochrane 9/2: 02-406: Mid-div, hdwy to chall 2f out, wknd fnl, eased.	9	53
824	**ROGUE SPIRIT** 21 [3] 4-9-8 Pat Eddery 5/1: 05-007: Chsd ldrs, no extra for press 2f out, sn btn.	6	45
2048}	**GIKO** 313 [8] 6-9-8 N Pollard 16/1: -000-8: Prom, rdn & wknd qckly fnl 2f: reapp: unplcd in 3 '99 starts (h'caps, rtd 58 at best): '98 wnr at Goodwood & Sandown (h'caps, rtd 68): eff at 1m/9f on fast, gd/soft & fibresand: handles any trk: with Jamie Poulton.	4	39
943	**WINDSHIFT** 9 [12] 4-9-8 (vis) J P Spencer 10/1: 531609: Mid-div, lost tch halfway, t.o.: see 381.	10	28
866	**CANADIAN APPROVAL** 15 [7] 4-9-5 M Tebbutt 11/1: -10440: Al last, t.o. in 10th: turf return.	dist	0
10 ran	Time 1m 59.9 (18.1) (Colin Weedon) C Weedon Chiddingfold, Surrey		

LONGCHAMP
THURSDAY APRIL 27TH   Righthand, Galloping Track

Official Going   HEAVY

1034   2.10 GR 3 PRIX D'HEDOUVILLE 4YO+   1m4f   Heavy
£21134 £7685 £3842 £2305   4 yo rec 1 lb

4417}	**FIRST MAGNITUDE** 173 A Fabre 4-9-4 O Peslier 28/10: 310-61: 4 ch c Arazi - Crystal Cup (Nijinsky) Settled rear, smooth hdwy 3f out, rdn to lead dist, pushed out, cosily: won 3 times in '99, incl a Gr 2 here at Longchamp (rtd 115): v eff at 12f on gd or hvy grnd: v smart colt, heads for the Coronation Cup at Epsom.		115
--	**CRILLON** E Lellouche 4-8-9 D Bonilla 9/2: 21-122: 4 br c Saumarez - Shanrila (Riverman)	¾	104

339

LONGCHAMP THURSDAY APRIL 27TH Righthand, Galloping Track

Trkd ldrs, hdwy to lead 3f out, hdd dist, kept on but al held by wnr: clr of rem: v useful, eff at 12f on hvy.
3796} **TURBOTIERE 235** E Libaud 5-8-6 L Huart 155/10: 641-33: 5 br m Turgeon - Victoria Dee (Rex Magna) *10* **88**
Prom, ev ch till well outpaced by front 2 fnl 2f.
7 ran   Time 2m 52.6   (D Wildenstein)   A Fabre France

SOUTHWELL TUESDAY APRIL 25TH Abandoned - Waterlogged

CATTERICK WEDNESDAY APRIL 26TH Abandoned - Waterlogged

BEVERLEY THURSDAY APRIL 27TH Abandoned - Waterlogged

RIPON SATURDAY APRIL 29TH Abandoned - Waterlogged

LEICESTER SATURDAY APRIL 29TH Abandoned - Waterlogged

WOLVERHAMPTON (Fibresand) FRIDAY APRIL 28TH Lefthand, Sharp Track

Official Going   STANDARD. Stalls: 7f - Outside, Rem - Inside.

1035   2.25 ARTHUR MED AUCT MDN 3YO (F)   7f aw rnd   Going 39 -17 Slow
£2254   £644   £322

837   **DIVERS PEARL 21** [6] J R Fanshawe 3-8-9 J Fanning 8/11 FAV: 63-21: 3 b f Prince Sabo - Seek The Pearl   **80a**
(Rainbow Quest): Sn cl-up, led over 3f out, rdn clr final 2f & eased nr line, cmftbly: value for double wng
margin: well bckd at odds-on: confirmed promise of reapp: plcd in '99 (auct mdn, rtd 87): apprec step up to 7f,
1m looks sure to suit: acts on fibresand, firm & gd/soft grnd: likes a sharp/undul trk: plenty in hand here.
549   **HOXTON SQUARE 69** [9] N P Littmoden 3-8-9 T G McLaughlin 8/1: 223-02: 3 ch f Case Law - Guv's Joy *8* **61a**
(Thatching): Led 3f, outpcd final 2f: op 7/1, 10 wk abs: caught a tartar, h'cap company will suit: see 549 (6f).
826   **TATE VENTURE 23** [8] S P C Woods 3-9-0 G Duffield 16/1: 03: 3 b g Deploy - Tasseled (Tate Gallery): *¾* **65a**
Chsd ldrs, rdn/outpcd halfway, kept on for press final 2f, no threat: op 10/1: a return to 1m+ will suit: see 826.
971   **SILVER ARROW 9** [4] B W Hills 3-8-9 A Eddery (5) 11/4: 4-04: Held up in tch, rdn/chsd ldrs 3f out, *3½* **55a**
sn held: AW bow, op 2/1: unplcd sole '99 start (rtd 73, fillies mdn): now qual for h'caps.
857   **DOROTHEA SHARP 18** [12] 3-8-9 D Young (7) 40/1: 000-05: Held up, mod gains: AW bow: unplcd in *5* **45a**
'99 (rtd 55, fillies mdn): with N P Littmoden.
4605} **SKELTON MONARCH 175** [3] 3-9-0 P M Quinn (5) 50/1: 0000-6: Rdn/bhd, mod prog: unplcd in '99 *shd* **50a**
(rtd 48 & 35a, mdns): has tried a t-strap prev: with R Hollinshead.
4040} **KINGS TO OPEN 220** [5] 3-9-0 J P Spencer 20/1: 0-7: Chsd ldrs 5f: 7 mth abs: unplcd sole '99 start *nk* **49a**
(rtd 64, auct mdn): now with J A Osborne.
909   **WINGED ANGEL 14** [2] 3-9-0 A Culhane 12/1: 408: Slowly away, al rear: op 10/1: AW bow: eyecatching *2* **45a**
in 909 & 804, will leave this bhd in h'cap company over 1m+: h'cap bow today.
--   **THE LONELY WIGEON** [1] 3-9-0 (t) Dale Gibson 14/1: 9: Dwelt/al outpcd: tchd 16/1, debut, with R Cowell. *1* **43a**
909   **NEEDWOOD TRIBESMAN 14** [10] 3-9-0 J Carroll 50/1: -00: Prom 5f: 10th: no form. *1* **41a**
892   **SOBER AS A JUDGE 15** [7] 3-9-0 S Drowne 50/1: 500-00: Chsd ldrs 4f: 11th: mod form. *4* **35a**
11 ran   Time 1m 30.1 (3.9)   (Cheveley Park Stud)   J R Fanshawe Newmarket, Suffolk.

1036   2.55 GALAHAD MDN CLAIMER 3YO+ (F)   5f aw rnd   Going 39 +17 Fast
£2219   £634   £317   3 yo rec 10lb

740   **GARTH POOL 32** [4] A Berry 3-9-2 J Carroll 4/1 FAV: 250-51: 3 b g Sri Pekan - Millionetta (Danehill):   **79a**
Made all & clr final 2f, unchall, easily: value for h'cap L+: op 3/1: best time of day: rnr-up in '99 (rtd 74, h'cap,
J Berry, blnks): eff at 5f on fast & fibresand, handles gd/soft: eff with/without blnks: enjoyed forcing tactics.
567   **NOBLE PATRIOT 66** [1] R Hollinshead 5-9-0 J P Spencer 14/1: 050002: 5 b g Polish Patriot - Noble *8* **44$**
Form (Double Form): Held up, rdn/chsd ldr 2f out, kept on tho' no impress: clr of rem: 2 mth abs: see 61 (sell).
869   **PICASSOS HERITAGE 17** [6] W Clay 4-9-0 F Norton 33/1: 650/03: 4 gr g Greensmith - Jane Herring *6* **32a**
(Nishapour): Dwelt, rdn/kept on final 2f, nrst fin: only mod form prev.
680   **JONATHANS GIRL 43** [11] J J Bridger 5-8-9 R Brisland (5) 25/1: -50404: Chsd ldrs, outpcd final 3f: abs. *hd* **27a**
930   **HOUT BAY 13** [9] 3-9-0 D Harrison 6/1: 40-645: Al outpcd: op 5/1: AW bow: see 781 (mdn). *3* **36a**
187   **LEMON STRIP 135** [3] 4-8-11 R Fitzpatrick (3) 14/1: 2440-6: In tch/hmpd halfway, sn btn: op 20/1: *nk* **22a**
5 mth abs: now with A G Juckes: see 63.
1021   **UNITED PASSION 4** [7] 3-8-11 I Mongan (5) 11/2: -207: Chsd ldrs 3f: qck reapp: see 740 (debut). *nk* **31a**
798   **CARMARTHEN 29** [5] 4-9-4 G Parkin 12/1: 44-008: Trkd ldrs 3f: op 10/1: see 235. *1¾* **24a**
4172} **TWICKERS 211** [10] 4-9-5 A Culhane 12/1: 4250-9: Dwelt, effort halfway, no impress: op 10/1, 7 mth *1¼* **23a**
abs: AW bow: rnr-up twice in '99 for R Guest (rtd 67, mdn): rtd 75 in '98 (fillies mdn): eff at 5f on firm & gd.
785   **WILLRACK TIMES 30** [8] 3-8-3 L Newman (5) 5/1: 04-500: Al outpcd: 10th: op 4/1: btr 706. *½* **16a**
883   **STEVAL 16** [2] 3-8-4 S Drowne 9/1: 000-40: Prom 3f: 11th: op 7/1: btr 883. *1¼* **14a**

877 **Perugino Pearl 17** [13] 3-8-7 D Mernagh (3) 33/1:   487 **Brief Call 79** [12] 3-8-3 G Duffield 14/1:
13 ran Time 1m 01.3 (1.1) (Lord Mostyn) A Berry Cockerham, Lancs.

1037 3.30 PERCEVAL HCAP 3YO+ 0-75 (E)   1m100y aw Going 39 -22 Slow [72]
£2814 £866 £433 £216 3 yo rec 14lb

711 **ROYAL ARTIST 36** [2] W J Haggas 4-10-0 (72) J P Spencer 1/1 FAV: 231-21: 4 b g Royal Academy - 78a
Council Rock (General Assembly): Cl-up till went on appr final 1f, hung left but drvn clr inside last: nicely bckd,
top weight: '99 scorer at Lingfield (mdn, rtd 69a), also plcd twice on turf (rtd 73): eff at 7f/8.5f, further could
suit: acts on fast, gd/soft, both AWs & a sharp trk: eff weight carrier: imprvg, should win more races.
*922 **MALCHIK 13** [1] P Howling 4-8-10 (54) R Winston 12/1: 033312: 4 ch c Absalom - Very Good (Noalto): 2½ 55a
Led to 6f out, hdwy to lead again over 2f out, sn hdd, not pace of wnr inside last: tchd 16/1, apprec further.
210 **PENGAMON 132** [6] M Wigham 8-9-1 (59) Dean McKeown 14/1: 2212-3: 8 gr g Efisio - Dolly Bevan ½ 59a
(Another Realm): Waited with, rdn to impr 3f out, styd on, nvr nrr: op 10/1, 4 mth abs: prev with D Thom: see 107.
921 **LORD EUROLINK 13** [8] C A Dwyer 4-9-9 (67)(tvi) D Holland 7/1: 111044: Cl-up, hdwy to lead ½ 66a
briefly 2f out, onepcd inside last: clr rem: loves to force the pace: see 817, 718.
923 **AUBRIETA 13** [12] 4-8-10 (54) S Drowne 16/1: 052045: Prom, gradually wknd final 3f: up in trip. 6 42a
907 **INTERNAL AFFAIR 14** [11] 5-9-10 (68) Lynsey Hanna (7) 13/2: 351566: Waited with, late gains. ¾ 54a
893 **NIGHT CITY 15** [7] 9-9-3 (61) N Callan 20/1: 602147: Dsptd lead till went on 6f out, drvn/hdd 2f 1½ 44a
out, wknd qckly, eased: unsuited by drop in trip, loves to dominate: see 893, 650.
2346} **COOL VIBES 303** [4] 5-9-10 (68) R Fitzpatrick (3) 33/1: /005-8: Dwelt, al bhd: long abs, new stable: 5 43a
unplcd in 3 '99 starts for J Pearce (h'caps, rtd 64): subs unplcd over timber for D Bridgwater (rtd 83h): shock
50/1 debut wnr at Newmarket in '98 (mdn, rtd 81): eff at 1m on firm, further should suit: with Mrs M Macauley.
4264} **ALMERINA 205** [3] 5-9-8 (66) J Carroll 33/1: 0060-9: Mid-div, lost tch final 4f: unplcd in 3 1¼ 39a
'99 Flat starts (h'caps, rtd 58), subs well btn in 3 hdle starts (novs, rtd 81h): ex-Irish, Oct '98 wnr at
Punchestown (mdn) & Cork (h'cap): eff at 7f/1m on gd/soft.
776 **SCISSOR RIDGE 30** [13] 8-8-12 (56) J Weaver 20/1: 242640: Al bhd, fin 10th: see 336. nk 29a
326 **Rayware Boy 105** [5] 4-8-11 (55)(bl) J Fanning 33/1:
866 **Royal Partnership 17** [9] 4-8-6 (50) Darren Williams (5) 14/1:
921 **The Imposter 13** [10] 5-9-4 (62) I Mongan (5) 20/1:
13 ran Time 1m 51.4 (5.2) (Tony Hirschfeld) W J Haggas Newmarket, Suffolk.

1038 4.00 LANCELOT CLASS STKS 3YO+ 0-60 (F)   7f aw rnd Going 39 -20 Slow
£2240 £640 £320 3 yo rec 13lb

854 **MANXWOOD 18** [1] D J S Cosgrove 3-8-8 C Rutter 16/1: 460-01: 3 b g Petorius - Eliza Wooding 66a
(Faustus): Made all, styd on strongly & rdn clr final 2f: first win: unplcd in mdns in '99 (rtd 67 &
68a): clearly relished forcing the pace over 7f: acts on fibresand & a sharp trk: can follow up.
3678} **TOP OF THE POPS 242** [3] C W Thornton 4-9-7 Dean McKeown 12/1: 4465-2: 4 b g Ballad Rock - 5 57a
Summerhill (Habitat): Trkd ldr, rdn/no extra final 2f: reapp: unplcd in '99 (mdns, rtd 69a): stays 7f on fibresand.
855 **CHAMPAGNE GB 18** [10] Andrew Reid 4-9-7 (BL) M Henry 33/1: 0-0503: 4 b g Efisio - Success Story shd 57a
(Sharrood): Sn outpcd, hung left & styd on well inside last, nrst fin: imprvd effort in first time blnks.
921 **ADOBE 13** [2] W M Brisbourne 5-9-9 A McCarthy (3) 5/1: 0-1024: Cl-up, rdn & outpcd appr final 2f. nk 58a
4510} **PETERS IMP 185** [12] 5-9-7 G Duffield 4/1: 0000-5: Rdn/rear, gd hdwy over 2f out, wknd ins last, 3 51a
eased: reapp: '99 scorer at Hamilton & Redcar (class stks, rtd 82, J Berry): '98 Haydock wnr (class stks, rtd
75): eff at 6/7f on soft & fibresand, suited by firm/fast: eff with/without blnks & can go well when fresh.
4341} **ABTAAL 198** [4] 10-9-7 (vis) R Fitzpatrick (3) 20/1: 6500-6: Sn rdn in tch, outpcd halfway, sn btn: 2½ 46a
'99 scorer at Southwell (sell) & W'hampton (2, clmr & h'cap, rtd 66a at best, rtd 56 on turf): '98 Brighton wnr
(2, class stks, R Hodges, also clmr for current stable) & Southwell (clmr, rtd 63a & 63): all 8 wins at 7f, has
tried further: acts on fast, soft & both AWs, likes fibresand: handles any trk, likes a sharp one: best held up.
930 **MAGIC SISTER 13** [5] 3-8-5 A Beech 10/1: 66-037: Dwelt, sn rdn in rear, eff 2f out, sn btn: AW bow. ½ 42a
*976 **NODS NEPHEW 9** [8] 3-8-10 J Carroll 11/4: 00-418: Prom, rdn & wknd qckly final 2f: op 2/1: 5 38a
well below best on today's AW bow: much btr 976 (stiff/undul 7.5f, hvy).
869 **MOUNT PARK 17** [7] 3-8-5 G Parkin 33/1: 53-009: Al outpcd: see 472. 1½ 30a
867 **C HARRY 17** [11] 6-9-7 J P Spencer 11/1: 265050: Nvr a factor, fin 10th: see 130 (sell). 1¾ 29a
881 **POLAR ICE 16** [6] 4-9-7 (tvl) T G McLaughlin 6/4 FAV: -00000: Waited with, rdn/hdwy 3f out, wknd 5 21a
qckly 2f out, fin 11th: well bckd, first time visor: reportedly suffering from an irregular heartbeat: see 881.
879 **BORDER GLEN 16** [9] 4-9-7 (bl) J Weaver 10/1: 362600: Chsd ldrs till wknd qckly 2f out, fin 8 7a
last: reportedly lost action & finished lame: see 292, 96.
12 ran Time 1m 30.3 (4.1) (Global Racing Club) D J S Cosgrove Newmarket, Suffolk.

1039 4.35 HOLY GRAIL APPR SELLER 4YO+ (G)   1m4f aw Going 39 -22 Slow
£1809 £517 £258 4 yo rec 1 lb

903 **HILL FARM DANCER 15** [4] W M Brisbourne 9-9-0 G Baker (3) 7/1: 314351: 9 ch m Gunner B - Loadplan 47a
Lass (Nicholas Bill) Held up in tch, prog after halfway to lead 3f out, readily: val 10L+, no bid: earlier won
here at W'hampton (C/D h'cap): '99 Southwell wnr (appr sell, rtd 54a & 30): '98 Musselburgh wnr (fill h'cap,
rtd 59): all wins at 12f, stays 2m: acts on firm, gd/soft & both AWs, likes W'hampton: goes well for an apprentice.
581 **BANNERET 64** [1] Miss S J Wilton 7-9-5 J Bosley 8/1: 210532: 7 b g Imperial Falcon - Dashing Partner 8 48a
(Formidable) Chsd ldrs, feeling pace 5f out, styd on fnl 2f, not trble wnr: blnkd hdles rnr since 866, see 561.
866 **MALWINA 17** [9] M G Quinlan 4-8-13 D Young (7) 6/1: 051253: 4 ch f Greinton - Mickys Pleasure ½ 42a
(Foolish Pleasure) Bhd, went past btn horses in str: op 5/1: holds form well, slightly better 561.
710 **ARTIC COURIER 36** [12] D J S Cosgrove 9-9-5 P Shea (3) 5/1: 0-1144: Chsd ldrs till fdd appr final 2f. 1 46a
866 **APPROACHABLE 17** [10] 5-8-13 K Dalgleish (3) 7/2 FAV: 324225: Handy, led 5f out till before 2f out, 5 33a
no extra: nicely bckd, stablemate 2nd: flattered last time but is capable of better: see 710, 45.e
855 **COLONEL CUSTER 18** [7] 5-9-5 R Cody Boutcher 5/1: 100506: Keen, front rank, led after 5f till 5f 2½ 35a
out, btn 3f out: op 14/1: see 408 (first time visor).
869 **ADIRPOUR 17** [3] 6-9-5 Stephanie Hollinshead (8) 20/1: 540037: Trkd ldrs till lost pl 4f out: see 556. 2 32a
641 **BEST PORT 53** [6] 4-8-12 R Farmer (5) 50/1: 006-08: Al bhd: stiff task, 8 wk abs, see 641. 1½ 24a
869 **SHAANXI ROMANCE 17** [8] 5-8-13 Hayley Turner (10) 8/1: 00-259: In tch 1m: new stable, longer trip. 5 17a
2438} **GLOW 300** [5] 4-8-7 J Mackay 6/1: /046-0: Nvr in tch: 10th, reapp, op 9/2: lightly rcd in '99 11 0a
(class stks, rtd 56, I Balding): lks flattered by a 73 in '98 for Lord Huntingdon: probably moderate.
922 **GENIUS 13** [11] 5-8-13 D Meah (5) 14/1: 004050: Al bhd: 11th, much longer trip, see 201. 0a
341

WOLVERHAMPTON (Fibresand)   FRIDAY APRIL 28TH   Lefthand, Sharp Track

918 **SAFE SHARP JO** 13 [2] 5-8-13 (vis) G Gibbons (7) 50/1: 060000: Led 5f, sn btn: last, stiff task. **0a**
12 ran   Time 2m 42.1 (8.5)   (M E Hughes)   W M Brisbourne Great Ness, Shropshire.

1040	5.10 EXCALIBUR HCAP 3YO 0-65 (F) 1m1f79y aw Going 39 -34 Slow	[69]
	£2247 £642 £321	

*613 **LORD HARLEY** 59 [9] B R Millman 3-9-5 (60) F Norton 6/4 FAV: 4-2211: 3 b c Formidable - Nanny Doon **70a**
(Dominion) Shkn up cl-up, led appr fnl 2f, sn in control, easing down: op evens: 8 wk abs since scored here at
W'hampton (h'cap): unplcd in '99 (rtd 32 & 51a): eff at 7f/9.3f: acts on both AWs, likes fibresand & W'hampton.

841 **CYBER BABE** 21 [1] Andrew Reid 3-8-4 (45) M Henry 10/1: 000-02: 3 ch f Persian Bold - Evvedya 2 **50a**
(Doyoun) Prom, eff 3f out, kept on but no ch with wnr: clr rem: stys 9.3f: goes on firm, gd grnd & fibresand.

744 **ARCTIC HIGH** 32 [7] M S Saunders 3-9-7 (62) J Weaver 13/2: 32303: 3 b f Polar Falcon - Oublier L'Ennui 4 **61a**
(Bellman) Led till appr fnl 2f, no extra: tchd 12/1: top-weight, nr to best: drop back to 1m may suit, see 658.

920 **FISHER ISLAND** 13 [8] R Hollinshead 3-8-10 (51) P M Quinn (5) 10/1: 50-634: Struggled to go pace till 1 **49a**
styd on/edged left final 2f: tchd 12/1: beginning to shape like a stayer: see 920, 709.

706 **BEWILDERED** 36 [6] 3-8-1 (42) Claire Bryan (5) 40/1: 4-0005: Prom till 3f out: see 365. 2½ **36a**

920 **CHARLEM** 13 [3] 3-8-5 (46) J Fanning 11/1: 00-66: Dwelt, nvr nr to chall: h'cap bow. nk **39a**

931 **PAPAGENA** 13 [10] 3-8-10 (51)(bl) Dean McKeown 11/1: 624307: Al same place: tchd 14/1, see 392. 1½ **41a**

409 **TAKE ACTION** 92 [2] 3-8-11 (52) A Culhane 16/1: 000-58: Nvr a factor: 3 mth abs, see 409. 5 **34a**

892 **JUMP** 15 [11] 3-9-5 (60) J P Spencer 13/2: 5-2609: In tch till 3f out: tchd 8/1, see 328. ½ **41a**

3345} **KNIGHTS RETURN** 259 [13] 3-7-10 (37)(7oh) R Brisland 5} 33/1: 000-0: Keen, well plcd till 5f out: 9 **2a**
10th: stiffish task on AW/h'cap bow/reapp for new stable: now with F Jordan.

887 **BERKELEY HALL** 16 [5] 3-9-1 (56) G Duffield 12/1: 003-00: Dwelt, al bhd: 11th on AW bow: 3rd 1¾ **17a**
final '99 start (auct mdn, rtd 63$): with B Palling.

909 **Shes Magic** 14 [4] 3-8-1 (42) D Mernagh (3) 33/1:   804 **Mcquillan** 28 [12] 3-7-13 (40) Dale Gibson 40/1:
13 ran   Time 2m 05.0 (6.8)   (H Gooding)   B R Millman Kentisbeare, Devon.

SANDOWN   FRIDAY APRIL 28TH   Righthand, Galloping Track, Stiff Finish

Official Going   SOFT (HEAVY In Places). Stalls: Sprint Course - Stands Side; Rem - Inside

1041	2.05 HARGREAVE HALE & CO STKS 3YO (C) 1m rnd Heavy 140 -11 Slow	
	£6307 £2332 £1166 £530	

972 **MEDICEAN** 9 [5] Sir Michael Stoute 3-8-10 K Fallon 10/11 FAV: -31: 3 ch c Machiavellian - Mystic **97+**
Goddess (Storm Bird) Waited with, imprvd to chall appr fnl 1f, styd on well to get up fnl stride: hvly bckd
tho' op 1/2: earlier a v promising 3rd in the Wood Ditton: eff at 1m, shld apprec 10f: acts on gd/soft &
hvy grnd, stiff/gall trks: progressive colt, likely to rate higher & win again.

*789 **MAN OMYSTERY** 29 [3] J Noseda 3-9-0 Pat Eddery 2/1: 0-12: 3 b c Diesis - Eurostorm (Storm Bird) shd **100**
In tch, closed 3f out, led 2f out, rdn ins last: worn down line: well bckd, clr rem: imprvd in defeat, giving
4lbs to this wnr: acts on gd & hvy grnd & is a useful colt: see 789.

-- **HIGHLAND REEL** [4] D R C Elsworth 3-8-7 N Pollard 5/1: 3: 3 ch c Selkirk - Taj Victory (Final Straw) 3½ **88**
Held up, prog to chall appr fnl 2f, not pace of front pair ins last: tchd 6/1, sound debut, clr rem: half-
brother to a 1m wnr: eff over a stiff 1m on hvy grnd: sure to improve, mdn looks a formality.

1032 **GRENADIER** 2 [2] W R Muir 3-8-10 Martin Dwyer 20/1: 4-54: Led till 2f out, wknd: tchd 14/1: qck reapp. 3½ **86**

4613} **DANDES RAMBO** 174 [1] 3-8-10 S Whitworth 50/1: -00-5: Prom till 3f out, sn lost tch: highly tried 18 **61**
on reapp: well btn both '99 starts: half-brother to sev wnrs, needs sell h'caps: with D R Arbuthnot.
5 ran   Time 1m 51.08 (12.08)   (Cheveley Park Stud)   Sir Michael Stoute Newmarket

1042	2.35 HEATHORNS RTD HCAP 4YO+ 0-95 (C) 1m rnd Heavy 140 -12 Slow	[95]
	£9883 £3748 £1874 £852 Came centre/stands side in str, stands rail prob riding slower	

733 **NIMELLO** 34 [5] P F I Cole 4-9-4 (85) J Fortune 8/1: 520-01: 4 b c Kingmambo - Zakota (Polish **91**
Precedent) Nvr far away, led 2f out, pushed out: bckd tho' op 6/1, blnks omitted: lightly rcd in '99, rnr-up
(stks, rtd 93): '98 Newmarket wnr (mdn, sole start, rtd 100): eff at 1m on firm & hvy grnd, stiff/gall trks:
best without blnks: still relatively unexposed, probably well h'capped.

851 **REGAL PHILOSOPHER** 18 [8] J W Hills 4-9-7 (88) M Hills 8/1: 420-62: 4 b g Faustus - Princess Lucy 1½ **91**
(Local Suitor) Mid-div, eff fnl 1f, styd on fnl 1f, not trouble wnr: op 6/1, fine run under top-weight.

747 **PHILATELIC LADY** 32 [7] M J Haynes 4-8-12 (79) S Carson (5) 8/1: 21-533: 4 ch f Pips Pride - Gold nk **81**
Stamp (Golden Act) Ran to best, headed twrds rear, gd hdwy & ev ch appr fnl 1f, onepace under
press ins last: ran to best, acts on fast, hvy & equitrack: see 593.

1409} **SLUMBERING** 345 [1] B J Meehan 4-9-1 (82) Pat Eddery 11/1: /006-4: Led till 2f out, no extra dist: 1 **82**
reapp, tchd 14/1: unplcd in 3 '99 starts (h'caps, rtd 83): '98 York wnr (mdn, rtd 89 at best): eff at 6/7f, stays
1m: acts on gd & hvy grnd, any trk: likes to force the pace: spot on back at 6/7f next time.

715 **PARKSIDE** 35 [3] 4-8-11 (78) J Reid 14/1: 130-05: Held up, prog to press ldrs 2f out, onepace 1f out: ½ **77**
'99 Warwick wnr (3 rnr mdn, rtd 80): unrcd juv: eff arnd 1m on fast & hvy grnd, any trk: with W Muir.

1015 **SILK ST JOHN** 4 [11] 6-9-7 (88) P McCabe 11/2: 00-006: Pulled hard twrds rear, eff 2f out, 2 **84**
no impress on ldrs: op 4/1, quick reapp: won this last year off 4lbs lower mark: see 1015.

875 **THE WHISTLING TEAL** 17 [10] 4-9-2 (83) J F Egan 10/3 FAV: 0-0037: Rear, prog to chase ldrs on 3 **74**
stands rail ent fnl 3, fdd bef fnl 1f: hvly bckd again but may have found the slowest ground: see 733.

4562} **SHARP REBUFF** 181 [2] 9-9-3 (84) S Sanders 10/1: 2350-8: Held up, badly bmpd & lost action/snatched 2½ **72**
up 3f out, position accepted: op 8/1 on reapp: '99 rnr-up (h'cap, here, rtd 87): '98 wnr here at Sandown (h'cap,
rtd 90): eff at 1m, best at 7f: acts on firm & soft grnd, likes Sandown: goes well fresh, this best forgotten.

-- **BARAGUEY** [4] 6-9-4 (85) R Hughes 16/1: 253/9: Prom till appr fnl 2f, fdd: 3 month hdles abs, plcd ½ **72**
both starts (stays 2m5.5f on soft, rtd 94h): ex-French mid-dist wnr (stays 2m on firm & soft, incl blnkd).

733 **NAVIASKY** 34 [9] 5-9-2 (83) Martin Dwyer 10/1: 016-00: Dwelt, al bhd: 10th: faster grnd suits, see 733. 1½ **68**
10 ran   Time 1m 51.14 (12.14)   (C Shiacolas)   P F I Cole Whatcombe, Oxon

SANDOWN FRIDAY APRIL 28TH Righthand, Galloping Track, Stiff Finish

1043 3.10 GR 2 KLM UK MILE 4YO+ (A) 1m rnd Heavy 140 -06 Slow
£36000 £13800 £6900 £3300 3 went stands side in str & were soon hard at work

*967 **INDIAN LODGE 9** [7] Mrs A J Perrett 4-9-0 M J Kinane 9/4 FAV: 211-11: 4 b c Grand Lodge - Repetitious (Northfields) Keen, bhd ldr, styd centre ent str, led 2f out, pushed out, cmftbly: hvly bckd: recent Newmarket wnr (Gr 3): '99 wnr at Newbury, Yarmouth & Newmarket (2, List, rtd 112): eff at 1m/9f: acts on fast & hvy grnd, handles firm, likes stiff trks, esp Newmarket: runs well fresh: v smart, progressive & genuine colt with a fine turn of foot: has earned a try in Group 1 company & should go well. **118**

4418} **TRANS ISLAND 194** [4] I A Balding 5-9-4 K Fallon 9/2: 1113-2: 5 b h Selkirk - Khubza (Green Desert) Led, styd centre in str, hdd 2f out, rallied but not pace of wnr: op 7/2, fine reapp: progressive hat-trick wnr in '99, at Leopardstown (h'cap), Newbury (List) & Longchamp (Gr 2, Gr 1 3rd on fnl start rtd 118): '98 wnr at Capannelle (Gr 2, subs plcd 2nd, rtd 112): eff at 7f/1m on firm, likes hvy grnd & stiff trks, esp Newbury: loves to force the pace & goes well fresh: prob still improving, lost nothing giving 4lbs to this wnr. *2* **118**

4399} **ALMUSHTARAK 195** [1] K Mahdi 7-9-0 R Cochrane 3/1: 4320-3: 7 b h Fairy King - Exciting (Mill Reef) Pulled hard, prom, came stands side in str, rdn & sn struggling with centre trio till ran on ins last: hvly bckd on reapp: plcd sev times last term (best when 3rd in this race, rtd 119): '98 wnr here at Sandown (Gr 2, by 5L), Gr 1 rnr-up (rtd 120): eff at 1m, stays 10f: acts on firm & hvy grnd, the latter prob suits: goes on any trk, likes Sandown: runs well fresh: high-class entire, jockey took wrong option, best forgotten *nk* **114**

952 **WARNINGFORD 10** [6] J R Fanshawe 6-9-0 T Quinn 10/1: 206-24: Keen, waited with, styd centre turning for home, shaken up 2f out, sn no extra: well bckd tho' op 8/1: 7f specialist, not disgraced, see 952. *2½* **110**

967 **MUJAHID 9** [3] 4-9-0 R Hills 8/1: 042-35: Pulled hard, rear, went stands side in str & was btn bef 2f out: tchd 10/1, quickish reapp: best forgotten on unfav'd side & is suited by faster grnd: see 967. *3½* **105**

12 **HANDSOME RIDGE 173** [2] 6-9-4 L Dettori 6/1: 0002-6: Pulled hard towards rear, came stands side turning for home, wknd bef fnl 2f: '99 wnr here at Sandown (this race, Gr 2) & Goodwood (rtd 120): '98 wnr at Doncaster & St Cloud (Gr 3, rtd 118): eff at 1m/10f: acts on fast, loves gd/soft & soft: goes on any trk & can run well fresh: smart entire at best, should pay to ignore this: with J Gosden. *3* **104**

6 ran Time 1m 50.69 (11.69) (Seymour Cohn) Mrs A J Perrett Pulborough, W Sussex

1044 3.40 HEATHORNS HCAP 4YO+ 0-85 (D) 2m78y Heavy 140 -34 Slow **[79]**
£7117 £2190 £1095 £547 4 yo rec 4 lb

4618} **RENZO 174** [1] J L Harris 7-8-9 (60) S Sanders 8/1: 0000-1: 7 b g Alzao - Watership (Foolish Pleasure) Mid-div, prog to lead ent str, sn clr, styd on strongly: op 6/1, 6 wk hdles abs, consistent this term: 98/99 debut wnr at Ascot (nov, rtd 132h, 2m, firm & gd/soft): unplcd on the Flat in '99 (rtd 80) & subs hobdayed: '98 wnr at Doncaster (h'cap, rtd 84): eff at 14f/2m: acts on firm & hvy grnd, any trk, likes Sandown: tried blnks, better without: enigmatic but v well h'capped gldg, winter wind op may have been the making of him. **65**

4467} **WONTCOSTALOTBUT 189** [3] M J Wilkinson 6-8-0 (51) A Nicholls (3) 11/4 FAV: /134-2: 6 b m Nicholas Bill - Brave Maiden (Three Legs) In tch, feeling pace ent str, styd on fnl 2f, no ch with wnr: 6 wks jmps abs, won at Newbury & Kempton (h'caps, 2m6f/3m, fast & hvy grnd, rtd 124h): won 1st of just 3 '99 starts at Folkestone (h'cap, rtd 54): no form in '98: eff at 2m on gd/soft & hvy grnd: goes v well fresh, any trk. *1½* **54**

*1023 **MY LEGAL EAGLE 4** [6] R J Price 6-8-11 (62)(5ex) P Fitzsimons (5) 5/1: 222213: 6 b g Law Society - Majestic Nurse (On Your Mark) Prom, eff 2f out, kept on same pace: qk reapp, clr rem: v consistent. *1¾* **63**

885 **JAMAICAN FLIGHT 16** [5] Mrs S Lamyman 7-9-10 (75) J Fortune 20/1: 443204: Led till 3f out, no extra: joint top-weight, back to near best with visor omitted: see 253. *6* **72**

4618} **GALAPINO 174** [2] 7-8-4 (55) R Mullen 12/1: 3400-5: Prom, rdn 3f out, fdd: 6 wk jumps abs, earlier won at Fontwell (2m2f h'cap, firm & gd, rtd 113h): '99 wnr here at Sandown (h'cap, rtd 61): '98 wnr at Goodwood (clm h'cap, rtd 70 & 66a, M Channon): eff at 14f/2m4f on any grnd/trk, best without visor: well h'capped. *6* **48**

963 **GRAND CRU 10** [4] 9-7-10 (47)(bl) Joanna Badger (7) 7/1: 000146: Held up, eff ent str, no impress. *1¼* **39**

726 **SALFORD FLYER 34** [9] 4-9-10 (79) N Pollard 5/1: 225-27: Al towards rear: well bckd tho' op 4/1: back up in trip, faster grnd suits: see 726. *21* **56**

885 **MISCHIEF 16** [7] 4-7-13 (53)(1ow) Martin Dwyer 25/1: 620308: Al bhd, btn 3f out: see 815 (12f, visor). *6* **27**

4370} **ROMERO 196** [8] 4-8-7 (62) T Quinn 6/1: 2360-W: Withdrawn at start, distressed: hdles fit, won 3 this season at Ascot (2 juv hdles & a nov h'cap, 2m, fast & soft, rtd 127h): dual '99 rnr-up (h'caps, rtd 70 at best, C Thornton): eff at 10f/12f: acts on gd/soft grnd: with J Akehurst. **0**

9 ran Time 3m 58.31 (28.51) (Cleartherm Ltd) J L Harris Eastwell, Leics

1045 4.15 APRIL FILLIES MDN 3YO (D) 1m2f Heavy 140 -64 Slow
£4524 £1392 £696 £348

-- **DREAM QUEST** [9] J L Dunlop 3-8-7 Pat Eddery 9/2: 1: 3 ch f Rainbow Quest - Dreamawhile (Known Fact) Nvr far away, led appr fnl 2f, hdd bef dist, rallied gamely under press to get up again line: bckd from 11/2, slow time: 340,000gns filly, related to a couple of gd sprinters: eff at 10f, 12f is going to suit (Oaks entry): goes on hvy grnd, stiff trk & runs well fresh: shld rate higher over further. **90+**

-- **REQUEST** [14] Sir Michael Stoute 3-8-7 K Fallon 5/2: 2: 3 b f Rainbow Quest - Highbrow (Shirley Heights) Prom, pushed into lead appr fnl 1f, drifted left, collared fnl stride: hvly bckd: half-sister to high-class mid-dist duo Blueprint & Fairy Godmother, dam a Grp performer: eff at 10f, 12f shld suit: acts on hvy grnd & runs well fresh: shld find similar before going on to better things. *shd* **89**

4194} **BURNING SUNSET 209** [7] H R A Cecil 3-8-11 T Quinn 2/1 FAV: -63-3: 3 ch f Caerleon - Lingerie (Shirley Heights) Bhd ldrs, prog & ev ch 2f out, onepace towards fin: hvly bckd, clr rem on reapp: 3rd on fnl '99 start (fill mdn, rtd 89): half-sister to smart French mid-dist wnr Linmos & 10f scorer Shiva: eff at 10f, bred for further: goes on fast & hvy grnd: shld find a maiden (Oaks entry). *1½* **91**

4614} **WHITE HOUSE 174** [1] W Jarvis 3-8-11 M Tebbutt 20/1: 0-4: Towards rear, shkn up ent fnl 3f, kept on nicely, nvr nr ldrs: eye-catching reapp: unplcd sole '99 start over 1m (rtd 58): half-sister to wnrs btwn 7f & 13.5f: dam 1m wnr juv: shld apprec this 10f trip: prob handles hvy grnd, faster will suit: one to keep in mind. *5* **84+**

3581} **ISLAND PRINCESS 246** [4] 3-8-11 N Pollard 7/1: 0020-5: Led till 2½f out, no extra: op 16/1 on reapp: '99 rnr-up (fill mdn, rtd 80): half-sister to a 7f wnr, dam a sprinter: goes on soft grnd. *1¾* **82$**

3640} **TITIAN ANGEL 243** [2] 3-8-11 R Morse 16/1: 2-6: Handy till 3f out: reapp: rnr-up sole '99 start (mdn auct, rtd 71): dam 12f wnr: eff at 1m, further shld suit: acts on gd grnd, with C Allen. *¾* **81**

884 **COCO LOCO 16** [6] 3-8-11 R Price 50/1: 0-67: Keen, nvr better than mid-div: longer trip. *5* **74$**

-- **HERSELF** [11] 3-8-7 S Sanders 14/1: 8: Nvr a factor: Hernado half sister to a useful styg h'capper. *6* **62**

915 **KOSMIC LADY 14** [8] 3-8-11 J F Egan 50/1: 09: Pld hard, al towards rear: Cosmonaut filly, up in trip. *2* **63$**

SANDOWN
FRIDAY APRIL 28TH   Righthand, Galloping Track, Stiff Finish

934   **MEDOOZA** 11 [10] 3-8-11 M Hills 50/1: 000: Rear, prog 6f out, wknd 3f out: 10th: Night Shift filly.   ¾   62$
850   **DIAMOND KISS** 18 [3] 3-8-11 S Whitworth 66/1: 0-00: Pulled hard, chsd ldrs till halfway: 11th.   1½   60$
--   **BLOSSOM WHISPERS** [12] 3-8-7 A Morris 20/1: 0: Pld hard, al bhd: 12th, Ezzoud half-sister to sev wnrs. 4   50
4473} **MELBA** 189 [5] 3-8-11 L Dettori 25/1: 00-0: Mid-div till 3f out: 13th on reapp.   3   49
13 ran   Time 2m 24.6 (20.5) (Hand Timed)   (Hesmonds Stud)   J L Dunlop Arundel, W Sussex

1046   4.45 BOW ST FILLIES MED AUCT MDN 2YO (E)   5f str   Heavy 140   -08 Slow
£3542   £1090   £545   £272

989   **ELSIE PLUNKETT** 6 [4] R Hannon 2-8-11 Dane O'Neill 7/1: -51: 2 b f Mind Games - Snow Eagle (Polar   87
Falcon) Cl-up, led appr fnl 1f, edged left under press dist, kept on well: nicely bckd: 6,500gns Feb foal, sire
a high-class sprinter: eff at 5f on hvy grnd: handles a gall trk: open to further improvement.
--   **AZIZ PRESENTING** [1] M R Channon 2-8-11 T Quinn 5/1: 2: 2 br f Charnwood Forest - Khalatara   ¾   85
(Kalaglow) Prom, went after wnr appr fnl 1f, sltly checked dist, ran on: well bckd, tho' op 7/2, clr of rem:
11,500gns Feb foal: sire 7f/1m performer: eff at 5f on hvy, further will suit: shld soon go one better.
--   **AMBER TIDE** [2] M L W Bell 2-8-11 M Fenton 7/1: 3: 2 ch f Pursuit Of Love - Tochar Ban (Assert)   3½   79
Chsd ldrs, outpcd 2f out, kept on nicely towards fin: op 5/1: 30,000gns Mar foal, half-sister to a 1m wng juv,
dam 10f wnr, sire 6-8f performer: promising, goes on hvy grnd, 6f is going to suit.
970   **OPEN WARFARE** 9 [5] M Quinn 2-8-11 J Fortune 7/2 FAV: -334: Led till ent fnl 2f, onepace: well   nk   78
bckd tho' drifted from 2/1, clr rem: shown enough to find a Northern mdn: see 886.
849   **SOONA** 18 [7] 2-8-11 L Dettori 8/1: 05: Chsd ldrs, no extra 2f out: nicely bckd from 10/1: see 849.   5   68
--   **ALNAHIGHER** [3] 2-8-11 K Fallon 9/2: 6: Al towards rear: hvly bckd tho' op 9/4: Mizoram sister   15   43
to juv sprint wnr Laabed, dam 6f wnr, sire 7f/1m performer: better expected, with M Johnston.
--   **THERESA GREEN** [8] 2-8-11 Kathleen McDermott (7) 16/1: 7: Dwelt, nvr troubled ldrs: IR 3,400gns   2   39
Charnwood Forest Jan foal, dam stoutly bred, sire 7f/1m performer: with Mrs Dutfield.
--   **IVANS BRIDE** [6] 2-8-11 S Sanders 10/1: 8: Slowly away, sn struggling: op 7/1: 5,000 gns   ½   38
Inzar Mar foal, dam 6f juv wnr: sire 6/7f performer: with G Margarson.
--   **KIRIWINA** [9] 2-8-11 J Reid 10/1: 9: V slow away, al bhd: 8,000 gns Tagula Mar foal, half-sister   9   22
to a 5f wnr in Italy: sire 6/7f performer: with Miss G Kelleway.
9 ran   Time 1m 07.0 (7.4) (Hand Timed)   (C J M Partnership)   R Hannon East Everleigh, Wilts

1047   5.20 SILVER CLEF RTD HCAP 3YO 0-100 (B)   5f str   Heavy 140   +14 Fast   [105]
£9335   £3540   £1770   £804

982   **KATHOLOGY** 8 [3] D R C Elsworth 3-8-7 (84) N Pollard 4/1 JT FAV: 223-21: 3 b c College Chapel -   89
Wicken Wonder (Distant Relative) Front rank, led after halfway, ran on, just lasted: hvly bckd tho' op 11/4, fast
time: 1st win, rnr-up 4 of 5 prev starts (mdn, rtd 86 & 78a): eff at 5/6f, stays 7f: goes on gd/soft, hvy grnd &
fibresand: best up with/forcing the pace, any trk: tough & consistent.
959   **ARGENT FACILE** 10 [1] D J S Cosgrove 3-8-5 (82)(t) J F Egan 16/1: 410-22: 3 b c Midhish -   shd   86
Rosinish (Lomond) Chsd ldrs, rdn 2f out, ran on strongly ins last, just failed: wnr in another 10y: has started
the season in fine style: acts on fast, hvy grnd & any trk: looks certain to apprec 6f next time: see 959.
935   **BARRINGER** 11 [2] M R Channon 3-8-11 (88) T Quinn 5/1: 00-453: 3 b g Nicolotte - Prosaic Star   2½   87
(Common Grounds) Held up, chsd ldrs 2f out, kept on but not pace of front rnr: op 7/2, back in trip, see 716.
3058} **SINGSONG** 272 [7] A Berry 3-8-13 (90) R Hughes 20/1: 1520-4: Dwelt, towards rear, prog/switched   3½   83
appr fnl 1f, nvr nr ldrs: reapp: '99 wnr at Doncaster (reapp) & Ripon (nov stks, rtd 93 in a nursery): eff at 5f,
tried 6f, shld suit: acts on firm & gd/soft grnd, sharp or gall trks: runs well fresh but shld be sharper for this.
4167} **POWER PACKED** 211 [10] P Robinson 3-9-3 (94) 4/1 JT FAV: 5212-5: Trkd ldrs, shaken up 2f out,   3   81+
fdd bef dist: nicely bckd from 5/1 on reapp: '99 nr Pontefract wnr (mdn, nurs rnr-up, rtd 90): eff at 5f, tried 6f:
acts on fast & gd grnd, stiff/gall trks: can force the pace. Grp entered colt, expect improvement on faster grnd.
4310} **NISR** 200 [5] 3-8-9 (86) R Cochrane 14/1: -002-6: V slow away, nvr a factor: reapp/h'cap bow: rnr-up   2   69
fnl of 3 '99 starts (mdn, rtd 87): eff at 6f, bred to apprec 7f/1m: goes on gd grnd: sharper over 6f+ soon.
988   **PIPADASH** 6 [4] 3-9-7 (98)(bl) K Darley 6/1: 150-27: Set gd clip till halfway, fdd: quick reapp, top-weight.   ¾   80
926   **COCO DE MER** 13 [8] 3-8-8 (85) M Roberts 20/1: 220-08: Not much room start, al bhd: '99 Chester   ¾   66
wnr, nurs rnr-up, rtd 89: eff at 5f: acts on firm & gd: suited by sharp trks: with R Fahey.
988   **LABRETTI** 6 [9] 3-8-13 (90)(bl) Pat Eddery 8/1: 000-09: Bhd from halfway: tchd 10/1, quick reapp.   1¼   69
652   **LOST IN HOOK** 51 [6] 3-8-6 (83) L Dettori 14/1: 452-30: Rear, btn halfway: 10th, 7 wk abs, nds faster grnd. 6   52
10 ran   Time 1m 05.91 (6.31)   (McDowell Racing)   D R C Elsworth Whitsbury, Hants

DONCASTER
SATURDAY APRIL 29TH   Lefthand, Flat, Galloping Track

Official Going   GOOD TO SOFT. Stalls Str Course - Stands Side, Round Course - Inside, Round Mile - Outside

1048   2.00 WILLOUGHBY MED AUCT MDN 2YO (F)   5f   Good/Soft 80   -02 Slow
£2912   £896   £448   £224

891   **BRAM STOKER** 16 [10] R Hannon 2-9-0 R Hughes 5/4 FAV: 21: 2 ch c General Monash - Taniokey (Grundy)   98
Made all, rdn over 1f out, styd on strongly, eased fnl line: hvly bckd, op 6/4: half brother to a 1m/12f wnr:
dam a 1m wnr: eff at 5f, 6f will suit: acts on gd/soft grnd & on any trk: can improve & win more races.
1000   **INNIT** 5 [11] M R Channon 2-8-9 S Drowne 12/1: 32: 2 b f Distinctly North - Tidal Reach (Kris S)   3   85
Trkd wnr halfway, rdn & kept on fnl 2f, nvr pace to chall: op 8/1, quick reapp: acts on gd/soft: win a race.
--   **THE NAMES BOND** [8] Andrew Turnell 2-9-0 W Supple 33/1: 3: 2 b c Tragic Role - Artistic Licence   2   85
(High Top) Cl-up halfway, rdn & kept on onepace fnl 2f: Feb foal, half brother to a 1m wnr: dam plcd over
10f/12f: sire a 12f wnr: looks sure to apprec much further in time: handles gd/soft grnd, pleasing thro.
--   **PHAROAHS GOLD** [4] W Jarvis 2-9-0 M Tebbutt 12/1: 4: In tch, rdn halfway, kept on fnl 2f, no   1½   81+
threat: op 8/1: Namaqualand, Feb foal, cost 28,000 IR gns: 6f+ will suit & sure to improve.
--   **TUMBLEWEED TENOR** [3] Pat Eddery 7/1: 5: Rdn chasing ldrs, btn fnl 2f: Mujadil gldg, Mar   1½   77
foal, cost 15,000 IR gns: dam plcd over 6f/1m as a 2yo: with B Meehan.
--   **RUSHBY** [6] 2-9-0 S Whitworth 12/1: 6: Dwelt, in tch halfway, sn outpcd: op 8/1: Fayruz colt, Apr   2½   71
foal, cost 45,000 IR gns: half brother to 4 juv wnrs: dam plcd over 10f: get further in time for Mrs P N Dutfield.
--   **SKITTLES** [9] 2-8-9 S Sanders 20/1: 7: Dwelt, sn rdn, nvr on terms: op 16/1: Topanoora filly, Jan   nk   65
foal, 2,300 gns purchase: half sister to a juv wnr abroad: dam unrcd, sire high-class 10/12f performer.

828   **IZZET MUZZY** 23 [5] 2-9-0 N Carlisle 50/1: 58: Dwelt, nvr on terms: see 828.   ½   68

--   **BAREFOOTED FLYER** [1] 2-8-9 C Lowther 12/1: 9: Went left start, al outpcd: op 8/1: Fly So Free   ½   61
filly, Apr foal, cost $20,000: dam a wnr at up to 9f in US, sire a champion US juv: 6f+ shld suit in time.

911   **HAMATARA** 15 [7] 2-9-0 K Darley 4/1: 40: In tch, rdn/btn 2f out: 10th: see 911.   nk   65

--   **ICEALION** [2] 2-9-0 T Lucas 50/1: 0: Dwelt, al outpcd: 11th: Lion Cavern gldg, May foal, cost   12   45
8,500 gns: dam 12f/2m wnr, sire a high-class 2yo: bred to need 6f+.

11 ran   Time 1m 02.3 (4.1)   (Alessandro Gaucci)   R Hannon East Everleigh, Wilts

---

1049   2.35 GR 3 LEICESTERSHIRE STKS 4YO+ (A)   7f str   Good/Soft 80   +03 Fast
£20300   £7700   £3850   £1750

4396} **SUGARFOOT** 196 [1] N Tinkler 6-9-1 R Cochrane 4/1: 1125-1: 6 ch h Thatching - Norpella (Northfields)   115
Cl-up, rdn over 2f out, styd on well to lead ins last, drvn out: best time of day: mkt drifter, op 9/4: reapp: in
fine form last term, wng at York (2, listed rtd h'cap & h'cap) & Doncaster (Gr 3, rtd 115): '98 scorer at Ascot &
York (2, val h'caps, rtd 104): eff at 6f, poss just best over a gall 1m: acts on firm & hvy: suited by a gall trk,
loves York & Doncaster: runs well fresh: tough & still progressive, continue to give a good account in Group races.

4396} **TUMBLEWEED RIDGE** 196 [4] B J Meehan 7-9-1 (tbl) M Tebbutt 7/2: 5210-2: 7 ch h Indian Ridge -   ½   114
Billie Blue (Ballad Rock) Led, rdn 2f out, hdd ins last, kept on tho' not pace of wnr: tchd 4/1, reapp: '99 wnr at
Leopardstown, Longchamp (Gr 3's) & Epsom (List, rtd 116): '98 Newmarket (rtd h'cap) & Leopardstown wnr (Gr 3, rtd
107): eff at 6f/1m, 7f specialist: acts on firm & soft, any trk, likes Newmarket: goes well fresh: eff with/without
blnks & t-strap: smart & tough entire, gd reapp & should win another Group 3.

4485} **GRANNYS PET** 189 [2] P F I Cole 6-8-12 Pat Eddery 5/2 FAV: 3121-3: 6 ch g Selkirk - Patsy Western   3   105
(Precocious) Held up in tch, eff 2f out, no impress on front pair: well bckd, tchd 3/1, reapp: '99 wnr at Chester
& twice at Goodwood (rtd h'caps) & Doncaster (C/D, stks, rtd 108 at best): '98 Haydock wnr (h'cap, rtd 101): suited
by 7f: handles any trk, likes Goodwood: acts on firm & soft grnd: has run well fresh: eff with/without blnks:
tough, very useful & progressive last term, fitter for this.

*952   **CRETAN GIFT** 11 [7] N P Littmoden 9-8-12 (vis) T G McLaughlin 5/1: -03514: Trkd ldrs, rdn/held over   ¾   104
1f out: op 4/1: 6f is his ideal trip: see 952 (Listed, 6f).

862   **ONE WON ONE** 20 [5] 6-8-12 G Duffield 9/2: 621-55: In tch, outpcd fnl 2f: op 5/1: '99 wnr at The   3½   97
Curragh (h'cap) & Leopardstown (List): eff at 5f/7f on firm & soft/hvy grnd: likes a gall trk.

5 ran   Time 1m 28.60 (5.4)   (Mrs D Wright)   N Tinkler Langton, N Yorks

---

1050   3.05 JAMES GUTTERIDGE HCAP 3YO+ 0-70 (E)   1m2f60y   Good/Soft 80   -20 Slow
£3926   £1208   £604   £302   3 yo rec 17lb   [70]

907   **DARK VICTOR** 15 [13] D Shaw 4-8-6 (47)(1ow) N Callan 14/1: 40501: 4 b g Cadeaux Genereux - Dimmer   54
(Kalaglow) Chsd ldrs, rdn fnl 3f, styd on well to lead ins last, drvn out: first win, plcd in a bmpr this winter:
improved for step up to 10.5f on gd/soft, 12f looks sure to suit: open to further improvement over further.

784   **ACHILLES WINGS** 31 [10] K R Burke 4-9-9 (65) J Weaver 4/1 FAV: 3442: 4 b c Irish River - Shirley   1¼   69
Valentine (Shirley Heights) Chsd ldr 4f out, rdn/led over 2f out, edged left & hdd ins last, no extra: hvly
bckd, op 6/1: h'cap debut: eff at 10f, handles gd/soft & equitrack: could find similar on this evidence.

931   **FEATHERTIME** 14 [5] Mrs G S Rees 4-8-12 (54) G Duffield 14/1: 14-533: 4 b f Puissance - Midnight Owl   2½   55
(Ardross) Handy, ev ch 2f out, rdn/no extra ins last: tchd 16/1: stays 10f: see 811.

991   **HIBERNATE** 7 [7] K R Burke 6-10-0 (70) D McGann 7/2 33/1: 000004: Led, rdn/hdd 2f out, no extra   1¼   69
ins last: imprvd eff, has slipped to a handy mark: loves to dominate & can find similar (all 4 wins at 12f).

918   **MURCHAN TYNE** 14 [3] 7-8-6 (50) W Supple 20/1: 50-005: Held up, rdn halfway, kept on fnl 2f for   hd   49+
press, nrst at fin: op 33/1: on a fair mark now & sure to relish a return to 12f+: see 788.

786   **YOUNG UN** 31 [1] 5-9-8 (64) P McCabe 14/1: 251-06: Held up, eff 3f out, no held: op 12/1: see 786.   ½   62

871   **GYPSY** 18 [9] 4-9-12 (68) S Sanders 14/1: 354437: Chsd ldrs, eff 3f out, no extra fnl 1f: op 12/1:   nk   65
acts on fast, soft & fibresand: clkr of rem here: 9f/sharp 10f poss ideal: see 871, 510 & 270.

889   **ROCK SCENE** 17 [20] 8-8-2 (44) P M Quinn (5) 14/1: 000/28: Dwelt/held up, eff 3f out, no impress.   9   29

889   **ACE OF TRUMPS** 17 [8] 4-8-11 (53)(t) N Kennedy 33/1: 0-1009: Prom 1m: btr 795 (9f, sell h'cap).   nk   37

854   **MALAKAL** 19 [2] 4-9-4 (60) J P Spencer 14/1: 00-000: Held up, eff 3f out, no held: 10th: op 12/1.   8   34

855   **PORT OF CALL** 19 [4] 5-8-5 (47) S Righton 25/1: 56000: Mid-div, hard rdn 4f out, no impress: 11th.   3½   16

943   **NOWELL HOUSE** 12 [15] 4-9-9 (65) G Parkin 10/1: 11-000: Chsd ldrs 9f: 12th: op 8/1: see 825.   5   27

965   **HINDI** 11 [18] 4-9-9 (65) R Cochrane 6/1: 56-020: Al towards rear: 15th: op 5/1: btr 965 (soft).   0

825   **OTAHUNA** 24 [19] 4-9-4 (60) K Darley 10/1: 600-30: Al bhd: 18th: op 12/1: btr 825.   0

842   Ertlon 22 [6] 10-8-13 (55) P Robinson 25/1:   3788} Royal Axminster 236 [12] 5-8-7 (49)(BL) S Whitworth 33/1:

1003   Hidden Enemy 5 [11] 4-9-9 (65) G Gibbons (7) 33/1:   890 Burning 17 [14] 8-8-9 (48)(3ow) T G McLaughlin 33/1:

825   Manzoni 24 [17] 4-8-10 (52) T Lucas 33/1:   835 Summer Bounty 22 [16] 4-9-9 (65)(t) A Culhane 20/1:

20 ran   Time 2m 16.68 (10.28)   (J C Fretwell)   D Shaw Averham, Notts

---

1051   3.35 ALDBOROUGH FILL MDN 3YO (D)   1m2f60y   Good/Soft 80   -94 Slow
£3874   £1192   £596   £298

4473} **UNSEEDED** 190 [1] J L Dunlop 3-8-11 Pat Eddery 7/4 FAV: 04-1: 3 ch f Unfuwain - Sesame (Derrylin)   87+
Made all, shaken up & pulled clr from over 1f out, eased nr fin, readily: val for 8L+: hvly bckd: promise on
2nd of 2 '99 starts (mdn, rtd 82): apprec step up to 10.5f, will relish 12f on gd/soft, soft grnd & a gall
trk: likes to force the pace: runs well fresh: plenty in hand here, can rate more highly & win more races.

--   **CLEPSYDRA** [5] H R A Cecil 3-8-11 W Ryan 4/1: 2: 3 b f Saddler's Wells - Quandary (Blushing   6   77
Groom) Chsd ldrs halfway, rdn/hung left 2f out, kept on tho' sn held by wnr: op 3/1: debut: mid-dist bred filly.

745   **ANASTASIA VENTURE** 33 [4] S P C Woods 3-8-11 N Callan 14/1: 53: 3 b f Lion Cavern - Our Shirley   nk   76
(Shirley Heights) Handy, rdn/edged left 2f out, & sn no extra: op 12/1: stays 10f: see 745 (1m).

--   **LIDAKIYA** [3] Sir Michael Stoute 3-8-11 D Holland 5/1: 4: Held up in tch, eff when no room 2f out,   shd   76+
kept on under hands & heels riding ins last: prob 2nd with a clr run: op 7/2: Kahyasi filly, will enjoy 12f.

--   **EXHIBITION GIRL** [2] 3-8-11 P Fessey 33/1: 5: Chsd ldrs, rdn/no impress wthn not much room   1½   75
over 1f out: Perugino filly, related to a 10f wnr abroad: with A Turnell.

--   **TALAQI** [7] 3-8-11 W Supple 16/1: 6: Rear/in tch, eff 3f out, no impress: op 12/1, debut: Nashwan   1½   74
filly: sister to a useful miler: with E A L Dunlop.

--   **DEVIL LANE** [9] 3-8-11 R Hughes 6/1: 7: Trkd ldrs, btn/hmpd over 1f out: bckd: Diesis filly.   4   70

826   **DIANEME** 24 [8] 3-8-11 J Carroll 10/1: 38: Slowly away, sn in tch, btn 3f out: op 10/1: jockey reported   13   61
filly lost her action: eyecatching effort in 826 (1m).

8 ran   Time 2m 19.17 (12.77)   (Christopher Spence)   J L Dunlop Arundel, W Sussex

DONCASTER **SATURDAY APRIL 29TH Lefthand, Flat, Galloping Track**

1052 **4.05 C B HUTCHINSON HCAP 4YO+ 0-90 (C) 2m110y Good/Soft 80 -67 Slow [84]**
£6838 £2104 £1052 £526 4 yo rec 4 lb

968 **WAVE OF OPTIMISM 10** [2] J Pearce 5-9-4 (74) G Bardwell 8/1: 130-01: 5 ch g Elmaamul - Ballerina Bay (Myjinski) Held up, keen, prog/chsd ldrs 4f out, styd on well fnl 2f to lead ins last, drvn out: op 7/1: '99 Sandown wnr (h'cap, rtd 75): '98 Nottingham wnr (mdn, rtd 75): suited by 2m on gd, likes gd/soft & soft grnd. **78**
997 **BRAVE TORNADO 7** [10] G B Balding 9-9-7 (77) S Carson (5) 4/1: 54/122: 9 ch g Dominion - Accuracy (Gunner B) Led, rdn/strongly prsd fnl 2f, hdd well ins last, just held: op 3/1: in fine form, likes soft grnd. *nk* **80**
876 **ROYAL EXPRESSION 18** [1] G M Moore 8-9-3 (73) J Weaver 8/1: 123163: 8 b g Sylvan Express - Edwins' Princess (Owen Dudley) Held up, rdn/outpcd 4f out, kept on well for press ins last, not pace of front pair: op 7/1: thorough stayer, will do better with a stronger pace: see 714 (2m2f). *2½* **74**
845 **PRINCE NICHOLAS 21** [7] K W Hogg 5-8-6 (62) J Bramhill 10/1: -02244: Held up, rdn to chall fnl 2f, sn onepace: op 8/1: eff at 10/14f, now stays 2m: see 779 (13f). *¾* **62**
*918 **PLEASANT MOUNT 14** [3] 4-8-5 (65) K Darley 9/4 FAV: 12-015: Cl-up, rdn/ch 2f out, no extra ins last. *nk* **65**
903 **EMBRYONIC 16** [6] 8-8-5 (61) G Carter 25/1: 60-006: Chsd ldrs, rdn/no extra fnl 2f: see 845. *5* **57**
845 **HOME COUNTIES 21** [4] 11-7-10 (52)(t) P Fessey 14/1: 232-07: In tch, outpcd over 3f out: op 12/1. *1¾* **47**
-- **TURNPOLE** [8] 9-10-0 (84) A Culhane 20/1: 1204/8: Prom, outpcd fnl 4f: op 14/1, long abs: 98/99 wnr over fences at Catterick & Sedgefield (novs, rtd 112c): '98 Flat wnr here at Doncaster (h'cap, rtd 88 at best): eff at 12f, suited by 2m & stays extreme dists: acts on fast & gd/soft, any trk: has run well fresh. *5* **75**
860 **CINDESTI 19** [5] 4-7-10 (56)(3oh) P M Quinn (5) 9/1: 011-09: Cl-up halfway, btn 3f out: op 8/1: see 860. *4* **44**
714 **BUSTLING RIO 36** [9] 4-8-0 (60) J Mackay (7) 20/1: 1-1500: Held up, rdn/btn 3f out: 10th: btr 428 (AW). *3* **45**
10 ran Time 3m 53.05 (24.25) (Wave Of Optimism Partnership) J Pearce Newmarket, Suffolk

1053 **4.35 V CHANDLER HCAP 3YO 0-75 (E) 1m rnd Good/Soft 80 -41 Slow [82]**
£4641 £1428 £714 £357

999 **FRENCH HORN 7** [3] M J Ryan 3-8-12 (66) P McCabe 4/1 FAV: 51-031: 3 b g Fraam - Runcina (Runnett) Keen/al prom, led going well over 1f out, drvn clr ins last, styd on strongly: op 9/2: '99 wnr on fnl start (nurs, rtd 69): eff at 7f/1m, stays 9f on gd/soft & soft, poss firm: likes a stiff/gall trk: shld win again. **77**
884 **KELTECH GOLD 17** [2] B Palling 3-8-10 (64) D Sweeney 14/1: 50-02: 3 b c Petorius - Creggan Vale Lass (Simply Great) Chsd ldrs, rdn & kept on fnl 2f, not pace of wnr: op 10/1, h'cap bow: eff at 1m on gd/soft. *4* **67**
976 **ENTITY 10** [6] T D Barron 3-8-10 (64) C Lowther 16/1: 0-0003: 3 ch g Rudimentary - Desert Ditty (Green Desert) Reared & slowly away, rdn/prog to chall 3f out, no extra ins last: op 14/1: lost many lengths at start, fine effort in circumstances: eff at 1m, tried further: interesting when obtaining a level break: see 967. *1* **65**
857 **CELEBES 19** [15] I A Balding 3-9-4 (72) K Darley 16/1: 4-3464: Chsd ldrs, rdn/kept on fnl 2f for press. *3½* **68**
*887 **BALFOUR 17** [12] 3-8-7 (61) P Robinson 9/1: 600-15: In tch, ch 2f out, sn held: op 8/1: see 887 (7f). *1¾* **55**
4614} **DESERT ISLAND DISC 175** [20] 3-9-1 (69) R Cochrane 20/1: 050-6: Mid-div, rdn/kept on fnl 2f, no threat: reapp/h'cap bow: unplcd in '99 (rtd 76, fill mdn). *1* **62**
920 **BAILEYS PRIZE 14** [19] 3-9-5 (73) D Holland 14/1: 45-27: Held up, rdn halfway, mod gains: see 920. *1½* **64**
4498} **ROMANTIC AFFAIR 187** [18] 3-9-3 (71) Pat Eddery 9/2: 013-8: Bhd halfway, mod gains fnl 3f under hands & heels riding, no threat: nicely bckd: h'cap debut/reapp: '99 Newcastle wnr (auct mdn, rtd 74): eff at 7f, 1m+ will suit: acts on soft grnd & a stiff/gall trk: not given a hard time here, can leave this bhd over further. *1½* **60**
*992 **MR COSPECTOR 7** [16] 3-9-3 (71) O Urbina 12/1: 400-19: In tch, rdn/btn 2f out: op 10/1: see 992. *½* **59**
976 **CARELESS 10** [24] 3-8-3 (57) G Duffield 12/1: 400-40: Wide/prom, held fnl 2f: 10th: op 10/1. *1¾* **43**
4107} **MIDDLETHORPE 216** [11] 3-8-1 (55) Dale Gibson 33/1: 3300-0: Towards rear, rdn/mod gains fnl 2f: 11th: plcd twice in '99 (rtd 59, nurs): stays 7f, 1m+ could yet suit: handles gd & gd/soft grnd, sharp/stiff trk. *3* **37**
930 **CUIGIU 14** [9] 3-8-9 (63) F Lynch 25/1: -05420: Cl-up, led over 2f out till over 1f out, fdd: 12th. *hd* **45**
701 **YOURE SPECIAL 37** [21] 3-9-7 (75) M Tebbutt 20/1: 02-100: In tch wide, btn 3f out: 13th: btr 319. *shd* **57**
841 **DOVES DOMINION 22** [8] 3-8-3 (56)(1ow) S Drowne 20/1: 000-50: In tch, outpcd fnl 3f: 14th: see 841 (7f). *½* **38**
887 **GLEN VALE WALK 17** [22] 3-8-6 (60) S Sanders 20/1: 003-00: Chsd ldrs 5f: 15th: see 887. *¾* **40**
827 **BEST EVER 24** [1] 3-8-2 (56) G Parkin 25/1: 000-00: Led 6f, sn btn: 16th: stablemate of 11th: rnr-up twice in '99 (rtd 66, nurs): eff at 7f/1m: acts on firm & gd grnd, sharp/gall trk. *½* **35**
*741 **Heathyards Mate 33** [23] 3-9-1 (69) P M Quinn (5) 25/1:
887 **Term Of Endearment 17** [5] 3-7-12 (52) G Bardwell 33/1:
807 **Alabama Wurley 29** [17] 3-8-9 (63) D McGaffin (6) 25/1
3272} **Rooftop Protest 262** [13] 3-9-0 (68) A Culhane 25/1:
4369} **Silk St Bridget 197** [4] 3-8-4 (58) M Baird 25/1:
4445} **Runin Circles 192** [10] 3-8-3 (57) T Lucas 25/1:
495 **Foxs Idea 79** [14] 3-9-5 (73) S Carson (5) 25/1:
3963} **Poker Polka 225** [7] 3-9-4 (72) J Tate 25/1:
24 ran Time 1m 45.77 (9.67) (The French Horn Hotel Ltd Sonning) M J Ryan Newmarket, Suffolk

1054 **5.05 REDMILE MDN 3YO+ (D) 1m2f60y Good/Soft 80 -38 Slow**
£4855 £1494 £747 £373 3 yo rec 17lb

-- **BLUE** [10] Mrs A J Perrett 4-9-10 Pat Eddery 7/4 FAV: 6622/1: 4 b c Bluebird - Watership (Foolish Pleasure) Handy, led over 4f out, styd on well ins last, rdn out: hvly bckd, op 11/4: long abs: missed last term: promise in '98 (rnr-up twice, rtd 86, mdn): eff at 1m, apprec step up to 10.3f, further shld suit: acts on fast & soft grnd, sharp/undul or gall trk: runs well fresh, gd weight carrier: op to further improvement. **88**
850 **FIRST OFFICER 19** [15] J R Fanshawe 3-8-7 R Cochrane 12/1: 02: 3 b c Lear Fan - Trampoli (Trempolino) Prom, chsd wnr fnl 3f, kept on, not pace to chall: left debut bhd: acts on gd/soft, going the right way. *1½* **85**
849} **EASY TO LOVE 382** [14] H R A Cecil 4-9-5 W Ryan 5/1: 5-3: 4 b f Diesis - La Sky (Law Society) Trkd ldrs, onepace fnl 2f: op 5/2, reapp: unplcd sole '99 start (mdn, debut, rtd 83): eff at 10f on fast & gd/soft. *1½* **78**
-- **LUXOR** [7] H R A Cecil 3-8-7 A McGlone 10/1: 4: Held up, keen, eff 3f out, kept on onepace: op 12/1, stablemate of 3rd: clr of rem: debut: stays gall 10.5f & handles gd/soft grnd. *1¾* **81**
843} **COURT OF JUSTICE 382** [8] 4-9-10 Dean McKeown 50/1: 0-5: Towards rear, mod late gains under hands & heels riding fnl 2f, no threat to ldrs: reapp: unplcd sole '99 start for P W Chapple Hyam (rtd 58): needs 12f+. *6* **73**
873 **ADAWAR 18** [1] 3-8-7 K Darley 9/1: 56: Unruly stalls, prom 1m: see 873. *¾* **71**
983 **UNDER THE SAND 9** [6] 3-8-7 P Robinson 50/1: 07: Held up, no room 4f out, sn outpcd: longer 10f trip. *1* **69**
840 **LOVE BITTEN 22** [2] 3-8-7 R Ffrench 33/1: 008: Led after 2f till 4f out, fdd: longer 10f trip. *½* **68**
-- **VICTORY ROLL** [9] 4-9-10 S Drowne 50/1: 9: Al rear: debut: with Miss E C Lavelle. *3½* **63**
-- **SCACHMATT** [5] 3-8-7 J P Spencer 33/1: 50: Chsd ldrs 7f: 10th: Brit debut, unplcd in a 7.5f mdn in Italy. *1* **61**
4605} **RAMPART 176** [16] 3-8-7 D Holland 5/1: 03-0: Chsd ldrs 7f: 11th: op 7/2, 6 month abs, plcd on 2nd of just 2 '99 starts (rtd 83, mdn): eff at 7f, bred to relish mid-dists: handles hvy grnd. *4* **55**

DONCASTER SATURDAY APRIL 29TH Lefthand, Flat, Galloping Track

WOODBASTWICK CHARM 19 [11] 3-8-7 G Bardwell 66/1: 0-00: Led 2f, btn 3f out: 15th: see 850. **0**
-- **Doctor John** [3] 3-8-7 C Lowther 50/1: -- **Cedar Grove** [12] 3-8-7 S Whitworth 14/1:
4495} **Salabue 187** [13] 3-8-7 G Carter 20/1:
15 ran   Time 2m 18.55 (12.15)   (K J Buchanan)   Mrs A J Perrett Pulborough, W Sussex

SANDOWN SATURDAY APRIL 29TH Righthand, Galloping Track, Stiff Finish.

Official Going HEAVY. Stalls: Inside.

1055 2.15 DAVID LLOYD HCAP 3YO 0-100 (C) 1m rnd Heavy 176 +00 Fast [105]
£14950 £4600 £2300 £1150

933 **PIPSSALIO 12** [2] Jamie Poulton 3-7-12 (75)(2ow)(12oh) F Norton 20/1: 000-21: 3 b c Pips Pride - Tesalia **82**
(Finissimo) Held up, rdn & plenty to do over 2f out, styd on well final 2f & squeezed thro' to lead on line despite
12oh: unplcd in 3 juv sprint starts: stays 8.3f well, further will suit: enjoys hvy & a stiff/easy trk: improving.
902 **EVEREST 16** [11] P F I Cole 3-8-5 (82) L Newman (5) 11/1: 2-232: 3 ch c Indian Ridge - Reine d'Beaute *shd* **88**
(Caerleon) Held up, hdwy 2f out, kept on despite slightly short of room over 1f out to chall inside last, just
tchd off: jockey rec a 1-day whip ban: op 9/1: another ½ plcd run & acts on firm & hvy: deserves a race.
999 **TUMBLEWEED TOR 7** [3] B J Meehan 3-8-6 (83) D R McCabe 33/1: 643-03: 3 b g Rudimentary - Hilly *shd* **89**
(Town Crier) Al prom, went on dist, kept on till collared nr line, just btn: stays a stiff 1m on gd/firm & hvy.
*912 **VINTAGE PREMIUM 15** [10] R A Fahey 3-9-3 (94) R Winston 5/2 FAV: 10-214: Led 2f, led again over 2f 1¼ **97**
out till dist, kept on same pace, not btn far: hvly bckd & another gd run on hvy, acts on gd/firm: see 912.
4197} **SMART RIDGE 210** [6] A Nicholls 3-9-7 (98) A Nicholls 33/1: 6110-5: Waited w, eff over 2f out, onepace fnl 1 **99**
1f: '99 Brighton (2, mdn & nursery h'cap) & Hamilton wnr (nursery h'cap, rtd 102 at best), with M Channon): eff at
5/6f, stays 1m: acts on firm, handles hvy & any trk: gd weight collect: tough & genuine, sharper for this.
4145} **KINGSDON 213** [7] Dane O'Neill 3-9-4 (95) Dane O'Neill 6/1: 1231-6: Prom, eff over 1f out, no extra ins last: ½ **95**
reapp: stays at Kempton (auct mdn) & Salisbury (nov stks, rtd 96): eff at 6/7f on fast, relishes soft, any trk.
4601} **FATHER JUNINHO 177** [1] J Fortune 11/1: 1012-7: Waited w, eff over 2f out, no impress: 1¾ **89**
'99 scorer at Redcar & Doncaster (nursery h'caps, rtd 92 at best): eff at 7f/8.3f on firm, gd/soft & on any trk.
912 **CHEMS TRUCE 15** [9] 3-8-13 (90) Martin Dwyer 13/2: 521-38: Cl-up, rdn & wknd over 1f out: btr 912. 2½ **83**
4272} **DARE HUNTER 205** [4] 3-8-11 (88) J Reid 20/1: -156-9: In tch, btn 2f out: juv scorer at Sandown 5 **73**
(mdn, debut, rtd 90): eff at 7f on firm/fast grnd.
*920 **SIR FERBET 14** [8] 3-8-10 (87) M Hills 6/1: 43-210: Led after 2f till hdd & wknd 2f out: 10th, btr 920 (aw). 13 **50**
*164 **TWICE BLESSED 141** [5] 3-7-10 (73)(1oh) M Henry 12/1: 0021-0: Prom, wknd qckly over 2f out: *dist* **0**
11th: abs, best 164 (mdn, equitrack).
11 ran   Time 1m 53.08 (14.08)   (Chris Steward)   Jamie Poulton Telscombe, East Sussex.

1056 4.10 GR 3 THRESHER CLASSIC TRIAL 3YO (A) 1m2f Heavy 176 -21 Slow
£36000 £13800 £6900 £3300

4215} **SAKHEE 210** [6] J L Dunlop 3-8-11 R Hills 11/4: -411-1: 3 b c Bahri - Thawakib (Sadler's Wells) **115**
Made all, qcknd over 2f out, kept on well for press ins last, gamely: well bckd on reapp: won fnl 2 of 3 juv
starts, at Nottingham (mdn) & Sandown (stks, rtd 102): dam smart 12f wnr: eff at 1m, relished step up to 10f
& further looks sure to suit: acts on fast, revels in hvy grnd & likes Sandown: likes to run up with/force
the pace: smart, genuine & improving, open to further improvement & well regarded.
*980 **PAWN BROKER 9** [2] D R C Elsworth 3-8-11 O Peslier 6/4 FAV: 61-12: 3 ch c Selkirk - Dime Bag 1 **113**
(High Line) Trkd wnr, eff to chall 2 out, hard rdn & no extra ins last, only btn 1L: clr of rem & ran to best
stepped up to Gr class: stays 10f on gd & hvy: see 980 (Listed).
*823 **GOING GLOBAL 24** [3] S P C Woods 3-8-11 J Reid 8/1: 31-13: 3 ch c Bob Back - Ukraine Girl 4 **107**
(Targowice) Cl-up, rdn over 2f out, onepace: gd run in better company, type to win races abroad: see 823.
4558} **WHITEFOOT 182** [1] G A Butler 3-8-6 L Dettori 12/1: 013-4: Waited w, eff over 2f out, no extra *nk* **101**
over 1f out: reapp, in '99 trained by J Pearce, scored at Sandown (fillies mdn) & plcd in List (rtd 100 at
best): eff at 1m, mid-dists should suit (dam 12f): acts on gd/soft, prob handles hvy: now with G Butler.
957 **ZAFONICS SONG 11** [5] 3-8-11 K Fallon 8/1: 4-35: Chsd ldr, hard rdn & btn 2f out: enjoy mdns. 3 **102**
864 **MONTE CARLO 20** [4] 3-8-11 Dane O'Neill 7/1: 311-06: In tch, effort over 2f out, sn btn: op 5/1. ½ **101**
6 ran   Time 2m 23.83 (19.73)   (Hamdan Al Maktoum)   J L Dunlop Arundel, West Sussex.

1057 4.45 GR 3 GORDON RICHARDS STKS 4YO+ (A) 1m2f Heavy 176 +11 Fast
£24000 £9200 £4600 £2200

4544} **LITTLE ROCK 183** [3] Sir Michael Stoute 4-8-10 K Fallon 5/2 FAV: 2401-1: 4 b c Warning - Much Too **113**
Risky (Bustino) Cl-up, styd on to lead over 1f out, drvn out to hold on ins last: hvly bckd, gd time on reapp:
in '99 won first & last, at Sandown (stks) & Newmarket (List, rtd 113): juv wnr at Leicester (mdn): v eff at 10f,
shld stay further: acts on fast, likes soft & hvy: runs well fresh on any trk, likes Sandown: smart & genuine.
967 **DIAMOND WHITE 10** [8] M J Ryan 5-8-12 J Reid 12/1: 11-012: 5 b m Robellino - Diamond Wedding ¾ **113**
(Diamond Shoal) Prom, eff 2f out, chall appr final 1f, sn no extra till kept on again cl-home, not btn far:
struck in face by rivals whip: back to best on favoured hvy grnd: most tough mare: see 967.
967 **BOMB ALASKA 10** [6] G B Balding 5-8-10 J F Egan 4/1: 21-443: 5 br g Polar Falcon - So True (So ½ **110**
Blessed) Keen, waited with, effort 2f out, styd on to chall final 1f, no extra cl-home, not btn far: nicely
bckd, smart, may improve again in a more strongly run race: see 967, 703.
3399} **COMMANDER COLLINS 259** [4] J H M Gosden 4-8-10 J Fortune 10/1: 1/04-4: Keen, waited with, eff 1¾ **108**
2f out, sn no impress till kept on again late: unplcd in 2 '99 starts for P Chapple Hyam (rtd 107): '98 wnr
at Newmarket (List) & Doncaster (Gr 1 Racing Post Trophy, rtd 115): eff at 1m, stays 10f & further shld suit:
acts on firm & hvy: runs well fresh: gd reapp, sharper for this & can win a Listed/Gr 3, prob over further.
10 **SOSSUS VLEI 175** [5] 4-8-10 M Roberts 10/1: /162-5: Keen, prom, hard rdn over 1f out, onepace: *nk* **107**
lightly rcd in '99, won at Bath (stks, rtd 110 when rnr-up in a Gr 3 in France): juv wnr at Newmarket (stks):
eff at 1m on firm & hvy: needs soft: v useful, enjoy a return to 1m?
4399} **GOLD ACADEMY 196** [2] 4-8-10 Dane O'Neill 6/1: 0134-6: Cl-up till wknd over 1f out: reapp: in fine 3½ **103**
'99 form, won at Chepstow (mdn) & York (List), also fine 3rd in a Gr 1 at Royal Ascot & 4th in Gr 1 Champion at
Newmarket (rtd 121$ & 114): eff at 1m/10f on firm, gd/soft & on any trk, likes gall ones: much better than this.
3399} **ALRASSAAM 259** [1] 4-8-13 L Dettori 10/3: 1612-7: Led over 1f out, wknd qckly & eased: reapp: 11 **94**

SANDOWN   SATURDAY APRIL 29TH   Righthand, Galloping Track, Stiff Finish.

'99 wnr at Newbury (mdn, reapp), Haydock (stks) & Chantilly (Gr 3, rtd 116 at best): stays 10f & acts on firm
& v soft grnd: v useful & progressive last term, much better than this.
1015 **KING PRIAM 5** [7] 5-8-10 (bl) D Harrison 50/1: 362008: Waited with, rdn & btn over 2f out: 13 76
out-classed, much better off in h'caps, see 967, 733.
8 ran   Time 2m 20.69 (16.59)   (J M Greetham)   Sir Michael Stoute Newmarket

---

1058   5.45 FLAT V JUMP JOCKS HCAP 4YO+ 0-80 (D)   1m rnd   Heavy 176 -11 Slow   [49]
£6779 £2086 £1043 £521

*942 **POLISH SPIRIT 12** [4] B R Millman 5-11-5 (68) T Quinn 9/4: 03-111: 5 b g Emarati - Gentle Star   82
(Comedy Star) Prom in the pack, smooth prog turning for home, led ent fnl 2f, shkn up, cmftbly: hvly bckd: earlier
won at Windsor (h'cap, crse rec) & Pontefract (class stks): '99 wnr again at Windsor (h'cap, rtd 63): '98 Warwick
wnr (mdn, rtd 65): eff at 1m, stays 10f on fast, hvy & any trk, likes Windsor: runs well fresh: improving.
*1007 **ROLLER 5** [12] J G Given 4-11-6 (69)(4ex) L Dettori 11/8 FAV: 5-3212: 4 b g Bluebird - Tight Spin   5 73
(High Top) Handy, outpcd 3f out, styd on to chase wnr appr fnl 1f, no impress: hvly bckd, qk reapp, clr rem.
817 **CAD ORO 26** [10] G B Balding 7-11-2 (65) A P McCoy 7/1: 200-03: 7 ch g Cadeaux Genereux - Palace   7 57
Street (Secreto) Towards rear, imprvd under press over 2f out, went 3rd inside last, nvr troubled ldrs: came out
best of those rdn by a jump jockey & prob not disgrcd against 2 imprvg sorts: likes soft & hvy: see 817.
4313} **TWIN TIME 201** [2] J S King 6-10-12 (61) N Williamson 16/1: 3500-4: Led chsg pack, prog 2f out,   3½ 47
sn rdn & no extra: reapp: '99 wnr at Bath (2, h'cap & fill h'cap, ddht, rtd 65 at best): '98 wnr again at Bath
(appr mdn h'cap, rtd 66): eff at 1m/10f on firm & gd/soft: runs well fresh, with/without t-strap: Bath specialist.
748 **FAMOUS 33** [13] 7-10-4 (53)(11oh) M Hills 25/1: 2-0005: Nvr troubled ldrs: stiffish task: see 90.   3 34
833 **JAVELIN 23** [1] 4-10-10 (59) J Fortune 25/1: 0-5406: Nvr better than mid-div: see 658.   3½ 34
786 **CHARTER FLIGHT 31** [3] 4-10-6 (55) K Fallon 16/1: -04007: Al bhd: see 383.   2 26
3743} **BIRTH OF THE BLUES 239** [11] 4-11-4 (67) R Johnson 20/1: 1000-8: Nvr in it: '99 Leicester wnr (h'cap,   ½ 37
rtd 69): unplcd in 3 '98 starts (rtd 67): eff at 1m, tried 12f: acts on soft/hvy, stiff trk: sharper next time.
842 **CONSULTANT 22** [7] 4-10-4 (53)(1oh) C Llewellyn 20/1: 320029: Led till ent fnl 2f, sn lost   2 19
place: op 14/1 on turf return, prob went off too fast, see 842, 175.
923 **PERUVIAN STAR 14** [6] 4-10-9 (58) J Reid 40/1: 0-0500: Rcd in 2nd till 2f out, sn wknd: 10th, lngr trip.   1¼ 22
4225} **STEP ON DEGAS 208** [5] 7-10-4 (53) A Maguire 33/1: 2200-0: Al towards rear: reapp: plcd in '99   21 0
(h'caps, rtd 56 & 55a): '98 Brighton wnr (h'cap, rtd 62 at best): eff at 6/7f, stays a sharp 1m: acts
on firm, gd/soft grnd, both AWs: can go well fresh: with Mrs King.
895 **PROSPECTORS COVE 16** [9] 7-11-7 (70) M A Fitzgerald 12/1: -30000: Al bhd: 12th: top weight, see 618. nk 3
12 ran   Time 1m 53.98 (14.98)   (Mrs Izabel Palmer)   B R Millman Kentisbeare, Devon.

WARWICK   MONDAY MAY 1ST   Lefthand, Sharp, Turning Track

Official Going   SOFT. Stalls: Inside, Except 7f 164yds - Outside.

1059   2.05 PRIMROSE FILLIES MDN 2YO (D)   5f rnd   Soft Inapplicable
£3556 £1094 £547 £273   Flag start, raced centre - stands side fnl 2f

-- **PARTY CHARMER** [4] C E Brittain 2-8-11 G Hall 100/30: 1: 2 b f Charmer - Party Game (Red Alert)   79
Chsd ldrs, prog/led over 1f out, styd on well despite wandering ins last, rdn out: op 9/4: Apr foal, sister to
tough sprint h'capper Passion For Life: dam a 6f 3yo wnr: eff over a sharp/turning 5f, shld get further: acts
on soft grnd & runs well fresh: ran gree, open to further improvement.
-- **CHURCH MICE** [1] M L W Bell 2-8-11 M Fenton 3/1 FAV: 2: 2 br f Petardia - Negria (Al Hareb):   5 69
Cl-up, led 2f out, rdn/hdd over 1f out & sn held: well clr of rem: Feb foal, cost 17,500 gns: sire smart 2yo,
subs high class at 1m: handles soft grnd & 6f+ should suit in time: ran green, improve.
-- **GENERAL JANE** [3] R Hannon 2-8-11 Dane O'Neill 7/2: 3: 2 ch f Be My Chief - Brave Advance (Bold   11 53
Laddie) Prom 4f: op 9/4: Apr foal, cost 3,700 gns: half-sister to formerly useful sprinter Venture Capitalist.
-- **DEGREE OF POWER** [5] A W Carroll 2-8-11 M Tebbutt 20/1: 4: Chsd ldrs, hmpd/outpcd 2f out, held   ½ 52
after: op 12/1: Sure Blade filly, Mar foal, half-sister to a 5f juv wnr: dam a 6f wnr, sire top class at 1m.
-- **JEWELLERY BOX** [6] 2-8-11 L Newman (5) 25/1: 5: Rdn/towards rear, wide over 2f out, sn held: nk 51
Kings Signet filly, May first foal, cost 5,000 gns: dam a NH mdn: sire a useful sprinter: with W G M Turner.
932 **FOREST MOON 14** [7] 2-8-11 J Fortune 5/1: 66: Led halfway, sn hdd & btn: see 932.   ¾ 50
836 **DRIPPING IN GOLD 24** [2] 2-8-11 S Carson (5) 14/1: 37: Led till halfway, sn btn: op 12/1: btr 836.   2½ 45
-- **PRINCESS PENNY** [8] 2-8-11 A Daly 16/1: R: Unruly bef start, whipped rnd start & refused to race: 0
op 14/1, stablemate of 5th: Kings Signet filly, dam a modest mdn: sire a useful sprinter.
8 ran   Time 1m 03.90   (Michael Clarke)   C E Brittain Newmarket, Suffolk.

1060   2.35 BATCHELOR CLASSIFIED STKS 3YO+ 0-80 (D)   6f168y rnd   Soft Inapplicable
£3768 £1159 £579 £289   3 yo rec 12lb   Raced centre - stands side fnl 2f

1011 **REDOUBTABLE 7** [5] D W Chapman 9-9-8 A Culhane 7/1: 143201: 9 b h Grey Dawn II - Seattle Rockette   80
(Seattle Slew): Dictated in front, styd on well when prsd final 2f, drvn out: op 6/1: earlier scored on sand
at Southwell & Lingfield (both h'cap, rtd 84a): '99 Thirsk wnr (h'cap, rtd 81): '98 Lingfield, Ayr & Newcastle wnr (h'caps,
rtd 79 & 78a): suited by 6/7f, stays a sharp 1m: acts on firm, soft & both AWs: tried blnks: likes a sharp one.
992 **CRISS CROSS 9** [2] R Hannon 3-8-7 Dane O'Neill 4/1: 6-222: 3 b c Lahib - La Belle Katherine (Lyphard)   ¾ 75
Trkd wnr, effort over 1f out, kept on for press, al just held: acts on soft/hvy: can find a race: see 884 (mdn).
1011 **SUSANS PRIDE 7** [4] B J Meehan 4-9-8 M Tebbutt 4/1: -41003: 4 b g Pips Pride - Piney Pass (Persian   1½ 76
Bold): Chsd ldrs, efft over 1f out, kept on, not able to chall: op 11/2: back to form here: see 780 (h'cap, fast).
4408} **RAVISHING 196** [6] W J Haggas 3-8-4 W Supple 11/4 FAV: 1-4: Keen in tch, onepace over 1f out: op   nk 69
2/1, 7 mth abs: sole start wnr last term at Pontefract (auct mdn, rtd 85): eff at 6f, this lngr 7f trip will suit, could
get further: acts on gd & soft grnd & likes a stiff/undul trk: has run well fresh.
2742} **COOL TEMPER 290** [3] 4-9-5 J Tate 6/1: 2222-5: Held up racing keenly, effort 2f out, not able to chall: ¾ 71
reapp: rnr-up all 6 starts last term (rtd 87, mdn, J Banks): eff at 6f on firm & any trk: eff in a t-strap.
905 **THE DOWNTOWN FOX 17** [1] 5-9-5 (bl) J Fortune 13/2: -10006: In tch, outpcd over 2f out: see 320.   5 64
6 ran   Time 1m 28.80   (David W Chapman)   D W Chapman Stillington, Nth Yorks.

1061

3.10 POLO CLUB HCAP 3YO 0-80 (D)   6f168y rnd   Soft   Inapplicable   [86]
£4277   £1316   £658   £329 Raced across track fnl 2f

994   **INFOTEC** 9 [4] H Akbary 3-9-0 (72) J Stack 12/1: 022-01: 3 b c Shalford - Tomona (Linacre):   79
Sn trkd ldr trav well, rdn/led 1f out, styd on well, drvn out: op 16/1: rnr-up twice in '99 (rtd 76, mdn): apprec
return to 7f: acts on gd/soft & soft grnd, handles a stiff/gall trk: open to improvement.

852   **BLACKPOOL MAMMAS** 21 [2] J M Bradley 3-8-7 (65) Claire Bryan (5) 14/1: 4-0102: 3 b f Merdon Melody 1¼   69
- Woodland Steps (Bold Owl) Led till 1f out, kept on: op 12/1: another gd run here at Warwick: see 813 (stks).

731   **IN THE ARENA** 37 [15] B W Hills 3-9-2 (74) J Weaver 7/4 FAV: 00-43: 3 ch c Cadeaux Genereux - Tajfah 3½   73
(Shadeed) Restrained rear, prog final 2f, nvr nrr to chall: hvly bckd: looks sure to do better with a positive ride.

4306} **BISHOPSTONE MAN** 203 [1] S Mellor 3-8-10 (68) A Daly 25/1: 0030-4: Slowly away & bhd, styd on well   1   66+
fnl 2f, nrst fin: clr rem: op 16/1: 7 mth abs: plcd in '99 (mdn, rtd 71): eff at 6/7f, further looks sure to
suit: handles soft grnd: made up some good late ground & one to keep tabs on over further.

4376} **NEVER DISS MISS** 199 [7] 3-9-1 (73) D McGaffin 20/1: 0300-5: Mid-div, late gains, no threat: op   5   64
14/1, 7 mth abs: '99 Sandown scorer (med auct mdn, R Williams, rtd 84): eff at 5f, 7f/1m shld suit: acts on soft.

852   **KINSMAN** 21 [5] 3-8-7 (65) M Fenton 20/1: 5-3006: Prom 6f, no extra: see 534 (AW).   ¾   55

4207} **PAYS DAMOUR** 212 [9] 3-9-1 (73) Dane O'Neill 25/1: 5610-7: Chsd ldrs 6f: op 10/1, 7 mth abs: ½   62
'99 Epsom scorer (4 rnr nursery, rtd 76): eff over a sharp/undul 6f, 7f should suit: acts on fast grnd.

884   **UP THE KYBER** 19 [13] 3-9-4 (76) J Fortune 8/1: 00-38: Prom 5f: h'cap bow: btr 884 (7mth, 7,8f).   2½   61

875   **BOANERGES** 20 [3] 3-9-7 (79) G Hind 33/1: 432-09: Mid-div at best: plcd twice in '99 (rtd 83, first time   9   54
visor, mdn, J Noseda): eff at 6/7f, bred to apprec further: handles soft grnd, sharp/stiff trk.

900   **GDANSK** 18 [14] 3-8-11 (69) J Carroll 25/1: 055-40: Mid-div, btn 2f out: 10th: h'cap bow: see 900.   nk   43

3652} **THORNCLIFF FOX** 246 [19] 3-9-5 (77) W Supple 33/1: 0330-0: Mid-div, btn 2f out: 11th: 8 mth abs: 2½   47
plcd twice in '99 (rtd 74a & 77, auct mdns): eff at 5f: handles gd/soft grnd & fibresand: has run well in blnks.

*888   **FOOTPRINTS** 19 [11] 3-9-4 (76) J Fanning 11/2: 021-10: Prom, struggling halfway: 19th: btr 888 (6f).   0

4600} Wilfram 179 [12] 3-8-10 (68) Darren Williams (7) 50/1: 4557} **Regardez Moi** 184 [6] 3-8-6 (64) C Rutter 25/1:
894   Doctor Dennis 18 [10] 3-8-9 (67)(bl) M Tebbutt 25/1: 773   Frampant 33 [8] 3-8-9 (67) R Winston 12/1:
4404} Caldey Island 196 [18] 3-8-1 (69) L Newman (5) 33/1:857   The Prosecutor 21 [16] 3-8-7 (65) P Mundy (7) 20/1:
188   La Tortuga 138 [20] 3-9-3 (75) D Griffiths 33/1:   888   Castlebar 19 [17] 3-9-8 (67) J Tate 25/1:
20 ran   Time 1m 28.40   (Michael C Whatley)   H Akbary Newmarket, Suffolk.

1062

3.40 LEAMINGTON FILL MDN DIV 1 3YO+ (D)   7f164y rnd   Soft   Inapplicable
£2913   £896   £448   £224   3 yo rec 13lb Raced centre -stands side fnl 2f

4555} **SERRA NEGRA** 184 [8] W J Haggas 3-8-8 J Fortune 4/1: 0-1: 3 b f Kris - Congress (Dancing Brave):   80
Mid-div, rdn/prog to lead over 1f out, styd on well inside last, rdn out: op 5/1, 6 mth abs: unplcd sole '99 start
(rtd 71, mdn): eff over a sharp/turning 1m, 10f sure to suit: acts on soft grnd & runs well fresh: can rate higher.

962   **SPELLBINDER** 13 [9] G B Balding 4-9-7 S Carson (5) 11/1: 0-32: 4 b f Magical Wonder - Shamanka   2½   75
(Shernazar): Rear/in tch, rdn & styd on well final 2f, not pace of wnr: op 6/1: styd lngr 7,8f trip, should get
further: acts on soft grnd: h'cap company will suit: see 962.

1010   **PENNYS PRIDE** 7 [4] Mrs M Reveley 5-9-7 A Culhane 3/1 FAV: 3023: 5 b m Pips Pride - Mursuma (Rarity)2½   71
Keen, trkd ldrs going well halfway, effort final 2f, onepace: see 1010, 759.

934   **LULLABY** 14 [5] J R Fanshawe 3-8-8 O Urbina 4/1: 0-34: Hndy, chllr over 1f out, no extra: op 5/2: btr 934.   3   67

--   **SATEEN** [1] 3-8-8 G Sparkes (7) 10/1: 5: Dwelt, held up in tch, onepace/held final 2f, rdn 5/1, debut: 3   63
half-sister to a 12f wnr: looks sure to apprec 1m+ in time, not knocked about here for L M Cumani, improve.

920   **SALVA** 16 [7] 4-9-7 J Weaver 12/1: 30-46: In tch rear, mod late gains, no threat: op 6/1: see 920.   2   60

909   **BRANSTON FIZZ** 17 [3] 3-8-8 J Fanning 5/1: 223-47: Cl-up, wknd over 1f out: op 11/4: btr 909 (6f).   ¾   59

915   **NUNKIE GIRL** 17 [6] 3-8-8 Dane O'Neill 25/1: 08: In tch, rdn halfway, sn struggling.   2   56

962   **BEACH BABY** 13 [2] 3-8-8 S Clancy (5) 100/1: -00009: Led till over 1f out, wknd qckly: mod form.   ½   55

313   **FOX STAR** 110 [10] 3-8-8 (bl) A Daly 50/1: 600-60: In tch wide, wknd 2f out, t.o: 10th: 4 mth abs.   14   39
10 ran   Time 1m 44.40   (Cyril Humphrics)   W J Haggas Newmarket, Suffolk.

1063

4.10 LEAMINGTON FILL MDN DIV 2 3YO+ (D)   7f164y rnd   Soft   Inapplicable
£2913   £896   £448   £224   3 yo rec 13lb Raced centre - stands side fnl 2f

877   **KANAKA CREEK** 20 [10] A Berry 3-8-8 J Carroll 7/2: 235-21: 3 ch f Thunder Gulch - Book Collector   73
(Irish River): Held up in tch, rdn to chall over 1f out, led inside last, styd on well, drvn out: op 5/1: plcd 4
times in '99 (mdns & h'cap, rtd 76 at best, J Berry): eff at 6f/1m on fast & hvy grnd, any trk: deserved this.

2287} **DANAMALA** 308 [5] R Hannon 4-9-7 Dane O'Neill 12/1: 0330-2: 4 b f Danehill - Carmelized (Key To The   1   71
Mint): Prom, led over 4f out, rdn/hdd inside last, kept on well: op 7/1: 10 mth abs: plcd twice in '99 (rtd
76, mdn): eff arnd 7f, 1m+ could suit: handles fast & soft grnd, sharp or stiff/gall trk.

915   **POLAR DIAMOND** 17 [1] M Morrison 3-8-10(2ow) D Griffiths 40/1: 03: 3 b f Polar Falcon - Bold Gem   2   70
(Never So Bold): Prom, kept on onepace for press final 2f: op 25/1: eff at 7,8f, could get further: acts on soft.

915   **TWIN LOGIC** 17 [8] J H M Gosden 3-8-8 J Fortune 15/8 FAV: 50-04: Prom, outpcd over 2f out, kept on   1¼   66
inside last, no threat: more expected after promising Newbury intro: ahead of todays 3rd in 915.

980   **SHADY POINT** 11 [9] 3-8-8 G Hall 9/1: 03-05: In tch, rdn/lost place halfway, kept on final 2f, not   nk   65
able to chall: op 8/1: plcd in '99 (rtd 77, mdn): eff arnd 7f, 1m+ should suit: prob handles firm & soft.

3834} **GABIDIA** 236 [2] 3-8-8 M Tebbutt 5/1: 3-6: Held up in tch, btn over 1f out: op 3/1, 8 mth abs: plcd   3   61
sole '99 start (rtd 81, stks): eff at 7f, should apprec 1m+: handles firm grnd.

840   **TARSHEEH** 24 [4] 3-8-8 W Supple 6/1: 07: Held up in tch, effort 3f out, sn btn: op 9/2: see 840.   5   54

--   **SILVER SPOON** [6] 3-8-8 A Rawlinson 12/1: 8: Keen/prom, btn 2f out: op 14/1, debut: dam styd   6   46
12f, should apprec further in time for R Guest.

808   **CAROLES DOVE** 30 [3] 4-9-7 N Carlisle 40/1: 0-09: Led 3f, sn btn: mod form, lngr 7,8f trip.   8   37
9 ran   Time 1m 46.20   (Mrs John Magnier)   A Berry Cockerham, Lancs.

1064 **4.45 R HACKETT HCAP 3YO 0-80 (D) 1m4f56y Soft Inapplicable [87]**
£4048 £1245 £622 £311 Raced towards centre fnl 2f

*832 **POMPEII 25** [1] P F I Cole 3-9-7 (80) J Fortune 7/4 FAV: 20-211: 3 b c Salse - Before Dawn (Raise A Cup): Led/dsptd lead thro'out, strongly prsd final 2f & styd on gamely to narrowly prevail, all-out: nicely bckd: earlier scored at Leicester (mdn, easily): plcd in '99 (rtd 79, earlier with P W Chapple Hyam): eff arnd 12f, could get further: acts on fast & soft grnd, stiff/gall or sharp trk: showed plenty of resolution here. **81**
850 **GUARD DUTY 21** [11] M P Tregoning 3-9-6 (79) A Daly 6/1: 33-62: 3 b g Deploy - Hymne d'Amour (Dixieland Band): Rear/in tch, prog to chall/narrow lead over 2f out, kept on, just held: op 4/1, stays 12f. *hd* **80**
850 **SKYE BLUE 21** [5] M R Channon 3-8-11 (70) M Fenton 10/1: 50-53: 3 b g Blues Traveller - Hitopah (Bustino): Keen, held up in tch, prog/trkd ldrs over 2f out, rdn & kept on inside last, not pace to chall: op 16/1, h'cap bow: styd lngr 12f trip well: handles gd & soft grnd: should find a race, poss over further: see 850. *1* **70**
833 **FAYRWAY RHYTHM 25** [2] M A Jarvis 3-9-6 (79) M Tebbutt 11/1: 244-44: Trkd ldrs, rdn/ch final 2f, kept on well for press: well clr rem, not btn far: op 7/1: styd lngr 12f trip well: see 833. *hd* **79**
892 **BROKENBOROUGH 18** [4] 3-7-13 (58) Dale Gibson 33/1: 060-05: Led 2f, lost place halfway, no impress after: unplcd in '99 (rtd 68, mdn): lngr 12f trip today. *8* **50**
4477} **NAJJM 192** [6] 3-9-6 (79) W Supple 7/1: 2233-6: Dwelt, rear/in tch, effort halfway, btn 3f out: op 6/1, 6 mth abs: plcd all 4 '99 starts (rtd 85, mdn): eff at 7f/1m, mid-dists should suit: handles firm & soft grnd. *6* **65**
827 **COSMIC BUZZ 26** [10] 3-8-5 (64) G Hind 25/1: 500-07: Prom 9f: '99 Salisbury wnr (clmr, rtd 77, unplcd on sand, rtd 28a): eff over a stiff/undul 7f, acts on gd/soft grnd: enjoys clmg grade. *14* **38**
3913} **RUSSIAN SILVER 230** [12] 3-8-13 (72) G Hall 20/1: 0340-8: Held up, effort 4f out, sn btn: 8 mth abs: plcd in '99 (rtd 71, fillies mdn): eff at 7f, bred to apprec this lngr 12f trip: handles firm & gd grnd. *nk* **46**
4114} **STORMDANCER 217** [3] 3-8-4 (63) L Newman (5) 20/1: 000-9: Sn rdn, al bhd: 7 mth abs, h'cap bow: unplcd from 3 starts at up to 10f last term (rtd 71): with R Hannon. *10* **27**
933 **TADREEJ 14** [7] 3-9-2 (75) C Rutter 20/1: 032-00: Mid-div, strugg 4f out: 10th: op 14/1, lngr 12f trip. *8* **31**
906 **SEA SQUIRT 17** [8] 3-9-5 (78) J Carroll 11/2: 22-230: Prom, wknd 4f out, t.o: 11th: btr 906, 720. *dist* **0**
11 ran Time 2m 52.40 (Highclere Thor'bred Racing Ltd) P F I Cole Whatcombe, Oxon.

1065 **5.15 KINGS HIGH HCAP 4YO+ 0-65 (F) 1m2f110y Soft Inapplicable [65]**
£2635 £753 £376 Raced across track fnl 2f

885 **DIABLO DANCER 19** [10] B R Millman 4-9-11 (62)(VIS) G Hind 8/1: 00-051: 4 b g Deploy - Scharade (Lombard): Prom & led halfway, clr over 2f out, held on gamely inside last, all-out: rnr-up in a mdn hdle this winter (rtd 99h): '99 rnr-up (h'cap, rtd 92): '98 Nottingham wnr (auct mdn) & Lingfield (nov, rtd 91): eff at 10/11.5f on firm & soft, any trk: has run well fresh: v well h'capped, suited by forcing tactics in hdgr today. **65**
1003 **ANNADAWI 7** [8] C N Kellett 5-8-5 (42) M Fenton 15/2: 546322: 5 b g Sadler's Wells - Prayers'n Promises (Foolish Pleasure): Chsd ldrs, rdn & styd on well final 2f, just held: threatening to win: see 1003. *hd* **44**
*889 **KINGFISHERS BONNET 19** [6] S G Knight 4-8-13 (50) L Newman (5) 10/1: 24-013: 4 b f Hamas - Mainmast (Bustino): Prom, rdn & kept on final 2f, not pace to chall: op 8/1: running well: see 889 (C/D). *1¼* **51**
890 **PIPS BRAVE 19** [18] M J Polglase 4-8-11 (48)(bl) J Weaver 7/1: -36024: Held up in tch, no room going well 3f out, swtchd & rdn/styd on final 1f, not pace to chall: op 5/1: on a handy mark: see 890, 473. *1¾* **47**
*1003 **PAS DE PROBLEME 7** [7] 4-9-11 (62)(6ex) Dale Gibson 10/1: 50-015: Held up, rdn & kept on final 3f, nrst at fin: op 8/1, 6lb pen for latest: ahead of todays rnr-up in 1003 (C/D). *hd* **60**
1050 **ROCK SCENE 2** [3] 8-8-7 (44) P Dobbs (5) 12/1: 00/206: Held up, prog 3f out, sn no threat: qck reapp. *2* **40**
890 **HATHNI KHOUND 19** [20] 4-8-11 (48) J Carroll 16/1: 200-67: Rear, rdn/mod late gains: btr 238 (C/D). *6* **38**
859 **CASHIKI 21** [1] 4-8-6 (43) Dane O'Neill 25/1: 000-68: Mid-div, lost place halfway, no threat after. *nk* **33**
811 **AHOUOD 30** [17] 4-8-11 (48) J Tate 20/1: 422569: Led 2f, btn/eased final 1f: btr 446 (mdn, AW). *2½* **36**
809 **MASTER BEVELED 30** [11] 10-10-0 (65)(bl) J Fortune 14/1: 6/0-30: Held up, effort 4f out, sn held: 10th: op 10/1, jumps fit (unplaced): see 809. *½* **52**
890 **DINAR 19** [19] 5-8-4 (41) A Daly 13/2 FAV: 200-30: Held up, keen, efft 4f out, btn 2f out: 11th: op 5/1. *1½* **27**
*890 **GABLESEA 19** [16] 6-9-2 (53) A Culhane 8/1: 024610: Rear, effort 2f out, no impress: 12th: op 5/1. *1¾* **37**
890 **KATIE KOMAITE 19** [5] 7-8-2 (39)(vis) C Rutter 11/1: 010-40: Dwelt & al rear, 13th: op 8/1: btr 890. *½* **22**
1038 **CHAMPAGNE GB 3** [2] 4-9-8 (59)(bl) M Henry 9/1: -05030: Led after 2f till 6f out, btn/hmpd 2f out & eased: 17th: qck reapp, op 12/1: see 1038, 516. **0**
750 **Noble Investment 34** [14] 6-8-9 (46) S Carson (5) 16/1: 775 **Inkwell 33** [15] 6-8-3 (40)(bl) J Fanning 20/1:
3639} **Browns Flight 246** [12] 4-8-11 (48) J Stack 25/1: 748 **Landican Lane 35** [9] 4-8-2 (39)(bl) A McCarthy (3) 40/1:
4602} **Game Tufty 179** [13] 4-9-12 (63) R Winston 25/1:
19 ran Time 2m 25.50 (Kentisbeare Quartet) B R Millman Kentisbeare, Devon.

1066 **5.45 LEVY BOARD APPR HCAP 3YO+ 0-60 (G) 7f164y rnd Soft Inapplicable [60]**
£1911 £546 £273 3 yo rec 13lb Raced across track fnl 2f.

4331} **PICCOLO CATIVO 202** [16] Mrs G S Rees 5-8-11 (43) Angela Hartley (3) 12/1: 4500-1: 5 b m Komaite - Malcesine (Auction Ring): Mid-div, rdn/prog to lead over 1f out, clear inside last, styd on well, pushed out cl-home: op 10/1: 7 mth abs: '99 reapp wnr at Catterick (appr class stks, rtd 64): '98 Hamilton (appr) & Carlisle wnr (h'caps, rtd 65): eff at 5/7.8f on gd, relishes soft grnd, handles fibresand: handles any trk: runs esp well fresh. **49**
1007 **LANDING CRAFT 7** [8] D Carroll 6-9-8 (54) K Dalgleish (3) 9/2: 4-0032: 6 ch g Zilzal - Dockage (Riverman): Rear, prog/chsd wnr over 1f out, kept on tho' al held: op 6/1, cl rem: eff arnd 7f/9f: see 1007. *2* **56**
973 **LEOFRIC 12** [6] M J Polglase 5-8-12 (44)(bl) Hayley Turner (7) 12/1: -35033: 5 b g Alhijaz - Wandering Stranger (Petong): Rear, swished & styd on well inside final 2f, nrst fin: op 10/1: see 973, 693. *5* **39**
218 **KUWAIT ROSE 132** [10] K Mahdi 4-10-0 (60) R Cody Boutcher 6/1: 3626-4: Led till over 1f out, no extra: op 10/1, 4 mth abs: see 73 (mdn). *¾* **54**
4581} **WARRING 182** [13] 6-9-4 (50) D Glennon (5) 25/1: 0540-5: Mid-div, onepace final 2f: 3 mth jumps abs (mod form): rnr-up twice in '99 (rtd 54, h'cap): '98 Windsor wnr (2, h'caps, rtd 61): eff arnd 1m on firm & gd/soft, has tried a t-strap: on a fair mark, sharper at Windsor. *¾* **43**
867 **GUEST ENVOY 20** [12] 5-9-3 (49) J Mackay (5) 7/2 FAV: 441126: Held up, kept on final 2f, no threat. *nk* **41**
*958 **MUDDY WATER 13** [2] 4-10-0 (60) R Naylor (5) 10/1: 62-017: Rear, kept on final 2f, no threat: op 8/1. *2* **49**
*896 **DANZAS 18** [19] 6-8-12 (44)(bl) Joanna Badger 10/1: 460618: Mid-div at best: op 7/1: see 896 (g/s). *½* **32**
942 **NAKED OAT 14** [9] 5-8-13 (45) J Bosley 12/1: 000009: Rear, mod gains final 2f: op 16/1: see 329 (AW). *hd* **32**
691 **ANNIE APPLE 44** [5] 4-9-6 (52) M Worrell (5) 20/1: 00-000: Chsd ldrs 6f: 10th: 6 wk abs: see 594 (AW). *1¼* **37**
96 **MYTTONS MISTAKE 160** [7] 7-9-3 (49) D Meah (5) 20/1: 5000-0: Trkd ldrs halfway when slightly hmpd, *½* **33**

onepace final 2f: 11th: 5 mth abs: '99 Brighton wnr (sell, rtd 53, unplcd on sand, rtd 43a): '98 Bath & Kempton wnr (h'caps, rtd 71): eff at 6/7f, stays 1m: acts on firm & gd/soft, both AWs: best without blnks & nay trk.

584	**Paarl Rock 66** [20] 5-8-13 (45) P Hanagan 25/1:			958	**Toblersong 13** [18] 5-9-6 (52)(t) Kristin Stubbs (5) 12/1:
336	**Caversfield 107** [1] 5-9-7 (53) D Watson (5) 20/1:			896	**Ones Enough 18** [4] 4-9-6 (52) S Clancy (3) 16/1:
787	**D W Mccee 33** [11] 4-9-1 (47) D Kinsella (5) 33/1:			65	**Lament 166** [14] 4-9-12 (58) M Pattinson (7) 20/1:
503	**Reachforyourpocket 79** [3] 5-8-13 (45) G Baker (3) 14/1:
647	**Kustom Kit Kevin 56** [17] 4-9-7 (53) N Mitchell (7) 20/1:

19 ran   Time 1m 43.20   (J W Gittins)   Mrs G S Rees Sollom, Lancs.

Official Going   GOOD/SOFT (GOOD places). Stalls: Str Crse - Stands Side; Rnd Crse - Ins, except Round 1m - Outside.

1067   1.50 WISETON NOV AUCT STKS 2YO (E)   5f str   Good/Soft 60   -14 Slow
£3396   £1045   £522   £261   Runners raced stands side

-- **DREAMS DESIRE** [5] J A Glover 2-7-12 D Mernagh (3) 7/1: -1: 2 b f Mind Games - Champenoise   **82+**
(Forzano) Nvr far away, led dist, styd on strongly under hands-&-heels riding: gamble from 14/1: 8,000gns Feb
foal: half-sister to sprint winning 2yo Bebe De Champ: dam scored over 1m: eff at 5f on gd/soft grnd, 6f will
suit: handles a gall trk, runs well fresh: op to plenty of improvement, shld rate more highly & win more races.

989 **FRANICA 9** [7] A Bailey 2-7-12 A Mackay 3/1 FAV: -2222: 2 b f Inzar - Comfrey Glen (Glenstal)   1   **78**
Tried to make all, collared dist, kept on but no ch with nearly wnr: nicely bckd: rnr-up on all 4 starts & sorely
due a change of luck: acts on gd/soft & hvy grnd: see 989, 812.

932 **TIMES SQUARE 14** [13] G C H Chung 2-8-4(1ow) Dean McKeown 9/1: -43: 2 b c Timeless Times -   1   **81**
Alaskan Princess (Prince Rupert) Prom, kept on fnl 1f, not pace to chall: attractive, eff at 5f on gd/soft, 6f will suit.

-- **GOLDEN WHISPER** [14] I A Balding 2-7-12 A Nicholls (3) 25/1: -4: Dwelt, recovered & sn in tch, kept   2   **69**
on fnl 1f: ndd this debut: Mar foal, cost IR 2,000gns: dam a 7/9f Irish wnr, sire a top-class miler: eff at
5f on gd/soft grnd, 6f will suit: tall filly who will learn from this & looks sure to improve.

-- **TRAVELLING BAND** [9] 2-8-7(1ow) K Fallon 8/1: -5: Slowly away & outpcd, fin v strongly fnl 1f, nvr   nk   **77+**
nrr: ndd this debut, shorter priced stablemate of 4th: 11,000gns purchase: Apr foal, half-brother to a mid-dists
wnr in France: scopey, ndd race: bred to apprec 6/7f+: most eye-catching, sure to improve & relish further.

-- **MISS VERITY** [4] 2-7-13(1ow) P Fessey 33/1: -6: Mid-div, late hdwy, nvr dngrs on debut: better   ¾   **66**
for race: cheaply bght Apr foal: dam a dual sprint wnr: with J Wainwright & sure to learn from this.

904 **DIVINE WIND 17** [10] 2-8-3 G Duffield 9/2: -147: Chsd ldrs till onepcd fnl 2f: swtg & boiled over   nk   **69**
in the prelimiaries: strong, scopey filly: see 904, 730 (C/D).

-- **CIRCUIT LIFE** [12] 2-8-3 G Carter 12/1: -8: Nvr btr than mid-div: ndd this debut: 9,000gns Mar   shd   **69**
foal: half-brother to 6f 2yo scorer: dam styd 1m: with A Berry, stocky gelding.

*865 **TICCATOO 20** [3] 2-8-1 P M Quinn (5) 12/1: -19: Trkd ldrs 3½f out, grad fdd: lkd well: see 865 (AW).   hd   **67**

-- **FALCON GOA** [11] 2-7-12 Kim Tinkler 33/1: -0: Nvr a factor in 10th on debut: ndd this.   4   **52**

700 **BOLD MCLAUGHLAN 39** [2] 2-8-12 A McGlone 16/1: -00: Prom 3f, fdd into 11th: see 700 (C/D).   ½   **65**

-- **TIRANA** [6] 2-8-12 J P Spencer 20/1: -0: Al bhd, fin 12th on debut.   6   **50**

-- **SON OF A PREACHER** [8] 2-8-6 O Pears 20/1: -0: Al rear, fin last: op 14/1.   shd   **44**

13 ran   Time m 01.91 (3.71)   (Sports Mania)   J A Glover Carburton, Notts.

1068   2.20 BAWTRY CLAIMER DIV 1 4YO+ (E)   6f str   Good/Soft 60   +09 Fast
£2535   £780   £390   £195   Runners raced stands side

680 **PRESS AHEAD 46** [8] S R Bowring 5-8-4 (VIS) Dean McKeown 20/1: -15501: 5 b g Precocious - By Line   **62**
(High Line) Broke well & made all, rdn clr fnl 1f despite drifting left: best time of day, 7 wk abs, first time visor:
prev trained by B McMahon to win at W'hampton (AW h'cap, rtd 57a): rnr-up in '99 (h'caps, rtd 51): '98 W'hampton
wnr (mdn auct, rtd 66a & 50): eff at 5/6f on gd/soft grnd & f/sand: handles a sharp or gall trk, likes W'hampton:
best up with or forcing the pace, runs well fresh: revitalised by change of stable & first time visor today.

881 **PALO BLANCO 19** [11] Andrew Reid 9-7-13 M Henry 10/1: 0-3342: 9 b h Kylian - Linpac Mapleleaf 2½   **51**
(Dominion) Prom, ev ch over 1f out, not pace of wnr ins last: gd effort back on turf: see 680 (AW seller).

941 **AGENT MULDER 14** [1] P D Cundell 6-9-2 (bl) D Holland 3/1 JT FAV: 00-233: 6 b g Kylian - Precious   1¾   **64**
Carloline (The Noble Player) Mid-div & eff halfway, kept on fnl 1f but not pace to chall: swtg, op 9/4, poor draw.

803 **SEVEN 31** [6] Miss S J Wilton 5-8-8 (bl) S Whitworth 20/1: 154004: Dwelt, recovered & in tch, not   1¼   **52**
pace of ldrs fnl 1f: mkt drifter: unplcd in a nov sell hdle since 803: see 414 (7f/AW).

1005 **JACKERIN 7** [9] 5-8-6 (bl) G Duffield 20/1: 00-655: Prom, onepcd fnl 1f: padd pick: best at 5f.   2½   **44**

691 **FRENCH GRIT 44** [7] 8-8-5(1ow) F Lynch 20/1: 060006: Rear, late hdwy, nvr nr to chall: 6 wk abs   shd   **43**
best held up for a late chall, hinted at a return to form here: see 166 (AW).

756 **TANCRED TIMES 34** [14] 5-7-13 Kimberley Hart (5) 25/1: -00037: Prom till fdd dist: lkd well.   1¾   **33**

1005 **BATALEUR 7** [2] 7-8-7(1ow) R Lappin 14/1: 1-6548: Chsd ldrs 3f, fdd over 1f out: qck reapp.   ¾   **38**

919 **SAMWAR 16** [4] 8-8-6 (vis) R Fitzpatrick (3) 14/1: 606329: Dwelt, nvr a factor: lost ch start today.   1   **34**

787 **ENCOUNTER 33** [13] 4-9-6 McGlone 10/1: 000-40: Nvr a factor in 10th: see 787.   1¾   **28**

787 **TRUMPET BLUES 33** [5] 4-8-4 O Pears 16/1: 6-0300: Chsd ldrs 4f, fdd into 11th: see 531 (7f, AW).   2½   **22**

4489} **ARIUS 190** [10] 4-9-10 G Bardwell 25/1: 2040-0: Slowly away, nvr a factor in 12th: top-weight: shd   **42**
fit from hdles, modest nov/h'cap form (rtd 68h at best): ex-French, dual wnr in native country in '99: eff at
1m/9f on soft & hvy grnd: with G Margarson & shld do better over 1m+.

4610} **ANSELLMAN 178** [3] 10-8-12 (bl) G Carter 11/1: 0300-0: Mid-div till btn 2f out: fin 13th, reapp: ¾   **27**
'99 Bath wnr (h'cap, rtd 75): '98 Redcar wnr (clmr, rtd 87 & 67 at best): '97 Ripon & Leicester wnr (clmr/h'cap,
rtd 88 & 83a): eff at 6f, just best at 5f: acts on any grnd & any trk: runs well fresh & best in blnks/visor.

824 **MALLIA 26** [12] 7-9-0 C Lowther 3/1 JT FAV: 164140: Al struggling, fin last: hvly bckd: something amiss?   1   **26**

14 ran   Time 1m 13.87 (3.07)   (Roland M Wheatley)   S R Bowring Edwinstowe, Notts.

1069   2.50 SPONSORSHIP COND STKS 3YO (C)   1m rnd   Good/Soft 60   -19 Slow
£6480   £2484   £1242   £594

4290} **SOBRIETY 205** [3] R F Johnson Houghton 3-8-12 J Reid 16/1: 124-1: 3 b c Namaqualand - Scanno's   **100**
Choice (Pennine Walk) Chsd ldrs, imprvd to lead dist, held on well fnl 1f, drvn out: reapp: lightly rcd juv,
Salisbury debut wnr (mdn auct, rtd 95 at best): half-brother to a 1m wnr: eff over a stiff 1m, 10f will suit:

acts on firm & gd/soft, runs well fresh: handles a gall trk: scopey & useful, worth a try in Listed company.
4102} **JALAD 218** [6] B Hanbury 3-9-1 (t) R Hills 6/1: -216-2: 3 b c Marju - Hamsaat (Sadler's Wells) *nk* **102**
Rcd keenly & prom, chall strongly fnl 1f, just btn in a driving fin: lkd well for reapp, op 9/2, 5L clr 3rd: '99 Leicester wnr (mdn), subs last of 6 at Ascot (Gr 2, rtd 102): eff over a stiff 1m, 10f will suit: acts on firm & gd/soft, handles soft: handles a gall trk, runs well fresh: wears a t-strap: useful colt, shld go one better.
765 **PARADISE GARDEN 37** [5] M Johnston 3-8-12 D Holland 9/1: 224-03: 3 b c Septieme Ciel - Water *5* **89**
Course (Irish River) Early ldr, remained prom & ev ch till outpcd by front 2 fnl 1f: lkd fit: '99 Newcastle wnr (nov auct), subs 2nd in List (rtd 100): eff at 1m, prob stays 10f: acts on gd & firm, handles soft: consistent.
955 **SHABLAM 13** [7] Sir Michael Stoute 3-9-3 K Fallon 4/5 FAV: 31-54: Outpcd, styd on fnl 1f, nvr nr ldrs: *nk* **93**
hvly bckd & rcd too keenly for own good in early stages: looks as tho' 10f will suit: most eye-catching in 955.
3919} **DECARCHY 229** [4] 3-9-1 W Ryan 9/2: 1-5: Led after 2f till dist, no extra: tchd 6/1, lkd fit for reapp: *hd* **91**
won at Yarmouth (mdn, rtd 90+) on sole juv start: half-brother to high-class 10f performer Chester House: dam scored over 9f: eff at 7f, bred to apprec 1m/10f: acts on gd/soft & runs well fresh: small colt.
4097} **VEIL OF AVALON 218** [2] 3-9-3 K Darley 14/1: 3116-6: Rear, outpcd halfway, rallied fnl 1f but no ch *1½* **90**
with ldrs: op 10/1, ndd this reapp: '99 wnr at Lingfield (mdn) & Newbury (stks), subs last of 6 in Gr 1 Fillies Mile (rtd 95): eff at 6/7f, shld stay 1m+: acts on gd & firm, prob handles gd/soft: can run well fresh.
*784 **AUCHONVILLERS 33** [1] 3-9-1 S Righton 33/1: 6-17: Dwelt, recovered & in tch racing keenly, short *2½* **83**
of room 3f out, no ch after: lkd fit, swtg & boiled over at the start: see 784 (mdn).
829 **SORBETT 25** [8] 3-9-3 J P Spencer 50/1: 1-68: Chsd ldrs 5f, sn btn: still better for race: see 829. *7* **71**
8 ran Time 1m 42.41 (6.31) (Anthony Pye-Jeary) R F Johnson Houghton Blewbury, Oxon.

1070 **3.25 PEGLER HCAP 3YO+ 0-90 (C) 1m2f60y Good/Soft 60 +06 Fast [86]**
£7345 £2260 £1130 £565

1015 **YAROB 7** [10] D Nicholls 7-9-10 (82) K Fallon 5/1: 5-0101: 7 ch g Unfuwain - Azyaa (Kris) **95**
Trkd ldrs till went on over 3f out, clr fnl 2f, kept on strongly under hands-&-heels riding: well bckd, gd time, jt top-weight: earlier scored at Pontefract (h'cap, made all): '99 Doncaster wnr (this h'cap, rtd 84): eff at 1m/11f, acts on firm, soft & f/sand: handles any trk, likes a stiff/gall one, esp Doncaster: best up with or forcing the pace & a gd weight carrier: must hold excellent chances under a penalty in the Thirsk Hunt Cup on Sat.
975 **MINDANAO 12** [5] Miss J A Camacho 4-9-10 (82) K Darley 9/2 FAV: 121-42: 4 b f Most Welcome - Salala *4* **87**
(Connaught) Mid-div, bmpd after 2f & lost pl, imprvd over 2f out, styd on well to take 2nd but no ch with wnr: nicely bckd, jt top-weight: not get the run of today's race: spot on next time, stable in gd form: see 975.
4574} **MCGILLYCUDDY REEKS 182** [6] Don Enrico Incisa 9-8-9 (67) Kim Tinkler 33/1: 0600-3: 9 b m Kefaah - *½* **71**
Kilvarnet (Furry Glen) Chsd ldrs, chsd wnr 2f out, kept on but caught for 2nd cl-home: ndd this reapp: '99 wnr at Beverley & here at Doncaster (h'caps, rtd 76): '98 wnr at Newcastle & Thirsk (h'caps, rtd 77): eff at 1m, suited by 10/12f: acts on firm & soft, handles any trk: eff with/without a t-strap: tough, on a wng mark.
*965 **ADMIRALS PLACE 13** [4] H J Collingridge 4-8-9 (67) G Carter 12/1: 122314: Mid-div, when hmpd after *1½* **69**
2f, styd on well fnl 2f, nrst fin: fair effort in the circumstances: see 965.
4475} **INTENSITY 192** [12] 4-9-6 (78) G Duffield 11/2: 5001-5: Rear, hmpd after 2f, hdwy halfway & in tch, *1* **78+**
onepcd fnl 2f: just better for reapp, tchd 9/1: '99 wnr at Newcastle (3 rnr mdn, reapp, with K Burke) & here at Doncaster (h'cap, rtd 79): eff at 9/10f, 12f may suit: acts on firm & soft grnd, handles a stiff/gall trk: lightly rcd gelding who did not get the run of today's race, spot on next time.
4264} **TYPHOON GINGER 208** [15] 5-8-3 (61) F Norton 14/1: 5243-6: Dwelt, styd on fnl 2f, nvr nr to chall: *6* **52+**
ndd this reapp: plcd sev times in '99 (h'caps, rtd 59 at best): plcd on a couple of '98 starts (h'cap, rtd 60): eff at 10f on firm & gd/soft grnd: can run well fresh: promising reapp & fitter next time.
1559} **COPPLESTONE 341** [9] 4-9-4 (76) D Holland 25/1: 43/4-7: Prom, grad fdd fnl 2f: reapp: 4th in a *2½* **64**
Folkestone h'cap (rtd 76) on sole '99 start: plcd in '98 (h'cap, rtd 80, first time visor): eff at 7f/1m, not stay 10f? handles gd, firm grnd & fibresand: has run well in a visor, not worn today.
*943 **WILTON 14** [11] 5-8-13 (71) Dean McKeown 10/1: -30118: Nvr better than mid-div: btr 943 (hvy). *½* **58**
986 **RAPIER 9** [2] 6-9-10 (82) J P Spencer 12/1: 010-49: Mid-div when hmpd & lost pl early on, rallied 4f *1* **67**
out, no impress fnl 2f: jt top-weight: this is best forgotten: see 986.
875 **ROYAL ARROW FR 20** [8] 4-9-7 (79) L Swift (7) 40/1: 000-00: Led till 3f out, fdd: fin 10th: lightly rcd *2½* **61**
& little form for F Murphy in '99: back in '98 won in native France at Deauville (List): eff at 6f on soft grnd.
975 **WUXI VENTURE 12** [3] 5-9-1 (73) A Nicholls (3) 16/1: 000000: Rear, late prog under a kind ride, nvr a *7* **45**
factor in 11th: longer priced stablemate of wnr: has slipped to a handy mark, primed for a return to form: see 601.
921 **LIGHT PROGRAMME 16** [14] 6-8-11 (69) R Perham 50/1: /00-00: Rear, prog to chase ldrs halfway, btn *1½* **39**
3f out: fin 12th: see 921 (sand).
1048} **LUCKY GITANO 368** [1] 4-9-9 (81) J Reid 11/1: 5/32-0: Nvr a factor in 13th: reapp. *1* **49**
4530} **ST HELENSFIELD 187** [7] 5-9-10 (82) R Hills 12/1: 3004-0: Dwelt, recovered to race mid-div, btn *1½* **48**
3f out: fin 14th, jt top-weight, reapp.
757 **DISPOL ROCK 34** [13] 4-9-0 (72) C Lowther 20/1: 160-00: Dwelt, brief effort halfway, sn btn: last. *9* **23**
15 ran Time 2m 11.90 (5.50) (Lucayan Stud) D Nicholls Sessay, N.Yorks.

1071 **3.55 JOE SIME HCAP 3YO 0-80 (D) 1m6f132y Good/Soft 60 -11 Slow [84]**
£4290 £1320 £660 £330

*937 **SAMSAAM 14** [5] J L Dunlop 3-9-3 (73) R Hills 4/5 FAV: 000-11: 3 b c Sadler's Wells - Azyaa (Kris) **81**
Mid-div, prog to chall going well appr final 2f, drvn to assert towards fin: hvly bckd: recent Windsor wnr (h'cap): promise in mdns in '99 (rtd 74): related to 7/10f wnr Yarob: imprvd since stepped up in trip, eff at 12/14.5f, shld get 2m: acts on gd/soft & hvy grnd & runs well fresh, sharp or gall trk: progressive, strong & lengthy colt.
937 **MERRYVALE MAN 14** [10] J G Given 3-8-12 (68) P Goode (3) 16/1: 312102: 3 b c Rudimentary - Salu *¾* **74**
(Ardross) Held up, gd prog to take narrow lead 2f out, hdd ins last, not btn far: 10L clr of 3rd, op 10/1: right back to form over longer trip, eff at 12f/14.5f: small, game colt, see 782.
420 **DOUBLE BANGER 93** [8] M Johnston 3-9-7 (77) D Holland 7/1: 341-33: 3 b c Ela Mana Mou - Penny *10* **69**
Banger (Pennine Walk) Waited with, rdn & hdwy 3f out, hmpd before 2f out, styd on but nvr nr ldrs: 3 mth abs & lkd backward, top-weight on h'cap bow: shld stay 14f+ & win similar: see 604 (10f AW mdn).
924 **SUNDAY RAIN 16** [1] P F I Cole 3-9-0 (70) K Fallon 6/1: 0-4224: Prom, ch 3f out, drifted left/no extra. *6* **53**
924 **RUNNING TIMES 16** [4] 3-8-6 (62)(BL) K Darley 12/1: 0-5035: Pulled hard, cl-up, led 4f out till 2½f *1* **43**
out, fdd: lkd well but raced too freely over lngr 14.5f trip in first time blnks: see 605.
*939 **OPEN GROUND 14** [9] 3-7-10 (52) A Nicholls(1) 16/1: 3-0016: Led after 6f till 4f out, gradually wknd. *16* **11**
4414} **TARA HALL 196** [6] 3-7-11 (53) T Williams 33/1: 0050-7: Handy till 4f out: bandaged & ndd this reapp: *14* **0**
unplcd over 1m last term, incl blnkd (with N Littmoden): bred for mid-dists: with W Brisbourne.
782 **CHIEF OF JUSTICE 33** [3] 3-8-13 (69) J P Spencer 12/1: 0-1138: Led till 1m out, wknd qckly 4f out. *4* **2**

36 **ROCK ON ROBIN 171** [7] 3-7-10 (52)(vis)(7oh) P M Quinn (5) 66/1: 6000-9: Prom till halfway: stiff task, reapp: failed to make the frame up to 10f as a juv (auct mdn, visored, rtd 53): not bred for long trips. *2½* **0**
827 **BLUE HAWAII 26** [2] 3-7-13 (55) F Norton 14/1: 000-20: Al bhd: 10th: lkd well, lngr trip, see 827 (10f). *14* **0**
10 ran Time 3m 13.40 (10.40) (Hamdan Al Maktoum) J L Dunlop Arundel, W Sussex

1072 **4.30 MAY DAY HOLIDAY MDN 3YO+ (D) 7f str Good/Soft 60 -21 Slow**
£4335 £1334 £667 £333 3yo rec 12lb Runners raced stands side

983 **PEACEFUL PROMISE 11** [4] E A L Dunlop 3-8-12 J Reid 11/10 FAV: 0-31: 3 b c Cadeaux Genereux - Island Wedding (Blushing Groom) Nvr far away, led 2f out, rdn out: hvly bckd: unplcd sole juv start (rtd 73): brother to a 1m/10f wnr, dam 7f/1m scorer: eff at 7f, shld get 1m: goes on gd/soft grnd, gall trks: strong colt. **86**
3646} **TAKE FLITE 246** [5] W R Muir 3-8-12 R Brisland (5) 5/1: 3034-2: 3 b c Cadeaux Genereux - Green Seed (Lead On Time) Pulled hard in tch, prog to go after wnr appr final 1f, kept on: tchd 6/1, fit: plcd last term (mdn, rtd 89): eff at 7f, bred to aprrec 1m+: goes on firm & gd/soft: shld find a minor trk maiden. *1¼* **82**
839 **BALI BATIK 24** [1] G Wragg 3-8-12 D Holland 8/1: 0-43: 3 b g Barathea - Miss Garuda (Persian Bold) Well plcd, chall 2f out, held towards fin: op 6/1, padd pick: imprvg, scopey gelding: see 839. *nk* **81**
-- **GINGKO** [14] J G Smyth Osbourne 3-8-12 R Perham 33/1: -4: Waited with, imprvd 3f out, onepcd dist: better for belated debut: dam 7f wnr: eff at 7f on gd/soft grnd. *2* **77**
972 **AMRITSAR 12** [7] 3-8-12 K Fallon 9/1: -05: Al arnd same place: lkd well: Indian Ridge colt. *1* **75**
909 **DAYLILY 17** [6] 3-8-7 G Parkin 100/1: -006: Led till 2f out, onepace: scopey: h'caps over further next. *nk* **69$**
804 **BURGUNDIAN RED 31** [15] 3-8-12 G Carter 20/1: 504-07: Nvr better than mid-div: op 12/1, needs h'caps. *4* **66**
983 **PRECIOUS LOVE 11** [10] 3-8-12 W Ryan 16/1: -08: Nvr trbld ldrs: bkwd, scopey colt. *¾* **64**
4473} **ON SHADE 192** [9] 3-8-7 G Duffield 100/1: 60-9: Pld hard, nvr a factor: ndd this reapp & now qual for h'caps: half-sister to sev wnrs, notably useful 1m/9f juv Andy Dufresne, dam 12f wnr: 1m+ going to suit. *3½* **52**
-- **PERCUSSION** [3] 3-8-12 S Whitworth 20/1: -0: Al rr: 10th, half-brother to useful stayer Orchestra Stall. *1¼* **54**
-- **SIMULCASTING** [2] 3-8-12 J P Spencer 20/1: -50: Swerved left & reign broke start, cl-up 5f: 11th. *1¼* **51**
826 **TOUGH TIMES 26** [13] 3-8-12 K Darley 20/1: -560: Al bhd: 12th, stablemate 6th, now qual for h'caps. *1* **49**
961 **Indiana Jones 13** [8] 3-8-12 F Lynch 20/1: 909 **Seahorse Boy 17** [11] 3-8-12 P Fessey 100/1:
2052} **Rimatara 318** [12] 4-9-10 T Lucas 50/1:
15 ran Time 1m 28.89 (5.69) (Maktoum Al Maktoum) E A L Dunlop Newmarket

1073 **5.00 BAWTRY CLAIMER DIV 2 4YO+ (E) 6f str Good/Soft 60 +01 Fast**
£2522 £776 £388 £194 Runners raced stands side

958 **MARENGO 13** [12] M J Polglase 6-8-6 K Darley 9/1: 622321: 6 b g Never So Bold - Born To Dance (Dancing Brave) Mid-div, prog over 2f out, led ins last, drifted left, styd on well, rdn out: lkd well: '99 wnr at Southwell, W'hampton, Epsom (h'caps, rtd 69a & 68) & Southwell again (J Akehurst, h'cap): eff at 6f, tried 7f: acts on firm, soft & f/sand: likes to race with/force the pace: likes Southwell: apprec drop to clmg grade. **60**
816 **RUSSIAN ROMEO 28** [3] B A McMahon 5-9-0 (bl) G Duffield 14/1: 552232: 5 b g Soviet Lad - Aotearoa (Flash Of Steel) Handy, drvn & ev ch over 1f out, kept on well, just held: lkd well: see 816, 40. *½* **66**
758 **FIRE DOME 34** [14] D Nicholls 8-9-4 K Fallon 8/11 FAV: 04-033: 8 ch g Salt Dome - Penny Habit (Habitat) Trkd ldrs, rdn to lead over 1f out till ins last, no extra: hvly bckd: stays 6f, prob just best at 5f. *1* **67**
622 **BEWARE 60** [10] D Nicholls 5-8-4 A Nicholls (3) 11/1: 366154: Prom, rdn & no room over 1f out, no extra inside last: op 6/1, 2 mth abs, lngr prcd stablemate of 3rd: see 559 (AW sell). *1¾* **48**
4034} **PLEASURE 223** [9] 5-8-9 (bl) Dean McKeown 25/1: 1500-5: Chsd ldrs, onepace over 1f out: lkd fit after 8 mth abs: '99 Beverley scorer (first time blnks, h'cap, rtd 61): '98 Doncaster wnr (appr h'cap, rtd 57): eff at 5/7f on gd & soft, likes a stiff/gall trk: goes well fresh & likes to force the pace: eff in blnks. *1* **50**
872 **BLUSHING GRENADIER 20** [5] 8-8-7 (bl) S Finnamore (5) 16/1: 301666: Led till over 1f out, no extra. *4* **36**
908 **SHARP EDGE BOY 17** [1] 4-9-0 L Swift(7) 33/1: -00007: Chsd ldrs, outpcd fnl 2f: lkd well: see 622. *½* **42**
763 **LORD HIGH ADMIRAL 34** [13] 12-8-4 (vis) F Norton 7/1: 04-148: Led/dsptd lead 5f: op 9/2: won this race in '99: not able to dominate today: see 673 (AW). *nk* **31**
4331} **SOUPERFICIAL 202** [7] 9-8-4 Kim Tinkler 40/1: 0100-9: Dwelt, nvr on terms: ndd this, 7 mth abs: '99 Newcastle scorer (h'cap, rtd 52): '98 wnr at Carlisle (clmr) & Hamilton (sell, rtd 65): eff at 5/6f, stays 7f: acts on firm, enjoys gd, hvy & fibresand: eff in blnks/vis, best without: best on a stiff trk & loves Hamilton. *1½* **27**
3027} **TRAPPER NORMAN 276** [2] 8-8-6 V Halliday 33/1: 3233-0: Prom 4f, sn outpcd: 9 mth abs: plcd 4 times in '99 (rtd 57, sell): rtd 49 in '98 (clmr): eff at 6/7f, stays 8.5f: handles firm & fast ground. *nk* **28**
-- **ANOTHER VICTIM** [4] 6-8-4 S Righton 100/1: 06/0: Mid-div, btn 2f out: 11th: long abs, mod form. *2* **20**
692 **Belle Of Hearts 42** [11] 4-7-13 J Lowe 100/1: 816 **Mikes Double 28** [8] 6-8-4 (vis) R Fitzpatrick(1) 40/1:
646 **Kings Chambers 56** [6] 4-8-4 (bl) A Whelan 100/1:
14 ran Time 1m 14.35 (3.55) (Brian Androlia) M J Polglase Southwell, Notts.

1074 **5.30 COAL MINER HCAP 3YO+ 0-85 (D) 6f str Good/Soft 60 -01 Slow** **[83]**
£4277 £1316 £658 £329 3yo rec 10lb Stalls 1-8 raced far side (at a big disadvantage)

1013 **DAAWE 7** [15] D Nicholls 9-8-13 (68)(bl) O Pears 16/1: 163061: 9 b h Danzig - Capo Di Monte (Final Straw) Led/dsptd lead thro'out on stands rail, narrow lead ins last, held on well, rdn out: lkd superb, op 12/1: earlier won at Southwell & W'hampton (2, h'caps, rtd 98a): '99 scorer at Pontefract & Newcastle (h'caps, rtd 71 & 68a): '98 Thirsk & Doncaster wnr (ltd stks, rtd 81 & 75a): suited by 5/6f, stays 1m: acts on firm, hvy & f/sand: handles any trk: eff with/without visor/blnks: has run well fresh: loves to force the pace: tough & genuine 9yo. **74**
824 **REX IS OKAY 26** [12] S R Bowring 4-8-12 (67)(bl) Dean McKeown 16/1: 664002: 4 ch g Mazilier - Cocked Hat Girl (Ballacashtal) Prom stands side, rdn & ev ch fnl 1f, kept on well, just held: win sn at 7f? see 824. *nk* **71**
*763 **FEARBY CROSS 34** [21] W J Musson 4-9-5 (74) J Reid 8/1: 006-13: 4 b g Unblest - Two Magpies (Doulab) Chsd ldrs stands side, rdn to chall final 1f, onepace nr fin: padd pick, in gd heart: see 763. *1* **75**
725 **ELLENS ACADEMY 37** [1] E J Alston 5-9-8 (77) D Holland 14/1: 000-04: Held up far side, prog & hung right to join stand side group 2f out, ch 1f out, no extra nr fin: sharper for this reapp: '99 wnr at Newbury & Newmarket (h'caps, rtd 83): rnr-up in '98 (stks, rtd 60): suited by 6f, stays 1m well: acts on firm & gd grnd, handles soft: best without blnks: fine effort in the circumstances (poor low draw), spot on next time on gd grnd. *nk* **77+**
4518} **THE GAY FOX 188** [20] 6-8-13 (68)(t) G Duffield 16/1: 5050-5: Prom stands side, rdn & kept on ins last: op 12/1, sharper for this reapp: plcd in '99 (rtd 71, h'cap): '98 wnr at Sandown (h'cap, rtd 94): eff at 6/7f, suited by 5f on any trk: handles firm, enjoys gd/soft or hvy grnd: gd weight carrier who has run well fresh: runs well in t-strap & with/without blnks: well h'capped. *shd* **68**
844 **DEMOLITION JO 23** [19] 5-9-5 (74)(vis) J P Spencer 16/1: 320-06: In tch stands side, kept on inside last, not pace to chall: plcd numerous times in '99 (rtd 75 & 65a): '98 Chester wnr (h'cap, rtd 79 & 71a): eff *nk* **73**

DONCASTER
MONDAY MAY 1ST   Lefthand, Flat, Galloping Track

at 5/7f on any grnd & trk, also handles fibresand: wears a visor: tough mare.

817   **DISTINCTIVE DREAM 28** [13] 6-9-1 (70) D Kilcourse (7) 25/1: 410367: Held up, nvr pace to chall.   ½   68

926   **VENIKA VITESSE 16** [16] 4-9-1 (70) T Williams 25/1: 310-08: In tch stands side, held over 1f out: lkd   ¾   65
superb: '99 wnr at Lingfield (AW auct mdn, rtd 70a), Carlisle & Nottingham (h'caps, rtd 72): eff at 5/6f, could get
further: likes fast grnd & equitrack, handles any trk: worth another chance on faster grnd.

1028   **BLUE STAR 5** [11] 4-9-6 (75)(vis) C Cogan(5) 14/1: 512209: In tch stands side, slightly hmpd 2f out,   shd   70
sn held: op 12/1: qck reapp: see 660 (AW).

746   **RED DELIRIUM 35** [18] 4-8-13 (68) K Fallon 3/1 FAV: 000-20: Held up stands side, effort 2f out, mod   ½   62
gains: 10th: hvly bckd, op 5/1: more expected after encouraging reapp: see 746 (fast).

3382}   **ABLE AYR 259** [6] 3-8-11 (76) Dawn Rankin (7) 66/1: 0450-0: In tch far side, nvr a factor: 11th, just   3½   60
better for reapp: '99 Carlisle wnr (auct mdn, rtd 81): eff at 5/6f on fast & gd grnd: 1st home on unfav side.

4572}   **STYLISH WAYS 182** [3] 8-8-11 (66) F Norton 9/1: 0050-0: Held up far side, effort 2f out, no impress   shd   50
with ldrs stands side: ddhtd for 12th, just sharper for reapp: plcd in '99 (rtd 83, h'cap), also rtd 102$ in a
List contest: '98 wnr at Newmarket & Haydock (h'caps, rtd 77): stays 7f, suited by 6f: acts on firm & gd, loves
soft or hvy grnd: handles any trk, likes a stiff one: nicely h'capped, forget this, poor low draw here.

941   **MISTER MAL 14** [9] 4-9-6 (75) K Darley 10/1: 13-050: Dwelt, in tch stands side, outpcd final 1f: 12th.   dht   59

926   **PIERPOINT 16** [14] 5-9-0 (69) Clare Roche(7) 16/1: 000-00: In tch stands side, hmpd over 1f out,   1   50+
sn held: 14th, op 12/1: stablemate of wnr: no luck in running here: keep in mind with headgear back on: see 926.

941   **SHARP GOSSIP 14** [7] 4-9-1 (70) S Whitworth 25/1: 622-00: Nvr on terms far side: 15th: ex-Irish.   ½   50

4572}   **TRINITY 182** [17] 4-9-4 (73) G Carter 25/1: 0000-0: In tch stands side 4f: 16th: reapp, needed this.   1¼   49

702   **PIPS MAGIC 39** [10] 4-10-0 (83) A McGlone 8/1: 000-00: Al towards rear centre: 20th: topweight.   0

905   **GAY BREEZE 17** [5] 7-9-10 (79) S Finnamore (5) 16/1: 445-30: Led far side 5f, sn btn: 21st: op 12/1.   0

4362} **Mr Stylish 200** [8] 4-9-2 (71) A Nicholls(3) 25/1:   926 **Uncle Exact 16** [22] 3-8-12 (77) F Lynch 33/1:

941 **Northern Svengali 14** [2] 4-9-6 (75) C Lowther 25/1:   1008 **Bedevilled 7** [4] 5-9-5 (74) Lynsey Hanna (7) 25/1:

22 ran   Time 1m 14.49 (3.69)   (Mrs Andrea M Mallinson)   D Nicholls Sessay, Nth Yorks.

KEMPTON
MONDAY MAY 1ST   Righthand, Flat, Fair Track

Official Going   GOOD/SOFT (SOFT in places). Stalls: Str - Far Side; Rem - Inside.

1075
2.10 BONUSPRINT HCAP 3YO 0-90 (C)   1m1f rnd   Good/Soft 90   +00 Fast   [95]
£7377   £2270   £1135   £567

*761   **BONAGUIL 34** [12] C F Wall 3-9-1 (82) R Mullen 100/30 FAV: 04-111: 3 b g Septieme Ciel -   90
Chateaubrook (Alleged) Waited with, short of room 3f out, switched & styd on well over 1f out to lead ins last, drvn
out, going away: well bckd tho' op 5/2: landed hat-trick after wins at Lingfield (mdn auct, rtd 77a) & Sandown
(h'cap): unplcd both '99 starts, subs gelded: stays 9f well, 10f looks sure to suit: acts on gd, gd/soft grnd
& equitrack & on a sharp or stiff trk: runs well fresh: useful & fast improving, could progress further.

4047} **MALLEUS 222** [3] R M Beckett 3-8-13 (80) R Cochrane 20/1: 5532-2: 3 ch g Hamas - Queen Warrior   nk   87
(Daring March) Chsd ldrs, eff 2f out, kept on to chall ins last, no extra cl-home, just btn: plcd on 2 of 4 '99
starts for P Walwyn (rtd 84): stays 9f on firm, soft & on a sharp & undul trk: tough, gd reapp, can win a race.

4601} **POLAR RED 179** [4] M J Ryan 3-8-6 (73) P McCabe 12/1: 123W-3: 3 ch g Polar Falcon - Sharp Top   ½   79
(Sharpo) Cl-up, went on 3f out, hard rdn & collared ins last, no extra, not btn far on reapp: juv scorer at
Windsor (nurs h'cap, rtd 73): eff at 1m/9f on fast, gd/soft & likes an easy trk: gd comeback.

800   **RED CANYON 32** [2] M L W Bell 3-7-10 (63) J Mackay (7) 9/2: 000-24: Handy, eff to chase ldr 5f out   2½   65
till no extra appr fnl 1f: clr rem, see 800.

701   **DIVINE PROSPECT 39** [7] 3-8-7 (74) S Drowne 12/1: 506-65: Rdn bhd, late gains: needs further.   7   65

3645} **STARLYTE GIRL 246** [10] 3-9-7 (88) R Hughes 25/1: 2310-6: Bhd, switched over 2f out, no impress: 6   70
top-weight on reapp: won 1 of 4 juv starts, at Warwick (fill mdn, rtd 86): stays 7.8f on gd & firm, any trk.

4550} **ASSURED PHYSIQUE 185** [5] 3-8-7 (74) P Robinson 33/1: 0600-7: Led 1f, handy till wknd well over   ¾   55
2f out: unplcd juv (rtd 71): bred to want mid-dists.

*877   **SWIFT DISPERSAL 20** [1] 3-8-8 (75) G Faulkner (3) 10/1: 0018: Bhd, came to race stands side alone   nk   55
in str, no dngr: much btr 877 (6f, fill mdn).

*880   **KATHAKALI 19** [9] 3-8-3 (70) Martin Dwyer 9/1: -21119: In tch, wknd 2f out: in fine equitrack form.   1½   48

933   **GRACE AND POWER 14** [11] 3-8-13 (80) Pat Eddery 20/1: 242-00: Handy till wknd over 3f out: 6   49
reapp: rnr-up on 2 of 3 juv starts (rtd 83): stays 7f on gd/firm, gd & a stiff track: shld do better on gd grnd.

*884   **MY RETREAT 19** [6] 3-9-1 (82) M Hills 4/1: 52-10: In tch, rdn & wknd qckly over 2f out, eased: 14   31
11th, reportedly lost action: see 884.

933   **CEDAR PRINCE 14** [8] 3-8-12 (79)(bl) S Sanders 33/1: 120-00: Led after 1f till 6f out, wknd over 3f out.   8   16

12 ran   Time 1m 58.1 (8.1)   (Mrs R M S Neave)   C F Wall Newmarket.

1076
2.40 TRIPLEPRINT HCAP 3YO+ 0-90 (C)   1m4f   Good/Soft 90   -19 Slow   [88]
£7182   £2210   £1105   £552   3 yo rec 19lb

1030   **BLUE STYLE 5** [7] P Mitchell 4-8-0 (60)(t) R Mullen 3/1 FAV: 0-6121: 4 ch g Bluebird - Style For   68
Life (Law Society) Held up, hdwy wide 3f out to lead dist, styd on well, rdn out: hvly bckd: qck reapp after
shade unlucky in 1030, earlier won at Brighton (clmr, with J Poulton): modest French/Irish form in '99 (blnks):
stays 12f well, further suit: wears a tongue-strap: likes gd/soft & hvy, sharp trk: tough & progressive.

4287} **FOREST FIRE 205** [8] B Hanbury 5-9-6 (80) M Roberts 16/1: 0560-2: 5 b m Never So Bold - Mango   1   85
Sampaquita (Colombian Friend) Waited with, hdwy 2f out to lead over 1f out, sn hdd & not pace of wnr: in '99
scored at Newmarket (2, h'caps, rtd 82), subs too highly tried: '98 Sandown scorer (2, clmr & fill h'cap, rtd
70): eff at 10f, stays 12f on firm, gd/soft & on any trk, likes a gall one: tough, fine reapp, spot-on for this.

*991   **SPRING PURSUIT 9** [15] R J Price 4-10-0 (88) P Fitzsimons (5) 7/1: -60213: 4 b g Rudimentary -   2½   89
Pursuit Of Truth (Irish River) Handy, eff & ev ch 2f out, onepace fnl 1f: nicely bckd & running well: see 991.

868   **THAMES DANCER 20** [12] K McAuliffe 4-8-10 (70) T E Durcan 33/1: 623-04: In tch, eff 3f out,   ¾   70
rdn & kept on fnl 1f, no dngr: encouraging, see 868.

968   **LEGAL LUNCH 12** [9] 5-8-8 (68)(vis) Pat Eddery 10/1: 3-4205: Keen, in tch, eff 2f out, no impress.   ½   67

968   **GENTLEMAN VENTURE 12** [4] 4-9-3 (77) S Sanders 11/2: 000-36: Prom, led over 3f out till over 2f   1   75
out, no extra: more promising in 968.

3982} **WASP RANGER 226** [1] 6-8-12 (72) N Callan 25/1: 0200-7: Dwelt, in tch, eff 2f out, sn no impress: 2   68
reapp: '99 scorer at Kempton (h'cap, rtd 75): missed '98, '97 wnr at Goodwood (mdn, with P Cole, rtd 93):

suited by 10f now on firm or gd/soft & on any trk: has run well in blnks: shld pinch another h'cap at 10f.
4284} **CONSPICUOUS 205** [16] 10-9-8 (82) A Clark 16/1: 0011-8: Waited with, hdwy 2f out, sn onepace: shd 78
reapp: won fnl 2 '99 starts, at Kempton & Ascot (amat h'caps, rtd 85): '98 Brighton scorer (h'cap, rtd 89): eff
at 1m/10f, stays a stiff 12f now: acts on firm & equitrack, revels in gd/soft & hvy: gets on well with Mr L Jefford.
968 **CLARENDON 12** [13] 4-9-3 (77) Martin Dwyer 8/1: 300-09: Chsd ldrs, eff & hmpd 2f out, onepace. 1¾ 71
1030 **WESTMINSTER CITY 5** [6] 4-7-10 (56)(3oh) J Mackay (7) 8/1: 3212U0: Bhd, eff over 4f out, wknd ½ 49
over 2f out: 10th, qck reapp, see 748.
968 **WAIT FOR THE WILL 12** [10] 4-9-3 (77) I Mongan (5) 33/1: 060-00: In tch, wknd over 3f out: 11th: nk 70
in '99 won at Salisbury (amat h'cap, rtd 72): rtd 79 for I Balding in '98: stays 12f on firm/fast, handles gd/soft.
868 **SAGAPONACK 20** [3] 4-9-6 (80) R Cochrane 16/1: 5140: Keen bhd, no dngr: 12th, see 868 & 643 (aw). 4 67
4103} Arabian Moon 218 [11] 4-9-13 (87) P Robinson 33/1: 845 **Bergamo 23** [2] 4-8-5 (65)(bl) S Drowne 16/1:
4467} Amezola 192 [14] 4-9-7 (81)(t) R Hughes 16/1:   747 **Direct Deal 35** [5] 4-9-3 (77) D Harrison 33/1:
16 ran   Time 2m 44.03 (13.03)   (M C Mason & D S Nevison)   P Mitchell Epsom, Surrey.

1077   3.15 DOUBLEPRINT HCAP 4YO+ 0-110 (B)   1m jub rnd   Good/Soft 90   +01 Fast   [106]
£29000 £11000 £5500 £2500

1015 **ESPADA 7** [11] M H Tompkins 4-8-7 (85) S Sanders 6/1: 50-621: 4 b c Mukaddamah - Folk Song (The 92
Minstrel) Chsd ldrs, hdwy for press to lead appr fnl 1f, styd on well, drvn out: well bckd, gd time: '99 scorer
at Thirsk (class stks) & Ayr (h'cap, rtd 88): '98 Ripon wnr (mdn auct, rtd 82): eff at 7f, stays an easy 1m well
on fast & soft grnd: handles a gall or easy trk: useful, in fine heart & improving.
*1015 **PULAU TIOMAN 7** [16] M A Jarvis 4-9-10 (102)(5ex) P Robinson 7/1: 00-212: 4 b c Robellino - Ella 1 107
Mon Amour (Ela Mana Mou) Waited with, hdwy for press 2f out, styd on well ins last, not rch wnr: well bckd under
a pen having btn this wnr by a neck when 5lb better off in 1015: in tremendous form.
966 **ADJUTANT 12** [17] N P Littmoden 5-9-1 (93) R Cochrane 12/1: 13-303: 5 b g Batshoof - Indian Love 2 95
Song (Be My Guest) Held up rear, hdwy under min press over 2f out, kept on fnl 1f, nvr nr to chall: all prev
wins at 7f, but stays 1m & will do better with a more positive ride (set plenty to do here): see 966, 725.
1015 **SMOOTH SAILING 7** [14] K McAuliffe 5-8-7 (85) N Callan 20/1: 020-04: Chsd ldrs, eff 2f out, 1½ 84
kept on ins last, nvr dngrs: see 1015.
1042 **SILK ST JOHN 3** [3] 6-8-10 (88) P McCabe 14/1: 0-0065: Waited with, kept on late, no dngr: now 2 84
on a winning mark & can go in again over a stiffer 1m: see 1015.
986 **CULZEAN 9** [13] 4-8-5 (83) P Fitzsimons (5) 12/1: 03-536: In tch, eff & short of room 2f out, onepace. ¾ 78
715 **TAFFS WELL 38** [9] 7-7-10 (74)(1oh) J Mackay (7) 9/1: 606-47: Bhd, eff 2f out, sn no impress: op shd 69
7/1: caught the eye in 715 & well worth another chance when stable returns to form: see 715.
687 **FLOATING CHARGE 45** [8] 6-7-13 (77) R Ffrench 9/1: 61-2U8: Led, clr over 3f out till hdd & no extra 1¾ 69
over 1f out: op 7/1: 6 wk abs: see 580 (fibresand).
875 **INDIUM 20** [4] 6-8-0 (78) R Mullen 14/1: 0-4049: Slow away, bhd, late gains: wants a stiff 1m. ¾ 69
1031 **STOPPES BROW 5** [6] 8-8-2 (80)(bl) P Doe 33/1: 00-400: Sn bhd, no dngr: 10th, see 1031. shd 71
733 **TAYSEER 37** [12] 6-8-8 (86) R Hughes 9/2 FAV: 111-00: Held up, eff 2f out, sn wknd: 11th, nk 76
hvly bckd from 8/1: see to hit form: see 733.
966 **WEALTHY STAR 12** [15] 5-8-8 (86)(t) J A Beech (5) 13/2: 0-0550: Cl-up, rdn 2f out, sn btn: nk 75
well bckd, 12th, jockey received a 1 day careless riding ban: btr 966 (7f), 895.
4470} **SMART SAVANNAH 192** [10] 4-9-1 (93) M Hills 10/1: 0500-0: Waited with, eff over 2f out, sn btn: 7 71
13th: '99 wnr at Ascot (h'cap, rtd 101): '98 scorer at Sandown (stks, rtd 97): v eff at 1m, poss just
stays 10f: acts on fast, gd/soft & likes a stiff trk: wears a t-strap: should do better.
*55 **BRILLIANT RED 167** [5] 7-9-10 (102)(t) Pat Eddery 14/1: 0021-0: Keen in tch, rdn & wknd over ½ 79
2f out: 14th, long abs since 55 (equitrack, 10f).
966 **SALTY JACK 12** [7] 6-8-6 (84) Martin Dwyer 33/1: 213000: In tch, rdn & btn over 3f out: 15th. 2½ 57
3028} **JUNO MARLOWE 276** [1] 4-9-4 (96) N Pollard 33/1: 0010-0: Chsd ldrs till wknd appr 2f out: won 5 61
1 of 4 '99 starts, at Newmarket (fill rtd h'cap, rtd 95): suited by 7f on firm, prob handles soft & any trk.
3872} **FOR YOUR EYES ONLY 233** [2] 6-9-7 (99)(bl) T E Durcan 33/1: 5006-0: In tch, wknd qckly over 2f out: 1½ 61
fin last on reapp: in '99 won a 1m h'cap in Dubai: '98 scorer at Sandown (2, rtd h'caps, with T Easterby) &
Goodwood (val h'cap, rtd 108): suited by 1m, stays 10f on firm or hvy & any trk, likes Sandown: wears blnks.
17 ran   Time 1m 43.96 (7.16)   (Mrs Janis Macpherson)   M H Tompkins Newmarket.

1078   3.45 EBF BONUSPHOTO FILL COND STKS 3YO (C)   6f str   Good/Soft 90   +04 Fast
£6090 £2310 £1155 £525

*956 **MAY CONTESSA 13** [5] D R C Elsworth 3-8-13 N Pollard 11/4: 35-11: 3 b f Bahri - Copper Creek 101
(Habitat) Keen, waited with, gd hdwy to lead on bit appr fnl 1f, pushed clr, readily: well bckd, gd time: earlier
scored at Newmarket (mdn): plcd in '99 (rtd 80): v eff at 6f, 7f will suit: acts on gd & gd/soft & handles a
sharp or stiff trk: runs well fresh: v useful & improved run today: warrants a try in Listed company.
2325} **JEZEBEL 309** [4] C F Wall 3-9-7 R Mullen 8/1: -11-2: 3 b f Owington - Just Ice (Polar Falcon) 3 101
Keen in tch, eff to chall over 1f out, kept on but not pace of wnr ins last: reapp: won both juv starts, at Sans
Siro (incl List, rtd 95): v eff at 6f on firm or gd/soft & on a stiff or easy trk: v useful & unexposed filly,
fine effort here conceding plenty of weight & shld win more races.
1016 **PRESENTATION 7** [6] R Hannon 3-8-13 R Hughes 7/4 FAV: 633-23: 3 b f Mujadil - Beechwood nk 93
(Blushing Groom) Led, hdd over 1f out, no extra: hvly bckd, clr of rem: better expected but this was a useful run.
4201} **SHANNON DORE 212** [3] B Hanbury 3-8-13 A Beech (5) 14/1: 2010-4: Chsd ldr, wknd well over 1f 7 78
out: juv scorer at Nottingham (mdn, rtd 82): eff at 6f, bred to stay further: acts on firm & gd, any trk.
4286} **IMPERIALIST 205** [8] 3-9-3 M Roberts 11/1: 4360-5: Waited with, rdn & btn well over 1f out: reapp: 1½ 79
tough juv, won at Sandown (fill mdn) & Salisbury (stks), plcd in List company (rtd 97): eff over 5/6f on firm & gd.
912 **ROO 17** [2] 3-8-13 S Sanders 10/1: 420-06: In tch, btn 2f out: see 912. 1 73
988 **KALINDI 9** [7] 3-9-3 S Drowne 12/1: 200-07: Handy, wknd over 2f out: in '99 scored at Royal Ascot 6 65
(Windsor Castle, rtd 82): v eff at 5f, tried 6f: acts on gd/firm & a stiff trk: do better on a sounder surface?
988 **KELSO MAGIC 9** [1] 3-8-13 Pat Eddery 7/1: 546-08: Al bhd: juv scorer at Salisbury (fill mdn) & 1 59
Brighton (nurs h'cap, rtd 94 when 4th in a Gr 3): v eff around 5.3f on firm, gd/soft & on any trk: useful at best.
8 ran   Time 1m 16.28 (5.18)   (DGH Partnership)   D R C Elsworth Whitsbury, Hants.

KEMPTON MONDAY MAY 1ST Righthand, Flat, Fair Track

1079 **4.20 BONUSFILM EBF MDN 2YO (D) 5f str Good/Soft 90 -50 Slow**
£3542 £1090 £545 £272

-- **GLORY DAYS** [2] R Hannon 2-9-0 R Hughes 7/4 FAV: 1: 2 ch c Lahib - Gloire (Thatching) **88+**
Led after 1f, styd on well over 1f out, pushed out, cmftbly: hvly bckd: Mar foal, cost Ffr 200,000: half-brother to a 5/7f wnr: eff at 5f, further will suit: runs well fresh on gd/soft: looks useful, win better races.
-- **SILCA LEGEND** [3] M R Channon 2-9-0 S Drowne 7/2: 2: 2 ch c Efisio - Silca Cisa (Hallgate) ¾ **85+**
Bmpd start but sn prom, eff to chase wnr 2f out, kept on ins last but not pace of wnr, hands-and-heels: nicely bckd, well clr of rem on debut: Apr foal: half-brother to Irish 1,000 Guineas rnr-up Golden Silca: dam 5f juv scorer: eff at 5f, 6f will suit: handles gd/soft: improve a bundle for this gd debut & win plenty of races.
-- **DRESS CODE** [1] W Jarvis 2-8-9 R Cochrane 4/1: 3: 2 b f Barathea - Petite Epaulette (Night Shift) Went left start, sn in tch, rdn & onepace over 1f out: debut, Jan foal, cost 47,000gns: half-sister to a couple of 5f juv wnrs: dam 5f juv scorer: bred to apprec 5/6f & shld come on for this. *5* **67**
-- **PRIYA** [4] C E Brittain 2-8-9 P Robinson 7/2: 4: In tch, wknd 2f out on debut: Mar first foal. *3½* **60**
993 **JACKS BIRTHDAY 9** [6] 2-9-0 S Sanders 20/1: 05: Handy till btn halfway: see 993. *5* **55**
-- **TROPICAL RIVER** [7] 2-9-0 D Harrison 12/1: 6: Led 1f, wknd over 2f out: debut: Mar first foal, dam useful 5/6f juv scorer: Lahib colt. *2½* **50**
-- **COUNTRYWIDE PRIDE** [8] 2-9-0 N Callan 14/1: 7: Al bhd on debut: Feb foal: dam 7f juv wnr. *2½* **45**
7 ran Time 1m 05.3 (7) (A F Merritt) R Hannon East Everleigh, Wilts.

1080 **4.50 FOTOCOLOR MDN 3YO (D) 1m jub rnd Good/Soft 90 -05 Slow**
£4758 £1464 £732 £366

972 **INGLENOOK 12** [14] J L Dunlop 3-9-0 Pat Eddery 2/1: -51: 3 b c Cadeaux Genereux - Spring (Sadler's Wells) In tch, eff & short of room well over 1f out, switched left & styd on strongly ins last, going away, readily: dam mid-dist wnr: stays 1m well, sure to relish 10f: acts on gd/soft: useful & has a turn of foot, win more races. **99+**
983 **MATERIAL WITNESS 11** [10] W R Muir 3-9-0 N Callan 7/4 FAV: -32-22: 3 b c Barathea - Dial Dream (Gay Mecene) Cl-up, eff to chase ldr 2f out, kept on ins last, not pace of wnr: hvly bckd: stays 1m: win a race. *3* **91**
4614} **CARENS HERO 177** [1] Mrs A J Perrett 3-9-0 R Hughes 14/1: 0-3: 3 ch g Petardia - Clearglade (Vitiges) Led, rdn & hdd just ins fnl 1f, no extra: clr of rem, op 10/1: full brother to a 1m scorer: eff at 1m on gd/soft. *1¼* **89**
4605} **FOOL ON THE HILL 178** [3] L G Cottrell 3-9-0 A Clark 33/1: 06-4: In tch, wknd over 1f out: unplcd both juv starts (rtd 69): half-brother to wnrs over 6f/1m: dam sprinter: better on a minor trk back at 7f? *6* **79**
-- **ROB LEACH** [6] 3-9-0 R Price 33/1: 5: Sn bhd, rdn over 2f out, no impress: cost 19,000gns: half-brother to a 12f wnr: bred to improve when stepped up to 10f+. *1* **77**
4524} **GREEN CASKET 187** [7] 3-9-0 D Harrison 13/2: 6-6: In tch, wknd 2f out: rtd 79 when unplcd sole juv start: half-brother to a couple of useful mid-dist performer: dam useful over 6/9f. *2½* **73**
956 **MAGIC EAGLE 13** [11] 3-9-0 I Mongan (5) 25/1: -67: Chsd ldr 4f, wknd over 2f out: see 956. *6* **63**
915 **HAZY HEIGHTS 17** [13] 3-8-9 D R McCabe 16/1: 68: Bhd, nvr plcd to chall: sure to relish further & gives the impression more is to come with a stronger ride, monitor her progress. *nk* **57+**
957 **AFTER THE BLUE 13** [9] 3-9-0 S Drowne 20/1: 6-09: Al bhd: rtd 75 when unplcd sole juv start. *1¾* **59**
983 **GOLDEN RETRIEVER 11** [8] 3-9-0 N Pollard 14/1: 0-00: Al bhd: 10th: dam 7f scorer & 1m shld suit. *½* **58**
759 **NIGHT SIGHT 34** [4] 3-9-0 M Roberts 9/1: 00: In tch, wknd over 2f out: 11th: with G Wragg. *1* **56**
729 **Cedar Light 37** [12] 3-9-0 S Sanders 50/1: 103 **Dr Cool 159** [5] 3-9-0 P Doe 16/1:
832 **Sibelius 25** [2] 3-9-0 T G McLaughlin 33/1: -- **Jimal** [15] 3-9-0 R Cochrane 33/1:
15 ran Time 1m 44.37 (7.57) (Seymour Cohn) J L Dunlop Arundel, W.Sussex.

NOTTINGHAM TUESDAY MAY 2ND Lefthand, Galloping Track

Official Going GOOD TO SOFT (SOFT places). Stalls: Str - Stands Side; Rem - Inside.

1081 **2.15 COME RACING SELLER 3YO (G) 6f Good/Soft 83 -19 Slow**
£2002 £572 £286 Field Raced in 2 Groups, first two home on far side

785 **CAPE COAST 34** [2] J A Osborne 3-8-12 R Cochrane 8/1: 26-001: 3 b c Common Grounds - Strike It Rich (Rheingold): In tch far side, rdn/prog to lead over 1f out, held on well when strongly prsd inside last, rdn out: bght in for 5,800 gns, first win: op 11/1: rnr-up on first of 2 '99 starts (rtd 77, auct mdn, D Marks): eff at 6f (dam a 10f wnr): acts on fast & gd/soft: likes a gall trk: best without blnks: apprec drop to sell grade. **62**
872 **SCHATZI 21** [1] D Moffatt 3-8-7 J Bramhill 11/1: 005-02: 3 gr f Chilibang - Fluorescent Flo (Ballad Rock): In tch far side, rdn to chall final 1f, just held: op 8/1, rest well covered here: mdn, see 872. *hd* **56**
659 **K ACE THE JOINT 52** [3] S R Bowring 3-8-12 Dean McKeown 40/1: 00-063: 3 ch g Savahra Sound - Be My Sweet (Galivanter): Held up far side, rdn/outpcd over 2f out, kept on fnl 1f: abs: eff at 6f on gd/soft. *3½* **53$**
515 **DIAMOND PROMISE 78** [14] P D Evans 3-8-13 J P Spencer 9/4 FAV: 35-204: Handy stands side, overall ldr halfway, rdn/hdd over 1f out & no extra nr fin: 11 wk abs: first home on stands side: see 357, 228 (AW). *nk* **53**
909 **ELLPEEDEE 18** [4] 3-8-12 (t) Kim Tinkler 8/1: 00-065: Handy far side, outpcd over 1f out: op 5/1. *1½* **49**
34 **BLUE SAPPHIRE 172** [15] 3-8-7 Kimberley Hart (5) 25/1: 0000-6: Prom stands side, onepace final 2f: 6 mth abs: unplcd in '99 (rtd 50 & 29a, has tried 7f prev). *1½* **40$**
929 **RED SONNY 17** [16] 3-8-12 J Carroll 12/1: 000-07: Led stands side 3f: op 10/1: unplcd in '99 (rtd 61). *nk* **44**
3713} **COMMONBIRD 244** [10] 3-8-7 M Henry 16/1: 0500-8: Prom stands side 4f: op 12/1: 8 mth abs: unplcd in '99 (tried blnks, rtd 57 & 45a at best). *1½* **35**
222 **PETRIE 132** [12] 3-8-12 P Fessey 6/1: 2256-9: In tch stands side, hung left, nvr factor: see 88, 42 (AW). *1½* **37**
841 **LYRICAL LEGACY 25** [11] 3-8-7 (VIS) R Mullen 33/1: 000-00: Cl-up stands side 4f: 10th: vis: mod form. *½* **30**
813 **LA BIRBA 29** [6] 3-8-7 (bl) D Holland 16/1: 004-00: Led far side 4f: 11th: op 12/1: blnks reapplied. *1½* **27**
783 **Blazing Pebbles 34** [7] 3-8-7 R Ffrench 50/1: 188 **Mademoiselle Paris 139** [17] 3-8-8(1ow) M Tebbutt 14/1:
-- **Minstrel Gem** [13] 3-8-12 T Williams 33/1: 887 **Risky Gem 20** [5] 3-9-4 G Bardwell 14/1:
827 **Proper Gent 27** [18] 3-8-12 F Lynch 33/1: 4112} **Mujoda 218** [9] 3-8-7 J Tate 50/1:
150 **Miss Roxanne 148** [8] 3-8-8(1ow) R Lappin 50/1:
18 ran Time 1m 16.9 (6.1) (Godiva) J A Osborne Lambourn, Berks.

1082   2.45 SPONSORSHIP FILLIES HCAP 3YO+ 0-70 (E)   6f   Good/Soft 83   +10 Fast   [70]
　　　　£3043　£869　£434   3 yo rec 10lb Raced centre - far side

941   **TALARIA** 15 [15] S C Williams 4-9-6 (62) G Faulkner (3) 33/1: 00-601: 4 ch f Petardia - Million At Dawn   67
(Fayruz): Held up, smooth prog to chall final 2f, rdn/led inside last, styd on well, rdn out: best time of day: '99
Newmarket wnr for G Wragg (mdn, rtd 86): rtd 87 in '98 (stks): eff at 6f on firm & gd/soft grnd: likes a stiff/gall
trk: eff with/without a t-strap: clearly on a fair mark & could win again.

931   **MY TESS** 17 [18] B A McMahon 4-9-7 (63) K Darley 8/1: 213242: 4 br f Lugana Beach - Barachois   hd   67
Princess (Barachois) Sn cl-up & led halfway, rdn/hdd inside last, kept on well, just held: op 5/1, best at further.

817   **COMPRADORE** 29 [9] M Blanshard 5-9-4 (60) R Cochrane 9/1: 030-03: 5 b m Mujtahid - Keswa (King's   1½   60
Lake) Hld up, rdn & kept on well final 2f, nrst fin: op 10/1: slipped down the weights & a return to 7f cld suit.

218   **HEAVENLY MISS** 133 [12] D Carroll 6-8-7 (49) (bl) R Hills 16/1: 5450-4: Sn led till 3f out, fdd cl home: abs.   1   47

1005   **STRATS QUEST** 8 [19] S Whitworth 16/1: 001005: Held up, efft halfway, onepace final 1f.   2½   43

958   **GRACE** 14 [1] 6-8-7 (49) D Mernagh (3) 4/1 FAV: 2-4466: Mid-div, efft/prog 2f out, held final 1f: op 7/1.   nk   39

4604}   **WAFFS FOLLY** 180 [6] 5-9-0 (56) D R McCabe 12/1: 3034-7: Keen/prom, no impress final 2f: op 10/1,   2   41
6 mths abs: plcd sev times in '99 for G F H Charles Jones (rtd 59): '98 reapp wnr at Folkestone (med auct mdn,
subs rtd 64 at best, h'cap): eff at 6f, tried 7f: acts on firm & soft grnd: runs well fresh: with D J S Ffrench Davis.

910   **CARRIE POOTER** 18 [14] 4-9-13 (69) C Lowther 16/1: 45-168: Chsd ldrs, outpcd over 2f out: op 10/1.   hd   53

*910   **AMBER BROWN** 18 [3] 4-9-4 (60) G Duffield 11/2: 50-019: Led 1f, chsd ldr 4f: op 9/2: btr 910 (soft).   1   42

4529}   **CIBENZE** 188 [13] 3-9-2 (68) P Fessey 33/1: 2653-0: Dwelt, mid-div, nvr on terms: 10th: 6 mth abs: hd   49
rnr-up in '99 (rtd 77, fillies mdn): eff at 5f, handles firm & gd/soft grnd.

746   **DAYS OF GRACE** 36 [7] 5-9-0 (56) J Weaver 6/1: 313220: Cl-up 4f: 11th: see 466 (AW).   ¾   35

910   **TANCRED ARMS** 18 [5] 4-8-13 (55) F Lynch 7/1: -02230: Mid-div, nvr on terms: 12th: see 910, 698.   nk   33

910   **CAUTION** 18 [10] 6-9-7 (63) D Holland 14/1: -60600: Al towards rear: 13th: tchd 16/1: see 645.   nk   40

4015}   **MILL END QUEST** 225 [4] 5-8-8 (50) T Lucas 10/1: 6000-0: Rear, no impress: 14th: op 9/1, 8 mth abs: 1   25
'99 Pontefract wnr (fill h'cap, rtd 59): rcd in '99 (rtd 56, h'cap): eff at 5/6f on fast & soft: tried blnks.

910   **Premium Princess** 18 [17] 3-9-2 (58) J Carroll 33/1:　416   **Leen** 95 [11] 3-9-2 (68) Jonjo Fowle (7) 33/1:

171   **Thirty Six Cee** 143 [2] 3-8-8 (60) M Tebbutt 25/1:　910   **Snap Cracker** 18 [16] 4-9-1 (57) O Pears 33/1:

328   **Sounds Special** 109 [20] 3-8-9 (61) Dean McKeown 33/1: 2626}   **Dawns Dancer** 295 [8] 3-9-3 (69) R Ffrench 25/1:

20 ran   Time 1m 15.2 (4.4)   (J W Lovitt)   S C Williams Newmarket, Suffolk.

1083   3.15 BAKERY NOV MED AUCT STKS 2YO (F)   5f   Good/Soft 83   -15 Slow
　　　　£2331　£666　£333   Raced towards centre

904   **MILLYS LASS** 18 [3] M R Channon 2-8-11 P Fessey 2/5 FAV: -3121: 2 b f Mind Games - Millie's Lady   80
(Common Grounds): Cl-up, shkn up/went on over 2f out & clr 1f out, rdn to hold on when prsd nr fin: nicely bckd:
earlier scored at Leicester (auct mdn): eff at 5f, 6f should suit: acts on fast & soft, any trk: tough.

--   **EASTERN PROMISE** [5] A Berry 2-8-7 J Carroll 5/1: 2: 2 gr f Factual - Indian Crystal (Petong):   ½   74
In tch, outpcd by wnr over 2f out, styd on well for press fnl 1f: op 2/1: Apr foal, sister to a 5f sell
juv wnr: dam a 5f wnr: eff at 5f on gd/soft grnd, should get 6f: penny dropped close home here, should improve.

*836   **NINE TO FIVE** 25 [1] R Brotherton 2-9-1 J P Spencer 11/2: 113: 3 b f Imp Society - Queen And Country   7   69
(Town And Country): Led till halfway, sn held: op 3/1: see 836 (clmr).

865   **FESTINO** 21 [6] N P Littmoden 2-8-7 D Holland 20/1: 04: Swerved start/rear, nvr on terms: op 14/1.   5   52

722   **BAYRAMI** 38 [4] 2-8-7 O Pears 50/1: 05: In tch till halfway: no form.   3½   44

--   **LIMBO DANCER** [2] 2-8-7 V Halliday 40/1: 6: Dwelt/al rear: Superlative filly, Mar foal, cost 500gns: ½   42
half-sister to a 5f juv wnr, dam a 5f juv wnr: with R M Whitaker.

6 ran   Time 1m 03.4 (4.9)   (Ken Lock Racing Ltd)   M R Channon West Isley, Berks.

1084   3.45 WEATHERBYS MDN 3YO (D)   1m54y rnd Good/Soft 83 -59 Slow
　　　　£3835　£1180　£590　£295

971   **SIPSI FAWR** 13 [13] M L W Bell 3-8-9 M Fenton 5/1: -01: 3 b f Selkirk - Sipsi Fach (Prince Sabo):   82
Chsd ldrs, prog to chall final 2f, styd on well inside last to lead nr line, rdn out: op 5/2: earlier mid-div in a
competitive Newmarket mdn: apprec step up to 1m, may get further: acts on gd/soft: should go the right way.

--   **BARTON SANDS** [1] L M Cumani 3-9-0 J P Spencer 14/1: 3 b c Tenby - Hetty Green (Bay Express):   ½   85
Trkd ldrs, rdn to chall/narrow lead over 1f out, hdd nr line: op 8/1: 30,000 gns purchase, dam an Irish
12f wnr: eff over 1m, mid-dists will suit: acts on gd/soft grnd & a gall trk: pleasing intro, shld win a race.

983   **KRISPIN** 12 [11] G Wragg 3-9-0 D Holland 11/2: 603: 3 ch c Kris - Mariakova (The Minstrel):   1   83
Unruly start, chsd ldrs, rdn/ch 2f out, kept on inside last: op 6/1: well-bred, should do btter: see 789.

--   **MUSALLY** [2] N A Graham 3-9-0 R Hills 5/4 FAV: 4: Handy, rdn/briefly led 2f out, ev ch inside last,   nk   82
no extra cl-home: hvly bckd on debut: 50,000 gns purchase: Muhtarram colt, dam a gd/soft grnd.

--   **TEE CEE** [8] 3-8-9 G Duffield 12/1: 5: In tch, outpcd by front quartet final 2f: op 7/1, debut: Lion   3½   70
Cavern filly, 18,000 gns purchase: dam a 7f wnr: with R Guest.

713   **INCA STAR** 39 [9] 3-9-0 J Reid 9/1: 3-56: Mid-div, rdn/held over 2f out: op 5/2: see 713 (10f).   1   73

826   **PENG** 27 [3] 3-9-0 (t) T Williams 66/1: 007: Led till 2f out, btn/eased inside last: saddle slipped: 3   67
shwd up well for a long way, only mod form prev, low grade h'caps should now suit.

956   **SMILE ITS SHOWTIME** 14 [6] 3-9-0 A Rawlinson 50/1: -08: Mid-div, rdn halfway, sn btn: mod form.   9   54

4379}   **BAJAN SUNSET** 200 [7] 3-9-0 R Lappin 50/1: 0-9: Keen/rear, strugg 3f out: 7 mth abs: no form in '99.   1¾   51

1989}   **FLINTSTONE** 322 [4] 3-9-0 K Darley 20/1: 03-0: Al rear: 10th: op 12/1, 11 mth abs: plcd 2nd of   ¾   50
2 '99 starts (rtd 72, auct mdn): eff at 7f, should stay 1m: acts on fast grnd & a sharp trk.

4557}   **Kelling Hall** 185 [5] 3-9-0 D R McCabe 66/1:　198   **Flight Refund** 137 [10] 3-9-0 P M Quinn (5) 50/1:

--   **Golden Oscar** [12] 3-9-0 C Lowther 25/1:

13 ran   Time 1m 51.2 (11.8)   (W H Joyce)   M L W Bell Newmarket, Suffolk.

1085   4.15 NOTTINGHAM HCAP 3YO 0-70 (E)   1m54y rnd Good/Soft 83 -29 Slow   [77]
　　　　£3283　£938　£469

1024   **TAKE MANHATTAN** 8 [2] M R Channon 3-8-8 (57) P Fessey 7/1: -00661: 3 b g Hamas - Arab Scimetar   66
(Sure Blade) Chsd ldrs, prog to lead over 2f out, duelled with rnr-up from over 1f out, styd on strongly to assert
ins last: first win: unplcd in '99 (rtd 64, mdn): eff at 1m, could get further: acts on gd/soft grnd & a gall trk.

789 **PILLAGER 33** [12] Mrs A J Bowlby 3-8-11 (60) P McCabe 7/1: 0-602: 3 b c Reprimand - Emerald Ring (Auction Ring): Mid-div, prog to chall final 2f, rdn/kept on well, held nr fin: op 12/1, h'cap debut: eff arnd 1m on gd/soft grnd: well clr of rem & clearly on a handy mark, should go one better. *2* **64**

887 **SEA EMPEROR 20** [9] Mrs G S Rees 3-8-6 (55) M Henry 33/1: 000-03: 3 br g Emperior Jones - Blumarin (Scenic): Chsd ldrs, rdn/ch 2f out, sn outpcd by front pair: unplcd in '99 (rtd 64, mdn): prob styd lngr 1m trip. *6* **50**

840 **DILETIA 25** [8] N A Graham 3-9-4 (67) R Cochrane 10/1: 60-04: Held up in tch, stdy gains under hands & heels riding fnl 3f, no threat: op 8/1, h'cap bow: not given hard time, improve, poss at 10f. *1¼* **60**

976 **HEATHYARDS LAD 13** [6] 3-9-0 (63) P M Quinn (5) 7/2: 406325: Led till 3f out, fdd: nicely bckd. *4* **48**

736 **PRETENDING 38** [14] 3-8-6 (55) D Harrison 25/1: 060-06: Held up, effort 3f out, sn onepace: rnr-up in '99 (rtd 73, 5f auct mdn): acts on fast grnd & a stiff trk. *hd* **39**

4081} **MISTY MAGIC 221** [3] 3-8-12 (61) D Holland 12/1: -030-7: Chsd ldrs 5f: op 20/1, 7 mth abs/h'cap bow: plcd in '99 (rtd 63, auct mdn): eff at 6f, could get further: acts on fast grnd & a sharp/undul trk. *1* **43**

4390} **WISHFUL THINKER 199** [5] 3-9-7 (70) S Whitworth 25/1: 0000-8: Rear, mod late gains: 7 mth abs, topweight: rnr-up in '99 (rtd 82, auct mdn): eff at 6f, bred to apprec 1m+: handles firm & gd: impr over further. *½* **51**

4290} **BALLISTIC BOY 206** [11] 3-9-1 (64) Dean McKeown 33/1: 000-9: Slowly away, mod prog from rear: 7 mth abs, h'cap bow: unplcd in '99 for A T Murphy (rtd 64): this lngr 1m trip should suit, now with J J O'Neill. *1* **43**

*929 **STARLIGHT 17** [10] 3-9-1 (64) J Reid 3/1 FAV: 545-10: Chsd ldrs 7f: 10th: op 7/4: see 929 (7f). *1* **41**

264 **BEDOUIN QUEEN 118** [16] 3-9-5 (68) K Darley 33/1: 005-00: Twds rear, no impress: 11th: 4 mth abs. *3½* **38**

976 **Sweet Haven 13** [18] 3-8-3 (52) G Duffield 33/1: 613 **Calko 63** [1] 3-8-12 (61)(bl) C Lowther 14/1:

857 **Marvel 22** [17] 3-9-2 (65) Kim Tinkler 25/1: 479 **Miss Skicap 84** [4] 3-9-3 (66)(BL) I Mongan (5) 25/1:

4461} **Lady Jones 194** [13] 3-8-4 (53) G Bardwell 25/1: 4061} **Comanche Queen 222** [15] 3-8-7 (52)(4ow) R Lappin 33/1:

17 ran Time 1m 48.7 (9.3) (M G St Quinton) M R Channon West Isley, Berks.

1086

4.45 ENJOYMENT FILLIES HCAP 3YO+ 0-80 (D) 1m2f Good/Soft 83 -18 Slow [76]
£4101 £1262 £631 £315 3 yo rec 15lb

692 **ALBERKINNIE 43** [4] J L Harris 5-7-10 (44)(13oh) K Dalgleish (7) 25/1: 253321: 5 b m Ron's Victory - Trojan Desert (Troy): Handy, chsd ldr 2f out, rdn/led inside last, held on well nr fin, rdn out: 6 wk abs: first win on 30th start!: eff arnd 1m/12f on fast, gd/soft & both AWs: handles a sharp or gall trk: runs well fresh. **47**

1007 **ITSANOTHERGIRL 8** [5] M W Easterby 4-9-8 (70) T Lucas 11/4 FAV: -00122: 4 b f Reprimand - Tasmin (Be My Guest): Held up rear, styd prog final 4f, kept on well ins last, not reach wnr: op 9/4: see 931 (1m, soft). *¾* **71**

859 **TEMPRAMENTAL 22** [10] S R Bowring 4-7-12 (45)(1ow) T Williams 13/2: -22533: 4 ch f Midhish - Musical Horn (Music Boy): Led & clr 3f out, rdn & hdd inside last, no extra cl-home: 1 win in 29 starts: see 859. *¾* **46**

943 **SHARP SPICE 15** [6] D J Coakley 4-9-0 (62) D Harrison 9/2: 334-44: In tch thro'out, rdn/ch 2f out, onepace when not much room inside last: op 7/2: see 943. *1* **61**

4619} **NORCROFT JOY 178** [3] 5-9-10 (72) J Reid 8/1: 6056-5: Held up, effort 3f out, kept on onepace inside last: op 7/1, 6 mth abs: '99 Warwick & Doncaster wnr (h'caps, rtd 77, M J Ryan): '98 wnr at Yarmouth, Hamilton & Beverley (h'caps, rtd 71): eff at 12/14f: acts on fast & soft, any trk: has run well fresh: sharper at 12f. *nk* **70**

965 **RIVER ENSIGN 14** [7] 7-8-5 (53) P M Quinn (5) 5/1: 601036: Cl-up, btn final 2f: op 4/1: btr 859. *8* **43**

973 **COLLEGE PRINCESS 13** [2] 6-7-10 (44)(12oh) A McCarthy (2) 33/1: 540-47: Held up, efft 4f out, sn held. *½* **33**

4579} **TWENTY FIRST 183** [1] 4-9-1 (63) D Holland 5/1: 5026-8: Held up, brief effort over 3f out, sn btn: op 6/1, 6 mth abs: rnr-up in '99 (rtd 63, stks): eff over a gall 10f: handles firm & gd/soft grnd. *¾* **51**

931 **SUNSET LADY 17** [8] 4-8-9 (57) K Darley 8/1: 504-09: Prom, fdd over 2f out: op 14/1: rnr-up in '99 (h'cap, rtd 71, P C Haslam, no sand form): '98 wnr at Thirsk (fillies sell), Pontefract (fillies nursery h'cap) & Ayr (nursery h'cap, rtd 71): eff at 7f/1m, stays 10f: acts on fast, hvy & any trk: best up with/forcing the pace. *½* **44**

3544} **LUVADUCK 252** [9] 4-9-8 (70) G Duffield 50/1: 5400-0: Chsd ldrs, rdn/hmpd 4f out, sn struggling: 8 mth abs: unplcd in '99 (rtd 75, M J Heaton Ellis, fillies mdn): stays 1m & handles fast grnd. *dist* **0**

10 ran Time 2m 12.4 (10.1) (Paddy Barrett) J L Harris Eastwell, Leics.

1087

5.20 NEXT MEETING HCAP 4YO+ 0-60 (F) 1m6f Good/Soft 83 -10 Slow [60]
£2530 £723 £361 4 yo rec 1 lb

860 **TOTEM DANCER 22** [12] J L Eyre 7-9-5 (51) D Holland 16/1: -00001: 7 b m Mtoto - Ballad Opera (Sadler's Wells): Held up in tch, smooth/stdy prog final 4f to lead over 2f out, rdn clr over 1f out, styd on strongly: op 14/1: plcd in h'caps in '99 (rtd 74): '98 Chester wnr (amat h'cap, rtd 83 at best & 63a): eff at 12/14f, tried 2m: acts on gd & soft, handles firm & fibresand: best without a vis: v well h'capped & could go in again. **62**

885 **SHAMPOOED 20** [2] R Dickin 6-9-0 (46) J Reid 13/2: 120/32: 6 b m Law Society - White Cap's (Shirley Heights): Held up, prog to chase wnr over 1f out, kept on tho al held: op 11/2: recent jumps wnr at Stratfor (h'cap, rtd 95h): a return to 2m will suit: see 885. *3½* **50**

51 **IRELANDS EYE 169** [14] J Norton 5-9-8 (54) J Weaver 16/1: 2360-3: 5 b g Shareef Dancer - So Romantic (Teenoso): Rear, prog 4f out, rdn/hung left 3f out, kept on onepace inside last: op 14/1, 6 mth abs: plcd twice in '99 (rtd 57, h'cap): 98/99 bmpr wnr at Catterick & Newcastle (soft): suited by 14f/2m & handles gd & soft grnd. *3* **54**

737 **SHARAF 36** [8] W R Muir 7-9-0 (46) D Harrison 25/1: 045-P4: Chsd ldrs, kept on onepace final 2f: place form in '99 (rtd 51 & 47a, h'caps): '98 Bath wnr (h'cap, rtd 52): eff at 14f/2m2f on fast & soft, handles fm: best without blnks/visor: has broken blood vessels prev. *2½* **43**

940 **PROTOCOL 15** [15] 6-9-3 (49)(t) P Goode (3) 9/2 JT FAV: -00235: Cl-up, ch 2f out, sn onepace & eased/held nr line: jockey given a 3-day ban for easing down prematurely and losing fourth: op 7/2: see 940. *hd* **46**

853 **RUBY LASER 22** [3] 4-8-10 (43) G Bardwell 33/1: 403-06: Chsd ldrs 13f: see 853 (12f). *3½* **36**

903 **SALVAGE 19** [17] 5-9-1 (47) F Lynch 9/2 JT FAV: 10-037: Rear, eff 3f out, sn held: see 903, 779. *½* **39**

3299} **BUSTOPHER JONES 264** [13] 6-9-3 (49) S Mitchell 12/1: 01/3-8: Cl-up 5f out, led over 3f out till over 2f out, fdd: op 10/1: 9 mth abs: plcd sole '99 start (h'cap, rtd 49): '98 sole start wnr at Southwell (mdn h'cap, rtd 47a): eff at 11f, prob stays 14f: acts on fibresand, prob handles gd: has run well fresh. *1¾* **39**

860 **OLD HUSH WING 22** [16] 7-9-4 (50) A Culhane 13/2: 10-569: Held up in tch, efft 3f out, no impress: thor' styr, considerately handled here, sure to relish a return to 2m+: see 714. *½* **39+**

853 **JOLI SADDLERS 22** [9] 4-9-1 (48) J Carroll 25/1: 600-00: Mid-div, btn 3f out: 10th: see 853. *1¼* **36**

*903 **HASTA LA VISTA 19** [18] 10-9-3 (49)(vis) T Lucas 11/1: 220-10: Led till 3f out, fdd: 11th: op 8/1. *1¼* **36**

4584} **KAGOSHIMA 182** [10] 5-9-3 (49) O Pears 33/1: 6/65-0: Held up, effort 4f out, no impress: 12th: 6 mth abs: h'cap bow: unplcd in '99 (rtd 53, mdn): rtd 78 on sole '98 start (L Cumani, mdn). *10* **29**

*963 **VERSATILITY 14** [5] 7-9-11 (57) G Duffield 11/2: 0-5310: Chsd ldrs 11f: 13th: op 9/2: btr 963 (soft). *1½* **36**

1052 **CINDESTI 3** [6] 4-9-6 (53) K Darley 8/1: 11-000: Chsd ldrs 13f: 14th: op 12/1, qck reapp: see 860. *hd* **32**

408 **Cohiba 96** [7] 7-8-10 (42) J Tate 25/1: 940 **Malian 15** [11] 4-9-10 (57)(VIS) C Lowther 25/1:

825 **Indigo Bay 27** [1] 4-9-11 (58) H Bastiman 33/1:

17 ran Time 3m 11.3 (13.0) (G Lloyd) J L Eyre Sutton Bank, Nth Yorks.

BATH TUESDAY MAY 2ND Lefthand, Turning Track with Uphill Finish

Official Going GOOD/SOFT. Stalls: Str Crse - Far Side; Rnd Crse - Inside.

1088 **2.00 PENSFORD AUCT MDN 2YO (E) 5f rnd Good 54 -24 Slow**
£2772 £792 £396

762 **QUANTUM LADY 35** [9] B R Millman 2-7-12 F Norton 9/2 JT FAV: -41: 2 b f Mujadil - Folly Finnesse (Joligeneration) Chsd ldrs, imprvd to lead ent fnl 1f, rdn clr despite edging left: op 3/1: dam a 6/7f wnr: eff over a sharp 5f, 6f will suit: acts on gd grnd: can continue to progress. **75**

-- **PICCOLO PLAYER** [11] R Hannon 2-8-6 Dane O'Neill 13/2: -2: 2 b c Piccolo - The Frog Lady (Al Hareb) Dwelt, imprvd 2f out, ran on well fnl 1f but no ch with wnr: tchd 9/2, debut: 12,000gns Mar foal: half-sister to 7f 2yo scorer The Frog Queen: eff at 5f, needs 6f &/or a more gall trk: sure to learn from this & improve. *3* **73**

849 **KALUKI 22** [7] W R Muir 2-8-6 R Brisland(5) 10/1: -63: 2 ch c First Trump - Wild Humour (Sayruz) Chsd ldrs, ch 2f out, not qckn fnl 1f: op 7/1: eff at 5f on gd grnd, 6f will suit: see 849 (C/D). *½* **72**

1019 **EVERMOORE 8** [1] J S Moore 2-7-12 A Nicholls(3) 33/1: -04: Chsd ldrs, imprvd to lead 2f out till hdd ent fnl 1f, no extra: Apr foal, cost 15,000gns: sire a top class sprinter: shwd gd speed today. *¾* **61**

1001 **JOINT INSTRUCTION 8** [5] 2-8-8 S Drowne 6/1: -45: Mid-div, keeping on when hmpd ent final 1f, rallied cl-home: ran well in the circumstances: stable in fine form at present, must be given another chance. *½* **70**

-- **JUSTELLA** [13] 2-7-12 A Daly 20/1: -6: Slowly away & bhd, styd on strongly fnl 1f, nrst fin: ran green, mkt drifter: cheaply bought Apr foal: half-sister to a wnr over hdles: already looks in need of 6f+: plenty to like about this debut, will improve considerably & one to keep in mind. *hd* **60+**

-- **THE MARSHALL** [14] 2-8-8 M Hills 6/1: -7: In tch till outpcd halfway, rallied fnl 1f but ch had gone: op 3/1 on debut: 15,000gns purchase: Mar foal, half-brother to sev wnrs: dam stayd mid-dists: improve. *¾* **67+**

-- **TOTAL MAGIC** [8] 2-8-6 K Fallon 9/2 JT FAV: -8: Rear, imprvg when hmpd dist, no ch after: nicely bckd: 15,000gns Mar foal: dam a multiple sprint wnr: sire a high class sprinter: I Balding colt, do better. *2* **59**

993 **MY FRIEND JACK 10** [6] 2-8-3 A Clark 5/1: -59: Led till 2f out, hmpd dist when held, eased: see 993. *2½* **49**

828 **BOHEMIAN SPIRIT 26** [2] 2-8-3 N Pollard 12/1: -540: Chsd ldrs & rdn, onepcd when hmpd dist: 10th. *1¼* **45**

-- **Insheen** [3] 2-8-3 J F Egan 20/1: -- **The Dark Lady** [12] 2-7-12 G Baker (7) 33/1:

-- **Bee King** [10] 2-8-11 S Sanders 14/1: -- **Monte Mayor Golf** [4] 2-7-12 Dale Gibson 20/1:

14 ran Time 1m 04.2 (3.9) (N W Lake) B R Millman Kentisbeare, Devon.

1089 **2.30 TATTENHAM CLASS STKS 3YO 0-95 (B) 1m2f46y Good 54 -37 Slow**
£10166 £3128 £1564 £782

925 **KING O THE MANA 17** [4] R Hannon 3-8-13 R Hughes 8/1: 16-041: 3 b c Turtle Island - Olivia Jane (Ela Mana Mou) Trkd ldrs, lost pl 4f out, gd hdwy to lead 1½f out, pushed clr despite edging left, eased: value for 3L: '99 wnr at Warwick (mdn auct) & Newcastle (nurs h'cap, rtd 99): half-brother to a 14f wnr: eff at 1m, apprec step up to 10f: acts on fast & soft, handles a turning trk: useful, deserves step up into List company. **106**

4515} **RIDDLESDOWN 189** [6] S P C Woods 3-8-11 L Dettori 13/2: 321-2: 3 ch c Common Grounds - Neat Dish (Stalwart) Led till 1½f out, sn outpcd by wnr: reapp: lightly rcd juv, won here at Bath (mdn auct, rtd 94): half-brother to a 10f wnr, dam a 6f wng 2yo: eff at 10f, shld stay 12f: acts on fast & soft grnd & on a gall or turning trk: can run well fresh: useful colt, can sn go one better. *1¼* **98**

4483} **OPTIMAITE 192** [3] B R Millman 3-9-2 R Perham 20/1: 2040-3: 3 b c Komaite - Leprechaun Lady (Royal Blend) Dwelt, sn recovered & mid-div, imprvd to chall 2f out, onepcd ins last: reapp: '99 wnr at Windsor (mdn auct, debut) & Ascot (val stks, rtd 99): related to sev wnrs, incl 14f wnr Goodbye Millie: dam a styr: prob stays 10f, 1m may prove ideal: acts on firm & gd/soft, handles a sharp or gall trk: can run well fresh & set the pace. *2½* **99**

*851 **SECRET AGENT 22** [2] Sir Michael Stoute 3-8-13 K Fallon 5/4 FAV: 12-14: Rear, effort & swtchd 2f out, kept on but not pace to chall: hvly bckd from 5/2: always struggling today up in class: see 851 (1m). *hd* **96**

810 **AL TOWD 31** [7] 3-8-11 W Supple 12/1: 123-05: Dwelt, effort from rear 2f out, sn onepcd: op 8/1: lkd in need of 12f+ here: see 810. *nk* **93**

912 **IMPERIAL ROCKET 18** [8] 3-8-11 Dane O'Neill 12/1: 011-46: In tch, ev ch 2f out, fdd final 1f: lngr trip. *2½* **89**

4462} **COLONIAL RULE 194** [5] 3-8-11 J Fortune 9/1: 0231-7: Chsd ldr, ev ch 2f out, grad fdd: op 6/1 on reapp: '99 Brighton wnr (A Foster, mdn, rtd 96): half-brother to a juv wnr, dam a smart wng juv: eff at 1m, mid-dists shld suit: acts on gd & soft grnd, handles any trk: likes to race up with/force the pace: now with J Gosden. *2* **85**

*171 **FORBEARING 143** [1] 3-8-11 S Sanders 7/2: 5611-8: Rcd keenly in tch, wknd 2f out: abs, lngr trip. *nk* **84**

735 **ROYAL EAGLE 38** [9] 3-9-0 Pat Eddery 20/1: 412-09: Rcd v freely, al towards rear: op 14/1: '99 wnr at Epsom (mdn auct, rtd 86): eff at 7f on firm & gd/soft grnd: handles a sharp or gall trk: can run well fresh: reportedly changed his legs thro'out & this explanation was noted by the stewards. *6* **78**

9 ran Time 2m 15.3 (9.3) (D Boocock) R Hannon East Everleigh, Wilts.

1090 **3.00 LISTED FILLIES STKS 3YO+ (A) 5f rnd Good 54 +16 Fast**
£12818 £4862 £2431 £1105 3yo rec 9lb

4377} **CASSANDRA GO 200** [1] G Wragg 4-9-0 M Roberts 12/1: 1460-1: 4 gr f Indian Ridge - Rahaam (Secreto) Chsd ldrs, imprvd to lead dist, ran on well, pushed out: best time of day, reapp: '99 wnr at Newmarket (2, mdn & stks, rtd 105), also plcd in List company: eff at 6f/1m, enjoyed drop to 5f: acts on gd & fast: runs v well fresh, eff with/without a t-strap: handles a turning or gall trk: v useful filly who can improve further. **109**

988 **SERAPHINA 10** [12] B A McMahon 3-8-5 W Supple 14/1: 04-062: 3 ch f Pips Pride - Angelic Sounds (The Noble Player) Rear, rdn to impr 2f out, ran on well fnl 1f but not rch wnr: eff at 5f, a return to 6f will suit. *2* **103**

4170} **CARHUE LASS 215** [7] Patrick O'Leary 6-9-4 K Fallon 8/1: 1200-3: 6 b m Common Grounds - Return Journey (Pennine Walk) Front rank, led halfway, hdd dist, no extra: Irish raider, successful here at Bath last term (this race, rtd 105): rnr-up at The Curragh in '98 (List h'cap, rtd 96): '97 Tipperary wnr (List): best at 5f on gd & soft: runs v well fresh & handles a turning trk: useful mare, likes to run up with or force the pace. *¾* **104**

3989} **KASHRA 227** [8] M Johnston 3-8-5 M Hills 14/1: 1146-4: Rdn in rear, hdwy when hmpd over 1f out, fin well but chance had gone: '99 wnr at Pontefract, Goodwood & Newmarket (nurs h'caps, rtd 96), also 4th in List: eff at 5f, crying out for a return to 6f: acts on firm & gd/soft grnd, handles any trk: spot-on next time at 6f. *¾* **97+**

988 **TARAS GIRL 10** [10] 3-8-5 J Fortune 8/1: 020-35: Rear, rdn to impr 1½f out, nrst fin: needs 6f. *nk* **96**

702 **DAMALIS 40** [4] 4-9-0 R Hughes 16/1: 440-46: Led till halfway, fdd final 1f: 6 wk abs: not disgrcd in this tougher company: caught the eye in 702 (h'cap). *1¼* **92**

1019} **KASTAWAY 371** [2] 4-9-0 Pat Eddery 20/1: 40/4-7: Rcd keenly in tch, btn fnl 1f: mkt drifter, reapp: 4th here at Bath (this race, rtd 85) on sole '99 start: '98 Lingfield, Thirsk, Doncaster & Windsor wnr (with J Berry, stks, rtd 94 & 81a): best up with/forcing the pace at 5f on firm, hvy & equitrack: can run well fresh. *1* **89$**

1331} **FLAVIAN 353** [9] 4-9-0 C Rutter 20/1: 21/0-8: In tch, rdn halfway, sn btn: reapp: unplcd sole '99 *shd* **89**

start: '98 Newmarket wnr (mdn, rtd 95): eff at 6f, 7f shld suit: acts on fast grnd, handles a gall trk.
3453} **ROWAASI 257** [11] 3-8-9 L Dettori 4/1: 2124-9: Al struggling in mid-div, nvr a factor: '99 Sandown wnr (List, rtd 107+), subs rnr-up at Ascot (Gr 3) & 4th at York (Gr 2): sprint bred, eff at 5f, has tried 6f & a return to that trip shld suit: acts on firm & gd grnd, handles gd/soft: capable of better. ½ 92
4377} **DEADLY NIGHTSHADE 200** [3] 4-9-0 N Pollard 11/10 FAV: 2/00-0: Rear, brief effort 2f out, sn btn: fin 10th, hvly bckd on reapp: unplcd on both '99 starts (reportedly broke blood vessels, rtd 102): '98 Bath & Goodwood wnr (stks), rnr-up in a Gr 3 (rtd 105): eff at 5/6f on fast & firm: handles any trk, can run well fresh. 1½ 84
*905 **AMBITIOUS 18** [5] 5-9-0 A Nicholls 20/1: 20-010: AL outpcd, fin 11th: much better in h'caps. 20 34
953 **MISTY MISS 14** [6] 3-8-12 J F Egan 25/1: 103-0P: Chsd ldrs till p.u. lame halfway: promising 953 (7f). 0
12 ran Time 1m 02.2 (1.9) (Trevor C Stewart) G Wragg Newmarket

1091 3.30 TOTE FILLIES HCAP 4YO+ 0-80 (D) 1m3f144y Good 54 -25 Slow [78]
£6711 £2065 £1032 £516

*853 **SURE QUEST 22** [2] D W P Arbuthnot 5-8-2 (52) J F Egan 13/2: 234111: 5 b m Sure Blade - Eagle's Quest (Legal Eagle) In tch, swtchd 2f out, ran on strongly to lead ins fnl 1f, drvn out: completed hat-trick after wins at W'hampton (AW sell, rtd 50a) & Windsor (fill h'cap): back in '98 won at Folkestone (mdn h'cap, rtd 61): eff at 10/12f on gd, firm & f/sand: likes a sharp/undul or turning trk: has tried a visor, best without: in fine form. 63
772 **PULAU PINANG 34** [11] G A Butler 4-9-4 (68) L Dettori 9/2: 310-22: 4 ch f Dolphin Street - Inner Pearl (Gulf Pearl) In tch, drvn to lead 2f out, collared ins last & not btn far: tchd 7/1, 6L clr 3rd: game run conceding 16lbs to today's wnr: acts on gd, firm grnd & equitrack: see 772 (AW). 1¼ 76
748 **FEE MAIL 36** [8] I A Balding 4-9-1 (65) K Fallon 2/1 FAV: 021-33: 4 b f Danehill - Wizardry (Shirley Heights) Rcd keenly & trkd ldrs, led briefly 2f out, left bhd fnl 1f: nicely bckd: slightly disapp after 748. 6 64
853 **AEGEAN DREAM 22** [6] R Hannon 4-10-0 (78) R Hughes 13/2: 05-234: Waited with, imprvd to chase ldrs when bmpd 2f out, no ch after: top weight: btr 853, see 747. 3½ 72
3480} **CHEEK TO CHEEK 256** [5] 6-9-1 (65) M Hills 33/1: 2325-5: Chsd ldr, led 3f out till 2f out, grad fdd: mkt drifter, reapp: failed to win in '99, plcd sev times (h'caps, rtd 65 at best): '98 wnr at W'hampton (AW mdn), here at Bath (fill h'cap) & Yarmouth (h'cap, rtd 65 & 65a): best up with/forcing the pace, eff btwn 12f & 2m: best on fast & firm grnd, also fibresand: gd weight carrier who can run well fresh. 4 53
889 **COURT CHAMPAGNE 20** [3] 4-7-10 (46)(6oh) R Brisland(5) 40/1: 00/006: Rear, imprvd 4f out, nrst fin. 4 28
4113} **WATER FLOWER 218** [7] 6-9-4 (68) R Perham 8/1: 1100-7: Nvr a factor: op 11/2, reapp: in gd form in '99, won at Salisbury (reapp) & Chepstow (2, h'caps, rtd 74): Jan '99 Exeter hdle wnr (nov, rtd 107h, eff arnd 2m on gd & gd/soft, with M Pipe): '97 Flat wnr at Newmarket (with J Fanshawe, clmr, rtd 71): eff at 10/12f, has tried 2m: acts on gd & firm, likes a stiff/undul or gall trk: gd weight carrier, can run well fresh: capable of better. ¾ 49
4546} **SECRET DROP 186** [1] 4-9-1 (65) T E Durcan 16/1: 0360-8: Slowly away, recovered to chase ldrs 1m, grad fdd: plcd at Lingfield (mdn, rtd 81) in '99: dam an 11f wnr: eff at 10f on hvy: tried an eyeshield. 2½ 43
705 **OVER THE MOON 40** [10] 6-7-11 (47)(1ow)(7oh) F Norton 13/2: 101409: Rear, effort 4f out, sn btn: bckd from 12/1, 6 wk abs: see 672 (AW). 7 15
-- **ACCOUNTING** [4] 4-9-3 (67) A Beech (5) 20/1: 4/03-0: Nvr a factor in 10th: fit from the jumps. 2½ 32
853 **I TINA 22** [9] 4-9-3 (67) Pat Eddery 11/1: 364-60: Led till 3f out, fdd into last: see 853. 7 22
11 ran Time 2m 34.2 (9.2) (Miss P E Decker) D W P Arbuthnot Upper Lambourn, Berks.

1092 4.00 TWERTON HCAP 3YO+ 0-70 (E) 5f rnd Good 54 +08 Fast [70]
£2758 £788 £394 3 yo rec 9 lb

763 **KHALIK 35** [8] Miss Gay Kelleway 6-9-8 (64)(t) K Fallon 7/2 FAV: 200-31: 6 b g Lear Fan - Silver Dollar (Shirley Heights) Dwelt, bhd, gd hdwy over 1f out, styd on strongly to lead cl-home, rdn out: nicely bckd, gd time: won first 2 in '99, at Salisbury & Lingfield (h'caps, rtd 64): wng form over 5/6f, stays 7f: acts on fast, likes gd & gd/soft, any trk: tried blnks & wears a t-strap. 70
1008 **BOWLERS BOY 8** [3] J J Quinn 7-8-7 (49) J Fortune 8/1: 35-0W2: 7 ch g Risk Me - Snow Wonder (Music Boy) In tch, eff over 1f out, kept on ins last: carries head high, but well h'capped & likes Pontefract. ¾ 53
802 **ORIEL STAR 32** [7] P D Evans 4-8-7 (49)(vis) J F Egan 20/1: 0-0063: 4 b f Safawan - Silvers Era (Balidar) Prom, kept on for press to lead dist, collared & no extra fnl 70y: back in a visor: best over an easy 5f. 1 50
881 **DIAMOND GEEZER 20** [6] R Hannon 4-9-6 (62) P Fitzsimons (5) 13/2: 3-5024: With ldr, went on over 2f out till just inside last, no extra: best form over a sharp 6f as in 881, see 113. ¾ 61
1008 **REGAL SONG 8** [15] 4-9-7 (63)(bl) Pat Eddery 7/1: 3203W5: Bhd, eff 2f out, onepace: needs 6f? 1 60
673 **OFF HIRE 49** [10] 4-8-11 (53)(vis) R Fitzpatrick (3) 25/1: 142106: In tch, eff to chall over 1f out, wknd. 1¾ 46
897 **BRAMBLE BEAR 19** [9] 6-8-7 (49) D Sweeney 8/1: 662607: Sn bhd, some late gains: see 691, 403. 1¾ 37
2304} **LADYCAKE 309** [2] 4-8-1 (43) F Norton 33/1: 0006-8: Led till over 2f out, wknd over 1f out: reapp: in '99 trained by J Berry, plcd twice (rtd 59a & 42 at best): '98 wnr at Musselburgh (2, auct mdn & sell, rtd 65): needs a sharp 5f & acts on gd, gd/soft & fibresand: has run well fresh at Musselburgh, tried blnks. 1¾ 26
3543} **SPLIT THE ACES 252** [5] 4-8-3 (44)(1ow) S Drowne 7/1: 0000-9: Chsd ldrs, wknd over 1f out: gamble from 16/1 on reapp: in gd early season '99 form, won at Bath (clmr, rtd 61), subs form t.o: eff at 5f, stays 6f on gd, possibly handles soft: has run well fresh: tried blnks to no avail. hd 27
2256} **MALAAH 311** [19] 4-8-13 (55)(bl) A Beech (5) 33/1: 0066-0: Nvr a factor on reapp: 10th: in '99 trained by R Armstrong, unplcd (rtd 54, tried blnks, sprint trips). ½ 36
3912} **DAME JUDE 231** [12] 4-9-1 (57) L Dettori 16/1: 4000-0: Al bhd: 11th: reapp: in '99 trained by W Muir, plcd (rtd 68): '98 wnr at Brighton & Sandown (nov auct, rtd 76): eff at 5/6f, prob stays 7f on firm & gd/soft. 1¼ 34
4050} **BREW 223** [13] 4-9-4 (60) R Hughes 14/1: 0060-0: Waited with, no dngr: 12th, reapp: best in '99 when rnr-up on reapp (h'cap, rtd 75): eff at 5f on gd/firm on a sharp/undul trk. ½ 36
774 **MANGUS 34** [11] 6-9-5 (61) S Sanders 20/1: 14-650: In tch, eased when btn fnl 1f: 13th, see 774 (AW). shd 36
4261} **SUPERBIT 210** [17] 8-9-4 (60) W Supple 20/1: 0031-0: Al bhd, 14th, reapp. 1¼ 31
1008 **EASTERN TRUMPETER 8** [14] 4-9-6 (62) Claire Bryan (5) 9/1: 141000: In tch, btn over 2f out: 18th. 0
175 **Purple Fling 143** [16] 9-9-0 (56) J D Smith 25/1: 4586} **Nickles 182** [18] 5-8-11 (53) A Daly 16/1:
631 **Catchthebatch 59** [1] 4-8-12 (54)(bl) S Carson (5) 16/1:
897 **Knockemback Nellie 19** [20] 4-9-7 (63) N Pollard 25/1:
816 **Democracy 29** [4] 4-10-0 (70)(bl) L Newman (5) 25/1:
20 ran Time 1m 02.6 (2.3) (A F Griffin) Miss Gay Kelleway Lingfield, Surrey.

1093	4.30 BLATHWAYT MDN 3YO (D) 1m2f46y Good 54 -38 Slow
	£3945 £1214 £607 £303

-- **FANTASY PARK** [5] Mrs A J Perrett 3-9-0 Pat Eddery 10/1: 1: 3 b c Sanglamore - Fantasy Flyer **89+**
(Lear Fan) Sn bhd, rdn 3f out, styd on well over 1f out to lead last strides, going away: op 7/1 on debut: eff
at 10.2f, 12f sure to suit: runs well fresh: improve plenty for this fine debut, go on & win more races.

972 **TRAHERN 13** [12] J H M Gosden 3-9-0 L Dettori 4/6 FAV: -42: 3 b c Cadeaux Genereux - Tansy shd **86**
(Shareef Dancer) Waited with, hdwy over 3f out, led over 1f out, kept on for press till collared last strides:
hvly bckd: lost little in defeat & stays 10.2f: must win sn: see 972.

4474} **SKIBO 193** [4] M P Tregoning 3-9-0 A Daly 8/1: 44-3: 3 b c Carnegie - Dyna Avenue (Northern 2½ **82**
Taste) Led aft 2f till over 1f out, no extra: reapp: rtd 84 when 4th on both juv starts (back-end mdns):
eff at 1m/10f, further could suit: acts on gd & soft grnd & on a stiff trk: should win a race.

936 **DESTINATION 15** [6] C A Cyzer 3-9-0 S Sanders 20/1: 0-524: Handy, rdn & no extra appr final 1f. ½ **81**

-- **MY LAST BEAN** [10] 3-9-0 J Stack 50/1: 5: Cl-up, ev ch appr 2f out, no extra over 1f out: 1 **79**
half-brother to a wng stayer & a sprint wnr: stays 10f & a gd debut.

4605} **ILJASOOR 179** [14] 3-9-0 W Supple 20/1: 0-6: In tch, rdn & no extra final 2f: rtd 69 sole juv 1½ **77**
start: dam 1m/12f wnr & mid-dists will suit later.

916 **MAZAARR 18** [3] 3-9-0 S Drowne 50/1: 67: In tch, wknd 2f out: see 916. ½ **76**

2932} **NEW FORTUNE 282** [2] 3-8-9 Martin Dwyer 50/1: 0-8: Dwelt, sn in tch, btn soon over 2f out: well 5 **64**
btn sole juv start: dam 7f wnr & 1m/10f should suit.

915 **ICON 18** [1] 3-8-9 T E Durcan 33/1: 09: Nvr a factor: see 915. 2 **61**

4338} **SHAPOUR 203** [9] 3-9-0 K Fallon 7/2: 02-0: Dwelt, sn bhd, effort over 3f out, sn wknd: rnr-up on 2½ **61**
2nd of only 2 juv starts (rtd 80, mdn): eff at 1m, bred to want mid-dists: handles gd/soft grnd.

-- **ALWAYS VIGILANT** [15] 3-8-9 R Hughes 14/1: 0: Led 2f, cl-up, wknd 2f out: sister to a 12f wnr. **0**

814 **Sioned Lyn 29** [8] 3-8-9 R Price 33/1: 850 **Blues Whisperer 22** [11] 3-9-0 R Perham 66/1:

884 **Silver Auriole 20** [13] 3-8-9 N Pollard 100/1:

14 ran Time 2m 15.4 (9.4) (K Abdulla) Mrs A J Perrett Pulborough, West Sussex.

1094	5.00 LEVY BOARD HCAP 3YO 0-75 (E) 1m2f46y Good 54 -34 Slow	**[82]**
	£2821 £806 £403	

4537} **BLESS THE BRIDE 187** [9] J L Dunlop 3-9-4 (72) L Dettori 6/1: 466-1: 3 b f Darshaan - Feather Bride **76**
(Groom Dancer) Waited with, hdwy 2f out, styd on well for press to lead cl-home, drvn out on reapp: jockey rec a
2-day whip ban: unplcd on 3 juv starts (rtd 75): sire won French Derby: runs well fresh & relished step up to
10f, further will suit: has improved since h'capped & stepped up to mid-dists, like so many J Dunlop 3yo's.

3736} **DISTANT PROSPECT 243** [8] J R Arnold 3-9-0 (68) S Sanders 33/1: 0030-2: 3 b c Namaqualand - hd **71**
Ukraine's Affair (The Minstrel) Waited with, eff 2f out, kept on well for press in last to lead cl-home, collared
last strides: reapp: plcd once as a juv (rtd 73): half-brother to a mid-dist/styg wnr: enjoyed this step up to
10f, further should suit: acts on gd/firm & gd grnd: open to further improvement.

3980} **PALUA 227** [13] Mrs A J Bowlby 3-9-7 (75) J Stack 25/1: 0030-3: 3 b c Sri Pekan - Reticent Bride ¾ **76**
(Shy Groom) In tch, gd hdwy to lead over 2f out, collared ins last, onepace, not btn far: reapp, top weight:
plcd on 1 of 4 juv starts (mdn, rtd 82): dam 6f wnr: eff at 7f, enjoyed step up to 10f: acts on gd/firm, gd
grnd & a stiff trk: fine reapp under top weight, spot-on for this.

*1055 **PIPSSALIO 3** [11] Jamie Poulton 3-9-1 (69)(6ex) O Urbina 9/4 FAV: 00-214: In tch, kept on for press ½ **69**
3f out, swtchd left & kept on for press appr fnl 1f, held when slightly hmpd cl-home: nicely bckd, stays 10f.

4061} **MILLIONS 222** [5] 3-8-7 (61) K Fallon 4/1: 000-5: Slow away, bhd, effort for press over 1f out when nk **61+**
slightly short of room, staying on in 4th, hmpd & snatched up cl-home: shade unlucky: reapp: unplcd in 3
juv starts over 1m: enjoyed step up to 10f: improve for this, just the type for a 12f h'cap.

4305} **WHENWILLIEMETHARRY 204** [12] 3-9-0 (68) N Pollard 16/1: 4500-6: Bhd, gd hdwy to chall appr final 1¾ **64**
1f, onepace & held when hmpd cl-home: reapp: unplcd juv (rtd 72 at best): eff at 7f, just stays 10f on gd & firm.

3803} **ELEGIA PRIMA 238** [6] 3-8-9 (63) M Roberts 25/1: 1600-7: Bhd, some late gains, no dngr: reapp: 3½ **53**
won debut as a juv, at Salisbury (med auct mdn, rtd 72), form subs t.o: eff at 7f on firm grnd, should
apprec further: has tried blnks: improve.

4257} **KISTY 210** [3] 3-9-4 (72) C Rutter 12/1: 054-8: Slow away, nvr a factor: reapp: unplcd in 3 juv ½ **61**
starts (rtd 77): dam 12f wnr: half-sister to a top class 1m/10f scorer: eff at 1m on soft grnd.

4305} **SWEET ANGELINE 204** [4] 3-9-1 (69) W Supple 16/1: 4030-9: In tch, eff to chall well over 2f out, wknd. 4 **52**

894 **EASTWOOD DRIFTER 19** [7] 3-9-0 (68) R Hughes 8/1: 600-30: In tch, wknd 2f out: 10th, btr 894 (1m). 1 **50**

892 **ESTABLISHMENT 19** [15] 3-9-0 (68) T G McLaughlin 7/1: 00-640: In tch, wknd over 3f out: 11th. hd **50**

800 **CLASSIC LORD 33** [14] 3-8-3 (57) J Fanning 9/2: 500-00: In tch, wknd over 2f out: 12th. 2½ **35**

833 **COWBOYS AND ANGELS 26** [10] 3-9-1 (69) A Daly 33/1: 0-3360: Led 6f out till over 2f out: 13th. 6 **38**

933 **Hard Days Night 15** [2] 3-7-11 (50)(1ow) Dale Gibson 40/1:

4516} **Titan Lad 189** [1] 3-7-10 (50)(7oh) R Brisland 25/1: 40/1:

15 ran Time 2m 15.0 (9) (Mrs Dan Abbott) J L Dunlop Arundel, West Sussex.

WINDSOR TUESDAY MAY 2ND Sharp Fig 8 Track.

Official Going GOOD TO SOFT (SOFT in places). Stalls: Inside; Rnd Crse realignment rendered pace figures inapplicable.

1095	5.30 BONUSPRINT MDN 2YO (D) 5f Good/Soft Inapplicable
	£3477 £1070 £535 £267

-- **IMPERIAL MEASURE** [4] B R Millman 2-9-0 P Robinson 3/1: 1: 2 b c Inchinor - Fair Eleanor (Saritamer) **77**
Pld hard cl-up, not much room & swtchd appr final 1f, kept on well to lead nr fin, drvn out: nicely bckd: 11,000
gns Feb foal, half-brother to 3 juv wnrs: eff at 5f, 6f will suit: goes on gd/soft, runs well fresh: gd debut.

984 **SOLDIER ON 12** [3] M R Channon 2-9-0 T Quinn 7/2: 02: 2 b c General Monash - Golden Form nk **76**
(Formidable) Handy, rdn to lead dist, cght fnl strides under hands & heels: op 5/2: acts on gd/soft grnd.

-- **WESTERN HERO** [2] R Hannon 2-9-0 Dane O'Neill 2/1 FAV: 3: 2 ch c Lake Coniston - Miss Pickpocket 3 **69**
(Petorius) Tried to make all, rdn appr final 1f, sn hdd, no extra: well bckd tho' op 13/8, clr rem: 26,000 gns
Mar 1st foal, dam 5f juv wnr, sire a sprinter: speedily bred newcomer, should improve & win a race.

-- **CHEVENING LODGE** [7] K R Burke 2-9-0 P Doe 20/1: 4: Held up, prog 2f out, sn hung left, onepace: op 14/1: 12,000 gns Eagle Eyed Mar foal, half-brother to useful sprint juv, Magical Times: dam 5f wnr. *5* **56**
-- **MER MADE** [6] 2-8-9 G Carter 14/1: 5: Missed break, nvr got in it: 2,700 gns Prince Sabo Feb 1st foal, dam a miler, sire a sprinter: with T Naughton. *1¼* **48**
932 **KINGS CREST 15** [8] 2-9-0 J Mackay (7) 33/1: 06: Chsd ldrs till edged left & outpcd 2f out: 17,000 gns Deploy Feb 1st foal, dam 11f wnr, sire 12f performer: needs more time & a lot further than 5f. *hd* **53**
-- **WESTON HILLS** [5] 2-9-0 N Callan 7/1: 7: Outpcd thro'out: stablemate 4th, op 5/1: 8,000 gns Robellino Apr foal, half-brother to 4 juv wnrs, notably useful sprinter Westcourt Magic, dam 1m wnr. *7* **35**
-- **THE WALL** [1] 2-8-9 A Polli (3) 40/1: 8: Cl-up till wknd qckly ent final 2f: cheaply bought Mistertopogigo Apr foal, half-sister to 2 sprinters, sire a sprinter: with J Gilbert. *4* **20**
8 ran Time 1m 03.0 (4.2) (Southern Cross Racing) B R Millman Kentisbeare, Devon.

1096

6.00 IRELAND CLASS STKS 3YO+ 0-60 (F) 1m3f135y Good/Soft Inapplicable
£2352 £672 £336 3 yo rec 19lb

939 **CROSS DALL 15** [1] Lady Herries 3-7-13 J Mackay (7) 13/2: 003-31: 3 b f Blues Traveller - Faapette (Runnett) Restrained in last, gd prog appr final 2f, led before dist, rdn out: bckd tho' op 5/1: btn fav on reapp (wore eyeshield): plcd in an AW mdn in late '99 for R Ingram (rtd 56a & 68$): eff at 11.5f on gd/soft grnd, handles equitrack, sharp trks: eff with/without visor, not blinks: best held up (forced it last time). **57**
937 **FLIQUET BAY 15** [3] Mrs A J Perrett 3-8-2 (BL) T Ashley 5/1 FAV: 600-42: 3 b g Namaqualand - Thatcherite (Final Straw) Chsd ldrs, und press from 3f out, styd on for 2nd but not pace of wnr: nicely bckd: eff at 11.5f on gd/soft: lazy sort, wore blnks here & shld find a race when puting best foot forward. *1½* **57**
892 **TWOS BETTER 19** [7] G L Moore 3-8-2 F Norton 14/1: 000-03: 3 br g Rock City - Miss Pin Up (Kalaglow) Mid-div, chsd ldrs 2f out, sn rdn, onepcd towards fin: op 10/1: apprec step up to 11.5f on gd/soft. *hd* **57**
937 **THE FROG QUEEN 15** [11] D W P Arbuthnot 3-7-13 A Nicholls (3) 12/1: 001-04: Rear, rdn 2f out, kept on but unable to chall: stays 11.5f, see 937. *1½* **52**
943 **PEKAY 15** [10] 7-9-7 (bl) J Bosley (7) 11/2: 2/0035: Held up, prog & ev ch appr final 2f, rdn & no extra before dist: nicely bckd tho' op 9/2: back up in trip, blnks reapplied: btr 943 (10f h'cap). *2½* **52**
4602} **DALBY OF YORK 180** [6] 4-9-7 J Fortune 6/1: 3000-6: Cl-up, led halfway till ent final 2f, onepcd: reapp: '99 wnr here at Windsor (reapp, h'cap) & Musselburgh (class stks, rtd 63): mdn prom in '98 (rtd 60): eff at 11.5f/14f, stays 15f: acts on firm/fast grnd, sharp trks, without blnks: sharper next time on qcker surface. *hd* **52**
892 **BLESS 19** [4] 3-7-13 G Baker (7) 16/1: 006-07: Led till halfway, ev ch till fdd 2f out: stays 11.5f? *2½* **46**
885 **FLETCHER 20** [9] 6-9-7 T Quinn 13/2: 00-008: Nvr a factor: see 182. *1* **48**
827 **FIFE AND DRUM 27** [8] 3-8-2 G Carter 9/1: 000-09: Chsd ldrs till 3f out: lngr trip, see 827. *nk* **47**
4284} **OSCIETRA 206** [2] 4-9-4 S Carson (5) 11/1: 4060-0: Rear, hdwy 4f out, btn 2f out: 10th, reapp: '99 Kempton wnr (appr h'cap, rtd 67): unrcd juv: eff over a sharp 9f on soft: drop back in trip likely to suit. *5* **39**
889 **JUST WIZ 20** [5] 4-9-7 (bl) R Smith (5) 10/1: 055300: Pld hard in tch, wknd 3f out: 11th: see 161. *2½* **39**
11 ran Time 2m 32.6 (Global Racing Club) Lady Herries Angmering, West Sussex.

1097

6.30 R WALTERS FILLIES HCAP 3YO+ 0-85 (D) 1m67y rnd Good/Soft Inapplicable [80]
£3965 £1220 £610 £305 3 yo rec 13lb

859 **DENS JOY 22** [5] Miss D A McHale 4-8-4 (56) R Mullen 20/1: 5-3001: 4 b f Archway - Bonvin (Taufan) Rear, rdn & had to be swtchd ent fnl 2f, led below dist, just lasted, rdn out: first win: plcd on '99 debut for H Collingridge (rtd 65): apprec drop back to a sharp 1m, poss stays 12f on gd/soft, fast & fibresand. **59**
3722} **UMBRIAN GOLD 243** [4] J A R Toller 4-9-10 (76) R Ffrench 8/1: 2210-2: 4 b f Perugino - Golden Sunlight (Ile de Bourbon) Handy, lost place 3f out, rallied before dist, not much room, strong run for press, just failed: op 6/1, reapp: '99 Ascot wnr (mdn, thrice rnr-up, rtd 81): eff at 7f/1m, shld stay 10f on this evidence: acts on fast & soft grnd, any trk: likes to force the pace: should go one better soon. *shd* **78**
847 **DORISSIO 24** [6] I A Balding 4-8-12 (64) A Nicholls (3) 15/8 FAV: 11-333: 4 b f Efisio - Floralia (Auction Ring) Trkd ldrs, pshd into lead appr final 1f, sn rdn/hdd & onepace: hvly bckd, return to 7f suit? *¾* **64**
4598} **SILK DAISY 180** [2] H Candy 4-8-12 (64) A McGlone 6/1: 3023-4: Chsd ldrs, led 2f out till bef fnl 1f, no extra: reapp: plcd thrice last term (mdns, rtd 69): eff at 7f/1m, goes on fast & gd/soft grnd, forcing it. *2* **60**
817 **TRUMP STREET 29** [7] 4-7-11 (48)(1ow) F Norton 6/1: 0-0025: Led till 2f out, fdd: unsuited up in trip? *9* **29**
739 **MY ALIBI 36** [1] 4-8-4 (56) N Callan 7/2: 56-126: Held up, effort 3f out, sn btn: nicely bckd, see 692. *8* **22**
601 **EPERNAY 64** [3] 4-9-4 (70) D Meah (7) 9/1: 25-157: Al bhd, struggling 2f out: op 7/1, 9 wk abs on turf return: surely something amiss: see 453 (fibresand, auct mdn). *6* **26**
7 ran Time 1m 46.5 (Miss D A McHale) Miss D A McHale Newmarket, Suffok.

1098

7.00 PRICEWATERHOUSE HCAP 3YO 0-80 (D) 5f Good/Soft Inapplicable [86]
£4101 £1262 £631 £315

105 **QUEEN OF THE MAY 160** [6] M R Channon 3-9-3 (75) S Drowne 14/1: 4413-1: 3 b f Nicolotte - Varnish (Final Straw) Trkd ldrs, rdn appr final 1f, burst thro' to lead below dist, shade readily: over 5 mth abs: '99 wnr at Brighton (debut, fill auct mdn, rtd 79) & Lingfield (nursery, rtd 77a): eff at 5f/6f on firm, gd/soft & equitrack, likes sharp/undul trks: runs well fresh: can force the pace: speedy, improving filly. **83**
883 **CORBLETS 20** [8] S Dow 3-8-7 (65) P Doe 14/1: 250-32: 3 b f Timeless Times - Dear Glenda (Gold Song) In tch, prog to chall appr final 1f, outpcd by wnr: gd run, goes on fast, gd/soft grnd & equitrack. *1¾* **67**
994 **BEST BOND 10** [15] N P Littmoden 3-8-8 (66) T G McLaughlin 20/1: 055-03: 3 ch c Cadeaux Genereux - My Darlingdaughter (Night Shift) Outpcd till strong run final 1f, nvr nrr: '99 mdn promise for J Dunlop (rtd 68 & 78$): eff at 5f, return to further sure to suit: handles gd/soft grnd & looks a future winner. *hd* **68**
994 **CD FLYER 10** [14] M R Channon 3-9-2 (74) T Quinn 9/2 FAV: 5-0644: Towards rear, styd on under press appr final 1f, nrst fin: well bckd, stablemate wnr: handled drop to 5f, return to 6f will suit: see 852. *nk* **75**
901 **LIZZIE SIMMONDS 19** [13] 3-7-10 (54)(t) Kim Tinkler 25/1: 00-455: Prom, effort 2f out, ev ch, onepace inside last: op 16/1: should find a race off this mark: see 777. *nk* **54**
960 **MARSHALL ST CYR 14** [11] 3-8-2 (59)(1ow) J F Egan 12/1: 5-0056: Well plcd/ev ch till no extra dist. *1* **57**
4250} **POPPYS SONG 210** [12] 3-9-0 (72) C Rutter 9/1: 3441-7: Handy, under press 2f out, unable to qckn: tchd 12/1, reapp: '99 Catterick wnr (mdn, rtd 74): half-sister to sprinter Speed On: eff at 5f on firm & soft. *nk* **68**
982 **JAMES STARK 12** [16] 3-9-7 (79) G Carter 25/1: 16-008: Al arnd same place: stablemate 3rd, top-weight. *nk* **74**
3373} **AROGANT PRINCE 262** [17] 3-7-12 (56) R Brisland (5) 33/1: 0460-9: Chsd ldrs, wknd under press appr final 1f: reapp: moderate 3rd on debut last term (mdn, rtd 58 & 73$): with J Bridger. *1¾* **47**
4476} **RED TYPHOON 193** [9] 3-9-5 (77) N Callan 20/1: 1610-0: Mid-div, not much room 2f out, nvr dngrs: 10th, reapp: '99 wnr at Haydock & Lingfield (clmrs, rtd 79, J Berry): eff at 6f, prob stays 7f: acts on *hd* **68**

WINDSOR   TUESDAY MAY 2ND   Sharp Fig 8 Track.

fast & soft grnd, prob any trk: best up with/forcing the pace: sharper next time at 6f: with M Kettle.

837	**DANCEMMA 25** [2] 3-9-4 (76) D Sweeney 16/1: 602-00: Chsd ldrs till 2f out: 11th, see 837.	hd	66

*652 **LICENCE TO THRILL 55** [10] 3-9-3 (75) R Price 6/1: 25-110: Led, drifted left ent final 2f, hdd — ½ 63
dist & btn: 12th, 8 wk abs: turf return: progressive on equitrack previously, worth another chance: see 652.
4167} **DUCIE 215** [3] 3-8-11 (69) A Nicholls (3) 9/1: 2020-0: Nvr in it: 13th on reapp, rtd 75/1: thrice — hd 57
rnr-up last term (fill mdn, rtd 82): eff at 5f, should get further: acts on fast & gd/soft grnd: with I Balding.
888 **CHORUS 20** [1] 3-9-3 (75) P Robinson 5/1: 544-20: Al towards rear: 16th, nicely bckd, dropped in trip. — 0
888 **Born To Rule 20** [4] 3-8-11 (69) L Newman (5) 25/1:   4491} **Absent Friends 192** [5] 3-8-10 (68) J Fortune 16/1:
808 **Prime Recreation 31** [7] 3-8-12 (70) Dale Gibson 33/1:
17 ran   Time 1m 02.1 (3.3)   (Miss Maggie Worsdell & Mrs Carolyn Wood)   M R Channon West Isley, Berks.

1099   7.30 STORACALL MDN 3YO (D)   1m67y rnd Good/Soft Inapplicable
£4530   £1394   £697   £348

983 **ELGHANI 12** [14] R W Armstrong 3-9-0 R Hills 12/1: 01: 3 br c Lahib - Fawaakeh (Lyphard) — 91
Led after 2f, rdn & found extra when prsd appr fnl 1f, kept on strgly: imprvd for debut: unrcd juv, dam 6f juv wnr:
apprec step up to 1m, may get further: goes on gd/soft grnd & a sharp trk: eff forcing the pace: progressive colt.
983 **BLUE MOUNTAIN 12** [11] R F Johnson Houghton 3-9-0 L Dettori 6/1: 235-52: 3 ch c Elmaamul - — 2 86
Glenfinlass (Lomond) Cl-up, rdn to chall appr fnl 1f, onepce ins last: eff at 7f/1m: in front of this wnr in 983.
4379} **GIVE THE SLIP 200** [2] Mrs A J Perrett 3-9-0 Pat Eddery 8/1: 34-3: 3 b c Slip Anchor - Falafil — ¾ 85+
(Fabulous Dancer) Pulled hard, handy, effort 2f out, styd on but not pace of front pair: hvly bckd, well
clr rem, reapp: ran well both '99 starts (hot Newmarket mdn, rtd 94): eff at 1m but is crying out for mid-dists:
goes on gd & gd/soft grnd: looks a sure-fire wnr when stepped up in trip.
972 **VALDERO 13** [16] W R Muir 3-9-0 R Brisland (5) 25/1: -04: Towards rear, shkn up & imprvd to go — 8 69
4th appr final 1f, nvr nr ldrs: Arazi colt, one more run for h'cap mark.
983 **JUMBO JET 12** [9] 3-9-0 (t) J Fortune 14/1: 405: Early ldr, no extra ent final 2f: see 983. — ½ 68
-- **LILLAN** [7] 3-8-9 T E Durcan 16/1: 6: Held up, late hdwy under hands-&-heels, nvr dngrs: — shd 63+
stablemate of 5th: Hernando filly, related to several wnrs: looks sure o improve for this: with G Butler.
4379} **TOORAK 200** [3] M Hills 10/1: 6-7: Al same place: reapp: 6th sole '99 start (rtd 86). — 1 66
972 **BLUE STATE 13** [1] 3-9-0 K Fallon 3/1: -08: Dwelt, chsd ldrs 3f out, wknd before dist: hvly bckd. — 2½ 62
-- **VANNUCCI** [13] 3-9-0 P Dobbs (5) 50/1: 9: Nvr got in it: debut: Perugino gelding, dam unrcd. — 1½ 59
4490} **TARCOOLA 192** [12] 3-9-0 R Cochrane 33/1: 04-0: In tch till 2f out: 10th, reapp: well btn 4th in '99 — hd 59
(rtd 57): Pursuit Of Love colt, dam related to smart sprinter Dazzle: apprec h'caps: with V Soane.
4600} **BUXTEDS FIRST 180** [15] J Mongan (5) 50/1: 00-0: Al towards rear: 11th, reapp: well btn in '99. — ½ 53
962 **MOBO BACO 14** [8] 3-9-0 O Urbina 50/1: 040: Chsd ldrs till 3f out: 12th: see 962. — shd 58
934 **PASADENA 15** [6] 3-8-9 R Hughes 20/1: 040: Al bhd: 13th: see 934. — hd 52
3562} **Swiss Alps 251** [4] 3-9-0 R Price 50/1:   814 **Ridgewood Bay 29** [5] 3-8-9 R Smith (5) 50/1:
4150} **Issara 216** [10] 3-9-0 (BL) T G McLaughlin 50/1:
16 ran   Time 1m 46.0   (Hamdan Al Maktoum)   R W Armstrong Newmarket.

1100   8.00 CASTLE HCAP 3YO+ 0-60 (F)   1m2f   Good/Soft Inapplicable   [60]
£2646   £756   £378   3 yo rec 15lb

*835 **ANOTHER MONK 25** [16] R Ingram 9-8-12 (44) L Newman (5) 20/1: -41411: 9 b g Supreme Leader - Royal — 51
Demon (Tarboosh) Led halfway, rdn appr fnl 1f, held on well, pshd out: in terrific form, earlier won at Lingfield
(2, sell & appr h'cap, rtd 47a): plcd in '99 for B Johnson (h'caps, rtd 44 & 51a): eff at 10f/2m: acts on gd/sft
grnd, both AWs, loves Lingfield: runs well fresh, with/without visor & likes to be up with/forcing the pace: game.
892 **SECOND PAIGE 19** [11] N A Graham 3-8-9 (56) R Cochrane 9/1: 00-402: 3 b g Nicolotte - My First Paige — ¾ 60
(Runnett): Rear, kept on well for press ent final 2f, held towards fin: tchd 12/1: apprec step up to 10f:
goes on fast & gd/soft grnd: gd run against elders, came from a long way back, shld win soon: see 744.
896 **MELLOW MISS 19** [13] R M Flower 4-9-6 (52) S Drowne 20/1: -56033: 4 b f Danehill - Like The Sun — 1¾ 54
(Woodman): U.r. & bolted before start, rear, prog 2f out, rdn to chall before dist, onepace: stays 10f, gd run.
880 **SAMMYS SHUFFLE 20** [17] Jamie Poulton 5-8-8 (40)(bl) O Urbina 25/1: 153064: Chsd ldrs, under — 1 40
press 2f out, styd on, unable to chall: gd turf return: handles gd/soft, loves equitrack/Lingfield & Brighton.
779 **TIME LOSS 34** [5] 5-9-2 (52) Pat Eddery 13/2 FAV: 000-05: Towards rear, short of room ent final 3f, — ¾ 51
drvn to chse ldrs bef dist, no extra ins last: bckd frm op 9/2: rnr-up on '99 reapp (appr h'cap, rtd 66):
'98 Chepstow wnr (mdn, rtd 84, H Candy): eff at 10/11f on fast & gd/soft grnd, prob any trk, without blnks.
854 **NAFITH 22** [20] 4-9-9 (55) S Whitworth 20/1: 321306: Bhd, some late prog under press, nvr on terms. — 2½ 50
749 **JESSINCA 35** [3] 4-8-8 (40) P Doe 25/1: 151007: Chsd ldrs, effort 3f out, no impression: longer trip. — nk 34
490 **BITTER SWEET 82** [18] 4-9-8 (54) G Hind 25/1: 20-048: Nvr a factor: not given a hard time: rnr-up — hd 48
in a v weak mdn last term (rtd 61, D Elsworth): eff at 9f on soft grnd: handles firm: interesting in a mdn h'cap.
647 **KOCAL 57** [21] 4-8-11 (43) K Fallon 9/1: 00-259: Nvr dngrs, wide into str: 8 wk abs, longer trip. — hd 36
4437} **IN THE STOCKS 196** [2] 6-9-6 (52) S Carson 9/1: 0561-0: Chsd ldrs, rdn appr final 2f, no impress: — ½ 44
10th: tchd 14/1, reapp: landed final '99 start at Lingfield (h'cap, rtd 51): '98 Bath wnr (sell h'cap, rtd 55):
eff at 1m/11.5f on fast & gd/soft grnd, prob soft, any trk: with L Cottrell.
880 **THATCHAM 20** [4] 4-9-4 (50) R Price 11/1: 00-320: Chsd ldrs, ev ch 2f out, wknd: 11th, see 880. — 2½ 39
854 **THE SHADOW 22** [8] 4-9-11 (57) A Nicholls (3) 12/1: 615-00: Al same place: 12th, top-weight, see 854. — 2 43
4366} **SILENT SOUND 201** [7] 4-9-8 (54) D Sweeney 11/1: 6020-0: Nvr troubled ldrs: 13th: reapp: '99 — ½ 39
Redcar wnr for P Calver (mdn h'cap, rtd 57 at best): eff at 10f, stays 12f, tried 2m: acts on fast &
soft grnd, any trk: best blnkd (not worn): likely to leave this bhd next time: with Mrs Perrett.
1058 **FAMOUS 3** [9] 7-8-10 (42)(bl) R Brisland (5) 7/1: -00050: Al towards rear: 16th, qck reapp, bckd from 9/1. — 0
887 **ISLAND THYMES 20** [10] 3-8-9 (56) R Hills 12/1: 06-300: Nvr on terms: 18th, see 813 (7f). — 0
890 **SILVERTOWN 20** [1] 5-9-9 (55) J P Spencer 9/1: 0-1100: Led till halfway, btn 3f out: 20th, drifted from 5/1. — 0
855 **Da Boss 22** [22] 5-9-8 (54) Dane O'Neill 25/1:   889 **Druridge Bay 20** [12] 4-8-9 (41) S Righton 33/1:
963 **Joli Flyers 14** [19] 6-8-9 (41) F Norton 25/1:   620 **Who Goes There 62** [6] 4-9-0 (46) N Callan 33/1:
568 **Ciel De Reve 70** [15] 6-8-10 (42) T G McLaughlin 33/1:
21 ran   Time 2m 10.0   (D G Wheatley)   R Ingram Epsom, Surrey.

Official Going   SOFT (GOOD/SOFT Places).   Stalls: Inside

1101   2.45 TIMEFORM SELL HCAP 3YO+ 0-60 (F)   **1m rnd   Good/Soft 98   -03 Slow**   [60]
£2488   £711   £355   3 yo rec 13lb

958   **LEONIE SAMUAL** 15 [20] R J Hodges 5-8-10 (42) F Norton 7/1: 00-431: 5 b m Safawan - Hy Wilma   46
(Jalmood) Held up, prog wide 2f out, styd on gamely ins last to lead line: lkd well, rdn ins 1st success: well btn
both '99 starts: eff at 6/7f, suited by 1m: acts gd & soft, sharp/undul or stiff trk: apprec drop to sell grade.
3779}   **SPECIAL K** 240 [2] J R Weymes 8-8-10 (42) D Holland 9/1: 04U0-2: 8 br m Treasure Kay - Lissi Gori   hd   45
(Bolkonski) In tch, chsd ldr over 1f out, styd on well & briefly led nr line, hdd post: reapp: '99 reapp wnr here
at Pontefract (clmr, rtd 46): rtd 53 in '98 (J R Turner): eff at 7/8.4f on any grnd/trk: runs well fresh.
675   **MUSTANG** 48 [7] J Pearce 7-8-7 (39)(vis) R Price 16/1: 002503: 7 ch g Thatching - Lassoo (Caerleon)   nk   41
Led, clr 2f out, hard rdn/hdd nr line: tchd 3/1, 7 wk abs: jockey given 3-day whip ban.
834   **MUTABARI** 27 [5] Mrs S Lamyman 6-8-12 (44) J Fanning 16/1: 304004: Hndy, chsd ldr 2f out, sn held.   4   38
907   **BLOOMING AMAZING** 19 [8] 6-9-10 (56) J Weaver 9/1: 060505: Chsd ldrs, onepace fnl 2f: see 176.   1½   47
907   **ZECHARIAH** 19 [13] 4-9-3 (49) J F Egan 5/1 FAV: 005-46: Chsd ldrs, outpcd fnl: lkd well, op 4/1.   ½   39
1050   **ACE OF TRUMPS** 4 [10] 4-9-7 (53)(t) M Fenton 14/1: -10007: Chsd ldrs, held fnl 2f: qck reapp.   1¼   40
859   **WATER LOUP** 23 [4] 4-8-11 (43) R Brisland (5) 20/1: 00-608: In tch, btn 2f out: op 14/1: see 692 (AW).   2½   25
942   **OAKWELL ACE** 16 [15] 4-8-8 (40) B Sooful (7) 11/1: 30-509: Mid-div at best: see 872.   nk   21
922   **ESPERTO** 18 [3] 7-9-1 (47) G Bardwell 20/1: 322/00: Dwelt/rear, rdn & mod gains fnl 3f: 10th: 2½   23
longer priced stablemate of 3rd, swtg: apprec return to 10f+: see 922.
2788] **CODICIL** 48 [14] 4-9-6 (52) T Williams 25/1: 0035-0: Mid-div at best: 11th: 10 month abs: unplcd   3   22
in '99 (rtd 56, stks): '98 Redcar wnr (auct mdn, rtd 68, Mrs J Ramsden): stays 10f, acts on fast & soft grnd.
942   **RED APOLLO** 16 [12] 4-8-8 (40)(vis) L Newton 25/1: -64000: Nvr factor, 12th: see 942, 544.   ½   9
846   **PURSUIVANT** 25 [19] 6-9-5 (51)(bl) R Fitzpatrick (3) 7/1: 0-0340: Mid-div, eff 3f out, sn held: 13th: bckd.   1¼   17
811   **GENERAL KLAIRE** 32 [17] 5-8-13 (45) J Reid 12/1: 136400: Nvr on terms: 14th: see 501 (AW, 7f).   2½   6
699   Try Paris 41 [1] 4-8-12 (44)(vis) J Carroll 33/1:   697   **Komaseph** 44 [16] 8-8-6 (38) P McCabe 25/1:
943   Sterling High 16 [9] 5-8-10 (42)(tbl) T E Durcan 33/1:   846   **Ultra Calm** 25 [6] 4-9-11 (57)(tbl) P Goode (3) 20/1:
624}   Grey Strike 420 [11] 4-8-8 (40) Darren Williams(5) 33/1:1073   **Belle Of Hearts** 2 [18] 4-8-7 (39) A Clark 33/1:
20 ran   Time 1m 49.9 (8.1)   (Mrs Carol Taylor)   R J Hodges Charlton Adam, Somerset

---

1102   3.15 TIMEF'M RACELINE MDN 2YO (D)   **5f rnd   Good/Soft 98   -06 Slow**
£3835   £1180   £590   £295

--   **ATMOSPHERIC** [7] P F I Cole 2-9-0 D Sweeney 8/15 FAV: 1: 2 ch c Irish River - Magic Feeling (Magical   89
Wonder) Made all, rdly asserted under hands & heels riding fnl 2f, styd on strongly: hvly bckd, on toes, lkd fit:
Jan first foal: dam multiple mid-dist Irish wnr, sire top-class 2yo/miler: eff at 5f, looks sure to relish 6f+:
acts gd/soft grnd & a stiff/undul trk: runs well fresh: can rate more highly & win again.
--   **AFFARATI** [8] J L Eyre 2-9-0 J F Egan 10/1: 2: 2 b g Emarati - Affairiste (Simply Great)   3   77
Chsd ldrs, rdn & chsd wnr over 1f out, kept on well ins last: 5L clr 3rd: Jan foal, cost 23,000gns: dam a once
rcd mdn, a half sister to a French Gr 3 wnr: eff at 5f, looks sure to relish 6f+: handles gd/soft grnd.
--   **HARRIER** [4] T D Easterby 2-9-0 W Supple 10/1: 3: 2 b c Prince Of Birds - Casaveha (Persian Bold)   5   68
Chsd wnr, outpcd fnl 2f: lkd well tho' just sharper for this: Jan foal, cost £4,000: dam unrcd, sire Irish 2,000
Guineas wnr: will apprec 6f+ in time & improve.
--   **MARKUSHA** [3] D Nicholls 2-9-0 F Norton 12/1: 4: In tch, onepcd fnl 2f: op 10/1, ndd this: 3½   60
Alahijaz colt, Feb foal, cost 6,000 gns: dam a 5f juv wnr, sire a smart 2yo: sure to apprec further in time.
--   **FRISCO BAY** [1] 2-9-0 R Winston 9/2: 5: Dwelt, rdn/in tch, no impress fnl 2f: op 4/1, stablemate of   1   58
3rd, sharper for this: Effisio colt, Feb foal, half brother to 10f wnr Dancing Bay: dam 10f/hdles wnr, sire 6f/1m
performer: sure to relish further in time & can leave this behind.
--   **HAMASKING** [5] 2-8-9 T E Durcan 16/1: 6: Sn rdn, nvr on terms: ndd this: Hamas filly, Mar foal: 1¼   51
dam unrcd, sire a high-class sprinter: scopey filly, shld improve in time for T D Easterby.
--   **MOUNT ROYALE** [6] 2-9-0 Kim Tinkler 16/1: 7: In tch, outpcd halfway: ndd this: Wolfhound colt,   2   52
Mar foal, cost 19,500 gns: half brother to numerous wnrs incl 3 juv wnrs, dam 12f 3yo wnr.
7 ran   Time 1m 06.5 (5.2)   (Highclere Thoroughbred Racing Ltd)   P F I Cole Whatcombe, Oxon

---

1103   3.50 SILVER TANKARD MDN 3YO (D)   **1m2f   Good/Soft 98   +07 Fast**
£7085   £2180   £1090   £545

957   **ST EXPEDIT** 15 [8] G Wragg 3-9-0 D Holland 11/8 FAV: 3-201: 3 b c Sadler's Wells - Miss Rinjani   94
(Shirley Heights) Keen, chsd ldr, led over 4f out, edged right fnl 2f & held on well: well bckd, padd pick, best
time of day: plcd in '99 (rtd 91, mdn): eff at 10f, 12f shld suit: handles gd & gd/soft & a stiff/undul trk:
trainer reported colt wore a ring-bit today & can rate more highly.
789   **STAR DYNASTY** 34 [3] E A L Dunlop 3-9-0 J Reid 6/4: 4-32: 3 b c Bering - Siwaayib (Green Desert)   ¾   90
Trkd ldrs, chsd wnr 3f out, rdn fnl 2f, kept on tho' al just held: well clr of rem: hvly bckd, op 2/1: styd this
longer 10f trip well: now qual for h'caps but could find a similar contest on this evidence.
957   **TAKWIN** 15 [2] B Hanbury 3-9-0 (t) J Weaver 20/1: 03: 3 b c Alzao - Gale Warning (Last Tycoon)   17   66
In tch halfway, outpcd over 2f out: wears a t-strap: again bhnd today's wnr in 957.
717   **WETHAAB** 40 [7] B W Hills 3-9-0 W Supple 12/1: 0-04: Held up, brief eff 3f out, sn btn: op 10/1, abs.   10   55$
2662} **MAYBEN** 294 [5] 3-9-0 G Parkin 100/1: U60-5: Prom till halfway, sn btn: 10 month abs: unplcd all   1   54
3 '99 starts for C Smith (rtd 72, mdn, poss flattered): now with Mrs P Sly.
701   **HAITHEM** 41 [6] 3-9-0 J Fanning 14/1: 420-06: Pulled hard/hung, led till halfway, sn btn: sharper   4   49
for this, abs: rnr-up in '99 (rtd 80, mdn): eff over 7f on firm, mid-dists shld suit but needs to learn restraint.
934   **ARIALA** 16 [1] 3-8-9 D Sweeney 14/1: 67: In tch 7f: op 10/1: btn 934 (1m).   3½   40
--   **TINKERS CLOUGH** [4] 3-9-0 R Lappin 100/1: 8: Sn bhd: debut, with A Senior.   dist   0
8 ran   Time 2m 17.2 (9.1)   (J L C Pearce)   G Wragg Newmarket

364

PONTEFRACT   WEDNESDAY MAY 3RD   Lefthand, Undulating Track, Stiff Uphill Finish

1104

4.20 TIMEFORM HCAP 3YO 0-85 (D)   **1m2f**   **Good/Soft 98   -09 Slow**   **[90]**
£7280   £2240   £1120   £560

*759   **DANCING BAY 36** [2] Miss J A Camacho 3-9-4 (80) J P Spencer 9/2: 50-11: 3 b g Suave Dancer - Kabayil   **89**
(Dancing Brave) Settled towards rear, prog fnl 3f & rdn to lead ins last, styd on strongly, pushed clr nr fin: op
3/1, h'cap bow: earlier scored at Newcastle (mdn): rtd 72 in '99: apprec step up to 10f, 12f+ will suit: acts
on gd/soft & soft grnd & a stiff/gall trk: has run well fresh: progressive gldg, one to keep on the right side.

924   **RHODAMINE 18** [9] J L Eyre 3-7-13 (61) P M Quinn (5) 20/1: -00042: 3 b g Mukaddamah - Persian   2½   63
Empress (Persian Bold) Rear, prog to lead 2f out, hdd ins last, not pace of wnr: stays 10f, handles firm & gd/soft.

*892   **SMOOTH SAND 20** [7] M A Jarvis 3-9-0 (76) P Robinson 4/1: 40-113: 3 b c Desert Secret - Baby   nk   77
Smooth (Apalachee) Chsd ldrs, prog to chall 2f out, rdn/no extra ins last: hvly bckd tho' op 3/1: clr of rem:
ran to form of latest tho' jockey reported mount boiled over in the stalls: see 892.

736   **DISTINCTLY EAST 39** [12] M H Tompkins 3-8-10 (72) S Sanders 33/1: 020-04: Rear, prog 3f out, outpcd12   61
fnl 2f: big step up in trip, prev eff at 5/6f: see 736 (7f h'cap, reapp).

745   **ALLEGRESSE 37** [6] 3-9-1 (77) W Supple 7/2 FAV: 36-35: Keen/held up, rdn halfway, mod late   8   58
prog: bckd tho' op 9/4, h'cap bow: longer 10f trip: 12f+ could suit on this evidence: see 745.

*606   **SHEER TENBY 70** [11] 3-9-2 (78) R Price 16/1: -4016: Chsd ldrs 3f out, sn held: ndd this, abs.   5   53

823   **CHAPEL ROYALE 28** [5] 3-9-7 (83) O Pears 50/1: 001-57: Keen & led/dsptd lead 1m, wknd: see 823 (9f).1¼   56

3930}   **DALYAN 231** [1] 3-8-8 (70) J Carroll 20/1: 0445-8: Keen/chsd ldrs 7f: ndd this on reapp: unplcd in   1½   41
'99 (rtd 76, nov stks): stays 1m & handles firm & gd grnd: scopey type, shld apprec mid-dists this term.

*827   **BOSS TWEED 28** [8] 3-8-4 (66) A Clark 5/1: 114319: Held up, eff over 3f out, sn held: nicely bckd.   nk   37

902   **STORMVILLE 20** [4] 3-8-7 (69) T Williams 40/1: 55-640: Chsd ldrs 7f: 10th: btr 736 (7f).   7   32

1002   **DONTBESOBOLD 9** [10] 3-8-1 (63)(VIS) F Norton 25/1: 662440: Led/dsptd lead racing keenly 6f, sn   4   21
btn: 11th: not settle in 1st time visor: btr 1002, 847.

*902   **ARIZONA LADY 20** [3] 3-8-6 (68) R Winston 14/1: 040-10: Cl-up 6f, sn struggling, 12th: op 20/1:   dist   0
trainer reported filly unsuited by grnd tho' handled it in 902 (9f, mdn).

12 ran   Time 2m 18.8 (10.7)   (Elite Racing Club)   Miss J A Camacho Norton, N Yorks

1105

4.50 BLACK BOOK MDN 3YO+ (D)   **6f rnd   Good/Soft 98   -14 Slow**
£3003   £924   £462   £231   3 yo rec 10lb

956   **SAN SALVADOR 15** [11] J Noseda 3-9-0 J Weaver 4/11 FAV: -321: 3 b c Dayjur - Sheer Gold (Cutlass)   83+
Prom, led halfway & rdly pulled clr fnl 1f under hands & heels riding, eased: value 5L+, well bckd, padd pick:
rnr-up to progressive May Contessa in 956: eff at 6f, 7f will suit: acts on gd & gd/soft & a stiff/undul trk.

962   **BILLY BATHWICK 15** [17] B Smart 3-9-0 (bl) D Holland 16/1: 6-5552: 3 ch c Fayruz - Cut It Fine   3   68
(Big Spruce) Led, hdd halfway, kept on fnl 2f, no ch with wnr: lkd well, op 14/1: see 804.

808   **GREY COSSACK 32** [15] M Brittain 3-9-0 T Williams 16/1: 4-63: 3 gr g Kasakov - Royal Rebeka   2   63
(Grey Desire) Held up, rdn & kept on fnl 2f, no threat: vis omitted: handles gd/soft: 7f+ & h'caps shld suit.

1018   **ASTRONAUT 9** [16] W J Haggas 3-9-0 J F Egan 20/1: 04: Rear, styd on well fnl 2f, nrst fin: op 14/1.   1   61

4588}   **WATERGOLD 182** [13] 3-9-0 O Pears 100/1: 000-5: Rear, rdn & styd on well fnl 2f, no threat: sharper   nk   60$
for this reapp: unplcd in '99 (rtd 54): eyecatching late hdwy, return to 7f+ & h'caps shld suit.

--   **TOYON** [7] 3-9-0 S Sanders 10/1: 6: Mid-div, nvr on terms: debut, ndd this: unruly in padd: nk   59
IR 29,000gns purchase, half brother to a smart mid-dist performer, dam nvr at up to 9f: improve over further.

877   **SAVANNAH QUEEN 22** [14] 3-8-9 M Fenton 16/1: 507: Chsd ldrs halfway, sn held: btt 794 (gd).   ¾   52

877   **CUPIDS CHARM 22** [8] 3-8-9 J Reid 16/1: 4-08: In tch all: op 33/1: see 877.   ½   50

826   **IT CAN BE DONE 28** [12] 3-9-0 P M Quinn (5) 50/1: 006-09: Rear, mod gains: unplcd in '99 (rtd 61).   1¾   51

707   **MERCHANT PRINCE 41** [4] 4-9-10 Dean McKeown 100/1: 000-50: In tch till halfway: 10th: 6 wk abs.   3   45$

790   **CASTLE BEAU 34** [3] 5-9-10 F Norton 50/1: 0/00: Al rear: 11th: no form.   3   0

4158}   **Mimandi 217** [9] 3-8-9 R Winston 100/1:   909 **Rudetski 19** [6] 3-9-0 C Teague 100/1:

884   **Joebertedy 21** [1] 3-9-0 A Clark 100/1:   3086} **Lucky Uno 275** [5] 4-9-10 R Fitzpatrick (3) 50/1:

740   **Above Board 37** [2] 5-9-10 (bl) S Righton 50/1:

16 ran   Time 1m 20.8 (6.7)   (Lucayan Stud)   J Noseda Newmarket

1106

5.20 TIMEFORM.COM HCAP 3YO 0-80 (D)   **1m4f   Good/Soft 98   -08 Slow**   **[87]**
£3916   £1205   £602   £301

4537}   **CEPHALONIA 188** [1] J L Dunlop 3-9-2 (75) W Supple 1/1 FAV: 004-1: 3 b f Slip Anchor - Cephira (Abdos)   85+
Trkd ldrs, al going well, led over 3f out & clr dist, eased nr line: hvly bckd on h'cap bow/reapp, padd pick:
promise fnl '99 start (rtd 80, mdn): apprec step up to 12f, 14f+ will suit: acts on gd/soft grnd & a stiff/undul
trk: runs well fresh: clrly expected here & did not let backers down, shld win more races as she steps up in trip.

939   **DAME FONTEYN 16** [2] M L W Bell 3-7-10 (55)(3oh) J Mackay (6) 16/1: 00-P22: 3 b f Suave Dancer -   1   58
Her Honour (Teenoso) Rear/in tch, rdn & kept on well fnl 2f, no threat to wnr: acts on gd/soft & hvy grnd.

*924   **SUDDEN FLIGHT 18** [5] E A L Dunlop 3-9-7 (80) J Reid 3/1: 130-13: 3 b c In The Wings - Ma Petite   4   78
Cherie (Caro) Held up in tch, prog to chall wnr over 2f out, no extra ins last: lkd well: tchd 7/2: topweight.

827   **PTAH 28** [3] J L Eyre 3-8-7 (65)(5oh) R Brisland (5) 33/1: 00-004: Settled rear, rdn & stdy gains fnl   1   52
3f, nrst fin: styd longer 12f trip, 14f may suit: acts on gd/soft grnd: could find similar: see 636.

782   **BOLLIN NELLIE 35** [10] 3-8-2 (61) R Winston 16/1: 354-45: Prom, no extra over 1f out: op 14/1.   3   54

978   **WINDMILL LANE 14** [7] 3-8-1 (60) F Norton 11/1: 505-06: Handy, led halfway till 3f out, fdd: op 8/1.   2   50

3272}   **WITCHS BREW 266** [4] 3-8-1 (60) P Fessey 50/1: 566-7: Dwelt/al rear: longer priced stablemate of 5th,   1   49
sharper for this: unplcd from 3 starts at up to 7.5f in '99 (rtd 59 & 50a): bred to apprec mid-dists this term.

979   **BOLD STATE 13** [6] 3-8-11 (70) S Sanders 20/1: 100-08: Chsd ldrs halfway, sn held: '99 York wnr   1   58
(auct mdn, rtd 78): eff at 1m, mid-dists shld suit: acts on firm & gd: has run well in a vis, disapp in blnks.

4327}   **PAPI SPECIAL 204** [8] 3-8-13 (72)(vis) J F Egan 12/1: 0422-9: Led till halfway, sn wknd: fin lame: dist   0
reapp: rnr-up fnl 2 '99 starts (rtd 74, auct mdn): stays 1m, get further: handles gd/soft & soft: eff in a visor.

2420}   **BOLD WILLY 305** [9] 3-7-10 (55)(10oh) P M Quinn (5) 100/1: 060-0: Chsd ldrs, struggling halfway: dist   0
10th: reapp, mod form at up to 7.5f last term.

10 ran   Time 2m 46.8 (12.7)   (Exors Of The Late Lord Howard de Walden)   J L Dunlop Arundel, W Sussex

Official Going   GOOD/SOFT (GOOD in places). Stalls: Str - Stands Side; Rnd - Inside.

1107   **2.00 GARTER STKS 2YO (B)**   **5f str**   **Good/Soft 79** **-33 Slow**
£9001   £3414   £1707   £776

*985 **SHOESHINE BOY** 13 [6] B J Meehan 2-9-1 Pat Eddery 4/1: 2111: 2 b g Prince Sabo - Susie Sunshine   **98**
(Waajib) Made all, al trav best, kept on over 1f out, rdn out ins last: nicely bckd: earlier scored at Warwick
(auct mdn) & Newmarket (stks): half-brother to a 7f wnr: dam 9f juv wnr: eff at 5f, 6f will suit: acts on fast,
soft & on any trk: proving tough & useful, likes to dominate & shld be back here for the Royal meeting.
  984   **DOMINUS** 13 [7] R Hannon 2-8-11 R Hughes 5/2 FAV: 22: 2 b c Primo Dominie - Howlin' (Alleged)   ¾ **92**
Prom, rdn 2f out, kept on ins last, not btn far: sure to apprec 6f & must win soon: see 984.
*974 **MEDIA MOGUL** 14 [3] T D Barron 2-8-11 C Lowther 12/1: 13: 2 b c First Trump - White Heat (Last   ¾ **90**
Tycoon) Prom, rdn halfway, outpcd over 1f out till kept on again ins last: sure to relish 6f & progressing well.
*1006 **TARAS EMPEROR** 9 [9] J J Quinn 2-9-1 A Culhane 10/1: 414: In tch on outer, rdn 2f out, kept on   ½ **93**
ins last: encouraging, sure to relish further & win again on a lesser trk: see 1006.
*993 **SHUSH** 11 [2] 2-9-1 O Peslier 11/2: 15: Waited with, eff 2f out, kept on same pace fnl 1f: see 993.   ½ **92**
*1000 **QUIZZICAL LADY** 9 [4] 2-8-6 Dane O'Neill 20/1: 0516: Bhd, rdn 2f out, kept on same pace fnl 1f.   1¼ **81**
1046 **AZIZ PRESENTING** 5 [5] 2-8-6 T Quinn 5/1: 27: In tch, eff 2f out, sn no extra: better off in mdns.   ¾ **79**
-- **ANIMAL CRACKER** [1] 2-8-6 S Drowne 33/1: 8: Slow away, nvr a factor: debut: Mar foal: 5 **69**
half-sister to a 7f/1m wnr: dam winning stayer/hdler: sure to enjoy 6f+ in time.
812 **SAWBO LAD** 30 [10] 2-8-11 K Darley 25/1: 69: In tch, btn halfway: stiff task: see 812.   nk **73**
*843 **TIME N TIME AGAIN** 25 [8] 2-9-1 K Fallon 9/1: 10: With wnr, wknd qckly over 1f out: btr 843 (gd).   shd **77**
10 ran   Time 1m 04.61 (5.61)   (Oneoneone Racing)   B J Meehan Upper Lambourn, Beks.

1108   **2.35 LISTED WOODCOTE STKS 3YO (A)**   **1m rnd**   **Good/Soft 79** **-34 Slow**
£14963   £4604   £2302   £1151

4257} **EMBRACED** 211 [5] J R Fanshawe 3-8-11 R Cochrane 5/1: 1-1: 3 b f Pursuit Of Love - Tromond   **106+**
(Lomond) Prom, styd on well to lead on bit dist, pushed clr, readily: reapp: won sole juv start, at Nottingham
(mdn): half-sister to smart 1m juv & subs French Derby rnr-up Nowhere To Exit: dam 9f wnr: eff at 1m, sure to
stay at least 10f: acts on gd/soft, soft & a stiff trk: runs well fresh: unbtn, potentially smart, win Gr races.
*745 **VERBOSE** 37 [11] J H M Gosden 3-8-11 J Fortune 4/1 FAV: 5-12: 3 b g Storm Bird - Alvernia (Alydar)   3 **100**
Prom, sltly hmpd over 2f out, sn led till dist, outpcd by wnr: bckd, clr rem: fine run up in class: see 745.
3843 **CIRCLE OF LIGHT** 237 [9] P W D'Arcy 3-8-11 K Darley 8/1: 10-3: 3 b f Anshan - Cockatoo Island   3½ **94**
(High Top) Led till over 2f out, no extra over 1f out: nicely bckd on reapp: won first of only 2 juv starts, at
Lingfield (med auct mdn, rtd 93): half-sister to a 7f wnr & also Champion Hdler Collier Bay: dam mid-dist wnr:
eff at 1m, bred to stay much further: acts on gd & gd/soft & has run well fresh: useful, rate higher over further.
4007} **SO PRECIOUS** 226 [12] N P Littmoden 3-8-11 K Fallon 16/1: -61-4: In tch, eff 2f out, kept on   1½ **92**
same pace over 1f out: reapp: won 2nd of only 2 juv starts, at Kempton (mdn, rtd 79): half-sister to a
7f juv wnr: stays 1m & acts on gd, handles hvy: encouraging reapp, sharper for this.
4091} **FUNNY GIRL** 221 [4] 3-8-11 Dane O'Neill 33/1: -45-5: In tch, eff over 2f out, onepace: reapp: unplcd   ½ **91**
both juv starts (rtd 85 at best): dam 9f wnr: eff at 1m on gd: sure to enjoy a drop into mdn company.
4555} **PREMIER PRIZE** 186 [10] 3-8-11 N Pollard 5/1: 61-6: Missed break, waited with, hdwy over 2f out,   nk **91**
no extra appr fnl 1f on reapp: op 3/1: won last of 2 juv starts, at Nemarket (back-end fill mdn, rtd 95): dam
5f juv scorer: stays a stiff 7f on soft grnd: shld rate more highly.
-- **PROMISING LADY** [2] 3-8-11 S Drowne 11/1: 1-7: Waited with, eff 2f out, onepace: reapp: ½ **90**
won sole juv start, at Tralee (mdn, with D Gillespie): eff at 1m on gd/soft grnd: some promise here.
3725} **CAFE OPERA** 244 [1] 3-8-11 R Hills 20/1: 42-8: Held up rear, plenty to do over 2f out, late   ½ **90**
gains: rnr-up as a juv (rtd 89): bred to enjoy mid-dists & will improve with a more positive ride, prob in h'caps.
4315} **THE WOODSTOCK LADY** 205 [8] 3-8-11 M Hills 7/1: 1-9: Prom, hung badly right over 2f out, wknd: 1½ **88**
reapp: won sole juv start at Leicester (back-end fill mdn, rtd 87): eff at 7f, shld stay further (dam 11f wnr):
acts on gd/soft & has run well fresh.
971 **MISS KIRSTY** 14 [3] 3-8-11 Pat Eddery 10/1: 3-60: Keen & al bhd: 10th.   2½ **84**
4555} **OUR FIRST LADY** 186 [7] 3-8-11 T Quinn 33/1: 0-0: Prom, wknd qckly 2f out: 11th, reapp.   7 **72**
-- **SILK STOCKINGS** [6] 3-8-11 O Peslier 33/1: 0-0: Slow away, al bhd: fin last.   12 **52**
12 ran   Time 1m 47.53 (9.03)   (Cheveley Park Stud)   J R Fanshawe Newmarket.

1109   **3.05 GR 3 SAGARO STKS 4YO+ (A)**   **2m45y**   **Good/Soft 79** **-12 Slow**
£25200   £9660   £4830   £2310   4 yo rec 3 lb

987 **ORCHESTRA STALL** 11 [1] J L Dunlop 8-8-12 K Darley 6/1: 121/61: 8 b g Old Vic - Blue Brocade   **116**
(Reform) Waited with, rdn over 3f out, appeared held appr 2f out but styd on well for press appr fnl 1f to get
up cl-home, drvn out: missed '99 & '98, in '97 won here at Ascot, The Curragh & Longchamp (all Gr 3s, rtd 121):
suited by 2m & handles gd/soft & handles hvy: likes gd/soft, enjoys a gall trk, esp Ascot: clearly still v smart
& a fine training performance, shld win another staying Group race if staying sound.
4608} **PERSIAN PUNCH** 180 [8] D R C Elsworth 7-8-12 T Quinn 6/1: 5401-2: 7 ch g Persian Heights - Rum   shd **115**
Cay (Our Native) Prom, kept on to lead 2f out, drvn out ins last, collared nr fin, just tchd off: well bckd on
reapp: below best in '99, since then 9f-plus start at Doncaster (5 rnrs, stks, rtd 110 at best): '98 scorer at Newmarket,
Sandown & York (Gr 3's), also plcd in Melbourne Cup (Gr 1, rtd 118): '97 wnr at Newbury & Sandown (again, Gr
3, rtd 120): eff at 12f, suited by 14f/2m & does stay 2m4f (but disapp in Ascot Gold Cup sev times): acts on
fm & hvy: runs well fresh up with the pace: primed for a big run in the Henry II (won that race twice prev).
4205} **CELERIC** 214 [6] J L Dunlop 8-9-1 Pat Eddery 11/2: 6133-3: 8 b g Mtoto - Hot Spice (Hotfoot)   4 **115**
Held up, gd hdwy 3f out, styd on to chall over 1f out, no extra ins last: reapp, stablemate wnr: '99 wnr at
Ascot (Gr 3, this race) & York (Gr 3), also 5½L 4th in Ascot Gold Cup: no wins in '98: '97 wnr at York (Gr
2) & R Ascot (Gr 1 Gold Cup, rtd 122, with D Morley): eff at 14f/2m, stays 2m4f: acts on gd/soft, prefers gd or
fm: runs well fresh & relishes a gall trk, loves York & Ascot: v tough & top-class stayer who loves to come
late through horses & will relish a faster surface in the Yorkshire Cup (tremendous record at that track).
4237} **SAN SEBASTIAN** 214 [5] J L Dunlop 6-8-12 (b) O Peslier 4/1: 5442-4: Led 6f out till over 2f out, no   3½ **109**
extra: reapp: in '99 trained by M Grassick, won at Royal Ascot (2m6f Queen Alexandra stks) & on fnl start rnr-up
in a Gr 1 (rtd 119): '98 wnr at Clonmel (h'cap), Gowran & Royal Ascot (h'caps): eff at 2m, relishes 2m4f/2m6f now:
acts on firm, enjoys gd/soft & hvy & a stiff trk: gd weight carrier who wears blnks: v smart, out-and-out stayer.
987 **ASHGAR** 11 [2] 4-8-9 G Duffield 16/1: 340-05: Prom, rdn over 2f out, wknd over 2f out: '99 wnr at   9 **101**

Redcar (mdn), subs 4½L 4th in a Gr 3 (rtd 111$): eff at 14f/2m on firm/fast: lightly rcd, apprec stks/Listed.

987   **RAISE A PRINCE 11** [3] 7-8-12 (t) N Callan 11/1: 033-56: Waited with, gd hdwy 3f out, rdn &   7   95
btn appr 2 out: loves soft grnd & will apprec stks company: see 987.

4596} **TRAVELMATE 183** [7] 6-8-12 R Cochrane 3/1 FAV: 2225-7: Waited with, gd hdwy trav well over 3f   21   79
out, rdn & btn qckly appr 2f out: hvly bckd on reapp: rnr-up on 3 of 4 '99 starts, incl Northumberland Plate
& Tote Ebor h'caps (rtd 110): '98 wnr at Newmarket (2, h'cap & rtd h'cap, rtd 97): eff at 12f, stays 2m & likes
fm/fast, handles gd/soft & likes Newmarket: runs well fresh: v useful, put this bhd him on a sounder surface.

3555} **ROYAL REBEL 234** [9] 4-8-9 K Fallon 10/1: 0010-8: In tchd, wknd over 3f out: reapp.   14   67

3796} **JASEUR 241** [4] 7-8-12 (BL) J Fortune 33/1: 0306-9: Led till 6f out, wknd over 3f out: tried blnks.   5   62

9 ran   Time 3m 40.69 (14.69)   (Sir David Sieff)   J L Dunlop Arundel, W.Sussex.

1110   3.40 VICTORIA CUP HCAP 4YO+ 0-110 (B)   7f str   Good/Soft 79   +06 Fast   [105]
£22750   £7000   £3500   £1750   Field raced in 2 Groups - no advantage

4401} **BOLD KING 200** [22] J W Hills 5-8-9 (86) M Hills 25/1: 1524-1: 5 br g Anshan - Spanish Heart   94
(King Of Spain) Handy in centre, hdwy over 1f out, sn led, rdn clr: gd time: '99 scorer at Newbury (rtd h'cap,
rtd 90) & plcd sev times: '98 wnr at Southwell (mdn auct, rtd 80a): suited by a stiff 7f, stays 10f: acts on
fast & soft, any trk: runs v well fresh & can carry big weights: v useful & tough.

935   **HORNBEAM 16** [2] J R Jenkins 6-8-13 (90) O Peslier 16/1: 05-022: 6 b h Rich Charlie -   2   94
Thinkluckybelucky (Maystreak) Prom stands side, hdwy to chall dist, kept on ins last, only 2L: in fine form.

966   **CARIBBEAN MONARCH 14** [17] Sir Michael Stoute 5-9-1 (92) K Fallon 11/4 FAV: 040-43: 5 b g Fairy   1½   94
King - Whos The Blonde (Cure The Blues) Waited with, tacked across to stands side halfway, hdwy to lead over
1f out till dist, onepace: hvly bckd: v useful & has plenty of ability, but winless for 2 years: see 966.

1015   **PRINCE BABAR 9** [16] R A Fahey 9-8-3 (80) P Hanagan (7) 16/1: 00-244: Chsd ldrs stands side,   2   79
eff over 1f out, kept on same pace: win a less competitive h'cap: see 1015, 875.

*935   **ALWAYS ALIGHT 16** [13] 6-9-0 (91) N Callan 33/1: 63-015: In tch stands side, kept on for press   2   87
over 1f out, no dngr: running well, all wins at 6f & relishes soft/hvy: see 935.

1028   **ELMHURST BOY 7** [11] 4-7-13 (76) P Doe 25/1: -54566: Slow away, bhd stands side, no room over   hd   72+
2f out & again over 1f out, styd on well ins last: no luck in running: looks poised to strike, esp with headgear.

1004   **MUCHEA 9** [3] 6-9-10 (101) T Quinn 14/1: 0-0227: Waited with stands side, eff 2f out, onepace.   shd   97

1077   **SMOOTH SAILING 2** [15] 5-8-8 (85) Dane O'Neill 20/1: 20-048: Chsd ldrs, wknd over 1f out.   1½   79

*966   **PRESENT LAUGHTER 14** [19] 4-8-11 (88) J Fortune 10/1: 00-419: Cl-up centre, btn over 1f out: btr 966.   ½   81

*977   **JO MELL 14** [7] 7-9-1 (92) K Darley 16/1: 50-010: Led over 2f out till over 1f out, no extra: 10th.   ¾   84

941   **EASTER OGIL 16** [6] 5-8-4 (81) Michael Doyle 33/1: 00-500: In tch stands side, rdn & badly   hd   72
hmpd well over 1f out, not recover: 11th, ignore this: see 941, 725.

935   **RETURN OF AMIN 16** [10] 6-9-6 (83) M Roberts 33/1: 0-0000: Al bhd stands side: 12th: see 935.   1¾   71

966   **NIGRASINE 14** [18] 6-9-9 (100)(bl) A Culhane 20/1: 00-030: Prom centre wknd over 2f out: 13th.   2   85

*900   **INDIAN PLUME 20** [12] 4-8-11 (78) G Duffield 33/1: 00-010: Prom centre wknd over 1f out: 14th.   ½   90

1015   **SECOND WIND 9** [4] 5-8-1 (78) A Beech (5) 12/1: 04-150: Overall ldr stands side till over 2f out: 15th.   2   59

4547} **TUMBLEWEED RIVER 187** [8] 4-8-8 (85) Pat Eddery 33/1: 4105-0: Al bhd, stands side: 16th: nk   66
reapp: '99 wnr at Haydock (mdn, rtd 76): likes to force the pace over a gall 7f on soft grnd.

1015   **INDIAN BLAZE 9** [14] 6-8-8 (85) N Pollard 33/1: 34-000: Al bhd stands side: 17th.   1½   64

935   **MIDHISH TWO 16** [5] 4-8-3 (80) N Mullen 50/1: 606-00: Cl-up stands side, wknd over 2f out: 18th.   3   55
'99 scorer at Lingfield (val sprint h'cap, rtd 89): '98 Newcastle wnr (mdn, rtd 85, with Sir M Stoute):
best at 6f on fast, soft grnd & on any trk: on a handy mark if returning to form.

4395} **HOLLY BLUE 200** [20] 4-9-3 (94) R Hughes 25/1: 4220-0: Al bhd centre, 19th: in fine '99 form,   3   65
won at Bath & Ascot (listed rtd h'cap, rtd 95 at best): eff at 7f/1m on fast, gd/soft & on a gall trk:
best with waiting tactics: useful at best, shld do much better.

966   **PREMIER BARON 14** [1] 5-8-5 (82) G Carter 10/1: 0-1400: Handy stands side, wknd over 2f out: 20th.   3½   48

966   **TAYIF 14** [9] 4-9-5 (96) R Cochrane 33/1: 510-00: Waited with, badly hmpd 2f out, not recover &   hd   62
eased: ignore this: in '99 won at Nottingham (mdn auct, reapp), Sandown & Newcastle (h'caps, rtd 97): v eff
at 7f on fast & soft, stiff trk: has run well fresh: useful colt with a turn of foot, this is best ignored.

21 ran   Time 1m 31.09 (5.09)   (The Farleigh Court Racing Partnership)   J W Hills Upper Lambourn, Berks

---

1111   4.10 LISTED PAVILION STKS 3YO (A)   6f str   Good/Soft 79   +09 Fast
£15470   £4760   £2380   £1190

955   **MOUNT ABU 15** [5] J H M Gosden 3-8-11 J Fortune 8/1: 526-41: 3 b c Foxhound - Twany Angel   113
(Double Form) Waited with, gd hdwy 2f out, squeezed thro' to lead nr fin, rdn out: nicely bckd, best time of day:
trained by P Chappel-Hyam in '99, won at Newbury (mdn), subs rnr-up in Gr 3 company in France (rtd 105): eff at
6f, stays 7f: acts on fast & gd/soft, likes a gall trk: smart sprinter who needs to be produced late.

+829   **SIR NICHOLAS 27** [2] J Noseda 3-8-11 O Peslier 10/11 FAV: 123-12: 3 b c Cadeaux Genereux - Final   hd   112
Shot (Dalsaan) Trkd ldrs, not much room 2f out, switched & hdwy to lead ins fnl 1f, no pace to repel wnr cl-
home: hvly bckd from 5/4, rider reportedly given a 1 day whip ban: smart sprinter who needs to be produced late.

969   **TRINCULO 14** [4] N P Littmoden 3-8-11 T G McLaughlin 20/1: 54-003: 3 b c Anita's Prince -   1¼   108
Fandangerina (Grey Dawn II) Dsptd lead, clr ldr 2f out till ins last, no extra: back to v best: see 969.

950   **MA YORAM 15** [7] M R Channon 3-8-11 T Quinn 5/1: 123-54: Dsptd lead, ev ch 1f out, no extra   1¼   104
fnl 100yds: 4L clr rem: see 950.

4294} **RUDIK 207** [8] 3-8-11 K Fallon 7/1: 2313-5: Rear, eff 2f out, not pace of ldrs: reapp: '99 Newcastle   4   92
wnr (mdn), subs 3rd at York (List, rtd 100): half brother to sev wnrs abroad: dam a smart sprinter in the USA:
eff at 6/7f: goes on fast, likes gd/soft & soft: handles a stiff/gall trk: reportedly held in high regard.

912   **ASAAL 19** [6] 3-8-11 R Hills 12/1: 110-56: Trkd ldrs till wknd fnl 1f: tchd 16/1: see 912 (1m h'cap).   6   76

950   **SEVEN NO TRUMPS 15** [1] 3-8-11 M Hills 10/1: 322-07: In tch, rdn & btn 2f out: see 950.   11   46

*837   **LOCHARATI 26** [3] 3-8-11 J Tate 20/1: -18: Led till 2f out, wknd qckly: poss went off to fast   7   26
but this was a puzzling eff up in grade after 837 (mdn auct).

8 ran   Time 1m 17.30 (4.20)   (Gary Seidler & Andy J Smith)   J H M Gosden Manton, Wilts

---

1112   4.40 MITSUBISHI STKS 4YO+ (C)   1m rnd   Good/Soft 79   -35 Slow
£7203   £2732   £1366   £621

3642} **SHARMY 248** [4] Sir Michael Stoute 4-8-12 K Fallon 7/2: 12-1: 4 b c Caerleon - Petticoat Lane   101
(Ela Mana Mou) Trkd ldrs, imprvd to lead ent fnl 1f, ran on strongly, rdn out: well bckd from 5/1, reapp: '99
Sandown wnr (mdn, debut), subs rnr-up at Yarmouth (stks, rtd 91 at best): 160,000gns purchase: eff at 1m, stays

ASCOT WEDNESDAY MAY 3RD Righthand, Stiff, Galloping Track

10f, mid-dist bred: acts on gd & gd/soft, runs well fresh: handles a stiff/gall trk: useful, can win more races.
4173} **CARDIFF ARMS 215** [7] M Johnston 6-8-12 M Hills 14/1: 3130-2: 6 b g Lowell - Shuzohra (Tom's Shu) *1½* **98**
Trkd ldrs, not much room 2f out, switched & kept on well fnl 1f, nrst fin: reapp: ex-NZ, reportedly won thrice in native land & plcd in their St Leger, unplcd at Newmarket (List) on sole Brit start in '99: eff at 1m, stays 10/12f: acts on firm & gd/soft grnd: poss a shade unlucky today, useful & deserves compensation over further.
4178} **TILLERMAN 215** [3] Mrs A J Perrett 4-9-3 Pat Eddery 10/11 FAV: 11-3: 4 b c In The Wings - Autumn *1½* **100**
Tint (Roberto) Rcd keenly rear, imprvd to lead 2f out, collared ent fnl 1f, no extra cl-home: hvly bckd, reapp, clr rem: unbtn in '99, won at Lingfield (mdn auct) & Newmarket (class stks, rtd 101): eff at 1m/9f, shld stay 10f: acts on fast & gd/soft, handles a stiff or sharp/undul trk: runs well fresh: useful, imprvg colt, spot on next time.
3752} **GREEN CARD 242** [2] S P C Woods 6-8-9 T Quinn 6/1: 5433-4: Trkd ldrs, ev ch 2f out, wknd fnl 1f: *4* **84**
plcd sev times in '99, best on reapp at Newmarket (Gr 3, rtd 110): '98 Nottingham & Doncaster wnr (stks, rtd 112), 3rd of 6 in a Gr 3: '97 Ripon wnr (mdn, rtd 109 at best): best at 1m, stays 10f & has tried 12f: acts on gd & firm, handles soft: handles any trk, has tried a visor, best without: smart at best.
4304} **TRIPLE DASH 205** [6] 4-9-3 G Duffield 6/1: 1343-5: Rear, eff 2f out, sn no impress: '99 Sandown *3½* **85**
wnr (stks, rtd 113), also plcd twice: '98 Newcastle wnr (mdn, rtd 103 at best): stays 1m well, shld get further: acts on fast & soft grnd: useful colt, capable of much better.
-- **MASTER HENRY** [1] 6-8-9 R Hughes 33/1: 024/6: Led 6f, wknd: longer priced stable-mate of 2nd: *5* **67**
6th of 7 bhd Monsignor here at Ascot (nov hdle) in Nov '99: ex-German Flat performer: eff at 1m/10f on soft.
920 **READING RHONDA 18** [5] 4-8-4 R Mullen 66/1: 5/57: Al towards rear, fin last: v stiff task: see 920. *4* **54**
7 ran Time 1m 47.65 (9.15) (Saeed Suhail) Sir Michael Stoute Newmarket

1113 **5.15 WHITE ROSE HCAP 3YO+ 0-80 (D) 1m str Good/Soft 79 -02 Slow [80]**
£7832 £2410 £1205 £602 3yo rec 13lb Raced towards centre

*1058 **POLISH SPIRIT 4** [10] B R Millman 5-9-7 (73)(5ex) T Quinn 9/4 FAV: 3-1111: 5 b g Emarati - Gentle **82**
Star (Comedy Star) In tch, rdn & styd on well fnl 2f to lead well ins last, all out, gamely: hvly bckd, op 3/1: quick reapp under a 5lb pen: earlier scored at Windsor (h'cap, course record), Pontefract (class stks) & Sandown (h'cap): '99 wnr again at Windsor (h'cap, rtd 63): '98 Warwick wnr (mdn, rtd 65): eff at 1m, stays 10f: acts on fast, relishes gd/soft & hvy grnd, any trk, likes Windsor: has run well fresh: tough & progressive gelding.
1058 **ROLLER 4** [6] J G Given 4-9-4 (70)(5ex) T G McLaughlin 8/1: -32122: 4 b g Bluebird - Tight Spin *nk* **78**
(High Top) Prom, rdn fnl 3f, led over 1f out till hdd well ins last, kept on well & just held: clr rem: tchd 10/1, 5lb pen: quick reapp: tough & progressive, also bhd this wnr in 1058.
3386} **IRON MOUNTAIN 261** [20] N A Callaghan 5-9-6 (72) A Beech (5) 33/1: 2260-3: 5 b g Scenic - Mertannah *4* **72**
(Shy Groom) Mid-div, rdn & kept on well fnl 2f, nrst fin: op 25/1, reapp: '99 Goodwood wnr (amat h'cap, rtd 75): '98 wnr at Yarmouth, Brighton, Beverley & Leicester (h'caps, rtd 73): eff at 1m, suited by 9/11f on firm & gd/sft grnd, not soft?: goes on any trk, without blnks: fine reapp, win again over 9f+.
857 **SAHARA SPIRIT 23** [19] E A L Dunlop 3-8-13 (78) K Darley 12/1: 40-224: Prom thr'out, ch 2f out, *½* **77**
no extra ins last: tchd 14/1: fine eff against elders: see 857, 761.
-- **CELTIC EXIT** [25] 6-9-7 (73)(t) K Fallon 20/1: 60-505: Dwelt, mid-div, kept on fnl 2f: op 14/1, 10 wk abs: *3* **66**
ex-French entire, '99 Longchamp wnr (h'cap): eff at 7f/1m, stays 10f: acts on gd/soft & hvy: wore a t-strap here.
4357} **HONEST BORDERER 202** [29] 5-9-11 (77) G Carter 20/1: 0036-6: In tch, eff over 2f out, kept on onepace: *nk* **69**
op 16/1, 7 month abs: plcd twice in '99 (rtd 84, reapp): '98 Ripon scorer (h'cap, rtd 83): eff at 9/10f on fast & soft grnd: handles any trk, best without blnks: encouraging reapp, will apprec a return to 9f+.
*1011 **MELODIAN 9** [12] 5-8-9 (61)(bl)(5ex) D Mernagh (3) 14/1: -02317: Prom, onepace over 1f out: bckd. *1½* **50**
854 **PATSY STONE 23** [3] 4-8-9 (61) Pat Eddery 10/1: 100-58: Held up, switched/eff over 2f out, held fnl 1f. *1* **48**
854 **LEGAL SET 23** [5] 4-9-4 (70) N Callan 10/1: 300-29: Prom 7f: tchd 12/1: see 854. *2* **53**
119 **QUEENS PAGEANT 158** [15] 6-9-4 (70) Dane O'Neill 33/1: 0050-0: Mid-div, rdn halfway, no impress: abs. *½* **52**
605 **KENNET 65** [22] 5-9-3 (69) D Harrison 50/1: 10-560: Chsd ldrs, outpcd fnl 2f: 11th: 2 month abs. *1½* **48**
725 **ANALYTICAL 39** [14] 4-9-6 (72) R Hughes 16/1: 300-00: Led overall till over 1f out, fdd/when hampered 1f *¾* **49**
out: 12th: op 12/1: '99 Nottingham wnr (auct mdn, rtd 80): eff around a gall 1m on fast grnd, handles gd/soft.
707 **BOBBYDAZZLE 41** [7] 5-8-4 (56) J Lowe 20/1: 3-2440: Chsd ldrs, no impress fnl 2f: 13th: 6 wk abs. *1½* **30**
1031 **SCENE 7** [18] 5-9-12 (78) J Fortune 20/1: -01000: Mid-div, eff/hmpd over 2f out, no ch after: 14th: *1½* **49**
op 14/1: won this race last term off an 8lb lower mark: see 831.
3670} **THE GREEN GREY 247** [11] 6-8-12 (64) M Roberts 50/1: 2200-0: Rdn/towards rear, mod gains: 15th: *2* **31**
reapp: lightly rcd in '99 (rnr-up, AW h'cap, rtd 66a, rtd 54 on turf): '98 wnr at Yarmouth (h'cap), Bath (sell), Brighton (clmr, W Muir), Kempton (h'cap, rtd 71) & Lingfield (AW h'cap, rtd 59a, D Morris): eff at 7f/1m on firm, gd/soft & eqtrk, handles any trk, likes Bath: best without a visor: gd weight carrier.
4481} **HARD LINES 193** [23] 4-9-9 (75) A Nicholls (3) 50/1: 1/0-0: Prom 5f: 16th: longer priced stable- *nk* **41**
mate of 5th, reapp: unplcd sole '99 start (rtd 50a, clmr): '98 sole start wnr at Newbury (debut, mdn, rtd 89): eff at 6f, 7f+ shld suit: acts on firm grnd & a stiff/gall trk: has run well fresh.
-1028 **CARLTON 7** [27] 6-9-13 (79) N Pollard 14/1: 21-420: Chsd ldrs 6f: 17th: op 10/1: btr 76 (6f). *hd* **45**
875 **GREAT NEWS 22** [8] 5-10-0 (80) M Hills 16/1: 30-000: Prom 5f: 18th: op 14/1: topweight: see 875. *¾* **44**
895 **TUMBLEWEED QUARTET 20** [1] 4-9-11 (77)(t) M Tebbutt 16/1: 00-560: In tch till halfway: 29th: btr 715. **0**
895 **MYSTIC RIDGE 20** [24] 6-9-6 (72) W Ryan 16/1: 0-4100: Mid-div, wknd qckly 2f out, t.o.: op 14/1: 30th. **0**
4562} **Hadleigh 186** [13] 4-9-6 (72) R Hills 40/1:
1033 **Windshift 7** [26] 4-9-1 (67)(vis) R Mullen 40/1:
746 **Anstand 37** [9] 5-8-11 (63) S Whitworth 50/1:
*462 **Kilmeena Lad 88** [16] 4-9-6 (72) S Carson (5) 25/1:
842 **April Ace 26** [2] 4-8-5 (57) S Drowne 50/1:
854 **Consort 23** [30] 7-8-8 (60) P Doe 25/1:
925 **Bebe De Cham 18** [4] 3-8-5 (70) A Culhane 50/1:
1033 **Giko 7** [17] 6-8-13 (65) O Urbina 25/1:
854 **Lough Swilly 23** [21] 4-8-4 (56) G Duffield 25/1:
4206} **Gemini Guest 214** [28] 4-9-12 (78) O Peslier 33/1:
30 ran Time 1m 45.19 (6.49) (Mrs Izabel Palmer) B R Millman Kentisbeare, Devon

LONGCHAMP SUNDAY APRIL 30TH Righthand, Galloping Track

Official Going HEAVY.

1114 **1.40 GR 3 PRIX VANTEAUX 3YO FILLIES 1m1f Heavy**
£21134 £7685 £3842

-- **AMERICA** [4] Mme C Head 3-9-0 O Doleuze 6/4 JT FAV: 31-11: 3 ch f Arazi - Green Rosy (Green Dancer) **112**
Trkd ldr, imprvd to lead dist, pushed out: eff at 9f on hvy, 10f will suit: smart filly, hds for French Oaks.
-- **HIDALGUIA** [1] J de Roualle 3-9-0 O Peslier 19/10: 1-12: 3 b f Barathea - Halesia (Chief's Crown) *1½* **109**

In tch, eff to chase wnr fnl 1f, no impress: earlier won reapp: eff at 9f on hvy grnd, 10f will suit: v useful.
-- **BEYOND THE WAVES** [7] J E Pease 3-9-0 T Jarnet 66/10: -13: 3 b f Ocean Crest - Excedent (Exceller)   1   **108**
Waited with, eff over 1f out, kept on under press: earlier won debut: eff at 9f on hvy, 10f will suit: v useful.
7 ran   Time 2m 10.0   (Wertheimer Brothers)   Mme C Head France

1115   2.10 GR 1 PRIX GANAY 4YO+   1m2f110y Heavy
£48031   £19212   £9606   £4803

*819   **INDIAN DANEHILL 28** [3] A Fabre 4-9-2 O Peslier 3/5 FAV: 632-11: 4 b c Danehill - Danse   **121**
Indienne (Green Dancer) Rear, eff when taken left 2f out, led ent fnl 1f, rdn out: recent reapp wnr at Longchamp
(Gr 2): '99 Longchamp wnr (Gr 3, reapp), subs plcd twice in Gr 1 company (rtd 116): eff at 1m/10.5f, loves soft
& hvy grnd: runs well fresh & likes Longchamp: high-class colt who will win more Group1 races this summer.
4399] **GREEK DANCE 197** [2] Sir Michael Stoute 5-9-2 K Fallon 5/1: 1265-2: 5 b h Sadler's Wells - Hellenic   2   **118**
(Darshaan) Held up, prog into 2nd 4f out, led dist till ent fnl 1f, not pace of wnr: reapp: '99 wnr at Haydock (Gr
3), subs 8L 2nd to Royal Anthem in Gr 1 Juddmonte at York (rtd 121): '99 Newmarket (mdn) & York wnr (stks, rtd
119): eff at 10f, stays 12f: acts on fast & hvy: handles any trk, runs well fresh: v smart, spot on next time.
819   **CHELSEA MANOR 28** [4] P Bary 4-9-2 T Thulliez 37/10: 41-023: 4 b c Grand Lodge - Docklands   3   **115**
(Theatrical) Trkd ldr, eff & edged left 2f out, onepcd fnl 1f: again bhnd today's wnr in 819.
768   **KABOOL 36** [1] Saeed bin Suroor 5-9-2 L Dettori 24/10: 334-44: Set pace till dist, wknd: see 768.   3   **112**
4 ran   Time 2m 27.2   (Baron Edouard de Rothschild)   A Fabre France

1116   3.15 GR 3 PRIX DE BARBEVILLE 4YO+   1m7f110y Heavy
£21134   £7685   £3842   4 yo rec 4 lb

665   **AMILYNX 50** A Fabre 4-9-4 O Peslier 16/10: 11-201: 4 gr c Linamix - Amen (Alydar)   **122**
In tch, hdwy to lead dist, ran on strongly, pushed clr: '99 wnr here at Longchamp (2, incl Gr 1 Prix Royal Oak,
rtd 123): eff at 2m on gd & hvy grnd: runs well fresh: tough, high-class young stayer.
2043] **KATUN 318** X Nakkachdji 7-8-11 T Thulliez 13/1: 30-242: 7 b h Saumarez - All Found (Alleged)   5   **108**
In tch, eff ent str, took 2nd cl home, no ch with wnr: lightly rcd in '99, won 1st 2, incl here at Longchamp (Gr 3),
subs 9th in Ascot Gold Cup (rtd 111 at best): eff at 2m on gd/soft & soft grnd: v useful stayer.
--   **MAGNUS** J M Beguigne 4-8-9 T Jarnet 51/10: 11-123: 4 b g Roakarad - Volcania (Neustrien)   ½   **110**
Chsd ldrs, led 3f out till dist, no extra & caught for 2nd cl home: prob stays 2m on hvy: v useful.
7 ran   Time 3m 40.2   (J-L Lagardere)   A Fabre France

Official Going   SOFT.

1117   3.00 GR 2 PREMIO REGINA 3YO FILLIES   1m   Heavy
£57630   £26143   £16128

4323] **XUA 203** [9] B Grizzetti 3-8-11 M Tellini 111/10: 223-1: 3 b f Fairy King - Bold Starlet (Precocious)   **108**
Mid-div, hdwy to lead dying strides: eff at 1m on soft grnd, 10f will suit: v useful filly.
--   **TIMI** [7] L Brogi 3-8-11 M Pasquale 82/10: 2: 3 b f Alzao - Timiram (Runnett)   ½   **107**
In tch, prog to lead 2f out, caught in shadow of post: eff at 1m on hvy grnd: v useful Italian filly.
913   **CRIMPLENE 16** [18] C E Brittain 3-8-11 P Robinson 39/10: 13-633: 3 ch f Lion Cavern - Crimson   1   **105**
Conquest (Diesis) Prom on outside, chall 2f out, no extra cl home: English raider, stays 1m: useful.
969   **EUROLINK RAINDANCE 11** [3] J L Dunlop 3-8-11 T Quinn 16/10: 125-30: Prom, ev ch 2f out, fdd into 11th.   94
18 ran   Time 1m 40.0   (B Grizzetti)   B Grizzetti Italy

1118   4.00 GR 2 PREMIO PARIOLI 3YO   1m   Soft
£57166   £25795   £15896

--   **DAVIDE UMBRO** [6] E Russo 3-9-2 S Dettori 86.6/1: -1: 3 b c In The Wings - Afreeta (Afleet)   **112**
Chsd ldrs, prog to lead 2f out, clr fnl 1f, readily: eff at 1m on soft grnd: smart Italian colt.
--   **GOLDEN INDIGO** [1] G Fratini 3-9-2 D Holland 183/10: -2: 3 ch c Miswaki - Curl And Set (Nijinsky)   3½   **109**
Nvr far away, chsd wnr fnl 2f, no impress: v useful colt.
--   **CALUKI** [2] L Camici 3-9-2 V Mezzatesta 47/10: -3: 3 b c Kris - Chevisaunce (Fabulous Dancer)   1   **105**
Rear, hdwy 2f out, kept on under press fnl 1f: eff at 1m on soft grnd, 10f will suit: v useful.
969   **CATCHY WORD 11** [13] E A L Dunlop 3-9-2 J Reid 25/10 FAV: 361-29: Rear, eff & btn 2f out: 9th: see 969.   97
982   **NOTHING DAUNTED 10** [3] 3-9-2 G Carter 79/10: 132-30: Early speed, btn 3f out: fin last: see 982 (6f).   83
13 ran   Time 1m 39.0   (Scuderia Colle Papa)   E Russo Italy

Official Going   GOOD.

1119   3.15 SUPER GRAND PRIX BMW 4YO+   1m4f83y Good
£7529   £3012   £2259   4 yo rec 1 lb

4619] **AKBAR 176** M Johnston 4-9-9 M J Kinane 6/4 FAV: 3230-1: 4 b c Doyoun - Akishka (Nishapour)   **99**
Mid-div, prog to lead 2f out, sn clr, pushed out: reapp: plcd sev times in '99 (trained mainly by J Oxx), incl
in List company (rtd 101): '98 Tipperary mdn wnr: eff at 10/14f on fast & hvy grnd.
--   **GALTEE** Germany 8-9-9 M Rulec 92/10: -2: 8 b h Be My Guest - Gandria (Charlottown)   2¾   **94**
--   **CANTERBURY** Switzerland 5-8-11 P Piatkowski 128/10: -3: 5 b c Acatenango - Clarissa (Priamos)   nk   **81**
12 ran   Time 2m 35.3   (Markus Graff)   M Johnston Middleham, N Yorks.

CURRAGH MONDAY MAY 1ST Righthand, Stiff, Galloping Track

Official Going SOFT

1120
3.00 GR 3 EBF TETRARCH STKS 3YO   7f   Soft
£32650   £9650   £4650

*770   **MONASHEE MOUNTAIN 36** A P O'Brien 3-8-11 M J Kinane 2/9 FAV: 11-11: 3 b c Danzig - Prospectors Delite   **115**
(Mr Prosepctor) Held up, smooth prog to lead 1f out, sn clr, readily: won twice at Curragh last term (List & Gr 3, rtd 105): eff at 7f, 1m will suit: acts
at the Curragh (List): won twice at Leopardstown last term (List & Gr 3, rtd 105): eff at 7f, 1m will suit: acts
on gd/soft and soft: runs well fresh: smart, win more Group races & the Irish 2000 Guineas looks the target.
947   **LEGAL JOUSTING 15** D K Weld 3-8-8 (BL) P J Smullen 4/1: 2-122: 3 b c Indian Ridge - In Anticipation   2½   **104**
(Sadler's Wells) Chsd ldr, kept on for press fnl 2f, no chance with wnr: op 5/2: tried blnks: see 947 (1m).
3396} **ANZARI 261** J Oxx 3-8-8 N G McCullagh 11/1: 4112-3: 3 b c Nicolotte -Anazara (Trempolino)   5   **96**
4 ran   Time 1m 33.4   (Michael Tabor)   A P O'Brien Ballydoyle, Co Tipperary

1121
4.00 LISTED EBF MOORESBRIDGE STKS 4YO+   1m2f   Soft
£19500   £5700   £2700

2320} **URBAN OCEAN 309** A P O'Brien 4-9-6 M J Kinane 1/1 FAV: /116-1: 4 ch h Bering - Urban Sea   **114**
(Miswaki) Made all & clr halfway styd on well fnl 3f, pushed out, unchall: reapp, hvly bckd: '99 wnr at Cork
(stks) & Curragh (Gr 3), subs 6th in Irish Derby (rtd 116): eff at 10f, 12f shld suit: acts on gd/soft & soft:
runs well fresh: likes a gall trk and front running: v smart entire, lightly raced & can win more Group races.
4030} **QUWS 225** K Prendergast 6-8-12 S Craine 5/1: 603-02: 6 b h Robellino - Fleeting Rainbow   5   **101**
(Rainbow Quest) Trkd ldr, rdn/outpcd 3f out, position accepted fnl 1f: op 4/1: plcd in Listed in '99 (rtd 102):
Curragh Gr 3 wnr in '98: stays 11f on gd & soft grnd: useful.
862   **WRAY 22** L Browne 8-8-12 K J Manning 9/1: 142-43: 3 ch g Sharp Victor - Faye (Monsanto)   4½   **96**
Trkd ldrs, efft 4f out, sn onepace/held: op 7/2: longer 10f trip: btr 862 (Gr 3,7f).
6 ran   Time 2m 19.5   (David Tsui)   A P O'Brien Ballydoyle, Co Tipperary

1122
5.30 LISTED EBF ATHASI STKS 3-4YO   7f   Soft
£19500   £5700   £2700   3 yo rec 12lb

1539} **DESERT MAGIC 344** C Collins 4-9-6 P Shanahan 16/1: 1000-1: 4 b f Green Desert - Gracieuse Majeste   **106**
(Saint Cyrien) Well Plcd, went on ent fnl 2f, not extended: op 12/1: '99 wnr here at The Curragh (fill h'cap, rtd 93
at best): eff at 7f on soft grnd, stiff/gall trk: goes well fresh: much improved here & a v useful effort.
3256} **YARA 267** K Prendergast 3-8-5 D P McDonogh 3/1: 220-22: 3 b f Sri Pekan - Your Village (Be My   5   **95**
Guest) Prom, eff 2f out, styd on but no ch with wnr: tchd 4/1: rnr-up 6 of last 7 starts, notably at Leopardstown
bhd Fasliyev (Gr. 1, rtd 104): eff at 6f, stays 7f: acts on fast & soft grnd: tough & useful filly.
948   **ARETHA 15** J S Bolger 3-8-8 (BL) K J Manning 7/4: 135-24: 3 b f College Chapel - Berenice (Unknown)   **96**
Rear, late hdwy und press, nvr nr ldrs: op 12/1, blnkd, btn over 7L: ran near to best, not quite up to this grade.
7 ran   Time 1m 31.7   (Mrs H D McCalmont)   C Collins Curragh, Co Kildare

SAINT CLOUD MONDAY MAY 1ST Lefthand, Galloping Track

Official Going HOLDING

1123
2.15 GR 2 PRIX DU MUGUET 4YO+   1m   Holding
£28818   £11527   £5764

*861   **DANSILI 26** A Fabre 4-8-11 C Soumillon 3/5 FAV: 133-11: 4 b c Danehill - Hasili (Kahyasi)   **121**
Made ev yd, readily: odds-on: earlier won here at St-Cloud in 3f, drvn out: '99 wnr at Chantilly & Deauville (Gr 3), rnr-up
in the French 2,000 Guineas: eff at 1m on gd & hvy grnd: can force the pace: high-class, improving.
768   **KINGSALSA 37** A Fabre 4-8-11 O Peslier 2/1: 35-132: 4 br c Kingmambo - Caretta (Caro)   2   **116**
Rear, prog to go 2nd bef dist, onepace und press ins last: good run up in grade against stablemate.
665   **DOUBLE HEART 51** Mlle V Dissaux 4-8-11 S Guillot 21/2: 331-33: 4 b c Akarad - Slanderous Facts   nk   **115**
(Slip Anchor) Last till kept on well ent fnl 2f, nvr nrr: dual winner last term: eff at 1m on soft grnd: improving.
5 ran   Time 1m 47.0   (K Abdulla)   A Fabre France

BRIGHTON THURSDAY MAY 4TH Lefthand, Very Sharp, Undulating Track

Official Going GOOD TO FIRM (GOOD in places). Stalls: 10f/12f - Outside; Rem - Inside.
Pace figures inapplicable due to strong following wind down home straight.

1124
2.30 PERTEMPS MDN 2YO (D)   5f59y rnd   Good/Firm   Slow
£2746   £845   £422   £211

985   **BLAKESHALL BOY 14** [9] M R Channon 2-9-0 S Drowne 9/4 FAV: 341: 2 b c Piccolo - Gigglleswick Girl   **79**
(Full Extent) With ldr, went on over 1f out, drvn out: Mar foal, dam a 6f wng juv: eff arnd 5f, 6f should
suit: acts on fast & gd/soft grnd: handles a sharp/undul trk: speedily bred, should win again.
891   **REPEAT PERFORMANCE 21** [7] W G M Turner 2-9-0 (t) A Daly 11/4: 42: 2 b c Mujadil - Encore   ¾   **77**
Une Fois (Shirley Heights) Broke well, led to over 1f out, rallied inside last, just held: clr rem: nicely
bckd tho' op 2/1: eff arnd 5f, 6f will suit on this evidence: acts on fast grnd & a sharp/undul trk: see 891.
--   **SANDAL** [1] R Hannon 2-8-9 R Hughes 11/4: 3: 2 b f Prince Sabo - Australia Fair (Without Fear)   4   **63**
Prom early, onepcd final 2f: nicely bckd on debut: Mar foal, half-sister to a smart sprinter: sharper for this.
--   **OPERATION ENVY** [2] R M Flower 2-9-0 Dane O'Neill 12/1: 4: Dwelt, bhd, modest late hdwy: 2½   **62**
tchd 20/1: Makbul colt, half-brother to a 1m wnr: should apprec 6f+ in time.
--   **PAT THE BUILDER** [6] 2-9-0 N Callan 16/1: 5: Chsd ldrs, rdn & btn final 2f: op 10/1: 8,000 gns first   ½   **60**

foal, sire high class juv/miler: should learn from this: with K Burke.
932 **LONDON EYE 17** [3] 2-8-9 J Reid 16/1: 06: Sn outpcd, modest late gains: see 932. *1½* **51**
891 **A B MY BOY 21** [8] 2-9-0 S Carson (5) 50/1: 67: Al outpcd: see 891. *5* **46**
849 **SEA RAY 24** [5] 2-9-0 J F Egan 50/1: 08: Al well bhd: cheaply bght half-brother to a 6f juv wnr. *2* **41**
932 **CEDAR JENEVA 17** [4] 2-8-9 P Doe 33/1: 0U: In tch when stumbled & u.r. halfway: see 932. **0**
9 ran Time 1m 01.6 (1.6) (M Bishop) M R Channon West Isley, Berks.

1125 **3.00 MILLENNIUM CLASS STKS 3YO 0-75 (D) 7f rnd Good/Firm Fair**
£3770 £1160 £580 £290

4312} **RENDITION 206** [6] W J Haggas 3-8-8 J F Egan 10/1: 530-1: 3 b f Polish Precedent - Rensaler **85**
(Stop The Music): Cl-up, rdn to lead appr final 1f, drvn clr: op 7/1 on reapp for new stable: plcd on
2nd of 3 '99 starts (fillies mdn, rtd 86, J Gosden): eff arnd 7f & clearly relishes fast or firm, 1m+ shld
suit in time: runs well fresh on a sharp/undul trk: fine effort for new connections, lightly raced.
933 **OMNIHEAT 17** [1] M J Ryan 3-8-8 P McCabe 5/2 FAV: 461-32: 3 b f Ezzoud - Lady Bequick *3* **77**
(Sharpen Up) Cl-up, hdwy to chall 2f out, ev ch until not pace of wnr inside last: acts on firm & hvy: 1m suit.
4355} **PEDRO JACK 203** [10] B J Meehan 3-8-11 J Fortune 13/2: 0110-3: 3 b g Mujadil - Festival Of Light *1½* **78**
(High Top): Prom, hdwy to lead over 2f out, hdd dist, no extra: up in trip: won twice in '99, at Nottingham
(2, auct mdn & nursery, rtd 77): eff at 6/7f on fast grnd: likes Nottingham: should win again.
4494} **AMORAS 194** [7] J W Hills 3-8-8 M Hills 10/1: 3154-4: Bhd, smooth hdwy over 2f out, rdn/onepace ins *1¾* **72**
last: '99 Bath wnr (nursery, rtd 76): eff at 7f/1m on firm & fast, handles gd/soft: sharper next time at 1m.
4480} **NOBLE SPLENDOUR 194** [3] 3-8-11 J P Spencer 13/2: 0350-5: Rear, rdn to impr over 2f out, no extra *¾* **73**
appr final 1f: op 5/1: plcd once in '99 (mdn, rtd 77): stays 7f on firm, handles gd/soft: fitter for this.
4277} **APLOY 209** [11] 3-8-8 J Reid 12/1: 2530-6: Cl-up, rdn & wknd final 2f: op 8/1: plcd twice as a juv *1¾* **67**
(mdns, rtd 78 at best): stays 6f, bred to apprec 7f+ in time: handles gd & fast grnd.
857 **GROESFAEN LAD 24** [4] 3-8-11 G Faulkner (3) 14/1: 00-047: Handy, lost tch final 2f: see 857. *3½* **64**
4516} **TWIST 191** [9] 3-8-11 Dane O'Neill 25/1: 064-8: Rcd wide in rear, hdwy to chall 2f out, wknd qckly *2* **60**
dist: rtd 79 at best from 3 '99 starts (auct mdn): eff at 1m on gd/soft grnd.
954 **BROMPTON BARRAGE 16** [5] 3-8-11 R Hughes 7/1: 640-09: Led, hdd 2f out, wknd qckly: tchd 10/1. *6* **50**
964 **SHARAVAWN 16** [8] 3-8-8 S Drowne 100/1: 000-60: Chsd ldrs to halfway, qckly lost tch, fin 10th. *9* **33**
3876} **NIGHT DIAMOND 236** [2] 3-8-11 K Fallon 8/1: 0530-0: Dwelt, al well bhd, t.o. in last: plcd once *dist* **0**
in '99 (mdn, rtd 78 at best): stays 6f, handles firm & gd/soft.
11 ran Time 1m 20.4 (0.6) (Pims UK Ltd) W J Haggas Newmarket.

1126 **3.30 EPSOM HCAP 3YO+ 0-80 (D) 6f rnd Good/Firm Fast** **[80]**
£4160 £1280 £640 £320 3 yo rec 10lb

226 **BLUNDELL LANE 129** [11] A P Jarvis 5-9-1 (67) J Fortune 10/1: 0000-1: 5 ch g Shalford - Rathbawn Realm **77**
(Doulab) Swtchd to ins & led after 2f (caused interference), made rest, rdn clr fnl 1f: fast time: jockey rec
a 4-day careless riding ban: bckd from 16/1, 4 mth abs: '99 scorer at Warwick (class stks, rtd 77): '98 Chester
wnr (h'cap, rtd 86), prev term scored at Redcar (nursery, rtd 76): all wins at 6f: acts on firm, fast &
fibresand: loves to force the pace on a sharp trk: runs esp well fresh: on a handy mark.
838 **IVORY DAWN 27** [3] K T Ivory 6-9-0 (66) C Carver (3) 14/1: 00-002: 6 b m Batshoof - Cradle Of Love *3* **70**
(Roberto) Bhd, swtchd wide & hdwy 2f out, styd on ins last, no ch wnr: op 10/1: h'capped to win, likes Brighton.
3790} **ALPEN WOLF 241** [2] W R Muir 5-9-11 (77) R Brisland (5) 9/1: 0105-3: 5 ch g Wolfhound - Oatfield *2* **76**
(Great Nephew): Handy, chsd ldrs over 1f out, no extra inside last: '99 wnr at Brighton & Bath (h'caps, rtd 79):
'98 scorer again at Brighton (3, sell, h'cap & class stks) & Folkestone (class stks, rtd 71 at best): eff at 5/7f
on fast/firm grnd: best on a sharp/undul trk, loves Brighton: gd weight carrier: spot-on next time.
879 **ELEGANT DANCE 22** [1] J J Sheehan 6-8-2 (54) R Ffrench 50/1: 000-64: Mid-div, eff 2f out, sn btn. *1½* **49**
958 **NINEACRES 16** [10] 9-8-2 (54)(bl) R Mullen 14/1: 401305: Cl-up, ev ch until no extra dist: op 12/1. *½* **47**
751 **BELIEVING 37** [12] 3-9-0 (76) R Hughes 14/1: 150-46: Bhd, late gains for press, nvr nrr: enjoy 7f. *1¼* **66**
1004 **FREDERICK JAMES 10** [8] 6-8-10 (62) J Reid 12/1: 0-4607: Handy, hmpd after 1f, rdn & wknd final 2. *¾* **50**
4518} **UPLIFTING 191** [4] 5-9-3 (69) M Roberts 13/2: 0300-8: Led early, cl-up till lost tch appr final *nk* **57**
1f: '99 scorer at Goodwood (h'cap, rtd 71): '98 Leicester wnr (mdn auct, rtd 75): eff at 5/6f on firm
& gd/soft grnd: runs well fresh on a sharp or stiff trk: has tried a visor, best without.
852 **SARENA PRIDE 24** [5] 3-9-0 (76) A Daly 14/1: 20-059: Dwelt, rear, late gains: tchd 20/1: btr 852. *1½* **60**
2989} **LUCY MARIELLA 281** [6] 4-9-0 (66) K Fallon 7/1: 0240-0: Al bhd, fin 10th: '99 Brighton scorer (mdn *½* **48**
h'cap, rtd 76 at best): eff at 5/6f on fast/firm grnd: usually wears a t-strap: has tried blnks, best without.
1028 **RESIST THE FORCE 8** [7] 10-10-0 (80) M Hills 12/1: 0-0200: Waited with, effort halfway, sn wknd, *4* **53**
fin 11th: reportedly broke blood vessel: qck reapp, top weight: much btr 895.
*881 **MISTER TRICKY 22** [9] 5-9-1 (67) J F Egan 2/1 FAV: 1-2010: Pulled v hard cl-up, badly hmpd after *dist* **0**
1f, wknd qckly & eased final 2f, fin last: reportedly broke a blood vessel: well bckd: forget this: see 881.
12 ran Time 1m 07.4 (Nick Coverdale) A P Jarvis Aston Upthorpe, Oxon.

1127 **4.00 DARLEY STALLIONS MDN 3YO (D) 1m2f Good/Firm Slow**
£4972 £1530 £765 £382

3588} **TRUMPET SOUND 251** [1] L M Cumani 3-9-0 J Reid 11/8 FAV: 4-1: 3 b c Theatrical - Free At Last **94**
(Shirley Heights): Waited with, gd hdwy to lead 2f out, edged right inside last, rdn out: hvly bckd, reapp:
up in trip: eye-catching sole '99 start (mdn, rtd 86+): half-brother to a 10f wnr: eff at 7f/10f, 12f will
suit: acts on firm & fast: runs well fresh on a sharp/undul trk: useful, open to further improvement.
4091} **PURPLE HEATHER 222** [7] R Hannon 3-8-9 Dane O'Neill 9/2: 642-2: 3 b f Rahy - Clear Attraction *¾* **87**
(Lear Fan): Keen cl-up, rdn to chall 2f out, drvn & no extra inside last: op 5/2 on reapp: 4th in a
Gr 3 on 2nd of 3 '99 starts (rtd 95), subs rnr-up when odds-on for a Nottingham fillies mdn: eff arnd
1m/10f, 12f will suit: acts on fast & gd grnd: looks certain to find similar sn.
-- **TORRID KENTAVR** [6] T G Mills 3-9-0 A Clark 25/1: 4-3: 3 b c Trempolino - Torrid Tango *2* **88**
(Green Dancer): Dwelt, rcd keenly in rear, short of room when progressed 3f out, styd on late, nvr nrr:
well btn 4th in Italy sole juv start (8.5f, hvy): stays 10f well & 12f will suit: handles fast: win a mdn.
606 **MUWAKALL 71** [3] R W Armstrong 3-9-0 R Price 33/1: 6-3534: Prom, hdwy to lead 5f out, hdd 2f out, *shd* **88$**
sn no extra: op 16/1, 10 wk abs: much imprvd here, treat rating with caution: see 606 (AW).
4452} **TOLSTOY 196** [4] 3-9-0 K Fallon 7/4: 22-5: Prom, chall ldrs 2f out, wknd appr final 1f: rnr-up both '99 *2* **84**
starts (mdns, rtd 88): eff at 7/8.3f, 10f should suit in time: acts on fast & gd/soft.
4526} **PROPER SQUIRE 190** [2] 3-9-0 J Fortune 8/1: 362-6: Al bhd: with A Foster in '99, rnr-up at *4* **78**

BRIGHTON THURSDAY MAY 4TH Lefthand, Very Sharp, Undulating Track

Yarmouth (mdn, rtd 84): eff at 1m on fast & gd/soft: now with J Gosden.
| 936 | CEDAR LORD 17 | [5] | 3-9-0 A Daly | 50/1: 0-67: Led to halfway, wknd qckly final 2f: stiff task. | 14 | 50 |

7 ran Time 2m 00.1 (2.3) (Gerald Leigh) L M Cumani Newmarket, Suffolk.

1128 4.30 TOM SMITH HCAP 3YO+ 0-60 (F) 1m3f196y Good/Firm Slow [60]
£2394   £684   £342   3 yo rec 19lb

835 **EVEZIO RUFO** 27 [4] N P Littmoden 8-8-9 (41)(vis) C Cogan (5) 12/1: 451151: 8 b g Blakeney - Empress 46
Corina (Free State): Mid-div, plenty to do appr final 3f, ran on strongly for press 2f out, all-out to lead
final strides: op 8/1: fit from a successful campaign on the AW, scored at W'hampton (3 h'caps) & Southwell
(amat h'cap): '99 wnr again at W'hampton (2, sell & h'cap, rtd 47a & 34): '98 Lingfield, Southwell & W'hampton
wnr (h'caps, rtd 61a & 56): last won on turf way back in '94: eff between 11f & 15f, suited by 12f: acts on
fast, hvy & equitrack, loves fibresand/W'hampton: suited by visor/blnks: loves coming late on a sharp trk.
772 **ORDAINED** 36 [3] Miss Gay Kelleway 7-8-12 (44) N Callan 33/1: -46042: 7 b m Mtoto - In The Habit shd 48
(Lyphard): In tch, gd to lead over 2f out, clr dist, wknd/hdd cl-home: gd turf return, acts on a gd mark.
671 **KIRISNIPPA** 51 [11] Derrick Morris 5-9-5 (51) C Carver (3) 16/1: 316053: 5 b g Beveled - Kiri Te 2 52
(Liboi): Held up, rdn & styd on well final 3f, nrst fin: 9 wk abs: eff at 11/12f on fast & fibresand.
748 **BONDS GULLY** 38 [7] R W Armstrong 4-9-9 (55) R Price 14/1: 0-3204: Cl-up, outpcd halfway, late gains. 2½ 52
2100} **ADMIRALS SECRET** 320 [6] 11-9-4 (50) R Mullen 12/1: 0060-5: Dwelt, bhd, late gains for press, nvr 3 43
nrr: long abs: unplcd in '99 (rtd 54 at best): '98 Lingfield wnr (2, appr & amat h'caps, rtd 68) & Brighton
(reapp, h'cap): eff at 12/14f on any grnd/trk, likes a sharp one, esp Lingfield: goes well fresh: well h'capped.
4519} **TWO SOCKS** 191 [15] 7-9-11 (57) I Mongan (5) 7/1: 6000-6: Cl-up, hdwy to lead 3f out, hdd 2f out ½ 49
& gradually wknd: reapp: '99 Kempton scorer (h'cap, rtd 72): '98 wnr at Warwick (h'cap, rtd 73 at best):
eff at 10/12f on firm, gd/soft & any trk: has tried blnks, best without: sharper next time.
1840} **TYROLEAN LOVE** 331 [5] 4-9-1 (47) R Hughes 50/1: /040-7: Bhd, late gains, no threat: 4th on 2nd 5 32
of 3 '99 starts (mdn, rtd 56$): rtd 51 at best in '98 (mdn).
*464 **DESERT SPA** 89 [16] 5-8-13 (45) A Clark 6/1 JT FAV: 02-118: Prom, ev ch until wknd qckly appr 1 26
final 1, eased: op 7/2, 3 mth abs: better expected on today's turf return: much btr 464 (AW h'cap).
4163} **OUR MONOGRAM** 218 [1] 4-9-7 (53) M Roberts 14/1: 0540-9: Dwelt, al bhd: rtd 74 on '99 debut hd 36
(mdn): stays 14f/2m on fast grnd.
1030 **SEA DANZIG** 8 [10] 7-9-11 (57) J F Egan 20/1: 221000: In tch to 4f out, 10th: needs to dominate. 1 38
1030 **GRIEF** 8 [9] 7-10-0 (60) J Fortune 20/1: 3-0000: Rear, late gains, fin 11th: top weight. ½ 40
748 **OCEAN LINE** 38 [18] 5-8-8 (40) A Beech (5) 6/1 JT FAV: 322040: Nvr a threat, fin 12th: nicely bckd. 3 15
407 **FOREST DREAM** 98 [12] 5-9-12 (58) A McCarthy (3) 50/1: 0-0000: Prom, fdd 4f out, 13th: 3 mnth abs. ¾ 32
963 **CLASSIC REFERENDUM** 16 [14] 6-9-1 (47)(bl) J P Spencer 8/1: 00-000: Led 5f-3f out, wknd: 14th. 1¼ 19
3449} **FULL EGALITE** 259 [2] 4-9-6 (52) Craig Williams 33/1: 6000-0: Al bhd, fin 15th: new stable. 11 9
3414} **POWER HIT** 261 [8] 4-9-10 (56)(bl) V Slattery 12/1: 3602-0: Led to halfway, sn lost tch, t.o.: 16th. 14 0
963 **MISTER MOP** 16 [17] 4-8-10 (42) A Daly 11/1: 540-60: Al well bhd, lost tch halfway, t.o, 17th. 7 0
943 **COURAGE UNDER FIRE** 17 [13] 5-9-2 (48)(VIS) K Fallon 9/1: /45-00: Prom to halfway, sn well bhd, 0
t.o. in 18th: not face first time visor?.
18 ran Time 2m 31.3 (3.1) (O A Gunter) N P Littmoden Newmarket.

1129 5.00 G L MOORE HCAP 3YO+ 0-70 (E) 1m rnd Good/Firm Fair [70]
£2947   £842   £421   3 yo rec 13lb

3854} **MOON AT NIGHT** 238 [3] L G Cottrell 5-9-8 (64) M Roberts 13/2: 0110-1: 5 gr g Pursuit Of Love - La 70
Nureyeva (Nureyev): Made all, styd on strongly final 2f, rdn out: reapp: '99 scorer at Chepstow & Brighton
(h'caps, rtd 66): '98 Goodwood wnr (clmg h'cap, rtd 56): likes to force the pace arnd 7f/1m: runs well fresh
on firm, gd/soft & any trk, likes Brighton: progressive, shld make a qck follow up.
890 **JUNIKAY** 22 [2] R Ingram 4-8-9 (51) K Fallon 4/1 FAV: 044-02: 6 b g Treasure Kay - Junijo (Junius): 2 52
Bhd, ran on well fnl 2f, nvr nrr: '99 Nottingham wnr (h'cap), plcd sev times (rtd 57 at best): '98 Brighton wnr
(h'cap, rtd 57): eff at 7f, suited by 1m/10f on firm, gd/soft & any trk: likes to come late, fairly h'capped.
842 **BEGUILE** 27 [7] R Ingram 6-8-6 (48)(t) R Mullen 16/1: 241063: 6 b g Most Welcome - Captivate nk 48
(Mansingh): Prom, drvn & not pace of wnr appr final 1f: may apprec a drop back to 7f: see 635.
332 **ARDENT** 110 [10] Miss B Sanders 6-8-7 (49) A Clark 9/1: 206-64: Chsd ldrs, drvn & no extra final 1¾ 46
2f: 3 mth abs: turf return: btr 100 (10f, equitrack).
895 **GULF SHAADI** 21 [12] 8-10-0 (70) J F Egan 11/2: 0-0405: In tch, eff 3f out, onepace: top-weight. shd 67
3721} **LYCIAN** 245 [4] 5-9-3 (59) R Ffrench 5/1: 1200-6: Mid-div, hdwy to chall halfway, drvn & no extra 1 54
final 2f: nicely bckd: reapp: '99 scorer at Lingfield (h'cap, rtd 70a) & Goodwood (h'cap, rtd 63): '98 wnr
at Brighton, Bath & Lingfield (h'cap, rtd 57 & 63a): eff at 1m/9.3f on firm, gd & both AWs, sharp/undul trk.
879 **DOLPHINELLE** 22 [1] 4-9-8 (64) O Urbina 12/1: 430347: In tch, short of room after 2f, prog 3f out, 3½ 53
wknd qckly final 1f: prev with R Hannon, now with J Poulton: see 754 (7f, AW).
612 **SHEER FACE** 65 [8] 6-9-6 (62) R Brisland (5) 14/1: -56548: Prom to halfway, sn btn: 9 wk abs. 2½ 47
1033 **MANSA MUSA** 8 [5] 5-9-11 (67) S Drowne 11/2: 0-0029: Cl-up, wknd qckly 2f out, eased when btn: nk 51
nicely bckd: much btr 1033 (stks, hvy).
620 **MASTER MAC** 64 [13] 5-8-12 (54) P Doe 20/1: 00-000: Dwelt, nvr a threat: fin 10th: 9 wk abs. 2½ 34
942 **INDIAN WARRIOR** 17 [15] 4-9-1 (57) L Newton 20/1: 666000: Dwelt, al in rear, fin 11th: see 942. 8 25
3369} **Green Turtle Cay** 264 [6] 4-9-4 (60) J Reid 25/1:
4196} **Super Monarch** 215 [11] 6-9-9 (65)(BL) R Hughes 16/1:
13 ran Time 1m 32.6 (0.6) (H C Seymour) L G Cottrell Dulford, Devon.

REDCAR THURSDAY MAY 4TH Lefthand, Flat, Galloping Track

Official Going GOOD/SOFT (SOFT in places). Stalls: Centre.

1130 2.20 BERNSTEIN MDN AUCT DIV 1 2YO (E) 5f Good/Soft 87 -03 Slow
£2535   £780   £390   £195

-- **MUJA FAREWELL** [12] T D Barron 2-8-0 W Supple 7/2: 1: 2 ch f Mujtahid - Highland Rhapsody (Kris) 79+
Cl-up, led appr final 1f, pshd out, narrowly but snugly: hvly bckd newcomer: 6,000gns Mar 1st foal, dam 6f wnr,
sire a sprinter: eff at 5f, should get 6f: acts on gd/soft grnd & runs well fresh: promising, should rate higher.

865　　**SHINNER** 23 [5] T D Easterby 2-8-0 P Fessey 20/1: 42: 2 b f Charnwood Forest - Trick (Shirley Heights)　¾　**75**
Mid-div, rdn & prog ent final 2f, kept on & not btn far: turf bow: left AW debut bhd & clr rem: eff at 5f, 6f
is going to suit: acts on gd/soft grnd, may find similar in the North: see 865.
821　　**MON SECRET** 29 [7] J L Eyre 2-8-8 R Lappin 9/1: 03: 2 b c General Monash - Ron's Secret (Efisio)　3　**74**
Dwelt, sn shkn up in mid-div, no impress till strong burst ent final 1f, nvr nr ldrs: op 7/1: acts on gd/soft
grnd but is clearly in need of further than 5f already: see 821.
--　　**LAUREL DAWN** [9] A Berry 2-8-8 J Carroll 9/2: 4: Prom & ev ch till hung left & no extra final 1f:　2½　**67**
drifted from 5/2: 8,200 gns Paris House Apr 1st foal: dam 6f wnr, sire a sprinter: prefer a sharper 5f for now?
796　　**BRIEF STAR** 35 [10] 2-8-0 D Mernagh (3) 25/1: -035: Led till 1½f out, fdd: see 796.　　nk　**58**
--　　**EL MAXIMO** [6] 2-8-8 J Stack 9/4 FAV: 6: Prom, rdn & no extra bef dist: bckd from 3/1: 8,000 gns　1　**63**
First Trump Apr foal, half-brother to decent sprinter Pips Magic, dam 7f wnr, sire a sprinter: likely to do better.
--　　**PATRICIAN FOX** [13] 2-8-8 G Bardwell 16/1: 7: Slow away, nvr got in it: debut: IR 3,400gns　　¾　**53**
Nicolotte Mar foal, half-sister to 2 wnrs, dam 10f wnr: sire a miler: with J J Quinn.
755　　**DISPOL LAIRD** 37 [4] 2-8-8 K Darley 12/1: 58: Al arnd same place: see 755.　　nk　**60**
--　　**ARRAN MIST** [1] 2-8-0 A Mackay 50/1: 9: Slow into stride, al towards rear: debut: 1,400 gns　　2　**46**
Alhijaz Mar foal, sister to a 5f juv wnr, sire a miler: with D Barker.
--　　**MAGNANIMOUS** [3] 2-8-8 Kim Tinkler 33/1: 0: Chsd ldrs 3f: 10th: 9,500 gns 2yo: Presidium Apr　nk　**53**
foal: brother to sprint h'capper Nineacres, dam a sprinter, sire a miler: with N Tinkler.
898　　**Nettles** 21 [11] 2-8-5 S Sanders 66/1:　　　　--　**Celtic Legend** [2] 2-8-0 T Williams 66/1:
12 ran　　　Time 1m 01.0 (4.5)　　　(T E Hollins)　　T D Barron Maunby, Nth Yorks.

1131　　2.50 BERNSTAIN MDN AUCT DIV 2 2YO (E)　　5f　　Good/Soft 87　-09 Slow
£2522　£776　£368　£194

--　　**PROMISED** [7] J A Glover 2-8-3 D Mernagh (3) 3/1 JT FAV: 1: 2 b f Petardia - Where's The Money　　**79**
(Lochnager) In tch, prog & pshd into lead 2f out, sn clr: bckd tho' op 9/4: IR 10,500gns Jan foal, half-sister to
a 6f juv wnr: dam 5f juv wnr, sire a sprinter/miler: eff at 5f, 6f will suit: acts on gd/soft: speedy filly.
--　　**WILSON BLYTH** [6] A Berry 2-8-5 J Carroll 11/2: 2: 2 b c Puissance - Pearls (Mon Tresor)　3½　**69**
Struggled to go pace till ran on strongly appr final 1f, nvr nrr: debut: 4,600 gns Puissance Feb 1st foal: dam
unrcd, sire a sprinter: handles gd/sft grnd: took a while to get the hang of things, 6f is going to suit.
898　　**FENWICKS PRIDE** 21 [5] B S Rothwell 2-8-8 M Fenton 3/1 JT FAV: -533: 2 b g Imperial Frontier -　shd　**72**
Stunt Girl (Thatching) Cl-up, tried to go with wnr appr final 1f, outpcd: tchd 4/1: shade btr 898.
989　　**PRINCESS OF GARDA** 12 [8] Mrs G S Rees 2-8-7 S Sanders 14/1: -U4: Well plcd, shkn up 2f out,　2½　**65**
outpcd till kept on cl-home: op 25/1: 14,500 gns Komaite Mar foal, sister to 3 wnrs, dam won over a mile.
898　　**DISPOL CHIEFTAN** 21 [4] 2-8-8 K Darley 10/1: 05: Led till 2f out, no extra: op 6/1: see 898.　　nk　**65**
--　　**HAULAGE MAN** [10] 2-8-8 A Culhane 12/1: 6: Dwelt & veered left, late prog, nvr a factor: 6,500gns　¾　**63**
Komaite Mar gldg: half-brother to prolific wng sprint h'capper Shadow Jury, dam won abroad, sire gets sprinters.
--　　**BOMBAY BINNY** [12] 2-8-0 W Supple 14/1: 7: Nvr on terms: 4,800 gns First Trump Mar 1st foal.　1¼　**51**
938　　**FAYZ SLIPPER** 17 [1] 2-8-0 P Fessey 8/1: 08: Chsd ldrs 3f: op 7/1, stablemate 7th, see 958.　2½　**45**
--　　**EDDIE ROYALE** [3] 2-8-5 O Pears 10/1: 9: Chsd ldrs till 2f out: op 8/1: IR 4,200gns Elbio Mar　¾　**48**
gldg, half-brother to 3 wnrs between 7f & 12f, dam a decent miler: sire a sprinter: with D Nicholls.
--　　**DOMINATE** [2] 2-8-5 G Parkin 66/1: 0: Dwelt, nvr dngrs: 10th: 2,000 gns Komaite Apr foal.　　nk　**47**
730　　**BANNINGHAM BLIZ** 40 [9] 2-8-0 T Williams 20/1: -00: Prom 3f: 11th.　　5　**32**
--　　**ARIES FIRECRACKER** [11] 2-8-8 F Lynch 25/1: 0: Al bhd: 12th.　　½　**39**
12 ran　　　Time 1m 01.3 (4.8)　　　(Paul J Dixon)　　J A Glover Carburton, Notts.

1132　　3.20 BERNSTEIN SELLER 3YO+ (F)　　7f str　　Good/Soft 87　-04 Slow
£2520　£720　£360　3 yo rec 12lb

778　　**MYBOTYE** 36 [14] A B Mulholland 7-9-3 (t) T Quinn 14/1: 000-41: 7 br g Rambo Dancer - Sigh　　**52**
(Highland Melody) Cl-up, led on the bit 2f out, pushed out: no bid: modest & lightly rcd in '99: plcd in '98
(h'cap, rtd 59): '97 Chepstow & Catterick wnr (subs disq, h'caps, rtd 61, R Bastiman): eff at 7f, tried 1m/10f:
acts on fast & soft, handles fibresand: can run well fresh, prob any trk: wears a t-strap.
520　　**UP IN FLAMES** 79 [11] Mrs G S Rees 9-9-3 (t) S Sanders 33/1: -00002: 9 b g Nashamaa - Bella Lucia　1½　**48$**
(Camden Town) Mid-div, no impress till styd on for press fnl 1½f, nvr nrr: 11 wk abs: eff at 7f/10f: see 405.
1004　　**HALMANERROR** 10 [7] G M McCourt 10-9-3 D Harrison 5/2 FAV: 00-653: 10 gr g Lochnager - Counter　½　**47**
Coup (Busted) Handy, chsd wnr ent final 2f, onepace inside last: bckd 4/1, clr rem: clearly flattered in 1004.
778　　**CYRAN PARK** 36 [2] W Storey 4-9-3 T Williams 12/1: 060-04: Trkd ldrs, drvn ent final 2f, unable　2½　**42**
to chall: tchd 16/1: eff at 7f, worth a try over further: handles fast & gd/soft grnd: see 778.
973　　**PLEASURE TRICK** 15 [8] 9-9-3 Kim Tinkler 33/1: 005005: Held up, late prog, nvr on terms: op 20/1.　2½　**36$**
4233]　**BY THE GLASS** 213 [23] 4-9-3 Suzanne France (7) 66/1: 0600-6: Chsd ldrs, onepce fnl 2f: st/mate 5th:　1½　**32**
reapp: moderate last year, '98 Leicester wnr for P Walwyn (5f auct mdn, rtd 73): acts on fast & gd, without blnks.
*778　　**DILETTO** 36 [16] 4-9-3 L Swift (7) 14/1: 602617: Al mid-div: this was more competitive than 778 (fast).　nk　**31**
899　　**SO WILLING** 21 [17] 4-9-3 (bl) A Culhane 10/1: 030568: Rear, late hdwy, nvr in it: op 8/1, blnks reapp.　½　**30**
844　　**JAYPEECEE** 26 [20] 4-9-8 R Lappin 9/1: 000-09: Front rank, ev ch appr final 2f, fdd: lngr trip, see 844.　nk　**29**
872　　**BIRCHWOOD SUN** 23 [21] 10-9-3 (vis) J Weaver 6/1: 3-3340: Nvr better than mid-div: 10th, st/mate 8th.　2½　**24**
803　　**MAMMAS BOY** 34 [1] 5-9-3 J Carroll 14/1: 400-00: Nvr troubled ldrs: 11th: see 803.　　½　**23**
684　　**SOUNDS COOL** 48 [18] 4-9-3 K Darley 33/1: 650400: In tch till 2f out: 12th: 7 wk abs, see 338.　¾　**21**
368　　**GUNNER SAM** 104 [22] 4-9-3 S Righton 16/1: 5-0000: Reared start, chsd ldrs till halfway: 13th, abs.　nk　**20**
929　　**GOOD EVANS ABOVE** 19 [4] 3-8-0 W Supple 14/1: 040-60: Nvr a factor: 14th: AW promise as a juv　1　**13**
(5f auct mdn, rtd 62a): eff at 5f on fibresand: with P Evans.
908　　**BERNARDO BELLOTTO** 20 [3] 5-9-3 O Pears 8/1: 0-0000: Al bhd: 19th, tchd 10/1: see 386.　　　**0**
795　　**CHOK DI** 35 [12] 4-9-3 C Teague 33/1: -40000: Led after 2f till 2½f out, sn btn: 20th, op 20/1, best at 6f.　**0**
--　　**Just Good Friends** [15] 3-8-5 M Fenton 50/1:　　973　**Time On My Hands** 15 [19] 4-9-3 (tbl) N Mitchell(7) 50/1:
908　　**Oddsanends** 20 [5] 4-9-8 (BL) C Lowther 14/1:　　872　**Cairn Dhu** 23 [10] 6-9-3 Kimberley Hart (5) 66/1:
--　　**Rudcroft** [6] 4-9-3 J Bramhill 66/1:　　　3771}　**Silver Bullet** 243 [13] 4-9-3 F Lynch 66/1:
973　　**Stamford Hill** 15 [9] 5-9-3 G Parkin 50/1:
23 ran　　　Time 1m 28.2 (6.4)　　　(J F Wright)　　A B Mulholland Hambleton, Nth Yorks.

1133　3.50 M B FILLIES HCAP 3YO+ 0-80 (D)　5f　Good/Soft 87　+07 Fast　[80]
£4829　£1486　£743　£371　3 yo rec 9 lb　All the pace was down the centre

941　**CARD GAMES** 17 [9] M W Easterby 3-9-0 (75) G Parkin 33/1: 0-0001: 3 b f First Trump - Pericardia　82
(Petong) Made just about all, held on well, drvn out: op 25/1, gd time: '99 wnr at Salisbury (nov auct stks)
& Pontefract (nursery, rtd 86, I Balding): eff at 5/6f, stays 7f: acts on firm & hvy grnd, any trk: has gone
well in a visor, likes to force the pace: well h'capped, type for a quick follow-up.

*1005　**WHIZZ KID** 10 [10] J M Bradley 6-8-10 (62)(6ex) Claire Bryan (5) 3/1 FAV: -00512: 6 b m Puissance -　nk　67
Panienka (Dom Racine) Front rank, rdn & ev ch when 2f out, al being held: well bckd: fine run, won this in '99.

2354}　**DAWN** 309 [4] J S Wainwright 3-8-9 (70) T Quinn 33/1: 634-3: 3 b f Owington - Realisatrice (Raja Baba)　1¾　71
Mid-div far side, shkn up & hdwy after halfway, onepace ins last: reapp/h'cap bow: cl-up 6th of 7 in a decent
fill mdn in '99 (rtd 77, N Graham): eff at 5f on gd/soft: gd run considering all the pace was down the centre.

4376}　**HONESTY FAIR** 202 [6] J A Glover 3-8-11 (72) K Darley 12/1: 3600-4: Trkd ldrs, effort ent final 2f,　nk　72
styd on but unable to chall: reapp/h'cap bow: plcd on debut last term (mdn, rtd 68 & 79S): eff at 5f,
return to 6f will suit: acts on fast & gd/soft grnd & should be sharper next time.

926　**SAPHIRE** 19 [18] 4-10-0 (80) K Hodgson 11/1: 000-05: In tch, styd on under press final 1½f, nvr nrr:　shd　80
highly tried last term (Listed 3rd of 5, rtd 94): '98 wnr at Newcastle (mdn) & York (nov stks, Listed rnr-up, rtd
102): eff at 5/6f: handles fast, loves gd/soft & hvy, any trk: v well h'capped, primed for a return to form.

1036　**TWICKERS** 6 [19] 4-8-10 (62) A Culhane 66/1: 250-06: Reared & bmpd start, prog 2f out, sn hung　¾　60
left, kept on without threatening: op 25/1, qck reapp: signs of a return to form: see 1036.

910　**PATSY CULSYTH** 20 [5] 5-9-7 (64) Kim Tinkler 20/1: 00-107: Towards rear far side, late hdwy, nvr　hd　45
dngrs: unsuited by drop back to 5f: see 756 (6f sell).

910　**AVONDALE GIRL** 20 [22] 4-9-2 (68) F Lynch 14/1: 000508: Rear, late prog, nvr nr ldrs: back in trip.　½　63

910　**RECORD TIME** 20 [23] 4-8-8 (60) L Swift (7) 12/1: 410-09: Al same place: '99 Newmarket wnr (h'cap,　½　54
rtd 63): sister to sprint h'capper Lago Dei Varano: eff at 5f, tried 6f: goes on gd & gd/soft grnd, any trk.

1005　**ROSES TREASURE** 10 [13] 4-7-10 (48)(vis)(5oh) C Adamson 33/1: 000-00: Chsd ldrs till appr fnl 1f: 10th.　½　40

2236}　**SOUNDS ACE** 314 [3] 4-8-5 (57) O Pears 16/1: 0006-0: Chsd ldrs, no extra dist: 11th, reapp: out　1½　45
of sorts last term: '98 wnr at Beverley (sell), Newmarket (nurs, rtd 68): eff at 5f, tried 6f: acts on fast, handles
gd/soft grnd, with/without blnks: suited by stiff/gall trks: can run well fresh: well h'capped now.

774　**FRILLY FRONT** 36 [17] 4-8-9 (61) C Lowther 11/2: 110160: Prom till appr final 1f: 12th, turf return.　1　46

--　**MUJAGEM** [8] 4-7-10 (48)(4oh) D Mernagh (1) 25/1: 0000/0: Nvr nr ldrs: 13th: stablemate wnr:　shd　33
stiffish task after nr 2 yr abs: failed to make the frame between 5f & 1m as a juv (mdn, rtd 64).

425　**APPLES AND PEARS** 94 [7] 4-7-13 (51) G Bardwell 14/1: 0-0500: Chsd ldrs till 2f out: 14th, 3 mth abs.　hd　35

739　**HAUNT THE ZOO** 38 [2] 5-7-12 (50)(2ow)(5oh) S Righton 20/1: 0-3000: Reared start, nvr a factor: 15th.　shd　34

910　**QUEEN SARABI** 20 [21] 5-8-0 (52)(bl) A Mackay 14/1: 4-0300: Al bhd: 16th, op 10/1, blnks reapplied.　nk　35

3440}　**BEVELENA** 260 [1] 4-9-11 (77) W Supple 10/1: 1500-0: Nvr troubled ldrs far side: 18th, reapp:　0
'99 Catterick wnr (h'cap, rtd 82): '98 Haydock wnr (nursery, rtd 77 & 56a): eff at 5f, stays 6f: acts on firm, soft
grnd & fibresand, any trk: best up with the pace: gd weight carrier: better than this.

910　**Piggy Bank** 20 [16] 4-8-6 (58) T Lucas 25/1:　910　**Tangerine** 20 [11] 3-8-9 (70) P Fessey 33/1:
*751　**E B Pearl** 37 [12] 4-7-10 (48)(7oh) J Bramhill 33/1:　2395}　**Hi Nicky** 307 [15] 4-9-4 (70) T Williams 66/1:
4514}　**Forest Queen** 191 [20] 3-7-12 (57)(2ow) N Kennedy 25/1: 62　**Emma Amour** 169 [14] 3-8-4 (65) P Goode(3) 66/1:
23 ran　Time 1m 00.5 (4)　(Guy Reed)　M W Easterby Sheriff Hutton, Nth Yorks.

1134　4.20 M B MED AUCT MDN DIV 1 3YO (E)　7f str　Good/Soft 87　-10 Slow
£2496　£768　£384　£192

3587}　**MYSTIFY** 251 [2] J H M Gosden 3-8-9 K Darley 4/6 FAV: -55-1: 3 b f Batshoof - Santa Linda (Sir Ivor)　90+
Bhd ldrs, led appr final 2f, sn clr, easily: hvly bckd, reapp: 5th at Newmarket final '99 start (fill mdn, rtd 92):
half-sister to smart mile-dist wnr Squeak: eff fresh at 7f, bred to apprec at least 10f: acts on firm & gd/soft grnd.

713　**PETEURESQUE** 41 [6] T D Barron 3-9-0 C Lowther 13/2: 25-62: 3 ch c Peteski - Miss Ultimo (Screen　13　73
King) Led after 2f till appr final 2f, easily outpcd by wnr: op 7/2, 6 wk abs: caught a tartar back in trip:
debut final juv start last term (mdn, rtd 78): eff at 7f, bred to apprec mid-dists: acts on firm grnd.

972　**BOLD GUEST** 15 [5] J W Hills 3-9-0 J Weaver 11/4: -03: 3 ch c Be My Guest - Cross Question (Alleged)　2½　68
Held up, prog & ev ch appr final 2f, sn wknd: bckd from 4/1: ran a similar race to debut, drop back in trip?

--　**FLOW BEAU** [3] G Woodward 3-8-9 R Lappin 66/1: 4: Outpcd on debut: Mtoto filly.　1¾　59

4164}　**WIGMAN LADY** 218 [7] 3-8-9 D Mernagh (3) 12/1: 3-5: Chsd ldrs till halfway: reapp: 3rd sole　2　55
juv start (7f auct mdn on soft grnd): stoutly bred Tenby filly with M Brittain.

976　**MR STICKYWICKET** 15 [1] 3-9-0 (BL) D Harrison 100/1: 006006: In tch till 3f out: blnkd, v stiff task.　hd　60$

1996}　**THE LAST RAMBO** 324 [4] 3-9-0 R Cody Boutcher(7) 66/1: 0-7: Early ldr, btn 3f out: btn sole juv start.　2½　55
7 ran　Time 1m 28.6 (6.8)　(Lord Hartington)　J H M Gosden Manton, Wilts.

1135　4.50 M B MED AUCT MDN DIV 2 3YO (E)　7f str　Good/Soft 87　-16 Slow
£2496　£768　£384　£192

--　**NOBLENOR** [4] L M Cumani 3-9-0 G Sparkes (7) 12/1: -01: 3 ch c Inchinor - Noble Flutter (The Noble　79
Player) Led after 3f, drifted & jnd final 2f, kept on narrowly under hands-&-heels: op 10/1 on Brit bow:
well btn in a 9f mdn in Italy last month: eff at 7f, should get further: goes on gd/soft grnd, gall trk.

4500}　**STILL IN LOVE** 192 [1] H R A Cecil 3-8-9 T Quinn 4/9 FAV: 3-2: 3 b f Emarati - In Love Again　nk　73
(Prince Rupert) Cl-up, chall fnl 2f, hard rdn, hung left, flashed tail, al being held: clr rem, hvly bckd, jockey
given 3 day whip ban: 3rd sole juv start (fill auct mdn, rtd 83): sprint bred, eff at 6/7f: acts on gd/soft & soft.

--　**SHALBEBLUE** [6] J G Given 3-9-0 K Darley 14/1: 3: 3 b g Shalford - Alberjas (Sure Blade)　7　64
Chsd ldrs feeling pace 3f out, late hdwy: debut: op 10/1: 10,000 gns Shalford yearling, brother to a 7f wnr.

837　**PROTECTOR** 27 [3] J W Hills 3-9-0 J Weaver 11/2: 50-04: Led 3f, btn 2f out: needs h'caps: see 837.　2　60$

4445}　**SOUTH LANE** 197 [2] 3-9-0 Kim Tinkler (5) 66/1: 00-5: Dwelt, nvr trbled ldrs: reapp, new stable, no form.　5　50$

--　**DIVA** [5] 3-8-9 S Sanders 5/1: 6: In tch till 3f out: debut: Exit To Nowhere filly with Sir M Prescott.　½　45
6 ran　Time 1m 29.0 (7.2)　(Il Paralupo)　L M Cumani Newmarket.

Official Going   STANDARD. Stalls: Inside

1136   2.10 BANKS'S MDN AUCT 2YO (F)   5f aw rnd Going 56   -08 Slow
£2240   £640   £320

1000 **BEVERLEY MACCA** 10 [5] A Berry 2-8-5 G Carter 5/4 FAV: 221: 2 ch f Piccolo - Kangra Valley (Indian   **76a**
Ridge) Prom travelling well, shaken up and led dist, readily pulled clr under hand and heels riding: val for 6L + :
well bckd: eff at 5f, 6f shld suit: acts on fibresand, prob handles hvy: likes a sharp trk: plenty in hand here.
928 **JOHN FOLEY** 19 [8] W G M Turner 2-8-7 P Fitzsimons (5) 16/1: -002: 2 b c Petardia - Fast Bay (Bay   3½   **67a**
Express) Led 1f, outpaced bef halfway, rdn and kept on inside last, no threat: op 20/1: handles fibresand.
-- **BLUE ORLEANS** [10] A G Newcombe 2-8-7 S Whitworth 5/2: 3: 2 b g Dancing Spree - Blues Player   hd   **66a**
(Jaazeiro) Rdn/outpcd towards rear early, styd on well for press ins last, nrst fin: bckd from 12/1: March foal,
cost 5,000gns: half brother to a 9/10f wnr, dam a 2m wnr: relish 6f soon and will stay much further.
-- **UNVEIL** [1] G M McCourt 2-8-0 F Norton 12/1: 4: Led till over 3f out, soon held: op 33/1: Rudimentary   1¾   **55a**
filly, Feb foal, 8,000gns 2yo: half sister to two juv wnrs, dam a mid-dist wnr: will apprec further later.
-- **EL HAMRA** [4] 2-8-5 G Duffield 10/1: 5: Chsd ldrs 4f: op 7/1: April foal, cost 4,400gns: dam a   1¼   **57a**
mdn, sire high class German miler: with B McMahon.
-- **MRS TIGGYWINKLE** [3] 2-8-2 J Tate 6/1: 6: Track ldrs, slightly hmpd halfway, soon outpcd: March   2   **49a**
foal, 3,000gns 2yo: dam Italian 3yo wnr: with N P Littmoden.
856 **SAND BANKES** [5] 2-8-3-7 S Finnamore (5) 7/1: 27: Dwelt, al bhd: op 5/1, stablemate of runner up.   8   **39a**
-- **MISS TOPOGINO** [7] 2-8-0 N Carlisle 33/1: 8: Slowly away and al rear: Mistertopogigo filly, May foal,   1¾   **28a**
cost 3,400gns: dam a 6f juv selling wnr: with Miss J F Craze.
8 ran   Time 1m 03.4 (3.2)   (Alan Berry)   A Berry Cockerham, Lancs

1137   2.40 AMAT CLAIMER DIV I 3YO+ (G)   6f aw rnd Going 56   -19 Slow
£1512   £432   £216   3 yo rec 10lb

1007 **TAKHLID** 10 [1] D W Chapman 9-11-12 Miss R Clark 7/4 FAV: 366501: 9 b h Nureyev - Savonnerie (Irish   **69a**
River) Dwelt, soon cl-up, led over 3f out & pushed clr over 1f out, readily: '99 wnr at Southwell (3), Lingfield
(2) & here at Wolverhampton (6, clmrs/h'caps, rtd 84a & 64): '98 Hamilton & Thirsk wnr (h'caps, rtd 74 & 64a):
eff btwn 6/8.4f on firm & soft, loves both AWs: gd wght carrier: relishes clmrs & Wolverhampton.
4133} **NAPIER STAR** 219 [10] A B Mulholland 7-10-13 (t) Miss A Elsey 20/1: 0/00-2: 7 b m Inca Chief -   5   **44a**
America Star (Norwich) Handy, outpcd bef halfway, kept on for press inside last, no threat: 7 mth abs: unplcd
in '99: '97 W'hampton wnr (fill h'cap, rtd 67a, Mrs M Macauley): eff over a sharp 5/6f on fibresand.
364 **NADDER** 105 [2] W M Brisbourne 5-11-0 (bl) Miss Diana Jones 20/1: 0-2503: 5 ch g Lion Cavern - Nadia   ½   **43$**
Nerina (Northern Dancer) Prom, one pace over 1f out: op 33/1, 3 month abs: see 276 (seller, 7f).
1081 **RED SONNY** 2 [5] A Berry 3-10-6 Mr A Evans 13/2: 00-004: Chsd wnr halfway, held 1f out: qck reapp.   1   **43a**
749 **NERONIAN** 37 [12] 6-11-0 Mr Ray Barrett (5) 33/1: 6-4305: Dwelt, never on terms: see 676, 554 (12f).   1¾   **37$**
691 **ALJAZ** 47 [6] 10-11-6 Mrs C Williams 4/1: 020646: Chsd ldrs, no impression final 2f: abs, op 3/1.   ½   **41a**
2550} **MAYDORO** 300 [11] 7-10-7 Miss K Rockey (5) 20/1: 0006-7: Chsd ldrs 5f: reapp: unplcd in '99 (rtd   hd   **27a**
45a & 23): '98 wnr here at W'hampton (C/D clmr) & Newcastle (seller, M Dods, rtd 56 & 52a): eff over 5/6f on
soft & fibresand, sharp/stiff track: runs well fresh & enjoys sell/claiming grade.
897 **CHAKRA** 21 [9] 6-11-4 Miss Hayley Bryan (7   14/1: 061068: Led 2f, btn 2f out: see 628.   nk   **37a**
2530} **FIRST GOLD** 301 [13] 11-10-12 Miss C Stretton (5) 50/1: /000-9: Al outpcd: 6 months jumps abs (mod   nk   **30a**
form): unplcd in '99 (rtd 22 & 39a): back in '97 scored at Leicester (J A Wharton, sell, rtd 51 & 57a): eff at
6/7f, stays a sharp 1m: acts on fast, soft & fibresand: eff with/without blinks: owner trained.
263 **WHATTA MADAM** 120 [4] 4-11-2 (t) Mr A Quinn (7) 13/2: 064-40: Prom 4f: 10th: 4 mth abs: see 154.   1½   **30a**
*883 **JAZZNIC** 22 [3] 4-10-9 Mr R C G Harris (7) 4/1: 5-6010: Al outpcd: 13th: btr 883 (5f).   **0a**
-- **Danni** [8] 7-10-9 Mr G O'Callaghan (7) 50/1:   1039 **Safe Sharp Jo** 6 [7] 5-11-0 (BL) Mr L Heath (7) 50/1:
13 ran   Time 1m 17.3 (4.5)   (S B Clark)   D W Chapman Stillington, N Yorks

1138   3.10 AIR FILLIES HCAP 3YO 0-85 (D)   6f aw rnd Going 56   -11 Slow   [90]
£3796   £1168   £584   £292

888 **DANCING EMPRESS** 22 [8] M A Jarvis 3-8-13 (75) P Robinson 100/30 FAV: 021-01: 3 b f Emperor Jones -   **81a**
Music Khan (Music Boy) Al handy, led over 1f out, held on well final 1f, rdn out: op 11/4: caught the eye when
apprentice rdn in 888: '99 Southwell scorer (auct mdn, rtd 76a & 78): eff at 5/6f: acts on firm, hvy & f/sand:
prob handles any track, likes a sharp/turning one: open to further improvement.
479 **STOP THE TRAFFIC** 86 [4] C N Allen 3-8-2 (64) J Mackay (7) 6/1: -42522: 3 b f College Chapel - Miss   ½   **67a**
Bagatelle (Mummy's Pet) Held up in touch, prog to chase wnr final 1f, kept on though al held: op 7/1: 12 wk abs.
870 **CAROLS CHOICE** 23 [7] D Haydn Jones 3-8-1 (63) C Rutter 10/1: -42033: 3 ch f Emarati - Lucky Song   1½   **62a**
(Lucky Wednesday) Prom, chance over 1f out, one pace: op 16/1: blinks ommitted after latest: see 870, 549.
888 **DESERT SAFARI** 22 [3] E J Alston 3-8-9 (71) G Duffield 9/1: 41-054: Rdn/twds rear, late gains.   ½   **68a**
544 **MAID TO LOVE** 75 [1] 3-7-13 (61) Joanna Badger (7) 12/1: 3-4225: Well bhd halfway, rdn/swtchd   nk   **57+**
& styd on strongly ins last, nrst fin: op 10/1, abs: eye catching late headway, sure to relish return to 7f +.
*901 **DISTINCTLY BLU** 21 [2] 3-8-1 (63) Iona Wands 10/1: 00-616: Chsd ldrs, held final 2f: see 901.   hd   **58a**
982 **KEBABS** 14 [12] 3-9-0 (76) G Carter 13/2: 0-5507: Mid-div/wide, held final 3f: op 5/1: AW bow: see 736.   1½   **68a**
852 **BAJAN BELLE** 24 [5] 3-8-13 (75) J Fanning 11/1: -31-08: Led over 3f out till over 1f out, faded: 1½   **63a**
h'cap/AW bow: '99 Carlisle wnr (auction mdn, rtd 81): eff over a stiff 5f, 6/7f will suit: acts on firm grnd.
4082} **BRANSTON LUCY** 223 [6] 3-7-11 (59) F Norton 11/1: 0531-9: Led 2f, btn 1f out: 7 month abs: '99   nk   **46a**
Redcar wnr (nursery, rtd 62 & 57a): eff at 5f: acts on firm & good grnd, any track.
901 **ITS ANOTHER GIFT** 21 [9] 3-7-11 (59) (bl) A Nicholls (0) 16/1: 00-030: Al bhd: 10th: AW bow: btr 901.   1¼   **43a**
1035 **HOXTON SQUARE** 6 [11] 3-8-1 (63) J Tate 12/1: 23-020: Sn bhd: 11th: op 10/1, qck reapp: btr 1035 (7f).   1½   **43a**
955 **STEALTHY TIMES** 16 [10] 3-9-7 (83) Dean McKeown 5/1: 1-00: Prom wide 4f: 12th: op 4/1, AW bow: 2   **58a**
'99 Nottingham wnr (fill auct mdn, rtd 86, sole start): eff at 6f, tried 7f: acts on good & runs well fresh.
12 ran   Time 1m 16.8 (4.0)   (The C H F Partnership)   M A Jarvis Newmarket

---

1139   **3.40 AMAT CLAIMER DIV II 3YO+ (G)**   **6f aw rnd Going 56 -22 Slow**
£1512   £432   £216   3 yo rec 10lb

756 **PALACEGATE TOUCH** 37 [2] A Berry 10-11-6 (bl) Mr A Evans 6/1: 420501: 10 gr g Petong - Dancing   **57a**
Chimes (London Bells) Track ldr halfway, rdn/led over 1f out, styd on well inside last, rdn out: op 5/1: '99 scorer
at Lingfield (2 claimers, rtd 75a & 62): '98 wnr again at Lingfield (clmr, rtd 76a), Warwick, Hamilton and Catterick
(2, clmr/slr, rtd 60): eff at 5/6f, stays 7f on firm, gd/soft & both aw: eff with/without blinks/visor: most tough.
879 **ITHADTOBEYOU** 22 [9] G L Moore 5-11-4 Mr H Poulton (7) 9/2: 600-22: 5 b h Prince Sabo - Secret   1½ **50a**
Valentine (Wollow) Handy, outpcd halfway, kept on inside last, not pace of wnr: see 879 (7f).
923 **FEATHERSTONE LANE** 19 [3] Miss L C Siddall 9-11-2 Mr R Douro (7) 9/2: 252223: 9 b g Siberian   1¾ **44a**
Express - Try Gloria (Try My Best) Bhd, rdn/styd on from over 1f out, nearest at 1f: likes W'hampton.
693 **SAN MICHEL** 45 [10] J L Eyre 8-11-0 (vis) Miss Diana Jones 16/1: 5-0054: Bhd, rdn/kept on final 2f,   1¼ **39a**
no threat: 6 week abs: visor reapplied: see 148.
778 **YOUNG BEN** 36 [8] 8-10-12 (vis) Mr P Childs (7) 40/1: 000-05: Led 2f, btn final 1f: visor reapp: 1¼ **34$**
unplcd in '99 (rtd 48): plcd in '98 (rtd 45 and 34a, h'caps): '97 Beverley wnr (h'cap, rtd 39): eff over 5/6f on
firm, good/soft and fibresand: best in blinks/visor, forcing the pace: has run well fresh.
923 **TROJAN HERO** 19 [4] 9-11-2 (VIS) Miss A Elsey 8/1: 453006: Led till halfway, faded: visor: btr 201.   1½ **34a**
414 **XSYNNA** 97 [12] 4-11-4 Mr A Carson (7) 100/30 FAV: 5-4267: Chsd ldrs 4f: op 3/1, abs: see 351 (C/D).   nk **35a**
867 **YORKIE TOO** 23 [7] 4-10-13 (bl) Miss J Feilden 14/1: 400-08: Mid-div at best: op 16/1: blinks reapp.   ¾ **28a**
753 **SING FOR ME** 37 [6] 5-10-9 Miss A Knobbs (7) 16/1: 042459: All outpcd: op 14/1: see 272.   ½ **22a**
1068 **FRENCH GRIT** 3 [11] 8-10-12 Mr J Bostock (7) 12/1: 600060: In touch whole 4f: 10th: qck reapp: see 166.   ½ **23a**
3163} **HI MUJTAHID** 273 [13] 6-11-0 Mr M Savage (7) 25/1: 3000-0: Prom 4f: 11th: op 33/1, 9 month abs: 2½ **18a**
plcd in '99 for Mrs H L Walton (rtd 32a, rtd 28 on turf): '98 Wolverhampton wnr (h'cap, rtd 40a): eff forcing pace
at 7f./8.5f on fast, soft and fibresand: handles a sharp or galloping track: eff with/without blinks: with J Bradley.
676 **RA RA RASPUTIN** 49 [1] 5-11-4 Miss S M Potts (7) 10/1: 100000: All bhd: 12th: on 16/1, jumps fit.   nk **21a**
12 ran   Time 1m 17.5 (4.7)   (A B Parr)   A Berry Cockerham, Lancs

---

1140   **4.10 ALLIED IRISH HCAP 3YO+ 0-85 (D)**   **5f aw rnd Going 56 +08 Fast**   **[83]**
£3783   £1164   £582   £291   3 yo rec 9 lb

*919 **PRIDE OF BRIXTON** 19 [11] Andrew Reid 7-8-9 (64) M Henry 6/1 JT FAV: 00-111: 7 b g Dominion -   **73a**
Caviar Blini (What A Guest) Handy and rdn/led halfway, clr over 1f out, eased down near fin, comfortably: value for
3L+: best time of day: completed a hat-trick, recent dual Wolverhampton wnr (seller and claimer, C/D): duel '99
rnr-up (clmr, rtd 73a): '98 wnr again at Wolverhampton (clmr, slr & h'cap for C Thornton and 2 h'caps for P Evans,
rtd 74a), also Carlisle (rtd 61): eff at 5f, suited by 5f on fast & soft, fibresand/Wolverhampton specialist.
1092 **EASTERN TRUMPETER** 2 [2] J M Bradley 4-9-2 (71) L Newman (5) 6/1 JT FAV: 410002: 4 b c First Trump   1¾ **71a**
- Oriental Air (Taufan) Rdn/towards rear till styd on final 2f, no threat: qck reapp: see 678 (C/D).
960 **DOUBLE O** 16 [3] W Jarvis 6-9-3 (72)(bl) F Norton 12/1: 0-4003: 6 b g Sharpo - Ktolo (Tolomeo)   3 **65a**
Rdn/bhd, styd on final 2f, no threat: op 8/1: on a fair mark: see 91.
897 **KING OF PERU** 21 [12] N P Littmoden 7-10-0 (83)(vis) D Young (7) 12/1: -55644: Prom, chsd wnr over shd **76a**
1f out, no impression inside last: op 10/1: see 660.
721 **KEEN HANDS** 40 [10] 4-9-5 (74)(vis) R Fitzpatrick (3) 14/1: 105055: Mid-div, no danger: abs, op 10/1.   nk **66a**
506 **MUKARRAB** 82 [8] 6-9-5 (74) G Duffield 7/1: 6-0436: Chsd ldrs, held final 2f: abs, op 5/1: see 191.   1¼ **63a**
774 **SOTONIAN** 36 [1] 7-8-3 (58) A Nicholls (3) 8/1: 050037: Led 1f, btn 2f out: see 394 (C/D).   nk **46a**
579 **JACKIES BABY** 70 [9] 4-9-5 (74) S Finnamore (5) 8/1: -04008: Led after 1f till halfway, faded: abs.   hd **61a**
3911} **TUSCAN DREAM** 233 [5] 5-9-4 (73) P Bradley (5) 8/1: 2014-9: Prom 3f: op 7/1, 8 mth abs: '99   1¼ **57a**
scorer at Musselburgh (seller), Wolverhampton (AW clmr), Lingfield and Epsom (h'caps, rtd 74 and 63a): thrice
plcd in '98 (rtd 68a and 65): likes to force the pace over a sharp 5f on firm, fast and fibresand: best without blinks.
960 **SUPREME ANGEL** 16 [7] 5-8-10 (65)(bl) T G McLaughlin 7/1: -31040: Chsd ldrs, outpcd fnl 2f: 10th.   hd **48a**
205 **ECUDAMAH** 138 [4] 4-8-12 (67) Dean McKeown 11/1: 1246-0: Rear, al outpcd: 11th: op 8/1, 5 month abs.   2½ **43a**
1074 **UNCLE EXACT** 3 [6] 3-8-13 (77) Iona Wands (5) 12/1: 20-000: Al rear: 12th: op 20/1, qck reapp: 2 **48a**
'99 Hamilton wnr (4 rnr auct mdn, rtd 83): eff at 5f, tried 6f: acts on fast and good grnd: AW bow today.
12 ran   Time 1m 02.6 (2.4)   (A S Reid)   Andrew Reid Mill Hill, London NW 7

1141   **4.40 MANCHESTER SELLER 3YO (F)**   **1m1f79y aw Going 56 -11 Slow**
£1813   £518   £259

1040 **CYBER BABE** 6 [1] Andrew Reid 3-8-6 M Henry 7/4: 00-021: 3 ch f Persian Bold - Ervedya (Doyoun)   **51a**
Made all & rdn clr over 2f out, held on well inside last, rdn out: sold for 3,200 gns: op 2/1, quick reapp:
rnr-up twice in '99 (rtd 58, M Tompkins): eff at 7f/1m, now suited by 9f, could get further: acts on fm, gd &
fibresand: eff forcing the pace and apprec this drop to selling grade.
869 **STANDIFORD GIRL** 23 [3] J G Given 3-8-6 Dean McKeown 14/1: 62: 3 b f Standiford - Pennine Girl   1½ **47a**
(Pennine Walk) Chsd wnr halfway, hung left/kept on inside last, al held: clr rem: op 10/1: styd longer 9.4f trip.
933 **KINGS GINGER** 17 [2] D J Wintle 3-8-11 Joanna Badger (7) 5/4 FAV: 003403: 3 ch g King's Signet   5 **42a**
- Cosset (Comedy Star) Keen, in touch, rdn/outpcd final 3f: well bckd, op 5/2: btr 540 (1m).
852 **PERFECT MOMENT** 24 [8] G M McCourt 3-8-11 G Carter 10/1: 000-04: Held up, eff 4f out, btn 2f out: 3 **36a**
op 6/1: '99 Leicester wnr (auction mdn, A P Jarvis, rtd 74): eff at 7f, 1m+ could suit: AW bow today.
555 **RITA MACKINTOSH** 73 [5] 3-8-6 (vis) F Norton 10/1: 30-305: In touch, btn 4f out: op 5/1, 10 wk abs.   1¾ **28a**
1035 **SKELTON MONARCH** 6 [9] 3-8-11 P M Quinn (5) 12/1: 000-66: Rdn/rear, struggling 3f out: op 10/1.   nk **32a**
841 **IRISH DANCER** 27 [4] 3-8-6 P Robinson 7/1: 004-07: In touch 5f: op 9/2: see 841.   2½ **22a**
971 **WROTHAM ARMS** 15 [6] 3-8-6 J Lowe 14/1: 0-08: Held up, btn 3f out: op 10/1: AW bow, no form.   11 **6a**
922 **SEASAME PARK** 19 [7] 3-8-11 G Duffield 8/1: 20-039: Prom 5f: op 6/1: see 806.   1¼ **8a**
9 ran   Time 2m 04.5 (6.3)   (A S Reid)   Andrew Reid Mill Hill, London NW7

1142   **5.10 TURCO HCAP 3YO 0-65 (F)**   **1m4f aw Going 56 -29 Slow**   **[72]**
£2233   £638   £319

597 **XELLANCE** 68 [7] M Johnston 3-7-12 (42) K Dalgleish (7) 6/1: 00-151: 3 b g Be My Guest - Excellent   **46a**
Alibi (Exceller) Waited with rear, smooth prog to lead over 1f out, edged right inside last, styd on well, rdn out:
op 10/1: 10 wk abs: earlier scored at Southwell (h'cap, first success): rtd 43 in '99 (unplcd): eff at 11/12f,
could get further: acts on fibresand & a sharp trk: runs well fresh.

WOLVERHAMPTON (Fibresand)   THURSDAY MAY 4TH   Lefthand, Sharp Track

832 **TUFTY HOPPER 28** [3] P Howling 3-8-12 (56) R Winston 10/1: 0-6442: 3 b g Rock Hopper - Melancolia ¾ 58a
(Legend Of France): In tch, rdn/lost place halfway, prog/ev cn 1f out, held nr fin: tchd 12/1: eff at 12f on
fibresand & gd/soft grnd, could apprec further: see 832 & 643.

*978 **ESTABELLA 15** [2] S P C Woods 3-9-5 (63) L Newman (5) 3/1: 05-213: 3 ch f Majtahid - Lady In Green 4 59a
(Shareef Dancer): Led, rdn/hdd over 1f out, no extra: op 2/1: AW bow: acts on gd/soft, hvy & fibresand: see 978.

1040 **FISHER ISLAND 6** [5] R Hollinshead 3-8-7 (51) P M Quinn (5) 12/1: 0-6344: Rear, prog 5f out, held ¾ 46a
final 2f: op 16/1, qck reapp: AW bow: unplcd at up in run in '99 (rtd 59): bred to apprec mid/styg dists this term.

799 **LE CAVALIER 35** [4] 3-9-7 (65) P Morse 11/1: 222266: Chsd ldr, btn over 1f out: op 7/1: btr 752. 4 54a

978 **ODYN DANCER 15** [8] 3-8-2 (46) G Baker (7) 25/1: 666206: Rear, mod late gains: see 537. 2½ 31a

978 **TYCOONS LAST 15** [12] 3-8-5 (49) J Fanning 25/1: 00-357: Mid-div, btn halfway: op 33/1: AW bow. 1½ 32a

4051} **DIVE 225** [11] 3-8-10 (54) G Duffield 5/4 FAV: -006-8: Mid-div, rdn halfway, btn 3f out: hvly bckd: shd 37a
reapp/h'cap debut, AW bow: unplcd at up in run in '99 (rtd 99): bred to apprec mid/styg dists this term.

858 **HORTON DANCER 24** [6] 3-8-11 (55)(VIS) G Carter 25/1: 4-609: Al bhd: visor: h'cap bow: btr 752. 3½ 33a

1040 **TAKE ACTION 6** [10] 3-8-8 (52) Dean McKeown 25/1: 00-500: Bhd 6f out: 10th: lngr 12f trip. 14 15a

523 Room To Room Magic 78 [1] 3-8-8 (52) D Sweeney 33/1:
978 High Capacity 15 [9] 3-7-11 (40)(bl)(1ow) F Norton 33/1:

12 ran   Time 2m 43.8 (10.2)   (T T Bloodstocks)   M Johnston Middleham, Nth Yorks.

MUSSELBURGH   FRIDAY MAY 5TH   Righthand, Sharp Track

Official Going   FIRM (GOOD/FIRM in places). Stalls: Inside, except 5f & 2m - Far side.

1143   2.15 ARMSTRONG AMAT HCAP 3YO+ 0-65 (F)   5f str   Good/Firm 40   +04 Fast   [37]
£2548   £728   £364   3 yo rec 9 lb   Field raced across the track

711 **COOL PROSPECT 43** [6] K A Ryan 5-10-10 (47)(bl) Miss Diana Jones 13/2 CO FAV: 050541: 5 b g Mon 52
Tresor - I Ran Lovely (Persian Bold) Handy, hdwy to lead ins 1f, kept on, pushed out: 6 wk abs, fair time:
'99 scorer at Redcar (h'cap, rtd 50 & 65a): eff at 5f, stays 1m on firm, gd/soft & fibresand: handles any trk &
eff with/without blnks: runs well fresh: 2nd win on 35th start.

798 **SWYNFORD DREAM 36** [10] J Hetherton 7-11-7 (58) Mr T Best (5) 13/2 CO FAV: 600-52: 7 b g Statoblest 1 59
- Qualitair Dream (Dreams To Reality) Prom, eff to chall ins last, kept on, only btn 1L: bckd & h'capped to win.

1008 **LEGS BE FRIENDLY 11** [12] D Nicholls 5-12-0 (65) Mr L Richardson (7) 16/1: 000-W3: 5 b g Fayruz - shd 66
Thalssa (Rusticaro) Handy, kept on onepace fnl 2f under a kind ride: out of sorts for K McAuliffe in '99 (rnr-up
once, rtd 72): lightly rcd since '97 wnr at Lingfield (rtd 81, blnkd first time): eff at 5f, stays a stiff 7f on
fm, soft & fibresand: tried blnks/visor: slipped right down the weights & his shrewd trainer can exploit it.

1068 **JACKERIN 4** [5] B S Rothwell 3-10-12 (49)(bl) Mr Nicky Tinkler (5) 12/1: 0-6554: Swtchd to race far 1¼ 47
side over 3f out, rdn 2f out, kept on same pace: qck reapp, see 777.

4331} **BIFF EM 206** [8] 6-10-3 (40) Mrs C Williams 20/1: 3000-5: Sn bhd, late gains on reapp: plcd sev 1 35
times in '99 (rtd 47): '98 wnr at Hamilton (amat h'cap, rtd 47): eff at 5/6f on fast or hvy grnd & loves Hamilton.

4471} **DAZZLING QUINTET 196** [2] 4-10-9 (46) Mr W Worthington (7) 12/1: 0020-6: In tch stands side, kept on nk 40
late, nvr nrr: reapp: mostly out of sorts in '99, rnr-up once (rtd 52S): '98 Beverley wnr (fillies auct mdn,
rtd 78): eff over 5/6f on firm, gd/soft & a stiff trk.

250 **SUE ME 123** [15] 8-11-9 (60)(bl) Mrs A Hammond (7) 12/1: 006-07: Led till just inside final 1f, no hd 53
extra: stablemate of 3rd, 4 mth abs: see 199 (sell).

3553} **IMPALDI 255** [7] 5-10-1 (38) Miss L Hanson (7) 14/1: 0050-8: Sn bhd, some late gains on reapp: 1½ 27
rnr-up once in '99 (rtd 44 at best): eff at 5/6f on firm & gd grnd: better off in sell h'caps over further.

777 **COLLEGE MAID 37** [14] 3-10-10 (56) Mr D Boyd (7) 8/1: 056-29: Nvr a factor: see 777. ¾ 43

867 **GRAND ESTATE 24** [4] 5-11-12 (63) Miss R Clark 9/1: 000030: Al bhd stands side: 10th. nk 49

673 **KALAR 52** [13] 11-10-5 (40)(bl)(2ow) Miss M Keuthern (0) 20/1: -00500: Cl-up till wknd 2f out: 11th. ¾ 26

897 **TINAS ROYALE 22** [11] 4-10-13 (50) Mrs L Pearce 13/2 CO FAV: 400-50: Al bhd: 12th: see 897. nk 33

910 Miss Grapette 21 [16] 4-10-8 (45) Mr S Hughes (7) 16/1:
901 Unmasked 22 [9] 4-9-10 (33)(3oh) Mr J J McShane (7) 40/1:
4409} Dinos Girl 200 [3] 3-9-10 (42) Miss K Walling (3) 50/1:
4059} Amber Go Go 225 [1] 3-9-11 (42)(1ow) Mr K Burke (0) 50/1:

16 ran   Time 59.3 (1.8)   (Mrs Candice Reilly)   K A Ryan Hambleton, N Yorks

1144   2.45 MCEWANS CLASS STKS 3YO+ 0-70 (E)   1m rnd   Good/Firm 40   +04 Fast
£3081   £948   £474   £237   3 yo rec 13lb

900 **LADY OF WINDSOR 22** [1] I Semple 3-8-4 (vis) R Winston 25/1: 404-51: 3 ch f Woods Of Windsor - North 71
Lady (Northfields) Made all, clr 3f out, kept on ins last, just held on for press: gd time: first win: plcd
sev times in '99 (rtd 74): eff at 6/7f, stays 1m on any trk: tried blnks, best in visor: well rdn.

*1037 **ROYAL ARTIST 7** [6] W J Haggas 4-9-9 J P Spencer 5/6 FAV: 31-212: 4 b g Royal Academy - nk 76
Council Rock (General Assembly) Dwelt, hld up, trav well but wnr had slipped clr 3f out, kept on well fnl 2f,
wld have won in one race: well bckd: most unlucky & prob wnr if asked for his effort earlier: see 1037.

999 **SPIRIT OF LIGHT 13** [3] M R Channon 3-8-7 S Drowne 4/1: 5-0023: 3 b g Unblest - Light Thatch (Thatch) 1 71
Chsd wnr, rdn over 2f out & outpcd by wnr, onepace over 1f out: in gd form: see 999.

908 **KASS ALHAWA 21** [7] D W Chapman 7-9-6 A Culhane 9/2: -20624: Keen, cl up, eff 2f out, onepace. 1½ 68

3429} **LADY LOVE 261** [8] 3-8-4 G Duffield 20/1: 1060-5: Prom, wknd over 2f out: won debut as a juv, at 1 63
Musselburgh (fill med auct mdn): dam 12f wnr: eff at 5f, poss stays 1m: acts on gd grnd.

*752 **MASSEY 38** [4] 4-9-9 G Bardwell 12/1: 16: Hld up, rdn over 3f out, mod late gains: needs 10f+. nk 68

900 **DISPOL JAZZ 22** [2] 3-8-4 K Darley 12/1: 410-37: Chsd ldrs, wknd over 2f out: see 900. 1½ 59

759 **DUNKELD CHAMP 38** [5] 3-8-7 A Daly 100/1: 00-08: Al bhd: dam 1m/9f wnr: modest. dist 0

8 ran   Time 1m 40.4 (2.9)   (Raeburn Brick Ltd)   I Semple Carlucke, S Lanarks

1145   3.20 OLD COURSE CLAIMER 4YO+ (F)   2m   Good/Firm 40   -07 Slow
£2769   £852   £426   £213   4 yo rec 3 lb

-- **MIDYAN BLUE** [3] P Monteith 10-8-6 R Winston 16/1: 0000/1: 10 ch g Midyan - Jarretiere (Star Appeal) 47
Made all, clr over 4f out, kept on: missed '99, prev term rtd 49 at best: last won back in '95 (rtd 92 at best):
eff at 12f, stays 2m on fast & hvy grnd: runs well fresh: gd training effort & another fine R Winston ride.

MUSSELBURGH **FRIDAY MAY 5TH Righthand, Sharp Track**

2417} **MONDRAGON 307** [4] Mrs M Reveley 10-8-12 A Culhane 11/10 FAV: 2/04-2: 10 b g Niniski - La Lutine (My Swallow) Hld up, eff over 2f out, not pace of wnr: well bckd: well btn both '99 starts: '98 wnr at Redcar & Beverley (h'caps, rtd 64 & 60a): 97/98 hdls wnr: eff at 14f/2m on fm, hvy & any trk. *7* **47**
822 **WAFIR 30** [9] D Nicholls 8-8-12 O Pears 2/1: 256-43: 8 b g Scenic -Taniokey (Grundy) Hld up, eff over 3f out, onepace: bckd tho' 6/4: stays 2m: see 822. *3* **44**
918 **XYLEM 20** [2] J Pearce 9-8-10 (vis) G Bardwell 12/1: 023054: In tch, rdn & no impress fnl 3f: flattered. *shd* **42$**
737 **SUDDEN SPIN 39** [8] 10-8-6 J Fanning 20/1: 05-065: In tch, eff to chase wnr over 2f out, sn btn. *5* **33$**
434} **ANOTHER ARTHUR 455** [7] 4-8-11 K Darley 33/1: 0/00-6: Chsd wnr till over 2f out, wknd: poor form. *5* **36$**
513 **TOTAL TROPIX 81** [6] 5-8-1 J McAuley (5) 40/1: 044/07: In tch, wknd 3f out: fell over hdls since 513. *1¾* **22$**
903 **BREYDON 22** [5] 7-8-6 P Hanagan (7) 10/1: 00-008: Al bhd. *nk* **27$**
3548} **CRAIGARY 255** [1] 9-8-10 G Duffield 14/1: /056-9: Prom, wknd over 4f out: rnr-up over hdls this winter (rtd 87h & 76c, stays 2m6.5f, fm & gd/soft): mod '99 form: last won in '97, at Hamilton (sell h'cap, rtd 42): 97/98 dual hdls wnr (sell h'caps, stays 2m3f, rtd 95h): eff at 12f on fm & gd, likes hvy: eff with/without blnks. *13* **19**
9 ran Time 3m 30.0 (7.5) (Mrs June Brown) P Monteith Rosewell, Midlothian

1146

3.55 MUSSELBURGH MED AUCT MDN 2YO (F) 5f str Good/Firm 40 -04 Slow
£2814 £804 £402

974 **UP TEMPO 16** [8] T D Easterby 2-9-0 K Darley 5/6 FAV: 21: 2 b c Flying Spur - Musical Essence (Song) Made all, kept on inside final 1f, rdn to assert cl-home: well bckd: cost IR 12,000gns, half-brother to 3 wnrs: v eff at 5f, 6f looks sure to suit: acts on fast & hvy grnd & on a stiff or easy trk: can rate more highly. **80**
700 **DENSIM BLUE 43** [2] J Pearce 2-9-0 G Bardwell 7/1: 02: 2 b c Lake Coniston - Surprise Visitor (Be My Guest) Cl-up, kept on for press final 1f, not btn far: Mar 1st foal: dam won over jumps: eff at 5f, will relish 6f: handles fast grnd & has the scope to go on & win a race. *½* **78**
-- **TICKER** [12] Denys Smith 2-9-0 J P Spencer 13/2: 3: 2 b c Timeless Times - Lady Day (Lightning) Handy, rdn 2f out, kept on inside last on debut: May foal: half-brother to a 1m juv wnr: dam mid-dist scorer: sure to relish 6f+ in time & shwd enough here to suggest he can win a race. *½* **76**
-- **NOT JUST A DREAM** [10] A Berry 2-8-9 O Pears 7/1: 4: Cl-up, kept on same pace for press over 1f out, hands-&-heels: Apr foal: bred to enjoy 6f/7f in time. *1* **68$**
-- **ORIENTAL MIST** [6] 2-9-0 C Lowther 12/1: 5: Went left start, sn bhd, 12L in arrears halfway, styd on well late: debut: Mar foal, cost 17,000 gns: half-brother to a 7f wnr: crying out for 6f, improve. *nk* **72+**
-- **NOWT BUT TROUBLE** [9] 2-9-0 N Kennedy 40/1: 6: In tch, effort 2f out, sn no impress: debut: Apr 1st foal: bred to apprec 6f in time. *½* **71**
898 **PHARAOH HATSHEPSUT 22** [1] 2-8-9 P Fessey 66/1: -407: Nvr dngr, some late gains: see 796. *hd* **65**
-- **ALICIAN SUNHILL** [5] 2-8-9 G Duffield 20/1: 8: Hmpd start, sn bhd, some late gains: debut: May 1st foal: dam 5f wnr: with Mrs A Duffield. *1¾* **61**
-- **EYES DONT LIE** [11] 2-9-0 R Winston 20/1: 9: Dwelt, al bhd. *3* **57**
-- **MONICA** [3] 2-8-9 T Williams 100/1: 0: Al bhd on debut: 10th. *3½* **42**
938 **Dance Queen 18** [4] 2-8-9 J Bramhill 20/1: -- **I Got Rhythm** [7] 2-8-9 A Culhane 100/1:
12 ran Time 59.7 (2.2) (T H Bennett) T D Easterby Great Habton, Nth Yorks.

1147

4.25 EAST LOTHIAN HCAP 3YO+ 0-80 (D) 1m4f Good/Firm 40 -05 Slow [73]
£4251 £1308 £654 £327

3575} **PLUTOCRAT 253** [7] L Lungo 4-9-10 (69) J P Spencer 9/4 JT FAV: 0231-1: 4 b g Polar Falcon - Choire Mhor (Dominion) Handy, eff to lead over 1f out, drvn out: reapp: '99 Musselburgh wnr (clmr, with J Noseda, rtd 76, claimed for £9,000): eff at 7f/9f, stays 12f well on fm & soft grnd: likes Musselburgh. **74**
4393} **SING AND DANCE 202** [6] J R Weymes 7-8-5 (50) G Sparkes (7) 9/1: 1202-2: 7 b m Rambo Dancer - Musical Princess (Cavo Dora) Hld up, eff to chall 2f out, hung left & no extra ins last: btn 1L: reapp: trained by E Weymes in '99, won at Musselburgh (h'cap) & Hamilton (appr h'cap, rtd 54): '98 wnr at Musselburgh, Newcastle & Catterick (h'caps, rtd 50): eff at 10/12f on fm, soft & any trk, likes Musselburgh: tried blnks/visor: tough. *1* **53**
903 **FREEDOM QUEST 22** [8] B S Rothwell 5-9-3 (62) M Fenton 11/2: 10-443: 5 b g Polish Patriot - Recherchee (Rainbow Quest) With ld, led after 4f till over 1f out, no extra: clr of rem: in gd form, see 903. *1* **63**
903 **FIELD OF VISION 22** [5] Mrs A Duffield 10-8-8 (53) G Duffield 6/1: 40-024: In tch, wknd over 2f out. *6* **47**
726 **GENEROUS WAYS 41** [2] 5-8-12 (57) L Swift (7) 10/1: 50-405: Nvr dngs under kind ride: abs, do better. *5* **44**
968 **LANCER 16** [1] 8-9-7 (66)(vis) G Bardwell 9/4 JT FAV: 0-6166: In tch, wknd 3f out: btr 815. *3* **49**
903 **DONE WELL 22** [3] 8-7-10 (41)(t)(14oh) J Bramhill 66/1: /0-007: Al bhd. *8* **14**
70 **ROMA 168** [4] 5-8-0 (45) A Daly 14/1: 1200-8: Led 4f, wknd 4f out: mod hdls form 3 months ago: '99 wnr at Musselburgh (fill h'cap, rtd 47): stays 12f on gd, gd/soft & fibresand: has run well fresh. *6* **10**
8 ran Time 2m 36.0 (5.4) (N A Bulmer) L Lungo Carrutherstown, D'fries & G'way

1148

5.0 GOLF COURSE HCAP DIV 1 3YO+ 0-65 (F) 7f30y rnd Good/Firm 40 -16 Slow [65]
£2842 £812 £406 3 yo rec 12lb

600 **SAGUARO 67** [6] K A Morgan 6-8-5 (42) P M Quinn (5) 9/1: 000-21: 6 b g Green Desert - Badawi (Diesis) Waited with, hdwy to lead over 1f out, kept on inside last, rdn out: abs: '99 wnr at Southwell & W'hampton (h'caps, rtd 79a), subs well btn on turf & over hdles: unplcd in '98 for J Gosden (tried visor): eff at 7/9.3f on fast, soft & fibresand: gd weight carrier who runs well fresh on an easy trk. **47**
908 **BOLLIN ROBERTA 21** [12] T D Easterby 4-9-8 (59) R Winston 11/2: 100-52: 4 b f Bob's Return - Bollin Emily (Lochnager) Bhd, eff 2f out, ev ch dist, kept on inside last, just btn: sole win over this C/D: see 908. *½* **62**
282 **ALMAZHAR 119** [5] J L Eyre 5-8-12 (49) T Williams 17/2: 26-223: 5 b g Last Tycoon - Mosaique Bleue (Shirley Heights) Chsd ldrs, effort to chall over 1f out, kept on inside last, not btn far: abs, on a fair mark. *hd* **52**
4593} **DETROIT CITY 184** [11] B S Rothwell 5-8-6 (43) M Fenton 6/1: 0000-4: Set pace till over 1f out, onepace on reapp: p.u. over hdles back in Dec: v busy on the Flat in '99, scored here at Musselburgh (h'cap, rtd 59): '98 wnr again here at Musselburgh (rtd mdn) & Beverley (clmr, rtd 64): suited by 7f on firm or soft grnd: handles any trk, loves Musselburgh: has tried a visor: h'capped to win. *2½* **41**
1011 **NOBALINO 11** [8] 6-9-11 (62)(vis) V Halliday 8/1: 135-05: Waited with, effort over 2f out, sn no impress: well bckd: only 2 wins in 34 starts: see 1011, 59. *3* **54**
931 **TAYOVULLIN 20** [4] 6-8-7 (44) F Lynch 10/1: 0-0006: In tch, effort 3f out, no impress under kind ride. *1* **34**
3947} **KIDZ PLAY 232** [9] 4-9-3 (54) A Culhane 16/1: 1024-7: Cl-up, btn 2f out: reapp: in '99 won at Hamilton (mdn h'cap, rtd 54): trained by M Johnson in '98, rtd 68: eff at 1m/10.8f on gd/firm & soft grnd. *nk* **43**
907 **TAKER CHANCE 21** [10] 4-8-10 (47) G Duffield 7/1: 0-0008: Prom, rdn & btn 2f out. *¾* **34**
1066 **TOBLERSONG 4** [2] 5-9-1 (52)(t) J P Spencer 11/1: 50-409: Al bhd: see 958 (6f, soft). *1½* **36**

MUSSELBURGH FRIDAY MAY 5TH Righthand, Sharp Track

929 **TECHNICIAN 20** [13] 5-9-5 (56)(bl) L Swift (7) 5/1 FAV: -00520: In tch, btn halfway: 10th: see 929. *1½* **37**
4589} **Granite City 184** [14] 3-8-2 (51) E Alston 25/1: 1024 **Threefortycash 11** [3] 3-8-2 (51) A Daly 33/1:
12 ran Time 1m 28.5 (3.9) (Roemex Ltd) K A Morgan Waltham-On-The-Wolds, Leics

1149 **5.30 GOLF COURSE HCAP DIV 2 3YO+ 0-65 (F) 7f30y rnd Good/Firm 40 -13 Slow [65]**
£2842 £812 £406 3 yo rec 12lb

749 **ETISALAT 38** [2] J Pearce 5-8-9 (46) G Bardwell 10/1: 312631: 5 b g Lahib - Sweet Repose (High Top) **51**
Slow away, bhd, hdwy for hard driving over 1f out to get up cl-home, typical never say die G Bardwell ride: earlier won at W'hampton (amat h'cap, rtd 57a): '99 Yarmouth wnr (sell h'cap) & Lingfield (h'cap, rtd 53 & 47a): unplcd in '98 for R Armstrong: eff at 7f/10f on fast, gd & both AWs: likes a sharp trk: likes to come late.
4450} **JACMAR 198** [14] Miss L A Perratt 5-8-5 (42) K Dalgleigh (7) 20/1: 0000-2: 5 br g High Estate - Inseyab *nk* **46**
(Persian Bold) In tch, gd hdwy to lead 2f out, rdn & collared cl-home: reapp: mostly out of sorts in '99, won at Hamilton (amat h'cap, rtd 63): no wins in '98, in '97 won again at Hamilton (3, rtd 95): eff at 5/6f, stays 7f: acts on fast & gd/soft: gd weight carrier: on a wng mark, should go in again at Hamilton.
899 **MR PERRY 22** [5] M D Hammond 4-9-3 (54)(BL) K Darley 7/1: 0-0023: 4 br g Perugino - Elegant Tune *1¼* **56**
(Alysheba) Keen, waited with, eff to chall 1f out, no extra: another gd run in blnks: acts on fast, fibresand & hvy.
67 **SWYNFORD PLEASURE 170** [3] J Hetherton 4-8-3 (40) J Fanning 50/1: 0000-4: Bhd, kept on late, nrst *nk* **41**
fin on reapp: plcd twice in '99 (rtd 55): rnr-up in '98 (rtd 66, with J Hetherton): eff over 7f/1m on fast & gd.
908 **JOHAYRO 21** [12] 7-9-10 (61) A Culhane 3/1: 0-0405: Prom, rdn & wknd over 1f out: twice below 798. *¾* **60**
749 **KESTRAL 38** [7] 4-8-5 (42) R Winston 10/1: 00-506: In tch, effort to chall over 1f out, sn btn: mdn. *shd* **41**
1068 **ENCOUNTER 4** [11] 4-8-13 (50) N Kennedy 9/1: 00-407: Prom till wknd over 1f out: see 787. *2* **45**
4616} **BETTYJOE 181** [4] 3-8-6 (55) P Fessey 25/1: 3000-8: Nvr a factor on reapp: plcd in '99 (rtd 64): *5* **42**
stays 6f on gd/firm & gd/soft.
795 **GO THUNDER 36** [1] 6-8-1 (38)(t) A Daly 16/1: 000-09: Al bhd. *nk* **24**
4447} **PERSIAN POINT 198** [10] 4-8-4 (41) R Lappin 50/1: 0000-0: Prom, wknd over 2f out: reapp: mod. *1* **25**
780 **CLADANTOM 37** [8] 4-9-1 (52) F Lynch 33/1: 06-000: Al bhd: 11th: see 156. *10* **18**
899 **LUNCH PARTY 22** [13] 8-9-7 (58) P Bradley (5) 13/8 FAV: 060-40: Dwelt, sn rushed up to lead till 2f *6* **14**
out, wknd & eased: 12th, well bckd, probably went off too fast, much btr 899.
674 **SQUIRE CORRIE 52** [6] 8-8-11 (48) G Parkin 50/1: 00-00P: In tch, wknd 3f out, p.u. & dismounted **0**
over 1f out: 7 wk abs, clearly something amiss.
13 ran Time 1m 28.6 (3.7) (Mrs E M Clark) J Pearce Newmarket, Suffolk

NEWMARKET (Rowley) FRIDAY MAY 5TH Righthand, Stiff, Galloping Track

Official Going GOOD. Stalls: Far Side.

1150 **2.05 DRAKEFORD CUP HCAP 3YO+ 0-85 (D) 1m2f Good/Firm 28 +06 Fast [83]**
£7826 £2408 £1204 £602 3yo rec 15lb

4295} **STAR TURN 209** [8] R M Flower 6-8-2 (57) F Norton 33/1: 1010-1: 6 ch g Night Shift - Ringtail **61**
(Auction Ring) Rear, imprvd 2f out, led ent fnl 1f, ran on strongly, drvn out: best time of day, reapp: lightly rcd in '99, won at Lingfield (h'cap, rtd 54a, reapp) & here at Newmarket (ladies h'cap, rtd 59): best at 10f on fast & soft grnd, handles equitrack, poss f/sand: runs v well fresh, handles any trk, likes Newmarket.
1031 **PINCHINCHA 9** [9] D Morris 6-9-6 (75) K Fallon 10/1: 23-402: 6 b g Priolo - Western Heights *½* **78**
(Shirley Heights) Waited with, imprvd to lead 2f out, hdd ent fnl 1f, rallied & only just btn: sound effort, well h'capped nowadays, but has not won since '97: see 786.
*907 **INCH PERFECT 21** [11] R A Fahey 5-9-1 (70) R Cochrane 11/4 FAV: 131-13: 5 b g Inchinor - Scarlet *¾* **71**
Veil (Tyrnavos) Rear, short of room 2f out, styd on well once clr fnl 1f, nrst fin: hvly bckd, not much luck in running here: gd run & poss unlucky: see 907.
4295} **SWEET REWARD 209** [17] J G Smyth Osbourne 5-8-13 (68) D Harrison 33/1: 0330-4: In tch, eff 2f out, *4* **63**
onepcd fnl 1f: 5th in a nov hdle in Jan '00 (rtd 101h): plcd sev times on the Flat in '99 (h'caps, rtd 73 at best): last won in '97, at Leicester (mdn auct, rtd 80): eff at 1m10f, acts on fast, loves soft & hvy grnd.
1031 **CAPTAINS LOG 9** [7] 5-9-3 (72) J Mackay(7) 7/1: 60-425: Rear, imprvd 3f out, onepcd fnl 1f: btr 1031. *2½* **63**
895 **HUGWITY 22** [16] 8-9-1 (70) M Hills 20/1: 300336: Chsd ldrs, imprvd to lead 3f out till 2f out, grad fdd. *1¾* **58**
1011 **TONIC 11** [15] 4-9-13 (82) D Holland 20/1: 100-07: Rdn in rear, styd on well fnl 1f, nrst fin: longer *3* **65**
10f trip, shapes as tho' even further will suit: slipping down the weights & one to keep in mind, see 1011.
22 **HERR TRIGGER 176** [5] 9-7-11 (52)(bl) J Lowe 40/1: 3405-8: Chsd ldrs till btn 2f out: reapp: see 22. *1* **33**
715 **WILD SKY 42** [6] 6-9-11 (80)(tvi) T Quinn 20/1: 000-09: Hdwy from rear 2f out, btn over 1f out: 6 wk *1¼* **59**
abs: '99 Leicester wnr (h'cap, rtd 86): plcd sev times in '98, also 5th in Cambridgeshire (rtd 82): '97 Newmarket wnr (h'cap, rtd 78): eff at 7f, suited by a stiff/str 1m, stays 9f: acts on firm & gd/soft grnd: eff with/without a visor, wears a t-strap: can run well fresh: gd weight carrier, capable of much better.
1050 **ACHILLES WINGS 6** [13] 4-8-10 (65) J Weaver 7/1: 34420: Chsd ldrs till btn 2f out: 10th: qck reapp. *1* **42**
4357} **SKY DOME 204** [2] 7-9-8 (77) S Sanders 25/1: 1060-0: Rear, eff 3f out, btn 2f out: fin 11th: p.u. on *1* **52**
sole hdle start last winter: '99 wnr here at Newmarket (amat h'cap, rtd 80): rnr-up in '98 (reapp, rtd 76): back in '96 won here at Newmarket (2) & Goodwood (h'caps, rtd 86): eff over 7f/1m, stays 10f: likes a stiff, gall trk, esp Newmarket, handles any: acts on firm & soft grnd: well h'capped now.
943 **ARCHIE BABE 18** [18] 4-8-11 (66) W Supple 16/1: 31-650: Hdwy from rear 3f out, btn dist: fin 12th. *¾* **40**
*975 **RINGSIDE JACK 16** [10] 4-9-2 (71) J Reid 16/1: 050-10: Drvn in mid-div, no impress fnl 2f: btr 975. *1½* **43**
986 **FREDORA 13** [14] 5-9-13 (82) Dale Gibson 25/1: 200-50: Chsd ldrs till wknd fnl 2f: fin 14th. *1½* **52**
2964} **FLAG FEN 283** [12] 9-8-13 (68) D McGaffin (7) 33/1: 1005-0: Clr ldr, hdd 3f out, fdd into 16th: reapp: **0**
'99 Yarmouth wnr (ladies h'cap, rtd 70): '98 wnr here at Newmarket (2, h'caps, rtd 65): '97 Ripon wnr (sell, J Parkes, rtd 57): best at 10f, stays 12f on firm, soft & f/sand: runs well fresh, likes a gall trk, esp Newmarket.
4442} **STORM HILL 198** [19] 4-9-9 (78) J Fortune 9/1: 3545-0: Prom 1m, wknd into last: reportedly choked. **0**
4477} **Got One Too 196** [4] 3-7-10 (66)(t)(11oh) A McCarthy (3) 100/1:
3871} **Simply Noble 237** [3] 4-9-6 (75) P Robinson 50/1:
18 ran Time 2m 04.32 (2.22) (K & D Computers Ltd) R M Flower Jevington, E.Sussex.

1151   **2.35 LISTED NEWMARKET STKS 3YO (A)**   **1m2f str   Good/Firm 28   -17 Slow**
£16392   £6061   £3030   £1377

3938} **BEAT HOLLOW 232** [5]   H R A Cecil 3-8-8 T Quinn   11/8 FAV: 1-1: 3 b c Sadler's Wells - Wemyss Bight **112**
(Dancing Brave) Nvr far away, went on after 4f, qcknd clr over 1f out, eased, cmftbly: hvly bckd, slow time: won
sole juv start, at Yarmouth (mdn, rtd 98): half-brother to a 10f wnr, dam won the Irish Oaks: eff at 10f, will stay
12f: acts on fast & soft, runs gd race fresh: highly rtd colt who is op to plenty of improvement: fav for the Derby.

4009} **SANDMASON 228** [4]   H R A Cecil 3-8-8 W Ryan   12/1: 1-2: 3 ch c Grand Lodge - Sandy Island (Mill   1½ **108**
Reef) Prom, chsd wnr fnl 1f, kept on under press: 9L clr 3rd, reapp: longer priced stablemate of wnr: Kempton mdn wnr
on sole '99 start (rtd 77): half-brother to wnrs over 7/12f, dam a useful mid-dist performer: sire a top-class
1m/10f performer: eff at 10f on fast & hvy, 12f will suit: runs well fresh: give a gd account in a Derby trial.

-- **ENTISAR** [3]   Saeed bin Suroor 3-8-8 R Hills   3/1: 3-3: 3 b c Nashwan - Fawaayid (Vaguely Noble)   9 **94**
Set slow pace 3f, remained prom till wknd dist: well bckd: plcd at Longchamp on sole '99 start (with D Loder,
9f, hvy): bred to apprec mid-dists, rcd too keenly for own gd here.

4466} **ETHMAAR 196** [2]   M P Tregoning 3-8-8 W Supple   15/2: -13-4: In tch till btn 2f out: reapp: '99 debut   4 **88**
wnr at Newbury (stks, rtd 103), plcd on sole subs outing: half-brother to a couple of 7f/1m wnrs, sire a high-
class miler: eff at 1m, mid-dists shld suit: acts on firm & on a gall trk, can run well fresh: capable of better.

9 **AKEED 182** [1]   3-8-8 J Fortune   7/2: -144-5: Prom 1m, wknd & eased: bckd from 5/1: reapp: '99 wnr   6 **79**
at York (mdn, debut, rtd 90+): $180,000 half-brother to a high-class 12f performer: dam won over 1m, sire won the
US Triple Crown: eff at 7f, bred to apprec mid-dists: acts on firm, handles hvy: with P Cole & capable of better.
5 ran   Time 2m 06.63 (4.53)   (K Abdulla)   H R A Cecil Newmarket.

1152   **3.10 GR 2 JOCKEY CLUB STKS 4YO+ (A)**   **1m4f   Good/Firm 28   +04 Fast**
£34800   £13200   £6600   £3000

3761} **BLUEPRINT 244** [3]   Sir Michael Stoute 5-8-9 K Fallon   9/2: 1142-1: 5 b h Generous - Highbrow (Shirley   **115**
Heights) Prom, imprvd to lead dist, styd on strongly, rdn out: hvly bckd, gd time, reapp: '99 wnr at Newmarket
(2, incl List, rtd 115) & R Ascot (val h'cap), also rnr-up in Gr 3 company: '98 wnr at Southwell, Lingfield & York
(h'cap, rtd 94, with Lord Huntingdon): eff at 12/14f on firm & gd/soft grnd, acts on both AWs: handles any trk,
likes a stiff/gall one, esp Newmarket: can force the pace: eff with/without a visor: tough, smart & progressive
entire who looks sure to run well in the Hardwicke stks at Royal Ascot.

3106} **CASAMASA 280** [11]   E Lellouche 4-8-9 O Peslier   33/1: 26-032: 4 b c Sadler's Wells - Millieme (Mill   1½ **112**
Reef) Rear & outpcd, short of room 2f out, switched & fin v strongly but too late: French chall: '99 Longchamp
wnr: eff at 12f, stays 2m: acts on fast & v soft grnd: v useful colt who looks sure to apprec a return to 14f+.

987 **LARGESSE 13** [8]   John Berry 6-8-9 J F Egan   25/1: 05-103: 6 b h Cadeaux Genereux - Vilanika (Top   ¾ **110**
Ville) Prom, kept 2f out, kept on under press fnl 1f: ran nr to best on this fast surface, loves gd & soft grnd:
all set for the Yorkshire Cup (nk 2nd in 110).

4173} **KAHTAN 217** [1]   J L Dunlop 5-8-9 R Hills   20/1: 3101-4: Tried to make all, collared dist, no extra: shd **110+**
reapp: '99 wnr at Chester (rtd h'cap) & here at Newmarket (List, rtd 110): '98 wnr again at Newmarket (List, rtd
106): '97 Newmarket mdn wnr: eff at 12f/2m2f, acts on gd & firm grnd: handles any trk, loves Newmarket: runs
well fresh: v useful entire, spot on over further next time.

4417} **LUCIDO 201** [9]   4-8-9 Pat Eddery   5/1: 1003-5: Rear, not much room over 2f out, kept on fnl 1f, nrst   nk **109**
fin: nicely bckd, reapp, stablemate of 4th: '99 wnr at Newbury (stks) & Lingfield (Gr 3 Derby trial), subs injured
in the Derby (rtd 114 at best): '98 Salisbury wnr (mdn, rtd 94): half-brother to high-class mid-dist wnr Leggera:
eff at 10/12f on firm & hvy: handles any trk, can run well fresh: smart colt, not much luck in running here.

1218} **BORDER ARROW 363** [5]   5-8-9 R Cochrane   12/1: 33/3-6: Held up going well, no room 4f out till 3f out,   3 **104+**
prog till fdd fnl 1f: reapp: 3rd at Goodwood (rtd 115+) on sole '99 start: '98 wnr at Newmarket (List, reapp),
subs fine 3rd in 2,000 Guineas & Epsom Derby (rtd 118): '97 Newmarket (mdn, rtd 104): eff at 10f, stays 12f well:
acts on fast & gd/soft grnd, runs well fresh: handles any trk, likes Newmarket: tough, high-class colt who ran
well for a long way here: spot on next time & one to keep in mind.

2043} **CHURLISH CHARM 323** [2]   5-8-12 J Reid   33/1: /310-7: Nvr trbld ldrs on reapp: '99 York wnr (Gr 2   2 **104**
Yorkshire Cup, rtd 115), subs unplcd in the Ascot Gold Cup: '98 Newmarket (mdn), Goodwood (stks) & Newbury wnr
(h'cap, rtd 104 at best): eff at 12/14f, stays 2m on fast & gd/soft grnd: handles a sharp/undul or gall trk, runs
well fresh: smart, lengthy colt who will be spot on for a repeat bid at the Yorkshire Cup.

*987 **YAVANAS PACE 13** [6]   8-8-9 D Holland   8/1: 06-018: Prom 10f, fdd: op 5/1: better on hvy grnd in 987.   5 **93**
767 **RHAGAAS 41** [7]   4-8-9 (vis) D O'Donohoe   12/1: 353-49: Hdwy from rear 2f out, sn btn: tchd 16/1, abs.   3½ **88**
3435} **ELA ATHENA 261** [10]   4-8-6 P Robinson   10/1: 1212-0: Chsd ldr 10f, fdd into 10th: reapp: '99 wnr at   3 **80**
Newbury (fill mdn, debut) & Chepstow (List), subs rnr-up at York (Gr 1 Yorkshire Oaks, rtd 115): eff at 12f, 14f
will suit: acts on fast & firm, can run well fresh: likes a stiff/undul & gall trk: smart, capable of better.

3873} **RAMRUMA 237** [4]   4-8-11 T Quinn   11/4 FAV: 1112-0: Chsd ldr till wknd qckly 2f out, eased, t.o. in   18 **60**
last: hvly bckd, reportedly fin sltly lame: '99 wnr at Newmarket (mdn), Lingfield (List), Epsom (Oaks), The Curragh
(Irish Oaks) & York (Gr 1, rtd 122 at best), also rnr-up in the St Leger: eff at 12f, stays 14f: acts on fast & hvy
grnd, handles any trk: runs v well fresh: top-class, tough & genuine filly, this much forgiven.
11 ran   Time 2m 31.72 (2.92)   (The Queen)   Sir Michael Stoute Newmarket.

1153   **3.40 H & K HCAP 3YO 0-100 (C)**   **7f str   Good/Firm 28   -17 Slow**   **[103]**
£7670   £2360   £1180   £590

*954 **RAYYAAN 17** [2]   N A Graham 3-8-10 (85) R Hills   11/2: 22-111: 3 ch c Cadeaux Genereux - Anam   **93**
(Persian Bold) Rear, imprvd 2f out, styd on strongly to lead on line, drvn out: well bckd: in terrific form, earlier
won at Southwell (mdn) & here at Newmarket (val h'cap): trained by P Walwyn in '99, dual rnr-up (mdn, rtd 86): eff
at 6/7f, will stay 1m: acts on fast & soft & on a sharp or gall trk, likes Newmarket: can run well fresh: progressive.

*982 **STRAHAN 15** [12]   J H M Gosden 3-9-2 (91) J Fortune   9/2 FAV: 321-12: 3 b c Catrail - Soreze (Gallic   shd **98**
League) Trkd ldr, imprvd to lead dist, worn down on line: nicely bckd, eff at 6f, stays a stiff 7f well: fine
run conceding this wnr 6lb: deserves similar, see 982 (6f here).

994 **CAIR PARAVEL 13** [8]   R Hannon 3-8-9 (84) Dane O'Neill   12/1: 11-53: 3 br c Dolphin Street - Queen's   1¼ **88**
Ransom (Last Tycoon) Rear, prog over 1f out, fin well but not rch front 2: stays 7f well: shld sn be winning.

794 **NIGHT EMPRESS 36** [19]   J R Fanshawe 3-8-0 (75) A Nicholls (3)   12/1: 230-24: Chsd ldrs, imprvd   ½ **78**
to lead briefly dist, sn no extra: gd effort from this consistent filly: see 794 (mdn).

689 **ZIETZIG 49** [9]   3-8-5 (80) N Callan   20/1: 420-05: Chsd ldrs, kept on under press fnl 1f: 7 wk abs: nk **82**
longer 7f trip, 1m may suit: see 689 (sand).

380

4611} **FRENCH LIEUTENANT 182** [10] 3-8-10 (85) K Fallon 10/1: -032-6: Slowly away, prog 1½f out, styd   ½   86+
on strongly, nrst fin: nicely bckd, reapp: thrice rcd in '99, rnr-up at Doncaster (stks, rtd 89): half-brother to a
winning miler in France, sire a top-class sprinter: stays 1m, acts on fast & hvy grnd: eye-catching h'cap debut,
one to keep a close eye on back over 1m next time.

4523} **ZIBELINE 191** [6] 3-7-13 (74) F Norton 20/1: 5450-7: Mid-div, styd on fnl 1f, nrst fin: reapp: 4th at   hd   75
Chepstow in '99 (mdn, rtd 82 at best): half-brother to a mid-dist wnr, dam scored over 12f: bred to apprec 1m+:
with C Brittain & shld improve further as he steps in trip.

4482} **LAGOON 195** [4] 3-9-7 (96) M Hills 20/1: 6135-8: Rear, kept on fnl 1f, nrst fin: reapp, top-weight: ½   96
'99 Pontefract wnr (mdn), subs 3rd here at Newmarket (nurs h'cap, rtd 93): eff at 5/6f on firm & gd/soft grnd:
runs well fresh, handles a gall/undul trk: sharper next time.

982   **LAS RAMBLAS 15** [13] 3-8-7 (82) J Reid 25/1: 100-09: Hdwy from rear halfway, no impress fnl 1f.   nk   81
982   **EASTWAYS 15** [1] 3-9-4 (93) J Weaver 10/1: 132-00: Rcd alone in centre & set pace 5f, no extra: nk   91
fin 10th: gd effort in the circumstances: see 982 (6f here).
982   **CHIQUITA 15** [7] 3-8-5 (80) R Ffrench 12/1: 211-50: Chsd ldrs till fdd fnl 1f: fin 11th: see 982.   shd   78
3954} **NIAGARA 231** [5] 3-8-5 (80) S Sanders 16/1: 1460-0: Nvr btr than mid-div, eased fnl 1f: reapp: '99   1¾   74
Ayr wnr (mdn auct, rtd 86): eff at 6/7f, poss stays 1m: acts on gd & firm grnd, handles a stiff/gall trk.
954   **LORD PACAL 17** [3] 3-9-0 (89) S Whitworth 40/1: 034-00: Rcd keenly rear, nvr a factor in 13th.   ½   82$
4616} **CHIMNEY DUST 181** [16] 3-8-10 (85) D Holland 20/1: 1204-0: Nvr troubled ldrs in 14th: reapp.   ½   77
3365} **LOVE LETTERS 265** [20] 3-8-7 (82) J Carroll 25/1: 3100-0: Chsd ldrs 6f, fdd: 15th, reapp, new stable.   nk   73
954   **RULE OF THUMB 17** [17] 3-8-7 (82) J F Egan 25/1: 16-00: Chsd ldrs 6f, fdd into 16th: see 954 (C/D).   hd   73
3191} **Molly Brown 273** [11] 3-8-11 (86) R Hughes 20/1:   4547} **Major Rebuke 189** [14] 3-8-11 (86) G Hall 33/1:
954   **Abuzaid 17** [15] 3-8-10 (85) W Supple 16/1:   3954} **Secret Conquest 231** [18] 3-8-7 (82) W Ryan 50/1:
20 ran   Time 1m 26.40 (3.20)   (Hamdan Al Maktoum)   N A Graham Newmarket.

1154   4.15 LISTED DAHLIA FILLIES STKS 4YO+ (A)   1m1f str   Good/Firm 28   -17 Slow
         £13746   £5214   £2607   £1185

1014 **CAPE GRACE 11** [4] R Hannon 4-8-9 Dane O'Neill 11/2: /44-61: 4 b f Priolo - Saffron (Fabulous Dancer)   104
Prom, imprvd to lead dist, kept on strongly, drvn out: nicely bckd: twice rcd in '99, 4th in List company (rtd 98):
'98 Ascot wnr (debut, fill mdn, rtd 103): eff at 9/10f on gd & fast, runs well fresh: apprec Group company abroad.
1014 **ANNAPURNA 11** [6] B J Meehan 4-8-9 Pat Eddery 25/1: 220-02: 4 b f Brief Truce - National Ballet   1¾   100
(Shareef Dancer) Rear, hdwy & ev ch dist, edged right ins fnl 1f & no extra cl-home: eff at 9/10f: ran to best.
-1057 **DIAMOND WHITE 6** [3] M J Ryan 5-9-3 J Reid 3/1: 10-023: 5 b m Robellino - Diamon Wedding (Diamond 1 106
Shoal) Rear, imprvd 3f out, not qckn fnl 1f: well bckd: rtd higher 1057 (10f, hvy).
967   **HASTY WORDS 16** [1] B W Hills 4-8-12 M Hills 11/2: 06-164: Set pace till dist, fdd: see 967, 703.   1½   98
967   **FAIRY GODMOTHER 16** [5] 4-8-12 R Hughes 6/5 FAV: 11-25: Chsd ldr 7f, fdd & eased, t.o.: hvly   17   73
bckd: puzzling effort, has reportedly broken blood vessels prev: see 967 (C/D).
3909} **ROSE OF MOONCOIN 234** [2] 4-8-9 J Tate 33/1: 5/00-6: Chsd ldrs 7f, fdd into last: well btn on both   ¾   68
'99 starts (List company): lightly rcd juv, won here at Newmarket (fill mdn, debut, rtd 102 at best): eff at
6f on fast grnd, can run well fresh: now with J Eustace.
6 ran   Time 1m 53.29 (4.09)   (George Strawbridge)   R Hannon East Everleigh, Wilts.

1155   4.50 PORTLAND LODGE MDN 3YO (D)   7f str   Good/Firm 28   -11 Slow
         £5226   £1608   £804   £402

--   **MEIOSIS** [9] Saeed bin Suroor 3-8-11 T E Durcan 7/2: -1: 3 b f Danzig - Golden Opinion (Slew   104+
O'Gold) Made all, rdn clr 2f out, v easily despite running green: hvly bckd, debut: bred in the purple, dam a
high-class miler: eff at 7f, 1m will suit: acts on fast grnd & on a gall trk, runs well fresh:
can only improve from here & looks well up to winning in Group company, holds sev big race entries.
4556} **PAPABILE 188** [10] W Jarvis 3-8-11 Pat Eddery 4/1: 52-2: 3 b f Chief's Crown - La Papagena (Habitat)   7   90
Chsd wnr thr'out, outpcd fnl 2f: tchd 6/1, reapp: twice rcd juv, rnr-up at Newmarket (fill mdn, rtd 92): full
sister to high-class miler Grand Lodge: eff at 7f on fast & soft grnd: caught a tartar today.
4473} **LAMEH 196** [8] R W Armstrong 3-8-11 R Hills 14/1: 405-3: 3 ch f Mujtahid - Tablah (Silver Hawk)   ½   89
Chsd ldrs till outpcd fnl 2f: flashed tail: trained by P Walwyn in '99, 5th at Doncaster (fill mdn, rtd 84):
eff at 1m on soft grnd: does not looks the easiest of rides.
4542} **ROSSE 189** [5] G Wragg 3-8-11 M Roberts 12/1: 0-4: Outpcd, some late hdwy, nvr nr ldrs: ran v   ¾   87
green: unplcd on sole '99 start (mdn, rtd 72): half-sister to sev wnrs, incl smart 1m performer Rebecca Sharp:
sire a top-class miler: shld apprec mid-dists & can only improve on this.
4473} **ENTAIL 196** [4] 3-8-11 J Fortune 5/2 FAV: 3-5: Dwelt, rcd keenly & sn chsd ldrs, wknd fnl 2f: hvly bckd   3½   80$
tho' op 2/1, reapp: plcd in a Doncaster fill mdn on sole '98 start (rtd 86): sire a top-class 1m/10f performer,
dam raced in France: eff at 1m, bred to apprec mid-dists: acts on soft grnd: rcd too keenly for own gd today.
--   **BELLA LAMBADA** [2] 3-8-11 K Fallon 10/1: -6: Slowly away, al outpcd: half-sister to high-class   2   76
10f wnr Stage Craft: sire a top-class mid-dist performer: with Sir M Stoute.
840   **SALIENT POINT 28** [7] 3-8-11 N Callan 33/1: -57: Prom 5f, fdd: see 840.   nk   75
--   **ADRIFT** [1] 3-8-11 W Ryan 16/1: -8: Al outpcd, nvr a factor on debut: half-sister to a couple   7   61
of useful peformers: with B Hanbury.
--   **BIRDSONG** [6] 3-8-11 S Sanders 33/1: -9: Ran green & al outpcd, t.o.: related to sev wnrs.   17   26
--   **FIORA** [3] 3-8-11 R Price 50/1: -0: Slowly away, al bhd, t.o. on debut.   19   0
10 ran   Time 1m 25.93 (2.73)   (Godolphin)   Saeed bin Suroor Newmarket.

1156   5.20 NEWMARKET CHALLENGE WHIP 3YO (G)   1m str   Good/Firm 28   -93 Slow
         £1

--   **MAY BALL** [2] J H M Gosden 3-8-9 J Fortune 2/7 FAV: 1: 3 b f Cadeaux Genereux - Minute Waltz   1
(Sadler's Wells) Made all, v cmftbly: drifted from 1/6: half-sister to 1m/9f wnr Daunt: sire a high-class
sprinter: eff at 1m on fast grnd: always toying with sole rival today.
--   **COUNTRYSIDE FRIEND** [3] M C Pipe 3-9-0 K Fallon 2/1: 2: 3 ch c Sabrehill - Well Proud (Sadler's   ¾   0
Wells) Trkd ldrs thr'out, ev ch halfway, sn outpcd: beaten by proximity to wnr: dam from a mid-dist family:
bred to apprec further & may be seen in juv nov hdles in due course.
2 ran   Time 1m 46.19 (9.69)   (Lord Hartington)   J H M Gosden Manton, Wilts.

THIRSK SATURDAY MAY 6TH Lefthand, Flat, Oval Track

Official Going GOOD (GOOD/FIRM places) Stalls: Str Course - stands side, Rnd Course - Inside

1157 2.05 SPRING MDN 3YO+ (D) 1m4f Good 54 -03 Slow
£4257 £1310 £655 £327 3 yo rec 19lb

--	**GARDEN SOCIETY** [7] J A R Toller 3-8-5 R Ffrench 9/1: 1: 3 ch c Caerleon - Eurobird (Ela Mana Mou)		96

Handy, led over 2f out, duelled with rnr-up over 1f out, styd on gamely to narrowly assert nr fin, drvn out: op 8/1: debut: effective at 12f, acts on gd grnd: holds a Derby entry, potentially useful.

951 **SOLITARY** 18 [2] B W Hills 3-8-5 Dean McKeown 4/11 FAV: 4-22: 3 b c Sanglamore - Set Fair (Alleged) 1¼ 94
Led/dsptd lead 1f, rdn to chall/narrow lead 2f out, no extra inside last: hvly bckd at odds on, well clr of rem: met a potentially useful rival, tho' better expected after 951 (working out well).

-- **FOLLOW LAMMTARRA** [1] M R Channon 3-8-5 P Fessey 12/1: 3: 3 ch g Lammtarra - Felawnah 9 84
(Mr Prospector) Trkd ldrs, outpcd fnl 3f: op 10/1, debut: sire a Derby wnr, this 12f trip will suit.

4315} **SEND ME AN ANGEL** 208 [3] S P C Woods 3-8-0 F Norton 25/1: 0-4: Mid-div, outpcd fnl 3f: op 20/1, 5 72
reapp: unplcd sole '99 start (rtd 63, mdn): bred to appreciate mid-dists, one more run needed for h'caps.

-- **KUWAIT MILLENNIUM** 5 [5] 3-8-5 W Ryan 11/2: 5: Rear, efft over 3f out, sn held: op 7/2, debut: 1¼ 75
strong, scopey colt: mid-dist bred colt, will know more next time for H Cecil.

- **ROVERETTO** [6] 5-9-10 A Culhane 20/1: 0/6: Chsd ldrs, btn 3f out: op 12/1, long Flat abs: jmps ½ 74
fit, earlier scored at Musselburgh (mdn hdle) & Catterick (nov hdle, rtd 117h at best, eff at 2m/2m4f, gd grnd): mod form sole '98 start on the level: likely to appreciate further & h'cap company.

-- **FORUM CHRIS** [4] 3-8-5 J Fanning 14/1: 7: Led after 1f till 2f out, fdd: op 12/1, debut. 3 70
4278} **WINDFALL** 211 [9] 3-8-5 D Sweeney 66/1: 0-8: Chsd ldrs 9f: reapp, no form sole '99 start. 15 54
-- **MICE DESIGN** [8] 3-8-5 C Cogan (4) 33/1: 9: Mid-div at best: debut, with N Littmoden. dist 0
1072 **RIMATARA** 5 [10] 4-9-10 G Parkin 100/1: 6-00: Sn bhd: 10th: lngr 12f trip: rtd 77 on sole '99 dist 0
start for I Balding (mdn, prob flattered): now with G P Kelly.

10 ran Time 2m 36.6 (6.8) (Duke Of Devonshire) J A R Toller Newmarket, Suffolk

1158 2.40 COXWOLD HCAP 3YO+ 0-90 (C) 7f rnd Good 54 -09 Slow [84]
£7247 £2230 £1115 £557 3 yo rec 12lb

4350} **NOOSHMAN** 206 [8] Sir Michael Stoute 3-8-13 (81) W Ryan 100/30 FAV: 252-1: 3 ch g Woodman - Knoosh 85
(Storm Bird) Hampered early & rear, strong run from 2f out to lead close home: nicely bckd, op 5/1: reapp, h'cap debut: plcd twice last term (rtd 85, mdn): eff at 7f, 1m+ looks sure to suit: acts on gd & hvy grnd & handles a stiff/gall track: runs well fresh: won this despite trouble in running, open to further improvement.

*803 **ABERKEEN** 36 [1] M Dods 5-8-9 (65) J F Egan 11/2: 212212: 5 ch g Keen - Miss Aboyne (Lochnager) ½ 68
Trkd ldrs, rdn/chall 2f out, kept on, not pace of wnr nr fin: jarred at heart, can win again: see 803.

1011 **SMART PREDATOR** 12 [15] J J Quinn 4-9-0 (70) J Stack 20/1: 06-003: 4 gr g Polar Falcon - She's Smart nk 72
(Absalom) Sn cl-up, rdn/led over 2f out, hdd ins last, no extra cl home: back to form, nicely h'capped: see 834.

715 **MANTLES PRIDE** 43 [4] J A Glover 5-9-12 (82)(vis) B Sooful(7) 14/1: 30-004: Hndy/chsd 2f out, kept on: abs. hd 83
1011 **AMBER FORT** 12 [10] 7-9-3 (73)(bl) Claire Bryan (5) 7/1: 00-325: Mid-div, efft wide fnl 3f, not pace to chall. ½ 73
725 **PEARTREE HOUSE** 42 [12] 6-9-12 (82) F Norton 6/1: 00-006: Mid-div, efft wide fnl 2f, nvr pace to chall: abs. 1 80
908 **DAY BOY** 22 [13] 4-8-13 (69) A Nicholls (3) 14/1: 430-37: Twds rear, efft wide fnl 2f, al held: see 908. ¾ 66
905 **LAGO DI VARANO** 22 [5] 4-8-9-7 (77)(vis) Dean McKeown 25/1: 4-0668: Prom, fdd fnl 2f: needs 5/6f. 1½ 71
*1060 **REDOUBTABLE** 5 [11] 9-10-1 (85)(6ex) A Culhane 14/1: 432019: Mid-div/wide, outpaced fnl 3f: op 12/1. 2½ 74
926 **CUSIN** 21 [6] 4-9-3 (73) J Fanning 8/1: 100-00: Chsd ldrs, efft over 2f out, sn held: 10th: see 926. nk 61
4195} **QUIET VENTURE** 217 [9] 4-6-9-5 (75) R Lappin 20/1: 3665-0: Led till over 2f out, fdd/eased fnl 1f: 11th, 1¼ 60
reapp: plcd form in '99 (rtd 81, h'cap): '98 Redcar, Musselburgh (class stks), Newcastle (h'cap) & W'hampton wnr (AW h'cap, rtd 88a & 81): suited by forcing tactics at 6f/1m on firm, fast & fibresand: handles any trk: has run well fresh: tried a visor, best without: eff in a tongue strap, not worn today.

1074 **Northern Svengali** 5 [7] 4-9-5 (75) D Sweeney 20/1: 926 **Euro Venture** 21 [16] 5-9-2 (72) O Pears 20/1:
3877} **Rich In Love** 238 [2] 6-10-0 (84) R Ffrench 20/1: 941 **Blakeset** 19 [14] 5-9-1 (71) C Lowther 16/1:
4510} **Perfect Peach** 193 [3] 5-8-13 (69) P Goode (3) 20/1:
16 ran Time 1m 27.3 (4.4) (Maktoum Al Maktoum) Sir Michael Stoute Newmarket

1159 3.15 WILGRO MDN 3YO (D) 7f rnd Good 54 -12 Slow
£4306 £1325 £662 £331

4528} **SALIM** 192 [1] Sir Michael Stoute 3-9-0 J F Egan 10/1: 0-1: 3 b c Salse - Moviegoer (Pharly) 86+
Trkd ldrs, swtchd & prog to lead over 1f out, styd on well, rdn out: op 6/1, reapp: unplcd sole '99 start (mdn, rtd 76): eff at 7f, 1m+ shld suit: acts on gd grnd & runs well fresh: open to improvement.

3802} **THERMAL SPRING** 242 [2] H R A Cecil 3-8-9 W Ryan 5/1: 5-2: 3 ch f Zafonic - Seven Springs ¾ 79
(Irish River) Rear, prog 3f out, rdn/kept on ins last, not pace of wnr: op 7/2, reapp: unplcd sole '99 start (rtd 71): eff at 7f, 1m will suit: acts on gd grnd: could improve & find similar in the north.

839 **WILLOUGHBYS BOY** 29 [9] B Hanbury 3-9-0 A Beech (5) 14/1: 03: 3 b c Night Shift - Andbell 1¼ 81
(Trojan Fen) Keen/chsd ldrs, efft 2f out, kept on ins last: eff at 7f on gd grnd, 1m+ will suit.

4292} **TIGRE** 210 [5] B W Hills 3-9-0 Dean McKeown 7/4 FAV: 2222-4: Led, rdn 3f out, hdd over 1f out, hd 80
no extra: well bckd, op 7/4: reapp: rnr-up on 4 of 5 '99 starts (rtd 89, mdn): eff at 7f/1m on fast & soft grnd: handles a gall trk: shown enough prev to find improvement but h'caps may now suit.

4569} **WATHBAT MUJTAHID** 187 [4] 3-9-0 N Carlisle 9/2: 032-5: Keen/chsd ldrs, onepace fnl 2f: reapp: nk 79
plcd fnl 2 '99 starts (rtd 86): eff at 7f, 1m+ shld suit: acts on gd & gd/sft, sharp/gall trk: pulled too hard today.

972 **LAST SYMPHONY** 17 [7] 3-9-0 M Tebbutt 7/2: -06: Dwelt, bhd, efft 2f out, no impress: op 9/2: h'caps 3 73
& 1m+ will suit: no luck in running on Newmarket debut previously.

4367} **SOLOIST** 204 [6] 3-8-9 R Lappin 100/1: 00-7: Al rear: reapp, no form in '99. 6 59$
902 **GENERAL DOMINION** 23 [8] 3-9-0 A Nicholls (3) 100/1: 08: Cl up 6f, btn/eased fnl 1f. 1½ 61$
3189} **WILLIAM THE LION** 274 [3] 3-9-0 C Lowther 100/1: 000-9: Chsd ldrs 5f: jockey given a 3-day ban for 1¾ 58$
irresponsible riding: reapp, no form last term.

4299} **SPIRIT OF KHAMBANI** 208 [11] 3-8-9 J Fanning 33/1: 03-0: Prom 5f: 10th: ndd this reapp: unplcd 1½ 50
in '99 (rtd 69, 6 furl mdn): poss not stay & worth a try at 5/6f: prob handles soft grnd: qual for h'caps.

2523} **WHITE SANDS** 303 [10] 3-8-9 R Ffrench 25/1: 0-0: Keen/chsd ldrs 5f: 11th: reapp. 5 40
11 ran Time 1m 27.5 (4.6) (Hamdan Al Maktoum) Sir Michael Stoute Newmarket

THIRSK SATURDAY MAY 6TH Lefthand, Flat, Oval Track

1160 **3.50 THIRSK HUNT CUP HCAP 3YO+ 0-95 (C) 1m rnd Good 54 +05 Fast [92]**
£11700 £3600 £1800 £900 3 yo rec 13lb

895 **VOLONTIERS 23** [9] P W Harris 5-8-12 (76) A Beech (5) 15/2: 25-041: 5 b g Common Grounds - Senlis (Sensitive Prince) Mid-div, prog/lead over 2f out, styd on strongly in last, drvn out: op 6/1: best time of day: plcd form in '99 (rtd 84a & 93): '98 wnr at Haydock (mdn) & Epsom (List, rtd 101): eff at 7f/easy 1m: acts on fast, gd/soft & equitrack: likes to race with/force the pace: handles any trk: nicely h'capped, could win again. **85**
846 **TONY TIE 28** [7] J S Goldie 4-8-13 (77) A Culhane 10/1: 10-622: 4 b g Ardkinglass - Queen Of The Quorn (Governor General) Chsd ldrs, rdn/kept on in last, not pace of wnr: in gd form, deserves a race: see 846, 715. *1¼* **82**
875 **KALA SUNRISE 25** [6] C Smith 7-8-10 (74) J Stack 14/1: 40-003: 7 ch h Kalaglow - Belle Of The Dawn (Bellypha) Bhd halfway, stdy prog fnl 3f, not reach ldrs: well h'capped, worth a try at 10? see 875. *2* **75**
4585} **DURAID 186** [17] Denys Smith 8-8-12 (76) A Nicholls (3) 20/1: 0401-4: Chsd ldrs, rdn/kept on wide fnl 2f, not pace to chall: op 16/1, reapp: '99 Beverley, Ripon & Catterick wnr (h'caps, rtd 79): unplcd '98 (rtd 76): eff at 7f/1m, tried 12f: acts on firm & soft, any trk: encouraging reapp, should win again in the North this term. *¾* **76**
900 **ROBZELDA 23** [14] 4-8-11 (75)(bl) J F Egan 14/1: 13-325: Twds rear, rdn/kept on fnl 2f, no threat. *½* **74**
539 **ADELPHI BOY 78** [1] 4-8-8 (72) D Mernagh (3) 20/1: -03146: Trkd ldrs, onepace fnl 3f: abs: see 480 (AW). *¾* **70**
1042 **SLUMBERING 8** [12] 4-9-3 (81) W Ryan 8/1: 006-47: Trkd ldrs, held fnl 2f: see 1042. *1* **77**
715 **WEETMANS WEIGH 43** [18] 7-8-12 (76) P M Quinn (5) 20/1: 464008: Mid-div, no threat: abs: see 49 (AW). *hd* **72**
1042 **NAVIASKY 8** [13] 5-9-3 (81) R Brisland (5) 14/1: 16-009: Dwelt/bhd, rdn/mod gains fnl 2f: op 12/1. *nk* **76**
4395} **VIRTUAL REALITY 203** [2] 9-9-9 (87) R Ffrench 10/1: 1230-0: Prom, briefly led over 2f out, fdd: 10th: op 12/1, reapp: '99 Warwick wnr (class stks, rtd 91): '98 Bath & Salisbury wnr (h'caps, rtd 89 at best): eff at 7.5f/10f on firm & gd, any track: best without vis: runs well fresh: gd weight carrier. *3½* **75**
875 **NOMINATOR LAD 25** [5] 6-8-13 (77) F Norton 20/1: 000-00: Chsd ldrs 6f: 11th: '99 Pontefract wnr (h'cap, rtd 83 at best): '98 h'cap wnr at W'hampton & Ayr (rtd 74a & 81): eff at 7/8.5f on firm, hvy and fibresand, any trk. *3* **59**
1011 **SUPREME SALUTATION 12** [4] 4-9-1 (79) C Lowther 7/2 FAV: 121-60: Prom 6f: bckd, op 9/2: see 1011. *nk* **60**
977 **NIGHT OF GLASS 17** [8] 7-9-10 (88) O Pears 11/1: 54-040: Mid-div, btn 2f out: 13th: op 14/1: btr 977. *1½* **66**
1110 **INDIAN PLUME 3** [3] 4-9-0 (78) Dean McKeown 50/1: 0-0100: Led 6f, wknd: 14th: qck reapp: btr 900. *¾* **55**
*1070 **YAROB 5** [15] 7-9-10 (88)(6ex) Clare Roche (7) 8/1: -01010: Prom, wide, btn 3f out: 15th: op 6/1. *shd* **65**
4101} **Fallachan 223** [16] 4-9-6 (84) M Tebbutt 12/1: 757 **Elvis Reigns 39** [10] 4-9-2 (80) J Fanning 50/1:
4266} **Jedi Knight 213** [11] 6-9-10 (88) T Lucas 25/1:
18 ran Time 1m 39.3 (3.9) (The Commoners) P W Harris Aldbury, Herts

1161 **4.25 EBF MARKET PLACE NOV STKS 2YO (D) 5f Good 54 -42 Slow**
£3591 £1105 £552 £276

*911 **INSPECTOR GENERAL 22** [1] P F I Cole 2-9-5 D Sweeney 11/8 JT FAV: 11: 2 b c Dilum - New Generation (Young Generation) Cl up, led 2f out, in command 1f out, styd on well: nicely bckd tho' op 8/11: earlier scored at Newbury (stks): eff at 5f, 6f will suit: acts on soft and gd grnd, easy/gall trk: has run well fresh: useful. **97**
*796 **NIFTY ALICE 37** [2] A Berry 2-8-9 F Norton 5/1: -12: 2 ch f First Trump - Nifty Fifty (Runnett) Cl up, ch 2f out, sn outpcd by wnr: op 6/1: acts on gd & gd/sft grnd: caught a tartar here; see 796 (auct mdn). *2½* **79**
843 **CO DOT UK 28** [6] K A Ryan 2-8-12 J F Egan 14/1: 53: 2 b g Distant Relative - Cubist (Tate Gallery) Bhd ldrs, rdn/kept on fnl 2f, not pace of wnr: op 20/1: see 843. *nk* **81**
*904 **REEDS RAINS 22** [4] T D Easterby 2-9-0 W Ryan 11/8 JT FAV: -14: Dwelt, bhd ldrs, rdn/outpcd fnl 2f: well bckd, op 2/1: better on soft grnd in 904 (debut). *½* **81**
-- **THEBAN** [5] 2-8-12 O Pears 66/1: 5: Chsd ldrs, fdd fnl 2f: ndd this: Inzar gelding, Apr foal: cost IR 12,000gns: dam Irish 12f wnr, sire class 6/7f performer: sure to appreciate further: with D Nicholls. *3* **72**
-- **ANGELAS HUSBAND** [3] 2-8-12 P Fessey 66/1: 6: Led 3f, sn btn: Feb foal, cost 8,200gns: dam a 13/15f wnr: stocky colt, showed gd early speed: ndd this & will know more next time. *½* **70**
1006 **STILMEMAITE 12** [7] 2-8-7 J Bramhill 33/1: -357: In tch, btn 2f out: op 12/1: btr 904 (sft). *hd* **64**
7 ran Time 1m 01.8 (4.8) (The Blenheim Parnership) P F I Cole Whatcombe, Oxon

1162 **4.55 BALDERSBY HCAP 3YO+ 0-85 (D) 5f Good 54 -02 Slow [85]**
£4862 £1496 £748 £374 3 yo rec 10lb Raced both sides, no advantage

1005 **SULU 12** [22] M W Easterby 4-8-6 (63) J F Egan 20/1: 3-0001: 4 b g Elbio - Foxy Fairy (Fairy King) Trkd ldrs stands side, styd on strongly to lead well in last, rdn out: op 16/1: 1st win: plcd sev times in '99 for I Balding (rtd 80, mdn): rtd 70 sole '98 start (auct mdn): eff at 5/7f on firm & gd/soft, any track. **70**
926 **BLESSINGINDISGUISE 21** [8] M W Easterby 7-9-3 (74)(bl) T Lucas 11/2 JT FAV: 10-502: 7 b g Kala Shikari - Blowing Bubbles (Native Admiral) Chsd ldrs far side, prog to lead overall 1f out, rdn/hdd well ins last: jockey given 2-day whip ban: stablemate of wnr: tough 7yo, can win more races: see 758. *1¾* **75**
573 **TORRENT 73** [1] D W Chapman 5-8-4 (61)(bl) D Mernagh (3) 16/1: -36553: 5 ch g Prince Sabo - Maiden Pool (Sharpen Up) Chsd ldrs far side, rdn/kept on fnl 1f, no threat: 10 wk abs: gd run, on a fair mark: see 205. *1* **60**
1140 **JACKIES BABY 2** [2] W G M Turner 4-10-0 (85) A Beech (5) 20/1: 040004: Led overall far side 4f. *nk* **83**
3869} **ZARAGOSSA 239** [3] 4-8-8 (65) P Bradley (5) 33/1: 4000-5: Chsd ldrs far side, onepace fnl 1f: op 25/1. *½* **61**
1008 **WILLIAMS WELL 12** [21] 6-8-7 (64)(bl) G Parkin 20/1: 004-06: Led stands side 4f, onepace fnl 1f: op 14/1. *¾* **58**
926 **STORYTELLER 21** [10] 6-10-0 (85) Dale Gibson 33/1: 244-07: Held up far side, prog 2f out, nvr pace to chall: '99 Doncaster (class stks) & Salisbury wnr (h'cap, rtd 90 at best): '98 Carlisle (appr h'cap), Ayr, Haydock, Beverley & Pontefract wnr (h'caps, rtd 87): eff at 6f, suited by a stiff 5f, stays 7f: acts on fast & soft ground: best in a visor: gd weight carrier: tough/progressive last two seasons, signs of a return to form here, keep in mind. *½* **77**
1008 **ANGEL HILL 12** [9] 5-8-4 (61) P Hanagan (7) 33/1: 00-008: Rear far far side, mod gains fnl 2f: see 1008. *¾* **51**
1008 **GORETSKI 12** [14] 7-9-0 (71) Kim Tinkler 25/1: 0-0009: Mid-div stands side, nvr on terms: see 926. *hd* **60**
1005 **POLLY GOLIGHTLY 12** [6] 7-8-7 (64)(bl) C Rutter 20/1: 044-00: Chsd ldrs far side 3f: 10th: see 1005. *hd* **52**
1133 **FRILLY FRONT 2** [24] 4-8-4 (61) D Sweeney 15/2: 101600: Chsd ldrs stnds side 3f: 11th: qck reapp. *hd* **48**
3350} **BAHAMIAN PIRATE 266** [23] 5-8-5 (62) Clare Roche (7) 12/1: 4321-0: Dwelt/bhd stands side, mod late gains under a kind ride: stewards found jockey guilty of taking insufficient measures to obtain best poss placing, 8-day ban: op 10/1, reapp: '99 Ripon wnr (mdn, rtd 72): eff at 5f, stays 7f: acts on gd & f/sand: has run well fresh: likes a sharpish track: shld leave this behind in similar contests & will benefit from stronger handling. *shd* **49+**
1074 **PIPS MAGIC 5** [13] 4-9-12 (83) A Culhane 12/1: 00-000: Dwelt, well bhd stds side, late gains, no threat: 13th: op 10/1: '99 Ascot wnr (val h'cap, rtd 93): '98 Ripon & Ayr wnr (mdn/nov, rtd 92 at best): eff at 5/6f on firm & soft: handles any trk, likes a stiff/gall one: slipping to a handy mark, primed for a return to form. *hd* **69+**
1008 **WATERFORD SPIRIT 12** [12] 4-9-1 (72) C Lowther 25/1: 0-00W0: Chsd ldrs stnds side 3f: 14th: '99 wnr *hd* **57**

THIRSK
SATURDAY MAY 6TH   Lefthand, Flat, Oval Track

here at Thirsk (C/D, h'cap, rtd 78 at best): eff at 5f, tried 6f: acts on fast & soft ground.
*1074 **DAAWE** 5 [17] 9-9-2 (73)(bl)(6ex) O Pears 11/2 JT FAV: 630610: Cl up stands side 3f: 20th: op 10/1.   **0**
3933} Royal Romeo 234 [11] 3-8-6 (73) W Ryan 33/1:   702 **Double Oscar 44** [7] 7-9-1 (72) T Hamilton (7) 25/1:
926   Zuhair 21 [18] 7-9-11 (82) A Nicholls (3) 14/1: 4391} Pleasure Time 203 [19] 7-9-2 (73)(vis) R Fitzpatrick (3) 12/1:
758   Sweet Magic 39 [15] 9-8-2 (59)(t) J Fanning 33/1:   1013 Mousehole 12 [16] 8-9-1 (72) R Ffrench 14/1:
4267} Flak Jacket 213 [4] 5-9-6 (77) M Tebbutt 14/1:   4471} Anthony Mon Amour 197 [5] 5-8-5 (62) F Norton 20/1:
1008 Sir Sandrovitch 12 [20] 4-8-9 (66) B McHugh (7) 16/1:
24 ran   Time 59.8 (2.8)   (Bodfari Stud Ltd)   M W Easterby Sheriff Hutton, N Yorks

HAYDOCK
SATURDAY MAY 6TH   Lefthand, Flat, Galloping Track

Official Going   GOOD. Stalls: 5f, 6f & 10f - Outside; 7f - Inside; 14f - Centre

1163
2.30 LISTED SPRING TROPHY 3YO+ (A)   7f30y rnd   Good/Firm 26   -11 Slow
£15665   £4820   £2410   £1205   3 yo rec 12lb

966   **ARCTIC CHAR 17** [3] B J Meehan 4-8-12 D R McCabe 9/1: 052-01: 4 br f Polar Falcon - Breadcrumb   **99**
(Final Straw) Led, hdd over 2f out, rall gamely ins last, drvn out to get up again fnl strides: won 1st 2 in '99,
at Leicester (fill mdn) & Kempton (fill stks), subs rnr-up in List company (rtd 104 at best): eff over 6/7f on
fast & soft grnd: acts on a stiff/gall or easy trk: has run well fresh: useful & genuine.
955   **SELKING 18** [2] K R Burke 3-8-5 N Callan 9/2: 402-32: 3 ch c Selkirk - Stay That Way (Be My Guest)   hd **103**
Cl-up till went on over 2f out, edged left & styd on well ins last, hdd cl-home: clr rem: sound run by this
3yo against elders here: tough, can win a 3yo Listed contest: see 955.
914   **NOW LOOK HERE 22** [4] B A McMahon 4-9-3 M Mullen 9/4: 33-233: 4 b g Reprimand - Where's Carol   3 **97**
(Anfield) Trkd ldrs, drvn & no extra appr fnl 1f: consistent form: see 914 (6f, h'cap).
4023} **RAMOOZ 231** [5] J W Hills 7-9-10 M Henry 11/2: 4446-4: Handy, rdn/btn from 2f out: reapp, cost   ½ **103**
current connections just 11,500gns: '99 scorer at Goodwood (List) & The Curragh (Gr 3, rtd 117, B Hanbury):
'98 wnr at York (List h'cap) & The Curragh (Gr 3, rtd 113): eff arnd 7f/1m on firm & soft grnd: acts on any
trk, likes The Curragh: best coming late off a strong pace: v smart entire at best, has a useful turn of foot.
*1004 **DESERT KNIGHT 12** [1] 4-9-3 J Weaver 2/1 FAV: 12-315: Settle rear, rdn 3f out & sn btn: nicely 1¾ **93**
bckd & much better expected after a smart effort in 1004 (6.7f stks, hvy).
5 ran   Time 1m 29.79 (2.69)   (Mis Gloria Abbey)   B J Meehan Upper Lambourn, Berks

1164
3.05 CROWTHER HOMES COND STKS 3YO+ (C)   6f   Good/Firm 26   +07 Fast
£6039   £2233   £1116   £507   3 yo rec 10lb

702   **GUINEA HUNTER 44** [5] T D Easterby 4-8-12 R Mullen 4/6 FAV: D03-01: 4 b g Pips Pride - Preponderance **95**
(Cyrano De Bergarac) Prom, went on over 1f out, rdn clr despite hanging left ins last, impressive: hvly bckd:
6 wk abs: '99 wnr of this very race here at Haydock (rtd 103): '98 Carlisle wnr (mdn, rtd 92 at best): suited
by 6f on firm, soft & any trk, likes Haydock: v useful, win in Listed company.
1016 **YORKIES BOY 12** [3] A Berry 5-8-12 S Drowne 6/1: 00-052: 5 ro h Clantime - Slipperose (Persepolis)   5 **87**
Cl-up, rdn & not pace of wnr appr fnl 1f: all wins have come at 5f: see 914.
988   **BRAVE BURT 14** [4] J Noseda 3-8-8 A J Weaver 15/2: 130-03: 3 ch c Pips Pride - Friendly Song (Song) 1 **90**
Led, hdd over 1f out, hung left & sn btn: shld apprec a return to own age group: see 988 (List).
1069 **SORBETT 5** [2] L M Cumani 3-8-12 G Sparkes (7) 16/1: 1-604: Handy, drvn, switched & no extra   nk **94$**
appr fnl 1f: qck reapp: seemingly much improved here but treat rating with caution: see 1069, 829.
*731 **LOOK HERE NOW 42** [1] 3-8-5 N Callan 4/1: -15: Prom, drvn/wknd fnl 2f: 6 wk abs: see 731. 1¾ **83**
5 ran   Time 1m 12.45 (1.15)   (M P Burke)   T D Easterby Great Habton, N Yorks

1165
3.35 CROWTHER FILLIES MDN 3YO (D)   1m2f120y   Good/Firm 26   -32 Slow
£4004   £1232   £616   £308

4400} **BROADWAY LEGEND 203** [6] J W Hills 3-8-11 M Henry 15/2: 30-1: 3 b f Caeleon - Tetradonna (Teenoso)   **86**
Made all, pressed ins last, drvn out: 3rd on '99 debut at Kempton (fill mdn, rtd 78): apprec this step up to
10.5f, further will suit (Oaks entry): acts on fast, handles hvy: can rate more highly & win again.
--   **LUCKY LADY** [4] Sir Michael Stoute 3-8-11 J Tate 5/2: 2: 3 ch f Nashwan - Jet Ski Lady (Vaguely   ¾ **85+**
Noble) Trkd ldrs, hdwy to chall ins last, styd on, just held: op 7/4 & clr rem on debut: half-sister to a 12f wnr:
sire won the Derby, dam won the Oaks: eff at 10.5f on fast: looks sure to relish 12f: will win similar.
4446} **GRANTED 199** [1] M L W Bell 3-8-11 R Mullen 11/2: 54-3: 3 b f Cadeaux Genereux - Germane   5 **77**
(Distant Relative) Handy, rdn/no extra over 2f out: up in trip: 4th at best in '99 (mdns, rtd 82 at best):
stays 7f, this longer 10f trip shld suit in time: handles gd/soft & fast.
4537} **SCARLETTA 191** [5] J H M Gosden 3-8-11 R Havlin 13/8 FAV: 22-4: Prom, hung badly left over 2f out,   6 **68**
sn no extra: rnr-up twice in '99 (fill mdns, rtd 86 A Foster): eff at 7f/8.3f on gd/sft: fitter next time.
3706} **LARAZA 248** [3] 3-8-11 J Weaver 8/1: 03-05: Waited with, rdn & outpcd over 2f out: up in trip so   3 **63**
reapp: plcd on 2nd of 2 '99 starts (auct mdn, rtd 72): acts on firm: mid-dists shld suit.
884   **SCRATCH THE DOVE 24** [2] 3-8-11 D McGaffin (7) 33/1: 006: Sn well in rear, t.o.: no form.   dist **0**
6 ran   Time 2m 16.09 (6.09)   (Freddy Bienstock And Martin Boase)   J W Hills Upper Lambourn, Berks

1166
4.05 CROWTHER EBF FILLIES MDN 2YO (D)   5f   Good/Firm 26   -39 Slow
£3867   £1190   £595   £297

1046 **OPEN WARFARE 8** [3] M Quinn 2-8-11 S Drowne 5/1: -3341: 2 b f General Monash - Pipe Opener   **78**
(Prince Sabo) Made all, hung left but styd on well ins last, rdn out: half-sister to a couple of wnrs, incl
an Irish juv scorer: eff over a gall 5f, 6f will suit: acts on fast & hvy grnd: improving.
--   **ZIETUNZEEN** [4] A Berry 2-8-11 J Weaver 7/4 FAV: 2: 2 b f Zieten - Hawksbill Special (Taufan)   1¾ **76**
Keen in tch, switched & hdwy ins last, kept on but not pace of wnr: clr rem: nicely bckd: 14,000gns Jan
foal, half-sister to a juv 5f wnr: eff at 5f, 6f shld suit: acts on fast grnd: pleasing debut, win similar.
--   **CHICARA** [--] T R Watson 2-8-11 N Callan 33/1: 3: 2 ch f Beveled - Chili Lass (Chilibang)   3½ **68**
Prom, rdn/outpcd over 2f out, hung left ins last: Mar foal, dam modest, sire decent in the US: speedily bred.
970   **BABY BUNTING 17** [2] M L W Bell 2-8-11 R Mullen 5/2: -44: Handy, rdn & no extra when carried   ½ **67**

left ins last: shade better on debut in 970 (gd/soft).
-- **BLOOM** [5] 2-8-11 T Williams 14/1: 5: Dwelt, in tch halfway, sn btn: Mar foal, half-sister to a winning stayer: dam 5/6f wnr: looks sure to apprec 6f in time, shld improve: with B J Meehan. *2* **62**
970 **CARRABAN 17** [1] 2-8-11 D R McCabe 4/1: -5W: Withdrawn after bolting to post. **0**
6 ran Time 1m 02.07 (3.27) (Open Warfare Partners) M Quinn Sparsholt, Oxon

1167 **4.40 CROWTHER HOMES HCAP 4YO+ 0-80 (D) 1m6f Good/Firm 26 +03 Fast [79]**
£6922 £2130 £1065 £532 4 yo rec 1 lb

885 **QUEDEX 24** [16] E L James 4-9-6 (72) I Mongan (5) 8/1: -60201: 4 b c Deploy - Alwal (Pharly) Waited with, smooth hdwy to lead over 2f out, drvn clr: gd time: '99 wnr at Goodwood (h'cap) & Bath (class stks, rtd 71): eff between 10f & 14f: acts on firm, soft & any trk: cld follow up. **79**
1023 **NEEDWOOD SPIRIT 12** [12] B C Morgan 5-8-9 (60) S Drowne 20/1: 345-02: 5 g b Rolfe - Needwood Nymph (Bold Owl) Rear, gd hdwy over 3f out, styd on but not pace of wnr: clr rem: sound effort: see 1023. *4* **62**
917 **HISTORIC 22** [2] W J Haggas 4-9-13 (79) J Weaver 8/1: 422-03: 4 b c Sadler's Wells - Urjwan (Seattle Slew) Led, hdd over 4f out, edged left & no extra fnl 2f: prob stys 14f: see 917. *3½* **78**
885 **SEGAVIEW 24** [15] Mrs P Sly 4-8-10 (62) R Havlin 12/1: 006-44: Cl-up, rdn, hung left & held fnl 2f: prefers good or softer grnd, on a handy mark: see 885. *nk* **61**
*845 **EXALTED 28** [1] 7-9-0 (65) A Daly 14/1: /40-15: Cl-up till no extra fnl 3f: see 845 (gd). *1* **63**
760 **LEDGENDRY LINE 39** [14] 7-8-9 (60) S Carson (5) 10/1: 240-56: Hmpd sn after start, gd hdwy to lead over 4f out, hdd 2f out, sn btn: on a fair mark: see 760. *1½* **56**
1052 **HOME COUNTIES 7** [8] 11-7-11 (48) N Kennedy 33/1: 32-007: Held up, nvr a dngr: qck reapp. *1¾* **42**
1044 **JAMAICAN FLIGHT 8** [13] 7-9-8 (73) K Dalgleish (7) 14/1: 432048: Handy, rdn/btn fnl 3f: see 1044. *nk* **67**
940 **LITTLE BRAVE 19** [6] 5-8-7 (58) J Tate 12/1: 24-469: Nvr a threat: see 940, 51. *¾* **51**
699 **DOUBLE BLADE 44** [3] 5-8-11 (62) S Finnamore (5) 4/1 FAV: 040-20: Held up, eff 4f out, carried head high & no extra fnl 3f: 10th: looked reluctant here: unplcd hdles rnr since 699. *¾* **54**
699 **URGENT SWIFT 44** [5] 7-9-1 (66) R Mullen 7/1: -51440: Nvr a factor, 11th: op 6/1: 6 wk abs. *¾* **57**
1044 **GRAND CRU 8** [9] 9-7-10 (47)(bl)(2oh) Joanna Badger (7) 20/1: 001460: Al in rear, fin 12th. *1¼* **36**
940 **CHARMING ADMIRAL 19** [11] 7-8-5 (56)(bl) D R McCabe 10/1: 5-0120: Sn bhd, 13th: btr 940 (2m5f). *1¼* **43**
876 **GIVE AN INCH 25** [7] 5-8-12 (63) T Williams 12/1: 10-000: Chsd ldrs, lost tch 2f out: 14th. *hd* **50**
671 **Yes Keemo Sabee 53** [10] 5-9-3 (68) N Callan 20/1: -- **Franchetti** [4] 4-10-0 (80) D O'Donohoe 33/1:
16 ran Time 3m 01.17 (3.17) (L Van Hijkoop) E L James East Garston, Berks

NEWMARKET (Rowley) SATURDAY MAY 6TH Righthand, Stiff, Galloping Track

Official Going GOOD. Stalls: Stands Side, except 1:50 - Far Side.

1168 **1.50 RUINART COND STKS 3YO (C) 1m4f Good/Firm 29 -26 Slow**
£6391 £2424 £1212 £551

*951 **WELLBEING 18** [6] H R A Cecil 3-9-0 T Quinn 7/4 FAV: 3-11: 3 b c Sadler's Wells - Charming Life (Sir Tristram) Cl-up, led appr fnl 1f, styd on strongly, pushed out: hvly bckd: recent reapp wnr here at Newmarket (mdn): 3rd of 5 sole juv start (stks, rtd 76): half-brother to a smart 10/12f wnr: eff at 12f, shld get 14f: acts on fast & gd grnd, stiff/gall trk, likes Newmarket: goes well fresh: useful & progressive, Derby hopeful, win a Group race. **106**
*833 **GARGALHADA FINAL 30** [2] J Noseda 3-9-0 Pat Eddery 3/1: 12: 3 b c Sabrehill - Secret Waters (Pharly) Held up, shkn up & prog 2f out, sn hung right, kept on to chase wnr ins last, onepace towards fin: imprvd up in grade on only 2nd start: apprec step up to 12f, acts on fast & gd/soft grnd: useful: see 833. *2½* **101**
998 **MISS LORILAW 14** [1] J W Hills 3-8-6 M Hills 16/1: 1-33: 3 b f Homme de Loi - Miss Lorika (Bikala) Held up in tch, feeling pace 2f out, kept on below dist, nvr able to chall: suited this step up to 12f & shld get further still: acts on fast & gd/soft grnd: see 998. *¾* **92**
957 **EJTITHAAB 18** [3] R W Armstrong 3-8-11 R Hills 20/1: 6-44: Well plcd, led 2½f out till bef dist, no extra: highly tried, longer trip: prob stays 12f on fast grnd, mdn a formaility. *2½* **93$**
*603 **SHAREEF 68** [4] 3-9-0 J Fortune 16/1: 15: Prom, led briefly ent fnl 3f, onepace: 10 wk abs, turf bow: acts on fibresand & prob fast grnd: not disgraced after winning an AW mdn on debut: see 603. *¾* **95**
3539} **ANSHAAM 259** [5] 3-8-11 J Carroll 5/2: 12-6: Led till 3f out, sn btn & eased: well bckd on reapp/Brit bow: recent rnr-up in a Godolphin trial: ex-French, '99 Deauville wnr & close rnr-up to Barathea Guest (List, rtd 108, D Loder): eff at 1m, shld stay 12f: goes on soft/hvy grnd, unsuited by this fast grnd: useful colt. *7* **84**
6 ran Time 2m 25.37 (6.57) (Exors Of The Late Howard de Walden) H R A Cecil Newmarket

1169 **2.25 MAYER PARRY MDN 2YO (D) 5f Good/Firm 29 -29 Slow**
£5525 £1700 £850 £425

-- **MIDNIGHT ARROW** [1] I A Balding 2-8-9 K Fallon 15/2: 1: 2 b f Robellino - Princess Oberon (Fairy King) Dwelt, held up last, shkn up 2f out, picked up well to lead below dist, readily: May foal, dam a sprint h'capper, sire a high-class juv: eff at 5f, will apprec 6f+: acts on fast grnd, stiff/gall trk: goes well fresh: useful debut, looks a potential Queen Mary contender on this showing. **89+**
-- **FIREWORK** [6] W J Haggas 2-9-0 M Hills 5/1: 2: 2 b c Primo Dominie - Prancing (Prince Sabo) Prom, eff & edged right appr fnl 1f, kept on but not pace of wnr: bckd from 8/1: 60,000gns Feb first foal, dam a 5f juv wnr, sire a sprinter: eff at 5f, shld get 6f: acts on fast grnd: shld go one better soon. *2½* **86**
-- **HAWK** [5] R Hannon 2-9-0 R Hughes 13/8 FAV: 3: 2 b c A P Jet - Miss Enjoleur (L'Enjoleur) Cl-up, led after halfway, under press & hdd below dist, onepace: hvly bckd: cost IR 61,000gns: half-brother to 1000 Guineas 2nd Oh Nellie, sire a miler: eff at 5f on fast grnd: can recoup losses. *¾* **84**
-- **PAN JAMMER** [2] M R Channon 2-9-0 T Quinn 5/1: 4: Dwelt, chsd ldrs, shkn up appr fnl 1f, outpcd: 11,500gns Piccolo Apr foal, half-brother to 10f/hdles wnr Kiss Me Kate: sire a sprinter: shld apprec 6f next time. *¾* **82**
-- **SPETTRO** [3] 2-9-0 J Fortune 4/1: 5: Sn handy, eff 2f out, unable to qckn: IR 50,000gns Spectrum first foal, dam 1m winning juv, sire 1m/10f performer: prob found this an inadequate test, with P Cole. *hd* **81**
-- **ARMAGNAC** [4] 2-9-0 G Duffield 33/1: 6: Led for 2½f, fdd bef dist: 19,000gns Young Ern April foal, half-brother to sev wnrs, notably smart sprint juv Green's Bid, sire a 7f performer: with D Sasse. *8* **61**
6 ran Time 1m 01.65 (3.45) (R P B Machaelson & Wafic Said) I A Balding Kingsclere, Hants.

NEWMARKET (Rowley) SATURDAY MAY 6TH Righthand, Stiff, Galloping Track

1170 3.00 COUNTRYWIDE RTD HCAP 4YO+ 0-100 (B) 1m2f str Good/Firm 29 -10 Slow [107]
£9941 £3770 £1885 £857

3982} **NATIONAL ANTHEM 231** [5] Sir Michael Stoute 4-9-3 (96) K Fallon 6/1 FAV: 3614-1: 4 b c Royal Academy - Heart's Harmony (Blushing Groom) Mid-div, prog 2f out, qcknd to lead ent fnl 1f, rdn & edged left, shade readily: hvly bckd, reapp: '99 Sandown wnr (mdn, rtd 97): rnr-up in '98 (stks, rtd 84): eff at 10f, may get 12f: acts on firm & gd/soft grnd, any trk: goes well fresh: useful, progressive colt, shld hold his own in in Listed/Gr 3. **105**

1031 **SUPPLY AND DEMAND 10** [1] J H M Gosden 6-8-7 (86)(bl)(3oh) J Fortune 7/1: 606-02: 2 b g Belmez - Sipsi Fach (Prince Sabo) Waited with, gd prog appr fnl 2f, chall bef dist, rdn & not pace of wnr: bckd tho' op 5/1: back to form with blnks reapp: goes on any trk, shld prove hard to beat at Goodwood later this month. *1½* **90**

3683} **GOLCONDA 250** [9] M L W Bell 4-8-7 (86) M Fenton 20/1: 2360-3: 4 br f Lahib - David's Star (Welsh Saint) Held up, prog & not much room 2f out, clr bef last & kept on, unable to chall: fine reapp: '99 wnr at W'hampton (mdn, rtd 67a), Kempton & Lingfield (h'caps, rtd 90 at best): eff at 10f, tried 12f: suited by firm/ fast, fibresand, prob handles soft: genuine filly, long term target is the John Smith's Cup at York in July. *1¼* **88**

*874 **JUST IN TIME 25** [17] T G Mills 5-8-12 (91) A Clark 15/2: 0-1414: Tried to make all, hdd appr fnl 1f, onepace: nicely bckd tho' op 6/1: remains in terrific form: see 874. *¾* **92**

1031 **FIRST FANTASY 10** [8] 4-8-7 (86)(3oh) R Cochrane 8/1: 411-05: Patiently rdn, closed on bit 2f out, shkn up & no extra ins last: bckd from 12/1, 5L clr: gd run shapes likes return to a sharper trk will suit: see 1031. *½* **86**

1031 **PRINCE OF MY HEART 10** [13] 7-8-7 (86) T Quinn 7/1: 0/6-66: Chsd ldrs, eff 2f out, outpcd: op 5/1. *5* **79**

4429} **ANOTHER TIME 200** [7] 8-8-7 (86)(3oh) W Woods 25/1: 2000-7: Towards rear, feeling pace 2f out, drfited right, nvr dngrs: reapp: '99 Leicester wnr (h'cap, rtd 87 & 66a): '98 wnr at Ascot (h'cap, rtd 91) & Lingfield (class stks): has tried hdles: eff at 1m/10f on firm, gd/soft grnd, suited by stiff trk, handles any. *1½* **76**

991 **THREE GREEN LEAVES 14** [12] 4-9-2 (95) M Roberts 25/1: /04-08: Cl-up, pushed along & lost pl 3f out, switched & kept on towards fin: worth a try in headgear now?: see 991. *nk* **85**

4224} **LAFITE 196** [3] 4-8-7 (86)(3oh)(t) R Hills 20/1: 0110-9: In tch, eff appr fnl 2f, no impress: sharper for reapp: '99 wnr at Chepstow, Newbury (fill h'cap) & Brighton (h'caps, rtd 84): plcd in '98 (mdn, rtd 77): eff at 1m/10f on firm & soft grnd, any trk: eff with/without t-strap: J Hills. *½* **75**

1031 **TARAWAN 10** [4] 4-8-7 (86)(1oh) K Darley 20/1: 10-000: Off the pace, nvr a factor: 10th: see 580. *hd* **75**

4116} **ROLLING STONE 222** [15] 6-8-11 (90) R Hughes 9/1: /431-0: Chsd ldrs till appr fnl 1f: 11th on reapp, h'cap bow: '99 wnr at Bath (mdn, rtd 86): missed '98 (fractured knee): plcd in '97 for Lady Herries (mdn, rtd 70): eff at 10f, tried further: acts on firm, suited by gd/soft: goes on sharp trks, forcing the pace. *hd* **78**

986 **MAKE WAY 14** [16] 4-8-7 (86)(3oh) Pat Eddery 20/1: 436-60: Chsd ldrs after halfway till 2f out: 12th. *nk* **74**

874 **PUNISHMENT 25** [14] 9-8-7 (86)(t)(6oh) G Duffield 50/1: -23550: Rr, prog 5f out, no extra 2f out: 13th. *¾* **72**

4619} **FLOSSY 182** [11] 4-8-8 (86)(1ow) O Peslier 9/1: 1621-0: Chsd ldrs, eff & btn 2f out, eased: 14th, bckd from 12/1 on reapp: '99 wnr at Beverley, Musselburgh, Newbury, Ripon (subs disq), Newcastle, Haydock & Doncaster (November h'cap, rtd 88): eff at 10f, suited by 12f: acts on firm & hvy grnd, any trk: tough. *1½* **70**

3734} **J R STEVENSON 247** [10] 4-9-7 (100) G Hind 25/1: 5150-0: Prom till ent fnl 3f: reapp, top-weight, 15th, h'cap bow: '99 Goodwood wnr (stks, first time visor, rtd 101 at best, P C Hyam): Chester mdn wnr in '98 (rtd 88): eff at 10f: acts on fast & soft grnd, sharp/undul trk: can go well fresh: best in a visor now (not worn). *½* **82**

4135} **EX GRATIA 221** [6] 4-8-9 (88) M Hills 9/1: 0214-0: Nvr in it, eased 3f out: 16th, fin distressed, reapp: '99 wnr at Haydock (mdn) & Doncaster (class stks, rtd 90): eff at 10/12f on fast & gd/soft grnd, likes gall trks. *22* **50**

16 ran Time 2m 05.95 (3.85) (Mrs Denis Haynes) Sir Michael Stoute Newmarket.

1171 3.40 GR 1 SAGITTA 2000 GUINEAS 3YO (A) 1m str Good/Firm 29 +13 Fast
£174000 £66000 £33000 £15000

981 **KINGS BEST 16** [12] Sir Michael Stoute 3-9-0 K Fallon 13/2: 115-21: 3 b c Kingmambo - Allegretta (Lombard) Restrained bhd, not much room appr fnl 2f, squeezed thro' & rapid hdwy bef fnl 1f, swept into lead dist, sn clr, impressive: hvy bckd, tchd 8/1, fast time: hit the front too sn in the Craven: '99 wnr at Newmarket (mdn) & York (List), subs too keen in the Dewhurst (rtd 112): half-brother to Arc wnr Ubrban Sea: eff at 1m, bred to get further: acts on gd/sft, suited by fast: goes on stiff/gall trks: nervy colt, awash with sweat today tho' settled much better in a noseband: top-class, fav for the Derby: has an electrifying turn on foot & may prove best kept to 1m. **127**

*862 **GIANTS CAUSEWAY 27** [17] A P O'Brien 3-9-0 M J Kinane 7/2 FAV: 111-12: 3 ch c Storm Cat - Mariah's Storm (Rahy) Prom, led appr fnl 1f, rdn & hdd ent fnl 1f, easily outpcd by wnr: hvly bckd Irish raider, tchd 9/2: ran to v best: eff at 7f/1m on fast & soft grnd: caught a tartar: high-class colt. *3½* **120**

*950 **BARATHEA GUEST 18** [10] G G Margarson 3-9-0 P Robinson 12/1: 11D-13: 3 b c Barathea - Western Heights (Shirley Heights) Rear, gd prog 2f out, kept on for press ins last: another cracking run from this v smart colt: shld get further than 1m: clrly goes on fast grnd but is the type to win a Gr 1/2 with some give. *1½* **117**

4468} **ZONING 197** [19] Saeed bin Suroor 3-9-0 J Carroll 50/1: 114-34: Well plcd, eff to chall 2f out, onepce bef dist: 11 wk abs since plcd in Dubai: '99 wnr at Yarmouth (mdn) & York (stks, Gr 3 4th, rtd 108, J Gosden): eff at 7f, stays 1m: goes on fast & gd/soft grnd, prob firm, likes gall trks: goes v well fresh: smart colt. *2* **113**

765 **COMPTON BOLTER 42** [3] 3-9-0 T Jarnet 100/1: 23-405: Waited with, not much room & switched 2f out, styd on, nvr nrr: 6 wk abs: fine run up in class: v useful, try 10f? *½* **112**

*981 **UMISTIM 16** [2] 3-9-0 Dane O'Neill 33/1: 151-16: Prom, rdn 2f out, unable to qckn: op 25/1: not disgraced considering grnd had gone against him: beat this wnr over C/D in 981 (gd/soft). *shd* **112**

4169} **PRIMO VALENTINO 219** [18] 3-9-0 Pat Eddery 16/1: 1111-7: Set strong pace, hdd appr fnl 1f, onepace: op 20/1 on reapp: most progressive last term, landed a 5-timer at Leicester (auct mdn), Goodwood (stks), Kempton (List), Newbury (Gr 2) & Newmarket (Gr 1 Middle Park, rtd 118): v eff at 6f, sprinting will be his game: acts on firm & soft, any trk: loves to force the pace: v smart, Group races to be won back in trip. *nk* **111**

950 **DISTANT MUSIC 18** [15] 3-9-0 M Hills 11/2: 111-28: In tch, prog to chase ldrs 2f out, edged right & rdn bef dist, no extra: hvly bckd from 7/1, winter favourite: has had an interrupted preparation tho' not a certain stayer over longer 1m trip: only btn a head by this 3rd in 950 (7f, here). *shd* **111**

*735 **SUMMONER 42** [7] 3-9-0 S Sanders 25/1: 61-19: Towards rear, gd prog to chase ldrs 2f out, sn hard rdn, fdd, eased towards fin: big step up in grade, probably suited by easier grnd: see 735 (cond, impressive). *2½* **106**

996 **LINCOLN DANCER 14** [6] 3-9-0 M Roberts 100/1: 310-40: Held up, prog & not much room 2f out, outpcd after: 10th: highly tried & far from disgraced, longer trip: see 996. *½* **105**

4197} **MILLENIUM MOONBEAM 217** [1] 3-9-0 G Hall 100/1: 614-0: Mid-div, green, shkn up, not much room 2f out, onepace: 11th on reapp: '99 Salisbury wnr (mdn, rtd 108 at best): eff at 6f, shld get further: acts on fast & gd/soft grnd, sharp or stiff trk: can run well fresh: big colt, win again in a lesser grade. *nk* **104**

*969 **CAPE TOWN 17** [20] 3-9-0 R Hughes 12/1: 12-10: Chsd ldrs, lost pl 2f out: 12th, stablemate 6th: shld get 1m, impressive on gd/soft grnd in 969 (7f, here). *1½* **101**

980 **WESTERN SUMMER 16** [13] 3-9-0 T Quinn 33/1: 1-40: Rear, wide effort over 2f out, no impress: 13th. *shd* **101**

945 **ONLYMAN 22** [5] 3-9-0 O Doleuze 33/1: 21-20: Nvr better than mid-div: French raider, '99 wnr at M-Laffitte (5½f on hvy grnd): stays 7f, first try on fast surface: with Mme C Head. *1¾* **97**
955 **FREE RIDER 18** [21] 3-9-0 R Cochrane 40/1: 221-20: Wide bhd, went past btn horses fnl 2½f: 15th: not given a hard time, well worth another try at this longer 1m trip: see 955 (gd grnd). *½* **96**
4169} **FATH 219** [14] 3-9-0 R Hills 16/1: 12-0: Chsd ldrs, rdn 2f out, fdd: 16th: recently won a Godolphin trial: '99 debut wnr at York (mdn), neck rnr-up to Primo Valentino sole subs start (Gr 1, rtd 117, M Tregoning): eff at 6f, styd 1m in the Dubai trial: acts on gd grnd, stiff/gall trks: drop back in trip likely to suit. *hd* **96**
-925 **FRENCH FELLOW 21** [23] 3-9-0 K Darley 16/1: 211-20: Chsd ldrs till 2f out: 17th: nds softer grnd? *nk* **95**
3332} **MANA MOU BAY 267** [8] 3-9-0 D Harrison 25/1: 21-0: Handy till 2f out: 18th, reapp, st/mate 6th: won fnl '99 start at Newbury (List, rtd 100): eff at 7f, bred to stay further: acts on fast grnd, gall trk. *nk* **95**
950 **SCARTEEN FOX 18** [26] 3-9-0 G Duffield 28/1: 110-40: Mid-div, wknd appr fnl 1f: 19th: longer trip. *1* **93**
-- **BROCHE** [24] 3-9-0 T E Durcan 33/1: 1-00: Well plcd till 2f out, eased: rnr-up to Fath in Dubai 2 weeks ago: won sole '99 start at The Curragh (7f mdn on gd grnd, J Oxx). *nk* **92**
950 **WINNING VENTURE 18** [9] 3-9-0 W Woods 50/1: 22D-30: Nvr troubled ldrs: 21st, much btr 950 (7f gd). *2½* **87**
+925 **RACE LEADER 21** [16] 3-9-0 J Reid 28/1: 132-10: In tch, btn when hmpd 2f out: 22nd, see 925 (sft). *nk* **86**
981 **SHAMROCK CITY 16** [27] 3-9-0 R Winston 66/1: 421-60: In tch wide till after halfway: 23rd. *3½* **80**
3055} **MASTERMIND 280** [25] 3-9-0 J Fortune 33/1: 21-0: Rear, rdn 3f out, sn btn & lost action: 24th on reapp: won fnl '99 start at Newmarket (mdn, rtd 96): half-brother to v smart 1m/12f performer Housemaster: eff at 6f, shld stay further: acts on firm grnd, stiff/gall trk: with P Cole. *1½* **77**
*955 **MISRAAH 18** [11] 3-9-0 W Supple 20/1: 41-10: In tch till halfway: 25th, stablemate wnr: btr 955 (gd). *1* **75**
4029} **BERNSTEIN 230** [22] 3-9-0 O Peslier 16/1: 115-0: Chsd ldrs till 3f out: 26th, nicely bckd Irish raider, stablemate rnr-up: won first 2 in '99 at The Curragh (mdn & Gr 3, rtd 117), found to have respiratory problem when btn at long odds-on other start (Gr 1): unproven beyond 6f on gd & gd/soft grnd. *15* **55**
4358} **ALFINI 205** [4] 3-9-0 N Pollard 25/1: 21-P: Al bhd, fatally broke leg appr fnl 1f: a sad loss. **0**
27 ran Time 1m 37.77 (1.27) (Saeed Suhail) Sir Michael Stoute Newmarket

1172 4.15 GR 3 PALACE HOUSE STKS 3YO+ (A) 5f Good/Firm 29 +03 Fast
£23200 £8800 £4400 £2000 3 yo rec 9 lb

*927 **PIPALONG 21** [4] T D Easterby 4-8-9 K Darley 9/1: 521-11: 4 b f Pips Pride - Limpopo (Green Desert) **110**
Chsd ldrs, hard rdn appr fnl 1f, kept on gamely to get up fnl strides: op 7/1, fair time: 3 wks ago won Thirsk reapp (stks): '99 wnr at Ripon (val h'cap) & Doncaster (List, rtd 107 at best): '98 wnr at Ripon (debut), York (nov fill) & Redcar (val 2yo Trophy, rtd 105): eff at 5/6f, prob stays 7f: goes on firm & hvy grnd, any trk: runs v well fresh: genuine, smart & still improving filly, hard to beat in the Duke of York stks next time.
4286} **KIER PARK 210** [3] M A Jarvis 3-8-6 P Robinson 11/2: 4211-2: 3 b c Foxhound - Merlannah (Shy Groom) Prom, tkd ldrs going well 2f out, pld out & qcknd to lead dist, ran on under press but collared cl-home: well bckd, reapp: '99 wnr at Lingfield (mdn) & Ascot (Gr 3, rtd 105): eff at 5f, stays 6f: acts on firm & soft grnd, any trk: goes well fresh: smart 3yo, sure to win more Group races, esp when held on to for a later challenge. *nk* **114+**
4620} **RAMBLING BEAR 182** [11] M Blanshard 7-9-1 R Cochrane 16/1: 0350-3: 7 ch h Sharrood - Supreme Rose (Frimley Park) Went right start & rear, plenty to do 2f out, ran on strongly, nrst fin: reapp: '99 wnr at Newmarket (this Gr 3, rtd 113 at best): '98 reapp wnr at Goodwood (stks, rtd 110 at best): eff at 5/6f: acts on firm & gd/soft, any trk, likes Goodwood & Newmarket: goes part well fresh, without blnks: smart entire. *½* **112**
-914 **LORD KINTYRE 22** [7] B R Millman 5-8-12 O Peslier 20/1: /50-24: Held up, prog appr fnl 1f, finished well, nvr nrr: fine run, prob back to juvenile best: v useful: see 914. *shd* **109$**
952 **HALMAHERA 18** [6] 5-8-12 M J Kinane 14/1: 6-5205: Well off the pace till strong run appr fnl 1f, nrst fin: back in trip & back to near best: see 734. *nk* **108**
927 **ROSSELLI 21** [12] 4-8-12 J Carroll 40/1: 050-46: Rear, hdwy under press appr fnl 1f, no extra nr fin: return to 5f & bounced back to form: goes on fast grnd, softer suits: see 927. *½* **106**
927 **EASTERN PURPLE 21** [5] 5-9-1 F Lynch 40/1: 00-037: Rear, prog appr fnl 1f, sltly short of room, kept on: gd run back in trip on grnd faster than ideal: see 734. *¾* **107**
952 **ARKADIAN HERO 18** [10] 5-8-12 Pat Eddery 3/1 FAV: 130-48: Outpcd, shkn up over 2f out, imprvd bef dist, no extra ins last: hvly bckd from 4/1: unsuited by drop back to 5f? see 952. *½* **103**
2} **BOLSHOI GB 546** [16] 8-8-12 T E Durcan 33/1: 4620/9: Rear, stdy late hdwy, nvr a threat: 2 yr abs: '98 hat-trick scorer at Beverley (stks), Sandown & R Ascot (Gr 2's, rtd 117): '97 wnr at Beverley (reapp, rtd 109): all wins over a stiff 5f, stays 6f: goes on firm & gd/soft grnd: loves to come late, with/without blnks. *½* **102**
952 **SUPERIOR PREMIUM 18** [19] 6-8-12 (BL) M Roberts 16/1: 10-000: Prom, no extra appr fnl 1f: 10th. *1* **99**
-- **BISHOPS COURT** [20] 6-8-12 (t) K Fallon 6/1: 2311/0: Held up, prog 2f out, hmpd & switched dist, no extra: 11th, hvly bckd, 2 yr abs: '98 wnr at Epsom (List h'cap), Newmarket (List) & Longchamp (Gr 3, rtd 115, Mrs Ramsden): '97 Chester wnr (h'cap): eff at 5f, stays 6f: acts on firm & hvy grnd, any trk, best coming late off a fast pace: smart at best: now with I Balding. *hd* **99**
914 **REPERTORY 22** [21] 7-8-12 R Price 40/1: 543-00: Prom till onepace appr fnl 1f: 12th, see 914. *½* **98**
952 **TEDBURROW 18** [22] 8-9-1 M Hills 20/1: 10-000: Rear, late hdwy, nvr a threat: 13th, back in trip. *hd* **101**
+702 **PERRYSTON VIEW 44** [2] 8-8-12 (bl) R Hughes 10/1: 401-10: Led till 2f out, fdd dist: 14th, well bckd from 14/1, 6 wk abs: best giving weight in h'caps: see 702. *¾* **98**
3905} **PROUD NATIVE 146** [15] 6-9-1 J Fortune 14/1: 3310-0: Nvr a factor: reapp: '99 wnr at Kempton (List), Leopardstown & Taby (Gr 3, Gr 1 3rd, rtd 114): '98 wnr at Doncaster, Haydock (h'caps) & Nottingham (stks, rtd 109): eff at 6f, prob best at 5f on firm & soft grnd, any trk: with D Nicholls. *1½* **95**
3875} **MRS P 238** [14] 3-8-6 J P Spencer 40/1: 3121-0: Nvr nvr ldrs: 16th on reapp: '99 wnr at Sandown (nurs) & Doncaster (Gr 2, rtd 102): eff at 5/6f on firm & gd/soft grnd, gall trks: highly tried, with Mrs Stubbs. *¾* **93**
1090 **CARHUE LASS 4** [13] 6-8-9 J Reid 33/1: 200-30: Prom till appr fnl 1f: 17th, Irish raider, see 1090. *½* **86**
4286} **THE TATLING 210** [8] 3-8-3 M Fenton 20/1: 1262-0: Held up, badly hmpd halfway, position accepted: 18th on reapp: '99 wnr at Yarmouth (mdn) & Brighton (stks, Gr 3 rnr-up, rtd 101): eff at 5/6f on fast & soft grnd. *nk* **88**
223 **AFAAN 136** [17] 7-8-12 (bl) T G McLaughlin 66/1: 4330-0: Prom, chall appr fnl 1f till wknd qckly below dist: 19th on reapp: stiff task: see 113. *1* **85**
4246} **MITCHAM 216** [1] 4-9-4 A Clark 25/1: 1040-0: Sn handy, fdd after halfway: 20th on reapp: '99 wnr at Newmarket (val sprint) & Royal Ascot (Gr 2, rtd 116): '98 wnr at Warwick (auct mdn): eff at 5/6f on fast grnd, handles soft: can go well fresh, any trk: high-class at best: with T Mills. *3½* **83**
4286} **VICTORY DAY 210** [18] 3-8-3 G Duffield 20/1: 2100-0: Bhd from halfway: 21st on reapp: '99 wnr at Windsor & Chester (stks, Gr 3 rnr-up, rtd 108, J Noseda): eff at 5f on firm & gd grnd, tight or gall track. *4* **67**
21 ran Time 59.5 (1.3) (T H Bennett) T D Easterby Great Habton, N.Yorks.

1173　　4.45 LADBROKES HCAP 3YO+ 0-95 (C)　　6f　　Good/Firm 29　-03 Slow　　[95]
£26000　£8000　£4000　£2000　3 yo rec 10lb　2 Groups, centre (high no's) prob favoured

914　**SARTORIAL** 22 [22]　P J Makin 4-10-0 (95) S Sanders 25/1: 32-141: 4 b g Elbio - Madam Slaney (Prince　**101**
Tenderfoot) Nvr far away in centre, qcknd to lead 1f out, drvn out: earlier won at Haydock (mdn): plcd all 3 '99
starts (rtd 89 & 78a): eff at 5/6f on firm, gd/soft, fibresand, any trk: runs well fresh: speedy, useful, progressive.
716　**CADEAUX CHER** 43 [30]　B W Hills 6-8-11 (78) R Cochrane 7/1: 040-22: 6 ch g Cadeaux Genereux -　½　**83**
Home Truth (Known Fact) Rear centre, imprvd ent fnl 2f, kept on strongly, just btn: 6 wk abs: has started the
season in fine form & shld not be long in winning tho' could do with being rdn a bit closer to the pace: see 716.
4296}　**PEPPERDINE** 210 [19]　D Nicholls 4-9-12 (93) K Fallon 6/1 FAV: 1002-3: 4 b g Indian Ridge - Rahwah　½　**96**
(Northern Baby) Held up centre, plenty to do 2f out, ran on, nvr nrr: hvly bckd, reapp: '99 York wnr (h'cap,
rtd 94): '98 wnr at Warwick (nurs, rtd 81, W Jarvis): eff at 6/7f on fast & gd/soft grnd, any trk: best without
blnks: runs well fresh & has a useful turn of foot: progressive, sure to win more races.
844　**MANORBIER** 28 [6]　K A Ryan 4-9-1 (82) F Lynch 16/1: 411204: Cl-up stands side, led that bunch bef　1　**82**
fnl 1f, kept on, al playing second fiddle to centre: right back to form after poor drawn: v tough: see 716.
1077　**TAYSEER** 5 [10]　6-9-5 (86) J Fortune 12/1: 11-005: Prom stands side, prog appr fnl 1f, styd on.　hd　**86**
844　**GET STUCK IN** 28 [20]　4-9-3 (84) R Hills 20/1: 140-06: Led centre till 1f out, onepace: see 844.　1½　**82**
1013　**DANIELLES LAD** 12 [27]　4-9-6 (87) K Darley 16/1: 00-047: Cl-up centre, eff 2f out, same pace dist.　nk　**82**
4530}　**DOWNLAND** 192 [24]　4-9-2 (83) M Roberts 25/1: 0620-8: Wide, mid-div, hmpd/lost grnd 2df out, late　shd　**78**
rally: reapp: '99 wnr at Lingfield (auct mdn, rtd 87): eff at 6f centre & gd grnd, sharp or gall trk.
728　**EMERGING MARKET** 42 [26]　8-9-7 (88) M J Kinane 12/1: 366-09: Rear centre, late hdwy, nvr a factor.　hd　**82**
4620}　**ALASTAIR SMELLIE** 182 [28]　4-9-8 (89) M Hills 20/1: 4004-0: Nvr better than mid-div in centre: plcd　hd　**82**
on reapp last term (h'cap, rtd 83, 4th in a Listed, rtd 101$): '98 Ayr wnr (nurs, rtd 83): eff at 6f, stays
7f: goes on fast & hvy grnd, any trk: stablemate of 2nd, with B Hills.
935　**HILL MAGIC** 19 [12]　5-9-4 (85) M Fenton 33/1: 005-00: Al same pl centre: 11th, see 935.　nk　**77**
977　**BOLDLY GOES** 17 [14]　4-8-13 (80) W Woods 40/1: 3-0060: Rear centre, late hdwy, nvr dbgrs: 12th.　nk　**71**
966　**MARSAD** 17 [3]　6-9-9 (90) O Peslier 20/1: 300-50: Nvr in it stands side: 13th: see 758.　nk　**80**
4296}　**GRACIOUS GIFT** 210 [15]　4-9-8 (89) R Hughes 16/1: 1230-0: Held up centre, hmpd halfway, nvr nr　nk　**78**
to chall: 14th, reapp: '99 wnr at Salisbury (fill mdn) & Windsor (fill h'cap, rtd 91): with Lord Huntingdon in
'98 (rtd 78): eff at 6/7f on firm & gd/soft grnd: can go well fresh & is a gd weight carrier: with R Hannon.
3827}　**LITERARY SOCIETY** 241 [21]　7-9-12 (93) S Whitworth 16/1: 3300-0: Rear centre, not much room　shd　**82**
2f out, nvr on terms: 15th, reapp: plcd thrice in '99 (Stewards Cup, rtd 94): '98 wnr at Newmarket (h'cap),
Yarmouth (class stks) & York (h'cap, rtd 97): eff at 5/6f on gd grnd, loves firm, handles gd/soft.
926　**NIGHT FLIGHT** 21 [23]　6-9-10 (91) R Winston 14/1: 6-0020: Held up, prog 2f out, not much room　shd　**79**
bef dist, onepace: 16th, not given a hard time: see 926.
1028　**CAUDA EQUINA** 10 [8]　6-8-13 (80) T Quinn 20/1: 0-0200: Nvr in it stands side: 17th, see 905.　¾　**66**
4093}　**CHAMPAGNE RIDER** 224 [5]　4-9-7 (88) T E Durcan 33/1: 0100-0: Al bhd stands side: 18th, reapp:　nk　**73**
'99 wnr at Leicester (rtd h'cap, rtd 91): '98 wnr at Kempton (2, mdn & stks, rtd 93): eff at 6f, tried 7f: goes
on firm & hvy grnd, any trk, likes Kempton: with K McAuliffe.
4144}　**RING DANCER** 220 [13]　5-9-1 (82) A Clark 25/1: 0/00-0: Al rear stands side: 19th, stablemate wnr,　½　**66**
reapp: unplcd in '99 (h'cap, rtd 83): '97 Ripon wnr (auct mdn, rtd 94): eff at 6f, stays 7f on fast & gd/sft.
1013　**PURE COINCIDENCE** 12 [17]　5-8-13 (80) W Supple 25/1: 00-300: Nvr on terms centre: 20th, see 678.　hd　**64**
*1013　**LIVELY LADY** 12 [16]　4-9-9 (90)(vis) Pat Eddery 12/1: 01-410: Nvr dngrs centre: 21st, nibbled from 16/1.　1¾　**70**
1388}　**MIZHAR** 354 [4]　4-9-9 (90) G Hind 33/1: /006-0: Led stands side till 2f out, sn btn: 25th, stablemate　**0**
3rd: unplcd in 3 '99 starts (incl visor): '98 wnr at Nottingham (mdn) & Newmarket (nurs, rtd 98, E Dunlop):
eff at 6/7f on firm & gd grnd, stiff/gall trks: now with D Nicholls.
3520} **Poles Apart** 258 [11] 4-9-4 (85)(t) G Duffield 25/1:　　881　**Bold Effort** 24 [1] 8-8-13 (80)(bl) N Pollard 50/1:
3770} **La Piazza** 245 [7] 4-9-1 (82) P Robinson 25/1:　　935　**Pax 19** [18] 3-8-12 (89) A McGlone 33/1:
1013　**The Puzzler** 12 [25] 9-9-2 (83) J Reid 25/1:　　702　**Threat** 44 [29] 4-10-0 (95) G Carter 33/1:
28 ran　　Time 1m 12.74 (1.94)　　(Mrs Greta Sarfaty Marchant)　　P J Makin Ogbourne Maisey, Wilts.

1174　　5.20 JOHN MOWLEM COND STKS 4YO+ (B)　　1m2f　　Good/Firm 129　-16 Slow
£10150　£3850　£1925　£875

4488}　**ISLAND HOUSE** 196 [5]　G Wragg 4-9-4 M Roberts 7/1: 4112-1: 4 ch c Grand Lodge - Fortitude (Last　**117**
Tycoon) Rear, prog ent fnl 2f, led below dist, held on well: reapp: '99 wnr at Pontefract (class stks) & Ayr
(stks, rtd 102 at best): rtd 81 in '98: eff at 1m/10f: acts on firm & hvy grnd, stiff/gall trk: goes well fresh:
a much imprvd performance from this v progressive, v smart colt, shld find a Group race.
709}　**MUTAMAM** 405 [3]　A C Stewart 5-8-7 R Hills 5/2: 14/0-2: 5 b h Darshaan - Petal Girl (Caerleon)　½　**104**
Trkd ldr, led 2f out till ent fnl 1f, kept on: hvly bckd tho' op 7/4, clr rem: reapp: unplcd sole '99 start in Dubai
for Godolphin: '99 wnr at Sandown (stks), Haydock & Goodwood (Gr 3's, Gr 1 4th, rtd 120): eff at 10f, tried 12f:
acts on firm, gd/soft grnd & any trk: best forcing the pace: better than this, v smart at best.
3667}　**HAPPY CHANGE** 250 [4]　M Johnston 6-9-1 J Reid 4/1: 5/21-3: 6 ch g Surumu - Happy Girl (Ginistrelli)　4　**106**
Prom, rdn 2f out, onepace: reapp: earlier rnr-up over hdles (2m, rtd 112h, Miss V Williams): '99 Epsom wnr
(stks, rtd 104): '98 wnr at Baden-Baden (Gr 3, rtd 115): eff at 10/12f on fast & soft grnd, sharp or undul trk.
767　**PEGNITZ** 42 [1]　C E Brittain 5-9-1 (BL) P Robinson 5/1: 053-04: Led till 2f out, same pace: op 4/1,　½　**105**
blnkd, 6 wk abs: '99 Epsom wnr (stks, rtd 109 in a Listed): '98 Windsor wnr (mdn, rtd 83): eff at 10f, tried
12f: acts on firm & gd grnd, handles equitrack, any trk: useful.
1014　**AZOUZ PASHA** 12 [2]　4-9-8 (vis) T Quinn 9/4 FAV: 121-55: Held up, eff 2f out, sn btn: bckd from 7/2.　1¾　**110**
1011　**NOUF** 12 [6]　4-8-2 W Supple 66/1: -00206: Cl-up till 3f out: v highly tried, back up in trip.　17　**70**
6 ran　　Time 2m 05.61 (4.61)　　(Mollers Racing)　　G Wragg Newmarket.

SALISBURY SUNDAY MAY 7TH Righthand, Galloping Track, Stiff Finish

Official Going GOOD TO FIRM (GOOD places). Stalls: Str Crse - Far Side, 10f - Inside, 12f - Stands Side.

1175 2.20 WOODFORD MDN DIV 1 3YO+ (D) 6f str Firm 04 +07 Fast
£3217 £990 £495 £247 3 yo rec 10lb Raced far side, favouring high no's

971 **ARABESQUE 18** [14] H R A Cecil 3-8-7 W Ryan 8/11 FAV: 32-31: 3 b f Zafonic - Prophecy (Warning) **91+**
Cl-up, went on over 1f out, sn clr, easily: val for 10L+: hvly bckd at odds on: gd time: confirmed promise of
reapp: twice rcd juv (rnr-up, fill mdn, rtd 93+): eff at 6/7f, 1m+ could suit: acts on firm & soft grnd, likes a
stiff/gall trk: can run well fresh: not inconvenienced by drop to 6f, useful filly, well regarded, one to follow.
915 **EFFERVESCENT 23** [5] I A Balding 3-8-7 A Nicholls (3) 14/1: 02: 3 b f Efisio - Sharp Chief (Chief **5 75+**
Singer) Rear, prog fnl 2f, styd on strongly ins last, no ch with wnr: op 12/1, reapp: unplcd sole '99 start (rtd 72,
fill mdn): eff at 6f, return to 7f+ shld suit: acts on firm grnd: eye-catching late hdwy, caught a tarter here.
956 **VILLA VIA 19** [15] J A R Toller 3-8-7 R Ffrench 8/1: -53: 3 b f Night Shift - Joma Kaanem (Double **1¼ 72**
Form) Chsd ldrs, kept on fnl 2f, no ch with wnr: progressed from debut, 7f+ could suit: handles firm: see 956.
956 **SUSSEX LAD 19** [20] R Hannon 3-8-12 R Hughes 6/1: 60-04: Led till over 1f out, no extra: see 956. **shd 77**
877 **POLAR LADY 26** [9] 3-8-7 D Harrison 10/1: 6-35: Keen/in tch, chsd ldrs 2f out, fdd fnl 1f: op 12/1. **3 64**
837 **TATTENHAM STAR 30** [18] 3-8-7 C Rutter 20/1: 350-36: Chsd ldrs 5f: see 837. **¾ 67**
-- **MALARKEY** [19] 3-8-12 G Duffield 25/1: 7: Dwelt, kept on fnl 2f, no threat: debut: half-brother to a **1 64**
wnr abroad at up to 10f: not given a hard time, sure to apprec further & can rate more highly for J Osborne.
-- **GASCON** [16] 4-9-8 G Carter 33/1: 8: Keen/rear, late gains, no threat: debut: dam a sprint wnr. **1¾ 60**
840 **LOUP CERVIER 30** [1] 3-8-12 O Urbina 33/1: 09: Dwelt, rear till mod gains fnl 2f: drpd in trip. **3 52**
839 **LITE A CANDLE 30** [6] 3-8-7 Dale Gibson 100/1: 00: Chsd ldrs 4f: 10th: drpd in trip. **1 44**
-- **LANDICAN LAD** [17] 3-8-12 S Sanders 25/1: 0: Chsd ldrs 3f: 11th: debut: half-brother to several wnrs. **1¾ 45**
1063 **POLAR DIAMOND 6** [4] 3-8-7 R Mullen 33/1: 030: Nvr a factor: 12th: op 14/1, qck reapp: btr 1063 (sft). **2 34**
2433} Many Happy Returns 309 [11] 3-8-7 S Carson (5) 100/1: 4507} Goldfaw 195 [8] 3-8-12 A Daly 100/1:
691 Deadly Samosa 50 [12] 4-9-8 N Pollard 25/1: 4493} St Ives 197 [7] 3-8-12 Martin Dwyer 66/1:
94 College Gallery 166 [3] 3-8-12 T E Durcan 66/1: 3318} Marwell Magnus 268 [13] 3-8-12 A Eddery (5) 66/1:
-- Piccalilli [10] 3-8-7 L Newman (5) 100/1: -- Touch The Sky [2] 3-8-7 G Hind 33/1: P
20 ran Time 1m 11.93 (u0.17) (K Abdulla) H R A Cecil Newmarket.

1176 2.55 SALISBURY FILLIES COND STKS 2YO (C) 5f str Firm 04 -07 Slow
£5544 £2103 £1051 £478

*932 **SECRET INDEX 20** [3] Mrs P N Dutfield 2-8-12 L Newman (5) 5/1: 11: 2 b f Nicolotte - Deerussa (Jareer) **90**
Handy, led over 1f out, held on well ins last, drvn out: earlier made a winning debut at Windsor (mdn):
eff at 5f, further looks sure to suit: has run well fresh: acts on firm & hvy grnd, sharp/stiff trk: progressive.
*938 **CELTIC ISLAND 20** [5] W G M Turner 2-8-9 A Daly 4/1: 212: 2 b f Celtic Swing - Chief Island (Be **1½ 82**
My Chief) Rdn chasing ldr, kept on ins last, al held by wnr: acts on firm & hvy grnd: see 938.
*1083 **MILLYS LASS 5** [2] M R Channon 2-8-9 Craig Williams 6/1: -31213: 2 b f Mind Games - Millie's Lady **2 77**
(Common Grounds) Led, rdn/hdd over 1f out, no extra: qck reapp: handles firm & soft, 6f needed now: see 1083.
-- **SECURON DANCER** [1] R Rowe 2-8-6 R Mullen 33/1: 4: Chsd ldrs, wknd fnl 1f: op 20/1: Emperor **1¼ 71**
Jones filly, Mar foal: dam a US wnr as a 3/4yo: sire high-class/progressive 1m/10f performer: needs further.
-- **RARE OLD TIMES** [8] 2-8-6 G Duffield 25/1: 5: Chsd ldrs, wknd fnl 1f: stablemate of wnr: Inzar **½ 69**
filly, Apr foal, cost Ir10,500gns: half-sister to an Italian juv wnr: dam 7f 3yo wnr, sire high-class 6/7f performer.
970 **PASHMEENA 18** [9] 2-8-9 R Hughes 11/8 FAV: -26: Rdn/bhd, switched halfway, sn btn: nicely bckd. **hd 72**
-- **FINAL PURSUIT** [7] 2-8-6 G Carter 14/1: 7: V slow away & al well bhd: op 12/1: Pursuit Of Love **12 44**
filly, Mar foal, 42,000gns 2yo: half-sister to 3 juv wnrs, including progressive sprinter Sir Nicholas: dam a useful
sprinter, wnr as a 2yo: sire high-class 6f/1m performer: can perform better in time for D Haydon Jones.
-- **PALACE AFFAIR** [6] 2-8-6 A Nicholls (3) 12/1: W: Refused to enter stalls, withdrawn: Pursuit Of **0**
Love filly, Apr foal: half-sister to 3 wnrs, incl 1m h'capper & mud lover Cad Oro: dam a 6/7f wnr: with G B Balding.
8 ran Time 1m 00.38 (0.58) (Index Storgae Systems Ltd) Mrs P N Dutfield Axmouth, Devon.

1177 3.30 WEATHERBYS HCAP 3YO 0-100 (C) 1m2f Firm 04 -07 Slow [100]
£6890 £2120 £1060 £530

4119} **WATER JUMP 223** [6] J L Dunlop 3-8-13 (85) D Harrison 6/1: -221-1: 3 b c Suave Dancer - Jolies Eaux **96**
(Shirley Heights) Held up, smooth prog fnl 3f to lead 2f out, rdn out: op 9/2, reapp/h'cap bow: '99 wnr on
fnl start at Hamilton (auct mdn), rnr-up twice prev, rtd 89 at best): eff at 1m, apprec step up to 10f, shld
get further: acts on firm & gd/soft grnd: loves a stiff/undul trk & runs well fresh.
1029 **BLUE GOLD 11** [8] R Hannon 3-9-7 (93) R Hughes 8/1: 133-42: 3 b c Rainbow Quest - Relatively Special **1 101**
(Alzao) Chsd ldrs, eff/hdd over 1f out, kept on tho' held: stays 10f on firm & gd/soft: see 1029 (hvy).
*999 **COMMON PLACE 15** [9] C F Wall 3-9-3 (89) R Mullen 11/2 FAV: -56113: 3 b g Common Grounds - One **1¼ 94**
Wild Oat (Shareef Dancer) Rear, eff/prog fnl 2f, kept on ins last tho' no impress: op 9/2: stays a stiff 10f:
acts on firm & soft/hvy grnd: consistent: see 999 (9f, soft).
727 **TRAVELLING LITE 43** [5] B R Millman 3-8-8 (80) G Hind 6/1: 260-34: Chsd ldrs, rdn/ch 3f out, no **2½ 80**
extra fnl 2f: 4w abs, shld stay this longer 10f trip: see 727 (stks).
4274} **DUCHAMP 213** [4] 3-8-12 (84) A Nicholls (3) 7/1: 6221-5: Led after 1f till over 2f out, sn onepace: op **¾ 82**
6/1, reapp: '99 wnr at York (nurs h'cap, rtd 84): eff at 1m, stays 10f: acts on fast & gd/soft grnd, poss firm.
1055 **FATHER JUNINHO 8** [3] 3-9-4 (90) D Duffield 8/1: 012-06: Rear, eff/switched 2f out, no impress. **¾ 86**
3830} **ROUSING THUNDER 242** [11] 3-8-6 (78) G Carter 10/1: -336-7: Keen/bhd, eff 2f out, mod late gains: **½ 72**
reapp/h'cap bow: plcd twice in '99 (rtd 83, mdn): eff at 7f, shaped as if this longer 10f trip will suit in time:
handles firm grnd & a stiff/gall trk: shld prove sharper for this: with E Dunlop.
2583} **MUCHANA YETU 302** [7] 3-7-12 (70) A Daly 20/1: 3055-8: Rider lost iron early, sn recovered/mid-div, **1¾ 61**
btn 2f out: op 16/1, reapp: plcd in '99 (rtd 76, debut): bred to apprec mid-dists this term: handles firm grnd.
4505} **THEATRELAND 195** [2] 3-8-5 (75)(2ow) S Sanders 6/1: 005-9: Rear, eff 2f out, no impress: reapp/h'cap **½ 66**
bow: unplcd in '99 (mdn, rtd 74): bred to apprec mid-dists: prob handles hvy, return to an easier surface may suit.
4487} **SILENT NIGHT 197** [10] 3-8-8 (80) N Pollard 16/1: -150-0: Led 1f, remained handy till 2f out: 10th: **6 59**
op 14/1, reapp: '99 debut wnr at Kempton (cond stks, rtd 89, subs disapp, incl in a t-strap): eff at 7f, bred to
get further: acts on firm grnd & has run well fresh: h'capper h'cap bow today: with D Elsworth.
979 **CRYSTAL FLITE 17** [1] 3-7-12 (70) Martin Dwyer 16/1: 063-00: Chsd ldrs, btn 2f out: 11th: op 12/1. **3 44**
11 ran Time 2m 05.6 (1.1) (The Earl Cadogan) J L Dunlop Arundel, W.Sussex.

389

SALISBURY SUNDAY MAY 7TH Righthand, Galloping Track, Stiff Finish

1178

4.00 WILTON RTD HCAP 3YO 0-100 (B) 6f str Firm 04 -03 Slow [103]
£9106 £3454 £1727 £785 Raced far side, high no's favoured

*994 **DUKE OF MODENA 15** [8] G B Balding 3-8-10 (85) S Carson (5) 9/1: 603-11: 3 ch g Salse - Palace Street (Secreto) Nvr far away, prog to lead below dist, rdn out: op 7/1: recent Kempton wnr on reapp (h'cap): plcd fnl '99 start (mdn, rtd 75), gelded since: half-brother to wng miler Cad Oro: eff at 6f on firm & soft/hvy, any trk. **93**

982 **DONT SURRENDER 17** [5] J L Dunlop 3-9-1 (90) G Carter 9/4 FAV: 211-02: 3 b c Zieten - St Clair Star (Sallust) Well plcd, led on bit 2f out, under press & hdd ins last: back to form: acts on firm & gd/soft. 1½ **93**

4355} **MISTER SUPERB 206** [7] V Soane 3-8-7 (82) S Sanders 14/1: 5640-3: 3 ch c Superlative - Kiveton Komet (Precocious) Off the pace till ran on well appr fnl 1f, nvr nrr: op 10/1, reapp: 4th of 15th in '99 (mdn, rtd 83): eff at 6f, further sure to suit (half-brother to a miler): goes on firm/fast grnd. 2½ **79**

982 **LAUNFAL 17** [1] R Hannon 3-9-3 (92) R Hughes 16/1: 325-04: Held up, imprvd ent fnl 2f, switched bef dist, no extra towards fin: '99 debut wnr at Windsor (mdn, Gr 3 3rd, rtd 97): eff at 5/6f, stays 7f: goes on firm & soft grnd, any trk: useful, sharper for this. ½ **88**

3856} **HERITAGE PARK 240** [4] 3-8-6 (81) L Newman (5) 16/1: 2156-5: Rear, prog & ev ch appr fnl 1f, sn onepace: reapp, stablemate 4th: '99 Sandown wnr (auct mdn, rtd 86): eff at 5/7f on fast & gd grnd, gall trk. 1½ **74**

994 **LAKELAND PADDY 15** [6] 3-8-1 (76)(1oh) Dale Gibson 9/2: 56-336: Al arnd same pl: bckd from 13/2. *1* **65**

105 **WAFFLES OF AMIN 165** [3] 3-8-4 (79) C Rutter 16/1: 2316-7: Mid-div, eff 3f out, late rally: over 5 mth abs. *nk* **69**

954 **ALPHILDA 19** [2] 3-8-5 (80) N Pollard 10/1: 220-08: Rear, nowhere to go from 2f out till 1f out, nvr dngrs. *hd* **70**

1098 **CHORUS 5** [12] 3-8-0 (77) Cheryl Nosworthy (7) 16/1: 44-209: Al towards rear: see 888. ¾ **63**

982 **HUNTING TIGER 17** [9] 3-8-10 (85) Craig Williams 14/1: 52-000: In tch till 3f out: 10th, see 792. *7* **58**

4214} **ENDYMION 218** [11] 3-8-0 (77) A Nicholls (3) 16/1: U030-0: Led till halfway, fdd: 11th, reapp: plcd in '99 (nurs, rtd 77): eff at 5f/6f, shld get further (half-sister to a 10f wnr): acts on firm/fast grnd. ½ **47**

*909 **EXORCET 23** [13] 3-8-13 (88) G Duffield 4/1: 00-10: Front rank, led after halfway till bef fnl 2f, sn btn: 12th on h'cap bow: much faster grnd than when scored in 909 (soft). 3½ **53**

12 ran Time 1m 12.53 (0.43) (Miss B Swire) G B Balding Fyfield, Hants.

1179

4.30 WINCANTON MDN 3YO (D) 1m4f Firm 04 +02 Fast
£3558 £1095 £547 £273

1017 **FILM SCRIPT 13** [3] R Charlton 3-8-9 R Hughes 7/2: 61: 3 b f Unfuwain - Success Story (Sharrood) Made ev yd, rdn appr fnl 1f, flashed tail, not extended: apprec step up to 12f on firm grnd with forcing tactics. **94**

1017 **MBELE 13** [6] W R Muir 3-9-0 Martin Dwyer 5/2 FAV: 2-32: 3 b c Mtoto - Majestic Image (Niniski) Chsd ldrs, lost pl 3f out, rallied bef dist: well bckd,clr rem, jockey given 2 day whip ban: eff at 12f on firm & soft. 1½ **94**

916 **BOX BUILDER 23** [2] M R Channon 3-9-0 Craig Williams 5/1: 33: 3 ch c Fraam - Ena Olley (Le Moss) Prom, keen, under press 2f out, no impress: tchd 6/1: better on debut in 916 (soft grnd). *7* **84**

1017 **ICE CRYSTAL 13** [4] H Candy 3-9-0 C Rutter 20/1: 004: Handy till 2f out: h'cap qualifying run. *hd* **84$**

-- **JARDINES LOOKOUT** [1] 3-9-0 R Mullen 33/1: 5: Ran in snatches, nvr troubled ldrs: debut: Ir 20,000gns Fourstars Allstar gelding with A Jarvis. *1* **82**

4142} **MORNINGSIDE 221** [11] 3-8-9 N Pollard 12/1: 6-6: Pld hard, nvr dngrs: reapp: 6th sole '99 start. *nk* **77$**

916 **RAINBOW SPIRIT 23** [10] 3-9-0 G Duffield 25/1: 0-57: Nvr troubled ldrs: h'caps next. ¾ **81$**

4556} **LANELLE 190** [7] 3-8-9 R Havlin 9/1: 0-8: Dwelt, imprvd & ev ch 4f out, wknd ent fnl 2f: 9th sole '99 start (rtd 83): related to smart stayer Landowner: type to do better in staying h'caps. ¾ **75**

1017 **LAFLEUR 13** [5] 3-8-9 A Daly 14/1: 0-09: Dwelt, brief effort 4f out: op 10/1, st/mate 3rd, now h'capped. *4* **69**

858 **MISTER WEBB 27** [9] 3-9-0 J Stack 33/1: 64-50: Pulled hard bhd ldrs, lost pl 3f out: 10th, nds sellers. 1½ **72$**

964 **BUSY LIZZIE 19** [8] 3-8-9 G Carter 4/1: 00-20: Al bhd: 11th, much btr 964 (soft). ½ **66**

11 ran Time 2m 34.64 (0.24) (The Queen) R Charlton Beckhampton, Wilts.

1180

5.05 WESSEX HCAP 4YO+ 0-90 (C) 1m6f Firm 04 -24 Slow [89]
£7572 £2330 £1165 £582 4 yo rec 1 lb

968 **AFTERJACKO 18** [12] D R C Elsworth 4-9-7 (83) N Pollard 3/1 FAV: 153-51: 4 ch g Seattle Dancer - Shilka (Soviet Star) Towards rear, imprvd appr fnl 2f, kept on gamely for press to lead ins fnl 1f, won on the nod: '99 Bath wnr (mdn, rtd 83): eff at 12f/14f on firm, gd/soft grnd, stiff trks: lightly rcd & improving. **88**

968 **TEMPLE WAY 18** [9] R Charlton 4-8-12 (74) S Sanders 10/1: 420-02: 4 b g Shirley Heights - Abbey Strand (Shadeed) Mid-div, imprvd to lead appr fnl 1f till below dist, rallied under press, just btn: '99 Chepstow wnr (1st time blnks, h'cap, rtd 76 at best): eff at 14f/2m, acts on firm/fast grnd, with/without blnks: any trk. *shd* **78**

791 **RARE GENIUS 38** [13] P W Harris 4-8-4 (66) G Duffield 13/2: 052-23: 4 ch g Beau Genius - Aunt Nola (Olden Times) Prom, led 2½f out till bef dist, no extra ins last: op 8/1: see 791. *2* **67**

714 **DANEGOLD 44** [18] M R Channon 8-7-13 (60) Martin Dwyer 7/1: 000-04: Rr, late hdwy, nvr a threat. 1½ **59**

3495} **SPY KNOLL 260** [1] 6-8-11 (72) O Urbina 14/1: /200-5: Prom, ev ch 2f out, same pace: rnr-up on reapp last term (h'cap, rtd 76, Mrs Richards): missed '98, '97 Chester wnr (mdn, rtd 93, Sir M Stoute): eff at 14f, gets 2m: acts on fast & gd/soft grnd, without visor: with J Poulton. *shd* **71**

4275} **ANGE DHONOR 213** [8] 5-7-11 (58) A Daly 12/1: 5300-6: In tch, eff 3f out, unable to chall: plcd last term (mdn, rtd 73 at best): rnr-up sole '98 start (mdn, rtd 79): tried hdles: eff at 12f, stays 14f on fast. ½ **56**

968 **ANGELS VENTURE 18** [2] 4-9-5 (81) R Hughes 16/1: 321-07: Al mid-div, '99 wnr at Yarmouth (mdn) & Brighton (appr h'cap, rtd 84, S Woods): rtd 88 sole juv start: eff at 12f on firm, soft, any trk: good weight carrier, goes well for an apprentice: now with J Jenkins. *2* **77**

1940} **TALES OF BOUNTY 330** [6] 5-7-13 (60) R Thomas (3) 25/1: /066-8: Rear, prog 3f out, nvr nr ldrs: stablemate of wnr: 11 wk jumps abs, scored at Exeter (2m1f nov on gd/soft grnd, rtd 113h): unplcd in '99 (h'cap, rtd 61): plcd in '98 (h'cap, rtd 68): eff at 12f on fast & gd grnd: with D Elsworth. *hd* **56**

4618} **MANE FRAME 183** [15] 5-8-5 (66) D Harrison 12/1: 4264-9: Led till appr fnl 2f, wknd: reapp: '99 wnr at Windsor (class stks), Warwick & Sandown (h'caps, rtd 68): '98 rnr-up (mdn, rtd 73): eff at 12f, stays 14f, stays 2m: acts on fast & hvy grnd, any trk, likes sharp ones/forcing the pace. 2½ **59**

714 **DISTANT STORM 44** [7] 7-7-10 (57)(bl)(4oh) A Polli (5) 16/1: 222-40: Rear, wide prog 4f out, wknd bef 2f out: 10th, 2 wks jumps absence, see 714. *nk* **50**

1044 **ROMERO 9** [11] 4-8-0 (62) P Doe 10/1: 360-W0: Prom till 2f out: 11th: see 1044. *shd* **55**

*860 **LE KHOUMF 27** [10] 9-7-10 (57) A Nicholls (3) 10/1: 0/5-10: In tch till 3f out: 12th: see 860 (gd/sft). *shd* **50**

714 **STAR RAGE 44** [16] 10-9-10 (85) R Ffrench 9/1: 131-60: Bhd fnl 4f: 13th, 6 wk abs, top-weight. 3½ **74**

-- **United Front** [5] 8-7-10 (57)(t)(2oh) Dale Gibson 50/1:

4113} **Mu Tadil 223** [4] 8-7-10 (57)(22oh) R Brisland(5) 66/1:

SALISBURY   SUNDAY MAY 7TH   Righthand, Galloping Track, Stiff Finish

3370} **Noteworthy 267** [3] 4-8-3 (65) C Rutter 25/1:   2640} **Sawlajan 299** [17] 9-7-10 (57)(5oh) P M Quinn (5) 50/1:
17 ran   Time 3m 01.96 (3.96)   (Sports Adviser)   D R C Elsworth Whitsbury, Hants.

1181   5.35 WOODFORD MDN DIV 2 3YO+ (D)   6f str   Firm 04   -23 Slow
£3233   £995   £497   £248   3 yo rec 10lb   Raced far side, high no's favoured

--   **WELCOME FRIEND** [20] R Charlton 3-8-12 W Ryan 7/4 FAV: 1: 3 b c Kingmambo - Kingscote (King's   **91 +**
Lake) Mid-div, jmpd path halfway, switched & qcknd to lead appr fnl 1f, cmftbly: debut: half-brother to a
Classic plcd colt: eff at 6f, will get further: acts on firm grnd, stiff trk: goes well fresh: promising.
4339} **EL GRAN PAPA 208** [18] J H M Gosden 3-8-12 R Havlin 6/1: 53-2: 3 b c El Gran Senor - Banner Hit   1¾   85
(Oh Say) Sn prom, prog & switched ent fnl 2f, sn carried left, kept on: reapp: plcd fnl '99 start (mdn, rtd 83):
eff at 6f, return to 7f will suit: acts on firm & gd/soft grnd: shown enough to win a maiden.
1021   **BUDELLI 13** [17] M R Channon 3-8-12 Craig Williams 10/1: 5-3623: 3 b c Elbio - Eves Temptation   1¼   81$
(Glenstal) Bhd ldrs, went left 2f out, kept on towards fin: tchd 14/1: 7f may suit: acts on firm & hvy grnd.
--   **THE ROXBURGH** [10] J A R Toller 3-8-12 R Ffrench 8/1: 4: Struggled to go pace till ran on   nk   81
fnl 1½f: debut: Known Fact IR 50,000gns colt: goes on firm grnd, 7f+ is going to suit.
4408} **STRAND OF GOLD 202** [6] 3-8-12 R Smith (5) 25/1: 0204-5: Feeling pace rear, some late hdwy, nvr   1½   77$
on terms: reapp: '99 mdn auct rnr-up (rtd 80$ & 63): half-brother to 3 wng sprinters: eff at 6f on gd/soft grnd.
--   **INDIAN DRIVE** [9] 3-8-12 R Hughes 11/1: 6: Dwelt & bhd till styd on/drifted left fnl 1½f: debut: nk   77
Indian Ridge brother to a 7f/1m wnr: with R Hannon.
1835} **CALIWAG 334** [14] 4-9-8 N Pollard 20/1: 4650-7: Prom, ev ch 2f out, fdd: reapp: 4th of 17   1   74
on debut last term (mdn, rtd 80$): half-brother to sprinters: yet to find a trip: with D Elsworth.
4600} **JAZZY MILLENNIUM 185** [11] 3-8-12 R Mullen 9/1: 4220-8: Cl-up, led briefly 1½f out, wknd: op 6/1   nk   74
on reapp: dual '99 rnr-up (mdn, rtd 86): eff at 7f on fast & gd grnd: with Miss G Kelleway.
837   **VIKING PRINCE 30** [8] 3-8-12 P Dobbs (5) 33/1: 00-009: Prom till 2f out: stiff task.   1½   70$
4171} **NATURAL 220** [12] 3-8-12 D Williamson (7) 25/1: 0-0: Nvr better than mid-div: 10th, reapp, new stable.   shd   70
837   **DESERT NORTH 30** [15] 3-8-12 O Urbina 14/1: 00: Front rank, led briefly 2f out: 11th, op 25/1.   nk   69
3985} **BLUE DOVE 232** [16] 3-8-7 D Harrison 33/1: 0-0: Led till 2f out, wknd qckly: 12th, reapp.   1¼   60
--   **SUAVE SHOT** [4] 3-8-7 G Duffield 12/1: 0: Al bhd: 18th.   0
--   Father Ted [3] 3-8-12 A Daly 50/1:   934   Napper Blossom 20 [13] 3-8-7 Kathleen McDermott (7) 50/1:
--   Mint Leaf [19] 3-8-7 C Rutter 16/1:   --   Ejder [1] 4-9-3 S Carson (5) 66/1:
--   To The Stars [7] 3-8-7 G Carter 33/1:
18 ran   Time 1m 13.76 (1.66)   (K Abdulla)   R Charlton Beckhampton, Wilts.

NEWMARKET (ROWLEY)   SUNDAY MAY 7TH   Righthand, Stiff, Galloping Track

Official Going   GOOD. Stalls: Stands Side, except 12f - Far Side.

1182   2.00 CURTIS RTD HCAP 4YO+ 0-110 (B)   6f   Firm 01   +01 Fast   [116]
£9439   £3580   £1790   £813   Raced stands side

2744} **DOCTOR SPIN 295** [2] R F Johnson Houghton 4-8-10 (98) J Reid 16/1: 6340-1: 4 b c Namaqualand -   108
Madam Loving (Vaigly Great) Trkd ldrs, al travelling well, led over 1f out, styd on strongly inside last, rdn out:
bckd from 20/1, reapp, fair time: plcd twice in '99 (rtd 99, Wokingham h'cap, subs suffered a chipped knee):
'98 wnr at Windsor (mdn) & Lingfield (nov auct stks, rtd 100): eff at 5/6f, stays a sharp 7f: acts on firm & gd
grnd, any trk: runs well fresh: decisive wnr today, v useful colt, progressive & can win in Listed company.
-702   **SHEER VIKING 45** [1] B W Hills 4-8-7 (95) M Hills 11/2 FAV: 000-22: 4 b g Danehill - Schlefalora   2   98
(Mas Media) Chsd ldrs, rdn/chsd wnr final 1f, al held: nicely bckd tho' op 4/1: 6 wk abs: acts on firm
& gd/soft: improved again & stays 6f but all wins at 5f & a return to that trip could suit: see 702.
4395} **HO LENG 204** [12] Miss L A Perratt 5-9-1 (103) M J Kinane 15/2: 0053-3: 5 b g Statoblest - Indigo Blue   hd   105
(Bluebird) Sn handy, rdn/kept on from over 1f out, not pace of wnr: reapp: '99 York wnr (rtd h'cap, rtd 106):
'98 wnr at York & also at Newmarket (val h'caps, rtd 109): suited by 6/7f, stays 1m: acts on firm & gd, prob
unsuited by softer: likes a stiff/gall trk, especially York & Hamilton: tough/genuine & useful performer.
1016   **HARMONIC WAY 13** [10] R Charlton 5-8-13 (101) J Fortune 8/1: 200-64: Held up, swtchd/kept on fnl 2f.   ¾   101
914   **FIRST MAITE 23** [7] 7-8-12 (100)(bl) J P Spencer 16/1: 324465: Led 4f, held 1f out: op 14/1: see 734.   1   98
1049   **CRETAN GIFT 8** [5] 9-9-7 (109)(vis) T G McLaughlin 10/1: 035146: Held up, effort 2f out, no impress.   1   105
1013   **ELLENS LAD 13** [9] 6-8-7 (95)(1oh) Pat Eddery 8/1: 12-057: Held up, outpcd 2f out, late gains, no threat.   ½   89
4469} **DELEGATE 196** [6] 7-8-12 (100) K Fallon 15/2: 3630-8: Hmpd start, held up in tch, rdn/no impress fnl   ½   92
2f: reapp: plcd twice in '99 for J E Banks (rtd 109, Listed): rtd 96 on sole '98 start (Brit bow): ex-French, won
sole juv start at Chantilly: eff at 5f, suited by 6f: acts on firm & gd: wore colt with N A Callaghan.
1004   **BON AMI 13** [11] 4-8-7 (95)(3oh) J Carroll 8/1: 0-0049: Prom 4f: bckd from 25/1: see 1004.   1   85
1016   **BLACKHEATH 13** [8] 4-8-7 (95)(1oh) S Whitworth 5/1: 330-00: Chsd ldrs 4f: 10th: tchd 14/1: see 1016.   1   83
702   **FURTHER OUTLOOK 45** [3] 6-8-10 (98) K Darley 14/1: 060-00: Slowly away, effort halfway, sn held: ½   84
11th: op 10/1, 6 wk abs: '99 h'cap scorer at Pontefract, Epsom & Doncaster (rtd h'cap, rtd 101): plcd in '98
(h'caps, rtd 84, Mrs A Perrett): stays 1m, suited by 5/6f: acts on firm, gd/soft & probably hvy: handles any trk:
likes to race with/force the pace & slow start definitely hindered him here, sharper next time: with D Nicholls.
728   **ROYAL RESULT 43** [13] 7-8-7 (95)(4oh) F Norton 12/1: 130-00: Chsd ldrs 4f: 12th: op 14/1, 6 wk abs.   1½   77
180   **OCKER 146** [4] 6-8-8 (94) R Fitzpatrick (3) 33/1: 4600-0: Bolted to post, chsd ldrs 3f: 13th: reapp.   6   67
13 ran   Time 1m 10.80 (0.0)   (Anthony Pye-Jeary)   R F Johnson Houghton Blewbury, Oxon.

1183   2.30 MAIL ON SUNDAY HCAP 3YO 0-90 (C)   1m str   Firm 01   -05 Slow   [95]
£15665   £4820   £2410   £1205   Majority racing centre always just ahead.

727   **ATAVUS 43** [25] W R Muir 3-8-12 (79) G Mosse 20/1: 531-41: 3 b c Distant Relative - Elysian (Northfields)   86
Trkd ldrs centre, led over 2f out, styd on gamely inside last, rdn out: op 16/1, 6 wk abs: h'cap bow: '99 scorer
at Lingfield (auct mdn, rtd 84): eff at 7f/1m, stays 9f & connections feel 10f will suit: acts on firm & gd, poss
soft: handles a sharp or stiff/gall trk: runs well fresh: progressive & potentially useful colt, rate more highly.
4558} **RED N SOCKS 190** [14] J L Dunlop 3-9-4 (85) T Quinn 14/1: 4510-2: 3 ch c Devil's Bag - Racing Blue   nk   91
(Reference Point) Mid-div centre, rdn/prog to chall final 2f, ev ch inside last, just held: op 12/1, reapp: '99
Yarmouth scorer (nursery, rtd 84): eff at 1m, tried 10f, could yet suit: acts on firm & fast grnd & a stiff/gall
trk: runs well fresh: progressive type, can find compensation.

*962   **MOON SOLITAIRE** 19 [9] E A L Dunlop 3-8-10 (77) M J Kinane 14/1: 6-413: 3 b c Night Shift - Gay   2   79
Fantastic (Ela-Mana-Mou): Prom stands side, led that group 3f out, rdn & styd on well inside last, not pace of
first 2 centre: nicely bckd, tchd 20/1: fine h'cap bow on unfavoured stands side: acts on firm & soft: see 962.

983   **FREDDY FLINTSTONE** 17 [6] R Hannon 3-8-8 (75) Dane O'Neill 12/1: 05-04: Chsd ldrs stands side,   nk   76
rdn & kept on well inside last: op 9/1: fine h'cap bow: outpcd in '99 (rtd 81, mdn): styd lngr 1m trip well, 10f +
could suit: acts on firm grnd & a stiff/gall trk: should find a race.

4569} **ALL THE GEARS** 188 [10] J H M Gosden 3-9-4 (85) K Fallon 9/1 FAV: 023-5: Stands side, rdn/ch over 1f out, kept on: 1¼   83
hvly bckd: reapp/h'cap bow: plcd twice in '99 (rtd 87, mdn): styd lngr 1m trip: acts on firm & soft grnd.

4583} **KAREEB** 187 [21] J Weaver 33/1: 2324-6: Held up centre, swtchd/eyecatching prog   shd   81
over 2f out, ch inside last, onepace: stablemate of wnr: reapp: rnr-up 3 times in '99 (rtd 84, mdn): styd lngr 1m
trip: acts on firm & gd, disapp sole soft grnd start: handles a sharp or stiff/gall trk: drop to 7f could suit.

954   **ROYAL INSULT** 19 [30] 3-9-3 (84) N Callan 25/1: 21-07: Prom centre, onepace final 2f: left reapp   1¼   79
bhd: '99 Redcar wnr (mdn, rtd 86): eff at 6f, stays stiff 1m: acts on firm, fast & handles soft, prob any trk.

3640} **INCHING CLOSER** 252 [24] 3-8-11 (78) J Mackay (7) 25/1: 524-8: Held up centre, effort/onepace final   1   71
2f: bckd at long odds, reapp/h'cap bow: outpcd in '99 (rtd 83, mdn): 1m will suit this term: handles gd grnd.

4380} **KELTIC BARD** 205 [20] 3-8-10 (77) R Fitzpatrick (3) 25/1: 2210-9: Led centre 5f, held 1f out: reapp: hd   69
'99 W'hampton wnr (AW nov auct stks, rtd 88a, rnr-up twice on turf, rtd 80): eff at 7f/8.5f on firm, fast & fibresand.

4041} **SOVEREIGN STATE** 229 [29] 3-8-7 (74) M Tebbutt 20/1: 6514-0: Prom side, onepace final 2f: 10th: ¾   65
reapp: '99 Thirsk wnr (mdn, rtd 81): eff at 1m on firm grnd, poss handles soft.

994   **INDIAN SUN** 15 [27] 3-8-12 (79) Pat Eddery 14/1: 10-460: Hld up cntre, mod gains, hands/heels ride: 11th. 1½   67

3632} **KATHIR** 253 [18] 3-9-4 (85) R Hills 10/1: 21-0: Chsd ldrs centre 7f: 12th: nicely bckd, op 12/1: reapp/   nk   72
h'cap bow: won 2nd of 2 '99 starts at Nottingham (mdn, rtd 84): eff at 1m, 10f + could suit: acts on fast & gd grnd.

912   **SCOTTISH SPICE** 23 [28] 3-9-7 (88) K Darley 20/1: 411-60: Held up centre, nvr pace to chall: 13th.   hd   74

4601} **MUST BE MAGIC** 185 [12] 3-8-2 (69) W Supple 33/1: 4300-0: Prom centre 6f: 14th: reapp.   nk   54

*717   **RUSHMORE** 44 [17] 3-8-13 (80) J Fortune 10/1: 3-10: Held up centre, rdn/held 2f out: 15th: abs.   ½   64

3758} **SHOTACROSS THE BOW** 246 [11] 3-8-10 (77) M Hills 16/1: 041-0: Stands side, nvr factor: 16th: reapp.   nk   60

954   **I PROMISE YOU** 19 [19] 3-8-6 (73) O Peslier 14/1: 35-100: Prom centre 6f: 17th: btr 792 (7f, gd).   1¼   53

4140} **KIND REGARDS** 222 [14] 3-9-5 (86) J Reid 14/1: 5214-0: Chsd ldrs 6f: 18th: tchd 16/1, reapp.   1   64

*1010   **ROSHANI** 13 [15] 3-8-11 (78) L Dettori 12/1: 30-210: Chsd ldrs centre halfway, sn held: 23rd: op 10/1.   0

884   **HYPERSONIC** 25 [2] 3-8-13 (80) M Roberts 25/1: 423-00: Led stands side 4f, sn btn: 25th: mdn.   0

4376} **PRINCIPLE ACCOUNT** 205 [8] 3-8-9 (76) J P Spencer 33/1: 2306-P: Stands side/sn rdn rear, bhd/p.u. 1f out.   0

4433} Azur 201 [3] 3-9-2 (83) R Cochrane 16/1:   804 Sutton Common 37 [7] 3-8-10 (77) J Carroll 12/1:
1053 Celebes 8 [13] 3-8-3 (70) D Sweeney 16/1:   4269} Top Of The Class 214 [5] 3-8-2 (68)(1ow) J F Egan 33/1:
954   Joey Tribbiani 19 [1] 3-8-0 (67) N Carlisle 50/1:   957 Sharp Risk 19 [26] 3-8-8 (75) A Clark 33/1:
994   Alawar 15 [22] 3-8-1 (68)(t) F Norton 33/1:
28 ran   Time 1m 36.95 (0.45)

(Stableside Racing Partnership II)   W R Muir Lambourn, Berks.

1184   3.05 LISTED PRETTY POLLY STKS 3YO (A)   1m2f   Firm 01   -18 Slow
£16240   £6160   £3080   £1400

--   **MELIKAH** [3] Saeed bin Suroor 3-8-8 L Dettori 5/4 FAV: 1: 3 ch f Lammtarra - Urban Sea (Miswaki)   106+
Chsd ldrs, pshd along 4f out, rdn & styd on strgly ins last to reel in ldr, led line: nicely bckd, Rules bow: recently
rnr-up in a Godolphin trial: bred in the purple: eff at 10f, 12f + will suit: acts on firm grnd, stiff/gall trk:
runs well fresh: well regarded Oaks entry, clearly v useful & will improve for a stronger gallop & further.

704   **CLOG DANCE** 45 [7] B W Hills 3-8-8 M Hills 6/1: 32-22: 3 b f Pursuit Of Love - Discomatic (Roberto)   hd   105
Chsd ldrs, led over 3f out, rdn inside last & hdd line: nicely bckd, tchd 7/1, 6 wk abs: clearly relished step up
to 10f, 12f may suit: acts on firm & gd/soft grnd: remarkably still a mdn but is a useful/progressive filly.

4326} **CLIPPER** 208 [2] B W Hills 3-8-8 J Reid 16/1: 01-03: 3 b f Salse - Yawl (Rainbow Quest)   2½   101
Held up, rdn/outpcd 2f out, kept on well inside last: op 14/1, stablemate of rnr-up: reapp: won 2nd of 2
'99 starts at Ayr (fillies mdn, rtd 89): eff over lngr 10f trip, stoutly bred & 12f + looks sure to suit: acts
on firm & soft grnd & a gall/stiff trk: fine reapp, useful filly, set to improve further when tackling 12f +.

3443} **NAVAL AFFAIR** 263 [6] Sir Michael Stoute 3-8-8 K Fallon 4/1: 31-4: Held up, rdn/chsd ldr 2f out,   shd   101
onepace/held inside last: hvly bckd, tchd 11/2: reapp: won 2nd of 2 '99 starts at Kempton (fillies mdn,
rtd 83): styd lngr 10f trip, may get further: handles firm & soft grnd & a gall/easy trk: useful filly.

4201} **EVERLASTING LOVE** 218 [8] 3-8-8 M Fenton 8/1: 4120-5: Held up, keen, rdn & kept on final 2f, not   nk   100
pace to chall: op 13/2, reapp: '99 Redcar wnr (nov med auct stks, subs rnr-up in a Gr 3, rtd 99): styd lngr 10f
trip, 12f + should suit (stoutly bred): useful, 12f + could bring more improvement.

3645} **HYPNOTIZE** 252 [1] 3-8-13 Pat Eddery 14/1: 6115-6: Held up, rdn/no impress final 2f: op 12/1,   6   96
stablemate of 4th: reapp: '99 wnr at Yarmouth (fillies mdn) & Sandown (conds stks, rtd 95): eff at 7f,
shld get further (dam a 10f wnr): acts on fast & gd grnd & a stiff/gall trk.

1045 **TITIAN ANGEL** 9 [5] 3-8-8 M Tebbutt 66/1: 2-67: Led 4f out, sn hdd/fdd final 2f: highly tried: mdn.   1¼   89$

4257} **CAUNTON** 215 [4] 3-8-8 R Cochrane 100/1: 040-8: Led 6f, btn 2f out: reapp: unplcd for M Bell in   11   77$
'99 (rtd 73, fillies mdn): mid-dist bred: highly tried here for P Howling.
8 ran   Time 2m 04.00 (1.9)   (Godolphin)   Saeed bin Suroor Newmarket.

1185   3.45 GR 1 SAGITTA 1000 GUINEAS 3YO (A)   1m str   Firm 01   +02 Fast
£145000   £55000   £27500   £12500 Field raced stands side

913   **LAHAN** 23 [10] J H M Gosden 3-9-0 R Hills 14/1: 11-41: 3 b f Unfuwain - Amanah (Mr Prospector)   120
Held up racing keenly, no room over 2f out, gd prog to lead over 1f out & rdn clr inside last, styd on strongly: hvly
bckd, gd time: put below-par soft grnd reapp firmly bhd her: unbtn juv, won at Redcar (fill mdn) & Newmarket
(Gr 2 Rockfel, rtd 109, flashed tail): eff at 7f/1m, reportedly likely to remain at such trips: acts on firm
& fast, disapp on soft: likes a stiff/gall trk: high class, take plenty of beating in the Coronation Stakes.

953   **PRINCESS ELLEN** 19 [5] G A Butler 3-9-0 K Darley 66/1: 105-02: 3 b f Tirol - Celt Song (Unfuwain)   1¼   116
Rdn chsg ldrs halfway, styd on well for press over 1f out, not reach wnr: eff at 7f/1m: acts on firm &
fast grnd: left reapp bhd: smart filly, sure to find a Group race: Irish Guineas is the next target: see 953.

+953 **PETRUSHKA** 19 [16] Sir Michael Stoute 3-9-0 K Fallon 6/4 FAV: 1-13: 3 ch f Unfuwain - Ballet Shoes   3   110
(Ela Mana Mou): Held up, rdn/bmpd over 2f out, no room over 1f out, styd on for press ins last, no threat: reportedly
in season: styd lngr 1m trip: acts on firm but was well below impressive win in '99 (7f, gd/soft), btn rnr-up).

953   **SEAZUN** 19 [15] M R Channon 3-9-0 J Reid 10/1: 121-24: Bhd ldrs, rdn/ch 2f out, kept on onepace: ½   109
tchd 12/1: stays 1m: could reoppose today's 2nd in Irish Guineas: also bhd todays 3rd in 953.

4201} **HIGH WALDEN** 218 [12] 3-9-0 T Quinn 9/1: W412-5: Held up, prog/rdn 2f out, sn onepace/held: reapp: ¾   108
'99 Leicester wnr (fillies mdn, subs rtd 103) rnr-up in a Listed contest): shld get further: acts on

firm & gd/soft grnd, stiff/gall trk: v useful filly who could improve when tackling further.
915 **VELVET LADY 23** [2] 3-9-0 J Fortune 50/1: 26: Led, rdn/hdd over 1f out & no extra inside last: *shd* **107**
styd lngr 1m trip, should get further: handles firm & soft grnd: mdn a formality on this evidence: see 915.
4137} **TORGAU 222** [7] 3-9-0 O Peslier 25/1: 6122-7: Trkd ldrs, lost pl 2f out, late rally: reapp: '99 wnr *1½* **105**
at Catterick (nov stks) & Newmarket (Gr 2, subs rnr-up in a Gr 1, rtd 112): eff at 6/7f, worth another try at 1m:
suit: acts on firm & gd grnd & has run well fresh: handles any trk: smart filly at best.
*948 **AMETHYST 21** [1] 3-9-0 M J Kinane 10/1: 243-18: Trkd ldrs, no extra final 1f: op 8/1: see 948 (soft). *nk* **104**
4245} **CHEZ CHERIE 217** [18] 3-9-0 G Mosse 66/1: 145-9: Held up, effort 2f out, held/eased fnl 1f: reapp: *hd* **103**
'99 Goodwood wnr (debut, fillies mdn, subs rtd 106 when unplcd in a Longchamp Gr 1 contest): eff at 7f, stays
1m: acts on firm & hvy grnd & handles a sharp/gall trk: prev with P W Chapple Hyam, now with L M Cumani.
4400} **ICICLE 204** [8] 3-9-0 R Cochrane 66/1: 6214-0: Held up, effort 2f out, sn held: 10th: reapp: *shd* **103**
'99 wnr at Folkestone (mdn, debut) & Goodwood (Gr 3, subs rtd 106 when 4th in a Gr 2): eff at 7f, shld stay
1m: acts on fast & gd grnd: has run well fresh: handles a stiff or sharp trk: with J Fanshawe.
*934 **CLARANET 20** [11] 3-9-0 F Norton 200/1: 4-3310: Chsd ldr, rdn/fdd final 1f: 11th: see 934 (hvy). *shd* **102$**
858 **MOSELLE 27** [4] 3-9-0 J P Spencer 100/1: 3-20: Dwelt/held up, rdn/no room 2f out, mod gains, no *nk* **101**
threat: 12th: no luck in running, return to 10f+ sure to suit: mdn a formality: highly tried after 858 (auct mdn).
4201} **AGRIPPINA 218** [9] 3-9-0 J Weaver 33/1: 211-0: Held up/keen, swtchd halfway, effort 2f out, btn/ *¾* **100**
eased final 1f: 13th: reapp: '99 wnr at Ayr (mdn) & Newmarket (Listed, rtd 104): eff at 7f, dam a 12f wnr & 1m+
should suit: acts on fast, likes gd/soft & soft & stiff/gall trks: worth another chance on an easier surface.
953 **HALLAND PARK GIRL 19** [14] 3-9-0 Dane O'Neill 66/1: 111-60: Held up, hmpd 2f out, btn/eased fnl 1f: 14th. *¾* **99**
953 **AUNTY ROSE 19** [3] 3-9-0 Pat Eddery 20/1: 130-30: Dwelt/held up, prog/no room over 2f out, btn *nk* **98**
final 1f: 15th: well bckd at long odds, op 33/1: btr 953 (7f, gd).
4245} **ISSEY ROSE 217** [6] 3-9-0 A Clark 66/1: 3140-0: Chsd ldrs 6f: 16th: reapp, highly tried. *1¾* **95**
4245} **MILETRIAN 217** [17] 3-9-0 M Roberts 66/1: 2514-0: Dwelt/held up, al towards rear: 17th: reapp. *3* **89**
-- **BINTALREEF** [13] 3-9-0 L Dettori 5/2: 1-0: Sn prom, rdn 3f out & btn/hmpd 2f out: 18th: hvly bckd: *3* **83**
stewards enquired into running, jockey reported filly nvr travelling: reapp: recent impressive wnr of a Godolphin
trial in Dubai: won sole '99 start in France (7f mdn, Deauville, D Loder): eff at 7f on gd grnd, 1m+ should suit
this term: something clearly amiss here, well regarded by powerful team & worth another chance.
18 ran Time 1m 36.38 (u0.12) (Hamdan Al Maktoum) J H M Gosden Manton, Wilts.

1186 **4.20 MAY CLASSIFED STKS 3YO 0-95 (B) 7f str Firm 01 -25 Slow**
£10286 £3165 £1582 £791

4310} **SPENCERS WOOD 209** [4] P J Makin 3-8-11 Pat Eddery 10/1: 1-1: 3 b c Pips Pride - Ascoli (Skyliner) **98**
Held up, prog to lead inside last, styd on well, rdn out: nicely bckd, op 12/1: reapp: sole start wnr in '99 at
Windsor (mdn, readily, rtd 89+): eff over lngr 7f trip, may get further (dam won up to 10f): acts on firm & gd grnd
& a stiff or sharp trk: runs well fresh: useful, prgreesive, unbeaten colt, type for the Gr 3 Jersey stks at Ascot.
955 **ACROBATIC 19** [9] J R Fanshawe 3-9-1 R Cochrane 100/30: 16-62: 3 br c Warning - Ayodhya (Astronef) *½* **100**
Handy, led 2f out, rdn/hdd inside last, kept on well for press: hvly bckd, tchd 4/1: useful colt: see 955.
4171} **QAMOUS 220** [7] E A L Dunlop 3-8-11 R Hills 2/1 FAV: 41-3: 3 gr c Bahri - Bel Ray (Restivo) *1¾* **93**
Held up, rdn/chsd ldrs over 1f out, hung right/held inside last: hvly bckd, tchd 5/2: reapp: won on 2nd of 2
'99 starts at Newmarket (mdn, rtd 91): eff at 7f, stays 1m: acts on firm & gd grnd, stiff/gall trk.
955 **LOVE YOU TOO 19** [3] S P C Woods 3-8-8 J Reid 33/1: 540-04: Led 5f, sn outpcd by front trio: '99 *4* **82**
debut wnr for A Kelleway at Doncaster (auct mdn, rtd 92 at best, Listed): eff at 5/6f, shld get 7f: acts
on fast & gd grnd & a gall trk: has run well fresh.
4137} **BAILEYS WHIRLWIND 222** [8] 3-8-9 M Fenton 14/1: 0110-5: Held up, rdn/ch 2f out, no extra inside *½* **82**
last: op 20/1, reapp: '99 wnr at Windsor (nov auct mdn) & Yarmouth (conds stks, rtd 92 at best): eff at 6f, this
lngr 7f trip should suit: acts on firm & soft grnd & a sharp/fair trk: has run well fresh.
4487} **MARAH 197** [1] 3-8-8 W Supple 9/1: 1306-6: Cl-up, fdd final 2f: op 8/1, reapp: '99 debut wnr at *4* **73**
Doncaster (4 rnr fillies mdn, subs rtd 92 at best, Listed): eff at 7f, bred for 1m+: acts on fast, poss hvy.
4286} **CONNECT 211** [2] 3-8-11 T Quinn 8/1: 2136-7: Held up, eff 2f out, sn btn: reapp: '99 Pontefract wnr *½* **75**
(med auct mdn, rtd 90 at best): eff at 5f, dam styd 11f so shld stay further: acts on fast & gd: has run well fresh.
4400} **PERUGIA 204** [5] 3-8-8 M Hills 13/2: 1200-8: Held up, effort 2f out, sn btn: op 7/1, reapp: '99 *5* **62**
Goodwood wnr (mdn, debut, rtd 93, Listed rnr-up): eff at 6/7f, tried 1m: acts on fast grnd & a stiff/sharp trk.
8 ran Time 1m 25.03 (1.83) (Four Seasons Racing Ltd) P J Makin Ogbourne Maisey, Wilts.

1187 **4.50 MARCH HCAP 4YO+ 0-100 (C) 1m4f Firm 01 -03 Slow [98]**
£6438 £2442 £1221 £555

3865} **RAINBOW WAYS 240** [14] B W Hills 5-10-0 (98) J Reid 10/1: 4165-1: 11875 b h Rainbow Quest - Siwaayib **106**
(Green Desert) Held up, prog final 3f & led over 1f out, styd on well inside last, drvn out: reapp: '99 York wnr
(rtd h'cap, rtd 101): won final 3 in '98, Newmarket (2, mdn & rtd h'cap) & Haydock (h'cap, rtd 93): eff at 12/14f,
stays 2m: acts on gd/soft, relishes fast/firm: prob handles any trk, loves a stiff/gall one: seems best without
blnks nowadays: gd weight carrier: runs well fresh: tough/v useful, hold his own in Listed/Group 3 company.
*997 **CAPTAIN MILLER 15** [2] N J Henderson 4-8-4 (74) J Mackay (7) 8/1: 210-12: 4 b g Batshoof - Miller's *½* **80**
Gait (Mill Reef) Prom, led 3f out, hdd over 1f out, rdn & kept on well inside last, just held nr fin: imprvd again
on drop to 12f, styd 2m well latest: clrly goes on any grnd: in great heart & can win again: see 997 (soft).
3211} **LIVIUS 274** [21] Major D N Chappell 6-8-10 (80) R Hills 20/1: /021-3: 6 b g Alzao - Maire de Beaujeu *nk* **85**
(Kenmare): Held up, prog when briefly no room over 2f out, styd on well for press ins last, no btn far: shade
unlucky in running on reapp: '99 wnr at Ascot (h'cap, rtd 83, lightly rcd): rtd 79 at best in '98: eff at 12f,
may get further: acts on firm & gd/soft grnd, any trk, likes a stiff one: best without blnks: progressive, win again.
-- **MARK OF PROPHET** [10] N A Callaghan 5-8-0 (70) F Norton 20/1: 1021/4: Held up, prog 3f out, kept *3* **71**
on onepace inside last: op 16/1, long abs: missed last term: '98 wnr at Leicester (classified stks) & Newmarket
(h'cap, rtd 77, J E Banks): eff at 12/14f on firm & gd grnd, likes a stiff/gall trk: fine comeback, win more races.
968 **ALBERICH 18** [7] 5-9-9 (93) K Fallon 8/1: 11-505: Chsd ldrs, led over 3f out, hdd 3f out, onepace. *1¾* **92**
968 **GALLERY GOD 18** [5] 4-9-0 (84) M Roberts 9/1: 316-06: Held up, prog/ch 3f out, no extra fnl 1f: bckd. *3½* **78**
1076 **SPRING PURSUIT 6** [12] 4-9-4 (88) P Fitzsimons (5) 16/1: 602137: Mid-div, rdn/lost place 2f out, *shd* **82**
late rally: op 14/1: qck reapp: prob handles firm & gd, relishes soft/hvy grnd: see 991 (hvy).
4608} **EMINENCE GRISE 184** [16] 5-9-8 (92) T Quinn 9/1: 4464-8: Held up, prog halfway, outpcd final 2f: *½* **85**
op 8/1, reapp: '99 Kempton wnr (h'cap, subs rtd 96 at best, stks): eff at 14f/2m, tried 2m6f: acts on firm &
gd/sft grnd: goes well fresh: prob handles any trk: has run well in blnks: appreciate a return to 14f+.
4545} **PAIRUMANI STAR 191** [4] 5-9-11 (95) Pat Eddery 20/1: 1200-9: Held up, eff 3f out, sn held: reapp: *1¼* **86**
'99 wnr at York (rtd h'cap), Salisbury (stks) & Newbury (h'cap, rtd 96): eff at 12/14f, stays a slowly run 2m well:

acts on firm, soft & any trk, likes Salisbury: has run well fresh: eff with/without blnks: tough/useful colt.

*805   **ACHILLES SKY 37** [13]   4-8-7 (77) J Weaver 6/1 FAV: 016-10: Held up, rdn3f out/sn held: 10th: hvly bckd.   2   65

4103}   **MUSICIAN 224** [11]   4-9-10 (94) R Cochrane 9/1: 1115-0: Held up, drvn/btn 2f out: 11th: tough/prog   nk   81
filly in '99, wng h'caps at Warwick, Thirsk, Newmarket & Doncaster (rtd 95): plcd in '98 (rtd 89): stays 12f well,
should get further: acts on firm, hvy & any trk: has run well fresh: with J Fanshawe.

3865}   **KNOCKHOLT 240** [3]   4-10-0 (98) M J Kinane 12/1: 4101-0: Held up, prog halfway, btn 2f out: 12th, reapp.   2   82

991   **HILL FARM BLUES 15** [6]   7-8-4 (74) Iona Wands (5) 33/1: 00-450: Prom halfway, btn 3f out: 13th.   2½   54

968   **NAUTICAL STAR 18** [17]   5-9-10 (94) M Hills 16/1: 202-00: Led 7f, btn 2f out: 14th..   2   71

4374}   Bid Me Welcome 205 [8] 4-8-11 (81) M Tebbutt 33/1: 633   **Mardani** 64 [18] 5-10-0 (98) J Carroll 20/1:

835   King Flyer 30 [9] 4-7-10 (66)(t) M Henry 25/1:   --   Divine Appeal [15] 5-8-12 (82) J F Egan 33/1:

18 ran   Time 2m 28.54 (u.26)   (Maktoum Al Maktoum)   B W Hills Lambourn, Berks.

1188   5.20 HASTINGS MDN 3YO (D)   1m   Firm 01   -22 Slow
     £6006   £1848   £924   £462   Raced stands side

972   **CHAMPION LODGE 18** [6]   J A R Toller 3-9-0 S Whitworth 6/1: -21: 3 b c Sri Pekan - Legit (Runnett)   95
Chsd ldrs, rdn/prog to lead inside last, edged right & styd on gamely, all out: confirmed
promise of C/D debut prev: eff at 1m on firm & gd/soft, handles a stiff/gall trk: clearly useful, win more races.

--   **HYMN** [11]   J H M Gosden 3-9-0 J Fortune 14/1: 2: 3 b c Fairy King - Handsewn (Sir Ivor)   hd   94
Dwelt/held up, prog & rdn/ev ch inside last, styd on well, just held: op 8/1, debut: half-brother to sev wnrs:
eff at 1m, may stay further: acts on firm grnd & a stiff/gall trk: fine intro, looks useful, mdn a formality.

4611}   **HER OWN WAY 184** [19]   J H M Gosden 3-8-9 J Carroll 16/1: 4-3: 3 b f Danzig - Formidable Lady   2   85
(Silver Hawk): Led, hdd inside last, no extra: op 12/1, reapp: stablemate of rnr-up: 4th on sole '99 start
(5 rnr stks, rtd 69): eff at 1m, may get further: acts on firm grnd & a stiff/gall trk.

--   **EXECUTIVE ORDER** [12]   Sir Michael Stoute 3-9-0 K Fallon 6/1: 4: Dwelt, rdn/towards rear, styd on   1¼   87+
well ins last under hands-&-heels: op 4/1, debut: Rainbow Quest half-brother to 2,000 Guineas wnr Entrepreneur:
eff at 1m, holds a Derby entry & mid-dists will suit: handles firm grnd & a stiff/gall trk: certain future winner.

--   **DESERT RAGE** [9]   3-9-0 J Reid 16/1: 5: Dwelt/chsd ldrs, kept on well from 2f out, not pace to chall: ¾   86
op 12/1, debut: half-brother to a top class miler, 10f+ will suit: stays 1m, acts on firm: improve over further.

4165}   **SAWWAAH 220** [17]   3-9-0 R Hills 9/4 FAV: 32-6: Trkd ldrs, ch 1f out, fdd final 1f: hvly bckd, tchd   nk   85
3/1, reapp: shorter priced stablemate of 5th: plcd both '99 starts (rtd 100, mdn): eff at 7f, stays this lngr 1m trip
should suit: acts on firm & gd grnd & a stiff/gall trk.

1012   **DANCE WEST 13** [18]   3-9-0 T Quinn 9/1: 07: Prom, ch over 1f out, no extra inside last: op 7/1.   1   83

--   **METRONOME** [15]   3-8-9 G Mosse 25/1: 8: In tch halfway, effort 2f out, no impression & position   1½   75+
accepted ins last: debut: half-sister to a 7f 2yo wnr: kind intro, will leave this behind: with L M Cumani.

--   **RHYTHMICALL** [3]   3-9-0 Pat Eddery 9/1: 9: Chsd ldrs 7f: op 8/1, debut: 18,000 gns purchase: shd   80
half-brother to a wnr abroad: likely to apprec 10f+ in time for Mrs A J Perrett.

4339}   **MANDOOB 208** [8]   3-9-0 W Supple 25/1: 5-0: reapp: rtd 70 on sole '99 start   4   72
(Leicester mdn): dam a useful 5/7f scorer: with A Stewart.

4524}   **COURT OF APPEAL 193** [7]   3-9-0 R Cochrane 25/1: 0-0: Chsd ldrs, ch 2f out, fdd: 11th: reapp.   nk   71

4613}   **GRAND ORO 183** [2]   3-9-0 J Weaver 25/1: 2-0: Chsd ldrs 6f: 12th: reapp.   hd   70

--   **NATIONAL PRINCESS** [20]   3-8-9 M Tebbutt 33/1: 0: Mid-div, btn 2f out: 13th: debut, with W Jarvis.   nk   64

--   **NEW IBERIA** [5]   3-9-0 Dane O'Neill 25/1: 0: Held up, btn 2f out: 14th: debut, stablemate of 4th.   1½   66

--   Shinghaar [14] 3-9-0 K Darley 33/1:   --   Mynah [16] 3-8-9 M Hills 25/1:

--   Scarlet Woman [10] 3-8-9 Darren Williams (7) 33/1:   --   Joondey [13] 3-9-0 O Peslier 25/1:

--   Dancing Dreams [1] 3-9-0 T G McLaughlin 66/1:

19 ran   Time 1m 38.33 (1.83)   (P C J Dalby)   J A R Toller Newmarket, Suffolk.

Official Going   GOOD/FIRM (GOOD in places). Stalls: Stands Side except 1m, 1m1f - Inside.

1189   2.10 EBF QUAL MDN 2YO (D)   5f str   Good/Firm 25   -25 Slow
     £4231   £1302   £651   £325

1048   **INNIT 8** [1]   M R Channon 2-8-9 P Fessey 10/3: -321: 2 b f Distinctly North - Tidal Reach (Kris):   87
Chsd ldrs, led ins fnl 1f, rdn out, narrowly: op 4/1: rnr-up at Doncaster prev: IR 12,500 gns Apr foal, dam a
1m juv wnr: eff at 5f, 6f will suit: handles gd/firm or gd/soft grnd: can imprv again & win more races.

-898   **BOUNCING BOWDLER 24** [5]   M Johnston 2-9-0 K Dalgleish (7) 3/1 FAV: -322: 2 b c Mujadil - Prima Volta½   90
(Primo Dominie): Took gd hold & tried to make all, hdd inside final 1f, not qckn, just btn: 5L clr of 3rd,
well bckd: sure to go one better sn: acts on fast or soft: see 898, 821.

928   **ORANGE TREE LAD 22** [3]   A Berry 2-9-0 O Pears 8/1: -023: 2 b g Tragic Role - Adorable Cherub (Halo)   5   75
Chsd ldrs, switched over 1f out, not trble front pair: op 6/1: handles gd/firm: up in class after 928 (clmr).

1146   **DENSIM BLUE 2** [10]   J Pearce 2-9-0 G Bardwell 11/1: -024: Trkd ldrs, rdn/wknd final 1f: drifter   1¼   71
from 6/1: qck reapp after 1146.

--   **PEREGIAN** [2]   2-9-0 A Culhane 14/1: -5: Slow start, nvr trbld ldrs: drifter from 6/1, stablemate of   ¾   68
2nd: IR 35,000 gns Apr foal, half-brother to 2 juv wnrs: dam 6f juv scorer: shld learn plenty from this.

--   **TRUSTED MOLE** [8]   2-9-0 R Winston 6/1: -6: Chsd ldrs, rdn over 2f out, btn over 1f out: debut, tchd   ¾   65
10/1: J Osborne May foal, cost IR 16,500 gns: half-brother to a mdn, dam 6f juv scorer: evidently better expected.

--   **SIR EDWARD BURROW** [6]   2-9-0 Dean McKeown 25/1: -7: Nvr went pace: M Todhunter Feb foal: 1½   61
first produce of a dam who won over 6/7f as a 2yo & later at 10f.

1067   **BOLD MCLAUGHLAN 6** [9]   2-9-0 A McGlone 16/1: -008: Chsd ldrs, btn 1½f out: rtd best 700 (debut).   nk   60

843   **CARTMEL PRINCE 29** [7]   2-9-0 J Bramhill 16/1: -69: Prom, rdn/btn over 2f out: btr 843 (C/D).   ¾   57

--   **SHATIN LAW** [4]   2-9-0 C Lowther 20/1: -0: Slowly away, al rear: Miss L Perratt Apr foal, cost   7   37
IR 11,500 gns: dam an Irish 1m wnr: sire a sprinter.

10 ran   Time 1m 00.6 (2.5)   (Tim Corby)   M R Channon West Isley, Berks.

1190 **2.40 NH JOCKEYS HCAP 4YO+ 0-70 (E)** **1m65y rnd** **Good/Firm 25** **-25 Slow** **[41]**
£3770 £1160 £580 £290

*1149 **ETISALAT 2** [15] J Pearce 5-10-5 (46)(6ex) M Brennan 4/1 FAV: 126311: 5 b g Lahib - Sweet Repose (High Top): Held up, prog 4f out, led 2f out, ran on well, rdn out: 6lb pen, qck reapp: 2 days ago scored at Musselburgh (h'cap): earlier won at W'hampton (amat h'cap, rtd 57a): '99 Yarmouth (sell h'cap) & Lingfield (h'cap) wnr: eff at 7f/1m, stays 10f: acts on gd & fast grnd, both AWs: likes a sharp trk, handles any: eff rdn from off the pace: in great heart & may complete the hat-trick. **52**
1065 **GABLESEA 6** [9] B P J Baugh 6-10-12 (53) Gary Lyons 12/1: 246102: 6 b g Beveled - Me Spede (Valiyar): Held up, prog 2f out, chsd wnr over 1f out, rdn & kept on: 3½L clr of 3rd & a gd run: see 890. *1½* **55**
3929} **CUTE CAROLINE 235** [13] A Berry 4-10-11 (52) D Parker 16/1: 0300-3: 4 ch f First Trump - Hissma (Midyan): Prog 3f out, rdn & kept on onepace inside final 2f: sound reapp: trained last term by C Thornton, plcd at Beverley from just 4 starts (7.5f mdn, rtd 65$): stays 8.3f on gd/firm: can prob find a small h'cap. *3½* **47**
786 **NOBLE CYRANO 39** [2] M D Hammond 5-11-1 (56) J Callaghan 12/1: -10004: Led over 6f, not qckn. *1½* **48**
875 **ATLANTIC CHARTER 26** [14] 4-11-10 (65) A Dobbin 5/1: 10-065: Held up rear, prog over 2f out, not trouble ldrs: top-weight: needs further: see 875. *shd* **57**
1101 **PURSUIVANT 4** [6] 6-10-10 (51)(bl) B Harding 9/1: -03406: In tch, rdn 3f out, onepcd fnl 2f: qck reapp. *1½* **40**
942 **BODFARI SIGNET 20** [11] 4-10-9 (50) E Husband 14/1: 50-007: Rdn over 3f out, not trouble ldrs: with M W Easterby last term (now B Baugh), won a mdn h'cap over this C/D here at Hamilton (rtd 58): dual rnr-up as a juv: eff over a stiff 8.3f, has tried 10f: acts on fast or soft grnd: eff in blnks (not worn this year). *¾* **37**
681 **DARE 52** [8] 5-11-6 (61)(vis) R Thornton 14/1: 000358: Took gd hold & prom, rdn 2f out, wknd: abs. *2* **44**
299 **BRANDONVILLE 118** [5] 7-10-7 (48)(t) Derek Byrne 50/1: 00-009: Eff over 2f out, nvr nr ldrs: abs. *1½* **28**
3932} **HAYSTACKS 235** [3] 4-11-1 (56)(vis) D J Moffatt 12/1: 2056-0: Rear, rdn 3f out, no dngr: fit from hdling, won at Kelso in Mar (juv nov, eff at 2m/2m2f): plcd form in '99, rnr-up at Ayr (h'cap, rtd 62): eff at 10/12f on fast or soft grnd: mdn on the Flat after 18 attempts. *¾* **34**
1149 **MR PERRY 2** [7] 4-10-13 (54)(bl) A S Smith 8/1: -00230: Chsd ldrs, rdn 3f out, wknd 2f out: qck reapp. *2* **28**
942 **KNAVES ASH 20** [4] 9-10-11 (52) Richard Guest 16/1: 023-00: Slow start, rear, nvr in it: fin 12th: trained last term by D Nicholls, won at Redcar (appr h'cap) & plcd sev times (rtd 56): '98 scorer at Thirsk (appr h'cap) & Newcastle (h'cap, rtd 67): eff at 1m-10f on gd & firm, handles gd/soft: now with M Todhunter. *2* **22**
847 **Sarmatian 29** [10] 9-10-9 (50)(t) A Scholes 100/1: 4502} **Align 195** [12] 4-10-9 (50) R Garritty 14/1:
-- **Najjar** [1] 5-11-2 (57) P Niven 25/1:
15 ran Time 1m 48.0 (4.2) (Mrs E M Clarke) J Pearce Newmarket.

1191 **3.10 CLASSIC CLAIMER DIV 1 3YO+ (E)** **1m1f36y** **Good/Firm 25** **-09 Slow**
£2444 £752 £376 £188 3yo rec 14lb

827 **WILL IVESON 32** [10] P C Haslam 3-8-9 P Goode (3) 2/1: -12101: 3 b g Mukaddamah - Cherlinoa (Crystal Palace): Took gd hold, prom, led inside final 3f, kept on well for press, narrowly: well bckd, jockey reportedly given 3-day whip ban: AW wnr at W'hampton & Lingfield in Jan (h'cap & appr h'cap): eff at 1m-1m1f on both AWs, firm & gd/soft, possibly not on soft: can force the pace. **47**
3140} **MERLY NOTTY 277** [6] W Storey 4-8-12 J Bramhill 66/1: 0005-2: 4 ch f Inchinor - Rambadale (Vaigly Great): In tch, eff over 2f out, ev ch ins fnl 1f, just held: 6L clr of rem & a gd reapp from this rank outsider (offic rtd 24): with J S Haldane in '99 (poor form, incl in sells): eff over a stiff 9f on gd/firm when fresh. *½* **34$**
822 **LOYAL TOAST 32** [1] N Tinkler 5-9-5 Kim Tinkler 25/1: 0-2003: 5 b g Lyphard - Lisieux (Steady Growth) Rdn 3f out, prog over 1f out, nvr nrr: see 670. *6* **32**
4096} **THREE CHERRIES 225** [7] R E Barr 4-9-0 Dean McKeown 20/1: 0050-4: Held up, rdn 3f out, no impress: reapp: unplcd last term for R Hannon over 6f. *1½* **25**
847 **FLOORSOTHEFOREST 29** [2] 4-9-9 C Lowther 7/4 FAV: 014-65: Prom, ev ch over 2f out, btn over 1f out: op 6/4: rtd much higher here in 847. *1* **32**
3779} **SECONDS AWAY 244** [5] 9-9-3 Dawn Rankin (7) 50/1: 3200-6: Held up, rdn 3f out, no prog: reapp: plcd form last term, incl in sells/clmrs (rtd 37 at best): in '98 won at Ayr (sell h'cap, rtd 36): eff at 1m/9f, stays 11f: acts on firm & gd/soft grnd: had no chance at these weights, fitter next time. *1¾* **24**
887 **WONDERLAND 25** [8] 3-8-5 P Fessey 8/1: 656-07: Lost place after 4f, no dngr subs: just thrice rcd as a juv, rtd 64 at best: eff at 5/6f on gd or firm: with J J O'Neill. *1¼* **24**
847 **COLLEGE DEAN 29** [4] 4-9-10 P Hanagan (7) 20/1: 00-608: Trkd ldrs, ev ch 3f out, wknd 1½f out. *1¾* **27**
4123} **MONACO 223** [3] 6-9-4 O Pears 20/1: 0030-9: Waited with, rdn over 3f out, nvr in it. *1¾* **19**
67 **AJJAE 172** [9] 4-9-6 (bl) V Halliday 14/1: 2600-0: Led until hdd inside final 3f, sn btn: reapp. *½* **20**
10 ran Time 1m 57.2 (3.1) (Lord Bolton) P C Haslam Middleham, Nth Yorks.

1192 **3.40 LILLEY HCAP 3YO+ 0-90 (C)** **6f str** **Good/Firm 25** **+12 Fast** **[86]**
£8931 £2748 £1374 £687 3yo rec 10lb

844 **XANADU 29** [10] Miss L A Perratt 4-7-10 (54)(1oh) D Mernagh(0) 33/1: 03-001: 4 ch g Casteddu - Bellatrix (Persian Bold): Led over 4f out, made rest, ran on well final 1f, cmftbly: '99 wnr over this C/D at Hamilton (sell) & Carlisle (h'cap, rtd 56): eff at 6f on fast/firm grnd: likes Hamilton. **63**
1074 **DISTINCTIVE DREAM 6** [13] A Bailey 6-8-12 (70) D Kilcourse(7) 11/1: 103602: 6 b g Distinctly North - Green Side (Green Dancer): Rdn to impr over 2f out, kept on, not trouble wnr: see 598 (7f, AW). *2½* **72**
+1028 **ABBAJABBA 11** [7] C W Fairhurst 4-9-7 (79) P Goode (3) 10/3 FAV: 0-3113: 4 b g Barrys Gamble - Bo' Babbity (Strong Gale): Prog 2f out, kept on final 1f: ran to best: see 1028. *½* **80**
1068 **MALLIA 6** [5] T D Barron 7-8-10 (68)(bl) R Winston 25/1: 641404: Slowly away, rear, prog 2f out, kept on, nr fin: see 719. *1* **66**
*1008 **INDIAN SPARK 13** [14] 6-10-0 (86) A Culhane 8/1: 0-0415: In tch, rdn over 2f out, styd on same pace: 8lb higher mark than 1008 (hvy). *½* **83**
1028 **FULL SPATE 11** [18] 5-8-7 (65) Claire Bryan(5) 6/1: 000-36: Prom, rdn/no extra appr final 1f. *nk* **61**
1074 **ABLE AYR 6** [3] 3-8-8 (76) Dawn Rankin (7) 33/1: 450-07: Dwelt, bhd, late prog, no dngr: see 1074. *1½* **68**
1011 **MAGIC MILL 13** [15] 7-8-7 (65) F Lynch 14/1: 40-408: Not trouble ldrs: see 844 (C/D). *1* **54**
1074 **DEMOLITION JO 6** [11] 5-9-2 (74)(vis) Joanna Badger (7) 14/1: 20-069: Dwelt, nvr troubled ldrs. *½* **62**
844 **NAISSANT 29** [8] 7-7-10 (54) K Dalgleish (7) 20/1: 000-50: Rdn after 3f, btn 2f out: fin 10th. *¾* **39**
1008 **UNSHAKEN 13** [12] 6-9-2 (74) Dean McKeown 6/1: 0-0240: Prom, rdn/btn 2f out: 11th, btr 1008. *hd* **59**
1149 **JOHAYRO 2** [16] 7-8-5 (61)(2ow) A McGlone 13/2: -04050: Early ldr, prom until btn 1½f out: 12th. *1½* **44**
4480} **HOWARDS LAD 197** [4] 3-8-10 (78) O Pears 50/1: 3400-0: Nvr troubled ldrs: fin 13th: reapp. *1½* **55**

4572} **ALBERT THE BEAR 188** [1] 7-8-6 (62) (2ow) C Lowther 14/1: 4600-0: Rcd stands side, rdn/btn　　**3**　**32**
halfway: fin 14th, reapp.
1133　**Forest Queen 3** [17] 3-7-10 (64) (7oh) J Bramhill 100/1: 3820} **Shalarise 242** [9] 3-8-1 (69) N Kennedy 50/1:
2013} **The Angel Gabriel 326** [6] 5-7-10 (54) (12oh) J McAuley(2) 150/1:
4120} **Six For Luck 223** [2] 8-7-10 (54) (t) (30oh) P Hanagan(2) 150/1:
18 ran　　Time 1m 10.6 (0.8)　　(David R Sutherland)　　Miss L A Perratt Ayr, Strathclyde.

1193

4.10 SUNDAY IS FUN DAY MDN 3YO+ (D)　**1m3f**　　**Good/Firm 25 -43 Slow**
£4914　£1512　£756　£378　　3yo rec 17lb

1017　**BANIYAR 13** [10] Sir Michael Stoute 3-8-9 F Lynch 2/7 **FAV**: 0-41: 3 ch c Alzao - Banaja (Sadler's　　**85**
Wells) Waited with, prog 3f out, led over 2f out, hard held: well bckd at long odds-on: promising 4th at
Kempton on reapp (rtd 87): unplcd sole juv start: half brother to wnrs over 10f/2m: eff at 11f, 12f+
shld suit: acts on fast or soft grnd: shld go on from here.
1032　**STORM WIZARD 11** [6] M R Channon 3-8-9 P Fessey 6/1: 0-342: 3 b g Catrail - Society Ball (Law　　¾　**78**
Society) Early ldr, led briefly again over 2f out, grossly flattered by losing margin: stays 11f: handles
gd/firm or hvy: sure to win a race: see 936.
1009　**DARK SHADOWS 13** [3] W Storey 5-9-12 T Williams 100/1: -53: 5 b g Machiavellian - Instant Desire　　¾　**77**
(Northern Dancer) Prog 4f out, ev ch over 2f out, rdn & kept on same pace: gd eff from this big outsider,
treat rating carefully: eff at 11f on gd/firm: see 1009.
1064　**SEA SQUIRT 6** [4] M Johnston 3-8-9 K Dalgleish (7) 8/1: 2-2304: Prom, rdn 3f out, btn over 2f　　2½　**74**
out: handles fast grnd: see 906, 720.
1024　**MANSTAR 13** [7] 3-8-9 N Kennedy 33/1: 0-5005: Rdn over 4f out, not trouble ldrs: stiff task,　　1　**72$**
dubious rating (offic 54): handles gd/firm: see 827.
--　　**HERACLES** [1] 4-9-12 O Pears 20/1: -6: Rear, some late prog under press: Flat debut: dual rnr-up　　hd　**72**
in NH Flat races in Feb (gd & gd/soft): with A Berry.
902　**LUCKY JUDGE 24** [2] 3-8-9 A Culhane 33/1: 0-57: Keen, held up, btn 3f out: see 902.　　18　**47**
--　　**WILLY BANG BANG** [5] 3-8-9 J Bramhill 100/1: -8: Al rear: W Storey half-brother to middle　　5　**40**
dist/styr Here Comes Herbie.
--　　**SPECTRE BROWN** [8] 10-9-12 K Sked 200/1: -9: Chsd ldrs, btn 4f out: Flat debut, poor 10yo jumper.　　½　**39**
902　**ROBIN HOOD 24** [9] 3-8-9 C Lowther 50/1: 0-00: Led after 2f until over 2f out, sn beat a retreat.　　2　**36**
10 ran　　Time 2m 26.3 (7.5)　　(H H Aga Khan)　　Sir Michael Stoute Newmarket.

1194

4.40 HASTE YE BACK HCAP 4YO+ 0-70 (E)　**1m5f**　　**Good/Firm 25 -04 Slow**　　**[69]**
£3818　£1175　£587　£293

4590} **BHUTAN 186** [2] Mrs M Reveley 5-9-10 (65) A Culhane 7/2 **FAV**: 0144-1: 5 b g Polish Patriot -　　**69**
Bustinetta (Bustino): Rear, not much room over 2f out, prog ins fnl 2f, led ins fnl 1f, drvn out: well bckd, reapp:
hat-trick scorer over hdles in 99/00 at M Rasen (mdn), Newcastle & Wetherby (h'caps, rtd 118h): '99 Flat scorer at
Newcastle (h'cap) & Catterick (class stks, rtd 66): eff at 10/14f on firm & soft, any trip: best held up.
809　**HUNTERS TWEED 36** [12] J D Bethell 4-10-0 (69) R Lappin 8/1: 505-02: 4 ch c Nashwan - Zorette　　shd　**72**
(Zilzal): Held up, prog 3f out, led briefly over 1f out, kept on, just btn: fine effort under 10-0: '99 wnr at
Doncaster (mdn, easily, rtd 58): goes well on fast, good/soft: deserves to go one better.
215　**ELSIE BAMFORD 138** [7] M Johnston 4-7-11 (38) K Dalgleish (7) 33/1: 3006-3: 4 b f Tragic Role - Sara　　2　**38**
Sprint (Formidable): Rdn over 4f out, kept on for press appr final 1f: reapp: stays 13f: see 215.
876　**HAPPY DAYS 26** [9] D Moffatt 5-7-10 (37) (6oh) J Bramhill 16/1: 0-0004: Not much room 3f out, prog　　1　**35**
& ev ch over 1f out, not qckn: bckd from 33/1 & a gd effort: should win back off his proper mark: see 552.
846　**OCEAN DRIVE 29** [13] 4-8-6 (47) C Lowther 14/1: 030-05: In tch, ev ch over 1f out, no extra: see 846.　　nk　**44**
4300} **FREETOWN 209** [4] 4-9-12 (67) O Pears 4/1: 41-6: Waited with, prog over 2f out, nvr nrr: 8 wk jumps　　hd　**64**
abs, plcd both hdle starts in Mar (rtd 103h): Flat scorer in '99 for P Cole (clmr, rtd 73, subs clmd by current
handler L Lungo for £20,000): eff at 11/12f, shld stay 14f: acts on gd & hvy, poss gd/firm: better expected.
1052　**PRINCE NICHOLAS 8** [5] 5-9-7 (62) Dean McKeown 8/1: 022447: Not much room over 2f out, onepcd.　　1¼　**57**
4275} **POLO VENTURE 213** [14] 5-9-5 (58) F Lynch 10/1: 50/0-8: Waited with, rdn 3f out, not trouble ldrs:　　1¼　**51**
3 mth jumps abs, rnr-up in Dec (rtd 94h): unplcd sole '99 Flat start: hdles wnr in 98/99: Flat wnr at
Lingfield back in May '98 (equitrack): stays 12f, acts on any grnd.
845　**MR FORTYWINKS 29** [11] 6-9-7 (62) R Winston 9/2: 300-29: Chsd ldrs, led 4f out till dist, wknd.　　¾　**54**
1023　**BOLD CARDOWAN 13** [6] 4-8-3 (44) N Kennedy 12/1: 60-000: Ev ch 3f out, wknd 1½f out: 10th.　　6　**27**
2450} **MILDON 309** [1] 4-8-6 (20w) A McGlone 66/1: /0000-0: Chsd ldrs 1m: 11th, reapp, chgd stables.　　7　**20**
--　　**PANOORAS LORD** [3] 6-7-10 (37) (17oh) P Hanagan(3) 100/1: 0000/0: Chsd ldrs 9f: 12th, reapp.　　1　**8**
4122} **LORD ADVOCATE 223** [10] 12-7-10 (37) (vis) (5oh) J McAuley(2) 20/1: 5060-0: Led until over 4f out,　　12　**0**
wknd: fin last: now 12yo, reapp.
13 ran　　Time 2m 49.3 (3.8)　　(P D Savill)　　Mrs M Reveley Lingdale, Nth Yorks.

1195

5.10 CLASSIC CLAIMER DIV 2 3YO+ (E)　**1m1f36y**　　**Good/Firm 25 -16 Slow**
£2444　£752　£376　£188　　3yo rec 14lb

1101　**ACE OF TRUMPS 4** [2] J Hetherton 4-9-3 (t) N Kennedy 5/1: 100001: 4 ch g First Trump - Elle Reef　　**53**
(Shareef Dancer): Rdn 3f out, led 2½f out, forged clr final 1f: qck reapp: made all at Musselburgh in Mar
(sell h'cap, rtd 55): '99 wnr at Nottingham (sell h'cap) & Warwick (clmr, with W Haggas, rtd 70): '98 Newmarket
wnr (sell): eff at 7f-10f on firm or soft in a t-strap: with/without blnks/vis: at home in sell/clmg grade.
806　**CHEZ BONITO 37** [8] J A Osborne 3-8-4 (1ow) R Winston 9/1: -52: 3 br f Persian Bold - Tycoon Aly　　5　**45**
(Last Tycoon): Rdn after halfway, ev ch when hmpd over 2f out, swtchd left over 1f out, not trouble wnr:
clmd by J M Bradley for £8,000: stays 9f, handles gd/firm: can probably win a sell/clmr over 9/10f.
1053　**ROOFTOP PROTEST 8** [7] Mrs M Reveley 3-8-5 A Culhane 11/2: 065-03: 3 b g Thatching - Seattle Siren　　2½　**42**
(Seattle Slew): Held up behind, styd on final 2f, too much to do: drifter from 4/1: hinted at ability in 3 juv
starts (rtd 67, 7.5f mdn): a step up to 10f+ shld suit: one to keep an eye on in similar modest grade.
--　　**ALABAMY SOUND 4** [4] K A Morgan 4-9-9 Dean McKeown 1/1 **FAV**: 441-4: Chsd ldrs, hung left 2f out,　　¾　**44**
no extra final 1f: well bckd from 5/4 on reapp: ex-French filly, last rcd over 12 mths ago when successful at
Chantilly (1m, gd): earlier ran respectively on soft: should be capable of better, possibly with more give.
973　**HOT POTATO 16** [6] 4-9-5 J McAuley(2) 20/1: 046005: Bhd, some late prog, nvr in it: see 298.　　1　**38$**
4129} **WESTERN VENTURE 222** [1] 7-9-4 K Dalgleish (7) 20/1: 0054-6: Led until 2½f out, btn 1f out:　　½　**36$**
jockey given 1-day ban - careless riding: shwd little in 4 starts last term when trained by M Wane: now
with I Semple: back in '97 scored here at Hamilton (sell h'cap, rtd 30): eff at 1m/9f on firm & gd/soft.

HAMILTON   SUNDAY MAY 7TH   Righthand, Undulating Track, Stiff Uphill Finish

795 **IMPULSIVE AIR 38** [9] 8-9-6 F Lynch 10/1: 05-507: Prom, wknd 1½f out: see 569. *2½* **34**
-- **TEEJAY N AITCH** [10] 8-9-6 (t) A McGlone 50/1: 0006/8: Al bhd. *1½* **32$**
756 **THE REPUBLICAN 40** [3] 3-8-3 T Williams 100/1: 00-09: Nvr troubled ldrs: seems poor. *9* **14**
1085 **COMANCHE QUEEN 5** [5] 3-8-6(1ow) R Lappin 20/1: 000-00: T.o. last to fin: seems of little account. *20* **0**
10 ran Time 1m 57.8 (3.7) (C D Barber-Lomax) J Hetherton Malton, Nth Yorks.

WINDSOR   MONDAY MAY 8TH   Sharp, Fig 8 Track

Official Going GOOD. Stalls: Inside.

1196

6.00 RODRIGO APPR HCAP 3YO+ 0-80 (E) 6f Good/Firm 21 -11 Slow [77]
£3104 £887 £443 3 yo rec 10lb Raced across track, mid-high no's dominated

941 **AT LARGE 21** [11] W J Musson 6-9-3 (66) P Shea (5) 11/2 FAV: 00-061: 6 b g Night Shift - Lady Donna **72**
(Dominion) Held up, no room over 2f out, no room when prog over 1f out, rdn/styd on well to lead nr line: hvly bckd from 10/1: '99 rnr-up at Sandown (h'cap, rtd 74, first time blnks, J Toller): eff at 5/7f on firm & soft, any trk: best without blnks: on a fair mark, won despite trouble in running & could score again.
844 **BLUE KITE 30** [24] N P Littmoden 5-8-10 (59) C Cogan 12/1: 451002: 5 ch g Silver Kite - Gold And Blue *shd* **63**
(Bluebird) Mid-div, rdn/prog to chall fnl 1f, kept on well, just btn in a thrilling fin: op 10/1: see 645 (AW).
844 **PALAWAN 30** [18] I A Balding 4-9-10 (73) N Chalmers (7) 7/1: 211203: 4 br g Polar Falcon - Krameria *½* **76**
(Kris) Gd speed to lead, rdn/hdd well ins last, no extra: pacey & a likely type for similar: see 728, 599.
1092 **DIAMOND GEEZER 6** [17] R Hannon 4-8-13 (62) P Fitzsimons (3) 7/1: -50244: Trkd ldrs, kept on fnl 1f. *nk* **64**
1008 **TEYAAR 14** [13] 4-9-12 (75) I Mongan 8/1: 101125: Prom, rdn/ch 1f out, just held nr fin: see 1008. *shd* **77**
4562} **LAW COMMISSION 191** [12] 10-9-3 (66) R Thomas (5) 25/1: 6000-6: Rear, prog when no room 1f out, *¾* **66+**
styd on well nr fin, nrst fin: op 20/1, reapp: '99 Newbury scorer (h'cap, rtd 87): unplcd in '98 (rtd 93, h'caps): eff at 6/7f, stays 1m: acts on hvy, suited by gd or firm, any trk, likes a sharp one: best coming late, no luck in running tonight & is a well h'capped 10yo who retains ability, one to note when T Quinn is aboard.
838 **BANDBOX 31** [21] 5-9-1 (64) R Studholme 16/1: -12007: Bhd, eff over 1f out, rdn/kept on, no threat. *shd* **64**
3969} **ZEPPO 233** [19] 5-8-8 (57) Cheryl Nosworthy (7) 12/1: 0600-8: Chsd ldrs, held fnl 1f: op 10/1, reapp: *nk* **56**
'99 Chepstow wnr (h'cap, rtd 61): '98 Lingfield wnr (h'cap, rtd 63): eff at 5/6f on firm & gd grnd: handles any trk: best without blnks: on a fair mark & shld prove sharper for this.
960 **CORNDAVON 20** [7] 4-9-3 (66) J Mackay (5) 11/1: 000-29: Held up in tch, rdn/not pace to chall. *½* **63**
82 **PRIX STAR 170** [5] 5-8-9 (58) P Goode 20/1: 2455-0: In tch, eff 2f out, sn held: 10th: 6 mth abs. *hd* **54**
1005 **SWINO 14** [16] 6-8-6 (55)(vis) Joanna Badger (5) 25/1: 2-4600: Reminders early, rear, nvr factor: 11th. *¾* **49**
1061 **DOCTOR DENNIS 7** [23] 3-8-8 (67) D Glennon (5) 33/1: 02-000: Mid-div, btn 2f out: 12th: rnr-up *nk* **60**
in '99 (rtd 69, nurs h'cap): eff over a sharp 7f, has tried 10f: handles gd/soft & firm: eff in blnks, not worn here.
4311} **DOUBLE MARCH 210** [22] 7-8-13 (62) C Catlin (5) 16/1: 0040-0: Chsd ldrs, held fnl 2f: 13th: op 12/1, *1* **53**
reapp: plcd in '99 (rtd 60, h'cap, H Candy): '98 wnr for current connections at Nottingham (2) & here at Windsor (h'caps, rtd 70): eff at 7f, suited by 6f: acts on fast & soft, any trk: has run well fresh.
881 **CHARGE 26** [10] 4-9-7 (70)(t) Darren Williams (3) 16/1: 022150: Chsd ldrs, rdn/btn/eased nr fin: 14th. *hd* **60**
1028 **COLD CLIMATE 12** [2] 5-8-11 (60) Gemma Jones (5) 14/1: 300-50: Dwelt/bhd, brief eff 2f out: 15th. *hd* **49**
926 **BRECONGILL LAD 23** [4] 8-9-11 (74) Iona Wands 7/1: 133-30: Chsd ldrs 4f: 16th: op 5/1. *hd* **62**
1036 **Jonathans Girl 10** [15] 5-7-10 (45)(15oh) R Brisland 66/1: 4604} **Derryquin 186** [6] 5-8-3 (52)(bl) R Lake (2) 40/1:
1005 **Rocklands Lane 14** [14] 4-7-10 (45)(7oh) D Kinsella (5) 50/1:
852 **Lady Noor 28** [25] 3-8-9 (68) Kathleen McDermott 33/1:
53 **Ronni Pancake 174** [1] 3-8-4 (63) N Farmer (7) 40/1: 64 **Dancing Mystery 173** [3] 6-9-12 (75) S Carson 25/1:
4471} **Sandpoint 199** [9] 4-7-10 (45)(6oh) Jonjo Fowle (0) 40/128 **Balanita 179** [20] 5-9-9 (72) S Finnamore (3) 25/1:
-- **Lady Dealer** [8] 5-7-10 (45)(10oh) G Baker (5) 66/1:
25 ran Time 1m 12.2 (1.9) (The Square Table) W J Musson Newmarket.

1197

6.25 VITTORIA FILLIES MDN AUCT 2YO (E) 5f Good/Firm 21 -17 Slow
£2982 £852 £426 Raced across track

1006 **KACHINA DOLL 14** [21] M R Channon 2-8-6 T Quinn 10/1: -3001: 2 b f Mujadil - Betelgeuse (Kalaglow) **83**
Led/dsptd lead thr'out, duelled with rnr-up fnl 1f, narrowly prevailed nr fin, drvn out: tchd 12/1: eff at 5f, 6f+ will suit: handles a sharp/gall trk: acts on fast & gd grnd, below par on hvy.
812 **FIAMMA ROYALE 35** [1] Mrs P N Dutfield 2-8-4 S Carson (5) 7/1: 42: 2 b f Fumo Di Londra - Ariadne *hd* **80**
(Bustino) Led/dsptd lead, just hdd/held nr fin: clr rem: acts on fast & soft grnd: can find similar: see 812.
-- **NUN LEFT** [17] R M Beckett 2-8-4 G Hind 25/1: 3: 2 b f Bishop Of Cashel - Salsita (Salse) *4* **70**
Mid-div, kept on well fnl 2f, no threat to front pair: op 20/1: Mar foal, cost 7,000gns: dam juv wnr abroad, sire high-class 7f/1m performer: will apprec 6f+ in time: handles fast grnd: encouraging intro.
-- **COPY CAT** [20] W R Muir 2-8-6 Martin Dwyer 12/1: 4: Went right start, sn handy, outpcd fnl 1f: op *¾* **70$**
10/1: Lion Cavern filly, Apr foal, cost 12,000gns: half-sister to high-class sprinter Averti: dam useful 5/6f performer, sire a high-class 2yo: promise here, acts on fast grnd & will know more next time.
-- **LOVE TUNE** [5] 2-8-2 R Ffrench 40/1: 5: Chsd ldrs, rdn/outpcd 2f out, kept on ins last: op 33/1: *nk* **65**
Alhijaz filly, first foal, cost 1,500gns: dam a modest mdn, sire a high-class miler: 6f+ shld suit in time.
-- **DISTINCTLY CHIC** [22] 2-8-6 R Mullen 25/1: 6: Dwelt, rear, eff when no room halfway, rdn/kept on *¾* **67**
ins last, no threat: May foal, cost IR 12,000gns: half-sister to useful 7f/1m juv wnr Hoh Steamer: 6f+ shld suit.
-- **BILLIE H** [18] 2-8-2 A Polli (3) 14/1: 7: Dwelt/towards rear, rdn & kept on from over 1f out, no threat: *nk* **62**
op 10/1: Cool Jazz filly, Mar foal, cost 800gns: dam a lightly rcd mdn, sire a smart sprinter: with C E Brittain.
-- **CHURCH BELLE** [8] 2-8-4 C Rutter 16/1: 8: Cl-up 4f: op 12/1: Apr foal, cost IR 9,000gns: *½* **62**
half-sister to sev wnrs incl a 6f juv wnr: dam a French wnr at up to 11f: apprec further in time.
-- **WINTER JASMINE** [9] 2-8-8 Pat Eddery 4/1 FAV: 9: Chsd ldrs, btn 2f out: hvly bckd: Robellino *nk* **65**
filly, Feb foal, cost 17,000gns: dam modest, sire a high-class 2yo: with B J Meehan.
-- **EBULLIENCE** [6] 2-8-6 S Drowne 9/1: 0: Dwelt/rear, mod late gains, no threat: 10th: op 4/1: *hd* **62**
12,500gns Feb foal: dam multiple wnr, incl as a juv: with R Charlton.
-- **HOT PANTS** [19] 2-8-2 C Catlin (7) 33/1: 0: Cl-up 4f: 11th: Rudimentary filly, Mar foal, cost *½* **56**
3,200gns: dam a 5/7f h'cap wnr: with K T Ivory.
970 **DELPHYLLIA 19** [10] 2-8-2 J Tate 20/1: -00: Chsd ldrs 3f: 12th: see 970. *1¼* **53**
-- **CHAWENG BEACH** [16] 2-8-2 Dale Gibson 25/1: 0: Dwelt, rear, nvr factor: 13th: op 14/1, debut. *hd* **52**
1067 **GOLDEN WHISPER 7** [11] 2-8-2 A Nicholls (3) 6/1: -40: Chsd ldrs, btn over 1f out: op 4/1: btr 1067 (g/s). **0**

WINDSOR   MONDAY MAY 8TH   Sharp, Fig 8 Track

--   **MISTY BELLE** [15] 2-8-4 P Robinson 9/1: 0: Chsd ldrs 4f: 18th: op 7/1, with B Millman.   0
--   **Broughtons Motto** [3] 2-8-2 L Newton 33/1:   849 **Easter Island 28** [14] 2-8-2 D O'Donohoe 33/1:
--   **Gold Air** [2] 2-8-4 D R McCabe 33/1:   -- **Silver Cloud** [7] 2-8-4 M Roberts 12/1:
1019 **Pertemps Gill 14** [4] 2-8-2 N Pollard 50/1:
20 ran   Time 1m 0.7 (1.9)   (Ridgeway Downs Racing)   M R Channon West Isley, Berks.

1198   6.55 FINANCIAL CLASS STKS 3YO+ 0-90 (C)   1m2f   Good/Firm 21 -04 Slow
£6695   £2060   £1030   £515   3 yo rec 15lb   92

851 **FERZAO 28** [2] Mrs A J Perrett 3-8-5 T Quinn 9/4 JT FAV: 01-31: 3 b c Alzao - Fer de Lance (Diesis)   92
Bhd ldrs, rdn/chsd ldr 2f out, kept on well to lead nr fin, drvn out: well bckd: won 2nd of 2 '99 starts, at
Leicester (mdn, rtd 91): eff at 1m/10f, further shld suit: acts on fast, gd/soft & sharp or gall trk: useful.
851 **KUSTER 28** [5] L M Cumani 4-9-3 L Dettori 11/4: 120-42: 4 b c Indian Ridge (Lomond)   nk 88
Led, qcknd over 3f out, rdn/strongly pressed from 2f out, hdd well ins last, just held: clr rem: well bckd:
styd longer 10f trip well: acts on fast & gd/soft: just bhd this wnr in 851.
851 **FRONTIER 28** [3] R Hannon 3-8-5 Dane O'Neill 7/1: 421-53: 3 b c Indian Ridge - Adatiya (Shardari)   4 85
Rear/in tch, eff over 2f out, no impress on front pair: op 5/1: also bhd today's first two in 851 (1m).
4318} **REFLEX BLUE 210** [4] J W Hills 3-8-2 M Henry 10/1: 2125-4: Rcd keenly/cl-up, rdn/outpcd fnl 3f: 1¼ 80
op 7/1, reapp: '99 Newmarket scorer (mdn, rtd 92 at best): eff at 7f/1m, shld get further: acts on firm & fast grnd.
4318} **BOW STRADA 210** [1] 3-8-5 Pat Eddery 9/4 JT FAV: 11-5: Bhd ldrs, rdn to close over 2f out, sn held: 2½ 79
nicely bckd tho' op 7/4: reapp: won both '99 starts, at Yarmouth (auct mdn) & Leicester (stks, rtd 89): eff at 1m/
10f on gd & gd/soft: handles a stiff/undul trk: has run well fresh: reportedly supplemented for the Derby.
5 ran   Time 2m 07.2 (2.5)   (Clive Batt & Mrs Elaine Batt)   Mrs A J Perrett Pulborough, W.Sussex.

1199   7.25 SPORTING INDEX HCAP 3YO 0-85 (D)   1m3f135y Good/Firm 21 -00 Slow   [92]
£7085   £2180   £1090   £545

906 **RIVER BANN 24** [10] P F I Cole 3-9-7 (85) J Fortune 6/1: 2-221: 3 ch c Irish River - Spiritual Star   90
(Soviet Star) Sn led & dictated pace, qcknd over 2f out, held on well ins last, rdn out: op 7/1, h'cap bow:
promise sole '99 start (rtd 90, mdn): 120,000gns purchase: eff around 11/12f on fast & gd grnd, prob handles
soft: handles a sharp or gall trk: responded well to front running tactics tonight & a fine J Fortune ride.
937 **BOX CAR 21** [5] G L Moore 3-8-1 (65) F Norton 7/1: 2-5322: 3 b g Blues Traveller - Racey Naskra   ½ 68
(Star de Naskra) Chsd ldrs, rdn/prog to chase wnr over 1f out, kept on: op 6/1: acts on fast, hvy & equitrack.
937 **KUWAIT TROOPER 21** [3] G A Butler 3-7-12 (62) J Mackay 7/1: 4/1 FAV: 0-4103: 3 b c Cozzene - Super   1½ 63
Fan (Lear Fan) Rear/in tch, eff wide fnl 3f, kept on tho' nvr a threat: hvly bckd: acts on fast & gd/soft grnd.
4380} **RAVENSWOOD 206** [6] M C Pipe 3-9-0 (78)(t) M Roberts 20/1: 6100-4: Rear, eff wide 3f out, stdy   1 78
late gains, no threat: op 16/1, reapp: '99 Brighton wnr (auct mdn, rtd 84): styd longer 11.7f trip tonight, further
could suit: acts on firm grnd & a sharp trk: wears a t-strap.
747 **FAIT LE JOJO 42** [7] J Reid 3-9-2 (80) J Reid 9/1: 313-45: Led 1f, remained handy, rdn/no extra over 1f   nk 79
out: 6 wk abs: prob styd longer 11.7f trip: fin clr of rem here: see 747.
*936 **MASTER GEORGE 21** [1] 3-9-2 (80) K Fallon 6/1: 2-16: Held up, eff 3f out, no impress: op 4/1.   5 72
4591} **WASEYLA 187** [4] 3-8-11 (75) L Dettori 9/1: 054-7: Twds rear, rdn/no impress fnl 3f: op 7/1, reapp: shd 67
unplcd in '99 for J Gosden (rtd 87, mdn): bred to apprec mid-dists: has tried a visor: with A Stewart.
701 **JATHAAB 46** [9] 3-9-2 (80) R Hills 5/1: 103-58: Keen/trkd ldrs, btn 2f out: bckd, abs, btr 701 (10f).   1½ 70
1002 **STAFFORD KING 14** [11] 3-7-10 (60)(4oh) R Brisland (5) 20/1: 0-0429: Mid-div, btn 3f out: btr 1002 (hvy).   ¾ 49
839 **HOME FORCE 31** [12] 3-8-3 (67) R Mullen 11/1: 40-00: Rear, eff 3f out, no prog: 10th: op 8/1,   1¼ 54
h'cap bow: longer 11.7f trip: 4th in a mdn in '99 (rtd 72): with C F Wall.
4432} **CYPRESS CREEK 202** [2] 3-7-10 (60)(4oh) M Henry 50/1: 0000-0: Mid-div, rdn/sltly hmpd 2f out,   2 44
sn struggling: 11th: reapp: unplcd in '99 (rtd 58): h'cap bow tonight.
1064 **SKYE BLUE 7** [8] 3-8-6 (70) T Quinn 9/1: 50-530: Prom early, btn 3f out: 12th: btr 1064 (soft).   1 53
12 ran   Time 2m 28.2 (2.4)   (HRH Prince Fahd Salman)   P F I Cole Whatcombe, Oxon.

1200   7.55 SALAMANCA MDN 3YO (D)   1m2f   Good/Firm 21 -12 Slow
£4316   £1328   £664   £332

--   **BEZZAAF** [10] M A Jarvis 3-8-9 P Robinson 16/1: 1: 3 b f Machiavellian - Maid Of Kashmir (Dancing   88
Brave) Prom, led over 3f out, styd on well ins last, rdn out: op 14/1, debut: dam a useful mid-dist performer:
eff at 10f, 12f+ shld suit: acts on fast grnd & a sharp trk: well run fresh: open to further improvement.
916 **TOTAL CARE 24** [13] H R A Cecil 3-9-0 T Quinn 5/6 FAV: 22: 3 br c Caerleon - Totality (Dancing Brave)   1¼ 89
Keen chasing ldrs, rdn/chsd wnr fnl 1f, kept on tho' al just held: hvly bckd: acts on fast & soft grnd: see 916.
4474} **ARDUINE 28** [18] J H M Gosden 3-9-0 L Dettori 9/2: 6-3: 3 ch f Diesis - Ardisia (Affirmed)   1½ 82
Keen/mid-div, prog fnl 2f, onepace ins last: well bckd, reapp, 5L clr rem: rtd 70 on sole '99 start (mdn): eff
at 10f, 12f will suit: handles fast grnd: encouraging reapp, shld win a mdn.
--   **EAST CAPE** [22] L M Cumani 3-9-0 G Sparkes (7) 33/1: 54: Mid-div, eff/bmpd 3f out, kept on   5 80+
well under hands-&-heels riding fnl 2f, no threat: reapp: last of 5 on debut in Milan recently: apprec step
up to 10f, 12f shld suit: prom handles fast grnd: eye-catching effort, improve with stronger handling.
3830} **GOLD QUEST 243** [19] 3-9-0 J Reid 20/1: 0-5: Chsd ldrs, held fnl 2f: op 14/1, reapp: unplcd sole   nk 79
'99 start (rtd 65, mdn): 10f+ shld suit this term.
--   **SEEK THE LIGHT** [17] 3-9-0 W Ryan 10/1: 6: Dwelt/twds rear, rdn & stdy gains fnl 3f, no threat to   2½ 75+
ldrs: op 7/1, debut: stablemate of rnr-up: dam a sister to Arc wnr Dancing Brave: looks sure to relish 12f+.
--   **PEPE GALVEZ** [3] 3-9-0 M Roberts 33/1: 7: Mid-div, onepace fnl 2f: half brother to a 1m/12f wnr.   shd 75
--   **HIGH DRAMA** [2] 3-9-0 Martin Dwyer 25/1: 8: Cl-up halfway, wknd over 1f out: debut: In The   ½ 74
Wings colt, 56,000gns purchase: mid-dist bred, entered in the Derby: with W R Muir.
4257} **MAGIC SUNSET 216** [9] 3-8-9 A Nicholls (3) 33/1: 00-9: Led 7f, fdd: reapp: unplcd both '99   shd 69$
starts (rtd 62, fill mdn): shld apprec mid-dists this term for h'capping, h'caps will suit.
1018 **QUIET READING 14** [21] 3-9-0 S Sanders 66/1: 00: Held up, eff 3f out, no impress: 10th: longer trip.   1¼ 72
4605} **SHAREEF KHAN 185** [7] 3-9-0 (bl) O Urbina 50/1: 0-0: Chsd ldrs, fdd over 1f out: 11th: reapp.   1¼ 70
--   **COLLINE DE FEU** [15] 3-8-9 R Havlin 50/1: 0: Held up, rdn/no impress fnl 3f: 12th: debut.   nk 64
--   **CHARTERHOUSE** [11] 3-9-0 M Hills 16/1: 0: Towards rear, rdn/mod prog: 13th: op 12/1, debut.   1 68
86   **EL ZITO 168** [14] 3-9-0 J P Spencer 33/1: 23-0: Keen/towards rear, nvr factor: 14th: nk 67
4315} **LA FAY 210** [1] 3-9-0 Pat Eddery 8/1: 24-0: Keen/prom 1m: 15th: reapp: rnr-up first of 2 '99 starts   1¼ 0
(rtd 82, stks): mid-dists will suit this term, handles firm grnd: can leave this bhd in h'cap company.
972 **POLLSTER 19** [16] 3-9-0 K Fallon 13/2: -00: Mid-div, strugg halfway: 21st: reportedly lost action: op 7/2.   0

398

WINDSOR   MONDAY MAY 8TH   Sharp, Fig 8 Track

--	**Able Seaman** [6] 3-9-0 G Hall 33/1:	--	**Red Lion Fr** [5] 3-9-0 D R McCabe 25/1:
--	**Betachance Dot Com** [8] 3-8-9 R Price 50/1:	--	**Lord Alaska** [4] 3-9-0 S Whitworth 25/1:
--	**Miss Amber Nectar** [12] 3-8-9 S Carson (5) 50/1:	--	**Habiba** [20] 3-8-9 (BL) G Faulkner (3) 50/1:

22 ran   Time 2m 08.00 (3.3)   (Sheikh Ahmed Al Maktoum)   M A Jarvis Newmarket.

1201   8.25 WATERLOO HCAP 3YO+ 0-70 (E)   1m67y rnd   Good/Firm 21   +04 Fast   [70]
£3136   £896   £448   3 yo rec 13lb

718   **DANAKIL** 44 [9] K R Burke 5-9-7 (63) N Callan 16/1: 635161: 5 b g Warning - Danilova (Lyphard)   68
Trkd ldrs, rdn/led over 1f out, held on well ins last, drvn out: best time of night, op 14/1, 6 wk abs: earlier
scored at W'hampton (h'cap, rtd 69a): '99 W'hampton wnr (mdn, rtd 77a & 64, J Banks): eff at 1m/9.5f on fast &
fibresand: handles gd & soft: likes a sharp trk: runs well fresh.
4472} **FUEGIAN** 199 [12] M Madgwick 5-8-13 (55) M Fenton 20/1: 2660-2: 5 ch g Arazi - Well Beyond (Don't   ¾   57
Forget Me) Rdn early to lead, hdd over 1f out, kept on well for press: reapp: '99 wnr here at Windsor (h'cap,
rtd 58): likes to force the pace over a sharp 1m, tried further: likes firm & fast: eff with/without a visor.
786   **ANEMOS** 40 [14] M A Jarvis 5-9-13 (69) P Robinson 11/2: 234263: 5 ch g Be My Guest - Frendly   hd   70
Persuasion (General Assembly) Trkd ldrs, rdn to chall over 1f out, kept on well: well bckd: eff at 1m/10f: abs.
1033 **ROGUE SPIRIT** 12 [15] P W Harris 4-9-11 (67) Pat Eddery 10/1: 5-0004: Mid-div, prog when briefly no   hd   67
room over 1f out, styd on well ins last when no room nr line: op 8/1: stays a sharp 1m: see 746.
3412} **TRICKS** 265 [18] 4-8-13 (55) D Harrison 20/1: 0060-5: Cl-up, kept on onepace fnl 2f for press: op   1¾   52
14/1, reapp: unplcd in '99 for I Balding (rtd 61, h'cap, tried blnks): '98 Lingfield wnr (Lord Huntingdon, AW mdn,
rtd 74a): eff at 7f, stays a sharp 1m: acts on both AWs & fast grnd: likes a sharp trk: now with D J Coakley.
4012} **PEPETA** 231 [8] 3-9-0 (69) K Fallon 7/1: 606-6: Cl-up, rdn/onepace fnl 1f: op 4/1, reapp/h'cap   ¾   65
bow: unplcd in '99 (rtd 74): this longer 1m trip shld suit: handles fast grnd.
4314} **ADMIRALS FLAME** 210 [2] 9-9-0 (56) R Mullen 12/1: 1400-7: Rear, prog fnl 2f, onepace ins last: shd   52
op 8/1, reapp: '99 Leicester wnr (h'cap, rtd 61): '98 scorer here at Windsor (h'cap, rtd 62): eff at 7f, suited
by 1m on firm & hvy grnd: handles any trk, loves Windsor: has run well fresh: fairly h'capped 9yo.
961   **BAHRAIN** 20 [17] 4-9-8 (64)(t) M Hills 16/1: /50-48: Rear, rdn/late gains, no threat: see 961 (7f, sft).   shd   59
1113 **CONSORT** 5 [13] 7-9-4 (60) Dane O'Neill 16/1: -00009: Slowly away, rear till kept on fnl 2f, nrst   nk   54
fin: op 20/1, qck reapp: v well h'capped, some signs of a return to form tonight: likes fibresand: see 208.
1058 **BIRTH OF THE BLUES** 9 [10] 4-9-9 (65) N Pollard 16/1: 000-00: Rear, eff wide 2f out, sn held: 10th.   shd   59
1050 **YOUNG UN** 9 [5] 5-9-7 (63) P McCabe 7/2 FAV: 51-060: Cl-up, btn/hmpd over 1f out: 11th: hvly bckd.   3   51
811   **CARINTHIA** 37 [1] 5-9-4 (60) S Sanders 12/1: 000-00: Cl-up wide 3f out, sn btn: 12th: op 10/1.   2½   43
965   **MY BOLD BOYO** 20 [16] 5-9-1 (57) O Urbina 12/1: -44050: Rear, rdn/held when bmpd over 1f out: 13th.   ¾   39
268   **Coughlans Gift** 124 [11] 4-9-5 (61) P Dobbs 16/1: 4309} **Lala Salama** 210 [3] 4-8-13 (55) J Fortune 14/1:
1037 **Almerina** 10 [4] 5-9-10 (66) I Mongan (5) 20/1:   784 **Commander** 40 [6] 4-9-9 (65) T Quinn 20/1:
4115} **Digon Da** 224 [7] 4-10-0 (70) A Clark 33/1:
18 ran   Time 1m 43.7 (1.4)   (The Danakilists)   K R Burke Newmarket.

SOUTHWELL (Fibresand)   MONDAY MAY 8TH   Lefthand, Sharp Track

Official Going   STANDARD.   Stalls: Inside, Except 5f - Outside.

1202   1.45 STILTON FILLIES HCAP 3YO 0-65 (F)   7f aw rnd   Going 37   -19 Slow   [68]
£2261   £646   £323

4570} **AFRICA** 189 [12] T D Barron 3-9-2 (56) C Lowther 8/1: 0330-1: 3 b f Namaqualand - Tannerrun (Runnett)   61a
In tch, hdwy ent str, edged left under press ins last but styd on to lead towards fin: op 6/1, AW bow, 6 month
abs: '99 Catterick wnr (sell, rtd 61 at best): eff at 7f, tried 1m: acts on firm, gd grnd & fibresand, suited
by sharp trks: best without blnks & runs well fresh: genuine, type to win again on sand.
62   **RIOS DIAMOND** 173 [10] M J Ryan 3-8-1 (41) G Bardwell 20/1: 0000-2: 3 b f Formidable - Rio   1   43a
Piedras (Kala Shikari) Well plcd, led after 3f, under press dist, worn down well ins last: near 6 month abs:
plcd in '99 (clmr, rtd 42a & 43): acts a sharp 7f on fibresand: tried a visor, eff without.
4   **PYJAMA GIRL** 182 [11] P R Chamings 3-9-6 (60) S Whitworth 20/1: 4506-3: 3 gr f Night Shift -   3½   55a
Permissible Tender (Al Hattab) Prom, rdn 2f out, outpcd by front rank: 6 month abs: prob flattered on turf
in '99 (fill mdn, rtd 75 & 52a): drop back to 6f likely to suit, prob handles fibresand.
870   **BILLYS BLUNDER** 27 [3] P D Evans 3-8-3 (43)(tvi) Joanna Badger (7) 10/1: 204454: Slow away &   hd   38a
shaken up, styd on wide up the str, nvr nr to chall: clr rank, tried 1m: see 493, 426.
1081 **MADEMOISELLE PARIS** 6 [14] 3-8-4 (44) F Norton 25/1: 400-05: Handy, chall 2f out, sn no extra: 3   33a
quick reapp: plcd on turf in '99 (clmr, rtd 84 & 48a): eff at 5f, tried 1m: handles fibresand, without blnks.
884   **MACHUDI** 26 [13] 3-9-1 (55) W Supple 16/1: 0-606: Nvr better than mid-div: AW/h'cap bow, see 804.   1   42a
1024 **DIAMOND OLIVIA** 14 [15] 3-8-13 (53) J F Egan 10/3 FAV: 40-347: Al same place: btr on turf 1024, 887.   ½   39a
870   **LYDIAS LOOK** 25 [8] 3-9-7 (61) J Fanning 20/1: 54108: Chsd ldrs till over 2f out: stays 7f?, see 740.   3   41a
2196} **NILOUPHAR** 319 [9] 3-8-0 (40)(BL) B Sooful (7) 25/1: 000-9: Hmpd start, in tch 5f: blnkd, new stable.   3   14a
899   **DENTON LADY** 25 [4] 3-8-4 (44) T Williams 20/1: 50-600: Struggling halfway: 10th, AW bow.   1¼   16a
1024 **DOUBLE FAULT** 14 [16] 3-9-0 (54) K Darley 7/2: 040-50: Wide, in tch 3f: 13th, tchd 6/1 on AW bow.   0a
1024 **GYMCRAK FIREBIRD** 14 [2] 3-9-1 (55) G Hind 12/1: 246-00: Dwelt, nvr in it: 14th: see 171.   0a
870   **HOT ICE** 27 [7] 3-8-8 (48) G Duffield 14/1: 310-00: Led till halfway, sn btn: 15th, op 10/1: see 870.   0a
933   **Flying Run** 21 [5] 3-9-5 (59) S Sanders 16/1:   4251} **Timeless Quest** 216 [6] 3-9-6 (60) L Newton 16/1:
930   **Kuuipo** 23 [1] 3-9-0 (54)(VIS) M Fenton 16/1:
16 ran   Time 1m 30.5 (3.9)   (Laurence O'Kane)   T D Barron Maunby, N Yorks

---

1203   2.15 LEICESTER CLAIMER 4YO+ (F)   1m4f aw   Going 37   -02 Slow
£2240   £640   £320

1070 **WILTON** 7 [13] J Hetherton 5-8-7 G Duffield 3/1 FAV: 301101: 5 ch g Sharpo - Poyle Amber (Sharrood)   60a
Waited with, prog to lead ent fnl 3f, rdn out: nicely bckd, qck reapp: earlier won at Hamilton (class stks) &
Pontefract (h'cap): lightly rcd since '98 wnr at Pontefract, Redcar (rtd 70) & Lingfield (h'caps, rtd 79a): eff
at 1m/sharp 12f: acts on gd, hvy, both AWs, likes Pontefract: eff with/without t-strap.
1145 **WAFIR** 3 [7] D Nicholls 8-8-9 (VIS) O Pears 6/1: 56-432: 8 b g Scenic - Taniokey (Grundy)   3   56a
Mid-div, prog to go 2nd 2f out, hung left, no ch wnr: op 8/1, qck reapp, vis, AW bow: eff on fast, hvy & f/sand.

399

871 **CHALCEDONY 27** [2] T D Barron 4-9-3 W Supple 4/1: 240403: 4 ch g Highest Honor - Sweet Holland 3½ **60a**
(Alydar) Well plcd, not clr run appr fnl 2f, onepace: tchd 6/1: back up in trip, see 508, 343.
1039 **APPROACHABLE 10** [10] Miss S J Wilton 5-8-11 I Mongan (5) 12/1: 242254: Mid-div, chsd ldrs 4f out 7 **45a**
till appr fnl 2f: op 7/1, stiff task, see 710, 45.
1039 **COLONEL CUSTER 10** [6] 5-8-13 (bl) G Bardwell 14/1: 005065: Prom, led halfway till 2½f out, fdd. 7 **38a**
1039 **BANNERET 10** [8] 7-8-5 P M Quinn (5) 8/1: 105326: Nvr nr ldrs: stiff task: see 581, 347. 3 **26a**
1091 **OVER THE MOON 6** [11] 6-8-6 T G McLaughlin 10/1: 014007: Nvr on terms: quick reapp, longer trip. 3 **23a**
1039 **ADIRPOUR 10** [9] 6-8-7 Stephanie Hollinshead (7) 33/1: 400308: Led till halfway, sn btn: see 556 (C/D) 2½ **21a**
*866 **JIBEREEN 27** [14] 8-9-7 R Mullen 6/1: 204319: Al towards rear: see 866 (11f, here). 5 **30a**
866 **PICKENS 27** [5] 8-8-7 Kim Tinkler 20/1: 4-0060: In tch till halfway: 10th, see 642. 10 **6a**
646 **North Ardar 63** [4] 10-8-5 F Norton 25/1: 893 **Socialist 25** [3] 4-8-11 (BL) J P Spencer 14/1:
922 **Bentico 23** [1] 11-8-7 (vis) Sarah Robinson (7) 20/1: 1100 **Da Boss 6** [12] 5-8-7 K Darley 12/1:
14 ran Time 2m 39.0 (4.7) (George A Moore) J Hetherton Malton, N Yorks

1204 **2.45 CHEDDAR MED AUCT MDN 3YO (F)** **1m aw rnd Going 37 +02 Fast**
£2219 £634 £317

1035 **TATE VENTURE 10** [4] S P C Woods 3-9-0 G Duffield 11/2: 031: 3 b g Deploy - Tasseled (Tate **70a**
Gallery) Mid-div, closed after 4f, rdn to lead below dist, just lasted: fair time: apprec return to 1m & further
shld suit (brother to mid-dist/stayer Deploy Venture): acts on fibresand, sharp trk: improving.
934 **MOST STYLISH 21** [8] C G Cox 3-8-9 S Sanders 9/2: 52: 3 ch f Most Welcome - Corman Style *shd* **64a**
(Ahonoora) Sn led, hdd 2½f out, again bef dist till ent fnl 1f, rallied, just failed: tchd 11/2, AW bow, clr rem:
eff at 1m, 10f+ looks sure to suit: goes on fibresand.
972 **SHATHER 19** [6] J W Hills 3-9-0 S Whitworth 4/5 FAV: -03: 3 b c Goofalik - Western Pride (Priamos) 3 **63a**
Trkd ldrs, led 2½f, hdd appr fnl 1f, no extra: op 1/2, clr rem AW bow: more expected down in grade after
9th in the Wood Ditton (had been working out): worth another chance back on turf.
920 **BELINDA 23** [9] K Bell 3-8-9 C Rutter 33/1: 04: Chsd ldrs wide, onepace appr fnl 2f: needs sells. 5 **48a**
1035 **THE LONELY WIGEON 10** [5] 3-9-0 (t) Dale Gibson 25/1: 05: Rear, eff after 4f, sn held: no form. 7 **39a**
858 **SHUFFLE 28** [3] 3-9-0 (BL) R Fitzpatrick (3) 50/1: 06: Nvr in it: blnkd on AW bow: First Trump colt. 12 **19a**
4597} **SWALDO 186** [10] 3-9-0 R Brisland (5) 11/1: 0023-7: Mid-div till halfway: reapp, op 8/1: plcd twice in 5 **11a**
'99 for G Chung (sell, rtd 65): eff at 1m on gd/soft grnd: now with N Berry.
804 **WAY OUT WEST 38** [1] 3-8-9 Dean McKeown 33/1: 08: Al towards rear: AW bow. 2 **2a**
1063 **SILVER SPOON 7** [7] 3-8-9 A Rawlinson 12/1: 09: Early ldr, lost place halfway: op 8/1, AW bow. 8 **0a**
696 **THE DIDDLER 49** [2] 3-9-0 D Harrison 50/1: 00: Chsd ldrs 3f: 10th, 7 wk abs. 9 **0a**
10 ran Time 1m 42.2 (2.8) (Dr Frank S B Chao) S P C Woods Newmarket

1205 **3.15 CAMEMBERT HCAP 3YO 0-70 (E)** **6f aw rnd Going 37 -01 Slow** **[77]**
£2804 £863 £431 £215

+1036 **GARTH POOL 10** [8] A Berry 3-9-9 (72) J Carroll 10/3 FAV: 50-511: 3 b g Sri Pekan - Millionetta **88a**
(Danehill) Made ev yard, clr & still on the bit 2f out, eased right down: any amount in hand: 10 days ago won in
similar style at W'hampton (mdn clmr): '99 rnr-up (h'cap, rtd 74, J Berry, blnkd): eff at 5/6f on fast grnd &
fibresand, handles gd/soft, with/without blnks: goes on sharp trks: a revelation with forcing tactics on fibresand.
909 **CRYFIELD 24** [7] N Tinkler 3-8-2 (51) J Fanning 20/1: 0502: 3 b g Efisio - Ciboure (Norwick) 4 **51a**
Prom, hung left ent fnl 2f, styd on but no ch with facile wnr: op 12/1 on AW/h'cap bow: eff at 6f on f/sand.
736 **ANTHEMION 44** [13] P C Haslam 3-9-3 (66) Dean McKeown 16/1: 300-03: 3 ch g Night Shift - New ¾ **64a**
Sensitive (Wattlefield) Rear, prog after 3f, drvn 2f out, same pace: AW bow, 6 wk abs: plcd last term
(mdn, rtd 70): 6f shld suit, handles fast grnd & fibresand.
736 **BULAWAYO 44** [9] B A McMahon 3-9-7 (70) W Supple 10/1: 6-1404: In tch, eff 2f out, nvr able to 1¼ **64a**
chall: 6 wk abs, unsuited by drop back to 6f: see 362 (7f mdn, forced it).
685 **MAJOR BART 52** [16] 3-8-1 (50) P Hanagan (7) 25/1: 00-05: Rear, wide prog 2f out, no extra: abs. *nk* **43a**
857 **PRICELESS SECOND 28** [10] 3-8-11 (60)(vis) D Mernagh (3) 16/1: 432206: Mid-div, under press appr ¾ **51a**
fnl 2f, no impress: unsuited by drop back to 6f?: see 417 (7f seller).
659 **POWER AND DEMAND 58** [14] 3-8-3 (52)(bl) F Norton 14/1: 025437: Al same pl: 8 wk abs, see 234. ½ **41a**
839 **SHOWING 31** [5] 3-8-11 (60) R Cochrane 11/2: 00-08: Chsd ldrs till fnl 2f: op 4/1, AW/h'cap bow. 3 **41a**
830 **UNFORTUNATE 32** [3] 3-8-1 (50) T Williams 20/1: 653069: Dwelt, nvr on terms: btr 181 (sell). 1¾ **27a**
1038 **MOUNT PARK 10** [15] 3-8-4 (53) N Pollard 33/1: 3-0000: Sn struggling: 10th, see 472. 1¼ **27a**
1033 **PEGGYS ROSE 12** [11] 3-9-3 (66) J F Egan 5/1: 140: Al bhd, 14th, tchd 7/1 on AW/h'cap bow. **0a**
300 **SIRENE 119** [2] 3-8-11 (60)(bl) D Harrison 8/1: 02-020: Chsd ldrs till halfway: 15th, op 10/1, 4 mnth abs. **0a**
887 **Phoebus 26** [4] 3-9-3 (66) J P Spencer 14/1: 909 **Secret Rendezvous 24** [12] 3-8-6 (55) O Pears 16/1:
976 **Bluegrass Mountain 19** [6] 3-9-3 (66) K Darley 16/1: 4570} **Claudius Tertius 189** [1] 3-8-0 (49) G Bardwell 14/1:
16 ran Time 1m 15.6 (2.3) (Lord Mostyn) A Berry Cockerham, Lancs

1206 **3.45 GLOUCESTER SELLER 2YO (G)** **5f aw str Going 37 -47 Slow**
£1813 £518 £259

828 **RUNNING FOR ME 32** [3] R Hollinshead 2-8-6 G Gibbons (7) 15/2: 61: 2 ch f Eagle Eyed - Running **61a**
For You (Pampabird) Nvr far away, led after halfway, rdn out: tchd 9/1 on AW bow, bght in for 5,000gns, slow time:
4,000 gns Feb foal, half-sister to a 5f wnr, dam 1m wnr: eff at 5f, 6f is going to suit: goes on fibresand, sharp trk.
1019 **ORCHARD RAIDER 14** [7] C A Dwyer 2-8-11 G Bardwell 12/1: -02: 2 b c Mujadil - Apple Brandy 1 **62a**
(Cox's Ridge) Prom, chall 2f out, kept on but held by wnr: op 20/1, AW bow: eff at 5f on fibresand, find similar.
1059 **PRINCESS PENNY 7** [5] W G M Turner 2-8-6 A Daly 12/1: R3: 2 ch f King's Signet - Princess Tallulah 2 **51a**
(Chief Singer) Led till after halfway, onepace bef dist: op 10/1, clr rem: gets a sharp 5f on fibresand.
-- **YOUNG MONASH** [2] B S Rothwell 2-8-11 M Fenton 3/1: 4: Prom, no extra ent fnl 2f: nicely bckd 4 **46a**
tho' op 2/1 on debut: 500 gns General Monash Apr gldg, half-brother to 2 juv wnrs, sire a sprinter.
856 **ROYLE FAMILY 28** [4] 2-8-11 O Pears 9/4 FAV: 45: Prom till hung violently left & ended up on 1¾ **41a**
far rail appr fnl 2f: well bckd: did similar on debut, could do with a rail to run against: see 856.
-- **SOOTY TIME** [8] 2-8-11 F Norton 16/1: 6: Prom till 2f out: 700 gns Timeless Times Mar gldg, 1st foal. 3½ **33a**
849 **DIAMOND MILLENNIUM 28** [6] 2-8-6 J F Egan 3/1: 57: Bhd from halfway: AW bow, see 849. 5 **18a**
1083 **BAYRAMI 6** [1] 2-8-6 R Winston 33/1: 058: Veered left start, al bhd: quick reapp. 1½ **14a**
-- **WHARFEDALE GHOST** [9] 2-8-11 T Williams 25/1: 9: Dwelt, sn struggling: 750 gns King Among 2 **14a**
Kings Mar foal, brother to a Danish 3yo wnr, sire moderate 11f scorer: with W Kemp.
9 ran Time 1m 02.0 (4.2) (R Hollinshead) R Hollinshead Upper Longdon, Staffs

SOUTHWELL (Fibresand) MONDAY MAY 8TH Lefthand, Sharp Track

1207 4.15 BRIE AMAT RDRS HCAP 4YO+ 0-70 (G) 1m aw rnd Going 37 -26 Slow [48]
£1939 £554 £277

890 **HOH GEM 26** [11] B R Millman 4-9-6 (40) Mr G Richards (1) 33/1: 000-01: 4 b g Be My Chief - Jennies' Gem (Sayf El Arab) Outpcd early, styd on ent fnl 2f, gd hdwy to lead below dist, sn clr: wng AW bow, well btn all 5 prev turf starts (rtd 54$): eff at 1m, tried 10f: goes on fibresand & a sharp trk & can pull hard. **48a**
846 **MIDNIGHT WATCH 30** [3] A G Newcombe 6-9-11 (45) Miss C Hannaford (5) 15/2: 132202: 6 b g Capote - Midnight Air (Green Dancer) Mid-div, wide into str, ch ent fnl 1f, outpcd by wnr: apprec the return to f/sand. *3* **47a**
*1137 **TAKHLID 4** [2] D W Chapman 9-11-8 (70)(5ex) Miss R Clark 9/1: 665013: 9 b h Nureyev - Savonnerie (Irish River) Nvr far away, chall 2f out, onepace dist: quick reapp with a pen back up in trip: see 1137 (6f clmr). *1½* **69a**
867 **MUTAHADETH 27** [8] D Shaw 6-10-1 (49)(bl) Mr T Best (3) 10/1: 446044: In tch, prog & ch appr fnl 1f, onepace under press: op 8/1: invariably thereabouts: see 183. *½* **47a**
*869 **KILLARNEY JAZZ 27** [1] 5-10-8 (56)(vis) Mr Paul J Morris (5) 6/1: 003015: Chsd ldrs, led ent fnl 2f till hung right & hdd below dist, no extra: btr 869 (seller, professionally ridden). *hd* **54a**
705 **SOPHOMORE 46** [12] 6-11-6 (68) Mrs Annette Harris (7) 9/1: 6/0306: Chsd ldrs wide over 2f out, nvr able to chall: tchd 14/1, 7 wk abs, see 599, 343. *1¼* **63a**
871 **SEPTEMBER HARVEST 27** [9] 4-9-7 (41) Mr S Dobson(4) 25/1: 644007: Nvr better than mid-div: see 261 *shd* **36a**
859 **SWING ALONG 28** [10] 5-11-0 (62) Mr V Coogan (5) 10/1: 533348: Nvr nr ldrs: back in trip, see 404. *hd* **56a**
749 **GODMERSHAM PARK 41** [7] 8-10-0 (48) Mr P Collington (7) 14/1: 441409: Led 3f out till bef fnl 1f, wknd. *nk* **41a**
822 **PREPOSITION 33** [14] 4-9-7 (41) Mrs C Williams 14/1: 524100: Sn led, hdd 3f out & btn: 10th, see 742. *nk* **33a**
866 **BE WARNED 27** [6] 9-10-12 (60)(vis) Miss E Folkes(5) 8/1: 501200: Bhnd halfway, broke bld vessel: 13th. **0a**
846 **MY TYSON 30** [13] 5-10-1 (49) Miss E Ramsden 9/2 FAV: 001360: Early ldr, lost pl halfway: 14th, see 676. **0a**
921 **Trojan Wolf 23** [15] 5-11-7 (69) Miss S Pocock(5) 16/1:
780 **Indian Dance 40** [5] 4-10-0 (48)(t) Mr W Worthington(7) 33/1:
248 **Butterscotch 126** [16] 4-9-8 (42) Miss Diana Jones 12/1: 1050 **Port Of Call 9** [4] 5-9-13 (47) Mrs M Morris (3) 20/1:
16 ran Time 1m 44.4 (5) (Brian Lovrey) B R Millman Kentisbeare, Devon

BRIGHTON TUESDAY MAY 9TH Lefthand, V Sharp, Undulating Track

Official Going: FIRM. Stalls: Inside, except 10f/12f - outside

1208 2.20 EBF/ASTAIRE MDN 2YO (D) 5f59y rnd Firm 05 -31 Slow
£3295 £1014 £507 £253

1095 **SOLDIER ON 7** [4] M R Channon 2-9-0 S Drowne 6/4 FAV: 021: 2 b c General Monash - Golden Form (Formidable) Cl-up & went on halfway, asserted fnl 1f, styd on well: hvly bckd: dam a 9f wnr: eff at 5f on firm & good/soft grnd, will get further: handles a sharp/undul track. **81**
1048 **TUMBLEWEED TENOR 10** [5] B J Meehan 2-9-0 D Holland 7/1: 52: 2 b g Mujadil - Princess Carmen (Arokar) Handy, rdn/chsd wnr fnl 1f, kept on, al held: op 5/1: acts on firm grnd & a sharp/undul track. *2½* **73**
1095 **WESTERN HERO 7** [6] R Hannon 2-9-0 Dane O'Neill 15/8: 33: 2 ch c Lake Coniston - Miss Pickpocket (Petorius) Dwelt, soon bhd ldrs, eff over 1f out, no impression: well bckd: closer to today's wnr in 1095 (g/s). *3½* **64**
-- **ASTAIREDOTCOM** [2] K R Burke 2-8-9 J Weaver 14/1: 4: Bhd/outpcd, rdn/kept on fnl 2f, no threat: op 10/1: Lake Coniston filly, Feb foal, cost IR 5,000gns: dam a juv wnr, sire progressive/top class sprinter. *1¼* **56**
828 **STORMING FOLEY 33** [1] 2-9-0 P Fitzsimons (5) 8/1: 425: Led till halfway, soon btn: op 6/1: btr 828. *½* **59**
-- **CEDAR TSAR** [3] 2-9-0 S Sanders 50/1: 6: Rdn/bhd, mod prog: Inzar colt, March foal, 9,500gns 2yo: dam a mdn, sire a high-class 6/7f performer: with R J O'Sullivan. *½* **57**
6 ran Time 1m 01.9 (1.9) (T S M Cunningham) M R Channon West Isley, Berks

1209 2.50 HARDINGS HCAP 4YO+ 0-70 (E) 1m4f Firm 05 +04 Fast [70]
£2915 £833 £416

1128 **TWO SOCKS 5** [12] J S King 7-9-1 (57) I Mongan (5) 6/1: 000-61: 7 ch g Phountzi - Mrs Feathers (Pyjama Hunt) Mid-div, rdn/prog to lead over 2f out, held on well inside last, drvn out: best time of day, tchd 7/1, quick reapp: '99 Kempton scorer (h'cap, rtd 72): '98 Warwick wnr (h'cap, rtd 73 at best): eff at 10/12f on firm, good/soft & any track: best without blinks: looks on a fair mark & could win again. **63**
1128 **KIRISNIPPA 5** [3] Derrick Morris 5-8-9 (51) C Carver (3) 7/1: 160532: 5 b g Beveled - Kiri Te (Liboi) Chsd ldrs, efft/drifted right from 3f out, styd on well ins last, not rch wnr: op 11/2, qck reapp: see 1128. *1¼* **54**
1076 **LEGAL LUNCH 8** [4] P W Harris 5-9-12 (68)(vis) J Weaver 5/1 FAV: -42053: 5 b g Alleged - Dinner Surprise (Lyphard) Trkd ldrs, rdn 3f out, kept on onepace: nicely bckd: see 6. *½* **70**
855 **FANDANGO DREAM 29** [10] M D I Usher 4-7-10 (38)(1oh) G Baker (7) 33/1: 000-04: Towards rear, rdn/late gains, no threat: stays 12f, prob handles firm grnd: see 855. *4* **34**
963 **RED BORDEAUX 21** [2] 5-8-7 (47)(BL)(2ow) S Sanders 16/1: /0-005: Rdn/rear, kept on fnl 2f for press, nrst fin: op 14/1, tried blinks: no form sole '99 start, 98/99 rnr up over timber (mdn hdle, rtd 90h, acts on soft): '98 Catterick wnr on the level (mdn, rtd 70, B Hills): eff at 12f, has tried 2m: acts on good/soft. *¾* **44**
607 **HURGILL DANCER 70** [17] 6-7-10 (38)(1oh) A Nicholls (0) 12/1: 4-3406: Chsd ldrs 3f out, sn held: abs. *nk* **32**
-- **PENNYS FROM HEAVEN** [14] 6-10-0 (70) Clare Roche (7) 14/1: 0034/7: Chsd ldrs, held final 3f: op 12/1, long Flat abs, Jumps fit (unplcd, Miss Venitia Williams): unplcd in '98 for L M Cumani (rtd 75, h'cap): '97 Bath wnr (rtd 80 at best, H Candy): eff at 12f, tried 14f: acts on firm & good/soft grnd: has run well in blinks. *1¼* **62**
835 **CEDAR FLAG 32** [6] 6-8-3 (45) L Newman (5) 16/1: 243108: Cl-up, led 5f out till over 2f out, faded. *1½* **35**
918 **QUAKERESS 24** [16] 5-7-10 (38)(10oh) J Mackay (7) 10/1: 345329: Mid-div, no impression final 3f. *8* **19**
*1086 **ALBERKINNIE 7** [8] 5-7-10 (38)(6ex)(1oh) K Dalgleish (7) 13/2: 533210: Mid div halfway, btn 3f out: 10th. *½* **18**
1003 **LOST SPIRIT 15** [18] 4-7-10 (38)(3oh) Joanna Badger (7) 33/1: 600350: Led till 5f out, soon btn: 11th. *6* **9**
1100 **SAMMYS SHUFFLE 7** [5] 5-7-12 (40)(bl) M Henry 7/1: 530640: Chsd ldrs 9f: 17th: op 6/1: see 1100 (10f). **0**
413 **Blowing Away 102** [11] 6-7-10 (38)(3oh) G Bardwell 20/1:
835 **War Baby 32** [15] 4-7-10 (38)(VIS) A McCarthy (1) 33/1:
333 **Max 115** [7] 5-7-10 (38)(1oh) R Brisland (5) 33/1: 489 **Lunar Lord 89** [13] 4-7-10 (38)(3oh) M Baird 33/1:
893 **Vegas 26** [9] 4-7-10 (38)(2oh) C Adamson 33/1:
17 ran Time 2m 28.3 (0.1) (Mrs Satu Marks) J S King Broad Hinton, Wilts

BRIGHTON   TUESDAY MAY 9TH   Lefthand, V Sharp, Undulating Track

1210   3.20 RENATE SELLER 3YO+ (G)   1m2f   Firm 05   -30 Slow
£1967   £562   £281   3 yo   rec 15lb

4467} **WILLIE CONQUER** 200 [11] D R C Elsworth 8-9-8 K Parsons (7) 11/8 FAV: 0540-1: 8 ch g Master Willie - Maryland Cookie (Bold Hour) Rear early, smooth/steady prog halfway, led 2f out & al holding rivals under hands-&-heels riding: nicely bckd tho' drifted from 8/13: sold to A Reid for 10,500gns: '99 reapp wnr here at Brighton (h'cap, rtd 88, t-strap): eff at 10/12f on firm & good/soft, handles any track, likes Brighton: runs well fresh.   63

1096 **JUST WIZ** 7 [9] R Hannon 4-9-8 Dane O'Neill 12/1: 553002: 4 b g Efisio - Jade Pet (Petong)   2½   56
In tch, rdn/outpcd 4f out, kept on for press final 2f, no threat: claimed by A Reid for £5000.

892 **COLLEGE ROCK** 26 [8] Mrs A E Johnson 3-8-2 (vis) A McCarthy (3) 8/1: -04263: 3 ch g Rock Hopper -   1¼   54
Sea Aura (Roi Soleil) Keen/prom, one pace fnl 2f: op 7/1: see 806.

893 **EI EI** 26 [7] G L Moore 5-9-8 I Mongan (5) 12/1: 246624: Dwelt, soon chsd ldrs, one pace fnl 2f.   1½   52$

4463} **GOLD LANCE** 201 [14] 7-9-8 R Miles (3) 33/1: 0060-5: Dwelt/rear, rdn/late gains, nrst fin: Flat reapp,   shd   52$
12 wk jumps abs (rtd 59h, sell h'cap): rnr up '99 (rtd 53, h'cap): rtd 45 in '98 (h'cap): '97 wnr at Pontefract, Chepstow (sell h'cap), Windsor & Goodwood (h'caps, rtd 61): eff at 7/9f, yet to convince at 10f+: acts on firm & gd/soft, handles equitrack: has run well fresh: eff with/without blinks.

-- **ALBINONA** [2] A Whelan 40/1: 000-6: Chsd ldrs, onepace fnl 2f: reapp: British debut, mod   nk   46
form in 7f/8.5f mdns in Ireland last term: with M H Tompkins.

893 **TWOFORTEN** 26 [16] 5-9-8 (bl) A Nicholls (3) 33/1: 5-0667: Prom 1m: blinks reapp: see 524.   1¾   49$

1065 **GAME TUFTY** 8 [19] 4-9-8 T G McLaughlin 16/1: 310-08: Mid-div, eff/no impress fnl 2f: '99 Windsor   1¼   47
wnr (sell, rtd 62): promise in '98 (stks, rtd 74$ & 67): eff at 1m/10f on gd & gd/soft, likes a sharp track.

1101 **ESPERTO** 6 [6] 7-9-8 G Bardwell 16/1: 22/009: Chsd ldrs 1m: quick reapp: see 922.   1¼   45

786 **THOMAS HENRY** 41 [10] 4-9-8 D Holland 9/2: 660550: Chsd ldrs, btn 3f out: 10th: op 6/1, abs.   3   41

822 **SATWA BOULEVARD** 34 [13] 5-9-3 P McCabe 50/1: 000000: Keen/prom 7f: 11th: see 326.   6   27

4232} **ARAGANT** 218 [4] 4-9-8 J Weaver 10/1: 5330-0: Led till 2f out, reapp: plcd in   ½   31
'99 (rtd 80, mdn, prob flattered, with P W Chapple Hyam): handles fast & good grnd.

775 **Gaelic Foray** 41 [12] 4-9-3 R Cochrane 50/1:   460 **Private Seal** 94 [17] 5-9-8 (t) A Beech (5) 50/1:
-- **Olly May** [5] 5-9-3 S Drowne 33/1:   3850} **Lady Wyn** 243 [3] 5-9-3 Darren Williams (7) 50/1:
896 **Corsecan** 26 [18] 5-9-8 R Brisland (5) 50/1:   1282} **The Bizz** 363 [15] 7-9-3 O Urbina 66/1:
18 ran   Time 2m 01.3 (3.5)   (Raymond Tooth)   D R C Elsworth Whitsbury, Hants

1211   3.50 HANNINGTONS MDN HCAP 3YO+ 0-70 (E)   6f rnd   Firm 05   -32 Slow   [58]
£2884   £824   £412   3 yo   rec 10lb

958 **ABSOLUTE FANTASY** 21 [16] E A Wheeler 4-9-0 (44)(bl) S Carson (5) 10/1: 260201: 4 b f Beveled - Sharp   49
Venita (Sharp Edge) Bhd ldrs, wide, rdn/prog to lead over 1f out, drifted left/styd on well inside last, rdn out: mod '99 turf form: eff at 6/7f, stays a sharp 1m: acts on fm, good & eqtrk, handles any track: eff in blinks.

634 **MAGIC BABE** 66 [13] Jamie Poulton 3-9-1 (55) O Urbina 14/1: 000-02: 3 b f Magic Ring - Head Turner   1½   56
(My Dad Tom) Rear/wide, rdn & styd on well fnl 2f, nrst fin: 2 month abs: handles firm & gd, return to 7f+ cld suit.

854 **ARZILLO** 29 [4] J M Bradley 4-9-9 (53) Claire Bryan (5) 20/1: 030-03: 4 b g Forzando - Titania's   shd   54
Dance (Fairy King) Prom, onepcd fnl 1f: plcd in '99 (rtd 59, h'cap, S Dow): eff at 6f/1m, handles firm grnd.

1098 **AROGANT PRINCE** 7 [12] J J Bridger 3-9-2 (56) R Brisland (5) 20/1: 460-04: Chsd ldrs, outpcd 2f   1¼   54
out, kept on inside last, not pace to chall: see 1098.

1137 **WHATTA MADAM** 5 [3] 4-9-12 (56)(t) I Mongan (5) 10/1: 64-405: Cl-up, led over 2f out, hard rdn/   ½   52
hdd over 1f out, no extra: op 14/1: see 154.

745 **BETTINA BLUE** 43 [9] 3-9-9 (63) J Weaver 11/1: 065-66: Mid-div, never pace to chall: 6 week abs.   ½   57

1024 **GROVE LODGE** 15 [6] 3-8-10 (50) S Whitworth 25/1: 0-0007: Rdn/towards rear, rdn & keeping on   ½   42+
well inside last when no room close home: a rtn to 7f+ cld suit on this evidence, interesting for similar.

2687} **DON QUIXOTE** 300 [17] 4-9-3 (47) A Nicholls (3) 6/1: 0030-8: Prom, ch 2f out, soon no extra: op   ¾   37
4/1, reapp: plcd in '99 (rtd 45, mdn h'cap, L Cumani): rtd 58 on sole '98 start: eff at 6f on fast grnd.

852 **SWING CITY** 29 [2] 3-9-5 (59) S Sanders 7/1: 400-09: Chsd ldrs, no impress fnl 1f: op 10/1.   hd   48

852 **LUSONG** 29 [10] 3-9-8 (62) Dane O'Neill 4/1 FAV: 226340: Rear/wide, mod prog: 10th: op 3/1.   shd   51

1092 **MALAAH** 7 [7] 4-9-11 (55)(bl) A Beech 12/1: 066-00: Led 4f, faded: 11th: op 10/1: see 1092.   1½   40

854 **NIGHT ADVENTURE** 29 [1] 4-9-1 (45) S Drowne 25/1: 30-000: Prom 2f, no room when held 1f out,   nk   29
eased near fin: 12th: plcd in '99 (L J Dunlop, mdn, rtd 69): stays 7f & handles firm grnd: with J M Bradley.

147 **Silver Sky** 155 [15] 4-8-10 (40) D Sweeney 33/1:   3883} **Fairytime** 241 [14] 4-8-10 (40)(BL) Martin Dwyer 20/1:
930 **Clear Crystal** 24 [5] 3-9-8 (62)(VIS) D Holland 12/1:   973 **Annijaz** 20 [18] 3-9-4 (58) D Harrison 16/1:
3895} **Blakey** 239 [11] 4-9-3 (47) Darren Williams (7) 20/1:345 **Kidnapped** 113 [8] 4-9-5 (49)(BL) T G McLaughlin 33/1:
18 ran   Time 1m 10.0 (2.2)   (The Red Square Partnership)   E A Wheeler Whitchurch on Thames, Oxon

1212   4.20 ALEXANDERS CLAIMER 3YO (F)   7f rnd   Firm 05   -29 Slow
£2284   £652   £326

654 **TEA FOR TEXAS** 62 [7] H Morrison 3-8-0 C Rutter 14/1: -35201: 3 ch f Weldnaas - Polly's Teahouse   53
(Shack) Led/dsptd lead throughout, asserted ins last & held on well, drvn out: claimed by J Akehurst for £9,000: 2 month abs: eff up with/forcing the pace at 6/7f on a sharp/undul trk: acts on firm & equitrack: runs well fresh.

165 **WELCOME SHADE** 151 [2] R Hannon 3-8-9 Dane O'Neill 100/30 JT FAV: 0014-2: 3 gr g Green Desert -   1½   58
Grey Angel (Kenmare) Rear, rh & prog dist, kept on ins last, not rch wnr: nicely bckd, abs: acts on firm & e/track.

514 **PERLE DE SAGESSE** 85 [1] Julian Poulton 3-8-4 A Morris 14/1: -05453: 3 b f Namaqualand - Pearl Of   hd   52
Dubai (Red Ransom) Rear, rh prog 3f out, kept on onepace from over 1f out: 12 week abs: see 155.

892 **ANNS MILL** 26 [11] J S Moore 3-8-6 L Newman 12/1: 100-04: Led/dsptd late till 1f out, faded: '99   1¼   51
Thirsk wnr (M Blanshard, rtd 63, seller): eff at 7f on firm grnd: enjoys selling grade.

1081 **COMMONBIRD** 7 [3] 3-7-12 M Henry 14/1: 500-05: Prom, looking held/hmpd over 1f out: see 1081.   hd   42$

*1081 **CAPE COAST** 7 [6] 3-8-11 R Cochrane 100/30 JT FAV: 6-0016: Chsd ldrs, btn final 1f: btr 1081 (6f).   1¼   47

1062 **FOX STAR** 8 [3] 3-8-0 A Beech 14/1: 00-007: Rdn/towards rear, never on terms: see 313 (AW).   1½   38

-- **GOLD RIDER** [4] 3-9-3 D Harrison 7/1: 8: Mid-div, outpcd final 2f: op 12/1, debut: with G M McCourt.   3   49

959 **PRINCESS VICTORIA** 21 [10] 3-8-0 J Mackay 7/2: 6-3339: Keen/chsd ldrs, faded fnl 2f: btr 959.   nk   31

459 **LUNAJAZ** 94 [9] 3-8-5 (VIS) R Price 33/1: 0-0500: Hmpd start, prom 3f: 10th: vs, 3 mth abs: see 241.   18   9

10 ran   Time 1m 22.2 (2.4)   (H Morrison)   H Morrison East Ilsley, Berks

402

BRIGHTON   TUESDAY MAY 9TH   Lefthand, V Sharp, Undulating Track

1213 4.50 LADBROKES HCAP 3YO+ 0-70 (E)   7f rnd   Firm 05 -04 Slow   [70]
£2905   £830   £415   3 yo rec 12lb

391 **BUTRINTO 105** [4] B R Johnson 6-8-4 (46) C Rutter 25/1: 0-5061: 6 ch g Anshan - Bay Bay (Bay Express)   55
Mid-div, rdn/prog over 1f out, lead ins last, styd on well, rdn out: 3 month abs: prev with J Pearce, rnr up in
'99 (rtd 74a, h'cap): '98 Newbury & Lingfield scorer (h'caps, rtd 75 & 75a): eff at 6f/1m on firm, gd & both
AW's: handles any track: best without blinks/visor: runs well fresh.

1082 **COMPRADORE 7** [7] M Blanshard 5-9-4 (60) R Cochrane 6/1: 30-032: 5 b m Mujtahid - Keswa (King's   1¼   64
Lake) Bhd ldrs, prog/rdn & briefly led inside last, not pace of wnr close home: nicely bckd: see 1082, 817.

587 **RAFTERS MUSIC 74** [14] D Nicholls 5-8-10 (52) Clare Roche (7) 12/1: 121603: 5 b g Thatching - Princess 1   54
Dixieland (Dixieland Band) Rdn/towards rear, prog when hung left 2f out, kept on well near fin: op 8/1, 10 wk abs.

1129 **GULF SHAADI 5** [9] Miss Gay Kelleway 8-10-0 (70) D Holland 7/1: -04054: Dwelt/towards rear, rdn   nk   71
& styd on well from 2f out, nrst fin: nicely bckd, op 8/1: quick reapp, topweight: see 169 (AW, 1m).

4206} **EVENTUALITY 220** [1] 4-9-13 (69) S Carson 25/1: 4146-5: Led after 1f & clear halfway, hard   2½   65
rdn/hdd ins last, fdd: well bckd, reapp: '99 wnr at Salisbury (fill h'cap) & Epsom (h'cap, rtd 69): plcd in '98
(rtd 66): eff at 7f, tried 10f: acts on firm/fast grnd, sharp/undulating or gall track.

3585} **KEE RING 257** [2] 4-9-12 (58) S Whitworth 25/1: 5035-6: Chsd ldrs, rdn/chsd ldr 2f out, soon held: ¾   53
reapp: plcd in '99 (rtd 56, mdn): rnr up in '98 on debut (rtd 79, auct mdn): eff at 6/7f, handles fast & good.

707 **VILLAGE NATIVE 47** [10] 7-8-12 (54)(bl) J Weaver 25/1: 000007: Led 1f, btn 1f out: abs: see 352 (AW).   4   41
852 **JACK DAWSON 29** [8] 3-8-7 (61) D Harrison 20/1: 000-08: Rdn/mid div, held over 1f out: see 852 (6f).   1¼   45
1032 **SPIRIT OF TENBY 13** [5] 3-8-13 (67) O Urbina 25/1: 005-69: Dwelt, rear, mod gains fnl 2f: see 1032 (1m).   1   49
879 **UNCHAIN MY HEART 27** [12] 4-9-0 (56) M Tebbutt 20/1: 0-1630: In touch 5f: 10th: btr 616 (AW).   shd   38
1092 **DAME JUDE 7** [13] 4-9-1 (57) S Sanders 20/1: 000-00: Rdn/rear, mod gains: 11th: op 14/1: see 1092.   nk   38
838 **AEGEAN FLAME 32** [11] 4-9-9 (65) S Drowne 12/1: 000-60: Rdn/mid div, no impression final 2f: 12th.   ½   45
1074 **RED DELIRIUM 8** [16] 4-9-12 (68) A Nicholls (3) 13/2: 00-200: In touch 4f: 15th: btr 746 (6f).   15
*153 **CRUISE 155** [18] 3-9-0 (68) Dane O'Neill 9/1: 51-0: In touch wide 4f: 17th: op 7/1, 5 month abs: see 153.   0
1058 Consultant 30 [3] 4-8-6 (48) L Newman (5) 33/1:   776 Bonnie Dundee 41 [15] 4-8-4 (46)(bl) D Kinsella (7) 20/1:
910 Milady Lillie 25 [17] 4-8-13 (55) C Carver (3) 16/1:   1058 Peruvian Star 10 [6] 4-8-13 (55) T G McLaughlin 33/1:
18 ran   Time 1m 20.4 (0.6)   (Miss Julie Reeves)   B R Johnson Epsom,Surrey

CHESTER   TUESDAY MAY 9TH   Lefthand, Very Sharp track

Official Going   GOOD (GOOD/FIRM in places). Stalls: Inside, except 1m2f - Stands Side.

1214 2.10 LILY AGNES COND STKS 2YO (B)   5f rnd   Good/Firm 20 -05 Slow
£8613   £3267   £1633   £742

*821 **ROMANTIC MYTH 34** [2] T D Easterby 2-8-8 K Darley 5/4 FAV: 11: 2 b f Mind Games - My First Romance   97
(Danehill) Bhd ldrs, rdn briefly appr fnl 1f, qcknd to lead ins last, readily: hvly bckd: unbtn, earlier won at
Ripon (mdn): 16,000gns Jan foal, half-sister to a 5f juv wnr, sire a sprinter: eff at 5f, shld get 6f: acts on fast
& soft grnd, sharp trks: goes well fresh: useful, imprvg & speedy, pencil her in for the Queen Mary.

755 **CHARLIE PARKES 42** [5] A Berry 2-8-10 J Carroll 6/1: 22: 2 ch c Pursuit Of Love - Lucky Parkes   ¾   94
(Full Extent) Tried to make all, under press dist, hdd & not pace of wnr final 100y: op 5/1, 6 wk abs, 5L clr rem:
clearly suited by this v sharp trk: acts on fast & soft grnd & suited forcing the pace: go one better sn.

985 **NEARLY A FOOL 19** [1] B A McMahon 2-8-13 T Quinn 9/1: 1433: 2 b g Komaite - Greenway Lady   5   82+
(Prince Daniel) Rear but in tch, not much room 2f out, styd on under hands-&-heels for 3rd: op 4/1, not given a
hard time once ldrs had skipped clr & is worth another chance on a more conventional trk: see 985, 700.

911 **Y TO KMAN 25** [4] R Hannon 2-8-13 R Hughes 10/3: 124: Chsd ldrs, effort appr final 1f, onepace.   ¾   80
1006 **STREGONE 15** [6] 2-8-13 (BL) Pat Eddery 14/1: 165: Dwelt, held up, outpcd 2f out: op 10/1, blnkd.   5   68
*878 **JUSTALORD 27** [7] 2-8-13 A Daly 25/1: -616: Prsd ldr till qckly lost pl 2f out: highly tried after 878.   1¾   63
-- **ITALIAN AFFAIR** [3] 2-8-5 G Duffield 40/1: 7: Sn struggling, t.o. on debut: IR 1,800gns Fumo Di   dist   0
Londra Mar 1st foal, dam moderate, sire a miler: with A Bailey & highly tried today.
7 ran   Time 1m 01.04 (1.24)   (T G Holdcroft)   T D Easterby Great Habton, Nth Yorks.

1215 2.40 STANLEY LEISURE HCAP 3YO 0-100 (C)   7f122y rnd   Good/Firm 20 +04 Fast   [107]
£18785   £5780   £2890   £1445 Low numbers have a big advantage here

735 **NICOBAR 45** [3] I A Balding 3-9-7 (100) K Fallon 9/2 FAV: 525-31: 3 b c Indian Ridge - Duchess Of Alba   108
(Belmez) Mid-div, imprvg when short of room appr fnl 2f, rall bef dist & kept on well to lead ins last, comfly: hvly
bckd, fair time, top-weight, 6 wk abs: '99 Haydock wnr (mdn, subs highly tried, rtd 100): eff at 7f/1m: acts on
fast & gd/soft, handles firm: goes on any trk, can force the pace: v useful, looks Listed/Gr 3 class.

954 **CAMBERLEY 21** [13] P F I Cole 3-8-7 (86) J Fortune 6/1: 62-322: 3 b c Sri Pekan - NSX (Roi Danzig)   ¾   91
Quckly across to trk ldrs on rail, shkn up to lead appr fnl 1f, sn hard rdn, collared well ins last: bckd tho'
op 4/1: fine run from a poor high draw, against this v useful wnr: eff at 6f/7.5f on fast & gd: sure to win sn.

884 **POLAR CHALLENGE 27** [14] Sir Michael Stoute 3-8-0 (79) R Ffrench 10/1: -54-03: 3 b c Polar Falcon -   1   82
Warning Light (High Top) In tch, prog over 2f out, rdn before dist, kept on but unable to chall: op 5/1 on
h'cap bow: gd run from a poor high draw, likely to apprec further than 7.5f: see 884.

810 **ATLANTIC RHAPSODY 38** [12] M Johnston 3-8-7 (86) M Hills 16/1: 32-104: Dwelt & outpcd, hemmed in   ½   88+
& last (going well) 2f out, found room & fin v fast, too late: blnks omitted, no luck today: see 894.

4591} **PEACOCK ALLEY 188** [2] A Berry 3-7-12 (77) P Fessey 20/1: 5023-5: Set gd pace, hdd appr final 1f, no extra   ½   78
inside last: drifter from 12/1 on reapp/h'cap bow: fillies mdn rnr-up last term (rtd 80): eff at 7f/1m, bred
for further: goes on fast & gd/soft grnd: should win races for W Haggas.

830 **MYTTONS AGAIN 33** [7] 3-7-10 (75)(bl) (6oh) J Bramhill 33/1: -40026: Mid-div, prog 2f out, sn onepace.   1½   73
4285} **MINKASH 213** [6] 3-9-0 (93) R Hills 10/1: 1220-7: Rear, imprvg on the bit when not clr run 2f out,   2½   86
kept on: tchd 14/1 on reapp: '99 York wnr (mdn, nursery rnr-up, rtd 95): eff at 7f/1m, bred to stay further:
acts on firm/fast grnd, stiff/gall trks: sharper for this, keep in mind: with B Hanbury.
4053} **GLENROCK 230** [5] 3-8-13 (92) J Carroll 16/1: 1103-8: Chsd ldrs, chall appr final 2f, fdd before dist: 3   79
reapp: '99 wnr at Lingfield (mdn auct) & here at Chester (4 rnr stks, rtd 91): eff forcing the pace at 5/6f,
stays 7f: goes on firm & hvy, sharp or gall trk: can run well fresh: with A Berry & return to 6f will suit.

403

727 **PIPS WAY** 45 [10] 3-7-11 (76) Dale Gibson 33/1: 040-69: Al mid-div: 6 wk abs: see 727. ½ 62
954 **PROUD CHIEF** 21 [8] 3-8-0 (78)(1ow) R Mullen 11/1: 00-260: Chsd ldrs till 2f out: 10th: see 792. 5 55
4033} **ZESTRIL** 231 [4] 3-8-3 (81)(1ow) G Duffield 20/1: 104-0: Prom, wknd fnl 2f: 11th on reapp/h'cap nk 57
bow: Carlisle debut wnr last term (mdn, rtd 81 at best): eff at 6f, shld get further: acts on fast, poss soft.
954 **OCEAN RAIN** 21 [11] 3-7-11 (76) F Norton 16/1: 05-050: Slow away, nvr got in it: 12th, visor omitted. 1 49
*704 **KOOKABURRA** 47 [16] 3-9-2 (95) Pat Eddery 15/2: 324-10: Al bhd: 15th: 7 wk abs, ignore, v poor draw. 0
933 **MENTIGA** 22 [1] 3-8-3 (81)(1ow) P Robinson 12/1: 13-050: Mid-div till 3f out: 16th, likes softer grnd, see 810. 0
954 Digital Image 21 [17] 3-8-4 (83) J F Egan 33/1: 977 **Cote Soleil** 20 [18] 3-8-9 (88) M Fenton 25/1:
690 Buggy Ride 52 [15] 3-8-8 (87) N Callan 50/1: *894 **Sporty Mo** 26 [9] 3-7-12 (77)(vis) D Mernagh (3) 14/1:
18 ran Time 1m 33.62 (1.22) (Robert Hitchins) I A Balding Kingsclere, Hants.

1216 3.10 GR 3 CHESTER VASE 3YO (A) 1m4f66y Good/Firm 20 +06 Fast
£36000 £13600 £6900 £3300

*916 **MILLENARY** 25 [4] J L Dunlop 3-8-10 Pat Eddery 8/1: -35-11: 3 b c Rainbow Quest - Ballerina 105
(Dancing Brave) In tch, shkn up 2f out, swtchd & drvn dist, kept on well to lead towards fin: op 6/1: gd time:
earlier won Newbury reapp (mdn): highly tried/ran well both '99 starts (stks, rtd 89): eff at 11f/12f, will stay
further: acts on firm & soft grnd, any trk: runs well fresh: v useful, lightly rcd & progressive.
4558} **WINDSOR BOY** 192 [2] P F I Cole 3-8-10 J Fortune 14/1: -165-2: 3 b c Mtoto - Fragrant Belle (Al ½ 103
Nasr) Waited with, pushed along to impr over 3f out, narrow lead dist, rdn & held final 50y: reapp: won '99 debut
at Beverley (auct mdn, highly tried after, rtd 99 when 6th in a Gr 1): clearly suited by step up to 12f: acts on
fast & gd grnd, handles soft: goes v well fresh: useful colt.
*713 **TANTALUS** 46 [3] B W Hills 3-8-10 M Hills 4/1: 2-13: 3 ch c Unfuwain - Water Quest (Rainbow Quest) ½ 102$
Chsd ldrs, prog to lead briefly appr final 1f, rdn & held towards fin: hvly bckd, 7 wk abs: imprvd in defeat
& clearly got this lngr 12f trip: acts on fast/gd/soft grnd, any trk: see 713.
765 **NIGHT STYLE** 45 [1] E A L Dunlop 3-9-0 J Reid 14/1: 11-604: Led till before final 1f, onepace: 6 wk hd 106
abs, not btn far: op 10/1: stays a sharp 12f & this was a v useful effort giving weight all round: see 656.
*996 **KINGSCLERE** 17 [6] 3-8-10 K Fallon 3/1 JT FAV: 323-15: Keen & restrained, eff but unable to get clr run 1¼ 101+
fnl 2f & eased nr fin: hvly bckd: wld have been 2nd at worst: gets 12f, give him another chance to prove himself.
*1017 **JOLLY SHARP** 15 [5] 3-8-10 T Quinn 3/1 JT FAV: 4-16: Handy, effort to chall 2f out, onepace before 1¼ 99
final 1f: hvly bckd: big step up in grade & not disgraced: acts on fast & soft grnd: see 1017.
4466} **IL CAPITANO** 200 [7] 3-8-10 R Hughes 16/1: 1662-7: Chsd ldrs till 3f out: stablemate 3rd, reapp: 8 91
'99 Ayr debut (mdn, stks rnr-up, rtd 96): eff at 7f/1m, bred to apprec 10f+: acts on gd & soft grnd, gall trks:
suited forcing the pace: needs his sights lowered.
1029 **GALLEON BEACH** 13 [8] 3-8-10 R Hills 8/1: 132-38: Mid-div, drpd away 4f out: op 6/1, nds stiff/gall trks. 30 66
8 ran Time 2m 38.11 (1.71) (L Neil Jones) J L Dunlop Arundel, West Sussex.

1217 3.40 WALKER HCAP 4YO+ 0-95 (C) 1m2f75y Good/Firm 20 00 Slow [93]
£12246 £3768 £1884 £942 A group of 5 were soon detached & nvr got into it

991 **NOUKARI** 17 [5] P D Evans 7-8-9 (74) J F Egan 16/1: 321401: 7 b g Darshaan - Noufryla (Top Ville) 80
In tch, hdwy 3f out, wide turning for home, kept on gamely under press to lead final strides: earlier won over hdls
at Ludlow (2m, firm & gd): prev Flat Catterick wnr (h'cap): '99 wnr at Lingfield (4), here at Chester (clmr),
Newmarket (h'cap) & Pontefract (stks, rtd 74 & 82a): '98 Southwell & Lingfield wnr (h'caps, rtd 63 & 63a): eff
at 10f/2m: goes on firm, soft, both AWs, any trk: likes Lingfield & Chester: ultra tough, genuine & consistent.
1160 **YAROB** 3 [9] D Nicholls 7-9-9 (88)(6ex) K Fallon 11/2: 010102: 7 ch g Unfuwain - Azyaa (Kris) nk 93
Nvr far away, led appr final 1f, hard rdn before reg, drifted right, hdd final strides: bckd tho' op 4/1: fine
run back at 10f with the Champion Jockey up, disappointing at 1m under an apprentice on Saturday: see 1070.
4456} **PENSION FUND** 201 [1] M W Easterby 6-9-1 (80) J Fortune 11/2: /106-3: 6 b g Emperor Fountain - 1¾ 82
Navarino Bay (Averof) Mid-div, prog 3f out, keeping on but booked for 3rd when squeezed for room-chome:
op 9/2, reapp: '99 Ripon wnr at York (h'cap, rtd 82): '98 Ripon wnr (h'cap, rtd 81): eff at 1m/10f, stays 12f:
acts on firm & soft, any trk: best without blnks & can carry big weights: runs well fresh, looks as gd as ever.
4410} **WARNING REEF** 204 [9] E J Alston 7-7-11 (62) F Norton 14/1: 4040-4: Mid-div, eff 2f out, styd on but 2 61
no threat: gd reapp: plcd sev times in '99 (h'caps, rtd 65): '98 wnr at Carlisle, Sandown & Ascot (h'caps, rtd
65 at best): eff at 10/12f, stays 14f: acts on firm, gd/soft grnd & fibresand, any trk: spot-on next time.
663 **GRALMANO** 59 [8] 5-8-6 (71) F Lynch 15/2: 25-145: Mid, plcd, led 3f out, no extra fnl 1f. 1½ 68
1037 **LORD EUROLINK** 11 [3] 6-8-2 (67)(tvi) R Ffrench 14/1: 110446: Chsd ldrs, effort 2f out, no impression. 1¾ 61
1077 **CULZEAN** 8 [12] 4-9-4 (83)(BL) Pat Eddery 10/1: 3-5367: Rcd in rear group (arnd 15L off ldrs), 2½ 73
late hdwy, nvr a factor: blnkd: see 733.
1031 **FORTY FORTE** 13 [4] 4-8-9 (74) N Callan 11/2: 441538: Led till 3f out, gradually wknd: see 786. ½ 63
695 **HANNIBAL LAD** 50 [10] 4-7-13 (64) Martin Dwyer 25/1: 311359: Well bhd, some late prog, nvr dngrs. shd 53
*1031 **NIGHT VENTURE** 13 [7] 4-9-10 (89) J Reid 5/1 FAV: 506-10: Hmpd start, al bhd: 10th, op 4/1, forget. 4 72
1011 **SALIGO** 15 [6] 5-7-13 (64) Kim Tinkler 25/1: 0-0000: Hmpd start, al bhd: 11th, tchd 40/1: dual 1½ 45
'99 rnr-up (h'cap, rtd 84): '98 wnr at Salisbury, Leicester & York (h'caps, rtd H, H Morrison): eff at 1m/10f
on firm & soft grnd, stiff/gall trk: best without blnks: v well h'capped now: with N Tinkler.
1031 **MARCHING ORDERS** 13 [11] 4-9-6 (85) J Carroll 50/1: 010-00: Mid-div, effort & btn 3f out: 12th: 8 56
ex-Irish, '99 wnr at Fairyhouse (mdn) & Cork (h'cap): eff at 1m/9f on gd & gd/soft grnd: with T Caldwell.
1042 **BARAGUEY** 22 [2] 6-9-1 (80) R Hughes 33/1: 253/00: Al well bhd: 13th: ignore, see 1042. 7 41
13 ran Time 2m 10.6 (2.1) (J E Abbey) P D Evans Pandy, Gwent.

1218 4.10 EVENING LEADER MDN 3YO (D) 1m2f75y Good/Firm 20 -33 Slow
£8125 £2500 £1250 £625

957 **AIR DEFENCE** 21 [4] B W Hills 3-9-0 M Hills 4/6 FAV: 2-21: 3 br c Warning - Cruising Height (Shirley 90
Heights) Trkd ldr, chall 2f out, rdn to take narrow lead ins last, pshd out: hvly bckd, slow time: rnr-up both
prev starts, incl sole '99 run (mdn, rtd 86): half-brother to a couple of smart mid-dist/styrs: eff at 10f, 12f will
suit: acts on fast & gd/soft grnd, sharp or gall trk: runs well fresh & shld prove better than the bare form.
4536} **DE TRAMUNTANA** 194 [1] W Jarvis 3-8-9 K Fallon 10/1: 00-2: 3 b f Alzao - Glamour Game (Nashwan) hd 83
Set moderate pace, wound it up 3f out, hard prsd 2f out, hdd inside last, rallied: reapp: unplcd in '99 (fill
mdn, rtd 76): apprec step up to 10f, (dam won over hdles): acts on fast grnd & a sharp trk, from the front.
979 **CRACOW** 19 [3] J W Hills 3-9-0 R Hills 6/4: 052-43: 3 b c Polish Precedent - Height Of Secrecy 1½ 86
(Shirley Heights) Bhd ldrs, went for a non-existent gap appr final 1f, sn swtchd & rdn, no impression: hvly bckd:
also found trouble in running on reapp: acts on fast & gd/soft grnd, must win a maiden sn: see 979.

CHESTER   TUESDAY MAY 9TH   Lefthand, Very Sharp track

4523} **MAMZUG** 195 [2] B Hanbury 3-9-0 G Faulkner (3) 33/1: 0-4: Pulled hard & chsd ldrs early, in tch   **5   78**
till pace qcknd appr final 2f: reapp: last sole '99 start: Hamas colt, dam 1m wnr: one more run for h'cap mark.
--   **BREAKIN GLASS** [5] 3-8-9 G Duffield 33/1: 5: Al bhd: highly tried on debut: Ardkinglass   **17   53**
half-sister to a couple of winning sprinters: with A Bailey.
5 ran   Time 2m 13.83 (5.33)   (K Abdulla)   B W Hills Lambourn, Berks.

1219   **4.40 PRINCE OF WALES HCAP 3YO 0-100 (C)**   **5f rd**   **Good/Firm 20   -18 Slow**   **[96]**
£8801   £2708   £1354   £677   Low numbers have a big advantage here

+1047 **KATHOLOGY** 11 [4] D R C Elsworth 3-9-7 (89) N Pollard 5/2 FAV: 23-211: 3 b c College Chapel - Wicken   **94**
Wonder (Distant Relative) Well plcd, rdn to lead 1f out, held on well: hvly bckd: recent Sandown wnr (rtd
h'cap): rnr-up 4 of 5 prev starts, thrice as a juv (mdn, rtd 86 & 78a): eff at 5/6f, stays 7f: acts on fast, hvy
grnd & fibresand, any trk: best up with/forcing the pace: tough, progressive & useful, made most of gd low draw.
926   **NIFTY MAJOR** 24 [1] A Berry 3-8-12 (80) O Pears 10/1: 150-02: 3 b g Be My Chief - Nifty Fifty   **nk   83**
(Runnett) Dwelt, sn pld himself prom, not clr run appr fnl 1f till below dist, hung up well: may have won
this with a clr run: '99 wnr at Musselburgh (2, auct mdn & nursery, rtd 82): eff at 5f, shld get 6f this term:
acts on fast & gd/soft grnd, likes sharp trks, esp Musselburgh: suited forcing the pace: should win soon.
4121} **SABRE LADY** 225 [5] Miss L A Perratt 3-8-13 (81) C Lowther 14/1: 1230-3: 3 ch f Sabrehill - Cal Norma's   **hd   83**
Lady (Lyphard's Special) Chsd ldrs, effort 2f out, not much impress till kept on well cl-home: clr rem, reapp:
'99 debut wnr at Hamilton (auct mdn, nursery plcd, rtd 84): eff at 5f, suited by 6f: acts on firm & gd/soft grnd,
prob any trk: goes well fresh: this should have put him spot-on for 6f next time.
4207} **KILBRANNAN SOUND** 220 [12] B A McMahon 3-8-10 (78) W Supple 20/1: 3210-4: Bhd, ran on fnl   **2½   74**
1½f, nvr nrr: gd reapp from poorest draw: '99 Doncaster wnr (val stks, rtd 81 at best): eff at 5f, suited by
6f: acts on firm & gd/soft, any trk: sister to useful sprinter Lord Kintyre, shld go close next time, esp back at 6f.
4612} **BLUE HOLLY** 186 [3] 3-8-8 (76) F Norton 13/2: 3123-5: Chsd ldrs & ev ch till no extra dist: tchd 8/1   **1¼   69**
on reapp: '99 Lingfield wnr (auct mdn, nursery plcd, rtd 79): eff at 5f on gd & hvy, poss fast: front-runner.
361   **WELCHS DREAM** 110 [8] 3-8-5 (73) J Bramhill 25/1: 424-56: Mid-div thro'out: 16 wk abs, new stable.   **hd   66**
1047 **LOST IN HOOK** 11 [2] 3-8-12 (80) R Mullen 7/1: 52-307: Sn led, hdd dist, fdd: see 652.   **½   72**
3461} **PALMSTEAD BELLE** 263 [6] 3-8-5 (73)(t) D Mernagh 3) 16/1: 0045-8: Early ldr, outpcd over 1f out: **1¾   61**
reapp, t-strap: '99 Nottingham wnr (fill stks, rtd 82 & 86$): eff forcing the pace at 5f on fast grnd, gall trk.
-1047 **ARGENT FACILE** 11 [9] 3-9-4 (86)(t) J F Egan 7/1: 10-229: Cl-up early, struggling to go pace   **hd   74**
by halfway: op 5/1, poor draw: now needs 6f: see 1047, 959.
3541} **LA CAPRICE** 259 [11] 3-8-10 (78) G Carter 14/1: 4521-0: Al bhd, 10th: badly drawn on reapp: **nk   65**
stablemate 2nd: won fnl '99 start at Lingfield (mdn, rtd 81): eff at 5f on firm & soft grnd: likes to force the pace.
959   **JUDIAM** 11 [10] 3-8-3 (71) P Fessey 20/1: 21-450: Nvr a factor: 11th: op 14/1, poor draw: see 652.   **1   55**
774   **AIRA FORCE** 41 [7] 3-8-13 (81) K Darley 11/2: 310-20: Chsd ldrs 2f: 12th, op 9/2, 6 wk abs: see 774.   **1½   62**
12 ran   Time 1m 01.72 (1.92)   (McDowell Racing)   D R C Elsworth Whitsbury, Hants.

CHESTER   WEDNESDAY MAY 10TH   Lefthand, Very Tight Track

Official Going   GOOD (GOOD/FIRM In Places). Stalls: Inside, Except 1m2f - Stands Side.

1220   **2.10 TESS GRAHAM HCAP 3YO 0-90 (C)**   **6f rnd**   **Good/Firm 23   -17 Slow**   **[92]**
£12506   £3848   £1924   £962   Low numbers have a big advantage here

888   **RAILROADER** 28 [6] G B Balding 3-8-10 (74) S Drowne 6/1: 340-61: 3 ch g Piccolo - Poyle Amber   **83**
(Sharrood) Bhd ldrs, shaken up to lead 1f out, rdn out: morning gamble from 14/1: 1st win, plcd thrice as a juv
(nurs, rtd 78): eff at 6f, shld get 7f: acts on fast & hvy grnd, tight or stiff trk: improving.
1028 **CHARLOTTEVALENTINA** 14 [1] P D Evans 3-9-2 (80) Joanna Badger (7) 25/1: 106-02: 3 ch f Perugino -   **1   85**
The Top Diesis (Diesis) Mid-div, prog & no room appr fnl 1f, switched & rdn, fin well: '99 Catterick wnr
(fill mdn, rtd 83): eff at 6f, 7f shld suit now: goes on fast grnd, sharp trks, without visor.
4033} **CORUNNA** 232 [5] A Berry 3-8-9 (73) J Carroll 12/1: 2406-3: 3 b g Puissance - Kind Of Shy (Kind Of   **1   75**
Hush) Unruly start, dsptd lead till dist, onepace: op 10/1, reapp: rnr-up sev times last term (mdn, rtd 84):
eff at 5/6f on firm/fast grnd, disapp on soft: suited up with/forcing the pace: consistent, deserves a race.
1021 **STAR PRINCESS** 16 [12] K T Ivory 3-8-9 (73) C Carver 3) 16/1: 324-64: Mid-div, eff ent fnl 2f,   **1   72**
styd on, nvr able to chall: gd run from a poor high draw: apprec this return to 6f: see 1021.
1181 **STRAND OF GOLD** 3 [2] 3-8-4 (68) A Daly 8/1: 204-55: Bmpd start, rear, kept on under press fnl 2f,   **¾   65**
nvr dngrs: h'cap bow, ran Sunday: lost any ch at the start, goes on fast & gd/soft grnd & is worth another ch at 6f.
534   **FEAST OF ROMANCE** 83 [3] 3-8-9 (73) S Whitworth 16/1: 3-1656: Chsd ldrs, eff appr fnl 1f, unable   **¾   68**
to qckn: 12 wk abs, turf return, back in trip: see 275.
3885} **ALJAWF** 240 [7] 3-9-7 (85) R Hills 5/1 FAV: 51-7: Slow away, mid-div, sltly hmpd 2f out, switched dist,   **hd   80**
kept on: hvly bckd tho' op 3/1 on reapp/h'cap bow: landed fnr of 2 '99 starts at Nottingham (mdn, rtd 92):
half-brother to v smart sprinter Arkadian Hero: eff at 6f, 7f will: suit next time: acts on fast grnd, gall trk.
*959 **BREEZY LOUISE** 22 [4] 3-8-4 (68)(bl) F Norton 8/1: 250-18: Led after 2f till 2f out, no extra: **1½   59**
nicely bckd tho' op 6/1: best at 5f as in 959 (clmr, 1st time blnks).
4616} **RYTHM N TIME** 186 [11] 3-8-13 (77) W Supple 16/1: 0430-9: Al same pl: reapp: '99 Beverley   **shd   68**
wnr (fill nurs, rtd 85 at best, T Easterby): eff at 5/6f, 7f, shld suit: goes on gd & gd/soft grnd, prob firm.
1047 **LABRETT** 12 [8] 3-9-7 (85) J Fortune 14/1: 00-000: Nvr dngrs, not given a hard time thro' fnl 2f: 10th: **nk   75**
jt top-weight, blnks omitted: useful at times last year & is now slipping down the weights, keep in mind: see 988.
*685 **LORD YASMIN** 54 [10] 3-8-4 (68) R Ffrench 10/1: 02-10: Chsd ldrs till wknd appr fnl 1f: 11th, abs.   **nk   57**
954   **BABY BARRY** 22 [16] 3-9-5 (83) G Duffield 20/1: 012-00: Chsd ldrs wide till 2f out: 12th, saddle slipped.   **¾   70**
736   **CHARMING LOTTE** 46 [9] 3-8-11 (75)(vis) Kim Tinkler 40/1: 315-00: Al rear: 13th, 7 wk abs: '99 Ayr   **¾   60**
wnr (nurs, rtd 74, P Shakespeare): eff at 6f, stays 7f: acts on gd, suited by soft/hvy, sharp/gall trk: wears a vis.
1098 **Red Typhoon** 8 [13] 3-8-13 (77) Pat Eddery 16/1:   4167} **Pertemps Fc** 223 [15] 3-8-3 (67) P Fessey 16/1:
736   **Golden Miracle** 46 [14] 3-9-4 (82) J Reid 20/1:
16 ran   Time 1m 15.48 (2.38)   (Peter Richardson)   G B Balding Fyfield, Hants.

CHESTER

WEDNESDAY MAY 10TH   Lefthand, Very Tight Track

1221   **2.40 BANK OF SCOTLAND MDN 2YO (D)   5f rnd   Good/Firm 23 -28 Slow**
£7085   £2180   £1090   £545

985   **KOMPLIMENT 20** [1] A Bailey 2-8-11 K Fallon 10/3: 51: 2 ch c Komaite - Eladale (Ela Mana Mou)   85
Sn setting moderate pace, qcknd appr fnl 1f, pshd out, cosily: well bckd: 16,000 gns Apr foal, half-brother
to a 1m wnr: eff forcing the pace over a sharp 5f, 6f will suit: acts on fast grnd: going the right way.

989   **RAGAMUFFIN 18** [7] T D Easterby 2-8-11 K Darley 7/1: -462: 2 ch c Prince Sabo - Valldemosa   ½ 80
(Music Boy) Chsd ldrs, chsd wnr appr fnl 1f, styd on but al being held: pulled clr of next & this was an
imprvd show: clrly suited by this faster surface & can win a Northern maiden.

984   **BANJO BAY 20** [6] B A McMahon 2-8-11 T Quinn 9/1: 53: 2 b c Common Grounds - Thirlmere   6 65
(Cadeaux Genereux) Struggled to go pace, kept on fnl 2f, nvr nr to chall: op 7/1: needs 6f now.

1001   **BARON CROCODILE 16** [9] A Berry 2-8-11 J Carroll 9/2: 224: Chsd ldrs, onepace appr fnl 1f: 2 59
had the worst of the draw & on much quicker grnd today: see 1001.

--   **PRINCE MILLENNIUM** [5] 2-8-11 R Hughes 11/4 FAV: 5: Trkd wnr, eff & no impress appr fnl 1f,   hd 59
eased: well bckd, fin lame: 30,000 gns First Trump Feb 1st foal, dam 6f wnr, well related: sire a sprinter.

--   **EMISSARY** [2] 2-8-11 D Holland 9/1: 6: Nvr in it: op 7/1: Primo Dominie Feb foal, dam 7f wnr,   3 51
sire a sprinter: stable haven't got going yet: with M Johnston.

1006   **PRINCE GRIGORI 16** [4] 2-8-11 W Supple 8/1: 047: Early ldr, lost tch 2f out: see 1006.   2 45

1020   **MAYSBOYO 16** [3] 2-8-11 Dale Gibson 33/1: -38: Chsd ldrs till halfway: see 1020.   9 25

8 ran   Time 1m 02.35 (2.55)   (Ray Bailey)   A Bailey Little Budworth, Cheshire

---

1222   **3.10 TOTE CHESTER CUP HCAP 4YO+ (B)   2m2f147y   Good/Firm 23   +01 Fast**   [114]
£65000   £20000   £10000   £50000   4 yo rec 4 lb

997   **BANGALORE 18** [4] Mrs A J Perrett 4-7-10 (86)(5oh) G Bardwell 16/1: 336-31: 4 ch h Sanglamore -   91
Ajuga (The Minstrel) Cl-up, went on 6f out, sn wound it up & stole 4L, hard rdn appr fnl 1f, just held on, gamely:
fair time: earlier won over hdles at Fontwell & Uttoxeter (nov, 2m/2½m, firm & gd, handles hvy, rtd 134h): '99
wnr at Pontefract (auct mdn, h'cap rnr-up, rtd 86, B Hills): eff at 12f, styd this sharp 2m2f well: goes on any
grnd, any trk: clrly a late maturer, now a useful stayer: given a fine ride by G Bardwell today.

--   **ANSAR** [3] D K Weld 4-7-11 (87) F Norton 11/1: 323-02: 4 b c Kahyasi - Anaza (Darshaan)   shd 91
Mid-div, stdy prog appr fnl 4f, sltly hmpd bef dist & switched, ran on strongly for press, just failed in a thrill
fin: Irish raider, bckd from 16/1: '99 Dundalk wnr (12th mdn): eff at 2m/2m2f: acts on firm & hvy grnd: useful.

917   **FANTASY HILL 26** [17] J L Dunlop 4-8-0 (90) G Carter 15/2: 302-53: 4 b g Danehill - Gay Fantasy   1 93
(Troy) Waited with, gd hdwy 4f out to chase wnr 2f out, sn rdn, kept on, unable to chall: tchd 9/1:
fine run from this tough, useful gelding, eff at 2m/2m2.5f: see 917.

997   **PRAIRIE FALCON 18** [5] B W Hills 6-7-13 (85) J Mackay (7) 8/1: 24-604: Mid-div, smooth prog 4f out,   1¼ 87
not much room 2f out, styd on, nvr trbld ldrs: nicely bckd, stablemate of fav: also 4th in this race in '99: see 917.

4205}   **RAINBOW HIGH 221** [18] S-9-13 (113) M Hills 9/2 FAV: 0321-5: Rear, eff & not much room 3f out,   1¾ 113
late hdwy, nvr a threat: hvly bckd from 11/2, gave 14lbs+ all round: '99 wnr at Newbury, here at Chester (this
race, off 10lbs lower mark) & Newmarket (3 rnr Gr 3, rtd 116): '98 Ripon wnr (mdn, rtd 94): eff at 2m/2m2.5f:
acts on firm & soft grnd, any trk: can force the pace: v useful weight carrying performance.

4467}   **TENSILE 201** [14] 5-7-12 (84) R Ffrench 20/1: 2530-6: Held up, prog 4f out, drvn 2f out, onepace: shd 84
6 mnth jumps abs, won hdles bow at Leicester (2m nov, gd grnd, rtd 110h): rnr-up in '99 (rtd h'cap, rtd 85):
'98 Beverley wnr (h'cap, rtd 87, L Cumani): eff at 14f, stays 2m2.5f on fast & soft grnd, prob any trk: clr rem.

991   **RUM POINTER 18** [6] 4-8-1 (91) W Supple 20/1: 100-07: Led till 6f out, fdd under press fnl 2f: 9 83
'99 wnr at Catterick (reapp), Ripon, Haydock & Ayr (h'caps, rtd 88): eff at 12f, stays 15f: acts on firm, suited
by soft grnd: goes on any trk & loves to force the pace: v tough, sure to apprec drop back in trip.

1052   **EMBRYONIC 11** [13] 8-7-10 (82)(21oh) P M Quinn (5) 100/1: 0-0068: Nvr better than mid-div, some late   3 71$
hdwy under a kind ride: v stiff task: keep in mind when back in h'cap proper: see 1052.

1052   **ROYAL EXPRESSION 11** [2] 8-7-10 (82)(9oh) Dale Gibson 33/1: 231639: Mid-div, eff 4f out, no impress.   1½ 70

4545}   **EILEAN SHONA 194** [15] 4-8-7 (97) A Nicholls (3) 7/1: 4311-0: Held up, closed 5f out, rdn 4f out,   2 83
grad wknd: 10th, stablemate 6th, reapp: landed fnl 2 in '99 at Redcar & Newmarket (rtd h'caps, rtd 96): '98
Redcar wnr (mdn, rtd 78): eff at 14f/2m: acts on firm & gd/soft grnd, stiff/gall trks: useful filly at best.

--   **STAGE PASS** [1] 7-8-4 (90) M Roberts 33/1: 1322/0: In tch, imprvd to trk ldrs 4f out, wknd qckly   shd 76
2f out: 11th: over 2 yr jmps abs, scored a Ludlow (nov hdle, 2m, gd grnd, rtd 110h): v long Flat abs, useful in
France for N Clement, scored at Evry, also Gr 3 rnr-up: eff at 12f/14f on gd & v soft grnd: with G Barnett.

--   **DATO STAR** [12] 9-8-7 (92)(1)(1ow) J Fortune 25/1: 0313/0: Chsd ldrs till 3f out: 12th: 8 wk jmps   2¼ 77
abs, hat-trick scorer at Newcastle, Kempton & Haydock (Gr1/2s, 2m, handles firm, loves hvy, rtd 171h): 2 yr
Flat abs, '98 Ayr wnr (h'cap, rtd 94): eff at 13f/2m on fast, suited by soft/hvy, gall trks: grnd against him here.

3723}   **BENATOM 251** [7] 7-8-10 (96) S Sanders 20/1: 2045-0: In tch till 3f out: 13th on reapp: '99   3 77
Newmarket wnr (h'cap, rtd 98 at best): plcd in '98 (rtd h'cap, rtd 97): former hdles wnr: eff at 1m6f/2½m:
suited by firm/fast grnd, handles gd/soft, any trk: can run well fresh, without visor: shld come on for this.

3817}   **FIRST BALLOT 246** [16] 4-8-0 (90) N Pollard 8/1: 1610-0: Handy, ran wide 5f out, lost place: 14th,   7 65
well bckd on reapp: '99 wnr at Newbury (mdn) & Ascot (h'cap, rtd 91 & 102$): eff at 12f/2m on firm/fast
grnd, stiff/gall trks: shld leave this bhd on a more galloping trk: with D Elsworth.

4374}   **SON OF SNURGE 208** [11] 4-7-10 (86)(7oh) P Fessey 16/1: 1203-0: Chsd ldrs till wknd qckly 4f out: ½ 61
15th on reapp: '99 wnr at Brighton (h'cap, rtd 81 at best & 72a): eff at 12f/2m:
acts on firm & gd grnd, equitrack, any trk: eff with/without blnks.

876   **MAZZELMO 29** [10] 7-7-10 (82)(20oh) C McCavish (7) 50/1: 01-050: Bhd halfway: 16th: v stiff task.   dist 0

1180   **STAR RAGE 3** [8] 10-7-13 (85) K Dalgleish (7) 25/1: 31-60F: Al bhd, pushed along, hmpd & fell 3f out.   0

4397}   **TOP CEES 207** [9] 10-8-13 (99) K Fallon 15/2: /411-P: Al last, broke down badly & p.u. 5f out: hvly bckd: 0
going for a 3rd win in this race: will now be retired after a distinguished if sometimes controversial career.

18 ran   Time 4m 03.0 (4.1)   (Mike Dawson)   Mrs A J Perrett Pulborough, W Sussex

---

1223   **3.45 LISTED CHESHIRE OAKS 3YO (A)   1m3f79y   Good/Firm 23   +01 Fast**
£28600   £8800   £4400   £2200

995   **SOLAIA 18** [1] P F I Cole 3-8-9 J Fortune 10/1: 555-41: 3 ch f Miswaki - Indian Fashion (General   102
Holme) Trkd ldrs, switched & rdn appr fnl 1f, styd on to lead ins last: bckd tho' op 8/1, fair time: '99 debut
wnr at Newmarket (h'cap, rtd mdn, fnl 6, Gr 3 5th of 6, rtd 100): eff at 1m, clrly suited by this step up to 11.5f:
acts on firm & soft/hvy grnd, any trk: useful & genuine filly, cld win a Group race abroad.

406

CHESTER   WEDNESDAY MAY 10TH   Lefthand, Very Tight Track

*873   **INFORAPENNY** 29 [4] R A Fahey 3-8-9 Pat Eddery 10/1: 40-12: 3 b f Deploy - Morina (Lyphard)   *1* 101
Waited with, briefly outpcd 3f out, styd on appr fnl 1f, checked below dist, kept on: tchd 12/1: much imprvd
up in grade, clrly suited by lngr 11.5f trip & further again will suit: acts on fast & soft grnd: useful filly.
995   **TANZILLA** 18 [3] C E Brittain 3-8-9 L Dettori 9/4 JT FAV: 123: 3 b f Warning - Tanz (Sadler's   *nk* 100
Wells) Led till ent fnl 1f, styd on for press: hvly bckd: not disgraced, big step up in trip: acts on
fast & soft/hvy grnd & stays 11.5f: see 995 (1m, soft).
4474}   **FAME AT LAST** 201 [2] B W Hills 3-8-9 M Hills 11/2: 1-4: Unruly bef start, cl-up, chall 1f out, held   *hd* 100
fnl 100y: well bckd, reapp: won sole '99 start at Doncaster (7f mdn, rtd 86): half-sister to a 10f wnr:
stays 11.5f: acts on fast & soft grnd, sharp or gall trk: runs well fresh: useful & well regarded.
3587}   **ABSCOND** 257 [5] J D Bethell 3-8-9 K Fallon 9/4 JT FAV: -22-5: Held up, unable to qckn: hvly   *2* 98
bckd tho' op 7/4 on reapp: rnr-up both '99 starts (fill mdns, rtd 100): eff at 7f, prob stays 11.5f: goes on
firm/fast grnd: more expected, may need a more galloping track: with Sir M Stoute.
5 ran   Time 2m 26.35 (2.55)   (Faisal Salman)   P F I Cole Whatcombe, Oxon

1224   4.15 DELVES BROUGHTON FILLIES MDN 3YO (D)   7f rnd   Good/Firm 23 -01 Slow
£6857   £2110   £1055   £527

971   **LAST RESORT** 21 [1] B W Hills 3-8-11 M Hills 5/2: -1-3: 3 ch f Lahib - Breadcrumb (Final Straw)   99+
Prom, led dist, rdn clr: well bckd tho' op 7/4: unrcd juv: eff at 7f, 1m is going to suit: acts on fast &
gd/soft grnd, stiff or sharp trk: going the right way & could be useful.
4542}   **INCREDULOUS** 194 [3] J R Fanshawe 3-8-11 D Harrison 20/1: 0-2: 3 ch f Indian Ridge - Fetlar   *3* 92
(Pharly) Led, under press 2f out, hdd 1f out, no extra: op 14/1, clr rem, reapp: no luck in running sole
'99 start: eff at 7f, has the pace for 6f: acts on fast grnd, sharp tck: shld find similar before long.
4606}   **JAWLA** 187 [7] J H M Gosden 3-8-11 R Hills 7/1: 0-3: 3 ch f Wolfhound - Majmu (Al Nasr)   *6* 80
Prom, ev ch ent fnl 2f, sn onepace: reapp: well btn sole '99 start: half-sister to top class miler
Mutathirm dam Gr 3 wng 1m juvenile: shld do better in time (Gr 1 entry).
4500}   **DANIYSHA** 198 [6] Sir Michael Stoute 3-8-11 K Fallon 5/4 FAV: 4-4: Held up, eff 3f out, same pace: *1½* 77
hvly bckd, reapp: 4th sole '99 start (fill auct mdn, rtd 82): eff at 6f, shld get further: handles soft grnd.
2380}   **TRIPLE WOOD** 314 [5] J Reid 13/2: 52-5: Slow away, al towards rear: nicely bckd on   *nk* 76
reapp: rnr-up fnl of 2 '99 starts (fill mdn, rtd 80): eff at 7f, bred for 1m+: goes on gd grnd.
4588}   **SLIP KILLICK** 189 [2] 3-8-11 M Roberts 33/1: 540-6: Nvr troubled ldrs: highly tried on reapp: *1* 74$
4th middle of 2 '99 starts (fill mdn, rtd 69): needs further & h'caps.
971   **BEADING** 21 [4] 3-8-11 T Quinn 25/1: 0-07: Chsd ldrs till 2f out: now qualified for h'caps.   *5* 64
7 ran   Time 1m 26.67 (1.67)   (H R H Prince Fahd Salman)   B W Hills Lambourn, Berks

1225   4.45 CHESHIRE REGIMENT HCAP 3YO 0-95 (C)   1m4f66y   Good/Firm 23 -01 Slow   [99]
£8391   £2582   £1291   £645

*701   **KAIAPOI** 48 [5] R Hollinshead 3-8-2 (73) P M Quinn (5) 5/1: 000-11: 3 ch c Elmaamul - Salanka   78
(Persian Heights) Rear, gd wide prog 3f out, led bef dist, rdly: 7 wk abs since won at Doncaster (h'cap): '99
wnr here at Chester (mdn, rtd 72): much imprvd at 10/12f: acts on fast & hvy, any trk, likes Chester: progressive.
4480}   **MICKLEY** 200 [8] J D Bethell 3-8-4 (75) R Lappin 20/1: 5400-2: 3 b g Ezzoud - Dawsha (Slip Anchor)   *2½* 76
Waited with, smooth wide prog appr fnl 2f, drvn & went 2nd ins last, not pace of wnr: fine reapp: '99
wnr at Musselburgh (auct mdn) & here at Chester (nurs, rtd 86): was eff at 7f/1m, suited by this step up
to 12f: acts on firm & soft grnd, prob any trk: goes well h'capped.
990   **UNAWARE** 18 [2] R Charlton 3-9-5 (90) Pat Eddery 14/1: 104-53: 3 b c Unfuwain - Rainbow Lake   *¾* 90+
(Rainbow Quest) In tch, going well but bhd a wall of horses 2f out, switched & ran on for press, not trble wnr:
eff at 12f, will apprec a more galloping trk: little luck today & can gain comp: see 990.
957   **ACCEPTING** 22 [7] J H M Gosden 3-8-12 (83) J Fortune 7/2 FAV: 02-64: Held up, prog & ev ch 2f   *½* 82
out, sn hung right, onepace ins last: hvly bckd on h'cap bow, clr rem: styd lngr 12f trip, poss unsuited by the trk.
979   **CONSTANT** 20 [1] W Supple 12/1: 005-05: Chsd ldrs, shaken up 3f out, not much room   *3* 68
2f out, onepace: op 8/1: this longer 12f trip shld suit: see 979.
979   **OSOOD** 20 [9] L Dettori 9/2: 161-66: Cl-up, narrow lead appr fnl 1f, sn hdd & btn: *6* 79
well bckd from 7/1: stays 12f?: see 979 (gd/soft).
990   **FIRST TRUTH** 18 [4] 3-9-7 (92) G Duffield 13/2: 5-6427: Chsd ldrs, led 2½f out till bef dist, wknd: *hd* 81
nicely bckd tho' op 11/2: unlikely to apprec this 12f trip on breeding: see 990, 735.
990   **ASTON MARA** 18 [3] 3-8-12 (83)(BL) D Holland 25/1: 154-08: Led till ent fnl 3f, lost pl: blnkd, lngr trip.   *6* 66
3957}   **FIRST MANASSAS** 236 [6] 3-8-13 (84) K Fallon 11/2: 5213-9: In tch, shkn up when squeezed for room   *12* 57
& snatched up appr fnl 1f, eased: nicely bckd tho' op 9/2 on reapp: '99 Haydock wnr (auct mdn, rtd 84):
eff at 7f/1m, worth another try at 12f: acts on fast & gd grnd, sharp or gall trk: usually forces the pace.
937   **DISTINCTLY WELL** 23 [10] 3-7-13 (70) Joanna Badger (7) 10/1: 00-230: Saddle slipped 3f, t.o.: 10th.   *dist* 0
10 ran   Time 2m 39.32 (2.92)   (J D Graham)   R Hollinshead Upper Longdon, Staffs

CHURCHILL DOWNS   SATURDAY MAY 6TH   Lefthand, Very Sharp, Oval Track

Official Going   DIRT - FAST

1226   10.27 GR 1 KENTUCKY DERBY 3YO   1m2f   Dirt   Inapplicable
£541585   £103659   £52829

--   **FUSAICHI PEGASUS** [15] N Drysdale 3-9-0 K Desormeaux 23/10 FAV: -11111: 3 b c Mr Prospector -   125a
Angel Fever (Danzig) -:
--   **APTITUDE** [2] R J Frankel 3-9-0 A Solis 118/10: 2-1232: 3 br c A P Indy - Dokki (Northern Dancer)   *1½* 121a
--   **IMPEACHMENT** [14] T Pletcher 3-9-0 C Perret 62/10: 444233: 3 b c Deputy Minister - Misconduct   *4* 115a
(Criminal Type)-:
*765   **CHINA VISIT** 42 [11] Saeed bin Suroor 3-9-0 L Dettori 237/10: 1-16: Mid-div, eff 3f out, no impress   110a
on leaders fnl 2f: 6th: abs: jockey reported colt didn't quite stay & likely to drop back in trip: see 765.
765   **CURULE** 42 [18] 3-9-0 M St Julien 237/10: -41337: Twds rear, prog/chsd ldrs 3f out, sn held: 7th: abs.   110a
19 ran   Time 2m 01.12   (F Sekiguchi)   N Drysdale America

SAN SIRO SUNDAY MAY 7TH Righthand, Stiff, Galloping Track

Official Going HEAVY

1227 3.25 LISTED PREMIO BAGGIO 3YO 1m2f Heavy Inapplicable
£22772 £10020 £5465

912 **SAILING** 23 [11] P F I Cole 3-8-8 F Jovine : 105-21: 3 ch f Arazi - Up Anchor (Slip Anchor)   **100**
Trkd ldrs, prog/led over 2f out, won readily: won 2 of 5 juv starts at Goodwood (fillies mdn) & Sandown (stks, rtd
100): eff at 1m, styd lngr 10f trip: acts on fast & heavy grnd, any trk: has run well fresh: useful performer.
--   **PERSIAN FILLY** [13] Italy 3-8-8 M Esposito : 2: 3 b f Persian Bold - Kafayef (Secreto)   4   **92**
--   **CASCINA BICOCCA** [8] Italy 3-8-8 G Forte : 3: 3 b f College Chapel - Nonna Rina (Bluebird)   3½   **87**
11 ran   Time 2m 13.4   (H R H Prince Fahd Salman)   P F I Cole Whatcombe, Oxon

1228 3.55 LISTED PREMIO EMANUELE FILIBERTO 3YO 1m2f Heavy Inapplicable
£22772 £10020 £5465

--   **SHIBUNIS FALCON** [6] M Guarnieri 3-9-5 M Monteriso : 1: 3 b c Polar Falcon - Shibuni (Damister)   **95**
980 **PRIESTLAW** 17 [10] J L Dunlop 3-9-2 F Jovine : 13-02: 3 ch c El Gran Senor - Schwanensee (Mr Leader) 1¾   **89**
Chsd ldrs, prog/ch over 1f out, one pace nr fin: eff at 10f on hvy grnd.
--   **FLUXUS** [8] Italy 3-9-2 G Bietolini : 3: 3 bc Night Shift - Fracassina (Rusticaro)   4   **83**
9 ran   Time 2m 13.6   (Scuderia Athena)   M Guarnieri, Italy

DUSSELDORF SUNDAY MAY 7TH Lefthand, Tight, Undulating Track

Official Going GOOD

1229 3.50 GR 2 GERMAN 1,000 GUINEAS 3YO 1m Good Inapplicable
£38710 £15484 £7742

1117 **CRIMPLENE** 7 [14] C E Brittain 3-9-2 P Robinson : 3-6331: 3 ch f Lion Cavern - Crimson Conquest   **114**
(Diesis) Wide, led after 2f, rdn clr fnl 2f: earlier in front of Lahan when plcd in the Fred Darling, '99 wnr
at Redcar (auct mdn) & Salisbury (stks, Gr 1 3rd, rtd 106): eff on firm, suited by good & hvy:
handles any trk: v useful, consistent filly, shld win more Group races.
948 **MARGAY** 21 [15] M J Grassick 3-9-2 E Ahern : 153-32: 3 b f Marju - Almarai (Vaguely Noble)   4   **104**
Trkd wnr, eff 2f out, styd on but no impression: Irish raider, ran to very best: eff at 7f, stays 1m: see 948.
--   **TURNING LEAF** [6] Germany 3-9-2 S Guillot : 3: 3 b f Last Tycoon - Tamacana (Windwurf)   2   **100**
Mid-div, prog and press 2f out, no extra dist: did best of the home contingent & is a useful filly.
955 **AREYDHA** 19 [12] M R Channon 3-9-2 S Drowne : 100-07: Chsd ldrs, fdd appr fnl 1f: btn 10L into 7th: **92**
Brit raider: '99 York debut wnr (fill stks, rtd 94): unproven beyond 5f, shld get at least 7f: acts on soft grnd:
15 ran   Time 1m 35.16   (Darley Stud Management)   C E Brittain Newmarket

KRANJI SUNDAY MAY 7TH -

Official Going GOOD

1230 2.15 EMIRATES SINGAPORE DERBY 4YO 1m2f Good Inapplicable
£141296 £49259 £25278

3873] **ALL THE WAY** 239 [13] Saeed bin Suroor 4-9-0 D Holland : 2154-1: 4 b c Shirley Heights - Future Past   **113**
(Super Concorde) Mid-div, wide, prog to lead bef dist, kept on strgly: '99 wnr at Newmarket (stks, 5th in the
Epsom Derby, rtd 113, T Mills): plcd sole juv start: eff at 10f/12f, tried 14f: acts on firm & good grnd:
goes well fresh & can force the pace: runs well fresh: Godolphin have got a v useful colt on their hands.
--   **SUPER GOLDLUCK** [1] Singapore 4-9-0 E Wilkinson : 2: 4 b c Fairy King - Perfect Welcome (Taufan)   2   **109**
--   **SET THE FASHION** [12] Singapore 4-9-0 (bl) D Brereton : 3: 4 br c Bellotto - Calculating (Last Tycoon)   nk   **108**
14 ran   Time 2m 03.2   (Godolphin)   Saeed bin Suroor Newmarket

CHANTILLY MONDAY MAY 8TH Righthand, Galloping Track

Official Going V SOFT

1231 3.10 GR 2 PRIX HOCQUART 3YO 1m3f V Soft Inapplicable
£33622 £13447 £6724 £3362

864 **LORD FLASHEART** 29 [2] A de Royer Dupre 3-9-2 G Mosse 5/2: 1D1-21: 3 b c Blush Rambler - Miss   **115**
Henderson Co (Silver Hawk) Settled rear, rdn to imprv 2f out, styd on strongly & drvn out to get up cl-home:
'99 wnr at Longchamp (Gr 3, 109), won 4 times in the Provinces: stays 11f on soft & hvy: smart & v consistent.
--   **CRIMSON QUEST** [6] A Fabre 3-9-2 O Peslier 1/1 FAV: 1-12: 3 ch c Rainbow Quest - Bex (Exploded) nse   **114**
Dsptd lead till went on for press, edged right & hdd cl-home: clr rem: recent Listed wnr:
eff at 11f on v soft grnd: smart, lightly raced colt: win sn in Gr company.
--   **HESIODE** [3] J C Rouget 3-9-2 T Jarnet 31/10: 12-113: 3 gr c Highest Honor - Elite Guest (Be My   3   **110**
Guest) Rear, styd on late, no ch with front 2: stays 11f, further shld suit: acts on v soft grnd.
6 ran   Time 2m 23.6   (J C Seroul)   A de Royer Dupre France

CORK   MONDAY MAY 8TH   --

Official Going   GOOD

1232   6.30 LISTED DAIRYGOLD CORK SPRINT 3YO+   6f   Good   Inapplicable
£16250   £4750   £2250

862   **NAMID** 29 J Oxx 4-9-6 J P Murtagh 10/3: /23-31: 4 b h Indian Ridge - Dawnsio (Tate Gallery)   **110**
Front rank, led over 1f out, rdn out, cosily: op 2/1: plcd on both '99 starts (rtd 107, Gr 3 & List):
'99 wnr at The Curragh (Gr 3, rtd 110): eff at 6/7f on gd & hvy grnd: v useful, win another Gr race sn.
*1122   **DESERT MAGIC** 7 C Collins 4-9-7 P Shanahan 12/1: 000-12: 4 br f Green Desert - Gracieuse   1   **106**
Majeste (Saint Cyrien) Led, drv/hdd appr fnl 1f, sn btn: qck reapp: poss better at 7f+: see 1122.
1049   **ONE WON ONE** 9 Mrs J Morgan 6-9-10 K J Manning 9/1: 21-553: 6 b g Naevus - Harvards Bay (Halpern   1   **106**
Bay) Waited with, hdwy 2f out, styd on, nvr nrr: qck reapp, will apprec a retun to 7f: see 1049.
9 ran   Time 1m 10.8   (Lady Clague)   J Oxx Currabeg, Co Kildare

WOLVERHAMPTON (Fibresand)   THURSDAY MAY 11TH   Lefthand, Sharp Track

Official Going: Standard. Stalls: Inside, except 7f - outside

1233   2.00 FREESIA FILLIES HCAP 3YO+ 0-65 (F)   6f aw rnd   Going 49   +04 Fast   [65]
£2261   £646   £323   3 yo rec 10lb

711   **PETITE DANSEUSE** 49 [10] D W Chapman 6-8-1 (38) J Mackay (7) 16/1: 001461: 6 b m Aragon - Let Her   **44a**
Dance (Sovereign Dancer) Mid-div, prog wide 2f out, styd on well ins last to lead near fin, rdn out: op 12/1,
7 wk abs: earlier scored at Southwell (sell h'cap): plcd in '99 (rtd 38 & 29a): eff at 5/7f on firm, soft & both
AWs, any trk: has run well in a visor, not blnks: runs well fresh: fairly h'capped and can win again.
1068   **PALO BLANCO** 10 [6] Andrew Reid 9-8-10 (47) M Henry 4/1 FAV: -33422: 9 b m Precocious - Linpac   ½   **50a**
Mapleleaf (Dominion) Rdn chasing ldrs, prog final 2f and led ins last, hdd near line: op 3/1: see 680 (C/D sell).
754   **OARE KITE** 44 [4] P S Felgate 5-8-0 (37)(bl) Dale Gibson 16/1: 542463: 5 b m Batshoof - Portvasco   1   **38a**
(Sharpo) Handy, rdn/briefly led inside last, not pace of front pair cl-home: op 12/1: abs: eff at 6/7f, stays 1m.
1073   **PLEASURE** 10 [9] A Smith 5-9-1 (52)(bl) Dean McKeown 8/1: 500-54: Handy, led over 2f out till ins   2   **48a**
last, no extra: op 10/1: see 1073 (claimer).
811   **BODFARI ANNA** 40 [11] 4-8-3 (40)(bl) R Mullen 7/1: -30545: Rdn/twds rear, kept on final 2f, no threat.   2½   **29a**
1137   **NAPIER STAR** 7 7-8-7 (44)(t) D Sweeney 14/1: /00-26: Cl-up 5f: op 12/1: see 1137.   ½   **31a**
1133   **HAUNT THE ZOO** 7 [3] 5-9-0 (51) N Callan 11/1: -30007: Rdn/twds rear, late gains, no threat: see 148.   ½   **36a**
1138   **STOP THE TRAFFIC** 7 [12] 3-9-3 (64) L Newman (5) 6/1: 425228: Rdn/towards the rear, mod gains.   1   **47a**
901   **MOY** 28 [8] 5-8-6 (42)(bl) (1ow) M Fenton 8/1: 530029: Led till over 2f out, faded: op 6/1: see 466.   hd   **25a**
739   **MUJAS MAGIC** 45 [7] 5-9-10 (61)(vis) R Fitzpatrick (3) 7/1: 402050: Rdn/al bhd: 10th: abs, topweight.   2   **38a**
*688   **BAYTOWN RHAPSODY** 55 [1] 3-8-13 (60) J Edmunds 7/1: 131310: Rear/hmpd halfway, nvr a factor: **0a**
12th: op 8/1, 8 wk abs: prev with P S McEntee, now with J Balding: see 688 (7f, seller).
1028   **Just For You Jane** 15 [2] 4-9-4 (55)(bl) S Sanders 20/1:1036 **Lemon Strip** 13 [5] 4-8-2 (39) P M Quinn (5) 12/1:
13 ran   Time 1m 15.5 (2.7)   (David W Chapman)   D W Chapman Stillington, N Yorks

1234   2.30 CAMELLIA CLAIMER 3YO (F)   1m100y aw   Going 49   -29 Slow
£2219   £634   £317

3263}   **RIDE THE TIGER** 274 [3] M D I Usher 3-8-13 S Sanders 20/1: 000-1: 3 ch c Imp Society - Krisdaline   **53a**
(Kris S) Chsd ldr, led 4f out, rdn/edged left inside last, held on for press cl-home: 9 month abs, AW bow:
unplcd in '99 on turf (rtd 47): apprec step up to 8.5f: acts on fibresand & a sharp track: runs well fresh.
937   **ALBERGO** 24 [1] M Blanshard 3-9-3 D Sweeney 25/1: 0-5002: 3 b g Deploy - River Dove (Riverman)   ½   **55$**
Rdn rear, prog fnl 3f & ch ins last, just held near fin: apprec drop to 1m & claiming grade: acts on f/sand.
971   **HOUNDS OF LOVE** 22 [9] R Guest 3-8-8 J Mackay (7) 10/1: 0-03: 3 b f Foxhound - Foolish Lady   4   **38a**
(Foolish Pleasure) Dwelt/rear, kept on final 2f, not pace to chall: op 8/1: rtd 60 on sole '99 start (mdn): styd
longer 8.5f trip on AW bow today, handles fibresand.
*1191   **WILL IVESON** 4 [5] P C Haslam 3-9-0 (vis) Dean McKeown 9/4 FAV: 121014: Prom, rdn to chall 2f out,   2   **40a**
held o'er 1f out: op 6/4, quick reapp: see 1191.
976   **NOWT FLASH** 22 [12] 3-9-3 M Fenton 8/1: 006105: Rear, mod gains fnl 2f: op 6/1: btr 589 (7f, sell).   6   **34a**
806   **RED KING** 41 [8] 3-8-7 (BL) G Carter 7/1: 000-66: Led 4f: blinks, op 10/1: 6 week abs: see 806.   6   **15a**
651   **CUPIDS DART** 64 [10] 3-9-7 R Winston 7/1: 235237: Towards rear, eff 3f out, no impress: 2 mth abs.   1   **27a**
882   **CROESO ADREF** 29 [2] 3-7-12 (BL) P M Quinn (5) 7/1: 364348: Chsd ldrs, btn 3f out: op 5/1, blnks.   3½   **0a**
1053   **ALABAMA WURLEY** 12 [4] 3-8-10 D McGaffin (7) 12/1: 03-009: Al towards rear: op 10/1: see 807.   1   **7a**
2595}   **SWEET TEDDY** 306 [7] 3-8-12 S Whitworth 4/1: 554-0: Mid-div, btn 2f out, eased: 10th: op 3/1,   nk   **8a**
reapp: AW bow: 4th on final '99 start (York auct mdn, rtd 80 at best): eff over a galld 6f & handles fast grnd.
1132   **GOOD EVANS ABOVE** 7 [11] 3-8-0 (BL) R Mullen 10/1: 40-600: Dwelt/al bhd: 13th: blinks: see 1132 (7f).   **0a**
1141   **Seasame Park** 7 [6] 3-8-2 M Henry 16/1:   3810} **Mystical Wisdom** 247 [13] 3-7-13(1ow) S Righton 14/1:
13 ran   Time 1m 52.8 (6.6)   (G A Summers)   M D I Usher Kingston Lisle, Oxon

1235   3.00 107.7. WOLF HCAP 3YO+ 0-70 (E)   7f aw rnd   Going 49   -12 Slow   [69]
£2785   £857   £428   £214   3 yo rec 11lb

1139   **FEATHERSTONE LANE** 7 [5] Miss L C Siddall 9-8-9 (50) N Callan 10/1: 522231: 9 b g Siberian Express -   **55a**
Try Gloria (Try My Best) Rdn rear, prog wide halfway, styd on well ins last to lead nr line: plcd sev times in
'99 (rtd 54 & 50): 4 times wnr here at W'hampton in '98 (2 clmrs, sell & h'cap, rtd 72a & 49): eff at 5/7f on
fast & gd/soft, loves both AW's, W'hampton specilist: eff with/without a visor: tough & genuine, deserved this.
908   **ROCK ISLAND LINE** 27 [4] G Woodward 6-9-9 (64) T G McLaughlin 11/2: 10-202: 6 b g New Express -   nk   **68a**
Gail's Crystal (Crofter) Chsd ldrs, rdn/led over 2f out, hdd near fin: back to form on return to sand: see 738.
600   **PIPPAS PRIDE** 73 [11] S R Bowring 5-9-9 (64) S Finnamore (5) 8/1: 311543: 5 ch g Pips Pride -   1¾   **65a**
Al Shany (Burslem) Twds rear, rdn, eff well final 2f, not able to chall: see 473 (1m).
*1038   **MANXWOOD** 13 [8] D J S Cosgrove 3-8-12 (64) J Mackay(7) 5/1: 60-014: Chsd ldrs/onepacd fnl 2f: op 3/1.   shd   **65a**
*687   **SANTANDRE** 55 [10] 4-10-0 (69) P M Quinn (5) 9/2 FAV: 064115: Chsd ldrs, no extra nr fin: see 687.   ½   **69a**

623 **PRIDEWAY 70** [12] 4-9-10 (65) R Mullen 10/1: 0 4406: Dwelt/rear, prog 2f out/held fnl 1f: abs, op 8/1. *nk* **64a**
1066 **MUDDY WATER 10** [7] 4-8-7 (48) D Harrison 5/1: 2-0107: Towards rear, eff 2f out, no impression. *hd* **46a**
1038 **ABTAAL 13** [3] 10-9-0 (55)(vis) R Fitzpatrick (3) 25/1: 500-68: Led after 3f till over 2f out, faded. *3½* **46a**
1126 **FREDERICK JAMES 7** [6] 6-8-10 (51) M Fenton 9/1: -46009: Al outpcd rear: op 8/1: see 262. *4* **34a**
3976} **ARBENIG 236** [2] 5-8-9 (50) D Sweeney 9/1: 6600-0: Led 3f, soon btn: 10th: op 12/1, 8 mth abs: *4* **25a**
plcd in '99 (rtd 57, h'cap): '98 Salisbury wnr (clmr, rtd 58 & 64a): eff at 7f/1m on firm, soft & f/sand: eff in blnks.
923 **DAHLIDYA 26** [9] 5-9-10 (65) I Mongan (5) 10/1: 031330: Dwelt/al bhd: 11th: tchd 12/1: btr 697 (6f). *1½* **37a**
11 ran Time 1m 30.5 (4.3) (Miss L C Siddall) Miss L C Siddall Colton, N Yorks

1236

3.30 TULIP AUCT MDN 2YO (F) 5f aw rnd Going 49 -31 Slow
£2233 £638 £319

-- **SANDLES** [10] S C Williams 2-8-7 G Faulkner (3) 9/1: 1: 2 b g Komaite - Miss Calculate (Mummy's **77a**
Game) Handy, rdn/styd on well inside last to lead near fin, rdn out: op 12/1: Feb foal, cost 10,000gns as a 2yo: dam a 6f juv wnr, subs won at 7f: eff at 5f, 6f+ will suit: acts on fibresand & a sharp track: runs well fresh.
993 **IF BY CHANCE 19** [4] D W P Arbuthnot 2-8-7 S Whitworth 9/4: 042: 2 ch c Risk Me - Out Of Harmony *2* **70a**
(Song) Prom, rdn & kept on well inside last, not pace of wnr: AW bow: handles soft & fibresand: see 993.
-- **NEW WONDER** [12] J G Given 2-7-13 R Ffrench 7/1: 3: 2 b f Presidium - Miss Tri Colour (Shavian) *hd* **61a**
Sn led & crossed to ins rail, clr over 1f out, rdn/wknd ins last & hdd nr fin: op 5/1: April foal, 9,200gns 2yo: dam a mdn, sire a miler: acts on fibresand: plenty of speed here, can find a race.
1136 **UNVEIL 7** [7] G M McCourt 2-8-1 D O'Donohoe 9/1: 44: Chsd ldr, held final 1f: op 8/1: see 1136. *1½* **59a**
970 **BLUE LADY 22** [8] 2-8-1 J Tate 6/4 FAV: -065: Chsd ldrs, held 1f out: op 5/4, AW bow: btr 970 (g/s). *2* **54a**
-- **ALIS IMAGES** [1] 2-8-3 G Carter 9/2: 6: Chsd ldrs, no impression fnl 2f: op 3/1: Mind Games *1* **54a**
filly, March foal, cost 6,000gns: dam a useful 6f juv wnr: with A Berry.
1019 **NAUGHTY KNIGHT 17** [2] 2-8-3 S Carson (4) 20/1: -057: Soon rdn, al outpcd: AW bow: btr 1019 (hvy). *3* **47a**
1095 **MER MADE 9** [3] 2-8-1(1ow) R Mullen 10/1: 58: Al outpcd: tchd 12/1: see 1095 (g/s). *shd* **45a**
-- **FLAMBE** [5] 2-8-6 Dale Gibson 10/1: 9: Al outpcd: Feb foal, 8,000gns 2yo: dam unraced, related *nk* **49a**
to a smart mid dist performer: apprec further in time for P C Haslam.
865 **RAISAS GOLD 30** [9] 2-7-12 C Adamson 16/1: 600: Al outpcd rear: 10th: op 12/1: mod form. *1* **39a**
-- **BORDER EDGE** [6] 2-8-8 N Callan 10/1: 0: Al outpcd, t.o.: 11th: op 8/1: Beveled colt, Feb foal, *19* **14a**
cost 5,500gns: half brother to a 5f juv wnr, dam unraced: with K McAuliffe.
-- **SOME DUST** [11] 2-8-3 L Newman (4) 16/1: U: Stumbled/u.r. leaving stalls: op 12/1: Kings Signet **0a**
colt, May foal, cost 500gns: dam a juv hdle wnr: sire a useful sprinter: with W G M Turner.
12 ran Time 1m 04.2 (4.0) (Chris Wright) S C Williams Newmarket

1237

4.00 BEGONIA SELLER 3YO+ (G) 5f aw rnd Going 49 -03 Slow
£1848 £528 £264 3 yo rec 9 lb

1068 **SAMWAR 10** [10] Mrs N Macauley 8-9-4 (vis) R Fitzpatrick (3) 2/1 FAV: 063201: 8 b g Warning - Samaza **54a**
(Arctic Tern) Dwelt, prog to lead dist & held on well well ins last, rdn out: no bid, op 6/4: '99 scorer here at Wolverhampton (3, sell & 2 h'caps) & Southwell (3, 2 clmrs & a h'cap, rtd 76a & 54): place form in '98 (rtd 74 & 71a, Miss G Kelleway): eff at 6/7f, suited by 5f: acts on firm, soft & e/track, f/sand specialist: has run well fresh: eff in blinks/visor: loves a sharp trk, esp W'hampton & Southwell: gd weight carrier.
753 **NOW IS THE HOUR 44** [7] P S Felgate 4-9-4 G Carter 20/1: 60-662: 4 ch g Timeless Times - Macs *½* **51$**
Maharanee (Indian King) Handy, rdn/outpcd 2f out, styd on well for press inside last, not reach wnr: op 16/1, 6 wk abs: blinks omitted after latest: eff at 5f on fibresand: mod form previously.
919 **YOUNG IBNR 26** [9] B A McMahon 5-9-9 L Newman (5) 8/1: 601443: 5 b g Imperial Frontier - Zalatia *nk* **55$**
(Music Boy) Led/dsptd lead till over 1f out, kept on for press ins last: also bhd today's wnr in 919: see 639.
1162 **SWEET MAGIC 5** [8] L R Lloyd James 9-9-4 (t) R Winston 5/1: 400404: Chsd ldrs, kept on fnl 1f. *hd* **49a**
1036 **NOBLE PATRIOT 13** [4] 5-9-4 Stephanie Hollinshead (7) 14/1: 500025: Late gains, nvr on terms: op 12/1. *1½* **46$**
263 **CELTIC VENTURE 127** [6] 5-9-4 I Mongan (5) 14/1: 000-66: Rdn/rear, mod gains: op 12/1, abs: see 263. *1½* **42a**
1073 **BLUSHING GRENADIER 10** [1] 8-9-9 (bl) S Finnamore (5) 7/1: 016667: Outpcd rear, never on terms. *1½* **44a**
674 **ARAB GOLD 58** [11] 5-9-9 S Sanders 12/1: 031448: Wide, never on terms: tchd 14/1, 2 month abs. *shd* **44$**
614 **GLASTONBURY 72** [13] 4-9-4 (VIS) N Callan 20/1: -00409: Chsd ldrs 4f: op 14/1, visor: 10 week abs. *nk* **38$**
956 **PRINCE NICO 23** [3] 3-8-9 D Harrison 10/1 -00: Led/dsptd lead after 1f till 2f out, wknd: 10th: AW bow. *½* **36a**
1036 **PICASSOS HERITAGE 13** [12] 4-9-4 S Carson (5) 16/1: 50/030: Dwelt/al bhd: 11th: see 1036. *1½* **33a**
1105 **MERCHANT PRINCE 8** [2] 4-9-4 (BL) P M Quinn (5) 20/1: 00-500: Al bhd/outpcd: 12th: blnks. *2½* **26a**
638 **SHAW VENTURE 68** [5] 3-8-9 D Sweeney 10/1: 060-60: Soon rdn/al outpcd: 13th: op 6/1, 10 wk abs. *5* **17a**
13 ran Time 1m 03.8 (2.6) (Andy Peake) Mrs N Macauley Sproxton, Leics

1238

4.30 MAGNOLIA HCAP 3YO 0-65 (F) 1m4f aw Going 49 -14 Slow **[72]**
£2212 £632 £316

1002 **HAMBLEDEN 17** [8] M A Jarvis 3-9-7 (65) G Carter 9/2: 00-031: 3 b g Vettori - Dalu (Dancing Brave) **79a**
Handy, led over 3f out & rdn clr over 2f out, eased down inside last, cmftbly: value for 20L+: AW bow: promise fnl '99 start (rtd 70, mdn): eff at 10f, apprec step up to 12f, shld get further: acts on fibresand & hvy, likes a sharp/turning trk: any amount in hand here, type to score again quickly under a penalty.
1142 **TUFTY HOPPER 7** [3] P Howling 3-8-12 (56) R Winston 3/1: -64422: 3 b g Rock Hopper - Melancolia *13* **56a**
(Legend Of France) Held up, rdn & prog to chase wnr 3f out, sn held: see 1142 (C/D).
937 **VANISHING DANCER 24** [2] K R Burke 3-9-1 (59) D Hayes (7) 20/1: 0-3W03: 3 ch g Llandaff - Vanishing *shd* **59a**
Prairie (Alysheba) Chsd ldrs, rdn/onepace & held 3f out: op 16/1: visor omitted after latest: see 523 (mdn).
1002 **TWEED 17** [1] R Charlton 3-8-13 (57)(VIS) D Harrison 5/1: 50-004: Led, hdd over 3f out & soon btn: *2* **54a**
unplcd in '99 (promise, rtd 74 , Leicester mdn): bred to appreac mid dist this term: also bhd this wnr in 1002.
1024 **PRESTO 17** [5] 3-8-13 (57) S Sanders 6/1: 000-05: Chsd ldr, btn 4f out: op 4/1: longer 12f trip. *6* **45a**
939 **DUN DISTINCTLY 24** [6] 3-8-3 (47) Dale Gibson 9/1: -42656: Rear, rdn/btn halfway: op 7/1: see 536. *1½* **33a**
1071 **BLUE HAWAII 10** [4] 3-8-11 (55)(t) L Newton 12/1: 00-207: Al rear: op 10/1: see 827 (10f). *15* **25a**
*1096 **CROSS DALL 9** [7] 3-8-13 (57)(6ex) J Mackay (7) 5/2 FAV: 03-318: V slowly away & bhd halfway: bckd *hd* **27a**
under a pen: tardy start did not help today but was well below 1096 (stks, g/s).
8 ran Time 2m 41.1 (7.5) (Stag & Huntsman) M A Jarvis Newmarket

Official Going FIRM (GOOD/FIRM in places). Stalls: Stands' Side; Except 1m & 1m1f - Inside.

1239 2.20 AMAT CLASSIFIED STKS 4YO+ 0-60 (F) 6f str Firm 15 -07 Slow
£2912 £832 £416 Majority of field raced far side

+1192 **XANADU 4** [13] Miss L A Perratt 4-11-10 Miss Diana Jones 5/2 FAV: 3-0011: 4 ch g Casteddu - Bellatrix (Persian Bold): Chsd ldrs till went on 4f out, pushed clr appr fnl 1f, cosily: nicely bckd, qck reapp: recently won here at Hamilton (h'cap): '99 scorer again at Hamilton (sell) & Carlisle (h'cap, rtd 56): eff over a stiff/ undul 6f on fast/firm grnd: loves Hamilton: in tremendous form, can complete hat-trick. 69

1126 **NINEACRES 7** [6] J M Bradley 9-11-13 (bl) Mr M Savage (7) 25/1: 013052: 9 b g Sayf El Arab - Mayor (Laxton): Chsd ldr thro'out, kept on fnl 1f, but no ch with wnr: qck reapp: gd effort at the weights: see 802. 2½ 64$

645 **YOUNG BIGWIG 66** [11] D W Chapman 4-11-7 Miss R Clark 6/1: 0-0603: 6 b g Anita's Prince - Humble Mission (Shack): Cl-up, kept on, not pace to chall: op 5/1, 9 wk abs: sharper next time: see 425 (h'cap). 1¾ 54

1149 **ENCOUNTER 6** [15] J Hetherton 4-11-7 Mr T Best (5) 10/1: 0-4004: Mid-div, rdn & styd on over 1f out, nvr nrr: qck reapp: needs h'caps: see 787. 2 48

*787 **BUNDY 43** [16] 4-11-10 Mrs C Williams 9/2: 000-15: Prom, btn fnl 2f: 6 wk abs: btr 787 (made all). shd 51

908 **GOLDEN BIFF 27** [2] 4-11-7 Mr W Peffers (7) 20/1: 106-06: Rear, styd on well fnl 2f, nvr nrr: see 908. 2½ 42

802 **MERANTI 41** [4] 7-11-7 Miss Hayley Bryan (7) 33/1: 000-07: In tch, rdn to impr over 2f out, onepcd fnl 2f: 6 wk abs: 4th at best in '99 (h'cap, rtd 52): '98 wnr at Salisbury & Thirsk (h'cap, rtd 66): eff at 6/7f on firm & gd, handles soft grnd: acts on any trk, likes Thirsk/Salisbury: well h'capped on old form. nk 41$

872 **SYCAMORE LODGE 30** [10] 9-11-7 Mr L Richardson (7) 8/1: 000-08: Rear, late gains, no dngr: keep in mind for a 7f h'cap at Catterick: see 872. ½ 40

896 **PRIORY GARDENS 28** [14] 6-11-7 Mr S Dobson (5) 50/1: 000449: Led early, prom, lost tch fnl 2f. 2½ 34

3601} **THWAAB 257** [3] 8-11-7 Miss A Deniel 20/1: /000-0: In tch stands side, wknd over 2f out, fin 10th: well btn in 4 '99 starts, prev firmer scored at Doncaster (h'cap, rtd 62): back in '96 won at Redcar & Ayr (2 h'caps, rtd 63): eff at 6/7f on firm & gd/soft grnd, with/without visor. shd 34

*1143 **COOL PROSPECT 6** [17] 5-11-10 (bl) Miss E Ramsden 8/1: 505410: Dwelt, al bhd, fin 11th: qck reapp: much btr 1143 (sharp 5f, amat h'cap). 1¼ 33

1139 Young Ben 7 [1] 8-11-7 (vis) Mr P Childs (7) 40/1:   1137 Nadder 7 [8] 5-11-7 (VIS) Miss K Rockey (5) 100/1:
4554} Johnny Staccato 195 [6] 6-11-7 Miss J Ellis (7) 50/1:   1143 Tinas Royale 6 [12] 4-11-4 Mrs L Pearce 16/1:
1192 Six For Luck 4 [5] 8-11-7 (t) Mr K Renwick 100/1:   1149 Go Thunder 6 [9] 6-11-7 (t) Mr M G Williams(7) 66/1:
17 ran Time 1m 11.1 (1.3) (David R Sutherland) Miss L A Perratt Ayr, Strathclyde.

1240 2.50 PAISLEY AUCT MDN QUAL 2YO (E) 5f str Firm 15 -17 Slow
£2821 £868 £434 £217

-- **HAMBLETON HIGHLITE** [3] K A Ryan 8-4-5(1ow) F Lynch 4/1: 1: 2 ch g Paris House - Sempreverde (Lear Fan): Dwelt, sn chsd ldrs, hdwy to lead appr final 1f, drvn out inside last: op 5/2: IR 4,200gns Apr foal, dam modest, sire a speedy juv: eff at 5f on firm grnd: acts on a stiff/undul trk: fine debut. 80

-- **SHATIN DOLLYBIRD** [1] Miss L A Perratt 8-4 2-7-13 D Mernagh (3) 7/1: 2: 2 ch f Up And At 'Em - Pumpona (Sharpen Up): Prom, rdn chall dist, duelled with wnr ins last, just held: 5L clr rem: 3,000 gns Apr foal, half-sister to 4 wnrs: eff over 5f on firm: pleasing debut, should land similar. hd 73

1131 **PRINCESS OF GARDA 7** [4] Mrs G S Rees 2-8-4 G Duffield 4/1: -U43: 2 b f Komaite - Malcesine (Auction Ring): Led, drvn over 2f out, edged left & hdd dist, sn btn: qck reapp: see 1131. 5 66

898 **DULCIFINGE 28** [5] J R Weymes 2-8-4 J Fanning 7/1: 04: Prom, rdn & no extra over 1f out: op 5/1 & looks in need of 6f now: see 898. 1½ 62

-- **CLANSINGE** [2] 2-7-13 G Bardwell 11/8 FAV: 5: Cl-up, swtchd & prog over 1f out, rdn & outpcd when ran green ins last: well bckd on debut: 4,500gns Clantime foal, half-sister to several 5f 2yo scorers: sure to learn from this experience & will improve for A Berry. nk 56

1131 **HAULAGE MAN 7** [6] 2-8-7 A Culhane 7/1: 66: Handy, rdn & onepcd final 2f: op 5/1: 6f now suit. shd 64
6 ran Time 59.7 (1.6) (Miss C M Barlow) K A Ryan Hambleton, Nth Yorks.

1241 3.20 UDDINGSTON SELL HCAP 3YO+ 0-60 (F) 1m4f Firm 15 -31 Slow [55]
£2898 £828 £414

*1039 **HILL FARM DANCER 13** [11] W M Brisbourne 9-8-6 (33) G Baker (7) 7/1: 143511: 9 ch m Gunner B - Loadplan Lass (Nicholas Bill): Mid-div, hdwy 3f out, drvn to lead dist, rdn out: no bid: recent W'hampton wnr (2, h'cap & appr sell): '99 Southwell wnr (appr sell, rtd 54a & 30): '98 Musselburgh wnr (fill h'cap, rtd 59): all wins at 12f, stays 2m on firm, gd/soft & both AWs, likes W'hampton: runs well for an appr: best in sellers. 38

2298} **OVERSMAN 318** [14] J G FitzGerald 7-9-6 (47) M Tebbutt 16/1: 2330-2: 7 b g Keen - Jamaican Punch (Shareef Dancer): Handy, rdn/hdwy over 2f out, styd on well for press ins last: op 12/1: 99/00 hdles wnr at Sedgefield (cj sell h'cap, rtd 96h, eff at 2m/2m2f on any grnd/trk): plcd sev times on the Flat in '99 (clmrs, rtd 58a & 52): last Flat win in '96 (auct mdn, rtd 79a): suited by 12/14f on firm/fast & fibresand, likes Southwell. 1 49

1147 **FIELD OF VISION 6** [3] Mrs A Duffield 10-9-12 (53)(bl) G Duffield 10/1: 0-0243: 10 b g Vision - Bold Meadows (Persian Bold): Held up, rdn to impr 3f out, ev ch when short of room over 1f out, no extra cl-home: op 7/1: in gd form, could land a sell h'cap sn: see 699. ½ 54

871 **COSMIC CASE 30** [7] J S Goldie 5-8-10 (37)(vis) Dawn Rankin (7) 10/1: 00-504: Waited with, smooth hdwy 2f out, swtchd & styd on appr final 1f, nvr nrr: op 8/1: eff at 1m/12f on firm & gd/soft: see 795. ¾ 36

822 **CAMAIR CRUSADER 36** [15] 6-8-7 (34) J P Spencer 5/1 FAV: 00-435: Rear, rdn/prog over 2f out, no extra inside last: handles firm/fast but will apprec softer grnd: see 822. nk 33

943 **TALECA SON 24** [6] 5-8-0 (27) K Dalgleish (7) 25/1: 540006: Settled rear, smooth hdwy halfway, ev ch until no extra for press over 1f out: op 14/1: visor omitted: see 211. ¾ 24

1147 **DONE WELL 6** [1] 8-8-0 (27)(t) A McCarthy (3) 33/1: 0-0007: Prom, led over 2f out, hdd dist, fdd. 2 21

737 **GROOMS GOLD 45** [18] 8-8-2 (29)(vis) G Bardwell 9/1: 422008: Handy, gd hdwy to lead 4f out, rdn/hdd 2 out, wkng/hmpd dist: op 7/1: drop in trip: btr 494 (AW, 2m). nk 23

3094} **MASTER HYDE 282** [16] 11-8-13 (40) P Fessey (7) 33/1: 4034-9: Nvr a threat: pt-to-pt fit: plcd once in '99 (amat h'cap, rtd 42), also rnr-up over timber (h'cap, rtd 101h, eff at 2½m/2m6f on firm & gd): rtd 38 at best on the level in '98 (h'cap): eff at 12f, stays 14f: acts on firm, gd/soft & equitrack: has run well fresh. 4 28

1044 **MISCHIEF 13** [9] 4-9-9 (50)(vis) Craig Williams 14/1: 203000: Led halfway-4f out, wknd fnl 2f: 10th. ½ 37

668 **ICE PACK 58** [17] 4-8-12 (39) Kim Tinkler 33/1: 20-600: Chsd ldrs, led after 4f to halfway, sn lost tch, fin 11th: prev with N Tinkler, now with D Enrico Incisa. 2½ 22

3729} **CHARITY CRUSADER 252** [10] 9-9-6 (47)(bl) A Culhane 10/1: 2400-0: Nvr a threat: 12th: reapp. 1¾ 27

1194 **LORD ADVOCATE 4** [4] 12-8-5 (32)(vis) V Halliday 16/1: 060-00: Led to 1m out, bhd fnl 4f, 13th. ¾ 10
859 **RIBBLE PRINCESS 31** [5] 5-8-11 (38) F Lynch 8/1: 000350: Rear, eff 4f out, sn wknd: 14th: btr 795. 1 14
2332} **PRIOLETTE 317** [2] 5-8-8 (35) R Lappin 20/1: 4040-R: Refused to race: new stable, reapp. 0
15 ran Time 2m 37.4 (5.6) (M E Hughes) W M Brisbourne Great Ness, Shropshire.

1242

3.50 MED AUCT MDN 3YO (E) 1m1f36y Firm 15 00 Slow
£2808 £864 £432 £216

1084 **BARTON SANDS 9** [5] L M Cumani 3-9-0 J P Spencer 15/8 FAV: 21: 3 b c Tenby - Hetty Green (Bay Express): Cl-up going well, hdwy to lead appr fnl 1f, edged left, rdn out, cosily: nicely bckd: cost 30,000gns, dam an Irish 12f wnr: eff at 1m/9f, mid-dists will suit: acts on firm, gd/soft & a gall or stiff/undul trk. 83
1080 **NIGHT SIGHT 10** [7] G Wragg 3-9-0 G Duffield 4/1: 002: 3 b c Eagle Eyed - El Hamo (Search For Gold): 1¼ 78
Settled in mid-div, gd hdwy to trk wnr over 1f out, not pace of wnr well inside last: nicely bckd: much imprvd effort here, stays 9f on firm grnd: now qual for h'caps & that sphere should suit.
976 **HAPPY HOOLIGAN 22** [3] M Johnston 3-9-0 J Fanning 7/2: 2-0533: 3 b c 3 b c Ezzoud - Continual 3 72
(Damascus): Cl-up, hdwy to lead briefly over 2f out, drvn/no extra inside last: nicely bckd, clr rem: acts on any grnd: will apprec a step up to 10f+: see 976 (h'cap).
1045 **WHITE HOUSE 13** [4] W Jarvis 3-8-9 M Tebbutt 9/4: 0-44: Prom, rdn & lost tch over 2f out: nicely 10 51
bckd tho' op 6/4: much better expected & prob not handle this firm grnd: much btr 1045 (hvy).
1053 **CUIGIU 12** [1] 3-9-0 K Dalgleish (7) 33/1: 054205: Led, hdd over 2f out, wknd qckly for press. 1¼ 54
-- **CELEBRE BLU** [6] 3-9-0 F Lynch 50/1: 6: Handy, rdn/wknd qckly final 3f: debut: Suave Dancer gldg. 10 38
1081 **PROPER GENT 9** [2] 3-9-0 Kimberley Hart (5) 100/1: 00-007: Prom, lost tch halfway, t.o: v stiff task. 24 0
7 ran Time 1m 55.4 (1.3) (Stanley W Clarke) L M Cumani Newmarket.

1243

4.20 D COOPER HCAP 3YO+ 0-70 (E) 1m65y rnd Firm 15 +03 Fast [68]
£3672 £1130 £565 £282

847 **PENTAGON LAD 33** [6] J L Eyre 4-9-9 (63) A Culhane 13/2: 00-051: 4 ch g Secret Appeal - Gilboa 70
(Shirley Heights): Mid-div, smooth hdwy to lead appr fnl 2f, hung left but sytd on strongly ins last, rdn out: best time of day: '99 h'cap scorer at Carlisle, Thirsk, Ripon & Chester (rtd 75): eff between 1m & 10.3f: acts on firm, gd/soft & any trk: on a fair mark, can make a qck follow-up.
1038 **ADOBE 13** [8] W M Brisbourne 5-8-9 (49) T Williams 6/1 JT FAV: -10242: 5 b g Green Desert - Shamshir 1¼ 54
(Kris): Settled rear, smooth hdwy 3f out, rdn & swtchd to chall over 1f out, kept on, just held: clr rem: gd run on return to turf, should find similar: see 921, 754.
975 **OCTANE 22** [13] W M Brisbourne 4-8-7 (47) A McCarthy (3) 16/1: 00-003: 4 b c Cryptoclearance - 4 45
Something True (Sir Ivor): Rear, styd on strongly fnl 2f, nvr nrr: s/mate of 2nd: shld relish return to 10f+.
899 **NORTHGATE 28** [11] M Brittain 4-8-4 (44)(bl) D Mernagh (3) 12/1: 00-054: Chsd ldrs, rdn & no ¾ 40
extra final 2f: op 8/1: see 754 (AW).
1190 **CUTE CAROLINE 4** [15] 4-8-12 (52) J Carroll 6/1 JT FAV: 300-35: Settled rear, smooth hdwy over ½ 47
2f out, rdn/btn inside last: tchd 8/1, qck reapp: see 1190.
1011 **DONNAS DOUBLE 17** [16] 5-9-10 (64) P Fessey 10/1: 10-056: Trkd ldrs, wknd final 2f: see 1011 (7f, hvy). 2 55
3253} **LINCOLN DEAN 275** [7] 4-8-8 (48) F Lynch 14/1: 5040-7: Led, rdn/hdd over 2f out, sn btn: reapp: 1¼ 37
early '99 scorer at Lingfield (h'cap, rtd 69a), subs unplcd on turf (rtd 60): rtd 72 on debut in '98: eff at 1m, has tried 10f: acts on equitrack, poss handles firm.
1058 **PROSPECTORS COVE 12** [4] 7-10-0 (68) G Bardwell 16/1: 300008: Dwelt, rear, smooth hdwy over ½ 56
3f out, kept on onepcd final 2f: nicely bckd, top weight: see 618 (10f, AW).
4372} **YOUNG ROSEIN 209** [2] 4-9-2 (56) M Tebbutt 12/1: 1U20-9: Nvr a threat on reapp: '99 scorer at shd 44
Musselburgh (h'cap, rtd 57, first win): unplcd in '98 (fill mdn, flattered, rtd 62): eff arnd a sharp 7f on fast.
1113 **APRIL ACE 8** [5] 4-9-3 (57) Craig Williams 33/1: 23-000: Chsd ldrs, lost tch final 2f, fin 10th. 2 41
1066 **LANDING CRAFT 10** [1] 6-9-0 (54) K Dalgleish (7) 9/1: -00320: Waited with, rdn & not qckn over 1¼ 35
3f out, sn btn, fin 11th: op 5/1: btr 1066 (soft).
1149 **PERSIAN POINT 6** [14] 4-8-2 (41)(1ow) G Duffield 33/1: 000-00: Handy, bhd 4f out: 12th: qck reapp. 3 18
4615} **RYEFIELD 187** [10] 5-9-4 (58) G Parkin 8/1: 0060-0: Al well bhd, fin 13th: '99 scorer at Newcastle ¾ 32
& Ayr (h'caps, rtd 68): '98 Carlisle scorer (mdn, rtd 80): eff at 7f/1m: acts on firm, gd/soft & a stiff/gall trk: runs well fresh, without blnks: back on a wng mark, shld be sharper next time.
931 **FALLS OMONESS 26** [3] 6-8-11 (51) L Swift (7) 9/1: 050-20: Rear, lost tch 3f out, eased when btn, 20 5
fin last: not handle firm grnd?: much btr 931 (soft).
14 ran Time 1m 44.8 (1.0) (Creskeld Racing) J L Eyre Sutton Bank, Nth Yorks.

1244

4.55 PANORAMA BAR HCAP 3YO+ 0-60 (F) 5f str Firm 15 +01 Fast [59]
£3120 £960 £480 £240 3 yo rec 9 lb Majority raced far side

1082 **HEAVENLY MISS 9** [15] D Carroll 6-9-4 (49)(bl) K Dalgleish (7) 6/1: 450-41: 6 b m Anita's Prince - 58
Heavenly Blessed (Monseigneur): Chsd ldrs far side, rdn to chall over 1f out, led ins last, drvn clr cl-home: nicely bckd: '99 wnr at Thirsk, W'hampton & Bath (h'caps, rtd 52 & 54a at best): plcd in '98 (rtd 50): eff at 5/6f on firm/fast, soft & both AWs: eff in blnks & handles any trk.
3578} **SUNSET HARBOUR 259** [10] J M Bradley 7-8-8 (39) G Bardwell 8/1: 0000-2: 7 br m Prince Sabo - 1¾ 42
City Link Pet (Tina's Pet): Prom far side, led dist till ins last, not pace of wnr: tchd 12/1: unplcd for S Kettlewell in '99 (rtd 39 & 38a, h'caps, tried visor): '98 wnr at W'hampton, Newcastle & Catterick (h'caps, rtd 52 & 44a): eff at 5/6f on firm, gd/soft & both AWs: eff with/without blnks: can run well fresh: win similar.
4267} **HIGH CARRY 218** [11] N Tinkler 5-9-8 (53) Kim Tinkler 12/1: 2400-3: 5 b m Forzando - Cam Maire 2 50
(Northern Prospect): Chsd ldrs far side, ev ch until no extra inside last: plcd thrice in '99 (h'caps, rtd 58 at best): '98 rnr-up (h'cap, rtd 83 at best), prev term scored at Beverley (clmr) & Sandown (nursery, rtd 86 at best): suited by a stiff 5f, stays a sharp 6f: acts on firm, soft, with/without blnks: well h'capped.
910 **BOW PEEP 27** [9] M W Easterby 5-9-12 (57)(bl) G Parkin 11/2 JT FAV: 00-124: Handy, rdn to impr hd 54
2f out, styd on inside last, nrst fin: in gd form, handles firm/fast, prefers gd/soft & soft grnd: see 798.
1068 **TANCRED TIMES 10** [3] 5-8-13 (44) Kimberley Hart (5) 33/1: 003505: Front rank stands side, rdn, 1¼ 37
hung right & onepcd over 1f out: poorly drawn & not disgrcd here, will apprec a return to 6f on softer grnd.
1149 **JACMAR 6** [8] 5-8-11 (42) D Mernagh (3) 11/2 JT FAV: 000-26: Mid-div, rdn & kept on onepcd over shd 35
1f out: tchd 7/1, qck reapp: btr 1149 (7f).
-- **BANDIDA** [12] 6-8-7 (38) R Lappin 100/1: 7: Well bhd, styd on strongly inside last, nvr nrr: ½ 30
8 mth jumps abs (modest form): sure to apprec much further than this on the Flat.
1143 **COLLEGE MAID 6** [17] 3-9-2 (56) A Culhane 10/1: 56-208: Prom, rdn/lost tch over 1f out: qck reapp. ¾ 46

1137 **CHAKRA** 7 [6] 6-8-7 (38) Claire Bryan (5) 14/1: 610609: Rear stands side, effort halfway, hung   **hd** **28**
right & onepcd over 1f out: qck reapp.
1005 **GARNOCK VALLEY** 17 [13] 10-9-7 (52) J P Spencer 20/1: -16400: Al bhd far side: 10th: btr 250.   **hd** **42**
1092 **ORIEL STAR** 9 [16] 4-9-4 (49)(vis) Joanna Badger (7) 7/1: -00630: Led far side, rdn/hdd over   **¾** **34**
1f out, wknd qckly, fin 11th: btr 1092.
756 **HENRY THE HAWK** 44 [14] 9-8-12 (43)(bl) F Lynch 16/1: 204-40: Prom, bhd fnl 2f: 12th: 6 wk abs.   **½** **26**
798 **BOWCLIFFE GRANGE** 42 [1] 8-8-7 (38) J Carroll 12/1: 0-0030: Led stands side, hdd over 2f out,   **0**
wknd qckly, fin 16th: 6 wk abs: trailblazer, poorly drawn here: see 798.
992 **INVISIBLE FORCE** 19 [4] 3-8-7 (47) J Fanning 12/1: -40-60: Rcd stands side, lost tch halfway,   **0**
fin 17th: op 7/1 on h'cap bow: poor low draw, shld be capable of better: see 992.
4364} **Calling The Shots** 210 [2] 3-8-13 (53) T Williams 33/1:   602 **Manolo** 73 [18] 7-9-7 (52)(bl) G Duffield 20/1:
4364} **Tartan Island** 210 [5] 3-8-13 (53) M Tebbutt 33/1:   634 **Facile Tigre** 68 [7] 5-9-4 (49) Craig Williams 33/1:
18 ran   Time 58.8 (0.7)   (E Gray)   D Carroll Southwell, Notts.

Official Going   GOOD (GOOD/FIRM in places). Stalls: Inside, except 1m2f - Stands Side.

1245   **2.10 HILL RTD HCAP 4YO+ 0-100 (B)**   **5f rnd**   **Firm 14**   **-06 Slow**   **[106]**
£9451   £3585   £1792   £814   Horses drawn low have a significant advantage here

1090 **DAMALIS** 9 [6] E J Alston 4-8-10 (88) W Supple 10/1: 40-461: 4 b f Mukaddamah - Art Age (Artaius):   **97**
Bhd ldr, led ent fnl 1f, rdn out: op 8/1: '99 Sandown wnr (rtd h'cap, rtd 96): '98 wnr here at Chester (fill mdn)
& Ripon (stks, rtd 98): all 4 wins at 5f, tried 6f: acts on firm & soft grnd, any trk, likes Chester: useful.
926 **SUNLEY SENSE** 26 [4] M R Channon 4-8-5 (83) S Drowne 10/1: 00-002: 4 b g Komaite - Brown Velvet   **¾** **88**
(Mansingh) Tried to make all, hdd below dist, kept on: right back to form: acts on firm & soft grnd, see 926.
941 **CRYHAVOC** 24 [1] D Nicholls 6-8-4 (82)(1oh) F Norton 7/1: 0-6003: 6 b g Polar Falcon - Sarabah   **1½** **83**
(Ela Mana Mou): Outpcd, short of room 2f out, ran on strongly fnl 1f, nvr nrr: op 5/1: gd run, see 716.
1090 **AMBITIOUS** 9 [11] K T Ivory 5-8-8 (84) C Catlin (7) 33/1: 0-0104: Held up, imprvd appr final 1f,   **nk** **84**
not trouble ldrs: op 20/1: fine run from poor high draw: see 905.
4120} **ACE OF PARKES** 227 [5] 4-8-7 (85) O Pears 12/1: 5506-5: Dwelt, short of room 2f out, prog dist,   **½** **83**
no extra towards fin: reapp: highly tried last term (5th of 8 in a List, rtd 90): '98 wnr at Hamilton (mdn auct)
& here at Chester (2, stks, rtd 113): eff at 5/6f: acts on firm & gd/soft grnd: likes to force the pace, any trk,
likes Chester: runs well fresh, has tumbled down the weights, should be spot-on for this.
926 **HENRY HALL** 26 [2] 4-8-9 (87) K Fallon 4/1 FAV: 00-606: Outpcd, late wide hdwy, nvr a threat: **1½** **81**
hvly bckd & clearly better expected with K Fallon up: not cope with this v tight track? see 702.
716 **CLASSY CLEO** 48 [3] 5-8-7 (85) J F Egan 7/1: 300007: Sn shkn up in mid-div, rdn dist, no impression.   **nk** **78**
1182 **FURTHER OUTLOOK** 4 [7] 6-9-6 (98) K Darley 14/1: 60-008: Prsd ldr till appr final 1f, no extra.   **nk** **90**
926 **ZIGGYS DANCER** 26 [10] 9-8-4 (82)(5oh) P Robinson 14/1: 043349: Nvr a factor: poor draw, see 223.   **3½** **65**
702 **ALMATY** 49 [9] 7-9-7 (99) Martin Dwyer 16/1: 603-00: Chsd ldrs, fdd appr final 1f: 10th, 7 wk abs: **¾** **80**
'99 rnr-up (List, rtd 109): '98 wnr at Beverley (stks), Newmarket (rtd h'cap, rtd 110): eff at 5f on any trk, likes
stiff ones: handles gd/soft, suited by firm/fast: best without visor, can force the pace: smart entire.
1162 **ZUHAIR** 5 [12] 7-8-4 (82) A Nicholls (3) 20/1: 0-0000: Al bhd: 11th: tchd 33/1, stablemate 3rd, poor draw.   **¾** **61**
1013 **PARADISE LANE** 17 [8] 4-8-6 (84) T Quinn 9/2: 000-20: Speed 2f, sn lost place: last, well bckd: **5** **53**
needs to dominate, didn't 'ping' from the stalls like he can, poor high draw: see 1013.
12 ran   Time 1m 00.82 (1.02)   (Liam & Tony Ferguson)   E J Alston Longton, Lancs.

1246   **2.40 LISTED DEE STKS 3YO (A)**   **1m2f75y**   **Firm 14**   **00 Fast**
£29737   £9150   £4575   £2287

955 **MERRY MERLIN** 23 [5] M L W Bell 3-8-8 T Quinn 25/1: 15-01: 3 b c Polar Falcon - Bronzewing (Beldale   **110**
Flutter): Trkd ldr, led just before dist, pushed clr: fair time: '99 debut wnr at Newmarket (mdn, subs last
in a Listed, rtd 100): eff at 7f, relished this step up to 10f & will stay further: likes firm grnd, goes on any
trk & can run well fresh: v useful colt, unfortunately not entered at Epsom or Ascot: should find a Group race.
980 **THREE POINTS** 21 [7] J L Dunlop 3-8-8 Pat Eddery 11/4 FAV: 113-32: 3 b c Bering - Trazi (Zalazl)   **2½** **105**
Pld hard bhd, plenty to do 3f out, styd on for press & went 2nd towards fin, nvr nr wnr: hvly bckd: another
useful run, appreciated this lngr 10f trip & is likely to get 12f: should find similar: see 980.
996 **ZYZ** 19 [8] B W Hills 3-8-8 M Hills 4/1: 13-233: 3 b c Unfuwain - Girette (General Assembly)   **½** **104**
Hld up, gd prog 2f out, drvn to chase ldrs bef dist, unable to chall: suited by step up to 10f, find a Gr race abroad.
1069 **SHABLAM** 10 [1] Sir Michael Stoute 3-8-8 K Fallon 11/2: 31-544: Chsd ldrs, prog & ch when hung   **nk** **103**
left appr final 1f, onepace under press: nicely bckd tho' op 9/2: styd lngr 10f trip: see 955.
980 **ISLAND SOUND** 21 [2] M Pollard 10/3: 411-25: Set gd clip, hdd appr final 1f, same pace: **shd** **103**
well bckd, clr rem: handles firm grnd but prob suited by softer: see 980 (9f, just in front of this rnr-up on gd/sft).
925 **SIR NINJA** 26 [6] 3-8-8 J Reid 20/1: 210-56: Al towards rear: highly tried, longer trip, not disgraced.   **5** **95**
4332} **THARI** 212 [3] 3-8-8 (BL) R Hills 10/1: 2136-7: Held up, hmpd about 2f, nvr got on terms: blnkd,   **3** **90**
tchd 12/1, reapp: '99 Chepstow wnr (mdn, rtd 96, P Walwyn): eff at 7f, should get further (brother & dam
won over 12f): acts on firm/fast grnd, handles soft & gd/undul trks: now with B Hanbury.
1069 **PARADISE GARDEN** 10 [4] 3-8-8 D Holland 16/1: 24-038: In tch till 4f out: stiff task: see 1069, 765.   **3** **85**
8 ran   Time 2m 10.0 (1.5)   (Sir Thomas Pilkington)   M L W Bell Newmarket.

1247   **3.10 GR 3 ORMONDE STKS 4YO+ (A)**   **1m5f89y**   **Firm 14**   **+11 Fast**
£36000   £13800   £6900   £3300

2912} **DALIAPOUR** 292 [1] Sir Michael Stoute 4-8-11 K Fallon 11/8 FAV: 2220-1: 4 b c Sadler's Wells - Dalara   **119**
(Doyoun) Pld hard, trkd ldrs, qcknd to lead appr fnl 1f, cosily: hvly bckd, fast time, reapp: '99 Epsom reapp
wnr (stks), rnr-up in both the English & Irish Derbys (rtd 118, L Cumani): '98 Chepstow (mdn) & Ascot wnr (List,
rtd 113): eff at 10f/13.5f on firm & soft, any trk: can force the pace, runs v well fresh: v smart, genuine colt.
987 **LIFE IS LIFE** 19 [2] M A Jarvis 4-8-8 P Robinson 11/1: 102-32: 4 b f Mansonnien - La Vie Immobile   **¾** **113**
(Alleged) Waited with, imprvd 3f out, went after wnr appr dist, clsd under hands-&-heels but was being held: clr
rem: acts on firm & hvy grnd: v progressive, smart filly, being aimed at the Gold Cup: must win a Group race.
3030} **DANISH RHAPSODY** 286 [6] Lady Herries 7-8-11 Pat Eddery 13/2: 5311-3: 7 b g Danehill - Ardmelody   **5** **110**

(Law Society) Set strong pace, hdd appr fnl 1f, no extra: bckd tho' op 11/2, reapp: won fnl 2 in '99 at Newbury (stks) & Goodwood (List rtd h'cap, rtd 116): '98 wnr at Haydock (reapp) & again at Goodwood (List, rtd 115): eff at 10/12f, not quite 13.5f?: acts on firm & gd/soft, any trk, esp Goodwood: likes to be up with/forcing the pace.

1152 **YAVANAS PACE 6** [7] M Johnston 8-9-0 D Holland 10/1: 6-0104: Ran in snatches, prom till dropped rear 5f out, styd on in the str, nvr dngrs: qck reapp, op 8/1: goes on firm grnd, suited by soft/hvy: see 987. — 4 108

3873} **ELMUTABAKI 243** [5] 4-8-11 R Hills 9/1: 1150-5: Mid-div, effort 2f out, onepace: reapp: '99 wnr at Royal Ascot (King George V H'cap) & Haydock (Listed, rtd 108): rnr-up sole '98 start: return to 12f should suit: acts on firm & gd/soft grnd, stiff/gall trks: v useful, with B Hills. — ½ 104

1109 **ASHGAR 8** [4] 4-8-11 J Fortune 25/1: 40-056: Held up, wide effort 3f out, no impression: see 1109. — 3 100

987 **TAUFANS MELODY 19** [3] 9-8-11 R Cochrane 25/1: 114/07: Al bhd: missed '99, '98 wnr at Baden Baden (Listed) & Caulfield (Gr 1), 4th in the Melbourne Cup (rtd 117): '97 wnr at Lingfield, Ascot (val h'cap, subs disq), Doncaster & France (List): eff at 12f, stays 2m on firm, likes soft grnd: stablemate of 3rd: smart 9yo. — 5 95

968 **BAY OF ISLANDS 22** [8] 8-8-11 (vis) K Darley 20/1: 123-08: Mid-div, rdn to chase ldrs 3f out, sn btn: tchd 33/1: '99 Nottingham wnr (h'cap, rtd 93 at best): '98 Doncaster wnr (h'cap, rtd 89): eff at 12f/14f, gets 2m: acts on firm & gd/soft grnd, any trk: eff with/without visor: highly tried: with D Morris. — 2½ 92

987 **CAPRI 19** [9] 5-9-2 T Quinn 5/1: 010-29: Cl-up till lost pl 3f out, eased right down: nds softer grnd. — dist 0

9 ran Time 2m 50.16 (0.36) (H H Aga Khan) Sir Michael Stoute Newmarket

---

1248 3.40 LISTED HUXLEY STKS 4YO+ 1m2f75y Firm 14 -10 Slow
£14170 £4360 £2180 £1090

1057 **SOSSUS VLEI 12** [2] G Wragg 4-8-12 M Roberts 1/1 FAV: 162-51: 4 b c Inchinor - Sassalya (Sassafras) Early ldr, prom, shkn up over 2f out, rdn dist, ran on & got up nr fin: jockey given 2 day whip ban: lightly rcd in '99, won at Bath (stks, Gr 3 rnr-up, rtd 110): v useful wnr at Newmarket (stks): eff at 1m/10.5f: acts on firm & hvy grnd, any trk: runs well fresh: v useful colt, win a Group race abroad. — 106

732 **RAIN IN SPAIN 47** [5] J Noseda 4-8-12 Pat Eddery 10/3: 113-32: 4 b c Unfuwain - Mana Isabella (Young Generation) Sn led, increased tempo 3f out, hard rdn ent final 1f, worn down towards fin: op 5/2, 7 wk abs: imprvd in defeat in this higher grade with forcing tactics: eff at 10f, return to 12f will suit: useful. — hd 105

1014 **MONSAJEM 17** [3] E A L Dunlop 5-8-12 (BL) J Reid 4/1: 3-6043: 5 ch c Woodman - Fairy Dancer (Nijinsky) Last, in tch, hard rdn appr final 1f, no impress till strong run towards fin: not btn far, op 3/1, blnkd: probably back to best here, return to 12f may suit now: useful: see 657. — ½ 104

1174 **PEGNITZ 5** [1] C E Brittain 5-8-12 P Robinson 9/2: 53-044: Bhd ldrs, appeared to be going best of all appr final 1f, sn rdn, unable to qckn: qck reapp, blnks omitted: different tactics, prob ran to best: see 1174. — ¾ 102

2320] **BEAT ALL 319** [4] 4-9-1 K Fallon 4/7: /134-W: 134-W: Bhdwin, appeared lame at start, returned sound: was an odds-on shot at the time: '99 reapp wnr at Newmarket (Listed, 3rd in the Epsom Derby, rtd 115): '98 wnr at Chepstow (mdn, rtd 92): eff at 10f/12f: acts on firm & gd/soft grnd, prob any trk: runs well fresh: smart colt. — 0

5 ran Time 2m 11.95 (2.45) (A E Oppenheimer) G Wragg Newmarket

---

1249 4.10 EBF SEFTON FILLIES MDN 2YO (D) 5f rnd Firm 14 -23 Slow
£6955 £2140 £1070 £535

1079 **DRESS CODE 10** [7] W Jarvis 2-8-11 R Cochrane 9/2: 31: 7 b f Barathea - Petite Epaulette (Night Shift) Bhd ldrs, hard rdn appr fnl 1f, grad wore down ldr, got up fnl strides: R Cochrane at his strongest: 47,000 gns Jan foal, half-sister to 7f juv wnr, sire 1m-10f performer: eff forcing the pace over a sharp 5f on firm. — 79

989 **MISS BRIEF 19** [6] P D Evans 2-8-11 J F Egan 14/1: -02: 2 b f Brief Truce - Preponderance (Cyrano de Bergerac) Tried to make all, drvn final 1f, collared nr line: a bold attempt: 8,200 gns May foal, half-sister to useful former Guinea Hunter, dam 5f juv wnr, sire 1m-10f performer: eff forcing the pace over a sharp 5f on firm. — nk 77

— **STRANGE DESTINY 1** [1] A Berry 2-8-11 K Darley 9/2: 3: 2 b f Mujadil - Blue Birds Fly (Rainbow Quest) Outpcd till ran on strgly fnl 1½f, too late: op 7/2, debut: 27,000 gns Feb foal, half-sister to a prolific sprinting juv: eff at 5f, looks sure to apprec 6f: acts on firm grnd: looks a certain future wnr. — ¾ 75+

1124 **SANDAL 7** [5] R Hannon 2-8-11 R Hughes 10/3 FAV: 34: Prom, lost grnd halfway, styd on final 1f, not trouble ldrs: nicely bckd, qck reapp: needs 6f, see 1124. — 1¾ 70

865 **REGAL AIR 30** [3] 2-8-11 W Supple 14/1: 35: Keen, chsd ldrs, onepace bef dist: clr rem, win a seller. — ¾ 68

1088 **JUSTELLA 9** [2] 2-8-11 A Daly 14/1: -66: Dwelt, nvr on terms: do better over further when h'capped. — 5 56

1067 **FRANICA 10** [9] A Mackay 4/1: -22227: Chsd ldrs, no extra appr final 1f, eased inside last: op 3/1: tricky draw & much quicker grnd today: consistent before, see 1067. — 3 47

— **CHANTAIGNE 11** [11] 2-8-11 K Fallon 7/1: 8: Al towards rear: stablemate 7th: 25,000 gns General Monash Feb foal, half-sister to a 7f juv wnr, sire a sprinter: had the worst of the draw. — 3 38

1019 **ELAINES REBECCA 17** [10] 2-8-11 J Fortune 20/1: -629: Mid-div till 2f out: poor draw, btr 1019 (hvy). — ½ 37

— **CELESTIAL POWER 8** [8] 2-8-11 J Weaver 20/1: 0: Sn struggling: 10th: 3,000 gns Superpower Feb foal, half-sister to 3 juv wnrs, sire a sprinter: another from the A Bailey stable. — 2½ 31

— **JEANNIES GIRL 4** [4] 2-8-11 J Bramhill 20/1: 0: Al bhd: 11th: 4th A Bailey rnr: 2,500 gns Superlative Mar 1st foal, dam & sire sprinters. — 3½ 23

11 ran Time 1m 01.64 (1.84) (Anthony Foster) W Jarvis Newmarket

---

1250 4.40 WYNN HCAP 4YO+ 0-90 (C) 7f122y rnd Firm 14 -05 Slow [86]
£9028 £2778 £1389 £694 Horses drawn low have a significant advantage

*895 **SILCA BLANKA 3** [3] A G Newcombe 8-9-9 (81) J Reid 13/2: 000-11: 8 b h Law Society - Reality (Known Fact) Well plcd, led dist, sn hard rdn, just held on: nicely bckd: 4 wks ago won Brighton reapp (h'cap): '99 wnr at Lingfield (h'cap, rtd 89a) & Epsom (h'cap, rtd 90): '98 Warwick wnr (stks, rtd 86): eff at 7f/1m on firm, soft grnd & equitrack: suited by sharp trks, Epsom specialist (3 wins): well h'capped. — 88

1011 **I CRIED FOR YOU 17** [1] J G Given 5-9-1 (73) Dean McKeown 13/2: 00-132: 5 b g Statoblest - Fall Of The Hammer (Auction Ring) In tch, prog & briefly short of room 2f out, styd on strgly for press, just failed: ran to best, clearly got this sharp 7.5f on firm grnd: progressive, will be winning again: see 1011, 838. — hd 79

49 **ARTERXERXES 178** [13] C G Cox 7-9-3 (75) S Drowne 25/1: 0200-3: 7 b g Anshan - Hanglands (Bustino) Led till 1f out, kept on: fine reapp considering drawn 13: '99 Kempton wnr (h'cap, rtd 77): '98 Folkestone wnr (h'cap rtd 80 & 80a): eff forcing the pace at 7f/1m: acts on firm, gd grnd & equitrack: goes well fresh, sharp trk specialist: best without visor: not badly h'capped, shld go close next time. — 1 79

1077 **TAFFS WELL 10** [9] B Ellison 7-9-1 (73) K Fallon 11/4 FAV: 06-404: Off the pace till gd hdwy ent fnl 2f, hmpd & snatched up nr fin: hvly bckd, wld have been 3rd: won this in '99 (off 10lbs lower), see 715. — shd 77

1015 **MISTER RAMBO 17** [2] 5-9-9 (81) R Hughes 10/1: 0-0105: Bhd, imprvng when short of room 2f out, kept on, nvr a threat: op 8/1: little luck in running despite favourable low draw: keep in mind, see 817. — 1½ 82

414

CHESTER THURSDAY MAY 11TH Lefthand, V Tight Track

-1192 **DISTINCTIVE DREAM 4** [12] 6-8-12 (70) R Cochrane 14/1: 036026: Rear, not clr run 2f out & swtchd, kept on but unable to chall: qck reapp, in form, gets 7.5f: see 598. *¾* **69**
1015 **LOVERS LEAP 17** [6] 4-9-8 (80) C Rutter 16/1: 120-07: Chsd ldrs, no extra appr final 1f: see 1015. *2* **75**
977 **NOMORE MR NICEGUY 22** [11] 6-9-11 (83) W Supple 20/1: 0-0008: Bhd, moderate late hdwy. *¾* **77**
1074 **BLUE STAR 10** [4] 4-9-2 (74)(vis) J Weaver 14/1: 122009: Prom till fdd appr fnl 1f: better at 6f, see 660. *2½* **63**
1158 **PERFECT PEACH 5** [5] 5-8-11 (69) T E Durcan 33/1: 100-00: Al mid-div: 10th, not given a hard time, qck reapp: '99 Musselburgh wnr (h'cap, rtd 72): back in '97 won at Thirsk (mdn) & Beverley (fill nurs, rtd 80, J Berry): eff at 5f, suited by 7f: acts on firm & gd/soft grnd, sharp or gall trks: best without blnks. *2* **54**
875 **TOPTON 30** [16] 6-9-4 (76)(bl) K Darley 16/1: 300200: Dwelt, nvr got in it from v poor draw: 11th. *shd* **61**
1160 **WEETMANS WEIGH 5** [7] 7-9-4 (76) T Quinn 14/1: 640000: In tch, effort ent final 2f, no impress & sn hmpd, eased: 12th, nicely bckd from 20/1, qck reapp: see 49. *¾* **60**
1160 **NOMINATOR LAD 5** [10] 6-9-5 (77) J Fortune 25/1: 00-000: Bhd, hmpd after halfway, nvr a factor: 13th. *1½* **58**
1158 **PEARTREE HOUSE 5** [17] 6-9-10 (82) A Nicholls (3) 14/1: 0-0060: Sn prom, wide, wknd appr final 1f: 14th, qck reapp, worth ignoring from stall 17: see 687. *hd* **63**
834 **Gift Of Gold 35** [8] 5-9-7 (79) A Mackay 16/1: 1192 **Demolition Jo 4** [14] 5-9-2 (74)(vis) Pat Eddery 20/1:
941 **Bodfari Pride 24** [15] 5-8-11 (69) F Norton 40/1:
17 ran Time 1m 33.81 (1.41) (Duckhaven Stud) A G Newcombe Huntshaw, Devon.

1251

5.10 COPYRITE HCAP 3YO+ 0-80 (D) 1m4f66y Firm 14 -17 Slow [79]
£7475 £2300 £1150 £575 3 yo rec 19lb

-- **VERIDIAN** [13] N J Henderson 7-9-11 (76) Pat Eddery 7/1: 2462/1: 7 b g Green Desert - Alik (Targowice) Rear, stdy prog 3f out, briefly short of room bef dist, kept on gamely under press to lead nr fin: jumps fit, 99/00 Kempton wnr (h'cap, 2m/2½m, firm & soft, rtd 126h, without blnks): nr 3 yr Flat abs, '97 wnr at Doncaster & here at Chester (h'caps, rtd 79): eff at 12f, tried 14f: acts on firm & gd/soft grnd, any trk, likes Chester. **84**
871 **BATSWING 30** [3] B Ellison 5-8-12 (63) F Norton 4/1 FAV: 06-002: 5 b g Batshoof - Magic Milly (Simply Great) Handy, rdn to lead below dist, hdd final 20y: big gamble just foiled: this return to form clearly expected, acts on firm & hvy grnd: see 699. *nk* **70**
1948} **PIPED ABOARD 334** [6] M C Pipe 5-10-0 (79)(vis) K Fallon 10/1: 6/00-3: 5 b g Pips Pride - Last Gunboat (Dominion) Mid-div, prog & slightly short of room 2f out, styd on without threatening: jumps fit, 99/00 Worcester wnr (amat h'cap, 2m/2m2f, firm & gd, visor, rtd 125h): lightly rcd since '98 wnr at Thirsk (rtd mdn, rtd 83 at best, J Dunlop): eff at 10/12f on firm & soft grnd, any trk, with/without blnks/visor. *1¾* **84**
1217 **HANNIBAL LAD 2** [8] W M Brisbourne 4-8-13 (64) T G McLaughlin 20/1: 113504: Rear, imprvd to chsd ldrs 3f out, nvr able to chall: better run than 48hrs ago: see 671, 605. *nk* **68**
1217 **WARNING REEF 2** [5] 7-8-11 (62) W Supple 7/1: 040-45: Waited with, styd on final 2f, nvr nr ldrs. *½* **65**
1044 **MY LEGAL EAGLE 13** [7] 6-9-0 (65) P Fitzsimons (5) 7/1: 222136: Bhd, moderate late hdwy: see 1023. *1* **66**
1190 **DARE 4** [10] 5-8-10 (61)(vis) S Drowne 20/1: 003507: Nvr trbld ldrs: qck reapp, back up in trip, see 83. *nk* **61**
809 **ENFILADE 40** [4] 4-9-8 (73)(t) W Ryan 9/2: 444-58: Led before halfway till 1f out, wknd: 6 wk abs. *¾* **72**
*1217 **NOUKARI 2** [12] 7-10-1 (80)(6ex) J F Egan 7/1: 214019: In tch, chsd ldrs 4f out till ent fnl 2f, fdd dist: probably came too soon after hard-fought win here 48hrs ago over 10f: see 1217. *shd* **79**
2562} **ANGIE MARINIE 307** [9] 4-8-13 (64) J Fortune 10/1: 2305-0: Held up, wide effort 5f out, nvr pace to chall: 10th, stablemate 3rd: 7 wk jumps abs, rattled up a 5-timer at N Abbot (2), Plumpton (2) & Aintree (juv nov, 2m1f, fast & gd/soft, forcing the pace, rtd 115h): '99 wnr at Nottingham (sell for R Fahey, appr h'cap plcd for current stable, rtd 67): eff at 1m/10f, stays 12f: goes on firm grnd, suited by soft. *shd* **63**
991 **LITTLE AMIN 19** [2] 4-9-8 (73) Martin Dwyer 25/1: 60-000: Led till bef halfway, lost pl 2f out: 11th. *13* **62**
1050 **SUMMER BOUNTY 12** [1] 4-9-0 (65) R Hughes 33/1: 002000: Sn prom, wknd qckly 2f out: 12th. *2* **52**
12 ran Time 2m 40.29 (3.89) (Thurloe Thor'breds III) N J Henderson Lambourn, Berks.

CARLISLE FRIDAY MAY 12TH Righthand, Stiff Track, Uphill Finish

Official Going FIRM. Stalls: Inside, except 1m4f - Outside.

1252

2.10 NATIONAL EXPRESS MDN 2YO (D) 5f rnd Firm 10 -24 Slow
£3737 £1150 £575 £287

1048 **THE NAMES BOND 13** [12] Andrew Turnell 2-9-0 W Supple 4/1: -31: 2 b g Tragic Role - Artistic Licence (High Top): Made all, kept on strongly fnl 1f, rdn out: drifted from 5/2: half-brother to a 1m wnr, dam styd mid-dists: eff over a stiff 5f, will stay 6f: can force the pace, acts on firm grnd, handles gd/soft: improving gelding who can rate more highly & win again. **78**
1088 **JOINT INSTRUCTION 10** [6] M R Channon 2-9-0 S Drowne 13/2: -452: 2 b c Forzando - Edge Of Darkness (Vaigly Great): Trkd ldrs, imprvd to chall final 1f, kept on & not btn far: op 9/1, rider reportedly given a 1-day whip ban: eff at 5f on firm grnd, 6f will suit: must sn go one better: see 1088. *½* **75**
989 **ONLY ONE LEGEND 20** [11] T D Easterby 2-9-0 J Carroll 6/1: -03: 2 b c Eagle Eyed - Afifah (Nashwan): Prom, kept on under press final 1f, only btn arnd 1L: bckd from 14/1: 14,000gns Mar foal: eff at 5f, 6f will suit: much imprvd on todays firm grnd: should find a small race. *nk* **74**
1048 **PHAROAHS GOLD 13** [14] W Jarvis 2-9-0 M Tebbutt 3/1 FAV: -44: Chsd ldrs, rdn & kept on fnl 1f, not pace of ldrs: eff at 5f, prob needs 6f now: handles firm & gd/soft grnd: btn just over 1L today, see 1048. *½* **73**
1046 **ALNAHIGHER 14** [8] 2-8-9 J Fanning 12/1: -65: Chsd ldrs, rdn & onepcd final 1f: see 1046. *1½* **64**
-- **JUST MURPHY** [2] 2-9-0 F Lynch 25/1: -6: Rear, stdy late prog, nvr nrr on debut: IR 3,700gns Feb foal: sire a useful miler: looks in need of 6f: eye-catching debut from a poor low draw, one to keep in mind. *1½* **65+**
821 **WHARFEDALE LADY 37** [10] 2-8-9 T Williams 12/1: -07: Rear, some late hdwy, nvr dngr: some promise here & could prove interesting in sell company: see 821. *¾* **57**
-- **WALLY MCARTHUR** [4] 2-9-0 K Darley 11/2: -8: Chsd ldrs, no impress final 2f: debut: first foal, Mar foal: A Berry colt, clearly thought capable of better & prob worth another ch, poor low draw today. *nk* **61**
821 **SIENA STAR 37** [5] 2-9-0 R Lappin 16/1: -09: Chsd ldrs till wknd over 1f out: poor low draw. *nk* **60**
1131 **DOMINAITE 8** [1] 2-9-0 G Parkin 33/1: -00: Slowly away, nvr a factor in 10th: poor low draw. *1½* **56**
843 **THORNTOUN DANCER 34** [15] 2-8-9 Dale Gibson 25/1: -00: Nvr a factor in 11th: see 843. *1¾* **46**
-- **LADY AMBITION** [13] 2-8-9 T Lucas 25/1: -0: Al rear, 12th on debut: reportedly hated firm grnd. *hd* **46**
-- **KUMAKAWA** [3] 2-9-0 V Halliday 16/1: -0: Swerved left start, al bhd: 13th, poor draw. *2* **45**
-- **BELANDO** [9] 2-9-0 L Newton 20/1: -0: Slowly away, al bhd: 14th. *½* **44**
-- **ECKSCLUSIVE STORY** [7] 2-8-9 A Culhane 25/1: -0: Mid-div, btn halfway: fin last, poor draw. *shd* **39**

15 ran   Time 1m 01.2 (1.7)   (Mrs Claire Hollowood)   Andrew Turnell Sandhutton, Nth Yorks.

1253   2.40 CUMBRIA CLASSIFIED STKS 3YO+ 0-65 (E)   1m4f   Firm 10 -04 Slow
£2821   £868   £434   £217   3yo rec 19lb

1091 **FEE MAIL** 10 [5] I A Balding 4-9-6 K Darley 4/5 FAV: 21-331: 4 b f Danehill - Wizardry (Shirley   70
Heights): Made all, clr fnl 1f, cmftbly: bckd tho' op 4/7, value for 8L+ : '99 Windsor wnr (h'cap, rtd 65): eff
at 12f on firm & gd/soft, handles a sharp or stiff trk: can force the pace: career best effort, cld follow up.
871 **SANTA LUCIA** 31 [3] M Dods 4-9-6 Dale Gibson 25/1: 020-02: 4 b f Namaqualand - Villasanta (Corvaro): 5   58
Chsd ldrs, styd on final 1f but no ch with wnr: lightly rcd in '99, rnr-up at Redcar (h'cap, rtd 65): eff
arnd 12f on firm & gd/soft grnd.
1086 **SUNSET LADY** 10 [6] J S Wainwright 4-9-6 J Carroll 20/1: 04-003: 4 b f Red Sunset - Lady Of Man   7   48
(So Blessed): Chsd wnr, ev ch 3f out, gradually fdd: see 1086.
779 **CADILLAC JUKEBOX** 44 [2] G M Moore 5-9-9 P Hanagan (7) 20/1: 105/04: Rear, effort halfway, btn   4   45
3f out: 6 wk abs: missed '99, prev term wnr at Pontefract (appr h'cap, rtd 71, with J Hills, first time blnks):
eff at 10/12f, acts on gd grnd & on a stiff trk: can front run.
1076 **BERGAMO** 11 [4] 4-9-9 (bl) S Drowne 11/4: 5-0005: Dwelt, recovered & in tch, btn 3f out: see 845.   6   36
827 **DEBS SON** 37 [1] 3-8-4 J Bramhill 11/2: 454-66: In tch, effort halfway, btn final 3f: see 827.   12   18
6 ran   Time 2m 32.5 (1.7)   (Gary Coull)   I A Balding Kingsclere, Hants.

1254   3.10 BET TAX FREE HCAP 3YO+ 0-70 (E)   1m1f61y   Firm 10 -24 Slow   [67]
£3302   £1016   £508   £254

*1190 **ETISALAT** 5 [15] J Pearce 3-8-13 (52)(6ex) G Bardwell 13/8 FAV: 263111: 5 b g Lahib - Sweet Repose   58
(High Top): Waited on, swtchd 2f out & gd prog to lead 1½f out, kept on gamely ins last, drvn out: well bckd
from 5/2, qck reappr, rider reportedly given a 3-day irresponsible riding ban: qck hat-trick, earlier scored at
Musselburgh & Hamilton (h'caps), prev at W'hampton (amat h'cap, rtd 57a): '99 Yarmouth (sell h'cap) & Lingfield
wnr (h'cap): eff at 7/10f on gd & firm, both AWs: handles any trk, likes to be held up for a late run.
3084} **SPARKY** 284 [2] M W Easterby 6-9-1 (54)(bl) T Lucas 16/1: 0/00-02: 6 b g Warrshan - Pebble Creek   ¾   58
(Reference Point): In tch, hdwy to chall 1f out, kept on under press & not btn far: 3L clr 2nd: jumps rnr this
winter, Feb '00 Catterick wnr (sell hdle, rtd 100h, eff at 2m on firm & gd/soft, blnkd): unplcd on both '99 Flat
starts: '97 Southwell wnr (h'cap, rtd 92h): eff at 1m/10f on firm & gd/soft & f/sand: blnks, well h'capped.
692 **PUPPET PLAY** 53 [16] E J Alston 5-8-9 (48) W Supple 25/1: 334203: 5 ch m Broken Hearted - Fantoccini 3   47
(Taufan): Cl-up, led after 4f till dist, no extra: 8 wk abs: see 845.
1149 **SWYNFORD PLEASURE** 7 [1] J Hetherton 4-8-1 (40) A Polli(3) 13/2: 000-44: Rear, imprvd 3f out, kept   1¼   37+
on final 1f, not pace to chall: op 9/2: returning to form & v well h'capped now: see 1149.
3202} **THATCHED** 279 [14] 10-8-6 (45) J Carroll 12/1: 0246-5: Rdn in rear, styd on fnl 1f, nvr nrr: reapp: ¾   41
plcd sev times in '99 (h'caps, rtd 46 at best): '98 Redcar wnr (h'cap, rtd 48): '97 wnr here at Carlisle (h'cap,
rtd 55): eff over 7/9f on hard & gd/soft grnd: handles any trk, likes Carlisle: has tried a visor, best without.
1007 **AMRON** 18 [11] 13-8-6 (45) P Bradley 20/1: 00-006: Prom, onepcd fnl 2f: 13yo, dual '99 wnr.   hd   41
1066 **LEOFRIC** 11 [10] 5-8-5 (44)(bl) L Newton 14/1: 350337: Rear, kept on final 2f, nvr nrr: mkt drifter.   1¾   38
2835} **ALAMEIN** 296 [6] 7-9-2 (55) T Williams 25/1: 2440-8: Nvr better than mid-div: modest form on 2 hdle   1¼   47
starts this winter: '99 Lingfield wnr (2, clmr & h'cap, rtd 77a, with D Nicholls, rtd 54 on turf): '98 Southwell
wnr (clmr, rtd 78a & 74): all wins at 7f, stays 1m: acts on firm both AWs & any trk, loves Lingfield: can run
well fresh: gd weight carrier who is eff with/without blnks: well h'capped for W Storey.
842 **HEVER GOLF GLORY** 35 [5] 6-8-2 (41) N Carlisle 20/1: 045039: Rear, effort 3f out, sn no impress.   ½   32
4090} **FUTURE COUP** 294 [9] 4-9-6 (59) A Culhane 16/1: 251D-0: Rear, prog to chase ldrs halfway, ev ch   2½   47
2f out, sn wknd into 10th: no form on 2 hdle starts this winter: '99 Beverley (clmr) & Nottingham wnr (sell
h'cap, subs disq, rtd 56, with W Haggas): eff at 7/10f on gd & fast, handles firm & gd/soft: now with J Norton.
1050 **NOWELL HOUSE** 13 [12] 4-9-10 (63) G Parkin 12/1: 1-0000: Led 4f, remnd prom till wknd 2 out: 11th.   hd   51
872 **STATE WIND** 31 [3] 4-7-11 (35)(vis)(1ow) Dale Gibson 33/1: 060500: Prom 7f, fdd into 12th: see 635.   2   21
943 **LAWNETT** 25 [13] 4-9-0 (53) K Darley 10/1: -05600: In tch 7f, wknd: fin 13th.   1   36
931 **RED CAFE** 27 [4] 4-8-12 (51) S Drowne 14/1: 03/360: Mid-div till btn halfway: fin 14th: btr 854.   2½   31
759 **ADULATION** 45 [8] 6-9-7 (60) M Tebbutt 16/1: 005-00: Al towards rear, fin last: 6 wk abs.   5   32
15 ran   Time 1m 58.6 (3.2)   (Mrs E M Clarke)   J Pearce Newmarket.

1255   3.40 BUS ADVERTISING HCAP 3YO 0-70 (E)   1m rnd   Firm 10 -06 Slow   [77]
£3198   £984   £492   £246

*1085 **TAKE MANHATTAN** 10 [13] M R Channon 3-8-13 (62)(6ex) S Drowne 5/2 FAV: 006611: 3 br g Hamas -   75
Arab Scimetar (Sure Blade): Prom, went on over 1f out, pushed clr fnl 1f, easily: well bckd: recent Nottingham
wnr (h'cap): eff at 1m on firm & gd/soft, likes a stiff or galt trk: fast impr gelding, shld complete hat-trick.
736 **SIGN OF THE TIGER** 48 [18] P C Haslam 3-9-5 (68) M Tebbutt 12/1: -11442: 3 b g Beveled - Me Spede   5   69
(Valiyar): Rear, imprvd 3f out, styd on fnl 1f but no ch with wnr: 7 wk abs: earlier in fine AW form: see 488.
4570} **DIHATJUM** 193 [2] T D Easterby 3-9-0 (63) G Parkin 11/1: 5026-3: 3 b g Mujtahid - Rosie Potts   shd   64
(Shareef Dancer): Tried to make all, collared over 1f out, no extra: op 8/1: plcd on sev '99 starts, incl at
Redcar (clmr, rtd 66): eff at 6f/1m on fast & firm grnd: has tried a visor, seems better without: likes to run
up with or force the pace: sharper next time.
1053 **CARELESS** 13 [12] T D Easterby 3-8-7 (56) J Carroll 6/1: 00-404: In tch, kept on final 2f, nrst fin: 1   55+
shorter priced stablemate of 3rd: crying out for 10f+ now: see 976 (reapp).
613 **JUMBOS FLYER** 73 [8] 3-8-11 (60) R Cody Boutcher (7) 25/1: 500-05: Rear, prog 2f out, staying on   shd   59+
when badly hmpd dist, no ch after: 10 wk abs: in the process of running best race to date, prob eff at 1m on
firm grnd: must be given another chance, see 613 (sand).
1022 **SAN DIMAS** 18 [14] 3-8-11 (60) C Lowther 20/1: 00-006: Rear, effort halfway, not pace to chall.   2½   54
894 **NUTMEG** 29 [5] 3-9-2 (65) Dale Gibson 12/1: 045-47: Prom, ev ch 2f out, sn onepcd: see 894.   1½   56
894 **WASEEM** 29 [15] 3-9-7 (70) J Fanning 14/1: -108: Nvr better than mid-div, short of room 3f out,   ¾   59
modest late hdwy: onepcd 10f: see 894.
4570} **NOBLE REEF** 193 [7] 3-9-0 (63) G Bardwell 20/1: 6060-9: Dwelt, late prog, nvr nr ldrs on reapp: 3rd   hd   52
at Chester in '99 (nurs h'cap, rtd 72): eff at 7f on firm grnd, 1m shld suit: with Mrs G Rees, capable of better.
929 **COMEX FLYER** 27 [16] 3-8-11 (60) A Nicholls (3) 11/1: 646-40: Nvr a factor in 10th: see 929.   1   47
929 **ONE DOMINO** 27 [17] 3-9-0 (63) A Culhane 14/1: 406-30: Rear, mod late gains, fin 11th: btr 929.   shd   50
887 **ALJAZIR** 30 [3] 3-8-11 (60) W Supple 11/1: 54-020: Nvr a factor in 12th: much btr 887 (hvy).   1¾   43
921 **ZABIONIC** 27 [4] 3-9-4 (67) P Fessey 20/1: 00-400: Mid-div till btn 2f out: fin 13th, mkt drifter.   1   48

1022 **STORMSWELL 18** [9] 3-8-5 (54) F Lynch 20/1: 060-00: Mid-div, no ch from halfway: fin 14th. *3* **29**
1061 **BLACKPOOL MAMMAS 11** [10] 3-9-2 (65) K Darley 6/1: -01020: Prom 6f, fdd into 15th: btr 1061. *2½* **35**
1053 **Glen Vale Walk 13** [6] 3-8-8 (57) Angela Hartley(7) 20/1: 3428} **Radical Jack 268** [11] 3-8-0 (49) J Bramhill 50/1:
857 **Fantasy Adventurer 32** [1] 3-8-11 (60) T Lucas 33/1:
18 ran Time 1m 40.1 (1.3) (M G St Quinton) M R Channon West Isley, Berks.

1256 **4.10 CUMBERLAND CLASS STKS 3YO+ 0-60 (F) 5f rnd Firm 10 +04 Fast**
£2562 £732 £366 3yo rec 9lb

1140 **EASTERN TRUMPETER 8** [3] J M Bradley 4-9-6 K Darley 7/1: 100021: 4 b c First Trump - Oriental Air **67**
(Taufan): Chsd ldrs, styd on strongly fnl 1f to force head in front on line: gd time: earlier won at W'hampton (2, h'caps, rtd 72a): '99 Folkestone (clmr) & Ayr wnr (h'cap, rtd 70 & 63a): stays a sharp 6f, all wins at 5f: acts on firm, soft & f/sand: handles any trk, likes W'hampton: tough & genuine colt, fine effort to defy a low draw here.
*1239 **XANADU 1** [11] Miss L A Perratt 4-9-9 D Mernagh (3) 5/4 FAV: -00112: 4 ch g Casteddu - Bellatrix *shd* **69**
(Persian Bold): Broke well & tried to make all, hdd on line: well bckd & just btn in a thrilling fin: in tremendous form, won at Hamilton 24hrs ago in 1239.
897 **QUITE HAPPY 29** [5] M H Tompkins 5-9-0 J Fanning 10/1: 400-03: 5 b m Statoblest - Four Legged Friend *½* **59$**
(Aragon): Dsptd lead, ev ch 1f out, kept on & just btn in a cl fin: 2L clr rem: shwd gd speed to overcome low draw: back to form here, well h'capped nowadays: see 897.
1133 **RECORD TIME 8** [12] E J Alston 4-9-0 W Supple 7/1: 10-004: Chsd ldrs, not qckn final 1f: acts *2* **53**
on firm & gd/soft grnd: see 1133.
1138 **ITS ANOTHER GIFT 8** [4] 3-8-6 (bl)(1ow) C Lowther 14/1: 0-0305: Rear, prog halfway, styd on fnl 1f, *¾* **51**
nrst fin: op 10/1, poor low draw: fair effort, see 901 (mdn h'cap, blnkd first time).
923 **SEALED BY FATE 27** [8] 5-9-3 (vis) J Carroll 7/1: 0-5066: Dwelt, late prog, nvr nr ldrs: see 697 (AW). *1* **50**
4508} **TICK TOCK 199** [10] 3-8-5 L Newton 16/1: 0020-7: In tch, onepcd final 1½f: reapp: in '99 rnr-up at *shd* **47**
Redcar (nursery h'cap, rtd 60): eff at 5f on firm grnd.
673 **TREASURE TOUCH 59** [1] 6-9-3 A Nicholls (3) 6/1: 020-08: Chsd ldrs on outside, wknd final 1f: 8 wk *½* **49**
abs: poor low draw, eff at 5f, a return to 6f will suit: well h'capped, see 673.
881 **WISHBONE ALLEY 30** [9] 5-9-3 (vis) Dale Gibson 9/1: 042039: Chsd ldrs till wknd final 1f: btr 881. *1* **46**
870 **DUNKELLIN HOUSE 31** [7] 3-8-8 P Hanagan (7) 25/1: 600-00: Nvr a factor in 10th: see 870 (sand). *2½* **39**
919 **RED SYMPHONY 27** [6] 4-9-0 O Pears 20/1: 030-50: Al towards rear, fin 11th: see 919. *shd* **36**
1005 **DISTANT KING 18** [2] 7-9-3 G Arnolda (7) 50/1: 000-00: Dwelt, al outpcd, fin last: poor low draw: *7* **19**
mainly modest '99 form, incl in blnks: '98 wnr here at Carlisle & Beverley (2, h'caps, rtd 61 at best): eff at 5f, has tried 10f: acts on soft, likes firm grnd: v well h'capped nowadays.
12 ran Time 59.8 (0.3) (R G G Racing) J M Bradley Sedbury, Gloucs.

1257 **4.40 TDI HCAP DIV 1 3YO+ 0-70 (E) 6f rnd Firm 10 -01 Slow [69]**
£3029 £932 £466 £233 3yo rec 10lb

1162 **BAHAMIAN PIRATE 6** [1] D Nicholls 5-9-7 (62) A Nicholls (3) 6/1: 321-01: 5 ch g Housebuster - **69**
Shining Through (Depity Minister): Prom on outside, went on 2f out, ran on strongly fnl 1f, drvn out: fine effort to overcome poor low draw, caught the eye on recent reapp: '99 Ripon wnr (mdn, rtd 72): eff at 5/6f, stays 7f: acts on gd, firm & f/sand: can run well fresh, handles a sharpish or stiff trk: cld follow up.
1073 **RUSSIAN ROMEO 11** [16] B A McMahon 5-9-5 (60)(vis) K Darley 4/1 FAV: 522322: 5 b g Soviet Lad - *nk* **66**
Aotearoa (Flash Of Steel): Chsd ldrs, swtchd left over 1f out, kept on strongly, not btn far: tchd 11/2: a string of gd recent plcd efforts, deserves a change of luck: acts on firm, soft & fibresand: see 1073, 816.
1196 **PRIX STAR 4** [6] C W Fairhurst 5-9-3 (58) J Fanning 8/1: 455-03: 5 ch g Superpower - Celestine *1½* **60**
(Skyliner): Set pace till 2f out, no extra inside last: qck reapp: gd front running effort from a poor low draw: well h'capped & deserves similar: see 82 (sand).
1196 **SWINO 4** [3] P D Evans 6-9-0 (55)(bl) S Drowne 16/1: -46004: V slowly away, imprvd over 1f out, fin *¾* **54**
v fast but too late: qck reapp, poor low draw: v eye-catching run from this well h'capped gelding: see 177 (AW).
1148 **TAYOVULLIN 7** [11] 6-8-4 (44)(1ow) F Lynch 9/1: -00065: Rdn in rear, styd on final 1f, nrst fin. *1½* **40**
1133 **E B PEARL 8** [13] 4-8-0 (41) J Bramhill 12/1: 065106: In tch till lost place halfway, rallied fnl 1f. *1½* **32**
1239 **PRIORY GARDENS 1** [10] 6-7-10 (37)(1oh) Claire Bryan(5) 11/1: 004407: Mid-div, effort 2f out, *2* **22**
sn no impress: op 8/1: see 896.
1132 **CYRAN PARK 8** [12] 4-8-12 (53) T Williams 20/1: 60-048: Rear, effort halfway, nvr a factor: see 1132. *nk* **37**
803 **FOREIGN EDITOR 42** [5] 4-9-10 (65) P Hanagan (7) 15/2: 133209: Prom till wknd final 1f: 6 wk abs. *shd* **49**
1149 **KESTRAL 7** [4] 4-8-1 (42)(t) Dale Gibson 10/1: 0-5060: Nvr btr than mid-div: fin 10th, poor low draw. *½* **25**
941 **SQUARE DANCER 25** [2] 4-10-0 (69) A Culhane 12/1: 100-00: Dwelt, modest late gains, nvr dngr in *½* **51**
11th: again badly drawn, could pop back to form in the nr future: see 941.
787 **THREE LEADERS 44** [8] 4-8-7 (48)(bl) W Supple 14/1: 5-0600: Rear, eff halfway, nvr dngrs: 12th, abs. *¾* **27**
1143 **BIFF EM 7** [9] 6-7-13 (40) D Mernagh (3) 8/1: 000-50: Chsd ldrs 4f, fdd: fin 13th: see 1143. *1* **16**
4018} **Printsmith 235** [15] 3-8-7 (58) O Pears 25/1: 930 **Get A Life 27** [14] 7-7-12 (39)(2ow)(14oh) N Kennedy 50/1:
3247} **Red Charger 277** [7] 4-9-11 (66) J Carroll 14/1:
16 ran Time 1m 12.8 (0.7) (H E Lhendup Dorji) D Nicholls Sessay, Nth Yorks.

1258 **5.10 TDI HCAP DIV 2 3YO+ 0-70 (E) 6f rnd Firm 10 +07 Fast [69]**
£3029 £932 £466 £233 3yo rec 10lb

85 **ARCHELLO 172** [14] M Brittain 6-8-2 (43) T Williams 25/1: 4000-1: 6 b m Archway - Golden Room **53**
(African Sky): Chsd ldr, imprvd to lead ent fnl 1f, styd on strongly, rdn out: long abs, best time of day: prob best in '99 when 4th at Newmarket (clmr, rtd 53): last won back in '97 at Ripon (mdn, rtd 69): eff at 5/6f on firm & soft: handles any trk, has tried a visor, best without: runs v well fresh: v well h'capped on old form.
1239 **NINEACRES 1** [10] J M Bradley 9-8-12 (53)(bl) P Fitzsimons (5) 9/2: 130522: 9 b g Sayf El Arab - Mayor *2½* **56**
(Laxton): Tried to make all, collared ent fnl 1f, not pace to repel wnr: rnr-up at Hamilton 24hrs ago in 1239.
4394} **EASTERN PROPHETS 209** [12] M Dods 7-9-4 (59)(vis) F Lynch 8/1: 3200-3: 7 b g Emarati - Four Love *2½* **55**
(Pas de Seul): In tch, kept on fnl 1f, not pace of ldrs: reapp: '99 Nottingham wnr (appr h'cap, rtd 66, first time visor), plcd numerous times subs: '98 Doncaster wnr (clmr, rtd 69 & 71a, with G Lewis): '97 Kempton wnr (h'cap, rtd 82): best forcing the pace over 5/6f, acts on firm, gd/soft & on both AWs: best in blnks/visor.
1244 **JACMAR 1** [15] Miss L A Perratt 5-8-1 (42) D Mernagh(3) 4/1 FAV: 00-264: Rear, ran on final 2f, *1½* **34**
nrst fin: qck reapp, ran 24hrs ago in 1244.
*1073 **MARENGO 11** [2] 6-9-7 (62)(6ex) K Darley 7/1: 223215: In tch, onepcd final 1f: not disgrcd under *2* **48**
a pen from a poor low draw: see 1073 (gd/soft).

CARLISLE FRIDAY MAY 12TH Righthand, Stiff Track, Uphill Finish

1074 **STYLISH WAYS** 11 [4] 8-9-11 (66) G Bardwell 10/1: 050-06: Mid-div, nvr nr ldrs: once again poorly *shd* 52
drawn: nicely h'capped & primed for a return to form: see 1074.
4302} **WESTGATE RUN** 214 [9] 3-8-7 (58) P Hanagan (7) 25/1: 0000-7: Rdn in rear, late hdwy, nvr nrr: 1 41
reapp: 2nd at Thirsk in '99 (clmr, rtd 75): eff at 7f on gd & firm: fitter next time & a return to 7f shld suit.
*781 **PISCES LAD** 44 [13] 4-9-7 (62) C Lowther 10/1: 000-18: Chsd ldrs, fdd fnl 1f: 6 wk abs since 781. 2½ 38
1239 **MERANTI** 1 [1] 7-7-10 (37) (1oh) Claire Bryan(5) 14/1: 00-009: Nvr better than mid-div: mkt drifter, 1½ 9
poor low draw, qck reapp: see 1239.
910 **HIGHLY FANCIED** 28 [6] 4-8-3 (44) Dale Gibson 20/1: 500-00: Nvr a factor in 10th: mkt drifter, ½ 15
poor draw: mainly modest form in '99 (h'caps, rtd 74 at best): eff at 6/7f on
firm & hvy grnd: v well h'capped nowadays.
3027} **PIPIJI** 287 [7] 5-7-10 (37) (2oh) Angela Hartley(4) 25/1: 2502-0: Al bhd, fin 11th: reapp: twice *hd* 8
rnr-up in '99 (h'cap, rtd 36): eff at 7f/1m on firm & soft grnd: still a mdn.
1005 **SAMMAL** 18 [11] 4-8-8 (49) O Pears 20/1: -00500: Prom 4f, fdd into 12th. 8 0
3744} **ZIBAK** 252 [8] 6-7-13 (40) P Fessey 12/1: 3000-0: Towards rear, fin 13th, reapp. 3 0
872 **VENTURE CAPITALIST** 31 [3] 11-9-11 (66) A Nicholls(3) 12/1: 450-00: No ch from halfway: fin 14th. 1½ 4
4439} **DOMINELLE** 205 [5] 8-9-2 (57) J Carroll 9/1: 0600-0: Chsd ldrs 4f, fdd: fin last, poor low draw. 3 0
15 ran   Time 1m 12.3 (0.2)   (Robert E Cook)   M Brittain Warthill, Nth Yorks.

LINGFIELD FRIDAY MAY 12TH Lefthand, Sharp, Undulating Track

Official Going   TURF - GOOD/SOFT (Gd Pl), AW - STANDARD: Stalls: Turf - Stds Side, AW 1m - Outside, Rem - Ins.

1259   2.20 BROOKS HCAP 3YO+ 0-80 (D)   1m aw rnd Standard Inapplicable   [75]
£3957   £1217   £608   £304   3 yo rec 13lb

67 **TAPAGE** 177 [6] Andrew Reid 4-7-13 (46) M Henry 7/1: 0030-1: 4 b g Great Commotion - Irena (Bold Lad) 50a
Unruly gait, sn led, strongly prsd 2f out, rdn & styd on gamely, all out: 6 mth abs: rnr-up twice in '99 (rtd 69
& 48a, clmr, W R Muir): '98 wnr at Lingfield (med auct mdn, D Gillsepie, rtd 78a): eff at 7f/1m: acts on firm,
fast & equitrack: handles any trk, likes Lingfield: best without blnks: likes to force the pace & runs well fresh.
875 **EASTERN CHAMP** 31 [12] S P C Woods 4-9-10 (71)(t) J Reid 9/1: 020-02: 4 ch c Star de Naskra - *shd* 74a
Dance Troupe (Native Charger) Wide, mid-div, rdn & prog to chall ins last, just held: '99 Redcar wnr (5 rnr med
auct mdn, rtd 75 & 73a): eff arnd 1m/9f on firm, fast & both AWs: handles a sharp or gall trk: eff in a t-strap.
1139 **ITHADTOBEYOU** 8 [5] G L Moore 5-8-3 (50) J F Egan 8/1: 00-223: 5 b h Prince Sabo - Secret Valentine ½ 52a
(Wollow) Trkd ldrs, rdn to chall over 1f out, ev ch ins last, just held nr line: eff at 5/7f, now stays a sharp 1m.
*842 **ELLWAY PRINCE** 35 [2] M Wigham 5-9-4 (65) Dean McKeown 11/8 FAV: 250114: Lost place/rdn early, *hd* 66+
trkg ldrs 3f out, no room repeatedly ins last on heels of ldrs: most unlucky, deserves compensation.
852 **AIR MAIL** 32 [8] 3-9-3 (77) J Tate 8/1: 2105: Led 1f, rem cl-up, ch over 1f out, fdd cl-home: stays 1¾ 75a
a sharp 1m, drop back to 7f could suit: see 651 (mdn).
881 **OTIME** 30 [7] 3-9-0 (74)(vis) P McCabe 20/1: 602066: Dwelt, sn handy, ev ch over 2f out, eff/no extra 2 68a
over 1f out: not quite get home over this longer 1m trip, a return to 6/7f shld prove ideal: see 165 (7f).
1037 **MALCHIK** 14 [1] 4-8-9 (56) M Roberts 10/1: 333127: Mid-div, nvr pace to chall: see 922 (sell). 1½ 47a
630 **KAMARAZI** 69 [10] 3-9-4 (78) S Sanders 14/1: -15008: Rdn/bhd & wide, nvr factor: abs: see 630 (7f). 1 67a
104 **MARMADUKE** 170 [11] 4-9-9 (70) N Callan 33/1: 4000-9: Chsd ldrs 6f: 6 month abs: '98 juv scorer 1¼ 56a
at San Siro (stks, rtd 80): eff at 5/7f, tried 10f: handles fast & soft grnd.
4499} **RENDITA** 200 [3] 4-8-12 (59) A Clark 20/1: 2000-0: Mid-div, btn 3f out: 10th: reapp: '99 Lingfield 3½ 38a
wnr (fill h'cap, rtd 61a, subs rnr-up on turf, rtd 54, h'cap): eff at 7f/1m, tried 10f: acts on equitrack & gd grnd,
handles a stiff/undul or sharp trk: best without a visor: has run well fresh.
3016} **Test The Water** 287 [4] 6-8-13 (60) D Kinsella (7) 33/1:60   **Sabot** 177 [9] 7-8-9 (56) B O'Leary (7) 33/1:
12 ran   Time 1m 37.63 (1.43)   (A S Reid)   Andrew Reid Mill Hill, London NW7

1260   2.50 EBF R R RICHARDSON MDN 2YO (D)   5f   Good/Soft 73 -15 Slow
£3493   £1075   £537   £268

-- **TRIPLE BLUE** [4] R Hannon 2-9-0 R Hughes 13/2: 1: 2 ch c Bluebird - Persian Tapestry (Tap On 88
Wood) Dwelt, sn handy, led over 2f out & rdly asserted fnl 1f, pushed out: op 9/2: Mar foal, cost 15,000gns:
half brother to a 5f wnr, dam a half sister to prog/top sprinter Lake Coniston: sire a top class sprinter: eff
at 5f on gd/soft, 6f will suit: looks potentially useful.
-- **IDLE POWER** [13] P W Harris 2-9-0 N Pollard 3/1 FAV: 2: 2 b c Common Grounds - Idle Fancy 1¾ 81
(Mujtahid) Sn prom, rdn/hung left over 1f out, kept on tho' al held: well bckd op 2/1: Mar foal, cost
33,000gns, 1st foal: dam a 1m wnr, sire high-class 2yo/miler: will apprec 6f+ in time: acts on gd/soft grnd.
-- **GILDED DANCER** [9] W R Muir 2-9-0 Martin Dwyer 20/1: 3: 2 b c Bishop Of Cashel - La Piaf *shd* 81
(Fabulous Dancer) Rdn/towards rear early, styd on well for press from 2f out, nrst at fin: op 16/1: May foal,
cost 9,900 gns: dam a juv French wnr at 7.5f, later won at up to 11f: handles gd/soft, looks sure to relish 6f+.
-- **WARLINGHAM** [1] Miss Gay Kelleway 2-9-0 J Reid 9/1: 4: Went left start, sn handy & led after 1f, 1½ 77
hdd over 2f out & no extra ins last: op 7/1: Catrail colt, Apr foal, 30,000 gns 2yo: half brother to a 5f juv wnr,
dam a mdn: sire high-class 6/7f performer: acts on gd/soft grnd, ran well for a long way, can improve.
-- **BOLINGBROKE CASTLE** [11] 2-9-0 (t) J F Egan 13/2: 5: Bhd ldrs, eff halfway, onepace: op 5/1: ¾ 75
Feb foal, cost 25,000 gns: half brother to 4 wnrs, incl a 5/6f juv wnr: sire high-class French juv 1m performer.
1124 **OPERATION ENVY** 8 [8] 2-9-0 C Rutter 9/1: 46: Towards rear, eff 2f out, mod gains: see 1124. 1 73
-- **OSO NEET** [6] 2-9-0 P Dobbs 25/1: 7: Sn handy, fdd fnl 1f: Teenoso colt, Apr foal, cost 2400gns: 5 64
half brother to a 6f juv wnr: dam multiple 5/7f wnr: sire a top-class 12f performer: shld get further in time.
-- **TUSCAN FLYER** [7] 2-9-0 J Fortune 5/1: 8: In tch, outpcd halfway: Clantime colt, Feb foal, cost 1¾ 61
24,000 gns: full brother to multiple wnr sprinter Tuscan Dawn: dam 9/13f wnr: may stay further.
1059 **DRIPPING IN GOLD** 11 [2] 2-9-0 J Tate 33/1: 309: Led 1f, sn btn: for btr 836. 4 47
-- **JACK SPRATT** [3] 2-9-0 L Newman (5) 8/1: 0: Sn handy, wknd qckly over 1f out, 10th: op 5/1: 1 50
longer priced stablemate of wnr: So Factual colt, Apr foal, cost IR 20,000gns: dam a useful 6f juv wnr.
-- **Geetee Eightyfive** [12] 2-9-0 S Carson (5) 33/1:   **Roxy Laburnum** [10] 2-8-9 M Roberts 16/1:
12 ran   Time 1m 01.20 (4.4)   (J C Smith)   R Hannon East Everleigh, Wilts

---

1261   3.20 WEATHERBYS MDN DIV 1 3YO+ (D)   7f str   Good/Soft 73   -17 Slow
£3282   £1010   £505   £252   3 yo rec 12lb

1072 **BALI BATIK** 11 [7] G Wragg 3-8-12 T E Durcan 5/1: 0-431: 3 b g Baratea - Miss Garuda (Persian Bold)   82
Chsd ldrs, rdn/prog to lead over 1f out, styd on well ins last, rdn out: op 3/1: unplcd sole '99 start (rtd 51,
mdn): eff over a sharp 7f, 1m+ shld suit: acts on gd/soft grnd & a sharp/undul trk: op to further improvement.
840 **BREAK THE GLASS** 35 [14] E A L Dunlop 3-8-12 J Reid 4/1 FAV: 44-32: 3 b g Dynaformer - Greek   1¾   78
Wedding (Blushing Groom) Chsd ldrs, rdn 3f out, styd on well from over 1f out, no threat to wnr: see 840.
4072} **CLOTTED CREAM** 231 [10] P J Makin 3-8-7 S Sanders 7/1: 03-3: 3 gr f Eagle Eyed - Seattle Victory   1½   70
(Seattle Song) Prom, rdn/chsd wnr over 1f out, not pace of wnr ins last: op 6/1, reapp: plcd fnl '99 start (rtd 80,
med auct mdn): stays longer 7f trip: handles gd/soft & soft grnd, now qual for h'caps.
1060 **CRISS CROSS** 11 [17] R Hannon 3-8-12 R Hughes 9/2: 6-2224: Led till over 1f out, onepace ins   nk   74
last: acts on gd/soft & hvy: see 1060, 884.
1066 **KUWAIT ROSE** 11 [4] 4-9-10 J Tate 50/1: 626-45: Prom, fdd fnl 1f: acts on gd/soft, soft & fibresand.   ¾   73$
4306} **DELAMERE** 214 [15] 3-8-7 J Fortune 10/1: 0-6: Chsd ldrs, eff 2f out, held fnl 1f: clr rem: op 6/1:   nk   67
reapp: unplcd sole '99 start (mdn, rtd 68, A G Foster): dam a 9f wnr, 7f+ will suit this term: handles gd/soft.
1054 **UNDER THE SAND** 13 [13] Dean McKeown 25/1: 007: Rear, rdn/late gains fnl 2f, no threat to   5   62
ldrs: dropped in trip: a return to 1m+ & h'cap company looks in order.
-- **PRINISHA** [18] 3-8-7 D Harrison 16/1: 8: Mid-div, held 2f out: op 12/1, debut: half-sister to a 1m wnr.   2½   52
1239} **NOCCIOLA** 370 [3] 4-9-5 S Sanders 10/1: 0-9: Chsd ldrs 5f: op 5/1, reapp: mod form sole '99 start   ½   51
(rtd 44): h'cap company & probably further will suit in time: with Sir M Prescott.
962 **SLIEVE BLOOM** 24 [11] 3-8-12 A Clark 14/1: 60: Chsd ldrs 5f: 10th: op 20/1: btr 962.   ½   55
-- **EUCALYPTUS** [8] 3-8-12 J F Egan 7/1: 0: Al rear: 11th: op 5/1, debut: 70,000gns 2yo, mid-dist bred.   ¾   54
2517} **Sibertigo** 309 [12] 4-9-10 C Rutter 50/1:   1072 **Percussion** 11 [16] 3-8-12 S Whitworth 25/1:
4430} **Mind The Silver** 206 [2] 3-8-12 Martin Dwyer 25/1:   4528} **Silken Fox** 198 [6] 3-8-12 N Callan 50/1:
-- **Pembroke Star** [9] 3-8-12 O Urbina 25/1:   -- **Harvy** [5] 3-8-12 A Eddery (5) 50/1:
17 ran   Time 1m 26.72 (6.32)   (J L C Pearce)   G Wragg Newmarket, Suffolk

---

1262   3.50 DURTNELL CLASS STKS 3YO+ 0-90 (C)   7f140y str   Good/Soft 73   -27 Slow
£6695   £2060   £1030   £515   3 yo rec 13lb

979 **EL CURIOSO** 22 [4] P W Harris 3-8-8 J Reid 6/1: 014-01: 3 b c El Gran Senor - Curious (Rare Performer)   95
Dwelt & held up bhd ldrs, prog & rdn/led ins last, styd on well, rdn out: op 5/1: '99 scorer at Salisbury (mdn) &
Warwick (nurs, rtd 93): eff at 7.5f/1m, tried 10f: acts on firm & soft, any trk: useful.
851 **WELSH WIND** 32 [2] R Ingram 4-8-4 J F Egan 5/1: 000-22: 4 b g Tenby - Bavaria (Top Ville)   ½   90
Handy, rdn/led over 1f out, hdd ins last, kept on well: acts on fast & gd/soft grnd, sharp trk.
966 **PERSIANO** 23 [1] J R Fanshawe 5-9-4 D Harrison 3/1 CO FAV: 050-03: 5 ch g Efisio - Persiandale   1¼   87
(Persian Bold) Keen & led till 5f out, led again 3f out, rdn/hdd over 1f out & no extra nr fin: op 2/1: handles
gd/soft & hvy, acts on fast & gd grnd: see 966.
1110 **HORNBEAM** 9 [5] J R Jenkins 6-9-4 R Hughes 3/1 CO FAV: 5-0224: Dwelt, rear/in tch, eff 2f out,   hd   86
briefly no room over 1f out, onepace ins last: op 5/2: better in a fast run race: btr 1110 & 935.
954 **ARETINO** 24 [6] 3-8-5 N Pollard 16/1: 203-05: Keen/trkd ldrs, btn 2f out: op 10/1, longer priced   9   73
stablemate of wnr: '99 debut wnr at Pontefract (auct mdn, subs rnr-up in a stks contest at Kempton, rtd 99): eff
at 6/7f on firm & gd/soft grnd, stiff/undul or easy trk: has run well form.
*961 **TAP** 24 [3] S Whitworth 3/1 CO FAV: 2-16: Keen/dsptd lead till 3f out, btn 2f out: well bckd,   2½   73
tchd 4/1: disapp after latest, needs more restraint in this better company: see 961 (mdn, easily, soft).
6 ran   Time 1m 35.48 (7.68)   (The Curious Twelve)   P W Harris Aldbury, Herts

---

1263   4.20 WEATHERBYS MDN DIV 2 3YO+ (D)   7f str   Good/Soft 13   -41 Slow
£3282   £1010   £505   £252   3 yo rec 12lb

979 **AUTUMN RAIN** 22 [2] E A L Dunlop 3-8-12 J Reid 5/2 FAV: 55-201: 3 br c Dynaformer - Edda (Ogygian)   74
Chsd ldrs, rdn fnl 2f, styd on gamely for press ins last to reel in ldr on line, all out: hvly bckd tho' op 2/1: rtd
77 at best in '99 (mdn): eff at 7f, return to 1m will suit, below par over 10f latest: acts on firm & soft, sharp/
gall trk: fine eff to overcome tricky low draw & can rate more highly back at 1m.
1012 **INNKEEPER** 18 [14] Miss Gay Kelleway 3-8-12 N Callan 12/1: 400-52: 3 b g Night Shift - Riyoom   shd   73
(Vaguely Noble) Led, rdn fnl 2f, kept on well, hdd line: op 10/1: stays a sharp 7f, acts on firm & gd/soft grnd.
1072 **SIMULCASTING** 11 [12] L M Cumani 3-8-12 R Hughes 12/1: -503: 3 ch c College Chapel - Simply The   1¼   70
Best (Lidhame) Prom, rdn/chsd ldr briefly 1f out, kept on ins last, not pace of wnr: op 10/1: unplcd both
starts in '99 (incl one in Italy): eff over a sharp 7f, 1m could suit: handles gd/soft grnd, h'caps shld suit.
-- **GLENDALE RIDGE** [1] Jamie Poulton 5-9-10 O Urbina 33/1: 4: Sn handy, onepace fnl 2f: Flat   3   64
debut: 4 month jumps abs, mod bmpr form on sole start: eff at 7f, shld apprec 1m+: handles gd/soft grnd.
1018 **SARENA SPECIAL** 18 [7] 3-8-12 D O'Donohoe 7/1: 426-25: Chsd ldr, held fnl 1f: op 10/1: see 1018.   ½   63
3594} **BIRDSAND** 259 [11] 3-8-7 D Harrison 14/1: 0-6: Mid-div, eff 2f out, sn outpcd by ldrs: op 12/1,   shd   58
reapp: rtd 50 sole '99 start (mdn): considerably handled here, h'caps will suit in time.
4515} **MOVING EXPERIENCE** 199 [8] 3-8-7 S Whitworth 25/1: 04-7: Twds rear, stdy gains fnl 2f, no threat: ¾   57
reportedly struck in & suffered injury to her off fore: reapp: 4th on 2nd of 2 '99 starts (rtd 64, med auct
mdn, M J Featherston Godley): bred to apprec mid-dists: worth another chance.
972 **YERTLE** 23 [3] R Ffrench 7/1: -08: Rdn along towards rear early, late gains under hands &   hd   61+
heels riding, no threat: op 6/1: drop to 7f & poor low draw against him, leave this bhd over 1m+: see 972.
1012 **PEKANESE** 18 [16] 3-8-12 M Roberts 11/4: 629: Trkd ldrs, hung left/btn over 1f out: nicely bckd.   nk   60
-- **THAMAN** [6] 3-8-12 J Tate 12/1: 0: Bmpd start & sn bhd, late gains, nvr factor: 10th: op 8/1, debut.   1   58
-- **LADY JEANNIE** [5] 3-8-7 S Carson (5) 50/1: 0: Chsd ldrs halfway, btn 2f out: 11th: debut.   ½   52
4277} **HARRY TASTERS** 217 [10] 3-8-12 N Pollard 14/1: 50-0: Mid-div, btn 2f out: op 12/1: unplcd in '99 (rtd   1¾   54
71, mdn): half brother to a 6f wnr: now qual for h'caps, with D Elsworth.
-- **Trysor** [15] 4-9-10 G Faulkner (3) 20/1:   8 **Betchworth Sand** 186 [9] 4-9-10 C Rutter 33/1:
-- **Wickham** [4] 4-9-5 A Clark 33/1:   1181 **Father Ted** 5 [17] 3-8-12 S Sanders 20/1:
1080 **Magic Eagle** 11 [1] 3-8-12 J F Egan 16/1:
17 ran   Time 1m 28.27 (7.87)   (Khalifa Sultan)   E A L Dunlop Newmarket, Suffolk

LINGFIELD FRIDAY MAY 12TH Lefthand, Sharp, Undulating Track

1264 4.50 TOTE HCAP 3YO+ 0-85 (D) 5f Good/Soft 73 +15 Fast [83]
£7410 £2280 £1140 £570 3 yo rec 9 lb

1140 **SUPREME ANGEL 8** [7] M P Muggeridge 5-8-4 (59) J F Egan 20/1: 310401: 5 b m Beveled - Blue Angel (Lord Gayle) Chsd ldrs, rdn fnl 2f & styd on well to lead ins last, drvn out: tchd 25/1, blnks omitted: earlier won at Southwell (AW h'cap, rtd 65a): unplcd in '99 (rtd 63): '98 Kempton wnr (h'cap, rtd 88): eff at 5/6f on firm, soft & f/sand: eff with/without blnks: likes a sharp/easy trk: well h'capped on best form & could win again. 68
1162 **POLLY GOLIGHTLY 6** [10] M Blanshard 7-8-9 (64)(bl) C Rutter 9/1: 44-002: 7 ch m Weldnaas - Polly's Teahouse (Shack) Al handy, rdn & kept on ins last, not pace of wnr: op 8/1, quick reapp: has now come to hand & is on a fair mark, likes Chester: see 1005. 1¾ 67
1013 **IVORYS JOY 18** [9] K T Ivory 5-9-8 (77) C Carver (3) 7/1: 0-5603: 5 b m Tina's Pet - Jacqui Joy (Music Boy) Handy, rdn/led over 1f out, hdd ins last & no extra cl-home: op 6/1: see 64. ½ 78
*1092 **KHALIK 10** [1] Miss Gay Kelleway 6-9-1 (70)(t)(6ex) N Callan 13/2 JT FAV: 00-314: Rdn/towards rear, kept on fnl 2f, not reach ldrs: remains in gd heart but a stiffer 5f shld suit: see 1092. ½ 69
4538} **COASTAL BLUFF 197** [5] 8-9-10 (79) T G McLaughlin 8/1: 0000-5: Sn trkg ldrs, no extra fnl 1f: op 10/1, reapp: unplcd last term (rtd 96, subs tried blnks & t-strap, stks): lightly rcd since '97 wnr for T D Barron at Newmarket (stks) & York (Gr1, ddht, rtd 118): eff at 5/6f on firm & gd/soft grnd, any trk: gd weight carrier who can go well fresh: reportedly tubed since last term: formerly v smart sprinter, has slipped to a lenient mark. *shd* 78
1013 **FORGOTTEN TIMES 18** [11] 6-8-12 (67)(vis) C Catlin (7) 7/1: 60-206: Prom, ch 1f out, no extra fnl 1f. *shd* 65
1196 **DANCING MYSTERY 4** [12] 6-9-6 (75) S Carson (5) 14/1: 010-07: Sn handy, onepace over 1f out. 1¼ 70
1092 **MANGUS 10** [8] 6-8-6 (61) N Pollard 20/1: 4-6508: Led till over 1f out, fdd: tchd 25/1: see 146. ½ 54
547 **RAINBOW RAIN 83** [3] 6-8-12 (67) O Urbina 16/1: -30229: Rear, late gains, nvr threat: op 12/1, abs. ½ 58
3545} **TIGER IMP 262** [4] 4-9-3 (72) J Fortune 13/2 JT FAV: 223-0: Mid-div, eff halfway, btn/eased fnl 1f: 10th: op 5/1, reapp/h'cap bow: plcd all 3 '99 starts (rtd 77, mdn): eff over a sharp/undul 6/7f on fast & gd grnd. 3 56
506 **AURIGNY 90** [6] 5-10-0 (83) S Sanders 20/1: 55-000: Rear, eff 2f out, no impress: 11th: 3 mth abs. 1¾ 63
1013 **THAT MAN AGAIN 18** [15] 8-9-4 (73)(bl) G Faulkner (3) 14/1: 60-000: Al towards rear: 12th: tchd 16/1: '99 h'cap scorer at Sandown & Newmarket (rtd 82): '98 wnr at Folkestone (h'cap, rtd 76) & Lingfield (clmr, rtd 74a): stays 6f, best at 5f: handles hvy, suited by fast/firm, any trk: best in blnks, tried vis: likes to force the pace. ½ 51
763 **BRUTAL FANTASY 45** [13] 6-8-9 (64) M Roberts 12/1: 306000: Al rear: 13th: 6 wk abs: see 288. 1 40
4538} **Kilcullen Lad 197** [2] 6-9-1 (70) D R McCabe 12/1: 4015} **Price Of Passion 235** [14] 4-9-4 (73) R Hughes 12/1:
15 ran Time 59.68 (2.88) (Least Moved Partners) M P Muggeridge Eastbury, Berks

1265 5.20 ARENA FILL HCAP 3YO+ 0-70 (E) 1m2f aw Standard Inapplicable [70]
£2758 £788 £394 3 yo rec 15lb

657} **LINGUISTIC DANCER 417** [4] G L Moore 5-7-10 (38)(12oh)(2ow)L Newman (0) 16/1: 0/30-1: 5 ch m Aragon - Linguistic (Porto Bello) Cl-up, led 4f out, styd on well, drvn out: 14 month abs: prev with A G Newcombe, plcd in '99 (rtd 32a, appr mdn h'cap): stays 10f, acts on both AWs & a sharp trk: runs well fresh. 44a
752 **PAPERWEIGHT 45** [8] Miss K M George 4-9-4 (60) N Callan 7/2 JT FAV: 230-42: 4 b f In the Wings - Crystal Reay (Sovereign Dancer) Handy, rdn/chsd wnr over 1f out, kept on tho' al held: 6 wk abs: well clr rem: acts on firm, hvy & equitrack: see 752 (mdn). 1¼ 63a
-- **HEIRESS OF MEATH** [7] M J Weeden 5-7-10 (38)(18oh) C Adamson 33/1: 0000/3: 5 ch m Imperial Frontier - Rich Heiress (Last Tycoon) Led after 2f till 4f out, no impress on wnr over 1f out: AW bow/long abs: no form prev. 7 31$
1065 **AHOUOD 11** [2] K Mahdi 4-8-0 (41)(1ow) J Tate 9/2: 225604: Trkd ldrs, lost pl 3f out, mod late gains. 1½ 33a
1053 **TERM OF ENDEARMENT 13** [1] 3-7-13 (56)(3ow)(8oh) R Ffrench 15/2: 60-005: Led 2f, rem handy 7f. ½ 46a
1096 **BLESS 10** [10] 3-7-10 (53)(2oh) J Lowe 14/1: 06-006: Rear, prog/chsd ldrs half way, btn 3f out. ½ 42a
1035 **DOROTHEA SHARP 14** [9] 3-7-10 (53)(8oh) C Catlin (4) 10/1: 00-057: In tch 7f: btr 1035 (7f, mdn). 5 35a
544 **WILD NETTLE 83** [5] 6-7-10 (38)(15oh) M Henry 33/1: 60-008: Wide/bhd, no impress: abs, blnks omitted: rnr-up twice in '99 (rtd 41a, mdn): plcd in '98 (rtd 34a & 33): eff at 7f/10f, handles eqtrk, gd & soft. *shd* 20a
4037} **EN GRISAILLE 234** [6] 4-8-6 (48) J F Egan 7/2 JT FAV: 6510-9: Chsd ldrs 6f: tchd 4/1, reapp: '99 Yarmouth scorer (clmr, rtd 48 at best): '98 Folkestone wnr (fills sell, rtd 62, Sir M Prescott): eff at 10f: acts on firm & gd grnd: goes well fresh & enjoys claming grade. *hd* 29a
1033 **CANADIAN APPROVAL 16** [3] 4-10-0 (70) Dean McKeown 4/1: 104400: In tch till halfway: 10th: op 5/2. ½ 50a
10 ran Time 2m 07.2 (4.4) (Mrs J Moore) G L Moore Woodingdean, E Sussex

NOTTINGHAM FRIDAY MAY 12TH Lefthand, Galloping Track

Official Going GOOD/FIRM. (Rnd crse appeared to ride slower than straight). Stalls: 5f & 6f - Stands Side; Rnd - Inside.

1266 2.00 WELCOME MED AUCT MDN 3YO (E) 6f Firm Fast
£3106 £887 £443 2 Groups, probably no advantage

4081} **BANAFSAJYH 231** [12] A C Stewart 3-8-9 R Hills 5/1: 623-1: 3 b f Lion Cavern - Arylh (Lyphard) Nvr far away stands side, led 2f out, pushed clr, readily: op 7/2, reapp: plcd final 2 '99 starts (fill mdn, rtd 78): eff at 6f, bred to get further: acts on firm/fast grnd, gall trks: goes well fresh. 77
4431} **PARKER 206** [3] B Palling 3-9-0 D Sweeney 25/1: 304-2: 3 b c Magic Ring - Miss Loving (Northfields) Cl-up far side, kept on but no ch with wnr on stands side: clr of next on his side, reapp: plcd on '99 debut (mdn auct, rtd 80): eff at 6/7f, related wng sprinters: acts on firm & soft grnd, sharp or gall trk: goes well fresh. 4 73
1021 **NEEDWOOD TRICKSTER 18** [11] B C Morgan 3-9-0 P Robinson 33/1: -033: 3 gr g Fayruz - Istaraka (Darshaan) Unruly before start, trkd ldrs stands side, unable to qckn appr final 1f: probably got this lngr 6f trip with t-strap omitted: handles firm & hvy grnd: see 1021. 1½ 69
909 **MI AMIGO 28** [19] L M Cumani 3-9-0 J P Spencer 2/1 FAV: 0-24: Front tank stands side till outpcd appr final 1f: well bckd from 10/3: rtd higher on soft grnd in 909. 1½ 65
1175 **MALARKEY 5** [10] 3-9-0 J Weaver 16/1: 05: Dwelt, went stands side, late hdwy, nvr a threat: qk reapp. 1¼ 61
888 **DOUBLE GUN 30** [8] 3-9-0 Dane O'Neill 10/1: 043-06: Chsd ldrs far side till 2f out: op 7/1: plcd final '99 start (auct mdn, rtd 76): may apprec a drop back to 5f: handles firm & gd grnd: with R Hannon. 1¼ 57
897 **QUEENSMEAD 29** [16] 3-8-9 A Daly 33/1: 625-07: Led stands side till ent final 2f, no extra: dual '99 rnr-up (mdn auct, rtd 73, R Hannon): eff at 5f on fast & gd grnd, without blnks: now with D Burchell. ½ 51
1105 **BILLY BATHWICK 9** [9] 3-9-0 (bl) Pat Eddery 16/1: -55528: Handy far side till 2f out: btr 1105 (g/s). *hd* 56

NOTTINGHAM   FRIDAY MAY 12TH   Lefthand, Galloping Track

4599} **PRETRAIL 190** [2] 3-9-0 A McCarthy (3) 10/1: 02-9: Wtdrs far side till lost place ent fnl 2f: op 7/1, nk 55
reapp, stablemate wnr: rnr-up final of 2 '99 starts (mdn, rtd 76): eff at 6f, bred to stay further: acts on gd/sft.
3231} **JOCKO GLASSES 277** [13] 3-9-0 R Mullen 50/1: 5-0: Dwelt, nvr got in it: 10th, reapp, no form. nk 54
1135 **DIVA 8** [6] 3-8-9 G Duffield 20/1: 60: Al bhd far side: 11th, market drifter, see 1135. shd 49
883 **SCAFELL 30** [1] 3-9-0 (VIS) R Fitzpatrick (3) 20/1: 50-020: Led far side till appr fnl 1f, wknd: 12th. 1 51
1098 **DANCEMMA 10** [20] 3-8-9 W Ryan 16/1: 02-000: Chsd ldrs stands side till 2f out: 13th. 1 43
956 **ALMASHROUK 24** [18] 3-9-0 F Norton 11/2: 0-6640: Al towards rear stands side: 14th, capable of more. 1 45
1021 Carew Castle 18 [7] 3-9-0 T Quinn 16/1:   --   **Gypsy Song** [4] 3-9-0 R Winston 25/1:
4536} Barton Miss 197 [14] 3-8-9 Mr I Mongan (4) 50/1:   --   **Mr Chrisbi** [5] 3-9-0 S Finnamore (5) 50/1:
--   Legal Tender [17] 3-9-0 V Slattery 50/1:   2976} **Jenin 290** [15] 3-8-9 R Cochrane 50/1:
20 ran   Time 1m 10.9 (0.1)   (Hamdan Al Maktoum)   A C Stewart Newmarket

---

1267   2.30 EBF NOV MED AUCT FILLIES STKS 2YO (F)   5f   Firm Fair
£2999   £657   £328

*1046 **ELSIE PLUNKETT 14** [7] R Hannon 2-9-0 Dane O'Neill 6/4 FAV: -511: 2 b f Mind Games - Snow Eagle 92
(Polar Falcon) Early ldr, again appr final 1f, qcknd clr: well bckd: last time won at Sandown (fill auct mdn):
6,500 gns Feb first foal, sire a sprinter: eff at 5f on firm & hvy grnd, gall trks: speedy, improving filly.
+898 **RED MILLENNIUM 29** [5] A Berry 2-8-12 F Norton 11/4: 12: 2 b f Tagula - Lovely Me (Vision) 6 75
Prom, effort appr final 1f, easily outpcd by wnr: caught a decent sort: handles firm grnd, wnr on gd/soft in 898.
1083 **NINE TO FIVE 10** [3] R Brotherton 2-9-2 J Mackay (7) 25/1: 1133: 2 b f Imp Society - Queen And Country 1¾ 74
(Town And Country) Led after 1f till before dist, no extra: not disgraced on this much qckr grnd: see 836.
1059 **CHURCH MICE 11** [1] M L W Bell 2-8-8 M Fenton 3/1: 24: Went left, outpcd thro'out: highly tried. 2 60
--   **SPICE ISLAND** [6] 2-8-8 G Duffield 12/1: 5: Hung left, nvr in it: op 11/2, debut: 6,000 gns Reprimand 3½ 52
Feb foal, dam a sprint wnr, sire a miler: highly tried: with J Glover.
--   **YUKA SAN** [4] 2-8-8 T Quinn 20/1: 6: Slowly away, chsd ldrs till halfway: debut, op 14/1: IR 6,000gns 1¾ 47
General Monash Mar 1st foal, dam 10f wnr, sire a sprinter: should do better in time, with C Cox.
6 ran   Time 59.0 (0.5)   (C J M Partnership)   R Hannon East Everleigh, Wilts.

1268   3.0 TRENT FILL MDN DIV 1 3YO (D)   1m54y rnd   Good/Firm Slow
£3488   £1078   £536   £268

4506} **COCO 200** [6] Sir Michael Stoute 3-8-11 K Fallon 10/1: 0-1: 3 ch f Storm Bird - Fondromance (Fappiano) 90
Nvr far away, went on halfway, sn hard prsd, al holding rnr-up despite edging right, pshd out: op 7/1: 7th on hvy
grnd sole '99 start (fill mdn, rtd 69): eff at 1m, 10f should suit: clearly suited by this fast grnd: runs well fresh.
915 **POETIC 28** [4] H R A Cecil 3-8-11 T Quinn 4/6 FAV: 32: 3 b f Nureyev - Draw Straws (Key To The Mint) hd 88
Hmpd start, cl-up, ev ch final 3f, carried right, hard rdn, al being held: well bckd: pulled clr of next & lost
nothing in defeat: acts on fast & soft grnd, should find similar soon.
4536} **CULTURED PEARL 197** [7] P F I Cole 3-8-11 Pat Eddery 8/1: 5-3: 3 ch f Lammtarra - Culture Vulture 6 76
(Timeless Moment) Well plcd, effort & swtchd ent final 2f, same pace: reapp: 5th of 13 sole '99 starts
(fill mdn, rtd 77): bred to apprec 10f+ & may do better once h'capped.
4555} **BREAKWATER 25** [2] L M Cumani 3-8-11 J P Spencer 7/2: 40-4: In tch, shkn up 3f out, no impress on 1 74+
ldrs: eye-catching h'cap qualifying run on reapp: 4th bhd Lahan on '99 debut (rtd 90 at best): eff at 7f,
1m should suit: handles fast grnd & is one to keep a close eye on in a decent h'cap later on.
1010 **SUMMER SONG 18** [10] 3-8-11 G Carter 25/1: 1-45: Dwelt, rear, moderate late hdwy: qual for h'caps. 1½ 71
936 **ORLANDO SUNRISE 25** [3] 3-8-11 G Hind 50/1: -06: Prom, fdd final 2f: needs a drop in grade. ¾ 70$
--   **KOINCIDENTAL** [1] 3-8-11 R Cochrane 50/1: 7: Nvr a factor: debut: stoutly bred Mtoto filly. 1 68$
--   **LADY TWO K** [12] 3-8-11 M Fenton 33/1: 8: Ran green, al rear: Grand Lodge filly, dam stoutly bred. 4 60
--   **BERZOUD** [8] 3-8-11 J Weaver 25/1: 9: Dwelt, al rear: Ezzoud newcomer with J Noseda. 1 58
4473} **WITH RESPECT 203** [11] 3-8-11 R Winston 50/1: 00-0: Keen, led till after halfway, lost place: no form. ¼ 57
1155 **SALIENT POINT 7** [9] 3-8-11 G Duffield 14/1: -500: Prom till 3f out: qck reapp, now qual for h'caps. nk 56
11 ran   Time 1m 45.8 (6.4)   (Philip Newton)   Sir Michael Stoute Newmarket

---

1269   3.30 TRENT FILL MDN DIV 2 3YO (D)   1m54y rnd   Good/Firm Slow
£3488   £1073   £536   £268

4555} **PLEASURE CENTER 195** [7] J H M Gosden 3-8-11 R Hills 11/2: 4-1: 3 ch f Diesis - Creaking Board 92
(Night Shift) Cmftbly made ev yd, easing down: tchd 13/2, slow time, reapp: promising 4th in a decent
Newmarket fill mdn sole '99 start (rtd 91): half-sister to a smart 9/11f wnr: eff at 7f/1m, should get 10f:
acts on fast & soft grnd, gall trks: runs well fresh, forcing the pace: potentially useful.
4556} **NEW ASSEMBLY 195** [6] Sir Michael Stoute 3-8-11 K Fallon 8/1: 00-2: 3 b f Machiavellian - Abbey Strand 2 85
(Shadeed) Rear, effort 3f out, kept on for 2nd but no ch wnr: op 6/1 on reapp: unplcd in 2 '99 mdns (rtd 85):
eff at 1m but is bred to apprec 10f+: goes on fast grnd: shwn enough to find similar tho' future prob lies in h'caps.
--   **SECOND AFFAIR** [8] C F Wall 3-8-11 R Mullen 25/1: 3: 3 b f Pursuit Of Love - Startino (Bustino) nk 84
Handy, kept on final 2f but not pace to chall: belated debut, clr rem: half-sister to 3 wnrs, dam useful up to
1m6f: eff at 1m, further is going to suit: handles fast grnd, should improve & find similar.
--   **SPORTING LADDER** [2] P F I Cole 3-8-11 T Quinn 11/2: 4: Prom, rdn 2f out, onepace: op 7/1 on 3 78
debut: Danzig sister to useful 7f h'capper Sporting Lad: prob handles fast grnd.
971 **MISS DORDOGNE 23** [11] 3-8-11 Pat Eddery 4/5 FAV: -25: Held up, wide prog appr final 3f, sn rdn, ½ 77
no extra: much to land the odds: unsuited by step up to 1m on fast grnd?: much btr 971 (7f, gd/soft).
4556} **POPPADAM 195** [12] 3-8-11 R Cochrane 25/1: 0-6: Well plcd till outpcd final 2f: reapp: unplcd sole 1¾ 73
'99 start for L Cumani (fill mdn, rtd 80): half-sister to an Irish 1000 Guineas wnr: one more run for h'cap mark.
--   **SHATTERED SILENCE** [3] 3-8-11 Dane O'Neill 50/1: 7: Nvr a factor: op 5/1: Cozzene newcomer. 3 67
4605} **BARDEN LADY 189** [5] 3-8-11 G Hind 66/1: 00-8: Chsd ldrs till 2f out: reapp, no form, stoutly bred. 1½ 64
992 **WELCOME ABOARD 20** [1] 3-8-11 R Winston 33/1: -39: Al bhd, not much room 5f out: see 992. 2½ 59
1010 **SUCH FLAIR 18** [10] 3-8-11 J Weaver 16/1: 0-30: Held up, brief effort 3f out: 10th: btr 1010 (hvy grnd). hd 59
971 Peaches 23 [4] 3-8-11 D Sweeney 50/1:   2421} Us And Them 314 [9] 3-8-11 (BL) R Fitzpatrick (3) 50/1:
12 ran   Time 1m 43.8 (4.4)   (George Strawbridge)   J H M Gosden Manton, Wilts.

421

1270	4.0 SPONSORSHIP HCAP 3YO 0-70 (E)	1m6f	Good/Firm	Slow	[77]
	£2854 £815 £407				

752 **BARCELONA** 45 [13] J Noseda 3-9-5 (68) J Weaver 12/1: 003-31: 3 b c Barathea - Pipitina (Bustino) 76
Mid-div, smooth prog 3f out, kept on well to get up inside last, rdn out: 6 wk abs, 1st win, h'cap bow: plcd final
'99 start (mdn, rtd 80): clearly apprec this step up to 14f: acts on fast & gd/soft grnd, sharp or gall trks.
1002 **SHRIVAR** 18 [3] M R Channon 3-8-13 (62) T Quinn 25/1: 5-0552: 3 b g Sri Pekan - Kriva (Reference   ½ 69
Point) In tch, prog to lead ent final 2f, worn down towards fin: clr rem, clearly apprec this big step up in
trip: eff at 14f, handles fast & gd/soft grnd: shld find similar from this lowly mark, see 894.
1106 **PTAH** 9 [11] J L Eyre 3-8-1 (50) F Norton 9/1: 0-0043: 3 b g Petardia - Davenport Goddess (Classic   3½ 53
Secret) Rear, styd on final 3f, nvr nrr: imprvd since stepped up in trip, try 2m?: handles fast & gd/soft.
1054 **LOVE BITTEN** 13 [2] M Johnston 3-9-5 (68) R Hills 20/1: 0004: Prom, effort appr final 2f, onepace: 1 70
h'cap bow, lngr trip, prob stays 14f on fast grnd.
1071 **SUNDAY RAIN** 11 [1] 3-9-7 (70) K Fallon 9/2: -42245: Led, shied from rails after 6f, hdd 3f out,   2½ 69
no extra: bckd from 6/1: drop back to 12f may suit: see 782, 701.
1106 **DAME FONTEYN** 9 [10] 3-8-3 (52) J Mackay 7/1: 2-0P226: Rear, late prog, nvr a threat: see 9/2.   hd 51
1071 **MERRYVALE MAN** 11 [12] 3-9-5 (68) R Winston 7/4 FAV: 121027: Front rank, led going well 3f out, sn   3½ 63
rdn, hdd before dist & wknd: well bckd: gets a gall 14.5f, may apprec drop back to 12f: see 1071, 782.
936 **DURLSTON BAY** 25 [4] 3-9-3 (66) A Daly 25/1: 0-308: Al same place: h'cap bow, lngr trip, see 832.   ½ 60
939 **NICIARA** 25 [14] 3-7-10 (45)(7oh) K Dalgleish (7) 33/1: 050049: Dwelt, nvr troubled ldrs: stiffish task.   ¾ 38
629 **FINERY** 69 [7] 3-9-2 (65) D McGaffin (7) 64240: Well plcd, chall 3f out, sn wknd: 10th,   3 54
10 wk abs, turf/h'cap bow: unsuited by step up to 14f?: see 545 (10f, AW).
1096 **FLIQUET BAY** 10 [6] 3-8-11 (60)(bl) T Ashley 8/1: 00-420: Cl-up till 3f out: 11th, op 6/1 not bred for 14f. 11 39
1064 **Brokenborough** 11 [5] 3-8-9 (58) D Sweeney 25/1:   937 **Established** 25 [9] 3-7-10 (45)(4oh) P M Quinn (5) 16/1:
658 **Sticiboots** 62 [8] 3-8-3 (52) G Carter 25/1:
14 ran   Time 3 06.0 (7.7)   (K Y Lim)   J Noseda Newmarket

1271	4.30 MEMBERS CLASS STKS 3YO+ 0-80 (D)	1m2f	Good/Firm	Fair	
	£3785 £1164 £582 £291	3 yo rec 15lb			

3956} **LADY ANGHARAD** 238 [3] J R Fanshawe 4-9-5 R Cochrane 10/3: 0200-1: 4 b f Tenby - Lavezzola (Salmon   83
Leap) Cl-up, led 2½f out, readily: wng reapp, fair time: '99 rnr-up for A Jarvis (h'cap, rtd 82): useful juv,
won at Epsom (Listed) & Salisbury (stks, rtd 100, tried Grp company): suited by 10f nowadays: acts on fast
& gd grnd, any trk: ran well once in a visor, prob best without: goes well fresh & is well h'capped.
1031 **CALLDAT SEVENTEEN** 16 [1] P W D'Arcy 4-9-8 Pat Eddery 11/2: 040-02: 4 b g Komaite - Westminster   1½ 82
Waltz (Dance In Time) Rear, prog ent fnl 2f, kept on but al being held by wnr: op 9/2: '99 Lingfield wnr (auct
mdn, rtd 75a) & Epsom (2, stks & h'cap, rtd 79): eff at 1m/10f on fast, gd/soft & equitrack, any trk, loves Epsom.
713 **FULL AHEAD** 49 [7] M H Tompkins 3-8-7 G Duffield 11/4: 45-33: 3 b c Slip Anchor - Foulard   3 77
(Sadler's Wells) Prom, hmpd & lost grnd appr fnl 2f, late hdwy: 7 wk abs: step up to 12f required, see 713.
3743} **COMMON CAUSE** 252 [6] C F Wall 4-9-5 R Mullen 7/1: 2310-4: Held up, prog to chall appr fnl 2f, no   nk 73
extra dist: op 5/1, reapp, clr rem: '99 wnr at Lingfield & Leicester (fill h'caps, rtd 80): eff at 12f on firm & gd.
1113 **GEMINI GUEST** 9 [2] 4-9-8 P Robinson 16/1: 300-05: Handy till fdd appr final 1f: '99 Thirsk wnr   5 68
(mdn, rtd 92 at best): unrcd juv: eff at 7f, not bred to apprec this lngr 10f trip: acts on fast grnd, gall trk.
705 **PRODIGAL SON** 50 [4] 5-9-8 K Fallon 5/2 FAV: 620-36: Sn shkn up, imprvd to chall appr final   4 62
2f, sn drifted left & btn, eased: tchd 7/2, 7 wk abs, stiffish task at the weights, see 119.
317 **COLONEL NORTH** 121 [5] 4-9-8 J Weaver 25/1: 640-07: Led till 2½f out, wknd: stiffish task, see 90.   4 56
7 ran   Time 2m 06.2 (3.9)   (Ian M Deane)   J R Fanshawe Newmarket

1272	5.05 CONF CENTRE HCAP 3YO+ 0-60 (F)	1m2f	Good/Firm	Slow	[59]
	£2625 £750 £375	3 yo rec 15lb			

1129 **JUNIKAY** 8 [15] R Ingram 6-9-6 (51) K Fallon 15/8 FAV: 44-021: 6 b g Treasure Kay - Junijo (Junius)   60
Trkd ldrs, qcknd to lead dist, v cmftbly: '99 wnr here at Nottingham (this h'cap, off 1lbs higher, rtd 57): '98
Brighton wnr (h'cap, rtd 57): eff at 1m/10f on firm, gd/soft grnd: likes Nottingham/coming with a late charge.
*871 **SMARTER CHARTER** 31 [1] Mrs L Stubbs 7-9-9 (54) Kristin Stubbs (7) 12/1: 463-12: 7 br g Master   2½ 57
Willie - Irene's Charter (Persian Bold) Waited with, stdy prog after 3f out to lead before 2f out, hdd dist
& outpcd by ready wnr: op 10/1, clr rem: remains in form form: see 871.
1100 **BITTER SWEET** 10 [11] J L Spearing 4-9-9 (54) G Hind 20/1: 0-0403: 4 gr f Deploy - Julie Flyte   3½ 52
(Drone) Chsd ldrs, effort 2f out, kept on well towards fin: clearly gets 10f, worth trying at 12f: see 1100.
1100 **TIME LOSS** 10 [13] J L Eyre 5-9-7 (52) Pat Eddery 13/2: 00-054: Handy, chall 3f out, sn onepace.   2½ 46
859 **CASSANDRA** 32 [4] 4-9-7 (52) G Carter 10/1: 500-25: Led till 2½f out, no extra before dist: op 8/1.   1¼ 44
-- **KELTECH STAR** [7] 4-9-9 (54) W Ryan 33/1: 0053-6: Cl-up till fdd appr fnl 1f: reapp/Brit bow: ex-Irish,   1 44
3rd of 6 in a '99 mdn (12f, soft, blnkd): half-sister to v smart miler Waajib & may do better herself back at 1m.
4270} **RIGHTY HO** 218 [8] 6-9-8 (53) K Hodgson 25/1: 6603-7: Chsd ldrs, outpcd final 2f: reapp: plcd fnl   1 42
'99 start (clmr, rtd 66$, only rtd 56 in h'cap company, C Booth): missed '98, '97 Salisbury & Epsom wnr for
P Walwyn (amat h'caps, rtd 70): eff at 1m/10f, prob stays 12f: acts on fast & soft, any trk, with/without visor.
4551} **CLASSIC EAGLE** 196 [18] 7-9-11 (56) M Fenton 50/1: /004-8: Mid-div thro'out: reapp: lightly rcd,   1 43
98/99 wnr over hdles at Huntingdon (h'cap, 2m, firm & soft, rtd 125h, Mrs D Haine): last won on the level in
'96 at Chepstow (mdn, rtd 90, R Harris): prob stays 12f on soft grnd: with Pat Mitchell.
4443} **RARE TALENT** 205 [5] 6-9-11 (56) T Quinn 8/1: 2000-9: Trkd ldrs till wknd qckly appr final 2f: reapp: 2½ 39
'99 wnr at Beverley (ladies h'cap) & Windsor (amat h'cap, rtd 61): '98 wnr at Doncaster (amat h'cap) & Chester
(h'cap, rtd 65): tried hdles: eff at 10f/11/15.5f: loves firm grnd, handles gd/soft, any trk: best without a visor.
793 **PRINCE DARKHAN** 43 [16] 4-10-0 (59) J Weaver 20/1: 450-00: In tch till 3f out: 10th, no form.   ¾ 41
3972} **CHEROKEE FLIGHT** 237 [3] 6-9-9 (54) Dane O'Neill 14/1: 0030-0: Bhd fnl 4f: 11th, reapp, new stable.   1¼ 34
1050 **Malakal** 13 [12] 4-9-10 (55) J P Spencer 16/1:   520 **Flush** 87 [17] 5-9-10 (55) I Mongan (5) 20/1:
568 **The Bargate Fox** 80 [14] 4-9-10 (55) G Duffield 16/1:   890 **Ferny Factors** 30 [6] 4-9-7 (52) R Cochrane 33/1:
893 **Tyra** 29 [2] 4-9-13 (58) N Esler (7) 40/1:   1058 **Charter Flight** 13 [10] 4-9-5 (50) R Winston 20/1:
890 **City Pursuit** 30 [9] 4-9-11 (56) P Robinson 50/1:
18 ran   Time 2m 07.1 (4.8)   (Ellangowan Racing Partners)   R Ingram Epsom, Surrey.

NOTTINGHAM   FRIDAY MAY 12TH   Lefthand, Galloping Track

1273   5.35 NEXT MEETING APPR HCAP 3YO+ 0-70 (G)   6f   Firm   Slow   [70]
£2198   £628   £314   3 yo rec 10lb

1040   **BERKELEY HALL** 14 [10]   B Palling 3-8-4 (56)(BL) D McGaffin (1) 20/1: 03-001: 3 b f Saddlers' Hall -   61
Serious Affair (Valiyar) Nvr far away, went on bef fnl 1f despite hanging right, ran on well: woken up by blnks:
3rd fnl '99 start (auct mdn, rtd 63\$): stoutly bred but suited by drop back to 6f: acts on firm & gd grnd, gall trks.
1066   **MYTTONS MISTAKE** 11 [17]   R J Baker 7-8-7 (49) G Sparkes (5) 16/1: 000-02: 7 b g Rambo Dancer -   1   50
Hi-Hunsley (Swing Easy) Prom, chall dist, held towards fin: back to form, well h'capped: see 1066.
834   **BINTANG TIMOR** 36 [12]   W J Musson 6-10-0 (70) P Shea (5) 11/2: 013-03: 6 ch g Mt Livermore - Frisky   nk   70
Kitten (Isopach) Dwelt, gd prog 2f out & ev ch till no extra well ins last: op 4/1, ran to best back in trip.
1196   **BLUE KITE** 4 [6]   N P Littmoden 5-9-3 (59) C Cogan 11/4 FAV: 510024: Struggled to go pace till ran on   1½   55
appr final 1f, ch below dist, sn onepace: bckd from 4/1, qck reapp, btr 1196, see 645.
781   **FOUND AT LAST** 44 [9]   4-9-0 (56) A Beech 13/2: -30035: Hmpd start, rear, imprvd & bmpd appr fnl   1   49
1f, unable to qckn: op 10/1, 6 wk abs, see 781, 273.
888   **SANTIBURI GIRL** 30 [15]   3-9-2 (68) R Studholme 14/1: 400-06: Prom, not clr run appr fnl 1f, unable   nk   60
to chall: '99 Salisbury wnr (nov auct, rtd 87, only 81 in nurseries): eff at 7f, tried 1m on fast & gd, prob soft.
1235   **DAHLIDYA** 1 [20]   5-7-13 (41) K Dalgleish (5) 11/1: 313307: Off the pace till kept on final 1½f,   ¾   31
nvr on terms: ran yesterday, turf return & is a tough mare: see 697.
1233   **HAUNT THE ZOO** 1 [19]   5-8-3 (45) Iona Wands 33/1: 300008: Al same pl: ran yesterday, see 148.   hd   35
1068   **SEVEN** 11 [8]   5-9-1 (57)(bl) I Mongan (7) 12/1: 540049: Went right & sn niggled, well plcd, drvn to   1½   43
lead briefly appr final 1f, fdd: jockey given 4 day whip ban: see 1068, 414.
--   **ISIT IZZY** [18]   8-7-10 (38) Joanna Badger (5) 50/1: 0360/0: Nvr dngrs: 10th, 2 yr abs since plcd   hd   24
for B McMahon in '98 (h'cap, rtd 43): disq rnr-up back in '96 (mdn, rtd 70): eff arnd 1m on fast & gd grnd.
499   **AJNAD** 91 [16]   6-9-1 (57) P Mundy (7) 25/1: 000050: Chsd ldrs till 2f out: 11th, 3 mth abs, turf return.   1   40
4581}   **ALFAHAAL** 193 [4]   7-8-4 (46) J Mackay (5) 12/1: 0040-0: Prom, chall 2f out, sn btn: 15th on   0
reapp, op 8/1: '99 Yarmouth wnr (h'cap, rtd 56): back in '97 won at Doncaster (h'cap) & Leicester (stks,
rtd 63, R J Houghton): eff at 7f/1m on fast, soft grnd & equitrack: with C Dwyer.
1005   **SEVEN SPRINGS** 18 [7]   4-8-3 (45) P M Quinn 8/1: -00620: Keen, trkd ldrs till wknd qckly 2f out: 16th.   0
1092   **PURPLE FLING** 10 [1]   9-9-0 (56) R Smith (3) 12/1: 316-00: Nvr in it: 17th, op 10/1, see 82.   0
838   **DELTA SOLEIL** 35 [5]   8-9-10 (66) R Brisland 12/1: 000-00: Led till 1½f out, sn lost place: last: '99   0
Kempton wnr (h'cap, rtd 78): '98 wnr at Salisbury & Newbury (h'cap, stks rnr-up, rtd 86): eff at 1m, unable
by 6f: acts on firm & gd/soft grnd, any trk: best when allowed to dominate: well h'capped, with V Soane.
1005   **Miss Bananas** 18 [14] 5-8-6 (48) D Meah (5) 16/1:   896   **Uncle Oberon** 29 [2] 4-8-2 (44)(VIS) P Clarke (2) 33/1:
1132   **Gunner Sam** 8 [3] 4-8-12 (54) G Baker (5) 33/1:
18 ran   Time 1m 12.1 (1.3)   (D Brennan)   B Palling Cowbridge, Vale Of Glamorgan.

BEVERLEY   SATURDAY MAY 13TH   Righthand, Oval Track With Stiff, Uphill Finish

Official Going   GOOD/FIRM. Stalls: Inside.

1274   2.20 STEVE DONOHUE SELLER 3YO (F)   1m2f   Firm 03   -27 Slow
£2450   £700   £350

869   **BONDI BAY** 32 [18]   J J O'Neill 3-8-7 J F Egan 13/2: 35-201: 3 b f Catrial - Sodium's Niece (Northfields)   53
Handy, hdwy to lead 2 out, drew clr for press fnl 1f: no bid: rtd 62 & 45a in '99: apprec this step up to
10f & acts on firm, gd, fibresand & stiff trk: has tried a t-strap & visor: likes sellers.
1071   **ROCK ON ROBIN** 12 [14]   C W Fairhurst 3-8-12 (vis) J Fanning 33/1: 000-02: 3 br g Rock City -   3½   51
Volcalmeh (Lidhame) In tch, hdwy over 2f out to chase wnr fnl 1f, no impress: stays 10f on firm & a stiff trk.
799   **UNICORN STAR** 44 [19]   J S Wainwright 3-8-12 R Winston 11/2: 040-43: 3 b g Persian Bold - Highland   1½   49
Warning (Warning) In tch, hdwy & not clr run appr fnl 1f, kept on ins last: 6 wk abs & enjoyed drop to selling
grade: eff at 10f, further could suit: acts on firm: shld find a selling h'cap.
1142   **HORTON DANCER** 9 [10]   M Brittain 3-8-12 (vis) D Mernagh (3) 33/1: 4-6004: Led over 3f out till 2f out.   nk   48
457   **WEST END DANCER** 98 [17]   3-8-7 O Urbina 40/1: 50-005: Bhd, eff & short of room 2f out, styd   2½   39
on late: 3 month abs with blnks discarded: best run to date & will apprec sell h'caps.
1148   **THREEFORTYCASH** 8 [11]   P Fessey 50/1: -45006: In tch, eff to chall 2f out, sn no extra.   nk   43
858   **INDIANA SPRINGS** 33 [16]   3-8-12 (vis) J Weaver 20/1: 005407: Nvr a factor: modest.   hd   42
976   **PIX ME UP** 24 [4]   3-8-7 F Lynch 6/1: 0-0008: In tch, eff 2f out, sn btn: see 976.   2   34
*806   **FRENCH MASTER** 43 [15]   3-8-12 (vis) S Finnamore (5) 3/1 FAV: -33319: Slow away, bhd, eff & short   hd   38
of room over 2f out, no impress: 6 wk abs, btr 806 (gd).
1040   **PAPAGENA** 15 [2]   3-8-7 (bl) F Norton 12/1: 243000: Chsd ldrs till wknd 2f out: 10th: see 1040 (aw).   1¾   30
1195   **THE REPUBLICAN** 6 [13]   3-8-12 (VIS) T Williams 50/1: 00-000: In tch, wknd over 2f out: 11th, visor.   5   28\$
536   **DR DUKE** 85 [7]   3-8-12 (bl) Dean McKeown 20/1: 406400: Led till over 3f out: 12th, with M Wigham.   shd   27
978   **Mountrath Rock** 24 [3] 3-8-7 (VIS) J Carroll 14/1:   1141   **Standiford Girl** 9 [12] 3-8-7 T G McLaughlin 12/1:
939   **The Final Word** 26 [6] 3-8-7 N Callan 33/1:   429   **Cinema Point** 103 [1] 3-8-12 S Sanders 16/1:
1022   **Needwood Trident** 19 [8] 3-8-7 G Hind 16/1:   3120}   **Highcal** 283 [5] 3-8-12 J Lowe 20/1:
286   **Queen For A Day** 126 [9] 3-8-7 A Beech 25/1:
19 ran   Time 2m 05.3 (3)   (A J Oliver)   J J O'Neill Skelton, Cumbria.

1275   2.55 LADY AMAT RDRS HCAP 3YO+ 0-70 (E)   7f100y rnd   Firm 03   -05 Slow   [49]
£3146   £968   £484   £242   3 yo rec 12lb

337   **CANTINA** 119 [10]   A Bailey 6-11-3 (66) Miss Bridget Gatehouse (5) 15/2: 020-01: 6 b m Tina's Pet -   72
Real Claire (Dreams To Reality) Made all, kept on fnl 1f, pushed out: 4 month abs: '99 wnr at Redcar (amat
stks, rtd 73 & 72a): '98 Chester wnr (2 yo, h'caps, disqual once, rtd 80): loves to force the pace over 7f/7.5f on
firm, gd/soft & on any trk: runs well fresh & took advantage of a handy mark today.
1150   **HUGWITY** 8 [7]   G C Bravery 8-11-7 (70) Mrs S Bosley 6/1: 003362: 8 ch g Cadeaux Genereux - Nuit   3   70
d'Ete (Super Concorde) In tch, eff to chase wnr appr fnl 1f, onepace: bckd from 9/1: acts on firm & both AWs.
857   **NOBLE PASAO** 33 [11]   Andrew Turnell 3-10-7 (68) Miss S Thomas (7) 33/1: -26003: 3 b g Alzao - Belle   nk   68
Passe (Be My Guest) Prom, eff to chase wnr 2f out, sn onepace: acts on firm, gd & fibresand: see 495.

423

684   **ERUPT** 57 [9] M Brittain 7-10-2 (51) Mrs S Eddery (5) 16/1: 06-204: In tch, rdn over 2f out, late *1* 49
gains: acts on firm, soft & fibresand: see 647, 60.
1148   **ALMAZHAR** 8 [12] 5-10-2 (51) Miss Diana Jones 7/4 FAV: 6-2235: Hld up, eff 2f out, no dngr, bhd. *hd* 49
867   **FOIST** 32 [13] 8-10-3 (52) Miss S Brotherston (5) 16/1: 50-006: Went left start, keen, bhd, late gains. *5* 41
3854} **SILVER TONGUED** 247 [2] 4-9-13 (48) Miss Hayley Bryan (7) 33/1: 0500-7: Chsd wnr, wkd 2f out: *¾* 35
in '99 trained by C Brittain (rtd 64): eff around 8.2f on firm grnd: now with J Bradley.
1192   **NAISSANT** 6 [5] 7-10-2 (51) Miss E Ramsden 12/1: 00-508: In tch, wknd 2f out: qck reapp, see 844. *1½* 35
1207   **SOPHOMORE** 5 [6] 6-11-7 (70) Mrs Annette Harris (7) 33/1: /03069: Bhd, btn over 2f out: see 599. *3* 49
1007   **LYNTON LAD** 19 [3] 8-10-13 (62) Miss Kim Jones (7) 16/1: 25-660: In tch, wknd over 2f out: 10th. *shd* 41
4196} **CHAMPAGNE N DREAMS** 224 [16] 8-10-7 (56) Mrs C Williams 8/1: 0410-U: Hmpd & u.r. after 1f: *0*
unfortunate reapp: with W Haigh in '99, won at Catterick (fill h'cap, rtd 57), also banned under 'non-triers'
Rule: '98 Chepstow wnr (ladies h'cap, with D Nicholls): eff at 7f/1m on fast, gd & on any track.
4593} **Knobbleeneeze** 192 [14] 10-9-12 (47)(vis) Ms T Dzieciolowska (7) 12/1:
676   **Bellas Gate Boy** 58 [8] 8-10-10 (59) Mrs L Pearce 14/1:
647   **Still Waters** 68 [4] 5-10-1 (50) Mrs S Moore (5) 33/1:
4527} **Russian Music** 199 [1] 7-11-2 (65)(t) Miss A Deniel 50/1:
4037} **Misalliance** 235 [15] 5-10-2 (51)(BL) Miss S Samworth 33/1:
16 ran   Time 1m 31.4 (0.6)   (R Kinsey)   A Bailey Little Budworth, Cheshire.

1276	3.25 SEALAND HCAP 4YO+ 0-75 (E) 2m35y Firm 03 -18 Slow	[68]
	£3087 £950 £475 £237 4 yo rec 3 lb	

1023   **SPA LANE** 19 [10] Mrs S Lamyman 7-8-0 (40) F Norton 13/2: 000-51: 7 ch g Presidium - Sleekit (Blakeney) *43*
In tch, hdwy over 2f out to lead ins last, styd on, rdn out: '99 scorer at Southwell & Pontefract (h'caps, rtd
38a & 48): '98 scorer here at Beverley (h'cap, rtd 52): eff at 12f, stays 2m2f on firm, hvy & fibresand:
handles any trk, likes a stiff fin: took advantage of a handy mark.
1087   **KAGOSHIMA** 11 [12] J Norton 5-8-7 (47)(VIS) O Pears 33/1: /65-02: 5 b g Shirley Heights - Kashteh *1½* 47
(Green Desert) Led 3f out till just ins last, not pace of wnr: improved for first time vis stepped up to 2m on fm.
1087   **IRELANDS EYE** 11 [2] J Norton 5-9-2 (56) J Weaver 10/1: 360-33: 5 b g Shareef Dancer - So Romantic *hd* 56
(Teenoso) Hld up, eff over 2f out, kept on ins last, not pace of wnr: stays 2m on firm & soft: running well.
1147   **GENEROUS WAYS** 8 [11] E J Alston 5-9-2 (56) T E Durcan 8/1: 0-4054: In tch, kept on for press *1¼* 55
fnl 2f: acts on firm/fast: on a winning mark: see 627.
797   **RIGADOON** 44 [17] 4-9-2 (59)(bl) G Parkin 7/2 FAV: 161-45: Prom, ev ch 1f out, onepcd: bckd, abs. *shd* 58
4078} **REGGIE BUCK** 232 [18] 6-7-11 (37) D Mernagh (2) 16/1: /000-6: Prom, onepace fnl 2f: last rcd over *1¾* 34
hdles 3 months ago, earlier won at Leicester & Catterick (h'cap hdles, rtd 106h, 2m, fast & gd/soft): 98/99 wnr at
Doncaster (nov h'cap): unplcd on the Flat last term for J L Harris: eff at 1m on fast, has tried blnks.
876   **NORTHERN MOTTO** 32 [9] 7-9-1 (55) J F Egan 12/1: 40-507: Waited with, eff over 2f out, onepace. *½* 51
963   **SHERIFF** 25 [5] 9-8-11 (53) M Henry 14/1: 24-028: Bhd, some late gains, no dngr: see 963, 788. *½* 46
940   **HIGHFIELD FIZZ** 26 [19] 8-8-2 (42) T Williams 33/1: 5-00P9: In tch, wknd 2f out: '99 Musselburgh *nk* 36
wnr (h'cap, rtd 47): '98 wnr at Pontefract & Musselburgh (rtd 53): stays 2m2f on fm, hvy & likes Musselburgh.
876   **HAYAAIN** 32 [8] 7-10-0 (68) M Roberts 8/1: /03-30: Nvr a factor: 10th: btr 876. *5* 57
1167   **YES KEEMO SABEE** 7 [16] 5-10-0 (68) L Newton 33/1: 0-6000: Al bhd: 11th: see 627. *nk* 56
3894} **FREE** 243 [4] 5-9-4 (58) A Culhane 6/1: 1223-0: In tch, wknd 3f out: 16th: long abs since nov chase *0*
wnr at Carlisle & Sedgefield (rtd 125c, stays 2m5f on fast & gd/soft): '99 Flat wnr at Newcastle (h'cap, rtd 59 at
best): 98/99 hdle wnr at Kelso & Catterick (rtd 117h): stays 2m on firm/fast & a stiff enuf track.
--   **SAINTLY THOUGHTS** [6] 5-10-0 (68) J P Spencer 16/1: 0421-0: Dsptd lead till 3f out, wknd: 17th, *0*
reapp: in '99 trained in Ireland, won at Downpatrick (h'cap): stays 2m1.5f on gd/firm.
832   **NAILER** 37 [14] 4-9-1 (58) N Callan 33/1: 00-60: Dsptd lead till wknd over 3f out: last, up in trip. *0*
668   **Turgenev** 60 [7] 11-7-11 (37)(1ow)(14oh) Dale Gibson 50/1:
1087   **Old Hush Wing** 11 [15] 7-8-11 (51) C Teague 14/1:
4458} **Bisquet De Bouche** 205 [1] 6-7-10 (36)(2oh) R Brisland (5) 16/1:
940   **Black Ice Boy** 26 [3] 9-7-12 (38) K Dalgleish (7) 33/1:
4587} **Simple Ideals** 193 [13] 6-8-11 (51) Kim Tinkler 33/1:
19 ran   Time 3m 33.7 (3.4)   (Sotby Farming Company Ltd)   Mrs S Lamyman Louth, Lincs.

1277	3.55 EAST RIDING COND STKS 3YO+ (C) 5f Firm 03 +05 Fast	
	£6264 £2376 £1188 £540 3 yo rec 9 lb	

4170} **FLANDERS** 226 [6] T D Easterby 4-9-3 R Winston 4/6 FAV: 5016-1: 4 b f Common Grounds - Family At *100*
War (Exploder) Cl-up, hdwy & sltly short of room 2f out, styd on well ins last to get up cl-home, rdn out on reapp:
gd time, hvly bckd: in '99 won at Doncaster (List) & rnr-up 3 times incl when btn a shd in the Kings Stand (rtd 113):
juv wnr at Beverley (2), Royal Ascot (stks) & Newbury (val sprint, rtd 105): suited by a stiff 5f on firm or gd/soft
& likes Ascot: runs well fresh: v useful & game, can rate more highly.
1164   **YORKIES BOY** 7 [3] A Berry 5-8-10 J Carroll 6/1: 0-0522: 5 ro h Clantime - Slipperose (Persepolis) *nk* 91
Set pace, rdn & hdd just ins last, rallied cl-home, just failed: game run back at best trip: acts on fm & gd/soft.
1074   **ELLENS ACADEMY** 12 [1] E J Alston 5-8-10 (bl) T E Durcan 12/1: 00-043: 5 b h Royal Academy - *shd* 91$
Lady Ellen (Horage) Dwelt, waited with, hdwy 2f out, styd on to lead just ins last, collared cl-home, just
btn: fine run tho' surely flattered (recently btn in h'cap off 77): see 1074 (6f).
--   **YORBA LINDA** [7] E J O'Neill 5-8-5 J F Egan 25/1: 2509-4: Waited with, eff well over 1f out, kept on *½* 85
for press ins last, not btn far on reapp: trained in Ireland in '99, won at The Curragh (h'cap): Curragh mdn
wnr in '97: suited by 5f, shld get further: acts on gd/firm & soft: encouraging reapp.
824   **FIRST MUSICAL** 38 [5] 4-8-5 D Mernagh 7/2: 004-05: Prom, rdn 2f out, onepace: better off in h'caps. *½* 84
1112   **MASTER HENRY** 10 [2] 6-8-10 J Fanning 33/1: 024/66: Prom, wknd 2f out: prob needs further. *9* 71
6 ran   Time 1m 01.2 (u0.1)   (Mrs Jean P Connew)   T D Easterby Great Habton, N.Yorks.

1278	4.30 WM HILL HCAP 3YO+ 0-70 (E) 5f Firm 03 -01 Slow	[69]
	£4836 £1488 £744 £372 3 yo rec 9 lb	

1008   **SHIRLEY NOT** 19 [20] S Gollings 4-9-10 (65) J F Egan 6/1: 00-031: 4 gr g Paris House - Hollia *73*
(Touchy Boy) Prom, hdwy wide over 1f out, rdn for press ins last to lead cl-home: dual '99 rnr-up (h'caps,
rtd 72): '98 scorer at Southwell (seller, with J Berry, rtd 60a) & Chester (nurs, rtd 77): suited by 5f on
firm, gd/soft & fibresand, prob hvy: runs well fresh on any trk: tough, well drawn today.
1008   **BODFARI KOMAITE** 19 [19] M W Easterby 4-9-6 (61) G Parkin 5/1 CO FAV: 066-W2: 4 b g Komaite - *shd* 69

Gypsy's Barn Rat (Balliol) Set pace, kept on for press ins last, collared cl-home, just btn: bckd from 10/1, clr of rem: in '99 scored at Musselburgh & Doncaster (h'caps, rtd 62): '98 Redcar scorer (nurs h'cap, rtd 62): all 3 wins at 5f on firm & gd, handles hvy & any trk: fine run.
1133 **WHIZZ KID 9** [10] J M Bradley 6-9-11 (66) Claire Bryan (5) 8/1: 005123: 6 b m Puissance - Panienka *3* **66**
(Dom Racine) Chsd ldrs, eff over 1f out, kept on ins last: in fine form: see 1133, 1005 (hvy).
1162 **SIR SANDROVITCH 7** [8] R A Fahey 4-9-10 (65) P Hanagan (7) 33/1: 0-0004: Bhd, eff & sltly short *nk* **65+**
of room 2f out, styd on ins last: back to form on fav'd firm grnd: h'capped to win soon: see 758.
4311} **BEYOND CALCULATION 215** [11] 6-9-10 (65) R Ffrench 20/1: 4000-5: In tch, rdn 2f out, kept on ins *shd* **65+**
last: reapp: in fine '99 form, won at Windsor, Bath, Thirsk & Brighton (h'caps): eff at 5.5/6f, stays 7f: likes firm, acts on gd/soft & fibresand, any trk: fine reapp, back on a wng mark & interesting next time over further.
1140 **SOTONIAN 9** [7] 7-9-9 (64) J Weaver 33/1: 500306: Prom, chall over 1f out, no extra ins last. *1* **61**
*1196 **AT LARGE 5** [14] 6-9-11 (66) L Newton 5/1 CO FAV: 0-0617: Bhd, some late gains, no dgnr: too sn? *¾* **61**
758 **ELVINGTON BOY 46** [9] 3-9-5 (69) Dale Gibson 40/1: 100-08: Prom, wknd over 1f out: 6 wk abs: *shd* **64**
'99 scorer at Ripon (mdn auct, rtd 81): eff at 5f on firm & gd grnd.
1162 **WILLIAMS WELL 7** [15] 6-9-7 (62)(bl) T Lucas 5/1 CO FAV: 04-069: Keen in tch, onepace fnl 2f. *nk* **56**
1258 **MARENGO 1** [13] 6-9-4 (59) D Harrison 14/1: 232150: Nvr a factor: 10th, unplcd yesterday in 1258. *shd* **53**
4267} **BOLLIN ANN 220** [12] 5-9-5 (60) R Winston 14/1: 0240-0: In tch,wknd well over 1f out: 11th: *hd* **53**
'99 wnr at Beverley (h'cap, rtd 58): '98 Ripon scorer (mdn, rtd 59): eff over 5/6f on fast, gd/soft & any trk.
908 **MALADERIE 29** [6] 6-9-1 (56)(vis) T Williams 40/1: 00-000: Al bhd: 12th: see 908. *1* **47**
1133 **TWICKERS 9** [16] 4-9-6 (61) A Culhane 10/1: 50-060: Slow away, al bhd: 13th: see 1133. *¾* **50**
1074 **VENIKA VITESSE 12** [4] 4-10-0 (69) C Lowther 25/1: 10-000: Switched right after start & al bhd: *1½* **54**
14th, poor draw: under top-weight: see 1074.
798 **AMERICAN COUSIN 44** [18] 5-9-2 (57) F Norton 9/1: 240-00: In tch, btn 2f out: 15th, abs, op 7/1: *shd* **42**
'99 wnr at Doncaster (2, appr h'caps, rtd 63 at best): rnr-up in '98 for R J Houghton (rtd 60): eff at 5/6f on fast, gd/soft & fibresand: best without blnks & likes Doncaster.
1005 **Polar Mist 19** [5] 5-9-1 (56)(tbl) Dean McKeown 40/1: 4331} **Sihafi 214** [2] 7-9-1 (56) T Hamilton (7) 33/1:
1005 **Aa Youknownothing 19** [1] 4-9-10 (65)(tvi) S Finnamore (5) 25/1:
4062} **Palvic Lady 233** [17] 4-9-5 (60) J Stack 25/1:
787 **Dil 45** [3] 5-9-5 (60) R Fitzpatrick (3) 33/1:
20 ran Time 1m 01.5 (0.2) (P Whinham, P Brown, J Stelling) S Gollings Scamblesby, Lincs.

1279

5.00 RACING W'FARE HCAP 3YO+ 0-85 (D) 1m100y Firm 03 +04 Fast [82]
£3900 £1200 £600 £300 3 yo rec 13lb

4196} **COURT EXPRESS 224** [7] W W Haigh 6-9-7 (75) F Lynch 16/1: 1500-1: 6 b g Then Again - Moon Risk **80**
(Risk Me) Waited with, hdwy to lead just ins fnl 1f, kept on well, drvn out: gd time on reapp: in '99 scored at Hamilton (2), Carlisle, Beverley & Redcar (h'caps, rtd 78): rtd 59 in '98: eff at 1m/10f on firm, gd/soft & on any trk, loves Carlisle: best without blnks: runs well fresh: v tough & progressive.
4479} **ITS OUR SECRET 204** [12] M H Tompkins 4-8-9 (63) S Sanders 16/1: 0000-2: 4 ch g Be My Guest - *hd* **67**
Lady Dulcinea (General) In tch, hdwy to chall appr fnl 1f, kept on for press ins last, just held: reapp: in early '99 scored at Nottingham (class stks, rtd 72), form subs t.o. & tried a visor: stays 8.5f on firm, gd/soft & on a gall trk: runs well fresh: fine reapp.
757 **COLWAY RITZ 46** [11] W Storey 6-9-6 (74) T Williams 12/1: 500-03: 6 b g Rudimentary - Million Heiress *½* **77**
(Auction Ring) In tch, hdwy to chall dist, no extra ins last, not btn far: reapp: in '99 scored at Ripon & Redcar (2, h'caps, rtd 84): '98 Beverley scorer (h'cap, rtd 75): eff over 1m/12f, suited by 10f: acts on gd/soft, relishes fast & firm & likes Redcar: tough & genuine, sharper next time over further, poss at Redcar.
*1243 **PENTAGON LAD 2** [16] J L Eyre 4-9-1 (69)(6ex) R Cody Boutcher (7) 3/1 FAV: 0-0514: Prom, eff *1¾* **68**
to lead over 1f out till just ins last, no extra: well bckd & another gd run after winning 2 days ago in 1243.
943 **TROIS 26** [13] 4-8-8 (62) T G McLaughlin 20/1: 103005: Slow away, bhd, kept on late, nrst fin: *½* **60**
apprec a return to further as in 271: handles firm & fibresand.
1074 **REX IS OKAY 12** [8] 4-9-2 (70)(bl) Dean McKeown 10/1: 640026: Led till dist, no extra: best at 7f. *1½* **66**
1007 **TIPPERARY SUNSET 19** [10] 6-8-8 (62) N Callan 12/1: 025-07: Slow away & bhd, btn 2f out. *3½* **51**
1007 **CYBERTECHNOLOGY 19** [4] 6-8-6 (60) J F Egan 25/1: 00-008: Bhd, some late gains: well h'capped. *5* **39**
834 **PLEADING 37** [2] 7-8-12 (66) J Carroll 10/1: 0-2339: Bhd, some late gains: btr 834 (gd/soft). *1¾* **41**
942 **ARC 26** [1] 6-8-11 (65) M Roberts 7/2: 424120: In tch, btn 2f out: 10th: btr 942. *1* **38**
1070 **WUXI VENTURE 12** [9] 5-9-1 (69) O Pears 14/1: 000000: In tch, wknd over 2f out: 11th: see 1070, 601. *1½* **39**
4274} **SPORTING GESTURE 219** [17] 3-8-8 (75) T Lucas 10/1: 6010-0: In tch, wkng when hmpd over 2f **0**
out: 15th: in '99 scored at Catterick (nurs h'cap, rtd 77): eff at 7f on gd/firm grnd & on a sharp track.
4199} **Edmo Heights 224** [3] 4-8-5 (59) R Winston 14/1: 1158 **Blakeset 7** [14] 5-9-0 (68) C Lowther 16/1:
4456} **Harlequin Dancer 205** [5] 4-10-0 (82) J P Spencer 16/1: 895 **Hormuz 30** [6] 4-9-9 (77) R Ffrench 25/1:
16 ran Time 1m 43.7 (u0.1) (Tim Hawkins) W W Haigh Melsonby, N.Yorks.

1280

5.30 LEVY BOARD MDN 3YO (D) 5f Firm 03 -03 Slow
£4189 £1289 £644 £322

1133 **HONESTY FAIR 9** [18] J A Glover 3-8-9 D Mernagh (3) 8/1: 600-41: 3 b f Reprimand - Truthful **79**
Image (Reesh) In tch, eff & switced left 2f out, kept on to lead ins last, rdn clr: op 6/1, joc rec a 4 day ban for irresponsible riding: plcd in '99 (rtd 68): eff over a stiff 5f, stays 6f on firm & gd/soft: improving.
1490} **FLY LIKE THE WIND 357** [8] M A Jarvis 3-8-9 P Robinson 8/1: 5-2: 3 br f Cyrano de Bergerac - Thulium *3* **70**
(Mansingh) Set pace, rdn over 1f out, collared ins, no extra: nicely bckd on reapp: rtd 66 sole juv start: eff at 5f on firm grnd: sharper for this.
740 **POP THE CORK 47** [17] R M Whitaker 3-9-0 Dean McKeown 33/1: 0-003: 3 ch g Clantime - Hyde *2½* **69$**
Princess (Touch Paper) Prom, eff to chall 2f out, not much room & switched appr fnl 1f, no extra: abs, handles fm.
4457} **NEEDWOOD TROOPER 205** [20] B C Morgan 3-9-0 G Hind 66/1: 0-4: In tch, eff to chall over 1f out, *½* **67**
no extra: reapp: well btn sole juv start: bred to apprec sprint trips.
3438} **SHINBONE ALLEY 269** [13] 3-9-0 J Carroll 11/10 FAV: 0205-5: Stumbled start but sn in tch, rdn *nk* **66**
& hung right over 1f out, onepace: hvly bckd on reapp: useful juv form, rnr-up twice & 5th in List (rtd 95 at best): eff over 5/6f on firm/fast grnd: plenty of ability, but costly to follow & worth a try in headgear.
1133 **DAWN 9** [19] 3-8-9 M Roberts 4/1: 634-36: In tch, eff & sltly hmpd 2f out, onepace: op 8/1: see 1133. *1* **58**
1072 **SEAHORSE BOY 12** [6] 3-9-0 T G McLaughlin 66/1: -007: Dwelt, bhd, some late gains: h'capped now. *1½* **59**
-- **ROZEL** [14] 3-8-9 D Harrison 20/1: 8: In tch, some late gains on debut: sprint bred, with R Guest. *nk* **53**
901 **APRILS COMAIT 30** [16] 3-8-9 V Halliday 66/1: 053309: Prom, wknd over 2f out: see 777, 696. *½* **51**
1035 **NEEDWOOD TRIBESMAN 15** [2] 3-9-0 J F Egan 66/1: -000: Nvr a factor: 10th: apprec further. *nk* **55**

BEVERLEY   SATURDAY MAY 13TH   Righthand, Oval Track With Stiff, Uphill Finish

--   **LOCH DIAMOND** [10] 3-8-9 J Weaver 5/1: 0: Slow away, bhd, brief eff over 1f out, nvr dngrs: ½   49
11th on debut: dam top-class sprinter.
1105 **TOYON** 10 [12] 3-9-0 S Sanders 20/1: 60: Keen, al bhd: 12th: see 1105.   ¾   52
1098 **Lizzie Simmonds** 11 [11] 3-8-9 (t) Kim Tinkler 33/1: 3893} **Paradise Yangshuo** 243 [4] 3-8-9 T E Durcan 50/1:
1062 **Branston Fizz** 12 [1] 3-8-9 J Fanning 12/1:   976 **Rum Lass** 24 [15] 3-8-9 A Culhane 25/1:
1021 **Rapidash** 19 [3] 3-9-0 (vis) R Fitzpatrick (3) 66/1:   2958} **Chin Up** 292 [9] 3-8-9 S Finnamore (5) 25/1:
18 ran   Time 1m 01.6 (0.3)   (P & S Partnership)   J A Glover Carburton, Notts.

LINGFIELD   SATURDAY MAY 13TH   Lefthand, Sharp, Undulating Track

Official Going GOOD TO SOFT (Good places). Pace figs inapp due to hvy rain after 3.10.
Stalls: Str - Stds Side, 10f - Ins, 11.5f - Outer.

1281   2.10 TESTERS MDN DIV 1 3YO+ (D)   1m2f   Good/Soft   Inapplicable
          £3107   £956   £478   £239   3 yo rec 15lb

957   **PENTAGONAL** 25 [3] Sir Michael Stoute 3-8-11 K Fallon 6/4 FAV: 0-01: 3 b c Dynaformer - Pent   82
(Mr Prospector) Trkd ldrs, rdn/prog to lead 2f out, styd on well fnl 1f, rdn to assert ins last, going away: hvly
bckd, reportedly struck into: rtd 77 sole '99 start (mdn): eff over 10f, further shld suit: acts on gd/soft.
1080 **ROB LEACH** 12 [1] R W Armstrong 3-8-11 G Carter 9/2: 52: 3 b g Robellino - Arc Empress Jane (Rainbow 2   77
Quest) Chsd ldrs, rdn/ch over 1f out, not pace of wnr ins last: op 7/2: eff at 10f on gd/soft: win at 12f.
884   **GIMCO** 31 [7] G C H Chung 3-8-11 L Dettori 7/1: 5-43: 3 b c Pelder - Valetta (Faustus)   1¼   75
Chsd ldrs, rdn/prog & ch 2f out, held ins last: bckd, tchd 8/1: styd longer 10f trip, prob handles gd & hvy.
4516} **BRIG OTURK** 200 [12] Mrs A J Perrett 3-8-11 R Hughes 8/1: 0-4: Keen & dsptd lead till over 1f out,   ¾   74
fdd nr fin: op 6/1: reapp: rtd 70 on sole '99 start (auct mdn): bred to stay 1m+: handles gd/sft.
4555} **MOUJEEDA** 196 [5] 3-8-6 J Reid 16/1: 0-5: Held up in tch, closed on ldrs over 3f out, rdn/held over 1f   3   65
out: op 12/1, reapp: unplcd sole '99 start for M Stoute (rtd 78, fill mdn): eff at 10f/12f wnr, mid-dists shld suit.
884   **EREBUS** 31 [6] 3-8-11 K Darley 25/1: 06: Keen, led 7f out till 4f out, fdd fnl 1f: longer 10f trip.   7   60
2852} **SADLERS SWING** 296 [4] 4-9-12 A Clark 33/1: 0-7: Rear, rdn/brief eff 2f out, no impress: 10 mth abs: 1¼   58
unplcd sole '99 start (rtd 63, mdn): mid-dists shld suit this term.
--   **BLUE STREET** 2 [4] 4-9-12 G Faulkner (3) 33/1: 8: Al rear: debut, with S Williams.   2½   54
832   **SINGLE CURRENCY** 37 [8] 4-9-12 D Sweeney 12/1: 3-09: Towards rear, btn 3f out: op 7/1: see 832.   7   44
771   **ESTUARY** 45 [10] 5-9-12 (t) A McCarthy (3) 14/1: 230: Chsd ldrs 7f: 10th: op 8/1, 6 wk abs.   ½   43
784   **TENACIOUS MELODY** 45 [11] 4-9-12 Dane O'Neill 33/1: 00: Led/dsptd lead after 1f till 7f out/sn btn: 11th*shd*   43
11 ran   Time 2m 13.81 (9.61)   (Sheikh Mohammed)   Sir Michael Stoute Newmarket.

1282   2.40 LISETD OAKS TRIAL 3YO (A)   1m3f106y   Good/Soft   Inapplicable
          £17400   £6600   £3300   £1500

*1179 **FILM SCRIPT** 6 [7] R Charlton 3-8-8 R Hughes 7/1: 611: 3 b f Unfuwain - Success Story (Sharrood)   98
Led/dsptd lead thr'out, rdn fnl 2f & duelled with rnr-up over 1f out, narrowly asserted nr fin, drvn out, gamely:
op 6/1: qck reapp: recent Salisbury wnr (mdn, made all): eff at 11.5f/12f, further shld suit: acts on firm,
gd/sft & any trk: likes to force the pace: tough & progressive filly, clearly useful.
979   **DOLLAR BIRD** 23 [1] J L Dunlop 3-8-8 M J Kinane 7/1: 610-32: 3 b f Kris - High Spirited (Shirley   ½   96
Heights) Chsd ldrs, rdn/switched for effort over 2f out, drvn to chall over 1f out, kept on well, just held nr fin:
op 6/1: jockey given 2 day ban for careless riding: styd 11.5f trip: tough & useful filly.
*1045 **DREAM QUEST** 15 [2] J L Dunlop 3-8-8 Pat Eddery 3/1: 13: 3 ch f Rainbow Quest - Dreamawhile (Known ¾   95
Fact) Chsd ldrs, prog/dsptd led 5f out till over 2f out, kept on onepace: jockey reported filly made a noise: nicely
bckd tho' op 2/1: styd longer 11.5f trip, further will suit: handles gd/soft & hvy: clr of rem, open to improvement.
*814   **BEDARA** 40 [5] B W Hills 3-8-8 J Reid 14/1: 02-14: Held up in tch, rdn/sltly hmpd over 3f out,   5   88
sn no impress on ldrs: op 8/1, 6 wk abs: see 814 (fill mdn).
1127 **PURPLE HEATHER** 9 [3] 3-8-8 Dane O'Neill 10/1: 642-25: Rear/in tch, hard rdn 2f out, no impress.   nk   87
3962} **KARALIYFA** 239 [4] 3-8-8 K Fallon 2/1 FAV: 3-6: Rear/in tch, eff/bmpd 3f out, rdn/no prog over 1f out   2   84
& position accepted: hvly bckd on reapp: plcd sole '99 start (stks, rtd 86+): eff at 7f, bred to apprec mid-dists
this term: handles firm grnd & gd/soft & jockey believes she will be suited by a return to faster conditions.
1017 **BANCO SUIVI** 19 [6] 3-8-8 M Hills 6/1: 5-27: Prom, rdn/btn 2f out: stablemate of 4th: see 1017 (mdn).   18   63
7 ran   Time 2m 32.36 (8.96)   (The Queen)   R Charlton Beckhampton, Wilts.

1283   3.10 LISTED FILLIES STKS 3YO+ (A)   7f str   Good/Soft   Inapplicable
          £13485   £5115   £2557   £1162   3 yo rec 12lb   Raced stands side, high no's favoured

927   **HOT TIN ROOF** 28 [8] T D Easterby 4-9-3 K Fallon 13/2: 230-21: 4 b f Thatching - No Reservations   102
(Commanche Run) Bhd ldrs, rdn/prog to lead over 1f out, in command ins last & pushed out cl-home: '99
Newcastle wnr (J Banks, fill mdn), sub plcd in List (rtd 103): eff at 6/7f on firm & soft, any trk: useful.
99   **SCARLETT RIBBON** 173 [3] P J Makin 3-8-5 A Clark 12/1: 10-2: 3 b f Most Welcome - Scarlett Holly   2½   96
(Red Sunset) Carried left start, in tch, kept on over 1f out, not pace of wnr: op 10/1, reapp: '99 debut Windsor
wnr (mdn, rtd 90): eff at 6/7f on gd/soft & a sharp/undul trk: runs well fresh: came from a tricky draw.
*1078 **MAY CONTESSA** 12 [1] D R C Elsworth 3-8-5 N Pollard 3/1 FAV: 35-113: 3 b f Bahri - Copper Creek   shd   97+
(Habitat) Hmpd start & settled towards rear, prog/switched left over 1f out, kept on ins last for press:
well bckd: styd longer 7f trip: poorly drawn & hmpd today, well worth another chance after 1078.
995   **FAIRY GEM** 21 [7] R Hannon 3-8-6(1ow) Dane O'Neill 20/1: 460-04: Settled towards rear, no room/   nk   97
switched over 1f out, rdn/styd on strongly ins last, nrst fin: op 16/1: acts on firm & gd/sft: worth another try at 1m.
1028 **THE FUGATIVE** 17 [12] 7-9-3 M Tebbutt 20/1: D0-045: Led, hung left & rdn/hdd over 1f out, sn held.   ½   95$
4400} **BOAST** 210 [11] 3-8-5 K Darley 8/1: 2416-6: Chsd ldrs, rdn/onepace fnl 2f: '99 Nottingham (nov,   shd   95
med auct stks) & Newmarket wnr (nov stks, rtd 99 at best): eff at 6f, stays 7f on gd/soft & firm & gd, any trk.
4201} **PEKANSKI** 224 [13] 3-8-5 R Hughes 12/1: 16-7: Dwelt, settled rear, eff 2f out, held fnl 1f: tchd 14/1,   ¾   94$
reapp: '99 Goodwood wnr (fill mdn, mdn), subs unplcd in List (rtd 96 at best, with P W Chapple Hyam): eff at
6f, 7f shld suit this term: acts on gd grnd & a sharp/undul trk: runs well fresh.
2233} **JEED** 323 [5] 3-8-5 W Supple 20/1: 1-8: Mid-div, eff 2f out, no impress: reapp: '99 sole start wnr at   1½   91$
Newmarket (6 rnr fill mdn, rtd 92+): eff at 6f, 7f+ shld suit: acts on fast & a stiff/gall trk: has run well fresh.
953   **ALHUFOOF** 25 [9] 3-8-5 R Hills 11/2: 31-49: Trkd ldrs, eff/drifted left & btn fnl 1f: op 9/2.   ½   90

913 **YAZMIN 29** [10] 3-8-5 Pat Eddery 16/1: 134-60: Mid-div, eff/btn 2f out: 10th: see 913. *2½* **85**
1158 **RICH IN LOVE 7** [6] 6-9-3 G Mosse 33/1: 000-00: Prom 5f: 11th: rnr-up in '99 (rtd 98, this race, flattered): '98 Ascot wnr (ladies h'cap) & Yarmouth (fill h'cap, rtd 83 at best): suited by 7f, stays 1m: acts on firm, gd & any trk, loves Yarmouth. *4* **77**
4294} **MISS ORAH 217** [4] 3-8-5 G Duffield 16/1: 124-0: Trkd ldrs 5f: 12th: reapp: '99 Salisbury wnr (fill mdn, debut, subs rtd 91, stks): eff at 7f, bred to apprec 1m+: acts on firm & a stiff/gall trk: runs well fresh. *2½* **72**
-- **AURATUM** [2] 3-8-6(1ow) L Dettori 7/2: 1-P: Unruly stalls, rider lost irons leaving gates, sn bhd, t.o./ p.u. nr fin: hvly bckd: recently reportedly disapp in a Godolphin 1m trial in Dubai: sole start wnr at Deauville in '99 for D Loder (6f, soft). **0**
13 ran Time 1m 25.33 (4.93) (Giles W Pritchard-Gordon) T D Easterby Great Habton, N.Yorks.

1284

3.40 GR 3 DERBY TRIAL 3YO (A) 1m3f106y Good/Soft Inapplicable
£34800 £13200 £6600 £3000

*998 **SADDLERS QUEST 21** [8] G A Butler 3-8-7 K Darley 100/30 FAV: 1-11: 3 b c Saddlers' Hall - Seren Quest (Rainbow Quest) Dwelt, settled towards rear, rdn/prog fnl 3f & drvn/strong chall ins last, narrowly prevailed, all out: well bckd: recent Kempton scorer (class stks): sole '99 start wnr at Bath (mdn, rtd 87+): apprec step up to 11.5f, half-brother to a 14f wnr & will get further: acts on gd/soft & soft/hvy grnd: likes a sharp/easy trk: runs well fresh: tough, useful & progressive, remains unbtn & heads next for the Epsom Derby. **109**
1056 **GOING GLOBAL 14** [4] S P C Woods 3-8-7 J Reid 12/1: 31-132: 3 ch c Bob Back - Ukraine Girl (Targowice) Trld ldrs, rdn/led 2f out, hard rdn ins last & hdd nr line, just held: tchd 14/1: stays 11.5f: useful. *nk* **108**
*1089 **KING O THE MANA 11** [7] R Hannon 3-8-7 R Hughes 14/1: 6-0413: 3 b c Turtle Island - Olivia Jane (Ela Mana Mou) Held up in tch, prog/rdn to chall 2f out, hard rdn ins last & held nr fin: op 12/1: stays 11.5f. *2* **105**
818 **APOLLO VICTORIA 42** [5] A P O'Brien 3-8-7 (VIS) M J Kinane 4/1: 1-24: Rear, in tch, eff/prog over 2f out, held 1f out: op 3/1, first time visor: 6 wk abs: this longer 11.5f trip will suit: see 818 (9f). *1¾* **103**
*1029 **ETERNAL SPRING 17** [1] 3-8-7 K Fallon 9/2: 132-15: Led/dsptd lead till 2f out: bckd, lngr trip. *7* **93**
-- **DUBAI TWO THOUSAND** [2] 3-8-7 L Dettori 7/2: 1-6: Led 1f, cl-up till 2f out: op 3/1: fin 5th in a 1m Godolphin trial in Dubai last month: sole '99 start wnr at Longchamp (4 rnrs, 1m, v soft, D Loder). *½* **92**
*1127 **TRUMPET SOUND 9** [6] 3-8-7 G Mosse 6/1: 4-17: Chsd ldrs, hard rdn 2f out, fdd: see 1127 (10f, mdn). *5* **85**
951 **BID FOR FAME 25** [3] 3-8-7 A Clark 33/1: 538: Towards rear when not handle bend 3f out, sn btn. *6* **76**
8 ran Time 2m 35.24 (11.84) (The Fairy Story Partnership) G A Butler Blewbury, Oxon.

1285

4.10 TOTE SCOOP6 HCAP 3YO 0-105 (B) 6f Good/Soft Inapplicable [107]
£32500 £10000 £5000 £2500 Raced stands side, high no's favoured

*1105 **SAN SALVADOR 10** [13] J Noseda 3-8-4 (83) A Nicholls (3) 2/1 FAV: -3211: 3 b c Dayjur - Sheer Gold (Cutlass) Trkd ldrs, prog to lead 2f out, sn rdn clr, easily: val for 10L+: hvly bckd, tchd 3/1: h'cap debut: recent Pontefract wnr (mdn): eff at 6f, 7f will suit: acts on gd & gd/soft grnd: handles a sharp or stiff/ undul trk: decisive wnr today, potentially v useful & can win in stronger class. **102**
988 **AWAKE 21** [8] M Johnston 3-9-5 (98) K Fallon 10/1: 2D-042: 3 ch c First Trump - Pluvial (Habat) Mid-div, rdn 2f out, kept on for press to take 2nd nr line, no ch with wnr: tchd 9/1: see 988 (List). *9* **98**
1153 **EASTWAYS 8** [12] M Johnston 3-8-12 (91) R Hills 8/1: 32-003: 3 ch c Efisio - Helens Dreamgirl (Caerleon) Trkd ldrs, rdn 2f out, kept on for press: see 982. *shd* **91**
3629} **NORFOLK REED 259** [7] R Hannon 3-8-8 (87) Dane O'Neill 20/1: 1020-4: Mid-div, briefly no room 2f out, rdn & kept on ins last, no threat: op 16/1, reapp: '99 debut wnr here at Lingfield (nov stks, subs rnr-up in a nurs, rtd 90 at best): eff at 5/6f, 7f+ could suit: acts on firm & fast & likes a sharp trk, has run well fresh. *1* **85**
1153 **ZIETZIG 8** [11] 3-8-1 (80) J Mackay (7) 8/1: 20-055: Towards rear, rdn & kept on fnl 2f, no threat. *nk* **77**
*1098 **QUEEN OF THE MAY 11** [17] 3-8-2 (81) S Drowne 8/1: 413-16: Trkd ldrs, held fnl 2f: tchd 10/1. *nk* **77**
4549} **CORRIDOR CREEPER 197** [1] 3-8-9 (88) Pat Eddery 12/1: 0221-7: Mid-div, eff 2f out, sn btn: poor low draw: reapp: '99 fnl start wnr at Brighton (mdn, rtd 88 at best): eff at 6f, dam a 1m wnr & 7f+ may yet suit: acts on firm & gd/soft grnd: handles a sharp/undul or gall track. *6* **73**
994 **SMOKIN BEAU 21** [10] 3-7-11 (76)(VIS) G Bardwell 16/1: 320028: Led & switched to stands rail, clr after 2f, rdn/hdd 2f out & fdd: op 14/1, showed usual early pace in first time visor: see 994, 275 & 127. *nk* **60**
3828} **ANSELLAD 248** [16] 3-8-11 (90) R Hughes 33/1: 0330-9: Trkd ldr till over 2f out, fdd: reapp: '99 Bath wnr for J Berry (nov stks, rtd 93 at best, nurs): eff at 5/5.5f, 6f shld suit: acts on firm & gd/soft, prob handles any trk: likes to race with/force the pace. *nk* **73**
982 **BLUE VELVET 23** [5] 3-8-7 (86) G Duffield 14/1: 024-60: In tch, btn 2f out: 10th: poor low draw. *4* **59**
1016 **DESERT FURY 19** [14] 3-9-7 (100) J Reid 12/1: 13-30: Struggling halfway: 11th: op 8/1: see 1016. *nk* **72**
988 **PUNCTUATE 21** [3] 3-9-3 (96) M Hills 8/1: 11-00: Al towards rear: 12th: poor low draw: see 988. *nk* **67**
1153 **LAS RAMBLAS 8** [9] 3-8-1 (80) D O'Donohoe 16/1: 00-000: Dwelt, al towards rear: 13th: op 12/1. *nk* **50**
1047 **Nisr 15** [2] 3-8-5 (84) A McGlone 25/1: 1186 **Connect 6** [4] 3-8-11 (90) K Darley 20/1:
953 **Bandanna 25** [15] 3-8-11 (90) G Carter 33/1:
16 ran Time 1m 12.87 (3.97) (Lucayan Stud) J Noseda Newmarket.

1286

4.45 HAVANA HORSE HCAP 4YO+ 0-105 (B) 7f str Soft Inapplicable [100]
£10920 £3360 £1680 £840 Majority racing stands side favoured.

1077 **ADJUTANT 12** [12] N P Littmoden 5-9-7 (93) M Tebbutt 5/2 FAV: 3-3031: 5 b g Batshoof - Indian Love Song (Be My Guest) Chsd ldrs halfway, switched & rdn to chall ins last, led nr fin, rdn out: hvly bckd: '99 Leicester wnr (stks, rtd 94): '98 wnr at Goodwood (h'cap, awdd race) & Haydock (h'cap, rtd 92): all wins at 7f, stays 1m: acts on firm, soft & any trk, likes Haydock: runs well fresh: useful performer. **96**
1250 **MISTER RAMBO 2** [1] B J Meehan 5-8-9 (81) R Hughes 5/1: -01052: 5 b g Rambo Dancer - Ozra (Red Alert) Prom, switched to stands rail & led over 4f out, strongly pressed ins last & hdd nr fin: qck reapp. *¾* **82**
966 **UNDETERRED 24** [9] C F Wall 4-9-7 (93) R Mullen 14/1: 400-03: 4 ch c Zafonic - Mint Crisp (Green Desert) Prom, ch over 1f out, kept on onepace for press: unplcd in '99 (rtd 109, list): '98 wnr at Yarmouth (mdn, ddht) & York (list, rtd 110): eff at 6/7f, could get further: dam 9/10f wnr: acts on firm & soft grnd, handles any trk: useful colt & slipping to a handy mark. *1½* **92**
4069} **PARISIEN STAR 232** [13] N Hamilton 4-8-10 (82) L Newman (5) 12/1: 6000-4: Held up, rdn & styd on fnl 2f, not pace to chall: op 10/1, reapp: rnr-up twice in '99 (rtd 90, class stks, G Lewis): '98 scorer at Epsom & Newbury (h'caps, rtd 94): eff at 6f/7.6f, stays a sharp 1m well: acts on fast & soft, any trk: nicely h'capped. *hd* **80**
1060 **COOL TEMPER 12** [11] 4-8-6 (78) J Tate 10/1: 222-55: Chsd ldrs, held fnl 2f: see 1060. *1¾* **74**
1110 **EASTER OGIL 10** [14] 5-8-8 (80)(vis) K Fallon 100/30: 0-5006: Chsd ldrs 5f: op 11/4: see 725. *14* **60**
1112 **TRIPLE DASH 10** [6] 4-10-0 (100) G Duffield 6/1: 343-57: Al towards rear: op 9/2: topweight. *3½* **75**

LINGFIELD SATURDAY MAY 13TH Lefthand, Sharp, Undulating Track

1110 **MIDHISH TWO 10** [4] 4-8-4 (76) G Carter 16/1: 06-008: Trkd ldrs 5f: op 14/1: see 1110.   nk   50
4357} **YEAST 212** [3] 8-8-11 (83) M Hills 14/1: 0100-9: Switched to race alone far side, btn 3f out: op 12/1,   19   37
reapp: '99 race at Chepstow (class stks), Salisbury (h'cap) & Ripon (clmr, rtd 89 at best): plcd in '98
(rtd 80): loves to force the pace at 1m, prob stays 12f: acts on firm, handles soft grnd: handles any trk.
2757} **DON BOSCO 301** [5] 4-8-0 (72) J Mackay (7) 16/1: /610-0: Led 2f, sn struggling: 10th: op 12/1,   dist   0
reapp: '99 Ripon scorer (h'cap, J Banks, rtd 75): eff at 6f, tried 1m: acts on firm grnd: now with N Callaghan.
725   **PETRUS 49** [7] 4-8-13 (85) A Nicholls (3) 16/1: 660-00: Bhd halfway: 11th: op 14/1, 7 wk abs: '99   7   0
wnr at Kempton, Yarmouth & Goodwood (h'caps, rtd 94 at best): eff at 7f, stays 1m: suited by fast & firm grnd.
11 ran   Time 1m 29.28 (8.88)   (J R Good)   N P Littmoden Newmarket.

1287

5.15 TESTERS MDN DIV 2 3YO+ (D)   **1m2f**   **Soft**   **Inapplicable**
£3087   £950   £475   £237   3 yo rec 15lb

--   **SPINNING TOP** [9] Sir Michael Stoute 3-8-6 K Fallon 4/6 FAV: 1: 3 b f Alzao - Zenith (Shirley Heights)   88
Trkd ldrs halfway, smooth prog to lead 3f out, rdn clr over 1f out, readily: val for 12L+: hvly bckd at odds on
on debut: half-sister to a 7f/9f wnr: eff at 10f, 12f+ could suit: acts on soft grnd & a sharp trk: runs well
fresh: entered in Ribblesdale stks at Royal Ascot, clrly well regarded & lks potentially useful on this evidence.
826   **SPEED VENTURE 38** [10] S P C Woods 3-8-11 G Duffield 6/1: 42: 3 b g Owington - Jade Venture   9   79
(Never So Bold) Led/dsptd lead till 3f out, sn held by wnr & position accepted ins last: clr rem, prob stays 10f.
4537} **SWEET CICELY 198** [4] D R C Elsworth 3-8-6 N Pollard 9/2: 00-3: 3 b f Darshaan - Glendora (Glenstal)   4   68
Prom, drvn/no impress over 3f out: bckd, op 6/1: unplcd in '99 (rtd 73, fill mdn): mid-dist h'caps shld suit.
1200 **ABLE SEAMAN 5** [1] C E Brittain 3-8-11 N Esler (7) 20/1: 04: Chsd ldrs, rdn/no impress 3f out: 1   72$
clr rem, qck reapp: well bhd on debut prev.
--   **HERBSHAN DANCER** [8] 6-9-12 Martin Dwyer 50/1: 5030/5: Mid-div, rdn/btn 3f out: long abs: 13   62
missed '99: rnr-up in '98 (rtd 45, amat h'cap): eff at 12f on fast & gd/soft grnd: best without blnks.
4505} **NO PASS NO HONOR 201** [12] 3-8-11 J Reid 33/1: 00-6: Mid-div, btn 4f out: reapp: rtd 60 at best   3½   59
last term (mdns): longer 10f trip today.
1045 **HERSELF 15** [2] 3-8-6 Dane O'Neill 10/1: 07: Rear, rdn/mod late gains: op 8/1: see 1045.   1½   53
4014} **TWICE 236** [5] 4-9-12 I Mongan (5) 8/1: 440-8: In tch, btn 3f out: Flat reapp, jumps fit (unplcd, rtd   3½   55
102h, flattered, juv nov): rtd 80 at best on the level last term for B Hills (mdn): mid-dist h'caps will suit.
--   **MANAGERIAL** [6] 3-8-11 G Bardwell 33/1: 9: Al towards rear: debut, with N Hamilton.   26   35
1032 **YAFA 17** [11] 4-9-12 K Darley 33/1: 00: Towards rear, bhd 4f out: 10th: longer 12f trip.   ¾   34
3961} **POLISH GIRL 239** [7] 4-9-7 D R McCabe 20/1: 0-0: Led after 1f till 4f out, sn btn: 11th: reapp.   1¼   28
--   **LINCONNU** [3] 5-9-12 (bl) J Tate 50/1: 0: Sn rdn, bhd 4f out: 12th: debut.   dist   0
12 ran   Time 2m 20.17 (15.97)   (The Queen)   Sir Michael Stoute Newmarket.

WINDSOR MONDAY MAY 15TH Sharp Fig 8 Track

Official Going   GOOD/FIRM. Stalls: Inside.

1288

6.10 SUADI CLASSIFIED STKS 4YO+ 0-75 (D)   **1m2f**   **Firm 08**   **-19 Slow**
£3926   £1208   £604   £302

4264} **TONIGHTS PRIZE 222** [11] C F Wall 6-9-0 S Sanders 10/1: 0035-1: 6 b g Night Shift - Bestow (Shirley   79
Heights) Pulled hard, handy, eff appr fnl 1f, led dist, kept on well: op 8/1, reapp: '99 rnr-up (h'cap, rtd 81):
'98 wnr at Pontefract (h'cap, rtd 90 at best): eff at 1m/10f: acts on firm & gd grnd, handles gd/soft: goes on
any trk, likes Pontefract: gd weight carrier, runs well fresh.
833   **PRINCE SLAYER 39** [5] T P McGovern 4-9-0 Pat Eddery 14/1: 352-02: 4 b g Batshoof - Top Sovereign   ¾   78
(High Top) Led till ent fnl 1f, ran on: 6 wk abs: dual '99 rnr-up (mdn, rtd 80, B Smart): rtd 77 sole juv start:
eff at 1m/10f on firm & hvy grnd: lightly rcd, shld shed mdn tag before long.
1150 **PINCHINCHA 10** [12] D Morris 6-9-0 J Tate 5/1: 3-4023: 6 b g Priolo - Western Heights (Shirley   shd   78
Heights) Midfield, boxed in ent fnl 2f, clr dist, ran on for press, not btn far: hvly bckd tho' op 7/2: would
have been at least 2nd with a clr passage but has become v difficult to win with: see 1150, 786.
4281} **TOTOM 220** [7] J R Fanshawe 5-8-11 D Harrison 9/1: 5145-4: Prom, rdn to chall appr fnl 1f, no extra   1¼   73
towards fin: tchd 12/1 on reapp: '99 wnr at Lingfield (2, turf & AW h'caps rtd 76a) & here at Windsor (2, stks
& h'cap, rtd 75): '98 wnr again at Lingfield (mdn, rtd 69a & 69, Lord Huntingdon): eff at 10f/11.5f: acts on
firm, gd grnd & equitrack, loves sharp trks, esp Lingfield & Windsor: eff with/without visor, can force the pace.
1113 **IRON MOUNTAIN 12** [13] 5-9-0 K Fallon 4/1 FAV: 260-35: Waited with, shkn up 2f out & not much   1¼   74
room, styd on, unable to chall: well bckd: not much luck in running & is worth another chance after 1113.
1086 **TWENTY FIRST 13** [10] 4-8-11 D Holland 25/1: 026-06: Front rank & ev ch till onepace appr fnl 1f.   2½   67$
975   **LADY ROCKSTAR 26** [3] 5-8-11 P McCabe 11/2: 05-027: Prom, imprvd after halfway, chall 2f out,   shd   67
sn rdn, no extra & eased towards fin: well bckd: see 975, 793.
3711} **MUYASSIR 257** [2] 5-9-0 M Roberts 8/1: 2140-8: Held up, eff & edged left 2f out, nvr dngrs: ½   69
reapp: '99 Newmarket wnr (h'cap, rtd 76 & 65a): '98 wnr at Lingfield (h'cap, rtd 72a & 72): eff at 1m/sharp
10f: acts on firm/fast grnd & equitrack, any trk: shld come on for this: with P Makin.
3081} **MISS FARA 287** [6] 5-8-11 R Hughes 15/2: 3/20-9: Well plcd, chall on bit 2f out, btn bef dist &   nk   65
eased: op 5/1, 5 wk hdles abs: earlier won at Taunton (2), Towcester & Cheltenham (2m/2m4f, h'cap, fast,
soft, rtd 126h): rnr-up first of 2 '99 starts (fill mdn, rtd 79): plcd thrice in '98 (mdn, rtd 80): eff at 10f,
shld apprec further: goes on fast & gd grnd: shown enough to find a race: with M Pipe.
1271 **COLONEL NORTH 3** [1] 4-9-0 M Henry 33/1: 40-0000: Held up, wide eff/bmpd ent fnl 2f, nvr dngrs: 10th.   1¼   66
1946} **GOODBYE GOLDSTONE 338** [9] 4-9-0 J F Egan 14/1: 1420-0: Rear, wide into str & rdn, sn bmpd &   hd   66
btn: 11th, op 10/1 on reapp: '99 Folkestone wnr (h'cap, rtd 75 at best & 53a): plcd sole '98 start (mdn,
rtd 72): eff at 10f, stays a sharp 12f: acts on gd & hvy grnd, handles gd/firm & fibresand: with T Naughton.
1201 **DIGON DA 7** [4] 4-9-0 D Sweeney 33/1: 400-00: Chsd ldrs 6f: plcd in'99 (1m mdn on firm, rtd 79).   15   51
12 ran   Time 2m 07.4 (2.7)   (Hintlesham Thoroughbreds)   C F Wall Newmarket.

1289 6.35 SPORTINGBET.COM HCAP 3YO 0-80 (D) 6f **Firm 08 -27 Slow** [84]
£4394 £1352 £676 £338 High numbers favoured in fast grnd sprints here

1125 **PEDRO JACK** 11 [15] B J Meehan 3-9-4 (74) Pat Eddery 3/1 FAV: 110-31: 3 b g Mujadil - Festival Of 81
Light (High Top) Made just about all but hard prsd thr'out, all out, on the nod: hvly bckd, tchd 4/1: '99
wnr at Nottingham (2, auct mdn & nurs, rtd 77): eff at 6/7f: goes on firm/fast grnd, sharp or gall trks,
likes Nottingham & being up with/forcing the pace: tough, lightly rcd & improving.
1061 **PAYS DAMOUR** 14 [14] R Hannon 3-9-2 (72) R Hughes 14/1: 610-02: 3 b c Pursuit Of Love - Lady Of shd 78
The Land (Wollow) With wnr, drvn appr fnl 1f, ev ch, just failed: clr rem, game effort: acts on firm & fast grnd.
1178 **ALPHILDA** 8 [18] B W Hills 3-9-7 (77) M Hills 6/1: 20-003: 3 gr f Ezzoud - Desert Delight (Green 3 74
Desert) Mid-div, styd on fnl 2f, nvr troubled ldrs: tchd 8/1, top-weight: acts on firm & gd/soft grnd.
1138 **BAJAN BELLE** 11 [11] M Johnston 3-9-5 (75) D Holland 16/1: 31-004: Prom, rdn ent fnl 2f, ¾ 70
unable to qckn: gets 6f, sole win at 5f: see 1138.
994 **WATERGRASSHILL** 23 [10] 3-8-1 (57) G Bardwell 10/1: 4-5205: In tch, hard rdn appr fnl 1f, kept 1 49
on cl-home, unable to chall: return to 7f may suit now, handles firm grnd, gd & equitrack: see 852.
1082 **CIBENZE** 3 [7] 3-8-9 (65) S Drowne 20/1: 653-06: Chsd ldrs, eff appr fnl 1f, same pace: prob stays 6f. shd 57
905 **POP SHOP** 31 [3] 3-9-5 (75) A McGlone 25/1: 62-007: Al mid-div: longer trip, slowly coming to hand. hd 66
1205 **SIRENE** 7 [17] 3-8-5 (60)(bl) (1ow) D Harrison 20/1: 2-0208: Slow into stride, late gains, nvr a threat. 1¾ 47
1125 **NIGHT DIAMOND** 11 [1] 3-9-5 (75) A Nicholls (3) 14/1: 530-09: Slow away, not much room 2f out, hd 61
nvr nr ldrs: poorly drawn, stiffer trk may suit: see 1125.
1061 **FRAMPANT** 14 [5] 3-8-9 (65) Martin Dwyer 25/1: 2-4300: In tch, w wide prog 2f out, fdd bef dist: 10th. nk 50
3921} **DANCING LILY** 243 [6] 3-7-10 (52)(3oh) R Brisland (5) 33/1: 5000-0: Wide, nvr a factor: 11th ¾ 35
on reapp/h'cap bow: unplcd juv (mdn auct, rtd 61$): with J Bridger, poor low draw here.
4018} **MISS FLIRTATIOUS** 238 [8] 3-8-8 (64) L Dettori 11/1: 4002-0: In tch till 2f out, btn & bmpd dist, nk 46
eased: 12th: rnr-up '99 start (vis, fill nurs, rtd 64, auct mdn, rtd 70): eff at 5/6f on fast & gd grnd.
1098 **JAMES STARK** 13 [16] 3-9-6 (76)(vis) J Mongan (5) 10/1: 6-0000: Front rank till wknd ent fnl 2f: 13th. hd 57
4355} **TINSEL WHISTLE** 214 [9] 3-9-6 (76) P Robinson 12/1: 1426-0: Mid-div till 2f out: 18th: '99 Yarmouth
wnr (2 sells, rtd 76): eff forcing the pace over a sharp 5/6f on firm & gd, likes Yarmouth: best without blnks.
744 **Muffin Man** 49 [4] 3-8-7 (63) R Hills 20/1: 3863} **Sea Haze** 248 [13] 3-9-4 (74) M Roberts 16/1:
4082} **Princess Aurora** 234 [2] 3-8-2 (58) R Mullen 16/1: 4380} **Ribbon Lake** 213 [20] 3-9-2 (72) S Whitworth 16/1:
887 **An Jolien** 33 [12] 3-8-4 (60) M Baird 14/1:
19 ran Time 1m 12.4 (2.1) (Michael F B Peart) B J Meehan Upper Lambourn, Berks.

1290 7.05 SUNLEY EBF COND STKS 2YO (B) 5f **Firm 08 -04 Slow**
£7308 £2772 £1386 £630

*984 **CERTAIN JUSTICE** 25 [6] P F I Cole 2-9-1 K Fallon 8/11 FAV: 11: 2 gr c Lit de Justice - Pure Misk 108+
(Rainbow Quest) Made all, drew clr under a tight rein ins last, easily: hvly bckd over evens, fair juv time:
earlier made a winning debut at Newmarket (mdn): 36,000gns Mar foal, half-brother to wnrs over 7/10f: eff at
5f, sure to get further: acts on firm & soft grnd, stiff or sharp trk: runs well fresh: likes to force the
pace: v useful & well regarded 2yo who will prove hard to beat in chosen Royal Ascot engagement.
*849 **THREEZEDZZ** 35 [5] J G Portman 2-8-13 Pat Eddery 12/1: 12: 2 ch c Emarati - Exotic Forest (Dominion) 5 91
Cl-up, ch appr fnl 1f, easily outpcd by wnr: op 8/1: not disgraced, cght a tartar: goes goes on firm & gd grnd.
1079 **SILCA LEGEND** 14 [1] M R Channon 2-8-11 S Drowne 7/2: 23: 2 ch c Efisio - Silca Cisa (Hallgate) nk 88
Prom, rdn appr fnl 1f, same pace: well bckd from 5/1: nds a return to mdns, prob handles firm & gd/soft grnd.
*1059 **PARTY CHARMER** 14 [7] C E Brittain 2-8-10 P Robinson 7/1: 14: Trkd ldrs, shkn up & btn appr ¾ 85
fnl 1f, saddle slipped: bckd tho' op 4/1, clr rem: prob worth another chance after 1059 (soft grnd fill mdn).
-- **SMITH AND WESTERN** [4] 2-8-8 L Newman 33/1: 5: Dwelt, in tch till ent fnl 2f: highly tried on debut: 6 68
6,200gns Factual Mar foal, half-brother to a hdles wnr & a wnr abroad: dam got 2m, sire a sprinter: with R Hannon.
-- **FOCUSED ATTRACTION** [2] 2-8-8 R Hughes 14/1: 6: Dwelt, nvr in it: op 8/1, stablemate 5th: 3 59
20,000gns Eagle Eyed Apr foal, half-brother to 7 wnrs, notably mid-dist/stayer Il Principe, dam 6f wnr.
-- **PAULAS PRIDE** [3] 2-8-3 M Baird 50/1: 7: Struggled thr'out: highly tried on debut: 8,500gns 3½ 45
Pivotal Apr foal, half-sister to 3 wnrs, dam got mid-dists, sire a sprinter: with M Ryan.
7 ran Time 59.4 (0.6) (The Blenheim Partnership) P F I Cole Whatcombe, Oxon.

1291 7.35 LISTED CORAL EUROBET STKS 3YO+ (A) **1m67y rnd Firm 08 +10 Fast**
£14885 £4580 £2290 £1145 3 yo rec 13lb

703 **SWALLOW FLIGHT** 53 [6] G Wragg 4-9-2 M Roberts 4/1: 124-21: 4 b c Bluebird - Mirage (Red Sunset) 114
Cl-up, pshd into lead appr fnl 1f, hard prsd ins last & had to be drvn out, gamely: fast time, tchd 5/1, 8 wk abs:
'99 wnr at York (h'cap) & Doncaster (stks, rtd 106c at best): plcd in '98: eff at 1m, stays 10f: acts on firm &
gd/soft grnd, any trk: can force the pace: tough, v useful & improving, shld win a Group race abroad.
1634} **KALANISI** 352 [8] Sir Michael Stoute 4-9-7 K Fallon 2/1 FAV: 111-2: 4 b c Doyoun - Kalamba (Green ½ 117
Dancer) In tch, niggled halfway, rdn bef dist, kept on well, not btn far: hvly bckd on reapp: unbtn in 3 for
L Cumani last term, at Folkestone (mdn), Newmarket (stks, rtd 112) & Kempton (List): eff at 1m: acts on firm
& soft grnd, any trk: runs well fresh: smart comeback beating wnr 5lbs: should win a Group race, probably at 10f.
768 **SHOWBOAT** 51 [6] B W Hills 6-9-2 M Hills 9/2: 10-063: 6 b h Warning - Boathouse (Habitat) nk 111
Prom, eff to press wnr appr fnl 1f, held towards fin: op 11/4, clr rem, 7 wk abs: ran to best back in trip.
764 **IFTITAH** 51 [1] Saeed bin Suroor 4-9-2 L Dettori 10/3: /5-324: Set good clip, hdd appr fnl 1f, no extra 4 103
& eased towards fin: well bckd from 5/1, 7 wk abs: gets 1m but has plenty of pace & will do better back at 7f.
967 **SERGEANT YORK** 26 [5] 4-9-2 J F Egan 100/1: 300-05: Bhd & struggled to go pace till went past 1 101$
btn horses ins last: highly tried, surely flattered again: dual '99 rnr-up (class stks, rtd 94): juv wnr at Hamilton
(auct mdn, rtd 94 at best): eff at 1m, tried 10f: acts on any grnd: with C Smith.
-- **NOBELIST** [2] 5-9-2 T E Durcan 25/1: 1234/6: Held up, nvr pace to chall: 2 yr abs, not given a hard ¾ 99
time on Brit bow: ex-French, 3rd in a Gr 3 in '98 (rtd 101, A Fabre): prev term won at M-Laffitte: eff at 1m/9f,
bred to apprec mid-dists: acts on gd & soft grnd: with C Brittain.
4501} **SPORTING LAD** 203 [7] 4-9-2 R Hughes 14/1: 0405-7: Keen, al bhd: not persevered with on reapp: 1 97
'99 Chester wnr (h'cap, rtd 103, List 4th, rtd 109): '98 wnr again at Chester (mdn, rtd 101): eff at 7/7.5f on
firm & gd grnd: goes on any trk but loves forcing the pace on sharp ones, esp Chester: useful, with P Cole.
1112 **CARDIFF ARMS** 12 [4] 6-9-2 R Hills 12/1: 130-28: Chsd ldrs, rdn/btn 2f out: stable yet to hit top gear. hd 97
8 ran Time 1m 42.1 (u0.2) (Mollers Racing) G Wragg Newmarket

WINDSOR   MONDAY MAY 15TH   Sharp Fig 8 Track

1292   8.05 LAING HCAP 3YO 0-70 (E)   1m3f135y Firm 08 -16 Slow   [76]
£3237   £925   £462

934   **FANFARE 28** [14] G A Butler 3-9-1 (63) L Dettori 15/2: 50-01: 3 b f Deploy - Tashinsky (Nijinsky)   70
Held up, hdwy under press ent fnl 2f, kept on well to lead below dist despite hanging left/flashing tail, readily:
op 6/1, h'cap bow: rtd 70 as a juv: clrly apprec step up to 12f on firm grnd, shapes like a thoro' styr: well placed.
1094   **MILLIONS 13** [12] Sir Michael Stoute 3-8-13 (61) K Fallon 5/2 FAV: 000-52: 3 b g Bering - Miznah   1½ 64
(Sadler's Wells) Held up, prog after 6f, imprvd to chall appr fnl 1f, not pace of wnr: hvly bckd: apprec
this step up to 12f: goes on firm & gd grnd: shld win soon.
937   **BORDER RUN 28** [11] B J Meehan 3-8-11 (59) R Hughes 25/1: 6-5003: 3 b g Missed Flight - Edraianthus   ½ 61
(Windjammer) Tried to make all, hdd ent fnl 1f, onepce: clr rem: back to form forcing the pace: stays 12f on fm/fast.
1075   **RED CANYON 14** [20] M L W Bell 3-9-1 (63) A Beech (5) 8/1: 00-244: Trkd ldrs, rdn & switched left 2f   3½ 61
out, onepace dist: nicely bckd from 11/1: gd run over lngr 11.5f trip, 10f may prove ideal: handles firm & gd/sft.
933   **GOOD FRIDAY 28** [18] 3-9-5 (67) S Whitworth 20/1: 530-65: Prom, hard rdn appr fnl 2f, unable to qckn: ¾ 64
bred to apprec this longer 11.5f trip, probably on an easier surface: see 933.
1096   **TWOS BETTER 13** [15] 3-8-12 (60) I Mongan (5) 16/1: 00-036: Sn cl-up & ev ch till rdn & went left   ½ 56
ent fnl 2f, ended up in centre: op 12/1: given a less than inspired ride, capable of better: see 1096 (C/D, gd/sft).
1022   **WADENHOE 21** [16] 3-8-12 (60) S Drowne 25/1: 000-67: Cl-up, ch 2f out, fdd under press: bred   1¼ 54
to get nothing back, may need softer grnd: see 1022.
*882   **SHAMAN 33** [4] 3-8-12 (60) N Callan 16/1: 41-218: Al in mid-div: lngr trip: see 882 (sand seller).   hd 54
937   **BARROW 28** [1] 3-9-4 (66) Pat Eddery 11/4: 034-09: Bhd, moderate late gains: hvly bckd back   hd 59
on faster grnd: lks v onepaced, shapes like further & a more galloping trk will suit: see 937.
1075   **KATHAKALI 14** [5] 3-9-3 (65) Martin Dwyer 16/1: 211100: In tch, rdn 2f out, no impress: 10th,   nk 58
yet to translate AW form to turf & this longer 11.5f trip not sure to suit: see 880.
1238   **CROSS DALL 4** [10] 3-8-12 (60) J F Egan 16/1: 3-3100: Nvr a factor: 11th, qck reapp, see 1096 (g/s).   1 52
1096   **THE FROG QUEEN 13** [7] 3-8-9 (57) D Holland 14/1: 01-040: Chsd ldrs, chall 3f out, btn 1f out: 12th: 1 48
3786]   **LEES FIRST STEP 252** [17] 3-9-2 (64) P Doe 33/1: 0020-0: Al bhd: 13th, reapp: '99 rnr-up (auct   5 50
mdn, rtd 69): eff at 7f on fast grnd: with P Murphy.
1064   Cosmic Buzz 14 [9] 3-8-10 (58) M Roberts 33/1:   395   Tormentoso 111 [8] 3-9-6 (68) A Daly 25/1:
1199   Cypress Creek 7 [2] 3-8-8 (56) Dane O'Neill 33/1:   701   Golden Rod 53 [13] 3-9-7 (69) M Hills 20/1:
815   Bolder Alexander 42 [3] 3-8-4 (52) N Pollard 40/1:   937   Maiysha 28 [19] 3-8-5 (53) A Clark 50/1:
1054   Woodbastwick Charm 16 [6] 3-8-6 (54) G Bardwell 33/1:
20 ran   Time 2m 28.6 (2.8)   (T D Holland-Martin)   G A Butler Blewbury, Oxon.

1293   8.35 SAVILL MED AUCT MDN 3YO (E)   1m2f Firm 08 -05 Slow
£3255   £930   £465

1099   **GIVE THE SLIP 13** [6] Mrs A J Perrett 3-9-0 Pat Eddery 4/5 FAV: 34-31: 3 b c Slip Anchor - Falafil   94
(Fabulous Dancer) Made all, drew clr fnl 2f, easily: hvly bckd, overdue success: ran well both '99 starts (hot
Newmarket mdn, rtd 94): suited by step up to 10f, shld get 12f: acts on firm & gd/soft grnd, prob any trk:
outclassed this field from the front today, can hold his own in better company: potentially useful colt.
4165]   **SOLO FLIGHT 228** [10] B W Hills 3-9-0 M Hills 7/2: 45-2: 3 gr c Mtoto - Silver Singer (Pharly)   10 78
Chsd ldrs, switched to chase wnr appr fnl 2f, sn no impress: reapp: promise both '99 mdn starts (rtd 91):
bred to apprec mid-dists, brother to stayer Busy Flight: h'caps next on the agenda & shld be kept in mind.
--   **MEMPHIS TEENS** [5] J R Jenkins 3-9-0 A McGlone 50/1: 3: 3 b c Rock City - Minteen (Teenoso)   6 69
Struggling till went past btn horses fnl 2f: debut, op 25/1: moderately bred, glimmer of promise.
4523]   **LION GUEST 201** [7] G G Margarson 3-9-0 P Robinson 10/1: 00-4: Well plcd till wknd qckly 2f out: 4 63
reapp, h'cap qualifying run, op 16/1: promise fnl '99 start (mdn, rtd 79): bred to apprec 10f.
1082   **THIRTY SIX CEE 13** [3] 3-8-9 J Tate 50/1: 000-05: Prom till 3f out: longer trip, needs sellers, see 171.   ½ 55
--   **ZERO GRAVITY** [12] 3-9-0 A Daly 40/1: 6: Nvr better than mid-div: debut: Cosmonaut first foal.   3 57
--   **VICTORIAN LADY** [8] 3-8-9 R Mullen 33/1: 7: Pulled hard in tch till 3f out: debut: Old Vic   ½ 51
half-sister to couple minor wnrs: with R Cowell.
1204   **SILVER SPOON 7** [13] 3-8-9 A Rawlinson 50/1: 008: Chsd ldrs 6f, qck reapp.   3 47
1200   **LORD ALASKA 7** [4] 3-9-0 S Whitworth 40/1: 09: Dwelt, al bhd: qck reapp: Sir Harry Lewis colt.   1 50
884   **ADRIANA 33** [11] 3-8-9 N Esler (5) 50/1: 000: Handy till 3f out: 10th.   1½ 43
--   **ROSAKER** [2] 3-9-0 L Dettori 7/2: W: Withdrawn start: Pleasant Tap colt, related to wnrs in the States.   0
4460]   Northern Life 207 [9] 3-8-9 J F Egan 50/1:   --   Wensum Dancer [15] 3-8-9 N Pollard 25/1:
1200   Habiba 7 [1] 3-8-9 (bl) G Faulkner (3) 50/1:
14 ran   Time 2m 06.0 (1.3)   (John E Bodie)   Mrs A J Perrett Pulborough, W.Sussex.

REDCAR   MONDAY MAY 15TH   Lefthand, Flat, Galloping Track

Official Going   GOOD/FIRM (GOOD in places back straight). Stalls: Str - Stands Side; Rem - Inside.

1294   2.00 CROW'S NEST NOV MED AUCT STKS 2YO (F)   5f   Firm 04 -22 Slow
£2299   £657   £328

*1136   **BEVERLEY MACCA 11** [6] A Berry 2-8-11 G Carter 2/1: 2211: 2 ch f Piccolo - Kangra Valley (Indian   80
Ridge) Led over 2f out, kept on well ins last, v cmftbly: val 4L+, well bckd: recently won at W'hampton (auct,
easily): v eff at 5f, shld stay further: acts on firm & fibresand, handles hvy & any trk: progressing v well.
989   **FANTASY BELIEVER 23** [7] J J Quinn 2-8-12 A Culhane 7/4 FAV: 2-32: 2 b g Sure Blade - Delicious   2 73
(Dominion) Handy, rdn 2f out, kept on despite edging left appr fnl 1f, not pace of wnr: handles firm & hvy.
1130   **ARRAN MIST 11** [8] D W Barker 2-8-7 F Lynch 20/1: 03: 2 b f Alhijaz - Saraswati (Mansingh)   1¼ 65
In tch, eff 2f out, onepace for press: imprvd for debut on this firm grnd & further will suit: see 1130.
--   **ALPHACALL** [5] T D Easterby 2-8-7 R Winston 9/1: 4: Chsd ldrs, rdn & no extra over 1f out: 2 59
Mar 1st foal, cost 4,000 gns: dam 1m/chase wnr: bred to need 6f+ in time.
1131   **DISPOL CHIEFTAN 11** [1] 2-8-12 W Supple 8/1: 055: Led till over 2f out, wknd over 1f out: needs sells.   ¾ 62
1102   **HAMASKING 12** [2] 2-8-7 K Darley 12/1: 66: Cl-up, wknd 2f out: see 1102.   1¼ 53
865   **DISGLAIR 34** [9] 2-8-7 J Fanning 33/1: 07: Chsd ldrs, btn halfway: Mar foal, cheaply bought.   1½ 49

-- **MISTER SANDERS** [10] 2-8-12 Dean McKeown 9/1: 8: Slow away & al bhd on debut: op 7/1: May *1¾* **50**
foal, half-brother to sev wng sprinters: dam 5f juv scorer: with R Whitaker.

-- **FAST BUCK** [4] 2-8-12 G Duffield 14/1: 9: Slow away & al bhd on debut: Apr foal, cost 15,000 gns. *¾* **48**

1146 **I GOT RHYTHM 10** [3] 2-8-9(2ow) C Teague 50/1: 00: Slow away & al well bhd: May foal: dam 12f wnr. *2½* **38**

10 ran Time 57.8 (1.3) (Alan Berry) A Berry Cockerham, Lancs.

1295

2.30 CLASSIC BOXES MDN 3YO (D) 1m2f Firm 04 -18 Slow
£2936 £839 £419

850 **BUCKMINSTER 35** [2] J H M Gosden 3-9-0 K Darley 4/9 FAV: 4-31: 3 br c Silver Hawk - Buckarina **88**
(Buckaroo) Made all, clr over 2f out, hands-&-heels, cmftbly: well bckd: rtd 83 when 4th on sole '99 start:
stays 10f, 12f looks sure to suit: acts on firm & gd grnd: useful, going the right way.

1054 **LUXOR 16** [4] H R A Cecil 3-9-0 W Ryan 2/1: 42: 3 ch c Grand Lodge - Escrime (Sharpen Up) *4* **80**
Keen cl-up, chsd wnr halfway, onepace final 2f: bckd tho' op 13/8: acts on firm & gd/soft: clr of rem.

3189} **LITTLE DOCKER 283** [6] T D Easterby 3-9-0 R Winston 12/1: 4-3: 3 b g Vettori - Fair Maid Of Kent *8* **70**
(Diesis) Chsd wnr to halfway, btn over 3f out: op 9/1: rtd 76 when 4th on sole juv start: dam miler:
eff at 7f, should stay at least 1m: acts on gd grnd.

972 **BALDAQUIN 26** [1] J H M Gosden 3-9-0 R Havlin 14/1: -04: Missed break & lost arnd 12L, stumbled *nk* **70**
after 2f, some late gains: longer priced stablemate of wnr: will go much closer with better stalls exit, see 972.

2632} **ALBARDEN 308** [5] 3-9-0 W Supple 33/1: 40-5: In tch, btn over 4f out: rtd 74 when 4th on 1st of only *13* **52**
2 starts: half-brother to wnrs over 6/12f: eff at 7f, should stay further: handles fast grnd.

1159 **GENERAL DOMINION 9** [3] 3-9-0 P Bradley (5) 66/1: 005: Keen in tch, btn 4f out: see 902. *5* **44**

6 ran Time 2m 04.5 (2.2) (Sheikh Mohammed) J H M Gosden Manton, Wilts.

1296

3.00 FAITHFUL HCAP 3YO+ 0-65 (F) 1m str Firm 04 -01 Slow **[63]**
£3211 £988 £494 £247 3 yo rec 13lb 2 Groups merged over 1f out

1196 **DERRYQUIN 7** [8] P L Gilligan 5-9-3 (52)(bl) D O'Donohoe 16/1: 400-01: 5 b g Lion Cavern - Top Berry **58**
(High Top) In tch in centre, eff 2f out, styd on to lead ins last, kept on, rdn out: unplcd in '99 (rtd 56 at best,
first time blnks): rtd 81 in '98: '97 wnr at Lingfield (mdn) & Doncaster (stks, rtd 100): suited by 1m on firm,
gd/soft & any trk: wears blnks now & has slipped right down the weights.

4570} **QUIDS INN 196** [2] T D Easterby 3-8-3 (51) P Fessey 20/1: 0000-2: 3 br g Timeless Times - Waltz On Air *1¾* **54**
(Doc Marten) Chsd ldrs centre, effort to chall inside last, not pace of wnr on reapp: unplcd as a juv (rtd
73 at best): stays 1m, handles firm/fast & a gall trk.

1086 **TEMPRAMENTAL 13** [17] S R Bowring 4-8-10 (45) Dean McKeown 16/1: 225333: 4 ch f Midhish - Musical *1* **46**
Horn (Music Boy) Cl-up centre, ev ch 3f out till no extra ins last: 1 win in 30 starts: see 1086 (10f, gd/soft, 859).

1113 **MELODIAN 12** [16] M Brittain 5-9-13 (62)(bl) D Mernagh (3) 9/1: 023104: Handy centre, onepcd *½* **62**
over 1f out: best at 7f as in 1011 (made all).

438 **SING CHEONG 103** [23] 4-9-6 (55) R Cochrane 20/1: 43-044: Led stands side group, no impress final *dht* **55**
1f: 3 mth abs & handles firm & equitrack: probably stays 1m: see 8.

1517} **WONDERFUL MAN 357** [1] 4-9-4 (53) R Winston 20/1: -460-6: Handy centre, led 2f out till hdd & *shd* **53**
wknd inside last: reapp: in '99 trained by M J Heaton Ellis, rtd 56 at best: stays 1m on firm & gd.

1101 **MUTABARI 12** [26] 6-8-8 (43) J Fanning 14/1: 040047: Cl-up stands side, rdn over 2f out, late gains. *1* **41**

1100 **KOCAL 13** [6] 4-8-5 (40) N Carlisle 20/1: 0-2508: Prom centre, wknd appr final 1f: mdn, see 584. *¾* **36**

1007 **A DAY ON THE DUB 21** [28] 7-8-12 (47) J P Spencer 12/1: 5-6449: Bhd stands side, some late gains. *shd* **43**

4593} **TORNADO PRINCE 194** [21] 5-9-12 (61) W Supple 14/1: 1000-0: Bhd stands side, no impress final 2f *½* **56**
on reapp: 10th: '99 scorer at Ripon, Thirsk & Pontefract (sells & sell h'caps, rtd 67): '98 Folkestone wnr
(h'cap, with N Callaghan): suited by 1m, stays 9.5f on gd & firm & any trk: will enjoy a return to sell grade.

1257 **CYRAN PARK 3** [12] 4-8-13 (48) T Williams 16/1: 0-0400: Held up centre, no impress over 2f out. *2* **39**

687 **OUT OF SIGHT 59** [15] 6-9-11 (60) K Darley 5/1 FAV: -21030: Al bhd centre: 12th: abs, btr 687. *¾* **49**

4342} **TROPICAL BEACH 215** [10] 7-9-1 (50)(vis) F Norton 12/1: 0004-0: Bhd, short of room 2f out, nrst *1* **37**
fin: 13th: reapp: in '99 scored at Newmarket & Lingfield (appr h'caps, rtd 52): '98 wnr at W'hampton (3,
h'caps, rtd 73a): eff at 5/6f, now suited by 7.5/9.5f: acts on firm & gd/soft, loves fibresand & any trk,
esp W'hampton: eff in blnks/visor & has run well fresh: best held up: will do better.

1254 **THATCHED 3** [25] 10-8-10 (45) W Ryan 11/1: 246-50: Nvr a factor stands side: 14th: qck reapp. *shd* **32**

1190 **KNAVES ASH 8** [9] 9-9-0 (49) G Duffield 33/1: 23-000: Al bhd stands side: 15th: see 1190. *nk* **35**

800 **HONG KONG 46** [7] 3-7-13 (47)(tbl) Dale Gibson 14/1: 002-00: Overall ldr centre till 2f out, wknd: *¾* **31**
16th: abs: rnr-up on fnl '99 start (sell nursery h'cap, rtd 47): stays 1m on firm & best run in first time blnks.

4574} **SWINGING THE BLUES 196** [22] 6-9-7 (56)(tvi) M Fenton 8/1: 4012-0: Al bhd stands side: 17th. *1¾* **36**

4459} **Scarlet Livery 207** [11] 4-9-5 (54) K Hodgson 33/1: 3862} **Silver Secret 248** [20] 6-8-5 (40) A Culhane 16/1:
1039 **Shaanxi Romance 17** [18] 5-9-0 (49) M Tebbutt 20/1: 4451} **Raased 208** [29] 8-8-7 (42)(t) P Goode (3) 33/1:
4002} **Altay 239** [4] 3-9-0 (62) P Hanagan (7) 16/1: 1258 **Pipiji 3** [19] 5-8-0 (35) A Mackay 16/1:
648 **Nice Balance 70** [24] 5-8-2 (37) Joanna Badger(7) 20/1:1133 **Roses Treasure 11** [5] 4-8-8 (43) J Bramhill 33/1:
1207 **My Tyson 7** [13] 5-8-6 (41) F Lynch 16/1: 1256 **Distant King 3** [27] 7-8-5 (33)(7ow) G Arnolda (0) 40/1:
584 **The Nobleman 80** [3] 4-7-11 (32)(t)(1ow)(6oh) N Kennedy 40/1:

28 ran Time 1m 35.2 (0.4) (Lady Bland) P L Gilligan Newmarket.

1297

3.30 TOTE FILLIES HCAP 3YO+ 0-80 (D) 7f str Firm 04 +00 Fast **[73]**
£7702 £2370 £1185 £592 3 yo rec 12lb

930 **MOTHER CORRIGAN 30** [1] M Brittain 4-8-9 (54)(VIS) D Mernagh (3) 33/1: 046-01: 4 gr f Paris House - **58**
Missed Opportunity (Exhibitioner) Made all, edged right fnl 2f but kept on well for press, just held on: fair time:
trained by L Cumani in '99 (mdn, rtd 69): enjoyed forcing tactics over this gall 7f on firm & enjoyed visor.

4435} **TOUS LES JOURS 209** [4] J S Goldie 4-9-1 (60) A Culhane 11/1: 0440-2: 4 b f Dayjur - Humility *shd* **63**
(Cox's Ridge) Cl-up, eff to chall over 1f out, kept on ins last, just held: in '99 trained by M Johnston, busy,
won at Catterick (class stks, rtd 65): '98 wnr at Beverley (rtd 76): eff arnd 7f/1m on fm, hvy & on any trk:
best without blnks: tough, fine reapp.

*1035 **DIVERS PEARL 17** [14] J R Fanshawe 3-9-5 (76) R Cochrane 9/4 FAV: 63-213: 3 b f Prince Sabo - Seek *¾* **77**
The Pearl (Rainbow Quest) Chsd ldrs, eff over 1f out, kept on inside last: gd run, see 1035 (mdn auct).

1196 **CORNDAVON 7** [7] M L W Bell 4-9-7 (66) M Fenton 9/1: 00-204: Chsd ldrs, effort to chall appr *½* **66**
final 1f, kept on same pace: stays 7f: see 960.

-1082 **MY TESS 13** [12] 4-9-8 (67) K Darley 7/1: 132425: In tch, kept on same pace for press over 1f out: *nk* **66**
handles firm, soft & fibresand, probably hvy: see 588.

1070 **TYPHOON GINGER 14** [8] 5-9-1 (60) F Norton 14/1: 243-66: Slowly away, bhd, swtchd right & kept on   ¾   57
over 1f out, nrst fin: encouraging run over an inadequate trip: mdn, but should go closer over further next time.
1213 **MILADY LILLIE 6** [21] 4-8-10 (55) C Catlin (7) 33/1: 3-6007: Bhd stands side, effort over 2f out,   ½   51
kept on inside last: no dngr: qck reapp: see 1213.
1250 **PERFECT PEACH 4** [10] 5-9-10 (69) J Fanning 25/1: 00-008: Waited with, brief effort 2f out, no impress.   ½   64
*1097 **DENS JOY 13** [6] 4-8-13 (58) M Tebbutt 12/1: -30019: Cl-up till btn over 1f out: btr 1097 (gd/soft).   1½   50
1082 **AMBER BROWN 13** [18] 4-9-0 (59) G Duffield 16/1: 0-0100: Prom, wknd 2f out: 10th, btr 910 (soft, 9f).   ½   50
877 **FLYING CARPET 34** [9] 3-8-1 (58) P Fessey 11/1: 0-0600: Al bhd: 11th: see 759.   1   47
1082 **CARRIE POOTER 13** [16] 4-9-8 (67) J P Spencer 16/1: 5-1600: In tch, btn 2f out: 12th: btr 910, 698.   hd   55
857 **OCEAN SONG 35** [13] 3-8-8 (65)(BL) Dale Gibson 33/1: 24600: In tch, btn over 2f out: 13th, blnkd.   1¼   50
910 **ROUGE ETOILE 31** [19] 4-9-1 (60) W Supple 25/1: 00-000: Al bhd: 14th: see 811.   1¾   42
777 **Blue Line Lady 47** [17] 3-7-13 (56) P Hanagan (7) 20/1:   1201 **Almerina 7** [15] 5-9-7 (66) R Winston 40/1:
1011 **On Till Morning 21** [3] 4-9-3 (62) F Lynch 25/1:   503 **Corn Dolly 93** [11] 4-8-4 (49) W Ryan 14/1:
1082 **Tancred Arms 13** [5] 4-8-9 (54) Kimberley Hart(5) 20/1:1138 **Maid To Love 11** [2] 3-8-5 (62) Dean McKeown 12/1:
4502} **Woore Lass 203** [20] 4-8-8 (53) Kim Tinkler 25/1:
21 ran   Time 1m 22.1 (0.3)   (M Brittain)   M Brittain Warthill, Nth Yorks.

1298   4.00 M MCCLELLAND CLAIMER 3YO+ (F)   6f Firm 04 -09 Slow
£2488   £711   £355   3 yo rec 10lb

1073 **FIRE DOME 14** [14] D Nicholls 8-9-12 F Norton 3/1 FAV: 4-0331: 8 ch g Salt Dome - Penny Habit   68
(Habitat) Outpcd, eff 2f out, strong run to lead on line, drvn out: '99 wnr at Sandown & here at Redcar (clmrs,
rtd 83, rtd 106$ in Gr 2 company): '98 Thirsk (stks) & Sandown wnr (List, rtd 107): stays 7f, suited by 5/6f: acts
on firm, hvy & f/sand: handles any trk, likes Sandown: has tried blnks, best without: 8yo, suited by clmg grade.
1068 **ANSELLMAN 14** [2] A Berry 4-9-10 (bl) G Carter 14/1: 300-02: 10 gr g Absalom - Grace Poole   hd   65
(Sallust) In tch, kept on strongly fnl 1f despite edging right, just btn: fine run from this 10yo, on fair mark.
1244 **TANCRED TIMES 4** [3] D W Barker 5-8-7 Kimberley Hart(5) 20/1: 035053: 5 ch m Clantime - Mischievous hd   47
Miss (Niniski) Tried to make all, just picked up on line: just btn in a thrilling fin, qck reapp: fine effort at
today's weights, wld meet today's 1st & 2nd on much better terms in h'caps: see 1244.
1143 **JACKERIN 10** [8] B S Rothwell 5-9-0 (bl) M Fenton 16/1: -65544: Prom, eff ent fnl 1f, not btn far: 1   51$
eff at 6f, poss just best at 5f: knocking on the door: see 1143, 798.
4363} **MAITEAMIA 214** [18] 7-9-8 (bl) K Darley 9/2: 3120-5: Chsd ldrs, kept on under press fnl 1f: btn   hd   58
just over 1L into 5th, reapp: '99 wnr at Southwell (2, AW h'caps, rtd 75a) & Redcar (appr h'cap, rtd 67): eff at
5f, suited by 6f, stays 1m on firm, soft/hvy & fibresand: runs well fresh in blnks: tough, spot-on next time.
*1068 **PRESS AHEAD 14** [5] 5-9-4 (vis) Dean McKeown 6/1: 155016: Prom, no extra cl-home: btn arnd 2L.   ¾   52
1133 **AVONDALE GIRL 11** [17] 4-9-1 F Lynch 7/1: 005007: Rear, imprvd 2f out, no impress inside last.   3   41
1139 **FRENCH GRIT 11** [9] 8-8-12 J P Spencer 16/1: 000608: Rear, late hdwy, nvr nrr: see 1068.   hd   37
790 **SOUND THE TRUMPET 46** [13] 8-8-12 (t) A Mackay 33/1: 060009: Mid-div, late prog, nvr nr ldrs: abs.   shd   37
1207 **INDIAN DANCE 7** [21] 4-8-12 (t) Joanna Badger (7) 33/1: 30-000: Rear, late prog, nvr dngrs in 10th: ¾   35
3rd of 4 at Epsom in '99, rtd 68$): eff at 7f on fast grnd, wears a t-strap: with M C Chapman.
1068 **TRUMPET BLUES 14** [1] 4-9-0 K Hodgson 25/1: -03000: Chsd ldrs, btn dist: 11th, s/mate of wnr.   hd   36
1073 **SOUPERFICIAL 14** [19] 9-9-2 Kim Tinkler 25/1: 100-00: Rear, prog 2f out, nvr nr ldrs: 12th: see 1073.   2½   31
1258 **VENTURE CAPITALIST 3** [6] 11-9-4 F Norton 12/1: 50-00W: Bolted on the way to start, slipped &   0
sadly broke leg, subs destroyed: likeable 11yo, a sad loss to all concerned.
1073 **Another Victim 14** [7] 6-9-0 S Righton 40/1:   1132 **Chok Di 14** [4] 4-8-12 (BL) A Culhane 25/1:
252} **Gad Yakoun 495** [10] 7-9-4 Angela Hartley (7) 40/1:   609 **Just Dissident 76** [11] 8-9-8 M Tebbutt 33/1:
1081 **Blue Sapphire 13** [20] 3-8-0 P Fessey 40/1:   800 **Miller Time 46** [12] 3-8-8 R Winston 20/1:
1133 **Tangerine 11** [16] 3-8-5 Dale Gibson 12/1:   1068 **Bateaur 14** [15] 7-9-2 R Lappin 25/1:
21 ran   Time 1m 09.7 (0.8)   (J M Ranson)   D Nicholls Sessay, Nth Yorks.

1299   4.30 COMERACING.CO.UK HCAP 3YO 0-70 (E)   1m2f Firm 04 -18 Slow   [77]
£2926   £836   £418

1053 **BAILEYS PRIZE 16** [15] M Johnston 3-9-7 (70) J Fanning 16/1: 45-201: 3 ch c Mister Baileys - Mar Mar   79
(Forever Casting) Gd hdwy to lead dist, drifted left, styd on well, pushed out: top weight: promise on both '99
starts (mdns, rtd 74): apprec this step up to 10f on firm, poss handles fibresand, 12f shld suit: gd weight
carrier: lightly rcd & open to further improvement.
1022 **LATE ARRIVAL 21** [13] D Morris 3-8-7 (56) R Cochrane 9/4 FAV: 040-42: 3 b g Emperor Jones - Try   2   61
Vickers (Fuzzbuster) Set pace till 2f out, rallied final 1f but not reach wnr: big gamble from 8/1: eff at
10f on firm grnd, 12f will suit: should sn go one better, see 1022.
4588} **YENALED 194** [12] J S Goldie 3-8-10 (59) A Culhane 16/1: 3563-3: 3 gr g Rambo Dancer - Fancy   ½   63
Flight (Arctic Tern) Rear, prog 2f out, styd on fnl 1f & nrst fin: reapp: plcd sev times in '99 (h'caps, rtd 64
at best): dam wnr over 10f: acts on gd & acts on gd grnd, prob handles soft: eff at 10f, may stay 12f: sharper next time.
883 **ALPHA ROSE 33** [2] M L W Bell 3-8-11 (60) M Fenton 10/1: 6-554: Chsd ldrs till outpcd 3f out,   ¾   62
rallied final 1f: h'cap debut: apprec this lngr 10f trip, may stay further: handles firm grnd: see 729.
4570} **MASTER SODEN 196** [8] 3-8-12 (61) K Lavelle (7) 7/1: 0001-5: Trkd ldr, led 2f out till hdd dist, eased   ¾   62
ins last & caught for 4th: reapp: '99 wnr here at Redcar (nursery h'cap, rtd 60): eff at 1m, will stay 10f: acts
on gd/soft, handles firm: prob in the frame with a stronger ride today & will do better when professionally rdn.
789 **GIVE NOTICE 46** [7] 3-9-1 (64) K Darley 9/2: 60-06: Chsd ldrs, onepcd final 2f: op 11/4, 7 wk sides: 2   62
twice rcd juv, (mdn, rtd 69): half-brother to a couple of wng milers also 12f scorer Tomos:
dam scored over 1m as a 2yo: with J Dunlop, 12f may suit.
1106 **BOLLIN NELLIE 12** [1] 3-8-8 (57) R Winston 14/1: 54-457: Nvr better than mid-div: see 782 (12f).   2   52
4157} **SMUDGER NORTH 229** [10] 3-9-0 (63) J P Spencer 20/1: 0200-8: Chsd ldrs, gradually fdd final 2f: 2   55
reapp: rnr-up at Newcastle in '99 (nov auct, rtd 76): eff at 1m on gd grnd, should stay 10f: with B Rothwell.
1255 **SAN DIMAS 3** [3] 3-8-11 (60)(BL) W Supple 14/1: 0-0069: Dwelt, effort 4f out, nvr nr ldrs: qck   1   51
reapp & tried blnks: see 1255 (1m).
1142 **LE CAVALIER 11** [6] 3-8-5 (54) W Ryan 14/1: 222650: Mid-div, effort 4f out, sn btn: 10th: see 752.   1½   42
1045 **COCO LOCO 17** [5] 3-9-2 (65) F Norton 10/1: 0-600: Rcd keenly in rear, nvr a factor in 11th.   1¾   50
3295} **Stepastray 277** [11] 3-8-5 (54) P Fessey 33/1:   1144 **Dispol Jazz 10** [16] 3-9-5 (68) G Duffield 16/1:
848 **The Walrus 37** [4] 3-8-10 (59) G Carter 12/1:   827 **Loblite Leader 40** [17] 3-8-7 (56) M Tebbutt 16/1:
1085 **Sea Emperor 13** [14] 3-8-4 (53) D Mernagh (3) 12/1:
16 ran   Time 2m 04.5 (2.2)   (Mrs Val Armstrong)   M Johnston Middleham, Nth Yorks.

1300	3.00 FAITHFUL HCAP 3YO+ 0-65 (F) **1m str Firm 04 +13 Fast**		[63]
	£3211 £988 £494 £247 3 yo rec 13lb		

*973 **WERE NOT STOPPIN 26** [7] R Bastiman 5-8-5 (40) W Ryan 16/1: 050511: 5 b g Mystiko - Power Take Off   **50**
(Aragon) Rear, prog halfway, styd on strongly to lead cl-home, drvn out: best time of day: recent Beverley
wnr (sell): eff arnd 1m, has tried further: acts on firm & hvy grnd, handles a gall trk: imprvg gelding.

871 **BOWCLIFFE 34** [3] E J Alston 9-9-5 (54) W Supple 10/1: 043602: 9 b g Petoski - Gwiffina (Welsh   2 **60**
Saint) Mid-div, gd hdwy to chall ent fnl 1f, kept on but not pace of wnr: apprec this return to 1m: see 447 (AW).

1259 **ELLWAY PRINCE 3** [17] M Wigham 5-8-13 (48) Dean McKeown 9/2 FAV: 501143: 5 b g Prince Sabo -   ½ **53**
Star Arrangement (Star Appeal) Led till ins last, no extra: tchd 7/1, qck reapp: sound effort back on turf.

1007 **STYLE DANCER 21** [22] R M Whitaker 6-9-11 (60) J P Spencer 14/1: 330-54: Rear, prog 2f out, kept   1 **63**
on fnl 1f & nrst fin: stays 1m well, possibly best at 6/7f: encouraging effort here, see 1007.

1033 **MISSILE TOE 19** [12] 7-8-10 (45) R Cochrane 10/1: 000-55: Rear, imprvg when short of room 2f out,   1 **46**
styd on fnl 1f but ch had gone: tchd 14/1: little luck in running here, worth another ch, esp at 10f: see 1033.

780 **ONLY FOR GOLD 47** [9] 5-9-7 (56) G Carter 14/1: 336-66: Prom, no extra fnl 1f: 7 wk abs: see 780.   2 **53**

1011 **DOUBLE ACTION 21** [23] 6-10-0 (63) K Darley 14/1: 6-4047: In tch, onepcd final 2f: top weight.   1½ **57**

3570} **FLAXEN PRIDE 264** [10] 5-8-5 (40) A Culhane 14/1: 0156-8: Mid-div, onepcd final 1f: '99 Leicester   ¾ **32**
wnr (fill h'cap, rtd 42): eff at 1m on fast grnd, likes a stiff/gall trk: with Mrs M Reveley.

*1066 **PICCOLO CATIVO 14** [6] 5-9-0 (49) Angela Hartley(7) 12/1: 500-19: Chsd ldrs, eff & ch 2f out, sn btn.   3 **35**

965 **TROIS ELLES 27** [5] 4-8-8 (43) A Mackay 33/1: 3-0360: Nvr better than mid-div: fin 10th: see 596 (sand).   ¾ **27**

1007 **OLLIES CHUCKLE 21** [20] 5-9-1 (50) J Fanning 25/1: 00-600: Nvr a factor in 11th: see 908 (reapp).   ½ **33**

1201 **CONSORT 7** [14] 7-9-7 (56) M Tebbutt 6/1: 000000: Rear, eff 3f out, nvr a factor in 12th: see 1201.   hd **38**

1101 **MUSTANG 12** [16] 7-8-5 (40)(vis) F Norton 16/1: 025030: Prom till wknd fnl 2f: 13th: see 1101.   2 **18**

646 **FLYING HIGH 70** [28] 5-7-10 (31)(bl)(3oh) N Kennedy 33/1: 640300: Nvr better than mid-div: fin 14th: 1¾ **5**
unplcd in a mdn hdle since 646: see 585.

1132 **UP IN FLAMES 11** [4] 9-8-3 (38)(t) G Duffield 14/1: 000020: In tch, eff & btn 3f out: 15th: btr 1132.   hd **11**

126 **Qualitair Survivor 167** [24] 5-7-13 (34) P Fessey 33/1:4066} **Silken Lady 234** [21] 4-8-2 (37) N Carlisle 33/1:
1007 Oriole 21 [13] 7-9-0 (49) Kim Tinkler 25/1:   907 Gymcrak Flyer 31 [26] 9-9-3 (52) R Winston 16/1:
1202 Kuuipo 7 [19] 3-8-6 (54)(t) M Fenton 33/1:   1007 High Sun 21 [8] 4-9-9 (58) F Lynch 14/1:
642 Winston 70 [25] 7-8-2 (37) R Lappin 33/1:   4409} Red September 210 [18] 3-8-7 (55) Dale Gibson 25/1:
4593} Tarradale 194 [1] 6-8-13 (48) K Hodgson 20/1:   1254 State Wind 3 [2] 4-8-0 (35)(vis) T Williams 33/1:
4447} Kingfisher Gold 208 [15] 4-8-11 (46) C Teague 33/1: 907 Bunty 31 [27] 4-8-10 (45) D O'Donohoe 33/1:
1707} College King 348 [11] 4-9-6 (55) D Mernagh (3) 25/1:
28 ran   Time 1m 34.1 (u0.7)   (I B Barker)   R Bastiman Cowthorpe, Nth Yorks.

Official Going   STANDARD. Stalls: Inside except 5f - Outside.

1301	1.45 ITALY HCAP 4YO+ 0-65 (F) **1m6f aw Going 47 -14 Slow**		[63]
	£2261 £646 £323 4 yo rec 1 lb Raced centre - stands side		

1167 **URGENT SWIFT 9** [15] A P Jarvis 7-10-0 (63) D Harrison 14/1: 514401: 7 ch g Beveled - Good Natured   **69a**
(Troy) Held up in tch, prog halfway & led over 2f out, rdn clr inside last & eased nr line: val for 5L+: earlier
won at Southwell (h'cap): '99 scorer at Salisbury & Haydock (rtd 78, plcd on sand, rtd 56a): unplcd in '98 (rtd 54,
h'cap): eff at 12/14f on fibresand, firm & gd, handles gd/soft & any trk, likes Southwell: tried blnks: tough.

860 **MANFUL 35** [5] R Brotherton 8-7-10 (31)(bl)(1oh) J Mackay (7) 10/1: 100302: 8 b g Efisio - Mandrian   3 **30a**
(Mandamus): Dwelt, prog final 3f, kept on, no impress: op 20/1: stays 14f, tried 2m, wng form at 10/12f.

1030 **SPOSA 19** [11] M J Polglase 4-9-12 (62) L Newton 8/1: 024063: 4 b f St Jovite - Barelyabride   shd **61a**
(Blushing Groom): Chsd ldrs wide, rdn/outpcd over 3f out, kept on for press fnl 2f, no threat: see 644.

1203 **BANNERET 7** [12] Miss S J Wilton 7-8-5 (40) P M Quinn (5) 14/1: 053264: Prom, outpcd 4f out, late   ¾ **38a**
gains for press: stays 14f: see 347 (12f, clmr).

918 **WESTERN COMMAND 30** [14] 4-9-9 (59) R Fitzpatrick (3) 9/1: 034645: Cl-up halfway, ch 2f out, no extra.   ½ **56a**

1203 **WAFIR 7** [3] 8-9-5 (54)(vis) K Fallon 2/1 FAV: 6-4326: Chsd ldrs, led 6f out till over 2f out, fdd fnl 1f: 7 **41a**
well bckd: trainer reported gelding moved feelingly after the race: see 1203, 1145 & 822.

855 **STEAMROLLER STANLY 35** [13] 7-9-11 (60) S Sanders 14/1: 246007: Chsd ldrs 10f: tchd 16/1:   3½ **42a**
jockey reported that gelding hung left throughout: see 380, 151.

1194 **ELSIE BAMFORD 8** [7] 4-8-2 (38) K Dalgleish (7) 8/1: 006-38: Held up, no impress: op 7/1: see 1194.   2½ **16a**

797 **ST LAWRENCE 46** [6] 6-8-13 (48) T E Durcan 8/1: 213309: Sn rdn mid-div, btn 3f out: op 6/1: jmps fit.   1½ **24a**

1039} **SHEPHERDS REST 383** [9] 8-8-11 (46) A Daly 11/1: 2320-0: Held up, eff halfway, btn 4f out: 10th: 10 **11a**
op 8/1, jumps fit (clmr, rtd 114c, h'cap): plcd 4 out of 5 starts in '99 (h'caps, rtd 40a & 39): eff arnd 12f/15.4f
on fibresand, gd/soft & hvy grnd: best without a visor: still a mdn on the level.

835 **KI CHI SAGA 38** [10] 8-7-11 (32)(bl)(1ow)(7oh) A Nicholls (0) 33/1: 600440: Led 1m, sn btn: 14th.   0a

482 **Nubile 97** [4] 6-7-10 (31)(tbl)(5oh) J Lowe 25/1:   608 Notation 76 [1] 6-7-10 (31)(13oh) Claire Bryan (5) 40/1:
642 Bobona 70 [2] 4-7-10 (32)(9oh) G Baker (7) 25/1:   3349} Courtledge 276 [8] 5-8-7 (42) J Carroll 11/1:
15 ran   Time 3m 08.3 (8.5)   (A P Jarvis)   A P Jarvis Aston Upthorpe, Oxon.

1302	2.15 SPAIN CLAIMER 2YO (F) **5f aw str Going 47 -09 Slow**	
	£2191 £626 £313	

*928 **UHOOMAGOO 20** [7] D Nicholls 2-8-12 K Fallon 4/5 FAV: -211: 2 b c Namaqualand - Point Of Law   **76a**
(Law Society): Sn handy, rdn/duelled with rnr-up from over 1f out, styd on well for press to narrowly prevail, all-
out: well bckd: earlier scored at Thirsk (clmr, rtd 76, earlier trained by R Fahey): eff at 5f, half-brother to a
7f wnr, should get further: acts on gd, soft & fibresand: handles a sharp/gall trk & enjoys sell/clmg grade.

1189 **ORANGE TREE LAD 8** [8] A Berry 2-8-12 J Carroll 7/2: -0232: 2 b g Tragic Role - Adorable Cherub   hd **75a**
(Halo): Handy, rdn/led 2f out, jnd by wnr & duelled inside last, just held: op 5/2: clr of rem: claimed for
£10,000: acts on fast, soft & fibresand: also bhd this wnr in 928: shld win similar soon.

974 **TIME MAITE 26** [1] M W Easterby 2-9-0 G Parkin 8/1: 43: 2 b g Komaite - Martini Time (Ardoon):   5 **63a**
Prom, rdn/outpcd by front pair final 1f: op 5/1: see 974.

SOUTHWELL (Fibresand) MONDAY MAY 15TH Lefthand, Sharp, Oval Track

-- **AMELIA** [3] J Cullinan 2-8-2 P M Quinn (5) 20/1: 4: Chsd ldrs, outpcd halfway, late gains, no threat: *shd* 51a
General Monash filly, Mar foal, 4,000 gns 2yo, first foal: dam a half-sister to sev wnrs, sire a speedy juvenile.
1136 **JOHN FOLEY 11** [4] 2-8-11 P Fitzsimons (5) 9/1: -0025: Prom & led halfway, sn hdd/fdd: op 7/1. 1 58a
755 **HOPGROVE 48** [5] 2-8-3 G Bardwell 14/1: 66: Led till halfway, rdn/wknd qckly: op 10/1, 7 wk abs. 8 35a
-- **CHILLI BOY** [6] 2-8-10 S Finnamore (5) 40/1: 7: Outpcd: Belfort gelding, Mar foal: sire smart at 7/9f. 5 33a
-- **MARKING TIME** [9] 2-9-0 N Callan 14/1: 8: Al outpcd: op 10/1: Goldmark gelding, Apr foal, cost 4 29a
10,000 gns: half-brother to an Italian juv wnr, dam unrcd: sire high-class French juv 1m performer: with K R Burke.
-- **TINY MIND** [2] 2-8-7 N Pollard 40/1: 9: Slowly away & al rear: Factual colt, Mar first foal: dam 13 0a
a lightly rcd mdn: sire a speedy/smart juv: with Miss A Stokell.
9 ran   Time 1m 0.6 (2.8)   (The David Nicholls Racing Club)   D Nicholls Sessay, Nth Yorks.

1303 2.45 FRANCE FILLIES HCAP 3YO+ 0-70 (E)   1m aw rnd Going 47 -01 Slow   [68]
£2756   £848   £424   £212   3 yo rec 13lb

1133 **MUJAGEM 11** [9] M W Easterby 4-8-4 (44) G Parkin 14/1: 000/01: 4 br f Mujadil - Lili Bengam (Welsh 47a
Saint): Cl-up halfway, led 3f out, drvn & just held on inside last: op 10/1: AW bow: missed '99: failed to make
the frame between 5f/1m as a juv in '98 (rtd 64): eff over a sharp 1m on fibresand: likes to race with/force the pace.
742 **STRAVSEA 49** [7] R Hollinshead 5-8-12 (52) P M Quinn (5) 5/1 JT FAV: 635042: 5 b m Handsome Sailor - hd 54a
La Stravaganza (Slip Anchor): Held up rear/in tch, rdn/prog wide from 2f out, styd on well inside last, just held.
1235 **MUDDY WATER 4** [5] D Marks 4-8-8 (48) D Harrison 5/1 JT FAV: -01003: 4 b f Salse - Rainbow Fleet 1 48a
(Nomination): Held up, prog/rdn & ch over 1f out, kept on onepace: op 9/2: qck reapp: clr rem: stays 1m well.
299 **CHINABERRY 126** [8] M Brittain 6-8-2 (42) G Bardwell 10/1: 064-04: Chsd ldrs, btn 1f out: 4 mth abs. 8 30a
867 **RED VENUS 34** [3] 4-8-13 (53)(bl) S Sanders 10/1: 533005: Held up, effort halfway, no impress. nk 40a
654 **DULZIE 68** [11] 3-8-0 (53) A Nicholls (3) 8/1: 60-246: Led 5f out till 3f out, fdd: abs: btr 654 (7f). 1¾ 37a
648 **TIME TEMPTRESS 70** [10] 4-9-1 (55) J Weaver 11/1: 506-07: Led after 2f till 5f out, sn btn: op 12/1: 8 27a
10 wk abs: '99 reapp wnr at Newcastle (h'cap, rtd 66): rtd 62 in '98: eff over 1m, tried 10f: acts on fast &
gd/soft grnd, stiff/gall sharpish trk: has run well fresh.
1082 **STRATS QUEST 13** [2] 6-7-10 (36)(2oh) J Mackay (7) 6/1: 010058: Prom/slightly hmpd 3f out, sn btn. 1½ 5a
1202 **MADEMOISELLE PARIS 7** [6] 3-7-10 (49)(6oh) J Lowe 20/1: 00-059: Led 1f, btn 3f out: op 14/1. nk 17a
*1141 **CYBER BABE 11** [4] 3-8-2 (55) L Newman (4) 11/2: 0-0210: Chsd ldrs 6f: 10th: op 4/1: now with 2½ 18a
A Newcombe: btr 1141 (sell, 9f, made all).
4115) **STARBOARD TACK 231** [1] 4-10-0 (68) J Carroll 14/1: 3354-0: Bhd halfway: 11th: op 8/1, AW bow: 1 29a
reapp: plcd twice last term for B W Hills (h'cap, auct mdn): eff arnd 10/12f, handles firm & gd/soft grnd.
11 ran   Time 1m 43.2 (3.8)   (C F Spence)   M W Easterby Sheriff Hutton, Nth Yorks.

1304 3.15 SWEDEN FILLIES AUCT MDN 2YO (F)   5f aw str Going 47 -11 Slow
£2233   £636   £319   Raced centre - stands side

1197 **BROUGHTONS MOTTO 7** [5] W J Musson 2-8-2 L Newton 14/1: 01: 2 b f Mtoto - Ice Chocolate (Icecapade) 68a
Rdn chasing ldrs halfway, drvn to lead ins last, just prevailed, all-out: op 10/1: Apr foal, cost 2,500 gns:
half-sister to 3 wnrs, incl a French 1m wnr: dam well related triple 1m wnr, sire a top class 10/12f performer:
eff at 5f, looks sure to appreciate much further in time: acts on fibresand & a sharp trk.
1067 **MISS VERITY 14** [13] J S Wainwright 2-8-1 C Rutter 4/1 JT FAV: -62: 2 ch f Factual - Ansellady hd 66a
(Absalom) Narrow lead till halfway, rdn/led again over 1f out & hdd inside last, styd on well, just held: op 3/1:
handles fibresand & gd/soft grnd.
1197 **LOVE TUNE 7** [8] K R Burke 2-8-1 R Ffrench 6/1: 53: 2 b f Alhijaz - Heights Of Love (Persian Heights): 1½ 62a
Al prom, rdn/lost pair of front pair inside last: mkt drifter, op 9/2: prob handles fast & fibresand, 6f+ will suit.
1136 **MRS TIGGYWINKLE 11** [1] N P Littmoden 2-8-4 D Young (7) 8/1: 64: In tch halfway, rdn & kept on ¾ 63a
onepace from over 1f out: bckd from 20/1: see 1136.
-- **WHITE STAR LADY** [4] 2-8-0 J Mackay (7) 25/1: 5: Chsd ldrs, outpcd over 1f out: So Factual filly, nk 58a
Apr foal, cost 1,000 gns: half-sister to a wnr abroad: dam a 10f wnr, apprec further in time for J R Weymes.
-- **FRENCH BRAMBLE** [2] 2-8-4 J Edmunds 25/1: 6: Prom 3f: General Monash filly, Apr foal, cost 2 57a
4,700 gns: dam unrcd, sire a speedy/well related juv: with J Balding.
865 **APRIL LEE 34** [3] 2-8-4 (e) T E Durcan 25/1: 67: Chsd ldrs 4f: eye-shield: see 865. shd 57a
1130 **BRIEF STAR 11** [14] 2-8-0 G Bardwell 20/1: -0358: Handy, briefly led halfway till over 1f out, fdd. 10 42a
1197 **BILLIE H 7** [6] 2-8-0 A Nicholls (3) 4/1 JT FAV: 09: Al outpcd: op 7/2: see 1197. nk 41a
1124 **LONDON EYE 11** [7] 2-8-0 L Newman (2) 25/1: 060: Al outpcd: 10th: see 932. 2½ 34a
-- **Worth A Ring** [12] 2-8-1 J Lowe 25/1:   1059 **Jewellery Box 14** [11] 2-8-0 A Daly 25/1:
974 **Tenerife Flyer 26** [9] 2-8-0 P M Quinn (5) 25/1:
13 ran   Time 1m 0.7 (2.9)   (Broughton Bloodstock)   W J Musson Newmarket, Suffolk.

1305 3.45 DENMARK SELLER 3YO+ (G)   7f aw rnd Going 47 -07 Slow
£1939   £554   £277   3 yo rec 13lb

1235 **ABTAAL 4** [9] Mrs N Macauley 10-9-8 (vis) R Fitzpatrick (3) 9/2: 00-601: 10 b g Green Desert - Stufida 52a
(Bustino): Dwelt, chsd ldrs halfway, rdn/prog to lead over 1f out, drvn out to hold on cl-home: op 11/2, no bid:
qck reapp: '99 scorer here at Southwell (sell) & W'hampton (2, clmr & h'cap, rtd 66a at best, rtd 56 on turf): '98
Brighton wnr (2, class stks, R Hodges, also clmr for current stable) & Southwell (clmr, rtd 63a & 63): all wins at
7f, tried further: acts on fast, soft & both AWs, fibresand: handles any trk, loves a sharp one: enjoys sell grade.
310 **SHARP STEEL 125** [7] Miss S J Wilton 5-9-8 C Rutter 9/1: 02-562: 5 ch g Beveled - Shift Over (Night nk 51a
Shift): Prom/led over 5f out, rdn/hdd over 1f out, styd on well, just held: op 7/1, abs: vis omitted after latest.
869 **WAITING KNIGHT 34** [4] Mrs N Macauley 5-9-8 (vis) Sarah Robinson (7) 9/1: 002223: 5 b h St Jovite - 2½ 46a
Phydilla (Lyphard): Prom, kept on final 2f, not pace of front pair: op 6/1, lngr prcd stablemate of wnr: see 178.
1205 **PRICELESS SECOND 7** [11] J A Glover 3-9-1 S Finnamore (5) 9/2: 322064: Chsd ldrs wide halfway, nk 50a
onepace final 2f: clr rem: see 1205, 417 (C/D).
1132 **ODDSANENDS 11** [13] 4-9-13 J Carroll 5/1: 510005: Prom wide 6f: tricky high draw: blnks omitted. 4 42a
1101 **KOMASEPH 12** [12] 8-9-8 D McCabe 20/1: 0-3606: Prom 6f: op 14/1: see 602. 3 31a
693 **SPRING BEACON 56** [5] 5-9-3 R Morse 20/1: 440/67: Outpcd rear, mod gains: 8 wk abs: see 693. 2½ 21a
905 **SIR JACK 31** [14] 4-9-8 J Weaver 4/1 FAV: 00-008: Mid-div wide halfway, btn 2f out: see 905 (5f). ¼ 25a
867 **DESERT INVADER 34** [5] 9-9-8 J Mackay (7) 33/1: 053-09: Al outpcd towards rear: rnr-up in '99 (rtd ¾ 24a
48a, h'cap): '98 wnr here at Southwell & also W'hampton (h'caps, rtd 63a, also rtd 28): eff at 6/7f, stays 1m:
acts on fast, fibresand/Southwell & W'hampton: runs well for an appr/amat.
922 **FLASHFEET 30** [1] 10-9-8 G Baker (7) 33/1: 000460: Prom till halfway, sn btn: 10th: see 398. 1 22a
434

SOUTHWELL (Fibresand) MONDAY MAY 15TH Lefthand, Sharp, Oval Track

584 **ROYAL SIX 80** [3] 7-9-8 T G McLaughlin 10/1: 600-00: Prom 5f: 12th: op 14/1, 12 wk abs: jockey given a 2-day ban for careless riding: see 584. **0a**
167} **GENERAL SONG 514** [6] 6-9-8 A Daly 25/1: 0000/0: Led 1f, btn 2f out: 13th: long abs: missed '99: no form in '98 (tried visor, rtd 42a): back in '96 scored in Italy (7.5f, gd). **0a**
1139 **Ra Ra Rasputin 11** [8] 5-9-13 D McGaffin (7) 16/1: 1203 **Adirpour 7** [2] 6-9-13 Stephanie Hollinshead (7) 33/1:
14 ran Time 1m 30.4 (3.8) (Andy Peake) Mrs N Macauley Sproxton, Leics.

1306 **4.15 GERMANY APPR HCAP 3YO+ 0-65 (F) 1m3f aw Going 47 +02 Fast [62]**
£2289 £654 £327 3 yo rec 17lb

975 **GENERATE 26** [12] M J Polglase 4-9-3 (51) A Beech 100/30 FAV: -162D1: 4 b f Generous - Ivorine (Blushing Groom): Prom, rdn/chsd ldr over 1f out, edged left, led inside last, styd on well, rdn out: best time of day: op 5/2: earlier scored at W'hampton (mdn, subs disq when rnr-up on turf, rtd 58, h'cap): ex-French mdn: eff at 9/10f, styd lngr 11f trip well, cld get further: acts on fibresand, hvy & any trk: has run well fresh. **57a**
4438} **WHISTLING DIXIE 208** [15] D Nicholls 4-8-2 (36) P M Quinn 4/1: 5600-2: 4 ch g Forest Wind - Camdens *1¾* Gift (Camden Town): Held up, prog 3f out, rdn & kept on onepace inside last: op 7/1, 7 mth abs: rnr-up in '99 (rtd 50, h'cap, T J Etherington): eff arnd 11/14f, tried 2m: acts on fast & fibresand: best without blnks. **38a**
742 **ACCYSTAN 49** [3] M D Hammond 5-9-7 (55) J Mackay (5) 5/1: 201633: 5 ch g Efisio - Amia (Nijinsky): *shd* Led/dsptd lead till rdn/hdd inside last, no extra cl-home: op 7/1, 7 wk abs: see 642 (12f). **57a**
*855 **BACHELORS PAD 35** [13] Miss S J Wilton 6-10-0 (62) J Bosley (5) 7/1: 121414: Held up, rdn & styd on *nk* well final 2f, nrst fin: only beaten around 2l & remains in gd heart: see 855. **63a**
1037 **ROYAL PARTNERSHIP 17** [5] 4-9-0 (48)(VIS) Darren Williams (3) 15/2: 020305: Held up, smooth prog *hd* to trk ldrs over 2f out, held inside last: visor: see 866, 455 (C/D, sell). **48a**
682 **ABLE PETE 59** [14] 4-8-5 (39) G Sparkes (5) 9/1: 502146: Held up, kept on fnl 2f/no threat: clr rem, abs. *2½* **35a**
1050 **MURCHAN TYNE 16** [11] 7-9-1 (49) P Mundy (7) 12/1: 0-0057: Chsd ldrs early, strugg 4f out: see 788. *7* **35a**
1003 **NOIRIE 21** [16] 6-8-8 (42) S Finnamore (3) 14/1: 00-238: Chsd ldrs 1m: op 10/1, AW bow: btr 1003 (hvy). *2* **25a**
742 **STATE APPROVAL 49** [9] 7-8-13 (47) D McGaffin (3) 14/1: 336059: Prom 9f: tchd 16/1, 7 wk abs. *¾* **29a**
513 **CAPTIVATING 91** [6] 5-7-11 (31) G Baker (5) 33/1: 030/00: Led 9f out till over 4f out, fdd: 10th: abs. *2½* **9a**
855 **PALAIS 35** [8] 5-8-2 (36)(vis) K Dalgleish (5) 16/1: 0-0000: Rdn/al rear: 11th: op 20/1: see 324 (C/D). *3½* **9a**
1207 **Swing Along 7** [2] 5-10-0 (62) D Meah (5) 16/1: 561 **River Captain 84** [7] 7-8-4 (38) P Fitzsimons (3) 20/1:
1023 **Evening Scent 21** [4] 4-8-11 (45) S Carson 12/1: 1014} **Exalt 384** [10] 4-9-12 (60)(BL) P Dobbs 33/1:
15 ran Time 2m 26.3 (5.0) (Dominic Racing) M J Polglase Southwell, Notts.

YORK TUESDAY MAY 16TH Lefthand, Flat, Galloping Track

Official Going GOOD/FIRM (FIRM places). Stalls: 5/6f - Stands Side, 7f & Round Course - Inside

1307 **2.05 YORKS LIFE HCAP 4YO+ 0-95 (C) 1m3f195y Good/Firm 21 -01 Slow [94]**
£11960 £3680 £1840 £920

1150 **INCH PERFECT 11** [2] R A Fahey 5-8-7 (73) R Cochrane 3/1 FAV: 31-131: 5 b g Inchinor - Scarlet Veil (Tyrnavos) Chsd lrs, prog to lead ins last & asserted near fin, drvn out: hvly bckd: earlier won at Thirsk (h'cap): '99 Southwell (reapp, sell), Redcar (with J Hetherton), Pontefract, Newcastle, Bath & W'hampton wnr (h'caps, rtd 63 & 63a): eff at 1m, suited by 10/12f on firm, soft, f/sand: runs well fresh: v tough & progressive, win again. **82**
1070 **MCGILLYCUDDY REEKS 15** [1] Don Enrico Incisa 9-8-1 (67) Kim Tinkler 20/1: 600-32: 9 b m Kefaah - *1¼* Kilvarnet (Furry Glen) Mid-div, rcd keenly, briefly outpcd 3f out, styd on well fnl 2f, not rch wnr: bckd, fine run. **72**
1076 **ARABIAN MOON 15** [5] C E Brittain 4-9-7 (87) J Reid 12/1: 300-03: 4 ch c Barathea - Excellent Alibi *½* (Exceller) Mid-div, prog to chall over 2f out, duelled with wnr over 1f out, no extra inside last: progressive in '99, scored at Rippon & Windsor (h'caps, rtd 89): rtd 74 in '98: eff at 12f, stays a stiff 2m: acts on firm & gd grnd, prob handles any track: spot on next time & shld win a val race, esp over further. **91**
1187 **ALBERICH 9** [8] M Johnston 5-9-12 (92) D Holland 6/1: 1-5054: Track ldrs, rdn fnl 3f, kept on onepace. *2* **93**
991 **INIGO JONES 24** [9] 4-10-0 (94) A Beech (5) 10/1: 33-145: Chsd ldrs, rapid prog wide to lead over *shd* 3f out, hdd 2f out & no extra fnl 1f: op 8/1: poss hit the front too soon here racing too wide: see 809. **95**
975 **FIORI 27** [3] 4-9-0 (80) M Tebbutt 20/1: -62006: Chsd-ldrs, rdn/briefly no room over 2f out, kept on. *¾* **80**
4135} **RADAS DAUGHTER 205** [10] 4-10-0 (94) K Fallon 16/1: 5610-7: Towards rear, raced keenly, rdn/kept on *½* fnl 3f, no threat: op 14/1, burly on reapp, top-weight: '99 scorer at Bath, Windsor, Ascot & Newmarket (h'caps, rtd 92): rtd 74 in '98 (mdn): eff at 10f, suited by 12f, may get further: goes on firm & soft, any track, suited by stiff ones: proved tough, progressive & useful last term, encouraging reapp & shld prove sharper for this. **93**
1170 **THREE GREEN LEAVES 10** [19] 4-9-12 (92) J Fanning 25/1: 04-008: Cl-up, rdn/outpcd fnl 3f: see 1170. *nk* **90**
1086 **ITSANOTHERGIRL 14** [4] 4-8-4 (70) G Parkin 20/1: 001229: Towards rear, prog 3f out, no hdwy fnl 1f. *¾* **67**
991 **LIGNE GAGNANTE 24** [22] 4-9-10 (90) L Dettori 12/1: 532-60: Held up, prog 3f out, no hdwy fnl 1f: 10th. *10* **76**
1031 **TOTAL DELIGHT 20** [18] 4-9-2 (82)(t) Pat Eddery 10/1: 20-100: Chsd-ldrs, btn 3f out: 11th: op 12/1. *1¼* **66**
*1306 **GENERATE 1** [13] 4-7-10 (62)(5oh) J Mackay(7) 25/1: 162D10: Cl-up 10f: 12th: won yesterday. *2½* **42**
*986 **CELESTIAL WELCOME 24** [17] 5-9-5 (85) A Culhane 16/1: 06-610: Al rear: 13th: btr 986 (hvy). *nk* **64**
4484} **SANDMOOR CHAMBRAY 206** [12] 9-8-7 (73) J Carroll 25/1: 1000-0: Led 1m, btn 2f out: 16th: reapp: '99 Pontefract scorer (h'cap, rtd 76): missed '98: eff at 10f, stays stiff 12f well: acts on firm & gd/soft grnd: handles any track, best up with or forcing the pace: eff with/without blinks, not worn today. **0**
1030 **FAIR WARNING 20** [16] 4-9-12 (92) M Hills 11/1: 412-50: Bhd fnl 4f: 17th: reportedly finished distressed. **0**
1187 **Spring Pursuit 9** [11] 4-9-8 (88) P Fitzsimons (5) 25/1: 1160 **Adelphi Boy 10** [7] 4-8-4 (70) D Mernagh (3) 33/1:
17 ran Time 2m 29.38 (2.58) (Tommy Staunton) R A Fahey Butterwick, North Yorks

1308 **2.35 WM HILL HCAP 3YO 0-105 (B) 7f rnd Good/Firm 21 +02 Fast [111]**
£22750 £7000 £3500 £1750

*1125 **RENDITION 12** [14] W J Haggas 3-7-10 (79) F Norton 11/2 FAV: 530-11: 3 b f Polish Precedent - Rensaler (Stop The Music) Settled rear, switched & smooth prog 3f out, led ins last, styd on strongly & pushed clr close home: fast time, hvly bckd: earlier won at Brighton (reapp, stks, first success): plcd on 2nd of 3 '99 starts (fill mdn, rtd 86, J Gosden): eff at 7f, shld stay 1m: relishes fast & firm grnd, handles a gall/sharp track: has run well fresh: v progressive & has a turn of foot, can win again in valuable h'cap company. **88+**
*1133 **CARD GAMES 12** [11] M W Easterby 3-7-11 (80) Dale Gibson 10/1: -00012: 3 b f First Trump - *1½* Pericardia (Petong) Al prom, rdn/led over 1f out, hdd inside last & no extra cl home: scopey, lengthy filly. **83**

3206} **SHATIN VENTURE 283** [3] Miss L A Perratt 3-8-11 (94) K Fallon 12/1: 1424-3: 3 b c Lake Coniston - Justitia (Dunbeath) Handy, rdn/chall 2f out, onepace fnl 1f: op 8/1, reapp, just needed this: '99 debut wnr at Ayr (nov stks, rtd 92): eff at 5f, stays 7f well, may get further: acts on fast & gd, likes a gall trk. *¾* **96**
969 **FULL FLOW 27** [7] B W Hills 3-9-6 (103) M Hills 12/1: 120-44: Dwelt, soon mid-div, prog to chall 2f out, not pace of front pair fnl 1f: op 10/1: useful colt, should win again: see 969 (List h'cap). *nk* **104**
1183 **KAREEB 9** [1] 3-8-0 (83) R Brisland (5) 7/1: 324-65: Held up, steady prog from 3f out, onepace fnl 1f. *½* **83**
1016 **DAY JOURNEY 22** [13] 3-9-7 (104) J Reid 14/1: 14-346: Mid-div, eff 3f out, styd on for press fnl 2f. *1½* **101**
979 **ROYAL CAVALIER 26** [4] 3-7-11 (80) P M Quinn (5) 33/1: 034107: Rear, mod late gains, no threat. *¾* **76**
954 **QUEENS BENCH 28** [10] 3-8-4 (87) W Ryan 8/1: 311-48: Rear, prog over 2f out, no hdwy fnl 1f: btr 954. *1¼* **80**
1285 **EASTWAYS 3** [9] 3-8-8 (91) R Hills 8/1: 2-0039: Held up, eff & repeatedly no room fnl 3f, nvr nrr: swtg, nicely bckd, qck reapp: no luck in running, this best forgotten: see 982. *shd* **84**
4583} **ITS ALLOWED 196** [16] 3-8-0 (83) W Supple 20/1: 0102-0: Tracked ldrs, fdd fnl 2f: 10th: reapp: '99 scorer at Thirsk (clmr), Lingfield (sell, M Channon) & Catterick (nursery h'cap, rtd 84): eff at 6/7f on firm, gd, handles gd/soft & any track, likes a sharp one: capable of better. *1¾* **73**
1153 **CAIR PARAVEL 11** [17] 3-8-3 (86) J Carroll 8/1: 11-530: In tch wide, btn 2f out, eased fnl 1f: 11th. *¾* **75**
874 **BELLA BELLISIMO 35** [15] 3-8-0 (83) R Ffrench 33/1: 535-00: Held up wide, eff 3f out/no prog: 12th. *nk* **71**
1153 **SECRET CONQUEST 11** [8] 3-7-10 (79)(1oh) J Mackay (7) 33/1: 100-00: Led 5f, fdd: 13th: '99 scorer at Haydock (sell) & Catterick (2, nurserys, rtd 85 at best): eff at 6/7f on fm & gd/sft, any track, likes Catterick. *¾* **66**
1192 **Able Ayr 9** [5] 3-7-10 (79)(5oh) P Fessey 20/1: 630 **Safranine 73** [2] 3-8-11 (94) Dean McKeown 33/1:
994 **Magelta 24** [6] 3-7-10 (79) G Bardwell 16/1: 1032 **Kind Emperor 20** [12] 3-7-11 (80)(1ow)(2oh) A Nicholls (0) 33/1:
17 ran Time 1m 22.63 (1.33) (Pims UK Ltd) W J Haggas Newmarket

1309

3.10 GR 3 MUSIDORA STKS 3YO (A) 1m2f85y Good/Firm 21 -27 Slow
£26100 £9900 £4950 £2250

4537} **KALYPSO KATIE 201** [9] J Noseda 3-8-8 M J Kinane 100/30: 1-1: 3 gr f Fairy King - Miss Toot (Ardross) Handy, rcd keenly, chsd ldr 2f out, styd on gamely for press to overhaul ldr near line, drvn out: well bckd, slow time: just sharper for this & reportedly hvly in season: '99 sole start wnr at Windsor (fill mdn, impressive, rtd 100+): suited by step up to 10.5f, 12f will suit: acts on fast & gd/soft grnd, sharp/gall trk: runs well fresh: hds next for Epsom Oaks where battling qualities & a stronger gallop/12f will bring further improvement. **114**
*995 **LADY UPSTAGE 24** [2] B W Hills 3-8-8 M Hills 14/1: 014-12: 3 b f Alzao - She's The Tops (Shernazar) Dictated pace, increased tempo fnl 3f, rdn/strongly pressed ins last, hdd nr line: stays 10f, acts on fast & hvy: nearly pinched this under a sound tactical ride: smart, reportedly reopposes this wnr in the Oaks. *hd* **113**
1185 **HIGH WALDEN 9** [5] H R A Cecil 3-8-8 W Ryan 5/2 FAV: 412-53: 3 b f El Gran Senor - Modena (Roberto) Held up in tch, eff fnl 2f, kept on ins last, not pace to chall: padd pick, hvly bckd: stays 10.5f, stronger gallop/12f+ will bring further improvement: v useful filly, may be supplemented for the Oaks: see 1185. *1½* **111**
1185 **MILETRIAN 9** [6] M R Channon 3-8-8 M Roberts 25/1: 514-04: In tch & rcd keenly, outpcd 3f out, kept on fnl 2f, nrst fin: '99 Redcar wnr (mdn), subs 4th in Gr 1 Prix Marcel Boussac at Longchamp (rtd 108): eff at 10f, lks sure to relish 12f+ & a stronger gallop: acts on firm & hvy: heads for the Oaks & can arte higher. *nk* **110+**
1184 **EVERLASTING LOVE 9** [8] 3-8-8 M Fenton 20/1: 120-55: Held up, prog to chall 2f out, sn onepace. *1* **109**
*1108 **EMBRACED 13** [3] 3-8-8 R Cochrane 11/4: 1-16: Chsd ldr 7f, rdn/fdd over 1f out: hvly bckd: warm & edgy in paddock: jockey felt filly did not stay longer 10.5f trip: btr 1108 (Listed 1m, gd/sft). *1½* **107**
4081} **ADAMAS 235** [1] 3-8-8 W Supple 50/1: 2-7: Chsd ldrs, btn 2f out: reapp: rnr up sole '99 start (rtd 80, fill mdn): eff at 6f, drop back to 1m shld suit: acts on firm grnd: must win her mdn. *3½* **102**
1185 **AGRIPPINA 9** [7] 3-8-8 Pat Eddery 20/1: 211-08: Held up, eff 3f out, sn held: bndgd, lngr 10f trip. *shd* **102**
4097} **MY HANSEL 233** [4] 3-8-8 J Reid 8/1: 13-9: Held up racing keenly, rdn/btn 2f out: op 7/1, reapp: '99 debut wnr at Newmarket (fill mdn, rtd 102), subs 3rd of 6 in Gr 1 Ascot Fillies Mile): stays 1m, mid dists shld suit: acts on firm & soft grnd, still/gall track: needs to learn more restraint. *1¼* **100**
9 ran Time 2m 12.32 (5.02) (M Tabor) J Noseda Newmarket

1310

3.40 NEWTON RATED HCAP 3YO 0-100 (B) 1m2f85y Good/Firm 21 -02 Slow [101]
£16504 £6260 £3130 £1422

*979 **KINGS MILL 26** [6] N A Graham 3-9-5 (92) R Cochrane 9/2 FAV: 23-111: 3 b c Doyoun - Adarika (King's Lake) Chsd ldrs, smooth prog to chall fnl 2f, styd on gamely to lead nr line, drvn out: hvly bckd: unbtn this term, earlier won at Southwell (auct mdn) & Newmarket (h'cap): eff arnd 10f, shld stay 12f: acts on fast & soft grnd, any trk: has run well fresh: useful & progressive colt, reportedly hds for King George V h'cap at R Ascot. **99**
1089 **SECRET AGENT 14** [15] Sir Michael Stoute 3-9-7 (94) K Fallon 6/1: 12-142: 3 b c Machiavellian - Secret Obsession (Secretariat) Rear, prog to lead dist, edged left ins last, hdd cl home: just btn in a thrilling fin: clr rem, swtg, hvly bckd: eff at 10f on fast & soft grnd, sharp/gall trk: useful colt, see 1089 & 851. *hd* **100**
*1075 **BONAGUIL 15** [5] C F Wall 3-9-0 (87) R Mullen 8/1: 4-1113: 3 b g Septieme Ciel - Chateaubrook (Alleged) Chsd ldr, outpcd 2f out, rdn & kept on ins last, not pace of front pair: stays 10f, acts on fast, gd/soft & equitrack: tough & progressive gelding: gd run here, shld relish 12f: see 1075. *3* **89**
1177 **DUCHAMP 9** [7] I A Balding 3-8-10 (83) K Darley 9/1: 221-54: Cl up, rdn fnl 3f, briefly led over 1f out, no extra inside last: nicely bckd: leggy colt, still sharper for this: see 1177. *hd* **84**
873 **MINGLING 35** [4] 3-8-7 (80) S Sanders 8/1: 450-35: Mid div, rdn/briefly outpcd over 2f out, switched & kept on for press inside last, no threat: h'cap bow, op 7/1: paddock pick: sure to relish 12f+: see 873. *¾* **80**
1215 **MINKASH 7** [9] 3-9-6 (93) R Hills 8/1: 220-06: Held up, rdn 3f out, kept on well fnl 1f, not pace to threaten: op 7/1: styd longer 10.5f trip, could appreciate further again on this evidence, see 1215. *shd* **93**
1089 **IMPERIAL ROCKET 14** [1] 3-9-3 (90) Dane O'Neill 20/1: 11-467: Mid-div, onepace fnl 2f: strong colt. *1¾* **88**
998 **BREATHLESS DREAMS 24** [13] 3-8-9 (82) M Fenton 33/1: 21-58: Cl-up, led over 4f out till over 1f out, fdd. *6* **71**
1055 **VINTAGE PREMIUM 17** [12] 3-9-7 (94) Pat Eddery 14/1: 0-2149: Held up, eff/repeatedly no room from over 2f out, no threat: op 12/1: trying longer 10f trip, no luck in running today, worth another chance: see 1055. *2* **80**
*1104 **DANCING BAY 13** [10] 3-9-1 (88) J P Spencer 7/1: 50-110: Prom, outpcd 2f out, soon btn: 10th: op 5/1. *1½* **72**
1183 **RUSHMORE 9** [2] 3-8-5 (78) D Sweeney 16/1: 3-100: Led 2f, cl-up till 2f out: 11th: btr 717 (7f). *nk* **61**
1075 **MY RETREAT 15** [8] 3-8-7 (80) M Hills 20/1: 52-100: Track ldrs, chance 2f out, fdd quickly: 12th: jockey reported colt choked in closing stages: see 884. *nk* **62**
850 **ARISTOCRAT 36** [3] 3-8-10 (83) R Hughes 14/1: 03-40: Cl-up, led after 2f till over 4f out, sn bhd: 13th. *¾* **64**
1094 **Pipssalio 14** [11] 3-8-5 (78) O Urbina 20/1: 4318} **Clear Prospect 218** [14] 3-8-11 (84) J Carroll 33/1:
15 ran Time 2m 09.64 (2.34) (First Millennium Racing) N A Graham Newmarket

YORK TUESDAY MAY 16TH Lefthand, Flat, Galloping Track

1311
4.10 STORAGE COND STKS 3YO (B) 1m5f194y Good/Firm 21 -24 Slow
£9222 £3498 £1749 £795

1199 **KUWAIT TROOPER** 8 [4] G A Butler 3-8-12 L Dettori 5/1: -41031: 3 b c Cozzene - Super Fan (Lear 93
Fan) Held up, prog to lead over 2f out, in command fnl 1f, pushed out: earlier won at Musselburgh (class stks):
eff at 12f, apprec step up to 14f: handles equitrack, likes fast & gd/soft, sharp/gall trks: runs well fresh:
tremendous eff at today's weights (wld have received 28lbs + in a h'cap): clearly imprvd for step up in trip.
1029 **MODISH** 20 [1] M H Tompkins 3-9-1 S Sanders 3/1: 114-22: 3 b c Tenby - Moorfield Daisy (Waajib) 3 91
Held up, prog to chase wnr over 1f out, al held: prob stays 14f: rtd just higher 1029 (14f hvy).
*1157 **GARDEN SOCIETY** 10 [3] J A R Toller 3-9-1 R Ffrench 5/2 FAV: 13: 3 ch c Caerleon - Eurobird ½ 90
(Ela Mana Mou) Al handy, led over 3f out till over 2f out, nicely bckd & eased ins last: nicely bckd, lkd well: jockey
given a 1-day careless riding ban: longer 14f trip: see 1157 (12f, gd).
*1009 **ALMOST FREE** 22 [6] M Johnston 3-9-1 J Reid 11/4: 14: Led after 2f till over 3f out, btn/slightly hmpd 4 84
2f out: nicely bckd tho' op 9/4: longer 14f trip: see 1009 (12f, hvy).
1179 **BOX BUILDER** 9 [2] 3-8-12 S Drowne 10/1: 335: Led 2f, btn 4f out: mdn: longer 14f trip. 3½ 76
5 ran Time 2m 59.59 (6.19) (Sheikh Khaled Duaij Al Sabah) G A Butler Blewbury, Oxon

1312
4.40 EBF NOV FILLIES STKS 2YO (D) 6f Good/Firm 21 -23 Slow
£7670 £2360 £1180 £590

-- **BARATHIKI** [2] P F I Cole 2-8-8 K Fallon 9/4 FAV: 1: 2 gr f Barathea - Tagiki (Doyoun) 88+
Rdn along early, prog halfway, rdn to lead ins last, pushed out cl home despite edging left: op 7/4, lkd fit:
April foal, 30,000gns purchase: dam a 7f juv wnr abroad, sire a top class miler: eff at 6f, 7f+ lks sure to suit:
acts on fast grnd & a gall track: runs well fresh: leggy & green filly, will know more next time, improve further.
1176 **CELTIC ISLAND** 9 [5] W G M Turner 2-8-12 A Daly 6/1: 2122: 2 b f Celtic Swing - Chief Island (Be My ½ 88
Chief) Led, rdn/edged left & hdd inside last, just held cl home: hvly bckd, op 8/1: well grown, lengthy filly
who lost little in defeat over longer 6f trip: can regain winning ways: see 1176, 938.
-- **SOFT BREEZE** [10] E A L Dunlop 2-8-8 J Reid 6/1: 3: 2 ch f Zafonic - Tropical (Green Desert) 2 79+
Dwelt & soon rdn along bhd, prog halfway & ch over 1f out, onepace ins last: op 4/1, ndd this debut: March foal,
dam half sister to high class miler Shake The Yoke: sire a top class 2yo/miler: eff at 6f, 7f+ shld suit: handles
fast grnd: stocky/scopey filly, not knocked about here, will improve & looks sure to find a race soon.
1161 **REEDS RAINS** 10 [8] T D Easterby 2-9-1 J Carroll 10/1: -144: Rdn & outpcd early, prog/chsd ldrs over ½ 84
1f out, never pace to chall: op 8/1: handles fast & soft grnd: see 904 (debut).
-- **LILS JESSY** [1] 2-8-8 Pat Eddery 100/30: 5: Handy, rdn/no extra over 1f out: op 8/1: handles 1½ 73
fast grnd: Feb foal, half sister to sev wnrs abroad: sire a top class miler: 7f+ shld suit, not knocked about here.
-- **LADY BEAR** [3] 2-8-8 R Winston 20/1: 6: V slowly away & bhd, kept on fnl 2f, nvr nrr: ndd this ½ 71+
debut: Grand Lodge filly, April foal, cost 81/2 Irish juv wnr, sire a top class 1m/10f performer:
lks sure to apprec 6f+ & will leave this bhd with a level break next time.
-- **QUEEN SPAIN** [9] S Drowne 10/1: 7: Dwelt/outpcd towards rear, never pace to chall: op 8/1, nk 70
ndd this: Mister Baileys filly, May foal, cost 19,000gns: half sister to several wnrs in US, dam a US well related
mdn: sire a high class 2yo & subesquent 2000 Guineas wnr: apprec 7f+ in time.
1107 **QUIZZICAL LADY** 13 [6] 2-8-12 Dane O'Neill 14/1: 05168: Chsd ldr 3f, btn 1f out: btr 1000 (5f, hvy). 5 65
8 ran Time 1m 12.01 (2.61) (Axom) P F I Cole Whatcombe, Oxon

SAINT CLOUD FRIDAY MAY 12TH Lefthand, Galloping Track

Official Going HOLDING

1313
2.25 GR 3 PRIX CLEOPATRE 3YO FILLIES 1m2f110y Holding
£21134 £7685 £3842 £2305

1027 **GOLD ROUND** 19 [4] Mme C Head 3-8-9 O Doleuze 21/10: 121-31: 3 b f Caerleon - Born Gold (Blushing 108
Groom) Led, hdd & dropped rear halfway, rall & styd on strongly over 2f out, led dist, rdn clr: up in trip:
won twice in '99: eff arnd 10.5f, 12f shld suit: acts on hvy grnd: tough, improving filly: Oaks entry.
-- **SEATTLE BAY** [9] J E Pease 3-8-9 T Jarnet 56/10: 413-2: 3 b f Opening Verse - Seattle Ways 2½ 104
(Seattle Slew) Mid-div, hdwy halfway, led over 2f out, hdd dist, not pace of wnr: landed one of 3 '99 starts
(mdn), subs third in a Gr 3: useful.
4245} **DARAKIYLA** 222 [5] A de Royer Dupre 3-8-9 G Mosse 17/10 FAV: -16-3: 3 b f Last Tycoon - Daralinsha 1½ 101
(Empery) Hld up, rdn/hdwy 3f out, kept on onepcd fnl 1f: reapp: '99 debut Chantilly wnr: stays 10.5f on hvy.
-- **PLAYACT** [7] N Clement 3-8-9 T Gillet 121/10: -514: Rear, styd on stdly fnl 2f, nvr nrr. 1 99
9 ran Time 2m 19.2 (Wertheimer Et Frere) Mme C Head France

LEOPARDSTOWN SUNDAY MAY 14TH Lefthand, Galloping Track

Official Going GOOD TO FIRM

1314
3.30 GR 3 DERRINSTOWN DERBY TRIAL 3YO 1m2f Good/Firm
£35750 £10450 £4950 £1650

949 **SINNDAR** 28 [3] J Oxx 3-9-4 (t) J P Murtagh 7/4 JT FAV: -11-21: 3 b c Grand Lodge - Sinntara 119
(Lashkan) Chsd ldr, hdwy to lead 2f out, strongly pressed dist, styd on well, drvn out: '99 wnr at The Curragh
(2, incl Gr 1 National, rtd 107): eff arnd 1m/10f, shld stay further: acts on fast & soft: wears a t-strap:
progressive & smart colt, fine run conceding weight here & can win more Group races.
*947 **BACH** 28 [4] A P O'Brien 3-8-11 J A Heffernan 7/4 JT FAV: -11-12: 3 b c Caerleon - Producer hd 111
(Nashua) Prom, drvn to chall over 1f out, styd on, just held: gd run up in class: stays 10f: see 947 (Listed).
-- **MUAKAAD** [1] D K Weld 3-8-11 P J Smullen 2/1: -13: 3 b c Muhtarram - Forest Lair (Habitat) 3½ 105
Settled last, hdwy 2f out, no threat to ldrs appr fnl 1f: recent Leopardstown mdn scorer (10f, soft).

LEOPARDSTOWN   SUNDAY MAY 14TH   Lefthand, Galloping Track

--   **SHAYADI** [2] J Oxx 3-8-11 N G McCullagh 25/1: -24: Led to 2f out, wknd: pacemaker for wnr.   7   94
4 ran   Time 2m 04.9   (H H Aga Khan)   J Oxx Currabeg, Co Kildare

---

1315   4.00 LISTED 1,000 GUINEAS TRIAL 3YO   1m   Good/Firm
£23750   £6650   £3150   £1050

3799} **PRESELI** 252 [3] M J Grassick 3-9-3 E Ahern 7/4 FAV: -111-1: 3 b f Caerleon - Hill Of Snow   113
(Reference Point) Trkd ldr, hdwy to lead appr fnl 1f, all out to hold on: reapp: landed all 3 '99 starts,
at Roscommon, Leopardstown (List) & The Curragh (Gr 1 Moyglare, rtd 113): eff at 7f/1m, further suit: acts on
gd & fast: reportedly best coming late off a strong pace: smart & unbeaten, heads for Irish 1000 Gns in gd form.
--   **STORM DREAM** [8] K Prendergast 3-8-10 S Craine 14/1: 23-2: 3 b f Catrail - Mamara Reef (Salse)   shd   105
Settled rear, gd hdwy over 2f out, chall wnr ins last, just failed: reapp: plcd in '99 (mdns): stays 1m on fast.
4242} **THEORETICALLY** 225 [6] D K Weld 3-9-1 P J Smullen 4/1: -411-3: 3 b f Theatrical - Aspern   2   106
(Riverman) Prom, drvn & not pace of ldrs fnl 1f: '99 wnr at Tralee (mdn) & The Curragh (Gr 3, rtd 102):
eff at 7f, stays 1m: useful, sharper next time.
770   **COIS CUAIN** 49 [7] J Oxx 3-8-10 J P Murtagh 10/1: 01-354: Handy, rdn & no extra fnl 2f: see 770.   hd   100
3554} **DANCE OF LOVE** 266 [9] 3-8-10 (t) F M Berry 10/1: 4316-5: In tch, hdwy when short of room over   hd   100
1f out, kept on ins last: 3rd in List company in '99 (rtd 97), subs won a Roscommon mdn: eff at 7f on gd & soft.
9 ran   Time 1m 41.6   (Neil Jones)   M J Grassick Pollardstown, Co Kildare

---

1316   4.30 LISTED AMETHYST STKS 3YO+   1m   Good/Firm
£16250   £4750   £2250   £750   3 yo rec 13lb

1120 **ANZARI** 13 [6] J Oxx 3-8-9 J P Murtagh 7/2: 112-31: 3 b c Nicolotte - Anazara (Trempolino)   105
Prom, short of room over 2f out, chall dist, all out to get up cl-home: '99 scorer at Roscommon (mdn) & Galway
(nurs h'cap), subs rtd 101 when rnr-up in a List race: eff at 7f/1m on gd & fast, not soft: tough & useful.
770   **JAMMAAL** 49 [3] D K Weld 3-8-9 P J Smullen 5/2 FAV: 13-212: 3 b c Robellino - Navajo Love Song   nk   104
(Dancing Brave) Cl-up, led 2f out, drvn/collared cl-home: acts on fast & soft: wnr at Cork (stks) since 770.
1232 **ONE WON ONE** 6 [4] Mrs J Morgan 6-9-11 T E Duncan 9/1: 1-5533: 6 b g Naevus - Harvard's Bay   hd   106
(Halpern Bay) Waited with, hdwy to chall dist, just held: gd weight-carrying performance: tough: see 1049.
--   **CATZ** [8] J S Bolger 3-8-6 N G McCullagh 9/1: 23-14: Mid-div, styd on fnl 2f, no dngr: clr rem.   1½   97
4533} **BASHKIR** 202 [7] 3-8-9 (bl) C O'Donoghue 6/1: 102-25: Cl-up, chall ldrs over 2f out, rdn & wknd   4   93
appr fnl 2f: recent rnr-up to Jammaal at Cork (stks): rtd 95 in '99 (rnr-up in Gr 3), prev won a Naas mdn.
9 ran   Time 1m 39.9   (H H Aga Khan)   J Oxx Currabeg, Co Kildare

---

LONGCHAMP   SUNDAY MAY 14TH   Righthand, Galloping Track

Official Going   VERY SOFT

1317   1.40 GR 1 PRIX LUPIN 3YO   1m2f110y   V Soft
£48031   £19212   £9606   £4803

864   **CIRO** 35 [6] A P O'Brien 3-9-2 M J Kinane 7/1: 211-31: 3 ch c Woodman - Gioconda (Nijinsky)   116
Front rank, chall over 2f out, sn led, styd on well, drvn out: '99 wnr at Galway (mdn), subs awarded the Gr 1
Grand Criterium at Longchamp (rtd 112): eff at 1m/11f on soft: v smart colt, shld go well in the French Derby.
*864 **KUTUB** 35 [4] F Head 3-9-2 D Bonilla 7/10 FAV: 1-12: 3 b c In The Wings - Minnie Habit   ¾   115
(Habitat) Waited with, gd hdwy to chall over 2f out, ev ch till no extra ins last: see 864 (beat today's wnr).
*1026 **RHENIUM** 21 [7] J C Rouget 3-9-2 T Jarnet 119/10: 11-113: 3 ch c Rainbows For Life - Miss   1   113
Mulaz (Luthier) Settled rear, styd on for press fnl 2f, nvr nrr: not btn far: in gd form: see 1026 (Gr 2).
--   **EPITRE** [2] A Fabre 3-9-2 O Peslier 86/10: -124: Trkd ldrs, styd on at onepce over 1f out: 1   111
recent rnr-up in Listed company at Chantilly (12f, hvy): will apprec a return to 12f.
--   **ALYZIG** [1] 3-9-2 O Doleuze 178/10: 21-25: Led early, with ldrs, held fnl 2f: Maisons-Laffitte   shd   111
mdn scorer in '99 (1m, hvy), prev rnr-up to highly rated Dubai Two Thousand on debut.
--   **RIVERS CURTAIN** [5] 3-9-2 L Dettori 27/10: 1-6: Led 2f to 2f out, fdd: landed sole juv start   2   107
in '99 for A Fabre (7f, hvy): now with Saeed bin Suroor & shld be capable of much better, sharper next time.
4322} **OCEAN OF WISDOM** 217 [3] 3-9-2 C Asmussen 154/10: 313-07: Al in rear.   8   95
7 ran   Time 2m 13.5   (Mr M Tabor, Mrs J Magnier & Mr R Santulli)   A P O'Brien Ballydoyle, Co Tipperary

---

1318   2.15 GR 1 FRENCH 2,000 GUINEAS 3YO   1m   V Soft
£96061   £38425   £19212   £9606

765   **BACHIR** 50 [5] Saeed bin Suroor 3-9-2 L Dettori 31/10: 33-121: 3 b c Desert Style - Morning   120
Welcome (Be My Guest) Led early, with ldrs till went on again over 1f out, drvn out: 7 wk abs: wnr in Dubai
prev this term, also rnr-up in the UAE Derby: smart juv, won at Chepstow (mdn auct) & broke juv course rec
at Goodwood (Gr 2, J Gosden, rtd 108 when Gr 1 plcd): eff at 6f/1m, stays 9f on firm, v soft & dirt: runs
well fresh on any trk: fast improving & potentially high-class colt, must be feared in the Irish 2,000 Guineas.
*1025 **BERINES SON** 21 [4] A Fabre 3-9-2 C Soumillon 32/10: 2-112: 3 b c Irish River - Berine   1½   118
(Bering) Waited with, hdwy & switched over 1f out, not pace of wnr: fine run, improved in defeat: see 1025.
4025} **VALENTINO** 239 [8] J H M Gosden 3-9-2 G Mosse 164/10: -14-3: 3 ch c Nureyev - Divine Danse (Kris)   1½   115
Rear, styd on strongly for press fnl 1f: reapp: '99 Ascot wnr (debut, mdn P Chapple Hyam), subs 4th in a Gr 1
at Longchamp (rtd 106): eff at 6f/1m, further sure to suit on this evidence: acts on fast & soft: win a Gr 2/3.
981   **EKRAAR** 24 [3] M P Tregoning 3-9-2 (bl) R Hills 89/10: 143-34: Dwelt, hdwy to lead after 1f,   1   113
hdd over 1f out, sn btn: gd run on this step up to Gr 1 class: prob wants further: see 981.
*1120 **MONASHEE MOUNTAIN** 13 [9] 3-9-2 M J Kinane 6/4 FAV: 11-115: Waited with, nvr a threat: nk   112
up in trip & lost unbeaten record here: btr 1120 (6f, 7f).
3107} **MON POTE LE GITAN** 288 [1] 3-9-2 D Boeuf 108/10: 5-2116: Prom, drvn/wknd over 1f out.   2   108
1025 **SLIPSTREAM KING** 21 [6] 3-9-2 O Peslier 73/10: -137: Handy, rdn/no extra fnl 2f: see 1025.   ¾   107
7 ran   Time 1m 39.4   (Godolphin)   Saeed bin Suroor Newmarket

LONGCHAMP SUNDAY MAY 14TH Righthand, Galloping Track

1319 3.25 GR 1 FRENCH 1,000 GUINEAS 3YO   1m   V Soft
£96061 £38425 £19212 £9606

946 **BLUEMAMBA 30** [3] P Bary 3-9-0 T Jarnet 184/10: 31-31: 3 b f Kingmambo - Black Penny (Private   112
Account) Trkd ldrs, led briefly 2f out, drvn to lead again ins last, all out: landed 2nd of 2 juv starts
(1m, gd grnd): eff at 1m, further shld suit: acts on gd & soft grnd: tough & smart filly.

*946 **PEONY 30** [1] D Sepulchre 3-9-0 C Asmussen 92/10: 11-112: 3 ch f Lion Cavern - Persiandale   nk 111
(Persian Bold) Waited with, no room 2f out, ran on well ins last, just failed: fine run & poss a shade unlucky
here: eff at 7f/1m: v useful, can win in Gr class shortly: see 946.

*971 **ALSHAKR 25** [4] B Hanbury 3-9-0 R Hills 183/10: 64-13: 3 b f Bahri - Give Thanks (Relko)   shd 110
Chsd ldrs, rdn to chall dist, no extra cl-home: eff at 7f/1m: big hike up in class & an excellent run by this
Brit raider: lks sure to win in Gr company sn: see 971 (mdn).

-- **ZARKIYA** [11] A de Royer Dupre 3-9-0 G Mosse 39/10: 1-24: Waited with, gd hdwy when no room   shd 110
over 1f out, switched left ins last & ran on strongly, unlucky: stays 1m on soft: deserves compensation.

*913 **IFTIRAAS 30** [8] 3-9-0 Pat Eddery 49/10: 142-15: Cl-up, hdwy to lead over 1f out, hdd   ½ 109
well ins last, no extra: up in trip, eff at 7.3f/1m: would enjoy a return to Gr 2/3 company: see 913.

*99 **ZEITING 174** [2] 3-9-0 S Maillot 597/10: 1611-6: Prom, held ins last: long abs: see 99.   ½ 108

3107} **CASTIYA 288** [10] 3-9-0 D Boeuf 33/1: 10-547: Rear, styd on well ins last, nvr nrr.   ½ 107

*1027 **LADY OF CHAD 21** [5] 3-9-0 M J Kinane 1/1 FAV: -11-18: Keen cl-up, drvn to lead over   1 105
1f out, hdd dist, wknd: ruined chance by racing too freely, can do better: see 1027.

-- **BLUE MOON** [9] 3-9-0 T Thulliez 33/1: 12-149: Nvr a factor.   hd 105

*1117 **XUA 16** [7] 3-9-0 O Peslier 33/1: 23-110: Al in rear: see 1117.   1 103

-- **SAONE ET LOIRE** [6] 3-9-0 N Jeanpierre 337/10: 006-60: Led, hdd/fdd 2f out: pacemaker.   0
11 ran   Time 1m 40.2   (Ecurie Skymarc Farm)   P Bary France

1320 4.00 GR 3 PRIX DE SAINT-GEORGES 3YO+   5f   V Soft
£21134 £7685 £3842   3 yo rec 9 lb

4246} **SAMPOWER STAR 224** [4] Saeed bin Suroor 4-9-2 L Dettori 5/1: 644-01: 4 b c Cyrano De Bergerac -   116
Green Supreme (Primo Dominie) Trkd ldr, switched & hdwy over 1f out, drvn out to lead cl-home: unplcd in Dubai
earlier this term: with R Hannon & v progressive in '99, win at Windsor (stks), Ascot (List) & York (Gr 3, also
Gr 1 plcd, rtd 116): '98 wnr at Folkestone (mdn auct) & Salisbury (nov, rtd 94, R Simpson): suited by 5/6f now,
stays 7f/1m: handles firm, suited by gd, hvy & any trk: v smart sprinter, win more Gr races this term.

*988 **WATCHING 22** [2] R Hannon 3-8-7 R Hughes 5/1: 23-212: 3 ch c Indian Ridge - Sweeping   nk 115
(Indian King) Led, drvn & hdd cl-home: gd run upped to Gr class: see 988.

4021} **SELTITUDE 240** [9] J E Hammond 4-9-3 T Gillet 34/1: 4110-3: 4 b f Fairy King - Dunoof (Shirley   1½ 112
Heights) Dwelt, rdn/hdwy over 1f out, no extra well ins last: reapp: won 3 times in '99 (incl Gr 3, rtd 108):
eff at 5f, poss best at 6f: acts on soft grnd: v useful.

*1016 **MONKSTON POINT 20** [1] D W P Arbuthnot 4-9-0 (vis) Pat Eddery 129/10: 00-117: Prom, wknd   3½ 102
fnl 2f, fin 7th: apprec a drop in grade: see 1016 (stks).
11 ran   Time 58.9   (Godolphin)   Saeed bin Suroor Newmarket

CAPANNELLE SUNDAY MAY 14TH Righthand, Flat, Galloping Track

Official Going GOOD

1321 4.30 GR 1 PREMIO PRESIDENTE 4YO+   1m2f   Good
£192261 £93772 £53840 £26920

2494} **TIMBOROA 315** [1] R Brogi 4-9-2 M Demuro : 4-1311: 4 b c Salse - Kisumu (Damister)   115
Handy, hdwy to lead over 1f out, drvn out to hold on: rtd 106 in '99 (List): eff at 10f on gd: v smart.

-- **CRISOS IL MONACO** [4] L Camici 5-9-2 F Jovine : 45-122: 5 b h Common Grounds - Gayshuka   nk 114
(Lord Gayle) Bhd, hdwy to chall over 1f out, no extra fnl strides: eff at 10f on gd: smart entire.

767 **CAITANO 50** [6] A Schutz 6-9-2 (bl) J Reid : 11-023: 6 b h Niniski - Eversince (Foolish   1 110
Pleasure) Cl-up, chall 2f out, wknd ins last: fin 4th, plcd 3rd: German raider: see 767.

1154 **DIAMOND WHITE 9** [9] M J Ryan 5-8-12 J Reid : 0-0234: Mid-div, eff 2f out, sn held: see 1154.   1 104

2982} **SUMITAS 294** [3] 4-9-2 T Hellier : 52443D: Settled rear, short of room & switched over 1f out,   112
styd on well ins last: fin 3rd, disqual & plcd 6th: German raider, stays 10f on gd grnd.

2493} **MUKHALIF 315** [8] 4-9-2 D O'Donohoe : 2210-9: Prom, wknd qckly fnl 2f, fin last: reapp: landed   90
the Gr 1 Italian Derby in '99 (rtd 110): unbeaten in 2 juv starts for D Loder, at Leicester (mdn) & Ascot
(stks, rtd 103+): eff at 10f/12f on firm grnd, handles soft: runs well fresh on stiff trks.
9 ran   Time 2m 00.6   (R Brogi)   R Brogi Italy

COLOGNE SUNDAY MAY 14TH Righthand, Fair Track

Official Going GOOD

1322 3.50 GR 2 GERMAN 2,000 GUINEAS 3YO   1m   Good
£61290 £24839 £12258

3020} **PACINO 289** [10] Saeed bin Suroor 3-9-2 Paul Eddery : 22-001: 3 b c Zafonic - June Moon (Sadler's   111
Wells) Led after 1f, rdn clr fnl 2f: recently well beaten in a couple of races in Dubai: with J Dunlop in '99,
rnr-up twice (mdns, rtd 86): eff at 7f/1m on fast & gd: much imprvd by new connections, win more Group races.

-- **DJIBOUTI** [9] M Trybuhl 3-9-2 A Helfenbein : 2: 3 b c Dashing Blade - Diana Dancer (Fabulous   3½ 104
Dancer) Bhd, styd on well fnl 2f but no chance with wnr.

-- **SIAMO** [6] D Richardson 3-9-2 L Hammer Hansen : 3: 3 gr c Java Gold - Suffinja (Windwurf)   nk 103
Mid-div till styd on strongly for press last, nrst fin.

COLOGNE   SUNDAY MAY 14TH   Righthand, Fair Track

3835} **GINOLAS MAGIC 249** [7] R Hannon 3-9-2 G Bocskai : 6305-7: Nvr a threat: reapp: '99 wnr at   **5   94**
Kempton (auct mdn) & Epsom (nov stks, rtd 98 at best): eff over 6/7f on gd & fast grnd: acts on a straight
or a turning/undul trk: useful at best, sharper next time with a drop in grade.
4 ran   Time 1m 36.12   (Sheikh Hamdan Bin Mohammed Al Maktoum)   Saeed bin Suroor Newmarket

JAGERSRO (SWEDEN)   SUNDAY MAY 14TH   --

Official Going   GOOD

1323   2.50 LISTED PRAMMS MEMORIAL 3YO+   1m143y   Good
£43860   £14620   £5848   £5848

1819} **STATO ONE 348** [10] Y Durant 8-9-6 Yvonne Durant 54/1: -2-1: 8 br g Statoblest - Million   **102**
Heiress (Auction Ring) -:
--   **BANZHAF** [9] Sweden 7-9-6 F Diaz 178/10: 2: 7 ch g Rare Performer - Hang On For Effer   **½   100**
(Effervescing) -:
1819} **HANGOVER SQUARE 348** [11] L Reuterskiold 6-9-6 M Larsen 11/10 FAV: -1-3: 6 ch h Jareer -   **nse   99**
Dancing Line (High Line) -:
4401} **TOUGH GUY 211** Sweden 4-9-6 J Brandt 84/10: 5010-3: Dead-htd for 3rd.   **dht   99**
1057   **KING PRIAM 15** [5] 5-9-6 (bl) R Price 25/1: 620005: Bhd, eff 2f out, sn btn, fin 5th.   **2   95**
1015   **PANTAR 20** [2] 5-9-6 K Darley 37/10: 321436: Prom, rdn/wknd final 2f, fin 6th.   **3   90**
2273} **CHINA RED 322** [12] 6-9-6 M Hills 123/10: 3100-7: In tch, fdd, fnl 3f, fin 7th: reapp.   **1   88**
11 ran   Time 1m 49.8   (Stall Rh)   Y Durant Sweden

YORK   WEDNESDAY MAY 17TH   Lefthand, Flat, Galloping Track

Official Going   FIRM Stalls: 5/6f - Stands Side, 7f - Round Course - Inside

1324   2.05 SONY HCAP 3YO+ 0-110 (B)   5f   Firm 14   -09 Slow   [107]
£19058   £5864   £2932   £1466   3 yo rec 8 lb   Field raced in 2 Groups

1182   **ELLENS LAD 10** [6] W J Musson 6-8-13 (92) Pat Eddery 11/1: 2-0501: 6 b g Polish Patriot - Lady Ellen   **99**
(Horage) Al handy far side, rdn/led 1f out, drvn/styd on well ins last, rdn out: op 10/1: '99 wnr at Newbury,
Haydock & Newmarket (h'caps, rtd 95): '98 Newmarket wnr (h'cap, rtd 86, E Alston): stays 6f, all wins at 5f: acts
on firm, soft & any trk, likes a stiff one, esp Newmarket: best without blnks: strong, tough & useful sprinter.
1245   **SUNLEY SENSE 6** [5] M R Channon 4-8-4 (83) S Drowne 16/1: 0-0022: 4 b g Komaite - Brown Velvet   **nk   88**
(Mansingh) Al handy far side, led over 1f out, sn hdd, kept on well: op 14/1, quick reapp: in fine form.
1182   **SHEER VIKING 10** [21] B W Hills 4-9-3 (96) M Hills 10/1: 00-223: 4 b g Danehill - Schlefalora   **¾   100**
(Mas Media) Held up stands side, no room over 1f out, rdn & styd on strongly ins last, not reach front pair
far side: back at 5f & a shade unlucky, deserves a nice prize: see 1182, 702.
941   **JUWWI 30** [4] J M Bradley 6-8-11 (90) Darren Williams (7) 20/1: 015144: Bhd far side, prog from over   **½   91**
1f out, nrst fin: customary late run, tough/ultra consistent, a credit to connections: win again at 6f?
1162   **JACKIES BABY 11** [2] 4-8-5 (84) A Daly 33/1: 400045: Led far side/overall 3f, kept on: pacey type.   **hd   84**
1172   **AFAAN 11** [23] 7-9-2 (95)(bl) T G McLaughlin 33/1: 330-06: Prom stands side, rdn/switched to lead   **nk   94**
that group ins last, held nr fin: gd run: loves Newmarket: see 113.
1245   **CRYHAVOC 6** [20] 6-8-2 (81) F Norton 9/2 FAV: -60037: Dwelt & held up stds side, no room halfway   **hd   79+**
& again over 1f out, switched & rdn/styd on well ins last, nrst fin: qck reapp, hvly bckd: must win at 6f.
1162   **BLESSINGINDISGUISE 11** [12] 7-7-11 (76)(bl) Dale Gibson 7/1: 0-5028: Bhd ldrs stands side, eff   **shd   74**
over 1f out, onepace: hvly bckd lkd well: on a handy mark, loves Ascot: see 758.
1245   **HENRY HALL 6** [10] 4-8-8 (87) K Fallon 10/1: 6-6069: Held up towards centre, switched/styd on fnl 1f.   **shd   84**
1172   **PERRYSTON VIEW 11** [13] 8-10-0 (107) K Darley 12/1: 01-100: Handy stds side, onepace fnl 1f: 10th.   **shd   104**
1245   **AMBITIOUS 6** [17] 5-8-4 (83) C Catlin (7) 25/1: -01040: Mid-div stands side, switched & styd on ins   **nk   79**
last, nvr able to chall: 11th: quick reapp: not disgraced: see 905 (soft).
1008   **TOM TUN 23** [11] 5-7-13 (78) T Williams 20/1: -52300: Unruly stalls, in tch centre, held fnl 1f: 12th.   **1¼   71**
905   **CARTMEL PARK 33** [22] 4-8-0 (78)(10w) G Carter 33/1: 01-050: Cl-up stands side, led that group   **shd   72**
over 1f out, hdd/no extra ins last: 13th: lkd superb: pacey: shld find another race in a lesser h'cap.
1173   **MIZHAR 11** [7] 4-8-6 (85) O Pears 33/1: 006-00: Held up far side, nvr on terms: 14th: see 1173 (6f).   **shd   70**
941   **REFERENDUM 30** [1] 6-7-13 (78) A Nicholls (2) 40/1: 0-0000: Chsd ldrs far side 3f: 15th: see 941.   **shd   70**
1173   **GET STUCK IN 11** [18] 4-8-4 (83) R Hills 14/1: 40-060: Led stands side 3f, fdd: 17th: see 844.   **0**
*1245   **DAMALIS 6** [15] 4-9-1 (94)(6ex) T E Durcan 16/1: 0-4610: Nvr on terms stands side: 18th: qck reapp.   **0**
1173   **NIGHT FLIGHT 11** [14] 6-8-11 (90) R Winston 10/1: -00200: Chsd ldrs twds centre 3f, eased/btn fnl 1f: 22nd.   **0**
1013   Midnight Escape 23 [9] 7-8-7 (86) R Mullen 25/1:   1245 **Further Outlook 6** [8] 6-9-3 (96) S Sanders 33/1:
1192   Indian Spark 10 [16] 6-8-7 (86) A Culhane 25/1:   4288} **Dashing Blue 221** [19] 7-10-0 (107) L Dettori 20/1:
1090   Deadly Nightshade 15 [3] 4-9-7 (100) M J Kinane 16/1:
23 ran   Time 57.93 (1.13)   (Mrs Rita Brown)   W J Musson Newmarket, Suffolk

1325   2.35 LISTED MIDDLETON STKS 4YO+ (A)   1m2f85y   Firm 14   -00 Slow
£15544   £5896   £2948   £1340

1170   **LAFITE 11** [3] J W Hills 4-8-9 (t) R Hills 20/1: 110-01: 4 b f Robellino - Gorgeous Dancer (Nordico)   **95**
Prom, rdn/briefly outpcd over 2f out, drvn/chsd ldr over 1f out, strong chall ins last & led on line, drvn out: bckd
at long odds, tchd 25/1: '99 wnr at Chepstow, Newbury (fillies h'cap) & Brighton (h'caps, rtd 84): plcd in '98 (mdn,
rtd 77): eff at 1m/10.5f on firm & soft, any trk, likes a gall one: eff with/without t-strap: useful & v progressive.
3627} **FANTAZIA 263** [6] J R Fanshawe 4-8-9 R Cochrane 11/2: 5111-2: 4 b f Zafonic - Trescalini (Sadler's   **shd   94**
Wells) Trkd ldrs, smooth prog to lead over 1f out, hard rdn/strongly prsd ins last & hdd line: nicely bckd: reapp:
rattled off a hat-trick of h'caps on fnl 3 '99 starts, at Redcar (2) & Newmarket (rtd h'cap, rtd 86): plcd in '98
(rtd 75, M Johnston): eff at 10/11f on firm & gd, stiff/gall trk, likes Redcar: tough & improving, fine reapp.
--   **BOISMORAND** [2] M F Mathet 4-8-9 Vincent Vion 20/1: 011-43: 4 ch f Sheikh Albadou - Coupole   **3½   89**
(Vaguely Noble) Held up, briefly no room 3f out, kept on for press fnl 2f, not pace of front pair: bckd at long odds:

440

lkd well: French raider, recent 4th in a Longchamp 10f h'cap: won twice in '99: eff at 1m/10.5f on firm & hvy grnd.

122 **LIMELIGHTING** 173 [5] J H M Gosden 4-8-9 L Dettori 11/4: 1212-4: Dwelt, sn handy, rdn/led over 2f out, hdd over 1f out & sn held: hvly bckd: 6 month abs: '99 wnr here at York (C/D mdn) & Doncaster (fill stks, rtd 95): stays 12f, both wins at 10f: acts on firm & hvy, any trk: not given hard time & proved tough/prog last term.	½	88
3907} **FARFALA** 247 [8] 4-8-12 K Fallon 9/2: 3010-5: Held up, eff over 2f out, no impress: bckd: ndd this on reapp: '99 scorer at M-Laffitte & also Chantilly (listed, rtd 108): eff at 10/12f on gd & soft grnd, prob handles firm: likes a gall trk & has run well fresh: prev with A Fabre, now P Cole & shld do better.	¾	90
1014 **SWEET SORROW** 23 [1] 5-8-9 S Sanders 5/2 FAV: 445-26: Held up, eff 4f out, sn btn: hvly bckd tho' op 2/1: disapp eff from this normally tough/consistent mare, rider reported she was unsuited by this firm grnd.	2½	83
1076 **FOREST FIRE** 16 [7] 5-8-9 M Roberts 10/1: 560-27: Cl-up, led over 3f out till over 2f out, sn btn.	3½	78
-- **MOULOUYA** [9] 5-8-9 R Mullen 33/1: 6/13-8: Led 7f, btn 2f out: jumps fit (recent Folkestone h'cap wnr, rtd 102h, eff at 2m/2m1.5f on gd & hvy): ex-French mare, '99 scorer at Saint Cloud (12f, hvy): with J Best.	14	62
8 ran Time 2m 08.79 (1.49) (Wood Hall Stud Ltd) J W Hills Upper Lambourn, Berks		

1326 3.10 GR 2 DANTE STKS 3YO (A)   1m2f85y   Firm 14   +09 Fast
£86275   £31900   £15950   £7250

*1056 **SAKHEE** 18 [3] J L Dunlop 3-8-11 R Hills 5/2 JT FAV: 411-11: 3 b c Badri - Thawakib (Sadler's Wells) Chsd ldr, rdn/prog to lead & hung right over 1f out, styd on resolutely ins last, drvn out: lkd superb, fast time: hvly bckd: earlier scored at Sandown (Gr 3): won fnl 2 of 3 juv starts, at Nottingham (mdn) & Sandown (stks, rtd 102): eff at 10f (dam smart 12f wnr) & further will suit: acts on firm & hvy, likes a stiff/gall trk, esp Sandown: likes to race with/force the pace: very smart & genuine, expect a big run in the Derby next month.		117
1056 **PAWN BROKER** 18 [4] D R C Elsworth 3-8-11 T Quinn 11/2: 61-122: 3 ch c Selkirk - Dime Bag (High Line) Rear/in tch, stdy prog fnl 3f & prsd wnr over 1f out, hung in bhd wnr ins ins last, held nr fin: well bckd: acts on firm & hvy, stays 10.5f: possibly distracted by whip of winning jockey & is smart/progressive like the wnr.	1¼	114
4102} **BEST OF THE BESTS** 234 [5] Saeed bin Suroor 3-8-11 L Dettori 5/2 JT FAV: 312-3: 3 ch c Machiavellian - Sueboog (Darshaan) Held up in tch, rdn fnl 3f, styd on ins last, not pace of front pair: hvly bckd tho' op 2/1: reapp, on toes in paddock, 2 handlers: '99 scorer at Sandown (C Brittain, Gr 3, rtd 112 & rnr-up in a Gr 2): styd longer 10.5f trip, shld stay 12f: acts on firm & soft, likes a stiff/gall trk: improve & shld win another Gr race.	¾	113
1171 **SHAMROCK CITY** 11 [1] P Howling 3-8-11 K Fallon 12/1: 21-604: Led, rdn fnl 3f, hdd over 1f out, onepace: bckd, op 16/1: styd longer 10f trip well, acts on firm & fast: posted seasonal best, Listed will suit.	nk	112
1025 **ROYAL KINGDOM** 24 [2] 3-8-11 M J Kinane 11/4: 115-55: Held up, left bhd fnl 3f: hvly bckd: surely something amiss here returning to longer 10f trip: not handle firm? see 1025 (1m).	11	100
5 ran Time 2m 07.81 (0.51) (Hamdan Al Maktoum) J L Dunlop Arundel, W Sussex		

1327 3.40 LISTED RTD HCAP 4YO+ 0-110 (A)   1m rnd   Firm 14   -04 Slow   [111]
£19957   £7570   £3785   £1720

1015 **MAYARO BAY** 23 [7] R Hannon 4-8-11 (94) R Hughes 14/1: 32-001: 4 b f Robellino - Down The Valley (Kampala) Cl-up, went on 2f out, clr ins last & always holding rivals after, rdn out: tchd 16/1: '99 Goodwood wnr (h'cap, rtd 98, plcd sev times): '98 Warwick wnr (mdn, rtd 84): eff at 7f/1m on gd/soft, relishes fast & firm grnd: acts on any trk: has run well fresh: tough/consistent & v useful filly, responded well to a positive R Hughes ride.		101
1110 **CARIBBEAN MONARCH** 14 [2] Sir Michael Stoute 3-5-8-10 (93) K Fallon 5/2 FAV: 40-432: 5 b g Fairy King - Whos The Blonde (Cure The Blues) Pulled hard/trkg ldrs, lost place halfway & no room over 2f out, switched & styd on well over 1f out, wnr had flown: hvly bckd, op 3/1: lkd well: acts on firm & soft grnd: again fin well.	1½	96
4560} **FREE OPTION** 200 [4] B Hanbury 5-8-11 (94) J Reid 10/1: 0610-3: 5 ch g Indian Ridge - Saneena (Kris) Chsd ldrs, rdn over 2f out, kept on onepace for press: op 8/1, reapp, padd pick: '99 scorer at Kempton (rtd h'cap), Chester (stks) & Newmarket (h'cap, rtd 96): '98 Lingfield (mdn) & Newbury wnr (h'cap, rtd 94 & 68a): eff at 7f/1m, stays a stiff 10f: suited by firm & gd, handles equitrack, any trk: best without t-strap: useful & tough, fine reapp.	¾	96
733 **RIVER TIMES** 53 [3] T D Easterby 4-8-8 (91) K Darley 7/1: 50-204: Dictated pace in lead 6f, fdd fnl 1f.	½	92
725 **THE PRINCE** 53 [13] 6-8-7 (90)(t) L Dettori 10/1: 03-105: Dwelt & held up rear, switched/kept on fnl 2f, no threat: fit after abs: prob best delivered late off a strong gallop, which never materialised here: see 663.	1	89
1112 **GREEN CARD** 14 [8] 6-8-9 (92) S Drowne 20/1: 433-46: Mid-div, rdn/onepace over 2f out: lkd well.	1½	88
1077 **JUNO MARLOWE** 16 [9] 4-8-12 (95) T Quinn 20/1: 010-07: Trkd ldrs halfway, fdd over 1f out: op 14/1.	½	90
966 **TAMMAM** 28 [10] 4-8-7 (90)(20h) J P Spencer 25/1: 34-008: Held up in tch, eff/no room 3f out till over 1f out, no impress: no luck in running, prob worth another ch: see 966.	1¼	82
3042} **ALFIE BOY** 291 [5] 4-9-3 (100) R Cochrane 20/1: 134-9: Held up, eff 3f out, no impress: reapp, ndd this: '99 Goodwood wnr (debut, auct mdn, rtd 87, subs rtd 103 in List company, poss flattered): unrcd juv: eff at 7f, stays a sharp 1m: handles firm & soft grnd: h'cap bow today.	½	91
1077 **BRILLIANT RED** 16 [11] 7-9-5 (102)(t) Pat Eddery 12/1: 021-00: Held up, eff 3f out, no impress: 10th.	3	87
1182 **HO LENG** 10 [6] 5-9-7 (104) M J Kinane 7/1: 053-30: Trkd ldrs pulling hard, rdn/btn 2f out: 11th.	shd	89
*1042 **NIMELLO** 19 [1] 4-8-7 (90) J Carroll 10/1: 20-010: Al rear: 12th: op 9/1: btr 1042 (hvy).	3½	68
*1110 **BOLD KING** 14 [12] 5-8-11 (94) M Hills 6/1: 524-10: Chsd ldrs 5f: 13th: much btr 1110 (7f, g/s).	5	62
13 ran Time 1m 37.27 (1.47) (J R Shannon) R Hannon East Everleigh, Wilts		

1328 4.10 BLUE BICYCLE MDN 2YO (D)   6f   Firm 14   -42 Slow
£7475   £2300   £1150   £575

984 **BARKING MAD** 27 [1] M L W Bell 2-9-0 M Fenton 11/4: 31: 2 b c Dayjur - Avian Assembly (General Assembly) Trkd ldrs, rdn/led over 1f out, styd on well ins last, rdn out: bandaged rear hind: confirmed eyecatching promise of Newmarket debut: Jan foal, cost $32,000: apprec step up to 6f, shld get further (dam smart at upto 9f): acts on firm & soft grnd a stiff/gall trk: useful juv, can win in better company & heads for Coventry Stks.		90+
1169 **FIREWORK** 11 [9] W J Haggas 2-9-0 M Hills 9/2: 22: 2 b c Primo Dominie - Prancing (Prince Sabo) Handy, rdn/chsd wnr over 1f out, kept on well: well bckd: lkd well: small, workmanlike colt: styd longer 6f trip & likes firm/fast grnd: capable clr of rem here & looks sure to find similar: see 1169.	1	86
911 **BARAKANA** 33 [6] B J Meehan 2-9-0 Pat Eddery 11/1: 33: 2 b c Barathea - Safkana (Doyoun) Chsd ldrs, rdn/kept on fnl 1f, not pace of front pair: bckd, op 12/1: jockey given a 1 day ban for excessive use of whip: shld find a race, handles firm grnd, going the right way after intro: see 911 (soft).	4	76
1124 **REPEAT PERFORMANCE** 13 [7] W G M Turner 2-9-0 (t) A Daly 20/1: 424: Led 2f, no extra fnl 1f: op 14/1: handles firm & gd/soft, eff at 6f but could find a race on a minor trk at 5f: see 1124, 891.	½	74
-- **ZANDEED** [11] 2-9-0 J Reid 14/1: 5: Sn pushed along in tch, hdwy fnl 2f, kept on, no threat: op 12/1: ndd this: May foal, cost 35,000 gns: half brother to a Gr1 plcd 7f/1m juv & a 6f juv wnr: relish 7f & win races.	hd	73+
-- **REEL BUDDY** [14] 2-9-0 R Hughes 20/1: 6: Dwelt, prog to lead halfway, hung left 2f out & hdd over	1¼	70

1f out, btn/eased fnl 1f: op 14/1, ndd this: Mr Greeley colt, Feb foal, cost 23,000 gns: Feb 1st foal, dam a 6f wnr: scopey, gd bodied colt, showed plenty of pace & will know more next time.

-- **MAGIC WATERS** [4] 2-9-0 M J Kinane 20/1: 7: Dwelt, rdn/towards rear early, styd on well from over ¾ 68+
1f out, nrst fin: op 16/1, edgy/green in paddock: Ezzoud gldg, Mar first foal, cost 22,000 gns: dam a 7f juv wnr.

-- **KHAYYAM** [13] 2-9-0 K Fallon 5/2 FAV: 8: Dwelt, mid-div, outpcd halfway, held after: hvly bckd hd 67
tho' op 2/1: paddock pick: Affirmed colt, Feb foal, cost 39,000 gns: well grown, will apprec 7f+ in time.

-- **PARTING SHOT** [10] 2-9-0 K Darley 12/1: 9: Dwelt, sn pushed along, nvr on terms: tchd 14/1, nk 66
shorter priced stablemate of 7th: reapp: Young Ern colt, May foal, cost 18,000 gns: dam a 5/6f juv wnr.

1161 **CO DOT UK 11** [12] 2-9-0 F Lynch 16/1: 530: Prom 4f: 10th: tchd 20/1: btr 1161 (5f, gd). 1½ 62

-- **STRETTON** [5] 2-9-0 L Dettori 16/1: 0: Chsd ldrs 4f, 11th: op 14/1: ndd this: Doyoun colt, Mar 2½ 55
foal, cost 26,000 gns: half brother to a 1m 3yo wnr, dam a 6f 3yo wnr: apprec 7f+, given a considerate intro here.

-- **Physical Force** [2] 2-9-0 R Mullen 40/1: -- **Missing Drink** [8] 2-9-0 G Duffield 50/1:
13 ran Time 1m 12.75 (3.35) (Christopher Wright) M L W Bell Newmarket, Suffolk

---

1329 4.40 PETERHOUSE HCAP 4YO + 0-90 (C) 1m5f194y Firm 14 -21 Slow [90]
£7865 £2420 £1210 £605

4397} **DOMINANT DUCHESS 214** [10] J W Hills 6-9-6 (82) M Hills 12/1: 4P22-1: 6 b m Old Vic - Andy's Find 88
(Buckfinder) Held up rear, switched & stdy run fnl 3f to lead well in last, drvn out: op 10/1, reapp: '99 Kempton
wnr (reapp, h'cap), subs rnr-up in Cesarewitch (rtd 85): eff at 14f, stays 2½m well: acts on firm & gd, handles
any trk: runs well fresh: tough & progressive mare, reportedly set for the 2m6f Queen Alexandra Stks at R Ascot.

*1180 **AFTERJACKO 10** [12] D R C Elsworth 4-9-12 (88) T Quinn 11/4 FAV: 53-512: 4 ch g Seattle Dancer - 1¼ 91
Shilka (Soviet Star) Held up, eff over 2f out & prog/drvn to lead over 1f out, held well in last & no extra: swtg:
hvly bckd, op 7/2: gd run under topweight, lengthy/progressive gldg: see 1180.

885 **WEET FOR ME 35** [4] R Hollinshead 4-8-13 (75) R Hughes 25/1: 02-003: 4 b c Warning - Naswara 1½ 76
(Al Nasr) Chsd ldrs, rdn/prog & chance over 1f out, onepace in last: padd pick: see 714.

1222 **SON OF SNURGE 7** [2] P F I Cole 4-9-3 (79) K Fallon 10/1: 203-04: Led, rdn/hdd over 1f out & no 1 79
extra cl-home: nicely bckd, tchd 12/1: prog physically from 3yo to 4yo: eff, reapp bhd, shld win again: see 1222.

968 **ALHAWA 28** [1] 7-9-7 (83) J Weaver 4/1: 006-25: Held up, rdn 2f out, kept on onepace: well bckd. hd 83

1980} **ROYAL CASTLE 337** [7] 6-8-13 (75) G Duffield 20/1: /530-6: Held up, rdn & styd on well from 2f out, hd 74+
nrst fin: tchd 25/1, fit on reapp, 6 wk jumps abs, 99/00 Towcester & Doncaster wnr (novs, rtd 104h), eff around 2½m
on firm & gd): lightly rcd on the Level last term (plcd, rtd 78, h'cap): back in '97 scored at Pontefract & Redcar
(h'caps, rtd 83, W Hern): eff at 12/14f, relish a return to 2m: acts on firm, prob bolt: should not be missed at 2m.

1167 **JAMAICAN FLIGHT 11** [8] 7-8-9 (71) J F Egan 25/1: 320407: Chsd ldrs, kept on onepace fnl 2f. nk 69

*1147 **PLUTOCRAT 12** [11] 4-8-12 (74) J Reid 7/1: 231-18: Bhd, eff 2f out, sn held: Ingr trip. ¾ 71

*1087 **TOTEM DANCER 15** [13] 7-7-11 (59) F Norton 7/1: 000019: Held up, eff/no room 3f out & again shd 56
over 1f out, switched & styd on ins last, no threat: bckd: no luck in running, this best forgotten: see 1087.

968 **WHO CARES WINS 28** [14] 3-9-3 (79) Pat Eddery 12/1: 120-00: Chsd ldrs, ch over 1f out, fdd fnl 1f: 2 73
10th: op 10/1, still ndd this: '99 Chester wnr (mdn, subs rtd 82, val h'cap): eff at 13/14f on fast & gd, sharp/gall trk.

3514} **SANDBAGGEDAGAIN 269** [3] 6-9-0 (76) G Parkin 20/1: 31/0-0: Held up, al towards rear, 11th: Flat 3½ 65
reapp, 6 month jumps abs (unplcd, rtd 69h): no form sole '99 Flat start: prog in '98, scored at Catterick, Ascot &
Chester (h'caps, rtd 78): eff arnd 2m on firm & hvy grnd & has run well fresh: best without blnks: handles any trk.

1086 **NORCROFT JOY 15** [15] 5-8-10 (72) J Reid 12/1: 056-50: Held up, prog 4f out, no hdwy fnl 2f: 12th. nk 69

757 **Parable 50** [17] 4-8-6 (68) F Lynch 33/1: 1251 **My Legal Eagle 6** [16] 6-8-3 (65) P Fitzsimons (5) 20/1:
*519 **High Policy 92** [9] 4-9-7 (83) L Dettori 16/1: *822 **Haya Ya Kefaah 42** [14] 8-7-11 (59)(1ow)(10oh) A Nicholls (0) 33/1:
16 ran Time 2m 58.29 (4.89) (Mrs Diana Patterson) J W Hills Upper Lambourn, Berks

---

Official Going FIRM (Watered). Pace Figs inapplicable due to high winds.

1330 2.25 HANNINGTONS HCAP 3YO+ 0-75 (E) 1m rnd Firm Inapplicable [75]
£2968 £848 £424 3 yo rec 12lb

4552} **NO EXTRAS 201** [14] G L Moore 10-9-6 (67) S Whitworth 12/1: 6040-1: 10 b g Efisio - Parkland Rose (Sweet 72
Candy) Patiently rdn, not much room 3f out, prog to lead over 1f out, held on well, rdn out, narrowly: reapp,
op 10/1: '99 scorer at Windsor (class stks, rtd 83): '98 scorer at Newmarket (h'cap): '97 wnr at Goodwood
(2, h'caps): stays easy 10f, v eff arnd 7f/1m on firm & soft, loves Goodwood: runs well fresh: tough 10yo.

1070 **COPPLESTONE 16** [4] P W Harris 4-9-13 (74) A Beech (5) 8/1: 3/4-02: 4 b g Second Set - Queen Of nk 78
The Brush (Averof) Dsptd lead from 1½f out, rdn on, just btn: fine run, shld win a race.

1066 **DANZAS 16** [7] J M Bradley 6-7-11 (44)(bl) Claire Bryan (5) 16/1: 606103: 6 b g Polish Precedent - nk 47
Dancing Rocks (Green Dancer) Towards rear, prog 2f out, rdn/ev ch fnl 1f, kept on, btn under ½L: gd eff.

539 **ITALIAN SYMPHONY 89** [12] P D Evans 6-8-11 (58)(vis) Joanna Badger (7) 14/1: 505004: Patiently ½ 60
rdn twds rear, eff/hdwy 2f out, chall fnl 1f, kept on, btn under 1L: abs, gd eff: tough (18 wins from 100 races).

1003 **SAMARA SONG 23** [8] 7-8-11 (58) R Fitzpatrick (3) 8/1: 00-005: Going well 2f out, onepcd fnl 1f. 2½ 56

3413} **MUTABASSIR 274** [5] 6-9-4 (65) I Mongan (5) 6/1: 4430-6: Hld up rr, styd on fnl 2f, nrst fin: stablemate: 2½ 58+
of wnr, promising after 9 mth abs: '99 scorer over C/D here at Brighton (h'cap, easily, rtd 72): '98 wnr again
at Brighton (mdn h'cap), Epsom, Folkestone (h'caps), Lingfield & Southwell (AW h'caps, rtd 56a): eff at 7f/1m,
stays 10f on firm & gd/soft, both AWs: likes a sharp trk: can go well fresh: back on a wng mark, keep in mind.

1066 **CAVERSFIELD 16** [9] 5-8-3 (50) R Ffrench 25/1: 00-007: Al prom, led over 2f out until over 1¾ 39
1f out, wknd: now with J M Bradley: see 336.

1243 **APRIL ACE 6** [3] 4-8-8 (55) C Rutter 25/1: 3-0008: Led until over 2f out, wknd over 1f out: ¾ 42
in '99 scored at Nottingham & Brighton (h'caps, rtd 59): juv wnr at Bath (mdn auct): eff at 7f/1m on
firm, gd/soft, any trk: tough sort, likes to front-run.

1213 **GULF SHAADI 8** [10] 8-9-7 (68) M Tebbutt 13/2: 040549: Rear, eff ins fnl 2f, nvr nrr: btr 1213 (7f here). 1 53

921 **DONE AND DUSTED 32** [2] 4-9-9 (70) J Mackay 16/1: 631560: Rdn/not qckn 2f out: 10th, see 583. 1 53

842 **SHAMWARI SONG 40** [6] 5-7-10 (43)(3oh) A McCarthy (0) 25/1: 030040: Nvr nr ldrs: 11th, see 505. 2½ 21

1076 **DIRECT DEAL 16** [1] 4-9-12 (73)(t) D Harrison 25/1: 13-000: Prom over 6f: fin 12th, see 747. 1½ 48

1094 **WHENWILLIEMETHARRY 15** [15] 3-8-8 (67) N Pollard 25/1: 500-60: Chsd ldrs, hmpd/wknd ent fnl 2f. 3 36

1113 **LEGAL SET 14** [11] 4-9-9 (70) N Callan 4/1 FAV: 00-200: Chsd ldrs, rdn/wknd 2f out: remote 19 9
last: reportedly not suited by the trk & fin distressed: twice before 854.

3413} MASTER MILLFIELD 274 [13] 8-8-0 (47) J Bramhill 33/1: /000-P: Prom over 3f, t.o./p.u. ins fnl 1f, lame.   **0**
15 ran   Time 1m 36.0 (4)   (K Higson)   G L Moore Woodingdean, E Sussex

---

1331   3.00 KIFFORD CLASS CLAIMER 3YO+ 0-60 (F)   1m2f   Firm   Inapplicable
      £2425   £693   £346   3 yo rec 14lb

1129 **SHEER FACE 13** [9] W R Muir 6-9-6 D Harrison 5/1: 565401: 6 b g Midyan - Rock Face (Ballad Rock)   **54**
Chsd ldrs, rdn to lead appr fnl 1f, styd on: well bckd, op 6/1: plcd form in '99 (h'cap, rtd 73, reapp):
'98 Goodwood wnr (h'cap, rtd 77 & 57a): eff at 7f/10f on firm & gd/soft, sharp/undul trk: well h'capped.
1210 **JUST WIZ 8** [7] Andrew Reid 4-9-7 M Henry 6/1: 530022: 4 b g Efisio - Jade Pet (Petong)   1¼   **52**
Led halfway until hdd over 1f out, kept on for press: gd eff: formerly with R Hannon: see 1210.
460 **FUERO REAL 102** [10] R J Hodges 5-9-4 O Urbina 25/1: 240-53: 5 b g Highest Honor - Highest Pleasure   ½   **48$**
(Foolish Pleasure) Rdn after halfway, styd on well ins fnl 2f, nrst fin: unplcd in a sell hdle since 460: 12f suit.
1101 **TRY PARIS 14** [14] H J Collingridge 4-9-0 (vis) N Callan 40/1: 0-0004: Chsd ldrs, rdn/not much   ½   **43**
room 3f out, kept on: stays 10f on firm, poor form prev: see 568.
2868} **MINJARA 299** [13] J A Morris 14/1: 0040-5: Held up rear, styd on fnl 2f, nrst fin: 10 month   shd   **55$**
abs, tchd 40/1: modest last term, 4th of 8 at Bath (1m h'cap, firm, rtd 36): treat this rating with caution.
4335} **PADDY McGOON 218** [16] 5-9-12 L Branch (7) 16/1: 5/00-6: In tch, rdn & kept on fnl 1f: reapp: no   nk   **54**
form just 2 runs last term: plcd once from 4 starts in '98 (10f h'cap, rtd 69): mdn, handles firm or gd/yldg.
1210 **COLLEGE ROCK 8** [4] 3-8-10 (vis) A McCarthy (3) 10/1: 042637: Gd hold, prom, drvn/btn over   1¼   **50**
1f out: formerly trained by Mrs A E Johnson, now R Brotherton: see 1210 (C/D).
775 **SASEEDO 49** [5] 10-9-0 G Bardwell 33/1: 004008: Dwelt, bhd, nvr nr ldrs: 7 wk abs: see 408.   3½   **35$**
632 **PHILISTAR 74** [2] 7-9-4 J Tate 4/1 FAV: -33609: Chsd ldrs, rdn/btn over 1f out: abs, see 452.   shd   **39**
1210 **TWOFORTEN 8** [11] 5-9-2 (bl) A Eddery (5) 33/1: -06000: Chsd ldrs over 3f out, btn over 1f out: 10th.   1   **35**
822 **AMAZING FACT 42** [8] 5-9-0 (BL) R Ffrench 33/1: 0-3600: Prom 7f, rdn/btn: blnkd, abs: see 607.   nk   **33$**
965 **LIONESS 29** [20] 4-9-1 Claire Bryan (5) 16/1: 30-000: Keen, restrained, rdn 3f out, no dngr: 12th.   8   **24**
1212 **FOX STAR 8** [12] 3-8-0 P Doe 25/1: 0-6000: Brief eff 3f out, nvr in it: 13th: see 313 (AW).   nk   **23**
871 **BADRINATH 36** [17] 6-9-4 G Faulkner (3) 10/1: -63200: Chsd ldrs over 1m: 14th: see 775, 360 (AW).   shd   **27**
1210 **EI EI 8** [3] 5-9-0 I Mongan (5) 8/1: 466240: Prom 1m, rdn/wknd: 16th, btr 1210 (C/D).   **0**
1209 **MAX 8** [6] 5-9-4 R Brisland (5) 40/1: -63200: Led until halfway, sn backpedalled: 18th.   **0**
896 **Emma Lyne 34** [19] 4-8-11 D Sweeney 40/1:   1128 **Ocean Line 13** [18] 5-9-2 A Beech (5) 11/1:
4473} **Petrisk 208** [1] 3-8-3 N Pollard 50/1:
19 ran   Time 2m 04.2 (6.4)   (A J de V Patrick)   W R Muir Lambourn, Berks

---

1332   3.30 FILLIES HCAP 3YO+ 0-70 (E)   1m3f196y   Firm   Inapplicable   [64]
      £2766   £790   £395   3 yo rec 17lb

855 **TUI 37** [7] P Bowen 5-7-10 (32)(2oh) Claire Bryan (5) 16/1: 000-51: 5 b m Tina's Pet - Curious   **37**
Feeling (Nishapour) Al up there, led 1½f out, styd on for press: unplcd on the Flat in '99 (rtd 38): '99
wnr over hdles at Sedgefield & Newmarket (rtd 97h): Flat scorer in '98 at Beverley & Newmarket (h'caps, rtd
55 at best): eff at 10/12f on firm & gd/soft, any trk: took advantage of a handy mark.
3718} **ELMS SCHOOLGIRL 259** [3] J M P Eustace 4-10-0 (64) J Tate 7/2: 1153-2: 4 ch f Emarati - Ascend   2   **65**
(Glint Of Gold) Prog 3f out, led briefly 2f out, onepace under press: gd eff, gave the wnr lumps
of weight on reapp: scored thrice here at Brighton in '99 (class stks & 2 h'caps, rtd 65): eff at 10/12f
on firm/fast grnd: Brighton specialist: shld scn go one better.
1128 **ORDAINED 13** [1] Miss Gay Kelleway 7-8-11 (47) N Callan 3/1 FAV: 460423: 7 b m Mtoto - In The   3½   **43**
Habit (Lyphard) Prog & chsd ldrs over 2f out, kept on onepace under press: just btr 1128 (C/D).
68 **NEEDWOOD MYSTIC 180** [10] B C Morgan 5-8-12 (48) S Whitworth 8/1: 5000-4: Led briefly over 2f out,   1¼   **42**
wknd over 1f out: gd eff after 6 month abs, just ndd this: in '99 scored twice at Warwick (mdn h'cap &
h'cap, rtd 51): eff around 12f on gd & firm, any trk, likes a sharp one, esp Warwick.
675 **MISS TAKE 62** [2] 4-8-2 (38) G Bardwell 25/1: 044005: Took gd hold, restrained, rdn 2f out,   3   **28**
no danger: 2 month abs: stays 12f? see 384.
4592} **ASHLEIGH BAKER 196** [8] 5-9-1 (51) J Fanning 9/2: 0053-6: Dsptd lead, rdn/btn over 2f out: reapp: 4   **36**
plcd last term (rtd 54 at best): '98 Ayr wnr (h'cap, with A Bailey): eff at 12f, tried 2m: acts on firm or soft.
1128 **FOREST DREAM 13** [9] 5-9-3 (53) A McCarthy (3) 33/1: -00007: Prom, wknd over 2f out: with L Dace.   4   **32**
4146} **INDIAN NECTAR 231** [4] 7-9-6 (56) J Mackay (7) 6/1: 1160-8: Eff & came wide over 3f out, sn held: 3½   **30**
reapp: last term scored at Nottingham, Lingfield (fillies' h'caps) & Chepstow (h'cap, rtd 58): 98/99 hdles
wnr at Worcester (nov) & Hereford (nov h'cap, rtd 84h): eff at 10/12f on gd/soft, any trk.
1265 **BLESS 5** [5] 3-7-10 (49)(1oh) J Lowe 25/1: 6-0069: Brief eff 3f out, sn held: see 1096, 892.   1   **22**
1091 **COURT CHAMPAGNE 15** [6] 4-8-4 (40) N Pollard 25/1: 0/0060: Chsd ldrs, rdn/btn: 10th, poor form.   9   **1**
3024} **SPONTANEITY 292** [11] 4-9-10 (60) W Supple 25/1: /000-0: Dsptd lead 9f, wknd, fin last: reapp.   nk   **21**
11 ran   Time 2m 34.2 (6)   (Dragon Racing)   P Bowen Letterston, Pembrokes

---

1333   4.00 DANNY BLOOR MDN 3YO+ (D)   7f rnd   Firm   Inapplicable
      £3818   £1175   £587   £293   3 yo rec 11lb

785 **MISTER CLINTON 49** [4] K T Ivory 3-8-12 D O'Donohoe 20/1: 000-41: 3 ch g Lion Cavern - Thewaari   **61**
(Eskimo) Held up rear, prog to lead over 1f out, ran on well, shade cmftbly: 7 wk abs, tchd 50/1: fin 4th off a
mark of 47 in a h'cap on reapp (6f): suited by this step up to 7f on firm: acts on a sharp/undul trk.
789 **THE ROBSTER 48** [6] B J Meehan 3-8-12 D R McCabe 14/1: 00-02: 3 ch c Woodman - Country Cruise   1½   **60**
(Riverman) Chsd ldrs, rdn/onepcd over 1f out: 7 wk abs, op 8/1: rtd 76 on fin of 2 juv starts (7f, soft/hvy),
made running): handled this firm grnd.
591 **LEGENDAIRE 81** [2] Miss Gay Kelleway 3-8-12 S Whitworth 14/1: 0-2243: 3 gr c Fly Till Dawn -   1   **58**
Iolani (Alzao) Held up bhd ldrs, not much room over 2f out, styd on fnl 1f: gd eff after an abs: acts on
gd & firm & equitrack: formerly trained by C Dwyer: needs h'caps: see 488, 355.
-- **MADURESE** [8] C E Brittain 3-8-12 D Harrison 10/1: 4: Slowly away & not go pace, styd on fnl 2f,   1¾   **54**
nrst fin: well bred newcomer, drifted from 6/1: will learn plenty from this & improve, stepped up to 1m.
1135 **STILL IN LOVE 13** [5] 3-8-7 W Ryan 7/2: 3-25: Dsptd lead until over 1f out: op 2/1, not handle fm?   1½   **46**
4310} **HARMONIC 219** [9] 3-8-7 N Pollard 8/11 FAV: 6624-6: Rdn/outpcd halfway: v hvly bckd on reapp: nk   **45**
shthd rnr-up after 4 juv starts (6f fill mdn, rtd 81): acts on gd & firm: shld suit: much better expected.
884 **LAHAAY 35** [3] 3-8-12 W Supple 40/1: 05-07: Dsptd lead until over 1f out, wknd: rtd 84 on fnl   1   **48**
of 2 juv starts at Doncaster (1m mdn auct, soft/hvy): bred for 7f/1m: with M Tregoning.
1212 **COMMONBIRD 8** [7] 3-8-7 M Henry 40/1: 00-058: Prom to halfway, wknd: see 1081 (sell).   14   **15**

961 **CEINWEN 29** [1] 5-9-4 R Ffrench 100/1: 009: Sn pushed along, btn 3f out: no form yet. *1* **13**
9 ran Time 1m 23.3 (3.5) (Miss Lilo Blum) K T Ivory Radlett, Herts

1334 4.30 LADBROKES SUSSEX HCAP 3YO 0-70 (E) 5f59y Firm Inapplicable [75]
£2829 £808 £404

1105 **CUPIDS CHARM 14** [2] R Guest 3-9-4 (65) D Harrison 5/1 FAV: 4-001: 3 b f Cadeaux Genereux - Chapka (Green Desert) In tch, prog from 2f out, led ins fnl 1f, shade cmftbly: well bckd, tchd 8/1: with P Chapple-Hyam sole juv start (rtd 76): eff at 5/6f on firm, prob not so eff on soft: can improve again & defy the h'capper. **73**
731 **PACIFIC PLACE 53** [8] M Quinn 3-8-3 (50) C Rutter 20/1: 00-02: 3 gr c College Chapel - Kaitlin (Salmon Leap) Chsd ldrs, styd on for press fnl 1f: abs, little form prev: eff over a sharp/undul 5.2f on firm, 6f shld suit. *¾* **55**
1211 **AROGANT PRINCE 8** [6] J J Bridger 3-8-5 (52) R Brisland (5) 6/1: 60-043: 3 ch c Aragon - Versaillesprincess (Legend Of France) Led until hdd ins fnl 1f: gd front-running eff: see 1211 (6f, here). *1* **54**
399 **WILLOW MAGIC 112** [5] S Dow 3-9-1 (62) P Doe 10/1: 02-504: Bhd, styd on ins fnl 2f, nrst fin: nr 4 month abs: caught the eye here: see 234 (equitrack). *1¼* **61+**
785 **ARCADIAN CHIEF 49** [7] 3-8-0 (47)(4ow)(5oh) N Pollard 33/1: 404-05: Dwelt, prog after 2f, onepcd appr fnl 1f: 7 wk abs: mod juv form (unplcd in sells). *nk* **45**
1220 **BREEZY LOUISE 7** [1] 3-9-7 (68)(bl) O Urbina 11/2: 50-106: Chsd ldrs, not much room over 2f out, wknd fnl 1f: best 959 (clmr). *2½* **59**
*870 **SERGEANT SLIPPER 36** [10] 3-8-8 (55)(vis) R Fitzpatrick (3) 7/1: 1-0017: Slow start, rdn to imprv 2f out, no real impress: much btr 870 (fibresand). *1½* **42**
961 **BALIDARE 29** [3] 3-7-13 (46) G Bardwell 16/1: 00-08: Sn rdn, nvr in it: no form prev: with M Weeden. *¾* **31**
1205 **POWER AND DEMAND 9** [4] 3-8-5 (52)(bl) N Callan 16/1: 254309: Rdn/btn ent fnl 2f: see 659. *½* **36**
592 **GREY FLYER 81** [9] 3-8-13 (60) A Mackay 8/1: -12050: Rdn over 2f out, sn held: 10th, abs: see 269. *hd* **43**
1098 **BORN TO RULE 15** [11] 3-9-5 (66)(BL) R Price 14/1: 44-000: Prom, rdn/wknd 2f out: 11th, blnks. *¾* **47**
1202 **HOT ICE 9** [13] 3-8-5 (52) A Beech (5) 10/1: 10-000: Nvr nr ldrs: 12th: see 870. *6* **19**
526 **KIRSCH 91** [12] 3-9-5 (66) W Supple 10/1: -31560: Sn outpcd: fin last: 3 month abs: see 361. *½* **32**
13 ran Time 1m 3.1 (3.1) (I Allan, Ming Yi Chen & Hung Chao Hong) R Guest Newmarket

1335 5.05 APPR H & H HCAP DIV I 3YO+ 0-60 (F) 7f rnd Firm Inapplicable [58]
£2194 £627 £313 3 yo rec 11lb

*1213 **BUTRINTO 8** [12] B R Johnson 6-9-8 (52)(6ex) P Shea 9/4 FAV: -50611: 6 ch g Anshan - Bay Bay (Bay Express) Waited with, prog to lead ent fnl 1f, came clr, cmftbly: v well bckd, tchd 10/3: overcame 15 wk abs when successful over this C/D at Brighton recently (h'cap, rtd 53): rnr-up for J Pearce in '99 (rtd 74a, h'cap): '98 scorer at Newbury & Lingfield (h'caps, rtd 75 & 75a): eff at 6f/1m, v eff at 7f: acts on gd, firm, both AWs: can go well fresh: in great heart, complete the hat-trick. **58**
1273 **MYTTONS MISTAKE 5** [10] R J Baker 7-9-3 (47) G Sparkes 100/30: 00-022: 7 b g Rambo Dancer - Hi Hunsley (Swing Easy) Rear, prog 3f out, styd on ins fnl 1f, no ch with wnr: shld go one better off this mark. *2½* **48**
1066 **REACHFORYOURPOCKET 16** [9] M D I Usher 5-8-13 (43) J Mackay 12/1: 461203: 5 b g Royal Academy - Gemaasheh (Habitat) Chsd ldrs, went 2nd 2f out, onepcd fnl 1f: ran close to best: acts on firm & equitrack. *½* **43**
1259 **SABOT 5** [2] T J Arnold 7-9-3 (47) B O'Leary (3) 14/1: 554-04: Dsptd lead, led over 2f out until ins fnl 1f: 4L clr of rem: reapp rnr-up in '99 when trained by C Thornton (clmr, rtd 59): sole win at Thirsk back in '96: eff at 7f/8.2f on firm, soft, fibresand: can prob win off this mark. *¾* **45**
896 **FLYING PENNANT 34** [7] 7-8-10 (40)(bl) M Worrell 12/1: 350-55: In tch, rdn 3f out, not trouble ldrs. *4* **31**
622 **GOLD EDGE 76** [16] 6-8-4 (34) G Gibbons 20/1: 0-0506: Rdn/wknd over 1f out: 11 wk abs, see 148. *3½* **20**
1210 **PRIVATE SEAL 8** [14] 5-8-2 (28)(t)(4ow) L Branch (0) 33/1: -56607: Styd on fnl 2f, nvr nrr: see 262. *nk* **13**
879 **GHAAZI 35** [5] 4-9-6 (50) M Pattinson (8) 25/1: 4-0008: Chsd ldrs over 4f: see 227, 109 (AW). *hd* **34**
316 **ENTROPY 126** [8] 4-8-6 (36) D Kinsella 20/1: 050-09: Rdn 3f out, nvr chall: 4 month abs since poor form on the AW: best in '99 when 5th of 9 at Goodwood (6f h'cap, rtd 64, with R Hannon): juv scorer at Bath (nurs): eff around 6f on firm & gd/soft: with B A Pearce. *1¾* **16**
1139 **HI MUJTAHID 13** [4] 6-8-1 (30)(1ow) S Clancy 16/1: 000-00: Chsd ldrs 5f, wknd: 10th: see 1139. *½* **9**
385 **IMARI 114** [11] 3-9-5 (60) D Young (3) 10/1: 40-250: Rdn after halfway, nvr in it: 14th: nr 4 month abs: see 303 (AW sell, J Given): now with N Littmoden. **0**
833 **Smarts Megan 41** [15] 4-8-4 (34) D Watson 25/1: 2075} **Mitie Access 334** [6] 4-8-5 (35) M Worrell 25/1:
439 **Queen Of The Keys 105** [3] 4-8-7 (37) M Howard (2) 33/1: 504 **Mujkari 95** [1] 4-8-11 (41)(vis) K Parsons 16/1:
896 **Robbies Dream 34** [13] 4-9-0 (44)(VIS) D Meah 16/1:
16 ran Time 1m 23.4 (3.6) (Miss Julie Reeves) B R Johnson Epsom, Surrey

1336 5.35 APPR H & H HCAP DIV II 3YO+ 0-60 (F) 7f rnd Firm Inapplicable [57]
£2194 £627 £313 3 yo rec 11lb

503 **MR CUBE 95** [8] J M Bradley 10-8-10 (39)(bl) D Watson 7/1: 000601: 10 ch g Tate Gallery - Truly Thankful (Graustark) Chsd ldrs, led ins fnl 1f, rdn out, shade cmftbly: 3 mth abs: plcd in '99 (rtd 39, h'cap): last won at Epsom back in '97 (h'cap): eff at 7f/1m on firm & gd/soft, any trk, likes a sharp/undul one: wears blnks. **44**
561 **IMBACKAGAIN 86** [3] N P Littmoden 5-9-4 (47) D Young (3) 20/1: 630002: 5 b g Mujadil - Ballinclogher (Creative Plan) Al prom, led over 2f out until ins fnl 1f, not fin pace of wnr: 12 wk abs: see 297. *1¾* **47**
896 **STITCH IN TIME 34** [1] G C Bravery 4-9-1 (44) J Mackay 11/4 FAV: 00-223: 4 ch g Inchinor - Late Matinee (Red Sunset) Chsd ldrs, dstpd lead over 1f out, not qckn ins fnl 1f: acts on firm or soft: see 896 (C/D). *½* **43**
155 **TALENTS LITTLE GEM 161** [11] A W Carroll 3-8-12 (52) P Shea 25/1: 0300-4: Rear, styd on ins fnl 2f, nvr nrr: reapp: modest form prev for V Soane, rtd 67$ here at Brighton as a juv (6f mdn, gd/soft). *¾* **49**
1066 **ANNIE APPLE 16** [14] 4-9-7 (50) M Worrell 16/1: 0-0005: Rear, prog 2f out, onepcd fnl 1f: see 594. *hd* **47**
803 **CEDAR WELLS 47** [7] 4-9-10 (53) K Parsons 12/1: 00-006: Outpcd halfway, styd on ins fnl 2f: abs. *1¾* **46**
934 **FRENCH FANCY 30** [9] 3-8-5 (45)(bl) R Naylor 14/1: 042407: Prog halfway, onepcd over 1f out. *½* **37**
1259 **ITHADTOBEYOU 5** [16] 5-9-7 (50) S Clancy 5/1: 0-2238: Lost pitch halfway, styd on again ins fnl 2f. *1* **40**
333 **PRINCESS MO 123** [6] 4-8-1 (30) G Sparkes 14/1: 005-09: Rear, hit rail over 4f out, no danger: abs. *¾* **18**
676 **KAFIL 62** [10] 6-8-7 (36)(BL) R Thomas 14/1: 0-2600: Chsd ldrs 5f, wknd: 10th, blnkd, abs: see 254. *hd* **23**
189 **TWO STEP 154** [2] 4-8-5 (34)(t) D Meah 9/1: 060-0: Led almost 5f, wknd: 11th: turf debut, poor AW. *1¾* **17**
867 **DARK MENACE 36** [4] 8-9-6 (49)(bl) D Kinsella (3) 7/1: -00060: Prom 5½f, wknd: 12th: see 159. *¾* **30**
-- **Balaclava** [12] 5-8-7 (36) D Glennon 33/1: 574 **Mariana 84** [15] 5-8-4 (33) G Gibbons 33/1:
1211 **Silver Sky 8** [13] 4-8-11 (40) A Hawkins 50/1: 1092 **Split The Aces 15** [5] 4-8-13 (42) O Kozak 14/1:
16 ran Time 1m 24.6 (4.8) (R Miles) J M Bradley Sedbury, Glos

YORK THURSDAY MAY 18TH Lefthand, Flat, Galloping Track

Official Going: FIRM Stalls: 5/6f - Stands Side, 7f/Round Course - Inside

1337 **2.15 GUILBERT UK RTD HCAP 4YO+ 0-105 (B) 6f Firm 19 -28 Slow [111]**
£17005 £6450 £3225 £1466 Raced stands side

1324 **JUWWI 1** [12] J M Bradley 6-8-7 (90) Darren Williams (7) 15/2: 151441: 6 ch g Mujtahid - Nouvelle Star (Luskin Star) Dwelt, prog finl 3f and switched to lead 4f out, styd on well, rdn clr: jockey given 3 day ban for irresponsible riding: hvly bckd: quick reapp: earlier won h'caps at Windsor & Thirsk: '99 wnr at Carlisle, Chepstow & Southwell (h'cap, rtd 85a & 79): '98 wnr at W'hampton (seller) & Lingfield (h'cap rtd 80a & 70): all wins at 5/6f, stays 7f on firm, hvy & both AWs, any trk: v tough & progressive, best held up for a late run. **97**
1182 **HARMONIC WAY 11** [9] R Charlton 5-9-4 (101) M J Kinane 7/2 FAV: 00-642: 5 ch h Lion Cavern - Pineapple (Superlative) Dwelt and held up, hdwy when no room 2f out till ins last, styd on well but wnr had flown: hvly bckd: unlucky, would have won with a clear run & shld win another valuable race: see 1182. *1* **106+**
1163 **NOW LOOK HERE 12** [16] B A McMahon 4-9-7 (104) T Quinn 10/1: 3-2333: 4 b g Repreimand - Where's Carol (Anfield) Bhnd ldrs, swtchd to chall going well 2f out, onepace: acts on firm and hvy: see 734. *nk* **106**
1110 **NIGRASINE 15** [6] J L Eyre 6-9-3 (100)(bl) J F Egan 12/1: 0-0304: Al prom, rdn halfway, kept on well. *hd* **101**
1324 **FURTHER OUTLOOK 1** [14] 6-8-13 (96) K Darley 20/1: -00005: Cl-up, narrow lead halfway, hdd 1f out, onepace: quick reapp, unplcd yesterday, showed more today: see 1182. *¾* **95**
1182 **DELEGATE 11** [15] 7-8-12 (95) Pat Eddery 11/1: 630-06: Held up, rdn/kept on fnl 2f, not pace to chall. *½* **92**
4296} **ALEGRIA 222** [4] 4-8-7 (90)(4oh) J Tate 12/1: 4530-7: Trkd ldrs, rdn/chance 2f out, wknd fnl 1f: reapp: plcd several times in '99 (rtd 86, h'cap) '98 Windsor wnr (fill mdn, rtd 78): eff at 5/6f on firm and gd. *2* **82**
1182 **BON AMI 11** [3] 4-8-7 (90)(BL) J Carroll 20/1: -00408: Chsd-ldrs, hung left/btn over 1f out: blnks. *½* **80**
4486} **RED LION GB 208** [2] 4-8-10 (93) R Cochrane 11/1: 5000-9: Rear, rdn 2f out, no impress: reapp: '99 reapp scorer at Leicester (stakes) and Yarmouth (h'cap, rtd '98): '98 wnr at Redcar (debut) & Windsor (nov auction, rtd 92 at best): suited by 6f, tried 7f: acts on fast & gd grnd, prob handles firm: handles any track and runs well fresh: good weight carrier: should do better. *nk* **82**
1182 **ROYAL RESULT 11** [13] 7-8-7 (90) F Norton 14/1: 30-000: Rdn mid div halfway, no impression: 10th. *hd* **78**
1173 **POLES APART 12** [7] 4-8-7 (90)(t)(7oh) S Finnamore (5) 33/1: 010-00: Led till halfway, btn over 1f out: 11th: '99 h'cap wnr at Doncaster (rtd 88): '98 Folkestone wnr (auction mdn, rtd 88): eff at 6f, tried 1m: acts on firm and gd, sharp/gall track: likes to race with/force the pace and suited by a tongue strap. *¾* **76**
1173 **LITERARY SOCIETY 12** [5] 7-8-9 (92) S Whitworth 7/1: 300-00: Held up towards centre, eff/no impress over 2f out: 13th: see 1173. **0**
1277 **First Musical 5** [11] 4-8-8 (91) D Mernagh (3) 14/1: 1173 **Alastair Smellie 12** [18] 4-8-7 (90)(2oh) M Hills 12/1:
1173 **Threat 12** [10] 4-8-8 (91) G Faulkner (3) 33/1:
15 ran Time 1m 12.2 (2.8) (J M Bradley) J M Bradley Sedbury, Gloucs

1338 **2.45 GR 3 DUKE OF YORK STKS 3YO+ (A) 6f Firm 19 -03 Slow**
£36000 £13800 £6900 £3300 3 yo rec 9 lb Raced towards centre

766 **LEND A HAND 54** [5] Saeed bin Suroor 5-9-5 L Dettori 100/30: 124-61: 5 b h Great Commotion - Janaat (Kris) Trkd ldrs, rdn over 2f out, prog to lead over 1f out, styd on strongly inside last, readily: hvly bckd, 8 wk abs: lkd superb, padd pick: '99 scorer in Dubai (List) & Newbury (Gr 3, rtd 120), also narrowly btn 4th in Breeders Cup Mile: rnr up in '98 for M Johnston (including 2,000 Guineas, rtd 119): smart btwn 6f/1m on firm, gd/soft & dirt: runs well fresh: tough & high class, Gr 2 Cork & Orrery at R Ascot shld be right up his street. **120**
*1172 **PIPALONG 12** [4] T D Easterby 4-9-2 K Darley 4/1: 21-112: 4 b f Pips Pride - Limpopo (Green Desert) Mid-div, switched/prog from halfway, rdn & kept on well fnl 2f, not pace of wnr: win another Group race: see 1172. *1½* **112**
766 **BOLD EDGE 54** [9] R Hannon 5-9-7 Dane O'Neill 8/1: 041-03: 5 ch h Beveled - Daring Ditty (Daring March) Led, rdn/hdd over 1f out, kept on: 8 week abs: in gd form, won the Gr 2 Cork & Orrery in '99 (rtd 118). *1* **115**
1172 **ARKADIAN HERO 12** [3] L M Cumani 5-9-1 K Fallon 9/4 FAV: 30-404: Held up rear, rdn/prog halfway, styd on inside last for press, not pace to chall: looked superb, hvly bckd: can rate more highly: see 952. *nk* **108**
*1182 **DOCTOR SPIN 11** [8] 4-9-1 J Reid 16/1: 340-15: Tracked ldrs, eff/hmpd over 1f out, kept on inside last: reportedly boiled over at start: lost momentum at crucial stage here & would have finished at least 3rd. *shd* **108+**
4201} **TABHEEJ 229** [10] 3-8-3 R Hills 12/1: 1313-6: Cl-up, rdn/fdd fnl 1f: tchd 14/1, reapp, fit: '99 wnr at Haydock (debut, fillies mdn) & Doncaster (stakes, rtd 101): eff at 5/6f, stays a stiff 7f: acts on firm and gd/sft grnd, stiff/gall trks: has run well fresh: useful filly who will appreciate an ease in grade. *2½* **98**
3841} **CUBISM 252** [2] 4-9-1 M Hills 25/1: 6064-7: Rear, eff over 2f out, no impression: reapp: '99 wnr at Salisbury and Haydock (rtd h'caps, rtd 101, subs rtd 110$ in List company): '98 Yarmouth (mdn) & Windsor (nursery rtd 90): eff at 6f on firm and fast grnd: has run well fresh: handles any track, likes a stiff/gall one. *½* **99**
1172 **TEDBURROW 12** [7] 8-9-5 T E Durcan 33/1: 0-0008: Mid-div, eff halfway, no impress: see 734 (lstd). *shd* **103**
1172 **PROUD NATIVE 12** [1] 6-9-5 J Fortune 20/1: 310-09: Held up rear, no impress: deadheated for 8th. *dht* **103**
952 **TEAPOT ROW 30** [6] 5-9-1 S Whitworth 12/1: 412-50: Dwelt, al bhd: 10th, needs further. *5* **90**
10 ran Time 1m 10.77 (1.37) (Godolphin) Saeed bin Suroor Newmarket

1339 **3.20 GR 2 YORKSHIRE CUP STKS 4YO+ (A) 1m5f194y Firm 19 +07 Fast**
£78300 £29700 £14850 £6750

4022} **KAYF TARA 243** [7] Saeed bin Suroor 6-9-0 L Dettori 15/8 FAV: 3111-1: 6 b h Sadler's Wells - Colorspin (High Top) Track ldrs, smooth prog to lead 3f out, readily pulled clr fnl 2f under hands and heels riding: fast time: reapp, lkd superb: hvly bckd: '99 scorer at Longchamp, Goodwood, Deauville (Gr 2's) & Curragh (Gr 1, rtd 127), also 4L 3rd in Ascot Gold Cup: '98 Haydock (stakes), Ascot (Gr 1 Gold Cup) & Curragh wnr (Gr 1, rtd 122): eff btwn 14f/2m4f on firm & hvy: runs well fresh: can force the pace: top class styr, take the beating in the Ascot Gold Cup. **125**
*1187 **RAINBOW WAYS 11** [3] B W Hills 5-8-9 M Hills 8/1: 165-12: 5 b h Rainbow Quest - Siwaayib (Green Desert) Held up, rdn/stdy prog fnl 3f, chsd wnr 1f out, kept on though no impression: well bckd, tchd 10/1: lkd well & is thriving physically: improving entire who shld land a Listed/Gr 3: see 1187 (h'cap). *4* **112**
1152 **CHURLISH CHARM 13** [8] R Hannon 5-8-12 J Reid 14/1: 310-03: 5 b h Niniski - Blushing Storm (Blushing Groom) Mid-div, rdn/styd on fnl 3f, no threat: op 16/1, lkd well: won this race last term (rtd 115). *1¾* **113**
1152 **KAHTAN 13** [6] J L Dunlop 5-8-9 R Hills 10/1: 101-44: Led, hdd 3f out, soon held: see 1152 (12f). *3½* **105**
1152 **LARGESSE 13** [2] 6-8-9 J F Egan 14/1: 5-1035: Tracked ldrs, rdn/no impression fnl 2f: needs soft. *3½* **100**
*140 **SINON 170** [4] 5-8-9 D Holland 16/1: 4/01-6: Cl-up, fdd fnl 3f: needed this: bckd at long odds, tchd 20/1: 6 month abs: '99 Saint Cloud wnr (Listed, rtd 113, no form sole British start): '98 wnr here at York (reapp, stakes, rtd 95): eff 14f/15f, stays 2m well: acts on firm & hvy grnd, likes a stiff/gall track: tall, rangy gelding. *½* **99**
1109 **CELERIC 15** [1] 8-8-9 Pat Eddery 9/2: 133-37: Settled rear, eff over 3f out, soon no impression *6* **90**

& position accepted fnl 1f: op 3/1: jockey reported gelding could not handle slippery conditions: btr 1109.
1109 **PERSIAN PUNCH 15** [5] 7-8-9 T Quinn 7/2: 401-28: Pushed along rear halfway, btn 3f out and eased *15* **75**
fnl 2f: hvly bckd, looked superb: jockey reported gelding disliked slippery conditions & slipped leaving stalls.
8 ran Time 2m 55.06 (1.66) (Godolphin) Saeed bin Suroor Newmarket

1340 **3.50 LISTED M SEELY GLASGOW STKS 3YO (A) 1m2f85y Firm 19 -08 Slow**
£15544 £5896 £2948 £1340

4411} **HATAAB 213** [5] E A L Dunlop 3-9-3 R Hills 10/1: 121-1: 3 ch c Woodman - Miss Mistletoes (The **111**
Minstrel) Dictated pace, quickened tempo over 5f out, styd on strongly for press fnl 3f to repel several challenges:
op 8/1, prob sharper for this on reapp: topweight: '99 debut wnr at Ascot (mdn) & Pontefract (Listed, rtd 101):
apprec step up to 10.5f, 12f should suit: acts on fast & gd, likes a stiff/gall track: goes well fresh: genuine
& progressive colt, very smart effort conceding weight today & can win when stepped up to Group class.
1151 **SANDMASON 13** [2] H R A Cecil 3-8-11 T Quinn 5/4 FAV: 1-22: 3 ch c Grand Lodge - Sandy Island *1½* **102**
(Mill Reef) Track ldr, rdn/kept on fnl 3f, al just held by wnr: hvly bckd: acts on firm & hvy, crying out for 12f.
4523} **FAST TRACK 204** [6] Sir Michael Stoute 3-8-11 K Fallon 3/1: 1-3: 3 b c Doyoun - Mannitika *1¾* **100**
(Kalamoun) Held up, eff 3f out, kept on onepace: bckd, tho' op 9/4: just better for this on reapp: impressive wnr
on sole '99 start at Yarmouth (mdn, rtd 98+): styd longer 10.5f trip, 12f should suit: acts on firm and gd/soft grnd
& a gall track: has run well fresh: smart colt, op to further improvement over 12f.
1171 **MASTERMIND 12** [3] P F I Cole 3-8-11 J Fortune 12/1: 21-04: Held up in tch, eff 2f out, never pace to *nk* **99**
chall: styd longer 10.5f trip, further may suit: lengthy, scopey colt who looked superb: see 1171 (1m).
-- **HATHA ANNA** [1] 3-8-11 L Dettori 4/1: 5: Held up, rdn/prog to briefly chase wnr till 2f out, fdd ins *3* **95**
last: racecourse bow, earlier reportedly showed up well in a private Godlophin trial in Dubai: mid-dists expected to
suit this scopey colt: should prove sharper for this, highly tried on intro & not disgraced, mdn would be a formality.
823 **COOL INVESTMENT 11** [4] 3-8-11 D Holland 16/1: 1-206: Trkd ldrs, btn 2f out: tall, rangy, needs a *7* **85**
drop in grade: unplcd in Swiss 2,000gns since 823 (9f).
6 ran Time 2m 10.14 (2.84) (Hamdan Al Maktoum) E A L Dunlop Newmarket, Suffolk

1341 **4.20 SCARBOROUGH HCAP 3YO 0-95 (C) 1m rnd Firm 19 -06 Slow** **[93]**
£8352 £2570 £1285 £642

1075 **MALLEUS 17** [3] R M Beckett 3-9-4 (83) M J Kinane 7/1: 532-21: 3 ch g Hamas - Queen Warrior **88**
(Daring March) Mid-div, switched and rdn/prog to lead over 1f out, styd on strongly inside last, rdn out to assert:
hvly bckd, tchd 10/1: confirmed reapp promise for 1st win: plcd twice in '99 (rtd 84, P Walwyn): eff at 1m, stays
9f: acts on firm, soft and a sharp/gall or undulating track: tall, lenghty & progressive, has thrived physically.
1153 **ZIBELINE 13** [14] C E Brittain 3-8-8 (73) T E Durcan 11/1: 450-02: 3 b c Cadeaux Genereux - Zia *1* **75**
(Shareef Dancer) Mid-div, eff/prog fnl 3f, styd on well inside last for press, not reach wnr: nicely bckd, op 14/1:
styd longer 1m trip well but this may not be far enough (dam scored over 12f): scopey colt, shld win a race.
1183 **ALL THE GEARS 11** [19] Sir Michael Stoute 3-9-6 (85) K Fallon 8/1: 023-53: 3 b c Gone West - Buckeye *½* **86+**
Gal (Good Counsel) Switched sharply left from start and settled rear, stdy gains fnl 3f & chasing ldrs when briefly
no room 1f out, styd on, hands & heels: op 6/1: shade unlucky in running from tricky high draw, win soon.
4477} **RESPLENDENT STAR 209** [9] P W Harris 3-9-3 (82)(BL) D Holland 25/1: 0010-4: Keen/chsd ldrs, rdn & *½* **82**
kept on fnl 2f, not pace of wnr: edgy/on toes for reapp: first time blinks: '99 Newcastle (nursery) & Southwell
wnr (nov auct stks, rtd 88 & 86a): eff at 1m, may stay further: acts on firm and fbrsnd, any trk: eff in blnks/vis.
986 **HADATH 26** [10] 3-8-10 (75)(VIS) J Carroll 50/1: 25-005: Led after 2f till over 1f out, no extra cl home: *nk* **74**
fine effort in first time visor: stays 1m: attractive gelding who should find a race: see 986.
*1062 **SERRA NEGRA 17** [5] 3-9-1 (80) J Fortune 7/1: 0-16: Dwelt, towards rear, prog/chsd ldrs over 1f *1* **77**
out, held inside last: hvly bckd, op 8/1: acts on firm & soft: see 1062 (mdn, soft).
1055 **SIR FERBET 19** [21] 3-9-5 (84) M Hills 20/1: 3-2107: Towards rear/wide, eff and hmpd 2f out, styd *1¾* **78+**
on well under hands & heels riding fnl 1f, never nearer: handles firm, gd and fibresand: worth another look.
1138 **DESERT SAFARI 14** [11] 3-8-5 (70) J Bramhill 25/1: 1-0548: Held up, keen, hmpd after 2f & again 2f *3½* **57+**
out when effort, styd on inside last, nearest fin: no luck in running trying longer 1m trip, worth another chance.
*857 **CELEBRATION TOWN 38** [2] 3-8-7 (72) R Cochrane 12/1: 505-19: Held up, eff 3f out, no impress. *shd* **59**
4477} **THE WIFE 209** [16] 3-9-2 (81) Pat Eddery 14/1: 2100-0: Settled rear, eff & short of room over 1f *1* **66**
out, no impress: 10th: op 16/1, better for this on reapp: '99 wnr at Beverley (fill auction mdn) & here at York
(nurs, rtd 87): eff at 7.5f/1m, may get further: acts on firm & gd, stiff/undul track: shld leave this behind.
1153 **NIAGARA 13** [15] 3-8-13 (78) R Hills 16/1: 460-00: Held up wide, eff 3f out, no impression: 11th. *shd* **63**
823 **CLEVER GIRL 43** [12] 3-9-7 (86) K Darley 16/1: 215-40: Track ldr, rdn 3f out, fdd fnl 2f: 12th: abs. *1½* **68**
1134 **PETEURESQUE 14** [8] 3-8-8 (73) J F Egan 25/1: 25-620: Chsd ldrs, fdd fnl 3f: 13th: btr 1134 (7f mdn). *nk* **54**
810 **SPIN A YARN 47** [1] 3-9-6 (85) J Reid 14/1: 441-00: Mid div, outpcd fnl 3f: 14: op 12/1, 7 wk abs. *1½* **63**
*1255 **TAKE MANHATTAN 6** [18] 3-8-4 (69)(5ex) P Fessey 4/1 FAV: 066110: Mid div/wide, eff 3f out, no *1* **45**
impression: 15th: hvly bckd under a pen: tricky high draw today: btr 1255.
983 **KNIGHTS EMPEROR 28** [17] 3-8-9 (74) F Norton 8/1: 0-400: Mid div/wide, btn 3f out: 17th: bckd. **0**
1084 **PENG 16** [6] 3-8-9 (74)(t) T Williams 14/1: 0000: Led 1f, cl up till 3f out: 19th: bckd, op 20/1: h'cap bow. **0**
931 **Zagaleta 33** [7] 3-8-11 (76) F Norton 33/1: 4411} **Jamestown 213** [20] 3-8-10 (75) R Fitzpatrick (3) 33/1:
566 **Lous Wish 86** [4] 3-7-12 (63)(bl) K Dalgleish (7) 40/1:
20 ran Time 1m 37.82 (2.02) (S W E J Slack) R M Beckett Lambourn, Berks

1342 **4.50 MICKLEGATE RTD HCAP 4YO+ 0-105 (B) 1m2f85y Firm 19 -11 Slow** **[110]**
£9720 £3687 £1843 £838

1031 **AMALIA 22** [1] P W Harris 4-9-2 (98) T Quinn 6/1: 10-041: 4 b f Danehill - Cheviot Amble (Pennine **105**
Walk) Held up racing keenly, no room 2f out and switched over 1f out, styd on well to lead well inside last, rdn out:
well bckd: '99 wnr at Redcar (mdn), Chester & Doncaster (h'caps rtd 99): eff at 7f/10f on firm & gd/soft, handles
hvy: likes a sharp/gall trk: can force the pace or come from bhd: small but v tough & useful filly.
3915} **WESTENDER 246** [6] W J Haggas 4-8-5 (87) M Hills 15/2: 2213-2: 4 b g In The Wings - Trude *½* **92**
(Windwurf) Dwelt/held up, prog fnl 3f and led over 1f out, rdn/hdd well inside last, no extra: nicely bckd on reapp:
'99 wnr at Yarmouth (reapp, mdn) & Ripon (h'cap, rtd 89): eff at 10f, half brother to a 15f scorer, could get further:
acts on firm & gd/soft grnd, sharpish or stiff/gall track: has run well fresh: leggy, attractive & lightly raced 4yo.
874 **ULUNDI 37** [3] Lady Herries 5-8-8 (90) Pat Eddery 6/1: 1133: 5 b g Rainbow Quest - Flit (Lyphard) *2½* **91**
Held up in tch, rdn/outpcd 3f out, staying on when hmpd over 1f out, kept on inside last, not pace to chall: acts on
firm, soft & fibresand: consistent, should relish 12f+: see 874, 747.
*1112 **SHARMY 15** [4] Sir Michael Stoute 4-9-4 (100) K Fallon 11/8 FAV: 12-14: Track ldr, rdn 3f out, *nk* **100**

YORK THURSDAY MAY 18TH Lefthand, Flat, Galloping Track

keeping on onepace when hmpd over 1f out: hvly bckd, paddock pick: acts on firm & gd/soft: see 1112 (stks, 1m).
1015 **TACTFUL REMARK** 24 [7] 4-9-7 (103) J P Spencer 25/1: 103-05: Led/clr halfway, hdd 2f out, no extra: ½ 102
jockey given 3-day ban for using whip with excessive force.
703 **WEET A MINUTE** 56 [5] 7-8-11 (93) L Dettori 12/1: 222256: Held up, eff 3f out, not able to chall: abs. 1 91
1170 **J R STEVENSON** 12 [2] 4-9-2 (98) F Norton 25/1: 150-07: Keen/prom, hmpd/no extra ins last, eased. ¾ 95
1170 **GOLCONDA** 12 [8] 4-8-5 (87) A Beech (5) 4/1: 360-38: In tch, rdn fnl 3f, fdd inside last: lkd superb. nk 83
8 ran   Time 2m 10.46 (3.16)   (Mrs P W Harris)   P W Harris Aldbury, Herts

SALISBURY   THURSDAY MAY 18TH   Righthand, Galloping Track, Stiff Finish

Official Going   GOOD (Watered). Stalls: Str - Far Side; 1m2f - Inside; 1m4f - Stands Side.

1343   1.30 NETHERHAMPTON FILL MDN DIV 1 3YO+ (D)   1m2f   Good 58 -26 Slow
£3243   £998   £499   £249   3 yo rec 14lb

4358} **REVIVAL** 217 [6] Sir Michael Stoute 3-8-7 F Lynch 6/1: 0-1: 3 b f Sadler's Wells - Fearless Revival 77
(Cozzene) Cl-up, led appr fnl 1f, pushed out: op 5/2, reapp: 9th sole '99 start (rtd 69): half-sister to high-class
sprinter Pivotal & miler Brave Revival: eff at 10f, may get further: goes well fresh on gd grnd & stiff trks.
-- **ARDANZA** [13] Lady Herries 3-8-7 M Roberts 12/1: 2: 3 b f Hernando - Arrastra (Bustino) 1 73+
Held up, closed appr fnl 2f, kept on under a kind ride: op 7/1, debut: half brother to a 7f wnr, dam 14f wnr:
eff at 10f on gd grnd but looks sure to apprec 12f & find a race.
961 **SALZGITTER** 30 [1] H Candy 3-8-7 C Rutter 6/1: 5-33: 3 b f Salse - Anna Of Brunswick (Rainbow nk 72
Quest) Chsd ldrs, eff 3f out, kept on ins last: tchd 10/1: apprec this step up to 10f, 12f sure to suit.
2774} **HAVANA** 306 [10] Mrs A J Perrett 4-9-7 G Carter 12/1: -33-4: In tch, shkn up fnl 2f, styd on nr fin: nk 72
op 7/1 on reapp: 3rd both '99 starts (fill mdn, rtd 69, J Banks): suited by step up to 10f: now qual for h'caps.
1051 **DEVIL LEADER** 19 [11] 3-8-7 R Hughes 14/1: 05: Well plcd, led 2½f out till bef dist, no extra fnl 1f. 1½ 69
964 **FAY** 30 [12] 3-8-7 D Sweeney 25/1: 656: Front rank, chall 2f out, onepace bef dist: back in trip. 1¼ 67
1846} **BONNIE FLORA** 344 [7] 4-9-7 R Perham 66/1: 00-7: Bhd, mod gains under a kind ride: reapp: unplcd 2 64+
both '99 starts for D Elsworth (fill mdn, rtd 68): one to keep an eye on now h'capped.
1054 **EASY TO LOVE** 19 [5] 4-9-7 W Ryan 11/8 FAV: 5-38: Led till appr fnl 2f, sn btn: hvly bckd from 1 63
9/4: unsuited forcing the pace?: see 1054 (gd/sft).
1179 **LANELLE** 11 [9] 3-8-7 R Havlin 5/1: 0-09: Nvr troubled ldrs: see 1179. 2 60
94 **RECOLETA** 177 [8] 3-8-7 N Pollard 33/1: 000-0: Chsd ldrs till wknd ent fnl 3f, eased: 10th, stiff task. 21 40
1200 **Miss Amber Nectar** 10 [4] 3-8-7 S Carson (5) 100/1:   1181 **To The Stars** 11 [2] 3-8-7 G Hind 66/1:
378 **Crack On Cheryl** 117 [3] 6-9-7 I Mongan (5) 100/1:
13 ran   Time 2m 12.85 (8.35)   (Cheveley Park Stud)   Sir Michael Stoute Newmarket, Suffolk

1344   2.05 NETHERHAMPTON FILL MDN DIV 2 3YO+ (D)   1m2f   Good 58 -14 Slow
£3243   £998   £499   £249   3 yo rec 14lb

4555} **LACE WING** 201 [3] B W Hills 3-8-7 R Hughes 10/1: 0-1: 3 ch f Caerleon - Capo Di Monte (Final Straw) 89
Rcd in 2nd, went on appr fnl 3f, drifted left, held on for press: tchd 14/1 on reapp: btn sole '99 start (fill mdn,
rtd 71): half-sister to sev wnrs: eff at 10f, 12f suit: acts on gd grnd, stiff/gall trk: goes well fresh.
-- **RIYAFA** [10] Sir Michael Stoute 3-8-7 F Lynch 9/1: 2: 3 b f Kahyasi - Riyama (Doyoun) nk 87+
Slow away, grad imprvd to press wnr ent fnl 1f, held nr fin: drifted from 9/2, well clr rem on debut:
fine run considering gave wnr around 10L start: eff at 10f, 12f suit on gd: must win soon.
873 **CABALLE** 37 [11] S P C Woods 3-8-7 G Duffield 7/1 FAV: 2-23: 3 ch f Opening Verse - Attirance 5 79
(Crowned Prince) Pulled hard, prom, ev ch 3f out, sn rdn, hung right, no extra: well bckd, btr 873 (soft).
-- **MASRORA** [9] M R Channon 3-8-7 Craig Williams 16/1: 4: Dwelt, mid-div halfway, eff 3f out, no 4 73
further impress on ldrs: op 12/1, debut: 100,000 gns Woodman yearling, rather green today, shld improve.
-- **VENTO DEL ORENO** [1] 3-8-7 G Sparkes (7) 14/1: -65: Held up, prog bef halfway, rdn appr 1¼ 70
fnl 2f, outpcd: tchd 20/1 on Brit bow: 6th on recent Italian debut: stoutly bred filly with L Cumani.
-- **NO FRILLS** [2] 3-8-7 W Ryan 9/1: 6: Mid-div, imprvd 3f out, btn & short of room 2f out: 3 66
op 9/2, stable-mate of rnr-up, debut: Darshaan filly out of a 10f wnr.
1265 **WILD NETTLE** 16 [13] 6-9-7 R Smith (5) 100/1: 0-0007: Pulled hard, nvr troubled ldrs: quick reapp. 8 56
4164} **THREE WHITE SOX** 232 [4] 3-8-7 M Fenton 50/1: 0-8: Nvr dangerous: reapp: unplcd sole '99 start. nk 55
4473} **REGAL CHARM** 209 [7] 3-8-7 R Havlin 14/1: 0-9: Mid-div till lost place 4f out: op 7/1 on reapp: 2 52
unplcd sole '99 start for A Foster (fill mdn, rtd 66): stoutly bred, now with J Gosden.
1093 **SIONED LYN** 16 [12] 3-8-7 R Price 50/1: 200: Bhd from halfway: 10th: surely flattered in 814. 3 48
1287 **POLISH GIRL** 5 [6] 4-9-7 D R McCabe 40/1: 0-00: Led till appr fnl 3f, sn btn: 12th, quick reapp. 0
-- **Dajam Vu** [8] 3-8-7 S Drowne 66/1:   896 **Mouton** 35 [5] 4-9-7 R Brisland (5) 100/1:
13 ran   Time 2m 11.71 (7.21)   (Maktoum Al Maktoum)   B W Hills Lambourn, Berks

1345   2.35 DRUIDS HCAP 3YO 0-70 (E)   1m str   Good 58 -39 Slow   [77]
£3107   £956   £478   £239

909 **TRICCOLO** 34 [13] A C Stewart 3-9-3 (66) M Roberts 11/2 FAV: 55-01: 3 b c Piccolo - Tribal Lady 78+
(Absalom) Confidently held up, prog on bit to lead appr fnl 1f, v cheekily, val 5L+: tchd 13/2 on h'cap bow:
5th in 2 '99 mdns (rtd 77+): 70,000 gns half brother to a wnr abroad: apprec step up to 1m, further shld suit:
goes on fast & soft grnd, stiff/gall trk: type to run up a quick sequence.
800 **RICH VEIN** 49 [10] S P C Woods 3-9-1 (64) N Callan 10/1: 500-42: 3 b g Up And At 'Em - Timissara ½ 71
(Shahrastani) Held up, prog under press 2f out, prsd wnr ins last but toyed with by wnr: op 8/1, clr rem:
7 wk abs: eff on gd & gd/sft grnd: caught a v leniently h'capped colt, qck reapp on the cards.
1213 **SPIRIT OF TENBY** 9 [7] S Dow 3-9-4 (67) P Doe 20/1: 05-603: 3 b g Tenby - Asturiana (Julio 4 66
Mariner) Towards rear, kept on fnl 1½f to go 3rd, no ch with ldrs: suited by return to 1m & shld get 10f.
837 **GRUINART** 41 [15] H Morrison 3-9-4 (67) D Griffiths 9/1: 0-004: Chsd ldrs, eff 2f out, unable to qckn. ¾ 64
1085 **DILETIA** 16 [9] 3-9-2 (65) G Duffield 10/1: 60-045: Handy, onepace when short of room appr fnl 1f. 2½ 57
4516} **AFRICAN PETE** 205 [12] 3-9-0 (63) G Hind 16/1: 036-6: Waited with, some wide hdwy 2f out, 1¾ 53
nvr on terms: op 12/1 on reapp/h'cap bow: plcd 16 in '99 (auct mdn, rtd 73 at best): with G Margarson.
1094 **SWEET ANGELINE** 16 [11] 3-9-3 (66) W Supple 16/1: 030-07: Trkd ldrs, wknd ent fnl 2f: plcd in ¾ 53
'99 (mdn, rtd 82 at best), prob flattered): stays 1m on firm grnd, without t-strap: with A Murphy.

SALISBURY   THURSDAY MAY 18TH   Righthand, Galloping Track, Stiff Finish

1125 **NOBLE SPLENDOUR** 14 [2] 3-9-7 (70) W Ryan 6/1: 350-58: Nvr in it: longer trip: see 1125. 3½ 51
1080 **GOLDEN RETRIEVER** 17 [18] 3-9-7 (70) N Pollard 10/1: 0-009: Chsd ldrs till 2f out: h'cap bawe. 2½ 46
894 **ANDYS ELECTIVE** 35 [17] 3-9-3 (66) A McGlone 16/1: 54-360: Chsd ldrs till wknd bef fnl 2f: 10th. shd 42
1255 **BLACKPOOL MAMMAS** 6 [4] 3-9-5 (68) R Ffrench 16/1: 010200: Led till fnl 2f, sn btn: 11th. hd 43
4494} **OARE PINTAIL** 208 [8] 3-9-4 (65) S Drowne 9/1: 6060-0: Mid-div till 3f out: 15th, reapp,
tchd 12/1: well btn all 4 '99 starts for P Walwyn (fill mdn, rtd 74): now with R Charlton. 0
4260} **NUTS IN MAY** 226 [1] 3-9-2 (65) G Carter 9/1: 020-0: Nvr troubled ldrs: 17th, op 6/1 on reapp:
rnr-up middle of 3 '99 starts (mdn, rtd 73): eff at 6f on fast grnd: with J Dunlop. 0
4515} Te Deum 205 [3] 3-9-4 (67) P Dobbs (5) 25/1:   933 Atylan Boy 31 [5] 3-9-6 (69) D R McCabe 25/1:
488 Royal Ivy 99 [6] 3-9-7 (70) S Carson (5) 14/1:   495 Storm Prince 98 [16] 3-9-7 (70) L Newman (5) 25/1:
17 ran   Time 1m 46.85 (7.75)   (Bruce Corman)   A C Stewart Newmarket, Suffolk

1346	3.10 CAPEL CURE SHARP MDN 2YO (D) 5f Good 58 -36 Slow
	£3542 £1090 £545 £272

1169 **PAN JAMMER** 12 [4] M R Channon 2-9-0 S Drowne 7/4 FAV: 41: 2 b c Piccolo - Ingerence (Akarad) 91
Well plcd, led 2f out, rdn out: hvly bckd from 11/4: confirmed debut promise (Newmarket mdn): 11,500 gns
Apr foal, half-brother to 10f/hdles wnr Kiss Me Kate: eff at 5f, will get 6f: goes on fast & gd grnd, stiff/gall trk.
-- **FLINT RIVER** [12] R F Johnson Houghton 2-9-0 S Sanders 11/4: 2: 2 b c Red Ransom - She's All ½ 88
Class (Rahy) Bhd ldrs, prog appr fnl 1f & ev ch, held towards fin: nicely bckd, debut: 20,000 IR gns
1st foal, dam a juv wnr in the States: eff at 5f, further in going to suit: shld go one better soon.
1048 **RUSHBY** 19 [7] Mrs P N Dutfield 2-9-0 L Newman (5) 16/1: 63: 2 b c Fayruz - Moira My Girl (Henbit) ¾ 86
Keen, mid-div prog under press ent fnl 2f, no extra towards fin: clr rem: gd run, eff at 5f on gd: gd run.
-- **MOONLIGHT DANCER** [1] R Hannon 2-9-0 R Hughes 8/1: 4: Cl-up & ev ch till outpcd appr fnl 1f: 3 77
10,000 gns Polar Falcon Mar foal, half brother to useful sprint juv Smart Ridge: improvement likely.
-- **FROMSONG** [2] G Hind 12/1: 5: Pulled hard, in tch, prog & ch appr fnl 2f, ran wide & nk 76
onepace: debut: 9,000 IR gnd Fayruz Apr foal, dam 6f wnr, sire a sprinter: with B Millman.
762 **NIGHT FALL** 51 [10] 2-8-9 M Roberts 16/1: 56: Bhd, late hdwy, nvr a threat: 7 wk abs, stablemate 4th. 4 61
-- **VINE COURT** [5] 2-8-9 A Clark 7/1: 7: Nvr dangerous: debut, op 7/2: IR£9,500 Turtle ¾ 59
Island May foal, half-sister to 4 wnrs, sire a miler: with T Mills.
1236 **SOME DUST** 7 [9] 2-9-0 A Daly 66/1: U8: Led till 2½f out, sn btn: see 1236. 6 49
1088 **THE MARSHALL** 16 [8] 2-9-0 M Henry 8/1: -09: Al bhd: seen 1088. ¾ 47
1260 **ROXY LABURNUM** 6 [6] 2-8-9 C Rutter 66/1: 00: Bhd when hmpd after 2f, nvr a threat: 10th, quick 3 34
reapp: 1,200 gns Eagle Eyed May 1st foal, dam unrcd, sire useful in the Staes: with R Flower.
10 ran   Time 1m 04.51 (4.71)   (Ms Lynn Bell)   M R Channon West Isley, Berks

1347	3.40 CLASSIFIED STKS 3YO 0-95 (B) 1m4f Good 58 +12 Fast
	£8681 £3209 £1604 £729

1089 **OPTIMAITE** 16 [2] B R Millman 3-9-3 G Hind 5/1: 040-31: 3 b c Komaite - Leprechaun Lady (Royal Blend) 104
Waited with, gd prog ent fnl 3f to lead bef dist, pushed clr: fast time: '99 wnr at Windsor (mdn auct) &
Ascot (val stks, rtd 99): was a sprinter as a juvenile, clrly relished this step up to 12f: acts on firm &
gd/soft grnd, any trk: can run well fresh & force the pace: tough, useful & on the upgrade.
1089 **RIDDLESDOWN** 16 [1] S P C Woods 3-9-1 G Duffield 11/8 FAV: 321-22: 3 ch c Common Grounds - Neat 5 97
Dish (Stalwart) Set gd pace, under press & hdd appr fnl 1f, onepace: hvly bckd: prob ran to best tho'
stamina poss stretched over this longer/stiff 12f trip: had this wnr 2½L in arrears in 1089 (10f).
1089 **ROYAL EAGLE** 16 [3] P F I Cole 3-9-0 D Sweeney 25/1: 12-003: 3 b c Eagle Eyed - Accountinquestion ¾ 95
(Classic Account) Prom, rdn to chall 3f out, no extra ent fnl 2f: shaped better over lngr 12f trip, sole win at 7f.
1089 **AL TOWD** 16 [5] J L Dunlop 3-9-0 W Supple 9/4: 23-054: Chsd ldrs, rdn appr fnl 2f, no impress: 2 92
nicely bckd from 3/1: would have been better off in a h'cap, also bhd this 1st & 2nd in 1089, see 810 (gd/soft).
4215} **MICHELE MARIESCHI** 229 [4] 3-9-3 R Hughes 9/1: 1622-5: Pulled hard in tch, brief eff appr fnl 2f, 12 83
btn & eased fnl 1f: drifted from 5/2 on reapp: '99 debut wnr at Newmarket (mdn, later 3½L rnr-up to Sakhee
in 1st time blnks, rtd 96): return to 1m will suit: acts on firm & hvy grnd, with/without blnks: with P Cole.
5 ran   Time 2m 37.91 (5.51)   (Always Hopeful Partnership)   B R Millman Kentisbear, Devon

1348	4.10 TRYON HCAP STKS 3YO+ 0-80 (D) 7f str Good 58 -18 Slow	[80]
	£4758 £1464 £732 £266 3 yo rec 11lb	

1213 **COMPRADORE** 9 [18] M Blanshard 5-8-9 (61) D Sweeney 11/2 JT FAV: 0-0321: 5 b m Mujtahid - Keswa 68
(King's Lake) Mid-div, trkd ldrs on bit 2f out, pld out & shkn up to lead below dist, cmftbly: plcd sev times in
'99 (h'cap, rtd 71): '98 Folkestone wnr (stks, rtd 72): eff at 6f/1m: acts on firm & hvy grnd, likes Salisbury.
4308} **FEATHER N LACE** 220 [6] C A Cyzer 4-8-10 (62) S Sanders 25/1: 4130-2: 4 b f Green Desert - Report 2 64
'Em (Staff Writer) Rear, prog & not much room appr fnl 2f, drvn & went 2nd ins last, no ch with wnr: reapp: '99
Newmarket wnr (claim, rtd 64 & 78$): plcd juv (rtd 79): eff at 7f/1m on firm & gd grnd, stiff trks, without blnks.
1012 **HOH HOH SEVEN** 24 [20] N E Berry 4-8-5 (57) N Callan 33/1: 500-03: 4 b g College Chapel - Fighting 2 55
Run (Runnett) Chsd ldrs, imprvd appr fnl 2f, styd on but unable to chall: plcd in '99 (clmr, rtd 72, mdn, rtd 78):
unrcd juvenile: stays 1m on firm grnd, without a visor: would enjoy mdn h'caps.
1158 **AMBER FORT** 12 [19] J M Bradley 7-9-7 (73)(bl) R Ffrench 11/2 JT FAV: 0-3254: Cl-up, led ent fnl 1f nk 70
till below dist, no extra: just best on a sharp trk: see 1011, 817.
1018 **CATAMARAN** 24 [16] S 5-9-7 (73) P Doe 11/1: 30-45: Hld up, hmpd after 2f, short of room fnl 2f & hd 70+
kept on nicely late: caught the eye & needs 1m+: not to be missed next time: see 1018.
1150 **SKY DOME** 13 [14] 7-9-9 (75) G Duffield 14/1: 060-06: Led till ent fnl 2f, onepace: see 1150. 1¾ 69
1213 **RED DELIRIUM** 9 [16] 4-9-2 (68) A Nicholls (3) 12/1: 0-2007: Chsd ldrs, rdn appr fnl 2f, not qckn. 2½ 57
1220 **STRAND OF GOLD** 8 [10] 3-8-5 (68) P Fitzimons (5) 7/1: 04-558: Al mid-div: op 10/1, see 1220, 1181. 1½ 54
1004 **BLUE ACE** 24 [1] 7-8-13 (65) A Culhane 8/1: 0-5009: Dwelt, nvr on terms: h'cap bow, see 927. 1¾ 48
1092 **DEMOCRACY** 16 [15] 4-8-12 (64) D Harrison 33/1: 300000: Pulled hard in mid-div, unable to qckn nk 46
2f out, eased towards fin: 10th, back up in trip, see 258.
761 **INSIGHTFUL** 51 [8] 3-9-0 (77) R Hughes 14/1: 312-50: Prom till ent fnl 2f, eased: 11th, abs, see 108. ½ 58
1181 **CALIWAG** 11 [11] 4-9-5 (71) N Pollard 13/2: 650-00: Bmpd start, nvr in it: 16th on h'cap bow. 0
*1061 **INFOTEC** 17 [7] 3-9-i (78) J Stack 10/1: 22-010: Prom 4f: 17th: see 1061 (soft). 0
485 Song Of Skye 99 [13] 6-9-6 (72) R Mullen 14/1:   1060 Susans Pride 17 [2] 4-9-12 (78) S Clancy (7) 14/1:
1213 Aegean Flame 9 [9] 4-8-13 (65) S Drowne 33/1:   381 Storm Cry 117 [17] 5-9-2 (68)(t) M Tebbutt 20/1:
1113 Kilmeena Lad 15 [3] 4-9-4 (70) S Carson (5) 20/1:   157 Apadi 162 [12] 4-9-8 (74) Martin Dwyer 25/1:

SALISBURY THURSDAY MAY 18TH Righthand, Galloping Track, Stiff Finish

3736} **Alpha Heights 259** [4] 3-8-10 (73) L Newman (5) 33/1:
20 ran   Time 1m 30.81 (5.31)   (C McKenna)   M Blanshard Upper Lambourn, Berks

1349 4.40 REDENHAM CLAIMER 3YO (F)   7f str   Good 58 -39 Slow
£2548   £728   £364

1094 **COWBOYS AND ANGELS 16** [12] W G M Turner 3-9-3 P Fitzimons (5) 8/1: -33601: 3 b c Bin Ajwaad - **71**
Halimah (Be My Guest) Nvr far away, led 2f out, pshd out: tchd 10/1, slow time: plcd twice in '99 (auct mdn,
rtd 79): eff at 7f, stays 9.4f: acts on fast & hvy grnd, prob handles fibresand: apprec drop back in trip.
311 **SONBELLE 128** [17] B Palling 3-9-3 P Doe 5/1 FAV: 064-02: 3 b f Son Pardo - Ty With Belle   3 **55**
(Pamroy) Led till 2f out, same pace: over 4 month abs: fav'd by weights on official ratings: see 149.
1081 **PETRIE 16** [22] M R Channon 3-8-7 S Drowne 12/1: 256-03: 3 ch g Fraam - Canadian Capers   3½ **52**
(Ballacashtal) Well plcd, rdn appr fnl 2f, no impress: stiffish task, unproven at 7f: see 42.
1211 **ANNIJAZ 9** [2] G M McCourt 3-8-2 D O'Donohoe 16/1: -50004: Held up, chsd ldrs appr fnl 2f, onepce. nk **46**
3442} **WALTER THE WHISTLE 274** [18] 3-8-7 G Duffield 20/1: 0-5: Rear, & unable to get a clr run till ent 1¾ **48**
fnl 2f, styd on, nvr a threat: reapp: unplcd sole '99 start for A Jarvis: prob capable of better: with J Osborne.
4457 **OUTSTANDING TALENT 210** [14] 3-8-6 A Culhane 14/1: 4300-6: Al same place: reapp: plcd in '99   1 **45**
(mdn, rtd 55, V Soane): now with A Carroll.
1212 **ANNS MILL 9** [5] L Newman (5) 12/1: 00-047: Rear, wide prog 3f out, no extra 2f out: see 1212. nk **42**
1212 **PERLE DE SAGESSE 9** [10] 3-8-5 A Daly 9/1: 054538: Nvr dangerous: tchd 12/1: see 155.   1 **41**
892 **GAVEL 35** [6] 3-9-3 (BL) S Sanders 12/1: 630-09: Held up, rdn appr fnl 2f, nvr a factor: blnkd: 1½ **50**
plcd in '99 (auct mdn, rtd 68): with out of form M Tompkins.
887 **BOTTELINO JOE 36** [9] 3-9-3 (BL) M Tebbutt 14/1: 045-00: Al towards rear: 10th, blnkd: rtd 66 in '99. ¾ **48**
813 **LADYWELL BLAISE 45** [13] 3-8-11 M Fenton 11/2: 314640: Chsd ldrs till 2f out: 11th, 6 wk abs. nk **41**
-- **WOODYATES** [3] 3-8-12 N Pollard 7/1: 0: Nvr dangerous: 13th on debut: stoutly bred Naheez filly.   **0**
4597} Sacred Heart **196** [16] 3-8-2 R Ffrench 25/1:   609 Lisa B **79** [8] 3-8-0 (vis) G Baker (7) 16/1:
1261 Silken Fox **6** [19] 3-8-0 (VIS) N Callan 50/1:   112 Shayzan **174** [4] 3-8-9 Martin Dwyer 16/1:
1021 Foxdale **24** [7] 3-8-12 D Griffiths 25/1:   3971} Musical Fruits **243** [15] 3-8-0 A Nicholls (3) 33/1:
62 Pardy Pet **183** [11] 3-8-6 A Clark 20/1:   1175 Goldfaw **11** [1] 3-9-7 A McGlone 40/1:
20 ran   Time 1m 32.29 (6.79)   (Mascalls Stud)   W G M Turner Corton Denham, Somerset

1350 5.15 LEVY BOARD HCAP 3YO+ 0-80 (D)   1m4f   Good 58 -12 Slow   [80]
£4218   £1298   £649   £324   3 yo rec 17lb

1076 **WAIT FOR THE WILL 17** [7] G L Moore 4-9-7 R Mullen 14/1: 60-001: 4 ch g Seeking The Gold - **78**
You'd Be Surprised (Blushing Groom) Waited with, imprvd ent fnl 3f, rdn dist, styd on to lead near fin: op
10/1, gd ride: '99 wnr at Salisbury (amat h'cap, rtd 82): eff at 12f on firm & gd/gd: loves Salisbury.
1199 **RAVENSWOOD 10** [9] M C Pipe 3-8-9 (78)(t) W Supple 5/1: 100-42: 3 b c Warning - Green Lucia nk **81**
(Green Dancer) Prom, led 2f out, hard rdn & worn down nr fin: bckd tho' op 7/2: in fine form: see 1199.
3535} **ROYAL MEASURE 269** [11] R Hannon 4-7-10 (48)(2oh) A McCarthy (3) 25/1: 0000-3: 4 b g Inchinor - ½ **50**
Sveltissima (Dunphy) Chsd ldrs, rdn ent fnl 2f no impress till styd on towards fin: reapp: 4th in a '99
mdn (rtd 78): unraced juv: stays 12f on gd grnd.
*1209 **TWO SOCKS 9** [8] J S King 7-8-9 (61)(6ex) I Mongan (5) 6/1: 00-614: Well plcd, ev ch 2f out, hd **63**
sn drvn, no extra nr fin: ran to best under a penalty for 1209.
1065 **KINGFISHERS BONNET 17** [6] 4-7-12 (50) L Newman (0) 20/1: 4-0135: Handy, led after 1m till 2f 1½ **50**
out, onepace bef dist: op 14/1: just about saw of this longer, stiff 12f, return to 10f will suit: see 889.
4148} **TOMMY CARSON 232** [11] 5-8-0 (52)(bl) M Henry 12/1: 2332-6: Led till 4f out, no extra till late hd **52**
rally: op 20/1, jumps fit (mdn, stays 2m6.5f on gd/soft in blnks or visor): dual '99 rnr-up (clmr, rtd 63 at
best, D Elsworth): mdn plcd in '98 (rtd 73): eff at 10f/14f, prob handles firm & hvy grnd, with/without blnks.
1209 **KIRISNIPPA 9** [14] 5-8-0 (51)(1ow) P Doe 6/1: 605327: Rear, some late hdwy, nvr nr ldrs: consistent. 1 **51**
1150 **STORM HILL 13** [5] 4-9-10 (76)(t) R Havlin 14/1: 545-08: Mid-div, rdn to chase ldrs 2f out, btn & ½ **74**
edged left ins last: op 10/1, t-strap reapplied after choking on reapp: '99 debut 3rd (mdn, rtd 91, A Foster):
eff at 10f on fast grnd: a drop back in trip will suit: with J Gosden.
565 **EUROLINK APACHE 86** [13] 5-8-11 (63) N Pollard 14/1: 2/249: Nvr a factor: 12 wk abs, h'cap bow. nk **60**
1096 **FLETCHER 16** [12] 6-8-0 (52) A Daly 20/1: 0-0000: Nvr nr ldrs: 10th, tricky ride, see 182. ½ **48**
1180 **ANGELS VENTURE 11** [2] 4-10-0 (80)(t) R Hughes 9/1: 21-000: In tch, pld hard, fdd fnl 2f: 11th. hd **76**
-- **HARIYMI** [3] 5-9-13 (79) A Clark 9/1: 214-0: Chsd ldrs till wknd appr fnl 2f: 12th, 10 wk jmps abs. 3 **70**
scored at Kempton (Gr2 nov, 2m, gd & soft, rtd 121h): ex-Irish, Flat wnr at Dundalk in '99 (10f on fast, J Oxx).
858 **PRINCE OMID 38** [10] 3-8-4 (72)(1ow) D Harrison 4/1 FAV: 05-340: Far too keen in tch, btn 3f out: 14th. **0**
889 **Vanborough Lad 36** [4] 11-7-10(48)(13oh) G Bardwell 50/1:
1100 **Famous 16** [15] 7-7-10 (48)(9oh) R Brisland (5) 50/1:
15 ran   Time 2m 40.81 (8.41)   (Richard Green (Fine Paitings)   G L Moore Woodingdean, E Sussex

THIRSK FRIDAY MAY 19TH Lefthand, Flat, Oval Track

Official Going   GOOD   Stalls: Str Course - Stands Side, Round Course - Inside

1351 2.00 MOWBRAY SELLER 3YO+ (G)   7f rnd   Good/Soft 82 +05 Fast
£3045   £870   £435   3 yo rec 11lb

872 **DANDY REGENT 38** [12] J L Harris 6-9-11 K Dalgleish (7) 10/1: 50-101: 6 b g Green Desert - Tahilla **65**
(Moorestyle) Led/dsptd lead thr'out, asserted from 2f out, in command was last, pushed out, rdly: val for 9L+:
no bid: earlier scored at Leicester (sell): rnr-up once in '99 (rtd 50): '98 Brighton wnr (h'cap, rtd 74 & 60a): eff
at 6f, suited by 7f/1m on firm, hvy & equitrack: handles any trk & runs well fresh: relishes sell grade.
1275 **ERUPT 6** [14] M Brittain 7-9-6 D Mernagh 7/1: 7-2042: 7 b g Beveled - Sparkingsovereign   7 **53**
(Sparkler) Mid-div, rdn/styd on fnl 2f, no threat to wnr: quick reapp: remains in gd heart: see 1275, 647.
1242 **CELEBRE BLU 8** [8] K A Ryan 3-8-9 F Lynch 14/1: 63: Chsd ldrs, rdn appr 2f out & kpt on: op 20/1: nk **52**
Held up, prog/swthed 2f out, styd on well, nrst fin: op 20/1: bandaged bhd: sure to appreciate 1m+.
1132 **MAMMAS BOY 15** [10] A Berry 5-9-6 J Carroll 10/1: 00-004: Mid-div, eff 2f out, kept on, no threat. nk **51**
1101 **OAKWELL ACE 16** [4] 4-9-1 R Cody Boutcher (7) 20/1: 0-5005: Mid-div, eff/switched 2f out, no impress. 1½ **43**
1132 **DILETTO 15** [16] 4-9-6 W Supple 14/1: 026106: Chsd ldrs, rdn/no impress fnl 2f: btr 1132 (fast). ¾ **47$**

449

1305 **ODDSANENDS** 4 [6] 4-9-11 Lynsey Hanna (7) 12/1: 100057: Led/dsptd lead 5f, grad fdd: qck reapp.   ½ 51
4476} **LAUND VIEW LADY** 210 [3] 3-8-4 O Pears 4/1 FAV: 1000-8: Keen/cl-up 5f: reapp, fit: '99 Ripon   1 39
scorer (auct mdn, rtd 82): eff at 6f, this longer 7f trip shld suit: acts on gd grnd on a sharpish trk.
1132 **JAYPEECEE** 15 [13] 4-9-6 D Holland 14/1: 00-009: Mid-div, btn 2f out: see 844 (6f).   nk 43
1239 **ENCOUNTER** 8 [11] 4-9-6 N Kennedy 5/1: -40040: Dwelt, nvr on terms: 10th: btr 1239, 787 (6f).   1¼ 40
1132 **SO WILLING** 15 [5] 4-9-6 (bl) A Culhane 8/1: 305600: Chsd ldrs halfway, drvn/held 2f out: 11th.   3½ 33
1256 **SEALED BY FATE** 7 [1] 5-9-6 (vis) R Winston 5/1: -50660: Strugg halfway, no impress: 13th: op 4/1.   0
1143 **Unmasked** 14 [2] 4-9-1 N Carlisle 33/1:   973 **Shontaine** 30 [9] 7-9-6 Kristin Stubbs (7) 16/1:
1132 **Pleasure Trick** 15 [7] 9-9-6 (vis) Kim Tinkler 14/1:   1149 **Cladantom** 14 [15] 4-9-1 Kimberley Hart (5) 25/1:
16 ran   Time 1m 28.3 (5.4)   (J L Harris)   J L Harris Eastwell, Leics

---

1352   2.30 JACK CALVERT MDN 3YO+ (D)   1m rnd   Good/Soft 82   -09 Slow
£4439   £1366   £683   £341   3 yo rec 12lb

1055 **EVEREST** 20 [1] P F I Cole 3-8-12 J Carroll 100/30: 2-2321: 3 ch c Indian Ridge - Reine d'Beaute   87
(Caerleon) Mid-div, prog to chall over 1f out, rdn/narrowly asserted nr fin: plcd all 4 starts prev incl sole '99 start
(rtd 89, mdn): eff at 1m, stays a sharp 6f, could get further: acts on gd & hvy grnd, sharp/stiff trk: consistent.
983 **PARAGON OF VIRTUE** 29 [8] Sir Michael Stoute 3-8-12 F Lynch 4/6 FAV: 02: 3 ch c Cadeaux Genereux   ½ 85
- Madame Dubois (Legend Of France) Chsd ldrs, smooth prog to lead over 1f out, rdn/strongly prsd ins last,
hdd nr fin: hvly bckd, nvr able to assert: jockey reported colt would prefer a faster surface: win sn.
-- **GOLDEN CHANCE** [7] M Johnston 3-8-12 D Holland 7/1: 3: 3 b c Unfuwain - Golden Digger (Mr   3½ 78
Prospector) Handy, led over 2f out till over 1f out, not pace of front pair ins last: burly on debut: dam a mdn
tho' well related: eff at 1m, handles gd/soft: scopey colt, should improve, prob over 10f+.
1051 **DIANEME** 20 [6] T D Easterby 3-8-7 R Winston 16/1: 304: Rdn/prsd ldrs 3f out, sn held: looks sure   5 64
to relish h'caps: lengthy, attractive filly who was eyecatching on debut in 826 (soft).
-- **GRAND AMBITION** [2] 4-9-10 R Cochrane 10/1: 5: Cl-up 6f: reapp, ndd this: ex-Irish, disq after   5 60
wng a 1m Galway mdn in '99 (D Weld): cost current connections 18,000 gns: eff at 1m, stays 11f: acts on fast grnd.
-- **SIERRA STORM** [10] 3-9-5 O Pears 50/1: 6: In 1cth 5f: Flat debut, 12 wk jumps abs (mod form).   7 44
1084 **GOLDEN OSCAR** 17 [9] W Supple 33/1: 07: Led 5f, sn btn.   1 47
4390} **BLUE HAWK** 216 [3] 3-8-12 P M Quinn 25/1: 0300-8: Bhd halfway: reapp, fit, unruly in paddock: 27 7
plcd last term, (rtd 72, mdn): stays 7f, tried 10f: handles firm grnd.
1193 **WILLY BANG BANG** 12 [5] 3-8-12 T Williams 50/1: -09: Slowly away, al bhd: mod form.   hd 7
961 **TALIBAN** 31 [4] 4-9-10 J F Egan 40/1: 600: Bhd halfway, virtually p.u.: 10th: see 784.   dist 0
10 ran   Time 1m 42.7 (7.3)   (H R H Prince Fahd Salman)   P F I Cole Whatcombe, Oxon

---

1353   3.00 STATION ROAD CLAIMER 4YO+ (E)   1m4f   Good/Soft 82   -18 Slow
£3038   £935   £467   £233

871 **DESERT FIGHTER** 38 [13] Mrs M Reveley 9-8-12 A Culhane 7/2: 14-001: 9 b g Green Desert - Jungle Rose   57
(Shirley Heights) Mid-div, smooth prog/trkd ldrs over 3f out & went on over 1f out, styd on well ins last, drvn out:
lkd well, op 7/2: '99 wnr here at Thirsk (this race), Haydock, Hamilton & Catterick (clmrs, rtd 66): plcd in '98
(h'caps, rtd 71): eff at 10/12f on firm & gd/soft, handles soft & any trk, likes Thirsk: enjoys claiming grade.
1065 **CASHIKI** 18 [15] B Palling 4-8-5 J F Egan 10/1: 00-602: 4 ch f Case Law - Nishiki (Brogan)   1¾ 47$
Trkd ldrs halfway, rdn/briefly led over 1f out, kept on, not pace of wnr: stays 12f: gd run on drop to clmg grade.
1209 **PENNYS FROM HEAVEN** 10 [2] D Nicholls 6-9-6 A Nicholls 33/1: 034/03: 6 gr g Generous -   1 61
Heavenly Cause (Grey Dawn II) Mid-div, prog fnl 3f, kept on ins last, not pace to chall: padd picks: improve.
676 **JATO DANCER** 64 [5] R Hollinshead 5-8-3 P M Quinn 50/1: 000054: Handy, rdn fnl 3f, kept on   nk 43$
onepace: 2 mth abs, fit: stays sharp 12f: handles fast, gd/soft & equitrack: see 359.
860 **I CANT REMEMBER** 39 [8] 6-8-12 S Finnamore (5) 5/2 JT FAV: 245405: Cl-up & saddle slipped forward,   ½ 51
led after 5f till over 2f out, no extra: nicely bckd, op 3/1: see 530, 428.
1209 **LOST SPIRIT** 10 [1] 4-9-0 Darren Williams (7) 33/1: 003506: Held up, keen, switched/late gains,   ¾ 52$
nvr nrr: significant change of tactics, likes to front run on sand: see 608 (AW h'cap).
-- **WRANGEL** [12] 6-8-12 J Carroll 8/1: 7: Handy, led over 2f out, hdd over 1f out & wknd: Flat debut,   ½ 49
jumps fit (99/00 Stratford wnr, nov h'cap, subs rtd 99h): eff around 2m/2m1.5f on firm & gd/soft grnd).
1191 **LOYAL TOAST** 12 [10] 5-8-10 Kim Tinkler 33/1: -20038: Handy 10f: looked well: see 1191, 670.   3½ 42$
1739} **BACKEND CHARLIE** 350 [6] 6-9-0 F Lynch 33/1: 65-9: Chsd ldrs 3f out, sn held: reapp, mod form.   14 31
70 **LOBUCHE** 182 [11] 5-8-12 (t) Joanna Badger (7) 33/1: 0000-0: Cl-up 9f: 10th: jumps fit (rnr-up   2 26
last term, rtd 79h): mod '99 Flat form: '98 Yarmouth wnr (h'cap, rtd 65, rnr-up on sand, rtd 59a): eff at 6f, stays
10f: acts on firm, soft & equitrack: has runs well fresh: best without blnks & a t-strap.
3974} **BAY OF BENGAL** 244 [4] 4-8-5 A Daly 12/1: 1040-0: Led 5f, btn 3f out: 14th: reapp: won 1st 2 starts   0
in '99 at Nottingham (sell h'cap) & Pontefract (h'cap, rtd 50): rtd 47 in '98 (sell, H Alexander): eff at 10/12f on
fast & gd, gall/undul trk: has run well fresh.
3025} **SITTING PRETTY** 294 [7] 4-8-9 T Williams 33/1: 000-P: U.r. sev times & bolted bef race, al bhd, p.u. 1f   0
reapp: mod form in '99 for D Nicholls, now with R Bastiman.
1241 **Charity Crusader** 8 [3] 9-9-1 (bl) T Eaves (7) 14/1:   1132 **Stamford Hill** 15 [14] 5-8-12 G Parkin 66/1:
1132 **Rudcroft** 15 [9] 4-8-6 J Bramhill 33/1:
15 ran   Time 2m 41.8 (12.0)   (A Frame)   Mrs M Reveley Lingdale, N Yorks

---

1354   3.30 BENEVOLENT MDN 3YO+ (D)   6f   Good/Soft 82   -18 Slow
£3737   £1150   £575   £287   3 yo rec 9 lb   Field raced stands side

3424} **MORGAN LE FAY** 275 [10] N Tinkler 5-9-2 Kim Tinkler 10/1: 5230-1: 5 b m Magic Ring - Melody Park   63
(Music Boy) Sn handy, narrow lead halfway, styd on gamely to just prevail, all out: tchd 12/1, burly on reapp:
rnr-up in '99 for D E Incisa (C/D h'cap, rtd 64): rnr-up thrice in '98 (fill mdn, rtd 69 at best, B Meehan): eff at
6/7f, tried 1m: acts on firm & soft grnd: strong mare who runs well fresh.
1220 **STAR PRINCESS** 9 [4] K T Ivory 3-8-7 C Catlin 5/2 FAV: 24-642: 3 b f Up And At 'Em - Princess   shd 63
Sharpenup (Lochnager) Sn cl-up, rdn/ev ch fnl 2f, kept on well, just held: bckd: btr 1220 (h'cap).
1036 **HOUT BAY** 21 [8] S E Kettlewell 3-8-12 A Culhane 10/1: 0-6453: 3 ch c Komaite - Maiden Pool   ½ 66
(Sharpen Up) Trkd ldrs halfway, rdn/prsd front pair fnl 1f, al just held: op 14/1: acts on gd & gd/soft grnd.
1061 **THORNCLIFF FOX** 18 [12] J A Glover 3-8-12 (VIS) O Pears 6/1: 330-04: Bhd ldrs, briefly no room   ½ 64
halfway, kept on ins last, not pace to chall: op 5/1: tried a visor: paddock pick: see 1061.
1256 **ITS ANOTHER GIFT** 7 [9] 3-8-7 (bl) J Carroll 10/1: -03055: Rear, prog/switched 2f out, no threat.   1½ 55
1261 **NOCCIOLA** 7 [7] 4-9-2 G Duffield 8/1: 0-06: Prom, outpcd fnl 2f: leave this bhd over further in h'caps.   1¼ 52

-- **BRITTAS BLUES** [5] 3-8-7 D Holland 4/1: 7: Cl-up, outpcd fnl 2f: op 7/2, debut: half sister to sev wnrs incl smart 6/7f performer Andreyev: lengthy, attractive filly who needed this: with M Johnston. ½ **50**
3941} **ABCO BOY 246** [11] 3-8-12 C Teague 40/1: 0-8: Rdn/outpcd, nvr on terms: reapp, no form. 3½ **47**
1205 **BLUEGRASS MOUNTAIN 11** [3] 3-8-12 R Winston 9/1: 60-009: Led 3f, sn btn: see 976. 3 **40**
246} **TAWN AGAIN 500** [6] 4-9-7 C Lowther 14/1: 6-0: Cl-up 4f: 10th: op 12/1: long abs, needed this: unplaced on sole '99 start (debut, rtd 50a, AW mdn). 5 **31**
2073} **Coming Up Roses 336** [1] 3-8-7 D Mernagh (3) 20/1: 3128} **Mawdsley 289** [2] 3-8-7 W Supple 25/1:
12 ran Time 1m 15.5 (6.0) (Don Enrico Incisa) N Tinkler Langton, N Yorks

1355 **4.00 HELMSLEY HCAP 4YO+ 0-90 (C) 2m Good/Soft 82 -26 Slow [83]**
£7046 £2168 £1084 £542 4 yo rec 2 lb

*1044 **RENZO 21** [4] J L Harris 7-8-12 (67) A Culhane 7/2: 000-11: 7 b g Alzao - Watership (Foolish Pleasure) In tch, rdn/led over 2f out, styd on strongly ins last, drvn clr: padd pick: recent jumps rnr (unplcd): earlier scored at Sandown (h'cap): back in 98/99 scored over timber at Ascot (debut, nov, rtd 132h): unplcd on the Level last term (rtd 80), subs hobdayed: '98 Doncaster wnr (h'cap, rtd 84): eff at 14f/2m: acts on firm & hvy, any trk, likes Sandown: best without blnks: enigmatic but well h'capped, enthusiasm seems rekindled at present. **73**
1222 **STAR RAGE 9** [2] M Johnston 10-10-0 (83) D Holland 3/1: 1-60F2: 10 b g Horage - Star Bound (Crowned Prince) Held up, pushed along 5f out, rdn/chsd wnr 1f out, al held: op 2/1: see 714. 5 **83**
903 **INDIANA PRINCESS 36** [5] Mrs M Reveley 7-9-0 (69) T Eaves (7) 9/2: 33-263: 7 b m Warrshan - Lovely Greek Lady (Ela Mana Mou) Led after 5f till halfway, again over 3f out till over 2f out, sn onepace/held: see 797. 7 **63**
1147 **FREEDOM QUEST 14** [6] B S Rothwell 5-8-7 (62) W Supple 11/2: 0-4434: Keen early, in tch, btn 2f out. ½ **55**
1180 **DANEGOLD 12** [3] 8-8-5 (60) P Fessey 2/1 FAV: 00-045: Dictated pace 5f, led again halfway till over 3f out, btn 2f out: op 9/4: not suited by this small field, likes to come late off a fast pace: best forgotten. *nk* **53**
5 ran Time 3m 40.0 (17.2) (Cleartherm Ltd) J L Harris Eastwell, Leics

1356 **4.30 D PEACOCK HCAP 3YO+ 0-75 (E) 6f Good/Soft 82 -11 Slow [74]**
£8489 £2612 £1306 £653 3 yo rec 9 lb Stands side group held advantage

1005 **DIAMOND DECORUM 25** [15] P D Evans 4-9-6 (66) Joanna Badger (7) 7/1: 000-61: 4 ch g Fayruz - Astra Adastra (Mount Hagen) Rdn/chsg ldrs stands side, prog/narrow lead over 1f out, styd on well, drvn out: nicely bckd, tchd 10/1: '99 Lingfield wnr (h'cap, rtd 81 & 66a): '98 Thirsk wnr (auct mdn, rtd 76): eff at 5/6f, stays 7f on fast & gd/soft, handles soft/hvy, any trk, likes a sharp/easy one: slipped to a handy mark. **71**
1126 **IVORY DAWN 15** [17] K T Ivory 6-9-8 (68) C Catlin (7) 10/1: 0-0022: 6 b m Batshoof - Cradle Of Love (Roberto) Rdn/chsd ldrs stands side, styd on well fnl 2f, nrst fin: op 8/1: win soon, prob at Brighton/Lingfield. ½ **70**
4298} **ANTONIO CANOVA 223** [20] Bob Jones 4-9-12 (72) D O'Donohoe 12/1: 6223-3: 4 ch g Komaite - Joan's Venture (Beldale Flutter) Cl-up stands side, ev ch fnl 1f, kept on well, just held nr fin: op 10/1, reapp, looked well: plcd fnl 3 '99 starts (rtd 75, stks): eff at 5/6f on fast & gd/soft grnd, sharp/stiff trk: fine h'cap bow. *nk* **73**
1239 **COOL PROSPECT 8** [21] K A Ryan 5-8-6 (52)(bl) F Lynch 16/1: 054104: Led stands side till over 1f out, no extra cl-home: op 20/1: see 1143. ½ **51**
1008 **PANDJOJOE 25** [2] 4-8-12 (58) R Winston 9/4 FAV: 00-055: Rdn chasing ldrs far side, led that group 1f out & rdn/pulled clr, no chance with ldrs stands side: hvly bckd: unlucky, v well h'capped, win soon. ½ **55+**
1158 **EURO VENTURE 13** [22] 5-9-9 (69) O Pears 8/1: -00006: Rdn in tch stands side, styd on strongly ins last, no room cl-home: imprvd eff back at fav 6f, now coming to hand, well h'capped & can win similar. *hd* **65+**
910 **SUGAR CUBE TREAT 35** [24] 4-8-11 (57) P Fessey 20/1: 010-07: Drvn/towards rear stds side, late gains. 2 **48**
1256 **WISHBONE ALLEY 7** [6] 5-8-6 (52)(vis) A Daly 25/1: 420308: Cl-up far side 4f, fdd: jockey given 4-day ban for careless riding: bandaged in front: see 312. ¾ **41**
1158 **SMART PREDATOR 13** [4] 4-9-10 (70) T Lucas 12/1: 6-0039: In tch far side, eff/hmpd over 1f out, switched & styd on ins last, no threat: op 10/1: eff at 6f, interesting next time over further (stays 1m). ½ **57+**
1158 **NORTHERN SVENGALI 13** [19] 4-9-12 (72) C Lowther 25/1: 040000: In tch stands side, held fnl 2f: 10th. *hd* **58**
780 **RETALIATOR 51** [18] 4-9-6 (66) Joanna Badger (7) 20/1: 000-00: Towards rear stands side, nvr pace to chall: 11th: longer priced stablemate of wnr, 7 wk abs: see 780. *nk* **51**
1192 **FULL SPATE 12** [3] 5-9-5 (65) A Nicholls (3) 14/1: 00-360: Led far side halfway, hdd 1f out/fdd: 12th. *hd* **49**
908 **KOSEVO 35** [11] 6-8-4 (50)(vis) Kimberley Hart (5) 33/1: -00000: Chsd ldrs towards centre 4f: 13th. *nk* **33**
-758 **MUNGO PARK 52** [10] 6-9-13 (73) D Holland 8/1: 200-20: In tch far side, eff 2f out/no impress: 14th: abs. 1½ **53**
+1082 **TALARIA 17** [9] 4-9-7 (67)(t) G Faulkner (3) 12/1: 0-6010: Chsd ldrs far side 4f: 16th: btr 1082. **0**
780 **ACID TEST 51** [12] 5-9-8 (68)(BL) J Carroll 14/1: -06630: Led far side 3f, btn 1f out: 20th: abs, blnks. **0**
1258 **Dominelle 7** [13] 8-8-11 (57) G Parkin 20/1: 1073 **Sharp Edge Boy 18** [23] 4-8-9 (55) W Supple 14/1:
2081} **Hakeem 335** [1] 5-9-1 (61) N Carlisle 33/1: 1257 **Square Dancer 7** [5] 4-9-9 (69) T Williams 25/1:
1008 **Mary Jane 25** [16] 5-8-10 (56) Kim Tinkler 25/1: 1192 **Johayro 12** [14] 7-9-0 (60) A McGlone 16/1:
1143 **Grand Estate 14** [8] 5-9-1 (61) A Culhane 16/1:
23 ran Time 1m 15.1 (5.6) (Diamond Racing Ltd) P D Evans Pandy, Gwent

1357 **5.00 KILBURN HCAP 3YO+ 0-80 (D) 5f Good/Soft 82 +02 Fast [80]**
£4595 £1414 £707 £353 3 yo rec 8 lb Stands side group held big advantage

1278 **BODFARI KOMAITE 6** [17] M W Easterby 4-8-9 (61) T Lucas 7/4 FAV: 66-W21: 4 b g Komaite - Gypsy's Barn Rat (Balliol) Made all stands rail, edged left when strongly prsd fnl 1f, just held on, all out: hvly bckd, op 2/1: quick reapp: '99 scorer at Musselburgh & Doncaster (h'caps, rtd 62): '98 Redcar scorer (nurs h'cap, rtd 62): all wins at 5f on firm & gd/soft, handles hvy & any trk: in good form. **64**
1278 **MALADERIE 6** [11] M Dods 6-8-4 (56)(vis) T Williams 25/1: 0-0002: 6 b g Thatching - Native Melody (Tudor Music) Bhd ldrs stands side, prog to chall fnl 1f, styd on well, just held: well h'capped, win soon: see 908. *hd* **58**
1074 **GAY BREEZE 18** [18] P S Felgate 7-9-11 (77) S Finnamore (5) 7/1: 45-303: 7 b g Dominion - Judy's Dowry (Dragonara Palace) Handy stands side, rdn & kept on ins last: op 6/1: gd run: see 905. 1 **77**
1245 **ZIGGYS DANCER 8** [14] E J Alston 9-9-11 (77) W Supple 16/1: 433404: In tch stands side, drvn & kept on fnl 2f, not pace to chall: looked superb, op 14/1: acts on firm, soft & both AWs: see 926, 223. *nk* **76**
1162 **DOUBLE OSCAR 13** [16] 7-9-4 (70) T Hamilton (7) 20/1: 0-0005: Rear stands side, styd on ins last, nrst fin: '99 Ayr wnr (h'cap, rtd 82 at best): '98 Lingfield, W'hampton, Goodwood & Ascot wnr (h'caps, rtd 89 & 89a): eff at 6f, just best at 5f, stays 7f: handles gd/soft & hvy, likes firm & gd & both AWs: suited by blnks, not worn today: gd weight carrier: now coming to hand, well h'capped & one to note, particularly with headgear reapplied. 1 **67+**
3911} **RIVER TERN 248** [13] 7-9-4 (70) D Holland 8/1: 6045-6: Towards rear stands side, switched/hung left over 1f out, kept on tho' al held: reapp: '99 h'cap wnr here at Thirsk (C/D) & York (rtd 73 at best): plcd sev times in '98 (rtd 66): eff at 6f, suited by 5f: acts on gd/soft, loves firm & fast: has run well fresh, handles *hd* **66**

FRIDAY MAY 19TH   **Lefthand, Flat, Oval Track**

any trk: eff with/without visor: best held up for a late run: fitter for this on faster ground.

1298 **JACKERIN** 4 [7] 5-7-10 (48)(bl)(1oh) Joanna Badger (7) 25/1: 655447: Keen/prom stands side 4f.	hd	43
787 **COLONEL SAM** 51 [9] 4-7-10 (48)(tbl)(3oh) P M Quinn (5) 33/1: -00008: Towards rear stands side, no impress: looked well, 7 wk abs: see 558 (mdn).	1½	39
1143 **SWYNFORD DREAM** 14 [8] 7-8-7 (59) J Carroll 14/1: 00-529: Prom stands side, btn/eased fnl 1f.	½	48
3944} **SURPRISED** 246 [15] 5-9-4 (70) R Winston 8/1: 2520-0: Held up stands side, no impress: op 6/1: reapp, ndd this: '99 wnr at Pontefract (h'cap, rtd 72): rtd 62 at best in '98 (J Ramsden): eff at 5f, suited by 6f & stays 7.4f: acts on firm & gd/soft, any trk: best without blnks: scopey gelding, sharper next time over 6f.	shd	59
1162 **TORRENT** 13 [6] 5-8-9 (61)(bl) Lynsey Hanna (7) 12/1: 365530: Dwelt, sn cl-up far side, led that group 2f out, no ch ins last: 11th: op 9/1, 1st time on unfav far side: prob best forgotten: see 205 (AW).	¾	48
1074 **PIERPOINT** 18 [10] 5-9-1 (67) A Culhane 20/1: 00-000: Rear stands side, no impress: 12th: see 1074.	nk	53
1245 **ZUHAIR** 8 [12] 7-10-0 (80) A Nicholls (3) 20/1: -00000: Sn rdn stands side, nvr on terms: 13th: see 716.	1	64
*777 **BENNOCHY** 51 [2] 3-8-1 (61) P Bradley (5) 20/1: 000-10: Held up far side, btn 2f out: 16th: abs, op 14/1.		0
1256 **TREASURE TOUCH** 7 [4] 4-8-7 (59)(BL) O Pears 20/1: 20-000: Led far side 3f, sn btn: 18th: blnks.		0
926 Miss Fit 34 [5] 4-9-8 (74) J F Egan (5)		
751 **Antonias Double** 52 [1] 5-9-9 (75) P Fessey 14/1:		
1162 Goretski 13 [3] 7-9-3 (69) Kim Tinkler 20/1:		

18 ran   Time 1m 01.00 (4.0)   (Bodfari Stud Ltd)   M W Easterby Sheriff Hutton, N Yorks

---

FRIDAY MAY 19TH   **Righthand, Undulating Track, Stiff Uphill Finish**

Official Going   GOOD TO FIRM. Stalls: 1m - Inside; Rem - Stands Side

1358	**6.30 VOLVO APPR HCAP 3YO+ 0-65 (F)** 5f **Good/Firm 34 +02 Fast**		[60]
	£2565 £733 £366 3 yo rec 8 lb		

1258 **JACMAR** 7 [2] Miss L A Perratt 5-8-12 (44) J Mackay 4/1 FAV: 0-2641: 5 br g High Estate - Inseyab (Persian Bold) In tch, rdn to improve 2f out, styd on strongly & drvn out to lead cl-home: qck reapp: '99 wnr here at Hamilton (amat h'cap, rtd 63): no wins in '98, '97 wnr again at Hamilton (3, rtd 95): eff at 5/6f, stays 7f: acts on firm & gd/soft grnd: eff weight carrier & v well h'capped on old form: all wins at Hamilton.		49
1007 **BEYOND THE CLOUDS** 25 [12] J S Wainwright 4-9-2 (48)(vis) R Farmer (5) 9/2: 65-002: 4 b g Midhish - Tongabezi (Shernazar) Led early, rdn to lead again appr fnl 1f, edged left & hdd fnl strides: gd eff in visor.	hd	52
1257 **BIFF EM** 7 [4] Miss L A Perratt 6-8-7 (39) M Scott (6) 10/1: 00-503: 6 ch g Durgan - Flash The Gold (Ahonoora) Cl-up, ev ch until short of room & held fnl 1f: loves Hamilton, on a fair mark: see 1143.	1¼	47
1143 **KALAR** 14 [13] D W Chapman 11-8-8 (40)(bl) D Egan (5) 10/1: 005004: Led after 1f, hdd over 1f out, not pace of ldrs ins last: very tough (14 wins from 167 runs): see 371 (AW).	½	39
1244 **FACILE TIGRE** 8 [10] 5-9-3 (49) D Meah (3) 50/1: 600005: Handy, rdn to chall appr fnl 1f, held fnl 1f.	nk	47
1275 **NAISSANT** 6 [3] 7-9-5 (51) Dawn Rankin (6) 16/1: 0-5006: Dwelt, bhd, late gains, no threat: lost ch with a tardy start here: well h'capped & interesting when stable return to form: see 844.	1	47
1133 **APPLES AND PEARS** 15 [11] 4-9-1 (47) P Shea 7/1: -05007: Nvr btr than mid-div: see 312.	hd	42
1148 **GRANITE CITY** 14 [8] 3-8-7 (47) B McHugh (5) 16/1: 560-08: Nvr a factor: plcd once in '99 (nurs h'cap, rtd 60 at best): stays 5/6f, handles firm grnd.	½	40
609 **SOUNDS LUCKY** 80 [5] 4-9-10 (56)(vis) D Young (6) 7/1: 044169: Al arnd same place: 11 wk abs.	hd	48
1255 **RADICAL JACK** 7 [1] 3-8-9 (49) D Watson (3) 100/1: 000-00: Dwelt, al bhd, fin 10th: quick reapp: unplcd as a juv (auct mdn, rtd 55 at best, tried blnks).	shd	41
1140 **MUKARRAB** 15 [4] 6-9-4 (50) G Gibbons (3) 6/1: -04360: Trkd ldrs, wknd fnl 2f, fin 11th: see 506.	1	40
3783} **PALLIUM** 256 [9] 12-7-12 (30)(tbl) D Kilcourse (2) 40/1: 0500-0: Lost tch halfway, fin 12th: last won back in '99 (rtd 27 at best): last won made in '99, at Hamilton (amat h'cap, rtd 54 at best): eff at 5/6f on firm & gd/soft grnd, handles gd/soft grnd: eff with/without blnks: now 12yo.	5	11
1257 **THREE LEADERS** 7 [6] 4-9-2 (48)(bl) L Swift (6) 14/1: -06000: Al bhd, fin last: see 648.	¾	27

13 ran   Time 59.70 (1.6)   (Marett-Sutherland-Hay)   Miss L A Perratt Ayr, Strathclyde

1359	**7.00 McGRATTAN AUCT MDN 2YO (E)** 5f **Good/Firm 34 -18 Slow**		
	£3146 £968 £484 £242		

1197 **DISTINCTLY CHIC** 11 [1] A P Jarvis 2-8-5 N Callan 2/1 JT FAV: 61: 2 b f Distinctly North - Dane's Lane (Danehill) Trkd ldrs, rdn to lead over 1f out, hung left but styd on well ins last, drvn out: IR 12,000gns May foal, half sister to a juv winner: acts on fast grnd & a stiff/undul trk.		75
1240 **SHATIN DOLLYBIRD** 8 [6] Miss L A Perratt 2-8-1 Dale Gibson 2/1 JT FAV: 22: 2 ch f Up And At 'Em - Pumpona (Sharpen Up) Trkd ldrs, led briefly over 2f out, ev ch till no extra well ins last: front 2 5L clr of rem: eff over a stiff/undul 5f on firm/fast grnd: deserves to land similar: see 1240.	½	68
1146 **ALICIAN SUNHILL** 14 [8] Mrs A Duffield 2-8-2(1ow) G Duffield 8/1: 03: 2 br f Piccolo - Midnight Spell (Night Shift) Chsd ldrs, rdn & not pace of front 2 fnl 1f: see 1146.	5	60
1146 **EYES DONT LIE** 14 [5] J Semple 2-8-8(1ow) M Tebbutt 50/1: 04: Dropped, rear, late gains: IR 5,800 gns Namaqualand half brother to sev wnrs: dam a juv 5f scorer: needs 6f.	1¾	62
-- **GAZETTE IT TONIGHT** [2] 2-8-0 D Mernagh (3) 6/1: 5: Trkd ldrs, dropped rear over 2f out, no threat after: cheaply bought filly, sister to a juv scorer in Italy, dam a 1m wnr: with A Berry, learn from this.	¾	52
1249 **ELAINES REBECCA** 8 [10] 2-8-0 G Bardwell 20/1: -6206: Prom, hdd appr fnl 1f: btr 1019 (sell, hvy).	1	50
1130 **NETTLES** 15 [3] 2-8-5 (BL) D Watson (7) 100/1: 007: Dwelt, al bhd: 1st time blnks: looks modest.	hd	54
1161 **ANGELAS HUSBAND** 13 [4] 2-8-9 P Hanagan (7) 16/1: 68: Led, hdd appr fnl 2f, wknd qckly: see 1161.	nk	57
-- **PILGRIM PRINCESS** [7] 2-8-5 J Bramhill 7/1: 9: Hmpd & dropped rear over 3f out, no ch after: IR12,000 gns 1st foal, dam plcd over 7f as a juv: with E J Alston.	6	42

9 ran   Time 1m 00.7 (2.6)   (Christopher Shankland)   A P Jarvis Aston Upthorpe, Oxon

1360	**7.30 POWER RENTAL HCAP 3YO+ 0-75 (E)** 1m65y **Good/Firm 34 +06 Fast**		[75]
	£3705 £1140 £570 £285 3 yo rec 12lb		

1243 **ADOBE** 8 [1] W M Brisbourne 5-8-2 (49) G Baker (7) 6/4 FAV: 102421: 5 b g Green Desert - Shamshir (Kris) Rear, prog ent fnl 3f to lead 2f out, rdn out: earlier won at W'hampton (h'cap, rtd 58a at best): '99 wnr at Bath (mdn h'cap) & Nottingham (h'cap, rtd 55 & 49a): plater for J Gosden in '98: eff at 7f suited by 1m on firm, gd grnd & fibresand, handles soft, any trk: eff with/without t-strap: runs well fresh.		54
1195 **IMPULSIVE AIR** 12 [2] J R Weymes 8-7-10 (43)(3oh) J Mackay (7) 20/1: 5-5002: 8 b g Try My Best -	1¼	44

452

Tracy's Sundown (Red Sunset) Rear, prog under press appr fnl 2f, not trouble wnr: back to form, win again.

*1254 **ETISALAT** 7 [3] J Pearce 5-9-2 (63)(6ex) G Bardwell 5/2: 631113: 5 b g Lahib - Sweet Repose   1   62
(High Top) Rear, smooth prog after 4f, rdn & onepace 2f out, late hdwy: quick reapp & a penalty: tough.

1300 **QUALITAIR SURVIVOR** 4 [10] J Hetherton 5-7-10 (43)(VIS)(9oh) J Bramhill 50/1: 045-04: Mid-div,   1   40$
eff fnl 3f, styd on but not pace to chall: quick reapp, stiffish task, visored: well btn 4th on Flat bow
last term (auct mdn, rtd 61$): former dual bmpr rnr-up.

1191 **FLOORSOTHEFOREST** 12 [8] 4-8-13 (60) Dale Gibson 16/1: 14-655: Chsd ldrs, chall 2f out, no extra.   ½   56

705 **KUWAIT THUNDER** 57 [5] 4-7-10 (43)(vis)(1oh) K Dalgleish (7) 10/1: 004406: Mid-div, chsd ldrs   1   37
appr fnl 2f, hung left & fdd fnl 1f: 8 wk abs, visor reapplied: see 368.

1148 **TAKER CHANCE** 14 [9] 4-7-11 (44) Iona Wands (5) 20/1: -00007: Led till 2f out, wknd: vis reapp.   nk   37

1085 **BALLISTIC BOY** 17 [4] 3-8-3 (62) P Hanagan (7) 25/1: 000-08: Al bhd: see 1085.   ¾   54

*1297 **MOTHER CORRIGAN** 4 [7] 4-8-13 (60)(vis)(6ex) D Mernagh (3) 13/2: 46-019: Keen, well plcd & ev ch   10   37
till wknd ent fnl 2f: longer trip, prob came too soon after 1297 (7f).

3984} **MEHMAAS** 244 [6] 4-9-11 (72) G Duffield 33/1: 1504-0: Bhd from halfway: 10th, reapp, top-weight: 11   34
'99 Brighton wnr (auct mdn, rtd 74): plcd prev term (rtd 80 & 78a): eff at 7f/1m on fast, gd/soft grnd &
fibresand, with/without blnks/visor: with R Barr.

10 ran   Time 1m 46.1 (2.3)   (P R Kirk)   W M Brisbourne Great Ness, Shropshire

---

1361   8.05 LUDDON SELL HCAP 3YO+ 0-60 (F)   1m3f   Good/Firm 34 -17 Slow   [55]
     £2926   £836   £418   3 yo rec 15lb

963 **MAJOR ATTRACTION** 31 [12] W M Brisbourne 5-8-2 (29) G Baker (7) 16/1: 060001: 5 gr g Major Jacko -   37
My Friend Melody (Sizzling Melody) Dwelt, imprvd after 1m, led dist, sn clr: first win: plcd for P Eccles in
'99 (AW sell, rtd 50a, prob flattered): eff over a stiff 11f, tried 2m: acts on fast grnd, without blnks/visor.

*1195 **ACE OF TRUMPS** 12 [7] J Hetherton 4-9-10 (51)(t) N Kennedy 7/1: 000012: 4 ch g First Trump -   5   52
Elle Reff (Shareef Dancer) Mid-div, prog to lead appr fnl 2f, hdd dist, onepace: prob ran to best under
a big weight tho' stiff 11f prob stretches his stamina: see 1195 (9f here).

1241 **CAMAIR CRUSADER** 8 [6] W McKeown 6-8-7 (34) G Duffield 6/1: 0-4353: 6 b g Jolly Jake - Sigrid's   1   34
Dream (Triple Bend) In tch, prog appr fnl 2f, styd on without threatening: see 1241, 822, 795.

1191 **MERLY NOTTY** 12 [16] W Storey 4-8-7 (34) J Mackay (7) 3/1 FAV: 005-24: Chsd ldrs, ev ch appr fnl   ¾   33
2f, sn onepace: nicely bckd, longer trip, see 1191 (9f here).

855 **GENUINE JOHN** 39 [4] 7-8-9 (36) D Mernagh (3) 7/1: 3-3245: Made most till ent fnl 3f, no extra.   hd   34

1210 **ESPERTO** 10 [9] 7-9-3 (44) G Bardwell 12/1: 2/0006: Held up, imprvd 3f out, sn rdn, no impress.   4   36

1195 **HOT POTATO** 12 [15] 4-8-0 (27) J McAuley (5) 10/1: 460057: Al around same place: see 298.   nk   18

1191 **SECONDS AWAY** 12 [17] 9-8-3 (30) Dawn Rankin (5) 16/1: 200-68: Nvr out of mid-div: see 1191.   ½   20

1241 **DONE WELL** 8 [10] 8-8-0 (27)(t) J Bramhill 20/1: -00009: Nvr nr ldrs: see 903.   ¾   16

1202 **DENTON LADY** 11 [11] 3-8-2 (44) P Hanagan 7/2 33/1: 0-6000: Mid-div till 3f out: 10th, longer trip.   hd   32

1191 **THREE CHERRIES** 12 [8] 4-9-6 (47) N Callan 33/1: 050-40: Chsd ldrs 1m: 11th, btr 1191 (9f).   ½   34

846 **PHILMIST** 41 [14] 8-9-4 (45)(bl) Dale Gibson 7/1: 164-00: Pld hard in mid-div, lost place 3f out: 6 wk   0
abs: '99 wnr here at Hamilton (2, sell h'cap & appr h'cap, rtd 49): '98 wnr again here at Hamilton h'cap,
rtd 51 & 47a): eff at 11f/14f on fast, soft grnd & fibresand, Hamilton specialist: wears blnks & is best coming late.

1190 **SARMATIAN** 12 [2] 9-8-13 (40)(t) K Dalgleish (7) 50/1: 30/000: Led 5f out till 3f out, sn btn: 15th   0
3f out, sn btn: 15th, see 847.

800 **WELCOME BACK** 50 [18] 3-8-2 (44) Iona Wands (5) 12/1: 006-00: Bhd from halfway, sadde slipped: last.   0

1191 **Ajjae** 12 [13] 4-8-12 (39)(bl) M Tebbutt 25/1:   848 **Alfahad** 41 [3] 7-8-11 (38) R Cody Boutcher (7) 16/1:
16 ran   Time 2m 24.4 (5.6)   (Positive Partners)   W M Brisbourne Great Nee, Shropshire

---

1362   8.35 A-PLANT MED AUCT MDN 3-5YO (E)   1m4f   Good/Firm 31 -01 Slow
     £3120   £960   £480   £240   3 yo rec 17lb

1084 **INCA STAR** 17 [1] M Johnston 3-8-9 R Winston 6/1: 3-561: 3 b c Trempolino - Inca Impress (Sovereign   79
Dancer) Waited with, prog & went 2nd halfway, led over 4f out, rdn 2f out, styd on well, eased nr fin: rtd 85 when
plcd sole juv start: suited by this step up to 12f, likely to stay 14f: acts on gd/firm or gd/soft grnd.

1271 **FULL AHEAD** 7 [8] M H Tompkins 3-8-9 G Duffield 1/1 FAV: 45-332: 3 b c Slip Anchor - Foulard   3   74
(Sadler's Wells) Led until hdd by wnr, rdn & kept on fnl 2f, nvr lkd likely: stays 12f, turn will come: see 713.

1179 **RAINBOW SPIRIT** 12 [7] A P Jarvis 3-8-9 N Callan 6/1: 0-503: 3 b g Rainbows For Life - Merrie   shd   74
Moment (Taufan) In tch, rdn 3f out, kept on fnl 2f: stays 12f, handles gd/fm: see 916.

1157 **FORUM CHRIS** 13 [6] M Johnston 3-8-9 A Culhane 25/1: 04: Waited with, rdn/outpcd 4f out,   2½   70$
kept on fnl 2f: 11L clr of rem, stablemate of wnr: one more run for h'caps.

1157 **MICE DESIGN** 13 [2] 3-8-9 C Cogan (5) 40/1: 05: Held up, outpcd 4f out, nvr in it: t.o. debut prev.   11   58

4076} **HUTOON** 238 [5] 3-8-9 G Bardwell 11/4: 043-6: Keen & prom, rdn over 3f out, btn over 2f out: 1   57
reapp: juv promise, 4th at Chepstow (1m mdn auct) & 3rd at Redcar (9f mdn, rtd 82): acts on gd &
fast/firm grnd: poss stay 12f, may be suited by 10f: with J Hills, much btr than this.

-- **DESERT MUSIC** [4] 4-9-7 M Tebbutt 33/1: 7: Slow start, al rear, t.o.: J Weymes half sister   27   12
to a couple of wnrs over 1m/12f: no immediate promise here.

1144 **DUNKELD CHAMP** 14 [3] 3-8-9 Dale Gibson 100/1: 00-008: Prom until 5f out, t.o.: no form yet.   11   15
8 ran   Time 2m 36.00 (4.2)   (Jaber Abdullah)   M Johnston Middleham, N Yorks

---

1363   9.05 CMPE GLASGOW HCAP 4YO+ 0-75 (E)   1m5f   Good/Firm 34 -07 Slow   [65]
     £3217   £990   £495   £247

552 **SWAGGER** 90 [5] A Dickman 4-9-7 (58) G Duffield 5/1: -11141: 4 ch g Generous - Widows Walk (Habitat)   61
Al up there, prog to lead over 2f out, styd on, rdn out: 3 mth abs: completed a fibresand hat-trick at Southwell
back in Jan (2 amat h'cap & a h'cap with Sir M Prescott, 63a): '99 wnr again at Southwell (amat h'cap): eff at
11/12f, stays 2m1f: acts on fast/firm, f'sand, any trk: eff up with the pace or forcing it, goes well fresh.

1194 **HAPPY DAYS** 12 [7] D Moffatt 5-7-12 (35) J Bramhill 7/1: -00042: 5 b g Primitive Rising - Miami   1¼   35
Dolphin (Derrylin) Rdn to improve 3f out, chsd wnr appr fnl 1f: another gd eff: see 1194 (C/D).

791 **ARTHURS KINGDOM** 50 [8] A P Jarvis 4-9-8 (59)(vis) N Callan 6/1: 006-03: 4 b g Roi Danzig - Merrie   ½   58
Moment (Taufan) Waited with, rdn to imprv 3f out, kept on for press fnl 1f: 5L clr rem: plcd last term (f'sand
mdn auct, 63a) & h'cap (rtd 66): eff at 10/11f, stays 13f: acts on gd & fast grnd & f'sand: wears a visor.

1194 **MR FORTYWINKS** 12 [9] J L Eyre 6-9-10 (61) F Lynch 3/1 FAV: 00-204: Led until hdd over 2f out,   5   53
rdn/btn: twice below 845.

1254 **LAWNETT** 7 [1] 4-9-2 (53) M Tebbutt 25/1: 056005: Some late hdwy, no dngr: stays 13f? see 437.   5   38

453

HAMILTON FRIDAY MAY 19TH Righthand, Undulating Track, Stiff Uphill Finish

1194 **OCEAN DRIVE 12** [3] 4-8-8 (45) Dale Gibson 9/1: 30-056: In tch, rdn/held 4f out: btr 1194 (C/D). ½ 29
845 **SPREE VISION 41** [4] 4-9-4 (55) R Winston 16/1: 00-007: Trkd ldr, ev ch over 2f out, rdn/wknd: nk 38
plcd in a Kelso mdn hdle recently: best in '99 when 6L rnr-up in a Doncaster h'cap (rtd 82, with S C Williams,
now P Monteith): 2yo scorer at Newcastle (mdn auct): stays 12f, acts on fast or hvy & on a gall trk.
*1128 **EVEZIO RUFO 15** [10] 8-8-8 (45)(vis) C Cogan (5) 7/2: 511518: No ch fnl 6f: best on sharp trks. 2 25
940 **CRESSET 32** [2] 4-9-5 (56)(bl) A Culhane 12/1: 212209: Bhd halfway, t.o.: see 868 (AW). 19 16
9 ran   Time 2m 50.8 (5.3)   (Mike Smallman)   A Dickman Burnhope, Co Durham

NOTTINGHAM FRIDAY MAY 19TH Lefthand, Galloping Track

Official Going   GOOD TO SOFT.   Stalls: 5f/6f - Stands Side; Rem - Inside.

1364
1.50 COME RACING HCAP DIV 1 3YO+ 0-70 (E)   1m2f   Good/Soft 63 -14 Slow   [68]
£3080   £880   £440   3 yo rec 14lb

1296 **A DAY ON THE DUB 4** [12] D Eddy 7-8-7 (47) J Fanning 8/1: -64401: 7 b g Presidium - Border Mouse 51
(Border Chief) Rear, hdwy to trk ldrs going well after halfway, led bef dist, edged left, held on well: '99
wnr at Southwell (auct mdn, rtd 44a), Newcastle (claim h'cap) & Redcar (clmr, rtd 56): stays 2m on gd/soft
over hdles (rtd 74h): eff at 1m/12f on fast, soft grnd & fibresand, any trk.
290 **DIVORCE ACTION 132** [11] P R Hedger 4-9-6 (60) D Sweeney 16/1: 150-02: 4 b g Common Grounds - hd 63
Overdue Reaction (Be My Guest) Mid-div, pulled hard, prog to trk ldrs appr fnl 1f, kept on, wnr wld not be denied:
jumps fit, in Mar won at Newbury (2m juv nov h'cap, fast grnd, rtd 95h): '99 Kempton wnr (clmr, rtd 68, P Cole):
eff at 9f/10f on firm & gd/soft grnd: runs well fresh & shld gd one better soon.
605 **SYLVA LEGEND 81** [7] C E Brittain 4-10-0 (68)(t) N Esler (7) 16/1: 4-5603: 4 b g Lear Fan - Likeashot 2 68
(Gun Shot) Front rank, led 2½f out till bef fnl 1f, onepace for press: 12 wks abs, top-weight: ran to best: mdn.
1217 **LORD EUROLINK 10** [3] C A Dwyer 6-9-13 (67) T G McLaughlin 13/2: 104464: Early ldr & again appr fnl 1¾ 65
3f till bef 2f out, no extra 1f out: visor omitted, probably better at 1m: see 718.
4057} **CITY GAMBLER 240** [8] 6-8-10 (50) J P Spencer 9/1: 0540-5: Held up, late hdwy, nvr a factor: reapp, nk 47
op 7/1: plcd in '99 (h'cap, rtd 61): '98 wnr at Leicester (h'cap, rtd 68 at best): eff over a stiff/gall
10/12f on fast & gd/soft, poss soft: slipped down the weights & sharper next time: likes Leicester.
850 **WAVERLEY ROAD 39** [2] 3-8-11 (65) R Hughes 14/1: 4-506: Held up, not much room appr fnl 2f, 3½ 57
nvr nr to chall: 6 wks abs, h'cap bow: see 704.
-- **TOMASZEWSKI** [16] 5-9-8 (62) R Havlin 14/1: 650/7: Nvr better than mid-div: 2 yr abs: op 10/1: 1 52
unplcd in 3 '98 starts (mdns, rtd 70): well bred, with P Harris.
1050 **HINDI 20** [1] 4-9-11 (65)(BL) O Urbina 10/1: 6-0208: Handy till fdd ent fnl 2f: too free in blinkers? 3½ 50
1254 **FUTURE COUP 7** [15] 4-9-5 (59) J Weaver 16/1: 51D-09: Nvr troubled ldrs: qck reapp, see 1254. 8 36
3745} **COY DEBUTANTE 259** [17] 6-8-9 (49) L Newton 9/1: 0053-0: Dwelt, at towards rear: 10th, reapp: plcd 6 18
fnl '99 start (amat h'cap, rtd 49): bmpr plcd for M Pipe prev term (2m1f, fast): stays 10f on fast grnd.
1201 **BAHRAIN 11** [10] 4-9-10 (64)(t) M Henry 4/1 FAV: 50-400: Held up, drvn 4f out, btn 2f out, eased: 11th. 2 30
1100 **NAFITH 17** [6] 4-8-12 (52) J Mongan (5) 10/1: 213060: Led bef halfway till over 3f out, wknd: 12th. nk 18
2752} **DANIEL DERONDA 307** [9] 6-9-4 (58) P McCabe 8/1: 5621-0: Struggling after halfway: last, reapp, op 8/1: 0
landed fnl '99 start here at Nottingham (h'cap, rtd 59, J Cullinan): rtd 71 in '98 for P Harris: eff at 10/11.5f
on firm & soft grnd, likes gall trks: with P Burgoyne.
699 **Rainbow Raver 57** [5] 4-8-5 (44)(1ow) R Lappin 33/1: 1050 **Burning 20** [14] 8-8-6 (46) L Newman (5) 33/1:
1003 **Cabaret Quest 25** [4] 4-9-1 (51) Claire Bryan 25/1: -- **Meridiana** [13] 4-9-9 (63) P Fitzimons (5) 14/1:
17 ran   Time 2m 10.0 (7.7)   (Revblayd)   D Eddy Ingoe, Northumberland.

1365
2.20 WELCOME SELL HCAP 3YO 0-60 (G)   1m54y rnd   Good/Soft 63 -54 Slow   [67]
£1976   £564   £282

1024 **SEDONA 25** [9] Andrew Turnell 3-8-8 (47) P Fitzsimons (5) 14/1: -5U301: 3 b g Namaqualand - Talahari 55
(Roi Danzig) Dwelt, imprvd 4f out, led appr fnl 2f, readily: bght in for 11,800 gns, slow time: earlier plcd on AW
(rtd 48a): unplcd both '99 starts: eff at 6f, imprvd at 1m on gd/soft grnd, handles fibresand: apprec drop in grade.
1141 **PERFECT MOMENT 15** [2] G M McCourt 3-8-13 (52) R Brisland (5) 7/1: 00-042: 3 b f Mujadil - Flashing 4 52
Raven (Maelstrom Lake) Nvr far away, eff 2f out, kept on but outpcd by wnr: stays 1m on fast & gd/soft grnd.
806 **TIMELESS CHICK 49** [17] Andrew Reid 3-8-9 (48)(bl) M Henry 10/1: 0-0043: 3 ch f Timeless Times - ½ 47
Be My Bird (Be My Chief) Prom, under press appr fnl 2f, kept on onepace: blnks reapplied: handles gd & gd/soft.
1274 **MOUNTRATH ROCK 6** [13] N Tinkler 3-9-0 (53)(vis) J Weaver 12/1: 0-0004: Rear, short of room bef nk 51
fnl 1f, styd on: visor: led fnl '99 rnr-up (sell, rtd 62): eff at 6f, worth another try at 1m: acts on firm & gd/soft.
1191 **WONDERLAND 12** [3] 3-8-9 (48)(VIS) J P Spencer 6/1 FAV: 56-005: Chsd ldrs, unable to qckn for ¾ 45
press fnl 2f: more expected in first time visor over longer trip: stays 1m?: see 1191.
1274 **DR DUKE 6** [7] 3-8-12 (51)(bl) Dean McKeown 8/1: 064006: Sn led, hdd halfway, hmpd 3f out, onepce. 2½ 43
4018} **BEE GEE 242** [16] 3-8-5 (44) D Sweeney 33/1: 0000-7: Held up, brief eff appr fnl 2f: reapp, no form. nk 35
799 **FOSTON FOX 50** [11] 3-8-8 (47) K Hodgson 33/1: 64-058: In tch, chsd ldrs 4f out till 2f out: 7wk abs. ½ 37
1053 **DOVES DOMINION 20** [15] 3-9-2 (55) Craig Williams 8/1: 00-509: Nvr better than mid-div: tchd 11/1. ½ 44
1234 **ALABAMA WURLEY 8** [18] 3-9-7 (60)(VIS) D McGaffin (7) 16/1: 3-0000: Nvr nr to chall: 10th, top-weight. 1½ 46
1081 **K ACE THE JOINT 17** [4] 3-9-0 (53) L Newton 9/1: 0-0630: Slowly away, nvr on terms: 11th, see 1081 (6f).3½ 33
1234 **CROESO ADREF 8** [1] 3-8-5 (44) L Newman (5) 12/1: 643400: Nvr in it: 15th, blnks omitted, see 257. 0
4570} **Wee Barney 200** [12] 3-8-4 (43) J Stack 25/1:   3928} **Dolfinesse 247** [6] 3-9-5 (58) Martin Dwyer 20/1:
1202 **Timeless Quest 11** [10] 3-8-11 (50) J Fanning 16/1: 688 **Lady Cyrano 63** [8] 3-8-12 (51) R Fitzpatrick (3) 14/1:
1234 **Seasame Park 8** [5] 3-8-7 (46) D Harrison 20/1:   1175 **College Gallery 12** [14] 3-8-6 (45) G Hind 33/1:
18 ran   Time 1m 49.1 (9.7)   (Mrs Claire Hollowood)   Andrew Turnell Sandhutton, N.Yorks.

1366
2.50 CLASSIFIED STKS 3YO 0-85 (C)   1m54y rnd   Good/Soft 63 -33 Slow
£6730   £2071   £1035   £517

1055 **TUMBLEWEED TOR 20** [1] B J Meehan 3-9-2 D R McCabe 3/1 FAV: 43-031: 3 b g Rudimentary - Hilly 90
(Town Crier) Made ev yd, drew clr fnl 2f: first win: highly tried first 2 in '99 (stks, rtd 89): eff at 1m on gd/soft
& hvy grnd, prob handles fast: much improved & useful here with forcing tactics.
1055 **DARE HUNTER 20** [7] B W Hills 3-9-2 J P Spencer 7/1: 156-02: 3 ch g Gulch - Dabaweyaa (Shareef 5 83
Dancer) Waited with, eff appr fnl 2f, styd on but wnr had flown: stays 1m on firm & gd/soft: see 1055.

4140} **RED LETTER 234** [6] R Hannon 3-8-13 R Hughes 12/1: 0040-3: 3 b f Sri Pekan - Never Explain (Fairy ¾ 78
King) Waited with, late prog, nvr nr to chall: reapp, op 8/1: '99 debut wnr at Ascot (nov fill stks, rtd 87):
eff at 6f, worth another try over further: acts on fast & prob gd/soft grnd, stiff/gall trks.

*921 **RISK FREE 34** [2] N P Littmoden 3-9-4 T G McLaughlin 6/1: 2-4214: Prom, rdn 3f out: fdd bef dist. ½ 82

1183 **KIND REGARDS 12** [4] 3-8-13 J Fanning 4/1: 214-05: Mid-div, short of room ent fnl 3f, nvr dngrs: 1¾ 74
'99 Beverley wnr (fill mdn, rtd 88): eff at 7f/1m on firm & gd/soft grnd: stable not firing at present.

*1135 **NOBLENOR 15** [3] 3-9-4 G Sparkes (7) 8/1: -016: Bhd ldrs, outpcd 3f out: btr 1135 (7f auct mdn). 4 71

810 **MAKASSEB 48** [5] 3-9-2 Craig Williams 10/1: 225-07: Chsd ldrs till wknd appr fnl 2f: op 8/1, 7 wk abs: hd 69
dual '99 rnr-up (mdn, rtd 89): eff at 1m on gd & gd/soft grnd: with M Channon.

4524} **KING SPINNER 205** [8] 3-9-2 D Harrison 7/1: 3451-8: Al bhd: reapp, tchd 9/1: '99 Yarmouth wnr (mdn, 7 57
rtd 89): eff forcing the pace at 1m on gd & soft grnd, stiff/gall track: with A Jarvis.

8 ran   Time 1m 47.4 (8)   (The Sixth Tumbleweed Partnership)   B J Meehan Upper Lambourn, Berks.

1367   3.20 EBF COLWICK NOV STKS 2YO (D)   6f   Good/Soft 63   -40 Slow
£3380   £1040   £520   £260

*1048 **BRAM STOKER 20** [5] R Hannon 2-9-0 R Hughes 8/13 FAV: 211: 2 ch c General Monash - Tanoikey 97
(Grundy) Cl-up, led ent fnl 2f, pushed clr, readily: well bckd, slow time: recent Doncaster wnr (auct mdn):
half-brother to a 1m/12f wnr, dam a miler: eff at 5f, apprec step up to 6f: acts on gd/soft grnd, gall trks:
suited being up with/forcing the pace: useful, improving colt, deserves to take his chance at Royal Ascot.

*1102 **ATMOSPHERIC 16** [1] P F I Cole 2-9-5 D Sweeney 2/1: 12: 2 ch c Irish River - Magic Feeling (Magical 2½ 92
Wonder) Prom, chall 2f out, not pace of cmftble wnr: well bckd: imprvd in defeat giving 5lbs to wnr over lngr 6f trip.

1166 **CARRABAN 13** [3] B J Meehan 2-8-7 D R McCabe 11/1: -5W3: 2 b f Mujadil - Bayazida (Bustino) 3 69
Led till hung left & hdd ent fnl 2f, no extra: op 7/1: stiffish task up in trip & a far from straightforward ride.

-- **ILLUSIONIST** [4] E A L Dunlop 2-8-12 J P Spencer 8/1: 4: Keen, chsd ldrs till wknd qckly 2f out: 7 58
op 6/1: 50,000gns Mujtahid Feb first foal, dam well related: sire a sprinter: will find easier tasks.

-- **BLUSHING SPUR** [2] 2-8-12 J Fanning 40/1: 5: In tch till halfway: highly tried on debut: 11 38
10,000gns Flying Spur Apr foal, dam unrcd, sire an Australian miler: with D Shaw.

5 ran   Time 1m 17.0 (6.2)   (Alessandro Gaucci)   R Hannon East Everleigh, Wilts.

1368   3.50 FINN CLASS STKS 3YO+ 0-65 (E)   6f   Good/Soft 63   +01 Fast
£3164   £904   £452   3 yo rec 9 lb

1278 **BEYOND CALCULATION 6** [9] J M Bradley 6-9-4 J P Spencer 4/1: 000-51: 6 ch g Geiger Counter - Placer 66
Queen (Habitat) Made ev yd, shkn up, held on well: fair time, qck reapp: '99 wnr at Windsor, Bath, Thirsk
& Brighton (h'caps, rtd 70 at best): eff at 5f, suited by 6f, stays 7f: acts on firm, gd/soft, handles
fibresand, any trk: best up with/forcing the pace: tough & in good form.

896 **JAMES DEE 36** [11] A P Jarvis 4-9-4 D Harrison 5/2 FAV: 022262: 4 b g Shalford - Glendale Joy ¾ 63
(Glenstal) Prom, prsd wnr appr fnl 1f, styd on but al being held: prob ran to best back in trip: see 462 (7f).

1196 **BANDBOX 11** [4] M Salaman 5-9-4 (bl) J Weaver 13/2: 120003: 5 ch g Imperial Frontier - Dublah ½ 61
(Private Account) Waited with, short of room over 2f out & 1f out, kept on, nvr nrr: shld rate higher, see 598.

1278 **MARENGO 6** [6] M J Polglase 6-9-7 R Fitzpatrick (3) 10/1: 321504: Chsd ldrs, eff 2f out, unable ¾ 62$
to chall: qck reapp, stiff task on official ratings ratings tho' tchd 14/1: see 1073 (clmr).

1196 **DOUBLE MARCH 11** [7] 7-9-4 Martin Dwyer 12/1: 040-05: Held up, switched ent fnl 2f, late hdwy. 1¼ 56

1092 **SUPERBIT 17** [5] 8-9-4 J Fanning 4/1: 031-06: Front rank & ev ch till fdd bef fnl 1f: stiffish task: ½ 55
landed fnl '99 start here at Nottingham (class stks, rtd 61 & 51a): (98 Ripon wnr (sell h'cap, rtd 59 at best):
eff at 5/6f on firm & fibresand, suited by gd or softer: likes Nottingham: best up with the pace, without blnks/visor.

1256 **TICK TOCK 7** [3] 3-8-6 L Newton 14/1: 020-07: Chsd ldrs, no extra appr fnl 1f: qck reapp, lngr trip. 3½ 44

1273 **ALFAHAAL 7** [8] 7-9-4 O Urbina 16/1: 040-08: Nvr a factor: v stiff task, qck reapp, suited by further. shd 47$

4404} **MARON 214** [1] 3-8-9 R Hughes 14/1: 3000-9: Chsd ldrs till after halfway: reapp: '99 Hamilton 10 27
wnr (auct stks, rtd 73): eff at 5f: acts on fast & gd grnd, poss handles soft.

1063 **CAROLES DOVE 18** [10] 4-9-1 D McGaffin (7) 66/1: 0-000: Al towards rear: 10th: highly tried. nk --

976 **Bond Diamond 30** [12] 3-8-9 J Stack 20/1:   4384} **Fairy Prince 216** [2] 7-9-4 D Sweeney 20/1:

12 ran   Time 1m 14.5 (3.7)   (E A Hayward)   J M Bradley Sedbury, Gloucs.

1369   4.20 CUP FINAL MDN 3YO+ (D)   1m6f   Good/Soft 63   +02 Fast
£3289   £1012   £506   £253   3 yo rec 20lb

1179 **MBELE 12** [14] W R Muir 3-8-6 Martin Dwyer 1/2 FAV: 2-321: 3 b c Mtoto - Majestic Image (Niniski) 89
Well plcd, hmpd 2f, led 2f out, rdn & hung left appr fnl 1f, narrowly: well bckd, best time of day: overdue win, rnr-up
sole '99 start (mdn, rtd 89): eff at 12f, suited by step up to 14f: acts on firm & soft grnd, sharp or gall trks: useful.

1068} **SILVER ROBIN 385** [1] N J Henderson 4-9-12 R Hughes 9/2: -2/3-2: 4 b g Silver Hawk - Wedge Musical nk 88
(What A Guest) Held up, gd prog to chall ent fnl 2f, just held: op 3/1 on reapp: plcd at Newmarket sole '99
start (List, rtd 103, L Cumani): rnr-up sole juv start (mdn, rtd 87): full brother to useful stayer Silver Wedge:
eff at 10/14f on firm & gd/soft grnd: cost new connections 14,000gns & has been gelded: must win a maiden.

1179 **JARDINES LOOKOUT 12** [9] A P Jarvis 3-8-6 D Sweeney 16/1: 53: 3 b g Fourstars Allstar - Foolish hd 87
Flight (Fool's Holme) Rear, imprvd ent str, styd on well towards fin: clr rem, again ran in snatches tho' suited
by step up to 14f on gd/soft grnd: shown enough to find a mdn: also bhd this wnr in 1179.

-- **SON OF A GUN** [6] J Neville 6-9-12 J Weaver 16/1: 4: Prom, led 3½f out tilll 2f out, held/hmpd bef 3 84
dist: op 10/1, Flat bow, 15 wk jmps abs: 99/00 M Rasen bmpr wnr (13.5f, stays 2m, firm & fast): stays 14f on gd/sft.

1127 **MUWAKALL 15** [12] 3-8-6 G Hall 10/1: -35345: Mid-div, chsd ldrs 3f out, no extra bef fnl 1f: flattered. 2½ 81$

1157 **FOLLOW LAMMTARRA 13** [2] 3-8-6 Craig Williams 12/1: 36: Chsd ldrs till fdd appr fnl 1f: see 1157. 6 76

1091 **SECRET DROP 17** [3] 4-9-7 O Urbina 16/1: 360-07: Made most fll appr fnl 3f, sn btn: op 12/1. 5 66$

848 **WELDUNFRANK 41** [13] 7-9-12 T G McLaughlin 50/1: 08: Nvr a factor: see 848. 11 61

850 **SHARVIE 39** [5] 3-8-6 R Lake (7) 50/1: 0-09: Al towards rear: 6 wk abs, no worthwhile form. 20 46

-- **REGAL HOLLY** [4] 5-9-7 (bl) J Fanning 16/1: 0: Prom, led bef halfway till 5f out, sn lost pl: ½ 40
10th on Flat bow, 15 wk jumps absence: landed 2 Worcester bmprs in 99/00, later plcd over hdles (rtd 104h, stays
2½m, firm & soft, with/without blnks): shld do better: with B McMahon.

567 **True Romance 87** [15] 4-9-12 (BL) Dean McKeown 50/1: -- Running Water [10] 7-9-12 I Mongan (5) 20/1:
1002 **Espere Dor 25** [7] 3-8-6 Sophie Mitchell 50/1:   826 **Quigleys Point 44** [8] 4-9-12 L Newton 66/1:

14 ran   Time 3m 06.9 (8.6)   (Mr & Mrs John Wilson)   W R Muir Lambourn, Berks.

1370   4.50 COME RACING HCAP DIV 2 3YO+ 0-70 (E)   1m2f   Good/Soft 63   -04 Slow   [68]
£3066   £876   £438   3 yo rec 14lb

889   **ZAHA 37** [13] J Pearce 5-8-12 (52) Dean McKeown 14/1: 0-6001: 5 b h Lahib - Mayaasa (Lyphard)   **63**
Cl-up, led appr fnl 2f, readily: '99 wnr at Southwell (auct mdn, rtd 66a) & Yarmouth (class stks, rtd 60): rtd 58 in
'98 for R Armstrong: eff at 10/11f: acts on gd, hvy, both AWs, prob handles firm: prob best without blnks/visor.

1065   **ANNADAWI 18** [7] C N Kellett 5-8-4 (44) C Rutter 11/2: 463222: 5 b g Sadler's Wells - Prayers'n   5   **47**
Promises (Foolish Pleasure) Held up, styd on fnl 2f, nvr nr wnr: op 7/1: remains a mdn, try 12f?: see 1065, 1003.

1033   **STROMSHOLM 23** [17] J R Fanshawe 4-9-12 (66) D Harrison 14/1: 2-4063: 4 ch g Indian Ridge -   ¾   **68**
Upward Trend (Salmon Leap) Waited with, imprvd appr fnl 3f: under press bef dist, not pace to chall: prob
styd this longer 10f trip: acts on gd & gd/soft grnd: see 685.

1201   **YOUNG UN 11** [6] 5-9-9 (63) P McCabe 9/2 FAV: 1-0604D: Rear, prog appr fnl 3f, switched appr fnl   ½   **63**
1f, sn onepace: fin 4th, disqual & placed last, jockey given a 5 day ban: see 786.

3815}   **RICCARTON 255** [12] J M Bradley 7-8-10 (50) J P Spencer 14/1: 000-4: Held up, prog ent fnl 3f,   ½   **51+**
switched & hmpd bef dist, styd on, nrst fin: fin 5th, plcd 4th, reapp: 99/00 hdles wnr at Taunton (mdn, 2m3f,
firm/fast grnd, rtd 93h): plcd reapp in '99 (h'cap, rtd 58): '98 wnr at Redcar, Hamilton & Doncaster (h'caps,
rtd 63, P Calver): eff at 9/11f on any grnd, any trk: can go well fresh: very interesting off this mark.

1007   **KHUCHN 25** [18] 4-9-0 (54) J P Spencer 25/1: -00505: Led till 2½f out, onepace: fin 6th, plcd 5th.   nk   **53**

793   **ACEBO LYONS 50** [5] 5-9-5 (59) R Hughes 12/1: 00-166: Held up, chsd ldrs 3f out, fdd ent fnl   2   **55**
2f: fin 7th, plcd 6th, 4 wk abs: new stable, gone to A Jarvis: see 705 (fast grnd).

*1065   **DIABLO DANCER 18** [8] 4-9-10 (64)(vis) G Hind 5/1: 0-0517: Prom, eff appr fnl 2f, btn & hmpd   ¾   **59**
bef fnl 1f: tchd 6/1: btr 1065 (first time visor, soft grnd).

1190   **GABLESEA 12** [9] 6-9-1 (55) T G McLaughlin 8/1: 461028: Held up, prog 3f out, wknd 2f out: see 890.   ½   **49**

965   **DR MARTENS 31** [10] 6-8-8 (48) L Newton 33/1: 006-09: Held up, eff 3f out, nvr dngrs: see 965.   2½   **39**

576   **MUTADARRA 85** [15] 7-9-11 (65) R Studholme (5) 16/1: -40000: Al bhd: 10th: recent jumps rnr, in   ¾   **55**
March won a Huntingdon mdn hdle (2m, firm, rtd 101h): see 292.

1065   **PIPS BRAVE 18** [14] 4-8-7 (47)(bl) R Lappin 15/2: 360240: Chsd ldrs till 3f out: 11th, see 1065, 890.   2½   **34**

1201   **Coughlans Gift 11** [3] 4-9-7 (61) P Dobbs (5) 20/1:   3807} **Double Destiny 255** [16] 4-9-6 (60) Martin Dwyer 25/1:

565   **Melvella 87** [2] 4-8-5 (45) L Newman (5) 33/1:   1037 **Cool Vibes 21** [14] 5-10-0 (68) R Fitzpatrick (3) 25/1:

1066   **Kustom Kit Kevin 18** [11] 4-8-7 (47) J Fanning 16/1:

17 ran   Time 2m 09.0 (6.7)   (Exclusive Three Partnership)   J Pearce Newmarket.

Official Going   GOOD/FIRM. Stalls: Str - Stands Side, Rnd - Inside.

1371   2.10 WOODCOTE COND STKS 3YO (B)   6f   Good 57   +09 Fast
£9198   £3489   £1744   £793

4482}   **JARN 209** [6] B Hanbury 3-9-0 (t) R Hills 11/2: 10-1: 3 b c Green Desert - Alkariyh (Alydar)   **106**
Held up, hdwy for press to lead appr fnl 1f, styd on well, drvn out on temp: won first of 2 juv starts, here at
Newbury (mdn, rtd 103), subs disapp on soft: v eff at 6f, shld stay 7f: acts on firm & gd & runs well fresh here
at Newbury: smart colt, wears a t-strap & open to further improvement.

1171   **WINNING VENTURE 13** [7] S P C Woods 3-9-2 L Dettori 4/1: 2D-302: 3 b c Owington - Push A Button   nk   **107+**
(Bold Lad) Waited with, hdwy & no room over 1f out till ins last, styd on strongly, too late, unlucky: fine
run back in trip with no luck in running: win a List/Gr 3 over 7f soon: see 950.

1172   **THE TATLING 13** [3] M L W Bell 3-9-0 M Fenton 7/1: 262-03: 3 b c Perugino - Aunty Eileen (Ahonoora)   1   **102**
Cl-up, hdwy to chall over 1f out, kept on same pace ins last: fine run: useful, see 4286.

4605}   **HOPEFUL LIGHT 196** [10] J H M Gosden 3-9-0 J Fortune 5/2 FAV: 1-4: Slow away, held up, short   1   **101+**
of room well over 1f out, switched left & styd on well fnl 1f, nrst fin: reapp: won sole juv start, at Doncaster
(back-end mdn, rtd 92): eff at 6/7f, 1m shld suit: has run well fresh on gd & hvy grnd: v useful, win soon.

4201}   **FLOWINGTON 230** [2] 3-8-6 T Quinn 20/1: 1300-5: Handy, ev ch 2f out, onepace: reapp: juv scorer   nk   **90**
at W'hampton (seller, rtd 65a) & Warwick (nov auct), subs 4L 3rd in a Gr 2 (rtd 97): eff over 5/6f on firm,
gd & fibresand: handles any trk.

3720}   **SEE YOU LATER 260** [4] 3-8-9 K Fallon 9/2: -133-6: Chsd ldr till went on 2f out, hdd appr fnl   nk   **92**
1f, no extra: reapp: won first of 3 juv starts, at Sandown (fill mdn), subs plcd in List (rtd 92): eff at
5f, just stays 6f: acts on gd/firm & gd & on a stiff trk: better off in h'caps at 5f?

969   **HUNTING LION 30** [9] 3-9-0 J Reid 9/1: 123-07: In tch, rdn 2f out, some late gains: see 969.   1   **94**

1028   **RUSSIAN FOX 23** [5] 3-9-0 Dane O'Neill 25/1: 201-08: Led till 2f out, no extra: see 1028 (h'cap).   4   **82**

4306}   **TOLERATION 221** [8] 3-8-9 N Pollard 20/1: 41-9: In tch, wknd 2f out: reapp: won 2nd of only   hd   **76**
2 juv starts at Windsor (mdn, rtd 85): eff at 6f, has the pace for 5f: acts on gd & gd/soft: find easier races.

9 ran   Time 1m 14.49 (2.89)   (Hamdan Al Maktoum)   B Hanbury Newmarket.

1372   2.40 HIGHCLERE FILLIES COND STKS 2YO (C)   5f34y   Good 57   -01 Slow
£5597   £2123   £1061   £482

*1267   **ELSIE PLUNKETT 7** [3] R Hannon 2-8-8 Dane O'Neill 4/6 FAV: -5111: 2 b f Mind Games - Snow   **92**
Eagle (Polar Falcon) Made all, qcknd appr fnl 1f, pushed out: hvly bckd: earlier scored at Sandown (fill auct
mdn) & Nottingham (auct fill): eff at 5.2f, 6f suit: acts on firm & hvy: useful & improving, Queen Mary type.

--   **FAIR PRINCESS** [6] B W Hills 2-8-5 M Hills 7/1: 2: 2 b f Efisio - Fair Attempt (Try My Best)   2   **82**
In tch, eff over 1f out, kept on to chase wnr ins last, not her pace: Mar foal, cost 12,500gns: half-sister
to a 5f juv wnr: plenty to like about this & must be winning shortly: improve.

*762   **MILLENNIUM MAGIC 52** [2] J G Portman 2-8-8 A Beech (5) 4/1: 13: 2 b f Magic Ring - Country Spirit   2   **82**
(Sayf El Arab) Cl-up, ev ch over 1f out, sn btn: 7 wk abs, prob ran to form of 762.

--   **SPIRIT OF SONG** [7] M R Channon 2-8-5 T Quinn 12/1: 4: Bhd, kept on late, nvr dngrs under   nk   **75**
hands-and-heels: Apr foal: Mar foal, cost 34,000gns: dam 7f juv scorer: sure to relish 6f next time & come on.

1107   **ANIMAL CRACKER 16** [4] 2-8-8 S Drowne 33/1: 05: In tch, rdn & outpcd over 1f out, late gains.   nk   **78**

*886   **SERVICEABLE 37** [1] J Tate 12/1: 316: Handy, btn well over 1f out: stiff task: see 886 (hvy).   nk   **80**

--   **DANZA MONTANA** [5] 2-8-5 Pat Eddery 12/1: 7: Keen bhd, rdn & btn 2f out on debut: Feb   shd   **74**

NEWBURY   FRIDAY MAY 19TH   Lefthand, Flat, Galloping Track

foal, cost 52,000gns: dam wnr in France: bred to relish 6f+: with J Osborne.
7 ran   Time 1m 03.31 (3.01)   (C J M Partnership)   R Hannon East Everleigh, Wilts.

1373   3.10 TOTE HCAP 3YO+ 0-90 (C)   1m4f   Good 57 -14 Slow   [86]
£7748   £2384   £1192   £596   3 yo rec 17lb

991 **CARLYS QUEST** 27 [6] J Neville 6-9-10 (82)(tvi) K Fallon 8/1: 302-31: 6 ch g Primo Dominie - Tuppy   89
(Sharpen Up) Waited with, gd hdwy 2f out, strong run to lead ins last, qcknd clr, readily: failed to win in '99,
plcd sev times (rtd 84 at best): '98 scorer at Newmarket & Warwick (h'caps): eff over 10/12f on firm, hvy & on
any trk: wears blnks/visor & a t-strap: best held up for a late run: v consistent & in top form.
845 **MORGANS ORCHARD** 41 [14] A G Newcombe 4-8-1 (59) N Pollard 20/1: 521552: 4 ch g Forest Wind -   3 60
Regina St Cyr (Doulab) Prom, styd on to lead 2f out, rdn & hdd ins last, not pace of wnr: abs, lightly rcd.
1070 **INTENSITY** 18 [3] M H Tompkins 4-9-6 (78) S Sanders 6/1: 001-53: 4 b g Bigstone - Brillante (Green   nk 79
Dancer) In tch, eff & switched left 2f out, kept on same pace over 1f out: stays 12f, win a h'cap: see 1070.
572 **MONO LADY** 86 [4] D Haydn Jones 7-8-10 (68)(bl) M Fenton 33/1: 0-0204: In tch, eff 2f out, kept   hd 69
on for press ins last, no dngr: 3 month abs & the sort to win another h'cap (7 wins from 48 starts): see 469.
997 **FINAL SETTLEMENT** 27 [13] H S-B-F (65) Pat Eddery 8/1: 33-165: Waited with, eff appr 2f out, short   1 64
of room over 1f out, onepace: gd run back at 12f, just best at 14f?: see 997, 726.
1076 **CONSPICUOUS** 18 [2] M H Tompkins 4-9-10 (82) S Carson (5) 16/1: 011-06: Waited with, eff to chall well over   1 80
1f out, sn onepace: clr of rem: interesting in an amat h'cap with Mr L Jefford: see 1076.
1170 **PUNISHMENT** 13 [5] J Reid 33/1: 235507: Chsd ldrs, rdn & btn well over 1f out.   4 71
1251 **BATSWING** 8 [9] 5-8-5 (63) F Norton 100/30 FAV: 6-0028: Slow away, sn chsd ldr & ev ch over   shd 55
3f out till over 1f out, wknd: well bckd & better expected after 1251.
*1076 **BLUE STYLE** 18 [1] 4-8-8 (66)(t) R Mullen 4/1: -61219: Bhd, rdn 2f out, sn btn: wants soft?   ½ 57
*791 **PUZZLEMENT** 50 [10] 6-9-3 (75) P Robinson 11/1: 333310: Keen bhd, eff to chall 2f out, sn wknd: 10th. 2½ 62
968 **ALS ALIBI** 30 [12] 7-8-4 (62) K Darley 14/1: 61/000: Handy, led over 3f out till 2f out, wknd qckly: ¾ 48
11th: missed '99, prev term won here at Newbury (h'cap, this race) & Bath (h'cap, rtd 75): eff at 12f on firm &
gd/soft: has run well fresh & likes Newbury: on a fair mark on past form.
1031 **CHIEF CASHIER** 23 [11] 5-9-7 (79) S Drowne 20/1: 48-500: Led till over 3f out, wknd: 12th: see 747.   2 61
-- **ALCAYDE** [8] 5-9-2 (74) A Clark 20/1: 1425/0: Al bhd, t.o. in last: something amiss on comeback?:   dist 0
last rcd on the Flat back in '98 for J Dunlop, won at Newcastle (h'cap, rtd 82 at best): suited by 10f &
handles gd/firm, like soft & a gall track.
13 ran   Time 2m 37.83 (8.53)   (Yorkeys Knob Racing)   J Neville Coedkernew, Monmouthshire.

1374   3.40 LISTED FILLIES TRIAL 3YO (A)   1m2f   Good 57 +01 Fast
£15275   £4700   £2350   £1175

1056 **WHITEFOOT** 20 [14] G A Butler 3-8-9 L Dettori 4/1: 013-41: 3 b f Be My Chief - Kelimutu (Top Ville)   102
Held up, hdwy over 2f out, styd on well to lead ins last, rdn to assert: nicely bckd: '99 scorer at Sandown
(fill mdn), rtd 100 at best for J Pearce: eff at 1m, stays 10f & 12f looks sure to suit (dam won at that trip):
acts on gd, prob handles hvy: tough & progressive, shld win a Group race & will reportedly be aimed at the Oaks.
1108 **CIRCLE OF LIGHT** 16 [8] P W D'Arcy 3-8-9 K Darley 16/1: 10-32: 3 b f Anshan - Cockatoo Island   1¼ 100
(High Top) Set strong pace, sn clr, rdn 2f out, hdd ins last, kept on same pace for press: clr of rem & a bold
front running effort stepped up to 10f, 12f looks sure to suit: big, gall sort who can win races over further.
1108 **PREMIER PRIZE** 16 [12] D R C Elsworth 3-8-9 N Pollard 14/1: 61-63: 3 ch f Selkirk - Spot Prize   5 92
(Seattle Dancer) Waited with, hdwy & short of room appr 2f out, kept on same pace for press over 1f out: op
10/1: useful run & stays 10f on gd & soft: debut eff in h'caps: see 1108.
1045 **REQUEST** 21 [3] Sir Michael Stoute 3-8-9 K Fallon 5/2: 24: In tch, eff for press 3f out,   1¾ 89
sn no impress: hvly bckd: acts on gd & hvy & must win a mdn soon: see 1045.
1185 **VELVET LADY** 12 [5] 3-8-9 J Fortune 9/2: 265: In tch, rdn over 3f out, onepace: shld stay   1¼ 87
10f & will gain some confidence with a mdn win: see 1185, 915.
1108 **PROMISING LADY** 16 [6] 3-8-9 S Drowne 25/1: 1-06: Bhd, some late gains, nvr dngrs: could prove   nk 86
interesting in h'cap company: see 1108.
1108 **THE WOODSTOCK LADY** 16 [10] 3-8-9 R Hills 25/1: 1-07: Bhd, brief effort over 2f out, no impression.   nk 85
*1165 **BROADWAY LEGEND** 13 [13] 3-8-9 M Hills 11/1: 30-18: Chsd ldr, rdn & wknd qckly over 1f out: see 1165. ¾ 84
1045 **BURNING SUNSET** 21 [7] 3-8-9 T Quinn 5/1: -63-39: Bhd, brief eff over 3f out, sn btn: nicely   2½ 80
bckd from 10/1: would enjoy a return to mdn company as in 1045.
*1051 **UNSEEDED** 20 [11] 3-8-9 Pat Eddery 11/2: 04-10: Handy, wknd over 1f out: 10th, nicely bckd.   8 70
1075 **STARLYTE GIRL** 18 [1] 3-8-9 J Reid 50/1: 310-60: Al bhd: 11th: see 1075.   4 64
4487} **CREAM TEASE** 209 [9] 3-8-9 S Whitworth 40/1: 1600-0: Keen, al bhd: 12th: '99 scorer at Salisbury 22 34
(fill mdn, rtd 85): eff at 7f, further shld suit: acts on gd, handles firm: highly tried here.
99 **GIRLS BEST FRIEND** 179 [2] 3-8-9 G Carter 40/1: 1040-0: Al bhd: 13th: juv scorer at Lingfield   14 14
(mdn, rtd 93 at best): eff at 6f/1m on soft grnd, handles fibresand & any track.
1185 **CLARANET** 12 [4] 3-8-9 F Norton 40/1: -33100: In tch, reportedly lost action over 2f out & virtually p.u.   ½ 13
14 ran   Time 2m 08.44 (5.64)   (Gary A Tanaka)   G A Butler Blewbury, Oxon.

1375   4.10 PEMBURY HCAP 3YO+ 0-80 (D)   1m2f   Good 57 -14 Slow   [79]
£4615   £1420   £710   £355   3 yo rec 14lb

1077 **INDIUM** 18 [17] W J Musson 6-9-11 (76) Pat Eddery 10/1: -40401: 6 b g Groom Dancer - Gold Bracelet   81
(Golden Fleece) Held up rear, gd hdwy & short of room 2f out, strong run ins last to get up cl-home, going
away: '99 scorer at Ascot (h'cap, rtd 81): '98 scorer at Newmarket (subs disqual) & Newbury (h'caps, rtd
79 & 38a): prev best at 1m, stays 10f well: acts on firm & hvy & handles any trk, likes a gall one, esp
Newbury: gd weight carrier who loves to come late & at the top of his form.
1070 **ADMIRALS PLACE** 18 [4] H J Collingridge 4-9-2 (67) G Carter 14/1: 223142: 4 ch c Perugino - Royal   ¾ 69
Daughter (High Top) Cl-up, led over 1f out, kept on for press ins last till collared cl-home: in gd form.
1065 **PAS DE PROBLEME** 18 [3] M Blanshard 4-8-11 (62) M Roberts 16/1: 0-0153: 4 ch g Ela Mana Mou - shd 64
Torriglia (Nijinsky) Handy, eff to chall over 1f out, no extra cl-home, btn less than 1L: in gd heart: see 1003.
1076 **GENTLEMAN VENTURE** 18 [14] J Akehurst 4-9-12 (77) T Quinn 13/2: 00-364: Waited with, gd hdwy   hd 78
over 1f out to chall ins last, no extra cl-home, btn around 1L: eff at 10/12f & knocking on the door.
*1002 **CASTLEBRIDGE** 25 [8] 3-8-10 (75)(vis) J Fortune 14/1: 011615: Set pace till over 1f out, onepace.   1¼ 74
4335} **CAPRIOLO** 220 [2] 4-9-6 (71) Dane O'Neill 20/1: 2001-6: In tch, kept on same pace for press   shd 70
ins last: reapp: '99 scorer at Salisbury (mdn h'cap) & Leicester (h'cap, rtd 73): plcd in '98 (rtd 90): stays 12f,

both wins at 10f: acts on firm & gd/soft, in blnks, not a visor: spot on next time back in blnks on a stiff track.
4470} **AMRAK AJEEB 210** [10] 8-9-2 (67) V Slattery 25/1: 4000-7: Slow away, bhd, styd on late, nrst fin on reapp: mostly out of sorts in '99 for M Channon, earlier won in Dubai (h'ap): missed '98, prev term with B Hanbury (rtd 108 at best): eff at 1m/10f & handles firm, likes gd or soft grnd: has run well fresh under big weights: best coming late: encouraging here & is thrown in on best prev form, keep in mind. *nk* **65+**
*1150 **STAR TURN 14** [13] 6-8-11 (62) F Norton 7/2: 010-18: Bhd, eff 2f out, sn short of room, kept on late. *½* **59**
1113 **THE GREEN GREY 16** [1] 6-8-10 (61) M Fenton 33/1: 200-09: Handy, rdn & btn over 1f out: see 1113. *¾* **57**
1150 **SIMPLY NOBLE 14** [18] 4-9-8 (73) T E Durcan 33./1: 630-00: Bhd, wide & effort well over 1f out, kept on ins last: 10th: plcd in '99 (h'caps, rtd 77): '98 wnr at Hamilton (auct mdn, rtd 78): stays 12f on fm & gd/soft. *shd* **69**
1113 **TUMBLEWEED QUARTET 16** [5] 4-9-10 (75)(tbl) J Reid 25/1: 0-5600: Chsd ldrs, ev ch over 2f out, wknd ins last: btr 715 (1m). *shd* **70**
1113 **GIKO 16** [12] 6-8-9 (60) P Doe 33/1: 00-000: In tch, hdwy over 2f out, wknd over 1f out; 12th, not stay? *1¾* **52**
1113 **KENNET 16** [21] 5-9-2 (67) L Dettori 14/1: 0-5600: Chsd ldrs, wknd over 1f out: 13th: see 512. *hd* **58**
1113 **GREAT NEWS 16** [22] 5-9-12 (77) M Hills 25/1: 0-0000: Bhd, modest late gains: 14th: see 1113 (1m). *½* **67**
1033 **SOVEREIGNS COURT 23** [11] 7-9-5 (70) A Clark 14/1: 020/30: Nvr a factor: 15th: see 1033. *1* **58**
4513} **KISS ME KATE 206** [6] 4-9-2 (67) R Hills 7/1: 0001-0: In tch, wknd 2f out: 16th: fit form hdlng, earlier won hdles at Plumpton & Huntingdon (mares mdn, rtd 108h, 2m, gd & gd/soft): in '99 won at Ripon (mdn auct) & Redcar (class stks, rtd 66): eff at 10f on firm & gd/soft, any trk: best with waiting tactics: with S Sherwood. *3½* **50**
1288 **LADY ROCKSTAR 4** [19] 5-9-9 (74) P Robinson 10/1: 5-0200: Bhd, slipped badly & rider lost iron over 4f out, not recover, fin last: ignore this: see 975. **0**
1097 **Umbrian Gold 17** [20] 4-9-12 (77) R Ffrench 14/1: 873 **Hint Of Magic 38** [15] 3-8-13 (78) N Pollard 20/1:
2806} **Taverner Society 304** [9] 5-9-7 (72) S Drowne 25/1: 1144 **Massey 14** [16] 4-9-3 (68) K Fallon 14/1:
4284} **Wadi 223** [7] 5-8-11 (62) S Sanders 33/1:
22 ran Time 2m 09.87 (7.07) (Magnificent Seven) W J Musson Newmarket.

1376

4.40 PLATINUM MDN DIV 1 3YO (D) 1m str Good 57 -07 Slow
£4043 £1244 £622 £311

-- **TAKRIR** [9] J L Dunlop 3-9-0 R Hills 20/1: 1: 3 b c Bahri - Ice House (Northfields) In tch, hdwy over 2f out, led over 1f out, styd on for press, drvn out on debut: cost IR 100,000gns: half-brother to wnrs over 1m/12f: stays 1m, further looks sure to suit: runs well fresh on gd: useful, win in better grade. **85**
2476} **GREY EMINENCE 318** [5] R Hannon 3-9-0 Dane O'Neill 33/1: 5-2: 3 gr c Indian Ridge - Rahaam (Secreto) Waited with, eff 2f out, kept on well ins last, not btn far: reapp: rtd 82 when 5th sole juv start: brother to useful 6/7f wnr Cassandra Go, dam 7f wnr: stays 1m well on gd: plenty to like about this & must win races. *¾* **82+**
1032 **GLORY QUEST 23** [6] Miss Gay Kelleway 3-9-0 J Fortune 9/2: 33-223: 3 b c Quest For Fame - Sonseri (Prince Tenderfoot) Handy, hdwy over 1f out, kept on ins last, btn around 1L: another gd plcd run: see 1032. *nk* **82**
-- **ALMIDDINA** [2] R Charlton 3-8-9 R Perham 25/1: 4: Waited with, eff & short of room well over 1f out, kept on nicely ins last, kind ride: half-sister to a couple of wnrs: stays 1m, further suit: caught the eye. *1¼* **75+**
-- **HOBB ALWAHTAN** [1] 3-9-0 L Dettori 15/8: 5: Cl-up, led over 2f out till over 1f out, no extra: hvly bckd tho' op 5/4 on debut: half-brother to top 1m/10f wnr Dubai Millenium: bred to relish 1m/10f: do better. *shd* **79**
1714} **AURA OF GRACE 352** [10] 3-8-9 R Price 50/1: 0-6: Keen, bhd, brief eff over 1f out, kept on same pace: rtd 57 sole juv start: promise here & shld stay further than 1m: apprec a mdn on a minor track. *¾* **72**
983 **ORIENT EXPRESS 29** [7] 3-9-0 J D Smith 50/1: 07: Keen in tch, onepace over 1f out: see 983. *1¾* **73**
4379} **RUM PUNCH 217** [3] 3-9-0 K Fallon 9/1: 0-8: In tch, rdn & btn over 1f out: rtd 75 when unplcd sole juv start: bred to apprec 1m: with Sir M Stoute. *hd* **72**
972 **BORDER SUBJECT 30** [15] 3-9-0 Pat Eddery 13/8 FAV: -69: Keen, handy, hmpd over 2f out, onepace: hvly bckd from 9/4: will rate more highly: see 972. *shd* **72**
3884} **GUARDED SECRET 249** [4] 3-9-0 S Sanders 25/1: 3-0: Bhd, btn 2f out: 10th: rtd 73 sole juv start: dam 7f scorer & 7f/1m will suit. *1* **70**
3881} **HALHOO LAMMTARRA 251** [8] 3-9-0 S Drowne 15/2: 2-0: Prom, wknd well over 1f out: 11th: rtd 87 when rnr-up sole juv start (mdn): dam 6/9f wnr: eff at 1m, bred to stay further: acts on fast grnd. *1* **68**
-- **GENERAL JACKSON** [13] 3-9-0 N Pollard 20/1: 0: Slow away & al bhd: 12th. *2* **64**
4453} **HELLO VEGAS 211** [14] 3-9-0 M Hills 20/1: 6-0: Slow away, al bhd: 13th. *hd* **63**
1175 **Lite A Candle 12** [12] 3-8-9 F Norton 66/1: 837 **Pieta 42** [11] 3-8-9 T E Durcan 66/1:
15 ran Time 1m 41.95 (5.15) (Hamdan Al Maktoum) J L Dunlop Arundel, W.Sussex.

1377

5.10 PLATINUM MDN DIV 2 3YO (D) 1m str Good 57 -04 Slow
£4017 £1236 £618 £309

3836} **FOREIGN SECRETARY 254** [3] Sir Michael Stoute 3-9-0 K Fallon 4/1: 4-1: 3 b c Kingmambo - Misinskie (Nijinsky) Waited with, hdwy & short of room over 2f out, styd on well ins last to lead cl-home, cosily: op 2/1: rtd 80 sole juv start: half-brother to smart 10/12f wnrs: eff at 1m, 10f looks sure to suit: one to follow. **92+**
4523} **ARGENTAN 205** [6] J H M Gosden 3-9-0 J Fortune 5/2 FAV: 33-2: 3 b c Gulch - Honfleur (Sadler's Wells) Handy, hdwy to chall & short of room over 1f out, kept on ins last, not pace of wnr: just btn: hvly bckd on reapp: plcd both juv starts for A Foster (back-end mdns, rtd 94): dam 13.5f list scorer: stays 1m, further shld suit: acts on gd & gd/soft: useful, must win a mdn. *½* **90**
-- **GLEDSWOOD** [5] Lady Herries 3-8-9 K Darley 20/1: 3: 3 ch f Selkirk - Horseshoe Reef (Mill Reef) Waited with, eff well over 2f out, sn short of room, staying on again when hmpd ins last, not btn far: shade unlucky: half-sister to mid-dists wnrs: eff at 1m, 10f/12f looks sure to suit: improve & win races over further. *hd* **84+**
992 **MORNINGS MINION 27** [13] R Charlton 3-9-0 R Perham 25/1: -44: In tch, hdwy over 2f out to lead over 1f out, hdd & onepcd ins last, not btn far: much imprvd for debut & stays 1m: win a minor trk mdn. *shd* **89**
-- **SHADOWBLASTER** [10] 3-9-0 M Roberts 10/1: 5: With ldr, squeezed out appr fnl 1f, staying on again when no room ins last under a kind ride: nicely bckd from 14/1: cost 15,000gns: half-brother to a useful mid-dists performer: looks sure to apprec 1m+ & must have gone close with a more forceful ride: promising. *1¼* **87+**
4285} **PYTHAGORAS 223** [2] 3-9-0 Pat Eddery 9/1: -40-6: Handy, eff to chall over 1f out, eased when held ins last: rtd 82 when 4th on debut last term: stays 1m on gd grnd: has ability. *¾* **85$**
1041 **HIGHLAND REEL 21** [8] 3-9-0 N Pollard 100/30: 37: In tch, eff to chall when short of room 2f out, kept on again ins last: bckd tho' op 9/4: can win a mdn on a minor trk: promising: see 1041. *½* **84+**
4040} **ZAFFIA 241** [12] 3-8-9 S Whitworth 33/1: 42-8: Made most till over 1f out, no extra: rtd 71 when rnr-up on 2nd of only 2 juv starts (mdn auct): prob stays 1m on gd & soft grnd. *hd* **78**
789 **AMJAD 50** [9] 3-9-0 L Dettori 9/1: 59: In tch, eff & staying on when not clr run over 1f out, eased ins last: shld do better, see 789. *1¼* **80$**
4600} **FALCONIDAE 197** [11] 3-9-0 S Sanders 20/1: 64-0: Bhd, eff over 2f out, onepace when hmpd over *¾* **78**

NEWBURY   FRIDAY MAY 19TH   Lefthand, Flat, Galloping Track

1f out, not recover: 10th: rtd 79 when 4th on 2nd of only 2 juv starts: 1m shld suit & will apprec h'caps.

4462} **CALLAS 211** [14] 3-8-9 S Carson (5) 20/1: 04-0: In tch, eff 2f out, sn btn: 11th, reapp.	4	65

1200 **Red Lion Fr 11** [7] 3-9-0 M Fenton 33/1:   4606} **Hoteliers Pride 196** [4] 3-9-0 A Clark 66/1:

--   **Aegean Flower** [1] 3-9-0 S Drowne 25/1:

14 ran   Time 1m 41.67 (4.87)   (W J Gredley)   Sir Michael Stoute Newmarket.

SAINT CLOUD   WEDNESDAY MAY 17TH   Lefthand, Galloping Track

Official Going   GOOD

1378   3.15 GR 3 PRIX CORRIDA 4YO+ FILLIES   1m2f110y   Good
£21134   £7685   £3842

2818} **SUPER TASSA 306** [4] V Valiani 4-8-9 T Thulliez 121/10: 02-411: 4 ch f Lahib - Center Moriches (Magical Wonder) -:		109
-- **WAR GAME** [1] A Fabre 4-8-9 O Peslier 3/5 FAV: 1-12: 4 b f Caerleon - Walensee (Troy)	½	108
1034 **TURBOTIERE 20** [3] E Libaud 5-8-11 L Huart 44/10: 41-333: 5 br m Turgeon - Victoria Dee (Rex Magna) -:	1½	107
*1154 **CAPE GRACE 12** [5] R Hannon 4-8-9 Dane O'Neill 11/5: 44-615: Trkd ldr, rnd/no extra	hd	104

appr fnl 1f, fin 5th: Brit raider, upped in class: not disgraced: see 1154 (List).

5 ran   Time 2m 16.5   (V Valiani)   V Valiani Italy

LONGCHAMP   THURSDAY MAY 18TH   Righthand, Galloping Track

Official Going   GOOD

1379   1.55 GR 3 PRIX DE GUICHE 3YO   1m1f   Good
£21134   £7685   £3842

-- **SUANCES** M Delcher-Sanchez 3-9-2 J L Martinez 107/10: 11-111: 3 ch c Most Welcome - Prayer Wheel (High Line) In tch, hdwy to lead dist, rdn clr: smart Spanish raider, v eff arnd 9f on gd grnd.		116
1026 **BOUTRON 25** P Costes 3-9-2 A Junk 13/10 FAV: 0-3322: 3 b c Exut To Nowhere - Vindelonde (No Lute)	2½	111

Led, hdd over 1f out, not pace of wnr: acts on gd & hvy grnd: see 1026 (Gr 2).

-- **BERISKAIO** A Fabre 3-9-2 O Peslier 16/10: -13: 3 b c Bering - Boubskaia (Niniski)	nk	110

Prom, drvn, hung left & no extra ins last: stys 9f on gd grnd: v useful.

6 ran   Time 2m 02.5   (Mme G Cabrero)   M Delcher-Sanchez Spain

1380   2.25 GR 3 PRIX LA FORCE 3YO   1m4f   Good
£21234   £7685   £3842   £2305

*990 **HOLDING COURT 26** M A Jarvis 3-9-2 O Peslier 29/10: 210-11: 3 b c Hernando - Indian Love		116

Song (Be My Guest) Made all, rdn & styd on strongly ins fnl 1f: earlier won at Haydock (rtd h'cap): trained by B Meehan to win again at Haydock in '99 (stks, rtd 97), subs unplcd in Gr 1 company: half-brother to high-class 6/7f performer Tomba: eff at 10.5f/12f: acts on good, hvy & a gall frk, likes Haydock: runs well fresh & likes to force the pace: prog & developing into a v smart performer, may be supplemented for the French Derby.

-- **BONNET ROUGE** E Lellouche 3-9-2 D Boeuf 3/5 FAV: -112: 3 b c Pistolet Bleu - French Free Star	3	110

(Carmarthen) Settled last, rdn/prog 2f out, styd on but no ch with wnr: eff at 12f on gd grnd.

-- **HERCULANO** Mme M Bollack Badel 3-9-2 A Badel 19/2: -51233: 3 b c Subotica - Hokey Pokey (Lead	2½	106

On Time) In tch, rdn & late gains, no threat: stays 12f on gd grnd, further shld suit.

-- **SNETTERTON** P Bary 3-9-2 (BL) T Thulliez 9/2: 1-244: Cl-up, rdn/wknd over 1f out: blnkd.	1½	104
1168 **GARGALHADA FINAL 12** 3-9-2 J Weaver 7/1: 125: Trkd ldr, chall briefly 2f out, wknd qckly appr	10	92

fnl 1f: capable of much better & reportedly may apprec a softer surface: see 1168, 833.

5 ran   Time 2m 34.9   (J R Good)   M A Jarvis Newmarket

THIRSK   SATURDAY MAY 20TH   Lefthand, Flat, Oval Track

Official Going: GOOD   Stalls: Straight Course - Stands Side, Round Course - Inside

1381   2.15 SKIPTON CLAIMER 2YO (E)   5f   Good 54   -32 Slow
£3006   £925   £462   £231   Raced towards stands side

1214 **JUSTALORD 11** [5] W G M Turner 2-8-6 A Daly 4/1: -6161: 2 b g King's Signet - Just Lady (Emarati)		73

Sn cl up, led over 1f out, styd on well, drvn out close home: op 7/2: earlier scored at Lingfield (3-runner AW mdn, rtd 71a): eff at 5f on equitrack & gd grnd: likes a sharp trk & enjoys claiming grade.

928 **WATERPARK 35** [10] M Dods 2-8-3 T Williams 11/1: -632: 2 b f Namaqualand - Willisa (Polar Falcon)	1	66

Chsd ldrs, rdn/briefly no room over 1f out, kept on inside last, not reach wnr: handles gd & soft grnd: see 928, 801.

1252 **DOMINAITE 8** [7] M W Easterby 2-8-11 G Parkin 50/1: -003: 2 b g Komaite - Fairy Kingdom (Prince	nk	73

Sabo) In tch towards centre, rdn & kept on fnl 1f, nearest fin: will apprec 6f & similar grade, handles gd grnd.

928 **PETIT TOR 35** [13] J Norton 2-8-4 O Pears 20/1: -04: Rdn chasing ldrs, kept on fnl 1f: see 928.	½	64
898 **DAM ELHANAH 37** [16] 2-8-3 R Winston 13/8 FAV: -245: Tracked ldrs 4f: hvly bckd: btr 898 (g/s).	½	61
1131 **BANNINGHAM BLIZ 16** [4] 2-8-0 A Beech (5) 100/1: -006: Outpcd early, styd on well fnl 1f, nrst fin.	nk	57
-- **SCREAMIN GEORGINA** [17] 2-8-4 G Carter 9/2: 0: Outpcd mid div halfway, no impression: well bckd,	½	59

op 14/1, paddock pick: Muhtarram filly, April foal, cost 1,800gns: half sister to a useful 6f juv wnr, dam a 5f juv wnr: sire a top class 10f performer: lengthy, scopey filly, 6f+ will suit in time, more expected here.

928 **DANCING PENNEY 35** [11] 2-8-4 (BL) F Lynch 25/1: -508: Led till over 1f out, wknd: ran freely in blnks.	1	57
-- **DOUBLE KAY** [6] 2-8-5 D Mernagh (3) 14/1: 9: Dwelt, rdn/rear, no impress: op 10/1: Treasure	1¼	55

Kay gelding, April foal, cost 2,800gns: dam modest, sire a smart sprinter: with J Glover.
1131 **FAYZ SLIPPER 16** [14] 2-8-1 W Supple 16/1: 000: Hmpd start, never on terms: 10th: see 938. *3½* **42**
1146 **MONICA 15** [15] 2-7-11 P Hanagan (4) 100/1: 00: Soon outpcd: 11th: mod form. *hd* **37**
1130 **Magnanimous 16** [2] 2-8-9 Kim Tinkler 50/1: -- **Flowing Rio** [3] 2-8-3 Dale Gibson 33/1:
-- **Diamond Murphy** [8] 2-7-13 N Kennedy 25/1:
14 ran Time 1m 01.3 (4.3) (Mrs M S Teversham) W G M Turner Corton Denham, Somerset

1382

2.45 DISHFORTH CLASS STKS 3YO 0-95 (B) 1m rnd Good 54 -05 Slow
£9717 £2990 £1495 £747

*1188 **CHAMPION LODGE 13** [2] J A R Toller 3-9-0 S Whitworth 9/4 JT FAV: -211: 3 b c Sri Pekan - Legit **97**
(Runnett) Trkd ldrs, no room/swtchd 2f out, rdn & styd on well fnl 1f to lead near fin: op 7/4: paddock pick: recent Newmarket wnr (mdn): eff at 1m on firm & gd/soft grnd, easy or stiff/gall track: useful colt, can win more races.
*1099 **ELGHANI 18** [1] R W Armstrong 3-9-0 W Supple 5/2: 012: 3 br c Lahib - Fawaakeh (Lyphard): *½* **94**
Led, rdn fnl 2f, hdd well inside last: well bckd, op 3/1: looked well: acts on gd & gd/soft grnd: see 1099.
1055 **KINGSDON 21** [3] R Hannon 3-8-12 D Holland 9/4 JT FAV: 231-63: 3 b c Brief Truce - Richly Deserved *¾* **91**
(King's Lake) Handy, rdn/every chance over 1f out, just held near fin: nicely bckd: see 1055 (h'caps).
1246 **PARADISE GARDEN 9** [4] M Johnston 3-8-12 J Carroll 5/1: 4-0304: Trkd ldrs, btn 3f out: op 4/1. *12* **73**
4 ran Time 1m 40.1 (4.7) (P C J Dalby) J A R Toller Newmarket, Suffolk

1383

3.15 BLACK CAT HCAP 4YO+ 0-95 (C) 6f Good 54 +04 Fast [94]
£8216 £2528 £1264 £632 Stalls 1-5 raced far side, no advantage

1173 **MANORBIER 14** [21] K A Ryan 4-9-2 (82) F Lynch 3/1 FAV: 112041: 4 ch g Shalford - La Pirouette **85**
(Kennedy Road) Bhnd ldrs, briefly no room 2f out, switched & rdn/prog to lead well inside last: hvly bckd, best time of day: earlier scored twice at W'hampton (sells, rtd 64a) & Doncaster (h'cap): missed '99, '98 Chepstow wnr (juv auction mdn, D Arbuthnot, rtd 83): suited by 6f, acts on fast, soft & fibresand: handles any track: tough/ rapidly progressing gelding, thriving physically & looks potentially useful.
1196 **TEYAAR 12** [19] D Shaw 4-8-9 (75) A Beech (5) 11/1: 011252: 4 b g Polar Falcon - Music In My Life *nk* **77**
(Law Society) Prom, rdn/narrow lead ins last, hdd near fin: jock given a 1-day ban for misuse of whip: see 1008.
1158 **LAGO DI VARANO 14** [2] R M Whitaker 8-8-9 (75)(bl) Dean McKeown 25/1: -06603: 8 b g Clantime - On *hd* **76**
The Record (Record Token) Al handy far side, rdn/briefly led inside last, kept on well, just held: right back to form with blinks reapplied, well h'capped for similar & all successes at 5f, shld win soon: see 758.
1173 **BOLDLY GOES 14** [1] C W Fairhurst 4-8-11 (77) P Goode (3) 25/1: -00604: Chsd ldrs far side, rdn to *shd* **78+**
chall over 1f out, styd on well, just held: thriving physically & well h'capped for similar: keep in mind.
*1337 **JUWWI 2** [4] 6-10-2 (96)(6ex) Darren Williams (7) 10/1: 514415: Far side first 2f, switched & prog to *shd* **96**
lead in centre 2f out, hdd fnl 1f, just held cl home: op 7/1, quick reapp under a pen: in great heart: see 1337.
1279 **BLAKESET 7** [6] 5-7-12 (64) P Fessey 50/1: 100006: Chsd ldrs, kept on fnl 1f, not pace to chall. *2* **59**
1250 **NOMORE MR NICEGUY 9** [11] 6-9-1 (81) W Supple 25/1: -00007: In tch, rdn/styd on fnl 1f: improved *shd* **76**
efforts recently: looks nicely h'capped, loves Chester, spot on at 7f: see 977.
1004 **BRAVE EDGE 26** [10] 9-9-5 (85) D Holland 14/1: 0-0338: Bhd ldrs, no impression fnl 1f: tchd 16/1: *1* **78**
jockey found guilty of careless riding & referred to Portman Square as a result of previous offences.
*824 **FRANCPORT 45** [18] 4-8-11 (77) G Carter 5/1: 00-519: Held up, no impress: 6 wk abs since 824. *3½* **61**
1279 **REX IS OKAY 7** [8] 4-8-4 (70)(bl) L Newton 20/1: 400260: Cl up stands side 3f, btn/hmpd 1f out. *½* **52**
1162 **PIPS MAGIC 14** [20] 4-9-0 (80) R Winston 8/1: 0-0000: Held up, switched/eff over 1f out, sn held: 11th. *shd* **62**
1158 **QUIET VENTURE 14** [5] 6-8-6 (72) R Lappin 40/1: 665-00: In tch far side 3f: 12th: see 1158. *¾* **52**
1256 **XANADU 8** [7] 4-7-12 (64) D Mernagh (3) 14/1: 001120: Led stand side 4f: 13th: op 12/1: btr 1256. *¾* **42**
905 **AMARANTH 36** [3] 4-8-11 (77)(t) J P Spencer 33/1: 6-0000: Chsd ldrs 4f: 14th: see 631. *½* **53**
1162 **STORYTELLER 14** [23] 6-9-3 (83)(vis) Dale Gibson 10/1: 44-000: Al rear: 19th: op 8/1: vis reapp. **0**
4572} **Double Splendour 201** [14] 10-9-2 (82) G Parkin 33/1:1162 **Flak Jacket 14** [12] 5-8-9 (75) O Pears 25/1:
3959} **Jeffrey Anotherred 246** [22] 6-8-10 (76) A Clark 25/1: 1158 **Redoubtable 14** [9] 9-9-2 (82) J Stack 25/1:
1028 **Selhurstpark Flyer 24** [15] 9-8-11 (77) J Carroll 20/1:
20 ran Time 1m 12.5 (3.0) (Uncle Jacks Pub) K A Ryan Hambleton, N Yorks

1384

3.45 EASINGWOLD HCAP 3YO 0-100 (C) 5f Good 54 -00 Slow [104]
£7241 £2228 £1114 £557

*1280 **HONESTY FAIR 7** [4] J A Glover 3-7-10 (72) D Mernagh (1) 4/1: 00-411: 3 b f Reprimand - Truthful **85**
Image (Reesh) Handy, led 2f out, rdn clr inside last, readily: looked well, nicely bckd: earlier won at Beverley (mdn): plcd in '99 (rtd 68): eff at 5f, stays 6f: acts on firm and gd/soft grnd: improving, should win again.
1219 **BLUE HOLLY 11** [1] J S Moore 3-7-13 (75) P M Quinn (5) 10/1: 123-52: 3 b f Blues Traveller - Holly *4* **76**
Bird (Runnett) Went left start, rdn/in tch centre, kept on fnl 1f, no impression on wnr: tchd 12/1: see 1219.
1219 **LA CAPRICE 11** [11] A Berry 3-8-2 (77)(1ow) G Carter 12/1: 521-03: 3 ch f Housebuster - Shicklah *1¼* **76**
(The Minstrel) Handy, outpcd 2f out, kept on inside last, no threat to wnr: see 1219.
1219 **SABRE LADY 11** [7] Miss L A Perratt 3-8-8 (84) D Holland 7/1: 230-34: Outpcd, late gains fnl 2f. *hd* **81**
988 **BOLEYN CASTLE 28** [8] 3-9-7 (97) A Clark 25/1: 165-05: Rdn bhd ldrs early, never pace to chall: still *nk* **93**
burly: '99 Windsor wnr (debut, mdn, rtd 86, subs rtd 97 at Ascot, Gr 3, flattered): eff at 5f on gd grnd.
1047 **POWER PACKED 22** [5] 3-9-3 (93) P Robinson 7/4 FAV: 212-56: Prom, no extra over 1f out: well bckd. *hd* **88**
3828} **EBBA 244** [9] 3-9-2 (92) A Beech (5) 14/1: 1505-7: In tch 4f: op 10/1: reapp: '99 wnr at Catterick *nk* **86**
(auction mdn), Yarmouth (2, nov auction & stakes, rtd 94 at best): eff at 5/6f, dam a 12f scorer, could get further: acts on firm & fast grnd: handles a sharp/fair track, likes Yarmouth: likes to dominate.
1164 **BRAVE BURT 14** [10] 3-9-4 (94) J Carroll 12/1: 30-038: Led 3f, faded: op 10/1: now with D Nicholls. *nk* **87**
1192 **HOWARDS LAD 13** [6] 3-7-11 (73) Dale Gibson 33/1: 400-09: Al outpcd: '99 Ayr wnr (mdn, rtd 86 at *2½* **59**
best): eff at 6f, tried 7f: acts on gd/soft grnd & a stiff/gall track: best without a vis: will apprec a return to 6f+.
1047 **COCO DE MER 22** [3] 3-8-4 (80) R Winston 20/1: 20-000: Cl up 4f, fdd: 10th: op 14/1: see 1047. *2½* **59**
1219 **NIFTY MAJOR 11** [2] 3-8-7 (83) O Pears 15/2: 50-020: Chsd ldrs 3f: 11th: btr 1219. *¾* **60**
11 ran Time 59.70 (2.7) (P And S Partnership) J A Glover Carburton, Notts

1385

4.20 EBF CARLTON FILLIES NOV STKS 2YO (D) 5f Good 54 -26 Slow
£4153 £1278 £639 £319 Raced centre - stands side

*1067 **DREAMS DESIRE 19** [5] J A Glover 2-9-0 D Mernagh (3) 15/8 FAV: -11: 2 b f Mind Games - Champenoise **90**
(Forzano) Made all, asserted from over 1f out, styd on well inside last, rdn out: hvly bckd: earlier made a winning
debut at Doncaster (nov auction stakes): eff at 5f, dam a 1m wnr, will get further: acts on gd & gd/soft grnd, gall/
sharpish track: has run well fresh: likes to dominate: reportedly well regarded.

*1130 **MUJA FAREWELL 16** [3] T D Barron 2-9-0 W Supple 3/1: 12: 2 ch f Mujtahid - Highland Rhapsody 1¾ **81**
(Kris) Handy, rdn/outpcd by wnr over 1f out: well bckd: acts on gd & gd/soft grnd: see 1130.

*1189 **INNIT 13** [2] M R Channon 2-9-3 P Fessey 3/1: -3213: 2 b f Distinctly North - Tidal Reach (Kris S) nk **83**
Handy, onepace over 1f out: bckd, though op 5/2: see 1189.

1161 **NIFTY ALICE 14** [6] A Berry 2-8-12 G Carter 11/2: -124: Dwelt, in tch, kept on fnl 2f: clr of rem. ½ **76**

-- **SENSIMELIA** [8] C Teague 50/1: 5: Dwelt, never on terms: Inzar filly, Feb foal, cost 3,000 6 **63**
IR gns: looked fit: dam a 5f juv wnr, sire a high class 6/7f performer: with M Wane.

938 **BEREZINA 33** [4] J Carroll 11/1: 56: Prom 3f, wknd quickly: op 8/1: btr 938. 7 **50**

989 **TOMAMIE 28** [1] O Pears 100/1: -07: Chsd ldrs 3f, soon struggling, mod form. 2½ **43**

-- **POLYPHONIC** [9] J A Lappin 100/1: 8: Al bhnd: burly: Binary Star filly, Feb foal, cost 500gns, 1½ **39**
a first foal: dam a 5f juv wnr: with G Woodward.

8 ran Time 1m 01.00 (4.0) (Sports Mania) J A Glover Carburton, Notts

1386

4.50 DARLINGTON MDN 3YO (D) 1m4f Good 54 -34 Slow
£4387 £1350 £675 £337

1051 **LIDAKIYA 21** [4] Sir Michael Stoute 3-8-9 F Lynch 4/1: 41: 3 b f Kahyasi - Lilissa (Doyoun) **85**
Trkd ldrs, rdn/chsd ldr over 2f out, styd on well to lead well inside last, going away: apprec this step up to 12f, shld
get further: acts on gd & gd/soft grnd: op to further improvement.

1054 **SCACHMATT 21** [1] L M Cumani 3-9-0 J P Spencer 20/1: 502: 2 b c Zafonic - Svanzega (Sharpen ¾ **86**
Up) Led/disputed lead till went on over 4f out, rdn/hdd well inside last & no extra: op 16/1: left British debut
bhnd: stays 12f & handles good grnd: see 1054.

-- **APPLE TOWN** [2] H R A Cecil 3-8-9 A McGlone 4/1: 3: 3 br f Warning - Applecross (Glint Of Gold) 3 **77**
Handy, rdn/outpcd over 2f out: needed this on debut: mid dist bred, Ribblesdale entry at Royal Ascot, stays 12f.

979 **ARANYI 30** [10] J L Dunlop 3-9-0 G Carter 4/6 FAV: 644-54: Keen, mid div, eff over 2f out, al held: 3½ **77**
hvly bckd: this longer 12f trip may yet suit, needs to learn more restraint: btr 979 (h'cap, 10f).

-- **NINNOLO** [6] 3-9-0 R Morse 33/1: 5: Rear, mod gains fnl 2f: 32,000gns purchase, dam a 6f juv wnr. 1 **76**

4277} **MILL EMERALD 225** [3] 3-8-9 R Winston 100/1: 0-6: Chsd ldrs, btn 3f out: reapp: well bhnd sole '99 5 **64**
start: bred to apprec this longer 12f trip for R Fahey.

1054 **DOCTOR JOHN 21** [8] 3-9-0 P Fessey 50/1: 07: Led/dspd lead till 4f out, btn 2f out: longer 12f trip. nk **68**

-- **HAAFEL** [7] 3-9-0 W Supple 10/1: 8: Trkd ldrs 4f out, btn 2f out: op 8/1, paddock pick, debut: 14 **52**
half-brother to sev wnrs, incl high-class miler Maroof: dam a 12f scorer: with R Armstrong.

3891} **ULSHAW 250** [7] 3-9-0 R Lappin 33/1: 05-9: Al bhnd: reapp: rtd 68 on 2nd of 2 '99 starts (auct mdn): 1 **51**
bred to apprc mid dists this term, now qual for h'caps: with J Bethell.

-- **BANK BUSTER** [5] 3-9-0 O Pears 100/1: 0: Keen, bhd 4f out: 10th: debut: with W Kemp. dist **0**

10 ran Time 2m 40.3 (10.5) (H H Aga Khan) Sir Michael Stoute Newmarket, Suffolk

1387

5.20 STANDARD HCAP 3YO 0-80 (D) 1m rnd Good 54 -25 Slow [85]
£4758 £1464 £732 £366

1183 **SOVEREIGN STATE 13** [3] M A Jarvis 3-9-2 (73) P Robinson 9/2 FAV: 514-01: 3 b g Soviet Lad - Portee **76**
(Slip Anchor) Chsd ldrs, prog to lead over 1f out, drvn and just held on near fin: looked well: '99 wnr here at Thirsk
(mdn, rtd 81): eff at 1m: acts on firm & gd grnd, poss handles soft: likes Thirsk.

1234 **NOWT FLASH 9** [6] B S Rothwell 3-8-0 (57) Joanna Badger (7) 33/1: 061052: 3 ch c Petardia - hd **59**
Mantlepiece (Common Grounds) Wide/towards rear, prog fnl 3f and styd on strongly inside last, just held:
eff at 6/7f, now stays 1m well: acts on fibresand & gd grnd: see 589 (7f seller).

1255 **SIGN OF THE TIGER 8** [7] P C Haslam 3-8-11 (68) P Goode (3) 7/1: 114423: 3 b g Beveled - Me Spede nk **69+**
(Valiyar) Towards rear, prog/no room over 2f out, styd on well inside last, just held: unlucky, can be rated wnr
here with a clr run: acts on both AWs, firm & gd grnd: deserves similar: see 1255, 450.

857 **MANA DARGENT 40** [7] M Johnston 3-9-5 (76) J P Spencer 12/1: 33-204: Chsd ldrs, kept on fnl 2f, 2½ **72**
not pace to chall: op 10/1, 6 week abs: stays 1m: see 717 (7f).

1255 **ALJAZIR 8** [9] 3-8-3 (60) W Supple 25/1: 4-0205: Trkd ldrs, onepace over 1f out: stays 1m, see 887. nk **55**

924 **DESRAYA 35** [12] 3-8-5 (62) (BL) F Lynch 33/1: 000-06: Led till over 1f out, faded: 1st time blnks. 4 **49**

1183 **INDIAN SUN 13** [10] 3-9-7 (78) G Carter 5/1: 0-4607: Twds rear, mod gains for press: nicely bckd. 2 **61**

1018 **LUCKY SWEEP 26** [15] 3-9-1 (72) D Holland 12/1: 64-58: Prom 6f: tchd 14/1, h'cap bow: see 1018. ¾ **54**

4107} **BENBYAS 237** [14] 3-8-3 (60) D Mernagh (3) 12/1: 0400-9: Mid div, no impression: op 14/1, reapp: ¾ **41**
needed this: unplcd in '99 (rtd 73, mid auction mdn): stays a stiff 1m & handles gd grnd.

900 **INDY CARR 37** [2] 3-9-3 (74) T Williams 25/1: 1-60: Mid div, btn 2f out: 10th: see 900 (7f). 1 **53**

1022 **EVER REVIE 26** [8] 3-7-10 (53)(bl) (1oh) P Fessey 25/1: 100-00: Prom 6f: 11th: see 1022. ¾ **31**

1104 **DALYAN 17** [1] 3-8-11 (68) J Carroll 25/1: 445-00: Al towards rear: 12th: see 1104. 2½ **27**

1035 **WINGED ANGEL 22** [4] 3-8-5 (62) R Winston 5/1: 4000: Towards rear, eff 3f out, no impression: 14th: **0**
nicely bckd, op 7/1: h'cap bow: more expected after eyecatching efforts earlier: see 1035.

1053 **ENTITY 21** [16] 3-8-7 (64) G Parkin 7/1: -00030: Reared & stuck in stalls, took no part: see 1053, 976. **0**

736 **Slick Willie 56** [13] 3-9-4 (75) R Winston 14/1: 909 **Northern Echo 36** [11] 3-8-8 (65) Dale Gibson 33/1:

16 ran Time 1m 41.7 (6.3) (Mrs G R Smith) M A Jarvis Newmarket, Suffolk

461

Official Going   STANDARD. Stalls: 7f - Outside: Rem - Inside.

1388

7.00 RED DEVIL MDN 3YO+ (D)   1m1f79y aw Going 33 +04 Fast
£2834   £872   £436   £218   3 yo rec 13lb

1105 **ASTRONAUT** 17 [12] W J Haggas 3-8-10 J F Egan 13/2: 041: 3 b g Sri Pekan - Wild Abandon (Graustark)   75a
Held up, prog halfway, led bef clsd drifts, rd on op 5/1, fair time: unrcd juv, apprec step up to 9.5f on fibresand bow.
1051 **ANASTASIA VENTURE** 21 [2] S P C Woods 3-8-5 N Callan 3/1 FAV: 532: 3 b f Lion Cavern - Our Shirley   2   66a
(Shirley Heights): Nvr far away, chall dist, not pace of wnr: AW bow, handles fibresand better both turf starts.
1265 **PAPERWEIGHT** 8 [8] Miss K M George 4-9-4 J Tate 8/1: 30-423: 4 b f In The Wings - Crystal Reay   ½   65a
(Sovereign Dancer) Led after 3f till 1½f out, same pace: tchd 10/1: stiff task, handles any grnd: see 1265.
909 **AIWIN** 36 [5] G C H Chung 3-8-10 (t) M Henry 66/1: -04: Waited with, prog & drifted left 2f   ¾   68a
out, nvr able to chall: AW bow for this Forzando colt: stays 9.3f & handles fibresand.
1266 **DIVA** 8 [9] 3-8-5 G Duffield 9/1: 605: Bhd, imprvd after 4f till no extra 2f out: op 6/1, AW bow, lngr trip.   1½   60a
1268 **CULTURED PEARL** 8 [11] 3-8-5 D Sweeney 4/1: 5-36: Prom, sn ran wide, chall 4f out till 3f out, fdd: 1¾   56a
op 11/4 on AW bow: up in trip & was reportedly unable to handle the trk: see 1268.
4047} **MUFFLED** 241 [7] 3-8-5 K Darley 6/1: 40-7: Mid-div till 3f out: reapp/AW bo: flattered 4th in a   11   41a
Leicester mdn on '99 debut (rtd 70): with J Dunlop.
1084 **SMILE ITS SHOWTIME** 18 [4] 3-8-10 A Rawlinson 40/1: -008: Al towards rear: AW bow.   ¾   45a
4339} **SHERZABAD** 221 [3] 3-8-10 (t) A Clark 9/2: 00-9: In tch till 3f out: reapp, AW bow, nicely bckd: 3½   39a
t-strap today: rtd 68 when unplaced on 2 juv starts: with Sir M Stoute.
326 **ABLE MILLENIUM** 127 [1] 4-9-9 R Price 20/1: 330-00: Early ldr, btn 4f out: 10th, 4 mth abs, see 122.   7   27a
-- **MYAHSMONT** [10] 5-9-9 S Whitworth 50/1: 0: Nvr in it: 11th, Flat bow, jumps fit: moderate.   ½   26a
11 ran   Time 2m 00.9 (2.7)   (Highclere Thor'bred Racing Ltd)   W J Haggas Newmarket, Suffolk.

1389

7.30 DIVE CLASS CLAIMER 4YO+ 0-60 (F)   1m4f aw Going 33 -09 Slow
£2219   £634   £317

1128 **DESERT SPA** 16 [8] P J Makin 5-9-3 A Clark 2/1 FAV: 2-1101: 5 b g Sheikh Albadou - Healing Waters   60a
(Temperance Hill) Cl-up, led 3f out, rdn clr before dist: nicely bckd: clearly suited by return to fav trk/surface:
earlier won here at W'hampton (2, h'caps): '98 wnr again here at W'hampton (h'cap, rtd 56a & 63, P Harris):
12f W'hampton fibresand specialist, handles fast & soft: best without blnks: tough.
918 **IRISH CREAM** 35 [7] Andrew Reid 4-8-4 (vis) M Henry 5/1: 201062: 4 b f Petong - Another Baileys   3   41a
(Deploy) In tch, prog appr final 2f, no ch with wnr: op 4/1: ran to best back in trip, see 668 (Southwell).
1203 **APPROACHABLE** 12 [3] Miss S J Wilton 5-8-8 I Mongan (4) 7/1: 422543: 5 b h Known Fact - Western   1   43a
Approach (Gone West) Well plcd, onepace under press appr final 1f: tchd 9/1, stiff task, best in claimers here.
*1241 **HILL FARM DANCER** 9 [2] W M Brisbourne 9-8-4 G Baker (7) 3/1: 435114: Bhd, imprvd after halfway,   3½   34a
rdn 3f out, no impress on ldrs: stiff task: better off in sell h'caps: see 1039.
-- **ZATOPEK** [5] 8-8-5 O Pears 50/1: 0400/5: Chsd ldrs 5f: stiff task, jumps fit, no form: nr 3yr Flat abs: 8   23a
rnr-up thrice in '97 (rtd 25): rtd 60 & 53a back in '96: eff at 1m, stays a sharp 12f on fast, soft & fibresand.
1037 **NIGHT CITY** 22 [4] 9-9-3 (VIS) N Callan 9/2: 021406: Led till 5f, sn btn: visored, op 5/2, see 650.   nk   35a
2769} **DRIVE ASSURED** 308 [6] 6-8-5 (t) P M Quinn (5) 20/1: 10/0-7: Al towards rear: 11 wk jumps abs,   18   3a
99/00 Uttoxeter wnr (sell h'cap, 2m, gd/soft grnd, t-strap, rtd 71): lightly rcd since '98 win at Brighton
(h'cap, rtd 73, C Brittain): eff at 1m, tried 14f on fast & gd/soft grnd: with K Morgan.
1272 **CITY PURSUIT** [1] 4-8-7 R Price 25/1: /0-00P: Al bhd, p.u. 4f out.   0a
8 ran   Time 2m 38.6 (5.0)   (D M Ahier)   P J Makin Ogbourne Maisey, Wilts.

1390

8.00 INTERCLASS HCAP 3YO 0-70 (E)   7f aw rnd Going 33 00 Slow   [77]
£2765   £851   £425   £212

1205 **ANTHEMION** 12 [7] P C Haslam 3-9-2 (65) Dean McKeown 8/1: 00-031: 3 ch g Night Shift - New Sensitive   71a
(Wattlefield) Rear, prog halfway, kept on gamely under press to lead nr fin: jockey given 2-day whip ban,
1st win: plcd in '99 (mdn, rtd 70): apprec return to 7f, shld get 1m: goes on fast grnd & fibresand, sharp trk.
1235 **MANXWOOD** 9 [6] D J S Cosgrove 3-9-2 (65) J F Egan 7/4 FAV: 0-0142: 3 b g Petorius - Eliza Wooding   hd   70a
(Faustus) Sn led, drvn appr final 1f, hdd final strides: well bckd from 3/1, clr rem: improving, see 1038.
887 **CHILI PEPPER** 38 [8] A Smith 3-8-9 (58) P M Quinn 7/1: 06-6103: 3 gr f Chilibang - Game Germaine   6   53a
(Mummy's Game) Bhd, late prog thro' btn horses, nvr nrr: appreciated return to fibresand: see 706.
1038 **NODS NEPHEW** 22 [10] Miss J A Camacho 3-9-1 (64) K Darley 5/1: 0-4104: Chsd ldrs, swtchd & no   2½   55a
impress ent final 2f: see 976 (hvy grnd).
1233 **STOP THE TRAFFIC** 9 [2] 3-9-3 (66) J Mackay (7) 12/1: 252205: Early ldr, fdd ent final 2f: btr 1138.   ¾   56a
870 **DIAMOND RACHAEL** 39 [5] 3-9-1 (64) (vis) R Fitzpatrick (3) 10/1: 012366: Mid-div, outpcd 2f out: 1   52a
op 8/1, 6 wk abs, visor reapplied: see 549.
4524} **ABLE NATIVE** 206 [1] 3-9-7 (70) R Price 14/1: 025-7: Nvr on terms: reapp/AW/h'cap bow: fillies mdn   1   56a
rnr-up last year (rtd 78): eff at 7f on hvy grnd: with R Armstrong.
420 **JOELY GREEN** 112 [11] 3-9-2 (65) T G McLaughlin 8/1: -23458: Nvr a factor: 16 wk abs, back in trip.   shd   51a
1212 **WELCOME SHADE** 11 [3] 3-9-5 (68) C Cogan (5) 12/1: 014-29: Sn bhd: new stable, btr 1212, 2 (e/trk).   3½   48a
1202 **MACHUDI** 12 [4] 3-8-3 (52) L Newman (5) 20/1: 0-6060: Al towards rear: 10th, op 12/1.   1¼   30a
870 **PADDYWACK** 39 [9] 3-8-11 (60)(bl) A Culhane 7/1: 112220: Dwelt, al bhd, eased 2f out: 11th,   dist   0a
6 wk abs, reportedly sulked after missing the break, see 654.
11 ran   Time 1m 28.5 (2.3)   (Lord Scarsdale)   P C Haslam Middleham, Nth Yorks.

1391

8.30 TOGGLE FILLIES HCAP 3YO+ 0-70 (E)   6f aw rnd Going 33 +03 Fast   [69]
£2775   £854   £427   £213   3yo rec 9 lb

1278 **WHIZZ KID** 7 [11] J M Bradley 6-7-10 (37) Claire Bryan (5) 9/1: 051231: 6 b m Puissance - Panienka   42a
(Dom Racine) In tch, imprvd after 3f, led ent final 1f, held on well: op 4/1: in fine heart, earlier won at
Warwick (h'cap, rtd 67): '99 wnr at Ripon, Redcar, Chepstow, Ayr & Newcastle (h'caps, rtd 62): suited
by 5f/sharp 6f: acts on firm & both AWs, likes gd/soft & hvy, any trk: tough mare, on a fair mark on a/w.
1138 **CAROLS CHOICE** 16 [5] D Haydn Jones 3-8-13 (63) Dean McKeown 12/1: 420332: 3 ch f Emarati -   ¾   65a
Lucky Song (Lucky Wednesday) Nvr far away, led 2f out till below dist, kept on: op 9/1: deserves to shed mdn tag.
1233 **PALO BLANCO** 9 [2] Andrew Reid 9-8-9 (50) M Henry 5/1: 334223: 9 b m Precocious - Linpac   hd   51a

WOLVERHAMPTON (Fibresand) SATURDAY MAY 20TH Lefthand, Sharp Track

Mapleleaf (Dominion) Prom, effort 2f out, styd on, not btn far: tchd 8/1: holding her form well, see 680.
*1244 **HEAVENLY MISS** 9 [12] D Carroll 6-8-4 (45)(bl) K Dalgleish (7) 5/1: 50-414: Wide towards rear, hdwy   1¾ 41a
final 1½f, unable to chall: back on AW, better on turf, see 1244.
1233 **MOY** 9 [6] 5-7-13 (40)(VIS) A McCarthy (3) 14/1: 300205: Chsd ldrs, unable to qckn appr final 1f: visor.   1 33a
1233 **PLEASURE** 9 [10] 5-8-9 (50) R Fitzpatrick (3) 9/1: 00-546: Unable to go early pace, late hdway: see 1073.nk 42a
1066 **GUEST ENVOY** 19 [8] 5-8-13 (54) L Newman (5) 11/1: 411267: Nvr nr ldrs: return to 7f?: see 811.   hd 46a
1137 **MAYDORO** 16 [3] 7-7-10 (37)(5oh) G Baker (7) 33/1: 006-08: Handy till 2f out: stiffish task, see 1137.   ½ 28a
1173 **LA PIAZZA** 14 [9] 4-10-0 (69) J F Egan 4/1 FAV: 300-09: In tch till ent final 2f: op 2/1: '99   3 52a
wnr here at W'hampton (auct mdn, rtd 68a) & Lingfield (2, turf h'caps, rtd 84 at best): eff at 5f, suited
by 6f: acts on firm, both AWs, likes sharp trks, especially Lingfield: not her form: with W Haggas.
1205 **MOUNT PARK** 12 [1] 3-7-12 (48)(BL) Iona Wands (4) 33/1: -00000: Led till 2f out, lost pl: 10th, blnkd.   3 24a
579 **YABINT EL SHAM** 86 [7] 4-10-0 (69) P M Quinn (5) 11/1: 520000: Al bhd: 11th, 12 wk abs.   nk 45a
872 **Hot Legs** 39 [13] 4-7-10 (37)(bl)(2oh) J Mackay (7) 33/1:1126 **Elegant Dance** 16 [4] 6-8-2 (43) P Bradley (5) 25/1:
13 ran   Time 1m 14.6 (1.8)   (B Paling)   J M Bradley Sedbury, Gloucs.

1392   **9.00 PARACHUTE SELLER 3YO+ (G)**   5f aw rnd   Going 33 -13 Slow
£1904   £544   £272   3 yo rec 8 lb

1237 **SWEET MAGIC** 9 [9] L R Lloyd James 9-9-4 (t) K Darley 7/2: 004041: 9 ch g Sweet Monday - Charm Bird   54a
(Daring March) Cl-up, led dist, held on well: he bid: '99 wnr here at W'hampton (sell) & Catterick (h'cap, rtd
62 & 65a): lightly rcd in '98 (rtd 58): eff at 5f on firm, soft & fibresand: likes W'hampton/sharp trks.
*1237 **SAMWAR** 9 [2] Mrs N Macauley 9-9-9 (vis) R Fitzpatrick (3) 4/1: 632012: 8 b g Warning - Samaza   ½ 57a
(Arctic Tern): Dwelt, imprvd by halfway, led 1½f out, sn hdd, held towards fin: op 5/2: tough, see 1237.
1008 **NIFTY NORMAN** 26 [4] D Nicholls 6-9-9 O Pears 9/4 FAV: 363463: 6 b g Rock City - Nifty Fifty (Runnett)   1 54a
Early ldr, front rank & ev ch till onepace inside last: see 440, 272 (beat rnr-up).
1273 **MISS BANANAS** 8 [3] C N Kellett 5-9-4 D Meah (7) 16/1: 015004: Led after 2f till appr fnl 1f, no extra.   2 44$
1237 **NOBLE PATRIOT** 9 [8] 5-9-4 J F Egan 12/1: 000255: Chsd ldrs, same pace after halfway: stiff task.   1½ 40a
1139 **SING FOR ME** 16 [1] 5-8-13 Stephanie Hollinshead (7) 20/1: 424506: Nvr dngrs, short of room 2f out.   1¾ 31a
1237 **PRINCE NICO** 9 [5] 3-8-10 A Rawlinson 20/1: -007: Mid-div till outpcd/hung left appr final 1f.   1¼ 33a
1237 **YOUNG IBNR** 9 [10] 5-9-9 L Newman (5) 13/2: 014438: Wide, prom till fnl 2f: clsr to front pair in 1237.   1 35a
1137 **RED SONNY** 16 [7] 3-8-10 P Bradley (5) 8/1: 0-0049: Chsd ldrs till halfway.   2½ 24a
919 **SUNRISE GIRL** 35 [6] 3-8-5 A McCarthy (3) 50/1: 060: Unruly before start, nvr in it: 10th, modest.   dist 0a
10 ran   Time 1m 02.5 (2.3)   (Miss Kate Waddington)   L R Lloyd James Malton, Nth Yorks.

1393   **9.30 GO RED HCAP 3YO+ 0-60 (F)**   1m100y aw rnd   Going 33 -09 Slow   [60]
£2289   £654   £327

1065 **CHAMPAGNE GB** 19 [6] Andrew Reid 4-9-9 (55)(bl) M Henry 12/1: 050301: 4 b g Efisio - Success Story   63a
(Sharrood) Held up, smooth prog 3f out, led before dist, rdly: '99 Leicester wnr (clmr, rtd 66, R Charlton): eff
at 1m/10f, tried 12f: acts on gd grnd & fibresand, with/without blnks: unexposed on sand, cld rate higher.
1259 **MALCHIK** 8 [3] P Howling 4-9-10 (56) R Winston 10/1: 331202: 4 ch c Absalom - Very Good (Noalto)   3 57a
Prom till halfway, kept on again final 1½f: back to best away from equitrack: win another seller: see 922.
869 **INDIAN SWINGER** 39 [13] P Howling 4-9-3 (49) N Callan 12/1: 522003: 4 ch c Up And At 'Em - Seanee 1¾ 47a
Squaw (Indian Ridge): Held up, chsd ldrs after halfway, same pace fnl 2f: abs: better at 6/7f?
*1207 **HOH GEM** 12 [2] B R Millman 4-9-4 G Hind 7/2 FAV: 00-014: Struggled to go pace, late hdwy.   2½ 44a
1213 **PERUVIAN STAR** 11 [12] 4-9-4 (50) J Tate 11/1: 050005: Chsd ldrs wide, led halfway till ent fnl 2f.   ½ 43a
1213 **CONSULTANT** 11 [11] 4-9-8 (54) L Newman (5) 11/1: 002006: Front rank till appr final 2f: see 842.   2 43a
1207 **MUTAHADETH** 12 [7] 6-9-2 (48)(bl) J Fanning 8/1: 460447: Nvr nr ldrs & hmpd appr dist: see 183.   3 32a
1037 **THE IMPOSTER** 22 [8] 5-10-0 (60) I Mongan (5) 16/1: 2-1008: Chsd ldrs till 2f out: C/D wnr in 707.   1¼ 42a
869 **DOMINO FLYER** 39 [9] 7-9-3 (49)(BL) G Duffield 8/1: 50-049: Led 4f, btn 2f out: too free in blnks?   3 34a
1243 **PROSPECTORS COVE** 9 [5] 7-9-12 (58) T G McLaughlin 8/1: 000000: Al towards rear: 10th, see 618.   1¾ 32a
1086 **RIVER ENSIGN** 18 [1] 7-9-4 (50) P M Quinn (5) 7/1: 010360: In tch till halfway: 11th, see 859.   9 10a
1038 **C HARRY** 22 [4] 6-9-3 (49) J F Egan 10/1: 650500: Nvr in it: 12th, up in trip, see 130 (sell).   10 0a
1100 **THATCHAM** 18 [10] 4-9-6 (52) R Price 8/1: 0-3200: Midfield till 4f out: 13th, see 880 (10f, equitrack).   3 0a
13 ran   Time 1m 49.8 (3.6)   (A S Reid)   Andrew Reid Mill Hill, London NW7.

LINGFIELD   SATURDAY MAY 20TH   Lefthand, Sharp, Undulating Track

Official Going   GOOD TO SOFT (SOFT in places). Stalls: Str Crse - Far Side; 9f - Inside; 2m - Outside.

1394   **6.05 COCKNEY NIGHT HCAP 4YO+ 0-75 (E)**   2m   Good 51 -33 Slow   [72]
£3094   £884   £442   4 yo rec 2 lb

1076 **THAMES DANCER** 19 [9] K McAuliffe 4-9-9 (69) T E Durcan 12/1: 23-041: 4 ch c Green Dancer - Hata   78
(Kaldoun): Cl-up, hdwy chall 2f out, sn led, drvn out: op 10/1: up in trip: first win: plcd twice in
'99 (rtd 71 & 62a, h'caps), prev term rtd 77 on debut: eff at 12f, clearly relished this step up to 2m,
even further bhd suit: acts on gd, gd/sft & gall or sharp/undul trk.
1087 **SHARAF** 18 [10] W R Muir 7-8-0 (42)(2ow) Sophie Mitchell 16/1: 45-P42: 7 b g Sadler's Wells - Marie   ½ 51
de Randre (Crystal Palace): Handy, ev ch until no extra well inside last: clr rem: costly 2lbs o/w: see 1087.
3509] **HAL HOO YAROOM** 272 [5] J R Jenkins 7-8-13 (57) F Norton 12/1: 1145-3: 7 b h Belmez - Princess   6 58
Nawaal (Seattle Slew): Mid-div, styd on well final 2f, no ch with front 2: 8 wks ago scored over timber at Fontwell
(h'cap, rtd 106h at best, eff at 2m1f/2m4f on firm & gd, runs well fresh, sharp trks): '99 Flat wnr at Bath &
Warwick (h'caps, rtd 63): also won over hdles: eff at 13f, suited by 2m/2m1f: acts on firm, gd & both AWs.
1044 **GALAPINO** 22 [7] Jamie Poulton 7-8-7 (51) P Doe 9/1: 400-54: Dwelt, settled rear, rdn to impr 3f   ¾ 51
out, kept on but no ch with ldrs: wknd by a return to a more gall trk: see 1044.
1817} **DUTCH DYANE** 348 [17] 7-7-10 (40)(6oh) D Kinsella (7) 14/1: 2/03-5: Sn in tch, hdwy to lead 3f out,   hd 40
hdd dist, wknd: '99/00 hdles scorer at Fontwell & Leicester (h'cap, rtd 99h at best, eff at 2m/2m6.5f on gd, hvy,
any trk): plcd 2nd of 2 '99 Flat starts (h'cap, rtd 36): '98 rnr-up (h'cap, rtd 36): eff at 12f/2m on firm & soft.
1023 **MEILLEUR** 26 [3] D Wallace (7) 16/1: -23606: Settled in tch, rdn to impr 3f out, sn btn.   nk 56
-- **LE TETEU** [12] 7-8-11 (55) Gemma Jones (7) 20/1: 1003/7: Bhd, late gains, no threat: plcd once   2 52
over timber in 99/00 (h'cap, rtd 102h, eff at 2m on gd & firm): Flat wnr way back in '96, at Haydock (1m h'cap, gd).

917   **TREASURE CHEST** 36 [11] 5-9-10 (68)(vis) D R McCabe 16/1: 250-08: Dwelt, nvr a threat, late gains: ½   64
plcd twice over timber in 99/00 (h'caps, rtd 85h, eff at 2m7f on hvy): plcd twice on the level in '99 (h'caps, rtd
77 at best): dual '98 rnr-up (h'caps, rtd 82, M Tregoning): eff at 2m/2m2.5f on fast: best in t-strap & visor.
1044   **WONTCOSTALOTBUT** 22 [20] 6-8-12 (56) K Fallon 5/2 FAV: 134-29: Rear, gd hdwy over 2f out,   1   51
wknd qckly appr final 1f: nicely bckd, reportedly in season: btr 1044 (hvy).
1180   **MU TADIL** 13 [6] 8-7-10 (40)(5oh) J Bramhill 40/1: 200-00: Rear, late gains, fin 10th: plcd   1   34
twice in '99 (h'caps, rtd 41 at best): eff at 2m2f on firm & gd/soft grnd.
1167   **NEEDWOOD SPIRIT** 14 [15] 5-9-4 (62) S Drowne 6/1: 45-020: Nvr a factor: 11th: tchd 10/1: btr 1167.   1½   54
--   **GIVE AND TAKE** [14] 7-8-1 (45) G Bardwell 25/1: 0355/0: Sn prom, rdn/fdd fnl 3f: 12th: jumps fit.   4   33
726   **WILD COLONIAL BOY** 56 [13] 5-7-10 (40)(1oh) C Adamson 33/1: 0-4400: Mid-div at best: 13th: abs.   2½   25
3925}   **DURHAM** 248 [1] 9-9-2 (60) S Clancy (7) 16/1: 2200-0: Prom, grad lost tch after halfway, fin 14th.   3   42
1087   **JOLI SADDLERS** 18 [16] 4-7-12 (44)(BL) R Brisland (5) 33/1: 00-000: Trkd ldrs till went on 5f   5   21
out, hdd 3f out, fdd, fin 15th: bnkd.
1209   **RED BORDEAUX** 11 [8] 5-8-0 (44)(bl) C Catlin (6) 14/1: 0-0050: Led, hdd 5f out, sn lost tch, fin 19th.   0
1065   **Browns Flight** 19 [19] 4-8-1 (45)(2ow) R Ffrench 33/1: 4154}   **Sure Future** 234 [18] 4-8-8 (54)(bl) C Urbina 20/1:
3315}   **Fujiyama Crest** 281 [4] 8-10-0 (72)(vis) J Lowe 20/1:   1180   **United Front** 13 [2] 8-8-4 (48)(VIS) S Carson (5) 25/1:
20 ran   Time 3m 38.73 (13.53)   (Delamere Cottage Racing Partners)   K McAuliffe Lambourn, Berks.

1395   6.35 T DAVIDFIELD HCAP 3YO+ 0-60 (F)   1m1f   Good 51   -44 Slow   [60]
£2772   £792   £396   3 yo rec 13lb

*1272   **JUNIKAY** 8 [12] R Ingram 6-9-11 (57) K Fallon 6/4 FAV. 4-0211: 6 b g Treasure Kay - Junijo (Junius):   64
Bhd, smooth hdwy 2f out, pshd into lead ins last, eased cl-home, cmftbly: nicely bckd: recent Nottingham wnr
(h'cap): '99 wnr of same race at Nottingham (rtd 57), prev term scored at Brighton (h'cap, rtd 57): loves to
come late over 1m/10f on firm, gd/soft & any trk, likes Nottingham: in fine form, can complete the hat-trick.
4579}   **THIHN** 201 [7] N E Berry 5-9-7 (53) Dane O'Neill 7/1: 0522-2: 5 ch g Machiavellian - Hasana   1½   54
(Private Account): Settled in tch, hdwy to chall 2f out, not pace of wnr well ins last: op 4/1 on reappr: rnr-up on
fnl 2 '99 starts (h'caps, rtd 55 at best): twice rcd in '98 (well btn): eff at 9f/10f on gd & soft grnd.
4314}   **WITH A WILL** 222 [4] H Candy 9-6-8 (54) C Rutter 9/1: 6040-3: 6 b g Rambo Dancer - Henceforth   nk   54
(Full Of Hope): Prom, drvn to lead over 1f out, hdd well ins last, no extra: reappr: 4th at best in '99 (h'caps,
rtd 62 at best): back in '98 scored at Kempton (appr h'cap) & Lingfield (h'cap, rtd 62), prev term won at Chepstow
(h'cap, rtd 64): suited by 9f, stays 10f: acts on fast & gd/soft, possibly soft: likes an easy/turning trk.
1076   **WESTMINSTER CITY** 19 [9] D R C Elsworth 4-9-7 (53) N Pollard 5/1: 212U04: Handy, rdn to chall   1½   50
over 1f out, sn btn: clr rem, op 4/1: drop in trip & will apprec a return to 10f+: see 748.
880   **MULLAGHMORE** 38 [8] 4-9-11 (57)(bl) Pat Eddery 5/1: -15155: Led, hdd appr final 1f, wknd   7   44
qckly: turf return: btr 620 (10f, equitrack).
--   **CLIFTON WOOD** [10] 5-9-7 (53) J Bramhill 25/1: 5600/6: Cl-up, ev ch until fdd appr final 1f: 1   38
9 wk jumps abs (modest form): rtd 64 on '98 Flat debut (mdn, rtd 66).
4522}   **TARSKI** 207 [2] 6-9-6 (52) S Carson (5) 14/1: 3650-7: In tch, effort 3f out, sn held: '99 Goodwood   hd   37
scorer (h'cap, rtd 58): rtd 79 at best in '98, prev term plcd once for H Cecil (rtd 92): suited by 10f, stays 12f,
has tried 12f: acts on fast & gd grnd: runs well fresh & handles any trk: well h'capped.
1259   **TEST THE WATER** 8 [11] 6-10-0 (60) B O'Leary (7) 25/1: 062-08: Sn outpcd, late hdwy: rnr-up fnl   4   38
'99 start (sell, rtd 70): '98 Sandown wnr (clmr, rtd 80): eff at 1m/9f on fast, gd/soft, any trk: without bnkrs.
1129   **INDIAN WARRIOR** 16 [3] 4-9-7 (53) P Shea 25/1: 660009: Al bhd, t.o.   21   6
1201   **LALA SALAMA** 12 [14] 4-9-6 (52) J Fortune 11/1: 000-00: Prom, wknd qckly fnl 3f, t.o.: 10th: op 8/1.   8   0
859   **ELBA MAGIC** 40 [13] 5-9-12 (58) D R McCabe 14/1: 00-000: Al well bhd, t.o. in 11th: 6 wk abs.   7   0
1129   **GREEN TURTLE CAY** 16 [5] 4-10-0 (60) T E Durcan 33/1: 006-00: Keen in tch, wknd qckly fnl 3f, last.   0
12 ran   Time 1m 58.15 (7.65)   (Ellangowan Racing Partners)   R Ingram Epsom, Surrey.

1396   7.10 APPLES & PEARS SELLER 2YO (G)   6f str   Good 51   -30 Slow
£1928   £551   £275

1197   **CHAWENG BEACH** 12 [11] R Hannon 2-8-6 Dane O'Neill 4/1: 01: 2 ro f Chaddleworth - Swallow Bay   62
(Penmarric): Cl-up, rdn to lead appr fnl 1f, styd on strongly, drvn out to hold on: bought in for 5,400gns:
cheaply bought Mar foal, dam juv 6f wnr: eff at 6f, 7f could suit: acts on gd grnd & a sharp/undul trk.
1208   **CEDAR TSAR** 11 [5] R J O'Sullivan 2-8-11 S Sanders 6/1: 62: 2 b c Inzar - The Aspecto Girl (Alzao)   shd   66
Cl-up, chall appr final 1f, styd on well, just failed: op 4/1, clr rem: eff at 6f on gd, win a sell: see 1208.
1304   **LONDON EYE** 5 [9] K T Ivory 2-8-6 (BL) C Catlin (7) 20/1: 0603: 2 b f Distinctly North - Clonavon   3½   52
Girl (Be My Guest): Led, hdd over 1f out, not pace of front 2: tried in bnkrs: qck reappr: see 932.
1206   **ORCHARD RAIDER** 12 [7] C A Dwyer 2-8-11 (t) G Bardwell 5/1: -024: Cl-up, eff appr final 1f,   2½   51
sn held: tchd 7/1: up in trip: see 1206 (5f, fibresand).
--   **PRESENTOFAROSE** [8] 2-8-6 F Norton 10/1: 5: Dwelt, ran green in rear, late hdwy: op 8/1, debut: 2½   40
cheaply bought Apr foal, half-sister to a 6f juv wnr: dam unrcd: with J S Moore, a glimmer of ability here.
1020   **SILKEN TOUCH** 26 [6] 2-8-6 Pat Eddery 9/4 FAV: -26: Bhd, nvr with ldrs: well bckd & much   7   25
better expected after a promising debut in 1020 (5f, hvy).
712   **HARRY JUNIOR** 57 [4] 2-8-11 (t) P Clarke (7) 16/1: 67: Nvr a threat after 8 wk abs: see 712.   hd   30
1206   **PRINCESS PENNY** 12 [3] 2-8-6 A Daly 12/1: R38: Prom, wknd rapidly fnl 2f: up in trip: see 1206.   2½   19
1124   **A B MY BOY** 16 [1] 2-8-11 S Carson (5) 25/1: 609: Sn outpcd: see 891.   2   18
856   **ELEANOR J** 40 [12] 2-8-6 R Ffrench (7): 460: Handy, rdn to impr halfway, sn btn: 10th: 6 wk abs.   ½   12
856   **Molly Irwin** 40 [2] 2-8-12 N Farmer (7) 20/1:   1260   **Dripping In Gold** 8 [10] 2-8-6 P Doe 16/1:
12 ran   Time 1m 13.69 (4.89)   (F Coen)   R Hannon East Everleigh, Wilts.

1397   7.40 PETTICOAT CLASSIFIED STKS 3YO 0-70 (E)   7f str   Good 51   -23 Slow
£3094   £884   £442

1273   **SANTIBURI GIRL** 3 [3] J R Best 3-8-8 R Mullen 11/2: 00-061: 3 b f Casteddu - Lake Mistassiu   66
(Tina's Pet): Rdn/rear, gd hdwy 2f out, led inside last, drvn out: nicely bckd tho' op 9/2: '99 Salisbury
wnr (nov auct, rtd 87): suited by 7f, has tried 1m: acts on fast & gd, poss soft: acts on a sharp/undul trk.
887   **DISTANT GUEST** 38 [9] G G Margarson 3-8-11 (BL) S Sanders 8/1: 00-202: 3 b c Distant Relative -   1   66
Teacher's Game (Mummy's Game): Cl-up, drvn to lead appr final 1f, hdd inside last, no extra cl-home:
clr rem: op 6/1 & a gd effort in first time bnkrs: acts on gd & soft grnd: see 813.
1175   **TATTENHAM STAR** 13 [1] M J Haynes 3-8-11 S Drowne 9/2 FAV: 50-363: 3 b c Mistertopogigo -   2½   62
Candane (Danehill): Keen in tch, chall 2f out, no extra fnl 1f: tchd 6/1: up in trip: see 837 (flattered).

LINGFIELD SATURDAY MAY 20TH Lefthand, Sharp, Undulating Track

740 **WELSH VALLEY** 54 [8] M L W Bell 3-8-8 M Fenton 11/2: 02-204: Sn clr ldr, hdd appr final 1f, wknd: ½ 58
8 wk abs: possibly not stay 7f: btr 685 (6f mdn, AW).
3958} **PREMIER FOIS** 246 [4] 3-8-8 R Cochrane 15/2: -15-5: Waited with, rdn/late gains, no threat: 1¼ 56
reapp, op 6/1: '99 debut scorer here at Lingfield (auct mdn, rtd 71): eff at 6f, this 7f trip & further
should suit in time: acts on fast grnd, runs well fresh on a sharp/undul trk.
1099 **MOBO BACO** 18 [5] 3-8-11 O Urbina 16/1: 0406: Dwelt, sn outpcd, late hdwy: needs 1m+?: see 1099. nk 59
1061 **BISHOPSTONE MAN** 19 [2] 3-8-11 A Daly 11/2: 030-47: Cl-up, drvn & wknd qckly appr final 1f: 6 49
well bckd from 12/1: btr 1061 (h'cap, soft).
1125 **BROMPTON BARRAGE** 16 [6] 3-8-11 (t) Dane O'Neill 6/1: 40-008: Front rank, dropped rear halfway. 2½ 45
1035 **SILVER ARROW** 22 [7] 3-8-8 J Reid 5/1: 4-049: In tch when short of room & dropped last over 3f 1½ 39
out, no ch after: disapp here: see 1035.
9 ran Time 1m 25.56 (5.16) (Alan Turner) J R Best Hucking, Kent.

1398 8.10 OASTWELL WINES HCAP 3YO+ 0-85 (D) 5f str Good 51 +10 Fast [82]
£4075 £1254 £627 £313

*1256 **EASTERN TRUMPETER** 8 [5] J M Bradley 4-8-8 (62) J Fortune 11/4 FAV: 000211: 4 b c First Trump - 67
Oriental Air (Taufan): Dsptd lead, went on over 2f out, prsd inside last, drvn to hold on: fast time: recent
W'hampton (2, h'caps, rtd 72a) & Carlisle wnr (class stks): '99 Folkestone (clmr) & Ayr wnr (h'cap, rtd 70 & 63a):
stays a sharp 5f, best at 5f on firm, soft, fibresand & any trk, likes W'hampton: tough & genuine, in fine form.
-1264 **POLLY GOLIGHTLY** 8 [2] M Blanshard 7-8-11 (65)(bl) C Rutter 9/2: 4-0022: 7 ch m Weldnaas - nk 69
Polly's Teahouse (Shack): Dsptd lead, chall ldr 2f out, duelled with wnr inside last, just failed:
op 3/1: in fine form, deserves to go one better: see 1264.
+1264 **SUPREME ANGEL** 8 [1] M P Muggeridge 5-8-12 (66) Pat Eddery 9/2: 104013: 5 b m Beveled - Blue ¾ 68
Angel (Lord Gayle) Handy, ev ch appr final 1f: rdn/late gains: op 4/1: bt rnr-up on 6lb better terms in 1264.
1074 **FEARBY CROSS** 19 [10] W J Musson 4-9-7 (75) P Shea 5/1: 06-134: Settled rear, edged left over 1½ 73
2f out, ran on strongly inside last, nvr nrr: suited by 6f & a return to that trip will suit: keep in mind: see 763.
1173 **BOLD EFFORT** 14 [3] 8-9-7 (75)(bl) J Reid 16/1: 001005: Mid-div, drvn appr fnl 1f, sn btn: btr 774. nk 72
1264 **AURIGNY** 8 [7] 5-9-10 (78) S Sanders 25/1: 5-0006: Bhd, late gains, no threat: jnt top weight: see 191. shd 75
1173 **PURE COINCIDENCE** 14 [5] 5-9-10 (78) K Fallon 7/1: 0-3007: Led to halfway, rdn & btn over 1f 1½ 71
out: op 5/1, jnt top weight: see 678 (AW).
1211 **MALAAH** 11 [9] 4-7-13 (50)(bl)(3ow) A Daly 20/1: 66-008: Cl-up, drvn & wknd over 1f out: see 1092. nk 45
1133 **BEVELENA** 16 [7] 4-9-7 (75) S Drowne 16/1: 500-09: Prom, wknd qckly over 1f out, eased: see 1133. 2½ 61
1162 **MOUSEHOLE** 14 [4] 8-9-2 (70) M Fenton 20/1: 0-0000: Al outpcd, fin 10th: see 1013. 2½ 50
10 ran Time 58,87 (2.07) (R G G Racing) J M Bradley Sedbury, Gloucs.

1399 8.40 M DE GUINGAND MDN 3YO (D) 6f str Good 51 00 Slow
£3298 £1015 £507 £253

1181 **BUDELLI** 13 [8] M R Channon 3-9-0 Craig Williams 15/2: -36231: 3 b c Elbio - Eves Temptation (Glenstal): 81
Led, hdd appr final 1f, rallied gamely for press inside last to lead cl-home, all-out: well bckd: plcd 3 times
prev this term: rtd 70 when unplcd sole '99 start: eff at 6f, 7f looks sure to suit: acts on firm & hvy
grnd, sharp/undul trk, probably handles any: in fine form.
1175 **VILLA VIA** 13 [2] J A R Toller 3-8-9 R Ffrench 5/1: -532: 3 b f Night Shift - Joma Kaanem (Double nk 75
Form): Trckd ldr, rdn to lead over 1f out, hdd well inside last, just held: op 4/1, clr rem: eff at 6f on
firm & gd: 7f will suit: see 1175.
1181 **JAZZY MILLENNIUM** 13 [14] Miss Gay Kelleway 3-9-0 K Fallon 7/2: 220-03: 3 ch c Lion Cavern - 3½ 71
Woodcrest (Niniski): Prom, rdn to impr 2f out, not pace of ldrs fnl 1f: mkt drifter: will apprec a return to 7f.
4358} **STRATTON** 219 [10] C F Wall 3-9-0 R Mullen 5/2 FAV: 6-4: Dwelt, sn in tch, drvn & no extra appr nk 70
fnl 1f: nicely bckd on reapp: rtd 82 when 6th on sole '99 juv start (mdn): will apprec 7f next time.
1266 **MALARKEY** 8 [20] 3-9-0 F Norton 8/1: 055: Rdn in mid-div, switched & ran on well fnl 2f, flew home, ½ 69+
nvr nrr: now qual for h'caps & looks sure to apprec 7f/1m in that sphere, keep in mind: see 1175.
1280 **TOYON** 7 [15] 3-9-0 S Sanders 16/1: 606: In tch, rdn & styd on appr final 1f, nrst fin: qck 1 66
reapp: sure to impr over further now qual for h'caps: see 1105.
1175 **LANDICAN LAD** 13 [1] 3-9-0 S Carson (5) 25/1: 07: Nvr better than mid-div: see 1175. 1¼ 63
924} **KINSAILE** 397 [11] 3-8-9 A Polli (3) 20/1: 0-8: Trckd ldrs, wknd qckly appr final 1f: rtd 62 on ¾ 56
sole '99 start (mdn, with R Charlton): now with P L Gilligan.
4542} **HANDSOME FANCY** 204 [9] 3-8-9 N Pollard 33/1: 00-9: Nvr a dngr: rtd 59 on 2nd of 2 '99 starts (6f mdn). hd 56
3998} **OUR MEMOIRS** 244 [18] 3-9-0 (t) R Perham 33/1: 0-0: Keen/rear, nvr with ldrs: 10th: mod juv form. 5 49
1175 **LOUP CERVIER** 13 [17] 3-9-0 P Doe 25/1: 000: Sn outpcd, modest late gains: fin 11th: see 1175. ¾ 47
961 **THE JAM SAHEB** 32 [16] 3-9-0 (t) O Urbina 25/1: 00-60: Nvr a factor: fin 12th: see 961. 1½ 43
-- **RETSKI** [6] 3-9-0 J Reid 9/1: 0: Veered right start, al bhd: fin 13th: S Dow newcomer. shd 43
794 **Bokay** 51 [5] 3-8-9 D R McCabe 33/1: 909 **Ozawa** 36 [12] 3-9-0 R Cochrane 33/1:
841 **Tabbettinna Blue** 43 [13] 3-8-9 M Fenton 20/1: -- **Miss Swift** [7] 3-8-9 M Howard (4) 33/1:
17 ran Time 1m 11.85 (3.05) (Mrs C Roper) M R Channon West Isley, Berks.

NEWBURY SATURDAY MAY 20TH Lefthand, Flat, Galloping Track

Official Going GOOD TO FIRM. Stalls: Rnd Crse - Inside; 3:10 - Stands Side; Rem - Centre.

1400 1.30 LONDON CUP RTD HCAP 3YO 0-100 (A) 1m4f Good/Firm 24 -10 Slow [97]
£9123 £3460 £1730 £786

*1106 **CEPHALONIA** 17 [8] J L Dunlop 3-9-2 (85) Pat Eddery 9/2: 004-11: 3 b f Slip Anchor - Cephira (Abdos) 94
Waited with, imprvd 3f out, rdn & qcknd clr appr fnl 1f, cmftbly: well bckd, from 11/2: recent reapp wnr at
Pontefract (h'cap): promise fnl '99 start (mdn, rtd 80): revelation since stepped up to 12f in h'caps, stay
further: acts on fast & gd/soft, stiff trks: runs well fresh: progressive, R Ascot King George V H'cap type.
1199 **MASTER GEORGE** 12 [2] I A Balding 3-8-11 (80) Martin Dwyer 25/1: 2-162: 3 b g Mtoto - Topwinder 2½ 83
(Topsider): Rear, imprvd & tried to go with wnr appr fnl 1f, styd on but nvr any impress: stays 12f on fast & hvy.
998 **KEW GARDENS** 28 [3] Mrs A J Perrett 3-9-5 (88) M J Kinane 11/4 JT FAV: 416-23: 3 ch c Arazi - Hatton 1½ 89
Gardens (Auction Ring) Mid-div, prog & ev ch appr fnl 2f, same pace ins last: well bckd: prob improved in

defeat: styd this longer 12f trip: goes on fast & gd/soft, prob hvy: see 998.
1198 **REFLEX BLUE 12** [1] J W Hills 3-9-4 (87) M Hills 14/1: 125-44: Patiently rdn, prog to chase ldrs 2f out, sn onepace: op 10/1: not disgraced over longer 12f trip: see 1198. *2½* **85**
979 **BOLD EWAR 30** [5] 3-8-10 (79)(bl) G Mosse 9/1: 1-5325: Led till appr fnl 1f, wknd: op 7/1, lngr trip. *3* **73**
*1064 **POMPEII 19** [4] 3-9-1 (84) T Quinn 5/1: 0-2116: Prom till fdd ent fnl 2f: faster grnd, hard race in 1064. *5* **73**
1089 **COLONIAL RULE 18** [6] 3-9-7 (90) J Fortune 14/1: 231-07: Handy till wknd 2f out: op 10/1: longer trip (bred to stay 12f) & top-weight on h'cap bow: see 1089. *1¼* **78**
1225 **FIRST MANASSAS 10** [7] 3-9-1 (84) K Fallon 11/4 JT FAV: 213-08: Held up, brief wide eff 3f out: nicely bckd, stablemate rnr-up: more expected after trble in running at Chester: unproven at 12f: see 1225. *2½* **69**
8 ran Time 2m 33.42 (4.12) (Exors of The Late Lord Howard de Walden) J L Dunlop Arundel, W.Sussex.

1401

2.00 LISTED ASTON PARK STKS 4YO+ (A) 1m5f61y Good/Firm 24 -14 Slow
£14625 £4500 £2250 £1125

657 **SEA WAVE 77** [3] Saeed bin Suroor 5-8-12 (t) L Dettori 7/4 FAV: 343-01: 5 b h Sadler's Wells - Three Tails (Blakeney) Well plcd, led 2f out, rdn briefly, shkn up nr fin, shade rdly: well bckd, 11 wk abs: plcd in a Gr 2 in '99 (rtd 118): prev term won at Lingfield (mdn), Leicester (stks) & York (Gr 2, rtd 123): eff at 12f/13.3f on firm & gd/soft grnd, any trk: runs well fresh: eff with/without t-strap: high-class at best, can rate higher. **114**
987 **LIGHTNING ARROW 28** [5] J L Dunlop 4-8-12 T Quinn 12/1: 430-02: 4 br g Silver Hawk - Strait Lane (Chieftain II) Led, under press appr fnl 2f, sn hdd, styd on: left dismal hvy grnd reapp bhd: dual '99 rnr-up (Gr 3, rtd 105 at best): '98 wnr at Newmarket (stks, rtd 103+): eff btwn 10f & 13.3f: acts on firm & gd/soft, not hvy: goes on any trk, without blnks & is best up with/forcing the pace: very useful. *1¾* **108**
1014 **ZAAJER 26** [6] E A L Dunlop 4-9-1 R Hills 15/2: 604-33: 4 ch c Silver Hawk - Crown Quest (Chief's Crown) In tch, rdn appr fnl 2f, styd on for 3rd: op 6/1: styd lngr 13f trip: acts on fast, suited by soft. *1½* **109**
987 **MAYLANE 28** [9] A C Stewart 6-9-1 M Roberts 10/1: 511-04: Restrained, keen in last, prog to chase front pair appr fnl 1f, sn onepace: clr of rem: goes on fast grnd but seems better on softer nowadays: see 987. *¾* **108**
4608} **MOWBRAY 197** [7] 5-8-12 J Fortune 7/1: 1305-5: Rear, eff 3f out, no impress: op 10/1 on reapp: '99 Goodwood wnr (h'cap, 3rd in the Ebor, rtd 102): '98 Leicester wnr (stks, rtd 103): eff at 12f/14f, tried 2½m: acts on firm & hvy grnd, any trk: can go well fresh, without blnks: stiff task at these weights. *8* **97**
1109 **RAISE A PRINCE 17** [2] 7-8-12 (t) N Callan 14/1: 33-566: Held up, wide prog 4f out, no extra 3f out. *5* **92**
*968 **MOWELGA 31** [1] 6-8-12 Pat Eddery 4/1: 110/17: Mid-div, rdn 4f out, fdd bef 2f out: well bckd: plenty on at the weights & slightly longer trip, also 2nd start back after long absence: see 968 (h'cap, gd/soft). *6* **86**
2194} **GENEROUS TERMS 331** [4] 5-8-12 K Fallon 12/1: /403-8: Prom, eff & btn 3f out, eased dist: stiff task on reapp: lightly rcd/unplcd in '99 (List, rtd 104): '98 wnr at Leicester (mdn) & Salisbury (stks, rtd 102): eff at 12/14f on fast & gd/soft, not firm?: can run well fresh, gall trks: useful but needs a drop in grade. *22* **70**
8 ran Time 2m 50.23 (5.13) (Godolphin) Saeed bin Suroor Newmarket.

1402

2.35 GR 1 LOCKINGE STKS 4YO+ (A) 1m str Good/Firm 24 +13 Fast
£81000 £31050 £15525 £7425

3795} **ALJABR 258** [1] Saeed bin Suroor 4-9-0 L Dettori 8/13 FAV: /214-1: 4 gr c Storm Cat - Sierra Madre (Baillamont) Set gd pace, prsd & rdn appr fnl 1f, kept on well to draw clr ins last: hvly bckd from evs, fast time, reapp: '99 Goodwood wnr (Gr 1 Sussex, rtd 125, broke crse rec): unbtn juv, won at Sandown (mdn), Goodwood (Gr 3) & Longchamp (Gr 1, rtd 119): v eff at 1m: acts on soft, suited by firm/fast: runs v well fresh & loves to force the pace on any trk, likes Goodwood: lightly raced & top-class, hard to beat in the top mile races. **122**
1043 **TRANS ISLAND 22** [2] I A Balding 5-9-0 K Fallon 13/2: 113-22: 5 b h Selkirk - Khubza (Green Desert) Keen in rear, prog 2f out, sn rdn, kept on for 2nd but no ch with wnr: op 5/1: another fine run from this v smart entire, sure to win again back in Gr 2/3 company: see 1043. *2* **117**
*1043 **INDIAN LODGE 22** [5] Mrs A J Perrett 4-9-0 M J Kinane 5/1: 11-113: 4 b c Grand Lodge - Repetitious (Northfields) Prom, chall 2f out, sn edged badly left & rdn, onepace below dist: lost nothing in defeat in this highest grade: goes on fast & hvy grnd, the latter poss suits best: high-class, can continue to give a gd account. *shd* **117**
768 **GOLDEN SILCA 56** [7] M R Channon 4-8-11 S Drowne 33/1: 022-04: In tch, rdn to improve 2f out, kept on but nvr able to chall: 8 wk abs: back to best at favourite track: smart, see 768. *½* **113**
*1049 **SUGARFOOT 21** [3] 6-9-0 R Cochrane 9/1: 125-15: Handy, pushed along when carr badly left ent fnl 2f, no impress dist: wld prob have been 1L or so closer but still a smart effort: relish a return to Gr 3. *¾* **114**
1043 **ALMUSHTARAK 22** [6] 7-9-0 G Mosse 12/1: 320-36: Bhd ldrs, rdn 2f out, unable to qckn: below best today & reportedly returned with a cut fore leg, rtd 118 when 3rd in this last year: see 1043 (just bhd this rnr-up). *2½* **109**
769 **WORLDLY MANNER 56** [4] 4-9-0 (vis) D O'Donohoe 14/1: 0-2D07: Prom till wknd qckly 3f out: 8 wk abs, stablemate wnr: '99 Nad Al Sheba rnr-up (List, subs disqual for banned substances, rtd 116 at best): top US 2yo in '98, winning thrice, joined Godolphin for $5,000,000: eff at 7f, stays 9f, wears blnks/vis: trained on? *10* **89**
7 ran Time 1m 37.64 (0.84) (Godolphin) Saeed bin Suroor Newmarket.

1403

3.10 KINGWOOD MDN 2YO (D) 6f Good/Firm 24 -31 Slow
£4576 £1408 £704 £352

-- **PATSYS DOUBLE** [6] M Blanshard 2-9-0 R Cochrane 20/1: 1: 2 b c Emarati - Jungle Rose (Shirley Heights) Mid-div going well, burst thro' to lead ent fnl 1f, cmftbly: tchd 33/1: 10,000gns May foal, half-brother to 4 wnrs, dam 10f wnr: eff at 6f, will get further: acts on fast grnd & a gall trk: win more races, Ascot bound. **101+**
-- **ECOLOGY** [8] J L Dunlop 2-9-0 M Roberts 16/1: 2: 2 b c Sri Pekan - Ecco Mi (Priolo) Outpcd early, gd prog over 2f out, sn hung left but kept on for 2nd, not touble wnr: tchd 20/1: 21,000gns Mar foal, dam stoutly bred, sire a sprinter: eff at 6f, 7f will suit: acts on fast grnd: winning turn merely delayed. *1¾* **94+**
-- **SNOW BUNTING** [11] R Charlton 2-9-0 S Drowne 6/1: 3: 2 ch c Polar Falcon - Marl (Lycius) Mid-div, short of room 2f out, clr bef dist & ran on, unable to chall: op 4/1: Mar first foal, dam smart 5f juv wnr, sire 6f/1m performer: eff at 6f, 7f will suit in time: goes on fast grnd, sure to improve & win a mdn. *¾* **92**
-- **HATA** [4] R W Armstrong 2-8-9 R Hills 9/4 FAV: 4: Well plcd, led ent fnl 2f till below dist, onepace: hvly bckd from 5/1: Hamas Mar foal, sister to a 6f wnr, dam 6f wnr: gets 6f, has the pace for 5f on fast grnd. *hd* **87**
-- **SIBLA** [10] 2-8-9 L Newman (5) 33/1: 5: Chsd ldrs, lost pl 2f out, rallied well towards fin: 8,000gns Piccolo Mar foal, half-sister to juv wnrs at 6/10f, dam 6f juv wnr, sire a sprinter: 7f lks sure to suit, pleasing. *2½* **80**
-- **TROUBLESHOOTER** [13] 2-9-0 Martin Dwyer 20/1: 6: Front rank & ev ch till onepace bef fnl 1f: tchd 33/1: 8,000gns Ezzoud Mar foal, half-brother to a useful 6f juv, dam NH wnr, sire 10f performer. *nk* **84**
-- **PREFERRED** [2] 2-9-0 R Hughes 12/1: 7: Handy, ev ch 2f out, not pace of ldrs dist & eased: IR£9,000 Distant Relative Feb foal, half-brother to a wnr abroad, sire a miler: with R Hannon. *nk* **83**
-- **AINTNECESSARILYSO** [12] 2-9-0 N Pollard 16/1: 8: Dwelt & bhd, late progress: So Factual *nk* **82+**

Apr foal, half-brother to a pair of modest sprinters, dam 7f wnr, sire a sprinter: will improve, with D Elsworth.
-- **KEEP THE PEACE** [9] 2-9-0 K Fallon 13/2: 9: Nvr a factor: 8,500gns Pertardia Feb foal, brother *1¼* **78**
to a juv wnr abroad, dam 1m/10f wnr, sire a sprinter/miler: with I Balding.
-- **ZELOSO** [5] 2-9-0 M J Kinane 7/1: 0: Dwelt, chsd ldrs wide halfway till 2f out: 10th, *½* **77**
op 9/2, stablemate rnr-up: 72,000gns Alzao Jan foal, half-brother to 4 wnrs: dam useful 7f/1m wnr.
-- **BAD AS I WANNA BE** [3] 2-9-0 Pat Eddery 11/2: 0: Well plcd, rdn & held when short of room bef dist, *¾* **75**
lost pl: 11th, tchd 7/1: 62,000gns Common Grounds Mar foal, brother to a 7f juv wnr: sire spinter/miler: B Meehan.
-- **ANALYZE** [7] 2-9-0 T Quinn 9/1: 0: Led till ent fnl 2f, no exrta: 12th: 37,000gns Anabaa Feb foal. *2* **69**
-- **COURT ONE** [1] 2-9-0 F Norton 33/1: 0: Sn struggling: 13th: Shareef Dancer Mar foal, brother *20* **39**
to a mid-dist h'capper, dam a hdles wnr, sire 12f performer, with M Quinn.
13 ran Time 1m 14.9 (3.3) (Mrs Patricia Buckley) M Blanshard Upper Lambourn, Berks.

1404

3.40 HATHERDEN MDN 3YO (D) 1m2f Good/Firm 24 -28 Slow
£4836 £1488 £744 £372

-- **SUBTLE POWER** [15] H R A Cecil 3-9-0 T Quinn 7/2: 1: 3 b c Sadler's Wells - Mosaique Bleue **92+**
(Shirley Heights) Towards rear, imprvd ent str, led bef dist, kept on strongly, pushed out: op 11/4, slow time, debut: IR 36,000gns colt: eff at 10f, will enjoy 12f+: acts on fast grnd & a gall trk, runs well fresh: potentially very useful colt, sure to rate higher & hold his own in better company, well regarded.
-- **RED EMPRESS** [7] Sir Michael Stoute 3-8-9 R Ffrench 33/1: 2: 3 b f Nashwan - Nearctic Flame *1¼* **83**
(Sadler's Wells) Prom, led 3f out, rdn 2f out, sn hdd, styd on: op 12/1, debut: regally bred half-sister to 3 smart mid-dist wnrs, dam v useful 10f wnr: eff at 10f, 12f suit: goes on fast grnd & mdn looks a formality.
1200 **ARDUINE 12** [5] J H M Gosden 3-8-9 L Dettori 11/4 FAV: 6-33: 3 ch f Diesis - Ardisia (Affirmed) *shd* **83**
Well plcd thr'out, rdn 2f out, styd on but not pace to chall: hvly bckd from 11/2: another gd run: see 1200.
-- **STAGE DIRECTION** [21] J H M Gosden 3-9-0 J Fortune 10/1: 4: Waited with, wide stdy hdwy in the *nk* **87+**
str, nrst fin: op 8/1, not given a hard time on debut, stablemate 3rd: Theatrical half-brother to high-class 7f/10f wnr Ryafan: eff at 10f, looks sure to improve over 12f: handles fast grnd: expect him to rate higher & win soon.
-- **RAGDALE HALL** [13] 3-9-0 R Havlin 33/1: 5: Mid-div, shkn up appr fnl 2f, styd on but nvr able to *1¼* **85**
chall: stablemate 3rd/4th, debut: $130,000 Bien Bien colt: handles fast grnd & will know more next time.
1012 **FINISHED ARTICLE 26** [20] 3-9-0 N Pollard 16/1: 50-46: Chsd ldrs, eff 2f out, kept on same pace: *½* **84**
probably styd longer 10f trip on fast grnd: see 1012.
-- **DALAMPOUR** [4] 3-9-0 K Fallon 11/2: 7: Off the pace, styd on thr' btn horses fnl 2f, nvr on terms: *1¼* **82+**
op 4/1, st/mate rnr-up, clr rem: Shernazar half-brother to high-class mid-dist colt Daliapour: relish 12f & win.
1099 **TOORAK 18** [9] 3-9-0 G Mosse 25/1: 6-08: Nvr btr than mid-div: longr trip, now qual for h'caps. *6* **74**
1168 **EJTITHAAB 14** [12] 3-9-0 R Hills 11/2: 6-449: Cl-up, led 3f out till 2f out, fdd: back in trip, see 1168. *shd* **74**
-- **LUCKY ARROW** [10] 3-8-9 M Roberts 50/1: 0: Nvr a threat: 10th: 16,000gns Indian Ridge filly. *nk* **68**
1093 **MAZAARR 18** [6] 3-9-0 S Drowne 50/1: 600: Same place thr'out, kind ride: better in h'caps, *1¼* **71**
1200 **HIGH DRAMA 12** [16] 3-9-0 Martin Dwyer 33/1: 00: In tch, eff 5f out, wknd 2f out: 12th. *1* **69**
-- **BOGUS MIX** [18] 3-8-9 N Callan 50/1: 0: Al bhd: 13th: Linamix half-sister to a cple of mid-dist wnrs. *1½* **62**
-- **BAYSWATER** [1] 3-8-9 M Hills 12/1: 0: Nvr in it: 14th: Caerleon sister to high-class 10f performer Tenby. *3½* **57**
1054 **Cedar Grove 21** [2] 3-9-0 R Hughes 50/1:
-- **Variety** [17] 3-8-9 R Cochrane 25/1:
4171} **Shaan Madary 233** [11] 3-8-9 J Reid 50/1:
1080 **Hazy Heights 19** [8] 3-8-9 Pat Eddery 50/1:
857 **Moose Malloy 40** [14] 3-9-0 P McCabe 50/1:
-- **Ramadanzen** [3] 3-8-9 F Norton 50/1:
20 ran Time 2m 07.99 (5.19) (The Thoroughbred Corporation) H R A Cecil Newmarket.

1405

4.10 HEADLEY FILLIES HCAP 3YO 0-80 (D) 7f str Good/Firm 24 -05 Slow [85]
£4693 £1444 £722 £361 Raced stands side

4495} **LA SPEZIANA 208** [13] D R C Elsworth 3-8-5 (62) N Pollard 12/1: 466-1: 3 b f Perugino - Election **73**
Special (Chief Singer) Cl-up, led going well 2f out, rdn out ins last: winning reapp/h'cap bow: mdn promise in '99 (rtd 71): eff at 7f, has the pace for 6f, tried 1m: acts on fast grnd & a gall trk: runs well fresh: lightly rcd.
1075 **SWIFT DISPERSAL 19** [23] S C Williams 3-9-3 (74) G Faulkner (3) 33/1: 00102: 3 gr f Shareef Dancer - *¾* **82**
Minsden's Image (Dancer's Image) Mid-div, prog to chase wnr appr fnl 1f, styd on for press but being held: apprec drop back in trip: eff at 6/7f on fast & soft grnd: shld win on turf, see 877.
1125 **OMNIHEAT 16** [22] M J Ryan 3-9-2 (73) P McCabe 7/2 FAV: 61-323: 3 b f Ezzoud - Lady Bequick *1¼* **78**
(Sharpen Up) Mid-div, boxed in 3f out till 2f out, styd on for press but not pace to chall: well bckd: tough sort, not much luck in running, worth another try at 1m?: see 933.
1289 **CIBENZE 5** [15] M R Channon 3-8-8 (65) S Drowne 33/1: 53-064: Mid-div, styd on fnl 1½f, nvr nr to *½* **69**
chall: qck reapp: apprec step up to 7f: see 1082.
1053 **FOXS IDEA 21** [17] 3-8-13 (70) R Hills 33/1: -13305: Rear, not clr run ent fnl 2f, switched dist, ran on: *1¼* **71+**
can win on turf off this mark: see 1053.
1063 **SHADY POINT 19** [5] 3-8-12 (69) L Dettori 10/1: 03-056: Rear, late prog, nvr dngrs: h'cap bow, *1* **68**
likely to do better at 1m when ridden closer to the pace: see 1063.
4506} **TIME VALLY 208** [1] 3-8-9 (66) P Doe 40/1: 006-7: Wide & towards rear, gd prog ent fnl 2f, no extra *hd* **65**
ins last: promise on reapp/h'cap bow from tricky draw: promise fnl '99 start (fill mdn, rtd 74): with S Dow.
794 **GOLDEN LOCKET 51** [24] 3-9-1 (72) N Callan 20/1: 500-48: Rear, some late prog, nvr on terms. *nk* **70**
857 **PINHEIROS DREAM 40** [11] 3-8-13 (70) Pat Eddery 14/1: 300-59: Well plcd till fdd appr fnl 1f: 6 wk abs. *¾* **66**
1061 **FOOTPRINTS 19** [19] 3-9-4 (75) M Roberts 14/1: 21-100: Led till 2f out, grad wknd: 10th, wants 6f. *4* **63**
1085 **MISTY MAGIC 18** [6] 3-8-1 (58) R Ffrench 33/1: 030-00: Prom till 2f out: 11th, see 1085. *1¼* **43**
1201 **PEPETA 12** [16] 3-8-10 (67) K Fallon 8/1: 606-60: Rear, nvr found a clr run: 12th, forget this, see 1201. *2* **48**
3798} **FIRST DRAW 258** [8] 3-8-11 (68) R Cochrane 12/1: -635-0: Pulled hard towards rear, briefly short *nk* **48+**
of room 2f out, nvr plcd to chall: 13th, reapp: ex-Irish, last of 5 in a '99 Listed (rtd 61): stewards looked into this eye-catching run, reportedly refused to settle & suffered a bump: sure to improve with a positive ride.
1126 **BELIEVING 16** [3] 3-9-2 (73) R Hughes 25/1: 50-460: Nvr dngrs, ran widest of all: 14th, longer trip. *shd* **53**
1012 **FAIR IMPRESSION 26** [7] 3-9-4 (75) J Reid 8/1: 02-00: Chsd ldrs wide, no extra 2f out, eased dist: 16th. **0**
4167} **KISSING TIME 233** [18] 3-9-7 (78) J Fortune 14/1: 1506-0: Chsd ldr, eff ent fnl 2f, sn btn: 18th, top-weight, **0**
reapp: '99 Bath wnr (mdn auct, rtd 82): eff at 5f on firm grnd: with P Cole.
4491} **TREWORNAN 210** [10] 3-9-6 (77) T Quinn 10/1: -516-0: Al towards rear: 23rd on reapp: '99 Brighton **0**
wnr (mdn, rtd 82, D Elsworth): eff at 6f, shld stay 7f: acts on gd/soft grnd, handles firm: with J Dunlop.
1061 **Regardez Moi 19** [14] 3-8-5 (62) R Havlin 33/1:
954 **Cinnamon Court 32** [2] 3-9-5 (76) Martin Dwyer 20/1:
4500} **In A Twinkling 208** [4] 3-8-11 (68) M Hills 33/1:
1082 **Leen 18** [12] 3-8-6 (63) F Norton 40/1:
1138 **Kebabs 16** [27] 3-9-4 (75) P Fitzimons (5) 20/1:
1220 **Charming Lotte 10** [26] 3-9-1 (72)(vis) G Mosse 25/1:
1196 **Lady Noor 12** [25] 3-8-7 (64) L Newman (5) 40/1:
1205 **Peggys Rose 12** [9] 3-8-8 (65) M J Kinane 25/1:

NEWBURY SATURDAY MAY 20TH Lefthand, Flat, Galloping Track

3145} **Dusky Virgin** 290 [20] 3-8-4 (61) D O'Donohoe 33/1:
4539} **Cumbrian Princess** 205 [21] 3-8-4 (61) D Sweeney 25/1:
27 ran   Time 1m 26.31 (2.01)   (Pampas Partnership)   D R C Elsworth Whitsbury, Hants.

1406   4.40 CARRIE HCAP 3YO 0-90 (C)   6f   Good/Firm 24   00 Fast   [95]
£7312   £2250   £1125   £562   Raced stands side

1060 **RAVISHING** 19 [11] W J Haggas 3-8-10 (77) M Hills 10/1: 1-41: 3 b f Bigstone - Dazzling Maid   81
(Tate Gallery) Towards rear, prog 2f out & grad switched to outside, ran on strongly to lead towards fin: op
12/1, fair time, h'cap bow: won sole '99 start at Pontefract (auct mdn, rtd 85): eff at 6f, tried 7f latest: acts
on fast & gd, handles soft, gall/undul trk: runs well fresh: only lightly raced, on the upgrade.
2661} **SALVIATI** 311 [8] Mrs A J Perrett 3-9-4 (85) M J Kinane 10/1: 31-2: 3 b c Lahib - Mother Courage   hd   88
(Busted) Held up, gd prog to lead appr fnl 1f, sn rdn, worn down nr fin: op 7/1 on reapp/h'cap bow: landed
fnl '99 start at Folkestone (mdn, rtd 83): eff at 6f, shld get further: acts on firm & gd/soft grnd, gall/undul.
982   **ILLUSIVE 30** [14] M Wigham 3-8-3 (70) (bl) F Norton 33/1: 411203: 3 b c Night Shift - Mirage (Red   ¾   71
Sunset) Mid-div, wide, prog & ev ch appr fnl 1f, not pace of front pair: acts on fast & both AWs, handles gd/soft.
1153 **MOLLY BROWN** 15 [13] R Hannon 3-9-2 (83) R Hughes 14/1: 105-04: Led stands side till dist, onepace: ½   82
'99 Haydock debut wnr (mdn, rtd 88): eff at 5f, stays 6f: acts on fast & gd grnd & suited up with/forcing the pace.
1285 **NORFOLK REED** 7 [9] L Newman 3-9-5 (86) L Newman 10/1: 020-45: Rear, gd prog & drifted left appr   hd   84
fnl 1f, unable to chall: stablemate 4th, qck reapp: reapp at 7f now: see 1285.
1220 **ALJAWF** 10 [18] R Hills 5/2 FAV: 51-06: Towards rear, boxed in 2f out, switched bef   shd   82
dist, ran on, nrst fin: hvly bckd from 4/1: no luck in running: interesting at 7f next time: see 1220.
*1289 **PEDRO JACK** 5 [1] 3-8-13 (80) Pat Eddery 6/1: 10-317: Rcd alone in centre till 2f out &   ½   76
prob overall ldr, brght right & hdd bef dist, no extra: tchd 8/1, qck reapp & penalty for 1289.
1178 **MISTER SUPERB** 13 [12] 3-9-1 (82) R Cochrane 4/1: 640-38: Waited with, nowhere to go appr fnl 2f   ¾   76
till bef dist, styd on: nicely bckd, tchd 10/1: needs a step up 7f/1m & a more positive ride: see 1178.
206   **PERUVIAN CHIEF** 154 [15] 3-9-7 (88) T G McLaughlin 33/1: 2113-9: Front rank, rdn ent fnl 2f, squeezed   ½   81
for room appr fnl 1f, onepace & eased nr fin: op 20/1, top-weight, reapp: worth another chance, see 1112
1285 **BLUE VELVET** 7 [10] 3-9-2 (83) L Dettori 12/1: 24-600: Bhd, late hdwy, nvr dngrs: 10th, see 982.   nk   75
1153 **CHIQUITA** 15 [7] 3-8-11 (78) J Fortune 11/1: 11-500: Bhd, not much room 2f out, mod late hdwy: 11th.   1   67
1178 **HUNTING TIGER** 13 [17] 3-9-1 (82) J Reid 25/1: 2-0000: Chsd ldrs till 2f out: 12th, see 792.   3½   62
4145} **FOLLOW SUIT** 234 [16] 3-9-0 (81) T Quinn 14/1: -15-0: Al bhd: reapp, h'cap bow: '99 debut wnr   0
at York (auct mdn, rtd 82): eff at 6f on fast grnd & can go well fresh: with J Dunlop.
*1220 **RAILROADER** 10 [14] 3-8-13 (80) S Drowne 8/1: 40-610: Prom till appr fnl 2f: 16th, disapp after 1220.   0
1261 Mind The Silver **8** [3] 3-7-12 (65) R Brisland (5) 33/1: 982 Loves Design **30** [5] 3-8-7 (74)(vis) D O'Donohoe 20/1:
1289 Frampant **5** [2] 3-7-12 (65) Martin Dwyer 33/1:   1220 Feast Of Romance **10** [6] 3-8-4 (71) R Havlin 25/1:
18 ran   Time 1m 13.04 (1.44)   (G C Johnston)   W J Haggas Newmarket.

NOTTINGHAM SATURDAY MAY 20TH Lefthand, Galloping Track

Official Going   GOOD. Stalls: 5/6f - Stands Side, Rem - Inside.

1407   2.00 CHANDLER CLASSIFIED STKS 3YO+ 0-70 (E)   1m54y rnd   Good 40   -33 Slow
£3038   £868   £434   3 yo rec 12lb

1275 **HUGWITY** 7 [2] G C Bravery 8-9-5 A Nicholls (3) 3/1: 033621: 8 ch g Cadeaux Genereux - Nuit d'Ete   75
(Super Concorde): Chsd ldrs, briefly no room 2f out, prog to lead over 1f out & in command inside last, pushed out
cl-home: op 7/2: earlier scored twice at Lingfield (AW clmrs, rtd 83a): '99 scorer again at Lingfield (h'cap, rtd
86a): eff between 7f/10f on fast, gd/soft & both AWs: handles any trk: loves Lingfield: tough & genuine.
4225} **MAGIC FLUTE** 229 [10] Lady Herries 4-9-2 S Sanders 7/1: 5P20-2: 4 ch f Magic Ring - Megan's Flight   2   69
(Welsh Pageant): Towards rear, rdn & styd on final 2f, no impress on wnr: op 6/1, reapp: rnr-up in '99 (rtd 71,
h'cap): eff at 1m, dam a wng styr, worth a try at 10f+: acts on firm grnd & a gall/easy trk: mdn, shld find a race.
794   **SADAKA** 51 [1] E A L Dunlop 3-8-4 G Duffield 12/1: 30-03: 3 ch f Kingmambo - Basma (Grey Dawn II):   3   63
Chsd ldrs, onepace fnl 2f: op 10/1, abs: plcd in '99 (debut, rtd 74, fill mdn): eff at 7f/1m, handles firm & gd.
1113 **QUEENS PAGEANT** 17 [8] J L Spearing 6-9-2 G Hind 8/1: 050-04: Held up, kept on fnl 2f, nrst fin.   ½   62
1075 **ASSURED PHYSIQUE** 19 [4] 3-8-7 D Harrison 10/1: 600-05: Led/dsptd lead 6f, fdd final 1f: op 12/1.   ¾   64
1150 **FLAG FEN** 15 [13] 9-9-5 D McGaffin (7) 12/1: 005-06: Held up, efft 3f out/no impress: op 10/1: see 1150.   1   62
842   **KEZ** 43 [12] 4-9-5 R Fitzpatrick (3) 16/1: 000-07: Prom, led 2f out, hdd/fdd over 1f out: abs, op 14/1.   1½   62
3860} **ARTFUL DANE** 253 [9] 8-9-5 (bl) J Weaver 50/1: 0004-8: Held up, effort 3f out, sn held: reapp: plcd   7   48$
form in '99 (rtd 51, h'cap): unplcd in '98 (rtd 84): '97 Doncaster reapp wnr (val h'cap, rtd 78): suited by 1m on
firm & gd/soft: best in a visor, tried binks: has run well fresh.
1195 **ALABAMY SOUND** 13 [7] 4-9-2 J F Egan 10/1: 441-49: Held up, effort 3f out, no impress: see 1195.   9   32
1144 **SPIRIT OF LIGHT** 15 [11] 3-8-7 M Tebbutt 5/1: -00230: Chsd ldrs 6f: 10th: op 7/2: btr 1144, 999.   ¾   34
*1144 **LADY OF WINDSOR** 15 [3] 3-8-7 (vis) M Fenton 9/1: 04-510: Led 1f, hdd 3f out, sn btn/eased: 11th.   22   2
11 ran   Time 1m 45.4 (6.0)   (Sawyer Whatley Partnership)   G C Bravery Newmarket, Suffolk.

1408   2.30 E-MAIL MED AUCT MDN 2YO DIV I (E)   6f str   Good 40   -33 Slow
£2646   £756   £378   Raced stands side

--   **PARVENUE** [12] E A L Dunlop 2-8-9 W Ryan 4/1: 1: 2 b f Ezzoud - Patria (Mr Prospector):   78
Bhd ldrs, swtchd 2f out & prog to lead 1f out, readily pulled clr ins last, readily: op 9/4: Feb foal, first foal:
dam a 7.5f juv wnr: eff at 6f, 7f+ will suit: acts on gd & a gall trk: runs well fresh: open to further improvement.
1048 **BAREFOOTED FLYER** 21 [9] T D Barron 2-8-9 C Lowther 8/1: 02: 2 ch f Fly So Free - Carmelita   4   66
(Mogambo) Held up, rdn/outpcd halfway, styd on well for press from over 1f out, no threat to wnr: left debut bhd:
eff at 6f, will apprec 7f+: acts on gd grnd: see 1048.
1130 **EL MAXIMO** 16 [9] M G Quinlan 2-9-0 J F Egan 7/2 FAV: 63: 2 b c First Trump - Kentucky Starlet   shd   71
(Cox's Ridge): Led, rdn/hdd 1f out, kept on onepace: op 5/2: stays 6f: see 1130 (5f).
1236 **BORDER EDGE** 9 [4] K McAuliffe 2-9-0 J Tate 33/1: 04: Prom, ch 2f out, onepace fnl 1f: see 1236.   nk   70
--   **YOUNG JACK** [11] 2-9-0 D McGaffin (7) 14/1: 5: Held up/rdn halfway, styd on inside last, no threat: nk   69
Reprimand colt, Feb foal, half-brother to a 7f AW wnr: dam a 7f wnr: should learn from this & apprec 7f+ in time.
1046 **IVANS BRIDE** 22 [8] 2-8-9 S Sanders 25/1: 06: Held up, effort halfway, onepace: see 1046 (5f).   1½   60

468

-- **SOMERS HEATH** [2] 2-8-9 K Darley 8/1: 7: Cl-up, wknd final 1f: Definite Article filly, Feb foal, cost ¾ 58
4,700 IR gns: first foal: dam a lightly rcd mdn, sire a high class 2yo, subs best at 10/12f: with T D Easterby.
1130 **PATRICIAN FOX 16** [3] 2-8-9 A Culhane 8/1: 08: Prom, fdd over 1f out: see 1130. 4 48
1067 **TIRANA 19** [5] 2-9-0 J Fanning 25/1: -09: Trkd ldrs, btn 1f out: bhd debut prev. 2½ 46
-- **TRAVELLERS DREAM** [1] 2-9-0 G Hind 12/1: 0: Dwelt, al rear, 10th: op 14/1: Blues Traveller colt, ¾ 44
Apr foal, cost 18,000 gns: dam an unrcd half-sister to a wnr abroad: sire high class 9/12f performer.
-- **SIMPLY REMY** [13] 2-9-0 D Williamson (7) 20/1: 0: Dwelt, nvr a factor: 11th: Chaddleworth gelding, ½ 42
Mar foal, cost 6,000 gns: first foal: dam unplcd abroad: with John Berry.
-- **Springborne Jasmin** [7] 2-8-9 (t) R Fitzpatrick (3) 50/1932 **Dance With Me 33** [6] 2-9-0 D R McCabe 16/1:
13 ran   Time 1m 15.2 (4.4)   (Hesmonds Stud)   E A L Dunlop Newmarket, Suffolk.

1409 3.00 AKINS CLASSIFIED STKS 3YO 0-85 (C) 6f str Good 40 -22 Slow
£8541 £2628 £1314 £657

*1285 **SAN SALVADOR 7** [7] J Noseda 3-9-4 J Weaver 1/5 FAV: -32111: 3 b c Dayjur - Sheer Gold (Cutlass): 94
Cl-up, niggled at halfway, shkn up to lead over 1f out & edged left inside last, al just holding rivals, pushed out:
bckd at long odds on: earlier scored at Pontefract (mdn) & Lingfield (val h'cap, by 9L, rtd 103): eff at 6f, could
stay 7f: acts on gd & gd/soft grnd: handles a sharp or stiff/undul trk: useful colt, shld rate higher.
1111 **LOCHARATI 17** [2] J M P Eustace 3-9-1 J Tate 16/1: -102: 3 ch c Emarati - Lochspring (Precocious): ¾ 87
In tch, rdn/outpcd briefly 2f out, styd on inside last, al just held: op 12/1: acts on gd & gd/soft: see 837.
1220 **BABY BARRY 10** [1] Mrs G S Rees 3-8-12 G Duffield 20/1: 12-003: 3 b c Komaite - Malcesine (Auction nk 84
Ring): Cl-up racing keenly, ch/edged left over 1f out, kept on: not btn far: see 1220, 954.
4081} **MELANZANA 239** [4] E A L Dunlop 3-8-9 M Tebbutt 8/1: 31-4: Held up, keen, briefly no room over 1f shd 81
out, onepace nr fin: op 7/1, reapp: '99 Redcar wnr (fill mdn): eff at 6f, 7f should suit: acts on fm & gd, gall trk.
1219 **KILBRANNAN SOUND 11** [5] 3-8-9 J F Egan 10/1: 210-45: Cl-up, rdn 2f out, sn no extra: op 8/1. 3½ 72
1205 **BULAWAYO 12** [3] 3-8-12 R Mullen 66/1: -14046: Led, rdn 2f out, hdd over 1f out, sn held: see 362 (AW). 1 73$
6 ran   Time 1m 14.5 (3.7)   (Lucayan Stud)   J Noseda Newmarket, Suffolk.

1410 3.30 LISTED KILVINGTON FILLIES STKS 3YO+ (A) 6f str Good 40 +12 Fast
£13862 £5258 £2629 £1195 3 yo rec 9 lb Raced stands side

*1283 **HOT TIN ROOF 7** [7] T D Easterby 4-9-6 K Darley 9/2: 30-211: 4 b f Thatching - No Reservations 108
(Commanche Run): Held up, rdn final 2f & prog to lead inside last, styd on strongly, rdn out: fast time: recent
Lingfield scorer (Listed fillies stks): '99 Newcastle wnr (J Banks, fillies mdn, subs plcd in a Listed contest, rtd
103): eff at 6/7f on firm & soft, any trk: tough, v useful & improving, worth a try in Group company.
1185 **HALLAND PARK GIRL 13** [11] R Hannon 3-8-11 Dane O'Neill 5/1: 11-602: 3 b f Primo Dominie - Katsina 1½ 103
(Cox's Ridge): Led, rdn/hdd inside last, no extra: apprec return to sprint trip: reportedly may drop to 5f next time.
4376} **MAGIC OF LOVE 218** [8] M L W Bell 3-8-7 M Fenton 8/1: 1131-3: 3 b f Magic Ring - Mistitled (Miswaki): hd 98
Prom, trav well, ev ch over 1f out, no extra inside last: op 13/2, reapp: '99 scorer at Beverley (fillies auct mdn),
Lingfield (fillies stks) & Newmarket (val auct stks, also plcd in Gr 2 company, rtd 100 at best): eff at 5/6f on firm
& gd grnd, sharp/stiff trk: useful filly who shld be plcd to effect.
*1175 **ARABESQUE 13** [9] H R A Cecil 3-8-7 W Ryan 9/4: 32-314: Cl-up, rdn/held 1f out: well bckd, op 9/2. 2 93
1078 **JEZEBEL 19** [5] 3-8-11 R Mullen 5/1: -11-25: Held up, effort over 1f out, sn onepace: see 1078. shd 97
1133 **SAPHIRE 16** [6] 4-9-2 K Hodgson 50/1: 00-056: Held up, rdn/mod late gains, no threat: likes 1¼ 90$
soft grnd & interesting back in h'caps off correct mark of 80: see 1133.
1090 **FLAVIAN 18** [10] 4-9-2 C Rutter 33/1: 1/0-07: Prom, wknd final 1f: see 1090. hd 89
1090 **KASHRA 18** [3] 3-8-7 J Fanning 9/1: 146-48: Bhd ldrs, effort over 1f out, sn btn: op 13/2: btr 1090. 10 70
988 **SUSIES FLYER 28** [1] 3-8-7 S Sanders 33/1: 11-59: Prom, wknd 2f out: see 988 (5f). 2 65
-1090 **SERAPHINA 18** [2] 3-8-7 G Duffield 15/2: 4-0620: Keen/prom 4f: 10th: op 13/2: btr 1090 (5f). shd 65
10 ran   Time 1m 12.5 (1.7)   (Giles W Pritchard-Gordon)   T D Easterby Great Habton, Nth Yorks.

1411 4.00 TOTE SCOOP6 HCAP 3YO+ 0-80 (D) 1m6f Good 40 -06 Slow [80]
£5694 £1752 £876 £438 3 yo rec 20lb

809 **KATHRYNS PET 49** [11] Mrs M Reveley 7-9-7 (73) A Culhane 13/2: 041-61: 7 b m Blakeney - Starky's Pet 78
(Mummy's Pet): Held up towards rear, stdy prog from over 3f out to lead 1f out, styd on well inside last, pushed
out cl-home: op 11/2, 7 wk abs: earlier won over timber at Kelso (h'cap, rtd 125h, 2m, firm & gd/soft): '99 Flat
wnr at Catterick & Newmarket (h'caps, rtd 72): '98 Flat wnr abroad at Catterick: eff at 12/14f, stays 2m well: acts
on fast & soft grnd, any trk: seems best held up for a late run: tough.
788 **MENTAL PRESSURE 52** [7] Mrs M Reveley 7-7-10 (4)(oh) J Mackay (7) 9/1: 000/32: 7 ch g Polar Falcon ¾ 51
- Hysterical (High Top): Held up, stdy prog wide 4f out & led over 1f out, sn hdd, kept on for press: op 8/1,
lngr prcd stablemate of wnr: 8 wk abs: shown enough to win a similar contest (mdn): see 788.
963 **NATURAL EIGHT 32** [3] Jamie Poulton 6-8-1 (53) M Henry 12/1: 1-6333: 6 b g In The Wings - Fenny ¾ 55
Rough (Home Guard): Towards rear, rdn & styd on steadily final 3f, not pace of wnr: op 10/1: see 168.
964 **SELIANA 32** [5] G Wragg 4-9-4 (70) J F Egan 11/2: /3-234: Chsd ldrs, led over 2f out till over 1f out, 3½ 69
no extra: stayed this lngr 14f trip: handles gd & soft grnd: see 832.
1167 **SEGAVIEW 14** [16] 4-8-8 (60) J Fanning 9/2 FAV: 06-445: Bhd ldrs, eff 3f out, sn no impress. 3½ 56
868 **CUPBOARD LOVER 39** [14] 4-8-6 (58) M Fenton 12/1: 10-656: Sn chsd ldrs racing keenly, led over 2 52
3f out till over 2f out, fdd final 1f: often takes a strong hold, a tricky ride who runs well for A Mackay: see 788.
1106 **SUDDEN FLIGHT 17** [13] 4-8-6 (78) M Tebbutt 15/2: 30-137: Held up, effort 3f out, no prog final 2f. ½ 71
1023 **ZINCALO 26** [6] 4-8-6 (58)(t) D Harrison 15/2: 00-048: Mid-div, chsd ldrs 2f out, sn held: see 1023, 835. 2½ 49
1180 **MANE FRAME 13** [2] 5-8-13 (65) D Griffiths 8/1: 264-09: Led 11f, fdd: see 1180. 10 49
1187 **BID ME WELCOME 13** [8] 4-10-0 (80) D McGaffin (7) 33/1: 151-00: Chsd ldrs 10f, sn btn: 10th: '99 2 62
h'cap wnr at Warwick, Nottingham (C/D) & Newmarket (rtd 82): 4th in '98 (mdn, rtd 63, M Johnston): eff at 12/15f
on fast & gd, gd grnd: both handles soft: likes to race off the pace on any trk: has run well fresh.
1276 **REGGIE BUCK 7** [10] 6-7-10 (48)(14oh) Claire Bryan (5) 25/1: 000-60: Chsd ldrs 11f: 11th: see 1276. ¾ 29
-- **Edipo Re** [15] 8-8-13 (65) W Ryan 33/1:   200 **Sudest 155** [13] 6-8-13 (65) S Sanders 16/1:
1087 **Cindesti 18** [4] 4-7-11 (49)(BL) N Carlisle 14/1:   917 **Il Principe 36** [9] 6-9-9 (75) G Hall 10/1:
15 ran   Time 3m 04.7 (6.4)   (Bill Brown)   Mrs M Reveley Lingdale, Nth Yorks.

1412   4.30 GEARHOUSE HCAP 3YO+ 0-70 (E)   5f str   Good 40 -02 Slow   [70]
£3055   £940   £470   £235   3 yo rec 8 lb Centre/far side group ahead at halfway

1278 **WILLIAMS WELL 7** [15] M W Easterby 6-9-4 (60)(bl) T Lucas 4/1 FAV: 4-0601: 6 ch g Superpower -   **68**
Catherines Well (Junius): Bhd ldrs stands side, no room/swtchd 2f out, rdn/strong run inside last to lead nr fin:
op 7/2: '99 wnr at Carlisle & Catterick (h'caps, rtd 70 at best): eff at 6f, all wins at 5f: acts on firm & soft,
likes Catterick, handles any trk: best in blnks: in fine form at present, could win again.

*1140 **PRIDE OF BRIXTON 16** [9] Andrew Reid 7-8-5 (47) M Henry 9/2: 0-1112: 7 b g Dominion - Caviar Blini 1¼ 49
(What A Guest): Al handy towards centre, rdn/led over 1f out, hdd well inside last & no extra: op 7/2, v tough.

2344 **HARVEYS FUTURE 325** [6] P L Gilligan 6-8-1 (43) A Polli (3) 20/1: 1020-3: 6 b g Never So Bold - Orba ½ 43
Gold (Gold Crest): Held up centre, swthd & styd on final 1f, not pace of wnr: reapp: '99 reapp scorer at Bath
(h'cap, rtd 40, unplcd on sand, rtd 34a): eff at 5f, stays 6f: acts on gd, soft & fibresand, prob handles any trk.

1244 **SUNSET HARBOUR 9** [1] J M Bradley 7-8-0 (42) Claire Bryan (5) 7/1: 000-24: Stumbled start, sn handy 1 40
far side, ev ch when briefly no room over 1f out, kept on inside last: remains in gd form & is on a handy mark.

1357 **COLONEL SAM 1** [16] 4-8-3 (45)(tb) A Nicholls (3) 25/1: 000005: Held up stds side, no room over shd 43
1f out, swtchd & strong run inside last, nrst fin: unplcd yesterday at Thirsk: mdn, but showed some promise here.

1133 **SOUNDS ACE 16** [11] 4-8-12 (54) J Fanning 16/1: 006-06: Held up stands side, effort 2f out, kept on. 1¼ 49

1143 **DAZZLING QUINTET 15** [7] 4-8-3 (45) R Fitzpatrick (3) 16/1: 020-67: Led far side till over 1f out, fdd. 1 38

1220 **PERTEMPS FC 10** [8] 3-9-1 (65) D Harrison 20/1: 160-08: In tch, held up final 1f: op 14/1: '99 wnr nk 57
at Newcastle (sell) & Beverley (nursery, rtd 68): eff over a stiff 5/6f on gd & firm grnd, best without blnks.

1162 **ZARAGOSSA 14** [13] 4-9-8 (64) P Bradley (5) 8/1: 000-59: Chds ldrs stands side, fdd final 1f: tchd 10/1. 1 54

1244 **CHAKRA 9** [4] 6-7-10 (38) K Dalgleish (7) 20/1: 106000: Held up far side, nvr pace to chall: 10th. nk 27

1073 **LORD HIGH ADMIRAL 19** [2] 12-8-12 (54)(vis) K Darley 12/1: 4-1400: Prom far side 4f: 11th: op 10/1. ½ 41

129 **BLACK ARMY 172** [14] 5-10-0 (70) J Tate 12/1: 3030-0: Cl-up stands side 4f: 12th: op 10/1, 6 mth abs. nk 56

1162 **WATERFORD SPIRIT 14** [12] 4-10-0 (70) C Lowther 10/1: -00W00: Chsd ldrs stands side 3f: 16th.   0

887 **AISLE 38** [18] 3-8-9 (59)(bl) S Finnamore (5) 5/1: 255050: Dwelt, sn rdn bhd stands side, nvr a factor: 0
17th: nicely bckd, op 16/1: more expected here: see 518.

518 **Bodfari Times 95** [10] 4-8-6 (48)(t) A McCarthy (3) 33/1: 826 **Precision 45** [17] 5-8-12 (54) J F Egan 33/1:
1138 **Branston Lucy 16** [5] 3-8-9 (59) J Weaver 16/1:   1098 **Prime Recreation 18** [3] 3-9-2 (66) G Duffield 25/1:
18 ran   Time 1m 0.6 (2.1)   (Mr K Hodgson & Mrs J Hodgson)   M W Easterby Sheriff Hutton, Nth Yorks.

1413   5.05 E MAIL AUCT MDN 2YO DIV II (E)   6f str   Good 40 -28 Slow
£2632   £752   £376   Raced towards centre

1252 **PHAROAHS GOLD 8** [11] W Jarvis 2-9-0 M Tebbutt 11/4 JT FAV: -441: 2 b c Namaqualand - Queen Nefertiti 80
(Fairy King): Chsd clr ldr 2f out, rdn & styd on well to lead nr fin: op 4/1: apprec this step up to 6f, will stay
further: acts on firm & gd/soft grnd, stiff/gall trk.

938 **EXTRA GUEST 33** [10] M R Channon 2-8-9 Craig Williams 4/1: 432: 2 b f Fraam - Gibaltarik (Jareer): nk 72
Led & clr mid-race, just hdd well inside last: op 3/1, rest well covered: stays 6f on gd & hvy grnd.

-- **NUMERATE** [9] M L W Bell 2-8-9 J Mackay (7) 8/1: 3: 2 b f Bishop Of Cashel - Half A Dozen (Saratoga 3 65
Six): Dwelt/outpcd early, styd on final 2f, not pace of front pair: op 6/1: Mar foal, cost 4,600 gns: half-sister
to a juv wnr abroad, dam plcd as a 2yo: sire a high class 7f/1m performer: stays 6f, will get further: handles gd.

984 **HOMELIFE 30** [6] D Sasse 2-9-0 W Ryan 11/2: 64: Dwelt, sn prom in chsg group, kept on inside shd 70
last: op 7/1: styd lngr 6f trip & handles gd grnd: see 984.

-- **MERIDEN MIST** [3] 2-8-9 A Culhane 11/4 JT FAV: 5: Chsd ldrs 2f out, onepace: op 2/1: Distinctly 1 63
North filly, Mar foal, cost 11,000 gns, first foal: dam a 5f juv wnr, sire a high class 2yo: with P W Harris.

1189 **TRUSTED MOLE 13** [2] 2-9-0 J Weaver 12/1: -66: Outpcd early, kept on final 1f, nrst fin: tchd 14/1. hd 67

730 **TROJAN PRINCE 56** [5] 2-9-0 A Eddery 5/1: -07: Trkd ldrs, wknd final 1f: op 6/1, abs: see 730 (5f). 1½ 63

984 **MEDIA BUYER 30** [4] 2-9-0 J D Smith 20/1: 08: Sn rdn, nvr on terms: op 14/1: see 984 (5f). 1¼ 60

1136 **EL HAMRA 16** [7] 2-9-0 G Duffield 20/1: 59: Chsd ldrs, strugg over 2f out: op 14/1: btr 1136 (AW, 5f). 2 55

-- **JANMO** [8] 2-8-9 D Harrison 33/1: 0: Al outpcd: 10th: Wolfhound filly, Feb foal, cost 9,400 gns: 3½ 41
half-sister to 4 wnrs incl 3 2yo wnrs: dam a mdn: sire high class 5/7f performer: with C Dwyer.

1067 **Son Of A Preacher 19** [12] 2-9-0 J Fanning 33/1:   1000 **Distant Dawn 26** [1] 2-8-9 G Hind 25/1:
12 ran   Time 1m 14.9 (4.1)   (Sales Race 2000 Syndicate)   W Jarvis Newmarket, Suffolk.

1414   5.35 APPR MDN HCAP 3YO+ 0-70 (G)   1m54yrnd   Good 40 -46 Slow   [68]
£2177   £622   £311   3 yo rec 12lb

4558} **XIBALBA 203** [15] C E Brittain 4-9-1 (67) N Esler (5) 13/2: 000-1: 3 b c Zafonic - Satanic Dance (Shareef 71
Dancer): Trkd ldrs, rdn/prog to lead over 1f out, held on for press cl-home: rtd 75 at best in '99 (highly tried,
Listed): eff at 1m, tried 10f, may yet suit: acts on gd grnd & a gall trk: runs well fresh.

4426} **COMPATRIOT 214** [18] P S Felgate 4-9-10 (64) S Finnamore (5) 10/1: 4304-2: 4 b g Bigstone - hd 67
Campestral (Alleged): Hld up, prog to lead 2f out till over 1f out, styd on well inside last, just held: tchd
14/1: reapp: topweight: rnr-up on reapp in '99 (M Callaghan, mdn, rtd 87): rnr-up in '98 (rtd 96): eff at
5f/1m on firm & soft: has run well in blnks: handles any trk: shwn enough to win similar for new connections.

1336 **STITCH IN TIME 3** [13] G C Bravery 4-8-4 (44) A Nicholls 5/2 FÁV: 0-2233: 4 ch g Inchinor - Late nk 46
Matinee (Red Sunset): Held up, rdn & prog from over 2f out, styd on well, post came too sn: op 7/2, qck reapp.

1211 **ARZILLA 11** [9] J M Bradley 4-8-13 (53) Claire Bryan (5) 11/2: 30-034: Keen/chsd ldrs, onepace fnl 1f. 2½ 50

1053 **DESERT ISLAND DISC 21** [14] 3-9-1 (67) C Halliwell (7) 14/1: 050-65: Dwelt/rear, late gains fnl 2f. shd 64

1085 **BEDOUIN QUEEN 18** [16] 3-8-11 (63) J Bosley (5) 14/1: 05-006: Towards rear, mod gains final 3f. nk 59

826 **THIEVES WELCOME 45** [10] 3-8-11 (63) G Sparkes (7) 6/1: -63-07: Held up, rdn/mod prog over 2f out, 4 51
sn held: h'cap bow, 6 wk abs: see 826.

4426} **BERBERIS 214** [12] 4-8-5 (45) K Dalgleish (5) 25/1: 000-8: Keen/prom, led over 3f out till 2f out, fdd: 2½ 28
h'cap bow, unplcd in '99 for C Brittain (rtd 62): now with J M Bradley.

1213 **JACK DAWSON 11** [5] 3-8-6 (58) D Williamson 9/1: 00-009: Trkd ldrs, led 4f out till over 3f out, fdd. 2 37

1275 **SILVER TONGUED 7** [8] 4-8-4 (44) Iona Wands (3) 20/1: 500-00: Trkd ldrs 7f: 10th: see 1275. ½ 22

1085 **WISHFUL THINKER 18** [1] 3-9-1 (67) Jonjo Fowle (5) 10/1: 000-00: Nvr factor: 11th: op 8/1: see 1085. 4 37

1058 **JAVELIN 21** [6] 4-9-1 (55) R Fitzpatrick 12/1: -54060: Cl-up/dsptd lead 6f: 12th: op 16/1: see 658. 6 16

4008} **KALAHARI FERRARI 243** [2] 4-8-10 (50) A McCarthy 10/1: 5330-0: Keen/chsd ldrs, wknd final 3f: 14th: 0
reapp: plcd numerous times last term (rtd 60, unplcd on sand, rtd 48a, J Berry): unplcd in '99 (rtd 77, mdn): eff
at 7f/9f: handles fast & gd/soft, any trk: now with A G Hobbs.

NOTTINGHAM   SATURDAY MAY 20TH   Lefthand, Galloping Track

1099 **Pasadena** 18 [7] 3-9-1 (67) R Smith (5) 14/1:
1211 **Blakey** 11 [3] 4-8-3 (43) D Glennon (7) 16/1:
16 ran   Time 1m 46.5 (7.1)   (R Meredith)

3150} **Who Da Leader** 289 [17] 3-9-3 (69) P Dobbs (3) 14/1:
C E Brittain Newmarket, Suffolk.

SOUTHWELL (Fibresand)   MONDAY MAY 22ND   Lefthand, Sharp, Oval Trak

Official Going   STANDARD. Stalls: Inside, Except 5f - Outside

1415
1.45 CLASS CLAIMER DIV 1 3YO+ 0-60 (F)   **1m3f aw**   **Going 41   -15 Slow**
£1848   £528   £264   3 yo rec 15lb

1203 **PICKENS** 14 [11]   Don Enrico Incisa 8-9-5 Kim Tinkler 16/1: -00601: 8 b g Theatrical - Alchi (Alleged) **44a**
Rdn/prom & wide thr'out, styd on gamely for press fnl 2f to prevail on line: '99 wnr here at Southwell (sell,
rtd 64a): '98 wnr here at Southwell (4, sell/h'caps, rtd 71a): eff at 11/12f, stays 14f: acts on firm &
gd/soft, f/sand/Southwell specialist who relishes sell/clmg grade.
1389 **APPROACHABLE** 2 [7]   Miss S J Wilton 5-9-5 M Tebbutt 6/4 FAV: 225432: 5 b h Known Fact - Western **hd 43a**
Approach (Gone West) Prom, chsd ldr after 2f, rdn/led 2f out, hdd nr line: hvly bckd: quick reapp, claimed by
K Morgan for £2,000: rarely runs a bad race but is now on a long losing run & wins over shorter: see 710, 45.
1234 **HOUNDS OF LOVE** 11 [9]   R Guest 3-8-7 A Beech (5) 5/1: 0-033: 3 b f Foxhound - Foolish Lady (Foolish ½ **45a**
Pleasure) Rear, prog halfway, kept on fnl 2f, not pace of wnr: styd longer 11f trip: see 1234 (8.5f).
1389 **NIGHT CITY** 2 [1]   K R Burke 9-9-13 N Callan 5/1: 214064: Led 9f, kept on ins last: qck reapp, clr rem. ½ **49a**
1241 **TALECA SON** 11 [3]   S K Dalgleish (7) 33/1: 400065: Held up, eff halfway, btn 1f out: see 943. 6 **32$**
1301 **BOBONA** 7 [4]   4-9-3 G Baker (7) 33/1: 026506: Struggling 4f out: stiff task, see 178 (C/D). 2½ **26$**
1275 **MISALLIANCE** 9 [2]   5-8-12 P Fessey 16/1: 400-07: Bhd early, mod gains: op 12/1: AW bow: plcd in ¾ **20a**
'99 (rtd 54, C F Wall): '97 Newcastle wnr (auct mdn, rtd 76 at best): eff at 7f/1m, handles firm & gd/soft.
1141 **KINGS GINGER** 18 [5]   3-8-10 S Finnamore (5) 9/2: 034038: Hmpd after 2f, al rear: see 540, 392 (9f) ½ **32a**
1353 **JATO DANCER** 3 [6]   5-9-0 P M Quinn (5) 14/1: 000549: Al rear: quick reapp: flattered 1353. 3½ **16a**
1301 **KI CHI SAGA** 7 [8]   8-9-3 (bl) P McCabe 33/1: 004400: Dwelt, al rear: 10th: see 219, 115. 6 **10a**
855 **LA CINECITTA** 42 [10]   4-9-2 K Hodgson 33/1: 000-00: Prom 7f: 11th: 6 wk abs: AW bow: mod form 8 **0a**
last term (rtd 39, tried blnks): unplcd in '98 (rtd 63, juv fills mdn): with C Booth.
11 ran   Time 2m 27.5 (6.2)   (Don Enrico Incisa)   Don Enrico Incisa Coverham, N Yorks

1416
2.15 BIRMINGHAM HCAP 4YO+ 0-65 (F)   **2m aw**   **Going 41   -45 Slow**   **[63]**
£2240   £640   £320   4 yo rec 2 lb

4127} **VINCENT** 237 [14]   J L Harris 5-8-11 (46) G Baker (7) 16/1: D344-1: 5 b g Anshan - Top Anna (Ela Mana **51a**
Mou) Rear, stdy prog fnl 6f & chall from over 1f out, led ins last, styd on well, rdn out: tchd 20/1: reapp: '99
wnr at Southwell & W'hampton (h'caps, rtd 52a), unplcd on turf, rtd 48, rtd 81h, h'cap): plcd in '98 (h'cap, rtd 55a, subs
tried visor): eff at 12f/2m on fast, fibresand specialist, poss handles eqtrk: loves a sharp trk & runs well fresh.
1301 **ST LAWRENCE** 7 [5]   B S Rothwell 6-8-13 (48) M Fenton 10/1: 133002: 6 gr g With Approval - Mingan 1 **50a**
Isle (Lord Avie) Led 2f, led again 6f out, rdn/strongly prsd from over 1f out, hdd ins last, no extra: see 542.
940 **HETRA HEIGHTS** 35 [3]   W J Musson 5-9-1 (50) L Newton 3/1 FAV: -61103: 5 b m Cox's Ridge - Top ¾ **51a**
Hope (High Top) Handy halfway, ev ch 2f out, rdn out/not pace of wnr ins last: op 9/2: clr rem: see 644 (C/D).
918 **TIME CAN TELL** 37 [11]   A G Juckes 6-8-12 (47) N Callan 6/1: -55134: Trkd ldrs, rdn/no extra fnl 2f. 4 **44a**
1306 **ACCYSTAN** 7 [6]   5-9-6 (55) A Beech (5) 8/1: 016335: Prom, fdd fnl 2f: op 7/2: see 642 (12f). ¾ **51a**
1301 **BANNERET** 7 [12]   7-8-5 (40)(vis) P M Quinn (5) 16/1: 532646: Trkd ldrs, eff 3f out, soon held: vis reapp. 3 **33a**
1276 **BLACK ICE BOY** 9 [13]   9-7-10 (40)(vis)(9oh) K Dalgleish (7) 16/1: 500007: Led after 2f, sn clr, hdd 6 **18a**
6f out, sn btn: visor reapplied, stiff task 9lbs o/h: see 1141.
1087 **SALVAGE** 20 [4]   5-8-12 (47) P McCabe 6/1: 0-0308: Rear, prog/chsd ldrs 6f out, sn btn: AW bow. 13 **24a**
492 **ROLE MODEL** 102 [10]   4-7-10 (33) P Fessey 10/1: 062-59: Al rear: jumps fit (rnr-up, sell, rtd 81h). 5 **5a**
-- **SIRINNDI** [9]   6-9-11 (60) D O'Donohoe 33/1: 0365/0: Al bhd: 10th: op 5/1, top-weight, Brit/AW bow, 8 **24a**
abs: ex-Irish, '97 wnr at The Curragh (mdn) & Cork (stks), tried hdles: eff at 12f, stays 2m on gd & hvy grnd.
1065 **Hathni Khound** 21 [2]   4-7-10 (31)(2oh) C Adamson 16/1:
1301 **Notation** 7 [1]   6-7-11 (32)(bl) (1ow)(14oh) S Righton 50/1:
-- **Members Welcome** [7]   7-7-10 (31)(1oh) Iona Wands (4) 33/1:   --   **Pianist** [8] 6-9-1 (50) J Tate 33/1:
14 ran   Time 3m 41.3 (15.3)   (P Caplan)   J L Harris Eastwell, Leics

1417
2.45 CLASS CLAIMER DIV 2 3YO+ 0-60 (F)   **1m3f aw**   **Going 41   -16 Slow**
£1848   £528   £264   3 yo rec 15lb

1306 **ROYAL PARTNERSHIP** 7 [7]   K R Burke 4-9-7 (vis) Darren Williams (7) 5/4 FAV: 203051: 4 b g Royal **59a**
Academy - Go Honey Go (General Assembly) Held up, hdwy to lead on bit over 2f out, sn clr, drvn out to hold on:
well bckd: clmd by Stan Moore for £5,000: prev won here at Southwell (C/D, sell): ex-Irish, plcd in '99
(mdn, with J Oxx): eff at 11f, tried 12f: acts on fibresand & likes Southwell: eff with/without visor.
1101 **ULTRA CALM** 19 [6]   P C Haslam 4-9-7 Dean McKeown 10/1: 006002: 4 ch g Doubletour - Shyonn ¾ **57a**
(Shy Groom) Mid-div, prog/ev ch 2f out, sn outpcd by wnr, kept on nr fin as wnr tired: clr rem: eff at 1m/11f.
1039 **GLOW** 24 [10]   M J Polglase 4-9-4 L Newton 16/1: 046-03: 4 b f Alzao - Shimmer (Bustino) 8 **45a**
Dwelt, kept on 2f out, hdd 4f out & sn outpcd, mod late rally to take 3rd: op 12/1: see 1039.
1305 **ADIRPOUR** 7 [3]   R Hollinshead 6-9-5 Stephanie Hollinshea 25/1: 030004: Chsd ldr, went on over 4f ¾ **45$**
out, hdd over 2f out, fdd/eased cl home: jockey given 5-day ban for easing down prematurely & losing 3rd pl.
407 **TEN PAST SIX** 116 [4]   8-9-5 (vis) P McCabe 11/1: /50-05: Chsd ldrs 1m: op 8/1, abs: vis reapp. 3½ **40a**
unplcd in '99 (rtd 53): '98 wnr at Southwell, Hamilton & Carlisle (clmrs, rtd 57 & 63a): eff at 1m/12f on any grnd/trk.
866 **POLISH PILOT** 41 [1]   5-9-3 D Harrison 16/1: 000-06: Held up, eff halfway, no impress: op 12/1, jumps 5 **31a**
fit (plcd, rtd 92h, sell hdle): claimed for £3,000: see 866.
1305 **SPRING BEACON** 7 [9]   5-8-12 J Weaver 25/1: 40/607: Prom 8f: stiff task: see 693. 10 **15a**
1241 **OVERSMAN** 11 [8]   7-9-13 M Tebbutt 5/2: 330-28: Held up, eff 3f out, no impress: op 7/4: btr 1241. 1¼ **28a**
-- **GIULIA MURIEL** [2]   4-9-2 O Pears 12/1: 9: Led 2f, btn 6f out: op 10/1, Brit/AW debut: reportedly dist **0a**
a wnr in Italy last term: with K Morgan.
2309} **MUMBAI** 328 [5]   4-9-3 S Finnamore (5) 50/1: 400-0: Sn rdn, al rear: jumps fit, AW bow: modest. 6 **0a**
10 ran   Time 2m 27.6 (6.3)   (Tendorra)   K R Burke Newmarket, Suffolk

471

SOUTHWELL (Fibresand)   MONDAY MAY 22ND   Lefthand, Sharp, Oval Trak

1418
3.15 CARDIFF MED AUCT MDN 2YO (F)   5f aw str   Going 41   -23 Slow
£2254   £644   £322   Raced across track, middle - high no's favoured

--   **ROUGH SHOOT** [7] T D Barron 2-9-0 (h) C Lowther 12/1: 1: 2 ch g King's Signet - Tawny (Grey Ghost) In tch, prog/rdn to chall over 1f out, styd on well to lead nr line: op 8/1: May foal, brother to a 5f juv wnr, dam a 5/6f juv wnr: eff at 5f, 6f shld suit: acts on fibresand & a sharp trk: runs well fresh.   **77a**
1267   **CHURCH MICE 10** [16] M L W Bell 2-8-9 (VIS) M Fenton 7/2 FAV: 242: 2 br f Petardia - Negria (Al Hareb) Sn led, rdn over 1f out, strongly prsd ins last & hdd/just held nr fin: clr rem: op 4/1: jockey given 1-day ban for excessive use of whip: gd run in 1st time visor: acts on firm, soft & fibresand.   nk   **71a**
1249   **REGAL AIR 11** [6] B I Case 2-8-9 T E Durcan 4/1: 353: 2 b f Distinctly North - Dignified Air (Wolver Hollow) Handy, ch 2f out, rdn/edged right & held ins last: op 11/4: see 1249, 865.   4   **61a**
730   **DENNIS EL MENACE 58** [13] W R Muir 2-9-0 D Harrison 16/1: -04: Prom, fdd 1f out: op 12/1, abs.   ½   **64a**
1131   **EDDIE ROYALE 18** [9] 2-9-0 O Pears 16/1: 05: Prom 4f: op 14/1: see 1131.   nk   **63a**
--   **TRUDIE** [5] 2-8-9 V Halliday 33/1: 6: Cl-up, fdd fnl 2f: Komaite filly, Mar foal, half-sister to 2 juv wnrs, dam a 6f juv wnr: with Miss J F Craze.   2½   **51a**
1304   **FRENCH BRAMBLE 7** [8] 2-8-9 J Edmunds 14/1: 67: Rdn/outpcd early, kept on fnl 2f: 6f+ will suit.   ¾   **49a**
--   **RIVER OF FIRE 11** [11] 2-9-0 J Tate 10/1: 8: Outpcd early, mod late gains: tchd 12/1: Dilum gelding, Mar foal, half-brother to 4 wnrs incl a 10f juv wnr: dam modest: looks sure to relish further for J M P Eustace.   2   **49a**
849   **INZACURE 42** [10] 2-9-0 M Tebbutt 12/1: 09: Went right start, bhd halfway, no impress: op 10/1, abs.   nk   **48a**
--   **DUSTY PRINCESS** [4] 2-8-9 Dean McKeown 20/1: 0: Al outpcd: 10th: Aragon filly, Feb foal, dam modest.   1   **41a**
1136   **BLUE ORLEANS 18** [1] 2-9-0 J Weaver 4/1: 30: Rcd alone early on far side, sn outpcd: 11th: op 11/2.   ½   **44a**
898   **Percy Verance 39** [12] 2-9-0 P Fessey 33/1:   **Fathers Footsteps** [3] 2-9-0 P McCabe 33/1:
--   **Coniston** [14] 2-9-0 J Lowe 25/1:   --   **Tobytoo** [2] 2-9-0 K Dalgleish (7) 16/1:
15 ran   Time 1m 01.00 (3.2)   (Harrowgate Bloodstock Ltd)   T D Barron Maunby, N Yorks

1419
3.45 LONDON FILLIES HCAP 3YO+ 0-70 (E)   1m aw rnd   Going 41   -03 Slow   [63]
£2814   £866   £433   £216   3 yo rec 12lb

1235   **PRIDEWAY 11** [1] W M Brisbourne 4-10-0 (63) J Tate 14/1: -44061: 4 b f Pips Pride - Up The Gates (Captain James) Mid-div, rdn/prog halfway & led 2f out, styd on strongly ins last, rdn out: op 12/1: '99 reapp wnr at W'hampton (h'cap, rtd 75, A Bailey), rnr-up twice on turf (h'cap & sell, rtd 70): plcd in '98 (rtd 71): eff at 6f, suited by 7f/1m: acts on fast, likes gd/soft, soft & fibresand: gd weight carrier: best in blnks.   **69a**
1303   **MUDDY WATER 7** [3] D Marks 4-8-12 (47) D Harrison 5/1: 010032: 4 b f Salse - Rainbow Fleet (Nomination) Trkd ldrs, rdn/hung left 2f out, kept on tho' al held: ran to best: see 1303, 958.   2½   **48a**
869   **TSUNAMI 41** [14] P D Evans 4-8-3 (38) L Newton 25/1: -06003: 4 b f Beveled - Alvecote Lady (Touching Wood) Dwelt/towards rear, drvn & kept on fnl 2f, nrst fin: abs: stays 1m, handles fast, hvy & fibresand.   1½   **36a**
*1303   **MUJAGEM 7** [10] M W Easterby 4-9-1 (50)(6ex) G Parkin 5/1: 00/014: Led till halfway, onepace over 1f out: not disgraced makeing a qk reapp with a 6lb penalty for 1303 (ahead of today's rnr-up).   ¾   **47a**
1391   **GUEST ENVOY 2** [6] 5-9-5 (54) J Bosley (7) 10/1: 112605: Twds rear, late gains, no threat: ran Saturday.   1   **49a**
1391   **MOUNT PARK 2** [5] 3-8-1 (48)(bl) K Dalgleish (7) 40/1: 000006: Chsd ldrs, led halfway, hdd 2f out.   2½   **38a**
1303   **STRAVSEA 7** [4] 5-9-3 (52) P M Quinn (5) 100/30 FAV: 350427: Rear halfway, nvr a threat: nicely bckd.   ½   **41a**
739   **CHASETOWN CAILIN 56** [9] 5-7-10 (31)(t) Kim Tinkler 14/1: 030-68: Prom/keen 6f: op 12/1, 8 wk abs.   ½   **19a**
882   **ARMENIA 40** [2] 3-8-11 (58) S Finnamore (5) 7/1: 214329: Chsd ldrs 6f: 6 wk abs, now with A Newcombe.   4   **38a**
1272   **FLUSH 10** [13] 5-8-7 (42) C Cogan (5) 25/1: 00-500: Dwelt, sn prom, btn 3f out: 10th: see 520.   shd   **22a**
1303   **Chinaberry 7** [12] 6-8-7 (42) Dean McKeown 14/1:   4575} **Marnie 203** [11] 3-8-6 (53) A Daly 16/1:
1297   **Maid To Love 7** [7] 3-8-13 (60) N Callan 12/1:   1175 **Polar Diamond 15** [8] 3-9-7 (68) D Griffiths 16/1:
14 ran   Time 1m 42.9 (3.5)   (Nev Jones)   W M Brisbourne Great Ness, Shropshire

1420
4.15 HULL SELLER 2YO (G)   6f aw rnd   Going 41   -44 Slow
£1834   £524   £262

1396   **PRINCESS PENNY 2** [3] W G M Turner 2-8-7 A Daly 9/2: R301: 2 ch f King's Signet - Princess Tallulah (Chief Singer) Made all, rdn/strongly prsd 2f out, styd on gamely ins last, drvn out: op 3/1: no bid: quick reapp: eff at 5/6f on fibresand & a sharp trk, likes to force the pace: apprec drop to sell grade/return to fibresand.   **60a**
974   **IMPISH LAD 33** [4] B S Rothwell 2-8-12 M Fenton 13/8 FAV: 052: 2 b g Imp Society - Madonna Da Rossi (Mtoto) Trkd ldr, rdn to chall fnl 2f, ch ins last, kept on well, just held: clr rem: stays 6f, handles fibresand.   hd   **64a**
--   **SWEET VELETA** [7] R M Whitaker 2-8-7 V Halliday 12/1: 3: 3 b f Cosmonaut - Redgrave Design (Nebbiolo) Cl-up, ch 2f out, sn hung left/btn: op 7/1: Feb foal, cost 900gns: dam a 5f juv wnr.   5   **50a**
928   **CITRUS 37** [1] P C Haslam 2-8-7 Dean McKeown 9/4: -04: Sn handy, rdn/held when hmpd over 1f out.   5   **41a**
836   **DECEIVES THE EYE 45** [2] 2-8-12 S Ritchie (7) 10/1: 345: Chsd ldrs 4f: abs: btr 836, 722 (5f).   3   **39a**
1020   **EXELLENT ADVENTURE 28** [5] 2-8-12 N Callan 12/1: -W6: Cl-up, badly hmpd over 1f out, sn btn: op 7/1.2   **34a**
1302   **TINY MIND 7** [6] 2-8-12 C Lowther 50/1: 07: Dwelt, sn bhd: no form.   14   **8a**
7 ran   Time 1m 18.4 (5.1)   (Mrs A F Horsington)   W G M Turner Corton Denham, Somerset

1421
4.45 LIVERPOOL HCAP DIV 1 3YO+ 0-60 (F)   6f aw rnd   Going 41   -41 Slow   [60]
£2261   £846   £323   3 yo rec 9 lb

4450}   **HIGH ESTEEM 215** [2] M A Buckley 4-9-7 (53) Dean McKeown 14/1: 0440-1: 4 b g Common Grounds - Whittle Woods (Emarati) Made all, rdn fnl 2f, styd on strongly, rdn out: op 12/1: reapp, AW bow: unplcd last term (rtd 68): unplcd in '98 (rtd 59): eff over a sharp 6f on gd, hvy & fibresand: runs well fresh: likes to dominate.   **59a**
923   **SUPERFRILLS 37** [1] Miss L C Siddall 7-8-7 (37)(2ow) N Callan 16/1: 006-02: 7 b m Superpower - Pod's Daughter (Tender King) Chsd wnr, ev ch 2f out, held in last: tchd 20/1: see 923.   2½   **37a**
*1305   **ABTAAL 7** [3] Mrs N Macauley 10-9-12 (58)(vis)(6ex) Sarah Robinson (7) 12/1: 0-6013: 10 b g Green Desert - Stufida (Bustino) Dwelt & rdn/twds rear, kept on fnl 2f, nrst fin: op 9/1, 6lb penalty: all wins at 7f.   ½   **54a**
1305   **KOMASEPH 7** [7] R F Marvin 8-8-3 (35) S Righton 11/1: -36064: Chsd ldrs, onepace fnl 1f: see 602.   nk   **30a**
1275   **FOIST 9** [5] 8-9-3 (49) G Parkin 9/2 JT FAV: 0-0065: Held up, prog halfway, held 2f out: op 6/1: see 587.   2   **39a**
1391   **MAYDORO 2** [14] 7-8-0 (32) J Tate 7/1: 06-006: Prom, onepace 1f out: bckd, op 14/1: qck reapp.   ½   **20a**
965   **THE THIRD CURATE 34** [6] 5-8-11 (43)(bl) D O'Donohoe 6/1: 000-07: Chsd ldrs 4f: tchd 12/1: see 187.   2½   **24a**
1305   **DESERT INVADER 7** [12] 9-8-9 (41) K Dalgleish (7) 20/1: 53-008: Mid-div, btn 2f out: see 1305.   2½   **16a**
1011   **PRESENT CHANCE 28** [15] 6-10-0 (60)(bl) L Newton 14/1: -00009: Prom 4f: op 16/1, topweight.   ¾   **32a**
4554}   **SKYERS FLYER 206** [4] 6-9-0 (46) J Lowe 14/1: 4503-0: Dwelt, eff halfway, sn held: 10th: reapp: '99   ¾   **16a**

472

SOUTHWELL (Fibresand)   MONDAY MAY 22ND   Lefthand, Sharp, Oval Trak

Carlisle wnr (h'cap, rtd 52 at best, unplcd on sand, rtd 35a): plcd form in '98 (rtd 66, M Wane): eff at 5/6f, stays
an easy 1m: handles gd/soft, likes gd or fast grnd, any trk: loves a stiff one: with R Thompson.
1273 **FOUND AT LAST 10** [9] 4-9-1 (47) P Goode (3) 5/1: 300350: Dwelt, al rear: 11th: see 781, 273.   4   **7a**
1092 **REGAL SONG 20** [10] 4-9-10 (56)(bl) K Hodgson 9/2 JT FAV: 203W50: Dwelt, sn rdn, bhd halfway: 14th: **0a**
reportedly lodged his head in stalls & missed the break: see 414.
4586} **Sea Minstrel 202** [13] 4-8-0 (37) P Fessey 33/1: 1205 **Secret Rendezvous 14** [11] 3-8-9 (50) P M Quinn (5) 16/1:
14 ran   Time 1m 15.8 (5.5)   (C C Buckley)   M A Buckley Upper Helmsley, N Yorks

---

1422   5.15 LIVERPOOL HCAP DIV 2 3YO+ 0-60 (F)   6f aw rnd Going 41   +04 Fast   [60]
£2261   £646   £323   3 yo rec 9 lb

*1233 **PETITE DANSEUSE 11** [8] D W Chapman 6-8-11 (43) Kimberley Hart (5) 7/1: 014611: 6 b m Aragon - Let   **48a**
Her Dance (Sovereign Dancer) Chsd ldrs, prog fnl 2f, rdn/led well ins last: best time of day: earlier won h'caps
here at Southwell (sell) & W'hampton (fillies): plcd in '99 (rtd 38 & 29a): eff at 5/7f on firm, soft & both AWs:
handles any trk: with/without visor, not blnks: has run well fresh: in great form.
1239 **NADDER 11** [12] W M Brisbourne 5-8-8 (40) C Cogan (5) 16/1: 250302: 5 ch g Lion Cavern - Nadia   ½ **42a**
Nerina (Northern Dancer) Handy, led 2f out, sn strongly prsd, hdd ins last & no extra: eff at 6/7f: see 1137, 276.
1273 **SEVEN SPRINGS 10** [1] R Hollinshead 4-8-2 (34) P M Quinn (5) 6/1: 006203: 4 b g Unblest - Zaydeen   ½ **34a**
(Sassafras) Held up, prog to chall fnl 2f, ev ch ins last, just held nr fin: tchd 9/1: clr of rem: see 1005, 647.
923 **GRASSLANDIK 37** [9] A G Newcombe 4-9-3 (49) D Griffiths 7/1: 535004: Chsd ldrs, ch over 1f out, fdd.   5 **40a**
674 **CHILLIAN 69** [15] 4-7-12 (30) N Carlisle 33/1: 000-05: Chsd ldrs, wide over 3f out, sn held: 10 wk abs.   nk **20a**
1105 **ABOVE BOARD 19** [3] 5-9-10 (56)(bl) P McCabe 20/1: 203306: Led/clr halfway, hdd 2f out & wknd.   nk **45a**
1205 **CRYFIELD 14** [2] 3-8-11 (52) J McAuley 13/2: 05027: Rear, late gains, nvr factor: op 5/1: see 1205.   nk **40a**
719 **VICE PRESIDENTIAL 58** [6] 5-9-4 (50) Dean McKeown 7/1: 500458: Dwelt, keen/trkd ldrs, btn 2f out.   2 **33a**
1237 **NOW IS THE HOUR 11** [16] 4-8-11 (43) P Goode (3) 12/1: 0-6629: Mid-div, btn 2f out: op 10/1.   ¾ **24a**
1368 **MARENGO 3** [14] 6-9-11 (57)(vis) R Price 5/1 FAV: 215040: Mid-div/wide, btn 2f out: 10th: vis reapp.   nk **37a**
3855} **Defiance 256** [7] 5-8-3 (35) Sophie Mitchell 16/1:   4445} **Bodfari Jet 215** [4] 3-8-13 (54) G Parkin 12/1:
1840} **Saint George 349** [11] 4-9-1 (47) D Hayes 25/1:1073 **Mikes Double 21** [10] 6-8-5 (37)(vis) K Dalgleish (7) 14/1:
1303 **Mademoiselle Paris 7** [5] 3-8-0 (41) J Tate 25/1:   808 **Lucky Cove 51** [13] 4-9-13 (59) Kim Tinkler 25/1:
16 ran   Time 1m 15.6 (2.2)   (David W Chapman)   D W Chapman Stillington, N Yorks

---

WINDSOR   MONDAY MAY 22ND   Sharp, Fig 8 Track

Official Going   GOOD TO SOFT. Stalls: Inside.

1423   6.15 ROUSSEAU CLAIMER 3YO+ (F)   6f str   Good/Soft   Inapplicable
£2509   £717   £358   3 yo rec 9 lb

*1298 **FIRE DOME 7** [2] D Nicholls 8-9-10 F Norton 11/8 FAV: -03311: 8 ch g Salt Dome - Penny Habit   **80**
(Habitat) Handy, rdn fnl 2f, led ins last & held on well cl-home, sold out: clmd by A Reid for £10,000, well bckd:
earlier won at Redcar (clmr): '99 wnr at Sandown & Redcar (clmrs, rtd 83, rtd 106$ in Gr 2 company): '98 Thirsk
& Sandown wnr (List, rtd 107): stays 7f, suited by 5/6f on firm, hvy & fibresand: handles any trk, likes Sandown:
best without blnks: gd weight carrier: tough (9 wins from 46) 8yo who is well suited by claiming grade.
1196 **DOCTOR DENNIS 14** [4] B J Meehan 3-8-1 D Glennon (7) 11/1: 2-0002: 3 b g Last Tycoon - Noble   nk **64**
Lustre (Lyphard's Wish) Bhd ldrs, prog fnl 2f, led ins last, kept on well, just held: eff at 6/7f.
1212 **CAPE COAST 13** [14] J A Osborne 3-8-9 J Reid 11/1: -00163: 3 b c Common Grounds - Strike It Rich   ½ **71**
(Rheingold) Towards rear, prog fnl 2f, styd on ins last, not reach front pair: op 9/1: sell h'caps will suit.
1066 **LAMENT 21** [10] Miss Gay Kelleway 4-8-7 Dane O'Neill 14/1: 000-04: Chsd ldrs, kept on fnl 1f: abs: 1½ **56**
'99 Pontefract wnr (clmr, rtd 60): '98 wnr for Mrs L Stubbs at Lingfield (clmr, rtd 67): eff at 6/7f, acts on
fast & gd/soft grnd: handles any trk: has run well fresh: encouraging run here.
3678} **PERIGEUX 266** [12] 4-9-10 C Carver (3) 20/1: 0200-5: Prom, ev ch over 1f out, no extra ins last: op   ¾ **71**
14/1, reapp: prev with J Berry, rnr-up thrice in '99 (rtd 69 & 74a, clmrs): '98 Southwell wnr (AW mdn) &
W'hampton (stks, rtd 85 & 89a): eff at 6/7f on firm, gd/soft & fibresand, handles any trk: eff with/without blnks.
867 **MAGIQUE ETOILE 41** [8] 4-8-9 T G McLaughlin 12/1: 32-006: Trkd ldrs, onepace fnl 1f: abs: see 114.   ½ **54**
1092 **KNOCKEMBACK NELLIE 20** [3] 4-9-1 (BL) N Pollard 16/1: 005007: Led 5f: blnks: op 12/1: unplcd   ¾ **58**
last term (rtd 73, mdn): rnr-up twice in '98 (rtd 75, mdns): eff at 6f, tried 7f: acts on firm: tried blnks.
1349 **LISA B 4** [11] 3-7-12 G Baker (7) 16/1: 0-2008: Mid-div, nvr pace to chall: qck reapp: btr 533 (5f).   ½ **48**
1213 **VILLAGE NATIVE 13** [18] 7-9-0 (bl) R Ffrench 33/1: 000009: Prom 4f: see 352.   ½ **54$**
1303 **STRATS QUEST 7** [1] 6-8-5 Martin Dwyer 8/1: 100500: In tch 4f: 10th: op 6/1: btr 816 (soft).   shd **44**
840 **CRAFTY PICK 45** [17] 3-8-2 P Fitzsimons (5) 20/1: 000: Mid-div at best: 11th: 6 wk abs, mod form.   ½ **48**
1263 **HARRY TASTERS 10** [16] 3-9-1 L Branch (7) 14/1: 50-00: Held up, eff 2f out, no impress: 12th.   1½ **56**
958 **Montendre 34** [15] 13-8-10 O Urbina 20/1:   1336 **Silver Sky 5** [9] 4-8-5 R Perham 40/1:
971 **Rose Of Hymus 33** [13] 3-8-6 W Ryan 14/1:   1062 **Beach Baby 21** [19] 3-8-0 C Adamson 40/1:
1068 **Arius 21** [5] 4-9-10 P Robinson 33/1:   1239 **Johnny Staccato 11** [21] 6-8-10 R Hughes 33/1:
459 **Cappucino Lady 107** [6] 3-7-10 R Brisland (5) 40/1:   2856} **Striding King 304** [20] 5-9-2 P Doe 40/1:
20 ran   Time 1m 12.6   (J M Ranson)   D Nicholls Sessay, N.Yorks.

1424   6.45 EBF FILLIES MDN 2YO (D)   5f str   Good/Soft   Inapplicable
£4504   £1386   £693   £346

-- **FLYING MILLIE** [17] R Hannon 2-8-11 R Hughes 9/2 FAV: 1: 2 b f Flying Spur - Sweet Pleasure   **87**
(Sweet Revenge) Bhd ldrs, shkn up/prog 2f out, rdn/narrow lead well ins last, styd on well: hvly bckd, tchd 7/1:
May foal, half-sister to sev wnrs, incl a French juv sprint wnr: dam a 6f juv wnr: eff at 5f, 6f will suit: acts
on gd/soft grnd & a sharp trk: runs well fresh: open to further improvement.
-- **SUPERSTAR LEO** [14] W J Haggas 2-8-11 L Dettori 11/2: 2: 2 b f College Chapel - Council Rock   hd **86**
(General Assembly) Al handy, rdn/led over 1f out, hdd well ins last, just held: op 5/1: Mar foal, cost 3,400gns:
half-sister to a 5f juv wnr: eff at 5f on gd/soft grnd, will suit fast grnd: pleasing intro & can find similar.
-- **AUTUMNAL** [18] B J Meehan 2-8-11 D R McCabe 7/1: 3: 2 b f Indian Ridge - Please Believe Me   1 **83**
(Try My Best) Prom, led over 1f out, rdn/edged left & sn hdd, no extra cl-home: op 6/1: Indian Ridge filly,
Apr foal, sister to a 5f juv wnr: dam a 5f juv wnr, sire a high-class sprinter: eff at 5f on gd/soft grnd.
-- **UPSTREAM** [9] Major D N Chappell 2-8-11 R Hills 15/2: 4: Slowly away, switched wide & prog fnl 2f,   3½ **75+**

473

styd on well, too late: op 6/1: Prince Sabo filly, Mar foal, half-sister to a 5f juv wnr & useful miler For Your Eyes
Only: dam a juv sprint wnr: eff at 5f, 6f+ will suit: handles gd/soft grnd: eye-catching late hdwy, will improve.

--   **MISTY EYED** [15] 2-8-11 L Newman (5) 8/1: 5: Dwelt/bhd, styd on fnl 2f, nrst at fin: Paris House   nk   74
filly, May foal, cost IR 3,200gns: half-sister to a dual 5f juv wnr: dam unrcd: shld improve & learn from this.

1079   **PRIYA 21** [3] 2-8-11 P Robinson 7/1: 46: Led till over 1f out, just held when badly hmpd dist: op 11/2.   1   72

--   **SHIRLEY FONG** [8] 2-8-11 M Hills 20/1: 7: Held up, eff halfway, onepace: Bluebird filly, May foal,   ½   71
cost IR 19,000gns: sire a top-class sprinter: 6f+ will suit, with J W Hills.

--   **ONCE REMOVED** [4] 2-8-11 P Doe 33/1: 8: Chsd ldrs, wknd fnl 1f: op 20/1: Distant Relative filly,   ½   69
May foal, cost 7,000gns: dam modest, sire a top-class miler: with S Dow.

--   **FAZZANI** [20] 2-8-11 T Quinn 8/1: 9: Chsd ldrs, btn over 1f out: op 6/1: Shareef Dancer filly, Mar   1   67
foal, cost 12,000gns: dam a 10/13f wnr, sire Irish Derby wnr: stoutly bred, sure to apprec much further in time.

--   **LADY KINVARRAH** [2] 2-8-11 Martin Dwyer 14/1: 0: Slowly away, mod gains: 10th: op 12/1: Brief   1¼   64
Truce filly, Apr foal, cost 23,000gns: half-sister to a useful 6/7f juv wnr Whyome: dam a 5f juv wnr: with J R Arnold.

--   **BRUNNHILDE** [7] 2-8-11 F Norton 20/1: 0: Towards rear, no impress: 11th: tchd 25/1, with J Berry.   hd   63

--   **MISS DAMINA** [13] 2-8-11 R Ffrench 33/1: 0: Held up, eff/btn 2f out: 12th: Apr foal, with J Pearce.   1   60

--   **QUIESCENT** [19] 2-8-11 Dane O'Neill 10/1: 0: Dwelt, nvr on terms: 15th: op 7/1, stablemate of wnr.   0

--   **Shirley Oaks** [12] 2-8-11 G Carter 20/1:   --   **Armida** [16] 2-8-11 R Brisland (5) 33/1:

--   **Jarv** [10] 2-8-11 R Mullen 33/1:   --   **Little Mouse** [6] 2-8-11 J Weaver 33/1:

--   **Divebomb** [1] 2-8-11 J Reid 14/1:

18 ran   Time 1m 0.4   (John E Guest)   R Hannon East Everleigh, Wilts.

1425   **7.15 FM GLOBAL HCAP 3YO 0-85 (D)**   **1m3f135y Good/Soft Inapplicable**   **[87]**
          £4004   £1232   £616   £308

3980} **STAR CAST 247** [3] Major D N Chappell 3-8-9 (68) R Hills 33/1: 0500-1: 3 ch f In The Wings - Thank   76
One's Stars (Alzao) Settled rear, rdn/prog 2f out, led appr fnl 1f, drvn clr ins last: first win, big step
up in trip: 5th at best from 4 juv starts in '99 (7f mdns, rtd 78 at best): clrly apprec this step up to 11.5f
& further shld suit: runs v well fresh on gd/soft grnd & a sharp/turning track.

*1362 **INCA STAR 3** [6] M Johnston 3-9-6 (79)(6ex) J Reid 4/1: 3-5612: 3 b c Trempolino - Inca Empress   2   84
(Sovereign Dancer) In tch, rdn to chall appr fnl 1f, no extra ins last: nicely bckd: qck reapp: in fine form.

1094 **DISTANT PROSPECT 20** [1] J R Arnold 3-8-10 (69) Martin Dwyer 9/1: 030-23: 3 b c Namaqualand -   nk   74
Ukraine's Affair (The Minstrel) Dwelt, rear, prog 2f out, styd on well: up in trip & stays 11.5f well: in gd form.

1093 **DESTINATION 20** [10] C A Cyzer 3-9-6 (79) G Carter 20/1: 0-5244: Waited with, gd hdwy 3f out,   3   80
ev ch but prob just held when hmpd appr fnl 1f, not recover: shade unlucky not to be plcd here: stays 11.5f.

1064 **FAYRWAY RHYTHM 21** [2] 3-9-7 (80) P Robinson 8/1: 44-445: Led early, cl-up after, chall again   ¾   80
3f out, wknd dist: see 1064.

1075 **DIVINE PROSPECT 21** [12] 3-8-13 (72) D Harrison 16/1: 06-656: In tch, rdn to impr 2f out, held   1½   70
fnl 1f: up in trip: see 701 (10f).

1009 **FRATERNITY 28** [11] 3-9-4 (77) L Dettori 8/1: 02-47: Rcd keenly cl-up, led 1m out, rdn/hdd appr   2   72
fnl 1f, wknd: tchd 12/1 on today's h'cap bow: see 1009 (10f, hvy).

*1094 **BLESS THE BRIDE 20** [9] 3-9-1 (74) Pat Eddery 7/2 FAV: 466-18: In tch, eff 3f out, rdn/fdd   1½   67
fnl 2f: well bckd tho' op 5/1: more expected on this step up to 11.5f: btr 1094 (10f, gd, h'cap bow).

1225 **CONSTANT 12** [7] 3-8-11 (70) M Hills 6/1: 05-059: Mid-div, lost tch fnl 2f: op 9/2: btr 1225 (fast).   2½   59

1017 **JEUNE PREMIER 28** [4] 3-8-9 (68) D R McCabe 20/1: 0-500: Rcd keenly in rear, nvr a threat, fin 10th.   2   54

1017 **PRINCE ELMAR 28** [13] 3-9-1 (74) R Hughes 12/1: 30-00: Cl-up, lost tch fnl 2f, fin 11th: h'cap bow.   1   58

1179 **LAFLEUR 15** [5] 3-8-9 (68) T Quinn 8/1: 0-0000: Settled rear, nvr a threat, fin 12th: op 6/1.   2½   48

4462} **FAGIN 214** [8] 3-9-2 (75) S Sanders 20/1: 636-0: Bhd, lost tch fnl 2f, t.o. in 13th: reapp: 15   33
up in trip: plcd once in '99 for B Meehan (mdn, rtd 81): now with M H Tompkins.

13 ran   Time 2m 29.5   (Mrs G C Maxwell)   Major D N Chappell Pulborough, W.Sussex.

1426   **7.45 BEECHCROFT COND STKS 2YO (B)**   **5f str Good/Soft Inapplicable**
          £7308   £2772   £1386   £630

1176 **RARE OLD TIMES 15** [1] Mrs P N Dutfield 2-8-6 L Newman 12/1: 51: 2 b f Inzar - Moona (Lear Fan)   82
Dwelt, chall halfway, led 2f out, edged left but styd on well, drvn out: IR 10,500gns Apr foal, half-sister to an
Italian juv wnr: eff at 5f, 6f will suit: acts on gd/soft & a sharp/turning track: going the right way, win again.

--   **JOHNNY REB** [6] R Hannon 2-8-8 R Hughes 7/2: 2: 2 b c Danehill - Dixie Eyes Blazing (Gone West)   ¾   81
Chsd ldr, ev ch appr fnl 1f, kept on, just held: nicely bckd on debut: 58,000gns first foal: dam a mdn: sire
top-class at 6f/1m: eff at 5f on gd/soft, 6f will suit: excellent debut, will win similar.

*1221 **KOMPLIMENT 12** [3] A Bailey 2-9-0 K Fallon 11/8 FAV: 513: 2 ch c Komaite - Eladale (Ela Mana Mou)   1¼   84
Dsptd lead, rdn/no extra well ins last: hvly bckd & not disgraced here: acts on fast & gd/soft: see 1221.

1312 **QUIZZICAL LADY 6** [2] M Quinn 2-8-6 Pat Eddery 7/1: 051604: Led, drvn/hdd 2f out, wknd: qck   3   68
reapp: btr 1000 (auct mdn, hvy grnd).

*1208 **SOLDIER ON 13** [5] 2-9-0 T Quinn 3/1: 0215: Dwelt, rear, eff 2f out, sn btn: can do better, see 1208.   4   67

--   **SAVING LIVES ATSEA** [4] 2-8-8 S Sanders 20/1: 6: Settled rear, lost tch halfway: debut: Dolphin   6   47
Street IR15,500gns Feb foal: sire top-class 6/7f performer: with M H Tompkins.

6 ran   Time 1m 01.0 (2.2)   (Graham Brown)   Mrs P N Dutfield Axmouth, Devon.

1427   **8.15 TOTE HCAP 3YO 0-85 (D)**   **5f str Good/Soft Inapplicable**   **[91]**
          £7592   £2336   £1168   £584

1334 **AROGANT PRINCE 5** [15] J J Bridger 3-7-10 (59)(6oh) R Brisland (5) 20/1: 0-0431: 3 ch c Aragon -   62
Versaillesprincess (Legend Of France) Made just about all, hard prsd appr fnl 1f, edged left, all out: qk reapp,
1st win: moderate 3rd on debut in '99 (mdn, rtd 58 & 73S): eff at 5f, gets 6f on firm & gd/soft grnd, sharp trks.

1098 **CORBLETS 20** [1] S Dow 3-8-3 (66) P Doe 8/1: 50-322: 3 b f Timeless Times - Dear Glenda (Gold Song)   ½   68
Held up, gd prog to chall appr fnl 1f, kept on under press, held nr fin: improving, see 883.

1220 **LORD YASMIN 4** [4] J Noseda 3-8-3 (66) G Carter 10/1: 02-103: 3 b c Lahib - Adieu Cherie (Bustino)   ¾   66
Mid-div, shkn up halfway & not clrst of runs, ran on for press ins last, nrst fin: op 14/1: clrly eff at
5f but a return to 6f looks sure to suit: acts on gd, gd/soft grnd & firebrand: see 685.

4149} **OUR FRED 236** [15] T G Mills 3-9-0 (77) A Clark 16/1: 3433-4: In tch, prog & ev ch appr fnl 1f, no   ½   75
extra ins last: reapp: plcd 3 out of 4 juv starts (nurs, rtd 79): eff at 5/6f on firm & gd/soft grnd: consistent.

1406 **ILLUSIVE 2** [8] 3-8-7 (70)(bl) F Norton 11/2: 112035: Chsd ldrs, eff appr fnl 1f, no impress till   nk   67
kept on towards fin: well bckd from 7/1: ran 48hrs ago & unsuited by the drop back to 5f here: see 1406, 592.

WINDSOR MONDAY MAY 22ND Sharp, Fig 8 Track

1178 **CHORUS** 15 [7] 3-8-10 (73) P Robinson 10/1: 4-2006: Trkd ldrs, rdn appr fnl 1f, unable to qckn. hd **69**
1098 **POPPYS SONG** 20 [10] 3-8-7 (70) C Rutter 9/1: 441-07: Well plcd, rdn appr fnl 1f, same pace. nk **65**
1219 **JUDIAM** 13 [3] 3-8-5 (68) L Newman (5) 20/1: 1-4508: Mid-div, chsd ldrs appr fnl 1f, no extra fnl 1f. ¾ **61**
1175 **SUSSEX LAD** 15 [9] 3-9-3 (80) R Hughes 9/2 FAV: 60-049: Front rank & ev ch till wknd ent fnl 1f: 1½ **69**
nicely bckd from 6/1 on h'cap bow: see 956.
1285 **SMOKIN BEAU** 9 [13] 3-8-13 (76)(vis) J Fortune 13/2: 200200: Chsd ldrs, outpcd appr fnl 1f: nk **64**
10th: disappointing, had lkd ready for this drop back to 5f: better without visor in 994.
1078 **SHANNON DORE** 21 [14] 3-9-7 (84) W Ryan 7/1: 010-40: Nvr troubled ldrs: 11th, well bckd from 9/1. ¾ **70**
1181 **Mint Leaf** 15 [6] 3-8-7 (70)(t) J Reid 16/1:   3712} **Clansman** 264 [2] 3-8-2 (65) D O'Donohoe 25/1:
4347} **Needwood Truffle** 222 [11] 3-9-1 (78) S Whitworth 25/1: 1021 **Onlyoneunited** 28 [12] 3-8-7 (70) D Sweeney 16/1:
15 ran   Time   (Miss Julie Self)   J J Bridger Liphook, Hants.

1428   **8.45 VOLTAIRE FILLIES MDN 3YO+ (D)**   **1m67yrnd**   **Good/Soft   Inapplicable**
£4277   £1316   £658   £329   3 yo rec 12lb

850 **SHAMAH** 42 [1] B W Hills 3-8-9 R Hills 7/4 FAV: 22-21: 3 ch f Unfuwain - Shurooq (Affirmed) **94**
Made all & pld clr fnl 2f, eased down: val 10L+: hvly bckd: overdue win, rnr-up all 3 prev starts, incl both in
'99 (fill mdn, rtd 96): eff forcing it at 7f/10f on firm & gd/soft, any trk: goes well fresh: useful & improving.
4194} **LATOUR** 233 [16] J W Hills 3-8-9 M Hills 10/1: -645-2: 3 b f Sir Pekan - Fenny Rough (Home Guard) 6 **80**
Handy, eff 3f out, went 2nd appr fnl 1f, outpcd by easy wnr: op 12/1 on reapp: 4th in a Newmarket fill mdn
in '99 (rtd 92): eff at 7f/1m on firm grnd, handles gd/soft: will not al meet one as useful, may win similar.
-- **YOUHADYOURWARNING** [14] Saeed bin Suroor 3-8-9 L Dettori 33/1: 3-3: 3 br f Warning - Youm Jadeed ½ **79**
(Sadler's Wells) Well plcd till kept on onepace appr fnl 2f: reapp, bckd, Brit bow: plcd on sole start
in France last year (hvy grnd): may appreciate a step up to 10f.
-- **TRIPLE SHARP** [10] L M Cumani 3-8-9 J Weaver 16/1: 4: Prom till no extra appr fnl 1f: op 12/1, 2 **76**
debut: Selkirk half-sister to a 9f AW wnr: has ability.
1269 **POPPADAM** 10 [5] 3-8-9 O Urbina 20/1: 0-65: Chsd ldrs till appr fnl 2f: clr rem, qual for h'caps. shd **76**
-- **CAPE LODGE** [13] 3-8-9 T Quinn 25/1: 6: Dwelt, nvr nr ldrs: debut: Lear Fan half-sister to 4 wnrs. 8 **64**
971 **SEEKING SUCCESS** 33 [6] 3-8-9 K Fallon 7/2: -07: Nvr a factor: well bckd from 9/2: btr 971. nk **64**
-- **BRIONEY** [3] 3-8-9 (t) J Fortune 14/1: 8: Nvr better than mid-div: Barathea half-sister to a 9f wnr. nk **64**
-- **HATHEETHAH** [9] 3-8-9 M Fenton 16/1: 9: Nvr dngrs: Machiavellian 1st foal out of a sprinter. 2 **61**
4306} **GOLDFINCH** 224 [15] 3-8-9 D Harrison 25/1: 0-0: Pulled hard in tch till 3f out: 10th, stablemate 5th, 4 **55**
reapp: unplcd sole '99 start (rtd 60): with J Fanshawe.
-- **Bamboozle** [7] 4-9-7 P Doe 25/1:   1181 **Ejder** 15 [12] 4-9-7 S Carson (5) 50/1:
1263 **Wickham** 10 [2] 4-9-7 A Clark 50/1:   1159 **White Sands** 16 [4] 3-8-9 S Sanders 33/1:
-- **Tasso Dancer** [8] 4-9-7 D Sweeney 50/1:
15 ran   Time 1m 43.6   (Hamdan Al Maktoum)   B W Hills Lambourn, Berks.

MUSSELBURGH MONDAY MAY 22ND Righthand, Sharp Track

Official Going   FIRM. Stalls: 5f/2m - Stands Side; Rem - Inside.

1429   **6.30 NEWS AUCT MDN 2YO (F)**   **5f str**   **Good/Firm 39   -15 Slow**
£2828   £808   £404

1249 **FRANICA** 11 [5] A Bailey 2-7-12 J Mackay (7) 7/1: 222201: 2 b f Inzar - Comfrey Glen (Glenstal) **77**
Rear, rdn to impr over 2f out, led dist, rdn clr fnl 50y: rnr-up 1st 4 starts this term: 2,200gns foal, half-sister
to 3 wnrs, dam styd 1m: eff at 5f on fast & hvy, 6f suit: handles a sharp or gall trk: consistent, deserved win.
1006 **CUMBRIAN HARMONY** 28 [7] T D Easterby 2-8-0 W Supple 25/1: 02: 2 b f Distinctly North - Sawaki 1½ **73+**
(Song) Sn outpcd, switched & ran on strongly fnl 2f, nvr nrr: stays 5f on fast, 6f suit: encouraging: see 1006.
1146 **NOWT BUT TROUBLE** 17 [8] D Nicholls 2-8-3 N Kennedy 11/1: 63: 2 ch g Midhish - Shinadeosee 1 **73$**
(Adonijah) Mid-div, hdwy/hung right over 1f out, no extra fnl 1f: stays 5f on fast, 6f will no w suit: see 1146.
1249 **MISS BRIEF** 11 [6] P D Evans 2-8-5 J Carroll 5/2 FAV: -024: Led, hdd dist, onepcd in last: shd **75**
nicely bckd tho' op 9/4: see 1249 (firm).
970 **COZZIE** 33 [1] 2-7-12 A McCarthy (3) 20/1: -305: In tch, kept on fnl 2f, no threat: see 970, 856. 1 **65**
-- **HENRY TUN** [3] 2-8-4(1ow) K Darley 11/1: 6: Ran green, nvr better than mid-div on debut: cheaply ½ **70**
bght Apr foal, half-brother to winning sprinter Sam Tun: dam a 6/7f wnr: shld improve for this debut run.
1249 **JUSTELLA** 11 [12] 2-7-12 Joanna Badger (7) 12/1: -667: Mid-div, short of room & switched (causing ½ **63**
interference) 2f out: kept on, nvr nrr: jockey rec a 6 day irresponsible riding ban: see 1249.
1130 **LAUREL DAWN** 18 [14] 2-8-10 P Bradley (5) 10/1: 48: Trkd ldrs, rdn/rdn appr fnl 1f: see 1130. ¾ **73**
1146 **PHARAOH HATSHEPSUT** 17 [11] 2-8-0 T Williams 25/1: -4009: Handy, lost tch fnl 2f: needs sellers. 1 **60**
-- **CARUSOS** [2] 2-8-3(1ow) G Hind 14/1: 0: Dwelt, rdn & hdwy when short of room 2f out, no dngr ½ **62**
after: 10th: IR 8,000gns Be My Guest foal, half-sister to 6f juv wnr Charming Lotte: will apprec 6f+ in time.
-- **AMAMACKEMMUSH** [9] 2-8-7 F Lynch 10/1: 0: Dwelt, with ldrs over 2f out, wknd qckly fnl 1f, hd **66**
fin 11th: op 7/1: May foal, sire a speedy juv: with K A Ryan.
-- **VENDOME** [10] 2-8-10 J P Spencer 3/1: 0: Prom, hmpd when wkng over 1f out, fin 12th: nicely 7 **54**
bckd on debut: 22,000gns General Monash first foal: with J A Osborne.
1206 **Wharfedale Ghost** 14 [4] 2-8-3 R Winston 100/1:   1083 **Limbo Dancer** 20 [13] 2-7-12 Dale Gibson 100/1:
14 ran   Time 1m 00.2 (2.7)   (Ms M A Rowlands)   A Bailey Little Budworth, Cheshire.

1430   **7.00 APPLEYARD SELLER 3YO+ (F)**   **5f str**   **Good/Firm 39   -03 Slow**
£2758   £788   £394   3 yo rec 8 lb

1143 **SUE ME** 17 [11] D Nicholls 8-9-4 (bl) A Nicholls (3) 11/2: 06-001: 8 b g Contract Law - Pink Fondant **56**
(Northfields) Mid-div, imprvd over 2f out, led dist, drvn out: op 4/1, no bid: '99 Southwell wnr (clmr, rtd 63a)
& Ayr (h'cap, rtd 62): '98 wnr again at Southwell (3, h'caps, rtd 61a), Pontefract & Doncaster (h'caps, rtd 72):
stays 1m, suited by 5/6f on fast, hvy, both A/Ws & any trk, loves Southwell: runs well fresh, with/without blnks.
1258 **PISCES LAD** 10 [12] T D Barron 4-9-9 J P Spencer 10/1: 00-102: 4 b g Cyrano de Bergerac - Tarnside ¾ **58**
Rosal (Mummy's Game) Settled rear, smooth hdwy over 2f out, styd on ins last, nvr nrr: gd run, best at 6f.
1256 **QUITE HAPPY** 10 [6] M H Tompkins 5-8-13 A Whelan 9/4 FAV: 00-033: 5 b m Statoblest - Four Legged 1 **45**
Friend (Aragon) Led, rdn/hdd dist, sn no extra: nicely bckd: loves a sharp 5f: see 1256, 897.

475

*1392 **SWEET MAGIC 2** [13] L R Lloyd James 9-9-9 (t) K Darley 8/1: 040414: Trkd ldrs, rdn to chall ½ 54
2f out, no extra ins last: ran 48hrs ago: remains in gd heart: see 1392 (AW).
1298 **JUST DISSIDENT 7** [8] 8-9-4 D Holland 20/1: -40005: In tch, rdn/styd on appr fnl 1f, nvr nrr: qck reapp. *nk* 49$
1081 **ELLPEEDEE 20** [2] 3-8-10 (t) W Supple 14/1: 0-0656: Handy, improving when hmpd over 1f out, 1½ 46
onepcd ins last: drop in trip: see 909 (6f, soft).
179 **PACK A PUNCH 161** [4] 3-8-5 M Scott (5) 33/1: 46-7: With ldr, rdn/wknd appr fnl 1f: long abs, turf bow. *2* 36
919 **PALACEGATE JACK 37** [3] 9-9-4 (bl) J Carroll 13/2: 253238: Chsd ldrs, sltly hmpd over 1f out, no dngr. *nk* 41
1140 **UNCLE EXACT 18** [10] 3-8-10 F Lynch 6/1: 0-0009: Cl-up, wknd 2f out, eased ins last: see 1140. 1½ 37
1358 **FACILE TIGRE 3** [14] 5-9-4 R Winston 16/1: 000050: Front rank, wknd over 1f out: 10th: qck reapp. ½ 36
1298 **CHOK DI 7** [16] 4-9-4 (bl) A Culhane 33/1: 000000: Nvr a factor: 11th: qck reapp, dubious rating. *shd* 36$
778 **TANGERINE FLYER 54** [9] 5-9-4 Joanna Badger (7) 25/1: 0/0600: Al outpcd, fin 12th, 8 wk abs. ½ 35
1358 **Pallium 3** [15] 12-9-4 (tbl) K Sked 66/1:
959 **Pape Diouf 34** [1] 3-9-1 (bl) G Hind 16/1:
1239 **Six For Luck 11** [7] 8-9-4 (t) J Mackay (7) 100/1:
930 **Royal Canary 37** [5] 3-8-10 (t) Dale Gibson 66/1:
16 ran Time 59.6 (2.1) (T G Meynell) D Nicholls Sessay, N.Yorks.

1431

7.30 APPLEYARD HCAP 3YO+ 0-70 (E) 7f30y rnd Good/Firm 39 -01 Slow [68]
£3003 £924 £462 £231 3 yo rec 11lb

1351 **ERUPT 3** [7] M Brittain 7-8-10 (50) R Winston 16/1: -20421: 7 b g Beveled - Sparklingsovereign 55
(Sparkler) Dwelt, rear, rdn to improve halfway, styd on to lead dist, drvn out: qck reapp: '99 wnr at Newcastle (h'cap, rtd 52), prev term won here at Musselburgh (h'cap, rtd 58): best at 7f/1m on firm, soft & fibresand: acts on any trk, likes Musselburgh: has tired visor, best without: in gd form.
3918} **THREE ANGELS 250** [4] M H Tompkins 5-10-0 (68) A Whelan 20/1: 2060-2: 5 b g Houmayoun - *nk* 72
Mullaghroe (Taboosh) In tch, imprvd 2f out, hung left & kept on for strong press ins last, held cl-home: jockey rec a 4 day careless riding ban & a 2 day whip ban: plcd sev times in '99 (h'caps & stks, rtd 77 at best): '98 wnr at Folkestone (auct mdn) & Haydock (h'cap, rtd 80 at best): suited by 6/7f, stays 1m: acts on fast & gd/soft grnd: handles any trk, eff with/without a visor: clrly goes well fresh: shld win again.
1213 **RAFTERS MUSIC 13** [1] D Nicholls 5-8-12 (52) A Nicholls (3) 11/2: 216033: 5 b g Thatching - Princess ¾ 55
Dixieland (Dixieland Band) Rear, styd on strongly for press ins last, closing at fin: tchd 7/1: stays 7f.
1275 **ALMAZHAR 9** [5] J L Eyre 5-8-11 (51) T Williams 13/2: -22354: Chsd ldrs, rdn to chall appr ¾ 53
fnl 1f, no extra for press fnl 100yds: consistent form: see 1148.
1330 **ITALIAN SYMPHONY 5** [13] 6-9-4 (58)(vis) Joanna Badger (7) 5/1 FAV: 050045: Rear, eff/short of 1½ 57
room over 1f out, kept on well ins last, nvr nrr: nicely bckd, qck reapp: unlucky in running, v tough: see 1330.
942 **RYMERS RASCAL 35** [11] 8-9-5 (59) W Supple 7/1: 500-56: Cl-up, rdn when no room appr fnl 1f, *nk* 57
no extra ins last: on a winning mark, keep in mind: see 942.
1356 **JOHAYRO 3** [9] 7-9-6 (60)(vis) A Culhane 10/1: 405007: Led, hdd dist, wknd: op 8/1. *nk* 58
1038 **PETERS IMP 24** [12] 5-9-11 (65) J Carroll 10/1: 000-58: Sn detached, styd on late: see 1038. 1½ 60
*1132 **MYBOTYE 18** [2] 7-8-8 (48)(t) J Fanning 12/1: 00-419: Dsptd lead, lkd held when badly *shd* 43
hmpd ent fnl 1f, not recover: see 1132 (sell, gd/soft).
1258 **EASTERN PROPHETS 10** [10] 7-9-5 (59)(vis) F Lynch 12/1: 200-30: Trkd ldrs, lost tch fnl 1f, fin 10th. ¾ 53
1190 **MR PERRY 15** [3] 4-9-0 (54)(VIS) D Holland 16/1: 002300: Nvr a threat, fin 11th: twice below 1149. *1* 46
1356 **WISHBONE ALLEY 3** [8] 5-8-11 (51) C Teague 20/1: 203000: Front rank, wknd qckly fnl 2f, fin ½ 42
12th: qck reapp: girth reportedly snapped shortly after start: see 1356 (6f).
1243 **YOUNG ROSEIN 11** [14] 4-9-1 (55) K Darley 13/2: U20-00: Rear, brief eff 3f out, no threat, fin 13th. 1¾ 43
1144 **LADY LOVE 17** [6] 3-9-2 (67) J P Spencer 20/1: 060-50: Mid-div, hmpd 5f out, no threat after: last. *5* 47
14 ran Time 1m 28.0 (3.1) (Sidney Eaton) M Brittain Warthill, N.Yorks.

1432

8.00 APPLEYARD TROPHY HCAP 3YO+ 0-65 (F) 1m4f Good/Firm 39 +07 Fast [62]
£5300 £1631 £815 £407 3 yo rec 17lb

1243 **OCTANE 11** [13] W M Brisbourne 4-8-12 (46) A McCarthy (3) 9/2: 0-0031: 4 b g Cryptoclearance - 52
Something True (Sir Ivor) Mid-div, rdn/ran on well appr fnl 1f, led ins last, rdn out: good time, first win: with H Cecil when fav for 1st 2 in '99 (rtd 80, debut, flattered): eff around 12f on fast: handles a sharp trk.
1741} **PICCADILLY 353** [9] Miss Kate Milligan 5-8-3 (37) G Hind 20/1: 1000-2: 5 ch m Belmez - Polly's Pear 1½ 39
(Sassafras) Led, clr 2f out, wknd/hdd ins last, no extra: tchd 33/1 on reapp: wnr at Ripon on '99 reapp (sell h'cap, rtd 41), plcd twice over hdles (sell h'caps, rtd 74h, stays 2m on fast): with T Etherington in '98 (rtd 63 at best): eff at 12f on fast & soft: has tried blnks, seems better without: gd run, win another sell h'cap.
975 **SANDABAR 33** [8] Mrs M Reveley 7-9-11 (59)(t) A Culhane 13/2: 04-003: 7 b g Green Desert - ¾ 60
Children's Corner (Top Ville) Settled rear, gd hdwy when short of room over 2f out, rallied appr fnl 1f, no extra fnl 100yds: tchd 10/1 & poss a shade unlucky here: styd this longer 12f trip: see 786.
1301 **ELSIE BAMFORD 7** [10] M Johnston 4-8-4 (38) J Fanning 14/1: 06-304: Cl-up, rdn & btn ins last. *shd* 39
1147 **SING AND DANCE 17** [7] 7-9-4 (52) R Winston 4/1 FAV: 202-25: Settled in tch, rdn to improve 1½ 50
5f out, ev ch till no extra ins last: op 3/1: won this race off a 4lb lower mark last year: see 1147.
1355 **FREEDOM QUEST 3** [2] 5-10-0 (62) W Supple 5/1: -44346: Front rank, drvn & not pace of ldrs appr ½ 59
fnl 1f: tchd 8/1: qck reapp: see 903, 793.
1065 **KATIE KOMAITE 21** [4] 7-8-4 (38)(vis) A Mackay 25/1: 10-407: Rear, late hdwy: mkt drifter, see 890 (hvy). *6* 26
1272 **CASSANDRA 10** [3] 4-9-4 (52) K Darley 14/1: 00-258: Handy, rdn/held fnl 2f: op 10/1: btr 859 (10f). ¾ 39
1272 **TIME LOSS 10** [14] 5-9-2 (50) J P Spencer 5/1: 0-0549: Nvr better than mid-div: see 1100. *hd* 37
1241 **COSMIC CASE 11** [12] 5-8-2 (36)(vis) T Williams 16/1: 0-5040: With ldr, fading/hmpd 2f out: 10th. *3* 18
1364 **Rainbow Raver 3** [5] 4-8-10 (44) R Cody Boutcher (7) 25/1:
1254 **Amron 10** [11] 13-8-8 (42) O Pears 25/1:
1147 **Roma 17** [1] 5-8-9 (43) J Carroll 33/1:
4444} **Diamond Crown 215** [6] 9-8-2 (36) A Whelan 33/1:
14 ran Time 2m 24.4 (3.8) (Christopher Chell) W M Brisbourne Great Ness, Shropshire.

1433

8.30 TOUN CLASS STKS 3YO+ 0-60 (F) 1m6f Good/Firm 39 -27 Slow
£3461 £1065 £532 £266 3 yo rec 20lb

1299 **ALPHA ROSE 7** [6] M L W Bell 3-8-0 J Mackay (7) 2/1 FAV: 6-5541: 3 ch f Inchinor - Philgwyn (Milford) 59
Cl-up, hdwy to lead over 2f out, prsd ins last, rdn out, shade cosy: qck reapp, nicely bckd: first win: unplcd on sole '99 start for R J R Williams (rtd 68): eff at 10f, stays 14f on firm/fast grnd.
1329 **TOTEM DANCER 5** [2] J L Eyre 7-9-8 D Holland 5/2: 000102: 7 b m Mtoto - Ballad Opera (Sadler's *nk* 59
Wells) Chsd ldrs, prog over 2f out, chall dist, no extra cl-home, just btn: clr rem, qck reapp: consistent.
793 **KILCREGGAN 53** [1] Mrs M Reveley 6-9-9 A Culhane 3/1: 610-03: 6 b g Landyap - Lehmans Lot (Oats) 3½ 55

MUSSELBURGH **MONDAY MAY 22ND Righthand, Sharp Track**

Settled last, rdn & styd on 2f out, not pace of front 2: 8 wk abs: '99 scorer at Redcar (h'cap, rtd 67 at best):
plcd in a bmpr in 98/99 (2m, gd/soft): eff at 14f, 2m+ shld suit: acts on fast grnd & a gall track.
*1145 **MIDYAN BLUE 17** [5] P Monteith 10-9-11 R Winston 7/1: 000/14: Led, rdn/hdd 2f out, sn btn. *¾* **56**
978 **CASTANEA SATIVA 33** [4] 3-8-0 (BL) W Supple 8/1: 20-045: Trkd ldrs, wknd qckly for press fnl *19* **31**
3f: op 5/1, first time blnks: prob not stay this longer 14f trip: see 978.
5 ran Time 3m 05.7 (9.2) (Richard I Morris Jnr) M L W Bell Newmarket.

1434 **9.00 EAST LOTHIAN HCAP 3YO 0-65 (F) 1m rnd Good/Firm 39 -04 Slow [69]**
£2814 £804 £402

1299 **YENALED 7** [5] J S Goldie 3-9-4 (59) A Culhane 6/1: 563-31: 3 gr g Rambo Dancer - Fancy Flight **67**
(Arctic Tern) Held up, hdwy to lead on bit over 1f out, rdn & easily went clr ins last, eased fnl 50yds, val 5/6L:
qck reapp, first win: plcd sev times in '99 (h'caps, rtd 64 at best): dam won over 10f: eff at 1m/10f, further
shld suit: acts on gd & firm, poss handles soft: v impressive here & shld make a qck follow up under a penalty.
1255 **JUMBOS FLYER 10** [10] J L Eyre 3-9-5 (60) D Holland 6/1: 00-052: 3 ch c Jumbo Hirt - Fragrant *1¾* **61**
Princess (Germont) Waited with, gd hdwy 2f out, styd on ins last but no ch with easy wnr: nicely bckd:
stays 1m on firm & fast: met an improving rival here, shld win similar soon: see 1255.
1361 **DENTON LADY 3** [3] W T Kemp 3-8-3 (44)(bl) O Pears 25/1: -60003: 3 br f Inchinor - Lammastide *1½* **42**
(Martinmas) Trkd ldrs, ev ch till not pace of wnr appr fnl 1f: qck reapp & an imprvd effort here out of sell grade.
1040 **JUMP 24** [9] J A Osborne 3-9-2 (57) J P Spencer 20/1: -26004: Led, hdd appr fnl 1f, sn btn: op 14/1. *1½* **52**
800 **COSMIC SONG 53** [2] 3-8-4 (45) Dale Gibson 7/1: 5-5635: Chsd ldrs, no extra for press appr fnl *shd* **40**
1f: 8 wk abs: may apprec a softer surface: see 800 (mdn h'cap).
1255 **COMEX FLYER 10** [12] 3-9-2 (57) A Nicholls (3) 25/1: 46-406: Front rank, rdn & fdd appr fnl 1f. *4* **45**
*1274 **BONDI BAY 9** [1] 3-9-0 (55) W Supple 6/1: 5-2017: Rcd keen in mid-div, rdn & no extra fnl 2f: *nk* **43**
shld apprec a return to 10f: see 1274 (seller).
800 **FLOATING EMBER 53** [13] 3-7-12 (39) T Williams 50/1: 600-08: Handy, grad fdd fnl 3f: 8 wk abs: *½* **26**
unplcd in '99 (mdns & nurs, rtd 56 at best): half-sister to a 6f wnr.
4505} **PARKERS PEACE 210** [8] 3-9-6 (61) J Carroll 10/1: 000-9: Prom, wknd qckly fnl 2f: reapp: unplcd *¾* **47**
in 3 juv starts (mdn, rtd 63 at best).
1296 **QUIDS INN 7** [7] 3-8-10 (51) K Darley 7/4 FAV: 000-20: Prom, drpd rear 4f out, no threat after, *nk* **37**
fin 10th: well bckd, qck reapp: much better expected after 1296.
1365 **WEE BARNEY 3** [6] 3-8-2 (43) N Kennedy 50/1: 000-00: Al rear, fin 11th: qck reapp. *1½* **26**
4251} **A BOB LIGHT 230** [11] 3-9-7 (62) A Whelan 12/1: 2450-0: Trkd ldrs, grad wknd halfway: 12th: reapp. *3½* **39**
1085 **CALKO 20** [4] 3-9-4 (59)(bl) R Winston 20/1: 111000: Nvr a threat, fin last: thrice below 540 (AW). *5* **28**
13 ran Time 1m 41.0 (3.5) (Martin Delaney) J S Goldie Uplawmoor, E.Renfrews

BATH **MONDAY MAY 22ND Lefthand, Turning Track With Uphill finish**

Official Going GOOD TO FIRM. Stalls: Str Course - Far Side; Round Course - Inside.

1435 **1.30 MED AUCT MDN DIV 1 3YO (F) 1m rnd Good/Firm 25 00 Fast**
£1876 £536 £268

1218 **MAMZUG 13** [2] B Hanbury 3-9-0 G Faulkner (3) 7/4 FAV: 0-41: 3 b c Hamas - Bellissi (Bluebird) **76**
Cmftbly made all: well bckd, fair time: finished last sole '99 start, clrly imprvd this term: eff at 1m, tried
10f on reapp: acts on fast grnd & a turning trk: improved for forcing tactics.
3804} **CHRISS LITTLE LAD 258** [4] W R Muir 3-9-0 Martin Dwyer 14/1: 040-2: 3 ch g Hamas - Jeema (Thatch) *3½* **67**
Prom, rdn 2f out, kept on for 2nd but no impress on wnr: op 10/1 on reapp, clr rem: 4th in an auct mdn last
term (rtd 67): half-brother to wnrs btwn 6f/1m, apprec step up to 1m: handles fast grnd.
1263 **YERTLE 10** [1] J A R Toller 3-9-0 R Ffrench 3/1: -003: 3 b c Turtle Island - Minatina (Ela Mana Mou) *4* **59**
Rcd in 2nd after 3f, under press 3f out, onepace bef dist: drifted from 7/4: flattered on debut (Wood Ditton).
4515} **BRISBANE ROAD 209** [3] I A Balding 3-9-0 K Fallon 11/4: 00-4: Cl-up, outpcd fnl 2f under kind *nk* **58**
ride: op 7/2, reapp: unplcd in '99 (rtd 60): type to improve now h'capped.
4432} **VICTORIET 216** [6] 3-8-9 A McGlone 14/1: 0000-5: Nvr a factor: reapp, op 10/1: 4th of 5 in a fill *¾* **51**
mdn in '99 (rtd 66): has tried blnks: a plater: with A Murphy.
1175 **ST IVES 15** [9] 3-9-0 R Cochrane 25/1: 006-06: Prom till wknd qckly 3f out: op 14/1: rtd 58 in '99. *10* **36**
1093 **SILVER AURIOLE 20** [7] 3-8-9 S Sanders 50/1: 007: Pulled hard, nvr in it: no form *2* **27**
4500} **JAYNES PRINCESS 210** [5] 3-8-9 D Sweeney 50/1: 0-8: Sn struggling: reapp: unplcd sole '99 start. *nk* **26**
1204 **THE LONELY WIGEON 14** [8] 3-9-0 (t) R Mullen 25/1: 059: Rear, brief eff 5f out: turf bow, modest. *¾* **29**
9 ran Time 1m 40.3 (2) (Christopher Cooke) B Hanbury Newmarket, Suffolk

1436 **2.00 MED AUCT MDN DIV 2 3YO (F) 1m rnd Good/Firm 25 -06 Slow**
£1869 £534 £267

1080 **CARENS HERO 21** [8] Mrs A J Perrett 3-9-0 R Hughes 1/2 FAV: 0-31: 3 ch g Petardia - Clearglade **77**
(Vitiges) Readily made all: hvly bckd to land the odds: unplcd sole '99 start (auct mdn, rtd 74): eff at 1m:
goes on fast & gd/soft grnd, forcing the pace on a turning track: lightly raced.
972 **LADY LUCHA 33** [9] B W Hills 3-8-9 M Hills 5/1: -02: 3 ch f Lord Avie - Sin Lucha (Northfields) *1½* **67**
Chsd wnr, feeling pace appr fnl 2f, rallied dist, al held: op 3/1: acts on fast & will relish 10f+.
1281 **EREBUS 9** [1] M H Tompkins 3-9-0 S Sanders 10/1: 063: 3 b c Desert Style - Almost A Lady (Entitled) *1¾* **68**
Mid-div, eff 3f out, styd on but nvr pace to chall: op 7/1: suited by this fast grnd, worth another try at 10f in h'caps.
972 **WORK OF FICTION 33** [4] R Hannon 3-9-0 Dane O'Neill 10/1: -04: In tch, prog ent fnl 3f, no extra *1¾* **64**
under press bef dist: op 6/1: may do better back at 7f when h'capped.
-- **MAIDEN AUNT** [6] 3-8-9 Martin Dwyer 16/1: 5: Nvr a factor: debut: Distant Relative filly with W Muir. *3½* **52**
1261 **PERCUSSION 10** [7] 3-9-0 S Whitworth 50/1: -006: Rear, shaken up 3f out, outpcd: nds mid-dist h'caps. *1½* **54**
1212 **GOLD RIDER 13** [5] 3-9-0 R Studholme (5) 40/1: 07: Prom till 2f out: Common Grounds gelding. *½* **53**
-- **AL AWAALAH** [2] 3-8-9 F Norton 50/1: 8: Dwelt, nvr dangerous: debut: Mukaddamah filly. *7* **34**
1266 **LEGAL TENDER 10** [3] 3-9-0 V Slattery 50/1: 09: Sn bhd: Contract Law gelding with D Burchell. *25* **14**
9 ran Time 1m 40.8 (2.5) (Mrs R Doel) Mrs A J Perrett Pulborough, W Sussex

1437

2.30 TROWBRIDGE NOV STKS 2YO (D)　5f rnd　Good/Firm 25　-33 Slow
£3212　£988　£494　£247

*1197　**KACHINA DOLL** 14 [1]　M R Channon 2-8-11 T Quinn 6/5 FAV: -30011: 2 b f Mujadil - Betelgeuse　　　　87
(Kalaglow) Cl-up, went on 2f out & easily pulled clr: well bckd, slow time: recent Windsor wnr (fill mdn auct):
11,500 gns Apr foal: eff at 5f, 6f going to suit: likes fast grnd, prob not hvy: improving fast, win more races.
*1088　**QUANTUM LADY** 20 [3]　B R Millman 2-8-11 F Norton 9/4: -412: 2 b f Mujadil - Folly Finnesse　　6　75
(Joligeneration) Chsd ldrs, eff 2f out, outpcd by wnr: op 13/8: cght a fair sort on this qckr grnd: see 1088.
*1166　**OPEN WARFARE** 16 [2]　M Quinn 2-9-0 J Fortune 11/4: -33413: 2 b f General Monash - Pipe Opener　1½　74
(Prince Sabo) Nvr going pace: op 2/1: reportedly unsuited by qck grnd tho' handled it well in 1166 (made all).
1267　**NINE TO FIVE** 10 [4]　R Brotherton 2-8-11 S Sanders 10/1: 11334: Led till 2f out, no extra: op 7/1.　hd　71
4 ran　　Time 1m 03.4 (3.4)　　(Ridgeway Downs Racing)　　　　　M R Channon West Isley, Berks

1438

3.00 MITIE GURKHA HCAP 3YO+ 0-70 (E)　5f161y rnd　Good/Firm 25　-01 Slow　　　[70]
£2847　£876　£438　£219　3 yo rec 9 lb

1258　**NINEACRES** 10 [17]　J M Bradley 9-9-0 (56)(bl) P Fitzsimons (5) 10/1: 305221: 9 b g Sayf El Arab -　　60
Mayor (Laxton) Rear, gd wide prog after halfway to lead dist, held on gamely: prev won at W'hampton (rtd 58a) &
Southwell (h'caps): '99 wnr again at W'hampton (clmr, rtd 59a, turf h'cap plcd, rtd 42): eff at 5/6f, stays
7f: acts on firm, gd grnd, both AWs, likes W'hampton: wears blnks or vis & can force the pace/run well fresh.
1074　**MR STYLISH** 21 [1]　I A Balding 4-9-12 (68) K Fallon 9/2: 404-02: 4 b g Mazilier - Moore Stylish　hd　71
(Moorestyle) Towards rear, switched appr fnl 1f, ran on strongly, pace came too sn: op 6/1: thrice rnr-up in
'99 (h'caps, rtd 71): unrcd juv: eff at 6f, stays 7f: acts on fast & hvy grnd, any trk: must shed mdn tag soon.
1196　**DIAMOND GEEZER** 14 [4]　R Hannon 4-9-6 (62) Dane O'Neill 4/1 FAV: 502443: 4 br c Tenby - Unaria　nk　64
(Prince Tenderfoot) Front rank, led bef 2f out till ent fnl 1f, styd on: in gd form: see 1092, 113.
1196　**ZEPPO** 14 [10]　B R Millman 5-9-1 (57) L Dettori 5/1: 600-04: Trkd ldrs, drvn/ev ch dist, onepace nr fin.　nk　58
1264　**KILCULLEN LAD** 10 [14]　6-10-0 (70)(vis) J F Egan 16/1: 060-05: Mid-div, wide, styd on fnl 1½f　¾　69
but not able to chall: clr rem, top-weight: '99 Brighton wnr (h'cap, rtd 74, R Ingram): '98 wnr at Redcar
(h'cap, rtd 85 & 85a, K Ivory): eff at 5/6f on firm, soft grnd & equitrack: prob best in a visor now, tried blnks.
1192　**ALBERT THE BEAR** 15 [18]　R Hughes 7-9-5 (61) 600-06: Well plcd & clr till no extra appr fnl 1f:　2　54
'99 wnr at Carlisle (sell, 1st time vis) & Pontefract (h'cap, rtd 69 at best): disq after plcd in '98 (h'cap,
rtd 86): eff at 6/7.5f on firm & gd/soft, handles hvy, likes Chester: well h'capped, best visored now (not worn).
958　**BALI STAR** 34 [6]　5-8-8 (50) Pat Eddery 16/1: 00-207: Outpcd, late prog into mid-div: not given　nk　42
a hard time & this lightly rcd gldg wld be interesting in a mdn h'cap: see 802.
41　**EARLEY SESSION** 191 [9]　3-8-0 (51)(4ow)(11oh) C Rutter 50/1: 000-8: Struggled to go pace, switched　1　40
appr fnl 1f & kept on: stiff task on reapp/h'cap bow: rtd 57 in '99: lks capable of better over further.
4490}　**BOLD SABOTEUR** 212 [2]　3-8-4 (55) N Pollard 16/1: 000-9: Nvr in it: h'cap bow: rtd 60 in '99.　½　42
4133}　**BAYONET** 237 [16]　4-9-0 (56) V Slattery 40/1: 4000-0: Chsd ldrs, onepace appr fnl 2f: , 10th on reapp:　nk　42
placed in a 6f mdn h'cap on fast grnd in '99 (rtd 58): with Jane Southcombe.
1105　**CASTLE BEAU** 19 [11]　5-8-6 (48) F Norton 25/1: 0/000: Al towards rear: 11th, yet to make the frame.　shd　34
1273　**DELTA SOLEIL** 10 [12]　8-9-7 (63) R Cochrane 14/1: 00-000: Al towards rear, not clr run 2f out: 12th.　2½　43
4280}　**CRUSTY LILY** 227 [3]　4-8-1 (43) Claire Bryan (5) 16/1: 5100-0: Led till appr fnl 2f, sn btn: 18th, st/mate wnr.　0
1140　Ecudamah 18 [7] 4-9-4 (60) T G McLaughlin 16/1:　1074 Sharp Gossip 21 [5] 4-9-11 (67) S Whitworth 16/1:
838　My Petal 45 [8] 4-9-8 (64)(BL) L Newman (5) 20/1:　3887} Sontime 252 [13] 3-9-1 (66) D Sweeney 25/1:
563　Calandrella 90 [15] 7-7-12 (40) G Sparkes (4) 20/1:
18 ran　　Time 1m 10.6 (1.5)　　(J M Bradley)　　　　　J M Bradley Sedbury, Glos

1439

3.30 CHEDDAR CLASSIFIED STKS 3YO 0-80 (D)　1m2f46y　Good/Firm 25　-03 Slow
£3701　£1139　£569　£284

979　**ECSTASY** 32 [1]　R M Beckett 3-8-9 Pat Eddery 9/2: 030-01: 3 b f Pursuit Of Love - Gong (Bustino)　　79
Held up in tch, imprvd to chall appr fnl 1f, hard rdn to get on top towards fin: op 10/3: '99 Warwick
wnr for P Walwyn (auct mdn, rtd 81 at best): eff at 7f/10f on fast, gd/soft grnd & any trk.
1310　**MINGLING** 6 [4]　M H Tompkins 3-8-12 S Sanders 4/5 FAV: 50-352: 3 b c Wolfhound - On The Tide　¾　80
(Slip Anchor) Well plcd, narrow lead 2f out, sn rdn, hdd fnl 50y: hvly bckd, qck reapp: more expected after 1310.
4339}　**MYTHICAL KING** 223 [5]　B Palling 3-8-12 K Fallon 10/1: 350-3: 3 b c Fairy King - Whatcombe (Alleged)　nk　79
Led till 2f out, onepace: tchd 14/1, reapp, clr rem: plcd last term (mdn, rtd 76): styd lngr 10f trip on firm/fast.
1094　**PALUA** 20 [6]　Mrs A J Bowlby 3-8-12 J Stack 6/1: 030-34: Pulled hard, prom till fdd/edged left bef fnl 1f.　4　73
1177　**SILENT NIGHT** 15 [2]　3-8-9 N Pollard 7/1: 150-05: In tch till fnl 2f: tchd 9/1, needs a drop back in trip.　8　60
4597}　**EDEIFF** 200 [3]　3-8-9 P Fitzsimons (5) 20/1: 601-6: Dwelt, brght to stands rail 4f out, sn struggling:　8　50
reapp: landed fnl '99 start at Windsor (sell, rtd 61): eff at 1m, bred to get 12f: acts on gd/soft & a sharp trk.
6 ran　　Time 2m 08.9 (2.9)　　(A D G Oldrey)　　　　　R M Beckett Lambourn, Berks

1440

4.00 SALLY LUNN FILLIES HCAP 3YO+ 0-80 (D)　1m5f22y　Good/Firm 25　-13 Slow　　　[76]
£3760　£1157　£578　£289　3 yo rec 19lb

1091　**PULAU PINANG** 20 [12]　G A Butler 4-9-10 (72)(t) L Dettori 2/1 FAV: 10-221: 4 ch f Dolphin Street - Inner　　79
Pearl (Gulf Pearl) Waited with, imprvd ent fnl 4f rdn to lead appr fnl 1f, styd on strgly: well bckd from 3/1:
'99 Lingfield wnr (auct mdn, rtd 71): eff at 12/13f, shld get 2m: acts on firm, gd & equitrack, with/without t-strap.
*1253　**FEE MAIL** 10 [4]　I A Balding 4-9-6 (68) K Fallon 4/1: 1-3312: 4 b f Danehill - Wizardry (Shirley　1¾　71
Heights) Tried to make all, under press ent fnl 2f, sn hdd, styd on: op 3/1, clr rem: stays 13f, v genuine.
853　**ROYAL PATRON** 42 [5]　J L Dunlop 4-9-9 (71) T Quinn 7/2: 562-23: 4 ch f Royal Academy - Indian Queen 3　70
(Electric) Handy, chsd ldr halfway till onepace 2f out: 6 wk abs: handles fast & gd/soft grnd, see 853.
1094　**ELEGIA PRIMA** 20 [3]　Major D N Chappell 3-7-11 (63)(2oh)(1ow) F Norton 14/1: 600-04: Mid-div, eff & 3　60
short of room 5f out, late hdwy, nvr a threat: well worth another try over mid-dists: see 1094.
1091　**CHEEK TO CHEEK** 20 [9]　6-9-1 (63) M Hills 9/1: 325-55: Mid-div thr'out: op 7/1: see 1091.　1½　57
1128　**TYROLEAN LOVE** 18 [7]　4-7-10 (44)(1oh) R Brisland (5) 25/1: 040-06: Nvr troubled ldrs: see 1128.　2½　35
1180　**NOTEWORTHY** 15 [6]　4-8-12 (60) R Cochrane 20/1: 345-07: Prom till appr fnl 2f: 3rd of 5 in '99　3　48
for J Noseda (fill mdn, rtd 74 at best): once rcd juv: eff at 12f, stays 14f on fast & gd grnd: with J Neville.
6　**LEGGY LADY** 196 [8]　4-7-13 (47) R Ffrench 14/1: 0604-8: Unplcd till wknd qckly 3f out: reapp:　nk　35
failed to make the frame in '99 (rtd 60): with J Toller.

BATH
MONDAY MAY 22ND   **Lefthand, Turning Track With Uphill finish**

4454} **BOSSY SPICE** 214 [1] 3-7-10 (63)(26oh) J Bramhill 100/1: 6000-9: Al towards rear: no form.　　nk　50$
--　　**HAPPY GO LUCKY** [10] 6-9-5 (67) O Urbina 25/1: 2001/0: In tch till 3f out: 10th, 2 year abs:　　1　53
'98 Folkestone wnr (class stks, rtd 70 at best): '97 Warwick wnr (ltd stks, rtd 87, R O'Sullivan): has tried
hdles: eff at 10/12f on firm, soft grnd, any trk: best forcing the pace: with M Weeden.
1023 **STREET WALKER** 28 [2] 4-8-3 (51) A Clark 12/1: 53-400: Nvr troubled ldrs: 11th, see 853.　　1½　35
635　**ANNELIINA** 79 [11] 4-8-10 (58) R Morse 33/1: 0-0000: Sn bhd: 12th, 11 wk abs, much longer trip.　　16　28
12 ran　　Time 2m 50.5 (5)　　　(Mrs A K H Ooi)　　　G A Butler Blewbury, Oxon

---

1441　　**4.30 LAVERTON CLASSIFIED STKS 3YO+ 0-80 (D)**　　**5f rnd**　　**Good/Firm 25　-01 Slow**
　　　　£3721　£1145　£572　£286　3 yo rec 8 lb

1126 **ALPEN WOLF** 18 [7] W R Muir 5-9-5 Martin Dwyer 13/2: 105-31: 5 ch g Wolfhound - Oatfield (Great　　79
Nephew) Front rank, led ent fnl 2f, drvn out, gamely: tchd 10/1: '99 wnr at Brighton & here at Bath (h'caps,
rtd 79): '98 scorer at Brighton (3, sell, h'cap & class stks) & Folkestone (class stks, rtd 71): eff at 5f/6f,
sharp 7f: acts on firm/fast grnd, any trk: loves Brighton, likes Bath: gd weight carrier: tough.
4413} **RUSHCUTTER BAY** 217 [3] P L Gilligan 7-9-5 A Polli (3) 10/1: 5050-2: 7 br g Mon Tresor - Llwy Bren　nk　77
(Lidhame) Outpcd early, gd hdwy ent fnl 2f, rdn to chall ins last, held nr fin: gd reapp: '99 Windsor wnr
(class stks, rtd 90): '98 Newmarket wnr (h'cap, rtd 84): eff at 5/6f on firm & gd grnd, without visor: best
up with/forcing the pace: back on a good mark now & this shld have put him spot on, especially back at 6f.
1264 **DANCING MYSTERY** 10 [11] E A Wheeler 6-9-5 S Carson (5) 20/1: 10-003: 6 b g Beveled - Batchworth　hd　76
Dancer (Ballacashtal) Well plcd, wide, chall on bit ent fnl 2f, ev ch, not quicken, just btn: back to form, see 64.
1286 **EASTER OGIL** 9 [9] I A Balding 5-9-5 (vis) K Fallon 5/1: -50064: Badly outpcd till strong burst　　1　73
fnl 1½f, nvr nrr: tchd 6/1: prob wants a bit further but back on a wng mark: see 941.
1173 **CAUDA EQUINA** 16 [4] 6-9-5 T Quinn 3/1: -02005: Mid-div, eff 2f out, not pace to chall: well bkcd　shd　73
from 9/2: rtd 82 when landed this race in '99 & has a fine record at this course: see 905.
1013 **SPEED ON** 28 [2] 7-9-5 C Rutter 8/1: 660-06: Outpcd towards rear, staying on fin but no threat: op 11/2.　1¼　70
*1012 **WILDFLOWER** 28 [5] 3-8-11 S Sanders 8/1: 17: Wide nvr trbld ldrs: unsuited by drop back to 5f on　nk　69
qckr grnd against a seasoned bunch on only 2nd ever start: well worth another eff after 1012 (7f soft, mdn).
4413} **RITAS ROCK APE** 217 [6] 5-9-2 F Norton 12/1: 2130-8: Led till ent fnl 2f, no extra: sharper for reapp:　½　64
v progressive last term, won at Brighton (2, 1 stks), here at Bath & Lingfield & Salisbury (h'caps/appr h'caps,
rtd 80): plcd in '98 (rtd 62 & 56a): loves forcing the pace at 5f on firm & gd grnd, handles gd/soft & fibresand.
1220 **CHARLOTTEVALENTINA** 12 [10] 3-8-8 J F Egan 8/1: 06-029: Bhd ldrs onepace when hmpd twice ins last.¾　60
763　**PRINCE PROSPECT** 55 [8] 4-9-5 Pat Eddery 5/1: 010220: Chsd ldrs till appr fnl 1f: 10th, 8 wk abs.　1¾　60
1264 **PRICE OF PASSION** 10 [1] 4-9-2 (vis) R Cochrane 20/1: 010-00: Struggling after halfway: stiffish　　7　43
task at the weights, visor reapplied: '99 Goodwood wnr (h'cap, rtd 74): '98 Folkestone wnr (nurs, rtd 85):
eff at 5f on firm/fast grnd, sharp/undul trk: eff with/without visor: with D Arbuthnot.
11 ran　　Time 1m 01.6 (1.3)　　　(R Haim)　　　W R Muir Lambourn, Berks

---

1442　　**5.00 LEVY BOARD HCAP 3YO+ 0-70 (E)**　　**1m rnd**　　**Good/Firm 25　+03 Fast**　　**[69]**
　　　　£2947　£842　£421　3 yo rec 12lb

*1259 **TAPAGE** 10 [3] Andrew Reid 4-8-10 (51) M Henry 14/1: 030-11: 4 b g Great Commotion - Irena (Bold Lad)　　57
Trkd ldr, rdn to chall appr fnl 1f, led ins last: fair time: 10 days ago scored at Lingfield (AW h'cap, rtd 50a):
dual '99 rnr-up (clmrs, rtd 69, W Muir): '98 Lingfield wnr (auct mdn, rtd 78a, D Gillespie): eff at 7f, suited
by 1m: acts on firm, fast grnd & equitrack, any trk, likes Lingfield: best without blnks, forcing the pace.
1058 **TWIN TIME** 23 [1] J S King 6-9-6 (61) J Fortune 6/1: 500-42: 6 b m Syrtos - Carramba (Tumble Wind)　½　65
Tried to make all, rdn 2f out, worn down ins last: nrly repeated last season's success in this race (off same mark).
1235 **ARBENIG** 11 [9] B Palling 5-9-7 (48) D Sweeney 20/1: 600-03: 5 b m Anita's Prince - Out On Her Own　¾　50
(Superlative) Mid-div, hdwy to chase ldrs appr fnl 1f, unable to chall: apprec return to 1m, eff with/without blnks.
1279 **ITS OUR SECRET** 9 [15] M H Tompkins 4-9-11 (66) S Sanders 10/1: 000-24: Rear, wide prog fnl 2f.　1¾　64
*1040 **LORD HARLEY** 24 [11] 3-8-7 (60) C Rutter 12/1: -22115: Midfield, late hdwy, nvr dngrs: turf return.　nk　57
1097 **DORISSIO** 20 [4] 4-9-9 (64) K Fallon 5/2 FAV: 1-3336: Rear, styd on fnl 2f, nvr nr to chall:　hd　61
well bckd from 9/2, jockey given 4 day ban for careless riding: see 841.
1129 **LYCIAN** 18 [10] 5-9-3 (58) S Whitworth 7/1: 200-67: Nvr better than mid-div: capable of better.　1¼　53
1129 **ARDENT** 18 [13] 6-8-7 (48) A Clark 16/1: 00-648: Rear, rdn to chase ldrs 3f out, fdd bef dist: see 23.　½　42
1190 **BODFARI SIGNET** 15 [5] 4-8-5 (46)(bl) A Polli (3) 33/1: 0-0009: Chsd front pair till 2f out: blnks reapp.　4　32
1201 **ROGUE SPIRIT** 14 [16] 4-9-13 (68) Pat Eddery 6/1: -00040: Nvr a factor: 10th, top-weight, tchd 8/1.　3½　48
1066 **WARRING** 21 [7] 6-8-8 (49) J F Egan 8/1: 540-50: Handy till 3f out: 11th, see 1066.　nk　28
1099 **TARCOOLA** 20 [8] 3-8-12 (65) R Cochrane 7/1: 04-0F: Rear, hmpd/fell ent fnl 4f: op 6/1 on h'cap bow.　0
111　Peruginos Malt 178 [6] 4-9-5 (60) A McGlone 33/1: 2841} **Research Master** 305 [12] 3-8-7 (60) S Carson (5) 33/1:
172　Mr Bergerac 163 [2] 9-9-9 (64) J Stack 20/1: B
15 ran　　Time 1m 40.1 (1.8)　　　(A S Reid)　　　Andrew Reid Mill Hill, London NW7

BEVERLEY
TUESDAY MAY 23RD   **Righthand, Oval Track, With Stiff, Uphill Finish**

Official Going: GOOD Stalls: Inside

1443　　**2.25 BEAVER SELLER 2YO (F)**　　**5f**　　**Good 57　-43 Slow**
　　　　£2296　£656　£328

1236 **NAUGHTY KNIGHT** 12 [11] G B Balding 2-8-11 A Nicholls (3) 20/1: -0501: 2 ch c King's Signet -　　67
Maid Of Mischief (Be My Chief) Chsd ldr halfway, rdn/led 1f out, styd on well, rdn out: no bid: op 14/1: only
mod form prev: eff over a stiff 5f, should get further: acts on gd grnd: apprec this drop to selling grade.
928　**WINDCHILL** 38 [10] T D Easterby 2-8-6 J Carroll 8/1: -002: 2 ch f Handsome Sailor - Baroness　　2　56
Gymcrak (Pharly) Trckd ldrs, rdn & styd on inside last, not pace of wnr: op 6/1: acts on gd grnd, needs 6f.
1267 **SPICE ISLAND** 11 [9] J A Glover 2-8-6 G Duffield 11/4 FAV: 53: 2 b f Reprimand - Little Emmeline　　1　54
(Emarati) Led, rdn/hung left & hdd 1f out, onepace: bckd, op 3/1: acts on gd grnd: see 1267.
928　**CHORUS GIRL** 38 [7] M W Easterby 2-8-6 T Lucas 4/1: -54: Bhd ldrs, styd on fnl 1f, never pace to　hd　53
chall: will apprec 6f & similar grade: clr of rem: see 928.
--　　**MISS EQUINOX** [6] 2-8-6 Kim Tinkler 20/1: 5: Chsd ldrs 4f: Presidium filly, April foal, cost 7,400gns　5　44
as a 2yo: sister to a 5/6f juv wnr: dam a multiple 5f wnr, including as a juv: with N Tinkler.

479

1136 **SAND BANKES 19** [2] 2-8-11 A Daly 12/1: 206: Chsd ldrs till halfway: op 10/1: btr 856 (AW, debut). *hd* **48**
-- **TOMMY SMITH** [1] 2-8-11 J McAuley (5) 20/1: 7: Went left start & bhnd, mod late gains: op 10/1: *hd* **47**
Timeless Times gelding, March foal, dam unraced: sire a speedy/multiple juv wnr: will know more next time.
*1206 **RUNNING FOR ME 15** [8] 2-8-11 G Gibbons (7) 3/1: 618: Cl up, hmpd when wkng over 1f out: btr 1206. *1* **45**
1249 **JEANNIES GIRL 12** [5] 2-8-6 K Hodgson 20/1: 09: Dwelt, al outpcd rear: op 10/1: no form. *9* **24**
1302 **HOPGROVE 8** [4] 2-8-6 T Williams 20/1: 660: Dwelt, soon handy, btn 2f out: 10th: btr 755. *1¾* **19**
928 **POPPYS CHOICE 38** [3] 2-8-6 G Parkin 10/1: -060: Al outpcd rear: 11th: see 928. *8* **4**
11 ran Time 1m 06.3 (5.0) (D F Lockyer, C A Parry, G B Balding) G B Balding Fyfield, Hants

1444

2.55 CONS CLUB MDN 3YO (D) 7f100y rnd Good 57 -04 Slow
£4143 £1275 £637 £318

1159 **WILLOUGHBYS BOY 17** [12] B Hanbury 3-9-0 W Ryan 9/4 FAV: 031: 3 b c Night Shift - Andbell **84**
(Trojan Fen) Handy, led over 1f out, in command inside last, pushed out: well bckd, op 3/1: eff at 7f/7.5f, 1m10f should suit: acts on gd & a stiff/undul trk: on the upgrade & shld win again.
1183 **SUTTON COMMON 16** [14] K A Ryan 3-9-0 J Carroll 5/1: 04-202: 3 b c Common Grounds - Fadaki *3* **77**
Hawaki (Vice Regent) Led 5f, kept on inside last, al held by wnr: return to h'cap company shld suit: see 804.
1105 **IT CAN BE DONE 20** [8] R Hollinshead 3-9-0 P M Quinn (5) 25/1: 06-003: 3 ch g Case Law - Breeze *1½* **74$**
Away (Prince Sabo) Rdn/rear, styd on fnl 2f, no threat to wnr: tchd 33/1: stays 7.5f, handles gd: mod form prev.
1099 **BLUE STREAK 21** [10] Sir Michael Stoute 3-9-0 F Lynch 100/30: -004: Held up, eff over 2f out and no *2* **68**
room over 1f out, onepace: op 3/1: return to 1m+ & h'cap company should suit: see 1099, 972.
936 **STALLONE 36** [13] 3-9-0 J Weaver 5/1: -45: Dwelt, rear, keeping on when no room over 1f out, nvr *½* **67**
plcd to chall: op 5/2: given a kind ride & unsuited by drop to 7.5f, sure to do better over 1m+ with positive ride.
972 **JAHMHOOR 34** [7] 3-9-0 G Carter 10/1: -06: Held up, eff 2f out, held fnl 1f: op 7/1. *½* **66**
1268 **ORLANDO SUNRISE 11** [1] 3-8-9 G Hind 25/1: -067: Prom, rdn/wknd over 1f out: see 1268, 936. *1½* **58**
-- **WHITEGATE WAY** [4] 3-8-9 J Bramhill 50/1: 8: Dwelt/rear, late gains, no threat: debut: sister to a *¾* **57**
5/9f wnr: 1m+ should suit: with A Bailey.
1134 **FLOW BEAU 19** [11] 3-8-9 R Lappin 25/1: 49: Held up, efft 3f out, rdn/wknd fnl 1f: btr 1134. *1½* **54**
1072 **PRECIOUS LOVE 22** [5] 3-9-0 R Hills 10/1: -000: Trkd ldr, wknd over 1f out: 10th: op 7/1. *2* **53**
3942} **Grantley 250** [3] 3-9-0 K Sked 50/1: 1204 **Way Out West 15** [9] 3-8-9 Dean McKeown 66/1:
-- **City Bank Dudley** [2] 3-9-0 Carolyn Bales (7) 66/1: -- **Annakaye** [6] 3-8-9 T Lucas 33/1:
14 ran Time 1m 35.4 (4.6) (Mrs G E M Brown) B Hanbury Newmarket, Suffolk

1445

3.25 DIGITAL RTD HCAP 3YO+ 0-95 (C) 1m100y rnd Good 57 +05 Fast **[97]**
£6014 £2281 £1140 £518 3 yo rec 12lb

1110 **JO MELL 20** [6] T D Easterby 7-9-8 (91) J Carroll 4/1: 0-0101: 7 b g Efisio - Militia Girl (Rarity) **97**
Made all, rdn fnl 2f, styd on well inside last, rdn out: best time of day: earlier scored here at Beverley (stakes): '99 Newcastle wnr (classified stakes, rtd 88): '98 wnr at Ascot (val h'cap, rtd 109), listed rnr up: eff at 7/8.5f on firm, likes gd & hvy, any trk, likes Ascot & Beverley: likes to race with/force the pace: v useful & tough .
1160 **DURAID 17** [5] Denys Smith 8-8-8 (78)(1oh) A Nicholls (3) 5/1: 401-42: 8 ch g Irish River - Fateful *2* **78**
Princess (Vaguely Noble) Held up, prog fnl 3f, no room over 1f out, switched/chsd wnr 1f out, kept on: see 1160.
1291 **SERGEANT YORK 8** [1] C Smith 4-8-11 (80) J F Egan 11/2: 00-053: 4 b c Be My Chief - Metaphysique *1½* **78**
(Law Society) Held up in tch, prog fnl 3f, onepace/held inside last: op 9/2: see 1291.
1271 **CALLDAT SEVENTEEN 11** [4] P W D'Arcy 4-8-8 (77) G Duffield 7/2 FAV: 40-024: Chsd ldrs, held fnl 2f. *2½* **70**
3993} **ICE 248** [7] 4-9-7 (90)(vis) J Fanning 8/1: 0040-5: Chsd wnr, rdn/fdd over 1f out: op 7/1: reapp: '99 *1* **81**
scorer in Swiss 2,000 Guineas & subs at York (h'cap, rtd 100, form subs t.o.): '98 wnr at Musselburgh & York (2, h'caps, rtd 94): eff at 1m/9f on fast, likes gd or hvy grnd, hndls any track, loves York: suited by a visor.
*1279 **COURT EXPRESS 10** [2] 6-8-10 (79) F Lynch 4/1: 500-16: Held up, eff 2f out, no impression: op 7/2. *hd* **69**
1279 **HARLEQUIN DANCER 10** [3] 4-8-10 (79) J P Spencer 10/1: 500-07: Chsd ldrs, btn 2f out: op 8/1: '99 *13* **49**
Leicester scorer (auct mdn, J H M Gosden, subs fine 3rd in val Britannia h'cap at Royal Ascot, rtd 87): eff at 1m, tried 10f: acts on firm & gd, loves a stiff/gall track: needs strong handling: eff with/without a visor.
7 ran Time 1m 48.2 (4.4) (C H Newton Jnr Ltd.) T D Easterby Great Habton, N Yorks

1446

3.55 R.CHANNEL HCAP 3YO 0-70 (E) 1m4f Good 57 -26 Slow **[74]**
£3048 £938 £469 £234

3849} **PENSHIEL 257** [6] J L Dunlop 3-8-10 (56) G Carter 6/1: 000-1: 3 b g Mtoto - Highland Ceilidh (Scottish **64**
Reel) Held up, rdn/prog fnl 3f, switched to chall over 1f out & drvn/led near line: op 4/1: reapp/h'cap bow: unplcd at up to 1m last term (rtd 60, debut): relished this step up to 12f, further should suit: acts on gd grnd & a stiff/undul track: runs well fresh: jockey reported gelding still green, shld win more races, prob over further.
1100 **SECOND PAIGE 21** [2] N A Graham 3-8-13 (59) J Weaver 4/1 FAV: 0-4022: 3 b g Nicolotte - My First *hd* **65**
Paige (Runnett) Chsd ldrs, prog to lead over 1f out, rdn/hdd near line: styd longer 12f trip well: see 1100, 744.
1299 **SMUDGER SMITH 8** [14] B S Rothwell 3-9-3 (63) W Supple 33/1: 200-03: 3 ch g Deploy - Parfait *1¾* **67**
Amour (Clantime) Chsd ldrs, rdn fnl 3f, staying on well & chance when hmpd 1f out, kept on near fin: op 20/1: shade unlucky, would have gone v close here: styd longer 12f trip well: can find compensation: see 1299.
1071 **RUNNING TIMES 22** [9] T D Easterby 3-9-0 (60) G Parkin 16/1: -50354: Led 6f, remained prom, no *hd* **63**
room/eff 2f out, hmpd over 1f out, kept on: stays 12f & handles gd grnd: blinks ommitted after latest.
1270 **LOVE BITTEN 11** [11] 3-9-7 (67) R Ffrench 9/1: 00045: Chsd ldr, led 5f out, hdd/no extra over 1f out. *3* **66**
1103 **MAYBEN 20** [4] 3-8-7 (53) A Culhane 33/1: U60-56: Bhnd, drvn/late gains fnl 3f, no threat: 14f+ suit. *1¾* **50**
1193 **MANSTAR 16** [15] 3-9-2 (62)(BL) N Kennedy 25/1: -50057: Bhd ldrs, held over 1f out: clr rem, blinks. *½* **58**
1292 **WADENHOE 8** [13] 3-9-0 (60) P Fessey 8/1: 00-608: Mid div halfway, btn 2f out: op 12/1: btr 1096, 827. *13* **42**
1096 **FIFE AND DRUM 21** [12] 3-8-9 (55) R Hills 10/1: 00-009: Twds rear halfway, btn 2f out: op 8/1: see 827. *3* **33**
978 **DOUBLE RED 34** [7] 3-9-2 (62) M Fenton 8/1: 22-230: Held up, eff 3f out, soon held: 10th: btr 978, 807. *shd* **40**
1200 **MAGIC SUNSET 15** [8] 3-9-5 (65) A Nicholls (3) 16/1: 00-00: Rear, btn 3f out: 11th: op 10/1, h'cap bow. *2* **40**
1094 **CLASSIC LORD 21** [5] 3-8-8 (54)(bl) J Fanning 10/1: 00-000: Chsd ldrs 10f: 12th: tchd 12/1: longer *¾* **28**
12f trip: rnr up in '99 (debut, rtd 70, subs disapp in blinks): bred to apprec mid-dists, handles gd/soft grnd.
1142 **ESTABELLA 19** [10] 3-9-3 (63) G Duffield 9/2: 5-2130: Cl up 10f: 13th: bckd: btr 1142, 978. *1½* **35**
1159 **Soloist 17** [3] 3-8-10 (56) R Lappin 20/1: 1045 **Medooza 25** [1] 3-8-6 (52) J Carroll 16/1:
15 ran Time 2m 41.2 (9.9) (Cyril Humphris) J L Dunlop Arundel West Sussex

BEVERLEY　　TUESDAY MAY 23RD　　Righthand, Oval Track, With Stiff, Uphill Finish

1447　4.30 DIGITAL FILLIES MDN 3YO+ (D)　1m2f　Good 57　-17 Slow
£4007　£1233　£616　£308　3 yo rec 14lb

1223　**ABSCOND** 13 [4] Sir Michael Stoute 3-8-10 F Lynch 11/10 FAV: 22-51: 3 b f Unbridled - Lemhi Go 　**88**
(Lemhi Gold) Made all & clr 3f out, al holding rivals inside last, shade cosily: rnr up both '99 starts (fill
mdns, rtd 100): eff around 10/11f: acts on firm & gd, sharp/stiff track: likes to force the pace: rate higher.
1188　**METRONOME** 16 [6] L M Cumani 3-8-10 J P Spencer 100/30: 02: 3 b f Salse - Rapid Repeat (Exactly 　1　**85**
Sharp) Held up, drvn/prog to chase wnr over 1f out, kept on well: nicely bckd: will enjoy 12f & win a race.
1063　**TWIN LOGIC** 22 [10] J H M Gosden 3-8-10 W Ryan 10/1: 543: 3 ch f Diesis - Indigenous (Lyphard) 　1¾　**83**
Held up, rdn & kept on fnl 2f, not pace to chall: op 8/1: eff at 10f, shld rate higher when stepped up in trip.
--　**WINDMILL** [9] T D Easterby 3-8-10 J Carroll 20/1: 4: Held up, kept on fnl 2f, nearest fin: op 10/1, 　¾　**82**
debut: Ezzoud filly, half sister to several wnrs: stays 10f & 12f+ could suit: handles gd grnd.
4556}　**MUTASADER** 206 [3] 3-8-10 R Hills 9/2: 0-5: Mid div, rdn/onepace fnl 2f: op 8/1, reapp: rtd 85 on 　1　**81$**
sole '99 start (fillies mdn): mid dists will suit this term.
--　**MOUNTAIN DANCER** [2] 3-8-10 J Fanning 10/1: 6: Chsd wnr halfway, btn 2f out: op 8/1, debut: 　2½　**77**
Rainbow Quest filly, sister to a 1m juv wnr: dam a 7f juv wnr: mid dists will suit.
1155　**ADRIFT** 18 [1] 3-8-10 W Supple 33/1: -07: Chsd ldrs 7f: longer 10f trip. 　11　**65**
1134　**WIGMAN LADY** 19 [5] 3-8-10 T Williams 50/1: 3-58: Chsd wnr 4f, soon btn: longer 10f trip: see 1134. 　7　**55**
--　**REDHILL** [8] 3-8-10 A Culhane 100/1: 9: Soon rdn/al rear: debut, with R Hollinshead. 　18　**35**
973　**BRIGMOUR** 34 [7] 4-9-10 Carolyn Bales (7) 100/1: 000: In tch 4f: 10th: no form. 　*dist*　**0**
10 ran　　Time 2m 09.7 (7.4)　　(Cheveley Park Stud)　　Sir Michael Stoute Newmarket, Suffolk

1448　5.05 ROSE AND CROWN HCAP 3YO 0-80 (D)　1m2f　Good 57　-18 Slow　　[84]
£4303　£1324　£662　£331

1061　**NEVER DISS MISS** 22 [16] W Jarvis 3-9-1 (71) D McGaffin (7) 14/1: 300-51: 3 b f Owington - Pennine 　**79**
Pink (Pennine Walk) Trkd ldrs, led over 1f out, held on well inside last, rdn out: '99 Sandown scorer (auct mdn,
R Williams, rtd 84): prev eff at 5f, well suited by this step up to 10f: acts on gd & soft grnd, stiff/undul trk.
1053　**ROMANTIC AFFAIR** 24 [6] J L Dunlop 3-9-1 (71) G Carter 17/2: 300-30 FAV: 013-02: 3 ch g Persian Bold - 　1　**77**
Broken Romance (Ela Mana Mou) Mid div racing keenly, lost place bef halfway, rdn/prog 3f out, switched to chse
wnr over 1f out, styd on well: styd longer 10f trip, should get further: acts on gd & soft: win soon: see 1053.
4613}　**NOBLE CALLING** 199 [15] N A Graham 3-8-7 (63) J Weaver 10/1: 0600-3: 3 b c Caller I D - Specificity 　hd　**68**
(Alleged) Prom, rdn/led 6f out, hdd over 1f out, kept on: op 7/1: reapp: unplcd last term (rtd 68, mdn): styd
longer 10f trip, should get further, acts on gd grnd: encouraging h'cap bow.
*1299　**BAILEYS PRIZE** 8 [11] M Johnston 3-9-6 (76)(6ex) J Fanning 11/2: 5-2014: Prom, briefly no room over 　hd　**80**
2f out, kept on well inside last: ran to best under 6lb pen: acts on firm & gd grnd, prob fibresand: see 1299.
1053　**MIDDLETHORPE** 24 [13] 3-7-11 (52)(1ow) Dale Gibson 33/1: 300-05: Held up, styd on onepace fnl 3f. 　3½　**52**
1104　**RHODAMINE** 20 [9] 3-8-8 (64) J F Egan 7/1: 000426: Rear, prog/forced wide over 1f out, kept on, nrst fin. 　1　**62**
976　**OLD FEATHERS** 34 [17] 3-8-9 (65) J P Spencer 33/1: 666-07: Prom, fdd fnl 2f: unplcd in '99 (rtd 71). 　1¾　**61**
1106　**BOLD STATE** 20 [14] 3-8-10 (66) A Whelan 16/1: 00-008: Chsd ldr 4f out, btn 2f out: see 1106. 　hd　**61**
999　**TOP HAND** 31 [4] 3-9-5 (75) R Hills 7/1: 61-49: Prom, rdn/fdd fnl 2f: h'cap bow, longer 10f trip: btr 999. 　5　**63**
1183　**CELEBES** 16 [7] 3-8-11 (67) G Duffield 12/1: 346400: Keen/chsd ldrs 1m: 10th: op 14/1: lngr 10f trip. 　1¾　**53**
701　**CITY FLYER** 61 [10] 3-8-3 (59)(t) R Lappin 25/1: 04-500: Held up, no room 3f out, soon held: 11th: abs. 　½　**44**
4601}　**ANGEL LANE** 201 [3] 3-7-12 (53)(1ow) T Williams 25/1: 0000-0: Held up, drvn 2f out, no impression: 12th: 2 　**36**
reapp: unplcd last term (rtd 63, stakes): longer 10f trip & h'cap bow today: has tried a tongue strap.
1279　**SPORTING GESTURE** 10 [8] 3-9-3 (73) T Lucas 20/1: 010-00: Led 3f, btn 2f out: 15th: op 14/1: lngr 10f trip. 　**0**
810　**BUYING A DREAM** 52 [1] 3-9-7 (77) W Supple 10/1: 124-30: Prom, btn/hmpd over 3f out: 17th: 7 wk abs. 　**0**
1024　**Pups Pride** 29 [2] 3-7-10 (52)(3oh) P Hanagan (3) 20/1:
1024　**Portia Lady** 29 [12] 3-7-10 (52)(4oh) P M Quinn (5) 50/1:
1064　**Tadreej** 22 [5] 3-9-2 (72) P Fessey 20/1:
17 ran　　Time 2m 09.8 (7.5)　　(Tim Fenner)　　W Jarvis Newmarket, Suffolk

GOODWOOD　　TUESDAY MAY 23RD　　Righthand, Sharpish, Undulating Track

Official Going　Straight - GOOD/SOFT; Round - GOOD. Stalls: Str - Stands Side; Round - Inside Except 1m4f - Outside.

1449　2.10 TREHEARNE & NORMAN MDN 3YO (D)　1m rnd　Good/Soft 67　-07 Slow
£5720　£1760　£880　£440

--　**REACH THE TOP** [7] J H M Gosden 3-9-0 L Dettori 4/1 JT FAV: 1: 3 b c Zafonic - Andaleeb (Lyphard) 　**92**
Held up, shaken up ent str, kept on well to lead appr fnl 1f, going away: nicely bckd from 6/1 on debut:
half-brother to Gr1 winning juv filly Prophecy, dam F2af wnr: eff at 1m, 10f will suit: goes well fresh on
a sharp/undul trk on gd/soft grnd: potentially v useful colt, likely to win again & rate higher.
1242　**NIGHT SIGHT** 12 [5] G Wragg 3-9-0 D Holland 13/2: 0022: 3 b c Eagle Eyed - El Hamo (Search For 　3½　**84**
Gold) Led appr fnl 1f, same pace: tchd 15/2: imprvd from the front: eff at 1m/9f on firm & gd/soft grnd.
1188　**DESERT RAGE** 16 [2] E A L Dunlop 3-9-0 J Reid 4/1 JT FAV: 53: 3 b c Polish Precedent - Shore Line 　1¼　**82**
(High Line) Handy, eff fnl 2f, unable to qckn till kept on nr fin: bckd tho' op 3/1: btr 1188 (firm).
983　**HAMLYN** 33 [4] D R C Elsworth 3-9-0 N Pollard 6/1: 50-64: Rcd in 2nd till no extra ent fnl 3f: lngr trip. 　¾　**80**
--　**TOUGH MEN** [1] 3-9-0 T Quinn 5/1: 5: Keen, in tch till onepace 3f out: op 7/2 on debut: 　2　**76**
350,000 gns Woodman colt, dam well related: with H Cecil.
1281　**ROB LEACH** 10[6] 3-9-0 R Price 10/1: 526: Al bhd: btr 1281 (10f). 　8　**62**
--　**TOUCH FOR GOLD** 9 [3] 3-9-0 K Fallon 5/1: 7: Chsd ldrs till wknd qckly 3f out: drifted from 3/1: 　½　**56**
on debut: Mr Prospector 1st foal out of a 6f/1m wnr: with Sir M Stoute.
7 ran　　Time 1m 43.28 (5.88)　　(K Abdulla)　　J H M Gosden Manton, Wilts

GOODWOOD TUESDAY MAY 23RD Righthand, Sharpish, Undulating Track

1450 **2.40 NEWTON HCAP 4YO+ 0-100 (C) 1m rnd Good/Soft 67 +00 Fast [97]**
£10920 £3360 £1680 £840

1262 **PERSIANO 11** [5] J R Fanshawe 5-9-5 (88) D Harrison 7/1: 50-031: 5 ch g Efisio - Persiandale (Persian Bold) Mid-div, qcknd to chall 2f out, narrow lead dist, rdn out: fair time: plcd twice in '99 (h'cap, rtd 101): '98 wnr at Warwick, Salisbury & Doncaster (h'caps, rtd 100): eff at 7f/sharp 1m: acts on firm & gd/soft, handles hvy: goes on any trk, without visor: useful at best & still on a fair mark, heads for the Royal Hunt Cup. **93**
1042 **REGAL PHILOSOPHER 25** [10] J W Hills 4-9-5 (88) M Hills 8/1: 20-622: 4 b g Faustus - Princess Lucy (Local Suitor) Mid-div, going well but not much room appr fnl 2f, clr bef dist & strong chall ins last, just held: nicely bckd: lost nothing in defeat & wnr got 1st run: has a turn of foot, go close in Whitsun H'cap at Sandown. *hd* **92**
1288 **IRON MOUNTAIN 8** [8] N A Callaghan 5-8-3 (72) A Beech (5) 8/1: 60-353: 5 b g Scenic - Merlannah (Shy Groom) Off the pace till brought widest of all & kept on strongly ent fnl 2f, nvr nrr: further suits best. *1¾* **72**
1160 **NAVIASKY 17** [9] W R Muir 5-8-11 (80) Martin Dwyer 10/1: 6-0004: Slow away, rear, prog & short of room 2f out, styd on for press, not trble front pair: ran to best back at fav trk: win another h'cap this term. *nk* **79**
1327 **TAMMAM 6** [6] 4-9-5 (88) Pat Eddery 16/1: 4-0005: Mid-div, eff & not clearest of runs appr fnl 2f, switched bef dist, unable to qckn: tchd 20/1, quick reapp: ran nr to best: hampered in running in 1327. *1½* **85**
1077 **STOPPES BROW 22** [11] 8-8-9 (78)(bl) J Mackay (7) 16/1: 0-4006: Slow away & at least 10L off ldrs till imprvd going well 2f out, short of room dist, styd on: eye-catching: sharp trk specialist, h'capped to win again. *½* **74+**
*1113 **POLISH SPIRIT 20** [2] 5-8-12 (81) T Quinn 3/1 FAV: -11117: Well plcd & ev ch till no extra 1f out: hvly bckd from 9/2 to complete a 5 timer: btr 1113 (beat this 3rd). *1½* **74**
1286 **PARISIEN STAR 10** [16] 4-8-13 (82) L Newman (5) 9/1: 000-48: Led till dist, fdd: just best at 7f? *½* **74**
669 **SILKEN DALLIANCE 70** [15] 5-8-11 (80)(BL) K Fallon 10/1: 00-009: Pulled hard bhd ldrs, shaken up & ch 2f out, sn onepace under press, hmpd nr fin: op 8/1, too keen in 1st time blnks after 10 wk abs: see 601. *½* **71**
935 **CHOTO MATE 36** [14] 4-9-6 (89) P Dobbs (5) 50/1: 046/W0: Reluctant to enter stalls, towards rear, prog over 2f out, no extra bef dist: 10th: withdrawn prev start after 2 year abs: '98 wnr here at Goodwood (mdn, rtd 86): unproven beyond 5f on firm grnd though is bred to stay at least 1m: with R Hannon. *¾* **78**
1217 **CULZEAN 14** [13] 4-8-11 (80)(bl) Dane O'Neill 16/1: -53600: Front rank till outpcd & badly hmpd appr fnl 1f: 11th, stable-mate 10th, back in trip: see 733. *nk* **68**
4485} **OMAHA CITY 213** [1] 6-9-12 (95) C Rutter 20/1: 3106-0: Well plcd, chall trav well 2f out, fdd appr fnl 1f: 12th: reapp: '99 wnr here at Goodwood (h'cap) & York (rtd h'cap, rtd 97): back in '97 won again here at Goodwood (rtd h'cap, awdd race, rtd 104): eff at 7f, stays a sharp/undul 1m: acts on firm & gd/soft, any trk, likes Goodwood: can carry big weights: fitter for this & will apprec a return to 7f with R Cochrane up. *2* **79**
1286 **TRIPLE DASH 10** [12] 4-10-0 (97) S Sanders 16/1: 43-500: Nvr troubled ldrs: 13th, top-weight. *¾* **80**
733 **COMPTON ARROW 59** [7] 4-9-9 (92)(t) L Dettori 11/1: 330-00: Mid-div, btn ent fnl 3f: 15th, 8 wk abs, t-strap: plcd twice in '99 (cond stks, rtd 98): '98 wnr at Haydock (mdn auct) & Ascot (nov, rtd 101): eff at 7f/1m on firm & soft grnd, any trk: better than this: with G Butler. **0**
1015 **Prince Du Soleil 29** [4] 4-9-2 (85) F Norton 50/1: 1160 **Slumbering 17** [3] 4-8-11 (80) D R McCabe 20/1:
16 ran Time 1m 42.74 (5.34) (Miss A Church) J R Fanshawe Newmarket, Suffolk

1451 **3.10 LISTED PREDOMINATE STKS 3YO (A) 1m1f192y Good/Soft 67 +05 Fast**
£22750 £7000 £3500 £1750

-- **ROSCIUS** [5] Saeed bin Suroor 3-8-8 L Dettori 9/2: 2-1: 3 b c Sadler's Wells - Rosefinch (Blushing Groom) Sn with ldr, went on appr fnl 3f, hard prsd & rdn bef dist, would not be denied, gamely: op 7/2, gd time: rnr-up sole '99 start in native France, earlier this year won one of the Dubai trials: eff at 10f, 12f shld suit: acts on gd/soft, sharp/undul trk: runs well fresh: v useful, genuine & lightly raced, front two well clr here. **109**
*1103 **ST EXPEDIT 20** [4] G Wragg 3-8-8 D Holland 10/1: 3-2012: 3 b c Sadler's Wells - Miss Rinjani (Shirley Heights) Restrained in last, gd prog appr fnl 3f, chall dist, ran on, just failed: much improved for fitting of a ring-bit, won a Pontefract mdn last time: 12f shld suit: useful, well clr of rem, win a Listed/Gr 3. *shd* **108**
996 **BOGUS DREAMS 31** [3] S P C Woods 3-8-8 J Reid 14/1: 113-53: 3 ch c Lahib - Dreams Are Free (Caerleon) Held up, prog 3f out, kept on same pace ent fnl 2f: ran to best over longer 10f trip: see 996. *6* **100**
1216 **TANTALUS 14** [1] B W Hills 3-8-8 M Hills 11/4 FAV: 2-134: Well plcd, eff appr fnl 2f, no impress: well bckd from 7/2: prob ran close to best back in trip tho' shade disappointing after 1216 (12f, fast grnd). *½* **99**
*1198 **FERZAO 15** [2] 3-8-8 Pat Eddery 9/1: 01-315: Trkd ldrs, rdn 2f out, fdd: stiffish task, see 1198 (fast). *3* **94**
1171 **MILLENIUM MOONBEAM 17** [8] 3-8-8 K Darley 6/1: 614-06: Short of room after 3f, in tch till wknd 2f out: not bred to apprec this longer 10f trip: tchd 7/1, see 1171 (2,000 Guineas). *2½* **91**
*1246 **MERRY MERLIN 12** [7] 3-8-11 T Quinn 10/3: 15-017: Set gd pace till hdd appr fnl 3f, sn btn: well bckd tho' op 9/4: Derby hopes sunk in this rain-softened grnd, worth another ch on firm: see 1246 (impressive). *1¾* **92**
4569} **NORTON 204** [6] 3-8-8 A Clark 16/1: 501-8: Al bhd: stiff task on reapp & reportedly hung right thr'out: landed fnl '99 start at Redcar (mdn, rtd 92): half brother to useful mid-dist/stayer Turtle Valley, dam a 12f wnr: eff at 7f last term, shld stay mid-dists: acts on gd/soft grnd, gall trk: with T Mills. *2* **86**
8 ran Time 2m 10.27 (6.17) (Godolphin) Saeed bin Suroor Newmarket

1452 **3.40 TOTE TRIFECTA HCAP 3YO 0-105 (B) 1m1f Good/Soft 67 -09 Slow [111]**
£32500 £10000 £5000 £2500

1183 **MOON SOLITAIRE 16** [11] E A L Dunlop 3-7-10 (79)(1oh) F Norton 7/1: 6-4131: 3 b c Night Shift - Gay Fantastic (Ela Mana Mou) Never far away, qcknd to lead approaching fnl 1f, pshd out, readily: bckd from 10/1: earlier won at Folkestone (mdn): promise sole juv start on (mdn , rtd 75): eff at 7f/9f (half-brother to a 12f wnr): acts on firm, soft grnd & any track: progressive colt with a turn of foot, well worth following. **91**
*1293 **GIVE THE SLIP 8** [15] Mrs A J Perrett 3-8-7 (90)(6ex) Pat Eddery 6/1: 34-312: 3 b c Slip Anchor - Falafil (Fabulous Dancer) Led till appr fnl 1f, kept on for press: nicely bckd: prob improved again in defeat under a penalty on h'cap bow: eff at 9/10f, 12f shld suit: genuine & useful, shld land a nice prize over further. *2* **98**
1310 **SECRET AGENT 7** [1] Sir Michael Stoute 3-8-11 (94) K Fallon 7/2 FAV: 2-1423: 3 b c Machiavellian - Secret Obsession (Secretariat) Bhd, good wide hdwy over 2f out to chase front pair bef dist, no impress & hung right ins last: hvly bckd from 5/1, qck reapp: difficult low draw: another useful run: see 1310, 851. *1¼* **100**
1215 **ATLANTIC RHAPSODY 14** [8] M Johnston 3-8-3 (86) R Winston 12/1: 2-1044: Mid div, shaken up 3f out, styd on bef fnl 1f, nvr dngrs: stays 1m1f: needs strong handling & re-application of blnks could suit. *1* **90**
1177 **FATHER JUNINHO 16** [12] 3-8-5 (88) D Harrison 25/1: 12-065: Bhd, switched & styd on fnl 2f, never near to chall: slowly coming to hand: looks sure to relish further: see 1055. *1¼* **90**
*1215 **NICOBAR 14** [10] 3-9-7 (104) K Darley 11/1: 25-316: Prom, no extra fnl 2f: top-weight, lngr trip. *2* **102**

1089 **FORBEARING 21** [16] 3-8-7 (90) S Sanders 20/1: 611-07: Mid div, hmpd on bend entering straight, no impression on leaders 2f out & not persevered with: worth keeping in mind when stable returns to form. *1¼* **86**
*1183 **ATAVUS 16** [4] 3-8-2 (85) P Doe 14/1: 31-418: Bhnd, hdwy into mid-div over 2f out, no further prog. *nk* **80**
921 **INVER GOLD 38** [9] 3-7-10 (79)(2oh) G Sparkes (5) 40/1: 24-139: Al around same place: turf return. *nk* **74**
761 **NOBLE PURSUIT 56** [6] 3-8-3 (85)(1ow) A Clark 25/1: 412-40: Rear, rdn & edged left appr fnl 2f, never dangerous: 10th, 8 week abs: longer trip: see 761. *3* **76**
1177 **BLUE GOLD 16** [5] 3-8-13 (96) J Reid 20/1: 33-420: In tch till fdd 2f out: 11th, btr 1177, 1029. *nk* **85**
1183 **RED N SOCKS 16** [3] 3-8-7 (90) T Quinn 10/1: 510-20: Mid-div, effort over 2f out, soon btn, eased dist: 12th, tchd 12/1: in front of this wnr in 1183 (firm grnd, 1m). *nk* **79**
*933 **SOLLER BAY 36** [19] 3-7-10 (79)(3oh) M Henry 25/1: 2-1310: Prom till appr fnl 2f: 13th: see 933. *½* **67**
*1261 **BALI BATIK 11** [14] 3-8-1 (84) A Beech (5) 12/1: 0-4310: Chasd ldrs, wknd & not much room: 14th: unsuited by step up to 9f on h'cap bow? see 1261 (7f mdn). *1¼* **70**
1183 **SCOTTISH SPICE 16** [13] 3-8-3 (86) R Mullen 25/1: 11-600: Al bhnd: 15th, up in trip on softer grnd. *1½* **70**
3671} **IDOLIZE 267** [2] 3-8-7 (89)(1ow) J Fortune 20/1: -021-0: Never in it: 16th on reapp/h'cap bow: landed fnl '99 start at Chepstow (1m fill mdn, gd grnd, rtd 95): sister to smart 9/12f wnr Riyadian: shld apprec mid-dists. *1¼* **72**
977 **PETIT MARQUIS 34** [7] 3-8-9 (92) O Urbina 14/1: 2-120: Rear, wide into straight, sn btn: 18th, h'cap bow. **0**
1055 **Chems Truce 24** [18] 3-8-6 (89) Martin Dwyer 25/1: 1159 **Tigre 17** [20] 3-8-2 (85) N Pollard 25/1:
1183 **Inching Closer 16** [17] 3-7-10 (79)(2oh) J Mackay (7) 16/1:
20 ran Time 1m 57.38 (6.88) (Maktoum Al Maktoum) E A L Dunlop Newmarket, Suffolk

1453

4.10 FOREST ALLIANCE COND STKS 3YO+ (C) 6f str Good/Soft 67 -01 Slow
£6148 £2332 £1166 £530

1172 **SUPERIOR PREMIUM 17** [5] R A Fahey 6-9-10 K Fallon 5/2: 0-0001: 6 br h Forzando - Devils Dinge (Song) Pld hard, prsd ldr till went on halfway, rdn out: nicely bckd: '99 wnr in Sweden (List), at Ascot & Newbury (h'caps, rtd 114): '98 wnr at Chester (rtd h'cap), Haydock & here at Goodwood (Stewards Cup, rtd 107): eff at 5f, best at 6f: acts on firm, hvy grnd & any trk: can go well fresh, carry big weights: tough & v smart. **111**
4418} **TOMBA 219** [6] M A Jarvis 6-10-0 M Tebbutt 7/2: 3010-2: 6 ch h Efisio - Indian Love Song (Be My Guest) Chsd ldrs, rdn appr fnl 1f, kept on but unable to chall: op 5/1: gd run conceding 4lbs to wnr on reapp: '99 wnr at Haydock (stks) & Munich (Gr 3, rtd 116, B Meehan): '98 wnr at Ascot (Gr 2), Munich (Gr 3) & Longchamp (Gr 1, rtd 118): eff at 6/7f, loves soft/hvy grnd, acts on firm: likes Haydock: v smart, spot on next time. *1¼* **111**
952 **DEEP SPACE 35** [1] E A L Dunlop 5-9-6 J Reid 9/4 FAV: 120-63: 5 br g Green Desert - Dream Season (Mr Prospector) In tch, outpcd 2f out, keeping on fin: well bckd tho' op 6/4: not disgraced, faster grnd suits. *hd* **103**
1324 **AFAAN 6** [2] R F Marvin 7-8-11 T G McLaughlin 15/2: 30-064: Not settle bhd, pld wide to improve 2f out, styd on for press, unable to chall: tchd 10/1, qck reapp: blnks omitted & new tactics: see 1324. *nk* **93**
952 **ANDREYEV 35** [4] 6-9-10 P Dobbs (5) 4/1: 0-1005: Slow away, held up, prog & ch ent fnl 2f, sn rdn, fdd ins last: well bckd from 6/1: consistency not his strong point: see 734. *1* **103**
1277 **MASTER HENRY 10** [3] 6-8-11 M Hills 25/1: 24/666: Led for 3f, sn btn: tchd 50/1, v highly tried. *9* **65**
6 ran Time 1m 14.07 (4.07) (J C Parsons) R A Fahey Butterwick, N Yorks

1454

4.45 ANNE FRANCES MDN 2YO (D) 5f str Good/Soft 67 -14 Slow
£4114 £1266 £633 £316

-- **BAARIDD** [1] M A Jarvis 2-9-0 L Dettori 11/2: 1: 2 b c Halling - Millstream (Dayjur) In tch, imprvd ent fnl 2f & ran on well to lead cl-home: tchd 7/1: Feb 1st foal, dam high-class sprinter, sire 10f performer: eff at 5f, further will suit: acts on gd/soft grnd, sharp/undul trk: runs well fresh: has a turn of foot. **90**
1290 **SILCA LEGEND 8** [9] M R Channon 2-9-0 T Quinn 4/1: 232: 2 ch c Efisio - Silca Cisa (Hallgate) Prsd ldr, hard rdn to lead dist, ran on but hdd nr fin: caught a decent newcomer: deserves to go one better. *hd* **88**
1169 **HAWK 17** [6] R Hannon 2-9-0 R Hughes 4/5 FAV: 33: 2 b c A P Jet - Miss Enjoleur (L'Enjoleur) Led till 1f out, same pace: hvly bckd: trainer felt there was something amiss: better on fast in 1169. *1* **85**
849 **LADY EBERSPACHER 43** [10] Mrs P N Dutfield 2-8-9 L Newman (5) 33/1: 04: Sn handy, eff 2f out, not pace of ldrs: left debut bhd after 6 wk abs: handles gd/soft grnd, 6f will suit now. *1¾* **75**
-- **PROUD REFLECTION** [7] 2-9-0 J Fortune 10/1: 5: Slow away, widest of all, nvr a threat: op 8/1, debut: 14,000 gns Petong Mar foal, v speedily bred half-brother to 4 wnrs, incl useful sprinter Mugello: with A Jarvis. *1¼* **76**
-- **PICCLED** [2] 2-9-0 S Drowne 25/1: 6: Lost sev length start, nvr got in it: op 16/1, forget this: 40,000 gns Piccolo Feb foal, half-brother to decent juv mdn Bee Eight, dam unrcd, sire a sprinter: with M Channon. *½* **75**
-- **JETHAME** [8] 2-8-9 Pat Eddery 14/1: 7: Well plcd till wknd qckly ent fnl 2f: debut: 7,000 gns Definite Article Mar foal, half-sister to 3yo wnrs abroad, sire 10f/12f performer: needs more time/further. *5* **57**
-- **CHISPA** [5] 2-8-9 Dane O'Neill 25/1: 8: In tch till 2f out: stablemate 3rd, debut, op 16/1: 8,000 gns Imperial Frontier Feb 1st foal, dam prolific wnr in Belgium. *¾* **55**
-- **MUJALIA** [3] 2-9-0 P Doe 25/1: 9: Sn struggling: debut: 13,000 gns Mujtahid Mar 1st foal, sprint bred. *10* **40**
9 ran Time 1m 01.76 (4.06) (Sheikh Ahmed Al Maktoum) M A Jarvis Newmarket, Suffolk

1455

5.20 GLORIOUSGOODWOOD.CO.UK MDN 3YO (D) 1m4f Good/Soft 67 -53 Slow
£4192 £1290 £645 £322

1151 **ENTISAR 18** [4] Saeed bin Suroor 3-9-0 L Dettori 4/5 FAV: 3-31: 3 b c Nashwan - Fawaayid (Vaguely Noble) Dictated slow pace, rdn over 2L clr appr fnl 1f, stride shortened ins last & just held on: hvly bckd, slow time: earlier over 10L bhd Beat Hollow on Brit bow: plcd at Longchamp sole '99 start for D Loder (9f, hvy): eff at 10f/sharp 12f: acts on fast, gd/soft & prob hvy & likes to force the pace: useful. **91**
1200 **TOTAL CARE 15** [5] H R A Cecil 3-9-0 T Quinn 5/4: 222: 3 br c Caerleon - Totality (Dancing Brave) In tch, chsd wnr 4f out, no impress 2f out till styd on towards fin: well bckd: stays 12f & shld win a mdn. *¾* **89**
1200 **PEPE GALVEZ 15** [3] B Hanbury 3-9-0 Dane O'Neill 20/1: 03: 3 br c Mango Express - Mango Sampaquita (Colombian Friend) Chsd ldrs, feeling pace 4f out, late hdwy: op 14/1, clr rem: apprec step up to 12f on gd/sft. *½* **88**
1179 **MORNINGSIDE 16** [2] D R C Elsworth 3-8-9 N Pollard 9/1: 6-64: Rcd in 2nd till bef halfway, btn 4f out. *28* **61**
4599} **PREMIERE VALENTINO 201** [1] 3-9-0 D Holland 20/1: 0-5: In tch till halfway: op 14/1, stiff task, reapp: well btn sole '99 start: half-brother to wnrs at 6/7f, dam 2m wnr: with D Arbuthnot. *10* **56$**
5 ran Time 2m 46.22 (14.42) (Godolphin) Saeed bin Suroor Newmarket, Suffolk

LONGCHAMP
SUNDAY MAY 21ST Righthand, Galloping Track

Official Going GOOD TO SOFT

1456
1.45 GR 2 PRIX VICOMTESSE VIGIER 4YO+ **1m7f110y Good/Soft**
£28818 £11527 £5764 £2882 4 yo rec 1 lb

*1116 **AMILYNX** 21 [6] A Fabre 4-9-4 O Peslier 1/2 FAV: 1-2011: 4 gr c Linamix - Amen (Alydar) ‡23
Settled in tch, smooth hdwy to lead 2f out, pshd out, comfortably: earlier won here at Longchamp (Gr 3):
'99 scorer again at Longchamp (2, incl Gr 1 Prix Royal Oak, rtd 123): suited by 2m: acts on gd & hvy grnd:
runs v well fresh & acts on a gall trk, loves Longchamp: tough & high-class stayer, win more Gr races.
-- **LE TINTORET** [5] Y de Nicolay 7-8-12 O Doleuze 104/10: 24-102: 7 b g Goldneyev - Akariya (Akarad) 1 112
Dwelt, raced keenly in rear, hdwy over 2f out, styd on but no ch with wnr: clr rem: stays 2m on gd/soft.
1247 **YAVANAS PACE** 10 [4] M Johnston 8-8-12 J Fanning 19/10: -01043: 8 ch g Accordion - Lady In Pace 4 108
(Burslem) Trkd ldr, drvn & no extra appr fnl 1f: not disgraced, apprec a drop back to Gr 3/List: see 1247.
1247 **ASHGAR** 10 [3] C E Brittain 4-8-12 D Harrison 191/10: 0-0564: Led, rdn/hdd 2f out, sn btn: see 1109. 2½ 106
6 ran Time 3m 27.2 (J-L Lagardere) A Fabre France

1457
2.55 GR 1 PRIX SAINT-ALARY FILLIES 3YO **1m2f Good/Soft**
£48031 £19212 £9606 £4803

944 **REVE DOSCAR** 39 [4] Mme M Bollack Badel 3-9-0 A Badel 96/10: 2-221: 3 gr f Highest Honor - Numidie 111
(Baillamont) Rear, plenty to do over 2f out, ran on strongly to chall dist, drvn to lead well ins last, going away:
1st win: rnr-up twice prev this term & also sole '99 start: eff arnd 10f on gd/soft: smart & improving.
-- **FOLIE DANSE** [7] Y de Nicolay 3-9-0 D Bonilla 17/1: 21-152: 3 b f Petit Loup - Folle Envie 1½ 109
(Un Desperado) Settled last, smooth hdwy to chall over 1f out, no extra well ins last: eff at 10f on gd/soft.
1114 **HIDALGUIA** 21 [1] J de Roualle 3-9-0 O Peslier 9/1: 1-123: 3 b f Barathea - Halesia (Chief's Crown) hd 109
Mid-div, rdn to lead 2f out, hdd well ins last, no extra: clr rem: stays 9/10f on gd/sft & hvy: see 1114.
4594} **GOLDAMIX** 203 [5] C Laffon Parias 3-9-0 D Boeuf 1/5 JT FAV: -11-4: Led, hdd 2f out, sn btn: 5 102
landed both '99 juv starts (incl Gr 1, rtd 108): eff at 10f, 12f shld suit: acts on hvy: useful at best.
995 **BLUSIENKA** 29 [3] 3-9-0 T Jarnet 69/10: -1-435: Nvr a threat: up in trip: see 995 (1m). 2 99
*1114 **AMERICA** 21 [2] 3-9-0 O Doleuze 1/5 JT FAV: 31-116: Chsd wnr, outpcd fnl 2f: btn 1114. 1 97
1108 **SO PRECIOUS** 18 [6] 3-9-0 T G McLaughlin 191/10: -61-47: Prom, drvn/wknd fnl 3f: highly tried. 4 91
7 ran Time 2m 08.0 (Mme G de Chatelperron) Mme M Bollack Badel France

1458
3.30 GR 1 PRIX D'ISPAHAN 4YO+ **1m1f Good/Soft**
£48031 £19212 £9606 £4803

3795} **SENDAWAR** 259 [5] A de Royer Dupre 4-9-2 G Mosse 4/5 FAV: 2111-1: 4 b c Priolo - Sendana (Darshaan) 125
Cl-up going well, pshd into lead 2f out, easily qcknd clr: reapp: '99 wnr at R Ascot (Gr 1 St James Palace)
& Longchamp (3, incl Gr 1 French 2,000 Guineas, rtd 126): rnr-up both '99 starts: suited by a stiff 1m/9f,
stays 10.5f: runs well fresh on fast & hvy grnd: tough, top-class colt, holds strong claims in the Eclipse.
*1115 **INDIAN DANEHILL** 21 [1] A Fabre 4-9-2 O Peslier 6/5: 32-112: 4 b c Danehill - Danse 3 118
Indienne (Green Dancer) Led, hdd ins fnl 2f, kept on but not pace of comfortable wnr: high-class colt: see 1115.
1115 **CHELSEA MANOR** 21 [2] P Bary 4-9-2 T Thulliez 72/10: 1-0333: 4 b c Grand Lodge - Docklands 1 116
(Theatrical) In tch, rdn/hdwy over 1f out, btn ins last: handles gd/soft & hvy: apprec drop to Gr 3 class.
1123 **DOUBLE HEART** 20 [3] Mlle V Dissaux 4-9-2 T Jarnet 109/10: 1-3434: Settled rear, styd on stdly snk 115
fnl 2f but no chance with ldrs: handles gd/soft & soft: see 1123.
1321 **DIAMOND WHITE** 7 [4] 5-8-13 J Reid 97/10: -02345: Chsd ldrs, drvn/no extra appr fnl 1f: highly 3 108
tried here: tough & genuine mare who will apprec a drop back to Gr 2/3: see 1057.
5 ran Time 1m 59.3 (H H Aga Khan) A de Royer Dupre France

SAN SIRO
SUNDAY MAY 21ST Righthand, Stiff, Galloping Track

Official Going GOOD

1459
3.25 GR 1 ITALIAN OAKS 3YO **1m3f Good**
£92390 £49123 £29278 £14639

1117 **TIMI** 21 [10] L Brogi 3-8-11 M Demuro 57/10: 21-121: 3 b f Alzao - Tramiram (Runnett) 107
Settled in tch, rdn/prog to chall ins last, drvn out to lead near line: eff at 1m/11f on gd & hvy: v useful.
-- **POLAR CHARGE** [11] B Grizzetti 3-8-11 G Bietolini 105/1: 1-1302: 3 b f Polar Falcon - Take Charge nk 106
(Last Tycoon) Trk ldrs, led well ins fnl 1f, hdd near fin: fine run from this rank outsider: eff at 11f on gd.
3906} **WELL MINDED** 251 [5] H Blume 3-8-11 M Esposito 87/10: 120-43: 3 br f Monsun - Well Proved (Prince ¾ 105
Ippi) Waited with, hdwy when no room over 1f out, ran on strongly ins last: German raider: eff at 11f on gd.
4245} **DIGNIFY** 231 [9] Saeed bin Suroor 3-8-11 L Dettori 44/10: 1310-4: Prom, rdn to lead over 3f out, shd 105
hdd well ins last, no extra cl-home: with D R Loder in '99, scored at Chantilly (Gr 3, rtd 102): eff at 7f/1m,
stays 11f: acts on fast & gd: shld apprec Listed company in Britain.
1168 **MISS LORILAW** 15 [15] 3-8-11 M Hills 17/2: 1-336: Raced wide mid-div, no extra over 1f out, fin 6th. 1½ 102
1184 **NAVAL AFFAIR** 14 [17] 3-8-11 K Fallon 4/1: 31-40: Handy, drvn & no extra 2f out, 10th: see 1184. 2 98
1223 **TANZILLA** 11 [7] 3-8-11 P Robinson 3/1 FAV: 1230: Al in rear, fin 12th: see 1223 (List). nk 97
953 **CROESO CARIAD** 33 [18] 3-8-11 T Quinn 56/10: 210-50: Eff from rear 3f out, sn btn: 14th, lngr trip. ½ 96
18 ran Time 2m 16.1 (Allevamento La Nuova Sbarra) L Brogi Italy

1460
4.25 GR 2 PREMIO EMILIO TURATI 3YO+ **1m Good**
£43877 £20302 £11366 £5683

764 **MUHTATHIR** 57 [3] Saeed bin Suroor 5-9-11 L Dettori 30/100 FAV: 414-31: 5 ch h Elmaamul - Mamju 119
(Al Nasr) Made all, pshd clr appr fnl 1f, comfortably: '99 wnr here at San Siro (Gr 1, rtd 118 at best),
prev term won at Doncaster, Newbury, Goodwood (Gr 2) & rnr-up at Longchamp (French 2,000 Guineas, rtd 120):

SAN SIRO   SUNDAY MAY 21ST   Righthand, Stiff, Galloping Track

loves to race up with/force the pace over 7f/1m on firm, gd & dirt: high-class miler, win more Gr races.
-- **EMBODY** [8] B Grizzetti 5-9-6 G Bietolini 79/10: 2: 5 b h Indian Ridge - Kamakha (Natroun)   5   106
Mid-div, hdwy & styd on fnl 2f, no chance with wnr: stays 1m on good grnd.
1232} **DANE FRIENDLY** 379 [1] O Pessi 4-9-6 D Zarroli 80/1: -00-3: 4 b c Danehill - Always Friendly   3   101
(High Line) Waited with, styd on late: well btn in 2 '99 mdn runs for P Chapple Hyam, now trained in Italy.
1057 **ALRASSAAM** 22 [5] M A Jarvis 4-9-6 P Robinson 57/10: 612-04: Cl-up, chall wnr 3f out, drvn &   ½   100
wknd appr fnl 1f: Brit raider, capable of better: see 1057.
8 ran   Time 1m 35.4   (Godolphin)   Saeed bin Suroor Newmarket

SAINT CLOUD   MONDAY MAY 22ND   Lefthand, Galloping Track

Official Going   SOFT

1461   1.55 GR 2 PRIX JEAN DE CHAUDENAY 4YO+   1m4f   Soft
£28818   £11527   £5764   £2882

*1034 **FIRST MAGNITUDE** 25 [1] A Fabre 4-9-2 O Peslier 9/10 FAV: 10-611: 4 ch c Arazi - Crystal   115
Cup (Nijinsky): Prom, chall over 1f out, led dist, pshd out, shade cosy: won 3 times in '99, incl a Longchamp
Gr 2 (rtd 115): v eff arnd 12f on gd & hvy grnd: tough, smart & consistent colt.
1034 **CRILLON** 25 [5] E Lellouche 4-8-12 D Bonilla 56/10: 1-1222: 4 br c Saumarez - Shangrila (Riverman)   shd   109
Cl-up, chall over 1f out, styd on, not btn far but al held: acts on soft/hvy: also bhd this wnr in 1034.
2490} **SPENDENT** 327 [2] P Bary 4-8-12 (bl) T Thulliez 7/1: 5114-3: 4 ch c Generous - Cattermole (Roberto)   1½   106
Rear, drvn/styd on fnl 2f, no ch with ldrs: '99 Chantilly wnr (Gr 3, rtd 111): eff at 12f on gd: eff in blnks.
*665 **RUSSIAN HOPE** 72 [3] H A Pantall 5-8-12 G Toupel 13/10: 12-114: Led till hdd ins fnl 1f,   snk   106
sn btn: smart at best, capable of better: see 665 (Gr 3, hvy).
5 ran   Time 2m 37.9   (D Wildenstein)   A Fabre France

BRIGHTON   WEDNESDAY MAY 24TH   Lefthand, V Sharp, Undulating Track

Official Going   RACES 1-3 - GOOD TO SOFT; RACES 4-6 - SOFT. Stalls: Inside except 1m2f & 1m4f - Outside.

1462   6.15 DONATELLO LADY RDRS HCAP 3YO+ 0-60 (F)   1m rnd   Good/Soft   Inapplicable   [37]
£2499   £714   £357   3 yo rec 12lb Majority raced centre fnl 3f

1336 **DARK MENACE** 7 [8] E A Wheeler 8-10-12 (49)(bl) Miss E Johnson Houghton 16/1: 000601: 8 br g Beveled - 53
Sweet And Sure (Known Fact): Chsd ldrs, led over 2f out till over 1f out, rallied well inside last for press to lead
again nr line: op 14/1: '99 wnr here at Brighton (h'cap) & Lingfield (AW sell, rtd 47 & 52a at best): '98 wnr at
Southwell (h'cap, rtd 41a, also rtd 47): eff at 6f/1m: acts on fm, gd/sft & both AWs: likes Brighton: suited by blnks.
1330 **DANZAS** 7 [11] J M Bradley 6-10-7 (44)(bl) Mrs S Moore (5) 6/1: 061032: 6 b g Polish Precedent -   nk   47
Dancing Brave (Green Dancer): Chsd ldrs 3f out, remnd far rail final 2f, led over 1f out, hdd well inside last
& no extra: op 7/1: continues to run well & likes Brighton: see 1330 & 896.
4057} **DOVEBRACE** 245 [9] A Bailey 7-10-1 (38) Miss Bridget Gatehouse 20/1: 3006-3: 7 b g Dowsing - Naufrage ½   40
(Main Reef): Mid-div, prog/ev 2f out, kept on onepace: op 16/1, reapp: place form in '99 (rtd 43, h'cap): rnr-up
in '98 (h'cap, rtd 62): back in '95 scored at Haydock, York & Chester (mdn/stks, rtd 100): eff at 6f/1m: acts on firm
& gd/soft: tried blnks & visor, prob best without: nicely h'capped.
*1335 **BUTRINTO** 7 [13] B R Johnson 6-11-1 (52) Miss L Sheen 5/2: 506114: Held up, prog/ch 2f   ¾   52
out, onepace inside last: nicely bckd tho' op 5/4: acts on firm, gd/soft & both AWs: see last 1335 (7f).
1431 **ITALIAN SYMPHONY** 2 [1] B 6-11-7 (58)(vis) Miss E Folkes 5/1: 500455: Mid-div, late gains fnl 2f.   3½   53
1296 **TROPICAL BEACH** 9 [3] 7-10-13 (50)(vis) Mrs L Pearce 12/1: 004-06: Rdn/mid-div, held final 2f: op 10/1.   3   40
686 **WAIKIKI BEACH** 68 [12] 9-10-0 (37)(bl) Mrs J Moore 16/1: -00047: Cl-up, led halfway till 2f out, wknd: 1¼   25
10 wk abs: blnks reapplied: see 136 (AW sell).
1275 **KNOBBLEENEEZE** 11 [6] 10-10-8 (45)(vis) Ms T Dzieciolowska (7) 12/1: 550-08: Led after 2f till   nk   32
halfway, sn btn: op 14/1: rnr-up in '99 (reapp, rtd 63, stks): '98 wnr at Newbury (h'cap, rtd 69 at best): eff at
7f/1m: handles firm, relishes gd/soft & hvy grnd: handles any trk, likes Newbury: best in a visor.
3850} **COSMO JACK** 258 [4] 4-10-13 (50)(vis) Miss J Allison 9/1: 4501-9: Rear, mod gains: Flat reapp, jmps   2½   33
fit, 99/00 wnr at Catterick, Ludlow (clmrs), Leicester (sell) & Taunton (juv nov h'cap, rtd 106h), eff at 2m/2m1f on gd
& hvy): '99 Flat wnr at Haydock & Chepstow (sells, rtd 62): '98 Bath wnr (sell, B Meehan) & Sandown (sell nursery,
rtd 73): eff at 7f/1m, tried 10/12f: acts on fast & gd/soft: suited by blnks, wore a vis today: enjoys sell grade.
890 **DELTA GEORGIA** 42 [10] 4-10-8 (45) Mrs S Bosley 20/1: 502-00: Prom 6f: 10th: abs: rnr-up in '99 (rtd   ½   27
50, sell, unplcd on sand, rtd 33a): stays a gall/undul 1m & handles fast grnd: h'cap bow today.
962 **Reken** 36 [2] 4-9-13 (36) Miss Donna Handley (7) 33/1:   650 **Rawi** 77 [5] 7-9-7 (30) Miss L J Harwood (7) 14/1:
1335 **Ghaazi** 7 [7] 4-10-13 (50) Mrs C Williams 25/1: 4037} **Indian Bazaar** 246 [15] 4-10-3 (40) Miss Hayley Bryan (7) 25/1:
14 ran   Time 1m 38.8 (6.8)   (M V Kirby)   E A Wheeler Whitchurch On Thames, Oxon.

1463   6.45 LONDON METRO MED AUCT MDN 2YO (E)   5f59y rnd   Good/Soft   Inapplicable
£2832   £809   £404   Raced centre - stands side fnl 3f

1189 **DENSIM BLUE** 17 [1] J Pearce 2-9-0 R Ffrench 8/1: -0241: 2 b c Lake Coniston - Surprise Visitor (Be   78
My Guest): Made all, drvn over 1f out, styd on strongly & pushed clr inside last: tchd 10/1: eff at 5.2f, 6f will
suit: acts on fast, relished gd/soft here: likes a sharp/undul trk & improved for front running tactics.
1197 **CHURCH BELLE** 16 [4] R Hannon 2-8-9 Dane O'Neill 5/2: 02: 2 gr f College Chapel - Siva (Bellypha)   3½   65
Dwelt, sn chsg ldrs, rdn & kept on inside last, al held by wnr: nicely bckd tho' op 2/1: handles gd/soft: see 1197.
1088 **KALUKI** 22 [7] W R Muir 2-9-0 Martin Dwyer 4/1: -633: 2 ch c First Trump - Wild Humour (Fayruz):   nk   69
Prom, rdn/outpcd 2f out, kept on inside last, no threat to wnr: handles gd & gd/soft grnd: see 1088.
1328 **REPEAT PERFORMANCE** 9 [9] W G M Turner 2-9-0 (t) A Daly 2/1 FAV: 4244: Prom, rdn/onepace   shd   69
fnl 2f: well bckd: acts on fast grnd & gd/soft: see 1328, 1124 (C/D).
1304 **APRIL LEE** 9 [3] 2-8-9 (e) T E Durcan 25/1: 605: Prom, outpcd 2f out, held after: see 865.   1   62
1236 **UNVEIL** 13 [2] 2-8-9 D O'Donohoe 25/1: 446: Cl-up halfway, hung left/btn 1f out, eased inside last.   3   56
-- **JUSTINIA** [5] 2-8-9 W Ryan 25/1: 7: Al outpcd rear: Inchinor filly, Feb foal, half-sister to a 5/6f juv   1½   53

485

wnr, dam only modest: sire a high class 7f performer: with E J O'Neill.

1260 **OPERATION ENVY** 12 [6] 2-9-0 S Drowne 12/1: 468: In tch 3f, sn held: op 10/1: btr 1260, 1124.   1¼   56
836 **CEDAR BILL** 47 [8] 2-9-0 S Sanders 33/1: 59: Sn outpcd: 7 wk abs: see 836.   2   52
--   **MACKEM BEAT** [10] 2-8-9 J D Smith 25/1: 0: Dwelt, sn outpcd/bhd: 10th: Aragon filly, Apr foal,   13   25
cost 3,000 gns: half-sister to 3 wnrs, dam a 10f wnr: sire high class 7f/1m performer: with A J McNae.
10 ran   Time 1m 04.2 (4.2)   (Double M Partnership)   J Pearce Newmarket, Suffolk.

1464	7.15 UKBETTING.COM HCAP 3YO+ 0-65 (F) 6f rnd Good/Soft Inapplicable [60]

£2990   £920   £460   £230   3 yo rec 9 lb Raced centre - stands side fnl 3f

1092 **BRAMBLE BEAR** 22 [5] M Blanshard 6-9-1 (47) D Sweeney 11/2: 626001: 6 b m Beveled - Supreme Rose   51
(Frimley Park): Hmpd start & rear, rdn/prog over 1f out, styd on well to lead nr fin, drvn out: op 7/1: place form
in '98 (rtd 62, h'cap): '98 Lingfield wnr (h'cap, rtd 73): eff at 5/6f on firm & soft grnd, handles equitrack.
1335 **ENTROPY** 7 [7] B A Pearce 4-8-4 (36) D R McCabe 33/1: 50-002: 4 b f Brief Truce - Distant Isle   ¾   38
(Bluebird): Chsd ldrs, hmpd/lost place halfway, rallied & styd on strongly inside last, nrst fin: gd run: see 1335.
1132 **HALMANERROR** 20 [6] G M McCourt 10-9-9 (55) D Harrison 9/2 FAV: 0-6533: 10 gr g Lochnager -   hd   56
Counter Coup (Busted): Towards rear, rdn & prog 2f out to chall inside last, onepace nr fin: nicely bckd, op 8/1.
*1211 **ABSOLUTE FANTASY** 15 [13] E A Wheeler 4-9-2 (48)(bl) S Carson (5) 11/2: 602014: Chsd ldrs,   ½   48
led halfway, hung left inside last, hdd nr fin: acts on firm, gd/soft & equitrack: remains in gd heart: see 1211.
958 **HALF TONE** 36 [11] 8-8-8 (40)(bl) C Rutter 14/1: 50-005: Outpcd rear, late gains, nvr nrr: see 958.   hd   39
1265 **TERM OF ENDEARMENT** 12 [10] 3-8-5 (46) F Norton 20/1: 0-0056: In tch, rdn 2f out, keeping on well   1¼   41
when hmpd inside last & eased nr fin: shade unlucky, would have gone clsr: handles gd & gd/soft: see 887.
1213 **KEE RING** 15 [8] 4-9-10 (56)(BL) S Whitworth 8/1: 035-67: Led after 1f till halfway, btn 1f out: blnks.   shd   51
1213 **DAME JUDE** 15 [9] 4-9-7 (53) P Robinson 10/1: 0-008: Prom 4f: op 8/1: see 1092.   1   45
4112} **LE LOUP** 240 [1] 3-9-7 (62) S Drowne 12/1: 0600-9: Led 1f, handy 4f: op 8/1, reapp: plcd in '99   1¼   51
(rtd 82, auct mdn): eff at 5f on soft grnd & a sharp/undul trk.
1335 **GOLD EDGE** 7 [4] 6-8-2 (34) G Sparkes (7) 8/1: -05060: Handy 2f out, wknd final 1f: 10th: op 14/1.   nk   22
1412 **CHAKRA** 4 [3] 6-8-3 (35) Claire Bryan (5) 10/1: 060000: Rear, efft halfway, btn 1f out: 11th: qck reapp.   ½   22
503 **BEVERLEY MONKEY** 102 [12] 4-8-7 (39) P Fitzsimons (5) 14/1: 55-000: Chsd ldrs 4f: 12th: abs, op 12/1.   nk   25
1336 **TWO STEP** 7 [2] 4-8-2 (34)(t) Dale Gibson 16/1: 060-00: Bhd halfway/eased final 1f: 13th: see 1336.   dist   0
13 ran   Time 1m 12.4 (4.6)   (G H S Bailey & N C D Hall)   M Blanshard Upper Lambourn, Berks.

1465	7.45 COURAGE SELL HCAP 3YO+ 0-60 (F) 1m4f Good/Soft Inapplicable [54]

£1968   £562   £281   3 yo rec 17lb Raced centre - stands side fnl 3f

1331 **FUERO REAL** 7 [6] R J Hodges 5-8-9 (35) S Drowne 5/1: 40-531: 5 b g Highest Honor - Highest   39
Pleasure (Foolish Pleasure): Chsd ldrs, drvn/led over 2f out, edged left inside last, held on gamely nr fin, all-out:
op 10/1, no bid: rnr-up twice in '99 (rtd 42, h'cap, subs mod jumps form): former Flat wnr in the French provinces:
eff arnd 10/12f on firm & good/soft grnd, likes a sharp/undul trk: apprec drop to sell h'cap grade.
1241 **GROOMS GOLD** 13 [18] J Pearce 8-8-0 (26)(vis) R Ffrench 14/1: 220002: 8 ch g Groom Dancer -   nk   29
Gortynia (My Swallow): Led till over 2f out, hard rdn/ch inside last when bumped left, kept on well, just held: op
12/1: shade unlucky here: op 12/1: eff in a visor, best prev without blnks: see 369.
4336} **DUELLO** 225 [17] M C Pipe 9-10-0 (54) Darren Williams (7) 7/2 FAV: 0521-3: 9 b g Sure Blade - Royal   ¾   56
Loft (Homing): Mid-div, prog/chsd ldrs 2f out, carried head high & to one side in last: nicely bckd: Flat reapp,
jumps fit (plcd, rtd 96h, h'cap): '99 Leicester clmr wnr (rtd 58, M Blanshard): '98 Nottingham wnr (h'cap, rtd 59):
eff at 12/14f on any grnd, fibresand, any trk, likes gall ones.
1209 **LUNAR LORD** 15 [3] J S Moore 4-8-6 (32) G Hind 20/1: 50-004: Chsd ldrs, onepace final 2f: unplcd   1½   32
last term (h'caps, rtd 40): rtd 50 at best in '98: stays a sharp/undul 12f & handles soft grnd.
1002 **UNIMPEACHABLE** 30 [4] 3-8-8 (51) P Fitzsimons (5) 16/1: 5-0005: In tch, kept on final 2f, onepace.   3   47
1210 **GOLD LANCE** 15 [1] 7-9-2 (42) S Sanders 12/1: 060-56: Prom, rdn/no extra over 1f out: see 1210 (10f).   1½   36
1332 **MISS TAKE** 7 [9] 4-8-12 (38) N Callan 14/1: 440057: Mid-div, onepace final 2f: op 10/1: see 1332, 384.   ¾   31
1394 **RED BORDEAUX** 4 [5] 5-9-4 (44)(bl) Dane O'Neill 10/1: -00508: Mid-div, efft 4f out, btn 2f out: op 7/1.   3   33
1332 **ORDAINED** 7 [2] 7-9-7 (47) T Quinn 11/2: 604239: Chsd ldrs, btn 2f out: btr 1332, 1128 (fast & firm).   4   31
1350 **VANBOROUGH LAD** 6 [13] 11-8-9 (35) C Rutter 12/1: 46-500: Rear, nvr factor: 10th: op 10/1, qck reapp.3½   15
1065 **INKWELL** 23 [11] 6-8-7 (33) S Whitworth 10/1: 525000: Al rear: 12th: tchd 12/1: see 260.   0
3323} **FROZEN SEA** 285 [8] 9-8-6 (32) J F Egan 10/1: 0022-0: Al rear: 14th: Flat reapp, jumps fit, no form: 0
rnr-up on final 2 of 4 '99 starts on the level (rtd 53a, sell, flattered & 34, C/D sell h'cap): back in '96 scored
at Yarmouth (ltd stks, rtd 67): eff at 14f, handles firm, gd & equitrack.
1128 **Power Hit** 20 [15] 4-10-0 (54) M Roberts 12/1:   1203 **Socialist** 16 [10] 4-8-6 (34) J P Spencer 20/1:
14 ran   Time 2m 38.50 (10.4)   (Grandstand Jockeys)   R J Hodges Charlton Adam, Somerset.

1466	8.15 WINDMILL MED AUCT MDN 3YO (F) 1m2f Soft Inapplicable

£2247   £642   £321 Raced centre - stands side fnl 3f

1293 **SOLO FLIGHT** 9 [8] B W Hills 3-9-0 M Hills 6/5 FAV: 45-21: 3 gr c Mtoto - Silver Singer (Pharly):   82
Cl-up halfway, led 2f out, hung left/asserted final 1f, pushed out cl-home: hvly bckd: rtd 91 in '99 (mdns): eff
at 10f, will stay further (brother to smart jumper Busy Flight): acts on firm & soft: win races over further.
1200 **EL ZITO** 16 [4] M G Quinlan 3-9-0 J F Egan 20/1: 23-02: 3 b g Mukaddamah - Samite (Tennyson):   2   79
Led, hard rdn/hdd 2f out, held final 1f: well clr rem: op 14/1: stays 10f, posted imprvd effort on soft grnd: see 86.
4516} **MUSCHANA** 211 [3] J L Dunlop 3-8-9 T Quinn 13/8: 532-3: 3 ch f Deploy - Youthful (Green Dancer):   9   65
Chsd ldrs 4f out, btn over 2f out: hvly bckd tho' op 11/8: reapp: plcd final 2 '99 starts (rtd 83, fillies mdn):
eff at 7f/1m, mid-dists shld suit: acts on gd/soft grnd, poss not soft?: shld do better.
1293 **WENSUM DANCER** 9 [4] R Guest 3-8-9 D Harrison 33/1: 04: Prom till halfway, no ch 3f out: no form.   21   45
4305} **BREMRIDGE** 226 [6] 3-9-0 J P Spencer 7/1: 5002-5: Prom, hard rdn/struggling 3f out: op 6/1, reapp: ¾   49
rnr-up final '99 start (rtd 78, nursery, A G Foster), earlier with P Chapple Hyam): stays a sharp 1m, acts on good.
--   **ONLY WORDS** [2] 3-9-0 M Roberts 12/1: 6: Rear, brief effort 3f out, sn btn: op 5/1, debut.   1½   48
1293 **VICTORIAN LADY** 9 [5] 3-8-9 Dale Gibson 33/1: 07: Sn bhd: see 1293.   11   32
7 ran   Time Not taken due to poor visibility.   (Lady Hardy)   B W Hills Lambourn, Berks.

BRIGHTON

WEDNESDAY MAY 24TH   **Lefthand, V Sharp, Undulating Track**

1467	8.45 LADBROKES CLASSIFIED STKS 3YO+ 0-65 (E) 7f rnd Soft Inapplicable

£2791   £797   £398   3 yo rec 11lb   Raced centre - stands side fnl 3f

*1348 **COMPRADORE 6** [2] M Blanshard 5-9-5 D Sweeney 9/4 JT FAV: -03211: 5 b m Mujtahid - Keswa (King's **68**
Lake): Rear, smooth prog final 2f & led inside last, pushed out cl-home, readily: value for 3L+: op 5/2, qck
reapp: recent Salisbury wnr (h'cap): plcd sev times in '99 (h'cap, rtd 71): '98 Folkestone wnr (stks, rtd 72):
eff at 6/7f, stays 1m: acts on firm & hvy, any trk, likes Salisbury: in gd heart.
1061 **KINSMAN 23** [5] I A Balding 3-8-9 (vis) K Fallon 11/2: -30062: 3 b g Distant Relative - Besito (Wassl) **1¼ 64**
Led, hard rdn/hdd inside last, held by wnr cl-home: tchd 7/1: imprvd effort with visor reapp: see 534 (AW).
1201 **COMMANDER 16** [3] M Kettle 4-9-6 (t) N Callan 12/1: 05-503: 4 b g Puissance - Tarkhana (Dancing **2½ 60**
Brave): Chsd ldr, onepace fnl 2f: tchd 16/1: t-strap: eff over a sharp 7f, return to 1m shld suit: handles soft.
1397 **DISTANT GUEST 4** [7] G G Margarson 3-8-11 R Hills (bl) P Robinson 9/2: 0-2024: Towards rear, onepace fnl 2f. **½ 59**
1330 **MUTABASSIR 7** [1] 6-9-6 T Quinn 9/4 JT FAV: 430-65: Towards rear, hdwy over 2f out, held over 1f **3½ 54**
out: nicely bckd tho' op 7/4: more expected after eyecatching latest, worth another ch on a faster surface.
3780} **AUNT DORIS 261** [8] 3-8-6 S Carson (5) 12/1: 0130-6: In tch, effort 3f out, sn held: op 8/1, reapp: **3½ 46**
'99 Leicester wnr (sell, J Berry, rtd 65): eff at 5/6f on fast & gd grnd, stiff/gall or sharpish trk: enjoys sell grade.
1297 **CORNDAVON 9** [9] 4-9-3 M Fenton 4/1: 0-2047: Chsd ldrs 5f: bckd: btr 1297, 960 (5f). **4 40**
1061 **WILFRAM 6** [6] 3-8-9 Darren Williams (7) 33/1: 040-08: Chsd ldrs, struggling halfway: unplcd last **9 33**
term (rtd 75, nov auct stks, flattered): with J M Bradley.
8 ran   Time Not Taken Due To Poor Visibility   (C McKenna)   M Blanshard Upper Lambourn, Berks.

GOODWOOD

WEDNESDAY MAY 24TH   **Righthand, Sharpish, Undulating Track**

Official Going   SOFT (GOOD TO SOFT in places). Stalls: Str crse - Stands Side; Rnd Crse - Inside, except 1m4f - Outside.

1468	2.10 METSA-SERLA FILLIES MDN 3YO (D) 7f rnd Good/Soft 62 -28 Slow

£5622   £1730   £865   £432

-- **DANCEABOUT** [2] G Wragg 3-8-11 D Holland 2/1 FAV: 1: 3 b f Shareef Dancer - Putupon (Mummy's Pet) **88**
Bhd ldrs, gd prog to lead ent final 2f, kept on strgly: well bckd on belated debut (cracked pelvis last year when
with P C Hyam): eff at 7f, shld get 1m: acts on gd/soft grnd, sharp/undul trk: goes well fresh & is well regarded.
1224 **JAWLA 14** [3] J H M Gosden 3-8-11 R Hills 9/2: 0-32: 3 ch f Wolfhound - Majmu (Al Nasr) **1¼ 84**
Led, under press & hdd appr final 1f, not pace of wnr: imprvg with each run, eff at 7f on gd grnd: see 1224.
1224 **DANIYSHA 14** [6] Sir Michael Stoute 3-8-11 K Fallon 3/1: 4-43: 3 b f Doyoun - Danishara (Slew O'Gold) **2 80**
Handy, effort 2f out, same pace: nicely bckd: shld stay further & apprec minor trks: see 1224.
-- **HAREEBA** [11] P J Makin 3-8-11 S Sanders 12/1: 4: Held up, nvr pace to chall: debut: Hernando **2½ 75**
half-sister to 3 wnrs: should know more next time.
1268 **BREAKWATER 12** [1] J P Spencer 3/1: 40-45: Cl-up, wknd qckly 2f out: bckd, promising 1268 (fast).7 **63**
-- **MOLLY MALONE** [9] 3-8-11 C Rutter 50/1: 6: Al bhd: op 25/1 on debut: with J Tuck. **1¾ 60**
6 ran   Time 1m 30.78 (6.28)   (Bloomsbury Stud)   G Wragg Newmarket, Suffolk.

1469	2.40 LISTED LUPE STKS 3YO (A) 1m2f Good/Soft 62 -01 Slow

£19500   £6000   £3000   £1500

4605} **LOVE DIVINE 201** [3] H R A Cecil 3-8-8 T Quinn 3/1: 2-1: 3 b f Diesis - La Sky (Law Society) **114**
Held up, prog going well over 3f out to lead before 2f out, shkn up, readily: hvly bckd, reapp: rnr-up sole '99
start (mdn, rtd 83+): apprec step up to 10f, 12f shld suit: acts on gd/soft grnd, handles hvy & any trk: goes well
fresh: smart & improving, yet to race on fast grnd but has leapt to the head of the Oaks betting in an open year.
*1287 **SPINNING TOP 11** [5] Sir Michael Stoute 3-8-8 K Fallon 11/8 FAV: 12: 3 b f Alzao - Zenith **4 106**
(Shirley Heights): Restrained, imprvd 3f out, sn rdn to chase wnr, hung right, onepace: hvly bckd: imprvd in
defeat, acts on gd/soft & soft grnd tho' connections believe she will apprec a faster surface in the Ribblesdale.
1223 **INFORAPENNY 14** [4] R A Fahey 3-8-8 Pat Eddery 12/1: 40-214: 3 b f Deploy - Morina (Lyphard) **1½ 104**
Bhd, und press 3f out, styd on well ins last, nvr nrr: gd run & sure to enjoy a return to 12f: see 1223.
*1227 **SAILING 17** [6] P F I Cole 3-8-11 J Fortune 10/1: 05-214: Chsd ldrs, ch ent final 3f, sn no extra. **1½ 105**
*1200 **BEZZAAF 16** [1] 3-8-8 L Dettori 10/1: 15: Cl-up, led 3f out, sn hdd, fdd: tchd 12/1: big step **1 100$**
up in grade on softer grnd, not disgraced: see 1200.
4097} **BRITANNIA 241** [2] 3-8-8 K Darley 4/1: 3322-5: Led till 3f out, btn & hmpd: nicely bckd from **5 93**
5/1 on reapp: plcd all 4 juv starts, incl at Ascot (Gr 1, rtd 103): eff at 1m, bred to apprec further: acts on fast
& soft grnd, stiff/undul trk: likes to force the pace: trainer felt she would need this first run.
6 ran   Time 2m 10.52 (6.32)   (Lordship Stud)   H R A Cecil Newmarket, Suffolk.

1470	3.10 ABN AMRO HCAP 3YO 0-110 (B) 7f rnd Good/Soft 62 -06 Slow	[113]

£35000   £10000   £5000   £2500

1215 **CAMBERLEY 15** [16] P F I Cole 3-8-3 (88) K Darley 7/2 FAV: 2-3221: 3 b c Sri Pekan - NSX (Roi **95**
Danzig) In tch going well, imprvd ent fnl 2f, qcknd below dist, drvn to lead towards fin: well bckd from 6/1:
overdue first win, plcd in v competitive h'caps earlier, rnr-up '99 start (conds, rtd 95, Miss G Kelleway):
eff at 7f/7.5f, shld get 1m: acts on fast & gd/soft grnd, any trk: useful, tough & progressive colt.
1153 **STRAHAN 19** [19] J H M Gosden 3-8-10 (95) L Dettori 9/2: 21-122: 3 b c Catrail - Soreze (Gallic **½ 100**
League): Handy, went on ent final 2f, kept on strongly but worn down well inside last: tchd 11/2: another
smashing run from this v useful, imprvg colt, should make up into a Listed/Gr 3 performer: see 1153, 982.
1405 **SWIFT DISPERSAL 4** [10] S C Williams 3-7-10 (81)(7oh) P M Quinlan (5) 12/1: 001023: 3 gr f Shareef **2 82**
Dancer - Minsden's Image (Dancer's Image): Held up, gd prog 3f out, kept on for 3rd below dist, no ch ldrs:
each-way gamble from 33/1 raced despite 7lbs o/h, ran Saturday: imprvg filly, win on turf bef long.
1153 **LAGOON 19** [1] B W Hills 3-8-10 (95) M Hills 16/1: 135-04: Rear, stdy wide prog final 2½f, nvr **nk 95+**
nrr: stays a sharp/undul 7f & shld land a nice prize with a more positive ride, prob over further: see 1153.
*1178 **DUKE OF MODENA 17** [11] 3-8-7 (92) S Carson 5/1: 03-115: Mid-div, some hdwy und press 2f out, **½ 91**
nvr nr ldrs: op 7/1, not clearest of passages over lngr 7f trip but clr rem: in-form, return to flatter trk may suit.
*1153 **RAYYAAN 19** [9] 3-8-5 (90) R Hills 8/1: 2-1116: Held up, smooth wide prog 3f out, rdn before **3 83**

487

dist, sn no extra: op 6/1: wng run ended on this rain-softened grnd, v progressive on fast earlier: see 1153.
1285 **ZIETZIG** 11 [15] 3-7-10 (81)(2oh) J Mackay (7) 14/1: 0-0557: Al arnd mid-div: op 10/1, up in trip. nk 73
1072 **TAKE FLITE** 23 [17] 3-7-10 (81)(1oh) R Brisland (5) 16/1: 034-28: Rcd in 2nd till lost place appr fnl nk 72
2f: op 12/1: goes on gd/soft but connections feel he needs a fast surface, worth a try at 1m?: see 1072.
1308 **EASTWAYS** 8 [4] 3-8-6 (91) K Fallon 12/1: -00309: In tch on outer, chsd ldrs 3f out, fdd bef fnl 1f. ½ 81
995 **TEODORA** 32 [3] 3-8-13 (98) Pat Eddery 25/1: 453-50: Bhd, prog into mid-div 3f out, no further hdwy: 10th.1¾ 85
1178 **LAUNFAL** 17 [8] 3-8-7 (91)(1ow) R Hughes 16/1: 25-040: Al towards rear: 11th, back up in trip. 1½ 76
954 **DIAMOND LOOK** 36 [6] 3-7-13 (84) G Carter 8/1: 2-130: Chsd ldrs till wknd 2f out: 12th: shd 68
much clsr to this wnr in 954 (gd grnd), see 839.
1220 **LABRETT** 14 [2] 3-7-10 (81) Dale Gibson 20/1: 0-0000: Al bhd: 13th, lngr trip, see 1220, 988. nk 64
913 **OUT OF AFRICA** 40 [18] 3-8-12 (97) Dane O'Neill 25/1: 111-00: Led till ent final 2f, sn btn: 14th. nk 79
1171 **FREE RIDER** 18 [13] 3-9-7 (106) T Quinn 10/1: 21-200: Mid-div, denied room appr final 3f till dist, nk 87
position accepted: 15th, top-weight, h'cap now: worth another chance: see 1171 (2,000 Guineas), 955.
1153 Rule Of Thumb 19 [12] 3-7-10 (81)(2oh) F Norton 33/1:4468} **Strasbourg** 215 [5] 3-8-12 (97) J Fortune 25/1:
1153 Major Rebuke 19 [14] 3-8-1 (83)(3ow) G Duffield 33/1:
18 ran   Time 1m 29.28 (4.78)   (HRH Sultan Ahmad Shah)   P F I Cole Whatcombe, Oxon.

1471 3.40 FAIRCLOUGH HCAP 3YO+ 0-95 (C)   6f   Good/Soft 62 +07 Fast   [92]
£7913   £2435   £1217   £608 All the pace was down the centre (mid-high no's)

1173 **DANIELLES LAD** 18 [8] B Palling 4-9-8 (86) K Darley 14/1: 0-0401: 4 b g Emarati - Cactus Road (Iron 94
Duke) Made all, pshd out, readily: dual '99 rnr-up (h'caps, rtd 91): '98 wnr here at Goodwood (mdn auct) &
Doncaster (nursery, rtd 88): eff at 5/6f on fast, likes gd/soft, hvy & Goodwood: qk follow-up?
1110 **RETURN OF AMIN** 21 [12] W R Muir 6-9-2 (80)(VIS) Martin Dwyer 16/1: -00002: 6 ch h Salse - 1¾ 83
Ghassanah (Pas de Seul) Dwelt, pushed along mid-div, hard rdn & hdwy before dist, not get to wnr: back to
form in first time visor & is well h'capped now: likes soft grnd & a stiffer trk: see 728.
1324 **CRYHAVOC** 7 [10] D Nicholls 6-9-4 (82) F Norton 7/2 FAV: 600303: 6 b g Polar Falcon - Sarabah 1 82
(Ela Mana Mou) Chsd ldrs, pushed along 2f out, squeezed thro' dist, not pace to chall: well bckd, see 716.
703 **DEBBIES WARNING** 62 [6] K Mahdi 4-10-0 (92) L Dettori 20/1: 30-064: Rcd towards stands side, nk 91
mid-div, prog appr fnl 1f, no extra nr fin: gd run, top weight, 9 wk abs, back in trip, away from the wnr.
4144} **LOCH LAIRD** 238 [16] 5-9-1 (79) J Reid 11/1: 6000-5: In tch, wide, chsd ldrs appr final 1f, sn onepace: ½ 77
reapp: '99 wnr at Salisbury (mdn, reapp) & here at Goodwood (h'cap, rtd 82): plcd in '98 (mdn, rtd 77):
eff at 5/6f, tried 7f on firm & soft, any trk: runs v well fresh & can carry big weights: with M Madgwick.
1173 **DOWNLAND** 18 [7] 4-9-4 (82) M Roberts 9/1: 620-06: Chsd ldrs, shkn up over 2f out, chsd wnr 1 77
briefly 2f out, onepace: should apprec a return to faster grnd: see 1173.
1173 **MARSAD** 18 [14] 6-9-10 (88) T Quinn 13/2: 0-5007: Hld up, imprvd 2f out, no extra 1f out: bckd, clr rem. shd 83
*1126 **BLUNDELL LANE** 20 [17] 5-8-12 (76) J Fortune 14/1: 000-18: Cl-up till wknd appr fnl 1f: nds faster grnd. 5 59
1126 **UPLIFTING** 20 [15] 5-8-3 (67) A Daly 14/1: 300-09: Front rank till lost place 2f out: won this on ½ 49
fast grnd in '99 off 1lbs lower mark: see 1126.
1173 **RING DANCER** 18 [5] 5-9-1 (79) A Clark 20/1: /00-00: Outpcd towards stands side: 10th: see 1173. ¾ 59
1173 **CADEAUX CHER** 18 [11] 6-9-3 (81) Pat Eddery 11/2: 40-220: Nvr got in it on stands side: 11th, shd 61
nicely bckd from 13/2, faster grnd suits: see 1173, 716.
1173 **HILL MAGIC** 18 [1] 5-9-4 (82) M Fenton 14/1: 05-000: Nvr a factor stands side: 12th. ½ 61
1153 **LORD PACAL** 19 [4] 3-8-13 (77) G Duffield 33/1: 34-000: Slow away, al bhd: 13th, back in trip: ¾ 54
'99 debut wnr at Newbury (mdn, Gr 3 4th, rtd 100): eff at 5f, should get 6f: acts on fast grnd & a stiff/gall trk.
1245 **CLASSY CLEO** 13 [13] 5-9-5 (83) J F Egan 20/1: 000000: Chsd ldrs till halfway: 14th, see 64. nk 59
1213 **EVENTUALITY** 15 [2] 4-8-4 (68) S Carson (5) 10/1: 146-50: Al bhd stands side: 15th, faster grnd suits. 3½ 36
1173 **GRACIOUS GIFT** 18 [9] 4-9-10 (88) R Hughes 12/1: 230-00: In tch till halfway: 16th, op 10/1: see 1173. 1 53
16 ran   Time 1m 13.28 (3.28)   (Mrs P K Chick)   B Palling Cowbridge, Vale Of Glamorgan.

1472 4.10 FESTIVAL THEATRE MDN 2YO (D)   6f   Good/Soft 62 -38 Slow
£4426   £1362   £681   £340

-- **CD EUROPE** [2] M R Channon 2-9-0 S Drowne 25/1: 1: 2 ch c Royal Academy - Woodland Orchid 94
(Woodman) Chsd ldrs, led appr final 1f, pshd clr: jockey given 4 day ban for irresponsible riding: IR£20,000
Mar foal, sire a sprinter/miler: eff at 6f, will get further: acts on gd/soft grnd & runs well fresh.
1328 **REEL BUDDY** 7 [7] R Hannon 2-9-0 R Hughes 4/1: 62: 2 ch c Mr Greeley - Rosebud (Indian Ridge) 3 85
Tried to make all, hdd dist & outpcd: tchd 5/1: imprvd in defeat from the front on this gd/soft: win in a race.
-- **ELGRIA** [12] R Hannon 2-9-0 Dane O'Neill 20/1: 3: 2 b c Distinctly North - Perfect Swinger 1¼ 82
(Shernazar) Wide, prom, ch appr final 1f, onepace: stablemate 2nd, debut: 7,000 IR gns Mar foal, dam
moderate, sire a sprinter: eff at 6f on gd/soft grnd & should improve.
-- **CRIPSEY BROOK** [3] R J O'Sullivan 2-9-0 S Sanders 33/1: 4: Chsd ldrs, swtchd & hdwy 2f out, ½ 81
no extra dist: debut: 8,000 gns Lycius Mar foal, dam a mdn, sire 6f/1m performer: pleasing debut.
-- **MARINE** [10] 2-9-0 K Fallon 9/4 FAV: 5: Dwelt & lost at least 10L, imprvd into mid-div by halfway, 1¼ 78
no extra fnl 1f: hvly bckd from 7/2 on debut: Marju May foal, half-brother to a 9f/11f wnr & a wng hdler, dam
11f wnr, sire 1m/12f performer: bred to apprec a lot further but obviously been shwg something, worth another ch.
-- **HAWKES RUN** [4] 2-9-0 D R McCabe 33/1: 6: Slow to stride & hung right thro'out, hard rdn halfway hd 78
kept on nicely in last: 13,000 gns Hernando Mar gldg, half-brother to 5 wnrs, incl high class mid-dist filly.
-- **ADJOURNMENT** [13] 2-9-0 J Fortune 6/1: 7: Chsd ldrs till 2f out: mkt drifter on debut: IR80,000 gns 6 66
Patton Mar foal, half-brother to a Champion 2yo in Italy, dam unrcd, sire a smart dirt sprinter in the States.
-- **FLOOT** [5] 2-9-0 Pat Eddery 10/1: 8: Prom, wide till lost place 2f out: debut: 31,000 gns hd 66
Piccolo Feb foal, half-brother to a 12f/NH wnr, dam stoutly bred, sire a sprinter: with J Dunlop.
-- **ATTORNEY** [8] 2-9-0 P Robinson 7/2: 9: Prom, losing place when hmpd before dist, eased: well 3 60
bckd from 5/1 on debut: Wolfhound Mar 1st foal, dam useful juv sprinter, sire 5f/7f performer: drop to 5f?
-- **LAI SEE** [6] 2-9-0 L Dettori 12/1: 0: Dwelt, al bhd: 10th, debut: IR 4,800 Tagula Mar foal, 4 52
half-brother to 3 wnrs, incl a 5f juv, dam a mdn, sire a sprinter: with A Jarvis.
-- **MENAS ERN** [1] 2-9-0 P Doe 20/1: 0: V slow away, sn struggling: 11th on debut: 18,000 gns 25 27
Young Ern Mar 1st foal, dam 7f/1m wng juv, sire 7f performer: with S Dow.
11 ran   Time 1m 15.98 (5.98)   (Circular Distributors Ltd)   M R Channon West Isley, Berks.

GOODWOOD   WEDNESDAY MAY 24TH   Righthand, Sharpish, Undulating Track

1473   4.45 MARRIOTT HCAP 3YO+ 0-80 (D)   1m rnd   Good/Soft 62 -31 Slow   [80]
£6012   £1850   £925   £462   3 yo rec 12lb

2622} **KANZ WOOD** 317 [15] W R Muir 4-8-10 (62) Martin Dwyer 33/1: /050-1: 4 ch g Woodman - Kanz   65
(The Minstrel) Mid-div, gd prog appr final 2f to lead 1f out, rdn out: first win, reapp: moderate & lightly rcd
since '98 when plcd in a Newmarket mdn (rtd 81): eff at 7f/1m, tried 12f: acts on fast & gd/soft grnd: runs
well fresh: reportedly had a wind operation since last year & could prove leniently h'capped.

*1201 **DANAKIL** 16 [6] K R Burke 5-9-0 (66) N Callan 6/1: 351612: 5 b g Warning - Danilova (Lyphard)   1¾ 65
Chsd ldrs thro'out, kept on und press for 2nd, not trble wnr: bckd: continues in terrific form, see 1201.

3721} **JUST NICK** 265 [3] W R Muir 6-8-12 (64) J Reid 14/1: 0000-3: 6 b g Nicholas - Just Never Know -   1   61
(Riverman) Handy, going well, prog to lead on bit ent final 2f till 1f out, no extra: reapp, shorter-priced
stablemate of wnr: missed '98, rtd 84 in '97, sole win in '96 at Folkestone
(auct mdn): eff at 7f/1m: acts on firm & hvy grnd, any trk: well h'capped now.

1330 **COPPLESTONE** 7 [4] P W Harris 4-9-8 (74) A Beech (5) 7/1: /4-024: Chsd ldrs, led 3f out, sn hdd,   2½ 67
fdd final 1f: qck reapp, handles gd/sft, prefers faster grnd?: see 1330, 1070.

4496} **MISS RIMEX** 212 [1] N Pollard 4-9-11 (77) N Pollard 12/1: 3501-5: Towards rear, some hdwy 2f out, nvr nr ldrs: 1¼ 68
op 10/1, top-weight, reapp: '99 wnr at Newmarket (h'cap) & Leicester (clmr, rtd 79 at best): '98 Kempton wnr
(nurs, rtd 80): eff at 1m, tried 10f on firm & soft grnd, any trk, likes stiff/gall ones: sharper for this.

1335 **REACHFORYOURPOCKET** 7 [12] 5-7-10 (48)(5oh) G Baker (7) 12/1: 612036: Nvr better than mid-div.   1½ 36
*1203 **WILTON** 16 [17] 5-9-4 (70) G Duffield 9/2: 011017: Bhd, effort & not clr run over 2f out, nvr dngrs.   2   54
1259 **KAMARAZI** 12 [8] 3-8-9 (73) P Doe 33/1: 150008: Hmpd start, not much room 3f out, nvr a factor.   shd 57
842 **ROGER ROSS** 47 [16] 5-7-11 (49) F Norton 7/1: 100-59: In tch till fdd 2f out: 7 wk abs, back in trip.   1¼ 31
1215 **PROUD CHIEF** 15 [9] 3-8-13 (77) D Harrison 10/1: 0-2600: Chsd ldrs till appr final 2f: 10th, see 792.   8   45
1442 **MR BERGERAC** 2 [2] 9-8-12 (64) D Sweeney 20/1: 556-B0: Mid-div till 3f out: 11th, blnks off, see 119.   7   20
*1129 **MOON AT NIGHT** 20 [7] 5-9-3 (69) M Roberts 10/3 FAV: 110-10: Stumbled start but led till 3f   5   17
out, sn btn: 12th, bckd: reportedly unsuited by the grnd: see 1129 (fast).

732 **WELODY** 60 [13] 4-9-3 (69)(bl) L Dettori 16/1: 42100: Cl-up till 3f out, btn & hmpd: 13th: 9 wk abs.   14   3
13 ran   Time 1m 44.8 (7.4)   (D J Deer)   W R Muir Lambourn, Berks.

1474   5.20 RACING CHANNEL COND STKS 4YO+ (B)   1m4f   Good/Soft 62 -38 Slow
£10753   £3498   £1749

1174 **MUTAMAM** 18 [1] A C Stewart 5-8-9 R Hills 4/9 FAV: 4/0-21: 5 b h Darshaan - Petal Girl (Caerleon)   112
Easily made all: well bckd to land the odds, sole wnr: unplcd sole '99 start in Dubai for Godolphin: '99 wnr
at Sandown (stks), Haydock & Goodwood (Gr 3's, Gr 1 4th, rtd 120): eff at 10f, stays a slow run 12f: acts on
firm, gd/soft grnd & any trk, likes Goodwood & forcing the pace: v smart, shld win another Group race.

1247 **TAUFANS MELODY** 13 [2] Lady Herries 9-8-9 K Darley 3/1: 14/002: 9 b g Taufan - Glorious Fate   9   103
(Northfields) Trkd wnr, outpcd turning for home: stiffish task at the weights: see 1247.

4135] **LOCOMBE HILL** 239 [3] M Blanshard 4-9-3 M Roberts 5/1: 0310-3: 4 b c Barathea - Roberts Pride   16   96
(Roberto) Al last, left bhd 3f out: stiff task on reapp: '99 Kempton wnr (class stks, rtd 98): '98 Newbury
wnr (2, mdn & nov, rtd 107 at best): eff at 12f on firm, suited by hvy, any trk, likes Newbury.
3 ran   Time 2m 43.77 (11.97)   (Hamdan Al Maktoum)   A C Stewart Newmarket, Suffolk.

NEWCASTLE   THURSDAY MAY 25TH   Lefthand, Galloping, Stiff Track

Official Going   GOOD (GOOD TO SOFT places). Stalls: Str Crse - Stands Side; Rnd Crse - Inside except 10f - Outside.

1475   2.20 TYNE BRIDGE NOV STKS 2YO (D)   5f   Good/Soft 62 -41 Slow
£3445   £1060   £530   £265   Raced stands side

1107 **MEDIA MOGUL** 22 [1] T D Barron 2-9-2 K Darley 5/2: 131: 2 b g First Trump - White Heat (Last Tycoon):   92
Chsd ldr, rdn to chall & briefly hung left over 1f out, hard drvn to get up cl home: nicely bckd: earlier scored
at Beverley (debut, mdn auct): eff at 5f, 6f suer to suit: acts on gd & hvy grnd, stiff/gall trk: has run well
fresh: potentially useful, should win more races at 6f+.

1214 **CHARLIE PARKES** 16 [3] A Berry 2-8-12 J Carroll 8/11 FAV: 222: 2 ch c Pursuit Of Love - Lucky Parkes   ½   85
(Full Extent): Led, strongly prsd from over 1f out, hdd well ins last & no extra: hvly bckd: not given hard race.

*1240 **HAMBLETON HIGHLITE** 14 [6] K A Ryan 2-9-2 F Lynch 8/1: 13: 2 ch g Paris House - Sempreverde   2½ 82
(Lear Fan) Bhd ldr, effort 2f out, not pace of front pair: op 6/1: acts on firm & gd/soft grnd: see 1240 (firm).

821 **BALL GAMES** 50 [5] D Moffatt 2-8-12 J Bramhill 10/1: 4: Trkd ldrs, outpcd final 2f: 7 wk abs, op 8/1.   3   71
-- **SMART DANCER** [2] 2-8-12 R Winston 5/1: 5: In tch 3f: op 8/1: Spectrum colt, Feb foal, cost   6   60
16,000 gns: half-brother to 2 wnrs abroad: dam a lightly rcd French mdn, sire a top class 1m/10f performer.
5 ran   Time 1m 03.35 (5.15)   (Mrs J Hazell)   T D Barron Maunby, Nth Yorks.

1476   2.50 ACCESS TO JUSTICE CLAIMER 2YO (F)   6f   Good/Soft 62 -70 Slow
£2733   £781   £390   Raced stands side

1302 **TIME MAITE** 10 [6] M W Easterby 2-9-0 G Parkin 100/30 FAV: 431: 2 b g Komaite - Martini Time (Ardoon):   64
Sn cl-up & led after 2f, clr over 1f out, post came just in time under hands & heels: op 5/1: styd lngr 6f trip,
suld get further: acts on gd/soft grnd, prob handles fibresand & hvy grnd: likes a stiff/gall trk & front running.

1381 **PETIT TOR** 5 [8] J Norton 2-8-9 O Pears 4/1: -042: 2 b f Rock City - Kinoora (Kind Of Hush):   hd 58
Mid-div & rdn halfway, styd on well for press from over 1f out, just failed: op 7/4: stays 6f, acts on gd & gd/soft.

-- **STICKS** [11] C B B Booth 2-8-9 K Hodgson 7/1: 3: 2 ch f Aragon - Petiller (Monsanto):   1   56+
Drvn/rear, styd on final 2f, nrst at fin: op 8/1: Apr foal, cost 3,800 gns: half-sister to 2 juv wnrs, dam a 3yo
Belgium wnr: stays 6f, looks sure to apprec further: acts on gd/soft grnd: win a race.

1294 **I GOT RHYTHM** 10 [2] Mrs M Reveley 2-8-9 A Culhane 33/1: 004: Rdn/towards rear, styd on final   2   51
2f, not pace of front pair: clr of rem: imprvd on step up to 6f, handles gd/soft grnd: stay further in nurseries.

-- **VODKA** [7] 2-8-8 Dean McKeown 14/1: 5: Chsd ldrs 4f: op 12/1: Inzar gelding, Apr foal, half-   8   41
brother to wnrs abroad: dam a French mdn, sire a 6/7f performer: with P C Haslam.

-- **CONSPIRACY THEORY** [12] J Carroll 11/2: 6: Dwelt, chsd ldrs 4f: op 5/2: Fraam filly, Apr   4   31

489

foal, cost 2,600 gns: half-sister to 3 juv wnrs: dam 6f 3yo wnr: speedily bred: with A Berry.
-- **JEZADIL** [5] 2-8-5 T Williams 14/1: 7: Mid-div, btn 2f out: op 12/1: Mujadil filly, Apr foal, cost 1½ 25
7,500 gns: half-sister to a 6f juv wnr: dam a mdn, half-sister to smart juv Torgau: with M Dods.
1019 **BOBANVI 31** [4] 2-8-5 R Winston 8/1: -548: Mid-div, drvn/btn 2f out: btr 1019, 856. hd 24
-- **DOCKLANDS ROLLER** [3] 2-8-8 Kim Tinkler 20/1: 9: In tch 4f: op 14/1: Inzar gelding, Apr foal, 1¾ 23
cost 7,000 Irish gns: half-brother to 2 juv wnrs: dam an unrcd half-sister to Oaks wnr Ginevra: will stay further.
1294 **DISGLAIR 10** [1] 2-7-10 K Dalgleish (7) 10/1: 000: Al outpcd rear: 10th: op 12/1: btr 1294 (firm). 2½ 4
1206 **BAYRAMI 17** [13] 2-7-11 N Kennedy 33/1: 0500: Led 2f, sn struggling: 11th: btr 1083. 1½ 1
-- **ROWENAS GIRL** [9] 2-8-5 T Lucas 14/1: 0: Slowly away & al rear: 12th: op 10/1: Sabrehill filly, 3½ 0
Apr foal, sister to a 1m juv wnr, dam a 5/7f juv wnr: sire a top class 10f performer: with M W Easterby.
12 ran Time 1m 19.2 (7.9) (T Beston & B Bargh) M W Easterby Sheriff Hutton, Nth Yorks.

1477

3.20 GREAT NORTH ROAD HCAP 3YO 0-70 (E) 1m str Good/Soft 62 -43 Slow [75]
£3120 £960 £602 £301 2 Groups - Stands side group held big advantage

1387 **SIGN OF THE TIGER 5** [13] P C Haslam 3-9-7 (68) P Goode (3) 6/1: 144231: 3 b g Beveled - Me Spede 72
(Valiyar): Rear stands side, prog final 2f & styd on well for press inside last to lead line: op 9/2, qck reapp:
earlier won AW h'caps at Southwell & W'hampton (rtd 74a): plcd in '99 (rtd 57a): eff at 7f/1m: acts on firm,
gd/soft & both AWs, any trk: has run well fresh: tough/progressive gelding, deserved this & can win again.
1387 **NOWT FLASH 5** [17] B S Rothwell 3-8-10 (57) Joanna Badger (7) 7/1: 610522: 3 ch c Petardia - hd 60
Mantlepiece (Common Grounds): Held up stands side, prog over 2f out & led 1f out, rdn/hdd line: qck reapp,
just ahead of today's wnr latest: acts on gd, gd/soft & fibresand: see 1387, 589 (sell).
1297 **FLYING CARPET 10** [1] T D Easterby 3-8-11 (58) K Darley 9/1: 0-6003: 3 b f Barathea - Flying Squaw 2½ 56+
(Be My Chief): Held up far side, prog/led that group over 2f out & sn drvn clr, drifted right inside last, styd on
well: op 8/1: ended up on stands side but clr best of those who rcd on far side: stays 1m, acts on gd/soft grnd:
can be considered unlucky here, shrewd trainer can find compensation in similar soon: see 759.
961 **HAIKAL 37** [11] N A Graham 3-9-4 (65) W Supple 20/1: 0-004: Mid-div stands side, rdn/prog to lead nk 62
briefly over 1f out, no extra nr fin: styd lngr 1m trip on h'cap bow: acts on gd/soft grnd: encouraging effort.
1104 **DONTBESOBOLD 22** [10] 3-9-1 (62)(vis) Dean McKeown 16/1: 624405: Stds side, led & clr halfway, hdd 1½ 56
over 1f out, no extra: again ran freely in first time visor: see 847, 278 (mdn).
*930 **ALPATHAR 40** [14] 3-8-13 (60) T Williams 12/1: 025-16: In tch stds side, chall over 1f out, sn held: abs. ¾ 53
1244 **CALLING THE SHOTS 14** [18] 3-8-2 (49) J Bramhill 33/1: 000-07: Held up stands side, outpcd over 2f ½ 41
out, rdn/late gains, nvr nrr: unplcd last term (rtd 55, mdn): 1m should suit, may get further.
1255 **ONE DOMINO 13** [20] 3-8-13 (60) A Culhane 14/1: 06-308: Chsd ldr stands side, ch 2f out, sn held. hd 51
1135 **SOUTH LANE 21** [15] 3-8-1 (48) J McAuley (5) 33/1: 00-59: Dwelt, towards rear stands side, mod prog. ½ 38
1085 **MARVEL 23** [16] 3-8-13 (60) Kim Tinkler 20/1: 10-000: In tch stands side, btn 2f out: '99 Ayr wnr (mdn, hd 49
rtd 76): eff at 7f on hvy grnd & a gall trk.
1053 **BEST EVER 26** [3] 3-8-5 (52) T Lucas 16/1: 00-000: In tch far side, nvr a factor: 11th: poor low draw. 1½ 38
*1333 **MISTER CLINTON 8** [9] 3-8-5 (52)(6ex) C Carver (3) 3/1 FAV: 00-410: Chsd ldrs stands side 6f: 12th. 2½ 33
1296 **HONG KONG 10** [7] 3-8-0 (47)(tbl) Dale Gibson 20/1: 02-000: Held up stands side, nvr a factor: 13th. 2 24
1105 **WATERGOLD 22** [5] 3-8-3 (50) O Pears 9/1: 000-50: Prom far side, btn 2f out & position accepted: 1½ 24
14th: poor low draw, this best forgiven: see 1105 (6f, mdn).
1202 **DOUBLE FAULT 17** [6] 3-8-7 (54) J Carroll 12/1: 40-500: Led far side grp over 3f out till over 2f out, 1½ 25
sn btn: 15th: op 10/1: poor low draw: btr 1024.
1183 **Top Of The Class 18** [12] 3-9-5 (66) N Kennedy 16/1: 873 **Dee Diamond 44** [19] 3-8-7 (53)(1ow) F Lynch 33/1:
1255 **Glen Vale Walk 13** [8] 3-8-5 (52) G Bardwell 20/1: 1072 **On Shade 24** [4] 3-8-3 (50) J Fanning 25/1:
942 **Rainworth Lady 38** [2] 3-7-12 (45) K Dalgleish (7) 33/1:
20 ran Time 1m 45.4 (8.4) (Mrs B M Hawkins) P C Haslam Middleham, Nth Yorks.

1478

3.50 SCOTCHHILLS HCAP 4YO+ 0-80 (D) 2m110y Good/Soft 62 -16 Slow [78]
£3916 £1205 £602 £301 4 yo rec 2 lb

115 **VIRGIN SOLDIER 181** [12] M Johnston 4-9-12 (78) J Fanning 10/1: 1112-1: 4 ch g Waajib - Never Been 86
Chaste (Posse): In tch, smooth prog 3f out & led over 2f out, held on well inside last, drvn out: tchd 11/1, abs,
top-weight: '99 scorer at Lingfield (h'caps, 2, rtd 84a), Musselburgh (h'cap, rtd 58), Southwell & W'hampton (AW
h'caps): plcd in '98 (mdn, rtd 62, T Etherington): eff at 12f/2m on gd, gd/soft & both AWs & any trk: runs well
fresh: best without blnks & a gd weight carrier: most tough & progressive gelding, should win again.
1194 **FREETOWN 18** [2] L Lungo 4-9-1 (67) K Darley 3/1 FAV: 41-62: 4 b g Shirley Heights - Pageantry ½ 73
(Welsh Pageant): Led/dsptd lead till over 2f out, styd on well for press final 1f: clr of rem: hvly bckd, op 4/1:
relished step up to 2m & a likely type for similar: see 1194.
1276 **KAGOSHIMA 12** [7] J Norton 5-7-10 (46)(vis)(1oh) G Bardwell 7/1: 65-023: 5 b g Shirley Heights - 5 47
Kashteh (Green Desert) Cl-up & ch over 2f out, kept on tho' not pace of front pair: op 6/1: handles firm & gd/sft.
1167 **LEDGENDRY LINE 19** [8] Mrs M Reveley 7-8-8 (58) A Culhane 9/1: 40-564: Settled towards rear, rdn & 4 55
late gains final 3f, no threat to ldrs: op 7/1: one win from 28 on the Flat: see 760.
1276 **TURGENEV 12** [1] 11-7-10 (46)(26oh) Joanna Badger (7) 50/1: 0-0005: Keen/handy, outpcd/lost place ½ 42
4f out, kept on final 2f, no threat: stiff task & a remarkably imprvd effort back on an easy surface: see 576.
4069} **PASS THE REST 244** [14] 5-8-12 (62) J Carroll 33/1: 0000-6: Rear, mod late gains, no threat: unplcd 2 56
last term (rtd 62a & 60a, tried blnks & visor): '98 Ripon wnr (h'cap, rtd 78) & W'hampton (rtd 89a, J Noseda):
eff at 7f/1m, lngr 2m trip could yet suit: acts on gd/soft, hvy & fibresand: handles a sharp/gall trk: well h'capped.
1301 **SPOSA 10** [4] 4-8-5 (57) R Fitzpatrick (3) 20/1: 240637: Mid-div, rdn/no impress final 3f: see 644, 556. 1½ 50
1276 **YES KEEMO SABEE 12** [10] 5-8-10 (60) L Newton 10/1: -60008: Rear, mod late gains: see 627. nk 53
1276 **NORTHERN MOTTO 12** [9] 7-8-0 (50) A Beech (3) 10/1: 0-5009: Held up, effort 4f out, no impress. 1 42
1167 **GIVE AN INCH 19** [5] 5-8-10 (60) T Williams 8/1: 0-0000: Held up, prog/chsd ldrs 3f out, sn btn: 10th. hd 52
1276 **GENEROUS WAYS 12** [13] 5-8-3 (53) W Supple 10/1: -40540: Hld up, prog/chsd ldrs 3f out, sn held: 11th. ½ 44
1276 **OLD HUSH WING 12** [3] 7-7-12 (48) Dale Gibson 5/1: -56000: Led after 1f, drvn/hdd 4f out & sn btn: 14th. 0
1276 **Highfield Fizz 12** [11] 8-7-10 (46)(11oh) K Dalgleish (7) 40/1:
1167 **Home Counties 19** [6] 11-7-10 (46)(2oh) N Kennedy 16/1:
14 ran Time 3m 39.52 (14.02) (J David Abell) M Johnston Middleham, Nth Yorks.

1479	4.20 FILLIES & MARES HCAP 3YO+ 0-75 (E) 5f Good/Soft 62 -08 Slow			[70]
	£3003 £924 £462 £231 3 yo rec 8 lb Far side group held clear advantage			

1278 **BOLLIN ANN** 12 [4] T D Easterby 5-9-2 (58) K Darley 9/1: 240-01: 5 b m Anshan - Bollin Zola (Alzao) **64**
Chsd ldrs far side, drvn & styd on well inside last to lead nr line: op 8/1: '99 Beverley wnr (h'cap, rtd 58): '98
Ripon scorer (gd, rtd 59): eff over 5/6f on fast, gd/soft & any trk, likes a stiff one.

1298 **TANCRED TIMES** 10 [1] D W Barker 5-7-12 (40) J McAuley (5) 4/1 FAV: 350532: 5 ch m Clantime - **hd 45**
Mischievous Miss (Niniski): Led far side, hdd nr line: well bckd: trailblazer, deserves similar: on a gd mark.

1358 **NAISSANT** 6 [2] J S Goldie 7-8-6 (48) A Beech (5) 11/2: -50063: 7 b m Shaadi - Nophe (Super Concorde):3 **46**
In tch far side, drvn & kept on final 2f, not pace to chall: qck reapp: win again at Hamilton &/or over further.

1244 **HIGH CARRY** 14 [11] N Tinkler 5-8-10 (52) Kim Tinkler 12/1: 400-34: Chsd ldrs far side, onepace fnl 1f. **nk 49**

1296 **ROSES TREASURE** 10 [8] 4-8-1 (43)(bl) Joanna Badger (7) 20/1: 0-0005: Bhd ldrs far side, kept on **3 33**
final 1f, not able to chall: slipped down the weights & not disgraced here: see 1005.

1298 **AVONDALE GIRL** 10 [13] 4-9-10 (66) F Lynch 16/1: 050006: Cl-up stands side, led that group over 2f **hd 55+**
out, kept on well, no ch with ldrs far side: op 14/1: first home on unfav stands side, will rate higher: see 214.

1162 **ANGEL HILL** 19 [9] 5-9-2 (58) R Winston 10/1: 0-0007: Swtchd/rcd stands side, chsd ldrs, no impress. **½ 45**

1256 **RECORD TIME** 13 [12] 4-9-0 (56) W Supple 8/1: 0-0048: Held up stands side, effort 2f out, no threat. **½ 41**

1082 **SNAP CRACKER** 23 [19] 4-8-10 (52) K Dalgleish (7) 25/1: 002009: Chsd ldrs stands side 3f: see 751. **½ 35**

275 **CAUTIOUS JOE** 140 [3] 3-9-10 (74) B McHugh (5) 20/1: 100-00: Prom far side 4f: 10th: see 202. **hd 56**

1162 **FRILLY FRONT** 19 [17] 4-9-3 (59) C Lowther 10/1: 016000: Dwelt, stds side, nvr factor: 11th: op 8/1. **½ 39**

1257 **E B PEARL** 13 [6] 4-7-11 (39) J Bramhill 16/1: 651060: Bhd far side, mod prog: 12th: btr 751 (AW). **½ 17**

1256 **RED SYMPHONY** 13 [18] 4-8-10 (52) O Pears 14/1: 30-500: Rear stds side, no impress: 13th: see 919. **¾ 28**

1278 **TWICKERS** 12 [16] 4-9-4 (60) A Culhane 12/1: 0-0600: Prom stands side 4f: 15th: op 7/1: btr 1133. **0**

1421 **SUPERFRILLS** 3 [15] 7-7-12 (40) G Bardwell 9/1: 06-020: Chsd ldrs stds side 3f: 19th: op 8/1, qck reapp. **0**

1133 **EMMA AMOUR** 21 [20] 3-8-10 (60) T Lucas 33/1: 205-00: Led stands side 3f: 20th: see 62. **0**

1280 Dawn 12 [7] 3-9-6 (70) R Cody Boutcher (7) 12/1:

232 Swynford Welcome 150 [14] 4-8-12 (54) Dean McKeown 20/1:

1082 Premium Princess 23 [10] 5-8-13 (55) J Carroll 16/1: 1192 **Shalarise** 18 [5] 3-9-2 (66) Dale Gibson 33/1:
20 ran   Time 1m 01.72 (3.52)   (Lady Westbrook)   T D Easterby Great Habton, Nth Yorks.

1480	4.55 NEWCASTLE MED AUCT MDN 3YO (E) 1m2f32y Good/Soft 62 +08 Fast		
	£2847 £876 £438 £219		

1084 **MUSALLY** 23 [2] N A Graham 3-9-0 W Supple 6/4 FAV: 41: 3 ch c Muhtarram - Flourishing (Trojan Fen): **84**
Handy, led 2f out & readily asserted, styd on strongly, readily: hvly bckd tho' op 4/5: gd time: 50,000
gns purchase: apprec step up to 10f, cld get further: acts on gd/soft & a stiff/gall trk: win again.

1281 **GIMCO** 12 [6] G C H Chung 3-9-0 O Urbina 4/1: 5-432: 3 b c Pelder - Valetta (Faustus): **5 75**
In tch, rdn/prog to chase wnr over 1f out, kept on, al held: op 7/2: clr of rem: see 1281, 884.

1362 **FORUM CHRIS** 6 [7] M Johnston 3-9-0 J Fanning 13/2: 043: 3 ch g Trempolino - Memory Green (Green **5 68**
Forest): Handy, led over 3f out, rdn/hdd 2f out & sn btn: qck reapp: dropped in trip, 12f/h'caps shld now suit.

4229} **FIRST BACK** 234 [9] C W Fairhurst 3-9-0 P Goode (3) 50/1: 006-4: Prom, ch 2f out, fdd: reapp: **2½ 64$**
unplcd last term (rtd 70, mdn).

1295 **LITTLE DOCKER** 10 [5] 3-9-0 R Winston 12/1: 4-35: Rear, hdwy 4f out, no prog final 2f: see 1295. **nk 63**

1300 **KUUIPO** 10 [8] 3-8-9 (t) Dean McKeown 50/1: 0-0006: In tch 1m: Ingr 10f trip: see 930. **2½ 54$**

1310 **CLEAR PROSPECT** 9 [3] 3-9-0 J Carroll 50/1: 643-07: Led 7f, sn btn: op 4/1: mdn promise last term **10 48**
for P W Chapple Hyam & A G Foster (rtd 84): stays a stiff/gall 10f & handles gd/soft: has been gelded.

1134 **THE LAST RAMBO** 21 [4] 3-9-0 R Cody Boutcher (7) 40/1: 0-08: Bhd halfway: Ingr 10f trip, mod form. **2½ 44**

1106 **PAPI SPECIAL** 22 [11] 3-9-0 (vis) O Pears 8/1: 422-09: In tch 7f: op 14/1: see 1106 (h'cap). **11 32**

-- **RIPPLE** 1 [1] 3-8-9 C Teague 25/1: 0: Slowly away & al rear: 10th: debut, with Mrs M Reveley. **2½ 23**
10 ran   Time 2m 12.00 (5.5)   (Hamdan Al Maktoum)   N A Graham Newmarket, Suffolk.

Official Going   SOFT. Stalls: Str Crse - Stands Side; Rnd Crse - Inside, except 1m4f - Outside.

1481	2.10 MOTABILITY FILLIES MDN 3YO (D) 1m1f Good/Soft 87 -32 Slow		
	£5330 £1640 £820 £410		

-- **BINA RIDGE** 9 [9] H R A Cecil 3-8-11 T Quinn 7/2: 1: 3 b f Indian Ridge - Balabina (Nijinsky) **99+**
Waited with, smooth prog after halfway, led before dist, readily pulled clr: op 5/2, impressive debut:
related to sev wnrs: eff at 9f, will get further (Ribblesdale entry): acts on gd/soft grnd & a sharp/undul
trk: runs well fresh: useful, win races in much better company.

*1156 **MAY BALL** 20 [6] J H M Gosden 3-8-11 J Fortune 5/1: 12: 3 b f Cadeaux Genereux - Minute Waltz **6 89**
(Sadler's Wells): Led till ent final 2f, sn outpcd by easy wnr: op 4/1: wnr of a meaningless match sole
prev start: stays 9f, acts on fast & gd/soft grnd: can win a mdn: see 1156.

915 **EUROLINK ARTEMIS** 41 [10] J L Dunlop 3-8-11 Pat Eddery 7/2: 43: 3 b f Common Grounds - Taiga **5 81**
(Northfields): Held up, effort turning for home kept on same pace for 3rd: well bckd, abs, shld stay this trip.

-- **AMELIAS FIELD** 3 [3] S P C Woods 3-8-11 G Duffield 20/1: 4: Handy, no extra appr final 2f: debut: **2½ 78**
dam stoutly bred: will find easier mdns.

4506} **MOSSY MOOR** 213 [8] 3-8-11 R Hughes 11/2: 4-5: In tch till hung left 2f out: reapp: 4th sole '99 **1¼ 76**
start (fill mdn, rtd 77): Sanglamore filly, dam 10f wnr: bred to apprec mid-dists, poss handles hvy grnd.

1062 **NUNKIE GIRL** 24 [4] 3-8-11 R Smith (5) 40/1: 006: Al bhd: up in trip, needs h'caps. **1¾ 74$**

1269 **SPORTING LADDER** 13 [7] 3-8-11 K Fallon 10/3 FAV: 47: Well plcd, wknd qckly 3f out: btr 1269 (fast). **9 62**

3724} **MARJORY POLLEY** 266 [2] 3-8-11 (BL) S Drowne 50/1: 400-8: Chsd ldrs till 3f out: stiff task: **12 54$**
reapp: rtd 58 & 50a for P Walwyn last term: tried blnkrs: now with Miss Newton Smith.
8 ran   Time 2m 01.19 (10.69)   (K Abdulla)   H R A Cecil Newmarket, Suffolk.

GOODWOOD THURSDAY MAY 25TH Lefthand, Sharpish, Undulating Track

1482 2.40 LISTED FESTIVAL STKS 4YO+ (A) 1m1f192y Good/Soft 87 -12 Slow
£22750 £7000 £3500 £1750

*1174 **ISLAND HOUSE 19** [3] G Wragg 4-8-12 M Roberts 6/4 FAV: 112-11: 4 ch c Grand Lodge - Fortitude (Last Tycoon) Led, grad wound it up ent str, hard prsd below dist, held on gamely despite edging right: hvly bckd from 2/1, jockey given 1-day ban for whip abuse: earlier won at Newmarket (conds): '99 wnr at Pontefract (class stks) & Ayr (conds, rtd 102 at best): rtd 81 in '98: eff at 1m, suited by 10f now: acts on firm & hvy grnd, any trk: runs well fresh: v progressive tough & smart colt, game from the front today, can win a Group 3. **113**

*1014 **RIGHT WING 31** [2] J L Dunlop 6-9-1 (vis) Pat Eddery 2/1: 01-312: 6 b h In The Wings - Nekhbet (Artaius) Waited with, imprvd to trk wnr on bit appr final 1f, shkn up to chall inside last, ran on but wnr wld not be denied: well bckd, clr rem: needs to come late but in the form of his life: v smart, likes soft: see 1014. *nk* **115**

1154 **ANNAPURNA 20** [1] B J Meehan 4-8-7 J Fortune 16/1: 20-023: 4 b f Brief Truce - National Ballet (Shareef Dancer) Handy, chsd wnr 2f out, outpcd 1f out: op 12/1, fine effort at the weights: goes on fast grnd, prob handles gd/soft: can win with a slight ease in grade: see 1014. *5* **100**

1057 **BOMB ALASKA 26** [5] G B Balding 5-9-1 J F Egan 7/2: 1-4434: Restrained rear, rdn to impr appr final 2f, sn no impress: op 11/4: better than this, suited by an end-to-end gallop: see 703. *4* **103**

1248 **MONSAJEM 14** [4] 5-8-12 (bl) J Reid 13/2: -60435: Pulled hard bhd wnr, rdn over 2f out, sn btn: op 11/2: puzzling run: see 1248 (first time blnks), 657. *12* **88**

5 ran Time 2m 14.13 (9.93) (Mollers Racing) G Wragg Newmarket, Suffolk.

1483 3.10 HLB KIDSONS HCAP 4YO+ 0-90 (C) 7f rnd Good/Soft 87 +04 Fast **[89]**
£11635 £3580 £1790 £895

1250 **GIFT OF GOLD 14** [2] A Bailey 5-9-2 (77) J Reid 25/1: -45001: 5 ch h Statoblest - Ellebanna (Tina's Pet) Nvr far away, trav well, cruised into lead appr fnl 1f, v cmftbly: gd time, tchd 33/1: '99 wnr at Goodwood (h'cap, rtd 85 & 59a): '98 Lingfield wnr (h'cap, rtd 83, A Kelleway): stays 1m, all 4 wins at 7f: acts on fast, likes gd/soft & soft, poss both AWs: goes on any trk but likes sharp ones, especially Goodwood: well h'capped. **86**

1004 **BOOMERANG BLADE 31** [15] B Smart 4-9-5 (80) J Stack 16/1: 0-0662: 4 b f Sure Blade - Opuntia (Rousillon) Front rank, narrow lead appr fnl 2f till bef dist, styd on but outpcd: likes gd/soft: see 935. *3½* **82**

1250 **PEARTREE HOUSE 14** [1] D Nicholls 6-9-4 (79) F Norton 11/1: -00603: 6 b g Simply Majestic - Fashion Front (Habitat) Bhd, plenty to do ent str, briefly short of room ent final 2f, ran on strongly, nvr a threat: op 8/1: back to form, well h'capped, shrewd trainer will place him to advantage soon: see 687. *shd* **81+**

1273 **BINTANG TIMOR 13** [8] W J Musson 6-8-10 (71) Pat Eddery 7/1: 13-034: Chsd ldrs, swtchd for effort appr final 1f, kept on same pace: nicely bckd from 9/1: back up in trip, running well in defeat: see 834. *¾* **71**

1110 **PRINCE BABAR 22** [3] 9-9-5 (80) K Fallon 7/1: 0-2445: Last, pushed along halfway, imprvg when short of room 2f out, kept on, nvr dngrs: set plenty to do: see 875. *1½* **77**

*434 **WELCOME GIFT 114** [14] 4-8-8 (69) J F Egan 14/1: 2-2216: Midfield, prog 2f out, no extra inside last, nr 4 mth abs, turf/h'cap bow: not disgrcd in this competitive heat: drop back to 6f may suit for now: see 434. *¾* **65**

1348 **AMBER FORT 7** [11] 7-8-12 (73)(bl) J Fortune 10/1: -32547: Mid-div, squeezed thro' appr final 1f, rdn, flashed tail & onepace final 1f: qck reapp: 7f specialist who likes Goodwood: see 1011, 817. *shd* **69**

1286 **MISTER RAMBO 12** [16] 5-9-8 (83) R Hughes 6/1 FAV: 010528: Prom, rdn 2f out, btn before dist, eased: nicely bckd: had a hardish race in soft grnd in 1286, see 817. *3½* **73**

1173 **CHAMPAGNE RIDER 19** [4] 4-9-12 (87) T E Durcan 25/1: 100-09: Al arnd same place: best at 6f. *¾* **76**

1196 **COLD CLIMATE 17** [5] 5-7-12 (59) A Daly 33/1: 00-500: Mid-div, rdn 2f out, no impress: 10th, up in trip. *nk* **47**

1110 **ELMHURST BOY 22** [13] 4-9-0 (75) P Doe 7/1: 545660: Rear, shkn up ent final 3f, some hdwy & short of room 2f out, position accepted: 11th: finding trouble in every race: stable out of sorts: see 239. *2* **59**

4426} **HYPERACTIVE 219** [17] 4-8-9 (70) M Roberts 10/1: 20/1-0: Led till appr final 2f, sn btn: 12th: op 7/1 on reapp/h'cap bow: landed sole '99 start at Yarmouth (mdn, rtd 75): '98 rnr-up (mdn, rtd 75): eff at 6/7f: goes on fast & gd grnd: can run well fresh, easy trk: worth another ch on a faster surface. *1½* **51**

1110 **SECOND WIND 22** [10] 5-9-2 (77) D O'Donohoe 10/1: 4-1500: Chsd ldrs till 2f out: 13th, op 8/1. *2* **55**

4562} **KARAMEG 208** [6] 4-9-4 (79) T Quinn 10/1: 3515-0: Hmpd early, nvr in it, eased bef fnl 1f: op 8/1, reapp: '99 wnr at Doncaster (fill h'cap) & Newmarket (h'cap, rtd 80): rtd 72 in '98: eff at 6f, suited by 7f, stays 1m: acts on firm & gd/soft grnd, any trk, likes gall ones: this is best forgotten: with P Harris. **0**

4562} **Tiger Talk 208** [12] 4-9-5 (80)(BL) D Holland 25/1: 966 **Chewit 36** [7] 8-9-8 (83) L Newman (5) 14/1:
4585} **Akalim 205** [9] 7-8-7 (68) P Fitzimons (5) 25/1:

17 ran Time 1m 30.34 (5.84) (Classic Gold) A Bailey Little Budworth, Cheshire.

1484 3.40 A & J BULL RTD HCAP 4YO+ 0-100 (B) 1m6f Good/Soft 87 +08 Fast **[107]**
£9785 £3711 £1855 £843

1187 **PAIRUMANI STAR 18** [8] J L Dunlop 5-9-2 (95) Pat Eddery 12/1: 200-01: 5 ch h Caerleon - Dawn Star (High Line) Chsd ldrs, hard rdn to chall appr fnl 1f, got on top ins last, almost cght by rnr-up's late rally: gd time: '99 wnr at York (rtd h'cap), Salisbury (stks) & Newbury (h'cap, rtd 96): eff at 12/14f, stays a slow run 2m: acts on firm, soft, any trk, likes Salisbury: can go well fresh with/without blnks: useful. **103**

917 **MURGHEM 41** [11] M Johnston 5-9-6 (99) D Holland 12/1: 0-2242: 5 b h Common Grounds - Fabulous Pet (Somethingfabulous) Set gd clip, und press appr fnl 1f, hdd ins last, rallied & nrly got back up: 6 wk abs, well clr rem: tough, useful entire, deserves another win & stable now coming back to form: see 695. *shd* **106**

1187 **GALLERY GOD 18** [5] G Wragg 4-8-4 (83)(1oh) M Roberts 7/1: 16-063: 4 ch c In The Wings - El Fabulous (Fabulous Dancer) In tch, effort 2f out, sn bumped, carried right, kept on for 3rd but no ch with ldrs: possibly saw out this lngr 14f trip tho' faster grnd would have suited: see 968. *6* **85**

*1167 **QUEDEX 19** [2] E L James 4-8-4 (83)(2oh) S Whitworth 12/1: 602014: Held up, prog under press & drifted right appr final 2f, kept on same pace: ran to best 2lbs 'wrong': see 1167. *hd* **85$**

4484} **MONTALCINO 215** [7] 4-8-13 (92) S Sanders 16/1: 5320-5: Bhd, prog into mid-div over 2f out, rdn & no further hdwy: reapp: '99 wnr here at Goodwood (mdn, rtd 93 in a rtd h'cap): rtd 73 sole '98 start: eff at 12/13f on firm & gd/soft grnd, prob any trk: has been gelded & should be sharper next time. *nk* **93**

*1030 **ZILARATOR 29** [13] 4-8-11 (90) T Quinn 6/1: 55-616: Hld up, shkn up 3f out, no impress: btr 1030 (12f, hvy). *1* **90**

732 **SALMON LADDER 61** [4] 8-9-7 (100)(bl) J Fortune 12/1: 133-47: Prom, ev ch 3f out, gradually wknd: top-weight, 9 wk abs: won this race in '99 (off 8lbs lower mark): see 732. *½* **100**

1222 **TENSILE 15** [9] 5-8-6 (84)(1ow) K Fallon 4/1 FAV: 530-68: Chsd ldrs, wknd ent final 2f: well bckd. *4* **82**

968 **LITTLE PIPPIN 36** [12] 4-8-6 (85) S Drowne 9/2: 140-49: In tch till 3f out: nicely bckd, lngr trip, see 968. *3½* **79**

997 **TURTLE VALLEY 33** [6] 4-8-11 (90) P Doe 12/1: 40-000: Al bhd: 10th, see 997, 695. *6* **79**

GOODWOOD THURSDAY MAY 25TH Lefthand, Sharpish, Undulating Track

10 ran   Time 3m 09.88 (11.08)   (Windflower Overseas Holding Inc)   J L Dunlop Arundel, West Sussex.

1485   4.10 LISTED CONQUEROR COND STKS 3YO+ (A)   1m rnd   Good/Soft 87 -02 Slow
£18183   £5595   £2797   £1398   3 yo rec 12lb

4487} **CORINIUM** 215 [4] H R A Cecil 3-8-5 T Quinn 10/11 FAV: -311-1: 3 br f Turtle Island - Searching Star   108
(Rainbow Quest) Held up, effort over 2f out, no impress till kept on well before dist, led final 100y, going away:
hvly bckd, reapp: '99 wnr at Warwick (fill mdn) & Newbury (Listed, rtd 109): half-sister to smart 7f/1m wnr
Fa Eq: eff at 1m, crying out for further on this evidence: acts on gd & hvy grnd, prob any trk: goes well fresh:
v useful & deserves to take her place in the Oaks & should go well granted easy grnd.
1117 **EUROLINK RAINDANCE** 25 [1] J L Dunlop 3-8-2 G Carter 5/1: 25-302: 3 b f Alzao - Eurolink Mischief   1¾ 102
(Be My Chief) Tried to make all, kept on well for press but hdd final 100y: op 4/1: game & useful, enjoy further.
*1224 **LAST RESORT** 15 [6] B W Hills 3-8-2 N Pollard 7/1: -413: 3 ch f Lahib - Breadcrumb (Final Straw)   1¼ 100
Waited with, imprvd 3f out, rdn bef dist, same pace: gd run in much tougher company: stays 1m: useful.
953 **DECISION MAID** 37 [3] G Wragg 3-8-2 F Norton 8/1: 51-04: Well plcd, shkn up & ev ch entr final 2f,   ½ 99
no extra final 1f: tchd 10/1: better run tho' possibly not quite see out this longer 1m trip: see 953
*1134 **MYSTIFY** 21 [5] 3-8-2 D O'Donohoe 8/1: -55-15: Chsd ldrs till appr final 1f: tchd 10/1, up in trip & grade.   4 91
*1327 **MAYARO BAY** 8 [2] R Hughes 4-9-3 7/1: 2-0016: Handy till fdd 2f out: well bckd, needs faster grnd.   5 84
6 ran   Time 1m 44.54 (7.14)   (Mr Derek & Mrs Jean P Clee)   H R A Cecil Newmarket, Suffolk.

1486   4.45 SUSSEX FILLIES MDN 2YO (D)   6f   Good/Soft 87 -27 Slow
£4397   £1353   £676   £338

-- **GOODIE TWOSUES** [6] R Hannon 2-8-11 Dane O'Neill 12/1: 1: 2 b f Fraam - Aliuska (Fijar Tango)   93
Well plcd, rdn ent final 2f, led dist, kept on well: op 8/1, debut: 7,000 gns Mar foal, dam a 5f juv wnr:
eff at 6f, 7f should suit: goes on gd/soft grnd, sharp/undul trk & runs well fresh: good debut.
-- **HEJAZIAH** [3] P F I Cole 2-8-11 J Fortune 6/4 FAV: 2: 2 b f Gone West - Toptrestle (Nijinsky)   ½ 91
Led till 1f out, styd on: hvly bckd newcomer: Mar foal, dam & sire milers: eff at 6f, stay further in time:
handles gd/soft grnd: learn plenty from this & can win a mdn before long.
-- **MAKBOOLA** [7] J L Dunlop 2-8-11 R Hills 3: 2 b f Mujtahid - Haddeyah (Dayjur)   1¾ 86
Held up, prog on outer to chase ldrs appr final 1f, no extra inside last: op 5/1: Jan foal, dam 6f juv wnr, sire
a sprinter: stays 6f, handles gd/soft grnd & will know more next time.
1046 **AMBER TIDE** 27 [5] M L W Bell 2-8-11 M Fenton 15/8: 34: Cl-up, rdn & onepace before final 1f: 1½ 82
well bckd from 5/2: see 1046.
-- **MAROMA** [4] 2-8-11 Pat Eddery 7/1: 5: In tch, effort & no impress 2f out: stablemate 3rd: 3 75
First Trump Feb foal, half-sister to a 6f wng juv, dam 6f wnr, sire a sprinter.
1346 **VINE COURT** 7 [2] 2-8-11 A Clark 7/1: 06: Chsd ldrs till wknd ent final 2f: qck reapp.   4 65
1197 **EASTER ISLAND** 17 [1] S Sanders 2-8-11 33/1: 007: Slow away, al bhd: little sign of ability yet.   6 50
7 ran   Time 1m 16.81 (6.81)   (Mrs Sue Crane & Lady Davis)   R Hannon East Everleigh, Wilts.

1487   5.20 ROYAL SUSSEX APPR HCAP 3YO+ 0-70 (E)   5f   Good/Soft 87 -19 Slow   [66]
£3705   £1140   £570   £285   3 yo rec 8 lb

1278 **POLAR MIST** 12 [1] M Wigham 5-9-0 (52)(tbl) J Mackay (5) 12/1: 0-0001: 5 b g Polar Falcon - Post   57
Mistress (Cyrano de Bergerac) Cl up, narrow lead & drifted right appr fnl 1f, sn hard rdn/prsd, held on gamely:
'99 wnr at Folkestone (stks, rtd 72) & W'hampton (3, sell, clm & h'cap, rtd 67a, Mrs Macauley): '98 W'hampton
wnr (mdn, rtd 78a, Sir M Prescott): stays 6f, suited to 5f on gd/soft & hvy, fibresand/Wolverhampton specialist:
wears blinks/visor/t strap & can run well fresh: back to form & well h'capped for new connections.
1264 **FORGOTTEN TIMES** 13 [9] K T Ivory 6-10-0 (66)(vis) C Catlin (5) 10/3 FAV: 0-2062: 6 ch m Nabeel   nk 70
Dancer - Etoile d'Amore (The Minstrel) Chsd ldrs, clsd 2f out, strong chall inside last, held near fin: well
bckd, top-weight: lost nothing in defeat, won this last year (off 23lbs lower mark!): see 897.
1464 **HALF TONE** 1 [5] R M Flower 8-8-2 (40)(bl) S Carson 5/1: 0-0053: 8 gr h Touch Of Grey -   1 41
Demillinga (Nishapour) Rear, styd on fnl 2f to go 3rd, no trouble ldrs: bckd, qk reapp, ran well last night.
1278 **SIHAFI** 12 [3] D Nicholls 7-9-2 (54) T Hamilton (7) 9/1: 000-04: Chsd ldrs, lost place halfway,   2½ 49
rallied & edged right appr fnl 1f, no extra inside last: tchd 12/1: plcd twice in '99 (h,caps, rtd 71): won
9 times in '98, at Lingfield (2), Windsor, Bath, Folkestone, Salisbury, Sandown, Haydock & W'hampton (h,caps rtd
71 & 81a): stays 6f, best at 5f: acts on both AW, handles gd/soft, prefers gd & firm: h'capped to win on faster.
1073 **BEWARE** 24 [4] R 5-9-13 (65) Clare Roche 11/2: 661545: Towards rear, kept on fnl 1f, never dngrs.   3½ 52
1358 **BEYOND THE CLOUDS** 6 [8] 4-8-10 (48)(vis) P Fitzimons 13/2: 5-0026: Led till 2f out, fdd: ½ 34
drifted from 9/2, quick reapp, needs faster grnd: see 1358, 1007.
82 **NIGHTINGALE SONG** 187 [10] 6-8-12 (50) Darren Williams (3) 11/1: 0600-7: Prom till 2f out: tchd 14/1,   3½ 29
reapp: '99 wnr at Lingfield, Leicester & Sandown (h,caps, rtd 53): lightly raced since '96 win at Windsor
(sell, rtd 64, M Meade): eff 5/6f, tried 1m: acts on firm & soft, handles gd/soft AW.
1289 **DANCING LILY** 10 [2] 3-8-3 (49) R Brisland 20/1: 000-08: Never a factor: see 1289.   1½ 25
1438 **ECUDAMAH** 3 [4] 4-9-8 (60)(t) J Bosley (5) 15/2: 46-009: Slow away, nvr dngrs: ran on Monday.   1½ 33
3921} **RUN MACHINE** 253 [11] 3-8-2 (48) L Newman 33/1: 000-0: Soon bhd: 10th, reapp/h'cap bow.   2 16
1422 **ABOVE BOARD** 3 [7] 5-7-13 (37)(bl) D Watson (2) 16/1: 033060: Bhnd halfway: 11th, op 25/1, qk reapp. 1¼ 2
11 ran   Time 1m 01.99 (5.29)   (Stephen Roots)   M Wigham Newmarket, Suffolk

HAYDOCK FRIDAY MAY 26TH Lefhthand, Galloping Track

Official Going   SOFT after 2nd Race (Rain throughout afternoon). Stalls; 1m - Inside; Rem - Outside.

1488   2.00 ASTLEY GREEN AUCT MDN 2YO (E)   5f   Good/Soft Inapplicable
£3024   £864   £432

1240 **PRINCESS OF GARDA** 15 [14] Mrs G S Rees 2-8-2(1ow) G Duffield 16/1: -U431: 2 b f Komaite - Malcesine   78
(Auction Ring) With ldr, styd on to lead over 1f out, rdn out ins last: op 12/1: cost 14,500gns: full sister
to 2 juv 5f wnrs: dam 1m scorer: best up with/forcing the pace at 5f on gd/soft.
-- **WHERES JASPER** [11] K A Ryan 2-8-9 J Carroll 14/1: 2: 2 ch g Common Grounds - Stifen (Burslem)   ¾ 83+

493

In tch, eff halfway, sn rdn, kept on well fnl 1f, not btn far on debut: cost 18,000gns: related to sev wnrs: eff at 5f, crying out for 6f: handles gd/soft: can win similar soon: encouraging.

-- **RIDGEWAY LAD** [13] T D Easterby 2-8-9 K Darley 4/1: 3: 2 ch g Primo Dominie - Phyliel (Lyphard) hd 82
Dwelt, in tch, kept on nicely over 1f out, nrst fin on debut: Apr foal, cost 16,500gns: dam useful 6f scorer as a juv: eff at 5f, 6f sure to suit: handles gd/soft: type to improve for this.

1294 **FANTASY BELIEVER 11** [15] J J Quinn 2-8-3 W Supple 2/1 FAV: -324: Set pace till appr fnl 1f, nk 76
onepace, not btn far: nicely bckd: rtd higher 1294.

-- **BIJAN** [6] 2-8-1 P M Quinn (5) 16/1: 5: Sn bhd, kept on nicely over 1f out, nrst fin on debut: shd 74+
Apr foal, cost IR 10,000gns: dam 6f juv wnr: bred to relish 6f & showed plenty of promise here, clr rem.

1418 **DENNIS EL MENACE 4** [10] 2-8-9 Martin Dwyer 16/1: -046: In tch, rdn & no impress well over 1f out. 5 72

-- **GALAXY RETURNS** [12] 2-8-3 O Pears 12/1: 7: Bhd, modest late gains on debut: Mar foal, cost nk 65
6,200gns: bred to need 6f+ & time: with A Berry.

-- **KALUGA** [2] 2-7-12 A Nicholls (1) 14/1: 8: Bhd, some late hdwy: debut: Mar foal, cost hd 59
52,000gns: half-sister to a 5/6f juv wnr: dam 7f juv scorer: will apprec further.

1236 **NEW WONDER 15** [3] 2-7-12 G Baker 7/1: 39: Keen, handy till wknd well over 1f out: see 1236 (AW). ¾ 57

-- **PRINCE NOR** [4] 2-8-6 M Roberts 12/1: 0: Dwelt & al bhd on debut: 10th: Mar first foal, dam 5f juv wnr. ½ 64

-- **DARWIN TOWER** [9] 2-8-3 J Fanning 25/1: 0: Nvr a factor: 11th on debut. shd 60

-- **TOTALLY COMMITTED** [1] 2-8-6 Dane O'Neill 9/1: 0: Carried left start & al bhd: op 6/1, fin 14th. 0

865 **Miss Progressive 45** [5] 2-7-12 Kim Tinkler 50/1: -- **Cricketers Club** [8] 2-8-6 S Whitworth 33/1:
1252 **Belando 14** [7] 2-8-3 J F Egan 25/1:
15 ran Time 1m 02.44 (3.64) (North West Racing Club) Mrs G S Rees Sollom, Lancs

---

1489 **2.30 LEAHURST COND STKS 3YO+ (C) 1m30y rnd Good/Soft Inapplicable**
£6069 £2244 £1122 £510 3 yo rec 12lb

2165} **DUCK ROW 338** [5] J A R Toller 5-8-13 S Whitworth 9/4: 0160-1: 5 ch g Diesis - Sunny Moment (Roberto) 106
Trkd ldr, went on over 2f out, kept on gamely for press on reapp: lightly rcd in '99, won at Ascot (stks, rtd 109, made all): no wins in '98, rtd 115 when plcd in a Gr 1 at Ascot: v eff around 1m on gd & gd/soft: likes a gall trk, esp Ascot & has run fresh up well:fin/forcing the pace: smart & genuine at best.

4195} **EXEAT 237** [1] J H M Gosden 4-8-13 L Dettori 10/11: 2353-2: 4 b c Dayur - By Your Leave (Private ¾ 103
Account) Waited with, hdwy trav well to chall 2f out, not pace of wnr ins last for press on reapp: well bckd, clr rem: smart but frustrating in '99, plcd sev times & 4L 8th in 2,000 Guineas (rtd 115): juv scorer at Haydock (mdn): eff at 7f/1m on firm, gd/soft & on a gall trk: has tried a visor: v useful but expensive to follow.

1445 **SERGEANT YORK 3** [2] C Smith 4-8-13 J F Egan 12/1: 0-0533: 4 b c Be My Chief - Metaphysique 11 78
(Law Society) Keen in tch, btn over 2f out: 1 win from 23 & needs h'caps: qck reapp.

1342 **TACTFUL REMARK 8** [4] J A Osborne 4-8-13 J P Spencer 9/2: 03-054: Led till over 2f out, no extra: 3 72
better of firm grnd in 1342.
4 ran Time 1m 45.6 (6.1) (Duke Of Devonshire) J A R Toller Newmarket.

1490 **3.00 TOTE HCAP 4YO+ 0-90 (C) 1m30y rnd Soft Inapplicable** [88]
£7377 £2270 £1135 £567

1077 **SILK ST JOHN 25** [7] M J Ryan 6-9-11 (85) G Faulkner (3) 4/1 JT FAV: -00651: 6 b g Damister - Silk 90
St James (Pas de Seul) Waited with, hdwy for press fnl 2f to get up cl-home: well bckd: '99 wnr at Sandown & Newbury (h'caps, rtd 97): '98 wnr at Chepstow (ltd stks), Haydock (val h'cap, subs disq), Windsor (2) & Newbury: suited by a gall 1m, stays 11f on firm, hvy & fibresand: v tough, genuine & useful, took advantage of handy mark.

1250 **TAFFS WELL 15** [2] B Ellison 7-8-13 (73) K Fallon 4/1 JT FAV: 6-4042: 7 b g Dowsing - Zahiah (So nk 77
Blessed) Waited with, hdwy to lead over 1f out, kept on for press till collared ins last: just held: well bckd: another fine run on grnd prob easier than ideal & deserves a win: see 1250, 715.

1160 **TONY TIE 20** [5] J S Goldie 4-9-7 (81) J Fanning 7/1: 0-6223: 4 b g Ardkinglass - Queen Of The nk 85
Quorn (General Governor) Chsd ldrs, kept on for press over 1f out to chall ins last, just held in a 3 way photo.

1160 **FALLACHAN 20** [1] M A Jarvis 4-9-8 (82) P Robinson 9/1: 220-04: Chsd ldrs, eff to chall well over ¾ 85
1f out, onepace ins last: clr of rem: '99 scorer at Musselburgh (mdn h'cap) & Nottingham (h'cap, rtd 85 at best): eff at 7f/1m on firm, gd/soft & on a stiff or easy trk: tough.

1250 **WEETMANS WEIGH 15** [12] 7-9-0 (74) J P Spencer 16/1: 400004: Hld up, eff 2f out, onepace: see 49. 4 71

*1160 **VOLONTIERS 20** [13] 5-9-9 (83) A Beech 5/1: 5-0416: Chsd ldrs, rdn & no extra appr fnl 1f: btr 1160. hd 79

1113 **SCENE 23** [18] 5-9-2 (76) T G McLaughlin 14/1: 010007: Bhd, modest late gains: best 831. 1¾ 69

715 **TOM DOUGAL 63** [1] 5-9-4 (78) J F Egan 16/1: 000-08: Waited with, eff to chall well over 2f out, 1 69
sn btn: 2 month abs: '99 scorer at Ayr (class stks, rtd 87): '98 wnr at Newmarket (val h'cap) & York (h'cap, rtd 92): suited by a gall 1m on firm, gd/soft, handles hvy & any trk: slipped back to a handy mark.

1062 **PENNYS PRIDE 25** [15] 5-8-13 (73) A Culhane 14/1: 30239: Waited with, rdn & no impress over 2f out. 6 54

1070 **ROYAL ARROW FR 25** [6] 4-8-13 (73) W Supple 50/1: 00-000: Led till over 2f out, no extra: see 1070. 5 46

859} **Open Arms 408** [11] 4-9-1 (75) M Roberts 33/1: 1217 **Marching Orders 17** [16] 4-9-6 (80) J Carroll 40/1:
1042 **Parkside 28** [14] 4-9-2 (76) Martin Dwyer 12/1: 1352 **Grand Ambition 7** [10] 4-9-9 (83) Rebecca Bolton (7) 66/1:
3506} **Initiative 28** [8] 4-9-13 (87) P McCabe 40/1:
15 ran Time 1m 49.69 (9.19) (C R S Partners) M J Ryan Newmarket.

1491 **3.30 EQUITABLE RTD HCAP 3YO 0-95 (C) 1m2f120y Soft Inapplicable** [97]
£5896 £2236 £1118 £508

1075 **POLAR RED 25** [3] M J Ryan 3-8-6 (75) G Faulkner (1) 100/30: 23W-31: 3 ch g Polar Falcon - Sharp Top 85
(Sharpo) Made all, kept on well for press to draw clr ins last: juv scorer at Windsor (nurs h'cap, rtd 73): eff at 1m/10.5f on fast, enjoyed soft here: handles a sharp or gall trk: on the up-grade.

1177 **COMMON PLACE 19** [1] C F Wall 3-9-7 (90) R Mullen 5/1: 561132: 3 b g Common Grounds - One Wild 3 94
Oats (Shareef Dancer) Dwelt, waited with, eff to chall trav well 2f out, onepace & edged left appr fnl 1f: tough.

1261 **BREAK THE GLASS 14** [2] E A L Dunlop 3-8-11 (80) J Reid 11/4: 44-323: 3 b g Dynaformer - Greek 1¼ 82
Wedding (Blushing Groom) Cl-up, rdn & onepcd fnl 2f: bckd: stays 10.5f on soft: worth a try in headgear.

1341 **ZIBELINE 8** [5] C E Brittain 3-8-4 (73) P Robinson 9/2: 50-024: Chsd ldrs, wknd 2f out: up in trip. 2 72

1225 **MICKLEY 16** [4] 3-8-8 (77) R Lappin 10/1: 400-25: Keen in tch, rdn but ev ch over 2f out, sn rdn & btn. nk 75

1448 **BAILEYS PRIZE 3** [6] 3-8-4 (73)(3ex) J Fanning 4/1: -20146: Prom till wknd 2f out: btr 1448, 1299 (firm). 1 70
6 ran Time 2m 19.48 (9.48) (M Byron) M J Ryan Newmarket.

1492 4.00 BICKERSHAW MDN CLAIMER 2YO (F)   5f   Soft Inapplicable
£2352   £672   £336

1381 **WATERPARK** 6 [8] M Dods 2-8-6 F Lynch 15/8 FAV: -6321: 2 b f Namaqualand - Willisa (Polar Falcon)   68
Chsd ldrs al trav best, styd on to lead over 1f out, drew clr, cmftbly: Jan first foal, cost 4,500gns: dam
7f wnr: eff at 5f on soft & gd: going the right way.
-- **CATCH THE CHRON** [5] N Tinkler 2-8-6(1ow) T Quinn 16/1: 2: 2 b f Clantime - Emerald Gulf (Wassl)   3   60+
Dwelt, bhd, eff over 1f out, kept on & ran green fnl 1f, no dngr on debut: Mar foal, cost 4,200gns: will improve.
1240 **CLANSINGE** 15 [7] A Berry 2-8-8 J Carroll 5/1: 53: 2 ch f Clantime - North Pine (Import)   2½   57
Cl-up, led 3f out till over 1f out, no extra: see 1240.
1381 **FAYZ SLIPPER** 6 [2] T D Easterby 2-8-5 K Darley 14/1: 0004: Prom, wknd well over 1f out.   1¾   50
1208 **ASTAIREDOTCOM** 17 [1] 2-8-11 K Fallon 3/1: 45: Al bhd, modest late gains: see 1208.   3   50
1420 **EXELLENT ADVENTURE** 4 [6] 2-8-10 J F Egan 25/1: -W66: In tch, btn halfway.   hd   48
1189 **CARTMEL PRINCE** 19 [4] 2-8-9 G Duffield 7/1: -607: Led till 3f out, no extra: see 1189.   nk   46
-- **DOUBLE DIGIT** [3] 2-8-3 A Mackay 25/1: 8: Dwelt, al bhd on debut: Apr foal, cost 3,000gns: 16   8
dam 7f juv wnr: with M Brittain.
-- **EASTER BONNET** [9] 2-8-2 S Righton 33/1: 9: Rdn & al bhd: debut: Apr foal: with N Babbage.   2   4
9 ran   Time 1m 02.86 (4.06)   (Russ Mould)   M Dods Piercebridge, Co.Durham.

1493 4.30 EAGLE PARK FILLIES MDN 3YO (D)   1m4f   Soft Inapplicable
£3809   £1172   £586   £293

1344 **RIYAFA** 8 [3] Sir Michael Stoute 3-8-11 K Fallon 1/2 FAV: 21: 3 b f Kahyasi - Riyama (Doyoun)   89
Cl-up, led over 2f out, v cheekily, val 4L+: hvly bckd: stays 12f well: handles gd & soft grnd: can rate
more highly & win in stronger company.
1051 **CLEPSYDRA** 27 [1] H R A Cecil 3-8-11 T Quinn 100/30: 22: 3 b f Sadler's Wells - Quandary (Blushing   ¾   81
Groom) Set stdy pace till after 4f, led again over 2f out, sn hdd & toyed with by wnr: clr rem & stays 12f on soft.
-- **EDHKERINI** [4] M A Jarvis 3-8-11 L Dettori 5/1: 3: 3 ch f Lammtarra - Walesiana (Star Appeal)   5   76
Waited wth, rdn & ev ch over 2f out, sn rdn & btn: op 3/1: bred to relish mid-dists & shld improve.
1184 **TITIAN ANGEL** 19 [2] C N Allen 3-8-11 M Dwyer 14/1: 2-604: Led to 4th till over 2f out, no extra.   1   75
4 ran   Time   (H H Aga Khan)   Sir Michael Stoute Newmarket.

1494 5.00 MONKS HEATH APPR HCAP 3YO 0-70 (E)   6f   Soft Inapplicable   [77]
£3290   £940   £470

1061 **THE PROSECUTOR** 25 [8] B A McMahon 3-8-13 (62) P Mundy (7) 9/1: 615001: 3 b c Contract Law - Elsocko   64
(Swing Easy) Handy, eff & hung left over 1f out but styd on well ins last to get up cl-home: op 5/1: earlier
scored at Southwell (h'cap, rtd 79a): '99 wnr at W'hampton (mdn, rtd 74a, 66): eff at 5f, suited by 6f on
fibresand or soft, prob handles fast: acts on any track.
1244 **COLLEGE MAID** 15 [7] J S Goldie 3-8-4 (53) Dawn Rankin (5) 10/1: 6-2002: 3 b f College Chapel - Maid   hd   55
Of Mourne (Fairy King) Set pace, rdn & collared cl-home, just btn: deserves a win: see 777.
41 **KATIES VALENTINE** 195 [23] R A Fahey 3-8-6 (55) B McHugh (7) 14/1: 045-3: 3 b f Balnibarbi - Ring   1   55
Side (Alzao) Bhd, hung badly left over 1f out but kept on, not btn far: long abs: stays 6f on soft: lightly rcd.
1193 **ROBIN HOOD** 19 [5] Miss L A Perratt 3-8-1 (50) Clare Roche (3) 20/1: 0-004: Prom, ev ch over   1   48
1f out, onepace ins last: op 12/1: apprec drop back to 6f on soft ground.
1213 **CRUISE** 17 [9] 3-9-2 (65) R Smith 9/1: 51-05: In tch, eff over 1f out, no impress: acts on soft & equitrack.   2½   58
1053 **BALFOUR** 27 [16] 3-8-12 (61) N Esler (3) 2/1 FAV: 00-156: Bhd, some late gains: see 1053.   hd   53
1061 **LA TORTUGA** 25 [12] 3-9-7 (70) G Baker (3) 14/1: 450-07: Nvr a factor: see 171, 108.   nk   61
1098 **DUCIE** 24 [3] 3-9-4 (67) Karen Peippo (7) 10/1: 020-08: Handy, btn over 1f out: see 1098.   ½   57
4009} **MISTY BOY** 249 [15] 3-8-5 (54) Darren Williams 8/1: 060-9: Al bhd on reapp: unplcd on 3 '99 starts.   5   34
1149 **BETTYJOE** 21 [22] 3-8-2 (51) G Gibbons (5) 12/1: 000-00: Handy till btn 2f out: 10th: see 1149.   nk   30
4514} **ABSINTHER** 213 [10] 3-9-1 (64) L Swift (5) 20/1: 0300-0: Slow away & al bhd: 11th on reapp: hd   42
plcd once as a juv (rtd 67, 7f, hvy).
3887} **BANGLED** 256 [6] 3-9-0 (63) P Bradley 20/1: 0450-0: Chsd ldrs, wknd 2f out: 12th: reapp, plcd   1   40
once as a juv (rtd 68 at best, 5f).
4347} **DANCING RIDGE** 226 [14] 3-8-5 (54) Joanna Badger (3) 16/1: 2060-0: Handy till wknd over 2f out: 1¼   29
13th: reapp: rnr-up once as a juv (clmr, 6f, gd/firm, rtd 69).
1159 **SPIRIT OF KHAMBANI** 20 [19] 3-8-7 (56) S Finnamore 10/1: 03-00: Handy till btn over 2f out: 14th.   1¾   28
1205 **MAJOR BART** 18 [11] 3-8-1 (50) P Hanagan (3) 10/1: 00-050: In tch, wknd 3f out: 15th, op 7/1.   3   16
15 ran   Time 1m 17.8 (6.5)   (Whiston Management Ltd)   B A McMahon Hopwas, Staffs.

Official Going   GOOD. Stalls: Inside.

1495 6.40 GORDONS GIN HCAP 3YO 0-85 (D)   1m rnd   Good 54 +07 Fast   [89]
£4111   £1265   £632   £316

*744 **SIGN OF HOPE** 60 [11] I A Balding 3-9-2 (77) J Fortune 11/2: 003-11: 3 ch g Selkirk - Rainbow's End   87
(My Swallow): Settled rear, smooth hdwy appr final 2f, led dist, rdn clr inside last, eased cl-home: gd time:
abs: earlier won on reapp at Windsor (h'cap, first win): plcd final '99 start (rtd 80): eff at 1m, bred for
further: acts on fast & gd: runs well fresh, with/without visor: progressive, should complete hat-trick.
924 **WINTZIG** 41 [2] M L W Bell 3-8-4 (65) M Fenton 16/1: 61-052: 3 b f Piccolo - Wrangbrook (Shirley   1¾   69
Heights) Waited wth, rdn to impr 2f out, styd on appr final 1f but no threat to wnr: 6 wk abs: apprec further.
1094 **EASTWOOD DRIFTER** 24 [4] W R Muir 3-8-5 (66) O Pears 20/1: 00-303: 3 ch c Woodman - Mandarina   2½   65
(El Gran Senor) Rear, hdwy when swtchd appr final 1f, styd on well, nvr nrr: well worth another try at 10f.
1061 **IN THE ARENA** 25 [7] B W Hills 3-8-13 (74) J Reid 3/1: 00-434: Cl-up, ev ch until slightly hmpd   1¼   71
& no extra appr final 1f: clr rem: prob stays longer 1m trip: see 1061, 731 (6f).

*1345 **TRICCOLO** 8 [10] 3-8-11 (72)(6ex) M Roberts 9/4 FAV: 55-015: Settled in tch, prog 4f out, ev ch   7   59
until wknd qckly inside last: disapp here, looked a useful prospect when scoring easily in 1345.
1341 **HADATH** 8 [6] 3-9-0 (75)(vis) J Carroll 6/1: 5-0056: Led, hdd appr final 1f, fdd: bckd: btr 1341 (firm)   ¾   60
840 **EYELETS ECHO** 49 [3] 3-8-9 (70) S Sanders 12/1: 6-007: In tch, wknd qckly fnl 2f: 7 wk abs, h'cap bow.   9   40
1072 **DAYLILY** 25 [9] 3-8-4 (65) W Supple 20/1: -0068: Rcd keenly with ldrs, wknd qckly fnl 2f: h'cap bow.   ½   54
990 **FAVORISIO** 34 [1] 3-9-7 (82) K Darley 11/1: 0-1169: Front rank, lost tch final 2f: top weight: ½   50
twice wkd below best on turf, much btr 709 (fibresand).
1341 **LOUS WISH** 8 [5] 3-8-2 (63) F Norton 66/1: 636000: Sn bhd, fin 10th: see 346.   hd   30
3320} **LOMOND DANCER** 287 [8] 3-8-4 (65) R Mullen 33/1: 4406-0: In tch, wknd rapidly final 2f, fin last: 0
reapp: 4th at best in '99 (auct mdns, rtd 72 at best): stays 7f, handles firm & gd grnd.
11 ran   Time 1m 45.6 (3.8)   (George Strawbridge)   I A Balding Kingsclere, Hants.

1496   7.05 GUINNESS FILLIES HCAP 3YO+ 0-70 (E)   1m2f   Good 54   -05 Slow   [67]
£3029   £932   £466   £233   3 yo rec 14lb

1296 **TEMPRAMENTAL** 11 [11] S R Bowring 4-8-6 (45) K Darley 12/1: 253331: 4 ch f Midhish - Musical Horn   50
(Music Boy): Made all, drvn out 2f out, drvn out to hold on: v consistent this term (plcd
5 out of 6 starts): plcd form in '99 (rtd 47, rtd 45a on sand, h'caps, prev term scored at Chepstow (nursery,
rtd 62, first time visor): eff at 5f, now suited by 1m/10f, stays 12f: acts on firm, gd/soft & both AWs:
has tried blnks, eff with/without a visor: handles any trk & likes to dominate.
1432 **CASSANDRA** 4 [6] M Brittain 4-8-13 (52) J F Egan 14/1: 0-2502: 4 b f Catrail - Circo (High Top):   ½   55
Mid-div, rdn/prog over 2f out, styd on strongly inside last, no btn far: qck reapp: acts on gd & gd/soft.
*1033 **INCHINNAN** 30 [3] C Weedon 3-9-1 (68) J Reid 4/1 FAV: 52-213: 3 b f Inchinor - Westering (Auction   nk   70
Ring): In tch, rdn/chsg wnr appr fnl 1f, kept on, no extra cl-home: clr rem: eff at 1m/10f: in gd form, see 1033.
1350 **KINGFISHERS BONNET** 8 [15] S G Knight 4-8-11 (50) L Newman (5) -01354: In tch, drvn & styd   6   42
on appr final 1f, nvr nrr: prob needs hvy: see 1350 (hvy).
1272 **BITTER SWEET** 14 [10] 4-8-13 (52) G Hind 9/1: -04035: Handy, rdn to impr over 2f out, sn no extra.   4   37
748 **AN SMEARDUBH** 60 [14] 4-8-1 (40) F Norton 16/1: 00-006: Dwelt, mid-div at best: see 603 (mdn).   3   20
1272 **KELTECH STAR** 14 [2] 4-9-1 (54) N Callan 9/1: 053-67: Trkd ldrs, rdn & grad wknd final 2f: see 1272.   1¼   32
1243 **FALLS OMONESS** 15 [7] 6-8-12 (51) W Supple 12/1: 50-208: Rcd keenly in rear, effort 2f out, no   1   28
dngr: up in trip: twice below a promising reapp in 931 (soft).
1253 **SUNSET LADY** 14 [8] 4-8-10 (49) J Carroll 25/1: 4-0039: Prom, lost tch fnl 2f: btr 1253 (12f, firm).   1   25
4148} **PATRITA PARK** 240 [13] 6-8-3 (42) J Mackay (7) 11/1: 3240-0: Bhd, eff/no room over 1f out, no dngr: shd   18
fin 10th: reapp: plcd 6 times for Mrs P Dutfield in '99 (h'caps, rtd 46 at best): won fnl '98 start, at Brighton
(amat h'cap, rtd 38, W G M Turner): eff between 10f & 14f: acts on firm & gd/soft grnd: now with Mrs M Reveley.
-- **YANKEE DANCER** [4] 5-9-2 (55) P M Quinn 33/1: 632/0: Al in rear, 11th: reapp: missed '99, shwd   5   23
promise when plcd in 2 Irish mdns back in '98 (12f, yldg & soft): with R Hollinshead & may be capable of better.
1288 **TWENTY FIRST** 11 [19] 4-9-1 (60) D Holland 9/1: 26-060: Chsd ldrs, lost tch final 2f, fin 12th.   2   27
2676} **MELODY LADY** 317 [16] 4-9-1 (54) J Fortune 14/1: 0202-0: Al in rear, fin 13th: rnr-up twice in   1½   15
'99 (rtd 56 at best): plcd once in '98 (clmr, first time blnks, rtd 61, Mrs L Stubbs): eff at 12f on gd & fast.
1101 **Codicil** 23 [18] 4-8-9 (48) A Culhane 25/1:   1040 **Bewildered** 28 [5] 3-8-0 (53) Kimberley Hart (5) 50/1:
1296 **Scarlet Livery** 11 [5] 4-9-1 (54) K Hodgson 33/1:   1300 **Silken Lady** 11 [17] 4-7-12 (37) O Pears 50/1:
1133 **Hi Nicky** 22 [1] 4-9-13 (66) T Williams 66/1:
18 ran   Time 2m 14.0 (5.9)   (Roland M Wheatley)   S R Bowring Edwinstowe, Notts.

1497   7.35 PARFETTS COND STKS 2YO (C)   6f rnd   Good 54   -29 Slow
£5974   £1133   £515   £257

1102 **AFFARATI** 23 [1] J L Eyre 2-8-11 J F Egan 9/4 FAV: 21: 2 b g Emarati - Affairiste (Simply Great):   79
Cl-up, no room/swtchd over 1f out, styd on well to lead ins last, drvn out: up in trip: 23,000 gns Jan foal,
dam half-sister to a French Gr 3 wnr: eff at 5/6f on gd, gd/soft grnd & a stiff/gall trk: going the right way.
1131 **WILSON BLYTH** 32 [3] A Berry 2-8-11 J Carroll 5/1: 22: 2 b c Puissance - Pearls (Mon Tresor):   ¾   76
Dwelt, bhd, smooth hdwy 2f out, led appr final 1f, hdd inside last, sn btn: another gd run, stays 6f.
828 **GALY BAY** 50 [5] D Morris 2-8-6 S Sanders 13/2: 33: 2 b f Bin Ajwaad - Sylhall (Sharpo):   1½   67
Dwelt, settled near, drvn & ran on strongly inside last, nvr nrr: 7 wk abs: improve again.
*1124 **BLAKESHALL BOY** 22 [4] M R Channon 2-9-1 S Drowne 100/30: 3414: Trkd ldr, rdn, hung left & wknd   nk   75
inside final 1f: top-weight: jockey rec a 1 day careless riding ban: up in trip: shade btr 1124.
1437 **OPEN WARFARE** 4 [2] 2-8-10 K Fallon 9/1: 334135: Led, hdd appr final 1f, fdd/hmpd dist: qck reapp.   6   58
1006 **SIGN THE TRUCE** 32 [6] 2-8-11 K Darley 6/1: 06: Chsg ldrs when hmpd halfway, rdn/wknd over 1f out.   3   52
6 ran   Time 1m 19.1 (5.0)   (David Scott)   J L Eyre Sutton Bank, Nth Yorks.

1498   8.05 STRONGBOW CLAIMER 4YO+ (F)   1m rnd   Good 54   -02 Slow
£2530   £723   £361

-- **SHARP PLAY** [5] M Johnston 5-9-2 J Fanning 15/8 FAV: 1163/1: 5 b g Robellino - Child's Play   67
(Sharpen Up) Cl-up till went on appr fnl 2f, sn clr, pushed out, cmftbly: reapp: missed '99, v useful in '98,
scored at Ripon (stks, reapp), Dielsdorf (Swiss 2,000 Guineas) & Thirsk (stks, rtd 107): eff at 1m/9f, poss not
stay 12f: acts on fast & gd/soft, can run from off the pace: tough & genuine, win more races if staying sound.
1286 **YEAST** 13 [15] W J Haggas 8-9-7 K Fallon 2/1: 100-02: 8 b g Salse - Orient (Bay Express)   6   61
Trkd ldr, kept on fnl 2f but no ch with easy wnr: top-weight: likely to meet a useful rival here: see 1286.
1254 **LEOFRIC** 14 [7] M J Polglase 5-8-7 (bl) R Fitzpatrick (3) 16/1: 503303: 5 b g Alhijaz - Wandering   1   45$
Stranger (Petong) Dwelt, sn in tch, eff 2f out, rdn/no extra appr fnl 1f: likes sell/claim grade: see 973.
1358 **THREE LEADERS** 7 [14] E J Alston 4-8-5 W Supple 33/1: 060004: Handy, late gains, nvr nrr.   1½   40
1235 **PIPPAS PRIDE** 15 [1] 5-8-9 S Finnamore (5) 10/1: 115435: Cl-up, outpcd when short of room 3f out,   1   42
rallied & styd on again fnl 2f: turf return: btr 1235 (7f, AW).
973 **KIERCHEM** 37 [13] 9-8-6 O Pears 16/1: 030/26: Nvr better than mid-div: recently p.u. over hdles.   2   35
1296 **CYRAN PARK** 11 [8] 4-8-5 T Williams 20/1: -04007: In tch, rdn to impr 3f out, wknd qckly ins last.   1½   31
4328} **NOBBY BARNES** 227 [10] 11-8-5 Kim Tinkler (5) 3000-8: Dwelt, rear, late gains: reapp: plcd once   1¾   28
in '99 (clmr, rtd 45$): '98 wnr at Hamilton (h'cap, rtd 45 & 32a): eff around 7/9f on fast & hvy, handles both AWs.
1300 **HIGH SUN** 11 [4] 4-9-2 D Holland 10/1: 1-4009: Prom, rdn & wknd qckly appr fnl 1f: see 1007.   ½   38
1037 **RAYWARE BOY** 28 [12] 8-8-6 L Newton 25/1: 00-000: Al bhd, 10th: well btn over timber since 1037.   4   22
1137 **NERONIAN** 22 [6] 6-8-9 C Cogan (5) 50/1: -43050: Led after 4f, hdd over 2f out, wknd qckly, fin 13th.   0
962 **FAIRFIELD BAY** 38 [3] 4-8-7 (bl) (2ow) R Lappin 33/1: 00/000: Led, hdd halfway, qckly lost tch, 15th.   0

PONTEFRACT FRIDAY MAY 26TH Lefthand, Undulating Track, Stiff Uphill Finish

1113 **Windshift** 23 [18] 4-9-2 N Callan 14/1:   --   **Valhalla Gold** [9] 6-8-11 R Winston 33/1:
890   **Ginner Morris** 44 [17] 5-8-7 M Roberts 20/1:   --   **Full Circuit** [16] 4-8-5 J F Egan 20/1:
16 ran   Time 1m 46.3 (4.5)   (Mrs I Bird)   M Johnston Middleham, N.Yorks.

1499   8.35 WALKERS HCAP 3YO+ 0-70 (E)   1m4f   Good 54   -01 Slow   [70]
        £3120   £960   £480   £240

1150 **ARCHIE BABE** 21 [1] J J Quinn 4-9-7 (63) A Culhane 10/1: 1-6501: 4 ch g Archway - Frensham Manor   70
(Le Johnstan) Mid-div, rdn/styd on 2f out, kept on to lead ins last, drvn out: '99 wnr at Pontefract & Redcar
(2, h'caps, rtd 70), prev term scored at Thirsk (auct mdn, rtd 75): suited by 10/12f on firm & soft grnd:
handles any trk, likes Redcar & Pontefract: tough & genuine.
4365} **JUST GIFTED** 225 [4] R M Whitaker 4-9-9 (65) K Fallon 6/1: 3605-2: 4 b g Rudimentary - Parfait   1   70
Amour (Clantime) Cl-up, went on appr fnl 1f, hdd ins last, no extra: reapp: plcd twice in '99 (h'cap, rtd 70 at
best): plcd as a juv (mdn, debut, rtd 75 at best): eff at 10/12f on fast & gd/soft: runs well fresh: gd reapp.
1432 **ELSIE BAMFORD** 4 [16] M Johnston 4-7-10 (38) K Dalgleish (7) 12/1: 6-3043: 4 b f Tragic Role -   ¾   41
Sara Sprint (Formidable) Front rank, chal ldr 2f out, drvn & no extra ins last: qck reapp: consistent mdn.
*1276 **SPA LANE** 13 [13] Mrs S Larnyman 7-8-0 (42) F Norton 9/2: 00-514: Led, hdd appr fnl 1f, onepcd.   hd   45
1180 **RARE GENIUS** 19 [15] 4-9-12 (68) J Fortune 4/1 FAV: 52-235: Front rank, btn appr fnl 1f: top-weight.   3   66
1023 **SKYERS A KITE** 32 [12] 5-8-3 (44)(1ow) J Fanning 12/1: 30-206: Bhd, prog 3f out, no extra appr fnl 1f.   ½   42
1128 **ADMIRALS SECRET** 22 [3] 11-8-5 (47) R Mullen 10/1: 060-57: Settled rear, hdwy 2f out, kept on, nvr nrr.   1   42
1272 **RIGHTY HO** 14 [11] 6-8-11 (53) K Hodgson 25/1: 603-08: Nvr a threat: see 1272.   1ᵏ   46
260 **REPTON** 143 [18] 5-7-12 (40) J Mackay (7) 16/1: 60-09: Dwelt, sn in tch, grad fdd fnl 3f: ½   32
5 month ago: '99 scorer at Southwell (appr h'cap, rtd 52a, rtd 54 on turf, Mrs A Duffield): '98 Redcar scorer
(h'cap, rtd 54): eff btwn 10f & 12f on gd/soft & fibresand, runs well fresh: has tried blnks, best without.
943 **NORTHERN ACCORD** 39 [7] 6-8-2 (42)(bl) (2ow) J F Egan 20/1: 4/0-60: Rear, prog over 3f out,   ¾   35
late gains, no threat: fin 10th.
889 **TAJAR** 44 [10] 8-7-12 (40) N Kennedy 16/1: 30-600: Al in rear, fin 11th: see 889, 705.   5   24
1332 **NEEDWOOD MYSTIC** 9 [5] 5-8-6 (48) S Whitworth 12/1: 000-40: In tch, wknd qckly fnl 2f, fin 16th.   0
4234} **Indian Rope Trick** 235 [9] 4-8-8 (50) O Pears 25/1:   1254 **Puppet Play** 14 [6] 5-8-6 (48) W Supple 16/1:
1254 **Alamein** 18 [8] 7-8-9 (51)(t) T Williams 50/1:   68 **Bolt From The Blue** 189 [14] 4-8-9 (51) Kim Tinkler 25/1:
560 **Rosies All The Way** 95 [2] 4-7-10 (38) P Fessey 25/1:   1087 **Indigo Bay** 24 [17] 4-8-11 (53) S Sanders 25/1:
18 ran   Time 2m 40.7 (6.6)   (Mrs K Mapp)   J J Quinn Settrington, N.Yorks.

1500   9.05 COCA COLA MDN 3YO (D)   6f rnd   Good 54   -01 Slow
        £3705   £1140   £570   £285

1261 **CLOTTED CREAM** 14 [12] P J Makin 3-8-9 S Sanders 11/4: 03-31: 3 gr f Eagle Eyed - Seattle Victory   78
(Seattle Song) Front rank, kept on to lead ins last, styd on strongly, rdn out: plcd fnl '99 start (rtd 80, auct mdn):
eff at 6f, stays 7f: acts on gd & soft grnd: handles a sharp/undul or stiff trk: could follow up in a h'cap.
1061 **GDANSK** 25 [10] A Berry 3-9-0 J Carroll 33/1: 55-402: 3 b g Pips Pride - Merry Twinkle (Martinmas)   1¾   76$
Led, hdd just ins last, not pace of wnr: eff over a stiff/undul 6f on gd grnd: imprvd effort today.
1175 **EFFERVESCENT** 19 [4] I A Balding 3-8-9 K Fallon 11/10 FAV: 023: 3 b f Efisio - Sharp Chief (Chief   ½   70
Singer) Cl-up, rdn & kept on onepace ins last: consistent form: handles firm & gd grnd: see 1175.
1105 **GREY COSSACK** 23 [1] M Brittain 3-9-0 T Williams 10/1: 4-634: Cl-up, ev ch till no extra for   hd   75
press ins last: well clr rem: handles gd & gd/soft grnd: gd reapp: better off in h'caps: see 1105, 808.
-- **FLEDGLING** [3] 3-8-9 M Roberts 10/1: 5: Dwelt, rear, late gains, no threat: took a while to get going here,   6   57
filly, with A C Stewart: took a while to get going here, will learn from this & shld improve.
1105 **RUDETSKI** 23 [2] 3-9-0 C Teague 100/1: -006: Mid-div, rdn/btn fnl 2f: see 909.   1   59$
-- **DID YOU MISS ME** [9] 3-8-9 J Weaver 5/1: 7: Dwelt, nvr a threat on debut: Indian Ridge filly,   2   49
dam useful at 10f: with J Noseda, will improve.
2718} **STREAK OF DAWN** 315 [8] 3-8-9 D Williamson (7) 100/1: 00-8: Dwelt, al in rear: reapp, new stable.   11   27
4369} **FOXY ALPHA** 224 [7] 3-8-9 J F Egan 100/1: 0-9: Mid-div, lost tch fnl 2f: now with J L Eyre.   hd   27
1354 **ABCO BOY** 7 [5] 3-9-0 R Lappin 100/1: 0-00: Al bhd, fin 10th: qck reapp, modest form.   5   22
1280 **Paradise Yangshuo** 13 [11] 3-8-9 W Supple 50/1:   1105 **Joebertedy** 23 [6] 3-9-0 J Fanning 100/1:
12 ran   Time 1m 17.4 (3.3)   (Dr Carlos E Stelling)   P J Makin Ogbourne Maisey, Wilts.

SOUTHWELL (FIBRESAND) FRIDAY MAY 26TH Lefthand, Sharp, Oval Track

Official Going   STANDARD   Stalls: 7f - Outside; Rem - Inside

---

1501   1.50 LION HCAP 3YO+ 0-60 (F)   1m6f aw   Going 27   -26 Slow   [60]
        £2254   £644   £322

1301 **WESTERN COMMAND** 11 [13] Mrs N Macauley 4-9-13 (59) R Fitzpatrick (3) 14/1: 346451: 4 b g Saddlers   62a
Hall - Western Friend (Gone West) Rear, prog to chall ent str, styd on well und press to assert ins last: op 10/1: prev
won here at Southwell (h'cap): '99 wnr again here at Southwell (2, h'caps, rtd 76a, Sir M Prescott) & W'hampton:
eff at 11/14f, stays 2m: acts on e/trk, fibresand/Southwell specialist: best without blnks/vis: gd weight carrier.
1416 **TIME CAN TELL** 4 [11] A G Juckes 6-9-1 (47) N Callan 10/1: 551342: 6 ch g Sylvan Express - Stellaris   ¾   49a
(Star Appeal) In tch, trkd ldrs going well 4f out, narrow lead 2f out & rdn, worn down ins last: qk reapp, clr rem.
1301 **MANFUL** 11 [12] R Brotherton 8-7-12 (30)(bl) J Mackay (7) 7/2: 350024: 8 b g Efisio - Mandrian   8   25a
(Mandamus) Rear & niggled, prog 4f out, styd on for 3rd, no ch ldrs: bckd again, in front of this wnr 1301.
1416 **ST LAWRENCE** 4 [9] B S Rothwell 6-9-2 (48) M Fenton 9/2: 330024: Cl-up, led 4f out-2f out, no extra.   1¾   42a
66 **DALLACHIO** 191 [7] 9-8-2 (34)(t) L Newman (4) 25/1: 0/00-5: Prsd ldr, ev ch till onepace appr fnl 1f: 3   25a
hdles fit (plcd), won back in 94/95 (2m4f, firm & gd/sft, t-strap, P Hobbs): ex-Irish, '94 Clonmel wnr (12f mdn).
1306 **WHISTLING DIXIE** 11 [8] 4-8-4 (36) F Norton 11/8 FAV: 600-26: Chsd ldrs, fdd 2f out: up in trip, bckd.   5   23a
1023 **SILENT VALLEY** 32 [3] 6-7-11 (29)(1ow)(2oh) J Bramhill 33/1: 00-007: Nvr dngrs: see 1023.   15   6a
940 **AMSARA** 39 [4] 4-7-10 (28)(7oh) K Dalgleish (7) 50/1: 060008: Chsd ldrs clr: stiff task.   3   2a
-- **AQUAVITA** [6] 6-8-8 (40) J Tate 33/1: 3005/9: Bhd fnl 4f: missed '99: '98 wnr at Lingfield   5   10a
(claim, rtd 52a, J Moore): prev term won over hdles at Hereford (sell, rtd 95h): rtd 48 in '97: eff at
12f, suited by 2m: acts on both AW, firm & gd, sharp trks: with Miss K George.
868 **WINSOME GEORGE** 45 [2] 5-9-1 (47) N Kennedy 12/1: 0-2330: Al bhd: 10th, 6 wk abs: see 868, 682.   3½   14a

SOUTHWELL (FIBRESAND) FRIDAY MAY 26TH Lefthand, Sharp, Oval Track

-- **QUALITAIR PRIDE** [5] 8-7-12 (30) Dale Gibson 33/1: 0000/0: Chsd ldrs, outpcd, fnl 3f: 11th, long abs: *11* **0a**
3 year abs, '97 wnr here at Sothwell (amat h'cap, rtd 40a, J Bottomley): plater over hdles (rtd 76h): eff at
12f on fibresand, handles firm & gd/sft: suited forcing the pace: entitled to need this: with C Dwyer.
1361 **ALFAHAD 7** [10] 7-8-6 (38)(VIS) T Williams 33/1: 00/000: Sn struggling: 12th, AW bow. *dist* **0a**
12 ran   Time 2m 07.2 (7.4)   (Andy Peake)   Mrs N Macauley Sproxton Leics

1502 2.20 GROUPER CLAIMER 3YO (F) 1m3f aw Going 27 -40 Slow
£2191 £626 £313

1270 **FINERY 14** [4] W Jarvis 3-8-13 M Tebbutt 7/4 FAV: 642401: 3 ch g Barathea - Micky's Pleasure **64a**
(Foolish Pleasure) Trkd ldrs, going well but short of room 4f out to 2f out, led bef dist, cmftbly: well bckd: apprec
return to sand, unraced juv: eff at 1m/11f, shld get further on both AW's.
1183 **SHARP RISK 19** [1] P Howling 3-9-1 R Winston 4/1: 53002: 3 ch c Risk Me - Dara Dee (Dara Monarch) ¾ **62a**
Trkd ldr, ev ch 2f out, onepace dist: op 5/2: suited by ease in grade: eff at 11f on fibresand: see 373.
1106 **WINDMILL LANE 23** [2] B S Rothwell 3-8-6 M Fenton 5/2: 05-263: 3 bf Saddlers Hall - Alpi Dora 1¼ **51a**
(Valiyar) Chsd ldrs, chall 2f out, same pace: AW bow, clr rem: handles firm, hvy & fibresand: see 978.
1274 **CINEMA POINT 13** [7] M H Tompkins 3-8-11 S Sanders 16/1: 0-0204: Nvr a factor: btr 429 (1m sell h'cap)7 **49$**
1204 **SHUFFLE 18** [6] 3-9-5 (bl) R Fitzpatrick (3) 33/1: 065: Al rear, wide: no form, flattered* 6 **51a**
771 **FOOLS PARADISE 58** [5] 3-9-5 G Carter 33/1: 0-66: Prom, rdn/btn 3f out: 8 wk abs: no form. nk **50a**
1234 **MYSTICAL WISDOM 15** [3] 3-7-12 F Norton 12/1: 606-07: Keen, led till 2f out, sn btn: flattered 5 **24a**
6th of 7 in a '99 mdn auct (rtd 63$): drop to 1m likely to suit, with P Chamings.
1188 **SCARLET WOMAN 19** [8] 3-9-0 D Hayes (7) 7/1: 08: Prom & chance till fdd 2f out: AW bow. 2 **38a**
8 ran   Time 2m 28.26 (7.36)   (The Finery Partnership)   W Jarvis Newmarket

1503 2.50 MINNOW MDN 2YO (D) 6f aw rnd Going 27 -33 Slow
£2697 £830 £415 £207

801 **DIM SUMS 56** [6] T D Barron 2-9-0 C Lowther 1/1 FAV: 21: 2 b g Repriced - Regal Baby (Northern **76a**
Baby) Keen, wide in tch, prog to lead ent fnl 2f, readily: 8 wk abs: Jan foal, half-brother to a wng US juv,
dam unrcd, sire a dirt miler: apprec step up to 6f, get further: acts on fibresand, sharp trk: improving.
1252 **ALNAHIGHER 14** [4] M Johnston 2-8-9 R Ffrench 9/2: -652: 2 b f Mizoram - Petite Butterfly 2 **61a**
(Absalom) Led till appr fnl 1f, onepce for press: AW bow, op 3/1: prob stays 6f on fibresand, see 1252, 1046.
1102 **MARKUSHA 23** [2] D Nicholls 2-9-0 F Norton 7/1: 43: 2 b c Aljihaz - Shafir (Shaadi) 1½ **62a**
Prsd ldr & ev ch till no extra appr fnl 1f: clr rem, AW bow: prob handles fibresand: see 1102.
1252 **SIENA STAR 14** [3] J L Eyre 2-9-0 J Fortune 10/1: -004: Chsd ldrs 4f: AW bow: 8,000 gns 3½ **53a**
Brief Truce May first foal, related to sev wnrs, sire got 10f: with J Eyre.
1067 **CIRCUIT LIFE 25** [5] 2-9-0 G Carter 5/1: -05: Chsd ldrs till 2f out: AW bow, see 1067. nk **52a**
821 **MR PERTEMPS 51** [1] 2-9-0 J Tate 14/1: 06: Slow away, al bhd: 7 wk abs, AW bow, op 10/1: 60,000 1¾ **48a**
gns Primo Dominie Feb foal, half-brother to wng juv Salamanca, dam juv wnr, sire a sprinter: with S Williams.
6 ran   Time 1m 16.9 (3.6)   (Harrowgate Bloodstock Ltd)   T D Barron Maunby, Yorks

1504 3.20 STAR HCAP 3YO+ 0-85 (D) 6f aw rnd Going 27 +01 Fast [83]
£3835 £1180 £590 £295 3 yo rec 9 lb

1140 **KEEN HANDS 22** [7] Mrs N Macauley 4-9-3 (72)(vis) R Fitzpatrick (3) 5/1: 050551: 4 ch g Keen - Broken **80a**
Vow (Local Suitor) Chsd ldrs, drvn to lead ent fnl 1f, ran on well: earlier won here at Southwell (2, C/D h'caps):
'99 wnr at W'hampton (sell) & here at Southwell (3, sells & h'cap, rtd 75a & 45): eff at 5/7f, suited by 6f:
fibresand/Southwell specialist: wears a visor, can carry big weights: tough (7 wins from 33 starts).
1383 **TEYAAR 6** [6] D Shaw 4-9-2 (71) N Callan 9/2 FAV: 112522: 4 b g Polar Falcon - Music In My Life 1 **75a**
(Law Society) Cl-up, led ent str, worn down below dist: tchd 16/1, qck reapp, back on sand, v tough, see 923.
1244 **GARNOCK VALLEY 15** [12] A Berry 10-9-4 (73) G Carter 7/1: 164000: 10 b Dowsing - Sunley 3½ **68a**
Sinner (Try My Best) Wide, rear, ran on late for 3rd: a return to form at favourite trk: see 218.
1192 **MALLIA 19** [2] T D Barron 7-9-1 (70)(bl) R Winston 11/1: 414044: Reared, hld up, late prog, nvr dngrs. hd **65a**
1140 **DOUBLE O 22** [1] 6-9-1 (70)(bl) S Sanders 12/1: -40035: Chsd ldrs, not qckn fnl 2f: bt wnr in 1140. 1 **62a**
1235 **ROCK ISLAND LINE 15** [3] 6-8-12 (67) D Holland 5/1: 0-2026: Chsd ldrs, onepce/edged right 1f out. ½ **58a**
1060 **THE DOWNTOWN FOX 25** [14] 5-10-0 (83)(bl) J Fortune 16/1: 100067: Prom & ch till fdd 2f out & bmpd. ¾ **72a**
*941 **PIPS SONG 39** [8] 5-9-8 (77) J Lowe 13/2: -24018: Nvr a factor: 6 wk abs: btr 941 (hvy). ¾ **64a**
1273 **DAHLIDYA 14** [13] 5-8-10 (65) Hayley Turner (7) 20/1: 133009: Lost many lenghts start & then bmpd 1½ **49a**
after 2f, nvr in it: losing chance at the stalls: see 697.
1421 **PRESENT CHANCE 4** [11] 6-8-5 (60)(bl) L Newton 25/1: 000000: Slow away & switched, nvr dngrs: 10th. hd **44a**
905 **BRANSTON PICKLE 42** [4] 3-9-4 (82) J Weaver 20/1: 1-2000: Led till 2f out, no extra: 12th, 6 wk abs. **0a**
1259 **Air Mail 14** [5] 3-8-11 (75) J Tate 14/1:   678 **Soaked 71** [10] 7-9-4 (73) G Parkin 33/1:
1162 **Anthony Mon Amour 20** [9] 5-8-11 (66) F Norton 16/1:
14 ran   Time 1m 14.87 (1.57)   (Andy Peake)   Mrs N Macauley Sproxton Leics

1505 3.50 CLOWN SELLER 3YO+ (G) 1m aw rnd Going 27 -01 Slow
£1946 £556 £278 3 yo rec 13lb

1305 **SHARP STEEL 11** [5] Miss S J Wilton 5-9-7 D Holland 6/1: 2-5621: 5 ch g Beveled - Shift Over Night **63a**
(Night Shift) Early leader, again appr fnl 3f, sn clr: op 9/2, bt in for 5,800 gns: plcd in '99 (stks, rtd 57a):
'98 wnr here at Southwell (sell, rtd 57a, G L Moore): eff at 7f/sharp 1m on both AWs, likes Southwell & sellers.
1265 **CANADIAN APPROVAL 14** [3] I A Wood 4-9-7 J Fortune 4/1: 044002: 4 ch f With Approval - Atasteforlace 9 **48a**
(Laomedonte) Prom, hmpd 4f out & rdn, styd on for 2nd, no ch wnr: back by est equitrack, see 336.
1393 **INDIAN SWINGER 6** [11] P Howling 4-9-7 R Winston 6/1: 220033: 4 ch c Up And At Em - Seanee 2½ **44a**
Squaw (Indian Ridge) In tch, styd on thro' btn horses, nvr able to chall: qck reapp, stiff task, btr 1393.
1305 **WAITING KNIGHT 11** [4] Mrs N Macauley 5-9-7 (vis) R Fitzpatrick (3) 7/2 FAV: 022234: Prom, chsd wnr hd **44a**
2f out, appeared to go lame dist & eased: op 7/1, clr rem, wld have been 2nd: remains in-form, see 178.
1300 **FLYING HIGH 11** [2] 5-9-7 F Norton 33/1: 403005: Nvr better than mid-div: stiff task. 5 **34$**
1421 **ABTAAL 4** [16] 10-9-12 (vis) Sarah Robinson 10/1: -60136: Dwelt, nvr nr ldrs: stablemate 4th. 1¼ **37a**
1305 **FLASHFEET 11** [1] 10-9-7 N Carlisle 50/1: 004607: Front rank, lost pl 2f out: v stiff task, see 398. 1½ **29$**
1237 **MERCHANT PRINCE 15** [12] 4-9-7 N Callan 9/1: 0-5008: In tch till over 2f out: stiff task. hd **29a**
1417 **SPRING BEACON 4** [15] 5-9-2 M Tebbutt 20/1: 0/6009: Nvr on terms: qck reapp, see 693. ½ **23a**

498

SOUTHWELL (FIBRESAND)   FRIDAY MAY 26TH   Lefthand, Sharp, Oval Track

1137 **DANNI** 22 [6] 7-9-2 S Sanders 33/1: 0/00: Al towards rear; 10th, no form.   *1*   **21a**
1190 **PURSUIVANT** 19 [7] 6-9-7 (bl) G Carter 6/1: 034060: Al bhd: 12th: see 446.   **0a**
976   **TOWER OF SONG** 37 [9] 3-8-9 (bl) Kimberley Hart (5) 14/1: 504000: Led 2f till appr fnl 3f, sn btn: 14th.   **0a**
790   **Puiwae** 57 [8] 5-9-2 J Bramhill 50/1:   1065 **Noble Investment** 25 [13] 6-9-7 L Newman (5) 25/1:
53   **Dinky** 192 [10] 3-8-4 J Mackay (7) 40/1:   1354 **Coming Up Roses** 7 [14] 3-8-4 L Newton 25/1:
16 ran   Time 1m 41.6 (2.2)   (John Pointon & Sons)   Miss S J Wilton Wetley Rocks Staffs

1506   4.20 ANGEL FILLIES HCAP 3YO+ 0-65 (F)   7f aw rnd   Going 27 -07 Slow   [65]
£2289   £654   £327   3 yo rec 11lb

1273 **HAUNT THE ZOO** 14 [5] J L Harris 5-8-12 (49) J Weaver 4/1: 000001: 5 b m Komaite - Merryhill Maid   **58a**
(M Double M) Hld up, smooth prog over 2f out to lead bef dist, easily went clr: op 6/1: '99 wnr here at Southwell
(fill h'cap) & Lingfield (h'cap, rtd 54a & 46): missed '98: eff at 6/7f, tried 1m: acts on both AW's, handles fast:
likes sharp trks, esp Southwell: can go well fresh: right back to form here.
1233 **OARE KITE** 15 [3] P S Felgate 5-8-2 (38) (10w) G Carter 7/1: 424632: 5 b m Batshoof - Portvasco   *6*   **39a**
(Sharpo) Well plcd, led halfway till bef fnl 1f, no ch with wnr: ran to best, clr rem, deserves a win on the AW.
*1419 **PRIDEWAY** 4 [11] W M Brisbourne 4-10-4 (69) (6ex) J Tate 4/1: 440613: 4 b f Pips Pride - Up   *4*   **61a**
The Gates (Captain James) Prom, ev ch 2f out, so onepace: too sn with a pen/big weight back in trip after 1419?
1391 **PLEASURE** 6 [4] A Smith 5-8-13 (50) (bl) R Fitzpatrick (3) 9/1: 0-5464: Lost sev lengths start,   *1*   **40a**
modearate prog & short of room 2f out, nvr dngrs: op 6/1: up in trip, see 1391, 1073.
1419 **GUEST ENVOY** 4 [7] 5-9-3 (54) L Newman (5) 7/1: 126055: Handy, chal 3f out, grad wknd: qk reappr.   ½   **43a**
*1422 **PETITE DANSEUSE** 4 [10] 6-8-12 (49) (6ex) Kimberley Hart (5) 7/2 FAV: 146116: Cl-up till lost pl   nk   **37a**
3f out: nicely bckd in search of a hat-trick but was back up in trip & prob came too soon after 1422 (6f)
1280 **CHIN UP** 13 [2] 3-8-12 (60) S Sanders 14/1: 005-07: Bhd from halfway: AW bow: 5th of 15 in a   2½   **43a**
6f mdn fnl '99 start (rtd 66): poss handles firm grnd: with M Tompkins.
1202 **NILOUPHAR** 18 [12] 3-7-10 (44) (bl) (9oh) J Mackay (7) 33/1: 000-08: Al towards rear: stiff task.   *3*   **22a**
1233 **BODFARI ANNA** 15 [8] 4-8-1 (38) (bl) T Williams 9/1: 305459: Dwelt, prom till 3f out: see 604.   2½   **12a**
1335 **SMARTS MEGAN** 9 [9] 4-7-12 (34) (10w) N Carlisle 25/1: 00-000: Sn bhd: 10th, no form, AW bow.   1¼   **6a**
4575) **BINT ALJOOD** 207 [1] 3-8-10 (58) J Fortune 10/1: 0545-0: Nvr in it: 11th, reappr, op 7/1: plcd in a   3½   **25a**
Haydock nursery in '99 (rtd 58): eff at 6f on firm & soft grnd: with B McMahon
4589) **Lady Tilly** 205 [6] 3-7-13 (47) F Norton 20/1:
12 ran   Time 1m 29.0 (2.4)   (R Atkinson)   J L Harris Eastwell Leics

BRIGHTON   FRIDAY MAY 26TH   Lefthand, V Sharp, Undulating Track

Official Going: SOFT   Stalls: 10/12f - Outside, remainder - inside. Pace Figs Inapplicable due to rain.

1507   2.10 EBF NOV MED AUCT STKS 2YO (E)   6f rnd   Good/Soft Inapplicable
£2717   £836   £418   £209   Raced stands side fnl 3f

1252 **JOINT INSTRUCTION** 14 [1] M R Channon 2-8-12 S Drowne 6/4 FAV: -4521: 2 b c Forzando - Edge Of   **77**
Darkness (Vaigly Great) Made most, shaken up & asserted fnl 1f, pushed out close home: well bckd, tchd 2/1:
apprec step up to a sharp 6f, stay further: acts on firm & hvy grnd, any trk: eff forcing the pace.
993   **THOMAS SMYTHE** 34 [5] N P Littmoden 2-8-12 D Sweeney 12/1: 02: 2 ch c Colllege Chapel - Red Barons 3   **68**
Lady (Electric) Cl up, outpcd/lost place 2f out, rdn & kept on inside last, no threat: op 10/1: longer 6f trip.
1367 **CARRABAN** 7 [4] B J Meehan 2-8-7 D R McCabe 11/4: -5W33: 2 b f Mujadil - Bayazida (Bustino)   1¼   **60**
Keen, held up bhnd ldrs, eff 2f out, soon held: nicely bckd though op 2/1: see 1367, 970.
--   **KNOCK** [3] R Hannon 2-8-12 R Hughes 3/1: 4: Cl-up, chsd wnr 2f out till fdd fnl 1f: market drifter,   ¾   **63**
op 6/4: Mujadil colt, April foal, brother to two 5f juv wnrs: dam a 3yo French wnr.
--   **FOLEY MILLENNIUM** [2] 2-8-12 A McCarthy (3) 9/1: 5: Cl up 3f, fdd over 1f out: op 7/1: Tagula   2½   **58**
colt, March foal, cost 6,800gns: dam a 5/7f juv wnr: with M Quinn.
5 ran   Time 1m 12.4 (4.6)   (Ridgeway Downs)   M R Channon West Isley, Berks

1508   2.40 PALACE PIER SELLER 3YO+ (G)   6f rnd   Good/Soft Inapplicable
£1901   £543   £271   3 yo rec 9 lb   Raced stands side fnl 3f

1423 **DOCTOR DENNIS** 4 [7] B J Meehan 3-8-10 D Glennon (7) 7/4 FAV: -00021: 3 b g Last Tycoon -   **60**
Noble Lustre (Lyphard's Wish)·Trckd ldrs, shaken up to chall over 1f out, led inside last, drifted left/drvn out:
bought in for 3,200gns: reapp: rnr up in '99 (rtd 69, nursery h'cap): eff at 6f/sharp 7f, tried 10f: acts
on firm & gd/soft grnd: eff with/without blinks: enjoys selling grade.
1305 **SIR JACK** 11 [2] D Nicholls 4-9-5 R Hughes 5/2: 0-0002: 4 b g Distant Relative - Frasquita (Song)   ½   **57**
Cl up, rdn/led over 1f out till inside last, kept on: op 7/2: acts on gd & gd/soft: see 905.
1298 **ANOTHER VICTIM** 1 [1] M R Bosley 6-9-5 D Sweeney 25/1: 06/003: 6 ch g Beveled - Ragtime Rose   1½   **53$**
(Ragstone) Handy, rdn & kept on onepace from over 1f out: only mod form prev: stys 6f & handles gd/soft grnd.
1336 **FRENCH FANCY** 9 [9] B A Pearce 3-8-5 (bl) O Urbina 9/1: 424004: Cl up till over 1f out: op 10/1.   1¼   **45**
3855) **MUTASAWWAR** 260 [10] 6-9-5 D R McCabe 12/1: 3500-5: Keen/held up, eff 2f out, soon held: op 10/1,   *3*   **44**
reapp: plcd twice last term (rtd 72a, claimer, unplcd on turf, rtd 49): '98 wnr at Lingfield (AW h'cap, rtd 67a at
best, Chepstow, h'cap, rtd 57): eff at 5/6f on fast, gd/soft & both AWs, sharp/undul trk: eff with/without blnks.
1237 **ARAB GOLD** 15 [6] 5-9-11 R Studholme (5) 33/1: 314406: Led till halfway, btn 1f out: btr 634 (AW).   nk   **49$**
1211 **WHATTA MADAM** 17 [5] 4-9-0 (t) I Mongan (5) 7/2: 4-4057: Led halfway till over 1f out, wknd qckly.   *3*   **32**
1139 **TROJAN HERO** 22 [8] 9-9-5 (t) J D Smith 20/1: 530068: Dwelt, btn 2f out: op 16/1, tongue strap.   *4*   **29**
887   **LEA VALLEY EXPRESS** 44 [4] 3-8-5 (tvi) A McGlone (5) 25/1: 305-09: Al rear: 6 week abs: plcd last   1½   **21**
term (rtd 55, seller, rtd 84a on sand): eff over a sharp 5f on soft grnd: eff in a visor.
1423 **JOHNNY STACCATO** 4 [3] 6-9-5 C Rutter 20/1: 30-000: Bhnd halfway: 10th: op 14/1: qck reappr: rnr   2½   **21**
up in '99 (rtd 56), claimer): '97 Sandown wnr (stakes, rtd 98, J Eustace): eff at 5/6f on fast & hvy grnd.
10 ran   Time 1m 12.2 (4.4)   (Mrs Judith Mendonca)   B J Meehan Upper Lambourn, Berks

BRIGHTON FRIDAY MAY 26TH Lefthand, V Sharp, Undulating Track

1509 3.10 FRIDAY AD HCAP 3YO+ 0-65 (F) 1m2f Good/Soft Inapplicable [65]
£2509 £717 £358 3 yo rec 14lb Raced stands side fnl 3f

890 **BRIERY MEC 44** [4] H J Collingridge 5-8-4 (41) G Bardwell 6/1: 233-01: 5 b g Ron's Victory - Briery 46
Fille (Sayyaf) Led/disputed lead till drvn/went on over 2f out, styd on well inside last, drvn out: op 4/1, abs,
first win: plcd thrice in '99 (rtd 43): eff at 10f on gd & soft, stiff/gall or sharp track: runs well fresh.
1209 **SAMMYS SHUFFLE 17** [11] Jamie Poulton 5-8-1 (38)(bl) M Henry 6/1: 306402: 5 b h Touch Of Grey - 2 39
Cabinet Shuffle (Thatching) Held up, prog fnl 3f, pressed wnr 1f out, held near fin: op 5/1: back on a gd mark.
748 **DION DEE 60** [8] Dr J R J Naylor 4-8-5 (42) N Pollard 25/1: 003003: 4 ch f Anshan - Jade Mistress 3 40
(Damister) Held up rear, rdn & kept on fnl 2f, no threat: abs: stays a sharp 10f & handles gd/soft: mod form prev.
1128 **BONDS GULLY 22** [6] R W Armstrong 4-9-2 (53) R Price 5/1: -32044: Trkd ldrs, no extra 1f out: op 7/2. 1 50
892 **LENNY THE LION 43** [2] 3-8-6 (54)(3ow) R Hughes 7/2 FAV: 065-05: Prom, lost place/rdn halfway, 1½ 52
switched/mod late gains: nicely bckd after 6 wk abs: this 10f trip shld suit: see 892 (C/D).
209 **CAPTAIN MCCLOY 160** [3] 5-8-3 (40) R Brisland (5) 16/1: 0050-6: Chsd ldrs, wknd 2f: abs: see 209 (AW). ½ 34
1128 **FULL EGALITE 22** [5] 4-8-10 (47) C Rutter 25/1: 000-07: Towards rear, mod gains fnl 3f: unplcd 1 40
last term for W J Haggas (rtd 63, subs disapp in a visor): '98 wnr at Brighton (mdn,rtd 70, R Simpson): eff over
a sharp/undulating 6f, handles soft grnd: with B R Johnson.
1332 **FOREST DREAM 9** [10] 5-9-2 (53) A McCarthy (3) 33/1: 000008: Led/disputed lead 1m, btn/eased fnl 1f. 6 39
618 **CONFRONTER 86** [1] 11-8-3 (40) P Doe 20/1: 5-0009: Handy till halfway, no chance after: 12 wk abs. 2 24
4578} **ZIDAC 207** [9] 8-10-0 (65) A Clark 6/1: 6013-0: Keen/held up, eff 3f out, btn/eased fnl 1f: 10th: shd 45
reapp: '99 scorer at Lingfield (AW stakes, rtd 62a), Bath (claimer) & Brighton (C/D selling h'cap, rtd 67 62a):
'98 Warwick wnr (claiming h'cap, rtd 65): eff at 10/11f on fast, soft & both AWs: handles any track, likes a sharp
one: runs well fresh & a gd weight carrier: enjoys selling/claiming grade.
1331 **PADDY MCGOON 9** [13] 5-9-5 (56) L Dettori 7/1: 7/1: /00-60: Trkd ldrs 7f: 11th: see 133 (clmr). 3½ 36
1183 **JOEY TRIBBIANI 19** [12] 3-8-11 (62) J D Smith 20/1: 64-000: Keen/trkd ldrs 7f: 12th: unplcd last 3 39
term (rtd 68): longer 10f trip today.
1293 **THIRTY SIX CEE 11** [7] 3-8-4 (55) J Stack 10/1: 00-050: Keen/held up, bhnd 3f out: 13th: op 5/1. shd 32
13 ran Time 2m 06.3 (8.5) (N H Gardner) H J Collingridge Exning, Suffolk

1510 3.40 SEASIDE RACING MDN 3YO+ (D) 1m4f Good/Soft Inapplicable
£3770 £1160 £580 £290 3 yo rec 17lb Raced stands side fnl 3f

1218 **CRACOW 17** [2] J W Hills 3-8-10 M Hills 4/9 FAV: 52-431: 3 b c Polish Precedent - Height Of 87
Secrecy (Shirley Heights) Cl up halfway & narrow lead over 3f out, rdn/asserted over 1f out & pushed clr inside
last, eased near fin: value for 5L+: hvly bckd: rtd 84 when rnr up on last of 3 juv starts in'99: eff at 10/12f,
could get further: acts on gd & gd/soft, any track: open to further imporvement back in h'cap company.
1200 **GOLD QUEST 18** [1] Sir Michael Stoute 3-8-10 (t) W Ryan 7/2: 0-52: 3 ch c Rainbow Quest - My 2 79
Potters (Irish River) Led halfway till over 3f out, every chance till no extra over 1f out: op 9/4: tongue strap:
styd longer 12f trip: prob handles fast & good/soft grnd.
1653} **STORMY SKYE 361** [3] G L Moore 4-9-13 (tbl) I Mongan (5) 8/1: /442-3: 4 b g Bluebird - Canna 3½ 76
(Caerleon) Cl up, rdn/outpcd over 2f out: clr rem: op 7/1, reapp: wore a tongue strap: rnr-up fnl '99 start (nov
stakes, first time blinks, A J McNae, rtd 82): plcd in '98 (listed, rtd 98): stays 12f: handles fast & soft.
1157 **SEND ME AN ANGEL 20** [7] S P C Woods 3-8-5 D Harrison 14/1: 0-44: Cl up 5f out, wknd qckly fnl 3f. 16 55
1529} **ORIENTAL PRIDE 367** [4] 4-9-13 D Sweeney 100/1: /000-5: Bhnd halfway: reapp: rtd 71 on reapp in 11 48
'99 for E Dunlop (sub tried blinks): rtd 66 in '98: now with J Cullinan.
920 **EVIYRN 41** [5] 4-9-13 A McGlone 50/1: 04-06: Led 1f, soon struggling: 6 week abs, longer 12f trip. 17 31
-- **LARAS DELIGHT 6** [6] 5-9-8 O Urbina 50/1: 7: Led after 1f till halfway, soon bhnd: Flat debut. 21 5
7 ran Time 2m 37.2 (9.0) (N N Browne) J W Hills Upper Lambourn, Berks

1511 4.10 FLANAGAN FILLIES HCAP 3YO+ 0-70 (E) 1m rnd Soft Inapplicable [60]
£2886 £888 £444 £222 3 yo rec 12lb Raced stands side fnl 3f

1100 **JESSINCA 24** [4] Derrick Morris 4-8-6 (38) D Sweeney 5/1: 510001: 4 b f Minshaanshu Amad - Noble 44
Soul (Sayf El Arab) Handy, rdn 3f out, prog/led over 1f out, held on gamely near line, all out: tchd 7/1: earlier
won AW h'caps at Southwell & W'hampton (rtd 53a): unplcd in '99 (rtd 45a & 25, R Phillips): eff around 1m on
fibresand & soft grnd: likes a sharp/undulating track: tough.
1201 **CARINTHIA 18** [6] C F Wall 5-9-9 (65) A McGlone 6/1: 00-002: 5 b m Tirol - Hot Lavender nk 62
(Shadeed) Cl up, led 3f out, rdn/hdd over 1f out, rallied well near fin, just held: clr rem: acts on firm & soft.
1099 **BUXTEDS FIRST 24** [13] G L Moore 3-8-11 (55) J D Smith 12/1: 00-003: 3 gr f Mystiko - Sea Fairy 11 49
(Wollow) Chsd ldrs, outpcd/held over 2f out: op 10/1: only mod prev, h'cap bow today.
1211 **MAGIC BABE 17** [1] Jamie Poulton 3-8-11 (55) O Urbina 6/1: 00-024: Chsd ldrs, no impression fnl 1f. 1 48
1336 **TALENTS LITTLE GEM 9** [12] 3-8-8 (52) Craig Williams 7/1: 50-045: Handy, lost pl halfway, held after. 1¼ 43
*1212 **TEA FOR TEXAS 17** [7] 4-8-10 (54) A Daly 10/1: 352016: Led 5f: btr 1212 (7f, firm, clmr, H Morrison). hd 45
1024 **ANTIGONEL 23** [3] 3-9-0 (58) D Harrison 3/1 FAV: 00-037: Sn hndy, wknd quickly over 1f out: btr 1024. 3 45
4414} **CORAL SHELLS 221** [11] 3-8-13 (57) D R McCabe 9/1: 6025-8: Soon struggling: reapp: rnr up in '99 1 45
for P Walwyn (nurs, rtd 57): eff at 7f, 1m shld suit: acts on soft grnd & a sharp/turning track: now with R M Flower.
654 **BROWNS DELIGHT 79** [5] 3-9-2 (60) R Perham 33/1: -04409: abs: vis omitted: see 287. ¾ 45
1335 **QUEEN OF THE KEYS 9** [9] 4-8-5 (37) G Bardwell 50/1: 030000: Slowly away, eff halfway, sn btn: 10th. 2½ 18
4146} Fairly Sure 240 [2] 7-8-1 (33) Sophie Mitchell 25/1:
1265 Heiress Of Meath 14 [10] 5-7-10 (28)(2oh) C Adamson 33/1:
1336 Princess Mo 9 [8] 4-7-13 (30)(1ow) A Whelan 14/1:
13 ran Time 1m 39.4 (7.4) (The Lambourn Racing Club) Derrick Morris Lambourn, Berks

1512 4.45 LADBROKES SUSSEX HCAP 3YO 0-70 (E) 5f59y rnd Soft Inapplicable [72]
£2731 £780 £390 Raced stands side fnl 3f

4376} **STONEY GARNETT 224** [7] M S Saunders 3-9-7 (65) A Daly 7/1: 3U30-1: 3 b f Emarati - Etourdie (Artic 69
Term) Chsd ldrs, rdn halfway, styd on gamely to lead near fin, drvn out: reapp: plcd sev times in '00 (rtd 68,
h'cap): eff at 5/6f on firm & soft, gall/sharp track: eff with/without blinks: gd weight carrier & runs well fresh.
1368 **TICK TOCK 7** [2] M Mullineaux 3-8-11 (55) A McCarthy (3) 7/2 JT FAV: 20-002: 3 ch f Timeless Times ¾ 55
- Aquiletta (Bairn) Led, rdn over 1f out, hdd inside last & no extra: eff at 5f on firm & soft: see 1256.

500

BRIGHTON FRIDAY MAY 26TH Lefthand, V Sharp, Undulating Track

1334 **WILLOW MAGIC 9** [4] S Dow 3-9-4 (62) P Doe 4/1: 2-5043: 3 b f Petong - Love Street (Mummy's Pet) Handy, rdn/ch over 1f out, onepace nr fin: nicely bckd: acts on equitrack, handles firm & soft: see 234. ½ **61**
1334 **PACIFIC PLACE 9** [3] M Quinn 3-8-6 (50) C Rutter 7/2 JT FAV: 00-024: Cl up 3f, onepace: op 5/2. 1½ **46**
1334 **ARCADIAN CHIEF 9** [1] 3-7-12 (42) C Catlin (7) 9/2: 04-055: Dwelt, sn handy, wknd 1f out: see 1334. 7 **27**
1289 **PRINCESS AURORA 11** [6] 3-9-0 (58) R Hughes 4/1: 020-06: Slowly away & well bhnd, eased/no chance 1f out: lost chance at start, this prob best forgotten: rnr up in '99 (C/D, h'cap rtd 62): eff at 5f on fast. dist **0**
6 ran Time 1m 06.7 (6.7) (David Chown) M S Saunders Haydon, Somerset

DONCASTER SATURDAY MAY 27TH Lefthand, Flat, Galloping Track

Official Going GOOD TO SOFT. Stalls: Str Crse - Stands Side; Rnd Crse - Inside; Rnd Mile - Outside.

1513 2.20 ZETLAND MDN 2YO (D) 6f Good 53 -43 Slow
£3558 £1095 £547 £273

-- **BLUEBERRY FOREST** [13] J L Dunlop 2-9-0 W Ryan 9/2: 1: 2 br c Charnwood Forest - Abstraction (Rainbow Quest): Settled rear, smooth hdwy 3f out, ran on well & rdn out to lead cl-home, going away: op 7/2 on debut, lkd well: IR 75,000gns purchase: half-brother to 3 wnrs abroad: eff at 6f, 7f shld suit: acts on gd grnd & a gall trk: fine debut, type to improve plenty for this & should win more races. **84+**
1413 **TROJAN PRINCE 7** [3] B W Hills 2-9-0 A Eddery (5) 20/1: -002: 2 b c Known Fact - Helen V (Slewacide): Trkd ldrs, led dist, kept on under hands-&-heels, collared cl-home: qck reapp, fit: eff at 6f on gd: win similar. ½ **80**
1189 **PEREGIAN 20** [11] M Johnston 2-9-0 R Ffrench 16/1: -53: 2 b c Eagle Eyed - Mo Pheata (Petorius): Front rank, chall/hung left ins last, no extra cl-home: op 12/1: prob still ndd this, stays 6f on gd: improve. ¾ **78**
1067 **FALCON GOA 26** [7] N Tinkler 2-8-9 Kim Tinkler 25/1: -04: Led, hdd just inside last, sn btn: better effort over this lngr 6f trip, handles gd grnd: improve further. 1½ **69**
1249 **SANDAL 16** [10] 2-8-9 L Newman (5) 7/2: 345: Prom, rdn to impr 2f out, held when short of room inside last: nicely bckd: styd this lngr 6f trip: see 1249. nk **68**
-- **DANCE ON THE TOP** [2] 2-9-0 G Carter 6/4 FAV: 6: Dwelt, sn mid-div, styd on under hands-&-heels final 2f, nvr nrr: well bckd: 100,000gns Mar foal, half-brother to a Listed 1m wnr in Germany, dam useful at 12f: burly, will come on for the run: not given a hard time here & will improve. 1½ **69**
-- **CANDOTHAT** [12] 2-9-0 R Mullen 14/1: 7: Rdn/rear, late gains, no threat: lkd v well: 11,000 gns Feb foal, dam a 6f juv wnr: with P W Harris, should improve. nk **69**
-- **STORM KING** [4] 2-9-0 C Lowther 10/1: 8: Dwelt, nvr a factor: 35,000 gns Jan foal, half-brother to 6 wnrs, incl a 7f scorer: with A Berry, sharper next time. 2½ **63**
-- **NISAN BIR** [8] 2-9-0 P Fessey 25/1: 9: Cl-up, wknd appr final 1f: debut: dam 10f wnr: needed this. nk **63**
-- **TIP THE SCALES** [1] 2-9-0 Dean McKeown 25/1: 0: Al bhd, 10th: half-brother to a 7f juv wnr. ½ **62**
-- **SANTISIMA TRINIDAD** [9] 2-8-9 G Parkin 16/1: 0: Handy, lost tch final 2f, fin 11th: 17,000 gns first foal: sire a high class juv: with T D Easterby, needed this. ½ **56**
-- **RAMESES** [6] 2-9-0 A Mackay 25/1: 0: Prom, wknd from halfway, last: lkd fit on debut: with Mrs Stubbs. 11 **41**
12 ran Time 1m 16.59 (5.79) (L Cashman) J L Dunlop Arundel, West Sussex.

1514 2.55 SAN ROSSORE HCAP 3YO+ 0-100 (C) 7f str Good 53 -31 Slow [100]
£7475 £2300 £1150 £575 3 yo rec 11lb

1158 **MANTLES PRIDE 21** [12] J A Glover 5-8-10 (82)(bl) O Pears 7/1: 0-0041: 5 br g Petong - State Romance (Free State): Settled in rear, smooth hdwy 2f out, rdn to lead dist, qcknd well, rdn out: lkd v well: '99 wnr at Carlisle, Redcar & Haydock (h'caps, rtd 84): plcd in '98 (rtd 86): seems suited by 7f, stays 1m: acts on firm, soft & any trk: runs well fresh & eff in blnks/visor: tough, shwd a decent turn of foot here. **87**
*1286 **ADJUTANT 14** [9] N P Littmoden 5-9-11 (97) M Tebbutt 2/1 FAV: -30312: 5 b g Batshoof - Indian Love Song (Be My Guest): Waited with, gd hdwy 3f out, dsptd lead until no extra well inside last: nicely bckd, lkd well: another sound effort: in fine form: see 1286. ¾ **100**
1356 **SMART PREDATOR 8** [17] J J Quinn 4-7-12 (70) A Mackay 5/1: -00303: 4 gr g Polar Falcon - She's Smart (Absalom): Trkd ldrs, kept on well ins last, held cl-home: stays 1m & may apprec a return to that trip. ½ **72**
3220} **LUANSHYA 293** [3] R M Whitaker 4-7-13 (71) K Dalgleish (7) 25/1: 0050-4: Rear, smooth hdwy to lead halfway, hdd dist, sn held: clr rem on reapp: '99 scorer at Catterick (med auct mdn, rtd 79): dual juv rnr-up: eff at 6/7f: handles gd & gd/soft, likes fast/firm grnd: fine reapp & should win similar sn. 1½ **70**
1337 **NIGRASINE 9** [5] 6-10-0 (100)(bl) D Sweeney 7/1: -03045: Led, hdd halfway, outpcd 2f out, late gains: top weight: likes fast/firm grnd: see 734. 4 **92**
1286 **UNDETERRED 14** [6] 4-9-7 (93) R Mullen 15/2: 00-036: Rear, prog 3f out, rdn to chall appr fnl 1f, wknd. ¾ **84**
1383 **REDOUBTABLE 7** [11] 9-8-8 (80) C Lowther 14/1: 201007: Prom, rdn & fdd appr final 1f: qck reapp. nk **71**
4456} **BERGEN 219** [2] 5-8-2 (74) A Nicholls (3) 12/1: 0020-8: Trkd ldrs, wknd qckly final 2f: op 8/1, edgy in prelims: rnr-up in '99 (h'cap, rtd 75, B Hills): rnr-up in '98 (h'cap, rtd 83, J Hanson): '97 Pontefract wnr (mdn auct, rtd 79): eff at 1m on firm & gd: runs well fresh: with D Nicholls, ndd this & sharper next time. 1¾ **62**
1015 **SURPRISE ENCOUNTER 33** [4] 4-8-10 (82) G Carter 8/1: 156-09: Rear, rdn to impr halfway, sn no extra: op 11/2: '99 reapp scorer at Kempton (mdn, rtd 87): lightly rcd in '98, highly tried on final start (stks, rtd 90): eff arnd 7f: acts on fast, handles gd/soft: can go well when fresh. 4 **63**
1286 **PETRUS 14** [14] 4-8-10 (82) N Esler (7) 25/1: 60-000: Nvr a factor: fin 10th: lkd v well. 1 **61**
1337 **THREAT 9** [7] 4-9-0 (86)(t) R Ffrench 25/1: 2-0000: Chsd ldrs, wknd from halfway, fin last: see 702. 3 **60**
11 ran Time 1m 29.14 (5.94) (Mrs Janis Macpherson) J A Glover Carburton, Notts.

1515 3.30 ROSEHILL COND STKS 3YO (B) 1m2f60y Good 53 +05 Fast
£9078 £3479 £1739 £832

1171 **BROCHE 21** [4] Saeed bin Suroor 3-9-0 D Holland 7/4 FAV: 1-001: 3 b c Summer Squall - Ribbonwood (Diesis): Trkd ldr, went on appr fnl 1f, pshd out: gd time, nicely bckd: recent 20th of 27 in 2,000 Guineas, also rnr-up in Dubai: won sole '99 start at The Curragh (7f mdn, gd, J Oxx): clearly apprec this step up to a gall 10f, 12f will suit: acts on gd grnd: potentially smart colt, should win in List/Gr 3 company. **111**
4483} **CORNELIUS 217** [3] P F I Cole 3-8-11 D Sweeney 100/30: 136-2: 3 b c Barathea - Rainbow Mountain (Rainbow Quest): Led, qcknd pace halfway, travelling well 2f out, hdd & found nil over 1f out: well clr rem on reapp, lkd v well: '99 debut scorer at York (mdn), subs 3rd in Gr 3 Coventry at R Ascot (rtd 106+): dam an 11.5f wnr: eff at 10f, further shld suit: acts on fast & soft: prob just ndd this & shld win a decent prize this term. 4 **101**

1069 **DECARCHY 26** [2] H R A Cecil 3-9-0 W Ryan 9/2: 1-53: 3 b c Distant View - Toussaud (El Gran Senor): *19* **80**
Settled last, rdn to impr 3f out, sn lost tch: small colt: much better on reapp in 1069.
4528} **SHAIBANI 213** [1] B W Hills 3-9-0 G Carter 5/2: 1-4: Handy, rdn/lost tch 3f out, t.o: lkd fit on reapp: *8* **70**
impressively scored at Yarmouth on sole '99 juv start (mdn, rtd 95): half-brother to a useful 6/7f juv wnr: eff
at 7f on gd/soft, 1m+ shld suit in time: can go well fresh: well regarded & something surely amiss here.
4 ran   Time 2m 11.38 (4.98)   (Godolphin)   Saeed bin Suroor Newmarket.

1516   4.00 MASTERCUTLER.COM MED AUCT MDN 3YO (E)   5f   Good 53 -28 Slow
£2899   £892   £446   £223

877 **JODEEKA 46** [1] J A Glover 3-8-9 D Holland 7/2: 51: 3 ch f Fraam - Gold And Blue - (Bluebird): **76**
Waited with, smooth hdwy to lead ins last, pushed out, readily: 6 wk abs: half-sister to wng 6/7f AW performers
Blue Kite & Blue Star: apprec drop back to 5f: acts on gd grnd & gd/soft trk: one to keep on the right side.
1280 **FLY LIKE THE WIND 14** [2] M A Jarvis 3-8-9 M Tebbutt 15/8 FAV: 5-22: 3 br f Cyrano de Bergerac - ½ **72**
Thulium (Mansingh): Cl-up, hdwy to lead appr final 1f, hdd inside last, kept on under hands-&-heels:
nicely bckd: rangy filly, reportedly hanging thro'out: acts on firm & gd grnd: interesting in h'caps.
1220 **CORUNNA 17** [7] A Berry 3-9-0 G Carter 5/1: 406-33: 3 b g Puissance - Kind Of Shy (Kind Of Hush): 1¾ **73**
Mid-div, hdwy when short of room over 1f out, styd on well, nrst fin: lkd well: acts on firm & gd grnd:
not much luck in running here: deserves to win sn: see 1220.
127 **SKYLARK 179** [6] R Hannon 3-8-9 L Newman (5) 7/1: 3000-4: Rear, rdn & ran on well fnl 1f: hd **68**
6 mth abs: plcd on 1st 3 '99 starts (mdns, rtd 84 at best): stays 5/6f on firm/gd: lengthy, unfurnished filly.
1266 **SCAFELL 15** [3] 3-9-0 (vis) P McCabe 16/1: 0-0205: Led, hdd appr final 1f, wknd: speedy, will 1¾ **69$**
apprec a sharper trk: see 883 (Lingfield).
901 **LAYAN 44** [10] 3-8-9 J Edmunds 50/1: 06-566: Rear, prog when hmpd over 1f out, no threat: no 1 **61$**
luck in running & imprvd eff here, needs low-grade h'caps: see 777.
1280 **POP THE CORK 14** [5] 3-9-0 V Halliday 7/1: 0-0037: Trkd ldrs, wknd qckly ins last: see 1280 (firm). nk **66$**
1354 **HOUT BAY 8** [4] 3-9-0 W Ryan 20/1: -64538: Mid-div, btn final 2f: needs a drop in grade: see 1354. 1 **63$**
1308 **KIND EMPEROR 11** [9] 3-9-0 Dean McKeown 10/1: 253009: Handy, fdd fnl 2f: swtg, needs to dominate. 1½ **59**
9 ran   Time 1m 02.25 (4.05)   (S J Beard)   J A Glover Carburton, Notts.

1517   4.30 MERLIN CLASSIFIED STKS 3YO+ 0-80 (D)   6f   Good 53 -17 Slow
£5668   £1744   £872   £436   3 yo rec 9 lb

1441 **EASTER OGIL 5** [13] I A Balding 5-9-2 (vis) G Hind 7/2: 500641: 5 ch g Pips Pride - Piney Pass **82**
(Persian Bold): Settled rear, prog/slightly hmpd over 1f out, weaved thro' to lead ins last, pshd out, cosily:
qck reapp: won just 1 of 16 '99 starts, at Bath (h'cap, rtd 85), prev term scored at Beverley (mdn) & Sandown
(stks, rtd 83): eff at 5/7f on firm & soft: runs well fresh on any trk, likes a stiff/gall one: eff in a visor.
1384 **LA CAPRICE 7** [6] A Berry 3-8-4 G Carter 10/1: 21-032: 3 ch f Housebuster - Shicklah (The Minstrel): nk **76**
Prom till went on 2f out, hung right & hdd inside last, no extra cl-home: jockey received a 2-day careless
riding ban: lkd fit & well: in gd form, deserves similar: eff at 5/6f: see 1384, 1219.
1383 **BOLDLY GOES 7** [9] C W Fairhurst 4-9-2 P Goode (3) 10/3 FAV: 006043: 4 b c Bold Arrangement - Reine ½ **77**
de Thebes (Darshaan): Rear, prog 3f out, chall inside last, no extra cl-home: lkd well, clr rem: gd effort: see 824.
4620} **ZIRCONI 203** [7] D Nicholls 4-9-2 W Ryan 8/1: 0640-4: Prom, rdn/no extra inside last: just needed 2 **72**
this: rtd 82 on '99 reapp (stks, 1st time blnks) with Mme C Head), subs jnd current connections: plcd numerous
times in '98 (rtd 111, Gr 1): eff arnd 6/7f on gd/soft & hvy grnd: encouraging reapp, spot-on next time.
1383 **LAGO DI VARANO 7** [1] 8-9-2 (bl) Dean McKeown 5/1: 066035: Led, hdd over 2f out, wknd inside last: ½ **71**
all wins at 5f & will apprec a return to that trip: see 1383.
1308 **SECRET CONQUEST 11** [8] 3-8-4 R Ffrench 14/1: 00-006: Sn rdn/rear, nvr a threat: should apprec 3 **61**
a return to 7f in a 3yo h'cap: see 1308.
1264 **COASTAL BLUFF 15** [5] 8-9-2 D Holland 6/1: 000-57: Prom, wknd/hmpd over 1f out: nicely bckd. 1 **61**
4448} **SYLVA PARADISE 220** [2] 7-9-2 (vis) N Esler (7) 16/1: 3500-8: Handy, wknd qckly final 2f: reapp: 13 **46**
plcd sev times in '99 (h'caps, rtd 84 at best): plcd form in '98 (h'caps, rtd 85), last won back in '96 (h'cap,
rtd 92): stays 7f, suited by 5/6f on firm, soft & with/without blnks: likes to race up with the pace.
8 ran   Time 1m 15.01 (4.21)   (G M Smart)   I A Balding Kingsclere, Hants.

1518   5.05 HARTINGTON HCAP 3YO+ 0-85 (D)   1m4f   Good 53 +11 Fast   **[82]**
£4231   £1302   £651   £325   3 yo rec 17lb

1209 **LEGAL LUNCH 18** [4] P W Harris 5-9-0 (68)(BL) A Culhane 11/2: 420531: 5 b g Alleged - Dinner Surprise **72**
(Lyphard): Settled rear, prog when short of room over 3f out, chall ins last, drvn out to get up cl-home: fast
time: lkd well, 1st time blnks (usually visored): plcd sev times in '99 (rtd 86, h'cap): '98 Haydock wnr (mdn,
rtd 91 at best): stays 2m, eff at 10.5/12f on firm, soft & equitrack: eff with/without visor, sharpened up by blnks.
1251 **HANNIBAL LAD 16** [12] W M Brisbourne 4-8-10 (64) Martin Dwyer 7/1: 135042: 4 ch g Rock City - nk **68**
Appealing (Star Appeal): Bhd, gd prog when 3f out, led inside last, styd on but collared cl-home: eff at
1m/12f on firm, gd & fibresand: may apprec another step up in trip.
1070 **ST HELENSFIELD 26** [8] M Johnston 5-9-11 (79) R Ffrench 16/1: 004-03: 5 ch g Kris - On Credit 1½ **80**
(No Pass No Sale): Mid-div, rdn to impr over 3f out, chall inside last, no extra cl-home: '99 Newcastle wnr
(h'cap, rtd 88): '97 Bath scorer (mdn, debut): plcd in Listed class (rtd 90): eff at 12f on firm & soft:
can go well fresh, eff weight carrier: handles a stiff/gall or undul trk: gd run, could win again sn.
1307 **FIORI 11** [3] P C Haslam 4-9-10 (78) M Tebbutt 7/2 FAV: 620064: Hdwy from rear over 3f out, rdn to ½ **78**
chall ins last, btn inside last: nicely bckd: see 1307.
1307 **MCGILLYCUDDY REEKS 11** [9] Kim Tinkler 9-9-2 (70) Kim Tinkler 4/1: 00-325: Cl-up, led going well over 2f out, 1 **68**
hdd inside last, wknd: genuine: see 1307.
1251 **WARNING REEF 16** [2] 7-8-7 (61) C Lowther 10/1: 40-456: Settled rear, rdn to impr 3f out, no dngr. 3 **54**
1307 **SANDMOOR CHAMBRAY 11** [6] 9-9-3 (71) G Parkin 20/1: 000-07: Led 4f out, rdn/hdd 2f out: burly. 9 **51**
1194 **HUNTERS TWEED 20** [7] 4-9-4 (72) R Lappin 12/1: 05-028: Bhd, nvr a factor: much btr 1194. 1¼ **50**
1373 **PUZZLEMENT 8** [1] 6-9-6 (74) N Esler (7) 12/1: 333109: Trkd ldrs, kept tch final 2f: twice below 791. 7 **42**
1353 **PENNYS FROM HEAVEN 8** [13] 6-8-6 (60) A Nicholls (3) 9/1: 34/030: Led to 4f out, wknd, 10th: burly. ½ **27**
-- **FAR AHEAD 11** [11] 8-10-0 (82) T Williams 20/1: 0021/0: Mid-div, lost tch final 3f, t.o. in last: reapp 11 **34**
after 3 yr abs: '97 Beverley (h'cap) & York wnr (val Ebor h'cap, rtd 88): useful hdler in 96/97 (rtd 122h, eff
at 2½/3m): dual Thirsk wnr in '96 (2, h'caps, rtd 82): eff at 10/14f on fast, gd/soft & equitrack: tough.
11 ran   Time 2m 34.86 (5.06)   (The Alleged Partnership)   P W Harris Aldbury, Herts.

DONCASTER SATURDAY MAY 27TH Lefthand, Flat, Galloping Track

1519 5.35 HANDS & HEELS APPR HCAP 4YO+ 0-70 (F) 7f str Good 53 -21 Slow [66]
£2278 £651 £325

1431 **RAFTERS MUSIC** 5 [17] D Nicholls 5-9-0 (52) T Hamilton (5) 9/2: 160331: 5 b g Thatching - Princess 56
Dixieland (Dixieland Band): Bhd stands side, rdn to impr 2f out, rdn/styd on strongly to lead fnl strides:
qck reapp: recent dual Southwell wnr (h'caps, rtd 68a): '99 wnr at Epsom (clmr, Mrs A Perratt, rtd 59):
eff at 6/7f on firm, hvy & fibresand: handles any trk, likes Southwell: eff with/without blnks, has tried t-strap.
1300 **ONLY FOR GOLD** 12 [21] A Berry 5-9-2 (54) D Allan (5) 10/1: 36-662: 5 b h Presidium - Calvanne Miss hd 57
(Martinmas): Led after 2f, styd on, collared cl-home: clr rem: imprvd eff, win a similar contest, well h'capped.
1239 **BUNDY** 16 [10] M Dods 4-9-8 (60) T Eaves 14/1: 00-153: 4 b g Ezzoud - Sanctuary Cove (Habitat): 2½ 58
Mid-div far side, hdwy to chall over 1f out, btn inside last: sound effort: see 787 (reapp).
1335 **MYTTONS MISTAKE** 10 [14] R J Baker 7-8-13 (51) G Sparkes 6/1: 0-0224: Cl-up stands side, rdn & ¾ 47
no extra inside last: consistent form: see 1335.
1101 **ZECHARIAH** 24 [8] A Hawkins 14/1: 05-465: Chsd ldrs stands side, rdn/held appr final 1f. 2 39
1148 **TOBLERSONG** 22 [16] 5-8-11 (49)(t) Kristin Stubbs 20/1: 0-4006: Rear, ran on strongly fnl 2f, nvr nrr. 1¼ 39
521 **PIPE DREAM** 102 [19] M Worrell 33/1: -33607: Handy stands side, wknd appr final 1f: 3 27
3 mth abs: see 353 (equitrack, mdn, flattered).
1498 **THREE LEADERS** 1 [13] 4-8-5 (43) D Glennon 33/1: 600048: Nvr a threat stands side: ran yesterday. 1¾ 24
*1258 **ARCHELLO** 15 [7] 6-9-0 (52) R Farmer 10/1: 000-19: In tch far side, styd on fnl 2f, no threat: btr 1258. 1½ 30
1504 **DAHLIDYA** 1 [9] 5-8-0 (38) Hayley Turner (5) 20/1: 330000: Dwelt, rear, late gains: 10th: ran 24hrs ago. ½ 15
1011 **VICTORIOUS** 33 [4] 4-9-10 (62) B McHugh (5) 11/1: 0-1100: Handy far side, rdn/onepace final 2f, hd 39
fin 11th: nicely bckd: twice below 908 (soft grnd).
*1358 **JACMAR** 8 [6] 5-8-10 (48) D Meah 10/1: -26410: Nvr a factor: fin 14th: btr 1358 (5f). 0
1235 **SANTANDRE** 16 [11] 4-9-4 (56) Stephanie Hollinshead 12/1: 641150: Hmpd 6f out, wknd fnl 2f: 16th. 0
1336 **IMBACKAGAIN** 10 [1] 5-8-10 (48) D Young 9/1: 300020: In tch, fdd final 2f, fin 20th: op 7/1, btr 1336. 0
1296 **Distant King** 12 [15] 7-7-12 (36)(2ow)(3oh) D Egan (0) 50/1:
1360 **Kuwait Thunder** 8 [18] 4-8-2 (40) G Gibbons 20/1:
1148 **Technician** 22 [2] 5-9-1 (53)(bl) L Swift 16/1:   1239 **Sycamore Lodge** 16 [3] 9-9-2 (54) Carolyn Bales 14/1:
1296 **Kocal** 12 [19] 4-8-0 (38) R Naylor 20/1:   973 **Bayard Lady** 38 [12] 4-7-10 (34)(BL)(2oh) D Kinsella 33/1:
4541} **Moon Dream** 212 [22] 4-8-1 (39) Shane Fordham (5) 33/1:
21 ran Time 1m 28.39 (5.19) (Mrs N F Thesiger) D Nicholls Sessay, Nth Yorks.

WARWICK SATURDAY MAY 27TH Lefthand, Sharp Track

Official Going HEAVY. Stalls: Inside

1520 6.30 HUNTINGDON AMAT HCAP 3YO+ 0-65 (G) 7f164y rnd Heavy Inapplicable [43]
£2136 £610 £305 3 yo rec 12lb Raced towards far side fnl 3f

1393 **HOH GEM** 7 [7] B R Millman 4-10-1 (44) Mr G Richards (5) 8/1: 0-0141: 4 b g Be My Chief - Jennies' 49
Gem (Sayf El Arab): Rear, stdy prog wide fnl 2f, led/went clr ins last, drvn out: earlier won at Southwell (AW amat
h'cap, rtd 48a): eff at 7f/1m, tried 10f: acts on hvy & f/sand, likes a sharp trk: runs well for an amateur.
1306 **SWING ALONG** 12 [5] R Guest 5-11-2 (59) Mr V Coogan (5) 16/1: 334002: 5 ch m Alhijaz - So It Goes 1½ 61
(Free State): Chsd ldrs, briefly no room 2f out, switched & styd on well ins last, not reach wnr: see 404 (AW).
*750 **RAMBO WALTZER** 60 [6] Miss S J Wilton 8-10-11 (54) Mr T Best (5) 9/1: 126113: 8 b g Rambo Dancer - 2 53
Vindictive Lady (Foolish Pleasure): Chsd ldrs, led over 2f out till ins last, no extra: 2 month abs: acts on fast,
hvy, fibresand/sharp track specialist: see 750 (clmr).
1257 **SWINO** 15 [19] P D Evans 6-10-11 (54) Mr A Evans 12/1: 460044: Rdn/bhd early, late gains for press. ½ 52
4311} **ROBELLION** 229 [1] 9-10-11 (54) Miss S Newby Vincent (3) 16/1: 0000-5: Mid-div, onepace fnl 2f: op 1 51
14/1, reapp: '99 reapp scorer at Lingfield (ladies h'cap, rtd 63, subs disapp in blnks): '98 wnr at Lingfield (2yo,
ltd stks & clmr, D Arbuthnot) & Southwell (amat h'cap, Mrs L Stubbs, rtd 66a & 68): eff at 7f, stays a sharp 10f:
acts on fast & gd/soft grnd, both AWs: has run well fresh for an amateur.
1462 **DANZAS** 3 [17] 6-10-2 (45)(bl) Mrs S Moore 6/1 JT FAV: 610326: Chsd ldrs, onepace/held fnl 1f. shd 42
*1336 **MR CUBE** 10 [3] 10-10-1 (44)(bl) Miss Hayley Bryan (7) 9/1: 006017: Chsd ldrs 2f out, onepace: op 7/1. ½ 40
560 **ON PORPOISE** 96 [14] 4-10-0 (43) Mr M D'Arcy (6) 33/1: 000-08: Rear, mod gains fnl 2f for press: nk 39
3 month abs: unplcd last term (rtd 62, mdn): mod form prev.
1190 **BRANDONVILLE** 20 [18] 7-9-13 (42)(t) Miss S Samworth 20/1: 0-0009: Dwelt/bhd, mod gains fnl 2f. 4 32
1296 **OUT OF SIGHT** 12 [2] 6-11-2 (59) Mrs S Bosley 9/1: 210300: Chsd ldrs 6f: 10th: see 539 (AW). hd 49
1235 **FREDERICK JAMES** 16 [8] 6-11-3 (60) Mr J J Best (7) 16/1: 460000: Chsd ldrs 6f: 11th: see 262 (AW). 2½ 46
1210 **THOMAS HENRY** 18 [13] 4-10-11 (54)(vis) Miss E Folkes 25/1: 605500: Chsd ldrs 5f, 12th: vis reapp. 3½ 35
754 **SHARP SHUFFLE** 60 [11] 7-11-3 (60) Mr D Dennis 16/1: 202400: Al bhd: 13th: op 12/1, 2 mth abs. 2 38
1275 **BELLAS GATE BOY** 14 [20] 8-11-0 (57) Mrs L Pearce 6/1 JT FAV: 10-000: Dwelt/al bhd: 14th: op ¾ 34
5/1: won this last term off a 8lb lower mark: see 676.
4343} **Miss Money Spider** 227 [4] 5-10-7 (50) Mr M Savage(7) 14/11272 **Tyra** 15 [12] 4-10-7 (50)(BL) Mr R Bailey(7) 20/1:
16 ran Time 1m 43.60 (Brian Lovrey) B R Millman Kentisbeare, Devbon

---

1521 7.00 MARKET RASEN HCAP 3YO 0-80 (D) 1m2f110y Heavy Inapplicable [82]
£4030 £1240 £620 £310 Raced towards far side fnl 3f

1414 **DESERT ISLAND DISC** 7 [7] N A Graham 3-8-12 (66) S Whitworth 5/1: 50-651: 3 b f Turtle Island - 70
Distant Music (Darshaan) Trkd ldrs, chsd ldr 5f out, led ins last, held on well, drvn out: 1st win: unplcd last
term (rtd 76, fill mdn): apprec step up to 10.5f, could get further: acts on gd, likes hvy & a sharp/turning trk.
1225 **DISTINCTLY WELL** 17 [8] P D Evans 3-9-2 (70) J F Egan 6/1: 0-2302: 3 b g Distinctly North - Brandywell ½ 72
(Skyliner) Rear, prog 5f out, switched to chall from over 1f out, styd on well, just held: op 5/1: see 937, 846.
1375 **CASTLEBRIDGE** 8 [2] M C Pipe 3-9-7 (75) J Carroll 3/1 FAV: 116153: 3 b g Batshoof - Super nk 76
Sisters (Call Report): Led, rdn/hdd ins last, just held nr fin: bckd: see 1002 (C/D).
937 **PINCHANINCH** 40 [10] J G Portman 3-8-2 (56) N Carlisle 33/1: 00-004: Rear, prog 3f out, switched nk 56
2f out & styd on well ins last: btn less than 1L: 6 wk abs: eff at 10.5f on hvy grnd: see 709.
1080 **DR COOL** 26 [1] 3-8-2 (56) F Norton 10/1: 03-05: Dwelt, chsd ldr, outpcd over 2f out, kept on for nk 55

503

press ins last: tchd 14/1, h'cap bow: clr of rem: styd longer 10.5f trip, handles hvy: worth a try at 12f: see 103.
1085 **PILLAGER** 25 [6] 3-8-9 (63) J Stack 4/1: 0-6026: Rear, eff 3f out, btn over 1f out: op 3/1: btr 1085 (1m).   6 56
1255 **ZABIONIC** 15 [4] 3-8-9 (63)(BL) W Supple 20/1: 0-4007: Keen, held up, eff 4f out, sn btn: blnks, op 14/1. 4 52
1348 **ALPHA HEIGHTS** 9 [5] 3-9-0 (68) L Newman (5) 20/1: 500-08: Chsd ldrs 7f: plcd on debut in '99 (rtd   7 50
75, mdn): eff at 5/6f, handles firm & fast grnd.
931 **EVERGREEN** 42 [3] 3-9-6 (74) R Hughes 12/1: 30-359: Keen/chsd ldrs, btn 2f out: op 10/1, 6 wk abs. shd 56
720 **MARJU GUEST** 63 [9] 3-9-1 (69) Craig Williams 10/1: 44-230: In tch 6f: 10th: op 8/1: 2 mth abs.   12 42
4076} **DARCY DANCER** 246 [12] 3-8-9 (63) J Fortune 16/1: 350-0: Bhd halfway: 11th: reapp/h'cap bow: dist 0
rtd 75 on debut last term (5 rnr mdn): bred to apprec mid-dists, prev with M Wane, now with A J McNae.
11 ran   Time 2m 24.90   (Flying Colours Racing)   N A Graham Newmarket, Suffolk

---

1522   **7.30 WWW.WARWICK NOV MED AUCT STKS 2YO (E)**   **5f rnd Heavy Inapplicable**
£2804   £801   £400   Raced across track fnl 3f

-- **FLUMMOX** [7] M Johnston 2-8-12 J Fanning 11/2: 1: 2 b c Rudimentary - Pluvial (Habat)   85
In tch, rdn & styd on well from over 1f out, led well ins last, drvn out: op 3/1: Apr foal, half brother to useful
'99 6f juv Awake: dam a half sister to a smart juv: sire a smart/prog miler: eff at 5f, 6f + will suit: acts on hvy
grnd & a sharp/turning trk: runs well fresh: open to further improvement.
1197 **FIAMMA ROYALE** 19 [8] Mrs P N Dutfield 2-8-7 L Newman (5) 5/4 FAV: 422: 2 b f Fumo Di Londra - ½ 77
Ariadne (Bustino) Led till halfway, drvn/ev ch from over 1f out, kept on well: hvly bckd: acts on fast & hvy grnd.
-- **MY LUCY LOCKET** [2] R Hannon 2-8-7 R Hughes 7/2: 3: 2 b f Mujadil - First Nadia (Auction Ring) hd 76
Led halfway, rdn/edged left over 1f out & ndd well ins last: op 4/1: Feb foal, 16,000gns 2yo: dam a lightly raced
mdn: sire a speedy juv: eff at 5f, shld stay further: acts on hvy grnd: encouraging intro.
-- **DUBAI SEVEN STARS** [5] M C Pipe 2-8-7 J Carroll 12/1: 4: Cl-up, onepace fnl 2f: op 14/1: 2½ 71
Suave Dancer filly, May foal, dam a 10/12f wnr: sire a top-class 12f performer: looks sure to relish much further.
-- **BLUE REIGNS** [6] 2-8-12 T G McLaughlin 10/1: 5: Chsd ldrs, held fnl 2f: Whittingham colt, Apr 3 70
foal, cost 7,500 gns: full brother to 6f wng h'capper Blue Star: half brother to a 5f juv wnr: dam lightly rcd.
-- **FOREVER MY LORD** [4] 2-8-12 J Fortune 6/1: 6: Dwelt/sn rdn, nvr pace to chall: op 4/1: Be My Chief 1¾ 67
colt, Feb foal, cost 11,000 gns: dam a multiple 5f wnr, sire top-class 7f/1m performer: stay further in time.
1088 **THE DARK LADY** 25 [3] 2-8-7 G Baker (7) 33/1: -07: In tch till halfway: mod on debut prev. 2 58
7 ran   Time 1m 02.70   (Lord Hartington)   M Johnston Middleham, N Yorks

---

1523   **8.00 NOTTINGHAM CLAIMER 4YO+ (F)**   **1m2f110y Heavy Inapplicable**
£2436   £696   £348   Raced stands side fnl 3f

965 **PLURALIST** 39 [2] W Jarvis 4-9-2 M Tebbutt 7/4 FAV: 21-241: 4 b c Mujadil - Encore Une Fois   64
(Shirley Heights) Chsd clr ldr 5f out, rdn & grad reeled in ldr to lead nr line, all out: nicely bckd tho' op 5/4:
claimed by K George for £15,000: '99 Southwell wnr (med auct mdn, rtd 58a), rnr-up on turf (rtd 77): rtd 76+ in
'98 (mdn): eff at 9/11f & further cld suit: acts on firm, hvy & f/sand: handles any trk: apprec drop to clmg grade.
922 **THE WILD WIDOW** 42 [1] Miss S J Wilton 6-8-0 (bl) C Cogan (3) 11/4: 00-022: 6 gr m Saddlers' Hall hd 47
- No Cards (No Mercy) Keen, led & clr halfway, rdn /ev ch from over 1f out, edged right ins last & hdd nr line: clr rem, abs: see 922.
965 **COL WOODY** 39 [7] J G Portman 4-8-4 A Nicholls (3) 12/1: 06-003: 4 ch g Safawan - Sky Fighter 7 44
(Hard Fought) Rear, drvn/late gains fnl 3f, no threat to front pair: recent jumps nr (unplcd, sell h'cap): see 710.
-- **JIMMY SWIFT** [11] P R Hedger 5-8-4 L Newman (5) 9/1: /300-4: Rear, rdn/mod gains fnl 3f: 5 39
jumps fit (mod form): ex-Irish: '98 Roscommon wnr (10f mdn): eff at 10f on gd/soft grnd.
4525} **NEEDWOOD MAESTRO** 213 [5] 4-8-9 J Carroll 25/1: 0040-5: Rear, mod gains: reapp: plcd form last 1¼ 43$
term (rtd 54, sell): eff at 1m, tried 14f: handles soft & hvy grnd.
890 **HAROLDON** 45 [9] 11-8-10 P Fitzsimons 20/1: 305-06: Rear, nvr on terms: 6 wk abs: plcd sev 4 40
times last term (rtd 42, h'cap): '98 Nottingham wnr (sell h'cap, rtd 54): eff at 10/11.5f on firm, soft & equitrack.
1393 **THE IMPOSTER** 7 [10] 5-8-8 S Whitworth 9/1: -10007: Chsd ldrs 7f: op 7/1: see 707 (1m, AW). 9 29
-- **TAL Y LLYN** [12] 6-8-3 Sophie Mitchell 33/1: 0000/8: Sn bhd: missed last term: rtd 40 & 25 in '98 28 4
(unplcd, tried blnks): '97 Newbury wnr (stks, rtd 74, B Hills): formerly eff at 7f: acts on gd & gd/soft grnd.
4576} **CLASSIC COLOURS** 208 [3] 7-8-9 (t) F Norton 25/1: 0000-9: Chsd ldrs 7f: reapp: plcd twice in '99 ¾ 9
(rtd 51, appr h'cap): rtd 54 in '98 (h'cap): eff around 10/11f on fast & hvy grnd, stiff/sharp trk: eff in a t-strap.
4258 **THE GROOVER** 235 [4] 4-8-8 D Harrison 20/1: -00-0: Chsd ldrs 6f: 10th: reapp: mod form. 1½ 7
2309} **Bold Conqueror** 333 [13] 4-8-2(3ow) J F Egan 50/1: -- **Princess Senorita** [6] 5-8-4 J Fanning 25/1:
12 ran   Time 2m 22.60   (The Pluralist Partnership)   W Jarvis Newmarket, Suffolk

---

1524   **8.30 E-MAIL WARWICK HCAP 3YO+ 0-70 (E)**   **1m6f135y Heavy Inapplicable**   [66]
£3005   £858   £429   3 yo rec 21lb 4 yo rec 1 lb   Raced stands side fnl 3f

1499 **ELSIE BAMFORD** 1 [12] M Johnston 4-7-13 (38) K Dalgleish (7) 9/1: -30431: 4 b f Tragic Role - Sara   44
Sprint (Formidable) Handy, chsd ldrs 7f out & led over 4f out, hdd over 3f out, rallied gamely ins last to lead nr
line, all out: op 7/1, fin 3rd last night at Pontefract: plcd in '99 (rtd 58 & 48a, h'caps): unplcd in '98 (rtd
62): suited by 12/14.7f on firm, hvy & fibresand: runs well for an appr: 1st win tonight.
1411 **MANE FRAME** 7 [9] H Morrison 5-9-10 (62) R Hughes 9/2: 64-002: 5 b g Unfuwain - Moviegoer (Pharly) hd 67
Trkd ldr, remained handy & led over 3f out, rdn/just hdd nr fin: op 7/2: see 1180.
1394 **DUTCH DYANE** 7 [4] G P Enright 7-8-2 (40) D Kinsella (7) 9/2: /03-53: 7 b m Midyan - Double Dutch 2 43
(Nicholas Bill) Keen, rear, prog/briefly no room 3f out, rdn & styd on ins last, not reach front pair: see 1394.
1306 **MURCHAN TYNE** 12 [10] B A McMahon 7-8-10 (48) W Supple 14/1: -00504: Settled rear, prog/rdn to 1½ 50
chase front pair over 2f out, held fnl 1f: op 8/1: see 788.
*1332 **TUI** 10 [3] 5-8-2 (40) G Baker (7) 6/1: 00-515: Mid-div, onepace/held fnl 3f: see 1332 (12f, firm). 3½ 39
1329 **MY LEGAL EAGLE** 10 [5] 6-9-12 (64) P Fitzsimons (5) 6/1: 213606: Chsd ldrs 3f out, held over 1f out. 3½ 60
1394 **NEEDWOOD SPIRIT** 7 [6] 5-9-10 (62) S Whitworth 8/1: 5-0207: Chsd ldrs 13f: op 10/1: btr 1167. 1 57
1394 **TREASURE CHEST** 7 [11] 5-10-0 (66)(vis) J Carroll 14/1: 50-008: Al rear: op 12/1: see 1394. hd 61
1368 **CAROLES DOVE** 8 [1] 4-8-3 (42) N Carlisle 16/1: 0-0009: Keen/chsd ldrs, btn 3f out: op 14/1. 9 28
1411 **EDIPO RE** 7 [13] 8-8-13 (51) M Tebbutt 20/1: 400/00: Chsd ldrs 5f out, sn btn: 99/00 hdles wnr at 3½ 34
Huntingdon (sell h'cap, rtd 69h): mod form on the level in recent seasons: dual Italian wnr in '94 (1m, sft/hvy).
1366} **BROCTUNE LINE** 376 [2] 6-7-12 (36) F Norton 33/1: 3005-0: Led till 4f out, sn btn: 11th: reapp: 10 9
plcd twice in '99 (rtd 59a, Mrs M Reveley, sell): '97 Southwell wnr (2 h'caps, rtd 59a): eff at 11f on fibresand.
11 ran   Time 3m 27.50   (Mrs Sheila Ramsden)   M Johnston Middleham, N Yorks

WARWICK SATURDAY MAY 27TH Lefthand, Sharp Track

1525
9.00 WINCANTON MDN 3YO+ (E) 6f168y rnd Heavy Inapplicable
£3818 £1175 £587 £293 3 yo rec 11lb

1215 **PEACOCK ALLEY** 18 [1] W J Haggas 3-8-8 J F Egan 13/8: 023-51: 3 gr f Salse - Tagiki (Doyoun) 82
Handy, led over 2f out, & sn in command, pushed clr ins last, cmftbly: val for 8L+: op evens: rnr-up last term
(fillies mdn, rtd 80): eff at 7f/1m, bred for further: acts on fast & hvy grnd, sharp/turning or stiff trk.

-- **KING SILCA** [7] M R Channon 3-8-8 Craig Williams 7/1: 2: 3 b g Emarati - Silca Cisa (Hallgate) 5 75
Chsd ldrs, drvn/ch over 2f out, sn outpcd by easy wnr: op 5/1, clr of rem: debut: half brother to 2 wnrs incl
smart 5f/1m performer Golden Silca: eff at 6.8f on hvy grnd.

-- **PSALMIST** [11] Noel T Chance 3-8-8 J Carroll 20/1: 3: 3 ch f Mystiko - Son Et Lumiere (Rainbow 4 63
Quest) Dwelt/rear, eff/chsd ldrs 2f out, held fnl 1f: op 14/1, debut: half sister to a hdles wnr, shld stay further.

4112} **TIME BOMB** 243 [4] B R Millman 3-8-8 G Hind 10/1: 0-4: Chsd ldrs, onepace fnl 3f: reapp: unplcd 1 62
sole '99 start (rtd 42, mdn): this longer 7f trip shld suit.

1266 **DOUBLE GUN** 15 [2] 3-8-13 R Hughes 6/1: 43-065: Dwelt, chsd ldr, led over 3f out till over 2f out, fdd. 1¾ 65
1181 **NATURAL** 20 [6] 3-8-13 D Williamson (7) 25/1: 0-06: In tch, btn 2f out: now qual for h'caps. ½ 64
1263 **TRYSOR** 15 [9] 4-9-10 G Faulkner (3) 16/1: 07: Rear, mod gains: op 10/1: bhd on debut prev. 1½ 62$
1281 **BLUE STREET** 14 [12] 4-9-10 T G McLaughlin 33/1: 08: Rear, mod gains: dropped in trip. shd 62
1263 **INNKEEPER** 15 [3] 3-8-13 D Holland 5/2: 00-529: Unruly stalls, led 4f: op 7/2: btr 1263, 1012. 2½ 58
9 ran Time 1m 28.80 (Mrs & Mrs G Middlebrook) W J Haggas Newmarket, Suffolk

KEMPTON SATURDAY MAY 27TH Righthand, Flat, Fair Track

Official Going SOFT (HEAVY places) Stalls: Str course - far side; 10f - outside, remainder - inside

1526
2.05 SPORTINGODDS COND STKS 2YO (C) 6f str Soft 129 -75 Slow
£5444 £2013 £1006 Raced towards centre

*1260 **TRIPLE BLUE** 15 [1] R Hannon 2-9-0 R Hughes 4/6 FAV: 11: 2 ch c Bluebird - Persian Tapestry (Tap On 94+
Wood) Trkd ldr, al trav well, led over 1f out, drew clr, easily : val for 10L+: Lingfield (mdn) debut wnr: apprec
step up to 6f, stay further: acts on gd/soft & soft: has run well fresh: looks v useful, win more races.

1328 **BARAKANA** 10 [5] B J Meehan 2-8-10 Pat Eddery 7/4: 332: 2 b c Barathea - Safkana (Doyoun) 7 77
Led, rdn halfway, hdd over 1f out & sn no ch with wnr: hvly bckd: prefer a faster surface as in 1328?

-- **DOUBLE BREW** [3] R Hannon 2-8-7 T Quinn 13/2: 3: 2 ch c Primo Dominie - Boozy (Absalom) 8 62
Trkd front pair, eff 2f out, sn btn & position accepted: op 5/1, longer priced stablemate of wnr: May foal, cost
10,000gns: half-brother to a 5f juv wnr, dam v useful sprinter: sire a high-class 2yo, will learn from this.
3 ran Time 1m 23.36 (12.26) (J C Smith) R Hannon East Everleigh, Wilts.

1527
2.35 SPREADMAIL.COM HCAP 3YO+ 0-95 (C) 2m Soft 129 -16 Slow [92]
£7215 £2220 £1110 £555 4 yo rec 2 lb Raced stands side fnl 3f

*1052 **WAVE OF OPTIMISM** 28 [12] J Pearce 5-9-1 (79) T Quinn 13/2: 30-011: 5 ch g Elmaamul - Ballerina Bay 84
(Myjinski) Keen, waited with rear, rdn/prog fnl 3f & styd on well for press ins last to lead nr line: op 11/2:
earlier scored at Doncaster (h'cap): '99 Sandown wnr (h'cap, rtd 75): '98 Nottingham wnr (mdn, rtd 75): suited
by 2m: acts on gd, relishes gd/soft & soft grnd, handles any trk: progressive & game stayer.

1484 **TURTLE VALLEY** 2 [6] S Dow 4-9-10 (90) P Doe 20/1: 0-0002: 4 b c Turtle Island - Primrose Valley hd 94
(Mill Reef) Trkd ldr, led over 3f out, rdn fnl 2f & hdd nr line: stays 2m & loves soft: back on a fair mark.

*1355 **RENZO** 8 [1] J L Harris 7-8-7 (71) S Sanders 9/2: 00-113: 7 b g Alzao - Waterfow (Foolish Pleasure) 2½ 73
Settled in tch, prog/chsd ldrs over 1f in, little room in last, onepace when switched nr fin: well bckd: see 1355.

1052 **BRAVE TORNADO** 28 [7] G B Balding 9-9-2 (80) S Drowne 4/1 JT FAV: 4/1224: Trkd ldrs, chsd ldr 2 80
3f out till over 1f out, rdn/no extra fnl 1f: well bckd: clr of rem here: also bhd today's wnr in 1052.

4397} **EASTWELL HALL** 224 [8] S-9-3 (81) Pat Eddery 7/1: /054-5: Keen/held up rear, eff over 2f out, no 8 75
impress: op 11/2, Flat reapp, rtd 84: '99 Warwick & Ascot wnr (novs, rtd 132h, eff at 2m/2½m on fast & soft, any
trk): plcd in '99 (val Cesarewitch h'cap, rtd 84): in '98 trained by R Curtis, scored at Bath, Folkestone & Warwick
(h'caps, subs plcd sev times, rtd 75): eff 10/12f, stays 2m1f well: acts on fast & soft, any trk: has run well fresh.

1076 **AMEZOLA** 26 [10] A 4-8-13 (79)(t) R Hughes 10/1: 206-06: Cl-up, wkng when hmpd 2f out: rnr-up in 2½ 71
'99 (h'cap, rtd 85, subs tried t-stap): '98 Bath wnr (auct mdn, rtd 79): stays a stiff/gall 14f: acts on gd & hvy.

4013} **KINGSTON VENTURE** 250 [5] 4-9-13 (93) G Duffield 25/1: 2105-7: Handy, rdn 3f out, fdd fnl 2f: Flat 1 84
reapp, jumps fit, 99/0 Hereford (juv nov, rtd 108h at best, eff at 2m/2½m on fast & soft): '99 Flat scorer at
Doncaster (h'cap) & Lingfield (stks, rtd 96): '98 Salisbury wnr (med auct mdn, rtd 75): eff at 10/12f: acts on firm
& gd/soft, gall/sharpish trk: likes to front run: will apprec a drop in trip.

4618} **JAWAH** 203 [13] 6-9-0 (78) Craig Williams 16/1: 0010-8: Dwelt/rear, rdn/btn 3f out: Flat reapp, jumps ¾ 68
fit (rtd 82h, amat nov): '99 Doncaster scorer (h'cap, K Mahdi, rtd 79): plcd fnl 2 '98 starts (h'caps, rtd 76 at
best): eff at 14f, stays 2m & tried further: acts on gd & soft, with/without visor, not blnks: gd weight carrier.

4545} **NICELY** 21 [11] 4-9-5 (85) M Henry 8/1: 0410-9: Keen, held up rear, eff 2f out, sn btn: reapp: Flat ¾ 74
Newbury wnr (h'cap, subs rtd 84, rtd h'cap): '98 Bath wnr (med auct mdn, rtd 77): prev eff at 1m/11.3f, now suited
by 2m: acts on firm & gd/soft, handles hvy: likes a gall track: fitter for this.

1167 **HISTORIC** 21 [2] 4-8-11 (77)(BL) D R McCabe 4/1 JT FAV: 22-030: Led till 3f out, fdd: 10th: jockey 1½ 65
given a 3 day ban for irresponsible riding: tried blnks, no improvement: see 917.
10 ran Time 3m 47.42 (23.22) (Wave Of Optimism Partnership) J Pearce Newmarket.

1528
3.10 FINSPREADS.COM HCAP 3YO+ 0-90 (C) 1m2f Soft 129 +10 Fast [90]
£7475 £2300 £1150 £575 3 yo rec 14lb Raced stands side fnl 3f

1310 **PIPSSALIO** 11 [11] Jamie Poulton 3-8-0 (76) M Henry 8/1: -21401: 3 b c Pips Pride - Tesalia (Finissimo) 82
Chsd ldrs, rdn/led 2f out, styd on gamely ins last, drvn out: op 7/1: fast time: earlier scored at Sandown (h'cap):
unplcd last term: eff at 1m/10f, could get further: acts on gd, relishes soft/hvy grnd: handles a sharp or stiff/
gall trk: progressive colt who shld win again in the mud.

1170 **SUPPLY AND DEMAND** 21 [2] J H M Gosden 6-9-13 (89)(bl) K Fallon 7/2 FAV: 06-022: 6 b g Belmez - ¾ 93
Sipsi Fach (Prince Sabo) Rear, gd hdwy 2f out, held by brave wnr ins last: hvly bckd: topweight: acts on

505

fast & soft: came with what looked like a wng run here & not go past, but is in good form: see 1170.

1170 **MAKE WAY 21** [3] B J Meehan 4-9-6 (82) D R McCabe 25/1: 36-603: 4 b g Red Ransom - Way Of The *3* **83**
World (Dance Of Life) Trkd ldrs, rdn & kept on onepace fnl 2f: op 16/1: acts on firm & soft grnd: see 896.

1091 **AEGEAN DREAM 25** [4] R Hannon 4-9-2 (78) R Hughes 10/1: 5-2344: Trkd ldrs, ch over 1f out, sn no *4* **75**
extra: prob handles hvy, prefers firm/fast grnd: see 853, 747.

1307 **SPRING PURSUIT 11** [8] 4-9-10 (86) P Fitzsimons (5) 13/2: 213005: Rear, hdwy 3f out, no prog fnl 1f. *4* **79**

1160 **ROBZELDA 21** [5] 4-8-13 (75)(bl) J F Egan 8/1: 3-3256: Bmpd start, rear, eff 3f out, no impress. *5* **63**

1042 **PHILATELIC LADY 29** [12] 4-9-3 (79) S Carson (5) 6/1: 1-5337: Rear, eff 3f out, no prog: see 1042, 593. *4* **63**

1375 **GREAT NEWS 8** [13] 5-8-11 (73) T Quinn 12/1: -00008: Trkd ldr, led 3f out till 2f out, fdd: op 10/1: *½* **56**
slipping down the weights & worth another chance at 1m: see 875.

1288 **PRINCE SLAYER 12** [1] 4-9-0 (76) Pat Eddery 9/1: 52-029: Led 7f: op 7/1: btr 1288 (firm). *3½* **56**

699 **PASSIONS PLAYTHING 65** [6] 4-8-8 (70)(BL) S Drowne 40/1: 44-600: Bhd 3f out: 10th: blnks: abs. *dist* **0**

*637 **TYLERS TOAST 84** [7] 4-8-3 (65) P Doe 10/1: -21110: Trkd ldrs, wknd 2f out: 11th, abs, a/w wnr. *3½* **0**

11 ran Time 2m 14.21 (11.91) (Chris Steward) Jamie Poulton Telscombe, E.Sussex.

1529

3.40 LISTED ACHILLES STKS 3YO+ (A) 5f str Soft 129 -33 Slow
£14755 £4540 £2270 £1135 3 yo rec 8 lb Raced towards centre

1320 **MONKSTON POINT 13** [1] D W P Arbuthnot 4-9-3 (vis) T Quinn 7/2: 0-1101: 4 b g Fayruz - Doon Belle **107**
(Ardoon) Sn handy, rdn/led over 1f out, styd on well ins last, rdn out: well bckd: earlier scored at Newbury (rtd
h'cap) & here at Kempton (stks): rnr-up once last term (rtd 97): '98 wnr at Bath (2) & Ayr (list, rtd 105): eff at
5/6f: acts on fast, relishes soft: handles any trk, likes Kempton: suited by a vis: v useful sprinter.

4286} **VITA SPERICOLATA 231** [6] J S Wainwright 3-8-8 G Bardwell 20/1: 5060-2: 3 b f Prince Sabo - Ahonita *2* **100**
(Ahonoora) Rear, styd on fnl 2f, not pace of wnr: '99 wnr at Musselburgh (seller, debut) & subs at Sandown
(List, rtd 102): eff at 5f, stays 6f: acts on firm & soft grnd, any trk: runs well fresh: useful, fine reapp.

1371 **SEE YOU LATER 8** [7] Major D N Chappell 3-8-4 G Duffield 7/1: 133-63: 3 b f Emarati - Rivers *½* **95**
Rhapsody (Dominion) Led till over 1f out, onepace ins last: tchd 8/1: acts on fast & soft grnd: see 1371.

1172 **LORD KINTYRE 21** [2] B R Millman 5-9-3 Pat Eddery 7/2: 50-244: Held up, eff 2f out, onepace: op 11/4. *½* **99**

1410 **SAPHIRE 7** [8] 4-8-12 K Hodgson 33/1: 0-0565: Chsd ldrs, outpcd over 1f out, kept on again *1¼* **91**
ins last: interesting back in a h'cap at 6f, on soft off around 82: see 1410.

1172 **HALMAHERA 13** [5] 5-9-7 K Fallon 3/1 FAV: -52056: Prom, rdn/held over 1f out: topweight: btr 820, 734. *½* **99**

1277 **YORBA LINDA 14** [4] 5-8-12 J F Egan 20/1: 509-47: Bhd over 1f out: highly tried: see 1277. *14* **70**

1371 **THE TATLING 8** [3] 3-8-9 R Hughes 9/2: 62-038: Chsd ldrs, btn over 1f out: btr 1371 (6f, gd). *6* **66**

8 ran Time 1m 06.38 (8.08) (Derrick C Broomfield) D W P Arbuthnot Upper Lambourn, Berks.

1530

4.15 LISTED HERON STKS 3YO (A) 1m jub Soft 129 +05 Fast
£14885 £4580 £2290 £1145 Raced stands side fnl 3f

*1080 **INGLENOOK 26** [3] J L Dunlop 3-8-12 Pat Eddery 3/1: -511: 3 b c Cadeaux Genereux - Spring (Sadler's **107**
Wells) Chsd ldrs, prog/led over 2f out, styd on strongly & rdn clr ins last: fast time: well bckd: eff at 1m,
10f+ shld suit: acts on gd/soft & soft: progressive & v useful colt, now deserves a crack at Group company.

1246 **SIR NINJA 16** [4] D J S Ffrench Davis 3-8-12 K Fallon 16/1: 10-562: 3 b c Turtle Island - The *3½* **100**
Poachers Lady (Salmon Leap) Rear/in tch, prog to chase wnr over 1f out, kept on but al held: stays 1m: see 925.

4468} **SUN CHARM 218** [2] Saeed bin Suroor 3-8-12 T E Durcan 6/1: 15-3: 3 b c Gone West - Argon Laser *2½* **96**
(Kris) Held up, eff 2f out, sn held: bckd tho' op 4/1: reapp: '99 wnr for Sir M Stoute at Leicester (stks, subs
unplcd in a Gr 3, rtd 102 at best): eff at 7f, further shld suit: acts on gd/soft & a stiff trk: goes well fresh.

1215 **KOOKABURRA 18** [1] B J Meehan 3-8-12 D R McCabe 25/1: 24-104: Led 6f: op 14/1: see 704 (fast). *10* **85**

1171 **UMISTIM 21** [6] 3-9-3 R Hughes 8/13 FAV: 51-165: Trkd ldr, hung left 4f out, sn btn & position *shd* **90**
accepted fnl 2f: hvly bckd at odds on: something clrly amiss here, connections mystified: see 1171, 981 (g/s).

5 ran Time 1m 46.69 (9.89) (Seymour Cohn) J L Dunlop Arundel, W.Sussex.

1531

4.45 SPORTINGODDS.COM HCP 3YO+ 0-90 (C) 6f str Soft 129 -22 Slow **[89]**
£7637 £2350 £1175 £587 3 yo rec 9 lb Majority raced far side

*1471 **DANIELLES LAD 3** [3] B Palling 4-10-3 (92)(6ex) P Fitzsimons (5) 7/1: -04011: 4 b g Emarati - Cactus **97**
Road (Iron Duke) Sn tracking ldrs, switched & shkn up ins last to lead nr fin, rdn out: op 5/1: qck reapp under a
6lb pen after recent Goodwood win (h'cap): rnr-up twice in '99 (h'caps, rtd 91): '98 Goodwood (auct mdn) &
Doncaster wnr (nurs h'cap, rtd 88): eff at 5/6f on fast, relishes gd/soft & hvy, any trk: gd weight carrier.

1126 **SARENA PRIDE 23** [15] R J O'Sullivan 3-8-4 (74) J F Egan 9/1: 0-0502: 3 b f Persian Bold - Avidal *½* **76**
Park (Horage) Chsd ldrs, drvn & kept on well ins last, not reach wnr: op 7/1: apprec drop back to 6f: see 727

1173 **LIVELY LADY 21** [8] J R Jenkins 4-10-0 (89)(vis) Pat Eddery 6/1: 1-4103: 4 b f Beveled - In The *½* **90**
Papers (Aragon) Rear, prog/briefly no room 2f out, ev ch ins last, no extra nr line: gd run: see 1013 (5f).

1324 **MIDNIGHT ESCAPE 10** [10] C F Wall 7-9-8 (83) S Sanders 16/1: 40-004: Dwelt/rear, rdn/kept on fnl 2f: *1¼* **82**
on a handy mark: see 1324.

4298} **ALMASI 231** [14] 8-8-13 (74) M Cotton (4) 16/1: 6030-5: Trkd ldrs, led over 2f out, hdd well ins last *2* **69**
& no extra: reapp: '99 Doncaster scorer (fill h'cap, rtd 79): rtd 82 in '98 (h'cap): eff at 6f, stays 7f: acts on
firm or soft, any trk, loves Doncaster: often best with a late run: sharper for this with a more experienced jockey.

1110 **PREMIER BARON 24** [4] 5-9-6 (81)(BL) J Tate 14/1: -14006: Chsd ldrs, no impress over 1f out: blnks. *5* **68**

1383 **FRANCPORT 7** [1] 4-9-2 (77) T E Durcan 15/2: 0-5107: Rear, eff halfway, no impress: op 10/1: btr 824. *2½* **59**

1178 **WAFFLES OF AMIN 20** [9] 3-8-8 (76)(2ow) R Hughes 16/1: 316-08: Mid-div, held 2f out: see 77 (mdn). *nk* **57**

1196 **PALAWAN 19** [6] 4-8-13 (74) N Chalmers (7) 10/1: 112039: Led 4f: not handle soft? see 599. *1¾* **52**

935 **PASSION FOR LIFE 40** [5] 7-9-13 (88) T Quinn 6/1: 61-100: Prom 3f, btn/eased fnl 1f: 10th: abs. *3* **60**

1357 **GORETSKI 8** [13] 7-8-6 (67) C Rutter 14/1: 000000: Al rear: 11th: op 12/1: see 926. *¾* **38**

1173 **THE PUZZLER 21** [7] 9-9-7 (82) G Duffield 11/2: 50-300: Reared start, mid-div, btn 2f out: 12th: bckd. *2½* **48**

1245 **PARADISE LANE 16** [2] 4-9-8 (83) Cheryl Nosworthy (7) 20/1: 00-200: Rcd alone centre, prom 2f: 13th. *½* **48**

13 ran Time 1m 20.16 (9.06) (Mrs P K Chick) B Palling Cowbridge, Vale Of Glamorgan.

1532   5.20 UPTIME COMMERCE MDN 3YO (D)   1m jub   Soft 129   -24 Slow
£4524   £1392   £696   £348 Raced centre - stands side fnl 3f

1188 **COURT OF APPEAL 20** [11] J R Fanshawe 3-9-0 Pat Eddery 25/1: 0-01: 3 ch c Bering - Hiawatha's Song   89
(Chief's Crown) Trkd ldr, rdn/led 2f out, held on gamely ins last, drvn out: unplcd both starts prev: eff
at 1m on soft grnd & an easy trk: has reportedly been racing too freely prev: op to further improvement.

-- **MAHFOOTH** [10] Saeed bin Suroor 3-9-0 T E Durcan 5/4 FAV: 3-02: 3 ch c Diesis - I Certainly Am   ¾   87
(Affirmed) Trkd ldrs, rdn/prog to chall over 1f out, just held nr fin: clr rem: hvly bckd: British debut, 2 mth
abs: ex-French, plcd on sole '99 start at Deauville (list): subs well btn in UAE Debry (12f): eff at 7f/1m, shld
stay further: handles gd/soft & soft grnd.

-- **SALIX DANCER** [12] Pat Mitchell 3-9-0 R Perham 50/1: 3: 3 b g Shareef Dancer - Willowbank (Gay   5   79
Fandango) Prom, ch 2f out, sn outpcd by front pair: debut, brother to a 10f wnr: handles soft, stays 1m, get further.

-- **EVE** [1] M L W Bell 3-8-9-0 M Fenton 16/1: 4: Rear, eff 2f out, late gains, nrst fin: op 14/1, debut: ½   73
half-sister to a 1m wnr: stays 1m & handles soft grnd: kind intro, can improve.

884 **DICKIE DEADEYE 45** [6] 3-9-0 S Carson (5) 25/1: 05: Keen/trkd ldrs, held fnl 2f: 6 wk abs: see 884.   1¼   76
-- **KRANTOR** [4] 3-9-0 T Quinn 4/1: 6: In tch, eff/held 2f out: bckd, op 5/1: 6: debut: Arazi colt, this   ¾   75
1m trip shld suit: could improve on a faster surface for H R A Cecil.

1263 **SARENA SPECIAL 15** [8] 3-9-0 P Doe 16/1: 26-257: Prom, ev ch 2f out, wknd over 1f out: op 14/1.   1¼   73
1376 **RUM PUNCH 8** [3] 3-9-0 K Fallon 5/1: 0-08: Rear, rdn 2f out, keeping on but no threat when no room   4   67+
over 1f out, position soon accepted: backed, op 8/1: tenderly handled, leave this bhd in h'cap company, one to note.
1376 **ORIENT EXPRESS 8** [9] 3-9-0 D R McCabe 25/1: 009: Chsd ldrs 6f: now quals for h'caps.   6   58
1376 **HALHOO LAMMTARRA 8** [7] 3-9-0 S Drowne 12/1: 2-00: Led 6f: 10th: op 10/1: see 1376.   6   49
-- **HEFIN** [5] 3-9-0 G Faulkner (3) 33/1: 0: Dwelt/rear, btn 3f out: 11th: debut, with S C Williams.   1   48
-- **RESILIENT** [13] 3-9-0 K W Marks 25/1: 0: Dwelt, al bhd: 12th: dam a Irish 13f wnr: with W J Haggas.   1¼   46
12 ran   Time 1m 49.05 (12.25)   (Mrs Susan Davis)   J R Fanshawe Newmarket.

Official Going   SOFT. Stalls: 7f & 1m - Inside; 14f - Centre: Rem - Outside.

1533   1.30 BE FRIENDLY HCAP 3YO+ 0-105 (B)   5f   Good/Soft 85   -03 Slow   [104]
£11154   £3432   £1716   £858   3 yo rec 8 lb   Field raced centre/stands side

1324 **INDIAN SPARK 10** [6] J S Goldie 6-8-9 (85) A Culhane 20/1: 041501: 6 ch g Indian Ridge - Annes   93
Gift (Ballymoss) Handy centre, styd on to lead just ins fnl 1f, rdn clr: earlier won in the mud at Newcastle
(h'cap): '99 York scorer (rtd h'cap, rtd 91): '98 scorer at Thirsk & Doncaster (2, h'caps): v eff at 5f, stays
6f: acts on firm, loves gd/soft & hvy & gall trks: gd weight carrier: tough, useful in these conditions.

1324 **SHEER VIKING 10** [21] B W Hills 4-9-7 (97) M Hills 11/2 FAV: 0-2232: 4 b g Danehill - Schlefalora   1½   101
(Mas Media) In tch stands side, rdn 2f out, styd on to chase wnr ins last, no threat: running well in defeat.
1337 **FURTHER OUTLOOK 9** [18] D Nicholls 6-9-4 (94) J Weaver 8/1: 000053: 6 gr g Zilzal - Future Bright   ½   97
(Lyphard's Wish) Led stands side, kept on till rdn & hdd ins last, onepace: can go in again (Epsom wnr in '99).
1337 **NOW LOOK HERE 9** [11] B A McMahon 4-10-0 (104) K Darley 10/1: -23334: From stands side, eff   nk   106
over 1f out, kept on same pace in last: another gd plcd run under top-weight: wants further: see 1337 (6f).
*1324 **ELLENS LAD 10** [13] 6-9-7 (97) P Shea (7) 10/1: -05015: Waited with stands side, eff over 1f   ½   98
out, kept on ins last: useful & tough: see 1324.
1324 **NIGHT FLIGHT 10** [19] 6-9-0 (90) R Winston 9/1: 002006: In tch stands side, eff over 1f out,   ½   90
keeping on when short of room cl-home: likes soft grnd & on a handy mark: see 926.
1192 **UNSHAKEN 20** [10] 6-7-11 (73) J Bramhill 20/1: -02407: Bhd stands side, staying on when hmpd   ¾   73+
over 1f out, kept on ins last: eye-catching: h'capped to win now, one to be with over 6f next time: see 1008.
1277 **ELLENS ACADEMY 14** [17] 5-8-6 (82)(bl) W Supple 11/1: 0-0438: Dwelt, bhd stands side, kept on   nk   81
late, nrst fin: gd run, both wins at 6f: see 1277, 1074.
*1164 **GUINEA HUNTER 21** [16] 4-9-0 (90) J Fortune 6/1: 03-019: Chsd ldr stands side, no extra fnl 1f: bckd.   ½   97
1182 **FIRST MAITE 20** [15] 7-9-8 (98)(bl) T G McLaughlin 12/1: 244650: Bhd stands side: 10th, can do better.   ½   94
1182 **OCKER 20** [1] 6-9-1 (91) R Fitzpatrick (3) 40/1: 600-00: Prom far side, btn over 1f out: 11th, see 47.   1   84
-1398 **POLLY GOLIGHTLY 7** [5] 7-7-10 (72)(bl) (4oh) Dale Gibson 20/1: -00220: Led far side 4f, no extra: 12th.   nk   64
1324 **HENRY HALL 10** [20] 4-8-10 (86)(VIS) J Reid 11/1: -60600: Waited with stands side, eff & hmpd   nk   78
2f out, not recover: 13th: first time visor: see 1245, 702.
1324 **REFERENDUM 10** [12] 6-7-13 (75) F Norton 33/1: -00000: Nvr a factor stands side: 14th.   ½   66
4296} **PRINCELY DREAM 231** [9] 4-8-10 (86) P Hanagan (7) 25/1: 1320-0: Cl-up far side, wknd over   ½   76
1f out: 15th on reapp: '99 scorer at Ayr (class stks, rtd 89 at best): '98 wnr at York (mdn, subs disqual) &
Pontefract (mdn, rtd 85): eff at 5f, suited by 6f on fast or soft, gall trk: has tried a visor & runs well fresh.
1277 **YORKIES BOY 14** [4] 5-9-0 (90) J Carroll 16/1: -05220: In tch far side, btn over 2f out: 16th, btr 1277.   1   78
4144} **Tussle 241** [2] 5-9-2 (92) D Harrison 33/1:   1383 **Flak Jacket 7** [7] 5-7-11 (72)(1ow) N Kennedy 33/1:
927 **Speedy James 42** [3] 4-9-4 (94) J Fanning 33/1:
19 ran   Time 1m 03.22 (4.42)   (Frank Brady)   J S Goldie Uplawmoor, E Renfrewshire.

1534   2.00 SANDY LANE LISTED RTD HCAP 3YO 0-110 (A)   6f   Good/Soft 85   -06 Slow   [112]
£13885   £5266   £2633   £1197   All bar 2 raced centre

1171 **LINCOLN DANCER 21** [1] M A Jarvis 3-9-7 (105) M Roberts 7/1: 10-401: 3 b c Turtle Island - Double   115
Grange (Double Schwartz) Handy, hdwy to lead over 1f out, pushed clr ins last, impressive: top-weight: earlier
11L 10th in 2000 Guineas: '99 wnr at York (mdn, debut) & York (stks, rtd 104, with G Lewis): relished drop
back to 6f: poss stays 1m: revels in gd/soft, any trk: smart effort, cld win a Gr 3 race on similar grnd.
1078 **PRESENTATION 26** [9] R Hannon 3-8-12 (96) J Weaver 13/2: 33-232: 3 b f Mujadil - Beechwood   4   97
(Blushing Groom) In tch, gd hdwy over 1f out, edged left ins last & kept on but not pace of wnr: will apprec 7f.
1178 **DONT SURRENDER 20** [11] J L Dunlop 3-8-10 (94) J Fortune 100/30 FAV: 11-023: 3 b c Zieten - St   nk   95
Clair Star (Sallust) In tch, eff over 2f out, onepace fnl 1f: well bckd: running well: see 1178, 982.
4294} **BALLY PRIDE 231** [15] T D Easterby 3-9-6 (104) K Darley 14/1: 3062-4: Led stands side over 4f, edged   ¾   104
left & kept on for press over 1f out: juv scorer at The Curragh (val stks, plcd in Gr 2, rtd 103 at best): half

brother to wnrs over 1m/mid-dists: v eff around 6.3f, 7f looks sure to suit: acts on gd/firm & gd/soft, gall trks & has run well in blnks: gelded since last term, useful & interesting next time over further.
1406 **PERUVIAN CHIEF 7** [6] 3-8-7 (91)(4oh) T G McLaughlin 25/1: 113-05: Led over 4f, onepace: see 1406. *1* **89**
1215 **GLENROCK 18** [10] 3-8-7 (91)(1oh) W Supple 20/1: 103-06: Prom, hard rdn & onepace over 1f out. *1* **87**
1285 **AWAKE 14** [12] 3-9-0 (98) J Fanning 9/2: D-0427: Prom, rdn & btn appr fnl 1f: well bckd: btr 1285. *1¼* **92**
1285 **PUNCTUATE 14** [13] 3-8-8 (92) F Norton 12/1: 11-008: Prom, wkng when hmpd ins last: see 988. *1¼* **84**
1111 **ASAAL 24** [7] 3-8-12 (96) R Hills 11/1: 10-569: Prom, wknd well over 1f out: btr 912. *2½* **83**
4197} **SUDRA 238** [4] 3-8-12 (96) J Carroll 14/1: 310-0: Nvr a factor: 10th on reapp: rcd 3 times as a juv, won at Thirsk (mdn, firm, rtd 94+): eff at 6f, shld stay further: acts on firm grnd & has run well fresh: shld prove a different proposition on a sounder surface. *nk* **82**
1090 **TARAS GIRL 25** [3] 3-9-2 (100) A Culhane 11/1: 20-350: With ldrs till wknd well over 1f out: 11th. *6* **74**
1410 **KASHRA 7** [14] 3-8-13 (97) M Hills 16/1: 46-400: Trkd ldrs stands side, wknd over 1f out: 12th, lost form. *3½* **64**
12 ran Time 1m 16.76 (5.46) (Michael Baker) M A Jarvis Newmarket.

1535

2.30 TOTE CREDIT HCAP 3YO 0-110 (B) 1m30y rnd Good/Soft 85 +09 Fast [111]
£43875 £13500 £6750 £3375 Field raced centre in straight

1452 **ATLANTIC RHAPSODY 4** [12] M Johnston 3-8-3 (86) J Fanning 11/1: -10441: 3 b g Machiavellian - First Waltz (Green Dancer) Waited with, gd hdwy 2f out, styd on to lead ins fnl 1f, rdn out: nicely bckd: gd time, qck reapp: earlier scored at Southwell (mdn, first time blnks, rtd 91a): plcd all 4 '99 starts (rtd 91, mdns): eff at 1m/9f & handles firm, likes gd/soft & any trk: has run well in blnks: proving tough & useful. **95**
1310 **VINTAGE PREMIUM 11** [16] R A Fahey 3-8-11 (94) R Winston 16/1: -21402: 3 b c Forzando - Julia Domna (Dominion) Led 2f, prom, kept on for press over 1f out, not pace of wnr: running v well & likes soft. *1¼* **100**
1080 **MATERIAL WITNESS 26** [11] W R Muir 3-8-5 (88) Martin Dwyer 16/1: 32-223: 3 b c Barathea - Dial Dream (Gay Mecene) Hld up, gd hdwy to lead over 1f out till ins last, no extra: another useful plcd run, win a mdn. *½* **93**
1155 **PAPABILE 22** [4] W Jarvis 3-8-3 (86) D Harrison 14/1: 52-24: Waited with, gd hdwy well over 1f out to chall, onepcd ins last: stays 1m: lightly rcd, type to win a nice contest: see 1155. *1½* **89**
*1158 **NOOSHMAN 21** [13] 3-8-2 (85) F Norton 5/2 FAV: 252-15: In tch, hdwy well over 1f out, onepace: well bckd: stays 1m & could rate more highly: see 1158 (turn of foot). *1* **87**
*1262 **EL CURIOSO 15** [8] 3-8-11 (94) K Darley 11/1: 14-016: Waited with, keen, eff over 2f out, sn no impress. *1¼* **94**
1055 **SMART RIDGE 28** [1] 3-9-1 (98) J Weaver 25/1: 110-57: Keen, 6f out till over 1f out, no extra. *½* **97**
1186 **QAMOUS 20** [15] 3-8-10 (93) W Supple 9/1: 41-38: Held up rear, gd hdwy over 1f out, sn short of room & onepcd: op 6/1: looks capable of more with a positive ride: see 1186. *hd* **91**
*1069 **SOBRIETY 26** [7] 3-9-5 (102) D O'Donohoe 14/1: 124-19: Waited with, rdn & no impress 2f out. *1* **98**
1308 **ROYAL CAVALIER 11** [14] 3-7-10 (79)(1oh) P M Quinn (5) 40/1: 341000: Waited with, eff over 2f out, wknd over 1f out: 10th: see 720 (fibresand, mdn). *½* **74**
1215 **COTE SOLEIL 18** [3] 3-8-3 (86) A Beech (5) 20/1: 4-3300: Prom, ev ch well over 1f out, sn wknd: 11th. *½* **80**
*1032 **TWEED MILL 31** [2] 3-8-5 (88) M Roberts 6/1: 3-210: Dwelt, sn rdn & handy, wknd over 1f out: 12th. *2½* **78**
1382 **Kingsdon 7** [6] 3-8-11 (94) J Carroll 16/1: 1069 **Jalad 26** [9] 3-9-7 (104)(t) R Hills 12/1:
1347 **Michele Marieschi 9** [17] 3-8-13 (96) J Fortune 16/1: 765 **Shouf Al Badou 63** [5] 3-9-0 (97) J Reid 12/1:
16 ran Time 1m 46.64 (6.14) (Atlantic Racing Ltd) M Johnston Middleham, N.Yorks.

1536

3.00 THWAITES HCAP 4YO+ 0-80 (D) 1m6f Good/Soft 85 +00 Fast [78]
£11154 £3432 £1716 £858 Field raced centre in straight

1251 **ENFILADE 16** [8] B Hanbury 4-9-7 (71)(t) R Hills 9/2 JT FAV: 44-501: 4 b g Deploy - Bargouzine (Hotfoot) Prom, led over 2f out, kept on well, rdn out: '99 scorer at Chester & Haydock (h'caps, rtd 80): winning form over 12/14f on firm & gd/soft, any trk: tough, slipped back to a winning mark. **78**
1350 **FLETCHER 9** [4] H Morrison 6-8-0 (50) F Norton 16/1: -00002: 6 b g Salse - Ballet Classique (Sadler's Wells) Hld up, eff for press over 2f out, onepace over 1f out: better run on favoured soft grnd. *2½* **53**
*1394 **THAMES DANCER 7** [11] K McAuliffe 4-10-0 (78) W Supple 6/1: 3-0413: 4 ch c Green Dancer - Hata (Kaldoun) Led 1f, led again 3f out, sn hdd but kept on onepace: clr rem: fine run, big weight: return to 2m suit. *1¼* **80**
4397} **FOUNDRY LANE 224** [5] Mrs M Reveley 9-9-10 (74) T Eaves (7) 8/1: 3440-4: Led after 1f till over 5f out, ev ch over 2f out, wknd appr fnl 1f: last rcd over jumps 4 months ago, won at Aintree (h'cap hdle, rtd 142h), Catterick & Huntingdon (h'cap chases, rtd 128c, stays 2m4f on gd & hvy): 98/99 Wetherby wnr (nov chase): plcd on the Flat in '99 (rtd 78): '98 scorer at York (h'cap, rtd 74): eff over 12f/2m on firm & soft, runs well fresh. *6* **70**
1329 **SANDBAGGEDAGAIN 10** [2] 6-9-10 (74) J Reid 11/1: 1/0-05: Waited with, eff 2f out, sn no impress. *2½* **67**
943 **SHAFFISHAYES 40** [3] 8-9-1 (65) A Culhane 10/1: 455-06: Hld up, eff 3f out, wknd dist: 6 wk abs. *nk* **58**
848 **DEEP WATER 49** [10] 6-9-6 (70) J Fortune 7/1: 253/27: Bhd, btn well over 3f out: unplcd over hdls. *10* **53**
1329 **WEET FOR ME 10** [7] 4-9-12 (76) F Lynch 9/1: 2-0038: Prom, wknd over 2f out: btr 1329 (firm). *1* **58**
1052 **PLEASANT MOUNT 28** [6] 4-9-0 (64) K Darley 9/2 JT FAV: 2-0159: Led over 5f out till 3f out, wknd: nicely bckd: much btr 918 (fibresand). *1* **45**
-- **ALPINE PANTHER** [9] 7-8-8 (58) D Harrison 25/1: 1360/0: Bhd fnl 4f: last rcd on the Flat in '98, won at Nottingham (h'cap, rtd 61): 98/99 hdle wnr at Plumpton (clmr), Newcastle & Bangor (rtd 130h, 3m, fast & soft): eff at 14f on the Flat on fast & soft grnd. *6* **33**
1187 **ACHILLES SKY 20** [1] 4-9-13 (77) J Weaver 7/1: 16-100: Bhd, brief effort over 2f out, sn wknd & eased: longer trip, twice below 805 (12f, gd, has broken blood vessels). *1¼* **51**
11 ran Time 3m 09.92 (11.92) (H Channon) B Hanbury Newmarket.

1537

3.35 STANLEY RACING MDN 3YO+ (D) 7f30y rnd Good/Soft 85 -41 Slow
£4004 £1232 £616 £308 3 yo rec 11lb Field raced centre in straight

1159 **LAST SYMPHONY 21** [9] M A Jarvis 3-8-13 M Roberts 11/2: -061: 3 b c Last Tycoon - Dancing Heights (High Estate) Held up, rdn 2f out, styd on strongly from unpromising position over 1f out to get up cl-home: showed promise earlier & eff at 7f, 1m sure to suit: acts on gd/soft: improve for this & interesting in h'caps over further. **81+**
-- **CAPRICHO** [1] W J Haggas 3-8-13 J Weaver 100/30 JT FAV: 2: 3 gr g Lake Coniston - Star Spectacle (Spectacular Bid) Hld up, hdwy to lead over 1f out, edged left & collared cl-home under hands-and-heels: gamble from 6/1: gd debut at 7f, shld stay further: handles gd/soft: prob have landed gamble with a stronger ride. *½* **79**
1268 **SUMMER SONG 15** [4] E A L Dunlop 3-8-8 J Reid 6/1: 1-453: 3 b f Green Desert - High Standard (Kris) Waited with, rdn 2f out, kept on ins last: type to do better now h'capped & shld apprec a return to 1m. *½* **73**
1072 **AMRITSAR 26** [6] Sir Michael Stoute 3-8-13 F Lynch 100/30 JT FAV: -054: Prom, rdn & sltly outpcd over 2f out, onepace fnl 1f: bckd tho' op 9/4: could do better over further. *2* **75**
1348 **STRAND OF GOLD 9** [8] 3-8-13 (BL) J Fortune 7/1: 4-5505: Led over 5f, wknd fnl 1f: tried blnks, *hd* **74$**

treat with caution: see 1220.
4361} **BARNIE RUBBLE 226** [7] 4-9-10 F Norton 25/1: 0-6: Chsd ldr, wknd fnl 1f: some promise here. *1* **72**
1072 **BURGUNDIAN RED 26** [2] 3-8-13 J Carroll 12/1: 04-007: Al bhd: see 804. *8* **60**
4500} **IPANEMA BEACH 215** [5] 3-8-8 R Hills 9/1: 6-8: In tch, eff to chall well over 1f out, sn wknd: op 7/1: *½* **54**
rtd 72 on sole juv start: dam 7f/1m wnr, styd 10.5f: shld apprec 7f+.
8 ran Time (R Leah) M A Jarvis Newmarket.

1538

4.05 ST HELENS FILLIES MDN 2YO (D) 5f Good/Soft 85 -36 Slow
£4212 £1296 £646 £324

-- **ASH MOON** [7] K R Burke 2-8-11 D Harrison 25/1: 1: 2 ch f General Monash - Jarmar Moon (Unfuwain) **83**
Waited with, hdwy 2f out, styd on well to lead nr fin, going away: Apr foal, cost 5,000gns: eff at 5f, further looks sure to suit: handles gd/soft: v pleasing debut, type to win a valuable race.
1372 **FAIR PRINCESS 8** [3] B W Hills 2-8-11 M Hills 1/1 FAV: 22: 2 b f Efisio - Fair Attempt (Try My Best) *½* **81**
Chsd ldr, led 2f out, kept on till collared ins last, just btn: well bckd & will win a race: handles gd/soft.
1166 **ZIETUNZEEN 21** [6] A Berry 2-8-11 J Weaver 11/2: 23: 2 b f Zieten - Hawksbill Special (Taufan) *2½* **76**
Handy, rdn & onepace over 1f out: win on a minor track: handles gd/firm & gd/soft: see 1166.
-- **EFFERVESCE** [2] M A Buckley 2-8-11 J Carroll 20/1: 4: In tch, eff over 1f out, onepcd, hands-and-heels: Feb foal, cost IR 34,000gns: half-sister to sev wnrs: speedily bred & showed some promise here. *2* **72**
-- **RUNAWAY BRIDE** [5] 2-8-11 R Fitzpatrick (3) 25/1: 5: Sn rdn & nvr a factor: debut: Apr foal, cheaply bght: dam 7f wnr: with C Smith. *3½* **65$**
1413 **EXTRA GUEST 7** [9] 2-8-11 J Reid 5/1: 4326: In tch, btn 2f out: see 1413. *½* **64**
1359 **PILGRIM PRINCESS 8** [1] 2-8-11 W Supple 33/1: 07: Led 3f, wknd over 1f out: see 1359. *1* **62**
-- **EASY FREE** [4] 2-8-11 R Winston 20/1: 8: Slow away & al bhd: debut: Mar foal, cheaply bght: dam 1m wnr: bred to need 6f+: with T D Easterby. *2½* **57**
-- **MISS BEADY** [10] 2-8-11 K Darley 9/1: 9: Slow away, sn in tch till wknd 2f out: debut: op 7/1: Mar first foal, cost 11,500gns: dam 6f juv wnr: speedily bred. *24* **17**
9 ran Time 1m 04.86 (6.06) (David H Morgan) K R Burke Newmarket.

1539

4.35 MTB GROUP MDN 3YO (D) 1m2f120y Good/Soft 85 -28 Slow
£4043 £1244 £622 £311 Field raced centre in straight

1054 **FIRST OFFICER 28** [2] J R Fanshawe 3-9-0 D Harrison 5/4 FAV: 021: 3 b c Lear Fan - Trampoli (Trempolino) In tch, hdwy to lead over 1f out, kept on ins last, rdn out: hvly bckd: dam mid-dist scorer: stays 10.5f, further shld suit: acts on gd/soft: going the right way. **87**
-- **DARARIYNA** [6] Sir Michael Stoute 3-8-9 F Lynch 8/1: 2: 3 b f Shirley Heights - Dararita (Halo) *1* **80**
Prom, eff to chase wnr fnl 1f, kept on on debut: op 6/1: eff at 10.5f, bred to stay further: handles gd/soft: clr of rem, v pleasing debut & the type to win races over further.
990 **PRINCE AMONG MEN 35** [5] M C Pipe 3-9-0 K Darley 4/1: 336-33: 3 b g Robellino - Forelino (Trempolino) Handy, hdwy to lead over 3f out till over 1f out, onepace: stays 10.5f, 1m/9f may prove ideal. 4 **80**
1268 **LADY TWO K 15** [9] J Mackie 3-8-9 J Fanning 25/1: 04: Held up rear, some late gains under kind ride. *1¾* **73**
902 **HIGH TOPPER 44** [3] 3-9-0 J Reid 5/1: 0-25: Prom, wknd well over 1f out: see 902. *2* **75**
1017 **STRAWMAN 33** [1] 3-9-0 M Hills 25/1: 006: Led over 4f, wknd over 1f out: see 704. *2* **73$**
934 **SAVE THE PLANET 40** [4] 3-8-9 F Norton 33/1: 007: Led 6f out till over 3f out, no extra: see 794. *8* **58**
-- **BOURKAN** [8] 3-9-0 M Roberts 9/1: 8: Slow away & al bhd: dam mid-dist scorer: with A Stewart. *1½* **62**
-- **BUTTERWICK CHIEF** [12] 3-9-0 R Winston 25/1: 9: Sn rdn & al bhd: jockey rec a 5 day whip ban. *nk* **62**
9 ran Time 2m 21.86 (11.86) (HRH Prince Fahd Salman) J R Fanshawe Newmarket.

LINGFIELD

SATURDAY MAY 27TH AW - LH, Very Sharp Track: Turf - LH, Sharp, Undulating Track

Official Going Turf - HEAVY; AW - STANDARD. Stalls: Turf; Str Crse - Far Side; Rnd Crse - Inside; AW - Inside.

1540

6.10 BEATLEMANIA SELLER 3YO (G) 1m4f aw Standard Inapplicable
£1834 £524 £262

1365 **BEE GEE 8** [3] M Blanshard 3-8-7 Dale Gibson 10/1: 000-01: 3 b f Beveled - Bunny Gee (Last Tycoon): **40a**
Front rank, went on 4f out, held on well fnl 1f, drvn out: bt in for 3,000gns: modest mdn form in '99, apprec this drop to sell grade: eff over a sharp 12f on equitrack: handles a sharp trk.
1210 **ALBINONA 18** [1] M H Tompkins 3-8-7 A Whelan 9/1: 000-62: 3 b f Distinctly North - Across The Ring *1¾* **37a**
(Auction Ring): Chsd ldrs, prog to chall 2f out, kept on fnl 1f: 9L clr 3rd: eff at 12f on equitrack: see 1210.
1415 **HOUNDS OF LOVE 5** [7] R Guest 3-8-7 J Mackay (7) 7/4 FAV: 0-0333: 3 b g Foxhound - Foolish Lady *9* **23a**
(Foolish Pleasure): Dwelt, recovered to chase ldrs, btn 2f out: well bckd, qck reapp: better expected after 1415.
-- **BIG E** [2] S P C Woods 3-8-12 (VIS) G Duffield 7/2: -4: Led till 4f out, fdd: op 5/2, first time visor on debut: dam won over middle dists: seems modest. 4 **22a**
1331 **FOX STAR 10** [6] 3-8-7 I Mongan(4) 10/1: -60005: Dwelt, prog 1m out, btn 3f out: see 313 (6f here). *1½* **15a**
-- **SEDUCTION** [5] 3-8-7 A Clark 5/1: -6: Chsd ldrs till halfway, sn bhd, t.o: debut, with C Cyzer. *12* **0a**
-- **NOVELLINI STAR** [4] 3-8-12 S Righton 12/1: -7: Dwelt, nvr nr ldrs, t.o. in last on debut: with N Babbage. *18* **0a**
7 ran Time 2m 35.44 (6.24) (Mara Racing) M Blanshard Upper Lambourn, Berks.

1541

7.10 EBF NASHVILLE FILL MDN 2YO (D) 6f str Soft 107 -08 Slow
£3594 £1106 £553 £276

-- **SILVER JORDEN** [10] J L Dunlop 2-8-11 T Quinn 11/8 FAV: -1: 2 gr f Imp Society - Final Call (Town Crier): Dwelt, styd prog 2f out, strong run to lead ins fnl 1f, pushed clr despite running green: nicely bckd: Jan foal, cost 17,000gns: related to numerous wnrs, incl 2yo scorers: dam a 5f juv wnr: eff at 6f, will stay 7f: acts on soft grnd & on a sharp trk, runs well fresh: sure to benefit from this, rate more highly & win more races. **84+**
1312 **QUEEN SPAIN 11** [3] M R Channon 2-8-11 S Drowne 11/4: -02: 2 b f Mister Baileys - Excellus (Exceller): *1¾* **77**
Prom, ev ch over 1f out, kept on fnl 1f but not pace of wnr: op 7/4: eff at 6f on soft grnd: imprvd for today's stiffer test of stamina, already looks in need of 7f: should find similar, see 1312.
-- **PIVOTABLE** [8] M L W Bell 2-8-11 M Fenton 11/2: -3: 2 ch c Pivotal - Lady Dowery (Manila): *½* **76**

Prom, led halfway till ins fnl 1f, no extra: op 7/2: 8,000gns Mar foal: half-sister to a couple of wnrs abroad: dam a mid-dist wnr in France, sire a high class sprinter: eff at 6f on soft grnd: sure to learn from this.
-- **PRIMA VENTURE** [2] S P C Woods 2-8-11 G Duffield 7/1: -4: Prom, onepcd final 1f on debut: first 2½ 70
foal, dam a 6f 2yo wnr: Feb foal, sire a high class 6f/1m performer: with S Woods.
-- **BULA ROSE** [13] 2-8-11 D McGaffin (7) 25/1: -5: Led till halfway, wknd over 1f out: IR 2,500gns Apr 3 63
foal: dam a mid-dist wnr in Ireland: with W G M Turner, apprec further.
-- **ORANGETREE COUNTY** [14] 2-8-11 D R McCabe 14/1: -6: Dwelt, outpcd, nvr nr ldrs on debut: cheaply 16 33
bought May foal, half-sister to sev wnrs abroad: sire a decent 6/7f performer: shld benefit from better grnd.
-- **ONE BELOVED** [4] 2-8-11 C Adamson 12/1: -7: Dwelt, no ch from halfway: op 8/1 & lngr pricd ¾ 31
stablemate of rnr-up: cheaply bought Apr foal: sister to 10f wnr Diamond Flame: dam a 7f/1m wnr.
7 ran Time 1m 17.34 (6.94) (Mr & Mrs Gary Pinchen) J L Dunlop Arundel, W Sussex

1542

7.40 DISCO INFERNO HCAP 3YO+ 0-75 (E) 7f str Soft 107 -31 Slow [72]
£3178 £908 £454

1297 **AMBER BROWN 12** [10] K T Ivory 4-9-0 (58)(BL) G Duffield 10/1: -01001: 4 b f Thowra - High Velocity 65
(Frimley Park) Rcd keenly in bhd ldrs, eff to lead ins fnl 1f, styd on strongly, drvn out: earlier won at Thirsk (h'cap): eff at 6/7f, wng form on soft: back to form on soft grnd & with first time blnks today.
1037 **SCISSOR RIDGE 29** [9] J J Bridger 8-8-0 (44) R Brisland (5) 12/1: 426402: 8 ch g Indian Ridge - Golden nk 50
Scissors (Kalaglow): Front rank, ev ch final 1f, ran on & not btn far: back to form, acts on firm, soft grnd & both AWs: well h'capped & should sn go one better: see 29 (AW).
1129 **DOLPHINELLE 23** [5] Jamie Poulton 4-9-4 (62) O Urbina 11/1: 303403: 4 b c Dolphin Street - Mamie's 1¾ 65
Joy (Prince Tenderfoot): Mid-div, imprvd to chall 1f out, not pace of front 2 cl-home: see 1129 (fast grnd).
1113 **MYSTIC RIDGE 24** [8] B J Curley 6-9-12 (70) M Fenton 11/1: -41004: Led till ins fnl 1f, no extra: 1¾ 70
drifted from 6/1, top weight: acts on soft, best form prev on gd & firm grnd: primed to win on a faster surface.
958 **CONTRARY MARY 39** [4] 5-8-11 (55) T Quinn 11/2: 45-005: Rear, smooth hdwy 2f out, eased & onepcd 1½ 52
ins fnl 1f: v well h'capped on best form, not given a hard time today: see 958.
1113 **ANSTAND 24** [18] 5-9-0 (58) S Drowne 20/1: 00-006: Mid-div, some late prog, nvr nr ldrs: 5th at ½ 54
Goodwood in '99 (h'cap, rtd 70): '98 Ripon (h'cap) & York wnr (stks, rtd 77, with Mrs J Ramsden): eff at 6f, tried 7f: acts on gd & fast, handles any trk: has tried blnks, can run well fresh: hinting at a return to form.
1330 **CAVERSFIELD 10** [6] 5-8-3 (47) S Righton 12/1: 0-0007: In tch, no impress final 2f: see 1330. 2 39
1462 **KNOBBLEENEEZE 3** [14] 10-8-1 (45)(vis) C Rutter 7/1: 50-008: Rear, bmpd 2f out, nvr nr ldrs: ¾ 35
op 7/1, qck reapp: see 1462.
1129 **SUPER MONARCH 23** [1] 6-9-7 (65) G Bardwell 33/1: 530-09: Chsd ldrs till btn 2f out: trained by K 1 53
Burke in '99, plcd at Goodwood (h'cap, rtd 66): '98 wnr at Lingfield (AW mdn, rtd 70a) & Newmarket (val h'cap, rtd 81): eff at 7f/1m, has tried 10f: acts on fast, soft grnd & equitrack.
4232} **GREEN GOD 236** [11] 4-9-10 (68) A Clark 14/1: 2620-0: Mid-div, outpcd halfway, eased fnl 1f: fin 5 48
10th, reapp: rnr-up in a couple of '99 starts (h'caps, rtd 72): eff at 7f on soft grnd, has tried 1m.
1279 **PLEADING 14** [17] 7-9-6 (64)(bl) R Mullen 4/1 FAV: -23300: Nvr trbld ldrs in 11th: btr 834. nk 43
867 **NEELA 46** [13] 4-9-0 (58) R Smith (5) 14/1: 040-00: In tch 5f, wknd: fin 12th, abs. 4 30
1414 **SILVER TONGUED 7** [16] 4-7-10 (40) Claire Bryan(5) 25/1: 00-000: Chsd ldrs till halfway, wknd: 13th. 7 0
1097 **TRUMP STREET 25** [3] 4-8-4 (48) Jonjo Fowle (7) 14/1: -00250: Dwelt, recovered & prom 5f, wknd. 3½ 0
471 **CITY REACH 110** [15] 4-9-4 (62)(vis) S Sanders 7/1: 2-4130: Rcd keenly in rear, hmpd 2f out, no ¾ 14
ch after: fin last, long abs: forget this: see 471, 367 (AW).
15 ran Time 1m 30.1 (9.7) Flag Start (K T Ivory) K T Ivory Radlett, Herts.

1543

8.10 ROLLING ROCK FILLIES HCAP 3YO+ 0-70 (E) 5f Soft 107 +08 Fast [66]
£2912 £832 £416 3yo rec 8lb

1423 **KNOCKEMBACK NELLIE 5** [6] D R C Elsworth 4-9-8 (60)(bl) S Sanders 9/2: 5-0001: 4 b f Forzando - Sea 67
Clover (Ela Mana Mou): Bmpd start, sn led & made all, kept on well fnl 1f, drvn out: best time of day, qck reapp: unplcd in '99 (mdn, rtd 73): rnr-up twice in '98 (mdns, rtd 75): eff at 5/6f, has tried 7f: acts on firm & soft grnd, wears blnks: can force the pace & gained first win today on 18th start.
*1391 **WHIZZ KID 7** [10] J M Bradley 6-10-0 (66) Claire Bryan (5) 9/4 FAV: 512312: 6 b m Puissance - Panienka 1¼ 68
(Dom Racine): In tch, kept on fnl 1f but not pace of wnr cl-home: well bckd, top weight: v tough & consistent.
774 **KAYO GEE 59** [9] L Montague Hall 4-9-11 (63)(VIS) N Callan 12/1: 00-603: 4 b f Komaite - Darling Miss 1½ 61
Daisy (Tina's Pet): Bmpd start, prom till outpcd halfway, rallied fnl 1f but ch had gone: 1st time visor, 8 wk abs.
1487 **NIGHTINGALE SONG 2** [2] L Montague Hall 6-8-12 (50) A Clark 7/2: 600-04: Prom till onepcd final 1f: 1½ 44
op 9/2, qck reapp, shorter prcd stablemate of 3rd: see 1487.
1423 **STRATS QUEST 5** [5] 6-8-12 (50) T Quinn 4/1: 005005: Prom till onepcd final 1f: qck reapp. shd 44
1344 **MOUTON 9** [1] 4-7-13 (37) G Bardwell 16/1: 500006: Al outpcd, nvr nr ldrs: see 314 (10f, sand). 6 19
1423 **BEACH BABY 5** [4] 3-7-10 (42)(6oh) C Adamson 20/1: 000007: Dwelt, recovered to chase ldrs 3f, 2½ 18
fdd: qck reapp: modest form.
1196 **LADY DEALER 19** [8] 5-7-11 (35) S Righton 25/1: 000/08: Badly hmpd leaving stalls, no ch after: 11 0
fin last, forget this: missed '99: lightly rcd & little mdn form prev term: with M Usher.
8 ran Time 1m 01.78 (4.98) (Notaproperjob Partnership) D R C Elsworth Whitsbury, Hants.

1544

8.40 FLOWER POWER HCAP 3YO 0-65 (F) 1m2f aw Standard Inapplicable [72]
£2257 £645 £322

1345 **RICH VEIN 9** [4] S P C Woods 3-9-9 (67) N Callan 7/2: 00-421: 3 b g Up And At 'Em - Timissara 71a
(Shahrastani) Chsd ldrs, prog to chall when flatered ins last, rallied to lead on line, all-out: rider reportedly given a 2-day careless riding ban: lightly rcd in '99 (rtd 71, mdn): related to a mid-dist wnr, dam scored over 1m/10f: eff at 1m/10f, shld stay 12f: acts on gd grnd & equitrack: could improve further.
1094 **ESTABLISHMENT 25** [3] C A Cyzer 3-9-7 (65) S Sanders 10/1: 0-6402: 3 b g Muhtarram - Uncharted shd 68a
Waters (Celestial Storm): Early ldr, led again 4f out till caught on line: 5L clr 3rd: acts on equitrack.
*1234 **RIDE THE TIGER 16** [6] M D I Usher 3-9-0 (58) T Quinn 6/1: 000-13: 3 ch g Imp Society - Krisdaline 5 53a
(Kris S): Chsd ldrs, ev ch when bmpd & eased 2f out, rallied inside last but ch had gone: probably stays 10f.
*1022 **RATIFIED 33** [7] H Candy 3-8-13 (57) C Rutter 9/4 FAV: 00-214: Rear, prog 4f out, no impress fnl 2f. 1½ 50a
3971} **YAHESKA 252** [1] 3-7-10 (40)(5oh) J Mackay (7) 16/1: 000-5: Rear, well bhd halfway, no ch after: 14 13a
stiffish task, reapp: lightly rcd & modest juv form in '99, incl in sells: with E O'Neill.
1292 **BORDER RUN 12** [5] 3-9-5 (63) D R McCabe 4/1: -50036: Chsd ldr, led after 2f till 4f out, fdd. 4 30a
892 **THE GIRLS FILLY 44** [2] 3-9-0 (58)(tBL) A Clark 6/1: -23007: Al bhd, effort 4f out, sn btn: tchd 2 22a

6/1, 6 wk abs: tried in blnks: see 615 (1m).
3177} **MIDNIGHT MAX 295** [8] 3-7-12 (42) J Lowe 20/1: 050-8: In tch 6f, sn btn: reapp: lightly rcd & ½ **5a**
modest '99 form: half-brother to a couple of wnrs over 6/9f: with C Dwyer.
8 ran   Time 2m 05.41 (2.61)   (Arashan Ali)   S P C Woods Newmarket.

LEICESTER   MONDAY MAY 29TH   Righthand, Stiff, Galloping Track

Official Going   SOFT. Stalls: Stands Side.

1545   **2.20 LCFC FOX LEISURE HCAP 3YO+ 0-75 (E)**   **6f**   **Soft 93**   **+01 Fast**   **[73]**
£4914 £1512 £756 £378   3 yo rec 9 lb   Raced towards centre

1278 **AT LARGE 16** [14] W J Musson 6-9-10 (69) L Newton 4/1: -06101: 6 b g Night Shift - Lady Donna   **76**
(Dominion): Held up, prog final 2f & led inside last, styd on well, pushed out cl-home: nicely bckd: earlier
scored at Windsor (appr h'cap): rnr-up in '99 (h'cap, first time blnks, J Toller): eff at 5/7f on firm & soft, any
trk: best without blnks: gd weight carrier: in fine form this term, on a fair mark & can go in again.
1237 **BLUSHING GRENADIER 18** [7] S R Bowring 8-8-5 (50)(bl) Dale Gibson 16/1: 166602: 8 ch g Salt Dome 2½ **51**
- La Duse (Junius): Led, rdn/prsd over 1f out, hdd inside last & hmpd nr fin: op 14/1: see 602 (sell h'cap, AW).
1421 **REGAL SONG 7** [6] T J Etherington 4-9-4 (63)(bl) J Weaver 12/1: 03W503: 4 b g Anita's Prince - Song 1½ **61**
Beam (Song): Chsd ldrs, drifted right 1f out, no extra inside last: op 10/1: handles fast, soft & fibresand.
1092 **BOWLERS BOY 27** [11] J J Quinn 7-8-7 (52) S Sanders 3/1 FAV: 5-0W24: Held up, effort 2f out, onepace. ½ **49**
1423 **PERIGEUX 7** [3] 4-9-3 (62) C Carver (3) 10/1: 200-55: Prom, fdd over 1f out: flattered 1423. 4 **51**
1296 **MUTABARI 14** [2] 6-7-12 (42) K Dalgleish (7) 16/1: 400406: Rdn/towards rear, late gains, nrst fin. 1½ **28**
1392 **MISS BANANAS 9** [12] 5-8-0 (45) D Meah (1) 16/1: 150047: Chsd ldr, wknd final 2f: op 14/1: see 872. 2½ **26**
1257 **RUSSIAN ROMEO 17** [1] 5-9-5 (64)(bl) P Mundy (7) 7/1: 223228: Prom 4f: op 8/1: blnks reapplied. 1¼ **24**
1421 **SKYERS FLYER 7** [8] 6-8-1 (46) J Lowe 20/1: 503-09: Nvr on terms: see 1421. shd **24**
1061 **CALDEY ISLAND 28** [10] 3-8-11 (65) G Hind 33/1: 600-00: Al outpcd: 10th: plcd last term (rtd 78, shd **42**
med auct mdn, subs disapp in a visor): eff at 6f on fast grnd & a stiff/undul trk.
1298 **PRESS AHEAD 14** [13] 5-8-13 (58)(vis) S Finnamore (5) 10/1: 550160: Prom 4f: 11th: btr 1068. ½ **34**
1082 **WAFFS FOLLY 27** [9] 5-8-10 (55) S Whitworth 9/1: 034-00: Prom, fdd over 2f out: 12th: tchd 11/1. 1 **29**
3502} **Charlie Sillett 282** [5] 8-9-6 (65) J D Smith 14/1: -- **Sailormaite** [4] 9-8-5 (50) R Fitzpatrick (2) 50/1:
14 ran   Time 1m 15.3 (5.5)   (The Square Table)   W J Musson Newmarket, Suffolk.

1546   **2.55 MICHAEL LANE SELL HCAP 3YO+ 0-60 (G)**   **1m2f**   **Soft 93**   **-13 Slow**   **[58]**
£2390 £683 £341   3 yo rec 14lb   Raced towards centre fnl 3f

1361 **ESPERTO 10** [3] J Pearce 7-8-7 (37) G Bardwell 11/1: /00061: 7 b g Risk Me - Astrid Gilberto (Runnett) **41**
Held up, rcd keenly, smooth prog to lead over 1f out, styd on well, drvn out: op 12/1, no bid: missed '99: plcd
all 3 '98 starts (sell, rtd 54): '97 Nottingham wnr (sell, rtd 53): eff at 10f, stays ⌐2f: acts on firm, soft &
handles fibresand: runs well fresh & handles any trk: enjoys sell grade.
1465 **LUNAR LORD 5** [10] J S Moore 4-8-3 (32)(1ow) G Hind 10/1: 0-0042: 4 b g Elmaamul - Cache (Bustino): ¾ **35**
Prom, led 3f out, rdn/hdd over 1f out, kept on: op 12/1: qck reapp: eff at 10/12f on soft grnd: see 1465.
1300 **UP IN FLAMES 14** [2] Mrs G S Rees 9-8-7 (37)(t) S Sanders 12/1: 000203: 9 b g Nashamaa - Bella Lucia ¾ **38**
(Camden Town): Held up, prog final 2f, kept on onepace for press: acts on firm, heavy & fibresand: well h'capped.
568 **BROUGHTONS MILL 97** [9] W J Musson 5-8-9 (39) L Newton 4/1 FAV: 03-004: Held up, prog/prsd ldrs 2 **38**
over 1f out, sn no extra: op 7/2, 3 mth abs: handles gd/soft & soft grnd: see 418.
1065 **ROCK SCENE 28** [1] 8-9-11 (41) P Doe 6/1: 0/2065: Held up, smooth prog/prsd ldrs 1f out, onepace. hd **40**
1306 **STATE APPROVAL 14** [5] 7-8-8 (38) I Mongan (5) 12/1: 360506: Held up, prog 2f out, held final 1f. 4 **33**
1203 **NORTH ARDAR 21** [9] 10-8-10 (40) N Callan 33/1: -50007: Prom 1m: see 178. 5 **30**
*1101 **LEONIE SAMUAL 26** [14] 9-9-1 (45) O Urbina 6/1: 0-4318: Led/dsptd lead 7f, sn btn: btr 1101 (1m, g/s). ½ **37**
1370 **PIPS BRAVE 10** [13] 4-9-1 (45)(bl) J Weaver 11/2: 602409: Held up, nvr a factor: see 890, 473. 2 **32**
1084 **KELLING HALL 27** [8] 3-8-6 (50) S Whitworth 33/1: 00-00: Led/dsptd lead 1m: 10th: h'cap bow, 1¾ **35**
Ingr 10f trip: rtd 60 on debut in '99 (mdn, no form subs).
1898} **CITY GUILD 353** [12] 4-9-12 (56) L Newman (5) 16/1: 00/0-0: Mid-div, btn 3f out: 11th: op 14/1, jmps 5 **36**
fit (no form): no other sole '99 Flat start: rtd 63 at best from 3 unplcd '98 starts.
1645} **KATIYMANN 364** [4] 8-8-13 (43)(t) M Fenton 12/1: 0001-0: Al rear: 12th: jumps fit (mod form): '99 1½ **22**
Leicester wnr (C/D sell h'cap, rtd 45): missed '98: eff at 10f in sell grade on gd grnd: suited by a t-strap.
581 **Sticks and Stones 95** [6] 8-8-3 (43) A Mackay 12/1: 1722} **Harnage 361** [11] 5-7-11 (27) D Kinsella (7) 40/1:
1203 **Over The Moon 21** [17] 6-8-8 (38) R Fitzpatrick (3) 14/1:
1741} **Gunboat Diplomacy Gb 360** [16] 5-8-3 (33) Dale Gibson 12/1:
1505 **Merchant Prince 3** [18] 4-8-10 (40)(VIS) T G McLaughlin 40/1:
17 ran   Time 2m 13.1 (10.6)   (Mrs Anne V Holman-Chappell)   J Pearce Newmarket, Suffolk.

1547   **3.25 BLUE ARMY HCAP 3YO+ 0-85 (D)**   **1m str**   **Soft 93**   **+02 Fast**   **[82]**
£7897 £2430 £1215 £607   3 yo rec 12lb   Raced towards centre

1113 **PATSY STONE 26** [1] M Kettle 4-8-7 (60)(1ow) S Sanders 5/1: 00-501: 4 b f Jester - Third Dam (Slip **70**
Anchor): Dwelt, held up, rdn/prog to lead over 1f out, sn in command, styd on strongly: '99 scorer at Yarmouth
(mdn h'cap, rtd 64, W Musson): place form in '98 (rtd 64): eff at 6f, suited by 1m on firm & soft, prob any trk.
1279 **TIPPERARY SUNSET 16** [5] D Shaw 6-8-6 (60) K Dalgleish (7) 9/2 CO FAV: 25-002: 6 gr g Red Sunset - 5 **60**
Chapter And Verse (Dancer's Image): Dwelt, held up, prog/led 2f out, rdn/hdd over 1f out & sn held by wnr.
1490 **PARKSIDE 3** [3] W R Muir 4-9-8 (76) R Brisland (5) 9/2 CO FAV: 0-0503: 4 b g Common Grounds - Warg 1½ **74**
(Dancing Brave): Held up, effort over 2f out, no extra: qck reapp: see 1042.
1414 **COMPATRIOT 9** [2] P S Felgate 4-8-12 (66) S Finnamore (5) 7/1: 304-24: Held up, effft 2f out, sn held. hd **63**
1348 **HOH HOH SEVEN 11** [6] 4-9-4 (57)(1ow) N Callan 8/1: 00-035: Held up, hdwy 4f out, held 2f out. ¾ **54**
1375 **GIKO 10** [8] 6-8-3 (57) P Doe 14/1: 0-0006: Cl-up, led over 3f out, wknd 2f out: op 16/1: see 1033. ½ **52**
1506 **PRIDEWAY 3** [7] 4-8-12 (66)(6ex) T G McLaughlin 7/1: 406137: Trkd ldrs 6f: qck reapp: btr 1419 (AW). nk **60**
1375 **UMBRIAN GOLD 10** [4] 4-9-9 (77) R Ffrench 9/2 CO FAV: 10-208: Led 4f, btn 2f out: bckd: btr 1097. 5 **64**
-- **STRACHIN** [9] 6-9-10 (78) J Weaver 14/1: 6213/9: In tch 4f: long Flat abs, Jumps fit, no form, missed 17 **46**
'99: '98 Carlisle wnr (mdn, L Cumani, rtd 88 at best): eff over a stiff 1m, stays 10f: acts on gd/soft & hvy grnd.
9 ran   Time 1m 41.7 (7.3)   (I Fraser, J Butt, B Goldsmith)   M Kettle Blewbury, Oxon.

1548 4.00 FILBERT FOX MED AUCT MDN 3YO (F) **1m str Soft 93 -23 Slow**
£2541 £726 £363 Raced towards centre

1269 **WELCOME ABOARD** 17 [4] J G Given 3-8-9 T G McLaughlin 7/1: -301: 3 ch f Be My Guest - Loreef 75
(Main Reef): Held up, prog 3f out & led over 1f out, in command inside last, styd on well, pushed out: op 13/2:
eff at 1m, 10f+ should suit: acts on soft grnd & a stiff/gall trk: clearly going the right way.
1261 **PRINISHA** 17 [8] H Candy 3-8-9 S Sanders 7/1: 02: 3 gr f Prince Sabo - Nisha (Nishapour): 2½ 71
Held up, keen, rdn/styd on final 2f, not pace of wnr: op 8/1: stays 1m: acts on soft grnd: shld pinch a race.
1266 **MI AMIGO** 17 [5] L M Cumani 3-9-0 M Fenton 5/4 FAV: 0-243: 3 b c Primo Dominie - Third Movement 1¾ 74
(Music Boy): Trkd ldrs, keen, rdn/led over 1f out, sn hdd & no extra inside last: hvly bckd, clr rem, stays 1m.
1263 **SIMULCASTING** 17 [7] L M Cumani 3-9-0 D O'Donohoe 7/2: -5034: Led 7f: op 9/4, lngr 1m trip. 6 67
1085 **PRETENDING** 27 [9] 3-9-0 I Mongan (5) 16/1: 60-065: Dwelt/held up, nvr able to chall: see 1085. 3½ 62$
1188 **NATIONAL PRINCESS** 22 [1] 3-8-9 D McGaffin (7) 11/2: 06: Chsd ldr 4f: btr 1188 (firm). 2 54
-- **ROSE TINA** [6] 3-8-9 S Carson (5) 33/1: 7: Held up, al towards rear: debut, with E Wheeler. 1½ 52
-- **HANOI** [3] 3-8-9 (BL) J Lowe 33/1: 8: Slowly away, al rear: blnks: debut, with Dr J D Scargill. 20 30
4614} **BENTYHEATH LANE** 205 [10] 3-9-0 S Whitworth 40/1: 00-9: Prom 4f: reapp, rtd 68 from 2 '99 starts 5 28
(auct mdn): half-brother to a 12f wnr.
1266 **MR CHRISBI** 17 [2] 3-9-0 L Newton 40/1: 00: Bhd halfway: 10th: lngr 1m trip, no form. *dist* 0
10 ran Time 1m 43.7 (9.3) (J W Rowles) J G Given Willoughton, Lincs.

1549 4.30 CUP WINNERS CLAIMER 2YO (F) **5f Soft 93 -03 Slow**
£2257 £645 £322 Raced towards centre

*1443 **NAUGHTY KNIGHT** 6 [1] G B Balding 2-8-3 L Newman (5) 2/1: -05011: 2 ch c King's Signet - Maid Of 65
Mischief (Be My Chief): Chsd ldrs, rdn/prog & hung right over 1f out, led inside last & styd on well, going away:
qck reapp: well bckd: recent Beverley wnr (sell): eff at 5f, 6f suit: acts on gd & soft, stiff/gall trk.
1302 **AMELIA** 14 [5] J Cullinan 2-8-2 Joanna Badger (7) 4/1: 42: 2 b f General Monash - Rose Tint (Salse) 1¼ 61
Handy, led halfway, rdn/hdd inside last & no extra: clr of rem: op 7/2: handles soft: see 1302.
*1476 **TIME MAITE** 4 [4] M W Easterby 2-9-3 G Parkin 13/8 FAV: 4313: 2 b c Komaite - Martini Time 5 66
(Ardoon): Rdn/outpcd early, effort over 2f out, held final 1f: nicely bckd, qck reapp: see 1476 (6f, made most, clmr).
1437 **NINE TO FIVE** 7 [2] R Brotherton 2-8-10 G Bardwell 100/30: 113344: Hmpd start, led 3f, sn btn: op 3/1. 14 39
1304 **JEWELLERY BOX** 14 [3] 2-7-12 G Baker (7) 20/1: 505: Chsd ldrs, hung right/btn 2f out: see 1059. 6 18
5 ran Time 1m 03.1 (4.8) (D F Lockyer, C A Parry, G B Balding) G B Balding Fyfield, Hants.

1550 5.05 CALKE ABBEY MED AUCT MDN 2YO (F) **5f Soft 93 -07 Slow**
£2488 £711 £355 Raced centre - stands side

1418 **CHURCH MICE** 7 [3] M L W Bell 2-8-9 (vis) M Fenton 6/4 FAV: 2421: 2 br f Petardia - Negria 75
(Al Hareb): Held up, rdn/prog final 2f, led inside last, drifted right, styd on well, rdn out: eff at 5f, 6f
should suit: acts on firm, soft & fibresand: handles a sharp or stiff/gall trk: eff in a visor.
-- **MISS DOMUCH** [1] R Hannon 2-8-9 R Smith (5) 5/1: 2: 2 ch f Definite Article - Eliza Orzeszkowa 2½ 69
(Polish Patriot): Chsd ldrs, rdn/prog on onepace final 2f: op 9/2: Mar foal, cost 5,500 Irish gns, a first foal:
dam a daughter of a smart juv, plcd herself as a 3yo at 7f: sire proved best at 10/12f: acts on soft grnd.
-- **CYRAZY** [6] J G Given 2-8-9 M McLaughlin 8/1: 3: 2 b f Cyrano de Bergerac - Hazy Kay hd 68
(Treasure Kay): Led after 1f, hung right/clr over 1f out, wknd & hdd in last: op 7/1: Jan foal, cost 4,500 gns:
half-sister to a 5f juv wnr: dam a mdn, sire a smart juv/sprinter: handles soft grnd, clr of rem here.
-- **EAGLES CACHE** [7] A Berry 2-9-0 S Sanders 4/1: 4: Chsd ldrs, btn 2f out: op 5/2: Eagle Eyed colt, 4 65
Jan foal, cost 10,000 gns: half-brother to a mid-dist wnr, dam modest: stay further in time.
1408 **SPRINGWOOD JASMIN** 9 [5] 2-8-9 (t) R Fitzpatrick (3) 25/1: 05: Led 1f, btn 2f out: jockey given 3-day 1¾ 57
ban for using whip with excessive force: dropped to 5f, bhd on debut prev.
1095 **CHEVENING LODGE** 27 [4] 2-9-0 N Callan 4/1: 46: Chsd ldrs, btn 2f out: op 3/1: see 1095. 5 54
6 ran Time 1m 03.3 (5.0) (R P B Michaelson) M L W Bell Newmarket, Suffolk.

1551 5.35 FILBERT APPR HCAP 4YO+ 0-65 (F) **1m3f183y Soft 93 -36 Slow** **[64]**
£2530 £723 £361 Raced stands side fnl 4f

1100 **JOLI FLYERS** 27 [8] R J Hodges 6-8-1 (37) D Kinsella (5) 9/1: 20-001: 6 gr g Joli Wasfi - Hagen's 38
Bargain (Mount Hagen): Dictated pace in front, held on well inside last, rdn out: op 7/1: plcd in 2m/2m1f novs
this winter (rtd 108h, soft): '99 rnr-up on the level (rtd 46, appr h'cap, V Soane): '98 Kempton wnr (h'cap, rtd
49): loves to force the pace at 12/14f, poss stays 2m: acts on gd/soft & soft grnd, any trk: nicely h'capped.
2880} **LEGEND** 311 [3] R Hannon 4-10-0 (64) R Smith 7/1: 3/34-2: 4 b f Belmez - Once Upon A Time (Teenoso):1 63
Held up, rdn/chsd wnr 2f out, kept on, not able to chall: op 6/1, reapp: top weight: unplcd last term for
I A Balding, rtd 57, 5 rnr h'cap: plcd in a mdn in '98 (rtd 80, Lord Huntingdon): stays 12f, handles gd/soft & soft.
1096 **PEKAY** 27 [7] B Smart 7-9-8 (58) (bl) P Shea (3) 4/1: /00353: 7 b g Puissance - K-Sera (Lord Gayle): 2 55
Held up, hdwy 3f out, edged right/onepace over 1f out: see 1096, 682.
1332 **ASHLEIGH BAKER** 12 [2] M Johnston 5-8-13 (49) K Dalgleish (3) 3/1: 053-64: Chsd wnr, rdn/btn 2f out. 3 43
1209 **FANDANGO DREAM** 20 [4] 4-7-12 (34) G Baker (3) 9/1: 00-045: Held up, rdn 4f out, mod late gains. 13¼ 27
1389 **IRISH CREAM** 9 [1] 4-7-10 (32)(vis)(1oh) D Glennon (3) 11/4 FAV: 010626: Chsd wnr halfway, hung ¾ 24
right/wknd final 2f: bckd, op 7/2: btr 1389, 668 (AW).
*1361 **MAJOR ATTRACTION** 10 [5] 5-8-2 (38) Joanna Badger (3) 6/1: 600017: Dwelt, held up, stumbled & 2½ 28
lost momentum 5f out, sn no impress: btr 1361 (fast).
1276 **NAILER** 16 [6] 4-9-0 (50) S Finnamore 25/1: 00-608: Held up, al bhd: see 832 (mdn, C/D). 11 32
8 ran Time 2m 43.6 (15.3) (Joli Racing) R J Hodges Charlton Adam, Somerset.

CHEPSTOW

MONDAY MAY 29TH   Lefthand, Undulating, Galloping Track

Official Going   HEAVY (SOFT in places). Stalls: Str Crse - Stands Side; Rnd Crse - Inside.

1552

2.30 ST MELLONS CLASS STKS 3YO+ 0-75 (D)   1m str   Heavy 132   -09 Slow
£3786   £1165   £582   £291   3yo rec 13lb

*1053 **FRENCH HORN** 30 [5] M J Ryan 3-8-10 N Esler (7) 8/15 FAV: 1-0311: 3 b g Fraam - Runcina (Runnett) **85**
Held up, imprvd 4f out, led bef 2f out, sn clr, v easily: hvly bckd: last month won at Doncaster (h'cap): '99
Leicester wnr (nurs, rtd 69): eff at 7f/1m, stays 9f: acts on gd/soft & hvy, poss firm, any trk: imprvg mud-lark.

4479} **BARABASCHI** 220 [3] J H M Gosden 4-9-6 J Fortune 11/2: 0322-2: 4 b g Elmaamul - Hills' Presidium 8 **70**
(Presidium) Led till appr final 2f, easily outpcd: op 4/1 on reapp: 4 times rnr-up in '99 for A Foster (auct
mdn, rtd 78): rtd 82 in '98: eff at 7f, handles fast & hvy grnd, without blnks.

1259 **MARMADUKE** 17 [1] Miss Gay Kelleway 4-9-6 D Harrison 12/1: 000-03: 4 ch g Perugino - Sympathy 2 **67**
(Precocious) Handy, effort 3f out, no impression: op 10/1: see 1259.

1375 **TAVERNER SOCIETY** 10 [2] M S Saunders 5-9-6 R Hughes 14/1: 003-04: Chsd ldrs, ch 3f out, sn btn: 5 **60**
tchd 20/1, stiffish task: well btn in '99 (tried t-strap & blnks): plcd in '98 (stks, rtd 104, R Armstrong): '97
Kempton wnr (mdn, rtd 92): eff at 1m/10f, tried 12f: acts on firm & gd/soft grnd, sharp or gall trk.

1012 **MONDURU** 35 [4] 3-8-8 Martin Dwyer 11/2: 0-035: Prom till appr halfway: op 4/1: btr 1012 (7f, sft) 2½ **58**
5 ran   Time 1m 43.2 (11.3)   (The French Horn Hotel Ltd Sonning)   M J Ryan Newmarket

1553

3.00 ST WEONARDS SELLER 2YO (F)   6f   Heavy 132   -46 Slow
£2194   £627   £313

1443 **SAND BANKES** 6 [3] W G M Turner 2-8-11 (VIS) P Fitzsimons (5) 3/1: 2061: 2 ch c Efisio - Isabella **70**
Sharp (Sharpo) Trkd ldrs, led halfway, pshd out, rdy: no bid, slow time, qck reapp: 5,000 gns Jan foal, dam
a sprinter, sire 6f/1m performer: apprec step up to 6f: acts on fibresand & hvy: sharpened up by visor.

1413 **DISTANT DAWN** 9 [1] B R Millman 2-8-6 D Harrison 6/1: 402: 2 b f Petong - Turbo Rose (Taufan) 4 **57$**
Keen, chsd ldrs, prsd wnr 3f out till 2f out: op 5/1: down in grade, poss handles hvy grnd.

-- **IMMACULATE CHARLIE** [2] A T Murphy 2-8-6 A McGlone 7/1: 3: 2 ch f Rich Charlie - Miner's Society 4 **49**
(Miners Lamp) Detached till ran on fnl 1½f: op 10/1 on debut: May foal, half-sister to a pt-to-pt wnr.

-- **MISSING A BIT** [5] J A Osborne 2-8-11 J Fortune 4/1: 4: Led till halfway, gradually wknd: debut: 1½ **51**
IR 6,000gns Petorius Jan 1st foal, sire a sprinter.

1396 **PRESENTOFAROSE** 9 [4] 2-8-7(1ow) R Hughes 7/4 FAV: 55: Handy till halfway: better expected. 2½ **42**
5 ran   Time 1m 19.5 (10.7)   (T Lightbowne)   W G M Turner Corton Denham, Somerset.

1554

3.30 ST ARVANS MDN 3YO (D)   1m4f23y   Heavy 132   -06 Slow
£3818   £1175   £587   £293

1017 **WAFFIGG** 35 [3] M A Jarvis 3-9-0 M Tebbutt 5/4 FAV: 51: 3 b c Rainbow Quest - Celtic Ring (Welsh **86**
Pageant) Nvr far away, led going well appr final 3f, cmftbly: hvly bckd tho' op 4/5: half-brother to French
Derby wnr Celtic Swing: eff at 12f, shld get further: acts on hvy grnd & an undul trk: imprvg, potentially useful.

-- **KADOUN** [1] L M Cumani 3-9-0 G Sparkes (7) 25/1: 2: 3 b c Doyoun - Kumta (Priolo) 1¾ **81**
Unruly start & rear, rdn & prog 2f out, styd on for 2nd but flattered by idling wnr: debut: bred to apprec
mid-dist & clearly stays a gall/undul 12f on hvy grnd: had the rest covered, should find similar.

-- **FRANGY** [5] L M Cumani 3-8-9 D Harrison 8/1: 3: 3 b f Sadler's Wells - Fern (Shirley Heights) 3 **73**
Chsd ldrs, outpcd fnl 4f, late rally: op 5/1, shorter-priced stablemate of rnr-up, clr rem: half-sister
to mid-dist wnrs: handles hvy grnd & looks capable of better.

1157 **KUWAIT MILLENNIUM** 23 [4] H R A Cecil 3-9-0 T Quinn 9/2: 54: Prom, led ent str till bef 3f out, fdd. 8 **71**
951 **CAPA** 41 [6] 3-9-0 R Hughes 6/4: 22-45: Led till over 4f out, btn appr final 2f: well bckd from 5/2, ¾ **70**
reportedly choked after 6 wk abs: first try on hvy, see 951.

1344 **REGAL CHARM** 11 [2] 3-8-9 J Fortune 20/1: 0-06: Nvr in it, btn 5f out & eased right down: dist **0**
jockey reported the filly was never travelling, Stewards ordered a routine test.
6 ran   Time 2m 47.7 (16.6)   (Sheikh Ahmed Al Maktoum)   M A Jarvis Newmarket

1555

4.05 ST ATHAN FILLIES HCAP 3YO+ 0-80 (D)   1m4f23y   Heavy 132   -26 Slow   [77]
£7150   £2200   £1100   £550   3 yo rec 17lb

1031 **APRIL STOCK** 33 [4] G A Butler 5-9-10 (73)(t) R Hughes 10/11 FAV: 410-51: 5 ch m Beveled - Stockline **80**
(Capricorn Line) Waited with, stalked ldr on bit 4f out, led below dist, easily: well bckd: '99 wnr at
Folkestone (fill mdn, Miss G Kelleway) & Windsor (stks, rtd 72): plcd sev times in '98 (rtd 76): eff at 12f,
stays 2m: goes on gd & hvy grnd, any trk: probably goes best with t-strap now.

*1091 **SURE QUEST** 27 [3] D W P Arbuthnot 5-8-10 (59) T Quinn 7/4: 341112: 5 b m Sure Blade - Eagle's 7 **59**
Quest (Legal Eagle) Pld hard, in tch, hdwy to lead 5f out, und press & hdd ent final 1f, eased fnl 100y: bckd,
clr rem: lost nothing attempting a 4-timer on this testing grnd: goes on firm, gd, hvy & fibresand: tough.

1344 **SIONED LYN** 11 [2] D Burchell 3-7-11 (63)(1ow)(3oh) C Cogan (0) 10/1: 2003: 3 b f Perpendicular - 14 **53**
Lady Spider (Ring Spider) Rcd in 2nd till halfway, fdd 4f out: op 14/1, h'cap dbut: see 814 (10f, sft).

1086 **SHARP SPICE** 27 [1] D J Coakley 4-8-13 (62) D Harrison 5/1: 34-444: Led till 5f out, wknd: unsuited 17 **39**
by step up to 12f with forcing tactics? see 943.
4 ran   Time 2m 50.0 (18.9)   (Stock Hill Racing)   G A Butler Blewbury, Oxon.

1556

4.35 ST BRIAVELS MDN 3YO+ (D)   1m str   Heavy 132   +02 Fast
£4013   £1235   £617   £308   3 yo rec 12lb

4606} **DIXIELAKE** 206 [1] H Candy 3-8-7 C Rutter 8/1: 0-1: 3 b f Lake Coniston - Rathvindon (Realm) **83**
Dwelt, grad imprvd & led bef fnl 1f, pshd out: fair time, reapp: mid-div sole '98 start (mdn, rtd 70): half-sister
to wnrs up to 11f, dam/sire sprinters: apprec step up to 1m: acts on hvy grnd, gall/undul trk: on the upgrade.

-- **CROWN LODGE** [3] L M Cumani 3-8-7 G Sparkes (7) 10/1: 2: 3 ch f Grand Lodge - Itqan (Sadler's nk **82**
Wells) Slow away, chsd ldrs halfway, led 2½f out till bef dist, kept on but held: op 14/1, clr rem on debut:
half-sister to a decent miler, dam suited by soft grnd: eff at 1m on hvy grnd: should improve & find similar.

1188 **JOONDEY** 22 [9] M A Jarvis 3-8-12 M Tebbutt 5/1: 03: 3 b c Pursuit Of Love - Blueberry Walk 6 **78**
(Green Desert) Slowly into stride, bhd, styd on under minimal press final 2f to go 3rd, nvr nr ldrs: op 6/1:

513

prob handled this hvy grnd & looks capable of better, most likely when h'capped.

1344	WILD NETTLE 11 [8] J C Fox 6-9-5 P Fitzsimons (5) 50/1: -00004: Prom, no extra appr fnl 2f: flattered:		7	59$

-- LION OF JUDAH [2] 3-8-12 D Harrison 6/4 FAV: 5: Cl-up, led after 3f till 2½f out, fdd: nicely bckd 1½ 62
stablemate of rnr-up, tchd 9/4 on debut: Caerleon half-brother to a high class 1m/12f performer in Japan.

1159 WATHBAT MUJTAHID 23 [7] 3-8-12 J Fortune 5/2: 032-56: Pulled hard prom, lost place 3f out. 10 52
1428 TASSO DANCER 7 [5] 4-9-5 R Havlin 33/1: 0/07: Led briefly after 2f, wknd qckly appr fnl 3f: no form. 3½ 43
1436 LEGAL TENDER 7 [4] 3-8-12 C Cogan (5) 50/1: 008: Early ldr, bhd final 4f: no form 2 45
1099 VALDERO 27 [6] 3-8-12 Martin Dwyer 6/1: -049: In tch 4f: tchd 8/1, now qual for h'caps. ½ 44

9 ran   Time 1m 42.3 (10.4)   (C G P Wyatt)   H Candy Wantage, Oxon.

1557   **5.10 ST BRIDES FILLIES HCAP 3YO+ 0-80 (D)   6f   Heavy 132   +04 Fast**   **[69]**
£3883   £1195   £597   £298   3 yo rec 9 lb

1542 TRUMP STREET 2 [1] S G Knight 4-8-7 (48) Jonjo Fowle (7) 14/1: 002501: 4 b f First Trump - Pepeke 53
(Mummy's Pet) Mid-div, gd prog to lead appr fnl 2f, rdn out: fair time, 1st win, ran 48hrs ago: plcd in '99 (auct
mdn, rtd 59, N Graham): mdn rnr-up in '98 (rtd 89): eff at 6/7.5f: acts on firm & hvy, sharp or gall/undul trks.
*1138 DANCING EMPRESS 25 [7] M A Jarvis 3-9-10 (74) P M Quinn (5) 7/2: 21-012: 3 b f Emperor Jones - ½ 78
Music Khan (Music Boy) Waited with, went after wnr appr fnl 1f, styd on: tchd 9/1, clr rem: in-form, see 1138 (AW).
1391 PALO BLANCO 9 [3] Andrew Reid 9-8-10 (53) M Henry 5/1: 342233: 9 b m Precocious - Linpac Mapleleaf 5 47
(Dominion) Mid-div, effort & hdwy 3f out, no extra 2f out: op 7/1: grnd prob softer than she wants: see 680.
1082 GRACE 27 [2] J M Bradley 6-8-6 (47) P Fitzsimons (5) 11/4 FAV: -44664: Dwelt, prom till 2f out. 4 33
1097 SILK DAISY 27 [8] 4-9-8 (63) A McGlone 9/2: 023-45: Nvr trbled ldrs: unsuited by drop to 6f on hvy? 2½ 45
-- WYN [6] 5-8-6 (47) Martin Dwyer 33/1: 6060/6: Prom till 3f out: 12 wk jmps abs (moderate): 2 year 1½ 26
Flat abs, '98 rnr-up for C Dwyer (auct mdn, rtd 60, prob flattered): eff at 6f on gd grnd, tried 1m: with M Usher.
1543 STRATS QUEST 2 [5] 6-8-9 (50) T Quinn 9/2: 050057: In tch till appr fnl 2f: too sn after 1543? hd 29
1266 QUEENSMEAD 17 [4] 3-8-10 (60) J Fortune 14/1: 25-008: Led till appr final 2f, sn lost place. 6 29

8 ran   Time 1m 16.5 (7.7)   (Richard Withers)   S G Knight West Hatch, Somerset.

Official Going GOOD/SOFT (SOFT in places). Stalls: Str - Stands Side; 14f - Centre; Round - Inside.

1558   **2.15 YARM NOV AUCT STKS 2YO (E)   5f   Good/Soft 76   +00 Fast**
£2847   £876   £438   £219 Field raced centre

1221 RAGAMUFFIN 19 [3] T D Easterby 2-8-8 K Darley 9/2: -4621: 2 ch c Prince Sabo - Valldemosa (Music Boy) 85
Keen, prom, rdn 2f out, kept on over 1f out to lead nr last, rdn out: cost 10,000 gns: dam multiple 5f
scorer: v eff at 5f on gd/firm, gd/soft & a sharp or gall trk: improving.
1385 MUJA FAREWELL 9 [8] T D Barron 2-8-5 W Supple 9/4: 122: 2 ch f Mujtahid - Highland Rhapsody nk 81
(Kris) Cl-up, led over 2f out, rdn & collared nr last, just btn: nicely bckd, scope, clr rem: going the right way.
*1131 PROMISED 25 [1] J A Glover 2-8-9 D Mernagh (3) 6/4 FAV: 13: 2 b f Petardia - Where's The Money 3 78
(Lochnager) Cl-up, ev ch well over 1f out, one-paced: well bckd & prob ran to form of 1131 (mdn auct).
*1294 BEVERLEY MACCA 14 [6] A Berry 2-8-11 G Carter 7/1: 22114: Led till halfway, wknd dist: been busy. ¾ 78
-- TEFI [7] 2-8-8 R Winston 33/1: 5: Slow away, bhd, some late gains: debut: Apr foal, cost 7,200gns: 5 65
dam 12f wnr: sure to relish a step up to 6f+ : stable-mate of wnr & will improve.
-- SPUR OF GOLD [9] 2-8-3 G Duffield 33/1: 6: In tch, bhd after 2f: ndd race on debut, tall: ½ 59
Apr 1st foal, cost IR 9,500gns: with J Wainwright.
-- ITIS ITIS [5] 2-8-8 P Fessey 40/1: 7: Nvr a factor: burly, stable-mate of wnr: Apr foal, cost IR 8,400gns. 5 54
730 AKATIB 65 [2] 2-8-3 J Fanning 66/1: -08: Nvr a factor: ndd race after abs: Apr 1st foal, 1½ 47
cost 10,000gns: bred to need 6/7f in time: with N Tinkler.
-- CATALAN BAY [4] 2-7-13 T Williams 33/1: 9: In tch, hung badly right 2f out & sn btn: scope, 5 33
ndd debut: Feb foal, cost 5,200 gns: full sister to a sprint wnr, dam 5/6f juv scorer: with R Bastiman.

9 ran   Time 1m 0.3 (3.8)   (Mrs Jennifer E Pallister)   T D Easterby Great Habton, N Yorks

---

1559   **2.45 BANK HOLIDAY SELLER 3-5YO (F)   7f str   Good/Firm 76   +00 Fast**
£2499   £714   £357   3 yo rec 11lb Field raced centre

1351 MAMMAS BOY 10 [16] A Berry 5-9-7 G Carter 6/1: 0-0041: 5 b g Rock City - Henpot (Alzao) 55
Waited with, hdwy 2f out, kept on for press nr last to get up cl-home: bt in for 4,000 gns: '99 scorer at Thirsk
(sell) & Musselburgh (clmr, rtd 62): '98 Doncaster wnr (mdn h'cap) & Sandown (clmr, rtd 72): eff at 5f, suited by
7f now on firm or hvy & on any trk: best without blnks & can carry big weights: enjoys sell/clmg company, tough.
1351 OAKWELL ACE 15 [15] J A Glover 4-9-2 K Darley 4/1: -50052: 4 b f Clantime - Fardella (Molvedo) shd 49$
Waited with, eff 2f out, styd on to chall nr last, just held: gd run: best off in sell h'caps: see 872.
1360 MEHMAAS 10 [19] R E Barr 4-9-7 (vis) G Duffield 10/1: 504-03: 4 b g Distant Relative - Guest 1¼ 52
List (Be My Guest) Cl-up, led over 2f out till ins last & no extra, not btn far: dropped in grade, see 1360.
1508 SIR JACK 3 [3] D Nicholls 4-9-7 F Norton 11/4 FAV: -00024: Prom, ev ch over 1f out, onepace: qk reapp. 1 50
1506 LADY TILLY 3 [8] 3-8-5 N Kennedy 33/1: 560-05: Chsd ldrs, rdn & onepace over 1f out: qk 2 42
reapp: plcd once in '99 (rtd 65$): prob stays 7f on gd/soft.
1357 JACKERIN 10 [17] 5-9-7 (bl) W Supple 13/2: 554406: Keen bhd, eff over 1f out, no impress: needs 5/6f. 4 40
1132 BY THE GLASS 25 [14] 4-9-7 Kim Tinkler 20/1: 600-67: Nvr a factor: see 1132. ½ 39$
1351 UNMASKED 10 [13] 4-9-2 Dawn Rankin (7) 25/1: -00008: Bhd, mod late gains: see 798. nk 33$
1132 SILVER BULLET 5 [1] 4-9-7 (VIS) F Lynch 66/1: 600-09: In tch, bhd 2f out: mod form. ½ 37$
790 CZAR WARS 60 [12] 5-9-7 P Goode (3) 25/1: 44-000: Al bhd: fin 10th, 2 month abs. 4 31
4481} SUSY WELLS 219 [5] 5-9-2 D Mernagh (3) 20/1: 0560-0: Nvr a factor: 11th on reapp: plcd in '99 nk 25
(rtd 55$ at best): stays 1m on firm & soft: has tried blnks.
1422 CHILLIAN 7 [9] 4-9-7 T Williams 33/1: 00-050: In tch, btn 2f out: 12th, see 674. 2 27
1434 DENTON LADY 7 [2] 3-8-5 (bl) O Pears 9/1: 600030: Cl-up, wknd over 2f out: 13th, btr 1434 (gd/firm). 1 20
1351 CLADANTOM 10 [11] 4-9-2 A Culhane 50/1: -00000: Led till over 2f out, wknd: fin last, blnks. 0

1305 Ra Ra Rasputin 14 [10] (bl) Iona Wands(5): 1351 So Willing 10 [4] 4-9-7 (bl) J Fanning 14/1:
1205 Unfortunate 21 [6] 3-8-5 V Halliday 25/1:   1519 Bayard Lady 2 [7] 4-9-2 (t) K Hodgson 66/1:
1132 Just Good Friends 25 [18] 3-8-10 R Winston 20/1:

19 ran Time 1m 27.1 (5.3) (G Tiribocchi) A Berry Cockerham, Lancs

1560 **3.20 CARLSBERG HCAP 3YO 0-80 (D) 1m3f Good/Soft 76 -12 Slow [86]**
£4914 £1512 £756 £378

1448 **RHODAMINE 6** [4] J L Eyre 3-8-6 (64) F Norton 9/2: 004261: 3 b c Mukaddamah - Persian Empress (Persian Bold) Dwelt, sn in tch, hdwy for press to lead over 1f out, kept on gamely: '99 scorer at Newcastle (auct mdn, rtd 73): eff at 1m, stays 11f on firm, gd/soft & likes a gall trk. **70**
1255 **WASEEM 17** [3] M Johnston 3-8-9 (67) J Fanning 12/1: -1002: 3 ch c Polar Falcon - Astolat (Rusticaro) Cl-up, hdwy trav best to chall over 2f out, rdn & kept on same pace over 1f out, just held: stays 10f: handles fibresand & gd/soft: shld win again, see 493. *nk* **72**
1446 **RUNNING TIMES 6** [2] T D Easterby 3-8-2 (60) W Supple 5/1: 503543: 3 b c Brocco - Concert Peace (Hold Your Peace) In tch, rdn & sltly outpcd over 2f out, kept on again fnl 1f: see 1446, 1071 (1st time blnks). *2½* **61**
1199 **FAIT LE JOJO 21** [7] S P C Woods 3-9-7 (79) G Duffield 3/1: 13-454: Led 4f out till well over 1f out, no extra: top weight: see 1199, 747 (gd/firm). *1¾* **78**
4495} **COUNT ON THUNDER 217** [6] 3-8-4 (62) G Carter 6/1: 000-5: In tch, btn 2f out: better for race, op 4/1: some promise in 3 unplcd juv starts (rtd 76 at best): shld apprec mid-dists. *5* **55**
*1434 **YENALED 7** [1] 3-8-7 (65)(6ex) A Culhane 11/4 FAV: 63-316: Waited with, eff 2f out, sn btn: well bckd: longer trip on softer grnd: btr 1434 (1m, gd/firm). *1¾* **55**
1434 **COMEX FLYER 7** [8] 3-7-13 (57) N Kennedy 33/1: 6-4067: Keen in tch, eff over 3f out, wknd 2f out. *3* **44**
3654} **MANX SHADOW 274** [5] 3-7-10 (54)(9oh) J Bramhill 66/1: 0050-8: Led till 4f out, wknd: v burly, poor. *dist* **0**
8 ran Time 2m 25.2 (9.7) (M Gleason) J L Eyre Sutton Bank, N Yorks

1561 **3.55 ZETLAND GOLD CUP HCAP 3YO+ 0-105 (B) 1m2f Good/Soft 76 +06 Fast [100]**
£11066 £3405 £1702 £851 3 yo rec 14lb

1291 **NOBELIST 14** [3] C E Brittain 5-9-9 (95) T E Durcan 14/1: 234/61: 5 b g Bering - Noble Peregrine (Lomond) Cl-up, gd hdwy to lead over 1f out, styd on strongly, shade cosily: gd time: ex-French, 3rd in a Gr 3 back in '98 (rtd 101, with A Fabre): eff at 1m, apprec step up to 10f & further could suit: acts on gd & soft grnd: lightly raced & useful, shld land another nice prize. **101**
1103 **STAR DYNASTY 26** [4] E A L Dunlop 3-7-10 (82) F Norton 4/1: 4-322: 3 b c Bering - Siwaayib (Green Desert) Keen, hld up, eff for press over 2f out, sltly short of room well over 1f out but kept on to chase wnr ins last: jockey received a 3 day irresponsible riding ban, scope: fine run from this 3yo, must win, poss at 12f. *1* **87**
*1307 **INCH PERFECT 13** [12] R A Fahey 5-8-7 (79) K Darley 15/8 FAV: 1-1313: 5 b g Inchinor - Scarlet Veil (Tyrnavos) Cl-up trav well, led 2f out, hdd over 1f out, onepace, nicely bckd: prob best coming late. *2½* **80**
1528 **ROBZELDA 2** [6] K A Ryan 4-8-3 (75) Iona Wands (5) 33/1: -32564: Prom, chall over 2f out, onepace. *1¼* **74**
1170 **ANOTHER TIME 23** [8] 8-8-11 (83) R Mullen 25/1: 000-05: Waited with, brief eff over 2f out, onepace: just better for race: could rate higher on a sounder surface: see 1170. *½* **81**
1279 **COLWAY RITZ 16** [5] 6-8-4 (76) T Williams 9/1: 00-036: In tch, rdn over 2f out, no impress: sure to go closer back on fast grnd: likes Redcar, see 1279. *1½* **72**
1373 **INTENSITY 10** [7] 4-8-6 (78) J Fanning 10/1: 01-537: Waited with, rdn 2f out, onepace: do better. *nk* **74**
1279 **PENTAGON LAD 16** [10] 4-7-11 (69) P Fessey 20/1: -05148: Led 4f out till 2f out: btr 1279 (1m). *1¾* **63**
1490 **SCENE 3** [1] 5-8-4 (76) D Mernagh (3) 16/1: 100009: Chsd ldrs, wkng when badly hmpd 2f out. *nk* **69**
1113 **ROLLER 26** [2] 4-8-5 (77) G Duffield 9/1: 321220: Led till 4f out, no extra: 10th, better than this at 1m. *1¼* **68**
1342 **J R STEVENSON 11** [9] 4-9-11 (97) O Pears 25/1: 50-000: Nvr a factor: 11th: see 1170. *¾* **87**
1307 **CELESTIAL WELCOME 13** [13] 5-8-11 (83) A Culhane 8/1: 6-6100: Hld up, rdn 3f out, sn btn: 12th. *2½* **69**
977 **SECRETS OUT 40** [14] 4-8-10 (82) W Supple 25/1: 100-50: In tch, wknd 3f out: last, abs. *28* **28**
13 ran Time 2m 09.3 (7) (H E Sheikh Rashid Al Maktoum) C E Brittain Newmarket

1562 **4.30 STOKESLEY MED AUCT MDN 3YO (E) 6f Good/Soft 76 -06 Slow**
£2800 £800 £400

1500 **GREY COSSACK 3** [3] M Brittain 3-9-0 D Mernagh (3) 3/1: 4-6341: 3 gr g Kasakov - Royal Rebeka (Grey Desire) Cl-up, hdwy to lead 1f out, kept on, rdn out: quick reapp: eff at 6f on gd/soft: tried visor. **78**
1266 **PRETRAIL 17** [8] A C Stewart 3-9-0 A McCarthy (3) 3/1: 02-02: 3 b c Catrail - Pretty Lady (High Top) Cl-up, eff & switched left over 1f out, kept on same pace ins last: stocky, still just better for race. *1¾* **75**
1351 **CELEBRE BLU 10** [7] K A Ryan 3-9-0 F Lynch 10/1: 633: 3 b g Suave Dancer - Taufan Blu (Taufan) Waited with, short of room 3f out till well over 1f out, kept on well ins last: bckd from 25/1: improved as market suggested back at 6f, further shld suit: acts on gd/soft: not given a hard time & can win a race. *½* **74**
1427 **OUR FRED 7** [4] T G Mills 3-9-0 T Williams 13/8 FAV: 433-44: Cl-up, eff over 1f out, sn no extra: clr rem. *1¾* **71**
-- **QUEEN MOLLY** [2] 3-8-9 (t) F Norton 7/1: 5: Set pace till over 1f out, wknd: op 9/2: speedily bred. *5* **56**
1105 **MIMANDI 26** [5] 3-8-9 G Duffield 50/1: 00-06: Al bhd. *1¾* **52**
696 **SHARP SMOKE 70** [6] 3-8-9 A Culhane 50/1: 4-67: Cl-up, wknd over 1f out: abs, see 696. *24* **4**
-- **REDS DESIRE** [1] 3-9-0 V Halliday 25/1: 8: Al bhd on debut: with Miss J Craze. *1¾* **5**
8 ran Time 1m 13.8 (4.9) (Robert E Cook) M Brittain Warthill, N Yorks

1563 **5.00 ROSE GARDEN HCAP 3YO+ 0-70 (E) 1m6f Good/Soft 76 -20 Slow [68]**
£3672 £1130 £565 £282 3 yo rec 20lb

1478 **HIGHFIELD FIZZ 4** [7] C W Fairhurst 8-7-11 (37)(1ow)(2oh) T Williams 5/1: 00P001: 8 b m Efisio - Jendor (Condorcet) Waited with, eff to lead 2f out, sn rdn clr: quick reapp, '99 wnr at Musselburgh (h'cap, rtd 47): '98 scorer at Pontefract & Musselburgh (rtd 53): eff at 14f, stays 2m2f on firm or hvy & on any trk, loves Musselburgh. **42**
1276 **SIMPLE IDEALS 16** [2] Don Enrico Incisa 6-8-6 (46) Kim Tinkler 7/2: 133-02: 6 b g Woodman - Comfort And Style (Be My Guest) In tch, eff over 2f out, sn onepace: '99 scorer at Haydock, Ayr & Redcar (h'caps, rtd 50): unplcd for N Tinkler in '99: stays 15f on firm, soft & on any trk, likes a gall one: gd reapp. *7* **44**
1039 **BEST PORT 31** [8] J Parkes 4-7-10 (36)(14oh) D Mernagh (0) 66/1: 06-003: 3 b g Be My Guest - Portree (Slip Anchor) Cl-up, eff to chall 2f out, onepace: boiled over in padd: treat rating with caution. *3½* **30$**
1194 **PRINCE NICHOLAS 22** [1] K W Hogg 5-9-7 (61) J Bramhill 5/1: 224404: Led till 3f out, no extra: bckd. *nk* **55**
1411 **MENTAL PRESSURE 9** [3] 7-9-0 (54) A Culhane 13/8 FAV: 00/325: Led till 3f out, wknd: btr 1411. *3* **45**
1194 **POLO VENTURE 22** [4] 5-9-0 (54) J Fanning 14/1: 0/0-06: Trkd ldr, led 3f out till 2f out, wknd. *¾* **44**
4584} **GREAT HOPPER 209** [5] 5-7-10 (36)(16oh) P Hanagan (4) 66/1: 000-7: Prom, wknd over 4f out: poor. *3* **23**
1329 **PARABLE 12** [6] 4-9-11 (65) K Darley 7/1: 513008: Bhd, btn 2f out: op 5/1, btr 671 (a/w). *dist* **0**

REDCAR MONDAY MAY 29TH Lefthand, Flat, Galloping Track

8 ran   Time 3m 11.2 (13.5)   (Mrs P J Taylor Garthwaite)   C W Fairhurst Middleham, N Yorks

SANDOWN MONDAY MAY 29TH Righthand, Galloping Track, Stiff Finish

Official Going HEAVY. Stalls: Sprint Crse - Far Side; Rem - Inside.

1564 2.05 BONUSPHOTO FILLIES HCAP 3YO+ 0-95 (C) 7f rnd Soft 111 +04 Fast [89]
£7020 £2160 £1080 £540 3yo rec 11lb

*1405 **LA SPEZIANA** 9 [4] D R C Elsworth 3-7-10 (68) J Mackay (7) 7/2: 466-11: 3 b f Perugino - Election 88
Special (Chief Singer) Made all, qcknd clr 2f out, ran on strongly, rdn clr: fast time: recent Newbury scorer
(fill h'cap, reapp): mdn promise in '99 (rtd 95+) at 7f, has tried 1m & that trip shld suit: acts on fast
& soft grnd handles a gall trk: runs well fresh, can force the pace: fast improving & progressive filly.
1341 **SERRA NEGRA** 11 [6] W J Haggas 3-8-8 (80) J F Egan 9/4 FAV: 0-162: 3 b f Kris - Congress (Dancing 10 80
Brave) Waited with, imprvd 2f out, took 2nd brief, no ch with impressive wnr: hvly bckd: met a fast improving rival.
4218} **MADAM ALISON** 240 [5] R Hannon 4-9-5 (80) P Dobbs (5) 10/1: 6526-3: 4 b f Puissance - Copper Burn hd 80
(Electric) Rear, imprvd 2f out, onepace fnl 1f: op 7/1, reapp: '99 Newmarket wnr (fill h'cap, rtd 83 at best):
'98 Leicester wnr (fill mdn auct, rtd 77): eff at 1m on fast & hvy, likes a stiff/gall trk: can run well fresh.
1063 **DANAMALA** 28 [1] R Hannon 4-8-11 (72) Dane O'Neill 13/2: 330-24: In tch till lost pl 2f out, no ch 3 67
after: shorter priced stablemate of 3rd: see 1063 (mdn).
1153 **NIGHT EMPRESS** 24 [2] A Nicholls (3) 4/1: 30-245: Rcd keenly & chsd wnr, wknd over hd 71
1f out: nicely bckd: see 1153, 794.
1154 **ROSE OF MOONCOIN** 24 [7] 4-9-10 (85)(BL) R Cochrane 20/1: /00-66: Rear, eff 2f out, sn btn: 2½ 76
tried in blnks: prob not handle these testing conditions: see 1154 (list).
3916} **WAX LYRICAL** 257 [3] 4-9-10 (85) P Robinson 10/1: 10-77: Rcd keenly & prom, wknd 2f out: fin last, 3 71
jt top-weight: twice rcd in '99, debut Salisbury wnr (mdn, rtd 95+, with J Toller): eff at 6f on firm grnd, handles
a stiff trk: can run well fresh: now with M Jarvis: rcd too freely for own gd here & better prev on firm grnd.
7 ran   Time 1m 33.9 (7.5) Hand Timed   (Pampas Partnership)   D R C Elsworth Whitsbury, Hants.

1565 2.35 GR 3 HENRY II STKS 4YO+ (A) 2m78y Soft 111 -33 Slow
£24000 £9200 £4600 £2200 4yo rec 2lb

1339 **PERSIAN PUNCH** 11 [5] D R C Elsworth 7-8-12 P Robinson 11/2: 01-201: 7 ch g Persian Heights - 114
Rum Cay (Our Native) Rcd keenly & made virtually all, briefly hdd 2f out, kept on gamely fnl 1f, drvn out: rider
reportedly given a 3 day whip ban, slow time: below best in '99, won fnl start at Doncaster (stks, rtd 110 at best),
4th in this v race: '98 wnr at Newmarket, here at Sandown (this race) & York (Gr 3's), also plcd in Melbourne Cup
(Gr 1, rtd 118): '97 wnr at Newbury & Sandown (again, this race, rtd 120): eff at 12f, suited by 14f/2m & does stay
2½m: acts on firm & hvy grnd, runs well fresh: best up with or forcing the pace: reportedly hds for the Ascot
Gold Cup (has disapp in that race thrice prev): high-class tough & v game stayer.
1339 **CHURLISH CHARM** 11 [4] R Hannon 5-9-3 Paul Eddery 5/1: 10-032: 5 b h Niniski - Blushing Storm (Blushing ½ 118
Groom) Trkd ldrs, chall 3f out, led briefly 2f out, kept on well & just btn in a close fin: acts on fast, likes
soft grnd: high-class effrt under top-weight here & clearly at the top of his form, win more Gr races in this form.
4532} **ARCTIC OWL** 218 [3] J R Fanshawe 6-9-1 R Cochrane 9/4 FAV: 2226-3: 6 b g Most Welcome - Short 1¾ 114+
Rations (Lorenzaccio) In tch, ch over 2f out, kept on fnl 1f under a kind ride, hung right cl home: well bckd, clr
rem: '99 wnr here at Sandown (this race, rtd 123), subs rnr-up Doncaster (Gr 2) & Newmarket, & incl Gr 3, rtd 121): '97 wnr at Windsor (mdn auct) & York (rtd h'cap): eff at
12f/2m on fast & hvy: runs well fresh, handles any trk: high-class gelding, spot on next time.
987 **BIENNALE** 37 [6] Sir Michael Stoute 4-8-10 K Fallon 7/1: /13-44: In tch, btn 2f out: first attempt beyond 5 106$
12f & not disgraced in this decent company: worth another ch on a faster surface, see 987 (12f).
1222 **EILEAN SHONA** 11 [8] 4-8-7 A Nicholls 16/1: 311-05: Dwelt, eff 3f out, sn no impress: longer 1 102$
priced stablemate of 3rd: highly tried & sharper for this in h'caps: see 1222.
1109 **SAN SEBASTIAN** 26 [2] 6-8-12 (bl) M J Kinane 4/1: 442-46: Chsd wnr till 3f out, grad fdd: thorough 1½ 103
stayer, unsuited by the slow pace today: twice a wnr at Royal Ascot: see 1109.
*13 **SPIRIT OF LOVE** 204 [7] 5-8-12 O Peslier 9/1: 0001-7: Al rear, eased when no ch fnl 1f: reapp: '99 6 97
wnr in Germany (List), also 4th at Ascot (Gr 3, rtd 113): progressive stayer in '98, won at Southwell (AW mdn),
Doncaster (2), Ascot (h'cap) & notably Newmarket (Cesarewitch H'cap, rtd 106): eff at 14f, stays 2m2f well: acts
on fast, v soft & f/sand: best up with or forcing the pace, likes a gall trk: useful stayer at best.
7 ran   Time 3m 53.45 (23.65)   (J C Smith)   D R C Elsworth Whitsbury, Hants.

1566 3.10 GR 2 TR'PRINT TEMPLE STKS 3YO+ (A) 5f str Soft 111 +14 Fast
£36000 £13800 £6900 £3300

1324 **PERRYSTON VIEW** 12 [10] J A Glover 8-9-3 J Reid 8/1: 1-1001: 8 b h Primo Dominie - Eastern Ember 116
(Indian King) Made all on far rail, rdn clr fnl 1f, cmftbly: best time of day, morning gamble from 16/1: earlier
won at Doncaster (h'cap, reapp): in '99 trained by P Calver to win at Newmarket (h'cap, reapp) & Doncaster (rtd
h'cap, rtd 99): '99 Ripon wnr (rtd h'cap, rtd 93): eff at 5/6f on firm & soft, handles any trk, loves Newmarket
& Doncaster: eff with/without blnks/visor, likes front-running tactics: gd weight carrier who can run well fresh:
career best effort today & improved by new trainer, sound claims in the King's Stand Stks at Royal Ascot.
1338 **PROUD NATIVE** 11 [8] D Nicholls 6-9-3 K Fallon 14/1: 10-002: 6 b g Imp Society - Karamana (Habitat) 5 108
Trkd ldrs far side, styd on well to take 2nd cl-home, no ch with wnr: op 10/1: win another Gr 3: see 1172.
1172 **RAMBLING BEAR** 23 [9] M Blanshard 7-9-3 R Cochrane 9/1: 350-33: 7 ch h Sharrood - Supreme Rose ¾ 105
(Frimley Park) Dwelt, prog to chase wnr halfway on far rail, ev ch 1f out, sn outpcd: 5L clr rem: best prev on
firm & gd/soft grnd in Gr 3/Listed: runs esp well fresh: see 1172.
4246} **IMPERIAL BEAUTY** 239 [1] P J Makin 4-9-0 Pat Eddery 9/2: 2012-4: Rear, switched far side over 1f out, 5 90+
no ch with front 3 & not given a hard time: well bckd, reapp: '99 wnr at York & Newbury (List), also fine snk 2nd
at Longchamp (Gr 1 Prix L'Abbye, rtd 116): '98 Salisbury wnr (stks), also rnr-up in Gr 1 Cheveley Park (rtd 109):
eff at 5/6f, has tried 1m: acts on firm & hvy, likes stiff trks: can run well fresh: smart filly who had little
ch from poor low draw: spot on next time & will prove a different prospect in the King's Stand stks at R Ascot.
*1320 **SAMPOWER STAR** 15 [3] 4-9-3 L Dettori 11/8 FAV: 44-015: Rcd centre & held up, eff halfway, no 3 86
impress when short of room dist, no ch after & eased: hvly bckd from 2/1: nvr competitive racing up the middle
of the trk: this must be forgotten: see 1320.

SANDOWN   MONDAY MAY 29TH   Righthand, Galloping Track, Stiff Finish

*1453 **SUPERIOR PREMIUM 6** [5] 6-9-3 M Roberts 9/1: -00016: Rcd centre & prom 2½f, sn btn: qck reapp: rcd up unfav'd centre of crse, forget this: see 1453 (stks).   1¾   82
1172 **ROSSELLI 23** [7] 4-9-3 J Carroll 14/1: 50-467: Chsd wnr till halfway, wknd: see 1172.   9   62
1172 **BOLSHOI GB 23** [6] 8-9-3 C Lowther 20/1: 620/08: Speed 3f, wkng when hmpd dist: see 1172.   8   44
1172 **EASTERN PURPLE 23** [2] 5-9-3 (bl) O Peslier 16/1: 0-0309: Prom till halfway centre, wknd into last: no ch racing on the worst of the grnd: see 927.   6   30
9 ran   Time 1m 04.45 (4.85)   (Mrs Janis Macpherson)   J A Glover Carburton, Notts.

1567   3.45 DOUBLEPRINT RATED HCAP 3YO+ 0-105 (B)   1m rnd   Soft 111   -18 Slow   [111]
£16269   £6171   £3085   £1402

+1291 **SWALLOW FLIGHT 14** [7] G Wragg 4-9-11 (108) M Roberts 5/1: 24-211: 4 b c Bluebird - Mirage (Red Sunset) Prom, led 2f out, kept on ins last, drvn out: well bckd, top-weight: recent Windsor wnr (List): '99 wnr at York (h'cap) & Doncaster (stks, rtd 106): eff at 1m, stays 10f: acts on firm & soft, handles any trk: likes to run up with or force the pace: gd weight carrier: tough, smart & improving, win another Listed race.   113
*1445 **JO MELL 6** [6] T D Easterby 7-8-11 (94)(3ex) J Carroll 13/2: -01012: 7 b g Efisio - Militia Girl (Rarity) Set pace till 2f out, rallied gamely fnl 1f, only just btn: fine run under 3lb pen: loves soft.   hd   98
1323 **PANTAR 15** [3] I A Balding 5-8-11 (94)(bl) M J Kinane 13/2: 214363: 5 b g Shirley Heights - Spring Daffodil (Pharly) Rcd keenly rear, eff over 1f out, no impress till fin well but too late: often fancied in big field h'caps, usually runs well but seldom wins: see 1015.   ½   97
1450 **REGAL PHILOSOPHER 6** [1] J W Hills 4-8-8 (91)(3oh) R Hills 5/1: 0-6224: Trkd ldrs, onepcd fnl 1f.   ¾   92
1342 **SHARMY 11** [9] 4-9-3 (100) K Fallon 11/4 FAV: 12-145: Trkd ldrs, no impress ins fnl 1f: well bckd from 4/1: not disgraced, btn under 2L: acts on firm & soft grnd: see 1342 (10f).   hd   101
1327 **THE PRINCE 12** [8] 6-8-8 (91)(1oh) O Peslier 10/1: 3-1056: Rear, eff 2f out, no impress fnl 1f.   1¾   89
1110 **ALWAYS ALIGHT 26** [5] 6-8-8 (91) J F Egan 20/1: 3-0157: Trkd ldrs, eff 2f out, fdd fnl 1f: btr 935.   2   85
1291 **CARDIFF ARMS 14** [4] 6-9-0 (97) L Dettori 9/1: 30-208: Rear, rdn to impr dist, sn btn: btr 1112.   6   79
1323 **KING PRIAM 15** [10] 5-8-9 (92)(bl) Pat Eddery 12/1: 200059: Prom till halfway, wknd qckly & eased: fin last: this is not his form: see 733, 448.   16   49
9 ran   Time 1m 49.35 (10.35)   (Mollers Racing)   G Wragg Newmarket.

1568   4.20 BONUSPRINT FILLIES MDN 2YO (D)   5f str   Soft 111   -71 Slow
£4290   £1320   £660   £330

1197 **GOLD AIR 21** [1] B J Meehan 2-8-11 Pat Eddery 8/1: -01: 2 b f Sri Pekan - Pebbledash (Great Commotion) Made virtually all, held on well fnl 1f, drvn out: slow time: 9,500gns Mar foal: dam modest tho' related to a useful sprinter in Ireland: sire a top-class juv: eff at 5f on soft grnd: plenty of speed in her pedigree, handles a stiff/gall trk: open to further improvement.   82
-- **ECSTATIC** [4] R Hannon 2-8-11 Dane O'Neill 3/1: -2: 2 ch f Nashwan - Divine Quest (Kris) Dwelt, recovered to press wnr halfway, kept on well fnl 1f despite running green, just btn in a driving fin: op 9/4: Mar first foal, dam a 7f wnr, related to sev wnrs: sire a top-class mid-dist performer: eff at 5f on soft grnd, 6f+ will suit: sure to benefit from today's experience & will sn go one better.   nk   81+
-- **FAST FOIL** [2] M R Channon 2-8-11 Craig Williams 12/1: -3: 2 b f Lahib - Fast Chick (Henbit) Dwelt, recovered to chase ldrs, styd on under hands-and-heels riding, nrst fin: drifted from 7/1: 9,000gns purchase: May foal, half-sister to 6f 2yo scorer Missile: dam a 9f/12f wnr, sire a top-class miler: eff at 5f on soft grnd, bred to apprec 6f+: most promising debut, sure to learn from this & win races.   1   78+
1424 **FAZZANI 7** [6] M R Channon 2-8-11 S Drowne 10/3: -04: Early ldr, short of room & lost pl halfway, ran on again ins fnl 1f but not rch ldrs: shorter priced stablemate of 3rd: once again suggested 6f+ will suit.   hd   78$
-- **BEE ONE** [3] 2-8-11 N Pollard 13/2: -5: Dwelt, eff halfway, no impress fin 1f: op 9/2: IR 21,000gns purchase: Feb foal, dam a 1m wnr: sire a high-class 6/7f performer: worth another chance on faster grnd.   3   70
-- **EARLY WISH** [5] 2-8-11 J Reid 11/4 FAV: -6: Front rank till btn dist: hvly bckd tho' op 7/4: Mar foal, cost 60,000gns: half-sister to sev useful wnrs in the USA: dam a winning juv in Ireland: sire smart around 1m: B Hanbury filly & much better was clrly expected: prob worth another chance on faster grnd.   5   58
6 ran   Time 1m 08.71 (9.11)   (Gold Group International Ltd)   B J Meehan Upper Lambourn, Berks.

1569   4.50 DOUBLEPRINT HCAP 3YO+ 0-80 (D)   7f rnd   Soft 111   -34 Slow   [84]
£5573   £1715   £857   £428

1341 **CELEBRATION TOWN 11** [5] D Morris 3-9-2 (72) R Cochrane 10/1: 05-101: 3 br g Case Law - Battle Queen (King Of Hush) Waited with, stdy prog halfway, strong run to lead cl-home, scored a shade cosily: earlier won at Southwell (reapp, h'cap): unplcd for J J O'Neill in '99 (rtd 73 at best): eff at 7f, has tried 1m & this trip will suit: acts on gd/soft & soft grnd, disapp on firm last time: handles a sharp or stiff/gall trk: runs well fresh: won cosily here & shld gain more successes when the grnd rides soft.   77
1348 **INSIGHTFUL 11** [9] R Hannon 3-9-4 (74) Dane O'Neill 20/1: 12-502: 3 b g Desert Style - Insight (Ballad Rock) Trkd ldrs, prog to chall despite edging right 1f out, kept on but not pace of wnr cl-home: see 108.   ¾   76
1345 **ATYLAN BOY 11** [13] B J Meehan 3-8-9 (65)(BL) D R McCabe 33/1: 50-003: 3 b g Efisio - Gold Flair (Tap On Wood) Led & tried to make all, worn down cl-home: 4L clr rem: fine front-running effort in first time blnks: eff over a stiff/gall 7f on soft grnd: see 933.   shd   67
1178 **LAKELAND PADDY 22** [10] M Blanshard 3-9-4 (74) D Sweeney 8/1: 6-3364: Chsd ldr till 2f out, outpcd till kept on again cl-home: nicely bckd: fair effort over this longer 7f trip, 1m could suit: see 994.   4   68
4433} **PAGEANT 223** [3] 3-9-4 (74) P Robinson 20/1: 443-5: Rcd keenly rear, kept on fnl 1½f, nrst fin on reapp: thrice rcd for R Williams in '99, plcd at Lingfield (mdn, rtd 78): eff at 7f, looks in need of 1m now: handles firm & hvy grnd: now with W Jarvis, spot on next time.   ½   67+
1183 **MUST BE MAGIC 22** [12] 3-8-10 (66) O Peslier 8/1: 300-06: Trkd ldrs, eff 2f out, onepcd fnl 1f: plcd at Goodwood in '99 (mdn, rtd 80): eff at 1m on soft grnd & a return to that trip will now suit: looks v well h'capped & worth another chance back over a longer trip.   1¼   56
3469} **SOCIAL CONTRACT 283** [2] 3-9-7 (77) J F Egan 25/1: 1410-7: Mid-div & rcd wide, onepace fnl 1f: stablemate of rnr-up, reapp: '99 wnr at Southwell (sell, rtd 80a, with T Stack) & Lingfield (nurs, with W Haggas, rtd 79): eff at 6/7f on fast, hvy grnd & fibresand: handles a sharp trk: tough gelding, now with R Hannon.   ¾   65
1406 **CHIQUITA 9** [14] 3-9-6 (76) J Mackay(7) 6/1: 1-5008: Rear, eff 2f out, late prog but nvr dngrs: nicely bckd from 9/1: not given a hard time, primed for a return to form: see 1406, 982.   nk   63
1405 **FOXS IDEA 9** [8] 3-8-13 (69) R Hills 12/1: 133059: Rear, eff 2f out, late prog but nvr dngrs: see 1405.   ¾   54
1387 **ALJAZIR 9** [11] 3-8-2 (58) A Nicholls(3) 10/1: -02050: Prom, ev ch 2f out, grad fdd into 10th.   1   41
4616} **TRIBAL PRINCE 205** [7] 3-9-4 (74) M J Kinane 10/1: 5025-0: Rear, eff 2f out, sn no impress: fin 11th,   1   55

517

reapp: failed to win in '99 (rnr-up twice, h'cap, rtd 74): eff at 7f on firm & hvy grnd: has tried a visor,
seems better without: with P Harris & capable of better.
1041 **GRENADIER** 31 [6] 3-9-3 (73) K Fallon 5/1 FAV: 4-540: Trkd ldrs, wknd fnl 1½f: fin 12th, well   ¾   52
bckd: better expected on h'cap debut, reportedly damaged off-hind heel: see 1041, 1032.
1333 **HARMONIC** 12 [16] 3-9-5 (75) N Pollard 16/1: 624-60: Front rank fnl wknd qckly dist: fin 13th.   3   49
1341 **DESERT SAFARI** 11 [1] 3-8-13 (69) S Drowne 20/1: -05400: Rear, nvr a factor in 14th: btr 1341.   5   35
1387 **SLICK WILLIE** 9 [4] 3-9-2 (72)(bl) Pat Eddery 12/1: 32-000: Al bhd, fin 11th: see 736.   1¼   35
1289 **BAJAN BELLE** 14 [15] 3-9-3 (73) J Reid 12/1: 1-0040: Rcd keenly & prom 5f, wknd qckly, t.o. in   17   6
last: rcd much too keenly for own gd here: see 1289 (6f, firm).
16 ran   Time 1m 36.6 (10.2) Hand Timed   (Meadowcrest Ltd)   D Morris Newmarket.

1570   5.25 TRIPLEPRINT HCAP 4YO+ 0-80 (D)   1m2f   Soft 111 -75 Slow   [72]
        £5369   £1652   £826   £413

1375 **PAS DE PROBLEME** 10 [4] M Blanshard 4-9-5 (63) M Roberts 13/8 FAV: -01531: 4 ch g Ela Mana Mou -   68
Torriglia (Nijinsky) Made all, kept on strongly fnl 1f, rdn out: hvly bckd, slow time: earlier won at Warwick (h'cap):
unplcd in '99, rnr-up prev term (stks, debut, rtd 79): eff at 9/10.5f, acts on fast, likes hvy grnd: improving gelding
who can force the pace: pulled out more keenly today.
1307 **GENERATE** 13 [5] M J Polglase 4-8-13 (57) N Pollard 9/2: 62D102: 4 b f Generous - Ivorine (Blushing   2   59
Groom) Mid-div, eff 3f out, no impress till styd on well to take 2nd cl-home, no ch with wnr: took too long
to get going today, needs further judged on this: see 1306 (11f, sand).
1251 **DARE** 18 [8] P D Evans 5-9-0 (58)(vis) J F Egan 9/2: 035003: 5 b g Beveled - Run Amber Run (Run   2   57
The Gantlet) Rcd keenly & prom, chsd wnr 2f out, caught for 2nd cl-home: nicely bckd: see 637 (AW).
1395 **WESTMINSTER CITY** 9 [7] D R C Elsworth 4-8-9 (53)(BL) L Branch (7) 11/2: 12U044: Mid-div,   3   47
switched & eff 2f out, no impression: tried in blnks: see 1395.
1419 **MUDDY WATER** 7 [1] 4-9-2 (60) D Sweeney 15/2: 100325: Rcd keenly in bhd wnr, ev ch 3f out,   6   46
btn 2f out: tchd 9/1: see 1419 (1m, sand).
3329} **TAKE A TURN** 290 [2] 5-8-9 (53) A Clark 25/1: 0000-6: Rear, hmpd 5f out, no ch after: trained by   6   31
Miss G Kelleway in '99 & mainly modest form: 98/99 Taunton & Plumpton hdle wnr (2m1f, firm): '98 Salisbury
wnr (h'cap, rtd 75 & 77a): '97 Chester wnr (nurs, rtd 82, with M Channon): eff at 1m/10f on fast, hvy grnd &
equitrack: can run well fresh: prob best when blnkd or visored: now with M Wilkinson.
1373 **ALCAYDE** 10 [6] 5-9-10 (68) Dane O'Neill 14/1: 425/07: Rear, hmpd 5f out, no ch after: forget this.   11   31
1370 **COUGHLANS GIFT** 10 [3] 4-8-13 (57) P Dobbs(5) 20/1: 5-000U: Mid-div, hit rail & u.r. 5f out: see 210.   0
8 ran   Time 2m 22.7 (18.6) Flag Start   (Captain Franic Burne)   M Blanshard Upper Lambourn, Berks.

Official Going: GOOD TO SOFT   Stalls: Stand Side

1571   2.15 JIG RACING HCAP 3YO 0-70 (E)   1m3f183y   Good/Soft 89 -11 Slow   [77]
        £3120   £960   £480   £240   Raced towards centre fnl 4f

850 **FIRECREST** 50 [8] J L Dunlop 3-9-0 (63) Pat Eddery 4/1 JT FAV: 00-01: 3 b f Darshaan - Trefoil   75
(Blakeney) Chsd ldrs, prog/led over 3f out, soon rdn clr & in command, eased down near line: val for 9L+: op
11/4, abs: h'cap type: relished this step up to 12f, shld get further: plenty in hand here, looks sure to go in again.
827 **SUAVE PERFORMER** 55 [1] S C Williams 3-8-3 (51)(1ow) N Pollard 5/1: 04542: 3 b g Suave Dancer -   7   52
Francia (Legend Of France) In tch, rdn/prog to chase wnr over 2f out, no impression & position accepted inside last:
nicely bckd, op 6/1: 8 week abs: styd longer 12f trip but caught a tartar here: acts on gd/soft & soft: see 827.
1094 **KISTY** 28 [10] H Candy 3-9-7 (70) L Newman (5) 8/1: 054-03: 3 b f Kris - Pine Ridge (High Top)   1   69
Held up, rdn/mod gains fnl 2f, no threat: op 7/1: stays 12f, may get further: see 1094.
1270 **SHRIVAR** 18 [6] M R Channon 3-9-4 (67) S Drowne 9/1: -05524: Prom, chsd wnr 3f out, held fnl 2f.   shd   66
1425 **DISTANT PROSPECT** 8 [7] 3-9-6 (69) S Sanders 4/1 JT FAV: 30-235: Held up, outpcd 5f out, no impress.   5   62
1041 **DANDES RAMBO** 32 [2] 3-8-9 (58) S Whitworth 20/1: 00-56: Rear/in tch, mod gains fnl 4f: see 1041.   6   44
278 **BLUE CAVALIER** 144 [4] 3-7-12 (47)(2ow)(6oh) P Doe 33/1: 60-07: Held up, never a factor: 5 month abs.   3   29
937 **NORTHERN TIMES** 43 [12] 3-8-12 (61) N Callan 33/1: 510108: Chsd ldrs, eff 4f out, sn btn: 6 wk abs.   8   34
936 **STRATEGIC DANCER** 43 [5] 3-9-1 (64) J Fortune 12/1: -6009: Led & quickened clr 5f out, rdn/hdd   hd   37
over 3f out, soon btn: op 10/1, 6 wk abs/h'cap bow: bred to appre this tougher 12f trip: only mod form prev.
1184 **CAUNTON** 23 [9] 3-9-2 (65) J Weaver 20/1: 040-00: Trck ldr, btn 3f out: 10th: see 1184 (10f).   dist   0
4508} **GREAT RICHES** 217 [13] 3-7-10 (45)(5oh) J Lowe 40/1: 000-0: Chsd ldrs, keen, struggling 4f out: 11th.   15   0
*1142 **XELLANCE** 26 [11] 3-7-10 (45) K Dalgleish (7) 6/1: 0-151U: Bmpd & u.r.start: op 11/2: see 1142 (AW).   0
12 ran   Time 2m 40.2 (11.9)   (Sir Thomas Pilkington)   J L Dunlop Arundel, West Sussex

1572   2.45 GARY WILTSHIRE CLAIMER 3YO (F)   1m str   Good/Soft 89 -01 Slow
        £2467   £705   £352   Raced centre - stands side

1196 **RONNI PANCAKE** 22 [5] J S Moore 3-8-5 N Callan 12/1: 606-01: 3 b f Mujadil - Funny Choice   54
(Commanche Run) Held up, prog to lead over 1f out, held on gamely inside last, all out: op 10/1, first win:
rnr-up last term (rtd 78 & 42a): apprec step up to 1m: acts on fast & gd/soft, stiff/undulating trk.
1017 **THE FLYER** 36 [8] P F I Cole 3-9-2 J Fortune 5/1: 6-602: 3 b c Blues Traveller - National Ballet   shd   64
(Shareef Dancer) Rdn/towards rear halfway, prog to chall under press fnl 1f, styd on well, just held: claimed by J
Pointon for £10,000: eff at 1m, tried further: handles gd/soft grnd: clr of rem & can win similar.
1141 **SKELTON MONARCH** 26 [6] R Hollinshead 3-8-4 P M Quinn 33/1: 00-663: 3 ch c Prince Of Birds   7   42
- Toda (Absalom) Held up, eff 3f out, late gains for press, no threat: see 1035.
1349 **WALTER THE WHISTLE** 12 [13] J A Osborne 3-8-9 Pat Eddery 4/1: 0-54: Towards rear, drvn early, drvn/   1   42
chsd ldrs 3f out & chance over 1f out, held inside last: op 7/2: see 1349.
1159 **WILLIAM THE LION** 24 [9] 3-9-0 J Carroll 20/1: 000-05: Chsd ldrs, briefly led over 1f out, fdd.   1½   47
1331 **COLLEGE ROCK** 13 [3] 3-8-10 (BL) S Drowne 12/1: 426306: Chsd ldrs 6f: blinks, op 10/1: see 1331.   hd   46
3810} **ERIN ANAM CARA** 266 [12] 3-8-9 C Rutter 12/1: 5443-7: Prom, wknd quickly fnl 1f: op 9/1: reapp: 2   38
plcd last term (rtd 60, sell h'cap, C/D, unplcd on sand, rtd 58a): eff at 1m, handles firm & gd grnd.
1234 **ALBERGO** 19 [14] 3-9-4 D Sweeney 11/1: -50028: Soon rdn, never on terms: op 10/1: see 1234, 395.   5   39

*1349 COWBOYS AND ANGELS 12 [1] 3-9-6 P Fitzsimons (5) 11/4 FAV: 336019: Cl up, led halfway, hdd/wknd ¾ **40**
over 1f out: nicely bckd though op 9/4: btr expected after 1349 (7f).
1293 NORTHERN LIFE 15 [10] 3-8-1 J F Egan 20/1: 000-00: Held up, prog/briefly led over 1f out, sn wknd: ¾ **20**
10th: longer priced stablemate of wnr, only mod form prev at up to 10f.
1422 MADEMOISELLE PARIS 8 [2] 3-8-1 S Righton 33/1: -05000: Led 4f, fdd fnl 2f: 11th: see 1202. 4 **13**
1415 Kings Ginger 8 [4] 3-8-10 (VIS) R Fitzpatrick (3) 12/1: 830 **Jensens Tale 54** [7] 3-8-8 N Pollard 50/1:
1106 Bold Willy 27 [11] 3-8-6 P Doe 33/1:
14 ran   Time 1m 41.6 (7.2)   (J Laughton)   J S Moore East Garston, Berks

---

1573	**3.15 CAPEL CURE SHARP MDN 2YO (D) 6f Good/Soft 89 -14 Slow**
	£3688 £1135 £567 £283 Raced towards stands side

-- **EARL GREY** [3] W Jarvis 2-9-0 M Tebbutt 2/1 JT FAV: 1: 2 b c Twining - Regal Peace (Known Fact) **75**
Dwelt, bhnd ldrs, bmpd 2f out & switched 1f out, drvn & styd on well to lead ins last: Feb foal, cost 35,000gns:
half-brother to two US wnrs, dam a juv 5f Irish wnr: eff at 6f, will get further: acts on gd/soft: goes well fresh.
-- **GRAND FIVE** [5] J S Moore 2-9-0 J F Egan 8/1: 2: 2 b c Spectrum - Iberian Dancer (El Gran Senor) nk **74**
Chsd ldrs, rdn/led over 1f out, edged left & hdd wi inside last, just held: op 6/1: Feb foal, 16,000gns 2yo, a
first foal, dam a 9f 3yo wnr: sire top class 1m/10f performer: eff at 6f, will get further, acts on gd/soft grnd.
1403 ANALYZE 10 [4] M R Channon 2-9-0 S Drowne 2/1 JT FAV: 03: 2 b c Anabaa - Bramosia (Forzando) 1½ **70**
Led 4f out, rdn/onepce inside last: bckd: acts on gd/soft grnd, going the right way after intro: see 1403.
-- **MOON MASTER** [1] J A Osborne 2-9-0 Pat Eddery 9/2: 4: 2 b c Primo Dominie colt, May foal, cost 26,000gns: nk **69**
onepace: op 3/1: Primo Dominie colt, May foal, cost 26,000gns: half brother to a German 3yo wnr, dam unrcd.
1048 IZZET MUZZY 31 [2] 2-9-0 J Weaver 8/1: 505: Chsd ldrs, outpcd fnl 2f: see 828 (5f). 7 **56**
5 ran   Time 1m 16.00 (6.2)   (The Tea Clippers)   W Jarvis Newmarket, Suffolk

---

1574	**3.45 MARTYN COND STKS 3YO+ (C) 7f str Good/Soft 89 -07 Slow**
	£6834 £2244 £1122 3 yo rec 11lb Raced towards far side

1049 GRANNYS PET 31 [2] P F I Cole 6-9-11 J Fortune 10/11 FAV: 121-31: 6 ch g Selkirk - Patsy Western **108**
(Precocious) Trck ldr, shaken up 1f out & led inside last, in command near fin, pushed out: '99 wnr at Chester,
Goodwood (2, rtd h'caps) & Doncaster (stakes, rtd 108 at best): '98 Haydock wnr h'cap, rtd 101): suited by 7f:
handles any track, likes Goodwood: acts on fm & sft, runs well fresh: eff with/without blinks: tough & useful.
2599} TISSIFER 325 [3] M Johnston 4-9-4 J Carroll 3/1: 0220-2: 4 b c Polish Precedent - Ingozi (Warning) 2½ **96**
Led, rdn/hdd ins last, not pace of wnr: op 9/4, reapp: '99 reapp wnr at Thirsk (stks, rtd 110, subs rnr up twice,
incl 1st time blinks), reapp: '98 wnr at Epsom (mdn) & Kempton (stakes, rtd 103 at best): eff at 1m, stys 10f: acts
on fast & soft, any trk: goes well fresh: v smart at best but has suffered injury problems, prob sharper for run.
4272} ON TIME 236 [1] J R Fanshawe 3-8-12 R Cochrane 5/2: 113-3: 3 b c Blues Traveller - Go Flightline ½ **100$**
(Common Grounds) Bhnd front pair, eff over 1f out, not pace to chall: op 9/4, reapp: won first two in '99 at Warwick
(auct mdn) & Goodwood (stks, rtd 97): eff at 7f, may get further: acts on gd & hvy, sharp/gall track: runs well fresh.
3 ran   Time 1m 28.7 (6.7)   (Mrs Denise Margot Arbib)   P F I Cole Whatcombe, Oxon

---

1575	**4.15 TOM FRUIT HCAP 3YO+ 0-70 (E) 1m2f Good/Soft 89 -10 Slow [69]**
	£3263 £1004 £502 £251 3 yo rec 14lb Raced towards centre fnl 4f

1370 ANNADAWI 11 [3] C N Kellett 5-8-4 (45) C Rutter 7/2 JT FAV: 632221: 5 b g Sadler's Wells - Prayers'n **49**
Promises (Foolish Pleasure) Towards rear, rdn/prog fnl 3f & led over 1f out, in command inside last, rdn out: op
5/2: first win in 17th start: mod form in '99, including over jumps: eff around 1m/10.5f on gd/soft, hvy &
any track: best without blnks/vis & a tongue strap: deserved this first success.
1370 KHUCHN 11 [6] M Brittain 4-8-11 (52) J Weaver 7/2 JT FAV: 005052: 4 b c Unfuwain - Stay Sharpe 2½ **52**
(Sharpen Up) Hndy, led over 2f out, rdn/hdd over 1f out & soon held: clr rem: nicely bckd: acts on gd & gd/soft.
1254 HEVER GOLF GLORY 18 [2] C N Kellett 6-7-10 (37) K Dalgleish (7) 14/1: 450303: 6 b g Efisio - Zaius 5 **31**
(Artaius) Held up, prog/led over 3f out, hdd over 2f out, no extra: longer priced stablemate of wnr: see 842, 383.
1496 BITTER SWEET 4 [7] J L Spearing 4-8-11 (52) Pat Eddery 4/1: 040354: Held up, eff 2f out, held fnl 1f. 2 **43**
1100 THE SHADOW 28 [5] 4-8-13 (54) J Reid 8/1: 15-005: Track ldrs, outpcd 3f out: op 6/1: see 854 (1m). ½ **44**
4522} BONELLI 217 [1] 4-8-5 (46) Martin Dwyer 11/1: 0460-6: Dwelt/held up, eff 4f out, mod late gains: 1½ **34**
reapp: unplcd last term (rtd 56, auction mdn): rtd 66 in '98.
608 PRIORS MOOR 91 [8] 5-8-0 (40)(1ow) P Doe 33/1: 00-007: Led 6f, soon btn: 3 month abs: see 608. 10 **18**
4584} TOTALLY SCOTTISH 210 [4] 4-8-13 (54) J Carroll 9/1: 004-8: Dwelt, al rear: op 6/1, reapp/h'cap bow. 4 **26**
3649} MUNGO DUFF 275 [9] 5-9-10 (65) S Whitworth 16/1: 0/50-9: Prom 7f: op 10/1, reapp: unplcd in '99 dist **0**
(rtd, 71, J R Fanshawe): unplcd both '98 starts for P Harris: topweight today & now with Mrs V C Ward.
9 ran   Time 2m 12.4 (9.9)   (Sean A Taylor)   C N Kellett Smisby, Derbys

---

1576	**4.45 CLINTON CLASS STKS 3YO 0-90 (C) 6f Good/Soft 89 +09 Fast**
	£6500 £2000 £1000 £500

1703} COTTON HOUSE 363 [1] M R Channon 3-8-8 S Drowne 5/1: 124-1: 3 b f Mujadil - Romanovna **100**
(Mummy's Pet) Handy, led over 2f out, readily pulled clr, pushed out inside last, comfortably: fast time: op 3/1,
reapp: '99 debut wnr at Warwick (auct fill mdn, rtd 89, subs sidelined by a fractured pelvis): eff at 5/6f, may get
further: acts on firm & gd/soft grnd, stiff/sharp track: runs well fresh: useful & improved from two-to-three.
1219 ARGENT FACILE 21 [4] D J S Cosgrove 3-8-11 (t) J F Egan 2/1 JT FAV: 0-2202: 3 b c Midhish - 6 **90**
Rosinish (Lomond) Chsd ldrs, rdn/outpcd by wnr fnl 2f: op 5/2: caught a tartar here: see 1047, 959.
3048} HAPPY DIAMOND 304 [3] M Johnston 3-8-11 J Reid 3/1: 21-3: 3 b c Diesis - Urus (Kris S) 1 **88**
Held up, eff 2f out, outpcd: reapp: '99 wnr on second of 2 starts at Thirsk (mdn, rtd 87): eff at 5f, this longer
6f trip will suit: acts on firm & fast grnd & a sharpish track: has run well fresh.
*1159 SALIM 24 [2] Sir Michael Stoute 3-8-13 R Hills 2/1 JT FAV: 0-14: Led 3f, btn over 1f out: well bckd. 5 **81**
4 ran   Time 1m 14.6 (4.8)   (Michael A Foy)   M R Channon West Isley, Berks

Official Going   GOOD TO SOFT (SOFT in places). Stalls: Str Crse - Stands Side; 1m6f - Centre; Rem - Inside.

1577
   2.00 EBF FILL MED AUCT MDN 2YO (E)   6f   Good/Soft 77 -48 Slow
£2990   £920   £460   £230

1413 **NUMERATE** 10 [3] M L W Bell 2-8-11 J Mackay (7) 2/1 FAV: 31: 2 b f Bishop Of Cashel - Half A Dozen   74
(Saratoga Six) Sn led, made rest, pshd out, shade cmftbly: well bckd from 7/2, lkd well, slow time: 4,600 gns Mar
foal, half-sister to a juv wnr: sire 7f/1m performer: eff forcing the pace at 6f on gd & gd/soft grnd, gall trks.

-- **CLASSY ACT** [6] A Berry 2-8-11 G Carter 6/1: 2: 2 ch f Lycius - Stripanoora (Ahonoora)   1   69
Struggled to go pace till kept on well final 1½f, nrst fin: op 4/1 on debut: 15,000 gns Mar foal, half-sister to
4 juv wnrs, sire sprinter/miler: eff at 6f, 7f will suit: goes on gd/soft grnd: scope to improve & win similar.

1429 **CUMBRIAN HARMONY** 8 [10] T D Easterby 2-8-11 K Darley 3/1: 023: 2 b f Distinctly North - Sawaki   ¾   67$
(Song) Nvr far away & ev ch, unable to qckn fnl 1f: bckd tho' op 5/2, clr rem, fit: stays 6f: handles fast & gd/sft.

1408 **IVANS BRIDE** 10 [2] G G Margarson 2-8-11 G Duffield 16/1: 064: Prom, effort 2f out, onepace: fit.   2   61

-- **ROYAL MUSICAL** [8] 2-8-11 T Williams 25/1: 5: Slow away, in tch halfway, no extra inl 2f: better   4   51
for race: 3,400IR gns Royal Abjar half-sister to sev wnrs, notably decent juv sprinter First Musical: small filly.

-- **KATIES DOLPHIN** [9] 2-8-11 A Culhane 16/1: 6: Al same place: debut, unfurnished filly: 2   45
2,400 gns Dolphin Street Apr foal, dam 12f wnr, sire 6/7f performer: with J Carr.

974 **SOMETHINGABOUTMARY** 41 [4] 2-8-11 T G McLaughlin 33/1: 07: Nvr trbld ldrs: small, needs sells.   2½   39

1429 **CARUSOS** 8 [12] 2-8-11 M Fenton 10/1: 08: Chsd ldrs till halfway: small filly, see 1429.   shd   39

938 **TUPGILL FLIGHT** 43 [14] 2-8-11 O Pears 66/1: 09: Struggling after 3f: 6 wk abs, strong, needs time.   nk   38

1197 **SILVER CLOUD** 22 [5] 2-8-11 A Nicholls (3) 20/1: 00: Mid-div till 2f out: 10th, lkd well, strong: ½   37
6,800 gns Petong Feb foal, half-sister to sev wnrs, dam 7f wnr, sire a sprinter: with W Jarvis.

1252 **WHARFEDALE LADY** 18 [13] 2-8-11 R Winston 20/1: -000: Sn bhd: 12th, op 8/1, small & plain.   0

1146 **Dance Queen** 25 [11] 2-8-11 J Bramhill 50/1:   1424 **Little Mouse** 8 [7] 2-8-11 M Baird 100/1:
13 ran   Time 1m 16.4 (7.5)   (Cheveley Park Stud)   M L W Bell Newmarket, Suffolk.

1578
   2.30 REDCAR AMAT MDN HCAP 3YO+ 0-60 (G)   6f   Good/Soft 77 -44 Slow   [25]
£2044   £584   £292   3 yo rec 9 lb

1422 **CRYFIELD** 8 [9] N Tinkler 3-11-3 (51) Mrs C Williams 14/1: 050201: 3 b g Efisio - Cibourne (Norwick)   59
In tch, kept on ent final 2f to lead below dist, pushed out: sweating, strong: unrcd juv: earlier rnr-up on
sand (h'cap, rtd 51a): eff over a sharp or gall 6f on gd/soft grnd & fibresand: well ridden by his amateur pilot.

825 **EASTERN RAINBOW** 55 [18] K A Ryan 4-10-8 (33)(bl) Miss E Ramsden 7/1: 00-002: 4 b g Bluebird -   1½   36
Insaf (Raise A Native) Nvr far away, led 2f out till ent fnl 1f, not pace of wnr: 8 wk abs: big drop in trip, 1st
time in the frame: rtd 60 & flattered on debut last term: suited to drop to 6f, handles gd/soft grnd & wears blnkrs.

1462 **INDIAN BAZAAR** 6 [11] J M Bradley 4-11-1 (40) Miss Hayley Bryan (7) 25/1: 230-03: 4 ch g Indian Ridge1¾   38
- Bazaar Promise (Native Bazaar) Handy, hard rdn appr 2f out, same pace: qck reapp, just burly: '99 rnr-up
(h'cap, rtd 40, Sir M Prescott): well btn juv: eff at 6f, tried 12f: handles firm & gd/soft grnd.

1295 **GENERAL DOMINION** 15 [8] Denys Smith 3-11-9 (57) Mrs S Eddery (5) 20/1: 0054: Chsd ldrs, hdwy   shd   55
for press 2f out, no extra ins last: big, lengthy & scopey, suited to drop to 6f on h'cap bow: handles gd/soft.

1139 **YORKIE TOO** 26 [25] Miss J Feilden 4-11-7 (46)(bl) Miss J Feilden (7) 00-005: Rear, late hdwy, nvr a threat: op 20/1.   2   38

1211 **DON QUIXOTE** 21 [3] 4-11-6 (45) Mr L Richardson (7) 4/1 FAV: 030-06: In tch, prog appr final 1f,   1½   33
nvr pace to chall: bckd from 8/1: should do better with stronger handling: see 1211.

1392 **PRINCE NICO** 11 [16] 3-10-6 (40) Mr V Coogan (4) 25/1: -0007: Al arnd same place: scope, h'cap bow.   ½   27

179 **SWYNFORD ELEGANCE** 169 [17] 3-10-10 (44) Mr S Dobson (5) 33/1: 6050-8: Nvr better than mid-div.   hd   30

1422 **DEFIANCE** 8 [26] 5-10-10 (35) Mr J J Best (7) 25/1: 050-09: Nvr troubled ldrs: lkd well: no form in   hd   21
'99 (tried blnks): plcd back in 2 mdn h'caps (rtd 79): eff at 7f on fast grnd: with A James.

1559 **DENTON LADY** 1 [6] 3-10-8 (42)(bl) Miss K Walling 7 20/1: 000300: Outpcd, moderate late hdwy: 10th.   ¾   26

1430 **CHOK DI** 8 [1] 4-10-8 (33)(bl) Miss L Hay (7) 16/1: 000000: Led till appr final 1f, sn btn: 11th, see 273.   1   14

1462 **DELTA GEORGIA** 6 [21] 4-11-6 (45) Miss Bridget Gatehouse (3) 20/1: 02-000: Nvr dngrs: 12th, qk reapp.   ½   25

1414 **ARZILLO** 10 [19] 4-12-0 (53) Mr M Savage (7) 12/1: 0-0340: Al towards rear: 17th: top-weight, op 8/1.   0

1239 **TINAS ROYALE** 19 [13] 4-11-4 (43) Mrs L Pearce 10/1: 0-5000: Nvr a factor: 18th, see 897.   0

1202 **BILLYS BLUNDER** 22 [15] Mr J Folkes (5) 3-10-4 (42)(tvi) Miss E Folkes (5) 12/1: 044540: Chsd ldrs till 2f out: 20th.   0

1422 **NADDER** 8 [5] 5-10-7 (32) Mr T Best (5) 11/2: 503020: Mid-div till ent final 2f: 21st, tchd 7/1, better on sand.   0

1391 **MOY** 10 [20] 5-10-7 (32)(vis) Miss K Rockey (5) 11/1: 002050: In tch till halfway: 22nd, op 8/1, see 466.   0

1244 **Tartan Island** 19 [10] 3-11-0 (48) Mr W Peffers (7) 33/1:
1365 **Timeless Quest** 11 [14] 3-10-11 (45) Mr F Windsor Clive (3) 33/1:
1349 **Outstanding Talent** 12 [24] 3-11-4 (52) Mr K Burke (7) 14/1:
145 **Dance Little Lady** 178 [23] 3-11-9 (57) Miss S Brotherton (5) 50/1:
1334 **Power And Demand** 13 [4] 3-11-0 (48)(bl) Mrs S Bosley 25/1:
2634‡ **Abstract** 323 [12] 4-10-12 (37) Miss Rachel Clark (7 33/1:
181 **Epona** 19 [22] 3-10-8 (42) Miss L J Harwood (7) 40/1:
1354 **Bluegrass Mountain** 11 [17] 3-11-12 (60) Mr Nicky Tinkler (5) 50/1:
25 ran   Time 1m 16.2 (7.3)   (Mr & Mrs G Middlebrook)   N Tinkler Langton, Nth Yorks.

1579
   3.00 CLASSIFIED STKS 3YO+ 0-70 (E)   7f str   Good/Soft 77 -03 Slow
£2899   £892   £446   £223   3 yo rec 11lb

1514 **SMART PREDATOR** 3 [7] J J Quinn 4-9-0 J Stack 11/4: 003031: 4 gr g Polar Falcon - She's Smart   73
(Absalom) Made ev yd, drew clr bef fnl 1f, readily: nicely bckd, ran well on Saturday, padd pick: '99 York wnr (mdn,
rtd 84): eff at 7f/1m: acts on firm & soft grnd, any trk: prob best forcing the pace: quick follow-up likely.

1431 **LADY LOVE** 8 [6] Denys Smith 3-8-0 (bl) A Nicholls (3) 20/1: 60-502: 3 b g Pursuit Of Love -   3   64
Lady Day (Lightning) Pulled hard, in tch, rdn appr final 1f, styd on well for 2nd but no trouble wnr: lkd
well: eff at 5f/7f: acts on gd & gd/soft grnd: back to form in first time blnks: lengthy filly: see 1144.

888 **MELLOW JAZZ** 48 [3] E A L Dunlop 3-8-0 G Carter 10/3: 1-03: 3 b f Lycius - Slow Jazz (Chief's Crown)   1¼   62
Chsd ldrs, rdn ent final 2f, unable to qckn: sturdy filly, needed this after 7 wk abs: prob stays 7f, see 888.

1399 **MALARKEY** 10 [4] J A Osborne 3-8-3 F Norton 9/4 FAV: 0554: Handy, under press 2f out, onepace.   hd   65

1405 **CHARMING LOTTE** 10 [1] 3-8-0 (vis) J Mackay (7) 12/1: 5-0005: Well plcd & ch 2f out, outpcd: v fit.   ½   61

1215 **MYTTONS AGAIN** 21 [2] 3-8-3 A Mackay 8/1: 400266: Prom till halfway: small, blnks omitted, see 158.   5   54

1144 **KASS ALHAWA** 25 [8] 7-9-0 A Culhane 40/1: 206247: Pulled hard bhd ldrs, lost place after halfway.   1¾   51

1354 **THORNCLIFF FOX** 11 [9] 3-8-3 (bl) O Pears 25/1: 30-048: Veered right, al bhd: lkd well, longer trip.   shd   51

REDCAR TUESDAY MAY 30TH Lefthand, Flat, Galloping Track

8 ran Time 1m 27.4 (5.6) (B Shaw) J J Quinn Settrington, Nth Yorks.

1580 **3.30 EVENING GAZETTE HCAP 3YO+ 0-90 (C) 5f Good/Soft 77 +13 Fast [84]**
£7475 £2300 £1150 £575 3 yo rec 8 lb

+1398 **EASTERN TRUMPETER 10** [4] J M Bradley 4-8-10 (66) K Darley 4/1: 002111: 4 b c First Trump - Oriental Air (Taufan) Well plcd, rdn & qcknd to lead below dist, ran on strgly: fast time: hat-trick landed: earlier won at W'hampton (2, h'caps, rtd 72a), Carlisle (class stks) & Lingfield (h'cap): '99 Folkestone (clmr) & & Ayr wnr (h'cap, rtd 70): all wins at 5f, stays 6f on firm, soft, fibresand, likes W'hampton: improving. **73**
1471 **CRYHAVOC 6** [2] D Nicholls 6-9-12 (82) F Norton 7/2 FAV: 003032: 6 b g Polar Falcon - Sarabah (Ela-Mana-Mou) Cl-up, rdn & ev ch appr final 1f, kept on, just held: bckd, qck reapp: knocking at the door. *nk* **87**
1196 **BRECONGILL LAD 22** [10] D Nicholls 8-9-2 (72) A Nicholls (3) 9/1: 33-303: 8 b g Clantime - Chikala (Pitskelly) Trkd ldrs, keen, prog to chase wnr appr final 1f, kept on & just held: stablemate 2nd, in form. *nk* **76**
*1412 **WILLIAMS WELL 10** [13] M W Easterby 6-8-10 (66)(bl) T Lucas 8/1: -06014: In tch, kept on final 1½f, not pace to chall: op 6/1, ran to best, in-form, see 1412. *¾* **68**
1357 **GAY BREEZE 11** [14] 7-9-7 (77) S Finnamore (5) 8/1: 5-3035: Cl-up, led after 2f till dist, no extra. *1½* **75**
1357 **DOUBLE OSCAR 11** [3] 7-8-13 (69) T Hamilton (7) 33/1: -00056: In tch, unable to pick up appr fnl 1f. *½* **66**
-- **RIOJA** [12] 5-8-9 (65) G Carter 9/1: 0000/7: Mid-div, feeling pace 2f out, late rally: boiled over in paddock after 2yr abs: '98 reapp wnr at Newmarket (h'cap, rtd 76): plcd twice as a juv (rtd 76): eff at 6f/7f: acts on gd/soft grnd, handles fast: can go well fresh: scopey gldg, go closer next time at 6f+. *1* **59**
*1384 **HONESTY FAIR 10** [8] 3-9-7 (85) D Mernagh (3) 13/2: 0-4118: Never out of mid-div: lkd well but was tackling older horses for the first time, see 1384. *hd* **79**
1357 **ZUHAIR 11** [7] 7-9-7 (77) Clare Roche (7) 33/1: 000009: Front rank till 2f out: lkd well, st/mate 2nd/3rd. *1* **68**
4612} **SEVEN OF SPADES 207** [9] 3-8-4 (68) P Hanagan (7) 50/1: 0035-0: In tch, outpcd 2f out: 10th: small, fit for reapp: juv rnr-up (auct mdn, rtd 75): eff at 5f, tried 6f: goes on gd & gd/soft grnd, prob hvy. *¾* **57**
1412 **WATERFORD SPIRIT 10** [5] 4-8-11 (67) T Williams 25/1: 00W000: Went right start, al bhd: 11th: *1¼* **53**
1479 **Swynford Welcome 5** [1] 4-7-12 (54)(BL) J Bramhill 50/1:
1479 **Twickers 5** [6] 4-8-4 (60)(BL) G Duffield 20/1: 4585} **Statoyork 210** [11] 7-8-5 (61) J Fanning 20/1:
14 ran Time 59.7 (3.2) (R G G Racing) J M Bradley Sedbury, Gloucs.

1581 **4.00 SKELTON MDN HCAP 3YO 0-60 (F) 1m6f Good/Soft 77 -12 Slow [67]**
£2404 £687 £343

1270 **DAME FONTEYN 18** [11] M L W Bell 3-9-5 (58) J Mackay (7) 4/1: -P2261: 3 b f Suave Dancer - Her Honour (Teenoso) Held up, steady prog after 5f out, led appr fnl 1f, hung left, rdly: fit: well btn all 3 '99 starts: eff at 12/14f, shld get 2m: acts on gd/soft & hvy grnd, stiff/gall tracks: improving filly. **63**
1270 **PTAH 18** [15] J L Eyre 3-8-11 (50) F Norton 5/1: -00432: 3 b g Petardia - Davenport Goddess (Classic Secret) Mid-div, prog to lead going well 4f out, shaken up & hdd bef fnl 1f, kept on: op 4/1, v fit, small, clr rem: improved again & is likely to get 2m: shld win a staying h'cap up north: also bhd wnr in 1270. *1* **52**
1296 **ALTAY 15** [9] R A Fahey 3-9-5 (58) R Winston 14/1: 506-03: 3 b g Erin's Isle - Aliuska (Fijar Tango) Mid div, prog to press ldrs 3f out, soon onepce: op 10/1, clr rem, better for race: unplcd juv (mdn, rtd 63): big gelding, prob stays 14f on gd/soft grnd. *5* **56**
1446 **SMUDGER SMITH 7** [16] B S Rothwell 3-9-7 (60) M Fenton 3/1 FAV: 00-034: Towards rear, wide prog to chase ldrs 3f out, soon onepace: nicely bckd from 4/1, rather small to be carrying top weight over longer trip. *8* **52**
1361 **WELCOME BACK 11** [7] 3-8-5 (44) F Lynch 16/1: 06-005: Held up, improved turning for home soon no further impression: longer trip, unplcd juv (aution mdn, rtd 56): with K Ryan. *½* **35**
1253 **DEBS SON 18** [14] 3-9-4 (57) J Bramhill 10/1: 54-666: Mid-div, chsd ldrs appr fnl 3f, grad wknd. *6* **43**
1142 **TYCOONS LAST 26** [3] 3-8-7 (46) T G McLaughlin 12/1: 0-3507: Never better than mid div: up in trip. *1½* **31**
807 **BITTY MARY 60** [2] 3-8-11 (50) G Carter 20/1: 050-08: In tch till 3f out: not given a hard time, 9 wk abs. *2* **33**
1299 **LOBLITE LEADER 15** [13] 3-8-11 (50) J Fanning 20/1: 50-009: Led till entering fnl 4f, soon btn: op 14/1, longer trip: prob flattered 5th of 14 in '99 (auct mdn, rtd 73): with G M Moore: not certain to get 14f. *hd* **33**
1435} **ROCKY ISLAND 375** [6] 3-8-5 (44) Dale Gibson 14/1: 000-0: Never dangerous: 10th, v burly on reapp/ h'cap bow: well btn in 3 sprints as a juv: bred to need mid-dists: with Mrs Reveley. *4* **24**
1433 **CASTANEA SATIVA 8** [5] 3-9-3 (56) K Darley 12/1: 0-0450: Chsd ldrs till halfway: 11th, blnks omitted. *12* **26**
1053 **Runin Circles 31** [8] 3-9-2 (55) G Parkin 20/1: 1293 **Silver Spoon 15** [4] 3-8-6 (45) G Duffield 20/1:
4263} **Dispol Miss Chief 237** [10] 3-8-9 (48) O Pears 20/1: 1143 **Amber Go Go 25** [1] 3-8-3 (42) R Lappin 33/1:
15 ran Time 3m 10.3 (12.5) (Frank A Farrant) M L W Bell Newmarket, Suffolk

1582 **4.30 KIRKLEATHAM MDN 3YO+ (D) 1m2f Good/Soft 77 -17 Slow**
£2964 £912 £456 £228 3 yo rec 14lb

1093 **TRAHERN 28** [4] J H M Gosden 3-8-10 K Darley 1/4 FAV: -421: 3 b c Cadeaux Genereux - Tansy (Shareef Dancer) In tch, trkd ldrs on bit 3f out, led dist, v easily, any amount in hand: hvly bckd to land the odds: earlier eye-catching 4th in the Wood Ditton (working out well): brother to a miler abroad: eff at 1m/10f on gd & gd/soft grnd, stiff/gall tracks: strong & scopey colt, should hold his own in better company. **88**
1054 **ADAWAR 31** [10] Sir Michael Stoute 3-8-10 F Lynch 10/1: 562: 2 b c Perugino - Adalya (Darshaan) Well plcd, led 3f out till 1f out, flatteredd by proximity to wnr: op 8/1, well clr rem, big & strong: stays 10f on gd/soft grnd: shown enough to find similar in the North though future is prob in h'caps: see 873. *1¼* **78**
-- **PERPETUO** [7] R A Fahey 3-8-5 P Hanagan (7) 50/1: 3: 3 b f Mtoto - Persian Fountain (Persian Heights) Rear, eff to go 3rd 2f out, no chance with ldrs: small, unfurnished newcomer: mid-dist bred. *9* **59**
-- **EMPIRE DREAM** [1] M Johnston 3-8-10 J Fanning 13/2: 4: Prom, led appr straight till 3f out, no extra: op 9/2: stocky Alzao newcomer, dam useful 7f/10f performer: should improve. *1¼* **62**
1369 **WELDUNFRANK 11** [3] 7-9-10 T G McLaughlin 100/1: 005: Led till went wide & hdd bef straight, fdd. *1¼* **60**
1193 **DARK SHADOWS 23** [9] 5-9-10 T Williams 20/1: -536: Never troubled ldrs: big, plain, jumping sort. *½* **59**
1054 **COURT OF JUSTICE 31** [5] 4-9-10 O Pears 16/1: 0-57: Mid div till 4f out: burly & bandaged all round. *8* **49**
772} **OCEAN VIEW 421** [8] 4-9-5 R Winston 66/1: 6-8: Al rear: last sole '99 start (rtd 55): half-sister to a 5f wnr. *6* **36**
86 **WILD FLIGHT 190** [11] 3-8-10 T Lucas 100/1: 00-9: Chsd ldrs till 4f out: sweating, lengthy & unfurnished. *24* **21**
9 ran Time 2m 11.7 (9.4) (Sheikh Mohammed) J H M Gosden Manton, Wilts

REDCAR TUESDAY MAY 30TH Lefthand, Flat, Galloping Track

1583 5.00 LEVY BOARD H'CAP 3YO+ 0-70 (E) 1m1f Good/Soft 77 -10 Slow [70]
£3198 £984 £492 £246 3 yo rec 13lb

+ 1300 **WERE NOT STOPPIN** 15 [4] R Bastiman 5-8-5 (47) O Pears 11/4 FAV: 505111: 5 b g Mystiko - Power Take 55
Off (Aragon) Chsd ldrs, led appr fnl 1f, rdn out: nicely bckd from 4/1, lkd well: qck hat-trick landed after wins
at Beverley (sell) & here at Redcar (h'cap): eff at 1m/9f, tried further: acts on firm & hvy grnd, gall trks.
4363} **BACCHUS** 229 [11] Miss J A Camacho 6-9-6 (62) F Norton 9/1: 5015-2: 6 b g Prince Sabo - Bonica nk 68
(Rousillon) Waited with, imprvd appr fnl 2, kept on under hands & heels (carried head high), just btn: attractive,
just better for reapp: '99 wnr at Beverley (2, sell h'cap & h'cap) & h'cap: '97 wnr at Newmarket (mdn, rtd 82,
A Stewart): eff at 7.5f/9f: acts on fast & gd/soft grnd, stiff/gall trks, likes Beverley: hard to beat next time.
1217 **SALIGO** 21 [6] N Tinkler 5-9-4 (60) Kim Tinkler 11/2: -00003: 5 b m Elbio - Doppio Filo (Vision) 1½ 64
Rear, imprvd 3f out & every chance 2f out, no extra under press inside last: nicely bckd from 14/1,
well clr rem: big run expected & delivered from this well h'capped mare: see 1217.
899 **PERCHANCER** 47 [13] P C Haslam 4-9-1 (57) P Goode (3) 9/1: 100134: Bhnd, some prog 3f out, soon 7 51
onepace: paddock pick, 7 week abs, sharper next time , see 846.
1370 **GABLESEA** 11 [8] Dale Gibson 12/1: 610205: Rear, mod late headway & edged left. 2½ 46
1348 **BLUE ACE** 12 [7] 7-9-4 (60) A Culhane 9/2: -50006: Mid div, effort 4f out, no impress: longer trip. 3½ 47
1254 **NOWELL HOUSE** 18 [5] 4-9-5 (61) G Parkin 25/1: -00007: Never trbld ldrs: slipping down the weights. ½ 47
1254 **SPARKY** 18 [16] 6-9-2 (58) (bl) T Lucas 12/1: /00-28: Held up, brief eff appr fnl 3f: see 1254 (firm). 1½ 42
4513} **LOVE KISS** 217 [15] 5-8-13 (55) T Williams 50/1: /600-9: Led till extr fnl 2f, sn btn: lightly rcd shd 39
& no form since pld as a 2yo in '97 (stks, rtd 86, M Johnston): prob stays 1m, handles gd & gd/sft grnd.
1279 **CYBERTECHNOLOGY** 17 [3] 6-9-1 (57) F Lynch 10/1: 0-0000: In tch till 3f out: 10th: op 8/1, lkd well. 2½ 38
847 **BOLD AMUSEMENT** 52 [1] 10-9-10 (66) A Nicholls (3) 8/1: 250-20: Chsd ldrs till 3f out: 11th, 7 wk abs. ½ 46
1477 **Dontbesobold** 5 [14] 3-8-7 (62) (vis) M Fenton 16/1: 1300 **College King** 15 [12] 4-8-10 (52) D Mernagh (3) 50/1:
-- **Flashtalkin Flood** [9] 6-8-7 (49) R Lappin 50/1:
14 ran Time 1m 56.6 (7.8) (I B Barker) R Bastiman Cowthorpe, N Yorks

---

SANDOWN TUESDAY MAY 30TH Righthand, Galloping Track, Stiff Finish

Official Going HEAVY. Stalls: Sprint Course - Far Side, Remainder - Inside

1584 6.15 CREDIT SUISSE MDN 3YO (D) 1m rnd Soft 112 -61 Slow
£4329 £1332 £666 £333

1188 **HYMN** 23 [3] J H M Gosden 3-9-0 J Fortune 8/11 FAV: -21: 3 b c Fairy King - Handsewn (Sir Ivor) 90
Press ldr till went on 3f out, hdd dist, rallied to regain lead ins last, held on gamely: hvly bckd from 5/4, slow
time: half brother to several wnrs: eff at 1m, shld stay 10f: acts on firm & soft grnd & on a stiff/gall trk:
battled on well today: useful & genuine, can rate more highly.
-1376 **GREY EMINENCE** 11 [1] R Hannon 3-9-0 Dane O'Neill 7/2: 5-22: 3 gr c Indian Ridge - Rahaam ½ 89
(Secreto) Prom, prog to lead dist, carried head on one side & hdd ins last, kept on but outbattled by wnr: nicely
bckd tho' drifted from 7/4: acts on gd & soft grnd: has shown enough to find similar: see 1376.
1377 **HIGHLAND REEL** 11 [2] D R C Elsworth 3-9-0 N Pollard 10/3: -303: 3 ch c Selkirk - Taj Victory 1¼ 87
(Final Straw) Waited with, eff & no impress 2f out, ran on fnl 1f but too late: now qual for h'caps, 10f will suit.
1376 **GENERAL JACKSON** 11 [4] D R C Elsworth 3-9-0 T Quinn 20/1: -04: Led till 3f out, soon btn: longer 7 75
priced stablemate of 3rd: sire a top class sprinter, dam mid-dist bred: again bhnd today's 2nd in 1376.
4 ran Time 1m 52.79 (13.79) (Mrs B V Sangster, Mrs J Magnier) J H M Gosden Manton Wilts

1585 6.45 WINTERTHUR HCAP 3YO 0-80 (D) 1m2f Soft 112 -33 Slow [83]
£4582 £1410 £705 £352

*1292 **FANFARE** 15 [1] G A Butler 3-9-3 (72) L Dettori 9/2: 50-011: 3 b f Deploy - Tashinsky (Nijinsky) 77
Waited with, imprvd 2f out, styd on strongly to lead ent fnl 1f, kept on strongly, rdn out: op 7/2: recent Windsor
wnr (h'cap): eff at 10f, stays 12f: acts on firm & soft grnd, handles a stiff/gall or sharp trk: improving filly.
1193 **STORM WIZARD** 23 [7] M R Channon 3-9-7 (76) T Quinn 7/1: 0-3422: 3 b g Catrail - Society Ball 1¼ 78
(Law Society) Trckd ldr, ev ch 2f out, kept on fnl 1f but not pace of wnr: op 10/1, top weight: deserves a race.
*1448 **NEVER DISS MISS** 7 [8] W Jarvis 3-9-7 (76)(5ex) D McGaffin (7) 5/1: 00-513: 3 b f Owington - Pennine shd 78
Pink (Pennine Walk) Rcd keenly in bhnd ldr, led 2f out to fnl 1f, kept on & not btn far: gd run under 7lb pen.
1261 **UNDER THE SAND** 18 [6] M A Jarvis 3-8-13 (68) P Robinson 4/1: -0004: Prom till outpcd 2f out, styd ½ 69
on again fnl 1f: well bckd, clr of rem: fair eff on h'cap debut: stays 10f, even better will suit: see 1261.
1425 **JEUNE PREMIER** 8 [9] 3-8-13 (68) D R McCabe 25/1: 0-5005: Led till 2f out, fdd: see 936. 8 57
1177 **MUCHANA YETU** 23 [4] 3-8-13 (68) L Newman (5) 16/1: 055-06: Trck ldrs, rdn & btn 2f out: see 1177. 3 52
4432} **NIGHT MUSIC** 224 [2] 3-8-9 (64) M Roberts 16/1: 40-7: Rcd wide & sn struggling, no ch fnl 2f: hd 48
reapp: 4th at Salisbury in '99 (mdn auct, debut, rtd 70+): related to sev mid-dist wnrs, sire a prog sprinter.
1511 **CORAL SHELLS** 4 [3] 3-8-2 (57) M Henry 25/1: 025-08: Rear, prog to chase ldrs 2f out, soon btn. shd 41
1292 **MILLIONS** 15 [5] 3-8-11 (66) K Fallon 5/2 FAV: 00-529: Trckd ldrs, ev ch 3f out, sn btn: hvly nk 49
bckd: disapp eff, not handle this testing grnd? much btr 1292 (12f, firm).
9 ran Time 2m 18.6 (14.5) (T D Holland-Martin) G A Butler Blewbury, Oxon

1586 7.15 LISTED NATIONAL STKS 2YO (A) 5f str Soft 112 -14 Slow
£11927 £3670 £1635 £917

1107 **TARAS EMPEROR** 27 [2] J J Quinn 2-9-1 J Fortune 6/1: -4141: 2 b g Common Grounds - Strike It Rich 104
(Rheingold) Prsd ldr, went on over 1f out, clr fnl 1f, pushed out: bckd from 9/1: earlier scored at Newcastle
(nov): dam scored over 10f, related to a 1m wnr: eff at 5f, will stay 6f: acts on gd/soft, winning form on soft
& hvy grnd: likes a stiff/gall track: fast improving & smart juv, strong claims at R Ascot given similar ground.
1214 **STREGONE** 21 [5] B J Meehan 2-9-1 L Dettori 25/1: -1652: 2 b g Namaqualand - Sabonis (The 3½ 96
Ministral) Held up & outpcd, ran on well to take 2nd cl home, no ch with wnr: acts on fast & soft grnd, crying
out for 6f now: best eff to date, shld regain winning ways judged on this: see 1214, 743 (debut).
*1372 **ELSIE PLUNKETT** 11 [3] R Hannon 2-8-12 Dane O'Neill 7/4 FAV: -51113: 2 b f Mind Games - Snow Eagle ½ 92

(Polar Falcon) Set pace till dist, no extra ins last & caught for 2nd cl home: hvly bckd tho' op 5/4: has won
on hvy, reportedly much better on faster grnd as in 1372: still on target for the Queen Mary.
1454 **SILCA LEGEND 7** [6] M R Channon 2-8-12 T Quinn 9/2: -2324: Track ldrs, outpcd fnl 1f: well bckd   ¾ **89**
from 6/1: has shown more than enough to win with a drop in grade: see 1454 (mdn).
*1169 **MIDNIGHT ARROW 24** [7] 2-8-10 K Fallon 15/8: -15: Rdn in rear, hmpd halfway, no ch after: hvly   3 **81**
bckd tho' op 5/4: lost all ch when hmpd & prob not at home in these testing conditions: see 1169 (fast grnd).
1346 **RUSHBY 12** [4] 2-8-12 L Newman 20/1: -636: Raced keenly & chsd ldrs, wknd when went right dist.   6 **71**
6 ran   Time 1m 05.89 (6.29)   (Tara Leisure)   J J Quinn Settrington, N Yorks

---

1587   **7.45 GR 3 BRIGADIER GERARD STKS 4YO+ (A)**   **1m2f**   **Soft 112** **+15 Fast**
       £24000   £9200   £4600   £2200

967   **SHIVA 41** [4] H R A Cecil 5-9-0 T Quinn 7/2 FAV: 102-01: 5 ch m Hector Protector - Lingerie (Shirley   **123**
Heights) Trkd ldr, led over 2f out, soon drew well clr & 7L in command when eased down from unlucky in running
2nd: hvly bckd, fast time: in '99 won at Newmarket (Gr 3) & Curragh (Gr 1, beat Daylami, rtd 121): '98 wnr at
Kempton (fill mdn): v eff over 8.5/10.5f on gd/firm or soft: runs well fresh on a gall track: top class mare,
clearly in tremendous heart & will take the beating in chosen Royal Ascot engagement.
1152 **BORDER ARROW 25** [3] I A Balding 5-8-10 R Cochrane 5/1: 3/3-62: 5 ch h Selkirk - Nibbs Point   1¾ **115**
(Sure Blade) Held up, in contention when slipped on bend over 4f out, soon well adrift, styd on well over 1f out to
chase eased down wnr ins last: well bckd, clr rem: acts on fast & soft: fine run, must win a Gr race in this form.
*1248 **SOSSUS VLEI 19** [6] G Wragg 4-8-10 M Roberts 8/1: 62-513: 4 b c Inchinor - Sassalya (Sassafras)   5 **106**
In tch, rdn over 3f out, onepace fnl 2f: not disgraced: see 1248 (Listed).
1248 **BEAT ALL 19** [8] Sir Michael Stoute 4-8-10 K Fallon 9/2: 134-W4: Cl up, eff to chase wnr over 1f out,   1½ **104**
soon wknd: bckd tho' op 7/2: reportedly ndd this & shld certainly rate more highly: see 1248.
4203] **LADY IN WAITING 226** [7] 5-8-12 J Fortune 9/1: 2015-5: Set gd pace, clr after 3f till hdd over 2f out,   1 **105**
no extra: reapp: in '99 won at York (List) & Newmarket (Gr 2, by 8L, rtd 111): '98 scorer at Chepstow (fill
stks) & Newmarket (List): stays 12f, suited by a gall 10f: acts on firm, gd/soft & on any trk, likes Newmarket:
loves to force the pace & has run well fresh: useful & geniune, sharper for this.
1458 **DIAMOND WHITE 9** [5] 5-8-12 J F Egan 9/1: 023456: In touch, brief eff over 3f out, wknd over 2f out.   1½ **103**
*12   **ELLE DANZIG 205** [2] 5-9-0 A Starke 7/1: 4141-7: Cl up, wknd 2f out: reapp: in '99 won twice in   4 **101**
Germany (Gr 3's) & at Capannelle (Gr 1, rtd 118): in '98 won the German 1,000 Guineas & Oaks: eff over 10/
11f & likes soft & hvy: has run fresh: German mare, smart at best.
768   **EASAAR 66** [9] 4-8-10 L Dettori 11/2: /0-128: Waited with, rdn over 2f out, eased when well btn   14 **83**
over 1f out: much better on gd grnd in 768.
8 ran   Time 2m 13.8 (9.7)   (Niarchos Family)   H R A Cecil Newmarket

---

1588   **8.45 EVENING MDN 3YO+ (D)**   **1m2f**   **Soft 115** **-72 Slow**
       £4368   £1344   £672   £336   3 yo rec 14lb

4528] **CANFORD 216** [8] W Jarvis 3-8-11 R Cochrane 6/4 FAV: 4-1: 3 b c Caerleon - Veronica (Persian   **88**
Bold) Made virtually all, drew clr over 1f out, v easily: hvly bckd tho' op 4/6 on reapp: rtd 90 when 4th on
sole juv start: dam 1m scorer: stays 10f, further looks sure to suit: revels in soft: useful, win in stronger grade.
1054 **VICTORY ROLL 31** [9] Miss E C Lavelle 4-9-11 S Drowne 10/1: 02: 4 b c In The Wings - Persian   11 **69**
Victory (Persian Bold) Cl up, eff to chase wnr over 1f out, sn btn: stays 10f on soft & showed some promise here.
1200 **QUIET READING 22** [7] C A Cyzer 3-8-11 S Sanders 11/2: 003: 3 b g Northern Flagship - Forlis Key   3 **66$**
(Forli) Cl up, rdn & onepace fnl 2f: prob stays 10f on soft: see 1200.
1263 **GLENDALE RIDGE 18** [6] Jamie Poulton 5-9-11 R Mullen 11/2: 44: Bhnd, mod late gains: see 1263 (7f). 1½ **64**
4180] **AUDACITY 242** [4] 4-9-11 L Newman (5) 33/1: 0500-5: Chsd wnr till 3f out, wknd: mod form.   6 **56$**
1287 **HERBSHAN DANCER 17** [5] 6-9-11 Martin Dwyer 20/1: 030/56: Cl up, wknd well over 2f out: see 1287.   3 **52**
1281 **SADLERS SWING 17** [1] 4-9-11 A Clark 14/1: 0-07: Keen, cl up till wknd over 2f out: see 1281.   1¾ **50**
--   **PENNY MUIR** [3] 3-8-6 J Lowe 20/1: 8: In tch, wknd over 3f out: dam a pt-to-pt wnr.   4 **41**
--   **KING OF THE WEST** [10] 4-9-11 A McGlone 25/1: 9: Keen, soon bhnd on debut: stoutly bred.   1½ **44**
1263 **BETCHWORTH SAND 18** [11] 4-9-11 C Rutter 33/1: 0-00: Al bhnd: 10th: mod form.   1½ **42**
--   **EAST ROSE** [2] 4-9-6 R Perham 10/1: 0: Al bhnd: finished last on debut: with M Usher.   6 **31**
11 ran   Time 2m 22.8 (18.7)   (Woodcote Stud)   W Jarvis Newmarket

---

NEWBURY   WEDNESDAY MAY 31ST   **Lefthand, Flat, Galloping Track**

Official Going GOOD/SOFT (SOFT places). Stalls: 5f - Stands Side; 6/7f - Centre; Rem - Outside.

1589   **6.30 EBF BOXFORD MDN 2YO (D)**   **5f34y**   **Good/Soft 71** **-18 Slow**
       £4446   £1368   £684   £342

1372 **ANIMAL CRACKER 12** [5] D Marks 2-8-9 S Drowne 9/2: 051: 2 gr f Primo Dominie - Child Star (Bellypha)   **84**
With ldr, kept on appr final 1f to lead ins last, hands-&-heels, cosily: bckd tho' op 9/4: Mar foal, cost 19,000gns:
half-sister to a 7f/1m wnr: dam wng styr/hdler: eff at 5f, further will suit: acts on fast & gd/soft: improve.
--   **GAME N GIFTED** [7] B J Meehan 2-9-0 J Carroll 7/4 FAV: 2: 2 b c Mind Games - Margaret's Gift   shd **88**
(Beveled) Handy, eff to chall over 1f out, kept on for press ins last, just held: hvly bckd on debut: Jan foal,
cost 33,000gns: dam 5/6f wnr: speedily bred & this was a useful eff at 5f on gd/soft: must win soon.
1260 **JACK SPRATT 19** [9] R Hannon 2-9-0 Dane O'Neill 10/1: 03: 2 b c So Factual - Raindancing (Tirol)   1 **85**
Led, rdn & hdd ins last, only btn 1L: improved for debut & eff at 5f on gd/soft: win a race on this form: see 1260.
--   **TEMPLES TIME** [3] R Hannon 2-8-9 R Hughes 11/2: 4: Slow away, sn in tch, effort over 1f out, eased   1½ **76**
when held inside last, not given hard time on debut: stablemate of 3rd: Mar foal, cost IR 7,500gns:
full sister to a 7f juv scorer: looks sure to apprec 6f in time.
--   **MAN OF DISTINCTION** [4] 2-9-0 N Pollard 5/1: 5: Slow away & bhd, kept on nicely over 1f out,   shd **81+**
nrst fin under hands-&-heels: op 7/2 on debut: Apr 1st foal, cost 25,000gns: dam Gr 3 6f juv wnr: eff at 5f,
sure to relish 6f: handles gd/soft: type to come on plenty for this, clr of rem & must be wng soon.
1260 **OSO NEET 19** [8] 2-9-0 P Dobbs 20/1: 06: Cl-up, rdn & btn over 1f out: see 1260.   4 **71**
1408 **BORDER EDGE 11** [1] 2-9-0 T E Durcan 16/1: 047: Al bhd: btr 1408 (6f).   6 **57**
--   **RAW SILK** [6] 2-9-0 A Clark 16/1: 8: Slow away & al bhd on debut: Mar foal, cost 8,000 gns: dam   5 **45**
multiple 1m scorer: will need 6f+: with M Ryan.

NEWBURY   WEDNESDAY MAY 31ST   Lefthand, Flat, Galloping Track

-- **POLISH PADDY** [2] 2-9-0 R Smith (5) 25/1: 9: Slow away, al bhd on debut: Mar foal, cost   10   23
IR 5,000gns: Priolo colt, stablemate of 3rd & 4th & will need further.
9 ran   Time 1m 04.83 (4.53)   (D Marks)   D Marks Lambourn, Berks.

1590   7.00 KINGSTON SMITH HCAP 4YO+ 0-85 (D)   7f str   Good/Soft 71   +08 Fast   [84]
£5434   £1672   £627   £627

1542 **DOLPHINELLE** 4 [12] Jamie Poulton 4-8-6 (62) O Urbina 11/1: 034031: 4 b c Dolphin Street - Marnie's   66
Joy (Prince Tenderfoot) Hld up, kept on nicely over 1f out to lead ins last, hands-&-heels, cosily: gd time, qk
reapp: Jan '99 Lingfield wnr (amat h'cap, rtd 61a, with R Hannon): '99 wnr at Brighton (h'cap, rtd 75 & 61a): eff
over 6/7f on firm, soft & equitrack: handles any trk & best without blnks/visor: cld win again in this form.
1383 **BRAVE EDGE** 11 [9] R Hannon 9-9-13 (83) Dane O'Neill 14/1: -03302: 9 b g Beveled - Daring Ditty   nk   84
(Daring March) In tch, hdwy & swtchd left over 1f out, kept on to lead ins last, collared cl-home, just btn:
fine run under top weight & remains on a handy mark: see 1383, 725.
1542 **SCISSOR RIDGE** 4 [16] J J Bridger 8-7-10 (52)(8oh) R Brisland (5) 14/1: 264023: 8 ch g Indian Ridge -   ¾   51
Golden Scissors (Kalaglow) Rcd alone stands side, cl-up, kept on fnl 1f, not btn far: qck reapp & in fine form.
1348 **SUSANS PRIDE** 13 [8] B J Meehan 4-9-7 (77) J Carroll 16/1: 100303: Handy, effort to lead over 1f   dht   76
out, collared inside last, no extra: see 1060, 780.
1286 **COOL TEMPER** 18 [7] 4-9-6 (76) R Hughes 11/1: 22-555: In tch, rdn 1f out, onepace: stays 7f.   nk   74
1250 **LOVERS LEAP** 20 [13] 4-9-8 (78) C Rutter 5/1: 20-006: Bhd, kept on over 1f out, nrst fin: nicely   ¾   75
bckd, clr of rem: returning to form: see 1015.
1113 **CARLTON** 28 [15] 6-9-6 (76) N Pollard 7/1: 1-4207: Bhd, late hdwy, no dngr: btr 1028 (hvy), 935.   3½   67
895 **PAGAN KING** 48 [10] 4-9-2 (72) S Whitworth 14/1: 156-08: Bhd, mod late gains, no dngr: likes Brighton.   1¾   60
937} **MAGIC POWERS** 407 [2] 5-8-5 (61) S Drowne 25/1: 03/0-9: Sn bhd, no dngr: reapp: well btn sole   1   47
'99 start: rtd 62 when plcd in '98: stays 7f on gd/soft.
1504 **THE DOWNTOWN FOX** 5 [11] 5-9-4 (74)(vis) J Reid 16/1: 000600: Bhd, nvr a factor: qck reapp, see 320. nk   59
*1467 **COMPRADORE** 7 [4] 5-9-4 (74)(6ex) D Sweeney 4/1 FAV: 032110: Handy, wknd over 1f out: 11th, too sn? 4   53
1450 **SLUMBERING** 8 [6] 4-9-10 (80)(BL) Pat Eddery 12/1: 6-4000: Led till over 1f out, wknd: 12th, blinkers.   6   44
1348 **APADI** 13 [5] 4-9-0 (70) Martin Dwyer 33/1: 600-00: In tch, btn 2f out: 13th: poor.   4   33
1126 **LUCY MARIELLA** 27 [1] 4-8-8 (64)(t) L Dettori 11/1: 240-00: Nvr a factor: 14th: see 1126.   11   11
14 ran   Time 1m 28.72 (4.42)   (Mrs G M Temmerman)   Jamie Poulton Telscombe, E Sussex

---

1591   7.30 TOTE HCAP 3YO+ 0-80 (D)   6f   Good/Soft 71   +08 Fast   [80]
£7832   £2410   £1205   £602   3 yo rec 9 lb

1398 **FEARBY CROSS** 11 [11] W J Musson 4-9-9 (75) Pat Eddery 7/2 FAV: 6-1341: 4 b g Unblest - Two Magpies   81
(Doulab) Hld up, hdwy over 1f out, styd on well for press to get up ins last, drvn out: nicely bckd, gd time:
earlier wnr at Sandown (h'cap), rtd 83 when unplcd for J Bethell in '99: '98 Ayr wnr (auct mdn, rtd 90): eff
over a stiff 5f, 6f suits: acts on fast & soft, without blnks: has run well fresh: in fine heart.
1398 **BOLD EFFORT** 11 [16] K O Cunningham Brown 8-9-7 (73)(bl) R Hughes 20/1: 010052: 8 b g Bold   ¾   76
Arrangement - Malham Tarn (Riverman) Sn bhd, kept on over 1f out, nrst fin, too late: well h'capped, win a gd sprint.
1074 **THE GAY FOX** 30 [7] B A McMahon 6-9-2 (68)(tVIS) J Reid 11/1: 050-53: 6 gr g Never So Bold - School   1½   68
Concert (Music Boy) In tch, eff 1f out, kept on same pace ins last: gd run in a visor but on a long losing run.
1471 **RETURN OF AMIN** 7 [12] W R Muir 6-10-0 (80)(bl) Martin Dwyer 11/2: 000024: Bhd, effort over 1f   shd   79
out, kept on same pace: well bckd: another well h'capped sprinter who is on a long losing run: see 1471, 728.
1398 **SUPREME ANGEL** 11 [8] 5-9-1 (67) C Cogan (5) 8/1: 040135: With ldr, onepace over 1f out: in form.   1   64
1441 **CAUDA EQUINA** 9 [6] 6-9-13 (79) Craig Williams 16/1: 020056: Cl-up, ev ch over 1f out, no extra   ¾   74
inside last: Bath specialist, see 1441, 905.
1061 **BOANERGES** 30 [2] 3-9-0 (75) N Pollard 33/1: 32-007: Swtchd right start, effort over 1f out, no impress.   hd   69
1068 **AGENT MULDER** 30 [3] 6-9-4 (70)(bl) L Dettori 8/1: 0-2338: Cl-up, wknd final 1f: see 1068, 941.   1¼   61
1483 **WELCOME GIFT** 6 [16] 4-9-3 (69) J Fortune 7/1: -22169: In tch, btn final 1f: see 1483, 434.   ½   59
763 **SHADY DEAL** 64 [4] 4-7-10 (48)(1oh) G Baker (7) 33/1: 003000: Led till just ins fnl 1f, wknd: 10th.   nk   37
1368 **DOUBLE MARCH** 12 [14] 7-8-6 (58)(BL) C Catlin (7) 10/1: 40-050: In tch, wknd over 1f out: 13th, blnks.   0
1405 Lady Noor 11 [1] 3-7-13 (60) P Doe 33/1:   1368 Bandbox 12 [10] 5-8-11 (63) S Whitworth 16/1:
1348 Kilmeena Lad 13 [15] 4-9-2 (68) S Carson (5) 14/1:   816 Astrac 58 [13] 9-9-12 (78) T Ashley 25/1:
1398 Bevelena 11 [5] 4-9-7 (73) N Callan 33/1:
16 ran   Time 1m 15.41 (3.81)   (Mrs Rita Brown)   W J Musson Newmarket.

1592   8.00 MILLENN'M PLATE COND STKS 4YO+ (C)   1m2f   Good/Soft 71   -18 Slow
£6128   £2266   £1133   £515

2790} **DEHOUSH** 317 [1] A C Stewart 4-8-7 L Dettori 5/4 FAV: 1204-1: 4 ch c Diesis - Dream Play (Blushing   111
Groom) Trkd ldr, went on over 2f out, styd on strongly despite flashing tail, pushed out: reapp: lightly rcd in
'99, Kempton reapp wnr (List), subs rnr-up at Sandown (Gr 3 Classic trial, rtd 112): '98 debut Newmarket wnr (mdn):
eff at 1m/10f, acts on firm & soft grnd, runs v well fresh (won first time out prev 2 seasons):
handles a gall or fair trk: smart colt who should win in Listed/Group company.
2967} **COMPTON ACE** 309 [2] G A Butler 4-9-5 (t) R Hughes 4/1: 2131-2: 4 ch c Pharly - Mountain Lodge   3½ 115+
(Blakeney) Rcd keenly bhd ldrs, imprvd to chase wnr fnl 1f, kept on under hands-&-heels riding: reapp: '99 wnr
at Newbury (h'cap) & Goodwood (Gr 3), reportedly broke a bone in his knee), also plcd at R Ascot (Gr 3, rtd 114 at
best): eff at 10/14f, stays 2m well: acts on firm & soft, handles any trk: suited by a t-strap, runs well fresh:
smart & progressive colt, this was a fine effort conceding today's wnr 12lbs: shld soon go one better over 12f+.
1248 **PEGNITZ** 20 [5] C E Brittain 5-9-1 P Robinson 5/1: 3-0443: 5 b h Lear Fan - Likely Split (Little   2½ 107
Current) Led till 2f out: returned to forcing tactics today: see 1248.
1482 **ANNAPURNA** 6 [4] B J Meehan 4-8-2 D R McCabe 100/30: 0-0234: Waited with, eff 3f out, no impress   3½   89
on ldrs: qck reapp: better than this & this prob came too sn after 1482 (List).
-- **LORD JIM** [3] 8-8-7 J Fortune 33/1: 0034/5: Chsd ldrs till lost place ent str, no ch after on comeback: 4   88
last rcd over hdles in Apr '99, rnr-up at Ascot (Gr 2, rtd 138h, with J Old), eff at 3m on firm & soft): 97/98 hdle wnr
at Chepstow, Cheltenham & Sandown: last rcd on the Flat in '98, trained by Lord Huntingdon & plcd at R Ascot
(Queen Alexandra Stks, rtd 97): '96 Flat wnr at Salisbury & Leopardstown (List, rtd 105): eff at 14f, stays 2m6f
on firm & hvy: usually wears blnks/visor, not today: lngr prcd stablemate of rnr-up, fitter next time.
5 ran   Time 2m 11.67 (8.87)   (Sheikh Ahmed Al Maktoum)   A C Stewart Newmarket.

NEWBURY

WEDNESDAY MAY 31ST   Lefthand, Flat, Galloping Track

1593   **8.30 SPY CLAIMER 3YO (E)**   **1m2f**   Good/Soft 71   -66 Slow
       £2843   £875   £437   £218

1238 **PRESTO** 20 [6] W J Haggas 3-8-5 (tBL) P Robinson 6/1: 00-051: 3 b g Namaqualand - Polish Dancer **60**
(Malinowski) Rear, imprvd 2f out, gamely forged ahead fnl strides: apprec this drop to clmg grade & first time
blnks: eff at 10f, shld stay 12f: acts on gd/soft grnd & on a stiff/gall trk: wears a t-strap.

1199 **SKYE BLUE** 23 [3] M R Channon 3-8-6 S Drowne 7/4 FAV: 0-5302: 3 b g Blues Traveller - Hitopah **nk 60**
(Bustino) Trkd ldrs, imprvd to chall dist, led ins last till caught nr fin: eff at 10/12f: should win similar.

1238 **VANISHING DANCER** 20 [8] K R Burke 3-9-0 N Callan 8/1: -3W033: 3 ch g Llandaff - Vanishing Prairie **2½ 64**
(Alysheba) Chsd ldrs, drvn to chall dist, not qckn cl-home: btn off a mark of 59 in a h'cap on the AW in 1238:
acts on gd/soft grnd: in front of today's wnr in 1238 (fibresand).

4047} **SUMMER CHERRY** 252 [1] P F I Cole 3-9-5 J Fortune 4/1: 00-4: Dwelt, gd hdwy to lead dist till ins **½ 68$**
last, no extra: reapp: twice rcd in '99 (rtd 73 in mdn company): $220,000 half-brother to a couple of wnrs in
the States: not disgrcd over this lngr 10f trip, 9f or a sharper trk may suit: sharper for this.

1175 **MANY HAPPY RETURNS** 24 [7] J A Nicholls (3) 10/1: 00-05: Rear, imprvg when short of room 2f **¾ 46**
out, not reach ldrs: lightly rcd in mdns over 6f: sire a high class 7f/1m performer: fair effort over this much
lngr 10f trip, not much luck in running here: with G Balding, apprec modest h'caps.

1343 **RECOLETA** 13 [10] 3-8-9 (BL) J Stack 20/1: 000-06: In tch, wknd over 1f out: tried blnks: little form. **6 46**

1349 **SILKEN FOX** 13 [2] 3-8-2 (BL) P Doe 33/1: 00-007: Led till over 1f out, wknd: first time blnks. **5 31**

1099 **RIDGEWOOD BAY** 29 [5] 3-8-2 C Rutter 40/1: 00-008: Al towards rear: see 814. **1½ 29**

701 **NO REGRETS** 69 [9] 3-9-0 J Carroll 20/1: 0-5009: Chsd ldr, ev ch 2f out, wknd qckly: 10 wk abs. **5 33**

1414 **BEDOUIN QUEEN** 11 [4] 3-8-3 S Carson 7/1: 5-0060: Hdwy from rear to chase ldrs 2f out, sn btn. **1 20**
10 ran   Time 2m 16.58 (13.78)   (Mr & Mrs Peter Lumley)   W J Haggas Newmarket.

1594   **9.00 K ROBERTSON HCAP 3YO+ 0-75 (E)**   **1m5f61y**   Good/Soft 71   -55 Slow   **[75]**
       £3071   £945   £472   £236   3 yo rec 19lb

4307} **TURTLE SOUP** 233 [2] Mrs L Richards 4-9-13 (74) Pat Eddery 8/1: 1204-1: 4 b c Turtle Island - Lisa's **77**
Favourite (Gorytus) In tch, chall strongly fnl 3f, forged ahead ins last, drvn out: reapp: in '99 trained by L
Cumani to win at Ayr (h'cap, rtd 76 at best): eff at 11/12f, stays an extended 13f well: acts on fast & soft grnd,
likes a stiff/gall trk: runs well fresh: fine first effort for new connections under a strong Pat Eddery ride.

1150 **ACHILLES WINGS** 26 [13] K R Burke 4-9-8 (69) J Weaver 4/1 FAV: 344202: 4 b c Irish River - Shirley **½ 71**
Valentine (Shirley Heights) Keen in rear, imprvd to lead 3f out, collared ins last, kept on & just btn: stays 13f.

3837} **KING OF MOMMUR** 266 [7] B R Millman 5-7-13 (46) A McCarthy (3) 10/1: 0060-3: 5 b g Fairy King - **¾ 47**
Monoglow (Kalaglow) Chsd ldrs, imprvd to chall 3f out, short of room & swtchd dist, kept on: won over hdles at
Exeter in Mar '00 (nov, rtd 108h, eff at 2m3f on gd/soft): trained by B Meehan in '99, plcd at Kempton (h'cap,
rtd 67): eff at 12/13f on firm & gd/soft: usually wears a t-strap, has worn a t-strap, not today: sound effort.

4465} **WENDS DAY** 223 [5] S E H Sherwood 5-9-4 (65) R Hughes 10/1: 45/3-4: Slowly away, well bhd over 4f **¾ 65+**
out, kept on nicely fnl 2f, too late: 4L clr rem, reapp: last rcd over hdls 11 wks ago, earlier won at Doncaster
(nov hdle, rtd 116h, eff at 2m on gd & soft): plcd sole '99 start (rtd 61): eff at 12/13.2f, further shld suit:
acts on gd/soft, soft over hdles: set too much to do & v interesting next time with a more positive ride.

1411 **NATURAL EIGHT** 11 [9] 6-8-11 (58) O Urbina 11/2: -63335: Dwelt, rdn & styd on fnl 2f, not rch ldrs. **4 54**

1292 **GOOD FRIDAY** 16 [11] 3-7-13 (65) P Doe 10/1: 30-656: Chsd ldrs, rdn & onepcd fnl 4f: see 1292 (12f). **5 56**

1271 **GEMINI GUEST** 19 [4] 4-9-11 (72) P Robinson 20/1: 00-057: Nvr a factor: see 1271. **1 62**

1375 **SIMPLY NOBLE** 12 [3] 4-9-10 (71) T E Durcan 30/1: 30-008: Nvr able to chall, nvr nr ldrs: see 1375. **2½ 58**

1551 **PEKAY** 2 [6] 7-8-11 (58) (bl) J Stack 8/1: 003539: Led after 3f till 3f out, fdd: too sn after 1551? **3 41**

1128 **COURAGE UNDER FIRE** 27 [10] 5-7-12 (45) Martin Dwyer 25/1: 45-000: Rear, effort halfway, btn **2½ 25**
final 3f: fin 10th: see 1128.

1272 **MALAKAL** 19 [12] 4-8-3 (50) D O'Donohoe 14/1: -00000: Chsd ldrs 9f, wknd: see 56 (AW mdn). **12 18**

1180 **TALES OF BOUNTY** 24 [8] 5-8-12 (59) N Pollard 12/1: 066-00: Chsd ldrs, ev ch 5f out, sn wknd, t.o. **dist 0**

1440 **FEE MAIL** 9 [1] 4-9-7 (68) A Nicholls 9/2: -33120: Led 3f, wknd qckly, t.o. in last: puzzling **1 0**
effort this is clearly not her form: much btr 1440 (gd/fm), 1253.
13 ran   Time 3m 01.92 (16.82)   (M K George)   Mrs L Richards Funtington, W Sussex

---

RIPON

WEDNESDAY MAY 31ST   Righthand, Sharpish Track

Official Going   GOOD. Stalls: Str Course/2m - Stands Side, Round Course - Inside

---

1595   **6.45 LISHMAN MDN 2YO (D)**   **5f**   Good 42   -14 Slow
       £3471   £1068   £534   £267

1189 **BOUNCING BOWDLER** 24 [8] M Johnston 2-9-0 J Fanning 5/6 FAV: -3221: 2 b c Majadil - Prima Volta **90**
(Primo Dominie) Made all & always in command, pushed out fnl 1f, easily: val for 4L+: hvly bckd: plcd 3 starts
prev: eff at 5f, 6f will suit: acts on fast & soft grnd, likes a sharp trk: running well.

1130 **MON SECRET** 27 [5] J L Eyre 2-9-0 J F Egan 8/1: 032: 2 b c General Monash - Ron's Secret (Efisio) **2½ 78**
Chsd wnr thr'out, rdn & no impress fnl 2f: op 11/2: handles fast & gd/soft grnd: see 1130.

1252 **WALLY MCARTHUR** 19 [3] A Berry 2-9-0 C Lowther 8/1: -03: 2 b c Puissance - Giddy (Polar Falcon) **3 71**
Chsd ldrs, kept on ins last, no impress: op 11/2, clr rem: handles fast grnd, see 1252.

-- **PASITHEA** [9] T D Easterby 2-8-9 K Darley 6/1: 4: In tch, hung right towards centre bef halfway, **4 55**
nvr pace to threaten: op 9/2: Celtic Swing filly, half sister to a 5f juv wnr: dam a 5f juv wnr.

-- **CLOONDESH** [2] J L Eyre 2-9-0 R Winston 6/1: 5: In tch, no impress fnl 2f: op 10/1: Forzando gldg, March **1 58**
foal, cost 21,000 gns: half brother to a 7f juv scorer: dam a French 6f wnr: apprec 6f+, with R A Fahey.

-- **WHARFEDALE CYGNET** [4] J L Eyre 2-8-9 O Pears 33/1: 6: Dwelt/bhd, mod gains fnl 2f: Kings Signet filly, **3 46**
May foal, dam a mdn: sire a useful sprinter: with W T Kemp.

-- **MISTER MIND** [7] J D Mernagh (3) 20/1: 7: Chsd ldrs 3f: Mind Games colt, Apr foal, cost **1¾ 47**
12,500 gns: half brother to 2 wng juvs, dam unrcd: sire high-class & precocious 2yo: with M Brittain.

865 **KEEP DREAMING** 50 [6] 2-8-9 F Norton 14/1: 08: Struggling halfway: 7 wk abs, op 20/1: see 865. **1¾ 39**

-- **SIMPLY BROKE** [1] 2-9-0 Dean McKeown 33/1: 9: Slowly away, al bhd: Simply Great gldg, Mar **hd 43**
foal: brother to a 1m/10f wnr, dam unrcd: sire high-class 10f performer: with P C Haslam.

9 ran Time 1m 0.6 (2.8) (Paul Dean) M Johnston Middleham, N Yorks

1596
7.15 RIPON FESTIVAL CLAIMER 3YO (F) 1m str Good 42 + 02 Fast
£2282 £652 £326

1274 **PIX ME UP** 18 [17] K A Ryan 3-8-0 Iona Wands (5) 10/1: -00001: 3 b f Up And At 'Em - Water Pixie 53
(Dance Of Life) Mid-div, rdn & prog fnl 3f, prsd ldr from 2f out & styd on well under press to lead nr line: op 8/1:
1st win: rcd twice in '99 (mdns, rtd 80): eff at 1m, tried 10f: acts on firm & gd, gall/sharp trk.
1024 **SEND IT TO PENNY** 37 [12] M W Easterby 3-8-2 G Parkin 16/1: 04-002: 3 b f Marju - Sparkish hd 54
(Persian Bold) Chsd ldrs, rdn/led 2f out, strongly prsd fnl 1f & hdd nr fin: clr rem: eff at 6f/1m on gd & fast.
1477 **DOUBLE FAULT** 6 [18] T D Easterby 3-8-6 (BL) R Winston 10/1: 0-5003: 3 br f Zieten - Kashapour 3 52
(Nishapour) Trkd ldrs, chsd front pair 2f out, held fnl 1f: op 8/1: blnks: see 1024.
1365 **MOUNTRATH ROCK** 12 [14] N Tinkler 3-7-12 (vis) F Norton 8/1: -00044: Rear, rdn/prog to chase 1¾ 41
ldrs 2f out, held fnl 1f: op 7/1: prob stays 1m: see 1365 (sell h'cap).
1365 **DOLFINESSE** 12 [11] D Mernagh (3) 25/1: 050-05: Chsd ldrs, onepace fnl 2f: unplcd '99 (rtd 62). 1½ 42
*1202 **AFRICA** 23 [9] 3-8-6 K Darley 2/1 FAV: 330-16: Mid-div, eff 2f out, wknd: bckd: btr 1202 (7f, a/w). ¾ 45
1365 **FOSTON FOX** 12 [10] J Bramhill 25/1: 4-0507: Mid-div, eff 2f out, held/no room 1f out: blnks.1½ 38
1439 **EDEIFF** 9 [15] J F Egan 12/1: 601-68: Rcd freely, led & clr 5f out, hdd 2f out, fdd: see 1439 (10f). ½ 43
48 **MIST OVER MEUGHER** 198 [16] P Fessey 50/1: 0000-9: Chsd ldrs 6f: reapp: unplcd last term. 7 22
1423 **HARRY TASTERS** 9 [6] 3-9-11 J P Spencer 20/1: 50-000: Mid-div at best: 10th: op 14/1: see 1263. 2½ 44
586 **COLOMBE DOR** 96 [4] 3-8-11 Dean McKeown 12/1: 6-2260: Al bhd: 11th: op 8/1, abs: btr 461, 311. shd 30
1349 **GAVEL** 13 [13] 3-8-11 (bl) W Supple 16/1: 30-000: In tch 5f: 12th: op 14/1: see 1349. 2 26
1299 **DISPOL JAZZ** 16 [7] 3-8-6 G Duffield 7/1: 0-3000: Mid-div at best: 13th: op 6/1: btr 900 (7f). ½ 20
1234 **SWEET TEDDY** 20 [5] 3-8-4 M Henry 9/1: 554-00: Bhd halfway: 17th: op 7/1: see 1234 (AW). ½ 20
1446 **Soloist** 8 [2] 3-8-2 K Dalgleish (7) 20/1: 1386 **Bank Buster** 11 [1] 3-8-7 O Pears 50/1:
1341 **Peng** 13 [8] 3-9-11 (t) H Bastiman 12/1:
17 ran Time 1m 40.7 (3.2) (Roses Racing Club) K A Ryan Hambleton, N Yorks

1597
7.45 FARM SERVICES HCAP 4YO+ 0-75 (E) 2m Good 42 -06 Slow [62]
£3549 £1092 £546 £273 4 yo rec 2 lb

4412} **KEEP IKIS** 226 [13] Mrs M Reveley 6-8-6 (40) D Mernagh (3) 10/1: 0023-1: 6 ch m Anshan - Santee Sioux 47
(Dancing Brave) Held up, rdn/prog fnl 4f & led ins last, styd on strongly, pushed out, going away: reapp: plcd
fnl 2 '99 starts (rtd 41, h'cap): formerly a bmpr rnr-up with S Gollings: eff at 2m/2m2f, marathon trips could
suit: acts on fast & gd, stiff/undul or sharpish trk: runs well fresh: thorough stayer, op to further improvement.
1276 **SHERIFF** 18 [6] J W Hills 9-8-10 (44) M Henry 12/1: 4-0202: 9 b g Midyan - Daisy Warwick 2½ 46
(Ribot) Handy, led over 3f out till ins last, onepace nr fin: on a fair mark for similar: see 963, 788.
1499 **SPA LANE** 5 [8] Mrs S Lamyman 7-8-8 (42) F Norton 11/2: 0-5143: 7 ch g Presidium - Sleekit ¾ 43
(Blakeney) Mid-div, rdn/prog to chall & ev ch fnl 2f, onepace nr fin: quick reapp: see 1499, 1276.
1411 **SEGAVIEW** 11 [4] Mrs P Sly 4-9-8 (58) J Fanning 9/2 FAV: 6-4454: Held up in tch, smooth prog 2½ 57
& ev ch over 1f out, no extra ins last: stays a sharpish 2m: shld find a race this term: see 885.
1350 **EUROLINK APACHE** 13 [14] T Quinn 5-9-13 (61) T Quinn 12/1: 2/2405: Slowly away & rear, styd on stdly 2½ 58
fnl 3f, no threat to ldrs: ran as if this longer 2m trip will suit: see 565, 519 (AW mdn, 12f).
1363 **HAPPY DAYS** 12 [3] 5-8-1 (35) J Bramhill 6/1: 000426: Prom, rdn/onepace over 2f out: see 1363, 552. nk 31
1478 **GIVE AN INCH** 6 [1] 5-9-12 (60) J Mackay (7) 9/1: -00007: Held up, eff 2f out, no impress: qck reapp. 2 54
1128 **OUR MONOGRAM** 27 [11] 4-8-13 (49) W Supple 12/1: 540-08: Led fnl 4f out, sn btn: see 1128. nk 42
1478 **TURGENEV** 6 [7] 11-7-10 (31)(11oh)(1ow) Dale Gibson 10/1: -00059: Mid-div, rdn fnl 3f, no impress. 3 21
1167 **CHARMING ADMIRAL** 25 [15] 7-9-8 (56)(bl) G Duffield 14/1: -01200: Mid-div, held 2f out: 10th: btr 876.nk 46
1194 **BOLD CARDOWAN** 24 [2] 4-8-7 (43) N Kennedy 14/1: 0-0000: Keen/held up rear, nvr factor: 11th. 2½ 31
1276 **RIGADOON** 18 [17] 4-9-6 (56)(bl) G Parkin 9/1: 61-450: Handy, led over 4f out till over 3f out, fdd: 13th. 0
3978} **The Blues Academy** 256 [16] 5-10-0 (62) K Darley 14/1: 1276 **Free** 18 [10] 5-9-6 (54) A Culhane 12/1:
1194 **Mildon** 24 [12] 4-8-1 (37) K Dalgleish (7) 33/1:
15 ran Time 3m 32.5 (7.7) (T McGoran) Mrs M Reveley Lingdale, N Yorks

1598
8.15 AMEC HCAP 3YO+ 0-85 (D) 1m str Good 42 +03 Fast [82]
£5401 £1662 £831 £415 3 yo rec 12lb

1160 **INDIAN PLUME** 25 [1] C W Thornton 4-9-8 (76) J P Spencer 20/1: -01001: 4 b c Efisio - Boo Hoo 81
(Mummy's Pet) Made all, drvn over 1f out, styd on strongly & in command/pushed out nr fin: best time of night:
earlier scored at Musselburgh (class stks, made all): place form in '99 (rtd 85): '98 Pontefract wnr (mdn, rtd 86):
eff at 7f/1m on fast, gd/firm & a gall/sharp trk: loves to force the pace: tough.
1356 **HAKEEM** 12 [11] M Brittain 5-8-5 (59) D Mernagh (3) 25/1: 020-02: 5 ch g Keffaah - Masarrah 1½ 61
(Formidable) Al prom, chsd wnr fnl 2f, held ins last: '99 Thirsk wnr (h'cap, rtd 63 at best, unplcd on sand, rtd
45a): with R Armstrong in '98 (h'cap, unplcd, rtd 75): eff at 6/7f, now suited by 1m on firm & gd/soft, without blnks.
1243 **DONNAS DOUBLE** 20 [18] D Eddy 5-8-8 (62) P Fessey 12/1: 0-0563: 5 ch g Weldnaas - Shadha shd 62
(Shirley Heights) Handy, rdn & kept on fnl 2f, not quite pace of wnr ins last: see 1011.
*1407 **HUGWITY** 11 [13] G C Bravery 8-9-7 (75) A Culhane 7/1: 336214: Chsd ldrs, kept on onepace fnl 2f. 2 71
1300 **DOUBLE ACTION** 16 [14] 6-8-7 (61) K Darley 10/1: -40405: Mid-div, rdn/onepace fnl 2f: see 1011, 623 1¼ 54
1561 **PENTAGON LAD** 2 [6] 4-9-1 (69) F Lynch 6/1: 051406: Mid-div, eff over 2f out, sn no extra: qck reapp. ½ 61
1360 **IMPULSIVE AIR** 12 [17] 8-7-10 (50)(7oh) J Mackay (7) 16/1: -50027: Mid-div, eff 2f out, no impress. ½ 41
1300 **STYLE DANCER** 16 [4] 6-8-6 (60) W Supple 11/1: 30-548: Held up, hdwy 3f out, no prog 1f out: see 1007.1 49
1473 **MISS RIMEX** 7 [10] 4-9-9 (77) T Quinn 9/1: 501-59: Chsd ldrs 6f: see 1473. nk 65
1348 **SKY DOME** 13 [9] 7-9-5 (73) S Sanders 12/1: 60-060: Chsd ldrs 7f: 10th: see 1150. shd 61
966 **TEMERAIRE** 42 [16] 5-10-0 (82) J F Egan 5/1 FAV: 0-0200: Twds rear, eff 2f out, no impress: 11th: abs. 4 62
1310 **BREATHLESS DREAMS** 15 [12] 3-8-12 (78) A McGlone 9/1: 21-500: Held up, effort/btn 2f out: 12th. 6 0
1341 **THE WIFE** 13 [15] 3-9-0 (80) R Winston 7/1: 100-00: Hampered start & slowly away, switched wide/eff 5f 0
out, no impress: 16th: lost chance at start here, this prob best forgotten: see 1341.
1183 **Keltic Bard** 24 [5] 3-8-10 (76) R Fitzpatrick (3) 12/1: 793 **Battle Warning** 62 [7] 5-8-4 (58) J Fanning 14/1:
1160 **Elvis Reigns** 25 [3] 4-9-5 (73) P Goode (3) 33/1:
3432} **Toshiba Times** 287 [2] 4-7-10 (50)(10oh) K Dalgleish (7) 50/1:
17 ran Time 1m 40.6 (3.1) (Guy Reed) C W Thornton Coverham, N Yorks

RIPON   WEDNESDAY MAY 31ST   Righthand, Sharpish Track

1599   8.45 ST AGNESGATE MDN 3YO+ (D)   1m2f   Good 42 -31 Slow
£3497   £1076   £538   £269   3 yo rec 14lb

1032 **FLITWICK** 35 [4] H R A Cecil 3-8-10 T Quinn 100/30: 01: 3 b c Warning - Flit (Lyphard)   83
Handy, led ins last & narrowly asserted nr fin under hands & heels riding nr fin: slow time: left hvy grnd debut
bhd: stays slowly run 10f, may get further: acts on gd grnd & a sharpish trk: open to further improvement.
-- **SENSE OF FREEDOM** [1] M Johnston 3-8-5 J Fanning 10/1: 2: 3 ch f Grand Lodge - Greatest Pleasure ½ 76
(Be My Guest) Dwelt, held up in tch, eff from 3f out, styd on well ins last despite flashing tail, not reach wnr:
eff at 10f, stronger gallop/further shld suit: acts on gd grnd: green on intro, shld know more next time, improve.
1404 **FINISHED ARTICLE** 11 [2] D R C Elsworth 3-8-10 S Sanders 8/13 FAV: 50-463: 3 b c Indian Ridge -   hd 80
Summer Fashion (Moorestyle) Handy, led over 3f out till ins last, no extra nr fin: see 1404, 1012.
1188 **MANDOOB** 24 [7] A C Stewart 3-8-10 W Supple 10/1: 5-04: In tch, onepace under a kind ride over   2½ 76
1f out, kind ride: will do better now h'capped: see 1188.
-- **DAME HATTIE** [6] 5-9-5 G Hind 50/1: 5: Held up, hdwy/chsd ldrs 3f out, held fnl 1f: Flat debut,   2 68
bmpr fit (stays 2m, handles gd & gd/soft).
1344 **VENTO DEL ORENO** 13 [3] 3-8-5 K Darley 10/1: -656: Held up, eff 3f out, held over 1f out: see 1344.   5 61
1352 **WILLY BANG BANG** 12 [8] 3-8-10 T Williams 100/1: -007: Prom, outpcd fnl 3f: mod form.   21 44
1582 **OCEAN VIEW** 1 [5] 4-9-5 R Winston 100/1: 6-08: Led 7f, sn btn: unplcd yesterday at Redcar.   4 33
8 ran   Time 2m 10.6 (7.3)   (K Abdulla)   H R A Cecil Newmarket, Suffolk

1600   9.15 ALLHALLOWGATE HCAP 3YO 0-70 (E)   6f   Good 42 -20 Slow   [77]
£3354   £1032   £516   £258   Majority racing far side always just ahead

1494 **COLLEGE MAID** 5 [22] M A Goldie 3-8-5 (53)(1ow) A Culhane 4/1 FAV: -20021: 3 b f College Chapel -   61
Maid Of Mourne (Fairy King) Handy far side, rdn/led ins last, styd on well, drvn out: quick reapp: '99
Musselburgh wnr (auct mdn, plcd sev times, rtd 74): eff at 5/6f on firm, soft & handles hvy: handles any trk.
976 **LORDOFENCHANTMENT** 42 [20] N Tinkler 3-8-9 (58)(vis) G Duffield 8/1: 66-052: 3 ch g Soviet Lad -   1¼ 61
Sauvignon (Alzao) Led far side till ins last, kept on well, not btn far: abs: acts on fast, gd & handles hvy.
1278 **ELVINGTON BOY** 18 [10] M W Easterby 3-9-3 (66) T Lucas 9/1: 00-003: 3 ch g Emarati - Catherines Well ½ 67+
(Junius) Cl-up stands side, styd on well ins last, not reach front far side: eff at 5/6f: clr of rem & a fine
effort in the circumstances: looks nicely h'capped & a likely type for similar contests, keep in mind: see 1278.
1494 **ROBIN HOOD** 5 [2] Miss L A Perratt 3-8-11 (50) K Dalgleish (7) 10/1: 0-0044: Prom stds side 5f: qck reapp. 4 41
1297 **BLUE LINE LADY** 16 [1] 3-8-3 (52)(BL) R Winston 9/1: 00-005: Prom stands side 5f: rnr-up   shd 43
twice last term (rtd 76, auct mdn): eff at 6f, fried 7f: handles firm & gd, any trk: tried blnks.
1387 **BENBYAS** 11 [19] 3-8-8 (57)(VIS) R Cody Boutcher 25/1 14/1: 400-06: Prom far side, held fnl 1f: vis.   nk 47
1578 **OUTSTANDING TALENT** 1 [7] F Norton 20/1: 00-607: Prom stands side, held over 1f out.   2½ 35
1098 **BEST BOND** 29 [3] 3-9-4 (67) J Mackay (7) 6/1: 55-038: Dwelt, twds rear stds side, mod gains fnl 2f.   ¾ 48
1387 **DESRAYA** 11 [9] 3-8-10 (59)(bl) F Lynch 16/1: 00-069: In tch far side, outpcd fnl 2f: see 1387, 924.   hd 39
1280 **NEEDWOOD TRIBESMAN** 18 [21] 3-8-4 (53) G Hind 16/1: -0000: Chsd ldrs far side 4f: 10th: h'cap bow.   1 31
1390 **PADDYWACK** 11 [11] 3-8-9 (58)(bl) Claire Bryan (5) 16/1: 122200: In tch far side 4f: 11th: see 654 (AW).   1 34
*1562 **GREY COSSACK** 2 [8] 3-9-13 (76)(6ex) D Mernagh (3) 10/1: -63410: In tch far side, btn 2f out: 12th: shd 52
quick reapp under a pen: see 1562 (auct mdn).
1494 **BETTYJOE** 5 [14] 3-8-2 (52) P Fessey 20/1: 00-000: Nvr on terms far side: 13th: qck reapp; see 1149.   2½ 20
1390 **CHILI PEPPER** 11 [18] 3-8-2 (52) P M Quinn (5) 12/1: 61030: Mid-div far side, held fnl 2f: 14th.   ½ 18
1412 **Pertemps Fc** 11 [6] 3-8-13 (62) W Supple 12/1:   3935) **Speedfit Free** 258 [13] 3-9-7 (70) J Fanning 25/1:
1341 **Peteuresque** 13 [12] 3-9-7 (70) K Darley 12/1:   1255 **Nutmeg** 19 [16] 3-8-13 (62) S Sanders 14/1:
1477 **Top Of The Class** 6 [15] 3-9-3 (66)(VIS) T Williams 20/1:   4230) **Silver Socks** 240 [17] 3-8-4 (53) G Parkin 25/1:
1422 **Bodfari Jet** 9 [4] 3-8-5 (54) Dale Gibson 20/1:
21 ran   Time 1m 13.7 (3.7)   (S Bruce)   J S Goldie Uplawmoor, East Renfrewshire

SOUTHWELL   WEDNESDAY MAY 31ST   Lefthand, Sharp, Oval Track

Official Going   SOFT.   Stalls: Inside.

1601   1.30 CLASSIFIED CLAIMER DIV 1 3YO+ 0-60 (F)   7f rnd   Soft 115 +06 Fast
£1918   £548   £274   3 yo rec 11lb

*1431 **ERUPT** 9 [3] M Brittain 7-9-10 D Mernagh (3) 7/2 FAV: 204211: 7 b g Beveled - Sparklingsovereign   58
(Sparkler) Trkd ldrs, no room & switched 2f out, led over 1f out, drvn out: gd time: clmd for £9,000: earlier
won at Musselburgh (h'cap): '99 wnr at Newcastle (h'cap, rtd 52), '98 wnr again at Musselburgh (h'cap, rtd 58):
suited by 7f/1m on firm, soft, fibresand & any trk, likes Musselburgh: best without visor: tough, in fine form.
1421 **MAYDORO** 9 [9] W M Brisbourne 3-8-7 G Baker (7) 16/1: 6-0062: 7 b m Dominion Royale - Bamdoro   2 37
(Cavo Doro) Dwelt, hdwy halfway, led briefly appr fnl 1f, sn no extra: turf return: eff at 5/7f: see 1137.
1335 **FLYING PENNANT** 14 [4] J M Brayshay 7-9-0 (bl) Pat Eddery 11/2: 50-553: 7 gr g Waajib - Flying   3½ 38
Beckee (Godswalk) Held up, plenty to do 3f out, ran on well, nrst fin: op 9/2: do better in h'caps: see 896.
1422 **VICE PRESIDENTIAL** 9 [12] J G Given 5-8-12 Dean McKeown 9/2: 004504: Prom, hdwy to lead over 2f   1 34
out, hdd over 1f out, onepace: tchd 6/1: see 32.
1213 **BONNIE DUNDEE** 22 [7] 4-9-5 (bl) S Carson (5) 16/1: 60-005: In tch, rdn/prog 2f out, onepcd fnl 1f.   2 37
1298 **SOUND THE TRUMPET** 16 [1] 8-8-10 (t) J Mackay (7) 16/1: 600006: V slow to start, hdwy over 2f   2 24
3f out, onepcd fnl 2f: lost all ch at start team: see 97.
1505 **TOWER OF SONG** 5 [6] 3-8-5 A Culhane 14/1: 040007: Rear, nvr a threat: qck reapp: btr 36 (seller).   ¾ 29
1335 **HI MUJTAHID** 14 [2] 6-8-12 Claire Bryan (5) 33/1: 00-008: Cl-up, wknd qckly fnl 2f: stiff task.   1 23
1207 **KILLARNEY JAZZ** 23 [5] 5-9-8 (vis) T G McLaughlin 11/2: 030159: Set fast pace to 2f out, fdd: btr 869.   2½ 29
1505 **ABTAAL** 5 [10] 10-9-2 (vis) R Fitzpatrick (3) 9/1: 601360: Dwelt, eff 3f out, bhd fnl 2f, 10th: qck reapp.   1 21
1237 **Picassos Heritage** 20 [8] 4-9-0 F Norton 16/1:   1298 **Gad Yakoun** 16 [11] 7-9-4 Angela Hartley (7) 33/1:
12 ran   Time 1m 34.6 (7.6)   (Sidney Eaton)   M Brittain Warthill, N.Yorks.

527

1602   2.00 EBF MDN 2YO (D)   6f rnd   Soft 115   -08 Slow
£3523   £1084   £542   £271

1328 **CO DOT UK** 14 [5] K A Ryan 2-9-0 F Lynch 7/1: 5301: 2 b g Distant Relative - Cubist (Tate Gallery)   **77**
Cl-up, rdn & ran on 2f out, drvn out to lead well ins last, going away: 6,500gns May foal: dam a 7f juv wnr,
sire top-class at 1m: eff at 6f, further could suit: acts on gd & soft grnd, sharp trks: going the right way.
1408 **YOUNG JACK** 11 [3] W Jarvis 2-9-0 D McGaffin (7) 8/1: 52: 2 b c Reprimand - Chadenshe (Taufan)   1¼   **72**
Dwelt, rdn/prog 3f out, led ins last fnl 1f, sn hdd & no extra: stays 6f on soft: shld win similar: see 1408.
-- **FLYING TURK** [7] J A Osborne 2-9-0 J P Spencer 16/1: 3: 2 ch c Flying Spur - Empress Wu (High   1   **69**
Line) In tch, hdwy when no room & switched over 1f out, ran on well for press ins last: jockey rec a 2 day whip
ban: 15,000gns Apr foal, half-brother to 3 juv wnrs: dam plcd at 7f: eff at 6f on soft, 7f will suit: encouraging.
1048 **HAMATARA** 32 [12] I A Balding 2-9-0 (t) K Darley 12/1: 404: Cl-up, led over 2f out, hdd ins last,   ½   **68**
sn btn: clr rem, op 8/1: up in trip, first time t-strap: see 911.
1260 **IDLE POWER** 19 [8] 2-9-0 Pat Eddery 8/11 FAV: 25: Rcd keenly cl-up, rdn to lead over 2f out,   3½   **61**
sn hdd & btn: nicely bckd: rcd too keenly for own gd here: btr 1260 (debut, 5f).
1221 **EMISSARY** 21 [4] 2-9-0 J Fanning 11/1: 66: Prom, rdn/held fnl 2f: op 7/1: see 1221.   5   **51**
1408 **TIRANA** 11 [6] 2-9-0 R Winston 33/1: -007: Dwelt, nvr a threat: modest prev form.   ¾   **50**
1208 **STORMING FOLEY** 22 [1] 2-9-0 G Duffield 9/1: 4258: Led to 2f out, wknd qckly: op 7/1: btr 828.   1¾   **46**
1424 **DIVEBOMB** 9 [10] 2-8-9 S Carson (5) 20/1: 09: Prom, fdd fnl 2f: see 1294.   3½   **34**
1294 **FAST BUCK** 16 [9] 2-9-0 J F Egan 25/1: 00: Sn rdn/rear, nvr a dngr, fin 10th.   nk   **38**
1367 **Blushing Spur** 12 [2] 2-9-0 O Pears 33/1:   1413 **Son Of A Preacher** 11 [11] 2-9-0 F Norton 66/1:
12 ran   Time 1m 21.5 (7.4)   (Tony Fawcett)   K A Ryan Hambleton, N.Yorks.

1603   2.30 CLASSIFIED CLAIMER DIV 2 3YO+ 0-60 (F)   7f rnd   Soft 115   -06 Slow
£1918   £548   £274   3 yo rec 11lb

1387 **EVER REVIE** 11 [7] T D Easterby 3-8-6 (bl) K Darley 4/1 JT FAV: 00-001: 3 b f Hamas - Lucy Limelight   **51**
(Hot Spark) Cl-up, rdn to lead appr fnl 1f, drvn out: clmd for £7,000: '99 scorer at Beverley (seller, rtd 68,
first time blnks): eff around 7f, has tried 10f: acts on gd/soft & soft grnd: handles any trk & eff in blnks.
3738} **KING TUT** 272 [3] W Jarvis 4-9-2 D McGaffin (7) 14/1: 6000-2: 4 ch g Anshan - Fahrenheit (Mount   ¾   **48**
Hagen) Held up, smooth hdwy over 2f out, ran on strongly, just held: clmd for £5,000: well btn all 4 '99
starts (mdns & h'cap, rtd 63 at best): half-brother to a smart sprinter: eff at 7f on soft grnd.
1207 **TAKHLID** 23 [10] D W Chapman 9-9-10 A Culhane (7) 4/1 JT FAV: 650133: 9 b h Nureyev - Savonnerie   ½   **55**
(Irish River) Sn led, hdd halfway, led again 2f out, hdd appr fnl 1f, onepcd in last: nicely bckd: see 1137.
1520 **MR CUBE** 4 [6] J M Bradley 10-8-12 (bl) D Watson (7) 8/1: 060104: Rear, prog when not room over   1¼   **41**
2f out, styd on, nvr nrr: op 7/1: qck reapp: handles firm & soft grnd: see 1136.
1296 **SHAANXI ROMANCE** 16 [1] 5-9-6 (tvi) J Fortune 12/1: -25005: Dwelt, hdwy over 2f out, no extra dist.   1   **47**
1542 **CAVERSFIELD** 4 [4] 5-9-0 Claire Bryan (5) 7/1: -00006: Prom, edged right 2f out, drvn & wknd: nk   **41**
jockey rec a 1 day careless riding ban: qck reapp: see 1330, 336.
4504} **ROFFEY SPINNEY** 219 [5] 6-9-4 D Hayes 16/1: 0006-7: Led early, with ldrs till wknd appr fnl 1f: 3   **39**
early '99 scorer at W'hampton (seller, rtd 62a, J Cullinan), subs well btn on turf (tried blnks/visor): '98
wnr at Folkestone & Leicester (clmr & sell h'cap, rtd 61 & 71a, R Hannon): eff at 7f/9.4f on firm, gd/soft &
both AWs: acts on any trk, likes Lingfield: best up with/forcing the pace: now with C Drew.
1273 **SEVEN** 19 [8] 5-9-2 (bl) T G McLaughlin 11/2: 400408: Prom, wknd appr fnl 1f: op 5/1: see 1273.   2   **33**
1371} **PROUD CAVALIER** 380 [11] 4-8-12 C Rutter 50/1: 0/00-9: Dwelt, sn prom, wknd qckly fnl 2f: stiff task.   6   **19**
1477 **HONG KONG** 6 [2] 3-7-13 (tbl) J Mackay (7) 8/1: 2-0000: Cl-up, led over 3f out, hdd 2f out,   ½   **16**
wknd, fin 10th: op 6/1, qck reapp: see 1296..
1422 **MIKES DOUBLE** 9 [12] 6-8-10 (vis) R Fitzpatrick (3) 20/1: 500000: Al well bhd, fin 11th.   12   **0**
11 ran   Time 1m 35.5 (8.5)   (Leeds United Racing Club Ltd)   T D Easterby Great Habton, N.Yorks.

1604   3.00 FAIRHAM BROOK HCAP 3YO+ 0-80 (D)   1m4f   Soft 115   -06 Slow   [80]
£3770   £1160   £580   £290   3 yo rec 17lb

-1518 **HANNIBAL LAD** 4 [6] W M Brisbourne 4-8-12 (64) T G McLaughlin 2/1 FAV: 350421: 4 ch g Rock City -   **69**
Appealing (Star Appeal) Held up, hdwy to lead over 2f out, drvn out: qck reapp: earlier won at
W'hampton & Southwell (2, h'caps, rtd 80a): '99 wnr again at W'hampton (seller, rtd 66a, P Evans): eff at 7f,
suited by 11/12f: acts on firm, gd & fibresand: likes a sharp trk, esp Southwell: runs well fresh: v tough.
1350 **STORM HILL** 13 [4] J H M Gosden 4-9-7 (73)(t) J Fortune 9/2: 45-002: 4 b c Caerleon - Jackie Berry   2   **75**
(Connaught) Waited with, hdwy over 3f out, chall appr fnl 1f, no extra: stays 10/12f on fast & soft: see 1350.
1306 **EVENING SCENT** 16 [9] J Hetherton 4-7-10 (48)(3oh) K Dalgleish (7) 16/1: 30-603: 4 b f Ardkinglass -   2   **47**
Fresh Line (High Line) Settled rear, hdwy midway, hung left fnl 2f, no extra in last: inadequate trip, see 1023.
1150 **TONIC** 2 [2] M Johnston 4-9-12 (78) J Fanning 11/2: 00-004: Waited with, prog over 2f out,   ½   **76**
chall when short of room over 1f out, sn btn: see 1150, 1011.
1417 **GLOW** 9 [3] 4-8-2 (54) L Newton 16/1: 46-035: Sn clr ldr, hdd appr fnl 2f, rallying when badly   nk   **52**
hmpd dist, sn held: styd 12f on soft grnd: see 1039.
3975} **PERADVENTURE** 256 [8] 5-9-11 (77) K Darley 5/1: 30/5-6: Prom, wknd qckly fnl 3f: op 4/1: 99/00   19   **56**
hdle scorer at Wetherby (rtd 120h, eff over a gall 2m on gd/soft & soft, runs well fresh): 5th of 5
sole '99 Flat start (h'cap, rtd 57), prev term scored for R Hannon at York (mdn, rtd 85 at best): eff forcing
the pace over a gall 10.5f, stays 12f: acts on fast, gd/soft & any trk, likes a gall one.
832 **MURJAN** 55 [7] 3-8-6 (75) G Carter 7/1: 434-57: Bhd, lost tch halfway: see 1150.   6   **46**
*1501 **WESTERN COMMAND** 5 [5] 4-8-0 (49)(3ow)(6ex) R Fitzpatrick (0) 11/1: 464518: Rcd keenly cl-up,   1¼   **21**
wknd qckly 3f out fn last: btr 1501 (fibresand).
8 ran   Time 2m 48.9 (14.5)   (John Pugh)   W M Brisbourne Great Ness, Shropshire.

1605   3.30 LEVY BOARD MDN 3YO+ (D)   6f rnd   Soft 115   -07 Slow
£3848   £1184   £592   £296   3 yo rec 9 lb

-- **NAJEYBA** [7] A C Stewart 3-8-7 M Roberts 11/4: 1: 3 ch f Indian Ridge - Innocence (Unfuwain)   **67**
Rcd keenly with ldrs, rdn to lead over 2f out, ran on well despite hanging left ins last, rdn out: op 4/1:
debut: eff at 6f, further could suit: runs well fresh on soft grnd & a sharp trk: gd debut, shld win again.
1175 **GASCON** 24 [5] D J Coakley 4-9-7 D Harrison 11/1: 02: 4 b g Beveled - Lady Roxanne (Cyrano de   1¼   **68**

Bergerac) Held up, gd hdwy over 2f out, chall wnr ins last, no extra cl-home: tchd 14/1: stays 6f on soft.

1211 **SWING CITY** 22 [3] R Guest 3-8-7 G Duffield 8/1: 00-003: 3 ch f Indian Ridge - Menomiee (Soviet   5   53
Star) Led, hdd appr fnl 2f, sn btn: op 6/1: needs 7f & h'caps: see 852.

--   **FLY MORE** [6] J M Bradley 3-8-12 J P Spencer 20/1: 4: Dwelt, hdwy when ran green over 2f out,   4   49
hung left & no extra sn after: 14,500gns Lycius gelding: shld learn plenty from this experience & will improve.

1399 **LANDICAN LAD** 11 [8] 3-8-12 Pat Eddery 10/1: 005: Prom, rdn/wknd appr fnl 1f: see 1175.   3   42

--   **SAPPHIRE MILL** [2] 3-8-7 P Robinson 6/1: 6: Prom, lost tch fnl 2f: mkt drifter on debut.   ¾   36

3443} **NICKS JULE** 287 [1] 3-8-7 F Norton 25/1: 50-7: Cl-up, drvn & wknd qckly fnl 2f: reapp: rtd 62   4   28
when 5th on first of 2 '99 starts (fill mdn, with A P Jarvis): now with J Osborne.

971   **BAILEYS ON LINE** 42 [9] 3-8-7 J Fanning 16/1: -08: Sn rdn, nvr a threat: mid-dist bred.   6   16

--   **AJYAAL** [4] 3-8-12 R Hills 9/4 FAV: 9: V unruly bef race, prom to halfway, sn lost tch, t.o.:   11   0
op 5/4 on debut: full brother to useful 6f performer Mutaakkid: with J Gosden.

9 ran   Time 1m 21.4 (7.3)   (Sheikh Ahmed Al Maktoum)   A C Stewart Newmarket.

1606   4.00 COCKER BECK FILLIES HCAP 3YO+ 0-70 (E)   7f rnd   Soft 115   +06 Fast   [68]
£3115   £890   £445   3 yo rec 11lb

1506 **BODFARI ANNA** 5 [14] J L Eyre 4-8-6 (46)(vis) J F Egan 14/1: 054501: 4 br f Casteddu - Lowrianna   52
(Cyrano de Bergerac) Waited with, gd hdwy over 3f out, led appr fnl 1f, rdn clr ins last: op 11/1: gd time:
'99 Haydock wnr (sell h'cap, rtd 50), prev term scored at Nottingham (seller, rtd 66, M Easterby): eff at
6/7f: acts on firm, soft & fibresand: acts on any trk & eff in blnks/visor.

1257 **TAYOVULLIN** 19 [9] K A Ryan 6-8-1 (41) Iona Wands (5) 9/1: 000652: 6 ch m Shalford - Fifth Quarter   2½   42
(Cure The Blues) Dwelt, rdn/prog over 3f out, led appr fnl 1f, hdd dist, not pace of wnr: on a fair mark: see 550.

1133 **PATSY CULSYTH** 27 [3] Don Enrico Incisa 5-8-6 (46) Kim Tinkler 16/1: 0-1003: 5 b m Tragic Role -   1¼   45
Regal Salute (Dara Monarch) Cl-up, rdn to chall 2f out, no extra appr fnl 1f: see 756 (reapp, seller).

4106} **SHINING STAR** 248 [13] J A Osborne 3-9-0 (65) J P Spencer 20/1: 0565-4: Held up, smooth hdwy   2   60
2f out, ran on strongly, nvr nrr: reapp, new stable: 5th at best in '99 (auct mdns, rtd 66 at best, J Berry):
sister to a 6f juv wnr: prob stays 7f, handles soft grnd: with J Osborne.

1506 **GUEST ENVOY** 5 [10] P M Quinn (5) 10/1: 260555: Dwelt, rdn/prog appr fnl 2f, btn   3½   39
over 1f out: op 13/2: qck reapp: see 811.

1419 **MUJAGEM** 9 [1] 4-8-8 (48) G Parkin 9/1: 0/0146: Led, hdd appr fnl 1f, wknd qckly: btr 1303 (1m, AW).   ½   37

513   **CRYSTAL LASS** 107 [6] 4-8-12 (52) J Edmunds 16/1: 04-057: Front rank, rdn/fdd fnl 2f: 3 month abs.   2   37

1557 **GRACE 2** [8] 6-8-7 (47) P Fitzsimons (5) 8/1: 446648: Cl-up, lost tch fnl 2f: ran 48hrs ago.   shd   32

1405 **PEPETA** 11 [11] 3-9-1 (66) K Darley 4/1 FAV: 06-609: Sn rdn in mid-div, eff 2f out, no dngr: 1¾   48
nicely bckd & better clearly expected here: see 1201.

1297 **CARRIE POOTER** 16 [2] 4-9-11 (65) C Lowther 14/1: -16000: Speed to 2f out, fdd: 10th: op 10/1.   ¾   46

1506 **OARE KITE** 5 [5] 5-8-8 (48)(bl) A Nicholls (3) 9/1: 246320: Dwelt, al rear: 13th: op 7/1, qck reapp.   0

4053} **PRINCESS RIA** 252 [7] 3-9-3 (68) A Mackay 7/1: 3500-0: Sn rdn rear, lost tch halfway, last: '99 debut   0
wnr at Haydock (nov stks, rtd 79): dam a 7f/1m wnr: eff over 6f, 7f shld suit: runs well fresh on gd/soft grnd.

1419 Mount Park 9 [15] 3-9-0 (65) A Culhane 25/1:   160   Violet 175 [12] 4-9-6 (60) T G McLaughlin 33/1:

1086 Luvaduck 29 [16] 4-10-0 (68) M Roberts 25/1:

15 ran   Time 1m 34.6 (7.6)   (The Haydock Badgeholders)   J L Eyre Sutton Bank, N.Yorks.

1607   4.30 TRENT MED AUCT MDN 3YO (F)   7f rnd   Soft 115   -02 Slow
£2268   £648   £324

1113 **SAHARA SPIRIT** 28 [5] E A L Dunlop 3-9-0 G Carter 4/7 FAV: 0-2241: 3 b g College Chapel - Desert   71
Palace (Green Desert) In tch, hdwy & pushed into lead appr fnl 1f, idled ins last & drvn out to hold on: nicely
bckd at odds on: twice rnr-up prev this term: plcd on debut in '99 (mdn auct, rtd 83): eff at 6/7f, stays
1m: acts on gd, soft & a stiff/undul or sharp trk: v consistent.

1444 **IT CAN BE DONE** 8 [10] R Hollinshead 3-9-0 P M Quinn (5) 16/1: 6-0032: 3 ch g Case Law - Breeze   nk   70
Away (Prince Sabo) Well bhd halfway, drvn/styd on well 2f out, fin well, just held: gd run, eff at 7f on gd & soft.

1204 **MOST STYLISH** 23 [9] C G Cox 3-8-9 G Duffield 8/1: 523: 3 ch f Most Welcome - Corman Style   ¾   64
(Ahonoora) Front rank, ev ch till not pace of wnr well ins last: op 6/1, clr rem: eff at 7f/1m on soft & fibresand.

1063 **GABIDIA** 30 [3] M A Jarvis 3-8-9 P Robinson 7/1: 3-64: Cl-up, rdn/held fnl 1f: see 1063.   4   57

1287 **ABLE SEAMAN** 18 [2] 3-9-0 Pat Eddery 9/1: 045: Led 5f out, rdn/hdd appr fnl 1f, fdd: btr 1287 (10f).   5   54

1035 **KINGS TO OPEN** 33 [4] 3-9-0 J P Spencer 25/1: 0-06: Bhd, nvr a factor: see 1035.   6   45

1204 **THE DIDDLER** 23 [1] 3-9-0 L Newton 66/1: 007: Led to 5f out, rdn/wknd fnl 2f.   ¾   44

1204 **BELINDA** 23 [11] 3-8-9 C Rutter 20/1: 048: Dwelt, nvr a dngr: turf bow: see 920.   ½   38

1269 **BARDEN LADY** 19 [6] 3-8-9 M Roberts 25/1: 00-09: Cl-up, rdn & wknd appr fnl 2f, eased when btn.   1   36

--   **MARTINS PEARL** [8] 3-9-0 D Harrison 25/1: 0: Sn rdn in tch, wknd qckly fnl 2f, fin 10th: Petong colt.   6   31

1195 **CHEZ BONITO** 24 [7] 3-8-9 Claire Bryan (5) 16/1: -520: Prom, lost tch halfway, fin 11th: prev with   nk   26
J Osborne, now with J M Bradley, btr 1195 (clmr).

11 ran   Time 1m 35.2 (8.2)   (Stars And Stripes)   E A L Dunlop Newmarket.

1608   5.00 LEMEN HCAP 3YO+ 0-75 (E)   1m2f   Soft 115   No Standard Time   [73]
£2926   £836   £418   3 yo rec 14lb

1393 **RIVER ENSIGN** 11 [8] W M Brisbourne 7-8-7 (52) P M Quinn (5) 8/1: 103601: 7 br m River God - Ensigns   55
Kit (Saucy Kit) Made all, pressed appr fnl 1f, styd on well, drvn out: earlier won at W'hampton (2, clmr & fill
h'cap, rtd 51a) & Southwell (h'cap): '99 W'hampton wnr (clmr, rtd 53a) & Chester (h'cap, rtd 47): suited by
forcing the pace over 1m/10f on gd, hvy & fibresand: likes a sharp trk, esp Southwell/W'hampton: runs well fresh.

1306 **BACHELORS PAD** 16 [11] Miss S J Wilton 6-8-13 (58) I Mongan (5) 10/3 FAV: 214142: 6 b g Pursuit Of   1¼   59
Love - Note Book (Mummy's Pet) Mid-div, smooth hdwy over 4f out, rdn to chall appr fnl 1f, no extra ins
last: v tough (not out of first 4 in prev 8 starts): acts on firm, soft & fibresand: tough, see 855.

1292 **GOLDEN ROD** 16 [10] P W Harris 3-8-6 (65) A Culhane 25/1: 00-003: 3 ch g Rainbows For Life - Noble   ½   65
Form (Double Form) Cl-up, rdn to chall over 1f out, btn ins last: 4th on first of 3 '99 starts (debut, auct
mdn, rtd 77): dam a 1m/10f wnr: eff at 10f on soft grnd & a sharp trk: gd run.

370   **TOPAZ** 131 [1] H J Collingridge 5-7-10 (41)(15oh) J Mackay 7/1: 50/1: 000-04: Sn rdn in mid-div,   3½   35
styd on well fnl 2f, nvr nrr: clr rem: well btn in '99, prob flattered when rtd 67 on '98 debut (mdn):
stays 10f on soft: seemingly much imprvd but treat rating with caution.

1300 **TROIS ELLES** 16 [7] 3-4-7-12 (43)(2ow)(3oh) A Mackay 16/1: -03605: Hdwy from rear halfway,   8   26
wknd qckly fnl 2f: see 596 (equitrack).

SOUTHWELL WEDNESDAY MAY 31ST Lefthand, Sharp, Oval Track

679 **SUPERSONIC 76** [12] 4-9-12 (71) Pat Eddery 7/2: 520-46: Prom, rdn/fdd fnl 3f: 11 wk abs: btr 679. 6 45
1100 **DRUIDGE BAY 29** [9] 4-7-10 (41)(5oh) S Righton 25/1: 00-007: Dwelt, hdwy halfway, lost tch 1¾ 12
fnl 2f: unplcd on turf in '99 (rtd 45 at best): rnr-up twice in '99 (sellers, rtd 73 & 55a at best): eff around 1m on soft grnd & fibresand: handles firm.
1303 **STARBOARD TACK 16** [3] 4-9-8 (67) G Carter 14/1: 354-08: Dwelt, nvr a factor: see 1303. 1¾ 35
1388 **PAPERWEIGHT 11** [4] 4-9-6 (65) M Tebbutt 15/2: 0-4239: Badly hmpd after 2f, no dngr after, t.o. 18 15
4602} **TIGER GRASS 209** [5] 4-8-13 (58) D Harrison 6/1: 0240-0: Al well bhd, t.o. in 10th: rnr-up once nk 8
in '99 (h'cap, rtd 61 at best, tried blnks): subs scored over hdles at Plumpton (juv mdn, rtd 106h, eff at 2m on hvy, sharp/undul trk): eff around 7/10f, has tried 13f: acts on gd & gd/soft grnd.
1498 **LEOFRIC 5** [6] 5-7-11 (42)(bl) K Dalgleish (7) 9/1: 033030: Rcd keenly cl-up, wknd qckly fnl 2f: 11th. 2 0
943 **RED ROSES 44** [14] 4-7-10 (41)(4oh) Kim Tinkler 25/1: 36-000: Handy, lost tch halfway, t.o.: 12th: abs. 5 0
12 ran Time 2m 20.4 (Crispandave Racing Associates) W M Brisbourne Great Ness, Shropshire.

YARMOUTH WEDNESDAY MAY 31ST Lefthand, Flat, Fair Track

Official Going GOOD. Stalls: Str Course - Far Side; 2m - Stands Side; Rem - Inside.

1609 1.50 HOWARDS MDN 3YO+ (D) 5f43y Good/Soft 68 +00 Fast
£3770 £1160 £580 £290

1280 **ROZEL 18** [3] R Guest 3-8-8 S Sanders 14/1: 01: 3 ch f Wolfhound - Noirmant (Dominion) 80
Keen bhd ldrs, led ent fnl 1f, readily drew clr: eff over an easy 5f on gd/soft, 6f will suit: improving.
1399 **VILLA VIA 11** [4] J A R Toller 3-8-8 R Ffrench 9/4: -5322: 3 b f Night Shift - Joma Kaanem (Double 2 73
Form) Prsd ldr, led 2f out till below dist, onepace: prob ran to best back in trip tho' will apprec a return to further: handles firm & gd/soft grnd, see 1399.
4400} **DOUBLE PLATINUM 228** [1] J H M Gosden 3-8-8 L Dettori 4/9 FAV: 20-3: 3 ch f Seeking The Gold - 1¼ 70
Band (Northern Dancer) Led till 2f out, no extra fnl 1f: nicely bckd, reapp: debut rnr-up last term, subs not btn far in a Gr 2 (rtd 94, A Foster): half-sister to Gr 2 wng juv Applaud: eff at 6f on gd/soft, prob fast.
4537} **BALLETS RUSSES 216** [2] H J Collingridge 3-8-8 M Hills 33/1: 500-4: Chsd ldrs till appr fnl 1f: stiff 8 50
task on reapp: well btn all 3 '99 starts at up to 1m (fill mdn, rtd 62): moderate.
4 ran Time 1m 03.5 (3.4) (Matthews Breeding & Racing) R Guest Newmarket

1610 2.20 COOPERS FILLIES HCAP 3YO 0-75 (E) 1m str Good/Soft 68 -11 Slow [80]
£3055 £940 £470 £235 Stalls 1 & 2 raced far side, rest in centre

1024 **MIDNIGHT ALLURE 37** [8] C F Wall 3-8-7 (59) R Mullen 7/1: 500-21: 3 b f Aragon - Executive Lady 71
(Night Shift) Towards rear, imprvd after halfway to lead bef 2f out, kept on strongly despite flashing tail: 1st win: thrice rcd juv (debut, mdn, rtd 62): half-sister to sprinter Midnight Escape: eff at 1m, may get further: acts on gd/soft & hvy grnd, stiff or gall trk: runs well fresh & is on the upgrade.
1405 **SHADY POINT 11** [7] C E Brittain 3-9-1 (67) L Dettori 5/2 FAV: 3-0562: 3 b f Unfuwain - Warning 2½ 73
Shadows (Cadeaux Genereux) Confidently held up, imprvd to go after wnr appr fnl 1f, unable to get on terms & no extra towards fin: bckd from 4/1, clr rem: again set a lot to do, see 1405, 1063.
1297 **OCEAN SONG 16** [3] S R Bowring 3-8-10 (62)(bl) S Finnamore (5) 20/1: 246003: 3 b f Savahra Sound - 4 60
Marina Plata (Julio Mariner) Well plcd, eff 2f out, onepace: longer trip, see 794.
1215 **PIPS WAY 22** [6] K R Burke 3-9-7 (73) N Callan 14/1: 40-604: Led centre grp till 3f out, no extra bef dist. ¾ 70
1105 **SAVANNAH QUEEN 28** [5] 3-8-13 (65) W Ryan 15/2: 5005: Towards rear, switched to far side appr 2 58
fnl 2f, nvr nr to chall: op 6/1 on h'cap bow/longer trip: mid-race manoeuvre appeared the wrong call: see 794.
1365 **ALABAMA WURLEY 12** [9] 3-8-4 (56) L Newman (5) 33/1: -00006: Chsd ldrs, outpcd appr fnl 1f: clr. nk 48
*1397 **SANTIBURI GIRL 11** [10] 3-9-3 (69) A Beech (5) 8/1: 0-0617: Handy till fdd ent fnl 2f: btr 1397 (7f stks). 5 53
1125 **AMORAS 27** [12] 3-9-7 (73) M Hills 11/2: 154-48: Nvr a factor: tchd 13/2, faster surface suits. ½ 56
813 **WOODWIND DOWN 58** [13] 3-8-6 (58) T Quinn 20/1: 0-2009: Al towards rear: 8 wk abs, see 651. ½ 40
1062 **LULLABY 30** [14] 3-9-4 (70) R Cochrane 11/2: 0-340: Speed 5f: 10th, op 9/2 on h'cap bow, see 934. ½ 51
1405 **GOLDEN LOCKET 11** [4] 3-9-4 (70) J Reid 10/1: 00-400: Well plcd till 3f out: 11th, lngr trip, see 794. ½ 50
807 **WILEMMGEO 61** [2] 3-8-4 (56) Sophie Mitchell 20/1: 121050: Rcd far side & led after halfway, btn 2f out. 0
1053 **SILK ST BRIDGET 32** [1] 3-8-1 (53) M Baird 14/1: 000-00: Rcd far side & overall ldr till appr appr fnl 3f, 0
sn btn: 15th: well btn in 3 '99 6f starts (fill mdn, rtd 59): stoutly bred sister to 1m/10f wnr Lady Rockstar.
1419 **Marnie 9** [15] 3-8-1 (53) R Ffrench 33/1: 4537} **Havent Made It Yet 216** [11] 3-7-10 (48)(13oh) D Glennon(4) 50/1:
15 ran Time 1m 41.4 (6.3) (Mervyn Ayers) C F Wall Newmarket

1611 2.50 PIER HOTEL HCAP 3YO+ 0-70 (E) 7f str Good/Soft 68 -18 Slow [70]
£3107 £956 £478 £239 3 yo rec 11lb

1393 **PROSPECTORS COVE 11** [5] J Pearce 7-9-9 (65) T Quinn 10/1: 000001: 7 b g Dowsing - Pearl Cove 70
(Town And Country) Waited with, imprvd appr fnl 2f, shaken up to lead ent fnl 1f, ran on well: '99 wnr at Newmarket & here at Yarmouth (h'caps, rtd 77 & 65a): '98 wnr at Brighton (rtd 63) & Lingfield (h'caps, rtd 62a): eff at 7f/10f, stays 2m: acts on firm, soft & both AWs: goes well fresh, any trk, likes Yarmouth: best without visor.
1330 **SAMARA SONG 14** [8] Ian Williams 7-9-0 (56) W Ryan 11/2 JT FAV: 0-0052: 7 ch g Savahra Sound - ¾ 59
Hosting (Thatching) Held up, weaved thro' appr fnl 1f, styd on under press, not reach wnr: tchd 7/1: now nearing peak fitness, return to 1m will suit: see 1003.
78 **BE MY WISH 193** [16] W A O'Gorman 5-8-10 (52) L Dettori 10/1: 0045-3: 5 b m Be My Chief - Spinner nk 54
(Blue Cashmere) Rear, gd prog to chall appr fnl 1f no extra towards fin: clrr em, reapp: best in '99 with 1st time blnks (class stks, rtd 55, S Woods): '98 wnr at Ascot (mdn, rtd 77 & 76a, Miss G Kelleway): eff at 7f, tried 11.5f: acts on firm/fast grnd & equitrack, handles gd/soft: prob best without blnks, well h'capped.
1393 **THATCHAM 11** [2] R W Armstrong 4-8-5 (47)(BL) G Hall 16/1: -32004: Prom, led ent fnl 3f, rdn/hdd 4 41
below dist, fdd: blnkd, back in trip: probably handles equitrack & gd/soft: see 880.
1431 **THREE ANGELS 9** [6] 5-9-12 (68) S Sanders 7/1: 060-25: Rear, kept on late: needs 1m. shd 62
4441} **MYLANIA 224** [4] 4-9-6 (62) J Weaver 16/1: 0420-6: Held up, imprvd 2f out, sn no extra: reapp: 3 50
'99 rnr-up (h'cap, rtd 63, M Tompkins): eff at 1m on soft grnd: now with J Given.
1370 **DOUBLE DESTINY 12** [15] 4-8-13 (55)(BL) C Carver (3) 33/1: 600-07: Struggled to go pace, not 1 41
much room appr fnl 1f, staying on fin: blnkd: unplcd in 3 '99 starts for H Candy (mdn, rtd 71, prob flattered): half-brother to a couple of wng sprinters tho' shapes like 1m will suit: with K Ivory.

1148	**NOBALINO** 26 [19] 6-9-4 (60) (vis) P Shea (7) 16/1: 35-058: Chsd ldrs, fdd appr fnl 1f: see 59.		hd	46
1297	**DENS JOY** 16 [9] 4-9-2 (58) J Reid 7/1: 300109: Al same place: tchd 16/1: btr 1097 (1m).		nk	43
1393	**PERUVIAN STAR** 11 [3] 4-8-5 (47) N Callan 20/1: 500050: Front rank for 5f: 10th, see 721.		shd	32
1383	**REX IS OKAY** 11 [1] 4-9-13 (69)(bl) S Finnamore (5) 12/1: 002600: Prom till 2f out: 13th, see 824.			0
*1351	**DANDY REGENT** 12 [20] 6-9-4 (60) R Mullen 11/2 JT FAV: 0-1010: Led till after halfway, grad wknd: 15th.			0
1368	**ALFAHAAL** 12 [10] 7-8-5 (45)(2ow) M Hills 10/1: 40-000: Nvr dngrs: 17th, won this in '99, see 1273.			0
*1148	**SAGUARO** 26 [17] 6-8-3 (45) L Newman (5) 7/1: 00-210: Handy 4f: 19th, btr 1148 (fast).			0

1050	**Ertlon** 32 [12] 10-8-8 (50) S Hitchcott (7) 33/1:	1100 **Who Goes There** 29 [13] 4-8-0 (42) A McCarthy(3) 33/1:
1097	**Epernay** 29 [14] 4-9-11 (67) R Cochrane 14/1:	1289 **An Jolien** 16 [7] 3-8-5 (58)(bl) G Faulkner (0) 16/1:
1237	**Glastonbury** 20 [11] 4-8-2 (44) R Ffrench 33/1:	4499} **Saifan** 219 [18] 11-9-0 (56) (vis) G Bardwell 16/1:

20 ran   Time 1m 28.6 (6)   (Saracen Racing)   J Pearce Newmarket, Suffolk

---

1612	3.20 WILTSHIRES NOV STKS 2YO (D) 6f Good/Soft 68 -55 Slow
	£3282 £1010 £505 £252

--	**GROVE DANCER** [6] M H Tompkins 2-8-7 S Sanders 20/1: 1: 2 b f Reprimand - Brisighella (Al Hareb)			70

In tch, feeling pace ent fnl 2f, styd on strgly for press ins last to get up dying strides: slow time, debut: Jan foal, sire a miler: eff at 6f, further is going to suit: goes well fresh on gd/soft: gd strong ride.

--	**CARNIVAL LAD** [5] Sir Michael Stoute 2-8-12 L Dettori 13/8 FAV: 2: 2 ch c Caerleon - Fun Crowd		nk	73

(Easy Goer) Held up, eff appr fnl 1f, strong run fnl 100y, not btn far: well bckd: $320,000 Feb 1st foal, dam unrcd, sire 10/12f performer: handles gd/soft grnd, shld get off the mark pretty soon & will apprec 7f+.

--	**SYLVAN GIRL** [2] C N Allen 2-8-7 W Ryan 20/1: 3: 2 ch f Case Law - Nordic Living (Nordico)		nk	67

Bmpd start, held up, gd prog to lead ent fnl 1f, hdd cl-home: drifted from 12/1: 17,000 gns Feb foal, sister to 2 juv wnrs, sire a sprinter: handles gd/soft grnd & gets 6f tho' has the pace for 5f & can win back at that trip.

1019	**HARD TO CATCH** 37 [1] K T Ivory 2-8-12 R Cochrane 14/1: -534: Chsd ldrs, rdn appr fnl 1f, unable		¾	70

to qckn: tchd 33/1: cost new stable £5,000: stays 6f, see 1029, 911.

*1507	**JOINT INSTRUCTION** 5 [3] 2-9-2 T Quinn 7/4: -45215: Led for 2f & again briefly appr fnl 1f,		nk	73

no extra: quick reapp: well bckd: consistent, see 1507.

--	**TEREED ELHAWA** [4] 2-8-7 J Reid 7/2: 6: Prom, led halfway till 1½f out, onepace: op 5/2: 40,000 gns		hd	64

Cadeaux Genereux Feb 1st foal, dam a wnr in France, sire a sprinter: with E Dunlop.

6 ran   Time 1m 17.6 (7.3)   (P H Betts)   M H Tompkins Newmarket

---

1613	3.50 LOVEWELL BLAKE CLAIMER 3YO (F) 2m Good/Soft 68 -12 Slow
	£2205 £630 £315

1071	**OPEN GROUND** 30 [6] P Howling 3-8-13 R Mullen 7/4 FAV: -00161: 3 ch g Common Grounds - Poplina			54

(Roberto) In tch, imprvd to lead 2f out, pushed out, rdly: nicely bckd: earlier won at Pontefract (sell): eff at 12f/2m on gd/soft & hvy grnd, stiff/undul or easy trks: suited by claimers & sellers.

4523}	**MAGENKO** 217 [1] M H Tompkins 3-8-9 S Sanders 7/1: 000-2: 3 ch g Forest Wind - Bebe Auction		3	47

(Auction Ring) Chsd ldrs, chall appr fnl 2f, outstyd by wnr: reapp: well btn all 3 '99 starts up to 7f (rtd 66, surely flattered): suited by this step up to 2m on gd/soft grnd.

1270	**NICIARA** 19 [2] M C Chapman 3-8-7 L Newman (5) 12/1: 500403: 3 b g Soviet Lad - Verusa (Petorius)		1¼	44$

Early ldr & again appr fnl 3f till brief 2f out, onepace: op 10/1, v stiff task, flattered over longer 2m trip.

1362	**MICE DESIGN** 12 [5] N P Littmoden 3-8-13 J Weaver 7/1: 054: Held up, chsd ldrs appr fnl 2f, onepace.		1¼	49
1292	**TORMENTOSO** 16 [3] 3-9-7 T Quinn 3/1: 0-4605: Sn led, hdd 3½f out, sn btn: unsuited by lngr trip?		30	37
892	**DIAMOND GEORGIA** 48 [4] 3-7-10 G Bardwell 12/1: 050006: Keen, al bhd: stiff task, 7 wk abs.		11	5
1540	**SEDUCTION** 4 [7] 3-8-12 M Hills 8/1: -67: Sn struggling: op 10/1, qck reapp, turf bow, no form.		dist	0

7 ran   Time 3m 36.1 (12.8)   (S J Hammond)   P Howling Newmarket

---

1614	4.20 AMAT RDRS HCAP 3YO+ 0-70 (F) 1m3f101y Good/Soft 68 -04 Slow	[31]
	£2404 £687 £343 3 yo rec 15lb	

1499	**ADMIRALS SECRET** 5 [16] C F Wall 11-11-3 (48) Miss H Webster (5) 10/1: 60-501: 11 ch g Secreto -			51

Noble Mistress (Vaguely Noble) Nvr far away, led appr fnl 1f, styd on well: qck reapp: unplcd in '99 (rtd 54): '98 wnr at Lingfield (2, appr & amat h'caps, rtd 68) & Brighton: eff at 12/14f on any grnd/trk, likes sharp ones, esp Lingfield: goes well fresh & is well h'capped.

1023	**NOSEY NATIVE** 37 [15] J Pearce 11-11-0 (45) Mrs L Pearce 4/1 FAV: -00322: 7 b g Cyrano de Bergerac -		1¼	46

Native Flair (Be My Native) Rear, hdwy ent str & ch till nth & hung left appr fnl 1f: op 7/1: hard to win with.

1394	**MEILLEUR** 11 [10] Lady Herries 6-11-13 (58) Miss R Woodman (7) 11/1: 236063: 6 b g Nordico - Lucy		½	58

Limelight (Hot Spark) Held up, kept on fnl 3f, not pace to chall: op 7/1, back in trip, consistent: see 68.

1100	**SILENT SOUND** 29 [7] Mrs A J Perrett 4-11-9 (54) Miss L J Harwood (7) 8/1: 020-04: Held up, prog &		hd	54

switched ent fnl 3f, onepace ins last: jockey given 1 day whip ban: clr rem, just best at 10f in blnks: see 1100.

791	**MAY KING MAYHEM** 62 [14] 7-10-9 (40)(bl) Mrs C Williams 7/1: 116-65: Well plcd, led ent fnl		9	31

3f till bef dist, fdd: 9 wk abs, blnks reapplied: see 791.

1393	**MALCHIK** 11 [1] 4-10-6 (37) Miss S Pocock (5) 11/1: 312026: Handy, eff 3f out, grad wknd: best at 9f.		1¾	26
1207	**SEPTEMBER HARVEST** 23 [3] 4-10-13 (44) (vis) Mr S Dobson (5) 16/1: 440007: Mid-div thr'out.		1¾	31
788	**URGENT REPLY** 63 [11] 7-10-5 (36) Miss Michelle Saunde 20/1: 400-08: Dwelt, nvr a factor: '99		shd	23

Warwick wnr (h'cap, rtd 43): '98 hat-trick scorer at Hamilton, Musselburgh & Chepstow (appr h'caps, rtd 54): eff at 12f/2m on fast & soft grnd, any trk: goes well for an appr, with/without t-strap: slipped down weights.

1209	**ALBERKINNIE** 22 [4] 5-11-2 (47) Miss Michelle Saunders (7) 10/1: 332109: Prom till 4f out: btr 1086 (10f).		2	32
1296	**NICE BALANCE** 16 [2] 5-10-5 (36) Mr W Worthington (7) 20/1: 565300: Chsd ldrs till 3f out: 10th, see 418.		3	18
1363	**ARTHURS KINGDOM** 12 [8] 4-12-0 (59) Mr S Sauce (7) 9/1: 06-030: Nvr dangerous: 11th, op 7/1.		shd	41
1022	**CHILLI** 37 [13] 3-10-7 (53) Mr B Hitchcott (3) 5/1: 332330: Led for fnl 1m, lost place: 10th, see 1022, 597.		2	33

3448}	**Caerdydd Fach** 286 [9] 4-10-0 (31) Miss C Lake(5) 33/1:1272	**Classic Eagle** 19 [12] 7-11-10 (55) Mr S Rees(7) 14/1:
201	**The Blue Brazil** 166 [5] 4-9-10 (27)(3oh) Mr T Doyle 20/1:	
1292	**Maiysha** 16 [6] 3-10-1 (47)(BL) Mr F Windsor Clive (5) 25/1:	

16 ran   Time 2m 31.1 (8.3)   (Mrs C A Wall)   C F Wall Newmarket

YARMOUTH WEDNESDAY MAY 31ST Lefthand, Flat, Fair Track

1615
4.50 R HARROD APPR HCAP 3YO+ 0-60 (F) 1m2f21y Good/Soft 68 +05 Fast [60]
£2264 £647 £323 3 yo rec 14lb

853 **SIFAT 51** [10] J R Jenkins 5-9-8 (54)(vis) D Glennon 8/1: 040-51: 5 b m Marju - Reine Maid (Mr **61**
Prospector) Trkd ldrs, ran on to lead well ins last, rdn out: gd time, 7 wk abs: plcd over jumps in late '99 (2m
nov, gd/soft, rtd 97h): unplcd in '99 for N Graham (h'caps, rtd 63, blnkd): '98 Pontefract wnr (mdn, rtd 74, M
Tregoning): eff at 1m/10f on fast & soft grnd, any trk: best in a visor, tried blinkers.
1509 **FOREST DREAM 5** [6] L A Dace 5-9-1 (47) G Sparkes 20/1: 000002: 5 b m Warrshan - Sirenivo ½ **51**
(Sir Ivor) Held up, switched & gd prog appr fnl 1f, hard rdn & ev ch ins last, not pace of wnr: quick reapp.
1272 **SMARTER CHARTER 19** [3] Mrs L Stubbs 7-9-9 (55) Kristin Stubbs 3/1 FAV: 63-123: 7 br g Master shd **59**
Willie - Irene's Charter (Persian Bold) Held up, prog when short of room appr fnl 1f, ran on for hands &
heels towards fin, nvr nrr: nicely bckd from 4/1: likely to have gone close with a clr passage: see 871.
*1496 **TEMPRAMENTAL 5** [15] S R Bowring 4-9-6 (52)(6ex) N Mitchell (8) 15/2: 533314: Led till well ins 1 **54**
last, no extra: tough filly, ran well out again qckly with a penalty for 1496.
1370 **ACEBO LYONS 12** [13] 5-9-13 (59) Miss Lisa Jones (8) 10/1: 0-1665: Held up, wide, prog to shd **61**
chase ldrs appr fnl 1f, kept on: op 8/1, top-weight, see 1370, 705.
855 **MICE IDEAS 51** [8] 4-8-12 (44) D Young (3) 8/1: 051236: Held up, prog appr fnl 1f, no extra ins last. 1½ **44**
1265 **EN GRISAILLE 19** [7] 4-9-0 (46) D Williamson (8) 14/1: 510-07: Rear, prog 4f out till onepce 2f out. 1¾ **43**
1293 **ADRIANA 16** [2] 3-7-10 (42) S Hitchcott (8) 20/1: 0008: Keen, cl-up, saddle slipped after 3f, held fnl 2f. ¾ **39**
1205 **CLAUDIUS TERTIUS 23** [1] 3-8-1 (47) Lindsey Rutty (8) 20/1: 000-09: Cl-up till short of room 3f out: nk **43**
longer trip: unplcd juv (mdn, rtd 64): this 10f trip shld suit: with M Jarvis.
4253} **BROKE ROAD 239** [9] 4-9-2 (48) P Mundy 15/2: 3614-0: Mid-div, not clr run 3f out, lost place: 10th, 5 **36**
jumps fit, won in March at Fakenham (c.j. mdn, 2m, gd & hvy, rtd 106h): '99 Hamilton wnr (h'cap, rtd 47 &
49a): eff around 1m, stays 10f: acts on firm, gd/soft & fibresand: eff with/without blnks: with Mrs V Ward.
1404 **MOOSE MALLOY 11** [12] 3-8-2 (48) D Kinsella 6/1: 00-000: Al towards rear; 13th: unplcd juv (mdn, 0
rtd 52): bred to apprec mid-dists: with M Ryan.
3918} Mezzoramio 259 [14] 8-9-0 (46) K Parsons 12/1:   1473 Roger Ross 7 [16] 5-9-3 (49) G Gibbons 14/1:
1725} Capercaillie 363 [11] 5-8-2 (34) R Lake (1) 12/1:   1417 Giulia Muriel 9 [4] 4-8-10 (42)(VIS) R Naylor 25/1:
15 ran   Time 2m 10.5 (6.3)   (Mr C N & Mrs J C Wright)   J R Jenkins Royston, Herts

BELMONT PARK WEDNESDAY MAY 24TH Lefthand, Easy Track

Official Going DIRT

1616
9.40 CHIEF HONCHO STKS 4YO+ 1m1f Dirt Inapplicable
£21585 £7195 £3957

769 **RUNNING STAG 60** P Mitchell 6-8-11 S Sellers 16/10 FAV: 22-201: 6 b h Cozzene - Fruhlingstag (Orsini) **115a**
Prom, led appr fnl 1f, readily: 9 wk abs: '99 wnr here at Belmont & Saratoga (Gr 2 h'caps, rtd 118a & 120):
'98 wnr at Lingfield (stks, rtd 107a) & Deauville (Gr 3, rtd 117): eff 7.5f, suited by 9/10f: acts on firm & gd/sft,
loves equitrack & dirt: runs well fresh, any trk, likes sharp ones: tough & v smart Atlantic-hopping entire.
-- **EARLY WARNING** United States 5-8-5 J Chavez 7/2: 2: 5 b h Summer Squall - Vid Kid (Pleasant Colony) 1½ **104a**
-- **WILD IMAGINATION** United States 6-8-2 A Gryder 15/1: 3: 6 b g Wild Again - La Fantastique (Le 3½ **95a**
Fabuleux) -):
6 ran   Time 1m 48.08   (J Cohen)   P Mitchell Epsom, Surrey

LONGCHAMP THURSDAY MAY 25TH Righthand, Stiff, Galloping Track

Official Going GOOD

1617
3.30 GR 3 PRIX DU PALAIS-ROYAL 3YO+ 7f Good Inapplicable
£21134 £7685 £3842 £2113 3 yo rec 11lb

9 **BLU AIR FORCE 202** B Grizzetti 3-8-7 O Peslier 71/10: 12-101: 3 b c Sri Pekan - Carillon Miss **112**
(The Minstrel) Held up, gd prog 2f out, hard rdn to get up nr fin: smart, imprvg colt, eff at 7f on gd grnd.
1043 **WARNINGFORD 27** J R Fanshawe 6-9-4 D Harrison 24/10: 06-242: 6 b h Warning - Barford Lady ½ **111**
(Stanford) Early ldr, prom, short of room appr fnl 1f, ran on well when clr ins last: ran well at best trip.
1049 **TUMBLEWEED RIDGE 26** B J Meehan 7-9-4 (bl) M Tebbutt 31/10: 210-23: 7 ch h Indian Ridge - Billie 1½ **108**
Blue (Ballad Rock) Sn led, worn down nr fin: lost a shoe & prob a sound run in the circumstances: see 1049.
861 **IRIDANOS 50** C Laffon Parias 4-9-4 D Boeuf 67/10: 2-3244: Rear till ran on strgly fnl 2f, nvr nrr. shd **108**
1110 **MUCHEA 22** 6-9-4 (VIS) C Asmussen 137/10: -02205: Chsd ldrs, chall appr fnl 1f, sn no extra: flattered? ½ **107$**
11 ran   Time 1m 20.4   (D Wildenstein)   B Grizzetti Italy

CAPANNELLE SUNDAY MAY 28TH Righthand, Flat, Galloping Track

Official Going GOOD/FIRM

1618
4.30 GR 1 ITALIAN DERBY 3YO 1m4f Good/Firm Inapplicable
£210544 £117569 £71439

-- **KALLISTO** H Blume 3-9-2 A Boschert 34/10: 32-111: 3 b c Sternkonig - Kalinikta (Konigsstuhl) **111**
Mid-div, imprvd 5f out, led appr fnl 2f, drew clr: v useful German raider, completed a hat-trick and is unbeaten
for the season: eff at 12f on fast grnd: clearly a fast improving colt.
1216 **WINDSOR BOY 19** P F I Cole 3-9-2 J Fortune 3/1 FAV: 165-22: 3 b c Mtoto - Fragrant Belle (Al Nasr) 6 **104**
Chsd ldrs, hard at work 4f out, no ch with wnr but styd on best of the rest: gd run, improved at 12f, see 1216.

CAPANNELLE   SUNDAY MAY 28TH   Righthand, Flat, Galloping Track

--	**PAOLINI** A Wohler 3-9-2 W Ryan 18/1: 03-113: 3 b c Lando - Prairie Darling (Stanford)	*shd*	**104**

In tch, gd prog ent fnl 3f, same pace bef dist: useful German raider, reopposes wnr in the German Derby.
1216 **NIGHT STYLE** 19 E A L Dunlop 3-9-2 J Reid 66/10: 1-6040: Chsd ldrs, wknd fnl 3f: 14th, btn arnd 18L.   **92**
1317 **RIVERS CURTAIN** 14 3-9-2 D O'Donohoe 13/2: 1-60: Slow away, midfield till 3f out: 19th, btn arnd 34L.   **78**
20 ran   Time 2m 27.1   (Gestut Rottgen)   H Blume Germany

CHANTILLY   TUESDAY MAY 30TH   Righthand, Galloping Track

Official Going   SOFT

1619	2.55 GR 3 PRIX DU CHEMIN 4YO+ 1m Soft Inapplicable
	£21134 £7685 £3842

1123 **KINGSALSA** 29 A Fabre 4-8-12 O Peslier 7/10 FAV: 5-1321: 4 br c Kingmambo - Caretta (Caro)   **115**
Held up, smooth prog 2f out to lead well ins last, readily: prev won reapp at Compiegne: '99 wnr at Longchamp,
plcd in French 2,000 Guineas (rtd 116): eff at 7f/9f, tried 10f: acts on good, hvy grnd & dirt: smart colt.
-- **BANYUMANIK** Mario Hofer 4-8-12 G Bocksai 114/10: 06-112: 4 b c Perugino - Bennetta (Top Ville)   ½ **112**
Led, clr appr str, drvn 2f out, collared well ins last: v useful German raider, eff at 1m/10f: acts on soft grnd.
1828} **LE ROI CHIC** 359 N Clement 4-8-12 G Mosse 121/10: 6-0253: 4 b c Balleroy - Chic Emilie (Policeman)   ¾ **111**
Led chsg pack, eff 2f out, kept on but not pace to chall: gd run & 3L clr rem: eff at 1m on soft & hvy grnd.
7 ran   Time 1m 41.5   (D Wildenstein)   A Fabre France

LEOPARDSTOWN   WEDNESDAY MAY 24TH   Lefthand, Galloping Track

Official Going   GOOD

1620	7.30 LISTED SAVAL BEG STKS 3YO+ 1m6f Good Inapplicable
	£16250 £4750 £2250

1109 **ROYAL REBEL** 21 M Johnston 4-9-10 (bl) M J Kinane 6/1: 010-01: 4 b g Robellino - Greenvera   **110**
(Riverman) Trk ldrs, rdn fnl 3f, prog to chase leader 1f out, styd on gamely to lead line, all out: op 4/1: '99 wnr
at Newcastle (mdn) & Leopardstown (stks, rtd 108): 5th in a Gr1 in '98 (rtd 102): eff at 14f on firm & gd/sft
grnd: likes a galloping trk, especially Leopardstown: eff with/without blnks: v useful stayer.
4022} **ENZELI** 249 J Oxx 5-10-1 J P Murtagh 4/7 FAV: /114-2: 5 b h Kahyasi - Ebaziya (Darshaan)   *shd* **114**
Trkd ldr, led over 1f out till line: reapp: '99 wnr at Leopardstown (Listed) & R Ascot (Gr 1 Gold Cup, rtd 121):
eff at 14f, revelation over 2m4f last term: acts on fast & gd/hvy: high-class stayer, sharper for this at Ascot.
-- **HIRAPOUR** D K Weld 4-9-6 P J Smullen 6/1: 21-013: 4 b g Kahyasi - Himaya (Mouktar)   2½ **102**
5 ran   Time 2m 57.1   (P D Savill)   M Johnston Middleham, N Yorks

CURRAGH   SATURDAY MAY 27TH   Righthand, Stiff, Galloping Track

Official Going   YIELDING

1621	2.45 LISTED MARBLE HILL STKS 2YO 5f Good/Soft Inapplicable
	£19500 £5700 £2700

-- **PYRUS** A P O'Brien 2-8-9 M J Kinane 11/10 FAV: 1: 2 b c Mr Prospector - Most Precious   **101**
(Nureyev) Trkd ldr, rdn/led over 1f out, styd on well: eff at 5f, looks sure to relish 6f: acts on gd/sft grnd
& a stiff/gall trk: runs well fresh: well regarded & useful, excellent debut & a Royal Ascot type.
-- **CONEY KITTY** D Hanley 2-8-6 N G McCullagh 12/1: -22: 2 ch f Lycius - Auntie Maureen (Roi   1½ **92**
Danzig) Bhd ldrs, efft & kept on ins last, not pace of wnr: op 10/1: must win a race.
-- **GALLITO CASTAO** E Lynam 2-8-9 J P Murtagh 10/1: -3253: 2 b c Furno Di Londra - Cut The Red   hd **95**
Tape (Sure Blade) Chsd ldrs, onepace fnl 1f.
1385 **INNIT** 7 M R Channon 2-8-11 L Dettori 5/1: -32135: Led till over 1f out, fdd: btn less than 2l in 5th.   nk **96**
6 ran   Time 1m 00.6   (Michael Tabor)   A P O'Brien Ballydoyle, Co Tipperary

1622	3.15 GR 3 GREENLANDS STKS 3YO+ 6f Good/Soft Inapplicable
	£27625 £8500 £4250 £1700 3 yo rec 9 lb

*1232 **NAMID** 19 J Oxx 4-9-4 J P Murtagh 3/1 FAV: 23-311: 4 b h Indian Ridge - Dawnsio   **115**
(Tate Gallery) Held up, prog/rdn to lead over 1f out, in command nr fin, pushed out, readily: op 5/1: recent Cork
wnr (List): plcd both '99 starts (Gr 3 & List, rtd 107): eff at 6/7f on gd & hvy: progressive, win another Gr race.
4415} **SOCIAL HARMONY** 224 D K Weld 6-9-4 P Shanahan 16/1: 124-02: 6 b g Polish Precedent - Latest   1½ **109**
Chapter (Ahonoora) Cl up, rdn/ev ch 2f out, not pace of wnr from over 1f out: eff at 6f/7f on gd/fm & soft.
981 **ROSSINI** 37 A P O'Brien 3-9-1 M J Kinane 7/2: 112-43: 3 b c Miswaki - Touch Of Greatness   ½ **114**
(Hero's Honour) Cl up, ev ch 2f out, kept on onepace: op 7/4: back in trip: see 981.
*1383 **MANORBIER** 7 K A Ryan 4-9-4 Dane O'Neill 16/1: 120414: Trkd ldrs, no room over 1f out till   hd **107**
inside last, styd on well nr fin: shade unlucky, prob plcd with a clr run: v progressive: see 1383 (h'cap).
952 **GORSE** 39 5-9-10 P Robinson 7/1: 125-36: Led, hdd over 1f out, no extra: op 5/1: fin 6th: see 952.   **110**
1111 **MA YORAM** 24 3-8-9 L Dettori 8/1: 23-548: Chsd ldrs, held fnl 2f, fin 8th: op 5/1: stiff task.   **100**
9 ran   Time 1m 12.5   (Lady Clague)   J Oxx Currabeg Co Kildare

1623   3.50 GR 1 IRISH 2,000 GUINEAS 3YO   1m   Good/Soft   Inapplicable
£116600 £40000 £20000 £8000

*1318 **BACHIR 13** Saeed bin Suroor 3-9-0 L Dettori 4/1: 3-1211: 3 b c Desert Style - Morning Welcome   **120**
(Be My Guest) Made all, drvn & hard pressed ins last, styd on well, drvn out: earlier won on reapp in Dubai &
Longchamp (French 2,000 Guineas): smart juv, won at Chepstow (mdn auct) & broke juv crse rec at Goodwood (Gr 2,
J Gosden, rtd 108 when Gr 1 plcd): effat 6f, suited by 1m & stays 9f: acts on firm, soft & dirt: runs well
fresh on any trk: high-class miler who shld be the one to beat in the St James Palace Stakes.

1171 **GIANTS CAUSEWAY 21** A P O'Brien 3-9-0 M J Kinane 9/10 FAV: 11-122: 3 ch c Storm Cat - Mariah's   nk **119**
Storm (Rahy) Cl-up, rdn & ran on to chall wnr ins last, styd on well for press, just held: high-class miler who
deserves another Gr 1 prize (rnr-up in Newmarket 2000 Gns last time) & likely to re-oppose today's wnr at R Ascot.

1171 **CAPE TOWN 21** R Hannon 3-9-0 Dane O'Neill 16/1: 12-103: 3 gr c Desert Style - Rossaldene   ¾ **117**
(Mummy's Pet) Chsd ldr, rdn to improve fnl 2f, kept on well, not pace of front 2: stays 1m & enjoys gd/soft.

1171 **BARATHEA GUEST 21** G G Margarson 3-9-0 P Robinson 11/4: 1D-134: Prom, slightly outpcd 3f out,   ¾ **115**
rallied & ran on strongly ins last: looks sure to relish a step up to 10f+ now: see 1171.

1171 **SCARTEEN FOX 21** N Pollard 20/1: 10-405: Prom, drvn/not pace of chall ldrs fnl 2f: needs Listed.   3 **109**
1120 **LEGAL JOUSTING 26** 3-9-0 P J Smullen 20/1: 2-1226: Waited with, no impress fnl 2f: up in class.   1 **107**
--   **GLAD MASTER** 3-9-0 J P Murtagh 20/1: D11-07: Front rank, rdn/wknd fnl 3f: stable-mate of wnr: **0**
smart German trained juv in '99, won a Gr 3 at Cologne: eff at 6f/1m on good & soft grnd.

--   **GREGORIAN** 3-9-0 K J Manning 200/1: 3-08: Al in rear: out of his depth.   **0**
8 ran   Time 1m 39.8   (Godolphin)   Saeed bin Suroor Newmarket

Official Going   GOOD TO YIELDING

1624   2.15 NAPOLINA EBF MDN 2YO   6f   Good/Soft   Inapplicable
£6900 £1600 £700

--   **DARWIN** A P O'Brien 2-9-2 M J Kinane 4/11 FAV: 1: 2 b c Danehill - Armorique (Top Ville)   **100+**
Chsd ldrs going well, cruised into lead 2f out, pshd clr, easily: debut: eff at 6f on gd/soft, further sure to suit:
v impressive here & highly regarded by powerful stable: looks a surefire future Listed/Group wnr, R Ascot next.

--   **VENTURA** C O'Brien 2-8-11 F M Berry 12/1: 2: 2 b f Spectrum - Wedding Bouquet (King's Lake)   7 **75**
Chsd ldr, rdn to improve 2f out, stayed on but no chance with facile wnr.

--   **WAYFARER** D Wachman 2-9-2 J A Heffernan 33/1: -03: 2 b c Blues Traveller - Holly Bird (Runnett)   1½ **76**
Prom, outpcd 3f out, switched & styd on late.
10 ran   Time 1m 14.7   (Michael Tabor)   A P O'Brien Ballydoyle, Co Tipperary

1625   3.15 GR 1 TATTERSALLS GOLD CUP 4YO+   1m2f110y Good/Soft   Inapplicable
£63000 £20000 £10000 £4000

123 **MONTJEU 182** J E Hammond 4-9-0 M J Kinane 1/3 FAV: 1114-1: 4 ch c Sadler's Wells - Floripedes   **127+**
(Top Ville) Held up going well, blocked in appr fnl 1f, squeezed thro' gap ins last, easily went clr, hard held:
'99 wnr at Longchamp (2 Gr 2s), Chantilly (Gr 1 French Derby, by 4L), Curragh (Gr 1 Irish Derby, by 5L) & most
notably the Gr 1 Arc at Longchamp (rtd 136): juv wnr at Longchamp & Chantilly: suited by 10/12f & likes gd &
hvy, handles fm: likes a gall trk: top-class colt with a terrific turn of foot, hard to beat in King George.

1115 **GREEK DANCE 28** Sir Michael Stoute 5-9-0 K Fallon 5/1: 265-22: 5 b h Sadler's Wells - Hellenic   1½ **121**
(Darshaan) Mid-div, hdwy to chall dist, styd on but no ch with easy wnr: not disgraced against a rival of
the very highest class & looks sure to win at least a Gr 2: see 1115.

3873} **MUTAFAWEQ 260** Saeed bin Suroor 4-9-0 L Dettori 8/1: 1541-3: 4 b c Silver Hawk - The Caretaker   1½ **119**
(Caerleon) Prom, chall 2f out, sn led, hdd ins, no extra: reapp: '99 wnr at Doncaster (reapp, stks), R Ascot
(Gr 2 King Edward) & again at Doncaster (Gr 1 St Leger, rtd 125): '98 Newmarket mdn wnr: eff at 12f, suited
by 14.6f, likes firm/fast, handles gd/soft: runs well fresh: high-class, gd reapp over an inadequate trip.

4399} **GOLDEN SNAKE 225** B W Hills 4-9-0 Pat Eddery 20/1: 2160-4: Front rank, chall ldrs 2f out, drvn   2 **116**
& btn ins fnl 1f: '99 scorer at Newmarket (Listed) & Chantilly (Gr 1, rtd 119): '98 Doncaster wnr (mdn, rtd 93+):
eff at 9f/10.4f on fast & gd/gall grnd: acts on stiff/gall trks & runs well fresh: apprec a drop to Gr 2/3 class.

*1121 **URBAN OCEAN 27** 4-9-0 D M Oliver 12/1: 116-15: Led, drvn/hdd 2f out, wknd fnl 1f: see 1121.   2½ **113**
5 ran   Time 2m 13.3   (Michael Tabor)   J E Hammond France

1626   4.15 GR 1 IRISH 1,000 GUINEAS 3YO   1m   Good/Soft   Inapplicable
£112600 £40000 £20000 £8000

*1229 **CRIMPLENE 21** C E Brittain 3-9-0 P Robinson 16/1: -63311: 3 ch f Lion Cavern - Crimson Conquest   **116**
(Diesis) Led, found extra for press appr fnl 1f, ran on strgly, gamely: 3 weeks ago landed the German 1,000 Guineas
at Dusseldorf (by 4L): '99 wnr at Redcar (auct mdn) & Salisbury (stks, Gr 1 3rd, rtd 106): v eff at 1m on firm,
suited by gd & hvy, any trk: likes to force the pace: v smart, tough & improving, Coronation Stakes next up.

1185 **AMETHYST 21** A P O'Brien 3-9-0 M J Kinane 7/1: 43-102: 3 b f Sadler's Wells - Zummerudd (Habitat)   1½ **112**
In tch, imprvd 3f out, rdn & ev ch appr fnl 1f, held fnl 100y: shwd English Guineas running to be all wrong
(reportedly in season) back on this softer grnd: will reportedly apprec a less testing 1m: see 948.

1315 **STORM DREAM 14** K Prendergast 3-9-0 S Craine 20/1: 23-23: 3 b f Catrail - Mamara Reef (Salse)   1½ **109**
Waited with, prog on outer 3f out, chall bef dist, onepce fnl 1f: v useful maiden, continues career in the USA.

1185 **SEAZUN 21** M R Channon 3-9-0 T Quinn 8/1: 21-244: Rear, hdwy for press appr fnl 1f, unable   hd **109**
to chall: v genuine Brit raider, goes on fast & gd/sft: see 1185 (also 4th in Newmarket Guineas).

1185 **PRINCESS ELLEN 21** 3-9-0 K Darley 7/1: 05-025: Prom, and press 2f out, unable to qckn: 2½ **104**
op 5/1: found to be 'in-season' & worth another chance after v promising rnr-up in Newmarket 2000 Guineas.

1315 **THEORETICALLY 14** 3-9-0 P J Smullen 9/1: 411-36: Nvr better than mid-div: needs a drop in grade.   ¾ **102**
1122 **YARA 27** 3-9-0 D P McDonogh 25/1: 20-227: Hld up, eff 3f out, nvr pace to chall: highly tried.   **0**
*863 **CHIANG MAI 49** 3-9-0 K Fallon 11/1: -11-18: Prom till 2f out: 7 wk abs, op 8/1: lost unbtn record.   **0**
*1155 **MEIOSIS 23** 3-9-0 L Dettori 7/2 FAV: -19: Chsd ldrs, rdn/btn 2f out, eased: tchd 9/2:   **0**

better expected but was asking a lot on only 2nd start over lngr trip & on softer grnd: found to be slightly lame.
-- **ALLURING** 3-9-0 D M Oliver 66/1: 24-150: Rear, hdwy 3f out, sn wknd: 10th, stablemate 2nd: 0
earlier won a Listowel mdn (1m, soft grnd): highly tried.
-- **PAPER MOON** 3-9-0 J A Heffernan 50/1: -100: Bhd from halfway: 11th, stablemate rnr-up: 0
earlier won a Leopardstown mdn on debut (1m, soft grnd).
*1315 **PRESELI** 14 3-9-0 E Ahern 5/1: 111-10: Chsd lrds, wknd qckly bef fnl 2f: 12th, op 7/2: listless   0
way to lose unbeaten record & was later found to be in season: gave 7lbs & a beating to this 3rd in 1315.
948 **BELLS ARE RINGING** 42 3-9-0 C O'Donoghue 50/1: 616-40: Sn bhd: 13th.   0
13 ran   Time 1m 39.8   (Sheikh Marwan Al Maktoum)   C E Brittain Newmarket

---

1627   4.50 LISTED AIRLIE STUD SILVER STKS 3YO   1m2f   Good/Soft Inapplicable
£21125 £6175 £2925

1316 **JAMMAAL** 14 D K Weld 3-8-12 (BL) P J Smullen 5/1: 3-2121: 3 b c Robellino - Navajo Love Song   107
(Dancing Brave) Rear, gd prog ent str, led bef dist, ran on well: earlier won at Cork (stks): juv wnr at
Leopardstown (mdn, Gr 1 3rd, rtd104): eff at 1m, suited by step up to 10f in blinkers on fast & soft grnd: v useful.
-- **KORASOUN** J Oxx 3-8-12 J P Murtagh 2/1 FAV: -12: 3 b c Darshaan - Kozana (Kris)   2   104
In tch, niggled 3f out, onepace till ran on fnl 1f, nvr nrr: clr rem: earlier made a wng debut at Navan:
eff at 10f, 12f is going to suit: acts on good/soft grnd: useful, lightly rcd & improving.
1246 **ISLAND SOUND** 17 D R C Elsworth 3-8-12 T Quinn 3/1: 11-253: 3 b g Turtle Island - Ballet   4   99
(Sharrood) Led chsg pack, imprvd to lead ent fnl 3f till bef dist, no extra: Brit raider, apprec a drop in trip?
1374 **PROMISING LADY** 9 M R Channon 3-8-9 W Supple 16/1: 1-067: Al bhd: highly tried Brit raider.   0
1284 **APOLLO VICTORIA** 15 (BL) M J Kinane 9/2: 1-248: In tch till 3f out, eased: blinkered, see 818.   0
8 ran   Time 2m 12.8   (Hamdan Al Maktoum)   D K Weld Curragh, Co Kildare

---

AYR   THURSDAY JUNE 1ST   Lefthand, Galloping Track

Official Going: GOOD/FIRM. Stalls: Rnd course - Inside, Straight Course - Stands Side

1628   2.20 EBF AYR MAY NOV STKS 2YO (D)   6f   Good/Firm 24 -19 Slow
£3474   £1069   £534   £267

*1492 **WATERPARK** 6 [8] M Dods 2-8-9 F Lynch 15/2: -63211: 2 b f Namaqualand - Willisa (Polar Falcon)   80
Held up, prog to press ldrs 2f out, led ins last & styd on well, rdn out: recent Haydock wnr (mdn clmr): suited
by step up to 6f, shld get further: acts on fast & soft grnd & likes a gall trk: prog filly, can win more races.
*1359 **DISTINCTLY CHIC** 13 [10] A P Jarvis 2-8-11 N Callan 7/2: 612: 2 b f Distinctly North - Dane's Lane   ¾   79
(Danehill) Prom, rdn/ev ch over 1f out, kept on well for press: bckd, tho' op 11/4: styd longer 6f trip: see 1359.
1006 **MAMMAS TONIGHT** 38 [11] A Berry 2-9-0 G Carter 3/1: 1333: 2 ch g Timeless Times - Miss Merlin   hd   81
(Manacle) Chsd ldrs, edged left/ch over 1f out, kept on for press: acts on fast, hvy & fibresand: see 1006, 801.
-- **BIG JOHN** [7] J S Goldie 2-8-12 A Culhane 8/1: 4: Twds rear, outpcd halfway, shkn up & styd on   2½   72+
well under hands & heels riding fnl 2f, nrst fin: op 5/1: Cadeaux Genereux colt, Feb foal, cost 42,000gns: half
brother to a 6f wnr/12m juv wnr: stays 6f, 7f shld suit: eyecatching, can improve & find a race.
-- **LOVE** [2] 2-8-12 M Hills 5/2 FAV: 5: Soon led, strongly pressed & edged left/hdd inside last, fdd cl-   2½   65
home: hvly bckd: Royal Academy colt, March foal, dam a French juv wnr: stay further in time for M Johnston.
-- **MILLIKEN PARK** [5] 2-8-7 C Lowther 9/1: 6: Rear, rdn, late gains, no threat: Fumo Di Londra filly,   hd   59
Feb foal, cost IR 11,000gns: half sister to a 6f wnr, dam a well related mdn, shld improve for Miss L A Perratt.
1161 **STILMEMAITE** 26 [9] 2-8-7 J Bramhill 66/1: -3507: Cl up 4f: btr 1006, 904 (5f, soft/hvy).   1¾   56
-- **MR SQUIGGLE** [4] 2-8-12 R Winston 50/1: 8: In tch towards centre, btn 2f out: Persian Bold   1½   57
colt, April foal, 15,500gns 2yo: dam unraced, sire a high class juv/miler.
1359 **ANGELAS HUSBAND** 13 [3] 2-8-12 P Fessey 66/1: 609: In tch 4f: btr 1161 (debut, 5f).   ¾   55
-- **QUIET TRAVELLER** [1] 2-8-12 Dale Gibson 50/1: 0: Dwelt, al bhd: 10th: Blues Traveller colt, May   5   46
foal, cost 17,000gns: dam a 1m/9f wnr, sire a high class 9f2f performer.
1131 **ARIES FIRECRACKER** 28 [6] 2-8-12 O Pears 100/1: 00: Bhd halfway: 11th: no form.   7   33
11 ran   Time 1m 11.85 (2.55)   (Russ Mould)   M Dods Piercebridge, Co Durham

---

1629   2.50 BELL GROUP HCAP 3YO+ 0-70 (E)   5f   Good/Firm 24 -11 Slow   [65]
£3010   £860   £430   3 yo rec 7 lb

1278 **SIR SANDROVITCH** 19 [10] R A Fahey 4-9-6 P Hanagan (7) 5/2 FAV: -00041: 4 b g Polish Patriot -   77
Old Downie (Be My Guest) Cl-up & al travelling best, led over 1f out & styd on strongly to assert inside last, rdn up:
hvly bckd: '99 Musselburgh wnr (mdn), sub rnr-up in h'cap (rtd 78): suited by 5f, tried 6f: handles a sharp or gall
trk: needs fast or firm grnd & best fresh: likes a French juv wnr & Flat run to follow when conditions suit.
1512 **TICK TOCK** 6 [11] M Mullineaux 3-8-7 (51) J F Egan 9/1: 0-0022: 3 ch f Timeless Times - Aquiletta   2½   54
(Bairn) Chsd ldrs, briefly no room/outpcd halfway, kept on for press inside last, no ch with wnr: quick reapp.
1487 **SIHAFI** 7 [12] D Nicholls 7-9-3 (54) A Nicholls (3) 100/30: 00-043: 7 ch g Elmaamul - Kit's Double   ¾   55
(Spring Double) Bhd ldrs, trav well, kept on inside last, not pace of wnr: well bckd tho' op 5/2: turn not far away.
1357 **SWYNFORD DREAM** 13 [5] J Hetherton 7-9-8 (59) J Carroll 14/1: 0-5204: Led till over 1f out, onepace.   1   58
1479 **E B PEARL** 7 [1] 4-8-2 (39) J Fanning 33/1: 510605: Cl up, outpcd fnl 1f: see 751 (AW).   ¾   36
1504 **GARNOCK VALLEY** 6 [9] 10-8-13 (50) G Carter 20/1: 640036: Outpcd rear, mod late gains for press.   nk   46
1357 **MALADERIE** 13 [7] 6-9-8 (59) (vis) T Williams 7/1: -00027: Driven bhd ldrs, btn 2f out: btr 1357.   shd   55
1431 **JOHAYRO** 10 [8] 7-9-7 (58) A Culhane 5/1: 050008: Cl-up, squeezed out when wkng 2f out: see 798.   3½   45
1258 **HIGHLY FANCIED** 20 [6] 4-8-3 (40) K Dalgleish (7) 66/1: 00-009: Dwelt, al outpcd: see 1258.   6   16
1358 **GRANITE CITY** 13 [2] 3-7-13 (43) J Mackay (7) 16/1: 60-000: Al outpcd: 10th: see 1358.   4   9
10 ran   Time 58.35 (1.75)   (W G Moore & G Winton)   R A Fahey Butterwick, N Yorks

1630   3.20 EBF CROSSHILL CLASSIFIED STKS 3YO 0-90 (C)   1m rnd Good/Firm 24 -17 Slow
£7598   £2882   £1441   £655

*1041 **MEDICEAN 34** [2] Sir Michael Stoute 3-8-13 F Lynch 1/1 FAV: -311: 3 ch c Machiavellian - Mystic   **111+**
Goddess (Storm Bird) Handy, briefly no room 2f out & switched dist, qcknd impressively to lead ins last, pushed
clr cl home: value for 3L+, hvly bckd: recent Sandown wnr (stks): eff at 1m, shld apprec 10f: acts on fast &
hvy, stiff/gall track: useful & prog colt, should make his mark in List company.
913 **OUT OF REACH 48** [6] B W Hills 3-8-8 M Hills 3/1: 1-52: 3 b f Warning - Well Beyond (Don't Forget Me) 1½ 99
Handy, led till over 1f out till inside last, soon held by easy wnr: bckd fro' op 2/1, 7 wk abs: acts on fast &
hvy grnd, styd longer 1m trip: caught a potentially smart rival here: see 913 (Gr 3).
4591} **LITTLEPACEPADDOCKS 211** [5] M Johnston 3-8-8 J Fanning 15/2: 1-3: 3 b f Accordion - Lady In Pace   ½ 98
(Burslem) Cl up, led over 2f out till dist, no extra ins last: '99 Musselburgh wnr (mdn): sister to smart Yavanas
Pace: eff at 1m, mid dists will suit: acts on gd & fast: runs well fresh: likely to improve over further.
1384 **EBBA 12** [4] M L W Bell 3-8-6 M Fenton 16/1: 505-04: Bhnd ldrs 3f out, eff & soon onepace: op 10/1:   3 90
this longer 1m trip shd suit (dam a 12f scorer): see 1384 (5f, h'cap).
995 **AL GHABRAA 40** [3] 3-8-8 J P Spencer 5/1: 1-65: Led till over 2f out, soon held: op 5/2, 6 week abs.   ½ 91
*1063 **KANAKA CREEK 31** [1] 3-8-10 J Carroll 33/1: 35-216: Prom, rdn/btn 2f out: see 1063 (soft, mdn).   4 85
6 ran   Time 1m 39.89 (3.29)   (Cheveley Park Stud)   Sir Michael Stoute Newmarket

1631   3.50 MACDONALDS HCAP 3YO+ 0-80 (D)   7f rnd Good/Firm 24 +06 Fast   [71]
£4485   £1380   £690   £345   3 yo rec 10lb

1011 **PERSIAN FAYRE 38** [14] A Berry 8-9-2 (59) J Carroll 8/1: 000-01: 8 b g Persian Heights - Dominion   63
Fayre (Dominion) Sn led, clr over 2f out, drvn ins last, just held on: gd time: '99 Redcar (sell), Carlisle
(clmr) & Ayr wnr (h'cap, this race, rtd 79): '98 Haydock wnr (stks, rtd 76): stays 1m, front running 7f specialist:
acts on firm & gd/soft, any track, likes a stiff/gall one: tough & genuine 8yo.
1431 **ALMAZHAR 10** [15] J L Eyre 5-8-8 (51)(vis) J F Egan 12/1: 223542: 5 b g Last Tycoon - Mosaique Bleue nk 54
(Shirley Heights) In tch wide, drvn & kept on well fnl 2f, just held: op 10/1: win sn, poss at 1m: see 143 (AW, 7f).
*1519 **RAFTERS MUSIC 5** [16] J A Nicholls 5-8-9 (52) A Nicholls (3) 5/1: 603313: 5 b g Thatching - Princess 1½ 52
Dixieland (Dixieland Band) Held up in tch wide, prog/edged left over 1f out, kept on ins last tho' held near fin.
1158 **DAY BOY 26** [4] Denys Smith 4-9-1 (68) R Winston 9/1: 30-304: Chsd ldrs, kept on for press fnl 2f.   hd 67
1519 **VICTORIOUS 5** [10] 4-9-5 (62)(t) M Fenton 14/1: -11005: Dwelt, eff wide 3f out, mod gains: op 16/1.   ¾ 60
1356 **NORTHERN SVENGALI 13** [9] 4-9-11 (68) J P Spencer 25/1: 400006: Held up, rdn/mod prog fnl 2f.   ½ 65
651 **TRAJAN 85** [5] 3-9-10 (77) N Callan 12/1: 25655-47: Chsd ldrs, outpcd fnl 2f: abs: see 651.   shd 74
1297 **TOUS LES JOURS 17** [8] 4-9-5 (62) A Culhane 8/1: 440-28: Mid div, drvn/held fnl 2f: op 7/1: see 1297. ½ 58
1479 **NAISSANT 7** [12] 7-8-5 (48) J Mackay (7) 10/1: 500639: Hld up, no impress fnl 2f: see 844 (Hamilton). ¾ 43
1286 **DON BOSCO 19** [2] 4-9-13 (70) G Carter 20/1: 610-00: Cl up 6f: 10th: see 1286.   ½ 64
1351 **ENCOUNTER 13** [3] 4-8-3 (46) N Kennedy 12/1: 400400: In tch 5f: 11th: tchd 14/1: see 787.   1½ 37
1356 **SUGAR CUBE TREAT 13** [11] 4-8-12 (55) J Bramhill 14/1: 10-000: Held up, no impression: 12th.   hd 45
1250 **DISTINCTIVE DREAM 21** [7] 6-10-0 (71) M Hills 9/2 FAV: 360260: Held up, no room halfway, sn held: 13th. 1 59
4298} **Friar Tuck 236** [13] 5-9-11 (68) C Lowther 20/1: 1360 **Mother Corrigan 13** [6] 4-9-0 (57)(vis) D Mernagh (3) 20/1:
1356 **Square Dancer 13** [1] 4-9-8 (65) T Williams 40/1:
16 ran   Time 1m 25.08 (1.28)   (Murray Grubb)   A Berry Cockerham, Lancs

1632   4.20 ARRAN RATING RELATED MDN 3YO 0-70 (E)   1m1f20y Good/Firm 24 -03 Slow
£2800   £800   £400

814 **SHAM SHARIF 59** [2] B W Hills 3-8-11 M Hills 4/1: 00-51: 3 b f Be My Chief - Syrian Queen (Slip   64
Anchor) Made all, strongly pressed ins last, held on gamely, all out: 2 month abs, crse rec time: unplcd both
'99 starts (rtd 72): eff at 9f, tried 10f, shld suit: acts on fast & a gall track: likes to force the pace.
1345 **NOBLE SPLENDOUR 14** [4] L M Cumani 3-9-0 J P Spencer 5/2 JT FAV: 50-502: 3 ch Grand Lodge -   hd 66
Haskeir (Final Straw) Chsd ldrs, rdn to chall over 1f out, drvn/kept on ins last, just held: well bckd: stays 9f.
1360 **BALLISTIC BOY 13** [5] J J O'Neill 3-9-0 J Fanning 14/1: 00-003: 3 ch g First Trump - Be Discreet   3½ 59
(Junius) Chsd ldrs, kept on fnl 2f, not pace of front pair: op 25/1: acts on fast grnd: see 1085 (h'cap).
4257} **SANGRA 240** [3] N A Callaghan 3-8-11 J F Egan 5/2 JT FAV: 356-4: Trkd ldrs, rdn/chance over 1f out, hd 55
no extra inside last: hvly bckd: op 7/2: reapp: plcd on debut in '99 (rtd 76): eff at 7f, stays 9f: handles fast.
1303 **DULZIE 17** [1] 3-8-11 N Callan 50/1: 0-2465: Prom, onepace fnl 2f: see 589 (AW seller, 7f).   ½ 54
954 **DATURA 44** [6] M Fenton 5/1: 400-06: Cl up, btn 2f out, eased: op 4/1, visor: 6 wk abs: 6 45
plcd last term for J H M Gosden (rtd 86, rnr up, fill mdn): eff at 6/7f, return to shorter trip should suit: handles
good grnd & a stiff/gall track: now with M L W Bell.
4107} **JIMGAREEN 249** [7] 3-8-11 C Lowther 14/1: 0490-7: Dwelt, bhnd halfway: op 5/1, reapp: rnr up on   10 30
debut last term (rtd 76, mdn): eff at 6f, tried 1m: handles gd grnd.
929 **CLEAR MOON 47** [8] 3-9-0 N Kennedy 50/1: 063-58: Bhd halfway: 7 week abs: see 929 (7f).   2 29
8 ran   Time 1m 52.8 (2.5)   (Wafic Said)   B W Hills Lambourn, Berks

1633   4.55 GALLOWAY HCAP 3YO 0-80 (D)   1m2f192y Good/Firm 24 +06 Fast   [84]
£3757   £1156   £578   £289

1292 **RED CANYON 17** [7] M L W Bell 3-8-6 (62) M Fenton 9/4 FAV: 0-2441: 3 b g Zieten - Bayazida (Bustino) 64
Led till over 1f out, drifted right & led again ins last, just prevailed, all out: well bckd tho' op 6/4, gd time:
1st success: rtd 66 at best in '99 (unplcd, mdns): eff at 1m, now suited by 11f, could get further: acts on firm
& gd/soft grnd, sharp/gall trk: consistent gelding, open to further improvement.
1446 **LOVE BITTEN 9** [5] M Johnston 3-8-11 (67) R Ffrench 5/1: 000452: 3 b g Darshaan - Kentmere   nk 68
(Galetto) Handy, led over 1f out till over 2f out, no extra inside last: op 4/1: eff around 11/14f on fast grnd.
1477 **ONE DOMINO 7** [4] M Dods 3-8-5 (60)(VIS)(1ow) A Culhane 16/1: 6-3003: 3 ch g Efisio - Dom One   nk 61
(Dominion) Prom, rdn/outpcd over 2f out, rallied well for press inside last, just held: first time vis: styd longer
11f trip: acts on fast & soft grnd: see 929 (rtd mdn).
1425 **DIVINE PROSPECT 10** [2] A P Jarvis 3-9-2 (72) N Callan 3/1: 6-6564: Chsd ldrs, onepace fnl 2f: op 4/1. 1½ 70
1310 **MY RETREAT 16** [8] 3-9-7 (77) M Hills 6/1: 2-1005: Cl up, btn over 1f out: op 9/2: btr 884 (1m, hvy). 5 68
1007 **GARGOYLE GIRL 38** [6] 3-7-11 (53) J Mackay (7) 16/1: 000-06: Rear, mod late gains: op 25/1:   ½ 43
unplcd last term (rtd 73, flattered, mdn): should apprec mid dists this term, handles gd/soft grnd.

AYR THURSDAY JUNE 1ST Lefthand, Galloping Track

1225 **ASTON MARA 22** [3] 3-9-7 (77)(bl) J Fanning 12/1: 54-007: Held up, rdn/btn 3f out: op 8/1.   11 55
1446 **MANSTAR 9** [1] 3-8-6 (62)(bl) N Kennedy 16/1: 500508: Prom, btn 3f out: op 12/1: see 1446, 1193.   12 27
8 ran   Time 2m 17.92 (1.92)   (Terry Neill)   M L W Bell Newmarket

GOODWOOD THURSDAY JUNE 1ST Righthand, Sharpish, Undulating Track

Official Going   Str - GOOD/SOFT; Rnd - GOOD. Stalls: Str - Stands side; Rnd - Inside; 1m4f - Outside.

1634
2.10 AVTRADE SELLER 2YO (E)   6f str   Good/Soft 90   -37 Slow
£3412   £1050   £525   £262

1429 **JUSTELLA 10** [6] W G M Turner 2-8-7 Pat Eddery 13/8 FAV: -6601: 2 b f Hollow Hand - Willabelle   72
(Will Somers) Made all, clr appr fnl 1f, styd on well, rdn out: nicely bckd, sold for 9,000gns: April foal, half
sister to a hdles wnr: eff at 6f, on gd/sft & a sharp/undulating trk: will now continue racing career in France.
--   **MYHAT** [5] M Blanshard 2-8-7 D Sweeney 6/1: 2: 2 ch f Factual - Rose Elegance (Bairn)   2 66
Dwelt, rear, drvn/hdwy 2f out, styd on well: clr rem, debut: sold to K Ivory for £6,000: Apr 1st foal: dam a 3yo
1m/12f wnr: eff at 6f on gd/sft, further suit: acts on a sharp/undul trk: gd debut, will improve, win a seller.
1396 **LONDON EYE 12** [3] K T Ivory 2-8-7 (bl) C Catlin (7) 9/2: 06033: 2 b f Distincly North - Clonavon   8 50
Girl (Be My Guest) Trkd ldrs, slightly hmpd bef halfway, wknd fnl 2f: op 7/2: shade btr 1396.
1463 **CEDAR BILL 8** [2] R J O'Sullivan 2-8-12 R Miles (4) 16/1: 504: Prom, no room halfway, wknd fnl 2f.   3 48
1463 **MACKEM BEAT 8** [4] 2-8-8(1ow) T G McLaughlin 16/1: 05: Front rank, hmpd after 2f, fdd fnl 2f.   ½ 43
1396 **A B MY BOY 12** [7] 2-8-12 S Carson (5) 25/1: 6006: Mid div, eff after halfway, sn btn: see 891.   1 44
1059 **GENERAL JANE 31** [1] 2-8-7 Dane O'Neill 3/1: 37: Prom, lost tch halfway: much btr 1059 (5f, soft).   8 23
7 ran   Time 1m 17.65 (7.65)   (Darren Coombes)   W G M Turner Corton Denham, Somerset

1635
2.40 AJ WALTER CLASSIFIED STKS 3YO+ 0-85 (C)   1m rnd   Good/Soft 90   +08 Fast
£6148   £2332   £1166   £530   3 yo rec 11lb

4357} **BLACK SILK 231** [3] C F Wall 4-9-2 R Mullen 8/1: 0503-1: 4 b g Zafonic - Mademoiselle Chloe   91
(Night Shift) Bhnd, rdn to imprv over 2f out, styd on to lead appr fnl 1f, rdn out: reapp, best time of day: '99
wnr at Warwick (mdn, also plcd sev times, rtd 88 at best): debut rnr-up in '98 (mdn, rtd 85): eff at 7f/1m on
firm & gd/soft grnd: handles a sharp or gall track: runs well fresh: tough & useful.
1153 **FRENCH LIEUTENANT 27** [4] G A Butler 3-8-6(1ow) Pat Eddery 11/10 FAV: 032-62: 2 b c Cadeaux   1 89
Genereux - Madame Crecy (Al Nasr) Bhd, rdn/prog 2f out, styd on well for press ins last, not rch wnr: hvly
bckd: ran as if another step up in trip may suit: gd run against elders here: see 1153.
*1490 **SILK ST JOHN 6** [2] M J Ryan 6-9-7 G Faulkner (3) 9/4: 006513: 6 b g Damister - Silk St James   1¾ 90
(Pas de Seul) Waited with, gd hdwy over 2f out, chsd wnr appr fnl 1f, held well ins last: nicely bckd, well
clr rem: quick reapp: loves coming late off a strong pace: see 1490.
1483 **CHEWIT 7** [5] G L Moore 8-9-2 I Mongan (5) 12/1: 35-604: Front rank, dsptd lead appr fnl 2f, wknd   8 71
quickly over 1f out: quick reapp: see 966, 1391.
151 **LAKE SUNBEAM 178** [1] 4-9-2 Martin Dwyer 14/1: 6045-5: Prom, rdn/dspt lead over 2f out, lost tch   ¾ 70
appr fnl 1f: op 10/1, reapp: '99 Salisbury wnr (stks, rtd 92, R Hannon), subs joined current connections & well
btn on hdls bow (2m1f juv nov, hvy, rtd 65h): rtd 93+ sole juv start in '98 (mdn): eff at 7f/1m: acts on firm,
fast & a stiff/gall track: can go well fresh & likes to force the pace: sharper next time on a sounder surface.
1015 **CRYSTAL CREEK 38** [7] 4-9-2 R Hughes 9/1: 250-06: Led, hdd appr fnl 2f, wknd quickly: '99 wnr at   3 65
Kempton (reapp, mdn) & Bath (h'cap, 89): eff up with or forcing the pace at 1m, stays a sharp 10.3f: acts on
firm or gd/soft grnd: can go well when fresh.
1450 **PRINCE DU SOLEIL 9** [6] 4-9-2 F Norton 16/1: 2-0007: In tch, wknd quickly fnl 2f, t.o.   12 49
7 ran   Time 1m 43.96 (6.56)   (S Fustok)   C F Wall Newmarket, Suffolk

1636
3.10 CASCO HCAP 3YO+ 0-80 (D)   6f str   Good/Soft 90   +02 Fast
£4368   £1344   £672   £336   3 yo rec 8 lb   [80]

1250 **BODFARI PRIDE 21** [5] D Nicholls 5-8-12 (64) F Norton 16/1: 0/0001: 5 b g Pips Pride - Renata's   68
Ring (Auction Ring) Made all, drvn/strongly prsd over 1f out, all out to hold on: gd time: missed '99, prev
term won at Redcar (auct mdn) & Chester (h'cap, rtd 86 at best, A Bailey): eff at 6f/7.5f on fast & hvy grnd:
eff on a sharp or gall trk, likes Chester: on a fair mark & can win more races for shrewd connections.
1464 **HALMANERROR 8** [10] G M McCourt 10-8-3 (55) D Harrison 10/1: -65332: 10 gr g Lochnager -   hd 58
County Coup (Busted) Dwelt, rear, gd hdwy appr fnl 1f, ran on strongly well inside last, just failed: very
tough veteran, prob best suited by 7f: see 790 (seller).
1438 **MR STYLISH 10** [4] I A Balding 4-9-2 (68) K Darley 3/1 FAV: 04-023: 4 b g Mazilier - Moore   shd 71
Stylish (Moorestyle) Cl up, chall ins last, styd on: nicely bckd: deserves a win: see 1438.
1356 **IVORY DAWN 13** [3] K T Ivory 6-9-4 (70) C Catlin (7) 6/1: -00224: Bhnd, gd hdwy appr fnl 1f, styd   1 70
on ins last, held cl home: op 4/1, clr rem: remains in gd heart, win sn: see 1356.
837 **COMPTON BANKER 55** [9] 3-9-6 (80) J Fortune 10/1: 605-05: In tch, short of room 2f out, rdn   2½ 74
& btn fnl 1f: op 7/1, 8 wk abs: may apprec a sounder surface: see 837.
1464 **KEE RING 8** [6] 4-8-4 (56)(bl) S Whitworth 25/1: 35-606: Held up, rdn/hdwy over 1f out, nvr nrr.   1¼ 47
1264 **KHALIK 20** [7] 6-9-3 (69)(t) Pat Eddery 5/1: 0-3147: Cl up, fdd appr fnl 1f: btr 1092 (5f, gd).   2 55
1438 **DIAMOND GEEZER 10** [2] 4-8-10 (62) R Hughes 11/2: 024438: Handy, grad wknd fnl 2f: btr 1438.   nk 48
*1464 **BRAMBLE BEAR 8** [1] 6-8-3 (54)(1ow)(7ex) D Sweeney 9/1: 260019: Cl up, bhd halfway, wknd.   7 27
--   **OGGI** [9] 9-9-13 (79) S Sanders 20/1: 0040/0: With ldrs, wknd qckly fnl 2f, fin last: reapp: missed   5 41
'99, 4th at best in '99 (h'cap & stks, rtd 86 at best): '97 wnr at Leicester & here at Goodwood (h'caps, rtd 90),
also 5th in val Stewards Cup: suited by 6f on firm & gd/soft, handles fibresand: acts on any trk, likes Haydock:
eff with/without blnks: has run well fresh but entitled to need this, sharper next time.
10 ran   Time 1m 15.3 (5.3)   (Bodfari Stud Ltd)   D Nicholls Sessay, N Yorks

1637   **3.40 INTALOGIK HCAP 3YO 0-95 (C)**   **1m4f**   Good/Soft 90 -13 Slow   [96]
£8346   £2568   £1284   £642

*1425 **STAR CAST 10** [9] Major D N Chappell 3-8-5 (73) (5ex) R Hills 11/1: 500-11: 3 ch f In The Wings - Thank   79
One's Stars (Alzao) Held up, gd hdwy over 2f out, rdn/led dist, styd on strongly, drvn out: recent Windsor wnr
(reapp, h'cap, first win): 5th at best from 4 juv starts (7f mdns, rtd 78 at best): now suited by 11/12f, further
could suit: runs well fresh on gd/soft & a sharp/turning track: improving, should complete a hat-trick.
*1491 **POLAR RED 6** [6] M J Ryan 3-8-12 (80) (5ex) G Faulkner (3) 9/2: 3W-312: 3 ch g Polor Falcon -   ½   84
Sharp Top (Sharpo) Cl up, rdn to lead 6f out, hdd dist, not pace of wnr well ins last: qck reapp, eff btwn 1m & 12f.
*1281 **PENTAGONAL 19** [4] Sir Michael Stoute 3-8-12 (80) J Reid 2/1 FAV: 0-013: 3 b c Dynaformer - Pent   nk   84
(Mr Prospector) Mid div, rdn to chall inside last, held cl home: hvly bckd on h'cap bow: stays 10/12f: see 1281.
*1199 **RIVER BANN 24** [7] P F I Cole 3-9-7 (89) J Fortune 8/1: 2-2214: Led, hdd 6f out, with ldrs till   1½   90
no extra appr fnl 1f: op 7/1: loves to dominate: see 1199.
1425 **DESTINATION 10** [2] 3-8-11 (79) S Sanders 16/1: -52445: Rear, rdn/kept on fnl 2f, no threat: clr rem.   1¾   78
1179 **BUSY LIZZIE 25** [8] Pat Eddery 14/1: 00-206: Rear, eff halfway, no threat: twice   8   67
below a promising reapp in 964 (fillies mdn, soft).
1310 **DUCHAMP 16** [5] 3-9-1 (83) K Darley 7/2: 21-547: Handy, lost tch fnl 3f: up in trip: btr 1310 (10f).   1½   67
*1238 **HAMBLEDEN 21** [3] 3-8-7 (75) P Robinson 8/1: 0-0318: Prom, wknd qckly fnl 3f: op 7/1: turf return,   1½   56
much better on the A/W in 1238 (fibresand, very easily).
1199 **BOX CAR 24** [1] 3-7-13 (67) F Norton 11/1: -53229: Raced very keenly in mid div, lost tch fnl 3f.   8   36
9 ran   Time 2m 44.18 (12.38)   (Mrs G C Maxwell)   Major D N Chappell Pulborough W Sussex

1638   **4.10 AAXICO MDN 3YO (D)**   **7f rnd**   Good/Soft 90 -17 Slow
£3900   £1200   £600   £300

-- **MODERN BRITISH** [6] G L Moore 3-9-0 R Hughes 14/1: 1: 3 ch g Indian Ridge - Touraya (Tap On   94 +
Wood) Settled rear, hmpd 3f out, rdn/styd on appr fnl 1f, led led ins last, shade cosily: debut: 80,000gns half
brother to a smart 5f/1m wnr: eff at 7f, 1m shld suit: runs well fresh on gd/soft grnd & a sharp/undul trk:
excellent debut against some experienced rivals here, should improve & win again.
1099 **BLUE MOUNTAIN 30** [4] R F Johnson Houghton 3-9-0 J Reid 100/30: 35-522: 3 ch c Elmaamul -   ¾   91
Glenfinlass (Lomond) Cl up, led appr fnl 2f, hdd well ins last, no extra: nicely bckd: deserves a win: see 1099.
4555 **SHALIMAR 215** [3] J H M Gosden 3-8-9 J Fortune 5/2 FAV: 26-3: 3 b f Indian Ridge - Athens Belle   1¼   83
(Groom Dancer) Keen mid div, rdn to chall over 1f out, lkd held in cl 3rd when squeezed for room well ins last:
hvly bckd on reapp: cl 2nd to subs 1,000 Guineas wnr Lahan on '99 debut (fill mdn, rtd 95, P Chapple Hyam), subs
trained by A G Foster: eff at 7f, 1m shld suit: acts on fast & gd/soft, handles soft grnd: capable of better.
1376 **GLORY QUEST 13** [1] Miss Gay Kelleway 3-9-0 Dane O'Neill 5/1: 3-2234: Chsd ldrs, dsptd lead   hd   88
2f out, no extra fnl 1f: frustrating mdn: flattered 1376.
-- **TAFFETA** [2] 3-8-11 Pat Eddery 9/2: 5: Dwelt, mid div, rdn to chall 3f out, wknd over 1f out: well clr   3½   77
rem: op 7/2 on debut: 90,000gns Barateea filly, 1m+ should suit in time: with J L Dunlop.
1263 **LADY JEANNIE 20** [5] S Carson 33/1: 06: Keen, prom, lost tch fnl 3f: see 1263.   16   52
1438 **BOLD SABOTEUR 10** [7] 3-9-0 N Pollard 25/1: 000-07: Led, hdd 2f out, wknd: needs a drop in grade.   12   41
7 ran   Time 1m 32.0 (7.5)   (Richard Green (Fine Paintings))   G L Moore Woodingdean E Sussex

1639   **4.45 B & H WORLDWIDE MED AUCT MDN 2YO (E)**   **5f str**   Good/Soft 90 -60 Slow
£3883   £1195   £597   £298

1454 **PICCLED 9** [5] M R Channon 2-9-0 S Drowne 9/4 FAV: 61: 2 b c Piccolo - Creme de Menthe   78
(Green Desert) Made all, strongly prsd appr fnl 1f, drvn out to hold on: nicely bckd: half-brother to decent
juv mdn Bee Eight: eff at 5f, 6f cld suit: acts on gd/soft, faster grnd will reportedly suit: improve & win again.
-- **STRUMPET** [2] R F Johnson Houghton 2-8-9 J Reid 7/2: 2: 2 bf Tragic Role - Fee (Mandamus)   ¾   70
Prom, rdn/chall over 1f out, ran on, just held: April foal, half-sister to 2 juv 1m wnrs: dam a 6/10f wnr: eff
at 5f on gd/soft, 6f sure to suit: acts on a sharp/undul trk: fine debut, shld go one better soon.
-- **MISS INFORM** [4] D R C Elsworth 2-8-9 N Pollard 8/1: 3: 2 b f So Factual - As Sharp As   ½   69
(Handsome Sailor) Dwelt, rear, gd hdwy over 2f out, every ch till held well ins last: 3,000gns April foal, half-
sister to a juv 6f wnr, dam scored over 7f: eff at 5f on gd/soft, 6f will suit.
-- **MAJESTIC QUEST** [1] J Neville 2-9-0 K Darley 12/1: 4: Prom, outpcd over 2f out, styd on again   1¾   69
ins last: 15,000gns Piccolo foal, dam a juv 6f wnr: should improve, prob over 6f.
-- **SAAFEND ROCKET** [3] 2-9-0 R Hughes 5/1: 5: Front rank, outpcd 2f out, not given a hard time: nk   68
op 7/2: 28,000gns half-brother to useful 6/7f juv wnr Ginolas Magic: with R Hannon, spot on at 6f next time.
1260 **WARLINGHAM 20** [6] 2-9-0 Pat Eddery 11/4: 46: Fly jumped & veered right start, pulled very hard   ½   67
in rear, never a threat: nicely bckd & needs to learn to settle: see 1260 (debut).
6 ran   Time 1m 04.19 (7.49)   (Captain J Macdonald-Buchanan)   M R Channon West Isley, Berks

1640   **5.15 ILS MDN 3YO (D)**   **1m2f**   Good/Soft 90 -20 Slow
£4231   £1302   £651   £325

1295 **BALDAQUIN 17** [5] J H M Gosden 3-9-0 R Hughes 7/4 JT FAV: -041: 3 b c Barathea - Nibbs Point (Sure   85
Blade) Cl up till went on over 2f out, pshd well clr appr fnl 1f, hvly eased ins last: val 5/6L: nicely bckd:
eff at 10f, further could suit: acts on gd/soft & a sharp/undul trk: impressive here & should win more races.
1287 **SPEED VENTURE 19** [2] S P C Woods 3-9-0 J Reid 5/2: 422: 3 b g Owington - Jade Venture   1¾   76
(Never So Bold) Led to 2f out, sn well outpcd, closed on eased rival ins last, no dngr: nicely bckd, clr rem:
had no answer winner's turn of foot here: stays 10f on gd/soft: see 1287. 826.
1344 **THREE WHITE SOX 14** [3] P W Harris 3-8-9 J Fortune 14/1: 0-03: 3 ch f Most Welcome - Empty Purse   4   64
(Pennine Walk) Prom, rdn/btn fnl 2f: poss stays 10f on gd/soft, lower grade h'caps should suit.
1099 **LILLAN 30** [4] G A Butler 3-8-9 K Darley 7/4 JT FAV: 64: Mid div, rdn/lost tch fnl 3f: up in trip: 6   54
better expected after an encouraging debut in 1099 (1m).
1287 **NO PASS NO HONOR 14** [1] 3-9-0 Pat Eddery 20/1: 00-65: Waited with, never a factor: see 1287.   shd   59$
-- **MISS MANETTE** [6] 3-8-9 J Lowe 33/1: 6: Al well bhnd, t.o.: debut: half sister to a 6f juv scorer.   16   34
6 ran   Time 2m 15.06 (10.86)   (Sheikh Mohammed)   J H M Gosden Manton Wilts

Official Going   Race 1-2 - GOOD/SOFT; Race 3-6 - SOFT. Stalls: 5f - Stands side; Rem - Inside.
Pace figures inapplicable due to rain throughout afternoon

1641   2.00 NSPCC FILLIES NOV AUCT STKS 2YO (F)   5f str   Good/Soft   Inapplicable
£2457   £702   £351

1267 **RED MILLENNIUM 21** [3] A Berry 2-8-6 K Darley 5/2: 121: 2 b f Tagula - Lovely Me (Vision) **92**
Made all, rdn & drew well clr ins last, cmftbly: earlier scored on debut at Musselburgh (auct mdn): 2,000gns
Feb foal, dam modest: eff at 5f, 6f will suit: handles firm, clearly well suited by an easy surface: runs well
fresh on a sharp or gall trk: much imprvd here, shld win more races.

-- **BALI ROYAL** [7] J M Bradley 2-8-2 P Fitzsimons (4) 40/1: 2: 2 b f King's Signet - Baligay (Balidar) **6 73**
Slow to stride, sn in tch, kept on fnl 1f but not pace of wnr: debut: inexpensive Feb foal, half sister to a juv
1m wnr, dam scored at 5/7f: stays 5f on gd/soft, 6f sure to suit: pleasing debut, win sn.

-- **PEYTO PRINCESS** [10] C W Fairhurst 2-8-4 P Doe 6/1: 3: 2 b f Bold Arrangement - Bo' Babbity **¾ 74**
(Strong Gale) Outpcd early, gd hdwy 2f out, edged left & kept on over 1f out: op 12/1: half-sister to sev wnrs,
incl a useful 5/6f juv wnr: sire smart at 8/10f: lks in need of 6f: acts on gd/sft: encouraging debut.

1372 **MILLENNIUM MAGIC 14** [1] J G Portman 2-8-10 A Beech (5) 2/1 FAV: 134: Prom, drvn & wknd appr **1 78**
fnl 1f: nicely bckd tho' op 6/4: below par here on grnd softer than prev experienced: btr 1372, 762.

-- **FACE D FACTS** [9] 2-8-9 R Mullen 20/1: 5: Dwelt, outpcd, late hdwy, no threat: op 12/1: 9,000gns **nk 77**
So Factual filly, half-sister to prolific sprinter Soaked: dam a 7f wnr: shld improve for C F Wall.

-- **VICTEDDU** [6] 2-8-2 G Bardwell 40/1: 6: Sn rdn in tch, fdd over 1f out: cheaply bought foal, **shd 70**
half-sister to a 10f wnr: 6f+ will suit: with M G Quinlan.

-- **EAU ROUGE** [4] 2-8-9 P Robinson 10/1: 7: Cl-up, wknd qckly fnl 2f: op 12/1: 7,500gns Grand **1 74**
Lodge filly, half-sister to juv wnrs abroad, dam a 6f wnr: shld improve for M A Jarvis.

-- **THATS JAZZ** [5] 2-8-2 J Mackay (7) 6/1: 8: Dwelt, outpcd, eff halfway, lost tch over 1f out: **1¼ 64**
cheaply bought & speedily bred filly: dam a juv 6f wnr.

1408 **SOMERS HEATH 13** [2] 2-8-6 T E Durcan 20/1: 09: Prom to halfway: see 1408. **3½ 60**
1067 **TICCATOO 32** [8] 2-8-8 P M Quinn (5) 16/1: -100: Handy, lost tch over 2f out, 10th: btr 865 (AW). **1 59**
10 ran   Time 1m 02.6 (4.1)   (The Red Shirt Brigade Ltd)   A Berry Cockerham, Lancs

1642   2.30 EBF CINDERHILL MDN 2YO (D)   5f str   Good/Soft   Inapplicable
£3396   £1045   £522   £261

1424 **QUIESCENT 11** [2] R Hannon 2-8-9 L Newman (5) 7/1: 01: 2 ch f Primo Dominie - Tranquility **90**
(Night Shift) Slow to start & veered left, sn prom, led halfway, pshd clr over 1f out: op 4/1: recently well btn
on debut: half-sister to 5f juv wnr The Bull McCabe, dam 1m wnr: eff at 5f on gd/sft, 6f suit: can follow up.

-- **AMIS ANGEL** [5] D Carroll 2-8-9 T E Durcan 16/1: 2: 2 b f Fayruz - Khunasira (Nishapour) **4 79**
Outpcd, styd on well ins last, no ch with wnr: clr rem: 3,500gns half-sister to two wnrs in Germany, dam a
mdn in France: stays 5f, 6f shld suit on this showing: took time to get the hang of things here, will improve.

1252 **ONLY ONE LEGEND 21** [1] T D Easterby 2-9-0 K Darley 6/4: -033: 2 b c Eagle Eyed - Afifah **3½ 76**
(Nashwan) Led, hdd bef halfway, fdd fnl 2f: nicely bckd: shade better on firm in 1252.

1083 **EASTERN PROMISE 31** [3] A Berry 2-8-9 J Weaver 11/8 FAV: 24: Cl-up, rdn/wknd appr fnl 1f, eased **2 66**
when btn: much better expected after a pleasing C/D debut in 1083.

-- **SO SOBER** [4] 2-9-0 R Mullen 9/1: 5: Dwelt, sn in ldrs, hung left & outpcd fnl 2f: op 6/1: **5 61**
Common Grounds Jan 1st foal, dam a decent 6f juv scorer: with C F Wall.
5 ran   Time 1m 03.5 (5.0)   (The Hon Sir David Sieff)   R Hannon East Everleigh, Wilts

1643   3.00 ROSELAND MDN 3YO (D)   1m54y rnd   Soft   Inapplicable
£3981   £1225   £612   £306

-- **PRINCE CASPIAN** [1] C E Brittain 3-9-0 P Robinson 6/1: 1: 3 ch g Mystiko - Real Princess (Aragon) **79**
Broke well & made all, drvn out to hold on cl-home: dam a 7f scorer: eff over a gall 1m, further shld suit:
runs well fresh on soft & loves to force the pace: enterprisingly ridden by P Robinson.

4528} **FOREST HEATH 219** [2] H J Collingridge 3-9-0 M Roberts 11/2: 00-2: 3 gr g Common Grounds - **hd 78**
Caroline Lady (Caro) Waited with, outpcd 4f out, switched & ran on well despite hanging left ins last, just
failed: unplcd both '99 starts (mdns, rtd 82, J E Banks): eff at 1m on soft: look out for next time at 10f+.

3755} **RIPARIAN 272** [5] Sir Michael Stoute 3-9-0 J Reid 1/1 FAV: -5-3: 3 b g Last Tycoon - La Riveraine **1½ 75**
(Riverman) Mid-div, rdn to imprv 2f out, not pace of wnr fnl 1f: nicely bckd on reapp: promising 5th on sole
'99 juv start (7f mdn, rtd 79): dam a dual 12f wnr: stays 7f/1m, further shld suit: handles firm & soft grnd.

794 **ANYHOW 64** [8] A Berry 3-8-9 M Henry 12/1: 3-04: Settled rear, gd hdwy halfway, drvn & wknd **4 63**
over 1f out: 9 wk abs: up in trip & poss stays 1m: see 794.

1261 **SLIEVE BLOOM 21** [6] 3-9-0 A Clark 12/1: 605: Trkd wnr, fdd fnl 2f: up in trip: see 962 (7f). **2 64$**
1532 **RESILIENT 6** [3] 3-9-0 K Darley 10/1: 06: Prom, dropped rear fnl 2f: qck reapp: see 1532. **hd 64**
-- **HAZIRAAN** [7] 3-9-0 D Harrison 6/1: 7: Fronk rank, wknd qckly 2f out: debut: Primo Dominie **5 56**
colt, dam scored between 7f & 12f: longer priced stablemate of 3rd & likely to do better in time.
-- **DONNINI** [4] 3-9-0 R Mullen 6/1: 8: Dwelt, al rear: op 4/1 on debut: Kris gelding, with P Harris. **8 44**
8 ran   Time 1m 51.8 (12.4)   (Lady Sieff)   C E Brittain Newmarket

1644   3.30 WAREHOUSE SELL HCAP 3YO 0-60 (G)   1m2f   Soft   Inapplicable   [65]
£1993   £569   £284

1365 **PERFECT MOMENT 14** [11] G M McCourt 3-9-2 (53) D Harrison 6/1: 0-0421: 3 b f Mujadil - Flashing **58**
Raven (Maelstrom) Trkd ldr, went on 2f out, styd on well, rdn out: bought in for 3,400gns: '99 Leicester wnr
(auct mdn, A Jarvis, rtd 74): now suited by 1m/10f: acts on fast & soft grnd: enjoyed recent drop to sells.

1465 **UNIMPEACHABLE 9** [15] J M Bradley 3-9-0 (51) P Fitzsimons (5) 13/2: -00052: 3 b f Namaqualand - **2 52**
Bourbon Topsy (Ile De Bourbon) Waited with, rdn/hdwy 2f out, sn chsg wnr, hung left & held fnl 1f: well clr rem:
styd this longer 10f trip: imprvd eff here: see 1002.

1274 **FRENCH MASTER 20** [13] P C Haslam 3-9-7 (58) P Goode (3) 12/1: 333103: 3 b g Petardia - Reasonably **9 46**
French (Resonable) Dwelt, rear, styd on late, no threat to front 2: op 7/1: btr 806 (non h'cap, gd grnd).

978 **HIGH BEAUTY 44** [10] M J Ryan 3-8-5 (42) A Clark 20/1: 0-0404: Bhd, prog over 2f out, no extra **½ 29**
appr fnl 1f: 6 wk abs: see 783.

NOTTINGHAM FRIDAY JUNE 2ND Lefthand, Galloping Track

4114} **LADY VIENNA 249** [12] 3-8-13 (50) A Daly 8/1: 0005-5: Mid-div, drvn 3f out, fdd over 1f out: *5* **30**
reapp: flattered when 5th on fnl '99 start (10f mdn, gd/soft, rtd 62$).
1274 **ROCK ON ROBIN 20** [1] 3-9-0 (51)(vis) M Roberts 11/2 FAV: 00-026: Prom to 4f out: btr 1274 (firm). *3* **27**
1292 **CYPRESS CREEK 18** [5] 3-9-0 (51) J Reid 10/1: 00-007: In tch, fdd over 2f out: see 1199. *shd* **27**
1572 **SKELTON MONARCH 3** [16] 3-8-9 (46) P M Quinn (5) 9/1: 0-6638: Dwelt, nvr a threat: qck reapp. *3* **18**
4353} **SUPER KIM 232** [8] 3-9-1 (52) A Polli (3) 25/1: 000-9: Cl-up, wknd fnl 2f: up in trip, h'cap bow: *hd* **24**
unplcd in 3 '99 starts (5/7f mdns, rtd 53 at best).
429 **TE ANAU 123** [9] 3-8-4 (41) L Newton 16/1: 00-000: Al bhd, fin 10th: 4 month abs. *nk* **12**
1274 **STANDIFORD GIRL 20** [4] 3-8-8 (45) S Sanders 14/1: 6200: Prom, wknd qckly 2f out: btr 1141 (A/W). *½* **15**
1365 **WONDERLAND 14** [2] 3-8-9 (46) K Darley 15/2: 6-0050: Led to over 2f out, wknd rapidly, eased: 15th. **0**
1142 **Take Action 29** [3] 3-8-8 (45) T Williams 14/1: 807 **Secretario 63** [6] 3-8-12 (49) J Weaver 12/1:
1349 **Musical Fruits 15** [14] 3-7-10 (33)(3oh) D Kinsella (7) 40/1:
1392 **Red Sonny 13** [7] 3-9-2 (53) P Bradley (5) 33/1:
16 ran Time 2m 14.5 (12.2) (Christopher Shankland) G M McCourt Letcombe Regis, Oxon

1645 4.00 HORSESMOUTH HCAP 3YO 0-85 (D) 1m54y rnd Soft Inapplicable [92]
£4290 £1320 £660 £330

1607 **IT CAN BE DONE 2** [6] R Hollinshead 3-7-10 (60)(3oh) P M Quinn (5) 9/4: -00321: 3 ch g Case Law - *nk* **65**
Breeze Away (Prince Sabo) Waited with, gd hdwy over 2f out, chall when hmpd ins last, just held: fin 2nd, awarded race: ran 48hrs ago: unplcd in '99 (rtd 61): imprvd form upped to 7/8.3f: acts on gd & soft.
1341 **CLEVER GIRL 15** [3] T D Easterby 3-9-5 (83) K Darley 6/1: 5-401D: 3 b f College Chapel - Damezao **89**
(Alzao) Led, drvn & hung right for press ins last, drvn out to hold on: disqual from 1st, plcd 2nd: clr rem, nicely bckd: back to form & disqualification looked a shade harsh here: can win similar: see 823.
*1263 **AUTUMN RAIN 21** [5] E A L Dunlop 3-9-4 (82) J Reid 2/1 FAV: 5-2013: 3 br c Dynaformer - Edda *5* **79**
(Ogygian) Raced keenly cl-up, fdd appr fnl 1f: imprvd in defeat: see 1263 (mdn).
1452 **NOBLE PURSUIT 10** [1] T G Mills 3-9-7 (85) A Clark 9/1: 12-404: Settled rear, eff 3f out, sn btn. *½* **81**
1348 **INFOTEC 15** [7] 3-8-13 (77) J Stack 8/1: 2-0105: Front rank, lost tch over 1f out: btr 1061 (6.7f). *3½* **68**
1215 **MENTIGA 24** [2] 3-9-1 (79) P Robinson 8/1: 3-0506: Prom to 3f out, sn bhd: op 6/1: see 810. *2½* **66**
1150 **GOT ONE TOO 28** [4] 3-7-10 (60)(t)(5oh) G Bardwell 33/1: 000-07: Dwelt, nvr with ldrs. *17* **27**
954 **GRAND BAHAMIAN 45** [8] 3-9-4 (82) J Weaver 10/1: 010P: Handy, wknd 2f out, sn p.u./dismounted. **0**
8 ran Time 1m 50.7 (11.3) (Michael R Oliver) R Hollinshead Upper Longdon, Staffs

1646 4.30 12TH JUNE APPR HCAP 3YO+ 0-70 (G) 1m54y rnd Soft Inapplicable [59]
£1858 £531 £265 3 yo rec 11lb

1201 **ADMIRALS FLAME 25** [7] C F Wall 9-9-10 (55) Lorna Ford (5) 100/30: 400-01: 9 b g Doulab - Fan **60**
The Flame (Grundy) Waited with, shaken up & prog 2f out, led ins last, rdn out: op 5/2: '99 Leicester wnr (h'cap, rtd 61), prev term scored at Windsor (h'cap, rtd 62): eff at 7f, suited by 1m & acts on firm & hvy grnd: can go well when fresh & handles any trk, loves Windsor: tough & fairly h'capped 9yo.
1065 **DINAR 32** [6] R Brotherton 5-8-9 (40) D Kinsella 11/2: 00-302: 5 b h Dixieland Band - Bold Jessie *¾* **43**
(Never So Bold) Keen/led, grabbed stands rail 4f out & sn clr, hdd ins last, no extra: 7L clr rem: eff at 1m/12f: gd run under an enterprising ride, will apprec a return to further & can land a similar event.
1395 **WITH A WILL 13** [5] H Candy 6-9-10 (55) R Naylor 2/1 FAV: 040-33: 6 b g Rambo Dancer - Henceforth *7* **47**
(Full Of Hope) Prom, not pace of ldrs fnl 3f: top weight: better on reapp in 1395 (9f, gd grnd).
1300 **PICCOLO CATIVO 18** [3] Mrs G S Rees 5-9-4 (49) M Worrell 11/2: 00-104: Chsd ldrs, saddle slipped *hd* **41**
6f out, kept on but no ch with ldrs after: unfortunate, ignore: see 1066.
1520 **BRANDONVILLE 6** [4] 7-8-11 (42)(t) S Clancy 10/1: -00005: Dwelt, eff 3f out, sn btn: qck reapp. *4* **27**
1085 **HEATHYARDS LAD 31** [2] 3-9-7 (63) A Hawkins 11/2: 063256: Front rank, lost tch fnl 2f: btr 976. *½* **47**
1611 **ERTLON 2** [1] 10-9-5 (50) S Hitchcott (5) 25/1: 6-0007: Prom to halfway: ran 48hrs ago. *2½* **30**
7 ran Time 1m 51.7 (12.3) (Mrs C A Wall) C F Wall Newmarket

BRIGHTON FRIDAY JUNE 2ND Lefthand, Very Sharp, Undulating Track

Official Going GOOD/FIRM. Stalls: Inside, except 1m2f & 1m4f - Outside.

1647 6.15 LADY RIDERS CLAIMER 4YO+ (F) 1m3f196y Good 48 -10 Slow
£2289 £654 £327

-- **NO LANGUAGE PLEASE** [11] R Curtis 6-10-9 Miss M Gunstone (7) 33/1: 1: 6 ch g Arapahos - Strong **51**
Language (Formidable) Sn bhd, plenty to do over 3f out, styd on strongly over 1f out to get up cl-home, going away: fit from a couple of hdle runs, rtd 74c & 91h in 99/00: former pt-to-pt wnr: stays 12f on gd grnd.
1462 **RAWI 9** [1] Mrs A J Perrett 7-10-1 Miss L J Harwood (7) 20/1: -06002: 7 ch g Forzando - Finally (Final *¾* **41$**
Straw) Chsd ldr after 5f, led over 1f out, kept on for press till collared cl-home: stays 12f: see 110.
4223} **ZIGGY STARDUST 242** [9] Mrs A J Bowlby 5-9-13 Mrs S Bosley 6/1: 3244-3: 5 b g Roi Danzig - Si *2* **36**
Princess (Coquelin) In tch chsg group, kept on late, nrst fin on reapp: plcd sev times in '99 (rtd 56$ at best): eff over 10/12f on firm & gd/soft: mdn after 20 starts.
1415 **NIGHT CITY 11** [5] K R Burke 9-10-13 Miss K Warnett (7) 2/1: 140644: Sn clr ldr, rdn & hdd over *1¾* **47**
1f out, no extra: bckd tho' op 6/4, clr of rem: 9yo, see 1389, btr 650.
1241 **MISCHIEF 22** [6] 4-10-13 Miss J Ellis (7) 20/1: 030005: In tch, btn over 3f out: see 815. *12* **35**
1415 **KI CHI SAGA 11** [8] 8-9-13 (tbl) Miss C Hannaford (5) 33/1: 044006: Waited with, btn 3f out, eased. *¾* **20**
1331 **AMAZING FACT 16** [2] 5-9-11 (bl) Miss Hayley Bryan (7 25/1: -36007: Al bhd: modest mdn. *3½* **14**
408 **ROMAN REEL 127** [3] 9-9-11 Mrs J Moore 12/1: 40-008: In tch, btn 3f out: 4 mth abs, see 408, 332. *1¼* **12**
576 **CHILDRENS CHOICE 99** [4] 9-9-12 (vis) Mrs L Pearce 15/8 FAV: -31349: In tch, brief effort over *1¼* **11**
3f out, sn wknd: nicely bckd after 3 mth abs: better than this, see 363 (sell).
52 **FOURDANED 199** [12] 7-9-13 Mrs K Hills (7) 25/1: 0005-0: Rcd wide & al bhd: 10th: modest '99 *2* **9**
form (rtd 35): rtd 44 & 60a back in '98: stays 12f on firm, soft & equitrack: tried blnks/eye-shield.
1210 **Lady Wyn 24** [10] 5-9-6 Mrs S Moore (5) 66/1: 963 **Grey Buttons 45** [7] 5-10-2 Mrs J Powell (5) 50/1:
12 ran Time 2m 35.2 (7) (Mrs G Fletcher) R Curtis Lambourn, Berks.

BRIGHTON   FRIDAY JUNE 2ND   Lefthand, Very Sharp, Undulating Track

---

1648   6.45 EBF MED AUCT MDN 2YO (E)   6f   Good 48 -15 Slow
£2886   £888   £444   £222

1507 **KNOCK 7** [6] R Hannon 2-9-0 R Hughes 5/2 FAV: 41: 2 b c Mujadil - Beechwood (Blushing Groom):   80
With ldr, went on over 2f out, styd on well inside last, drvn out: Apr foal: full brother to a couple of 5f
wnrs: improved for debut & stays 6f on gd grnd.
1507 **THOMAS SMYTHE 7** [5] N P Littmoden 2-9-0 D Sweeney 11/4: 022: 2 ch c College Chapel - Red   2½ 73
Barons Lady (Electric) Set pace till over 2f out, not pace of wnr: not disgraced, but in front of this wnr in 1507.
1413 **TRUSTED MOLE 13** [3] J A Osborne 2-9-0 (BL) S Carson 5/2: -663: 2 b c Eagle Eyed - Orient Air   3 65
(Prince Sabo): Cl-up, rdn & no extra appr final 1f: tried blnks: see 1189.
1463 **KALUKI 9** [4] W R Muir 2-9-0 I Mongan (5) 7/2: -6334: In tch, rdn 2f out, no impress: btr 1463 (5f).   ½ 63
-- **DAWN ROMANCE** [8] 2-8-9 P Fessey 4/1: 5: Slow away, nvr a factor on debut: Apr 1st foal, cost   4 47
4,500 IR gns: dam juv 6/1m scorer: with M Channon.
-- **ONKAPARINGA** [1] 2-8-9 P Doe 14/1: Al bhd, sadly collapsed & died after line.   20 0
6 ran   Time 1m 11.6 (3.8)   (Mrs Suzanne Costello-Haloute)   R Hannon East Everleigh, Wilts.

1649   7.15 RENDEZVOUS FILLIES HCAP 3YO 0-75 (E)   1m2f   Good 48 -08 Slow   [81]
£2808   £864   £432   £216

1405 **OMNIHEAT 13** [5] M J Ryan 3-9-7 (74)(BL) G Faulkner (3) 2/1 FAV: 1-3231: 3 b f Ezzoud - Lady Bequick   77
(Sharpen Up) Waited with, gd hdwy to lead over 1f out, rdn clr, eased cl-home: value for 4L+: won last of 7 juv
starts, at Doncaster (nursery h'cap, rtd 71): eff at 7f, relished this step up to 10f & first time blnks: handles
firm, likes gd & hvy & any trk: unexposed at this trip, should go in again.
1390 **ABLE NATIVE 13** [3] R W Armstrong 3-9-1 (68) R Price 8/1: 025-02: 3 b f Thatching - Native Joy (Be   2½ 65
My Native) Handy, eff over 2f out, keeping on when short of room appr final 1f, kept on again cl-home: stays 10f.
1292 **THE FROG QUEEN 18** [2] D W P Arbuthnot 3-7-12 (51) J Mackay (7) 5/1: 1-0403: 3 b f Bin Ajwaad -   shd 48
The Frog Lady (Al Hareb) Cl-up, rdn & onepace final 2f: not disgraced: see 1096, 937.
1521 **EVERGREEN 6** [11] R Hannon 3-9-7 (74) R Hughes 7/1: 0-3504: Hld up, late gains, nvr dngr: stays 10f.   ¾ 70
1165 **LARAZA 27** [4] 3-8-13 (66)(BL) L Newman (5) 20/1: 03-55: Keen, handy, led over 2f out, sn hdd   hd 61
& wknd: tried blnks, see 1165.
1345 **DILETIA 15** [9] 3-8-9 (62)(BL) S Carson (5) 10/1: 0-0456: Led 4f out till over 2f out, wknd: blnks.   1¾ 54
1425 **LAFLEUR 11** [1] 3-9-1 (68) P Fessey 16/1: 0-0007: Prom, btn over 2f out: see 1179.   4 54
853 **SILVER QUEEN 53** [8] 3-9-5 (72) N Esler (5) 10/1: 440-08: Prom, btn over 2f out: 7 wk abs: 7 48
rtd 79 in '99 (unplcd): should stay 10f: acts on firm grnd.
1265 **DOROTHEA SHARP 21** [7] 3-7-10 (49)(4oh) G Baker (7) 25/1: 0-0509: Al bhd: see 1035.   1¼ 23
1388 **CULTURED PEARL 13** [6] 3-9-6 (73) D Sweeney 8/1: 5-360: In tch, btn over 2f out: 10th, see 1388, 1268.nk 46
4614} **SPARK OF LIFE 209** [10] 3-8-6 (59)(bl) S Whitworth 33/1: 060-0: Keen, led till 4f out, wknd: rtd 64   4 26
in first time blnks when unplcd as a juv (1m): bred to stay mid-dists.
11 ran   Time 2m 03.4 (5.6)   (Mrs E Delaney)   M J Ryan Newmarket.

1650   7.45 CITY INDEX DASH HCAP 3YO+ 0-80 (D)   5f59y rnd   Good 48 +17 Fast   [78]
£6818   £2098   £1049   £524   3 yo rec 7 lb

1264 **IVORYS JOY 21** [5] K T Ivory 5-9-13 (77) C Carver (3) 13/2: -56031: 5 b m Tina's Pet - Jacqui Joy   86
(Music Boy) Cl-up, led over 1f out, sn rdn clr, cmftbly: fast time: in '99 won at Thirsk, Haydock (h'caps, rtd
82) & W'hampton (h'cap, rtd 87a): plcd in '98: '97 wnr at Goodwood (2, sells) & Newbury (nursery): v eff at 5f,
stays 6f on firm & fibresand, runs gd & hvy, best without blnks/a visor: tough, in fine heart, qck follow-up?
1487 **FORGOTTEN TIMES 8** [3] K T Ivory 6-9-2 (66)(vis) C Catlin (7) 11/2: -20622: 6 ch m Nabeel Dancer -   3 66
Etoile d'Amore (The Minstrel) Chsd ldrs, eff over 1f out, chsd wnr ins last, no impress: stablemate of wnr: tough.
1441 **DANCING MYSTERY 11** [4] E A Wheeler 6-9-9 (73) S Carson (5) 11/2: 0-0033: 6 b g Beveled - Batchworth1   70
Dancer (Ballacashtal): Sn bhd, hdwy 2f out, onepace final 1f: gd run: see 1441, 64.
1398 **AURIGNY 13** [1] S Dow 5-9-12 (76) P Doe 10/1: -00064: Handy, styg on when hmpd dist, not recover: 2 68
probably would have been plcd & has slipped right down the weights: see 191.
*1368 **BEYOND CALCULATION 14** [7] 6-9-2 (66) R Hughes 9/2 FAV: 00-515: Led, rdn & hdd over 1f out, no   1¼ 55
extra: went off too fast today: best at 6f as in 1368.
*1427 **AROGANT PRINCE 11** [8] 3-8-2 (59)(6ex) J Mackay (7) 8/1: -04316: Handy, rdn & btn 2f out: btr 1427.   3½ 39
*1441 **ALPEN WOLF 11** [9] 5-10-4 (82)(6ex) R Brisland (5) 11/2: 05-317: Handy, rdn & no extra over 1f out.   hd 61
1196 **CHARGE 25** [2] 4-9-3 (67)(tBL) D Sweeney 9/1: 221508: Cl-up, ev ch 2f out, hmpd over 1f out, no   nk 45
extra: blnks, best 691 (equitrack).
3360} **GREY PRINCESS 293** [6] 4-10-0 (78) A Beech (5) 10/1: 0000-9: Slow away, al bhd: reapp, top weight: 7 42
plcd once in early '99 (rtd 89): juv scorer at Windsor, Salisbury & Brighton (2, nursery h'caps, rtd 94): wng form
at 5/6f on gd & firm, loves to force the pace at Brighton: has run well fresh: well h'capped when returning to form.
9 ran   Time 1m 01.6 (1.6)   (K T Ivory)   K T Ivory Radlett, Herts.

1651   8.15 MARINA CLASS STKS 3YO 0-70 (E)   6f rnd   Good 48 -04 Slow
£2728   £779   £389

1427 **LORD YASMIN 11** [4] J Noseda 3-9-0 L Newman (5) 5/2 FAV: 2-1031: 3 b c Lahib - Adieu Cherie   73
(Bustino) Prom, hdwy to lead dist, just held on for press ins last: bckd from 9/2: earlier won at Southwell (AW,
mdn, rtd 77a): rtd 67 in a sell as a juv: v eff at 6f on gd, gd/soft, fibresand & a sharp trk: has run well fresh.
*1512 **STONEY GARNETT 7** [1] M S Saunders 3-8-11 A Daly 9/2: U30-12: 3 b f Emarati - Etourdie (Arctic Tern) nk 69
Set pace, rdn & hdd over 1f out, kept on gamely for press ins last, just held: genuine & in gd heart.
1405 **KEBABS 13** [8] J A Osborne 3-8-8 D Sweeney 5/1: 550003: 3 b f Catrail - Common Rumpus (Common   nk 65
Grounds) With ldrs, ev ch over 1f out, kept on for press inside last, just held: see 736.
1406 **FRAMPANT 15** [5] M Quinn 3-8-8 S Carson (5) 10/1: 430004: In tch, rdn over 2f out, sn btn: see 689.   3½ 56
1427 **CORBLETS 11** [2] 3-8-8 P Doe 4/1: 0-3225: Dwelt, bhd, some late gains, no dngr: btr 1427, 883.   ¾ 54
1406 **FEAST OF ROMANCE 13** [3] 3-8-11 R Hughes 12/1: 165606: With ldr, wknd over 1f out: see 1220, 275.   ½ 56
1405 **DUSKY VIRGIN 3** [7] 3-8-8 I Mongan (5) 11/1: 651-07: In tch, wknd over 2f out: '99 scorer at   1½ 49
Brighton (sell, rtd 63, with M Quinn): stays 7f on firm grnd in sell grade.
1202 **PYJAMA GIRL 25** [6] 3-8-8 S Whitworth 7/1: 506-38: Slow away, al bhd: btr 1202 (fibresand).   7 35
8 ran   Time 1m 10.9 (3.1)   (L P Calvente)   J Noseda Newmarket.

541

BRIGHTON FRIDAY JUNE 2ND Lefthand, Very Sharp, Undulating Track

1652

8.45 SOUTHERN FM HCAP 3YO+ 0-80 (D) 7f rnd Good 48 -06 Slow [76]
£3835 £1180 £590 £295 3 yo rec 10lb

1483 **ELMHURST BOY 8** [3] S Dow 4-9-13 (75) P Doe 7/2: 456601: 4 b c Merdon Melody - Young Whip 79
(Bold Owl) Hld up, hdwy to lead ins last, carried head high but styd on, rdn out: caught the eye earlier: '99
scorer at Epsom (mdn, rtd 80) & Lingfield (h'cap, rtd 84a): eff at 6f, suited by 7f & stays 1m: likes a
sharp/undul trk & handles firm, likes gd, hvy & equitrack: eff with/without blnks or a visor: on a gd mark.
1297 **MILADY LILLIE 18** [7] K T Ivory 4-8-5 (53) C Carver (3) 5/1: -60002: 4 b f Distinctly North - Millingdale 1½ 53
Lillie (Tumble Wind) Handy, led 2f out till ins last, not pace of wnr: should pinch a race here at Brighton.
1542 **KNOBBLEENEEZE 6** [2] M R Channon 10-7-11 (45) P Fessey 11/1: 0-0003: 10 ch g Aragon - Proud nk 44
Miss (Semi-Pro) Handy, lost place over 2f out, kept on again cl-home: op 7/1, qck reapp: loves soft.
1531 **WAFFLES OF AMIN 6** [4] R Hannon 3-9-4 (76) L Newman (5) 9/1: 16-004: Led till 3f out, onepace. ½ 74
1483 **AMBER FORT 8** [5] R Hughes 3/1 FAV: 325405: Keen in tch, staying on when short of nk 69
room over 1f out, not recover: on a fair mark: best of 7f: see 1483.
1473 **REACHFORYOURPOCKET 9** [1] 5-7-10 (44)(1oh) G Baker (7) 6/1: 120366: Prom, wknd over 1f out. 1½ 38
1464 **ABSOLUTE FANTASY 9** [6] 4-8-0 (48)(bl) S Carson (2) 9/2: 020147: Keen cl-up, wknd over 1f out. ½ 41
7 ran Time 1m 23.6 (3.8) (R E Anderson) S Dow Epsom, Surrey.

AYR FRIDAY JUNE 2ND Lefthand, Galloping Track

Official Going GOOD/FIRM. Stalls: Round Course - Inside, Str Course - Stands Side

1653

2.20 G MIDDLETON ISA MED AUCT MDN 2YO (E) 6f Good/Firm 29 -17 Slow
£2925 £900 £450 £225

-- **CELTIC SILENCE** [3] M Johnston 2-9-0 J Fanning 7/2: 1: 2 b c Celtic Swing - Smart N Noble (Smarten) 97+
Sn prom, led 2f out & rdly asserted ins last, cmftbly: val for 5L+, op 2/1: Feb foal, cost 60,000gns, a 1st
foal: dam multiple wnr in USA: sire high-class mid-dist performer: eff at 6f, 7f+ will suit: acts on fast
grnd & a gall trk: runs well fresh: heads for Chesham stakes at R Ascot & a potentially smart colt.
-- **SNOWSTORM** [6] M L W Bell 2-9-0 M Fenton 3/1 JT FAV: 2: 2 gr c Environment Friend - Choral 3½ 84+
Sundown (Night Shift) Slowly away, rdn & kept on fnl 2f, no threat to wnr: bckd tho' op 2/1: Feb foal, cost
30,000gns: half brother to a 6f juv wnr: dam 1m/10f wnr: eff at 6f, 7f+ sure to suit: acts on fast grnd & a
gall trk: met a potentially smart rival here, sure to leave this bhd & find similar with a level break.
-- **QUEENS MUSICIAN** [7] M Dods 2-9-0 A Culhane 12/1: 3: 2 b c Piccolo - Queens Welcome (Northfields) nk 83
Prom halfway, rdn/hung left over 2f out, kept on ins last, no ch with wnr: op 8/1: May foal, cost 23,000gns:
half brother to 2 juv wnrs at 6/7f: 7f shld suit: acts on fast grnd, encouraging intro.
1146 **ORIENTAL MIST 28** [4] L A Perratt 2-9-0 C Lowther 13/2: 54: Cl-up, rdn/no extra over 1f out. 1¾ 79
-- **IRISH DISTINCTION** [5] 2-9-0 J F Egan 3/1 JT FAV: 5: Rdn/chsd ldrs 2f out, sn held: bckd from 8/1: ½ 77
Distinctly North colt, Mar foal, cost IR 14,000gns: brother to a dual 7f juv wnr Father Juninho: better expected.
1146 **TICKER 28** [9] 2-9-0 J Carroll 7/1: 36: Bhd ldrs, outpcd from halfway: btr 1146 (5f). 2½ 70
-- **NAMLLAMS** [8] 2-9-0 R Winston 20/1: 7: U.r. & bolted bef start, led 4f, wknd qckly: op 12/1: Magic 5 61
Ring colt, Mar foal, 40,000gns 2yo: dam a mdn, a half sister to sev wnrs: sire speedy/precocious 2yo: lost ch
with unruly antics bef start & prob worth another chance.
1359 **EYES DONT LIE 14** [2] 2-9-0 Dale Gibson 50/1: 048: Dwelt, nvr on terms: btr 1359 (5f). 6 50
1628 **ARIES FIRECRACKER 1** [1] 2-9-0 G Parkin 33/1: 009: Sn bhd: ran yesterday: mod form. 18 20
9 ran Time 1m 12.05 (2.75) (P D Savill) M Johnston Middleham, N Yorks

1654

2.50 ST VINCENT HCAP 3YO+ 0-85 (D) 6f Good/Firm 29 -01 Slow [81]
£4017 £1236 £618 £309 3 yo rec 8 lb

1383 **AMARANTH 13** [10] J L Eyre 4-9-7 (74) R Cody Boutcher (7) 33/1: -00001: 4 b g Mujadil - Zoes Delight 80
(Hatim) Chsd ldrs, led over 1f out, styd on strongly ins last, rdn out: t-strap omitted: '99 wnr at Newcastle &
Newmarket (h'caps, rtd 83): '98 juv wnr at Redcar (auct mdn, rtd 76): eff at 5/6f on firm or soft: loves a stiff/
gall trk: eff with/without a t-strap: has slipped to a handy mark & gd follow-up.
1422 **MARENGO 11** [4] M J Polglase 6-8-8 (61) R Fitzpatrick(3) 25/1: 150402: 6 b g Never So Bold - Born To 1 64
Dance (Dancing Brave) Chsd ldrs, rdn & kept on ins last, not pace of wnr: back to form on turf with visor omitted.
1011 **PEPPIATT 39** [9] N Bycroft 6-8-6 (59) J Fanning 16/1: -03403: 6 ch g Efisio - Fleur Du Val (Valiyar) nk 61
Trkd ldrs, rdn & kept on fnl 2f, not pace of wnr: not btn far: see 908, 802 & 667.
2014] **MISTER WESTSOUND 352** [11] Miss L A Perratt 8-8-3 (56)(bl) N Kennedy 50/1: 3100-4: Rear, prog to ½ 56
chase ldrs over 1f out, onepace nr fin: reapp: '99 wnr here at Ayr (h'cap, rtd 57): '98 Ayr wnr (h'cap, rtd 49):
eff at 6/7f on any grnd/trk, loves Ayr: suited by blnks/visor: has reportedly had cancer & a brave comeback.
1519 **JACMAR 6** [6] 5-7-10 (49)(1oh) Dale Gibson 25/1: 264105: Chsd ldrs, rdn/outpcd 2f out, styd on nk 48
well for press nr fin: quick reapp, stablemate of 4th: in gd heart & will relish a return to Hamilton: see 1358.
1356 **PANDJOJOE 14** [14] 4-8-5 (58) R Winston 7/4 FAV: 0-0556: Held up in tch, badly hmpd halfway, ¾ 55
styd on fnl 1f, ch had gone: hvly bckd: this best forgotten, worth another ch: see 1356, 1008.
1356 **EURO VENTURE 14** [8] 5-9-2 (69) M Fenton 6/1: 000067: Led till over 1f out, fdd: see 1356, 645. ½ 64
1631 **DISTINCTIVE DREAM 1** [13] 6-9-4 (71) K Hodgson 8/1: 602608: Mid-div, not pace to chall: ran yesterday. ½ 64
888 **INDIAN MUSIC 51** [15] 3-8-13 (74) J Carroll 25/1: 001-09: Rear, no impress: 7 wk abs: '99 Doncaster 1 65
wnr over 1f out over a gall 5f on hvy grnd.
1215 **ZESTRIL 24** [2] 3-9-5 (80) C Lowther 50/1: 104-00: Prom centre till over 1f out: 10th: see 1215 (7.5f). 1 69
*1354 **MORGAN LE FAY 14** [5] 5-8-10 (63) Kim Tinkler 25/1: 230-10: Prom towards centre 5f: 11th. 1¼ 49
1471 **BLUNDELL LANE 9** [7] 5-9-9 (76) J F Egan 8/1: 00-100: Cl-up 4f: 12th: op 14/1: btr 1126 (made most). 2½ 55
1383 **PIPS MAGIC 13** [12] 4-9-0 (77) A Culhane 5/1: -0000W: Refused to ent stalls & withdrawn: see 1162. 0
4510] **Lady Boxer 220** [3] 4-9-7 (74) P Hanagan (7) 40/1: 1384 **Howards Lad 13** [16] 3-8-7 (68)(BL) D Mernagh (3) 100/1:
15 ran Time 1m 11.1 (1.8) (M Gleeson) J L Eyre Sutton Bank, N Yorks

---

1655   **3.20 PRIVATE PENSION MDN 3YO+ (D)**   **1m2f**   **Good/Firm 29 -07 Slow**
£3770   £1160   £580   £290   3 yo rec 13lb

1452 **INCHING CLOSER 10** [5] N A Callaghan 3-8-11 J F Egan 5/2: 24-001: 3 b g Inchinor - Maiyaasah (Kris)   **82**
Chsd ldr, rdn/led over 1f out, styd on well nr fin: drvn out: nicely bckd: rnr-up in '99 (rtd 83, mdn): eff at 1m,
styd longer 10f trip well today: acts on fast & gd grnd & likes a gall trk.

-- **TAKAMAKA BAY** [8] M Johnston 3-8-11 J Fanning 2/1 JT FAV: 2: 3 ch c Unfuwain - Stay Sharpe   *1*   **80**
(Sharpen Up) Dictated pace in front, qcknd tempo over 2f out, hdd over 1f out, kept on for press: well clr of rem:
debut, cost IR 58,000gns as a yearling: eff at 10f, could stay further: acts on fast grnd.

1165 **GRANTED 27** [1] M L W Bell 3-8-6 (VIS) M Fenton 2/1 JT FAV: 54-33: 3 b f Cadeaux Genereux - Germane   *7*   **68**
(Distant Relative) Chsd front pair 3f out, sn no impress: well bckd in 1st time visor: clr of rem: btr 1165.

4373} **PHILAGAIN 231** [6] Miss L A Perratt 3-8-6 N Kennedy 100/1: 000-4: Chsd ldrs, btn 3f out: new stable.   *8*   **59$**
-- **KELBURNE** [7] 3-8-11 A Culhane 20/1: 5: Held up, outpcd fnl 3f: debut, dam a 7f/1m AW wnr.   *1*   **63**
-- **LITTLE LES** [3] 4-9-10 R Winston 100/1: 6: Held up, btn 3f out: Flat debut, jumps fit (no form).   *1½*   **61**
4292} **SISTER KATE 237** [2] Kim Tinkler 25/1: 6-7: Chsd ldrs, struggling 4f out: reapp, no form.   *14*   **41**
-- **MABSHUSH** [4] 4-9-10 G Parkin 33/1: 8: Dwelt, bhd halfway: debut, cost 1,000gns as a 3yo.   *2½*   **42**
8 ran   Time 2m 08.04 (3.64)   (Gallagher Equine Ltd)   N A Callaghan Newmarket

---

1656   **3.50 STOCKBROKERS CUP HCAP 3YO+ 0-95 (C)**   **1m2f**   **Good/Firm 29 +13 Fast**   **[90]**
£6773   £2084   £1042   £521   3 yo rec 13lb

1490 **TONY TIE 7** [5] J S Goldie 4-9-5 (81) A Culhane 7/2: -62231: 4 b g Ardkinglass - Queen Of The Quorn   **86**
(Governor General) In tch, rdn/led 1f out, styd on well in last, drvn out: best time of day: '99 Doncaster wnr
(lady riders h'cap, rtd 74): '98 wnr at Salisbury (stks) & Chester (nurs, rtd 89, W Turner): eff at 1m, suited
by this step up to 10f: acts on firm & hvy: handles any trk & has run well fresh: tough & genuine colt.

1007 **CHIEF MONARCH 39** [1] R A Fahey 6-8-10 (72) J Carroll 4/1: 0-2502: 6 b g Be My Chief - American   *1½*   **74**
Beauty (Mill Reef) Chsd ldrs, briefly outpcd 3f out, rdn to chall over 1f out, not pace of wnr: bckd: see 757.

4571} **LITTLE JOHN 214** [2] Miss L A Perratt 4-7-10 (58) Dale Gibson 16/1: 3446-3: 4 b g Warrshan - Silver   *1*   **59**
Venture (Silver Hawk) Keen & cl-up, led 3f out till over 1f out, no extra: reapp: plcd twice last term (rtd 69, mdn):
rtd 80 at best in '98 (mdn): eff at 9/12f, handles fast & soft grnd.

1450 **IRON MOUNTAIN 10** [4] N A Callaghan 5-8-10 (72) J F Egan 7/4 FAV: 0-3534: Chsd ldrs, ch over 1f out,   *1*   **72**
onepace ins last: hvly bckd: see 1113 (1m).

733 **LATALOMNE 69** [6] 6-10-0 (90) M Fenton 3/1: 00-005: Led till 3f out, btn 1f out: jumps fit (unplcd).   *6*   **81**
1187 **DIVINE APPEAL 26** [3] 5-8-13 (75) J Fanning 100/1: 260-06: Prom, btn 2f out: ex-French, 99   *4*   **60**
Chantilly wnr: eff at 12f on soft grnd: prev won at Criquette Head, cost current connections 7,000gns.
6 ran   Time 2m 06.03 (1.63)   (Frank Brady)   J S Goldie Uplawmoor, E Renfrews

---

1657   **4.20 CLASSIFIED STKS 3YO+ 0-60 (F)**   **1m5f**   **Good/Firm 29 -27 Slow**
£2341   £669   £334   3 yo rec 17lb

*1433 **ALPHA ROSE 11** [4] M L W Bell 3-8-5 M Fenton 9/4 FAV: -55411: 3 ch f Inchinor - Philgwyn (Milford)   **58**
Trkd ldrs, rdn/led over 2f out, drvn out to maintain narrow advantage ins last: hvly bckd: recent Musselburgh wnr
(class stks): unplcd for R Williams in '99 (rtd 68): eff at 10/14f: acts on firm & fast grnd & a sharp or gall trk.

1518 **PENNYS FROM HEAVEN 6** [1] D Nicholls 6-9-9 J F Egan 11/2: 4/0302: 6 gr g Generous - Heavenly   *½*   **57**
Cause (Grey Dawn II) Chsd ldrs, rdn to chall over 1f out, kept on well ins last, just held: qck reapp: see 1209.

1433 **KILCREGGAN 11** [9] Mrs M Reveley 6-9-9 A Culhane 3/1: 10-033: 6 b g Landyap - Lehmans Lot   *2½*   **53**
(Oats) Chsd ldrs halfway, onepace fnl 2f: op 9/4: also bhd this wnr in 1433.

1363 **SPREE VISION 14** [7] P Monteith 4-9-9 R Winston 16/1: 0-0004: Rear/in tch, kept on fnl 2f, no   *1¼*   **51**
threat: imprvd eff, poss coming to hand & is v well h'capped: see 1363.

1478 **SPOSA 8** [6] 4-9-6 R Fitzpatrick (3) 6/1: 406305: Held up in tch, eff over 2f out, sn onepace/held.   *1¼*   **46**
1253 **SANTA LUCIA 21** [2] 4-9-6 Dale Gibson 7/1: 20-026: Trkd ldrs, outpcd over 2f out: see 1253.   *½*   **45**
1501 **WINSOME GEORGE 7** [8] 5-9-9 (BL) N Kennedy 10/1: -23307: Held up, eff 3f out, sn held: blnks.   *2½*   **44**
1241 **ICE PACK 22** [5] 4-9-6 Kim Tinkler 50/1: 0-6008: Prom early, no impress fnl 4f: see 1241, 556.   *1½*   **39$**
2636} **SWANDALE FLYER 326** [3] 8-9-9 D Mernagh (3) 100/1: /050-9: Dictated pace 11f, sn btn: Flat reapp,   *5*   **35$**
jumps fit (no form): unplcd on the level last term (rtd 30, h'cap): back in 97/98 scored over timber at Sedgefield.

331 **MISTER GILL 140** [11] 3-8-6 J Fanning 14/1: 300-00: Cl-up, led over 3f out till over 2f out, wknd qckly: *6*   **26**
10th: 5 month abs: plcd in '99 for A T Murphy (rtd 63, nurs h'cap, t-strap): eff at 5f, handles firm & fast grnd.
10 ran   Time 2m 51.88 (7.28)   (Richard I Morris Jr)   M L W Bell Newmarket

---

1658   **4.50 PRIVATE CLIENT HCAP 3YO+ 0-65 (F)**   **1m rnd**   **Good/Firm 29 -06 Slow**   **[60]**
£2593   £741   £370   3 yo rec 11lb

1631 **ALMAZHAR 1** [6] J L Eyre 5-9-5 (51) J F Egan 2/1 FAV: 235421: 5 b g Last Tycoon - Mosaique Bleue   **57**
(Shirley Heights) Chsd ldrs, rdn fnl 2f & styd on well ins last to lead nr line, rdn out: hvly bckd: tchd 3/1: rnr-up
24 hrs prev: '99 scorer at Redcar, Southwell (2) & W'hampton (2, h'caps, rtd 78a & 52 at best): eff at 6f, suited
by 7f/1m: acts on fast & fibresand, sharp/gall trk: best without blnks/visor: tough & consistent.

1243 **NORTHGATE 22** [11] M Brittain 4-9-10 (42)(bl) D Mernagh (3) 8/1: 0-0542: 4 b c Thatching - Tender   *nk*   **47**
Time (Tender King) Led, clr over 2f out, rdn/hdd nr line: fine front running eff, can find similar: see 754.

497 **BRANDON MAGIC 112** [3] D Nicholls 7-9-1 (47) N Kennedy 20/1: 01-003: 7 ch g Primo Dominie - Silk   *2*   **48**
Stocking (Pardao) Prom, kept on onepace fnl 2f: 4 month abs, op 14/1: nicely h'capped for similar: see 497.

4232} **THORNTOUN GOLD 242** [15] J S Goldie 4-8-13 (45) Dawn Rankin (7) 50/1: 3000-4: Rear, kept on fnl 2f,   *¾*   **45**
nrst fin: reapp: '99 Thirsk wnr (sell h'cap, rtd 51 at best): rtd 78 in '98: eff around 7f/1m, tried 10f: acts on
firm & soft, sharp/gall trk: enjoys sell grade: encouraging reapp, sharper next time in similar.

3243} **BROCTUNE GOLD 298** [5] 9-8-10 (42) A Culhane 16/1: 0060-5: Mid-div, briefly no room halfway,   *nk*   **41**
styd on for press fnl 2f, nrst fin: reapp: unplcd last term (rtd 43, h'cap): '98 wnr at Musselburgh & Catterick
(h'caps, rtd 61): eff at 6f/1m, tried 10f: acts on firm & soft: handles any trk, likes Musselburgh.

1608 **LEOFRIC 2** [1] 5-8-10 (42)(bl) R Fitzpatrick (3) 14/1: 330306: Mid-div, hmpd 3f out, kept on ins   *½*   **40**
last: qck reapp, op 10/1: would have fin closer here with a clr run: enjoys sell/clmg grade: see 973.

1519 **KUWAIT THUNDER 6** [17] 4-8-8 (40)(vis) R Cody Boutcher (7) 16/1: 440607: Rear, mod gains fnl 2f.   *nk*   **37**
1243 **LINCOLN DEAN 22** [14] 4-8-13 (45) R Winston 6/1: 040-08: Keen/held up, eff 2f out, sn held: op 8/1.   *¾*   **41**
1448 **PUPS PRIDE 10** [13] 3-8-6 (49) G Parkin 16/1: 0-5009: Chsd ldrs, outpcd fnl 2f: op 14/1: see 800.   *½*   **44**

1297 **WOORE LASS** 18 [4] 4-9-4 (50) Kim Tinkler 20/1: 404-00: Rear, mod gains fnl 2f: 10th: '99 wnr at   ½   44
Brighton (fill h'cap, R Hannon, rtd 70): '98 Salisbury wnr (auct mdn, rtd 80): eff at 1m, stays 10f: acts on
firm & gd/soft, any trk: acts on firm, gd/soft grnd & handles equitrack.
1243 **CUTE CAROLINE** 22 [9] 4-9-4 (50) J Carroll 8/1: 00-350: In tch, btn 2f out: 11th: btr 1243, 1190.   2½   39
1243 **RYEFIELD** 22 [10] 5-9-10 (56) C Lowther 10/1: 060-0R: Refused to race: op 16/1: see 1243.   0
1296 **Raased** 18 [7] 8-8-8 (40)(tvi) P Hanagan (7) 14/1:   1361 **Ajjae** 14 [8] 4-8-4 (36)(bl) Dale Gibson 14/1:
831 **Isle Of Sodor** 57 [12] 4-8-13 (45) R Lappin 16/1:   1598 **Toshiba Times** 2 [1] 4-8-8 (40) M Fenton 33/1:
1434 **Bondi Bay** 11 [16] 3-8-12 (55) J Fanning 20/1:
17 ran   Time 1m 39.4 (2.8)   (Sunpak Potatoes 2)   J L Eyre Suttong Bank, N Yorks

---

Official Going   GOOD. Stalls: Inside.

1659   2.10 STAPLETON FILLIES AUCT MDN 2YO (F)   5f rnd   Good 52   -20 Slow
      £2310   £660   £330

1424 **SUPERSTAR LEO** 11 [2] W J Haggas 2-8-4 T Quinn 4/11 FAV: -21: 2 b f College Chapel - Council Rock   88+
(General Assembly): Made all, clr over 1f out, eased down: val for 5L+, well bckd: half-sister to a 5f 2yo
wnr: eff at 5f on gd & gd/soft, sharp trk: speedy filly who can force the pace, win stronger races.
886 **WANNA SHOUT** 51 [11] R Dickin 2-8-4 G Hind 14/1: -552: 2 b f Missed Flight - Lulu (Polar Falcon):   ¾   73
Mid-div, kept on well to chase wnr final 1f, flattered by proximity to eased down wnr: 3L clr rem, 7 wk abs, op
10/1: eff at 5f on gd grnd, 6f will suit: will not always meet one so useful: see 812 (debut).
1408 **PATRICIAN FOX** 13 [7] J J Quinn 2-8-4 R Ffrench 33/1: -003: 2 b f Nicolotte - Peace Mission (Dunbeath): 3   64
Prom, rdn & onepcd final 2f: worth a try in sells, eff at 5f on gd grnd: see 1130 (debut).
-- **MADAME ROUX** [6] J G Smyth Osbourne 2-8-10 F Norton 14/1: -4: Chsd ldrs, onepcd fnl 2f: op   2   64
8/1: 12,000gns Feb foal: half-sister to sev wnrs, incl a 1m 2yo scorer: sire a smart miler: will learn from this.
-- **CHARTLEYS PRINCESS** [4] J J Quinn 2-8-4 N Callan 16/1: -5: Chsd ldrs, effort 2f out, no impress on debut: ½   57
Apr foal, cost 1,600gns: related to sev wnrs, incl 2yos: sire a high class juv: with K Burke.
1236 **ALIS IMAGES** 22 [8] 2-8-7 G Carter 25/1: -66: Chsd ldrs, eff halfway, no ch with ldrs: see 1236 (AW).   ¾   57
-- **LADY ROCK** [10] O Pears 10/1: -7: Rear, mod late prog, nvr dngr on debut: 13,500gns Mar   2   54
foal: half-sister to a couple of 5f 2yo wnrs: sire a useful spint h'capper: with R Bastiman.
1359 **ALICIAN SUNHILL** 14 [3] 2-8-4 G Duffield 20/1: -038: Outpcd, nvr nr ldrs: see 1236 (AW).   hd   48
-- **VIOLENT** [12] 2-8-4 Dean McKeown 25/1: -9: In tch 3f, wknd: racecourse bow, op 12/1: Mar foal, cost   1   45
1,400gns: dam a wnr over 7f as a juv: sire a high class mid-dist performer: likely to apprec further given time.
1304 **MRS TIGGYWINKLE** 18 [5] 2-8-4 W Supple 16/1: -640: Prom 3½f, fdd into 10th: see 1304 (sand).   ½   44
1488 **MISS PROGRESSIVE** 7 [13] 2-8-7 J McAuley (5) 50/1: -6000: Nvr a factor, fin 11th.   1   44
-- **Pentagon Lady** [1] 2-8-7 F Lynch 33/1:   -- **Captains Folly** [9] 2-8-4 V Halliday 33/1:
13 ran   Time 1m 00.9 (3.6)   (The Superstar Leo Partnership)   W J Haggas Newmarket.

1660   2.40 CROFT SELLER 4YO+ (F)   1m5f175y   Good 52   -23 Slow
      £2257   £645   £322

2372 **HULLBANK** 337 [7] W W Haigh 10-8-12 G Carter 3/1: 1255-1: 10 b g Uncle Pokey - Dubavarna (Dubassoff):   57
Waited with, imprvd 3 out, went on appr final 1f, kept on well, drvn out: reapp, no bid: '99 Redcar wnr (h'cap,
rtd 68), also rnr-up once: '98 Southwell & Redcar wnr (h'caps, rtd 60a & 70): '97 Beverley scorer (h'cap): eff
btwn 14f & 2m2f, acts on gd, firm grnd & fibresand: handles any trk, best held up for a late run: gd weight
carrier who runs v well fresh: 10yo who apprec this drop into sell company.
1241 **FIELD OF VISION** 22 [8] Mrs A Duffield 10-8-12 G Duffield 11/4 FAV: -02432: 10 b g Vision - Bold   nk   56
Meadows (Persian Bold): Trkd ldrs, ev ch when short of front-rank pos, kept on well & just btn in a cl fin: see 1241.
-- **ALL ON MY OWN** [3] J S Wainwright 5-8-12 J McAuley (5) 25/1: -3: 5 ch g Unbridled - Someforall   2½   53
(One For All): Chsd ldrs till lost pl 4f out, rallied fnl 1f but not rch ldrs: recent jumps rnr, unplcd in a mdn
hdle: some bmpr form (gd/soft): eff at 14f, will stay 2m: acts on gd grnd & on a sharp trk: cld find a seller.
1301 **WAFIR** 18 [4] D Nicholls 8-8-12 (bl) F Norton 10/3: -43264: Rear, effort 2f out, kept on but not pace   ½   52
to chall: op 5/2: see 1203 (AW).
1498 **RAYWARE BOY** 7 [1] N Callan 4-8-12 (bl) 14/1: 0-0005: Early ldr, remnd prom & regained lead 2f out,   1   50$
hdd dist, no extra: offic rtd just 40, so treat this rating with caution: in early '99 won at Southwell (2, h'caps,
rtd 68a): eff at 1m, much lngr 14f trip here: acts on fibresand & can run well fresh: wears blnks: with D Shaw.
1597 **TURGENEV** 2 [5] P Ears 11-8-12 O Pears 9/2: 000506: Led after 2f till 2f out, wkng when hmpd ins last.   nk   49$
4370 **STOLEN MUSIC** 231 [6] 7-8-7 Dean McKeown 14/1: 000007: Rear, effort 2f out, nvr nr ldrs on reapp: 1½   42
'99 wnr at Redcar & here at Catterick (h'caps, rtd 48), also rnr-up once: '98 wnr at Beverley (2) & Redcar
(h'caps, rtd 38): eff at 10f, stays 2m, suited by 14f: acts on firm & hvy grnd: has tried a visor, best without:
handles any trk, likes Beverley & Redcar: will apprec a return to h'cap company & fitter next time.
-- **MAREMMA** [2] 6-8-7 G Hind 20/1: 4441/8: Chsd ldrs till lost pl 4f out, no ch after, fin last: missed   ½   41$
'99 on the Flat: prev term trained by Don Enrico Incisa to win at Doncaster (sell, rtd 48): '97 Redcar wnr (mdn
sell, rtd 48): eff over 11/12f, prob stays 14f: acts on fast & soft grnd: now with Miss Kate Milligan.
8 ran   Time 3m 06.0 (10.6)   (Mrs V Haigh)   W W Haigh Melsonby, Nth Yorks.

1661   3.10 BARTON MDN 3YO+ (D)   1m4f   Good 52   +02 Fast
      £2772   £792   £396   3yo rec 15lb

951 **MORNING LOVER** 45 [5] K R Burke 3-8-8 N Callan 3/1: 0-51: 3 b c Ela Mana Mou - The Dawn Trader   76
(Naskra): Trkd ldrs, hard rdn to lead inside final 1f, kept on strongly, drvn out: 6 wk abs, gd time, op 2/1:
shwd some promise at Newmarket on reapp: dam a 7f wnr: eff at 12f, should stay 14f: acts on gd grnd & on a
sharp trk, runs well fresh: lightly rcd, should progress further.
1386 **APPLE TOWN** 13 [4] H R A Cecil 3-8-4(1ow) T Quinn 4/11 FAV: -32: 3 br f Warning - Applecross   ½   71
(Glint Of Gold): Tried to make all, worn down inside final 1f, just btn in a cl fin: 4L clr of 3rd, hvly bckd:
1lb o/w probably proved v costly: should stay 14f: acts on gd grnd: see 1386.
1193 **HERACLÈS** 26 [2] A Berry 4-9-9 G Carter 16/1: -63: 4 b g Unfuwain - La Masse (High Top):   4   69
In tch, rdn & ch 2f out, onepcd final 1f: op 12/1: eff at 12f, stays 2m in NH Flat races: see 1193.
453 **BLAIR** 119 [1] W W Haigh 3-8-8 F Lynch 66/1: 0-004: Rear, prog & ch 2f out, sn btn: long abs: 5   61$

offic rtd just 40, so treat this rating with caution: Ingr 12f trip here: see 328.
1362 **DESERT MUSIC 14** [7] 4-9-4 G Hind 66/1: -05: In tch till outpcd 4f out, no ch after: see 1362. *5* **47**
1287 **HERSELF 20** [6] 3-8-3 G Duffield 12/1: -006: Nvr a factor: op 8/1: see 1287, 1045 (soft/hvy). *½* **46**
1299 **THE WALRUS 18** [3] 3-8-8 J P Spencer 25/1: 03307: Front rank till wknd qckly 2f out: flattered 848. *1½* **48**
7 ran Time 2m 37.3 (6.1) (D & M Cased Hole) K R Burke Newmarket.

1662

3.40 WENSLEY SPRINT HCAP 3YO+ 0-85 (D) 5f rnd Good 52 -04 Slow [78]
£4329 £1332 £666 £333 3yo rec 7lb

*1357 **BODFARI KOMAITE 14** [6] M W Easterby 4-9-3 (67) T Lucas 4/1: 6-W211: 4 b g Komaite - Gypsy's Barn Rat (Balliol): Prom, went on halfway till hdd dist, rallied well to lead again cl-home, drvn out: recent Thirsk wnr (h'cap): '99 Musselburgh & Doncaster wnr (h'caps, rtd 62): '98 Redcar wnr (nurs h'cap, rtd 62): all wins at 5f on firm & gd/soft grnd, handles hvy: handles any trk: suited by running up with or forcing the pace: in form. **73**
1580 **BRECONGILL LAD 3** [1] D Nicholls 8-9-8 (72) F Norton 7/2 FAV: 3-3032: 8 b g Clantime - Chikala (Pitskelly): Prom, led dist till ins last, just btn in a driving fin: well bckd, qck reapp: deserves to go one better. *nk* **77**
1430 **QUITE HAPPY 11** [8] M H Tompkins 5-8-4 (54) W Supple 11/1: 0-0333: 5 b m Statoblest - Four Legged Friend (Aragon): Mid-div, styd on to chase front 2 final 1f, not quite get there: tchd 14/1: change of tactics, usually forces the pace: well h'capped now: see 1430, 897. *2* **54**
1357 **TORRENT 14** [7] D W Chapman 5-8-10 (60)(bl) Lynsey Hanna (7) 9/1: 655304: Dwelt & hmpd start, late hdwy, nvr rchd ldrs: has shwn enough to win similar, prob needs stronger handling: see 1357, 1162. *½* **59**
1324 **TOM TUN 16** [5] 5-9-13 (77) S Finnamore (5) 12/1: 523005: Rear, styd on final 1f, nrst fin: top-weight. *shd* **76**
1278 **SOTONIAN 20** [9] 7-8-12 (62) N Callan 8/1: 003066: Trkd ldrs till fdd dist: tchd 11/1: won this race off a 2lb lower mark last year: see 774. *1¾* **56**
1278 **AMERICAN COUSIN 20** [3] 5-8-4 (54) Clare Roche (7) 16/1: 40-007: Al mid-div: stablemate of 2nd. *½* **47**
1398 **MOUSEHOLE 13** [12] 8-9-3 (67) G Duffield 16/1: -00008: Rear, modest late hdwy, nvr dngrs: gradually slipping down the weights & one to keep in mind when encountering favoured fast grnd: see 1013. *1* **57**
1357 **RIVER TERN 14** [11] 7-9-5 (69) R Ffrench 11/2: 045-69: Rear, effort 2f out, btn final 1f: btr 1357. *½* **58**
1516 **POP THE CORK 6** [4] 3-8-6 (63) Dean McKeown 33/1: -00300: Prom 3½f, fdd into 10th: qck reapp. *½* **51**
1580 **WATERFORD SPIRIT 3** [10] 4-9-3 (67) J P Spencer 25/1: 0W0000: In tch till fdd dist: qck reapp. *1½* **51**
1324 **CARTMEL PARK 16** [2] 4-9-12 (76) O Pears 9/1: 1-0500: Led till halfway, fdd into last: see 1324. *½* **59**
12 ran Time 1m 00.1 (2.8) (Bodfari Stud Ltd) M W Easterby Sheriff Hutton, Nth Yorks.

1663

4.10 PEN HILL CLAIMER DIV 1 3YO+ (F) 6f rnd Good 52 -06 Slow
£1897 £542 £271 3yo rec 8lb

1545 **BLUSHING GRENADIER 4** [9] S R Bowring 8-8-13 (bl) S Finnamore (5) 9/2: 666021: 8 ch g Salt Dome - La Duse (Junius): Chsd ldrs till outpcd 2f out, styd on well to lead ins fnl 1f, won going away: qck reapp, value for 2/3L: earlier won at Southwell (sell h'cap): '99 Redcar & Carlisle wnr (clmrs, rtd 67 & 55a): '98 W'hampton (sell, rtd 55a), Warwick (clmr, with M Fetherston Godley), Haydock & Newcastle wnr (h'caps, rtd 63): eff btwn 5f & 1m, all wins at 6f: acts on gd, fast & on both AWs: suited by blnks/visor: tough gelding, best in sell/claimers. **45**
921 **ROYAL CASCADE 48** [10] B A McMahon 6-9-3 (bl) W Supple 20/1: 630202: 6 b g River Falls - Relative Stranger (Cragador): Rear, fin v well but too late: 7 wk abs: back to form on return to clmg grade: see 667. *¾* **42**
1257 **PRIORY GARDENS 21** [6] J M Bradley 6-8-11 R Ffrench 14/1: 044003: 6 b g Broken Hearted - Rosy O'Leary (Majetta): Rear, imprvd 1f out, kept on under press, nrst fin: meet today's wnr on better terms in h'caps. *½* **35**
1479 **TANCRED TIMES 8** [5] D W Barker 5-8-8 Kimberley Hart (5) 3/1 FAV: 505324: Led 2f, remnd prom & ev ch inside last, no extra cl-home: well bckd: see 1479 (h'cap). *¾* **29**
1257 **GET A LIFE 21** [1] 7-8-5(1ow) N Callan 50/1: 0-0505: Dwelt, effort 2f out, kept on final 1f & nrst fin. *nk* **25**
1559 **JACKERIN 4** [7] 5-8-13 (vis) Dean McKeown 7/1: 544066: Chsd ldrs, onepcd final 1f: qck reapp. *½* **32**
*1430 **SUE ME 11** [2] 8-9-1 (bl) F Norton 7/2: 6-0017: Led after 2f till collared inside last, no extra: possibly went off too fast here: see 1430 (sell). *hd* **34**
1430 **PISCES LAD 11** [3] 4-9-1 J P Spencer 7/2: 0-1028: Chsd ldrs, onepace final 1½f out: btr 1430 (sell). *½* **33**
1298 **FRENCH GRIT 18** [8] 8-8-11 F Lynch 14/1: 006009: In tch, no impress final 1f: see 1068. *nk* **28**
1266 **GYPSY SONG 21** [4] 3-8-11 O Pears 25/1: -00: Dwelt, nvr a factor: looks modest. *¾* **33**
10 ran Time 1m 13.8 (3.5) (S R Bowring) S R Bowring Edwinstowe, Notts.

1664

4.40 PEN HILL CLAIMER DIV 2 3YO+ (F) 6f rnd Good 52 +07 Fast
£1897 £542 £271 3yo rec 8lb

1357 **TREASURE TOUCH 14** [2] D Nicholls 6-8-11 Iona Wands (5) 6/1: 0-0001: 6 b g Treasure Kay - Bally Pourri (Law Society): Broke well & made all, clr fnl 1f, cmftbly: op 9/2, best time of day: rnr-up in '99 (class stks, rtd 60): '97 wnr at Southwell, Nottingham (2), Newmarket & Thirsk (rtd 71a & 89): eff at 5f, suited by 6f: acts on firm, gd/soft & f/sand: handles any trk: has tried blnks, seems best without: v well h'capped. **61**
1074 **BEDEVILLED 32** [6] T D Barron 5-9-5 J P Spencer 5/2 FAV: 510W02: 5 ch g Beveled - Putout (Dowsing): Mid-div, styd on under press fnl 1f, not rch wnr: did not get the best of runs, back to form: see 758. *1¾* **62**
1519 **SYCAMORE LODGE 6** [3] D Nicholls 9-9-1 F Norton 11/2: 0-0003: 9 ch g Thatching - Bell Tower (Lyphard's Wish): Rear, hmpd after 2f, prog 2f out, no impress final 1f: qck reapp, shorter prcd stablemate of wnr: usually runs well here at Catterick, poss better at 7f: back to form & well h'capped: see 872 (sell). *2* **52**
1258 **SAMMAL 21** [5] J A Glover 4-8-13 O Pears 25/1: 005004: Rear, kept on under press final 1f, nrst fin. *½* **49**
1298 **ANSELLMAN 18** [9] 10-9-9 (bl) G Carter 7/2: 00-025: Chsd wnr till fdd final 1f: 10yo, btr 1298. *4* **47**
1351 **LAUND VIEW LADY 14** [1] 3-8-2 K Dalgleish(7) 11/2: 000-06: Rear, eff when hmpd halfway, no ch after. *1½* **30**
1358 **APPLES AND PEARS 14** [4] 4-8-10 G Duffield 10/1: 050007: Prom till wknd dist: see 312 (sand). *1* **27**
1479 **RED SYMPHONY 8** [8] 4-8-12 N Callan 25/1: 0-5008: Prom 4f, gradually fdd: see 919. *2½* **22**
1464 **BEVERLEY MONKEY 9** [7] 4-8-4 Claire Bryan (5) 25/1: 5-0009: Dwelt, some hdwy halfway, sn btn: lost ch at the start today: capable of better, see 436. *2* **8**
1298 **INDIAN DANCE 18** [10] 4-8-11 G Hind 25/1: 0-0000: Chsd ldrs 4f, wknd: fin last. *nk* **14**
10 ran Time 1m 13.0 (2.7) (J P Honeyman) D Nicholls Sessay, Nth Yorks.

CATTERICK FRIDAY JUNE 2ND Lefthand, Undulating, V Tight Track

1665

5.10 GRINTON HCAP 3YO 0-70 (E) 6f rnd Good 52 -03 Slow [72]
£3150 £900 £450

*1600 **COLLEGE MAID 2** [2] J S Goldie 3-9-1 (59)(6ex) A McGlone 9/4 FAV: 200211: 3 b f College Chapel - **68**
Maid Of Mourne (Fairy King): Trkd ldrs, qcknd into lead dist, rdn clr: qck reapp: recent Ripon wnr (h'cap): '99
Musselburgh wnr (mdn auct, rtd 74): eff at 5/6f on firm & soft: handles any trk: in fine form.
*1273 **BERKELEY HALL 21** [5] B Palling 3-9-5 (63)(bl) F Norton 6/1: 3-0012: 3 b f Saddlers' Hall - Serious 1½ **66**
Affair (Valiyar): In tch, hmpd & lost pl after 2f, ran on strongly fnl 1f but nr rch wnr: poss a shade unlucky.
1334 **GREY FLYER 16** [3] Mrs L Stubbs 3-8-13 (57) J P Spencer 14/1: 120503: 3 gr g Factual - Faraway Grey 1¼ **56**
(Absalom): Led till dist, no extra: front rnr: eff at 5/6f: see 269, 242 (sand).
*1494 **THE PROSECUTOR 7** [10] B A McMahon 3-9-4 (62) W Supple 7/2: 150014: Rdn in rear & hmpd after hd **61**
2f, styd on fnl 2f, nrst fin: eff at 6f on soft, may need further on this faster grnd: bt this wnr in 1494.
192 **NATSMAGIRL 170** [1] 3-8-7 (51) G Carter 20/1: 0050-5: Dwelt, imprvd 2f out, no extra when short of 1¾ **45**
room inside last: reapp: some promise here, a return to 7f should suit: see 74 (6f sell, first time visor).
*785 **TONDYNE 65** [9] 3-8-3 (57) D Duffield 4/1: 00-016: Prom, rdn & btn 2f out: 9 wk abs: btr 785. 3½ **41**
1494 **DANCING RIDGE 7** [6] 3-8-10 (54) N Callan 16/1: 060-07: In tch 4f, sn btn: see 1494. 2½ **31**
570 **BOOMSHADOW 100** [7] 3-9-2 (60) F Lynch 25/1: 00-68: Dwelt, nvr a factor: long abs: see 570. 1 **34**
1494 **MAJOR BART 7** [4] 3-8-6 (50) O Pears 16/1: 0-0509: Prom 4f, fdd: modest form, see 1696. 4 **12**
1021 **DANAKIM 39** [8] 3-9-7 (65) G Hind 11/1: 000240: In tch, slightly hmpd after 2f, btn fnl 2f: btr 1021. 4 **15**
10 ran Time 1m 13.6 (3.3) (S Bruce) J S Goldie Uplawmoor, East Renfrews.

BATH FRIDAY JUNE 2ND Lefthand, Turning Track With Uphill Finish

Official Going GOOD/SOFT. Stalls: Str Course - Far Side; Round Course - Inside.

1666

6.35 BOLLINGER AMAT HCAP 4YO+ 0-70 (G) 1m2f46y Good/Soft 65 -30 Slow [40]
£2345 £670 £335

1375 **SOVEREIGNS COURT 14** [14] L G Cottrell 7-11-13 (67) Mr L Jefford 7/1: 20/301: 7 ch g Statoblest - **72**
Clare Celeste (Coquelin): Held up, prog 3f out, & switched, ran on well to lead appr fnl 1f, rdn clr: missed '99,
plcd in '98 (h'caps, rtd 77): '97 wnr at Nottingham (2, h'caps, rtd 74): eff at 1m, suited by 10f: acts on fast,
likes gd/soft & hvy grnd, gall trks, likes Nottingham: goes well fresh.
1465 **VANBOROUGH LAD 9** [11] Dr J R J Naylor 11-9-10 (36)(1oh) Mr Ray Barrett (2) 14/1: 6-5002: 11 b g 3½ **36**
Precocious - Lustrous (Golden Act) Rear, smooth hdwy to trk ldrs 2f out, eff bef dist, unable to qckn: op 10/1:
fair attempt to repeat last season's success in this race (rtd 49), reserves his best for this trk: see 889.
4284} **BOATER 237** [16] A T Murphy 6-11-6 (60) Mr A Jones (3) 8/1: -420-3: 6 b g Batshoof - Velvet Beret 1¾ **58**
(Dominion) Pulled hard, led after 5f till appr fnl 1f, onepace: missed fir, 99/00 wnr at N Abbot (2, h'caps, 2m1f,
firm & hvy, rtd 110h): '99 rnr-up (amat h'cap, rtd 62): last won in '97 at Brighton (h'cap, rtd 77, D Morley):
stays 10f, best at 1m/9f: best up with/forcing the pace on firm, hvy grnd, equitrack, like sharp trks.
*1511 **JESSINCA 7** [2] Derrick Morris 4-10-3 (43)(5ex) Mr M Foley 6/1 JT FAV: 100014: Rear, wide prog 1¾ **39**
4f out, same pace fnl 2f: not disgraced back up in trip with a penalty so soon after 1511 (1m).
1096 **OSCIETRA 31** [3] 4-11-3 (57) Mr T Best (5) 14/1: 060-05: Rear, mod late prog, nvr a factor: see 1096. nk **52**
3889} **IL DESTINO 263** [1] 5-11-8 (62) Mr C B Hills (3) 6/1 JT FAV: 1262-6: Al around same place: reapp: ¾ **56**
'99 wnr here at Bath (h'cap, rtd 65 & 70a, P Makin): plcd in '98 (h'caps, rtd 63 & 68a): eff at 1m, suited
by 10f: acts on firm/fast grnd & equitrack, sharp or gall trk: now with B Hills.
-- **BALLYKISSANN** [18] 5-9-10 (36)(bl) Mr G Carenza (3) 50/1: 0030/7: Handy till no extra appr ¾ **29**
fnl 2f: hdles fit (plater): missed '99, plcd in '98 for D Ffrench Davies (h'cap rtd 41): stays 1m on firm without blnks.
1570 **DARE 4** [5] 5-11-4 (58)(vis) Mr A Evans 13/2: 350038: Nvr troubled ldrs: quick reapp, tchd 8/1. 3 **47**
1496 **KINGFISHERS BONNET 7** [5] 4-10-12 (52) Mr G Richards (5) 10/1: 013549: Prom till wknd 2f out. 5 **34**
2167} **OLD SCHOOL HOUSE 345** [10] 7-10-5 (45) Mr G Browitt (7) 40/1: /000-0: Nvr nr ldrs: 10th, reapp: 10 **17**
lightly rcd & no form since '96 wnr at W'hampton, Doncaster, here at Bath (h'caps, rtd 59) & Lingfield (ltd stks,
rtd 71a): eff at 14f/2m on fast, hvy grnd, both AWs: goes on any trk: with T Naughton.
1330 **DIRECT DEAL 16** [15] 4-12-0 (68) Mr A Bradley (5) 14/1: 3-0000: Well plcd, lost pl ent str: 11th. 1¾ **38**
*1465 **FUERO REAL 9** [4] 5-10-4 (44)(5ex) Mr T Tibbatts (7) 10/1: 0-5310: Al towards rear: 15th, see 1465. 0
1065 **Landican Lane 32** [17] 4-9-10 (36)(4oh) Mr T Radford (5) 66/1:
1465 **Inkwell 9** [13] 6-9-10 (36)(tbl)(3oh) Mr A Quinn (7) 25/1:
1201 **Birth Of The Blues 25** [9] 4-11-9 (63) Mr J Gee (5) 12/1: 1287 **Twice 20** [6] 4-11-13 (67)(t) Mr H Poulton (7) 20/1:
92 **Lucayan Beach 192** [7] 6-11-6 (60) Mr A Honeyball (5) 25/1:
3414} **Alminstar 290** [12] 4-9-11 (37) Mr J J Best (0) 25/1:
18 ran Time 1m 15.6 (9.6) (E Gadsden) L G Cottrell Dulford, Devon

1667

7.05 EBF FILLIES MDN 2YO (D) 5f161y rnd Good/Soft 65 +08 Fast
£3562 £1096 £548 £274

1176 **FINAL PURSUIT 26** [5] D Haydn Jones 2-8-11 T Quinn 10/1: 01: 2 b f Pursuit Of Love - Final Shot **94**
(Dalsaan): Prom, led 2f out, drvn out (flashed tail): op 33/1, front 2 clr, fast juv time: missed break on debut
last month: 42,000 gns Mar foal, half-sister to 3 juv wnrs, notably Sir Nicholas, dam useful sprinter: eff
at 5.7f, sure to get further: acts on gd/soft grnd, up with the pace: potentially useful, Queen Mary possible.
-- **AL IHSAS** [3] J H M Gosden 2-8-11 R Hills 2/1 FAV: 2: 2 b f Danehill - Simaat (Mr Prospector) ¾ **91**
Mid-div, switched & gd prog to chall bef dist, held nr fin: nicely bckd, clr rem, debut: Mar foal, sister to 7f juv
Samut, dam a miler: eff over extended 5f, 6f+ sure to suit: handles gd/soft, can win soon.
-- **NASHIRA** [4] C R Egerton 2-8-11 J Reid 10/1: 3: 2 ch f Prince Sabio - Aldevonie (Green Desert) 3½ **82**
Mid-div, kept on ent fnl 2f, not pace to chall: tchd 14/1 on debut: 15,000 gns Feb 1st foal, sire a sprinter:
prob handles gd/soft grnd & met a couple of decent fillies: 6/7f will suit next time.
1372 **SPIRIT OF SONG 14** [7] M R Channon 2-8-11 Craig Williams 5/1: 44: Chsd ldrs, eff 2f out, onepace 1 **79**
till styd on nr fin: tchd 6/1: rtd higher on debut, see 1372.
-- **SINGLE HONOUR** [8] 2-8-11 Dane O'Neill 25/1: 5: Dwelt, imprvd over 2f out, rdn bef dist, shd **79**
onepace: unfancied on debut: Mark Of Esteem May foal, half sister to 2 wnrs, notably 7/12f Arabian Story:
dam wng miler as a 2yo, sire a miler: attractively bred, shld improve in time: with R Hannon.

546

-- **GREEK DREAM** [13] 2-8-11 M Hills 11/2: 6: Rear, wide prog 2f out, nvr able to chall: op 4/1, clr of next on debut: Distant View Jan 1st foal, dam smart mid-dist performer, sire a miler: likely improver. 1¾ 75+
1454 **JETHAME 10** [6] 2-8-11 D R McCabe 20/1: 07: Prom, eff & short of room appr fnl 2f, no extra. 3 67
-- **STARRY MARY** [14] 2-8-11 S Sanders 66/1: 8: Nvr in it: 3,000 gns Deploy Apr foal: stoutly bred. 1¼ 64
-- **SILLA** [12] 2-8-11 W Ryan 10/1: 9: Prom till 2f out: op 6/1 on debut: Gone West Jan foal, dam sprint bred, sire a miler: with I Balding. hd 64
-- **DOMINIQUE** [11] 2-8-11 P Dobbs (5) 33/1: 0: Wide, in tch till not much room 2f out: 10th, stalbemate 5th: 6,200 gns Primo Dominie Mar foal, half-sister to 2 wnrs, dam useful juv, sire a sprinter. 1½ 61
-- **BRING PLENTY** [17] 2-8-11 J Fortune 14/1: 0: Dwelt, nvr in it: 11th, stalbemate 2nd, debut: Southern Halo Mar foal, half-sister to a pair of 7f/1m wng juvs, dam 5f juv wnr, later got 10f. ½ 60
1197 **COPY CAT 25** [1] 2-8-11 Martin Dwyer 6/1: 40: Bhd from halfway: 16th, tchd 8/1, btr 1197 (fast).   0
1046 Theresa Green 35 [10] 2-8-11 Kathleen McDermott (7) 66/1 **Maid Of Arc** [16] 2-8-11 D Harrison 20/1:
-- Annie Ruan [15] 2-8-11 C Rutter 66/1: 1059 Forest Moon 32 [2] 2-8-11 M Roberts 33/1:
891 Bluebel 50 [9] 2-8-11 A Nicholls (3) 66/1:
17 ran   Time 1m 12.3 (3.2)   (Jack Brown (Bookmaker) Ltd)   D Haydn Jones Efail Isaf, Rhondda C Taff

---

1668   7.35 NEWTON MED AUCT MDN 3YO (D)   1m2f46y   Good/Soft 65   -18 Slow
£3750   £1154   £577   £288

1188 **RHYTHMICALL 26** [6] Mrs A J Perrett 3-9-0 M Roberts 3/1: 01: 3 b c In The Wings - Rhoman Ruby (Rhoman Rule): Prom, led bef 2f out, canter: op 2/1, any amount in hand: 18,000 gns half-brother to a wnr abroad: apprec step up to 10f, should get 12f: acts on gd/soft grnd: impressive here, could be useful. 84
1127 **PROPER SQUIRE 29** [1] J H M Gosden 3-9-0 J Fortune 4/1: 362-62: 3 b c Bien Bien - La Cumbre (Sadler's Wells) Chsd ldrs, under press ent fnl 3f, kept on for 2nd but nvr any hope with facile wnr: nds h'caps. 7 72
1134 **BOLD GUEST 29** [5] J W Hills 3-9-0 M Hills 9/1: -033: 3 ch c Be My Guest - Cross Question (Alleged) Rear, closed 4f out, went 2nd bef 2f out, sn onepace: op 7/1: longer trip, now qual for h'caps. ½ 71
1218 **DE TRAMUNTANA 24** [2] W Jarvis 3-8-9 T Quinn 1/1 FAV: 00-24: Led till appr fnl 2f, grad wknd: well bckd: unsuited by this easier surface? see 1218 (prob flattered, dictated slow pace around Chester). 5 59
1293 **LORD ALASKA 18** [3] 3-9-0 A Nicholls (3) 50/1: 005: Nvr in it: ndd this for h'cap mark. ¾ 63$
-- **STRECCIA** [4] 3-8-9 C Rutter 16/1: 6: Prom till 3f out: Old Vic filly out of a miler. 6 50
-- **SWEMBY** [7] 3-8-9 Martin Dwyer 33/1: 7: Sn struggling: debut: Mizoram filly out of a 6f wnr. 5 43
7 ran   Time 2m 14.4 (8.4)   (Sunday School)   Mrs A J Perrett Pulborough, W sussex

---

1669   8.05 EBF AND RSW FILLIES MDN 3YO (D)   1m rnd   Good/Soft 65   -13 Slow
£6955   £2140   £1070   £535

915 **LET ALONE 49** [3] B W Hills 3-8-11 J Fortune 25/1: 01: 3 b f Warning - Mettlesome (Lomond) Rear, hdwy after halfway, drvn appr fnl 1f & kept on gamely to put head in front on line: come on plenty for debut: sister to a 7f scorer, dam 1m/9f wnr: apprec this step up to 1m, likely to get 10f: acts on gd/soft grnd. 81
1428 **SEEKING SUCCESS 11** [6] Sir Michael Stoute 3-8-11 R Reid 8/1: -002: 3 b f Seeking The Gold - Testy Trestle (Private Account) Prom, eff to lead appr fnl 1f, sn rdn, worn down line: op 9/2: ran a decent race in defeat: eff at 1m on gd/soft grnd: shown enough to land similar. shd 80
1428 **LATOUR 11** [5] J W Hills 3-8-11 M Hills 3/1: 645-23: 3 b f Sri Pekan - Fenny Rough (Home Guard) Well plcd, led 3f out till bef fnl 1f, no extra towards fin: bckd from 9/2: drop back to 7f may suit: see 1428. 1¼ 78
1159 **THERMAL SPRING 27** [1] H R A Cecil 3-8-11 T Quinn 6/4 FAV: 5-24: Mid-div, chsd ldrs & not much room appr fnl 2f, styd on but unable to chall: bckd, op 2/1: stays 1m, acts on gd & gd/soft & is worth another ch. nk 77
1344 **MASRORA 15** [8] 3-8-11 Craig Williams 8/1: 45: Chsd ldrs, rdn & onepace appr fnl 1f. 1¾ 74
971 **POWERLINE 44** [9] 3-8-11 Dane O'Neill 10/1: -06-06: Rear, wide eff 2f out, nvr dngrs: op 6/1, abs. 2½ 70
4315} **TOWN GOSSIP 235** [4] 3-8-11 S Sanders 50/1: 0-7: Nvr a factor: reapp, unplcd sole '99 start. 2 66
2741} **CHELONIA 32** [10] 3-8-11 R Hills 9/1: 3-8: Led till 3f out, fdd: op 6/1, stalbemate of wnr, reapp: plcd sole '99 start (fill mdn, rtd 80): 30,000gns half sister to a 12f wnr: capable of better. nk 65
1436 **MAIDEN AUNT 11** [2] 3-8-11 Martin Dwyer 25/1: 59: Nvr in it: see 1436. 1¼ 63$
1444 **WHITEGATE WAY 10** [7] 3-8-11 R Mullen 50/1: 00: Dwelt, al towards rear: 10th. 3½ 57
10 ran   Time 1m 44.5 (6.2)   (K Abdulla)   B W Hills Lambourn, Berks

---

1670   8.35 ASM BIG DADDA CLAIMER 3YO (F)   5f rnd   Good/Soft 65   -11 Slow
£2275   £650   £325

1081 **DIAMOND PROMISE 31** [5] P D Evans 3-8-4 R Mullen 9/2: 5-2041: 3 b f Fayruz - Cupid Miss (Anita's Prince) Rear, prog halfway, rdn to lead dist, held on well: op 7/2: '99 wnr at Thirsk, Leicester & Lingfield (clmrs, rtd 75, sand rnr-up, rtd 70a): eff at 5/6f gd, soft, both AWs: best forcing the pace in claimers. 58
1289 **JAMES STARK 18** [8] N P Littmoden 3-9-7 (vis) J Fortune 7/1: -00002: 3 b g Up And At 'Em - June Maid (Junius) In tch, prog to chall appr fnl 1f, kept on under press, held nr fin: op 5/1: ran to best back in trip giving weight all round: acts on both AWs, handles gd & gd/soft grnd: see 275, 105. nk 74
1427 **CHORUS 11** [13] B R Millman 3-9-2 D Harrison 5/1: -20063: 3 b f Bandmaster - Name That Tune (Fayruz) Prom, led 2½f out till 1f out, no extra: op 3/1: btr 1427, 888. 2½ 63
841 **ITSGOTTABDUN 56** [4] K T Ivory 3-8-11 (bl) S Sanders 12/1: 423664: Rear, gd prog to chase ldrs 2f out, same pace bef dist: 8 wk abs, back in trip, see 527. ¾ 56
1349 **PETRIE 15** [12] 3-8-11 T Quinn 4/1 FAV: 56-035: Rear, wide prog 2f out, rdn & onepace fnl 1f: came in from 10/1 despite having a stiffish task on official ratings: see 42. nk 55$
1334 **BREEZY LOUISE 16** [9] 3-8-8 N Pollard 13/2: 0-1066: Nvr troubled ldrs: see 959. 1½ 49
1430 **ELLPEEDEE 11** [6] 3-8-13 (t) C Rutter 8/1: -06567: Prom till appr fnl 1f: op 16/1: see 909. 2 48
1036 **BRIEF CALL 35** [7] 3-8-8 D McGaffin (6) 25/1: 5-0608: Nvr on terms: turf return, see 487. nk 42
1423 **LISA B 11** [3] 3-8-4 (bl) Craig Williams 14/1: -20009: Chsd ldrs, not cl run 3f out till bef dist & btn. 1 35
959 **MINIMUS TIME 45** [14] 3-8-2 (bl) A Nicholls (3) 20/1: 014640: Flyjmpd start, prom, led briefly 3f out, fdd: 10th, 6 wk abs, see 357. 2½ 27
1436 Gold Rider 11 [1] 3-9-5 D O'Donohoe 33/1: 1557 Queensmead 4 [10] 3-8-8 C Cogan (5) 16/1:
1392 Sunrise Girl 13 [2] 3-8-0 A McCarthy (3) 40/1: 4430} Wild Magic 227 [11] 3-8-0 Martin Dwyer 33/1:
14 ran   Time 1m 03.8 (3.8)   (Diamond Racing Ltd)   P D Evans Pandy, Gwent

BATH   FRIDAY JUNE 2ND   Lefthand, Turning Track With Uphill Finish

1671   9.05 LORDSWOOD HCAP 3YO 0-70 (E)   1m rnd   Good/Soft 65   + 01 Fast   [75]
£2849   £814   £407

1053 **KELTECH GOLD 34** [7] B Palling 3-9-4 (65) D Harrison 6/1: 50-021: 3 b c Petorius - Creggan Vale **71**
Lass (Simply Great), Prom, hard rdn appr fnl 1f, ran on to lead towards fin, narrowly: tchd 10/1, fair time, 1st
win: 5th on debut last term (mdn auct, rtd 69): cost IR 14,000 gns: eff at 1m on gd/soft: on the upgrade.

*1024 **BOLD RAIDER 39** [8] I A Balding 3-9-1 (62) A Nicholls (3) 9/2: 000-12: 3 b g Rudimentary - Spanish   shd **67**
Heart (King Of Spain) Sn led, drvn appr fnl 1f, worn down well ins last, just failed: op 6/1, clr rem, 6 wk
abs: acts on gd/soft & hvy grnd & is proving tough: see 1024.

*1564 **LA SPEZIANA 4** [4] D R C Elsworth 3-9-13 (74)(6ex) R Thomas (7) 1/1 FAV: 66-113: 3 b g Perugino -   2½ **75**
Election Special (Chief Singer) Mid-div, prog & ev ch appr fnl 1f, onepace ins last: well bckd from 9/4:
winning run ended but was giving plenty of weight away & it poss came too sn after 1564.

1521 **PILLAGER 6** [14] Mrs A J Bowlby 3-9-2 (63) J Reid 12/1: -60264: Well plcd, rdn & ev ch appr fnl 1f,   3½ **58**
edged left & no extra: quick reapp: drop back to 7f may suit: see 1085.

1495 **WINTZIG 7** [5] 3-9-4 (65) R Mullen 8/1: 1-0525: Dwelt, late prog, nvr a threat: clr rem, worth another ch.   nk **59**

1080 **AFTER THE BLUE 32** [2] 3-9-1 (62) Craig Williams 8/1: 6-006: Chsd ldrs, fdd appr fnl 1f: tchd 5/1.   4 **49**

1435 **CHRISS LITTLE LAD 11** [9] 3-9-2 (63) Martin Dwyer 12/1: 040-27: Early ldr, wknd under press appr   ½ **49**
fnl 1f: tchd 16/1, h'cap bow, see 1435 (C/D auct mdn on fast).

1002 **STRICTLY SPEAKING 39** [11] 3-8-11 (58)(bl) J Fortune 14/1: 5-0668: Nvr in it: blnks reapp.   ½ **43**

937 **TITUS BRAMBLE 46** [12] 3-8-7 (54) N Pollard 33/1: 00-009: Dwelt, nvr nr ldrs: 7 wk abs, drop in trip.   shd **39**

1464 **LE LOUP 9** [15] 3-9-1 (62) Dane O'Neill 40/1: 600-00: Mid-div till 3f out: 10th, big step up in trip.   2 **44**

1093 **Blues Whisperer 31** [13] 3-8-6 (53) A McCarthy(3) 33/1:
4185} **Flyover 245** [10] 3-9-2 (63) Cheryl Nosworthy(7) 33/1:
1397 **Mobo Baco 13** [3] 3-9-1 (62) O Urbina 33/1:   1397 **Bishopstone Man 13** [16] 3-9-4 (65) C Rutter 25/1:
4184} **Rosetta 245** [1] 3-8-8 (55) Jonjo Fowle(7) 40/1:   1094 **Hard Days Night 31** [6] 3-7-13 (46) D Glennon(7) 40/1:
16 ran   Time 1m 43.4 (5.1)   (D Brennan)   B Palling Cowbridge, Vale Of Glamorgan

---

LINGFIELD (MIXED)   SATURDAY JUNE 3RD   Lefthand, Sharp, Undulating Track

Official Going   GOOD/SOFT (GOOD Places); AW - STANDARD. Stalls: Turf - Stands Side; AW - Inside.

1672   2.20 OCS LADY AMAT HCAP 3YO+ 0-75 (F)   7f str   Good 47   -37 Slow   [53]
£2324   £664   £332   3 yo rec 10lb

1520 **ROBELLION 7** [5] Miss E C Lavelle 9-10-1 (54) Miss S Newby Vincent (1) 4/1: 000-51: 9 b g Robellino -   **56**
Tickled Trout (Red Alert) Prom, eff 2f out, kept on to lead towards fin: qck reapp, slow time: '99 reapp wnr here
at Lingfield (this ladies h'cap, rtd 63): '98 wnr again here at Lingfield (2, ltd stks & clmr, D Arbuthnot) &
Southwell (amat h'cap, rtd 66a & 68, Mrs Stubbs): best at 7f/1m, stays 10f: acts on fast, gd/sft, both AWs:
loves Lingfield: best without blinkers & goes well for lady riders: well h'capped & tough.

3313} **MY EMILY 295** [2] G L Moore 4-11-5 (72) Mrs J Moore 5/1: 1200-2: 4 b f King's Signet - Flying Wind   ½ **72**
(Forzando) Cl-up, led appr fnl 2f, kept on but collared well ins last: sound reapp: '99 Brighton wnr (mdn h'cap,
rtd 70 at best): plcd prev term (rtd 65): eff at 7f: acts on firm & gd, handles gd/sft, any trk: goes well fresh.

1520 **BELLAS GATE BOY 7** [8] J Pearce 8-10-1 (54) Mrs L Pearce 9/1: 0-0003: 8 b g Doulab - Celestial   2 **50**
Air (Rheingold) Dwelt, rear, styd on 2f out to go 3rd below distr, ran on finish: qk reapp: see 676.

1505 **FLASHFEET 8** [9] P D Purdy 10-9-6 (45) (3ow)(22oh) Miss A Purdy (0) 66/1: 046004: Led till bef fnl 2f.   ½ **40$**

705 **FINAL DIVIDEND 72** [4] 4-11-7 (74) Miss Joanna Rees (7) 6/1: 100-45: Al mid-div: back in trip.   hd **69**

4282} **ALHUWBILL 239** [1] 5-9-3 (42)(9oh) Miss C Hannaford (5) 33/1: 0000-6: In tch, fdd fnl 1f: abs,   3 **31**
stiff task: flattered when well btn 5th in '99 (mdn rtd 57): has tried hdles: with J Bridger.

1348 **CATAMARAN 16** [7] 5-11-5 (72) Miss R Woodman (7) 2/1 FAV: 30-457: In tch, outpcd 2f out: nicely   1¼ **59**
bckd: needs 1m+ & really caught the eye in last 1348.

1207 **TROJAN WOLF 26** [10] 5-10-4 (57) Miss S Pocock (5) 12/1: 530008: Prom till 2f out: op 16/1, see 255.   ¾ **43**

1289 **RIBBON LAKE 19** [6] 3-10-6 (69) Miss C Stretton (5) 12/1: 600-09: Nvr in it: '99 wnr here at   ¾ **53**
Lingfield (auct mdn, rtd 79): eff at 6/7f: acts on firm & gd grnd, any trk: better than this, with Mrs Dutfield.

1196 **JONATHANS GIRL 26** [3] 5-9-3 (42)(12oh) Miss J Ellis (7) 50/1: 040400: Handy, wknd qckly fnl 2f: 10th.   ½ **25**
10 ran   Time 1m 26.27 (5.87)   (The Forty Ninth Partnership)   Miss E C Lavelle Hatherden Hants

1673   2.50 DON CLARK NOV AUCT STKS 2YO (E)   6f str   Good 47   -05 Slow
£2966   £848   £424

-- **SHE ROCKS** [1] R Hannon 2-8-4 D Harrison 10/1: 1: 2 b f Spectrum - Liberty Song (Last Tycoon)   **82**
Chsd ldrs, shkn up to lead 2f out, sn rdn clr, readily: less fancied stablemate of fav, debut: 11,000lr gns Feb foal:
dam won in France: sire 1m/10f performer: eff over a sharp 6f on gd, will stay further: runs well fresh: win again.

1437 **QUANTUM LADY 12** [5] B R Millman 2-8-7 G Hind 7/2: -4122: 2 b f Mujadil - Folly Finnesse   4 **75**
(Joligeneration) Cl-up, rdn 2f out, styd on same pace: prob ran to best up in trip, stays 6f: see 1437, 1088.

1497 **OPEN WARFARE 8** [2] M Quinn 2-8-9 Martin Dwyer 8/1: 341353: 2 b f General Monash - Pipe Opener   1½ **74**
(Prince Sabo) Led till 2f out, no extra for press: return to 5f likely to suit: see 1437, 1166.

*1304 **BROUGHTONS MOTTO 19** [4] W J Musson 2-8-5 L Newton 9/2: 014: Rear, some prog 2f out, nvr   2 **64**
any impress on ldrs: op 3/1, clr rem: longer trip back on turf: btr 1304.

1088 **INSHEEN 32** [7] 2-8-6 J F Egan 25/1: -05: Chsd ldrs till 2f out: 3,500lr gns Inzar Apr foal.   4 **55**

-- **CHANGE OF IMAGE** [3] 2-8-1 R Mullen 12/1: 6: Nvr on terms: 6,000gns Spectrum Apr foal,   hd **50**
half-sister to a 6f juv wnr, dam 7f juv wnr: sire 1m/10f performer: with J Eustace.

1463 **CHURCH BELLE 10** [6] 2-8-5(1ow) Dane O'Neill 2/1 FAV: 027: Cl-up till lost pl 2f out: well bckd   ½ **53**
stablemate of winner: longer trip, only placing class form to date: see 1463 (gd/sft).

-- **EMMA CLARE** [10] 2-8-2(1ow) G Carter 14/1: 8: Al bhd: debut: 2,800gns Namaqualand Apr foal, sister   6 **38**
to a 1m5f wnr, dam 12f/2m scorer: sire sprinter/miler.

1396 **CEDAR TSAR 14** [9] 2-8-6 M Henry 7/1: 629: In tch till halfway: new stable, much btr 1396.   5 **32**

-- **FATHER SEAMUS** [8] 2-8-6 R Winston 20/1: 0: Lost many lengths start, al detached: 10th, debut: ½ **31**
1,500gns Bin Ajwaad Apr foal, half-brother to 2 wng 5f juvs, dam 6f juv wnr, sire 7f/1m performer: with P Butler.
10 ran   Time 1m 11.92 (3.12)   (M Mulholland)   R Hannon East Everleigh, Wilts

---

1674   3.20 LISTED LEISURE STKS 3YO+ (A)   6f str   Good 47   +08 Fast
   £15718   £5962   £2981   £1355   3 yo rec 8 lb

*1111 **MOUNT ABU 31** [5] J H M Gosden 3-8-10 R Havlin 6/1: 26-411: 3 b c Foxhound - Tawny Angel **112**
(Double Form) Hld up, prog to trk ldrs 2f out, switched & rdn to chall dist, led nr fin, drvn out: nicely bckd, gd
time: prev won at Ascot (Listed): '99 wnr at Newbury (mdn, Gr 3 rnr-up, rtd 105, P C Hyam): stays 7f, improving
fast at 6f: acts on fast & gd/sft, any trk: smart, genuine colt with a good turn of foot, shld win a Group race.
+1410 **HOT TIN ROOF 14** [6] T D Easterby 4-8-13 K Darley 9/4 FAV: 0-2112: 4 b f Thatching - No   hd   **107**
Reservations (Commanche Run) Chsd ldrs, niggled after 3f, drvn to lead 1f out, hdd cl-home: hvly bckd to
complete a hat-trick: lost nothing in defeat against a much improved sprinter: v tough/useful filly, see 1410.
1371 **WINNING VENTURE 15** [4] S P C Woods 3-8-6 D Harrison 10/3: D-3023: 3 b c Owington - Push A Button ¾   **106**
(Bold Lad) Pld hard, mid-div, shkn up & imprvd to chall appr fnl 1f, sn rdn & hung right, held nr fin, just btn: well
bckd: fair run tho' becoming frustrating & is probably worth a try in headgear now: see 1371, 950.
1111 **TRINCULO 31** [8] N P Littmoden 3-8-7(1ow) T G McLaughlin 9/1: 4-2004: Prom, edn & ev ch ent fnl 2f,   nk   **106**
carried bef dist, onepace towards fin: ran to best & pulled clr of next: also bhd wnr in 1111, see 969.
1453 **DEEP SPACE 11** [1] 5-9-0 G Carter 6/1: 20-635: Prom, wide, ch bef fnl 1f, outpcd: likes fast.   3   **97**
4469} **EASY DOLLAR 225** [2] 8-9-0 (bl) C Rutter 33/1: 2106-6: Cl-up, widest of all, led halfway till 2f out,   nk   **96**
fdd fnl 1f: prob flattered on reapp: '99 Nottingham wnr (h'cap, rtd 91): out of sorts in '98, Listed plcd in '97 (rtd
109): eff at 6/7f, stays 1m: acts on firm & gd, handles hvy: best forcing the pace in blnks or visor: apprec h'caps.
1168 **SHAREEF 28** [9] 3-8-6 J F Egan 25/1: 157: Detached till kept on nicely appr fnl 1f: big drop in trip   ½   **95+**
after running over 12f: sure to relish a return to 1m+: keep an eye on: see 1168, 603.
1453 **ANDREYEV 11** [7] 6-9-4 Dane O'Neill 12/1: -10058: Nvr on terms: see 1453, 734.   1¾   **94**
4620} **GAELIC STORM 210** [3] 6-9-4 R Winston 6/1: 0126-9: In tch, prog 3f out, sn hung left, btn bef fnl 1f: 1½   **90**
op 5/1, reapp: '99 wnr at Goodwood (stks), Sweden (2, 1 Listed) & Newmarket (Listed, rtd 115): '98 wnr at York
(2), Newcastle & Newbury (h'caps, rtd 114): eff at 6/7f: acts on firm, suited by gd or softer: smart at best.
1111 **SEVEN NO TRUMPS 31** [10] 3-8-6 (BL) R Mullen 25/1: 22-000: Led till halfway, fdd: 10th, blinkered.   2   **80**
10 ran   Time 1m 11.16 (2.36)   (Gary Seidler & Andy J Smith)   J H M Gosden Manton, Wilts

---

1675   3.55 NICHOLSON GRAHAM & JONES MDN 3YO+ (D)   7f str   Good 47   -30 Slow
   £3731   £1148   £574   £287   3 yo rec 10lb

1562 **PRETRAIL 5** [1] A C Stewart 3-8-13 R Mullen 4/5 FAV: 02-021: 3 b c Catrail - Pretty Lady (High Top)   **76**
Cl-up, led bef fnl 2f, sn rdn & edged left, held on well under press: hvly bckd from 3/1, slow time, qk reapp: rnr-up
fnl '99 start (mdn, rtd 76): eff over a sharp 6/7f: acts on fast & gd grnd, sharp trks: improving.
814 **REEMATNA 61** [4] M A Jarvis 3-8-8 J F Egan 7/2: 0-42: 3 b f Sabrehill - Reem Albaraari (Sadler's   hd   **70**
Wells) Keen, rear, pld out & gd hdwy to chall appr fnl 1f, kept on for press, just held: nicely bckd, 9 wk abs:
suited by the drop back to 7f on gd grnd, likely to get 1m: shld find similar in the north, see 814.
-- **MOON GOD** [3] E A L Dunlop 3-8-13 G Carter 15/8: 6223-3: 3 b c Thunder Gulch - Lyric Fantasy (Tate   1¾   **72**
Gallery) Keen, bhd ldrs, eff 2f out, unable to qckn: nicely bckd on reapp/Brit bow: ex-Irish, dual '99 rnr-up for
A O'Brien (mdns): cost current connections 44,000gns: eff at 6f, stays 7f on gd & soft: do better from the front?
1377 **AEGEAN FLOWER 15** [6] R M Flower 3-8-13 (BL) C Rutter 33/1: 04: Prom till 3f out: blinkered.   19   **47**
4404} **COST AUDITING 229** [5] 3-8-8 M Henry 33/1: 2000-5: Led, carried head awkwardly, hdd ent fnl 3f &   nk   **41**
btn: reapp, reportely lost her action early on: '99 rnr-up (nurs, rtd 65a, Sir M Prescott): eff at 5f on fast & f/sand.
1175 **PICCALILLI 27** [2] 3-8-8 S Whitworth 33/1: 06: Sn struggling: no form.   3½   **36**
6 ran   Time 1m 25.82 (5.42)   (S J Hammond)   A C Stewart Newmarket, Suffolk

---

1676   4.25 RUINART HCAP 3YO+ 0-85 (D)   6f str   Good 47   -03 Slow   **[85]**
   £4082   £1256   £628   £314   3 yo rec 8 lb

*1423 **FIRE DOME 12** [8] Andrew Reid 8-9-4 (75) M Henry 5/1: 033111: 8 ch g Salt Dome - Penny Habit   **82**
(Habitat) Chsd ldrs, rdn appr fnl 1f, picked up well to lead ins last, going away: op 4/1: qck hat-trick landed
after wins at Redcar & Windsor (clmrs, for D Nicholls, clmd out of last one for £10,000): '99 wnr at Sandown &
Redcar (clmrs, rtd 83): '98 Thirsk & Sandown wnr (List, rtd 107): stays 7f, eff at 5/6f: acts on firm, hvy &
fibresand: goes on any trk, likes Sandown: gd weight carrier, best without blinkers: well h'capped 8yo.
1517 **COASTAL BLUFF 7** [12] N P Littmoden 3-8-9-6 (77) T G McLaughlin 10/1: 00-502: 8 gr g Standaan -   1½   **79**
Combattente (Reform) Grabbed stands rail & made most, edged left 1f out, hdd & no extra ins last: gd run.
1590 **BRAVE EDGE 3** [1] R Hannon 9-9-12 (83) Dane O'Neill 4/1: 033023: 9 b g Beveled - Daring   hd   **85**
Ditty (Daring March) Wide, in tch, drvn to chall appr fnl 1f, outpcd nr fin: bckd from 6/1: gd run from stall 1.
*1542 **AMBER BROWN 7** [2] K T Ivory 4-8-5 (62)(bl) J F Egan 8/1: 010014: Prom, rdn & ev ch ent fnl 2f,   nk   **63**
no extra towards fin: tchd 10/1: back in trip: tough & in form, ideally suited by soft grnd: see 1542.
1531 **MIDNIGHT ESCAPE 7** [4] 7-9-11 (82) R Mullen 13/2: 0-0045: Mid-div, eff 2f out, not pace to chall.   nk   **82**
1483 **BINTANG TIMOR 9** [9] 6-9-0 (71) L Newton 8/1: 3-0346: Badly outpcd, styd on appr fnl 1f: needs 7f.   nk   **58**
1543 **KAYO GEE 7** [5] 4-8-4 (61)(vis) C Rutter 16/1: 0-6037: Dsptd lead after 3f till appr fnl 1f, btn ins last.   ½   **58**
4144} **SARSON 248** [7] 4-9-12 (83) P Dobbs (5) 33/1: 5000-8: Hld up, rdn 2f out, onepace: reapp, jt top-weight,   hd   **79**
stablemate 3rd: unplcd in '99 (List, rtd 97): useful juv, won at Sandown (List, rtd 108, Gr 2 rnr-up): eff
at 5f, stays 6f: acts on fast & gd/sft grnd: best held up: well h'capped if recapturing 2yo form.
1591 **RETURN OF AMIN 3** [10] 6-9-11 (82) Martin Dwyer 11/2: 000249: Hld up, pshd along to improve   ½   **77**
over 2f out, no ch with ldrs when not much room ins last: bckd, qck reapp: btr 1471.
1471 **LOCH LAIRD 10** [3] 5-9-7 (78) P Doe 8/1: 000-50: Nvr on terms: 10th: see 1471.   4   **63**
1438 **SHARP GOSSIP 12** [11] 4-8-6 (63)(bl) S Whitworth 8/1: 2-0000: Prom till halfway: 11th, blnks   2   **43**
reapp, tchd 12/1: ex-Irish mdn, dual '99 rnr-up (off mark of 70) : eff at 6/7f on soft grnd: with J Toller.
2860} **SHAFAQ 316** [6] 3-9-5 (84) R Price 12/1: -13-0: Sn out the back: 12th, reapp/h'cap bow: 2½   **58**
'99 debut wnr her at Lingfield (mdn, rtd 85): eff forcing the pace over a sharp 6f on fast grnd.
12 ran   Time 1m 11.78 (2.98)   (A S Reid)   Andrew Reid Mill Hill, London, NW7

1677   5.0 GUINEA PIG HCAP 3YO+ 0-85 (D)   1m4f aw   Standard   Inapplicable   **[80]**
   £3789   £1166   £583   £291   3 yo rec 15lb

*1523 **PLURALIST 7** [5] Miss K M George 4-9-4 (70) J F Egan 7/1: 1-2411: 4 b c Mujadil - Encore Une Fois   **75a**
(Shirley Heights) In tch, eff 3f out, styd on dourly to lead cl-home: last week won at Warwick (clmr, W Jarvis, cost
current connections £15,000): '99 Southwell wnr (mdn auct, rtd 58a & 77): eff at 9f/12f on any grnd, both AW's.

LINGFIELD (MIXED)　　SATURDAY JUNE 3RD　　Lefthand, Sharp, Undulating Track

*1100 **ANOTHER MONK** 32 [3]　R Ingram 9-7-10 (48)(2oh) M Henry 9/2: 414112: 9 b g Supreme Leader　　nk　52a
- Royal Demon (Tarboosh) Cl-up, led halfway till bef fnl 2f, again ins last till fnl strides: in terrific form.
1288 **TOTOM** 19 [2]　J R Fanshawe 5-9-7 (73) D Harrison 4/1 FAV: 145-43: 5 b m Mtoto - A Lyph (Lypheor)　　1　75a
Led 5f, again appr fnl 2f, hard rdn, hdd & no extra ins last: bckd, clr rem: stays 12f, best at slightly shorter?
1307 **TOTAL DELIGHT** 18 [9]　Lady Herries 4-10-0 (80) P Doe 7/1: 0-1004: Handy, eff 3f out, onepace bef dist.　4　78a
1373 **MONO LADY** 15 [1]　7-9-0 (66)(bl) C Rutter 7/1: -02045: Rear, gd prog 5f out, same pace fnl 3f: bckd.　1　63a
1604 **WESTERN COMMAND** 3 [8]　4-8-8 (60) R Fitzpatrick (3) 12/1: 645106: Rear, wide prog 5f out, sn onepace. 2　54a
1292 **KATHAKALI** 19 [10]　3-8-10 (77) Martin Dwyer 7/1: 111007: Nvr trbld ldrs: tchd 10/1: lngr trip, btr 880.　2½　68a
1375 **ADMIRALS PLACE** 15 [6]　4-8-13 (65) G Carter 11/2: 231428: Al towards rear: op 9/2, see 1070, 965.　½　55a
1518 **ST HELENSFIELD** 7 [7]　5-9-13 (79) R Winston 9/2: 04-039: Prom 7f: bckd, qk reapp, AW bow: see 1518.3½　68a
880 **FULHAM** 52 [4]　4-7-10 (48)(bl) (5oh) D Kinsella (7) 33/1: 0-4200: Pld hard, bhd from halfway: 10th, abs.　15　19a
10 ran　　Time 2m 31.75 (2.55)　　(Exterior Profiles Ltd)　　Miss K M George Princes Risborough, Bucks

---

CATTERICK　　SATURDAY JUNE 3RD　　Lefthand, Undulating, Very Tight Track

Official Going　SOFT. Stalls: Inside.

1678　2.25 MED AUCT FILLIES MDN 3-4YO (E)　6f rnd　Soft 129　-18 Slow
£2730　£840　£420　£210 Raced stands side fnl 3f

1036 **STEVAL** 36 [6]　R Guest 3-8-10 P M Quinn (3) 12/1: 00-401: 3 ch f Efisio - Vannozza (Kris):　　58
Held up in tch, rdn/prog over 2f out & led 1f out, styd on well, rdn out: rtd 57 at best in '99 (debut, mdn): eff
at 6f on a sharp/turning trk: acts on soft grnd.
1562 **QUEEN MOLLY** 5 [4]　R M H Cowell 3-8-10 (t) Dale Gibson 3/1: 52: 3 b f Emarati - Tiszta Sharok　1¼　54
(Song): Trkd ldr, led over 2f out, rdn/hdd 1f out, no pace of wnr: qck reapp, op 2/1: see 1562.
3890} **DAKOTA SIOUX** 264 [5]　R A Fahey 3-8-10 M Tebbutt 1/1 FAV: 3-3: 3 ch f College Chapel - Batilde　1½　51
(Victory Piper): Handy, hard rdn 2f out, held final 1f: hvly bckd, op 7/4: reapp: plcd sole '99 start (med auct
mdn, rtd 711): eff at 5f, this lngr 6f trip should suit: handles fast grnd, not soft here?
3854} **LITTLE CHAPEL** 268 [1]　G H Yardley 4-9-4 A Nicholls (3) 6/1: 0050-4: Trkd ldrs, outpcd over 1f　hd　58$
out: reapp: unplcd last term for D J S ffrench Davis (rtd 67, h'cap): eff at 6f, tried 7f: handles firm/fast.
1500 **FOXY ALPHA** 8 [2]　3-8-10 A Culhane 10/1: 0-05: Chsd ldrs, bhd final 2f: op 14/1: mod form.　11　34
4607} **PETERS PRINCESS** 211 [3]　3-8-10 J Carroll 10/1: 0650-6: Led 4f, sn btn: tchd 12/1: reapp: unplcd　5　26
last term for J Berry (rtd 47).
6 ran　　Time 1m 19.1 (8.8)　　(Mrs Lesley Mills)　　R Guest Newmarket, Suffolk.

1679　2.55 SKIPTON-ON-SWALE SELLER 2YO (F)　6f rnd　Soft 129　-14 Slow
£2299　£657　£328 Raced stands side fnl 3f

1294 **HAMASKING** 19 [4]　T D Easterby 2-8-6 J Carroll 11/4 FAV: 661: 2 b f Hamas - Sialia (Bluebird):　　60
Dwelt, sn in tch, rdn/chsd ldr over 2f out, styd on well for press inside last to lead nr fin: well bckd: no bid:
apprec this step up to 6f, will get further: acts on soft grnd, poss handles firm: apprec this drop to sell grade.
*1553 **SAND BANKES** 5 [8]　W G M Turner 2-9-3 (vis) S Finnmore (5) 7/2: 20612: 2 ch c Efisio - Isabella　¾　68
Sharp (Sharpo): Led after 2f & clr halfway, rdn/strongly prsd final 1f & hdd nr fin: bckd, op 4/1: qck reapp.
1443 **CHORUS GIRL** 11 [2]　M W Easterby 2-8-6 T Lucas 3/1: -543: 2 ch f Dancing Spree - Better Still　3　51
(Glenstal): Rdn/mid div, kept on final 2f, not pace of front pair: clr of rem: clmd by D Nicholls for £6,000.
-- **MASTER COOL** [9]　G M Moore 2-8-11 Dale Gibson 20/1: 4: Dwelt/outpcd early, mod late prog: op　8　44
14/1: Mar foal, a first foal, cost 15,000 gns: dam a hdles wnr, sire a smart sprinter: stay further in time.
1206 **DIAMOND MILLENNIUM** 26 [7]　2-8-6 J Stack 7/1: 505: Keen, chsd ldrs, held fnl 2f: op 4/1: see 849 (5f). nk　38
-- **HOLBECK** [5]　2-8-6 A Culhane 7/1: 6: Mid-div, no impress final 2f: bckd, op 10/1: Efisio filly, May　2　34
foal, cost 90,000 gns: dam unrcd: sire tough 6f/1m performer: with T Nikoler.
1420 **DECEIVES THE EYE** 12 [10]　2-8-11 Dean McKeown 20/1: 3457: Led 2f, btn 2f out: btr 836, 722 (5f).　½　38
-- **IMPREZA** [11]　2-8-6 D Mernagh (3) 33/1: 8: Sn bhd: Mistertopogigo filly, Mar first foal, dam a mdn.　8　21
1476 **BAYRAMI** 9 [6]　2-8-6 P Goode (3) 50/1: 05009: Cl-up, wknd qckly 2f out: mod form.　½　20
-- **PROPERTY ZONE** [1]　2-8-11 G Parkin 16/1: 0: Slowly away, al bhd: 10th: lngr prcd stablemate of　7　14
3rd: Cool Jazz gelding, Apr foal, dam a minor 6f 3yo wnr.
1420 **TINY MIND** 12 [3]　2-8-11 A Nicholls (3) 66/1: 000: Bhd halfway: 11th: no form.　1　12
11 ran　　Time 1m 18.9 (8.6)　　(Ryedale Partners No 3)　　T D Easterby Great Habton, Nth Yorks.

1680　3.25 CALDERPRINT HCAP 3YO+ 0-85 (D)　7f rnd　Soft 129　-01 Slow　　[80]
£4673　£1438　£719　£359　3 yo rec 10lb　Raced stands side fnl 3f

1445 **DURAID** 11 [8]　Denys Smith 8-9-12 (78) A Nicholls (3) 7/2 FAV: 01-421: 8 ch g Irish River - Fateful　84
Princess (Vaguely Noble): Mid-div, rdn final 2f & narrow lead inside last, styd on well, rdn out: well bckd, op 5/1:
'99 Beverley, Ripon & Catterick wnr (h'caps, rtd 79): unplcd in '98 (rtd 76): eff at 7f/1m, tried 12f: acts on
firm & soft, any trk, likes Catterick: genuine gelding, at the top of his form at 8yo.
1431 **PETERS IMP** 12 [7]　A Berry 5-8-10 (62) J Carroll 12/1: 00-502: 5 b g Imp Society - Catherine Clare　nk　66
(Sallust): Bhd, prog to chall inside last, styd on well, just held: op 10/1: nicely h'capped, win on stiffer trk.
1598 **DOUBLE ACTION** 3 [11]　T D Easterby 6-8-9 (61)(bl) G Parkin 6/1: 404053: 6 br g Reprimand - Final　1½　63
Shot (Dalsaan): Chsd ldrs, kept on onepace final 2f: op 8/1: qck reapp: blnks reapplied: see 1011, 623.
*1275 **CANTINA** 21 [5]　A Bailey 6-9-6 (72) G Faulkner (3) 8/1: 20-014: Led, remnd centre final 3f, hdd/no　1¼　72
extra inside last, op 6/1: see 1275 (firm)
1514 **LUANSHYA** 7 [4]　4-9-5 (71) Dean McKeown 9/1: 050-45: Chsd ldrs, hard rdn/onepace final 2f: see 1514. 1　70
1160 **SUPREME SALUTATION** 28 [12]　4-9-11 (77) M Tebbutt 13/2: 21-606: Held up in tch, eff 3f out, mod gains. ½　75
1519 **SANTANDRE** 7 [2]　4-8-2 (54) P M Quinn (3) 11/1: 411507: Mid-div, no impress final 2f: see 687 (AW).　nk　51
1153 **CHIMNEY DUST** 29 [9]　3-9-8 (84) O Urbina 12/1: 204-08: Mid-div, held final 2f: '99 Warwick wnr　4　75
(auct mdn, rtd 87 at best, h'cap): eff at 7f on firm & hvy grnd, sharp/gall trk.
1431 **MR PERRY** 12 [3]　4-8-0 (52)(bl) R Ffrench 20/1: 023009: Prom 5f: op 14/1: see 1149, 846.　2　40
1356 **MARY JANE** 15 [10]　5-8-1 (53) Kim Tinkler 25/1: -00000: Prom 5f: 10th: see 844 (8f).　½　40
1419 **CHINABERRY** 12 [15]　6-7-10 (48)(4oh) D Mernagh (3) 25/1: 4-0400: Nvr on terms: 11th: see 299.　1¾　33
1356 **ACID TEST** 15 [6]　5-9-0 (66) Dale Gibson 10/1: 066300: Al rear: 12th: op 8/1: blnks omitted: see 525.　½　50
1496 **Hi Nicky** 8 [13]　4-8-8 (60) T Williams 33/1:　　907 **Hyde Park** 50 [14] 6-8-6 (58) A Culhane 16/1:

CATTERICK   SATURDAY JUNE 3RD   Lefthand, Undulating, Very Tight Track

1383 **Quiet Venture** 14 [1] 6-9-3 (69) R Lappin 20/1:
15 ran   Time 1m 32.1 (9.1)   (A Suddes)   Denys Smith Bishop Auckland, Co Durham.

1681
4.00 MOULTON CLASSIFIED STKS 3YO+ 0-60 (F)   7f rnd   Soft 129   -01 Slow
£2352   £672   £336   3 yo rec 10lb   Raced stands side fnl 3f

1431 **MYBOTYE** 12 [13] A B Mulholland 7-9-9 (t) G Faulkner (3) 10/1: 0-4101: 7 br g Rambo Dancer - Sigh **60**
(Highland Melody): Held up in tch, smooth prog over 3f out, rdn/led over 1f out, in command when rdn out nr
fin: earlier scored at Redcar (sell): modest form/lightly rcd in '99: plcd in '98 (h'cap, rtd 59): eff at 7f,
tried 1m/10f: acts on east & soft, handles fibresand, any trk: has run well fresh: suited by a t-strap.
1257 **PRIX STAR** 22 [11] C W Fairhurst 5-9-6 P Goode (3) 9/2: 55-032: 5 ch g Superpower - Celestine 1¼ **53**
(Skyliner): Trkd ldrs, drvn/ch over 1f out, kept on for press: op 7/2: in gd form: see 1257, 82.
1255 **STORMSWELL** 22 [3] R A Fahey 3-8-7 T Lucas 20/1: 60-003: 3 ch f Persian Bold - Stormswept (Storm nk **49**
Bird): Prom, drvn over 1f out, kept on for press: op 14/1: unplcd last term (rtd 62, mdn): eff at 7f on soft.
1664 **SYCAMORE LODGE** 1 [1] D Nicholls 9-9-6 A Nicholls (3) 7/1: -00034: In tch, onepace fnl 2f: qck reapp. 2½ **48**
1477 **NOWT FLASH** 9 [12] 3-8-6 Dean McKeown 11/4 FAV: 105225: Prom, rdn/no extra final 1f: nicely bckd. hd **47**
1275 **CHAMPAGNE N DREAMS** 21 [5] 8-9-3 Kim Tinkler 9/1: 410-U6: Twds rear, nvr pace of ldrs: see 1275. 2 **41**
1239 **GOLDEN BIFF** 23 [4] 4-9-6 R Lappin 13/2: 06-067: Keen/led over 1f out, sn held: see 908. shd **44**
4164} **PHARAOHS HOUSE** 248 [6] 3-8-10 G Parkin 14/1: 3000-8: Always rear: op 10/1: reapp: plcd in '99 11 **32**
(rtd 79, mdn, subs disapp in blnks): eff over a sharpish 6f on gd/soft grnd.
1447 **BRIGMOUR** 11 [2] 4-9-3 S Finnamore (5) 33/1: 0009: Sn bhd: mod form. 4 **23**
804 **DOM MIGUEL** 64 [9] 3-8-10 A Culhane 7/1: 05-00: Cl-up, wknd qckly 2f out: 10th: nicely bckd, abs. 6 **17**
10 ran   Time 1m 32.1 (9.1)   (J F Wright)   A B Mulholland Hambleton, Nth Yorks.

1682
4.30 SINDERBY MED AUCT MDN 3YO (F)   7f rnd   Soft 129   +02 Fast
£2646   £756   £378   1st & 3rd raced stands side fnl 3f, remainder centre

837 **HAND CHIME** 57 [3] W J Haggas 3-9-0 K W Marks 8/1: 01: 3 ch g Clantime - Warning Bell (Bustino): **63**
Chsd ldrs, rdn/chall over 1f out, rdn & narrowly asserted well inside last: tchd 10/1, 8 wk abs: well bhd on
debut dbt: apprec step up to 7f, should get further: acts on soft grnd & a sharp/turning trk: runs well fresh.
1583 **DONTBESOBOLD** 4 [1] B S Rothwell 3-9-0 Dean McKeown 4/1: 440502: 3 b g River Falls - Jarmar 1 **61**
Moon (Unfuwain): Keen, clr over 3f out, remnd centre fnl 3f, hdd nr fin: clr rem: eff arnd 7f/10.5f: see 1002.
4197} **WOODLANDS** 245 [6] N A Graham 3-9-0 J Carroll 8/1 FAV: -030-3: 3 b g Common Grounds - Forest Of 8 **52**
Arden (Tap On Wood): Chsd ldr, drvn/no extra final 2f: hvly bckd: jockey reported gelding unable to act on soft
grnd: reapp: plcd last term (rtd 81, med auct mdn, R McGhin): eff at 6f on firm grnd & a sharp trk.
-- **JANETTE PARKES** [5] A Berry 3-8-9 D Mernagh 4/1: 4: Dwelt, nvr on terms: op 3/1, debut. 2 **44**
4081} **ANNESPRIDE** 253 [7] 3-8-9 A Culhane 12/1: 0-5: Dwelt, sn bhd: op 16/1, reapp: no form. 28 **12**
5 ran   Time 1m 31.9 (8.9)   (Mrs M M Haggas)   W J Haggas Newmarket, Suffolk.

1683
5.05 PICKHILL HCAP 4YO+ 0-70 (E)   1m5f175y   Soft 129   -38 Slow   [66]
£3965   £1220   £610   £305   Raced stands side fnl 3f

*1524 **ELSIE BAMFORD** 7 [6] M Johnston 4-8-3 (41) R Ffrench 2/1 FAV: 304311: 4 b f Tragic Role - Sara Sprint **49**
(Formidable): Mid-div, smooth/stdy prog 4f out, rdn/led 1f out, in command/pushed out nr fin: well bckd, op 3/1:
recent Warwick wnr (h'cap, first win): plcd in '98 (rtd 58 & 48a, h'caps): unplcd in '98 (rtd 62): suited by 12f/
14.7f: acts on firm & fibresand, relishes soft/hvy grnd: likes a sharp/turning trk, prob handles any: tough filly.
1087 **HASTA LA VISTA** 32 [5] M W Easterby 10-8-9 (47)(vis) T Lucas 5/1: 20-102: 10 b g Superlative - Falcon 1¼ **51**
Berry (Bustino): Led 2f, remnd cl-up & led again 2 out, rdn/hdd 1f out, kept on: op 4/1: see 903.
871 **DESERT RECRUIT** 53 [14] D Nicholls 4-8-4 (42) A Nicholls (3) 10/1: 14-553: 4 b g Marju - Storm Gayle ½ **45**
(Sadler's Wells): Led after 2f & clr 3f out, rdn/hdd 2f out, kept on: clr rem: op 7/1, abs: acts on east & soft.
1432 **FREEDOM QUEST** 12 [12] B S Rothwell 5-9-8 (60) R Lappin 12/1: 443464: Prom, held fnl 2f: op 10/1. 6 **57**
1536 **SHAFFISHAYES** 7 [10] 8-9-10 (62) A Culhane 6/1: 55-065: Held up, hdwy 4f out, held fnl 2f: see 943. nk **59**
1361 **MERLY NOTTY** 15 [3] 4-7-12 (36)(2ow) T Williams 11/1: 05-246: Chsd ldrs, btn 2f out: op 8/1. shd **32**
1253 **BERGAMO** 22 [9] 4-9-6 (58) J Carroll 14/1: -00057: Bhd, mod gains final 3f: op 10/1: see 845. 5 **49**
1499 **BOLT FROM THE BLUE** 8 [1] 4-8-11 (49) Kim Tinkler 25/1: 240-08: Mid-div, btn 3f out: rnr-up twice 6 **34**
in '99 (rtd 57, clmr): rtd 64 in '98 (clmr): suited by 10/11f, tried 2m: handles gd/soft & hvy, best without blnks.
1416 **ACCYSTAN** 12 [16] 5-9-2 (54) Dale Gibson 14/1: 163359: Mid-div, btn 3f out: op 10/1: see 642 (AW). nk **38**
855 **ONCE MORE FOR LUCK** 54 [2] 9-9-11 (63) C Teague 7/1: 4-060: Bhd, mod gains fnl 3f: op 6/1: see 779. 3½ **44**
1009 **Royal Reprimand** 40 [15] 5-7-12 (36)(vis) Kimberley Hart (2) 25/1:
1499 **Rosies All The Way** 8 [7] 4-7-10 (34)(t) S Righton 25/1:
4584} **Minalco** 214 [4] 4-7-11 (35)(1ow)(3oh) N Carlisle 33/1: 1496 **Yankee Dancer** 8 [13] 5-9-0 (52) P M Quinn (3) 20/1:
14 ran   Time 3m 18.5 (23.1)   (Mrs Sheila Ramsden)   M Johnston Middleham, Nth Yorks.

MUSSELBURGH   SATURDAY JUNE 3RD   Righthand, Sharp Track

Official Going: FIRM   Stalls: Inside, except 5f/2m - Stand Side

1684
2.10 SHERATON SELLER 2YO (F)   5f   Firm -01   -33 Slow
£2590   £740   £370   Raced stands side

1429 **COZZIE** 12 [6] J G Given 2-8-6 V Halliday 9/4 JT FAV: -3051: 2 ch f Cosmonaut - Royal Deed (Shadeed) **65**
Dsptd lead halfway, narrowly asserted inside last, styd on well, drvn out: well bckd though op 9/4: bought in for
4,200gns: eff at 5f, may get further: acts on firm & fibresand, likes a sharp track: apprec drop to sell grade.
1214 **ITALIAN AFFAIR** 25 [1] A Bailey 2-8-6 J Bramhill 4/1: 02: 2 ch f Fumo Di Londra - Sergentti nk **64**
(Common Grounds) Led, joined halfway, kept on well for press, just held nr fin: op 7/4: clr of rem: acts on fm.
1476 **CONSPIRACY THEORY** 9 [3] A Berry 2-8-6 O Pears 9/2: 63: 2 b f Fraam - Dewberry (Bay Express) 4 **54**
Cl up, outpcd fnl 2f: see 1476 (6f, claimer).
1381 **MONICA** 14 [7] W T Kemp 2-8-6 F Norton 50/1: 004: Prom, outpcd fnl 2f: no form. 3½ **45**
1381 **DOUBLE KAY** 14 [2] 2-8-11 D McGaffin (7) 9/4 JT FAV: 05: Bhd ldrs, strugg fnl 2f: bckd: see 1381. 3 **43**
1549 **JEWELLERY BOX** 5 [5] 2-8-6 G Baker (7) 16/1: 5056: Soon bhd: quick reapp: btr 1059 (debut, soft). 24 **2**

6 ran   Time 59.1 (1.6)   (D Bass)   J G Given Willoughton, Lincs

1685   2.40 TERRACE REST'NT CLAIMER 4YO+ (F)   7f30y rnd Firm -01 -42 Slow
£2380   £680   £340

*1559 **MAMMAS BOY 5** [5] A Berry 5-9-3 T E Durcan 9/4 FAV: -00411: 5 b g Rock City - Henpot (Alzao)   55
Held up in tch, prog to lead inside last, styd on well, rdn out: well bckd, op 9/2: recent Redcar wnr (sell): '99
wnr at Thirsk (sell) & Musselburgh (clmr, rtd 62): '98 Doncaster wnr (mdn h'cap) & Sandown (clmr, rtd 72): eff at
5/6f, suited by 7f: acts on firm & hvy, any track, likes Musselburgh: best without blinks & enjoys sells/clmrs.
1148 **DETROIT CITY 29** [13] B S Rothwell 5-8-11 J Bramhill 5/1: 000-42: 5 b g Distinctly North - Moyhora   1¼ 45
(Nashamaa) Led, rdn fnl 3f, hdd inside last, edged left/not pace of wnr cl home: on a fair mark: see 1148.
1603 **MR CUBE 3** [6] J M Bradley 10-8-7 (bl) D Watson (7) 11/2: 601043: 10 ch g Tate Gallery - Truly   1 39
Thankful (Graustark) Prom, rdn & kept on one pace fnl 2f: quick reapp: see 1336 (appr h'cap).
1601 **MAYDORO 3** [7] W M Brisbourne 7-8-0 G Baker (7) 11/1: -00624: Held up, kept on fnl 2f, not pace to chall. 1½ 29
1663 **PRIORY GARDENS 1** [8] 6-8-7 P Fitzsimons (5) 9/1: 440035: Pressed ldr 2f out, sn held: 3rd yesterday. hd 35
1258 **ZIBAK 22** [12] 6-8-13 F Lynch 14/1: 000-06: Keen/cl up 6f, op 12/1: '99 wnr at Ayr & Thirsk (sell   3½ 34
h'caps): rnr up '98 (mdn h'cap, rtd 42): eff at 6/7f on firm & gd/soft: runs well for appr/amat in selling company.
1191 **MONACO 27** [3] 6-8-7 P Hanagan (7) 20/1: 030-07: Rear, mod gains: plcd in '99 (rtd 41, seller):   1¾ 25
only mod form since '97 when rtd 72 for L Cumani: eff around 1m/9f on firm & gd/soft: return to further will suit.
1631 **ENCOUNTER 2** [1] 4-8-9 N Kennedy 8/1: 004008: Prom 6f: op 6/1, quick reapp: btr 787 (6f).   ¾ 26
4123} **POWER GAME 250** [4] 7-8-11 D McGaffin (7) 50/1: 0000-9: In tch, btn 2f out: reapp: rtd 50   3½ 21
last term (unplcd): '97 wnr at Musselburgh (2, h'caps, rtd 57, J Berry): eff at 1m on fast & gd/soft blinks, tried vis.
-- **SWOOSH** [11] 5-8-11 J Fanning 50/1: 4400/0: Cl up 4f, soon struggling: 10th: long flat abs, 8 mth   7 10
jmps abs (mod form): '98 wnr on the level at Nottingham (sell h'cap, J A Glover, rtd 58, unplcd on sand, rtd 56a): eff
at 1m, stays 10f: acts on fast & gd/soft grnd, prob fibresand: likes a stiff/gall track: best without blinks/visor.
824 **ROCK FALCON 59** [9] 7-9-7 O Pears 7/2: -000RR: Again ref to race: 2 mth abs, blnks omitted: plcd   0
form in '99 (rtd 101, Lady Herries, h'cap): '98 wnr at Kempton, Goodwood (h'caps) & Bath (stakes, rtd 102): ref to
race twice in '97: loves to dominate at 7f/1m on any track: acts on firm & hvy: best in blinks & has run well fresh.
11 ran   Time 1m 27.8 (2.9)   (Mrs J M Berry)   A Berry Cockerham, Lancs

1686   3.10 SHERATON GRAND HCAP 3YO+ 0-85 (D)   2m   Firm -01 -64 Slow   [83]
£6347   £1953   £976   £488   3 yo rec 21lb4 yo rec 1 lb

732 **CHRISTIANSTED 70** [5] F Murphy 5-9-9 (78) A Daly 2/1 FAV: 152-61: 5 ch g Soviet Lad - How True   82
(Known Fact) Chsd ldrs, prog to lead inside last & in command/pushed out cl home: slow time: nicely bckd: 10
wk abs: '99 Ripon (reapp) & Nottingham wnr (h'caps, rtd 75): 98/99 hurdles wnr at Catterick, Doncaster &
Musselburgh (juv nov h'cap, rtd 120h): eff at 12f/2m on firm & soft, any trk: gd weight carrier: runs well fresh.
1355 **STAR RAGE 15** [7] M Johnston 10-9-11 (80) J Fanning 9/4: -60F22: 10 b g Horage - Star Bound   1 82
(Crowned Prince) Led after 5f, pressed/rdn 3f out, hdd inside last, kept on: nicely bckd: v tough, see 714.
1478 **NORTHERN MOTTO 9** [4] J S Goldie 7-7-11 (52)(1ow)(4oh) F Norton 4/1: -50003: 7 b g Mtoto -   2 52
Soulful (Zino) Chsd ldr 5f out, one pace over 1f out: bckd: on a fair mark & likes Chester & Musselburgh.
1433 **TOTEM DANCER 12** [6] J L Eyre 7-8-6 (61) F Lynch 7/2: 001042: Held up, prog to press ldrs 3f out,   1¼ 60
held 1f out: tchd 4/1: prob stays a sharp 2m, best at 12/14f with more ease in the grnd: see 1087 (g/s, 14f).
1355 **INDIANA PRINCESS 15** [2] 7-8-13 (68) T Eaves (7) 5/1: 3-2635: Dictated the pace 5f, outpaced fnl 2f. 1¾ 65
4108} **SEATTLE ART 251** [1] 6-8-2 (55)(2ow) O Pears 50/1: 0/66-6: Held up, bhnd 3f out: reapp, jumps fit   24 36
(mod form): mod form since plcd in mdns in '97 (rtd 83, H Cecil): formerly eff at 12/14f, handles firm & gd/soft.
6 ran   Time 3m 32.6 (10.1)   (John Duddy)   F Murphy West Witton, N Yorks

1687   3.40 SCOTTISH SPRINT HCAP 3YO+ 0-95 (C)   5f   Firm -01 +09 Fast   [90]
£15210   £4680   £2340   £1170   3 yo rec 7 lb Raced across track, no advantage

1383 **XANADU 14** [9] Miss L A Perratt 4-8-2 (64) Iona Wands (5) 14/1: 011201: 4 ch g Casteddu - Bellatrix   69
(Persian Bold) Made all far side, rdn/held on gamely inside last: fast time (course record): earlier scored
twice at Hamilton (h'cap & classified stakes): '99 scorer again at Hamilton (seller) & Carlisle (h'cap, rtd 56): eff
at 5/6f: relishes fast/firm grnd, stiff/undulating or sharp track, loves Hamilton: likes to force the pace.
*1654 **AMARANTH 1** [2] J L Eyre 4-8-12 (74)(t)(6ex) R Cody Boutcher (7) 9/1: 000012: 4 b g Mujadil -   shd 78
Zoes Delight (Hatim) Soon prom, rdn & chall/drifted right over 1f out, styd on well, just held: op 6/1: quick
reapp & a fine effort under a 6lb pen having won at Ayr yesterday: see 1654 (6f).
1047 **SINGSONG 36** [1] A Berry 3-9-5 (88) D Allan (7) 20/1: 520-43: 3 b g Paris House - Miss Whittingham   ¾ 90
(Fayruz) Prom stands side, rdn & kept on inside last: op 16/1: see 1047 (firm h'cap).
1324 **JACKIES BABY 17** [15] W G M Turner 4-9-8 (84) A Daly 8/1: 000454: Cl up far side, onepace fnl 1f. nk 85
1529 **YORBA LINDA 7** [4] 5-9-10 (86) J Fanning 20/1: 09-405: Cl up stds side, onepace fnl 1f: op 12/1. ½ 85
1662 **RIVER TERN 1** [3] 7-8-7 (69) P Fitzsimons (5) 10/1: 45-606: In tch 4f: unplcd yesterday at Catterick. ½ 66
1412 **ZARAGOSSA 14** [8] 4-8-0 (62) P Fessey 16/1: 00-507: Prom centre 4f: plcd on reapp last term, (rtd   nk 58
77, h'cap): debut wnr in '98 (juv mdn, rtd 77 at best): suited by 5f on firm & gd/soft: runs well fresh.
*1629 **SIR SANDROVITCH 2** [16] 4-8-9 (71)(6ex) P Hanagan (7) 5/2 JT FAV: 000418: Slowly away & well bhnd   ¾ 65
far side, late gains, nrst fin: hvly bckd under 6lb pen: lost all chance at start, this is best forgotten.
104 **CROWDED AVENUE 192** [12] 8-9-9 (85) D Sweeney 12/1: 2040-9: Chsd ldrs far side 4f: op 10/1, 6 mth   ½ 77
abs: lightly raced last term (rtd 87, stakes): plcd twice in '98 (rtd 93): back in '96 scored at Sandown (h'cap):
suited by 5f on firm & good grnd, any track: best held up for a late run.
1629 **JOHAYRO 2** [13] 7-7-10 (58)(vis) J McAuley (4) 10/1: 500000: In tch far side 4f: 10th: qck reapp. ¾ 48
1384 **NIFTY MAJOR 14** [5] 3-9-0 (83) T E Durcan 20/1: 0-0200: Dwelt, al bhnd centre: 11th: see 1219. nk 72
1580 **TWICKERS 4** [11] 4-7-10 (58)(bl) G Baker (7) 33/1: 060000: Dwelt, in tch 3f: 12th, qck reapp: see 1580. 1 60
1140 **TUSCAN DREAM 30** [10] 5-8-11 (73) P Bradley (5) 12/1: 014-00: Cl up far side 4f: 13th: tch 40/1. 1¼ 57
-1580 **CRYHAVOC 6** [6] 6-9-6 (82) F Norton 5/2 JT FAV: 030320: Centre, never on terms: 14th: hvly bckd,   nk 65
tchd 4/1: quick reapp: eff at 5f, but needs a stiffer track on this trip, 6f ideal: see 716.
14 ran   Time 57.00 (u.5)   (David R Sutherland)   Miss L A Perratt Ayr, Strathclyde

MUSSELBURGH   SATURDAY JUNE 3RD   Righthand, Sharp Track

1688   **4.15 ERROL MDN 3YO+ (D)**   **5f**   **Firm -01   +03 Fast**
£2795   £860   £430   £215   3 yo rec 7 lb   Raced stands side

1516 **CORUNNA** 7 [1] A Berry 3-8-12 T E Durcan 11/8 FAV: 06-331: 3 b g Puissance - Kind Of Shy (Kind Of   **79**
Hush) Handy, rdn/led over 1f out, always holding rival, rdn out: nicely bckd: rnr up sev times last term (mdn, rtd
84): eff at 5/6f on firm & gd, dissap on soft: likes to race with/force the pace on a sharp/gall track: deserved this.
4476} **POLAR HAZE** 225 [1] Miss S E Hall 3-8-12 F Norton 15/8: 2026-2: 3 ch g Polar Falcon - Sky Music   1½ **74**
(Absalom) Chsd ldrs, chsd wnr over 1f out, not pace to chall: op 5/4, reapp: rnr up twice last term (rtd 79,
C/D mdn): eff at 5f, tried 6f, should now suit: acts on firm & gd grnd, sharp track.
1516 **SCAFELL** 7 [6] C Smith 3-8-12 (vis) J McAuley (5) 5/1: -02053: 3 b c Puissance - One Half Silver   4 **64**
(Plugged Nickle) Cl up, onepace fnl 2f: mdn after 13 starts: see 883.
901 **DUBAI NURSE** 51 [3] A R Dicken 6-9-0 A Daly 50/1: /00-04: Led till over 1f out, sn held: 7 wk abs.   2 **54$**
1578 **MOY** 4 [8] 5-9-0 (vis) J Fanning 10/1: 020505: Chsd ldrs, never on terms: qck reapp: see 1391, 466.   ½ **52$**
1430 **ROYAL CANARY** 12 [4] 3-8-12 C Lowther 50/1: 5-0006: Dwelt, soon outpcd: see 848.   6 **44**
901 **MISS SINCERE** 51 [7] 3-8-7 J Bramhill 16/1: 044047: Dwelt, al outpcd: abs: op 14/1: see 357 (sell).   5 **32**
1192 **THE ANGEL GABRIEL** 27 [2] 5-9-5 D McGaffin (7) 20/1: 000-08: Soon outpcd: no form.   8 **22**
8 ran   Time 57.3 (u0.2)   (Chris & Antonia Deuters)   A Berry Cockerham, Lancs

1689   **4.45 COCKATOO HCAP 3YO+ 0-60 (F)**   **1m1f**   **Firm -01   -12 Slow**   [60]
£2618   £748   £374   3 yo rec 12lb

1148 **KIDZ PLAY** 29 [13] J S Goldie 4-9-7 (53) F Lynch 9/2: 024-01: 4 b g Rudimentary - Saka Saka (Camden   **58**
Town) Made all & clr over 3f out, held on well inside last, rdn out: op 7/1: '99 Hamilton wnr (mdn h'cap, rtd 54):
rtd 68 in '98 (M Johnston): eff at 1m/10.8f on firm & gd: suits stiff/undul or sharp track: likes to force the pace.
1360 **FLOORSOTHEFOREST** 15 [1] Miss L A Perratt 4-9-11 (57) C Lowther 12/1: 4-6552: 4 ch g Forest Wind -   1¾ **58**
Ravensdale Rose (Henbit) Handy, outpcd 3f out, hung left/kept on well fnl 1f: op 10/1: acts on firm, poss soft.
*1432 **OCTANE** 12 [9] W M Brisbourne 4-9-3 (49) J Fanning 3/1 FAV: -00313: 4 b g Cryptoclearance -   **49**
Something True (Sir Ivor) Rear, styd on fnl 3f, nrst fin: op 4/1: acts on firm/fast: needs 10f+: see 1432 (12f).
1361 **SECONDS AWAY** 15 [8] J S Goldie 9-7-10 (28) (3oh) J McAuley (5) 20/1: 00-604: Held up, kept on fnl 2f.   shd **28**
1331 **MINJARA** 17 [15] 5-8-6 (38) D Sweeney 4/1: 040-55: In tch, held over 1f out: op 3/1: see 1331.   1¾ **35**
1360 **QUALITAIR SURVIVOR** 15 [16] 5-8-7 (39)(vis) J Bramhill 14/1: 45-046: Mid div, onepace fnl 2f: see 1360.   ¾ **35**
*1365 **SEDONA** 15 [5] 3-8-12 (56) P Fitzsimons (5) 9/1: 5U3017: Dwelt/rear, mod gains fnl 2f: op 7/1.   nk **51**
1414 **STITCH IN TIME** 14 [11] 4-8-13 (45) T E Durcan 6/1: -22338: In tch, rdn/btn 1f out: op 4/1: mdn.   ½ **39**
1361 **DONE WELL** 15 [10] 8-7-10 (28)(t) (6oh) P Hanagan (4) 50/1: 000009: Held up, nvr factor: see 903 (14f).   2 **18**
1241 **LORD ADVOCATE** 23 [14] 12-7-10 (28)(vis)(1oh) P Fessey 66/1: 60-000: Chsd ldrs, outpcd fnl 3f: 10th: 5 **8**
plcd form last term (rtd 37, h'cap): '98 Hamilton wnr (h'cap, rtd 46 at best): eff at 11/15f: front rnr, loves firm
& gd, Hamilton & Musselburgh: suited by vis/blinks: return to further & front running tactics will suit.
1416 **NOTATION** 12 [12] 6-7-10 (28)(bl)(10oh) G Baker (7) 66/1: 040000: Dwelt, eff 3f out, no impress: 11th.   ¾ **7**
1361 **ACE OF TRUMPS** 15 [6] 4-9-5 (51)(t) N Kennedy 14/1: 002100: In tch 6f: 14th: op 8/1: btr 1195 (clmr).   0
1300 **FLAXEN PRIDE** 19 [3] 5-8-7 (39) F Norton 10/1: 156-00: In tch 6f: 15th: op 14/1: see 1300.   **0**
1361 **Sarmatian** 15 [4] 9-8-0 (30)(t) (2ow) A Daly 66/1:   1241 **Ribble Princess** 23 [7] 5-8-4 (36) Iona Wands (5) 20/1:
855 **Irsal** 54 [2] 6-7-10 (28)(bl)(3oh) Claire Bryan (5) 33/1:
16 ran   Time 1m 51.7 (1.0)   (W M Johnstone)   J S Goldie Uplawmoor, E Renfrews

NEWMARKET (Rowley)   SATURDAY JUNE 3RD   Righthand, Stiff, Galloping Track

Official Going GOOD/FIRM. Stalls: Far Side.

1690   **2.00 WATES GROUP AMAT HCAP 4YO+ 0-70 (E)**   **1m str**   **Good/Firm 24   -33 Slow**   [42]
£5486   £1688   £844   £422   Stalls 1-6 & 8 raced stands side

*1330 **NO EXTRAS** 17 [19] G L Moore 10-12-0 (70) Mr R L Moore (5) 10/1: 040-11: 10 b g Efisio - Parkland   **74**
Rose (Sweet Candy) Held up far side, prog 2f out, led ent fnl 1f, ran on strongly, rdn out: op 7/1, top-weight:
recent reapp wnr here at Brighton (h'cap): '99 Windsor wnr (class stks, rtd 83): '98 wnr again here at Newmarket (h'cap)
& in '97 scored at Goodwood (2, h'caps): stays an easy 10f, v eff arnd 7f/1m: acts on firm & soft grnd, handles
any trk, loves Goodwood & Newmarket: runs well fresh: tough 10yo who is a fine mount for an amateur.
1520 **RAMBO WALTZER** 25 [25] Miss S J Wilton 8-10-12 (54) Mr T Best (5) 10/1: 261132: 8 b g Rambo Dancer -   ¾ **56**
Vindictive Lady (Foolish Pleasure) Chsd ldrs far side, rdn & styd on well fnl 1f, only just btn: in fine form.
4481} **PADHAMS GREEN** 224 [12] B W Hills 4-11-6 (62) Mr C B Hills (3) 20/1: 0600-3: 4 b g Aragon - Double   shd **64**
Dutch (Nicholas Bill) Hld up far side, imprvd 2f out, ran on fnl 1f & nrst fin: reapp: in '99 trained by M Tompkins
to win at Salisbury (appr h'cap, rtd 69): eff at 7f/1m on gd & firm grnd: handles a gall trk: sharper next time.
1300 **MISSILE TOE** 19 [4] D Morris 7-10-2 (44) Mr Paul J Morris (5) 10/1: 00-554: Prom on stands side,   nk **45**
rdn & drifted to far side fnl 1f, fin v well & only just btn: fine eff in the circumstances: turn not far away.
1296 **SILVER SECRET** 19 [22] 6-9-10 (38) Mr M Murphy(5) 25/1: 463-05: Prom far side, outpcd 2f out,   hd **39**
rallied fnl 1f: only btn arnd 1L: '99 wnr here at Newmarket (amat h'cap, rtd 45): '97 Folkestone wnr (mdn auct,
M Heaton Ellis, rtd 52): acts on gd & firm: well h'capped & hinted at a return to form.
1611 **SAMARA SONG** 3 [1] Mr A Jones(3) 8/1 FAV: --00526: Prom stands side, styd on under   shd **57**
press fnl 1f: qck reapp: not disgraced running on prob the 'wrong side': see 1611.
1370 **KUSTOM KIT KEVIN** 15 [26] 4-9-12 (40)(t) Mr S Dobson(5) 33/1: 010007: Chsd ldrs far side, led   shd **41**
briefly dist, no extra in last: far from disgraced, btn only around 1L: back to form: see 584 (AW mdn h'cap).
1203 **JIBEREEN** 26 [8] 10-8 (50) Mr M Foley (5) 25/1: 043108: Rear far side, kept on fnl 2f, nrst fin.   ½ **50**
1520 **ON PORPOISE** 7 [10] 4-9-13 (41) Mr M D'Arcy (5) 50/1: 00-009: Dwelt far side, styd on fnl 1f   ½ **40**
despite edging left, nrst fin: see 1520.
1498 **PIPPAS PRIDE** 8 [13] 5-10-0 (42) Mr S Drake(5) 33/1: 154350: Chsd ldrs far side, onepcd fnl 1f: 10th.   ¾ **39**
*1520 **HOH GEM** 7 [16] 4-10-7 (49) Mr G Richards (5) 11/1: -01410: Rear, imprvd 2f out, not qckn fnl 1f: 11th.   1 **44**
*1296 **DERRYQUIN** 19 [3] 5-11-2 (58)(bl) Mr M Nicolls (5) 14/1: -00-010: Prom far side, outpcd fnl 1f: nk **52**
fin 12th: prob had the worst of the draw & shld be given another chance after 1296.
1348 **RED DELIRIUM** 16 [11] 4-11-10 (66) Mr J Gee (5) 20/1: -20000: Prom far side, onepcd fnl 1½f: 13th.   2 **56**
1442 **ITS OUR SECRET** 12 [27] 4-11-10 (66) Mr R Walford 10/1: 00-240: Led far side, drifted left & hdd dist,   3 **50**

553

fdd into 14th: reportedly lost both front shoes & not disgraced in the circumstances: see 1442, 1279.
1496 **CASSANDRA 8** [7] 4-10-13 (55) Mr W Fearon (7) 25/1: -25020: Front rank 4f far side, wknd dist: 15th. *1* **37**
1615 **ROGER ROSS 3** [5] 5-10-3 (45)(bl) Mr G Carenza(7) 25/1: 0-5000: Dwelt, recovered & prom till 3f *nk* **26**
out stands side: fin 16th, qck reapp: see 102 (AW).
1520 **SWING ALONG 7** [8] 5-11-5 (61) Mr V Coogan (5) 12/1: 340020: Dwelt, nvr trbld ldrs on stands side: 17th. *1* **40**
*1393 **CHAMPAGNE GB 14** [15] 4-11-0 (56)(bl) Mr J Unett(7) 14/1: 503010: Dwelt & bhd far side, nvr dngrs: 24th. **0**
1422 **Saint George 12** [20] 4-10-0 (42) Mr L Phillips (5) 50/1:1261 **Sibertigo 22** [14] 4-10-13 (55) Mr J J Best (7) 33/1:
1498 **Neronian 8** [17] 6-9-10 (38)(5oh) Mr S Rees (7) 40/1: 1300 **Consort 19** [24] 7-10-12 (54) Mr J Darby(6) 33/1:
1393 **Consultant 14** [9] 4-10-1 (43) Mr P Collington(7) 25/1:
1570 **Coughlans Gift 5** [18] 4-11-1 (57) Mr M Nakauchida(5) 33/1:
1272 **The Bargate Fox 22** [21] 4-10-10 (52) Mr Nicky Tinkler (5) 33/1:
1139 **Xsynna 30** [2] 4-10-12 (54) Mr A Carson(7) 25/1: 1611 **Alfahaal 3** [6] 7-10-3 (45) Mr V Lukaniuk(3) 33/1:
27 ran Time 1m 41.10 (4.60) (K Higson) G L Moore Woodingdean, E Sussex

1691

2.30 MIX-IT MDN 2YO (D) 6f str Good/Firm 24 -27 Slow
£5252 £1616 £808 £404

-- **VOLATA** [2] M H Tompkins 2-9-0 S Sanders 25/1: -1: 2 b c Flying Spur - Musianica (Music Boy) **92+**
Dwelt, gd hdwy from rear 2f out, ran on strongly to lead ins fnl 1f, rdn out & won going away: 37,000gns Feb foal: half-brother to sev wnrs, inc a couple of useful mid-dist scorers: dam a 6f winning 2yo: eff over a stiff 6f, 7f suit: acts on fast, runs well fresh: has a turn of foot, potentially v smart & takes his ch in the Coventry Stks.
-- **ARHAAFF** [8] M R Channon 2-8-9 J Fortune 4/1 JT FAV: -2: 2 b f Danehill - Mosaique Bleue *¾* **83+**
(Shirley Heights) Nvr far away, ev ch fnl 1f, not pace to repel wnr cl-home: bckd from 8/1, drvn & flashed tail on debut: Mar foal, cost 170,000gns: half-sister to sev wnrs, incl 10f scorer Subtle Power: sire a top-class sprinter/miler: eff over a stiff 6f on fast, 7f suit: held in some regard & turn is merely delayed.
1403 **ZELOSO 14** [13] J L Dunlop 2-9-0 Pat Eddery 10/1: -03: 2 b c Alzao - Silk Petal (Petorius) *1½* **84+**
Chsd ldrs, sltly outpcd 2f out, styd on eye-catchingly under hands-&-heels riding ins last: eff over a 6f on fast grnd, 7f will suit: most encouraging effort & shld not be missed next time: see 1403.
-- **PAGLIACCI** [10] Sir Michael Stoute 2-9-0 T Quinn 6/1: -4: Front rank, ev ch 2f out till ins last, no *nk* **83**
extra cl-home: op 4/1, racecourse bow: Mar foal, dam a high-class juv wnr: sire a top-class miler in the USA: eff at 6f on fast grnd, prob already needs 7f: sure to learn plenty from this & pick up a mdn.
-- **CAUSTIC WIT** [17] 2-9-0 J Reid 16/1: -5: Rcd keenly in mid-div, styd on nicely under hands-&-heels *shd* **83+**
riding fnl 1f: Mar foal, dam a 1m wnr in France: first foal, sire a top-class sprinter: plenty to like about this most encouraging debut: eff at 6f & fast grnd, 7f sure to suit: one to keep a close eye on.
1426 **JOHNNY REB 12** [6] 2-9-0 R Hughes 4/1 JT FAV: -26: Set pace till 2f out, no extra: well bckd: not *½* **82**
disgraced in an above-average mdn: will find easier tasks & be plcd to effect: see 1426 (debut).
-- **TRUSTTHUNDER** [15] 2-8-9 J Weaver 50/1: -7: Slowly away, fin well after struggling earlier on, nvr *2* **71**
nrr: cost 7,000gns as a 2yo: Mar foal, sire a top-class miler: N Littmonden filly who will learn from this.
-- **LOST AT SEA** [7] 2-9-0 N Callan 50/1: -8: In tch, onepcd fnl 2f on debut: 10,000gns Mar foal, *nk* **75**
half-brother to sev wnrs, incl over 10f: dam a sprint winning 2yo, sire a top-class miler: with K Burke.
-- **SWEET PROSPECT** [9] 2-8-9 N Pollard 50/1: -9: Dwelt, recovered & in tch, no impress fnl 2f: Apr *1½* **66**
foal, cost 30,000gns: half-sister to a couple of sprinters: dam a 6f juv scorer, sire a top-class mid-dists performer.
-- **MAYTIME** [4] 2-8-9 M Fenton 12/1: -0: Rear, eff 2f out, nvr nr ldrs & fin 10th. *¾* **63**
-- **TORTUGUERO** [11] 2-9-0 M Hills 10/1: -0: Rear, eff halfway, nvr nr to chall: fin 11th, mkt drifter. *1* **65**
-- **SHARP ACT** [3] 2-9-0 R Hills 16/1: -0: Prom 4½f, fdd into 12th. *hd* **65**
-- **WARDEN WARREN** [12] 2-9-0 P Robinson 16/1: -0: Slowly away, not recover on debut: fin 13th. *1* **62**
-- **Jamila** [16] 2-8-9 W Ryan 50/1: -- **Tamiami Trail** [1] 2-9-0 D R McCabe 40/1:
-- **Carraca** [14] 2-9-0 J P Spencer 16/1:
16 ran Time 1m 13.91 (3.11) (J Ellis) M H Tompkins Newmarket.

1692

3.05 BRITISH HOLIDAYS MDN 3YO (D) 1m str Good/Firm 24 -15 Slow
£5200 £1600 £800 £400

4606} **JATHAABEH 211** [12] M A Jarvis 3-8-9 P Robinson 9/1: 0-1: 3 ch f Nashwan - Pastorale (Nureyev) **90+**
Trkd ldrs racing keenly, qcknd to lead ent fnl 1f, ran on strongly, rdn out: tchd 14/1: unplcd in a Doncaster mdn on sole juv start: half-sister to sev wnrs, incl a smart 7f 2yo scorer: dam won over 7f: eff over a stiff 1m, will stay further: acts on fast grnd & runs well fresh: showed a gd turn of foot today, win in stronger company.
-- **ASLY** [3] Sir Michael Stoute 3-9-0 R Hills 7/1: -2: 3 br c Riverman - La Pepite (Mr Prospector) *1* **92+**
Waited with, gd hdwy to press wnr ent fnl 1f, pulled clr with wnr but al 2nd best: debut: $400,000 purchase: dam from a smart American family: eff over a stiff 1m on fast grnd, mid-dist bred: sure to benefit from today's experience & looks nailed on to win in mdn company.
-- **DEXTROUS** [4] H R A Cecil 3-9-0 W Ryan 12/1: -3: 3 gr c Machiavellian - Heavenley Cause (Grey *3½* **85+**
Dawn II) Slowly away, gd hdwy from rear 2f out, ran on nicely under hands-&-heels riding, no ch with front 2: dam high-class juv in the USA: sire a top-class miler: eff at 1m, looks in need of 10f: handles fast grnd & a gall trk: v promising debut, sure to rate more highly & win at least a maiden.
1188 **DANCE WEST 27** [13] H R A Cecil 3-9-0 T Quinn 9/2: -004: Chsd ldrs, went on 2f out till hdd ent *hd* **85**
last, no extra: shorter priced stablemate of 3rd: see 1188, 1012.
-- **DIVULGE** [8] 3-9-0 J Fortune 9/4 FAV: -5: Dwelt, hdwy from rear to lead 3f out till 2f out, eased when *¾* **83**
held ins fnl 1f: well bckd, debut: bred to apprec 1m/10f: clrly showing ability at home & worth another chance.
-- **CLASSY IRISH** [7] 3-9-0 J P Spencer 20/1: -6: Rear, switched & some late hdwy, nvr nr ldrs on debut: *1¾* **79**
half-brother to a useful mid-dist wnr: bred to apprec 10f+: not given a hard ride & sure to improve considerably.
-- **CHOCSTAW** [11] 3-9-0 J Reid 33/1: -7: Trkd ldrs till wknd over 1f out: longer priced stablemate *5* **69**
of rnr-up: sire a top-class mid-dist performer: Sir M Stoute colt who is mid-dist bred.
-- **KATIYPOUR** [10] 3-9-0 Pat Eddery 9/1: -8: Prom 6f, fdd: tchd 12/1, debut: longer priced stablemate *½* **68**
of rnr-up: half-brother to a smart mid-dist wnr: will apprec 10f+ now.
4379} **BLINDING MISSION 232** [1] 3-8-9 J Weaver 16/1: 50-9: Rcd keenly rear, nvr a factor: twice rcd juv, *1½* **60**
prom in mdn company (rtd 78): sister to a 5f juv scorer: with J Noseda & now quals for h'caps.
4432} **BAJAN BROKER 228** [5] 3-8-9 A Clark 33/1: 43-0: Effort from rear 3f out, btn over 1f out: fin 10th. *6* **48**
4607} **POLAR STAR 211** [2] 3-9-0 S Sanders 12/1: 02-0: Trkd ldrs & rcd keenly, eased when btn fnl 2f: 11th. *5* **43**
4600} **ROCCIOSO 212** [6] 3-9-0 R Smith (5) 66/1: 00-0: Set pace 4f, grad wknd: fin last, reapp. *5* **33**
983 **DANDILUM 44** [9] 3-9-0 R Hughes 8/1: 022-4W: Withdrawn, not under starter's orders: see 983. **0**
13 ran Time 1m 39.62 (3.12) (Sheikh Ahmed Al Maktoum) M A Jarvis Newmarket.

1693	**3.35 LISTED KING CHARLES II STKS 3YO (A)** **7f str Good/Firm 24 +12 Fast**
	£14616 £5544 £2772 £1260

*983   **SHIBBOLETH** 44 [7] H R A Cecil 3-8-12 (t) T Quinn 2/1 FAV: -11: 3 b c Danzig - Razyana (His Majesty)   **115+**
Trkd ldrs, qcknd into lead 1f out, styd on strongly under hands-&-heels riding, cmftbly: hvly bckd, val for 3L+,
gd time, 6 wk abs: recent debut wnr here at Newmarket (mdn): brother to a high-class miler, dam 10f performer:
eff at 7f, will stay 1m: acts on fast & gd/soft, runs well fresh: handles a stiff trk: wore a t-strap today: smart,
lightly rcd & fast improving colt who could develop into a top-class miler: earned his place in the St James's Palace.

4428}   **OBSERVATORY** 228 [6] J H M Gosden 3-8-12 J Fortune 12/1: 141-2: 3 ch c Distant View - Stellaria   1¼   108
(Roberto) Slowly away, rdn to impr 2f out, fin v well but no ch with wnr: reapp: '99 Yarmouth wnr (2, mdn &
stks, rtd 100): eff over a stiff 7f, 1m will suit: acts on gd & fast, runs well fresh: useful, improving colt who
reportedly heads for the Jersey Stks at R Ascot, however may be seen to greater effect when stepped up to 1m.

1470   **FREE RIDER** 10 [9] I A Balding 3-8-12 M Hills 14/1: 1-2003: 3 b c Inchinor - Forever Roses   shd   108
(Forzando) Nvr far away, led briefly dist, not pace of front 2 cl-home: bckd to form in this tougher company.

--   **MAKAAREM** [3] Saeed bin Suroor 3-8-12 R Hills 9/2: 1-4: Chsd ldrs, ev ch 2f out, not qckn fnl 1f: 1¾   104
op 7/2, reapp: won sole juv start at M-Laffitte (6f, gd): half-brother to top-class miler Aljabr: eff at 7f:
handles fast grnd, acts on gd: useful colt, spot on next time & prob has a decent prize in him.

4175}   **TOUGH SPEED** 246 [4] 3-8-12 J Reid 9/2: -214-5: Mid-div, eff 2f out, no impress fnl 1f: nicely bckd,   1½   101
reapp: '99 Doncaster wnr (stks, rtd 109), subs 4th here at Newmarket (List): $230,000 purchase: eff at 7f, will
apprec 1m+: acts on gd & fast, handles a gall trk: not given a hard time today, sharper next time.

1530   **KOOKABURRA** 7 [5] 3-8-12 D R McCabe 50/1: 4-1046: Pushed along in rear, no impress fnl 1f.   nk   100
4175}   **MEADAAAR** 246 [8] 3-8-12 Pat Eddery 9/1: -213-7: Led till dist, no extra: reapp: '99 Yarmouth   1¼   97
wnr (stks), subs plcd in List (rtd 100): eff at 7f, 1m will suit: acts on gd & firm, handles a stiff/gall trk.

*1371   **JARN** 15 [1] 3-8-12 (t) W Supple 8/1: 10-18: Nvr nr ldrs: puzzling effort after 1371.   1½   94
1078   **IMPERIALIST** 33 [2] 3-8-7 R Hughes 50/1: 360-59: Chsd ldrs 5f, wknd qckly, fin last: poss not stay   29   49
7f, but this is not her form: see 1078.

9 ran   Time 1m 24.08 (0.88)   (K Abdulla)   H R A Cecil Newmarket.

1694	**4.10 CORAL HCAP 3YO 0-105 (B)** **6f Good/Firm 24 +01 Fast**	**[111]**
	£26000 £8000 £4000 £2000 Field raced in 2 Groups	

1371   **HUNTING LION** 15 [16] M R Channon 3-9-7 (104) Craig Williams 50/1: 23-001: 3 b c Piccolo - Jalopy   107
(Jalmood) In tch far side, ran on strongly to lead nr fin, rdn out: top-weight: '99 Bath wnr (mdn), subs rnr-up
in a Gr 2 (rtd 99+): eff over a stiff 6f, has tried 7f & shld stay: acts on fast & firm grnd, handles any trk:
can run well fresh & a gd weight carrier: genuine, very useful effort under joint top-weight in this valuable h'cap.

1534   **PERUVIAN CHIEF** 7 [18] N P Littmoden 3-8-4 (87) C Cogan(5) 33/1: 13-052: 3 b c Foxhound - John's   nk   88
Ballad (Ballad Rock) Held up far side, prog over 1f out, weaved his way thro' & fin well, just btn in a v cl fin:
rider reportedly given a 4 day careless riding ban: acts on fast grnd & on both AWs: useful sprinter, see 112.

1285   **CORRIDOR CREEPER** 21 [25] P W Harris 3-8-3 (86) A Beech (5) 16/1: 221-03: 3 ch c Polish Precedent - hd   87
Sonia Rose (Superbly) Chsd ldrs far side, went on 2f out till worn down cl-home: just btn in a thrilling fin.

*1219   **KATHOLOGY** 25 [26] D R C Elsworth 3-8-10 (93) N Pollard 12/1: 3-2114: Prom far side, ev ch fnl 1f,   shd   94
just btn in a bunched fin: far from disgraced on hat-trick bid: see 1219.

1534   **GLENROCK** 7 [8] 3-8-5 (88) A McGlone 40/1: 03-065: Front rank stands side, led that group 2f out,   ½   88
ran on well despite edging right, only just btn: sound run, again bhd today's 2nd in 1534, see 1215.

1406   **PEDRO JACK** 14 [20] 3-7-11 (80) D Glennon(7) 20/1: 0-3106: Chsd ldrs far side, led after 2f till   nk   79
2f out, rallied well & btn under 1L: loves to force the pace: see 1289.

1285   **LAS RAMBLAS** 21 [7] 3-7-10 (10h) G Sparkes(5) 40/1: 0-0007: Rear stands side, styd on well   shd   78
fnl 1f, nrst fin: only btn arnd 1L & right back to form here: worth another chance over further: see 982 (C/D).

1406   **NORFOLK REED** 14 [12] 3-8-3 (86) L Newman (5) 20/1: 20-458: Held up far side, ran on well fnl 1f,   shd   85
nrst fin: only btn arnd 1L: once again suggested that 7f will now suit: see 1406, 1285.

1534   **PUNCTUATE** 7 [1] 3-8-6 (89) M Hills 20/1: 1-0009: Held up stands side, styd on well fnl 1f, nvr nrr: ½   87
prob had the worst of the draw today: one to keep in mind for a decent h'cap when better drawn: see 1285, 988.

1406   **BLUE VELVET** 14 [15] 3-7-12 (81) G Bardwell (5) 33/1: 4-6000: Held up far side, styd on fnl 1f, nrst   shd   79
fin: fin 10th: fair effort & shld be plcd to win sprint h'caps this term: see 1285, 982.

1410   **ARABESQUE** 14 [13] 3-8-11 (94) T Quinn 4/1 JT FAV: 2-3140: Held up far side, nvr nr ldrs: fin 11th,   ¾   89
hvly bckd: highly tried in 1410, see 1175 (mdn).

1384   **BOLEYN CASTLE** 14 [19] 3-8-12 (95) A Clark 33/1: 65-050: Prom far side, not qckn fnl 1f: 12th.   nk   89
1406   **SALVIATI** 14 [24] 3-8-5 (88) Pat Eddery 7/1 JT FAV: 31-20: In tch far side, prog held when short   ½   81
of room in last: tchd 9/1, fin 13th: better expected after 1406.

1186   **BAILEYS WHIRLWIND** 27 [14] 3-8-10 (93) M Fenton 33/1: 110-50: Prom far side, onepcd fnl 1f: 14th.   hd   86
*1406   **RAVISHING** 14 [3] 3-7-12 (81) J Mackay(7) 8/1: 1-410: Held up stands side, nvr ldr ldrs: fin 15th.   shd   74
1470   **ZIETZIG** 10 [27] 3-7-10 (79)(10h) J Lowe 33/1: -05500: Held up far side, late prog fnl' nvr dngrs: 16th.   shd   72
1470   **EASTWAYS** 10 [4] 3-8-6 (89) R Hills 20/1: 003000: Chsd ldrs stands side, outpcd over 1f out,   nk   81
rallied cl-home: fin 17th: see 1308 (7f).

1285   **DESERT FURY** 21 [30] 3-9-0 (97) J Reid 25/1: 13-300: Led 2f far side, rem prom till wknd fnl 1f: 18th.   ¾   86
953   **JEMIMA** 46 [21] 3-9-7 (104) J Fortune 20/1: 100-00: Chsd ldrs far side, keeping on when hmpd ent   hd   93
fnl 1f, no ch after: fin 19th, 7 wk abs, jt top-weight: this is prob best forgotten: see 953 (7f here, Gr 3).

1285   **CONNECT** 21 [10] 3-8-3 (86) P Robinson 33/1: 36-000: Chsd ldrs 4f stands side, fin 20th: see 1186.   nk   74
1285   **RUSSIAN FOX** 15 [22] 3-8-9 (92) R Hughes 33/1: 01-000: Led 3f stands side, wknd fnl 1f: fin 21st.   hd   80
*1266   **BANAFSAJYH** 22 [23] 3-7-10 (79)(10h) A McCarthy (3) 8/1: 623-10: Trkd ldrs far side, short of room in   0
dist, eased when btn: well bckd, fin high in regard & better expected after impressive mdn win in 1266.

2042} Alfie Lee 352 [11] 3-8-10 (93) W Ryan 66/1:   1384 Blue Holly 14 [17] 3-7-10 (79)(3oh) A Polli (3) 50/1:
1470 Take Flite 10 [22] 3-7-10 (79) R Brisland (5) 33/1:   4507} Jailhouse Rocket 222 [29] 3-8-9 (92) M Worrell(7) 50/1:
1047 Pipadash 36 [28] 3-8-13 (96) J P Spencer 25/1:   4428} Dorchester 228 [9] 3-9-3 (100) S Sanders 33/1:
1371 Flowington 15 [5] 3-8-11 (94) J Weaver 33/1:   4140} Kamareyah 249 [6] 3-8-2 (85) W Supple 50/1:
30 ran   Time 1m 12.23 (1.43)   (Jaber Abdullah)   M R Channon West Isley, Berks.

1695   4.40 WATES CLASSIFIED STKS 3YO+ 0-90 (C)   1m4f   Good/Firm 24 -25 Slow
£7046   £2168   £1084   £542   3yo rec 15lb

1307 **THREE GREEN LEAVES** 18 [3] M Johnston 4-9-4 R Hills 9/2: 4-0001: 4 ch f Environment Friend - Kick   90
The Habit (Habitat) In tch, rdn into lead dist, held on, all out: tchd 6/1: twice rcd in '99, 4th at Newbury (List,
rtd 98): '98 wnr at Beverley (2), Newcastle, Cork & Pontefract (List, rtd 99): eff at 10/12f, may stay further:
acts on firm & soft, handles a stiff/gall trk: can force the pace & has run well fresh: game, can rate higher.
1342 **WESTENDER** 16 [4] W J Haggas 4-9-7 M Hills 9/4 FAV: 213-22: 4 b g In The Wings - Trude (Windwurf)   hd   92
Dwelt, no room over 1f out, ran on strongly under hands & heels ins last, just failed: hvly bckd: eff at 10f,
stays a stiff 12f well: rider looked confident he would get there, but just lost out: deserves to go one better.
*1373 **CARLYS QUEST** 15 [7] J Neville 6-9-9 (tvi) T Quinn 7/1: 02-313: 6 ch g Primo Dominie - Tuppy (Sharpen 1½   91
Up) Waited with, eff 2f out, styd on well but not pace of first 2: needs to be held up for a late run: see 1373.
1170 **FLOSSY** 28 [6] C W Thornton 4-9-4 J Fortune 7/1: 621-04: Held up, imprvd 2f out, not qckn ins last: ½   85
tough filly, back to form here: see 1170.
*1054 **BLUE** 35 [5] 4-9-9 Pat Eddery 7/2: 622/15: Trkd ldrs, led 2f out till dist, no extra: well bckd.   ¾   88
*848 **HIDDEN BRAVE** 56 [1] 3-8-8 J Reid 14/1: 2-16: Led till 2f out, no extra: 8 wk abs: not disgraced.   hd   88
1325 **FOREST FIRE** 17 [2] 5-9-4 W Ryan 12/1: 60-207: Rcd keenly & trkd ldr, ev ch 3f out till 2f out, fdd.   1¼   81
7 ran   Time 2m 34.70 (5.90)   (R N Pennell)   M Johnston Middleham, N.Yorks.

1696   5.15 NGK/FMI MDN STKS 3YO (D)   1m4f   Good/Firm 24 -18 Slow
£4758   £1464   £732   £366

1404 **DALAMPOUR** 14 [2] Sir Michael Stoute 3-9-0 Pat Eddery 2/5 FAV: -01: 3 b c Shernazar - Dalara   96+
(Doyoun) Dwelt, recovered to trk ldrs, went on 2f out, pushed clr fnl 1f, eased, cmftbly: val for 4L+, well bckd:
half-brother to high-class mid-dist wnr Daliapour: apprec this step up to 12f, 14f will suit: acts on fast grnd
& on a gall trk: improving, potentially useful stayer, win in better company.
1103 **TAKWIN** 31 [5] B Hanbury 3-9-0 (t) R Hills 20/1: -032: 3 b c Alzao - Gale Warning (Last Tycoon)   2   88
Trkd ldrs, eff 2f out, kept on fnl 1f but no ch with cmftble wnr: eff at 12f on fast: win a race: see 1103.
916 **ANDROMEDES** 50 [6] H R A Cecil 3-9-0 T Quinn 11/4: 3-43: 3 b c Sadler's Wells - Utr (Mr Prospector)   hd   88
Set pace till collared 2f out, no extra: nicely bckd, 7 wk abs: acts on fast & hvy, stays a stiff 12f: see 916.
1404 **CEDAR GROVE** 14 [1] A C Stewart 3-9-0 R Hughes 50/1: -004: Chsd ldr till wknd 3f out, well bhd: 16   64
well btn in mdns at Doncaster & Newbury prev: mid-dist bred colt.
1200 **CHARTERHOUSE** 26 [4] 3-9-0 M Hills 16/1: -05: Nvr a factor, btn fnl 2f, t.o.: see 1200.   15   42
-- **MILA** [3] 3-8-9 J Reid 50/1: -6: Slowly away, al bhd, t.o. fnl 2f on debut: dam a 7f winning   17   12
2yo in France: sire a high-class miler: with Miss I Foustok.
6 ran   Time 2m 33.86 (5.06)   (HH Aga Kan)   Sir Michael Stoute Newmarket.

1697   5.45 WATES GROUP MDN 3YO+ (D)   1m2f str   Good/Firm 24 +01 Fast
£4160   £1280   £640   £320   3yo rec 13lb

4277} **RASM** 239 [8] A C Stewart 3-8-11 W Supple 5/1: 3-1: 3 b c Darshaan - Northshiel (Northfields)   100
Chsd ldrs, prog to lead dist, ran on strongly, rdn out: gd time, reapp: plcd at Lingfield (mdn, rtd 89+) on sole
'99 start: 100,000gns half-brother to a 1m wnr: dam scored over 7f: appr this step up to 10f, may stay 12f: acts
on fast & soft, runs well fresh: handles a gall trk: useful, improving colt who looks sure to win more races.
1374 **BURNING SUNSET** 15 [5] H R A Cecil 3-8-6 T Quinn 11/4: 63-302: 3 ch f Caerleon - Lingerie (Shirley   1½   91
Heights) In tch, imprvd to chall 1f out, kept on ins last: nicely bckd: apprec this return to mdn company &
has shown enough to win similar: acts on fast & hvy grnd: shld relish 12f+: see 1045.
957 **TARBOUSH** 46 [3] H R A Cecil 3-8-11 W Ryan 16/1: -03: 3 b c Polish Precedent - Barboukh (Night   ¾   94
Shift) Prom, led 3f out till collared dist, no extra cl-home: longer priced stablemate of rnr-up, 7 wk abs, clr of 4th:
eff at 10f on fast grnd: half-brother to smart 10f French wnr Barbola: has shown enough to win a mdn, see 957.
1404 **STAGE DIRECTION** 14 [16] J H M Gosden 3-8-11 J Fortune 15/8 FAV: -44: Rcd keenly in mid-div, imprvd 3   89
2f out, not pace fnl 1f: bckd from 5/2: looks in need of 12f: again showed promise & must win in mdn company.
-- **POLI KNIGHT** [2] 3-8-6 M Hills 20/1: -5: Rear, rdn to impr 2f out, styd on nrst fin: cost 85,000gns: 1¼   82
related to a couple of useful wnrs: bred to apprec 10/12f: with J Hills & sure to learn from this.
-- **KIFTSGATE** [1] 3-8-11 Pat Eddery 16/1: -6: Held up, eye-catching hdwy under a kind ride 2f out,   ¾   86+
eased ins fnl 1f: drifted from 8/1 on debut: half-brother to smart mid-dist wnr Rambling Rose: mid-dist bred,
caught the eye in some style today: with Sir M Stoute & shld not be missed next time.
-- **TIKRAM** [12] 3-8-11 A McGlone 25/1: -7: Mid-div, not pace to chall on debut: stablemate of 2nd   2½   82
& 3rd: brother to 12f wnr Taming: with H Cecil.
789 **THUNDERING SURF** 65 [13] 3-8-11 A Clark 33/1: 5-08: Bhd, styd on nicely fnl 2f, nvr plcd to chall: ½   81+
9 wk abs: plenty to like about this h'cap qual run: one to keep a close eye on when tried in h'caps: see 789.
1281 **MOUJEEDA** 21 [7] 3-8-6 Craig Williams 33/1: 0-59: Prom 1m, fdd: see 1281.   1¼   74
378 **SALORY** 133 [15] 4-9-10 L Newman(5) 100/1: 000-30: Led till 3f out, fdd into 10th: long abs,   7   69$
top-weight: offic rtd just 48, treat this rating with caution: see 378 (sand).
1188 **NEW IBERIA** 27 [10] 3-8-11 J Reid 25/1: -00: Nvr a factor, btn fnl 2f: see 1188 (1m here).   4   63
1466 **WENSUM DANCER** 10 [4] 3-8-6 M Fenton 100/1: -040: Nvr better than mid-div, btn fnl 2f: fin 12th.   1   56$
-- **ALNAAMI** [1] 3-8-11 R Hills 10/1: -0: Chsd ldrs 7f, fdd: fin 17th, debut: dam a 7f wnr, from a   0
high-class family: sire a top-class mid-dist performer: with J Gosden.
1404 **High Drama** 14 [19] 3-8-11 R Birsland(5) 50/1:   1155 **Birdsong** 29 [14] 3-8-6 N Pollard 50/1:
-- **Republican Lady** [6] 8-9-5 P Shea (7) 100/1:   -- **Burning Daylight** [17] 3-8-11 S Sanders 33/1:
1466 **Only Words** 10 [11] 3-8-11 R Hughes 66/1:   1188 **Shinghaar** 27 [9] 3-8-11 J Weaver 33/1:
19 ran   Time 2m 04.41 (2.31)   (Hamdan Al Maktoum)   A C Stewart Newmarket.

Official Going   SOFT (HEAVY in places). Stalls: Inside, except 2m1f - Centre.

1698   **2.15 FURNITURE AUCT MDN DIV 1 2YO (F)**   **5f rnd**   **Soft 90**   **+00 Fast**
   £3152   £970   £485   £242

1513 **FALCON GOA 8** [13] N Tinkler 2-8-0 Kim Tinkler 4/1: -041: 2 b f Sri Pekan - Minden (Bluebird)   76
Cl up, led halfway, clr dist, readily: well bckd, fair juv effort: 5,500lr gns first foal, sire a sprinter:
apprec drop back to 5f, stays 6f: handles gd & soft grnd: improving.
--   **HARD TO LAY** [1] D J S Cosgrove 2-8-0 C Rutter 7/1: 2: 2 brf Dolphin Street - Yavarro (Raga   3½ 67
Navarro) Prom, eff 2f out, keeping on fin: debut, tchd 10/1: 8,000lr gns March foal, half-sister to 2 wnrs,
notably sprinter/fair miler Pelham, sire 6/7f performer: prob handles soft grnd & should apprec step up to 6f.
1102 **HARRIER 32** [9] T D Easterby 2-8-3 K Darley 6/4 FAV: 33: 2 b c Prince Of Birds - Casaveha (Persian   ½ 69
Bold) Led till halfway, one pace: nicely bckd: prob handles soft but more expected: see 1102.
--   **TOMTHEVIC** [4] J J Quinn 2-8-5 G Duffield 9/2: 4: Slow away, prom till fdd appr fnl 1f: debut: 1¼ 68
6,500lr gns Emarati March gelding, half-brother to 2 wnrs, dam a 1m/10f wnr:
1359 **GAZETTE IT TONIGHT 16** [3] P Fessey 14/1: 55: Handy till 2f out: op 7/1: see 1359.   1¾ 58
1385 **POLYPHONIC 15** [6] F Norton 40/1: 06: Bhnd from halfway: see 1385.   6 46
--   **JUST MISSED** [12] G Parkin 25/1: 7: Dwelt, never in it: op 16/1 on debut: 6,000gns   hd 51
Inchinor March foal, half-sister to 3 wnrs, dam 10f wnr, sire 7f performer.
--   **EL UNO** [2] 2-8-3 (BL) O Pears 33/1: 8: Dwelt, soon struggling: op 16/1 on debut: 3, 200lr gns   23 4
Elmaamul March foal, half-brother to 1m wnr Elghani, dam 6f juv wnr, sire 10f/12f performer: tried blnks.
8 ran   Time 1m 05.8 (4.5)   (Racingclubcouk)   N Tinkler Langton, N Yorks

---

1699   **2.45 ARENA LEISURE SELLER 3YO+ (E)**   **1m2f**   **Soft 90**   **-19 Slow**
   £3591   £1105   £552   £276   3 yo rec 13lb

1434 **FLOATING EMBER 6** [3] J L Eyre 3-8-0 F Norton 10/1: 00-001: 3 b f Rambo Dancer - Spark (Flash Of   39
Steel) Well plcd, led bef fnl 2f, ran on: no bid: unplcd in '99 (mdn, rtd 56): apprec 10f trip on soft in a sell.
1361 **HOT POTATO 16** [4] J S Wainwright 4-9-4 J McAuley (5) 10/1: 600502: 4 b c Roman Warrior - My Song   3½ 38
Of Songs (Norwick) Chsd ldrs, chsd wnr appr fnl 2f, same pace: op 16/1: stays 10f, handles soft & fibresand.
1496 **CODICIL 9** [9] M Dods 4-8-13 T Williams 9/2: 35-003: 2 ch f Then Again - Own Free Will   1 32
(Nicholas Bill) Mid div, prog to chall appr fnl 2f, soon onepace: clr of rem: see 1101.
--   **MISS CASH** [7] J R Turner 3-8-0 W Supple 40/1: 4: Hld up, imprvd 3f out, fdd 2f out: Rock Hopper filly.   8 23
1353 **LOYAL TOAST 16** [2] Kim Tinkler 7/1: 200305: Led till 2.5f out, wknd: stiff task, faster grnd suits.   ¾ 27
--   **BLACK MARK** [1] 4-9-4(4ow) N Pollard 33/1: 6: Al around mid div: Flat bow, jumps fit, no form.   ½ 26
3604} **TOEJAM 281** [14] 7-9-4 G Duffield 12/1: 5040-7: Held up, headway to press ldrs 3f out, wknd quickly   nk 26
2f out: reapp: flattered & well btn 5th in '99 (mdn, rtd 63).
846   **NAVAN PROJECT 57** [5] 6-9-4 P Fessey 14/1: 050-08: Never trbld ldrs: hdles fit, in March won at   1½ 24
Sedgefield (2m1f sell h'cap, gd & hvy, rtd 65h): lightly raced since '97 Tipperary win (9f h'cap on gd grnd, rtd 74).
2465} **PCS EUROCRUISER 335** [6] 4-9-4 D Mernagh (3) 16/1: 004U-9: Chsd ldrs till 3f out: reapp, no   ¾ 23
worthwhile form up to 1m last term, rtd $59 as a juv: prob handles gd/soft grnd.
1272 **FERNY FACTORS 23** [8] 4-9-4 K Fallon 7/2 FAV: -00000: Chsd ldrs, wknd quickly 3f out: 10th, bckd.   hd 23
4574} **Chrysolite 216** [11] 5-9-4 (tbl) O Pears 12/1:   301 **Little Lottie 146** [16] 4-8-13 G Baker (7) 20/1:
1353 **Sitting Pretty 16** [17] 4-8-13 R Winston 20/1:
13 ran   Time 2m 19.0 (10.9)   (Martin West)   J L Eyre Sutton Bank, N Yorks

---

1700   **3.15 CORAL NOV FILLIES STKS 2YO (D)**   **6f rnd**   **Soft 90**   **-02 Slow**
   £3640   £1120   £560   £280

--   **SAUDIA** [1] P F I Cole 2-8-11 K Darley 4/5 FAV: 1: 2 b f Gone West - Blint Pasha (Affirmed)   85+
Cl up, led appr fnl 1f, easily went clr: nicely bckd, debut: 540,000gns April foal, half-sister to 6 wnrs, dam
high-class at mid-dists: eff at 6f, 7f+ suit: acts on soft & runs well fresh: looks onew to follow.
--   **FORUM FINALE** [7] M Johnston 2-8-11 J Fanning 7/2: 2: 2 b f Silver Hawk - Silk Masque (Woodman)   5 72
Led till appr fnl 1f, outpcd: debut: $50,000 April 1st foal, dam 6f juv wnr, sire a miler: caught a useful sort.
1146 **NOT JUST A DREAM 30** [2] A Berry 2-8-11 J Carroll 12/1: 43: 2 b f Mujadil - Red Cloud (Taufan)   4 64
Chsd ldrs, unable to quicken fnl 2f: see 1146.
1408 **BAREFOOTED FLYER 15** [4] T D Barron 2-8-11 K Fallon 6/1: 024: Handy till 2f out: see 1408.   shd 63
--   **JELBA** [3] 2-8-11 W Supple 14/1: 5: Bhd from halfway: debut: 16,000gns Pursuit Of Love Feb   21 60
foal, half-sister to 4 wnrs, including 2 7f/1m juv scorers: sire 6f/1m performer: with N Littmoden.
5 ran   Time 1m 19.7 (5.6)   (H R H Prince Fahd Salman)   P F I Cole Whatcombe, Oxon

---

1701   **3.45 STANLEY LEISURE HCAP 3YO+ 0-80 (D)**   **2m1f22y**   **Soft 90**   **+04 Fast**   [79]
   £2571 £2571 £605   £302

1478 **LEDGENDRY LINE 10** [5] Mrs M Reveley 7-8-4 (55) A Culhane 9/2: 0-5641: 7 b g Mtoto - Elder (Niniski)   58
Waited on, stdy progress after 4f out, led bef 2f out, hard rdn, joined fnl stride: op 7/2, fair time, jockey given
3 day whip ban: earlier won nov chases at Kelso & Sedgefield (stays 3m1f, firm & hvy, rtd 115c): plcd sev times
in '99 (h'caps, rtd 62): sole prev Flat win in '97 at Ayr (mdn h'cap rtd 75): eff at 12f/2m1f: acts on firm & hvy.
1597 **GIVE AN INCH 4** [3] W Storey 5-8-7 (58) T Williams 4/1 JT FAV: 000001: 5 b m Inchinor - Top   dht 61
Heights (High Top) Held up, prog after 3f out, chsd ldr bef fnl 1f, kept on strongly to share the spoils:
quick reapp: '99 wnr here at Pontefract & Ayr (h'caps, rtd 71): '98 Redcar wnr (mdn sell) & Ayr wnr (2,
h'caps, rtd 64): eff at 2m/2m2f: acts on fast, likes gd/soft & hvy grnd, gall tracks, likes Ayr : well h'capped.
1597 **CHARMING ADMIRAL 4** [6] Mrs A Duffield 7-8-5 (56)(bl) G Duffield 11/2: 012003: 7 b g Shareef   1½ 57
Dancer - Lilac Charm (Bustino) Held up, rdn 3f out, late gains, no dngr: likes soft grnd & Pontefract: see 876.
1416 **BLACK ICE BOY 13** [7] R Bastiman 9-7-10 (47)(vis)(19oh) D Mernagh (0) 14/1: 000004: Led/dspd head   2 46$
till over 2f out, same pace: stiff task & surely flattered though loves Pontefract: see 141.
1087 **PROTOCOL 33** [8] 6-7-11 (47)(t)(1ow) F Norton 4/1 JT FAV: 002355: Prom, fdd rfnl 2f: hdles runner.   10 39
1329 **JAMAICAN FLIGHT 18** [2] 7-9-8 (55) K Fallon 5/1: 204006: Bhd ldrs till lost place appr fnl 3f: bckd.   16 48
1478 **YES KEEMO SABEE 10** [1] 5-8-5 (56)(VIS) A Nicholls (3) 7/1: 600007: Pulled hard & led halfway   10 25
till appr fnl 3f, wknd quickly: too free in visors, see 627

7 ran   Time 3m 54.9 (14.6)   (Black Type Racing)   Mrs M Reveley Muggleswick, Co Durham

1702 4.15 WILLIAM HILL HCAP 3YO+ 0-95 (C)   6f rnd   Soft 90   -03 Slow   [93]
£7540   £2320   £1160   £580   3 yo rec 8 lb

1262 **HORNBEAM** 23 [13] J R Jenkins 6-10-0 (93) M Tebbutt 4/1: -02241: 6 b h Rich Charlie - Thinkluckybelucky   97
(Maystreak) Well plcd, led appr fnl 1f, shade cmftbly: top-weight: 4th at York in '99 (val h'cap rtd 95): '98 Doncaster
wnr (List, rtd 107): eff at 6f/1m: handles firm, suited by gd/soft & hvy: runs well fresh, likes gall trks: useful.
*1517 **EASTER OGIL** 8 [7] I A Balding 5-9-1 (80)(vis) K Fallon 15/8 FAV: 006412: 5 ch g Pips Pride -   2½   80
Piney Pass (Persian Bold) Held up in tch, under press 3f out, styd on but no ch with wnr: shade btr 1517.
1504 **PIPS SONG** 9 [12] Dr J D Scargill 5-9-6 (85) J Lowe 3/1: 240103: 5 ch g Pips Pride - Friendly   ¾   83
Song (Song) Led till over 1f out, onepace: op 9/4: better held up: see 941 (C/D).
1383 **STORYTELLER** 15 [1] M Dods 6-9-1 (80)(vis) Dale Gibson 9/1: 4-0004: Chsd ldrs, chall 2f out, soon   1½   75
no extra: op 6/1: just best over a stiff 5f & giving weight to lesser rivals: see 1162.
1337 **ALASTAIR SMELLIE** 17 [11] 4-9-7 (86) N Pollard 9/2: 04-005: Al bhd: see 1173.   nk   80
5 ran   Time 1m 19.7 (5.6)   (K C Payne)   J R Jenkins Royston, Herts

1703 4.45 TOTE CLASSIFIED STKS 3YO 0-90 (C)   1m2f   Soft 90   +06 Fast
£6792   £2090   £1045   £522

3041} **CAROUSING** 309 [1] M Johnston 3-8-9 K Darley 4/1: 611-1: 3 b c Selkirk - Moon Carnival (Be My   92
Guest) Cl up, led appr fnl 1f, drvn out: op 3/1, gd time, reapp: '99 wnr at Lingfield (mdn) & Goodwood (nurs,
rtd 91): suited by step up to 10f (dam 12f wnr): runs well fresh on firm & soft, sharp/undulating tracks.
*1377 **FOREIGN SECRETARY** 16 [5] Sir Michael Stoute 3-8-13 K Fallon 5/4 FAV: 4-12: 3 b c Kingmambo -   ½   95
Misinskie (Nijinsky) Held up, prog to lead briefly appr fnl 1f, rallied, held near fin: nicely bckd, clr rem:
lost little in defeat over this longer trip, eff at 1m/10f: acts on gd & soft grnd: see 1377.
4536} **COEUR DE LA MER** 220 [2] J H M Gosden 3-8-8 J Carroll 5/2: 31-3: 3 b f Caerleon - Cochineal   5   83
(Vaguely Noble) Set gd pace till bef fnl 1f, no extra: reapp: landed fnl '99 start at Windsor (fill mdn,
rtd 88 A Foster): eff at 1m, bred to apprec mid-dists: acts on gd/soft & soft grnd, sharp trk.
990 **MISBEHAVE** 43 [4] M L W Bell 3-8-8 A Culhane 5/1: 10-044: Chsd ldrs, chall 2f out, sn btn, eased.   26   49
4 ran   Time 2m 16.5 (8.4)   (P D Savill)   M Johnston Middleham, N Yorks

1704 5.15 FURNITURE AUCT MDN DIV 2 2YO (F)   5f rnd   Soft 90   -20 Slow
£2136   £965   £482   £241

-- **DA VINCI** [4] J A Osborne 2-8-5 F Norton 9/2: 1: 2 b c Inzar - Tuft Hill (Grundy)   74
Prom, led below dist, rdn & hung left, just held on: debut: 7,600gns Feb foal: half-brother to 2 juv wnrs,
dam juv wnr: sire 6f/7f performer: eff at 5f on soft grnd & runs well fresh.
1381 **DOMINAITE** 15 [10] M W Easterby 2-8-3 G Parkin 7/4 FAV: -0032: 2 b g Komaite - Fairy Kingdom   nk   71
(Prince Sabo) Dwelt, mid div, switched & kept on fnl 1f, too late: well bckd from 5/2: acts on firm & soft, win at 6f.
1197 **GOLDEN WHISPER** 27 [12] I A Balding 2-7-12 A Nicholls (0) 7/2: -403: 2 b f Priolo - Gold Wind   2   61
(Marju) Never far away, led 2f out & short of room entering fnl 1f, one pace: handles gd/soft & soft.
1252 **ECKSCLUSIVE STORY** 23 [6] J J Quinn 2-8-3 G Duffield 16/1: -04: Well plcd & every ch till no   3   60
extra dist: Ir£9,200 Definite Article Feb foal, half-sister to a 7f wnr, sire act 12f.
1381 **BANNINGHAM BLIZ** 15 [9] 2-7-12 D Mernagh (2) 15/2: -0065: Never dangerous: see 1131.   2½   50
1476 **JEZADIL** 10 [8] 2-8-0 T Williams 14/1: 06: Prom till 2f out: op 10/1: see 1476.   nk   51
-- **FLINT** [11] 2-8-4(1ow) T Lucas 16/1: 7: Dwelt, improved halfway, wknd quickly appr fnl 1f: op 10/1   ¾   53
on debut: 2,000gns Fayruz April foal, sire a sprinter: with M Easterby.
-- **GRACEFUL EMPEROR** [3] J R Winston 20/1: 8: Rear, not much room appr fnl 1f, soon beaten: 8   36
debut: 7,000gns Emperor Jones April foal, half-brother to sev wnrs abroad, incl 1 juv, sire act 10f: with D Eddy.
1418 **FATHERS FOOTSTEPS** 13 [5] 2-8-3 J McAuley (5) 33/1: 09: Led till 2f out, soon btn: Clantime colt.   15   6
9 ran   Time 1m 06.8 (5.5)   (Andy Miller)   J A Osborne Lambourn, Berks

1705 5.45 PONTEFRACT APPR HCAP 3YO+ 0-70 (F)   1m2f   Soft 90   -14 Slow   [67]
£3360   £1034   £517   £258   3 yo rec 13lb

1570 **GENERATE** 6 [4] M J Polglase 4-9-4 (57) Hayley Turner (7) 9/2 JT FAV: 2D1021: 4 b f Generous -   63
Ivorine (Blushing Groom) In tch, prog 3f out, led appr fnl 1f, rdn out: quick reapp: earlier won at W'hampton,
(mdn, rtd 64a) & Southwell (appr h'cap): ex-French mdn: eff at 9/10f, stys 11f: acts on soft/hvy grnd &
fibresand, any track: gd ride for an inexperienced jockey.
1615 **SMARTER CHARTER** 4 [5] Mrs L Stubbs 7-9-2 (55) Kristin Stubbs (5) 9/2 JT FAV: 3-1232: 7 br g   ¾   59
Master Willie - Irene's Charter (Persian Bold) Hld up, improved 3f out & went 2nd dist, held towards fin: clr ren.
1207 **BUTTERSCOTCH** 27 [17] J L Eyre 4-8-10 (49) R Cody Boutcher 14/1: 00-003: 4 b g Aragon - Gwiffina   5   48
(Welsh Saint) Well plcd, led 4f out till appr fnl 1f, one pace: op 10/1: handls firm & soft: mdn, see 248.
*1364 **A DAY ON THE DUB** 16 [7] D Eddy 7-8-12 (51) P Hanagan 5/1: 644014: Pulled hard, bhd ldrs, chall   ½   49
2f out, soon no extra: tchd 6/1: btr 1364 (12f).
1104 **BOSS TWEED** 32 [2] 3-9-0 (66) J Mackay 7/1: 143105: In tch, chsd ldrs 3f out till 2f out: op 5/1, see 827.   4   60
1300 **OLLIES CHUCKLE** 20 [12] 5-8-8 (47) G Baker 14/1: 0-6006: In tch, prog/ch over 2f out, grad wknd.   hd   40
1432 **KATIE KOMAITE** 13 [9] 7-7-11 (36) Angela Hartley 7/1: 0-4007: Dwelt, never better than mid-div.   hd   29
1306 **ABLE PETE** 20 [18] 4-7-12 (37) G Sparkes (5) 1/1: 021468: Al towards rear: mdn, see 608.   2   28
822 **JAMMIE DODGER** 60 [14] 4-7-12 (37) Clare Roche 20/1: 40-009: Led till 4f out, lost place: 9 wk abs: 5   23
plcd in '99 (sell h'cap, rtd 43 & $60): unraced 2yo: stays 1m on gd grnd, handles gd/soft: with R Whitaker.
4340} **SUAVE FRANKIE** 235 [15] 4-8-9 (48) D Watson (3) 50/1: 4200-0: Mid div with 4f out: 10th on reapp   3½   30
dual '99 rnr up (h'cap, rtd 51, class stks, rtd 56, S Williams): eff at 12f, stays 2m on firm & gd, poss best blnkd.
1353 **STAMFORD HILL** 16 [3] 5-7-10 (35)(11oh) D Allan (1) 50/1: 0000: Behind fnl 4f: 11th, stiff task.   20   0
1432 **TIME LOSS** 13 [6] 5-8-8 (47) R Naylor (5) 9/1: -05400: Soon prom, lost tch appr str: 12th, st/mate 3rd.   8   1
12 ran   Time 2m 18.5 (10.4)   (Dominic Racing)   M J Polglase Southwell, Notts

Official Going   GOOD TO SOFT (GOOD in places). Stalls: Inside.

1706   2.25 KENILWORTH FILL MED AUCT MDN 2YO (E)   5f rnd   Good/Soft   Inapplicable
£3042   £936   £468   £234

1249 **STRANGE DESTINY** 24 [8] A Berry 2-8-11 G Carter 5/6 FAV: 31: 2 b f Mujadil - Blue Birds Fly   82
(Rainbow Quest): Veered left start but sn led, styd on strongly inside last, rdn out: nicely bckd: 27,000 gns
Feb foal, half-sister to a sprint juv wnr: eff at 5f, 6f sure to suit: acts on gd/soft: could rate higher.
1541 **PIVOTABLE** 8 [7] M L W Bell 2-8-11 M Fenton 100/30: -32: 2 ch f Pivotal - Lady Dowery (Manila):   2   76
Dwelt, sn chsg ldrs, no extra final 1f: gd run down in trip: eff at 5/6f on gd & soft: shld win similar sn.
1197 **MISTY BELLE** 27 [3] B R Millman 2-8-11 A McCarthy (3) 25/1: 03: 2 gr f Petong - La Belle Dominique   ¾   74
(Dominion): Front rank, rdn/not pace of wnr appr fnl 1f: left debut run bhd: dam a sprinter: stays 5f on gd/soft.
-- **ISLAND QUEEN** [6] R Hannon 2-8-11 R Hughes 7/1: 4: Dwelt, sn mid-div: hmpd halfway, ran green   2   70
but styd on inside last: 11,500 gns Turtle Island half-sister to a 6f 2yo wnr: dam plcd in Ireland: will improve.
-- **SEANS HONOR** [2] 2-8-11 T G McLaughlin 25/1: 5: Bhd, hdwy over 2f out, edged right & not pace   ¾   68
of wnr ins last: 5,500 gns Apr foal, sister to 5f 3yo scorer Ecudamah: dam prolific wnr in the US: 6f shld suit.
-- **CHERRY FLYER** [5] 2-8-11 G Faulkner (3) 16/1: 6: Dwelt, bhd, nvr a threat: Formidable Feb foal,   2½   62
half-sister to a 5/6f 2yo wnr: with S C Williams, better for race.
-- **WESTLIFE** [4] 2-8-11 R Mullen 25/1: 7: Prom, rdn/lost tch final 2f: Mar 1st foal: dam plcd   6   50
over 5f as a juv: speedily bred filly, with H Collingridge.
1124 **CEDAR JENEVA** 31 [9] 2-8-11 P Doe 33/1: 0U8: Mid-div, lost tch halfway: modest efforts so far.   6   38
1385 **TOMAMIE** 15 [10] 2-8-11 J Weaver 50/1: -009: Keen cl-up, rdn/fdd over 2f out, fin last: no form.   1½   35
9 ran   Time 1m 01.1   (Team Valor)   A Berry Cockerham, Lancs.

1707   2.55 RADLETT SELL HCAP 3YO+ 0-60 (G)   1m2f110y   Good/Soft   Inapplicable   [53]
£2270   £648   £324   3 yo rec 13lb

1666 **VANBOROUGH LAD** 2 [8] Dr J R J Naylor 11-8-6 (31) M Hills 7/1: -50021: 11 b g Precocious - Lustrous   35
(Golden Act): Mid-div, gd hdwy 2f out, styd on strongly & drvn out to lead line: op 5/1, no bid, qk reapp: busy
in '99, won at Bath (reapp) & Haydock (amat h'caps, rtd 50), prev term won at Windsor (h'cap): suited by 10f, stays
11.5f on firm, hvy & any trk, likes Bath: runs well fresh & goes well for an amat: tough & well h'capped 11yo.
1546 **BROUGHTONS MILL** 6 [12] W J Musson 5-9-0 (39) R Hughes 7/2 FAV: 3-0042: 5 gr g Ron's Victory -   shd   42
Sandra's Desire (Grey Desire): Trkd ldrs till went on ins last, styd on for press, hdd line: plcd on fnl '99
start (h'cap, rtd 40, also rtd 47a): eff arnd 10f: handles gd/soft & soft grnd: could land a sell h'cap.
1546 **NORTH ARDAR** 6 [4] R Brotherton 10-9-1 (40) N Callan 25/1: 500003: 10 b g Ardar - Langwaite   1   42
(Seaepic): Led, rdn/hdd just ins last, held cl-home: qck reapp: best run this term: see 178 (AW clmr).
1209 **CEDAR FLAG** 26 [1] R J O'Sullivan 6-9-1 (40) R Miles (6) 20/1: 431004: Front rank, hdwy to lead   ½   41
appr final 1f, hdd inside last, sn btn: previously appeared a return to 12f: see 682 (AW amat h'cap).
1546 **ROCK SCENE** 6 [19] 8-9-2 (41) P Dobbs (5) 7/1: /20655: Waited in, hdwy over 3f out, kept on.   3   38
1644 **UNIMPEACHABLE** 2 [10] 3-8-8 (47) D Sweeney 13/2: 000526: Slow start, sn chsg ldrs, rdn/lost tch   4   38
appr final 1f: ran 48hrs ago, btr 1644.
1274 **WEST END DANCER** 22 [16] 3-8-1 (40) M Henry 7/1: 0-0057: Held up, nvr a factor: btr 1274 (firm).   1½   29
1353 **CASHIKI** 16 [15] 4-8-13 (38) D Harrison 8/1: 0-6028: Prom, lost tch fnl 2f: op 6/1: btr 1353 (12f).   3½   24
1331 **MAX** 18 [11] 5-8-5 (30) R Brisland 33/1: -60009: Mid-div, fdd final 2f: see 256.   1½   14
1203 **COLONEL CUSTER** 27 [2] 5-8-9 (34) (bl) G Bardwell 20/1: 050650: Led, hdd over 1f out, wknd: 10th.   ¾   17
1465 **GOLD LANCE** 11 [14] 7-9-1 (40) S Sanders 10/1: 60-560: Hmpd after 2f, nvr a threat, 11th: see 1210.   1¼   21
1254 **RED CAFE** 23 [3] 4-9-10 (49) T G McLaughlin 20/1: 3/3600: Dwelt, sn in tch, fdd fnl 3f, 11th: up in trip.   1¾   28
1647 **Lady Wyn** 2 [9] 5-8-0 (25) Claire Bryan (5) 40/1:   1442 **Bodfari Signet** 13 [18] 4-9-3 (42)(bl) J Weaver 20/1:
2284] **La Petite Flameche** 342 [17] 5-9-4 (43) G Carter 40/1: 1505 **Noble Investment** 9 [7] 6-9-1 (40) M Fenton 25/1:
3823] **Essie** 270 [20] 3-9-1 (54)(bl) S Whitworth 33/1:   1292 **Cosmic Buzz** 20 [6] 3-8-12 (51)(VIS) M Roberts 20/1:
1423 **Silver Sky** 13 [13] 4-8-8 (33) Martin Dwyer 33/1:   4316] **California Son** 237 [5] 4-8-11 (36) R Thomas (7) 25/1: U
20 ran   Time 2m 19.7   (Mrs S P Elphick)   Dr J R J Naylor Shrewton, Wilts.

1708   3.25 SUNDAY MDN 3YO+ (D)   6f168y rnd   Good/Soft   Inapplicable
£4030   £1240   £620   £310   3 yo rec 10lb

1525 **KING SILCA** 8 [4] M R Channon 3-8-12 Craig Williams 7/2: 21: 3 b g Emarati - Silca-Cisa (Hallgate):   78
Trkd ldrs, went on ins fnl 1f, rdn out, shade cosy: half-brother to 2 wnrs incl smart 5f/1m performer Golden Silca:
eff arnd 6.8f, further should suit: acts on gd/soft & hvy grnd, likes a sharp trk: imprvg & could follow up.
-- **GWENDOLINE** [11] J R Fanshawe 3-8-7 O Urbina 7/1: 2: 3 b f Polar Falcon - Merlins Charm   1¾   71
(Bold Bidder): Mid-div, hdwy & ran green 2f out, styd on well inside last: nicely bckd on debut: dam
a 7f Gr 3 wnr as a 3yo: eff at 6.8f on gd/soft, further sure to suit: good debut & can win similar.
4306] **TERRA NOVA** 237 [12] R W Armstrong 3-8-7 R Price 10/1: 5246-3: 3 ch f Polar Falcon - Tarsa (Ballad   1   69
Rock): Trkd ldrs, led appr final 1f, hdd ins last, sn btn: op 7/1, clr rem on reapp: rnr-up twice in '99 (mdns,
rtd 79 at best): half-sister to a 6/7f juv wnr: eff at 6.7f on firm & gd/soft, handles soft.
1537 **BARNIE RUBBLE** 8 [1] A Bailey 4-9-8 G Carter 25/1: 0-64: Mid-div, rdn to impr 2f out, sn btn: 4   67
1444 **STALLONE** 12 [7] 3-8-12 J Weaver 10/1: -455: Dwelt, rear, prog appr final 1f, no threat to ldrs: 1½   64+
now qual for h'caps & will do better at 1m+ in that sphere: see 1444.
1525 **BLUE STREET** 8 [5] 4-9-8 G Faulkner (3) 50/1: 006: Mid-div at best: needs further.   ¾   62
1263 **BIRDSAND** 23 [2] 3-8-7 D Harrison 14/1: 0-67: Cl-up, rdn/wknd appr final 1f: see 1263.   nk   56
133 **LEVEL HEADED** 186 [6] 5-9-3 S Carson 66/1: 0050-8: Rcd keenly in mid-div, effort 2f out,   1   54S
no dngr: 6 mth abs, new stable: failed to make the frame for E Wheeler in '99 (mdns, rtd 40 at best):
rtd 40 on h'cap debut in '98: stays 1m, handles hvy: now with P W Hiatt.
-- **PROFOUND** [8] 4-9-8 R Hughes 25/1: 9: Dwelt, effort 2f out, short of room dist & sn held: debut.   nk   58
-- **DAWN TRAVELLER** [3] 3-8-7 R Mullen 33/1: 0: Rear, eff/no room over 1f out, sn btn: 10th: debut.   nk   52
1468 **HAREEBA** 11 [10] 3-8-7 S Sanders 5/1: 40: In tch, wknd qckly final 1f, fin 11th: btr 1468.   hd   51
956 **ALASAN** 47 [9] 3-8-12 F Lynch 3/1 FAV: 3-00: Chsd ldrs, wknd qckly appr final 1f, eased when btn,   1¾   52
fin last: drifted from 7/4 after 7 wk abs: twice well below best for new connections: see 956.
12 ran   Time 1m 24.8   (Tim Corby)   M R Channon West Isley, Berks.

1709   **3.55 WARWICK OAKS STKS 3YO+ (C)**   **1m2f110y Good/Soft Inapplicable**
£7035   £2310   £1155   3 yo rec 13lb

1170 **FIRST FANTASY** 29 [2] J R Fanshawe 4-9-0 M Hills 4/6 FAV: 11-051: 4 b f Be My Chief - Dreams   **84**
(Rainbow Quest): Rcd keenly chsg ldr, hdwy to lead 2f out, styd on well despite flashing tail ins last, rdn out:
nicely bckd at odds-on: '99 Warwick, Yarmouth (2) & Folkestone wnr (h'caps, rtd 82): eff arnd 10f on firm &
gd/soft grnd: acts on a sharp or fair trk, likes Yarmouth: genuine & tough.
*1343 **REVIVAL** 17 [1] Sir Michael Stoute 3-8-4 F Lynch 6/4: 0-12: 3 b f Sadler's Wells - Fearless Revival   1½ **82**
(Cozzene): Led, qcknd over 3f out, hdd 2f out, swtchd/styd on, not pace of wnr: acts on gd & gd/soft: see 1343.
1108 **SILK STOCKINGS** 32 [3] C E Brittain 3-8-0 P Doe 10/1: 0-03: 3 b f Trempolino - Waaria (Shareef   4 **72**
Dancer) Settled rear, rdn/no extra appr final 1f: up in trip.
3 ran   Time 2m 26.0 (11.8)   (Aylesfield Farms Ltd)   J R Fanshawe Newmarket.

1710   **4.25 FILLIES HCAP 3YO 0-75 (E)**   **6f168y rnd Good/Soft Inapplicable**   **[80]**
£3198   £984   £492   £246

1257 **PRINTSMITH** 23 [13] J Norton 3-8-1 (53) G Bardwell 33/1: 300-01: 3 br f Petardia - Black And Blaze   **58**
(Taufan): Trkd ldrs, rdn to lead final 1f, rdn out: '99 scorer at Catterick (sell, rtd 61): dam a 7f wnr: eff
at 5f, styd this lngr 6.8f trip well: acts on gd/soft, gd & a sharp/turning trk.
1405 **FOOTPRINTS** 15 [3] M Johnston 3-9-7 (73) M Hills 9/2 FAV: 1-1002: 3 b f College Chapel - Near Miracle   ¾ **76**
(Be My Guest): Mid-div, rdn/hdwy 2f out, styd on well inside last, just held: back to best here: eff at 5/6.8f.
1600 **TOP OF THE CLASS** 4 [7] Martyn Wane 3-8-10 (62) R Lappin 20/1: 0-0003: 3 b f Rudimentary -   1½ **63**
School Mum (Reprimand): Waited with, imprvg when short of room over 2f out, fin well, nrst fin: qck
reapp: '99 wnr at Ayr (nursery h'cap, rtd 71): eff at 6f/7.5f on gd & gd/soft grnd: runs well fresh on
a gall trk: shade unlucky in running here, should apprec a return to 7f+ & is on a fair mark.
1405 **MISTY MAGIC** 15 [1] P W Harris 3-8-2 (54) R Mullen 8/1: 30-004: Dwelt, rear, hdwy & styd on well   nk **54**
over 1f out, nvr nrr: further will suit: see 1085.
1390 **STOP THE TRAFFIC** 15 [5] 3-8-12 (64) R Morse 14/1: 522055: Mid-div, rdn/styd on appr fnl 1f, nrst fin.   shd **64**
1345 **BLACKPOOL MAMMAS** 17 [14] 3-9-0 (66) Claire Bryan (5) 7/1: 102006: Cl-up, rdn to lead appr final   ½ **65**
1f, hdd dist, sn btn: tchd 10/1: shade btr 1061.
1487 **DANCING LILY** 10 [11] 3-7-7 (48)(3oh) R Brisland (5) 25/1: 00-007: Rear, styd on fnl 1f, no dngr: up in trip.3 **39**
1397 **WELSH VALLEY** 15 [6] 3-9-0 (66) M Fenton 11/2: 2-2048: Prom, rdn/led 3f out, hdd over 1f out, wknd.   7 **49**
994 **GRANDMA ULLA** 43 [12] 3-8-12 (64) S Sanders 16/1: 00-009: Hmpd start, sn mid-div, bhd fnl 3f: abs.   2½ **43**
4490} **PAMELA ANSHAN** 225 [10] 3-7-10 (48)(6oh) A Polli 33/1: 000-0: Bhd, drvn/short of room 3f out,   1¼ **25**
no dngr, fin 10th: shwd little in 3 '99 mdn starts (rtd 45).
1397 **SILVER ARROW** 15 [15] 3-8-13 (65) R Hughes 12/1: 4-0400: Rcd wide in lead, came stands side &   1 **40**
hdd over 3f out, sn wknd, fin 11th: see 1035.
1202 **Flying Run** 27 [9] 3-8-5 (57) Martin Dwyer 33/1:   1405 **Cumbrian Princess** 15 [2] 3-8-7 (59) D Sweeney 20/1:
2471} **T Gs Girl** 335 [4] 3-8-8 (60) R Smith (5) 11/1:
14 ran   Time 1m 25.6 (1.6)   (Ecosse Racing)   J Norton High Hoyland, Sth Yorks.

1711   **4.55 SID HCAP 3YO+ 0-70 (E)**   **1m7f181y Good/Soft Inapplicable**   **[69]**
£3068   £944   £472   £236   3 yo rec 21lb4 yo rec 1 lb

1524 **MANE FRAME** 8 [2] H Morrison 5-9-10 (65) R Hughes 11/2 JT FAV: 4-0021: 5 b g Unfuwain - Moviegoer   **67**
(Pharly): Settled rear, smooth hdwy 5f out, swtchd & led dist, pushed out, cosily: '99 scorer at Windsor (stks),
Warwick & Sandown (h'caps, rtd 68), rnr-up prev term (mdn, rtd 73): now suited by 14f/2m & even further should
suit: acts on fast, hvy & any trk, likes a sharp one, esp Warwick: tough & improving, can go in again.
1276 **IRELANDS EYE** 22 [3] J Norton 5-8-13 (54) J Weaver 7/1: 60-332: 5 b g Shareef Dancer - So   1¼ **53**
Romantic (Teenoso): Held up, rdn to impr over 1f out, styd on inside last but no ch with cmftble wnr: in gd form.
1394 **SHARAF** 15 [1] W R Muir 7-8-10 (51) Sophie Mitchell 12/1: 5-P423: 7 b g Sadler's Wells - Marie de   shd **50**
Flandre (Crystal Palace): Front rank, rdn to lead appr final 1f, hdd dist, kept on, not pace of wnr: op 8/1, clr rem.
1023 **DOUBLE RUSH** 41 [10] G A Ham 8-8-3 (44)(t) G Carter 10/1: -61234: Settled rear, gd hdwy over   5 **38**
3f out, ev ch until outpcd inside last: rk wk abs: new stable, prev with T Keddy: see 1023.
1087 **VERSATILITY** 33 [18] 7-8-12 (53) M Hills 10/1: -53105: Led, hdd over 2f out, drvn/wknd: tchd 14/1.   6 **42**
1501 **MANFUL** 9 [13] 8-8-5 (46)(bl) N Callan 14/1: 030236: Dwelt, sn mid-div, rdn/lost tch fnl 3f: tchd 25/1.   1¼ **34**
1411 **SELIANA** 15 [15] 4-10-0 (70) M Roberts 11/2 JT FAV: 3-2347: Prom till went on appr final 2f,   ¾ **57**
hdd over 1f out, fdd: up in trip: see 1411 (14f).
1499 **REPTON** 1 [5] 5-7-11 (38)(1ow)(3oh) N Carlisle 20/1: 00-008: Dwelt, rear, hdwy when short of   1 **24**
room 3f out, no dngr: up in trip: see 1499.
1524 **NEEDWOOD SPIRIT** 8 [16] 5-9-5 (60) S Whitworth 12/1: -02009: Nvr a factor: btr 1167.   3 **43**
4577} **SHARAZAN** 216 [7] 7-9-0 (55) Claire Bryan (5) 8/1: 6060-0: Bhd, modest late gains, fin 10th: nk **38**
landed a hat-trick over hdles in 99/00, at Newbury, Towcester & Huntingdon (h'caps, rtd 104h, eff at
2m3f/3m2f on any grnd/trk): unplcd on the Flat in '99 (h'caps, rtd 60 at best): last won back in '97
in native Ireland (h'cap, J Oxx): eff at 12f/2m on gd & gd/soft: usually wears blnks, not today.
1440 **NOTEWORTHY** 13 [14] 4-8-12 (54) M Fenton 33/1: 45-000: Trkd ldrs, lost tch final 3f, fin 11th.   5 **31**
1614 **Urgent Reply** 4 [17] 7-7-10 (37)(t)(2oh) G Bardwell 25/1:
876 **Maknaas** 54 [6] 4-9-4 (60) A Clark 14/1:
1394 **United Front** 15 [4] 8-7-11 (38)(t) D Kinsella (7) 50/1:   1524 **My Legal Eagle** 8 [5] 6-9-7 (62) P Doe 12/1:
1276 **Hayaain** 22 [8] 7-9-10 (65) D Harrison 14/1:   608 **Brynkir** 96 [9] 6-7-12 (39) A Polli (3) 33/1:
*1416 **Vincent** 13 [12] 5-8-6 (47) S Sanders 14/1:
18 ran   Time 3m 34.0   (A J & M Arbib)   H Morrison East Ilsley, Berks.

1712   **5.25 BANBURY MDN STKS 3YO**   **5f**   **Good/Soft Inapplicable**
£3965   £1220   £610   £305

1500 **GDANSK** 9 [5] A Berry 3-9-0 G Carter 5/2 FAV: 5-4021: 3 b g Pips Pride - Merry Twinkle (Martinmas).   **72**
Made all, rdn & styd on strongly inside last: unplcd as a juv (mdns, rtd 70 at best): eff at 6f, apprec this
drop back to the minimum trip: acts on gd & gd/soft, stiff/undul or sharp trks: improved today.
1266 **DANCEMMA** 23 [6] M Blanshard 3-8-9 D Sweeney 7/1: 2-0002: 3 ch f Emarati - Hanglands (Bustino):   2 **64**
Front rank, rdn & kept on inside last, no threat to wnr: likes gd or softer grnd: see 837.

WARWICK   SUNDAY JUNE 4TH   Lefthand, Sharp, Turning Track

1479 **DAWN** 10 [2] J S Wainwright 3-8-9 M Roberts 9/1: 4-3603: 3 b f Owington - Realisatrice (Raja Baba): ½ 63
Prom, rdn & no extra inside final 1f: op 12/1 & apprec this softer surface today: see 1133.
1098 **ABSENT FRIENDS** 33 [9] J Cullinan 3-9-0 N Callan 20/1: 300-04: Mid-div, rdn to impr 2f out, sn 2½ 63
held: plcd once in '99 (nov stks, rtd 81), modest form subs: eff at 5f on soft.
1376 **PIETA** 16 [7] 3-8-9 O Urbina 14/1: 0005: Rdn in mid-div, no threat to ldrs: first sign of form 1 56$
but treat rating with caution, (offic only 50): see 729.
1516 **SKYLARK** 8 [8] 3-8-9 R Hughes 7/2: 000-46: Bhd, styd on late, no threat to ldrs: see 1516. hd 55
3634} **CRYSTAL CANYON** 281 [4] 3-8-9 S Sanders 12/1: 60-7: Dwelt, sn outpcd, modest late gains: 1¾ 51
unplcd in 2 juv starts (mdns, rtd 67 at best): 6f should suit.
558 **ELTARS** 104 [3] 3-8-9 (BL) S Righton 50/1: 0-008: Handy, rdn/fdd final 3f: long abs, blnkd. 4 46
1280 **LOCH DIAMOND** 22 [10] 3-8-9 J Weaver 5/1: 09: Unruly at start, al in rear: see 1280. shd 41
-- **MAVIS** [1] 3-8-9 D Harrison 20/1: 0: Prom, lost tch final 2f, fin 10th: speedily bred, with B Palling. 2½ 36
10 ran   Time 1m 0.3 (2.5)   (Chris & Antonia Deuters)   A Berry Cockerham, Lancs.

THIRSK   MONDAY JUNE 5TH   Lefthand, Flat, Oval Track

Official Going   SOFT. Stalls: Str Course - Stands Side, Round Course - Inside

1713   6.45 PICKERING FILLIES SELLER 2YO (E)   6f   Good/Soft 70 -60 Slow
£2892   £890   £445   £222

928 **LASTOFTHEWHALLEYS** 51 [8] K A Ryan 2-8-9 F Lynch 25/1: -001: 2 b f Noble Patriarch - Pride Of Whalley 62
(Fayruz) Sn prom, switched 1f out, rdn to lead ins last, styd on well: no bid, 7 wk abs: modest form prev, incl
on sand: apprec step up to 6f, will get further: acts on gd/soft: runs well fresh & enjoys sell grade.
1443 **WINDCHILL** 13 [5] T D Easterby 2-8-9 K Darley 4/7 FAV: -0022: 2 ch f Handsome Sailor - Baroness 2 56
Gymcrak (Pharly) Sn prom, rdn/ch fnl 1f, held nr fin: hvly bckd: acts on gd & gd/soft: apprec step up to 6f.
1443 **HOPGROVE** 13 [6] M Brittain 2-8-9 D Mernagh (3) 20/1: 6603: 2 b f So Factual - Awham (Lear Fan) hd 55
Chsd ldrs, rdn/led over 1f out, hdd ins last & no extra cl-home: clr rem, op 12/1: eff at 6f on gd/sft grnd.
1679 **IMPREZA** 2 [9] Miss A Stokell 2-8-9 (VIS) P Fessey 50/1: 04: Dwelt, bhd, mod prog: visor: qck reapp. 10 35
1136 **MISS TOPOGINO** 32 [7] 2-8-9 V Halliday 25/1: 05: Chsd ldrs, btn 2f out: see 1336. 2 31
1418 **DUSTY PRINCESS** 14 [2] 2-8-9 Dean McKeown 11/2: 06: Led till over 1f out, wknd qckly: see 1418 (5f). hd 30
1396 **ELEANOR J** 16 [1] 2-8-9 (VIS) R Ffrench 14/1: 4607: Bhd 2f out: visor, op 14/1: btr 856, 722 (AW). shd 30
-- **BELLS BEACH** [4] 2-8-9 O Pears 9/2: 8: Dwelt, sn well bhd: op 7/2: General Monash filly, Mar 29 0
foal, cost 3,000gns: dam unrcd, sire a speedy juv & a half brother to high-class miler King Of Kings.
8 ran   Time 1m 17.3 (7.8)   (Mrs C M Barlow)   K A Ryan Hambleton, N Yorks

1714   7.15 NAGS HEAD HCAP 3YO+ 0-80 (D)   5f   Good/Soft 70 -10 Slow   [76]
£4413   £1358   £679   £339   3 yo rec 7 lb   Raced centre - stands side

1358 **MUKARRAB** 17 [8] D W Chapman 6-8-0 (48) D Mernagh (3) 12/1: 043601: 6 b g Dayjur - Mahassin (Biscay) 53
Led/dsptd lead & went on over 1f out, held on well nr fin, drvn out: '99 wnr at Lingfield (4 h'caps, rtd 87a & 54):
'98 wnr again at Lingfield (2, h'caps, rtd 55a) & Thirsk (mdn h'cap, rtd 53): eff at 5/6f on fast, soft & both
AWs, Lingfield specialist: best without blnks, gd weight carrier: nicely h'capped & cld win again.
1356 **COOL PROSPECT** 17 [7] K A Ryan 5-8-4 (52)(bl) F Lynch 10/1: 541404: 5 b g Mon Tresor - I Ran Lovely ¾ 54
(Persian Bold) Sn rdn, led/dsptd lead till over 1f out, kept on for press ins last: op 8/1: see 1143 (amat h'cap).
1580 **WILLIAMS WELL** 6 [5] M W Easterby 6-9-4 (66)(bl) T Lucas 7/2: 060143: 6 ch g Superpower - shd 68
Catherines Well (Junius) Chsd ldrs, eff over 1f out, kept on ins last, not reach wnr: op 4/1, qck reapp: see 1412.
1662 **TORRENT** 3 [9] D W Chapman 5-8-12 (60)(bl) J G Duffield 6/1: 553044: Rdn/prom, ch 1f out, no extra. 2 58
4361} **BENZOE** 235 [11] 10-8-9 (57) Iona Wands 5/5 16/1: 0000-5: Rear/sltly hmpd start, chsd ldrs, held over 1 53
1f out: op 12/1, reapp: '99 Leicester wnr (h'cap, A Turnell, rtd 66): in '98 trained by Mrs Ramsden to win at Thirsk
& Redcar (h'caps, rtd 76): eff at 5f, suited by 6f: acts on soft & hvy, suited by gd & firm grnd: best without blnks:
handles any trk, loves Thirsk: now with sprint master D Nicholls & should prove sharper for this.
1412 **PRECISION** 16 [6] 5-8-1 (49) W Supple 25/1: 0/0006: Rear, late gains fnl 2f, no threat: see 1005. ½ 44
1422 **SEVEN SPRINGS** 14 [3] 4-7-11 (45) P M Quinn 12/1: 062037: Held up, nvr pace to chall: see 1005. ½ 39
*1278 **SHIRLEY NOT** 23 [10] 4-9-10 (72) K Darley 5/2 FAV: -0318: Mid-div, rdn/held fnl 2f: hvly bckd. nk 65
780 **ARPEGGIO** 68 [1] 5-9-6 (68) O Pears 9/1: 00-009: Mid-div, held fnl 2f: 10 wk abs: see 780 (7f). nk 60
1244 **ORIEL STAR** 25 [2] 4-8-2 (50)(bl) R Ffrench 10/1: 006300: Chsd ldrs 3f: 10th: blnks reapp, op 8/1. 1½ 39
1422 **Lucky Cove** 14 [4] 4-8-11 (59) Kim Tinkler 50/1:   1662 **Waterford Spirit** 3 [12] 4-9-5 (67)(BL) C Lowther 14/1:
12 ran   Time 1m 01.00 (4.0)   (Ian Armitage)   D W Chapman Stillington, N Yorks

1715   7.45 TOTE HCAP 3YO+ 0-100 (C)   1m4f   Good/Soft 70 +09 Fast   [100]
£7052   £2170   £1085   £542   3 yo rec 15lb

1484 **GALLERY GOD** 11 [3] G Wragg 4-8-9 (80) K Darley 9/4 FAV: 6-0631: 4 ch c In The Wings - El Fabulous 88
(Fabulous Dancer) Trkd ldr, rdn/prog to lead 2f out, in command ins last, rdn out: well bckd, fast time: '99 wnr
at Newcastle (class stks, rtd 86): eff at 12/14f on firm & gd/soft, handles hvy & any trk: can force the pace.
1222 **RUM POINTER** 26 [6] T D Easterby 4-9-1 (87) J Carroll 6/1: 00-002: 4 b g Turtle Island - Osmunda 3 90
(Mill Reef) Led, rdn/hdd 2f out, kept on for press ins last: front rnr who is back on a fair mark: see 1222.
-- **KUMATOUR** [1] C E Brittain 5-10-0 (100) T E Durcan 14/1: /163-3: 5 b h Batshoof - Runelia (Runnett) ½ 102
Chsd ldrs, prog to press front pair 2f out, held ins last: reapp: '99 wnr in Dubai: '98 Windsor (auct mdn) &
San Siro wnr (stks, rtd 102, L Cumani): eff at 10/12f well: acts on firm & hvy, any trk, runs well fresh.
1484 **MONTALCINO** 11 [4] P J Makin 4-9-6 (92) K Fallon 4/1: 320-54: Held up in tch, rdn/mod gains fnl 2f. 2½ 91
1030 **MONTECRISTO** 40 [2] 7-9-4 (90) A Beech 9/1: 11/2: 100-35: Held up, eff 3f out, no impress: 6 wk abs. 3½ 85
1401 **GENEROUS TERMS** 16 [7] 5-9-10 (96)(t) C Rutter 12/1: 403-06: Chsd ldrs 9f: 10th: op 10/1: t-strap. 3½ 90
*1499 **ARCHIE BABE** 10 [5] 4-7-10 (68)(1oh) G Baker (7) 7/1: -65017: Trkd ldrs, btn 2f out: btr 1499. hd 61
1499 **JUST GIFTED** 10 [8] 4-7-10 (68)(2oh) K Dalgleish (7) 7/1: 605-28: Chsd ldrs, btn 3f out: op 6/1. 1½ 0
8 ran   Time 2m 37.1 (7.3)   (Takashi Watanabe)   G Wragg Newmarket

1716   8.15 CALVERTS CLASSIFIED STKS 3YO+ 0-80 (D)   7f rnd   Good/Soft 70   -20 Slow
£4127   £1270   £635   £317   3 yo rec 10lb

4395) **A TOUCH OF FROST 233** [2] G G Margarson 5-9-2 (bl) K Darley 2/1: 0150-1: 5 gr m Distant Relative -   85
Pharland (Bellypha) Trkd ldrs, prog/lead over 1f out & readily asserted under hands & heels riding ins last: hvly
bckd, reapp: '99 wnr at Salisbury (2, clmr & fill h'caps, rtd 83) & York (h'cap): '98 Salisbury wnr (fill mdn, rtd
70): eff at 1m, 7f specialist: acts on firm & gd/sft grnd: suited by blnks.
1483 **BOOMERANG BLADE 11** [1] B Smart 4-9-2 J Stack 4/5 FAV: -06622: 4 b f Sure Blade - Opuntia (Rousillon) 3   80
Led, jnd over 2f out, hdd over 1f out & sn held: hvly bckd: btr 1483 (h'cap).
1645 **INFOTEC 3** [3] H Akbary 3-8-12 K Fallon 7/2: -01053: 3 b c Shalford - Tomona (Linacre)   6   74
Trkd ldrs, rdn/bmpd over 1f out, sn held by front pair: op 4/1: qck reapp: btr 1061 (sft).
1559 **MEHMAAS 7** [4] R E Barr 4-9-5 (vis) G Duffield 25/1: 04-034: Bhd 3f out: highly tried: see 1360.   8   60
4 ran   Time 1m 29.2 (6.3)   (Mrs Patricia J Williams)   G G Margarson Newmarket

1717   8.45 SPROXTON MDN 3YO+ (D)   1m rnd   Good/Soft 70   -44 Slow
£4179   £1286   £643   £321   3 yo rec 11lb

1268 **POETIC 24** [1] H R A Cecil 3-8-8 T Quinn 1/2 FAV: 321: 3 b f Nureyev - Draw Straws (Key To The Mint)   72
Led, rdn/hdd over 2f out, led again over 1f out & forged clr ins last: well bckd at odds on: eff at 1m, 10f shld suit:
acts on fast & gd/sft grnd, gall/sharpish trk: shld rate more highly in better company.
--   **DOUBLE BID** [4] T P Tate 3-8-13 T Lucas 50/1: 2: 3 b g Rudimentary - Bidweaya (Lear Fan)   2½   72
Dwelt/bhd, styd on fnl 2f to take 2nd cl home, no threat to wnr: dam a 1m wnr: eff at 1m on gd/sft grnd.
1352 **GOLDEN OSCAR 17** [2] Andrew Turnell 3-8-13 P Fessey 50/1: 003: 3 ch g Primo Dominie - Noble   shd   72
Destiny (Dancing Brave) Trkd wnr, lead over 2f out, held over 1f out & no extra cl home: only mod form prev.
1309 **ADAMAS 20** [3] Andrew Turnell 3-8-8 W Supple 6/4: 2-04: Trkd ldrs 6f: op 11/10: flattered 1309.   3   62
--   **STEEL TRADER** [5] 3-8-13 D Mernagh (3) 66/1: 5: In tch, rdn/btn 2f out: debut, dam a 7f wnr.   7   56
5 ran   Time 1m 44.5 (9.1)   (The Thoroughbred Corporation)   H R A Cecil Newmarket

1718   9.15 SALTERSGATE HCAP 3YO+ 0-70 (E)   1m rnd   Good/Soft 70   -31 Slow   [70]
£3425   £1054   £527   £263   3 yo rec 11lb

759 **GRUB STREET 69** [9] M Brittain 4-8-8 (50) D Mernagh (3) 33/1: 50-01: 4 b c Barathea - Broadmara   53
(Thatching) Handy, led over 1f out, styd on well ins last, drvn out: 10 wk abs, h'cap bow: rtd 58 from two starts
last term (unplcd, mdns): eff at 1m, may get further: acts on gd/sft grnd & a sharpish trk: runs well fresh.
1477 **BEST EVER 11** [3] M W Easterby 3-7-12 (51) Dale Gibson 4/1: 0-0002: 3 ch g Rock City - Better Still   ¾   52
(Glenstal) Trkd ldrs, drvn/kept on fnl 2f, not pace of wnr: op 5/1: acts on firm & gd/sft: see 1053.
4295) **AIR OF ESTEEM 240** [2] P C Haslam 4-9-13 (69) P Goode (3) 7/1: 0260-3: 4 b g Forzando - Shadow   1¼   68
Bird (Martinmas) In tch, prog to chall over 1f out, rdn/no extra ins last: op 5/1, reapp: '99 wnr at Lingfield
(AW mdn, rtd 69a) & Haydock (h'cap, rtd 81): rtd 66 in '98: eff arnd 1m, tried 10f: acts on gd, gd/sft & both
AWs: has run well fresh: encouraging reapp & looks on a handy mark for similar.
1498 **CYRAN PARK 10** [7] W Storey 4-8-0 (42)(BL) T Williams 11/1: 040004: Held up, keen, hdwy fnl 3f,   ¾   40
onepace/held ins last: op 10/1, tried blnks: eff at 7f/1m: see 1132.
1542 **PLEADING 9** [10] 7-9-5 (61)(bl) J Carroll 10/1: 233005: Dwelt/bhd, mod gains: op 8/1: see 454 (AW).   1   57
1519 **ZECHARIAH 9** [4] A Beech 5/1: 5-4656: Led, rdn/hdd over 1f out, fdd: op 5/2: btr 907.   nk   40
1473 **DANAKIL 12** [8] 5-9-12 (68) Darren Williams (7) 3/2 FAV: 516127: In tch, rdn/btn 1f out: bckd: btr 1473.   1   61
1361 **THREE CHERRIES 17** [6] 4-8-3 (44)(1ow) G Duffield 20/1: 50-408: Keen, held up, nvr threaten: see 1191. ¾   37
1559 **SUSY WELLS 7** [1] 5-7-10 (38)(3oh) P Fessey 33/1: 560-09: Mid-div, btn 3f out: see 1559.   2½   26
1351 **PLEASURE TRICK 17** [5] 9-7-10 (38)(6oh) Kim Tinkler 33/1: 500500: Al rear: 10th: see 496.   3½   20
10 ran   Time 1m 43.5 (8.1)   (Mel Brittain)   M Brittain Warthill, N Yorks

Official Going   SOFT (HEAVY Places).   Stalls: 1m4f - Outside; Rem - Inside

1719   2.15 THWAITES MED AUCT MDN 2YO (E)   5f rnd   Good/Soft 60   -62 Slow
£2834   £872   £436   £218

--   **CARK** [4] A Berry 2-9-0 O Pears 5/6 FAV: 1: 2 b c Farfelu - Precious Girl (Precious Metal)   68
Trkd ldrs, led appr fnl 1f, rdly despite bit slipping/hanging left ins last: well bckd, slow time, debut: Apr first
foal, dam wng sprint juv, sire a sprinter: eff over a stiff 5f, shld get 6f: acts on gd/sft grnd, runs well fresh.
--   **FIRST SIGHT** [1] J J O'Neill 2-9-0 C Lowther 11/2: 2: 2 ch g Eagle Eyed - Madaraka (Arctic Tern)   3½   60$
Went left, cl-up, led appr fnl 1f, sn hdd, outpcd: longer prced stablemate of 4th, op 7/1: IR 12,500gns Mar
gldg: dam 10f wnr, sire well-related Grade 2 winner: 6f+ shld suit, poss handles gd/soft grnd.
--   **NEERUAM STAR** [3] D Moffatt 2-9-0 J Bramhill 8/1: 3: 3 b c Cool Jazz - Bay Meadows Star (Sharpo)   1¼   57
Led till bef fnl 1f, no extra: op 5/1: Apr foal, dam modest, sire a sprinter.
--   **OLYS WHIT** [2] J J O'Neill 2-9-0 K Darley 2/1: 4: Well plcd till fdd ent fnl 2f: op 6/4, stablemate   4   47
of rnr-up: 4,800gns Whittingham Mar gldg: half-brother to a 3yo wnr abroad, sire a sprinter.
4 ran   Time 1m 05.6 (6.1)   (Andrew Gorton)   A Berry Cockerham, Lancs

1720   2.45 THWAITES SMOOTH CLAIMER 3YO+ (F)   1m4f   Good/Soft 60   -04 Slow
£2268   £648   £324   3 yo rec 15lb

1660 **FIELD OF VISION 3** [6] Mrs A Duffield 10-9-8 G Duffield 7/4: 024321: 10 b g Vision - Bold Meadows   54
(Persian Bold) Rear, imprvd after halfway, led bef dist, drifted right, held on well, drvn out: qk
reapp: lightly rcd, incl over hdles since '98 wnr at Hamilton & Beverley (h'caps, rtd 72 & 67a): eff at 12/14f:
acts on firm, gd/sft, both AW's, any trk, likes stiff finishes: 10yo, in gd heart.
1660 **WAFIR 3** [4] D Nicholls 8-9-2 A Culhane 13/8 FAV: 432642: 8 b g Scenic - Taniokey (Grundy)   ¾   48
Mid-div, clsd after 7f, led appr 2f out till bef fnl 1f, styd on: clr rem, nicely bckd, clmd by T Cuthbert for £3,000:

ran near to best tho' expected to beat this wnr after 1720 (6lbs better off here for 3L).

1433 **MIDYAN BLUE** 14 [5] P Monteith 10-9-6 O Pears 10/3: 00/143: 10 ch g Midyan - Jarretiere (Star Appeal) Sn in long lead, no extra/hdd appr fnl 2f: tchd 9/2: set off too fast on rain-softened grnd: see 1145.   8   44

1353 **LOST SPIRIT** 17 [3] P W Hiatt 4-9-10 Darren Williams (7) 10/1: 035064: Pld hard, nvr a factor: stiff task.   9   40$

1145 **CRAIGARY** 31 [1] 9-9-4 J Carroll 50/1: 056-05: Led chsg pack for 7f, btn 4f out: stablemate wnr.   16   20

797 **MIDDAY COWBOY** 67 [7] 7-9-2 J McAuley (5) 150/1: 00-006: Al bhd: hdles rnr, offic. rtd 15.   4   14$

563 **GREAT HOPPER** 7 [2] 5-9-9 P Hanagan (7) 100/1: 000-07: Hld up, lost tch 4f out: imposs task, qk reapp. 6   15

7 ran   Time 2m 38.5 (7.7)   (Mrs J L Tounsend)   Mrs A Duffield Constable Burton, N Yorks

---

1721   3.15 THWAITES SMOOTH HCAP 3YO+ 0-75 (E)   1m rnd   Good/Soft 60   -38 Slow   [68]
£2912   £896   £448   £224   3 yo rec 11lb

1279 **ARC** 23 [2] G M Moore 6-9-10 (64) K Darley 11/10 FAV: 241201: 6 b g Archway - Columbian Sand (Salmon Leap) Nvr far away, led going well 2f out, cmftbly: well bckd, slow time: earlier won at Musselburgh (h'cap): '99 wnr at W'hampton (stks, rtd 67a) & here at Carlisle (stks, rtd 64, F Jordan): eff at 1m/10f: acts on firm, hvy & fibresand, any trk, likes Carlisle: gd weight carrier, goes best for K Darley.   69

1498 **NOBBY BARNES** 10 [1] Don Enrico Incisa 11-7-13 (36)(3ow) Kim Tinkler 8/1: 000-02: 11 b g Nordance - Loving Doll (Godswalk) Sn setting slow pace, hdd 2f out, same pace: 1016, clr rem: new tactics, ran to best.   4   36

1442 **WARRING** 14 [3] M S Saunders 6-8-6 (46) A Culhane 10/3: 40-503: 6 b g Warrshan - Emerald Ring (Auction Ring) Early ldr, lost tch appr 3f out: yet to come to hand, see 1066.   7   33

*749 **WELLCOME INN** 69 [4] G Woodward 6-7-10 (36)(t)(2oh) D Mernagh (3) 3/1: 233414: Bhd fnl 4f: 10 wk abs, turf return: in gd form on fibresand earlier, capable of better: see 749.   ½   22

4 ran   Time 1m 46.6 (7.8)   (Mrs A Roddis)   G M Moore Middleham, N Yorks

---

1722   3.45 THWAITES BREWERY HCAP 3YO 0-70 (E)   1m1f61y   Good/Soft 60   +01 Fast   [77]
£2977   £916   £458   £229

1434 **COSMIC SONG** 14 [7] R M Whitaker 3-7-10 (45)(1oh) D Mernagh (0) 13/2: -56351: 3 b f Cosmonaut - Hotaria (Sizzling Melody) Pulled hard & led early, regained lead bef halfway, kept on strongly, pushed out: fair time, first win: unplcd in '99 (rtd 50 & 54a): eff at 1m/9.3f: suited by gd/soft grnd, prob any trk.   51

1477 **MARVEL** 11 [6] Don Enrico Incisa 3-8-8 (57) Kim Tinkler 9/1: 0-0002: 3 b f Rudimentary - Maravilla (Mandrake Major) Rear, rdn turning for home, no impress till kept on strongly fnl 1f, nvr nrr: suited by step up to a stiff 9.3f: acts on gd/soft & hvy grnd: see 1477.   2   59

4570] **SAANEN** 217 [4] Mrs A Duffield 3-8-11 (60) G Duffield 11/2: 0400-3: 3 b g Port Lucaya - Ziffany (Taufan) Chsd ldrs, eff appr fnl 1f, not pace to chall: reapp: 4th of 13 in an auction mdn in '99 (rtd 63, Mrs Duffield): suited by step up to 9.3f, handles firm & gd/soft grnd.   1¼   60

1434 **JUMBOS FLYER** 14 [1] J L Eyre 3-8-12 (61) R Cody Boutcher (7) 9/4 FAV: 0-0524: Chsd ldrs, chall ent fnl 2f, onepace and press: nicely bckd: in front of this wnr in 1434 (1m, fast).   nk   60

1572 **WILLIAM THE LION** 6 [3] 3-8-6 (55) J Carroll 20/1: 00-055: Handy til no extra ent fnl 2f: qk reapp.   ¾   53

1300 **RED SEPTEMBER** 21 [3] 3-8-2 (51) Dale Gibson 12/1: 665-06: Prom, fdd 2f out: tchd 20/1: unplcd juv auct mdn, rtd 62, probabl;y flattered): with G M Moore.   6   41

1477 **CALLING THE SHOTS** 11 [9] 3-7-11 (46) T Williams 8/1: 00-007: Held up, short of room 2f out, sn btn.   3½   32

1053 **MR COSPECTOR** 37 [2] 3-9-7 (70) Rebecca Bolton(7) 5/1: 00-108: Al rear: op 7/2, btr 992 (7f mdn, hvy). 10   42

4408] **DOUBLE ENTRY** 231 [8] 3-7-10 (45)(15oh) J Bramhill 25/1: 000-9: Sn led, hdd bef halfway, wknd qckly 2f out: stiff task on reapp/h'cap bow: no form for D Nicholls last term: brother to a 13f/hdles wnr.   15   2

9 ran   Time 2m 01.0 (5.6)   (R M Whitaker)   R M Whitaker Scarcroft, W.Yorks.

1723   4.15 RATING RELATED MDN 3YO 0-60 (F)   6f rnd   Good/Soft 60   -17 Slow
£2352   £672   £336

1600 **BENBYAS** 5 [8] J L Eyre 3-9-0 (vis) R Cody Boutcher (7) 12/1: 00-061: 3 b g Rambo Dancer - Light The Way (Nicholas Bill) Well plcd, led ent fnl 2f, ran on well despite drifting right: op 10/1, qck reapp: unplcd in '99 (auct mdn, rtd 73): stays 1m, suited by drop back to a stiff 6f: acts on gd & gd/soft 6f: prob best visored now?   60

1494 **KATIES VALENTINE** 10 [7] R A Fahey 3-8-11 K Darley 4/1 FAV: 045-32: 3 b f Balnibarbi - Ring Side (Alzao) Rear, sn hard at work, styd on fnl 1½f, nvr nrr: bckd from 11/4: acts on gd/soft & soft, return to 7f?   2   52

1548 **PRETENDING** 7 [2] J D Bethell 3-9-0 R Lappin 16/1: 0-0653: 3 b g Primo Dominie - Red Salute (Soviet Star) Wide rear, late prog, nvr a threat: qck reapp, back in trip, handles fast & gd/soft grnd: see 1085.   ¾   53

1600 **ROBIN HOOD** 5 [5] Miss L A Perratt 3-9-0 C Lowther 10/1: -00444: Prom, rdn to chall 2f out, sn onepace: op 8/1, qck reapp: stiff task at the weights, ran nr to best: see 1494.   3½   46

1387 **NORTHERN ECHO** 16 [6] 3-9-0 (BL) F Lynch 14/1: 0-0005: Led till appr fnl 1f, fdd: op 10/1, blinkered.   2   41

992 **MADAME GENEREUX** 44 [13] 3-8-11 G Duffield 4/1: 0-456: Well plcd & ch till wknd dist: 6 wk abs.   1¾   35

4230] **RED MITTENS** 245 [3] 3-8-11 C Teague 50/1: 5600-7: Wide, mid-div, nvr troubled ldrs: reapp: down the field a4 '99 starts (rtd 68, prob flattered): sprint bred, with M Wane.   ¾   33

1038 **MAGIC SISTER** 38 [11] 3-8-11 J Fanning 13/2: 6-0308: Dwelt, nvr in it: see 930.   hd   33

118 **JEPAJE** 191 [12] 3-9-0 G Faulkner (3) 10/1: 2040-9: Front rank till 2f out: abs, op 8/1: see 105.   hd   35

2606] **CONSIDERATION** 331 [9] 3-8-11 J Carroll 14/1: 6244-0: In tch till halfway: 10th, op 10/1, reapp: '99 rnr-up (clmr, rtd 61 & 44a): eff at 5f on soft grnd: with A Berry.   1   29

1081 **SCHATZI** 34 [10] 3-8-11 J Bramhill 10/1: 05-020: Chsd ldrs 3f: 12th: see 10881, 872.   0

1477 **Watergold** 11 [1] 3-9-0 (VIS) O Pears 16/1:   1560 **Comex Flyer** 7 [4] 3-9-0 (BL) A Culhane 20/1:

13 ran   Time 1m 16.7 (4.6)   (C H Stephenson & Partners)   J L Eyre Sutton Bank, N.Yorks.

1724   4.45 THWAITES APPR HCAP 3YO+ 0-65 (F)   5f rnd   Good/Soft 60   +04 Fast   [62]
£2632   £752   £376   3 yo rec 7 lb

1545 **BOWLERS BOY** 7 [5] J J Quinn 7-9-4 (52) P Hanagan (5) 5/1: -0W241: 7 ch g Risk Me - Snow Wonder (Music Boy) Mid-div, rdn 2f out, kept on strongly despite drifting right to get up fnl stride: op 4/1, best time of day, qck reapp: plcd in '99 (1st time blnks, h'cap, rtd 49): '98 Pontefract wnr (2, h'caps) & Redcar (stks, rtd 76): eff at 5/6f: acts on fast, loves gd/soft & fibresand grnd: prob handles fibresand: likes Pontefract/stiff finishes.   57

1412 **DAZZLING QUINTET** 16 [1] C Smith 4-8-9 (43) J McAuley 14/1: 20-602: 4 ch f superlative - Miss Display (Touch Paper) Tried to make all, switched halfway, ran on but worn down line: a bold attempt.   shd   47

*1139 **PALACEGATE TOUCH** 32 [4] A Berry 10-8-11 (45)(bl) D Allan (7) 14/1: 205013: 10 gr g Petong - Dancing Chimes (London Bells) Chsd ldrs, eff & hung violently left bef fnl 1f, ended up on stands rail, kept on.   1½   45

CARLISLE MONDAY JUNE 5TH Righthand, Stiff Track, Uphill Finish

1631 **NAISSANT 4** [2] J S Goldie 7-9-0 (48) Dawn Rankin (5) 7/1: 006304: Mid-div, feeling pace halfway, late hdwy: tchd 9/1, qck reapp: back in trip, has won here twice over 7f: see 844. ½ 47
1479 **FRILLY FRONT 11** [3] 4-9-9 (57) Lynsey Hanna (5) 14/1: 160005: Outpcd till kept on fnl 1½f: see 631. *hd* 56
1487 **BEWARE 11** [8] 5-10-0 (62) Clare Roche (5) 9/1: 615456: Held up, eff & hung right 2f out, unable to chall. ¾ 59
1508 **MUTASAWWAR 10** [9] 6-8-11 (45) Darren Williams (3) 14/1: 500-57: Dwelt, prog 2f out, no extra dist. *shd* 42
*1487 **POLAR MIST 11** [6] 5-9-8 (56)(tbl) G Faulkner 5/2 FAV: -00018: Well plcd, no extra appr fnl 1f: nicely bckd to complete a qck double but all winning form on much sharper tracks than this: see 1487. *nk* 52
1358 **BIFF EM 17** [12] 6-8-5 (39) R Cody Boutcher (5) 7/1: 0-5039: Hmpd sn after start, chsd ldrs till 2f out. *nk* 35
1244 **HENRY THE HAWK 25** [7] 9-8-7 (41)(bl) P Goode 12/1: 04-400: Nvr a factor: 10th: see 756. ½ 36
1559 **UNMASKED 7** [11] 4-7-10 (30)(4oh) Kimberley Hart 33/1: 000000: Al rear: 11th, qck reapp, stiff task. ½ 24
1438 **ALBERT THE BEAR 14** [10] 7-9-11 (59)(vis) P Bradley (3) 8/1: 00-060: Bhd ldrs, hmpd halfway, lost pl ent fnl 2f: 12th, visor reapplied: stablemate of 3rd, better than this: see 1438. ¾ 51
12 ran Time 1m 02.3 (2.8) (Bowlers Racing) J J Quinn Settrington, N.Yorks.

WINDSOR MONDAY JUNE 5TH Sharp Fig 8 Track

Official Going GOOD. Stalls: Inside. Pace Figs inapplicable due to course re-alignment.

1725 6.30 DESIRE IS A MED AUCT MDN 3YO (E) 1m2f Good Inapplicable
£2996 £856 £428

1404 **RAGDALE HALL 16** [11] J H M Gosden 3-9-0 R Havlin 4/6 FAV: 51: 3 b c Bien Bien - Gift Of Dance (Trempolino) Prom, hdwy to lead over 1f out, kept on well ins last, shade cosily: hvly bckd: cost $130,000: stays 10f well, further shld suit: handles fast & gd: going the right way. 82
1556 **JOONDEY 7** [10] M A Jarvis 3-9-0 P Robinson 7/1: 032: 3 b c Pursuit Of Love - Blueberry Walk (Green Desert) Cl-up, led over 2f out till over 1f out, kept on but not pace of wnr: op 5/1: eff at 10f & handles gd & hvy: shown enough to win a race & open to improvement. 1¼ 78
1386 **NINNOLO 16** [12] C N Allen 3-9-0 R Morse 14/1: 53: 3 b c Perugino - Primo Stampari (Primo Dominie) Keen in tch, hdwy over 2f out, kept on same pace: not given a hard time & stays 10f on gd: could improve. 2½ 74
1093 **NEW FORTUNE 34** [3] W R Muir 3-8-9 R Brisland (5) 33/1: 0-04: Waited with, eff 2f out, sn onepace: stays 10f on gd grnd: see 1093. 1½ 67$
1266 **JOCKO GLASSES 24** [1] 3-9-0 R Mullen 20/1: 5-05: Sn bhd, late gains, nvr dngrs: encouraging h'cap qual run stepped up to 10f on gd grnd: open to further improvement & shld stay 12f. 1¼ 70
395 **AROB PETE 132** [14] 3-9-0 T G McLaughlin 50/1: 0-006: Made most till over 2f out, no extra: flattered? 2 67$
1293 **MEMPHIS TEENS 21** [2] 3-9-0 A McGlone 9/1: 37: In tch, rdn & btn over 2f out: op 6/1: see 1293. 3½ 62
1377 **RED LION FR 17** [7] 3-9-0 Pat Eddery 20/1: 008: Keen, with ldrs, wknd over 2f out: bred to stay 1m. 2 60
1548 **ROSE TINA 7** [15] 3-8-9 S Carson (5) 50/1: 09: Prom, wknd over 2f out. 2½ 51
1436 **AL AWAALAH 14** [4] 3-8-9 S Whitworth 50/1: 00: Prom, btn over 3f out, eased: 10th: see 1436. ¾ 50
-- **BROMEIGAN** [5] 3-8-9 N Pollard 20/1: 0: Dwelt, al bhd: 11th: bred for mid-dists. 2½ 46
-- **SPOT** [8] 3-8-9 M Henry 10/1: 0: Al bhd: 12th: dam 7f scorer: with A Reid. 1¾ 43
1425 **Prince Elmar 14** [6] 3-9-0 Martin Dwyer 14/1: 4536} **Tarrifa 221** [9] 3-8-9 F Norton 33/1:
1399 **Miss Swift 16** [13] 3-8-9 M Howard (1) 50/1:
15 ran Time 2m 08.2 (Ragdale Racing) J H M Gosden Manton, Wilts.

1726 7.00 INDESIT SILVER HCAP 3YO 0-75 (E) 1m67y rnd Good Inapplicable [82]
£3202 £915 £457

1390 **MANXWOOD 16** [4] D J S Cosgrove 3-8-6 (60) J F Egan 8/1: -01421: 3 b g Petorius - Eliza Wooding (Faustus) Prom, eff to chall 2f out, kept on ins last to get up cl-home, rdn out: earlier scored at W'hampton (class stks, made all, rtd 66a): unplcd in '99 (rtd 67 & 68a): best up with/forcing the pace over 7f/8.3f on fibresand & gd grnd: likes a sharp track: on the up-grade. 65
933 **EASTERN SPICE 49** [2] R Hannon 3-9-7 (75) L Newman (5) 14/1: 035-02: 3 b c Polish Precedent - Mithl Al Hawa (Salse) Prom, led over 2f out, edged left over 1f out but kept on till collared cl-home, just btn: fine run after a 7 wk abs: plcd twice as a juv (rtd 82): eff at 7f/8.3f on firm & gd: shown enough to win. *hd* 79
1345 **GRUINART 18** [16] H Morrison 3-8-11 (65) D Griffiths 14/1: 0-0043: 3 br g Elbio - Doppio Filo (Vision) Hld up, hdwy over 2f out, kept on ins last, nrst fin: best effort to date over 8.3f on gd & worth a try over further. ¾ 67
4498} **COMMONWOOD 224** [3] J G Smyth Osbourne 3-8-9 (63) N Pollard 25/1: 4406-4: Dwelt, bhd, hdwy 2f out, kept on onepace ins last, eased cl-home & lost 3rd pl: plcd twice as a juv (rtd 85): eff around 5.7f, stays 8.3f on firm & gd grnd: has worn a t-strap. *shd* 65
1405 **PINHEIROS DREAM 16** [15] 3-9-0 (68) J Fortune 10/1: 00-505: Prom, sltly hmpd over 5f out, eff 2f out, onepace: stays 8.3f: see 857. ¾ 68
1405 **REGARDEZ MOI 16** [5] 3-8-4 (58) F Norton 25/1: 33-006: Pressed ldr till over 2f out, onepace: plcd sev times in '99 (rtd 66): eff over 5f/1m on gd & soft grnd. ¾ 57
1390 **WELCOME SHADE 16** [9] 3-8-7 (61) T G McLaughlin 25/1: 14-207: Bhd, some late gains: see 1212. 2 56
1341 **TAKE MANHATTAN 18** [10] 3-9-4 (72) Craig Williams 13/2: 661108: Sn handy, eff over 2f out, no extra. ½ 66
1473 **KAMARAZI 12** [11] 3-9-0 (68) W Ryan 16/1: 500009: Held up, modest late gains: see 630. 1¼ 60
1345 **SPIRIT OF TENBY 18** [6] 3-8-11 (65) P Doe 9/1: 5-6030: Bhd, short of room over 2f out, some late gains: 10th: worth a try over 10f: see 1345. *hd* 56
1333 **THE ROBSTER 19** [8] 3-8-11 (65) Pat Eddery 6/1 FAV: 00-020: Made most till over 2f out: 11th. ½ 55
1448 **CELEBES 13** [14] 3-8-8 (62)(VIS) G Hind 12/1: 464000: Keen, in tch till btn over 2f out: 12th, visor. *1* 50
1350 **PRINCE OMID 18** [17] 3-9-2 (70)(VIS) D Harrison 10/1: 5-3400: Keen, prom till wknd & hmpd ins last: 13th, visor, see 1350, btr 858 (7f). *hd* 57
4425} **LIVELY MILLIE 230** [1] 3-8-2 (56) R Mullen 33/1: 5000-0: Slow away & al bhd: 14th: modest form. ¾ 41
1407 **SPIRIT OF LIGHT 16** [13] 3-9-1 (69) A Daly 8/1: 002300: Lost pl when hmpd after 1f, btn 2f out: 15th. *nk* 53
1405 **Cinnamon Court 16** [18] 3-9-6 (74) Martin Dwyer 20/1: 1293 **Lion Guest 21** [12] 3-9-0 (68) P Robinson 11/1:
1390 **Joely Green 16** [7] 3-8-8 (62) M Fenton 25/1:
18 ran Time 1m 43.7 (1.4) (Global Racing Club) D J S Cosgrove Newmarket.

1727   7.30 INDESIT EBF NOV STKS 2YO (D)   5f   Good Inapplicable
£5005   £1540   £770   £385

1424 **MISTY EYED** 14 [7] Mrs P N Dutfield 2-8-7 L Newman (5) 11/2: 51: 2 gr f Paris House - Bold As Love   89
(Lomond) Prom, hdwy to lead fnl 1f, rdn clr, going away: May foal, cost IR 3,200gns: half-sister to a dual
5f scorer: eff at 5f on gd grnd, 6f shld suit: useful effort here & shld go in again.
1346 **FLINT RIVER** 18 [2] R F Johnson Houghton 2-8-12 J Reid 2/1 FAV: 22: 2 b c Red Ransom - She's   3   85
All Class (Rahy) Cl-up, led over 2f out till ins fnl 1f, not pace of wnr: hvly bckd: shld win similar: see 1346.
1522 **MY LUCY LOCKET** 9 [1] R Hannon 2-8-7 R Hughes 5/1: 33: 2 b f Mujadil (Auction Ring)   nk   79
Handy, hung left 2f out, flashed tail but kept on for press ins last: nicely bckd: handles gd & hvy grnd: see 1522.
1197 **WINTER JASMINE** 28 [6] B J Meehan 2-8-7 Pat Eddery 10/1: 04: Led till over 2f out, onepace: op   ¾   77
6/1: better for debut & will stay further: see 1197.
932 **ROMANTIC POET** 49 [4] G Hind 10/1: 35: In tch, btn fnl 1f: op 7/1, abs, see 932 (hvy).   2½   75
743 **SPEEDY GEE** 70 [3] 2-8-12 P Robinson 100/30: 36: Cl-up, btn fnl 1f: 10 wk abs, see 743.   nk   74
932 **FIENNES** 49 [9] M Fenton 7/1: 57: Cl-up, wknd over 1f out: 7 wk abs, see 932.   3   66
-- **LIGHT EVIDENCE** [8] J Reid 33/1: 8: Sn bhd on debut: Mar foal, dam 6f juv wnr: bred for speed.   6   45
-- **BEDFORD FALLS** [10] 2-8-7 M Hills 20/1: 9: Slow away & al bhd: debut: Apr foal, cost 3,000gns: 10   17
half-sister to sev wnrs, dam 5f juv scorer: speedily bred, with A McNae.
-- **GLOBAL EXPLORER** [5] 2-8-12 J F Egan 25/1: 0: Slow away & al bhd: 10th: Feb foal, cost   1½   20
22,000gns: dam 1m scorer: with P Mitchell.
10 ran   Time 59.8 (1)   (Mrs Jan Fuller)   Mrs P N Dutfield Axmouth, Devon.

1728   8.00 A-RATED CLASS STKS 3YO+ 0-90 (C)   6f   Good Inapplicable
£6418   £1975   £987   £493   3 yo rec 8 lb

1337 **ALEGRIA** 18 [4] J M P Eustace 4-8-13 J Tate 9/2: 530-01: 4 b f Night Shift - High Habit (Slip Anchor)   91
Front rank, went on dist, styd on well despite edging right, rdn out: plcd sev times in '99 (h'caps, rtd 86): '98
wnr here at Windsor (fill mdn, rtd 78): eff at 5/6f on gd & firm: handles any trk, likes a sharp one, esp Windsor.
1576 **ARGENT FACILE** 6 [1] D J S Cosgrove 3-8-8 (t) J F Egan 8/1: -22022: 3 b c Midhish - Rosinish   1½   90
(Lomond) Trkd ldrs, imprvd to chall fnl 1f, no extra cl-home: op 6/1: qck reapp: deserves a change of luck.
1531 **LIVELY LADY** 9 [3] J R Jenkins 4-9-5 (vis) Pat Eddery 9/4 FAV: -41033: 4 b f Beveled - In The Papers   1¼   90
(Aragon) Rear, gd prog 2f out, short of room 1f out, not qckn ins last: well bckd: not disgraced under top-weight.
1450 **CHOTO MATE** 13 [7] R Hannon 4-9-2 P Dobbs 12/1: 46/W04: Front rank, eff when short of room   1½   83
dist, no ch after: op 8/1: prob btn'd a few strides 6f: must be given another chance, see 1450 (likes Goodwood).
1078 **ROO** 35 [6] S Carson 3-8-5 S Carson 5/1: 10: 20-065: Front rank, edged right dist, onepace 3rd when hit rail   ¾   78
& rider lost irons ins fnl 1f: likes soft grnd: see 912.
1441 **RUSHCUTTER BAY** 14 [5] 7-9-2 A Polli 4/1: 050-26: Set pace till dist, fdd: stiff task: see 1441.   1½   77
1337 **LITERARY SOCIETY** 18 [2] S Whitworth 7-9-3 S Whitworth 5/1: 00-007: Stumbled start, no ch after: see 1173.   3   69
7 ran   Time 1m 11.4   (J C Smith)   J M P Eustace Newmarket.

1729   8.30 ARISTON DIGITAL HCAP 3YO+ 0-85 (D)   1m2f   Good Inapplicable   [83]
£4179   £1288   £643   £321

1150 **CAPTAINS LOG** 31 [18] M L W Bell 5-9-6 (75) M Fenton 6/1: 0-4251: 5 b g Slip Anchor - Cradle Of   80
Love (Roberto) Chsd ldrs, eff 2f out, forged ahd ins last, drvn out: nicely bckd: rnr-up in '99 (rtd 80 at best):
'98 wnr at Warwick (mdn) & Newcastle (h'cap, rtd 82): eff at 10/12f, handles any grnd: handles any trk & can
run well fresh: tough gelding who could win again.
1528 **MAKE WAY** 9 [10] B J Meehan 4-9-11 (80) S Clancy(7) 10/1: 6-6032: 4 b g Red Ransom - Way Of The   ½   83
World (Dance Of Life) Mid-div, imprvd to lead dist, not pace to repel wnr cl-home: deserves to go one better.
1375 **AMRAK AJEEB** 17 [12] R J Baker 8-8-12 (67) J Reid 12/1: 000-03: 8 b h Danehill - Noble Dust   nk   69
(Dust Commander) Led after 1f till dist, kept on: tchd 16/1: 8yo who clrly retains ability: best held up for a
late run, unlucky & should be entered again: see 1375.
1150 **SWEET REWARD** 31 [13] J G Smyth Osbourne 5-8-13 (68) F Norton 9/1: 330-44: Mid-div, eff 3f out,   shd   70
styd on under press fnl 1f & nrst fin: well h'capped: acts on fast, loves soft & hvy: bt today's wnr in 1150.
1547 **GIKO** 7 [17] 6-8-2 (57)(BL) M Henry 33/1: -00065: Chsd ldrs, kept on under press fnl 2f: stays an easy   nk   58
10f: gd effort in first time blnks, only btn arnd 1L: see 1033.
1375 **THE GREEN GREY** 17 [16] 6-8-5 (60) W Ryan 16/1: 00-006: Nvr far away, short of room & lost pl dist,   1¾   59+
rallied ins last: stays an easy 10f, best prev at 7f/1m: fairly h'capped & looks primed to win: see 1113.
1375 **KENNET** 17 [8] 5-8-10 (65) D Harrison 14/1: -56007: Prom till lost pl over 2f out, rallied dist, onepcd.   hd   58
1364 **BAHRAIN** 17 [1] 4-8-6 (61)(t) M Hills 16/1: 0-4008: Rear, imprvd to chase ldrs 3f out, eased when btn.   1¾   58
1150 **FREDORA** 31 [6] 5-9-10 (79) D Sweeney 20/1: 00-509: Early ldr, rem prom & ch 2f out, fdd ins last.   nk   75
-- **FORZA FIGLIO** [5] 7-9-8 (77) R Mullen 33/1: 2040/0: Mid-div, onepcd fnl 2f: fin 10th on comeback: ¾   72
missed prev 2 seasons, in '97 trained by Miss G Kelleway & rnr-up on a couple of starts (rtd 88): '96 Goodwood
wnr (mdn, rtd 87+): eff at 1m/12f on firm & gd/soft: handles a gall or sharpish trk.
1373 **PUNISHMENT** 17 [7] 9-9-6 (75)(t) N Pollard 25/1: 355000: Rear, imprvd to chase ldrs 3f out,   shd   70
btn dist: fin 11th: see 374 (sand).
4520} **SKI RUN** 223 [15] 4-9-8 (77) R Hughes 7/1: 001-0: Mid-div, no impress fnl 2f on reapp: fin 12th: shd   72
lightly rcd in '99, trained by R Johnson Houghton to win at Bath (mdn, rtd 78): eff at 11.6f on gd/soft grnd.
1070 **LUCKY GITANO** 35 [9] 4-9-9 (78) Pat Eddery 13/2: /32-00: Rear, eff 2f out, no impress: fin 13th: hd   73
twice rcd in '99, rnr-up at Brighton (mdn auct, rtd 87): rnr-up in '98 (mdn auct, rtd 76): half-brother to a
couple of wnrs abroad: eff at 1m/10f on firm & gd/soft: can run well fresh: with J Dunlop & capable of better.
*1375 **INDIUM** 17 [11] 6-9-10 (79) J Fortune 9/2 FAV: 404010: Rear, nvr nr ldrs: fin 14th, bckd from 6/1:   1¾   72
much better expected after 1375 (stiff trk).
-- **Ionian Spring** 5 [2] 5-9-10 (79) Dane O'Neill 20/1: 1170 **Tarawan** 30 [19] 4-10-0 (83) Leanne Masterton(7) 20/1:
-- **Fantail** [3] 6-10-0 (83) S Sanders 25/1:   56 **Final Lap** 202 [20] 4-9-5 (74) D McGaffin (7) 20/1:
18 ran   Time 2m 06.1 (1.4)   (Christopher Wright)   M L W Bell Newmarket.

WINDSOR MONDAY JUNE 5TH   Sharp Fig 8 Track

1730

9.00 DIAMOND LINE HCAP 3YO+ 0-60 (F)   1m3f135y Good Inapplicable   [60]
£2758   £788   £394   3yo rec 15lb

4519} **COURT SHAREEF** 223 [16] R J Price 5-9-8 (54) P Fitzsimons (5) 10/1: 4405-1: 5 b g Shareef Dancer - **65**
Fairfields Cone (Celtic Cone) Mid-div, smooth prog to lead dist, sn clr, cmftbly despite drifting right, eased down:
val for 3L+: rnr-up in a nov hdle in Nov '99 (rtd 103h, eff at 2m on gd grnd): trained by R Dickin in '99 & rtd
61 at best (h'cap): '98 winr here at Windsor & Leicester (h'cap, rtd 74 at best): eff at 12/14f on gd & fast grnd:
handles any trk, likes Windsor: runs well fresh: fairly h'capped for new connections & cld follow up.
1521 **PINCHANINCH** 9 [1] J G Portman 3-8-9 (56) A Nicholls (3) 16/1: 0-0042: 3 ch g Inchinor - Wollow Maid ¾ **60**
(Wollow) Rear, prog when hmpd 2f out, styd on under press fnl 1f, not rch winr: little luck, stays 11.6f on gd & hvy.
890 **LEGENDARY LOVER** 54 [4] J R Jenkins 6-9-6 (52)(vis) J Fortune 7/1: 066-53: 6 b g Fairy King - Broken 1¼ **54**
Romance (Ela Mana Mou) Rear, switched & prog over 1f out, styd on well, nrst fin: well bckd, 8 wk abs: see 890.
1521 **DR COOL** 9 [8] W Jarvis 3-8-9 (56) F Norton 10/1: 03-054: Prom, not qckn ins last: stays 11.6f. ½ **56**
1292 **CROSS DALL** 21 [2] 3-8-8 (55)(e) J F Egan 14/1: -31005: Dwelt, well bhd till imprvd 2f out, nrst fin: ½ **55**
best held up for a late run, tho' waiting tactics prob overdone here: tried in an eye-shield: see 1096 (C/D).
1375 **WADI** 17 [11] S Sanders 25/1: 100-06: Front rank, ev ch 2f out, fdd ins last: in '99 3½ **53**
trained by G McCourt to win at Warwick (sell h'cap) & Salisbury (clmr, rtd 70): '98 Pontefract winr for H Cecil
(mdn, rtd 81): eff at 10/12f on firm, soft grnd & equitrack: has worn blnks/t-strap, seems best without: loves
to run-up with/force the pace: when for Dr J Naylor, on a fair mark.
4551} **COMMON CONSENT** 220 [18] 4-9-8 (54) S Whitworth 25/1: 0303-7: Mid-div, short of room 5f out, imprvd ¾ **48**
& ev ch 2f out, fdd: reapp: plcd in a couple of '99 starts (h'cap, rtd 62): eff at 11/12f, acts on fast & gd/soft.
1180 **ANGE DHONOR** 29 [19] 5-9-12 (58) A Daly 12/1: 300-68: Chsd ldrs, onepcd fnl 1½f: see 1180 (14f). nk **51**
1100 **IN THE STOCKS** 34 [13] 6-9-6 (52) S Carson(5) 12/1: 561-09: Chsd ldrs, btn dist: see 1100 (10f here). ¾ **44**
1677 **ANOTHER MONK** 2 [20] 9-9-3 (49) L Newman (5) 4/1 FAV: 141120: Set pace till dist, no extra: fin 1 **39**
10th, well bckd, qck reapp: too soon after 1677 (sand)?
3528} **FIERY WATERS** 287 [6] 4-9-12 (58) J Mackay (7) 33/1: 3000-0: Dwelt, switched & hdwy 2f out, eased nk **47+**
when btn fnl 1f: fin 11th, reapp: lightly rcd in '99, plcd at Ripon (mdn auct, rtd 74): eff at 10f on firm.
4095} **KING FOR A DAY** 254 [14] 4-9-1 (47)(vis) P McCabe 33/1: 0000-0: Effort from rear 3f out, sn no 1¼ **34**
impress: fin 12th: recent sell hdle form (rtd 72, tried a visor): rtd 68 when 6th of 13 on
reapp in '99 (h'cap): eff at 9f, handles firm & hvy: wears blnks/visor: with Bob Jones.
1199 **STAFFORD KING** 28 [10] 3-8-8 (55) W Ryan 20/1: -04200: Rcd keenly rear, btn 2f out: fin 13th. nk **41**
889 **SACREMENTUM** 54 [12] 5-9-4 (50) J P Spencer 12/1: 020640: Rear, eff 2f out, sn btn: fin 14th, abs. nk **35**
1292 **TWOS BETTER** 21 [5] 3-8-11 (58) I Mongan (5) 9/1: 0-0360: Mid-div, imprvd to chase ldrs 4f out, nk **42**
wknd fnl 2f: fin 15th, nicely bckd: much btr 1096.
1364 **COY DEBUTANTE** 17 [3] 6-9-3 (49) Pat Eddery 8/1: 053-00: Effort from rear 3f out, sn btn & eased. ¾ **32**
1364 **Daniel Deronda** 17 [7] 6-9-12 (58)(BL) M Fenton 25/1: 1050 **Royal Axminster** 37 [9] 5-8-13 (45) R Havlin 25/1:
4276} **Latin Bay** 241 [17] 5-8-13 (45) P Doe 25/1:   1428 **Wickham** 14 [15] 4-9-4 (50) A Clark 14/1:
20 ran   Time 2m 28.8 (3.0)   (Derek & Cheryl Holder)   R J Price Ullingswick, H'fordshire.

LEICESTER   MONDAY JUNE 5TH   Righthand, Stiff, Galloping Track

Official Going   GOOD/SOFT.   Stalls: Stands Side.

1731

1.30 LAZY DAZE CLAIMER DIV 1 3YO+ (F)   1m str   Good/Soft 70   +08 Fast
£2030   £580   £290   3 yo rec 11lb

1275 **SOPHOMORE** 23 [3] J L Harris 6-9-6 K Dalgleish (7) 14/1: 030601: 6 b g Sanglamore - Livry (Lyphard) **66**
Prom, hdwy to lead appr fnl 1f, styd on well, drvn out: best time of day: 4th over hdles in 99/00 (2m sell
h'cap, soft, rtd 66h): last rcd on the Flat back in '97 (unplcd, rtd 89 for B Hills): mdn winr on sole juv start
in '96 (rtd 86): has tried further: acts on gd, gd/soft & a stiff/gall trk.
1523 **THE WILD WIDOW** 9 [4] M C Pipe 6-8-7 (VIS) R Hughes 9/4 FAV: 0-0222: 6 g rm Saddlers' Hall - ½ **52**
No Cards (No Mercy) Led, clr 4f out, rdn/hdd appr fnl 1f, rallied well ins last: well clr rem, 1st time visor,
new stable: fine run for new connections, shld find compensation in similar: see 1523.
1520 **THOMAS HENRY** 9 [10] J S Moore 4-9-0 Pat Eddery 8/1: 055003: 4 br g Petardia - Hitopath (Bustino) 7 **48**
Waited wth, hdwy over 2f out, kept on but not pace of front 2: see 786.
892 **LAGO DI LEVICO** 53 [6] A P Jarvis 3-8-9 D Harrison 8/1: 0-154: Mid-div, rdn to improve 2f out, 1 **52**
sn no extra: 8 wk abs: see 892 (h'cap).
1407 **ARTFUL DANE** 16 [1] 8-8-12 J Weaver 20/1: 004-05: Rear, late gains, nvr nrr: see 1407. nk **44**
1434 **A BOB LIGHT** 14 [11] 3-8-4 W Supple 10/1: 450-06: Mid-div, eff 2f out, kept on, no threat: rnr-up hd **47**
once in '99 (fill mdn, rtd 72): dam 10f winr: stays 1m, further shld suit: acts on gd/soft, handles fast grnd.
4155} **COUNTESS PARKER** 250 [12] 4-8-9 A Daly 7/1: 204-7: Dwelt, al in rear: reapp, new stable: rnr-up 7 **31**
on 1st of 3 '99 starts for H Cecil (mdn, rtd 87): eff at 1m on gd, poss not soft: now with J M Bradley.
1545 **CHARLIE SILLETT** 7 [9] 8-8-12 J D Smith 20/1: 000-08: Nvr a threat: qck reapp: well btn all 4 '99 6 **25**
starts (h'caps, rtd 74 at best): back in '97 scored at Chester (clmr, rtd h'cap, rtd 88): eff at 6/7f on gd grnd, suited
by soft or hvy: acts on any trk & gd weight carrier: fairly h'capped on old form.
1572 **THE FLYER** 6 [5] 3-9-3 I Mongan (5) 13/2: 6-6029: Dwelt, al bhd: quick reapp, new stable. 1 **39**
1336 **MARIANA** 19 [2] 5-8-7 T G McLaughlin 50/1: 505000: Trkd ldrs, wknd ldist tch fnl 2f, fin 10th. 2 **14**
1210 **ARAGANT** 27 [8] 4-9-0 F Norton 16/1: 330-00: Handy, wknd qckly fnl 2f, 11th. nk **21**
163 **ARANA** 178 [7] 5-9-1 R Havlin 50/1: 0000-0: In tch, wknd rapidly fnl 2f, t.o. in 12th: long abs. 21 **0**
12 ran   Time 1m 39.4 (5.0)   (J L Harris)   J L Harris Eastwell, Leics

1732

2.00 LAZY DAZE CLAIMER DIV 2 3YO+ (F)   1m str   Good/Soft 70   -27 Slow
£2016   £576   £288   3 yo rec 11lb

1442 **ARBENIG** 14 [1] B Palling 5-9-1 D Sweeney 9/4 FAV: 00-031: 5 b m Anita's Prince - Out On Her Own **39**
(Superlative) Led early, remained with ldrs, led again appr fnl 1f, styd on well, rdn out: plcd in '99 (rtd 57,
rtd h'cap): '98 Salisbury winr (clmr, rtd 58 & 64a): eff at 7f/1m on firm, soft & fibresand: acts on a stiff/gall
trk & eff in blnks: can rate more highly.
1556 **WILD NETTLE** 7 [5] J C Fox 6-8-11 R Smith (5) 8/1: 000042: 6 ch m Beveled - Pink Pumpkin ½ **33**

(Tickled Pink) Mid-div, rdn & gd hdwy appr fnl 1f, kept on for press: op 6/1, qck reapp: gd run at the weights.
1417 **ADIRPOUR 14** [2] R Hollinshead 6-8-12 Stephanie Hollinshead (7) 8/1: 300043: 6 gr g Nishapour - Adira (Ballad Rock) Waited with, prog halfway, hung right & no extra for press ins last: clr rem: see 1417. ¾ 33
1407 **ALABAMY SOUND 16** [12] K A Morgan 4-9-3 L Newman (5) 7/1: 41-404: Cl-up, led halfway, hdd appr fnl 1f, wknd: shade btr 1195. 2½ 34
1331 **PHILISTAR 19** [11] 7-9-0 C Cogan (5) 4/1: 336005: Mid-div, prog 2f out, kept on, no dngr. ¾ 30
1415 **LA CINECITTA 14** [7] 4-8-7 K Hodgson 50/1: 00-006: Rdn/rear, imprvd 2f out, drvn/no extra ins last. ¾ 22
1462 **REKEN 12** [3] 4-8-12 P McCabe 50/1: 00-007: Dwelt, rear, eff 2f out, no threat: no form. 4 20
1032 **CARNAGE 40** [10] 3-8-9 R Havlin 20/1: 000-08: Prom, rdn/lost tch fnl 2f: 6 wk abs. nk 28
1210 **OLLY MAY 27** [9] 5-8-11 F Norton 50/1: 09: Al bhd: mod form. 1 17
1349 **SACRED HEART 18** [6] 3-7-10 (t) Claire Bryan (5) 14/1: 0-00: Rcd keenly cl-up, wknd fnl 2f, fin 10th. ¾ 12
3592] **BE THE CHIEF 283** [4] 4-8-12 P C Coppinger 50/1: /005-0: Prom, rdn/fdd fnl 3f, fin 11th: op 8/1: jumps fit (mod form): prev with T G Mills, now with W Clay. 9 8
1498 **FAIRFIELD BAY 10** [8] 4-8-12 (E) G Bardwell 50/1: 0/0000: Rcd keenly & led after 2f, hdd halfway, sn wknd, eased, t.o. in 12th: 1st time eye-shield: no form. 21 0
12 ran   Time 1m 42.2 (7.8)   (Andrew Smallwood)   B Palling Cowbridge, Vale Of Glamorgan

---

1733

2.30 TIGER BEST CONDITION STKS 3YO (C)   **7f str**   **Good/Soft 70**   **-13 Slow**
£6032   £2288   £1144   £520

953 **BEDAZZLING 48** [5] J R Fanshawe 3-8-9 P Robinson 11/2: 120-01: 3 gr f Darshaan - Dazzlingly Radiant (Try My Best) Waited with, hdwy/switched over 2f out, rdn to lead over 1f out, strongly prsd ins last, drvn out to hold on: 7 wk abs: '99 Kempton wnr (fill mdn), subs rnr-up in a val Newmarket stks race (rtd 99): eff arnd 7f, 1m shld suit: acts on firm, hvy & a stiff/gall or fair trk: runs well fresh: useful & prog, win more races. 104
913 **TOTAL LOVE 52** [7] E A L Dunlop 3-8-5 T Quinn 3/1 JT FAV: 233-02: 3 ch f Cadeaux Genereux - Favorable Exchange (Exceller) Mid-div, rdn to chall dist, styd on for press, just held: 7 wk abs: clr rem: eff at 7f/1m: usual, back to near best here & shld win similar, poss in headgear: see 913 (Gr 3). shd 99
1283 **BOAST 23** [4] R F Johnson Houghton 3-8-9 J Reid 13/2: 416-63: 3 ch f Most Welcome - Bay Bay (Bay Express) Led, hdd 2f out, not pace of front 2 ins last: op 5/1: v consistent, deserves another race: see 1283. 2½ 99
*1268 **COCO 24** [3] Sir Michael Stoute 3-8-9 K Fallon 11/2: 0-14: Cl-up, rdn & kept on fnl 2f, not pace of ldrs: clr rest & imprvd in defeat: see 1268. ¾ 98
1376 **AURA OF GRACE 17** [2] 3-8-5 R Price 25/1: 0-65: Dwelt, sn cl-up, fdd fnl 2f: highly tried: see 1376. 7 83$
1283 **FAIRY GEM 23** [6] 3-8-5 Dane O'Neill 50/1: 60-046: Dwelt, settled rear, switched/eff 2f out, no danger to ldrs: much btr 1283 (List). nk 82
2405] **DANDY NIGHT 339** [1] 3-8-5 F Norton 8/1: 1402-7: Prom, rdn/lost tch fnl 2f: reapp: '99 debut scorer at Newmarket (mdn, rtd 101 at best): eff around 5f on firm & gd/soft grnd: runs well fresh on a gall trk: shld be sharper next time & may apprec a drop back to 6f. shd 82
7 ran   Time 1m 27.8 (5.8)   (B McAllister)   J R Fanshawe Newmarket

---

1734

3.00 ORIGINAL SELL HCAP 3-5Y 0-60 (G)   **6f str**   **Good/Soft 70**   **-08 Slow**   **[54]**
£2170   £620   £310   3 yo rec 8 lb

1559 **UNFORTUNATE 7** [13] Miss J F Craze 3-8-12 (46)(bl) V Halliday 40/1: 306001: 3 ch f Komaite - Honour And Glory (Hotfoot) Sn rdn & outpcd, weaved thro' fnl 1½f, drvn out to lead nr fin, going away: no bid, qck reapp: jockey rec a 2 day whip ban: unplcd on turf in '99 (rtd 35), subs won at Southwell (AW sell, rtd 55a): suited by 6f: acts on gd/soft & fibresand: eff with/without blnks: well rdn by V Halliday today. 51
1438 **BAYONET 16** [16] Jane Southcombe 4-9-11 (51) A Nicholls (3) 20/1: 000-02: 4 b f Then Again - Lambay (Lorenzaccio) Cl-up, rdn to lead appr fnl 1f, kept on but hdd cl-home: handles fast & gd/soft grnd. 1½ 52
1423 **CRAFTY PICK 14** [10] R Hannon 3-9-2 (50) Dane O'Neill 12/1: 0003: 3 b f Thatching - Lucky Pick (Auction Ring) Mid-div, prog over 1f out, styd on, nrst fin: h'cap bow: stays 6f on gd/soft, further shld suit. nk 51
1351 **JAYPEECEE 17** [11] J L Eyre 4-9-8 (48)(VIS) J Mackay (7) 16/1: 0-0004: Handy, rdn/prog 2f out, styd on ins last: imprvd eff in 1st time visor: handles gd & gd/soft: see 844. ½ 48
1336 **SPLIT THE ACES 19** [19] 4-8-12 (38) O Urbina 20/1: 00-005: Rear, styd on fnl 2f, nvr nrr: handles gd & gd/soft grnd, worth another try at 7f: see 1092. shd 38
1664 **SAMMAL 3** [15] 4-9-6 (46) D Harrison 11/1: 050046: Mid-div, rdn/kept on onepce fnl 2f: qck reapp. nk 45
1037 **AUBRIETA 38** [18] 4-9-8 (48)(bl) Pat Eddery 9/2 FAV: 520457: Led after 1f, hdd appr fnl 1f, fdd. 1¼ 44
1438 **CASTLE BEAU 14** [2] 5-9-4 (46) F Norton 16/1: 0/0008: Mid-div, eff halfway, nvr a threat: mod form 5 28
1143 **MISS GRAPPETTE 31** [12] 4-9-0 (40) A Daly 20/1: 00-009: Led early, with ldrs till wknd qckly fnl 2f: '99 reapp scorer at Catterick (mdn, rtd 71): plcd 4 times as a juv (rtd 75): eff up with the pace over 6f, handles firm & gd/soft grnd: can go well when fresh: with A Berry. ½ 23
1578 **DON QUIXOTE 6** [3] 4-9-5 (45)(BL) K Fallon 5/1: 30-060: Nvr a threat, 10th, qck reapp, blnkd. nk 27
1479 **SNAP CRACKER 11** [21] 4-9-7 (47) G Baker (7) 11/1: 020000: Al bhd, fin 11th: see 751. 1¼ 26
1601 **VICE PRESIDENTIAL 5** [14] 5-9-6 (46) Dean McKeown 10/1: 045040: Front rank, wknd qckly fnl 2f, fin 12th: tchd 14/1, quick reapp: see 32 (AW). nk 24
1336 **ITHADTOBEYOU 19** [6] 5-9-8 (48) I Mongan 25/1: -22300: Handy, fdd fnl 2f, 13th: op 6/1, see 1259. shd 26
1578 **YORKIE TOO 6** [22] 4-9-6 (46) J Reid 14/1: 0-0050: Rcd far side, prom, wknd fnl 2f, 14th: qck reapp. nk 23
1412 Bodfari Times 16 [8] 4-9-2 (42)(t) P M Quinn (3) 20/11572 Jensens Tale 6 [1] 3-8-12 (46)(BL) D Sweeney 33/1:
176 Positive Air 175 [17] 5-9-4 (44) W Supple 33/1: 1690 Xsynna 2 [4] 4-10-0 (54)(bl) C Cogan (5) 33/1:
1559 So Willing 7 [7] 4-9-2 (42)(vis) J Weaver 16/1: 1273 Gunner Sam 24 [9] 4-9-7 (47) K Dalgleish (7) 25/1:
1233 Lemon Strip 25 [5] 4-8-12 (38)(BL) L Newman(5) 40/1: 1395 Green Turtle Cay 16 [20] 4-9-13 (53) T E Durcan 33/1:
22 ran   Time 1m 14.5 (4.7)   (P T Walton)   Miss J F Craze Elvington, N Yorks

---

1735

3.30 EVERARDS HCAP 3YO 0-80 (D)   **1m2f**   **Good/Soft 70**   **-20 Slow**   **[85]**
£4628   £1424   £712   £356

934 **ORIGINAL SPIN 49** [4] J L Dunlop 3-9-6 (77) T Quinn 15/8 FAV: 42-21: 3 b f Machiavellian - Not Before Time (Polish Precedent) Cl-up, rdn into lead appr fnl 1f, jnd dist, all out to get up fnl stride: nicely bckd, 7 wk abs, h'cap bow: rtd 83 when rnr-up on 2nd of only 2 '99 starts (mdns): acts at 8.4f, stays 10f well: acts on gd/sft, hvy & a stiff/gall trk: runs well fresh: lightly raced & open to further improvement, could follow up. 84
1491 **BAILEYS PRIZE 13** [3] M Johnston 3-9-5 (76) J P Spencer 6/1: 201462: 3 ch c Mister Baileys - Mid Mar (Forever Casting) Waited with, gd hdwy over 2f out, rdn to chall dist, duelled with wnr last, hdd line: clr rem: acts on firm, gd/soft & fibresand: fine run, shld win similar: see 1299. hd 82
1439 **MYTHICAL KING 14** [10] B Palling 3-9-7 (78) D Harrison 10/1: 350-33: 3 b c Fairy King - Whatcombe 3 79

567

(Alleged) Led, qcknd pace over 3f out, hdd appr fnl 1f, not pace of ldrs: handles firm & gd/soft: see 1439 (stks).
*1414 **XIBALBA** 16 [7] C E Brittain 3-8-13 (70) N Esler (7) 7/1: 000-14: Front rank, rdn/no extra over   nk   71
1f out: poss stays 10f: ran to form of 1414 (mdn h'cap).
1364 **WAVERLEY ROAD** 17 [8] 3-8-6 (63) D Sweeney 14/1: 4-5065: Prom, rdn/outpcd 2f out: see 702 (mdn).   1½   62
1177 **THEATRELAND** 29 [5] 3-9-3 (74) (VIS) K Fallon 6/1: 005-06: Waited with, rdn/hdwy & hung right   nk   73
2f out, sn no extra: visored: may apprec another step up in trip: see 1177.
1104 **SHEER TENBY** 33 [2] 3-9-4 (75) R Price 25/1: -40167: Nvr a threat: see 606.   nk   73
1452 **INVER GOLD** 13 [1] 3-9-6 (77) S Whitworth 10/1: 4-1308: Al bhd: longer 10f trip: btr 278 (7f AW mdn).   2½   71
1142 **FISHER ISLAND** 32 [9] 3-7-10 (53) P M Quinn (3) 14/1: -63449: Rear, hdwy halfway, lost tch fnl 2f.   nk   47
1414 **WISHFUL THINKER** 16 [6] 3-8-6 (63) Jonjo Fowle (7) 33/1: 00-000: Mid-div, fdd fnl 2f, 10th: up in trip.   ½   56
10 ran   Time 2m 11.5 (9.0)   (R Barnett)   J L Dunlop Arundel, W Sussex

---

1736   4.00 BEACON FILLIES HCAP 3YO+ 0-70 (E)   1m3f183y   Good/Soft 70   +01 Fast   [69]
£3071   £945   £472   £236   3 yo rec 15lb

*1571 **FIRECREST** 6 [6] J L Dunlop 3-8-13 (69) (6ex) T Quinn 11/8 FAV: 00-011: 3 b f Darshaan - Trefoil   85
(Blakeney) Trkd ldrs, led 3f out, easily went clr appr fnl 1f, hvly eased ins last: val 8/10L: nicely bckd, qck
reapp: earlier won here at Leicester on h'cap bow (easily): unplcd on 3 mdn starts prev: suited by recent step
up to 12f, further shld suit: runs well fresh on gd/soft & gall trk: v prog now & looks sure to win more races.
*1683 **ELSIE BAMFORD** 2 [7] M Johnston 4-8-6 (47) (6ex) K Dalgleish (7) 7/2: 043112: 4 b f Tragic Role -   4   50
Sara Sprint (Formidable) Led, hdd over 3f out, kept on but not pace of easy wnr: unfortunate to come up
against a very prog rival on todays hat-trick bid: shld regain wng ways sn: see 1683.
1524 **MURCHAN TYNE** 9 [5] B A McMahon 7-8-7 (48) W Supple 12/1: 005003: 7 ch m Good Thyme -   1¾   48
Ardnamurchan (Ardross) Mid-div, rdn to improve 3f out, no extra appr fnl 1f: see 788.
1524 **TUI** 9 [3] P Bowen 5-7-12 (39) Claire Bryan (5) 14/1: 0-5154: Dsptd lead to halfway, ev ch till   1¼   37
fdd fnl 2f: consistent recent form: see 1332 (firm).
1499 **SKYERS A KITE** 10 [13] 5-8-2 (43) A Nicholls (3) 20/1: 0-2065: Waited with, prog when short of room   ½   40
over 2f out, kept on, no danger: see 1023, 822.
1496 **PATRITA PARK** 10 [10] 6-8-1 (42) J Mackay (7) 7/1: 240-06: Held up, late gains, no threat: see 1496.   hd   39
885 **RENAISSANCE LADY** 54 [11] 4-8-4 (45) Dean McKeown 16/1: 200-07: Front rank, drvn/lost tch fnl 2f: 1¾   40
8 wk abs: '99 scorer at Brighton (med auct mdn, rtd 55): stays a sharp/undul 12f on fast grnd.
1501 **SILENT VALLEY** 10 [4] 6-7-10 (37) (13oh) Iona Wands (5) 50/1: 0-0008: Dwelt, nvr a factor: stiff task.   ½   31
1585 **MUCHANA YETU** 6 [9] 3-8-12 (68) R Havlin 20/1: 55-069: Al bhd: quick reapp: see 1177.   2   59
1440 **BOSSY SPICE** 14 [12] 3-7-10 (52) (15oh) G Baker (7) 40/1: 000-00: Prom 6f, lost tch fnl 4f, 10th.   ½   42
248 **Lady Irene** 154 [14] 4-8-1 (42) L Newman (5) 40/1:   1440 **Tyrolean Love** 14 [8] 4-7-12 (39) F Norton 20/1:
863} **Fly Like A Bird** 418 [2] 4-9-0 (55) R Fitzpatrick (3) 16/1:
13 ran   Time 2m 36.4 (8.1)   (Sir Thomas Pilkington)   J L Dunlop Arundel, W Sussex

---

1737   4.30 TRIPLE GOLD FILL MDN 2YO (D)   5f str   Good/Soft 70 -12 Slow
£3796   £1168   £584   £292

--   **DANCE ON** [5] Sir Michael Stoute 2-8-11 K Fallon 4/9 FAV: 1: 2 ch f Caerleon - Dance Sequence   89+
(Mr Prospector) Outpcd early, prog over 2f out, led dist, pushed clr ins last, cmftbly: well bckd at odds-on:
Apr 1st foal, dam a 6f Gr 2 wnr as a 2yo: sire high-class at 10/12f: eff at 5f, 6f+ lks sure to suit: runs
well fresh on gd/soft & a stiff/gall trk: fine debut & can only improve: potentially smart Queen Mary prospect.
--   **KARITZA** [2] M R Channon 2-8-11 T Quinn 3/1: 2: 2 b f Rudimentary - Desert Ditty (Green Desert)   3   77+
Dwelt, sn in tch, led over 2f out, hdd dist, kept on under hands & heels: 8,800gns sister to a juv wnr in France:
dam 6f wnr: eff at 5f on gd/soft: held in high regard, not given a hard time here: will go one better soon.
--   **MULLING IT OVER** [6] T D Easterby 2-8-11 J Reid 25/1: 3: 2 b f Blues Traveller - Wonderment   2½   71
(Mummys Pet) Rdn/rear, late gains under hands & heels, nrst fin: op 16/1: 26,000gns Mar foal, half sister to
a juv scorer abroad: 6f looks sure to suit, given a kind intro today.
1424 **ONCE REMOVED** 14 [4] S Dow 2-8-11 P Doe 14/1: 04: Prom, led & saddle slipped 3f out, sn hdd,   ¾   69
fdd fnl 2f: ignore this run: see 1424.
--   **ALINGA** [7] 2-8-11 A Beech 14/1: 5: Dwelt, nvr a threat: King's Theatre Feb 1st foal: dam a   2   64
dual juv 5f scorer: shld improve.
1424 **LADY KINVARRAH** 14 [1] 2-8-11 D Harrison 20/1: 06: Led early, lost tch fnl 2f: see 1424.   shd   64
--   **POWDER** [3] 2-8-11 W Supple 14/1: 7: Al outpcd: op 7/1: Mar 1st foal, dam a 7f scorer: 6   53
with M Tompkins & shld improve when stepped up in trip.
7 ran   Time 1m 02.4 (4.1)   (Cheveley Park Stud)   Sir Michael Stoute Newmarket

---

1738   5.00 LEVY BOARD MDN 3YO (D)   1m3f183y   Good/Soft 70 -31 Slow
£3984   £1226   £613   £306

--   **MARIENBARD** [5] M A Jarvis 3-9-0 M Tebbutt 11/2: 1: 3 b c Caerleon - Marienbad (Darshaan)   86
Dwelt, hdwy & hung left 2f out, ran on stongly for press to lead ins last, rdn out, eased nr fin: op 3/1: half
brother to 12f wnr Gensher: eff over a undul/gall 12f on gd/soft: runs well fresh: ran v green, improvement likely.
1455 **PEPE GALVEZ** 13 [7] B Hanbury 3-9-0 K Fallon 4/9 FAV: 032: 3 br c Mango Express - Mango   1¾   82
Sampaquita (Colombian Friend) Led, rdn/edged left appr fnl 1f, hdd ins last: well bckd: btr 1455.
3802} **JAMAIEL** 272 [3] C E Brittain 3-8-9 N Esler (7) 33/1: 0-3: 3 b f Polish Precedent - Avice Caro (Caro)   3   72
Cl-up, chald over 2f out, hung left & held appr fnl 1f: reapp: t.o. in last sole '99 juv start (7f fill
mdn, saddle slipped): styd this longer 12f trip & handles gd/soft: sharper next time.
1200 **COLLINE DE FEU** 28 [1] Mrs P Sly 3-8-9 J Weaver 20/1: 04: Dwelt, rdn/hdwy 2f out, no threat: see 1200.   2   69
4338} **ROMNEY** 237 [2] 3-9-0 G Parkin 100/1: 00-5: Cl-up, drvn & fdd fnl 2f: reapp: mod form in 2 '99 starts.   5   67$
--   **BOULDER** [4] 3-9-0 J P Spencer 9/1: 6: Dwelt, eff halfway, lost tch fnl 2f: Bigstone colt,   shd   67
dam a 7f/1m wnr in Ireland: shld improve for L Cumani.
1103 **ARIALA** 33 [6] 3-8-9 D Sweeney 10/1: 607: Chsd ldrs, lost tch fnl 3f: tchd 25/1: btr 934 (1m).   15   42
7 ran   Time 2m 40.2 (11.9)   (Saif Ali)   M A Jarvis Newmarket

LINGFIELD TUESDAY JUNE 6TH Lefthand, V Sharp Track

Official Going Tufr: GOOD (GD/SFT Pl), AW - STANDARD. Stalls: 9f - Ins, 11f - Outside: AW - Inside, except 5f (outside)

1739 **1.45 VIGO CLAIMER DIV 1 3YO+ (E) 7f aw rnd Going 30 -01 Slow**
£2403 £686 £343 3 yo rec 10lb

1734 **AUBRIETA 1** [6] D Haydn Jones 4-9-2 (bl) K Fallon 9/4 FAV: 204501: 4 b f Dayjur - Fennel (Slew O'Gold) **63a**
Held up, prog 3f out, led ins last, sn clr: qck reapp: '99 wnr here at Lingfield (mdn, rtd 59a & 62): plcd in '98 (rtd 79, C Brittain): eff at 6/7f, tried 1m: acts on fast, gd & equitrack, likes Lingfield: best in blinks.
1349 **PERLE DE SAGESSE 19** [2] Julian Poulton 3-8-4 A Daly 9/2: 545302: 3 b f Namaqualand - Pearl of Dubai (Red Ransom) Led, hdd inside last, sn held: op 3/1: see 155 (C/D). *4* **52a**
1464 **ENTROPY 13** [3] B A Pearce 4-8-12 O Urbina 6/1: 0-0023: 4 b f Brief Truce - Distant Isle (Bluebird) Rdn chasing ldrs 3f out, kept on tho' al held: eff arnd 6/7f on firm, gd/soft & equitrack: see 1335. *½* **49$**
1552 **TAVERNER SOCIETY 8** [5] M S Saunders 5-9-13 S Carson (5) 9/2: 03-044: Rdn/rear halfway, mod gains *2½* **59a**
1611 **GLASTONBURY 6** [7] 4-8-13 F Norton 20/1: 040005: Cl up halfway, wknd over 1f out: see 425. *1¾* **42$**
1511 **PRINCESS MO 11** [1] 4-8-10 (bl) A Polli (3) 25/1: 5-0006: Trkd ldrs, drvn halfway, sn held: blnks reapp. *1½* **36$**
1423 **VILLAGE NATIVE 15** [9] 7-9-3 (bl) S Sanders 10/1: 000007: In tch, rdn/btn 3f out: see 352. *3½* **36a**
1508 **ARAB GOLD 11** [8] 5-9-1 Martin Dwyer 12/1: 144068: Prom 4f: btr 634 (6f, h'cap). *½* **33a**
1511 **HEIRESS OF MEATH 11** [4] 5-8-8 P Doe 16/1: 00/309: Dwelt, soon bhd: see 1255 (10f). *9* **13a**
9 ran Time 1m 24.95 (2.15) (P F Crowley) D Haydn Jones Efail Isaaf, Rhondda C Taff

1740 **2.15 SAN SEBASTION MED AUCT MDN 2YO (F) 5f aw rnd Going 30 -02 Slow**
£2215 £633 £316

1429 **LAUREL DAWN 15** [9] A Berry 2-9-0 R Hughes 100/30: 401: 2 gr c Paris House - Madrina (Waajib) **76a**
Showed gd speed to cross to inside rail & make all, clr over 1f out, readily: value for 6L+: op 4/1: eff at 5f, 6f may suit: acts on eqtrk & gd/soft grnd: fine AW bow, speedy type, looks sure to win more races.
1302 **JOHN FOLEY 22** [7] W G M Turner 2-9-0 A Daly 8/1: -00252: 2 b c Petardia - Fast Bay (Bay Express) *4* **67a**
Hard rdn chasing wnr after 1f, outpcd fnl 2f: clr of rem: handles both AWs: shld find a race: see 1136, 812.
1206 **SOOTY TIME 29** [6] J S Moore 2-9-0 Martin Dwyer 33/1: 63: 2 ch g Timeless Times - Gymcrak Gem (Don't Forget Me) Rdn chasing ldrs halfway, no impression fnl 2f: see 1206 (seller). *5* **58a**
1463 **OPERATION ENVY 13** [4] R M Flower 2-9-0 J Fortune 5/1: 4604: Wide/bhd halfway, late gains for pressure, nrst fin: needs 6f+: see 1260, 1124. *nk* **57a**
1095 **THE WALL 35** [3] 2-8-9 A Polli (3) 33/1: 05: Chsd ldrs, held 2f out: see 1095. *½* **50a**
-- **BILLYJO** [2] 2-9-0 K Fallon 3/1 FAV: 6: Outpcd rear & soon switched wide, no impression: op 5/2: *6* **44a**
Idris gelding, May foal, cost IR4,700gns: dam unraced, sire a prog 7f/10f Irish performer: with B J Meehan.
-- **OUR LITTLE CRACKER** [5] 2-8-9 F Norton 8/1: 7: Soon bhd/wide: Petong filly, March foal, cost *hd* **38a**
4,500gns: sister to a 7f juv wnr, dam only modest: with M Quinn.
-- **INVESTMENT FORCE** [8] 2-9-0 J Fanning 7/2: 8: V slowly away, al bhd: op 5/2: Imperial Frontier *¾* **41a**
colt, May foal, cost IR 28,000gns: brother to a 7f juv wnr: dam a top class juv abroad: lost chance at start today.
1346 **ROXY LABURNUM 19** [1] 2-8-9 C Rutter 33/1: 009: Soon outpcd rear: mod form. *5* **27a**
9 ran Time 59.42 (1.62) (Laurel (Leisure) Ltd) A Berry Cockerham, Lancs

1741 **2.45 VIGO CLAIMER DIV 2 3YO+ (E) 7f aw rnd Going 30 -08 Slow**
£2391 £683 £341 3 yo rec 10lb

1603 **TAKHLID 6** [3] D W Chapman 9-9-11 A Culhane 4/5 FAV: 501331: 9 b h Nureyev - Savonnerie (Irish **62a**
River) Held up in tch, drvn to chall dist, led ins last, drvn out: well bckd, qck reapp: earlier won at W'hampton (amat clmr): '99 wnr at Southwell (3), Lingfield (2) & W'hampton (6, clmrs/h'cap, rtd 84a & 64): '98 Hamilton & Thirsk wnr (h'caps, rtd 74 & 64a): eff btwn 6/8.4f on firm & soft, loves both AWs: a credit to all concerned.
1423 **MAGIQUE ETOILE 15** [4] M P Muggeridge 4-8-12 T G McLaughlin 4/1: 2-0062: 4 b f Magical Wonder *1½* **45a**
- She's A Dancer (Alzao) Cl up, led over 4f out, drvn/hdd inside last, kept on: op 6/1: see 114, 25 (6f, mdn)
1210 **GAELIC FORAY 28** [2] R P C Hoad 4-8-10 K Fallon 20/1: 0-003: 4 b f Unblest - Rich Heiress *3½* **36a**
(Last Tycoon) Chsd ldr halfway, hard rdn/onepace over 1f out: mod form prev.
1137 **ALJAZ 33** [8] Miss Gay Kelleway 10-9-3 Dane O'Neill 15/2: 206464: Prom 5f: op 6/1: see 44 (6f). *1½* **40a**
1596 **EDEIFF 6** [1] 3-8-8 A Daly 8/1: 01-605: Led 2f, btn 2f out: qck reapp: see 1439. *7* **30a**
4277} **TUCSON 242** [7] 3-8-7 C Rutter 33/1: 0-6: Dwelt, al bhd: reapp: mod form. *½* **28a**
1601 **BONNIE DUNDEE 6** [6] 4-9-0 (bl) S Carson (5) 10/1: 0-0057: Al outpcd rear: blinks reapp: see 776. *1½* **22a**
1210 **CORSECAN 28** [5] 5-9-1 I Mongan (5) 33/1: 00/008: Cl up 5f: missed '99: '98 wnr here at Lingfield *2½* **18a**
(h'cap, S Dow, rtd 66a & 42): eff at 1m, tried 10f: acts on equitrack & fast grnd.
8 ran Time 1m 25.43 (2.63) (S B Clark) D W Chapman Stillington, N Yorks

1742 **3.15 THEHORSESMOUTH HCAP 3YO 0-60 6f aw rnd Going 30 -16 Slow** **[67]**
£2320 £663 £331

1508 **FRENCH FANCY 11** [3] B A Pearce 3-8-6 (45)(bl) P M Quinn (3) 8/1: 240041: 3 gr f Paris House - **50a**
Clipping (Kris) Chsd ldrs, styd on gamely ins last to lead nr line: 1st success: plcd form in '99 (rtd 61, sell, C Dwyer): eff at 6/7f, tried 1m: acts on fast, soft & eqtrk: handles a gall or sharp/undul trk: eff in blnks.
1600 **PADDYWACK 6** [13] D W Chapman 3-9-7 (60)(bl) Claire Bryan (5) 8/1: 222002: 3 b g Bigstone - *½* **62a**
Millie's Return (Ballard Rock) Handy, rdn/led over 1f out, hard rdn/hdd near line: op 6/1: loves Lingfield: see 654.
1670 **ITSGOTTABDUN 4** [10] K T Ivory 3-9-5 (58)(bl) C Catlin (7) 7/1 JT FAV: 236643: 3 b g Foxhound - *3½* **51a**
Lady Ingrid (Taufan) Rdn/bhd, late gains, no threat to front pair: quick reapp: see 527 (C/D, seller).
1244 **INVISIBLE FORCE 26** [2] M Johnston 3-8-3 (42) J Fanning 9/1: 40-604: Led till over 1f out, wknd fnl 1f. *nk* **34a**
1578 **POWER AND DEMAND 7** [7] 3-8-13 (52)(bl) F Norton 10/1: 430005: Chsd ldrs 2f out, no impression. *½* **42a**
1349 **ANNIJAZ 19** [11] 3-8-12 (51) D O'Donohoe 10/1: 500046: Rdn/bhd, mod wide gains: see 973, 773. *nk* **40a**
617 **PARKSIDE PROSPECT 97** [5] 3-8-12 (51) I Mongan (5) 9/1: -45007: Chsd ldrs, btn 2f out: bckd, abs. *1½* **37a**
1494 **BANGLED 11** [9] 3-9-5 (58) D Harrison 12/1: 450-08: Towards rear, mod gains: see 1494. *nk* **43a**
1670 **LISA B 4** [4] 3-8-11 (50)(bl) Craig Williams 7/1 JT FAV: 200009: Trkd ldrs 4f: well bckd: qck reapp. *1* **33a**
1080 **CEDAR LIGHT 36** [1] 3-8-13 (52) S Sanders 14/1: 0-000: Chsd ldrs 4f: 10th: h'cap/AW bow. *shd* **35a**
1428 **WHITE SANDS 15** [14] 3-8-11 (50) K Fallon 11/1: 0-000: Wide/al bhd: 11th: h'cap/AW bow. *shd* **32a**
1435 **ST IVES 15** [8] 3-8-8 (47) G Hind 12/1: 06-060: Al towards rear: 12th: op 8/1: AW/h'cap bow. *nk* **28a**
4132} **Playinaround 252** [6] 3-8-13 (52) A Daly 16/1: 1508 **Lea Valley Express 11** [12] 3-8-11 (50)(vis) S Whitworth 33/1:

LINGFIELD   TUESDAY JUNE 6TH   Lefthand, V Sharp Track

14 ran   Time 1m 13.18 (2.78)   (Richard J Gray)   B A Pearce Newchapel, Surrey

1743   3.45 MOSEY ON DOWN HCAP 3YO+ 0-75 (E)   1m3f106y Good Inapplicable   [75]
£2842   £812   £406   3 yo rec 15lb

1614 **MAY KING MAYHEM 6** [12] Mrs A L M King 7-7-10 (43)(bl)(4oh) P M Quinn (3) 10/1: 16-651: 7 ch g Great   50
Commotion - Queen Ranavalona (Sure Blade) Keen, rear, prog 4f out, rdn to lead dist, styd on gamely, drvn out:
'99 Leicester (appr h'cap) & Newmarket wnr (amat h'cap, rtd 43): '98 scorer at Haydock & Pontefract (appr h'cap,
rtd 43): suited by 11.5/12f, stys 15f: acts on fast, gd/soft & handles f/sand, any trk: suited by blnks.
1076 **WASP RANGER 36** [9] G L Moore 6-9-11 (72) I Mongan (5) 6/1: 200-02: 6 b g Red Ransom - Lady   ¾ 77
Climber (Mount Hagen) Mid div, rdn/prog to chall fnl 2f, styd on well, just held: op 8/1: stays 11.5f: see 1076.
*1395 **JUNIKAY 17** [6] R Ingram 6-9-1 (62) K Fallon 3/1 FAV: -02113: 6 b g Treasure Kay - Junijo (Junius)   2½ 63
Mid div, drvn & kept on fnl 2f, not pace of front pair: hvly bckd: stays 11.5f: see 1395 (9f).
1608 **GOLDEN ROD 6** [8] P W Harris 3-8-5 (66)(1ow) A Culhane 10/1: 0-0034: Chsd ldr, drvn/briefly led   3 64
over 2f out, fdd fnl 1f: op 8/1, quick reapp: acts on gd/soft & soft grnd, not quite see out this longer 11.5f trip.
1416 **SIRINNDI 15** [5] 6-8-10 (57) J P Spencer 12/1: 365/05: Rear, drvn/mod late gains: see 1416 (2m).   1½ 52
1509 **DION DEE 11** [14] 4-7-10 (43)(2oh) S Righton 20/1: 030036: Keen/held up wide, outpcd over 3f out.   1½ 36
699 **MUKHLLES 75** [2] 7-8-3 (50) Gemma Jones 11/1: 500-07: Held up, outpcd over 3f out: abs: '99 wnr   ½ 42
here at Lingfield (h'cap, reapp, rtd 51): rtd 32 & 42a in '98 (h'caps): eff at 10f, handles firm & fast.
1395 **THIHN 17** [1] 5-8-7 (54) Dane O'Neill 13/2: 522-28: Trckd ldrs, fdd fnl 2f: op 11/2: btr 1395 (9f).   ½ 45
577 **SHY PADDY 103** [4] 8-7-10 (43)(20oh) G Baker (7) 50/1: 22/009: Prom early, btn 3f out: 3 month abs.   nk 33
1373 **BLUE STYLE 18** [13] 4-9-5 (66)(t) R Mullen 100/30: 612100: Chsd ldrs wide 3f out, held 2f out: 10th.   2½ 52
1483 **TIGER TALK 12** [7] 4-10-0 (75) J Weaver 16/1: 000-00: Led 9f, wknd: 13th: '99 scorer at Folkestone   0
(auct mdn) & Sandown (h'cap, B W Hills, rtd 90): rnr up fnl 2 '98 starts (rtd 81): eff at 7f/1m, may get further:
acts on gd/soft & hvy grnd, gall or sharp track: likes to force the pace & runs well fresh: with N Littmoden.
1395 Test The Water 17 [11] 6-8-9 (56) B O'Leary (3) 33/1:
2835} One In The Eye 321 [10] 7-7-11 (44)(1ow)(23oh) M Henry 66/1:
3888} Petane 267 [3] 5-7-10 (43)(21oh) C Catlin (4) 66/1:
14 ran   Time 1m 32.22 (8.82)   (S J Harrison)   Mrs A L M King Wilmcote, Warwicks

1744   4.15 ARENA LEISURE HCAP 3YO+ 0-90 (C)   1m1f   Good Inapplicbale   [88]
£7117   £2190   £1095   £547   3 yo rec 12lb

1445 **ICE 14** [2] M Johnston 4-10-0 (88)(vis) K Fallon 5/1: 040-51: 4 b g Polar Falcon - Sarabah (Ela Mana   93
Mou) Held up, outpcd over 3f out, drvn past its last, led near line: '99 wnr Swiss 2,000 Guineas
& at York (h'cap, rtd 100): '98 wnr at Musselburgh & York (2, h'caps rtd 94): eff at 1m/9f on fast, likes gd or
hvy, handles any trk, loves York: carries head high & needs strong handling.
1370 **YOUNG UN 18** [9] M J Ryan 5-8-2 (62) J Tate 6/1: -06042: 5 b h Efisio - Stardyn (Star Appeal)   nk 66
Chsd ldrs, rdn/led over 1f out, kept on well inside last, hdd near line: see 786.
1450 **TAMMAM 14** [5] Mrs L Stubbs 4-9-12 (86) J P Spencer 5/1: -00053: 4 b g Priolo - Bristle (Thatch)   hd 89
Held up in tch, prog & rdn to chall over 1f out, styd on well inside last, just held: op 4/1: acts on firm & gd/soft,
prob handles soft: shown enough to win similar: see 1450, 966.
1473 **COPPLESTONE 13** [7] P W Harris 4-9-2 (76) A Culhane 9/1: 4-0244: Chsd ldrs, hmpd/lost place after   2½ 74
3f, drvn & kept on inside last, not pace to chall: op 8/1: eff at 7/9f, worth another try at 10f: see 1070.
1528 **TYLERS TOAST 10** [4] 4-8-5 (65) P Doe 12/1: 211105: Held up in tch, prog wide to chall over 3f out,   ¾ 62
rdn/hdd over 2f out & soon no extra: see 637 (AW).
1473 **CONSPICUOUS 18** [1] 10-9-6 (80) S Carson (5) 10/1: 11-066: Rear, rdn/late gains, nrst fin: bckd.   ¾ 76
*1436 **CARENS HERO 15** [6] 3-9-0 (86) R Hughes 7/2 FAV: 0-317: Led 2f, hard rdn/fdd dist: well bckd.   3½ 75
*1473 **KANZ WOOD 13** [3] 4-8-8 (68) Martin Dwyer 5/1: 050-18: Handy 3f out, briefly led over 2f out, fdd.   3½ 50
1075 **CEDAR PRINCE 36** [8] 3-8-3 (75)(bl) F Norton 16/1: 20-009: Led after 2f till over 3f out, wknd: '99   6 48
Ascot wnr (h'cap, 1st time blinks, rtd 82 at best): eff at 7f on a stiff/sharp track, on fast & gd: suited by blinks.
9 ran   Time 1m 56.30 (5.8)   (J David Abell)   M Johnston Middleham, N Yorks

1745   4.45 COUNTRY&WESTERN CLASS STKS 3YO 0-65 (E)   7f aw rnd Going 30 +04 Fast
£2816   £804   £402

1569 **ATYLAN BOY 8** [2] B J Meehan 3-8-11 Dane O'Neill 5/1: 0-0031: 3 b g Efisio - Gold Flair (Tap On   78a
Wood) Handy, rdn/prog 2f out & soon clr, readily: value for 8L+: op 9/2, first win, AW bow: unplcd as
a juv (rtd 78 at best): eff at 7f, tried 1m, should suit: acts on equitrack & soft grnd, sharp or stiff/gall trk:
ran well in similar though admittedly today: plenty in hand here, took to this surface well, can win again.
1388 **DIVA 17** [5] Sir Mark Prescott 3-8-8 G Duffield 3/1: 6052: 3 b f Exit To Nowhere - Opera Lover   7 62a
(Sadler's Wells) Rdn/chsd ldrs over 2f out, soon outpcd by wnr: hvly bckd: '98 scorer & 1m+ should suit.
1467 **KINSMAN 13** [1] I A Balding 3-8-11 (vis) K Fallon 2/1 FAV: 300623: 3 b g Distant Relative - Besito   shd 65a
(Wassl) Led after 1f till over 2f out, soon outpcd by easy wnr: hvly bckd: see 1467, 534.
*636 **LUCKY STAR 94** [6] D Marks 3-8-8 J Fortune 5/1: 6-1314: Chsd ldrs, btn 3f out: abs: btr 636.   6 53a
1345 **ANDYS ELECTIVE 19** [4] 3-8-11 M Tebbutt 14/1: 4-3605: Chsd ldrs 5f: op 10/1: see 717 (mdn).   3 50a
1349 **LADYWELL BLAISE 19** [7] 3-8-8 M Fenton 8/1: 146406: Dwelt, al wide/rear: bckd, op 10/1: see 334 (mdn).3 41a
1349 **SHAYZAN 19** [8] 3-8-11 (t) Martin Dwyer 25/1: 046-07: Dwelt, al rear: t-strap: unplcd in '99 (rtd 72).   hd 43a
1040 **ARCTIC HIGH 39** [3] 3-8-8 J Weaver 9/1: 323038: Led 1f, btn halfway: btr 1040, 610 (fbrsnd, 9f ,mdn).   12 22a
8 ran   Time 1m 24.61 (1.81)   (Mrs Sheila Tucker)   B J Meehan Upper Lambourn, Berks

---

BADEN-BADEN   FRIDAY JUNE 2ND   Lefthand, Sharpish, Turning Track

Official Going   GOOD TO SOFT

BADEN-BADEN   FRIDAY JUNE 2ND   Lefthand, Sharpish, Turning Track

1746   3.25 GR 3 BENAZET-RENNEN 3YO+   6f   Good/Soft
£24194   £9677   £4839   3 yo   rec 8 lb

-- **SKIP** [6] U Suter 6-9-6 T Mundry 196/10: 1: 6 b g Distinctly North - Etching (Auction Ring) **117**
Chsd ldrs, ran on well for press to lead cl-home, drvn out: v eff at 6f on gd/soft grnd: smart German gelding.
2492} **SUPER LOVER** 335 [5] W Baltromei 4-9-6 P Van de Keere 225/10: 1D4-2: 4 ch c Dashing Blade - **nk 116**
Superlativa (Superlative) Hdwy from rear halfway, led briefly ins last, held nr fin: eff at 6f on gd/soft.
4325} **TERTULLIAN** 236 [8] P Schiergen 5-9-6 T Hellier 49/10: 3132-3: 5 ch h Miswaki - Turbaine **nk 115**
(Trempolino) Cl-up, rdn to lead appr fnl 1f, hdd ins last, no extra: eff arnd 6f on gd & soft grnd.
1171 **PRIMO VALENTINO** 27 [3] P W Harris 3-8-10 Pat Eddery 1/2 FAV: 111-06: Led, hdd over 1f out, fdd: **3¾ 103**
btn nrly 4L into 6th: reportedly unsuited to the 'sticky' grnd here: v smart at best: see 1171.
1453 **TOMBA** 10 [2] 6-9-6 M Tebbutt 42/10: 010-27: Trkd ldrs, wknd from halfway, fin 7th: well below **½ 104**
best on favoured grnd here, reportedly possibly dehydrated: btr 1453.
9 ran   Time 1m 12.19   (L Plietzsch)   U Suter Baden-Baden, Germany

CHANTILLY   SATURDAY JUNE 3RD   Righthand, Galloping Track

Official Going   GOOD TO SOFT

1747   1.50 GR 2 PRIX DU GROS-CHENE 3YO+   5f   Good/Soft
£28818   £11527   £5764   3 yo   rec 12 lb

4531} **NUCLEAR DEBATE** 174 [5] J E Hammond 5-9-2 G Mosse 7/1: 120-61: 5 b g Geiger Counter - I'm An **116**
Issue (Cox's Ridge) Settled last, gd hdwy over 1f out, drvn out to lead cl-home: dual '99 scorer, incl a List
race at Deauville (rtd 104): ex-Mrs Ramsden, in '98 won at Thirsk (mdn) & Newcastle (h'cap, rtd 100 at best):
suited by 5/6f on gd/soft & soft, handles fast &gd : smart & improving, may take his chance in the King's Stand.
1320 **WATCHING** 20 [1] R Hannon 3-8-9 T Jarnet 3/1: 3-2122: 3 ch c Indian Ridge - Sweeping (Indian **hd 115**
King) Led, hdd 2f out, rall to lead again well ins last, hdd nr fin: another smart run: v tough, see 1320.
1320 **SELTITUDE** 20 [4] J E Hammond 4-8-12 O Peslier 9/10 FAV: 110-33: 4 b f Fairy King - Dunoof **¾ 109**
(Shirley Heights) Trkd ldrs, went on 2f out, hdd/no extra well ins last last: see 1320.
5 ran   Time 58.7   (J R Chester)   J E Hammond France

1748   2.55 GR 3 PRIX DE ROYAUMONT 3YO FILLIES   1m4f   Good/Soft
£21134   £7685   £3842

944 **SADLERS FLAG** 52 [6] Mme C Head 3-9-0 O Doleuze 3/1: -13211: 3 b f Sadler's Wells - Animatrice **107**
(Alleged) Raced keenly in rear, switched & hdwy 2f out, styd on well for press, drvn to lead cl-home: recent
C/D scorer: eff around 10/12f on gd/soft grnd: useful
-- **FLAWLY** [2] E Lellouche 3-9-0 C Soumillon 73/10: 46-512: 3 b f Old Vic - Flawlessly (Rainbow **hd 106**
Quest) Led 5f, led again 2f out, kept on well for press, hdd fnl strides: eff at 12f on gd/soft, further suit.
-- **MAEANDER** [1] A Fabre 3-9-0 O Peslier 9/10 FAV: -213: 3 ch f Nashwan - Massaraat (Nureyev) **3 101**
Waited with, switched & hdwy 2f out, drvn/no extra fnl 1f.
*964 **SKIMRA** 46 [3] R Guest 3-9-0 G Duffield 86/10: 26-15: Prom, led after 5f, hdd appr fnl 2f, **7½ 91**
fdd, fin 5th: highly tried Brit raider, will apprec a drop in grade: see 964 (fillies mdn).
6 ran   Time 2m 32.0   (Wertheimer Et Frere)   Mme C Head France

SUFFOLK DOWNS (USA)   SATURDAY JUNE 3RD   --

Official Going   FAST (DIRT)

1749   10.40 GR 2 MASSACHUSETTS HCAP 3YO+   1m1f   Fast
£243902   £60976   £30488

*1616 **RUNNING STAG** 10 [9] P Mitchell 6-8-4 J R Velazquez : 2-2011: 6 b h Cozzene - Fruhlingstag **115a**
(Orsini) Trkd ldrs, went on appr fnl 1f, kept on well, rdn out: recent wnr at Belmont (stks): '99 wnr at
Belmont & Saratoga (Gr 2 h'caps, rtd 118a & 120), prev term scored at Lingfield (stks, rtd 107a) & Deauville
(Gr 3, rtd 117): eff at 7.5f, well suited by 9/10f on firm & gd/soft, loves equitrack & dirt: runs well fresh
on any trk, likes a sharp one: v tough & smart globe-trotting dude.
-- **OUT OF MIND** [6] United States 5-8-2 E Delahoussaye : 2: 5 br h Sestero - Optativa (Janus II) **2 111a**
-- **DAVID USA** [7] United States 4-8-1 A Gryder : 3: 4 ch c Mt Livermore - Fateful Beauty (Turkoman) **2 108a**
8 ran   Time 1m 49.45   (Richard J Cohen)   P Mitchell Epsom, Surrey

NAAS   SATURDAY JUNE 3RD   Lefthand, Stiff, Galloping Track

Official Going   YIELDING

1750   2.30 MUJADIL EBF FILLIES MDN 2YO   6f   Yielding
£6900   £1800   £700

-- **RED CORAL** [16] A P O'Brien 2-9-0 M J Kinane 8/13 FAV: 1: 2 b f Fairy King - Coral Fury (Mill **98**
Reef) Cl-up, prog to lead 2f out, styd on well, rdn out, comfortably: half-sister to wng juv Pink Coral:
eff at 6f, further shld suit: acts well on gd/sft grnd: well-regarded, R Ascot bound if cut in the grnd.
-- **LADY OF KILDARE** [4] T J Taaffe 2-9-0 F M Berry 25/1: -02: 2 b f Mujadil - Dancing Sunset (Red **1½ 91**
Sunset) Prom, hdwy to chall 3f out, hdd 2f out, not pace of wnr ins fnl 1f: stays 6f on gd/soft.

NAAS   SATURDAY JUNE 3RD   Lefthand, Stiff, Galloping Track

--   **MARSEILLE EXPRESS** [11] M J Grassick 2-9-0 E Ahern 9/1: 3: 2 cf f Caerleon - Sweet Soul Dream   1½   87
(Conquistador Cielo) In tch, gd hdwy over 1f out, held ins last: debut, stays 6f on gd/soft.
15 ran   Time 1m 14.0   (Manchester United Racing Club)   A P O'Brien Ballydoyle, Co Tipperary

1751   3.00 SUPPORTING NAAS RACE 3YO+   7f   Yielding
£5865   £1360   £595

4029} **MURAWWI** 258 [5] D K Weld 3-9-2 (bl) P J Smullen 1/1 FAV: 042-21: 3 b c Perugino - Pheopotstown   107
(Henbit) Led to 5f out, sn led again, rdn clr over 1f out, cmftbly: recent rnr-up on reapp: '99 Curragh mdn wnr,
subs head rnr-up at 50/1 in Gr 1 National Stks (rtd 107): eff at 7f/1m on gd/sft & soft: win a Listed/Gr race.
3699} **SAND PARTRIDGE** 279 [6] K Prendergast 3-8-11 S Craine 5/1: 510-02: 3 b f Desert Style - Pipe Opener   5   91
(Prince Sabo) Prom, drvn & not pace of wnr over 1f out: '99 Punchestown mdn wnr (7.5f, gd/yldg).
--   **PLURABELLE** [2] J S Bolger 3-8-11 K J Manning 5/1: 14-3: 3 b f Irish River - Wild Bluebell   1   89
(Bluebird) Handy, no extra for press appr fnl 1f: reapp: '99 scorer at Gowran Park (7f mdn, gd/yldg).
6 ran   Time 1m 25.1   (Hamdan Al Maktoum)   D K Weld Curragh, Co Kildare

CHANTILLY   SUNDAY JUNE 4TH   Righthand, Galloping Track

Official Going   VERY SOFT

1752   3.05 GR 1 PRIX DU JOCKEY CLUB 3YO   1m4f   V Soft
£240154   £96061   £48031   £24015

*1380 **HOLDING COURT** 17 [14] M A Jarvis 3-9-2 P Robinson 61/10: 10-111: 3 b c Hernando - Indian   122
Love Song (Be My Guest) Made all, clr 3f out, qcknd 2f out & styd on powerfully in clr lead for an impressive win:
earlier won at Haydock (reapp, rtd h'cap) & Longchamp (Gr 3): '99 wnr again at Haydock (stks, rtd 97, B Meehan):
half brother to high-class 6/7f performer Tomba: stays 12f well, further shld suit: acts on gd, loves soft/hvy
& a gall trk: loves to dominate & runs well fresh: most progressive & high-class colt, given a fine positive
ride here, may be supplemented for the Irish Derby & would prove hard to beat with cut in the ground.
*1231 **LORD FLASHEART** 27 [13] A de Royer Dupre 3-9-2 G Mosse 12/1: D1-212: 3 b c Blush Rambler -   6   116
Miss Henderson Co (Silver Hawk) Waited with, hdwy 2f out, styd on but no ch with wnr: tough & smart: see 1231.
--   **CIRCUS DANCE** [11] A Fabre 3-9-2 O Peslier 44/10cp: 64-13: 3 b c Sadler's Wells - Dance By Night   2   113+
(Northfields) Dwelt, bhd, hdwy 2f out, styd on well, too late: stays 12f on soft: nvr yet competitive, will improve.
1317 **KUTUB** 21 [10] F Head 3-9-2 (BL) D Bonilla 21/10cp: 1-124: Settled rear, gd hdwy over 2f out,   nk   112
no extra ins last: 1st time blnks: shade below best: see 1317 (10f), 864.
*1515 **BROCHE** 8 [1] 3-9-2 C Soumillon 108/10cp: 1-0015: Mid-div, rdn & kept on onepace over   nk   111
2f out: upped in class & not disgraced, appce a drop to Gr 3/List company.
*1317 **CIRO** 21 [6] 3-9-2 M J Kinane 44/10cp: 11-316: Handy, eff over 2f out but well bhd wnr,   nse   111
wknd fnl 1f: Irish raider: reportedly unsuited by the grnd here but did win on soft in 1317 (10f).
*1451 **ROSCIUS** 12 [3] 3-9-2 R Hills 108/10cp: 2-17: Dwelt, sn in mid-div, hdwy over 2f out,   2   108
wknd qckly ins last: up in trip/grade: better in Listed company in 1451 (9.8f, gd/sft).
*1216 **MILLENARY** 26 [9] 3-9-2 Pat Eddery 133/10: 35-118: Nvr better than mid-div: highly   1   106
tried, may apprec a sounder surface: see 1216 (Gr 3, fast grnd).
4594} **COSMOGRAPHE** 217 [4] 3-9-2 T Jarnet 21/1: 2-1130: Nvr a threat, fin 10th: see 1231.   hd   106
1231 **HESIODE** 27 [12] 3-9-2 S Guillot 21/1: 2-1130: Nvr a threat, fin 10th: see 1231.   nk   105
864   **PETROSELLI** 56 [2] 3-9-2 J Reid 48/1: 2-2450: Al bhd, fin 11th.   0
1340 **MASTERMIND** 17 [5] 3-9-2 J Fortune 51/1: 21-040: Trkd ldrs, wkng when hmpd over 1f out, fin 12th: 0
reportedly unsuited by the soft grnd here: better on firm in 1340 (10.5f, Listed).
1326 **PAWN BROKER** 18 [7] 3-9-2 T Quinn 114/10: 1-1220: Al in rear: 13th, much btr 1326 (Gr 2, 10f).   0
1314 **MUAKAAD** 21 [8] 3-9-2 P J Smullen 21/1cp: -130: Al last, fin 14th: Irish raider, btr 1314.   0
14 ran   Time 2m 31.8   (J R Good)   M A Jarvis Newmarket

1753   3.45 GR 1 PRIX JEAN PRAT 3YO   1m1f   V Soft
£38425   £15370   £7685   £3842

*1379 **SUANCES** 17 [2] M Delcher-Sanchez 3-9-2 G Mosse 26/10: 1-1111: 3 ch c Most Welcome -   119
Prayer Wheel (High Line) Prom, hdwy & qcknd into lead appr fnl 1f, rdn/drew well clr ins last: unbeaten this term,
incl at Longchamp (Gr 3): v eff arnd 9f on gd & soft: high-class spanish trained colt, shld win more valuable races.
1314 **BACH** 21 [7] A P O'Brien 3-9-2 M J Kinane 4/1: 11-122: 3 b c Caerleon - Producer (Nashua)   6   109
Mid-div, hdwy 2f out, styd on, wnr had flown: not disgraced: tough/consistent: see 1314.
*1322 **PACINO** 21 [6] Saeed bin Suroor 3-9-2 R Hills 53/10: 2-0013: 3 b c Zafonic - June Moon   snk   109
(Sadler's Wells) Cl-up, went on 2f out, sn hdd, btn ins last: poss handles soft, acts on fast: see 1322.
1246 **THREE POINTS** 24 [4] J L Dunlop 3-9-2 Pat Eddery 139/10: 13-324: Led, hdd 2f out, fdd: prob   3   104
poss unsuited by this drop in trip, bred to apprec mid-dists: see 1246 (10f, List, firm).
1318 **LOYAL TARTARE** [1] 3-9-2 T Jarnet 191/10: 2-6445: Mid-div, eff 2f out, sn btn.   1½   101
1318 **BERINES SON** 21 [5] O Peslier 13/10 FAV: 2-1126: Rear, nvr with ldrs: much btr 1318, 1025.   2½   97
7 ran   Time 1m 53.4   (J Cohen)   M Delcher-Sanchez Spain

1754   4.55 GR 3 PRIX DE SANDRINGHAM 3YO FILLIES   1m   V Soft
£21134   £7685   £3842

1319 **ZARKIYA** 21 [3] A de Royer Dupre 3-8-12 G Mosse 1/1 FAV: 1-241: 3 b f Catrail - Zarkana (Doyoun)   112
Waited with, gd hdwy over 2f out, drvn out to get up cl-home: eff arnd 1m on soft: v useful & lightly raced.
--   **PENNYS GOLD** [6] P Bary 3-8-12 S Guillot 145/10: 4-152: 3 b f Kingmambo - Penny's Valentine   hd   111
(Storm Cat) Trkd ldrs, rdn to chall ldst, kept on, just held: useful effort, eff at 1m on soft.
--   **DEVON HEIGHTS** [12] A Fabre 3-8-12 O Peslier 27/10: 0-113: 3 ch f Mt Livermore - Devon Diva   ½   110
(The Minstrel) Led to halfway, led again appr fnl 1f, styd on, hdd nr fin: eff at 1m on soft.
13 ran   Time 1m 41.7   (H H Aga Khan)   A de Royer Dupre France

TOKYO SUNDAY JUNE 4TH Lefthand Track

Official Going FIRM

1755 7.35 GR 1 YASUDA KINEN 3YO+ 1m Firm
£581037 £230201 £144787

-- **FAIRY KING PRAWN** [12] P F Yiu 4-9-2 R Fradd : 1 : 5 b g Danehill - Twiglet (Twig Moss) 121
4418} **DIKTAT 21** [10] Saeed bin Suroor 5-9-2 D O'Donohoe : 115-62: 5 br h Warning - Arvola (Sadler's nk 120
Wells) Bhd, gd hdwy 3f out, ev ch ins last, just failed: up in trip: 6th here over 7f 3 wks ago: won 1st 4
in '99, at Goodwood (stks), Newmarket (Gr 1), Deauville (Gr 1) & Haydock (Gr 1 Sprint Cup, rtd 124): '98 wnr
at Newmarket (mdn), Leicester (stks) & R Ascot (Gr 3, rtd 117): eff at 6/7f, styd this longer 1m trip v well:
runs well fresh on firm, soft & any trk: high-class & tough, win more Group races.
-- **KING HALO** [9] Japan 5-9-2 Y Fukunaga : 3: 5 b h Dancing Brave - Goodbye Halo (Halo) ¾ 119
18 ran Time 1m 33.9 (Mr & Mrs Lau Sak Hong) P F Yiu Hong Kong

LEOPARDSTOWN MONDAY JUNE 5TH Lefthand, Galloping Track

Official Going YIELDING

1756 3.00 LISTED ROCHESTOWN STKS 2YO 6f Yielding
£16250 £4750 £2250

-- **PIRATE OF PENZANCE** A P O'Brien 2-8-12 M J Kinane 5/2 FAV: 1: 2 br c Southern Halo - Stolen 101
Pleasures (Marfa) Cl-up, gd hdwy over 1f out, sn led, readily drew clr: eff at 6f on gd/sft: win more races.
*1346 **PAN JAMMER 18** M R Channon 2-9-2 J P Murtagh 7/2: 412: 2 b c Piccolo - Ingerance 2½ 94
(Akarad) Led, drvn & edged left appr fnl 1f, sn hdd, not pace of wnr: clr rem: handles fast & gd/soft: useful.
-- **BALADEUR** K Prendergast 2-9-2 D P McDonogh 3/1: -213: 2 b c Doyoun - Singing Filly (Relkino) 5 84
Prom, hdwy to chall 2f out, wknd appr fnl 1f: recent Navan scorer (5.7f mdn, hvy).
5 ran Time 1m 17.2 (Mrs John Magnier) A P O'Brien Ballydoyle, Co Tipperary

1757 3.30 GR 3 BALLYOGAN STKS 3YO+ 5f Yielding
£22750 £6650 £3150 £1050 3 yo rec 7 lb

2965} **RUDIS PET 176** D Nicholls 6-9-6 S Sanders 4/1: 2116-1: 6 ch g Don't Forget Me - Pink Fondant 115
(Northfields) Cl-up, went on over 2f out, styd on well, drvn out: made rapid improvement in '99, wng at Thirsk,
Newcastle (h'caps), Ascot (rtd h'cap) & Goodwood (Gr 3, rtd 118): unplcd in '98 (Mrs Ramsden), prev term won at
Sandown & Doncaster (rtd h'caps, rtd 87, R Hannon): stays 6f, suited by racing up with/forcing the pace over 5f:
acts on firm & hvy, eff with/without blnks: tough v smart sprinter, seems set for another successful campaign.
+1090 **CASSANDRA GO 34** G Wragg 4-9-0 M Roberts 13/2: 460-12: 4 gr f Indian Ridge - Rahaam ½ 107
(Secreto) Prom, rdn & ran on well ins last, al held by wnr: acts on fast & gd/sft: smart, win another List race.
*1529 **MONKSTON POINT 9** D W P Arbuthnot 4-9-3 (BL) S Craine 4/1: -11013: 4 b g Fayruz - Doon 3 102
Belle (Ardoon) Handy, rdn to imprv over 1f out, kept on, no dngr: gd run in blnks (usually visored): see 1529.
-- **ZILINA** C Collins 5-8-11 P Shanahan 16/1: 42-104: Mid-div, eff over 1f out, no threat. nk 96
1173 **PEPPERDINE 30** 4-9-3 J P Murtagh 7/2 FAV: 002-35: Dwelt, rear, styd on for press fnl 2f, no dngr: 1½ 99
stablemate of wnr: up in class, progressive h'capper prev & shld relish a return to 6f in that sphere.
1172 **MRS P 30** 3-8-12 E Ahern 10/1: 121-09: Al last: highly tried: see 1172. 0
9 ran Time 1m 00.4 (G H Leatham) D Nicholls Sessay, N Yorks

BEVERLEY WEDNESDAY JUNE 7TH Righthand, Oval Track With Stiff, Uphill Finish

Official Going GOOD TO SOFT Stalls: Inside

1758 6.40 RACING PAGES HCAP 3YO 0-60 (F) 1m4f Good/Soft 83 -30 Slow [66]
£3835 £1180 £590 £295

1448 **MIDDLETHORPE 15** [8] M W Easterby 3-8-13 (51) Pat Eddery 100/30 FAV: 00-051: 3 b g Noble Patriarch - 57
Prime Property (Tirol) Towards rear, stdy prog fnl 3f, rdn/led ins last, styd on well, drvn out: 1st win: plcd form
in '99 (rtd 59, h'cap): well suited by this step up to 12f, may get further: acts on gd & gd/soft, sharp/stiff trk.
1633 **ONE DOMINO 6** [13] M Dods 3-9-5 (57)(vis) A Culhane 13/2: -30032: 3 ch g Efisio - Dom One ¾ 61
(Dominion) Mid-div, rdn/prog to chall fnl 1f, just held nr fin: styd this longer 12f trip: acts on fast & soft grnd.
4606} **TYPHOON TILLY 215** [3] C F Wall 3-8-12 (50) R Mullen 12/1: 000-3: 3 b g Hernando - Meavy (Kalaglow) 1¼ 52
Chsd ldrs, rdn/led over 1f out, hdd ins last & no extra cl-home: op 14/1: h'cap bow, reapp: unplcd at up
to 1m last term (rtd 60, mdn): relished this step up to 12f, may get further: acts on gd/soft grnd.
1571 **SUAVE PERFORMER 8** [1] S C Williams 3-8-13 (51) G Faulkner (3) 7/2: 045424: Towards rear, no 1¼ 51
room 3f out & switched 2f out, prog/chsd ldrs 1f out, held nr fin: op 3/1: see 1571, 827.
3686} **SADLERS SONG 282** [9] 3-9-1 (53) S Drowne 14/1: 6005-5: In tch, rdn/ch over 1f out, sn held: reapp: 1¾ 51
h'cap bow: unplcd last term for P C Haslam (rtd 58, mdn): mid-dists looks sure to suit this term for M R Channon.
1274 **UNICORN STAR 25** [15] 3-8-12 (50) J McAuley (5) 12/1: 40-436: Chsd ldrs, onepace fnl 2f: op 10/1. ½ 47
1103 **WETHAAB 35** [4] 3-9-3 (55) W Supple 10/1: 0-047: Handy, led over 2f out, hdd over 1f out & wknd: 6 44
tchd 14/1, h'cap bow/longer 12f trip: see 1103, 717.
1274 **HORTON DANCER 25** [14] 3-8-11 (49)(vis) D Mernagh (3) 20/1: -60048: Handy, led 4f out till 2f out, fdd. 2 35
1615 **CLAUDIUS TERTIUS 7** [11] 3-8-9 (47) N Callan 6/1: 00-009: In tch 10f: op 8/1: lngr 12f trip: see 1615. 7 24
1657 **MISTER GILL 5** [12] 3-9-7 (59) J Fanning 25/1: 00-000: Mid-div at best: 10th: see 1657. ½ 35
827 **SORRENTO KING 63** [2] 3-8-12 (50)(bl) G Parkin 33/1: 400-00: Led 1m, bhd fnl 2f: 14th: unplcd 0
last term (rtd 62, 1st time blnks, h'cap): stays a sharp 7f, bred to apprec mid-dists: handles fast grnd.
1615 Moose Malloy 7 [6] 3-8-10 (48) P McCabe 12/1: 1274 Highcal 25 [7] 3-8-12 (50) F Lynch 66/1:
1581 Bitty Mary 8 [10] 3-8-12 (50) G Carter 50/1: 1480 First Back 13 [5] 3-9-5 (57) P Goode (3) 12/1:
15 ran Time 2m 44.8 (13.5) (J H Quickfall & A G Black) M W Easterby Sheriff Hutton, N Yorks

BEVERLEY WEDNESDAY JUNE 7TH Righthand, Oval Track With Stiff, Uphill Finish

1759 7.10 HILARY NEEDLER COND STKS 2YO (B) 5f Good/Soft 83 +03 Fast
£8763 £3324 £1662 £755

-- **FREEFOURRACING** [6] B J Meehan 2-8-5 Pat Eddery 11/1: 1: 2 b f French Deputy - Gerri N Jo Go (Top Command) Rdn & towards rear, switched & strong run for press from over 1f out, led nr fin: fast juvenile time: Mar foal, half sister to a 6f juv wnr & subs useful 6/7f h'cap performer Al Muallim: dam a 6/7f wnr: eff at 5f, 6f sure to suit: acts on gd/soft & a stiff trk: runs well fresh: fine debut, v useful & worth following. **100+**
*1641 **RED MILLENNIUM 5** [8] A Berry 2-8-8 G Carter 11/4: 1212: 2 b f Tagula - Lovely Me (Vision) Led, clr over 1f out, wknd & hdd well ins last: nicely bckd: confirmed improvement of latest: tough & useful. ½ **100**
1486 **HEJAZIAH 13** [9] P F I Cole 2-8-8 T Quinn 8/13 FAV: 23: 2 b f Gone West - Toptrestle (Nijinsky) Cl-up, rdn/onepace fnl 2f: hvly bckd: well clr of rem: acts on gd/soft: a return to 6f shld suit: see 1486. ¾ **98**
1621 **INNIT 11** [1] M R Channon 2-8-12 S Drowne 10/1: 321354: Sltly hmpd start & went badly left, bhd, mod late gains: op 8/1: lost chance at start today, prob best forgiven: see 1621, 1189. 7 **91**
*1429 **FRANICA 16** [3] 2-8-8 R Mullen 20/1: 222015: Chsd ldrs till halfway: op 12/1: see 1429 (fast). 4 **79**
886 **ASTER FIELDS 56** [2] 2-8-8 N Callan 100/1: 06: Went left start, sn bhd: highly tried, abs: see 886. 7 **68**
1558 **PROMISED 9** [4] 2-8-8 D Mernagh 14/1: 137: Al bhd: op 10/1: see 1558, 1131. *nk* **67**
1426 **QUIZZICAL LADY 16** [5] 2-8-8 J Carroll 14/1: 516048: Prom till halfway: op 20/1: see 1000 (hvy). *nk* **66**
8 ran Time 1m 05.3 (4.0) (Roldvale Ltd) B J Meehan Upper Lambourn, Berks

1760 7.40 TOTE EXACTA HCAP 3YO+ 0-70 (E) 7f100y rnd Good/Soft 83 +02 Fast **[66]**
£5018 £1544 £772 £386 3 yo rec 10lb

1296 **MELODIAN 23** [11] M Brittain 5-9-10 (62)(bl) D Mernagh (3) 6/1: 231041: 5 b f Grey Desire - Mere Melody (Dunphy) Chsd ldrs, prog/rdn to lead ins last, styd on strongly, rdn clr: earlier scored at Newcastle (h'cap, made all): '99 wnr here at Beverley, also Doncaster & Catterick (h'caps, rtd 56): '98 Newcastle wnr (h'cap, rtd 44): eff at 7f, stays 1m well: acts on firm & hvy, any trk: suited by blnks: likes Beverley: tough & improving. **71**
1724 **NAISSANT 2** [13] J S Goldie 7-8-10 (48) A Culhane 8/1: 063042: 7 b m Shaadi - Nophe (Super Concorde) Chsd ldrs, rdn/led over 1f out, hdd ins last & no extra: quick reapp: see 844 (6f). 6 **48**
1658 **LEOFRIC 5** [2] M J Polglase 5-8-5 (43)(bl) G Carter 16/1: 303063: 5 b g Alhijaz - Wandering Stranger (Petong) Towards rear, rdn & prog fnl 3f, onepace/held ins last: quick reapp: see 973 (sell). 1¾ **40**
1718 **ZECHARIAH 2** [9] J L Eyre 4-8-7 (45) F Lynch 14/1: -46564: Cl-up, rdn/ch over 1f out, sn no extra: qck reapp: handles fast, gd/soft & fibresand: see 907. *nk* **41**
3462} **RIVER BLEST 292** [15] 4-9-5 (57) J Fanning 33/1: 0336-5: Led till over 1f out, no extra: reapp: plcd in '99 (rtd 59, class stks): eff at 6f, styd this longer 7.5f trip: handles fast & gd/soft grnd. 1 **51**
1462 **TROPICAL BEACH 14** [7] 7-8-9 (47)(vis) G Bardwell 10/1: 04-066: Dwelt, sn rdn/bhd, mod late gains. 1½ **39**
1498 **HIGH SUN 12** [5] 4-9-2 (54) N Callan 33/1: -40007: Mid-div, held fnl 2f: see 942. ¾ **45**
1132 **BERNARDO BELLOTTO 34** [1] 5-8-10 (48) K Hodgson 33/1: -00008: Bhd, mod prog fnl 2f for press. *hd* **38**
*1606 **BODFARI ANNA 7** [4] 4-9-0 (52)(vis)(6ex) T Quinn 8/1: 545019: Rear, mod gains: btr 1606 (sft). 1¼ **40**
1631 **VICTORIOUS 6** [3] 4-9-9 (61)(t) K Darley 5/1: 110050: Mid-div, no prog fnl 2f: 10th: quick reapp. 1½ **47**
879 **ROI DE DANSE 56** [10] 5-8-4 (42) S Drowne 50/1: 250250: Mid-div, btn 2f out: 11th: abs: see 227, 203. ¾ **27**
1448 **SPORTING GESTURE 15** [8] 3-9-7 (69) Pat Eddery 4/1 FAV: 10-000: Al bhd: 12th: see 1279. 2½ **50**
*1506 **HAUNT THE ZOO 12** [12] 5-8-4 (42) K Dalgleish (7) 25/1: 000010: Mid-div, btn 2f out: 14th: btr 1506 (AW). **0**
1421 **Foist 16** [6] 8-8-10 (48) T Lucas 13/2: 1423 **Arius 16** [16] 4-9-3 (55)(bl) G Hind 40/1:
1718 **Pleading 2** [14] 7-9-9 (61) J Carroll 12/1:
16 ran Time 1m 36.9 (6.1) (Mel Brittain) M Brittain Warthill, N Yorks

1761 8.10 BRIAN YEARDLEY COND STKS 2YO (B) 5f Good/Soft 83 -05 Slow
£8752 £3319 £1659 £754

1628 **MAMMAS TONIGHT 6** [9] A Berry 2-8-9 G Carter 13/2: 13331: 2 ch g Timeless Times - Miss Merlin (Manacle) Rdn/bhd halfway, strong run for press from over 1f out, led nr fin: quick reapp: earlier scored on debut at Southwell (auct mdn, rtd 79a): eff at 5f, stays 6f & a return to further will suit: acts on fast, hvy & fibresand: handles any trk, loves a stiff one: has run well fresh: tough & improving. **101**
*1595 **BOUNCING BOWDLER 7** [3] M Johnston 2-8-13 J Fanning 11/4: -32212: 2 b c Mujadil - Prima Volta (Primo Dominie) Sn led, hard rdn ins last & hdd nr fin, no extra: brave front running performance: useful. 1 **102**
*1146 **UP TEMPO 33** [7] T D Easterby 2-8-9 K Darley 2/1 FAV: 213: 2 b c Flying Spur - Musical Essence (Song) Chsd ldr halfway, rdn/held ins last: well clr of rem: gd run: see 1146. 1½ **94**
*1252 **THE NAMES BOND 26** [8] Andrew Turnell 2-8-13 W Supple 14/1: -314: In tch, outpcd fnl 2f: see 1252. 6 **89$**
1426 **SOLDIER ON 16** [5] 2-8-13 S Drowne 16/1: 02155: In tch, held 2f out: see 1208 (firm). 1¼ **87$**
*1497 **AFFARATI 12** [1] 2-9-1 T Quinn 4/1: 216: Bhd halfway, no impress: see 1497 (stks, 6f). 3½ **82$**
1475 **HAMBLETON HIGHLITE 13** [2] 2-8-11 F Lynch 12/1: 137: In tch, btn 2f out: see 1475, 1240. 5 **70**
1443 **TOMMY SMITH 15** [6] 2-8-9 J Carroll 100/1: 08: Bhd 2f out: highly tried: see 1443 (sell, C/D). 5 **60**
8 ran Time 1m 05.70 (4.4) (J K Brown) A Berry Cockerham, Lancs

1762 8.40 KINGSTON HCAP 3YO+ 0-80 (D) 1m110y rnd Good/Soft 83 -12 Slow **[76]**
£4576 £1408 £704 £352

1251 **LITTLE AMIN 27** [6] W R Muir 4-9-8 (70) K Darley 12/1: 0-0001: 4 b g Unfuwain - Ghassanah (Pas de Seul) Trkd ldr, rdn/led over 2f out, styd on well ins last, rdn out: '99 reapp Newcastle wnr (mdn, J Bethell), subs scored for current connections at Haydock (h'caps, rtd 80): plcd in '98 (rtd 79): eff over a gall 12f, well suited by drop to a stiff 1m tonight: loves gd/soft & soft grnd & can force the pace. **76**
1217 **GRALMANO 29** [7] K A Ryan 5-9-8 (70) F Lynch 3/1: 0-1452: 5 b g Scenic - Llangollen (Caerleon) Dictated pace till over 2f out, rdn & kept on fnl 1f, not pace of wnr: see 551 (AW). 1¼ **72**
1547 **TIPPERARY SUNSET 9** [2] D Shaw 6-8-12 (60) N Callan 4/1: 5-0023: 6 gr g Red Sunset - Chapter And Verse (Dancers Image) Rear/in tch, eff over 2f out & prog/no room over 1f out, onepace ins last: see 1007. 1½ **59**
1583 **SALIGO 8** [4] N Tinkler 5-8-12 (60) J Fanning 5/2 FAV: 000034: Bhd ldrs, onepace fnl 2f: bckd. *hd* **58**
1579 **KASS ALHAWA 8** [5] 7-9-7 (69) A Culhane 10/1: 062405: Bhd ldrs, rdn/held over 1f out: see 908, 38 5 **59**
1575 **KHUCHN 8** [3] 4-8-4 (52)(t) D Mernagh (3) 5/1: 050526: Trkd ldr, rdn/btn 2f out: btr 1575 (10f) 1 **40**
1490 **OPEN ARMS 12** [1] 4-9-10 (72) W Supple 25/1: 3/3-07: Rear/in tch, left bhd fnl 2f: plcd sole '99 start (h'cap, rtd 74): plcd in '98 (rtd 76, nurs, C Brittain): stays 1m, get further: acts on firm & gd grnd. 14 **40**
7 ran Time 1m 51.9 (8.1) (Sheikh Amin Dahlawi) W R Muir Lambourn, Berks

BEVERLEY   WEDNESDAY JUNE 7TH   Righthand, Oval Track With Stiff, Uphill Finish

1763   9.10 ARTHUR CAMPBELL MDN 3YO+ (D)   7f100y rnd   Good/Soft 83   -29 Slow
£3477   £1070   £535   £267   3 yo rec 10lb   Raced centre fnl 3f

1444 **SUTTON COMMON** 15 [3] K A Ryan 3-8-11 F Lynch 10/1: 4-2021: 3 b c Common Grounds - Fadaki Hawaki   74
(Vice Regent) Led/dsptd lead till went on halfway, rdn/strongly prsd from 2f out, held on gamely nr fin, all out:
rtd 73 in '99 (mdn): eff at 7f/7.5f, tried 1m: acts on gd & gd/soft grnd, sharp/stiff trk: can force the pace.
1352 **GOLDEN CHANCE** 19 [4] M Johnston 3-8-11 J Fanning 11/2: 32: 3 b c Unfuwain - Golden Digger   hd   75
(Mr Prospector) Bhd ldrs, prog to chall fnl 2f, rdn/duelled with wnr ins last, just held: eff at 7.5f/1m: see 1352.
3962 **FLUME** 264 [1] B W Hills 3-8-6 W Supple 9/2: 44-3: 3 br f Zafonic - Rainy Sky (Rainbow Quest)   5   62
Led/dsptd lead till halfway, outpcd fnl 2f: reapp: 4th on both '99 starts (rtd 95, fills mdn, debut): eff at 6/7f,
mid-dist bred & sure to apprec 1m+: handles firm & fast: leave this bhd in h'caps over further.
1224 **INCREDULOUS** 28 [2] J R Fanshawe 3-8-6 D Harrison 4/9 FAV: 0-24: Pulled hard bhd ldrs, left bhd   19   34
over 2f out: needs to learn to settle: btr 1224 (gd/fm).
4 ran   Time 1m 39.2 (8.4)   (The North Broomhill Racing Syndicate)   K A Ryan Hambleton, N Yorks

NEWCASTLE   WEDNESDAY JUNE 7TH   Lefthand, Galloping, Stiff Track

Official Going   SOFT (HEAVY in places). Stalls: Str Crse - Stands Side; Rnd Crse - Inside; 1m2f - Outside.

1764   2.20 THEHORSESMOUTH MDN 2YO (D)   5f   Heavy 167   -40 Slow
£3493   £1075   £537   £268   Field tacked over to far side.

-- **RUMORE CASTAGNA** [6] S E Kettlewell 2-9-0 A Culhane 8/1: 1: 2 ch g Great Commotion - False Spring   78
(Petorius): Prom, hdwy to lead appr final 1f, rdn out ins last: op 6/1, debut: Apr foal, cost 11,000 gns:
half-brother to a 7f/9f scorer: eff at 5f, 6f will suit: clearly enjoys hvy grnd & runs well fresh: pleasing.
1131 **BOMBAY BINNY** 34 [4] T D Easterby 2-8-9 K Darley 6/1: 02: 2 b f First Trump - Bombay Sapphire   3½   65
(Be My Chief) Led over 2f out till appr final 1f, sn slightly short of room, not pace of wnr: handles hvy.
-- **SIAMO DISPERATI** [3] C B B Booth 2-9-0 A McKeown K Hodgson 4/1: 3: 2 ch c Aragon - Jambo (Rambo Dancer): 1½   67
Sn bhd, effort over 1f out, onepace: debut: Feb 1st foal, cost 5,200 gns: dam 7f juv wnr: bred for 6/7f.
-- **OLYS GILL** [5] J J O'Neill 2-9-0 C Lowther 16/1: 4: In tch, bhd 2f out: Mar foal, cost 7,200 gns.   5   52
-- **PROCEED WITH CARE** [1] 2-9-0 J Fanning 4/7 FAV: 5: Led till over 2f out, wknd over 1f out: bckd   hd   57
on debut: Apr foal, half-brother to a useful 6/7f juv wnr: dam 1m scorer: with M Johnston, do better on gd?
-- **HANDSOME LAD** [2] 2-9-0 A McGlone 11/1: 6: Missed break & al well bhd on debut: Apr foal, cost   16   27
11,000 IR gns: half-brother to a 5f juv wnr: with A Scott.
6 ran   Time 1m 08.57 (10.37)   (Middleham Park Racing XXIV)   S E Kettlewell Middleham, Nth. Yorks.

1765   2.50 BET TAX FREE HCAP 3YO 0-85 (D)   1m rnd   Heavy 167   -14 Slow   [91]
£3802   £1170   £585   £292

1610 **PIPS WAY** 7 [4] K R Burke 3-8-10 (73) N Callan 13/2: 0-6041: 3 ch f Pips Pride - Algonquin Park   80
(High Line) Keen, handy, led 2f out, rdn clr ins last: won '99 debut at Ripon (mdn, rtd 84): eff at 6f, suited
by 1m now & handles fast, revels in hvy: prob handles any trk & has tried a vis to no avail: has run well fresh.
1387 **INDIAN SUN** 18 [1] J L Dunlop 3-8-13 (76) K Darley 7/2: -46002: 3 ch g Indian Ridge - Star Tulip   3½   77
(Night Shift) Led till 3f out, rallied for press over 1f out, not pace of wnr ins last: handles firm, acts on
hvy & stays 1m, well worth a try over further now: see 994, 792.
1183 **KATHIR** 31 [2] A C Stewart 3-9-7 (84) R Hills 11/8 FAV: 21-03: 3 ch c Woodman - Alcando (Alzao)   1½   83
Keen, handy, rdn 3f out, swtchd & kept on over 1f out, btn ins last: acts on fast, prob handles hvy: see 1183.
1387 **INDY CARR** 18 [5] M Dods 3-8-7 (70) F Lynch 12/1: 1-604: In tch, rdn over 3f out, no impress: see 900.   2½   65
1387 **MANA DARGENT** 18 [3] 3-8-11 (74) J P Spencer 3/1: 3-2045: Led 3f out till 2f out, no extra: btr 1387.   8   59
5 ran   Time 1m 53.5 (14.5)   (Paul James McCaughey)   K R Burke Newmarket.

1766   3.20 ST JAMES SELLER 3YO+ (G)   5f   Heavy 167   -04 Slow
£1961   £556   £283   3 yo rec 7 lb   Field raced far side except Nifty Norman

1664 **RED SYMPHONY** 5 [8] J Semple 4-9-0 (VIS) N Callan 14/1: -50001: 3 b f Merdon Melody - Woodland   45
Steps (Bold Owl) Handy, styd on over 1f out to lead ins last, rdn out: qck reapp: plcd twice in '99 (rtd 58
at best): '98 wnr at W'hampton (sell, rtd 60a) & Musselburgh (2, sell & nursery, with J Berry, rtd 70): all
4 wins a 5f, revels in hvy & on fibresand: handles any trk: relished drop to sell grade & visor.
1298 **SOUPERFICIAL** 23 [7] Don Enrico Incisa 9-9-5 Kim Tinkler 10/1: 00-002: 9 gr g Petong - Duck Soup   1½   47
(Decoy Boy): Slow away, bhd, kept on over 1f out, nrst fin: gd run, will apprec sell h'caps: see 1073.
1479 **AVONDALE GIRL** 13 [3] M Dods 4-9-0 F Lynch 7/4 FAV: 500063: 4 ch f Case Law - Battle Queen   1   40
(Kind Of Hush) Cl-up, went on over 1f out till ins last, no extra: bckd tho' op 5/4: should rate higher (off 64).
1663 **JACKERIN** 5 [1] B S Rothwell 5-9-5 M Roberts 8/1: 440664: Bhd, kept on over 1f out, nrst fin.   1   43
1724 **HENRY THE HAWK** 2 [4] 9-9-5 (bl) C Teague 16/1: 4-4005: Chsd ldrs, onepace over 1f out: clr of   ½   42
rem, qck reapp: would apprec sell h'cap company: see 756.
1244 **BANDIDA** 27 [9] 6-9-0 R Lappin 20/1: 06: Bhd, no impress final 2f: see 1244.   10   19
1430 **SWEET MAGIC** 16 [13] 9-9-10 (t) K Darley 8/1: 404147: Prom, btn over 1f out: btr 1392 (fibresand).   1   27
1392 **NIFTY NORMAN** 18 [14] 6-9-10 (bl) O Pears 9/2: 634638: Bhd alone on stands side: ignore this.   1¼   25
3783 **BLAZING IMP** 275 [6] 7-9-5 T Williams 33/1: 0000-9: In tch, wknd over 1f out: in '99 trained by   ¾   18
Mrs J Jordan: modest form term: '98 wnr at Hamilton (sell, rtd 50): eff at 5f on fast & gd/soft.
1578 **CHOK DI** 8 [2] 4-9-5 (bl) T Eaves (7) 33/1: 000000: Led far side till over 1f out, wknd: 10th.   2   14
1137 **JAZZNIC** 34 [12] 4-9-5 A Daly 10/1: -60100: In tch, btn halfway: 11th, twice well below 883 (equitrack).   4   6
1479 Roses Treasure 13 [10] 4-9-0 J P Spencer (7)   1562 Reds Desire 9 [5] 3-8-12 V Halliday 50/1:
1430 Palacegate Jack 16 [11] (bl) D Allan (7) 12/1:
14 ran   Time 1m 06.75 (8.55)   (W Edward)   I Semple Carluke, Sth Lanarks.

NEWCASTLE WEDNESDAY JUNE 7TH Lefthand, Galloping, Stiff Track

1767
3.50 TAX CLASSIFIED STKS 3YO+ 0-60 (F) 1m4f93y Heavy 167 -02 Slow
£2649 £757 £378 3 yo rec 15lb

1363 **MR FORTYWINKS** 19 [1] J L Eyre 6-9-7 R Cody Boutcher (7) 3/1: 0-2041: 6 ch g Fool's Holme - Dream On **60**
(Absalom) Made all, kept on well for press over 1f out, hdd briefy ins last, gamely: op 7/4: '99 wnr at
Hamilton, Ripon (lady riders) & Carlisle (h'caps, rtd 70): '98 wnr at W'hampton, Southwell & Nottingham (rtd 63
& 71a): best up with/forcing the pace over 11/13f on firm, hvy or fibresand: genuine, stable in tremendous heart.
848 **LASTMAN** 60 [2] J J O'Neill 5-9-7 J P Spencer 13/2: 4/5-52: 5 b g Fabulous Dancer - Rivala 1 **59**
(Riverman) In tch, hdwy on bit to chall over 3f out, jockey looking round for dangers, rdn over 1f out, led briefly
ins last, no extra: abs & stays 12.3f on hvy: found less than expected, but given an over-confident ride on hvy.
*1581 **DAME FONTEYN** 8 [3] M L W Bell 3-8-5 J Mackay (7) 4/6 FAV: P22613: 3 b f Suave Dancer - Her 12 **48**
Honour (Teenoso) Handy, rdn & wknd well over 1f out: btr 1581 (mdn h'cap).
1581 **LOBLITE LEADER** 8 [5] G M Moore 3-8-6 J Fanning 16/1: 0-0004: Chsd wnr till wknd 4f out. dist **0**
1295 **ALBARDEN** 24 [4] J A Carroll 11/1: 40-55: Prom, btn over 4f out: see 1295. dist **0**
5 ran Time 2m 58.78 (20.88) (Miss Nuala Cassidy) J L Eyre Sutton Bank, Nth Yorks.

1768
4.20 THEHORSESMOUTH HCAP 3YO 0-85 (D) 6f Heavy 167 +04 Fast [90]
£3932 £1210 £605 £302 Field tacked over to far side

1162 **ROYAL ROMEO** 32 [3] T D Easterby 3-8-8 (70) J P Spencer 12/1: 531-01: 3 ch g Timeless Times - Farinara **76**
(Dragonara Palace) Chsd ldrs, hdwy & not clr runn 2f out till over 1f out, styd on well ins last to get up cl home,
rdn out: best time of day: '99 wnr at Beverley (mdn, rtd 76): eff at 5f, stays 6f well on gd/soft & hvy.
1600 **LORDOFENCHANTMENT** 7 [6] N Tinkler 3-7-10 (58) Kim Tinkler 7/1: 6-0522: 3 ch g Soviet Lad - ¾ **62**
Sauvignon (Alzao) Dwelt, sn in tch, hdwy to lead appr fnl 1f, collared cl-home, not btn far: visor discarded.
1495 **DAYLILY** 12 [12] T D Easterby 3-8-0 (62) P Fessey 12/1: -00603: 3 ch f Pips Pride - Leaping Water 2½ **61**
(Sure Blade) Waited with, effort 2f out, sn onepace: better back at 6f on hvy grnd: see 909.
1557 **DANCING EMPRESS** 9 [8] M A Jarvis 3-8-12 (74) M Roberts 5/2 FAV: 1-0124: Cl-up, led briefly over nk **72**
1f out, no extra: see 1557, 1138.
1308 **ABLE AYR** 22 [4] 3-8-12 (74) A Culhane 16/1: 0-0005: Sn rdn bhd, some late gains: clr of rem: ¾ **70**
handles fast & hvy & slipping down the weights: see 1074.
4512 **LORD OMNI** 225 [9] 3-8-8 (70) C Lowther 14/1: 604-6: Bhd, btn 2f out: reapp: fin 4th on last 7 **54**
of 3 juv starts (64): stays 6f on fast grnd.
1406 **MOLLY BROWN** 18 [10] 3-9-7 (83) K Darley 5/1: 05-047: Led halfway till over 1f out, wknd: btr 1406. 1½ **64**
3973 **WELCOME TO UNOS** 263 [11] 3-8-10 (72) F Lynch 33/1: 502-8: Al bhd: reapp: rnr-up on last of 3 3 **47**
juv starts (mdn, rtd 74): eff at 6f on fast grnd.
1406 **LOVES DESIGN** 18 [2] 3-8-9 (71)(vis) L Newman (5) 11/2: -30009: Prom, btn over 2f out: see 736. ½ **45**
1516 **HOUT BAY** 11 [5] 3-8-1 (63) A Daly 14/1: 645300: In tch, not clr run 2f out, no extra: 10th. 2 **33**
*1205 **GARTH POOL** 30 [7] 3-9-1 (77) J Carroll 13/2: 0-5110: Led 4f, no extra: 11th: not handle hvy? 19 **5**
1220 **GOLDEN MIRACLE** 28 [1] 3-9-4 (80)(BL) J Fanning 14/1: 15-000: Prom, btn 3f out: last, blnks. 4 **0**
12 ran Time 1m 21.1 (9.8) (Peter C Bourke) T D Easterby Great Habton, Nth Yorks.

1769
4.55 BORDER MINSTREL HCAP 3YO+ 0-75 (E) 1m2f32y Heavy 167 +01 Fast [75]
£2804 £863 £431 £215

1715 **ARCHIE BABE** 2 [5] J J Quinn 4-9-6 (67) A Culhane 5/1: 650101: 4 ch g Archway - Frensham Manor **77**
(Le Johnstan) Prom, led 2f out, sn rdn clr, cmftbly: qck reapp, earlier scored at Pontefract (h'cap): '99 scorer
again at Pontefract & Redcar (2, h'caps, rtd 70): '98 Thirsk scorer (auct mdn, rtd 75): suited by 10/12f on firm
or hvy: handles any trk, likes a gall one, esp Redcar or Pontefract: tough & genuine.
1306 **NOIRIE** 23 [4] M Brittain 6-7-11 (44)(1ow)(2oh) N Garbutt Jnr 6/1: 0-2302: 6 br g Warning - Callipoli 7 **44$**
(Green Dancer) Handy, rdn 3f out, rallied 2f out but not pace of wnr: nicely bckd: gd run, but 1 win in 29 starts.
4444 **CAMARADERIE** 231 [9] Mrs M Reveley 4-8-1 (48) J Fanning 3/1: 0034-3: 4 b g Most Welcome - Secret 1 **47**
Valentine (Wollow): Led 4f out till 2f out, no extra: nicely bckd & clr of rem on reapp: plcd once last
term (rtd 49 at best): eff at 10f, stays 12f on gd/soft & hvy grnd: worth a try in blnks.
1499 **NORTHERN ACCORD** 12 [2] M Dods 6-7-12 (45)(bl) (2ow)(7oh) T Williams 12/1: /0-604: Prom, outpcd 12 **32**
over 4f out, no impress: see 943.
1190 **ATLANTIC CHARTER** 31 [1] 4-9-2 (63) J P Spencer 9/2 FAV: 0-0655: Al bhd: hvly bckd: unsuccessful 18 **32**
gamble over lngr trip & on grnd yet to prove effective on: see 875.
1689 **FLOORSOTHEFOREST** 4 [8] 4-8-10 (57) C Lowther 6/1: -65526: Led 2f, led 6f out till 4f out, wknd: hd **26**
not handle hvy?: btr 1689 (9f, firm).
1656 **DIVINE APPEAL** 5 [7] 5-10-0 (75) C Teague 14/1: 60-067: Bhd, effort over 3f out, no extra: top-weight. 12 **32**
1685 **SWOOSH** 4 [6] 5-8-3 (50)(bl) O Pears 25/1: 400/08: Led after 2f till 6f out, no extra: see 1685. 17 **0**
4584 **KIDOLOGY** 218 [3] 4-7-11 (44)(t)(1ow)(3oh) N Kennedy 25/1: 000-9: Sn bhd: modest form. 1¾ **0**
9 ran Time 2m 23.3 (16.8) (Mrs K Mapp) J J Quinn Settrington, Nth Yorks.

YARMOUTH WEDNESDAY JUNE 7TH Lefthand, Flat, Fair Track

Official Going GOOD. Stalls: Str Crse - Far Side; Rem - Inside.

1770
2.10 SPONSORSHIP HCAP 3YO 0-80 (D) 1m3f101y Good 41 -01 Slow [84]
£3867 £1190 £595 £297

*807 **FANTASTIC FANTASY** 68 [5] J L Dunlop 3-9-1 (71) Pat Eddery 7/4 FAV: 300-11: 3 b f Lahib - Gay Fantasy **76**
(Troy) Held up, prog ent fnl 4f, led bef dist, hard rdn, just held on: well bckd, 10 wk abs: prev won Southwell
reapp (fill h'cap): rtd 80 in '99 (fill mdn): eff at 10/11.5f: acts gd grnd, sharp trks: runs v well fresh.
1362 **FULL AHEAD** 19 [3] M H Tompkins 3-9-7 (77) S Sanders 12/1: 5-3322: 3 b c Slip Anchor - Foulard hd **81**
(Sadler's Wells) Rear, ran on strongly under press ent fnl 2f, just failed: overdue a win: see 1362, 713.
1407 **ASSURED PHYSIQUE** 18 [4] C E Brittain 3-8-11 (67) D Harrison 16/1: 00-053: 3 b c Salse - Metaphysique 1¾ **69**
(Law Society) Held up, prog 3f out, ch appr fnl 1f, rdn & same pace: apprec step up to 11.5f & more patient tactics.
1238 **TUFTY HOPPER** 27 [2] P Howling 3-8-9 (65) J Fortune 25/1: 644224: Chsd ldrs, feeling pace 4f out, hd **67**

576

short of room & switched 2f out, styd on: clr rem, ran to best back on turf: acts on gd, gd/soft & fibresand.
1446 **ESTABELLA 15** [8] 3-8-4 (60) N Pollard 14/1: -21305: Led till ent fnl 2f, no extra: see 1142, 978. *8* **54**
1199 **HOME FORCE 30** [11] 3-8-8 (64) J Reid 16/1: 40-006: Handy, chall appr fnl 2f, grad wknd: drop in trip? *½* **57**
1448 **NOBLE CALLING 15** [1] 3-8-8 (64) J Weaver 6/1: 600-37: Prom, rdn & held when not clr run 2f out. *1¼* **55**
1299 **LATE ARRIVAL 23** [9] 3-8-1 (57) J Tate 13/2: 40-428: Well plcd till 3f out: tchd 8/1, longer trip. *3½* **45**
1404 **MAZAARR 18** [10] 3-9-4 (74) Craig Williams 16/1: 6009: Held up, chsd ldrs halfway till appr fnl 3f. *hd* **62**
*1502 **FINERY 12** [6] 3-8-4 (60) A Beech (5) 16/1: 424010: Al towards rear: 10th, new stable, see 1502 (AW). *1½* **46**
1585 **MILLIONS 8** [7] 3-8-10 (66)(BL) K Fallon 11/2: 0-5200: Reluctant to race, al detached: 11th, blnkd. *dist* **0**
11 ran Time 2m 27.6 (4.8) (Windflower Overseas Holdings Inc) J L Dunlop Arundel, W Sussex

1771

2.40 WEATHERBYS MDN 3YO+ (D) 1m str Good 41 +01 Fast
£3997 £1230 £615 £307 3 yo rec 11lb 2 groups that merged 2f out

1535 **PAPABILE 11** [14] W Jarvis 3-8-8 Pat Eddery 5/2 FAV: 52-241: 3 b f Chief's Crown - La Papagena **91**
(Habitat) Well plcd stands side, led appr fnl 2f, readily: nicely bckd, best time of day: overdue success, juv rnr-up at Newmarket (fill mdn, rtd 92): sister to high-class miler/10f performer Grand Lodge: eff at 1m on fast & soft grnd, any trk: useful filly, yet to run a bad race & can win again.
-- **RAINBOW HILL** [16] Sir Michael Stoute 3-8-13 K Fallon 4/1: 2: 3 b c Rainbow Quest - Hill Hopper *3½* **88+**
(Danehill) Rear stands side, imprvd after halfway, chall 2f out, not pace of wnr: op 5/2 on debut: 1st foal, dam useful 6/7f performer: eff at 1m, bred to get further: runs well fresh on gd grnd & similar looks a formality.
1344 **CABALLE 20** [5] S P C Woods 3-8-8 J Reid 7/1: 2-233: 3 ch f Opening Verse - Attirance (Crowned *2½* **78**
Prince) Prom in centre, eff appr fnl 1f, same pace: clr rem & prob ran to best back in trip: acts on gd & soft.
764 **THUNDER SKY 74** [2] C E Brittain 4-9-10 D O'Donohoe 14/1: 540/04: Cl-up centre, under press 2f out, *4* **75**
no impress: op 10/1, 11 wk abs: highly tried juv back in '98, not btn far into 4th in a Gr 2 (rtd 106): handles firm grnd but has yet to find a trip that suits.
-- **FLYING TREATY** [10] 3-8-13 J Fortune 11/1: 5: Held up centre, nvr pace to chall: op 8/1, debut: *¾* **74+**
You And I half-brother to sev wnrs, notably smart juv Silver Wizard & a 12f wnr: win races over further.
-- **ALL THE LUCK** [1] 3-8-8 T Quinn 4/1: 6: Dwelt centre, nvr on terms: tchd 11/2: Mr Prospector *½* **68**
sister to a 1m wnr, dam high-class 1m/10f performer: certain to improve for this: with H Cecil.
-- **SINCERITY** [6] 3-8-8 D Harrison 20/1: 7: Towards rear centre, nvr dngrs: debut: Selkirk *2½* **63**
half-sister to sev wnrs up to 12f: with J Fanshawe.
1428 **GOLDFINCH 16** [12] 3-8-8 D Meah (7) 33/1: 0-08: Prom stands side 6f: st/mate 7th, abs, turf bow. *¾* **62**
661 **HARVEY LEADER 88** [7] 5-9-10 O Urbina 33/1: 39: Prom centre till 3f out, fdd: st/nate 7th/8th. *1¾* **64**
1099 **SWISS ALPS 36** [4] 3-8-13 R Price 50/1: 0-00: Led centre till 3f out, fdd: 10th. *1½* **61**
1532 **Salix Dancer 11** [11] 3-8-13 M Fenton 16/1: 1532 **Hefin 11** [9] 3-8-13 N Pollard 50/1:
839 **Luckys Son 61** [3] 3-8-13 M Hills 14/1: 4607} **Satzuma 215** [8] 3-8-13 S Sanders 50/1:
1287 **Yafa 25** [13] 4-9-10 J Weaver 66/1: -- **Executive Ghost** [15] 3-8-13 K W Marks 50/1:
16 ran Time 1m 38.3 (3.2) (Exors of the late Lord Howard de Walden) W Jarvis Newmarket.

1772

3.10 YARMOUTH SELL HCAP 3YO+ 0-60 (G) 1m str Good 41 -39 Slow **[51]**
£2075 £593 £593 £296 3 yo rec 11lb

1335 **IMARI 21** [4] N P Littmoden 3-9-7 (55) M Tebbutt 16/1: 0-2501: 3 b f Rock City - Misty Goddess **60**
(Godswalk) Nvr far away, eff appr fnl 1f, ran on well to lead ins last: op 12/1, bght in for 4,250gns: unplcd in '99 (nov fill stks, rtd 70, J Given): eff over an easy 1m on fast, soft grnd, prob fibresand: apprec return to sell grade.
1331 **BADRINATH 21** [10] H J Collingridge 6-9-11 (48) A Beech (5) 10/1: 632002: 6 b g Imperial Frontier - *1½* **50**
Badedra (King's Lake) Prom, led 1½f out till well ins last, onepace: back in trip & back to form: see 360.
1505 **PURSUIVANT 12** [15] Mrs N Macauley 6-9-10 (47)(bl) J Weaver 12/1: 340603: 6 b g Pursuit Of Love - *1¾* **46**
Collapse (Busted) In tch, styd on fnl 2f, nrst fin: back to form for new connections, see 803.
1614 **CAERDYDD FACH 7** [16] Mrs A E Johnson 4-8-7 (30) A McCarthy (3) 16/1: 650-04: Held up, kept on *2* **25**
well fnl 1f, nvr nrr: qck reapp: unplcd last term for J Gilbert (clmr, rtd 45, mdn rtd 47a): turf promise in '98 (rtd 60, K Wingrove): stays 1m, tried 11f: handles gd & fast grnd.
1545 **MUTABARI 9** [14] 6-9-5 (42) J Fortune 10/1: 004065: Dwelt, rdn & prog appr fnl 2f, no extra fnl 1f. *nk* **36**
1300 **MUSTANG 23** [3] 7-9-3 (40)(bl) G Bardwell 14/1: 250306: Prom, onepace fnl 2f: blnks reapp, see 59. *1¾* **31**
1365 **TIMELESS CHICK 19** [12] 3-9-0 (48)(bl) M Henry 10/1: -00437: Handy till fdd appr fnl 1f: btr 1365, 806. *1¾* **36**
*1462 **DARK MENACE 14** [6] 8-10-0 (51)(bl) S Carson (5) 12/1: 006018: Cl-up, led 2½f out till bef fnl 1f. *¾* **38**
585 **KOOL JULES 103** [2] 4-8-2 (25)(t) N Pollard 33/1: 00609: Rcd alone far side, in tch till 2f out: abs. *2½* **7**
1129 **BEGUILE 34** [19] 6-9-11 (48)(t) K Fallon 11/4 FAV: 410630: Mid-div, rdn appr fnl 2f, no impress: 10th. *nk* **29**
261 **SOUHAITE 155** [18] 4-9-5 (42) Pat Eddery 10/1: 303-00: Al towards rear: 12th, 5 mnth abs, shorter trip. **0**
1101 **WATER LOUP 35** [17] 4-9-3 (40) J Reid 16/1: 0-6000: Prom till halfway: 16th, see 692. **0**
1739 **GLASTONBURY 1** [5] 4-9-7 (44) W Ryan 33/1: 400050: Led till 3f out, sn btn: 17th, ran yesterday. **0**
1608 **Druridge Bay 7** [20] 4-8-13 (36) S Righton 33/1: 555 **Could Be Expensive 107** [8] 3-8-11 (45) S Sanders 16/1:
841 **Miss Springfield 61** [13] 3-8-5 (39) J Tate 12/1: 1496 **Silken Lady 12** [7] 4-8-7 (30) M Baird 25/1:
1351 **Shontaine 19** [11] 7-9-2 (39) A Mackay 25/1: 787 **Hunan Scholar 70** [9] 5-9-2 (39)(t) M Fenton 33/1:
1603 **Mikes Double 7** [1] 6-8-11 (34) D Harrison 25/1:
20 ran Time 1m 41.5 (6.4) (J R Good) N P Littmoden Newmarket.

1773

3.40 ROYAL ANGLIAN FILL MDN 3YO+ (D) 6f Good 41 -26 Slow
£3802 £1170 £585 £292

1569 **PAGEANT 9** [2] W Jarvis 3-8-11 M Tebbutt 13/2: 443-51: 3 br f Inchinor - Positive Attitude (Red **76**
Sunset) Well plcd, rdn appr fnl 1f, ran on to lead towards fin: thrice rcd in '99, plcd once for R Williams (mdn, rtd 76): eff at 7f, apprec drop back to 6f: goes on firm & hvy grnd, prob any track.
1108 **OUR FIRST LADY 35** [6] D W P Arbuthnot 3-8-11 J Reid 11/2: 0-02: 3 b f Alzao - Eclipsing (Baillamont) *nk* **74**
Prom, led appr fnl 2f, worn down fnl 100y: unplcd sole '99 start (hot mdn, rtd 76): half-sister to a 6f wnr & useful 12f wnr Vagabond Chanteuse: eff up with/forcing the pace at 6f, tried 1m & shld stay: acts on gd grnd.
-- **EMANS JOY** [4] J R Fanshawe 3-8-11 D Harrison 11/2: 3: 3 b f Lion Cavern - Carolside (Music *2½* **67**
Maestro) Chsd ldrs, lost pl 2f out, rallied fnl 1f: debut, op 7/1: 10,000 half-sister to minor wnrs: 7f needed.
877 **BETHESDA 57** [1] J M P Eustace 3-8-11 J Tate 2/1 FAV: 265-64: Mid-div, keen, eff appr fnl 1f, onepce. *1¾* **63**
1500 **DID YOU MISS ME 12** [8] 3-8-11 J Weaver 8/1: 05: Held up, pushed along 2f out, unable to qckn. *½* **62**
-- **ETIENNE LADY** [3] 3-8-11 J Fortune 9/2: 6: Al bhd: debut: Imperial Frontier half-sister to a sprinter. *2½* **56**
4312} **SEEKING SANCTUARY 240** [7] 3-8-11 J Lowe 40/1: 0-7: Chsd ldrs till after 3f: well btn sole '99 start. *5* **44**
4376} **LUNALUX 236** [5] 3-8-11 M Fenton 33/1: 4550-8: Keen in lead, hdd appr fnl 2f, wknd: stiff task, reapp: *1¼* **41**

plcd in '99 (fill auct mdn, rtd 70 & 57a): eff forcing the pace at 5f, with/without visor: goes on firm grnd.
8 ran   Time 1m 14.4 (4)   (R J R Williams)   W Jarvis Newmarket.

1774   4.10 BRECKLAND MDN 2YO (D)   6f   Good 41 -69 Slow
£3493   £1075   £537   £268

-- **NORCROFT LADY** [7] N A Callaghan 2-8-9 Pat Eddery 11/2: 1: 2 b f Mujtahid - Polytess (Polish		86

Patriot) Prom, shkn up appr fnl 1f, kept on strongly to lead towards fin: slow time: Feb first foal, dam styd
10f, sire a sprinter: eff at 6f, will get 7f: goes well fresh on gd grnd & cld do better again with a faster pace.
--   **PALATIAL** [1] J R Fanshawe 2-8-9 D Harrison 3/1: 2: 2 b f Green Desert - White Palace (Shirley   ½ 84
Heights) Mid-div, hdwy to lead appr fnl 1f, hdd towards fin: nicely bckd from 5/1 on debut: Apr foal, sire a
sprinter/miler: eff at 6f on gd grnd: shld improve & find similar.
--   **RASOUM** [5] E A L Dunlop 2-9-0 J Reid 14/1: 3: 2 gr c Miswaki - Bel Ray (Restivo)   hd 88+
Keen, rear, imprvd 2f out, chsd ldrs & sltly short of room in last, kept on : drifter from 7/1, clr rem: $50,000
May foal, half-brother to 7f juv wnr Qamous, dam prolific wnr in the States: eff at 6f, step up to 7f will suit.
--   **SHADOWLESS** [4] C E Brittain 2-9-0 D O'Donohoe 11/2: 4: Towards rear, shkn up/switched appr fnl 1f,   3 79
not pace to trble ldrs: op 4/1: Alzao Apr foal, dam useful 7f/10f performer: likely improver over 7f/1m later.
1612 **CARNIVAL LAD 7** [2] 2-9-0 K Fallon 6/4 FAV: 25: Chsd ldrs & ev ch till wknd appr fnl 1f: well bckd,   1½ 75
qck reapp: expected to go one better than last week's debut, but that was less competitive: see 1612.
--   **DUSTY CARPET** [8] 2-9-0 P Clarke (7) 33/1: 6: Nvr going pace: 18,500gns Pivotal Mar foal,   3 66
half-brother to a 2m wnr, dam 10f wnr, sire a sprinter: with C Dwyer.
--   **ALBURACK** [6] J M Baird 12/1: 7: Cl-up, keen & ev ch till wknd bef dist: op 33/1: Rock City   1¾ 62
Apr foal, half-brother to a 3 juv wnrs, dam unrcd, sire a sprinter: drop back to 5f for now? with G Margarson.
--   **COLLEGE FACT** [9] 2-9-0 W Ryan 33/1: 8: Al bhd: 8,000gns Se Factual Mar first foal, sprint bred.   2 56
--   **CHOCOLATE FOG** [3] 2-8-9 M Hills 16/1: 9: Led till ent fnl 2f, wknd: op 10/1: Mt Livermore   ½ 50
Apr foal, sister to a wnr in the States, dam prolific wnr in N America: sire top-class on dirt: with R Cowell.
9 ran   Time 1m 17.0 (6.6)   (Norcroft Park Stud)   N A Callaghan Newmarket.

1775   4.45 HANDS&HEELS APPR HCAP 3YO+ 0-70 (F)   1m2f21y   Good 41 -39 Slow   [65]
£2163   £618   £309   3 yo rec 13lb

*1615 **SIFAT 7** [6] J R Jenkins 5-9-9 (60)(vis)(6ex) D Glennon 5/1: 40-511: 5 b m Marju - Reine Maid (Mr   67
Prospector) Mid-div, keen, imprvd to lead appr fnl 2f, cmftbly: slow time, qck reapp: defied 6lb pen for last
week's win here at Yarmouth (appr h'cap): plcd over jumps in late '99 (2m nov, gd/soft, rtd 97h): unplcd in '99
for N Graham (h'caps, rtd 63, blnkd): '98 Pontefract wnr (mdn, rtd 74, M Tregoning): eff at 1m/10f, tried further:
acts on fast & soft grnd, any trk, likes Yarmouth: best in a visor & is in cracking form.
1705 **SMARTER CHARTER 3** [8] Mrs L Stubbs 7-9-4 (55) Kristin Stubbs (3) 2/1 FAV: -12322: 7 br g Master   1¾ 58
Willie - Irene's Charter (Persian Bold) Held up, kept on fnl 2f to go 2nd below clsr, nvr nr wnr: nicely bckd,
qck reapp: deserves a change of luck: also bhd wnr in 1615, see 871.
1615 **FOREST DREAM 7** [7] L A Dace 5-8-10 (47) G Sparkes (3) 4/1: 000023: 5 b m Warrshan - Sirenivo (Sir   2 47
Ivor) Rear, imprvd 3f out, dsptd 2nd appr fnl 1f, onepcd ins last: see 1615 (clsr to this wnr & in front of rnr-up).
1331 **TRY PARIS 21** [2] H J Collingridge 4-7-12 (35)(vis) D Kinsella (3) 12/1: -00044: Rear, wide prog   shd 35
fnl 2f, nvr nrr: flattered in a clmr last time but beginning to show signs of ability: stays 10f.
--   **CRUAGH EXPRESS** [10] 4-9-3 (54) R Lake (5) 25/1: 3355-5: Held up, late prog, nvr dngrs: abs,   ½ 53
Brit bow: plcd twice in native Ireland last term (7f, gd/soft grnd): stays a slow run 10f.
1646 **ERTLON 5** [3] 10-8-13 (50) S Hitchcott (8) 25/1: -00006: Keen, chsd ldrs till no extra ent fnl 2f: qck   3 44
reapp: plcd thrice in '99 (h'cap, rtd 64a): lightly rcd since '97 wnr at Lingfield (clmr, rtd 79a & 71): eff at
7f/1m, unproven at 10f: acts on firm/fast, equitrack, handles soft & fibresand: best forcing the pace without blnks.
1434 **PARKERS PEACE 16** [1] 3-8-7 (57) Gemma Sliz (8) 25/1: 000-07: Pulled hard bhd ldrs, lost pl 2f out.   2 48
1575 **HEVER GOLF GLORY 8** [5] 6-8-0 (37) D Meah (3) 12/1: 503038: Pulled hard in lead, hdd 2½f out,   nk 28
wknd qckly: tchd 16/1, needs a drop back to 1m: see 383.
1375 **MASSEY 19** [4] 4-10-0 (65) D Watson (3) 6/1: 1609: Keen, handy, wknd fnl 2f: see 752 (12f AW mdn).   1 55
b1104 **DISTINCTLY EAST 35** [9] 3-9-5 (69) M Worrell (3) 14/1: 20-040: Al bhd: 10th, see 736.   ½ 58
10 ran   Time 2m 12.2 (8)   (Mrs C N & Mrs J W Wright)   J R Jenkins Royston, Herts.

Official Going   GOOD/SOFT. Stalls: 1m2f - Outside, Rem - Inside.

1776   6.30 ERNST & YOUNG MDN 2YO (D)   5f rnd   Good/Soft 69 -38 Slow
£3562   £1096   £548   £274

--   **PROUD BOAST** [5] Mrs G S Rees 2-8-9 Dean McKeown 12/1: -1: 2 b f Komaite - Red Rosein (Red Sunset)   73
Pulled hard & sn led, ran on strongly, rdn out: op 8/1: 9,500 gns Apr foal, half-sister to a juv wnr, dam
decent sprinter: eff forcing the pace over a sharp 5f on gd/soft grnd: runs well fresh.
1346 **MOONLIGHT DANCER 20** [6] R Hannon 2-9-0 R Hughes 6/4 FAV: -42: 2 b c Polar Falcon -   ¾ 75
Guanhumara (Caerleon) Front rank early, rdn, kept on to chase wnr appr final 1f, held towards fin: bckd tho'
drifted from 4/9: acts on gd/soft grnd & looks sure to appreciate a step up to 6f.
--   **PERTEMPS JARDINE** [3] R A Fahey 2-9-0 P Hanagan (7) 20/1: -3: 2 b c General Monash - Indescent   2½ 68
Blue (Bluebird) Dwelt & prom in rear, late hdwy, nvr dngrs: 7,000 gns Mar 1st foal, dam a mdn, sire a sprinter
(half-brother to King Of Kings): handles gd/soft grnd & should improve.
1429 **MISS BRIEF 16** [2] P D Evans 2-8-9 J F Egan 7/4: -0244: Prom, chall appr fnl 1f, sn onepace: bckd.   ½ 62
1260 **TUSCAN FLYER 26** [4] 2-9-0 T E Durcan 10/1: -05: Wide, chsd ldrs till appr final 1f: see 1260.   3 58
--   **GEMTASTIC** [7] 2-8-9 Dane O'Neill 25/1: -6: Handy till 2f out: 2,500 gns Tagula Mar 1st foal,   2½ 46
dam 7f wnr, sire a sprinter: with P Evans.
--   **PAT PINKNEY** [1] 2-8-9 G Duffield 12/1: -7: Slowly away, not much room 2f out, al bhd: op 8/1:   shd 46
3,000gns Imp Society Feb 1st foal: dam stoutly bred mdn, sire prolific on dirt in the States: with E Alston.
7 ran   Time 1m 05.15 (5.35)   (J W Gittins)   Mrs G S Rees Sollom, Lancs.

CHESTER WEDNESDAY JUNE 7TH Lefthand, V Tight Track

1777
7.00 SHELL CHEMICALS HCAP 3YO+ 0-80 (D) 1m2f75y Good/Soft 69 -20 Slow [80]
£4348 £1338 £669 £334

1373 **BATSWING** 19 [2] B Ellison 5-9-0 (66) K Fallon 10/3 FAV: -00201: 5 b g Batshoof - Magic Milly (Simply 74
Great) Bhd ldrs, shkn up to lead dist, sn clr, cmftbly: nicely bckd: plcd in '99 (h'cap, rtd 75, B Millman):
98/99 Taunton hdles wnr (mdn, rtd 104h, 2m3.5f soft): back in '97 won at Lingfield (mdn, M Meade, rtd 94):
eff at 10f, stays 12f: handles fast, likes gd/soft & hvy, any trk: eff with/without blnks: shld run well at York.
1251 **NOUKARI** 27 [4] P D Evans 7-9-12 (78) J F Egan 11/2: 140102: 7 b g Darshaan - Noufiyla (Top Ville) 3½ 80
In tch, eff 3f out, imprvg & not much room dist, swtchd & kept on, wnr had flown: tchd 13/2, jumps rnr 4-days ago.
*1608 **RIVER ENSIGN** 7 [5] W M Brisbourne 7-8-6 (58)(6ex) P M Quinn (3) 5/1: 036013: 7 b m River God - nk 59
Ensigns Kit) Led, under press appr fnl 1f, hdd dist, onepace: qck reapp & ran to best with a pen.
1666 **DARE** 5 [10] P D Evans 5-8-6 (58)(vis) Dane O'Neill 14/1: 500304: In tch, wide prog appr final 2 56
2f, sn onepace: qck reapp: see 1570, 83.
1518 **WARNING REEF** 11 [8] 7-8-7 (59) G Duffield 7/1: 0-4565: Chsd ldrs, no impress appr final 2f. nk 56
1251 **ANGIE MARINIE** 27 [7] 4-8-10 (62) R Hughes 12/1: 305-06: Cl-up & ch till wknd qckly dist: see 1251. 3 54
1528 **GREAT NEWS** 11 [1] 5-9-4 (70) Martin Dwyer 7/1: 000007: Pld hard, al towards rear: see 1528, 875. 2½ 59
1583 **GABLESEA** 8 [9] 6-8-3 (55) R Brisland (5) 7/1: 102058: Pulled hard, nvr troubled ldrs: see 890. 3½ 39
1279 **TROIS** 25 [3] 4-8-9 (61) T G McLaughlin 10/1: 030059: Nvr a factor: op 8/1, see 1279, 271. 3½ 40
9 ran Time 2m 17.72 (9.22) (Ashley Carr Racing(4)) B Ellison Lanchester, Co Durham.

1778
7.30 PEEPING TOM HCAP 3YO+ 0-95 (C) 7f rnd Good/Soft 69 +09 Fast [88]
£11066 £3405 £1702 £851 3yo rec 10lb

*1250 **SILCA BLANKA** 27 [2] A G Newcombe 8-9-10 (84) J Reid 4/1 FAV: 00-111: 8 b h Law Society - Reality 94
(Known Fact) Mid-div, hdwy 2f out, ran on strongly to lead dist, easily qcknd clr: fast time, hat-trick landed
after wins at Brighton & here at Chester (h'caps): '99 wnr at Lingfield (rtd 89a) & Epsom (h'caps, rtd 90): '98
Warwick wnr (stks, rtd 86): eff 7f/1m, connections toying with dropping on to 6f next time: acts on firm, soft
& equitrack, suited by sharp trks, loves Chester & Epsom: useful entire in the form of his life.
1383 **NOMORE MR NICEGUY** 18 [5] E J Alston 6-9-5 (79) K Fallon 9/2: 000002: 6 b h Rambo Dancer - Lariston 5 81
Gale (Pas de Seul) Keen, in tch, kept on fnl 2f, not pace of wnr: likes Chester, keep in mind when stable hit form.
1519 **ONLY FOR GOLD** 11 [4] A Berry 5-7-11 (57) Iona Wands(5) 5/1: 6-6623: 5 b h Presidium - Calvanne 1¼ 56
Miss (Martinmas) Front rank, led briefly appr final 1f, onepcd: ran to best, should win soon: see 1519, 780.
1531 **PREMIER BARON** 11 [7] P S McEntee 5-9-5 (79) T G McLaughlin 7/1: 140064: Bhd, not much room ½ 77
appr final 2f, kept on, nvr a threat: blnks omitted & a better run back over 7f, see 725.
1514 **BERGEN** 11 [3] 5-8-12 (72) A Nicholls (3) 9/1: 020-05: Towards rear, nvr nr to chall: not given a nk 69
hard time, stable probably priming him for a big h'cap: see 1514.
1547 **PRIDEWAY** 9 [1] 4-8-0 (60) P M Quinn (3) 12/1: 061306: Set gd pace till eff final 2f, fdd: prefers 3 51
giving weeght to lesser rivals: see 1419 (fill h'cap).
1453 **MASTER HENRY** 15 [6] 6-8-10 (70) R Ffrench 14/1: 4/6667: Mid-div, rdn & btn appr final 1f: h'cap bow. 4 53
1215 **DIGITAL IMAGE** 29 [11] 3-8-8 (78) R Hughes 25/1: 0-6008: Al towards rear, eased final 1f: '99 debut 4 53
wnr here at Chester (rtd 89): eff at 5f on firm grnd & a sharp trk: poor high draw today.
1654 **DISTINCTIVE DREAM** 5 [8] 6-8-11 (71) J F Egan 8/1: 026009: In tch kept 2f out, eased final 1f: qk reapp. 1 44
1533 **FLAK JACKET** 11 [9] 5-8-8 (68) G Duffield 12/1: 0-0000: Sn struggling: 10th, stablemate 5th: 24 16
rnr-up in '99 for B Meehan (h'cap, rtd 82): landed final 2 in '98 at Kempton & Haydock (h'caps, rtd 86): eff at
6f on firm & soft grnd, any trk: best without blnks: poor draw, now v well h'capped.
10 ran Time 1m 29.20 (4.20) (Duckhaven Stud) A G Newcombe Huntshaw, Devon.

1779
8.00 STUD CLASSIFIED STKS 3YO 0-75 (D) 1m2f75y Good/Soft 69 -09 Slow
£6272 £1930 £965 £482

1466 **EL ZITO** 14 [2] M G Quinlan 3-9-0 K Fallon 4/1: 23-021: 3 b g Mukaddamah - Samite (Tennyson) 86
Made ev yd, clr appr final 1f, unchall: deserved, rnr-up in '99 in Italy: eff at 1m/10.5f: acts on gd/soft,
soft & prob fibresand: likes to force the pace on sharp trks: appears to be on the upgrade.
1585 **NEVER DISS MISS** 8 [6] W Jarvis 3-8-13 D McGaffin (7) 11/4 FAV: 0-5132: 3 b f Owington - Pennine 4 77
Pink (Pennine Walk) Rear, styd on enf fnl 2f to op 2nd dist, held & eased nr fin: in-form, see 1448.
1439 **PALUA** 16 [5] Mrs A J Bowlby 3-9-0 (BL) J Reid 8/1: 30-343: 3 b c Sri Pekan - Reticent Bride (Shy ¾ 76
Groom) Chsd ldrs, eff 3f out, unable to qckn: blnkd & prob ran to best, see 1094.
4432} **PRINCIPLE** 232 [4] Sir Mark Prescott 3-9-0 G Duffield 4/1: 624-4: Pld hard, trkd ldr, fdd appr fnl 1f: 2½ 73
reapp: '99 rnr-up (med auct, rtd 79 at best): eff at 7f/1m, bred to apprec further: acts on fast & gd grnd.
810 **TRUE OBSESSION** 67 [1] 3-9-0 J Mackay 12/1: 600-05: Held up, nvr troubled ldrs: 10 wk abs, 7 63
longer trip: '99 Southwell wnr (mdn, rtd 80a, dual turf rnr-up, nurs, rtd 84): eff at 7f, not certain to get 10f:
acts on firm grnd & fibresand, up with/forcing the pace: with P Cole.
1521 **DISTINCTLY WELL** 11 [3] 3-9-0 J F Egan 4/1: -23026: Pld hard, chsd ldrs, stumbled after 3f, fdd fnl 2f. ¾ 62
6 ran Time 2m 16.55 (8.05) (Mario Lanfranchi) M G Quinlan Newmarket

1780
8.30 RON HARRIS CLAIMER 3YO (E) 6f rnd Good/Soft 69 -18 Slow
£3718 £1144 £572 £286 Low draw is a big advantage

1579 **CHARMING LOTTE** 8 [1] N Tinkler 3-8-3 (vis) C Rutter 7/2: -00051: 3 b f Nicolotte - Courtisane 65
(Persepolis) Trkd ldrs, led ent fnl 1f, pshd clr, v cmftbly: '99 Ayr wnr (nurs, rtd 74, P Shakespeare): eff at 6f,
stays 7f: acts on gd, suited by soft, any trk: wears a visor: enjoyed the ease in grade & favoured No 1 stall.
1405 **PEGGYS ROSE** 18 [2] P D Evans 3-8-5 J F Egan 6/1: 14002: 3 b f Shalford - Afrique Noir (Gallic League) 6 55
Led/dsptd lead, rdn appr fnl 1f, sn hdd, outpcd: better run back at 6f: suited by gd/soft grnd, see 830 (sell, debut).
1578 **BLUEGRASS MOUNTAIN** 8 [4] T D Easterby 3-8-10 (BL) G Duffield 16/1: -00003: 3 b g Primo Dominie 2 55$
- Florentynna Bay (Aragon) Mid-div, feeling pace 2f out, nvr able to chall: blnkd: see 976.
1651 **FRAMPANT** 5 [6] M Quinn 3-9-3 Martin Dwyer 25/1: 300044: Dsptd lead till 2f out, fdd: stiffish task. 1 59$
1579 **MYTTONS AGAIN** 8 [3] 3-8-6 J Mackay 3/1 FAV: 002665: Nvr better than mid-div: capable of better. ½ 47
1494 **LA TORTUGA** 12 [7] 3-8-7 C Cogan(5) 8/1: 50-006: Chsd ldrs till halfway: poor draw: see 108. 1¾ 43
1504 **BRANSTON PICKLE** 12 [5] 3-8-12 J Reid 9/2: -20007: Prom, wknd qckly appr fnl 1f: see 62. nk 47
1334 **KIRSCH** 21 [8] 3-8-7 (vis) T G McLaughlin 14/1: 315608: Nvr troubled ldrs: better on sand, see 361. 8 24
1368 **MARON** 19 [9] 3-8-12 T E Durcan 25/1: 000-09: Al bhd: poor high draw: see 1368. 2½ 23

579

CHESTER WEDNESDAY JUNE 7TH Lefthand, V Tight Track

9 ran   Time 1m 18.34 (5.24)   (Mike Gosse)   N Tinkler Langton, N Yorks

1781 9.00 DOGE OF VENICE HCAP 3YO+ 0-85 (D)   5f rnd   Good/Soft 69 -01 Slow   [85]
£4407 £1356 £678 £339   3yo rec 7lb   Low draw is a big advantage

*1636 **BODFARI PRIDE** 6 [1] D Nicholls 5-8-13 (70)(6ex) A Nicholls (3) 2/1 FAV: /00011: 5 b g Pips Pride - 79
Renatas Ring (Auction Ring): Led bef halfway, clr appr dist, easily defied a penalty: plenty in hand, quick reapp:
last week scored at Goodwood (h'cap): missed '99, prev term won at Redcar (auct mdn) & here at Chester (h'cap,
rtd 86, A Bailey): stays 7.5f, revelation since returned to sprinting: acts on fast & hvy grnd, any trk, likes
Chester: suited forcing the pace: well h'capped & shld make it 3 on the bounce.
1356 **RETALIATOR** 19 [3] P D Evans 4-8-6 (63) Dane O'Neill 11/1: 00-002: 4 b f Rudimentary - Redgrave   3 64
Design (Nebbiolo): Towards rear, shaken up & short of room 2f out, ran on fnl 1f, no ch wnr: back to form
at fav trk, won on this card last year: return to 6f will suit & is h'capped to win: see 780.
1517 **LAGO DI VARANO** 11 [6] R M Whitaker 8-9-4 (75)(bl) Dean McKeown 13/2: 660353: 8 b g Clantime - On   1 73
The Record (Record Token): Chsd ldrs wide, outpcd 2f out, styd on und press: back to form at best trip: see 1383.
1471 **CLASSY CLEO** 14 [5] P D Evans 5-9-9 (80) J F Egan 7/1: 000004: Chsd ldrs, onepace appr fnl 1f.   ¾ 75
1687 **TUSCAN DREAM** 4 [7] 5-9-2 (73) P Bradley (5) 16/1: 14-005: Led till halfway, fdd: faster grnd suits.   1½ 64
1533 **POLLY GOLIGHTLY** 11 [9] 7-8-11 (68)(bl) Dale Gibson 7/1: 002206: Prom, wide till wknd appr fnl 1f.   3 50
1257 **RED CHARGER** 26 [8] 4-8-8 (65) R Hughes 16/1: 001-07: V slow away, al bhd: stable mate wnr: won   ½ 46
fnl '99 start at Thirsk (h'cap, 1st time blnks, rtd 68): '98 wnr at Redcar, Catterick (auct mdn, rtd 84) & York
(sell): eff at 5/7f on firm & gd/soft, handles soft & f/sand: poss best in blnks (not worn): poor draw here.
1479 **CAUTIOUS JOE** 13 [2] 3-8-6 (57) P Hanagan (7) 20/1: 00-008: Stdd start, bhd: negative from gd draw. shd 51
1162 **DAAWE** 32 [10] 9-9-1 (72)(bl) Clare Roche (7) 11/1: 306109: Wide, outpcd halfway: stablemate of wnr. 10 28
1357 **ZIGGYS DANCER** 19 [11] 9-9-6 (77) K Fallon 7/1: 334040: Sn bhd, eased fnl 1f: 10th, poor draw,   5 21
reportedly lost action, see 1357, 223.
10 ran   Time 1m 03.33 (3.53)   (Bodfari Stud Ltd)   D Nicholls Sessay, N Yorks

NEWBURY THURSDAY JUNE 8TH Lefthand, Flat, Galloping Track

Official Going   GOOD/FIRM (GOOD places). Stalls: 5/6f - Stands Side; 7f/1m - Centre; Rnd Crse - Inside.

1782 6.30 ILSLEY MDN 2YO (D)   5f34y   Good/Firm 21 +04 Fast
£3776 £1162 £581   £290   Raced towards centre

886 **OH SO DUSTY** 57 [10] B J Meehan 2-8-9 Pat Eddery 7/2 FAV: 61: 2 b f Piccolo - Dark Eyed Lady   89
(Exhibitioner): Made all, strongly prsd nr fin, drvn & held on gamely, all-out: hvly bckd from 8/1, fast juv
time, 8 wk abs: eff at 5f, 6f shld suit: acts on fast grnd & a gall trk: runs well fresh: clearly going the
right way, reportedly could head for Queen Mary Stks at Royal Ascot.
-- **ZILCH** [8] R Hannon 2-9-0 R Hughes 7/2: 2: 2 ch c Zilzal - Bunty Boo (Noalto):   shd 93
Dwelt, sn in tch, grad reeled in wnr fnl 1f, just failed in a thrilling fin: op 5/1: Apr foal, cost 11,000gns:
dam a wng sprinter, sire high class miler: eff at 5f, 6f+ will suit: acts on fast grnd: compensation awaits.
-- **SANTA ISOBEL** [12] I A Balding 2-8-9 K Fallon 8/1: 3: 2 ch f Nashwan - Atlantic Record (Slip Anchor):   3 79+
Chsd ldrs, rdn & kept on final 2f, not pace of front pair: op 5/1: Apr foal, cost 50,000gns: dam unrcd, sire
high class 1m/12f performer: eff at 5f, bred to stay much further given time: must improve.
1568 **BEE ONE 10** [18] D R C Elsworth 2-8-9 N Pollard 10/1: -54: Rear, styd on well from 2f out, not   nk 78
pace to chall: tchd 12/1: left hvy grnd debut bhd: handles fast grnd, will apprec 6f+.
1197 **HOT PANTS 31** [9] 2-8-9 C Catlin (7) 33/1: 05: Chsd ldrs, no extra final 1f: see 1197.   1¾ 74
-- **AVERY RING** [5] 2-9-0 D Sweeney 20/1: 6: Towards rear, rdn & styd on well final 2f, nrst fin: op 14/1:   ½ 77+
Magic Ring colt, Apr foal, cost 6,800gns: dam a 5f juv wnr, sire a speed influence: promising.
-- **PARKSIDE PURSUIT** [15] 2-9-0 S Drowne 14/1: 7: In tch, onepace final 2f: op 12/1: Pursuit Of Love shd 77
colt, Mar foal: dam a 6f juv wnr, sire high class 6f/1m performer: with M R Channon & 6f will suit.
-- **KINGS BALLET** [17] 2-9-0 S Sanders 9/2: 8: Mid-div, effort 2f out, held wnr no room over 1f   3½ 68
out: bckd: Imperial Ballet colt, Apr foal: brother to a 6f juv wnr: dam unrcd: with P J Makin.
1403 **TROUBLESHOOTER 19** [14] 2-9-0 Martin Dwyer 10/1: 69: Mid-div, nvr pace to chall: see 1403 (6f).   ½ 66
-- **THAILAND** [1] 2-8-9 R Hills 16/1: 0: Keen/rear, mod late gains: 10th: op 12/1: Lycius filly, Apr   nk 60
foal, cost 16,000 gns: half-sister to a 7f juv wnr, dam a mdn: sire a top class 2yo at 6f/1m: with B W Hills.
-- **PAY THE SILVER** [19] 2-9-0 N Callan 20/1: 0: Dwelt/bhd, mod late gains: 11th.   ¾ 63
1260 **GEETEE EIGHTYFIVE** 27 [13] 2-9-0 R Brisland (5) 50/1: 00: Chsd ldrs 3f: 12th: no form on debut.   ½ 61
-- **BACCURA** [4] 2-9-0 W Ryan 25/1: 0: Rdn/bhd, styd on/no room over 1f out, position accepted: 13th: nk 60
May foal, cost 6,000 gns: half-brother to a juv wnr abroad: dam an Italian juv wnr: must be given another chance.
-- **GONE WITH THE WIND** [7] 2-8-9 M Hills 13/2: 0: Struggling halfway, 17th: op 4/1, stablemate of 10th: 0
Common Grounds filly, cost IR 35,000gns: sister to 3 wnrs incl smart 5f performer Flanders: dam a 5f juv wnr.
-- **Batchworth Lock** [11] 2-9-0 S Carson (5) 33/1:   -- **Agile Dancer** [6] 2-8-9 J Weaver 16/1:
1346 **The Marshall 21** [2] 2-9-0 (t) S Whitworth 25/1:   -- **Count Calypso** [16] 2-9-0 D O'Donohoe 25/1:
18 ran   Time 1m 01.17 (0.87)   (J S Gutkin)   B J Meehan Upper Lambourn, Berks.

1783 7.00 DISABLED ASSOCIATION MDN 3YO (D)   6f   Good/Firm 21 -00 Slow
£4498 £1384 £692   £346   Field raced centre - stands side

1569 **LAKELAND PADDY** 10 [11] M Blanshard 3-9-0 D Sweeney 6/1: -33641: 3 b c Lake Coniston - Inshad   79
(Indian King): Al handy, led/dsptd lead final 3f & styd on well for press to narrowly prevail nr line, all-out: op
5/1: rnr-up in '99 (rtd 81 at best, mdn): eff at 6/7f: acts on firm & soft grnd: handles any trk.
1406 **MISTER SUPERB** 19 [2] V Soane 3-9-0 S Sanders 7/2 FAV: 40-302: 3 ch c Superlative - Kiveton Komet nk 79
(Precocious): Led 3f, dsptd lead fnl 3f, drifted right 1f out, drvn/just held: bckd: see 1406, 1178 (h'caps).
839 **DESAMO 62** [7] J Noseda 3-9-0 Pat Eddery 4/1: 33: 3 br c Chief's Crown - Green Heights (Miswaki):   hd 78
Sn cl-up, rdn/ev ch inside last, just held nr fin: nicely bckd, 2 mth abs: handles fast & gd/soft: eff at 6/7f.
-- **ULYSSES DAUGHTER** [3] G A Butler 3-8-9 (t) T Quinn 4/1: 4: Mid-div, swtchd & rdn/pressed ldrs fnl   1 71
1f, kept on tho' al just held: op 3/1, debut: IR15,500gns purchase: eff at 6f, 7f+ suit: handles fast & a gall trk.
1261 **CRISS CROSS** 27 [5] 3-9-0 R Hughes 5/1: -22245: Sn handy & ev ch 2f out, edged left/no extra nr   ¾ 74
fin: well clr rem: op 4/1: acts on fast & hvy grnd: see 1261, 884.
4007} **POLISHED UP** 262 [4] 3-8-9 G Hind 20/1: 0-6: Chsd ldrs, held 2f out: op 12/1, reapp: unplcd sole 10 50

'99 start (rtd 58, fillies mdn, P T Walwyn): bred to apprec 1m this term: now with R M Beckett.
1399 **RETSKI 19** [10] 3-9-0 J F Egan 40/1: 07: In tch 4f: mod form. ¾ **53**
1607 **MARTINS PEARL 8** [6] 3-9-0 Martin Dwyer 50/1: 08: Chsd ldrs 4f: mod form. 1½ **49**
1399 **STRATTON 19** [12] 3-9-0 R Mullen 6/1: 6-49: Reared start, keen, in tch, rdn/wknd 2f out: see 1399. ¾ **47**
1399 **KINSAILE 19** [9] 3-8-9 D O'Donohoe 25/1: 0-00: Keen, outpcd halfway: 10th: op 12/1: see 1399. *hd* **41**
1181 **BLUE DOVE 32** [3] 3-8-9 R Hills 40/1: 0-00: In tch 4f: 11th: h'caps shld suit. *hd* **40**
1399 **OUR MEMOIRS 19** [1] 3-9-0 (t) S Whitworth 50/1: 0-00: Prom 3f: 12th: see 1399. 9 **29**
12 ran Time 1m 12.86 (1.26) (Mrs R G Wellman) M Blanshard Upper Lambourn, Berks.

1784

7.30 MITSUBISHI HCAP 3YO+ 0-85 (D) 1m5f61y Good/Firm 21 -30 Slow [84]
£4628 £1424 £712 £356 3 yo rec 17lb

1350 **RAVENSWOOD 21** [1] M C Pipe 3-8-6 (78)(t)(1ow) R Hughes 9/2 FAV: 00-421: 3 b c Warning - Green Lucia (Green Dancer): Rear, prog & repeatedly no room 3f out till dist, rdn/styd on strongly to lead cl home, going away: '99 Brighton wnr (auct mdn, rtd 84): eff at 12/13f, will stay further: acts on firm, gd & a stiff or sharp trk: eff in a t-strap: progressive styg type, value for more than winning margin tonight & is one to follow. **86+**
*1350 **WAIT FOR THE WILL 21** [3] G L Moore 4-9-5 (75) R Mullen 8/1: 0-0012: 4 ch g Seeking The Gold - You'd Be Surprised (Blushing Groom): Rear, prog/no room 3f out, led dist, not pace to repel wnr: bt this wnr in 1350. *1* **78**
*84 **SHARP STEPPER 199** [10] J H M Gosden 4-9-7 (77) J Fortune 6/1: 3321-3: 4 b f Selkirk - Awtaar (Lyphard): Held up rear, no room 3f out & prog/hmpd 2f out, squeezed thro' gap inside last & styd on, not pace of wnr: op 5/1: 7 mth abs: acts on fast, gd/soft & fibresand, eff at 13f: should win more races: see 84. 1½ **78**
1350 **KIRISNIPPA 21** [2] Derrick Morris 5-7-12 (52)(2ow) A Daly 16/1: 053204: Cl-up, rmnd prom & led 3f out, sn hard rdn & hdd 1f out, no extra: op 14/1: eff at 11/13f: consistent: see 1209, 1128 & 474 (AW). *1* **54**
1411 **BID ME WELCOME 19** [12] 4-9-7 (77) J Reid 25/1: 51-005: Led, hdd 3f out, remnd handy till fnl 1f. 1½ **75**
1076 **CLARENDON 38** [6] 4-9-7 (77) T Quinn 7/1: 00-006: Chsd ldrs, fdd final 2f: op 5/1: see 968 (12f). 3 **71**
*1301 **URGENT SWIFT 24** [8] 7-8-9 (65) Pat Eddery 9/1: 144017: Settled rear, effort 3f out, mod hdwy. *1* **58**
1394 **GALAPINO 19** [13] 7-7-10 (52)(1oh) M Henry 10/1: 00-548: Dwelt/rear, prog/ch 3f out, outpcd: see 1044. ¾ **44**
1411 **IL PRINCIPE 19** [7] 6-9-0 (70) J F Egan 20/1: -00009: Twds rear, eff over 3f out, btn/eased fnl 1f. 5 **55**
1509 **BONDS GULLY 13** [4] 4-7-10 (52)(1oh) R Brisland (5) 20/1: 320440: Chsd ldrs 10f: 10th: see 620, 547. 1½ **35**
3838} **PARADISE NAVY 274** [9] 11-8-2 (58)(bl) G Sparkes(7) 33/1: 6460-0: Rear, eff 4f out, sn held: 11th: '99 Lingfield wnr (AW h'cap, rtd 63a & 66): '98 Nottingham, Salisbury (rtd 70), Southwell & W'hampton wnr (h'caps, rtd 64a): eff at 14f/2m2f: acts on firm, hvy & both AWs: suited by binks: tricky ride, runs well for an amateur. 4 **35**
1594 **ACHILLES WINGS 8** [11] 4-8-13 (69) J Weaver 6/1: 442020: Chsd ldrs, keen, btn 2f out: 12th: bckd. 3 **42**
1329 **WHO CARES WINS 22** [5] 4-9-6 (76)(vis) K Fallon 8/1: 20-000: Mid-div, btn 3f out: 15th: visor, op 7/1. **0**
2628} **Prince Kinsky 332** [15] 7-8-1 (57) N Pollard 20/1: 1423} **Mole Creek 385** [14] 5-9-12 (82) G Faulkner (3) 25/1:
15 ran Time 2m 51.87 (6.77) (Lord Donoughmore) M C Pipe Nicholashayne, Devon.

1785

8.00 DOCKLANDS FILLIES HCAP 3YO+ 0-90 (C) 1m2f Good/Firm 21 -26 Slow [82]
£7319 £2252 £1126 £563 3 yo rec 13lb

*1386 **LIDAKIYA 19** [12] Sir Michael Stoute 3-8-12 (79) K Fallon 11/4 FAV: 411: 3 b f Kahyasi - Lilissa (Doyoun) Mid-div, styd on well fnl 1f to lead nr fin, going away: hvly bckd, h'cap bow: recent Thirsk wnr (mdn): eff at 10/12f, will relish further: acts on fast & gd/soft, gall/sharpish trk: progressive, can win again, esp over further. **88**
1555 **SURE QUEST 10** [15] D W P Arbuthnot 5-8-5 (59) Martin Dwyer 9/1: 411122: 5 b m Sure Blade - Eagle's Quest (Legal Eagle): Chsd ldrs, rdn/led over 2f out, hdd over 1f out, kept on well for press: tough performer. ½ **63**
1528 **AEGEAN DREAM 12** [5] R Hannon 4-9-8 (76) R Hughes 5/1: -23443: 4 b f Royal Academy - L'Ideale (Alysheba): Trkd ldrs, smooth prog & ev ch fin al 2f, narrow lead over 1f out till inside last, held cl-home: op 9/1: prob needs holding up till last moment: see 1528, 853 & 747. *hd* **79**
1271 **COMMON CAUSE 27** [2] C F Wall 4-9-9 (77) S Sanders 10/1: 310-44: Mid-div, rdn & styd on final 2f, not pace to chall: op 9/1: gd run, eff at 10f, 12f ideal: can find similar soon over further: see 1271. 2½ **76**
1287 **SWEET CICELY 26** [7] 3-8-1 (68) N Pollard 9/1: 00-35: Chsd ldr, onepace final 2f: op 7/1, h'cap bow. *nk* **66**
400 **LADY JO 134** [1] 4-8-6 (60) P Doe 20/1: 60-666: Rear, chsd ldrs 2f out, held final 1f: op 14/1, abs. 2 **55**
1375 **LADY ROCKSTAR 20** [13] 5-9-6 (74) G Faulkner (3) 9/1: -02007: Held up, swtchd/effort 3f out, sn held. 3½ **64**
727 **SEEKING UTOPIA 75** [4] 3-8-10 (77) N Callan 16/1: 205-58: Rear, mod gains fnl 3f: abs: see 727 (9f). ½ **66**
1608 **SUPERSONIC 8** [11] 4-9-3 (71) J Reid 20/1: 20-469: Led 1m, fdd: op 14/1: see 679 (AW). ½ **59**
745 **NABADHAAT 73** [14] 3-8-9 (76) R Hills 13/2: 40-40: In tch 1m: 10th: op 5/1, h'cap bow: 10 wk abs. ¾ **63**
1112 **READING RHONDA 36** [9] 4-8-4 (58) R Mullen 33/1: 5/500: Dwelt, al bhd: 11th: see 920 (mdn). 3½ **40**
1332 **ELMS SCHOOLGIRL 22** [3] 4-9-0 (68) J Tate 10/1: 153-20: Al bhd: 12th: op 8/1: see 1332. 4 **44**
4000} **Daniella Ridge 263** [8] 4-9-0 (68) Dane O'Neill 20/1: 1343 **Bonnie Flora 21** [10] 4-9-2 (70) R Perham 25/1:
14 ran Time 2m 07.47 (4.67) (H H Aga Khan) Sir Michael Stoute Newmarket

1786

8.30 DIDCOT CLASSIFIED STKS 3YO 0-80 (D) 1m str Good/Firm 21 -05 Slow
£4316 £1328 £664 £332 Field raced towards centre

1181 **EL GRAN PAPA 32** [8] J H M Gosden 3-9-0 J Fortune 5/2: 53-21: 3 b c El Gran Senor - Banner Hit (Oh Say): Rear, prog 2f out & qcknd to lead 1f out, pushed out cl-home: bckd from 9/2, 1st win: plcd in '99 (rtd 83, mdn): apprec step up to 1m, may get further: acts on firm & gd/soft, stiff/gall trk: shld improve further. **88**
1177 **TRAVELLING LITE 32** [1] B R Millman 3-9-0 G Hind 10/1: 60-342: 3 b c Blues Traveller - Lute And Lyre (The Noble Player): Led, shkn up over 2f out, hdd over 1f out, kept on for press: op 8/1: apprec return to 1m. 1½ **84**
1215 **POLAR CHALLENGE 30** [2] Sir Michael Stoute 3-9-0 K Fallon 2/1 FAV: 54-033: 3 b c Polar Falcon - Warning Light (High Top): Chsd ldrs, drvn/prsd ldr over 1f out, held ins last: hvly bckd: stays a gall 1m: see 1215. *1* **82**
*1018 **BIG FUTURE 45** [4] Mrs A J Perrett 3-9-2 Pat Eddery 7/2: 14: Rear, drvn & styd on onepace final 2f: bckd, op 4/1: 6 wk abs: stays 1m, acts on fast & soft grnd: see 1018 (mdn, 7f, soft). 1½ **81**
1377 **FALCONIDAE 20** [5] 3-9-0 S Sanders 12/1: 64-05: Rear, effort 2f out, not pace to chall: see 1377. *1* **77**
*1649 **OMNIHEAT 6** [3] 3-8-13 (bl) G Faulkner (3) 8/1: -32316: Chsd ldrs, hung left/btn 1f out: op 7/1. 1½ **73**
1569 **SOCIAL CONTRACT 10** [9] 3-9-0 J F Egan 20/1: 410-07: Keen/rear, efft 2f out, no impress: see 1569. 1½ **71**
810 **DILSAA 68** [6] 3-9-0 T Quinn 14/1: 525-58: Keen/rear, held 2f out: op 12/1, 10 wk abs: btr 810. 1½ **68**
1470 **MAJOR REBUKE 15** [11] 3-9-0 N Callan 33/1: 40-009: In tch, held 3f out: '99 debut wnr at Goodwood (4 rnr mdn, subs rtd 94, stks): eff at 6/7f, 1m should suit: handles fast & soft, sharp/stiff trk: has run well fresh. 2½ **63**
979 **SCOTTY GUEST 49** [7] 3-9-0 (t) M Fenton 12/1: 01-00: Chsd ldr, wknd qckly 2f out: abs: see 979. 1½ **60**
10 ran Time 1m 38.86 (2.06) (Thomas P Tatham) J H M Gosden Manton, Wilts.

NEWBURY

THURSDAY JUNE 8TH   Lefthand, Flat, Galloping Track

1787	9.00 MARSH BENHAM HCAP 3YO 0-75 (E) 7f str Good/Firm 21 -00 Slow	[82]
	£3302 £1016 £508 £254 Field raced towards centre	

1511 **MAGIC BABE** 13 [21] Jamie Poulton 3-8-1 (55) M Henry 16/1: 0-0241: 3 b f Magic Ring - Head Turner   **60**
(My Dad Tom): In tch, prog 2f out & led over 1f out, gamely held on nr fin, all-out: first success: unplcd in
'99 for D Elsworth (rtd 64, mdn): eff at 6/7f, tried 1m: acts on firm & gd, poss handles soft: prob handles any trk.
1405 **CIBENZE** 19 [16] M R Channon 3-8-11 (65) S Drowne 6/1: 3-0642: 3 b f Owington - Maria Cappuccini *shd*   **69**
(Siberian Express): Rear, prog final 2f & strong run inside last, just held: op 9/2: shaped as if 1m will suit.
1477 **MISTER CLINTON** 14 [11] K T Ivory 3-8-3 (57) D O'Donohoe 9/1: 0-4103: 3 ch g Lion Cavern - Thewaari *hd* **60+**
(Eskimo): Rear, eff/hmpd & lost momentum over 2f out, swtchd & styd on well ins last, just held: op 7/1: most
unlucky: apprec this return to 7f & can find compensation: see 1333 (mdn).
1266 **PARKER** 27 [8] B Palling 3-9-5 (73) K Fallon 5/1 FAV: 304-24: Chsd ldrs, drvn/ch 1f out, onepace cl   1¼ **73**
home: op 8/1: encouraging h'cap bow: see 1266 (auct mdn).
1345 **ROYAL IVY** 21 [10] T Quinn 3-8-13 (67) T Quinn 25/1: 231005: Rear, prog/chsd ldrs 1f out, held nr fin: see 421. 1¼ **64**
1569 **INSIGHTFUL** 10 [15] Dane O'Neill 3-9-6 (74) 2-5026: Rear, mod gains fnl 2f: op 9/2: see 108 (AW). nk **70**
1215 **OCEAN RAIN** 30 [7] 3-9-6 (74)(vis) M Fenton 14/1: 5-0507: Led till over 1f out, fdd: op 12/1: vis reapp. 1 **68**
1061 **UP THE KYBER** 38 [9] J Reid 20/1: 00-308: Rear, no room/hmpd over 2f out, kept on onepace   1 **66**
ins last: prob handles fast & hvy grnd, worth another look in similar: see 884.
1610 **SANTIBURI GIRL** 8 [17] 3-9-1 (69) Pat Eddery 14/1: -06109: Drvn/cl-up 2f out, fdd: op 16/1: see 1397. nk **60**
1377 **ZAFFIA** 20 [18] 3-9-7 (75) S Whitworth 7/1: 42-00: Chsd ldrs, outpcd final 2f: 10th: op 20/1: see 1377. nk **65**
1610 **SILK ST BRIDGET** 8 [14] 3-7-13 (53) M Baird 33/1: 00-000: Keen/rear, drvn/held fnl 2f: 11th: see 1610. 1¼ **40**
1494 **BALFOUR** 13 [6] 3-8-6 (60)(VIS) R Hughes 7/1: 0-1560: Rear, mod gains fnl 2f: visor: btr 887 (hvy). ½ **46**
1377 **CALLAS** 20 [3] 3-9-7 (75) J Stack 33/1: 04-00: Rear, effort 2f out, no impress: 13th: h'cap bow: 2½ **56**
4th of 2 '99 starts (rtd 79, mdn): bred to apprec mid-dists.
1442 **TARCOOLA** 17 [20] 3-8-11 (65) G Hind 20/1: 04-0F0: Chsd ldrs 5f: 14th: op 14/1: see 1442, 1099. 1 **44**
1289 **Sirene** 24 [19] 3-8-3 (57) A Beech (5) 14/1:   1399 **Loup Cervier** 19 [13] 3-8-2 (56) P Doe 33/1:
1289 **Muffin Man** 24 [4] 3-8-4 (58) G Baker (7) 33/1:   1263 **Magic Eagle** 27 [5] 3-8-8 (62) J F Egan 20/1:
962 **Distant Flame** 51 [22] 3-8-0 (54)(BL) R Mullen 20/1:   1726 **The Robster** 3 [12] 3-8-11 (65)(BL) D R McCabe 14/1:
999 **Chilworth** 47 [2] 3-8-3 (57)(bl) A Nicholls (3) 33/1:
21 ran   Time 1m 25.79 (1.49)   (Mrs J Wotherspoon)   Jamie Poulton Telscombe, East Sussex.

HAYDOCK

THURSDAY JUNE 8TH   Lefthand, Flat, Galloping Track

Official Going   GOOD/SOFT. Stalls: Outside, except 7f -Inside.

1788	2.30 GALLOWS HALL CLAIMER 3YO+ (E) 1m4f Good/Soft 79 -17 Slow	
	£2870 £820 £410 3 yo rec 15lb	

1070 **RAPIER** 38 [8] M D Hammond 6-9-8 Pat Eddery 9/4: 10-401: 6 b g Sharpo - Sahara Breeze (Ela   **77**
Mana Mou) Rear, prog 2f out, led cl home, rdn out: 99 Ayr wnr (h'cap, rtd 84) : in 98/99 won at Ayr (nov hdle,
rtd 100h, eff at 2m): '98 York Flat wnr (h'cap, rtd 90): eff at 1m/10f, stays 12f well: acts on firm, soft grnd
& on any trk: can run well fresh: has broken blood vessels: lightly rcd, apprec this drop to claiming grade.
1462 **COSMO JACK** 15 [6] M C Pipe 4-9-3 (vis) K Darley 14/1: 501-02: 4 b g Balla Cove - Foolish Law   *hd* **71$**
(Law Society) Rear, imprvd to lead 2f out, worn down cl home: amazing run at todays weights, wld have recieved
32lbs from today's wnr in a h'cap: stys a stiff 12f well: see 1462.
1604 **TONIC** 8 [2] M Johnston 4-9-8 J Fanning 6/4 FAV: 0-0043: 4 b g Robellino - Alyara (Alydar)   1¼ **75**
Prom, every ch dist, kept on & not btn far: well bckd: has shown enough to win a race this year: see 1604, 1150.
2915} **SUPLIZI** 320 [9] P Bowen 9-9-8 K Fallon 11/2: 000P-4: Hdwy from rear 2f out, every ch dist, no extra   1½ **73**
cl home: well clr of rem, reapp: lightly rcd & little form in val h'caps in '99: with B Llewellyn in '98, plcd
in 2 of 3 starts (rtd h'cap, rtd 97): back in '96 trained by L Cumani to win at Ripon (stks, rtd 98): eff at
10/12f on firm & hvy grnd: can run well fresh: unlucky h'capped on old form nowadays.
626 **QUIET ARCH** 98 [4] A Culhane 7-9-4 (vis) A Culhane 33/1: /40-05: In tch, outpcd final 2f: unplcd in a   8 **61$**
selling hdle 10 days ago: see 626 (A W seller).
1415 **JATO DANCER** 17 [5] 5-8-11 P M Quinn (3) 40/1: 005406: Led till 5f out, again 3f out till 2f out, fdd. 5 **49$**
1480 **KUUIPO** 14 [7] 3-8-2 J Bramhill 25/1: -00067: Al towards rear: see 930. 1¼ **54$**
1608 **RED ROSES** 8 [1] 4-8-12 Kim Tinkler 50/1: 6-8-008: Prom 1m, fdd: flattered. ½ **48$**
1329 **HAYA YA KEFAAH** 22 [3] 8-9-3 (VIS) J Mackay(7) 16/1: /00109: Dwelt & sadled slipped, recovered   28 **25**
& sn prom, led 5f out till 3f out, wknd & t.o.: tried a visor: lost all ch at the start: see 822 (sell h'cap).
9 ran   Time 2m 39.29 (11.49)   (Mrs A Kane)   M D Hammond Middleham, N Yorks

1789	3.00 RED CLOSE MDN 3YO (D) 7f30y rnd Good/Soft 79 -12 Slow	
	£4173 £1284 £642 £321	

1500 **FLEDGLING** 13 [3] A C Stewart 3-8-9 K Fallon 11/2: 51: 3 b f Efisio - Nest (Sharpo)   **82**
Made all, held on well fnl 1f, hands & heels: eff over a stiff 7f, will stay 1m: acts on gd/soft & a gall trk.
1377 **ARGENTAN** 20 [1] J H M Gosden 3-9-0 J Fortune 1/2 FAV: 33-22: 3 b c Gulch - Honfleur (Sadler's   1 **85**
Wells) Trckd wnr thro'out, chall halfway, kept on but not quite pace of wnr: hvly bckd, 7L clr 3rd: a return
to 1m will suit: should find similar, see 1377.
1562 **CELEBRE BLU** 10 [4] K A Ryan 3-9-0 F Lynch 5/1: 6333: 3 b g Suave Dancer - Taufan Blu (Taufan)   7 **71**
Al in 3rd, outpcd 2f out, eased fnl 1f: see 1562 (6f, mdn aution).
1436 **WORK OF FICTION** 17 [2] R Hannon 3-9-0 J Carroll 11/1: -044: Chsd ldrs till btn 2f out: op 7/1. 9 **57**
4 ran   Time 1m 33.54 (6.44)   (Racing For Gold)   A C Stewart Newmarket

1790	3.30 TOTE PLACEPOT HCAP 3YO+ 0-95 (C) 1m2f120y Good/Soft 79 -14 Slow	[95]
	£7182 £2210 £1105 £552 3 yo rec 14lb	

986 **MANTUSIS** 47 [7] P W Harris 5-9-5 (86) Pat Eddery 7/4 FAV: 01-321: 5 ch g Pursuit Of Love - Mana   **89**
(Windwurf) Prom, led after 4f, hld on well fnl 1f, rdn out: hvly bckd, 7 wk abs: '99 Yarmouth wnr (h'cap, rtd
85): rnr up in '98 (h'cap, rtd 94): '97 Haydock wnr (mdn, rtd 87): eff at 7/10f, stays 12f well: acts on firm

& hvy grnd, runs well fresh: handles any trk, can set the pace: tough & consistent gelding.

1518 **MCGILLYCUDDY REEKS 12** [4] Don Enrico Incisa 9-8-3 (70) Kim Tinkler 5/1: 0-3252: 9 b m Kefaah - Kilvamet (Furry Glen) Rcd keenly in tch, kept on fnl 1f & only just btn: fairly h'capd mare, best coming from off the pace in a strongly run race: should run well at Beverley next week: see 1307, 1070. ½ 72

1539 **PRINCE AMONG MEN 12** [3] M C Pipe 3-7-13 (80) J Mackay (7) 6/1: 36-333: 3 b g Robelline - Forelino (Trempolino) Trck ldrs, eff 2f out, kept on ins last & not btn far: see 1539 (C/D, mdn). 1 80

1561 **ROBZELDA 10** [5] K A Ryan 4-8-7 (74) F Lynch 6/1: 325644: Prom, one pace inside fnl 1f: clr rem. ¾ 73

1718 **AIR OF ESTEEM 3** [6] 4-8-2 (69) P M Quinn (3) 7/1: 260-35: Rear, prog entering straight, wknd dist: not stay 10f? much better around 1m prev: on a winning mark: qck reapp since 1718 (reapp). 6 60

1490 **MARCHING ORDERS 13** [2] 4-8-8 (75) K Fallon 6/1: 0-0009: Rear, no impression fnl 2f: see 1217. 9 54

4488} **THROUGH THE RYE 229** [1] 4-9-12 (93)(t) O Pears 40/1: 0104-7: Set pace 4f, wknd 3f out, fin last 4 66
on reapp, top weight: dual hdls wnr at Folkestone in early '00 (juv reapp rtd 130h, eff at 2m1f on soft/hvy): '99 Flat wnr for B Hills at Newcastle (mdn, rtd 82+): eff at 1m/11f on firm & hvy: wears a t-strap: now with M Pipe.

7 ran   Time 2m 19.75 (9.75)   (The Romantics)   P W Harris Aldbury, Herts

---

1791	4.00 SHANK LANE HCAP 4YO+ 0-100 (C)	2m45y	Good/Soft 79 -09 Slow		[96]
	£7117 £2190 £1095 £547 4 yo rec 1 lb				

1715 **RUM POINTER 3** [5] T D Easterby 4-9-4 (87) J Carroll 5/2 FAV: 0-0021: 4 b g Turtle Island - Osmunda (Mill Reef) Keen, made all, rdn clr appr fnl 1f, eased cl home: val 6L: qk reapp: '99 wnr at Catterick (reapp), Ripon, Haydock & Ayr (h'caps, rtd 88): eff at 12f, stays 2m well & loves gd/soft & soft, acts of firm & any trk: loves to dominate: v tough, game & open to further improvement at this trip. 93

1536 **FOUNDRY LANE 12** [9] Mrs M Reveley 4-8-7 (72) J Mackay (7) 15/2: 440-42: 9 b g Mtoto - Eider (Niniski) Handy, eff 2f out to chase wnr ins last, no impression: gd run & should be plcd to win another h'cap. 4 73

1527 **TURTLE VALLEY 12** [7] S Dow 4-9-10 (93) P Doe 6/1: -00023: 4 b c Turtle Island - Primrose Valley (Mill Reef) Chsd wnr, rdn & wknd appr fnl 1f: useful, likes gd grnd: see 1527, 997. 2 92

3197} **KAROWNA 307** [3] S A Brookshaw 4-7-13 (68) A Nicholls (2) 16/1: 3450-4: In tch, rdn & onepace 2f 2 66
out: recently rnr-up in a nov hdle (rtd 110h, stays 2m4.5f on fast & gd/soft): plcd for B McMahon in '99 (rtd 71): eff at 7f, poss stays 2m: acts on firm, gd/soft on hdles.

1527 **NICELY 12** [2] 4-8-13 (82) Pat Eddery 6/1: 410-05: In tch, gd hdwy to chall 2f out, no extra 4 77
appr fnl 1f: some promise here, see 1527.

1052 **TURNPOLE 40** [4] 9-8-12 (80) A Culhane 16/1: 204/06: Never a factor: see 1052. 1½ 74

1109 **JASEUR 36** [8] 7-9-10 (92)(vis) D Harrison 14/1: 306-07: Bhnd, eased when well btn over 1f out: 5 82
plcd sev times in '99, including in a Gr2 (rtd, 113S), also btn off a mark of 96 in h'caps: rtd 96 in '98: eff over 13f/2m on firm, soft & on any trk, likes Ascot: best in a visor & can carry big weights: enigmatic but useful.

1187 **HILL FARM BLUES 32** [6] 7-8-1 (69) T Williams 14/1: 0-4508: Bhd, btn over 2f out: see 879. 1½ 58

*1527 **WAVE OF OPTIMISM 12** [1] 5-9-1 (83) G Bardwell 9/2: 0-0119: V slow away & never a factor: nk 72
progressive earlier & could pay to ignore this: see 1527.

9 ran   Time 4m 41.23 (14.23)   (M P Burke)   T D Easterby Great Habton, N Yorks

---

1792	4.30 DEAN MOOR HCAP 3YO+ 0-80 (D)	5f	Good/Soft 79 +21 Fast		[76]
	£4043 £1244 £622 £311 3 yo rec 7 lb				

1781 **LAGO DI VARANO 1** [2] R M Whitaker 8-9-13 (75)(bl) Dean McKeown 11/2: 603531: 8 b g Clantime - On The Record (Record Token) Made all, kept on despite edging right ins last, rdn out: fast time: plcd 80
last night: top weight: '99 scorer at York & Sandown (h'caps, rtd 87): '98 scorer at Rippon (h'cap, rtd 93), also plcd in the Ayr Gold Cup: eff at 6f, all wins at 5f: acts on firm & soft, any trk: wears blinks/visor & loves to dominate: extremely tough & genuine gelding, slipped to a handy mark & a credit to connections.

787 **SHARP HAT 71** [1] D W Chapman 6-8-10 (58) A Culhane 4/1: 424402: 6 b g Shavian - Madam Trilby (Grundy) Handy, rdn 2f out, kept on to go 2nd inside last, no threat to wnr: well bckd from 7/1: encouraging 1¾ 58
run after 10 wk abs & on a very handy turf mark now: should be winning over 6f soon: see 91.

1631 **SUGAR CUBE TREAT 7** [4] M Mullineaux 4-8-7 (55) J Bramhill 20/1: 0-0003: 4 b f Lugana Beach - Fair Eleanor (Saritamer) Bhd, kept on late, never dangerous: wants further: see 910. hd 54

1714 **SHIRLEY NOT 3** [6] S Gollings 4-9-10 (72) K Darley 5/1: -03104: Bhd, brief eff 2f out, onepace. hd 71

1781 **DAAWE 1** [5] 9-9-10 (72)(bl) Clare Roche 10/1: 061005: Prom, btn fnl 1f: unplcd last night. 1 69

*1781 **BODFARI PRIDE 1** [3] 5-9-8 (70)(6ex) A Nicholls (3) 11/10 FAV: 000116: Prom, ev ch appr fnl 1f, no hd 66
extra & eased cl home: hvly bckd: won at Chester last night & this poss came just too soon: see 1781.

6 ran   Time 1m 01.69 (2.89)   (The Pbt Group)   R M Whitaker Scarcroft, W Yorks

---

1793	5.05 COME RACING HCAP 3YO 0-70 (E)	7f30y rnd	Good/Soft 79 -13 Slow		[75]
	£3248 £928 £464				

*1390 **ANTHEMION 19** [2] P C Haslam 3-9-4 (65) Dean McKeown 7/2 FAV: 0-0311: 3 ch g Night Shift - New 72
Sensitive (Wattlefield) In tch, hdwy to lead over 1f out, kept on ins last, rdn out: hvly bckd: earlier scored at W'hampton (h'cap, rtd 71a): plcd in '99 (rtd 70): suited by 7f on fast, gd/soft, fibresand & on any track.

1578 **SWYNFORD ELEGANCE 9** [9] J Hetherton 3-7-11 (44) G Bardwell 20/1: 050-02: 3 ch f Charmer - 2 47
Qualitairess (Kampala) Hld up, eff & hung badly left 2f out, kept on ins last no threat to wnr: stays 7f on gd/soft.

*1578 **CRYFIELD 9** [1] N Tinkler 3-8-10 (57)(6ex) J Fanning 5/1: 502013: 3 b g Efisio - Ciboure ¾ 59
(Norwick) Waited with, hdwy 2f out, soone one pace: mdn h'cap wnr in 1578 (6f), stys 7f.

1183 **ALAWAR 32** [8] C G Cox 3-9-2 (63)(t) D Harrison 14/1: 0-0004: Bhd, late gains, no danger: 3 60
stays 7f on firm & gd/soft: see 852.

1646 **HEATHYARDS LAD 6** [16] 3-9-2 (63) P M Quinn (3) 12/1: 632565: Wide, bhd, late gains, no danger. 1 59

1477 **ALPATHAR 14** [3] 3-8-11 (58) T Williams 12/1: 25-166: Waited with, effort 2f out, soon no impress. ¾ 52

1600 **BLUE LINE LADY 8** [14] 3-8-5 (52)(bl) K Darley 16/1: 0-0057: In tch, rdn 2f out, no impression. 1¼ 44

1682 **DONTBESOBOLD 5** [6] 3-9-0 (61)(vis) A Culhane 10/1: 405028: Missed break & all bhd: quick reapp. ¾ 52

884 **TAXMERE 57** [12] 3-7-11 (44) K Dalgleish 40/1: 60-09: Never a factor: abs. nk 34

1275 **NOBLE PASAO 26** [11] 3-9-7 (68) C Lowther 14/1: 260030: Led over 3f out from over 1f out, 1 56
wknd: 10th, top weight: btr 1275 (firm, 495).

2392} **OSTARA 342** [4] 3-8-11 (58) F Lynch 20/1: 0240-0: Led till over 3f out, wknd: 11th: reapp: 1½ 43
plcd once in '99 (seller, first time blinks, rtd 61, 6f, fast grnd).

1537 **STRAND OF GOLD 12** [13] 3-9-4 (65)(bl) J Carroll 14/1: -55050: Prom till wknd 2f out: 12th, see 1537. 1 48

1596 **SEND IT TO PENNY 5** [5] 3-7-11 (44)(BL) P Fessey 6/1: 4-0020: Al bhd: 15th: tried blinks, btr 1596. 0

1723 **Jepaje 3** [10] 3-8-13 (60) J Bramhill 14/1:   1496 **Bewildered 13** [15] 3-7-13 (46)(BL) J Mackay (7) 40/1:

1710 **Cumbrian Princess** 4 [7] 3-8-12 (59) M Tebbutt 20/1:
16 ran   Time 1m 33.77 (6.67)   (Lord Scarsdale)   P C Haslam Middleham, N Yorks

CHEPSTOW   THURSDAY JUNE 8TH   Lefthand, Undulating, Galloping Track

Official Going   GOOD (GOOD/SOFT in places). Stalls: Str Crse - Stands Side; Rnd Crse - Inside.

1794	**1.40 JACK BROWN HCAP DIV 1 3YO+ 0-70 (E)** **7f str** **Good/Soft 61** **-25 Slow** **[70]** £2919 £834 £417 3 yo rec 10lb

*1547 **PATSY STONE** 10 [19] M Kettle 4-9-10 (66)(6ex) S Sanders 8/1: 0-5011: 4 b f Jester - Third Dam   **70**
(Slip Anchor) Held up, rdn appr final 2f, kept on ins last to lead nr fin, rdn out: recent Leicester wnr (h'cap,
by 5L): '99 wnr at Yarmouth (mdn h'cap, rtd 64, W Musson): plcd in '98 (rtd 64): eff at 7f, 1m suits: acts on
firm & soft, any trk: can carry big weights & appears to be on the upgrade.
1611 **WHO GOES THERE** 8 [1] T M Jones 4-8-0 (42) A Polli (3) 33/1: -50002: 4 ch f Wolfhound - Challanging   nk **44**
(Mill Reef) Dwelt, imprvd appr fnl 2f to lead below dist, hdd fnl strides, back to form: see 265.
132 **WHITE EMIR** 190 [13] L G Cottrell 7-9-0 (56) A Clark 33/1: 4000-3: 7 b g Emarati - White African   ½ **57**
(Carwhite) Rear, prog 3f out, styd on for press: plcd in '99 (h'cap, rtd 72, B Millman): last won in '97 at
Sandown & Salisbury (rtd 83, B Meehan): eff at 5/6f, stays 7f on firm & hvy, with/without blnks: well h'capped.
1636 **HALMANERROR** 7 [7] G M McCourt 10-9-0 (56) R Hughes 7/2 FAV: 653324: Held up, swtchd & hdwy   nk **56**
appr final 2f, styd on, not btn far: nicely bckd, qck reapp: consistent but hard to win with this term.
1542 **GREEN GOD** 12 [14] 4-9-9 (65) J Reid 20/1: 620-05: Held up, chsd ldrs fnl 2f, al held: see 1542.   hd **65**
1591 **BANDBOX** 8 [2] 5-9-7 (63) J Weaver 12/1: 000306: Cl-up, led 2½f out till ins ent fnl 1f, no extra: best at 6f.   1¼ **61**
776 **DAPHNES DOLL** 71 [12] 5-8-8 (50) L Newman (5) 25/1: 1-0007: Chsd ldrs, outpcd towards fin: 1¼ **46**
10 wk abs, turf return: suited by further: see 209 (AW).
1336 **ANNIE APPLE** 22 [20] 4-8-7 (49) A Daly 14/1: -00058: Al same place: see 594.   1 **43**
1438 **ZEPPO** 17 [6] 5-9-2 (58) M Fenton 14/1: 00-049: Held up, chsd ldrs 3f out till 2f out: prefers sprinting.   ¾ **50**
1438 **BALI STAR** 17 [17] 5-8-7 (49) N Callan (5) 12/1: 0-2000: Trkd ldrs, wknd 2f out: 10th, lngr trip, see 1438, 802.   ¾ **40**
1348 **DEMOCRACY** 21 [11] 4-9-4 (60) S Drowne 20/1: 000000: Nvr troubled ldrs: 11th: see 258.   shd **51**
*1732 **ARBENIG** 3 [15] 5-8-13 (55)(6ex) D Sweeney 7/1: 0-0310: Mid-div till 2f out: op 10/1, too sn after 1732?   **0**
1542 **MYSTIC RIDGE** 12 [3] 6-9-13 (69) J P Spencer 7/1: 410040: Handy till 2f out: 15th, top-weight, see 476.   **0**
*1557 **TRUMP STREET** 10 [4] 4-8-10 (52)(6ex) Jonjo Fowle (7) 12/1: 025010: Chsd ldrs 4f: 17th, op 8/1: btr 1557.   **0**
960 **Shudder** 51 [16] 5-9-9 (65) O Urbina 14/1:   1721 **Warring** 3 [8] 6-8-4 (46) R Price 20/1:
1297 **Corn Dolly** 24 [9] 4-8-5 (47) S Carson(5) 20/1:   1520 **Miss Money Spider** 12 [10] 5-8-6 (48) P Fitzimons(5) 20/1:
1336 **Cedar Wells** 22 [18] 4-8-9 (51) D Mernagh (3) 20/1:   1481 **Marjory Polley** 14 [5] 3-8-3 (55) Martin Dwyer 33/1:
20 ran   Time 1m 25.8 (6)   (I Fraser, J Butt, B Goldsmith)   M Kettle Blewbury, Oxon.

1795	**2.10 ENTERTAIN AT CHEPSTOW HCAP 3YO 0-85 (D)** **5f** **Good/Soft 61** **-23 Slow** **[91]** £3900 £1200 £600 £300

1694 **BLUE HOLLY** 5 [13] J S Moore 3-8-13 (76) R Hughes 7/1: 3-5201: 3 b f Blues Traveller - Holly Bird   **83**
(Runnett) Rear, swtchd & smooth prog 2f out, led dist, v cmftbly: tchd 12/1, qck reapp: '99 Lingfield wnr (auct
mdn, rtd 79): eff at 5f, tried 6f: acts on gd & hvy, poss fast: imprvd for being held up, can follow up.
1289 **SEA HAZE** 24 [1] R J Baker 3-8-8 (71) M Roberts 20/1: 340-02: 3 ch g Emarati - Unveiled (Sayf El Arab)   2 **70**
Nvr far away, ev ch appr 1f, outpcd by wnr: '99 Bath wnr (auct mdn, rtd 74): eff at 5/6f on firm & gd/soft.
1391 **CAROLS CHOICE** 19 [2] D Haydn Jones 3-7-13 (62) Dale Gibson 7/1: 203323: 3 ch f Emarati - Lucky   nk **60**
Song (Lucky Wednesday) Led till dist, onepace: turf return, holds form well, see 1391, 549.
*773 **FINE MELODY** 71 [3] B W Hills 3-9-3 (80) J Reid 5/1: 3114: Pld hard, held up, swtchd appr fnl 1f, styd   ¾ **76**
on but unable to chall: turf bow & ran well enough but found this drop back to 5f against her: win again at 6f+.
1712 **DANCEMMA** 4 [4] 3-8-6 (69) D Sweeney 10/1: -00025: Chsd ldrs, no extra appr final 1f: qck reapp,   ½ **64**
1651 **STONEY GARNETT** 6 [11] 3-8-5 (68) A Daly 7/1: 30-126: Held up, feeling pace 2f out, moderate hdwy.   1¼ **60**
1670 **JAMES STARK** 6 [14] 3-8-11 (74)(vis) J Fortune 7/1: 000027: Bhd, not much room 2f out, ran on fnl 1f.   shd **66**
1670 **BREEZY LOUISE** 6 [10] 3-8-3 (66)(bl) S Drowne 12/1: -10668: Nvr a factor: qck reapp, blnks reapplied.   ¾ **56**
1427 **CLANSMAN** 17 [9] 3-7-11 (60) A Polli (3) 20/1: 045-09: Chsd ldrs till 2f out: flattered juv (mdn, rtd 73).   ½ **49**
1694 **PEDRO JACK** 5 [12] 3-9-3 (80) D R McCabe 7/2 FAV: -31060: Nvr dngrs: 10th, tchd 9/2, qck reapp: 1¾ **65**
suited by further & faster grnd: see 1694 (in front of this wnr), 1289.
1219 **PALMSTEAD BELLE** 30 [5] 3-8-7 (70)(t) R Mullen 8/1: 045-00: Speed 3f: 11th.   ¾ **53**
2601 **COLLISION TIME** 334 [6] 3-7-13 (62) Martin Dwyer 20/1: 4430-0: Bhd from halfway: 12th, reapp: 1 **42**
plcd in '99 (mdn, rtd 72): eff at 5/6f on gd & gd/soft, has tried a visor: with P Evans.
1410 **SUSIES FLYER** 19 [7] 3-9-7 (84) S Sanders 7/1: 15-500: Mid-div till 2f out: 13th, top weight.   hd **64**
13 ran   Time 1m 01.0 (4.2)   (Alan Chatfield)   J S Moore East Garston, Berks.

1796	**2.40 CASTLE BINGO FILLIES MDN 3YO+ (D)** **1m2f36y** **Good/Soft 61** **-12 Slow** £3965 £1220 £610 £305 3 yo rec 13lb

1428 **TRIPLE SHARP** 17 [2] L M Cumani 3-8-8 J P Spencer 3/1 JT FAV: 41: 3 ch f Selkirk - Drei (Lyphard)   **83**
In tch, eff 3f out, kept on well to lead towards fin, rdn out: has come on for debut: half-sister to a 9f AW wnr:
apprec step up to 10f, shapes like further will suit: acts on gd/soft grnd, gall/undul trk: improving.
1447 **TWIN LOGIC** 16 [8] J H M Gosden 3-8-8 J Reid 3/1 JT FAV: 5432: 3 ch f Diesis - Indigenous (Lyphard)   ½ **82**
Trkd ldrs, hmpd appr final 2f, ran & hdd below dist, kept on (flashed tail): clr rem: another
gd run, acts on gd & gd/soft grnd, should find similar.
1669 **POWERLINE** 6 [14] R Hannon 3-8-8 R Hughes 6/1: 06-063: 3 b f Warning - Kantikoy (Alzao)   3½ **78**
Cl-up, led 3f out, sn hdd, same pace: tchd 8/1, qck reapp: styd lngr 10f trip on gd/soft grnd: see 971.
-- **MARENKA** [5] H Candy 3-8-8 C Rutter 8/1: 4: Mid-div, hdwy 3f out till 1f out: debut: Mtoto half-   ½ **77**
sister to an Irish 9f wnr: likely to apprec a step up in trip: probs handles soft grnd.
1428 **CAPE LODGE** 17 [4] 3-8-8 J D Smith 14/1: 65: Held up, hdwy 3f out, nvr nr ldrs: better when h'capped.   2½ **74**
-- **CELTIC BAY** [13] 3-8-8 M Hills 8/1: 6: Slow away, nvr better than at fin: debut, well clr rem: ¾ **73+**
Green Dancer half-sister to sev wnrs up to 12f & that trip looks likely to suit: with J Hills.
3293 **CAPPELLINA** 301 [11] 3-8-8 S Drowne 33/1: 00-7: Nvr dngrs: reapp: mid-div when rtd 60 last term: 7 **65$**
bred to be suited by trips shorter than 10f: with P Murphy.
-- **LADY ABAI** [9] 3-8-8 Craig Williams 50/1: 8: Nvr a factor: op 20/1: Bin Ajwaad filly, dam stoutly bred.   ¾ **64**

CHEPSTOW THURSDAY JUNE 8TH Lefthand, Undulating, Galloping Track

1447 **MUTASADER 16** [1] 3-8-8 R Hills 9/2: 0-59: Well plcd, led 4f out-3f out, fdd: op 7/2: btr 1447 (gd). 1¾ 62
962 **CROSS LUGANA 51** [6] 4-9-7 N Callan 33/1: 0/00: In tch till 4f out: 10th: 7 wk abs. 2 59
1555 **SIONED LYN 10** [12] 3-8-8 M Roberts 33/1: 20030: Led till 4f out, wknd: 11th: stiffish task. ½ 58
1344 **Dajam Vu 21** [7] 3-8-8 R Havlin 50/1: 1404 **Ramadanzen 19** [3] 3-8-8 N Pollard 33/1:
-- **Risky Dream** [10] 3-8-8 Joanna Badger (7) 33/1:
14 ran Time 2m 11.5 (7.4) (Robert H Smith) L M Cumani Newmarket

---

1797 3.10 COMERACING CLASS STKS 3YO+ 0-90 (C) 1m2f36y Good/Soft 61 00 Slow
£6425 £1977 £988 £494 3 yo rec 13lb

1452 **IDOLIZE 16** [4] P F I Cole 3-8-1 L Newman (5) 4/1: 021-01: 3 ch f Polish Precedent - Knight's Baroness 92
(Rainbow Quest) Held up, imprvd appr fnl 3f, led bef 2f out, pushed clr, easily: op 11/4: landed fnl '99 start
here at Chepstow (fill mdn, rtd 95): sister to smart 9/12f wnr Riyadian: suited by step up to 10f, likely to
get 12f: acts on gd/soft grnd, likes this undulating/gall Chepstow trk: useful filly.
1031 **KOMISTAR 43** [3] P W Harris 5-9-5 M Roberts 7/2: 610-02: 5 ch g Komaite - Rosie's Gold (Glint 6 87
Of Gold) Led till appr final 2f, rallied for 2nd but no ch with wnr: 6 wk abs, ran to best, see 1031.
4204} **PRAIRIE WOLF 250** [5] M L W Bell 4-9-3 M Fenton 9/4 FAV: 3210-3: 4 ch g Wolfhound - Bay Queen ¾ 84
(Damister) Well plcd, ev ch 2f out, sn no extra: drifter from 5/4, reapp, clr of next: '99 wnr at W'hampton (mdn,
rtd 76a), Ripon, Nottingham (h'caps) & Yarmouth (class stks, rtd 91): unplcd both '98 starts: eff at 1m/10f:
acts on firm, soft, fibresand, any trk: can run well fresh but should be sharper for this.
733 **ZANAY 75** [1] Miss Jacqueline S Doyle 4-9-7 T G McLaughlin 7/2: -11104: Held up, effort 4f out, no 10 76
impress: tchd 6/1, 11 wk abs: yet to translate v useful/progressive winter AW form to turf: see 690.
1374 **GIRLS BEST FRIEND 20** [2] 3-8-3 Martin Dwyer 25/1: 040-05: Al bhd, lost tch 4f out: see 1374. 9 59
5 ran Time 2m 10.3 (6.2) (HRH Prince Fahd Salman) P F I Cole Whatcombe, Oxon.

1798 3.40 MOTOR MDN AUCT 2YO (E) 6f Good/Soft 61 -06 Slow
£2961 £846 £423

-- **BLUE GODDESS** [11] R Hannon 2-8-5 Dane O'Neill 14/1: 1: 2 b f Blues Traveller - Classic Goddess 97+
(Classic Secret) Mid-div, swtchd & imprvd 2f out, drifted left dist, led inside last, readily: debut: IR 15,000gns
Mar foal, half-sister to 2 wnrs abroad: sire 9/12f performer: eff at 6f, further is going to suit: acts on gd/
soft grnd, undulating trk & goes well fresh: potentially useful filly, worth following.
1001 **FACTUAL LAD 45** [4] B R Millman 2-8-7 A McCarthy (3) 6/1: 2332: 2 b c So Factual - Surprise Surprise 2 88
(Robellino) Tried to make all, clr ent fnl 2f, onepace & hdd ins last: plcd yet again & got this lngr 6f trip.
-- **PEACEFUL PARADISE** [1] J W Hills 2-8-6 M Hills 16/1: 3: 2 b f Turtle Island - Megdale (Waajib) shd 87
Dwelt, in tch, eff 2f out, styd on: debut: 16,000 gns Apr foal, bred to apprec 1m: handles gd/soft grnd.
-- **MONTANA MISS** [7] B Palling 2-8-0 D Mernagh (3) 16/1: 4: Chsd ldrs, unable to qckn 2f out: clr of ½ 80
rem on debut: 2,800 gns Earl Of Barking Mar foal, half-sister to 4 wnrs: dam juv wnr: stays 6f on gd/soft grnd.
1088 **MONTE MAYOR GOLF 37** [5] 2-8-1 Dale Gibson 33/1: -05: Chsd ldrs, outpcd appr final 1f: 15,000 gns 5 71
Case Law Apr foal, sister to 9/14f wnrs Cashiki & Lisa B, dam hdles wnr, sire a sprinter.
-- **MONSIEUR LE BLANC** [17] 2-8-11 Martin Dwyer 12/1: 6: Bhd, late gains: debut: 15,000 nk 80
gns Alzao Mar foal, dam & half-brother wnrs in France: with I Balding, will improve & relish further.
1522 **FOREVER MY LORD 12** [10] 2-8-9 J Reid 8/1: 67: Al same place: up in trip, see 1522. ¾ 76
1641 **BALI ROYAL 6** [6] 2-7-13 A Daly 11/2 JT FAV: 28: Chsd ldrs till 2f out: op 3/1, qck reapp, up in trip. 1½ 63
932 **WATTNO ELJOHN 52** [2] 2-8-9 S Whitworth 33/1: 09: Handy till 2f out: 5,000lrgns Namaqualand colt. shd 73
1328 **PHYSICAL FORCE 22** [8] 2-8-7 R Mullen 33/1: 00: Nvr in it: 10th: 6,400 gns Casteddu Mar foal, 4 61
half-brother to 3 wnrs in Germany, sire 7f performer: with J Best.
1472 **LAI SEE 15** [14] 2-8-6 N Callan 12/1: 00: Al towards rear: 11th, see 1472. 1¼ 57
1107 **SAWBO LAD 36** [16] 2-8-4 M Fenton 6/1: 600: Al bhd: 12th, op 8/1, see 812. ¾ 53
-- **LIONEL ANDROS** [15] 2-8-6 N Pollard 6/1: 0: Dwelt, sn btn: 14th on debut: 6,200 gns Lion Cavern 0
May foal, half-brother to useful sprint juv Midnight Blue, dam uncrd, sire 6/7f performer: with R Hodges.
1290 **SMITH AND WESTERN 24** [12] 2-8-7 R Hughes 11/2 JT FAV: 50: Bhd from halfway, eased appr final 1f: 0
15th, shorter prcd stablemate of wnr, see 1290 (firm).
-- **Vislink** [9] 2-8-10 D Sweeney 25/1: -- **No Name City** [13] 2-8-9 R Hills 14/1:
-- **Only When Provoked** [3] 2-8-5 R Havlin 25/1:
17 ran Time 1m 12.8 (4) (David Mort) R Hannon East Everleigh, Wilts.

1799 4.10 JACK BROWN HCAP DIV 2 3YO+ 0-70 (E) 7f str Good/Soft 61 +01 Fast [70]
£2908 £831 £415 3 yo rec 10lb

854 **GOODENOUGH MOVER 59** [14] J S King 4-8-5 (45)(2ow) R Havlin 33/1: 600-01: 4 ch g Beveled - Rekindled 54
Flame (Kings Lake) Led, clr 2f out, cmftbly: fair time, val 5L+, 8 wk abs: 1st win: with G Charles Jones in '99
(mdn, rtd 64): eff at 7f, tried 1m: acts on gd/soft: runs well fresh, udul trk: imprvd for new connections.
1519 **MYTTONS MISTAKE 12** [17] R J Baker 4-8-8 (50) G Sparkes (7) 9/1: -02242: 7 b g Rambo Dancer - Hi 3 51
Hunsley (Song Easy) Held up, kept on to go 2nd dist, no ch with easy wnr: remains in form, see 1066.
*1601 **ERUPT 8** [8] Miss S J Wilton 7-9-3 (59)(6ex) D Mernagh (3) 15/2: 042113: 7 b g Beveled - ¾ 59
Sparklingsovereign (Sparkler) Chsd ldrs, drvn appr fnl 1f, onepace: ran to best for new stable with a pen: tough.
1467 **MUTABASSIR 15** [10] G L Moore 4-8-6 (62) I Mongan (5) 7/1: 30-654: Trkd ldrs, unable to qckn 2f out. 2 58
1483 **AKALIM 14** [9] P Fitzsimons (5) 14/1: 210-05: Mid-div, hdwy to chase wnr briefly 2f out, no 3 56
extra: top-weight: '99 wnr at Newbury (appr h'cap, rtd 69): '98 wnr here at Chepstow (h'cap, rtd 63): eff at
6/7f, tried 1m: acts on firm, hvy, both AWs: prob best without visor now.
1297 **ROUGE ETOILE 24** [6] 4-8-13 (55) W Supple 16/1: 0-0006: Well plcd till 2f out: op 12/1: see 811. ½ 44
1652 **KNOBBLEENEEZE 6** [20] 10-8-0 (42) Craig Williams 12/1: -00037: Chsd ldrs till appr fnl 1f: qk reapp. nk 30
1590 **SCISSOR RIDGE 8** [11] 8-8-5 (47) R Brisland (5) 15/2: 640238: Handy till 2f out: op 10/1, see 1542, 29. ½ 34
4521} **ADDITION 226** [13] 4-9-2 (58) Sophie Mitchell 25/1: 0060-9: Nvr better than mid-div: reapp: '99 ¾ 43
Warwick wnr (fill h'cap, rtd 57): rtd 69 as a juv: eff at 6f/sharp 7f: acts on fast & gd/soft grnd.
1368 **JAMES DEE 20** [16] 4-9-8 (64) N Callan 5/1 FAV: 222620: Prom 5f: 10th, tchd 8/1, better at 6f this term. 2½ 44
1082 **DAYS OF GRACE 18** [18] 5-9-0 (56) Martin Dwyer 12/1: 132200: Nvr able to chall: 11th, see 466. ½ 35
1058 **CAD ORO 40** [19] 7-9-9 (65) F Keniry 12/1: 00-030: Nvr in it: 17th, 6 wk abs, op 9/1, see 1058, 817. 0
1542 **ANSTAND 12** [12] 5-8-13 (55) S Drowne 10/1: 0-0060: Chsd ldrs 4f: 19th, tchd 14/1: see 1542. 0
1511 **Antigonel 13** [4] 3-8-6 (58) Dane O'Neill 14/1: 3533} **Fionn De Cool** [1] 9-8-7 (49) A McGlone 20/1:
1113 **Lough Swilly 36** [7] 4-8-9 (51) G Hind 16/1: 4472} **Stridhana 230** [15] 4-9-9 (65) N Pollard 14/1:
1414 **Berberis 19** [3] 4-7-13 (41) Claire Bryan (5) 25/1: 1557 **Strats Quest 10** [5] 6-8-4 (46)(vis) M Roberts 16/1:

585

THURSDAY JUNE 8TH **Lefthand, Undulating, Galloping Track**

1344 **Polish Girl 21** [2] 4-8-7 (49) D R McCabe 20/1:
20 ran   Time 1m 24.0 (4.2)   (D Goodenough Removals & Transport)   J S King Broad Hinton, Wilts.

1800		4.40 THEHORSESMOUTH HCAP 3YO+ 0-85 (D) 2m2f Good/Soft 61 +02 Fast	[83]
		£3874 £1192 £596 £298 3 yo rec 23lb4 yo rec 2 lb	

1527 **EASTWELL HALL** 12 [6] T P McGovern 5-9-9 (78) L Newman (5) 6/1: 054-51: 5 b g Saddlers' Hall - **83**
Kinchenjunga (Darshaan) Rear, imprvd & short of rm 5f out, rdn to lead ins last, shade rdly: 99/00 hdles wnr at
Warwick & Ascot (novs, rtd 132h, 2m/2½m, fast & soft): plcd in '99 (Cesarewitch h'cap, rtd 84): '98 wnr at
Bath, Folkestone & Warwick (h'caps, rtd 75, R Curtis): eff at 12f/2m2f on fast & soft, any trk: can go well fresh.
1510 **STORMY SKYE** 13 [8] G L Moore 4-9-5 (76)(tbl) I Mongan (5) 8/1: 442-32: 4 b g Bluebird - Canna   1½ **78**
(Caerleon) In tch, prog to chall fnl 2f, no extra ins last: op 20/1 on reapp: likely to suited by this step up to 2m2f, likely improver.
1711 **SHARAZAN** 4 [9] O O'Neill 7-8-0 (55) Sophie Mitchell 9/1: 060-03: 7 b g Akarad - Sharaniya (Alleged)   1¼ **56**
Rear, kept on well final 2f, nvr nrr: qck reapp: clearly gets 2m2f, nicely h'capped, see 1711.
1524 **TREASURE CHEST** 12 [3] M C Pipe 5-8-9 (64)(vis) R Hughes 7/1: 0-0004: Held up, prog 4f out, led   ½ **65**
1½f out till ins last, onepace: clr of next: handles gd/soft, suited by fast: see 1394.
1527 **BRAVE TORNADO** 12 [2] 9-9-10 (79) F Keniry (5) 9/2: /12245: Early ldr & again appr final 4f till bef   3 **78**
dist, fdd: not disgrcd over this slightly lngr trip: in front of this wnr in 1527, see 917.
194 **DANGER BABY** 176 [4] 10-7-10 (51)(bl) Claire Bryan (5) 10/1: 3140-6: Chsd ldrs, no extra 2f out: 1 **49**
op 20/1 on reapp: '99 Bath wnr (h'cap, rtd 52): formerly a useful tho' temperamental chsr, 98/99 Sedgefield wnr
(h'cap, 2½m, any grnd, rtd 128c): eff at 2m/2m2f on gd & gd/soft, handles fast: poss best without blnks.
1394 **FUJIYAMA CREST** 19 [13] 8-9-0 (69) J Lowe 25/1: 043-07: Nvr a factor: 3rd of 7 final '99 start (h'cap,   5 **63**
rtd 75): 97/98 Stratford hdle wnr (nov, 3m, firm & gd, rtd 108h): lightly rcd on the level since '96 Ascot win
(h'cap, rtd 90, Sir M Stoute): eff at 14f/2m on firm & gd: best out in front in a visor: with R Curtis.
973} **FAST FORWARD FRED** 412 [12] 9-8-0 (55) Martin Dwyer 25/1: 10/0-8: Chsd ldrs till 3f out: reapp: 3½ **46**
unplcd sole '99 start, prev term won here at Chepstow (mdn h'cap), Bath & Sandown (h'caps, rtd 57): eff at
2m/2m2f on firm & gd grnd, likes gall trks & being up with the pace: with L Montague Hall.
1394 **MU TADIL** 19 [1] 8-7-10 (51)(16oh) R Brisland (5) 50/1: 00-009: Nvr troubled ldrs: stiff task, see 1394.   1¼ **41**
1030 **KINNESCASH** 43 [14] 7-9-10 (79) J Reid 9/1: 001-00: Trkd ldrs, wknd fnl 3f: hdles 2nd since 1030.   ½ **68**
1394 **WONTCOSTALOTBUT** 19 [10] 6-8-1 (56) Dale Gibson 7/2 FAV: 34-200: Held up, clsd halfway, went   hd **45**
out tamely 4f out: 11th, bckd from 9/2: reportedly in season when flopped latest, see 1044.
1527 **Jawah** 12 [11] 6-9-6 (75)(vis) G Faulkner (3) 14/1:   --   **Old Irish** [5] 7-8-10 (65) C Rutter 25/1:
1369 **Secret Drop** 20 [7] 4-8-3 (60) T E Durcan 16/1:
14 ran   Time 4m 02.5 (10.7)   (Eastwell Manor Racing)   T P McGovern Lewes, East Sussex.

SOUTHWELL (Fibresand)   **FRIDAY JUNE 9TH**   **Lefthand, Sharp, Oval Track**

Official Going   STANDARD. Stalls: 5f - Outside; Rem - Inside.

1801		2.20 FARNDON HCAP 3YO+ 0-65 (F) 7f aw rnd Going 33 -01 Slow	[63]
		£2359 £674 £337 3 yo rec 10lb	

439 **SOLLYS PAL** 128 [12] P J Makin 5-8-10 (45)(VIS) A Clark 9/1: 04-531: 5 gr g Petong - Petriece   **49a**
(Mummy's Pet) In tch, hdwy over 1f out, styd on to lead ins last, rdn out: long abs, 1st win, op 9/1: rtd 53
when unplcd in '99: eff at 7f on both AW's: runs well fresh: has flashed tail in past but apprec visor today.
*1505 **SHARP STEEL** 14 [13] Miss S J Wilton 5-9-7 (56) I Mongan (5) 7/2: -56212: 5 ch g Beveled - Shift   ½ **59a**
Over (Night Shift) Cl-up, led 2f out, edged left & hdd just ins fnl 1f, just btn: jock rec 1 day careless riding ban.
1275 **STILL WATERS** 27 [6] I A Wood 5-8-10 (45) G Hind 20/1: -06003: 5 b g Rainbow Quest - Krill (Kris)   shd **48a**
Led over 3f out till 2f out, ev ch ins last, btn less than 1L: eff at 7f/1m: slipped down the weights, see 172.
1654 **MARENGO** 7 [5] M J Polglase 6-9-8 (57) T G McLaughlin 7/1: 504024: Cl-up, hdwy & not clr run   1 **58a**
2f out, kept on same pace fnl 1f: prob just stays a sharp 7f, all 5 wins at 6f: see 654, 1073.
923 **FRANKLIN D** 55 [15] 4-8-9 (44) S Whitworth 20/1: -23406: Led 2f, cl-up, wknd appr fnl 1f & short   shd **45a**
of room ins last: clr of rem after a 7 wk abs: see 58.
*1235 **FEATHERSTONE LANE** 29 [16] 9-9-5 (54) M Tebbutt 12/1: 222316: Bhd, mod late gains: btr 1235.   4 **47a**
802 **ELTON LEDGER** 70 [8] 11-9-10 (59)(vis) R Price 20/1: 203507: In tch, wknd over 2f out: 10 wk abs.   hd **51a**
1601 **ABTAAL** 9 [1] 10-9-8 (57)(vis) P McCabe 10/1: 013608: Slowly away, nvr a factor: best in sell/clmrs.   nk **48a**
1419 **STRAVSEA** 18 [7] 5-9-5 (54) P M Quinn (3) 8/1: 504209: Nvr a factor: op 6/1: best 1303.   1¼ **43a**
1421 **DESERT INVADER** 18 [14] 9-8-1 (36) P Fessey 25/1: 3-0000: Al bhd: fin 10th.   4 **18a**
1354 **NOCCIOLA** 21 [4] 4-9-6 (55) G Duffield 100/30 FAV: 0-060: Dwelt, sn in tch, short of room & lost   **0a**
place 5f out, no impress: fin 14th, nicely bckd, see 1354.
1066 **D W Mccee** 39 [3] 4-8-7 (42) A Daly 33/1:   1614 **Nice Balance** 9 [9] 5-8-4 (39) Joanna Badger (7) 14/1:
1190 **Align** 33 [2] 4-9-1 (50) D Mernagh (3) 16/1:   624} **Bold Aristocrat** 457 [10] 9-9-7 (56) F Lynch 20/1:
1864} **Moonridge** 366 [11] 3-9-3 (62)(t) K Dalgleish (7) 33/1:
16 ran   Time 1m 29.0 (2.4)   (Mrs Paul Levinson)   P J Makin Ogbourne Maisey, Wilts

---

1802		2.55 ASLOCKTON CLAIMER 4YO+ (F) 2m aw Going 33 -77 Slow	
		£2191 £626 £313 4 yo rec 1 lb Very slow run race	

1393} **DJAIS** 388 [5] J R Jenkins 11-8-12 (vis) S Whitworth 13/2: 60/6-1: 11 ch g Vacarme - Dame de Carreau   **74a**
(Targowice) In tch, gd hdwy to lead over 2f out, held on for press in a slow run race ins last: recent well btn
3rd in a h'cap hdle, in 99/00 won at Huntingdon (h'cap, rtd 88h) & prev term at Warwick (h'cap, stays 3m2f on fm
& gd/soft): mod Flat form since French wnr back in '93: stays 2m: acts on fast & soft grnd & in a visor.
*327 **NOUFARI** 147 [4] R Hollinshead 9-8-12 P M Quinn 4/7 FAV: 11-512: 9 b g Kahyasi - Noufiyfa   ½ **73a**
(Top Ville) Hld up, eff to chase wnr 2f out, kept on, just held: fine run after a 4 month abs: v tough & genuine.
1415 **MISALLIANCE** 18 [3] M E Sowersby 5-7-13 P Fessey 25/1: 00-003: 5 ch m Elmaamul - Cabaret Artiste   12 **48a**
(Shareef Dancer) Cl-up, ev ch over 2f out, sn outpcd: stiff task, see 1415.
1301 **STEAMROLLER STANLY** 25 [1] D W Chapman 7-8-10 G Duffield 3/1: 460004: Led till over 2f out, wknd. hd **59a**
649 **ZOLA** 93 [2] 4-9-1 G Hind 12/1: 210-05: Cl-up, btn over 3f out: p.u. over hdles since 649.   22 **45a**
5 ran   Time 3m 43.6 (17.6)   (Christopher Shankland)   J R Jenkins Royston, Herts

---

SOUTHWELL (Fibresand) FRIDAY JUNE 9TH Lefthand, Sharp, Oval Track

1803
3.30 FILLIES MDN HCAP 3YO+ 0-75 (E) **1m aw rnd Going 33 -02 Slow** [67]
£2756 £848 £424 £212 3 yo rec 11lb

1610 **SHADY POINT** 9 [8] C E Brittain 3-9-3 (67)(VIS) T E Durcan 8/11 FAV: -05621: 3 b f Unfuwain - **70a**
Warning Shadows (Cadeaux Genereux) Cl-up, eff over 1f out to lead ins last, hands & heels: well bckd: rtd 77 in
'99: eff at 7f/1m on gd/firm, gd/soft & fibresand: enjoyed 1st time visor & poss best with kid-glove handling.
306 **ANNANDALE** 150 [3] M C Chapman 4-7-10 (35)(1oh) Joanna Badger (7) 14/1: 05-002: 4 ch f Balla Cove nk **35a**
- Gruinard Bay (Doyoun) Led, edged right appr fnl 1f & collared well ins last, just held: gd run after a long
abs for new stable (prev with D Nicholls): unplcd in '99: in '98 rtd 56: stays 1m on fast & fibresand.
1608 **STARBOARD TACK** 9 [6] R Brotherton 4-10-0 (67) I Mongan (5) 16/1: 54-003: 4 b f Saddlers' Hall - nk **67a**
North Wind (Lomond) Slow away, bhd, eff 2f out, kept on, just btn: op 8/1: handles firm, gd/soft & fibresand.
1268 **SALIENT POINT** 28 [4] S P C Woods 3-9-3 (67) G Duffield 11/2: -5004: Chsd ldr, onepace fnl 2f: ¾ **65a**
clr of rem: stays 1m on fibresand, prob gd/soft: see 840.
1509 **THIRTY SIX CEE** 14 [2] 3-8-2 (52) J Tate 12/1: 0-0505: In tch, wknd well over 1f out: op 9/1, see 1293. 7 **38a**
1658 **CUTE CAROLINE** 7 [5] 4-8-11 (50) P Bradley (5) 9/2: 0-3506: Al bhd: btr 1243, 1190. 5 **26a**
1211 **CLEAR CRYSTAL** 31 [1] 3-8-8 (58) F Lynch 14/1: 60-607: Chsd ldrs, wknd over 2f out: op 8/1: 5 **24a**
reportedly lost a shoe: see 1211.
7 ran Time 1m 42.2 (2.8) (Sheikh Marwan Al Maktoum) C E Brittain Newmarket

1804
4.05 THEHORSESMOUTH HCAP 3YO 0-60 (F) **1m aw rnd Going 33 -26 Slow** [62]
£2275 £650 £325

1793 **SEND IT TO PENNY** 1 [11] M W Easterby 3-8-10 (44)(bl) G Parkin 9/2 FAV: -00201: 3 b f Marju - **54a**
Sparkish (Persian Bold) Cl-up, led over 2f out, kept on well rdn out: unplcd yesterday: 1st win: rtd 54
in '99: eff at 6f, apprec step up to 1m & acts on fast grnd & fibresand: wears blnks.
1644 **RED SONNY** 7 [8] A Berry 3-8-11 (45) P Bradley (5) 14/1: 004002: 3 ch g Foxhound - Olivia's Pride 4 **46a**
(Digamist) Bhd, eff 2f out, kept on, no impress on wnr: stays 1m on fibresand: mdn h'caps will suit.
1614 **CHILLI** 9 [2] C E Brittain 3-9-6 (54)(VIS) T E Durcan 7/1: 323303: 3 br g Most Welcome - So Saucy 2½ **51a**
(Teenoso) Bhd, eff 2f out, no impress: 1st time visor: plcd numerous times prev: back in trip, see 1614.
1242 **CUIGIU** 29 [10] D Carroll 3-9-2 (50) K Dalgleish (7) 12/1: 542054: Led till over 2f out, no extra: btr 930. hd **46a**
1610 **WILEMMGEO** 9 [14] 3-9-6 (54) Joanna Badger (7) 10/1: 210505: In tch, btn 2f out: best 514 (sell). 4 **43a**
1399 **TABBETINNA BLUE** 20 [12] 3-8-3 (37) A McGlone 16/1: -00206: Prom, btn 2f out: twice below 841 (sell). ¾ **25a**
1434 **JUMP** 18 [13] 3-9-7 (55) G Duffield 10/1: 260047: In tch, btn 2f out: see 1434, 1040. 3 **38a**
976 **JUST THE JOB TOO** 51 [4] 3-9-7 (55) P Goode (3) 5/1: 641068: Al bhd: thrice below 555. 3 **33a**
1202 **RIOS DIAMOND** 32 [3] 3-8-10 (44) P McCabe 11/2: 000-29: Chsd ldrs till wknd over 2f out: btr 1202 (7f). 6 **13a**
1742 **LEA VALLEY EXPRESS** 3 [9] 3-9-2 (50)(vis) D Glennon 25/1: 5-0000: Slow away & al bhd: 10th. ½ **18a**
1596 Mist Over Meugher 9 [5] 3-8-2 (36) P Fessey 33/1: 1610 **Havent Made It Yet** 9 [1] 3-8-1 (35)(VIS) S Righton 25/1:
1578 Billys Blunder 10 [6] 3-8-8 (42)(tvi) S Whitworth 12/1:
13 ran Time 1m 44.1 (4.7) (Guy Reed) M W Easterby Sheriff Hutton, N Yorks

1805
4.35 FARNSFIELD SELLER 2YO (G) **6f Going 33 -43 Slow**
£1834 £524 £262

1396 **ORCHARD RAIDER** 20 [3] C A Dwyer 2-8-11 P Clarke (7) 6/4 FAV: -0241: 2 b c Mujadil - Apple Brandy **67a**
(Cox's Ridge) Cl-up, led over 2f out, sn rdn clr, easily: 1st win, bt in for 7,800 gns: Mar 1st foal: bhd this
rnr-up earlier: stays 6f & likes fibresand & sell grade.
1443 **RUNNING FOR ME** 17 [2] R Hollinshead 2-8-11 G Gibbons (7) 4/1: 6102: 2 ch f Eagle Eyed - Running 6 **56a**
For You (Pampabird) Keen, prom, not clr run over 1f out, kept on ins last, no impress: bt this wnr in 1206.
*1420 **PRINCESS PENNY** 18 [5] W G M Turner 2-8-12 A Daly 3/1: R3013: 2 ch f King's Signet - Princess nk **55a**
Tallulah (Chief Singer) Led till over 2f out, no extra: see 1420.
1420 **SWEET VELETA** 18 [4] R M Whitaker 2-8-6 D Mernagh (3) 6/1: 34: Cl-up, wknd over 1f out: see 1420. 1¼ **46a**
1492 **EXELLENT ADVENTURE** 14 [1] 2-8-11 S Whitworth 8/1: -W665: Al bhd: see 1492. 7 **33a**
5 ran Time 1m 17.8 (4.5) (Cedar Lodge 2000 Syndicate) C A Dwyer Newmarket

1806
5.05 WELLOW HCAP 3YO+ 0-60 (F) **5f aw str Going 33 +03 Fast** [58]
£2296 £656 £328 3 yo rec 7 lb

1506 **PLEASURE** 14 [15] A Smith 5-9-4 (48)(hbl) K Hodgson 12/1: -54641: 5 ch m Most Welcome - Peak Squaw **52a**
(Icecapade) Chsd ldrs, hdwy 2f out, edged left but kept on to lead ins last, rdn out: fair time: '99 wnr at
Beverley (1st time blnks, h'cap, rtd 61): '98 Doncaster scorer (appr h'cap): eff over 5/7f on gd, soft &
fibresand: handles any trk & runs well fresh in blnks & a hood.
1392 **SAMWAR** 20 [6] Mrs N Macauley 8-9-11 (55)(vis) P McCabe 8/1: 320122: 8 b g Warning - Samaza ½ **58a**
(Arctic Tern) Handy, eff to lead over 1f out, hdd ins last, no extra, no btn far: gd run out of sell grade: see 1392.
1739 **ARAB GOLD** 3 [7] M Quinn 5-8-9 (39)(BL) G Hind 33/1: 440603: 5 b g Presidium - Parklands Belle 1 **39a**
(Stanford) Prom, ev ch appr fnl 1f, no extra ins last: better run in 1st time blnks back at 5f: handles both A/Ws.
1412 **LORD HIGH ADMIRAL** 20 [14] C G Cox 12-10-0 (58)(vis) A Daly 14/1: -14004: Dsptd lead till over 1f out, 1¼ **54a**
no extra: op 10/1: joint top-weight: tough: see 673.
1629 **E B PEARL** 8 [5] 4-9-0 (44) J Bramhill 20/1: 106055: Handy, btn appr fnl 1f: see 751. 1 **37a**
1543 **WHIZZ KID** 13 [2] 6-8-11 (41) Claire Bryan (5) 5/1: 123126: In tch, onepace over 1f out: see 1391 (6f). nk **33a**
1092 **OFF HIRE** 38 [13] 4-10-0 (58)(vis) P Fitzsimons (5) 20/1: 421067: In tch, no impress over 1f out: see 614. ½ **49a**
1479 **SUPERFRILLS** 15 [8] 7-8-9 (39) M Tebbutt 16/1: 6-0208: In tch, no impress over 1f out: see 1421. nk **29a**
1421 **KOMASEPH** 18 [1] 8-8-4 (34) S Righton 20/1: 360649: In tch, wknd over 1f out: see 602 (6f). 1½ **20a**
1391 **HEAVENLY MISS** 20 [4] 6-9-1 (45)(bl) K Dalgleish (7) 5/1 FAV: 0-4140: In tch, wknd 2f out: 10th. nk **30a**
1504 **PRESENT CHANCE** 14 [3] 6-9-12 (56)(bl) L Newton 10/1: 000000: Al bhd: 11th: see 674. nk **40a**
1714 **SEVEN SPRINGS** 4 [9] 4-8-6 (36) P M Quinn (3) 7/1: 620300: Nvr a factor: 12th: btr 1422 (6f). 2½ **14a**
1487 **HALF TONE** 15 [11] 8-9-11 (55)(bl) A Clark 7/1: -00530: Al bhd: 13th, btr 1487 (turf). 5 **23a**
63 Tong Road 205 [12] 4-8-10 (40) G Parkin 25/1: 1392 **Young Ibnr** 20 [16] 5-9-4 (48) P Mundy (7) 20/1:
1244 Bowcliffe Grange 29 [17] 8-8-5 (35) D Mernagh (3) 14/3156) **Bally Cyrano** 309 [10] 3-9-6 (57)(BL) T E Durcan 16/1:
17 ran Time 59.3 (1.5) (The Rufus Partnership) A Smith Beverley, E Yorks

GOODWOOD FRIDAY JUNE 9TH Righthand, Sharpish, Undulating Track

Official Going GOOD. Stalls: Str Crse - Stands Side, Rnd Crse - Inside, except 12f - Outside.

1807

6.30 NEWS AMAT HCAP 3YO+ 0-70 (E)   1m1f   **Good/Soft 65**   **-50 Slow**   [47]
£3753   £1155   £577   £288   3 yo rec 12lb

477   **BARBASON 122** [9]   G L Moore   8-11-4 (65)   Mr R L Moore (5)   12/1: 0-2551: 8 ch c Polish Precedent -   **70**
Barada (Damascus) Held up, prog to lead dist, pushed out cl-home: slow time, 4 mth abs: '99 wnr at Lingfield
(2, clmr & class stks, rtd 76a), Newbury (amat h'cap), Sandown & Brighton (clmr, rtd 76): '98 wnr at Lingfield
& Brighton (h'caps, rtd 76a & 71): eff at 7f/10f on firm, gd/soft & equitrack: handles any trk, loves Lingfield:
eff with/without blnks & runs well fresh: genuine 8yo who runs well for an amateur.
1509   **SAMMYS SHUFFLE 14** [16]   Jamie Poulton   5-9-7 (40)(bl)   Mr H Poulton (7)   7/1: 064022: 5 b h Touch Of   2   **40**
Grey - Cabinet Shuffle (Thatching) Chsd ldrs, rdn/led over 2f out till over 1f out, kept on: see 1100, 575 (AW).
854   **EIGHT 60** [10]   C G Cox   4-11-3 (64)   Miss Joanna Rees (7)   33/1: 300-03: 4 ch g Thatching - Up To You   ¾   **63**
(Sallust) Handy, kept on onepace fnl 2f: 2 month abs: plcd in '99 (rtd 75, mdn, M J Heaton Ellis): eff around
1m/9f, handles firm & gd/soft grnd, sharp/gall track.
*1583   **WERE NOT STOPPIN 10** [18]   R Bastiman   5-10-6 (53)(6ex)   Miss R Bastiman (7)   4/1: 051114: Dwelt & rear, ¾   **51**
kept on fnl 2f, nrst fin: nicely bckd under a pen, op 11/4: in gd heart, apprec a return to professional handling.
100   **LITTLE TUMBLER 198** [14]   Miss R Woodman (7)   20/1: 1000-5: Dwelt/towards rear, prog/   ¾   **44**
ch over 2f out, held ins last: 7 month abs: '99 Brighton scorer (h'cap, rtd 50): '98 Lingfield wnr (h'cap, rtd 61):
eff at 1m/10f on fast & gd/soft grnd: likes a sharp/undul trk & has gone well fresh: looks nicely h'capped.
245   **HALF TIDE 159** [19]   6-9-6 (39)   Mr D H Dunsdon (1)   14/1: 133-06: Twds rear, mod prog fnl 2f: abs.   1   **34**
1442   **ROGUE SPIRIT 18** [12]   4-11-7 (68)   Miss A Elsey   14/1: 000407: Chsd ldrs, held fnl 2f: see 1201, 746 (6f).   ¾   **62**
1614   **SILENT SOUND 9** [13]   4-10-6 (53)   Miss L J Harwood (7)   6/1: 20-048: Cl-up over 2f out, sn no extra.   shd   **47**
1395   **TARSKI 20** [17]   6-10-3 (50)   Mr L Jefford   3/1 FAV: 650-09: Towards rear, briefly no room 2f out, sn   nk   **43**
onepace/held: op 5/1: likes Goodwood but needs a faster surface: see 1395.
1331   **TWOFORTEN 23** [5]   5-9-3 (36)(vis)(2oh)   Mr A Quinn (7)   25/1: 066000: Rear, mod gains: 10th: vis reapp.   1½   **26**
4365}   **GOLD MILLENIUM 239** [4]   6-9-9 (42)   Mrs Anna Scrase (7)   20/1: 0040-0: Chsd ldrs 7f: 11th: reapp: ¾   **31**
plcd but well btn last term (rtd 43, 14f h'cap).
1336   **KAFIL 23** [15]   6-9-3 (36)(4oh)   Miss R Illman (0)   33/1: -26000: Chsd ldrs 7f: 12th: blnks omitted.   3½   **19**
1672   **HUHWBILL 6** [6]   5-9-3 (36)(3oh)   Miss C Hannaford (5)   33/1: 000-60: Mid-div, btn 3f out: 13th: qck reapp.   1¼   **16**
1666   **LANDICAN LANE 7** [7]   4-9-3 (36)(4oh)   Mr T Radford (3)   50/1: 000000: Led 7f, fdd: 14th: plcd thrice   3½   **10**
in '99 (rtd 59, h'cap): '98 Brighton wnr (sell, R F Johnston Houghton, rtd 66): eff at 5/6f on gd & hvy grnd:
suited by blnks, not worn here: with T M Jones.
1100   **MELLOW MISS 38** [1]   4-10-5 (52)(bl)   Mr F Windsor Clive (3)   9/1: 560330: Rear, hard rdn/btn 3f out: 16th.   **0**
1672   **Trojan Wolf 6** [11]   5-10-10 (57)   Miss S Pocock (5)   20/1:
1462   **Waikiki Beach 16** [2]   9-9-3 (36)(2oh)   Mr A Keeley (7)   25/1:
793   **Alcove 71** [3]   9-10-8 (55)   Miss E Johnson Hough   20/1:
124   **Barossa Valley 192** [8]   9-9-8 (41)   Mr R Lucey Butler (7   50/1:
19 ran   Time 2m 0.87 (10.37)   (A Moore)   G L Moore Woodingdean, E.Sussex.

1808

7.00 WEALD & DOWNLAND MDN 3YO (D)   1m4f   **Good/Soft 65**   **-29 Slow**
£4134   £1272   £636   £318

--   **TALAASH** [5]   M R Channon   3-9-0   S Drowne   8/1: 1: 3 b c Darshaan - Royal Ballet (Sadlers Wells)   **94**
Bhd ldrs & al trav well, led & readily pulled clr under hands-and-heels riding fnl 3f, eased right: val for 12L+,
debut: 380,000gns purchase: eff at 12f, shld stay further: acts on gd/soft grnd & a sharp/undul trk: runs well
fresh: most impressive intro, looks useful & shld make his mark in better company.
1539   **DARARIYNA 13** [1]   Sir Michael Stoute   3-8-9   K Fallon   8/11 FAV: 22: 3 b f Shirley Heights - Dararita   8   **79**
(Halo) Niggled along halfway bhd ldrs, kept on for press fnl 3f, no ch with wnr: well bckd: lngr 12f trip shld suit.
1293   **ZERO GRAVITY 25** [2]   D J S ffrench Davis   3-9-0   R Studholme (5)   50/1: 63: 3 b g Cosmonaut - Comfort   1   **83**
(Chief Singer) In close tch, eff/outpcd fnl 3f: longer 12f trip: see 1293.
1386   **SCACHMATT 20** [4]   L M Cumani   3-9-0   J P Spencer   2/1: 5024: Led till over 3f out, sn held: well bckd.   1¾   **81**
1404   **BOGUS MIX 20** [3]   3-8-9   Dane O'Neill   20/1: 05: Cl-up, btn 3f out: see 1404 (10f).   22   **52**
5 ran   Time 2m 43.11 (6.61)   (Sheikh Ahmed Al Maktoum)   M R Channon West Isley, Berks

---

1809

7.30 EBF GEORGE BENTINCK MDN 2YO (D)   6f   **Good/Soft 65**   **+01 Fast**
£4173   £1284   £642   £321

1472   **MARINE 16** [4]   R Charlton   2-9-0   K Fallon   11/10 FAV: 51: 2 b c Marju - Ivorine (Blushing Groom)   **102**
Bhd ldrs, briefly no room over 2f out, rdn to lead well ins last & in command cl-home: hvly bckd, gd juv time:
eff at 6f, will relish step up to 7f+: acts on gd/soft & a sharp/undul trk: improving & can win in better company.
--   **BANNISTER** [5]   R Hannon   2-9-0   R Hughes   9/4: 2: 2 ch c Inchinor - Shall We Run (Hotfoot)   ¾   **98**
In tch, narrow lead 1f out, hdd ins last: nicely bckd: Apr foal, cost 66,000gns: half-brother to a 5/6f juv
wnr: sire high-class 7f performer: eff at 6f on gd/soft, shld get further: pleasing intro.
--   **GIVE BACK CALAIS** [7]   P J Makin   2-9-0   S Sanders   8/1: 3: 2 b c Brief Truce - Nichodoula (Doulab)   1½   **94**
Prom centre, rdn/led over 2f out till 1f out, kept on well: clr of rem, op 6/1: Apr foal, cost 24,000gns: half-
brother to a 1m juv wnr, dam a 7f/1m 3yo wnr: sire top-class 1m/10f performer: acts on gd/soft: encouraging intro.
1526   **DOUBLE BREW 13** [3]   R Hannon   2-9-0   Dane O'Neill   14/1: 34: Chsd ldrs, outpcd by front trio fnl 2f.   3   **87**
1573   **ANALYZE 10** [2]   2-9-0   S Drowne   7/1: 035: Led till over 2f out, sn held: op 6/1: btr 1573.   7   **74**
--   **UNCLE FOLDING** [6]   2-9-0   J P Spencer   14/1: 6: Rear/in tch, outpcd fnl 2f: Danehill colt, Apr foal,   2½   **67**
70,000gns 2yo: half-brother to a French 3yo wnr, dam useful at around 1m: stay further in time for J A Osborne.
6 ran   Time 1m 13.81 (3.81)   (K Abdulla)   R Charlton Beckhampton, Wilts.

1810

8.00 SUSSEX HCAP 3YO+ 0-90 (C)   7f rnd   **Good/Soft 65**   **+03 Fast**   [88]
£11163   £3435   £1717   £858   3 yo rec 10lb

1113   **CELTIC EXIT 37** [15]   I A Balding   6-8-13 (73)(t)   K Fallon   7/1: 0-5051: 6 b g Exit To Nowhere - Amour   **80**
Celtique (Northfields) Mid-div, briefly no room 2f out, switched & styd on strongly to lead ins last, going away:
ex-French, '99 Longchamp wnr (h'cap): eff at 7/10f on gd/soft & hvy, sharp/stiff trk: eff in a t-strap.
1676   **BINTANG TIMOR 6** [16]   W J Musson   6-8-11 (71)   Pat Eddery   7/2 JT FAV: -03462: 6 ch g Mt Livermore -   1½   **73**
Frisky Kitten (Isopach) Keen, towards rear, rdn/styd on fnl 3f, not pace of wnr: well bckd, qck reapp: see 1273, 834.

*1483 **GIFT OF GOLD 15** [12] A Bailey 5-9-10 (84) J Reid 7/2 JT FAV: 450013: 5 ch h Statoblest - Ellebanna   nk   85
(Tinas Pet) Chsd ldrs, rdn/led over 1f out till ins last, not pace of wnr: op 5/1: remains in gd heart: see 1483 (C/D).
1598 **TEMERAIRE 9** [10] D J S Cosgrove 5-9-8 (82) J F Egan 11/2: -02004: Chsd ldrs, briefly led over 1f out,   hd   82
onepace/held ins last: bckd from 12/1: see 834, 104 (AW).
1077 **SALTY JACK 39** [14] 6-9-6 (80) Dane O'Neill 20/1: 130005: Rear, switched/kept on well fnl 2f, nrst fin.   ½   79
1473 **JUST NICK 16** [3] 6-8-4 (64) Martin Dwyer 11/1: 000-36: Rear, rdn/late gains, nrst fin: tricky low draw.   ½   62
875 **REDSWAN 59** [13] 5-8-13 (73)(tbl) W Ryan 8/1: 401-07: Pulled hard in rear, slipped over 3f out, prog   ¾   70
2f out, held fnl 1f, eased nr fin: abs: '99 Leicester & Doncaster wnr (h'caps, rtd 74): '98 Newmarket wnr (clmr,
rtd 74 & 71a): eff at 7f/1m on firm/fast, handles fibresand: likes a stiff/gall trk: suited by blnks & a t-strap.
*1514 **MANTLES PRIDE 13** [2] 5-9-12 (86)(bl) K Darley 8/1: -00418: Mid-div, held fnl 2f: op 13/2: btr 1514.   2½   78
1514 **THREAT 13** [6] 4-9-6 (80) G Faulkner (3) 33/1: -00009: Handy, led 2f out till over 1f out, fdd: see 702.   1½   69
1635 **CHEWIT 8** [7] 8-9-7 (81) J P Spencer 9/1: 5-6040: Chsd ldrs halfway, wknd over 1f out: 10th: see 137.   1½   67
725 **TEOFILIO 76** [11] 6-8-13 (73)(bl) J Weaver 12/1: 60-160: Mid-div, btn 2f out: 11th: abs: see 459 (AW). shd 59
1013 **SAILING SHOES 46** [5] 4-9-10 (84) R Hughes 20/1: 050-00: Led 5f, sn btn: 13th: 6 wk abs: rnr-up in   0
'99 (rtd 98, cond stks): '98 Chester wnr (juv mdn), subs plcd in a Gr 2 at York (rtd 109): eff at 6f on firm & gd/soft.
1450 **COMPTON ARROW 17** [1] 4-10-0 (88)(tBL) J Fortune 16/1: 30-000: Dwelt, al twds rear: 12th: blnks.   0
829 **Moonlight Song 64** [4] 3-8-0 (70) P Doe 20/1:   1483 **Champagne Rider 15** [8] 4-9-11 (85) N Callan 25/1:
15 ran   Time 1m 28.86 (4.36)   (Action Bloodstock)   I A Balding Kingsclere, Hants.

1811   8.30 SPIRIT FM FILLIES MDN 3YO (D)   1m rnd   Good/Soft 65   -05 Slow
£4465   £1374   £687   £343

1108 **MISS KIRSTY 37** [2] G A Butler 3-8-11 (t) K Darley 5/1: 3-601: 3 ch f Miswaki - Spit Curl   87
(Northern Dancer) Chsd ldrs, rdn/prog to lead 2f out, held on gamely when strongly pressed fnl 1f, all out: wore a
t-strap: plcd form sole juv start (rtd 92): eff at 1m, may get further: acts on gd/soft grnd & a stiff/sharp trk.
1269 **MISS DORDOGNE 28** [5] G Wragg 3-8-11 Pat Eddery 9/4 FAV: -252: 3 b f Brief Truce - Miss Bergerac   nk   86
(Bold Lad) Mid-div, sltly hmpd & briefly no room 2f out, switched & drvn to strongly press wnr ins last, styd on well,
just held: well bckd: apprec this return to an easier surface: can find similar: see 1269, 971.
1481 **MOSSY MOOR 15** [10] Mrs A J Perrett 3-8-11 R Hughes 20/1: 4-53: 3 ch f Sanglamore - Moss (Alzao)   1¼   83
Held up, no room over 2f out till over 1f out, styd on strongly ins last, not reach front pair: no luck in running,
would have bustled up first 2 here: handles hvy & gd/soft: see 1481 (9f).
1261 **DELAMERE 28** [7] J H M Gosden 3-8-11 J Fortune 8/1: 0-064: Chsd ldrs, kept on onepace fnl 2f: op   nk   82
6/1: stays 1m & handles gd/soft grnd: going the right way: see 1261.
-- **TANGO TWO THOUSAND** [9] 3-8-11 R Havlin 16/1: 5: In tch, kept on fnl 2f, not pace of ldrs: debut.   2   78
-- **TARABAYA** [17] 3-8-11 K Fallon 5/1: 6: Chsd ldrs, kept on onepace fnl 2f: debut, op 4/1: Warning   hd   77
filly, this 1m trip will suit: shld improve for this intro: with Sir M Stoute.
-- **MUSALLIAH** [4] 3-8-11 J Reid 8/1: 7: Rear, eye-catching prog fnl 3f under minimal pressure, nrst   3   71+
fin: debut: Nureyev filly, 1m+ looks sure to suit: sure to leave this kind intro behind for J L Dunlop.
-- **WHITGIFT ROSE** [3] 3-8-11 W Ryan 20/1: 8: Mid-div, nvr a threat: debut, op 14/1, with Lady Herries.   nk   70
1481 **AMELIAS FIELD 15** [15] 3-8-11 N Callan 20/1: 49: In tch, onepace/held fnl 2f: see 1481.   nk   69
-- **APLESTEDE** [13] 3-8-11 J F Egan 50/1: 0: Mid-div at best: 10th: debut, with I Wood.   shd   69$
4265} **RAVINE 247** [8] 3-8-11 Dane O'Neill 16/1: 6-0: Prom fdd: reapp: unplcd sole '99 start (rtd 65).   nk   68
-- **FFYNNON GOLD** [11] 3-8-11 N Pollard 33/1: 0: Dwelt/rear, mod gains: 12th: debut, with J Portman.   1¼   65
957 **FOREST FRIENDLY 52** [16] 3-8-11 M Hills 8/1: 4-00: Led 6f, fdd: 13th: op 6/1, 8 wk abs.   hd   64
1525 **Psalmist 13** [19] 3-8-11 J P Spencer 25/1:   1268 **Koincidental 28** [12] 3-8-11 J Weaver 50/1:
1468 **Molly Malone 16** [6] 3-8-11 C Rutter 50/1:   -- **Magic Symbol** [14] 3-8-11 P Doe 20/1:
2149} **Monawara 352** [1] 3-8-11 S Drowne 12/1:
18 ran   Time 1m 42.97 (5.57)   (D R Windebank)   G A Butler Blewbury, Oxon

---

1812   9.00 TOTALBET.COM HCAP 3YO 0-80 (D)   1m1f192y   Good/Soft 83   -08 Slow   [85]
£4387   £1350   £675   £337

1735 **MYTHICAL KING 4** [3] B Palling 3-9-7 (78) K Darley 10/1: 50-331: 3 b c Fairy King - Whatcombe   85
(Alleged) Made all & clr 4f out, hard rdn fnl 2f, held on gamely ins last, all out: qck reapp: op 12/1, 1st win: plcd
last term (mdn, rtd 76): eff forcing the pace at 10f, could get further: acts on firm & gd, gd/soft/stiff trk.
1735 **BAILEYS PRIZE 4** [11] M Johnston 3-9-5 (76) J Reid 7/4 FAV: 014622: 3 ch c Mister Baileys - Mar   nk   82
Mar (Forever Casting) Chsd ldrs, styd on well for press, just held: well bckd: ahd of wnr in 1735.
1537 **AMRITSAR 13** [5] Sir Michael Stoute 3-9-0 (71) K Fallon 5/1: -0543: 3 ch c Indian Ridge - Trying For   1½   75
Gold (Natroun Baby) Chsd ldr, no room over 1f out & switched, staying on when hampered nr fin: h'cap bow,
op 4/1: stays 10f, may get further: handles gd/soft grnd: a likely type for similar.
1671 **AFTER THE BLUE 7** [8] M R Channon 3-8-5 (62) S Drowne 16/1: 6-0064: Towards rear, rdn/kept on   ½   65
fnl 2f, nrst fin: stays 10f: handles gd/soft grnd.
1449 **ROB LEACH 17** [4] 3-9-4 (75) R Price 14/1: 5265: Chsd ldr halfway, rdn/ch 2f out, held ins last.   nk   77
1495 **EASTWOOD DRIFTER 14** [2] 3-8-9 (66) Martin Dwyer 14/1: 0-3036: Rear, eff 3f out, no impress ldrs.   1¼   66
1183 **FREDDY FLINTSTONE 33** [7] 3-8-9 (66) Dane O'Neill 13/2: 05-047: Rear, mod gains fnl 2f: lngr 10f trip.   hd   75
1135 **PROTECTOR 36** [9] 3-8-9 (66) J Fortune 16/1: 50-048: Twds rear, rdn/held over 2f out: h'cap bow.   1½   63
4257} **INTRUM MORSHAAN 248** [6] 3-9-0 (71) Pat Eddery 14/1: 063-9: In tch, btn 3f out: reapp, op 3/1:   5   61
plcd fnl '99 start (mdn, rtd 72): stays 1m, bred to apprec mid-dists: acts on soft & a gall trk: h'cap bow today.
1405 **IN A TWINKLING 20** [1] 3-8-8 (65) R Hughes 25/1: 440-00: Rear, eff/hung left & btn over 2f out: 10th: 3   51
longer 10f trip: unplcd sole British start in '99 (auct fill mdn, rtd 54): ex-Irish, plcd once from 6 starts prev.
4425} **FAHAN 234** [10] 3-9-1 (72) S Sanders 12/1: 0430-0: Chsd ldrs, bhd fnl 3f: 11th: reapp, op 10/1:   dist   0
plcd in '99 (rtd 78, fill mdn): stays a stiff 7.5f, 1m+ may suit: handles gd/soft grnd.
11 ran   Time 2m 11.43 (7.23)   (Glyn & Albert Yemm)   B Palling Cowbridge Vale Of Glamorgan

FRIDAY JUNE 9TH   Lefthand, Undulating, V Tight Track

Official Going   GOOD/SOFT, SOFT IN PLACES. Stalls: Inside

1813 2.30 EBF NOV STKS 2YO (D)   5f rnd   Good/Soft 70 -30 Slow
£3705   £1140   £570   £285

*1659 SUPERSTAR LEO 7 [3] W J Haggas 2-8-9 R Mullen 8/13 FAV: -211: 2 b f College Chapel - Council **100**
Rock (General Assembly) Trkd ldrs, led 2f out, pshd clr, easily: hvly bckd: 7 days ago won here at Catterick
(fill auct mdn): eff at 5f, shld get 6f: acts on good & soft grnd, likes Catterick: speedy, useful, imprvg filly.
*1488 PRINCESS OF GARDA 14 [4] Mrs G S Rees 2-8-11 Dean McKeown 16/1: -U4312: 2 b f Komaite - 5 **87**
Malcesine (Auction Ring) Prsd ldr, ch 2f out, outpcd by wnr: imprvd in defeat, settled for sft/sft, see 1488.
*1522 FLUMMOX 13 [2] M Johnston 2-9-2 J Fanning 11/4: 13: 2 b c Rudimentary - Pluvial (Habat) 1½ **89**
Trkd ldrs, eff 2f out, no impress: shade disappointing after debut win in 1522 (hvy grnd).
1385 NIFTY ALICE 20 [5] A Berry 2-8-9 C Lowther 9/1: -1244: Led, rdn & hdd 2f out, sn btn: see 796. 3 **75**
-- SIPTITZ HEIGHTS [1] 2-8-7 J Carroll 6/1: 5: Lost many lengths start, al detached: op 9/2, green 10 **53**
debut: 21,000gns Zieten Feb foal, dam 7f juv wnr, sire a sprinter: shown something at home, do better next time.
5 ran   Time 1m 02.3 (5)   (The Superstar Leo Partnership)   W J Haggas Newmarket, Suffolk

1814 3.05 SCORTON CLAIMER 4YO+ (F)   1m5f175y   Good/Soft 70 -47 Slow
£2341   £669   £334

1647 NIGHT CITY 7 [3] K R Burke 9-8-13 D Sweeney 13/8: 406441: 9 b g Kris - Night Secret (Nijinsky) **48**
Led, keen & clr till 5f out, rdn & kept on strgly in the str, unchall: qk reapp: earlier won at Lingfield (claim,
rtd 68a): '99 wnr at Hamilton, York (clmrs), Brighton (h'cap, rtd 74) & Lingfield (clmr, rtd 82a): '98 Lingfield
(4, AW clmrs/hcap & turf h'cap), Hamilton (2), Thirsk, Catterick, Brighton & York (h'cap/clmrs, rtd 80 & 86a):
eff at 1m/13.7f on any grnd/trk, loves Lingfield: needs to have his own way in front: a credit to connections.
1432 DIAMOND CROWN 18 [6] Martyn Wane 9-8-3 J McAuley (5) 16/1: 000-02: 9 ch g Kris - State Treasure 2 **35**
(Secretariat) Rear, prog 3f out, styd on, no trble wnr: recent jmps rnr (modest): '99 Hamilton wnr (h'cap, rtd 46):
'98 wnr at Ayr & Newcastle (sell, rtd 53, 1st time visor): eff btwn 11f & 2m on firm & soft, with/without visor.
1660 STOLEN MUSIC 7 [4] R E Barr 7-8-4 Dean McKeown 8/1: 200-03: 7 b m Taufan - Causa Sua (Try My ½ **35**
Best) Trkd ldrs, chsd wnr ent str, no impress: qk reapp, stayed on at the weights, see 1660.
1657 PENNYS FROM HEAVEN 7 [1] D Nicholls 6-9-3 A Nicholls (3) 11/10 FAV: /03024: Led chsg pack, v 2½ **46**
keen, eff 3f out, no extra, eased dist: nicely bckd, rcd far too freely, see 1657, 1353.
1718 SUSY WELLS 4 [5] 5-7-12 N Carlisle 20/1: 60-005: Pld hard, hld up, fdd fnl 3f: longer trip, see 1718. 5 **23**
1660 MAREMMA 7 [2] 6-7-10 Iona Wands (5) 11/1: 441/06: Prom till 3f out: qk reapp, see 1660. 3½ **18**
6 ran   Time 3m 11.8 (16.4)   (Nigel Shields)   K R Burke Newmarket

1815 3.40 LIONWELD HCAP 3YO 0-70 (F)   6f rnd   Good/Soft 70 +10 Fast   [70]
£3900   £1200   £600   £300   3 yo rec 8 lb 2 groups in straight

*1664 TREASURE TOUCH 7 [10] D Nicholls 6-9-4 (60)(6ex) Iona Wands (5) 9/2 FAV: -00011: 6 b g 67
Treasure Kay - Bally Pourri (Law Society) Cl-up, came stands side in str, led appr fnl 1f & drvn, just held on:
tchd 6/1: last week won here at Catterick (C/D clmr): rnr-up in '99 (class stks, rtd 60): '97 wnr at Southwell,
Nottingham (2), Newmarket & Thirsk (rtd 71a & 89): suited by 6f: acts on firm, good/sft & fibresand, without blnks.
*1724 BOWLERS BOY 4 [14] J J Quinn 7-8-10 (52) P Hanagan (7) 11/2: 0W2412: 7 ch g Risk Me - Snow ½ 57
Wonder (Music Boy) In tch, styd centre in str, hard rdn, drifted right & ran on strgly appr fnl 1f, just failed: op 11/2,
qk reapp, clr rem: continues in terrific form, see 1724.
1662 SOTONIAN 7 [9] P S Felgate 7-9-6 (62) A Nicholls (3) 12/1: 030663: 7 br g Statoblest - Visage 3½ 59
(Vision) In tch, styd centre in str, kept on, not pace to chall: ran well, see 774.
1504 ANTHONY MON AMOUR 14 [2] D Nicholls 5-9-3 (59)(t) O Pears 20/1: 40-004: Prom, stands side in str, ½ 55
unable to qckn: stablemate of wnr: '99 rnr-up (h'cap, rtd 66 & 68a): '98 wnr at Chepstow (mdn h'cap) &
Southwell (class stks, rtd 69 & 66a): eff at 6f, just stays 7f: acts on fast, soft & fibresand: wears t-strap.
1356 GRAND ESTATE 21 [8] 5-9-2 (58) A Culhane 14/1: 003005: Outpcd, came stands side, nvr nr ldrs. ½ 53
1606 PATSY CULSYTH 9 [2] 5-8-4 (48) Kim Tinkler 7/1: -10036: Bhd, late hdwy far side: see 1606, 756. nk 40
1243 LANDING CRAFT 29 [1] 5-9-0 (56) D Sweeney 10/1: 003207: Nvr on terms: btr 1066, 1007 (7f/1m). nk 50
1601 SOUND THE TRUMPET 9 [11] 8-7-12 (40)(t) A Mackay 25/1: 000068: Al towards rear: see 97. ¾ 33
*1421 HIGH ESTEEM 18 [13] 4-8-12 (54) Dean McKeown 11/2: 440-19: Led till halfway, no threat after. ¾ 45
1545 SKYERS FLYER 11 [5] 6-8-2 (44) T Williams 7/1: 03-000: Nvr dngrs: 10th, see 1421. nk 34
1724 PALACEGATE TOUCH 4 [12] 10-8-3 (45)(bl) D Allan (7) 9/1: 050130: Led after 3f, far side, hdd bef dist. 1 33
1724 FRILLY FRONT 4 [6] 4-9-1 (57) C Lowther 7/1: 600050: Lost sev lengths start, al bhd: 13th, qk reapp. 0
1278 Venika Vitesse 27 [3] 4-9-11 (67) Lynsey Hanna (7) 12/1: 1479 Emma Amour 15 [4] 3-8-3 (53) T Lucas 20/1:
14 ran   Time 1m 13.9 (3.6)   (J P Honeyman)   D Nicholls Sessay, N Yorks

1816 4.15 LESLIE PETCH HCAP 3YO+ 0-70 (E)   1m4f   Good/Soft 70 -11 Slow   [67]
£4046   £1245   £622   £311 Field came stands side in straight

1683 HASTA LA VISTA 6 [12] M W Easterby 10-8-8 (47)(vis) T Lucas 5/1: 0-1021: 10 b g Superlative - 51
Falcon Berry (Bustino) Cl-up, drvn & chall strongly fnl 2f, won on nod: qk reapp: earlier won at Musselburgh
(reapp, h'cap) (rtd 45): '99 wnr at Musselburgh, Catterick & Beverley (h'caps, rtd 60): eff at
12f/2m: acts on firm & soft grnd, sharp trks: wears blnks or visor & runs well fresh: v tough.
1604 EVENING SCENT 9 [7] J Hetherton 4-8-6 (45) Dean McKeown 9/1: 0-6032: 4 b f Ardkinglass - Fresh shd 48
Line (High Line) Prom, strong chall fnl 2f, just btn: eff at 12f, return to 2m will suit, see 1023.
1736 SKYERS A KITE 4 [1] Ronald Thompson 5-8-4 (43) T Williams 8/1: -20653: 5 b m Deploy - Milady Jane 3 43
(Drumalis) Rear, hdwy und press fnl 4f, unable to chall: qk reapp, ran to best: see 822.
1563 BEST PORT 11 [11] J Parkes 4-7-11 (35)(13oh)(1ow) N Carlisle 25/1: 6-0034: Bhd, styd on stdly up the str. 1 35
1657 SPREE VISION 7 [13] 4-8-10 (49) O Pears 7/2: -00045: Prom, onepce fnl 2f: qk reapp, flattered 1657. 2½ 46
1683 DESERT RECRUIT 6 [2] 4-8-3 (42) A Nicholls (3) 5/1: 4-5536: Led till 2f out, no extra: qk reapp. hd 39
1523 NEEDWOOD MAESTRO 13 [8] 4-7-10 (35)(3oh) A McCarthy (2) 16/1: 040-57: Chsd ldrs till 2f out. 2 40
1563 SIMPLE IDEALS 11 [6] 8-7-8 (47) Kim Tinkler 7/1: 33-028: Bhd, nvr dngrs: btr 1563. ¾ 40
*1769 ARCHIE BABE 2 [10] 4-10-6 (73)(6ex) S Finnamore (5) 5/2 FAV: 501019: Chsd ldrs, wknd qckly hd 67
2f out: nicely bckd but this prob came too soon under a welter burden after 1769.
1432 PICCADILLY 18 [9] 5-7-12 (37) Iona Wands (5) 10/1: 000-20: In tch till ent str: 10th, btr 1432 (fast). ¾ 30

CATTERICK   FRIDAY JUNE 9TH   Lefthand, Undulating, V Tight Track

*1353 DESERT FIGHTER 21 [3] 9-9-4 (57) A Culhane 6/1: 4-0010: Al bhd, virt p.u.: 13th, lost action, see 1353.   0
1496 Melody Lady 14 [5] 4-8-13 (52) R Cody Boutcher (7) 25/1:
3242} Phase Eight Girl 305 [4] 4-7-13 (38) N Kennedy 20/1:
13 ran   Time 2m 41.0 (9.8)   (Mr K Hodgson)   M W Easterby Sherriff Hutton

---

1817	4.50 JERVAULX HCAP 3YO 0-65 (F) 5f rnd Good/Soft 70 -10 Slow	[70]
	£2478 £708 £354 Field came stands side	

1280 LIZZIE SIMMONDS 27 [3] N Tinkler 3-8-11 (53) N Kennedy 12/1: -45501: 3 b f Common Grounds - Able   59
Susan (Formidable) Chsd ldrs, drvn to lead entr fnl 1f, ran on well: 1st win, plcd in '99 (mdn, rtd 73): eff at
5/6f on fast & gd/sft grnd: tried a t-strap, best without: suited by sharp tracks.
*1665 COLLEGE MAID 7 [14] J S Goldie 3-9-6 (62)(6ex) A Culhane 1/1 FAV: 002112: 3 b f College Chapel   nk   67
- Maid Of Mourne (Fairy King) Dwelt, rdn to chse ldrs appr fnl 1f, kept on, just failed: well bckd, in-form.
1412 PRIME RECREATION 20 [2] P S Felgate 3-9-4 (60) Dale Gibson 33/1: 3-0003: b g Primo Dominie -   ½   64
Night Transaction (Tina's Pet) Led, und press & hdd below dist, kept on: plcd fnl '99 start (mdn, rtd 74):
eff forcing the pace over a sharp 5f on gd/sft grnd.
1098 MARSHALL ST CYR 38 [12] J G Given 3-9-2 (58) Dean McKeown 5/1: -00564: Prom, no extra fnl 1f: 2   56
prev trained by P Evans: see 1098.
1357 BENNOCHY 21 [8] 3-9-3 (59) O Pears 12/1: 00-105: Towards rear, prog appr fnl 1f, nv nr to chall: ½   56
acts on fast grnd, handles gd/sft, see 777 (class stks, here).
1742 INVISIBLE FORCE 3 [13] 3-8-0 (42) R Ffrench 10/1: 0-6046: Outpcd, late prog, nvr dngrs: qk reapp.   2½   33
1512 PRINCESS AURORA 14 [7] 3-8-10 (52) R Mullen 14/1: 20-067: Chsd ldrs till appr fnl 1f: see 1512.   1½   39
1280 APRILS COMAIT 27 [9] 3-8-7 (49)(BL) V Halliday 16/1: 533008: Prom, saddle slipped/outpcd fnl 2f.   shd   36
1605 SWING CITY 9 [6] 3-9-0 (56) C Lowther 8/1: 0-0039: In tch till appr dist: btr 1605 (6f, sft).   1½   40
1670 ELLPEEDEE 7 [15] 3-8-8 (50)(t) Kim Tinkler 16/1: 065600: Al bhd, short of room entr str: 10th, see 909.   nk   33
1430 PACK A PUNCH 18 [10] 3-8-3 (45) Iona Wands 7/1: 46-00: Hmpd start, nvr in it: 13th, h'cap bow.   0
1479 Shalarise 15 [4] 3-9-6 (62)(bl) J Fanning 20/1:   --   Just On The Market [1] 3-9-7 (63) D Sweeney 25/1:
527 Shouldhavegonehome 114 [5] 3-8-5 (47) J Edmunds 20/1:
14 ran   Time 1m 01.3 (4)   (Mike Goss)   N Tinkler Langton N Yorks

---

1818	5.25 RATING RELATED APPR MDN 3YO+ 0-60 (G) 7f rnd Good/Soft 70 -33 Slow	
	£1855 £530 £265 3 yo rec 10lb	

1723 COMEX FLYER 4 [5] D Nicholls 3-8-8 T Hamilton (3) 15/2: 406001: 3 ch g Prince Of Birds - Smashing   55
Pet (Mummy's Pet) Cmftbly made all: op 5/1: qk reapp: unplcd juv for J Berry (flattered 4th of 5 in a mdn,
rtd 71): eff forcing the pace over a sharp 7f on gd/sft grnd, tried further.
1421 FOUND AT LAST 18 [1] J Balding 4-9-4 G Baker 4/1: 003502: 4 b g Aragon - Girton (Balidar)   3½   50
Dwelt & bhd till kept on stdly fnl 2f, not bother wnr: op 6/1: styd this sharp 7f on gd/sft, see 781.
1596 DOUBLE FAULT 9 [10] T D Easterby 3-8-5 (bl) M Worrell (3) 3/1 FAV: -50033: 3 br f Zieten -   shd   47
Kashapour (Nishapour) Handy, feeling pace 2f out, same pace: op 4/1: unsuited by drop back to 7f?.
1559 LADY TILLY 11 [4] B Ellison 3-8-5 P Hanagan 7/1: 60-054: Pld hard, prom, no extra appr fnl 1f.   nk   46$
1632 CLEAR PEAK 8 [9] 3-8-8 M Scott (5) 7/1: 63-505: Mid-div, imprvd 3f out, sn onepace: back in trip.   nk   48
3350} EMLEY 300 [2] 4-9-1 D Allan (5) 6/1: 563-6: Nvr trbld ldrs: reapp: plcd fnl '99 start for   ½   44
D Nicholls (mdn, rtd 58): eff at 5f, shld get 7f: acts on good grnd, sharp track: now with A Berry.
1578 ABSTRACT 10 [3] 4-9-1 R Farmer (3) 40/1: 006-07: Chsd ldrs till 2f out: mid-div, ran flat, flattered.   1   42$
832 HOWABOYS QUEST 64 [8] 3-8-8 R Cody Boutcher 7/1: 440-08: Mid-div, no extra appr fnl 2f: 9 wk abs.   2½   41
1678 LITTLE CHAPEL 6 [7] 4-9-1 J Bosley 8/1: 050-49: Prom till 3f out: qk reapp, back up in trip.   7   28
1101 BELLE OF HEARTS 37 [6] 4-9-1 D Meah (3) 40/1: 0-0000: Al bhd: 10th, of little account.   13   10
10 ran   Time 1m 30.2 (7.2)   (Neil Smith)   D Nicholls Sessay, N Yorks

---

HAYDOCK   FRIDAY JUNE 9TH   Lefthand, Flat, Galloping Track

Official Going   GOOD/SOFT. Stalls: 7f & 1m - Inside; 6f & 1m2f - Outside; 1m6f - Centre. ALL TIMES SLOW.

1819	6.40 RADIO CITY AMAT HCAP 3YO+ 0-70 (G) 1m2f120y Soft Inapplicable	[30]
	£2023 £578 £289 3 yo rec 14lb	

1690 SILVER SECRET 6 [8] S Gollings 6-10-8 (38) Mr M Murphy (5) 9/1: 63-051: 6 ro g Absalom - Secret   44
Dance (Sadler's Wells) Held up, stdy prog ent the str, led appr fnl 1f, going away: '99 wnr at Newmarket (amat
h'cap, rtd 45): '97 Folkestone wnr (mdn auct, M H Ellis, rtd 52): eff at 1m/10f, stays 12f: acts on firm &
soft grnd, any trk: likes stiff/gall ones: gd ride for an amteur: well h'capped.
4571} BIG AL 221 [14] M D Hammond 4-11-5 (49) Mr D Dickenson (7) 20/1: 6000-2: b g Shalford - Our Pet   5   49
(Mummy's Pet) Rear, kept on fnl 2f, not trouble wnr: 10 wk jumps abs (stays 2m on gd, rtd 101h, t-strap): unplcd
for R Fahey last term (h'cap, rtd 63): '98 Haydock wnr (6f sell, rtd 74, R Hannon): stays 10.5f on fast & soft.
1608 BACHELORS PAD 9 [1] Miss S J Wilton 6-12-0 (58) Mr T Best (5) 9/2: 141423: 6 b g Pursuit Of Love -   2½   56
Note Book (Mummy's Pet) In tch, prog to lead appr fnl 2f till bef dist, no extra: see 855.
1722 MR COSPECTOR 4 [6] T H Caldwell 3-11-12 (70) Mr B Wharfe (7) 16/1: 0-1004: Prom, onepace 2f out.   1½   67
1209 BLOWING AWAY 31 [16] 6-10-0 (30) Mrs L Pearce 25/1: 0-0005: Chsd ldrs, outpcd appr fnl 2f: lightly   3   24
rcd & little form since plcd in '98 (h'caps, rtd 49, M Tompkins): 97/98 Uttoxeter wnr (hdle, 2m, gd & soft, rtd
76h): '97 Flat wnr at Leicester (clmr, rtd 48): eff at 1m/12f on firm & soft, tried a visor.
1777 DARE 2 [3] 5-12-0 (58)(vis) Miss E Folkes (5) 7/1: 003046: Keen, rear, chsd ldrs 2f out, sn onepace.   1   51
*1707 VANBOROUGH LAD 5 [7] 11-10-6 (36)(5ex) Mr Ray Barrett (5) 7/2 FAV: 500217: Mid-div, prog & not   2½   27
much room 3f out, no threat: qck reapp, won this race in '99 (11lbs lower today), see 1707.
1499 TAJAR 14 [17] 8-10-4 (34) Mrs H Keddy (5) 20/1: 0-6008: Chsd ldrs till appr fnl 2f: see 705.   shd   25
1296 KNAVES ASH 25 [11] 9-11-2 (46) Mr T Scudamore 20/1: 3-0009: Cl-up till wknd qckly 2f out: see 1190.   3½   34
1498 KIERCHAN 14 [13] 9-10-7 (37) Mrs F Needham 14/1: 30/260: Prom, lost pl appr fnl 2f: 10th, jumps rnr.   ½   24
1690 ON PORPOISE 6 [9] 4-10-11 (41) M R Darcy (7) 10/1: 0-0000: Al towards rear: 11th, qck reapp.   1¾   27
3914} DANZIG FLYER 268 [5] 5-10-8 (38)(12ow)(13oh) Miss S M Potts (6) 100/1: 0000-0: Early ldr, sn btn: 12th.   0
1583 Flashtalkin Flood 10 [2] 6-11-5 (49) Mr J A Richardson(7) 33/1:
1705 Time Loss 5 [15] 5-11-3 (47) Miss Diana Jones 9/1:
4057} Acquittal 261 [12] 8-10-5 (35) Miss C Foster (6) 25/1:

3745} **Averham Star** 280 [10] 5-9-10 (26)(vis)(6oh) Mr S Dobson (4) 100/1:
1707 **Red Cafe** 5 [4] 4-11-5 (49)(BL) Mrs C Williams 12/1:
17 ran   Time 2m 26.76 (16.76)   (J Robson)   S Gollings Scamblesby, Lincs.

1820 **7.10 EBF ROSTHERNE CLASS STKS 3YO+ 0-90 (C)** **7f30y rnd Soft Inapplicable**
£7477   £2653   £1326   £603   3 yo rec 10lb

733 **WAHJ** 76 [2] C A Dwyer 5-9-1 J Carroll 4/1: 040-01: 5 ch g Indian Ridge - Sabaah (Nureyev)   92
Made all, rdn 2f out, kept on well, unchall: plcd in '99 (List, rtd 100, Sir M Stoute): '98 wnr at Windsor (mdn) &
Chepstow (stks, rtd 109): eff at 7f/1m on fast & soft, goes well fresh & suited by forcing the pace: useful at best.
998 **BLUE SUGAR** 48 [3] J R Fanshawe 3-8-5 D Harrison 7/4 FAV: 1-42: 3 ch c Shuailaan - Chelsea My Love   2   88
(Opening Verse) Chsd ldrs, keen, toward centre in str, chsd wnr appr fnl 1f, drifted lft & sn onepace:
7 wk abs: acts on gd & soft grnd & appreciated the drop back to 7f: see 998.
1327 **GREEN CARD** 23 [4] S P C Woods 6-9-1 G Duffield 2/1: 33-463: 6 br h Green Dancer - Dunkellin (Irish   3   83
River) Keen, prom, centre ent str, outpcd fnl str, hung left: unsuited by drop back to 7f on soft grnd: see 1112.
1778 **PREMIER BARON** 2 [1] P S McEntee 5-9-6 P Shea (7) 11/2: 400644: Al bhd: bckd from 7/1, stiff task.   2   84$
4 ran   Time 1m 37.19 (10.09)   (S B Components)   C A Dwyer Newmarket.

1821 **7.40 OH! DE MOSCHINO HCAP 3YO 0-85 (D)** **1m6f Soft Inapplicable**   [88]
£3867   £1190   £595   £297

*1071 **SAMSAAM** 39 [2] J L Dunlop 3-9-7 (81) W Supple 4/5 FAV: 00-111: 3 b c Sadler's Wells - Azyaa (Kris)   93
Cl-up, led going well appr fnl 2f, sn clr, impressive: hat-trick landed after wins at Windsor & Doncaster (h'caps):
mdn promise last term (rtd 74): a revelation since since stepped up to 12/14.5f in h'cap company: acts on
gd/soft & hvy grnd, prob any trk, runs well fresh: wng run may not be at an end, potentially useful stayer.
1440 **ELEGIA PRIMA** 18 [1] Major D N Chappell 3-8-0 (60) A Nicholls (3) 12/1: 00-042: 3 ch f Mon Tresor -   5   60
Miss Milton (Young Christopher) Keen, trkd ldrs, rdn appr fnl 2f, same pace: stays a gall 14f on firm & soft grnd.
1480 **FORUM CHRIS** 15 [5] M Johnston 3-8-9 (69) J Fanning 11/1: 0433: 3 ch g Trempolino - Memory Green   3   68
(Green Forest) Led till appr fnl 2f, no extra: h'cap bow, longer trip, return to 12f may suit, see 1480.
1362 **RAINBOW SPIRIT** 21 [3] A P Jarvis 3-8-13 (73) G Duffield 11/1: 0-5034: Well plcd till lost pl appr   nk   72
fnl 2f: longer trip, poss non-stayer in this soft grnd on h'cap bow, see 1362.
1270 **MERRYVALE MAN** 28 [4] 3-9-0 (74) Dean McKeown 6/1: 210205: Prom, wknd under press appr fnl 2f: 3½   70
got to within a length of this wnr in 1071 (gd/soft).
*1225 **KAIAPOI** 30 [6] 3-9-6 (80) P M Quinn (3) 9/2: 00-11U: U.r. start: see 1225.   0
6 ran   Time 3m 17.63 (19.63)   (Hamdan Al Maktoum)   J L Dunlop Arundel, W.Sussex.

1822 **8.10 FELICITY HCAP 3YO 0-70 (E)** **1m30y rnd Soft Inapplicable**   [74]
£2996   £856   £428

1085 **LADY JONES** 38 [8] J Pearce 3-8-5 (50)(1ow) Dean McKeown 50/1: 100-01: 3 b f Emperor Jones - So   59
Beguiling (Woodman) Dwelt, rear, smooth hdwy over 2f out, led dist, pushed clr, eased cl-home: '99 scorer
at Brighton (sell, rtd 61 at best): dam a 7f juv sell wnr: eff at 7f/1m on fast & soft grnd: acts on a gall or
sharp/undul trk: prev forced the pace, a revelation here with waiting tactics, shld follow up.
*1596 **PIX ME UP** 9 [5] K A Ryan 3-9-0 (60)(6ex) Iona Wands (5) 11/1: 000012: 3 b f Up And At Em - Water   7   58
Pixie (Dance Of Life) Rear, hdwy to lead 2f out, hdd dist, no pace of easy wnr: clr rem: acts on firm & soft.
1671 **BOLD RAIDER** 7 [7] I A Balding 3-9-2 (62) A Nicholls (3) 4/5 FAV: 00-123: 3 b g Rudimentary -   5   52
Spanish Heart (King Of Spain) Chsd ldrs, went on over 3f out, hdd over 2f out, edged left & sn held: qck reapp
& much better expected: prob needs to dominate throughout: see 1671 (gd/soft).
*1603 **EVER REVIE** 9 [4] Miss S J Wilton 3-8-9 (55)(6ex) D Mernagh (3) 14/1: 0-0014: Led, hdd appr fnl   1   43
3f, sn rdn & onepcd: new stable, prev with T Easterby: see 1603 (clmr).
1500 **RUDETSKI** 14 [9] 3-8-10 (56) C Teague 20/1: -0065: Mid-div, eff 3f out, sn held: up in trip on   1   42
h'cap bow: mid-dists could suit: see 909.
1477 **ON SHADE** 15 [6] 3-7-13 (45) Dale Gibson 50/1: 60-006: Handy, rdn/wknd fnl 2f: see 1072.   nk   30
1113 **BEBE DE CHAM** 37 [3] 3-9-7 (67) R Cody Boutcher (7) 20/1: -00607: Held up, rdn/lost tch fnl 2f.   ¾   51
4305] **BINT HABIBI** 242 [1] 3-9-2 (62) Craig Williams 8/1: 4200-8: Chsd ldrs, wknd rapidly fnl 3f: reapp   7   36
rnr-up once in 99/00 (med auct mdn, rtd 69): eff at 7f, has tried 1m: acts on firm.
1681 **NOWT FLASH** 6 [2] 3-9-1 (61) Joanna Badger (7) 7/1: 052259: Prom, rdn/fdd fnl 2f: qck reapp.   nk   34
1632 **BALLISTIC BOY** 8 [11] 3-8-12 (58) J Fanning 7/1: 0-0030: Prom, wknd fnl 3f, 10th: btr 1632 (fast).   nk   30
10 ran   Time 1m 51.06 (10.56)   (Mrs Jean Routledge)   J Pearce Newmarket.

1823 **8.40 EBF WEAVER MDN 2YO (D)** **6f Soft Inapplicable**
£4465   £1374   £343

1488 **WHERES JASPER** 14 [4] K A Ryan 2-9-0 J Carroll 5/2: 21: 2 ch g Common Grounds - Stifen (Burslem)   85
Made all, rdn/drew clr ins last: cost 18,000gns, related to sev wnrs: eff at 5f, suited by this step up to 6f,
further could suit: handles gd/soft, soft & a gall trk: loves to dominate: going the right way, win again.
-- **RUDDER** [7] B W Hills 2-9-0 A McGlone 9/1: 2: 2 ch c Deploy - Wave Dancer (Dance In Time)   5   73
Sn rdn in tch, styd on well appr fnl 1f, no threat to wnr: half-brother to a useful 9f wnr: dam related to a
high-class stayer: gd debut over what is surely an inadequate trip, sure to relish 7f/1m+ in time.
-- **GILLS DIAMOND** [6] J J O'Neill 2-9-0 G Duffield 16/1: 3: 2 ch f College Chapel - Yafford (Warrshan)   ¾   66
Front rank, rdn/not pace of wnr fnl 1f: 12,000gns 2nd foal, dam a mdn, sire high-class at 6/7f: gd debut.
-- **THE FANCY MAN** [2] N Tinkler 2-9-0 Craig Williams 12/1: 4: Dwelt, sn prom, rdn & no extra fnl   ½   69
2f: Feb first foal, sire high-class at 10/12f: ran green here & shld improve on this pleasing debut.
-- **KIMOE WARRIOR** [3] 2-9-0 Dean McKeown 20/1: 5: V slow to start, in tch halfway, wknd ins last,   3½   63
Mar foal, half-brother to dam 7f wnr Mister Clinton, dam high-class at start here & shld improve.
-- **THE LOOSE SCREW** [10] 2-9-0 R Cody Boutcher (7) 14/1: 6: Prom, drvn/wknd qckly fnl 1f: 1   61
Bigstone gelding, dam unrcd: with J L Eyre.
1513 **PEREGIAN** 13 [5] 2-9-0 J Fanning 2/1 FAV: -537: Handy, rdn/lost tch appr fnl 1f: disapp here &   ½   60
prob not appr this softer surface: much btr 1513 (gd).
1221 **MAYSBOYO** 30 [1] 2-9-0 G Parkin 50/1: -308: Sn outpcd: see 1020.   8   48
-- **SHEER FOCUS** [8] 2-9-0 W Supple 7/1: 9: Mid-div, lost tch halfway: Mar first foal, dam Irish   1   46
Irish 9f wnr: with B W Hills & shld improve over further given time.

--   **EAGLET** [9] 2-9-0 O Pears 20/1: 0: Prom, wknd rapidly halfway, t.o.: 10th: debut, with A Scott.   *dist*   0
10 ran   Time 1m 20.11 (8.81)   (Jimm Racing)   K A Ryan Hambleton, N Yorks

1824	**9.10 VACUUM POUCH MDN 3YO+ (D)** **1m6f** **Soft** Inapplicable

       £4192   £1290   £645   £322   3 yo rec 19lb

1369 **FOLLOW LAMMTARRA 21** [7] M R Channon 3-8-7 Craig Williams 8/1: 361: 3 ch g Lammtarra - Felawnah   84
(Mr Prospector) Led to halfway, remained with ldrs, rdn to lead again fnl 1f, styd on strongly, rdn out: loves
to race up with/force the pace over 14f, 2m shld suit: acts on soft, poss handles gd: improving, win more races.
1369 **SON OF A GUN 21** [1] J Neville 6-9-12 Dean McKeown 100/30: 42: 6 b g Gunner B - Sola Mia (Tolomeo) 3   80
Front rank, went on halfway, hdd appr fnl 1f, not pace of wnr: stays 14f on gd/soft & soft grnd: win similar.
--   **POT LUCK** [2] H Morrison 3-8-7 D Griffiths 12/1: 3: 3 b c Be My Guest - Cremets (Mummy's Pet) 5   75
Prom, rdn to impr 2f out, sn not pace of front 2: encouraging debut, prob stays 14f on soft grnd: improve.
1386 **MILL EMERALD 20** [3] R A Fahey 3-8-3 P Hanagan (7) 16/1: 0-64: Rear, late hdwy, no threat: up in trip. 4   66
1599 **DAME HATTIE 9** [9] 5-9-7 O Pears 14/1: 55: Mid-div, drvn/lost tch fnl 2f: up in trip: see 1599.   ½   65
1369 **JARDINES LOOKOUT 21** [8] 3-8-7 D Sweeney 11/8 FAV: 536: Prom, rdn, hung left & wknd appr fnl 2f: 3   67
reportedly unsuited by the grnd but ran well on gd/soft in 1369.
1539 **BOURKAN 13** [4] 3-8-7 W Supple 6/1: 07: Prom, hdwy 3f out, wknd rapidly 2f out: up in trip   11   57
& will prob apprec a return to 10/12f: see 1539.
3212} **REVENGE 307** [5] 4-9-12 Jonjo Fowle (7) 16/1: 04-8: Handy, lost tch fnl 4f, fin last: 12 wk jumps 7   50
abs, plcd twice in 99/00 (juv mdn hdles, rtd 99h, R Phillips, stays 2m on hvy): 4th on 2nd of 2 '99 Flat
starts (12f mdn, gd/soft, rtd 78): now with C G Cox.
8 ran   Time 3m 18.11 (20.11)   (Sheikh Ahmed Al Maktoum)   M R Channon West Isley, Berks.

Official Going   GOOD. Stalls: 1m4f - Centre, Rem - Inside.

1825	**2.05 LISTED VICTRESS STKS 3YO+ (A)** **1m114y rnd** **Good/Soft 63** **-02 Slow**

       £22750   £7000   £3500   £1750   3yo rec 12lb   Runners came stands side home straight

1402 **GOLDEN SILCA 20** [3] M R Channon 4-9-6 S Drowne 11/4 FAV: 22-041: 4 ch f Inchinor - Silca Cisa   112
(Hallgate) In tch, short of room & squeezed thro' 2f out, led dist, idled in front & just held on: hvly bckd: rnr-up
in 3 of 4 '99 starts, incl Gr 1 Irish 1,000 Guineas & Coronation Stakes (Gr 115): v tough juv, won at Newbury (4,
incl Gr 2) & also in Germany: eff at sprint trips, stays 8.5f well: acts on firm & hvy grnd, handles any trk, likes
Newbury: runs v well fresh: tough & v smart filly who is prob value for more than today's wng margin.
1309 **HIGH WALDEN 24** [4] H R A Cecil 3-8-8 T Quinn 4/1: 12-532: 3 b f El Gran Senor - Modena (Roberto) shd 111
Rcd keenly & nvr far away, led 2f out till dist, rallied gamely cl-home & just btn in a thrilling fin: nicely bckd,
5L clr 3rd: best eff on this drop back in trip, stays 10f & return to that trip will suit: smart, shld win a Listed.
1185 **ICICLE 33** [7] J R Fanshawe 3-8-13 D Harrison 10/1: 214-03: 3 br f Polar Falcon - Blessed Honour 5 106
(Ahonoora) Waited with, rdn & styd on fnl 2f, took 3rd cl-home, no ch with front 2: stays an easy 8.5f, will get
further judged on this: acts most ind & gd/soft grnd: win a nice race abroad: see 1185.
*1269 **PLEASURE CENTER 28** [8] J H M Gosden 3-8-8 C McCarron 14/1: 4-14: Set pace till 2f out, no extra: 1   99
not disgraced in today's stiffer company: see 1269 (reapp, fill mdn).
1108 **VERBOSE 37** [2] 3-8-8 J Fortune 9/2: 5-125: Trkd ldrs, eff 2f out, grad fdd ins last: shorter 3   93
priced stable-mate of 4th: see 1108.
1309 **EVERLASTING LOVE 24** [5] 3-8-8 M J Kinane 9/1: 20-556: Prom, rdn & fdd fnl 2f: prob not apprec 3½   86
this drop back in trip: stays 10f, see 1184 (firm, reapp).
1184 **HYPNOTIZE 33** [1] 3-8-11 K Fallon 12/1: 115-67: Prom, ev ch when bmpd 2f out, grad fdd: form on ¾   87
gd & fast grnd prev: see 1184.
1327 **JUNO MARLOWE 23** [10] 4-9-6 M Roberts 33/1: 10-008: Rear, not come down hill, nvr a factor: nvr 6   72
travelling on today's undul trk: see 1077.
1592 **ANNAPURNA 9** [6] 4-9-6 Pat Eddery 20/1: -02349: Rear, imprvd to chase ldrs 2f out, wknd qckly fnl 1f. 5   62
966 **KUWAIT DAWN 51** [9] 4-9-6 K Darley 90/1: 00-000: In tch till halfway, fin last: 7 wk abs: highly tried, 5   52
well btn off a mark of 86 in h'caps earlier: '99 reapp wnr at Doncaster (stks, rtd 99), mainly out of form subs:
eff at 7f/1m on fast & gd/soft grnd: can run well fresh: with K Mahdi.
10 ran   Time 1m 47.40 (5.60)   (Aldridge Racing Ltd)   M R Channon West Isley, Berks

1826	**2.40 VODAFONE NETWORK HCAP 3YO 0-100 (C)** **7f rnd** **Good/Soft 63** **-18 Slow** [101]

       £22750   £7000   £2500   £1750

*1525 **PEACOCK ALLEY 13** [1] W J Haggas 3-8-4 (77) J F Egan 5/1 FAV: 23-511: 3 gr f Salse - Tagiki   85
(Doyoun) Nvr far away, imprvd to lead dist, kept on strongly, rdn out: well bckd: recent Warwick wnr (mdn,
cmftbly): eff at 7f/1m, bred to stay further: acts on fast, likes gd/soft & hvy, any trk: fast improving.
*1535 **ATLANTIC RHAPSODY 14** [4] M Johnston 3-8-5 (92) M Hills 6/1: 104412: 3 b g Machiavellian - First 1¼   96
Waltz (Green Dancer) Bhd, imprvd 2f out, styd on well fnl 1f but not quite rch wnr: seems suited by waiting
tactics: eff at 7f, return to 1m will suit: useful gelding who is still improving: see 1535.
1535 **QAMOUS 13** [6] E A L Dunlop 3-9-5 (92) R Hills 13/2: 41-303: 3 gr c Bahri - Bel Ray (Restivo) 1¼   93
Prom, eff & ev ch over 1f out, no extra cl-home: acts on firm & gd/soft grnd: ran to v best here: see 1186.
1531 **SARENA PRIDE 13** [9] R J O'Sullivan 3-8-3 (76) P Doe 12/1: -05024: Dwelt, drvn to improve from rear ½   76
2f out, styd on fnl 1f & nrst fin: sound eff, eff at 6/7f: see 1531, 727.
4207} **KNOCKTOPHER ABBEY 251** [16] 3-8-9 (82) M J Kinane 20/1: 1600-5: Prom, eff ent str & lost place, hd 82+
rallied fnl 1f: reapp: '99 Chepstow wnr (mdn auct, rtd 77): eff at 6/7f on firm & gd/soft, handles soft grnd:
handles a stiff or sharp trk: promising reapp, looks as tho' 1m will suit now.
1694 **ZIETZIG 6** [10] 3-8-5 (78) N Callan 14/1: 055006: In tch, ev ch dist, no extra ins last: qck reapp: ¾   76
poss stays 7f, seems best at 6f: handles gd/soft, likes fast & firm grnd: see 689 (AW).
1104 **CHAPEL ROYALE 37** [3] 3-8-7 (80) R Hughes 33/1: 01-507: Mid-div, eff 2f out, not pace to reach shd 78
ldrs: prev trained by D Nicholls, now with K Mahdi: see 823.
1471 **LORD PACAL 16** [17] 3-8-8 (81) J Mackay(7) 25/1: 4-0008: Mid-div, switched & eff 2f out, not pace to chall. hd 79
1289 **PAYS DAMOUR 25** [2] 3-8-4 (77) Dane O'Neill 8/1: 10-029: Prom, eff 2f out, grad fdd ins last. hd 75
1183 **I PROMISE YOU 33** [3] 3-7-13 (72) N Pollard 1/1: 5-1000: Led till dist, wkng when short of room 1½   67

ins last: fin 10th: best on reapp in 792.

4505} **MASTERPIECE USA 228** [15] 3-8-12 (85) K Fallon 7/1: -01-0: Rear, nvr nr to chall: fin 11th, reapp: 1 78
twice rcd juv, won at Lingfield (mdn, rtd 84): $250,000 half brother to a wnr in the USA: eff at 7f on hvy grnd,
bred to apprec 1m ᵃ : handles a sharp/undul trk: with Sir M Stoute & capable of btr.

829   **IYAVAYA 64** [11] 3-9-5 (92) S Drowne 40/1: 055-00: Slowly away, nvr a factor in 12th: 9 wk abs.   2 81

1535   **SHOUF AL BADOU 13** [13] 3-9-7 (94) J Reid 25/1: 11-000: Trkd ldrs till wknd over 1f out: fin 13th.   ½ 82

4476} **OGILIA 231** [8] 3-8-13 (86) K Darley 14/1: 3303-0: Al towards rear, fin 14th: reapp: '99 Bath wnr   shd 74
(fill mdn auct), subs plcd sev times, incl in a val Doncaster event (rtd 91 at best): eff at 6/6.5f on firm &
soft grnd: runs well fresh: capable of much better.

1470   **STRASBOURG 16** [14] 3-9-6 (93) J Fortune 20/1: 120-00: Al bhd, fin 15th: '99 debut wnr at Chepstow   3 75
(mdn, with P Chapple-Hyam), subs rnr-up in stks company (rtd 93) & tried in List company: related to sev wnrs,
dam scored over 7/10f: eff at 7f on fast & gd/soft grnd, shld stay 1m: now with J Gosden & capable of better.

1473   **PROUD CHIEF 16** [12] 3-8-2 (75)(VIS) B Brisland(5) 33/1: -26000: Prom 5f, fdd & fin last: tried a visor.   1½ 54
16 ran   Time 1m 25.77 (5.67)   (Mr & Mrs G Middlebrook)   W J Haggas Newmarket

---

1827   3.15 GR 1 CORONATION CUP 4YO+ (A)   1m4f   Good/Soft 63 +07 Fast
    £150000 £57500 £28750 £13750

+1247 **DALIAPOUR 29** [2] Sir Michael Stoute 4-9-0 K Fallon 11/8 FAV: 220-11: 4 b c Sadler's Wells - Dalara   121
(Doyoun) Made all, styd on strongly once in command fnl 1f, drvn out: hvly bckd, best time of day: recent reapp
wnr at Chester (Gr 3): '99 wnr here at Epsom (reapp, stks), subs rnr-up in both the English & Irish Derby's (rtd
118, with L Cumani): '98 Chepstow (mdn) & Ascot wnr (List, rtd 113): eff at 10/13.5f on both firm & soft grnd:
handles any trk, likes Epsom: can force the pace & runs v well fresh: high-class & genuine colt, who should
win more top-class mid-dist races this term & will give a gd account in the King George.

*767   **FANTASTIC LIGHT 76** [4] Saeed bin Suroor 4-9-0 C McCarron 7/4: 110-12: 4 b h Rahy - Jood (Nijinsky)   ¾ 120
In tch, imprvd to trk wnr over 4f out, kept on well cl-home but nvr going to rch wnr under a quiet ride: 11 wk
abs, hvly bckd, prev trained by Sir M Stoute: clearly runs v well fresh: jockey's inexperience around this
tricky course showed: may reoppose this wnr in the King George & can rate higher: see 767.

-1587 **BORDER ARROW 10** [3] I A Balding 5-9-0 J Fortune 6/1: /3-623: 5 ch h Selkirk - Nibbs Point (Sure   ¾ 119
Blade) Waited with, imprvd to chase wnr despite edging left from 2f out, no extra cl-home: rider reportedly given
a 4 day careless riding ban: high-class colt who shld win Group races this term: see 1587, 1152.

767   **SAGAMIX 76** [1] Saeed bin Suroor 6-9-0 O Peslier 13/2: /44-04: Chsd wnr till halfway, wknd & eased   7 109
fnl 1f: longer priced stable-mate of rnr-up, 11 wk abs: '98 Arc winner, capable of better: see 767.
4 ran   Time 2m 41.63 (6.83)   (H H Aga Khan)   Sir Michael Stoute Newmarket

---

1828   4.00 GR 1 VODAFONE OAKS 3YO (A)   1m4f   Good/Soft 63 -06 Slow
    £191400 £72600 £36300 £16500

*1469 **LOVE DIVINE 16** [3] H R A Cecil 3-9-0 T Quinn 9/4 FAV: 2-11: 3 b f Diesis - La Sky (Law Society)   121
In tch, prog to lead 2f out & kicked clr, ran on strongly, rdn out: hvly bckd, time 1.5 secs slower than 4 rnr
Coronation Cup: prev scored at Goodwood (List, reapp): eff at 10/12f, may stay further: acts on gd/soft grnd,
handles hvy & any trk, likes a sharp/undul one, runs v well fresh: top-class & improving filly, only lightly
raced & a fine run having reportedly suffered plenty of training problems: take the beating in the Irish Oaks.

*1309 **KALYPSO KATIE 24** [15] J Noseda 3-9-0 M J Kinane 7/2: 1-12: 3 gr f Fairy King - Miss Toot (Ardross)   2 116
Chsd ldrs, rdn to chase wnr fnl 1½f, no real impress ins last & just held on for 2nd: hvly bckd: eff at 10/12f,
handles a gall or sharp/undul trk: v smart filly who will reappose today's wnr in the Irish Oaks, see 1309.

*1184 **MELIKAH 33** [7] Saeed bin Suroor 3-9-0 C McCarron 10/1: -13: 3 ch f Lammtarra - Urban Sea (Miswaki)   nk 115+
Trkd ldrs, lost pl round Tattenham corner, ran on strongly fnl 1f under a kind ride, not get to wnr: eff at 10/12f
on firm & gd/soft grnd: tremendous eff on only 2nd start, may well have taken 2nd if jockey had been a little
stronger: open to plenty of improvement & looks sure to win mid-dist Group races this term: see 1184.

1185   **PETRUSHKA 33** [1] Sir Michael Stoute 3-9-0 K Fallon 9/2: 1-134: Trkd ldrs till lost place after 5f,   1½ 113
imprvd when sltly short of room over 2f out, kept on but not pace to chall: hvly bckd, 4L clr rem: did not
really get the run of today's race, stays 12f: acts on firm & gd/soft grnd: may reappose today's front 2 in the
Irish Oaks & that more gall trk will suit: see 1185, 953.

1309   **LADY UPSTAGE 24** [4] 3-9-0 M Hills 25/1: 14-125: Led after 3f till 2f out, grad fdd: fine front   4 107
running eff, prob stays 12f: again bhd today's 2nd in 1309, see 1995: relish a return to Listed/Gr 3.

*1485 **CORINIUM 15** [17] 3-9-0 W Ryan 16/1: 311-16: Prom, outpcd fnl 2f: well clr of rem: longer priced   1½ 105
stable-mate of wnr: reportedly not stay this longer 12f trip & will drop back to 10f next time: see 1485 (1m, List).

*1223 **SOLAIA 30** [13] 3-9-0 J Fortune 50/1: 55-417: Chsd ldrs till outpcd fnl 2f: see 1223 (List).   10 90

1282   **DOLLAR BIRD 27** [16] 3-9-0 G Carter 40/1: 10-328: Trkd ldrs, came wide into str, btn 2f out.   nk 89

1184   **CLIPPER 33** [18] 3-9-0 Pat Eddery 40/1: 01-039: Early ldr, rem prom till wknd over 2f out: longer   1 87
priced stable-mate of 5th: up in class & tried: see 1184 (again bhd today's 3rd. 10f).

1184   **CLOG DANCE 33** [12] 3-9-0 J Reid 33/1: 32-220: Chsd ldrs, came wide into str, sn btn & fin 10th.   ½ 86

*1313 **GOLD ROUND 28** [12] 3-9-0 O Doleuze 16/1: 21-310: Nvr better than mid-div: fin 11th: disapp run   4 80
from this French raider: much better expected after 1313 (10f).

625   **BLUEBELL WOOD 99** [11] 3-9-0 R Hughes 150/1: -11140: Al bhd, mod late prog, nvr dngrs in 12th: 4 74
long abs: v highly tried: see 625, 509 (AW h'cap).

*1374 **WHITEFOOT 21** [8] 3-9-0 O Peslier 9/1: 13-410: Rear, eff ent str, sn no ch: fin 13th, bckd from   hd 74
12/1: better expected & something clrly amiss: see 1374 (10f).

1457   **SO PRECIOUS 19** [6] 3-9-0 J Weaver 200/1: 61-400: Nvr a factor in 14th: once again highly tried.   16 52

1374   **PREMIER PRIZE 21** [14] 3-9-0 N Pollard 100/1: 61-630: Rear, some eff ent str, sn btn & fin 15th.   nk 51

1309   **MILETRIAN 24** [5] 3-9-0 M Roberts 25/1: 14-040: Chsd ldrs till wknd qckly ent str, fin last: 4 45
much better expected after 1309 (much closer to today's rnr-up).
16 ran   Time 2m 43.11 (8.31)   (Lordship Stud)   H R A Cecil Newmarket

---

1829   4.40 DISTRIBUTION HCAP 3YO+ 0-100 (C)   1m114yr rnd   Good/Soft 63 -11 Slow   [100]
    £22750 £7000 £3500 £1750

1528   **PRINCE SLAYER 13** [3] T P McGovern 4-8-4 (76) L Newman (5) 33/1: 2-0201: 4 b g Batshoof - Top   83
Sovereign (High Top) Trkd ldrs, imprvd to lead over 2f out, styd on well fnl 1f, drvn out: 1st win: single run
in '99 (mdn, rtd 80, B Smart): eff at 1m/10f on firm & hvy: handles a sharp/undul or gall trk: sound eff today.

1050   **HIBERNATE 41** [10] K R Burke 6-7-11 (69) J Mackay (7) 12/1: 000042: 6 ch g Lahib - Ministra (Deputy   ¾ 74
Minister) Nvr far away, chsd wnr fnl 2f, drifted in bhd wnr & onepcd ins last: 4L clr 3rd, 6 wk abs: on a wng

mark & fine eff over this inadequate 1m trip: all prev wins at 12f: likes a sharp trk: see 1050.

1173 **TAYSEER** 34 [16] D Nicholls 6-9-0 (86) K Fallon 9/2 JT FAV: 1-0053: 6 ch g Sheikh Albadou - Millfit | 4 | 83
(Blushing Groom) Slowly away, imprvg when short of room 2f out, kept on fnl 1f but no ch with front 2: nicely
bckd tho' op 7/2: has proved v costly to follow this term but a well h'capped gldg at best: see 733.

1490 **FALLACHAN** 14 [2] M A Jarvis 4-8-10 (82) M Roberts 9/2 JT FAV: 20-044: Prom, rdn & onepcd fnl | 1 | 77
2f: hvly bckd: did not seem completely at home on this sharp/undul trk: see 1490.

1567 **CARDIFF ARMS** 11 [8] 6-9-11 (97) D M Oliver 25/1: 0-2005: Mid-div, onepcd fnl 2f: best 1112. | 3½ | 85

1483 **MISTER RAMBO** 15 [7] 5-8-10 (82) R Hughes 16/1: 105206: Rcd keenly in bhd ldrs, grad fdd fnl 2f. | 3 | 64

1323 **CHINA RED** 26 [5] 6-9-0 (86) R Hills 16/1: 100-07: Set pace till 2f out, eased when btn: '99 wnr | 1½ | 65
at Lingfield (2, AW h'caps, rtd 98a): '98 Goodwood wnr (2, h'caps, rtd 88): '97 Nottingham wnr (mdn, rtd 85):
loves to force the pace over 1m on gd, firm grnd & equitrack: handles any trk, loves a sharp one, esp Lingfield
& Goodwood: gd weight carrier who runs well fresh: tough & capable of better.

1015 **CALCUTTA** 46 [1] 4-9-11 (97) M Hills 10/1: 106-08: Rear, eff 2f out, nvr nr ldrs & not given a hard | 1½ | 73+
time: 7 wk abs: '99 wnr at Newmarket & Doncaster (h'caps, rtd 102): '98 Ayr mdn wnr (rtd 90): v eff at 1m,
has tried further: acts on gd/soft, enjoys fast or firm grnd: likes a gall trk & runs well fresh: has a fine
turn of foot & loves to come with a late run: much more interesting back on fast grnd & on a gall trk next time.

1259 **EASTERN CHAMP** 28 [9] 4-7-13 (71) [t] N Pollard 16/1: 20-029: Mid-div, prog to chase ldrs 3f out, | 1½ | 44
wknd fnl 1f: better on fast or firm grnd: see 1259.

1450 **NAVIASKY** 17 [11] 5-8-8 (80) Martin Dwyer 15/2: -00040: Dwelt, eff 3f out, sn no impress: fin 10th. | shd | 53

1561 **SCENE** 11 [6] 5-8-2 (74) (vis) G Bardwell 14/1: 000000: Rdn in rear, nvr any ch: fin 11th, nicely | 1¼ | 44
bckd: won this race off the same mark as today last term: see 1113, 831.

1348 **SONG OF SKYE** 22 [12] M Henry 16/1: -03600: Mid-div, struggling fnl 3f, fin 12th: | 9 | 22
reportedly hung in today's soft grnd: see 423 (AW).

1567 **PANTAR** 11 [13] 5-9-8 (94) (bl) K Darley 6/1: 143630: Prom, rdn & btn over 2f out, eased considerably: | 2 | 42
fin 13th: reportedly lost his action: see 1567.

1979} **PYTHIOS** 360 [4] 4-10-0 (100) T Quinn 6/1: /131-0: Al bhd, lost tch fnl 3f, fin last: lightly rcd in '99, | ¾ | 46
won at Doncaster (mdn, reapp) & notably R Ascot (Britannia h'cap, rtd 103+): eff at 1m, shld stay further: all
form on fast or firm grnd on stiff/gall trks: usually wears a t-strap, not today: can run well fresh: v useful
colt who was reportedly nvr travelling in today's rain softened grnd: must be given another chance.

14 ran   Time 1m 48.16 (6.36)   (Ahmed Abdel-Khaleq)   T P McGovern Lewes, E Sussex

---

1830   5.10 LISTED VODAFONE SURREY STKS 3YO (A)   7f rnd   Good/Soft 63 -20 Slow
£22750 £7000 £3500 £1750

1452 **NICOBAR** 17 [5] I A Balding 3-8-11 K Fallon 11/4: 5-3161: 3 b c Indian Ridge - Duchess of Alba | | 112
(Belmez) Nvr far away, went on 2f out, sprinted clr fnl 1f, v easily: hvly bckd: earlier scored at Chester (h'cap):
'99 Haydock wnr (mdn, rtd 100), subs highly tried: eff at 7f/1m, acts on fast & gd/soft grnd,
handles firm: can force the pace, handles any trk: smart, fast imprvg colt who heads for the Jersey Stks at R
Ascot & will prove hard to beat if reproducing this.

1535 **SMART RIDGE** 13 [9] K R Burke 3-8-11 J Weaver 16/1: 10-502: 3 ch c Indian Ridge - Guanhumara | 7 | 99
(Caerleon) Rcd keenly in rear, imprvg when no room 2f out, fin fast to take 2nd but wnr in another parish: acts
on firm & gd/soft grnd, handles lvy: fast & fast imprvg rival here: see 1055.

1410 **MAGIC OF LOVE** 20 [2] M L W Bell 3-8-6 M Fenton 7/1: 131-33: 3 b f Magic Ring - Mistitled (Miswaki) | 2 | 90
Trkd ldrs, eff 2f out, onepcd fnl 1f: longer 7f trip & below best here: best prev on gd & firm grnd: see 1410.

1163 **SELKING** 34 [1] K R Burke 3-8-11 N Callan 10/1: 02-324: Led over 2f out, wkng when badly hmpd | 1¼ | 92
cl-home: shorter priced stable-mate of rnr-up: may have held on for 3rd if not hmpd: see 1163.

1118 **CATCHY WORD** 40 [3] 3-8-11 J Reid 15/2: 61-205: Trkd ldrs, eff 2f out, keeping on when hit rail ins | shd | 92
fnl 1f, stumbled badly & did well not to unseat jockey: op 6/1: 6 wk abs: 1m &/or a more gall trk will suit:
not disgraced in the circumstances & shld be given another chance: see 969.

1530 **SIR NINJA** 13 [10] 3-8-11 (VIS) T Quinn 8/1: 0-5626: Rear, nvr any impress on ldrs: tried a visor. | 1¼ | 89

1470 **TEODORA** 16 [11] 3-8-6 Pat Eddery 16/1: 53-507: Rear, eff 2f out, nvr nr ldrs: see 995. | 1¼ | 81

1371 **HOPEFUL LIGHT** 21 [6] 3-8-11 J Fortune 9/4 FAV: 1-48: Prom, not handle Tattenham corner, wknd & | 10 | 66
eased fnl 1f: hvly bckd: encouraging reapp in 1371, not handle today's trk & worth another chance.

1374 **CLARANET** 21 [7] 3-8-6 K Darley 25/1: 331009: Prom 5f, wknd into last: flattered 1185, see 934. | 5 | 51

9 ran   Time 1m 25.92 (5.82)   (Robert Hitchins)   I A Balding Kingsclere, Hants

---

1831   5.45 VODAFONE PAGING HCAP 3YO 0-100 (C)   1m2f   Good/Soft 63 -18 Slow   [105]
£22750 £7000 £3500 £1750

1452 **FORBEARING** 17 [1] Sir Mark Prescott 3-8-11 (88) S Sanders 10/1: 11-001: 3 b c Bering - For | | 104
Example (Northern Baby) Trkd ldrs, qcknd into lead 2f out, clr fnl 1f, easily: '99 wnr at Lingfield (mdn) &
W'hampton (nov, rtd 95a): eff at 1m, stays 10f well: acts on all AWs & on gd/soft & hvy grnd: handles a gall
or sharp/undul trk: useful & fast imprvg, can follow up: a welcome return to form for Sir M Prescott.

1452 **FATHER JUNINHO** 17 [14] A P Jarvis 3-8-11 (88) K Darley 8/1: 2-0652: 3 b c Distinctly North - Shane's | 3½ | 96
Girl (Marktingo) Held up, eff 2f out, styd on well into 2nd fnl 1f, no ch with wnr: stays 10f: bt this wnr in 1452.

*1452 **MOON SOLITAIRE** 17 [7] E A L Dunlop 3-8-12 (89) J Reid 15/8 FAV: -41313: 3 b c Night Shift - Gay | nk | 96
Fantastic (Ela Mana Mou) Rear, imprvd to chase wnr 2f out, wandered ins last & caught for 2nd cl-home:
hvly bckd, 7L rem: beat today's 1st & 2nd in 1452: stays 10f: useful.

1340 **COOL INVESTMENT** 22 [5] M Johnston 3-9-1 (92) M J Kinane 9/1: 1-2064: Rear, not handle Tattenham | 7 | 89+
corner, kept on well fnl 1f but no ch with ldrs: tchd 12/1: lkd all at sea on this sharp/undul trk: worth
another chance on a more conventional course, see 823.

1369 **MUWAKALL** 21 [4] 3-8-6 (83) G Carter 25/1: 353455: Held up, eff over 2f out, late prog but nvr | ½ | 79
dangerous: mdn, rcd as tho' 12f will suit: tried 14f in 1369, see 1127.

1400 **FIRST MANASSAS** 20 [3] 3-8-5 (82) Martin Dwyer 12/1: 13-006: Prom, led 3f out till over 2f out, fdd. | 1¼ | 76

*1387 **SOVEREIGN STATE** 20 [12] 3-8-1 (78) J Mackay (7) 15/2: 14-017: Trkd ldrs racing wide, struggling | 14 | 52
fnl 2f & well btn: much btr 1387 (1m, gd grnd).

1452 **TIGRE** 17 [6] 3-8-5 (82) M Roberts 20/1: 22-408: Nvr nr ldrs: see 1159 (7f mdn). | 2½ | 53

980 **ALVA GLEN** 50 [11] 3-9-7 (98) C McCarron 11/1: 421-69: Prom till lost place ent str, sn eased: | nk | 68
7 wk abs, top weight: not at home on this sharp/undul trk & this is best forgotten: see 980 (List).

1400 **BOLD EWAR** 20 [13] 3-8-2 (79) (bl) N Pollard 11/1: -53250: Chsd ldrs racing wide, wknd fnl 2f, 10th. | 1 | 47

1310 **IMPERIAL ROCKET** 24 [8] 3-8-10 (87) J Weaver 12/1: 1-4600: Led till 3f out, wknd & eased: fin 11th. | 3 | 50

1585 **STORM WIZARD** 10 [2] 3-7-13 (76) P Doe 8/1: -34220: Chsd ldrs till halfway, wknd qckly & t.o. | dist | 0
in last: reportedly broke a blood vessel: see 1585, 1193.

EPSOM FRIDAY JUNE 9TH Lefthand, Very Sharp, Undulating Track

12 ran   Time 2m 11.90 (8.10)   (Eclipse Thoroughbreds - Osborne House IV)   Sir Mark Prescott Newmarket

HAYDOCK SATURDAY JUNE 10TH Lefthand, Flat, Galloping Track

Official Going GOOD/SOFT (SOFT places). Stalls: Outside; Except 7f/1m - Inside.

1832

1.50 DOUGLAS RTD HCAP 3YO 0-100 (B)   1m4f   Good/Soft 79 -06 Slow   [107]
£9179   £3481   £1740   £791

1347 **RIDDLESDOWN** 23 [7] S P C Woods 3-9-3 (96) G Duffield 10/1: 21-221: 3 ch c Common Grounds - Neat   102
Dish (Stalwart) Trkd ldr till went on over 3f out, styd on well fnl 1f, drvn out: deserved win: '99 wnr at Bath (mdn
auct, rtd 94): eff at 10/12f, acts on fast & soft grnd: handles a gall or turning trk: can run well fresh & likes
to race up with or force the pace: useful & consistent colt who cld win a List event abroad.

1374 **THE WOODSTOCK LADY** 22 [2] B W Hills 3-8-8 (87) J P Spencer 11/1: 1-002: 3 ch f Barathea - Howlin'   ¾ 91
(Alleged) Rear, steady hdwy when short of room 3f out, ev ch 1f out, kept on & not btn far: 4L clr 3rd: back to
form on this drop in grade: eff at 12f on gd/soft grnd: handles a gall trk: see 1106 (List).

1451 **NORTON** 18 [1] T G Mills 3-8-11 (90) L Carter 6/1: 501-03: 3 ch c Barathea - Primrose Valley (Mill   4 88
Reef) Held up, hdwy & ev ch 2f out, not qckn fnl 1f: longer 12f trip & drop in grade: see 1451 (10f List).

1674 **SHAREEF** 7 [3] P F I Cole 3-9-0 (93) D Sweeney 8/1: -1504: Prom till fdd fnl 1f: h'cap bow: had the   5 83
speed not to be disgraced over 6f (List) in 1674: 1m/10f could prove ideal & worth another chance: see 1674 (gd).

*1400 **MASTER GEORGE** 21 [8] 3-8-3 (82) M Roberts 7/1: 2-1625: Waited with, switched & eff 3f out, fdd fnl 1f.   1 70
*1400 **FIRST OFFICER** 21 [6] 3-9-0 (93) S Sanders 10/11 FAV: 04-116: Mid-div, eff 3f out, sn outpcd by ldrs: ¾ 80
hvly bckd from 6/4: progressive prev & something amiss here? see 1400.
*1539 **FIRST OFFICER** 14 [4] 3-8-8 (87) D Harrison 11/2: -0217: Trkd ldrs till wknd 2f out: btr 1539 (10f).   11 59
1400 **COLONIAL RULE** 21 [5] 3-8-7 (86) J Carroll 20/1: 31-008: Set pace 9f, wknd into last: see 1400.   ¾ 57
8 ran   Time 2m 38.10 (10.30)   (The Storm Again Syndicate)   S P C Woods Newmarket

1833

2.20 LISTED CECIL FRAIL STKS 3YO+ (A)   6f   Good/Soft 79 +11 Fast
£15665   £4820   £2410   £1205   3yo rec 8lb

1338 **PIPALONG** 23 [4] T D Easterby 4-9-7 M Roberts 10/11 FAV: 1-1121: 4 b f Pips Pride - Limpopo (Green   115
Desert) Waited with, hdwy over 1f out, led cl home, shade cosily: well bckd, best time of day: earlier won at
Thirsk (reapp, stks) & Newmarket (Gr 3 Palace House): '99 Ripon (val h'cap) & Doncaster wnr (List, rtd 107): '98
wnr at Ripon (debut), York & Redcar (val 2yo Trophy, rtd 105): eff at 5/6f, prob stays 7f: acts on firm & hvy
grnd & on any trk: runs v well fresh: smart & genuine filly who shld run well in chosen R Ascot engagement.

-- **ROMANYLEI** [1] J G Burns 3-8-6 E Ahern 12/1: 11-62: 3 gr f Blues Traveller - Krayyalei (Krayyan)   ½ 103
Broke well & tried to make all, overhauled cl home: 8 wk abs: Irish raider, game front running effort: won both
juv starts, at Cork & Naas (h'cap): eff at 5/6f on fast & gd/soft grnd: useful, speedy filly, land a nice prize.
1410 **SERAPHINA** 21 [3] B A McMahon 3-8-6 G Duffield 12/1: -06203: 3 ch f Pips Pride - Angelic Sounds (The 2½ 97
Noble Player) Rear, styd on under press fnl 1f, not pace to chall: not disgraced, but rtd higher in 1090.
1283 **AURATUM** 28 [6] Saeed bin Suroor 3-8-6 J Carroll 9/2: 1-P4: Prom, fdd ins fnl 1f: tchd 6/1: see 1283.   1¾ 92
*1576 **COTTON HOUSE** 11 [2] 3-9-6 S Drowne 9/2: 124-15: Front rank 4f, wknd: see 1576 (stks).   shd 92
1470 **OUT OF AFRICA** 17 [5] 3-8-10 Dane O'Neill 14/1: 11-006: Prsd ldrs 4f, sn outpcd: tchd 25/1.   5 81
6 ran   Time 1m 15.42 (4.12)   (T H Bennett)   T D Easterby Great Habton, N Yorks.

1834

2.50 LISTED JOHN OF GAUNT STKS 4YO+ (A)   7f30y rnd   Good/Soft 79 -12 Slow
£15730   £4840   £2420   £1210

1316 **ONE WON ONE** 27 [2] Ms J Morgan 6-9-3 E Ahern 16/1: 553301: 6 b g Naevus - Harvaro's Bay (Halpern   114
Bay) Held up, stdy hdwy to lead ent fnl 1f, held on well, drvn out: Irish raider, rider reportedly given a 4-day
whip ban: '99 wnr at The Curragh (h'cap) & Leopardstown (List): eff btwn 5f, suited by 6/7f, stays 1m on fast,
likes gd/soft, hvy & a gall trk: has plenty of speed: smart & tough, should win more Listed events.
1077 **PULAU TIOMAN** 13 [5] M A Jarvis 4-8-12 M Roberts 4/1: -21242: 4 b c Robellino - Ella Mon Amour   nk 108
(Ella Mana Mou) Nvr far away, led briefly dist, chall strongly fnl 1f & just btn in a thrilling fin: nicely bckd:
4th in Italy (7f, fast, List) since 1077: another fine run, deserves to go one better: see 1015.
1674 **HOT TIN ROOF** 7 [7] T D Easterby 4-8-12 R Winston 7/2: -21123: 4 b f Thatching - No Reservations   ½ 107
(Commanche Run) Trkd ldrs going well, led briefly over 1f out, kept on well & not btn far: op 9/2: rider given
a 2-day whip ban: in-form, smart & tough filly: rtd just higher in 1674, 1410.
1617 **MUCHEA** 16 [3] M R Channon 6-8-12 (vis) S Drowne 10/1: 022054: Prom, eff & onepcd fnl 2f: see 1617.   2 102
1533 **NOW LOOK HERE** 14 [10] 4-8-12 G Duffield 12/1: 233345: Chsd ldrs, no impress fnl 2f: see 1533 (5f).   ½ 102
1617 **WARNINGFORD** 16 [8] 6-9-5 D Harrison 3/1 FAV: 6-2426: Mid-div, eff 2f out, btn fnl 1f: well bckd: 3½ 102
better expected over favoured 7f trip on rain-softened grnd: see 1617, 952.
*1163 **ARCTIC CHAR** 35 [4] 4-8-12 D R McCabe 14/1: 52-017: Set pace till dist, no extra: btr 1163.   ¾ 93
1482 **BOMB ALASKA** 16 [1] 5-9-3 Dane O'Neill 11/1: -44348: Front rank till wknd fnl 1½f: see 1057 (10f).   hd 98
1622 **MANORBIER** 14 [6] 4-8-12 F Lynch 12/1: 204149: Mid-div, eff & btn 2f out: flattered 1622.   2½ 88
1514 **ADJUTANT** 14 [9] 5-8-12 J P Spencer 9/1: 303120: In tch, outpcd fnl 3f: fin last: btr 1514, 1286.   2½ 83
10 ran   Time 1m 33.50 (6.40)   (Heavenly Syndicate)   Ms J Morgan Ballivor, Co Meath

1835

3.25 EBF MDN 2YO (D)   5f str   Good/Soft 79 -11 Slow
£3526   £1085   £542   £271

1424 **AUTUMNAL** 19 [8] B J Meehan 2-8-9 D R McCabe 4/6 FAV: -31: 2 b f Indian Ridge - Please Believe Me   80
(Try My Best) Nvr far away, went on dist, kept on well despite edging left, rdn out: hvly bckd from 6/5: sister
to a 5f juv wnr: dam a 5f 2yo wnr, sire a high-class sprinter: eff at 5f on gd/soft: can rate more highly.
1472 **ATTORNEY** 17 [7] M A Jarvis 2-9-0 M Roberts 9/1: -02: 2 ch c Wolfhound - Princess Sadie (Shavian)   ½ 82
Set pace till collared dist, rallied & only just btn: 4L clr 3rd: eff at 5f on gd/soft, 6f will suit: win similar.
1385 **SENSIMELIA** 21 [3] Martyn Wane 2-8-9 C Teague 20/1: -53: 2 b f Inzar - In The Papers (Aragon)   4 67
Nvr far away, outpcd by front 2 fnl 1f: op 12/1: 6f will now suit: see 1385.
1602 **EMISSARY** 10 [5] M Johnston 2-9-0 J Fanning 33/1: -664: Chsd ldrs, onepcd fnl 1½f: see 1221.   1¼ 67
-- **VAIL PEAK** [1] 2-9-0 G Duffield 10/1: -5: Prom till grad fdd fnl 1½f: mkt drifter: May foal, half   nk 67

596

brother to sev wnr in the States: shld apprec 6f: with J Noseda & shld improve.
-- **LOVE THING** [9] 2-8-9 R Winston 14/1: -6: Rcd stands side & outpcd, v green & hung to far side *nk* **61+**
fnl 2f, late gains: op 10/1: April foal, cost 3,000gns: sister to 6f 2yo wnr Lament & half sister to useful sprinter Superior Premium: shld apprec 6f+: ran v green today, sure to improve considerably & one to keep in mind.
-- **ALBANECK** [4] 2-9-0 J P Spencer 14/1: -7: Chsd ldrs despite running green, kept on late: op 8/1: *hd* **66**
Feb foal, dam a 5f winning 2yo: with T Easterby & speedily bred.
-- **KIRKBYS TREASURE** [6] 2-9-0 J Carroll 15/2: -8: Slowly away, no ch after: tchd 10/1: May foal, *13* **41**
half brother to winning sprinters: dam a sprinter, sire a high-class juv: with A Berry, lost all chance at the start.
1249 **CELESTIAL POWER 30** [10] 2-8-9 S Sanders 33/1: -09: Al outpcd on stands side, t.o.: see 1249. *23* **0**
9 ran Time 1m 03.30 (4.50) (Paul & Jenny Green) B J Meehan Upper Lambourn, Berks.

1836

4.20 LADBROKE HCAP 3YO+ 0-95 (C) 1m30y rnd Good/Soft 79 -07 Slow [95]
£7182 £2210 £1105 £552 3yo rec 11lb

1635 **SILK ST JOHN 9** [4] M J Ryan 6-9-7 (88) P McCabe 4/1 FAV: 065131: 6 b g Damister - Silk St James **94**
(Pas de Seul) Rear, prog 2f out, strong run to lead ins fnl 1f, rdn out: bckd from 11/2: earlier won here at Haydock (h'cap): '99 Sandown & Newbury wnr (h'caps, rtd 97): '98 wnr at Chepstow (ltd stks), here at Haydock (val h'cap, subs disqual), Windsor (2) & Newbury: stays 11f, suited by 1m on a gall trk, likes Haydock & Newbury: acts on firm, hvy grnd & f/sand: v tough, genuine & useful: likes to come with a late challenge & in fine form.
1450 **SILKEN DALLIANCE 18** [7] I A Balding 5-8-11 (78) M Roberts 11/1: 0-0002: 5 b m Rambo Dancer - A *¾* **81**
Sharp (Sharpo) Dwelt, hdwy 2f out, fin strongly but too late: blnks omitted: back to form & on a handy mark.
786 **THE EXHIBITION FOX 73** [2] B A McMahon 4-8-9 (76) S Sanders 25/1: 100-03: 4 b g Be My Chief - *1¼* **76**
Swift Return (Double Form) Prom, went on dist, not pace to repel wnr ins last: 10 wk abs: apprec retrun to 1m.
1561 **ROLLER 12** [6] J G Given 4-8-10 (77) D Harrison 9/2: 212204: Front rank, no extra fnl 1f: well bckd. *1½* **74**
1680 **PETERS IMP 7** [8] 5-7-12 (65) J Bramhill 10/1: 0-5025: Held up, hdwy 2f out, no impress ins fnl 1f. *½* **61**
*1744 **ICE 4** [5] 4-9-13 (94)(vis)(6ex) J Fanning 9/2: 40-516: In tch till wknd over 1f out: top-weight: qck *2* **86**
reapp under a pen after 1744 (9f).
1015 **DANGEROUS FORTUNE 47** [1] 4-9-0 (81) Dane O'Neill 10/1: 215-67: Trkd ldrs, rdn & btn 2f out: abs. *shd* **73**
1645 **CLEVER GIRL 8** [3] 3-8-10 (88) J Carroll 13/2: -401D8: Set pace till dist, fdd: see 1645. *1¼* **77**
1450 **TRIPLE DASH 18** [9] 4-9-12 (93) G Duffield 16/1: 3-5009: Nvr a factor: slipping down the weights. *7* **67**
1110 **TUMBLEWEED RIVER 38** [11] 4-9-2 (83)(BL) D R McCabe 25/1: 105-00: Chsd ldrs till wknd 3f out: fin *6* **45**
10th, first time blnks: likes to force the pace over 7f: see 1110.
1483 **PRINCE BABAR 16** [10] 9-8-12 (79) R Winston 7/1: -24450: Nvr a factor, t.o. in last: btr 1015. *15* **11**
11 ran Time 1m 47.40 (6.90) (C R S Partners) M J Ryan Newmarket

1837

4.55 WARRINGTON MDN 3YO (D) 1m30y rnd Good/Soft 79 -16 Slow
£3984 £1226 £613 £306

1556 **CROWN LODGE 12** [4] L M Cumani 3-8-9 J P Spencer 3/1: -21: 3 ch f Grand Lodge - Itqan (Sadler's **90**
Wells) Prom, drvn into lead dist, wandered but kept on well, drvn out: nicely bckd: half sister to a useful miler: eff at 1m on gd/soft & hvy grnd, 10f will suit: handles a gall trk: improving filly.
1584 **GREY EMINENCE 11** [5] R Hannon 3-9-0 Dane O'Neill 9/4: 5-222: 3 gr c Indian Ridge - Rahaam (Secreto) *2* **89**
Nvr far away, styd on under press fnl 1f, not pace of wnr: nicely bckd tho' op 11/8: deserves a change of luck.
1352 **PARAGON OF VIRTUE 22** [3] Sir Michael Stoute 3-9-0 D Harrison 15/8 FAV: -023: 3 ch c Cadeaux *2* **85**
Genereux - Madame Dubois (Legend Of France) Trkd ldr, led over 3f out till dist, no extra: bckd from 9/4.
1376 **HELLO VEGAS 22** [6] J H M Gosden 3-9-0 J Carroll 11/1: 6-04: Rear, nvr nr ldrs: tchd 14/1: 6th *11* **65**
at Nottingham (mdn, rtd 70) on sole '99 start: half brother to a useful miler: mid-dists may suit.
1388 **AIWIN 21** [1] 3-9-0 M Roberts 20/1: -045: Led till 3f out, wknd qckly: see 1388 (sand). *shd* **65**
1655 **SISTER KATE 8** [2] 3-8-9 G Duffield 16/1: 6-06: Rcd keenly in rear, btn 2f out: see 1655. *8* **44**
6 ran Time 1m 48.10 (7.60) (Robert H Smith) L M Cumani Newmarket

DONCASTER SATURDAY JUNE 10TH Lefthand, Flat, Galloping Track

Official Going GOOD/FIRM. Stalls: Str Crse - Stands Side: Round Course - Inside.

1838

2.15 DERBY DAY AUCT MDN DIV 1 2YO (E) 6f Good/Firm 27 -50 Slow
£3136 £965 £482 £241

-- **WITNEY ROYALE** [8] J S Moore 2-8-5 Dean McKeown 25/1: 1: 2 ch g Royal Abjar - Collected (Taufan) **74**
Dwelt & bmpd, imprvd halfway, kept on well & led towards fin: IR 6,400gns April foal: dam a mdn, sire a miler: eff at 6f, 7f is going to suit: acts on fast grd & runs well fresh on a gall track.
1408 **EL MAXIMO 21** [2] M G Quinlan 2-8-5 R Mullen 7/1: 632: 2 b c First Trump - Kentucky Starlet *nk* **72**
(Cox's Ridge) Nvr far away, led appr fnl 1f, rdn & worn down ins last: eff at 6f on gd & fast grnd.
1550 **EAGLES CACHE 12** [12] A Berry 2-8-5 G Carter 11/1: 43: 2 b c Eagle Eyed - Cache (Bustino) *nk* **71**
Cl up, drifted left & ev ch appr fnl 1f, held towards fin: apprec step up to 6f on fast grnd, see 1550.
1513 **NISAN BIR 14** [10] T D Easterby 2-8-5 G Parkin 14/1: 04: Rear, drvn appr fnl 1f, no impress till ran *1¾* **67$**
on cl home: already needs 7f: handles fast grnd.
1513 **TROJAN PRINCE 14** [6] 2-8-8 A Eddery(5) 11/10 FAV: -0025: Keen, rear, chsd ldrs fnl 1f, no dngr. *shd* **70**
821 **GOLDEN DRAGONFLY 66** [7] 2-8-8 F Norton 20/1: 006: Front rank, no extra dist: 9 wk abs: see 821. *¾* **68**
1443 **MISS EQUINOX 18** [3] 2-8-0 Kim Tinkler 33/1: 57: Led till appr fnl 1f, one pace: longer trip. *nk* **59**
1443 **SPICE ISLAND 18** [1] 2-8-0 D Mernagh (3) 16/1: 538: With ldrs, chall ent fnl 2f, hung left, outpcd. *1¼* **56**
-- **BYO** [4] 2-8-5 Joanna Badger (7) 40/1: 9: Prom till 2f out: IR 1000gns Paris House Mar first foal. *½* **59**
1088 **BEE KING 39** [5] 2-8-11 C Rutter 50/1: -00: In tch till appr fnl 1f: 10th, 6 wk abs: 10,000gns First *2½* **59**
Trump March foal, half-brother to sev wnrs up to 10f, dam & sire sprinters : with M Quinn.
-- **BY DEFINITION** [9] 2-8-3 N Pollard 7/1: 0: Went left start, nvr trbld ldrs: 11th, op 5/1 on debut, *½* **50**
v green: 12,000gns Definite Article April foal, half-sister to sev wnrs, sire 10/12f performer.
-- **LADY IN LOVE** [11] 2-8-0 W Supple 11/1: 0: Dwelt, al bhd: 12th, debut: 6,000gns Robellino March *5* **37**
foal, half-sister to a 5f winning juv, dam wnr in the States: with R Fahey.
12 ran Time 1m 15.99 (5.19) (Ernie Houghton) J S Moore East Garston, Berks

1839

2.45 STANLEY RACING HCAP 4YO+ 0-90 (C) 1m4f Good/Firm 27 -02 Slow [84]
£7182 £2210 £1105 £552

*1604 **HANNIBAL LAD** 10 [7] W M Brisbourne 4-8-11 (67) T G McLaughlin 4/1: 504211: 4 ch g Rock City - 75
Appealing (Star Appeal) In tch, imprvd entr str, led appr fnl 1f, pushed clr, rdly: earlier won at W'hampton &
Southwell (2 AW & 1 turf h'cap, rtd 80a): '99 wnr again at W'hampton (sell, rtd 66a, P Evans): eff at 11/12f:
acts on firm, gd grnd & f/sand: likes sharp or gall trk, esp Southwell: runs well fresh & is improving & tough.
779 **FATEHALKHAIR** 73 [1] B Ellison 8-8-4 (60) F Norton 7/1: 30-402: 8 ch g Kris - Midway Lady 3 63
(Alleged) Rear, hdwy 2f out, chsd wnr fnl 1f, no threat: op 11/2: unplcd over stks since 779, see 456.
+1518 **LEGAL LUNCH** 14 [4] P W Harris 5-9-1 (71)(bl) A Culhane 3/1 FAV: 205313: 5 b g Alleged - Dinner 1½ 72
Surprise (Lyphard) Led till appr fnl 1f, onepace: ran well tho' beat this wnr in 1st time blks in 1518.
633 **TAMING** 98 [2] I A Balding 4-9-10 (80) A McGlone 12/1: 3/1-04: Chsd ldrs, unable to quicken fnl 1f: ¾ 80
hdles rnr up for D Bridgewater 3 months ago (stys 2m on gd & gd/soft grnd, t strap): try further now? see 633.
809 **GREEN BOPPER** 70 [8] 7-8-11 (67) C Lowther 10/1: 342105: Well plcd & ev ch till rdn no extra 1¾ 65
appr fnl 1f: drifter from 7/1, 10 wk abs: gets a sharp 12f, drop back to 10f likely to suit, see 695.
1715 **JUST GIFTED** 5 [3] 4-8-10 (66) J Weaver 9/2: 05-206: Bhd, no room 3f out till appr fnl 1f, nvr dngrs. 1¾ 62
61518 **FAR AHEAD** 14 [6] 8-9-8 (78) T Williams 16/1: 021/07: Cl up till fdd appr fnl 1f: op 12/1: see see 1518. 3½ 71
779 **RAKEEB** 73 [5] 5-8-13 (69)(bl) P Goode (3) 9/2: 3D-148: Slowly into stride, chsd ldrs 5f out till 2f 10 52
out: op 3/1: btn twice over hdles, including at odds on, since 779, see 699 (C/D appr h'cap).
8 ran Time 2m 33.28 (3.48) (John Pugh) W M Brisbourne Great Ness, Shropshire

1840

3.20 COMERACING.CO.UK HCAP 3YO+ 0-80 (D) 7f str Good/Firm 27 -11 Slow [80]
£4719 £1452 £726 £363 3 yo rec 10lb

1250 **I CRIED FOR YOU** 30 [17] J G Given 5-9-9 (75) Dean McKeown 11/4 FAV: 0-1321: 5 b g Statoblest - 81
Fall Of The Hammer (Auction Ring) Mid div, prog & hung left appr fnl 1f, led below dist, rdn out: op 9/2:
earlier won at Lingfield (class stks): '99 wnr at Nottingham (class stks) & Windsor (h'cap, rtd 76): eff at 6f,
best arnd 7f: acts on firm & soft grnd, any trk: tried blnks/visor, prob best without: improving.
1483 **HYPERACTIVE** 16 [19] W H Brisbourne 4-9-2 (68) D O'Donohoe 9/1: 0/1-02: 4 b c Perugino - Hyannis ¾ 71
(Esprit Du Nord) Well plcd, led ent fnl 2f till ent fnl 1f, kept on but held: op 12/1: right back to form at
this faster surface: lightly raced, will win again soon: see 1483.
1158 **CUSIN** 35 [15] D Nicholls 4-9-5 (71) F Norton 16/1: 00-003: 4 ch g Arazi - Fairy Tern (Mill Reef) nk 73
Chsd ldrs, rdn towards well nr: ready to strike soon: see 926.
1483 **KARAMEG** 16 [5] P W Harris 4-9-12 (78) A Beech (5) 10/1: 515-04: Towards rear, not clr run & switched ¾ 78
right ent fnl 2f, styd on, unable to chall: ran to best, go close next time: see 1483.
1250 **TOPTON** 30 [16] 6-9-8 (74)(bl) R Mullen 10/1: 002005: Held up, rdn ent fnl 2f, kept on, nvr trbld ½ 73
ldrs: not far off best here, won this race last term off a 9lbs lower mark: see 463.
1490 **WEETMANS WEIGH** 15 [1] 7-9-6 (72) W Supple 16/1: 000046: Towards rear, wide, prog 2f out, rdn ¾ 70
& same pace inside fnl 1f: ran well from a poor low draw: see 448.
1590 **COOL TEMPER** 10 [9] 4-9-10 (76) J Tate 14/1: 2-5557: Chsd ldrs, eff appr fnl 1f, onepace: stays 7f. hd 74
1646 **DINAR** 8 [10] 5-7-10 (48)(5oh) K Dalgleish (7) 20/1: 0-3028: Front rank, no extra appr fnl 1f: stiff task. ½ 45
1520 **OUT OF SIGHT** 14 [21] 6-8-5 (57) N Pollard 20/1: 103009: At same pace: see 539. hd 54
1113 **HARD LINES** 38 [4] 4-9-4 (70) A McGlone 20/1: 1/0-00: Never better than mid div: 10th: not given 1 65
a hard time, op 14/1: worth another try at 7f: see 1113.
1383 **DOUBLE SPLENDOUR** 21 [12] 9-10-0 (80) S Finnamore (5) 33/1: 000-00: Slow away, not clr run 2f shd 75
out, nvr dngrs: 11th, top-weight: '99 reapp wnr at Newmarket (h'cap, rtd 89): '98 reapp wnr at Newmarket (rtd h'cap,
rtd 103): eff at 6f on firm & fast grnd, hndls soft & equitrack: likes Newmarket: nicely h'cappd bck at 6f.
*1579 **SMART PREDATOR** 11 [14] 4-9-7 (73) J Stack 12/1: 030310: Cl-up, led 3f out till over 1f out, fdd: 12th. hd 67
*1760 **MELODIAN** 3 [7] 5-9-2 (68)(6ex) D Mernagh (3) 8/1: 310410: Nvr trbld ldrs: 13th: btr 1760 (gd/soft). 1½ 59
1514 **REDOUBTABLE** 14 [6] 9-9-12 (78) A Culhane 25/1: 010000: Never a factor: 14th: see 1060. 1 67
1158 **ABERKEEN** 35 [11] 5-9-0 (66) J Weaver 8/1: 122120: Dwelt, bhd, not clr run 2f out, never in it: 17th. 0
1600 **PERTEMPS FC** 10 [22] 3-7-11 (59) Dale Gibson 25/1: 0-0000: Led till 3f out: 22nd, lngr trip, see 1412. 0
1300 Oriole 26 [13] 7-7-10 (48)(vis)(2oh) Kim Tinkler 33/1:
1652 Reachfouryourpocket 8 [2] 5-7-10 (48)(5oh) G Baker(7) 33/1:
1716 Infotec 5 [3] 3-8-13 (75) H Gind 20/1: 1330 April Ace 24 [18] 4-8-0 (52) R Brisland (5) 25/1:
1383 Jeffrey Anotherred 21 [20] 6-9-9 (75) T Williams 20/1: 1545 Regal Song 12 [8] 4-8-10 (62) O Pears 20/1:
22 ran Time 1m 25.84 (2.64) (One Stop Partnership) J G Given Willoughton, Lincs

1841

4.15 WORTHINGTON COND STKS 3YO+ 1m2f60y Good/Firm 27 +05 Fast
£6890 £2120 £1060 £530 3 yo rec 13lb

2967} **KING ADAM** 319 [1] Sir Michael Stoute 4-9-7 F Lynch 5/4 FAV: 1/16-1: 4 b c Fairy King - Sailor's Mate 113
(Shirley Heights) Held up, switched & smooth prog 2f out to lead dist, cleverly: gd time, val 3L+, hvly bckd on
reapp: '99 reapp wnr at Kempton (List, rtd 115), fin lame other start: '98 wnr at Goodwood (mdn, rtd 95+): eff
at 1m/10.3f, tried further & shld stay: acts on firm & gd/soft grnd, sharp/undul or gall trks: runs particularly
well fresh: v smart colt, can make up for lost time this Summer & win a Group race.
1574 **TISSIFER** 11 [2] M Johnston 4-9-0 A Culhane 9/2: 220-02: 4 b c Polish Precedent - Ingozi ¾ 104
(Warning) Held up, boxed in 3f out, clr & chsd wnr when rider dropped whip dist, kept on but al being held:
pulled clr of next & this was a v useful effort, apprec return to 10f: see 1574.
1311 **GARDEN SOCIETY** 25 [4] J A R Toller 3-8-4 R Ffrench 16/1: 133: 3 ch c Caerleon - Eurobird (Ela 4 101
Mana Mou) Early ldr, sn hmpd & mid div, rdn to chall 2f out, soon onepace: op 11/1: lightly rcd & progressive
colt: acts on fast & gd grnd: eff at 10f, nursery at 12f+ will suit: see 1157.
1248 **RAIN IN SPAIN** 30 [5] J Noseda 4-9-3 J Weaver 5/1: 13-324: Keen, led after 3f till appr fnl 1f, no extra. 1 100
*1481 **BINA RIDGE** 16 [3] 3-8-2(3ow) A McGlone 11/2: 15: Held up, shaken up & imprvd to chall 2f out, 1¾ 96
fdd dist: up in trip & grade after impressive gd/soft grnd debut in 1481 (fill mdn).
4497} **BASMAN** 229 [6] 6-9-0 J Stack 50/1: 40/5-6: Well plcd & ch till wknd appr fnl 1f: stiff task, 7 wk jmps 5 87
abs (rtd 126h): 5th sole '99 start (stks, rtd 79): 98/99 hdles wnr at Wincanton (mdn, 2m, gd & gd/soft, t-strap):
rtd 92 in '98, '97 Nottingham wnr: eff at 10/11.5f on gd & soft, prob handles fast: often wears a t strap.
6 ran Time 2m 0.66 (2.26) (Lord Weinstock) Sir Michael Stoute Newmarket

---

1842 4.50 COME BEHIND FILLIES HCAP 4YO+ 0-80 (D)   6f   Good/Firm 27 -04 Slow   [76]
　　　　　　£4485　£1380　£690　£345

1467 **CORNDAVON** 17 [3] M L W Bell 4-9-4 (66) J Mackay (7) 16/1: -20401: 4 b f Sheikh Albadou - Ferber's   81
Follies (Saratoga Six) Trkd ldrs, led appr fnl 1f, drifted right, qknd clr: '99 Warwick wnr (mdn, rtd 76, M F Godley):
plcd in '98 (nurs, rtd 77): stays 7f, apprec drop bck to 6f: acts on firm & gd, poss soft: quick follow up likely.
4267} **GLOWING** 248 [6] J R Fanshawe 5-9-12 (74) D O'Donohoe 12/1: 0110-2: 5 ro m Chillibang - Juliet   6 77
Bravo (Glow) Front rank, led after 3f till bef fnl 1f, outpcd: jt topweight, reapp: '99 wnr at Nottingham
(fill h'cap) & here Doncaster (h'cap, rtd 76): '98 Folkestone wnr (aution mdn, rtd 72): eff at 5/6f on firm,
gd/soft grnd, any track: runs well fresh, spot on next time.
1531 **ALMASI** 14 [22] C F Wall 8-9-12 (74) R Mullen 5/2 FAV: 030-53: 8 b m Petorius - Best Niece (Vaigly   1 74
Great) Held up, kept on well fnl 2f, nvr nr to chall: nicely bckd from 7/2: won this in '99 off same mark.
1680 **LUANSHYA** 7 [9] R M Whitaker 4-9-8 (70) Dean McKeown 16/1: 50-454: Prom rdn & unable to qckn dist. nk 69
1479 **PREMIUM PRINCESS** 16 [14] 5-8-4 (52) D Mernagh (3) 20/1: -00005: Bhd, not clr run after halfway,   ½ 50
styd on steadily fnl 2f, nvr dngrs: signs of a return to form back on fav grnd: well h'capped: see 802.
1479 **ANGEL HILL** 16 [10] 5-8-7 (55)(bl) A Culhane 10/1: -00006: Chsd ldrs, onepace appr fnl 1f: blnks.   1¼ 50
*1479 **BOLLIN ANN** 16 [13] 5-9-3 (65) J Weaver 11/2: 40-017: Mid-div thro'out: op 8/1, btr 1479 (5f, g/s).   1¾ 56
1519 **ARCHELLO** 14 [7] 6-8-4 (52) T Williams 16/1: 00-108: Prom till appr fnl 1f: best on reapp in 1258.   hd 43
1680 **MARY JANE** 7 [17] 5-8-2 (50) Kim Tinkler 33/1: 000009: Rear, not much room 2f out, styd on: see 844.   nk 40
3570} **SAFFRON** 290 [8] 4-8-9 (57) F Norton 25/1: 4000-0: Bhd, late prog into mid-div: 10th: unplcd in '99 for   ¾ 45
J Glover (fill h'cap, rtd 65): '98 Catterick wnr (nurs, rtd 77): eff at 7f, tried 1m on firm, soft & fibresand.
1297 **PERFECT PEACH** 26 [2] 5-9-5 (67) P Goode (3) 20/1: 0-0000: Wide, chsd ldrs till ent fnl 2f: 11th.   nk 54
1356 **DOMINELLE** 22 [1] 8-8-5 (53) W Supple 14/1: 00-000: Led 3f, grad wknd: 12th: '99 rnr up (fill h'cap,   ¾ 38
rtd 66): '98 wnr here at Doncaster (fill h'cap), Pontefract, Redcar & Ripon (h'caps, rtd 69): eff at 5/6f just
gets 7f: acts on firm & gd/soft, any trk, likes a stiff finish: best without blinks, well h'capped.
1606 **CARRIE POOTER** 10 [5] 4-9-1 (63) C Lowther 16/1: 160000: Al towards rear: 13th: see 698.   ½ 47
1806 **HEAVENLY MISS** 1 [19] 6-8-9 (57)(bl) K Dalgleish(7) 12/1: -41400: Chsd ldrs till 2f out: 14th, qck reapp. nk 40
1471 **EVENTUALITY** 17 [21] 4-9-3 (65) S Carson (5) 9/1: 46-500: Chsd ldrs till hung left 2f out: 20th, op 7/1.   0
1506 Petite Danseuse 15 [11] 6-7-10 (44)(4oh) Claire Bryan(5) 16/1:
1244 1244 Bow Peep 30 [12] 5-8-8 (56)(bl) G Parkin 14/1:
1412 Sounds Ace 21 [4] 4-8-3 (51) O Pears 25/1:　　　　4372} Turtles Rising 239 [16] 4-9-4 (66) A McCarthy(3) 25/1:
1391 Yabint El Sham 21 [18] 4-9-4 (66) N Pollard 25/1:　1356 Talaria 22 [15] 4-9-5 (67)(t) J Tate 14/1:
21 ran　　　Time 1m 12.64 (1.84)　　　(Anne Lady Scott)　　　M L W Bell Newmarket

---

1843 5.25 ST JOHN MDN 3YO+ (D)   5f   Good/Firm 27 -17 Slow
　　　　　　£4309　£1326　£663　£331   3 yo rec 7 lb

1280 **SHINBONE ALLEY** 28 [6] A Berry 3-9-0 G Carter 8/13 FAV: 205-51: 3 b c Lake Coniston - Villota   85
(Top Ville) Trkd ldrs, led appr fnl 1f, hard held: hvly bckd, any amount in hand, simple task: rnr up
twice & fifth in a Listed in '99 (rtd 95): eff at 5/6f on firm/fast grnd, any track.
1512 **PACIFIC PLACE** 15 [9] M Quinn 3-9-0 F Norton 7/1: 0-0242: 3 gr c College Chapel - Kaitlin   8 55
(Salmon Leap) Front rank & ev ch but easily outpcd appr fnl 1f: op 5/1, ran to best at these weights, see 1334.
1579 **THORNCLIFF FOX** 11 [10] J A Glover 3-9-0 (vis) O Pears 7/1: 0-0403: 3 ch g Foxhound - Godly Light   nk 54
(Vayrann) Led till appr fnl 1f, no extra: back in trip & different tactics with visor reapplied: see 1334.
1280 **NEEDWOOD TROOPER** 28 [5] B C Morgan 3-9-0 G Hind 7/1: 0-44: Well plcd till fdd appr fnl 1f.   1¼ 51
777 **LAMMOSKI** 73 [7] 3-9-0 Joanna Badger (7) 50/1: 005005: Never going pace: 10 week abs, stiff task.   nk 50
1688 **DUBAI NURSE** 7 [8] 6-9-2 (BL) Dean McKeown 16/1: 00-046: In tch till halfway: blnkd, op 33/1.   hd 45$
1525 **TRYSOR** 14 [4] 4-9-7 T G McLaughlin 33/1: 007: Al bhd: needs sell h'caps.   4 40
759 **NEWRYMAN** 74 [2] 5-9-7 T Lucas 66/1: 08: Al out the back: 11 week abs, highly tried.   18 10
1354 **TAWN AGAIN** 22 [3] 4-9-7 C Lowther 20/1: 6-09: Soon struggling: see 1354.   dist 0
9 ran　　　Time 1m 00.39 (2.19)　　　(J Hanson)　　　A Berry Cockerham, Lancs

---

1844 5.55 DERBY DAY AUCT MDN DIV 2 2YO (E)   6f   Good/Firm 27 -29 Slow
　　　　　　£3120　£960　£480　£240

-- **DOWN TO THE WOODS** [3] M Johnston 2-8-8 R Ffrench 2/1 FAV: 1: 2 ch c Woodman - Riviera Wonder   96+
(Batonnier) Made every yrd, pshd clr appr fnl 1f, rdly: well bckd: 18,000gns Jan foal, dam wnr in N America, sire
top class juv: eff at 6f on fast, 7f shld suit: goes well fresh on a gall trk: looks R Ascot material.
1568 **FRAST FOIL** 12 [9] M R Channon 2-8-0 Craig Williams 3/1: -32: 2 b f Lahib - Fast Chick (Henbit)   5 78
Mid div, rdn 2f out, styd on for 2nd, nvr nr wnr: stays 6f, handles fast & sft: caught a tartar, see 1568.
1488 **BIJAN** 15 [6] R Hollinshead 2-8-0 P M Quinn (3) 5/1: 53: 2 b f Muqaddamah - Alkariyh (Alydar)   1½ 74
Bmpd start, held up, wide prog to chse wnr briefly 2f out, same pace: tchd 7/1: shld win a fill mdn.
-- **LUNAR LEO** [7] S C Williams 2-8-5 G Faulkner (0) 20/1: 4: Keen, rear, imprvd 2f out, kept on onepce: 1½ 75
clr of next: 6,000gns Muhtarran Feb first gldg, dam a miler, sire 10f performer: 7f+ is going to suit, promising.
-- **HIDDEN LAKE** [11] 2-8-8 S Carson (5) 16/1: 5: Chsd ldrs, no extra 2f out: debut: 17,000gns Lake   5 66
Coniston Feb foal, dam a 12f wnr, sire a sprinter: with Mrs Bowlby.
-- **STRICTLY PLEASURE** [10] 2-8-5 D Mernagh (3) 25/1: 6: Never troubled ldrs, edged bck 2f out: 2 58
4,000gns Reprimand Feb foal, sire a sprinter/miler: with M Brittian.
1577 **CUMBRIAN HARMONY** 11 [1] 2-8-0 W Supple 4/1: 0237: Prom till 2f out: interesting in a seller.   1¾ 49
1429 **HENRY TUN** 19 [8] 2-8-5 T Lucas 10/1: 68: Handy till hung left appr fnl 1f: btr 1429 (5f).   3½ 46
1252 **KUMAKAWA** 29 [2] 2-8-5 V Halliday 33/1: -09: Chsd ldrs till fdd appr fnl 2f: 5,800gns Dancing   ½ 45
Spree March foal half-brother to a 7f wnr, sire & dam sprinters.
-- **MUJALINA** [4] 2-8-5 G Hind 25/1: 0: Dwelt, al bhd: 10th, IR 6,600gns Mujadil foal, dam 2m/hdles wnr.   1 42
1602 **FAST BUCK** 10 [5] 2-8-8 (BL) J Stack 33/1: 000: Green, well plcd till halfway: 11th, blinkered.   2 40
11 ran　　　Time 1m 14./16 (3.36)　　　(Miller/Richards Partnership)　　　M Johnston Middleham, N Yorks

EPSOM

SATURDAY JUNE 10TH   Lefthand, Very Sharp, Undulating Track

Official Going   GOOD (Good/Soft places first 3 races). Stalls: 5f - Stands Side; 6f - Outside; 12f - Centre; Rem - Inside.

1845

2.00 EDS HCAP 4YO+ (B)   1m2f   Good 46   +00 Fast   [107]
£29000   £11000   £5500   £2500

-1528 **SUPPLY AND DEMAND** 14 [14] J H M Gosden 6-8-11 (90)(bl) K Fallon 4/1 FAV: 6-0221: 6 b g Belmez -   101
Sipsi Fach (Prince Sabo) Hld up bhd, hdwy & not clr run over 2f out, strong run to lead appr fnl 1f, sprinted clr,
easily: plcd once for G L Moore in '99 (rtd 92): '98 wnr at Goodwood (h'cap, rtd 102, first time blnks): 97/98
hdles wnr at Newbury & Lingfield (rtd 117h): v eff at 10f on fast & soft, loves sharp/undul trks, esp Epsom:
eff with/without blnks: consistent & classy at times, but this was a useful & most convincing success.
  1375 **GENTLEMAN VENTURE** 22 [7] J Akehurst 4-7-13 (78) P Doe 14/1: 0-3642: 4 b g Polar Falcon - Our   7 78
Shirley (Shirley Heights) In tch, eff 2f out, kept on to take 2nd plce, no ch with impressive wnr: eff at
10/12f & knocking at the door: handles any trk: see 1375, 968.
-1656 **CHIEF MONARCH** 8 [6] R A Fahey 6-7-10 (75)(3oh) P Hanagan (6) 20/1: -25023: 6 b g Be My Chief -   1 74
American Beauty (Mill Reef) Bhd, eff over 2f out, kept on late, nrst fin: gd run, must be worth a try over 12f.
-- **HIMSELF** [4] H R A Cecil 5-8-11 (90) T Quinn 11/1: 6014-4: In tch, eff over 2f out, slightly short   shd 89
of room over 1f out, kept on same pace: in '99 trained by J Pease in France, won at St Cloud (stks): won fnl
2 '98 starts for current trainer back in '98, at Newcastle & Doncaster (h'caps, rtd 96): eff over 10.5f on fast,
gd grnd & likes a gall trk: useful, clearly still retains ability.
  1288 **GOODBYE GOLDSTONE** 26 [1] 4-7-10 (75)(4oh) P Fessey 16/1: 420-05: Cl-up, rdn & onepace final 2f.   2 71
  1217 **YAROB** 32 [12] 7-8-12 (91) O Peslier 9/1: 101026: Led till over 1f out, no extra: btr 1217.   4 82
  1373 **CHIEF CASHIER** 22 [13] 5-7-12 (76)(1ow) A Daly 16/1: 8-5007: Handy, rdn & wknd 2f out: likes soft.   ½ 67
  1342 **GOLCONDA** 23 [3] 4-8-8 (87) M Fenton 12/1: 60-308: Handy, btn over 2f out: twice below 1170.   shd 77
  1170 **JUST IN TIME** 35 [9] 5-8-12 (91) A Clark 10/1: -14149: Chsd ldr, wknd over 1f out: btr 1170, 874.   ¾ 80
*1498 **SHARP PLAY** 15 [8] 5-9-2 (95) M Hills 16/1: 163/10: Handy, rdn & wknd 2f out: 10th: btr 1498 (clmr).   shd 84
*1325 **LAFITE** 24 [2] 4-8-12 (91)(t) R Hills 10/1: 10-010: In tch, rdn when hmpd over 2f out, wknd: 1 78
11th, nicely bckd after wng 1324 (Listed fillies).
*1561 **NOBELIST** 12 [10] 5-9-10 (103) T E Durcan 9/1: 34/610: Al bhd, rdn & btn over 3f out: 12th: ½ 89
topweight & possibly not handle this trk: much btr in 1561.
  1561 **ANOTHER TIME** 12 [11] 8-8-3 (82) L Newman (5) 16/1: 00-050: Bhd, no impress final 3f: 13th, btr 1561.   ½ 67
  1561 **INTENSITY** 12 [5] 4-7-13 (78) G Bardwell 16/1: 1-5300: Nvr a factor, last: btr 1561, 1373.   10 51
14 ran   Time 2m 06.38 (2.58)   (Action Bloodstock)   J H M Gosden Manton, Wilts.

1846

2.30 LISTED WOODCOTE STKS 2YO (A)   6f rnd   Good 46   -29 Slow
£32500   £10000   £5000   £2500

  1367 **ATMOSPHERIC** 22 [8] P F I Cole 2-9-0 J Fortune 9/2: 121: 2 ch c Irish River - Magic Feeling   102
(Magical Wonder) Led after 1f, made rest, styd on strongly appr final 1f, rdn out: won debut at Pontefract (mdn):
Jan 1st foal, dam multiple mid-dist wnr: eff at 5/6f, further will suit: acts on gd, gd/soft & prob any trk:
has run well fresh: progressive & useful juv, should go in again a Group race.
  1586 **STREGONE** 11 [2] B J Meehan 2-9-0 Pat Eddery 9/1: -16522: 2 b g Namaqualand - Sabonis (The   1¼ 96
Minstrel) In tch, hdwy 2f out, styd on to chase wnr appr final 1f, kept on but al just held: enjoyed step up to
6f & further will suit: should land a nice prize on this form: see 1586, 743.
*1526 **TRIPLE BLUE** 14 [7] R Hannon 2-9-2 R Hughes 11/4 FAV: 113: 2 ch c Bluebird - Persian Tapestry   1½ 94
(Tap On Wood) Led wnr till appr final 1f, onepace: hvly bckd tho' ovr 2/1: ran to form of 1526 (3 rnrs, soft).
  1169 **ARMAGNAC** 35 [3] D Sasse 2-8-11 W Ryan 33/1: 64: Sn bhd, hdwy 2f out, kept on same pace ins last: 1¼ 85
enjoyed step up to 6f on this gd grnd & will win a mdn if reproducing this: see 1169.
  1522 **FIAMMA ROYALE** 14 [1] 2-8-6 L Newman 11/1: 4225: Handy, no extra appr fnl 1f: win a minor trk mdn.   hd 79
  1107 **SHUSH** 38 [5] 2-9-0 P Robinson 4/1: 156: Prom, rdn & btn 2f out: btr expected after 1107 (5f, gall trk).   1¾ 83
*1249 **DRESS CODE** 30 [4] 2-8-9 K Fallon 7/2: 317: Dwelt, bhd, rdn & btn over 1f out: find easier races.   nk 77
7 ran   Time 1m 11.13 (3.33)   (Highclere Thoroughbred Racing Ltd)   P F I Cole Whatcombe, Oxon.

1847

3.05 GR 3 VODAFONE DIOMED STKS 3YO+ (A)   1m114y rnd   Good 46   -02 Slow
£30000   £11500   £5750   £2750

-1402 **TRANS ISLAND** 21 [2] I A Balding 5-9-9 K Fallon 5/4 FAV: 13-221: 5 b h Selkirk - Khubza (Green Desert)   117
Set pace, hard rdn & briefly hdd over 1f out, rallied gamely to lead again & held on resolutely in a stirring fin:
hvly bckd: deserved Gr win after rnr-up in Gr 2 & Gr 1 earlier: '99 scorer at Leopardstown (h'cap), Newbury (Listed)
& Longchamp (Gr 2, rtd 118): '98 wnr at Capannelle (Gr 2, subs demoted): eff at 7f/sharp 8.5f on firm, likes gd/soft
& hvy & handles any trk, likes Newbury: loves to force the pace & runs well fresh: very smart, tough & genuine.
*1489 **DUCK ROW** 15 [3] J A R Toller 5-9-4 S Whitworth 4/1: 160-12: 5 ch g Diesis - Sunny Moment (Roberto)   hd 110
In tch, hdwy to lead over 1f out, hard rdn & hdd ins last, just held in a pulsating fin: stays 8.5f on any trk.
  1163 **RAMOOZ** 13 [6] J W Hills 7-9-7 R Hughes 11/1: 46-453: 7 b h Rambo Dancer - My Shafy (Rousillon)   2½ 109
Waited with, eff over 2f out, onepace, no dngr: nicely bckd: has won Gr 3 races at the Curragh in prev 3 seasons.
  137 **YAKAREEM** 192 [5] K Mahdi 4-9-4 J Fortune 25/1: 0000-4: Held up bhd, no impress over 2f out: 6 94
in '99 scored at W'hampton (stks, rtd 100a) & probably flattered when rtd 111S in this race (rnr-up): eff over
8.5/10f on firm, hvy & fibresand: has run well fresh on any trk.
  768 **FLY TO THE STARS** 77 [4] 6-9-11 C McCarron 2/1: 100-05: Chsd wnr till over 3f out, sn wknd: top-   ½ 100
weight, well bckd: tame run here: probably best on soft grnd on a gall trk: see 768.
5 ran   Time 1m 44.15 (2.35)   (Nagy Azar)   I A Balding Kingsclere, Hants.

1848

3.50 GR 1 VODAFONE DERBY STKS 3YO (A)   1m4f   Good 46   +10 Fast
£609000   £231000   £115500   £52500

*1314 **SINNDAR** 27 [15] J Oxx 3-9-0 (t) J Murtagh 7/1: 11-211: 3 b c Grand Lodge - Sinntara (Lashkari)   128
Cl-up, hdwy to chase wnr 2f out, styd on strongly over 1f out to lead ins last, drvn out: gd time, well bckd:
earlier won at Leopardstown (Gr 3, conceding weight): '99 wnr at the Curragh (2, incl Gr 1 National): eff at 1m,
stays 12f well on fast grnd: handles a sharp/undul & gall trk: wears a t-strap: most progressive, high-class
& genuine, set for an intriguing clash with Holding Court (impress French Derby wnr, soft grnd) in Irish Derby.
*1326 **SAKHEE** 24 [7] J L Dunlop 3-9-0 R Hills 4/1: 11-112: 3 b c Bahri - Thawakib (Sadler's Wells)   1 126
Al prom, went on over 3f out, styd on strongly for press till collared by wnr ins last, only btn 1L: hvly bckd:

600

tremendous run: stays 12f well on any trk: front two well clr of rem here & this top class colt can win a Gr 1.
*1151 **BEAT HOLLOW 36** [10] H R A Cecil 3-9-0 T Quinn 7/2 FAV: 1-13: 3 b c Sadler's Wells - Wemyss Bight (Dancing Brave) Keen, waited with, hdwy 4f out, slightly short of room over 2f out, kept on despite hanging left appr fnl 1f, not pace of front 2: hvly bckd tho' op 11/4: smart run & stays 12f, will reportedly drop back to 10f next time: only thrice rcd & open to improvement, esp on a more gall trk & should be plcd to win Gr races. 5 **120**
1326 **BEST OF THE BESTS 24** [3] Saeed bin Suroor 3-9-0 C McCarron 12/1: 312-34: Prom, left in lead after 5f till over 3f out, no extra over 1f out: up in trip & far from disgrcd: apprec step back to 10f in Gr 2/3. 4 **114**
*1168 **WELLBEING 35** [14] 3-9-0 W Ryan 7/1: 3-115: Prom, rdn & wknd over 1f out: well bckd, stablemate of 3rd: ran to form of 1168 in this top class contest & Listed company looks sure to suit: see 1168. 3 **110**
1340 **HATHA ANNA 23** [9] 3-9-0 K Darley 66/1: 56: Handy, rdn & btn 2f out: should stay 12f in lesser grade. ½ **109**
1451 **ST EXPEDIT 18** [4] 3-9-0 R Hughes 28/1: -20127: Handy travelling well, rdn & btn 2f out: lngr trip: reportedly will have a break now & will relish a return to Listed company as in 1451, see 1103. ½ **108**
1623 **BARATHEA GUEST 14** [6] 3-9-0 P Robinson 12/1: D-1348: Outpcd early, settled & hdwy when hmpd over 4f out, nvr dngr after: nicely bckd: lngr trip: things did not go his way today, could pay to forgive at 10f. 1½ **106**
1246 **ZYZ 30** [11] 3-9-0 J Fortune 100/1: 3-2339: Bhd, bmpd over 4f out, no impress: lngr trip, btr 1246. 2½ **102**
*1026 **ARISTOTLE 48** [8] 3-9-0 M J Kinane 5/1: 11-1D0: Handy, rdn & btn appr 2f out, eased appr final 1f: 10th, hvly bckd: better expected & something slightly amiss? veered badly & disq over 10.5f in 1026 (hvy). nk **102**
4136} **INCHLONAIG 256** [13] 3-9-0 Pat Eddery 16/1: 1-40: Held up rear, nvr a factor: 11th: 4th in Dubai back in Mar: won sole '99 start for R Charlton, at Newmarket (val stks, rtd 107+): eff at 7f, bred to stay arnd 1m/10f: has run well fresh on gd grnd & a gall trk: stablemate of 4th. 1½ **100**
1752 **BROCHE 6** [2] 3-9-0 C Soumillon 40/1: -00150: In tch, wknd over 3f out: 12th: see 1752. 7 **90**
1284 **GOING GLOBAL 28** [5] 3-9-0 J Reid 25/1: 1-1320: Al bhd: 13th: btr 1284 (gd/soft), 1056. ¾ **89**
*1510 **CRACOW 15** [16] 3-9-0 M Hills 66/1: 2-4310: Al bhd: 14th, needs h'caps, see 1510. hd **89**
1216 **KINGSCLERE 32** [12] 3-9-0 O Peslier 16/1: 23-150: Bolted to start, led & ran wide, hdd after 5f, wknd, t.o.: fin last: something amiss? much btr 1216, 996. *dist* **0**
15 ran Time 2m 36.75 (1.95) (H H Aga Khan) J Oxx Currabeg, Co Kildare.

1849

4.35 LISTED RTD DASH HCAP 3YO+ 0-110 (A) 5f str Good 46 +00 Fast [121]
£29000 £11000 £5500 £2500 3 yo rec 7 lb

3992} **ASTONISHED 266** [3] J E Hammond 4-9-2 (109) K Fallon 11/4 FAV: 110-11: 4 ch g Weldnaas - Indigo (Primo Dominie) Waited with, swtchd right & gd hdwy over 1f out, strong run ins last to get up cl-home, going away: hvly bckd, fair time: recently won at Cologne (Listed): in '99 scored at Deauville & impressive 4L wnr of Portland H'cap at Doncaster (rtd 116+): '98 wnr at Carlisle & Doncaster (nursery h'cap, with Mrs J Ramsden): eff at 5/6f on fast & soft, handles hvy: runs well fresh: v smart & given a fine ride here, should be plcd to win in Gr company. **113**
1566 **PROUD NATIVE 12** [1] D Nicholls 6-9-3 (110) O Peslier 7/1: 0-0022: 6 b g Imp Society - Karamana (Habitat) Handy, gd hdwy to lead over 1f out, rdn & collared cl-home, not btn far: fine run under joint top-weight in this smart contest & can win another Listed/Gr 3: see 1566, 1172. ¾ **111**
1172 **REPERTORY 35** [12] M S Saunders 7-8-10 (103) R Price 11/2: 43-003: 7 b g Anshan - Susie's Baby (Balidar) Led after 1f till over 1f out, onepcd: well bckd: ran well in this race prev & has speed to burn: useful. 1½ **100**
1529 **VITA SPERICOLATA 14** [11] J S Wainwright 3-8-2 (102) G Bardwell 8/1: 060-24: Sn rdn bhd, hdwy & short of room over 1f out, kept on ins last: would have gone closer without interference: tough, win a nice prize. nk **98+**
1172 **BISHOPS COURT 35** [13] 6-9-3 (110)(t) J Fortune 4/1: 311/05: Cl-up, eff to chall over 1f out, no extra ins last: owned by connections of wnr & landed this race 2 season's ago off an 8lb lower mark: useful. nk **105**
1090 **KASTAWAY 39** [5] 4-8-5 (98)(2ow)(15oh) Pat Eddery 25/1: 0/4-06: Hld up, late hdwy, nvr dngr: stiff task. 1 **90**
1687 **SINGSONG 7** [9] 3-7-10 (96)(7oh) P Fessey 14/1: 20-437: Bhd, eff & short of room over 1f out, onepace. *shd* **88**
1324 **DAMALIS 24** [7] 4-8-3 (96)(2oh) P Robinson 16/1: -46108: With ldrs till wknd appr final 1f: best 1245. ½ **87**
1245 **ALMATY 30** [4] 7-8-4 (97) K Darley 20/1: 03-009: In tch, eff & short of room over 1f out, wknd. 1½ **84**
1687 **JACKIES BABY 7** [6] 4-8-3 (96)(12oh) A Daly 33/1: 004540: Led 1f, wknd fnl 1f: 10th, stiff task: see 1687. 3 **75**
1453 **AFAAN 18** [2] 7-8-3 (96)(2oh)(bl) S Righton 16/1: 0-0640: In tch, btn over 1f out, 11th: btr 1453 (6f). 3½ **66**
4286} **TRAVESTY OF LAW 245** [8] 3-8-3 (103) J F Egan 20/1: 4050-0: In tch, wkng when hmpd over 1f out, eased: fin last on reapp: in '99 scored at Salisbury & Windsor (nov stks), also 2L 5th in a Gr 2 (rtd 100): speedy, eff arnd 5f on firm/fast grnd & on any trk. *shd* **73**
12 ran Time 55.59 (1.29) (D R Brotherton) J E Hammond France.

1850

5.10 VODAFONE INT'L RTD HCAP 4YO+ 0-105 (B) 1m4f Good 46 -08 Slow [111]
£29000 £11000 £5500 £2500

1484 **MURGHEM 16** [4] M Johnston 5-9-7 (104) R Hughes 9/1: -22421: 5 b h Common Grounds - Fabulous Pet (Somethingfabulous) Chsd clr ldr, went on over 1f out, held on well for press ins last under top weight: in '99 won at Sandown (h'cap, rtd 100, with B Hanbury): '98 scorer at Kempton (mdn, rtd 105): eff at 12f, stays 2m on firm, soft & fibresand: best up with/forcing the pace on any trk: has run well fresh & best without blnks: can carry big weights: smart, typically genuine & progressive M Johnston stayer. **110**
1307 **LIGNE GAGNANTE 25** [2] W J Haggas 4-8-7 (90)(2oh) J F Egan 6/1: 32-602: 4 b g Turtle Island - Lightino (Bustino) Cl-up, eff to chall appr fnl 1f, kept on, btn less than 1L: nicely bckd: fine run: useful & improving. ¾ **95**
*1342 **AMALIA 23** [1] P W Harris 4-9-6 (103) T Quinn 13/2: 0-0413: 4 b f Danehill - Cheviot Amble (Pennine Walk) Waited with, hdwy & slightly short of room 2f out, kept on over 1f out, nrst fin: nicely bckd: stays 12f well, go closer next time with a more positive ride: see 1342. ½ **107**
1484 **SALMON LADDER 16** [9] P F I Cole 8-8-13 (96) L Newman (5) 16/1: 33-404: Sn led, rdn & hdd over 1f out, onepace: tough & useful: see 732. 2 **97**
-- **HUDOOD** [8] 5-8-9 (92) T E Durcan 25/1: 1-1335: Waited with, hdwy 3f out, onepace over 1f out: prev trained in Dubai, 10f wnr: won again in Dubai in '99: eff at 1m/12f on gd, soft & dirt. nk **93**
1401 **MOWBRAY 21** [10] 5-9-3 (100) J Fortune 10/1: 305-56: Chsd ldrs, hung 3f out, no impress: btr 1401. 2 **98**
1307 **RADAS DAUGHTER 25** [6] 4-8-11 (94) K Fallon 3/1 FAV: 610-07: In tch, brief effort over 2f out, sn no impress & eased inside last: hvly bckd & more expected after promising in 1307. ¾ **91**
1217 **NIGHT VENTURE 32** [5] 4-8-7 (90)(1oh) J Reid 8/1: 06-108: Waited with, effort & no impress final 2f. ¾ **86**
*1695 **THREE GREEN LEAVES 7** [11] 4-8-7 (90)(1oh) R Hills 9/1: -00019: Handy, rdn & btn over 2f out: possibly too soon after 1695 (gall trk). ½ **85**
1187 **NAUTICAL STAR 34** [12] 5-8-8 (91) M Hills 12/1: 02-000: Cl-up, wknd 2f out: 10th: rnr-up thrice in '99 (rtd 96 when nk rnr-up in this race): '98 wnr at Newmarket & Epsom (h'caps, rtd 95): eff at 10/12f on fast & gd/soft & on any trk: has run well fresh & tried a visor, better without: best up with/forcing the pace: will do better when stable returns to form. 5 **79**
1187 **MARDANI 34** [3] 5-8-13 (96) M J Kinane 25/1: 20-000: Al bhd: stablemate of wnr: 11th, see 633. 5 **77**

EPSOM SATURDAY JUNE 10TH Lefthand, Very Sharp, Undulating Track

1401 **RAISE A PRINCE 21** [7] 7-8-13 (96)(t) N Callan 14/1: 3-5660: In tch, wknd over 2f out: 12th. 3½ 72
12 ran Time 2m 38.85 (4.04) (A Al-Rostamani) M Johnston Middleham, Nth Yorks.

1851 **5.45 DATA NETWORK HCAP 3YO+ 0-100 (C) 6f rnd Good 46 -04 Slow [96]**
£32500 £10000 £5000 £2500 3 yo rec 8 lb

*1676 **FIRE DOME 7** [14] Andrew Reid 8-8-12 (80) M Henry 11/1: 331111: 8 ch g Salt Dome - Penny Habit (Habitat) Handy, gd hdwy to lead appr fnl 1f, rdn clr ins last: 4 timer, earlier won at Redcar, Windsor (clmrs for D Nicholls, cost current connections £10,000) & Lingfield (h'cap, this trainer): '99 wnr at Sandown & Redcar (clmrs, rtd 83): '98 Thirsk & Sandown wnr (Listed, rtd 107): stays 7f, suited by 6f on firm, hvy or fibresand: handles any trk & can carry big weights: best without blnks: v tough, well h'capped on '98 form. 88
1533 **FURTHER OUTLOOK 14** [10] D Nicholls 6-9-13 (95) K Darley 11/2: 000532: 6 gr g Zilzal - Future Bright (Lyphard's Wish) With ldr, went on over 2f out till appr final 1f, not pace of wnr: nicely bckd: won this race by ½L from a 7lb lower mark last term & is clearly still improving & v tough: see 1533, 1337. 1¾ 97
1337 **ROYAL RESULT 23** [3] D Nicholls 7-9-5 (87) A Nicholls (3) 16/1: 0-0003: 7 b g Gone West - Norette (Northfields) In tch, hdwy over 2f out, kept on over 1f out, nrst fin: lesser fancied stablemate of rnr-up: looks poised to land another val h'cap: see 728. ½ 88
1337 **DELEGATE 23** [4] N A Callaghan 7-9-10 (92) Pat Eddery 8/1: 30-064: Sn bhd, kept on nicely over 1f out, nvr dngrs: nicely bckd: win a val sprint h'cap off this mark & looks sure to apprec a stiffer trk. 2½ 87
1324 **GET STUCK IN 24** [5] 4-8-13 (81) R Hills 10/1: 0-0605: Set pace till over 2f out, no extra 1f: gd run. 1½ 72
1283 **THE FUGATIVE 28** [7] 7-9-7 (89) M Tebbutt 15/2: 0-0456: In tch, effort well over 1f out, kept on inside last: likes Epsom, but high in the weights now: see 1028. hd 79
1778 **NOMORE MR NICEGUY 3** [15] 6-8-11 (79) J F Egan 16/1: 000027: Sn bhd, kept on late, nvr dngr: on a handy mark, interesting when stable returns to form, probably over 7f: see 1778 (Chester). nk 68
1383 **JUWWI 21** [8] 6-10-0 (96) Darren Williams (7) 12/1: 144158: Dwelt, sn well bhd, late gains, no dngr. ¾ 83
1471 **DEBBIES WARNING 17** [6] 4-9-10 (92) J Fortune 14/1: 0-0649: Sn bhd, nvr dngr: see 1471, 703. 1¾ 75
1694 **RUSSIAN FOX 7** [2] 3-9-0 (90) R Hughes 25/1: 1-0000: Prom, wknd 2f out: 10th: see 1028. 1 70
1533 **FIRST MAITE 14** [9] 7-10-0 (96)(bl) K Fallon 11/1: 446500: Al bhd: 11th, reportedly not handle trk. ½ 75
*1652 **ELMHURST BOY 8** [12] 4-8-10 (78) P Doe 14/1: 566010: Al bhd: 12th, btr 1652 (7f). shd 57
*1778 **SILCA BLANKA 3** [16] 8-9-7 (89)(5ex) J Reid 4/1 FAV: 0-1110: Handy, rdn & btn 2f out: 13th, hvly bckd: impressive in 1778 (7f) & this possibly came too sn. shd 67
1702 **ALASTAIR SMELLIE 6** [13] 4-9-1 (83) M Hills 20/1: 4-0050: Slow away & bhd, well held when not clr run over 1f out, eased: 14th: see 1173. ¾ 59
1564 **WAX LYRICAL 12** [17] 4-9-0 (82) P Robinson 20/1: 10-00: In tch, wknd qckly over 2f out: 15th, see 1564. 3 50
4093} **SURVEYOR 259** [11] 5-9-6 (88) R Morse 33/1: 5-00-0: Dwelt, al bhd, fin last: in '99 unplcd on 2 starts for J Dunlop (rtd 82): rtd 98 in '98: juv wnr at Lingfield & Kempton: eff at 6f on fast, soft/hvy & any trk. 1½ 52
16 ran Time 1m 09.63 (1.83) (A S Reid) Andrew Reid Mill Hill, London.

NEWMARKET SUNDAY JUNE 11TH Righthand, Stiff, Galloping Track

Official Going GOOD/FIRM. Stalls: Stands Side, except 12f - Far Side.

1852 **2.00 LADIES DERBY HCAP 4YO+ 0-60 (F) 1m4f Firm 05 -09 Slow [44]**
£5128 £1578 £789 £394

*1743 **MAY KING MAYHEM 5** [34] Mrs A L M King 7-9-9 (39)(bl)(4ex) Mrs C Williams 7/2 FAV: 6-6511: 7 ch g Great Commotion - Queen Ranavalona (Sure Blade) Prom halfway, led over 3f out & rdn clr dist, in command nr fin: hvly bckd: 4lb pen for recent Lingfield success (h'cap): '99 scorer at Leicester (appr h'cap) & Newmarket (this race, rtd 43): '98 scorer at Haydock & Pontefract (appr h'cap, rtd 43): all wins at 12f, stays 15f, acts on firm, gd/soft & handles fibresand, handles any trk, likes a gall one, esp Newmarket: tried a visor, suited by blnks. 45
1536 **FLETCHER 15** [36] H Morrison 6-10-9 (53) Mrs S Bosley 14/1: 000022: 6 b g Salse - Ballet Classique (Sadler's Wells) Held up, prog/chsd wnr 2f out, kept on but al held: op 16/1: v well h'capped for similar. ¾ 56
1819 **TAJAR 2** [25] T Keddy 8-9-4 (34) Mrs H Keddy (5) 25/1: -60003: 8 b g Slew O'Gold - Mashaarif (Mr Prospector) Held up, rdn & styd on fnl 2f, not pace of wnr: qck reapp: see 705. 1¾ 35
1647 **ZIGGY STARDUST 9** [13] Mrs A J Bowlby 5-9-4 (34) Mrs V Smart (4) 25/1: 244-34: Prom halfway, cl-up/ev ch 3f out, kept on onepace: see 1647 (clmr). 1½ 33
*1509 **BRIERY MEC 16** [30] 5-10-3 (47) Miss A L Hutchinson(7) 14/1: 33-015: Held up, prog halfway, held fnl 1f: op 12/1: stays 12f, best at 10f: handles firm & soft: see 1509 (10f, gd/soft). 3½ 41
1614 **NOSEY NATIVE 11** [17] 7-10-1 (45) Mrs L Pearce 7/1: 003226: Held up, rdn/late gains, no threat. 1½ 37
1551 **FANDANGO DREAM 13** [7] 4-9-1 (31) Mrs A Usher (5) 33/1: 0-0457: Held up, eff 3f out, held fnl 2f. nk 22
1615 **ACEBO LYONS 11** [23] 5-11-0 (58) Mrs J Powell (5) 20/1: -16658: Rear, late gains, nrst fin: see 705. 1 48
*1614 **ADMIRALS SECRET 11** [9] 11-10-7 (51) Miss H Webster (5) 12/1: 0-5019: Held up, mod gains fnl 3f. hd 40
1501 **TIME CAN TELL 16** [31] 6-10-1 (45) Miss S Talbot (7) 20/1: 513420: Mid-div, btn 2f out: 10th. ¾ 33
1819 **ACQUITTAL 2** [35] 8-10-0 (35)(vis)(9ow) Miss C Foster (0) 33/1: 000-00: Mid-div, held 2f out: 11th: qck reapp: plcd form in '99 (rtd 43, clmr): rnr-up in '98 (sell h'cap, rtd 36): '95 Musselburgh wnr (appr h'cap): eff at 10/12f on firm, hvy & fibresand: suited by visor/blnks. hd 31
1705 **ABLE PETE 7** [33] 4-9-2 (32) Miss C Hannaford (5) 16/1: 214600: Chsd ldrs 10f: 12th: op 25/1. ½ 18
1296 **SWINGING THE BLUES 27** [1] 6-10-12 (56) Miss Michelle Saunders(7) 33/1: 012-00: Rear, mod gains: 13th: '99 Redcar wnr (h'cap, rtd 56): rtd 93h over hdles in 98/99: '98 Flat wnr at Nottingham (h'cap) & Redcar (h'cap, rtd 68 at best): eff at 1m/9f, prob stays 10f: acts on firm & gd/soft, any trk: eff with/without a visor. 1½ 40
650 **RONQUISTA DOR 95** [32] 6-10-4 (48) Miss Diana Jones 20/1: 3-6040: Held up, btn 2f out: 14th: abs. nk 31
1353 **I CANT REMEMBER 23** [28] 6-10-10 (54) Mrs C Ford 20/1: 454050: Led/dsptd lead 9f, sn btn: 15th. ¾ 36
1614 **MEILLEUR 11** [22] 6-10-13 (57) Miss R Woodman (7) 12/1: 360630: Held up, eff 4f out, sn held: 16th. 3½ 38
1128 **MISTER PQ 38** [10] 4-9-10 (40) Marchioness Blandford(5) 25/1: 40-600: Mid-div at best: 17th: see 963. nk 16
1588 **AUDACITY 12** [19] 4-9-7 (37) Miss Elizabeth Neyens (7) 50/1: 500-50: Mid-div, btn 2f out: 18th. hd 12
1272 **RARE TALENT 30** [27] 6-10-12 (56) Miss S Samworth 20/1: 000-00: Mid-div, rdn/btn 2f out: 19th. hd 30
1736 **TUI 6** [15] 5-9-9 (39) Miss L Friend (7) 16/1: -51540: Held up, nvr land blow: 20th: op 14/1, qck reapp. 12
1509 **FULL EGALITE 16** [24] 4-9-13 (43) Miss L Sheen (5) 33/1: 00-000: Led after 5f till over 4f out: 30th. 0
889 **Count Frederick 60** [4] 4-10-1 (45) Miss Bridget Gatehouse(3) 50/1:
748 **Hawksbill Henry 76** [8] 6-9-10 (40) Mrs A Perrett 16/1:
1128 **Sea Danzig 38** [21] 7-10-8 (52) Miss R Illman (5) 33/1:

1501 **Whistling Dixie 16** [29] 4-10-0 (43) (1ow) Miss J Allison 14/1:
1614 **Alberkinnie 11** [11] 5-10-1 (45) Miss E Folkes (5) 33/1:
1499 **Needwood Mystic 16** [3] 5-10-1 (45) Miss S Phizackerlea (5) 33/1:
1546 **Sticks And Stones 13** [12] 8-9-8 (38) Mrs A Hvosief (5) 40/1:
1588 **Herbshan Dancer 12** [5] 6-9-5 (35) Mrs S Moore (5) 25/1:
1370 **Melvella 23** [2] 4-9-10 (40) Mrs S Eddery (5) 33/1:
1598 **Battle Warning 11** [6] 5-10-12 (56) Mrs A Hammond(7) 25/1:
1614 **Malchik 11** [18] 4-9-4 (34) Miss S Pocock (1) 40/1:   842 **Billichang 65** [26] 4-9-10 (40) Miss A Elsey 33/1:
--   **Lucy Tuffy** [20] 9-9-3 (33) Miss L McIntosh (7) 50/1:
34 ran   Time 2m 30.51 (1.71)   (S J Harrison)   Mrs A L M King Wilmcote, Warwickshire.

1853

2.35 BRECKLAND BINGO HCAP 3YO 0-95 (C)   1m str Firm 05 +06 Fast   [101]
£7377 £2270 £1130 £567

1341 **SIR FERBET 24** [1] B W Hills 3-8-10 (83) M Hills 11/2 JT FAV: -21001: 3 b c Mujadil - Mirabiliary (Crow)   **87**
Rdn chasing ldrs 3f out, switched & rdn/prog to lead well ins last, styd on well, rdn out: fast time: well bckd:
earlier scored at W'hampton (AW mdn, rtd 90a): plcd in '99 (rtd 89, mdn): suited by 1m, may get further: acts on
firm, gd & f/sand, has disapp on hvy: likes a stiff/gall or sharp trk: op to further improvement.
1366 **RED LETTER 23** [9] R Hannon 3-8-9 (82) R Hughes 12/1: 040-32: 3 b f Sir Pekan - Never Explain   1 **83**
(Fairy King) Bhd ldrs, chsd wnr well ins last, kept on well: op 10/1: stays 1m: acts on firm, fast & prob gd/soft.
1449 **NIGHT SIGHT 19** [7] G Wragg 3-8-12 (85) M Roberts 13/2: 00223: 3 b c Eagle Eyed - El Hamo (Search ½ **85**
For Gold) Handy, led 2f out, rdn/hdd well ins last & no extra: op 11/2: encouraging h'cap bow: see 1449.
*1435 **MAMZUG 20** [11] B Hanbury 3-8-6 (79) W Ryan 6/1: 0-414: Chsd ldrs, onepace fnl 2f: acts on 1¾ **76**
firm & fast: hcap debut, ran to form of latest: see 1435 (mdn).
1341 **SPIN A YARN 24** [6] J Reid 14/1: 41-005: Held up, eff 2f out, no impress: stablemate of wnr. hd **78**
957 **MONKEY BUSINESS 54** [5] 3-7-10 (69) J Mackay (7) 25/1: 34-06: Rdn/bhd early, prog when no room ¾ **64**
over 1f out, switched & styd on well ins last: abs, h'cap bow: unplcd in '99 (rtd 72): apprec 10f+ & similar company.
1598 **KELTIC BARD 11** [12] R Mullen 14/1: 10-007: Led halfway, hdd 2f out & sn held: see 1183. nk **67**
1535 **EL CURIOSO 15** [4] 3-9-7 (94) T Quinn 11/2 JT FAV: 4-0168: Chsd ldrs, held fnl 2f: see 1262 (7.5f). 1 **86**
1153 **ABUZAID 37** [10] 3-8-8 (81) W Supple 14/1: 01-009: Held up, eff 2f out, sn held: '99 Newcastle wnr 3 **67**
(mdn, made all): eff at 6f, 7f+ shld suit: acts on gd/soft & prob handles firm: likes stiff/gall trk & has run well fresh.
1366 **RISK FREE 23** [2] 3-8-12 (85) J Weaver 25/1: -42140: Cl-up, fdd over 1f out: 10th: btr 1366. 3 **65**
1535 **MICHELE MARIESCHI 15** [8] 3-9-5 (92) D Sweeney 33/1: 22-500: Led 4f, sn held: 13th: see 1347.   **0**
3989] Asturian Lady 267 [13] 3-9-7 (94) N Callan 25/1:   1183 Shotacross The Bow 35 [3] 3-8-3 (76) G Carter 12/1:
1164 Sorbett 36 [14] 3-9-5 (92) J Fortune 25/1:
14 ran   Time 1m 36.4 (u0.10)   (International Plywood plc & R Upton)   B W Hills Lambourn, Berks.

1854

3.10 LISTED FAIRWAY STKS 3YO (A)   1m2f Firm 05 -00 Slow
£6127 £3063 £1392 £696

1326 **SHAMROCK CITY 25** [5] P Howling 3-8-12 P Robinson 100/30: 1-6041: 3 b c Rock City - Actualite   **115**
(Polish Precedent) Made all, keen early, increased tempo 3f out, edged left & al holding rivals ins last, rdn out:
hvy bckd tho' op 11/4: '99 Doncaster wnr (mdn, rtd 101): eff at 1m, suited by 10f, 12f will suit: loves fast/
firm grnd & a stiff/gall trk: can force the pace: smart colt shld win a Gr 3, poss abroad.
*1404 **SUBTLE POWER 22** [1] H R A Cecil 3-8-12 T Quinn 11/8 FAV: 12: 3 b c Sadler's Wells - Mosaique Bleue 1½ **111**
(Shirley Heights) Trkd ldrs, outpcd 3f out, styd on well ins last, not pace of wnr: hvy bckd: step up to 12f will suit.
4398] **PORT VILA 239** [4] J H M Gosden 3-8-12 W Supple 10/1: 114-3: 3 b c Barathea - Girouette (Nodouble) nk **110**
Held up, eff/eff over 2f out, kept on onepace: op 8/1, reapp: won first 2 starts in '99, at Newbury (mdn) &
Kempton (stks), subs 4th of 5 in Gr 1 Dewhurst (rtd 108): eff at 7f, stays 10f well: acts on firm & fast.
1284 **TRUMPET SOUND 29** [3] L M Cumani 3-8-12 R Hughes 20/1: 4-104: Cl-up/keen, no extra fnl 1f. 2½ **106$**
1515 **CORNELIUS 15** [7] 3-8-12 J Fortune 12/1: 136-25: Pulled hard, handy, btn over 1f out: see 1515 (stks). 4 **100**
1340 **FAST TRACK 24** [8] 3-8-12 J Reid 5/1: 1-36: Rcd keenly bhd wnr, wknd over 1f out: bckd: btr 1340. 2 **97**
*1382 **CHAMPION LODGE 22** [6] 3-9-1 S Whitworth 12/1: -2117: Held up, eff 3f out, sn held: btr 1382 (1m). 5 **93**
7 ran   Time 2m 02.61 (0.51)   (Liam Sheridan)   P Howling Newmarket.

1855

3.40 EBF FILLIES HCAP 3YO 0-85 (D)   7f str Firm 05 -06 Slow   [89]
£7182 £2210 £1105 £552

1405 **TIME VALLY 22** [7] S Dow 3-8-3 (64) P Doe 6/1: 006-01: 3 ch f Timeless Times - Fort Vally (Belfort)   **72**
Held up in tch, switched right & rdn/prog to lead over 1f out, styd on strongly & rdn clr nr fin: op 5/1: rtd 74
in '99 (fill mdn): eff over a stiff/gall 7f, shld get 1m: acts on firm: first success, op t'further improvement.
4487] **LARITA 232** [6] J H M Gosden 3-9-6 (81) J Fortune 7/2 JT FAV: 310-2D: 3 ch f Arazi - Lypharita 2 **83**
(Lightning) Held up, hdwy when bmpd rival over 1f out, kept on ins last, nc with wnr: disqual & plcd last:
jockey given 5-day ban for irresponsible riding: nicely bckd tho' op 11/4: reapp: '99 Redcar wnr (fill mdn, rtd 88):
eff at 6/7f, 1m may suit: acts on firm & fast, prob handles soft: likes a stiff/gall track.
1632 **SANGRA 10** [4] N A Callaghan 3-8-4 (65) J Mackay (7) 7/2 JT FAV: 356-42: 3 b f El Gran Senor - Water 2 **63**
Song (Clever Trick) Handy, onepace from over 1f out: fin 3rd, plcd 2nd: well bckd: see 1632.
1569 **BAJAN BELLE 13** [8] M Johnston 3-8-11 (72) R Ffrench 9/1: -00403: Led/dsptd lead till over 1f out, 2 **66**
no extra: fin 4th, plcd 3rd: stays 7f, drop to 5/6f could suit: see 1289, 1138.
1289 **ALPHILDA 27** [2] 3-9-2 (77) M Hills 9/2: 0-0034: Bhd ldrs, eff/hmpd over 1f out, sn held: see 1289 (6f). 1 **69**
*54 **SAFARI BLUES 208** [5] 3-9-7 (82) Dane O'Neill 7/1: 5211-5: Prom, wknd over 1f out: 7 month abs. ½ **73**
1082 **DAWNS DANCER 40** [1] 3-8-5 (66) O Urbina 25/1: 342-06: Led/dsptd lead 5f, sn btn: 6 wk abs. 3 **51**
1649 **CULTURED PEARL 9** [3] 3-8-9 (70) D Sweeney 16/1: 5-3607: Cl-up, wkng/hmpd over 1f out: btr 1268. ¾ **54**
8 ran   Time 1m 23.98 (0.78)   (Mrs M Lingwood)   S Dow Epsom, Surrey.

1856

4.15 EBF FRANK BUTTERS FILLIES MDN 2YO (D)   6f Firm 05 -22 Slow
£5164 £1589 £794 £397

--   **MILLENIUM PRINCESS** [8] R Hannon 2-8-11 R Hughes 8/1: 1: 2 b f Eagle Eyed - Sopran Marida   **92**
(Darshaan) Led 2f, remained handy & led again dist, styd on strongly, rdn out: Mar foal, cost IR 20,000gns:
first foal, dam a wnr in Italy: eff at 6f, 7f+ will suit: acts on firm grnd & a stiff/gall trk: runs well
fresh: fine intro, likely to head for Royal Ascot & looks potentially useful.

-- **RASHAS REALM** [1] J L Dunlop 2-8-11 T Quinn 5/6 FAV: 2: 2 ch f Woodman - Performing Arts (The   2½   84
Minstrel) Dwelt, held up, switched & rdn to chase wnr over 1f out, al held: hvly bckd: Mar foal, cost 270,000gns:
half-sister to 3 juv wnrs: dam a useful miler: eff at 6f, 7f+ will suit: acts on firm grnd & a stiff/gall trk:
met a potentially useful rival & shld find a mdn on this evidence.
-- **BOIS DE CITRON** [2] R Hannon 2-8-11 Dane O'Neill 5/1: 3: 2 b f Woodman - Lemon Souffle (Salse)   nk   83
Held up, styd on fnl 2f, not pace to chall: op 4/1, shorter priced stablemate of wnr: Apr foal, cost Ffr 4,400,000:
half-sister to a useful 6f Irish juv: dam a won 5/7f juv scorer: eff at 6f, 7f+ will suit: acts on firm grnd.
-- **BOGUS PENNY** [4] S P C Woods 2-8-11 J Reid 20/1: 4: Rdn/rear, styd on well fnl 2f, nrst fin: op   2½   76+
14/1: Pennekamp filly, Mar foal, cost 38,000gns: half-sister to 2 juv wnrs: dam a 10f wnr: looks sure to relish 7f+.
-- **FADHAH** [9] J L Fortune 16/1: 5: Dwelt/held up, eff 2f out, sn held: Mukaddamah filly, Feb   1¼   73
foal, dam a 5f juv wnr: sire high-class 7f/1m performer: with L M Cumani.
1424 **SHIRLEY FONG** 20 [5] 2-8-11 N Callan 10/1: 06: Bhd ldrs, wknd 2f out: op 8/1: see 1424 (5f).   2½   66
-- **GUARDIA** [7] 2-8-11 G Carter 25/1: 7: Dwelt, al outpcd: Grand Lodge filly, Feb foal, half-sister to a   ¾   64
2m wnr: dam a 10f List wnr, sire top-class performer at 1m/10f: stablemate of rnr-up, apprec much further in time.
1372 **DANZA MONTANA** 23 [10] 2-8-11 W Ryan 10/1: 08: Led 4f out, rdn/hdd & wknd over 1f out: op 8/1.   ½   62
-- **MISTY DIAMOND** [3] 2-8-11 J Mackay (7) 33/1: 9: Dwelt, al outpcd rear: cheaply bght first foal.   1¼   59
-- **MI FAVORITA** [6] 2-8-11 P Robinson 14/1: 0: Prom 4f: 10th: op 10/1: Feb first foal, dam unrcd.   2½   52
10 ran   Time 1m 12.4 (1.6)   (Major A M Everett)   R Hannon East Everleigh, Wilts.

1857	**4.45 CECIL BOYD ROCHFORT MDN 3YO (D) 1m2f Firm 05 -49 Slow**
	£5027 £1547 £773 £386

1188 **MYNAH** 35 [4] A C Stewart 3-8-11 W Supple 33/1: 01: 3 b f Selkirk - Reyah (Young Generation)   86
Held up, rdn/hmpd 2f out, prog to lead ins last, styd on well, rdn out: slow time: apprec this step up to 10f,
12f shld suit: acts on firm grnd & a stiff/gall trk: círly going the right way.
-- **ZIBILENE** [6] L M Cumani 3-8-11 R Hughes 6/1: 2: 3 b f Rainbow Quest - Brocade (Habitat)   ½   84
Cl-up, ev ch fnl 2f, kept on well: op 8/1: debut: half-sister to top-class miler Barathea, dam a 7f/1m wnr: eff at
10f, 12f shld suit: acts on firm grnd & a stiff/gall trk: mdn a formality on this evidence.
1282 **PURPLE HEATHER** 29 [2] R Hannon 3-8-11 L Newman (5) 9/4: 42-253: 3 b f Rahy - Clear Attraction (Lear   nk   83
Fan) Trkd ldrs, hard rdn & kept on ins last, no extra: op 10/1: see 1127.
-- **SHAMAIEL** [5] C E Brittain 3-8-11 P Robinson 16/1: 4: Led, rdn/hdd over 1f out, kept on onepace: 1¾   81
op 12/1, debut: dam a useful 14f performer: eff at 10f, shld get further: handles firm grnd.
1428 **HATHEETHAH** 20 [7] 3-8-11 G Sparkes 33/1: 05: Held up, prog/led over 1f out, wandered & hdd   ¾   80
ins last, no extra: longer priced stablemate of rnr-up: see 1428.
1404 **RED EMPRESS** 22 [9] J Reid 1/1 FAV: 26: Bhd ldrs, keen, rdn/btn 1f out: hvly bckd: btr 1404.   3   76
4473} **TOWN GIRL** 233 [1] 3-8-11 (t) D Harrison 25/1: 0-7: Held up, rdn/btn over 3f out: reapp: rtd 59 on   5   69
sole '99 start (mdn): bred to apprec mid-dists this term.
-- **BEAU DUCHESS** [11] 3-8-11 M Roberts 25/1: 8: Held up, al rear: debut, with P W Harris.   5   62
1081 **BLAZING PEBBLES** 40 [8] 3-8-11 R Ffrench 66/1: 000009: Keen/prom, wknd over 2f out: 6 wk abs.   22   29$
9 ran   Time 2m 07.53 (5.43)   (Hamish Leslie-Melville & Lord Hartington)   A C Stewart Newmarket.

Official Going   GOOD TO SOFT. Stalls: Inside.

1858	**2.20 GORACING SELLER 3YO+ (E) 1m rnd Good 40 -12 Slow**
	£2873 £884 £442 £221 3yo rec 11lb

1207 **GODMERSHAM PARK** 34 [18] P S Felgate 8-9-8 K Darley 14/1: 414001: 8 b g Warrshan - Brown Velvet   45
(Mansingh) Trkd ldr, led 3f out, strongly pressed fnl 1f, just held, all out: no bid: op 12/1: earlier won at
Southwell (h'cap, rtd 51a): rnr-up in '99 (rtd 71a, h'cap): '98 wnr thrice at Southwell (h'caps) & also once at
W'hampton (h'cap, rtd 78a & 57): eff at 7f/1m on fast & gd, fibresand/Southwell specialist: best without vis/blnks.
1705 **JAMMIE DODGER** 7 [19] R M Whitaker 4-9-3 V Halliday 25/1: 0-0002: 4 b f Ardkinglass - Ling Lane   nk   39
(Slip Anchor) Handy, rdn/chall over 1f out, styd on well ins last, just held: see 1705.
1721 **NOBBY BARNES** 6 [17] Don Enrico Incisa 11-9-3 Kim Tinkler 16/1: 00-023: 11 b g Nordance - Loving   ¾   37
Doll (Godswalk) Towards rear, styd gains fnl 3f & took 3rd nr fin, not reach front pair: op 14/1: qck reapp.
1699 **CODICIL** 7 [10] M Dods 4-8-12 T Williams 12/1: 53-004: In tch, prog/ch over 1f out, no extra ins last.   1   30
1685 **MR CUBE** 8 [14] 10-9-3 (bl) D Watson 7) 11/1: 010435: Chsd ldrs, onepace fnl 2f: see 1336.   hd   35
1705 **OLLIES CHUCKLE** 7 [5] 5-9-3 A Culhane 7/1: -60066: Twds rear, kept on fnl 3f, no threat: see 908.   ½   34
1370 **COOL VIBES** 23 [3] 5-9-3 (VIS) R Fitzpatrick (3) 16/1: 05-007: Dwelt/rear, mod prog: op 14/1, visor.   ½   33
3049} **OTTERINGTON GIRL** 316 [15] 4-8-12 S Sanders 40/1: 0000-8: Chsd ldrs over 1f out, sn held: Flat   hd   28
reapp, 9 month jumps abs (no form): mod form on the level prev: prev with Miss S Hall, now with Mrs A Duffield.
1685 **DETROIT CITY** 8 [8] 5-9-3 M Fenton 7) 00-429: Mid-div, held 3f out: btr 1685, 1148 (7f).   nk   32
1081 **MINSTREL GEM** 40 [16] 3-8-6 J Bramhill 50/1: -00: Mid-div, btn 3f out: 10th: abs, longer 1m trip.   2   28
1707 **BODFARI SIGNET** 7 [20] 4-9-3 (bl) G Parkin 20/1: 000000: Led 5f, fdd: 11th: see 1190.   hd   28
1101 **BLOOMING AMAZING** 39 [2] 6-9-3 T G McLaughlin 10/1: 605050: In tch, rdn/btn over 1f out: 12th.   1½   25
1589} **JAY OWE TWO** 380 [12] 6-9-3 Dean McKeown 66/4 FAV: 2405-0: Chsd ldrs halfway, btn 2f out: 16th: 0
hvly bckd: reapp: rnr-up in '99 (rtd 78, h'cap): '98 scorer at Ayr (h'cap, rtd 79 at best) & W'hampton (AW h'cap,
rtd 81a): eff at 7f/8.5f on fast, hvy & fibresand: has run well fresh: eff with/without visor: handles any track.
800   **Four Men** 73 [1] 3-8-6 P Bradley (5) 20/1:   1699 **Toejam** [6] 7-9-3 G Duffield 14/1:
1699   **Hot Potato** 7 [9] 4-9-3 J McAuley (5) 25/1:   1689 **Ribble Princess** 8 [4] 5-8-12 (BL) F Lynch 14/1:
1353   **Rudcroft** 23 [7] 4-9-3 J Fanning 50/1:   1274 **The Republican** 29 [11] 3-8-6 N Kennedy 50/1:
19 ran   Time 1m 41.7 (4.2)   (P S Felgate)   P S Felgate Grimston, Leics.

1859	**2.55 CATHEDRAL MDN 2YO (D) 6f str Good 40 -26 Slow**
	£4273 £1315 £657 £328

1403 **ECOLOGY** 22 [5] J L Dunlop 2-9-0 K Darley 1/2 FAV: -21: 2 b c Sri Pekan - Ecco Mi (Priolo)   88
Sn handy, rdn/led over 1f out, hung right/in command nr fin, pushed out: hvly bckd at odds on: confirmed
promise of debut: eff at 6f, shld get further: acts on fast & gd grnd, sharpish/gall track: can improve.
1541 **QUEEN SPAIN** 15 [7] M R Channon 2-8-9 S Drowne 11/4: -022: 2 b f Mister Baileys - Excellus (Exceller)   2   75

Dwelt, sn in tch & led over 4f out, rdn/hdd over 1f out, held nr fin: well clr rem: acts on gd & soft grnd.

1503 **CIRCUIT LIFE 16** [1] A Berry 2-9-0 S Sanders 14/1: -053: 2 ch g Rainbows For Life - Alicedale (Trempolino) Chsd iront pair over 1f out, al held: op 14/1: see 1067.   7   60

-- **PERTEMPS THATCHER** [9] S C Williams 2-8-9 G Faulkner (3) 16/1: -4: In tch, held fnl 2f: Petong filly, May foal, 10,000gns 2yo: half-sister to 4 wnrs: dam unrcd: sire sprinter.   2   49

-- **ARJAY** [4] 2-9-0 C Lowther 20/1: -5: Dwelt/bhd, mod gains: Shaamit gelding, Apr foal, dam modest.   2½   48

-- **RED RIVER REBEL** [6] 2-9-0 O Pears 33/1: -6: Drvn/towards rear, mod gains: Inchinor colt, Apr foal, dam a dual 1m wnr: sire a smart high-class 7f performer: with J Norton.   nk   47

1550 **CHEVENING LODGE 13** [10] 2-9-0 D Hayes (7) 33/1: -467: Chsd ldrs, btn 2f out: btr 1095.   shd   47

974 **EURO IMPORT 53** [8] 2-9-0 F Norton 50/1: -008: Chsd ldrs 4f: 8 wk abs: see 974.   4   35

1130 **CELTIC LEGEND 38** [3] 2-8-9 T Williams 50/1: -09: Led early, btn 2f out: mod form.   1¼   26

1418 **TOBYTOO 20** [2] 2-9-0 R Fitzpatrick (3) 50/1: -00: Dwelt, al rear: 10th: no form.   11   0

10 ran   Time 1m 14.0 (4.0)   (Hesmonds Stud)   J L Dunlop Arundel, W.Sussex.

1860   **3.30 MIDDLEHAM HCAP 3YO+ 0-85 (D)   1m2f   Good 40 +09 Fast**   **[79]**
£4901 £1508 £754 £377

1561 **COLWAY RITZ 13** [9] W Storey 6-9-10 (75) T Williams 7/2: 0-0361: 6 b g Rudimentary - Million Heiress (Auction Ring) Held up, rdn/prog 3f out & led over 1f out, styd on well, rdn out: gd time: '99 scorer at Ripon (this race) & Redcar (2, h'caps, rtd 75): '98 Beverley scorer (h'cap, rtd 75): eff at 1m/12f, suited by 10f: acts on gd/soft, relishes gd & firm & likes Redcar/Ripon: gd weight carrier: tough & genuine performer.   81

1683 **FREEDOM QUEST 8** [2] B S Rothwell 5-8-7 (58) M Fenton 16/1: 434642: 5 b g Polish Patriot - Recherchee (Rainbow Quest) Towards rear, drvn & styd on fnl 2f, not pace of wnr: see 793.   ¾   61

1677 **ST HELENSFIELD 8** [5] M Johnston 5-10-0 (79) J Fanning 7/1: 4-0303: 5 ch g Kris - On Credit (No Pass No Sale) Handy, led over 3f out, rdn/hdd over 1f out, no extra: clr of rem: topweight: see 1518.   ¾   80

1683 **SHAFFISHAYES 8** [10] Mrs M Reveley 8-8-9 (60) A Culhane 7/1: 5-0654: Rear, drvn 3f out, styd on fnl 2f, no threat: slipped to a handy mark, 12f is ideal: see 943.   4   55

1762 **KHUCHN 4** [1] 4-8-1 (52) D Mernagh (3) 10/1: 505265: Keen, led after 2f till over 3f out, held fnl 2f.   hd   47

1150 **RINGSIDE JACK 37** [8] 4-9-5 (70) P Goode 10/1: 50-106: In tch, rdn/briefly no room 2f out, sn held.   3   60

3496} **KEWARRA 295** [7] 6-9-7 (72) K Dalgleish(7) 14/1: 0050-7: Bhd 3f out: Flat reapp, 4 month jumps abs (rnr-up, rtd 94h, mdn hdle): plcd on reapp on the level in '99 (B Millman, rtd 83, h'cap, subs disapp & tried in blnks): '98 Epsom wnr (reapp, rtd 93): eff at 7f, all 4 wins at 10f, tried 12f: acts on firm & soft: likes to dominate, handles any trk, likes Chepstow: has run well here: v well h'capped for A Streeter.   11   46

1658 **BRANDON MAGIC 9** [1] 7-7-11 (47)(1ow) F Norton 11/4 FAV: -0038: Keen, in tch, btn 2f out & eased fnl 1f: hvly bckd: longer 10f trip: see 497 (AW, 1m).   ½   21

1279 **HORMUZ 29** [6] 4-9-7 (72) K Darley 16/1: 50-009: Led 2f, ev ch 3f out, sn wknd & eased fnl 1f: '99 wnr for M Johnston at Lingfield (2, AW, mdn & h'cap, rtd 83a), Ripon (stks) & Beverley (h'cap, rtd 90): eff at 8.5f/10f on firm, gd/soft & equitrack, any trk, goes well fresh & likes to force the pace: with J M Bradley.   7   35

1790 **ROBZELDA 3** [4] 4-9-9 (74)(bl) F Lynch 15/2: 256440: Unruly stalls, chsd ldrs, drvn/btn 3f out, eased: 10th: qck reapp: blnks reapplied: too soon after 715.   17   12

10 ran   Time 2m 06.4 (3.1)   (Mrs M Tindale & Tom Park)   W Storey Muggleswick, Co.Durham.

1861   **4.00 TOTE TRIFECTA HCAP 3YO+ 0-90 (C)   5f str   Good 40 +12 Fast**   **[88]**
£7150 £2200 £1100 £550   3yo rec 7lb Majority racing far side - always just ahead.

+1580 **EASTERN TRUMPETER 12** [13] J M Bradley 4-8-10 (70) K Darley 7/2 FAV: 021111: 4 b c First Trump - Oriental Air (Taufan) Bhd ldrs far side, prog to lead ins last, held on gamely, drvn out: gd time: earlier scored at W'hampton (2, h'caps, rtd 72a), Carlisle (class stks), Lingfield & Redcar (h'caps): '99 Folkestone (clmr) & Ayr wnr (h'cap, rtd 70): all wins at 5f, stays 6f: acts on firm, soft & fibresand, handles any trk: most tough colt.   74

1662 **BRECONGILL LAD 9** [12] D Nicholls 8-9-2 (76) A Nicholls (3) 5/1: -30322: 8 b g Clantime - Chikala (Pitskelly) Trkd ldrs far side, rdn to chall wnr ins last, styd on well, just held: also just bhd wnr in 1580.   nk   78

1533 **HENRY HALL 15** [15] N Tinkler 4-9-11 (85) Kim Tinkler 12/1: 606003: 4 b c Common Grounds - Sovereign Grace (Standaan) Chsd ldrs far side, prog to chall ins last, just held nr fin: op 10/1: visor omitted after latest: turn not far away, a stiff 5f ideal: h'capped to win with similar effort: see 702.   hd   87

1714 **TORRENT 14** [14] D W Chapman 5-7-13 (59)(bl) D Mernagh (3) 12/1: 530444: Held up far side, briefly no room over 1f out, styd on strongly ins last, nrst fin: qck reapp: see 205.   shd   61

+1792 **LAGO DI VARANO 3** [6] 8-9-7 (81)(bl)(6ex) Dean McKeown 7/1: 035315: Prom stands side, led that group ins last, al just held by ldrs far side: qck reapp under a pen: not btn far on unfav'd side: see 205.   nk   82

1766 **NIFTY NORMAN 4** [2] 6-7-13 (59) N Kennedy 25/1: 346306: Led stands side 4f, kept on: qck reapp.   nk   59

1792 **DAAWE 3** [11] 9-8-12 (72)(bl) Clare Roche (7) 16/1: 610057: Prom far side, onepace fnl 1f: qck reapp.   nk   71

1533 **OCKER 15** [3] 6-9-13 (87) R Fitzpatrick (3) 25/1: 00-008: Chsd ldrs stands side, no ch to chall.   nk   85

-1792 **SHARP HAT 3** [8] K Dalgleish (7) 9/1: 244029: Bolted to start, prom far side 4f: qck reapp: ran away with apprentice jockey in preliminaries, prob needs stronger handling: see 91 (AW).   ½   55

1806 **WHIZZ KID 2** [10] 6-8-7 (67) S Drowne 14/1: 231260: Rear far side, nvr on terms: 10th: qck reapp.   ½   63

1591 **SUPREME ANGEL 11** [4] 5-8-7 (67) T G McLaughlin 10/1: 401350: Rear stds side, nvr on terms: 11th.   ½   62

1357 **ANTONIAS DOUBLE 23** [1] 5-9-0 (74) P Fessey (7) 10/1: 10-500: Stds side, nvr factor: 12th: see 751.   ¾   66

1580 **SEVEN OF SPADES 12** [16] 3-7-11 (64) P Hanagan(4) 16/1: 035-00: Dwelt/rear far side, nvr factor: 13th.   nk   55

3075} **ATLANTIC VIKING 314** [7] 5-10-0 (88) F Norton 16/1: 0141-0: Led till ins last, wknd: 14th: op 14/1, reapp: '99 wnr at Pontefract (h'cap) & here at Ripon (rtd h'cap): plcd in '98 (rtd 91, M Johnston): eff at 5/6f, stays 7f: acts on firm & gd/soft, any trk: blnks reapplied to win/force the pace: eff with/without blnks.   ½   78

1533 **UNSHAKEN 15** [9] 6-8-11 (71) S Sanders 8/1: 024000: Far side, nvr near to chall: 15th: worth another chance when stable returns to form (no wins from last 50 runners) & needs 6f: see 1533.   1¼   57

1264 **THAT MAN AGAIN 30** [5] 8-8-10 (70)(bl) G Faulkner (3) 25/1: 0-0000: Al bhd stds side: 16th: see 1264.   7   36

16 ran   Time 59.2 (1.4)   (R G G Racing)   J M Bradley Sedbury, Gloucs.

1862   **4.35 GARDEN HCAP 3YO 0-85 (D)   1m4f60y   Good 40 -05 Slow**   **[89]**
£4784 £1472 £736 £368

1425 **INCA STAR 20** [4] M Johnston 3-9-7 (82) R Winston 9/4 JT FAV: -56121: 3 b c Trempolino - Inca Empress (Sovereign Dancer) Cl-up till wknd 4f out, strongly pressed 2f out, styd on strongly & drvn clr ins last: earlier won at Hamilton (med auct mdn): rtd 85 when plcd sole juv start: apprec recent step up to 12f, 14f shld suit: acts on fast or gd/soft grnd: in fine form & on the up-grade, win again.   86

1585 **UNDER THE SAND 12** [1] M A Jarvis 3-8-7 (68) M Tebbutt 9/4 JT FAV: -00042: 3 b c Turtle Island -   2½   67

Occupation (Homing) Waited with, gd hdwy to chall wnr 2f out, ev ch till fdd ins last: nicely bckd, up in trip: prob styd this longer 12f trip: see 1585, 1261.

1581 **PTAH 12** [3] J L Eyre 3-7-10 (57)(4oh) D Mernagh (3) 5/1: 004323: 3 b g Petardia - Davenport Goddess 1 54$
(Classic Secret) Cl-up, rdn to chall 3f out, sn outpcd, late gains ins last: fair eff, will apprec return to 14f+.

1491 **MICKLEY 16** [6] J D Bethell 3-9-1 (76) K Darley 5/1: 00-254: Mid-div, rdn/prog 3f out, kept on, no threat. 1½ 71

1064 **NAJJM 41** [6] 3-9-2 (77) S Sanders 9/1: 233-65: Rear, rdn/prog 4f out, onepcd fnl 2f: see 1064. 1¾ 70

1581 **SMUDGER SMITH 12** [5] 3-8-2 (63) J Bramhill 12/1: 0-0346: Led to 4f out, wknd: see 1581, 1446. 2½ 52

1502 **WINDMILL LANE 16** [2] 3-7-11 (58)(VIS) Joanna Badger (7) 20/1: 5-2637: Rcd keenly in rear, rdn 8 35
/lost tch appr fnl 3f: 1st time visor: see 1502.

7 ran   Time 2m 39.1 (5.6)   (Jaber Abdullah)   M Johnston Middleham, N.Yorks.

1863
5.05 GO SUNDAY RACING MDN 3YO (D)   1m1f   Good 40   -05 Slow
£4257   £1310   £655   £327

1386 **ARANYI 22** [2] J L Dunlop 3-9-0 K Darley 1/1 FAV: 44-541: 3 gr c El Gran Senor - Heather's It (Believe It) 83
Cl-up, rdn to lead appr fnl 1f, styd on strongly ins last, drvn out: well bckd: rtd 92 at best when 4th on 2nd of 3 juv starts: eff at 9/10f, further could suit: acts on gd & gd/soft, sharpish or gall trks: on the up-grade.

1655 **TAKAMAKA BAY 9** [6] M Johnston 3-9-0 J Fanning 3/1: -22: 3 ch c Unfuwain - Stay Sharpe (Sharpen nk 82
Up) Led, hdd appr fnl 1f, rall ins last, just failed: well clr of rem: gd run, eff at 9/10f on fast & gd: win sn.

1344 **NO FRILLS 24** [5] Sir Michael Stoute 3-8-9 F Lynch 4/1: -63: 3 b f Darshaan - Bubbling Danseuse 8 64
(Arctic Tern) Mid-div, rdn to chase ldrs 2f out, sn outpcd: see 1344.

--   **PIES AR US** [3] C W Fairhurst 3-9-0 P Goode (3) 40/1: -4: Handy, rdn/lost tch over 4f: Perpendicular 9 53
gelding, half-brother to a winning stayer: may apprec further given time.

--   **FREE WILL** [7] 3-9-0 M Fenton 7/1: -5: Dwelt, bhd, no threat: half-brother to a 12f scorer. 4 46

1444 **FLOW BEAU 19** [8] 3-8-9 T G McLaughlin 66/1: -406: Dwelt, al bhd: up in trip: see 1134. ½ 40

1051 **EXHIBITION GIRL 43** [1] 3-8-9 P Fessey 14/1: -57: Prom, lost tch fnl 3f, fin last: 6 wk abs: see 1051. nk 39

7 ran   Time 1m 54.1 (4.1)   (Benny Andersson)   J L Dunlop Arundel, W.Sussex.

Official Going   Stalls: Inside, except 2m1f - Centre

1864
6.55 SYCAMORE FILLIES AUCT MDN 2YO (E)   6f rnd   Good 40   -13 Slow
£3737   £1150   £575   £287

1130 **SHINNER 39** [6] T D Easterby 2-8-0 W Supple 4/1: 421: 2 b f Charnwood Forest - Trick (Shirley Heights) 69
Chsd ldrs, rdn/led over 1f out, held on well nr fin, rdn out: nicely bckd: dam 10f: apprec this step up to 6f, 7f will suit: acts on gd & gd/soft grnd, stiff/undul or gall track.

1413 **MERIDEN MIST 23** [14] P W Harris 2-8-4 K Darley 9/2: 52: 2 b f Distinctly North - Bring On The Choir 1 70
(Chief Singer) Cl-up, rdn/led over 2f out till over 1f out, not pace of wnr: bckd, op 5/1: acts on gd: see 1413.

1312 **TEDDY BEAR 27** [7] R A Fahey 2-8-2 R Winston 3/1 FAV: 63: 2 b f Grand Lodge - Boristova (Royal shd 68
Academy) Chsd ldrs, styd on despite hanging left fnl 2f, closing well nr line, not given hard time: hvly bckd tho' op 2/1: acts on gd grnd: will improve & shld find similar, 7f sure to suit: see 1312.

--   **CAVERNARA** [8] T D Barron 2-8-0 P Fessey 20/1: 4: Held up, styd on held fnl 2f, no threat to front trio: 3 59+
op 16/1: Lion Cavern filly, May foal, cost 1,000gns: half-sister to a 5f juv wnr: dam lightly rcd: sire smart 6/7f wnr: stays 6f, 7f sure to suit: handles gd: eyecatching introduction & can rate more highly.

1698 **HARD TO LAY 8** [2] 2-8-2 G Carter 11/2: 25: Cl-up till over 1f out: bckd: btr 1698 (5f, soft). 1 59

904 **EASTERN RED 59** [10] 2-8-0 Iona Wands 50/1: -056: Mid-div, held over 1f out: abs: longer 6f trip. 1½ 53

1492 **CATCH THE CHRON 17** [3] 2-8-0 Kim Tinkler 10/1: 27: Dwelt, sn mid-div, held over 1f out: op 8/1. 1¼ 51

--   **PICTURE MEE** [4] 2-8-0 R Ffrench 20/1: 8: Rear/rdn halfway, late gains, no threat: op 25/1: Aragon 1¼ 48
filly, Feb foal, cost 2,200gns: half-sister to a 5f juv wnr, dam a 5f juv wnr: sire high-class 7f/1m performer.

974 **SLIPPER ROSE 54** [17] 2-8-0 P M Quinn (3) 20/1: -439: Chsd ldrs till over 1f out: abs: see 730. 1¼ 45

--   **STRATH FILLAN** [11] 2-8-2(2ow) L Newton 25/1: 0: Dwelt, rear, mod gains: 10th: Dolphin Street hd 46
filly, Feb foal, cost 2,200gns: dam a wnr abroad: sire top-class 6/7f performer: with W Musson.

1488 **KALUGA 17** [9] 2-8-0 F Norton 9/1: 00: In tch 4f: 11th: see 1488. ½ 42

1538 **MISS BEADY 16** [1] 2-8-4 J Carroll 20/1: 00: Led till over 2f out, wknd: 15th: op 33/1: mod form. 0

1577 **Somethingaboutmary 13** [12] 2-8-2 J McAuley (5) 50/1: 1577 **Royal Musical 13** [13] 2-8-2 T Williams 25/1:

--   **Light Of Aragon** [15] 2-8-1(1ow) J Fanning 25/1:   1476 **I Got Rhythm 18** [16] 2-8-0 D Mernagh (3) 33/1:

16 ran   Time 1m 17.3 (3.2)   (Sandal Racing)   T D Easterby Great Habton, N.Yorks.

1865
7.25 BEECH SELLER 3YO (F)   1m rnd   Good 40   -05 Slow
£2478   £708   £354

*1644 **PERFECT MOMENT 10** [3] G M McCourt 3-9-1 K Fallon 11/8 FAV: -04211: 3 b f Mujadil - Flashing Raven 63
(Maelstrom Lake) Sn handy, led over 1f out & sn readily pulled clr under hands & heels riding, eased nr line: val 8L+: well bckd, op 2/1: recent Nottingham wnr (sell h'cap): '99 Leicester wnr (auct mdn, A Jarvis, rtd 74): suited by 1m/10f on fast & soft, stiff/undul or gall trk: relishes selling grade.

1596 **DOLFINESSE 12** [10] M Brittain 3-8-9 (VIS) D Mernagh (3) 8/1: 50-052: 3 ch f Dolphin Street - 6 48$
Gortadoo (Sharpen Up) Led till over 1f out, sn held by easy wnr: op 7/1, first time visor: see 1596.

1804 **RED SONNY 3** [13] A Berry 3-9-0 P Bradley (5) 16/1: 040023: 3 ch g Foxhound - Olivia's Pride 1¾ 48$
(Digamist) Held up, prog to chall over 1f out, sn outpcd by wnr: op 14/1, qck reapp: see 1804, 1081.

1822 **PIX ME UP 3** [2] K A Ryan 3-9-1 Iona Wands (5) 7/2: 000124: In tch 2f out, sn onepace: op 3/1. nk 48

1731 **A BOB LIGHT 7** [9] 3-8-9 A Whelan (5) 9/1: 50-065: Chsd ldrs, held over 1f out: see 1731. 3 36

--   **RUNAWAY STAR** [8] 3-8-9 L Newton 33/1: 6: Held up, mod gains: debut, with W J Musson. ¾ 35

1644 **SKELTON MONARCH 10** [1] 3-9-0 P M Quinn (3) 20/1: -66307: Held up, nvr a threat: see 1035. 1 38

1505 **DINKY 17** [14] 3-8-9 P McCabe 100/1: 000-08: Rdn in rear halfway, no impress: no form. 3 27$

1596 **MOUNTRATH ROCK 12** [6] 3-8-9 (BL) Kim Tinkler 12/1: 000449: Dwelt/keen, mid-div, btn 2f out: blnks. ½ 26

1274 **THREEFORTYCASH 30** [7] 3-9-0 P Fessey 20/1: 450006: Cl-up till over 1f out: 10th: see 427. 6 22

1596 **Soloist 12** [12] 3-9-0 J F Egan 33/1:   1480 **Ripple 18** [5] 3-8-9 A Culhane 33/1:

3774} **Double Style 282** [11] 3-9-0 R Lappin 33/1:   1578 **Epona 13** [4] 3-8-9 K Darley 20/1:

14 ran   Time 1m 45.4 (3.6)   (Christopher Shankland)   G M McCourt Letcombe Regis, Oxon.

1866

7.55 WILLOW HCAP 3YO 0-80 (D)　　1m2f　　Good 40　-05 Slow　　[83]
£7345　£2260　£1130　£565

1560 **WASEEM** 14 [10] M Johnston 3-9-1 (70) J Fanning 6/1: -10021: 3 c ch Polar Falcon - Astolat (Rusticaro)　76
Made all, strongly pressed ins last, rdn & held on gamely cl-home: earlier scored at W'hampton (7f AW mdn, rtd 68a):
suited by front running at 10/11f, may get further: acts on gd, gd/soft & fibresand, sharp or stiff/gall trk.
1532 **RUM PUNCH** 16 [8] Sir Michael Stoute 3-9-4 (73)(t) K Fallon 11/4 JT FAV: 0-002: 3 b c Shirley　　nk　78
Heights - Gentle Persuasion (Bustino) Keen, held up, prog to chall fnl 1f, rdn/styd on well, just held nr fin:
apprec this step up to 10f on h'cap bow: acts on gd grnd.
936 **JUDICIOUS** 56 [11] G Wragg 3-8-13 (68) M Roberts 11/4 JT FAV: 00-03: 3 b c Fairy King - Kama Tashoof　2　70
(Mtoto) Dwelt, prog to chall 1f out, not pace of front pair ins last: 8 wk abs, gd h'cap bow: eff at 10f on gd grnd.
*1560 **RHODAMINE** 14 [7] J L Eyre 3-8-13 (68) F Norton 9/1: 042614: Dwelt, bhd, kept on fnl 2f, not　　2½　66
able to chall: apprec a return to further: see 1560.
1435 **BRISBANE ROAD** 21 [5] 3-8-7 (62)(t) K Darley 7/1: 00-45: Prom, onepace fnl 2f: h'cap bow: see 1435.　nk　59
1535 **ROYAL CAVALIER** 16 [9] 3-9-7 (76) P M Quinn (3) 25/1: 410006: Held up, eff 3f out, sn held: see 720.　4　67
*1548 **WELCOME ABOARD** 14 [6] 3-9-3 (72) Dean McKeown 10/1: -3017: Cl-up till over 1f out: see 1548 (1m).　1½　61
1104 **ALLEGRESSE** 40 [3] 3-9-6 (75) W Supple (5) 16-358: Prom 1m: 6 wk abs: btr 745 (1m, fast).　7　54
1569 **SLICK WILLIE** 14 [1] 3-8-13 (68) J Carroll 25/1: 2-0009: Held up, no impress: longer 10f trip: see 736.　½　46
1448 **TOP HAND** 20 [2] 3-9-3 (72) G Carter 17/2: 61-400: Chsd wnr, wknd 3f out: 10th: btr 999 (9f, soft).　10　39
10 ran　　Time 2m 13.1 (5.0)　　　(A Al-Rostamani)　　　M Johnston Middleham, N.Yorks.

1867

8.25 TONY BETHELL HCAP 4YO+ 0-70 (E)　　2m1f22y　Good 40　-24 Slow　　[67]
£3575　£1100　£550　£275　4 yo rec 1 lb

1478 **KAGOSHIMA** 18 [9] J Norton 5-8-6 (45)(vis) O Pears 7/1: 5-0231: 5 b g Shirley Heights - Kashteh　　53
(Green Desert) Handy, led 2f out, styd on strongly ins last, rdn out: unplcd in '99 (rtd 53): rtd 78 on sole '98
start for L Cumani (mdn): eff at 2m/2m1f, marathon trips may suit: acts on firm & gd/soft grnd, likes a stiff/gall
trk: suited by a visor: consistent colt, deserved this first success.
548 **BAISSE DARGENT** 114 [12] D J S Cosgrove 4-8-10 (50) J F Egan 11/1: 0-3232: 4 b g Common Grounds -3　54
Fabulous Pet (Somethingfabulous) In tch, rdn to chase wnr fnl 1f, kept on but al held: 4 month abs: gd run.
1597 **SPA LANE** 12 [3] Mrs S Lamyman 7-8-4 (43) F Norton 6/1: -51433: 7 ch g Presidium - Sleekit (Blakeney) 2½　45
Chsd ldrs, rdn/led over 4f out till over 2f out, onepace/held ins last: in fine form tho' ahd of this wnr in 1276.
*1597 **KEEP IKIS** 12 [8] Mrs M Reveley 6-8-7 (46) D Mernagh (3) 5/2 FAV: 023-14: Held up, rdn & kept on　　¾　47
fnl 2f, not pace to chall: see 1597.
*1701 **LEDGENDRY LINE** 8 [5] 7-9-4 (57) A Culhane 6/1: -56415: Held up, prog to chall 2f out, sn no extra.　1　57
*1563 **HIGHFIELD FIZZ** 14 [4] 8-8-3 (42) T Williams 12/1: 0P0016: Chsd ldrs halfway, held fnl 2f: btr 1563 (14f).　½　41
1478 **OLD HUSH WING** 18 [11] 7-8-6 (45) Dale Gibson 20/1: 560007: Led 5f, handy till wknd over 1f out.　1¼　43
1701 **YES KEEMO SABEE** 8 [2] 5-9-1 (54) L Newton 14/1: 000008: Held up, eff 2f out, no impress: vis omitted.　3　49
1416 **HETRA HEIGHTS** 21 [13] 5-7-10 (35)(3oh) A McCarthy (3) 14/1: 611039: Al rear: btr 644 (AW).　3　27
*940 **IMAD** 56 [7] 10-8-12 (51)(t) T G McLaughlin 14/1: 1-3410: In tch, outpcd fnl 3f: 10th: btr 940 (hvy).　hd　43
1701 **BLACK ICE BOY** 8 [10] 9-8-5 (44)(vis) Dean McKeown 14/1: 000040: Led after 5f till 4f out, sn btn: 11th.　nk　35
4397} Salska 240 [6] 9-10-0 (67) G Bardwell 20/1:　　1657 Santa Lucia 10 [1] 4-9-3 (57) A Clark 40/1:
13 ran　　Time 3m 51.22 (10.92)　　　(Keep On Running)　　　J Norton High Hoyland, S Yorks

1868

8.55 CEDAR CLASSIFIED STKS 3YO+ 0-65 (E)　　5f rnd　Good 40　+06 Fast
£2899　£892　£446　£223　3 yo rec 7 lb

1357 **PIERPOINT** 24 [4] D Nicholls 5-9-3 A Nicholls (3) 5/1: 0-0001: 5 ch g Archway - Lavinia (Habitat)　　67
In tch, rdn fnl 3f & styd on gamely for press ins last to lead nr line, all out: best time of night: '99 wnr at
Southwell (AW), Redcar & Pontefract (h'caps, rtd 67a & 73): plcd in '98 (rtd 73, R Fahey): suited by 5/6f, prob
stays 1m: acts on firm, gd/soft & fibresand, any trk: eff with/without blnks, has tried a vis: gd weight carrier.
1766 **AVONDALE GIRL** 5 [12] M Dods 4-9-0 F Lynch 7/1: 000632: 4 ch f Case Law - Battle Queen (Kind Of　nk　63
Hush) Mid-div, rdn/prog to chall ins last, styd on well, just held: qck reapp: see 214 (AW).
1768 **DAYLILY** 5 [1] T D Easterby 3-8-7 K Darley 4/1 FAV: 006033: 3 ch f Pips Pride - Leaping Water　　nk　62
(Sure Blade) Cl-up, led over 2f out, styd on well, just hdd nr line: acts on gd & hvy grnd: not btn far: see 1768.
1664 **ANSELLMAN** 10 [2] A Berry 10-9-3 (bl) G Carter 9/2: 0-0254: In tch, onepace fnl 2f: see 1068.　2　60
1806 **PRESENT CHANCE** 3 [3] 6-9-3 (bl) L Newton 16/1: 000005: Rear, styd on fnl 2f, not able to chall.　¾　58
1273 **AJNAD** 31 [11] 6-9-3 T G McLaughlin 20/1: 000506: Twds rear, kept on fnl 1f, nrst fin: see 282 (AW).　hd　57
1264 **BRUTAL FANTASY** 31 [6] 6-9-3 M Roberts 7/1: 060007: Led till over 2f out, hung right/sn btn: btr 288.　½　55
1545 **RUSSIAN ROMEO** 14 [7] 5-9-3 (bl) W Supple 5/1: 232208: Prom, held over 1f out: btr 1257, 816 & 40.　1¼　52
1795 **COLLISION TIME** 4 [10] 3-8-7 J F Egan 20/1: 430-09: Wide, prom 3f: qck reapp: see 1795.　1　47
1578 **DEFIANCE** 13 [5] 5-9-3 F Norton 50/1: 50-000: Chsd ldrs 4f: 10th: see 1578 (dim h'cap).　1　48
1519 **Distant King** 16 [8] 7-9-3 T Hamilton (7) 50/1:　　1714 **Lucky Cove** 7 [9] 4-9-3 Kim Tinkler 33/1:
12 ran　　Time 1m 03.00 (1.7)　　　(J H Knight)　　　D Nicholls Sessay, N.Yorks.

1869

9.25 WALNUT HCAP 3YO+ 0-70 (E)　　6f rnd　Good 40　-15 Slow　　[69]
£3094　£952　£476　£228　3 yo rec 8 lb

1519 **BUNDY** 16 [10] M Dods 4-9-5 (60) A Clark 10/1: 0-1531: 4 b g Ezzoud - Sanctuary Cove (Habitat)　　66
Prom, rdn/led over 1f out, held on gamely nr fin, all out: earlier made a winning reapp at Nottingham (h'cap):
plcd in '99 (h'cap, rtd 71): '98 wnr at Newcastle (seller) & Warwick (h'cap, rtd 73): stays 7f, suited by 6f: acts
on fast & hvy grnd, sharp/gall trk: best without blnks: runs well fresh: goes well for A Clark.
1680 **DOUBLE ACTION** 9 [14] T D Easterby 6-9-6 (61)(bl) K Darley 7/1: 040532: 6 b g Reprimand - Final　shd　66
Shot (Dalsaan) Rear, prog fnl 2f & styd on well ins last, just held: frustrating type but v well h'capped.
1580 **DOUBLE OSCAR** 13 [8] D Nicholls 7-9-12 (67) F Norton 8/1: 000563: 7 ch g Royal Academy - Broadway　¾　70
Rosie (Absalom) Dwelt, sn chsd ldrs, rdn/chsd wnr 1f out, held nr fin: eff at 6f, just best at 5f: on a handy mark.
1368 **FAIRY PRINCE** 24 [12] Mrs A L M King 7-9-2 (57) P M Quinn (3) 33/1: 200-04: Prom wide, onepace　1½　56
fnl 1f: left reapp bhd: rnr-up 4 times last term (rtd 62, h'cap, incl in a visor): '98 Beverley wnr (stks, rtd 74 in
a h'cap): eff at 5/6f on firm & gd/soft grnd any trk, likes an uphill finish: slipped to a handy mark.
1792 **SUGAR CUBE TREAT** 4 [16] 4-8-12 (53) J Bramhill 14/1: --0035: Rear, styd on fnl 2f, nrst fin: qck reapp.　3　45
1520 **SWINO** 16 [5] 6-8-12 (53)(vis) J F Egan 12/1: 600446: Rdn/twds rear, no room/hampered 2f out till　¾　43+

inside last, kept on nr fin: vis reapplied: no luck in running, much closer with a clear passage: worth another look.
1297 **ON TILL MORNING** 28 [15] 4-9-4 (59) F Lynch 33/1: 0-0007: Rear, mod late prog: see 910. ¾ 47
1724 **ALBERT THE BEAR** 7 [9] 7-9-4 (59)(vis) J Carroll 16/1: 0-0608: In tch, no room fnl 1f, position accepted: 1¼ 43
another to have no room in the closing stages of what proved a messy contest: capable of more: see 1438.
1356 **SHARP EDGE BOY** 24 [13] 4-8-11 (52) J Fanning 33/1: 000009: Led till over 1f out: fdd: see 622. hd 35
1490 **ROYAL ARROW FR** 17 [7] 4-9-13 (68) W Supple 33/1: 0-0000: Rear, mod late gains: 10th: see 1070. 2 46
1357 **SURPRISED** 24 [4] 5-10-0 (69) K Fallon 9/4 FAV: 520-00: Mid-div, eff/little room 2f out, sn held: 11th. 1¼ 44
1714 **BENZOE** 7 [1] 10-9-2 (57) A Nicholls (3) 12/1: 000-50: Keen, in tch, hmpd over 1f out, sn held: 15th: 0
prob best forgotten, capable 10yo, on a fair mark & loves Thirsk: see 1714.
1580 **Swynford Welcome** 13 [3] 4-8-8 (49) G Bardwell 25/1:
1631 **Mother Corrigan** 11 [6] 4-9-2 (57)(BL) D Mernagh (3) 14/1:
1082 **Caution** 41 [11] 6-9-2 (57) A Culhane 14/1:
15 ran   Time 1m 16.4 (3.3)   (A H Henderson)   M Dods Piercebridge, Co.Durham.

Official Going   GOOD/FIRM. Stalls: Inside, except 5f (new crse) - Stands Side.

1870	**2.00 EBF MDN 2YO (D)** 5f **Good 50 -22 Slow**
	£3380 £1040 £520 £260

1403 **PREFERRED** 23 [6] R Hannon 2-9-0 R Hughes 7/4: 01: 2 b c Distant Relative - Fruhlingserwachen (Irish 76
River) Sn prom, rdn to chall & carr left ent fnl 2f, kept on to lead towards fin: well bckd from 5/2: IR 9,000gns
Feb foal, half-brother to a wnr abroad, sire a miler: apprec drop back to 5f: acts on gd grnd & a gall track.
1639 **MAJESTIC QUEST** 11 [8] J Neville 2-9-0 K Darley 16/1: 42: 2 b c Piccolo - Teanarco (Kafu) hd 74
Rear, prog, drifted left & ran green 2f out, strong chall till no extra nr fin: op 12/1: eff at 5f on gd grnd.
1639 **WARLINGHAM** 11 [5] Miss Gay Kelleway 2-9-0 K Fallon 14/1: 463: 2 b c Catrail - Tadjnama (Exceller) ½ 72
Tried to make all, hdd well ins last: op 7/1: better run, eff at 5f on gd grnd.
-- **ITS SMEE AGAIN** [10] B W Hills 2-8-9 M Hills 25/1: 4: Prom, chall appr fnl 1f, onepce ins last: 1 64
op 16/1 on debut: 650gns Mizoram Feb foal, dam unrcd, sire 7f/1m performer: gets 5f on gd grnd.
1737 **KARITSA** 7 [7] 2-8-9 T Quinn 5/6 FAV: 25: Prsd ldrs & ev ch till fdd bef dist: well bckd, clr 2½ 57
rem, qck reapp: more expected, possibly came too soon after 1737 (gd/soft).
1550 **SPRINGWOOD JASMIN** 14 [9] 2-8-9 (t) L Newman 50/1: 056: Chsd ldrs till 2f out: Midhish 5 42
Mar foal, half-sister to 2 wnrs, incl a 7f juv, dam 2m wnr: sire a sprinter: with D Carroll.
1302 **ORANGE TREE LAD** 28 [2] 2-9-0 Dale Gibson 20/1: -02327: Chsd ldrs for 3f: op 12/1, new stable. 1 44
-- **MINIME** [3] 2-9-0 D Young (7) 50/1: 8: Nvr going pace: IR 6,600gns Mujtahid Jan foal. 5 29
-- **FOREST KITTEN** [1] 2-8-9 J Reid 10/1: 9: Slowly away, handy, wide, wknd qckly 2f out: op 7/1 on 3½ 15
debut: Marju May first foal, dam 6f juv wnr, sire 1m/12f performer: with E Stanners.
712 **NEVER FEAR** 80 [4] 2-8-9 J F Egan 100/1: 00: Al bhd: 10th, 11 wk abs: Mistertopogigo Apr first foal. 16 0
10 ran   Time 1m 02.1 (3.6)   (R J Brennan & N J Hemmington)   R Hannon East Everleigh, Wilts.

1871	**2.30 THEHORSESMOUTH HCAP 3YO+ 0-85 (D)** 5f **Good 50 +00 Fast** [85]
	£3965 £1220 £610 £305 3 yo rec 7 lb

1676 **COASTAL BLUFF** 9 [9] N P Littmoden 8-9-7 (78) K Fallon 11/4 FAV: 0-5021: 8 gr g Standaan - 83
Combattente (Reform) Trkd ldrs, switched to chall appr fnl 1f, kept on under press to lead fnl 100y, narrowly:
op 4/1, fair time: unplcd last term (stks, rtd 96, subs tried blnks & t-strap): lightly rcd since '97 wnr for T Barron
at Newmarket (stks) & York (Gr 1, ddht, rtd 118): eff at 5/6f on firm & gd/soft grnd, any trk: gd weight carrier
who can go well fresh: has been tubed: formally v smart sprinter, on a v lenient mark.
1662 **MOUSEHOLE** 10 [1] R Guest 8-8-7 (64) S Drowne 12/1: 000002: 8 b g Statoblest - Alo Ez (Alzao) hd 68
Rear, imprvd halfway, drvn & hmpd dist, ran on strgly, just failed: most unlucky, win soon on fast grnd, see 1013.
1441 **SPEED ON** 21 [6] H Candy 7-9-6 (77) C Rutter 10/1: 60-063: 7 b g Sharpo - Pretty Poppy (Song) nk 80
Cl-up, led 1½f out, hdd & drifted right ins last: op 7/1, clr rem, return to form: see 1013.
1517 **SYLVA PARADISE** 16 [2] C E Brittain 7-9-3 (74)(vis) P Robinson 33/1: 500-04: Towards rear, wide 2½ 70
prog appr fnl 1f, rdn & onepace ins last: slowly coming to hand, see 1517.
1356 **KOSEVO** 24 [10] 6-7-10 (53)(vis)(5ow) K Dalgleish (7) 33/1: 000005: Chsd ldrs, unable to qckn fnl 1f. ¾ 47
1162 **PLEASURE TIME** 37 [3] 7-9-1 (72)(vis) A Clark 20/1: 300-06: Led till ent fnl 2f, no extra: '99 Bath 1 63
wnr (class stks, rtd 80): '98 wnr here at Nottingham & Thirsk (h'caps, rtd 71): eff forcing the pace at 5/5.7f:
acts on firm & gd/soft grnd, gall trk, likes Nottingham: best visored, has tried blnks: with C Smith.
1591 **THE GAY FOX** 12 [7] 6-8-11 (68)(t) W Supple 7/1: 50-537: Mid-div, rdn & no impress appr fnl 1f. nk 58
728 **MUQTARB** 79 [4] 4-10-0 (85)(t) L Newton 33/1: /40-08: Slow away, some wide prog 2f out, nvr hd 75
on terms: top-weight: lightly rcd last term for M Tregoning, 4th of 5 (stks, rtd 91): '98 debut wnr at Ascot
(mdn, rtd 98, tried Listed, rtd 101): eff at 6f on fast grnd: now with W Musson.
1580 **HONESTY FAIR** 13 [12] 3-9-6 (84) D Mernagh (3) 10/1: -41109: Slow into stride, grad imprvd & chasing 1 71
ldrs when saddle slipped appr fnl 1f, eased right down: tchd 12/1: well worth another chance, see 1384.
1580 **GAY BREEZE** 13 [14] 7-9-6 (77) K Darley 13/2: -30350: Prom till no extra appr fnl 1f: 10th: see 905. shd 64
1728 **RUSHCUTTER BAY** 7 [15] 7-9-6 (77) G Duffield 13/2: 50-260: Al towards rear, (5th, qck reapp, back in trip. 0
1441 **RITAS ROCK APE** 21 [5] 5-9-5 (76) P Shea 11/1: 130-00: Prsd ldr till fdd ent fnl 2f: 13th, see 1441. 0
1650 **AURIGNY** 10 [13] 5-9-3 (74) S Sanders 12/1: 000640: Al bhd: 14th: see 1650, 191. 0
1531 **The Puzzler** 16 [8] 9-9-9 (80) M Hills 20/1:   1591 **Bevelena** 12 [11] 4-8-12 (69)(BL) J F Egan 33/1:
15 ran   Time 1m 01.0 (2.5)   (Paul J Dixon)   N P Littmoden Newmarket.

1872	**3.00 WAREHOUSE-UK COND STKS 3YO+ (C)** 1m54y rnd **Good 50 +04 Fast**
	£6110 £2317 £1158 £526 3 yo rec 11lb

2751} **SACRED SONG** 331 [7] H R A Cecil 3-8-4(2ow) T Quinn 5/2: 1-1: 3 b f Diesis - Ruby Ransom (Red 101
Ransom) Held up, niggled halfway, kept on appr fnl 2f, flashed tail bef dist, led well ins last, pshd out: nicely
bckd, gd time, reapp: won sole '99 start here at Nottingham (fill mdn, rtd 94): eff at 1m, shld get 10f: acts on
firm & gd grnd, likes this gall Nottingham trk: runs v well fresh: useful, unbtn, earned a tilt in Listed/Grp comp.
1186 **ACROBATIC** 36 [2] J R Fanshawe 3-8-7 D Harrison 7/4 FAV: 16-622: 3 br c Warning - Ayodhya 1½ 100
(Astronef) Prom, rdn to lead appr fnl 1f, hdd & no extra towards fin: gr run, gets 1m on firm & gd grnd, acts on

NOTTINGHAM   MONDAY JUNE 12TH   Lefthand, Galloping Track

1402 **WORLDLY MANNER 23** [4] Saeed bin Suroor 4-9-1 (vis) D O'Donohoe 5/2: -2D003: 4 b c Riverman - *2½* **92**
Lady Pastor (Flying Paster) Set gd pace & clr till 2f out, hdd bef fnl 1f & no extra: worth a try back at 7f?.
1744 **TAMMAM 6** [5] Mrs L Stubbs 4-9-1 K Fallon 10/1: 000534: Held up, eff 3f out, not pace to chall. *1½* **89$**
1029 **CEDAR MASTER 47** [6] 3-8-4 P Doe 20/1: 24-055: Led chasing pack, fdd ent fnl 3f: see 1029. *3* **83**
1489 **SERGEANT YORK 17** [3] 4-9-1 J F Egan 33/1: -05336: Al bhd: see 1291. *4* **75**
6 ran Time 1m 43.2 (3.8) (Niarchos Family) H R A Cecil Newmarket.

1873   **3.30 TURF 2000 FILLIES HCAP 3YO 0-80 (D) 1m54y rnd Good 50 -20 Slow [86]**
£3981 £1225 £612 £306

*1610 **MIDNIGHT ALLURE 12** [4] C F Wall 3-8-9 (67) R Mullen 11/8 FAV: 00-211: 3 b f Aragon - Executive Lady **77**
(Night Shift) Pld hard rear, imprvd appr fnl 2f, rdn bef fnl 1f & flashed tail, led ins last, edged left, pshd out: well bckd: recent Yarmouth wnr (fill h'cap): thrice rcd juv (mdn, rtd 62): half-sister to sprinter Midnight Escape: eff at 1m, likely to get 10f: acts on gd & hvy grnd, stiff or gall trk: goes well fresh & is improving.
1428 **POPPADAM 21** [3] J R Fanshawe 3-9-1 (73) D Harrison 10/1: 0-652: 3 ch f Salse - Wanton (Kris) *1* **80**
Prom, led 2½f out till below dist, kept on: op 7/1, well clr rem on h'cap bow: stays 1m on gd, shld find a race.
4260} **RESOUNDING 251** [2] A C Stewart 3-9-7 (79) M Roberts 9/4: 51-3: 3 b f Elmaamul - Echoing (Formidable) *4* **78**
Rear, prog & ch appr fnl 1f, outpcd: op 3/1 on reapp/h'cap bow: '99 wnr here at Nottingham (fill mdn, rtd 81): half-sister to useful 6f/1m performer Calcutta: eff at 6f, shld get 1m: acts on soft, handles firm, gall trk.
1606 **PEPETA 12** [12] I A Balding 3-8-7 (64)(1ow) K Fallon 11/2: 6-6004: Well plcd & ev ch till no extra *¾* **63**
appr fnl 1f: unsuited by longer 1m trip?: see 1201.
3659} **PHEISTY 287** [10] 3-9-2 (74) J Reid 25/1: 3600-5: Held up, not clr run & switched 2f out, nvr nr ldrs: *1½* **70**
reapp: '99 Leicester debut wnr (auct mdn, rtd 75): eff at 5f on gd & soft, shld get 1m (dam stoutly bred).
1511 **BROWNS DELIGHT 17** [9] 3-7-10 (54)(2oh) G Bardwell 50/1: 044006: Prom, led 3f out, sn hdd, onepce. *1* **48**
1649 **EVERGREEN 10** [11] 3-9-0 (72) Dane O'Neill 10/1: -35047: Nvr a factor: op 7/1: back in trip, see 794. *1* **64**
1710 **STOP THE TRAFFIC 8** [8] 3-8-5 (63) L Newman (5) 14/1: 220558: Keen, mid-div, fdd appr fnl 1f: *nk* **54**
will have to settle better to get longer 1m trip, see 397, 289.
1649 **LAFLEUR 10** [7] 3-8-5 (63)(VIS) S Drowne 16/1: -00009: Led & keen, hdd 3f out, sn btn: back in trip *½* **53**
& visored: yet to make the frame, rtd 79 sole juv start: half-sister to smart 7f juv/11f wnr Crown Of Light.
1405 **TREWORNAN 23** [5] 3-9-3 (75) T Quinn 14/1: 516-00: Chsd ldrs till ent fnl 3f: 10th, longer trip. *16* **40**
1649 **Dorothea Sharp 10** [6] 3-7-10 (54)(VIS)(11oh) K Dalgleish (7) 66/1:
4185} **Burn Park 255** [1] 3-7-13 (57) Claire Bryan (5) 33/1:
12 ran Time 1m 45.2 (5.8) (Mervyn Ayers) C F Wall Newmarket.

1874   **4.00 CONF CENTRE HCAP 3YO+ 0-70 (E) 1m6f Good 50 -16 Slow [69]**
£2930 £837 £418 3 yo rec 19lb

1411 **ZINCALO 23** [4] C E Brittain 4-9-1 (56)(t) P Robinson 16/1: 0-0401: 4 gr g Zilzal - Silver Glitz (Grey **60**
Dawn II) Sltly hmpd start, rear, hmpd 4f out & plenty to do, switched & kept on ent fnl 2f, nrst fin: fin ½L 2nd, plcd 1st: 1st win, rnr-up twice in '99 (mdn, rtd 85, flattered): eff around 14f on fast & hvy in a t-strap, not visor.
1301 **NUBILE 28** [14] W J Musson 6-7-10 (37)(tbl)(17oh) J Lowe 50/1: 0-6002: 6 b m Pursuit Of Love - *nk* **40$**
Trojan Lady (Irish River) Rear, styd on late & wide, nvr nrr: fin 3rd, plcd 2nd: jumps rnr 9 days ago: stays 14f.
1329 **NORCROFT JOY 26** [12] N A Callaghan 5-10-0 (69) J Reid 8/1: 56-503: 5 b m Rock Hopper - Greenhills *½* **71**
Joy (Radetzky) Held up, prog 3f out, drvn to chall appr fnl 1f, held towards fin: fin 4th plcd 3rd: ran to best.
554 **YATTARNA 114** [8] 4-8-13 (54) K Fallon 11/1: 010054: In tch, imprvd to lead 2f out, sn hdd, onepace: *½* **55**
fin 5th, plcd 4th, op 8/1: jmps fit, March wnr at M Rasen (juv nov, 2m1f, made all, firm, rtd 102h): see 5.
1187 **KING FLYER 36** [1] 4-9-7 (62)(t) A Beech(5) 16/1: 20-605: Hmpd start, late prog, nvr dngrs: 6th, plcd 5th. *½* **62**
1657 **KILCREGGAN 10** [13] 6-8-12 (53) A Culhane 3/1 JT FAV: 0-0337: Hld up, chsd ldrs 3f out till 1f out. *¾* **52**
1499 **RARE GENIUS 17** [10] 4-9-12 (67) K Darley 3/1 JT FAV: 2-2358: Prom, led appr str till bef 3f out. *hd* **66**
1701 **PROTOCOL 8** [15] 6-8-4 (45)(t) J F Egan 10/1: 023559: Led till appr fnl 4f, fdd bef 2f out: see 1701, 699. *2* **42**
4031} **GLOBAL DRAW 265** [2] 4-7-10 (37)(9oh) Claire Bryan (5) 10/1: 3000-0: Hmpd start, nvr troubled ldrs: *1* **33$**
jumps fit: plcd in '99 (first time blnks, clmr, rtd 48, J Parkes): unplcd juv (rtd 59): stays 10f on gd grnd.
1551 **LEGEND 14** [11] 4-9-12 (67) R Hughes 10/3: /34-20: Handy till 3f out: 13th, bckd from 6/1, lngr trip. **0**
860 **PRASLIN ISLAND 63** [7] Miss Gay Kelleway 4-8-7 (48) N Callan 12/1: 23001D: Taken left out of stalls, **52**
trkd ldrs, rdn to lead dist, styd on well: fin 1st, disqual & plcd last, jockey given 6 day ban for irresponsible riding, connections may appeal: tchd 16/1, new stable: goes on fast, gd grnd, best on AWs.
1730 **King For A Day 7** [5] 4-8-6 (47)(vis) D O'Donohoe 40/1: 1546 **Lunar Lord 14** [9] 4-7-10 (37) T Williams 14/1:
1306 **Palais 28** [3] 5-7-10 (37)(8oh) K Dalgleish (7) 33/1: 1608 **Topaz 12** [6] 5-7-10 (37)(3oh) G Bardwell 20/1:
15 ran Time 3m 07.5 (9.2) (C E Brittain) C E Brittain Newmarket

1875   **4.30 APPR CLASS STKS 3YO+ 0-70 (F) 1m2f Good 50 -04 Slow**
£2278 £651 £325 3 yo rec 13lb

-- **JULIUS** [5] M Johnston 3-8-1 K Dalgleish (5) 11/4: 0336-1: 3 b f Persian Bold - Babushka (Dance **67**
Of Life) Prom, led appr fnl 1f, rdn out: op 10/3, reapp/Brit bow: ex-Irish, plcd in a couple of Fairyhouse mdns (7f, gd grnd): eff over a gall 10f on gd grnd & runs well fresh.
1407 **FLAG FEN 23** [3] H J Collingridge 9-9-3 D McGaffin (5) 7/2: 05-062: 9 b g Riverman - Damascus Flag *1½* **65**
(Damascus) Led, under press & hdd appr fnl 1f, kept on: op 5/2, clr rem: ran to best at the weights, see 1150.
1775 **SMARTER CHARTER 5** [7] Mrs L Stubbs 7-9-5 Kristin Stubbs (7) 9/2: 123223: 7 br g Master Willie - *5* **59**
Irene's Charter (Persian Bold) Held up, chsd ldrs ent str till onepace bef fnl 1f: qk reapp, nicely bckd from 7/1 despite stiffish task on official ratings: consistent: see 871.
1332 **INDIAN NECTAR 26** [2] R Brotherton 7-9-0 I Mongan (3) 11/1: 160-04: Mid-div, prog 3f out, sn onepace. *nk* **53**
1050 **GYPSY 44** [4] 4-9-3 A Beech (3) 9/4 FAV: 544305: Chsd ldr 1m: op 7/4, 6 wk abs: see 1050, 270. *5* **49**
-- **RAKE HEY** [6] 6-9-3 J Bosley (5) 33/1: 0026/6: Held up, brief eff appr fnl 0f: op 16/1, 8 wk jmps abs: *¾* **48**
98/99 wnr at Hereford (2, 1 for S Mellor) & Kempton (2m1f, firm & soft, rtd 96h, with/without vis, up with/forcing the pace): 4 yr Flat abs, rnr-up in a rtd mdn (rtd 68, 1st time blnks, R J Houghton): stays 1m on firm grnd.
1690 **RAMBO WALTZER 9** [1] 8-9-7 G Sparkes (7) 8/1: 611327: Handy 6f: op 6/1: not a certain styr, see 750. *nk* **51**
7 ran Time 2m 07.7 (5.4) (Mrs K E Daley) M Johnston Middleham, N.Yorks.

Official Going GOOD/FIRM. Stalls: Inside.

1876 **6.40 COME RACING AUCT MDN 2YO (E)** 6f Good/Firm Inapplicable
£3234 £924 £462

1088 **PICCOLO PLAYER 41** [16] R Hannon 2-8-9 L Newman (5) 7/2 FAV: -21: 2 b c Piccolo - The Frog Lady 93
(Al Hareb) Made virtually all, drew clr fnl 1f, v cmftbly: abs: 12,000 gns Mar foal: half brother to a 7f juv wnr:
improved for debut & apprec step up to 6f, further will suit: acts on gd/firm & runs well fresh: win again.

-- **CAUVERY** [10] S P C Woods 2-8-10 G Duffield 11/1: 2: 2 ch c Exit To Nowhere - Triple Zee (Zilzal) 3½ 84
Prom, eff to chase wnr appr fnl 1f, no impress: nicely bckd on debut: Apr 1st foal, cost 13,000gns: encouraging
debut & eff at 6f, 7f will suit: acts on fast grnd: will improve & find a race.

828 **PASO DOBLE 67** [19] B R Millman 2-8-9 G Hind 11/1: 03: 2 b c Dancing Spree - Delta Tempo (Bluebird) 1 80
With wnr 4f, onepace over 1f out: 10 wk abs & showed promise here over 6f on gd/firm: see 828.

-- **MILLTIDE** [17] R Guest 2-7-13 J Mackay (7) 20/1: 4: Sn bhd, kept on for press over 1f out, nrst fin shd 70+
on debut: Feb foal, cheaply bought: half sister to sev wnrs: dam 1m scorer: 7f will suit: improve.

1472 **CRIPSEY BROOK 19** [6] 2-8-9 S Sanders 8/1: 45: Cl-up, rdn & btn appr fnl 1f: btr 1472 (gd/soft). 1½ 76

-- **MISSING YOU TOO** [8] 2-8-4 D Sweeney 16/1: 6: In tch, eff over 1f out, kept on same pace: ¾ 69
Feb foal, cost IR 13,000gns: half sister to a 6f juv wnr: showed some promise here & type to improve.

1648 **DAWN ROMANCE 10** [13] 2-8-1 Craig Williams 16/1: 07: Prom, rdn & no impress over 1f out: see 1648. ¾ 64

-- **TRUMPINGTON** [18] 2-8-1(1ow) R Mullen 16/1: 8: In tch, rdn & no impress fnl 2f: May foal, 1 61
cost 4,000 gns: dam 6f scorer: speedily bred, with I Balding.

-- **BOLSHOI BALLET** [20] 2-8-7 D Harrison 8/1: 9: Sn outpcd, some late gains: op 6/1: Apr 1st foal, shd 67
cost 6,200 gns: dam 7f juv scorer, later stayer: bred to need 7f+ & will do better: with J Dunlop.

-- **GOLDEN BEACH** [12] 2-8-2 P Doe 16/1: 0: In tch, btn over 1f out: 10th, debut: Mar foal, cost ½ 61
8,000 gns: half sister to wnrs over 6/7f: with Mrs P Dutfield.

-- **ACHILLES SPIRIT** [2] 2-8-12 J Weaver 20/1: 0: Dwelt, sn in tch, no impress over 1f out: 11th: hd 70
Apr foal, cost 18,000 gns: Deploy colt: shld rate higher with time & over further.

-- **ALAGAZAM** [15] 2-8-8 T E Durcan 33/1: 0: In tch, btn over 1f out: 12th: Feb foal, cost ¾ 64
10,000 gns: Alhajaz gldg, with P Case.

-- **ADWEB** [3] 2-7-13 Joanna Badger (7) 33/1: 0: Handy, btn 2f out: 13th, debut. 1¾ 50

-- **CHAUNTRY GOLD** [5] 2-8-8 Pat Eddery 10/1: 0: Slow away, sn in tch, wknd over 2f out: 14th. 1½ 55

-- **SAAFEND FLYER** [14] 2-8-9 Dane O'Neill 9/1: 0: Dwelt, al bhd: 17th on debut. 0

-- **Queens College** [9] 2-8-7 M Fenton 14/1: -- **Nelsons Flagship** [7] 2-8-6 M Hills 25/1:
1577 **Silver Cloud 13** [4] 2-8-2 (BL) J Tate 33/1: 1673 **Insheen 9** [21] 2-8-5 D R McCabe 25/1:
-- **Mr Ed** [11] 2-8-7 N Pollard 20/1: -- **Bosra Badger** [1] 2-8-4 R Perham 33/1:
21 ran Time 1m 11.7 (1.4) (Park Walk Racing) R Hannon East Everleigh, Wilts

---

1877 **7.10 MLL TELECOM FILLIES HCAP 3YO 0-75 (E)** 6f Good/Firm Inapplicable [82]
£3164 £904 £452

1739 **PERLE DE SAGESSE 6** [15] Julian Poulton 3-7-13 (53) A Daly 12/1: 453021: 3 b f Namaqualand - Pearl 55
Of Dubai (Red Ransom) Handy, hdwy to lead over 3f out, styd on well ins last, rdn out: in '99 won at Windsor (sell,
rtd 65, with P Cole) & Lingfield (2, sell & clmr, rtd 65a): eff at 5/7f on firm, gd & equitrack, sharp trks.

1670 **CHORUS 10** [18] B R Millman 3-9-2 (70) G Hind 13/2: 200632: 3 b f Bandmaster - Name That Tune 1¾ 66
(Fayruz) Prom, eff to chall 2f out, not pace of wnr ins last: still a mdn & worth a try in headgear: see 888.

1399 **FLEETING FANCY 23** [17] S Dow 3-8-3 (56)(1ow) G Duffield 16/1: 00-03: 3 b f Thatching - Fleetwood ¾ 51
Fancy (Taufan) Handy, eff & short of room over 2f out till over 1f out, onepace: eff over 6f on gd/firm.

4457} **WATER BABE 235** [16] J W Payne 3-8-6 (60) N Pollard 16/1: 050-4: In tch, hdwy 2f out, sn onepace: ¾ 52
reapp: rtd 64 when unplcd on 3 juv starts: eff at 6f on gd/firm.

1804 **RIOS DIAMOND 3** [7] 3-7-10 (50)(11oh) J Mackay (7) 25/1: 00-205: Bhd, eff & edged left appr fnl nk 41
1f, kept on same pace: quick reapp: apprec a return to 7f: acts on fibresand & gd/firm: see 1202.

1610 **MARNIE 12** [19] 3-7-10 (50)(3oh) G Baker (7) 11/1: 50-006: Bhd, some late gains: nvr dangerous: shd 41
best juv run on debut when rtd 74 (plcd): eff at 6f on gd/firm.

*1334 **CUPIDS CHARM 26** [6] 3-9-3 (71) D Harrison 11/2 JT FAV: 4-0017: Bhd, wknd & eased ins last. 2½ 56

1494 **DUCIE 17** [14] 3-8-10 (64) J Fortune 11/2 JT FAV: 20-008: In tch, wknd appr fnl 1f: see 1098. 1½ 45

1467 **AUNT DORIS 19** [1] 3-8-8 (62) J Stack 14/1: 130-69: Bhd, brief eff over 2f out, no impress: see 1467. ¾ 41

4517} **LADY STALKER 230** [4] 3-8-4 (58) M Henry 25/1: 4660-0: With ldrs till wknd over 1f out: 10th: 1 34
in '98 trained by M Fetherston Godley, rtd 69 (unplcd).

1220 **RED TYPHOON 33** [13] 3-9-6 (74) S Sanders 20/1: 10-000: Led till over 3f out, no extra: 11th, see 1698. 1 47

1651 **KEBABS 10** [3] 3-8-13 (67)(BL) D Sweeney 9/1: 00030: Dwelt, sn in tch, wknd 2f out: nvr enjoy blnks? 53

1710 **Dancing Lily 8** [5] 3-7-10 (50)(6oh) R Brisland (5) 33/11178 **Endymion 36** [8] 3-9-4 (72) L Newman (5) 20/1:
1435 **Silver Auriole 21** [9] 3-7-10 (50)(BL) (15oh) C Adamson 40/1994 **Night Shifter 51** [11] 3-8-13 (67) R Mullen 16/1:
4 **Zoena 217** [12] 3-8-9 (63) R Hughes 20/1:
17 ran Time 1m 11.3 (1) (Russell Reed & Gerald West) Julian Poulton Lewes, E Sussex

---

1878 **7.40 FRENCH HORN HCAP 3YO+ 0-85 (D)** 1m2f Good/Firm Inapplicable [83]
£4101 £1262 £631 £315 3 yo rec 13lb

1729 **THE GREEN GREY 7** [8] L Montague Hall 6-8-5 (60) G Duffield 7/1: 0-0061: 6 gr g Environment Friend - 68
Pea Green (Try My Best) Made all, kept on well for press & drew clr ins last: lightly rcd in '99 (rtd 66a & 54):
'98 scorer at Yarmouth (h'cap), Bath, Brighton (clmr, with W Muir), Kempton (rtd 71) & Lingfield (h'cap, rtd 59a,
with D Morris): eff at 7f/1m, stays 10f well on firm, gd/soft & equitrack: handles any trk, likes Bath: best
without a visor & can carry big weights: took advantage of slip in the weights, quick follow up?

1729 **FREDORA 7** [12] M Blanshard 5-9-10 (79) D Sweeney 8/1: 0-5002: 5 ch m Inchinor - Ophrys (Nonalaco) 4 83
Keen, bhd, eff 2f out, not pace of wnr fnl 1f: gd run under top weight: likes fast & slipped down the weights.

*1730 **COURT SHAREEF 7** [1] R J Price 5-8-5 (60)(6ex) P Fitzsimons (5) 3/1 FAV: 405-13: 5 b g Shareef Dancer 1 62
- Fairfields Cone (Celtic Cone) Waited with, eff over 2f out, onepace over 1f out: gd run: apprec return to 12f.

1450 **CULZEAN 20** [5] R Hannon 4-9-9 (78) R Hughes 8/1: 536004: Hld up, eff 2f out, sn onepace. hd 80

1364 **DIVORCE ACTION 24** [14] 4-8-8 (63) L Newman (5) 7/1: 50-025: Waited with, hdwy 2f out, no impress. nk 64

1729 **GIKO 7** [10] 4-9-13 (54)(bl) M Henry 10/1: 000656: Handy, eff to chase wnr after 4f till 2f out, wknd. hd 55

209 **REDOUBLE 177** [9] 4-8-3 (58) R Mullen 14/1: 4550-7: Handy, wknd 2f out: reapp: in '99 trained 13 43
by R O'Sullivan, plcd (rtd 64): stays 12f on firm & gd/soft.

1271 **PRODIGAL SON 31** [11] 5-9-3 (72) N Pollard 10/1: 20-368: Handy, wknd 2f out: see 1271, 119. *1½* **55**
1677 **KATHAKALI 9** [4] 3-7-10 (64)(4oh) R Brisland (5) 20/1: 110009: Handy, not handle bend 6f out, sn no impress: btr 880 (equitrack). *½* **46**
1744 **TYLERS TOAST 6** [13] 4-8-10 (65) P Doe 14/1: 111050: Bhd, btn 2f out: 10th, best 637 (A/W). *6* **39**
1590 **SLUMBERING 12** [6] 4-9-7 (76) Pat Eddery 16/1: -40000: Al bhd, 11th: see 1590, 1042 (1m). *¾* **49**
1666 **DIRECT DEAL 10** [2] 4-8-10 (65) G Baker (7) 20/1: -00000: Chsd wnr 4f, wknd 2f out: 12th, see 747. *shd* **38**
1528 **PASSIONS PLAYTHING 16** [7] 4-8-9 (64)(bl) D M Oliver 33/1: 4-6000: Al bhd: 13th: see 1528, 486. *11* **23**
13 ran Time 2m 04.6 (J Daniels) L Montague Hall Tadworth, Surrey

1879

8.10 HAMMOND CLASSIFIED STKS 3YO+ 0-80 (D) 1m67y rnd Good/Firm Inapplicable
£3770 £1160 £580 £290 3yo rec 11lb

1564 **MADAM ALISON 14** [4] R Hannon 4-9-3 Dane O'Neill 10/3 FAV: 526-31: 4 b f Puissance - Copper Burn (Electric) Front rank, rdn into lead dist, pushed clr, eased down: val for 3L+: '99 Newmarket wnr (fill h'cap, rtd 83 at best): '98 Leicester wnr (fill mdn auct, rtd 77): eff at 1m on fast & hvy grnd: handles a sharp/undul or stiff/gall trk: can run well fresh: well rdn by Dane O'Neill today. **82**
1826 **CHAPEL ROYALE 3** [1] K Mahdi 3-8-9 R Hughes 10/1: 1-5002: 3 gr c College Chapel - Merci Royale (Fairy King) Waited with, chall 3f out, sn onepace till styd on cl-home: qck reapp: stays 8.3f on fast & soft. *1¼* **81**
4357} **ZULU DAWN 242** [3] J W Hills 4-9-6 M Hills 9/2: 0164-3: 4 b g El Gran Senor - Celtic Loot (Irish River) Set pace till hdd dist, kept on: reapp: '99 Newbury wnr (mdn, rtd 83): eff at 1m on firm & gd/soft grnd: has tried blnks, seems best without: handles a sharp or stiff/gall trk: sharper next time. *hd* **81**
1829 **NAVIASKY 3** [2] W R Muir 5-9-6 D M Oliver 4/1: 000404: Rcd keenly in rear, rdn to improve 2f out, onepace ins last: quick reapp: see 1450. *½* **80**
1786 **OMNIHEAT 4** [6] 3-8-9 (bl) Pat Eddery 7/2: 323165: Rear, eff 3f out, not pace to chall: do better. *1¼* **77**
4357} **MINETTA 242** [5] 5-9-3 M Fenton 5/1: 2110-6: Chsd ldrs till lost pl ent str, no ch after on reapp: '99 wnr here at Windsor (2) & Thirsk (fill h'cap, rtd 77): '98 Newmarket (h'cap) & Bath wnr (stks, rtd 77): eff arnd 1m: likes fast & firm grnd, poss handles gd/soft & fibresand: acts on any trk, likes Windsor: has tried blnks, best without: gd weight carrier who is capable of better & fitter next time. *5* **64**
6 ran Time 1m 45.8 (William J Kelly) R Hannon East Everleigh, Wilts

1880

8.40 SWAN CLAIMER 3YO+ (F) 1m3135y Good/Firm Inapplicable
£2362 £675 £337 3yo rec 15lb

1788 **TONIC 4** [14] M Johnston 4-10-0 M Hills 11/4 FAV: -00431: 4 b g Robellino - Alyara (Alydar) Waited with, prog 3f out, rdn into lead dist & sn clr, easily: quick reapp, top weight: '99 reapp wnr at Ripon (mdn, rtd 88): eff at 1m, stays 12f well: acts on fast & hvy grnd, can run well fresh: handles a gall or sharp trk: gd weight carrier who was claimed for £15,000. **72**
1370 **MUTADARRA 24** [7] G M McCourt 7-9-4 D Harrison 5/1: 400002: 7 ch g Mujtahid - Silver Echo (Caerleon) In tch, went on 2f out till collared dist, sn outpcd by easy wnr: eff at 10/11.6f: see 1370, 292. *6* **53**
3631} **MONUMENT 289** [1] J S King 8-9-5 R Havlin 10/1: 1450-3: 8 ch g Cadeaux Genereux - In Perpetuity (Great Nephew) Trkd ldrs, led 3f out till over 2f out, ev ch till onepace fnl 1f: '99 Bath wnr (clmg h'cap, rtd 63): '98 Kempton wnr (appr h'cap, rtd 62 at best): '97 Nottingham wnr (ltd stks, rtd 62): eff btwn 1m & 12f, acts on gd & firm grnd: sharper next time in h'caps. *1½* **52$**
1023 **DIZZY TILLY 49** [13] A J McNae 6-9-6 P Fitzsimons (5) 12/1: 0-0004: Prog from rear 4f out, no impress 2f out, rallied cl-home: 7 wk abs: offic rtd just 40, so treat this rating with caution: see 748 (C/D). *1¼* **51$**
*1814 **NIGHT CITY 3** [12] 9-9-7 N Callan 4/1: 064415: Chsd ldr, led 5f out till 3f out, grad wknd: qck reapp. *3* **47**
4603} **SYRAH 221** [5] 4-8-13 D M Oliver 25/1: 0000-6: Trkd ldrs till onepace fnl 2f: reapp: trained by G Lewis & R Phillips in '99, little form: prev term 4th at W'hampton (AW sell, rtd 44a): now with W Muir & seems mod. *1* **37**
1523 **JIMMY SWIFT 16** [9] 5-9-4 L Newman (5) 14/1: 300-47: Mid-div, eff & btn 3f out: eased: rnr-up in a sell h'cap hdle at Fakenham (2m, gd) since 1523. *6* **33**
1544 **YAHESKA 16** [8] 3-8-0 J Mackay (7) 40/1: 000-58: Nvr a factor: see 1544 (sand). *1¼* **28**
1570 **WESTMINSTER CITY 14** [4] 4-9-9 (bl) L Branch (7) 11/2: 2U0449: Trkd ldrs, rdn & wknd qckly 2f out. *1* **35**
1739 **PRINCESS MO 6** [11] 4-8-11 (bl) C Rutter 40/1: -00060: Al bhd, fin 10th: quick reapp. *nk* **22**
791 **Multi Franchise 74** [6] 7-9-2 (vis) R Perham 33/1: 1510 **Oriental Pride 17** [3] 4-9-7 R Hughes 25/1:
1614 **The Blue Brazil 12** [10] 4-9-2 (VIS) J Lowe 33/1: 1593 **Silken Fox 12** [2] 3-8-2 (bl) M Henry 40/1:
14 ran Time 2m 28.4 (R Robinson) M Johnston Middleham, N Yorks

1881

9.10 RAFFLES CLASSIFIED STKS 3YO+ 0-75 (D) 5f Good/Firm Inapplicable
£3802 £1170 £585 £292 3yo rec 7lb

1531 **PALAWAN 16** [1] I A Balding 4-9-2 N Chalmers (7) 11/2: 120301: 4 br g Polar Falcon - Krameria (Kris) Front rank, went on halfway, held on well cl-home, hand & heels riding: earlier won at W'hampton (mdn) & Southwell (amat h'cap, rtd 76a): rnr-up sev times in '99 (mdn, rtd 75): eff at 5f, stays 7f well: acts on fast, gd & f/sand: handles a stiff or sharp trk: likes to run up with or force the pace & a gd weight carrier. **76**
1140 **KING OF PERU 39** [2] N P Littmoden 7-9-2 (vis) R Hughes 8/1: 556442: 7 b g Inca Chief - Julie's Star (Thatching) Trkd ldrs going well, chall strongly fnl 1f, not pace of wnr cl-home: see 660 (AW h'cap). *nk* **74**
1005 **FAUTE DE MIEUX 49** [9] M Kettle 5-9-5 N Callan 6/1: -60103: 5 ch g Beveled - Supreme Rose (Frimley Park) Chsd ldrs, eff 2f out, styd on under press & nrst fin: 7 wk abs, top weight: prev trained by E Wheeler: won this race last year: see 1005, 960. *1* **74**
4518} **ANGIE BABY 230** [4] R Ingram 4-8-13 J Weaver 5/1: 0600-4: Led till halfway, no extra on reapp: '99 Ripon wnr (clmr, reapp), subs plcd sev times (rtd 80 at best): '98 wnr at Redcar (mdn auct), Nottingham (fill nov), Hamilton (nov) & Lingfield (stks, rtd 89 at best): all wins at 5f, acts on firm & hvy grnd: runs well fresh: loves to force the pace & handles any trk: has slipped to a fair mark & fitter next time. *¾* **65**
*1516 **JODEEKA 16** [8] 3-8-9 G Duffield 9/4 FAV: -515: Chsd ldrs, onepace fnl 1f: rtd higher 1516. *3* **59**
1487 **ECUDAMAH 18** [5] 4-9-2 J Bosley (7) 20/1: 6-0006: Nvr nr to chall: see 40 (AW). *1¼* **55**
1175 **DEADLY SERIOUS 36** [3] 4-9-2 N Pollard 25/1: 433007: Nvr nr ldrs: see 558 (AW mdn). *1¾* **50**
*1021 **HELEN ALBADOU 49** [6] 3-8-9 J Tate 4/1: 3-18: Sn struggling & t.o., virtually p.u.: 7 wk abs. *dist* **0**
8 ran Time 59.2 (Crse Record) (Westenders) I A Balding Kingsclere, Hants

SALISBURY TUESDAY JUNE 13TH Righthand, Galloping Track, Stiff Finish

Official Going GOOD TO FIRM (FIRM places) Stalls: Str Course - Far Side, 10f - Inside, 12f - Stands Side

1882

1.30 E REAVEY FILL MDN AUCT DIV 1 2YO (F) 6f Good/Firm 35 -20 Slow
£2600 £800 £400 £200

-- **IN THE WOODS** [10] D J S Cosgrove 2-8-7 J F Egan 8/1: 1: 2 br f You And I - Silent Indulgence **93+**
(Woodman) Chsd ldrs, rdn/prog to lead 1f out, styd on well & in command/eased nr fin: val for 5L+: op 12/1: Feb foal, cost 11,000 gns: eff at 6f, will get further: acts on fast: runs well fresh: v encouraging, win again.
1403 **SIBLA 24** [1] Mrs P N Dutfield 2-8-3 L Newman (5) 5/2 FAV: 52: 2 b f Piccolo - Malibasta (Auction Ring) Chsd ldrs, led over 2f out & sn hung badly right, hdd 1f out, sn held by wnr: clr rem: nicely bckd: acts on fast grnd, needs to correct steering problems to find similar: see 1403. *3* **79**
1550 **MISS DOMUCH 15** [11] R Hannon 2-8-3 P Fitzsimons (5) 7/2: 23: 2 ch f Definite Article - Eliza Orzeszkowa (Polish Patriot) Led till over 2f out, wknd ins last: op 11/4: handles fast & soft grnd: see 1550 (5f). *4* **69**
1568 **FAZZANI 15** [8] M R Channon 2-8-7 S Drowne 7/2: -044: Chsd ldrs, rdn/drifted left over 2f out, sn held: bckd tho' op 11/4: btr 1568 (5f, soft). *¾* **71**
-- **PERSIAN CAT** [3] 2-8-7 S Sanders 6/1: 5: Dwelt/rear, kept on late under hands & heels riding, nrst fin: Persian Bold filly, Jan foal, cost 8,500 gns: half sister to a juv wnr abroad, dam an 11f French wnr: looks sure to relish 7f+: eyecatching late hdwy, sure to leave this bhd over further for Sir M Prescott. *¾* **69+**
1046 **KIRIWINA 46** [7] 2-8-3 S Whitworth 25/1: 06: Held up in tch, no impress fnl 2f: 6 wk abs: see 1046. *5* **56**
1659 **VIOLENT 11** [9] 2-8-0 M Henry 33/1: -07: Cl-up, fdd over 1f out: see 1659. *shd* **53**
1673 **EMMA CLARE 10** [5] 2-8-3 F Norton 33/1: 08: Cl-up, fdd fnl 2f: see 1673. *3½* **48**
1553 **PRESENTOFAROSE 15** [6] 2-8-0 N Farmer (7) 50/1: 559: Sn outpcd/bhd: see 1396 (5f). *7* **33**
1740 **ROXY LABURNUM 7** [2] 2-8-0 C Rutter 66/1: 0000: Al outpcd rear, 10th: mod form. *6* **22**
-- **ROCHAMPBEAU** [4] 2-8-0 S Righton 40/1: 0: Sn outpcd rear, 11th: Apr foal, cost 1,000 IR gns: half sister to a 1m/10f 3yo wnr, dam a mdn: with N M Babbage. *17* **0**
11 ran Time 1m 15.42 (3.32) (Global Racing Club) D J S Cosgrove Newmarket, Suffolk

1883

2.0 E REAVEY FILL MDN AUCT DIV 2 2YO (F) 6f Good/Firm 35 -31 Slow
£2600 £800 £400 £200

1197 **EBULLIENCE 36** [2] R Charlton 2-8-7 T Quinn 1/1 FAV: 01: 2 b f Makbul - Steadfast Elite (Glenstal) **78**
Led after 1f & increased tempo halfway, duelled with rnr-up ins last, narrowly prevailed under hands & heels: hvly bckd: left debut bhd: Feb foal, dam a multiple wnr: eff at 6f, 7f shld suit: acts on fast: can improve.
1641 **EAU ROUGE 11** [9] M A Jarvis 2-8-3 P Robinson 9/2: 02: 2 ch f Grand Lodge - Tarsa (Ballad Rock) *hd* **73**
Led 1f, remained handy & rdn/duelled with wnr ins last, drvn/just hdd line: eff at 6f on fast grnd: see 1641.
1667 **THERESA GREEN 11** [1] Mrs P N Dutfield 2-8-0 L Newman (5) 33/1: 003: 2 b f Charnwood Forest - In Your Dreams (Suave Dancer) Chsd ldrs, kept on fnl 1f, not pace to chall front pair: op 20/1: stays 6f on fast. *1½* **66**
1673 **CHANGE OF IMAGE 10** [5] J M P Eustace 2-8-3 J Tate 20/1: 64: Bhd ldrs, outpcd 2f out, kept on nr fin. *2* **64**
1639 **MISS INFORM 12** [4] 2-8-0 N Pollard 7/2: 35: Bhd ldrs, outpcd 2f out, onepace fnl 1f: see 1639. *nk* **60**
-- **MUSIC MAID** [3] 2-8-0 A Nicholls (3) 33/1: 6: Held up in tch, outpcd halfway, kept on ins last, no threat: op 20/1: Apr foal, cost 2,800 gns: half sister to 2 wnrs abroad: dam unrcd: sire 6/7f performer. *1½* **56**
1424 **JARV 22** [8] 2-8-3 P Doe 33/1: 07: Bhd ldrs, outpcd/sn held over 2f out: bhd on debut prev. *hd* **58**
-- **SHIMLA** [10] 2-8-7 Dane O'Neill 9/1: 8: Chsd ldrs, btn 2f out: op 6/1: Rudimantary filly, Feb foal, cost 11,000 gns: half sister to smart 7f/1m juv wnr King O The Mana: dam unrcd: shld apprec 7f+ in time. *1¼* **59**
1486 **EASTER ISLAND 19** [6] 2-8-3 D O'Donohoe 33/1: 0009: Held up, keen early, btn over 2f out: mod form *1¾* **51**
-- **BEAUTIFUL BUSINESS** [7] 2-8-0 F Norton 33/1: 0: Rear/in tch, struggling over 2f out: 10th: Deploy filly, Feb foal, cost 4,000 gns: half sister plcd at 7f as a 2yo: dam a mid-dist mdn. *2½* **41**
10 ran Time 1m 16.03 (3.93) (Beckhampton Partnership) R Charlton Beckhampton, Wilts

1884

2.30 SHERBORNE CLAIMER 3YO+ (F) 7f str Good/Firm 35 -10 Slow
£2618 £748 £374 3 yo rec 10lb

1672 **MY EMILY 10** [14] G L Moore 4-9-1 I Mongan (5) 9/4 FAV: 200-21: 4 b f King's Signet - Flying Wind **67**
(Forzando)Chsd ldrs, prog to lead over 1f out, styd on well & in command near fin, cmftbly: hvly bckd tho' op 7/4: '99 Brighton wnr (mdn h'cap, rtd 70 at best): plcd previous term (rtd 65): eff at 6/7f on firm & gd grnd, handles gd/sft & any track: goes well fresh: appreciated this drop to claiming grade.
1520 **SHARP SHUFFLE 17** [20] Ian Williams 7-9-3 K Fallon 5/1: 024002: 7 ch g Exactly Sharp - Style (Traffic Judge) Held up, lost place & drpd rear halfway, prog/no room over 2f out till over 1f out, styd on well ins last, wnr had flown: much closer to this wnr with a clr run: can win another seller/claimer in this form: see 138. *1¼* **64**
1794 **SHUDDER 5** [12] R J Hodges 5-9-2 S Drowne 9/1: 0-4303: 5 b g Distant Relative - Oublier L'Ennui (Bellman) Chsd ldrs, rdn/chsd wnr over 1f out, al held: op 8/1, quick reapp: see 838. *1½* **60**
1734 **CRAFTY PICK 8** [11] R Hannon 3-8-3 L Newman (5) 12/1: 00034: Cl up, rdn/led over 2f out, soon hdd & onepace: handles fast & gd/soft grnd: eff at 6/7f: see 1734 (sell h'cap). *1½* **54**
1794 **DEMOCRACY 5** [9] 4-9-5 D Harrison 12/1: 000005: Held up, rdn/late gains, no threat: quick reapp. *2* **56**
1572 **NORTHERN LIFE 14** [18] 3-8-0 A Nicholls (3) 50/1: 00-006: Rear, rdn/mod gains for press fnl 2f. *shd* **47$**
1610 **WOODWIND DOWN 13** [2] 3-8-2 Craig Williams 20/1: -20007: Chsd ldrs, held fnl 2f: see 651 (mdn). *2½* **44**
1508 **ANOTHER VICTIM 18** [3] 6-9-1 D Sweeney 33/1: 6/0038: Chsd ldrs till over 1f out: see 1508 (sell). *3* **41**
-- **ANNO DOMINI** [6] 4-9-12 D Griffiths 50/1: 5152/9: Keen/prom, held fnl 2f: reapp after long abs under topweight: missed '99: '98 Pontefract scorer (auction mdn, rtd 98 at best): eff at 5/6f on fast & gd. *1¾* **49**
1543 **BEACH BABY 17** [16] 3-7-13 A McCarthy (3) 50/1: 000000: Chsd ldrs 6f: 10th: see 1543. *1¼* **29**
1423 **CAPE COAST 22** [10] 3-8-9 J Reid 8/1: 001630: Bhd ldrs, btn 2f out: 11th: btr 1423, 1081 (6f). *1½* **36**
1760 **ROI DE DANSE 6** [15] 5-9-5 F Norton 25/1: 502500: Led till over 2f out, fdd: 15th: qck reapp: see 227. **0**
1543 **LADY DEALER 17** [19] 5-8-9 R Perham 50/1: 00/00U: Chsd ldrs, twds rear/no room when hmpd & u.r. 2f out. **0**
1181 **Napper Blossom 37** [1] 3-8-6 S Whitworth 25/1: 164 **Ubitoo 186** [13] 3-8-9 C Rutter 66/1:
1741 **Bonnie Dundee 7** [7] 4-8-12 (bl) S Carson (5) 33/1: 1423 **Striding King 22** [4] 5-9-3 P Doe 50/1:
1732 **Olly May 8** [8] 5-8-11 Jonjo Fowle (7) 50/1: 1741 **Edeiff 7** [5] 3-7-13 G Baker (7) 12/1:
19 ran Time 1m 28.65 (3.15) (B V & C J Pennick) G L Moore Woodingdean, E Sussex

---

1885   3.00 EBF CLASSIFIED STKS 3YO 0-85 (C)   1m2f   Good/Firm 35   +01 Fast
£7187   £2657   £1328   £604

1374 **STARLYTE GIRL** 25 [4] R Hannon 3-8-11 J Reid 8/1: 10-601: 3 b f Fairy King - Blushing Storm   84
(Blushing Groom) Made all, rdn when pressed fnl 2f, held on well inside last, rdn out: gd time: '99 Warwick
wnr (fill mdn, rtd 86): eff at 10f, should get further: acts on firm & gd, dissap on gd/soft: handles any track.
1400 **REFLEX BLUE** 24 [3] J W Hills 3-9-0 M Hills 4/1: 25-442: 3 b g Ezzoud - Briggsmaid (Elegant Air)   ¾   85
Held up in tch, rdn/chsd wnr fnl 1f, kept on, btn less than 1L: eff over a stiff 10f, return to 12f+ should suit.
*1588 **CANFORD** 14 [2] W Jarvis 3-9-2 M Tebbutt 5/2: 4-13: 3 b c Caerleon - Veronica (Persian Bold)   3½   82
Handy, rdn/chall 2f out, soon held: hvly bckd: handles fast grnd, impressive on soft in 1588 (mdn, made all).
1637 **POLAR RED** 12 [5] M J Ryan 3-9-2 G Faulkner (3) 2/1 FAV: W-3124: Chsd wnr, no extra fnl 1f: well bckd.   ½   81
1599 **FINISHED ARTICLE** 13 [1] 3-9-0 T Quinn 9/2: 0-4635: Rear/in tch, eff 3f out, no prog: see 1404, 1012.   7   69
5 ran   Time 2m 07.86 (3.36)   (Mohammed Suhail)   R Hannon East Everleigh, Wilts

---

1886   3.30 LAVERSTOCK MDN 3YO (D)   7f str   Good/Firm 35   -18 Slow
£3796   £1168   £584   £292

1638 **SHALIMAR** 12 [2] J H M Gosden 3-8-9 J Fortune 13/8 FAV: 26-31: 3 b f Indian Ridge - Athens Belle   75
(Groom Dancer) Towards rear early, keen, smooth prog to trck ldrs 2f out, rdn/led inside last, duelled with rnr-up,
narrowly prevailed: hvly bckd: rnr up to subs 1,000 Guineas wnr Lahan in '99 debut (fillies mdn, rtd 95, P Chapple
Hyam), subs trained by A G Foster: eff at 7f, 1m may suit: acts on gd & gd/soft grnd, handles a sharp/stiff track.
1569 **HARMONIC** 15 [1] D R C Elsworth 3-8-9 K Fallon 6/1: 24-602: 2 b f Shadeed - Running Melody   hd   74
(Rheingold) Held up, prog halfway & drvn/led briefly over 1f out, duelled with wnr inside last, just held: op 7/1.
1084 **TEE CEE** 42 [9] R Guest 3-8-9 S Sanders 11/2: 53: 3 b f Lion Cavern - Hawayah (Shareef Dancer)   1½   71
Chsd ldrs, every ch 1f out, rdn/not pace of front pair near fin: op 8/1, 6 week abs: apprec drop to 7f on fast.
-- **CAPRICCIO** [13] C G Cox 3-9-0 S Drowne 25/1: 4: Mid div & rdn 3f out, kept on well inside last, never   shd   76
not reach ldrs: debut: half brother to a mid dist performer: stays 7f, 1m+ looks sure to suit: acts on fast grnd.
1605 **FLY MORE** 13 [5] 3-9-0 P Fitzsimons (5) 33/1: 45: Chsd ldrs, onepace fnl 1f: see 1605 (6f).   3   70
1449 **HAMLYN** 21 [4] 3-9-0 N Pollard 100/30: 50-646: Keen/rear, rdn & mod gains fnl 3f: nicely bckd   1¾   67
though op 5/2, shorter priced stablemate of rnr up: btr 983.
1525 **DOUBLE GUN** 11 [11] 3-9-0 Dane O'Neill 16/1: 3-0657: Led till over 1f out, fdd: op 14/1: see 1266.   1   65
1675 **AEGEAN FLOWER** 10 [10] 3-9-0 (bl) C Rutter 66/1: 048: Chsd ldrs 5f: needs 10f+ h'caps.   3   59$
1525 **TIME BOMB** 17 [7] 3-8-9 G Hind 14/1: 0-49: Keen/chsd ldrs 5f: btr 1525 (hvy).   1½   51
915 **PRIM N PROPER** 60 [8] 3-8-9 R Hughes 12/1: 00: Held up, btn 2f out: 10th: op 10/1, 2 month abs.   5   41
1675 Piccalilli 10 [12] 3-8-9 S Whitworth 66/1:   1263 **Father Ted** 32 [3] 3-9-0 J F Egan 50/1:
1261 Harvy 32 [6] 3-9-0 A Eddery (5) 66/1:
13 ran   Time 1m 29.23 (3.73)   (Lady Banford)   J H M Gosden Manton, Wilts

---

1887   4.00 TOTE JACKPOT HCAP 3YO+ 0-90 (C)   6f   Good/Firm 35   +01 Fast   [85]
£7735   £2380   £1190   £595   3 yo rec 8 lb

1591 **BOLD EFFORT** 13 [18] K O Cunningham Brown 8-9-5 (76)(bl) R Hughes 10/1: 100521: 8 b g Bold   82
Arrangement - Malham Tarn (Riverman) Rear, no room/switched left 2f out, rdn/styd on strongly fnl 1f to lead nr
fin, rdn out: gd time: op 8/1: earlier scored at Lingfield (AW h'cap, rtd 81a): '99 scorer at Lingfield (h'cap,
rtd 97a & rtd 83): '98 wnr at Sandown & Kempton (h'caps, rtd 96 & 87a): eff at 5/6f, stays 1m: acts on firm,
gd/soft & both AWs, never fresh: suited by blinks & has run well fresh: on a fair mark, could win again.
1438 **KILCULLEN LAD** 22 [13] Lady Herries 6-8-13 (70)(vis) J F Egan 14/1: 60-052: 6 b g Fayruz - Royal   ½   73
Home (Royal Palace) Keen/held up, no room over 2f out, strong run inside last, not pace of wnr cl home.
1728 **ROO** 8 [17] R F Johnson Houghton 3-9-11 (90) S Carson (5) 33/1: 0-0653: 3 b f Rudimentary -   nk   92
Shall We Run (Hotfoot) Chsd ldrs, drvn/led over 1f out, hdd/onepace nr fin: acts on firm & fast, relishes soft grnd.
4439} **POINT OF DISPUTE** 237 [9] P J Makin 5-9-8 (79)(vis) S Sanders 6/1: 0001-4: Trkd ldrs trav well   hd   80
halfway, forced left over 1f out, kept on onepace inside last: op 7/1, reapp: '99 scorer at Lingfield & Nottingham
(h'caps, rtd 80): '98 Salisbury wnr (mdn, rtd 86): eff at 6/7f, likes fast & gd, any track: suited by a visor.
1702 **EASTER OGIL** 9 [12] 5-9-9 (80)(vis) K Fallon 100/30 FAV: 00-6205: Rear, switched 2f out, styd on   1½   77
inside last, not reach ldrs: hvly bckd: can rate higher: see 1517 (6f, classified stakes).
1794 **ZEPPO** 5 [6] 3-8-1 (58) A McCarthy (3) 20/1: 0-0406: Chsd ldrs, onepace fnl 1f: quick reapp.   shd   55
1676 **LOCH LAIRD** 10 [15] 5-9-6 (77) J Reid 12/1: 00-507: Mid div, not pace to chall: see 1471.   shd   73
1652 **WAFFLES OF AMIN** 11 [3] Dane O'Neill 3-8-9 (74) 25/1: 6-0048: Rear/drvn halfway, mod late gains.   2   65
1264 **RAINBOW RAIN** 32 [2] 6-8-8 (65) P Doe 33/1: 302209: Rear, eff 2f out, mod late gains: see 28.   ½   54
1650 **BEYOND CALCULATION** 11 [16] 6-8-8 (65) J Fortune 7/1: 0-5150: Cl up 5f: 10th: btr 1368.   shd   54
1591 **CAUDA EQUINA** 13 [8] 6-9-5 (76) S Drowne 20/1: 200560: Rear, never factor: 11th: see 1591, 905.   hd   64
*1438 **NINEACRES** 22 [4] 9-8-2 (59)(bl) Claire Bryan (5) 14/1: 052210: Chsd ldrs 5f: 12th: op 12/1.   shd   47
1810 **SAILING SHOES** 4 [10] 4-9-13 (84)(BL) P Dobbs (5) 33/1: 50-000: Led & clr after 2f, hdd over 1f out,   0
wknd quickly: 14th: blinks: quick reapp: see 1810.
1471 **CADEAUX CHER** 20 [5] 6-9-10 (81) M Hills 6/1: 0-2200: Chsd ldrs 5f: 15th: btr 1173, 716.   0
1652 Milady Lillie 11 [14] 4-7-10 (53) C Catlin (7) 25/1:   1286 Midhish Two 31 [14] 4-9-1 (72) D Harrison 16/1:
3408} Central Coast 301 [7] 4-9-12 (83) J Tate 12/1:   1591 Astrac 13 [11] 9-9-2 (73) T Ashley 66/1:
1371 Toleration 25 [19] 3-9-5 (84) N Pollard 25/1:
19 ran   Time 1m 14.16 (2.06)   (A J Richards)   K O Cunningham Brown Stockbridge, Hants

---

1888   4.30 BOLLINGER AMAT RDRS HCAP 4YO+ 0-70 (E)   1m4f   Good/Firm 35   +05 Fast   [36]
£2989   £854   £427

4154} **NORTH OF KALA** 258 [6] G L Moore 7-9-10 (32)(8oh) Mr A Quinn (7) 3/1 FAV: 0500-1: 7 b g Distinctly   39
North - Hi Kala (Kampala) Held up, smooth prog to lead over 1f out, sn pushed clr, rdly: val for 10L+: well bckd,
best time of day: op 9/4: Flat reapp, jumps fit, recent Fontwell wnr (h'cap, rtd 102h, eff at 2m/2m3f on fast & gd):
mod form on the Level last term (tried blnks): eff at 12f on fast & a stiff/gall trk: looks nicely h'capped.
1350 **TOMMY CARSON** 26 [7] Jamie Poulton 5-11-2 (52)(bl) Mr H Poulton (7) 7/1: 332-62: 5 b g Last Tycoon   6   52
- Ivory Palm (Sir Ivor) Chsd ldrs, led over 4f out, hdd over 1f out, kept on: nicely bckd: see 1350 (C/D).
1465 **DUELLO** 20 [2] M C Pipe 9-11-4 (54) Mr T Scudamore 6/1: 521-33: 9 b g Sure Blade - Royal Loft (Homing) 2   51
Chsd ldrs 2f out, kept on onepace: nicely bckd: see 1465 (sell h'cap).

613

SALISBURY TUESDAY JUNE 13TH Righthand, Galloping Track, Stiff Finish

1730 **ROYAL AXMINSTER 8** [9] Mrs P N Dutfield 5-10-9 (45) Mr L Jefford 12/1: 06-004: Rear, drvn/late gains 2 39
fnl 2f: unplcd last term (rtd 62, mdn): no form prev.
1666 **IL DESTINO 11** [8] 5-11-11 (61) Mr C B Hills (3) 9/2: 262-65: Chsd ldrs/rdn 3f out, sn held: see 1666 (10f). 4 49
1440 **HAPPY GO LUCKY 22** [3] 6-12-0 (64) Mr A Honeyball (5) 20/1: 001/06: Bhd halfway, mod late gains. 1¾ 50
4525} **CLASSIC CONKERS 230** [1] 6-9-12 (34) Mr S Rees (7) 33/1: 5460-7: Rear, mod gains: reapp: 6 wk 5 13
jmps abs (mod form): rtd 48 last term: '98 Yarmouth wnr (sell h'cap, rtd 58 at best): eff at 11/14f on fast & soft.
1350 **FAMOUS 26** [4] 7-10-3 (39) Mr W Worthington (7) 25/1: 005008: Al rear: see 90 (10f, AW). 2½ 14
66 **SLAPY DAM 209** [5] 8-10-7 (43) Mr R Bailey (7) 41/1: 0050-9: Chsd ldr, led over 5f out till over 4f out, 4 12
sn btn: 4 month jumps abs (mod form): '99 scorer at Brighton & Chepstow (clmrs, current connections, rtd 59, subs
with J M Bradley): eff at 10/12f on firm & soft, any trk: best without a visor.
1350 **ROYAL MEASURE 26** [11] 4-10-13 (49) Mr G Richards (5) 9/2: 000-30: Chsd ldrs 7f: 10th: see 1350. 1¾ 16
*1551 **JOLI FLYERS 15** [10] 6-10-6 (42) Mr T Best (5) 10/1: 0-0010: Led 7f, sn btn: 11th: btr 1551. dist 0
11 ran   Time 2m 36.02 (3.62)   (B Lennard)   G L Moore Woodingdean, E Sussex

---

1889 5.00 LEVY BOARD HCAP 3YO 0-65 (F) 7f str Good/Firm 35 -07 Slow [72]
£2786   £796   £398

1787 **MISTER CLINTON 5** [16] K T Ivory 3-8-13 (57) D O'Donohoe 5/2 FAV: -41031: 3 ch g Lion Cavern - 63
Thewaari (Eskimo) Rear, prog/switched 2f out, styd on strongly to lead nr fin, shade cosily: nicely bckd: quick
reapp: earlier scored at Brighton (mdn): suited by 7f, tried 1m: acts on firm & fast, sharp/stiff trk.
1259 **OTIME 32** [14] M Wigham 3-9-7 (65)(BL) F Norton 20/1: 020662: 3 b g Mujadil - Kick The Habit ½ 67
(Habitat) Chsd ldrs, led over 4f out, kept on well fnl 2f, hdd well ins last, no extra: acts on firm, fast & eqtrack:
eff at 6/7f: suited by blnks/visor: prev with Mrs N Macauley, gd run for new connections: see 1675.
1671 **BISHOPSTONE MAN 11** [15] S Mellor 3-9-4 (62) C Rutter 16/1: 0-4003: 3 b g Piccolo - Auntie Gladys shd 64
(Great Nephew) Chsd ldrs, rdn/chall over 1f out, kept on for press: handles fast & soft grnd: see 1061.
1787 **CHILWORTH 5** [4] T M Jones 3-8-13 (57)(VIS) R Price 50/1: 005604: Cl-up, ch 1f out, onepace: 1¼ 56
visor, quick reapp: eff at 7f, handles fast & gd grnd: see 998.
1435 **VICTORIET 22** [18] 3-8-8 (52) S Sanders 33/1: 000-55: In tch, kept on onepace fnl 2f: see 1435 (mdn). 1½ 48
1787 **CIBENZE 5** [6] 3-9-7 (65) S Drowne 4/1: -06426: Rear, styd on fnl 1f, not reach ldrs: quick reapp. 1 59
1345 **AFRICAN PETE 26** [2] 3-9-5 (63) G Hind 12/1: 036-67: Chsd ldrs, no extra fnl 1f: see 1345. ¾ 56
1511 **TEA FOR TEXAS 18** [1] 3-8-8 (52) P Doe 14/1: 520168: Rear, kept on fnl 2f, no threat: op 20/1. 1 43
1610 **ALABAMA WURLEY 13** [9] 3-8-8 (52) J F Egan 14/1: 000069: Chsd ldrs, keen, rdn/held & eased ins ¾ 42
last: jockey reported filly injured herself bhd: op 12/1: see 807.
1651 **PYJAMA GIRL 14** [20] 3-9-2 (60) S Whitworth 50/1: 06-300: In tch, no impress fnl 2f: 10th: see 1202. ½ 49
1494 **CRUISE 18** [11] 3-9-5 (63) R Hughes 14/1: 51-050: Led till over 4f out, btn 2f out: 11th: op 12/1. nk 51
1289 **MISS FLIRTATIOUS 29** [19] 3-9-4 (62)(BL) K Fallon 13/2: 002-00: Sn bhd, virt p.u. fnl 2f: 18th: blnks. 0
961 **FINAL KISS 16** [3] 3-8-8 (52)(t) A Whelan 50/1: 000-PF: Rear, broke blood vessel & fell 3f out: 8 wk abs. 0
1467 Wilfram 20 [8] 3-9-0 (58) P Fitzsimons (5) 50/1:   1045 Diamond Kiss 46 [12] 3-9-0 (58) L Newman (5) 50/1:
1710 Blackpool Mammas 9 [7] 3-9-7 (65) Claire Bryan (5) 20/1:1181 Viking Prince 31 [3] 3-8-11 (55) J Fortune 20/1:
1397 Brompton Barrage 24 [17] 3-9-5 (63) Dane O'Neill (5)   1606 Shining Star 13 [13] 3-9-5 (63) J Reid 12/1:
19 ran   Time 1m 28.46 (2.96)   (Miss Lilo Blum)   K T Ivory Radlett, Herts

---

REDCAR TUESDAY JUNE 13TH Lefthand, Flat, Galloping Track

Official Going   GOOD (GOOD/FIRM places). Stalls: Straight Course - Far side: 2m - Centre: Round - Inside.

1890 2.15 MAGNUM SELLER 2YO (G) 7f str Good 40 -13 Slow
£1855   £530   £265

1713 **WINDCHILL 8** [7] T D Easterby 2-8-6 K Darley 4/1: -00221: 2 ch f Handsome Sailor - Baroness 63
Gymcrak (Pharly) Rear, improved after halfway, led entering fnl 1f, pushed out: no bid: rnr-up in similar
last twice: suited by step up to 7f: acts on gd/soft grnd, sharp or gall tracks: likes selling grade.
1541 **BULA ROSE 17** [3] W G M Turner 2-8-6 A Daly 11/4 FAV: -52: 2 ch f Alphabatim - Titled Dancer ¾ 61
(Where to Dance) Led to below dist, kept on but held: nicely bckd: suited by step up to 7f on gd grnd.
1420 **IMPISH LAD 22** [8] B S Rothwell 2-8-11 (BL) M Fenton 13/2: 0523: 2 b g Imp Society - Madonna 2 62
Da Rossi (Mtoto) Well picd & ev ch till one pace appr fnl 1f: blnkd, lngr trip: stays 7f on gd, btr 1420 (6f).
1679 **MASTER COOL 10** [4] G M Moore 2-8-11 Dale Gibson 20/1: 44: In tch, feeling pace over 2f out. 2½ 57
1476 **DOCKLANDS ROLLER 19** [5] Kim Tinkler 50/1: 05: Al same place: see 1476. ½ 56
*1713 **LASTOFTHEWHALLEYS 8** [1] 2-8-11 F Lynch 7/2: -0016: Prom till 2f out: bckd from 9/2: 9 40
unsuited by longer 7f trip?: beat this wnr in 1713 (6f, gd/sft).
1713 **IMPREZA 8** [9] 2-8-6 (vis) P Fessey 66/1: 047: Bhd from halfway: no form. 6 25
-- **ITSAKINDOFMAGIC** [6] 2-8-6 G Bardwell 16/1: 8: In tch 3f: Presidium May foal, halfsister to a 1¼ 23
couple of 1m wnrs, dam unraced, sire a miler: B Murray.
1476 **STICKS 19** [2] 2-8-6 K Hodgson 4/1: 3P: Handy till p.u. halfway, sadly died. 0
9 ran   Time 1m 25.5 (3.7)   (Mrs Bridget Tranmer)   T D Easterby Great Habton, N Yorks

---

1891 2.45 JEROBOAM HCAP 3YO 0-70 (E) 6f Good 40 -02 Slow [77]
£3315   £1020   £510   £255

1578 **DANCE LITTLE LADY 14** [13] M W Easterby 3-8-3 (52) G Parkin 25/1: 064-01: 3 b f Common 56
Grounds - Kentucky Tears (Cougar) Front rank, led & edged right 2f out, drvn out: first win/time in the
frame: rtd 63 & 48a in '99: eff at 5/6f: acts on gd grnd, handles fibresand, sharp or gall track.
1138 **DISTINCTLY BLU 40** [3] K A Ryan 3-9-0 (63) F Lynch 16/1: 0-6162: 3 b f Distinctly North - Stifen ¾ 66
(Burslem) Led till 2f out, kept on under press: 6 week abs: eff at 5/6f on gd & gd/soft grnd, see 901.
1787 **BALFOUR 5** [4] C E Brittain 3-8-11 (60) T E Durcan 11/1: -15603: 3 b c Green Desert - Badawi ½ 61
(Diesis) In tch, eff 2f out, styd on nicely ins last: tch 14/1, qk reapp, vis omitted: eff at 6f, return to 7f?
1255 **FANTASY ADVENTURER 32** [17] J J Quinn 3-8-8 (55) J Stack 16/1: 0-0004: Prom, shaken up 2f out, nk 53
styd on but not pace to chall: promise on 2nd of 3 3 '99 starts (auct mdn, rtd 71): eff at 5/6f on fast & gd.
1817 **COLLEGE MAID 4** [11] 3-9-2 (65) A McGlone 2/1 FAV: 021125: Chsd ldrs, one pace fnl 1f: nk 64
well bckd from 7/2, quick reapp: remains in-form: see 1665.
1723 **PRETENDING 8** [10] 3-8-3 (52) G Duffield 14/1: -06536: Rear, late hdwy, never a threat: see 1723, 1085 nk 50

1768 **LORDOFENCHANTMENT 6** [15] 3-8-12 (61) Kim Tinkler 9/1: -05227: Prom & ev ch till onepace dist. *hd* **59**
1723 **KATIES VALENTINE 8** [6] 3-8-7 (56)(VIS) K Darley 7/1: 45-328: Al around same place: visored, bckd. *1¾* **50**
1804 **WILEMMGEO 4** [14] 3-8-4 (53) Joanna Badger (7) 33/1: 105059: Dwelt, never better than mid div. *1* **44**
1219 **WELCHS DREAM 35** [9] 3-9-7 (70) W Supple 20/1: 24-560: Prom till appr fnl 1f: 10th, top-weight. *shd* **61**
1464 **TERM OF ENDEARMENT 20** [7] 3-7-10 (45) G Bardwell 9/1: -00560: Never troubled ldrs: 11th. *1¾* **31**
1742 **PADDYWACK 7** [12] 3-8-7 (56)(bl) D Mernagh (3) 8/1: 220020: Handy till 2f out: 12th, quick reapp. *1¾* **37**
1427 **Judiam 22** [2] 3-9-3 (66) J Carroll 16/1: 1651 **Feast Of Romance 11** [8] 3-9-2 (65) R Mullen 16/1:
198 **Capacoostic 179** [18] 3-8-0 (49) Dale Gibson 50/1: 1710 **Top Of The Class 9** [5] 3-8-13 (62) C Teague 14/1:
731 **Nite Owl Mate 80** [1] 3-9-1 (64) C Lowther 50/1:
1822 **Bebe De Cham 4** [16] 3-9-4 (67)(VIS) R Cody Boutcher (7) 33/1:
18 ran Time 1m 11.4 (2.5) (G B Stuart) M W Easterby Sheriff Hutton, N Yorks

1892

3.15 ANDERSONS FILL HCAP 3YO+ 0-70 (E) 1m str Good 40 +07 Fast [70]
£3981 £1225 £612 £306 3 yo rec 11lb

1615 **TEMPRAMENTAL 13** [7] S R Bowring 4-8-9 (51) K Darley 15/2: 333141: 4 ch f Midish - Musical Horn (Music Boy) Set gd pace, hdd appr fnl 1f, rallied most gamely under press to get up again fnl strides: gd time: earlier won at Pontefract (fill h'cap): plcd in '99 (h'caps, rtd 47 & 45a): prev term scored at Chepstow (nurs, rtd 62, 1st time visor): eff at 1m/10f, stys 12f: acts on firm, gd/soft & both AW: has tried blinks, eff with/without visor: goes on any track & likes to dominate: very genuine. **56**
1606 **TAYOVULLIN 13** [4] K A Ryan 6-8-1 (43) Iona Wands (5) 12/1: 006522: 6 ch m Shalford - Fifth Quarter (Cure The Blues) In tch, prog to lead appr fnl 1f, hard rdn & worn down near fin: clr rem: gd run. *nk* **46**
1490 **PENNYS PRIDE 18** [6] Mrs M Reveley 5-10-0 (70) J Carroll 16/1: 302303: 5 b m Pip's Pride - Mursuma (Rarity) Rear, prog to go 2nd 1f out, no further hdwy: top-weight: acts on gd & hvy, see *2* **69**
1735 **FISHER ISLAND 8** [3] R Hollinshead 3-8-0 (53) P M Quinn (3) 33/1: 634404: Bhd till ran on fnl 1f. *nk* **51**
1559 **OAKWELL ACE 15** [13] 4-8-0 (42) D Mernagh (3) 9/1: 500525: In tch, styd on fnl 1f but not pace to chall: suited by return to 1m: acts on gd & soft, see 872. *½* **39**
1596 **FOSTON FOX 13** [8] 3-7-10 (49)(bl)(8oh) K Dalgleish (7) 100/1: -05006: Prom, eff 2f out, not quicken. *¾* **44**
1254 **SWYNFORD PLEASURE 32** [1] 4-7-11 (39) G Bardwell 25/1: 00-447: Chsd ldrs till appr fnl 1f: see 1149. *1¾* **31**
1649 **SILVER QUEEN 11** [2] 3-9-0 (67) T E Durcan 20/1: 40-008: Handy, one pace fnl 2f: see 1649. *½* **58**
1658 **THORNTOUN GOLD 11** [15] 4-8-4 (45)(1ow) A McGlone 10/1: 000-49: Al mid div: see 1658. *shd* **37**
1799 **ROUGE ETOILE 5** [12] 4-8-13 (55) W Supple 16/1: -00060: Front rank till 2f out: 10th, longer trip. *½* **45**
4441} **LEGACY OF LOVE 237** [5] 4-9-6 (62) A Beech (5) 9/1: 1044-0: Never trbld ldrs: 12th, reapp, bckd from 14/1: '99 Lingfield wnr (auct mdn, rtd 68, B Hills): unraced juv: eff at 7.5f/10f on firm & gd/soft: with Miss Hall. **0**
1631 **TOUS LES JOURS 12** [10] 4-9-6 (62) J Fanning 9/1: 40-200: Well plcd till wknd quickly 2f out: 13th. **0**
1511 **CARINTHIA 18** [17] 5-9-5 (61) R Mullen 7/2 FAV: 0-0020: Al bhd: 15th, drawn well away from the pace. **0**
1718 **Three Cherries 8** [9] 4-8-2 (44) P Fessey 33/1: 1606 **Crystal Lass 13** [11] 4-8-5 (47) J Edmunds 20/1:
1793 **Bewildered 5** [18] 3-7-10 (49)(3oh) T Hamilton (7) 100/1: 1658 **Woore Lass 11** [16] 4-8-5 (47) Kim Tinkler 14/1:
1689 **Flaxen Pride 10** [14] 5-7-10 (38)(1oh) J Lowe 12/1: 1649 **Laraza 11** [19] 3-8-11 (64)(bl) G Duffield 16/1:
19 ran Time 1m 37.4 (2.6) (Roland M Wheatley) S R Bowring Edwinstowe, Notts

1893

3.45 METHUSELAH MED AUCT MDN 2YO (E) 6f Good 40 -17 Slow
£2887 £825 £412

1486 **MAKBOOLA 19** [8] J L Dunlop 2-8-9 W Supple 4/7 FAV: 31: 2 b f Mujtahid - Haddeyah (Dayjur) Prom, led entering fnl 2f, drvn inside last, just held on: well bckd: Jan foal, dam & sire sprinters: eff at 6f, prob has enough toe for 5f: goes on gd & gd/soft grnd, gall or undulating track: should improve. **85**
-- **RIVER RAVEN** [11] Sir Mark Prescott 2-9-0 G Duffield 11/2: 2: 2 b c Efisio - River Spey (Mill Reef) Prom, eff appr fnl 1f, kept on strongly towards fin, just failed: April half-brother to sev wnrs, notably useful mid dist/stayers Jahafil & Mondschein: dam 7f juv wnr, sire 6f/1m performer: eff at 6f but looks a sure-fire wnr/improver when stepped up in trip: acts on gd grnd, gall track: promising. *shd* **89+**
-- **GENERAL HAWK** [10] R A Fahey 2-9-0 P Hanagan (7) 20/1: 3: 2 b c Distinctly North - Sabev (Saber Thrust) Well plcd & every ch, not pace of front pair inside last: tchd 50/1 on debut: 4,000 IR gns March foal, brother to a hdls wnr, dam multiple wnr in the States sire a sprinter: eff at 6f on gd grnd. *2½* **82**
1488 **NEW WONDER 18** [5] J G Given 2-8-9 Dean McKeown 25/1: 304: Keen, mid div, eff appr fnl 1f, unable to quicken: apprec this step up to 6f on gd grnd, acts on fibresand: shown enough to find a race. *1* **74**
1706 **PIVOTABLE 9** [2] 2-8-9 R Mullen 5/1: -325: Chsd ldrs, rdn 2f out, no impress: op 7/2, see 1706. *nk* **73**
-- **AMY DEE** [7] 2-8-9 Kim Tinkler 33/1: 6: Chsd ldrs, one pace fnl 2f: Be My Chief May foal, half-sister to smart sprinter Don Puccini, dam 6f juv wnr, sire 7f/1m performer: with N Tinkler. *1¼* **69**
-- **KOMALUNA** [9] 2-9-0 S Finnamore (5) 33/1: 7: Well plcd till 2f out: debut: Komaite April foal, brother to prolific winning juv sprinter Lunar Mist, dam 6/7f wnr: with S Bowring. *3* **65**
-- **CYNARA** [3] 2-8-9 Dale Gibson 33/1: 8: In tch till 2f out: debut: 4,200gns Imp Society Apr foal, half-sister to 2 wnrs, incl a 5f juv, dam a mdn, sire useful dirt performer in the States: with G M Moore. *1¾* **55**
1740 **INVESTMENT FORCE 7** [6] 2-9-0 J Fanning 16/1: 09: Led till 2f out, wknd: op 12/1, turf bow. *nk* **59**
-- **THEWHIRLINGDERVISH** [4] 2-9-0 K Darley 16/1: 0: Dwelt, never in it: 10th, op 12/1 on debut: 4,800gns Definite Article Feb first foal, dam plcd as a juv, sire high class juv & later 10/12f performer. *nk* **58**
10 ran Time 1m 12.3 (3.4) (Khalil Alsayegh) J L Dunlop Arundel, W Sussex

1894

4.15 HALF BOTTLE CLAIMER 4YO+ (F) 2m Good 40 -30 Slow
£2205 £630 £315 4 yo rec 1 lb

1802 **NOUFARI 4** [1] R Hollinshead 9-8-12 P M Quinn (3) 5/6 FAV: 1-5121: 9 b g Kahyasi - Noufiyla (Top Ville) Nvr far away, led 3f out, pshd out: well bckd, qk reapp: earlier won at Southwell (clmr, rtd 72a): '99 wnr at Nottingham, Thirsk (h'caps, rtd 76) & W'hampton (clmr, rtd 83a): '98 wnr at Southwell (2), W'hampton (2) & Newcastle (h'caps, rtd 81a & 71): eff at 14f/2m, stys 2m4f: acts on firm & gd/soft, loves fibresand, any trk. **52**
1814 **STOLEN MUSIC 4** [4] R E Barr 7-8-5 G Duffield 10/1: 00-032: 7 b m Taufan - Causa Sua (Try My Best) Well plcd, led 4f out till 3f out, kept on but held: qk reapp: ran to best at these weights: likes Redcar. *1½* **35**
1657 **ICE PACK 11** [2] Don Enrico Incisa 4-8-3 Kim Tinkler 50/1: -60003: 4 gr f Mukaddamah - Mrs Gray (Red Sunset) Early ldr, feeling pace 4f out, styd on late for third: v stiff task at the weights, stays 2m. *1* **33$**
1416 **SALVAGE 22** [7] W W Haigh 5-9-2 F Lynch 8/1: -03004: Soon led, hdd 4f out, same pace: see 779. *¾* **44**
1145 **MONDRAGON 39** [5] 10-8-10 K Darley 11/4: /04-25: Al bhd: capable of better: see 1145. *12* **28**
1660 **TURGENEV 11** [6] 11-8-9 O Pears 10/1: 005066: Never in it: stiff task, reportedly unsuited by the gd grnd *10* **19**
6 ran Time 3m 36.0 (11.2) (Ed Weetman) R Hollinshead Upper Longdon, Staffs

REDCAR TUESDAY JUNE 13TH Lefthand, Flat, Galloping Track

| **1895** | 4.45 SALMANAZAR HCAP 3YO 0-65 (F) 1m2f Good 40 -04 Slow | [69] |
| | £2457   £702   £351 | |

4461} **BAHAMAS** 236 [12] Sir Mark Prescott 3-9-3 (58) G Duffield 3/1 FAV: 0000-1: 3 b g Barathea - Rum Cay **64**
(Our Native) With ldrs, led 2f out, drvn out: reapp: only beat 4 horses home in 4 '99 starts (mdn, rtd 61):
110,000gns half-brother to smart styr Persian Punch: eff at 10f, 12f+ is going to suit: acts on gd & gall trk:
runs well fresh: typical M Prescott 3yo, improved for big step up in trip & can continue on the up-grade.
1722 **SAANEN** 8 [16] Mrs A Duffield 3-9-5 (60) R Ffrench 12/1: 400-32: 3 b g Port Lucaya - Ziffany ½ **63**
(Taufan) Handy, rdn to chall 2f out, held towards fin: improved since stepped up to 9/10f: see 1722.
1607 **ABLE SEAMAN** 13 [11] C E Brittain 3-9-7 (62) T E Durcan 16/1: 0453: 3 b g Northern Flagship - nk **64**
Love At Dawn (Grey Dawn II) In tch, shaken up 3f out, no impression till ran on below dist, btn less than
1L: op 12/1 on h'cap bow: eff at 10f, 12f is going to suit: handles gd grnd & can find similar.
*1722 **COSMIC SONG** 8 [5] R M Whitaker 3-8-9 (50)(6ex) D Mernagh (3) 7/1: 563514: Chsd ldrs, prog 1 **50**
to chall appr fnl 1f, soon onepace: op 11/2, quick reapp with a penalty & prob ran to form of 1722 (9.3f).
1299 **BOLLIN NELLIE** 29 [3] 3-8-13 (54) J Carroll 10/1: 4-4505: Rear, prog 3f out, styd on but no threat. 2½ **51**
1581 **ALTAY** 14 [4] 3-9-0 (55) R Winston 33/1: 06-036: Led till 2f out, no extra: big drop in trip, see 1581. 1¼ **50**
1610 **OCEAN SONG** 13 [10] 3-9-5 (60)(bl) S Finnamore (5) 10/1: 460037: Never near to chall: see 794. 1¾ **53**
1299 **STEPASTRAY** 29 [13] 3-8-9 (50) P Fessey 33/1: 000-08: Never better than mid-div: well btn in '99 (rtd 52). 1 **42**
1722 **MARVEL** 8 [15] 3-9-2 (57) Kim Tinkler 10/1: -00029: Never nr ldrs: in front of this rnr-up in 1722 (g/s). 12 **37**
*1593 **PRESTO** 13 [17] 3-9-0 (55)(tbl) K Darley 10/3: 0-0510: Dwelt, never on terms: 10th, nicely 6 **28**
bckd: much btr 1593 (claimer, first time blinks, gd/soft).
1610 **SAVANNAH QUEEN** 13 [1] 3-9-7 (62) F Lynch 10/1: 50050: In tch till 3f out: 13th, longer trip, see 1610, 794. **0**
1414 **JACK DAWSON** 24 [8] 3-8-13 (54) R Mullen 10/1: 0-000W: Withdrawn at start: see 852. **0**
1299 **San Dimas** 29 [2] 3-9-1 (56) W Supple 25/1:   1758 **Mister Gill** 6 [14] 3-9-0 (55) J Fanning 33/1:
14 ran   Time 2m 06.7 (4.4)   (Eclipse Thoro'breds)   Sir Mark Prescott Newmarket, Suffolk

---

GOWRAN PARK WEDNESDAY JUNE 7TH Righthand, Undulating Track

Official Going   GOOD/SOFT

| **1896** | 6.00 EBF MDN 2YO 7f Good/Soft |
| | £5865   £1360   £595 |

-- **HONOURS LIST** [2] A P O'Brien 2-9-2 M J Kinane 4/9 FAV: 1: 2 b c Danehill - Gold Script **96**
(Script Ohio) Made all, ran green but pushed well clr fnl 2f, easily: eff arnd an undul 7f on gd/soft grnd,
1m will suit: yet another smart colt from this very strong juvenile string, looks sure to win in better grade.
-- **EPIC PURSUIT** [4] D K Weld 2-9-2 P J Smullen 6/1: 2: 2 b c Salse - Perils Of Joy (Rainbow Quest) 7 **80**
Trkd wnr, rdn & well outpcd appr fnl 1f: shld stay well.
-- **FINE FEATHER** [1] J S Bolger 2-8-11 K J Manning 6/1: -43: 2 b f Bluebird - Majakerta (Unknown) 4½ **68**
Raced with wnr till hdd 4f out, ev ch till outpcd appr fnl 2f.
7 ran   Time 1m 30.9   (Mrs John Magnier)   A P O'Brien Ballydoyle, Co Tipperary

---

MAISONS LAFFITTE FRIDAY JUNE 9TH Left & Righthand, Sharpish Track

Official Going   SOFT

| **1897** | 3.40 LISTED PRIX DU CARROUSEL 4YO+ 1m7f Soft |
| | £13449   £5379   £4035 |

3011} **THREE CHEERS** 316 [4] J H M Gosden 6-9-4 S Guillot : /262-1: 6 b g Slip Anchor - Three Tails **110**
(Blakeney) Trkd ldr till went on appr halfway, hdd 3f out, rall & led again over 1f out, drvn out: reapp: rnr-up
twice in '99 (stks, rtd 114 in Gr 2): smart stayer in '98, fine 3rd in Gr 1 Ascot Gold Cup (rtd 119): last win
back in '97, at Newmarket (2, mdn & List) & Longchamp (Gr3, rtd 115): eff at 14f/2m, stays 2½m: acts on firm
& soft: eff with/without blnks/visor & t-strap: smart but quirky gelding, win a Gr race if in the mood.
-- **MR ACADEMY** [3] A Fabre 4-8-12 C Soumillon : 2: 4 b c Royal Academy - Miss d'Ouilly (Bikala) 1 **104**
-- **THEATRE KING** [2] France 6-8-12 A Badel : 3: 6 b g Old Vic - Draft Board (Rainbow Quest) 1 **103**
5 ran   Time 3m 15.1   (Sheikh Mohammed)   J H M Gosden Manton, Wilts

---

CORK FRIDAY JUNE 9TH --

Official Going   GOOD

| **1898** | 6.30 LOW LOW EBF RACE 3YO+ 1m2f Good |
| | £7400   £1600   £700 |

949 **SHAKESPEARE** 54 A P O'Brien 3-9-5 J A Heffernan 2/7 FAV: 1-41: 3 b c Rainbow Quest - Silver Lane **109**
(Silver Hawk) Trkd ldr, hdwy to chall 2f out, sn led, rdn & drew well clr ins last: 8 wk abs: returned
distressed when fin last on reapp: won sole '99 start at The Curragh (mdn, rtd 90): suited by
10f & 12f will suit: runs well fresh on fast & gd: useful & well regarded, can hold his own in Group company.
-- **RICKISON** D K Weld 3-9-2 P J Smullen 3/1: -12: 3 b c Sadler's Wells - Natuschka (Authi) 9 **90**
Set pace, drvn/hdd appr fnl 1f, sn well outpcd: 8 wks ago won at Listowel (debut, 12f appr mdn, gd/soft).
-- **SPIRITO DI PUNTO** A Leahy 3-8-7 N G McCullagh 50/1: -053: 3 b f Namaqualand - Hotel Du Lac 10 **66**
(Lomond) Raced in 3rd, lost tch fnl 2f: modest mdn, well outclassed here.
3 ran   Time 2m 10.2   (Mrs John Magnier)   A P O'Brien Ballydoyle, Co Tipperary

CURRAGH   SATURDAY JUNE 10TH   Righthand, Stiff, Galloping Track

Official Going   SOFT

1899   4.10 GR 3 GALLINULE STKS 3YO+   1m2f   Soft
£22750   £6650   £3150   £1050   3 yo rec 13lb

-- **GLYNDEBOURNE** [2] A P O'Brien 3-8-9 J A Heffernan 5/1: -211: 3 b c Sadler's Wells - Heaven Only   **118**
Knows (High Top) Cl-up, hdwy to lead 3f out, sn led, styd on strongly & rdn clr ins last: recent Curragh wnr (10f
mdn, gd/soft grnd): eff at 10/12f on soft: smart, lightly raced & improving, fully deserves ch in Irish Derby.
1482 **RIGHT WING 16** [3] J L Dunlop 6-9-8 (BL) K J Manning 7/4 JT FAV: 1-3122: 6 b h In The Wings -   3½ **113**
Nekhbet (Artaius) Settled rear, gd hdwy 3f out, styd on fnl 1f but no ch with wnr: 1st time blnks (usually
visored): ran to best upped to Gr company: likes coming late off a strong pace: see 1482, 1014.
-- **MEDIA PUZZLE** [5] D K Weld 3-8-9 P J Smullen 7/4 JT FAV: 3-113: 3 ch c Theatrical - Market Slide   ½ **112**
(Gulch) Prom, drvn/not pace of wnr fnl 2f: recent scorer at The Curragh (mdn) & Cork (stks, beat today's wnr):
eff at 10/12f: acts on soft grnd & a stiff/gall trk: v useful: win a List/Gr 3.
-- **TAKALI** [4] J Oxx 3-8-9 N G McCullagh 7/1: -2144: Handy, prog 3f out, rdn/no extra appr fnl 1f: hd **112**
earlier this term won at Cork (mdn): eff at 10/12f on soft grnd.
-- **MYTHOLOGICAL** [1] 3-8-9 P J Scallan 10/1: 1-5: recent winner of wnr.   15 **97**
5 ran   Time 2m 12.2   (Michael Tabor)   A P O'Brien Ballydoyle, Co Tipperary

CHANTILLY   SUNDAY JUNE 11TH   Righthand, Galloping Track

Official Going   GOOD TO SOFT

1900   2.00 GR 3 PRIX DE LA JONCHERE 3YO   1m   Good/Soft
£21134   £7685   £3842

-- **CAYOKE** H A Pantall 3-8-11 S Guillot 32/10: 132111: 3 b c Always Fair - Sarah Annita (Pharly)   **110**
Mid-div, rdn to chall over 2f out, switched appr fnl 1f, led ins last, drvn out: winner of 3 of his 5 starts
prev this term: eff over a gall 1m on good/soft grnd: v useful & improving.
-- **INDIAN PROSPECTOR** A Fabre 3-8-11 C Soumillon 81/10: 1-542: 3 b c Machiavellian - Danse Indienne   ¾ **108**
(Green Dancer) Led at fast pace, hdd ins last, no extra cl-home: eff at 1m on gd/soft grnd.
1025 **CRYSTAL DASS 49** T Clout 3-8-11 (bl) T Gillet 107/10: 2-1453: 3 b c Northern Crystal - Asslana   ½ **107**
(Al Nasr) Trkd ldrs, rdn to chall over 1f out, no extra for press ins last: consistent: see 1025.
8 ran   Time 1m 39.9   (Mme P-D Beck)   H A Pantall France

1901   3.15 GR 1 FRENCH OAKS 3YO FILLIES   1m2f110y   Good/Soft
£134486   £53794   £26897   £13449

-- **EGYPTBAND** [12] Mme C Head 3-9-0 D Doleuze 57/10cp: 1-11: 3 b f Dixieland Band - Egyptown (Top   **123**
Ville) Held up, smooth hdwy 2f out, led appr fnl 1f, rdn clr: recent scorer at Saint-Cloud (reapp, stks):
won sole juv start: eff at 10.5f on gd/soft, 12f shld suit: v smart & fast improving, win more Gr races.
*944 **VOLVORETA 60** [1] C Lerner 3-9-0 T Thulliez 4/5 FAV: 11-12: 3 ch f Suave Dancer -   3 **118**
Robertiya (Don Roberto) Mid-div, hdwy to lead 2f out, sn hdd, not pace of wnr ins last: clr rem: 7 wk abs:
not disgraced against a v progressive rival, acts on gd/soft & soft: shld stay 12f: win again in Gr 2/3.
1457 **GOLDAMIX 21** [9] C Laffon Parias 3-9-0 D Boeuf 57/10cp: -11-43: 3 gr f Linamix - Gold's Dance   3 **113**
(Goldneyev) Cl-up, led briefly over 2f out, no extra over 1f out: acts on hvy, handles gd/soft: see 1457.
*1457 **REVE DOSCAR 21** [15] Mme M Bollack Badel 3-9-0 A Badel 73/10cp: 2-2214: Settled rear,   1 **111**
styd on for press fnl 2f, not reach ldrs: Gr1 scorer in 1457 (ahead of today's 3rd).
1457 **FOLIE DANSE 21** [8] 3-9-0 D Bonilla 261/10: 11-1525: Waited with, late hdwy, nvr nrr: see 1457.   ¾ **110**
4245} **NEW STORY 252** [3] 3-9-0 C Soumillon 203/10: 452-16: Chsd ldrs, rdn to imprv over 1f out, sn held: shd **110**
recent wnr here at Chantilly: 3L rnr-up in a Longchamp Gr 1 in '99 (1m, hvy, rtd 109).
1319 **LADY OF CHAD 28** [14] 3-9-0 G Mosse 67/10: 11-107: Nvr a threat: longer trip, btr 1027 (1m).   ½ **109**
1319 **XUA 28** [13] 3-9-0 O Peslier 178/10: 3-1108: Bhd, mod late gains: Italian raider: see 1117.   shd **109**
1459 **TANZILLA 21** [6] 3-9-0 J P Murtagh 68/1: 12300: Prom, rdn/wknd fnl 2f, fin 12th: btr 1223 (List).   0
1404 **ARDUINE 22** [10] 3-9-0 C Asmussen 235/10: 6-330: Front rank, fdd fnl 2f, 13th: mdn: see 1404 (gd/fm).   0
14 ran   Time 2m 08.5   (Wertheimer Et Frere)   Mme C Head France

1902   4.25 GR 2 GRAND PRIX DE CHANTILLY 4YO+   1m4f   Good/Soft
£33622   £13449   £6724   £3362

4238} **DARING MISS 253** [4] A Fabre 4-8-8 C Soumillon 31/10 FAV: 12-411: 4 b f Sadler's Wells - Bourbon   **110**
Girl (Ile De Bourbon) Led at slow pace, hdd after 3f, led over 2f out, strongly, pressed ins last, drvn out,
just prevailed: dual wnr in '99, subs an unlucky rnr-up in a Longchamp Gr 2 (prematurely eased when jockey
mistook winning post, rtd 103): eff at 12f on gd/soft & hvy: smart & progressive, win more Gr races.
*1461 **FIRST MAGNITUDE 20** [1] A Fabre 4-9-2 O Peslier 6/1: 0-6112: 4 ch c Arazi - Crystal Cup   hd **117**
(Nijinsky) Rear, gd hdwy over 1f out, strong chall ins last, just held: v smart run conceding weight: see 1461.
2980} **BEN EWAR 323** [5] F Doumen 6-8-11 D Bonilla 97/10: -13423: 6 b b Old Vic - Sunset Reef (Mill Reef)   1½ **109**
Waited with, styd on well fnl 2f, not reach ldrs: consistent form this term, won on reapp: 4th in a val rtd
h'cap at Goodwood in '99 (rtd 109): thrice a wnr in France in '98: eff at 10/13f on gd & hvy: v useful.
1152 **LUCIDO 37** [3] J L Dunlop 4-8-11 Pat Eddery 62/10: 003-54: Trkd ldr till qcknd & went on after   ¾ **108**
4f, hdd 2f out, sn onepcd: unsuited by the slow early pace here: see 1152.
2980} **LUCKY DREAM 323** [2] 6-9-2 T Jarnet 78/10: 115-55: In tch, drvn/no extra appr fnl 2f.   ½ **111**
+1057 **LITTLE ROCK 43** [6] 4-8-11 K Fallon 38/10: 401-16: Led briefly after 3f, with ldrs till   ½ **106**
short of room & dropped rear over 1f out, no threat after: 6 wk abs: no luck in running here: see 1057.
6 ran   Time 2m 34.8   (K Abdulla)   A Fabre France

FRAUENFELD (SWITZERLAND)　　MONDAY JUNE 12TH　--

Official Going　　GOOD

1903　　2.45 GROSSER PREIS DER KAELIN 4YO+　　1m4f　　Good
£5647　£2259　£1694

*1119 **AKBAR** 43 M Johnston 4-9-9 M J Kinane : 230-11: 4 b c Doyoun - Akishka (Nishapour)　　　　　99
Made all, styd on well ins last, comfortably: recent scorer in Switzerland (stks): mainly with J Oxx in '99,
plcd sev times, incl in List company (rtd 101): eff at 10/14f on fast & hvy grnd: useful & consistent.
-- 　**HARISHON** Switzerland 4-9-9 C Brechon : 2 : 4 b c Waajib - Chenya (Beldale Flutter)　　　　1　95
-- 　**ACANTHUS** Switzerland 4-8-9 P Coppin : 3 : 4 ch c Hondo Mondo - Abundantia (Surumu)　　4¼　75
6 ran　　Time 2m 31.5　　　　(Markus Graff)　　　M Johnston Middleham, N Yorks

1904　　4.15 GROSSER PREIS DER SIA 4YO+　　1m1f55y　　Good
£1882　£753　£565

795 **CELESTIAL KEY** 74 M Johnston 10-9-11 M J Kinane : -20021: 10 br g Star De Naskra - Casa Key　　62
(Cormorant) Chsd ldrs, hdwy to lead dist, drvn out to hold on: plcd in Germany in '99 (unplcd in Britain,
rtd 52a, h'cap): '98 miss at Dielsdorf (amat rdrs stks, rtd 90, unplcd on sand, rtd 75a): eff arnd 7/9.3f on
firm, soft & fibresand: acts on any trk & best without a t-strap: tough 10yo.
-- 　**FOR PLEASURE** Switzerland 5-9-11 Ms Marlies Gloor : 2 : 5 b h Dashing Blade - Full Board (Fabulous　hd　61
Dancer) -:
-- 　**LION DOR** Switzerland 4-9-13 P Coppin : 3 : 4 b c Deploy - La Joie (Acatenango)　　　　　1　61
9 ran　　Time 1m 55.2　　　　(Markus Graff)　　　M Johnston Middleham, N Yorks

HAMILTON　　WEDNESDAY JUNE 14TH　　Righthand, Undulating Track, Uphill Finish

Official Going　　GOOD (GOOD/SOFT Places). Stalls: Stands Side, Except 1m - Inside

1905　　6.45 HAMILTON AMAT CLASSIFIED STKS 3YO+ 0-70　　6f　　Good/Firm 28　-32 Slow
£3607　£1110　£555　£277　　3 yo rec 8 lb

1869 **SURPRISED** 2 [4] R A Fahey 5-11-8 Miss S Brotherton (5) 4/1: 20-001: 5 b g Superpower - Indigo　　69
(Primo Dominie) Cl-up, led over 2f out, rdn & just held on nr fin: op 7/2, qck reapp: '99 wnr at Pontefract (h'cap,
rtd 72): eff at 5/6f & stays 7.4f: acts on firm & gd/soft, any trk: best without blnks: runs well for an amateur.
1631 **FRIAR TUCK** 13 [1] Miss L A Perratt 5-11-8 Miss Diana Jones 5/1: 000-02: 5 ch g Inchinor - Jay Gee　hd　68
Ell (Vaigly Great) Held up, rdn/styd on well ins last, just held: rnr-up in '99 (h'cap, rtd 87): '98 wnr at York
(val h'cap, rtd 101): eff at 5/6f on fast, loves soft: likes a sharp or gall trk: runs well fresh: v well h'capped.
1836 **PETERS IMP** 4 [6] A Berry 5-11-8 Mrs C Williams 2/1 FAV: -50253: 5 b g Imp Society - Catherine Clare　1¼　65
(Sallust) Held up in tch, prog/ch 1f out, held nr fin: op 5/2, quick reapp: see 1038.
1778 **DISTINCTIVE DREAM** 7 [5] A Bailey 6-11-8 Miss Bridget Gatehouse (3) 3/1: 260004: In tch, ch 1f out,　½　63
sn no extra: op 5/2: see 1250, 598.
1869 **ROYAL ARROW FR** 2 [2] 4-11-8 Mr A Honeyball(5) 8/1: -00005: Led 4f, sn held: qck reapp.　　5　54
3248} **THE CASTIGATOR** 309 [3] 3-11-0 Miss R Bastiman (7) 50/1: 004-6: Prom till halfway: reapp: unplcd　14　33
last term (rtd 61, auct mdn, J J O'Neill): now with R Bastiman.
6 ran　　Time 1m 13.4 (3.6)　　　(D R Brotherton)　　　R A Fahey Butterwick, N Yorks

1906　　7.15 BRYANT AUCT MDN QUALIFIER 2YO (E)　　5f　　Good/Firm 28　-34 Slow
£3510　£1080　£540　£270

-- **BECKY SIMMONS** [2] A P Jarvis 2-8-1 D Mernagh (3) 9/1: 1: 2 b f Mujadil - Jolies Eaux (Shirley Heights)　81
Handy, led 1f out, styd on well, rdn out: Apr foal, cost 6,000gns: half sister to 2 juv wnrs: eff at 5f, shld get
further: acts on fast & a stiff/undul trk: runs well fresh: open to further improvement.
1488 **FANTASY BELIEVER** 19 [4] J J Quinn 2-8-7 G Duffield 11/4 FAV: -3242: 2 b g Sure Blade - Delicious　½　84
(Dominion) Keen/handy, narrow lead over 1f out, sn hdd, kept on: well bckd: acts on fast & hvy: can find similar.
1653 **ORIENTAL MIST** 12 [9] Miss L A Perratt 2-8-12 C Lowther 6/1: 543: 2 gr c Balla Cove - Donna Katrina　1¾　85
(King's Lake) Trkd ldrs, rdn & styd on fnl 1f, not pace to chall: return to 6f shld suit: see 1653.
1595 **MON SECRET** 14 [6] J L Eyre 2-8-7 J Fanning 3/1: 0324: Cl-up, ch over 1f out, held ins last: op　1¾　76
7/2: handles fast & gd/soft grnd: see 1595, 1130.
-- **KELETI** [5] 2-8-7 J Carroll 8/1: 5: Dwelt/rear, mod late gains: op 7/1: Efisio colt, May foal, cost　3　69
8,000gns: half brother to 2 juv wnrs: sire 6f/1m performer: apprec 6f+ & shld improve for M Johnston.
730 **KANDYMAL** 81 [3] 2-8-2 P Hanagan (7) 14/1: -06: In tch, btn over 1f out: 12 wk abs: see 730.　　nk　63
1684 **ITALIAN AFFAIR** 11 [7] 2-7-13 J Bramhill 10/1: 027: Narrow lead till over 1f out, fdd: btr 1684 (fm).　nk　59
1659 **LADY ROCK** 12 [8] 2-8-5 O Pears 11/1: -08: Dwelt, al rear: see 1659.　　　　　5　56
-- **GOLGOTHA** [1] 2-8-0 P Fessey 20/1: 9: Slowly away & al rear: op 14/1: Presidium filly, Jan foal,　1¼　48
cost 3,200gns: sire a useful miler: with A Berry.
9 ran　　Time 1m 01.2 (3.1)　　　(Mrs D B Brazier)　　　A P Jarvis Aston Upthorpe, Oxon

1907　　7.45 WALTER SCOTT MDN HCAP 3YO+ 0-65 (F)　　1m65y rnd　Good/Firm 28　-01 Slow　　[63]
£3835　£1180　£590　£295　　3 yo rec 11lb

1681 **STORMSWELL** 11 [8] R A Fahey 3-8-3 (49) R Winston 7/1: 0-0031: 3 ch f Persian Bold - Stormswept　　53
(Storm Bird) Al handy, narrow lead ins last, held on gamely, all out: rtd 62 in '99 (unplcd, mdn): eff at 7f/1m:
acts on fast & soft grnd, stiff/undul trk.
1603 **KING TUT** 14 [11] J G Given 4-8-13 (48) Dean McKeown 11/2: 000-22: 4 ch g Anshan - Fahrenheit　nk　50
(Mount Hagen) Dwelt/towards rear, styd on well from over 1f out, just held: eff at 7f/1m, handles fast & soft
grnd: gd run for new connections, prev with W Jarvis: see 1603 (clmr).
1446 **CLASSIC LORD** 22 [10] M Johnston 3-8-3 (49) J Fanning 5/1: 0-0003: 3 b g Wolfhound - Janaat　hd　50
(Kris) Mid-div, prog to chall fnl 1f, just held nr line: handles fast & gd/soft grnd: eff around 1m: see 1446 (12f).

1499 **PUPPET PLAY** 19 [14] E J Alston 5-8-11 (46) J Carroll 10/1: 420304: Led, rdn/hdd ins last, just held   hd **46**
cl-home: beaten less than 1L: acts on both AWs & fast grnd: see 293.
--   **SOCIETY TIMES** [9] 7-7-11 (32)(1ow)(2oh) J Bramhill 33/1: 606/5: Twds rear, prog 3f out & ch fnl 1f,   1¾ **28**
held nr fin: reapp, long abs: unplcd/mod form from 3 starts when last rcd in '97: stays a stiff 1m & handles fast.
4513} **BURNING TRUTH** 232 [16] 6-10-0 (63) G Duffield 7/1: 3044-6: Mid-div, eff 2f out, held ins last: 7 mnth   nk **59**
jumps abs (unplcd, rtd 74h), top-weight: plcd thrice in '99 (rtd 67 & 57a, h'caps): 2nd twice in '98 (rtd 68,
class stks): eff at 1m/9f, prob stays 10f: handles firm & gd/soft, prob fibresand, likes a stiff/gall trk.
1793 **SWYNFORD ELEGANCE** 6 [13] 3-7-10 (42)(1oh) N Kennedy 4/1 FAV: 50-027: Rear, mod gains fnl 2f.   1 **36**
346 **LIONS DOMANE** 148 [12] 3-8-1 (47) Dale Gibson 14/1: 00-268: Prom 7f: abs: see 257 (AW, 7f).   ½ **40**
1681 **PHARAOHS HOUSE** 11 [4] 3-8-4 (49)(bl)(1ow) K Darley 20/1: 000-09: Chsd ldrs, held 1f out: blnks reapp.¾ **41**
1388 **SMILE ITS SHOWTIME** 25 [2] 3-8-3 (49) P Fessey 20/1: -0000: In tch 6f: 10th: h'cap bow: mod form.   ¾ **40**
1723 **WATERGOLD** 9 [7] 3-8-2 (48)(vis) P Hanagan (7) 16/1: 0-5000: Al rear: 11th: flattered 1105 (6f).   4 **31**
1658 **TOSHIBA TIMES** 12 [6] 4-7-13 (34)(VIS) D Mernagh (3) 10/1: 00-000: Dwelt, mid-div halfway, rdn/btn   **0**
2f out: 15th: visor: unplcd in '99 (rtd 61, mdn, prob flattered): no form since '98 start.
1444 Way Out West 22 [15] 3-7-10 (42) S Righton 25/1: -- Take Notice [5] 7-7-11 (31)(4oh) G Baker (7) 100/1:
1685 Monaco 11 [3] 6-7-11 (32)(1ow)(4oh) D Egan (0) 16/1: 1596 Peng 14 [1] 3-9-3 (63)(t) O Pears 20/1:
16 ran   Time 1m 46.2 (2.4)   (Exors Of The Late M J Paver)   R A Fahey Butterwick, N Yorks

---

HAMILTON WEDNESDAY JUNE 14TH Righthnad, Undulating Track, Uphill Finish

Official Going   GOOD (Good To Soft Places) Stalls, Except - Inside

1908	8.15 FAMOUSE GROUSE HCAP 3YO+ 0-75 (E) 1m4f Good/Firm 28 +01 Fast [73]
	£5447 £1676 £838 £419 3 yo rec 15lb

1816 **SPREE VISION** 5 [13] P Monteith 4-8-4 (49) K Darley 9/1: 000451: 4 b g Suave Dancer - Regent's   **55**
Folly (Touching Wood) Held up, rdn/prog to lead over 1f out, held on well: quick reapp, best
time of night: plcd over timber in 99/00 (mdn hdle): rtd 82 in '99 (rnr-up, h'cap, S C Williams): '98 Newcastle
wnr (juv auct mdn): eff at 12f, tried further: acts on fast grnd & a stiff/gall trk: v well h'capped, win again.
1689 **OCTANE** 11 [1] W M Brisbourne 4-8-4 (49) A McCarthy (3) 7/2 JT FAV: 003132: 4 b g Cryptoclearance - nk **54**
Something True (Sir Ivor) Held up, prog/no room over 2f out & again over 1f out, styd on ins last,
just held: no luck in running, wnr with a clr run: shld win again sn: see 1689, 1432.
1683 **ONCE MORE FOR LUCK** 11 [2] Mrs M Reveley 9-9-1 (60) T Eaves (7) 7/1: 4-0603: 9 b g Petorius -   1½ **63**
Mrs Lucky (Royal Match) Held up rear, prog when no room over 2f out & again over 1f out, kept on ins last,
not pace to chall: imprvd effort here, looks nicely h'capped & turn not far away: see 779.
1656 **LITTLE JOHN** 12 [8] Miss L A Perratt 4-8-13 (58) Dale Gibson 8/1: 446-34: Mid-div, prog/ch over 1f   1¼ **59**
out, held nr fin: see 1656.
1839 **GREEN BOPPER** 4 [9] 7-9-8 (67) C Lowther 9/1: 421055: Handy, led 3f out, sn hdd & held fnl 1f.   5 **61**
1689 **LORD ADVOCATE** 11 [7] 12-7-10 (41)(vis)(18oh) P Fessey 50/1: 0-0006: Led 7f, wknd over 1f out.   2 **32**
1816 **EVENING SCENT** 5 [6] 4-8-0 (45) N Kennedy 7/2 JT FAV: -60327: Hndy, led over 2f out till over 1f out, fdd. 1½ **34**
1683 **ACCYSTAN** 11 [3] 5-8-5 (50) G Duffield 20/1: 633508: Mid-div, no prog over 2f out: see 642 (AW).   3 **35**
4444} **GENSCHER** 238 [11] 4-8-10 (55) J Fanning 14/1: 1460-9: Mid-div, no impress fnl 2f: flat reapp, jmps   2 **37**
fit (rtd 85h, h'cap): '99 Hamilton scorer (C/D h'cap, rtd 58): eff at 12f on firm & fast grnd, likes a stiff/undul trk.
1546 **KATIYMANN** 16 [4] 8-7-10 (41)(tVI) D Mernagh (1) 20/1: 001-00: Al rear: 10th: visor: see 1546 (sell).   ¾ **22**
1788 **QUIET ARCH** 6 [5] 7-8-10 (55)(vis) P Hanagan (7) 33/1: 40-050: Led 5f out till over 2f out, fdd: 11th.   hd **35**
1563 **PRINCE NICHOLAS** 16 [10] 5-8-13 (58) Dean McKeown 8/1: 244040: In tch 9f: 12th: see 1052, 779.   2 **35**
1432 Roma 23 [14] 5-7-10 (41)(BL)(2oh) G Baker (7) 20/1: 1769 Divine Appeal 7 [12] 5-9-10 (69) C Teague 50/1:
14 ran   Time 2m 35.00 (3.2)   (I Bell)   P Monteith Lothian

HAMILTON WEDNESDAY JUNE 14TH Righthand, Undulating Track, Uphill Finish

Official Going   GOOD (Good To Soft Places) Stalls, Except - Inside

1909	8.45 CLASSIFIED CLAIMER 3YO 0-70 (E) 1m3f Good/Firm 28 -57 Slow
	£3445 £1060 £530 £265

1195 **ROOFTOP PROTEST** 38 [7] Mrs M Reveley 3-9-0 K Darley 9/4: 65-031: 3 b g Thatching - Seattle Siren   **59**
(Seattle Slew) Trkd ldrs, rdn/hung left over 1f out, led ins last, styd on well, drvn out: slow time: unplcd in '99
(rtd 67): apprec step up to 11f, could get further: acts on fast grnd & a stiff/undul trk: enjoys claiming grade.
1480 **PAPI SPECIAL** 20 [5] I Semple 3-8-10 (vis) R Winston 8/1: 22-002: 3 b g Tragic Role - Practical   ¾ **54**
(Ballymore) Led 2f, remained handy, kept on for press ins last: handles fast & soft: stays a slowly run 11f.
1644 **FRENCH MASTER** 12 [6] P C Haslam 3-8-1 (vis) G Baker (7) 2/1 FAV: 331033: 3 b g Petardia - Reasonably ¾ **44**
French (Reasonable) Led after 2f, rdn/hdd ins last & no extra cl-home: visor reapplied: see 806 (sell, 10f).
1193 **LUCKY JUDGE** 33 [3] W W Haigh 3-9-10 F Lynch 33/1: 0-504: Held up, rdn/ch & hung left over 1f out,   ½ **66$**
not pace of front pair cl-home: off but just 55, treat rating with caution: see 902 (mdn).
1632 **DULZIE** 13 [1] 3-8-7 D Mernagh (3) 5/1: -24655: Held up, prog/ch 1f out, fdd ins last: see 589 (7f, sell).   1 **48$**
1780 **LA TORTUGA** 7 [2] 3-8-8 A McCarthy (3) 7/1: 0-0006: In tch, ch over 1f out, fdd: see 108.   2 **46**
1730 **STAFFORD KING** 9 [4] 3-9-8 P Hanagan (7) 10/1: 042007: Al rear: btr 1002, 933 (hvy).   1¼ **58$**
7 ran   Time 2m 28.2 (9.4)   (P D Savill)   Mrs M Reveley Lingdale, N Yorks

1910	9.15 HERE AGAIN HCAP 3YO+ 0-60 (F) 5f Good/Firm 28 -00 Slow [58]
	£3818 £1175 £587 £293 3 yo rec 7 lb Quartet racing stands side soon struggling.

1487 **BEYOND THE CLOUDS** 20 [12] J S Wainwright 4-9-6 (50) R Winston 13/2: -00261: 4 b g Midnish -   **55**
Tongabezi (Shernazar) Chsd ldrs far side, prog to lead ins last, styd on well, rdn out: plcd last term (rtd 54,
h'cap): eff at 5f, stays 6f: acts on fast grnd & a stiff/undul trk: eff in a visor, 1st win here tonight without.
1412 **HARVEYS FUTURE** 25 [9] P L Gilligan 6-9-0 (44) G Duffield 5/1: 020-32: 6 b g Never So Bold - Orba   1½ **44**
Gold (Gold Crest) Towards rear far side, prog to chase wnr fnl 1f, kept on: acts on fast, soft & fibresand: see 1412.
1578 **EASTERN RAINBOW** 15 [14] K A Ryan 4-8-6 (36)(bl) F Lynch 7/2 FAV: 0-0023: 4 b g Bluebird - Insaf   shd **36**

HAMILTON WEDNESDAY JUNE 14TH Righthand, Undulating Track, Uphill Finish

(Raise A Native) Bmpd start & bhd, drvn & styd on well from over 1f out, nrst fin: eff at 5f, return to 6f shld prove ideal: handles fast & gd/soft grnd: can find similar on this evidence: see 1578 (mdn h'cap).
1724 **BIFF EM 9** [7] Miss L A Perratt 6-8-9 (39) C Lowther 12/1: -50304: Chsd ldrs far side, held fnl 1f. *3* **32**
1734 **MISS GRAPETTE 9** [11] 4-8-10 (40) J Carroll 25/1: 0-0005: Far side, led after 2f till hdd/fdd ins last. *hd* **32**
2550} **CLOHAMON 341** [10] 5-8-7 (37) K Hodgson 33/1: 0000-6: Led 2f far side, wknd over 1f out: reapp: *nk* **28**
mod form/unplcd last term (rtd 30, 1st time visor).
1298 **BATALEUR 30** [17] 7-9-1 (45) P Fessey 12/1: 654007: In tch far side, held over 1f out: see 1005, 499. *1½* **33**
1868 **DISTANT KING 2** [13] 7-8-3 (33) D Egan (5) 33/1: 000008: Bhd far side, mod gains: quick reapp. *¾* **19**
1663 **PISCES LAD 12** [3] 4-9-13 (57) K Darley 8/1: -10209: Stands side, held 2f out: see 1430, 781 (mdn) *¾* **41**
1766 **BANDIDA 7** [16] 6-8-5 (35) R Lappin 16/1: 060: Bhd far side, mod late gains: 10th: see 1244 (C/D). *hd* **18**
1629 **TICK TOCK 13** [15] 3-9-4 (55) Dean McKeown 5/1: -00220: Chsd ldrs far side 4f: 11th: see 1512, 1256. *shd* **38**
1233 **Napier Star 34** [6] 7-8-3 (33)(t) G Baker (7) 25/1:
1843 **Dubai Nurse 4** [4] 6-8-5 (35)(bl) P Hanagan (7) 20/1:
1143 **Impaldi 40** [8] 5-8-6 (36) N Kennedy 14/1:
1766 **Chok Di 7** [5] 4-8-3 (33)(bl) J Fanning 20/1:
1081 **Lyrical Legacy 43** [18] 3-8-5 (42)(vis) D Mernagh (3) 20/1:
1766 **Red Symphony 7** [2] 4-9-7 (51)(vis)(6ex) O Pears 11/1:
17 ran Time 59.5 (1.4) (Peter Charalambous) J S Wainwright Pennythorpe, N Yorks

LINGFIELD (MIXED) WEDNESDAY JUNE 14TH Lefthand, Sharp, Undulating Track

Official Going Turf: FIRM. AW: STANDARD. Stalls: AW: 5f/1m - Outside, Rem - Inside; Turf: 9f - Inside, 11f - Outside.

1911

1.30 AUSTRALIA HCAP DIV 1 3YO 0-60 (F) 1m3f106y Firm V Slow [67]
£2362 £675 £337

*1446 **PENSHIEL 22** [1] J L Dunlop 3-9-7 (60) Pat Eddery 4/9 FAV: 000-11: 3 b g Mtoto - Highland Ceilidh **69**
(Scottish Reel) Prom, eff to lead appr fnl 1f, sn in command, easing down: val 5L, hvly bckd, sow time: prev won reapp at Beverley (h'cap): unplcd at up to 1m last term (rtd 60): imprvd since stepped up to 12f, will get further: acts on firm & gd grnd, prob any trk: runs well fresh: imprvg & unexposed, rate higher & win again.
789 **ST GEORGES BOY 76** [2] H Morrison 3-7-11 (36)(1ow)(9oh) J Lowe 40/1: 0-6002: 3 b c Inchinor - *2½* **39**
Deanta In Eirinn (Red Sunset) Prom, rdn 2f out, styd on for 2nd but no ch with wnr: 11 wk abs: stiff task 9lbs o/h & best run yet for new connections: apprec step up to 11.5f on firm grnd: see 555.
1141 **IRISH DANCER 41** [6] Miss Gay Kelleway 3-8-6 (45) Dane O'Neill 20/1: 04-003: 3 ch f Lahib - Mazarine *nk* **47**
Blue (Chief's Crown) Bhd till ran on fnl 2f, nrst fin: 6 wk abs: suited by step up to 11.5f on firm grnd.
315 **LAGO DI COMO 154** [5] T J Naughton 3-9-5 (58) J Fortune 12/1: 00-304: Set slow place till hdd *nk* **60**
appr fnl 1f, no extra: 5 month abs: just about stays a slow run/sharp 11.5f, handles firm & equitrack.
1661 **THE WALRUS 12** [8] 3-8-10 (49) J Tate 10/1: 033005: Chsd ldrs, same pace appr fnl 1f: op 8/1. *nk* **50**
1671 **HARD DAYS NIGHT 12** [7] 3-8-1 (40) R Mullen 40/1: 0-0006: Nvr nr to chall: unplcd juv (nurs, rtd 51). *2½* **38**
1607 **KINGS TO OPEN 14** [3] 3-9-0 (53) F Norton 14/1: 0-067: Mid-div thr'out: big step up in trip on h'cap bow. *1* **50**
1730 **CROSS DALL 9** [12] 3-9-2 (55)(vis) T G McLaughlin 6/1: 310058: Lost 20L start, nvr in it: visor reapplied. *8* **44**
1332 **BLESS 28** [11] 3-8-4 (43) A Nicholls (3) 20/1: -00609: Mid-div, fdd appr fnl 2f: see 1096, 892. *¾* **31**
36 **COOL LOCATION 215** [10] 3-7-10 (35)(5oh) M Henry 50/1: 0000-0: Al towards rear: 10th, no form. *11* **13**
2808} **New Earth Maiden 330** [4] 3-7-10 (35)(2oh) G Bardwell 50/1:
1099 **Issara 43** [9] 3-7-10 (35)(10oh) R Brisland (5) 33/1:
12 ran Time 2m 30.91 (7.51) (Cyril Humphries) J L Dunlop Arundel, W Sussex

1912

2.00 SPONSOR MDN 3YO (D) 1m1f Firm Slow
£3776 £1162 £581 £290

1269 **NEW ASSEMBLY 33** [9] Sir Michael Stoute 3-8-9 K Fallon 8/13 FAV: 00-21: 3 b f Machiavellian - Abbey **85**
Strand (Shadeed) Cl-up, led halfway, made rest, pushed out, shade cmftbly: nicely bckd to land the odds: unplcd in 2 '99 mdns (rtd 85): eff at 1m/9f & will get further: acts on firm/fast grnd, sharp/undul or gall trks.
1449 **TOUGH MEN 22** [5] H R A Cecil 3-9-0 T Quinn 7/2: -52: 3 b c Woodman - Rhumba Rage (Nureyev) *¾* **87**
Bhd ldrs, shaken up to chase wnr appr fnl 1f, styd on nicely nr fin: tchd 5/1, clr rem: apprec step up to 9f on firm grnd & will apprec further: improving, shld win a maiden.
1157 **WINDFALL 39** [6] C A Cyzer 3-9-0 S Sanders 50/1: 0-03: 3 b g Polish Precedent - Captive Heart *4* **77$**
(Conquistador Cielo) Well plcd & ev ch till outpcd 2f out: suited by drop back to 9f on firm grnd & clr of rem.
-- **CITRUS MAGIC** [3] K Bell 3-9-0 J Bosley (7) 33/1: -4: Slow away & off the pace, late hdwy past *4* **69**
btn horses: debut: Cosmonaut colt who will find easier mdns.
-- **OPTION** [1] 3-8-9 F Norton 16/1: -5: In tch, rdn & onepace 3f out: Red Ransom filly out of a useful mare *1½* **61**
-- **CALDIZ** [7] 3-9-0 (t) Pat Eddery 5/1: -6: Nvr on terms: op 3/1: Warning colt, dam a useful 10f wnr. *8* **50**
1771 **HEFIN 7** [4] 3-9-0 G Faulkner (3) 50/1: -007: Pld hard, wide, al towards rear: quick reapp, no form. *½* **49**
421 **MISTER HAVANA 137** [8] 3-9-0 S Carson (5) 50/1: -08: Slow away, sn ran wide, nvr dngrs: absence. *shd* **49**
1640 **MISS MANETTE 13** [2] 3-8-9 J Lowe 25/1: -69: Led, ran wide after 2f, hdd & btn 5f out: see 1640. *21* **14**
9 ran Time 1m 54.58 (4.18) (The Queen) Sir Michael Stoute Newmarket

1913

2.30 COME RACING CLAIMER 3YO+ (F) 6f aw rnd Standard Inapplicable
£2341 £669 £334

*1739 **AUBRIETA 8** [3] D Haydn Jones 4-9-4 (bl) K Fallon 10/11 FAV: 045011: 4 b f Dayjur - Fennel (Slew O' **63a**
Gold) Trkd ldrs, led appr fnl 1f, easily pulled clr: well bckd: recent wnr again here at Lingfield (clmr): '99 wnr again at Lingfield (mdn, rtd 59a & 62): plcd in '98 (rtd 79, C Brittain): eff at 6/7f, tried 1m: acts on fast, gd grnd, equitrack/Lingfield specialist: best blinkered in claimers & has struck top form.
1557 **PALO BLANCO 16** [8] Andrew Reid 9-8-8 M Henry 3/1: 422332: 9 b m Precocious - Linpac Mapleleaf *5* **41a**
(Dominion) Chsd ldrs, styd on for 2nd fnl 1f but rdly outpcd by wnr: bckd from 4/1: oft plcd but 3 yrs since won.
1772 **GLASTONBURY 7** [5] P Howling 4-8-9 F Norton 20/1: 000503: 4 b g Common Grounds - Harmonious *2½* **35a**
(Sharood) Led till appr fnl 1f, no extra: qck reapp, stiff task at the weights: apprec drop back to 6f: see 425.
1881 **ECUDAMAH 2** [6] Miss Jacqueline S Doyle 4-9-3 (BL) L Newman(5) 7/1: -00064: Outpcd: blnkd, qck reapp *1¾* **38a**
1741 **GAELIC FORAY 8** [4] 4-8-8 S Drowne 12/1: 0-0035: Nvr on terms: stiff task, btr 1741 (7f). *1* **26a**
1508 **TROJAN HERO 19** [7] 9-8-13 (t) T G McLaughlin 14/1: 300606: Prom till halfway: see 201 (fibresand). *shd* **31a**
1741 **ALJAZ 8** [2] 10-9-1 Dane O'Neill 12/1: 064647: Handy 3f: op 10/1: see 44. *¾* **31a**
1732 **FAIRFIELD BAY 9** [1] 4-8-11 G Bardwell 50/1: /00008: Al bhd: v stiff task, AW bow. *9* **9a**

8 ran Time 1m 12.24 (1.84) (P F Crowley) D Haydn Jones Efail Isaf, Rhondda C Taff

1914

3.00 AUSTRALIA HCAP DIV 2 3YO 0-60 (F) 1m3f106y Firm V Slow [67]
£2362 £675 £337

1615 **ADRIANA 14** [3] C E Brittain 3-8-0 (39) A Nicholls (3) 11/2: 00001: 3 b f Tragic Role - Beatle Song (Song) **44**
Chsd ldrs, led appr fnl 1f, edged right, rdn out: op 8/1, v slow time: 1st win, suited by step up to 11.5f on firm.
103 **CROWN MINT 203** [5] R T Phillips 3-8-12 (51) K Fallon 8/1: 000-2: 3 gr c Chief's Crown - Add Mint *1½* **53**
(Vigors) Off the pace till kept on/hung right fnl 2f: reapp/h'cap bow: apprec step up to 11.5f on firm.
1270 **ESTABLISHED 33** [8] J R Best 3-7-12 (37)(BL) M Henry 12/1: 0-0503: 3 b g Not In Doubt - Copper *½* **38**
Trader (Faustus) Cl-up, led 4f out till appr fnl 1f, onepace: blnkd, back in trip: stays 11.5f on firm grnd.
*1540 **BEE GEE 18** [7] M Blanshard 3-8-1 (40) R Mullen 11/2: 00-014: Mid-div, chsd ldrs 4f out, no *½* **40**
impress fnl 1f: op 4/1: handles equitrack & firm grnd: see 1540 (sell).
1495 **LOMOND DANCER 19** [1] 3-9-7 (60) J Fortune 11/2: 406-05: Bhd, under press 3f out, late hdwy, nvr *½* **59**
a threat: op 4/1, top weight: prob styd this longer 11.5f trip: see 1495.
1274 **INDIANA SPRINGS 32** [2] 3-8-6 (45)(vis) J Tate 10/1: 054006: Bhd, chsd ldrs 4f out till 2f out. *1½* **42**
1477 **DEE DIAMOND 20** [4] 3-8-9 (48) A Daly 12/1: 40-007: Made most till appr fnl 4f, grad wknd: lngr trip. *2½* **42**
1758 **SADLERS SONG 7** [6] 3-9-0 (53) S Drowne 3/1 FAV: 005-58: Handy till 3f out, eased fnl 1f: qck reapp. *5* **42**
1572 **WALTER THE WHISTLE 15** [11] 3-8-7 (46)(BL) F Norton 10/1: 0-549: Pld hard bhd ldrs, lost pl 3f out. *13* **25**
1442 **RESEARCH MASTER 23** [10] 3-9-2 (55) S Whitworth 20/1: 004-00: Cl-up 1m: 10th, up in trip: *9* **26**
flattered 4th in '99 (auct mdn, rtd 66$): with P Chamings.
204 **TIC TAC MAC 179** [9] 3-7-10 (35)(5oh) G Bardwell 50/1: 0000-0: Sn bhd: 11th, stiff task, no form. *dist* **0**
11 ran Time 2m 30.54 (7.14) (R A Pledger) C E Brittain Newmarket

1915

3.30 SUSSEX HCAP 3YO+ 0-70 (E) 1m aw rnd Standard Inapplicable [69]
£2828 £808 £404 3yo rec 11lb

*1442 **TAPAGE 23** [7] Andrew Reid 4-8-7 (48) M Henry 9/4 FAV: 30-111: 4 b g Great Commotion - Irena (Bold **53a**
Lad) Early ldr, again halfway, clr bef dist, rdn out: well bckd: hat-trick after wins here at Lingfield (C/D) &
Bath (h'caps): dual '99 rnr-up (clmrs, rtd 69, W Muir): '98 Lingfield wnr (auct mdn, rtd 78a, D Gillespie): eff at
7f, 1m suits: acts on firm, fast grnd, likes equitrack/Lingfield: best without blnks, forcing the pace.
1348 **FEATHER N LACE 27** [6] C A Cyzer 4-9-9 (64) S Sanders 6/1: 130-22: 4 b f Green Desert - Report 'Em *1¾* **65a**
(Staff Writer) Wide, in tch, shaken up halfway, styd on well ins last, not trouble wnr: sound AW bow:
acts on firm, gd & equitrack: deserves another race: see 1348.
1511 **QUEEN OF THE KEYS 19** [8] S Dow 4-7-11 (37)(1ow) A Nicholls (0) 16/1: 300003: 4 b f Royal Academy - *¾* **38a**
Piano Belle (Fappiano) Dwelt, bhd, ran on for press fnl 2f, nvr nrr: return to form back on favourite surface.
1542 **SUPER MONARCH 18** [1] L A Dace 6-9-7 (62) G Bardwell 16/1: 30-004: Held up, prog after 4f, sn *1¾* **59a**
rdn, onepace appr fnl 1f; see 1542.
1519 **PIPE DREAM 18** [9] 4-8-9 (50) D R McCabe 20/1: 336005: Wide, nvr in it: see 353. *2½* **42a**
1552 **MARMADUKE 16** [4] 4-9-10 (65)(VIS) Dane O'Neill 14/1: 00-036: Nvr better than mid-div: visored. *nk* **56a**
1801 **FRANKLIN D 5** [12] 4-8-3 (44) S Whitworth 16/1: 234067: Chsd ldrs till 2f out, saddle slipped: see 58. *9* **21a**
1697 **SALORY 11** [2] 4-8-3 (44) L Newman (5) 11/2: 00-308: Chsd ldrs 4f: tchd 14/1: flattered in mdns earlier. *¾* **20a**
*1742 **FRENCH FANCY 8** [10] 3-7-13 (51)(bl)(6ex) R Brisland(5) 9/1: 400419: Dwelt, al bhd: op 7/1: btr 1742 (6f). *1½* **25a**
1852 **MALCHIK 3** [11] 4-9-3 (58) F Norton 20/1: 202600: Nvr on terms: 10th, quick reapp, see 922 (f/sand). *1¾* **29a**
776 **SUPERCHIEF 77** [5] 5-9-3 (58)(tbl) M Hills 7/1: 211150: Led after 2f till halfway, sn btn: 11th, 11 wk abs. *shd* **29a**
842 **BAAJIL 68** [3] 5-8-5 (46) N Callan 7/1: -00000: Bhd from halfway: 12th, 10 wk abs, see 3. *7* **7a**
12 ran Time 1m 39.94 (3.74) (A S Reid) Andrew Reid Mill Hill, London NW7

1916

4.00 TRACKSIDE SELLER 2YO (G) 5f aw rnd Standard Inapplicable
£1844 £527 £263

*1684 **COZZIE 11** [6] J G Given 2-8-11 T G McLaughlin 9/4 FAV: -30511: 2 ch f Cosmonaut - Royal Deed **65a**
(Shadeed) Rcd in 2nd, ran on well to reel in ldr ins last, going away: well bckd, bght in for 4,600gns: recent
Musselburgh wnr (sell): eff at 5f, shld get 6f: acts on firm/fast, both AWs, sharp trks, win more sellers.
1346 **SOME DUST 27** [2] W G M Turner 2-8-11 A Daly 16/1: -U02: 2 ch c King's Signet - Some Dream (Vitiges) *3½* **55a**
Led & 4L clr bef 2f out, sn onepace & hdd ins last: imprvd over this sharp 5f on equitrack, forcing the pace.
1197 **PERTEMPS GILL 37** [8] A D Smith 2-8-6 S Whitworth 33/1: -003: 2 b f Silca Blanka - Royal Celerity *4* **40a**
(Riverman) In tch, wide, outpcd turning for home, late rally: AW bow, 6f will suit: see 1019.
1206 **ROYLE FAMILY 37** [7] A Berry 2-8-11 R Hughes 7/2: -454: Rcd in 3rd, onepace ent str: see 1206, 856. *1½* **41a**
1549 **NINE TO FIVE 16** [3] 2-8-11 N Callan 7/2: 133445: Outpcd: AW bow, see 1267, 836. *3½* **33a**
-- **CROSS FINGERS** [5] 2-8-6 S Sanders 5/1: -6: Al bhd: debut: Idris Apr foal, half-sister to a useful *2½* **22a**
7f juv, dam 10f wnr, sire 7f/10f performer: with M Tompkins.
1740 **SOOTY TIME 8** [1] 2-8-11 Pat Eddery 6/1: -637: Sn struggling: op 8/1, btr 1740 (auct mdn). *¾* **25a**
-- **QUEENS SONG** [4] 2-8-6 S Drowne 8/1: -8: Dwelt, al out the back: debut: King's Signet Apr foal, *1¾* **16a**
sister to a 1m wnr, dam 5f juv wnr, sire a sprinter: with R Hodges.
8 ran Time 59.99 (2.19) (D Bass) J G Given Willoughton, Lincs

1917

4.30 LINGFIELD FILLIES HCAP 3YO+ 0-85 (D) 1m1f Firm V Slow [61]
£3848 £1184 £592 £296 3yo rec 12lb

1611 **DENS JOY 14** [4] Miss D A McHale 4-9-10 (57) D McGaffin (7) 9/2: 001001: 4 b f Archway - Bonvin **61**
(Taufan) 2nd, rdn appr fnl 2f, kept on gamely to lead dist, just lasted: prev won at Windsor (fill h'cap): plcd
in '99 for H Collingridge (rtd 65): eff at 1m/9f, poss stays 12f: acts on firm, gd/soft & fibresand, sharp trks.
*1775 **SIFAT 7** [2] J R Jenkins 5-9-9 (56)(vis) D Glennon (7) 1/2 FAV: 0-5112: 5 b m Marju - Reine Maid *nk* **59**
(Mr Prospector) Held up in tch, rdn ent fnl 2f, kept on well ins last, not quite get there: well bckd, qk reapp:
unsuited by drop back to 9f on hat-trick attempt: acts on firm & soft & can recoup losses at 10f: see 1775.
1511 **BUXTEDS FIRST 19** [3] G L Moore 3-8-7 (52) F Norton 7/1: 00-033: 3 gr f Mystiko - Sea Fairy (Wollow) *1½* **52**
Led till 1½f out, no extra when hmpd towards fin: op 4/1: stays 9f on firm grnd.
1064 **RUSSIAN SILVER 44** [1] C E Brittain 3-9-9 (68) P Robinson 9/2: 340-04: In tch till 3f out: 6 wk abs. *5* **60**
4 ran Time 1m 57.63 (7.13) (N T Davies & M Watmore) Miss D A McHale Newmarket

BEVERLEY WEDNESDAY JUNE 14TH Righthand, Oval Track with Stiff Uphill Finish

Official Going GOOD/FIRM. Stalls: Inside.

1918 2.20 LINCOLNSHIRE BUSINESS CLAIMER 2YO (F) 5f Firm 08 -36 Slow
£2352 £672 £336

1492 **CLANSINGE 19** [5] A Berry 2-8-10 J Carroll 6/1: 531: 2 ch f Clantime - North Pine (Import): 69
Made all, drvn over 1f out, held on well for press inside last, op 9/2: eff at 5f, half-sister to sev 5f 2yo wnrs: acts on firm, prob handles soft: likes a stiff trk & front running tactics: going the right way.
1492 **FAYZ SLIPPER 19** [2] T D Easterby 2-8-0 W Supple 8/1: 00042: 2 b f Fayruz - Farriers Slipper 1½ 54
(Prince Tenderfoot): In tch, prog 2f out, rdn/styd on inside last, not pace of wnr: op 4/1: handles firm.
1549 **AMELIA 16** [7] J Cullinan 2-8-4 Joanna Badger (7) 13/8 FAV: 423: 2 b f General Monash - Rose Tint ½ 57
(Salse): Trkd ldrs, bmpd/no room dist, swtchd & kept on onepace nr fin: hvly bckd: handles firm & soft grnd.
1761 **TOMMY SMITH 7** [3] J S Wainwright 2-8-11 R Winston 14/1: 004: Sn prom, wknd 1f out: op 12/1. ¾ 62
1713 **HOPGROVE 9** [9] 2-8-4 D Mernagh (3) 5/1: 66035: In tch, held 1f out: op 7/1: see 1713 (6f, g/s). 1½ 50
1476 **VODKA 20** [4] 2-9-2 Dean McKeown 13/2: 56: Cl-up, wknd over 1f out: op 8/1: see 1476. ½ 60
-- **SHADALHI** [8] 2-8-6 F Lynch 10/1: 7: In tch, btn 2f out: op 6/1: Alhijaz filly, Apr foal, cost 2,100gns: 1½ 46
dam a 5/6f juv wnr: sire a high class miler: with K A Ryan.
1659 **CAPTAINS FOLLY 12** [6] 2-8-4 N Carlisle 50/1: -08: Chsd ldrs till over 1f out: mod form. 2½ 37
-- **RAINBOW RIVER** [1] 2-9-3 P Goode (3) 20/1: 9: Al rear: Rainbows For Life gelding, Feb foal, 5 36
5,500 gns 2yo: half-brother to a 6f juv wnr, dam a mdn: with P C Haslam.
9 ran Time 1m 03.5 (2.2) (The Monkey Partnership) A Berry Cockerham, Lancs.

1919 2.50 E NORRIS HCAP 3YO 0-75 (E) 1m4f Firm 08 -12 Slow [82]
£3841 £1182 £591 £295

*1779 **EL ZITO 7** [1] M G Quinlan 3-9-12 (80)(5ex) J Mackay (7) 5/2 FAV: 3-0211: 3 b g Mukaddamah - Samite 84
(Tennyson): Led after 1f & sn clr, rdn/hung left inside last, held on well: well bckd: 5lb pen for recent Chester success (class stks, first win): rnr-up in '99 in Italy: eff at 1m/10.5f, styd this stiff 12f well, may get further: acts on firm, soft & prob fibresand: likes to force the pace on a sharp or stiff trk: progressive gelding.
1539 **HIGH TOPPER 18** [7] M Johnston 3-9-6 (74) J Reid 9/2: 0-252: 3 b c Wolfhound - Blushing Barada 1½ 75
(Blushing Groom): Chsd wnr, rdn & kept on final 1f, al just held: op 6/1, h'cap bow: styd this lngr 12f trip well, handles firm & gd/soft grnd: a likely type for a similar contest: see 902.
1571 **KISTY 15** [5] H Candy 3-9-2 (70) C Rutter 9/2: 54-033: 3 b f Kris - Pine Ridge (High Top): nk 70
Held up, rdn/prog final 2f, onepace/held inside last: handles firm & gd/soft grnd: see 1571 & 1094.
1480 **LITTLE DOCKER 20** [4] T D Easterby 3-9-0 (68) K Darley 11/2: 4-354: Led 1f & remnd handy, drvn/ch shd 68
1f out, no extra nr fin: styd lngr 12f trip: handles firm & gd: see 1295.
1448 **PORTIA LADY 22** [2] 3-7-10 (50)(bl)(4oh) P Fessey 33/1: 20-005: Chsd ldrs, onepace fnl 2f: see 1024. 3½ 45
1448 **OLD FEATHERS 22** [6] 3-8-7 (61) F Lynch 10/1: 66-006: Chsd ldrs 10f: op 8/1: see 1448 (10f). ¾ 55
*1758 **MIDDLETHORPE 7** [3] 3-8-2 (56)(5ex) G Parkin 7/2: 0-0517: Held up, prog halfway, rdn/btn 3f out: 8 38
nicely bckd: jockey reported gelding unsuited by faster grnd: see 1758 (g/s).
1644 **ROCK ON ROBIN 12** [9] 3-7-11 (51)(vis)(1ow)(2oh) T Williams 16/1: 0-0268: Al rear: see 1274 (10f). 10 19
1477 **RAINWORTH LADY 20** [8] 3-7-10 (50)(12oh) K Dalgleish (7) 50/1: 0-5009: Rear, nvr a factor: see 638. 1 17
9 ran Time 2m 33.7 (2.4) (Mario Lanfranchi) M G Quinlan Newmarket, Suffolk.

1920 3.20 ELTHERINGTON HCAP 3YO+ 0-70 (E) 7f100y rnd Firm 08 +05 Fast [68]
£4576 £1408 £704 £352 3 yo rec 10lb

1716 **MEHMAAS 9** [9] R E Barr 4-9-6 (60)(vis) J Reid 33/1: 4-0341: 4 b g Distant Relative - Guest List (Be My 62
Guest): Mid-div, prog & rdn to lead 1f out, styd on well, drvn out: gd time: '99 Brighton wnr (auct mdn, rtd 74, M Channon): plcd prev term (rtd 80 & 78a): eff at 7f/1m on firm, gd/soft & fibresand: eff with/without blnks/visor.
4196} **FUTURE PROSPECT 256** [12] M A Buckley 6-9-8 (62) D Holland 16/1: 2000-2: 6 b g Marju - Phazania nk 63
(Tap On Wood): Held up, prog/no room 1f out, swtchd & styd on well ins last, just held: reapp: no luck in running, prob wnr with a clr run: '99 wnr at Hamilton & Redcar (h'caps, rtd 67): '98 Pontefract wnr (reapp, clmr) & W'hampton (clmr, rtd 77 & 74a): eff at 7.5f/9f, tried further: acts on firm, soft & fibresand: runs well fresh & is a gd weight carrier: best without blnks & handles any trk: can find compensation.
1431 **RYMERS RASCAL 23** [5] E J Alston 8-9-3 (57) W Supple 9/1: 00-563: 8 b g Rymer - City Sound (On nk 57
Your Mark): Mid-div, rdn/prog & ev ch 1f out, kept on tho' just held nr fin: fine run: see 942.
1762 **KASS ALHAWA 7** [7] D W Chapman 7-10-0 (68) K Darley 7/1: 624054: Held up, prog/ch 1f out, onepace. 1 66
1858 **BLOOMING AMAZING 3** [14] 6-9-0 (54) R Fitzpatrick (3) 10/1: 050505: Handy, led over 2f out & sn clr, ¾ 50
rdn/hdd 1f out & no extra: qck reapp: on a handy mark: see 176 (AW).
1762 **TIPPERARY SUNSET 7** [13] 6-9-6 (60) J Mackay (7) 3/1 FAV: -00236: Missed break & bhd, late 2½ 52
gains for press, no threat: hvly bckd, op 4/1: acts on firm, loves gd/soft & soft grnd: see 1547, 1007.
1681 **CHAMPAGNE N DREAMS 11** [11] 8-9-1 (55) Kim Tinkler 12/1: 10-U67: Chsd ldrs 2f out, sn no extra. ¾ 45
1760 **HIGH SUN 7** [8] 4-9-0 (54) A Beech (5) 25/1: 400008: Rear, mod gains: see 942. ¾ 42
1840 **MELODIAN 4** [4] 5-10-0 (68)(bl)(6ex) D Mernagh (3) 6/1: 104109: In tch, effort 2f out, sn held: op 5/1. 1½ 53
1663 **ROYAL CASCADE 12** [15] 6-8-6 (46)(bl) T E Durcan 12/1: 302020: Al towards rear: 10th: op 10/1. 2 27
1434 **QUIDS INN 23** [6] 3-8-4 (54) P Fessey 12/1: 00-200: Al rear: 11th: op 10/1: btr 1296. ¾ 33
1680 **SANTANDRE 11** [16] 4-8-12 (52) P M Quinn (3) 10/1: 115000: Cl-up 5f: 12th: btr 687 (AW). 1½ 28
1615 **MEZZORAMIO 14** [2] 8-8-6 (46)(t) R Winston 16/1: 150-00: Mid-div, wide over 3f out, sn held: 13th: 3 16
op 12/1: '99 wnr at Warwick (sell h'cap) & Yarmouth (h'cap, rtd 48 at best): plcd in '98 (rtd 52, h'cap): suited by 7f/1m on firm, gd & fibresand: eff with/without blnks or vis & handles any trk, likes Yarmouth.
1718 **CYRAN PARK 9** [10] 4-8-2 (42)(bl) T Williams 12/1: 400040: Chsd ldrs 5f: 14th: btr 1718 (g/s). 3 6
1760 **ZECHARIAH 7** [3] 4-8-5 (45) F Lynch 14/1: 465640: Led, hdd 3f out & sn btn/eased: 15th: op 12/1. shd 9
15 ran Time 1m 31.0 (0.2) (J C Garbutt) R E Barr Seamer, Nth Yorks.

1921 3.50 LINCS & H'SIDE HCAP 3YO+ 0-70 (E) 1m2f Firm 08 -05 Slow [70]
£4628 £1424 £712 £356 3 yo rec 13lb

1615 **MICE IDEAS 14** [15] N P Littmoden 4-8-1 (43) P M Quinn (3) 12/1: 512361: 4 ch g Fayruz - Tender 47
Encounter (Prince Tenderfoot): Settled rear, smooth hdwy over 3f out, swtchd to chall dist, styd on to lead cl-home, drvn out: prev won at Southwell (2, appr mdn & sell): prev with S Mellor (rtd 70h over hdles): unplcd

in '99 (rtd 66 & 53a): suited by 10/11f on gd, firm & a sharp or stiff/undul trk, likes fibresand/Southwell.
1370 **STROMSHOLM 26** [6] J R Fanshawe 4-9-10 (66) D Harrison 10/1: -40632: 4 ch g Indian Ridge - Upward *nk* **69**
Trend (Salmon Leap): Rear, rdn/prog 3f out, rdn to chall dist, styd on, not btn far: acts on firm & gd/soft.
1583 **BACCHUS 15** [18] Miss J A Camacho 6-9-11 (67) K Darley 7/4 FAV: 015-23: 6 b g Prince Sabo - Bonica *¾* **69**
(Rousillon): Mid-div, smooth hdwy 3f out, styd on well inside last, well bckd: eff at 7.5/10f on firm & gd/sft.
*1370 **ZAHA 26** [7] J Pearce 5-9-5 (61) Dean McKeown 8/1: -60014: In tch, rdn/prog 2f out, kept on *hd* **62**
inside last, not pace of ldrs: see 1370 (gd/soft).
1718 **BEST EVER 9** [16] 3-7-10 (51) J Mackay (7) 5/1: -00025: Cl-up, rdn to chall 2f out, led dist, hdd well *1* **50**
inside last, wknd: up in trip, probably stays 10f: see 1718.
4441} **LOKOMOTIV 238** [17] 4-8-12 (54) P Fitzsimons (5) 33/1: 5300-6: Settled rear, effort 2f out, kept on, *2½* **49**
nvr nrr: reapp: rnr-up in '99 (h'cap, rtd 57, P D Evans): trained by M Channon in '98, won at Yarmouth (7f sell,
rtd 75 at best): eff at 7f/1m on firm & gd/soft: has tried blnks/visor, best without.
1744 **YOUNG UN 8** [9] 5-9-6 (62) P McCabe 5/1: 060427: Handy, rdn/no extra appr final 1f: btr 1744. *1½* **54**
1689 **QUALITAIR SURVIVOR 11** [8] 5-7-10 (38)(vis) J Bramhill 14/1: 5-0468: Rear, late hdwy: up in trip. *hd* **29**
1683 **ROYAL REPRIMAND 11** [1] 5-7-10 (38)(vis)(5oh) P Fessey 50/1: 45-009: Led, hdd appr final 1f, wknd. *1¾* **26**
1361 **GENUINE JOHN 26** [12] 7-7-10 (38)(4oh) N Carlisle 25/1: -32450: Rear, modest late gains, fin 10th. *nk* **25**
1769 **NORTHERN ACCORD 7** [14] 6-7-10 (38)(bl) T Williams 33/1: 0-6040: Prom, fdd fnl 2f, 11th: qck reapp. *hd* **25**
1775 **HEVER GOLF GLORY 7** [2] 6-7-10 (38)(4oh) K Dalgleish (7) 50/1: 030300: Nvr a dngr in 12th: qck reapp. *1½* **22**
1705 **A DAY ON THE DUB 10** [3] 7-8-9 (51) J Fanning 12/1: 440140: Rear, effort 3f out, sn wknd, fin 13th. *¾* **33**
1415 **Approachable 23** [11] 5-7-12 (40) Joanna Badger(7) 20/1: 965 **Swing Bar 57** [13] 7-8-4 (46) Claire Bryan(5) 16/1:
-- **Taking** [5] 4-9-9 (65)(t) C Rutter 50/1: 1279 **Edmo Heights 32** [4] 4-9-0 (56) W Supple 16/1:
1769 **Noirie 7** [10] 6-8-0 (42) D Mernagh (3) 25/1:
18 ran Time 2m 03.6 (1.3) (Mice Group Plc) N P Littmoden Newmarket.

1922 **4.20 BUSINESS SCHOOL MDN 3YO+ (D) 7f100y rnd Firm 08 +04 Fast**
£3893 £1198 £599 £299 3 yo rec 10lb

1582 **ADAWAR 15** [4] Sir Michael Stoute 3-8-11 F Lynch 11/4: 5621: 3 b c Perugino - Adalya (Darshaan): **80**
Cl-up, hdwy to chall dist, drvn out to lead final strides: nicely bckd, gd time: plcd once in 3 10f mdns prev:
clearly apprec this drop back to 7.5f, stays 10f: acts on firm & gd/soft grnd, gall or stiff/undul trk: tough.
1763 **GOLDEN CHANCE 7** [5] M Johnston 3-8-11 J Reid 7/4 FAV: 322: 3 b c Unfuwain - Golden Digger *nk* **79**
(Mr Prospector): Set fast pace, drvn appr final 1f, hdd nr fin: nicely bckd, clr rem: qck reapp:
acts on firm & gd/soft: will win similar sn, esp over further: see 1763, 1352.
4158} **ZIG ZIG 259** [6] Mrs A Duffield 3-8-11 W Supple 100/1: 0-3: 3 b g Perugino - Queen Of Erin (King Of *3* **73**
Clubs): Prom, rdn to impr 2f out, styd on but not pace of front 2 final 1f: reapp: well btn sole '99 juv
start (6f mdn, soft): clearly apprec step up to a stiff/undul 7.5f on firm grnd.
1377 **AMJAD 26** [3] C E Brittain 3-8-11 T E Durcan 5/2: 504: Dwelt, rear, rdn to impr over 3f out, styd *1½* **70**
on, no ch with ldrs: shade btr 1377 (1m, gd).
4092} **EL EMPERADOR 263** [2] 3-8-11 D Harrison 5/1: 6-5: Prom, hdwy 2f out, sn btn, flashed tail inside *nk* **69**
last: rtd 74 on sole '99 juv start (6f mdn, gd): half-brother to a 7/9f juv wnr abroad.
1447 **REDHILL 22** [7] 3-8-6 Dean McKeown 100/1: 06: Dwelt, al rear: looks modest. *8* **48**
1444 **ANNAKAYE 22** [1] 3-8-6 G Parkin 100/1: 07: Chsd ldrs, wknd rapidly fnl 2f, fin last: poor form so far. *7* **34**
7 ran Time 1m 31.1 (0.3) (H H Aga Khan) Sir Michael Stoute Newmarket.

1923 **4.50 ULH FILLIES HCAP 3YO+ 0-70 (E) 5f Firm 08 -02 Slow** **[69]**
£3107 £956 £478 £239 3 yo rec 7 lb

1724 **DAZZLING QUINTET 9** [13] C Smith 4-8-2 (43) J McAuley (5) 6/4 FAV: 0-6021: 4 ch f Superlative - Miss **49**
Display (Touch Paper) Made all, rdn out: well bckd: '99 rnr-up (clmr, rtd 52$): '98 wnr here at Beverley
(fill auct mdn, rtd 78): eff forcing the pace at 5/6f on firm & gd/soft grnd, likes this stiff Beverley trk.
3855} **MARINO STREET 279** [16] B A McMahon 7-8-5 (46) T E Durcan 12/1: 2560-2: 7 b m Totem - Demerger *1½* **48**
(Dominion) Well plcd, squeezed for room by wnr & swtchd below dist, kept on: reapp: '99 wnr at Warwick
(fill h'cap) & Haydock (h'cap, rtd 50 at best): plcd in '98 (h'caps, rtd 44 & 29a, P Evans): eff at 5f, stays 7.5f:
acts on firm, gd grnd & fibresand, with/without visor/blnks: goes well fresh, spot on next time.
1842 **SOUNDS ACE 4** [2] D Shaw 4-8-10 (51)(bl) J Mackay (7) 25/1: 6-0603: 4 ch f Savahra Sound - Ace Girl *1½* **49**
(Stanford) Prom centre, rdn ent final 2f, edged right, styd on but no impress on front pair: qck reapp, blnks
reapplied, acts on firm/fast, handles gd/soft: gd run back at 5f: v well h'capped: see 1133.
1842 **DOMINELLE 4** [11] T D Easterby 8-8-12 (53) W Supple 7/1: 0-0004: Chsd ldrs, onepace final 1f. *¾* **49**
1842 **PREMIUM PRINCESS 4** [9] 5-8-11 (52) D Holland 5/1: 000055: Mid-div, prog 2f out, onepace ins last: *nk* **47**
tchd 7/1, qck reapp: back in trip, grnd now in her favour: see 802.
1606 **GRACE 14** [1] 6-8-2 (43)(Vis) P Fitzsimons (5) 20/1: 466406: Rear & widest of all, late hdwy, nvr dngrs. *1½* **34**
1545 **MISS BANANAS 16** [7] 5-8-4 (45) D Meah (7) 20/1: 500407: Chsd ldrs, hung left 2f out & no extra. *1½* **32**
1815 **PATSY CULSYTH 5** [15] 5-8-5 (46) Kim Tinkler 14/1: 100368: Nvr better than mid-div: back in trip. *hd* **32**
1815 **SKYERS FLYER 5** [17] 6-8-2 (43) T Williams 14/1: 3-0009: Al same place: qck reapp, back in trip. *hd* **28**
1392 **SING FOR ME 25** [10] 5-7-10 (37)(1oh) N Carter (7) 33/1: 245060: Nvr on terms: 10th, turf return. *½* **21**
1175 **POLAR LADY 38** [3] 3-9-5 (67)(VIS) D Harrison 8/1: 6-350: Swtchd to far side start, al bhd: 14th, **0**
tchd 12/1 on h'cap bow: reportedly not face first time visor, back in trip: see 877.
1278 **Palvic Lady 32** [4] 4-9-2 (57) R Fitzpatrick (3) 33/1: 1687 **Twickers 11** [8] 4-8-12 (53) G Parkin 20/1:
573 **Ring Of Love 112** [6] 4-10-0 (69) R Cody Boutcher (7) 20/1: 1723 **Schatzi 9** [14] 3-8-7 (55) J Stack 16/1:
15 ran Time 1m 01.8 (0.5) (Roman Bath V) C Smith Temple Bruer, Lincs.

KEMPTON WEDNESDAY JUNE 14TH Righthand, Flat, Fair Track

Official Going GOOD TO FIRM (FIRM in places). Stalls: Str Crse - stands Side; Rnd Crse - Inside.

1924 **6.30 RUINART AUCT MDN 2YO (E) 6f str Good/Firm 24 -13 Slow**
£3883 £1195 £597 £298 Field split into 2 groups, stands side favoured.

1589 **MAN OF DISTINCTION 14** [2] D R C Elsworth 2-8-10 T Quinn 3/1 JT FAV: 51: 2 b c Spectrum - Air Of **84**
Distinction (Distinctly North): Dwelt, rear, smooth hdwy over 2f out, rdn to lead dist, styd on strongly,
drvn out: well bckd tho' op 9/4: dam a Gr 3 6f juv wnr: eff at 5f, apprec this step up to 6f & 7f could suit:

acts on fast & gd/soft grnd: well regarded, should improve & win again.
1776 **MOONLIGHT DANCER 7** [6] R Hannon 2-8-7 R Hughes 3/1 JT FAV: -422: 2 b c Polar Falcon - Guanhumara (Caerleon): Trkd ldrs till went on briefly appr final 1f, not pace of wnr well inside last: well bckd, qck reapp: eff at 5/6f, 7f will suit: acts on fast & gd/soft: win a race: see 1776. ¾ 78
1488 **TOTALLY COMMITTED 19** [11] R Hannon 2-8-7 Dane O'Neill 33/1: 03: 2 b c Turtle Island - Persian Light (Persian Heights) Bhd, hdwy & swtchd over 1f out, ran on well ins last, not reach wnr: stablemate of rnr-up: Apr foal, cost 9,500 gns: apprec this step up to 6f on faster grnd, 7f will suit: can improve & win similar. ½ 76+
984 **MAGIC BOX 55** [13] A P Jarvis 2-8-7 J Fortune 10/1: 644: Mid-div, rdn to impr over 1f out, styd on well inside last: op 8/1, 8 wk abs: eff at 6f on fast: see 700. *hd* 76
-- **ROOFER** [19] 2-8-2 Craig Williams 16/1: 5: Waited with far side, hdwy to lead that group over 1f out, ran on well under hands-&-heels inside last, not reach ldrs: first home on unfav far side: 14,500 gns Apr foal, dam unrcd: eff at 6f on fast, 7f should suit: v encouraging debut & one to keep a close eye on. 1 68+
1513 **CANDOTHAT 18** [12] 2-8-5 S Drowne 14/1: 06: Prom, rdn/not pace of ldrs over 1f out: see 1513. *hd* 70
1727 **WINTER JASMINE 9** [3] 2-8-2 D R McCabe 6/1: 047: Hdwy from rear halfway, kept on inside last, nvr nrr: op 9/2: will apprec 7f+ in nurseries: see 1727, 1197. 1¼ 63
1798 **LAI SEE 6** [21] 2-8-4(1ow) D Sweeney 33/1: 008: Led far side group till hdd & fdd over 1f out: qck reapp & an imprvd effort here on this faster surface: see 1472 (gd/soft). *hd* 65
-- **CIRCLE OF WOLVES** [9] 2-8-6(1ow) O Urbina 33/1: 9: Mid-div at best: Feb foal, half brother to sev 3yo+ wnrs: dam scored between 1m & 2m2f: with B Jones. *nk* 66
-- **BROWSER** [14] 2-8-5 N Callan 33/1: 0: Front rank, rdn/fdd over 1f out, fin 10th: IR8,000 gns Feb 1st foal: dam related to a high class styr: with K R Burke, sure to apprec further given time. ½ 64
1079 **JACKS BIRTHDAY 44** [10] 2-8-5 S Sanders 66/1: 050: Led, hdd appr final 1f, wknd, fin 11th: 6 wk abs. *nk* 63
1691 **SHARP ACT 11** [5] 2-8-10 R Hills 20/1: -00: Nvr a threat, fin 12th: 32,000 gns Alydeed colt, half-brother to a couple of wnrs in the States: with J W Hills. 1¼ 64
-- **TROUBADOUR GIRL** [1] 2-7-12 M Henry 16/1: 0: Dwelt, nvr with ldrs, fin 13th: Mar foal, half-sister to a 5f 2yo scorer: dam won over 6f: with M A Jarvis. 1¼ 48
-- **Carefully** [7] 2-8-5 P Robinson 20/1:
-- **My Very Own** [17] 2-8-3 J Tate 33/1:
762 **Kwaheri 78** [16] 2-8-2 L Newman (4) 33/1:
932 **Spirit Of Texas 58** [4] 2-8-7 Pat Eddery 33/1:
1429 **Vendome 23** [20] 2-8-5 F Norton 20/1:
-- **Halcyon Magic** [18] 2-8-4(1ow) R Perham 66/1:
1403 **Keep The Peace 25** [15] 2-8-7 K Fallon 16/1:
1589 **Raw Silk 14** [8] 2-8-5 G Carter 33/1:
21 ran Time 1m 13.3 (2.2) (Nicholas Cooper) D R C Elsworth Whitsbury, Hants.

1925

7.00 SPELTHORNE HCAP 3YO 0-85 (D) 6f str Good/Firm 24 +09 Fast [92]
£4543 £1398 £699 £349 Field raced stands side

1638 **BLUE MOUNTAIN 13** [15] R F Johnson Houghton 3-9-6 (84) J Reid 7/1: 5-5221: 3 ch c Elmaamul - Glenfinlass (Lomond): Settled rear, swtchd wide & hdwy appr final 1f, styd on strongly to lead inside last, drvn out: best time of day: first win: plcd on 2 of 3 juv starts (mdns, rtd 89): eff at 5/6f, stays 7f: acts on firm, gd/soft & any trk: consistent form this term, deserved this. 88
*1399 **BUDELLI 25** [9] M R Channon 3-9-0 (78) Craig Williams 9/1: 362312: 3 b c Elbio - Eves Temptation (Glenstal): Front rank, rdn to lead dist, hdd inside last & no extra cl-home: tough & consistent, see 1399 (mdn). ½ 80
1795 **PEDRO JACK 6** [1] B J Meehan 3-9-2 (80) Pat Eddery 5/1 FAV: 310603: 3 b g Mujadil - Festival Of Light (High Top): Chsd ldrs, went on 2f out, hdd dist, sn held: nicely bckd: qck reapp: apprec this return to 6f. ¾ 80
1470 **LABRETT 21** [4] B J Meehan 3-8-13 (77)(bl) R Hughes 9/1: -00004: Waited with, rdn & styd on inside last, not reach wnr: clr rem: stablemate of 3rd & improved run back in blnks: see 1220, 988. *hd* 77
1427 **ILLUSIVE 23** [11] 3-8-7 (71)(bl) F Norton 6/1: 120355: Rear, gd hdwy appr final 1f, not pace of ldrs. 2½ 64
1289 **TINSEL WHISTLE 30** [6] 3-8-10 (74) P Robinson 20/1: 426-06: Mid-div, hdwy & short of room 2f out, onepace under hands & heels fnl 1f: could do better: see 1289. ¾ 65
1651 **CORBLETS 12** [8] 3-8-4 (68) P Doe 16/1: -32257: Held up, rdn/hdwy over 1f out, sn not pace of ldrs. 1 56
1262 **ARETINO 33** [5] 3-9-7 (85) N Pollard 20/1: 03-058: Led, hdd 2f out, wknd: unsuited by drop in trip?. *nk* 73
1178 **HERITAGE PARK 38** [7] 3-9-1 (79) Dane O'Neill 10/1: 156-59: Nvr a threat: see 1178. 2 62
1600 **BEST BOND 14** [12] 3-8-2 (66)(BL) J Tate 12/1: 5-0300: Prom, lost tch final 2f, fin 10th: first time blnks: twice below 1098 (5f, gd/soft). *hd* 49
1289 **NIGHT DIAMOND 30** [3] 3-8-8 (72) A Nicholls (3) 11/1: 30-000: Dwelt, nvr a dngr, 11th: see 1289, 1125. 2½ 49
1517 **LA CAPRICE 18** [16] 3-8-12 (76) G Carter 7/1: 1-0320: Mid-div, rdn/wknd appr final 1f, 13th: btr 1517. 51
1183 **Hypersonic 38** [14] 3-8-13 (77) M Roberts 16/1:
1138 **Stealthy Times 41** [13] 3-9-5 (83) T G McLaughlin 33/1:
14 ran Time 1m 12.0 (0.9) (Mrs C J Hue Williams) R F Johnson Houghton Blewbury, Oxon.

1926

7.30 LEE & PEMBERTONS HCAP 3YO+ 0-80 (D) 1m rnd Good/Firm 24 +04 Fast [80]
£7507 £2310 £1155 £577

1288 **MUYASSIR 30** [12] P J Makin 5-9-8 (74) S Sanders 11/1: 140-01: 5 b h Brief Truce - Twine (Thatching): Trkd ldrs, gd hdwy appr final 1f, drvn out to hold on inside last: gd time: '99 wnr at Newmarket (h'cap, rtd 76 & 65a), prev term scored at Lingfield (h'cap, rtd 72a & 72): eff at 1m/sharp 10f, reportedly best suited by 9f: acts on firm/fast grnd & equitrack: handles any trk: back to best today on fav fast grnd. 82
1598 **SKY DOME 14** [15] M H Tompkins 7-9-5 (71) A Beech (5) 20/1: 0-0602: 7 ch g Bluebird - God Speed Her (Pas De Seul): Settled rear, prog when short of room over 1f out, swtchd & styd on strongly inside last, just failed, too much to do: clr rem: would have won if asked for effort earlier: h'capped to win. *nk* 78
1442 **TWIN TIME 23** [10] J S King 6-8-12 (64) Pat Eddery 12/1: 00-423: 6 b m Syrtos - Carramba (Tumble Wind) Led, hdd appr final 1f, not pace of front 2 inside last: gd run, keep in mind for Bath: see 1058. 2½ 66
1201 **ANEMOS 37** [7] M A Jarvis 5-9-4 (70) P Robinson 8/1: 342634: Mid-div, rdn/hdwy 2f out, no extra final 1f: consistent form this term, see 1201. ¾ 70
1514 **SURPRISE ENCOUNTER 18** [1] 4-9-12 (78) J Reid 16/1: 56-005: Waited with, rdn & styd on well inside last, not reach ldrs: eye-catching late hdwy here, keep in mind: see 1514. *hd* 78+
*1590 **DOLPHINELLE 14** [13] 4-8-12 (64) O Urbina 12/1: 340316: Rear, short of room & swtchd 2f out, styd on strongly inside last, nvr nrr: stays 1m & more interesting with a positive ride: see 1590. ¾ 63
1690 **SAMARA SONG 11** [16] 7-8-7 (59) W Ryan 6/1 FAV: 005267: Sn bhd, styd on well final 2f, nvr nrr. *shd* 58
1012 **FLIGHT SEQUENCE 51** [11] 4-9-10 (76) D Wallace (7) 25/1: 424-68: Rear, hdwy when short of room 2f out, no extra appr final 1f: 7 wk abs: see 1012 (mdn, banned for 30 days for 'schooling in public'). *nk* 74
1462 **BUTRINTO 21** [18] 6-8-8 (60) C Rutter 20/1: 061149: Mid-div, rdn/no extra appr final 1f: twice below best at 1m, btr 1335 (7f, firm). 2½ 53
1840 **TOPTON 4** [17] 6-9-8 (74)(bl) K Fallon 15/2: 020050: Nvr a factor, fin 10th: qck reapp. ¾ 66
1201 **FUEGIAN 37** [9] 5-8-4 (56)(vis) F Norton 20/1: 660-20: Front rank, rdn/wknd over 1f out, eased, 11th. 1¾ 45

1498 **YEAST 19** [8] 8-9-6 (72) J Fortune 16/1: 00-020: Cl-up wide, wknd final 2f, fin 12th: see 1286.   1¼   58
*1611 **PROSPECTORS COVE 14** [5] 7-9-4 (70) T Quinn 10/1: 000010: Rcd keenly in mid-div, rdn/lost tch   55
final 2f, fin 14th: much btr 1611 (7f, gd/soft).
1250 **ARTERXERXES 34** [3] 7-9-9 (75) S Drowne 10/1: 200-30: Trkd ldrs, wknd qckly over 2f out: 16th, see 1250.   52
1407 **MAGIC FLUTE 25** [2] 4-9-4 (70) R Hughes 12/1: P20-20: In tch, wknd/eased fnl 2f, 13th: lost action.   0
1672 **Catamaran 11** [14] 5-9-4 (70) P Doe 20/1:   1395 **Mullaghmore 25** [4] 4-8-4 (55)(bl)(1ow) N Callan 25/1:
875   **Young Precedent 64** [6] 6-9-13 (79) M Roberts 33/1:
18 ran   Time 38.62 (1.62)   (William Otley)   P J Makin Ogbourne Masey, Wilts.

1927   8.00 GET MARRIED HCAP 3YO+ 0-75 (E)   1m4f   Good/Firm 24 -19 Slow   [73]
£4387   £1350   £675   £337

1350 **TWO SOCKS 27** [5] J S King 7-9-1 (60) I Mongan (5) 6/1: 0-6141: 7 ch g Phountzi - Mrs Feathers   64
(Pyjama Hunt): In tch, gd hdwy over 2f out, rdn to lead dist, styd on well, drvn out: earlier won at Brighton
(h'cap): '99 wnr at Kempton (h'cap, rtd 72), prev term scored at Warwick (h'cap, rtd 73 at best): eff at 10/12f
on firm, gd/soft & any trk, likes Kempton: has tried blnks, best without: in fine form, shld win again.
4284} **MY PLEDGE 249** [8] C A Horgan 5-8-10 (55) T Quinn 14/1: 0450-2: 5 b g Waajib - Polluys Glow (Glow):   ¾   58+
Rcd keenly bhd, hdwy when hmpd appr final 1f, styd on for press inside last: reapp: 4th at best in '99 (h'caps,
rtd 59 at best): '98 Windsor wnr (h'cap, rtd 71): eff at 10/12f on fast & gd/soft grnd: fine reapp & poss
unlucky in running here & h'capped to go one better sn.
1373 **FINAL SETTLEMENT 26** [9] J R Jenkins 5-9-6 (65) L Newman (5) 11/2: 3-1653: 5 b g Soviet Lad - Tender   ½   67
Time (Tender King): Waited with, gd hdwy over 3f out, chall dist, no extra inside last: apprec a return to 14f.
*1570 **PAS DE PROBLEME 16** [2] M Blanshard 4-9-6 (65) M Roberts 6/1: 015314: led early, remnd with ldrs,   1¼   65
led again final 2f, hdd dist, sn held: gd run up in trip & on unfavd fast grnd: see 1570 (10f, soft).
1518 **PUZZLEMENT 18** [7] 6-9-13 (72) N Esler (7) 14/1: 331005: Trkd ldrs, rdn/onepcd inside last: see 791.   1   70
1411 **CUPBOARD LOVER 25** [6] 4-8-10 (55) K Fallon 5/1 FAV: 0-6566: Rcd v keenly & pulled into lead   2   50
after 3f, hdd appr final 2f, wkng when short of room dist: ruined ch by failing to settle: see 1411.
1730 **WADI 9** [10] 5-8-13 (58) S Sanders 16/1: 00-067: Mid-div, rdn/lost tch appr final 1f: see 1730.   ¾   52
1272 **PRINCE DARKHAN 33** [3] 4-8-11 (56) S Drowne 33/1: 50-008: Bhd, nvr with ldrs: failed to make   1¼   47
the frame in 4 '99 starts (rtd 67, 10f mdn, gd grnd).
*1677 **PLURALIST 11** [1] 4-10-0 (73) N Callan 7/1: -24119: Handy, rdn/fdd appr final 1f: shade disapp   ½   63
on todays hat-trick bid: see 1677 (equitrack).
1604 **STORM HILL 14** [4] 4-10-0 (73)(t) J Fortune 11/2: 5-002U: Virtually ref to race & u.r. leaving stalls.   0
10 ran   Time 2m 35.15 (5.15)   (Mrs Satu Marks)   J S King Broad Hinton, Wilts.

1928   8.30 HH CLASSIFIED STKS 3YO+ 0-75 (D)   1m6f92y   Good/Firm 24 -35 Slow
£4075   £1254   £627   £313   3 yo rec 19lb

*1270 **BARCELONA 33** [2] J Noseda 3-8-7 J Fortune 11/4: 03-311: 3 b c Barathea - Pipitina (Bustino):   80
Trkd ldrs till went on appr final 2f, styd on well inside last, rdn out: recent scorer at Nottingham
(h'cap, first win): plcd final '99 start (mdn, rtd 80): apprec recent step up to 14f, further could suit:
acts on fast, gd/soft & a sharp or gall trk: progressive, can complete a hat-trick.
1784 **WAIT FOR THE WILL 6** [4] G L Moore 4-9-12 K Fallon 2/1 FAV: -00122: 4 ch g Seeking The Gold -   1   78
You'd Be Surprised (Blushing Groom): Mid-div, gd hdwy over 2f out, rdn to chase wnr dist, styd on inside last,
just held: styd this Ingr 14f trip well: gd run against a progressive rival, likes Salisbury: see 1350.
1637 **HAMBLEDEN 13** [1] M A Jarvis 3-8-7 P Robinson 14/1: -03103: 3 b g Vettori - Dalu (Dancing Brave):   2½   74
Bhd, rdn to impr 3f out, drvn & kept on inside last, not pace of front 2: prob stays 14.4f: btr 1238 (12f, AW).
1677 **TOTOM 11** [7] J R Fanshawe 5-9-7 W Ryan 5/1: 45-434: Rear, hdwy when short of room 2f out, kept on   nk   69
extra inside last: unlucky not to fin clsr: apprec a return to 10/12f in h'caps: see 1677.
1329 **ROYAL CASTLE 28** [3] 6-9-10 S Sanders 9/1: 530-65: Trkd ldrs, rdn/wknd over 1f out: see 1329.   ¾   71
1527 **AMEZOLA 18** [5] 4-9-10 (t) T Quinn 10/1: 06-066: Set stdy pace, hdd/wknd 2f out: see 1527.   9   61
1800 **JAWAH 6** [6] 6-9-10 Pat Eddery 20/1: 10-007: Dwelt, al last: qck reapp: see 1527.   8   51
7 ran   Time 3m 11.25 (8.45)   (K Y Lim)   J Noseda Newmarket.

1929   9.00 CRITERION ASSET MDN 3YO (D)   1m4f   Good/Firm 24 -13 Slow
£4192   £1290   £645   £322

1455 **TOTAL CARE 22** [4] H R A Cecil 3-9-0 T Quinn 10/11 FAV: 2221: 3 br c Caerleon - Totality (Dancing   87
Brave): Made all, clr 2f out, rdn/styd on well in last, cosily: rnr-up all 3 prev starts: dam a 14f wnr: eff
at 11/12f, 14f suit: runs well fresh on fast, soft & a gall or sharp trk: useful, win races over further.
4338} **ARMEN 246** [7] M C Pipe 3-9-0 R Hughes 33/1: 0-2: 3 b c Kaldoun - Anna Edes (Fabulous Dancer):   1   83
Trkd wnr, rdn/styd on inside last but not pace of wnr: reapp: well btn on sole '99 start (1m mdn,
gd/soft): clearly apprec this step up to 12f on fast grnd: clr of rem today & will win a mdn sn.
1439 **MINGLING 23** [5] M H Tompkins 3-9-0 S Sanders 3/1: 0-3523: 3 b c Wolfhound - One The Tide   5   76
(Slip Anchor): Chsd front 2, rdn/no extra appr final 2f: up in trip, needs h'caps: see 1439.
1554 **KADOUN 16** [3] L M Cumani 3-9-0 Pat Eddery 3/1: 24: Waited with, hdwy 6f out, drvn/no extra fnl 4f.   5   69
4605} **AEGEAN WIND 222** [6] 3-9-0 G Carter 20/1: 0-5: Bhd, lost tch final 5f: reapp, big step up in trip: ½   68
well btn sole '99 juv start (7f mdn, hvy).
--   **ARTHUR K** [2] 3-9-0 D Griffiths 33/1: 6: Al well bhd: debut: Greensmith gelding, with H Morrison.   21   48
--   **GEETEE** [1] 3-9-0 K Fallon 33/1: 7: Dwelt, sn t.o: N Callaghan newcomer.   dist   0
7 ran   Time 2m 34.45 (4.45)   (K Abdulla)   H R A Cecil Newmarket.

Official Going: FIRM   Stalls: Inside, except 10f/12f - Outside

1930

6.35 DONATELLO LADIES HCAP 3YO+ 0-75 (E)   7f rnd   Good/Firm 39   -24 Slow   [37]
£2877   £822   £411   3 yo rec 10lb

1690 **NERONIAN** 12 [3] Miss D A McHale 6-9-10 (33) Miss L Johnston (7) 12/1: 305001: 6 ch g Mujtahid   35
- Nimieza (Nijinsky) Held up, prog 2f out, styd on well ins last to lead near line, going away: rnr up in '99 for K
R Burke (rtd 65, claimer, first time visor, rtd 43a on sand): back in '97 won at Beverley (limited stakes, rtd 72, B
W Hills): eff at 7f/10f on fast & gd: best without blinks/visor & handles a stiff or sharp track.
1519 **IMBACKAGAIN** 19 [6] N P Littmoden 5-10-10 (47) Miss L Sheen (5) 8/1: 000202: 5 b g Mujadil -   nk   48
Ballinclogher (Creative Plan) Handy, rdn/led 1f out, hdd nr line: op 5/1: apprec return to Brighton: see 1336, 297.
1540 **FOX STAR** 19 [4] Julian Poulton 3-9-11 (44)(bl) Ms D Goad (7) 25/1: 600053: 3 b f Foxhound - Our   1   43
Pet (Mummy's Pet) Chsd ldrs, kept on fnl 2f, not pace of front pair cl home: blinks reapp: eff at 5f, stays a sharp 7f.
1794 **ANNIE APPLE** 7 [10] N Hamilton 4-10-12 (49)(vis) Miss Elisabeth Neyen 11/1: 000504: Dwelt/towards   nk   47
rear, styd on fnl 2f, nrst fin: op 8/1: visor reapp: both wins in selling grade: see 594.
1793 **NOBLE PASAO** 7 [5] 3-11-7 (68) Miss S Thomas (7) 10/1: 600305: Led 4f out till 1f out, held nr fin.   nk   65
1542 **SILVER TONGUED** 19 [16] 4-9-12 (35) Miss Hayley Bryan (7) 33/1: 0-0006: Prom, onepace fnl 1f.   1½   29
1462 **ITALIAN SYMPHONY** 22 [11] 6-11-6 (57)(vis) Miss E Folkes (5) 7/2 FAV: 004557: Chsd ldrs 3f out, sn held.   ½   50
1601 **FLYING PENNANT** 15 [1] 7-10-1 (38)(bl) Mrs S Bosley 6/1: 0-5538: Dwelt/rear, mod gains: see 896.   nk   31
1672 **BELLAS GATE BOY** 12 [12] 8-11-2 (53) Mrs L Pearce 7/1: -00039: Dwelt/rear, mod gains: op 4/1.   5   45
418 **ROBBER RED** 139 [7] 4-11-2 (53) Miss E J Jones 20/1: 0-0000: Mid div, btn 2f out: 10th: see 336.   1½   41
1710 **GRANDMA ULLA** 11 [13] 3-10-12 (59) Miss Belinda Fisher 14/1: 0-0000: Rear, wide 3f out, sn btn: 11th.   1¼   44
1349 **ANNS MILL** 28 [9] 3-10-5 (52) Mrs S Moore (5) 16/1: 0-0400: Led 3f, btn/edged left over 1f out: 1¼   34
12th: jockey given a 6 day ban for careless riding: op 14/1: see 1212 (C/D, claimer).
1066 **ONES ENOUGH** 45 [15] 4-10-10 (47)(t) Mrs A Perrett 9/1: 00-000: Rear/hmpd early, eff/no room   0
over 1f out, no impression: 15th: op 6/1: 6 week abs: tongue strap: see 896.
934 **Swiftur** 59 [2] 3-9-9 (42)(BL) Miss D Pantall (7) 25/1:
1807 **Landican Lane** 6 [8] 4-9-9 (32) Miss S A Karlsson (5) 33/1:
1734 **Yorkie Too** 10 [14] 4-10-7 (44)(bl) Miss J Feilden 16/1:
16 ran   Time 1m 24.2 (4.4)   (Mrs Susan Mountain)   Miss D A McHale Newmarket

1931

7.05 EUROTOURS CLAIMER 2YO (F)   6f rnd   Good/Firm 39   -31 Slow
£2247   £642   £321

730 **YOUNG ALEX** 82 [4] K R Burke 2-9-3 S Carson (5) 3/1 JT FAV: -01: 2 ch g Midnish - Snipe Hunt   70
(Stalker) Dwelt, prog/led over 2f out, rdn clr over 1f out & eased ins last, readily: val for 5L+: op 4/1, 12 wk
abs: eff at 6f, bred to apprec further: acts on fast & a sharp track: runs well fresh: plenty in hand here.
1882 **PRESENTOFAROSE** 2 [5] J S Moore 2-8-2 J Mackay (7) 7/1: 5502: 2 b f Presenting - Little Red   3½   44
Rose (Precocious) Cl up over 2f out, soon held by easy wnr: quick reapp: see 1396 (seller).
1679 **DIAMOND MILLENNIUM** 12 [2] P D Evans 2-8-7 Joanna Badger (7) 4/1: 5053: 2 ch f Clantime -   nk   39
Innocent Abroad (Viking) Cl up halfway, every ch 2f out, soon held: op 9/4: see 849.
1553 **MISSING A BIT** 17 [1] J A Osborne 2-8-9 (BL) F Norton 7/2: 44: Keen/prom, briefly led halfway,   2   45
held 2f out: op 4/1, first time blinks: see 1553 (hvy).
1805 **PRINCESS PENNY** 6 [3] A Daly 3/1 JT FAV: R30135: Led, hdd/drvn 3f out, soon held: op 5/2.   6   31
-- **PERTEMPS JACK** [6] 2-8-5 R Perham 16/1: 6: Cl up, wknd over 2f out & eased: op 12/1: jockey   14   7
reported bit slipped through mouth: Silca Blanka gelding, April foal: dam unraced, sire 7/1m winning h'capper.
6 ran   Time 1m 12.00 (4.2)   (D G & D J Robinson)   K R Burke Newmarket, Suffolk

1932

7.35 EBF METRO FILLIES HCAP 3YO+ 0-65 (F)   5f59y rnd   Good/Firm 39   -04 Slow   [64]
£3419   £1052   £526   £263   3 yo rec 7 lb

1412 **SUNSET HARBOUR** 26 [3] J M Bradley 7-8-6 (42) Claire Bryan (5) 7/2 FAV: 00-241: 7 br m Prince Sabo -   50
City Link Pet (Tina's Pet) Bhd ldrs, rdn/led 1f out, styd on well, rdn out: bckd, op 4/1: unplcd for S Kettlewell
in '99 (rtd 39 & 38a, h'caps, tried visor): '98 wnr at W'hampton, Newcastle & Catterick (h,caps, rtd 52 & 44a): eff
at 6f, all wins at 5f: acts on firm, gd/soft & both AWs, any track: eff with/without blinks: has run well fresh.
*1543 **KNOCKEMBACK NELLIE** 19 [6] D R C Elsworth 4-10-0 (64)(bl) S Sanders 5/1: -00012: 4 b f Forzando   1   68
- Sea Clover (Ela Mana Mou) Prom, hard rdn/ch over 1f out, not pace of wnr near fin: op 7/2: ran to form of 1543.
1652 **ABSOLUTE FANTASY** 13 [8] E A Wheeler 4-10-12 (48)(bl) S Carson (5) 4/1: 201403: 4 b f Beveled -   ¾   50
Sharp Venita (Sharp Edge) Rear, switched wide bef halfway, kept on for press fnl 1f, not able to chall: op 6/1.
4221} **BOXBERRY** 255 [7] N A Callaghan 3-7-12 (41) J Mackay (7) 16/1: 0000-4: Dwelt, rear, styd on fnl 2f   1   41
for press, nearest fin: reapp, op 12/1: unplcd last term, (rtd 54, subs tried blinks): eff at 5f, 6f suit?
at 6f: prob handles fast grnd & a sharp/undulating track.
1662 **QUITE HAPPY** 13 [5] 5-9-3 (53) A Whelan 4/1: -03335: Led till 1f out, held/eased cl home: op 5/2.   1   51
1670 **MINIMUS TIME** 13 [1] 3-7-11 (40)(bl) A McCarthy (3) 20/1: 146406: Chsd ldrs, onepace fnl 2f: see 357.   ¾   36
1464 **GOLD EDGE** 22 [4] 6-7-10 (32)(2oh) G Sparkes (4) 12/1: 050607: Al outpcd: op 14/1: see 148.   1½   24
1512 **WILLOW MAGIC** 20 [9] 3-9-4 (61) P Doe 6/1: -50438: Chsd ldrs, fdd over 1f out: op 5/1: btr 1512.   ½   51
1795 **BREEZY LOUISE** 7 [2] 3-9-6 (63)(bl) S Drowne 14/1: 106609: Prom till halfway: btr 959 (clmr, soft).   11   33
9 ran   Time 1m 02.3 (2.3)   (Mrs Kay Blanford)   J M Bradley Sedbury, Gloucs

1933

8.05 POSTURITE SELLER 3-5YO (G)   1m2f   Good/Firm 39   -02 Slow
£1943   £555   £277   3 yo rec 13lb

1066 **NAKED OAT** 45 [9] B Smart 5-9-4 J Bosley 7/1: 14/1: 000001: 5 b g Imp Society - Bajina (Dancing   52
Brave) Keen, towards rear, rdn fnl 2f & styd on well to lead inside last, in command near fin: no bid: op 10/1: 6
wk abs: '99 wnr at W'hampton (mdn, rtd 65a) & Warwick (apprentice h'cap, rtd 60): plcd in '98 (mdn, rtd 68a): eff
at 1m/10f on fast & fibresand, sharp/turning or undulating track: runs well fresh: apprec this drop to sell grade.
1331 **JUST WIZ** 29 [13] Andrew Reid 4-9-4 M Henry 1/1 FAV: 300222: 4 b g Efisio - Jade Pet (Petong)   1½   49
Keen, prom, rdn fnl 2f, kept on, no extra: claimed by N Littmoden for £5,000: hvly bckd, op 6/4.
1807 **TWOFORTEN** 6 [7] M Madgwick 5-9-4 (vis) L Newman (3) 20/1: 660003: 5 b g Robellino - Grown At   ½   48$
Rowan (Gabitat) Dwelt, towards rear, rdn & kept on fnl 2f, no threat to wnr: op 14/1, quick reapp: see 524.
1880 **WESTMINSTER CITY** 3 [10] D R C Elsworth 4-9-10 (bl) L Branch (7) 8/1: U04404: Cl up going well   1¾   52$

BRIGHTON   THURSDAY JUNE 15TH   Lefthand, V Sharp, Undulating Track

3f out, rdn/fdd over 1f out: quick reapp: see 1570, 748.
1331 **EI EI** 29 [4] 5-9-4 I Mongan (5) 16/1: 662405: Keen/rear, eff 3f out, al held: op 14/1: see 404 (AW, 9f).   3   42
1332 **SPONTANEITY** 29 [2] 4-8-13 D Sweeney 20/1: 000-06: Mid div, outpcd over 4f out, mod late gains: ½   36
op 12/1: unplcd in '99 (rtd 60, h,cap): '98 Thirsk wnr (auct mdn, rtd 74): eff at 7f, bred to apprec 1m+: acts on fast.
1331 **LIONESS** 29 [12] 4-8-13 P Fitzsimons (5) 25/1: 0-0007: Chsd ldrs till over 1f out: see 965.   2½   32
1644 **LADY VIENNA** 13 [5] 3-8-0 A Daly 12/1: 005-58: Led 1f, handy 1m: see 1644.   4   26
1731 **ARAGANT** 10 [6] 4-9-4 (BL) S Drowne 20/1: 30-009: Mid div, btn 2f out, blinks: op 14/1: see 1210.   nk   30
380 **MAKARIM** 145 [8] 4-9-4 P Doe 12/1: 65-050: Strugg 3f out: 10th: op 10/1, jumps fit (mod form).   6   21
1364 **MERIDIANA** 27 [14] 4-8-13 F Norton 9/1: 441-00: Keen, prog/led after 1f, hdd 4f out & soon btn: 14th: 0
op 6/1: ex French, '99 wnr in the Provinces (12f, gd): now with J M Bradley.
3908} **Scenic Lady** 275 [1] 4-8-13 A Morris 20/1:   1212 **Lunajaz** 37 [3] 3-8-5 R Price 33/1:
1502 **Fools Paradise** 20 [11] 3-8-5 S Sanders 33/1:
14 ran   Time 2m 02.9 (5.1)   (The Dyball Partnership)   B Smart Lambourn, Berks

1934   8.35 CLASSIFIED STKS 4YO+ 0-65 (E)   1m3f196y   Good/Firm 39   -02 Slow
£2776   £793   £396

4602} **COPYFORCE GIRL** 224 [2] Miss B Sanders 4-8-13 (t) S Carson (5) 11/2: 0040-1: 4 b f Elmaamul -   58
Sabaya (Seattle Dancer) Prom, rdn fnl 4f & led over 2f out, always holding rivals inside last, rdn out: reapp, 6 mth
jump abs (mod form): rnr up in '99 (rtd 63, mdn h'cap, no sand form, rtd 24a): plcd once in '98 (fill mdn, rtd 81,
also rtd 49a): eff around a sharp/undul 11/12f on firm & fast: runs well fresh: first win tonight.
1407 **KEZ** 26 [3] S P C Woods 4-9-2 N Callan 2/1 FAV: 00-002: 4 b g Polar Falcon - Briggsmaid (Elegant   2   57$
Air) Held up, drvn/prog to chse wnr fnl 2f, kept on tho' held inside last: well bckd tho' op 5/4: see 842.
*1647 **NO LANGUAGE PLEASE** 13 [5] R Curtis 6-9-5 J Lowe 5/1: 13: 6 ch g Arapahos - Strong Language   2   57
(Formidable) Rear/in tch, eff over 3f out, kept on once pace: op 3/1: acts on fast & gd: see 1647 (C/D clmr).
1509 **PADDY MCGOON** 20 [4] D R C Elsworth 5-9-2 L Branch (7) 8/1: 00-604: Keen/chsd ldrs, onepace fnl 2f. hd   53
1666 **TWICE** 13 [6] 4-9-2 (t) I Mongan (5) 14/1: 40-005: Keen/led till over 2f out, soon btn: see 1287 (mdn).   13   39
1582 **WELDUNFRANK** 16 [1] 7-9-2 S Drowne 12/1: 0056: Keen/prom 9f: op 14/1: see 848.   nk   38
377 **BECKON** 145 [7] 4-8-13 C Rutter 4/1: 3-5457: In tch 9f: 5 month abs: see 111 (AW sell, 10f).   5   28
7 ran   Time 2m 33.1 (4.9)   (Copy Xpress Ltd)   Miss B Sanders Epsom, Surrey

1935   9.05 SUSSEX HCAP 3YO 0-70 (E)   1m3f196y   Good/Firm 39   +03 Fast   [72]
£2927   £836   £418

1544 **ESTABLISHMENT** 19 [2] C A Cyzer 3-9-7 (65) S Sanders 5/2 FAV: -64021: 3 b g Muhtarram - Uncharted   70
Waters (Celestial Storm) Keen, in tch, drvn & pressed ldr from over 2f out, gamely forged ahead near fin: nicely bckd,
tho' op 7/4: best time of night: first success: rtd 88 in '99 (mdn, flattered): apprec step up to 12f, shld get
further: acts on fast grnd & equitrack, likes a sharp/undulating track: open to further improvement.
1895 **JACK DAWSON** 2 [4] John Berry 3-8-10 (54) P Doe 7/2: -000W2: 3 b g Persian Bold - Dream Of Jenny   ½   57
(Caerleon) Handy, rdn/led over 3f out, strongly pressed inside last & hdd near fin, no extra: clr rem: op 4/1: qck
reapp: styd this longer 12f trip well: acts on fast grnd: see 852.
1613 **MICE DESIGN** 15 [1] N P Littmoden 3-8-8 (52) L Newman (3) 9/2: 0543: 3 b g Presidium - Diplomatist   6   46
(Dominion) Chsd ldrs, outpcd by front pair over 2f out: op 5/1: h'cap bow.
1581 **TYCOONS LAST** 16 [5] W M Brisbourne 3-7-11 (41) J Mackay (7) 9/1: -35004: Keen/rear, bhd halfway,   1   34
mod late gains: op 6/1: see 978, 799.
1914 **ESTABLISHED** 1 [7] 3-7-10 (40)(BL)(3oh) M Henry 9/2: -05035: Keen, rear, outpcd fnl 3f: op 7/2, blnks: 2   30
finished 3rd at Lingfield yesterday: tried blinks tonight: see 1914, 835.
1697 **WENSUM DANCER** 12 [3] 3-8-5 (49) N Pollard 12/1: -0406: Led till over 3f out, sn btn: op 8/1, h'cap bow. 8   30
1804 **JUMP** 6 [6] 3-8-11 (55) F Norton 14/1: 600407: In tch 9f: op 12/1: quick reapp: see 328 (AW mdn, 1m). 19 15
7 ran   Time 2m 32.5 (4.3)   (R M Cyzer)   C A Cyzer Maplehurst, W Sussex

HAMILTON   THURSDAY JUNE 15TH   Righthand, Undulating Track, Stiff Uphill Finish

Official Going: GOOD Stalls: Stands Side, except 1m/9f - Inside

1936   2.20 DOMINION BAR HCAP 4YO+ 0-60 (F)   1m5f   Good/Firm 25   +08 Fast   [58]
£3003   £924   £462   £231

1908 **EVENING SCENT** 1 [4] J Hetherton 4-9-1 (45) Dean McKeown 12/1: 603201: 4 b f Ardkinglass - Fresh   50
Line (High Line) Chsd ldrs, rdn/prog to lead over 1f out, styd on well near fin, rdn out: best time of day: unplcd
here at Hamilton last night: '99 Catterick wnr (sell, rtd 60): eff at 12/13f, stys a sharp 2m: acts on fast & soft
grnd, sharp or stiff/undulating track: can run well fresh.
1597 **HAPPY DAYS** 15 [9] D Moffatt 5-8-5 (35) J Bramhill 9/1: 004262: 5 b g Primitive Rising - Miami   1¼   38
Dolphin (Derrylin) Held up, rdn & styd on fnl 2f, not pace to chall: op 8/1: eff at 13f/2m: see 552.
1736 **ELSIE BAMFORD** 10 [12] M Johnston 4-9-6 (50) K Dalgleish (7) 9/4 FAV: 431123: 4 b f Tragic Role -   1½   51
Sara Sprint (Formidable) Mid div, rdn & kept on fnl 2f, not pace to chall: hvly bckd: running well: see 1683 (soft).
1614 **ARTHURS KINGDOM** 15 [2] A P Jarvis 4-10-0 (58) D Mernagh (3) 12/1: 6-0304: Held up, prog/chsd ldrs   1   57
over 1f out, onepce/held inside last: see 1363 (C/D).
1389 **HILL FARM DANCER** 26 [16] 9-8-8 (38) G Baker (7) 10/1: 351145: Dwelt/rear, prog/chsd ldrs over 1f shd 37
out, soon held: op 8/1: see 1241 (12f).
1816 **DESERT RECRUIT** 6 [7] 4-9-2 (46) J Fanning 10/1: -55366: Handy, led over 4f out till over 1f out   hd   45
fdd: op 8/1: quick reapp: see 1683, 779.
1432 **COSMIC CASE** 24 [18] 5-8-3 (33) Dawn Rankin (1) 25/1: -50407: Mid div, never plcd to chall: recent   1¾   29
jumps rnr, (unplcd, rtd 76h, rank h'cap): see 1241, 795.
1699 **LOYAL TOAST** 11 [14] 5-8-0 (30) Kim Tinkler 16/1: 003058: Rear halfway, mod late gains: op 14/1:   1¼   25
1686 **SEATTLE ART** 12 [8] 6-9-6 (50) R Winston 66/1: /66-69: Held up, eff 3f out, sn held: see 1686 (2m).   1   44
1814 **DIAMOND CROWN** 6 [17] 9-8-2 (32) A McAuley (5) 11/2: 00-020: Rear, mod gains: 10th: quick reapp.   1¾   24
1551 **MAJOR ATTRACTION** 17 [11] 5-8-7 (37) S Finnamore (3) 16/1: 000100: Rear, eff 3f out, sn held: 11th.   ¾   28
1499 **RIGHTY HO** 20 [15] 6-9-4 (48) K Hodgson 20/1: 03-000: Mid div, no prog fnl 3f: 12th: op 14/1.   1   38
1908 **LORD ADVOCATE** 1 [3] 12-7-10 (26)(vis)(3oh) P Fessey 25/1: -00060: Led till 4f out, soon btn: 15th.   0
1720 **Craigary** 10 [1] 9-7-10 (26)(bl)(1oh) N Kennedy 40/1:

627

1546 **Gunboat Diplomacy Gb 17** [5] 5-7-12 (28) T Williams 25/1:
1361 **Philmist 27** [10] 8-8-10 (40)(bl) C Lowther 12/1:   1499 **Indian Rope Trick 20** [6] 4-9-3 (47) O Pears 25/1:
1496 **Keltest Star 20** [13] 4-9-6 (50) J Carroll 33/1:
18 ran   Time 2m 47.7 (2.2)   (N Hetherton)   J Hetherton Malton, N Yorks

---

1937   2.50 BONNIE PRINCE CLAIMER 2YO (E)   5f   Good/Firm 25 -53 Slow
£2730   £840   £420   £210

-- **LAST IMPRESSION** [5] A P Jarvis 2-8-6 D Mernagh (3) 11/8 FAV: -1: 2 b f Imp Society - Figment   71
(Posse) Al handy, led over 1f out, pushed out to maintain advantage near fin, readily: value for 5L+: claimed by
J Goldie for £8,000: nicely bckd: April foal, cost 4,500gns: dam a sprint wnr: eff at 5f, will stay further:
acts on fast grnd & a stiff/undulating track: runs well fresh & open to improvement.
1492 **CARTMEL PRINCE 20** [1] D Moffatt 2-8-11 O Pears 5/1: -6002: 2 b c Prince Daniel - Oh My Oh My   ¾ 58
(Ballacashtal) Held up, switched & prog to press wnr over 1f out, kept on tho' flattered by margin of defeat: had
the rest well covered: acts on fast grnd: only mod form previously: see 843.
-- **SUNRIDGE ROSE** [2] P C Haslam 2-8-7 Dean McKeown 5/1: 3: 2 b f Piccolo - Floral Spark (Forzando)   3½ 47
Prom, ch 2f out, soon outpcd by front pair: op 5/2: March foal, cost 2,200gns: dam a 5f wnr: shld apprec 6f+.
1684 **CONSPIRACY THEORY 12** [6] A Berry 2-8-5 J Carroll 5/1: 634: Cl up, ch 2f out, soon held: op 5/2.   ¾ 43
1679 **HOLBECK 12** [4] 2-8-2 J Fanning 12/1: 65: Led till over 1f out, fdd: op 7/1: see 1679 (seller).   4 30
-- **DAVEYSFIRE** [3] 2-9-2 Dale Gibson 12/1: 6: Dwelt, al rear: op 6/1: Gildoran filly, June foal, half   5 30
sister to a winning hdler: dam a 6f juv wnr, sire a top class stayer: looks sure to apprec 1m+ in time.
6 ran   Time 1m 02.9 (3.9)   (Christopher Shankland)   A P Jarvis Aston Upthorpe, Oxon

---

1938   3.20 TATTS FILLIES MDN AUCT 2YO (E)   6f   Good/Firm 25 -43 Slow
£3526   £1085   £542   £271

1381 **FLOWING RIO 26** [6] P C Haslam 2-8-5 Dean McKeown 100/1: 01: 2 b f First Trump - Deanta In Eirinn   75
(Red Sunset) Held up, prog to lead over 1f out, styd on well inside last, pushed out: left debut bhd: half sister
to a 5f juv wnr, dam only modest: eff at 6f, 7f+ should suit: acts on fast grnd & a stiff/undulating track.
1577 **KATIES DOLPHIN 16** [5] J L Eyre 2-8-2(1ow) J Fanning 25/1: 62: 2 ch f Dolphin Street - Kuwah (Be   2 67
My Guest) Cl up, rdn/led over 2f out, hdd over 1f out, no pace of wnr: eff over a stiff 6f on fast.
1577 **CLASSY ACT 16** [3] A Berry 2-8-7 J Carroll 1/1 FAV: 23: 2 ch f Lycius - Stripanoora (Ahonoora)   1¼ 68
Trck ldrs, rdn/ev ch 2f out, hadn't much to offer in last: reportedly hung & not handle fast grnd: bt today's 2nd in 1577 (g/s).
1659 **PATRICIAN FOX 13** [8] J J Quinn 2-8-1 D Mernagh (3) 8/1: -0034: Held up, kept on fnl 2f, no threat: ¾ 60
op 5/1: prob handles fast & gd grnd: see 1659 (5f).
1538 **RUNAWAY BRIDE 19** [7] 2-8-0 J McAuley (5) 9/2: 55: Led till over 2f out, fdd: see 1538.   3 50
1304 **LOVE TUNE 31** [4] 2-8-0 T Williams 5/1: 536: In tch, btn 2f out: btr 1304, 1197 (5f).   shd 50
1764 **BOMBAY BINNY 8** [1] 2-8-2 P Fessey 10/1: 027: Al rear: op 7/1: btr 1764 (5w, 5f).   2 46
1659 **MISS PROGRESSIVE 13** [2] 2-8-2 Kim Tinkler 66/1: -60000: Cl up 4f: mod form.   hd 46
8 ran   Time 1m 13.4 (4.1)   (Rio Stainless Engineering Limited)   P C Haslam Middleham, N Yorks

---

1939   3.50 KIDSONS FILLIES HCAP 3YO+ 0-75 (E)   1m1f36y Good/Firm 25 -17 Slow   [62]
£3542   £1090   £545   £272   3 yo rec 12lb

1892 **SWYNFORD PLEASURE 2** [2] J Hetherton 4-8-5 (39) J Fanning 7/1: 0-4401: 4 b f Reprimand -   44
Pleasuring (Good Times) Rear, eff & came with a well time run fnl 2f to lead towards fin: tchd 9/1, fine ride,
ran 48hrs ago: first win, rnr-up in '99 (class stakes, rtd 55) & '98 (mdn auct, rtd 66): eff at 1m, suited by step
up to 9f: acts on fast & gd grnd, prob firm, any track: needs to be held up.
1762 **SALIGO 8** [6] N Tinkler 5-10-0 (62) J Carroll 3/1 JT FAV: 000342: 5 b m Elbio - Doppio Filo (Vision)   nk 66
Prom, led appr fnl 1f, collared well ins last: bckd: in sound form now, see 1583, 1217.
1353 **BAY OF BENGAL 27** [10] J S Wainwright 4-8-9 (43) J McAuley (5) 33/1: 040-03: 4 ch Persian Bold -   ¾ 45
Adjamiya (Shahrastani) Mid div, rdn to press ldrs appr fnl 1f, no extra near fin: drifted from 12/1:
back in trip & acts at 9/12f: see 1353.
*1765 **PIPS WAY 8** [9] K R Burke 3-10-2 (77)(6ex) Darren Williams (7) 6/1: -60414: Towards rear, improving   1 77
& briefly short of room over 1f out, not qckn ins last: op 7/2, top-weight & penalty: see 1765 (1m, hvy).
1778 **PRIDEWAY 8** [3] 4-10-0 (62) G Baker 9/1: 613065: Wide rear, prog & hung left bef fnl 1f, onepace.   nk 61
1632 **JIMGAREEN 14** [4] 3-9-2 (62) C Lowther 33/1: 490-06: Bhd, struggling & hard rdn 3f out, late   ½ 60
hdwy, never a threat: bred to apprec this kind of trip: see 1632.
1551 **ASHLEIGH BAKER 17** [12] 5-8-12 (46) K Dalgleish (7) 3/1 JT FAV: 53-647: Chsd ldrs feeling pace 3f   2 40
out, no threat after: bckd, unsuited by drop bck to 9f?: see 1332.
4454} **BLUE LEGEND 238** [5] 3-8-2 (48) D Mernagh (3) 33/1: 6000-8: Led till appr fnl 1f, fdd: reapp: '99   3½ 36
Brighton wnr (claimer, rtd 62 & 53a, J S Moore): eff at 7f on firm & gd/soft grnd: now with B Mactaggart.
1496 **SCARLET LIVERY 20** [11] 4-8-13 (47) K Hodgson 33/1: 60-009: Chsd ldrs till 2f out: plcd but prob   2 31
flattered in '99 (mdn, rtd 73$, R Cowell): eff at 7f on fast grnd: with W Tinning.
1268 **WITH RESPECT 34** [7] 3-8-12 (58) Dean McKeown 16/1: 00-00: Al towards rear: 10th on h'cap bow,   nk 42
rtd 65 last term & was prob flattered: with J Given.
1655 **PHILAGAIN 13** [8] 3-7-10 (42)(3oh) N Kennedy 33/1: 000-40: Prom, ch appr fnl 1f, sn btn, eased: 11th. shd 26
1658 **ISLE OF SODOR 13** [1] 4-8-6 (40) R Lappin 16/1: -00500: Al bhd: 12th, see 831.   2 20
12 ran   Time 1m 57.9 (3.8)   (Qualitair Holdings Limited)   J Hetherton Malton, N Yorks

---

1940   4.20 CIRCLE BAR CLASS STKS 3YO+ 0-60 (F)   1m65y   Good/Firm 25 +08 Fast
£2632   £752   £376   3 yo rec 11lb

*1360 **ADOBE 27** [5] W M Brisbourne 5-9-9 G Baker (7) 9/2: 024211: 5 b g Green Desert - Shamshir (Kris)   66
Held up, prog to lead dist, pshd out: op 7/2: gd time: earlier won at W'hampton (rtd 58a) & here at Hamilton
(h'caps): '99 wnr at Bath & Nottingham (h'caps, rtd 55 & 49a): plater for J Gosden in '99: eff at 7f, suited by
ext 1m: acts on firm, gd & f/sand, handles soft, any trk, likes Hamilton: eff with/without t-strap, runs well fresh.
1297 **TYPHOON GINGER 31** [1] G Brown 5-9-2 R Lappin 9/2: 43-662: 5 ch m Archway - Pallas Viking   ¾ 58
(Viking) Rear, ran on for press to chse wnr ins last, held nr fin: tchd 6/1: apprec return to 1m & is threatening to win.
1583 **CYBERTECHNOLOGY 16** [4] M Dods 6-9-5 J Carroll 10/1: -00003: 6 b g Enviroment Friend -   3½ 55
Verchinina (Star Appeal) Bhd, late hdway for press, never led ldrs: op 8/1: ran near to best, see 907.
*1689 **KIDZ PLAY 12** [2] J S Goldie 4-9-7 F Lynch 15/8 FAV: 24-014: Set gd pace till hdd appr fnl 1f, no extra. nk 56

HAMILTON THURSDAY JUNE 15TH Righthand, Undulating Track, Stiff Uphill Finish

1769 **FLOORSOTHEFOREST 8** [6] 4-9-5 C Lowther 6/1: 655265: Prom, ch appr fnl 1f, fdd: btr 1689. *1* **52**
1722 **JUMBOS FLYER 10** [3] 3-8-8 R Cody Boutcher (7) 5/1: -05246: Never trbld ldrs: btr 1722, 1434 (h'caps). *¾* **50**
1689 **DONE WELL 12** [7] 8-9-5 (t) R Winston 50/1: 000007: Prom till 3f out: impossible task, tchd 200/1. *10* **32**
3686} **IRANOO 290** [8] 3-8-8 (t) J Fanning 66/1: 4002-8: Well plcd till wknd quickly appr fnl 2f: reapp: *1* **30**
rnr up fnl '99 start for S Williams (claimer, rtd 55): eff at 1m on gd grnd, without t strap & blinks.
8 ran Time 1m 45.2 (1.4) (P R Kirk) W M Brisbourne Great Ness, Shropshire

1941 4.50 RAILWAY AMAT HCAP 3YO+ 0-60 (F) 6f Good/Firm 25 -25 Slow [29]
£2898 £828 £414 3 yo rec 8 lb

-1815 **BOWLERS BOY 6** [14] J J Quinn 7-11-9 (52) Miss E Ramsden 9/4 FAV: W24121: 7 ch g Risk Me - Snow **57**
Wonder (Music Boy) Mid-div, prog to lead dist, rdn out: well bckd from 7/2, qck reapp: recent Carlise wnr (appr h'cap): plcd in '99 (1st time blinks, h'cap, rtd 49): '98 Pontefract (2, h'caps) & Redcar wnr (stakes, rtd 76): eff at 5/6f: acts on fast, loves gd/soft & hvy, prob handles fibresand: suited by stiff finishes & is in fine form.
1654 **JACMAR 13** [11] Miss L A Perratt 5-11-5 (48) Miss Diana Jones 9/2: 641052: 5 br g High Estate - *nk* **52**
Inseyab (Persian Bold) Rear, improved entering fnl 2f, kept on well, not beaten far: back to best at fav trk.
1139 **SAN MICHEL 42** [10] J L Eyre 8-11-3 (46)(vis) Mrs J M Hill (7) 20/1: -00543: 8 b g Scenic - The Top *¾* **48**
Diesis (Diesis) Rear, switched & stdy prog fnl 2f, unable to chall: 6 week abs, jockey banned for irresp. riding.
1910 **NAPIER STAR 1** [13] A B Mulholland 7-10-4 (33)(t) Miss A Elsey 20/1: 0-2604: Rear, styd on late. *½* **34**
1760 **NAISSANT 8** [6] 7-11-3 (46) Mrs C Williams 6/1: 630425: In tch, styd on but not pace to chall: see 844. *1½* **43**
1685 **ZIBAK 12** [8] 6-10-7 (36) Mr D Boyd (7) 20/1: 00-065: Prom, onepace 1f out: see 1685. *dht* **33**
1815 **PALACEGATE TOUCH 6** [18] 10-11-2 (45)(bl) Mr A Evans 14/1: 501307: Led till dist, fdd: qk reapp. *hd* **41**
1910 **DISTANT KING 1** [1] 7-10-4 (33) Miss L Bradburne (5) 50/1: 000008: Nvr better than mid-div: ran yesterday. *1½* **25**
1681 **SYCAMORE LODGE 12** [2] 9-11-8 (51) Mr L Richardson (7) 12/1: 000349: Never on terms: back in trip. *½* **41**
1818 **ABSTRACT 6** [3] 4-10-5 (34)(vis) Miss Rachel Clark (5) 50/1: 06-000: In tch till 2f out: 10th, qk reapp. *hd* **23**
1662 **AMERICAN COUSIN 13** [7] 5-11-8 (51) Mr W Beasley (7) 16/1: 0-0000: Never on terms, hmpd fnl 1f: 11th. *1* **37**
1654 **MISTER WESTSOUND 13** [5] 8-11-13 (56)(bl) Mr T Best (5) 16/1: 100-40: Dwelt, rear, badly hmpd *3½* **33**
entering fnl 2f, no threat: 12th, stablemate rnr-up: see 1654.
1760 **River Blest 8** [12] 4-12-0 (57) Mr S Walker (5) 12/1: 1681 **Golden Biff 12** [15] 4-11-7 (50) Mr W Peffers (7) 16/1:
1663 **French Grit 13** [4] 8-10-13 (42) Mr J Bostock (7) 25/1:
3288} **Time For The Clan 309** [16] 3-11-0 (51) Miss R Bastiman (7) 50/1:
16 ran Time 1m 12.8 (3) (Bowlers Racing) J J Quinn Settrington, N Yorks

NEWBURY THURSDAY JUNE 15TH Lefthand, Flat, Galloping Track

Official Going GOOD/FIRM. Stalls: Str Crse - Far Side; Rnd Crse - Inside.

1942 2.00 BOLLINGER AMAT HCAP 4YO+ 0-75 (E) 1m2f Good/Firm 21 -27 Slow [44]
£3107 £956 £478 £239

1731 **THE WILD WIDOW 10** [5] M C Pipe 6-10-6 (50)(vis) Mr T Scudamore 6/1: -02221: 6 gr m Saddler's Hall - **71**
No Cards (No Mercy) Made all, sn well clr, 30L+ clr over 2f out, eased down: val 25L+: rnr-up earlier for Miss S Wilton: in '99 won at W'hampton (sell, H Collingridge, rtd 59a) & Warwick (sell, rtd 52): eff at 1m, suited by 10f, further shld suit: acts on fast, soft & fibresand: handles any trk: tried blnks, big improvement today in 2nd time visor with a very positive ride & shld make a qk follow-up.
1743 **WASP RANGER 9** [1] G L Moore 6-12-0 (72) Mr R L Moore (5) 5/4 FAV: 00-022: 6 b g Red Ransom - *16* **73**
Lady Climber (Mount Hagen) Hld up, rdn 3f out, went 2nd over 2f out but wnr was in another parish: well bckd.
1807 **TARSKI 6** [3] L G Cottrell 6-10-6 (50) Mr L Jefford 5/1: 50-003: 6 ch g Polish Precedent - Illusory *½* **50**
(King's Lake) Waited with, eff over 3f out, onepace: better run on fast grnd: likes Goodwood: see 1395.
1807 **GOLD MILLENIUM 6** [6] C A Horgan 6-9-12 (42) Mr B Hitchcott 20/1: 040-04: Chsd wnr till over 4f out. *hd* **42**
1555 **SHARP SPICE 17** [4] 4-11-2 (60) Mr M Bradburne 13/2: 4-4445: Handy chasing group, chsd clr wnr over *6* **51**
4f out till over 2f out: see 1555, 943.
1690 **PADHAMS GREEN 12** [2] 4-11-5 (63) Mr C B Hills (3) 6/1: 600-36: Hld up, eff over 3f out, wknd over 1f out. *1* **53**
1690 **SIBERTIGO 12** [8] 4-10-6 (50) Mr J J Best (7) 33/1: 00-007: Al bhd: poor form. *5* **32**
1807 **MELLOW MISS 6** [7] 4-10-8 (52)(bl) Mr F Windsor Clive(3) 20/1: 603308: Keen bhd, btn & hmpd 3f out. *2* **31**
1690 **SWING ALONG 12** [9] 5-11-3 (61) Mr V Coogan (5) 20/1: 400209: Bhd, btn 4f out: btr 1520 (hvy, 1m). *10* **25**
9 ran Time 2m 07.68 (4.88) (Mrs Pam Pengelly) M C Pipe Nicolashayne, Devon

1943 2.30 AEGON UK MDN 2YO (D) 6f str Good/Firm 21 -27 Slow
£4602 £1416 £708 £354

-- **FORWOOD** [14] M A Jarvis 2-9-0 P Robinson 16/1: -1: 2 b c Charnwood Forest - Silver Hut (Silver **98+**
Hawk) Bhd, hdwy over 1f out, styd on strongly fnl 1f to get up cl home, going away: Mar foal, cost 58,000 gns: half brother to a useful 1m wnr: dam juv 1m wnr: eff at 6f, 7f/1m will suit: acts on fast: promising, worth following.
-- **KINGS IRONBRIDGE** [11] R Hannon 2-9-0 Dane O'Neill 5/1: -2: 2 b c King's Theatre - Dream Chaser *hd* **96**
(Record Token) Slow away, bhd, hdwy over 1f out, kept on for press to lead ins last till collared last strides: bckd from 10/1: Mar foal: half brother to sprint/1m wnrs: dam 6f scorer: eff at 6f on fast grnd: win soon.
-- **CEEPIO** [6] T G Mills 2-9-0 A Clark 12/1: -3: 2 b c Pennekamp - Boranwood (Exhibitioner) *¾* **93**
Cl up, led 3f out till ins last, not btn far under hands & heels riding: Mar foal, cost 72,000 gns: half brother to a 5f juv wnr: dam 6f juv wnr: eff at 6f on fast grnd: can win a race on this evidence.
-- **GOGGLES** [3] H Candy 2-9-0 C Rutter 14/1: -4: Hld up, eff over 1f out, kept on ins last: Jan foal, *1½* **89**
cost 20,000 gns: half brother to a 6f juv wnr: eff at 6f, 7f will suit: handles fast: will improve for this.
-- **POTARO** [15] 2-9-0 D R McCabe 16/1: -5: Prom, rdn & onepace over 1f out: debut: Feb first foal, *1¾* **84**
cost 20,000 gns: Catrail colt: eff at 6f on fast grnd: gd first run.
1691 **TORTUGUERO 12** [12] 2-9-0 J Fortune 14/1: -06: Sn bhd, kept on fnl 1f, nrst fin: Apr foal, cost *2* **78+**
110,000 gns: brother to Gr 3 6f juv wnr & Irish 2000 Guineas scorer Verglas: dam 7f wnr: eff at 6f, will relish 7f/1m: acts on fast grnd: looks sure to rate higher & win a race.
1639 **STRUMPET 14** [13] 2-8-9 J Reid 8/1: -27: Bhd, eff 2f out, sn onepace: btr 1691. *¾* **70**
1403 **AINTNECESSARILYSO 26** [2] 2-9-0 N Pollard 8/1: -08: In tch, rdn 2f out, no impress. *shd* **75**
-- **LOGIC LANE** [7] 2-9-0 K Darley 9/2 FAV: -9: Chsd ldrs, wknd over 1f out: op 7/4: Feb foal, *½* **74**
cost IR£45,000: half brother to wnrs over 7f/2m: dam 5/7f juv wnr: bred to do better.

--	**TUDOR REEF** [9] 2-9-0 R Havlin 25/1: -9: Slow away, nvr a factor: Apr foal, cost 52,000 gns:	*dht*	74

half brother to Gr wng miler Almushtarak: bred to apprec 6f+: with M Channon.

1782 **PARKSIDE PURSUIT** 7 [17] 2-9-0 S Drowne 12/1: -00: Nvr dangrs: fin 11th, btr 1782. — *shd* 74
-- **MAINE LOBSTER** [8] 2-8-9 Pat Eddery 8/1: -0: In tch, no impress fnl 2f: fin 12th, op 5/1. — *nk* 68
-- **RICHENDA** [10] 2-8-9 S Sanders 50/1: -0: Slow away, al bhd: fin 13th on debut. — 1½ 64
-- **LIMBURG** [5] 2-9-0 R Brisland(5) 33/1: -0: Led to 3f out, no extra: fin 14th. — 3½ 59
-- **Junior Brief** [16] 2-9-0 T E Durcan 40/1: -- **Amarone** [1] 2-9-0 P McCabe 50/1:
-- **Dumaran** [4] 2-9-0 K Fallon 12/1:
17 ran   Time 1m 14.49 (2.89)   (Mr & Mrs Raymond Anderson Green)   M A Jarvis Newmarket

---

1944 3.00 AEGON UK COND STKS 2YO (C) 6f str Good/Firm 21 -33 Slow
£7639 £2824 £1412 £642

+1809 **MARINE** 6 [1] R Charlton 2-9-3 K Fallon 2/1 FAV: -511: 2 b c Marju - Ivorine (Blushing Groom) — 102
In tch, imprvd to lead dist, styd on strongly, rdn out: well bckd, qck reapp: recent Goodwood wnr (mdn): eff at
6f, 7f will suit: acts on fast & gd/sft grnd: handles a sharp/undul or gall trk: improving & v useful.
*1513 **BLUEBERRY FOREST** 19 [2] J L Dunlop 2-9-3 W Ryan 9/4: -12: 2 br c Charnwood Forest - 1 98
Abstraction (Rainbow Quest) Rear, prog over 1f out, styd on despite edging left, not quite rch wnr: well bckd:
acts on gd & fast grnd: 7f will now suit: useful colt who met a useful rival today: see 1513.
*1486 **GOODIE TWOSUES** 21 [5] R Hannon 2-8-12 Dane O'Neill 9/2: -13: 2 b f Fraam - Aliuska (Fijar Tango) *hd* 93
Prom, ev ch dist, held by wnr when eased cl home, caught for 2nd: rider given a 5 day ban: acts on fast & gd/soft.
*1774 **NORCROFT LADY** 8 [4] N A Callaghan 2-8-12 Pat Eddery 7/2: -14: Chsd ldrs, wkng when hmpd ins 3½ 83
fnl 1f: bckd from 5/1: not disgraced in this better company: see 1774 (mdn, debut).
*1589 **ANIMAL CRACKER** 15 [3] 2-8-12 D Sweeney 10/1: -0515: Set pace till dist, wknd: see 1589. 2 77
5 ran   Time 1m 14.85 (3.25)   (K Abdulla)   R Charlton Beckhampton, Wilts.

1945 3.30 LISTED BAL'MACOLL STUD STKS 3YO (A) 1m2f Good/Firm 21 +05 Fast
£14430 £4440 £2220 £1110

1630 **LITTLEPACEPADDOCKS** 14 [1] M Johnston 3-8-9 K Fallon 6/1: 1-31: 3 b f Accordion - Lady In Pace — 107
(Burslem) Trkd ldrs till lost place halfway, rallied to chall 2f out, rdn to lead cl home: fair time: '99 wnr at
Musselburgh (mdn) on sole start: sister to smart Yavanas Pace: apprec step up to 10f, 12f will suit: acts on gd
& fast grnd, can run well fresh: held in high regard & may tackle the Irish Oaks next.
1485 **EUROLINK RAINDANCE** 21 [4] J L Dunlop 3-8-9 G Carter 7/2 FAV: 5-3022: 3 b f Alzao - Eurolink *nk* 105
Mischief (Be My Chief) Rear, prog to lead dist, caught cl home & not pace of wnr: bckd from 9/2: stays 10f well.
1374 **CIRCLE OF LIGHT** 27 [8] P W D'Arcy 3-8-9 K Darley 4/1: 10-323: 3 b f Anshan - Cockatoo Island 3½ 100
(High Top) Rcd keenly in bhnd ldr, led 4f out till dist, sn no extra: op 5/2, 5L clr of rem: rcd too freely today.
1185 **CHEZ CHERIE** 39 [9] L M Cumani 3-8-9 Pat Eddery 9/2: 145-04: Mid-div, eff 4f out, btn 2f out: see 1185. 5 92
1469 **INFORAPENNY** 22 [2] 3-8-9 S Sanders 9/1: 0-1235: Nvr nr ldrs: btr 1469, 1223. ½ 91
*1344 **LACE WING** 28 [7] 3-8-9 J Reid 16/1: 0-16: Nvr a factor: up in class, see 1344 (mdn). 5 83
3843} **WARDAT ALLAYL** 280 [5] 3-8-9 Craig Williams 33/1: 3100-7: Chsd ldrs till btn 2f out: reapp: '99 8 71
wnr here at Newbury (stks, rtd 92), highly tried on 2 subs starts: half sister to high-class juv Bint Allayl: eff
at 7f on firm grnd, 1m shld suit: not stay 10f today?
*1797 **IDOLIZE** 7 [6] 3-8-9 J Fortune 15/2: 21-018: Nvr better than mid-div: btr 1797 (gd/soft). 10 56
1469 **BEZZAAF** 22 [3] 3-8-9 P Robinson 15/2: -15P: Saddle broke leaving stalls & rider lost irons, led 0
till 4f out, eased & p.u. over 1f out: bckd from 16/1: ignore this: see 1469, 1200.
9 ran   Time 2m 04.48 (1.68)   (Mrs Joan Keaney)   M Johnston Middleham, N Yorks.

1946 4.00 AEGON UK RTD HCAP 3YO+ 0-105 (B) 7f str Good/Firm 21 +17 Fast [108]
£13044 £4628 £2314 £1052 3yo rec 10lb

1470 **DUKE OF MODENA** 22 [2] G B Balding 3-8-2 (92) S Drowne 5/2: 3-1151: 3 ch g Salse - Palace Street — 98
(Secreto) Chsd ldr till went on 2f out, styd on strongly, rdn out: nicely bckd, best time of day: earlier won at
Kempton (reapp) & Salisbury (h'caps), no luck in running at Goodwood subs: eff at 6/7f on firm & soft/hvy grnd:
handles any trk: likes to run up with the pace: fast improving, useful gldng who nds for the Wokingham at R Ascot.
1851 **DELEGATE** 5 [4] N A Callaghan 7-8-12 (92) Pat Eddery 2/1 FAV: 0-0642: 7 ch g Polish Precedent - 2 93
Dangora (Sovereign Dancer) Dwelt, hdwy from rear 2f out, styd on but not rch wnr: well bckd, qck reapp: see 1851.
1327 **BOLD KING** 29 [3] J W Hills 5-9-0 (94) K Fallon 3/1: 24-103: 5 br g Anshan - Spanish Heart (King Of 3 89
Spain) In tch, eff 2f out, fdd fnl 1f: op 9/4: poss best caught fresh: see 1110 (C/D, reapp).
4195} **KUMAIT** 257 [1] E A L Dunlop 6-9-7 (101) J Reid 4/1: 0221-4: Set pace 5f, fdd: reapp: '99 wnr at 7 84
Redcar (stks, rtd 100), also plcd sev times: '98 Yarmouth wnr (stks, rtd 108), plcd in val h'caps & List: eff at 6/7f,
stays 7f: acts on gd/soft, loves gd & firm: best without a t-strap, loves to dominate: useful at best.
4 ran   Time 1m 24.59 (0.29)   (Miss B Swire)   G B Balding Fyfield, Hants.

1947 4.30 GEORGE SMITH MDN 3YO (D) 7f str Good/Firm 21 -11 Slow
£4342 £1336 £668 £334

837 **HILLTOP WARNING** 69 [5] S P C Woods 3-9-0 J Reid 3/1: 223-01: 3 b c Reprimand - Just Irene (Sagaro) — 78
Prom, led 2f out, edged left & hdd ins last, rallied gamely to regain lead nr line, all-out: well bckd, 10 wk debs:
plcd on all 3 '99 starts (mdn, rtd 88): eff at 6/7f on firm & soft grnd: runs well fresh: game eff here.
1080 **FOOL ON THE HILL** 45 [4] L G Cottrell 3-9-0 Pat Eddery 3/1: 06-42: 3 b g Reprimand - Stock Hill Lass *shd* 77
(Air Trooper) Chsd ldrs, rdn to lead ins fnl 1f, overhauled on line: abs: shld go one better: stays 7f on fast.
1584 **GENERAL JACKSON** 16 [3] D R C Elsworth 3-9-0 N Pollard 11/1: -043: 3 ch c Cadeaux Genereux - Moidart 2 73
(Electric) Chsd ldr till went on 3f out, hdd 2f out, ev ch when hmpd dist, no ch after: poss unlucky: see 1584.
-- **FLYING BACK** [1] R Hannon 3-9-0 R Smith (5) 20/1: -4: Mid-div, prog 3f out, onepcd fnl 1f: mkt 3 67
drifter on debut: half brother to sev wnrs, incl useful Flying brave: shld learn from this.
1181 **INDIAN DRIVE** 39 [7] 3-9-0 Dane O'Neill 11/4 FAV: -65: Nvr nr to chall: s/mate of 4th: see 1181. 4 59
-- **PING ALONG** [8] 3-8-9 K Fallon 9/2: -6: Slowly away, nvr nr ldrs: op 5/2: half sister to sev sprinters: 7 40
incl Unshaken: with M Pipe & shld be capable of better.
-- **FLAMEBIRD** [6] 3-8-9 D Sweeney 33/1: -7: Dwelt, eff halfway, sn btn: related to mid-dist wnrs. ¾ 38
4145} **HURRICANE STORM** 260 [2] 3-9-0 S Clancy 33/1: 06-8: Led till 3f out, wknd: reapp: twice rcd 14 13
juv (rtd 71): brother to a 9f wnr, dam a 6f juv scorer: sire a top-class sprinter: with B Meehan.

NEWBURY   THURSDAY JUNE 15TH   Lefthand, Flat, Galloping Track

8 ran   Time 1m 26.59 (2.29)   (G Noble)   S P C Woods Newmarket.

1948   5.00 THEHORSESMOUTH.CO.UK HCAP 3YO 0-85 (D)   1m4f   Good/Firm 21 -12 Slow   [87]
£3965   £1220   £610   £305

*1736 **FIRECREST 10** [4] J L Dunlop 3-9-9 (82)(6ex) Pat Eddery 1/1 FAV: 0-0111: 3 b f Darshaan - 90
Trefoil (Blakeney) Rear, smooth prog to lead 2f out, styd on well, cmftbly: well bckd: completed qck hat-trick
after wins at Leicester (2, h'caps): much imprvd for recent step up to 12f, 14f will suit: acts on fast & gd/soft
grnd, handles a gall trk: runs well fresh: progressive staying filly & winning run may not be at an end.
1779 **PALUA 8** [3] Mrs A J Bowlby 3-9-2 (75)(bl) J Reid 8/1: 0-3432: 3 b c Sri Pekan - Reticent Bride (Shy   1½ 78
Groom) Rcd keenly & chsd ldr, led 3f out till 2f out, not pace of wnr: op 5/1, 13L clr 3rd: stays 12f.
1790 **PRINCE AMONG MEN 7** [2] M C Pipe 3-9-7 (80) K Fallon 7/2: 6-3333: 3 b g Robellino - Forelino   13 63
(Trempolino) Set pace till 3f out, wknd: op 5/1: longer 12f trip: btr 1790 (10f).
*1661 **MORNING LOVER 13** [1] K R Burke 3-9-4 (77) N Callan 3/1: 0-514: Chsd ldrs 10f, wknd: btr 1661.   3½ 55
1521 **ALPHA HEIGHTS 19** [5] 3-8-4 (63) L Newman (3) 20/1: 00-005: Nvr a factor: see 1521.   2 38
5 ran   Time 2m 33.34 (4.04)   (Sir Thomas Pilkington)   J L Dunlop Arundel, W Sussex

YARMOUTH   THURSDAY JUNE 15TH   Lefthand, Flat, Fair Track

Official Going   GOOD/FIRM. Stalls: Inside.

1949   2.10 LEVY BOARD HCAP 3YO 0-70 (E)   1m6f   Good/Firm 26 -04 Slow   [74]
£2899   £892   £446   £223

1299 **GIVE NOTICE 31** [9] J L Dunlop 3-9-2 (62) T Quinn 8/1: 60-061: 3 b c Warning - Princess Genista   75
(Ile de Bourbon) Waited with, imprvd to lead 2f out, readily: 1st win, 2nd h'cap start: twice rcd juv (mdn, rtd
69): stoutly bred on dam's side, relished this step up to 14f on fast grnd: win more staying h'caps.
*1657 **ALPHA ROSE 13** [2] M L W Bell 3-8-10 (56) J Mackay (7) 4/1: 554112: 3 ch f Inchinor - Philgwyn   2½ 63
(Milford) Well plcd, led briefly appr fnl 2f, styd on but readily held by wnr: nicely bckd, well clr rem:
continues in fine form: see 1657, 1299 (10f, ahd of this wnr).
1770 **TUFTY HOPPER 8** [4] P Howling 3-9-5 (65) R Mullen 12/1: 442243: 3 b g Rock Hopper - Melancolia   13 62
(Legend Of France) Held up, imprvd 4f out, hung left & onepace bef fnl 2f: lngr trip & faster grnd: see 1770, 1142.
4151} **SPECTROMETER 260** [6] Sir Mark Prescott 3-9-6 (66) G Duffield 7/2 FAV: 506-4: Chsd ldrs, led   4 59
appr fnl 3f till bef 2 out, no extra: well bckd on reapp/h'cap bow: promise up to 1m as a juv (mdn, rtd 72).
1804 **CHILLI 6** [1] 3-8-4 (50) A Nicholls (3) 14/1: 233035: Chsd ldrs till 3f out: longer trip, visor omitted.   1¾ 41
1571 **SHRIVAR 16** [3] 3-9-7 (67) R Hughes 7/1: 055246: Led till appr fnl 4f, grad wknd: btr 1270 (held up).   6 53
1571 **XELLANCE 16** [8] 3-7-13 (45) R Ffrench 8/1: -151U7: Handy 10f: btr 1142 (12f, fibresand).   4 27
1661 **HERSELF 13** [7] 3-8-2 (48) G Bardwell 25/1: -0068: Bhd fnl 4f: h'cap bow, longer trip.   4 26
1862 **PTAH 4** [5] 3-8-7 (53) J F Egan 11/2: 043239: Cl-up, led ent fnl 5f till 3½f out, wknd qckly: see 1581.   1½ 30
9 ran   Time 3m 02.0 (4.2)   (I H Stewart Brown)   J L Dunlop Arundel, W.Sussex.

1950   2.40 TOLLHOUSE SELLER 2YO (G)   7f str   Good/Firm 26 -44 Slow
£1823   £581   £260

1679 **SAND BANKES 12** [5] W G M Turner 2-9-2 (vis) A Daly 2/1 FAV: 206121: 2 ch c Efisio - Isabella Sharp   74
(Sharpo) Easily made all: bght in for 3,750gns, well bckd, v slow time: earlier won at Chepstow (seller): Jan foal,
dam a sprinter, sire got 1m: eff at 6/7f on fast, hvy grnd & fibresand: improved forcing the pace in a visor.
1673 **CEDAR TSAR 12** [1] Andrew Reid 2-8-11 M Henry 9/2: 6202: 2 b c Inzar - The Aspector Girl (Alzao)   3 61
2nd thro'out, nvr any impress on wnr: poss styd this longer 7f trip, handles fast & gd grnd tho' rtd higher in 1396.
-- **SEL 4** [4] Sir Mark Prescott 2-8-6 G Duffield 9/4: 3: 2 b f Salse - Frog (Akarad)   2½ 51
Bhd, some prog when hung left appr fnl 1f, nvr dngrs: op 7/4: Apr first foal, dam 9f/12f wnr, sire 6f/1m performer.
1408 **DANCE WITH ME 26** [2] B J Meehan 2-8-11 (BL) R Hughes 6/1: 004: Chsd ldrs till 2f out: blnkd: 4 48
4,200gns Dancing Spree Feb gelding, dam a stayer, sire a sprinter.
1396 **HARRY JUNIOR 26** [3] 2-8-11 P Clarke (7) 25/1: 605: Nvr troubled ldrs: River Falls Feb first foal.   40
5 ran   Time 1m 27.5 (4.9)   (T Lightbowne)   W G M Turner Corton Denham, Somerset.

1951   3.10 KITCHENS FILLIES MDN 3YO (D)   7f str   Good/Firm 26 +00 Fast
£3542   £1090   £545   £272

1155 **ROSSE 41** [2] G Wragg 3-8-11 M Roberts 7/2: 0-41: 3 ch f Kris - Nuryana (Nureyev)   88
Well plcd, led appr fnl 1f, qcknd clr: tchd 13/2, fair time, 6 wk abs: unplcd sole '99 start (mdn, rtd 68): half-
sister to miler Rebecca Sharp: eff at 7f, shld apprec 1m: acts on fast grnd, easy trk: impressive, improving.
-- **MUNEEFA** [4] Saeed bin Suroor 3-8-11 D O'Donohoe 9/4 FAV: 2: 3 b f Storm Cat - By Land By   5 79
Sea (Sauce Boat) Early ldr & again 3f out till bef dist, sn outpcd by wnr: hvy bckd tho' op 5/4: half-sister to
smart 6/12f performer Fahal, dam high-class in the States: eff at 7f, shld suit: handles fast grnd, find similar.
4315} **LAND AHEAD 248** [11] H R A Cecil 3-8-11 T Quinn 5/1: 5-3: 3 ch f Distant View - Nimble Folly   1½ 76
(Cyane) Handy, feeling pace ent fnl 2f, staying on fin: 5th of 19 sole '99 starts (fill mdn, rtd 73):
half-sister to smart 10f performer Skimble: sure to apprec 1m+, prob handles fast grnd.
-- **JABUKA** [1] J A R Toller 3-8-11 C Carver (3) 14/1: 4: Chsd ldrs, same pace appr fnl 1f: debut: shd 76$
Shareef Dancer half-sister to fair mdn sprinter Bun Alley, dam 12f wnr: prob handles fast & will find easier mdns.
3634} **SEA DRIFT 292** [9] 3-8-11 J P Spencer 14/1: 0-5: Chsd ldrs, outpcd appr fnl 1f: reapp: mid-div   1¼ 74
sole '99 start (jt-fav, fill mdn, rtd 61): half-sister to wnrs at 7f/10f, dam a smart sprinter: h'capped after next run.
1609 **DOUBLE PLATINUM 15** [10] 3-8-11 R Hughes 6/1: 20-36: Keen & held up, shkn up & not much room   1¾ 71
2f out, nvr dngrs: op 9/2: rcd v freely & still green: had some decent juv form, try headgear?: see 1609.
1638 **TAFFETA 14** [3] 3-8-11 G Duffield 8/1: 57: Nvr on terms: tchd 10/1: not given a hard time.   2 67
-- **SAHAYB** [12] 3-8-11 R Hills 11/1: 02-8: Al towards rear: reapp/Brit bow: ex-French, rnr-up 2nd   3 61
of 2 '99 starts (7.5f on v soft grnd, D Loder): now with R Armstrong.
1605 **BAILEYS ON LINE 15** [7] 3-8-11 D Holland 25/1: -009: Chsd ldrs till appr fnl 2f: nds mid-dists h'caps.   3 55$
1773 **SEEKING SANCTUARY 8** [5] 3-8-11 J Lowe 50/1: 0-00: Al bhd: 10th, no form.   10 37
1293 **HABIBA 31** [8] 3-8-11 G Faulkner (3) 50/1: 000: Led after 1f till 3f out, sn btn: 11th: moderate.   6 27

631

11 ran   Time 1m 24.4 (1.8)   (A E Oppenheimer)   G Wragg Newmarket.

1952 | 3.40 RADIO NORFOLK COND STKS 3YO+ (C)   6f   Good/Firm 26   +03 Fast
£6090   £2310   £1155   £525   3 yo rec 8 lb

1514 **NIGRASINE** 19 [1] J L Eyre 6-8-9 (bl) J F Egan 3/1: 030451: 6 b h Mon Tresor - Early Gales **101**
(Precocious) Led till appr fnl 1f, rallied most gamely under press to regain lead ins last, ran on strongly:
nicely bckd tho' op 5/2, best time of day: '99 wnr at Thirsk & this v race here at Yarmouth (stks, rtd 112):
'98 Haydock scorer (Listed, rtd 107): eff at 6/7f, tried 1m: acts on gd/soft, suited by firm/fast: best up
with/forcing the pace, any trk, likes Yarmouth: wears blnks or visor: v tough & smart at best.
1849 **AFAAN** 5 [2] R F Marvin 7-8-9 T G McLaughlin 14/1: -06402: 7 ch h Cadeaux Genereux - Rawaabe   1 **99$**
(Nureyev) Trkd ldr, squeezed through to lead appr fnl 1f, sn rdn, hdd & no extra towards fin: ran v near to best,
got a perfect tow along from the wnr & prob suited by omission of blnks: sole 6f win 3 years ago: see 113.
1338 **CUBISM** 28 [9] J W Hills 4-8-9 (t) M Hills 9/4 FAV: 064-03: 4 b h Miswaki - Seattle Kat (Seattle   ¾ **97**
Song) Held up, hdwy & rdn appr fnl 1f, unable to chall: well bckd tho' op 7/4, t-strap: can do better, see 1338.
594} **FLYING OFFICER** 354 [8] Sir Mark Prescott 4-8-9 G Duffield 11/2: 2150-4: Chsd ldrs, ch appr fnl   shd **97**
1f, onepace towards fin: bckd from 7/1 on reapp: '99 wnr at W'hampton (3, h'cap & 2 stks, rtd 109a): '98
Lingfield wnr (auct mdn, rtd 85a): suited forcing the pace at 6/7f, stays a sharp 1m: acts on fast, both AWs.
1182 **CRETAN GIFT** 39 [6] 9-9-12 (vis) R Hughes 10/1: 351465: Held up in tch, no room appr fnl 1f till   ¾ **111**
below dist, unable to qckn: not disgraced giving many of these plenty of weight: see 952 (List).
1674 **GAELIC STORM** 12 [7] 6-9-12 D Holland 13/2: 126-06: Held up, keen, stumbled appr fnl 2f,   1¼ **107**
styd on ins last, nvr nr to chall: tchd 8/1, not far off best giving lots of weight away: see 1674.
1283 **MISS ORAH** 33 [3] 3-8-0 A Nicholls (3) 10/1: 124-07: Nvr dngrs: a big ask against seasoned sprinters.   3 **80**
4297} **SEA DEER** 250 [4] 11-8-9 R Hills 25/1: 1100-8: Prom till ent fnl 2f: stiff task, reapp: won 2 races   7 **61**
in 24hrs here at Yarmouth in '99 (sell & appr h'cap, rtd 78): '98 Newmarket wnr (h'cap, rtd 72): eff at 5f, suited
by 6/7f now: acts on firm, soft, both AWs, any trk, likes Newmarket & Yarmouth: sharper next time in a h'cap.
966 **LONE PIPER** 57 [5] 5-8-9 (t) D Harrison 16/1: 0-4009: Prom till halfway: 8 wk abs, see 660.   6 **46**
9 ran   Time 1m 11.8 (1.4)   (Sunpak Potatoes)   J L Eyre Sutton Bank, N.Yorks.

1953 | 4.10 GREAT YARMOUTH HCAP 3YO+ 0-70 (E)   6f   Good/Firm 26   -11 Slow   [69]
£2938   £904   £452   £226   3 yo rec 8 lb   Raced in 2 Groups that merged ent fnl 2f

1611 **THATCHAM** 15 [10] R W Armstrong 4-8-5 (46)(bl) R Hills 11/1: 320041: 4 ch g Thatching - Calaloo   **59**
Sioux (Our Native) Prom far side, led going well 2f out, sn clr, cmftbly: first win, unplcd in '99 (rtd 60):
suited by drop back to 6f: acts on fast, handles equitrack & gd/soft: best up with/forcing the pace in blnks on an easy trk.
1611 **BE MY WISH** 15 [9] W A O'Gorman 5-8-13 (54) M Roberts 3/1 FAV: 045-32: 5 b m Be My Chief - Spinner   5 **57**
(Blue Cashmere) Rear far side, styd on for press appr fnl 1f, nvr nr wnr: well bckd from 5/1: ran well tho'
unsuited by the drop back to 6f: in front on this wnr on reapp in 1611 (7f, here).
+1815 **TREASURE TOUCH** 6 [13] D Nicholls 6-9-8 (63)(6ex) Iona Wands (5) 7/2: 000113: 6 b g Treasure   2 **60**
Kay - Bally Pourri (Law Society) Front rank stands side & ev ch, onepace bef fnl 1f: drifter from 9/4, qck
reapp & hat-trick attempt: race possibly came too qckly: see 1815.
1842 **TALARIA** 5 [12] S C Williams 4-9-12 (67)(t) G Faulkner (3) 20/1: 601004: Rear stands side,   1¼ **61**
imprvd appr fnl 1f, nvr on terms: qck reapp: btr 1082 (fill h'cap).
1398 **MALAAH** 26 [5] 4-8-7 (48)(bl) D O'Donohoe 25/1: 6-0005: Prom side, onepace appr fnl 1f.   nk **41**
1868 **AJNAD** 3 [3] 6-9-0 (55) T G McLaughlin 14/1: 005066: Chsd ldrs far side, no extra bef fnl 1f.   ¾ **46**
4448} **BREVITY** 239 [7] 5-9-6 (61)(t) K W Marks 20/1: 5060-7: Nvr on terms far side on reapp: op 14/1:   hd **52**
'99 Newbury wnr (appr h'cap, rtd 60 & 56a): rtd 64 for J Gosden in '98: stays 10f, suited by 5/6f: acts
on firm, gd/soft & fibresand, gall trk: wears a t-strap: with D Sasse.
1631 **DON BOSCO** 14 [4] 4-9-13 (68) J F Egan 14/1: 10-008: Al mid-div far side: top-weight, back in trip.   1 **56**
1545 **PERIGEUX** 17 [14] 4-9-7 (62) C Carver (3) 12/1: 00-559: Led stands side till 2f out: op 8/1, see 1423.   ½ **49**
1438 **DELTA SOLEIL** 24 [11] 8-9-5 (60) G Hind 14/1: 0-0000: Chsd ldrs stands side till 2f out: 10th, see 1273.   ½ **46**
*879 **RAIN RAIN GO AWAY** 64 [2] 4-9-5 (60) R Ffrench 4/1: 143110: Led far side till after halfway, sn btn,   **0**
eased: 13th, bckd, 9 wk abs, turf return: progressive on sand previously over 7f: see 879.
1431 Wishbone Alley 24 [6] 5-8-7 (48)(vis) J P Spencer 20/1:   1690 Alfahaal 12 [1] 7-7-13 (40) G Bardwell 16/1:
4221} Rosslyn Chapel 255 [8] 3-7-10 (45)(4oh) M Baird 33/1:
14 ran   Time 1m 12.6 (2.2)   (Mrs John Davall)   R W Armstrong Newmarket.

1954 | 4.40 EBF NOV MED AUCT STKS 2YO (E)   6f   Good/Firm 26   -21 Slow
£3266   £1005   £502   £251

*1541 **SILVER JORDEN** 19 [7] J L Dunlop 2-9-1 T Quinn 8/11 FAV: -11: 2 gr f Imp Society - Final Call   **89**
(Town Crier) Well plcd, led 2f out, pushed clr, cmftbly: hvly bckd from 11/8: earlier made a winning debut
at Lingfield (fill mdn): 17,000gns Jan foal, related to sev wnrs, incl juvs: dam 5f juv wnr: eff at 6f, shld get 7f:
acts on fast & soft grnd, sharp trks: runs well fresh: unbeaten & looks pretty useful, win in better company.
1612 **SYLVAN GIRL** 15 [6] C N Allen 2-8-7 M Hills 11/2: 32: 2 ch f Case Law - Nordic Living (Nordico)   5 **67**
Waited with, hdwy to chase wnr appr fnl 1f, drifted left & no impress in last, eased: op 9/2: handles fast & gd/soft.
*1612 **GROVE DANCER** 15 [3] M H Tompkins 2-9-1 J F Egan 8/1: 13: 2 b f Reprimand - Brisighella (Al Hareb)   2 **69**
Chsd ldrs, struggling 2f out, late rally for 3rd: op 11/2: not disgraced under a pen on this much faster
grnd, had this rnr-up in arrears in 1612 (gd/soft, C/D).
-- **ALEXANDER STAR** [5] J A R Toller 2-8-7 S Whitworth 25/1: 4: Rear, chsd ldrs halfway till no   shd **61**
extra appr fnl 1f: op 16/1 on debut: 10,000gns Inzar Feb foal, dam a mdn, sire 6/7f performer.
*1648 **KNOCK** 13 [2] 2-9-4 R Hughes 11/2: 415: Led till 2f out: fdd: op 9/2: btr 1648 (gd grnd).   ½ **71**
-- **RED RYDING HOOD** [4] 2-8-7 J P Spencer 10/1: 6: Chsd ldrs for 3f, stiff task on debut: 3½ **52**
14,000gns Wolfhound Mar foal, half-sister to useful sprint juv Arethusa, dam & sire sprinters: with C Dwyer.
-- **PATHAN** [1] 2-8-12 G Duffield 20/1: 7: Cl-up till lost pl 2f out: debut: 5,200gns Pyramus Apr   1½ **53**
foal, half-brother to 5 wnrs, incl fair sprinter Sylvan Breeze & a 7f juv wnr: dam unrcd, sire 7f performer.
7 ran   Time 1m 13.7 (3.3)   (Mr & Mrs Gary Pinchen)   J L Dunlop Arundel, W.Sussex.

YARMOUTH THURSDAY JUNE 15TH Lefthand, Flat, Fair Track

1955
5.10 EVENING FILLIES HCAP 3YO 0-70 (E)   1m2f   Good/Firm 26 -01 Slow   [77]
£2990   £920   £460   £230

4537} **ALEXANDRINE 231** [9] Sir Mark Prescott 3-8-3 (52) G Duffield 6/4 FAV: 060-1: 3 b f Nashwan - Alruccaba   **61**
(Crystal Palace) Chsd ldrs, led appr fnl 2f, held on well: hvly bckd on reapp/h'cap bow: unplcd in 3 back-end
fillies mdns in '99 (rtd 56): half-sister to smart 6/7f juv wnr Last Second & mid-dist/styr Arrikala: suited
by step up to 10f, shld get 12f: goes on fast grnd & runs well fresh: at right end of h'cap, shld win again.

*1875 **JULIUS 3** [17] M Johnston 3-9-7 (70) D Holland 4/1: 336-12: 3 b f Persian Bold - Babushka (Dance   ¾ **75**
Of Life) Prom, chsd wnr fnl 2f, styd on but al being held: bckd from 6/1, qck reapp: imprvd again on h'cap
bow: acts on fast & gd grnd & shld be winning again soon.

*1772 **IMARI 8** [11] N P Littmoden 3-8-12 (61)(6ex) M Tebbutt 14/1: -25013: 3 b f Rock City - Misty   1½ **64**
Goddess (Godswalk) Rear, imprvd 2f out, styd on without getting to front pair: fine run over this longer 10f
trip with a penalty: eff at 1m/10f: see 1772 (sell h'cap, here).

1607 **MOST STYLISH 15** [3] C G Cox 3-9-3 (66) J P Spencer 8/1: 5234: Chsd ldrs, unable to qckn appr   2 **66**
fnl 1f: sound h'cap bow, styd this longer 10f trip: handles fast, soft & fibresand.

1345 **SWEET ANGELINE 28** [1] M Roberts 25/1: 30-005: Dwelt & bhd till gd late wide hdwy.   3 **58**
1600 **NUTMEG 15** [12] 3-8-9 (58) J F Egan 20/1: 5-4006: Nvr on terms with ldrs: up in trip, see 894.   1¾ **51**
1200 **LA FAY 38** [2] 3-9-7 (70) T Quinn 8/1: 24-07: Mid-div thr'out, not much room in last: h'cap bow.   1¾ **61**
*1632 **SHAM SHARIF 14** [6] 3-9-3 (66) M Hills 5/1: 00-518: Led after 3f till bef fnl 2f, fdd: h'cap bow.   2 **54**
1726 **PINHEIROS DREAM 10** [13] 3-9-5 (68) R Hughes 8/1: 0-5059: In tch till 2f out: longer trip, btr 1726 (1m).   3 **52**
1644 **SUPER KIM 13** [10] 3-7-13 (48) G Bardwell 40/1: 000-00: Nvr troubled ldrs: 10th, see 1644.   2 **29**
1671 **WINTZIG 13** [15] 3-9-4 (67) R Mullen 12/1: -05250: Al towards rear: 13th, see 1495, 924.   **0**
*1699 **FLOATING EMBER 11** [14] 3-7-10 (45)(7oh) Iona Wands (4) 16/1: 0-0010: Early ldr, prom till wknd   **0**
3f out: 15th, stiffish task after winning a seller in 1699 (soft).

1644 **Cypress Creek 13** [5] 3-7-12 (47) D Glennon (2) 33/1: 1446 **Medooza 23** [7] 3-7-11 (46) A Nicholls (0) 25/1:
1571 **Caunton 16** [4] 3-8-11 (60) T G McLaughlin 33/1:
1710 **Pamela Anshan 11** [16] 3-7-10 (45)(3oh) P M Quinn (3) 33/1:
1605 **Nicks Jule 15** [8] 3-8-4 (52)(1ow) D Harrison 20/1:
17 ran   Time 2m 06.9 (2.7)   (Miss K Rausing)   Sir Mark Prescott Newmarket.

GOODWOOD FRIDAY JUNE 16TH Righthand, Sharpish, Undulating Track

Official Going   GOOD/FIRM. Stalls: Str Crse - Stands Side; Rnd Crse - Inside; except 12f - Outside.

1956
6.25 CANACCORD MDN 3YO (D)   1m4f   Good/Firm Slow
£3900   £1200   £600   £300

-- **SHUWAIB** [5] M R Channon 3-9-0 S Drowne 7/2: 1: 3 b c Polish Precedent - Ajab Alzamaan   **88**
(Rainbow Quest) Handy, chsd ldr bef halfway, led over 1f out, held on well, rdn out: debut, bckd from 8/1: eff
at 12f, may get further: acts on fast grnd & a sharp trk: runs well fresh: open to further improvement.

1599 **SENSE OF FREEDOM 16** [3] M Johnston 3-8-9 J Reid 9/4: 22: 3 ch f Grand Lodge - Greatest Pleasure   nk **82**
(Be My Guest) Held up, prog to chase wnr fnl 1f, kept on despite swishing tail, just held: op 7/4: stays 12f.

957 **TROILUS 59** [4] J H M Gosden 3-9-0 J Fortune 2/1 FAV: 50-03: 3 ch c Bien Bien - Nakterjal (Vitiges)   3 **83**
Led, wide on bend 5f out, rdn/hdd over 1f out, held ins last: abs, op 11/8: stays a slowly run 12f: see 957 (10f).

1200 **POLLSTER 39** [2] Sir Michael Stoute 3-9-0 R Hills 5/1: -004: Held up, eff 2f out, onepace: lngr 12f trip.   ¾ **82**
1585 **NIGHT MUSIC 17** [1] 3-8-9 M Roberts 25/1: 400-05: Chsd ldrs early, btn 4f out: see 1585 (h'cap, 10f).   12 **64**
5 ran   Time 2m 39.70 (7.9)   (Sheikh Ahmed Al Maktoum)   M R Channon West Isley, Berks

1957
6.55 EBF COVERS FILLIES MDN 2YO (D)   6f   Good/Firm Slow
£3900   £1200   £600   £300

1667 **BRING PLENTY 14** [4] J H M Gosden 2-8-11 J Fortune 7/2: 01: 2 b f Southern Halo - Alcando (Alzao)   **94**
Rear/rdn halfway, prog over 1f out, styd on strongly to lead nr fin, won going away: bckd from 8/1: half-sister
to 2 7f/1m juv wnrs: eff at 6f, 7f+ looks sure to suit: acts on fast & a sharp trk.

-- **CYCLONE CONNIE** [2] C A Cyzer 2-8-11 R Hills 20/1: 2: 2 ch f Dr Devious - Cutpurse Moll (Green   1¼ **87**
Desert) Prom, led over 1f out, hdd ins last, not pace of wnr: Feb foal, cost 23,000gns: half-sister to a 7f
juv wnr: dam a 7f wnr, sire a Derby wnr: eff at 6f on fast, will get further: acts on a sharp trk: encouraging.

1612 **TEREED ELHAWA 16** [5] E A L Dunlop 2-8-11 J Reid 8/1: 63: 2 b f Cadeaux Genereux - Dimakya   3 **80**
(Dayjur) Led till over 1f out, held ins last: op 6/1: acts on fast & gd grnd, eff at 6f: see 1612.

-- **MIN MIRRI** [7] M R Channon 2-8-11 S Drowne 3/1 FAV: 4: Dwelt, in tch, prog to chall over 1f out,   hd **79**
held ins last: Selkirk filly, Apr foal, cost 18,500gns: sister to a 1m wnr, dam a 5f juv wnr: shld appreciate 7f+.

-- **DANCING VENTURE** [6] 2-8-11 Pat Eddery 12/1: 5: Chsd ldrs, no extra over 1f out: Shareef Dancer   1¼ **76**
filly, Feb foal, a first foal: dam a multiple French wnr, sire an Irish Derby wnr: 7f+ will suit.

-- **ANDROMEDAS WAY** [8] 2-8-11 S Sanders 13/2: 6: In tch, rdn/held over 1f out: op 9/2: Kris filly,   ½ **74**
Mar foal, cost 40,000gns: dam a 7f/1m wnr, sire top-class at 1m: likely to appreciate further for R Charlton.

-- **AKER WOOD** [1] 2-8-11 D Harrison 20/1: 7: Held up, nvr on terms with ldrs: Apr foal, a first foal: 3 **67**
dam a 14f/2m wnr, sire high-class at 7f/1m: looks sure to need 1m+ in time.

1176 **SECURON DANCER 40** [9] 2-8-11 P Doe 6/1: 48: Cl up 5f: 6 wk abs: op 4/1: btr 1176 (5f).   nk **66**
-- **EUROLINK SUNDANCE** [3] 2-8-11 T Quinn 5/1: 9: Dwelt, al rear: op 7/2: Mar foal, dam a 6/7f juv wnr.   ½ **64**
9 ran   Time 1m 13.21 (3.21)   (Anthony Speelman)   J H M Gosden Manton, Wilts

1958
7.25 CORAL HCAP 3YO 0-90 (C)   1m1f192y Good/Firm Slow   [95]
£9750   £3000   £1500   £750

*1831 **FORBEARING 7** [5] Sir Mark Prescott 3-9-13 (94)(6ex) S Sanders 1/1 FAV: 1-0011: 3 b c Bering - For   **103**
Example (Northern Baby) Chsd ldr, went on 3f out, drvn & strongly pressed fnl 1f, always just holding rivals, drvn
out: well bckd: 6lb pen for recent Epsom win (h'cap): 99 wnr at Lingfield (mdn) & Wolverhampton (nov, rtd 95a):
eff at 1m, stays 10f well: acts on both AWs, fast & hvy grnd, sharp/undul or gall trk: tough, cld complete hat-trick.

1812 **BAILEYS PRIZE 7** [1] M Johnston 3-8-9 (76) R Ffrench 3/1: 146222: 3 ch c Mister Baileys - Mar Mar   1 **82**

633

(Forever Casting) Prom, ev ch fnl 3f, held nr fin: op 9/4: tough & consistent: see 1812, 1735.
*1084 **SIPSI FAWR** 45 [4] M L W Bell 3-8-9 (76) J Mackay (7) 6/1: -013: 3 b f Selkirk - Sipsi Fach (Prince Sabo) *nk* **81**
Chsd ldrs, ch over 1f out, onepace/held nr fin: clr rem, op 9/1, abs, h'cap bow: stays 10f, acts on fast & gd/sft.
4561} **MARAHA** 230 [3] J L Dunlop 3-9-0 (81) R Hills 12/1: 610-4: Trkd ldrs, onepace fnl 2f: reapp: '99 Haydock 5 **79**
wnr (mdn, rtd 78): eff at 1m, mid-dists shld suit this term: acts on soft grnd & a gall trk: h'cap bow tonight.
1532 **HALHOO LAMMTARRA** 20 [6] 3-8-6 (73) S Drowne 12/1: 2-005: Hld up, eff/held fnl 2f: lngr 10f trip. *1¾* **69**
4136} **DANCING MIRAGE** 262 [2] 3-9-6 (87) J Reid 14/1: 2310-6: Held up in tch, rdn 3f out, no hdwy: reapp: 4 **77**
'99 Salisbury wnr (mdn, rtd 97): eff at 6/7f, half-sister to a 2m1f wnr & 1m + shld suit: acts on firm/fast & a stiff trk.
999 **FIELD MASTER** 55 [7] 3-8-5 (72) T Quinn 25/1: 322107: Led 7f, sn btn: 8 wk abs: btr 771 (AW). 7 **52**
7 ran   Time 2m 08.39 (4.19)   (Eclipse Thoroughbreds - Osborne House IV)   Sir Mark Prescott Newmarket

---

1959	**7.55 CHANDLER HCAP 3YO+ 0-85 (D)**	**1m6f**	**Good/Firm Slow**	**[83]**
	£3900 £1200 £600 £300	3 yo rec 17lb		

1784 **URGENT SWIFT** 8 [2] A P Jarvis 7-8-10 (65) D Harrison 100/30: 440101: 7 ch g Beveled - Good Natured **68**
(Troy) Rear, prog to lead dist, styd on well, rdn out: earlier won at Southwell (2, AW h'caps, rtd 69a): '99 wnr
at Salisbury & Haydock (h'caps, rtd 78 & 56a): eff at 12/14f on fibresand, firm & gd, handles gd/sft & any trk,
likes Southwell: tried blnks, best without: best with waiting tactics.
--   **AMANCIO** [5] Mrs A J Perrett 9-8-13 (68) T Quinn 5/1: 4130/2: 9 b g Manilla - Kerry Ring (Ack Ack) *¾* **69**
Handy, kept on fnl 3f, not pace of wnr: op 7/1: 8 wk jmps abs, wnr in 99/00 at Sandown (2m h'cap chase, rtd
134c): eff arnd 2m on fast & hvy, likes to dominate: last rcd on the level in '95, won at Epsom (stks): eff
at 12/14f on fast grnd & a sharp/easy trk: capable chaser, looks on a fair mark for a mid-dist/staying h'cap.
1695 **FOREST FIRE** 13 [1] B Hanbury 5-10-0 (83) M Roberts 3/1: 0-2003: 5 b m Never So Bold - Mango 1 **83**
Sampaquita (Colombian Friend) Prom, led over 2f out till over 1f out, held ins last: topweight: see 1076 (12f).
3838} **NORTHERN FLEET** 282 [3] Mark Campion 7-8-13 (68) J Fortune 13/2: 5100-4: Led 3f, handy till btn 3½ **63**
2f out: op 11/2: 8 wk jumps abs (unplcd, h'cap): '99 wnr for Mrs A J Perrett, at Salisbury (h'cap, rtd 71): eff
at 14f/2m on firm & soft, handles any trk, likes a stiff one.
*1594 **TURTLE SOUP** 16 [4] 4-9-8 (77) Pat Eddery 2/1 FAV: 204-15: Lead after 3f till over 2f out, no extra. *hd* **71**
5 ran   Time 3m 06.35 (7.55)   (A P Jarvis)   A P Jarvis Aston Upthorpe, Oxon

---

1960	**8.25 SUNLEY MDN 3YO (D)**	**1m rnd Good/Firm Slow**
	£3900 £1200 £600 £300	

1692 **DIVULGE** 13 [2] J H M Gosden 3-9-0 J Fortune 4/7 FAV: -51: 3 b c Diesis - Avira (Dancing Brave) **93**
Made all, shaken up ins last to maintain advantage, cmftbly: val for 5L+, well bckd: eff at 1m, shld get further:
acts on fast grnd & sharp/undul or stiff track: plenty in hand here, can rate more highly & win again.
1532 **KRANTOR** 20 [5] H R A Cecil 3-9-0 T Quinn 100/30: 62: 3 ch c Arazi - Epagris (Zalazl) 1 **81**
Handy, rdn/chsd wnr over 1f out, al held & flattered by margin of defeat: clr of rem: acts on fast: see 1532.
3998} **DIAMOND ROAD** 271 [3] C A Horgan 3-9-0 J Reid 20/1: 0-3: 3 b c Dolphin Street - Tiffany's Case 7 **70**
(Thatching) Held up, rdn/effort over 2f out, no ext, held over 1f out: reapp: well bhd on sole start last term in a Newbury
mdn: shld appreciate 1m this term: h'cap company will suit in time.
2200} **HAIL THE CHIEF** 358 [4] R Hannon 3-9-0 R Hughes 9/1: 0-4: Rear/in tch, rdn/held 2f out: reapp: *nk* **69**
op 10/1: unplcd sole '99 start (rtd 55, auct mdn): bred to appreciate 1m+ this term.
1399 **JAZZY MILLENNIUM** 27 [1] 3-9-0 D Holland 5/1: 20-035: Chsd wnr, btn over 1f out: op 4/1. *1¾* **66**
5 ran   Time 1m 41.27 (4.87)   (K Abdulla)   J H M Gosden Manton, Wilts

---

1961	**8.55 ST LOUIS RAMS HCAP 3YO 0-80 (D)**	**6f**	**Good/Firm Fair**	**[87]**
	£3900 £1200 £600 £300			

1591 **BOANERGES** 16 [8] R Guest 3-8-13 (72) D Holland 6/1: 2-0001: 3 br c Caerleon - Sea Siren (Slip **80**
Anchor) Trkd ldrs, led over 1f out, in command ins last & eased nr line: op 9/2: plcd twice in '99 (rtd 83,
1st time vis, mdn, J Noseda): eff at 6/7f: handles fast & soft grnd, sharp/stiff trk: 1st win tonight.
1308 **MAGELTA** 31 [1] R Hannon 3-9-2 (75) R Hughes 7/1: 43-002: 3 b c Magic Ring - Pounelta (Tachypous) *1¼* **76**
Cl up, rdn/kept on from over 1f out tho' not pace of wnr: acts on fast & gd/sft grnd: see 994.
1795 **JAMES STARK** 8 [5] N P Littmoden 3-9-1 (74) (vis) Pat Eddery 9/2: 000203: 3 b g Up And At 'Em - *hd* **74**
June Maid (Junius) Rdn/bhd, prog 2f out, no hdwy fnl 1f: handles both AWs, fast & gd/sft: see 1670, 275 & 105.
1694 **LAS RAMBLAS** 13 [6] R F Johnson Houghton 3-9-7 (80) J Fortune 9/4 FAV: -00004: Nvr pace to chall. *½* **78**
444 **DACCORD** 135 [4] 3-9-7 (80) S Sanders 9/1: 11-535: Held up, onepace fnl 2f: abs: new stable. *nk* **77**
1427 **SUSSEX LAD** 25 [2] 3-9-4 (77) L Newman (3) 6/1: 0-0406: Chsd ldrs, outpcd fnl 2f: btr 1175 (mdn). *½* **72**
1650 **AROGANT PRINCE** 14 [3] 3-8-3 (62) R Brisland (5) 16/1: 043167: Led till over 1f out, sn held: btr 1427 (5f)*1¾* **71**
1406 **HUNTING TIGER** 27 [7] 3-9-5 (78) J Reid 6/1: -00008: Prom 4f: see 792. 7 **56**
8 ran   Time 1m 12.36 (2.36)   (P A & D G Sakal)   R Guest Newmarket

---

SANDOWN   FRIDAY JUNE 16TH   Righthand, Galloping Track, Stiff Finish

Official Going   GOOD/FIRM (FIRM places). Stalls: Str - Stands Side; Rem - Inside.

1962	**2.00 EBF MDN 2YO (D)**	**5f**	**Good 43 -01 Slow**
	£3412 £1050 £525 £262		

1727 **SPEEDY GEE** 11 [3] M R Channon 2-8-11 S Drowne 4/1: 361: 2 b c Petardia - Champagne Girl (Robellino) **83**
Prom, styd on to lead dist, kept on well, pushed out: Feb foal, cost IR 55,000gns: brother to smart sprinter
Halmahera: dam 5f juv wnr: speedily bred & eff at 5f on gd grnd: improved today.
1586 **RUSHBY** 17 [6] Mrs P N Dutfield 2-8-11 L Newman (3) 5/1: -6362: 2 b c Fayruz - Moria My Girl *1¼* **77**
(Henbit) Led till over 1f out, not pace of wnr: op 7/2: shown enough to win on a minor track: see 1346, 1048.
--   **VALDESCO** [2] M A Jarvis 2-8-11 P Robinson 4/1: 3: 2 ch c Bluebird - Allegheny River (Lear Fan) *hd* **76+**
Sn rdn in tch, eff over 1f out, kept on for hands & heels: nicely bckd on debut: Feb foal, cost IR£47,000:
half-brother to a smart sprinter: dam 7f wnr: f6 sure to suit & showed promise here: rate higher next time.
--   **PAIRING** [5] H Morrison 2-8-11 J Fortune 10/1: 4: Slow away, in tch, ran green & onepace over *1¾* **71**
1f out: op 7/1, debut: Mar foal, cost 5,500gns: dam 5/6f scorer: bred to apprec 6f: promise here.

1639 **SAAFEND ROCKET 15** [4] 2-8-11 R Hughes 7/2 FAV: 55: With ldr till over 1f out: well bckd, see 1639. *1¾* **66**
-- **BEE J GEE** [1] 2-8-11 T Quinn 6/1: 6: Bhd after 1f on debut: Feb first foal, cost 10,000gns: *8* **50**
dam 7f juv scorer: speedily bred, with J Pearce.
-- **LAW BREAKER** [7] 2-8-11 K Fallon 8/1: 7: Slow away & al bhd on debut: op 5/1: Apr foal, cost *1¾* **46**
IR£4,500: dam 7f scorer: bred for 6/7f in time: with J Cullinan.
7 ran Time 1m 01.79 (2.19) (John Guest) M R Channon West Isley, Berks.

1963 **2.35 M. SIMMONDS MDN 3YO (D) 7f rnd Good 43 -05 Slow**
£4114 £1266 £633 £316

-- **RADIO STAR** [4] J R Fanshawe 3-9-0 D Harrison 11/2: 1: 3 b c Storm Cat - Andover Way (His Majesty) **82**
Held up, eff over 2f out, squeezed thr' ins last & styd on well to lead cl-home, rdn out: debut, jockey rec a
3-day irresponsible riding ban: half-brother to sev wnrs over 1m/12f: eff at 7f, 1m sure to suit: runs well
fresh on gd grnd & a stiff trk: shld improve plenty for this & win again.
1692 **DANCE WEST 13** [1] H R A Cecil 3-9-0 T Quinn 2/7 FAV: -0042: 3 b c Gone West - Danzante (Danzig) *¾* **81**
Led over 3f out, rdn 2f out, kept on for hands & heels till collared cl-home, not btn far: hvly bckd at odds on:
clearly better expected on drop back to 7f & worth a try in headgear: see 1692.
1532 **SARENA SPECIAL 20** [2] R J O'Sullivan 3-9-0 (BL) J F Egan 11/1: 6-2503: 3 b c Lucky Guest - *1¼* **79$**
Lariston Gale (Pas de Seul) Keen, waited with, eff over 2f out, kept on same pace: blnks, treat rating with caution.
1811 **RAVINE 7** [3] R Hannon 3-8-9 R Hughes 12/1: 6-04: Led till 3f out, wknd appr fnl 1f: op 8/1, see 1811. *2* **70**
4 ran Time 1m 29.75 (3.35) (Joseph Allen) J R Fanshawe Newmarket.

1964 **3.05 BAILEYGOMM HCAP 3YO 0-80 (D) 1m rnd Good 43 -01 Slow [86]**
£7442 £2290 £1145 £572

1495 **TRICCOLO 21** [2] A C Stewart 3-9-2 (74) M Roberts 5/2: 5-0151: 3 b c Piccolo - Tribal Lady (Absalom) **81**
Waited with, gd hdwy over 2f out, kept on to lead ins last, idled cl-home & just held on: impressive h'cap wnr
at Salisbury earlier: rtd 77+ in '99: stays 1m well, could get further: acts on fast & gd, handles soft &
a stiff trk: looks best coming as late as possible & shld go in again.
4278} **KIROVSKI 252** [6] P W Harris 3-8-10 (68) D Holland 12/1: 060-2: 3 b c Common Grounds - Nordic Doll *shd* **73**
(Royal Academy) Set pace, kept on for press till collared ins last, rallied cl-home & just held on reapp: rtd 71
when unplcd on 3 juv starts: stays 1m well on gd, could get further: lightly rcd, win a race on this form.
1726 **SPIRIT OF TENBY 11** [1] S Dow 3-8-7 (65) P Doe 12/1: -60303: 3 b g Tenby - Asturiana (Julio Mariner) *1¾* **66**
Held up, eff & short of room over 1f out, onepace: mdn: see 1726, 1345.
1787 **INSIGHTFUL 8** [5] R Hannon 3-9-4 (76) Dane O'Neill 7/2: -50264: Prom, onepace fnl 2f: btr 1569 (7f). *½* **76**
1786 **POLAR CHALLENGE 8** [3] 3-9-7 (79) K Fallon 13/8 FAV: 4-0335: Prom, ev ch 2f out, sn btn: well bckd: *nk* **78**
clearly better expected after 1786.
1435 **YERTLE 25** [4] 3-8-11 (69) R Ffrench 10/1: -0036: With ldr, wknd 2f out: see 1435. *8* **52**
6 ran Time 1m 42.54 (3.54) (Bruce Corman) A C Stewart Newmarket.

1965 **3.40 SBJ GROUP HCAP 3YO+ 0-100 (C) 1m2f Good 43 -01 Slow [95]**
£10725 £3300 £1650 £825 3 yo rec 12lb

1452 **BLUE GOLD 24** [7] R Hannon 3-9-2 (95) J Reid 9/1: 3-4201: 3 b c Rainbow Quest - Relatively Special **98**
(Alzao) Cl-up, led over 2f out till dist, rallied ins last & got up again last strides, gamely: in '99 won here at
Sandown (mdn, rtd 92): stays 10f well on firm, gd/soft & likes Sandown: useful, progressive & game.
1729 **MAKE WAY 11** [5] B J Meehan 4-8-13 (80) Pat Eddery 11/2: -60322: 4 b g Red Ransom - Way Of The *shd* **82**
World (Dance Of Life) Cl-up, eff to lead dist, kept on for press ins last but just hdd cl-home in a thrilling duel.
4203} **DASHIBA 258** [6] D R C Elsworth 4-9-10 (91) K Fallon 13/2: 0110-3: 4 ch f Dashing Blade - Alsiba *1¼* **90**
(Northfields) Waited with, hdwy & sltly short of room over 1f out, kept on ins last, nvr dngrs under hands & heels:
in '99 scored at Sandown (fill mdn) & Goodwood (h'cap, rtd 94): rtd 97 as a juv: eff over 1m/10f on firm, gd/soft
& on any trk: has run well fresh: useful, v encouraging reapp, closer next time with a stronger ride.
1288 **PINCHINCHA 32** [3] D Morris 6-8-10 (77) J F Egan 11/2: -40234: Waited with, eff over 2f out, *hd* **75**
kept on same pace ins last: plcd numerous times in recent seasons: see 1288, 1150.
137 **BRAZILIAN MOOD 198** [9] 4-8-3 (70) P Robinson 12/1: 0210-5: Chsd ldrs till over 3f out, wknd over *2½* **64**
1f out: op 8/1: long abs: sharper for this: see 56.
1729 **PUNISHMENT 11** [1] 9-8-8 (75)(t) R Hughes 33/1: 550006: Waited with, eff over 2f out, onepace. *½* **68**
1829 **HIBERNATE 7** [4] 6-8-2 (69) J Mackay (7) 7/2: 000427: Led till over 2f out, no extra, eased ins *½* **61**
last: bckd tho' op 5/2: has won over 12f but best on a sharp trk?: see 1829, 1050.
*1709 **FIRST FANTASY 12** [8] 4-9-5 (86) T Quinn 100/30 FAV: 1-0518: Slow away, keen, sn in tch till wknd *3* **74**
over 1f out: well bckd: raced too keenly: btr 1709 (3 rnrs, gd/soft).
*1210 **WILLIE CONQUER 38** [2] 8-9-3 (84) S Sanders 12/1: 540-19: Al bhd: now with A Reid, btr 1210 (slr). *½* **71**
9 ran Time 2m 08.5 (4.4) (Mohamed Suhail) R Hannon East Everleigh, Wilts

1966 **4.15 SBJ GROUP CLAIMER 3YO+ (E) 5f Good 43 +05 Fast**
£3493 £1075 £537 £268 3 yo rec 6 lb

1932 **KNOCKEMBACK NELLIE 1** [5] D R C Elsworth 4-8-13 (bl) N Pollard 9/2: 000121: 4 b f Forzando - **67**
Sea Clover (Ela Mana Mou) Cl-up, led 2f out, hard pressed ins last but kept on for press: fair time: claimed for
£10,000: rnr-up at Brighton last night: earlier scored at Lingfield (fill h'cap): unplcd in '99 (mdn, rtd 73):
eff at 5/6f on firm, soft & on any trk: best in blnks & can force the pace: in fine heart at present.
1881 **KING OF PERU 4** [3] N P Littmoden 7-9-5 (vis) R Hughes 100/30: 564422: 7 b g Inca Chief - Julie's *½* **72**
Star (Thatching) Waited with, eff to chall just ins fnl 1f, no extra for press, not btn far: qck reapp, well bckd.
1687 **CROWDED AVENUE 13** [6] P J Makin 8-9-4 S Sanders 15/8 FAV: 040-03: 8 b g Sizzling Melody - Lady *shd* **71**
Bequick (Sharpen Up) Prom, eff to chall just ins fnl 1f, not btn far: hvly bckd, shld rate higher: see 1687.
4261} **MISTER JOLSON 255** [1] R J Hodges 11-8-12 S Drowne 9/1: 0000-4: Bhd, eff over 1f out, sn onepace *2* **59**
on reapp: op 7/1: rnr-up thrice in '99 (rtd 67): '98 wnr at Bath (ltd stks, rtd 84), multiple scorer in prev
years: eff over 5/6f on firm, hvy & equitrack: has run well fresh on any trk, has tried blnks: v tough 11yo.
1734 **SPLIT THE ACES 11** [2] 4-8-11 O Urbina 25/1: 0-0055: Bhd, eff over 1f out, no impress: flattered. *hd* **57$**
1654 **BLUNDELL LANE 14** [4] 5-9-4 (vis) J Fortune 7/2: 0-1006: Led till 2f out, no extra: best 1126. *¾* **62**
6 ran Time 1m 01.49 (1.89) (Notaproperjob Partnership) D R C Elsworth Whitsbury, Hants.

SANDOWN FRIDAY JUNE 16TH Righthand, Galloping Track, Stiff Finish

1967 **4.50 THAMES DITTON HCAP 3YO 0-75 (E) 1m3f91y Good 43 +04 Fast [82]**
£4524 £1392 £695 £348

1448 **ROMANTIC AFFAIR 24** [9] J L Dunlop 3-9-5 (73) Pat Eddery 7/4 FAV: 13-021: 3 ch g Persian Bold - Broken Romance (Ela Mana Mou) Waited with, eff over 2f out, styd on to lead over 1f out, rdn clr: hvly bckd, fair time: '99 scorer at Newcastle (auct mdn, rtd 74): eff at 1m, enjoyed this step up to 11.4f, further suit: acts on gd & soft, stiff trk: type to progress again & win a nice h'cap. **83**
1640 **THREE WHITE SOX 15** [10] P W Harris 3-8-8 (62) D Holland 9/1: 0-032: 3 ch f Most Welcome - Empty Purse (Pennine Walk) In tch, eff & short of room over 2f out, kept on over 1f out, no impress on wnr: stays 11.3f on gd & gd/soft: shld win a race: see 1640. *3* **64**
1571 **DANDES RAMBO 17** [1] D W P Arbuthnot 3-8-0 (54)(1ow) P Doe 33/1: 00-563: 3 gr g Rambo Dancer - Kajetana (Caro) Hld up, hdwy to lead over 2f out till over 1f out, onepace: stays 11.4f on gd grnd: see 1041. *1½* **54**
1436 **PERCUSSION 25** [7] J A R Toller 3-8-0 (54) R Ffrench 14/1: -0064: In tch, rdn over 3f out, onepace over 1f out: stays 11.4f on gd grnd: will stay further: see 1436. *hd* **53**
1812 **ROB LEACH 7** [5] 3-9-7 (75) R Price 10/1: 52655: Prom, eff over 2f out, switched right, wknd. *1½* **72**
1770 **ASSURED PHYSIQUE 9** [6] 3-8-13 (67)(t) P Robinson 7/1: 0-0536: In tch, wknd over 1f out: op 5/1. *shd* **64**
1726 **JOELY GREEN 11** [8] 3-8-8 (62) T G McLaughlin 33/1: 345007: Bhd, brief eff over 1f out, no impress. *1½* **57**
*1585 **FANFARE 17** [4] 3-9-7 (75) T Quinn 3/1: 0-0118: Bhd, brief eff over 2f out, sn saddle slipped: well bckd: ignore this, see 1585. *2½* **66**
1544 **BORDER RUN 20** [11] 3-8-7 (61) R Hughes 10/1: 500369: Led 4f, ev ch 2f out, no extra over 1f out. *6* **43**
1585 **JEUNE PREMIER 17** [2] 3-8-8 (62) D R McCabe 20/1: -50050: Keen in tch, eff & short of room over 2f out, hmpd again over 1f out, eased: prob best to ignore this: see 1485 (10f). *7* **34**
1594 **GOOD FRIDAY 16** [3] 3-8-9 (63) L Newman (3) 14/1: 0-656U: Led after 4f till over 2f out, wkng when hmpd, stumbled & u.r. over 1f out: see 1594. **0**
11 ran Time 2m 26.32 (4.32) (The Earl Cadogan) J L Dunlop Arundel, W.Sussex.

CHEPSTOW FRIDAY JUNE 16TH Lefthand, Undulating, Galloping Track

Official Going Str Crse - GOOD TO FIRM; Rnd Crse - FIRM. Stalls: Str Crse - Stands Side; Rnd Crse - Inside.

1968 **6.35 EBF NOV STKS 2YO (D) 6f str Good 42 -36 Slow**
£3419 £1052 £526 £263

-- **LADY LAHAR** [4] M R Channon 2-8-7 R Havlin 7/1: 1: 2 b f Fraam - Brigadiers Bird (Mujadil): Sn rdn & outpcd, drvn & gd hdwy 2f out, led dist, styd on well, pushed out: Feb 1st foal, dam unrcd: sire smart miler: eff at 6f, 7f will suit: runs well fresh on good & a gall/undul trk: shld improve, can win again. **93**
1586 **SILCA LEGEND 17** [2] M R Channon 2-8-12 Craig Williams 8/15 FAV: -23242: 2 ch c Efisio - Silca Cisa (Haligate): Cl-up, led appr fnl 1f, sn hdd, onepcd: clr rem: hvly bckd stablemate of wnr: stays 6f: see 1586. *1½* **91**
-- **RORKES DRIFT** [3] T J Naughton 2-8-7 A McGlone 16/1: 3: 2 ch f Royal Abjar - Scanno's Choice (Pennine Walk): Dwelt & sn outpcd, rdn & styd on final 1f but no ch with front 2: IR 20,000 Mar foal, half-sister to a 1m scorer, dam modest 12f performer: will apprec 7f+. *4* **76**
1463 **REPEAT PERFORMANCE 23** [1] W G M Turner 2-8-12 (t) A Daly 3/1: 42444: Led to over 1f out, fdd. *shd* **81**
4 ran Time 1m 13.4 (4.6) (Barry Walters Catering) M R Channon West Isley, Berks.

1969 **7.05 UNIVERSITY HCAP 3YO+ 0-80 (D) 7f str Good 42 +05 Fast [77]**
£3916 £1205 £602 £301 3 yo rec 9 lb

*1799 **GOODENOUGH MOVER 8** [2] J S King 4-8-4 (51)(2ow)(6ex) R Havlin 9/2 CO FAV: 00-011: 4 ch g Beveled - Rekindled Flame (King's Lake): Sn led, rdn well clr final 2f, hvly eased inside last, value 7/8L: op 7/2, gd time: earlier won here at Chepstow (h'cap, 1st win, easily): with G Charles Jones in '99 (mdn, rtd 64): eff forcing the pace over 7f on gd & gd/soft, has tried 1m: runs well fresh on a gall/undul trk, likes Chepstow: land qk hat-trick. **67**
1799 **CAD ORO 8** [6] G B Balding 7-9-2 (65) S Carson (5) 25/1: 0-0302: 7 ch g Cadeaux Genereux - Palace Street (Secreto): Chsd wnr, hdwy & styd on final 2f, no ch with easy wnr: gd run on grnd faster than ideal. *2½* **66**
1356 **FULL SPATE 28** [3] J M Bradley 5-9-1 (64) P Fitzsimons (5) 8/1: 0-3603: 5 ch h Unfuwain - Double River (Irish River): Cl-up, rdn & not pace of wnr final 2f: tchd 10/1: see 1028. *1½* **63**
1590 **SUSANS PRIDE 16** [13] B J Meehan 4-10-0 (77) S Clancy (7) 12/1: 003034: Rear, late gains for press appr final 1f, no threat to ldrs: jnt top weight: gd run: see 780. *nk* **76**
1810 **BINTANG TIMOR 7** [9] 6-9-8 (71) P Shea (7) 9/2 CO FAV: 034625: Dwelt, rear, rdn to impr appr final 1f, styd on, no threat: op 7/2, qck reapp: left himself with too much to do here, shade btr 1810. *1½* **68**
1787 **PARKER 8** [12] 3-9-1 (73) K Fallon 9/2 CO FAV: 04-246: Rear, rdn/prog final 2f, kept on, no dngr. *¾* **69**
1547 **HOH HOH SEVEN 18** [5] 4-8-7 (56) Dane O'Neill 25/1: 0-0357: Nvr a threat: see 1348. *3½* **46**
4196} **LUCKY ARCHER 258** [8] 7-9-8 (71) J P Spencer 12/1: 55W0-8: Front rank, rdn/fdd final 2f: reapp: '99 scorer at Yarmouth & Bath (h'caps, rtd 74), prev term landed a hat-trick at Nottingham (app mdn h'cap), Yarmouth & Carlisle (h'caps, rtd 73): eff at 7f/1m on firm & gd grnd: has tried blnks, best without: acts on any trk, likes Yarmouth: back on a winning mark & sharper next time. *shd* **61**
1840 **REACHFORYOURPOCKET 6** [1] 5-7-10 (45)(VIS)(2oh) G Baker (7) 25/1: 036609: Prom 4f, wknd: visor. *hd* **35**
1799 **AKALIM 8** [7] 7-9-3 (66) A Daly 14/1: 10-050: Cl-up, lost tch final 2f, fin 10th: see 1799. *½* **55**
1799 **ERUPT 8** [11] 7-8-6 (55) A Beech (5) 10/1: 421130: Al rear, fin 11th: btr 1799, 1601. *1¾* **41**
1672 **FLASHFEET 13** [4] 10-7-12 (47)(2ow)(5oh) N Carlisle 66/1: 460040: In tch, wknd from halfway, fin 12th. *2* **29**
1590 **LOVERS LEAP 16** [10] 4-10-0 (77)(VIS) C Rutter 5/1: 0-0060: V keen, al bhd, fin last: jt top-weight: nicely bckd but failed to settle in first time visor: much btr 1590, see 1015. *2½* **55**
13 ran Time 1m 22.4 (2.6) (D Goodenough Removals & Transport) J S King Broad Hinton, Wilts.

1970 **7.35 FRIDAY NIGHT FILL MDN 3YO (D) 1m4f23y Good 42 +02 Fast**
£3737 £1180 £575 £287

1165 **LUCKY LADY 41** [2] Sir Michael Stoute 3-8-11 K Fallon 4/7 FAV: 21: 3 ch f Nashwan - Jet Ski Lady (Vaguely Noble): Cl-up, rdn into lead 2f out, styd on well for press, drvn out: nicely bckd, 6 wk abs: gd time: rnr-up prev on debut: half-sister to a 12f wnr: sire won the Derby, dam won the Oaks: eff at 10/12f on fast & **89**

gd grnd, further shld suit: runs well fresh on fast/gd & a gall/undul trk: potentially v useful, win more races.
1447 **METRONOME 24** [3] L M Cumani 3-8-11 J P Spencer 2/1: 022: 3 b f Salse - Rapid Repeat (Exactly Sharp): Led early, led again 4f out, hdd appr final 2f, not pace of wnr inside last: tchd 3/1: stays 12f on gd. *2½* **84**
1669 **MASRORA 14** [1] M R Channon 3-8-11 Craig Williams 9/1: 453: 3 br f Woodman - Overseas Romance (Assert): Settled last, hdwy 4f out, sn drvn & not pace of front 2: up in trip, poss stays 12f: h'caps suit. *3½* **79**
1668 **STRECCIA 14** [4] M Blanshard 3-8-11 C Rutter 33/1: 64: Rcd keenly & led after 2f, hdd 4f out, wknd qckly, t.o: longer 12f trip: see 1668 (debut, 10f). *dist* **49**
4 ran Time 2m 36.0 (4.9) (Maktoum Al Maktoum) Sir Michael Stoute Newmarket.

1971

8.05 SMOBY TOYS MDN HCAP 3YO+ 0-70 (E) 6f str Good 42 -05 Slow [70]
£2940 £840 £420 3 yo rec 7 lb

1734 **BAYONET 11** [11] Jane Southcombe 4-8-9 (51) J P Spencer (3) 7/1: 00-021: 4 b f Then Again - Lambay (Lorenzaccio): Cl-up, rdn to lead dist, styd on well, drvn out: tchd 10/1: plcd in a mdn h'cap in '99 (rtd 58): suited by racing up with/forcing the pace over 6f: acts on fast, gd/soft & a gall/undul trk. **55**
1578 **INDIAN BAZAAR 17** [8] J M Bradley 4-7-12 (40) Claire Bryan (5) 6/1: 30-032: 4 ch g Indian Ridge - Bazaar Promise (Native Bazaar): Keen/dsptd lead, hdd dist, no extra nr fin: tchd 12/1: win a mdn/sell h'cap. *1* **41**
1636 **MR STYLISH 15** [6] I A Balding 4-10-0 (70) K Fallon 6/4 FAV: 4-0233: 4 b g Mazilier - Moore Stylish (Moorestyle): Handy, rdn to impr 2f out, styd on to chall inside last, no extra cl-home: nicely bckd, clr rem. *shd* **71**
1578 **ARZILLO 17** [13] J M Bradley 4-8-9 (51) P Fitzsimons (5) 11/1: -03404: Prom, hdwy 2f out, btn fnl 1f. *2* **47**
1211 **LUSONG 38** [16] 3-8-12 (61) R Smith (5) 14/1: 263405: Rear, rdn/prog 2f out, styd on, no dngr to ldrs. *nk* **56**
1092 **BREW 45** [7] 4-9-1 (57) Dane O'Neill 10/1: 060-06: Dsptd lead, hdd dist, fdd: abs: unproven beyond 5f. *¾* **51**
1884 **ANOTHER VICTIM 3** [9] 6-8-0 (42) G Baker (7) 25/1: /00307: Mid-div, rdn ran on final 1f, no threat: qck reapp: twice below 1508 (sell, gd/soft, flattered). *½* **35**
1877 **MARNIE 4** [17] 3-7-13 (47)(1ow) C Rutter 14/1: 0-0068: Veered right leaving stalls, sn prom, rdn/btn appr final 1f: qck reapp: see 1877. *hd* **41**
1233 **JUST FOR YOU JANE 36** [18] 4-8-11 (53)(bl) A McGlone 16/1: 23-009: Hmpd start, nvr a factor: plcd early in '99 (AW sell/clmr, rtd 61a): plcd in '98 (rtd 69, blnkd): eff arnd 6/7f on firm, soft & fibresand. *1* **43**
152 **LADY BREANNE 193** [12] 4-8-13 (55) I Mongan (5) 20/1: 2636-0: Mid-div at best, fin 10th: 6 mth abs. *nk* **44**
1636 **KEE RING 15** [4] 4-8-11 (53)(bl) S Whitworth 14/1: 5-6060: Rear, effort halfway, no dngr, fin 11th. *½* **41**
1794 **BALI STAR 8** [1] 5-8-7 (49) N Callan 14/1: -20000: Al bhd, 12th: bckd from 25/1: see 1438, 802. *½* **35**
1671 **MOBO BACO 14** [15] 3-8-10 (59) S Carson (5) 25/1: 040600: In tch to halfway, sn bhd, 13th: see 1397. *1* **42**
1670 **Petrie 14** [2] 3-8-3 (52) Craig Williams 20/1:
1734 **Castle Beau 11** [5] 5-8-2 (44) Jonjo Fowle (7) 40/1:
1670 **Gold Rider 14** [3] 3-8-1 (50) A Daly 25/1:
1742 **Cedar Light 10** [19] 3-8-3 (52) A Beech (5) 40/1:
4360} **Fastrack Time 246** [14] 3-9-5 (68) W Hutchinson (7) 50/1:
1734 **Bodfari Times 11** [10] 4-8-0 (42) P M Quinn (3) 40/1:
1414 **Blakey 27** [20] 4-7-12 (39)(1ow) N Carlisle 20/1:
20 ran Time 1m 11.6 (2.8) (Mark Savill) Jane Southcombe Chard, Somerset.

1972

8.35 SEVERN CROSSING CLAIMER 3YO (F) 7f str Good 42 -18 Slow
£2446 £699 £349

1822 **BINT HABIBI 7** [13] M R Channon 3-8-4 Craig Williams 13/2: 200-01: 3 b f Bin Ajwaad - High Stepping (Taufan): Cl-up, led after 2f, styd on gamely when prsd ins last, drvn out: bckd from 10/1, qck reapp: rnr-up once in 99/00 (auct mdn, rtd 69): eff over a gall/undul 7f on firm & good, has tried 1m: apprec drop to clmrs. **49**
1600 **OUTSTANDING TALENT 16** [8] A W Carroll 3-8-4 A Beech (5) 16/1: 0-6002: 3 gr f Environment Friend - Chaleureuse (Final Straw): Mid-div, hdwy 2f out, ran on well fnl 1f, just held: eff at 7f on gd: win a sell/clmr. *¾* **47**
1649 **SPARK OF LIFE 14** [14] P R Chamings 3-7-12 (bl) S Righton 33/1: 060-03: 3 b f Rainbows For Life - Sparkly Girl (Danehill): Dwelt, rear, hdwy 2f out, ran on strongly for press inside last, just failed: stays 7f. *hd* **41**
1671 **LE LOUP 14** [2] Miss E C Lavelle 3-8-13 Dane O'Neill 12/1: 00-004: In tch, hdwy to chall wnr appr final 1f, no extra cl-home: stays 5/7f on gd & soft: see 1464. *shd* **56**
257 **PONTIKONISI 164** [20] 3-8-9 T E Durcan 25/1: 545-05: Hdwy from rear when hung left 2f out, styg on when hung left again appr final 1f, kept on: long abs: acts on gd grnd: see 150 (AW sell). *¾* **50$**
1237 **SHAW VENTURE 36** [3] 3-8-7 D Sweeney 12/1: 60-606: Front rank, rdn/no extra final 1f: op 9/1. *nk* **47**
1405 **LEEN 27** [5] 3-8-4 Jonjo Fowle (7) 12/1: -00007: Prom, edged left & fdd final 1f: see 275. *nk* **44**
1726 **CELEBES 11** [18] 3-8-7 (vis) K Fallon 5/2 FAV: 640008: Cl-up, drvn/no extra dist, eased: see 591. *½* **46**
1742 **PLAYINAROUND 10** [4] 3-8-2 A Daly 12/1: 530-09: Led 2f, with ldrs till fdd final 1f: '99 scorer at Brighton (sell, rtd 61): eff arnd a sharp/undul 6f: acts on firm grnd, likes sells. *1½* **38**
1884 **NORTHERN LIFE 3** [15] 3-7-12 P M Quinn (3) 8/1: 0-0060: Prom, held fnl 2f: op 16/1, qck reapp. *¾* **32**
1732 **SACRED HEART 11** [16] 3-8-0 (t) Claire Bryan (5) 25/1: 0-000: Sn outpcd, fin 11th: modest form. *1* **32**
1745 **SHAYZAN 10** [12] 3-8-7 (t) N Callan 11/1: 46-000: Handy, rdn/lost tch final 2f, 12th: see 1745. *3* **33**
1671 **ROSETTA 14** [17] 3-8-0 S Carson (5) 9/1: 550-00: Al rear, fin 13th: plcd once in '99 (sell, rtd 69 at best): stays a sharp 6f on fast & firm grnd. *shd* **26**
1022 **Little Tara 53** [1] 3-8-2 C Rutter 33/1:
4263} **Calebs Boy 254** [19] 3-8-9 S Whitworth 16/1:
1094 **Titan Lad 45** [6] 3-8-9 I Mongan (5) 16/1:
1502 **Mystical Wisdom 21** [11] 3-7-12 P Fitzsimons (5) 20/1:
-- **Topless In Tuscany** [10] 3-8-2 Sophie Mitchell 33/1:
-- **Chiaro** [9] 3-8-8 R Perham 16/1:
1796 **Risky Dream 8** [7] 3-8-2 Joanna Badger (7) 33/1:
20 ran Time 1m 24.0 (4.2) (A Merza) M R Channon West Isley, Berks.

1973

9.05 ROUND COURSE HCAP 3YO+ 0-80 (D) 1m2f36y Good 42 -01 Slow [77]
£3835 £1180 £590 £295 3 yo rec 12lb

1729 **AMRAK AJEEB 11** [6] R J Baker 8-9-4 (67) G Sparkes (7) 11/2: 00-031: 8 b h Danehill - Noble Dust (Dust Commander): Settled rear, smooth hdwy over 3f out, led 2f out, styd on well, rdn out: mostly out of sorts in '99 for M Channon, earlier won in Dubai (h'cap): missed '98, prev term with B Hanbury (rtd 108 at best): last win came in '96: eff at 1m/10f: handles firm, likes gd or soft grnd: runs well fresh on any trk, likes a stiff/gall or undul one: eff weight carrier & best coming late: v well h'capped on old form & could follow up. **75**
1784 **CLARENDON 8** [3] V Soane 4-10-0 (77) G Hind 11/2: 0-0062: 4 ch c Forest Wind - Sparkish (Persian Bold): Bhd, hdwy halfway, chsd wnr final 2f, styd on but al held: tchd 7/1: gd run under top weight: see 968. *1½* **81**
-- **REAL ESTATE** [5] J S King 6-9-7 (70) I Mongan (5) 8/1: 2113/3: 6 b g High Estate - Haitienne (Green Dancer): Rear, gd hdwy 2f out, ev ch until no extra final 1f: bckd from 12/1, clr rem: v long abs: hdles scorer back in 98/99 (h'cap, rtd 124h, eff at 2m on gd/soft, soft & any trk): progressive when last seen on the Flat in '97, won at Windsor & Ripon (h'caps, rtd 81): eff at 10/12f on firm & gd/soft *2½* **70**

CHEPSTOW
FRIDAY JUNE 16TH **Lefthand, Undulating, Galloping Track**

grnd: likes a sharp trk, handles any: fine reapp & on a fair mark, win again in this form.
4225) **HARMONY HALL 256** [8] J M Bradley 6-8-11 (60) P Fitzsimons (5) 16/1: 3040-4: Rear, prog halfway, 4 53
drvn/no extra final 2f: reapp: reapp sev times in '99 (h'caps, rtd 69 at best), subs won over timber
at Stratford (mdn, rtd 122h at best, eff arnd 2m on firm & gd/soft): '98 Flat wnr at Nottingham (h'cap,
rtd 69, J Fanshawe): eff at 1m/12f on firm & gd/soft: runs well fresh, eff weight carrier.
1666 **OSCIETRA 14** [1] 4-8-7 (56) Dane O'Neill 12/1: 60-055: Rear, hdwy for press final 2f, no threat. hd 49
1666 **BOATER 14** [9] 6-8-11 (60) A McGlone 12/1: 420-36: Rcd keenly & sn prom, rdn/fdd final 2f: op 8/1. 1¾ 50
1570 **TAKE A TURN 18** [2] 5-8-2 (51) C Rutter 33/1: 000-67: Nvr a factor: see 1570. ¾ 40
4459) **ASCARI 239** [10] 4-8-13 (62) K Fallon 10/3 FAV: 0631-8: Rcd keenly & led early, led again 4f out, 3½ 46
hdd 2f out, wknd qckly: bckd from 5/1: recently well btn 6th over timber: '99 Flat scorer for P W Harris
at Nottingham (h'cap, rtd 61): promise on '98 debut (med auct mdn, rtd 76 & 52a): eff at 10f on firm &
gd/soft grnd: loves to force the pace on a galt trk: now with W Jarvis, capable of better.
1362 **HUTOON 28** [11] 3-9-0 (75) S Whitworth 10/1: 043-69: Sn led, hdd 4f out, fdd: see 1362. 6 49
1860 **HORMUZ 5** [7] 4-9-9 (72) J P Spencer 20/1: 0-0000: Prom, lost tch final 2f, fin 10th: qck reapp. 9 34
1521 **CASTLEBRIDGE 20** [4] 3-9-0 (75)(vis) Craig Williams 7/2: 161530: Handy, wknd rapidly final 3f, 11th. 2½ 33
11 ran   Time 2m 08.4 (4.3)   (B P Jones)   R J Baker Stoodleigh, Devon.

SOUTHWELL (FIBRESAND)
FRIDAY JUNE 16TH **Lefthand, Sharp, Oval Track**

Official Going   STANDARD. Stalls: 5f - Outside; Rem - Inside.

1974
2.20 PLAY GOLF MDN 2YO (D)   6f aw rnd   Going 29   +07 Fast
£2785   £857   £428   £214

-- **SEA VIXEN** [5] Sir Mark Prescott 2-8-9 G Duffield 4/6 FAV: 1: 2 ch f Machiavellian - Hill Hopper 80a
(Danehill) Prom, led 2f out, rdn to repel rnr-up: wng debut, hvly bckd, gd time: Feb foal, dam useful 6/7f
performer, sire a miler: eff at 6f, 7f will suit: acts on fibresand: goes well fresh on a sharp track.
1691 **JAMILA 13** [7] E J O'Neill 2-8-9 G Carter 16/1: -02: 2 b f Green Desert - Virelai (Kris) ½ 77a
Handy, wide, rdn to chall appr fnl 1f, held towards fin: well clr rem: 20,000gns Mar foal, half-sister to useful
7f/1m performer Verzen, dam 12f wnr, sire sprinter/miler: eff over a sharp 6f on fibresand: shld find a fillies mdn.
1700 **BAREFOOTED FLYER 12** [4] T D Barron 2-8-9 J Tate 4/1: 0243: 2 ch f Fly So Free - Carmelita (Mogambo)9 57a
Led till ent fnl 2f, no extra: AW bow: prob ran to form of last 2 turf starts & prob handles fibresand, see 1408.
-- **WOLF VENTURE** [3] S P C Woods 2-9-0 R Fitzpatrick (3) 10/1: 4: In tch till appr fnl 1f: debut: op 11/2: 1½ 58a
Wolfhound Apr foal, brother to a 7f wnr, dam & sire sprinters.
1573 **IZZET MUZZY 18** [6] 2-9-0 G Hind 20/1: 5055: Nvr going pace: AW Bow, see 828. 5 46a
1095 **KINGS CREST 45** [1] 2-9-0 G Faulkner (3) 33/1: 066: V Slow away, outpcd: 6 wk abs, AW bow. 5 36a
1648 **TRUSTED MOLE 14** [2] 2-9-0 (bl) M Tebbutt 9/1: -6637: Cl-up 4f, wknd qckly: AW bow. 1½ 32a
-- **FORTUNA** [9] 2-9-0 C Nutter 16/1: 8: Slow to stride, nvr in it: debut, stablemate of wnr, op 12/1: 6 17a
50,000gns Fairy King Apr foal, related to top 2yo Revoque & useful miler Lonesome Dude, dam 7f wnr.
1429 **LIMBO DANCER 25** [8] 2-8-9 V Halliday 16/1: 609: Sn struggling: AW bow, see 1083. ¾ 10a
9 ran   Time 1m 14.6 (1.3)   (Cheveley Park Stud)   Sir Mark Prescott Newmarket, Suffolk

1975
2.55 CLASS CLAIMER 3YO+ 0-70 (E)   1m6f aw   Going 29   -47 Slow
£2705   £773   £386   3 yo rec 17lb

1802 **STEAMROLLER STANLY 7** [4] D W Chapman 7-9-6 R Studholme (5) 7/2: 600041: 7 b g Shirley Heights 58a
- Miss Demure (Shy Groom) Prd ldr, went on 6f out, clr ent str: qck reapp, tchd 9/2: '99 wnr at W'hampton (h'cap)
& here at Southwell (clmr, rtd 93a, no turf form, K Burke): '98 wnr at Lingfield (2, stks, rtd 100a, rtd 78 on turf in
1st time blnks, C Cyzer): eff at 10f/2m on firm/fast, loves both AWs, handles hvy: likes to dominate on sharp trks.
1604 **GLOW 16** [7] M J Polglase 4-9-5 G Carter 3/1 FAV: 6-0352: 4 b f Alzao - Shimmer (Bustino) 6 47a
Led till 6f out, styd on for 2nd under press but no ch wnr: ran to best at weights, stays 14f on fibresand, see 1039.
1501 **AQUAVITA 21** [6] Miss K M George 4-9-5 J Tate 25/1: 005/03: 6 b m Kalglow - Aigua Blava (Solford) 11 33a
Chsd ldrs, rems 6f out, onepace: stiff task, btn over hdles since 1501.
1711 **MANFUL 12** [5] R Brotherton 8-9-9 (bl) I Mongan (5) 7/2: 302364: Held up, rdn after 7f, no impress. 6 35a
-- **SIPOWITZ** [3] 6-9-13 A Clark 6/1: 1103/5: In tch till 4f out: 2 year abs, op 4/1: 3rd of 6 in '98 3½ 36a
(h'cap rtd 60a): '97 wnr at Pontefract (2, h'caps), W'hampton & Lingfield (2, turf & AW h'cap, rtd 63 & 53a):
eff at 2m/2m2f on fast, gd/sft grnd, both AWs, poss not soft: goes on any trk: with C Cyzer.
1613 **MAGENKO 18** [2] 3-8-6 G Duffield 9/2: 000-26: Prom till 6f out: AW bow, rtd 1613 (gd/sft). nk 31a
190 **FRONTIER FLIGHT 184** [2] 10-9-6 J Bosley (7) 40/1: 0560-7: Al bhd: reapp: lightly rcd/no form hd 28$
since 95/96 hdles wnr at Worcester (2, nov h'caps, 2m1f, firm & gd/sft, rtd 102h): sole win on the Flat in '92
for R Charlton at W'hampton (mdn): acts on firm & gd grnd: with P Hiatt.
1819 **DANZIG FLYER 7** [8] B-9-5 R Perham 40/1: 000-08: Lost many lengths start, nvr in it: qk reapp dist 0a
modest & tried blinkers in '99, plcd back in '97 (h'cap, rtd 72 & 75a): eff at 7f on gd/sft grnd & equitrack.
8 ran   Time 3m 10.5 (10.7)   (David W Chapman)   D W Chapman Stillington, N Yorks

1976
3.25 JAMES LATHAM HCAP 3YO+ 0-70 (E)   5f aw   Going 29   -07 Slow [68]
£2737   £782   £391   3 yo rec 6 lb

1324 **AMBITIOUS 30** [5] K T Ivory 5-9-8 (62) C Catlin (7) 7/4 FAV: 010401: 5 b m Ardkinglass - Ayodhya 75a
(Astronef) Trkd ldrs, led appr fnl 1f, easily came clr on the bit: earlier won at Thirsk (class stks): '99 wnr here
at Southwell (fill h'cap, rtd 65a, J Fanshawe), Sandown (2, h'cap & clmr), Redcar (class stks) & York (h'cap, rtd 79):
eff at 6f, suited by 5f: acts on firm grnd & fibresand, loves soft: goes on any trk, runs well for an apprentice.
1871 **KOSEVO 4** [2] D Shaw 6-8-10 (50)(vis) I Mongan (5) 12/1: 000052: 6 b g Shareef Dancer - Kallista 5 50a
(Zeddaan) In tch, styd on for press fnl 2f, no ch with wnr: qk reapp: back to form at fav trk, see 673.
1036 **UNITED PASSION 49** [3] D Shaw 3-8-8 (54) A Clark 16/1: -2003: 3 b f Emarati - Minam (Forzando) nk 53a
Well plcd & ev ch till outpcd fnl 1f: 7 wk abs, op 12/1: better run, prefers this Southwell surface? see 740.
1806 **OFF HIRE 7** [4] C Smith 4-9-4 (58)(vis) G Faulkner (3) 12/1: 210604: Dsptd lead till 2f out, no extra. ¾ 55a
1806 **SAMWAR 7** [1] A Bailey 4-9-1 (55)(vis) R Fitzpatrick (3) 3/1: 201225: Slow away, nrst fin: btr 1237 (seller). ¾ 51a
1724 **POLAR MIST 11** [9] 5-9-9 (63)(tbl) G Hind 8/1: 000106: Chsd ldrs till dist: ran well, see 1487. ¾ 57a
1504 **SOAKED 21** [7] 7-10-0 (68) R Studholme (5) 20/1: -00007: Dsptd lead till halfway: out of sorts, see 394. 2 56a
1766 **JACKERIN 9** [6] 5-8-5 (45) J Bramhill 16/1: 406648: Nvr dngrs: belated AW bow, see 1143, 798. ½ 32a

638

SOUTHWELL (FIBRESAND) FRIDAY JUNE 16TH Lefthand, Sharp, Oval Track

1815 **HIGH ESTEEM** 7 [8] 4-9-6 (60) G Duffield 11/2: 40-109: In tch 2f: qk reapp, see 1421 (6f, here). 5 37a
1817 **JUST ON THE MARKET** 7 [11] 3-9-3 (63) S Finnamore (5) 50/1: 000-00: Al bhd: ex-Irish clmr rnr-up. 1¾ 37a
1801 **MOONRIDGE** 7 [10] 3-9-2 (62) (tbl) K Dalgleish (7) 50/1: 00-000: Reared start, al bhd: moderate, ex-Irish. 6 26a
11 ran   Time 59.6 (1.8)   (Dean Ivory)   K T Ivory Radlett, Herts

1977   4.00 MED AUCT MDN 3YO (E)   1m aw rnd   Going 29 -29 Slow
£2737   £782   £391

1607 **BELINDA** 16 [5] K Bell 3-8-9 J Bosley (7) 33/1: 0401: 3 ch f Mizoram - Mountain Dew (Pharly) 65a
Held up, eff & hung left ent str, kept on well bef dist, got up dying strides: left prev form well bhd: unraced
juvenile: eff over a sharp 1m, shld get further on this evidence: acts on fibresand: may prove hard to place.
1376 **GUARDED SECRET** 28 [2] P J Makin 3-9-0 A Clark 15/8: 3-02: 3 ro c Mystiko - Fen Dance (Trojan Fen) hd 69a
Rcd in 2nd, led halfway, hard rdn/prsd fnl 2f, worn down post: fair AW bow, stays 1m on fibresand: win similar.
1837 **AIWIN** 6 [3] G C H Chung 3-9-0 (t) l Mongan (5) 4/1: -0453: 3 b c Forzando - Great Aim (Great Nephew) nk 68a
In tch, switched to far rail & prog 2f out, ran on, just btn: bckd from 6/1: gd run, return to 9f+ will suit.
1675 **REEMATNA** 13 [4] M A Jarvis 3-8-9 M Tebbutt 6/4 FAV: 0-424: Trkd ldrs, rdn & ev ch 2f out, held below ½ 62a
dist: well bckd: more expected on AW bow, worth a try in headgear?: see 1675.
4373} **SATIRE** 245 [7] 3-8-9 G Duffield 33/1: 0-5: Chsd ldrs 4f: reapp/AW bow: no form, stoutly bred. 14 42a
1771 **SALIX DANCER** 9 [6] 3-9-0 R Perham 12/1: 306: Unruly bef start, led 4f, sn btn: AW bow, see 1532. 14 27a
-- **THEWAYSHEWALKS** [1] 3-8-9 K Dalgleish (7) 50/1: 7: V slow away, al detached: belated debut. 4 15a
7 ran   Time 44.0 (4.6)   (North Farm Stud)   K Bell Lambourn, Berks

1978   4.35 SOUTHWELL SELLER 3YO+ (G)   1m3f aw   Going 29 -27 Slow
£1876   £536   £268   3 yo rec 13lb

1505 **CANADIAN APPROVAL** 21 [8] I A Wood 4-9-7 M Tebbutt 9/1: 440021: 4 ch f With Approval - Atasteforlace 53a
(Laomedonte) Led & clr till ent str, sn rdn, hung on grimly: op 9/2, bt in for 3,700gns: earlier won at Lingfield
(AW h'cap): plcd in '99 (val h'cap, rtd 78): '98 Lingfield wnr (auct mdn, rtd 78): eff at 1m, styd this lngr 11f
trip: acts on firm, gd grnd & both AW's, likes equitrack/Lingfield: goes well fresh, likes to force the pace.
1417 **ULTRA CALM** 25 [7] P C Haslam 4-9-7 Dean McKeown 9/4 FAV: 060022: 4 ch g Doubltour - Shyonn ¾ 51a
(Shy Groom) Chsd ldrs, prog & ch appr fnl 1f, rdn, flashed tail & no extra: clmd for £5,000, clr rem, in-form.
1707 **NORTH ARDAR** 12 [10] R Brotherton 10-9-7 l Mongan (5) 7/1: 000033: 10 b g Ardar - Lanwaite (Seaepic) 6 44a
In tch, prog into 3rd ent str, no further impress: rtd 50a when won this in '99, see 178.
1546 **OVER THE MOON** 18 [6] Mrs N Macauley 6-9-7 (vis) R Fitzpatrick (3) 10/1: 400004: Prom, onepace ent str.2 41a
1540 **BIG E** 20 [4] 3-8-8 G Duffield 16/1: -45: Wide, rear, moderate late progress whilst hanging left. 2 39a
1732 **ADIRPOUR** 11 [9] 6-9-12 Stephanie Hollinshead (7) 14/1: 000436: In tch, outpcd ent str: stiff task. 2½ 41$
1505 **INDIAN SWINGER** 21 [1] 4-9-7 G Faulkner (3) 7/1: 200337: Mid-div till 4f out: not stay?: btr 1505 (1m). 1¾ 35a
1660 **ALL ON MY OWN** 14 [3] 5-9-7 J McAuley (5) 16/1: -38: Al bhd: AW bow, see 1660. ½ 34a
1546 **STATE APPROVAL** 18 [5] 7-9-7 R Studholme (5) 7/1: 605069: Rcd in 2nd for 5f, sn btn: op 11/2, stiff task.½ 33a
1575 **BONELLI** 17 [2] 4-9-7 A Clark 8/1: 460-60: Chsd ldrs till halfway: AW bow, longer trip. 15 18a
10 ran   Time 2m 44.5 (6.2)   (Nigel Shields)   I A Wood Upper Lambourn, Berks

1979   5.10 RACELINE AMAT HCAP 3YO+ 0-65 (G)   7f aw rnd   Going 29 -25 Slow   [38]
£1918   £548   £274   3 yo rec 9 lb

1801 **STILL WATERS** 7 [16] I A Wood 5-10-7 (45) Mr A Evans 13/2: 060031: 5 b g Rainbow Quest - Krill 51a
(Kris) Cl-up, led 3f out, rdn out: tchd 8/1: '99 wnr here at Southwell (h'cap, rtd 66a, K Bell): plcd in '98 for
R Charlton (mdn, rtd 69): eff at 7f/1m, tried 10f: acts on fast, takes fibresand/Southwell, being up with the pace
1207 **MIDNIGHT WATCH** 39 [8] A G Newcombe 6-10-7 (45) Miss C Hannaford (5) 8/1: 322022: 6 b g Capote - 2 46a
Midnight Air (Green Dancer) In tch, prog appr fnl 2f, not trble wnr: clr rem, op 11/2: eff at 7f, return to 1m+?
1801 **FEATHERSTONE LANE** 7 [15] Miss L C Siddall 4-11-2 (54) Mr R Douro (7) 14/1: 223163: 9 b g Siberian 4 47a
Express - Try Gloria (Try My Best) Prom, eff 2f out, no impress: qk reapp, btr 1235 (W'hampton).
1239 **YOUNG BIGWIG** 36 [6] D W Chapman 6-11-6 (58) Miss R Clark 7/1: -06034: Chsd ldrs, no extra 2f out. 1¾ 48a
1801 **SHARP STEEL** 7 [3] 5-11-4 (56) Mr T Best (5) 9/4 FAV: 562125: Handy, onepace fnl 3f: btr 1505 (1m sell). 1½ 43a
1793 **DONTBESOBOLD** 8 [7] 3-11-2 (63) (vis) Mr Nicky Tinkler (5) 12/1: 050206: Led till 3f out, fdd: see 1002. 2 46a
1804 **CUIGIU** 7 [2] 3-10-3 (50) Mrs C Williams (7) 12/1: 420547: Front rank till appr fnl 2f: op 9/1, qk reapp. ¾ 32a
896 **TOP BANANA** 64 [12] 9-11-7 (59) Mrs C Dunwoody (7) 20/1: 620-08: In tch 4f: op 14/1, abs. 3 35a
2432} **MARTON MERE** 349 [4] 4-10-2 (40) Miss A Deniel 25/1: 2056-9: Nvr on terms: reapp: 2nd of 4 on turf ½ 15a
in '99 (mdn, rtd 58, 714 & 43a, T Easterby): needs sell h'caps (officially rtd 40): with A Lockwood.
1772 **MUTABARI** 9 [13] 6-10-12 (50) Mr S Dobson (5) 7/1: 040650: Wide, nvr better than mid-div: 10th. nk 24a
675 **Dream Carrier** 92 [1] 12-9-4 (28) (1ow)(3oh) Mrs C Peacock (0) 33/1:
872 **Bratby** 66 [2] 4-10-4 (42) Mr W Worthington (7) 40/1:
1952} **Time Is Money** 368 [14] 8-11-1 (36) (17ow) Mr M Jenkins (0) 50/1:
1615 **Giulia Muriel** 16 [11] 4-9-6 (30) Mr P Ferguson (2) 50/1:
14 ran   Time 1m 30.4 (3.8)   (Neardown Stables)   I A Wood Upper Lambourn, Berks

YORK   FRIDAY JUNE 16TH   Lefthand, Flat, Galloping Track

Official Going   GOOD. Stalls: 5f & 6f - Stands Side: 7f & Round Course - Inside.

1980   2.10 FAWCETT HCAP 3YO+ 0-100 (C)   5f   Good/Firm 23 -06 Slow   [97]
£7507   £2310   £1155   £577   3yo rec 6lb   Low Numbers (racing centre) prob favoured

1861 **HENRY HALL** 5 [5] N Tinkler 4-9-2 (85) Kim Tinkler 10/1: 060031: 4 b c Common Grounds - Sovereign 94
Grace (Standaan) Nvr far away, went on over 1f out, ran on strongly, rdn out: qck reapp, well bckd: rnr up 4
times in '99 (h'cap, rtd 100 at best): '98 Beverley (nov), Thirsk (clmr) & Doncaster wnr (stks, rtd 98): eff at
6f, suited by a stiff 5f: acts on firm & soft & on any trk: loves a gall one: fairly h'capped & cld follow up.
1869 **DOUBLE OSCAR** 4 [4] D Nicholls 7-7-12 (67) F Norton 8/1: 005632: 7 ch g Royal Academy - Broadway ¾ 73
Rosie (Absalom) Mid div, imprvd 2f out, ran on well fnl 1f, nrst fin: qck reapp: eff with/without blnks, win soon.
1702 **STORYTELLER** 12 [2] M Dods 6-8-9 (78) (vis) Dale Gibson 14/1: -00043: 6 b g Thatching - Please nk 83

639

Believe Me (Try My Best) Chsd ldrs, kept on under press fnl 1f, not pace of wnr cl home: nicely bckd: fine run: suited by a stiff 5f & h'capped to win soon: see 1702, 1162.

1781 **POLLY GOLIGHTLY 9** [8] M Blanshard 7-7-13 (68)(bl) C Rutter 25/1: 022064: Chsd ldrs, kept on under press fnl 1f: likes to run up with or force the pace, hndls any trk, prob best at Chester: see 1398, 1005.   1 70

1851 **FURTHER OUTLOOK 6** [22] 6-9-12 (95) K Darley 4/1 FAV: 005325: Prom, led 2f out till dist, no extra: qck reapp, shorter plcd stablemate of rnr-up: unfav high draw: just better over 6f in 1851 (sharp trk).   ½ 96

+1650 **IVORYS JOY 14** [9] 5-9-3 (86) C Carver (3) 8/1: 560316: Rear, improving when short of room dist, fin well but too late: won good faster than ideal: acts on firm & f/sand, loves gd & hvy: see 1650.   ½ 86

1792 **SHIRLEY NOT 8** [6] 4-8-3 (72)(BL) T Williams 20/1: 031047: Mid div, some late hdwy, nvr dngrs in first time blinks: see 1278.   shd 72

1533 **REFERENDUM 20** [19] 6-8-3 (72) A Nicholls (3) 25/1: 000008: Chsd ldrs, fdd ins fnl 1f: longer priced stablemate of rnr-up: unfav high draw: yet to hit form this term, subs very well h'capped now: see 941.   1 69

4391} **WESTCOURT MAGIC 244** [1] 7-8-8 (77) J Carroll 25/1: 6100-9: Set pace 3f, no extra on reapp: '99 wnr at Chester (h'cap, rtd 79): '98 wnr at Newcastle & Chester (again, 2, h'caps, rtd 90): won again at Chester in '97 (h'cap, rtd 89): stays 6f, loves to force the pace at 5f: acts on any grnd & on any trk, a real Chester specialist: gd weight carrier, runs well fresh: well h'capped front rnr, one to keep in mind back at Chester.   nk 73

1687 **RIVER TERN 13** [20] 7-7-12 (67) D Mernagh (3) 14/1: 5-6060: Rear, short of room 2f out till 1f out, ran on but ch had gone: no luck in running today, unfav high draw: see 1357.   nk 62

1861 **ANTONIAS DOUBLE 5** [16] 5-8-5 (74) P Fessey 25/1: 0-5000: Chsd ldrs 4f, fdd: qck reapp.   nk 68

1861 **LAGO DI VARANO 5** [17] 8-8-13 (82)(bl)(7ex) Dean McKeown 12/1: 353150: Rdn in rear, no room 2f out, no ch after: fin 12th, qck reapp: won this race off a 5lb lower mark last term: see 1861, 1792.   ¾ 73

1533 **ELLENS LAD 20** [14] 6-10-0 (97) L Newton 9/1: 050150: Nvr better than mid div: fin 13th, top-weight.   shd 88

1533 **NIGHT FLIGHT 20** [15] 6-9-6 (89) R Winston 12/1: 020060: Prom till wknd dist: 14th: see 1533.   1 77

1357 Miss Fit 28 [18] 4-8-4 (73) W Supple 25/1:   1861 **Atlantic Viking 5** [7] 5-9-5 (88) A Culhane 16/1:

1529 Saphire 20 [11] 4-9-6 (89) K Hodgson 33/1:   1694 **Connect 13** [13] 3-8-8 (83) W Ryan 25/1:

1533 Speedy James 20 [21] 4-9-5 (88) O Pears 33/1:

19 ran   Time 58.23 (1.48)   (Mike Gosse)   N Tinkler Langton, N Yorks

---

1981   2.45 HALIFAX SELLER 2YO (E)   6f   Good/Firm 23 -46 Slow
£7410   £2280   £1140   £570

1641 **SOMERS HEATH 14** [6] T D Easterby 2-8-6 K Darley 10/1: -001: 2 b f Definite Article - Glen Of Imaal (Common Grounds) Waited with, gd hdwy to lead ent fnl 1f, ran on strongly, rdn out: nicely bckd, bt in for 8,200gns: IR 4,700gns purchse: eff over a stiff 6f on fast grnd, hndls a gall trk: apprec this drop into selling company.   68

1612 **JOINT INSTRUCTION 16** [14] M R Channon 2-8-11 W Supple 4/5 FAV: 452152: 2 b c Forzando - Edge Of Darkness (Vaigly Great) Prom, led briefly dist, not pace of wnr ins fnl 1f: hvly bckd: consistent, eff on firm & hvy grnd: likes to run up with or force the pace: better expected on drop to selling company: see 1507.   1¾ 70

-- **UNLIKELY** [3] J A Osborne 2-8-11 F Norton 10/1: -3: 2 ch c Aragon - Homebeforemidnight (Fool's Holme) In tch, chall dist, not qckn ins last on debut: 3L clr rem: Jan foal, cost 2,000gns: sire a high-class 7f/1m performer: eff at 6f, will stay 7f: hndls fast grnd & a gall trk: sure to learn from this & find a seller.   ½ 69

1628 **STILMEMAITE 15** [12] N Bycroft 2-8-6 J Fanning 16/1: -35004: Prom, ev ch dist, fdd ins last: dropped into selling grade: see 974 (soft grnd, debut).   3 55

1549 **TIME MAITE 18** [10] 2-8-6 G Parkin 6/1: -43135: Just in lead till hdd dist, no extra: nicely bckd.   1 57

1698 **GAZETTE IT TONIGHT 12** [11] 2-8-6 J Carroll 16/1: -556: In tch, rdn & one pace fnl 2f: see 1359.   2½ 46

-- **CHRISTMAS MORNING** [1] 2-8-11 Dale Gibson 20/1: -7: Rdn in rear, late hdwy, nvr dngrs on debut: May foal, cost 2,600gns: dam a 6f wnr, sire a top class 1m/10f performer: already looks in need of 7f: with M W Easterby & sure to improve considerably on this.   nk 50

1679 **CHORUS GIRL 13** [13] 2-8-6 F Lynch 16/1: -5438: Chsd ldrs 4f, wknd: new stable: see 1679 (soft).   nk 44

1918 **HOPGROVE 2** [4] 2-8-6 D Mernagh 25/1: 660359: Mid div, eff over 2f out, btn dist: qck reapp.   nk 43

1381 **MAGNANIMOUS 27** [5] 2-8-11 Kim Tinkler 40/1: -000: Slowly away, never a factor in 10th: see 1130.   2 42

1492 **ASTAIREDOTCOM 21** [9] 2-8-6 (VIS) N Callan 10/1: -450: Bmpd start, al bhd: fin 11th, tried a visor.   ½ 36

1698 **JUST MISSED 12** [8] 2-8-6 T Lucas 25/1: -00: Slowly away & al bhd: see 1698 (mdn aution).   hd 36

1719 **FIRST SIGHT 11** [7] 2-8-11 C Lowther 9/1: -20: Hmpd start, al bhd: much btr 1719 (debut, gd/soft).   2 35

13 ran   Time 1m 13.56 (4.16)   (Mrs P E Needham)   T D Easterby Great Habton, N Yorks

---

1982   3.15 SHEPHERD RTD HCAP 4YO+ 0-95 (C)   1m5f194y   Good/Firm 23 +02 Fast   [102]
£9396   £3564   £1782   £810

1561 **INCH PERFECT 18** [1] R A Fahey 5-8-7 (82)(1oh) R Winston 6/1: -13131: 5 b g Inchinor - Scarlet Veil (Tyrnavos) Waited with, gd hdwy to lead 2f out, kept on strongly, drvn out: gd time, nicely bckd: earlier won at Thirsk & here at York (h'caps): '99 Southwell (reapp, sell), Redcar (with J Hetherton), Pontefract, Newcastle, Bath & W'hampton wnr (h'caps, rtd 63 & 63a): eff at 1m, suited by 10/14f: acts on firm, soft grnd & f/sand: runs well fresh: best held up for a late run: v tough & progressive gelding, a credit to all concerned.   88

1187 **EMINENCE GRISE 40** [9] H R A Cecil 5-9-4 (92) W Ryan 9/2: 464-02: 5 b g Sadler's Wells - Impatiente (Vaguely Noble) Trkd ldrs, imprvd to lead 3f out, collered 2f out, kept on but not pace of wnr: well bckd, 6 wk abs, 3L clr 3rd: sound run, a return to 2m+ will now suit: 4th at R Ascot in '99 (2m6f): see 1187.   1 97

1247 **BAY OF ISLANDS 36** [2] D Morris 8-9-2 (90)(vis) K Darley 8/1: 23-003: 8 b g Jupiter Island - Lawyer's Wave (Advocator) Trkd ldrs, short of room & lost place 3f out, rallied 2f out, kept on well but unable to rechall: clr rem: not much luck in running here: useful, sharper next time, see 1247.   3 90

1187 **LIVIUS 40** [3] Major D N Chappell 6-8-9 (83) M Hills 7/2 FAV: 021-34: Rear, prog to ch ldrs 3f out, one pace fnl 2f: well bckd, 6 wk abs: more expected over this longer 14f trip: best at 12f? see 1187.   4 77

1307 **ARABIAN MOON 31** [8] 4-9-1 (89) J Weaver 9/2: 00-035: In tch, chall 3f out, wknd qckly ins fnl 1f.   5 75

-- **HERITAGE** [5] 6-8-7 (83)(2oh) A Nicholls (3) 33/1: 000/46: Rear, eff 3f out, no impression fnl 2f: fell in a h'cap chase in Ireland 6 wks prev: lightly rcd on the Flat in recent seasons, back in '97 won at Haydock (mdn) & R Ascot (val King George V h'cap, with J Gosden, rtd 91): won a nov h'cap chase at Musselburgh in Feb '00 (with Mrs S Bramall, rtd 93c, eff at 2m on fast & gd/soft): eff at 12f on gd & fast grnd, hndls gd/soft over fences.   ½ 66

1791 **JASEUR 8** [10] 7-9-4 (92)(vis) L Vickers(2) 25/1: 06-007: Prom till wknd over 2f out: see 1791 (2m).   1¾ 75

1009 **MAJESTIC BAY 53** [6] 4-8-10 (84)(BL) A Culhane 20/1: 423-38: Prom till wknd over 3f out: 8 wk abs, first time blinks: longer 14f trip: see 1009 (12f mdn, reapp).   8 55

*1791 **RUM POINTER 8** [7] 4-9-2 (90)(3ex) J Carroll 4/1: -00219: Set pace 11f, wknd: much btr on soft.   ½ 60

1474 **LOCOMBE HILL 23** [4] 4-9-7 (95) D Sweeney 20/1: 310-30: Rear, eff 3f out, soon lost tch & t.o.   19 35

10 ran   Time 2m 56.43 (3.03)   (Tommy Staunton)   R A Fahey Butterwick, N Yorks

1983	**3.50 BLUE BICYCLE RTD HCAP 4YO+ 0-100 (B) 6f str Good/Firm 23 +10 Fast**				**[105]**
	£9622	£3649	£1824	£829	Low Numbers (racing centre) prob favoured

*1533 **INDIAN SPARK 20** [4] J S Goldie 6-9-0 (91) A Culhane 9/1: 415011: 6 ch g Indian Ridge - Annes   **102**
Gift (Ballymoss) Trkd ldrs, qcknd into lead 2f out, clr fnl 1f, cmftbly: nicely bckd, best time of day: recent
Haydock wnr (h'cap), earlier scored at Newcastle (h'cap): '99 wnr here at York (this race, rtd 91): '98 Thirsk
& Doncaster wnr (2, h'caps): v eff at 5/6f: acts on firm, loves gd/soft & hvy grnd: suited by a gall trk, loves
York & Doncaster: gd weight carrier: tough, useful sprint h'capper who is in top form.

423 **KAYO 139** [1] M Johnston 5-9-2 (93) M Hills 20/1: 0-0002: 5 b g Super Power - Shiny Kay (Star   **3   95**
Appeal) Prom, chsd wnr fnl 1f, kept on tho' no ch: long abs: eff at 6f, a return to 7f/1m will suit: runs v
well fresh: fine eff from an unfav high draw today: see 7 (AW), 1m.

1851 **FIRST MAITE 6** [3] S R Bowring 7-9-5 (96)(vis) K Darley 10/1: 465003: 7 b g Komaite - Marina Plata   **¾   95**
(Julio Mariner) Mid div, imprvd to chase wnr 1f out, no extra ins last & caught for 2nd cl home: tchd 16/1, qck reapp.

1514 **UNDETERRED 20** [12] C F Wall 4-9-0 (91) R Mullen 16/1: 0-0364: Hdwy from rear 2f out, kept on under   **nk   89**
press & nrst fin: unfav high draw: fine run & a return to 7f shld suit: see 1286.

1851 **JUWWI 6** [14] 6-9-5 (96) Darren Williams (7) 9/1: 441505: Dwelt, imprvd form rear over 1f out, fin   **1¼   90**
well but too late: nicely bckd, qck reapp: unfav high draw, best held up for a late run: see 1337 (C/D).

1687 **AMARANTH 13** [11] 4-8-7 (84)(1oh) R Cody Boutcher (7) 10/1: 000126: Mid div, no impression fnl 1f.   **½   77**

1533 **GUINEA HUNTER 20** [10] 4-9-7 (98) J Carroll 10/1: 3-0107: Chsd ldrs, onepace fnl 1f: top-weight.   **2   85**

1324 **MIZHAR 30** [1] 4-8-7 (84)(2oh) F Norton 10/1: 06-008: Rear, improved 2f out, no impression fnl 1f: **½   70**
with D Nicholls & slipping down the h'cap now: see 1173.

*1851 **FIRE DOME 6** [8] 8-8-7 (84)(3ex)(1oh) M Henry 11/4 FAV: 311119: Chsd ldrs till wknd fnl 1f: well   **½   69**
bckd, qck reapp: 5 timer foiled: in tremendous form earlier: see 1851.

1533 **PRINCELY DREAM 20** [6] 4-9-7 (84) P Hanagan(7) 12/1: 320-00: Never a factor in 10th: see 1533.   **shd 69**

1245 **ACE OF PARKES 36** [5] 4-8-7 (84) O Pears 14/1: 506-50: Front rank 4f, wknd: disappointing   **shd 69**
after promising reapp in 1245 (sharp track, 5f).

1337 **BON AMI 29** [7] 4-8-9 (86) P Bradley(5) 16/1: 004000: Rear, no room 2f out, improving when hmpd   **nk   70**
dist, no ch after: fin 12th: no luck in running, forget this: tried in blinks in 1337, see 1004.

1337 **POLES APART 29** [16] 4-8-7 (84)(1oh) W Ryan 20/1: 10-000: Mid div till btn fnl 1f: see 1337 (C/D).   **1¼   64**

966 **MAGIC RAINBOW 58** [9] 5-8-7 (84) M Fenton 16/1: -10600: Led 4f, wknd & fin last: 8 wk abs.   **1¼   60**

14 ran   Time 1m 10.18 (0.78)   (Frank Brady)   J S Goldie Uplawmoor, East Renfrewshire

1984	**4.25 MAJESTIC CLASS STKS 3YO+ 0-75 (D) 1m3f195y Good/Firm 23 -109 Slow**				
	£5265	£1620	£810	£405	V slow early pace

*1729 **CAPTAINS LOG 11** [3] M L W Bell 5-9-9 M Fenton 6/4 FAV: -42511: 5 b g Slip Anchor - Cradle Of   **82**
Love (Roberto) Settled well in bhd ldr, qcknd to lead 2f out, sn clr, cmftbly: hvly bckd, slow time: recent Windsor
wnr (h'cap): rnr up in '99 (rtd 80 at best): '98 Warwick (mdn) & Newcastle wnr (h'cap, rtd 82): eff at 10/12f,
hndls any grnd & any track: can run well fresh: tough, in good form.

1536 **ACHILLES SKY 20** [4] K R Burke 4-9-9 J Weaver 4/1: 6-1002: 4 b c Hadeer - Diva Madonna   **5   75**
(Chief Singer) In tch, chsd wnr fnl 1f, no impression: prob unsuited by this v slow pace: see 850 (reapp).

1790 **MCGILLYCUDDY REEKS 8** [1] Don Enrico Incisa 9-9-4 Kim Tinkler 7/2: -32523: 9 b m Kefaah -   **¾   68**
Kilvarnet (Furry Glen) Pulled v hard & set slow pace, hdd 2f out, no extra: nicely bckd: completely unsuited
by today's tactics, best coming from off the pace in a strongly run race: see 1790, 1307 & 1070.

4308} **GREYFIELD 249** [2] M R Channon 4-9-7 P Fessey 10/3: 3306-4: Dwelt, rcd keenly in rear, btn 2f out: **9   56**
nicely bckd: won a mdn hdle at Wincanton in March '00 (rtd 125h, eff at 2m on soft): '99 Flat wnr at Folkestone,
Beverley (dhtd) & Chester (h'cap, rtd 76): eff at 9/12f on firm & gd/soft grnd, soft over hdles: hndls any trk:
capable of much better, completely unsuited by this very slow pace today.

4 ran   Time 2m 42.75 (15.95)   (Christopher Wright)   M L W Bell Newmarket

1985	**5.00 BATLEYS MDN 3-4YO (D) 1m2f85y Good/Firm 23 -06 Slow**				
	£5642	£1736	£868	£434	3yo rec 12lb

1155 **BELLA LAMBADA 42** [7] Sir Michael Stoute 3-8-6 K Darley 9/4 FAV: -61: 3 ch f Lammtarra - Bella   **85**
Colora (Bellypha) In tch, rdn to lead dist, styd on well, drvn out: well bckd, 6 wk abs: half sister to high
class mid-dist wnr Stage Craft: sire a top class mid-dist performer: eff at 10f on fast grnd: hndls a stiff/
gall trk: improving filly who runs well fresh.

-- **HELENS DAY** [2] W Jarvis 4-9-4 F Norton 13/2: -2: 4 ch f Grand Lodge - Swordlestown Miss   **¾   82**
(Apalachee) Chsd ldr, ev ch over 1f out, kept on but not btn far: nicely bckd, 4L clr 3rd on debut: 35,000gns
purchase: eff at 10f on fast grnd, hndls a gall track: should find a mdn.

-- **SALUEM** [1] R Guest 3-8-6 W Ryan 15/2: -3: 3 b f Salse - Pat Or Else (Alzao)   **4   76**
Reared start, rdn to improve over 2f out, kept on but not pace to ch all on debut: op 5/1: related to top class
stayer Classic Cliche: looks in need of 12f+: hndls fast grnd: sure to learn from this.

1481 **MAY BALL 22** [3] J H M Gosden 3-8-6 J Carroll 5/2: -124: Set pace till hdd dist, no extra.   **2   73**

1771 **THUNDER SKY 9** [8] 4-9-9 J Weaver 4/1: 40/045: Rear, eff over 2f out, sn btn: see 1771 (1m).   **7   68**

1084 **BAJAN SUNSET 45** [4] 3-8-11 W Supple 33/1: 0-06: Prom, wknd qckly 3f out, t.o. in last: abs.   **18   41**

6 ran   Time 2m 10.32 (3.02)   (Helena Springfield Ltd)   Sir Michael Stoute Newmarket

SANDOWN   SATURDAY JUNE 17TH   Righthand, Galloping Track, Stiff Finish

Official Going   GOOD/FIRM (FIRM places); Stalls: Str - Centre, except Race 1986 (Stands); 14f - Outside; Rem - Inside.

1986	**1.50 EBF FILLIES MDN 2YO (D) 5f Good/Firm 32 -11 Slow**				
	£3542	£1090	£545	£272	

970 **MISE EN SCENE 59** [6] P Howling 2-8-11 P Robinson 10/1: -01: 2 b f Lugana Beach - Meeson Times   **88**
(Enchantment) Cl up, led over 1f out, kept on, pushed out: op 14/1: 2 month abs: Feb first foal, cost 6,200 gns:
dam 5/6f wnr: eff at 5f & clearly enjoyed this fast grnd: runs well fresh: well regarded & shld win more races.

-- **FOODBROKER FANCY** [5] D R C Elsworth 2-8-11 T Quinn 9/1: 2: 2 ch f Halling - Red Rita (Kefaah)   **½   86+**

SANDOWN SATURDAY JUNE 17TH Righthand, Galloping Track, Stiff Finish

Dwelt, bhd, well outpcd over 2f out, styd on well & ran green over 1f out, fin fast, just held: debut, op 6/1:
Mar 2nd foal, cost IR 75,000gns: half sister to a juv 6f Listed wnr: dam useful 6f juv: 6f+ will suit, v promising.
1667 **SILLA 15** [7] I A Balding 2-8-11 K Fallon 9/2: 03: 2 b f Gone West - Silver Fling (The Minstrel) 1½ 82
Led 2f out till over 1f out, onepace: improved for debut: handles fast: shown enough to win on a minor trk.
1424 **UPSTREAM 26** [3] Major D N Chappell 2-8-11 M Hills 11/10 FAV: 44: Led till over 2f out, wknd fnl 1f: 2½ 75
massive gamble from 11/8: better expected after pleasing debut run on good/soft grnd in 1424.
-- **MAURI MOON** [2] 2-8-11 M Roberts 8/1: 5: Slow away, bhd, some late gains: Apr foal: half sister 1½ 71
to wnrs over 7f/mid-dists: dam 7f/11f scorer: sure to relish 7f+ in time: with G Wragg.
-- **CAYMAN EXPRESSO** [4] 2-8-11 Dane O'Neill 8/1: 6: Cl up, wknd over 1f out: debut, op 6/1: Apr 3½ 62
foal, cost 24,000gns: half sister to a 7f wnr: dam won over 7f: with R Hannon.
-- **EAGALITY** [1] 2-8-11 D R McCabe 12/1: 7: Swerved left & hit rails after start, not recover: debut: 12 30
Apr foal, cost IR 9,500gns: half sister to a mid-dist wnr: with B Meehan.
7 ran Time 1m 01.74 (2.14) (J J Amass) P Howling Newmarket

1987 2.25 JOHN EGGINTON COND STKS 3YO+ (C) 5f Good/Firm 32 +23 Fast
£6148 £2332 £1166 £530 3 yo rec 6 lb

1849 **BISHOPS COURT 7** [6] I A Balding 6-8-11 (t) K Fallon 11/8 FAV: 11/051: 6 ch g Clantime - Indigo 109
(Primo Dominie) In tch, gd hdwy to lead appr fnl 1f, pushed clr, cosily: hvly bckd, fast time: missed '99, '98
wnr at Epsom, Newmarket (List) & Longchamp (Gr 3, rtd 115, min & Mrs J Ramsden): eff at 5/6f on firm & hvy: wears
a t-starp: loves to come late: very smart, win more races & escapes a penalty in a Listed race here next month.
1849 **REPERTORY 7** [8] M S Saunders 7-8-11 R Price 11/2: 3-0032: 7 b g Anshan - Susie's Baby (Balidar) ½ 104
Led till appr fnl 1f, kept on but held by wnr: clr rem: v fast from the gate & in top form: see 1849, 914.
1529 **SEE YOU LATER 21** [7] Major D N Chappell 3-8-0 W Supple 11/2: 33-633: 3 b f Emarati - Rivers 2½ 92
Rhapsody (Dominion) Chsd ldr to 2f out, onepace: nicely bckd: lightly raced, apprec h'cap company.
1533 **YORKIES BOY 21** [9] A Berry 5-8-11 J Fortune 16/1: 052204: Bhd, eff 2f out, onepace: well h'capped. shd 97
2745) **DON PUCCINI 336** [4] 3-9-2 J Stack 12/1: 3161-5: In tch, onepace fnl 2f: reapp: won 2 of 4 juv 2 102
starts, at Kempton & Newbury (val Super Sprint, rtd 110): eff over 5/6f & likes firm/fast grnd: handles a stiff
or easy trk: v good reapp under a big weight for a 3yo, keep an eye on him.
1534 **PRESENTATION 21** [3] 3-8-0 P Doe 8/1: 3-2326: In tch, eff 2f out, sn no impress: stiff task, see 1534. ¾ 84
1694 **ALFIE LEE 14** [5] 3-8-6(1ow) Dane O'Neill 33/1: 100-07: Slow away, bhd, no impress: needs h'caps. nk 89
1687 **YORBA LINDA 14** [2] 5-8-6 W Ryan 20/1: 9-4058: Handy, wknd over 1f out: stiff task, see 1687. 3 74
1693 **IMPERIALIST 14** [1] 3-8-1(1ow) R Mullen 12/1: 60-509: Slow away, sn in tch, wknd 2f out: see 1078. 3½ 66
9 ran Time 1m 0.06 (0.46) (D R Brotherston) I A Balding Kingsclere, Berks

1988 2.55 GROSVENOR SQUARE MDN 2YO (D) 7f rnd Good/Firm 32 -45 Slow
£4192 £1290 £645 £322

1472 **ADJOURNMENT 24** [5] P F I Cole 2-9-0 J Fortune 3/1 FAV: 01: 2 b c Patton - Miss Cabell Co (Junction) 87
Made all, ran on gamely for press over 1f out, rdn out: hvly bckd: Mar foal, cost IR 80,000gns: half brother
to sev wnrs: apprec step up to 7f & further will suit: acts on fast & a stiff trk: game, open to improvement.
-- **CASPIAN** [1] B W Hills 2-8-9 M Hills 9/2: 2: 2 b f Spectrum - Sinking Sun (Danehill) 1¾ 77
Keen, hld up, eff 2f out, kept on same pace: Jan first foal: stays 7f on fast grnd: very pleasing debut run.
-- **BLACK KNIGHT** [2] S P C Woods 2-9-0 T Quinn 8/1: 3: 2 b c Contract Law - Another Move (Farm Walk) ¾ 80+
Slow away, hld up, rdn 2f out, kept on well over 1f out, nrst fin: op 6/1: Apr foal, cost 8,200 gns: half brother
to wnrs over 7f/10f: dam 12f wnr: eff at 7f on fast, further sure to suit: improve plenty for this & win.
-- **POUNCE** [7] J A Osborne 2-8-9 J P Spencer 16/1: 4: Hld up, eff 2f out, kept on same pace: Apr foal, hd 74
cost IR 30,000gns: Grand Lodge filly who showed promise for the future here: stays 7f on fast.
1046 **SOONA 50** [8] 2-8-9 W Ryan 14/1: 055: Prom, rdn 2f out, onepace: 7 wk abs, stays 7f on fast. ¾ 72
1526 **BARAKANA 21** [4] 2-9-0 D R McCabe 7/2: 3326: Chsd wnr till no extra 2f out: bckd, up in trip. ½ 76
1413 **HOMELIFE 28** [3] 2-9-0 J Stack 6/1: 647: In tch, no extra fnl 2f: see 1413 (6f). 6 64
1876 **SAAFEND FLYER 5** [6] 2-9-0 Dane O'Neill 11/1: 08: Al bhd, qk reapp: May foal, cost 12,000 gns: shd 64$
half brother to two 7f juv wnr: dam 1m/12f scorer: with R Hannon.
8 ran Time 1m 31.8 (5.4) (The Blandford Partnership) P F I Cole Whatcombe, Oxon

1989 3.25 TOTE HCAP 3YO+ 0-100 (C) 7f rnd Good/Firm 32 -09 Slow [93]
£14218 £4375 £2187 £1093 3 yo rec 9 lb

1728 **CHOTO MATE 12** [10] R Hannon 4-9-7 (86) P Dobbs (5) 25/1: 6/W041: 4 ch c Brief Truce - Greatest 91
Pleasure (Be My Guest) Prom, qcknd over 1f out to lead ins last, pushed out, cosily: missed '99, '98 wnr at
Goodwood (mdn, rtd 86): eff at 5f, apprec step up to 7f & likes firm/fast grnd, any trk: unexposed at this trip.
1810 **TEMERAIRE 8** [11] D J S Cosgrove 5-9-3 (82) J Fortune 9/1: 020042: 5 b h Dayjur - Key Dancer 1½ 84
(Nijinsky) Led ins last, not hold on top of wnr: fine front-running eff, same tactics cld pay off on a sharp trk.
1851 **ELMHURST BOY 7** [9] S Dow 4-8-13 (78) P Doe 16/1: 660103: 4 b c Merdon Meldoy - Young Whip (Bold ½ 79
Owl) Hld up, carried head high but hdwy & switched ins over 1f out, short of room ins last, kept on: gd run.
*1716 **A TOUCH OF FROST 12** [12] G G Margarson 5-9-5 (84)(bl) P Robinson 5/1: 150-14: Chsd ldr 1¼ 83
till over 3f out, wknd fnl 1f: nicely bckd: not disgraced: see 1716.
*1810 **CELTIC EXIT 8** [3] 6-8-13 (78)(t) K Fallon 3/1 FAV: -50515: Hld up rear, kept on over 1f out, slightly 1½ 74
short of room dist but too late: well bckd: closer next time will rdn more positively: see 1810.
1810 **THREAT 8** [7] 4-8-10 (75) Dane O'Neill 33/1: 000006: Prom, rdn & switched right over 1f out, no extra: 1¼ 69
jockey rec a 2-day careless riding ban: rnr-up for J Gosden in '99 (rtd 98): '98 wnr at Goodwood (mdn, rtd 102):
stays 6f on gd & fast grnd: has run well fresh.
1810 **TEOFILIO 8** [8] 6-8-7 (71)(bl) J P Spencer 15/2: 0-1607: Hld up, rdn 2f out, no impress: jockey shd 64
rec a 2-day careless riding ban: won race last year off a 3lb lower mark: see 1810.
1490 **VOLONTIERS 22** [5] 5-9-4 (83) A Beech 10/1: -04168: Keen, prom, wknd over 1f out: btr 1490. 1½ 73
1810 **REDSWAN 8** [1] 5-8-7 (72)(tbl) W Ryan 6/1: 01-009: Keen cl up, wknd 2f out: bckd, too keen, see 1810. 2½ 57
1836 **TRIPLE DASH 7** [5] 4-9-10 (89) D Sweeney 20/1: -50000: Hld up, rdn 2f out, no impress: 10th, top-weight. 3 68
7 **DILKUSHA 222** [2] 5-8-12 (77) T Quinn 12/1: 3066-0: Keen, bhd, not handle bend over 4f out, short 3 50
of room over 1f out, no extra: fin 11th: '99 wnr at Kempton (h'cap, reapp) & Newbury (h'cap, rtd 78): '98 Brighton
wnr (rtd 75): stays 7f on firm & any trk: best without blnks: has run well fresh: best with hold up tactics.
11 ran Time 1m 29.25 (2.85) (Vernon Carl Matalon) R Hannon East Everleigh, Wilts

642

SANDOWN
SATURDAY JUNE 17TH   Righthand, Galloping Track, Stiff Finish

---

1990
4.00 BERKELEY SQUARE HCAP 3YO 0-95 (C)   1m1f   Good/Firm 32   -03 Slow   [99]
£7085   £2185   £1090   £545

1491 **COMMON PLACE** 22 [2]   C F Wall 3-9-5 (90) R Mullen 11/4: 611321: 3 b g Common Grounds - One Wild   **96**
Oat (Shareef Dancer) Dwelt, hld up, hdwy over 1f out, kept on despite hanging right to lead ins last, rdn out: well
bckd: earlier won at Kempton (2, class stks & h'cap): '99 Goodwood wnr (nurs h'cap): eff at 7f, stays 10.5f:
acts on firm & soft/hvy grnd: handles a stiff or easy trk, likes Kempton: tough, useful & still improving.
1697 **BURNING SUNSET** 14 [1]   H R A Cecil 3-9-1 (86) T Quinn 11/8 FAV: 3-3022: 3 ch f Caerleon - Lingerie   ½   **91**
(Shirley Heights) Led, rdn & collared ins last, not btn far: hvly bckd: useful, can win a race: see 1697.
*1439 **ECSTASY** 26 [4]   R M Beckett 3-8-7 (78) D Sweeney 11/2: 30-013: 3 b f Pursuit Of Love - Gong   1¾   **79**
(Bustino) Cl up, eff 2f out, onepace fnl 1f: ran to form of 1439.
1366 **DARE HUNTER** 29 [5]   B W Hills 3-9-0 (85) M Hills 7/1: 56-024: Chsd ldr to over 2f out, wknd &   3½   **80**
short of room 1f out: longer trip: btr 1366 (1m).
1125 **TWIST** 44 [6]   3-7-13 (70) R Brisland (5) 16/1: 064-05: Keen cl up, wknd over 1f out: abs, longer trip.   nk   **64**
1186 **MARAH** 41 [3]   3-9-7 (92) W Supple 5/1: 306-66: Dwelt, hld up, btn 2f out: abs, lngr trip, see 1186.   7   **74**
6 ran   Time 1m 54.35 (3.15)   (Induna Racing Partners Two)   C F Wall Newmarket

---

1991
4.30 JOHNSTONE HCAP 3YO+ 0-80 (D)   1m6f   Good/Firm 32   -42 Slow   [80]
£4231   £1302   £651   £325

1677 **TOTAL DELIGHT** 14 [1]   Lady Herries 4-10-0 (80)(t) P Doe 11/2: -10041: 4 b g Mtoto - Shesadelight   **83**
(Shirley Heights) Made all, kept on gamely over 1f out, rdn out: top-weight: earlier won at Leicester (h'cap):
plcd in '99 (rtd 77): eff at 10f, relished step up to 14f & forcing tactics: acts on gd/firm & gd/soft: runs
well fresh in a t-strap: genuine, carried a big weight today & unexposed at this trip.
1440 **CHEEK TO CHEEK** 26 [6]   C A Cyzer 6-8-7 (59) M Hills 11/2: 25-552: 6 b m Shavian - Intoxication (Great 1¼   **60**
Nephew) Hld up, eff 2f out, kept on for press despite flashing tail: likes fast grnd & back on a fair mark.
1784 **WHO CARES WINS** 9 [5]   C E Brittain 4-9-9 (75) K Fallon 7/2: 0-0003: 4 ch c Kris - Anne Bonny (Ajdal) shd   **76**
Chsd wnr 7f, eff 2f out, kept on same pace: well bckd: better run with visor discarded: see 1329.
1730 **ANGE DHONOR** 12 [3]   E L James 5-8-4 (56) D Sweeney 6/1: 00-604: Hld up, eff over 2f out, onepace.   ½   **56**
1440 **ROYAL PATRON** 26 [2]   4-9-5 (71) T Quinn 11/4 FAV: 62-235: Prom, rdn & no extra 2f out: bckd, see 1440.1   **70**
1784 **GALAPINO** 9 [4]   7-7-12 (50) D Glannon (7) 11/2: 0-5405: Slow away, bhd, btn over 2f out: see 1394.   13   **37**
6 ran   Time 3m 05.31 (10.31)   (D Heath)   Lady Herries Angmering, W Sussex

---

1992
5.05 LEICESTER SQUARE MDN 3YO (D)   1m2f   Good/Firm 32   -26 Slow
£4270   £1314   £657   £328

1697 **TARBOUSH** 14 [3]   H R A Cecil 3-9-0 T Quinn 1/2 FAV: -031: 3 b c Polish Precedent - Barboukh (Night   **83**
Shift) Made all, kept on well over 1f out, rdn out: well bckd: half brother to a 10f wnr: stays 10f on fast
ground: acts on a stiff trk: open to improvement in h'caps.
1692 **KATIYPOUR** 14 [5]   Sir Michael Stoute 3-9-0 K Fallon 3/1: -02: 3 ch c Be My Guest - Katiyfa (Auction   3   **76**
Ring) Cl up, wandered under press over 1f out, not pace of wnr: well bckd: eff at 10f on fast: win a race.
--   **VETORITY** [2]   B Smart 3-8-9 J Stack 33/1: 3: 3 b f Vettori - Celerite (Riverman)   1   **69+**
Bhd, rdn over 3f out, kept on late, nrst fin: op 14/1: plenty to like about this & 12f will suit: improve plenty.
--   **JOHNNY OSCAR** [6]   J R Fanshawe 3-9-0 P Robinson 10/1: 4: Cl up, rdn over 2f out, sn onepace: nk   **73**
half brother to a 7f wnr & maiden stayer Arctic Owl: bred to relish 12f+ & will learn from this.
1554 **KUWAIT MILLENNIUM** 19 [1]   3-9-0 W Ryan 12/1: 545: Chsd wnr 3f, no extra over 1f out: op 9/1.   1½   **70**
1045 **BLOSSOM WHISPERS** 50 [4]   3-8-9 M Hills 50/1: 06: Dwelt, bhd, rdn & no impress fnl 2f: abs, see 1045.   ½   **64**
6 ran   Time 2m 09.92 (5.82)   (Wafic Said)   H R A Cecil Newmarket

---

BATH
SATURDAY JUNE 17TH   Lefthand, Turning Track With Uphill Finish

---

Official Going   GOOD TO FIRM. Stalls: Str Crse - Far Side; Rnd Crse - Inside.

1993
2.00 CHARLCOMBE AUCT MDN 2YO (E)   5f rnd   Firm -06   -30 Slow
£2828   £808   £404

1667 **NASHIRA** 15 [8]   C R Egerton 2-8-4 L Newman (3) 4/5 FAV: 31: 2 ch f Prince Sabo - Aldevonie (Green   **80**
Desert) Prom, narrow lead below dist, drvn out: well bckd: 15,000gns Feb first foal, sire a sprinter: eff
at 5f, 6f will suit: acts on firm, prob handles gd/soft, turning track: going the right way.
1706 **MISTY BELLE** 13 [1]   B R Millman 2-8-2 A McCarthy (3) 11/1: 032: 2 gr f Petong - La Belle Dominique   hd   **76**
(Dominion) Led, hdd & edged right ent fnl 1f, kept on, just btn: imprvd, eff forcing the pace at 5f on firm grnd.
1667 **DOMINIQUE** 15 [9]   R Hannon 2-8-4 P Fitzsimons (5) 10/1: 03: 2 ch f Primo Dominie - Tender Loving   hd   **77**
Care (Final Straw) Chsd ldrs, eff appr fnl 1f, styd on & not btn far: tchd 12/1: imprvd drpd back to 5f on firm.
1737 **ONCE REMOVED** 12 [6]   S Dow 2-8-2 A Clark 8/1: 044: Mid-div, styd on ins last, nvr able to chall: 2   **69**
op 6/1: prob handles firm grnd, 6f nurseries will suit now: see 1737.
1221 **BARON CROCODILE** 38 [3]   2-8-7 P Bradley (5) 7/1: 2245: Prom, no extra fnl 1f: btr 1001, 849.   ¾   **72**
1838 **EL MAXIMO** 7 [2]   2-8-7 R Hughes 9/2: 6326: Prom, onepace appr fnl 1f: op 6/1, qck reapp.   1   **69**
--   **JASMICK** [5]   2-8-2 N Pollard 25/1: 7: Dwelt, nvr on terms: debut: 6,500gns Definite Article   2½   **58**
Mar foal, half-sister to a couple of sprinters, sire 10/12f performer: further will suit: with H Morrison.
1418 **BLUE ORLEANS** 26 [7]   2-8-5 S Whitworth 20/1: 308: Al bhd: turf bow, see 1136.   ¾   **59**
1782 **COUNT CALYPSO** 9 [4]   2-8-5 D Harrison 33/1: 09: Bhd from halfway: 7,000gns King's Signet   2   **53**
Feb foal, half-brother to sev wnrs, dam 10f wnr, sire a sprinter: with D J Coakley.
--   **RAMBLIN MAN** [10]   2-8-5 G Hind 33/1: 0: Dwelt, nvr in it: 10th, debut: 2,400gns Blues   3½   **44**
Traveller Apr first foal, sire best over mid-dists: with V Soane.
10 ran   Time 1m 01.5 (1.2)   (Mrs R F Lowe)   C R Egerton Chaddleworth, Berks.

1994 **2.30 JUNE SELL HCAP 3YO+ 0-60 (F) 5f161y rnd Firm -06 -15 Slow [55]**
£2310 £660 £330 3 yo rec 7 lb

1930 **ONES ENOUGH 2** [8] G L Moore 4-9-6 (47)(t) R Hughes 8/1: 0-0001: 4 b g Reprimand - Sea Fairy (Wollow) In tch, prog ent fnl 2f, hard rdn to lead below dist, ran on well: ran 48hrs ago: modest '99 form (incl blnkd): '98 Folkestone (mdn auct) & Lingfield wnr (stks, rtd 85): eff at 5/6f, tried 7f: acts on firm & hvy grnd & can force the pace: has tried an eye-hood (only has one eye): v well h'capped. **52**
1591 **SHADY DEAL 17** [18] M D I Usher 4-9-2 (43) G Baker (7) 12/1: 030002: 4 b g No Big Deal - Taskalady (Touching Wood) Led after halfway till ins last, kept on: back to form: acts on firm, gd/soft & equitrack. ½ **46**
1196 **SANDPOINT 40** [17] L G Cottrell 4-8-12 (39) S Drowne 16/1: 060-03: 4 b f Lugana Beach - Instinction (Never so Bold) In tch, prog & edged right appr fnl 1f, kept on for press: 6 wk abs: first time in the frame, flattered when rtd 51 in '99 (mdn): eff at 5.7f on firm grnd. ¾ **39**
1685 **PRIORY GARDENS 14** [9] J M Bradley 6-8-12 (39) P Fitzsimons (5) 9/1: 400354: Chsd ldrs, eff appr fnl 1f, kept on but not pace to chall: tchd 12/1: back in trip, see 1663, 262. ¾ **37**
1430 **JUST DISSIDENT 26** [15] 8-8-13 (40) G Hind 10/1: 400055: Sn led, hdd 2½f out, no extra: see 91. *1¼* **35**
1739 **VILLAGE NATIVE 11** [11] 7-9-10 (51)(bl) S Carson (5) 12/1: 000006: Rear, late wide hdwy: op 16/1. *shd* **46**
1734 **DON QUIXOTE 12** [7] 4-8-13 (40)(bl) O Pears 7/1 JT FAV: 0-0607: Nvr better than mid-div: see 1211. *nk* **34**
1724 **MUTASAWWAR 12** [4] 6-9-2 (43) Darren Williams (7) 7/1 JT FAV: 00-508: Mid-div thr'out, see 1508. *nk* **36**
1423 **MONTENDRE 26** [14] 13-9-4 (45) M Henry 14/1: 0-0009: Nvr dngrs: see 816. ½ **36**
4040} **ORLANDO SUNSHINE 270** [2] 3-9-10 (58) S Whitworth 16/1: 0000-0: Chsd ldrs, fdd appr fnl 1f: 10th: jt top-weight: debut rnr-up in '99 (auct mdn, rtd 69): eff at 5.7f on firm grnd. ¾ **47**
1793 **JEPAJE 9** [19] 3-9-7 (55)(BL) D Griffiths 20/1: 40-000: Dwelt, wide, nvr nr ldrs: 11th, blnkd, see 105. ½ **42**
1766 **HENRY THE HAWK 10** [6] 9-9-0 (41)(vis) A Clark 10/1: -40050: Prom 3f: 14th, tchd 12/1, visor repplied. **0**
1795 **Clansman 9** [13] 3-9-8 (56) D O'Donohoe 16/1: 1036 **Willrack Times 50** [1] 3-9-10 (58) L Newman (3) 20/1:
961 **Larimar Bay 60** [12] 4-8-13 (40) N Pollard 33/1: 1966 **Split The Aces 1** [16] 4-8-11 (38) S Drowne 12/1:
1578 **Tinas Royale 18** [3] 4-8-12 (39) T G McLaughlin 16/1: 4553} **Nitwitty 232** [5] 6-9-6 (47) P McCabe 25/1:
1766 **Jazznic 10** [10] 4-9-9 (50)(VIS) A Daly 20/1:
19 ran Time 1m 09.6 (0.5) (Heart Of The South Racing 3) G L Moore Woodingdean, E.Sussex.

1995 **3.05 PUMP ROOM NOV STKS 2YO (D) 5f rnd Firm -06 -30 Slow**
£3376 £1039 £519 £259

1214 **NEARLY A FOOL 39** [5] B A McMahon 2-9-5 N Pollard 4/1: 14331: 2 b g Komaite - Greenway Lady (Prince Daniel) Prom, rdn to lead appr fnl 1f, pushed out: 6 wk abs: earlier won the Brocklesby at Doncaster: first foal, dam hdles wnr: eff at 5f, shld get further: acts on firm & soft, gall trks: goes v well fresh: useful. **91**
1727 **MY LUCY LOCKET 12** [7] R Hannon 2-8-7 R Hughes 3/1 FAV: 332: 2 b f Mujadil - First Nadia (Auction Ring) Went right start, in tch, kept on under press & ch appr fnl 1f, held towards fin: nicely bckd: acts on firm & hvy grnd & must shed mdn tag soon, see 1522. ½ **77**
*1001 **IMPERIAL DANCER 54** [1] M R Channon 2-9-5 S Drowne 4/1: 4213: 2 b c Primo Dominie - Gorgeous Dancer (Nordico) Rear, not clr run & switched appr fnl 1f, kept on but no threat to ldrs: 8 wk abs: prob ran to best, acts on firm & hvy grnd: will apprec 6f: see 1001. *1¼* **86**
*1463 **DENSIM BLUE 24** [6] J Pearce 2-9-2 T G McLaughlin 8/1: -02414: Prom, led 2½f out till bef dist, no extra: op 6/1: ran well & clr of rem, handles firm & gd/soft grnd: see 1463. ¾ **80**
1381 **JUSTALORD 28** [2] 2-9-9 A Daly 20/1: -61615: Led till appr fnl 2f, fdd: difficult task after 1381 (clmr). 4 **77$**
1006 **SIR FRANCIS 54** [3] 2-9-5 L Newman (3) 9/2: 52106: In tch till hung right ent fnl 2f: 8 wk abs, see 891. *nk* **72**
*1704 **DA VINCI 13** [4] 2-9-0 D Harrison 13/2: 17: Pulled hard, handy till after halfway: btr 1704 (soft) 6 **52**
7 ran Time 1m 01.5 (1.2) (Nearly A Fool Partnership) B A McMahon Hopwas, Staffs.

1996 **3.35 PAT SCOTT HCAP 4YO+ 0-80 (D) 2m1f34y Firm -06 -30 Slow [69]**
£3740 £1151 £575 £287 4 yo rec 1 lb

1597 **SHERIFF 17** [9] J W Hills 9-8-5 (46) M Henry 11/2: -02021: 9 b g Midyan - Daisy Warwick (Ribot) Prom, led appr fnl 2f, styd on for press, pshd out nr fin: '99 rnr-up (h'cap, rtd 77a), won over hdles at N Abbot (3m, firm & gd/soft, rtd 118h at his peak): '98 hat-trick scorer at Lingfield (h'caps, rtd 76a & 55): eff at 2m/2m1f: acts on firm & gd/soft grnd, equitrack/Lingfield specialist: can cope with big weights: well h'capped. **50**
1394 **HAL HOO YAROOM 28** [1] J R Jenkins 7-9-3 (58) A Clark 6/1: 145-32: 7 b h Belmez - Princess Nawaal (Seattle Slew) Mid-div, prog to chase ldrs 3f out, kept on under press but al being held: in form, likes Bath. ½ **60**
1936 **ELSIE BAMFORD 2** [4] M Johnston 4-8-9 (51) K Dalgleish (7) 3/1 JT FAV: 311233: 4 b f Tragic Role - Sara Sprint (Formidable) Waited with, gd prog 5f out, rdn to chall 2f out, onepace towards fin: nicely bckd from 4/1, ran 48hrs ago: holds her form v well: eff at 12f/2m1f: see 1683. ½ **52**
1355 **DANEGOLD 29** [12] M R Channon 8-9-4 (59) R Hughes 3/1 JT FAV: 0-0454: Held up, feeling pace 4f out, kept on appr fnl 1f, nvr dngrs: well h'capped, see 1355, 714. 2 **58**
1440 **LEGGY LADY 26** [8] 4-8-4 (46) S Whitworth 12/1: 604-05: Pulled hard in mid-div, chsd ldrs 4f out till onepace appr fnl 1f: tchd 16/1, back up in trip: stays 2m1f on firm grnd. ¾ **44**
1711 **VERSATILITY 13** [6] 7-8-9 (50) N Pollard 10/1: 531056: Cl-up, led 6f out till appr fnl 2f, no extra. ¾ **47**
1800 **FUJIYAMA CREST 9** [11] 8-9-7 (62) J Lowe 16/1: 43-007: Nvr troubled ldrs: see 1800. *3½* **56**
1791 **HILL FARM BLUES 9** [10] 7-9-10 (65) L Newman (3) 16/1: -45008: Nvr better than mid-div: top-weight. ½ **58**
1784 **PARADISE NAVY 9** [13] 11-9-0 (55)(bl) G Sparkes (7) 16/1: 460-09: Al towards rear: still ndd this? *3½* **45**
1800 **MU TADIL 9** [7] 8-7-10 (37)(2oh) A McCarthy (3) 40/1: 0-0000: Al bhd, ran wide 3f out: 10th, see 1394. *shd* **27**
1802 **ZOLA 8** [2] 4-7-13 (41)(BL) A Daly 40/1: 10-050: Led till 6f out, grad wknd: 11th, blnkd, see 649. **0**
1711 **Noteworthy 13** [3] 4-8-5 (47) Claire Bryan (5) 20/1: 1711 **Brynkir 13** [5] 6-7-10 (37)(4oh) G Baker (7) 40/1:
13 ran Time 3m 45.0 (4.1) (The Sheriff Partnership) J W Hills Upper Lambourn, Berks.

1997 **4.05 CLASSIFIED STKS 3YO 0-65 (E) 1m3f144y Firm -06 -40 Slow**
£2730 £780 £390

1730 **PINCHANINCH 12** [6] J G Portman 3-8-11 L Newman (3) 15/8 FAV: -00421: 3 ch g Inchinor - Wollow Maid (Wollow) Bhd ldrs, led 2f out, shkn up & kept on well: nicely bckd, slow time, first win: unplcd in 3 '99 mdns (rtd 73): eff at 11.5f on firm & hvy grnd, without blnks on a turning track. **67**
1510 **SEND ME AN ANGEL 22** [7] S P C Woods 3-8-8 S Drowne 8/1: 0-442: 3 ch f Lycius - Niamh Cinn Oir (King Of Clubs) Led till 2f out, styd on but held: op 6/1: stays 11.5f on firm grnd & gd: see 1157. *1¼* **62**

BATH SATURDAY JUNE 17TH Lefthand, Turning Track With Uphill Finish

4452} **FLITE OF ARABY 240** [1] W R Muir 3-8-11 O Pears 12/1: 000-3: 3 b c Green Desert - Allegedly Blue (Alleged) Mid-div, pulled hard, not clr run 2f out & switched, hard rdn to chase ldrs dist, sn onepace: clr rem, reapp: unplcd in 3 '99 mdns (rtd 71): bred to apprec mid-dists & further: stays 11.5f on firm grnd. ¾ **64**
978 **DANCING MARY 59** [8] B Smart 3-8-8 J Bosley (7) 12/1: 303504: Prom, eff & went left appr fnl 2f, same pace: 8 wk abs, prob handles firm, gd/soft & fibresand: see 500. 3½ **56**
1377 **HOTELIERS PRIDE 29** [5] 3-8-11 A Clark 20/1: 00-05: Nvr troubled ldrs: yet to make the frame, flattered when rtd 70 in a '99 mdn: dam a 2m wnr: with L Cottrell. ¾ **59**
1588 **QUIET READING 18** [4] 3-8-11 R Hughes 3/1: 0036: Rear, imprvd 6f out, fdd appr fnl 1f: return to 10f? *nk* **58**
1745 **LUCKY STAR 11** [2] 3-8-8 (e) D Harrison 6/1: -13147: Pulled hard, handy, eff & onepace when sltly hmpd 2f out, eased: turf return, big step up in trip, wore an eye-shield: see 636. 2½ **52**
1726 **WELCOME SHADE 12** [3] 3-8-11 T G McLaughlin 8/1: 4-2008: Al rear, t.o.: longer trip, see 1212. *dist* **0**
8 ran Time 2m 29.0 (4) (A S B Portman) J G Portman Compton, Berks.

1998 **4.40 M. RUSSELL HCAP 3YO+ 0-75 (E) 1m rnd Firm -06 +08 Fast [75]**
£2884 £824 £412 3 yo rec 10lb

*1940 **ADOBE 2** [4] W M Brisbourne 5-8-12 (59)(6ex) T G McLaughlin 5/2 FAV: 242111: 5 b g Green Desert - Shamshir (Kris) Al going well bhd ldrs, rdn to lead ent fnl 1f, ran on strongly: nicely bckd from 7/2, crse rec, hat-trick landed: earlier won at W'hampton (rtd 58a) & Hamilton (2, h'caps): '99 wnr here at Bath & Nottingham (h'caps, rtd 55 & 49a): plater for J Gosden in '98: eff at 7f, suited by 1m: acts on firm, gd grnd & fibresand, handles soft, any trk, likes Hamilton & Bath: eff with/without t-strap & runs well fresh: tough & improving. **68**
1840 **DINAR 7** [3] R Brotherton 5-7-10 (43) K Dalgleish (7) 9/1: -30202: 5 b h Dixieland Band - Bold Jessie (Never So Bold) Nvr far away, led bef fnl 2f till dist, not pace of wnr: pld clr, qck reapp, ran to best. 1½ **48**
1473 **MOON AT NIGHT 24** [6] L G Cottrell 5-9-8 (69) A Clark 5/1: 10-103: 5 gr g Pursuit Of Love - La Nureyeva (Nureyev) Set gd pace till 2½f out, onepace: tchd 6/1: better run on more suitable grnd: see 1229. *3* **68**
621 **PARISIAN LADY 108** [10] A G Newcombe 5-8-4 (50)(1ow) S Whitworth 11/1: 6-6344: Outpcd till kept on well fnl 2f, nvr nrr: op 7/1, 15 wk abs, turf return: sharper next time: see 528, 152. *2* **46**
1930 **ITALIAN SYMPHONY 2** [5] 6-8-10 (57)(vis) P McCabe 12/1: 045505: Rear, late prog, nvr dngrs. ¾ **51**
1611 **PERUVIAN STAR 17** [1] 4-7-11 (44) A McCarthy (3) 25/1: 000506: Pulled hard, prom till appr fnl 1f. 2½ **33**
1731 **ARTFUL DANE 12** [14] 8-7-13 (43)(bl)(3ow) A Daly 12/1: 04-057: Nvr a factor: see 1407. 2½ **30**
1840 **HARD LINES 7** [9] 4-9-7 (68) R Hughes 7/1: /0-008: Mid-div thr'out: tchd 12/1, unproven beyond 6f. *nk* **51**
1666 **LUCAYAN BEACH 15** [12] 6-8-8 (55) S Drowne 33/1: 003-09: Dwelt, nvr threatened ldrs: see 92. 1¾ **35**
1395 **CLIFTON WOOD 28** [11] 5-8-2 (49) G Sparkes (7) 20/1: 600/60: Prom 5f: 10th, see 1395. *3* **23**
1794 **WARRING 9** [8] 6-7-10 (43)(1oh) D Kinsella (7) 10/1: -50300: In tch till 3f out: 11th, see 1066. 2½ **13**
1598 **HUGWITY 17** [13] 8-10-0 (75) D Harrison 8/1: 362140: Nvr on terms: 12th, top-weight, see 1407. 1½ **42**
1666 **Ballykissann 15** [7] 5-7-10 (43)(bl)(7oh) G Baker(7) 50/1:
1799 **Berberis 9** [2] 4-7-10 (43)(8oh) Claire Bryan (5) 50/1:
1840 **April Ace 7** [16] 4-8-1 (48) N Pollard 25/1:
15 ran Time 1m 37.2 (u1.2) (P R Kirk) W M Brisbourne Great Ness, Shropshire.

1999 **5.15 LEVY BOARD HCAP 3YO+ 0-85 (D) 5f161y Firm -06 +04 Fast [84]**
£3838 £1181 £590 £295 3 yo rec 7 lb

1887 **NINEACRES 4** [4] J M Bradley 9-8-3 (59)(bl) P Fitzsimons (5) 12/1: 522101: 9 b g Sayf El Arab - Mayor (Laxton) Mid-div, prog 2f out, rdn to lead ent fnl 1f, ran on: qck reapp: earlier won at W'hampton (rtd 58a), Southwell & here at Bath (h'caps): '99 wnr again at W'hampton (clmr, rtd 59a & 42): eff at 5/6f, stays 7f: acts on firm, gd grnd, both AWs, likes W'hampton & Bath: wears blnks or visor & can force the pace. **66**
1650 **ALPEN WOLF 15** [5] W R Muir 5-9-8 (78) D Harrison 7/1: 5-3102: 5 ch g Wolfhound - Oatfield (Great Nephew) Prom, led ent fnl 2f till below dist, onepace: back to form, loves firm/fast grnd & Bath: see 1441. 1½ **81**
1887 **KILCULLEN LAD 4** [7] Lady Herries 6-9-0 (70)(vis) T G McLaughlin 7/2 JT FAV: 0-0523: 6 b g Fayruz - Royal Home (Royal Palace) Towards rear, gd prog to chase wnr dist, no extra nr fin: tchd 5/1, qck reapp. *shd* **73**
1887 **CAUDA EQUINA 4** [12] M R Channon 6-9-6 (76) S Drowne 7/1: 005604: Bhd, imprvd appr fnl 1f, styd on but nvr able to chall: qck reapp: likes Bath: see 905. *1* **76**
1591 **KILMEENA LAD 17** [3] 4-8-9 (65) S Carson (5) 16/1: 410005: Stumbled start, mid-div, kept on towards fin, nvr a threat: signs of return to form: h'capped to win over 6/7f: see 462. 1½ **61**
1781 **CLASSY CLEO 10** [11] 5-9-8 (78) P McCabe 20/1: 000046: Chsd ldrs wide, outpcd appr fnl 1f: see 64. ½ **73**
1887 **EASTER OGIL 4** [6] 5-9-10 (80)(vis) R Hughes 7/2 JT FAV: 641257: Bhd, not clr run appr fnl 1f, position accepted: nicely bckd again, qck reapp: luckless gelding, see 1517. ¾ **73**
1795 **SEA HAZE 9** [8] 3-8-9 (72) G Hind 7/1: 40-028: Prom, ev ch 2f out, fdd: see 1795. *nk* **64**
3879} **PETARGA 280** [9] 5-9-6 (76) S Whitworth 12/1: 0300-9: Nvr going pace, reapp: '99 Folkestone wnr (h'cap, rtd 80): plcd twice in '98 (h'cap, rtd 80): eff at 5/6f on firm & gd grnd, sharp or gall trks. 1½ **65**
1849 **JACKIES BABY 7** [2] 4-10-0 (84) Darren Williams (7) 8/1: 045400: Led till ent fnl 2f, no extra: 10th. 2½ **67**
1629 **MALADERIE 16** [13] 6-8-3 (59)(vis) A Clark 12/1: 000200: Wide, nvr in it: 13th, won this in '99 (off 7lbs higher). **0**
1724 **Beware 12** [10] 5-8-4 (60) O Pears 16/1: 923 **Moocha Cha Man 63** [1] 4-9-0 (70) N Pollard 20/1:
13 ran Time 1m 08.5 (u0.6) (J M Bradley) J M Bradley Sedbury, Glos.

YORK SATURDAY JUNE 17TH Lefthand, Flat, Galloping Track

Official Going GOOD TO FIRM. Stalls: 5/6f - Stands Side, 7f/Rnd Crse - Inside.

2000 **2.10 CHARLES HENRY HCAP 3YO+ 0-80 (D) 6f Firm 10 -08 Slow [78]**
£5291 £5291 £1245 £622 3 yo rec 9 lb Field raced towards centre

1905 **FRIAR TUCK 3** [6] Miss L A Perratt 5-8-13 (65) R Hills 9/1: 00-021: 5 ch g Inchinor - Jay Gee Ell (Vaigly Great): Held up in tch, no room 2f out, rdn & strong run inside last to join ldr on line: nicely bckd, op 10/1: qck reapp: rnr-up in '99 (rtd 87, h'cap): '98 wnr here at York (val h'cap, rtd 101): eff at 5/6f on firm & soft grnd, sharp/galloping trk, loves York: has run well fresh: has suffered breathing problems but is now well h'capped. **70**
1517 **BOLDLY GOES 21** [12] C W Fairhurst 4-9-12 (78)(BL) J Fanning 14/1: 060431: 4 b c Bold Arrangement - Reine de Thebes (Darshaan): Sn handy, rdn/led inside last, strongly prsd nr fin & jnd on line: 1st time blnks: unplcd from 2 '99 starts (rtd 91, stks): '98 wnr at Pontefract, W'hampton (rtd 86a), Thirsk (stks) & Ripon (list, rtd 104): eff at 6/7f on firm, heavy & fibresand: has run well fresh in blnks. *dht* **83**

1533 **ELLENS ACADEMY 21** [13] E J Alston 5-10-0 (80)(bl) T E Durcan 15/2 FAV: -04303: 5 b h Royal Academy - Lady Ellen (Horage): Dwelt, sn mid-div, rdn/prog to chall over 1f out, held nr fin: hvly bckd, gd eff back at 6f. *1½* **82**
1504 **MALLIA 22** [10] T D Barron 7-9-1 (67)(bl) D Holland 20/1: 140444: Al cl-up, led 2f out till inside last, just held cl-home: fine run & clearly in good heart at present: see 719 (AW). *shd* **69**
1840 **SMART PREDATOR 7** [3] 4-9-6 (72) R Winston 20/1: 303105: Held up in tch, briefly no room over 2f out, drvn/kept on inside last, not reach ldrs: eff at 6/7f, stays 1m well: on a handy mark: see 1579 (made all, 7f). *nk* **73**
1714 **WILLIAMS WELL 12** [18] 6-9-2 (68)(bl) Pat Eddery 10/1: 601436: Bhd, kept on fnl 2f, no threat: improve. *½* **67**
1391 **LA PIAZZA 28** [8] 4-10-0 (80) J F Egan 20/1: 00-007: Mid-div, rdn/kept on fnl 2f, not pace to chall. *shd* **79**
*1356 **DIAMOND DECORUM 29** [14] 4-9-4 (70) N Callan 14/1: 00-618: Rdn/chsd ldrs 2f out, held fnl 1f. *½* **67**
1654 **EURO VENTURE 15** [1] 5-9-2 (68) F Norton 25/1: 000609: Chsd ldrs, held final 1f: see 1356, 645. *½* **63**
1842 **LUANSHYA 7** [16] 4-9-3 (69) J Reid 25/1: 0-4540: Mid-div, nvr pace to chall: 10th: see 1514 (7f). *1½* **60**
1531 **FRANCPORT 21** [5] 4-9-10 (76) J Carroll 16/1: -51000: Chsd ldrs, held over 1f out: 11th: btr 824 (sft). *shd* **67**
-1861 **BRECONGILL LAD 6** [17] 8-9-11 (77) A Nicholls (3) 8/1: 303220: Chsd ldrs 5f: 12th: nicely bckd. *shd* **67**
1636 **IVORY DAWN 16** [4] 6-9-4 (70) C Catlin (7) 14/1: 002240: Held up, effort 2f out, no impress: 13th. *½* **58**
1654 **PIPS MAGIC 15** [22] 4-9-11 (77) A Culhane 14/1: 0000W0: Rear, some hdwy 2f out, no prog: 14th. *hd* **64**
1662 **TOM TUN 15** [2] 5-9-9 (75) S Finnamore (5) 14/1: 230050: Chsd ldrs, held over 1f out: 15th: op 12/1. *nk* **61**
4439} **GREEN GINGER 241** [11] 4-9-9 (75) Craig Williams 33/1: 3100-0: Led till 2f out, fdd: 16th: reapp: '99 Nottingham wnr (auct mdn, rtd 80): rtd 82 when unplcd in '98: stays 7f, suited by 6f on firm & gd on a gall trk. *½* **59**
1517 **ZIRCONI 21** [20] 4-9-11 (77) K Darley 10/1: 640-40: Prom 4f: 20th: op 9/1: btr 1517. **0**
1840 **Jeffrey Anotherred 7** [19] 6-9-7 (73) F Lynch 33/1:
1580 **Zuhair 18** [15] 7-9-8 (74) N Kennedy 20/1:
1840 **Double Splendour 7** [7] 10-9-11 (77) P Fessey 20/1:
1840 **Redoubtable 7** [21] 9-9-10 (76) D Mernagh (3) 33/1:
1815 **Venika Vitesse 8** [23] 4-8-12 (64) C Lowther 20/1:
910 **Bollin Rita 64** [9] 4-9-2 (68) G Parkin 25/1:
23 ran Time 1m 10.45 (1.05) (Cree Lodge Racing Club) Miss L A Perratt Ayr, Strathclyde.

2001

2.40 CADOGAN HCAP 3YO+ 0-100 (C) 1m1f rnd Firm 10 +15 Fast **[99]**
£5221 £2610 £1305 3 yo rec 11lb

1836 **ICE 7** [2] M Johnston 4-9-5 (90)(vis) D Holland 10/1: 0-5161: 4 b g Polar Falcon - Sarabah (Ela Mana Mou): Made all, rdn & strongly prsd over 1f out, rdn/styd on gamely & holding rivals nr fin: fast time: tchd 12/1: earlier scored at Lingfield (h'cap): '99 wnr of Swiss 2,000 Guineas & at York (h'cap, rtd 100): '98 wnr at Musselburgh & York (2, h'caps, rtd 94): eff at 1m/9f on firm & hvy, any trk, loves York (unbeaten here from 4 starts): suited by a visor: eff held up or forcing the pace: carries head high but tough/useful at best. **95**
1160 **JEDI KNIGHT 42** [13] M W Easterby 6-9-1 (86) K Darley 16/1: 140-02: 6 b g Emarati - Hannie Caulder (Workboy): Cl-up, drvn/strong chall 1f out, kept on tho' held nr fin: 6 wk abs, op 14/1: '99 wnr at Beverley (h'cap), York & Hamilton (rtd h'caps, rtd 90): plcd form in '98 (h'caps, rtd 71): eff at 1m/10f on firm, g/s & any trk, loves a stiff/gall one: best without blnks: likes to race with/force the pace: useful & tough. *¾* **89**
1598 **THE WIFE 17** [3] T D Easterby 3-7-10 (78)(1oh) P Fessey 14/1: 00-003: 3 b f Efisio - Great Steps (Vaigly Great): In tch, prog to press front pair final 2f, kept on tho' al just held: back on a winning mark: see 1341. *¾* **80**
1845 **SHARP PLAY 7** [8] M Johnston 5-9-7 (92) J Fanning 20/1: 63/104: Trkd ldrs, kept on fnl 2f, held nr fin. *1* **93**
1762 **GRALMANO 10** [6] 5-8-2 (72)(1ow) F Lynch 12/1: -14525: Held up, rdn final 3f & kept on, no threat. *1½* **72**
1144 **ROYAL ARTIST 43** [7] 4-8-3 (74) J F Egan 9/2: 1-2126: Drvn chsg ldrs 2f out, held final 1f: op 3/1, abs. *1* **71**
1217 **PENSION FUND 39** [16] 6-8-10 (81) Pat Eddery 4/1 FAV: 106-37: Held up, eff 3f out, no impress: bckd. *½* **78**
+1656 **TONY TIE 15** [15] 4-9-0 (85) A Culhane 8/1: 622318: In tch, rdn/held over 1f out: op 6/1: see 1656. *¾* **81**
1015 **INVADER 54** [10] 4-9-0 (85) J Reid 14/1: 5-5509: Keen, in tch, btn over 1f out: abs: bckd: see 690. *1* **80**
1567 **REGAL PHILOSOPHER 19** [11] 4-9-6 (91) R Hills 9/1: -62240: Rear, mod gains when no room 1f out, position accepted: 10th: op 7/1: see 1450. *¾* **85**
1840 **CUSIN 7** [17] 4-8-1 (72) F Norton 10/1: 0-0030: Chsd ldrs till over 1f out, 11th: op 8/1: see 926. *2* **63**
1656 **IRON MOUNTAIN 15** [5] 5-7-13 (70) J Tate 7/1: -35340: Held up, drvn 3f out, mod gains: 12th: well bckd. *6* **52**
1788 **Suplizi 9** [1] 9-8-3 (74) R Ffrench 25/1:
1342 **Weet A Minute 30** [18] 7-9-7 (92) J Carroll 20/1:
1490 **Initiative 22** [9] 4-8-9 (80) J McAuley (5) 40/1:
1561 **Secrets Out 19** [14] 4-8-5 (76)(BL) R Winston 33/1:
16 ran Time 1m 48.35 (u.45) (J David Abell) M Johnston Middleham, Nth Yorks.

2002

3.10 QUEEN MUM AMAT LADIES HCAP 3YO+ 0-95 (C 1m3f195y Firm 10 -21 Slow **[74]**
£10958 £3376 £1687 £843 3 yo rec 14lb

1637 **PENTAGONAL 16** [11] Sir Michael Stoute 3-9-8 (82)(VIS) Mrs S Eddery (3) 4/1 FAV: 0-0131: 3 b c Dynaformer - Pent (Mr Prospector): Led/dsptd lead till went on before halfway, strongly prsd final 1f, rdn & held on gamely: first time visor, hvly bckd: earlier scored at Lingfield (mdn): rtd 77 on sole '99 start (mdn): eff at 10/12f on firm & gd/soft grnd, sharp/gall trk: can force the pace & runs well for a lady rider: well suited by hdgr today. **88**
*1777 **BATSWING 10** [2] B Ellison 5-9-13 (73) Miss E Ramsden 6/1: 002012: 5 b g Batshoof - Magic Milly (Simply Great): Mid-div, rdn & stdy prog final 3f, styd on well inside last, post came too sn: op 5/1: reportedly lost a shoe: fine effort, acts on firm & hvy: see 1777. *nk* **77**
1839 **FATEHALKHAIR 7** [4] B Ellison 8-9-2 (62) Mrs S Bosley 10/1: 0-4023: 8 ch g Kris - Midway Lady (Alleged): Chsd ldrs, rdn/prsd wnr over 1f out, held nr fin: clr rem & a gd run: likes Catterick: see 456. *1¾* **64**
1518 **FIORI 21** [6] P C Haslam 4-10-4 (78) Miss A Armitage (3) 7/1: 200644: Sn handy, briefly led over 3f out, fdd over 1f out: hvly bckd: see 380, 302. *5* **73**
1536 **SANDBAGGEDAGAIN 21** [7] 6-9-11 (71) Miss J Foster (3) 16/1: /0-055: Prom, onepace final 2f: op 14/1. *hd* **65**
*1194 **BHUTAN 41** [1] 5-9-8 (68) Mrs C Williams 9/2: 144-16: Held up, prog fnl 2f, held 1f out: well bckd, abs. *2½* **58**
1598 **ELVIS REIGNS 17** [15] 4-9-5 (65) Mrs A Hammond (6) 33/1: 0-0007: Held up, mod prog 3f out, no impress on ldrs: unplcd sole '99 start (Saint Cloud, Listed): '98 Ayr wnr (mdn, rtd 87, Mrs J R Ramsden): prob stays 1m4f: handles fast, suited by soft grnd & a gall trk: with M Hammond. *1¾* **53**
1561 **CELESTIAL WELCOME 19** [3] 5-10-7 (81) Miss E Johnson Houghton 16/1: -61008: Held up, bhd halfway, mod late gains: op 14/1: needs easy grnd: see 986 (hvy). *hd* **68**
1777 **NOUKARI 10** [9] 7-10-4 (78) Miss E Folkes (3) 9/1: 401029: Chsd ldrs, btn 2f out, recent jmps rnr. *3* **61**
1807 **SILENT SOUND 8** [10] 4-8-10 (56)(4oh) Miss L J Harwood (6) 33/1: 0-0400: Slowly away, nvr factor: 10th. *¾* **38**
1147 **LANCER 43** [14] 8-9-6 (66)(bl) Mrs L Pearce 10/1: -61660: Keen/held up, efft 3f out, sn btn: 11th: op 8/1: 6 wk abs, blnks reapplied: runner-up last term in this event off a 5lb higher mark: see 815 (soft). *1¾* **46**
1845 **CHIEF MONARCH 7** [13] 6-10-2 (76) Miss S Brotherton (3) 9/1: 250230: Chsd ldrs, btn 2f out: 12th. *1¾* **54**
1839 **Far Ahead 7** [16] 8-10-0 (74) Miss Diana Jones 25/1:
1373 **Morgans Orchard 29** [17] 4-9-0 (60) Miss C Hannaford (3) 12/1:
1784 **Kirisnippa 9** [12] 5-8-10 (56)(4oh) Miss M Gunstone (3) 25/1:
-- **Star Selection** [5] 9-10-1 (75) Miss P Robson 20/1:
1841 **Basman 7** [8] 6-11-0 (88) Mrs V Smart (3) 33/1:

YORK

SATURDAY JUNE 17TH   Lefthand, Flat, Galloping Track

17 ran   Time 2m 30.45 (3.65)   (Sheikh Mohammed)   Sir Michael Stoute Newmarket, Suffolk.

2003	3.45 W HILL HCAP 3YO 0-105 (B) 6f **Firm 10 + 05 Fast**	[110]
	£38532 £11856 £5928 £2964	

1833 **COTTON HOUSE** 7 [8] M R Channon 3-8-13 (95) Craig Williams 25/1: 24-151: 3 b f Mujadil - Romanovna   **101**
(Mummy's Pet): Chsd ldrs, rdn over 2f out & prog to lead inside last, styd on well, rdn out: fast time: earlier
scored on reapp at Leicester (class stks, readily): '99 debut wnr at Warwick (auct fillies mdn, rtd 89, subs sidelined
by a fractured pelvis): eff at 5/6f on firm & gd/soft grnd, stiff/sharp trk: has run well fresh: progressive/useful.
1406 **RAILROADER** 28 [7] G B Balding 3-7-12 (80) D Mernagh (3) 20/1: 0-6102: 3 ch g Piccolo - Poyle Amber ½ **83**
(Sharrood): Handy, rdn/led over 1f out till inside last, kept on: fine effort: acts on firm & hvy: see 1220.
*1308 **RENDITION** 32 [4] W J Haggas 3-8-5 (87) J F Egan 5/2 FAV: 30-113: 3 b f Polish Precedent - Rensaler hd **89**
(Stop The Music): Chsd ldrs, rdn over 2f out, kept on well for press inside last, not pace of wnr: hvly bckd,
tchd 7/2: eff at 6/7f: most tough & progressive filly, keep on the right side: see 1308.
1409 **BABY BARRY** 28 [6] Mrs G S Rees 3-8-1 (83) J Fanning 25/1: 2-0034: Chsd ldrs, drvn & kept on final 1f. 1½ **81**
1733 **BOAST** 12 [21] D Holland 3-9-1 (97) D Holland 25/1: 16-635: Rear, rdn & styd on well final 2f, nrst fin: acts on hd **94**
firm & gd/soft: eff at 6f, encouraging here & worth another try at 7f on this evidence: see 1283 (Listed, 7f).
+289 **RED REVOLUTION** 161 [9] 3-7-11 (79) P Fessey 10/1: -32-16: Cl-up 5f: over 5 mth abs, h'cap bow. ½ **74**
1694 **CORRIDOR CREEPER** 14 [17] 3-8-5 (87) A Culhane 10/1: 21-037: Chsd ldrs, rdn/onepace over 1f out. shd **82**
1384 **BRAVE BURT** 28 [14] 3-8-9 (91) A Nicholls (3) 25/1: 0-0308: Led till over 1f out, fdd: see 1384, 988. nk **85**
1534 **BALLY PRIDE** 21 [11] 3-9-7 (103) T E Durcan 20/1: 062-49: Chsd ldrs till over 1f out: see 1534. 1 **95**
1308 **SHATIN VENTURE** 32 [12] 3-8-13 (95) R Hills 17/2: 424-30: Chsd ldrs, rdn/held over 1f out: 10th. ¾ **85**
1694 **RAVISHING** 14 [10] 3-7-12 (80) F Norton 10/1: 1-4100: Chsd ldrs, rdn final 2f, not pace to chall: 11th. ½ **68**
1694 **PERUVIAN CHIEF** 14 [20] 3-8-7 (89) Pat Eddery 10/1: 3-0520: Bhd, rdn/mod gains: 12th: see 1694, 112. ½ **75**
1694 **JEMIMA** 14 [22] 3-9-6 (102) K Darley 20/1: 05-000: Rear, drvn/mod gains: 13th: see 953 (7f, Gr 3). nk **87**
1308 **SAFRANINE** 32 [18] 3-8-8 (90) R Cody Boutcher (7) 33/1: 20-000: Rear, drvn/mod gains: 14th: see 630. ½ **73**
1694 **BLUE VELVET** 14 [5] 3-7-12 (80) G Bardwell 25/1: -60000: Twds rear, nvr on terms: 15th: see 982. 1¾ **59**
1694 **GLENROCK** 14 [19] 3-8-6 (88) J Carroll 12/1: 3-0650: Twds rear, rdn/no impress form halfway: 16th. shd **67**
1409 Locharati 28 [1] 3-8-5 (87) J Tate 16/1:   1694 Dorchester 14 [15] 3-9-0 (96) M Worrell (7) 33/1:
1694 Jailhouse Rocket 14 [16] 3-8-7 (89) C Nutter 33/1:   1694 Desert Fury 14 [13] 3-8-12 (94) J Reid 25/1:
1441 Charlottevalentina 26 [3] 3-8-0 (82) Joanna Badger (7) 33/1:
1534 Taras Girl 21 [23] 3-9-1 (97) S Finnamore (5) 33/1:
1576 Happy Diamond 18 [2] 3-8-2 (84) R Winston 25/1:
23 ran   Time 1m 09.69 (.29)   (Michael A Foy)   M R Channon West Isley, Berks.

2004	4.15 PRENN RTD HCAP 3YO 0-100 (B) 1m2f85y Firm 10 -40 Slow	[104]
	£10891 £4131 £2065 £938	

1831 **ALVA GLEN** 8 [3] Sir Michael Stoute 3-9-4 (94) Pat Eddery 9/2: 21-601: 3 b c Gulch - Domludge (Lyphard) **102**
Made most, dictated pace, increased tempo final 3f & drvn/forged clr from over 1f out, styd on strongly: well bckd,
op 6/1: slow time: '99 Nottingham wnr (mdn, rtd 96): eff at 1m/slowly run 10f, could get further: acts on firm &
soft grnd, likes a gall trk: can force the pace.
1535 **VINTAGE PREMIUM** 21 [6] R A Fahey 3-9-7 (97) R Winston 7/1: 214022: 3 b c Forzando - Julia Domna 1½ **101**
(Dominion): Trkd ldrs, rdn & kept on final 2f, not pace of wnr: op 6/1: handles firm & fast, loves soft/hvy:
stays a slowly run 10f: see 912 (1m).
1831 **FATHER JUNINHO** 8 [5] A P Jarvis 3-9-0 (90) D Mernagh (3) 5/2: -06523: 3 b c Distinctly North - hd **93**
Shane's Girl (Marktingo): Trkd ldrs, rdn & kept on final 3f, not pace of wnr: nicely bckd tho' op 2/1: see 1831.
1491 **ZIBELINE** 22 [4] C E Brittain 3-8-4 (80)(5oh) A Nicholls (3) 7/1: 0-0244: Rear/in tch, eff/briefly ¾ **82$**
no room over 1f out, nvr pace to chall: handles firm & gd grnd: prob stays a slowly run 10f: see 1341 (1m).
*1703 **CAROUSING** 1 [1] 3-9-3 (93) J Reid 2/1 FAV: 611-15: Cl-up, rdn/briefly led over 3f out, wknd over 1f out. 1 **94**
1366 **MAKASSEB** 29 [7] 3-8-6 (82) Craig Williams 11/1: 25-006: Held up, eff 2f out, no prog: op 12/1: see 1366.¾ **82**
6 ran   Time 2m 12.52 (5.22)   (Sheikh Mohammed)   Sir Michael Stoute Newmarket, Suffolk.

2005	4.45 L SAINER MDN 2YO (D) 6f Firm 10 -15 Slow	
	£5564 £1712 £856 £428 Raced towards centre	

-- **CHIANTI** [3] J L Dunlop 2-9-0 Pat Eddery 8/11 FAV: 1: 2 b c Danehill - Sabaah (Nureyev): **91**
Led after 2f, rdn & pulled clr with rnr-up final 2f, drvn to assert inside last, styd on well: hvly bckd at odds on:
Mar foal, cost EIR500,000: half-brother to a 7f/1m wnr: dam a lightly rcd mdn: eff over a gall 6f, further will
suit: acts on firm grnd & runs well fresh: looks sure to further impr, particularly when tackling further.
1691 **LOST AT SEA** 14 [7] K R Burke 2-9-0 N Callan 16/1: -02: 2 b c Exit To Nowhere - Night At Sea 1¾ **85**
(Night Shift): Cl-up/dsptd lead, rdn & pulled clr with wnr final 2f, kept on tho' held inside last: acts on firm
grnd: eff at 6f, will stay further: clearly going the right way: see 1691.
-- **AMBER ROSE** [8] M Johnston 2-8-9 R Ffrench 20/1: 3: 2 ch f Royal Academy - La Fille de Cirque 3 **73+**
(Cadeaux Genereux): Dwelt & bhd/outpcd early, styd on well final 2f under hands-&-heels riding, nvr nrr: Mar
foal, cost 17,000 gns, a first foal: dam 3yo 1m wnr, sire top class sprinter/miler: eff at 6f, looks sure to apprec
7f+: handles firm & a gall trk: eye-catching late hdwy, not knocked about, will impr & find a northern mdn.
1782 **PAY THE SILVER** 9 [5] A P Jarvis 2-9-0 D Mernagh (3) 16/1: 04: Chsd ldrs, no impress final 2f: mid- 2 **73**
div on debut prev, Jan foal, cost 12,000 gns: dam a 5f juv wnr, sire progressive/high class sprinter: with A Jarvis.
1700 **FORUM FINALE** 13 [2] E Dunlop 2-9-0 D Holland 5/1: 25: Cl-up, outpcd/held 2f out: op 11/4: 8th 1700 (soft). 1¾ **64**
-- **SNOWEY MOUNTAIN** [6] 2-9-0 J F Egan 16/1: 6: Bhd halfway, mod late gains: op 12/1: Inchinor Mar 2 **64**
foal, cost 23,000 gns: half-brother to a 6f wnr: likely to need further on this evidence: with N Callaghan.
1628 **BIG JOHN** 16 [4] 2-9-0 A Culhane 11/2: 47: Cl-up 4f: bckd, op 10/1: btr 1628. 1½ **60**
-- **COTTONTAIL** [1] 2-9-0 J Reid 25/1: 8: Sn bhd: Alzao colt, Feb foal, cost 60,000 gns: half-brother 10 **41**
to sev wnrs, incl a smart 6f juv wnr: dam a mdn: with N Tinkler.
-- **LORD EFISIO** [9] 2-9-0 F Norton 33/1: 9: Sn outpcd & bhd: Efisio colt, Feb foal, half-brother to 19 **0**
sev 5/6f juv wnrs: dam a sprinter: with D Nicholls.
9 ran   Time 1m 10.9 (1.5)   (Wafic Said)   J L Dunlop Arundel, West Sussex.

YORK

SATURDAY JUNE 17TH   Lefthand, Flat, Galloping Track

2006

5.20 M SOBELL MDN STKS 3YO (D)   1m rnd   Firm 10   -05 Slow
£6857   £2110   £1055   £527

1692 **ASLY** 14 [3] Sir Michael Stoute 3-9-0 R Hills 1/2 FAV: -21: 3 b c Riverman - La Pepite (Mr Prospector):   89
Made all, prsd final 2f, rdn & al holding rivals inside last, styd on well: hvly bckd at odds-on: confirmed promise
of debut: $440,000 purchase: eff over a stiff/gall 1m, should stay further: acts on firm & fast grnd.
1377 **GLEDSWOOD** 29 [2] Lady Herries 3-8-9 K Darley 5/2: 32: 3 ch f Selkirk - Horseshoe Reef (Mill Reef):   1¼ 80
Prsd wnr & ev ch final 2f, held inside last: op 9/4, well clr of rem: handles firm & gd grnd: see 1377.
4605} **HIGHLAND GOLD** 225 [4] Miss L A Perratt 3-9-0 Pat Eddery 10/1: 65-3: 3 ch c Indian Ridge - Anjuli   9 71$
(Northfields): Chsd ldrs, outpcd/btn over 2f out: op 14/1, reapp: unplcd both '99 starts (rtd 70, mdn).
1280 **SEAHORSE BOY** 35 [1] J S Wainwright 3-9-0 D Holland 20/1: -0004: In tch till halfway, sn left bhd.   29 21
4 ran   Time 1m 37.00 (1.2)   (Hamdan Al Maktoum)   Sir Michael Stoute Newmarket, Suffolk.

NOTTINGHAM

SATURDAY JUNE 17th   Lefthand, Galloping Track

Official Going   GOOD TO FIRM (FIRM In Places) Stalls: 5f, 6f & 14f - Stands side: Rem - Inside.

2007

1.45 CHILLY MDN HCAP DIV 1 3YO+ 0-70 (E)   1m2f   Good 57 -04 Slow   [66]
£2968   £848   £424   3 yo rec 12lb

1446 **FIFE AND DRUM** 25 [4] E A L Dunlop 3-8-2 (50)(BL) (2ow) G Carter 4/1: 0-0001: 3 b g Rahy - Fife   58
(Lomond) Made all, rdn clr appr fnl 1f, styd on strongly: blnkd: first time in the frame: unplcd juv (rtd 69
at best): eff at 10f, bred to apprec middle dist: acts on gd grnd & a gall track: improved form in blinks.
1788 **KUUIPO** 9 [7] B S Rothwell 3-7-12 (48)(t) J Bramhill 20/1: 000602: 3 b f Puissance - Yankee Special   4 47
(Bold Lad) Cl up, outpcd over 3f out, no room 2f out, styd on, no threat: op 14/1: eff at 10f on gd: see 930.
1569 **MUST BE MAGIC** 19 [5] H J Collingridge 3-8-13 (63) R Perham 3/1 JT FAV: 00-063: 3 b c Magic Ring - shd 62
Sequin Lady (Star Appeal) Prom, rdn/eff appr fnl 1f, soon held: prob styd longer 10f trip on gd grnd: see 1569.
1415 **TALECA SON** 26 [3] D Carroll 5-7-10 (34)(9oh) S Righton 20/1: 000654: Dwelt, rear, raced keenly,   ½ 32
prog appr fnl 1f, hung left & soon btn: no disgraced from 9lb o/h: see 943, 211.
1807 **EIGHT** 8 [10] 4-9-12 (64) G Duffield 3/1 JT FAV: 00-035: Prom, rdn/fdd appr fnl 1f: btr 1807.   2 58
1299 **COCO LOCO** 33 [11] 3-8-10 (60) Dean McKeown 10/1: 0-6006: Mid div, rdn/one pace fnl 2f: see 884.   nk 54
1523 **CLASSIC COLOURS** 21 [2] 7-7-10 (34)(5oh) Jonjo Fowle (1) 50/1: 000-07: Prom, rdn/wknd appr fnl 1f.   nk 27
4366} **MILL AFRIQUE** 247 [8] 4-8-7 (45) J Mackay (7) 9/1: 4000-8: Bhd, eff after halfway, lost tch fnl   ¾ 37
2f: rnr up once in '99 (fillies h'cap, rtd 56): eff around 10f on fast & gd grnd: has previously tried blinks.
907 **KAFI** 64 [6] 4-9-3 (55)(VIS) R Havlin 12/1: 000-09: Handy, fdd over 2f out: 9 wk abs: 1st time visor: 3½ 42
unplcd as a juv in '99 (mdn, rtd 72 at best).
4367} **MACHE** 246 [9] 3-7-11 (47)(1ow)(2oh) Dale Gibson 33/1: 000-0: Never a threat, fin last: new stable.   9 21
10 ran   Time 2m 07.6 (5.3)   (Gainsborough Stud)   E A L Dunlop Newmarket

2008

2.20 GARY & SARAH SELL HCAP 3YO+ 0-60 (G)   1m6f   Good 57 -09 Slow   [56]
£2018   £576   £288   3 yo rec 17lb

1394 **DURHAM** 28 [4] G L Moore 9-10-0 (56)(bl) I Mongan (5) 7/1: 200-01: 9 ch g Caerleon - Sanctuary   58
(Welsh Pageant) Settled rear, gd hdwy appr fnl 3f, led dist, styd on strongly, drvn out: no bid: '99 wnr at
Goodwood (h'cap, rtd 64 at best): prev term scored at Sandown (h'cap, rtd 68): suited by 14f, stays 2m: acts
on soft & equitrack, likes firm & gd grnd: hndls any track & eff in blinks.
1707 **CASHIKI** 13 [14] B Palling 4-8-7 (35) D McGaffin (5) 12/1: -60202: 4 ch f Case Law - Nishiki (Brogan ½ 36
Settled rear, hdwy halfway, rdn to lead over 2f out, hdd dist, kept on, just held: op 10/1: eff at 12/14f.
1816 **BEST PORT** 8 [3] J Parkes 4-8-4 (32) P M Quinn (3) 13/2: -00343: 4 b g Be My Guest - Portree   nk 33
(Slip Anchor) Bhd, gd hdwy over 3f out, rdn/chall dist, styd on, not btn far: stys 14f on gd: see 1563, 641.
1852 **FANDANGO DREAM** 6 [16] M D I Usher 4-8-0 (28) C Rutter 10/1: -04504: Rear, prog fnl 3f, styd on   ¾ 28
well inside last: clr rem: quick reapp: stys 12/14f on firm & gd grnd: see 1209, 853.
2793} **TOP OF THE CHARTS** 334 [2] 4-8-9 (37) G Carter 7/1: 4044-5: Waited with, rdn to improve 4f out,   3½ 33
switched/hdwy over 1f out, kept on, nvr nrr: reapp: stys 14f, half brother to a 2m scorer: hndls fast & gd grnd: with Mrs M Reveley.
1852 **I CANT REMEMBER** 6 [15] 6-9-8 (50) G Duffield 5/1 FAV: 540506: Prom, rdn to lead 4f out, hdd   hd 46
appr fnl 2f, wknd: quick reapp: stys 12/14f on firm & gd grnd.
1465 **ORDAINED** 24 [9] 7-9-2 (44) M Tebbutt 14/1: 042307: Bhd, rdn/prog over 2f out, soon btn: see 1128.   1 39
1647 **CHILDRENS CHOICE** 15 [7] 9-8-12 (40) Dean McKeown 7/1: 313408: Cl up, drpd rear 7f out, late hdwy.   2½ 32
1647 **MISCHIEF** 15 [13] 4-8-11 (39)(vis) J Weaver 16/1: 300059: Dwelt, never a factor: see 815.   1½ 29
1644 **TAKE ACTION** 15 [8] 3-7-10 (41)(BL)(1oh) J Mackay (7) 33/1: -50000: Prom, rdn/btn fnl 2f, 10th: blnkd.2½ 28
1730 **LATIN BAY** 12 [5] 5-8-12 (40) R Havlin 16/1: 300-00: Nvr a dngr, fin 11th: dual Lingfield wnr in   1 26
'99 (sell h'caps, S Williams & G Lewis, rtd 50a), subs plcd on turf (rtd, 45), also trained briefly by D Nicholls
& D Wintle: eff arnd 12/13f on firm grnd & equitrack, likes to force the pace: now with P G Murphy.
1145 **XYLEM** 43 [11] 9-7-11 (25)(vis) Dale Gibson 10/1: 230540: Al bhd, finished 15th: tchd 16/1.   0
1736 **BOSSY SPICE** 12 [18] 3-7-10 (41)(4oh) S Righton 20/1: 00-000: Keen, led appr fnl 5f, sn hdd/wknd: 16th.   0
1040 **KNIGHTS RETURN** 50 [1] 3-7-10 (41)(11oh) Iona Wands 66/1: 000-00: Led to halfway, wknd, fin last.   0
2333} Bold Feliciter 354 [6] 4-8-6 (34)(vis) J Bramhill 33/1: 973 **Brilliancy** 59 [10] 5-8-9 (37)(t) C Cogan (5) 25/1:
1465 Socialist 24 [12] 4-7-11 (24)(1ow) N Carlisle 33/1:   1593 Ridgewood Bay 17 [17] 3-7-10 (41)(5oh) M Baird 66/1:
18 ran   Time 3m 07.6 (9.3)   (Wessex House Racing)   G L Moore Woodingdean, E Sussex

2009

2.50 ADRIAN ALLEN MED AUCT MDN 2YO (F)   5f   Good 57 -17 Slow
£2488   £711   £355

1589 **GAME N GIFTED** 17 [1] B J Meehan 2-9-0 J Weaver 1/3 FAV: 21: 2 b c Mind Games - Margaret's Gift   84
(Beveled) Dsptd lead, hung right & led appr fnl 1f, rdn clr inside last: nicely bckd at odds on: 33,000gns
Jan foal: dam a 5/6f wnr: speedily bred colt: eff at 5f on gd & gd/soft: rate more highly.
1782 **TROUBLESHOOTER** 9 [9] W R Muir 2-9-0 G Carter 7/1: 602: 2 b c Ezzoud - Oublier L'Ennui   3½ 74
(Bellman) Rear, no room/outpcd 3f out, switched/hdwy 2f out, ran on well, no dngr: apprec a return to 6f.

-- **CRIMSON RIDGE** [3] R Hollinshead 2-8-9 P M Quinn (3) 50/1: 3: 2 b f Kings's Signet - Cloudy Reef (Cragador) Front rank, rdn to improve over 1f out, soon not pace of wnr: Feb foal, dam a mdn: sire useful sprinter: speedily bred filly, should improve for experience. ¾ **67**

1706 **SEANS HONOR 13** [5] C N Kellett 2-8-9 C Rutter 12/1: 54: Dspd lead, led 2f out, sn hdd, no extra. *nk* **66**

-- **SAVANNA MISS** [6] 2-8-9 G Duffield 14/1: 5: Chsd ldrs, outpcd 3f out, rall/short of room over 1f out, sn no extra: April first foal, dam a juv 6f scorer: with B Palling, signs of ability here. *shd* **66$**

-- **RACHEL GREEN** [7] 2-8-9 R Morse 16/1: 6: Led 3f, fdd: 10,000gns 3rd foal: speedily bred. *2½* **60**

-- **RED FANFARE** [2] 2-8-9 M Tebbutt 20/1: 7: Handy, drvn & fdd fnl 2f: op 12/1: March foal, dam modest: sire high juv: with J A Osborne. *1¼* **56**

1859 **CHEVENING LODGE 6** [4] 2-9-0 D Hayes (7) 50/1: -4608: Cl up, short of room over 2f out, sn wknd. *1½* **57**

1577 **LITTLE MOUSE 18** [8] 2-8-9 M Fenton 50/1: 009: Soon outpcd, late eff when hung right over 1f out. *1* **49**

9 ran Time 1m 02.2 (3.7) (Margaret's Partnership) B J Meehan Upper Lambourn, Berks

2010

3.20 P HARVEY AUCT FILLIES MDN 2YO (E) 6f Good 57 -24 Slow
£2980 £851 £425

-- **SILK LAW** [5] A Berry 2-8-4 G Carter 9/4 FAV: 1: 2 ch f Barathea - Jural (Kris) Cl-up, hdwy/no room dist, drvn out to lead well ins last: 6,200gns 1st foal: dam a Gr 3 juv 1m wnr: eff at 6f, 7f+ sure to suit: runs well fresh on gd grnd & a gall track: fine debut, rate more highly when upped in trip. **77**

-- **YETTI** [2] H Candy 2-8-0 C Rutter 7/1: 2: 2 ch f Aragon - Willyet (Nicholas Bill) Cl up, chsg ldr when hmpd dist, styd on well, just held: Apr foal, dam unrcd: gd debut, eff over a gall 6f on gd. *½* **71**

-- **ALQUID NOVI** [3] J S Moore 2-8-8 Dean McKeown 5/1: 3: 2 ch f Bluebird - Persian Myth (Persian Bold) Hmpd leaving stalls, sn prom, rdn to lead appr fnl 1f, hdd well ins last, held cl home: 15,000gns Mar foal: half-sister to several wnrs: dam related to a high class sprinter: gd debut: eff at 6f on gd. *nk* **78**

1667 **STARRY MARY 15** [9] E L James 2-8-0 Dale Gibson 3/1: 04: Hmpd start, raced very keenly cl up, rdn, edged right & no extra inside last: clr rem: see 1667. *¾* **68**

1698 **POLYPHONIC 13** [1] 2-8-0 J Bramhill 33/1: 065: Switched right & caused interference after start, soon led, hdd 2f out, wknd: see 1385. *3* **61$**

-- **THE CHOCOLATIER** [4] 2-8-4 M Fenton 16/1: 6: Nvr a threat: 11,000gns Apr foal: with P Gilligan. *3* **58**

1641 **VICTEDDU 15** [8] 2-8-0 J Mackay (7) 9/2: 67: Rear, rdn/hdwy over 1f out, staying on well when badly hmpd inside last, not recover: ran a lot better than finishing position suggests: see 1641. *hd* **54**

-- **SKUKUSA** [7] 2-8-0 P M Quinn (3) 8/1: 8: Hmpd start, never a threat: Emarati 1st foal. *hd* **54**

-- **PRIDE OKILMARNOCK** [6] 2-8-4 G Duffield 7/2: W: Withdrawn before start. **0**

8 ran Time 1m 15.7 (4.9) (Kangaroo Courtiers) A Berry Cockerham, Lancs

2011

3.55 CHILY MDN HCAP DIV 2 3YO+ 0-70 (E) 1m2f Good 57 -05 Slow [65]
£2968 £848 £424 3 yo rec 12lb

1743 **DION DEE 11** [5] Dr J R J Naylor 4-8-2 (39) G Duffield 9/2: 300361: 4 ch f Anshan - Jade Mistress (Damister) Settled rear, smooth hdwy over 3f out, led dist, rdn clr ins last: mod form last term: eff arnd a sharp or gall 10f: acts on gd & gd/soft grnd: open to improvement, could follow up. **44**

1772 **PURSUIVANT 10** [10] Mrs N Macauley 6-8-10 (47)(bl) R Fitzpatrick (3) 7/1: 406032: 6 b g Pursuit Of Love - Collapse (Busted) Bhd, imprvd 3f out, styd on well, no ch with wnr: eff at 1m/10f on gd grnd. *3½* **46**

1708 **LEVEL HEADED 13** [1] P W Hiatt 5-8-0 (36)(1ow) C Rutter 16/1: 050-03: 5 b m Beveled - Snowline (Bay Express) Keen cl up, dsptd lead 4f out, no extra appr fnl 1f: op 12/1: stys 1m/10f on gd & hvy: see 1708. *½* **35**

1593 **SUMMER CHERRY 17** [11] P F I Cole 3-9-0 (63) M Tebbutt 3/1 FAV: 00-44: Front rank, rdn/no extra fnl 2f: h'cap debut: btr 1593 (claimer). *1¼* **59**

1603 **PROUD CAVALIER 17** [3] 4-7-10 (33)(8oh) M Baird 50/1: /00-05: Soon clr ldr, hdd over 1f out, wknd. *¾* **28**

1775 **CRUAGH EXPRESS 10** [7] 4-9-2 (53) J Weaver 5/1: 355-56: Settled rear, rdn/eff over 2f out, sn held. *1* **46**

1611 **MYLANIA 17** [2] 4-9-10 (61) Dean McKeown 11/2: 420-67: Raced v keenly with ldrs, fdd appr fnl 1f. *nk* **54**

1644 **HIGH BEAUTY 15** [6] 3-7-10 (45)(5oh) J Mackay (7) 14/1: -04048: Rear, drvn/prog over 2f out, sn wknd. *5* **30**

4438} **PARISIENNE HILL 241** [8] 4-7-10 (33)(13oh) Iona Wands (4) 50/1: 0000-9: Mid div, rdn/lost tch halfway. *5* **11**

1332 **COURT CHAMPAGNE 31** [9] 4-7-10 (33) P M Quinn (3) 5/1: /00600: Prom, rdn/wknd quickly fnl 2f, fin last, op 4/1: recent Stratford hdles wnr (nov, rtd 80h, eff at 2m on gd & a sharp track): only mod Flat form. *4* **5**

10 ran Time 2m 08.5 (6.2) (B C Mills) Dr J R J Naylor Shrewton, Wiltshire

2012

4.25 CENTURY CLASSIFIED STKS 3YO 0-60 (F) 1m2f Good 57 +06 Fast
£2425 £693 £346

1812 **AFTER THE BLUE 8** [8] M R Channon 3-9-0 R Havlin 6/1: -00641: 3 b c Last Tycoon - Sudden Interest (Highest Honor) Waited with, smooth hdwy appr fnl 1f, styd on strongly for press, drvn out to get up fnl strides: op 5/1, best time of day: 6th on sole '99 juv start (mdn, rtd 75): eff at 10f, 12f likely to suit in time: acts on gd grnd & a gall track: likes to come late off a strong pace. **64**

*1895 **BAHAMAS 4** [4] Sir Mark Prescott 3-9-2 G Duffield 4/5 FAV: 000-12: 3 b g Barathea - Rum Cay (Our Native) Trckd ldrs, hung left over 3f out, went on 2f out, edged right inside last, collered fnl strides: quick reapp: remains in gd form: see 1895 (reapp, h'cap). *nk* **65**

1255 **NOBLE REEF 36** [11] Mrs G S Rees 3-9-0 Dean McKeown 16/1: 060-03: 3 b c Deploy - Penny Mint (Mummy's Game) Chsd ldrs, rdn to improve 3 out, every ch dist, no extra well inside last: up in trip: 3rd at Chester in '99 (nursery h'cap, rtd 72): eff at 7f, stys 10f: acts on firm & gd: gd run & clr rem, win similar. *1* **61**

1632 **DATURA 16** [12] M L W Bell 3-8-11 J Mackay (7) 16/1: 00-064: Mid div, rdn/hdwy 2f out, short of room & wknd dist: up in trip & not quite get home over 10f?: see 1632 (9f). *4* **52**

*1572 **RONNI PANCAKE 18** [5] 3-8-13 I Mongan (5) 9/1: 06-015: Bhd, hdwy when hung left over 1f out, kept on, never nearer: bckd from 14/1: up in trip: btr 1572 (1m, gd/soft, claimer). *¾* **53**

1560 **COUNT ON THUNDER 19** [10] 3-9-0 G Carter 10/1: 000-56: Rear, late gains, never nearer: see 1560. *nk* **54**

1895 **OCEAN SONG 4** [1] 3-8-11 (bl) R Fitzpatrick (3) 12/1: 600307: Hmpd/drpd rear after 2f, no dngr after. *½* **50**

1544 **RATIFIED 21** [9] 3-9-2 C Rutter 8/1: 0-2148: Rear, rdn/wknd fnl 2f: btr 1022 (hvy). *4* **49**

1521 **ZABIONIC 21** [3] 3-9-0 (bl) Dale Gibson 25/1: -40009: Led, hdd 3f out, soon lost tch: see 717. *1½* **44**

4390} **CROOKFORD WATER 245** [2] 3-9-0 J Weaver 25/1: 000-0: Chsd ldrs, wknd quickly fnl 2f, finished 10th: unplcd in 3 juv starts (6f/1m mdns, rtd 59). *hd* **44**

1770 **LATE ARRIVAL 10** [7] 3-9-0 (BL) M Tebbutt 14/1: 0-4200: Cl up, led briefly 3f out, wknd, 11th: blnks. *1½* **41**

1796 **SIONED LYN 9** [6] 3-8-11 C Cogan (5) 50/1: 200300: Never a threat, finished last: see 1555. *6* **29**

12 ran Time 2m 07.4 (5.1) (Timberhill Racing Partnership) M R Channon West Isley, Berks

NOTTINGHAM   SATURDAY JUNE 17th   Lefthand, Galloping Track

2013   5.00 STEVE JORDAN HCAP 3YO 0-70 (E)   1m54y rnd   Good 57   -44 Slow   [75]
£3159   £972   £486

1448 **BOLD STATE** 25 [1] M H Tompkins 3-9-2 (63) G Duffield 9/2: 0-0001: 3 b g Never So Bold - Multi **67**
Softt (Northern State) Front rank, went on appr fnl 1f, strongly prsd ins last, drvn out & just prevailed: '99
scorer at York (auct mdn, rtd 78): eff at 1m, further should suit: acts on firm, gd & a gall track: eff with/
without a visor, has disappointed in blinks.
1525 **NATURAL** 21 [6] John Berry 3-9-1 (62) M Fenton 10/1: 0-062: 3 b g Bigstone - You Make Me Real   hd **65**
(Give Me Strength) Front rank, outpcd halfway, rall when no room over 1f out, found gap & ran on well ins last,
just failed: up in trip: eff at 1m on gd: excellent h'cap bow & a shade unlucky in running, go one better soon.
1710 **MISTY MAGIC** 13 [7] P W Harris 3-8-6 (53) R Lappin 5/1: 0-0043: 3 b f Distinctly North - Meadmore   1¼ **54**
Magic (Mansingh) Cl up, every ch until no extra well ins last: bckd from 8/1: eff at 6f/1m on fast & good.
1407 **SADAKA** 28 [10] E A L Dunlop 3-9-6 (67) G Carter 9/2: 30-034: Prom, led 6f out, hdd appr fnl 1f, wknd.   ¾ **66**
1569 **FOXS IDEA** 19 [5] 3-9-7 (68) Dale Gibson 3/1 FAV: 330505: In tch, rdn/late gains, nvr nrr: op 5/2.   1¼ **65**
1708 **BIRDSAND** 13 [2] O Urbina 6/1: 0-606: Bhd, rdn/prog over 3f out, sn onepcd: h'cap bow.   ½ **55**
1448 **ANGEL LANE** 25 [4] 3-8-1 (48) J Mackay 7/1 33/1: 000-07: Dwelt, rear, late gains, no dngr: see 1448.   1 **42**
1404 **HAZY HEIGHTS** 28 [3] 3-8-11 (58) S Clancy (7) 16/1: 6008: Dwelt, sn prom, wknd qckly fnl 2f: op 10/1.   2 **48**
1544 **MIDNIGHT MAX** 21 [8] 3-7-10 (43) (1oh) J Bramhill 50/1: 050-09: Keen in rear, nvr a factor: see 1544.   nk **33**
1053 **HEATHYARDS MATE** 49 [9] 3-9-5 (66) P M Quinn (3) 14/1: 042100: Rear, effort 2f out, sookn fdd,   7 **45**
fin 10th: 7 wk abs: btr 741 (AW seller).
2693} **COUNT TIROL** 338 [11] 3-9-2 (63) J Weaver 16/1: 003-0: Led early, with ldrs till wknd qckly fnl 2f: 11th,   7 **31**
op 10/1: plcd on final of 3 starts for M Heaton Ellis in '99 (5.7f auction mdn, firm, rtd 65): with C G Cox.
11 ran   Time 1m 47.8 (8.4)   (The Toy Boy Partnership)   M H Tompkins Newmarket

CARLISLE   SUNDAY JUNE 18TH   Righthand, Stiff Track, Uphill Finish

Official Going   FIRM Stalls: Inside.

2014   2.20 NEWS & STAR NOV AUCT STKS 2YO (E)   6f rnd   Firm 17   -34 Slow
£3542   £1090   £545   £272

*1538 **ASH MOON** 22 [4] K R Burke 2-8-10 N Callan 8/11 FAV: -11: 2 ch f General Monash - Jarmar Moon   **85+**
(Unfuwain) Trkd ldr, trav well, led inside fnl 1½f, qcknd clr, readily: bckd at odds-on: debut scorer at Haydock
(fillies mdn, rtd 90): 5,000gns April foal: eff at 5f, stays a stiff 6f well, further will suit: acts on firm
or gd/soft: promising filly, reportedly now steps up to listed class & is sure to win more races.
1488 **GALAXY RETURNS** 23 [5] A Berry 2-8-7 J Carroll 6/1: -02: 2 ch c Alhijaz - Naulakha (Bustino)   3 **70**
Bhd & rdn halfway, kept on inside fnl 2f, nearest fin: encouraging, needs 7f shld be plcd to advantage: see 1488.
1558 **TEFI** 20 [2] T D Easterby 2-8-9 K Darley 9/2: -53: 2 ch c Efisio - Masuri Kabisa (Ascot Knight)   ¾ **69**
Chsd ldrs, went 2nd over 1f out, kept on under pace: stays 6f on firm: see 1558.
1189 **SIR EDWARD BURROW** 42 [3] R F Fisher 2-8-7 R Winston 20/1: -04: In tch halfway, soon rdn & held: 5 **52**
6 wk abs, formerly with M Todhunter: see 1189.
1776 **PAT PINKNEY** 11 [7] 2-8-0 J Bramhill 33/1: -05: Led until hdd over 1f out, fdd: see 1776.   1 **42**
1558 **SPUR OF GOLD** 20 [6] 2-8-6(2ow) A Culhane 10/1: -66: Struggling from halfway, well bhd: see 1558.   13 **18**
6 ran   Time 1m 15.2 (3.1)   (David H Morgan)   K R Burke Newmarket, Suffolk

2015   2.50 UNION BRIGADE HCAP 3YO+ 0-70 (E)   6f rnd   Firm 17   -01 Slow   [70]
£4030   £1240   £620   £310   3yo rec 7lb

1519 **TECHNICIAN** 22 [13] E J Alston 5-8-7 (49)(bl) W Supple 20/1: 052001: 5 ch g Archway - How It Works   **56**
(Commanche Run) Chsd ldrs, led well over 1f out, ran on, rdn out: belated first success at 47th attempt:
rnr-up 11 times previously: eff around 6f/1m on firm, soft & fibresand, any track: wears blnks/visor.
1734 **SAMMAL** 13 [18] J A Glover 4-8-3 (45) O Pears 16/1: 500462: 4 b g Petardia - Prime Site (Burslem)   1½ **47**
Held up rear, not much room 2f out & again over 1f out, styd on for press: see 1664 (claimer), 639.
1869 **ALBERT THE BEAR** 6 [16] A Berry 7-9-0 (56)(vis) J Carroll 12/1: -06003: 7 b g Puissance -   shd **58**
Florentynna Bay (Aragon) Held up, not much room halfway, prog & not clr run over 1f out, styd on: see 1438.
1351 **SEALED BY FATE** 30 [11] J S Wainwright 5-8-7 (49)(vis) J McAuley(5) 20/1: 506604: Waited with, prog   1 **48**
halfway, rdn/onepace fnl 2f: one win in 45 starts: see 697.
1861 **SHARP HAT** 7 [10] 6-9-2 (58) A Culhane 9/1: 440205: Mid div, rdn 2f out, ran on fnl 1f: see 1792, 91.   1½ **53**
1869 **DOUBLE ACTION** 6 [20] 6-9-5 (61)(bl) K Darley 4/1: 405326: Bhd, prog 2f out, hmpd 1f out, kept on.   1 **53**
1680 **QUIET VENTURE** 15 [3] 6-9-9 (65) P Goode (3) 25/1: 5-0007: Prom, rdn 2f out, wknd over 1f out: ¾ **54**
best run this term: has dropped in the weights: see 1158.
1654 **PANDJOJOE** 16 [12] 4-9-2 (58) R Winston 10/1 8 FAV: -05568: Chsd ldrs, rdn 2f out, soon held: shd **47**
hvly bckd & can do much better: see 1654.
1941 **AMERICAN COUSIN** 3 [14] 5-8-9 (51) N Kennedy 10/1: -00009: Mid div, eff 2f out, onepcd 1f out.   nk **39**
1842 **CARRIE POOTER** 8 [7] 4-9-4 (60) C Lowther 25/1: 600000: Not trouble ldrs: 10th: best 910, 698.   1 **45**
*1714 **MUKARRAB** 13 [9] 6-8-10 (52) D Mernagh (3) 10/1: 436010: Made most until well over 1f out: 11th.   1¼ **33**
1412 **COLONEL SAM** 29 [19] 4-8-1 (43)(tbl) J Fanning 9/1: 000050: In tch, rdn 2f out, soon held: 12th.   shd **24**
1842 **ARCHELLO** 8 [15] 6-8-9 (51) P Robinson 20/1: 0-1000: Dsptd lead 4f, wknd: 13th, best 1258 (C/D).   shd **32**
1431 **EASTERN PROPHETS** 27 [4] 7-9-1 (57) F Lynch 20/1: 00-300: Mid div, rdn/btn 2f out: 14th.   1½ **24**
1806 **SEVEN SPRINGS** 9 [8] 4-8-1 (43) P M Quinn (3) 25/1: 203000: Soon bhd: fin last: see 1422 (AW).   1¾ **16**
15 ran   Time 1m 13.2 (1.1)   (All Saints Racing)   E J Alston Longton, Lancs.

2016   3.20 CALDERPRINT HCAP 3YO+ 0-80 (D)   1m6f32y   Firm 17   -25 Slow   [64]
£4153   £1278   £639   £319

4467} **GOLDEN CHIMES** 240 [5] D Nicholls 5-9-10 (60) A Culhane 7/2: 0030-1: 5 ch g Woodman - Russian Ballet   **68**
(Nijinsky) Chsd ldrs, led well over 2f out, ran on well, comfortably: fit from hurdling, won a 2m5f mdn event at
Sedgefield when trained by E Tuer (rtd 101h). Flat scorer in native Ireland back in '98 (mdn): eff at 1m6f,
will stay 2m: hndls soft, goes well on firm: should win again.

CARLISLE   SUNDAY JUNE 18TH   Righthand, Stiff Track, Uphill Finish

1686 **TOTEM DANCER 15** [1] J L Eyre 7-9-10 (60) K Darley 5/4 FAV: 010242: 7 b m Mtoto - Ballad Opera 5 60
(Sadler's Wells) Waited with, prog & dsptd lead well over 2f out, not pace of wnr: well bckd: 5L clr of rem.
*797 **BATOUTOFTHEBLUE 80** [4] W W Haigh 7-8-10 (46) F Lynch 5/2: 443-13: 7 br g Batshoof - Action Belle 5 38
(Auction Ring) Held up, prog & ev ch 2½f out, rdn/onepace: abs: likes Musselburgh: btr 797 (gd/soft).
-- **HOMBRE** [3] M D Hammond 5-9-8 (58) W Supple 7/1: 550/4: Led until 2½f out, fdd: hdles fit, rnr-up 7 40
to today's wnr Golden Chimes at Sedgefield in May (2m5f, firm, 88h): only thrice rcd prev on Flat back in '97.
1705 **STAMFORD HILL 14** [2] 5-7-11 (33) (1ow) (9oh) D Allan (0) 50/1: 00005: Chsd ldrs, chall 3f out, wknd. 2½ 12
5 ran   Time 3m 05.8 (6.0)   (G Tuer)   D Nicholls Sessay, N Yorks

2017   3.50 J NOBLE FILLIES HCAP 3YO 0-70 (E)   7f rnd Firm 17 +03 Fast   [76]
£3526   £1085   £542   £271

1569 **DESERT SAFARI 20** [1] E J Alston 3-9-5 (67) W Supple 10/1: 054001: 3 b f Desert Style - Dublah 73
(Private Account) Waited with, prog over 2f out, led inside fnl 1f, ran on well, rdn out, nicely bckd, tchd 16/1:
won fnl juv start at Musselburgh (fillies mdn auction mdn, rtd 74): stays a stiff 7f, should last 1m: hndls
hvy, goes on well on firm/fast grnd: has worn blnks, eff without: useful stable right back to form, win again.
1407 **LADY OF WINDSOR 29** [8] I Semple 3-9-7 (69) (vis) R Winston 20/1: 4-5102: 3 ch f Woods Of Windsor - 1¼ 71
North Lady (Northfields) Led until hdd over 1f out, battled on well: bold front-running eff: acts on firm & soft.
1865 **DOLFINESSE 6** [2] M Brittain 3-8-2 (50) (vis) D Mernagh (3) 14/1: 0-0523: 3 ch f Dolphin Street - 1¼ 49
Gortadoo (Sharpen Up) Never far away, kept on fnl 1f: mdn, last time finished 6L rnr-up in a Pontefract
seller: eff at 7f/1m on gd & firm: visored the last twice: should win a seller.
1793 **ALPATHAR 10** [3] M Dods 3-8-8 (56) F Lynch 12/1: 5-1664: Held up, rdn for eff 2f out, styd on, nk 54
nearest fin: hndls firm & soft grnd: see 930 (soft).
*1804 **SEND IT TO PENNY 9** [9] 3-8-4 (52) (bl) G Parkin 9/2: 002015: Led briefly over 1f out, rdn/no extra. nk 49
1892 **BEWILDERED 5** [7] 3-7-10 (44) (4oh) P Fessey 33/1: 050006: Chsd ldrs, drvn/btn 2f out: poor prev. 4 33
1596 **AFRICA 18** [11] 3-8-6 (54) K Darley 9/2: 30-167: Under press 3f out, nvr nr ldrs: best 1292 (reapp). 1¼ 40
1607 **GABIDIA 18** [4] 3-9-3 (65) P Robinson 2/1 FAV: 3-648: In tch, eff 2f out, soon held: well bckd on shd 51
h'cap debut & btr expected: see 1063.
1664 **LAUND VIEW LADY 16** [6] 3-8-6 (54) O Pears 25/1: 00-069: Al bhd: not trained on? see 1351 (sell). 2½ 35
1818 **DOUBLE FAULT 9** [5] 3-8-2 (50) (bl) J Fanning 9/1: 500330: Sn bhd: 10th: btr 1818 (rtd mdn, gd/sft). 5 21
1224 **SLIP KILLICK 39** [10] 3-8-9 (57) N Callan 10/1: 540-60: In tch for 5f, wknd: fin last: see 1224. 4 20
11 ran   Time 1m 26.5 (1.0)   (The Burlington Partnership)   E J Alston Longton, Lancs

2018   4.20 STRONGBOW CLASS STKS 3YO+ 0-75 (D)   1m rnd Firm 17 -05 Slow
£4212   £1296   £648   £324   3yo rec 10lb

1193 **SEA SQUIRT 42** [3] M Johnston 3-8-9 J Fanning 4/1: -23041: 3 b g Fourstars Allstar - Polynesian Goddess 74
(Salmon Leap) Made ev yard, quickened 3f out, styd on for press fnl 1f, narrowly: 6 wk abs, back in trip: thrice
rnr-up prev: eff out in front over a stiff 1m, stays 1m4f: acts on firm & soft: suited by forcing tactics.
1680 **SUPREME SALUTATION 15** [2] T D Barron 4-9-5 K Darley 13/8 FAV: 1-6062: 4 ch g Most Welcome - ½ 73
Cardinal Press (Sharrood) Trkd wnr, rdn over 2f out & ev ch ent fnl 1f, kept on, just btn: shld win again, see 1011.
1160 **KALA SUNRISE 43** [1] C Smith 7-9-5 J Stack 5/2: 0-0033: 7 ch h Kalaglow - Belle Of The Dawn ½ 72
(Bellypha) In tch, rdn 2f out, kept on, no pace to chall, but only btn 1L: on a fair mark: see 1160.
1840 **WEETMANS WEIGH 8** [4] R Hollinshead 7-9-5 N Callan 3/1: 000464: In tch, rdn 2f out, kept on fnl nk 71$
1f, btn just over 1L: see 1840, 49.
4 ran   Time 1m 40.6 (1.8)   (M J Pilkington)   M Johnston Middleham, N Yorks

2019   4.50 FATHERS DAY MDN 3YO (D)   1m1f61y Firm 17 -00 Slow
£4231   £1302   £651   £325

1425 **FAYRWAY RHYTHM 27** [4] M A Jarvis 3-9-0 P Robinson 7/4: 4-4451: 3 b c Fayruz - The Way She Moves 82
(North Stoke) Made all, chall strongly from over 2f out, styd on well for press fnl 1f: deserved success: eff
out in front over a stiff 9.3f, stays 12.2f: acts on firm or soft & on a sharp/turning or stiff track.
1200 **EAST CAPE 41** [1] L M Cumani 3-9-0 J P Spencer 4/5 FAV: -542: 3 b c Bering - Reine de Danse 1½ 80
(Nureyev) Chsd wnr over 2f out, hung right fnl 1f, no extra: hvly bckd: hndls firm, may prefer gd: shld go one better.
1447 **MOUNTAIN DANCER 26** [2] M Johnston 3-8-9 J Fanning 9/2: -63: 3 b f Rainbow Quest - Jammaayil 1½ 73
(Lomond) Outpcd 3f out, kept on fnl 1f: easier grnd should suit: see 1447 (debut, 10f).
1655 **KELBURNE 16** [3] J M Jefferson 3-9-0 A Culhane 33/1: -54: Rear, under press 3f out, soon held. 5 70
4 ran   Time 1m 57.0 (1.6)   (Yusof Sepiuddin)   M A Jarvis Newmarket, Suffolk

SALISBURY   SUNDAY JUNE 19TH   Righthand, Galloping Track, Stiff Finish

Official Going   GOOD/FIRM (FIRM in places). Stalls: Str - Far Side; 12f - Stands Side.

2020   2.00 EBF NOV FILLIES STKS 2YO (D)   5f Firm 07 -02 Slow
£3120   £960   £480   £240

1107 **AZIZ PRESENTING 46** [1] M R Channon 2-8-8 S Drowne 6/4 FAV: 201: 2 br f Charnwood Forest - Khalatara 81
(Kalaglow) Made all, kept on well over 1f out, pushed out: nicely bckd after a 6 wk abs: 11,500 gns Feb foal:
eff at 5f on firm, hvy & a stiff trk: runs well fresh: going the right way.
1641 **MILLENNIUM MAGIC 16** [4] J G Portman 2-9-1 A Beech (5) 7/2: 1342: 2 b f Magic Ring - Country Spirit 1¾ 80
(Sayf El Arab) Chsd ldr, outpcd over 2f out, kept on fnl 1f to take 2nd ins last: see 1372.
-- **ROYAL ASSAY** [2] Mrs P N Dutfield 2-8-8 L Newman (3) 8/1: 3: 2 ch f Goldmark - Glenista (Glenstal) ½ 72
Sn bhd, ran green but kept on over 1f out despite short of room ins last, nrst fin on debut: Feb foal, cost
9,000 IR gns: half-sister to a 5f juv scorer: eff at 5f, sure to relish 6f: learn from this & improve.
-- **NEARCTIC LADY** [3] R Hannon 2-8-8 R Hughes 7/4: 4: With wnr, btn over 1f out, eased cl-home: 1½ 68
well bckd: Feb foal, cost 18,000 IR gns: half-sister to a useful 6f juv wnr: bred to apprec 6f in time.
4 ran   Time 1m 0.25 (0.45)   (Coriolan Partnership)   M R Channon West Isley, Berks.

2021   2.30 THEHORSESMOUTH RTD HCAP 3YO 0-95 (C)   1m6f   Firm 07   -21 Slow   [100]
£6409   £1972   £986   £493

1560 **FAIT LE JOJO** 20 [2] S P C Woods 3-8-5 (77) G Duffield 9/2: 3-4541: 3 b g Pistolet Bleu - Pretty Davis   80
(Trempolino): Led over 3f out, kept on inside last, shade cosily: '99 scorer at W'hampton (mdn, rtd 83a): eff
at 10f, apprec this step up to 14f & likes firm/fast & fibresand: best up with/forcing the pace on any trk.
1695 **HIDDEN BRAVE** 15 [1] M Johnston 3-9-2 (88) R Ffrench 6/4: 2-162: 3 b c Bin Ajwaad - Fire Lily   1½   88
(Unfuwain): Led over 6f out till over 4f out, led again briefly over 3f out, kept on onepace for press
over 1f out: nicely bckd, jockey received a 2 day whip ban: probably stays 14f on firm & gd: see 848.
1510 **GOLD QUEST** 23 [4] Sir Michael Stoute 3-8-9 (81)(t) K Fallon 1/1 FAV: 0-523: 3 ch c Rainbow Quest -   10   71
My Potters (Irish River): Led after 1f till ran wide & hdd bend over 6f out, led again over 4f out till over 3f
out, sn wknd & eased ins last: hvly bckd, reportedly punctured a sole & this is best ignored: see 1510, 1200.
3 ran   Time 3m 01.94 (3.94)   (G A Roberts)   S P C Woods Newmarket.

2022   3.00 TOTE PLACEPOT HCAP 3YO+ 0-85 (D)   5f   Firm 07   +14 Fast   [80]
£7475   £2300   £1150   £575   3 yo rec 6 lb

1861 **THAT MAN AGAIN** 7 [9] S C Williams 8-9-0 (66)(bl) G Faulkner (3) 5/1: -00001: 8 ch g Prince Sabo -   72
Milne's Way (The Noble Player) Made virtually all, kept on for press ins last: gamble from 33/1 in the morning,
best time of day: shown little earlier this term on unsuitable grnd: '99 wnr at Sandown & Newmarket (h'caps, rtd
82): '98 wnr at Folkestone & Lingfield (rtd 76 & 74a): stays 6f, all wins at 5f & loves firm/fast grnd, handles
hvy & any trk: best in blnks, tried a visor: took advantage of favourable grnd conditions & a slip in the weights.
1356 **MUNGO PARK** 30 [7] M Dods 6-9-5 (71) K Fallon 11/2: 00-202: 6 b g Selkirk - River Dove (Riverman):   1   74
Hld up, eff over 2f out, chall ins last, flashed tail & not go past: plenty of temperament as well as ability.
+1861 **EASTERN TRUMPETER** 7 [12] J M Bradley 4-9-7 (73) P Fitzsimons (5) 5/1: 211113: 4 b c First Trump -   1¼   73
Oriental Air (Taufan): Sn cl-up, ev ch over 1f out, no extra ins last: op 3/1: proving v tough, landed 4 timer in 1861.
4554J **GOLDEN POUND** 233 [11] Miss Gay Kelleway 8-7-10 (48) G Baker (7) 25/1: 5056-4: Bhd, eff 2f out,   1   45
onepace fnl 1f: reapp: unplcd in '99 (rtd 57): '98 wnr at Leicester (h'cap, rtd 78): stays 1m, all wins at 6f:
acts on firm, soft & both AWs: handles any trk & best in blnks, has tried a visor: v well h'capped on best form,
interesting at 6f with blnks reapplied.
1650 **DANCING MYSTERY** 16 [1] 6-9-9 (75) S Carson (5) 9/1: -00335: Prom, eff over 2f out, sn no impress.   1¼   68
1871 **RITAS ROCK APE** 6 [5] 5-9-10 (76) T G McLaughlin 14/1: 30-006: Prom, btn final 1f: top weight.   nk   68
1980 **RIVER TERN** 2 [8] 7-9-1 (67) T Quinn 11/2: -60607: Dwelt, sn bhd, modest late gains: qck reapp.   nk   58
1871 **MOUSEHOLE** 6 [10] 8-8-12 (64) S Drowne 9/4 FAV: 000028: Sn bhd, late gains, no dngr: well bckd,   ½   54
likes this grnd & should do better: see 1871, 1013.
1672 **JONATHANS GIRL** 15 [4] 5-7-10 (48)(18oh) R Brisland (5) 100/1: 404009: Sn rdn & al bhd: see 358.   2   32
3694J **DOUBLE M** 292 [2] 3-9-8 (80) S Whitworth 33/1: 1404-0: Chsd wnr till wknd over 1f out, eased ins last: 3½   55
10th: in '99 won at Nottingham (mdn, rtd 81, first time visor): eff at 5f on fast & fibresand in a visor.
1650 **GREY PRINCESS** 16 [6] 4-9-9 (75) G Duffield 25/1: 000-00: Chsd wnr till wknd qckly 2f out: fin last.   7   36
11 ran   Time 59.46 (u0.34)   (J T Duffy & R E Duffy)   S C Williams Newmarket.

2023   3.30 CITY BOWL FILLIES HCAP 3YO+ 0-80 (D)   1m4f   Firm 07   -22 Slow   [78]
£4173   £1284   £642   £321   3 yo rec 14lb

1091 **WATER FLOWER** 47 [1] B R Millman 6-9-4 (68) K Fallon 3/1: 100-01: 6 b m Environment Friend - Flower   71
Girl (Pharly): Prom, stdd after 3f, hdwy to lead 2f out, edged right dist but kept on, idls out: '99 Salisbury (reapp)
& Chepstow wnr (2, h'caps, rtd 74): Jan '99 Exeter hdle wnr (nov, gd, rtd 107h, stays 2m on gd & gd/soft, with M
Pipe): eff at 10/12f, has tried 2m: acts on gd & firm: likes a stiff/undul trk, esp Salisbury: gd weight carrier.
1888 **HAPPY GO LUCKY** 5 [7] M J Weeden 6-9-0 (64) S Drowne 20/1: 01/062: 6 ch m Teamster - Meritsu   1¼   64
(Lyphard's Special): Led till over 2f out, kept on same pace: qck reapp: gd run, could win a mares h'cap: see 1440.
1880 **DIZZY TILLY** 6 [5] A J McNae 6-7-10 (46)(6oh) P Fitzsimons (5) 15/2: -00043: 6 b m Anshan - Nadema   1½   44
(Artaius): With ldr, onepace over 1f out: qck reapp: see 1880.
1785 **SEEKING UTOPIA** 10 [4] S P C Woods 3-8-9 (73) L Newman (3) 9/1: 05-504: Keen in tch, onepace over   nk   70
1f out: probably stays 12f: see 727.
1785 **COMMON CAUSE** 10 [2] 4-9-11 (75) S Sanders 7/4 FAV: 10-445: In tch, effort over 2f out, sn btn.   9   58
*295 **DREAM ON ME** 162 [6] 4-8-0 (50) Sophie Mitchell 25/1: 350-16: Chsd ldr till wknd qckly 4f out,   dist   0
virtually p.u. over 1f out, t.o: reportedly has a breathing problem, long abs since 295 (AW).
6 ran   Time 2m 35.9 (3.5)   (Avalon Surfacing Ltd)   B R Millman Kentisbeare, Devon.

2024   4.00 TISBURY FILLIES MDN 3YO (D)   1m str   Firm 07   -12 Slow
£3835   £1180   £590   £295

971 **SECRET DESTINY** 60 [7] J H M Gosden 3-8-11 R Hughes 7/4 FAV: 033-51: 3 b f Cozzene - Dramatrix   92
(Forty Niner) Cl-up, carried left when chall over 1f out, led ins last, styd on, rdn out: well bckd tho' op 5/4
after 2 mth abs: trained by A Foster in '99, plcd twice (rtd 92+): dam 10f wnr: apprec step up to 1m, 10f looks
sure to suit: acts on firm & soft grnd: useful, open to further improvement.
1669 **SEEKING SUCCESS** 16 [13] Sir Michael Stoute 3-8-11 K Fallon 9/4: -0022: 3 b f Seeking The Gold - Testy   1   90
Trestle (Private Account): Led, hung left over 1f out & hdd ins last, only btn 1L: clr rem: acts on firm & gd/soft.
--   **SHEER SPIRIT** [9] D R C Elsworth 3-8-11 N Pollard 11/2: 3: 3 b f Caerleon - Sheer Audacity (Troy):   7   79
Well bhd, kept on over 1f out, no threat: clr of rem: half-sister to Derby wnr Oath: will relish a step up to
10f+ & sure to do better with a more positive ride over further: v pleasing.
1811 **AMELIAS FIELD** 9 [1] S P C Woods 3-8-11 G Duffield 25/1: 404: In tch, brief eff over 3f out, no impress.   6   69
1669 **TOWN GOSSIP** 16 [8] S Sanders 33/1: 0-05: In tch, rdn 3f out, no impress: bred for 1m+.   2   65$
--   **NO TOMORROW** [2] 3-8-11 (t) Sophie Mitchell 33/1: 6: Bhd, some late gains: bred for 7f+.   hd   64
4012J **ALZITA** 272 [3] 3-8-11 S Whitworth 20/1: 0-7: Slow away & bhd, no impress over 2f out: rtd 67 when   hd   63
unplcd on sole juv start: half-sister to 2,000 Guineas wnr Island Sands: bred for 1m+: with J Toller.
1548 **PRINISHA** 20 [10] 3-8-11 R Ffrench 6/1: 028: Chsd ldr 4f out till 3f out, wknd: btr 1548 (soft).   7   51
1725 **ROSE TINA** 13 [11] S Carson (5) 50/1: 009: Handy, wknd over 2f out: see 1548.   15   23
1343 **TO THE STARS** 13 [12] 3-8-11 R Perham 50/1: 000: Chsd ldr till 4f out, wknd qckly: 10th, with B Millman.   1   21
1811 **FFYNNON GOLD** 9 [5] A Nicholls 25/1: 00: Prom, wknd halfway: 11th: see 1811.   10   3
--   **ABERNANT LADY** [4] 3-8-11 S Drowne 50/1: 0: Slow away & al bhd: 12th: half-sister to a 7f/1m wnr.   14   0

SALISBURY SUNDAY JUNE 19TH Righthand, Galloping Track, Stiff Finish

12 ran Time 1m 40.61 (1.51) (R E Sangster & Mr B V Sangster) J H M Gosden Manton, Wilts.

2025 **4.30 AXMINSTER APPR HCAP 3YO 0-70 (E) 1m str Firm 07 -19 Slow [77]**
£2884 £824 £412

1726 **GRUINART 13** [9] H Morrison 3-9-3 (66) L Newman (3) 5/2 FAV: -00431: 3 br g Elbio - Doppio Filo (Vision) Prom, eff to lead over 1f out, drvn clr: first win: stays 8.3f & enjoyed this firm grnd, acts on gd & a stiff or easy trk: gd confidence booster. **75**
1572 **COWBOYS AND ANGELS 19** [18] W G M Turner 3-9-7 (70) P Fitzsimons (3) 6/1: 360102: 3 b c Bin Ajwaad - Halimah (Be My Guest): Cl-up, kept on to chase wnr ins last, no impress: clr of rem & bckd from 10/1: back to form & acts on firm & hvy, handles fibresand: see 1349. *3* **73**
1742 **ANNIJAZ 12** [10] J G Portman 3-8-2 (51) A Beech (3) 16/1: 000463: 3 b f Alhijaz - Figment (Posse): With ldr, led over 4f out till over 1f out, no extra: prev with G McCourt & improved for step up to 1m on firm. *4* **47**
1444 **ORLANDO SUNRISE 26** [1] J L Spearing 3-9-0 (63) R Cody Boutcher (5) 14/1: -0604: Led till 4f out, no extra over 1f out: see 1268, 936. *¾* **57**
1414 **WHO DA LEADER 29** [16] 3-9-1 (64) R Smith (5) 20/1: 006-05: In tch, outpcd halfway, late gains, nvr dngrs: rnr-up once in '99 (rtd 84): eff at 5f on firm/fast grnd & has tried blnks. *shd* **58**
1544 **RIDE THE TIGER 22** [5] 3-8-9 (58) G Baker (5) 14/1: 00-136: In tch, outpcd halfway, modest late gains. *nk* **51**
1671 **FLYOVER 16** [7] 3-8-9 (58) Cheryl Nosworthy (7) 9/2: 000-07: Dwelt, in tch, btn over 2f out: gamble from 16/1: in '99 scored at Salisbury (fillies mdn auct, rtd 74): eff at 6f on gd/firm & gd & likes this stiff trk. *1* **49**
1726 **COMMONWOOD 13** [17] 3-9-1 (64) Shane Fordham (7) 11/2: 406-48: Bhd, rdn 2f out, no impress. *¾* **53**
1521 **MARJU GUEST 22** [2] 3-9-2 (65) G Faulkner 12/1: 4-2309: Waited with, rdn & btn over 2f out: btr 720. *2½* **49**
1671 **BLUES WHISPERER 16** [13] 3-8-0 (49) C Cogan (3) 20/1: 0-0000: Slow away & al bhd: 10th. *6* **21**
188 **Sofisio 186** [6] 3-9-5 (68) R Brisland(3) 14/1: 1672 **Ribbon Lake 15** [12] 3-9-2 (65) Kathleen McDermott(7) 20/1:
1593 **Many Happy Returns 18** [3] 3-7-13 (48) S Carson (0) 20/1:
1399 **The Jam Saheb 29** [4] 3-8-1 (50)(t) Jonjo Fowle (5) 20/1:
1345 **Golden Retriever 31** [11] 3-9-4 (67) R Thomas (7) 14/11571 **Northern Times 19** [15] 3-8-9 (58) A Nicholls 14/1:
16 ran Time 1m 41.2 (2.1) (The Gruinart Partnership) H Morrison East Ilsey, Berks

LEICESTER SUNDAY JUNE 18TH Righthand, Stiff, Galloping Track

Official Going GOOD TO FIRM. Stalls: Stands Side.

2026 **2.10 SPORTING BLUE HCAP 3YO 0-75 (E) 7f str Firm 01 +01 Fast [82]**
£3263 £753 £753 £251

1786 **SOCIAL CONTRACT 10** [16] R Hannon 3-9-7 (75) J F Egan 20/1: 10-001: 3 b g Emarati - Just Buy Baileys (Formidable) Held up, prog fnl 2f, rdn & styd on well to get up close home: '99 Southwell wnr (seller, rtd 80a, T Stack) & Lingfield (nurs, W Haggas, rtd 79): eff at 6f, suited by 7f on firm, hvy & fibresand, sharp/stiff track. **80**
1889 **CHILWORTH 5** [17] T M Jones 3-7-13 (50)(vis)(3ow) A Daly 6/1: 056042: 3 ch g Shalford - Close The Till (Formidable) Prom, rdn/led over 1f out, hdd nr fin: nicely bckd: eff at 7f on firm & gd grnd in a visor. *nk* **56**
*1773 **PAGEANT 11** [13] W Jarvis 3-9-4 (72) M Tebbutt 4/1 JT FAV: 43-512: 3 br f Inchinor - Positive Attitude (Red Sunset) Cl-up, ev ch fnl 1f, styd on well, just btn: ddhtd for 2nd: well bckd, op 11/2: eff at 6/7f. *dht* **75**
1341 **JAMESTOWN 31** [5] C Smith 3-9-4 (72) A Clark 25/1: 516-04: Prom, rdn/edged right over 1f out, kept on tho' just held nr fin: '99 Warwick wnr (auct mdn, rtd 78): eff at 6/7f on firm & soft, sharp/stiff track. *1½* **72**
1889 **OTIME 5** [12] 3-8-11 (65)(bl) Dean McKeown 7/1: 206625: Chsd ldrs, ch over 1f out, onepace nr fin. *¾* **63**
*1889 **MISTER CLINTON 5** [10] 3-8-12 (66)(6ex) D O'Donohoe 4/1 JT FAV: 410316: Held up, prog over 1f out, not pace to chall: op 7/2, 6lb pen: qck reapp: see 1889. *1½* **61**
4333} **LATINO BAY 250** [8] 3-8-4 (58) J Tate 20/1: 000-7: Mid-div, rdn/not pace to chall fnl 2f: reapp/h'cap bow: unplcd last term (rtd 66): half-brother to a 13f Irish wnr, 1m+ could suit this term. *nk* **52**
1569 **TRIBAL PRINCE 20** [15] 3-9-4 (72) J Weaver 16/1: 025-08: Sn prom, led over 2f out, hdd over 1f out, fdd. *nk* **65**
1234 **CUPIDS DART 38** [2] 3-8-11 (65) D Holland 25/1: 352309: Prom till over 1f out: see 615, 373 & 80. *2½* **53**
661 **SILCA FANTASY 99** [18] 3-7-11 (50)(1ow) N Carlisle 33/1: -44460: Led 4f, btn over 1f out: 10th: abs. *1½* **36**
1787 **SILK ST BRIDGET 10** [11] 3-7-10 (50)(2oh) J Mackay(7) 33/1: 0-0000: Mid-div at best: 11th: see 1610. *1½* **32**
4550} **ESCALADE 233** [19] 3-8-9 (63) Lindsey Rutty (7) 33/1: 0630-0: Chsd ldrs till over 1f out: 12th: reapp: plcd in '99 (rtd 65, nurs h'cap): eff at 7f, bred to apprec 1m+. handles gd/soft & a sharp/undul track. *1½* **42**
1889 **MISS FLIRTATIOUS 5** [7] 3-8-8 (62)(bl) Pat Eddery 10/1: 02-000: Held up, eff halfway, no impress: 14th. **0**
1467 **DISTANT GUEST 25** [9] 3-8-13 (67)(bl) G Bardwell 14/1: -20240: Sn rdn, nvr on terms: 15th: op 12/1. **0**
1545 **Caldey Island 20** [6] 3-8-6 (60) G Hind 33/1: 1607 **The Diddler 18** [4] 3-7-10 (50)(5oh) K Dalgleish(7) 66/1:
4409} **Jenko 244** [3] 3-7-13 (53) Dale Gibson 33/1: 694 **Nineteenninetynine 90** [1] 3-8-9 (63)(vis) R Fitzpatrick (3) 33/1:
18 ran Time 1m 22.0 (0.0) (J G Lambton) R Hannon East Everleigh, Wilts.

2027 **2.40 TIPSTERS HCAP DIV I 3YO+ 0-65 (F) 1m str Firm 01 -10 Slow [65]**
£2499 £714 £357 3yo rec 10lb

1772 **SOUHAITE 11** [3] W R Muir 4-8-3 (40) P Doe 20/1: 03-001: 4 b g Salse - Parannda (Bold Lad Ire): Dwelt, sn handy, led 4f out & clr over 2f out, hung right over 1f out, held on gamely inside last, all-out: '99 Southwell scorer (h'cap, first win, rtd 45a): eff at 1m/12f, has tried 2m: acts on fibresand & firm grnd: handles a stiff/gall or sharp trk & runs well fresh: best without a t-strap. **43**
1690 **DERRYQUIN 15** [17] P L Gilligan 5-9-7 (58)(bl) D O'Donohoe 11/1: 0-0102: 5 b g Lion Cavern - Top Berry (High Top): Chsd ldrs, rdn final 2f, styd on well inside last, just held: acts on gd/soft, relishes firm: see 1296. *nk* **60**
1690 **KUSTOM KIT KEVIN 15** [5] S R Bowring 4-8-4 (40)(t)(1ow) Dean McKeown 12/1: 100003: 4 b g Local Suitor - Sweet Revival (Claude Monet): Hmpd start/towards rear, styd on well from over 1f out, not reach wnr: btn under 1L, op 10/1: acts on firm grnd & fibresand: see 584 (AW mdn h'cap). *½* **42**
1598 **STYLE DANCER 18** [2] R M Whitaker 6-9-8 (59) Pat Eddery 4/1 FAV: 0-5404: Held up, styd on well final 2f, not reach ldr: op 7/2, btn less than 1L: see 1300, 79. *shd* **60**
1921 **HEVER GOLF GLORY 4** [14] 6-7-10 (33) J Mackay(7) 16/1: 303005: Prom, rdn/outpcd halfway, kept on. *1½* **31**
1547 **COMPATRIOT 20** [12] 4-10-0 (65) S Finnamore (5) 20/1: 04-246: Held up, styd on final 2f, no threat. *¾* **61**
1680 **ACID TEST 15** [1] 5-9-13 (64) M Hills 20/1: 663007: Chsd ldrs, no impress over 1f out: see 525 (7f). *2½* **55**
1611 **DOUBLE DESTINY 18** [4] 4-9-1 (52)(bl) C Carver (3) 20/1: 00-008: Chsd wnr halfway, btn over 1f out. *1¾* **39**
162 **DARYABAD 193** [13] 8-8-12 (49) Dale Gibson 8/1: 0116-9: Mid-div, drvn/no impress final 2f: op 7/1, *1½* **33**

6 mth abs: now with N Graham: see 28 (7f, AW).
1739 **ENTROPY 12** [8] 4-8-2 (38)(1ow) D R McCabe 14/1: -00230: Held up, nvr on terms: 10th: op 12/1. ½ **22**
1575 **PRIORS MOOR 19** [6] 5-7-12 (34)(1ow) N Carlisle 50/1: 0-0000: Al towards rear: 11th: see 608 (AW). 3 **12**
1799 **KNOBBLEENEEZE 10** [7] 10-8-7 (44) Craig Williams 16/1: 000300: Prom 6f: 12th: op 14/1: see 1462. 1½ **18**
1364 **FUTURE COUP 30** [20] 4-9-5 (56) J Weaver 14/1: 1D-000: Dwelt, al towards rear: 13th: see 1254. *hd* **30**
1360 **ETISALAT 30** [16] 5-9-10 (61) G Bardwell 5/1: 311130: Sn prom, rdn/strugg 3f out: 14th: btr 1360. 3½ **28**
1395 **Elba Magic 29** [11] 5-9-4 (55) R Fitzpatrick (3) 20/1: 1300 **Gymcrak Flyer 34** [15] 9-8-13 (50)(vis) G Hind 20/1:
-- **Queens Stroller** [19] 9-7-10 (33) Claire Bryan(5) 66/1:
17 ran Time 1m 35.3 (0.9) (J Bernstein) W R Muir Lambourn, Berks.

2028

3.10 LISTED LEICESTER STKS 4YO+ (A) 1m3f183y Firm 01 +11 Fast
£12945 £4910 £2455 £1116

*1850 **MURGHEM 8** [3] M Johnston 5-8-12 D Holland 3/1: 224211: 5 b h Common Grounds - Fabulous Pet **113**
(Somethingfabulous) Led after 4f, made rest, rdn dist, held on well, pushed out nr fin: fast time: last week scored at Epsom (rtd h'cap): '99 wnr at Sandown (h'cap, rtd 100, B Hanbury): '98 scorer at Kempton (mdn, rtd 105): eff at 12f, stays 2m: acts on firm, soft & fibresand, best up with/forcing the pace on any trk: can go well fresh, best without blnks: can carry big weights: smart, genuine & imprvg, win a Group race abroad.
1339 **RAINBOW WAYS 31** [6] B W Hills 5-9-1 J Reid 7/4 FAV: 65-122: 5 b h Rainbow Quest - Siwaayib ½ **115**
(Green Desert) Waited with, gd prog to chall 1f out, held towards fin: nicely bckd, 5L clr rem: imprvd in defeat, loves firm grnd: smart: see 1187 (h'cap).
3878} **ZINDABAD 281** [5] B Hanbury 4-9-4 R Hills 10/1: 1115-3: 4 b h Shirley Heights - Miznah (Sadler's 5 **110**
Wells) Prom & ev ch till no extra appr fnl 1f: op 7/1, reapp: '99 hat-trick scorer at Newmarket (h'cap), Ascot (rtd h'cap) & Windsor (Gr 3, rtd 114): '98 Pontefract wnr (mdn, rtd 103): eff at 10f, prob stays 12f: acts on soft, loves firm/fast: likes to force the pace on any trk: v useful run against in-form/race fit rivals, go close next time.
1401 **LIGHTNING ARROW 29** [1] J L Dunlop 4-8-12 Pat Eddery 3/1: 30-024: Early ldr, cl up till fdd bef dist. 2 **101**
4173} **HELVETIUS 261** [7] 4-8-12 Dane O'Neill 50/1: 3560-5: Chsd ldrs, outpcd 3f out: stiff task, reapp: 13 **81**
'99 Brighton wnr (3 rnr mdn at 1/16, Listed 3rd of 4, first time blnks, rtd 99, C Brittain): '98 rnr-up (stks, rtd 76): eff at 10/12f on firm & gd/soft, prob any trk: needs h'caps: now with P Ritchens.
1401 **MAYLANE 29** [2] 6-9-1 M Hills 7/1: 11-046: Reluctant to start, al bhd: see 1401, 987. 14 **64**
6 ran Time 2m 27.0 (u1.3) (A Al-Rostamani) M Johnston Middleham, Nth Yorks.

2029

3.40 PROPERTY MED AUCT MDN 2YO (E) 6f str Firm 01 -07 Slow
£3120 £960 £480 £240

-- **SANTOLINA** [8] J H M Gosden 2-8-9 R Hills 5/1: -1: 2 b f Boundary - Alamosa (Alydar) **87**
Mid-div, prog to lead appr fnl 1f, readily: op 3/1 on debut: Apr foal, half-sister to sev wnrs, incl smart miler Etizaaz, sire smart sprinter on dirt: eff at 6f, will get 7f: acts on firm grnd, stiff trk: runs well fresh, lks useful.
1538 **EXTRA GUEST 22** [12] M R Channon 2-8-9 Craig Williams 5/1: -43262: 2 b f Fraam - Gibaltarik (Jareer) 4 **73**
Chsd ldrs, styd on appr final 1f for 2nd, no ch with wnr: consistent, goes on firm & hvy grnd.
1667 **ANNIE RUAN 16** [11] D Haydn Jones 2-8-9 Dean McKeown 40/1: -03: 2 b f So Factual - Sans Diablo ½ **72**
(Mac's Imp) Sn led, hdd appr final 1f, one pace: May foal, sire a sprinter: eff at 6f on firm grnd: can win a race.
-- **FASTINA** [6] R Guest 2-8-9 D Harrison 50/1: -4: Slow away & off the pace till ran on well appr 2 **66+**
final 1f, nvr dngrs: Dunphy Apr foal, dam a wnr abroad: 7f is going to suit, promising.
-- **PRINCE OF BLUES** [2] 2-9-0 J Tate 33/1: -5: Mid-div, imprvd & drifted right appr final 1f, sn onepce: ½ **70**
10,500 gns Prince Of Birds Feb foal, half-brother to 6/7f juv wnr Inchalong, dam 6/7f juv wnr, sire a miler.
-- **FORMAL PARTY** [17] 2-8-9 Pat Eddery 15/2: -6: Slow away, sn prom, wide, no extra appr final 1f 1½ **61**
& eased: Formidable Feb first foal, dam unrcd: not given a hard time, sharper for this: with J Dunlop.
-- **BIBLE BOX** [9] 2-8-9 G Bardwell 40/1: -7: Rear, some late prog, nvr a factor: Bin Ajwaad Jan foal, ½ **60**
first produce of a 1m juv wnr, sire 7f/1m performer: with J Pearce.
1691 **MAYTIME 15** [15] 2-8-9 M Fenton 12/1: -08: Early ldr, fdd appr final 1f: Pivotal Apr foal, half- ½ **59**
sister to 5f juv wnr Hinton Rock, dam 6f juv wnr, sire a sprinter: with M Bell.
1328 **ZANDEED 32** [14] 2-9-0 J Reid 9/4 FAV: -59: Prom till ent final 2f: nicely bckd: rtd higher 1328. ½ **63**
-- **XIPE TOTEC** [13] 2-9-0 Dane O'Neill 20/1: -0: Nvr troubled ldrs: 10th, 16,000 gns Pivotal Apr 3½ **53**
foal, dam 6/7f wnr, sire a sprinter: with R Fahey.
1424 **BRUNNHILDE 27** [16] 2-8-9 M Tebbutt 16/1: -00: Al towards rear: 11th: 6,500 gns Wolfhound Feb foal, ¾ **45**
half-sister to 4 wnrs, notably 5f juv, later useful mid-dist performer Largesse, dam a miler: with John Berry.
1602 **FLYING TURK 18** [5] 2-9-0 M Hills 12/1: -30: Speed 4f: 12th: tchd 16/1: see 1602 (soft). ¾ **47**
-- **OUR DESTINY** [18] 2-9-0 J F Egan 12/1: -0: Dwelt, al bhd: 14th: 22,000 gns Mujadil Feb first foal. **0**
-- **Bishops Secret** [7] 2-9-0 A Whelan 20/1: -- **Sholto** [4] 2-9-0 D R McCabe 16/1:
-- **Essence** [10] 2-8-9 R Fitzpatrick (3) 50/1:
16 ran Time 1m 10.3 (0.5) (H Lascelles Indian Creek & A Stroud) J H M Gosden Manton, Wilts.

2030

4.10 MERCURY CLASS STKS 3YO+ 0-80 (D) 1m2f Firm 01 +05 Fast
£6792 £2090 £1045 £522 3yo rec 12lb

*1271 **LADY ANGHARAD 37** [6] J R Fanshawe 4-9-6 D Harrison 9/4 FAV: 200-11: 4 b f Tenby - Lavezzola **87**
(Salmon Leap): Settled rear, rdn/prog over 2f out, led dist, rdn clr: gd time: earlier won on reapp at Nottingham (stks): '99 rnr-up for A Jarvis (h'cap, rtd 82): useful juv, won at Epsom (Listed) & Salisbury (stks, rtd 100, tried Gr company): now suited by 10f: acts on fast, gd & any trk: ran well once in a visor, probably best without: goes well fresh & is nicely h'capped on juv form: useful filly.
1860 **ST HELENSFIELD 7** [4] M Johnston 5-9-6 (VIS) D Holland 11/4: -03032: 5 ch g Kris - On Credit 2½ **81**
(No Pass No Sale): Front rank, chall over 1f out, sn not pace of wnr: nicely bckd, qck reapp: visor: see 1518.
*1655 **INCHING CLOSER 16** [1] N A Callaghan 3-8-11 J Mackay (7) 5/1: 4-0013: 3 b g Inchinor - Maiyaasah 1½ **82**
(Kris): Waited with, rdn/hdwy 3f out, no extra inside last: acts on firm & gd grnd: see 1655.
*1812 **MYTHICAL KING 9** [2] B Palling 3-8-11 J Reid 11/2: 0-3314: Led, hdd appr final 1f, sn wknd: ¾ **81**
op 4/1: consistent, shade btr 1812 (gd/soft).
1599 **MANDOOB 18** [5] 3-8-8 R Hills 7/1: 5-045: Dwelt, rear, nvr a dngr: op 5/1, see 1599. 5 **70**
1635 **LAKE SUNBEAM 17** [3] 4-9-6 Dane O'Neill 12/1: 045-56: Prom, rdn/lost tch final 2f: up in trip & 2 **67**
should apprec a drop back to 1m: see 1635.
6 ran Time 2m 02.1 (u0.4) (Ian M Deane) J R Fanshawe Newmarket.

LEICESTER   SUNDAY JUNE 18TH   Righthand, Stiff, Galloping Track

2031
4.40 MERCURY FILLIES HCAP 3YO+ 0-75 (E)   6f str   Firm 01   -02 Slow   [70]
£3068   £944   £472   £236   3yo rec 7lb

1606 **OARE KITE** 18 [7] P S Felgate 5-8-4 (46)(bl) Dale Gibson 8/1: 463201: 5 b m Batshoof - Portvasco 53
(Sharpo): Made all, clr inside last, rdn out: '99 scorer at Leicester (sell, G L Moore, rtd 50, also rtd 43a):
'98 wnr again at Leicester (appr mdn, rtd 68): eff at 6/7f, stays 1m: acts on firm, soft & fibresand: handles
any trk, all three wins at Leicester: eff in blnks/visor.
1787 **SANTIBURU GIRL** 10 [10] J R Best 3-9-3 (66) Pat Eddery 7/1: 061002: 3 b f Casteddu - Lake Mistassiu 2 66
(Tina's Pet): Rear, styd on well final 2f, not reach wnr: gd run, will apprec a return to 7f: acts on firm & gd.
1760 **HAUNT THE ZOO** 11 [4] J L Harris 5-7-11 (39) K Dalgleish (7) 11/1: 000103: 5 b m Komaite - Merryhill ½ 38
Maid (M Double M): Front rank, rdn/outpcd over 2f out, rall ins last, no threat to wnr: btr 1506 (7f, fibresand).
1636 **BRAMBLE BEAR** 17 [5] M Blanshard 6-8-8 (50) D Sweeney 6/1: 600104: Waited with, rdn/ran on nk 48
well final 1f, nrst fin: see 1464 (gd/soft).
1842 **PETITE DANSEUSE** 8 [6] 6-7-12 (40) Iona Wands(5) 5/1 FAV: 611605: Rear, hdwy when swtchd ½ 37
over 2f out, ev ch till outpcd inside last: see 1506, 1422.
1923 **GRACE** 4 [8] 6-8-1 (43)(vis) Claire Bryan (5) 11/1: 664066: Cl-up, rdn/no extra appr fnl 1f: qck reapp. ¾ 37
1606 **VIOLET** 18 [1] 4-8-11 (53)(vis) D Holland 33/1: 000-07: Prom, rdn/btn over 1f out: early '99 2½ 40
scorer at W'hampton (mdn, rtd 78a), unplcd on turf (rtd 67): eff at 7f/8.5f on both AWs, handles soft &
sharp trks: has tried visor, probably best without.
1810 **MOONLIGHT SONG** 9 [9] 3-9-2 (65) M Tebbutt 16/1: 40-008: Handy, rdn/lost tch final 2f. ½ 51
1794 **WHO GOES THERE** 10 [3] 4-8-2 (44) P Doe 13/2: 500029: Dwelt, nvr a factor: btr 1794 (7f, gd/soft). 5 15
1953 **TALARIA** 3 [12] 4-9-10 (66)(t) J Mackay (7) 13/2: 010040: Dwelt, sn prom, wknd fnl 2f, 10th: qck reapp. 1½ 33
1731 **Arana** 13 [11] 5-7-10 (38)(6oh) S Righton 66/1:   399   **Rajmata** 144 [13] 4-8-11 (53)(vis) R Fitzpatrick (3) 33/1: R
12 ran   Time 1m 10.0 (0.2)   (Foreneish Racing)   P S Felgate Grimston, Leics.

2032
5.10 TIPSTERS HCAP DIV II 3YO+ 0-65 (F)   1m str   Firm 01   +04 Fast   [65]
£2499   £714   £357   3yo rec 10lb

*1942 **THE WILD WIDOW** 3 [17] M C Pipe 6-9-5 (56)(vis)(6ex) J Mackay (7) 1/1 FAV: 022211: 6 gr m Saddlers' Hall - 67
No Cards (No Mercy): Sn led & set fast pace, clr appr final 2f, styd on well, rdn out: gd time, hvly bckd: recent
pillar-to-post win at Newbury (10f h'cap): '99 wnr at W'hampton (sell, H Collingridge, rtd 59a) & Warwick (sell,
1st time blnks, rtd 52, Miss S Wilton): plcd in '98 (h'cap, rtd 69, J Eustace): loves to force the pace at 1m/11f
on firm, soft & fibresand: acts on any trk & eff with/without blnks/visor: in fine form for new connections.
1730 **SACREMENTUM** 13 [11] J A Osborne 5-8-4 (48) Pat Eddery 9/1: 206402: 5 b g Night Shift - Tantum 4 49
Ergo (Tanfirion): Sn outpcd, styd on well final 2f, no ch with wnr: bckd from 16/1: apprec a return to 10f.
1743 **THIHN** 12 [1] N E Berry 5-9-2 (53) Dane O'Neill 14/1: 22-203: 5 ch g Machiavellian - Hasana hd 54
(Private Account): Chsd ldr, hung right over 3f out, styd on but not pace of wnr: see 1395.
4449} **MAY QUEEN MEGAN** 242 [7] Mrs A L M King 7-8-3 (40) A Daly 20/1: 5504-4: Waited with, hdwy/hung 2 37
left over 1f out, sn held: placed form in '99 (h'cap, rtd 48 at best): '98 Nottingham (h'cap) & Lingfield wnr
(fill h'cap, rtd 55 at best): eff at 7/9f on firm & soft, stays 10f: best without blnks: likes Lingfield.
2011 **LEVEL HEADED** 1 [2] 5-7-13 (36) D Kinsella(7) 16/1: 50-035: Prom, rdn/no extra when hmpd ¾ 31
inside last: op 12/1: plcd yesterday in 2011.
*1731 **SOPHOMORE** 13 [3] 6-10-0 (65) K Dalgleish (7) 8/1: 306016: Front rank, wknd ins last: btr 1731 (clmr). 5 50
1772 **WATER LOUP** 11 [5] 4-7-13 (35)(1ow) P Doe 33/1: -60007: Led early, remnd chsg ldrs, rdn/fdd final 2f. 1¾ 17
1233 **MUJAS MAGIC** 38 [10] 5-8-13 (50)(vis) R Fitzpatrick (3) 33/1: 020508: Sn rdn, nvr a threat. 2 27
1364 **CABARET QUEST** 30 [9] 4-8-13 (50) Claire Bryan (5) 6/1: 0-0009: Dwelt, nvr a dngr. 2½ 25
4535} **PURPLE DAWN** 234 [8] 4-8-1 (34)(4ow) D R McCabe 33/1: 6000-0: Al rear, 10th: '99 Nottingham wnr 2 6
(sell h'cap, rtd 47, J S Moore), unplcd over hdles (novs, rtd 74h): eff at 10f on fast & gd: now with B A Pearce.
1772 **DRURIDGE BAY** 11 [18] 4-7-10 (33)(1oh) S Righton 50/1: -00000: Prom, rdn/lost tch final 2f: fin 11th. 3 0
1732 **WILD NETTLE** 13 [15] 6-7-12 (35) N Carlisle 14/1: 000420: Mid-div, eff 2f out, sn wknd: 12th: btr 1732. 2½ 0
1760 **LEOFRIC** 11 [20] 5-8-4 (41)(bl) J F Egan 12/1: 030630: Sn rdn in rear, al bhd: fin 15th: btr 1760. 0
1775 **Massey** 11 [4] 4-9-9 (60) J Reid 20/1:   1364 **Burning** 30 [13] 8-8-3 (40) A Clark 40/1:
1275 **Russian Music** 36 [16] 7-9-7 (58) G Bardwell 50/1:   1690 **Consultant** 15 [19] 4-8-1 (38) J Tate 33/1:
1772 **Hunan Scholar** 11 [6] 5-7-11 (33)(tbl)(1ow) Dale Gibson 50/1:
18 ran   Time 1m 34.1 (u0.3)   (Mrs Pam Pengelly & Mrs Helen Stoneman)   M C Pipe Nicholashayne, Devon.

WARWICK   MONDAY JUNE 19TH   Lefthand, Sharp, Turning Track

Official Going   GOOD TO FIRM. Stalls: Inside.

2033
6.50 GALLOWS HILL APPR HCAP 3YO+ 0-60 (G)   1m2f110y Good/Firm   Inapplicable   [58]
£2279   £651   £325   3yo rec 12lb

1258 **WESTGATE RUN** 38 [7] R A Fahey 3-8-11 (54) P Hanagan (5) 5/2 FAV: 000-01: 3 b f Emperor Jones - 58
Glowing Reference (Reference Point): Held up, rdn final 3f, hung left & styd on well for press to lead nr fin: hvly
bckd, op 4/1, first win: rnr-up in '99 (rtd 75): eff at 7f, apprec step up to 10f: acts on firm & gd, sharp trk.
1875 **INDIAN NECTAR** 7 [14] R Brotherton 7-9-9 (53) L Newman (3) 15/2: 60-042: 7 b m Indian Ridge - Sheer ½ 55
Nectar (Piaffer): Chsd ldrs, rdn/ev ch final 1f, styd on well, just held: back on a fair mark: see 1875.
1509 **CAPTAIN MCCLOY** 24 [10] N E Berry 5-8-10 (40)(bl) R Brisland (3) 16/1: 050-63: 5 ch g Lively One - shd 42
Fly Me First (Herbager): Chsd ldr, rdn/led over 1f out, edged left inside last & hdd nr line: op 12/1: gd
effort with blnks reapplied, likes Warwick and relishes a fast surface: see 209.
1707 **UNIMPEACHABLE** 15 [1] J M Bradley 3-8-11 (54) Claire Bryan (5) 16/1: 005264: Sn prom, rdn & kept 1¾ 53
on onepace final 2f: op 12/1: acts gd & hvy: see 1644, 1002.
1523 **THE IMPOSTER** 23 [9] 5-9-0 (44) I Mongan 25/1: 100005: Led, hdd over 1f out, no extra: see 707. 2½ 40
*1921 **MICE IDEAS** 5 [2] 4-9-5 (49)(6ex) P M Quinn 6/1: 123616: Held up, late gains: 6lb pen, op 9/2. 1½ 43
115 **JOIN THE PARADE** 206 [12] 4-10-0 (58) D McGaffin (5) 25/1: 3100-7: Held up, rdn/mod gains, no nk 51
threat: 7 mth abs: '99 Leicester wnr (appr h'cap, first win, rtd 59): eff at 10f, tried 14f: acts on firm & gd.
1058 **STEP ON DEGAS** 51 [5] 7-9-7 (51) S Carson (3) 33/1: 200-08: Held up, no room 3f out, held 1f out: abs. shd 44
1760 **TROPICAL BEACH** 12 [11] 7-9-1 (45)(vis) D Watson (7) 14/1: 4-0669: H.U, prog 4f out, no hdwy fnl 2f. 1 37

655

637   **MYSTERIUM 107** [6] 6-9-0 (44) D Young (7) 20/1: 212400: Chsd ldrs 9f: 10th: 4 mth abs: see 383 (AW).nk   35
1707   **CEDAR FLAG 15** [13] 6-8-11 (41) S Finnamore (5) 14/1: 310040: Mid-div, held 2f out: 11th: op 12/1.   1¾   30
1546   **PIPS BRAVE 21** [4] 4-8-13 (43) A Beech (3) 12/1: 024000: Held up, nvr land blow: 12th: op 8/1.   2   29
1745   **LADYWELL BLAISE 13** [17] 3-8-12 (55) J Mackay (5) 14/1: 464060: Prom 1m: 13th, op 12/1, see 334 (6f).   2   37
1788   Haya Ya Kefaah 11 [3] 8-9-5 (49)(vis) R Cody Boutcher (5) 20/1:
1775   Forest Dream 12 [16] 5-9-3 (47) G Sparkes (7) 14/1:
682   Alnajashee 94 [8] 4-10-0 (58)(t) G Baker (5) 40/1:   2011 Pursuivant 2 [19] 6-9-3 (47)(bl) R Fitzpatrick 14/1:
1416   Hathni Khound 28 [15] 4-9-1 (45) J Bosley (5) 25/1:   1546 City Guild 21 [20] 4-9-6 (50) F Keniry (3) 33/1:
1775   Ertlon 12 [18] 10-9-0 (44) S Hitchcott (7) 25/1:
20 ran   Time 2m 15.00   (Mark A Leatham)   R A Fahey Butterwick, Nth Yorks.

2034   **7.20 EBF FILLIES MDN 2YO (D)   5f rnd   Good/Firm   Inapplicable**
£3211   £988   £494   £247

--   **DANEHURST** [8] Sir Mark Prescott 2-8-11 G Duffield 9/2: 1: 2 b f Danehill - Miswaki Belle (Miswaki):   81+
Rdn along chsg ldrs, briefly outpcd over 1f out, drvn & strong run inside last to lead nr fin: op 11/4: Mar foal,
dam lightly rcd mdn: sire a top class sprinter/miler: acts at 5f, 6f looks sure to suit: acts on fast grnd & a
sharp/turning trk: runs well fresh: jockey reported filly sure to impr for this, can rate more highly.
1846   **FIAMMA ROYALE 9** [5] Mrs P N Dutfield 2-8-11 L Newman (3) 15/8 FAV: 42252: 2 b f Fumo Di Londra -   ½   78
Ariadne (Bustino): Led, rdn/prsd & hung right inside last, hdd nr fin: well bckd & clr of rem: see 1522 (C/D).
--   **RENEE** [2] M L W Bell 2-8-11 M Fenton 15/2: 3: 2 b f Wolfhound - Montserrat (Aragon):   4   68+
Dwelt/outpcd in rear, styd on under hands-&-heels riding fnl 2f, no threat to front pair: op 6/1: Jan foal, a 1st foal:
dam a dual 5f juv wnr: handles fast grnd: eye-catching late prog, sure to learn from this & can rate more highly.
1870   **ITS SMEE AGAIN 7** [6] B W Hills 2-8-11 M Hills 100/30: 44: Chsd ldr, rdn/held over 1f out: op 11/4.   1¾   64
1774   **CHOCOLATE FOG 12** [9] 2-8-11 M Roberts 20/1: 05: Dwelt, effort halfway, no impress: see 1774 (6f).   1   62
--   **SIMAS GOLD** [3] 2-8-11 R Brisland (5) 25/1: 6: Chsd ldrs, btn over 1f out: Goldmark filly, Jan foal,   ½   60
cost 10,000 gns, first foal: dam unrcd: sire a high class French 2yo at 1m: with W R Muir.
1424   **MISS DAMINA 28** [1] 2-8-11 G Bardwell 33/1: 07: Chsd ldrs till over 1f out: bhd debut prev.   1¾   56
1166   **CHICARA 44** [7] Craig Williams 25/1: 38: In tch till halfway: op 14/1, 6 wk abs: btr 1166.   5   45
--   **UTMOST** [4] 2-8-11 N Callan 33/1: 9: Dwelt, bhd 2f out: Most Welcome filly, Apr foal: dam a lightly   nk   44
rcd mdn, sire top class at 1m/12f: looks sure to apprec further in time for P Evans.
9 ran   Time 59.70   (Cheveley Park Stud)   Sir Mark Prescott Newmarket, Suffolk.

2035   **7.50 NUFFIELD CLASSIFIED STKS 3YO+ 0-80 (D)   6f rnd   Good/Firm   Inapplicable**
£3753   £1155   £577   £288   3 yo rec 7 lb

1999   **ALPEN WOLF 2** [5] W R Muir 5-9-7 T Quinn 4/1: -31021: 5 ch g Wolfhound - Oatfield (Great Nephew):   85
Led/dsptd lead till went on over 1f out, always holding pursuer inside last, pushed out cl-home: qck reapp:
earlier scored at Bath (class stks): '99 wnr at Brighton & again at Bath (h'caps, rtd 79): '98 scorer at Brighton (3,
sell, h'cap & class stks) & Folkestone (class stks, rtd 71): eff at 5f/sharp 7f: acts on firm & fast grnd, loves a
sharp/undul trk, especially Brighton: gd weight carrier: can force the pace: tough/genuine gelding.
*1842   **CORNDAVON 9** [3] M L W Bell 4-9-4 J Mackay (7) 5/4 FAV: 204012: 4 b f Sheikh Albadou - Ferber's   ¾   80
Follies (Saratoga): Chsd ldrs, rdn/chsd wnr inside last, kept on tho' al held: see 1842 (6f, fillies h'cap).
*1708   **KING SILCA 15** [1] M R Channon 3-8-12 Craig Williams 4/1: 213: 3 b g Emarati - Silca-Cisa (Hallgate):   2   77
Chsd ldrs, rdn/held over 1f out: handles fast grnd, poss best suited by easy grnd: see 1708 (g/s).
1999   **CLASSY CLEO 2** [6] P D Evans 5-9-1 N Callan 12/1: 000464: Held up, rdn/held 2f out: qck reapp.   3½   66
1871   **SYLVA PARADISE 7** [2] 7-9-4 G Duffield 8/1: 00-045: Held up, rdn/no impress final 2f: see 1517.   1¼   66
1564   **ROSE OF MOONCOIN 21** [4] 4-9-1 (bl) J Tate 14/1: 00-666: Led/sn clr, rdn/wknd & hdd over 1f out.   5   53
6 ran   Time 1m 21.30   (R Haim)   W R Muir Lambourn, Berks.

2036   **8.20 VOLVO FILLIES HCAP 3YO 0-65 (F)   6f168y rnd   Good/Firm   Inapplicbale**   [69]
£2436   £696   £348

1877   **RIOS DIAMOND 7** [3] M J Ryan 3-7-12 (39) J Mackay (7) 11/4 FAV: 0-2051: 3 b f Formidable - Rio   42
Piedras (Kalashikari): Held up in tch, rdn/prog to lead inside last, styd on well, rdn out: plcd in '99 (clmr, rtd
42a & 43): eff at 6f, suited by a sharp 7f: acts on fast & fibresand: best without a visor: first win tonight.
1365   **LADY CYRANO 31** [7] Mrs N Macauley 3-8-6 (47) R Fitzpatrick (3) 20/1: 620602: 3 b f Cyrano de   ¾   48
Bergerac - Hazy Kay (Treasure Kay) Hld up, rdn & styd on fnl 2f, not pace of wnr: mdn: see 555, 514 & 283.
1609   **BALLETS RUSSES 19** [2] H J Collingridge 3-8-9 (50) G Carter 8/1: 500-43: 3 b f Marju - Elminya   hd   50
(Sure Blade): Chsd ldrs, styd on onepace final 1f: eff at 7f, return to 1m may suit: handles fast: h'cap bone.
1772   **MISS SPRINGFIELD 12** [5] D Morris 3-8-0 (38)(VIS)(3ow) J Tate 16/1: 00-304: Rdn/towards rear, kept   nk   37
on for press final 2f, no threat: visor: handles fast & gd/soft: see 841.
1780   **KIRSCH 12** [1] 3-9-3 (58)(vis) Craig Williams 12/1: 156005: Rear, late gains final 2f, no threat.   ¾   56
1803   **CLEAR CRYSTAL 10** [4] 3-8-11 (52) M Hills 14/1: 0-6006: Chsd ldrs, onepace 1f out: see 1803, 930.   1½   47
1726   **LIVELY MILLIE 14** [1] 3-8-11 (52) G Duffield 10/1: 000-07: Chsd ldr, no extra over 1f out: see 1726.   hd   46
1438   **SONTIME 28** [8] 3-9-7 (62) M Roberts 7/1: 000-08: Led, hdd/fdd inside last: '99 wnr twice at   nk   55
Lingfield (sell & clmr, rtd 73): eff at 5/6f, return to sprint trips could suit: acts on fast & gd/soft, gall/undul or
sharp trk, likes Lingfield: can force the pace & enjoys sell/claiming grade.
*1710   **PRINTSMITH 15** [6] 3-9-2 (57) G Bardwell 9/2: 00-019: Rdn/prom, btn over 1f out: btr 1710 (C/D, g/s).   5   40
1266   **JENIN 38** [10] 3-7-10 (37)(2oh) G Baker (7) 20/1: 00-00: Held up, keen, al rear: 10th: h'cap bow.   7   9
1334   **BALIDARE 33** [9] 3-8-1 (42) L Newman (3) 9/1: 00-000: Prom, rung right/btn 3f out: 11th: mod form.   24   0
11 ran   Time 1m 23.10   (Rettendon Racing)   M J Ryan Newmarket, Suffolk.

2037   **8.50 THEHORSESMOUTH HCAP 3YO+ 0-65 (F)   1m7f181y   Good/Firm   Inapplicable**   [60]
£3131   £894   £447   3 yo rec 19lb

1736   **RENAISSANCE LADY 14** [2] T R Watson 4-8-10 (42) Craig Williams 12/1: 00-001: 4 ch f Imp Society -   50
Easter Morning (Nice Havrais): Held up, prog to lead over 1f out, readily asserted inside last, pushed out: '99
Brighton scorer (auct mdn, rtd 55): eff at 12f, well suited by this step up to a sharp 2m: loves fast grnd & a sharp/
undul trk: plenty in hand here, could score again in similar company.
1800   **DANGER BABY 11** [11] P Bowen 10-9-2 (48) M Fenton 7/1: 140-62: 10 ch g Bairn - Swordlestown Miss   4   49
(Apalachee): Held up, rdn & styd on final 3f, no threat to wnr: recent jumps rnr (ref, h'cap chase): see 1800.

656

WARWICK MONDAY JUNE 19TH Lefthand, Sharp, Turning Track

1852 **TUI 8** [3] P Bowen 5-8-6 (38) Claire Bryan (5) 9/1: 515403: 5 b m Tina's Pet - Curious Feeling (Nishapour): Chsd ldrs, rdn/led 2f out, sn hdd & held inside last: prob stays a sharp 2m, wng form at 10/12f. 1¾ **37**
2314} **REMEMBER STAR 356** [9] R J Baker 7-7-10 (28) G Sparkes (6) 12/1: 0/00-4: Chsd ldr, cl-up/ev ch over 2f out, held final 1f: Flat reapp, Jumps fit, dual 99/00 Exeter wnr (sell h'cap & nov sell, rtd 70h): only mod form on the level prev, incl with A G Newcombe. *shd* **27**
1874 **NUBILE 7** [10] 6-7-10 (28)(tbl)(8oh) J Lowe 11/2: -60025: Held up, efft wide 4f out, nvr pace to chall. 1½ **25**
1711 **URGENT REPLY 15** [7] 7-7-10 (28)(1oh) J Bramhill 11/1: 0-0006: Chsd ldrs, btn over 1f out: see 1614. 1½ **24**
1800 **SECRET DROP 11** [6] 4-10-0 (60) T E Durcan 25/1: 0-0007: Dwelt/rear, mod late gains: topweight. ¾ **55**
-- **RIVER FRONTIER** [5] 5-8-4 (36) G Baker (7) 9/1: 6516/8: Held up, nvr land blow: Flat reapp, jumps fit, recent N Abbot wnr (sell h'cap, rtd 77h, eff at 2m/2m6f on firm & hvy): missed '99 on the level: '98 Ripon wnr (sell h'cap, rtd 35, rnr-up on sand, rtd 38a, h'cap): eff at 10f on fast & both AWs: has run well fresh. ¾ **30**
1306 **CAPTIVATING 35** [4] 5-7-10 (28)(2oh) J Mackay (7) 50/1: 30/009: Led till 2f out, sn btn: lngr 2m trip. *2* **21**
1465 **GROOMS GOLD 26** [8] 8-7-10 (28)(vis)(1oh) G Bardwell 8/1: 200020: Prom 14f: 10th: btr 1465 (12f). ¾ **20**
1800 **FAST FORWARD FRED 11** [12] 9-9-6 (52) M Roberts 20/1: 0/0-00: Held up, effort 5f out, btn 3f out: 11th: jockey reported gelding finished distressed: see 1800. **0**
1852 **Audacity 8** [13] 4-8-2 (34) L Newman (3) 14/1: 1874 **Global Draw 7** [1] 4-7-10 (28) P M Quinn (3) 5/1 FAV:
13 ran Time 3m 28.10 (Alan A Wright) T R Watson Lambourn, Berks.

2038 9.20 JUHANNAS MDN 3YO+ (D) 1m4f56y Good/Firm Inapplicable
£3107 £956 £478 £239 3 yo rec 14lb

1696 **ANDROMEDES 16** [5] H R A Cecil 3-8-9 T Quinn 8/15 FAV: 3-431: 3 b c Sadler's Wells - Utr (Mister Prospector): Trkd ldr, led over 1f out, rdn clr inside last & eased nr fin, readily: rtd 86 when plcd on sole '99 start: eff at 12f, get further: acts on fast & hvy, sharp/turning or stiff/gall trk: op to further improvement. **82**
1554 **CAPA 21** [4] B W Hills 3-8-9 M Hills 7/4: 22-452: 3 b c Salse - Pippas Song (Reference Point): Led, rdn/hdd over 1f out, position accepted & eased when held inside last: see 1554, 951. *7* **71**
3385} **RYELAND 308** [1] Mrs P Sly 4-9-4 R Perham 25/1: 00-3: 4 b f Presidium - Ewe Lamb (Free State): Keen/prom, outpcd/held final 2f: reapp: rtd 60 at best from 2 starts in '99: lngr 12f may suit in h'caps. *13* **52**
1697 **REPUBLICAN LADY 16** [2] C Drew 8-9-4 P Shea (7) 33/1: -04: Slowly away, left bhd final 2f: lngr trip. *4* **46$**
4 ran Time 2m 41.90 (Mr M Tabor & Mrs John Magnier) H R A Cecil Newmarket, Suffolk.

BRIGHTON MONDAY JUNE 19TH Lefthand, V Sharp, Undulating Track

Official Going FIRM. Stalls: Inside except 1m2f - Outside.

2039 2.15 EURO 2000 MDN AUCT 2YO (F) 5f59y rnd Firm Slow
£2278 £651 £325

-- **DECEITFUL** [6] Sir Mark Prescott 2-8-4 S Sanders 9/2: 1: 2 ch g Most Welcome - Sure Care (Caerleon) Made ev yd, drvn out: op 3/1, debut: 1,000 gns May foal, dam 12f wnr, sire 1m/12f performer: eff over an extended 5f, 6f+ sure to suit: acts on firm grnd & a sharp/undul trk, forcing the pace. **64**
1634 **LONDON EYE 18** [2] K T Ivory 2-7-13 (bl) C Catlin (7) 10/1: 060332: 2 b f Distinctly North - Clonavon Girl (Be My Guest) Prsd wnr & ev ch till onepace inside last: ran to best, eff at 5f on firm grnd in blnks. 1¼ **55**
1577 **CARUSOS 20** [5] E J O'Neill 2-8-6 W Ryan 12/1: 003: 2 b f Be My Guest - Courtisane (Persepolis) Held up, shkn up 2f out, styd on inside last, nrst fin: acts on firm grnd, return to 6f in a seller will suit. *hd* **62**
1124 **PAT THE BUILDER 46** [4] K R Burke 2-8-11 J F Egan 6/1: 54: Prom, ch appr final 1f, same pace & drifted left for press: op 12/1, 7 wk abs: handles firm grnd. *nk* **66**
1507 **FOLEY MILLENNIUM 24** [8] 2-8-8 S Drowne 11/4 FAV: 55: Chsd ldrs, outpcd appr fnl 1f: tchd 6/1: better expected despite finishing last on gd/soft grnd debut: see 1507. 1½ **59**
-- **TIMELESS FARRIER** [7] 2-8-9 J Stack 3/1: 6: Slow away, chsd ldrs halfway, sn not handle camber & btn: op 9/4 on debut: 6,000 gns Timeless Times Mar foal, sprint bred, with B Smart. 1½ **56**
-- **BRITTAS BAY** [3] 2-8-3 P Robinson 7/1: 7: Stumbled 1f, al bhd: op 5/1,debut: 4,500lr gns ldris Mar foal, half-sister to a 6f wnr, sire 7f/10f performer: reportedly not handle the trk: with M Tompkins. *7* **34**
7 ran Time 1m 03.0 (3) (A S Reid) Sir Mark Prescott Newmarket, Suffolk.

2040 2.45 GOLF SELLER 3YO+ (G) 1m rnd Firm Slow
£1943 £555 £277 3 yo rec 10lb

1772 **MUSTANG 12** [10] J Pearce 7-9-4 (bl) T G McLaughlin 14/1: 503061: 7 ch g Thatching - Lassoo (Caerleon) In tch, hdwy 2f out, chall below dist, hard rdn & got up fnl strides: no bid, op 10/1: best in 1st time visor in '99 (h'cap, rtd 49a): rnr-up sev times in '98 (h'caps, rtd 52 & 54a, C Thornton): '97 wnr at W'hampton & Lingfield (h'caps, rtd 49a): eff at 7f/1m: acts on firm, gd/soft, both AWs: best in headgear on sharp trks. **44**
1462 **DOVEBRACE 26** [13] A Bailey 7-9-4 J Bramhill 7/1: 006-32: 7 b g Dowsing - Naufrage (Main Reef) Dwelt, gd prog 3f out & narrow lead ent final 1f, edged left under press, hdd post: clr rem, see 1462. *shd* **43**
1884 **DEMOCRACY 6** [8] P G Murphy 4-9-4 D Harrison 3/1 FAV: 000053: 4 ch g Common Grounds - Inonder (Belfort) Prom, led ent final 2f till below dist, no extra: tchd 5/1, qck reapp: better at shorter?: see 258. 2½ **38**
1819 **RED CAFE 10** [3] P D Evans 4-8-13 J F Egan 9/1: 360004: Well plcd, rdn & ev ch appr final 1f, unable to qckn & hmpd ent final 1f: op 14/1: back in trip, best 854 (h'cap, gd grnd, after 2 yr abs). ½ **32**
1726 **KAMARAZI 14** [9] 3-8-13 P Doe 4/1: 000004: Mid-div, checked appr final 2f, rdn before final 1f, styd on, nvr nr to chall: op 5/2: favoured by the weights on offic ratings but appeared ill at ease on the trk. *dht* **42**
1731 **LAGO DI LEVICO 14** [2] 3-8-13 W Ryan 9/2: 0-1546: Held up, short of room halfway, prog under press 2f out, sn no extra: well clr rem, clmd by D Morris for £5,000: suited by easier grnd?: see 892. 1½ **40**
1884 **BONNIE DUNDEE 6** [14] 4-8-13 (bl) S Carson (5) 14/1: 005007: Keen & led till ent final 2f, fdd. *10* **10**
1511 **TALENTS LITTLE GEM 24** [11] 3-8-3 F Norton 10/1: 00-458: Nvr a factor: see 1336. *3* **4**
1858 **BODFARI SIGNET 8** [7] 4-9-4 (bl) N Pollard 16/1: 000009: Chsd ldrs till appr final 2f: see 1190. ¾ **8**
1732 **REKEN 14** [4] 4-9-4 P McCabe 25/1: 0-0000: Dwelt, nvr in it: 10th: stiff task, no form. 1½ **5**
1889 **VIKING PRINCE 6** [12] 3-8-8 R Mullen 10/1: -00000: In tch till 3f out, eased, fin lame: 11th, qck reapp. 1½ **2**
1884 **Ubitoo 6** [5] 3-8-8 C Rutter 25/1: -- **Just Try Me** [6] 6-9-4 (t) I Mongan (5) 20/1:
1502 **Cinema Point 24** [1] 3-8-8 (BL) S Sanders 14/1:
14 ran Time 1m 35.0 (3) (Chris Marsh) J Pearce Newmarket, Suffolk.

BRIGHTON MONDAY JUNE 19TH Lefthand, V Sharp, Undulating Track

2041 **3.15 ON CLASSIFIED STKS 3YO+ 0-60 (F) 1m2f Firm Slow**
£2331 £666 £333 3 yo rec 12lb

1292 **SHAMAN 35** [2] G L Moore 3-8-10 I Mongan (5) 9/2: 1-2101: 3 b g Fraam - Magic Maggie (Beveled) **63**
Pulled hard, prom, led 2f out, sn hard rdn/prsd, held on gamely: op 7/1: earlier won at Lingfield (AW sell, rtd 66a): '99 wnr at Folkestone (rtd 71, M Channon) & again at Lingfield (sells, rtd 66a): eff at 1m/sharp 10f, tried further: acts on firm, gd grnd, likes equitrack/Lingfield, sharp trks: improving.
1942 **SHARP SPICE 4** [5] D J Coakley 4-9-3 S Sanders 7/1: -44452: 4 b f Lugana Beach - Ewar Empress *shd* **57**
(Persian Bold) Bhd, gd prog on inside rail 2f out & strong chall final 1f, wnr would not be denied: qck reapp, ran close to best: acts on firm & hvy grnd: see 943.
*1331 **SHEER FACE 33** [4] W R Muir 6-9-8 D Harrison 9/4 JT FAV: 654013: 6 b g Midyan - Rock Face (Ballad *1¾* **59**
Rock) Pld hard in tch, rdn ent str, styd on, no impress on ldrs: nicely bckd, fine run at the weights.
951 **CHATER FLAIR 62** [7] A P Jarvis 3-8-8 W Ryan 11/1: -00-04: Prom, no extra appr final 1f: 9 wk abs, *nk* **56**
clr rem: prob stays 10f on firm grnd.
1770 **ESTABELLA 12** [8] 3-8-7 (VIS) N Pollard 8/1: 213055: Pld hard, led, hdd 2f out, fdd: too free in visor. *5* **48**
1730 **COMMON CONSENT 14** [6] 4-9-3 S Whitworth 10/1: 303-06: In tch till ent final 2f, eased: back in trip. *1½* **44**
1785 **LADY JO 11** [3] 4-9-3 P Doe 9/4 JT FAV: 0-6667: In tch wide till 2f out: reportedly not handle firm grnd. *½* **43**
1745 **ARCTIC HIGH 13** [1] 3-8-5 J F Egan 16/1: 230308: Al bhd: see 1040, 610. *¾* **42**
8 ran Time 2m 03.2 (4.4) (Mrs S M Redjep) G L Moore Woodingdean, East Sussex.

2042 **3.45 VICTORCHANDLER HCAP 3YO 0-75 (E) 6f rnd Firm Fair** **[82]**
£2899 £892 £446 £223

1745 **KINSMAN 13** [3] I A Balding 3-8-9 (63)(vis) K Fallon 7/4 FAV: 006231: 3 b g Distant Relative - Besito **68**
(Wassl) Made just about all, found extra when joined appr final 1f: well bckd from 11/4: '99 wnr here at Brighton (nursery, rtd 70 & 62a): eff at 6/7f on firm & soft grnd, prob handles both AWs: suited forcing the pace on this sharp/undulating Brighton trk: wears blnks or visor.
*1508 **DOCTOR DENNIS 24** [6] B J Meehan 3-8-6 (60) D Glennon (7) 4/1: 000212: 3 b g Last Tycoon - Noble *1¼* **61**
Lustre (Lyphard's Wish) Chsd ldrs, prog & strong chall appr final 1f, sn rdn, onepace: in-form, see 1508 (C/D).
1932 **WILLOW MAGIC 4** [5] S Dow 3-8-7 (61) J F Egan 9/1: 504303: 3 b f Petong - Love Street (Mummy's *nk* **61**
Pet) Held up, kept on fnl 1½f, nvr nr to chall: op 6/1, qck reapp, clr rem: eff at 5f/sharp 6f, see 1512, 234.
1783 **CRISS CROSS 11** [4] R Hannon 3-9-7 (75) R Hughes 3/1: 222454: Trkd ldrs, shkn up & slightly short *5* **63**
of room 2f out, unable to qckn, eased dist: bckd from 4/1: btr 1783, see 884.
1891 **TERM OF ENDEARMENT 6** [1] 3-7-11 (51)(1ow)(6oh) F Norton 10/1: 005605: Chsd ldrs 3f: tchd 20/1. *3½* **31**
1925 **TINSEL WHISTLE 5** [2] 3-9-6 (74) P Robinson 3/1: 26-066: Prom, ch 2f out, sn hung badly left & btn. *2* **48**
6 ran Time 1m 09.4 (1.6) (Miss A V Hill) I A Balding Kingsclere, Hants.

2043 **4.15 VC C4 TELETEXT HCAP 3YO+ 0-70 (E) 1m rnd Firm Slow** **[64]**
£2982 £852 £426 3 yo rec 10lb

1496 **TWENTY FIRST 24** [2] G Wragg 4-9-10 (60) D Holland 2/1: 6-0601: 4 ch f Inchinor - Picnicing **62**
(Good Times) Cl-up, led 3f out, hard prsd inside last, rdn out: nicely bckd, slow time, first win: '99 rnr-up (stks, rtd 63): eff at 1m/10f: goes on firm & gd/soft grnd, sharp/undul or gall trk, up with the pace.
1210 **SATWA BOULEVARD 41** [4] P Mitchell 5-7-10 (32)(t)(5oh) D Glennon (5) 33/1: 000002: 5 ch m *hd* **33$**
Sabrehill - Winnie Reckless (Local Suitor) Prom, jnd wnr appr final 1f, sn rdn, edged left, held towards fin: 6 wk abs, stiff task: fine run for new connections, apprec drop back to 1m on firm grnd: see 326.
*1822 **LADY JONES 10** [6] J Pearce 3-8-13 (59) T G McLaughlin 11/10 FAV: 00-013: 3 b f Emperor Jones - *1¾* **56**
So Beguiling (Woodman) Bhd, feeling pace ent str, kept on well final 1f: nicely bckd from 7/4: goes on firm & soft grnd, will probably appreciate a step up to 10f now: see 1822.
1739 **HEIRESS OF MEATH 13** [5] M J Weeden 5-7-11 (33)(1ow)(10oh) F Norton 50/1: 0/3004: Pulled hard, *½* **29**
chsd ldrs, onepace 2f out, styg on fin: stiff task: handles firm grnd: see 1265.
1873 **BROWNS DELIGHT 7** [3] 3-8-6 (52) R Perham 16/1: 440065: Led/dsptd lead till 3f out, fdd: qck reapp. *1½* **45**
93 **FEEL NO FEAR 209** [7] 7-8-12 (48) K Fallon 7/2: 0126-6: Al bhd: new stable, jmps abs (stays 2m on firm). *2½* **36**
1585 **CORAL SHELLS 20** [1] 3-8-6 (52) S Drowne 10/1: 25-007: Chsd ldrs till appr final 2f, drifted left. *¾* **39**
7 ran Time 1m 36.5 (4.5) (Bloomsbury Stud) G Wragg Newmarket, Suffolk.

2044 **4.45 VICTORCHANDLER MDN HCAP 3YO 0-70 (E) 7f rnd Firm Fair** **[74]**
£3178 £908 £454

1745 **ANDYS ELECTIVE 13** [10] J R Jenkins 3-9-0 (60)(VIS) S Whitworth 20/1: -36051: 3 b c Democratic - **64**
English Mint (Jalmood) Made ev yd, came stands rail in str, drvn out: op 14/1, 1st win, unplcd in '99 (rtd 70): eff at 7f on firm & gd grnd: suited forcing the pace on a sharp/undul trk: woken up by visor.
4613} **COLNE VALLEY AMY 226** [4] G L Moore 3-8-4 (50) P Doe 10/1: -000-2: 3 b f Mizoram - Panchellita *1½* **50**
(Pancho Villa) Prom, rdn 2f out, kept on but not get to wnr: tchd 16/1: reapp/h'cap bow: unplcd in '99 (mdn, rtd 58): eff over a sharp/undul 7f on firm grnd.
1855 **DAWNS DANCER 8** [2] G C H Chung 3-9-2 (62) O Urbina 14/1: 42-003: 3 b f Petardia - Cree's Figurine *1* **60**
(Creetown) Chsd ldrs, prog appr final 1f, onepace towards fin: op 10/1: plcd twice in '99 (nov auct stks, rtd 72): half-sister to useful sprinter Royale Figurine: stays 7f, drop back to sprinting should suit: acts on firm/fast grnd.
1789 **WORK OF FICTION 11** [6] R Hannon 3-9-3 (63) R Hughes 12/1: -0444: Held up, rdn 2f out, styd on, *1¾* **57**
nvr dngrs: op 8/1 on h'cap bow: prob handles firm grnd.
1787 **THE ROBSTER 11** [7] 3-9-0 (60) D R McCabe 7/1: -02005: Chsd ldrs, rdn, hung left & onepace appr *½* **53**
final 1f: blnks omitted, tchd 14/1: btr 1333 (C/D mdn).
1333 **LEGENDAIRE 33** [9] 3-9-0 (60) D Holland 5/1: -22436: Al same place: see 1333, 355. *1½* **50**
1889 **CIBENZE 6** [1] 3-9-7 (67) S Drowne 13/8 FAV: 064267: In tch, effort 2f out, no impress: nicely bckd. *1½* **54**
1211 **GROVE LODGE 41** [11] 3-8-1 (47) F Norton 14/1: -00008: Al towards rear: 6 wk abs, op 8/1, see 1024. *1* **32**
1925 **BEST BOND 5** [12] 3-9-6 (66) K Fallon 6/1: -03009: Nvr in it, eased below dist: op 4/1, longer trip. *1* **49**
1388 **MUFFLED 30** [5] 3-9-4 (64) P Robinson 8/1: 40-00: Handy till 2f out, eased towards fin: 10th, h'cap bow. *2½* **42**
720 **EMERALD IMP 86** [3] 3-8-9 (55) R Perham 25/1: 04-60: Sn bhd: 11th, op 14/1, 3 mth abs, h'cap bow. *1½* **30**
11 ran Time 1m 21.7 (1.9) (Mrs Stella Peirce) J R Jenkins Royston, Herts.

Official Going FIRM. Stalls: 5f/2m - Stands Side; Rem - Inside.

2045
2.00 EBF FILLIES MED AUCT MDN 2YO 5f str Firm 19 -05 Slow
£2795 £860 £430 £215

1642 **EASTERN PROMISE** 17 [5] A Berry 2-8-11 J Carroll 9/4: 241: 2 gr f Factual - Indian Crystal (Petong) **71**
Led, strongly prsd appr fnl 1f, styd on gamely & all out to hold on: Apr foal, sister to a 5f sell juv wnr, dam
scored over 5f: eff at 5f on firm & gd/soft, 6f shld suit: handles a sharp trk: battled well today.
1641 **PEYTO PRINCESS** 17 [3] C W Fairhurst 2-8-11 A Culhane 4/5 FAV: 32: 2 b f Bold Arrangement - hd **70**
Bo Babbity (Strong Gale) Chsd wnr, rdn to chall appr fnl 1f, held nr fin: nicely bkcd: acts on firm & gd/soft,
6f shld suit now: capable of wng similar: see 1641.
1659 **CHARTLEYS PRINCESS** 17 [6] K R Burke 2-8-11 W Supple 4/1: -53: 2 b f Princes Sabo - Ethel Knight ½ **69**
(Thatch) Cl-up, joined wnr dist, no extra cl-home: clr rem: imprvd eff here, eff on 5f on firm: see 1659.
1595 **WHARFEDALE CYGNET** 19 [4] W T Kemp 2-8-11 O Pears 20/1: 64: In tch, wknd fnl 2f: see 1595. 10 **49**
1684 **MONICA** 16 [1] 2-8-11 Dale Gibson 50/1: 0045: Al outpcd in last: no form. 6 **37**
5 ran Time 58.7 (1.2) (Mrs B A Matthews) A Berry Cockerham, Lancs.

2046
2.30 MARDI GRAS CLAIMER 3YO+ (F) 7f30y rn Firm 19 -29 Slow
£2394 £684 £342 3 yo rec 9 lb

*1685 **MAMMAS BOY** 16 [13] A Berry 5-9-8 P Bradley (5) 5/2: 004111: 5 b g Rock City - Henpot (Alzao) **53**
Cl-up, led appr fnl 1f, easily went clr ins last, eased cl-home: val 4/5L, nicely bckd: hat-trick completed
after scoring at Redcar (sell) & here at Musselburgh (clmr): '99 wnr at Thirsk (sell) & again at Musselburgh (clmr,
rtd 62), '98 Doncaster (mdn h'cap) & Sandown wnr (clmr, rtd 72): eff at 5/6f, suited by a sharp 7f: acts on firm,
hvy & any trk, loves Musselburgh: best without blnks: in tremendous form, win more sell/clmrs.
1858 **DETROIT CITY** 8 [9] B S Rothwell 5-9-0 W Supple 5/1: 0-4202: 5 b g Distinctly North - Moyhora 2 **38**
(Nashamaa) Chsd ldr, went on appr fnl 2f, hdd over 1f out, not pace of easy wnr: clr rem: tchd 7/1: see 1685.
1724 **UNMASKED** 14 [12] J S Goldie 4-8-7 G Parkin 33/1: 000003: 4 ch f Safawan - Unveiled (Sayf El Arab) 3½ **24**
Trkd ldr, rdn/no extra appr fnl 1f: fair run at the weights, stays 7f on firm: see 798.
1685 **POWER GAME** 16 [11] D A Nolan 7-9-2 V Halliday 66/1: 000-04: Mid-div, rdn to impr 3f out, no extra ¾ **32$**
over 1f out: handles firm & gd/soft: treat rating with caution (offic only 24): see 1685.
3928 **THEOS LAD** 278 [14] 3-8-3 Dale Gibson 25/1: 5060-5: Led, hdd appr fnl 2f, sn wknd: reapp, new ½ **27**
stable: scored on '99 debut at Catterick (seller, rtd 68, R Guest): eff over a sharp 6f, mid-dist bred: runs well
fresh on firm grnd: has prev tried blnks: now with R Allan.
1559 **JUST GOOD FRIENDS** 21 [4] 3-8-3 D Mernagh (3) 50/1: 006: In tch, outpcd 3f out, mod late gains. nk **27**
1629 **GRANITE CITY** 18 [1] 3-8-9 A Culhane 20/1: 0-0007: Sn outpcd, ran on ins last: op 14/1: see 1358. 1 **31**
1760 **BERNARDO BELLOTTO** 12 [6] 5-9-4 (bl) K Hodgson 8/1: 000008: Chsd ldrs, btn fnl 2f: see 386. 1½ **28**
1907 **MONACO 5** [2] 6-8-12 F Lynch 50/1: 0-0009: Dwelt, al in rear: qck reapp. ½ **21**
1578 **DENTON LADY** 20 [3] 3-8-2 (bl) O Pears 16/1: 003000: Front rank, wknd qckly fnl 3f, fin 10th. 9 **6**
2265† **TILER** 359 [7] 8-9-4 J Carroll 5/4 FAV: 1054-P: Prom when broke down badly & p.u. 3f out. **0**
-- **Priestrig Brae** [10] 4-8-7 K Dalgleish (7) 66/1: -- **Serial** [8] 6-8-12 R Lappin 66/1:
13 ran Time 1m 28.4 (3.5) (Mrs J M Berry) A Berry Cockerham, Lancs.

2047
3.00 WIMPEY FANFARE HCAP 3YO 0-70 (E) 5f str Firm 19 +03 Fast [73]
£2938 £904 £452 £226

1662 **POP THE CORK** 17 [13] R M Whitaker 3-9-1 (60) K Dalgleish (7) 10/1: 003001: 3 ch g Clantime - **63**
Hyde Princess (Touch Paper) Trkd ldrs, rdn to lead appr fnl 1f, styd on well, drvn out: bckd from 16/1, best
time of day: 1st win: eff arnd a sharp 5f, has tried 6f: acts on firm & likes to race up with/force the pace.
1817 **MARSHALL ST CYR** 10 [11] J G Given 3-8-12 (57) Dean McKeown 7/1: 005642: 3 ch g Emarati - St nk **59**
Helena (Monsanto) Led, hdd appr fnl 1f, rall ins last, just held: op 5/1: gd run, eff at 5f on firm & gd/soft.
1781 **CAUTIOUS JOE** 12 [8] R A Fahey 3-9-7 (66) R Ffrench 9/2 FAV: 0-0003: 3 b f First Trump - Jomel hd **67**
Amou (Ela Mana Mou) Led stands side, chall ldrs dist, styd on, just held: acts on firm/fast, sharp or gall trk.
1500 **PARADISE YANGSHUO** 24 [12] E J Alston 3-8-1 (46) W Supple 12/1: 00-004: Mid-div, rdn/hdwy ½ **46**
over 2f out, ev ch till no extra well ins last: rnr-up thrice in '99 (seller & clmr for M Channon & nurs, rtd
63 at best): eff around 5f on firm & gd/soft grnd: looks fairly h'capped & could win soon.
1817 **APRILS COMAIT** 10 [4] 3-8-4 (47)(bl) (2ow) V Halliday 12/1: 330005: Front rank, edged right & 1¼ **45**
onepcd appr fnl 1f: tchd 20/1: see 777, 217.
*1817 **LIZZIE SIMMONDS** 10 [6] 3-8-12 (57) N Kennedy 7/1: 455016: Chsd ldrs, rdn/held ins last: see 1817. nk **52**
1817 **BENNOCHY** 10 [14] 3-8-12 (57) O Pears 9/1: 0-1057: Handy, rdn, edged right & onepcd over 1f out. shd **52**
1412 **BRANSTON LUCY** 30 [2] 3-8-12 (57)(hBL) F Lynch 9/1: 31-008: Dwelt, sn outpcd, styd on for press 1 **49**
ins last, nvr nrr: op 7/1 first time blnks: lost chance with slow start here, can do better: see 1138.
1665 **GREY FLYER** 17 [15] 3-8-11 (56) A Culhane 11/2: 205039: Chsd ldrs, btn appr fnl 1f: op 4/1: btr 1665. ½ **47**
1815 **EMMA AMOUR** 10 [5] 3-8-4 (49)(BL) G Parkin 20/1: 5-0000: Mid-div, lost tch halfway, fin 10th: blnkd. 4 **30**
1600 **SPEEDFIT FREE** 19 [3] 3-9-6 (65) J Carroll 16/1: 604-00: Al rear, fin 11th: '99 Yarmouth wnr (nov stks, 1 **43**
G Margarson, rtd 83): likes to force the pace around 6f on fast grnd: has tried blnks: now with M A Buckley.
1742 **Power And Demand** 13 [10] 3-7-13 (44)(bl) D Mernagh (3) 16/1:
1817 **Pack A Punch** 10 [7] 3-7-12 (41)(2ow) Dale Gibson 50/1:
1430 **Pape Diouf** 28 [1] 3-8-2 (47) A Nicholls (3) 16/1: 1562 **Mimandi** 21 [9] 3-7-12 (43)(VIS) P Fessey 25/1:
15 ran Time 58.3 (0.8) (Country Lane Partnership) R M Whitaker Scarscroft, W.Yorks.

2048
3.30 E'BURGH GOLD CUP HCAP 3YO+ 0-75 (E) 1m4f Firm 19 -23 Slow [72]
£8658 £2664 £1332 £666 3 yo rec 14lb

1955 **JULIUS** 4 [5] M Johnston 3-8-12 (70) K Dalgleish (7) 3/1: 36-121: 3 b f Persian Bold - Babushka **80**
(Dance Of Life) Trkd ldrs, hdwy to lead over 2f out, qcknd clr despite hanging badly ins last, pushed out:
nicely bckd, qck reapp: earlier won at Nottingham (stks, reapp/Brit bow): ex-Irish, plcd in a couple of
Fairyhouse mdns (7f, gd grnd): eff at 10/12f on firm & gd, 14f shld suit: runs well fresh on a sharp or gall
trk: showed a useful turn of foot despite still running green, remains on the upgrade & shld win more races.
1432 **SANDABAR** 28 [11] Mrs M Reveley 7-9-1 (59)(t) A Culhane 9/2: 4-0032: 7 b g Green Desert - 5 **60**
Children's Corner (Top Ville) Prom, rdn to chall 2f out, not pace of wnr ins last: gd run against a prog rival.

659

MUSSELBURGH MONDAY JUNE 19TH Righthand, Sharp Track

1777	**WARNING REEF** 12 [7] E J Alston 7-8-13 (57) W Supple 13/2: -45653: 7 b g Warning - Horseshoe Reef (Mill Reef) Mid-div, rdn/hdwy 3f out, held appr fnl 1f: on a fair mark now, but no wins in 2 years.	1¾	55
1936	**COSMIC CASE** 4 [2] J S Goldie 5-7-10 (40)(7oh) Iona Wands (4) 40/1: 504004: Settled rear, rdn to imprv halfway, kept on, nvr with ldrs: clr rem: qck reapp & not disgraced from 7lb o/h: see 1936.	¾	37$
1363	**OCEAN DRIVE** 31 [3] 4-7-13 (43) Dale Gibson 16/1: 0-0565: Chsd ldrs, rdn/not pace of ldrs fnl 3f.	3	36
*1936	**EVENING SCENT** 4 [10] 4-8-10 (54)(6ex) Dean McKeown 10/1: 032016: Set pace, hdd over 2f out, sn hung right & wknd: reportedly lost action: op 7/1, qck reapp: see 1936.	hd	47
1908	**OCTANE** 5 [8] 4-8-5 (49) C Cogan (5) 5/4 FAV: 031327: Prom, saddle slipped early stages, no extra fnl 3f: well bckd, qck reapp: ignore this run, in fine form prev: see 1908.	¾	41
1583	**BOLD AMUSEMENT** 20 [6] 10-9-7 (65) O Pears 25/1: 50-208: Nvr a factor: up in trip: btr 847.	1	55
1860	**RINGSIDE JACK** 8 [4] 4-9-10 (68) P Goode (3) 25/1: 0-1069: Rear, lost tch fnl 3f: top-weight: see 975.	1½	55
1908	**KATIYMANN** 5 [1] 8-7-11 (41)(tBL) D Mernagh (2) 50/1: 01-00P: Bhd 5f out, t.o./p.u. 2f out: sadly died.		0
10 ran	Time 2m 35.7 (5.1) (Mrs K E Daley) M Johnston Middleham, N.Yorks.		

2049	4.00 WIMPEY RIVA HCAP 3YO+ 0-70 (E) 1m1f Firm 19 +01 Fast		[63]
	£2925 £900 £450 £225 3 yo rec 11lb		
963	**AGIOTAGE** 62 [8] S C Williams 4-9-1 (50) F Lynch 7/1: 0-0001: 4 br g Zafonic - Rakli (Warning) Led, qcknd clr over 4f out, styd on strongly despite hanging left ins last, drvn out: bckd from 14/1 after 9 wk abs: 4th at best in '99 for H Cecil (h'cap, rtd 79, tried blnks): '98 Redcar wnr (mdn, rtd 93): eff at 7f/9f, has tried up to 2m: likes to force the pace on firm, gd/soft & a sharp or gall trk: runs shd fresh.		57
-1300	**BOWCLIFFE** 35 [1] E J Alston 4-9-7 (56) W Supple 5/4 FAV: 436022: 9 b g Petoski - Gwuiffina (Welsh Saint) Settled mid-div, rdn/prog 3f out, styd on well appr fnl 1f, held well ins last: nicely bckd, gd run.	¾	61
1583	**SPARKY** 20 [9] M W Easterby 6-9-8 (57)(bl) G Parkin 5/1: 00-203: 6 b g Warrshan - Pebble Creek (Reference Point) Cl-up, drpd rear 3f out, rallied & styd on strongly appr fnl 1f, kept on: op 3/1: see 1583.	¾	60
1777	**TROIS** 12 [7] J G Given 4-9-10 (59) Dean McKeown 8/1: 300504: Settled rear, rdn/late gains, nvr nrr.	2	58
1860	**BRANDON MAGIC** 8 [6] 7-8-12 (47) A Nicholls (3) 5/1: -00305: Front rank, rdn/not pace of ldrs fnl 2f: will apprec a drop back to 1m: see 1860, 497.	1	44
1296	**THATCHED** 35 [3] 10-8-8 (43) P Fessey 8/1: 46-506: Chsd ldrs, rdn/wknd fnl 2f: see 1254.	½	39
1104	**ARIZONA LADY** 47 [2] 3-9-8 (68) O Pears 15/1: 40-107: Keen in rear, nvr a dngr: see 1254.	1¾	61
1921	**QUALITAIR SURVIVOR** 5 [5] 5-8-3 (38)(vis) D Mernagh (3) 10/1: -04608: Handy, fdd fnl 2f: qck reapp.	1	29
1658	**LINCOLN DEAN** 17 [4] 4-8-8 (43) A Culhane 4/1: 40-009: Bhd, lost tch 3f out: nicely bckd: see 1243.	9	19
9 ran	Time 1m 52.3 (1.6) (Stuart C Williams) S C Williams Newmarket.		

2050	4.30 WIMPEY TEMPO APPR HCAP 3YO+ 0-60 (F) 1m6f Firm 19 -40 Slow		[51]
	£2268 £648 £324 3 yo rec 17lb		
1949	**XELLANCE** 4 [3] M Johnston 3-8-5 (45) K Dalgleish (5) 4/1: 151U01: 3 b g Be My Guest - Excellent Alibi (Exceller) Mid-div, rdn to lead appr fnl 1f, pushed clr ins last: nicely bckd, qck reapp: earlier won at Southwell & W'hampton (AW h'caps, rtd 46a): rtd 43 in '99 (unplcd): eff at 11/12f, stays 14f well: acts on firm, fibresand & a sharp trk: runs well fresh.		52
1936	**HILL FARM DANCER** 4 [4] W M Brisbourne 9-9-1 (38) C Cogan (3) 4/1: 511452: 9 ch m Gunner B - Loadplan Lass (Nicholas Bill) Chsd ldr, led over 2f out, hdd over 1f out, not pace of wnr: qck reapp: consistent.	4	39
1686	**NORTHERN MOTTO** 16 [6] J S Goldie 7-10-0 (51) Dawn Rankin (7) 3/1 FAV: 500033: 7 b g Mtoto - Soulful (Zino) Cl-up, drpd rear 3f out, drvn/late hdwy: nicely bckd tho' op 5/2: apprec a return to a sharp 2m.	nk	52
1657	**WINSOME GEORGE** 17 [5] C W Fairhurst 5-9-6 (43)(vis) P Goode (5) 9/1: 233004: Led after 3f, hdd 2f out, wknd: op 7/1: visor reapplied, tried blnks in 1657.	3½	40
1936	**DESERT RECRUIT** 4 [1] 4-9-7 (44) A Nicholls (3) 7/2: 553665: Badly hmpd after 3f, pulled hard & dsptd lead sn after, wknd qckly fnl 3f: op 3/1: qck reapp: ruined chance by refusing to settle here: btr 1683.	9	32
1720	**MIDYAN BLUE** 14 [2] 10-9-5 (42) D Mernagh 10/3: 0/143P: In lead when sadly broke leg & p.u. after 3f.		0
6 ran	Time 3m 04.8 (8.3) (T T Bloodstocks) M Johnston Middleham, N.Yorks.		

WINDSOR MONDAY JUNE 19TH Sharp Fig 8 Track

Official Going GOOD/FIRM. Stalls: Inside. Rnd Crse re-alignment rendered pace figs inapplicable.

2051	6.40 WATERFORD HCAP 3YO+ 0-75 (E) 1m67yrnd Inapplicable Good/Firm		[72]
	£3010 £860 £430 3 yo rec 10lb		
1926	**FUEGIAN** 5 [1] M Madgwick 5-8-12 (56) J Reid 11/2: 60-201: 5 ch g Arazi - Well Beyond (Don't Forget Me) Made all, keeping on for press when saddle slipped ins last, hung on despite jockey being unable to ride a fin cl-home: well bckd: '99 scorer here at Windsor (h'cap, rtd 58): loves to force the pace over a sharp 8.3f, esp here at Windsor: likes firm/fast grnd & eff with/without a visor.		58
*1917	**DENS JOY** 5 [13] Miss D A McHale 4-9-5 (63)(6ex) R Mullen 7/1: 010012: 4 b f Archway - Bonvin (Taufan) Handy, eff to chall just ins fnl 1f, kept on but just failed: fine run under a pen & loves an easy trk.	hd	64
1330	**LEGAL SET** 33 [9] K R Burke 4-9-12 (70) Dane O'Neill 6/1: 0-2003: 4 gr g Second Set - Tiffany's Case (Thatching) Prom, eff to chall over 1f out, kept on for press ins last, just held off in a 3-way photo: gd run.	nk	70
*1794	**PATSY STONE** 11 [12] M Kettle 4-9-11 (69) S Sanders 11/2: -50114: Keen, waited with, eff over 2f out, edged left for press & flashed tail dist, no extra: shade better on easier grnd in 1794 (7f).	1¼	67
3670}	**NO MERCY** 294 [11] 4-9-11 (69)(t) R Hills 9/2 FAV: 3334-5: Prom, eff to chall over 1f out, sn no extra: well bckd on reapp: won reapp in '99, at Lingfield (mdn auct mdn, rtd 77a, plcd on turf, rtd 71): eff at 1m/10f on firm, hvy & equitrack, any trk: has run well fresh & wore a t-strap today: clr of rem, gd reapp.	¾	65
1288	**COLONEL NORTH** 35 [10] 4-9-11 (69) M Henry 11/1: 0-0006: Sn bhd, modest late gains: see 90.	5	56
1666	**BIRTH OF THE BLUES** 17 [6] 4-9-2 (60) N Pollard 14/1: 0-0007: Hld up, eff 3f, no impress: see 1058.	nk	46
1891	**WILEMMGEO** 6 [5] 3-7-13 (53) Joanna Badger (7) 25/1: 050508: Sn bhd, no dngr: best 514 (blnks).	1½	38
1645	**GOT ONE TOO** 17 [4] 3-7-12 (52)(t) A McCarthy (3) 33/1: 00-009: Prom, wknd over 2f out: modest.	¾	33
4518}	**PRINCE OF ARAGON** 237 [2] 4-8-2 (40)(6ow) A Daly 25/1: 0400-0: Al bhd: 10th: in '99 trained by K Ivory, won at Thirsk (mdn, rtd 61): tried blnks & a visor: stays 7f on fast, gd/soft & fibresand.	3½	20
1543	**Mouton** 23 [3] 4-7-10 (40)(8oh) D Kinsella (7) 33/1: 1743 **Tiger Talk** 13 [7] 4-10-0 (72) J Weaver 16/1:		
1606	**Luvaduck** 19 [8] 4-9-5 (63)(VIS) S Drowne 33/1:		
13 ran	Time 1m 42.7 (D Knight) M Madgwick Denmead, Hants.		

WINDSOR   MONDAY JUNE 19TH   Sharp Fig 8 Track

2052   7.05 DAILY TELEGRAPH SELLER 2YO (G)   6f   Good/Firm   Inapplicable
£1865   £533   £266

1667 **FOREST MOON** 17 [6] P D Evans 2-8-6 J F Egan 7/2: 6601: 2 b f Charnwood Forest - Moon Watch (Night   57
Shift) Cl-up, led over 1f out, sn pushed clr, easily: nicely bckd: May foal, cost 10,000gns: enjoyed this
drop into sell grade at 6f on gd/firm grnd.
1553 **IMMACULATE CHARLIE** 21 [5] A T Murphy 2-8-6 A McGlone 9/2: 32: 2 ch f Rich Charlie - Miner's   3 47
Society (Miners Lamp) Chsd ldrs, rdn 2f out, onepace: will appreciate 7f in sell grade: see 1553.
1931 **DIAMOND MILLENNIUM** 4 [3] P D Evans 2-8-6 D Sweeney 10/1: 50533: 2 ch f Clantime - Innocent   hd 46
Abroad (Viking) Cl-up, eff to chall over 1f out, sn onepace: qck reapp, see 1931.
1740 **OUR LITTLE CRACKER** 13 [4] M Quinn 2-8-6 F Norton 20/1: 04: Prom, no impress appr fnl 1f: see 1740. 1 43
1931 **MISSING A BIT** 4 [2] 2-8-11 (bl) J P Spencer 8/1: 445: Led till over 1f out, wknd: qck reapp, see 1554. ¾ 42
1740 **BILLYJO** 13 [7] 2-8-11 Pat Eddery 4/1: 66: In tch, btn 2f out: see 1740.   1¾ 42
1798 **ONLY WHEN PROVOKED** 11 [9] 2-8-11 (VIS) R Havlin 10/1: 07: Slow away & al bhd: Apr foal,   3½ 32
cost IR 3,000gns: tried a visor: with A Streeter.
1589 **OSO NEET** 19 [8] 2-8-11 P Dobbs (5) 5/2 FAV: 068: Prom, rdn & wknd halfway: well bckd & clrly   3 23
better expected on drop to sell grade after 1589 (gd/soft), 1260.
8 ran   Time 1m 14.1   (Mrs Claire Massey)   P D Evans Pandy, Gwent.

2053   7.35 EL CAMINO-REAL HCAP 3YO 0-80 (D)   1m2f   Good/Firm   Inapplicable   [82]
£4179   £1286   £643   £321

1466 **MUSCHANA** 26 [2] J L Dunlop 3-9-5 (73) Pat Eddery 100/30: 532-31: 3 ch f Deploy - Youthful   82
(Green Dancer) Made all, pushed clr over 1f out, easily: plcd fnl 2 '99 starts (rtd 83): eff at 1m, stays 10f
well & 12f will suit: acts on gd/soft, likes gd/firm: lightly raced, qck follow-up likely.
1812 **EASTWOOD DRIFTER** 10 [5] W R Muir 3-8-10 (64) K Fallon 9/4 FAV: -30362: 3 ch c Woodman -   4 65
Mandarina (El Gran Senor) Hld up, eff over 2f out to chase wnr over 1f out, sn outpcd: stays 10f on fast & gd/soft.
1955 **PINHEIROS DREAM** 4 [6] B J Meehan 3-9-0 (68)(BL) D R McCabe 14/1: -50503: 3 ch f Grand Lodge -   2 66
Nikki's Groom (Shy Groom) Chsd wnr till over 1f out, no extra: not disgraced in first time blnks at 10f on fast.
1668 **BOLD GUEST** 17 [3] J W Hills 3-9-7 (75) R Hills 7/1: -0334: Waited with, eff & hung left over 2f   shd 73
out, onepaced: top-weight: prob stays 10f on fast & gd/soft: see 1134.
1935 **JACK DAWSON** 4 [4] 3-8-0 (54) P Doe 3/1: 000W25: Handy, btn over 2f out: btr 1935.   3 48
640 **SPANISH STAR** 107 [1] 3-9-6 (74) F Norton 8/1: 3-5136: Handy, wknd 3f out: long abs, see 640.   15 46
6 ran   Time 2m 06.8   (Aylesfield Farms Ltd)   J L Dunlop Arundel, W.Sussex.

2054   8.05 TOTE SPRINT HCAP 3YO+ 0-80 (D)   6f   Good/Firm   Inapplicable   [77]
£7767   £2390   £1195   £597   3 yo rec 7 lb

*1999 **NINEACRES** 2 [3] J M Bradley 9-9-2 (65)(bl)(6ex) P Fitzsimons (5) 14/1: 221011: 9 b g Sayf El   70
Arab - Mayor (Laxton) Hld up, hdwy over 1f out, sn led, kept on for press to hold on ins last: earlier scored at
Bath (2), W'hampton & Southwell (rtd 58a, h'caps): '99 scorer at W'hampton (clmr, rtd 59a & 42): eff at 5/6f,
stays 7f: likes firm & gd, both AWs, likes W'hampton & Bath: wears blnks or a visor & can force the pace: game
& tough, at the top of his form as a 9yo & a fine credit to his trainer.
1258 **STYLISH WAYS** 38 [8] J Pearce 8-9-0 (63) K Fallon 12/1: 50-062: 8 b g Thatching - Style Of Life   nk 67
(The Minstrel) Switched to stands side, bhd, eff over 1f out, chall ins last, just failed: back to form after
badly drawn twice & h'capped to win off this mark: see 1258, 1074.
2000 **IVORY DAWN** 2 [12] K T Ivory 6-9-7 (70) C Carver (3) 14/1: 022403: 6 b m Batshoof - Cradle Of Love   shd 74
(Roberto) Sn bhd, eff over 1f out, kept on, just held: qck reapp & deserves another win: loves Lingfield/Brighton.
1559 **SIR JACK** 21 [17] D Nicholls 4-8-7 (56) F Norton 12/1: 000244: Handy, effort & slightly short of   2 55
room over 1f out, kept on inside last: acts on fast & gd/soft & on a handy mark: see 905.
1969 **FULL SPATE** 3 [10] 5-9-1 (64) Pat Eddery 15/2: -36035: Slow away & bhd, sn swtchd to stands side,   shd 62
effort & short of room 2f out, late gains: qck reapp on a v handy mark: see 1028.
2000 **DIAMOND DECORUM** 2 [18] 4-9-7 (70) J F Egan 6/1 FAV: 0-6106: Handy, rdn & onepace over 1f out.   hd 67
1794 **BANDBOX** 11 [16] 5-8-13 (62) J Weaver 20/1: 003067: In tch, effort over 1f out, onepace: see 1368.   nk 58
1887 **MIDHISH TWO** 6 [15] 4-9-9 (72) D Harrison 10/1: -00008: In tch, rdn 2f out, modest late gains.   1½ 64
1356 **ANTONIO CANOVA** 31 [5] 4-9-10 (73) P McCabe 10/1: 223-39: Keen cl-up, led over 2f out till over 1f out.   ½ 64
1196 **LAW COMMISSION** 42 [20] 10-9-3 (66) N Pollard 15/2: 000-60: In tch, btn 2f out: 10th, abs, see 1196.   nk 56
1878 **SLUMBERING** 7 [13] 4-9-13 (76)(bl) S Clancy (3) 40/1: 400000: Prom, wknd over 1f out: 11th.   nk 65
1690 **RED DELIRIUM** 16 [11] 4-9-1 (64)(BL) S Drowne 16/1: 200000: In tch, btn 2f out: 12th, tried blnks.   ¾ 51
1953 **BREVITY** 4 [7] 5-8-12 (61)(t) K W Marks 25/1: 060-00: Al bhd: 13th, qck reapp.   ½ 46
*1877 **PERLE DE SAGESSE** 7 [14] 3-8-3 (59)(6ex) A Daly 12/1: 530210: With ldr over 2f out till btn   shd 43
over 1f out: 14th, btr 1877 (fillies h'cap).
1842 **GLOWING** 4 [6] 5-9-12 (75) D O'Donohoe 13/2: 110-20: Nvr a factor: 16th, btr 1842 (fillies h'cap).   0
1953 **DELTA SOLEIL** 4 [19] 8-8-11 (60)(VIS) G Hind 12/1: -00000: Led till over 2f out, wknd qckly into   0
last: 17th, tried a visor, qck reapp: see 1273.
1887 **Rainbow Rain** 6 [9] 6-9-2 (65) P Doe 33/1:   1887 **Loch Laird** 6 [4] 5-10-0 (77) J Reid 16/1:
1471 **Ring Dancer** 26 [1] 5-9-13 (76) A Clark 33/1:
19 ran   Time 1m 11.5   (J M Bradley)   J M Bradley Sedbury, Gloucs.

2055   8.35 DUN & BRADSTREET COND STKS 2YO (C)   5f   Good/Firm   Inapplicable
£5253   £1942   £971   £441

1558 **MUJA FAREWELL** 21 [4] T D Barron 2-8-8 K Darley 2/1 FAV: 1221: 2 ch f Mujtahid - Highland Rhapsody   83
(Kris) Made all, kept on gamely for press fnl 1f, just held: well bckd: earlier scored at Redcar (mdn auct):
dam 6f scorer: enjoyed forcing tactics today at 5f on fast, acts on gd/soft: proving tough & genuine.
1906 **FANTASY BELIEVER** 5 [2] J J Quinn 2-8-11 K Fallon 7/2: -32422: 2 b g Sure Blade - Delicious   nk 85
(Dominion) Chsd ldrs, eff to chall ins last, kept on for press, just held: clr of mrn: qck reapp & improved.
1589 **JACK SPRATT** 19 [3] R Hannon 2-8-11 Dane O'Neill 11/4: 033: 2 b c So Factual - Raindancing (Tirol)   4 75
Chsd wnr, ev ch till onepcd appr final 1f: rtd higher on gd/soft in 1589.
1813 **FLUMMOX** 10 [1] M Johnston 2-8-13 J Fanning 3/1: 134: Sn rdn & nvr a factor: btr 1813, 1522 (hvy).   5 63
1328 **MISSING DRINK** 33 [5] 2-8-11 Joanna Badger (7) 66/1: 05: Al bhd: Apr foal, half-brother to a 1m wnr.   3½ 52

661

WINDSOR MONDAY JUNE 19TH Sharp Fig 8 Track

5 ran   Time 59.4   (T Hollins, P Huntbach, D Rutter, W Carson)   T D Barron Maunby, Nth Yorks.

2056   9.05 DUNLOE MDN 3YO+ (D)   1m2f   Good/Firm   Inapplicable
£2951   £908   £454   £227   3 yo rec 12lb

1565} **JANET 390** [10] G C H Chung 3-8-8 O Urbina 7/2: 52-1: 3 b f Emperor Jones - Bid Dancer (Spectacular   74
Bid) Led 1f, led again 4f out, drew clr appr fnl 1f, eased cl-home: val 5L+ on reapp: in '99 trained by A Kelleway,
rnr-up (rtd 74): dam 1m scorer: apprec this big step up to 10f, further will suit: acts on gd/firm grnd: runs
well fresh: open to further improvement & should go in again in this form.
1062 **SPELLBINDER 49** [5] G B Balding 4-9-6 S Drowne 7/4 FAV: 0-322: 4 b f Magical Wonder - Shamanka   1¾   70
(Shernazar) In tch, eff over 2f out, sn hung left & not pace of wnr: 7 wk abs & stays 10f: acts on gd/soft & soft.
1200 **SHAREEF KHAN 42** [6] N A Graham 3-8-13 D Holland 6/1: 0-03: 3 b g Alzao - Sharenara (Vaigly Noble)   ½   74
Cl-up, rdn over 1f out, onepace: 6 wk abs & prob stays 10f: dam stoutly bred & mid-dist h'caps will suit.
4524} **BOLD PRECEDENT 236** [12] P W Harris 3-8-13 J Weaver 8/1: 0-4: Slow away, bhd, eff over 3f out,   hd   73
onepace: clr of rem on reapp: well btn sole jur start: half-brother to a useful 10f wnr: come on plenty for this.
1697 **SHINGHAAR 16** [1] 3-8-13 K Darley 14/1: -005: Led after 1f till 4f out, no extra: mid-dist bred gelding.   7   61
-- **WESTERN BAY** [7] 4-9-11 S Whitworth 25/1: 0-6: In tch, no impress final 3f: well btn in Sweden   3   56
on sole '99 start: with D Arbuthnot.
-- **QUEEN OF FASHION** [4] 4-9-6 D R McCabe 50/1: 7: Nvr a factor: Barathea filly.   2   48
-- **HOPEFUL** [13] 3-8-8 A McGlone 7/1: 8: Dwelt, al bhd: Elmaamul filly, with H Candy.   4   42
1281 **TENACIOUS MELODY 37** [9] 4-9-11 T G McLaughlin 66/1: 009: Al bhd: see 1281.   4   41
-- **SHERVANA** [11] 4-9-6 R Studholme (5) 33/1: 0: Prom, wknd 3f out: 10th: well btn in a recent bmpr.   ¾   35
-- Into The Clouds [8] 4-9-6 R Price 33/1:   1523 Princess Senorita 23 [3] 5-9-6 J Fanning 40/1:
-- Herring Green [2] 3-8-13 S Carson (5) 25/1:
13 ran   Time 2m 09.4   (Osvaldo Pedroni)   G C H Chung Newmarket.

THIRSK TUESDAY JUNE 20TH Lefthand, Flat, Oval Track

Official Going: FIRM. Stalls: Round Course - Inside, Straight Course - Stands side

2057   2.15 J COWAP MED AUCT MDN 2YO (F)   7f rnd   Good/Firm 23   -30 Slow
£3006   £925   £462   £231

1882 **PERSIAN CAT 7** [12] Sir Mark Prescott 2-8-9 S Sanders 13/8 FAV: 51: 2 b f Persian Bold - Echo Cove   72
(Slip Anchor) Soon cl up, rdn/led 3f out, styd on well fnl 1f, drvn out: hvly bckd: confirmed promise of debut:
apprec this step up to 7f, bred to apprec further: acts on fast grnd: going the right way.
1667 **MAID OF ARC 18** [1] M L W Bell 2-8-9 A Culhane 11/2: 02: 2 b f Patton - Holy Speed (Afleet)   1¼   68
Chsd ldrs, rdn/prog to ch wnr 2f out, kept on for press Wd' al just held: bckd: left debut bhd over this longer
7f trip: April foal, cost $37,000: dam a North American wnr: apprec this step up to 7f, handles fast grnd.
1602 **YOUNG JACK 20** [5] W Jarvis 2-9-0 D McGaffin (5) 5/1: 523: 2 b c Reprimand - Chadenshe (Taufan)   1¾   70
Chsd ldrs, rdn to chase front pair fnl 2f, held inside last: op 4/1: styd longer 7f trip, handles fast & soft grnd.
1503 **SIENA STAR 25** [3] J L Eyre 2-9-0 R Cody Boutcher (7) 14/1: -0044: Mid div, rdn & kept on fnl 2f,   ½   69
not pace to threaten: styd this longer 7f trip, handles fast grnd: nursery h'caps should suit.
1476 **PETIT TOR 26** [2] 2-8-9 O Pears 9/1: -0425: Prom, onepace fnl 2f: op 8/1: see 1476 (6f).   3   58
-- **NO SURRENDER** [8] 2-8-9 R Winston 14/1: 6: Dwelt, rear, hdwy 3f out, no prog fnl 1f: Brief Truce   shd   58
filly, March foal, cost 11.000gns: half sister to a 10f wnr, dam a mdn: sire top class at 1m/10f: will need 1m+.
1870 **SPRINGWOOD JASMIN 8** [14] 2-8-9 (t) K Dalgleish (7) 33/1: 0567: Chsd ldrs 5f: longer 7f trip.   5   48
-- **LATE AT NIGHT** [4] 2-9-0 T E Durcan 6/1: 8: Dwelt/bhd, late prog: op 9/2: March foal, cost   1¼   50
$6,000: half brother to 2 juv US wnrs: dam a mdn, sire useful 7f/1m Irish performer: with T D Barron.
-- **RISING PASSION** [6] 2-9-0 F Norton 16/1: 9: Prom, fdd fnl 2f: op 14/1: General Monash gelding,   2½   45
April foal, 7,000gns 2yo: dam half sister to high class sprinter Soba, sire a speedy juvenile.
-- **MARY HAYDEN** [10] 2-8-9 A Daly 14/1: 0: Led 4f, soon btn: 10th: Imp Society filly, March foal, dam   4   32
unraced, a half sister to a smart 1m/10f performer: with W G M Turner.
1503 **ALNAHIGHER 25** [11] 2-8-9 D Holland 11/2: -6520: Al bhd: 13th: op 4/1: btr 1503, 1252 (5/6f).   0
1488 **Darwin Tower 25** [7] 2-9-0 J Fanning 25/1:   1659 Pentagon Lady 18 [9] 2-8-9 G Parkin 20/1:
13 ran   Time 1m 26.6 (3.7)   (Mrs C R Phillipson)   Sir Mark Prescott Newmarket

2058   2.50 DAVID AND ELLY MDN 3YO (D)   7f rnd   Good/Firm 23   -04 Slow
£4205   £1294   £647   £323

1495 **HADATH 25** [4] M A Buckley 3-9-0 Dean McKeown 13/2: -00561: 3 br g Mujtahid - Al Sylah (Nureyev)   80
Made all, rdn/strongly prsd fnl 2f, al just holding rival, drvn out: '99 rnr up for M Tregoning (rtd, 91 nov stks):
eff at 7f on firm, soft & a gall/flat track: can force the pace & has run well fresh: eff with/without a visor.
1853 **NIGHT SIGHT 9** [3] G Wragg 3-9-0 D Holland 1/4 FAV: 002232: 3 b c Eagle Eyed - El Hamo (Search   ¾   78
For Gold) Bhd ldrs, chall 2f out going best, soon rdn & held inside last: hvly bckd at long odds on: see 1853 (1m).
-- **CONDOR HERO** [1] W Jarvis 3-9-0 F Norton 7/1: 3: 3 b g Catrail - Rince Deas (Alzao)   5   68
Dwelt, soon in tch, outpcd by front pair fnl 2f: op 5/1: debut: half brother to wnrs between 6f/1m.
-- **SUPER DOMINION** [2] M J Quinn (3) 25/1: 4: Bhd 3f out: debut: dam a 12f   9   54
hurdles wnr: half brother to winning 5/7f h'capper Santante.
1922 **ANNAKAYE 6** [5] G Parkin 50/1: 005: Cl up, hung right/btn 3f out: mod form.   1¼   46$
5 ran   Time 1m 24.8 (1.9)   (Mrs D J Buckley)   M A Buckley Upper Helmsley, N Yorks

2059   3.25 THEHORSESMOUTH SELLER 2YO (G)   6f   Good/Firm 23   -40 Slow
£2702   £772   £386

1876 **MILLTIDE 8** [6] R Guest 2-8-6 J Mackay (7) 4/5 FAV: 41: 2 b f Pyramus - Sea Farer Lake (Gairloch)   67
Dwelt & held up, steady prog halfway, led over 1f out, took command cl home, pushed out: sold for 7,200gns, will
join J Eyre: hvly bckd: eff at 6f, 7f+ shld suit: acts on fast grnd & appreciated this drop to selling grade.
1838 **MISS EQUINOX 10** [3] N Tinkler 2-8-6 Kim Tinkler 10/1: 502: 2 b f Presidium - Miss Nelski (Most   2½   61
Secret) Prom, rdn & kept on fnl 1f, not pace of wnr: op 8/1: eff at 6f on fast, could find one of these: see 1838.

662

1890 **BULA ROSE 7** [1] W G M Turner 2-8-6 A Daly 5/2: -523: 2 ch f Alphabatim - Titled Dancer (Where To Dance) Towards rear/rdn bef halfway, kept on fnl 2f, no threat to wnr: well bckd, op 3/1: eff at 6f, return to 7f should suit: acts on fast & gd grnd: see 1890. *nk* **60**
928 **PREMIER LASS 66** [4] B S Rothwell 2-8-6 J Bramhill 33/1: -004: Chsd ldrs, ch/hung left over 1f out, soon held: 2 month abs: improved eff at 6f on fast grnd: only mod form prev. *shd* **60**
1918 **SHADALHI 6** [2] 2-8-6 S Sanders 20/1: 05: Led till over 1f out, no extra: clr rem: op 14/1. *hd* **59**
1937 **CONSPIRACY THEORY 5** [8] 2-8-6 O Pears 10/1: 6346: Bhd halfway: op 8/1: btr 1684 (5f). *13* **35**
1359 **NETTLES 32** [5] 2-8-11 (bl) R Winston 50/1: 0007: Prom, wknd 2f out: longer 6f trip, mod form. *1½* **37**
1679 **PROPERTY ZONE 17** [9] 2-8-11 G Parkin 25/1: 08: Slowly away, al bhd: no form. *7* **24**
-- **SILK SOUK** [7] 2-8-6 P Bradley (5) 12/1: 9: Dwelt, soon bhd: op 25/1: Dancing Spree filly, March foal, a first foal: dam a lightly raced mdn with R D Wylie. *1½* **15**
9 ran Time 1m 13.3 (3.8) (C J Mills) R Guest Newmarket

2060

4.00 LADY AMAT RIDERS HCAP 3YO 0-70 (E) 6f Good/Firm 23 -22 Slow [48]
£2827 £870 £439 £217

1768 **LORD OMNI 13** [13] T D Barron 3-11-5 (67) Mrs F Needham 6/1: 604-61: 3 ch c El Prado - Muskoka Ice (It's Freezing) Mid div, prog halfway, styd on well to lead inside last, rdn out: op 8/1: first win: 4th on last of 3 juv starts in '99 (rtd 64): eff at 6f on fast grnd. **72**
1600 **DESRAYA 20** [14] K A Ryan 3-10-6 (54)(bl) Miss P Robson 9/1: 0-0602: 3 b g Desert Style - Madaraya (Shahrastani) Handy, led halfway till inside last, held cl home: eff at 6f, handles fast & gd/soft: eff in blinks. *¾* **56**
1780 **MARON 13** [6] A Berry 3-10-7 (55) Miss E J Jones 25/1: 00-003: 3 b g Puissanace - Will Be Bold (Bold Lad) Chsd ldrs, prog & every ch inside last, held near fin: eff at 5/6f: see 1368. *½* **55**
*1734 **UNFORTUNATE 15** [3] Miss J F Craze 3-10-3 (51)(bl) Miss H Webster (5) 9/1: 060014: Chsd ldrs, no extra inside last: op 8/1: acts on fast, gd/soft & fibresand: see 1734 (selling h'cap). *hd* **50**
1891 **DISTINCTLY BLU 7** [4] 3-11-1 (63) Miss E Ramsden 11/4: -61625: Led 3f, fdd fnl 1f: op 9/4, shorter priced stablemate of rnr up: see 1891, 901 (5f). *3½* **53**
1768 **WELCOME TO UNOS 13** [10] 3-11-7 (69) Miss E Folkes (5) 25/1: 502-06: In tch, outpcd halfway, kept on fnl 1f, no threat: 7f+ could suit on this evidence: see 1768. *1½* **55**
2017 **BEWILDERED 2** [1] 3-9-6 (40) Miss A Deniel 25/1: 500067: Mid div, held 2f out: qck reapp: see 2017. *¾* **24**
*1723 **BENBYAS 15** [9] 3-11-1 (63)(vis) Miss Diana Jones 9/1: 0-0618: Dwelt, nvr factor: op 8/1: btr 1723. *½* **45**
1891 **COLLEGE MAID 7** [5] 3-11-3 (65) Mrs C Williams 9/2: 211259: In tch, wknd 1f out: op 10/3: btr 1665. *hd* **46**
4476} **PRIDE OF PERU 242** [11] 3-10-4 (52) Mrs S Eddery (5) 20/1: 0000-0: Mid div, btn 2f out: 10th: reapp: unplcd last term (rtd 67, mdn): h'cap bow today. *1½* **30**
*1818 **COMEX FLYER 11** [12] 3-10-8 (56) Mrs S Bosley 6/1: 060010: Dwelt, al rear: 13th: op 5/1: btr 1818 (7f). **0**
1349 **Pardy Pet 33** [2] 3-9-11 (45)(BL) Miss Joanna Rees (7) 25/1:
1606 **Mount Park 20** [8] 3-10-10 (58)(bl) Miss R Clark 20/1:
13 ran Time 1m 12.2 (2.7) (Peter Jones) T D Barron Maunby, N Yorks

2061

4.35 RACINGPOST.CO.UK HCAP 3YO+ 0-80 (D) 1m4f Good/Firm 23 -47 Slow [66]
£3971 £1222 £611 £305 3 yo rec 14lb

2002 **FATEHALKHAIR 3** [2] B Ellison 8-9-10 (62) F Norton 4/5 FAV: -40231: 8 ch g Kris - Midway Lady (Alleged) Bhd ldrs, qcknd to lead over 1f out, styd on well, rdn out: slow time, hvly bckd from 11/10, qck reapp: rtd 120h over timber in 99/00 (Gr 2): '99 Flat wnr at Redcar, Catterick (2) & Thirsk, (h'caps, rtd 64 & 46a): plcd in '98 (rtd 38): gd weight carrier: suited by 12/13f on firm, soft & fibresand, any trk. **66**
3728} **ILE DISTINCT 292** [3] Mrs A Duffield 6-9-8 (60) S Sanders 6/1: 2403-2: 6 b g Dancing Dissident - Golden Sunlight (Ile de Bourbon) In tch, prog to chase wnr fnl 1f, kept on: rnr up last term (rtd 67, h'cap): '97 wnr at Musselburgh (rtd mdn) & Nottingham (ltd stks, rtd 73): eff at 1m/12f on fast & a sharp/stiff trk. *1½* **61**
1705 **BUTTERSCOTCH 16** [5] J L Eyre 4-8-11 (49) R Lappin 6/1: 0-0033: 4 b g Aragon - Gwiffina (Welsh Saint) Held up, switched for eff over 1f out, kept on but not pace of wnr: op 9/2: see 1705, 248 (mdn). *1½* **48**
*1816 **HASTA LA VISTA 11** [4] M W Easterby 10-8-12 (50)(vis) G Parkin 3/1: -10214: Led, drvn fnl 3f & hdd over 1f out, sn held: op 7/4: see 1816. *hd* **48**
1683 **BOLT FROM THE BLUE 17** [1] 4-8-6 (44) Kim Tinkler 12/1: 40-005: Cl up, outpcd/held over 1f out. *1½* **40**
5 ran Time 2m 38.2 (8.4) (R Wagner) B Ellison Lanchester, Co Durham

2062

5.10 JULIA BOOTH FILLIES HCAP 3YO+ 0-90 (C) 1m rnd Good/Firm 23 -10 Slow [75]
£6500 £2000 £1000 £500 3 yo rec 10lb

1873 **POPPADAM 8** [2] J R Fanshawe 3-9-2 (73) O Urbina 13/8 FAV: 0-6521: 3 ch f Salse - Wanton (Kris) Chsd ldrs, rdn/prog to lead inside last, styd on well & pushed out cl home: hvly bckd though op 5/4: 1st win: eff at 1m on fast & gd grnd: op to further improvement. **79**
1496 **FALLS OMONESS 25** [4] E J Alston 6-8-2 (49) J Bramhill 8/1: 0-2002: 6 b m River Falls - Sevens Are Wild (Petorius) Dwelt, waited with rear, steady prog for press fnl 2f, nrst fin: acts on fast & firm, enjoys soft/hvy. *¾* **51**
4110} **PICTURE PUZZLE 268** [1] W J Haggas 4-9-11 (72) J P Spencer 9/2: 0616-3: 4 b f Royal Academy - Cloudslea (Chief's Crown) Cl up, led over 2f out, rdn/hdd inside last & no extra: reapp: '99 wnr here at Thirsk (mdn), Yarmouth (fill h'cap) & Newcastle (h'cap, rtd 74): eff at 7f/1m on firm, fast, stiff/gall or fair track. *shd* **74**
1842 **PERFECT PEACH 10** [5] C W Fairhurst 5-9-4 (65) J Fanning 10/1: -00004: Dwelt, held up in tch, eff/prog 2f out, held fnl 1f: stays 1m, suited by 7f: see 1250. *2* **63**
1879 **MINETTA 8** [3] 5-10-0 (75) J Mackay (7) 7/2: 110-65: Chsd ldrs, rdn/no prog over 1f out: op 4/1. *1½* **70**
1308 **BELLA BELLISIMO 35** [6] 3-9-9 (80) R Winston 9/1: 35-006: Held up, rdn/btn 2f out: see 874. *1½* **72**
1680 **HI NICKY 17** [7] 4-8-7 (54) A Culhane 14/1: 0-0007: Led till over 2f out, fdd: unplcd last term (rtd 83, Listed, M J Ryan): '98 sole start wnr at Newmarket (fill mdn): eff at 6f on fast grnd: has run well fresh. *½* **45**
1303 **TIME TEMPTRESS 36** [8] 4-8-13 (60) K Dalgleish (7) 12/1: 06-008: Cl up 6f: op10/1: see 1303 (AW). *½* **50**
8 ran Time 1m 38.00 (2.6) (Lady Halifax) J R Fanshawe Newmarket

2063

5.40 N YORKS TONIGHT HCAP 3YO+ 0-70 (E) 7f rnd Good/Firm 23 +04 Fast [68]
£3646 £1122 £561 £280 3 yo rec 9 lb

1296 **TORNADO PRINCE 36** [13] E J Alston 5-9-6 (60) T E Durcan 12/1: 000-01: 5 ch g Caerleon - Welsh Flame (Welsh Pageant) Rear, stdy prog fnl 2f & led ins last, styd on well, rdn out: best time of day: '99 scorer at Ripon, Thirsk & Pontefract (sells & sell h'cap, rtd 67): '98 Folkestone wnr (h'cap, N Callaghan): suited by 7f/ **65**

THIRSK TUESDAY JUNE 20TH Lefthand, Flat, Oval Track

1m, stays 9.5f: needs firm & gd grnd, handles any trk: did well to overcome poor high draw & cld follow up.
1598 **HAKEEM 20** [2] M Brittain 5-9-7 (61) D Mernagh (3) 9/2 FAV: 20-022: 5 ch g Kefaah - Masarrah *1½* **62**
(Formidable) Chsd ldrs, prog to lead over 1f out, hdd inside last & no extra: nicely bckd, op 7/1: see 1598.
2027 **ACID TEST 2** [8] M A Buckley 5-9-10 (64) R Fitzpatrick (3) 14/1: 630003: 5 ch g Sharp - Clunk *hd* **64**
Click (Star Appeal) Chsd ldrs, prog/ch 1f out, not pace of wnr: quick reapp: see 525 (AW, 7f).
1887 **MILADY LILLIE 7** [9] K T Ivory 4-8-13 (53) Dean McKeown 12/1: 000204: Mid div, kept on fnl 2f for press. *½* **52**
1603 **SHAANXI ROMANCE 20** [3] 5-8-7 (47)(vis) R Price 11/1: 250055: Dsptd lead 2f out, fdd fnl 1f: op 7/1. *1¼* **43**
1011 **INTRICATE WEB 57** [1] 4-9-12 (66) S Sanders 12/1: 1-6006: Dwelt/towards rear, prog to chase ldrs *5* **52**
over 1f out, no hdwy fnl 1f: op 10/1, stablemate of wnr, 8 wk abs: see 623.
1387 **ENTITY 31** [11] 3-9-1 (64)(BL) J P Spencer 8/1: 000307: Mid div, no hdwy 2f out: blinks: op 10/1. *nk* **49**
1213 **UNCHAIN MY HEART 42** [7] 4-8-13 (53)(bl) D Holland 12/1: -16308: Handy, led over 2f out till over *nk* **37**
1f out, no extra: 6 week abs: blinks reapp: btr 616 (AW).
1611 **DANDY REGENT 20** [6] 6-9-6 (60) K Dalgleish (7) 10/1: -10109: Led till over 2f out, fdd: see 1351 (C/D). *2* **40**
1778 **ONLY FOR GOLD 13** [15] 5-9-3 (57) J Mackay (7) 7/1: -66230: Rear, never on terms: 10th: see 780. *shd* **37**
2015 **MUKARRAB 2** [16] 6-8-12 (52) A Culhane 12/1: 360100: Bhd, mod gains: 11th: qck reapp: needs 5/6f. *¾* **31**
*1920 **MEHMAAS 6** [4] 4-9-12 (66)(vis)(6ex) R Winston 9/1: -03410: Mid div at best: 12th: 6lb pen for 1920. *2½* **40**
1583 **LOVE KISS 21** [5] 5-8-10 (50) J Fanning 12/1: 600-00: Chsd ldrs 6f: 16th: broke a blood vessel: op 9/1. **0**
1842 **Saffron 10** [10] 4-9-0 (54) F Norton 14/1: 1920 **Santandre 6** [12] 4-8-12 (52) P M Quinn (3) 14/1:
1680 **Hyde Park 17** [14] 6-9-0 (54) O Pears 11/1:
16 ran Time 1m 24.2 (1.3) (Mrs J R Ramsden) E J Alston Longton, Lancs

ROYAL ASCOT TUESDAY JUNE 20TH Righthand, Stiff, Galloping Track

Official Going GOOD TO FIRM. Stalls: Straight Course - Stand Side, Round Course - Inside.
A class adjustment of +20 was added to each pace figure to compensate for the high-class of runners at this meeting.

2064

2.30 GR 2 QUEEN ANNE STKS 3YO+ (A) 1m str Good 45 +13 Fast
£72000 £27600 £13800 £6600 3 yo rec 10lb

-1291 **KALANISI 36** [11] Sir Michael Stoute 4-9-2 K Fallon 11/2: 111-21: 4 b c Doyoun - Kalamba (Green **122**
Dancer) Bhd, rdn after 3f, prog appr fnl 2f, ran on strongly to lead fnl 100y: fast time, nicely bckd: unbtn
in 3 '99 starts for L Cumani, at Folkestone (mdn), Newmarket (stks, rtd 112) & Kempton (List): eff at 1m, 10f shld
suit: acts on firm & soft, any trk: runs well fresh: high-class, lightly raced colt, should win in Group 1 company.
*1123 **DANSILI 50** [5] A Fabre 4-9-5 O Peslier 10/3: 33-112: 4 b c Danehill - Hasili (Kahyasi) *½* **123**
Chsd ldrs, rdn to lead appr dist, hdd fnl 100y, kept on, just btn: hvly bckd French raider, 7 week abs: ran to
best in defeat giving wnr 3lbs: high class & most consistent colt: see 1123.
*1567 **SWALLOW FLIGHT 22** [2] G Wragg 4-9-2 M Roberts 11/1: 4-2113: 4 b c Bluebird - Mirage (Red *shd* **120**
Sunset) Mid-div, hdwy 2f out, every ch inside last, held towards fin: clr rem: taking a big step up in grade
& much improved: must win a Group race in this form: see 1567 (rtd h'cap).
+1402 **ALJABR 31** [4] Saeed bin Suroor 4-9-7 R Hills 9/4 FAV: 214-14: Trkd ldr, led briefly 2f out, no extra *3½* **119**
& drifted right: hvly bckd under top-weight: ideally suited by firm/fast, made all in 1402 (Gr 1).
1402 **SUGARFOOT 31** [3] 6-9-2 Pat Eddery 14/1: 25-155: Chsd ldrs, eff over 2f out, not clr run & rdn *2½* **109**
bef dist, no impression: op 11/1: return to Group 3 will suit: loves Doncaster & York: see 1402, 1049.
*1460 **MUHTATHIR 30** [7] 5-9-7 W Supple 20/1: 14-316: Set gd clip till hdd 2f out, fdd & hmpd: clr rem. *nk* **113**
1402 **INDIAN LODGE 31** [10] 4-9-5 M J Kinane 12/1: 1-1137: Well plcd, eff appr fnl 2f, soon btn: *7* **99**
nicely bckd: not his form: possibly needs a break: see 1402 (Gr 1), 1043.
*1825 **GOLDEN SILCA 11** [8] 4-8-13 S Drowne 14/1: 2-0418: Never near ldrs: op 9/1, see 1825 (Listed). *2½* **88**
1847 **RAMOOZ 10** [6] 7-9-2 R Hughes 50/1: 6-4539: Al bhd: highly tried, see 1163. *½* **90**
1291 **SHOWBOAT 36** [1] 6-9-2 M Hills 20/1: 0-0630: Al towards rear: 10th, stable not firing. *3* **84**
1154 **HASTY WORDS 46** [9] 4-8-13 J Reid 66/1: 6-1640: Soon struggling: last, 7 week abs, stiff task, see 703. *19* **51**
11 ran Time 1m 39.68 (0.98) (H H Aga Khan) Sir Michael Stoute Newmarket, Suffolk

2065

3.05 GR 2 KING'S STAND STKS 3YO+ (A) 5f Good 45 -18 Slow
£81000 £31050 £15525 £7425 3 yo rec 6 lb 2 Groups, centre always holding stands side

*1747 **NUCLEAR DEBATE 17** [22] J E Hammond 5-9-2 G Mosse 16/1: 20-611: 5 b g Geiger Counter - I'm An **122**
Issue (Cox's Ridge) Mid-div centre, prog 2f out, led below dist, rdn out, readily: nicely bckd French raider:
earlier won at Chantilly (Gr 2): '99 wnr at M Laffitte, Deauville (List) & San Siro (Gr 3, rtd 113): in '98 won
at Thirsk (mdn) & Newcastle: v eff at 5f, stays 6f on gd & hvy, handles fast: high-class, keep on your side.
4246} **AGNES WORLD 261** [23] Hideyuki Mori 5-9-5 Y Take 16/1: 112-32: 5 b h Danzig - Mysteries (Seattle *1½* **120**
Slew) Prom centre, prog & every ch dist, kept on but not pace of wnr: nicely bckd Japanese raider, 3 mnth abs:
won 4 last term, notably at Longchamp (Gr 1, rtd 120): eff at 5/6f on firm & hvy: v tough & smart.
766 **BERTOLINI 87** [8] Saeed bin Suroor 4-9-2 (vis) J Bailey 7/1: 320-23: 4 b h Danzig - Aquiliegia *¾* **115**
(Alydar) Prom stands side, rdn & hung right 1f out, kept on: well bckd tho' op 11/2, 3 month abs: fair run
over what was an inadequate trip, win more Group races at 6f+: see 766 (dirt).
1566 **IMPERIAL BEAUTY 22** [4] P J Makin 4-8-13 Pat Eddery 7/1: 012-44: In tch stands rail, not clrst of *hd* **112**
runs 2f out, switched & ran on und press, nvr nrr: nicely bckd: better run: will relish Listed/Gr 3.
1566 **EASTERN PURPLE 22** [5] 5-9-2 F Lynch 66/1: -03005: Chsd ldrs stands side, rdn ent fnl 2f, *hd* **114**
kept on well towards fin: highly tried & ran to very best: all 3 wins at 6f & can score again at that trip.
1757 **CASSANDRA GO 15** [9] 4-8-13 M Roberts 20/1: 60-126: In tch centre, kept on fnl 1f, nvr dngrs: gd run. *hd* **111**
3798} **WARRIOR QUEEN 227** [21] 3-8-7 M J Kinane 20/1: 3610-7: Mid div centre, eff 2f out, no impression *1* **108**
on leaders: Irish raider, '99 wnr at Leopardstown (debut, mdn) & Curragh (Listed, rtd 104): eff at
5/6f on fast & gd grnd: runs well fresh on a gall track: can set the pace: useful filly.
1529 **LORD KINTYRE 24** [20] 5-9-2 G Hind 66/1: 0-2448: Well plcd centre, led appr fnl 1f, soon hdd & *shd* **111**
no extra: highly tried & a fine run: back to juvenile form & Listed/Gr 3 will suit.
1566 **RAMBLING BEAR 22** [7] 7-9-2 T Quinn 20/1: 50-339: Bhd stands side, late hdwy, never a threat. *¾* **109**
1566 **BOLSHOI GB 22** [11] 8-9-2 C Lowther 66/1: 20/000: Outpcd centre till kept on fnl 1f: 10th, won this in '98. *¾* **107**
1747 **WATCHING 17** [1] 3-8-10 R Hughes 14/1: -21220: Front rank stands side till 2f out, eased dist: 11th: *shd* **107**
ideally suited by testing grnd, only a head bhd this wnr in 1747, see 988.
*1277 **FLANDERS 38** [14] 4-8-13 K Darley 14/1: 016-10: Chsd ldrs in centre, no extra appr fnl 1f: 12th: *hd* **103**
capable of better, btn a short head in this last year (rtd 113), see 1277.

1529 **THE TATLING 24** [10] 3-8-10 (t) M Fenton 66/1: 2-0300: Al same place in centre: 13th, highly tried. ¾ **104**
1338 **TABHEEJ 33** [16] 3-8-7 R Hills 20/1: 313-60: Speed in centre till lost place 2f out: 14th, back in trip. ½ **100**
1833 **SERAPHINA 10** [17] 3-8-7 G Duffield 50/1: 062030: Dwelt, never in it: 15th: better off at 6f in Listed. *nk* **99**
1674 **TRINCULO 17** [19] 3-8-10 T G McLaughlin 50/1: -00340: Never dngrs centre: 16th, much btr 1674 (6f). *shd* **102**
1747 **SELTITUDE 17** [13] 4-8-13 O Peslier 20/1: 10-330: Dwelt, stands side, never a factor: 17th, st/mate of wnr. ¾ **97**
1566 **ROSSELLI 22** [3] 4-9-2 J Carroll 66/1: 0-4600: Prom stands side till 2f out: 18th, see 1172. *shd* **100**
+1566 **PERRYSTON VIEW 22** [12] 8-9-2 (bl) J Reid 14/1: -10010: Keen in centre & led, edged over to far rail 2f out, soon hdd & btn: 19th, nicely bckd from 20/1: had several of these bhd in 1566, can do better. *nk* **99**
*1757 **RUDIS PET 15** [6] 6-9-2 (bl) K Fallon 7/2 FAV: 116-10: Soon leading stands side group, hdd entering fnl 2f, soon btn, lost action dist & eased: 20th, hvly bckd: clearly something amiss, see 1757. 1½ **95**
1849 **PROUD NATIVE 10** [15] 6-9-2 D Harrison 14/1: -00220: Soon outpcd: 21st, much btr 1849, see 1172. *2* **89**
4246} **Dojima Muteki 261** [18] 10-9-2 K Take 150/1: 1849 **Travesty Of Law 10** [2] 3-8-10 D R McCabe 100/1:
23 ran Time 1m 01.13 (2.13) (J R Chester) J E Hammond France

2066

3.45 GR 1 ST JAMES PALACE STKS 3YO (A) 1m rnd Good 45 -26 Slow
£156600 £59400 £29700 £13500

1623 **GIANTS CAUSEWAY 24** [3] A P O'Brien 3-9-0 M J Kinane 7/2 FAV: 1-1221: 3 ch c Storm Cat - Mariah's Storm (Rahy) Made most till below dist, hard rdn & kept on gamely to regain lead near fin: hvly bckd Irish raider, deserved this after rnr-up in both the English & Irish Guineas, earlier won at the Curragh (Gr 3): won all 3 juv starts, at Naas, Curragh (Gr 3) & Longchamp (Gr 1, rtd 118): eff at 7f/1m, may get 10f: acts on fast & soft, any track: runs well fresh: best up with/forcing the pace: high-class, v tough & genuine colt. **120**
1318 **VALENTINO 37** [11] J H M Gosden 3-9-0 (t) G Mosse 16/1: -14-32: 3 ch c Nureyev - Divine Danse (Kris) Bhd, gd progress & switched 2f out, rdn to lead ins last, idled & hdd fnl strides: nicely bckd: high class run from this lightly raced colt: improved with t-strap: can use his turn of foot to win top races. *hd* **119**
*1630 **MEDICEAN 19** [10] Sir Michael Stoute 3-9-0 K Fallon 16/1: -3113: 3 ch c Machiavellian - Mystic Goddess (Storm Bird) Keen, bhd ldrs, slightly short of room appr fnl 1f till below dist, ran on: not btn far: v smart effort from this much improved colt: sure to win a Group race, possibly at 10f: see 1630 (class stks). ¾ **117**
+1693 **SHIBBOLETH 17** [9] H R A Cecil 3-9-0 (t) T Quinn 9/2: -114: Well plcd, rdn appr fnl 1f (flashed tail), kept on onepace: well bckd: lost unbtn record but much improved up in trip/grade: stays 1m, see 1693. ½ **116**
3857} **SARAFAN 284** [5] 3-9-0 G Duffield 12/1: 1221-5: V keen, mid-div, rdn 2f out, kept on ins last but unable to chall: well bckd, reapp: tough juv, won at Hamilton (mdn), Pontefract, Beverley (stks) & Goodwood (List, rtd 111): eff at 7f/1m, 10f may suit: acts on firm & gd/soft: runs v well fresh: will be plcd to advantage. ½ **115**
*1623 **BACHIR 24** [1] 3-9-0 J Bailey 6/1: -12116: Keen, cl-up wide, led halfway till 2f out, fdd fnl 1f: capable of much better & raced wide of the field here: beat this wnr a neck in 1623 (Irish gns, set a steady pace). *hd* **115**
*1530 **INGLENOOK 24** [2] 3-9-0 Pat Eddery 12/1: -5117: Held up, wide, eff appr fnl 2f, never any impression: supplemented for this & will relish a return to Listed/Gr 3 class: see 153 (Listed). 1½ **112**
*972 **FANAAR 62** [8] 3-9-0 J Weaver 16/1: -18: Last, passed 3 horses fnl 1f, nvr dngrs: bckd, 9 wk abs: highly tried on 2nd start after winning the Wood Ditton (beat this 3rd): clearly useful, will win more races: see 972. 1½ **109**
1171 **COMPTON BOLTER 45** [4] 3-9-0 T Jarnet 33/1: 3-4059: Chsd ldrs till 3f out: 6 week abs, see 765. ½ **108**
1226 **CHINA VISIT 45** [6] 3-9-0 J Velazquez 11/2: 1-160: Prom till 3f out: 10th, well bckd, stablemate of 6th. ¾ **107**
1623 **CAPE TOWN 24** [7] 3-9-0 R Hughes 20/1: 2-1030: Handy 5f: 11th, less than 1L bhd this wnr in 1623 & surely something amiss. *shd* **107**
11 ran Time 1m 42.61 (4.11) (Mrs John Magnier & Mr M Tabor) A P O'Brien Ballydoyle, Co Tipperary

2067

4.20 GR 3 COVENTRY STKS 2YO (A) 6f Good 45 -40 Slow
£36000 £13800 £6900 £3300

*1472 **CD EUROPE 27** [5] M R Channon 2-8-12 S Drowne 8/1: 11: 2 ch c Royal Academy - Woodland Orchid (Woodman) Prom, eff ent fnl 2f, styd on strongly under press to lead towards fin: slow time: earlier won debut at Goodwood (mdn): Ir£20,000 March foal, sire a sprinter/miler, dam a mdn: eff at 6f, 7f is sure to suit: acts on gd & gd/soft, prob any track: runs well fresh: unbeaten, v useful & progressive, win another Gr race. **107**
*1367 **BRAM STOKER 32** [9] R Hannon 2-8-12 R Hughes 4/1: 2112: 2 ch c General Monash - Taniokey (Grundy) Cl-up going well, led 2f out & looked the likely wnr dist, soon hard rdn, worn down cl-home: nicely bckd: improved in defeat: acts on gd & gd/soft grnd: v useful, shld win a Group race: see 1367. ½ **104**
-- **MODIGLIANI** [11] A P O'Brien 2-8-12 M J Kinane 7/2 FAV: 13: 2 b c Danzig - Hot Princess (Hot Spark) Cl up, feeling pace appr fnl 1f, kept on ins last: hvly bckd Irish raider, 3 mnth abs since landing a Curragh mdn: half-brother to top class miler Rodrigo De Triano: eff at 5/6f, further will suit: acts on gd & soft grnd: useful. *1* **101**
*1573 **EARL GREY 21** [3] W Jarvis 2-8-12 M Tebbutt 20/1: 14: Prom, shkn up appr fnl 1f & outpcd, kept on well towards fin: nicely bckd at big odds: useful run: acts on gd & gd/soft: much improved, interesting at 7f. ½ **99**
1846 **TRIPLE BLUE 10** [12] 2-8-12 Dane O'Neill 14/1: 1135: In tch, prog & ch 2f out, onepace dist: op 10/1: useful colt, not disgraced, acts on gd & soft grnd: see 1526. ¾ **96**
*1328 **BARKING MAD 34** [10] 2-8-12 M Fenton 13/2: 316: Keen in mid div, eff halfway, no impression till kept on near fin: nicely bckd from 9/1: needs 7f, see 1328. *hd* **96**
1774 **SHADOWLESS 13** [8] 2-8-12 P Robinson 25/1: 47: Never a factor though keeping on fin: win at 7f+. ¾ **93**
1846 **STREGONE 10** [1] 2-8-12 Pat Eddery 10/1: 165228: Nvr nr ldrs tho' staying on fin: see 1846, 743. *shd* **93**
*1586 **TARAS EMPEROR 21** [7] 2-8-12 K Fallon 13/2: -41419: Pulled hard in lead, hdd 2f out, fdd: unsuited by step up in trip & quicker grnd, see 1586 (soft). *2* **87**
1995 **IMPERIAL DANCER 3** [4] 2-8-12 Craig Williams 33/1: 42130: Al bhd: 10th, ran on Saturday, see 1001. 1½ **83**
*1426 **RARE OLD TIMES 29** [2] 2-8-7 L Newman 20/1: 510: Chsd ldrs till halfway: 11th, btr 1426 (5f gd/sft). *9* **53**
1846 **ARMAGNAC 10** [6] 2-8-12 T Quinn 50/1: 640: Soon struggling: 12th, highly tried mdn, see 1846. *shd* **58**
12 ran Time 1m 16.97 (3.87) (Circular Distributors Ltd) M R Channon West Isley, Berks

2068

4.55 GR 3 QUEEN'S VASE STKS 3YO (A) 2m45y Good 45 -39 Slow
£36000 £13800 £6900 £3300

*1696 **DALAMPOUR 17** [13] Sir Michael Stoute 3-8-11 K Fallon 3/1 FAV: -011: 3 b c Shernazar - Dalara (Doyoun) Mid-div, imprvd appr str, led 2f out & soon clr, readily: hvly bckd, slow time: recent Newmarket wnr (mdn): unraced juv: half-brother to high class mid dist wnr Daliapour: eff at 12f, relished this step up to 2m: acts on fast & gd grnd, stiff/gall trks: v useful & improving colt, sure to win more Group staying races. **109**
-- **DUTCH HARRIER** [2] K Prendergast 3-8-11 S Craine 33/1: 03122: 3 ch c Barathea - Fanny Blankers (Persian Heights) Veered right start, towards rear, improved appr fnl 2f, drvn bef dist, kept on but no ch wnr: jockey given 5 day ban (irresponsible ride/whip use): qck reapp, Irish raider: earlier won at Leopardstown *4* **102**

(mdn): unraced juvenile: eff at 12f/2m on fast & gd grnd: useful.

*1821 **SAMSAAM 11** [1] J L Dunlop 3-8-11 R Hills 11/2: 0-1113: 3 ch c Sadler's Wells - Azyaa (Kris) nk 101
Trkd ldrs, drpd into mid div appr straight, rall to dispute 2nd appr fnl 1f, no extra near fin: well bckd, clr rem:
first reverse this term but far from disgraced stepping out of h'cap company: eff at 14f, stays 2m on gd & hvy.

*1784 **RAVENSWOOD 12** [5] M C Pipe 3-8-11 (t) T Quinn 14/1: 0-4214: Bhd, some hdway though plenty 3½ 98$
to do when short of room 2f out, styd on: gets 2m & looks capable of better: improving: see 1784 (h'cap).

1216 **IL CAPITANO 42** [4] 3-8-11 R Hughes 33/1: 662-05: Led for 1m, prom when hmpd/snatched up 1 97$
appr fnl 2f, soon rdn & no extra: 1m week abs: longer trip, return to 12f will suit: see 1216.

*1369 **MBELE 32** [11] 3-8-11 Pat Eddery 14/1: 2-3216: Bhd, hdwy & hung right appr fnl 2f, one pace after: nk 97
bckd from 20/1, clr rem: not disgraced on only 5th ever start, longer trip: see 1369 (14f mdn).

1284 **DUBAI TWO THOUSAND 38** [9] 3-8-11 J Bailey 12/1: 1-67: Pulled hard, prom till fdd appr fnl 2f. 6 92

*1311 **KUWAIT TROOPER 35** [6] 3-8-11 K Darley 12/1: 410318: Towards rear, wide into str, never dngrs. 2½ 90

+1347 **OPTIMAITE 33** [7] 3-8-11 G Hind 7/1: 40-319: Hmpd start, pulled hard, al bhd: nicely bckd: ½ 89
another step up in trip for this former useful sprinting juvenile: see 1347 (12f).

*1554 **WAFFIGG 22** [8] 3-8-11 P Robinson 12/1: 510: Pulled hard in mid div, prog to lead after 1m till 2f ½ 89
out, wknd, edged right, 10th: only 3rd ever start, see 1554 (hvy grnd mdn).

1400 **KEW GARDENS 31** [12] 3-8-11 M J Kinane 20/1: 16-230: Bhd from halfway: 11th, up in trip/grade. 10 81

1459 **MISS LORILAW 30** [10] 3-8-6 M Hills 14/1: 1-3360: Pld hard, rear, brief eff 4f out: 12th, see 1168, 998. nk 75

*1832 **RIDDLESDOWN 10** [3] 3-8-11 G Duffield 14/1: 1-2210: Keen in tch, chsd ldrs 6f out till 3f out: 13th. 15 70
13 ran   Time 3m 36.27 (10.27)   (H H Aga Khan)   Sir Michael Stoute Newmarket, Suffolk

---

2069   5.30 DUKE OF EDINBURGH HCAP 3YO+ 0-105 (B)   1m4f   Good 45   +03 Fast   [105]
£35750   £11000   £5500   £2750   3 yo rec 14lb

4595} **KATIYKHA 233** [7] J Oxx 4-9-9 (100) J Murtagh 10/1: 2-2411: 4 b f Darshaan - Katiyfa (Auction Ring) 109
Bhd, gd hdwy ent str, hard rdn appr fnl 1f, wore down ldr near fin: tchd 12/1, gd time: Irish raider, 13 days ago
scored at Gowran Park (List): '99 wnr at Newmarket (2 mdn & rtd h'cap) & Leicester (stks, rtd 105, L Cumani): eff
at 12f, shld get further: acts on gd & soft grnd, likes stiff tracks: runs well fresh: v useful & progressive.

*1715 **GALLERY GOD 15** [6] G Wragg 4-8-9 (86) Y Take 14/1: -06312: 4 ch c In The Wings - El Fabulous shd 94
(Fabulous Dancer) Soon well plcd, led ent str, rdn appr fnl 1f, kept on, collared nr fin: fine run, progressive.

*1251 **VERIDIAN 40** [9] N J Henderson 7-8-4 (81) Pat Eddery 12/1: 462/13: 7 b g Green Desert - Alik 2½ 85
(Targowice) Rear, niggled halfway, kept on under press fnl 2f, never nearer: nicely bckd, 6 week abs:
fine run from this 7yo, another try at 14f+: see 1251.

*1170 **NATIONAL ANTHEM 45** [13] Sir Michael Stoute 4-9-12 (103) K Fallon 5/2 FAV: 614-14: Handy, briefly ½ 106
short of room ent str, chsd ldrs 2f out, soon rdn, same pace: hvly bckd from 4/1, 6 week abs: eff at 10f, stays 12f .

1695 **WESTENDER 17** [20] M Hills 13/2: 13-225: Well plcd & ch till one pace appr fnl 1f: nk 94
nicely bckd: tough sort, ran to best, see 1695, 1342.

1784 **SHARP STEPPER 12** [10] 4-8-1 (78) G Duffield 11/1: 321-36: Pulled hard held up, bmpd appr straight 1¼ 79
wide eff 2f out, styd on, never near leaders: ran well: see 1784, 84.

1329 **AFTERJACKO 34** [8] 4-9-0 (91) T Quinn 12/1: 3-5127: In tch, chsd ldrs ent straight, wknd bef dist. 1¼ 91

1841 **RAIN IN SPAIN 10** [2] 4-10-0 (105) R Hughes 33/1: 3-3248: Bhd, ran on into mid-div up the str, nvr ½ 104
dangerous: top-weight, h'cap bow: worth a try at 2m: see 732.

1850 **MOWBRAY 14** [14] 5-9-8 (99) D Sweeney 25/1: 05-569: Al same place: see 1401. 1½ 96

1222 **FIRST BALLOT 41** [18] 4-8-13 (90) P Robinson 25/1: 610-00: Prom till appr fnl 2f: 10th, 6 wk abs. nk 86

*1903 **AKBAR 8** [5] 4-9-12 (103)(4ex) M J Kinane 16/1: 30-110: In tch till 2f out: 11th, too soon after 1903? 1 98

1695 **CARLYS QUEST 17** [12] 6-8-13 (90)(tvi) S Drowne 25/1: 2-3130: Never dngrs: 12th, see 1695, 1373. 3 82

1342 **ULUNDI 33** [15] 5-8-13 (90) J Reid 20/1: 11330: Chsd ldrs till 3f out: 13th, up in trip, see 1342, 747. ¾ 81

*1555 **APRIL STOCK 22** [19] 5-8-1 (78)(t) G Carter 20/1: 10-510: Al towards rear: 14th, see 1555 (4-rnr fillies). 5 64

2271} **ZALAL 359** [1] 5-9-4 (95) W J Smith 50/1: 01D-00: Soon handy, fdd under press in the straight: 15th: 4 77
Irish raider: with L Cumani in '99, won at Goodwood (class stks, rtd 98): '98 wnr at Bath (mdn) & York (class stks,
rtd 95): eff at 10/12f on fast & gd grnd & any track: can go well fresh: useful at best, now with Luke Comer.

1850 **SALMON LADDER 10** [4] 8-9-4 (95) L Newman (3) 25/1: 3-4040: Set gd clip, hdd appr fnl 2f, wknd: 16th. 5 72

1620 **HIRAPOUR 27** [11] 4-9-8 (99)(BL) P J Smullen 20/1: 1-0130: Nvr trbld ldrs: 17th: blinkered Irish 2 74
raider: earlier won at Listowel: '99 wnr at Fairyhouse (mdn): eff at 12/13f on gd & soft grnd: with D Weld.

1850 **RADAS DAUGHTER 10** [17] 4-9-3 (94) K Darley 12/1: 10-000: Prom till halfway, soon btn: 18th. 12 59

1965 **Willie Conquer 4** [3] 8-8-7 (84) M Henry 66/1:   1784 **Mole Creek 12** [16] 5-8-1 (78) A Beech (5) 66/1:
20 ran   Time 2m 31.68 (2.68)   (H H Aga Khan)   J Oxx Currabeg, Co Kildare

---

LEOPARDSTOWN   WEDNESDAY JUNE 14TH   Lefthand, Galloping Track

Official Going   GOOD

2070   7.45 GR 3 BALLYCORUS STKS 3YO+   7f   Good
£22750   £6650   £3150   £1050   3 yo rec 10lb

1617 **TUMBLEWEED RIDGE 20** B J Meehan 7-9-12 (t) M Tebbutt 5/4 FAV: 10-231: 7 ch h Indian Ridge - 116
Billie Blue (Ballad Rock) Made all, rdn clr fnl 2f, easily: registered 3rd successive victory in this race: '99
wnr at Leopardstown (this race), Longchamp (Gr 3's) & Epsom (List, rtd 116): '98 Newmarket (rtd h'cap) &
Leopardstown (Gr 3) wnr: effective at 6f/1m, 7f specialist: acts on firm, soft & any
trk, likes Leopardstown/Newmarket: runs well fresh: with/without blnks/t-strap: most smart, tough & genuine.

1316 **BASHKIR 31** A P O'Brien 3-8-10 (bl) M J Kinane 8/1: 02-252: 3 b c Nureyev - Palestrina (Al Nasr) 3 100
Chsd wnr, rdn & kept on till 2f out, no ch with comfortable wnr: stays 7f on good: see 1316 (List).

4241} **POCO A POCO 256** E Lynam 3-8-7 K J Manning 8/1: 2251-3: 3 b f Imperial Frontier - Cut The Red hd 97
Tape (Sure Blade) Settled rear, hdwy over 2f out, rdn/no extra appr fnl 1f: reapp: '99 scorer at The Curragh
(List, rtd 105): eff at 6f, prob stays 7f: handles gd & soft: not disgraced here, sharper next time.

1172 **MITCHAM 39** T G Mills 4-9-12 A Clark 6/1: 040-04: Settled in tch, eff 2f out, not pace of ldrs 2½ 100
sn after: upped in trip & will apprec a return to 5/6f: see 1172.
7 ran   Time 1m 30.4   (The Tumbleweed Partnership)   B J Meehan Upper Lambourn, Berks

LEOPARDSTOWN   WEDNESDAY JUNE 14TH   Lefthand, Galloping Track

2071   **8.15 LISTED GLENCAIRN STKS 4YO+   1m1f   Good**
£16250   £4750   £2250

--   **ANNIEIRWIN** F Ennis 4-8-8 F M Berry 14/1: 314-61: 4 ch f Perugino - Elasca (Unknown)   **100**
Settled last, rdn/hdwy 2f out, ran on well ins last to lead cl-home, drvn out: in '99 scored at The Curragh
(mdn): eff at 1m/9f on gd & gd/soft grnd: handles a gall trk: useful & improving.
3696} **FREE TO SPEAK 292** D K Weld 8-9-0 (bl) P Shanahan 1/1 FAV: 10-022: 8 ch h Be My Guest - Love   **hd 105**
For Poetry (Lord Gayle) In tch, rdn/prog to lead dist, hdd fnl strides: recent rnr-up in a Leopardstown h'cap:
'99 wnr at The Curragh (val h'cap) & Tralee (List), rtd 113): wears blnks.
--   **ATACAT** J Oxx 4-8-11 J P Murtagh 5/2: -213: 4 b h Catrail - Atsuko (Mtoto)   **1½ 99**
Cl-up, rdn/dropped rear 2f out, styd on well ins last, held/hmpd nr fin: recent Dundalk wnr (9f mdn, gd/soft).
5 ran   Time 1m 57.1   (M E McElroy)   F Ennis Curragh, Co Kildare

LONGCHAMP   THURSDAY JUNE 15TH   Righthand, Stiff, Galloping Track

Official Going   GOOD

2072   **3.30 GR 3 LA COUPE 4YO+   1m2f   Good**
£21134   £7685   £3842

3795} **SLICKLY 284** Saeed bin Suroor 4-8-11 S Guillot 9/10 FAV: 4125-1: 4 gr h Linamix - Slipstream   **118**
Queen (Conquistador Cielo) Made all, rdn & ran on stongly fnl 2f: reapp/new stable: '99 wnr at Longchamp
(2, Gr 2 & Gr 1, rtd 119, A Fabre): '98 scorer at Chantilly (Gr 2, rtd 110): eff at 10/12f on gd & soft
grnd: handles a stiff/gall trk: high-class at best, open to further improvement for new connections.
--   **AGOL LACK** A Fabre 4-8-11 O Peslier 31/10: 12-512: 4 ch c Gulch - Garvin's Gal (Seattle Slew)   **2 113**
Chsg wnr thro'out, drvn/no extra appr fnl 1f: eff at 10f on gd grnd: v useful.
--   **KERRYGOLD** P Bary 4-8-11 C Soumillon 133/10: 110-33: 3 ch c Tel Quel - Star System (Northern   **snk 113**
Treat) Mid-div, rdn to imprv 2f out, held over 1f out: stays 10f well on gd grnd.
8 ran   Time 2m 04.7   (Godolphin)   Saeed bin Suroor Newmarket

SAN SIRO   SUNDAY JUNE 18TH   Righthand, Stiff, Galloping Track

Official Going   GOOD/FIRM

2073   **2.55 GR 3 PREMIO MARIO INCISA 3YO+   1m4f   Good/Firm**
£31679   £14683   £8227   3 yo rec 14lb

1469 **SAILING 25** P F I Cole 3-8-6 F Jovine : 5-2141: 3 ch f Arazi - Up Anchor (Slip Anchor)   **105**
Front rank, went on over 2f out, styd on well, rdn out: earlier won here at San Siro (List): '99 Goodwood
(fill mdn) & Sandown (stks, rtd 100) wnr: eff at 1m/12f on fast, hvy & any trk: runs well fresh: v useful.
*122 **DANGEROUS MIND 205** H Blume 4-9-5 A Starke : 1-2: 4 b f Platini - Desert Squaw   **2 100**
(Commanche Run) Handy, hdwy/short of room over 1f out, no extra ins last: eff at 10/12f on gd/fm & hvy.
*1378 **SUPER TASSA 32** V Valiani 4-9-5 T Thulliez : 2-4113: 4 ch f Lahib - Center Moriches   **½ 99**
(Magical Wonder) Cl-up, dropped rear 2f out, ran on well ins last: eff at 10.5f/12f on gd & gd/fm.
11 ran   Time 2m 34.0   (H R H Prince Fahd Salman)   P F I Cole Whatcombe, Oxon

2074   **3.55 GR 1 GRAN PREMIO DI MILANO 3YO+   1m4f   Good/Firm**
£100685   £50302   £29197

2494} **ENDLESS HALL 42** L M Cumani 4-9-6 F Jovine : 31-501: 4 b c Saddler's Hall - Endless Joy (Law   **117**
Society) Made all, rdn & went well clr 2f out, eased nr fin: won here at San Siro in '99 (List, rtd 110),
prev trained in Italy: eff forcing the pace at 10/12f on fast grnd: a much improved & v smart run here.
--   **CATELLA** P Schiergen 4-9-3 T Hellier : 11-122: 4 ch f Generous - Crystal Ring (Kris)   **5½ 106**
Trkd wnr, chall briefly 3f out, sn not pace of easy wnr: clr rem: German raider: eff at 12f on fast.
1461 **SPENDENT 27** P Bary 4-9-6 (bl) T Thulliez : 114-33: 4 ch c Generous - Cattermole (Roberto)   **4 103**
Held up, hdwy/hmpd over 2f out, styd on but no ch with ldrs: French challenger: see 1461 (13f).
9 ran   Time 2m 28.6   (Il Paralupo)   L M Cumani Newmarket

WOLVERHAMPTON (Fibresand)   WEDNESDAY JUNE 21ST   Lefthand, Sharp Track

Official Going   STANDARD. Stalls: Inside.

2075   **2.20 HYLTON FILLIES HCAP 3YO+ 0-75 (E)   1m4f aw   Going 38 -04 Slow**   **[67]**
£2684   £767   £383   3 yo rec 14lb

1677 **MONO LADY 18** [5] D Haydn Jones 7-9-12 (65)(bl) Dean McKeown 9/2: 020451: 7 b m Polish Patriot -   **70a**
Phylella (Persian Bold) Al handy, rdn/chsd ldr 2f out, led ins last, styd on well, rdn out: '99 wnr at Chester (h'cap,
rtd 72 at best): '98 wnr at Leicester (h'cap, rtd 73): eff at 10/12f on firm, gd/soft & both AWs: runs well fresh &
handles any trk: eff with/without blnks: gd weight carrier.
1551 **IRISH CREAM 23** [2] Andrew Reid 4-8-1 (40)(vis) M Henry 7/2: 106262: 4 b f Petong - Another Baileys   **2½ 41a**
(Deploy) Chsd ldr, led over 3f out, pressed/rdn fnl 2f, hdd ins last & held nr fin: clr rem: op 5/2: see 668.
2023 **DIZZY TILLY 3** [3] A J McNae 6-8-1 (40) P Fitzsimons (2) 5/1: 000433: 6 b m Anshan - Nadema (Artaius)   **7 31a**
Led 1m, outpcd by front pair fnl 2f: op 7/2: qck reapp: 4 years since sole prev AW start: see 748.
1736 **FLY LIKE A BIRD 16** [1] S P C Woods 4-8-8 (47) I Mongan (5) 12/1: /60-04: Held up, rdn/outpcd   **¾ 37a**

WOLVERHAMPTON (Fibresand) WEDNESDAY JUNE 21ST Lefthand, Sharp Track

fnl 2f: op 6/1: AW bow: unplcd last term (rtd 62, h'cap): plcd in '98 (rtd 63): eff at 10f on hvy grnd.
*1705 **GENERATE** 17 [4] 4-9-4 (57) S Sanders 11/10 FAV: D10215: Held up, eff/held 2f out: reportedly choked. 2 **44a**
5 ran Time 2m 38.6 (5.0) (Monolithic Refractories Ltd) D Haydn Jones Efail Isaf, Rhondda C Taff.

2076 2.55 MOTORING CLAIMER 4YO+ (F) 2m46y aw Going 38 -68 Slow
£2184 £624 £312

*1894 **NOUFARI** 8 [3] R Hollinshead 9-9-1 P M Quinn (3) 8/13 FAV: -51211: 9 b g Kahyasi - Noufiyla (Top **76a**
Ville) Held up, prog/rdn to chase ldr over 2f out, led over 1f out & rdn to maintain narrow advantage ins last:
slow time: nicely bckd at odds on: earlier scored at Southwell & Redcar (clmrs): '99 Nottingham, Thirsk (h'caps,
rtd 76) & W'hampton wnr (clmr, rtd 83a): '98 wnr at Southwell (2), W'hampton (3) & Newcastle (h'caps, rtd 81a & 71):
eff at 14f/2m, stays 2½m: acts on firm & gd/soft, loves fibresand & any trk: at home in claimers.
*1802 **DJAIS** 12 [5] J R Jenkins 11-8-13 S Whitworth 7/4: 0/6-12: 11 ch g Vacarme - Dame de Carreau nk **73a**
(Targowice) Held up, prog to lead over 2f out, hdd over 1f out, drvn & styd on well but al just held: op 5/4,
clr rem: acts on fibresand, fast & soft grnd: see 1802 (beat this winner at Southwell).
1802 **MISALLIANCE** 12 [2] M E Sowersby 5-7-12 P Fessey 20/1: 0-0033: 5 ch m Elmaamul - Cabaret Artiste 4 **54$**
(Shareef Dancer) Prom, cl-up till outpcd by front pair fnl 2f: op 14/1: stays slowly run 2m, best form at 7f/1m.
-- **WHITE WILLOW** [4] R Brotherton 11-8-7 (bl) I Mongan (4) 50/1: U440/4: Chsd ldr halfway, led 12 **54a**
over 4f out, hdd & wknd over 2f out: Flat reapp after long abs, points fit (mod form): last rcd on the level in
'97 (mod form): '94 Southwell wnr (14f h'cap): prev eff around 11/14f on fibresand, gd & soft, stiff/sharp trk.
-- **MORNING SUIT** [1] 6-8-9 M Henry 12/1: 5: Led 12f, btn 2f out: Flat debut, jumps fit (rtd 69h, sell). 29 **34a**
5 ran Time 3m 46.4 (17.2) (Ed Weetman) R Hollinshead Upper Longdon, Staffs.

2077 3.30 HATCHBACK MDN 2YO (D) 6f aw rnd Going 38 -10 Slow
£2795 £860 £430 £215

-- **BRAVADO** [8] Sir Mark Prescott 2-9-0 S Sanders 4/9 FAV: 1: 2 b c Zafonic - Brave Revival (Dancing **85a**
Brave) Sn handy & al going best, led over 1f out & asserted under hands-and-heels riding ins last: well bckd
at odds on: Jan foal, half-brother to a 7f juv wnr: dam 1m 2/3yo wnr: eff at 6f, will get further: acts on
fibresand & a sharp trk: runs well fresh: stable has won this race for 4 consecutive seasons: improvement likely.
-- **SEBULBA** [3] J G Given 2-9-0 Dean McKeown 10/1: 2: 2 b g Dolphin Street - Twilight Calm (Hatim) 3 **73a**
Led, rdn/hdd over 1f out, sn held by wnr: op 8/1: Mar foal, 5,500gns 2yo: dam unrcd: eff at 6f, handles fibresand.
1413 **EL HAMRA** 32 [5] B A McMahon 2-9-0 N Pollard 20/1: 503: 2 gr c Royal Abjar - Cherlinoa (Crystal 1 **71a**
Palace) Dwelt/outpcd towards rear, mod gains for press fnl 2f, no threat: op 14/1: handles fibresand.
1740 **JOHN FOLEY** 15 [4] W G M Turner 2-9-0 P Fitzsimons (5) 10/1: 002524: Chsd ldrs 4f: op 6/1. 4 **61a**
1974 **FORTUNA** 5 [6] 2-9-0 C Nutter 20/1: 05: Al outpcd: longer priced stablemate of wnr: see 1974. 1¼ **58a**
1727 **FIENNES** 16 [7] 2-9-0 T G McLaughlin 6/1: 506: Chsd ldrs 4f: op 7/1, AW bow: btr 932 (5f). 7 **45a**
-- **A TEEN** [1] 2-9-0 R Morse 33/1: 7: Slowly away & al bhd: Presidium colt, Feb foal, 6,000gns 2yo: 7 **32a**
half-brother to a minor juv 1m wnr, dam modest: with C N Allen.
-- **SOBER HILL** [2] 2-9-0 I Mongan (5) 16/1: 8: Slowly away & rear: op 14/1: Komaite gelding, March 10 **13a**
foal, cost 5,500gns: dam unrcd: with D Shaw.
8 ran Time 1m 15.7 (2.9) (Cheveley Park Stud) Sir Mark Prescott Newmarket.

2078 4.05 PCS HCAP 3YO+ 0-80 (D) 5f aw rnd Going 38 +10 Fast [80]
£3848 £1184 £592 £296 3 yo rec 6 lb

1662 **CARTMEL PARK** 19 [3] A Berry 4-9-8 (74) O Pears 16/1: -05001: 4 b g Skyliner - Oh My Oh My **83a**
(Ballacashtal) Made all & clr halfway, styd on strongly fnl 1f, rdn out: best time of day: '99 Sandown (1st time
vis) & Catterick wnr (h'caps, rtd 80): '98 Musselburgh & Newcastle wnr (nov, rtd 84): suited by 5f on firm, soft &
fibresand, handles any trk: eff with/without a visor: pacey geldng, loves to dominate, can win again.
1504 **TEYAAR** 26 [6] D Shaw 4-9-5 (71) I Mongan (5) 5/1: 125222: 4 b g Polar Falcon - Music In My Life 2½ **77a**
(Law Society) Rdn chasing wnr thr'out, kept on tho' nvr pace to chall: tough, eff at 5f, all 3 wins at 6f: see 1008.
1923 **RING OF LOVE** 7 [5] J L Eyre 4-8-7 (59) G Baker (7) 16/1: 365303: 4 b f Magic Ring - Fine Honey 1¼ **57a**
(Drone) Chsd ldrs, rdn & kept on onepace from over 1f out: op 10/1: see 372 (equitrack).
1815 **SOTONIAN** 12 [8] P S Felgate 7-8-4 (56) P M Quinn (3) 10/1: 306634: Chsd ldrs 4f: see 394. 1¼ **51a**
1795 **CAROLS CHOICE** 13 [11] 3-8-7 (65) Dean McKeown 10/1: 033235: Chsd ldrs till over 1f out: op 8/1. ½ **58a**
1976 **SAMWAR** 5 [2] 8-8-6 (58)(vis) A Beech 8/1: 012256: Held up, no room halfway, nvr pace to chall. hd **50a**
1766 **SWEET MAGIC** 14 [4] 9-7-13 (51)(t) S Righton 20/1: 041407: Mid-div at best: see 1392 (C/D, seller). 2½ **36a**
*1504 **KEEN HANDS** 26 [12] 4-10-0 (80)(vis) R Fitzpatrick (3) 11/1: 505518: Drvn/rear, outpcd: op 7/1. 5 **63a**
1953 **TREASURE TOUCH** 6 [9] 6-8-3 (55) A Clark 7/2 FAV: 001139: Dwelt, sn handy, btn 2f out: op 3/1. 1¼ **35a**
1768 **DANCING EMPRESS** 14 [7] 3-9-8 (80) M Tebbutt 7/1: -01240: Chsd ldrs 4f: 10th: op 6/1: see 1138 (6f). 1½ **58a**
1412 **PRIDE OF BRIXTON** 32 [10] 7-9-7 (73) M Henry 14/1: -11120: Sltly hmpd start, al rear: 11th: btr 1140. 3 **44a**
1842 Yabint El Sham 11 [13] 4-9-0 (66) N Pollard 25/1: 1868 **Brutal Fantasy** 9 [1] 6-8-10 (62) S Sanders 25/1:
13 ran Time 1m 01.6 (1.4) (P G Airey & R R Whitton) A Berry Cockerham, Lancs.

2079 4.40 STEERING WHEEL SELLER 2YO (G) 6f aw rnd Going 38 -44 Slow
£1813 £518 £259

1679 **DECEIVES THE EYE** 18 [2] J G Given 2-8-11 G Baker (7) 14/1: 34501: 2 b g Dancing Spree - Lycius **60a**
Touch (Lycius) Led over 1f, remained handy & led again over 1f out, held on well nr fin, rdn out: no bid: op
10/1: first win: eff at 6f, could get further: acts on fibresand & a sharp trk: best without blnks in sells.
1805 **RUNNING FOR ME** 12 [4] R Hollinshead 2-8-11 A Hawkins (7) 9/2: 61022: 2 ch f Eagle Eyed - Running 1 **56a**
For You (Pampabird) Prom, chsd wnr over 1f out, rdn & kept on, al just held: clr rem: eff at 5/6f on fibresand.
1713 **BELLS BEACH** 16 [5] A Berry 2-8-6 Dean McKeown 12/1: 03: 2 ch f General Monash - Clifton Beach 9 **35a**
(Auction Ring) Led over 4f out till over 1f out, wknd qckly fnl 1f: op 8/1: clr rem: see 1713.
1870 **MINIME** 9 [1] N P Littmoden 2-8-11 T G McLaughlin 7/2: 04: Outpcd, mod late gains: see 1870. 5 **31a**
1634 **MACKEM BEAT** 20 [6] 2-8-6 T Ashley 12/1: 055: Chsd ldrs, btn/hung hght 2f out: op 8/1: see 1463. 7 **13a**
1931 **PERTEMPS JACK** 6 [7] 2-8-11 R Parham 16/1: 66: Struggling halfway: op 14/1: see 1931. 5 **9a**
1931 **PRINCESS PENNY** 6 [8] 2-8-11 P Fitzsimons (5) 11/2: 301357: Al outpcd: qck reapp: btr 1420. 2½ **2a**
-- **RIVER ALN** [3] 2-8-6 S Sanders 2/1 FAV: 8: Sn outpcd/bhd: Inchinor filly, Mar foal, full sister to a 5 **0a**
5/6f juv wnr who later won at 7f/1m abroad: dam a 10f wnr: bred to apprec 1m+ for Sir Mark Prescott.
8 ran Time 1m 17.7 (4.9) (Mrs Trude Cutler) J G Given Willoughton, Lincs.

668

WOLVERHAMPTON (Fibresand) WEDNESDAY JUNE 21ST Lefthand, Sharp Track

2080 **5.15 FUEL HCAP 3YO 0-65 (F) 1m1f79y aw Going 38 -05 Slow [69]**
£2226 £636 £318

*1865 **PERFECT MOMENT 9** [8] C A Dwyer 3-9-0 (55)(6ex) A Beech (5) 3/1: 042111: 3 b f Mujadil - Flashing Raven (Maelstrom Lake) Al handy, drvn/led ins last, held on gamely nr fin: op 7/4: defied 6lb pen, earlier won at Nottingham (sell h'cap) & Pontefract (seller, G McCourt, rtd 65, subs sold to current connections for 13000gns): '99 Leicester wnr (auct mdn, A Jarvis, rtd 74): suited by 1m/10f on fast, soft & fibresand, sharp or stiff/gall trk. **60a**
1745 **DIVA 15** [12] Sir Mark Prescott 3-9-6 (61) S Sanders 11/8 FAV: 60522: 3 b f Exit To Nowhere - Opera Lover (Sadler's Wells) Held up, rdn & prog to chall fnl 1f, styd on well, al just held: hvly bckd, op 5/2: h'cap bow: eff at 9f on fibresand, prob handles equitrack: encouraging effort and could find a similar event: see 1745. ½ **64a**
1758 **CLAUDIUS TERTIUS 14** [7] M A Jarvis 3-8-0 (41) M Henry 12/1: 0-0003: 3 b g Rudimentary - Sanctuary Cove (Habitat) Trkd ldrs, rdn/prog to lead 2f out, hdd ins last & no extra cl-home: op 7/1: eff at 9f on fibresand. ¾ **43a**
850 **SWINGING TRIO 72** [4] T G Mills 3-9-7 (62) L Carter 12/1: 0-004: Led over 4f out till 2f out, onepace/ held over 1f out: clr rem: op 10/1, h'cap/AW bow: 10 wk abs: unplcd at up to 10f previously. 2½ **59a**
1911 **THE WALRUS 7** [5] 3-8-8 (49) J Tate 8/1: 330055: Chsd ldrs 7f: op 7/1: see 848, 806. 7 **35a**
1817 **INVISIBLE FORCE 12** [3] 3-7-13 (40) J Lowe 14/1: -60466: Chsd ldrs 7f: op 12/1: see 992 (mdn). ½ **25a**
1644 **STANDIFORD GIRL 19** [1] 3-8-11 (52) Dean McKeown 14/1: 62007: Led 5f, btn/hmpd 2f out: op 12/1. 1¾ **34a**
1419 **ARMENIA 30** [13] 3-8-13 (54) I Mongan (5) 12/1: 143208: Drvn early, nvr on terms: op 10/1: see 1419. 8 **24a**
1889 **PYJAMA GIRL 8** [10] 3-9-3 (58) P Fitzsimons (5) 20/1: 6-3009: Dwelt, al rear: btr 1202 (7f). 1¾ **25a**
1914 **RESEARCH MASTER 7** [11] 3-9-0 (55) S Righton 33/1: 04-000: Al rear: 10th: see 1914. ¾ **21a**
1369 **Espere Dor 33** [2] 3-7-10 (47)(10oh) C Adamson 50/1: 1419 **Maid To Love 30** [9] 3-9-2 (57) M Tebbutt 12/1:
1480 **The Last Rambo 27** [6] 3-8-1 (42) G Baker (7) 20/1:
13 ran Time 2m 02.2 (4.0) (Casino Racing Partnership) C A Dwyer Newmarket.

KEMPTON WEDNESDAY JUNE 21ST Righthand, Flat, Fair Track

Official Going GOOD TO FIRM, GOOD places. Stalls: Inside, except Str Crse - Stands Side.

2081 **6.35 F NAGLE APPR HCAP 3YO+ 0-75 (E) 1m4f Good/Firm 38 -23 Slow [58]**
£3334 £1026 £513 £256

*1852 **MAY KING MAYHEM 10** [5] Mrs A L M King 7-9-3 (47)(bl) Iona Wands 5/2: -65111: 7 ch g Great Commotion - Queen Ranavalona (Sure Blade) Held up, rdn/styd on from 2f out to lead nr line: well bckd: completed a hat-trick, earlier scored at Lingfield (h'cap) & Newmarket (lady riders h'cap): '99 scorer at Leicester (appr h'cap) & Newmarket (lady riders h'cap, rtd 43): '98 scorer at Haydock & Pontefract (appr h'cap, rtd 43): all win at 12f, stays 15f: acts on firm, gd/soft & handles fibresand, any trk, likes a gall one, esp Newmarket: tried a visor, suited by blnks. **50**
1875 **SMARTER CHARTER 9** [1] Mrs L Stubbs 7-9-13 (57) Kristin Stubbs 8/1: 232232: 7 br g Master Willie - Irene's Charter (Persian Bold) Held up, prog to lead 2f out, hdd nr line: stays 12f, all wins at shorter. nk **59**
*1888 **NORTH OF KALA 8** [4] G L Moore 7-8-0 (30)(6ex) Joanna Badger 4/5 FAV: 500-13: 7 b g Distinctly North - Hi Kala (Kampala) Mid-div, prog when no room over 2f out till over 1f out, styd on well ins last, not reach front pair: unlucky in running at a crucial stage, shld have gone close: hvly bckd, clr of rem here: shld find comp. 1¾ **30+**
1819 **BACHELORS PAD 12** [8] Miss S J Wilton 6-10-0 (58) Lynsey Hanna 10/1: 414234: Keen/prom 10f. 7 **48**
1888 **TOMMY CARSON 8** [3] 5-9-8 (52)(bl) Clare Roche 12/1: 32-625: Led 10f: op 10/1: see 1350. ½ **41**
1852 **ADMIRALS SECRET 10** [6] 11-9-6 (50) Lorna Ford 10/1: -50106: Hld up, prog over 2f out, sn held. 2½ **36**
1511 **FAIRLY SURE 26** [9] 7-8-2 (32) Cheryl Nosworthy (5) 33/1: 160-07: Keen/prom 10f: '99 Bath scorer (fill h'cap, rtd 34, unplcd on sand, rtd 33a): eff at 10f on firm grnd: has run well fresh. 5 **10**
747 **SUEZ TORNADO 86** [2] 7-10-0 (58) Hayley Turner 20/1: 650-08: Bhd 3f out: 7 wk jump abs (mod form). 5 **28**
1743 **MUKHLLES 15** [7] 7-9-3 (47) Gemma Jones 25/1: 00-00P: Broke down/p.u. 5f out: see 1743. **0**
9 ran Time 2m 37.39 (7.39) (S J Harrison) Mrs A L M King Wilmcote, Warwicks.

2082 **7.05 BISTRO MDN 2YO (D) 5f str Good/Firm 38 +07 Fast**
£3445 £1060 £530 £265

1602 **IDLE POWER 21** [4] P W Harris 2-9-0 Pat Eddery 6/1: -251: 2 b c Common Grounds - Idle Fancy (Mujtahid) Held up in tch, pushed along over 2f out, strong run for press ins last to lead nr line: op 7/1, gd juv time: eff at 5f (dam a 1m wnr), return to 6f+ shld suit: acts on fast & gd/soft grnd, sharp/easy trk. **89**
1835 **ATTORNEY 11** [3] M A Jarvis 2-9-0 P Robinson 4/5 FAV: -022: 2 ch c Wolfhound - Princess Sadie (Shavian) Led, rdn over 1f out, hdd nr line: hvly bckd: acts on fast & gd/soft grnd: see 1835. hd **88**
1798 **FACTUAL LAD 13** [8] B R Millman 2-9-0 A McCarthy (3) 8/1: -23323: 2 b c So Factual - Surprise Surprise (Robellino) Prom & ev ch over 1f out, onepace cl-home: op 6/1: acts on fast & gd/soft grnd, poss hvy. 1¼ **84**
1642 **SO SOBER 19** [2] C F Wall 2-9-0 R Mullen 25/1: -54: Held up, prog/chall over 1f out, held nr fin: not btn far: eff at 5f on fast grnd: clearly going the right way after debut: see 1642. 1¼ **80**
1290 **FOCUSED ATTRACTION 37** [6] 2-9-0 R Hughes 13/2: -65: Keen, trkd ldrs, ch over 1f out, sn held. ½ **79**
1870 **WARLINGHAM 9** [7] 2-9-0 S Drowne 8/1: -4636: Cl-up, rdn/btn over 1f out: see 1870. nk **78**
-- **KENTUCKY BOUND** [5] 2-9-0 J P Spencer 12/1: -7: Dwelt, nvr able to chall: Charnwood Forest colt, Feb first foal, cost 68,000gns: dam lightly rcd, sire progress 7f/1m performer: with J W Payne. 3 **69**
-- **FIRE BELLE** [1] 2-8-9 N Pollard 33/1: -8: Dwelt, al rear: Lake Coniston filly, May foal, cost 1,400gns: dam a dual 5f juv sell wnr: with H Howe. 23 **14**
8 ran Time 59.88 (1.58) (The Dreamers) P W Harris Aldbury, Herts.

2083 **7.35 EBF NOV STKS 2YO (D) 6f str Good/Firm 38 +01 Fast**
£4095 £1260 £630 £315

*1859 **ECOLOGY 10** [4] J L Dunlop 2-9-5 Pat Eddery 4/9 FAV: -211: 2 b c Sri Pekan - Ecco Mi (Priolo) Prom, rdn/outpcd halfway, drvn & rallied strongly to lead 1f out, in command cl-home, rdn out: gd time: earlier scored at Ripon (mdn): eff at 6f, shld get further: acts on fast & gd grnd, any trk: useful. **99**
1809 **DOUBLE BREW 12** [3] R Hannon 2-8-12 P Dobbs (5) 8/1: -342: 2 ch c Primo Dominie - Boozy (Absalom) Handy, led over 2f out till 1f out, held nr fin: improved performance on fast grnd: eff at 6f: see 1526. ¾ **87$**
*1020 **DAYGLOW DANCER 58** [5] M R Channon 2-9-5 S Drowne 8/1: -13: 2 b c Fraam - Fading (Pharly) 3 **85**

Led till 4f out, rdn/wknd ins last: 8 wk abs: acts on fast & hvy grnd, stays 6f: see 1020.

-- **SHINING OASIS** [1] P F I Cole 2-8-3 J Mackay (7) 7/2: -4: Led 4f out, rdn/hdd over 1f out & no   ½ **68**
extra: Mujtahid filly, Mar foal, cost 26,000gns: dam a 6f 3yo wnr: with P F I Cole.

-- **CAPTAIN GIBSON** [2] 2-8-8 S Whitworth 33/1: -5: Slowly away & al bhd: Beveled colt, Mar foal,   23 **23**
cost 3,000gns: dam a multiple wnr abroad at 4/5yo: with D J S Ffrench Davis.

5 ran   Time 1m 13.34 (2.24)   (Hesmonds Stud)   J L Dunlop Arundel, W.Sussex.

2084   8.05 SUMMER FILLIES HCAP 3YO 0-90 (C)   1m rnd Good/Firm 38 -08 Slow   [90]
£7020 £2160 £1080 £540

1811 **MOSSY MOOR** 12 [8] Mrs A J Perrett 3-9-7 (83) Pat Eddery 13/2: 4-531: 3 ch f Sanglamore - Moss   **89**
(Alzao) Chsd ldrs, prog to lead 2f out, rdn/styd on well & in command/eased cl home: h'cap debut, first win: rtd 77
on sole '99 start: eff at 1m, (dam a 10f wnr) further may suit: acts on fast & hvy grnd, stiff or sharp/easy trk.

1655 **GRANTED** 19 [9] M L W Bell 3-9-4 (71) (73) M Fenton 16/1: 54-332: 3 b f Cadeaux Genereux - Germane   ½ **77**
(Distant Relative) Held up, prog over 2f out, sltly squeezed by wnr over 1f out, kept on tho' al just held: visor
omitted after latest: eff at 7f/1m, 10f may yet suit: encouraging h'cap bow: see 1165.

1826 **SARENA PRIDE** 12 [2] R J O'Sullivan 3-9-0 (76) J F Egan 11/2: 050243: 3 b f Persian Bold -   1¾ **76**
Avidal Park (Horidge) Held up, kept on fnl 2f, not pace to chall: stays 1m, prev best at 6/7f, see 1826, 727.

1855 **LARITA** 10 [7] J H M Gosden 3-9-7 (83) R Hughes 2/1 FAV: 10-2D4: Chsd ldrs, kept on onepace   ½ **82**
fnl 2f: stays an easy 1m: see 1855.

-- **YOUR THE LADY** [4] 3-8-10 (72) S Drowne 25/1: 0-085: Led/dsptd lead 6f: h'cap bow: ex-Irish,   ½ **70**
unplcd from 3 starts prev: eff around an easy 1m on fast grnd.

*1873 **MIDNIGHT ALLURE** 9 [1] 3-8-11 (73)(6ex) R Mullen 3/1: 0-2116: Keen in tch, onepace/held 1f out.   1½ **68**

1826 **OGILIA** 12 [6] 3-9-7 (83) G Duffield 10/1: 303-07: Held up, rdn/nvr pace to chall: see 1826 (7f).   ¾ **76**

1855 **SAFARI BLUES** 10 [10] 3-9-4 (80) P Dobbs (5) 16/1: 211-58: Led till 2f out, sn held: see 1855, 54 (AW).   1¾ **69**

*1855 **TIME VALLY** 10 [3] 3-8-9 (71) P Doe 5/1: 06-019: U.r./ran loose bef start, al rear: this best forgotten.   3½ **53**

9 ran   Time 1m 40.70 (3.70)   (K Abdulla)   Mrs A J Perrett Pulborough, W.Sussex.

2085   8.35 RICHMOND HCAP 3YO+ 0-85 (D)   1m1f rnd Good/Firm 38 -00 Slow   [79]
£5668 £1744 £872 £436 3yo rec 11lb

*2032 **THE WILD WIDOW** 3 [14] M C Pipe 6-8-5 (56)(vis)(6ex) J Mackay (7) 7/4 FAV: 222111: 6 gr m Saddlers'   **63**
Hall - No Cards (No Mercy) Sltly hmpd after 1f, chsd ldrs, prog to lead over 3f out & clr 2f out, strongly pressed
ins last, held on well, drvn out: completed hat-trick under a 6lb pen: earlier made all in h'caps at Newbury &
Leicester, prev with Miss S J Wilton: '99 wnr at W'hampton (seller, H Collingridge, rtd 59a) & Warwick (seller, 1st
time blnks, rtd 52, Miss J Wilton): plcd in '98 (rtd 69, h'cap, J Eustace): loves to force the pace at 1m/11f on
firm, soft & fibresand: acts on any trk & eff with/without blnks or visor: tough/progressive mare.

1743 **JUNIKAY** 15 [5] R Ingram 6-8-10 (61) S Drowne 9/2: 021132: 6 b g Treasure Kay - Junijo (Junius)   nk **66**
Held up, prog & drvn to strongly press wnr fnl 1f, styd on well, al just held: rest well covered: see 1743.

1729 **FORZA FIGLIO** 16 [8] M Kettle 7-9-10 (75) R Mullen 20/1: 040/03: 7 b g Warning - Wish You Well   3½ **74**
(Sadlers Wells) Chsd ldrs, rdn & kept on onepace fnl 2f: sole win at Goodwood: see 1729 (10f).

1878 **FREDORA** 9 [6] M Blanshard 5-9-11 (76) D Sweeney 6/1: -50024: Chsd wnr 3f, no extra over 1f out.   ½ **74**

1729 **INDIUM** 16 [4] 6-10-0 (79) Pat Eddery 4/1: 040105: Rear, mod gains fnl 2f: see 1375.   1 **75**

*1690 **NO EXTRAS** 18 [10] 10-9-8 (73) S Whitworth 12/1: 40-116: Dwelt/towards rear, eff 2f out, no impress.   4 **62**

1786 **DILSAA** 13 [3] 3-8-13 (75) M Fenton 16/1: 25-507: Chsd ldrs, btn 2f out: see 801.   1¼ **62**

1729 **KENNET** 16 [13] 5-8-12 (63)(BL) D Harrison 20/1: 560008: Led 1f, wknd fnl 2f: blnks, no improvement.   ½ **49**

1576 **SALIM** 22 [12] 3-9-8 (84) R Hills 10/1: 0-149: Held up, eff/no room 2f out, sn held: see 1159 (7f, mdn).   hd **70**

1878 **GIKO** 9 [11] 6-8-6 (57)(bl) N Pollard 20/1: 006560: Prom 6f: 10th: see 1729, 1033.   2 **40**

*1878 **THE GREEN GREY** 9 [7] 6-9-0 (65)(6ex) M Roberts 6/1: -00610: Led after 1f till 5w over 3f out, sn held: fin   4 **41**
last: much better expected after 1878.

11 ran   Time 1m 53.44 (3.44)   (Mrs Pam Pengelly & Mrs Helen Stoneman)   M C Pipe Nicholashayne, Devon.

2086   9.05 JUNE MDN 3YO (D)   1m1f rnd Good/Firm 38 -54 Slow
£4231 £1302 £651 £325

1811 **TARABAYA** 12 [3] Sir Michael Stoute 3-8-9 R Hills 3/1: -61: 3 b f Warning - Tarakana (Shahrastani)   **83**
Led 3f, remained prom & led again 2f out, in command fnl 1f, pushed out: confirmed promise of debut: eff at
9f, could get further: acts on fast & easy trk: open to further improvement.

1811 **TANGO TWO THOUSAND** 12 [4] J H M Gosden 3-8-9 R Havlin 13/8 FAV: -52: 3 b f Sri Pekan - Run   2½ **78**
Bonnie (Runnett) Handy, rdn/outpcd over 2f out, kept on ins last, not pace of wnr: stays slow run 9f, handles fast.

1692 **BLINDING MISSION** 18 [5] J Noseda 3-8-9 Pat Eddery 7/1: 50-03: 3 b f Marju - Blinding (High Top)   ½ **77$**
Keen/held up, qcknd to lead after 3f, hdd 2f out, onepace: handles fast grnd, stays an easy 9f: h'caps shld suit.

4606} **ORANGEVILLE** 229 [7] J H M Gosden 3-9-0 R Hughes 5/2: 2-4: Dwelt, sn in tch, kept on onepace fnl 2f: 2 **78**
reapp: rnr-up sole '99 start (mdn, rtd 86): eff at 1m, handles fast & hvy grnd, gall/easy track.

1669 **CHELONIA** 19 [8] 3-8-9 M Roberts 9/1: 3-05: Dwelt/towards rear, mod late gains: bred to apprec   ½ **72$**
10f+ & h'caps, likely to improve in such company: see 1669.

3986} **VERDURA** 277 [1] 3-8-9 N Pollard 16/1: 0-6: Towards rear, eff 2f out, no impress: reapp: unplcd sole   1 **70**
'99 start (mdn, B W Hills): now with G A Butler.

-- **WINGS AS EAGLES** [6] 3-9-0 G Hind 25/1: -7: Mid-div, btn 1f out: debut: with R M Beckett.   1½ **72**

-- **DIZZIE LIZZIE** [9] 3-8-9 G Duffield 20/1: -8: Keen/trkd ldrs, btn over 1f out: debut, with T J Naughton.   6 **57**

8 ran   Time 1m 58.29 (8.29)   (H H Aga Khan)   Sir Michael Stoute Newmarket.

ROYAL ASCOT WEDNESDAY JUNE 21ST Righthand, Stiff, Galloping Track

Official Going GOOD/FIRM. Strong Headwind. Stalls: Str - stands Side; Rnd - Inside.
A class adjustment of +20 was added to the pace figure of each race to compensate for the high-class of runners.

2087 **2.30 GR 3 JERSEY STKS 3YO (A) 7f str Good 60 -02 Slow**
£42000 £16100 £8050 £3850

-1693 **OBSERVATORY 18** [9] J H M Gosden 3-8-11 K Darley 11/2: 141-21: 3 ch c Distant View - Stellaria (Roberto) Al prom, qckn to lead ins last, styd on strongly for press: well bckd: '99 Yarmouth wnr (2, mdn & stks, rtd 100): v eff over a stiff 7f, 1m shld suit: acts on gd & fast: runs well fresh: smart, progressive & his turn of foot can gain him more Gr race wins. **115**

1530 **UMISTIM 25** [17] R Hannon 3-9-3 Dane O'Neill 16/1: 1-1652: 3 ch c Inchinor - Simply Sooty (Absalom) Prom, hdwy to lead over 1f out till just inside last, kept on but not pace of wnr: back to best after disapp on v soft grnd in 1530 & should be plcd to win another Gr 3: see 1171 (1m), 981. 1½ **116**

*1694 **HUNTING LION 18** [1] M R Channon 3-8-11 Craig Williams 25/1: 3-0013: 3 b c Piccolo - Jalopy (Jalmood) Handy, hdwy 2f out, kept on ins last, only btn 2L: v useful run stepped up to 7f & acts on firm & gd: in fine heart, win a Listed race: see 1694. ½ **109**

1753 **THREE POINTS 17** [7] J L Dunlop 3-8-11 Pat Eddery 14/1: 3-3244: Set pace till appr final 1f, kept on samepace: op 10/1: fine run on big drop down to 7f, return to 1m/9f will suit: see 17533, 1246. ½ **108**

*1468 **DANCEABOUT 28** [16] 3-8-6 D Holland 10/1: 15: In tch, hdwy 2f out, kept on for hands & heels riding: acts on gd & gd/soft: v encouraging on only 2nd start: one to follow in stks/Listed: see 1468. 1 **101**

1171 **FATH 46** [2] 3-8-11 R Hills 9/1: 12-06: Keen, handy, no extra fnl 1f: op 6/1, abs, needs 6f? ½ **105**

1830 **SELKING 12** [14] 3-8-11 J Bailey 50/1: 2-3247: Bhd, effort over 2f out, kept on same pace: useful. 1¾ **101**

*1830 **NICOBAR 12** [13] 3-9-0 K Fallon 8/1: -31618: Sn bhd, effort 2f out, onepace: bckd tho' op 6/1: better expected after 1830 (sharp/undul trk, gd/soft). 1 **102**

1693 **FREE RIDER 18** [10] 3-8-11 M Hills 25/1: -20039: In tch, wknd over 1f out: shd bhd this wnr in 1693. 1½ **97**

*1617 **BLU AIR FORCE 27** [8] 3-9-3 O Peslier 25/1: 2-1010: Slow away, bhd, nvr dngrs: 10th: see 1617. ½ **102**

1623 **SCARTEEN FOX 25** [18] 3-9-0 T Quinn 16/1: 0-4050: Bhd, rdn & not much room 2f out, held over 1f out: 11th: see 1623 (1m), 950. ¾ **97**

1171 **RACE LEADER 46** [11] 3-9-0 J Reid 25/1: 32-100: In tch, wknd 2f out: 12th, abs: see 1171, 925 (1m). 1¾ **93**

1318 **MONASHEE MOUNTAIN 38** [12] 3-9-3 M J Kinane 9/2 FAV: 1-1150: Keen bhd, rdn over 2f out, sn btn: 13th: hvly bckd from 13/2: reportedly nvr moving well & capable of better: see 1318, 1120. ½ **95**

*1751 **MURAWWI 18** [4] 3-8-11 (bl) P J Smullen 20/1: 42-210: With ldrs, wknd appr fnl 1f: 14th, btr 1751. 1 **87**

1693 **MAKAAREM 18** [6] 3-8-11 W Supple 20/1: 1-40: In tch, wknd well over 1f out: 15th, see 1693. 3½ **80**

1825 **EVERLASTING LOVE 12** [3] 3-8-6 M Fenton 33/1: 0-5560: Bhd after 3f: 16th, see 1825 & 1184 (10f). 1½ **72**

1451 **MILLENIUM MOONBEAM 29** [15] 3-8-11 G Hall 33/1: 14-060: Al bhd: 17th. 4 **69**

*1692 **JATHAABEH 18** [19] 3-8-6 P Robinson 16/1: 0-10: Al bhd: 18th, nicely bckd, btr 1692 (mdn, 1m). 1 **62**

1830 **SMART RIDGE 12** [5] 3-8-11 J Weaver 66/1: 0-5020: In tch, wknd over 2f out: fin last, see 1830. 5 **57**

19 ran Time 1m 28.93 (2.93) (K Abdulla) J H M Gosden Manton, Wilts.

2088 **3.05 GR 3 QUEEN MARY STKS 2YO (A) 5f str Good 60 -35 Slow**
£33000 £12650 £6235 £3025

*1214 **ROMANTIC MYTH 43** [21] T D Easterby 2-8-8 K Darley 4/1 FAV: 111: 2 b f Mind Games - My First Romance (Danehill) Cl-up, went on over 2f out, qcknd clr appr fnl 1f, readily, hands-&-heels: hvly bckd, 6 wk abs: earlier scored at Ripon (mdn) & Chester (stks): 16,000 gns Jan foal: half-sister to a 5f juv wnr: v eff at 5f, 6f shld suit: acts on fast & soft grnd & on a stiff or sharp trk: has run well fresh: smart & v speedy filly with a turn of foot, the 6f Gr 2 Lowther at York should be right up her street. **107+**

-1667 **AL IHSAS 19** [19] J H M Gosden 2-8-8 R Hills 11/2: 22: 2 b f Danehill - Simaat (Mr Prospector) Slightly hmpd start, keen, cl-up, effort to chase wnr over 1f out, kept on but not her pace: well bckd: acts on gd & gd/soft: v useful filly who looks sure to relish 6f & win gd races at that trip: see 1667. 2½ **99**

-- **LITTLE FIREFLY** [12] A P O'Brien 2-8-8 M J Kinane 7/1: -13: 2 b c Danehill - Tootling (Pennine Walk) Waited with, eff over 2f out, kept on over 1f out: bckd tho' op 6/1: earlier scored at Leopardstown (mdn): Feb foal, cost IR£120,000: half-sister to a smart sprinter: return to 6f will suit: has a promising future. ½ **97**

*1706 **STRANGE DESTINY 17** [15] A Berry 2-8-8 J Bailey 25/1: 314: Went right start, bhd, hdwy & not clr run over 1f out, kept on well ins last under hands-&-heels riding: fine effort on this big step up in grade & would have gone much closer with a more positive ride: keep on your side, especially over further: see 1706. nk **96+**

*1176 **SECRET INDEX 45** [18] 2-8-8 L Newman 20/1: 115: Slightly hmpd start, sn handy, rdn 2f out, onepace: 6 wk abs: useful, ran to form of 1176 (stks). 1¾ **92**

*1424 **FLYING MILLIE 30** [11] 2-8-8 R Hughes 8/1: 16: Dwelt, bhd, qcknd over 1f out, no impress ins last: well bckd: acts on gd & gd/soft: encouraging here, looks sure to relish 6f & land a nice race: see 1424. ½ **90**

*1737 **DANCE ON 16** [9] 2-8-8 K Fallon 6/1: 17: Prom, eff & short of room 2f out till appr fnl 1f, onepace. ½ **89**

1782 **BEE ONE 13** [4] 2-8-8 D Holland 50/1: -548: With ldrs till btn appr final 1f: mdns will suit, see 1782. ½ **87**

1290 **PARTY CHARMER 37** [10] 2-8-8 P Robinson 50/1: 149: Sn bhd, some late gains: see 1290, 1059. nk **86**

1586 **MIDNIGHT ARROW 22** [14] 2-8-8 J Murtagh 20/1: -150: In tch, effort & short of room over 1f out, sn no impress: 10th: see 1586, 1169 (mdn). ½ **84**

+1782 **OH SO DUSTY 13** [16] 2-8-8 Pat Eddery 11/1: 610: Hmpd start, in tch, no impress over 1f out: 11th. ½ **82**

*2020 **AZIZ PRESENTING 3** [7] 2-8-8 S Drowne 40/1: 2010: Handy, btn appr final 1f: 12th, qck reapp. 1¾ **78**

1538 **FAIR PRINCESS 25** [6] 2-8-8 M Hills 25/1: 220: Prom, btn appr final 1f: 13th, stiff task, see 1538. nk **77**

1813 **SIPTITZ HEIGHTS 12** [13] 2-8-8 M Fenton 100/1: 50: Prsd ldr till wknd 2f out: 14th, stiff task, see 1813. 1½ **73**

*1568 **GOLD AIR 23** [17] 2-8-8 D R McCabe 40/1: -010: Bmpd leaving stalls, al bhd: 15th, see 1568. hd **72**

*1385 **DREAMS DESIRE 32** [3] 2-8-8 J Reid 20/1: -110: With ldrs till wknd over 2f out: 16th, see 1385. 3½ **62**

-- **MOUNTAIN GREENERY** [8] 2-8-8 F M Berry 33/1: -610: Slow away & al bhd: 17th: Apr foal, half-sister to a hdle scorer: dam 10f wnr: earlier won at Tipperary (mdn, 5f, soft). nk **61**

*1776 **PROUD BOAST 14** [20] 2-8-8 G Duffield 50/1: -10: Led till over 2f out, wknd: 18th, see 1776. ½ **59**

+1667 **FINAL PURSUIT 19** [2] 2-8-8 T Quinn 12/1: 010: Sn rdn & al bhd: 19th: btr 1667 (gd/soft, fill mdn). nk **58**

-- **DOUBLE FANTASY** [1] 2-8-8 C Asmussen 16/1: 0: Dwelt, in tch till wknd halfway: 20th on debut: bckd 25/1: Feb foal, cost 36,000 gns: half-sister to a juv 5/6f scorer: bred for speed, with B Smart. ½ **56**

20 ran Time 1m 02.75 (3.75) (T G Holdcroft) T D Easterby Great Habton, Nth Yorks.

2089 3.45 GR 1 PRINCE OF WALES STKS 4YO+ (A) 1m2f Good 60 +05 Fast
£156600 £59400 £29700 £13500

*769 **DUBAI MILLENNIUM 88** [7] Saeed bin Suroor 4-9-0 J Bailey 5/4: 11-111: 4 b c Seeking The Gold - Colorado Dancer (Shareef Dancer) Made all, qcknd clr 3f out, unchall for a famous win: val 10L+: well bckd tho' op 1/1, gd time: 3 mths ago landed Gr 1 Dubai World Cup by 6L (rtd 134a), earlier won again in Dubai (Listed): most progressive & high class in '99, won at Doncaster (stks), Goodwood (Listed), M Laffitte (Gr 2), Deauville & Ascot (Gr 1, rtd 128), met sole career defeat over 12f in Epsom Derby: '98 Yarmouth mdn wnr: v eff over 1m/10f, poss not stay 12f: handles firm, likes gd, soft & dirt: runs well fresh on any trk: can force the pace: colt out of the very highest draw & ran rivals ragged today, very hard to beat in the top global 1m/10f races. **133**
1321 **SUMITAS 38** [8] P Schiergen 4-9-0 T Hellier 66/1: 44-3D2: 4 b c Lomitas - Subia (Konigsstuhl) In tch, outpcd after 4f, kept on over 1f out to take 2nd ins last, but wnr in another league: Gr 2 Cologne wnr in '99. *8* **117**
1587 **BEAT ALL 22** [3] Sir Michael Stoute 4-9-0 K Fallon 14/1: 34-W43: 4 b h Dynaformer - Spirited Missus (Distinctive) Dwelt, in tch, outpcd after 4f, kept on just over 1f out, nvr dngrs: op 20/1: ran to best up in class & will enjoy a return to Listed/Gr 3 as in 1587, 1248. *½* **116**
*1458 **SENDAWAR 31** [4] A de Royer Dupre 4-9-0 G Mosse 6/5 FAV: 111-14: Trkd wnr, outpcd over 3f out, wknd over 1f out: hvly bckd: prob stays 10.5f but paid the price for keeping close tabs on this outstanding wnr & can win more top races when avoiding him: see 1458 (impress, Gr 1, 9f). *2½* **113**
*1841 **KING ADAM 11** [1] 4-9-0 M J Kinane 9/1: /16-15: Keen in tch, outpcd after 4f, no impress fnl 2f. *nk* **111**
*768 **RHYTHM BAND 88** [6] 4-9-0 T E Durcan 50/1: 1-3216: Waited with, al bhd: stablemate of wnr: fin 4th in a Gr 1 in the US 7 wks ago, btr 768 (Gr 3). *5* **104**
6 ran Time 2m 07.48 (3.48) (Godolphin) Saeed bin Suroor Newmarket.

2090 4.20 ROYAL HUNT CUP HCAP 3YO+ (B) 1m str Good 60 +00 Fast **[114]**
£69600 £26400 £13200 £6000 3 yo rec 10lb

1327 **CARIBBEAN MONARCH 35** [28] Sir Michael Stoute 5-8-10 (96) K Fallon 11/2: 0-4321: 5 b g Fairy King - Whos The Blonde (Cure The Blues) Hld up far side, gd hdwy over 2f out, qcknd to lead ins last, just held on for press: hvly bckd, fair time: promise all 3 prev starts this term: rtd 84 when 4th in '99: '98 wnr at Newmarket (mdn) & Windsor (h'cap, rtd 99): wng form over 6f/1m on firm, soft & on any trk: has run well fresh: loves to come late & not an easy ride, but clearly v useful & progressive, with a turn of foot. **107**
*733 **JOHN FERNELEY 88** [11] P F I Cole 5-8-9 (95) K Darley 12/1: 33-312: 5 b g Polar Falcon - I'll Try (Try My Best) In tch centre, gd hdwy to chall appr final 1f, styd on well inside last, just held: 3 mth abs & another tremendous run: loves a stiff 1m & continues to improve: Lincoln H'cap wnr in 733. *nk* **104**
*1450 **PERSIANO 29** [10] J R Fanshawe 5-8-6 (92) D Harrison 14/1: 0-0313: 5 ch g Efisio - Persiandale (Persian Bold) Prom, eff well over 1f out, kept on for press ins last, not btn far: excellent run & in top form. *½* **100**
1829 **PYTHIOS 12** [1] H R A Cecil 4-9-0 (100)(t) T Quinn 16/1: 131-04: Cl-up stands side, swtchd over 2f out & gd hdwy when not clr run appr final 1f, swtchd left & styd on ins last: right back to best & a shade unlucky here: acts on firm & gd & apprec return of t-strap: should land a val prize in this form: see 1829. *nk* **107+**
1112 **TILLERMAN 49** [24] 4-9-0 (100) Pat Eddery 5/1 FAV: 11-35: Held up far side, gd hdwy 2f out to chall 1f out, kept on inside last, eased slightly cl-home & lost 4th: hvly bckd: 7 wk abs & a v useful effort on only 4th start: looks one to keep on the right side: see 1112. *nk* **106**
*1635 **BLACK SILK 20** [13] 4-8-4 (90)(5ex) R Mullen 14/1: 503-16: Dwelt, waited with centre, gd hdwy 2f out & ev ch inside last, not btn far: op 10/1: at the top of his form: see 1635. *shd* **96**
-- **SPEEDFIT TOO** [18] 5-8-12 (98)(vis) T E Durcan 50/1: -15047: Cl-up far side, overall ldr 2f out till ins last, no extra: been racing in Dubai, last rcd 3 mth ago & earlier won over 7.5f: in '98 trained by G Margarson to win at Kempton (List, rtd 104): eff at 6f/1m on firm, prob soft, dirt & any trk: wears visor. *1¾* **100**
1327 **RIVER TIMES 35** [3] 4-8-5 (91) M Roberts 33/1: 0-2048: Cl-up stands side, led that group over 2f out & ev ch till no extra ins last: gd run & won at the Newmarket July meeting last term off this mark: see 663. *2½* **88**
1797 **ZANAY 13** [8] 4-8-4 (90)(BL) F Norton 66/1: 111049: Overall ldr centre till over 2f out: blnks. *2½* **82**
1450 **OMAHA CITY 29** [31] 6-8-7 (93) C Rutter 66/1: 106-00: Bhd far side, some late gains: 10th: much better at 7f arnd Goodwood: see 1450. *2½* **80**
1489 **EXEAT 26** [17] 4-9-5 (105)(vis) M J Kinane 20/1: 353-20: Hld up centre, eff 2f out, sn impress: 11th. *nk* **91**
1567 **THE PRINCE 23** [23] 6-8-4 (90)(tBL) P Robinson 40/1: -10560: With ldrs far wide, wknd over 1f out: 12th, tried blnks, see 1327. *¾* **74**
1567 **KING PRIAM 23** [4] 5-8-6 (92)(bl) D Holland 50/1: 000500: Bhd stands side, modest late gains: 13th. *nk* **75**
1485 **MAYARO BAY 27** [26] 4-9-0 (100) Dane O'Neill 25/1: -00160: Handy far side, rdn & no extra well over 1f out: 14th: beat this wnr on 3lb better terms in 1327, can do better. *1¼* **81**
764 **SLIP STREAM 88** [27] 4-9-11 (111) J Velazquez 33/1: 5-5400: With ldrs far side, wknd 2f out: 15th: 3 mth abs: in '99 scored at Goodwood (Listed, rtd 118) & just tchd off in a Gr 1 at Chantilly: '98 Leicester mdn scorer for D Loder: eff at 10f, suited by forcing tactics at 1m on firm & soft grnd: has run well fresh: v smart at best, should do better in a smaller field. *¾* **90**
1820 **GREEN CARD 12** [9] 6-8-4 (90)(BL) Craig Williams 50/1: 3-4630: Bhd centre, no dngr: 16th, blnks. *¾* **67**
1834 **MUCHEA 11** [16] 6-9-1 (101)(vis) S Drowne 33/1: 220540: Bhd far side, no impress final 2f: 17th. *1* **76**
1567 **JO MELL 23** [2] 7-8-10 (96) J Weaver 20/1: 010120: Led nr side group till over 2f out, no extra: 18th. *2½* **66**
1587 **EASAAR 22** [12] 4-10-0 (114) R Hills 25/1: 0-1200: Prom centre till wknd 2f out: 19th, btr 768. *2½* **79**
1829 **CARDIFF ARMS 12** [21] 6-8-11 (97) D M Oliver 33/1: -20050: Nvr a factor far side: 20th: btr 1829. *3½* **55**
1829 **PANTAR 12** [19] 5-8-8 (94)(bl) J Murtagh 25/1: 436300: In tch far side, btn well over 1f out: 21st. *1* **50**
1327 **FREE OPTION 35** [15] 5-8-8 (94) J Reid 25/1: 610-30: In tch centre till wknd 2f out: 22nd, btr 1327. *1* **48**
1489 **TACTFUL REMARK 26** [14] 4-9-0 (100) J P Spencer 50/1: 3-0540: Al bhd centre: 23rd: see 1489, 1342. *1* **52**
1834 **BOMB ALASKA 11** [29] 5-9-9 (109) L Newman (3) 33/1: 443400: In tch far side till wknd 2f out: 24th. *1¼* **59**
*1077 **ESPADA 51** [7] 4-8-5 (91) G Duffield 20/1: 0-6210: Handy stands side till wknd over 2f out: 25th, progressive earlier, see 1077. *½* **40**
1829 **CALCUTTA 12** [5] 4-8-11 (97) M Hills 16/1: 06-000: In tch stands side, wknd qckly 2f out: 26th, stable not firing at present: caught the eye in 1829. *½* **45**
*1702 **HORNBEAM 17** [6] 6-9-0 (100)(7ex) O Peslier 33/1: 022410: Cl-up stands side, wknd 2f out: btr 1702. *nk* **47**
1841 **TISSIFER 11** [30] 4-9-8 (108) J Carroll 25/1: 20-220: Prom far side till wknd qckly 2f out: 28th, btr 1841. *2* **51**
1262 **WELSH WIND 40** [20] 4-8-4 (90) J F Egan 25/1: 00-220: Chsd ldrs far side till wknd over 2f out: 29th. *2* **29**
1110 **HOLLY BLUE 49** [32] 4-8-7 (93) R Hughes 14/1: 220-00: Bhd far side, eased appr final 1f: 30th: reportedly lost action: see 1110. *½* **31**
1845 **YAROB 11** [22] 7-8-5 (91) A Nicholls (3) 25/1: 010260: With ldrs till wknd over 2f out: 31st, do better. *½* **28**
1656 **LATALOMNE 19** [25] 6-8-4 (90)(VIS) J Mackay (7) 33/1: 0-0050: Led far side group till over 2f *½* **26**

out, wknd qckly: fin last: tried a visor, see 733, 580.
32 ran Time 1m 41.91 (3.21) (Pierpont Scott & C H Scott) Sir Michael Stoute Newmarket.

2091 **4.55 LISTED CHESHAM STKS 2YO (A) 7f str Good 60 -25 Slow**
£24375 £7500 £3750 £1875

*1653 **CELTIC SILENCE 19** [7] M Johnston 2-8-12 K Fallon 15/8 FAV: 11: 2 b c Celtic Swing - Smart 'N Noble **106+**
(Smarten) Waited with, rdn 3f out, hdwy 2f out, styd on for press to lead ins last, shade cosy: hvly bckd: won debut at Ayr (med auct mdn, easily): Feb 1st foal, cost 60,000 gns: dam multiple wnr in the USA: sire won French Derby: eff at 6f, relished step up to 7f & further is sure to suit: acts on fast & gd grnd, gall trk: runs well fresh: v smart juv, open to any amount of further improvement as he steps up in trip & one to keep on the right side.
*1454 **BAARIDD 29** [14] M A Jarvis 2-9-0 P Robinson 7/1: 12: 2 b c Halling - Millstream (Dayjur) *1* **105**
Keen in tch, hdwy to lead appr fnl 1f, rdn & collared ins last, kept on, only btn 1L: well bckd: excellent run stepped up in class: acts on gd & gd/soft: stays 7f, further sure to suit in time & sure to win in Listed/Gr class.
-- **LEOPARD SPOT** [15] A P O'Brien 2-8-12 M J Kinane 13/2: 3: 2 b c Sadler's Wells - Savoureuse Lady *2* **99+**
(Caerleon) Waited with, hdwy over 2f out, kept on for press over 1f out, no impress on front 2: hvly bckd tho' op 5/1 on debut: Mar foal, cost 6,000,000Ffr: half-brother to a 12f wnr: dam smart over 10f: excellent debut at 7f on gd, sure to relish 1m+ in time: type to improve with racing & win gd races.
*1673 **SHE ROCKS 18** [16] R Hannon 2-8-7 D Harrison 9/1: 14: Handy, hdwy to lead over 2f out till appr *¾* **92**
final 1f, onepace: nicely bckd from 14/1: stays 7f: win again with an ease in grade: see 1673 (wng debut).
1522 **DUBAI SEVEN STARS 25** [8] 2-8-7 M Roberts 33/1: 45: Sn bhd, effort over 2f out, kept on inside last, *nk* **91**
nrst fin: relished step up to 7f on gd grnd & further sure to suit in time: must win a mdn over this trip.
1653 **SNOWSTORM 19** [5] 2-8-12 M Fenton 14/1: 26: Sn handy, rdn 2f out, onepace: stays 7f on gd & fast *1½* **94**
grnd: also bhd this wnr in 1653 & must win a mdn.
-- **ACADEMIC ACCURACY** [4] 2-8-7 R Hughes 25/1: 7: Bhd, rdn & edged right 2f out, hung right but kept *4* **81+**
on inside last: debut: Feb foal: half-sister to wnrs over 6/7.5f: stays 7f on gd grnd, further will suit in time: very green but promising here, will improve.
1312 **CELTIC ISLAND 36** [10] 2-8-7 A Daly 25/1: 21228: In tch, eff to chall over 2f out, wknd appr fnl 1f. *2½* **76**
-- **ARCHDUKE FERDINAND** [11] 2-8-12 K Darley 10/1: 9: In tch, wknd 2f out on debut: Jan foal, cost *½* **80**
56,000 gns: half-brother to sev juv wnrs: bred to need 1m+ in time: with P Cole.
1691 **ZELOSO 18** [3] 2-8-12 Pat Eddery 10/1: -030: Chsd ldrs, wknd over 2f out: 10th: btr 1691. *1½* **78**
1573 **GRAND FIVE 22** [12] 2-8-12 J F Egan 33/1: 20: In tch, wknd over 2f out: 11th: nicely bckd, see 1573. *2½* **73**
1846 **SHUSH 11** [6] 2-9-0 J Reid 25/1: 1560: Made most till over 2f out, no extra: 12th, see 1107. *1* **73**
1413 **MEDIA BUYER 32** [9] 2-8-12 D R McCabe 100/1: 000: Bhd from halfway: 13th, stiff task, see 984. *1½* **69**
1761 **THE NAMES BOND 14** [13] 2-9-0 M Hills 50/1: -3140: With ldrs till wknd over 2f out: 14th, best 1252. *1½* **69**
-- **SILVER INFERNO** [1] 2-8-12 R Havlin 100/1: 0: Al bhd: 15th: Feb foal, cheaply bought. *dist* **0**
15 ran Time 1m 30.59 (4.59) (P D Savill) M Johnston Middleham, Nth Yorks.

2092 **5.30 ASCOT HCAP 4YO+ 0-95 (C) 2m4f Good 60 +00 Fast** **[89]**
£29900 £9200 £4600 £2300 4 yo rec 2 lb

-- **BARBA PAPA** [22] A J Martin 6-9-7 (82)(t) J Murtagh 10/1: 0204-1: 6 b h Mujadil - Baby's Smile **95**
(Shirley Heights) In tch, hdwy 3f out, styd on over 1f out to chall ins last, drvn to lead cl-home: gd time: landed a 2m hdle at Roscommon 5 wks ago: last rcd on the Flat in '99, rnr-up in a Listed h'cap: eff at 12f, stays 2m4f on gd/firm & soft: wears a t-strap & can carry big weights: another successful A J Martin raid.
1711 **SELIANA 17** [16] G Wragg 4-8-5 (68) F Norton 25/1: -23402: 4 b f Unfuwain - Anafi (Slip Anchor) *1½* **79**
Al prom, led over 2f out, kept on over 1f out, flashed tail sev times & collared inside last, not btn far: clr of rem: stays 2m4f: clearly has her quirks, but shown enough to win a race: see 1411.
4397} **HEROS FATAL 249** [18] M C Pipe 6-9-7 (82) R Hughes 9/4 FAV: 5453-3: 6 ch g Hero's Honor - Femme *7* **87**
Fatale (Garde Royale) Cl-up, eff over 2f out, onepace over 1f out: big gamble from 4/1: last rcd over hdles 3 mths ago, earlier won at Cheltenham (2) & M Rasen (h'cap, rtd 146h at best, stays 2m5f on gd & hvy): on the Flat in '99 plcd in the Cesarewitch (rtd 85): in '98 won at Toulouse (Listed): stays 2m4f on fast & gd/soft.
1536 **THAMES DANCER 25** [24] K McAuliffe 4-9-2 (79) T E Durcan 16/1: -04134: In tch, effort over 2f out, *1½* **83**
onepace: probably stays 2m4f & continues in fine heart: see 1536, 1394 (2m).
*1800 **EASTWELL HALL 13** [8] 5-9-8 (83) L Newman (3) 10/1: 54-515: Bhd, hdwy when hurdled fallen *1½* **86+**
horse over 3f out, kept on fnl 2f, nvr nr to chall: stays 2m4f & would have gone closer with a positive ride.
*1880 **TONIC 9** [19] 4-9-0 (77)(3ex) J P Spencer 33/1: 004316: Waited with, effort over 3f out, sn onepace: *1½* **79**
now with J Osborne & possibly stays 2m4f: see 1880.
*1222 **BANGALORE 42** [14] 4-9-13 (90) M J Kinane 10/1: 36-317: Prom, wknd 2f out: see 1222. *3* **89**
1527 **HISTORIC 25** [2] 4-8-12 (75)(bl) J F Egan 25/1: 2-0308: Led till over 2f out, wknd: lngr trip, see 1527. *1* **73**
1800 **TREASURE CHEST 13** [21] 5-8-2 (63)(vis) A Nicholls (3) 40/1: -00049: Bhd, hmpd 3f out, late gains. *hd* **61**
*1711 **MANE FRAME 17** [10] 5-8-10 (71) J Reid 12/1: -00210: Handy, wknd over 2f out: 10th, best at 2m. *shd* **69**
664 **BE GONE 102** [11] 5-9-13 (88) D Holland 50/1: 0-1300: Bhd, effort over 3f out, no impress: 11th, *4* **82**
lngr trip, recently 3rd in a 2m6.5f h'cap hdle.
1980} **RAINBOW FRONTIER 372** [15] 6-9-10 (85) D M Oliver 25/1: 22/0-0: In tch, eff & short of room 4f out, *1½* **77**
no impress: 12th, stablemate of 3rd: last rcd over hdles back in Mar, earlier scored at Ascot (h'cap, rtd 145h, stays 2m on fast & hvy): tried blnks when rtd 143h in 98/99: well btn in this race sole '99 Flat start: rnr-up in this contest in '98 (rtd 85): stays 2m4f on gd & hvy.
1187 **CAPTAIN MILLER 45** [1] 4-9-1 (78) J Mackay (7) 7/1: 10-120: In tch, hmpd bend over 3f out, sn *nk* **70**
btn: 13th, well bckd, lngr trip, apprec a return to 12f/2m as in 1187 & 997.
1329 **SON OF SNURGE 35** [5] 4-9-2 (79) T Quinn 16/1: 03-040: Chsd ldr, ev ch till wknd 2f out: 14th. *3* **68**
1991 **GALAPINO 4** [13] 7-7-11 (58)(1ow)(8oh) N Carlisle 50/1: -54050: Slow away & al bhd: 15th. *12* **35**
1800 **SHARAZAN 13** [7] 7-8-2 (63)(6ow)(8oh) C Rutter 14/1: 60-030: Al bhd: 16th: see 1800. *8* **32**
1394 **WILD COLONIAL BOY 32** [6] 5-7-10 (57)(22oh) D Kinsella (7) 100/1: -44000: Al bhd: 17th, stiff trk. *7* **19**
1527 **RENZO 25** [3] 7-8-10 (71) J Weaver 20/1: 0-1130: In tch, wkng when badly hmpd over 3f out, eased: 18th. *15* **18**
1980} **DARAYDAN 372** [17] 8-9-9 (84) Dane O'Neill 50/1: 30/0-0: Al bhd: 19th. *1½* **30**
1329 **ALHAWA 35** [4] 7-9-8 (83) K Fallon 12/1: 06-25B: Bhd, effort & short of room 4f out, b.d. bend **0**
over 3f out: see 1329, 968.
1594 **NATURAL EIGHT 21** [20] 6-7-12 (59)(2ow)(3oh) A Daly 33/1: 63335B: Bhd, rdn but in tch when b.d. **0**
bend over 3f out: see 1594, 1411.
1222 **PRAIRIE FALCON 42** [12] 6-9-12 (87) M Hills 14/1: 4-604F: Waited with, hdwy & in 6th, travelling **0**
well when stumbled & fell bend over 3f out: may have been in the shake up: see 1222, 917.
1657 **SPOSA 19** [23] 4-7-10 (59)(12oh) G Bardwell 100/1: 06305P: Cl-up, wknd 5f out, well held when **0**

badly hmpd over 3f out, p.u: see 644.
--   **GENEROSA** [9] 7-8-9 (70) J A Heffernan 14/1: 0013/U: Waited with, held when hmpd & u.r. over 3f out.   **0**
24 ran   Time 4m 25.91 (7.91)   (Glen Devlin)   A J Martin Kildalkey, Co Meath.

HAMILTON   WEDNESDAY JUNE 21ST   Righthand, Undulating Track

Official Going   GOOD/FIRM. Stalls: Stands Side, except 1m/1m1f - Inside.

2093

2.10 MEIKLE CLASSIFIED STKS 3YO 0-65 (E)   **1m65y rnd**   **Firm 14**   **-21 Slow**
£2716   £776   £388

*2013 **BOLD STATE 4** [5] M H Tompkins 3-8-13 Dale Gibson 2/1: -00011: 3 b g Never So Bold - Multi Sofft   **65**
(Northern State) Well plcd, led appr final 2f, held on well: 4 days ago won at Nottingham (h'cap): '99 York wnr
(auct mdn, rtd 78): eff arnd 1m on firm, gd grnd, stiff/gall trks: eff with/without visor, has disapp in blnks.
1895 **SAANEN 8** [3] Mrs A Duffield 3-8-11 R Ffrench 4/1 FAV: 00-322: 3 b g Port Lucaya - Ziffany   hd   **62**
(Taufan) Cl-up, ev ch final 2f, just btn: nicely bckd, clr rem: in form, eff at 1m/10f: see 1722.
1735 **WISHFUL THINKER 16** [4] N Tinkler 3-8-11 Kim Tinkler 8/1: 0-0003: 3 b g Prince Sabo - Estonia   3½   **55**
(King's Lake) Chsd ldrs, feeling pace after 4f, styd on inside last: new stable: stays 1m: see 1085.
1939 **JIMGAREEN 6** [6] Miss L A Perratt 3-8-8 C Lowther 9/1: 90-064: Dwelt but sn prom & led halfway till   4   **44**
appr final 2f, no extra: nicely bckd, qck reapp: see 1939, 1632.
1593 **NO REGRETS 21** [1] 3-8-11 A Culhane 33/1: -50005: Led 4f, gradually wknd: yet to make the frame.   3½   **41**
1909 **LA TORTUGA 7** [2] 3-8-11 S Finnamore (5) 10/1: -0066W: Unruly before start & in stalls & withdrawn: **0**
trainer reported that the gelding will not run on the Flat again from his yard: see 108.
6 ran   Time 1m 46.7 (2.9)   (The Toy Boy Partnership)   M H Tompkins Newmarket, Suffolk.

2094

2.45 RAEBURN BRICK HCAP 3YO+ 0-75 (E)   **1m1f36y**   **Firm 14**   **-25 Slow**   **[65]**
£3558   £1095   £547   £273   3 yo rec 11lb

*2033 **WESTGATE RUN 2** [4] R A Fahey 3-8-6 (54) R Winston 6/4 FAV: 00-011: 3 b f Emperor Jones - Glowing   **58**
Reference (Reference Point) Nvr far away, rdn to lead ent final 1f, ran on strongly: well bckd: 48hrs ago
scored at Warwick (appr h'cap): '99 rnr-up (clmr, rtd 75): imprvd since stepped up to 9/10.5f: acts on
firm & gd grnd, prob any trk: improving & should notch a quick hat-trick.
1940 **FLOORSOTHEFOREST 6** [9] Miss L A Perratt 4-9-6 (57) C Lowther 10/1: 552652: 4 ch g Forest Wind -   1   **58**
Ravensdale Rose (Henbit) Set stdy pace, wound it up 3f out, hdd below dist, not pace of wnr: op 6/1,
qck reapp: back to best with new tactics, see 1689, 847.
*1939 **SWYNFORD PLEASURE 6** [6] J Hetherton 4-8-8 (45)(6ex) J Fanning 8/1: -44013: 4 b f Reprimand -   nk   **45**
Pleasuring (Good Times) Mid-div, rdn appr fnl 2f, styd on, not trble ldrs: op 11/2, qck reapp/pen & ran to best.
1583 **PERCHANCER 22** [8] P C Haslam 4-9-5 (56) P Goode (3) 6/1: 001344: Held up, feeling pace & short of   ¾   **55**
room after 5f, swtchd & ran on final 1f, nvr nrr: not much luck: see 846.
1920 **FUTURE PROSPECT 7** [2] 6-9-11 (62) A Culhane 11/2: 000-25: Dwelt, chsd ldrs 3f out, same pace.   hd   **61**
1939 **PRIDEWAY 6** [5] 4-9-9 (60) S Finnamore (5) 20/1: 130656: Chsd ldrs, no impress ent final 2f: nk   **58**
qck reapp, grnd faster than ideal: see 1778, 1419.
1858 **OLLIES CHUCKLE 10** [3] 5-8-4 (41) Dale Gibson 16/1: 600667: Chsd ldrs, no extra 2f out: see 908.   3½   **34**
1858 **NOBBY BARNES 10** [7] 11-7-13 (36) Kim Tinkler 14/1: 0-0238: Mid-div, chsd ldrs appr fnl 2f, fdd.   hd   **29**
1907 **CLASSIC LORD 7** [1] 3-8-1 (49) R Ffrench 15/2: -0003U: U.r. start: see 1907.   **0**
9 ran   Time 1m 57.7 (3.6)   (Mark A Leatham)   R A Fahey Butterwick, Nth Yorks.

2095

3.20 CASTLE 2000 CLAIMER 3YO+ (F)   **5f**   **Firm 14**   **-06 Slow**
£2324   £664   £332   3 yo rec 6 lb

1663 **TANCRED TIMES 19** [9] D W Barker 5-8-9 Kimberley Hart 3/1 JT FAV: 053241: 5 ch m Clantime -   **46**
Mischievous Miss (Niniski) Cl-up, led 2f out, sn clr: rnr-up in '99 (rtd 48 & 40a): '98 wnr at Carlisle (h'cap,
rtd 65 & 47a): eff at 5/6f, stays 7f: acts on firm, soft & f/sand, prob equitrack, any trk: has tried blnks.
1773 **LUNALUX 14** [7] C Smith 3-8-7 J Fanning 6/1: 550-02: 3 b f Emarati - Ragged Moon (Raga Navarro)   3   **41**
Led till 2f out, edged right & no extra: tchd 8/1: flattered last year, handles firm grnd: see 1773.
1941 **PALACEGATE TOUCH 6** [6] A Berry 10-9-6 (bl) P Bradley 3/1 JT FAV: 013003: 10 gr g Petong -   1   **45**
Dancing Chimes (London Bells) Outpcd, styd on late, nvr dngrs: tchd 5/1, qck reapp: see 1139 (6f).
1806 **ARAB GOLD 12** [8] M Quinn 5-9-0 (bl) A Culhane 13/2: 406034: Prom, onepace appr fnl 1f: stiff task.   ¾   **37**
1910 **IMPALDI 7** [2] 5-8-5 R Winston 8/1: 50-005: Chsd ldrs 3f: tchd 10/1, stiff task, qck reapp, see 1143.   2½   **22**
1430 **FACILE TIGRE 30** [4] 5-9-2 D Mernagh (3) 8/1: 000506: Handy till halfway: op 4/1: see 146.   nk   **32**
1430 **PALLIUM 30** [1] 12-9-0 (tbl) V Halliday 33/1: 00-007: Bhd from halfway: of little account nowadays.   5   **20**
1766 **BLAZING IMP 14** [3] 7-8-10 G Parkin 33/1: 000-08: Dwelt, nvr dngrs: see 1766.   1   **13**
8 ran   Time 59.1 (1)   (D W Barker)   D W Barker Scorton, Nth Yorks.

2096

3.55 LYNETTE MED AUCT MDN 3-5YO (F)   **5f**   **Firm 14**   **-16 Slow**
£2401   £686   £343   3 yo rec 6 lb

1688 **SCAFELL 18** [4] C Smith 3-8-13 (vis) R Winston 10/11 FAV: 020531: 3 b c Puissance - One Half Silver   **64**
(Plugged Nickle) Led, prsd appr final 1f, held on well, drvn out: nicely bckd: plcd 4 times in '99 (mdn, rtd
79): eff forcing the pace 5/6f: acts on firm, gd grnd & equitrack: eff with/without visor.
1723 **CONSIDERATION 16** [2] A Berry 3-8-8 P Bradley (5) 12/1: 244-02: 3 ch f Perugino - Reflection Time   ½   **57$**
(Fayruz) Prom, ev ch & drifted right appr final 1f, held towards fin: flattered tho' acts on firm & soft grnd.
1843 **PACIFIC PLACE 11** [3] M Quinn 3-8-13 A Culhane 5/2: -02423: 3 gr c College Chapel - Kaitlin   2½   **55**
(Salmon Leap) Chsd ldrs, onepace appr final 1f: prob ran to best: see 1334.
1678 **QUEEN MOLLY 18** [1] R M H Cowell 3-8-8 (t) Dale Gibson 3/1: 524: Prom & ch till no extra appr   nk   **49**
final 1f: unsuited by drop back in trip on much qckr grnd than in 1678.
4 ran   Time 59.6 (1.5)   (Mr & Mrs T I Gourley)   C Smith Temple Bruer, Lincs.

2097	4.30 YELLOW PAGES HCAP 3YO+ 0-80 (D) 6f **Firm 14 +06 Fast**	[70]
	£4043 £1244 £622 £311 3 yo rec 7 lb	

1941 **JACMAR 6** [11] Miss L A Perratt 5-8-6 (48) Dale Gibson 7/2 JT FAV: 410521: 5 br g High Estate - Inseyab **51**
(Persian Bold) Mid-div, rdn ent fnl 2f, ran on well to get up ins last: fair time, qck reapp: earlier won here at
Hamilton (appr h'cap): '99 wnr again at Hamilton (amat h'cap, rtd 63): back in '97 won thrice here at Hamilton
(rtd 95): eff at 5/6f, stays 7f: acts on firm & gd/soft grnd, can carry big weights: all wins at Hamilton.
1687 **JOHAYRO 18** [9] J S Goldie 7-8-13 (55) P Goode (3) 13/2: 000002: 7 ch g Clantime - Arroganza   ½ **56**
(Crofthall) Set decent clip, hdd below dist, kept on: tchd 8/1: back to form on fav surface, well h'capped, see 798.
1941 **NAISSANT 6** [7] J S Goldie 7-8-6 (48) K Dalgleish (7) 6/1: 304253: 7 b m Shaadi - Nophe (Super   hd **48**
Concorde) Well plcd, hung right appr fnl 1f, ran on well, not btn far: stablemate rnr-up, ran to best: see 844.
1815 **GRAND ESTATE 12** [8] D W Chapman 5-8-13 (55) A Culhane 7/2 JT FAV: 030054: Mid-div, kept on fnl 2f. ½ **54**
1631 **SQUARE DANCER 20** [5] 4-9-6 (62) G Parkin 33/1: -00005: Front rank, onepace appr final 1f: op 20/1. ¾ **59**
1765 **MANA DARGENT 14** [3] 3-9-10 (73) R Ffrench 10/1: -20456: Chsd ldrs till 2f out: top-weight, back in trip. ¾ **68**
1868 **ANSELLMAN 9** [6] 10-9-7 (63)(bl) P Bradley (5) 20/1: -02547: Not go pace till kept on fnl 1f: op 9/1. hd **58**
1766 **SOUPERFICIAL 14** [10] 9-8-8 (50) Kim Tinkler 7/1: 0-0028: Dwelt, nvr on terms: btr 1766 (5f, hvy). 2 **39**
1654 **HOWARDS LAD 19** [1] 3-8-13 (62) R Winston 20/1: 0-0009: Bhd from halfway: see 1384. 2½ **45**
1297 **TANCRED ARMS 37** [4] 4-8-11 (53) Kimberley Hart 12/1: 223000: Al rear: 10th, see 910, 698. 1¾ **32**
1941 **MISTER WESTSOUND 6** [2] 8-9-0 (56)(bl) N Kennedy 8/1: 00-400: Slow to start, al towards rear: 11th. 3½ **28**
11 ran   Time 1m 10.3 (0.5)   (Marett-Sutherland-Hay)   Miss L A Perratt Ayr, Strathclyde.

2098	5.05 HAMILTON APPR HCAP 4YO+ 0-65 (F) 1m5f **Firm 14 -24 Slow**	[60]
	£2632 £752 £376	

1908 **ONCE MORE FOR LUCK 7** [3] Mrs M Reveley 9-10-0 (60) T Eaves (5) 9/4: -06031: 9 b g Petorius -   **67**
Mrs Lucky (Royal Match) Waited wth, gd prog 2f out, sn led, shkn up: op 6/4, qck reapp, top-weight: earlier
won over hdles at Wetherby & Sedgefield (h'caps, 2m/2m5f, firm & hvy, rtd 131h): plcd in '99 (h'cap, rtd 77):
'98 wnr at York, Musselburgh (h'caps) & Catterick (appr clmr, rtd 76): eff at 10/14f on firm, soft grnd &
fibresand: best held up for a late run & was ridden with some aplomb by young T Eaves.
903 **PIPE MUSIC 69** [2] P C Haslam 5-8-3 (35)(vis) P Goode 14/1: 205002: 5 b g Mujadil - Sunset Cafe 1¾ **37**
(Red Sunset) Well plcd, ran out appr fnl 3f till bef dist, styd on: op 7/1, 7 wk jumps ago: goes on firm & gd/soft.
1996 **ELSIE BAMFORD 4** [1] M Johnston 4-9-4 (50) K Dalgleish 3/1: 112333: 4 b f Tragic Role - Sara 1 **51**
Sprint (Formidable) Nvr far away, led over 4f out till before 3f out, styd on: qck reapp, grnd faster than ideal.
*1720 **FIELD OF VISION 14** [4] Mrs A Duffield 10-9-4 (50) D Mernagh 8/1: 243214: Prom, unable to qckn dist. ½ **50**
1936 **HAPPY DAYS 6** [5] 5-8-3 (35) P Bradley (5) 2/1 FAV: 042625: Held up, effort 4f out, onepace: tchd 11/4. 3½ **31**
1936 **LORD ADVOCATE 6** [6] 12-8-3 (35)(vis)(7ow)(12oh) Dawn Rankin (0) 33/1: 000606: Led 1m, sn btn. ¾ **30$**
6 ran   Time 2m 50.5 (5)   (The Mary Reveley Racing Club)   Mrs M Reveley Lingdale, Nth Yorks.

Official Going   GOOD TO FIRM.   Stalls: Str Crse - Stands Side; Rnd Crse - Inside

2099	7.00 APPR SELL HCAP 3YO+ 0-60 (F) 1m rnd **Good/Firm 29 -17 Slow**	[60]
	£2352 £672 £336 3yo rec 10lb	

1819 **KIERCHEM 19** [19] C Grant 9-8-2 (34) T Hamilton (5) 12/1: 0/2601: 9 b g Mazaad - Smashing Gale   **37**
(Lord Gayle) Rear, prog entering fnl 2f, took narrow lead ins last, pshd out: no bid: missed 4 years on on the
Flat, 98/99 hdles wnr at Sedgefield (cj h'cap, gd/soft, suited by fast, rtd 102h): last won in '93 on debut:
eff at 1m, stays a sharp 12f goes on fast, hvy grnd & fibresand, any track.
1520 **DANZAS 25** [17] J M Bradley 6-8-13 (45)(bl) Claire Bryan 5/1 FAV: 103262: 6 b g Polish Precedent - ¾ **45**
Dancing Rocks (Green Dancer) Rear, stdy wide prog appr fnl 2f, strong chall dist, unable toward to chall: consistent.
1273 **ISIT IZZY 40** [12] A Streeter 8-8-3 (35) S Clancy(3) 12/1: 360/03: 8 b m Crofthall - Angie's Girl 1 **33**
(Dubassoff) Chsd ldrs, rdn & chance dist, unable to quicken: apprec this return to 1m: see 1273.
1819 **FLASHTALKIN FLOOD 12** [13] J L Eyre 6-8-10 (42) R Cody Boutcher 16/1: 00/004: Front rank, led 2f nk **39**
out till 1f out, onepace: lightly raced/no form since '98 Hamilton win (h'cap, rtd 60, Mrs Reveley): previous
term won at Nottingham, (sell h'cap, rtd 65, C Dwyer): eff at 1m on firm & hvy grnd, likes stiff/gall tracks.
1858 **MR CUBE 10** [8] 10-8-9 (41)(bl) D Watson (5) 14/1: 104355: Chsd ldrs, no impression appr fnl 1f. 1½ **35**
1994 **PRIORY GARDENS 4** [20] 6-8-7 (39) Darren Williams 8/1: 003546: Held up, prog & not clr run shd **33**
over 1f out, styd on for press, unable to chall: stablemate of 2nd & 5th: poss plcd with a clr run: see 262.
1664 **INDIAN DANCE 19** [5] 4-8-6 (38)(t) B McHugh(6) 25/1: -00007: Towards rear, wide into straight, 1 **30**
styd on but not pace of ldrs: back up in trip, see 1298.
1722 **CALLING THE SHOTS 16** [11] 3-8-1 (43) G Sparkes(5) 16/1: 0-0008: Al around mid div & hmpd 2f out. nk **34**
1603 **CAVERSFIELD 21** [16] 5-8-9 (41) N Esler(3) 12/1: 000069: Prom till outpcd appr fnl 1f: stablemate 2nd. shd **32**
1858 **JAMMIE DODGER 10** [3] 4-8-5 (37) D McGaffin 11/1: -00020: Front rank, led 4f out till 2f out, fdd: 10th. 1 **26**
1499 **ALAMEIN 26** [18] 7-9-0 (46)(t) J Bosley 16/1: 40-000: Never troubled ldrs: 11th, op 10/1, back in trip. 2½ **30**
1732 **PHILISTAR 16** [9] 7-9-1 (47)(bl) P Clarke 10/1: 360050: Chsd ldrs 6f: 12th, now with N Littmoden. 1¾ **27**
1690 **PIPPAS PRIDE 18** [14] 5-8-9 (41) S Finnamore (5) 9/1: 543500: Never a factor: 13th, see 473. hd **21**
59 **FIRST LEGACY 72** [2] 4-8-1 (33) D Egan(5) 40/1: 0/0-00: Led till halfway, lost place: 16th, 10 wk absence. 0
1658 **BROCTUNE GOLD 19** [6] 9-8-10 (42) Jonjo Fowle 9/1: 060-50: Mid-div till 2f out: 18th, op 7/1. 0
1793 **BLUE LINE LADY 13** [1] 3-8-6 (48)(bl) P Hanagan (3) 9/1: -00500: Al towards rear: 19th, up in trip, see 1600. 0
648 **Victoire 107** [7] 4-10-0 (60) P Shea (3) 33/1:
1869 **Swynford Welcome 9** [15] 4-9-3 (49)(bl) W Hutchinson (3) 16/1:
1892 **Three Cherries 8** [10] 4-8-9 (41) R Farmer(2) 33/1:   1132 **Cairn Dhu 48** [4] 6-8-0 (32) R Naylor(4) 50/1:
20 ran   Time 1m 41.2 (3.7)   (Mrs H Hunter)   C Grant Wolviston, C.Durham

2100 7.25 ODGERS NOV MED AUCT STKS 2YO (E) 5f str Good/Firm 29 -09 Slow
£2765 £851 £425 £212

1838 **BYO 11** [4] M C Chapman 2-8-12 S Carson(5) 20/1: -01: 2 gr c Paris House - Navan Royal (Dominion Royale) Cl up, led dist, pushed out: left debut well bhd: IR1,000gns March first foal: apprec the drop back to 5f: acts on fast grnd, sharpish track: going the right way. **79**
1429 **AMAMACKEMMUSH 30** [7] K A Ryan 2-8-12 F Lynch 8/1: -02: 2 b g General Monash - Paganina (Galetto) Narrow lead till entering fnl 1f, kept on: op 10/1: eff forcing the pace over a sharp 5f on fast grnd. ¾ **76**
1067 **DIVINE WIND 51** [10] B A McMahon 2-8-13 W Supple 5/1: -1403: 2 ch f Clantime - Breezy Day (Day Is Done)Trkd ldrs, rdn appr fnl 1f, kept on: 7 wk abs: 6f may suit now, acts on fast & gd: see 730. ¾ **74**
*1719 **CARK 16** [2] A Berry 2-9-4 O Pears 9/2: -14: Slow away, improved to chase ldrs halfway, one pace after: poss improved in defeat here: handles fast & gd/soft grnd, see 1719 (4 rnrs). 1¾ **74$**
*1418 **ROUGH SHOOT 30** [6] 2-9-2 C Lowther 7/2 JT FAV: -15: Keen, in tch, ran green appr fnl 1f, one pace: turf bow: 6f is going to suit: prob handles fast, acts on fibresand. *hd* **72**
1835 **ALBANECK 11** [3] 2-8-12 P Fessey 7/2 JT FAV: -06: Rear, styd on fnl 1f: see 1835. *shd* **68**
1653 **NAMLLAMS 19** [5] 2-8-12 R Winston 10/1: -07: Chsd ldrs till 2f out: op 14/1, see 1653. 1¾ **63**
-- **FLYING ROMANCE** [8] 2-8-7 J Stack 16/1: -8: Dwelt, never in it: Flying Spur filly, related to 2 sprinters. 1½ **54**
1893 **KOMALUNA 8** [9] 2-8-12 S Finnamore (5) 25/1: -09: Al bhd: see 1893. ¾ **56**
1764 **HANDSOME LAD 14** [1] 2-8-12 G Hills 20/1: -60: Soon struggling: 10th: see 1764. *16* **26**
10 ran Time 59.7 (1.9) (Jalons Partnership) M C Chapman Market Rasen, Lincs

2101 7.55 N WELLS HCAP 3YO 0-95 (C) 6f str Good/Firm 29 +09 Fast **[101]**
£7228 £2224 £1112 £556

1406 **ALJAWF 32** [1] E A L Dunlop 3-8-11 (84) W Supple 5/4 FAV: 51-061: 3 gr c Dehere - Careles Kitten (Caro) Chsd ldrs, hdwy to lead 2f out, rdn clr inside last: fast time: landed fnl of 2 '99 starts, at Nottingham (mdn, rtd 92): half brother to v smart sprinter Arkadian Hero: eff at 6f, 7f should suit: acts on fast grnd & a gall or sharpish track: useful, lightly raced & improving, win more races. **95**
1887 **ROO 8** [3] R F Johnson Houghton 3-9-1 (88) S Carson (5) 4/1: -06532: 3 b f Rudimentary - Shall We Run (Hotfoot) Hmpd start, soon cl-up, chall appr fnl 1f, soon not pace of wnr: in good form. 2 **92**
*1688 **CORUNNA 18** [5] A Berry 3-8-3 (76) G Carter 11/1: 6-3313: 3 b g Puissance - Kind Of Shy (Kind Of Hush) Mid div, rdn to improve 2f out, not pace of wnr appr last: consistant form: see 1688 (mdn). 2½ **73**
1654 **INDIAN MUSIC 19** [6] A Berry 3-7-13 (72) J Bramhill 16/1: 01-004: Soon outpcd, late hdwy for press, never nearer: worth a try over 7f now: see 1654. ¾ **66**
1430 **UNCLE EXACT 30** [2] 3-7-10 (69)(1oh) P Hanagan(4) 50/1: -00005: Led, hdd 2f out, wknd: see 1140. 1¾ **59**
1654 **ZESTRIL 19** [9] 3-8-4 (77) R Winston 25/1: 04-006: Prom, rdn/fdd fnl 2f: see 1215. ½ **66**
1308 **ITS ALLOWED 36** [10] 3-8-9 (82) P Fessey 16/1: 102-07: Soon outpcd, late hdwy, no dngr: see 1308. 1¾ **66**
1768 **ABLE AYR 14** [4] 3-7-13 (72) N Kennedy 12/1: -00058: Hmpd start, never a threat: btr 1768 (hvy). ½ **55**
1409 **KILBRANNAN SOUND 32** [11] 3-8-2 (75) P M Quinn (3) 14/1: 10-459: Mid div, rdn/lost tch fnl 1f. ½ **57**
1795 **FINE MELODY 13** [7] 3-8-6 (79) Dale Gibson 8/1: 31140: Chsd ldrs, wknd quickly appr fnl 1m, finished 10th: prefer an easier surface?: see 1795,773. 1½ **57**
1694 **PIPADASH 18** [8] 3-9-7 (94) K Darley 7/1: 0-2000: Front rank, wknd quickly fnl 2f, finished last: capable of more than this, best recent form has come on an easy surface: btr 988 (List, hvy). 2 **66**
11 ran Time 1m 11.2 (1.2) (Hamdan Al Maktoum) E A L Dunlop Newmarket, Suffolk

2102 8.25 PRICEWATERHOUSE HCAP 3YO+ 0-85 (D) 1m2f Good/Firm 29 -49 Slow **[79]**
£4030 £1240 £620 £310 3yo rec 12lb

*1860 **COLWAY RITZ 10** [2] W Storey 6-9-13 (78) J Stack 9/4 JT FAV: -03611: 6 b g Rudimentary - Million Heiress (Aution Ring) Settled rear, smooth hdwy to lead inside last, drvn out: slow time: earlier won here at Ripon (h'cap): '99 scorer at Ripon & Redcar (2, h'caps, rtd 84), previous term won at Beverley (h'cap, rtd 75): eff between 1m & 12f, suited by 10f: acts on gd/soft, loves gd & firm grnd: acts on any trk, likes Redcar & Ripon: good weight carrier: tough, genuine & in fine form. **83**
1177 **ROUSING THUNDER 45** [5] E A L Dunlop 3-9-0 (77) G Carter 9/4 JT FAV: 336-02: 3 b g Theatrical - Moss (Woodman) Cl-up, led 2f out, hdd ins last, sn not pace of wnr: gd run, eff at 10f on firm/fast: see 1177. ½ **80**
1084 **KRISPIN 50** [3] G Wragg 3-9-1 (78) K Darley 7/2: -6033: 3 ch c Kris - Mariakova (The Minstrel) Raced keenly cl up, rdn to chall appr fnl 1f, kept on, held cl home: up in trip, stays 1m/10f on fast & gd/soft. *1* **79**
1845 **ANOTHER TIME 11** [4] S P C Woods 8-10-0 (79) W Supple 3/1: 0-0504: Settled last, hdwy to chall appr fnl 1f, wknd: top weight: see 1561, 1170. 1¾ **78**
1490 **GRAND AMBITION 26** [1] 4-9-10 (75) O Pears 25/1: 40-505: Set steady pace, quickened 3f out, hdd 2f out, soon btn: see 1352. *nk* **72**
5 ran Time 2m 11.1 (7.8) (Mrs M Tindale & Tom Park) W Storey Muggleswick, Co Durham

2103 8.55 LEYBURN MDN 3YO+ (D) 1m4f60y Good/Firm 29 -27 Slow
£3696 £1056 £528 3yo rec 14lb

1857 **RED EMPRESS 10** [3] Sir Michael Stoute 3-8-5 F Lynch 4/7 FAV: -261: 3 b f Nashwan - Nearctic Flame (Sadler's Wells) Cl-up, went on 3f out, easily went clr: up in trip: prev rnr-up on debut: half-sister to 3 smart mid-dist wnrs: eff at 10f, suited by step up to 12f: acts on fast grnd & a sharp or gall track: simple task today. **80**
1480 **GIMCO 27** [4] G C H Chung 3-8-10 O Urbina 7/2: 5-4322: 3 b c Pelder - Valetta (Faustuf) Bhd, chsd wnr fnl 3f, outpcd appr fnl 1f: up in trip, poss stays 12f: h'cap company should suit: see 1480, 1281. *6* **75**
4543} **SUNSET GLOW 236** [2] B W Hills 3-8-10 K Darley 7/2: 4-3: 3 gr c Rainbow Quest - Oscura (Caro) Set stdy pace, hdd 3f out, wknd, eased when btn: reportedly lost a shoe & lost action: reapp, up in trip: rtd 85 when 4th on sole '99 start (1m, mdn, gd/soft): should be sharper next time. *22* **55**
3 ran Time 2m 40.4 (6.9) (Chevely Park Stud) Sir Michael Stoute Newmarket, Suffolk

RIPON

WEDNESDAY JUNE 21ST   **Righthand, Sharpish Track**

2104

9.25 COVERDALE MDN 3YO (E)   **1m rnd**   **Good/Firm 29 -31 Slow**
£3458   £1064   £532   £266

1771 **RAINBOW HILL 14** [7] Sir Michael Stoute 3-9-0 F Lynch 3/10 FAV: -21: 3 b c Rainbow Quest - **85**
Hill Hopper (Danehill) Made all, ran wide after 3f, strongly pressed inside last, drvn out to hold on:
rtd higher when rnr up on recent debut (mdn): eff at 1m, bred to apprec further: runs well fresh on
fast, gd & an easy or sharpish track: still green here & should improve further.
983 **WOODLAND RIVER 62** [1] J R Fanshawe 3-9-0 O Urbina 12/1: -002: 3 ch c Irish River - Wiener   nk **84**
Weld (Woodman) Settled rear, gd hdwy to chall appr fnl 1f, held cl home: first sign of form here after
9 week abs & imprvd on today's sounder surface: eff at 1m, further will suit: on fast grnd: win similar.
1343 **DEVIL LEADER 34** [2] B W Hills 3-8-9 K Darley 5/1: -053: 3 ch c Diesis - Shihama (Shadeed)   2½ **74**
Raced keenly, trckd wnr, ev ch till not pace of wnr appr fnl 1f: drop in trip: stys 1m on fast: see 1051.
-- **BIGGLES** [3] Andrew Turnell 3-9-0 W Supple 50/1: -4: Mid div, outpcd 3f out, styd on for press   2½ **74**
inside last: Desert Style gelding: encouraging debut.
1444 **JAHMHOOR 29** [4] 3-9-0 G Carter 14/1: -065: Front rank, wknd appr fnl 1f: see 972.   nk **73**
-- **PORAK** [5] 3-9-0 J Stack 33/1: -6: Dwelt, al rear: debut: half-brother to mid-dist/hdle wnr Kinnescash.   ½ **72**
1717 **GOLDEN OSCAR 16** [6] 3-9-0 P Fessey 25/1: -0037: Al rear, t.o.: stablemate of 4th: btr 1717.   13 **47**
7 ran   Time 1m 42.3 (4.8)   (Cheveley Park Stud Ltd)   Sir Michael Stoute Newmarket, Suffolk

RIPON

THURSDAY JUNE 22ND   **Righthand, Sharpish Track**

Official Going   GOOD/FIRM (GOOD in places). Stalls: Str Crse - Stands Side; Rnd Crse - Inside.

2105

2.10 THEHORSESMOUTH MED AUCT MDN 2YO (E)   **1m2f**   **Good/Firm 32 -31 Slow**
£2824   £869   £434   £217

1436 **LADY LUCHA 31** [4] B W Hills 3-8-9 A Culhane 5/2: -021: 3 ch f Lord Avie - Sin Lucha (Northfields)   **72**
Early ldr, remnd prom & regained lead 3f out, kept on well fnl 1f & rdn clr cl-home: bckd from 7/2: apprec
this step up to 10f, 12f will suit: acts on fast grnd & on a sharpish trk: should progress further.
1009 **LANNTANSA 59** [7] E A L Dunlop 3-9-0 W Ryan 14/1: 062: 3 b c Dolphin Street - Antakiya (Ela Mana   3½ **71**
Mou) In tch, went after wnr 2f out, ev ch till no extra ins last: 8 wk abs, 11L clr 3rd: apprec this drop back
to 10f: acts on fast grnd: should find a mdn judged on this, see 1009, 873.
-- **SANDROS BOY** [8] P D Evans 3-9-0 P McCabe 33/1: 3: 3 b g Alhijaz - Bearnaise (Cyrano de Bergerac)   11 **55**
In tch, eff over 3f out, chsd front 2 fnl 2f but no impress on debut: possibly handles fast: learn from this.
-- **MILLENNIUM SUMMIT** [6] J R Fanshawe 3-9-0 O Urbina 5/1: 4: Slowly away, mod late prog, nvr   1¾ **52**
dngrs on debut: mid-dist bred colt, a modicum of ability hinted at here: should learn from this.
1099 **JUMBO JET 51** [1] 3-9-0 (t) R Winston 7/4 FAV: 4055: Rear, eff & drifted left 3f out, no impress: 11 **36**
well bckd from 5/2, 7 wk abs: better clearly expected, lngr trip & faster grnd: rtd higher 1099, 840 (7f, gd/soft).
-- **SNATCH** [10] 3-9-0 J P Spencer 7/1: 6: Dwelt, effort 4f out, sn btn: debut: mid-dist bred, with M Bell.   ¾ **30**
4557> **CENTAUR SPIRIT 236** [5] 3-9-0 Craig Williams 33/1: 0-7: Led after 1f till last, wknd 3f out: unplcd   7 **25**
in a Newmarket sell on sole juv start: cost 50,000 gns: with A Streeter.
1771 **LUCKYS SON 15** [3] 3-9-0 J Weaver 10/1: 008: Rcd keenly in bhd ldrs, led after 3f till 3f out, wknd: nk **25**
rcd too keenly for own gd here: has shwn little so far, with J Dunlop.
4582> **BURCOT GIRL 233** [9] 3-8-9 R Cody Boutcher 33/1: 000-9: Effort from rear 4f out, sn btn & fin last.   8 **10**
9 ran   Time 2m 09.6 (6.3)   (K Abdullah)   B W Hills Lambourn, Berks.

2106

2.45 RICHMOND MDN 2YO (D)   **6f**   **Good/Firm 32 -05 Slow**
£3601   £1108   £554   £277

1764 **PROCEED WITH CARE 15** [1] M Johnston 2-9-0 J Fanning 5/1: 51: 2 b c Danehill - Ultra Finesse (Rahy)   **96+**
Made virtually all, ran on well fnl 1f despite drifting right, cmftbly: val for 3L+: half-brother to a useful
5/6f 2yo wnr: dam won over 1m: eff over an easy 6f, 7f will suit: acts on fast grnd, can force the pace:
reportedly held in some regard, useful effort today, can continue to progress & win a decent race.
1968 **SILCA LEGEND 6** [4] M R Channon 2-9-0 Craig Williams 5/6 FAV: 232422: 2 ch c Efisio - Silca Cisa   1¾ **88**
(Hallgate) With wnr, ev ch till no extra ins last: hvly bckd from 11/4, qck reapp: tough & consistent colt.
1328 **STRETTON 36** [10] J D Bethell 2-9-0 R Lappin 11/1: 03: 2 br c Doyoun - Awayil (Woodman)   2½ **81**
Prom, rdn & onepace fnl 1f: prob met a couple of above average rivals: has shwn enough to win, poss over 7f.
-- **LOVE LADY** [2] M Johnston 2-8-9 R Ffrench 12/1: 4: Chsd ldrs, onepcd fnl 1f under a kind ride: 1½ **72+**
clr of rem on debut, lngr prcd stablemate of wnr: Jan foal, dam a modest performer: sire a high-class juv:
likely to apprec 7f/1m given time: handles fast grnd: sure to improve considerably on this.
-- **MEA CULPA** [6] 2-8-9 J P Spencer 16/1: 5: Dwelt, recovered & in tch 2f out, sn no impress & not   5 **60**
given a hard time: debut: Jan foal, cost 10,000gns: half-sister to 7f/1m wnr Menas Gold: with T Easterby.
-- **IRON DRAGON** [3] 2-9-0 (t) J Weaver 6/1: 6: Dwelt, some late gains, nvr dngrs on debut: wore   3½ **55**
a t-strap: IR 50,000gns: Mar foal, dam a 6f juv wnr, sire a top class miler: lost all ch at the start today.
1737 **MULLING IT OVER 17** [9] 2-8-9 T E Durcan 9/1: 37: In tch till btn 2f out: btr 1737 (gd/soft).   1½ **46**
-- **LEATHERBACK** [8] 2-9-0 J Carroll 12/1: 8: Slowly away, nvr a factor on debut: IR 26,000gns Feb   1 **48**
foal: half-brother to a 6f 2yo wnr: sire top class miler: lost all ch at the start, reportedly lost his action.
1859 **CIRCUIT LIFE 11** [11] 2-9-0 A Clark 25/1: -0539: Prom 4f, fdd: btr 1859.   nk **47**
-- **SOLDIER POINT** [7] 2-9-0 Dale Gibson 25/1: 0: Nvr a factor, fin 10th on debut: cost 14,000gns: 5 **33**
Mar foal, half brother to a couple of wnrs: dam a 5f scorer, sire a top class 10f performer: with P Haslam.
-- **SOME WILL** [5] 2-9-0 R Winston 14/1: 0: Al bhd, fin last on debut: op 10/1: Apr foal, sire sprinter.   8 **11**
11 ran   Time 1m 12.2 (2.2)   (Maktoum Al Maktoum)   M Johnston Middleham, Nth Yorks.

2107

3.20 MIDDLEHAM HCAP 3YO+ 0-80 (D)   **5f**   **Good/Firm 32 +08 Fast**   **[74]**
£4208   £1295   £647   £323   3 yo rec 6 lb

1781 **TUSCAN DREAM 15** [5] A Berry 5-9-10 (70) P Bradley (5) 10/1: 4-0051: 5 b g Clantime - Excavator Lady   **76**
(Most Secret) Made virtually all, held on well fnl 1f, rdn out: gd time: '99 wnr at Musselburgh (sell), W'hampton
(AW clmr), Lingfield & Epsom (h'caps, rtd 74 & 63a): loves to force the pace over a sharp/easy 5f: best on fast,

677

firm grnd & f/sand: has tried blnks, better without: likes to run up with the pace & a gd weight carrier: tough.
1842 **BOLLIN ANN** 12 [2] T D Easterby 5-9-4 (64) J Weaver 7/2: 0-0102: 5 b m Anshan - Bollin Zola (Alzao)   nk 68
Nvr far away, ev ch final 1f, just btn in a cl fin: well bckd: eff at 6f, apprec return to 5f: likes a stiff trk.
1714 **COOL PROSPECT** 17 [1] K A Ryan 5-8-8 (54)(bl) F Lynch 100/30 FAV: 410423: 5 b g Mon Tresor - I Ran hd 57
Lovely (Persian Bold) In tch, rdn to chase ldrs 2f out, kept on & just btn in a cl fin: bckd from 9/2:
another sound run from this tough & consistent gelding: see 1714, 1143.
1861 **TORRENT** 11 [6] D W Chapman 5-9-0 (60)(bl) A Culhane 6/1: 304444: Trkd ldrs, ev ch inside final   ½ 62
1f, no extra cl-home: sound run, btn under 1L: see 1861 (C/D).
1980 **SHIRLEY NOT** 6 [9] 4-9-12 (72)(bl) J P Spencer 8/1: 310405: Mid-div, styd on final 1f, not pace   1¼ 70
to chall ldrs: qck reapp, top weight: see 1980 (first time blnks), 1278.
1714 **ORIEL STAR** 17 [7] 4-8-2 (48)(bl) P M Quinn (3) 16/1: 063006: Mid-div, not pace of ldrs: see 1092.   2½ 40
1714 **WATERFORD SPIRIT** 17 [11] 4-9-2 (62)(t) T E Durcan 16/1: 000007: Bhd, some late hdwy, nvr dngrs: ½ 52
little form this term, subs slipped down the weights: hinted at a return to form here: see 1162.
1545 **PRESS AHEAD** 24 [4] 5-8-9 (55) R Winston 16/1: 501608: Chsd ldrs 4f, fdd: btr 1068 (gd/soft, 6f).   nk 44
1953 **DON BOSCO** 7 [9] 4-9-8 (68)(BL) J Carroll 20/1: 0-0009: Prom 3f, fdd: first time blnks & rcd keenly.   ¾ 55
1976 **KOSEVO** 6 [10] 6-8-2 (48)(vis) D Mernagh (3) 10/1: 000520: Nvr a factor: qck reapp after 1976 (AW).   1 32
1580 **STATOYORK** 23 [8] 7-8-12 (58) J Fanning 6/1: 000-00: Slowly away, al bhnd & fin last: '99 wnr at   1¼ 38
Carlisle (class stks) & here at Ripon (2, h'caps incl this race, rtd 73): '98 Pontefract wnr (h'cap, rtd 49 & 53a):
eff btwn 5/7f, suited by 5f: acts on firm, soft & f/sand: best held up for a late run: broke a blood vessel here.
11 ran   Time 59.0 (1.2)   (Chris & Antonia Deuters)   A Berry Cockerham, Lancs.

2108   3.55 R.L. DAVISON HCAP 3YO 0-90 (C)   1m rnd   Good/Firm 32 -02 Slow   [95]
        £6987   £2150   £1075   £537

1645 **NOBLE PURSUIT** 20 [5] T G Mills 3-9-2 (83) A Clark 7/1: 2-4041: 3 b c Pursuit Of Love - Noble   89
Peregrine (Lomond) Made all, kept on well for press over 1f out, drvn out: '99 scorer at Salisbury (auct mdn,
rtd 87): eff arnd 1m on fast & gd, any trk: genuine.
1826 **STRASBOURG** 13 [1] J H M Gosden 3-9-7 (88) J Carroll 6/1: 20-002: 3 ch c Dehere - Pixie Erin (Golden   ½ 93
Fleece) Trkd wnr, eff to chall appr fnl 1f, just went down in a driving fin: top weight & clr of rem, stays 1m.
*1863 **ARANYI** 11 [4] J L Dunlop 3-9-2 (82) J Weaver 5/2: 4-5413: 3 gr c El Gran Senor - Heather's It (Believe   5 78
It) Waited with, hdwy over 2f out, sn no impress: nicely bckd: better expected after winning 1863 (mdn, gd).
1826 **MASTERPIECE USA** 13 [3] Sir Michael Stoute 3-9-2 (83) F Lynch 6/4 FAV: 01-04: Waited with, eff over   2 75
3f out, sn no impress: hvly bckd & clearly better expected, tho' poss nvr like this faster grnd: see 1826.
1811 **FOREST FRIENDLY** 13 [6] 3-8-10 (77) A Culhane 10/1: 4-005: In tch, btn well over 2f out: rtd   3 64
91 + when 4th on sole juv start: half-sister to an 11f scorer: dam 6f wnr: eff at 7f on soft.
*1645 **IT CAN BE DONE** 20 [2] 3-8-0 (67) P M Quinn (3) 13/2: 003216: Bhd, stumbled bend over 4f out,   5 46
no dngr: probably best to ignore this: see 1645 (soft).
6 ran   Time 1m 40.2 (2.7)   (Mrs Stephanie Merrydew)   T G Mills Headley, Surrey.

2109   4.30 LADY AMAT RIDERS HCAP 3YO+ 0-70 (E)   1m4f60y   Good/Firm 32 -38 Slow   [39]
        £2804   £863   £431   £215   3 yo rec 14lb

1852 **TAJAR** 11 [9] T Keddy 8-9-9 (34) Mrs H Keddy (5) 11/2: 600031: 8 b g Slew O'Gold - Mashaarif   38
(Mr Prospector) Waited with, gd hdwy to lead 3f out, kept on, pushed out: '99 scorer at Windsor (h'cap, rtd 53):
'98 Pontefract scorer (ladies h'cap) & Warwick (class stks): suited by arnd 12f on firm, handles soft: best
without blnks & has run well fresh on any trk: runs well for lady riders: slipped to a handy mark.
1852 **NOSEY NATIVE** 11 [10] J Pearce 7-10-5 (44) Mrs L Pearce 100/30: 032262: 7 b g Cyrano de Bergerac -   1 46
Native Flair (Be My Native) Hld up, eff & swtchd left 2f out, kept on ins last, no impress cl-home: bckd, tough.
*1767 **MR FORTYWINKS** 15 [3] J L Eyre 6-11-7 (60) Miss Diana Jones 13/8 FAV: -20413: 6 ch g Fool's Holme -   ½ 61
Dream On (Absalom): Led till 3f out, kept on same pace: hvly bckd: continues in gd form: see 1767.
1852 **ACQUITTAL** 11 [4] P L Clinton 8-9-7 (32)(vis) Mrs S Owen (5) 20/1: 00-004: Waited with, kept on final   ½ 32
2f, kind ride: 1 win in 42: see 1852.
1361 **CAMAIR CRUSADER** 34 [6] 6-9-8 (33) Miss P Robson 8/1: -43535: Waited with, effort & short of room   ¾ 32
over 2f out, onepace: op 6/1, see 1361.
737 **MR MORIARTY** 87 [5] 9-9-5 (30)(t) Mrs M Morris (3) 14/1: 5/0-06: Prom, slipped bend over 4f   2½ 25
out, ev ch well over 2f out, sn btn: unplcd over hdles since 737.
2008 **I CANT REMEMBER** 5 [2] 6-10-11 (50) Miss E Folkes (5) 8/1: 405067: Prom, btn 2f out: qck reapp.   1¼ 43
1816 **PICCADILLY 13** [8] 5-9-12 (37) Mrs F Needham 12/1: 00-208: Prom, wknd over 2f out: btr 1432.   6 22
1007 **ROOFTOP 59** [7] 4-11-1 (54)(vis) Mrs S Bosley 20/1: 650009: Al bhd: unplcd over hdles since 1007.   1½ 37
1657 **SWANDALE FLYER 20** [1] 8-9-3 (28)(1oh) Mrs C Williams 50/1: 050-00: Bhd from halfway, t.o.   dist 0
10 ran   Time 2m 42.1 (8.6)   (The Veg Chef Partnership)   T Keddy Alfrick, Worcs.

2110   5.05 LEVY BOARD HCAP 3YO 0-80 (D)   1m4f60y   Good/Firm 32 -21 Slow   [87]
        £4241   £1305   £652   £326

1770 **MAZAARR** 15 [1] M R Channon 3-8-8 (67) Craig Williams 10/1: 60001: 3 ch c Woodman - River Missy   71
(Riverman) Chsd ldrs, eff to chall over 2f out, kept on to lead ins last, rdn out: first win: stays 12.3f on fast.
*1633 **RED CANYON** 21 [2] M L W Bell 3-8-4 (63) W Ryan 11/2: -24412: 3 b g Zieten - Bayazida (Bustino)   hd 66
Led after 1f, rdn & hard prsd fnl 2f, collared cl-home, just btn: continues in gd heart & stays 12.3f: see 1633.
1821 **KAIAPOI 13** [3] R Hollinshead 3-9-7 (80) P M Quinn (3) 8/1: 0-103: 3 ch c Elmaamul - Salanka   1½ 81
(Persian Heights) Hld up, eff 3f out, kept on same pace final 1f, no dngr: proving consistent: see 1225.
1919 **HIGH TOPPER 8** [6] M Johnston 3-9-1 (74) J Fanning 5/1: 0-2524: Led 1f, ev ch again 2f out, no   shd 75
extra inside last: see 1919.
1862 **MICKLEY** 11 [5] 3-8-13 (72)(BL) R Lappin 9/1: 0-2545: Waited with, rdn & slightly outpcd over   nk 72
2f out, late gains: op 6/1, tried blnks: see 1225.
*1770 **FANTASTIC FANTASY** 15 [4] 3-9-2 (75) J Weaver 10/11 FAV: 00-116: Waited with, effort over 3f out,   2½ 72
sn wknd: hvly bckd: much better expected after 2 wins earlier: see 1770 (gd grnd).
6 ran   Time 2m 40.0 (6.5)   (Sheikh Ahmed Al Maktoum)   M R Channon West Isley, Berks.

RIPON
THURSDAY JUNE 22ND **Righthand, Sharpish Track**

2111
5.40 BEDALE CLASSIFIED STKS 3YO+ 0-70 (E)   **1m2f**   **Good/Firm 32**   **-22 Slow**
£2746   £845   £422   £211   3yo rec 12lb

*2048   **JULIUS 3** [5]   M Johnston 3-8-6 R Ffrench 4/7 FAV: 6-1211: 3 b f Persian Bold - Babushka (Dance Of Life):   **80**
Led till 7f out, led again 4f out, clr over 1f out, eased right down: val 8L+, hvly bckd: earlier scored at
Nottingham (stks) & Musselburgh (h'cap, easily): ex-Irish, plcd in mdns last term: eff at 10/12f on firm & gd:
has run well fresh on a sharp or gall trk: fast progressing, should land a quick fire hat-trick.
1598   **PENTAGON LAD 22** [6]   J L Eyre 4-9-7 A Culhane 10/1: 514062: 4 ch g Secret Appeal - Gilboa   2½   **71**
(Shirley Heights) Led 7f out till 4f out, no impress on easy wnr: tough, won off a higher mark than this in '99.
1632   **NOBLE SPLENDOUR 21** [7]   L M Cumani 3-8-7 J P Spencer 8/1: 0-5023: 3 ch c Grand Lodge - Haskeir   2   **66**
(Final Straw): In tch, effort over 3f out, no impress: op 6/1: see 1632.
1692   **BAJAN BROKER 19** [3]   N A Callaghan 3-8-4 W Ryan 20/1: 43-04: Bhd, effort over 3f out, held &   7   **53**
saddle slipped over 2f out: op 14/1: rtd 73 when plcd in '99: eff at 7f on gd & soft grnd.
1352   **DIANEME 34** [2]   3-8-4 R Winston 20/1: -3045: In tch, hung right & wknd over 2f out: see 1352, 826.   6   **44**
1837   **HELLO VEGAS 12** [4]   3-8-7 J Carroll 11/4: 6-04P: Waited with, p.u. & dismounted 3f out, lame: bckd.   **0**
6 ran   Time 2m 08.7 (5.4)   (Mrs K E Daley)   M Johnston Middleham, Nth Yorks.

ROYAL ASCOT
THURSDAY JUNE 22ND   **Righthand, Stiff, Galloping Track**

Official Going   GOOD TO FIRM. Strong Headwind Stalls: Str Crse - Stands Side; Rnd Crse - Inside.
A class adjustment of +20 was added to the pace figure of each race to compensate for the high-class of runners

2112
2.30 GR 2 RIBBLESDALE STKS 3YO FILL (A)   **1m4f**   **Good 52**   **-04 Slow**
£81000   £31050   £15525   £7425

1828   **MILETRIAN 13** [8]   M R Channon 3-8-8 M Roberts 10/1: 4-0401: 3 b f Marju - Warg (Dancing Brave)   **110**
Hld up, gd hdwy ent str, rdn to lead below dist, styd on strongly: op 8/1: bounced right back to best after
fin last in the Oaks: '99 Redcar wnr (mdn), 4th in a Longchamp Gr 1 (rtd 108): eff at 10f/12f: acts on firm
& gd, handles hvy: suited by stiff/gall trks & a strong pace: smart filly, shld win another Group race.
4097}   **TEGGIANO 270** [3]   Saeed bin Suroor 3-8-8 J Velazquez 7/2 JT FAV: 4111-2: 3 b f Mujtahid - Tegwen   1¼   **108**
(Nijinsky): Prom, chall 2f out, drifted right, but ev ch till no extra towards fin: well bckd from 9/2 on reapp:
rnr-up in a Godolphin trial this winter: progressive for C Brittain last term, won at Newbury (fill mdn),
Doncaster (Gr 3) & here at Ascot (Gr 1 Fillies Mile, rtd 110): eff at 1m, stayed this stiff/gall 12f well:
acts on fast & soft grnd: runs v well fresh: smart filly, should rate higher & win more Group races.
4473}   **INTERLUDE 244** [6]   Sir Michael Stoute 3-8-8 R Hughes 7/2 JT FAV: 1-3: 3 b f Sadler's Wells - Starlet   shd   **108+**
(Teenoso) Mid-div, smooth prog to trk ldrs 2f out, sn short of room until ins last, rdn & kept on: well bckd tho'
op 9/4 on reapp: landed sole '99 start at Doncaster (fill mdn, rtd 90+): eff at 1m/12f on gd & soft, stiff trk:
runs v well fresh: smart eff on only 2nd ever start, must have gone close with a clear run & sure to win a Gr race.
1459   **CROESO CARIAD 32** [9]   M L W Bell 3-8-8 T Quinn 12/1: 10-504: Well plcd, led 2½f out till ent   ¾   **107**
final 1f, onepace: nicely bckd from 20/1: big run expected & delivered after apparently unlucky in
running in the Italian Oaks: well clr rem: eff over a stiff/gall 12f tho' 10f may prove ideal: see 953.
1828   **WHITEFOOT 13** [1]   3-8-8 K Darley 9/2: 3-4105: Rear, feeling pace appr str, late hdwy, nvr a threat: 7   **98**
well bckd: better expected, probably worth a try in headgear: btr 1374 (10f, Listed).
1374   **UNSEEDED 34** [7]   3-8-8 Pat Eddery 7/1: 04-106: Keen in rear, nvr on terms with ldrs: nicely bckd   1   **97$**
from 10/1: up in trip & highly tried, treat rating with caution: see 1051 (fill mdn).
*1447   **ABSCOND 30** [5]   3-8-8 J Reid 14/1: 22-517: Keen in rear, gd hdwy final 2f, fdd: stablemate 3rd: ¾   **96$**
not disgraced but a drop in trip & grade are likely to suit: see 1447 (10f, mdn).
1828   **CLIPPER 13** [2]   3-8-8 (BL) D Holland 14/1: 01-308: Rcd in 2nd till appr str, sn btn: blnkd: better   14   **82**
than this, stable going through a lean patch & withdrew remaining runners from this card: see 1184.
1709   **SILK STOCKINGS 18** [10]   3-8-8 P Robinson 25/1: 0-039: Sn struggling: outclassed maiden.   16   **67**
9 ran   Time 2m 33.35 (4.35)   (Miletrian Plc)   M R Channon West Isley, Berks.

2113
3.05 GR 3 NORFOLK STKS 2YO (A)   **5f**   **Good 52**   **-52 Slow**
£33000   £12650   £6325   £3025

*1813   **SUPERSTAR LEO 13** [9]   W J Haggas 2-8-7 T Quinn 5/1: -2111: 2 b f College Chapel - Council Rock   **107**
(General Assembly) In tch, prog to lead appr fnl 1f, hands & heels, cosily: bckd tho' op 5/2: hat-trick landed
after 2 wins at Catterick (fill auct mdn & nov stks): eff at 5f, 6f will suit: acts on gd & soft, any trk: v
useful, progressive & speedy, looks thrown in for the Weatherbys Sprint at Newbury next month.
1761   **BOUNCING BOWDLER 15** [4]   M Johnston 2-8-12 D Holland 14/1: 322122: 2 b c Mujadil - Prima Volta   1¼   **106**
(Primo Dominie) Nvr far away, chall appr final 1f, kept on but not pace of wnr: well bckd, v tough & useful.
1756   **PAN JAMMER 17** [8]   M R Channon 2-8-12 S Drowne 9/1: 4123: 2 b c Piccolo - Ingerence (Akarad)   nk   **105**
Mid-div, hdwy when briefly short of room appr final 1f, kept on strongly, for press, nvr nrr: nicely bckd:
useful effort back in trip: can win in Listed/Group class with a return to 6f: see 1756, 1346.
--   **KEATS** [6]   A P O'Brien 2-8-12 M J Kinane 4/1: 14: Front rank & ev ch till onepace below dist: well   ½   **103**
bckd Irish raider, 8 wk abs: scraped home in a Cork mdn sole prev start: $280,000 Hennessy Feb foal: dam
a mdn: sire a top class juv: eff at 5f on gd & gd/soft grnd, stiff/gall trks: useful.
*1761   **MAMMAS TONIGHT 15** [5]   M R Channon 2-8-12 G Carter 16/1: 133315: In tch, shkn up 2f out, sn hmpd, hard rdn,   ½   **101**
unable to qckn: ran well tho' doubtful he wld have made the frame: return to 6f will suit: see 1761.
1290   **THREEZEDZZ 38** [7]   2-8-12 K Darley 33/1: 126: Bhd ldrs, effort 2f out, same pace: imprvd, see 1290, 849.   ½   **99**
*1727   **MISTY EYED 17** [2]   2-8-7 L Newman 14/1: 517: Dwelt, imprvd 2f out, rdn & sn edged right, no extra.   1   **91**
1107   **TIME N TIME AGAIN 50** [10]   2-8-12 W Supple 33/1: 108: Dwelt, bhd, eff 2f out, no impress ins last: 1½   **91**
will find easier races: stable out of form in 1107, see 843.
*1107   **SHOESHINE BOY 50** [11]   2-8-12 Pat Eddery 3/1 FAV: 21119: Led till appr final 1f, sn btn: hvly bckd   3½   **81**
to land a 4 timer after 7 wk abs: surely something amiss: see 1107 (C/D).
1727   **FLINT RIVER 17** [3]   2-8-12 J Reid 33/1: 220: Al bhd: 10th, highly tried mdn, see 1727, 1346.   1   **78**
1426   **KOMPLIMENT 31** [1]   2-8-12 G Duffield 20/1: 5130: Towards rear, lost tch appr fnl 1f: 11th, nicely bckd.   5   **63**
11 ran   Time 1m 03.18 (4.18)   (The Superstar Leo Partnership)   W J Haggas Newmarket, Suffolk.

2114   3.45 GR 1 GOLD CUP 4YO+ (A)   2m4f   Good 52   -01 Slow
£121800   £46200   £23100   £10500   4 yo rec 2 lb

*1339 **KAYF TARA** 35 [6] Saeed bin Suroor 6-9-2 M J Kinane 11/8 FAV: 111-11: 6 b h Sadler's Wells - Colorspin **122**
(High Top) Confidently held up, prog 4f out, loomed upsides & lkd set for a cmftble win 2f out, sn jinked sharply
right & had to be rdn to get on top towards fin: hvly bckd, survived a Stewards Enquiry: earlier won at York
(Gr 2): '99 wnr at Longchamp, Goodwood, Deauville (Gr 2) & Curragh (Gr 1, rtd 127), plcd in this race: '98
wnr at Haydock (stks), here at Ascot (this Gr 1) & Curragh (Gr 1, rtd 122): eff at 14f/2m4f, may make an
ambitious drop back to 12f for the King George: acts on firm & hvy, likes Ascot: top-class & thoroughly genuine.
4397 **FAR CRY** 250 [9] M C Pipe 5-9-2 K Darley 20/1: 2115-2: 5 b g Pharly - Darabaka (Doyoun)   hd **120**
Well plcd, led ent final 2f, sn rdn, hard prsd & carr right, worn down ins last, just btn: 14 wk jmps abs, late '99
Newbury wnr (nov hdle, 2m, gd & soft, rtd 153h): '99 Flat wnr at Southwell, W'hampton (rtd 90a, Sir M Prescott),
Kempton, Newcastle (Northumberland Plate h'cap) & Doncaster (Gr 3, rtd 114): '98 Southwell wnr (3): eff at 2m/2½m:
acts on firm, gd grnd & fibresand, any trk: goes v well fresh: high-class, tough & progressive stayer, looks on handy
mark of 111 for a repeat bid in the Northumberland Plate H'cap.
1592 **COMPTON ACE** 22 [1] G A Butler 4-9-0 (t) R Hughes 11/1: 131-23: 4 ch c Pharly - Mountain Lodge   1¾ **118**
(Blakeney) Waited with, gd prog ent str, hard rdn & ch appr fnl 1f, no extra nr fin: imprvd in this highest
grade: eff at 10f/2m4f: a most versatile, v smart colt, looks tailor-made for the Irish St Leger: see 1592.
1565 **SAN SEBASTIAN** 24 [5] J L Dunlop 6-9-2 (bl) D M Oliver 20/1: 42-464: Mid-div, imprvd 3f out, had   1¾ **116**
just been rdn & lkd onepcd when knocked sideways by eventual wnr & rider lost whip, held on for 4th: game run.
-1247 **LIFE IS LIFE** 42 [10] 4-8-11 P Robinson 14/1: 02-325: Waited with, hdwy appr final 2f, rdn bef   ¾ **112**
dist, styd on but unable to chall: 6 wk abs & ran to v best over this lngr 2m4f trip: must win a Gr 2/3: see 1247.
*1565 **PERSIAN PUNCH** 24 [2] 7-9-2 J Reid 20/1: 1-2016: Early ldr, again 5f out till ent final 2f, onepace: nk **115**
4th try in this race & showed he stays 2m4f, but is probably suited by a shorter trip: see 1565 (2m).
1565 **ARCTIC OWL** 24 [12] 6-9-2 D Harrison 10/1: 226-37: Al around same pl: longer trip, prob stays 2m4f.   ¾ **114**
1620 **ENZELI** 29 [3] 5-9-2 J Murtagh 9/2: 114-28: Rear, feeling pace ent straight, styd on late, nvr dngrs: 1½ **112**
nicely bckd Irish raider, clr rem: capabable of better, rtd 121 when winning this last term: see 1620.
1339 **CELERIC** 35 [7] 8-9-2 Pat Eddery 16/1: 33-309: Held up, brief eff ent straight: won this in '97, see 1109.   17 **98**
3108 **ENDORSEMENT** 326 [11] 4-8-11 T Quinn 13/2: 3116-0: Chsd ldrs, wknd quickly appr fnl 2f: 10th,   6 **90**
nicely bckd on reapp despite stiff task on official ratings: '99 wnr at Thirsk (fill mdn) & here at R Ascot
(Gr 3, rtd 101): eff at 2m: acts on fast & soft grnd, stiff/gall track: lightly raced, worth another ch at 2m.
1456 **ASHGAR** 32 [8] 4-9-0 (VIS) D Holland 66/1: -05640: Led after 3f till 5f out, btn 2f out: 11th, visored.   5 **88**
11 ran   Time 4m 24.53 (6.53)   (Godolphin)   Saeed bin Suroor Newmarket, Suffolk

---

2115   4.20 GR 2 CORK AND ORRERY STKS 3YO+ (A)   6f   Good 52   +03 Fast
£72000   £27600   £13800   £6600   3 yo rec 7 lb

1566 **SUPERIOR PREMIUM** 24 [17] R A Fahey 6-9-0 J Murtagh 20/1: 000161: 6 br h Forzando - Devils Dirge   **121**
(Song) Chsd ldrs, ran on to lead dist, rdn clr: nicely bckd, gd time: earlier won at Goodwood (stks): '99 wnr
in Sweden (List), Ascot & Newbury, (h'caps, rtd 114): '99 wnr at Chester (rtd h'cap), Haydock & Goodwood
(Steward's Cup, rtd 107): eff at 5f, suited by 6f: acts on firm, hvy grnd, any track, likes Ascot: tough & v smart.
1566 **SAMPOWER STAR** 24 [1] Saeed bin Suroor 4-9-0 J Velazquez 14/1: 4-0152: 4 b c Cyrano de Bergerac -   2 **115**
Green Supreme (Primo Dominie) Nvr far away, ch appr fnl 1f, kept on for 2nd but no ch with wnr: op 10/1:
back to nr best though is ideally suited by give in the grnd: v smart: see 1320.
*1338 **LEND A HAND** 35 [6] Saeed bin Suroor 5-9-0 J Bailey 7/4 FAV: 24-613: 5 b h Great Commotion -   ¾ **113**
Janaat (Kris) Well plcd & ev ch, drifted right ins last, onepcd c'home: hvly bckd: shorter preced stablemate
of 2nd & may have fin 2nd with a stronger ride: may be best suited by firm/fast grnd: see 1338.
1338 **BOLD EDGE** 35 [18] R Hannon 5-9-4 Dane O'Neill 8/1: 41-034: Set gd pace till hdd ent fnl 1f, no   hd **117**
extra: not far off best with Group 2 penalty, won this last term (rtd 118): v smart: see 766.
1952 **GAELIC STORM** 7 [5] 6-9-0 D Holland 14/1: 26-065: Bhd & way off the pace this flew ins fnl 1f, nvr nrr: 1 **110+**
qck reapp: maintains plenty of ability but becoming a tricky ride as he gets older: one to keep in mind at 7f.
1111 **SIR NICHOLAS** 50 [19] 3-8-8(1ow) G Mosse 11/1: 23-126: Rear, hdwy entering fnl 2f, no further   ¾ **109**
impression inside last: op 8/1, 7 wk abs: shade btr 1111 (C/D) & 829 (gd/soft).
1952 **CRETAN GIFT** 7 [16] 9-9-0 (vis) R Hughes 33/1: 514657: Prom, shaken up & no extra appr fnl 1f.   nk **107**
734 **LOTS OF MAGIC** 89 [9] 4-9-0 T Quinn 25/1: 140-68: Front rank 4f: clr rem, st/mate 4th, abs, 7f suits.   ¾ **105**
2065 **BOLSHOI GB** 2 [10] 8-9-0 C Lowther 50/1: 0/0009: Mid div throught, eased below dist: ran 48hrs ago.   5 **93**
1830 **MAGIC OF LOVE** 13 [11] 3-8-4 M Fenton 33/1: 31-330: Rear, shkn up halfway, held/hmpd bef dist: 10th.1¾ **86**
2070 **MITCHAM** 8 [15] 4-9-4 L Carter 25/1: 40-040: Never on terms: 11th: rtd 116 when won K Stand (5f) in '99. 2 **87**
+1833 **PIPALONG** 12 [13] 4-8-11 K Darley 9/2: -11210: Chsd ldrs till lost place appr fnl 1f: 12th, hvly bckd,   nk **79**
surely something amiss in this normally most consistent filly: see 1833.
1622 **ROSSINI** 26 [3] 3-8-11 M J Kinane 11/1: 12-430: Mid div till 2f out: 13th: Irish raider, btr 1622, 981.   1¼ **82**
1834 **NOW LOOK HERE** 12 [12] 4-9-0 W Supple 33/1: 333450: Chsd ldrs 4f: 14th, stiff task: see 1337, 734.   3 **70**
1525 **INNKEEPER** 26 [5] 3-8-7 S Drowne 100/1: 0-5200: Al bhd: 15th, impossible task, see 1263, 1012.   1¼ **66**
1757 **MONKSTON POINT** 17 [2] 4-9-0 (vis) J Reid 25/1: 110130: Sn bhd: 16th, progressive over 5f on soft prev. ½ **65**
16 ran   Time 1m 14.83 (1.73)   (J C Parsons)   R A Fahey Butterwick, N Yorks

---

2116   4.55 KING GEORGE V HCAP 3YO 0-105 (B)   1m4f   Good 52   +10 Fast   [105]
£35750   £11000   £5500   £2750

1452 **GIVE THE SLIP** 30 [5] Mrs A J Perrett 3-9-4 (95) Pat Eddery 8/1: 4-3121: 3 b c Slip Anchor - Falafil   **105**
(Fabulous Dancer) Rcd in 2nd, prog to lead ent str & drvn, just hdd dist, rall most gamely & sn regained lead,
ran on well: nicely bckd, fast time: prev won at Windsor (auct mdn): ran well both '99 starts (Newmarket mdn,
rtd 94): eff at 10f, relished step up to 12f: acts on firm & gd/soft, any trk, up with/forcing the pace: useful.
*1177 **WATER JUMP** 46 [3] J L Dunlop 3-8-13 (90) T Quinn 11/2 FAV: 221-12: 3 b c Suave Dancer - Jolies   ¾ **98**
Eaux (Shirley Heights) Waited with & still nearer last than first ent str, smooth hdwy 2f out, put head in front
dist, sn hdd, styd on: well bckd: fine run, eff at 10f/12f: useful & improving, win more races.
*1282 **FILM SCRIPT** 40 [6] R Charlton 3-9-5 (96) R Hughes 10/1: 6113: 3 b f Unfuwain - Success Story   1¼ **102**
(Sharrood) Settled in tch, closed 5f out, rdn 2f out, ch bef dist, no extra towards fin: op 8/1, 6 wk abs: useful
weight-carrying performance on h'cap bow: eff at 10f/12f, acts on gd grnd, genuine, useful filly: see 1282 (Oaks trial).
1310 **BONAGUIL** 37 [18] C F Wall 3-8-10 (87) R Mullen 14/1: -11134: Held up, hdwy ent straight, edged   1¼ **91**
left under press, unable to chall: gd run over this longer 12f trip & clearly stays: see 1310, 1075.

680

*1640 **BALDAQUIN** 21 [16] 3-8-8 (85) R Hills 13/2: -0415: In tch, prog on rails appr fnl 2f, soon rdn & no `1¾` **88**
further hdway: ran to best on h'cap bow: eff at 10f stays 12f on gd & gd/soft grnd: see 1640.

1703 **FOREIGN SECRETARY** 18 [7] 3-9-4 (85) J Bailey 16/1: 4-126: Towards rear, styd on fnl 2f, nrst fin `1` **97+**
under a kind ride: h'cap bow: well worth another try at 12f, win more races, esp given a more forceful ride.

1832 **MASTER GEORGE** 12 [12] 3-8-5 (82)(VIS) Martin Dwyer 33/1: -16257: Bhd, last entering straight, `1½` **82**
sn eff & not clr run, late hdwy, never a threat: not far off best in a visor, see 1400, 936.

*1310 **KINGS MILL** 37 [13] 3-9-7 (98) D Holland 10/1: 3-1118: Towards rear, v wide into straight, never `2½` **95**
on terms: longer trip, not the most inspired ride: see 1310 (beat this 4th).

1857 **PURPLE HEATHER** 11 [9] 3-8-10 (87)(BL) Dane O'Neill 25/1: 2-2539: Early ldr, prom, fdd 2f out: blnks. `½` **83**

1948 **PALUA** 7 [10] 3-7-12 (75)(bl) A Nicholls (3) 20/1: -34320: Chsd ldrs, wknd 2f out: 10th, nicely bckd, `2½` **68**
quick reapp: stays 12f, return to 10f may suit: see 1094.

1668 **PROPER SQUIRE** 20 [4] 3-7-13 (76) F Norton 25/1: 62-620: Mid div till wknd appr fnl 2f: 11th, h'cap bow. `7` **62**

1828 **BLUEBELL WOOD** 13 [2] 3-8-8 (85) M Fenton 50/1: 111400: Rear, wknd-4f out, styd on: 10th. `7` **64**

*1919 **EL ZITO 8** [1] 3-8-10 (87)(4ex) J F Egan 33/1: -02110: Soon led, hdd ent fnl 3f & btn: 13th, see 1919. `3` **63**

*850 **COVER UP** 73 [14] 3-9-1 (92) M J Kinane 7/1: 3-02-10: Al bhd: 14th, op 5/1, 10 wk abs. `4` **67**

*1295 **BUCKMINSTER** 38 [8] 3-8-10 (87) K Darley 8/1: 4-310: Pld hard, mid-div 3f out: 15th, h'cap bow, lngr trip.`¾` **61**

*1862 **INCA STAR** 11 [17] 3-8-8 (85) J Reid 12/1: 56121P: Soon pulled up, lame: nicely bckd from 16/1. **0**

16 ran   Time 2m 31.65 (2.65)   (John E Bodie)   Mrs A J Perrett Pulborough, W Sussex

---

2117	5.30 BRITANNIA HCAP 3YO 0-105 (B)	1m str	Good 52 -08 Slow	**[109]**
	£35750 £11000 £5500 £2750			

*1786 **EL GRAN PAPA** 14 [15] J H M Gosden 3-8-4 (85) F Norton 4/1 FAV: 53-211: 3 b c El Gran Senor - Banner **96**
Hit (Oh Say): Held up, gd progress 3f out, rdn & quickened appr fnl 1f, held on gamely, drvn out: hvly bckd
on h'cap bow: earlier won at Newbury (class stakes): plcd in '99 (mdn, rtd 83): eff at 1m on firm & gd/soft
grnd, stiff/gall tracks: progressive, useful colt, shld win again.

*1495 **SIGN OF HOPE** 27 [8] I A Balding 3-8-5 (86) J F Egan 14/1: 03-112: 3 ch g Selkirk - Rainbow's `nk` **96**
End (My Swallow) Mid div, wknd up halfway, imprvd 2f out, hard rdn to press wnr below dist, just btn: nicely bckd,
clr rem: failed to notch hat-trick tho' much imprvd in defeat: should stay 10f & deserves compensation: see 1495.

1693 **KOOKABURRA** 19 [16] B J Meehan 3-8-12 (93) G Mosse 25/1: -10463: 3 b c Zafonic - Annoconnor `2½` **98**
(Nureyev) Buried in the pack, improved 2f out, rdn to go 3rd dist, not pace of front pair: tchd 33/1:
not far off best back in h'cap company giving weight to 1st & 2nd: useful colt, see 704.

1041 **MAN OMYSTERY** 55 [30] J Noseda 3-8-13 (94) Pat Eddery 12/1: 0-124: Held up, switched & hdwy `1½` **96**
towards far rail appr fnl 2f, styd on, not trble ldrs: nicely bckd from 16/1, 8 week abs, h'cap bow: useful effort.

1826 **ATLANTIC RHAPSODY** 13 [11] 3-9-0 (95) D Holland 12/1: 044125: Bhd, clr run denied throughout `shd` **97+**
fnl 3f till inside last, finished strongly, never nearer: his turn of foot shld see further success: see 1535.

1535 **SOBRIETY** 26 [26] R Hughes 50/1: 24-106: Chsd ldrs, short of room & shuffled into mid-div `hd` **101**
appr fnl 2f, soon drvn, kept on well ins last: fine run under a big weight: worth a try at 10f: see 1069.

1452 **RED N SOCKS** 30 [17] 3-8-9 (90) T Quinn 12/1: 10-207: Prom, going well & every ch 2f out, sn shkn up `hd` **91**
& no extra: bckd tho' op 10/1: eff at 1m but shaped like may do better back at 7f: acts on firm & gd: see 1183.

1535 **NOOSHMAN** 26 [13] 3-8-4 (85) L Newman (3) 16/1: 52-158: Chsd ldrs & every ch till rdn & same pace `shd` **86**
appr fnl 1f: nicely bckd from 25/1, return to 7f may suit: see 1158.

1535 **KINGSDON** 26 [19] 3-8-11 (92)(t) Dane O'Neill 50/1: 1-6309: Bhd, nowhere to go 3f out so `nk` **92+**
switched from centre over to far rail, kept on, nrst fin: eye-catching, keep in mind: see 1055.

1831 **MOON SOLITAIRE** 13 [32] 3-8-10 (91)(VIS) J Reid 14/1: 413130: Mid div, chase ldrs 2f out, `1` **89**
no extra ins last: 10th well bckd, visored bck in trip: shade btr 1831, 1452 (bt todays 5th & wnr of prev race).

3957} **KINGDOM OF GOLD** 279 [6] 3-8-1 (81)(1ow) G Duffield 20/1: 416-0: Chsd ldrs, one pace for press appr `nk` **79**
fnl 1f: 11th on reapp: '99 Hamilton wnr (mdn, rtd 85): eff at 1m, bred to get 10f: acts on firm grnd, stiff track.

1854 **CORNELIUS** 11 [21] 3-9-7 (102) D Sweeney 50/1: 36-250: Mid div, going easily but bhd a wall of `¾` **97**
horses 3f out, sn shkn up, no impress: 12th, top-weight on h'cap bow: return to 10f will suit, see 1515 (led).

1789 **ARGENTAN** 14 [25] 3-8-5 (86)(VIS) P Robinson 50/1: 33-220: Reared, soon hmpd, prog to chase ldrs `½` **80**
2f out, no extra/eased inside last: 13th, stablemate wnr, visored, h'cap bow: should win a mdn, see 1377.

*1366 **TUMBLEWEED TOR** 34 [29] 3-8-13 (94) D R McCabe 50/1: 3-0310: Front rank till fdd appr fnl 1f: 14th. `hd` **88**

*1341 **MALLEUS** 35 [3] 3-8-6 (87) M J Kinane 12/1: 32-210: Bhd, shkn up into mid-div 3f out, onepce: 15th. `½` **80**

1535 **COTE SOLEIL** 26 [24] 3-8-3 (84)(BL) R Mullen 50/1: -33000: Chsd ldrs, wknd dist: 16th, blnkd. `shd` **77**

1826 **PAYS DAMOUR** 13 [18] 3-7-10 (78)(1oh) M Baird 50/1: 0-0200: Led till over 1f out, sn btn: 17th, lngr trip. `¾` **69**

*1675 **PRETRAIL** 19 [22] 3-7-13 (80) C Rutter 40/1: 2-0210: Never a factor: 18th, up in trip, h'cap bow. `3` **66**

1535 **MATERIAL WITNESS** 26 [20] 3-8-9 (90) Martin Dwyer 25/1: 2-2230: Al bhd: 19th, btr 1535, see 983. `shd` **76**

1069 **AUCHONVILLERS** 52 [7] 3-8-2 (83) A Nicholls (3) 50/1: 6-100: Front rank till 2f out, eased: 20th. `3½` **63**

1635 **FRENCH LIEUTENANT** 21 [23] 3-8-6 (87) K Darley 16/1: 32-620: Slow away, never near ldrs: 21st. `5` **57**

*1552 **FRENCH HORN** 24 [1] 3-8-5 (86) J Mackay (7) 20/1: -03110: Never dangerous: 27th, see 1552 (hvy). **0**

1341 **ALL THE GEARS** 35 [28] 3-8-5 (86) J Bailey 10/1: 23-530: Well plcd till eff & btn appr fnl 2f, eased: 28th, bckd. **0**

1452 Chems Truce 30 [5] 3-8-6 (87)(BL) D Harrison 66/1: 1308 Cair Paravel 37 [9] 3-8-5 (86) M Roberts 50/1:
1826 Qamous 13 [10] 3-8-12 (93) R Hills 25/1: 1879 Chapel Royale 10 [27] 3-7-11 (78) J Lowe 50/1:
1786 Travelling Lite 14 [14] 3-7-13 (80) M Henry 25/1: 1404 Ejtithaab 33 [31] 3-8-9 (90)(BL) W Supple 50/1:
1308 Kareeb 37 [12] 3-8-1 (82) R Brisland (5) 50/1: *1607 Sahara Spirit 22 [2] 3-7-11 (78) G Bardwell 33/1:
1377 Pythagoras 34 [4] 3-8-4 (85) P Doe 66/1:

32 ran   Time 1m 41.91 (3.21)   (Thomas P Tatham)   J H M Gosden Manton, Wilts

---

Official Going   STANDARD. Stalls: 5f - Outside: Rem - Inside.

2118	2.20 SKEGBY CLASSIFIED STKS 3YO+ 0-60 (F)	6f aw rnd	Going 53 +03 Fast
	£2261 £646 £323 3 yo rec 7 lb		

1097 **MY ALIBI** 51 [1] K R Burke 4-8-13 Darren Williams (7) 7/2 JT FAV: 6-1261: 4 b f Sheikh Albadou - **64a**
Fellwaati (Alydar) Rear, gd hdwy appr fnl 1f, strong run to lead ins last, rdn out: op 5/1, gd time, 7 wk abs:
earlier won here at Southwell (fill h'cap): prev with E Dunlop, unplcd in '99 (rtd 57, h'cap): eff btwn 6f & 1m,
has tried 10f: acts on gd, soft, likes fibresand/Southwell: runs well fresh: eff weight carrier: in fine form.

2015 **SHARP HAT** 4 [5] D W Chapman 6-9-2 G Parkin 11/2: 402052: 6 b g Shavian - Madam Trilby (Grundy) `1¼` **63a**

Cl up till went on over 3f out, rdn/hdd inside last, no extra: clr rem, qck reapp: see 1861, 91.

1979 **FEATHERSTONE LANE 6** [14] Miss L C Siddall 9-9-5 M Tebbutt 16/1: 231633: 9 b g Siberian Express - Try Gloria (Try My Best) Rear, hdwy 2f out, edged left & styd on well inside last, no threat to front pair: op 10/1, quick reapp: will apprec a return to 7f: see 1235.   4   56a

1976 **OFF HIRE 6** [9] C Smith 4-9-2 (vis) K Dalgleish (7) 16/1: 106044: Set gd pace, hdd over 3f out, wknd inside last: quick reapp: suited by 5f: see 614.   ½   52a

1542 **CITY REACH 26** [6] 4-9-2 (vis) S Sanders 9/1: -41305: Prom, no extra for press appr fnl 1f: btr 367.   4   44a

1801 **ELTON LEDGER 13** [12] 11-9-2 (vis) R Fitzpatrick (3) 16/1: 035006: Soon rdn in mid div, late gains.   shd   44a

1806 **SUPERFRILLS 13** [13] 7-8-13 O Pears 33/1: -02007: Trckd ldrs, fdd appr fnl 1f: see 923.   1¾   37a

1801 **MARENGO 13** [2] 6-9-5 T G McLaughlin 7/2 JT FAV: 040248: Dwelt, hdwy from rear halfway, lost tch appr fnl 1f: disappointing, can do better, see 1801.   1¾   39a

1771 **SWISS ALPS 15** [4] 3-8-9 (BL) R Price 16/1: 0-009: Handy, rdn/wknd fnl 2f: op 12/1, blnkd: AW bow.   1½   33a

1868 **PRESENT CHANCE 10** [7] 6-9-2 (bl) S Finnamore (5) 10/1: 000050: Never a threat, fin 10th.   ½   32a

1822 **EVER REVIE 13** [10] 3-8-9 (bl) I Mongan (5) 14/1: -00140: Dwelt, al bhd, 11th: btr 1603 (clmr, 7f, soft).   1   29a

4361] **BALLINA LAD 252** [8] 4-9-2 J Stack 11/1: 0000-0: Front rank, wknd qckly fnl 2f, fin last: op 7/1, reapp: '99 reapp scorer at Ripon (h'cap, rtd 67 at best): won '98 debut at Newcastle (mdn auct, rtd 69 at best): eff at 5/6f, has tried 7f: acts on fast, gd/soft & has gone well when fresh: has prev tried blnks.   0a

785   **Christopherssister 85** [15] 3-8-6 J Bramhill 25/1:   1603 **Roffey Spinney 22** [11] 6-9-2 N Carlisle 40/1:

1787 **Loup Cervier 14** [3] 3-8-9 R Perham 25/1:

15 ran   Time 1m 16.3 (3.0)   (L F S Associates Ltd)   K R Burke Newmarket

---

2119   2.55 MARKHAM MOOR CLAIMER 3YO+ (F)   1m3f aw   Going 53   -20 Slow
£2226   £636   £318   3 yo rec 13lb

*1978 **CANADIAN APPROVAL 6** [10] J A Wood 4-9-4 M Tebbutt 2/1 FAV: 400211: 4 ch f With Approval - Atasteforlace (Lamedonte) Sn led, clr halfway, styd on well, rdn out: qck reapp: recent Southwell wnr (sell), earlier won at Lingfield (AW h'caps): plcd in '99 (val h'cap, rtd 78): prev term scored again at Lingfield (auct mdn, rtd 78): eff btwn 1m & 11f on firm, gd, likes both AWs: runs well fresh & best forcing the pace: in form.   61a

1373 **ALS ALIBI 34** [9] W R Muir 7-9-12 O Pears 5/1: 1/0002: 7 b g Alzao - Lady Kris (Kris) Rear, taken wide & lost grnd bend after 2f, gd hdwy after halfway, styd on fnl 2f, no threat to wnr: poss a shade unlucky not to fin closer, acts on firm, gd/soft & fibresand: see 1373.   2½   65a

1978 **OVER THE MOON 6** [7] Mrs N Macauley 6-9-1 (vis) R Fitzpatrick (3) 10/1: 000043: 6 ch m Beveled - Beyond The Moon (Ballad Rock) Carried wide after 2f, rear, rdn/late gains, nvr nrr: clr rem, qck reapp.   3   49a

*1415 **PICKENS 31** [2] Don Enrico Incisa 8-9-4 Kim Tinkler 7/1: 006014: Soon outpcd, rdn/late hdwy, no threat to ldrs: better over C/D in 1415.   6   44a

1978 **NORTH ARDAR 6** [8] 10-9-5 I Mongan (5) 14/1: 000335: Hmpd after 2f, gd hdwy halfway, wknd qckly fnl 2f: op 8/1: treat rating with caution (offic only 29): see 1978, 178.   hd   45$

1417 **TEN PAST SIX 31** [4] 8-9-4 C Teague 25/1: 50-056: Led early, rdn/wknd fnl 4f: hdles rnr.   14   29a

34] **SAKHAROV 586** [1] 11-9-2 Claire Bryan (5) 25/1: 4050/7: Trck ldrs, wknd qckly fnl 4f: long abs: missed '99, prev term scored for P Eccles at Lingfield & W'hampton (h'caps): suited by 9/10f on fast & both AW's: has run well fresh & likes a sharp trk, handles any: has tried blinks, better without: see J Neville.   9   17a

1880 **SYRAH 10** [5] 4-9-1 S Sanders 25/1: 000-68: Cl up, lost tch fnl 4f: see 1880.   ½   15a

1770 **FINERY 15** [11] 3-9-1 S Finnamore (5) 9/4: 240109: Dwelt, soon with ldrs, wknd quickly fnl 4f: nicely bckd: twice below a comfortable C/D sucess in 1502.   1¼   26a

1699 **BLACK MARK 18** [3] 6-9-2 J Tate 33/1: 0000-0: Prom, wknd rapidly 5f out, fin 10th.   22   0a

1978 **ADIRPOOL 6** [6] 6-9-4 Stephanie Hollinshead (7) 25/1: 004360: Never dngrs, fin last: qck reapp.   7   0a

11 ran   Time 2m 29.7 (8.4)   (Nigel Shields)   I A Wood Upper Lambourn, Berks

---

2120   3.30 RETFORD FILL AUCT MDN 2YO (F)   5f aw str   Going 53   -15 Slow
£2261   £646   £323

1304 **MISS VERITY 38** [11] H Akbary 2-8-0 A Whelan 6/5 FAV: -621: 2 ch f Factual - Ansellady (Absalom) Made all, qcknd & went clr appr fnl 1f, rdn out: new stable: Apr foal, dam a dual sprint wnr: eff forcing the pace over a sharp 5f on fibresand, handles gd/soft: speedy filly, fine run for new connections.   73a

-- **TUPGILL TIPPLE** [1] S E Kettlewell 2-8-0 A Beech (5) 10/1: 2: 2 b f Emperor Jones - Highest Baby (Highest Honor) Trkd wnr, rdn/no extra appr fnl 1f: op 6/1: 4,000gns March first foal, dam French 2yo wnr: encouraging debut & showed plenty of pace here.   5   62a

1938 **PATRICIAN FOX 7** [6] J J Quinn 2-8-2 D O'Donohoe 13/2: -00343: 2 b f Nicolotte - Peace Mission (Dunbeath) Front rank, rdn/not pace of wnr appr fnl 1f: clr rem, op 5/1: qck reapp: handles fast, gd & f/sand.   1¾   58a

-- **DANITY FAIR** [3] R Bastiman 2-8-0 P Fessey 12/1: 4: Dwelt, outpcd, late hdwy: cheaply bought half-sister to 5f scorer Silk Cottage: dam 2yo 5f wnr: got the hang of things late in the day here, improve.   4   48a

1906 **GOLGOTHA 8** [5] 2-8-2 O Pears 20/1: 05: Prom, rdn/fdd fnl 2f: market drifter: see 1906.   1   47a

1706 **WESTLIFE 18** [4] 2-8-2 G Baker (7) 16/1: 06: In tch, wknd appr fnl 2f: see 1706.   3   40a

-- **MONICA GELLER** [9] 2-8-7 K Dalgleish (7) 8/1: 7: Dwelt, al outpcd: debut: 8,500gns Komaite filly, dam an Irish 10f wnr: with C N Allen, improve at 6f.   1½   42a

1740 **THE WALL 16** [8] 2-8-0 A Daly 33/1: 058: Handy, rdn/lost tch fnl 2f: see 1095.   hd   35a

1764 **OLYS GILL 15** [7] 2-8-7 S Sanders 6/1: 49: Prom, wknd quickly after halfway: bckd from 12/1.   hd   42a

-- **HIGH SOCIETY LADY** [2] 2-8-2 J Bramhill 25/1: 0: Dwelt, al bhd, 10th: Feb 1st foal, dam 10f wnr.   ¾   36a

1883 **CHANGE OF IMAGE 9** [10] 2-8-4 J Tate 6/1: 640: Al outpcd, fin 11th: op 4/1.   2   33a

1706 **TOMAMIE 18** [12] 2-8-0 N Carlisle 33/1: -0000: Sn well bhd, fin last.   6   19a

12 ran   Time 1m 01.2 (3.4)   (Charles Alan McKechnie)   H Akbary Newmarket

---

2121   4.05 FCL & PAYPLAN HCAP 3YO+ 0-70 (E)   1m aw rnd   Going 53   +06 Fast   [69]
£2863   £881   £440   £220   3 yo rec 10lb

143 **GUILSBOROUGH 201** [1] J G Smyth Osbourne 5-9-10 (65) M Tebbutt 14/1: 6060-1: 5 br g Northern Score - Super Sisters (Call Report) Trkd ldrs, ran on well to lead dist, drvn out: op 12/1, best time of day: 6 month abs: '99 wnr here at Southwell (h'cap, rtd 68a & rtd 57, D Morris): plcd in '99 (h'cap, rtd 57): eff at 7f/1m on fast & gd/soft, likes Southwell/fibresand: runs esp well fresh: fine eff for new stable.   72a

907 **MAI TAI 69** [11] D W Barker 5-9-1 (56) Kimberley Hart 10/1: 504102: 5 b m Scenic - Oystons Propweekly (Swing Easy) Rear, gd hdwy 2f out, styd on well fnl 1f, no threat to wnr: not disgraced after abs.   1½   59a

1979 **SHARP STEEL 6** [8] Miss S J Wilton 5-9-3 (58) I Mongan (5) 7/2: 621253: 5 ch g Beveled - Shift Over (Night Shift) Prom, went on appr fnl 3f, hdd dist, no extra: quick reapp: gd run, apprec a return to sells.   ¾   60a

SOUTHWELL (Fibresand) THURSDAY JUNE 22ND Lefthand, Sharp, Oval Track

2063 **SHAANXI ROMANCE 2** [13] M J Polglase 5-8-3 (44)(vis) R Fitzpatrick (0) 12/1: 500554: Mid div, rdn/ styd on inside last, no threat to wnr: op 8/1, clr rem: ran 48 hrs ago: see 869, 778. ¾ **44a**
1504 **ROCK ISLAND LINE 27** [15] 6-9-12 (67) T G McLaughlin 14/1: -20265: Front rank, rdn/fdd fnl 2f. 5 **59a**
749 **AREISH 86** [7] 7-9-3 (58) J Edmunds 8/1: 121356: Settled rear, late gains for press, no threat to ldrs: 3 month abs & should be sharper next time when returning to further: see 611. 1¼ **48a**
1790 **AIR OF ESTEEM 14** [9] 4-10-0 (69) P Goode (3) 3/1 FAV: 60-357: Rear, mod late gains: bckd from 6/1: better expected on this return to sand: see 1718. ½ **58a**
353 **ONE QUICK LION 155** [2] 4-9-5 (60) R Price 14/1: 65-048: Trckd ldrs, wknd qckly fnl 3f: 7 month abs. ¾ **48a**
1801 **NICE BALANCE 13** [14] 5-7-10 (37) K Dalgleish (7) 20/1: 530009: Never a threat. 1¾ **22a**
1606 **MUJAGEM 22** [16] 4-8-6 (47)(BL) G Parkin 12/1: /01460: Raced keenly & led, hdd 3f out, wknd fnl 2f, fin 10th: op 8/1 & failed to settle in first time blinks: better without headgear in 1303. nk **32a**
1819 **DARE 13** [3] 5-9-8 (63)(vis) Joanna Badger (7) 12/1: 030460: Dwelt, al bhd, fin 11th: op 9/1. 2 **44a**
1807 **TROJAN WOLF 13** [4] 5-9-12 (67) A Daly 12/1: 000000: Dwelt, soon with ldrs, wknd quickly fnl 3f, 12th. ½ **47a**
1690 **CHAMPAGNE GB 19** [12] 4-9-8 (63)(bl) S Sanders 7/1: 030100: Never in it, 13th: twice below 1393. 2 **39a**
1801 **Stravsea 13** [5] 5-8-12 (53) J Stack 12/1: 1519 **Kocal 26** [10] 4-8-2 (43) N Carlisle 20/1:
15 ran Time 1m 43.2 (3.8) (Mason Racing Limited) J G Smyth Osbourne Adstone, Northants

2122 **4.40 H/H APPR SELL HCAP 3YO+ 0-60 (G) 7f aw rnd Going 53 -11 Slow [55]**
£1830 £523 £261 3 yo rec 9 lb

1930 **IMBACKAGAIN 7** [11] N P Littmoden 5-8-3 (30) L Paddock (3) 7/2 FAV: 002021: 5 b g Mujadil - Ballinclogher (Creative Plan) Patiently rdn, prog 2f out, strong run to lead inside last, rdn out: qck reapp: rnr-up in '99 (rtd 59a, clmr): '98 wnr here at Southwell (h,cap, reapp, rtd 64a & 58): eff at 6f, suited by 7/9f, has tried 10f: acts on fast, soft, likes fibresand/Southwell: runs well fresh & likes coming late on a sharp trk. **38a**
1601 **KILLARNEY JAZZ 22** [4] G C H Chung 5-10-0 (55)(bl) M Worrell 9/2: 301502: 5 b g Alhijaz - Killarney Belle (Irish Castle) Prom, went on over 3f out, hdd over 2f out, led again appr fnl 1f, hdd/no extra inside last: top weight & 8L clr of rem: sound eff, win again soon: see 1207, 869. 1½ **59a**
1392 **NOBLE PATRIOT 33** [10] R Hollinshead 5-8-13 (40) Stephanie Hollinshead 20/1: 002553: 5 b g Polish Patriot - Noble Form (Double Form) Dsptd lead till went on appr fnl 2f, hdd over 1f out, wknd: op 14/1: up in trip: better though prob flattered in 1036 (mdn claimer). 8 **31a**
1707 **COLONEL CUSTER 18** [9] R Brotherton 5-8-10 (37) R Naylor 11/1: 506504: Rear, late hdwy for press, no dngr: unsuited by drop in trip here, apprec a return to 10f+: much btr 408 (sell h'cap, 1st time visor). 1½ **25a**
1801 **DESERT INVADER 13** [16] 9-8-5 (32) T Hamilton 16/1: -00005: Soon/rear, late hdwy, no dngr: op 10/1. 1¼ **18a**
1801 **ABTAAL 13** [8] 10-10-0 (55)(vis) Sarah Robinson (5) 12/1: 136006: Dwelt, soon outpcd, late hdwy for press: op 8/1, top weight: see 1305. 3½ **35a**
1422 **NOW IS THE HOUR 31** [15] 4-9-2 (43) G Gibbons 14/1: -66207: Prom, lost tch fnl 2f: see 1237. nk **23a**
1771 **YAFA 15** [5] 4-8-13 (40)(BL) C Halliwell (5) 12/1: 0008: Handy, fdd fnl 2f: op 7/1: blnkd, AW bow. 1½ **17a**
2032 **LEOFRIC 4** [12] 5-8-13 (40)(bl) Hayley Turner 6/1: 306309: Never a threat: qck reapp: btr 1760. ½ **16a**
1806 **E B PEARL 13** [14] 4-9-1 (42) D Meah 16/1: 060550: Mid div, btn fnl 2f, fin 10th. *shd* **18a**
1772 **DARK MENACE 15** [2] 8-9-2 (43)(bl) D Kinsella 9/2: 060100: Held up, nvr a factor, 11th: btr 1462. ½ **18a**
1601 **GAD YAKOUN 22** [3] 7-8-4 (31) D Allan (5) 25/1: /0-000: Led, hdd over 3f out, soon lost tch, fin 15th. **0a**
1923 **Sing For Me 8** [6] 5-8-11 (38) Carrie Jessop (5) 33/1: 1559 **Ra Ra Rasputin 24** [7] 5-8-7 (34)(bl) D Watson 16/1:
1601 **Picassos Heritage 22** [1] 4-8-10 (37) A Hawkins 33/1: 1391 **Hot Legs 33** [13] 4-8-6 (33)(bl) P Mundy 16/1:
16 ran Time 1m 31.1 (4.5) (Turf 2000 Limited) N P Littmoden Newmarket

2123 **5.15 RUFFORD HCAP 3YO 0-65 (F) 1m4f aw Going 53 -15 Slow [72]**
£2254 £644 £322

*2050 **XELLANCE 3** [1] M Johnston 3-8-4 (48) K Dalgleish (7) 6/4 JT FAV: 51U011: 3 b g Be My Guest - Excellent Alibi (Exceller) Rear, prog 3f out, styd on strongly despite hanging left ins last, drvn out: nicely bckd, qck reapp: earlier won here at Southwell, W'hampton & Musselburgh (h'caps): rtd 43 when unplcd in '99: eff btwn 11/14f: acts on firm & f/sand: runs well fresh & likes a sharp trk, esp Southwell: tough, in fine form. **53a**
1862 **WINDMILL LANE 11** [8] B S Rothwell 3-8-8 (52) Joanna Badger (7) 16/1: -26302: 3 b f Saddlers' Hall - Alpi Dora (Valiyar) Cl up, went on 2f out, styd on well ins last, hdd nr fin: op 12/1 improved form with the visor ommitted: eff at 12f on firm, hvy & fibresand: see 978. hd **56a**
1613 **NICIARA 22** [6] M C Chapman 3-7-11 (41)(bl) P Fessey 16/1: 004033: 3 b g Soviet Lad - Verusa (Petorius) Led, hdd 2f out, not pace of front pair inside last: flatted 1613 (2m clmr, gd/soft). 2½ **41a**
1571 **BLUE CAVALIER 23** [7] S Dow 3-7-12 (41)(1ow) N Carlisle 33/1: 60-004: Dsptd lead, drvn/fdd fnl 2f. 1½ **40a**
1949 **ALPHA ROSE 7** [5] 3-8-9 (53) A Beech (5) 6/4 JT FAV: 541125: Mid div, hung left & lost tch fnl 2f: mkt drifter from 4/5, qck reapp: more expected on this return to the AW: much btr 1949, 1657 (turf). 8 **39a**
1040 **CHARLEM 55** [4] 3-8-1 (44)(VIS)(1ow) O Pears 14/1: 00-666: Mid div, lost tch fnl 2f: 8 wk abs: visor. 2 **28a**
1142 **ODYN DANCER 49** [2] 3-8-2 (46) G Baker (7) 20/1: 662067: Never a threat: 7 wk abs: see 537. 3 **25a**
1779 **TRUE OBSESSION 15** [3] 3-9-7 (65) M Tebbutt 9/2: 00-058: Prom, rdn/wknd quickly 3f out, eased when btn, t.o.: tchd 7/1: up in trip: see 1779. *dist* **0a**
8 ran Time 2m 42.5 (8.2) (T T Bloodstocks) M Johnston Middleham, N Yorks

GOODWOOD FRIDAY JUNE 23RD Righthand, Sharpish, Undulating Track

Official Going Str - GOOD, GD/FIRM places & on Rnd Crse. Stalls: Str - Stands; Rnd Crse - Ins, except 12f - Outside.

2124 **6.35 COFFEE APPR HCAP 3YO+ 0-70 (E) 6f str Good/Firm 36 -12 Slow [70]**
£3250 £1000 £500 £250 3 yo rec 7 lb High no's towards centre favoured

3806} **MY BROTHER 290** [14] Dr J R J Naylor 6-7-10 (38)(4oh) Michael Doyle (7) 33/1: P000-1: 6 b g Lugana Beach - Lucky Love (Mummy's Pet): Rdn/towards rear till prog final 2f, styd on well for press to lead well ins last, edged left cl-home: reapp, 1st win/time in the frame: unplcd at up to 1m in '99 for P Eccles (tried visor, rtd 50 & 20a): rtd 38 from 2 starts in '98 (S Earle): eff at 6f on fast grnd & a sharp trk: runs well fresh. **40**
1464 **CHAKRA 30** [11] J M Bradley 6-7-10 (38)(7oh) G Baker (5) 33/1: 600002: 6 gr g Mystiko - Maracuja (Riverman): Prom, rdn/led over 1f out, hdd well inside last, just held: likes a sharp trk: see 628. nk **39**
1806 **HALF TONE 14** [13] R M Flower 8-7-13 (41)(bl) A Beech 14/1: 005303: 8 gr h Touch Of Grey - Demilinga (Nishapour): Rdn, outpcd early, styd on well final 1f, nrst fin: typical late flourish, well h'capped: see 958. nk **41**

2031 **GRACE** 5 [17] J M Bradley 6-8-1 (43) Claire Bryan (3) 14/1: 640664: Prom, kept on well fnl 1f: vis omitted. ½ 41
1869 **FAIRY PRINCE** 11 [4] 7-9-7 (57) R Smith (3) 12/1: 00-005: Held up, no room over 2f out till over 1f shd 55
out, swtchd left & styd on well inside last: no luck in running, gd run from unfav low draw: keep in mind.
1799 **SCISSOR RIDGE** 15 [15] 8-8-5 (47) S Clancy (5) 10/1: 402306: Prom, onepace fnl 1f: see 1542, 29 (AW). 2 40
1953 **PERIGEUX** 8 [8] 4-9-6 (62) C Catlin (5) 14/1: 0-5507: Prom, ch over 1f out, onepace: see 1423. hd 54
1915 **FRENCH FANCY** 9 [6] 3-7-10 (45) (bl) (20h) Joanna Badger (5) 25/1: 004108: Mid-div, held over 1f out. ½ 35
1971 **INDIAN BAZAAR** 7 [18] 4-7-12 (40) P Fitzsimons 11/2: 0-0329: Prom 5f: see 1578 (mdn h'cap). ¾ 28
1629 **SIHAFI** 22 [19] 7-8-11 (53) T Hamilton (5) 9/2 JT FAV: 0-0430: Prom 5f: 10th: nicely bckd: see 1487. ½ 39
2051 **MOUTON** 4 [10] 4-7-10 (38)(6oh) D Cosgrave (3) 50/1: 000600: Rear, eff/no room over 1f out: 11th. hd 23
763 **SEREN TEG** 87 [1] 4-8-10 (52) R Studholme 10/1: -14400: Prom 4f: 12th: 12 wk abs: see 440 (5f, AW). 3 30
1543 **NIGHTINGALE SONG** 27 [16] 6-8-5 (47) P Dobbs 7/1: 00-040: Led halfway till over 1f out, fdd: 13th. ¾ 23
1976 **POLAR MIST** 7 [12] 5-9-0 (56)(tbl) I Mongan 5/1: 001060: Led 3f, sn held: 14th: see 1487 (5f). shd 32
1971 **MR STYLISH** 7 [2] 4-10-0 (70) N Chalmers (5) 9/2 JT FAV: -02330: Held up, held when no room 1f out: 16th. 0
1438 **Calandrella** 32 [7] 7-7-10 (38) G Sparkes (3) 20/1:   1999 **Kilmeena Lad** 6 [5] 4-9-9 (65) S Carson 14/1:
1932 **Gold Edge** 8 [3] 6-7-10 (38)(8oh) D Kinsella 5) 40/1:
18 ran   Time 1m 12.85 (2.85)   (Robert & Cora Till)   Dr J R J Naylor Newmarket.

2125 **7.05 MENZIES EBF MDN 2YO (D) 7f str Good/Firm 36 -49 Slow**
£4056   £1248   £624   £312

1346 **NIGHT FALL** 36 [3] R Hannon 2-8-9 P Fitzsimons (5) 6/1: 561: 2 ch f Night Shift - Tumble (Mtoto): 80
Trkd ldr, led inside last & readily asserted, pushed out: slow time: Ir46,000 gns first foal: clrly apprec
this step up to 7f, 1m will suit: acts on fast grnd & a sharp/undul trk: improving.
1859 **QUEEN SPAIN** 12 [5] M R Channon 2-8-9 S Drowne 6/4: -0222: 2 b f Mister Baileys - Excellus 2½ 73
(Exceller, clr 2f out, rdn/hdd inside last & no extra: clr rem: acts on fast & soft grnd: stays a sharp 7f.
1408 **TRAVELLERS DREAM** 34 [2] B R Millman 2-9-0 G Hind 16/1: 03: 2 b c Blues Traveller - Helen's Dream 5 68$
(Troy) Trkd ldrs, held over 1f out: longr 7f trip, likely to need further still: see 1408.
-- **PERSUADE** [1] J H M Gosden 2-9-0 R Havlin 5/4 FAV: 4: Dwelt, sn in tch, hung left/btn over 2f 3 62
out: heavily bckd: Lure colt, Apr foal: dam a 7f juv wnr, sire a top class 1m US performer.
-- **UNDERCOVER GIRL** [4] 2-8-9 Martin Dwyer 3/1: 5: Keen/dwelt, al rear: op 10/1: Barathea filly, Feb 2 53
foal, cost Ffr750,000, a first foal: dam a wnr abroad, sire a top class miler: improve in time for W R Muir.
5 ran   Time 1m 30.44 (5.94)   (Jubert Family)   R Hannon East Everleigh, Wilts.

2126 **7.35 FESTIVAL HCAP 3YO+ 0-85 (D) 1m rnd Good/Firm 36 +12 Fast** [84]
£4387   £1350   £675   £337

*1998 **ADOBE** 6 [4] W M Brisbourne 5-8-3 (59)(6ex) G Baker (7) 9/4 FAV: 421111: 5 b g Green Desert - Shamshir 66
(Kris): Trkd ldrs, rdn/led over 1f out, styd on well inside last, pushed out cl-home: gd time: well bckd: completed
a 4-timer under a 6lb pen after earlier winning twice at Hamilton (h'cap & class stks) & Bath (h'cap), earlier won on
sand at W'hampton (rtd 58a, h'cap): '99 wnr at Bath & Nottingham (h'caps, rtd 55 & 49a): eff at 7f/1m on firm, gd &
fibresand, handles soft & any trk: likes Hamilton & Bath: eff with/without a t-strap: tough, at the top of his form.
1552 **BARABASCHI** 25 [9] J H M Gosden 4-9-2 (72) K Darley 7/1: 322-22: 4 b g Elmaamul - Hills' Presidium ½ 77
(Presidium): Keen/chsd ldrs, ev ch 1f out, kept on tho' al just held: eff at 7f/1m: see 1552.
1926 **SKY DOME** 9 [3] M H Tompkins 7-9-1 (71) A Beech (5) 11/2: -06023: 7 ch g Bluebird - God Speed Her 1½ 73
(Pas de Seul): Rear, styd on from over 1f out, not reach front pair: waiting tactics again overdone: see 1926, 1150.
1973 **HARMONY HALL** 7 [7] J M Bradley 6-8-4 (60) P Fitzsimons (5) 16/1: 040-44: Mid-div, kept on onepace. ½ 61
1450 **STOPPES BROW** 31 [5] 8-9-8 (78)(bl) I Mongan (5) 9/2: 440405: Dwelt/rear, late gains for press. shd 79
1879 **NAVIASKY** 11 [8] 5-9-10 (80) Martin Dwyer 15/2: 004046: Rear, no room over 2f out till over 1f out, 1¼ 78
mod late gains, no threat to leaders: likes to come late, needs luck in running, worth another chance: see 733.
1744 **KANZ WOOD** 12 [2] 4-8-11 (67) N Pollard 14/1: 50-107: Dwelt, nvr on terms: btr 1473 (C/D, g/s). 2 61
1113 **ANALYTICAL** 51 [6] 4-8-13 (69) R Hughes 9/1: 00-008: Led till over 1f out, fdd: 7 wk abs: see 1113. ¾ 62
1037 **PENGAMON** 56 [1] 8-8-3 (59) G Hind 16/1: 212-39: Chsd ldr till over 1f out, fdd: 8 wk abs: see 1037, 107. nk 56
1794 **GREEN GOD** 15 [10] 4-8-9 (65) S Drowne (5) 16/1: 20-050: Mid-div, btn 2f out: 10th: see 1542 (7f). 1¾ 54
1744 **COPPLESTONE** 17 [11] 4-9-5 (75) A Culhane 10/1: -02440: Keen/prom 6f: 11th: see 1744, 1070. 2½ 59
11 ran   Time 1m 39.33 (1.93)   (P R Kirk)   W M Brisbourne Great Ness, Shropshire

---

2127 **8.05 JAGUAR HCAP 3YO+ 0-95 (C) 1m4f Good/Firm 36 -06 Slow** [82]
£10578   £3255   £1627   £813   3 yo rec 14lb

1878 **COURT SHAREEF** 11 [5] R J Price 5-8-9 (63) P Fitzsimons 12/1: 05-131: 5 b g Shareef Dancer - 73
Fairfields Cone (Celtic Cone): Dwelt/rear, prog final 3f & styd on well for press inside last to lead nr fin: earlier
made a wng reapp at Windsor (h'cap): rnr-up in a nov hdle in Nov '99 (rtd 103h): rtd 61 at best on the level in '99
(h'cap, R Dickin): '98 wnr at Windsor & Leicester (h'caps, rtd 74 at best): suited by 12/14f on fast & gd grnd, any trk,
likes Windsor: has run well fresh: looks fairly h'capped at present, could win again.
*1785 **LIDAKIYA** 15 [6] Sir Michael Stoute 3-9-2 (84) K Darley 7/1: 4112: 3 b f Kahyasi - Lilissa ¾ 93
(Doyoun) Chsd ldr, led over 3f out, hard rdn final 1f & hdd nr line: hvly bckd: imprvg, win again: see 1785 (10f).
1928 **WAIT FOR THE WILL** 9 [4] G L Moore 4-9-9 (77) I Mongan (5) 5/1: 001223: 4 ch g Seeking The Gold ¾ 85
- You'd Be Surprised (Blushing Groom): Held up, smooth prog/chall fnl 2f, edged left/no extra nr fin: clr rem.
*1839 **HANNIBAL LAD** 13 [2] W M Brisbourne 4-9-7 (75) T G McLaughlin 6/1: 042114: Nvr a factor: btr 1839. 10 72
1839 **LEGAL LUNCH** 13 [1] 5-9-3 (71)(bl) A Culhane 15/2: 053135: Held up, btn 2f out: btr 1518. 7 56
1744 **CONSPICUOUS** 17 [7] 10-9-10 (78) S Carson (5) 10/1: 1-0666: Chsd ldrs, held 2f out: see 1373, 1076. 2 62
1729 **SWEET REWARD** 18 [3] 5-9-0 (68) F Norton 12/1: 30-447: Keen/prom, hmpd 3f out, sn btn: see 1150. 9 41
1845 **GOODBYE GOLDSTONE** 13 [8] 4-9-3 (71) R Hughes 9/1: 20-058: Pulled hard & sn clr ldr, hdd over 3f 21 20
out & sn btn: op 6/1: too free, see 1288 (10f).
8 ran   Time 2m 36.78 (4.98)   (Derek & Cheryl Holder)   R J Price Ullingswick H'fords

---

2128 **8.35 LUFTHANSA FILLIES HCAP 3YO+ 0-85 (D) 7f rnd Good/Firm 36 -05 Slow** [81]
£4251   £1308   £654   £327   3 yo rec 9 lb

1557 **SILK DAISY** 25 [1] H Candy 4-8-7 (60) A McGlone 12/1: 23-451: 4 b f Barathea - Scene Galante (Sicyos) 63
Held up, prog final 2f, rdn/led nr fin: 1st win: op 10/1: plcd thrice in '99 (rtd 69): eff at 7f/1m on fast & gd/sft.
*1787 **MAGIC BABE** 15 [4] Jamie Poulton 3-7-10 (58) M Henry 5/1: -02412: 3 b f Magic Ring - Head Turner nk 60

GOODWOOD
FRIDAY JUNE 23RD   Righthand, Sharpish, Undulating Track

(My Dad Tom) Prom, rdn/ev ch final 1f, styd on well, just held: in gd form: see 1787.
1680 **CANTINA** 20 [5] A Bailey 6-9-5 (72) I Mongan (5) 4/1 JT FAV: 0-0143: 6 b m Tina's Pet - Real Claire   ½   73
(Dreams To Reality) Led, rdn final 1f, edged left/hdd well ins last/no extra: joc given 2 day careless ride ban.
1787 **ROYAL IVY** 15 [2] J Akehurst 3-8-4 (66) F Norton 12/1: 310054: Rear, styd on final 2f, held nr fin.   hd   66
2027 **ENTROPY** 5 [10] 4-7-10 (49)(11oh) G Baker (7) 40/1: 002305: Held up, kept on onepace fnl 2f: qck reapp.   ¾   48$
1716 **BOOMERANG BLADE** 18 [3] 4-10-0 (81) J Bosley (7) 7/1: 066226: Prom, onepace when hmpd inside last. ½   79
1829 **SONG OF SKYE** 14 [12] 6-9-1 (68) R Hughes 8/1: 036007: Held up, effort 2f out, no impress: see 169.   ¾   65
2084 **SARENA PRIDE** 2 [9] 3-9-0 (76) R Ffrench 4/1 JT FAV: 502438: Towards rear, effort 3f out, no impress.   1   71
1971 **LADY BREANNE** 7 [8] 4-8-3 (55)(1ow) S Drowne 20/1: 636-09: Al rear: see 109 (mdn).   4   43
4486} **SHAROURA** 244 [11] 4-9-13 (80) A Nicholls (3) 10/1: 0100-0: Chsd ldr, btn over 1f out: 10th: reapp: ½   66
'99 wnr at Doncaster (reapp, mdn) & Yarmouth (h'cap, K Mahdi, rtd 82): rtd 72 in '98: eff between 5/7f on
fast & gd/sft grnd: has run well fresh on a gall or fair trk: now with D Nicholls.
1542 **NEELA** 27 [7] 4-8-0 (53) Martin Dwyer 25/1: 40-000: Chsd ldrs, btn 2f out: 11th: rtd 62 in '99 (mdn):   1¼   36
no form subs: eff at 6f on gd/soft grnd & a sharp trk: with R Hannon.
1855 **ALPHILDA** 12 [6] 3-9-0 (76) K Darley 11/2: -00340: Al rear: 12th, tchd 7/1: btr 1855, 1289.   3½   52
12 ran   Time 1m 27.37 (2.87)   (Mrs C M Poland)   H Candy Wantage, Oxon

---

2129	**9.05 LUFTHANSA MDN 3YO+ (D)** **1m1f** **Good/Firm 36** **-48 Slow**
	£4212 £1296 £648 £224 3 yo rec 11lb

1726 **EASTERN SPICE** 18 [6] R Hannon 3-8-12 R Hughes 11/4: 35-021: 3 b c Polish Precedent - Mithl Al Hawa   81
(Salse) Led 1f & again over 2f out, styd on well inside last, rdn out: slow time: plcd twice in '99 (rtd 82):
eff at 7t/9f on firm & gd grnd, likes a sharp trk & being up with/forcing the pace.
1771 **FLYING TREATY** 16 [1] J H M Gosden 3-8-12 K Darley 2/1 FAV: 52: 3 br c You And I - Cherie's Hope   1½   77
(Flying Paster) Dwelt, in tch, rdn/outpcd 3f out, kept on inside last, al held: well bckd: stays 9f on fast.
1960 **DIAMOND ROAD** 7 [3] C A Horgan 3-8-12 S Drowne 20/1: 0-33: 3 b c Dolphin Street - Tiffany's Case   2   73
(Thatching) Prom, rdn & kept on onepace final 2f: stays 9f on fast grnd, h'caps will suit now: see 1960.
1588 **GLENDALE RIDGE** 24 [5] Jamie Poulton 5-9-9 M Henry 25/1: 444: Keen/led after 1f till over 2f out,   3½   66
wknd ins last: op 14/1: now qualified for h'caps: see 1588, 1263.
--   **CIRCUS PARADE** [2] 3-8-12 R Havlin 10/1: 5: Never pace debut: 57,000gns Night Shift colt.   4   58
--   **NAJMAT JUMAIRAH** [4] 3-8-7 S Drowne 7/2: 6: Al rear: op 2/1, Mr Prospector filly, related to a smart styr.*   ½   52
--   **SILK GLOVE** [7] 3-8-12 A McGlone 4/1: 7: Held up, effort 3f out, sn held: op 2/1, debut: Hernando   8   45
half-brother to high-class miler Enrique: with H R A Cecil.
7 ran   Time 1m 58.02 (7.52)   (Mohamed Suhail)   R Hannon East Everleigh, Wilts.

NEWMARKET (July)
FRIDAY JUNE 23RD   Righthand, Stiff, Galloping Track

Official Going   GOOD TO FIRM. Stalls: Stands Side.

2130	**6.45 HALF MOON APPR HCAP 3YO+ 0-70 (E)** **1m str** **Good/Firm 21** **-08 Slow**	**[70]**
	£4030 £1240 £620 £310 3 yo rec 10lb	

1690 **MISSILE TOE** 20 [6] D Morris 7-8-3 (45) Jonjo Fowle (3) 9/2 FAV: 0-5541: 7 b g Exactly Sharp - Debach   51
Dust (Indian King) Mid-div, swtchd/hdwy appr final 1f, led ins last, rdn out: '99 wnr here at Newmarket (h'cap,
rtd 46): plcd in '98 (rtd 55$): eff at 1m/10f on fast, hvy, fibresand & any trk, likes Newmarket: in gd form.
1973 **ASCARI** 7 [4] W Jarvis 4-9-6 (62) D McGaffin (3) 16/1: 631-02: 4 br g Presidium - Ping Pong (Petong)   2   63
Cl-up, ev ch until no pace of wnr inside last: qck reapp: eff between 1m & 10f, apprec a return to the latter.
1920 **MEZZORAMIO** 9 [5] K A Morgan 4-8-4 (46)(t) D Allan (7) 20/1: 50-003: 8 ch g Cadeaux Genereux -   1   45
Hopeful Search (Vaguely Noble) Led to over 1f out, sn not pace of wnr: back to nr best with forcing tactics.
1519 **TOBLERSONG** 27 [11] Mrs L Stubbs 5-8-4 (46)(t) Kristin Stubbs (5) 16/1: -40064: V slow to start,   1   43
rear, styd on well for press final 1f, nrst fin: lost ch with slow start, did well to fin as cl as he did: see 958.
1772 **BADRINATH** 16 [2] 6-8-9 (51) C Cogan 8/1: 320025: Waited with, gd hdwy to lead appr final 1f,   ½   47
hdd inside last, wknd: shade btr 1772.
1967 **ASSURED PHYSIQUE** 7 [9] 3-9-1 (67)(VIS) N Esler (5) 14/1: -05366: Trkd ldrs, rdn/held appr final   ½   62
1f: qck reapp, first time visor: drop back to 1m: see 1772 (1m 11.15f).
1394 **BROWNS FLIGHT** 34 [12] 4-8-5 (40)(t)(7ow) D Young (0) 50/1: 40-007: Rear, eff over 2f out, no room   shd   42
& onepcd appr fnl 1f: recent hdles 2nd (2½m nov, gd, rtd 66h): 4th at best in '99 (h'caps, rtd 59 at best,
tried blnks/visor): plcd in '98 (rtd 81): eff at 6f, tried up to 12f: handles fast, gd/soft & a sharp/undul trk.
1690 **JIBEREEN** 20 [7] 8-8-8 (50) A Eddery 9/1: 431008: Chsd ldrs, btn appr final 1f: btr 866 (11f, AW).   ½   44
1777 **GABLESEA** 16 [16] 6-8-9 (51) S Finnamore (3) 12/1: 020509: Rear, late gains for press: btr 809.   1   43
*1726 **MANXWOOD** 18 [8] 3-8-11 (63) R Thomas (5) 5/1: 014210: Front rank, rdn, wknd/no room ins last, 10th.   ¾   54
1915 **PIPE DREAM** 9 [3] 4-7-12 (40) G Gibbons (0) 50/1: 360050: Handy, short of rm/wknd appr fnl 1f: 11th.   1½   28
2027 **ETISALAT** 5 [19] 5-9-5 (61) D Watson (5) 10/1: 111300: Nvr a factor, fin 12th: qck reapp: btr 1360.   shd   49
2051 **DENS JOY** 4 [17] 4-9-7 (63)(6ex) D Glennon (5) 11/2: 100120: Rear, lost tch fnl 2f, fin 17th: qck reapp.   0
2099 Swynford Welcome 2 [13] 4-8-7 (49) R Brisland 33/1: 1570 **Muddy Water** 25 [10] 4-9-4 (60) R Naylor (5) 14/1:
1281 **Estuary** 41 [14] 5-8-11 (53) P Clarke (3) 33/1:   4578} **Italian Rose** 235 [20] 5-7-10 (38)(1oh) A Hall (2) 50/1:
4152} **Uzy** 268 [15] 4-8-7 (49) K Parkin (5) 33/1:
18 ran   Time 1m 39.52 (2.32)   (Stag & Huntsman)   D Morris Newmarket.

2131	**7.15 INDUSTRIAL HCAP 3YO+ 0-80 (D)** **1m4f** **Good/Firm 21** **-13 Slow**	**[78]**
	£5564 £1712 £856 £428 3 yo rec 14lb	

999 **YOU DA MAN** 62 [2] R Hannon 3-8-9 (73) Dane O'Neill 10/1: 241251: 3 b c Alzao - Fabled Lifestyle   76
(King's Lake) Settled rr, gd hdwy appr final 2f, styd on to lead well ins last, drvn out: 9 wk abs, up in trip:
earlier won at Lingfield (AW mdn, rtd 79a): unplcd in '99 (rtd 66): eff at 10f, stays 12f well: acts on fast
& equitrack: handles a sharp or stiff/gall trk & runs well fresh: has tried blnks, best without: needs to come late.
1839 **JUST GIFTED** 13 [1] R M Whitaker 4-9-1 (65) D Holland 2/1 FAV: 5-2062: 4 b g Rudimentary - Parfait   ½   67
Amour (Clantime) Led early, hdwy to lead again over 3f out, sn hdd, led again dist, hdd ins last, no extra: see 1874.
1874 **NORCROFT JOY** 11 [5] N A Callaghan 5-9-5 (69) J Reid 9/4: 6-5033: 5 b m Rock Hopper - Greenhills   ¾   70
Joy (Radetzky) Cl-up, rdn to lead appr final 2f, hdd dist, sn no extra for press: clr rem: on a gd mark.
1350 **ANGELS VENTURE** 36 [4] J R Jenkins 4-9-13 (77)(t) Pat Eddery 11/4: 1-0004: Rear, rdn to impr final   3   73

2f, no extra inside last: nicely bckd, top-weight: see 1180.
-- **WOODYS BOY** [3] 6-9-1 (65) A Daly 20/1: 5231/5: Front rank, rdn/fdd final 2f: reapp, op 14/1: *nk* **61**
missed '99, prev term won 2 here at Newmarket (h'caps, incl reapp, rtd 66, M Heaton Ellis): eff at 14f/2m on firm & gd/soft: acts on a stiff or sharp trk, likes Newmarket: now with C G Cox, sharper next time over further.
2002 **LANCER 6** [6] 8-9-2 (66)(vis) G Bardwell 12/1: 616606: Sn led, hdd over 3f out, sn lost tch: qck reapp. *6* **54**
6 ran Time 2m 32.26 (4.06) (Buddy Hackett) R Hannon East Everleigh, Wilts.

2132

7.45 NGK SPARK PLUGS MDN 2YO (D) 6f str Good/Firm 21 -09 Slow
£4891 £1505 £752 £376

1691 **WARDEN WARREN 20** [10] M A Jarvis 2-9-0 P Robinson 16/1: -01: 2 b c Petong - Silver Spell (Aragon) **94**
Led early, remnd prom, led again ins last, edged left & drvn out: 20,000 gns Feb first foal: dam 2yo 5f wnr: half-sister to a useful sprinter: eff over a stiff/gall 6f on fast: left debut run bhd & could improve further.
-- **PALANZO** [5] P W Harris 2-9-0 Pat Eddery 7/4 FAV: 2: 2 b c Green Desert - Karpacka (Rousillon) *nk* **93**
Cl-up, went on appr final 2f, hdd inside last, just held: Feb first foal, dam useful in Italy, won as a juv: eff over a stiff/gall 6f on fast: gd debut, go one better soon.
1700 **JELBA 19** [8] N P Littmoden 2-8-9 J F Egan 33/1: 53: 2 b f Pursuit Of Love - Gold Bracelet (Golden Fleece): Prom, ev ch until no extra for press final 1f: imprvd form on this sounder surface: stays 6f on fast. *1½* **84**
-- **NOBLE DOBLE** [9] B W Hills 2-9-0 D Holland 20/1: 4: Waited with, gd hdwy over 2f out, fdd inside last: drifter from 12/1 on debut: 15,000 gns Feb 1st foal: dam an 11f wnr: bred to get 7f+ in time. *2½* **83**
-- **CEZZARO** [6] 2-9-0 M Roberts 6/1: 5: Dwelt, sn rdn, late gains, nrst fin: 60,000 gns Ashkalani foal, reportedly well regarded by connections (first 2yo rnr this term): will improve for A C Stewart. *1½* **80**
-- **HOSSRUM** [7] 2-9-0 J Reid 9/1: 6: Rear, rdn to impr halfway, sn btn: op 6/1: 38,000 gns Definite Article Feb foal, half-brother to decent juv 5f scorer Pipadash: expect better: with E Dunlop. *¾* **78**
-- **TOP NOLANS** [2] 2-9-0 S Sanders 7/1: 7: Veered right start, sn prom, rdn/wknd final 2f: Topanoora May foal, half-brother to a 6f juv scorer: with M H Tompkins. *¾* **77**
-- **SABANA** [4] 2-9-0 T Quinn 11/4: 8: Hmpd start, rear, nvr a factor: 120,000gns Sri Pekan half-brother to a Gr 3 juv scorer: should be capable of better for N Callaghan. *shd* **77**
1856 **MISTY DIAMOND 12** [3] 2-8-9 J Mackay (7) 33/1: 09: Hmpd start, led after 2f, hdd 2f out, wknd/eased. *26* **42**
9 ran Time 1m 12.77 (1.77) (John E Sims) M A Jarvis Newmarket.

2133

8.15 H & K HCAP STKS 3YO+ 0-95 (C) 7f str Good/Firm 21 +13 Fast [95]
£7865 £2420 £1210 £605 3 yo rec 9 lb

1483 **SECOND WIND 29** [10] C A Dwyer 5-8-8 (75)(t) J Mackay (7) 16/1: -15001: 5 ch g Kris - Rimosa's Pet **84**
(Petingo): Dsptd lead, went on over 3f out, rdn clr appr final 1f, readily: fast time: earlier won on reapp at Leicester (h'cap): '99 wnr at Brighton (clmr, Miss G Kelleway) & Epsom (current stable, h'cap, rtd 74): rnr-up for P Cole in '98 (rtd 85): eff at 6f/1m, suited by 7f now: acts on firm, soft & any trk: runs well fresh & now best in a t-strap: useful performance here in a fast time, should make a quick follow up.
1825 **JUNO MARLOWE 14** [14] P W Harris 4-9-13 (94) T Quinn 14/1: 0-0002: 4 b f Danehill - Why So Silent *3½* **95**
(Mill Reef): Waited with, rdn/hdwy appr final 1f, styd on inside last, no threat to wnr: v useful: see 1077.
1983 **KAYO 7** [11] M Johnston 5-9-12 (93) D Holland 5/2 FAV: -00023: 5 b g Superpower - Shiny Kay *hd* **94**
(Star Appeal) Led, hdd over 3f out, rdn, no extra & edged left inside last: well bckd from 4/1, in gd heart.
1926 **SURPRISE ENCOUNTER 9** [18] E A L Dunlop 4-8-11 (78) J Reid 8/1: 6-0054: Dwelt, rear, late hdwy for *½* **78+**
press, nrst fin: eye-catching again, running into form & worth another look at 1m: see 1926, 1514.
1810 **JUST NICK 14** [16] 6-7-10 (63) R Brisland (5) 14/1: 00-365: Waited with, gd hdwy inside last, nvr *¾* **61**
nrr: will apprec a return to 1m & is on a fair mark: see 1473.
1810 **MANTLES PRIDE 14** [13] 5-9-5 (86)(bl) O Pears 10/1: 004106: Prom, rdn/not pace of ldrs over 1f out. *nk* **84**
1840 **HYPERACTIVE 13** [4] 4-8-3 (70) M Roberts 7/2: /1-027: Rcd v keenly in tch, hung left & no extra *¾* **67**
appr final 1f: failed to settle here & can do better, see 1840.
1926 **TOPTON 9** [7] 6-8-7 (74)(bl) R Mullen 14/1: 200508: Rear, late gains for press, no dngr: see 1840. *½* **70**
1989 **TEOFILIO 6** [2] 6-8-4 (71)(bl) P Doe 14/1: -16009: Nvr a threat: qck reapp: won this race *nk* **67**
last term off a 2lbs lower mark: see 1989, 594.
1150 **WILD SKY 49** [17] 6-8-9 (76)(tvi) S Sanders 20/1: 00-000: Rear, hdwy when short of room over *¾* **70**
1f out, swtchd & no extra inside last: fin 10th: 7 wk abs: see 1150.
1952 **SEA DEER 8** [8] 11-8-10 (77) O Urbina 33/1: 100-00: Prom, wknd qckly final 1f: fin 11th: see 1952. *shd* **71**
1729 **IONIAN SPRING 18** [9] 5-8-10 (77) Dane O'Neill 33/1: 221/00: Dwelt, nvr a threat: 12th: missed '99, *½* **70**
prev term plcd all 3 turf starts (rtd 80), subs won at W'hampton (AW auct mdn, rtd 81a, Lord Huntingdon): eff at 10f, bred to be suited by mid-dists: acts on gd, fast & fibresand: handles a gall or sharp/turning trk.
1620} **KINAN 391** [5] 4-9-4 (85) J Weaver 33/1: 0050-0: Handy, fdd fnl 2f: 13th: reapp, unplcd in '99 (h'caps *hd* **78**
rtd 85 at best, R Armstrong): won fnl '98 start, at Nottingham (mdn, rtd 91): eff at 6/7f on fast, gd & a gall trk.
1493} **Gudlage 398** [3] 4-9-10 (91) W Ryan 33/1:
1611 **Three Angels 23** [6] 5-8-3 (70) Craig Williams 14/1:
1110 **Tayif 51** [12] 4-10-0 (95) J P Spencer 16/1:
1514 **Petrus 27** [15] 4-8-12 (79) P Robinson 14/1:
1851 **Surveyor 13** [19] 5-9-1 (82) R Morse 33/1:
18 ran Time 1m 24.36 (0.46) (John Purcell) C A Dwyer Newmarket.

2134

8.45 HENNINGER CLAIMER 3YO (E) 1m str Good/Firm 21 -16 Slow
£3776 £1162 £581 £290

1263 **THAMAN 42** [13] B Hanbury 3-9-10 J Mackay (7) 8/1: 01: 3 b c Sri Pekan - Shaping Up (Storm Bird) **73**
Waited with, gd hdwy when hung left over 2f out, led appr final 1f, drvn out: 6 wk abs, op 5/1, clmd for £15,000: eff over a stiff/gall 1m on fast grnd: runs well fresh: fine effort conceding weight here, prob better than a clmr.
1972 **SPARK OF LIFE 7** [7] P R Chamings 3-8-3 (bl) S Righton 11/1: 60-032: 3 b f Rainbows For Life - *1½* **49**
Sparkler Girl (Danehill): Dwelt, hdwy from rear over 3f out, led appr final 1f, sn hdd, no extra well inside last: qck reapp, op 7/1: eff at 7f/1m on fast/firm: gd effort & 5L clr rem here, win a sell/clmr.
1726 **REGARDEZ MOI 18** [6] A W Carroll 3-8-9 Craig Williams 12/1: 3-0063: 3 b f Distinctly North - Tomard *5* **46**
(Thatching): Led, hdd appr final 1f, not pace of front pair: see 1726.
2017 **DOLFINESSE 5** [3] M Brittain 3-8-9 (vis) P Robinson 14/1: -05234: Front rank, rdn/no extra appr fnl 1f. *nk* **46**
2036 **MISS SPRINGFIELD 4** [17] 3-7-13 (vis) J Tate 14/1: 0-3045: Mid-div, rdn to impr 2f out, btn over 1f out. *2* **32**
1865 **RUNAWAY STAR 11** [16] 3-8-5 L Newton 12/1: 66: Dwelt, styd on well for press final 1f, nvr nrr: *1¼* **36**
glimmer of ability here & may apprec a step up in trip: see 1865.
-- **CONCIERGE** [5] 3-9-10 Pat Eddery 1/1 FAV: 7: Prom, ev ch until fdd appr final 1f: joint top-weight *nk* **55**
on debut & hvly bckd: Catrail colt, with P Cole: bred to be better than a plater & clrly more expected.

NEWMARKET (July) FRIDAY JUNE 23RD Righthand, Stiff, Galloping Track

1572 **ERIN ANAM CARA 24** [18] 3-8-5 J F Egan 6/1: 443-08: Nvr better than mid-div: see 1572. *1* **34**
1035 **SOBER AS A JUDGE 56** [9] 3-8-4 O Pears 40/1: 00-009: Chsd ldrs, lost tch final 2f: mod prev form. *1* **31**
-- **HTTP FLYER** [1] 3-8-7 S Whitworth 20/1: 0: Rear, late gains, no dngr: 10th: debut, with W Musson. *1½* **31**
1873 **STOP THE TRAFFIC 11** [12] 3-8-9 R Morse 14/1: 205500: Dwelt, rear, eff over 2f out, sn btn: fin 11th. *½* **32**
527 **Katie King 128** [4] 3-8-1 J Lowe 50/1: 1419 **Polar Diamond 32** [11] 3-8-9 L Newman (3) 14/1:
2026 **Cupids Dart 5** [14] 3-8-10 R Mullen 14/1: 2025 **Who Da Leader 5** [2] 3-9-6 Dane O'Neill 14/1:
1955 **Cypress Creek 8** [10] 3-7-13 (VIS) D Glennon (7) 33/1:1596 **Gavel 23** [8] 3-8-6 S Sanders 40/1:
1495 **Lous Wish 28** [15] 3-8-10 (bl) R Fitzpatrick (3) 20/1:
18 ran Time 1m 40.2 (3.0) (B Hanbury) B Hanbury Newmarket.

2135 **9.15 LINDEMANS MDN 3YO (D) 1m2f Good/Firm 21 +02 Fast**
£5050 £1554 £777 £388

1295 **LUXOR 39** [1] H R A Cecil 3-9-0 T Quinn 7/2: 421: 3 ch c Grand Lodge - Escrime (Sharpen Up) **92**
Made all, rdn & ran on strongly inside last, readily: fair time, nicely bckd: eff over a stiff/gall 10f on fast & gd/soft grnd, 12f shld suit: useful effort here, should improve further & win more races.
1188 **EXECUTIVE ORDER 47** [3] Sir Michael Stoute 3-9-0 P at Eddery 4/9 FAV: 42: 3 b c Rainbow Quest - *1¾* **87**
Exclusive Order (Exclusive Native): Dwelt, sn with ldr, ev ch until not pace of wnr inside last: 7 wk abs & nicely bckd at odds on: eff at 1m/10f: sure to win similar sn: see 1188.
1127 **TORRID KENTAVR 50** [8] T G Mills 3-9-0 A Clark 10/1: 4-33: 3 b c Trempolino - Torrid Tango *shd* **87**
(Green Dancer): Mid-div, rdn/hdwy appr fnl 1f, sn onepcd: clr rem, 7 wk abs: another gd run, win a mdn sn.
-- **PRECIOUS POPPY** [5] Sir Michael Stoute 3-8-9 Dane O'Neill 12/1: 4: Dwelt, rear, swtchd/hdwy *4* **75**
over 2f out, sn held: op 7/1: dam a 7f/1m wnr: stablemate of rnr-up & should improve for experience.
956 **SHARP LIFE 66** [4] 3-9-0 W Ryan 14/1: -05: Keen cl-up, no extra appr fnl 1f: 9 wk abs: up in trip. *2* **76**
1738 **JAMAIEL 18** [7] 3-8-9 P Robinson 16/1: 0-36: Sn prom, fdd final 2f: see 1738 (11/5f, gd/soft). *1* **69**
-- **TRIPPITAKA** [6] 3-8-9 J Weaver 25/1: 7: Dwelt, rear, nvr a factor: debut, with N Graham. *6* **59**
1200 **BETACHANCE DOT COM 46** [2] 3-8-9 G Bardwell 66/1: 08: Dwelt, al bhd: 7 wk abs. *10* **43**
-- **TALENT STAR** [9] 3-9-0 S Righton 50/1: 9: Slow to start, al well bhd, fin last: highly tried on debut. *1* **46**
9 ran Time 2m 03.79 (1.89) (Exors of the late Lord Howard De Walden) H R A Cecil Newmarket.

AYR FRIDAY JUNE 23RD Lefthand, Galloping Track

Official Going GOOD. Stalls: Str - Stands Side; Rnd - Inside.

2136 **2.20 AYRSHIRE SELL HCAP 3YO+ 0-60 (G) 1m rnd Good 44 -06 Slow [50]**
£2107 £602 £301 3 yo rec 10lb

2040 **DOVEBRACE 4** [7] A Bailey 7-9-2 (38) J Bramhill 5/1: 06-321: 7 b g Dowsing - Naufrage (Main Reef) **49**
Hld up, hdwy 3f out, sn short of room till 2f out, led ins last, rdn clr ins last: no bid, deserved win: plcd in '99 (rtd 43): last won back in '95, at Haydock, York & Chester (mdn/stks, rtd 100): eff at 6f, suited by 1m on firm & gd/soft: tried blnks/visor: win another sell h'cap.
1689 **SECONDS AWAY 20** [13] J S Goldie 9-8-7 (29) K Dalgleish (7) 11/2: 0-6042: 9 b g Hard Fought - Keep *5* **32**
Mum (Mummy's Pet) Hld up, eff over 1f out, kept on, no threat to wnr: shld win another sell h'cap: see 1191.
1330 **SHAMWARI SONG 37** [5] K A Ryan 5-9-4 (40) F Lynch 3/1 FAV: 300403: 5 b g Sizzling Melody - Spark *½* **42**
Out (Sparkler) Led 4f out till over 1f out, no extra: nicely bckd: slipped down weights: prev with Mrs Jewell.
1690 **SAINT GEORGE 20** [14] K R Burke 4-9-1 (37) D Sweeney 8/1: 00-004: In tch, eff 2f out, kept on: first form. *½* **38**
1546 **UP IN FLAMES 25** [9] 9-9-4 (40)(t) G Duffield 8/1: 002035: Cl up, wknd over 1f out: see 1546. *1½* **39**
1865 **RED SONNY 11** [11] 3-9-0 (46) P Bradley (5) 10/1: 400236: Cl up, wknd well over 1f out: btr 1865. *½* **44**
1559 **SILVER BULLET 25** [10] 4-8-7 (29)(vis) C Lowther 16/1: 00-007: Bhd, some late gains, no threat: mod. *hd* **26**
1351 **DILETTO 35** [12] 4-9-1 (37) L Swift (7) 8/1: 261068: Bhd, late gains, nvr plcd to chall: do better. *1¾* **30**
2099 **CAIRN DHU 2** [3] 6-8-10 (32) Kimberley Hart 33/1: 0-0009: Al bhd: qk reapp, see 159. *2* **21**
1907 **WATERGOLD 9** [8] 3-9-0 (46)(vis) Dale Gibson 20/1: -50000: In tch, wknd over 2f out: 10th. *1* **33**
1891 **KATIES VALENTINE 10** [15] 3-9-10 (56) P Hanagan (7) 5/1: 5-3200: Al bhd: fin 13th, longer trip. **0**
2553} **Tragic Lady 350** [6] 4-9-4 (40) M Fenton 33/1: 585 **Broughton Belle 119** [4] 4-7-10 (18) Clare Roche (7) 50/1:
1722 **Double Entry 18** [2] 3-8-1 (33) Dawn Rankin (0) 66/1: -- **Playmaker** [1] 7-8-13 (35) J Fanning 66/1:
15 ran Time 1m 40.64 (4.04) (Dovebrace Ltd Air-Conditioning-Projects) A Bailey Little Budworth, Cheshire

2137 **2.55 AYR FOR LIFE MED AUCT MDN 2YO (E) 6f Good 44 -40 Slow**
£3009 £926 £463 £231

1737 **ALINGA 18** [4] M L W Bell 2-8-9 M Fenton 2/1: 51: 2 b f King's Theatre - Cheyenne Spirit (Indian Ridge) **79**
Dwelt, sn handy, eff to chall appr fnl 1f, drvn to get up ins last: Feb first foal, cost 31,000IR gns: dam 5/6f wnr: apprec step up to 6f, further will suit: put experience to good use & responded well to press.
-- **XALOC BAY** [1] K R Burke 2-9-0 D Sweeney 7/4 FAV: 2: 2 br c Charnwood Forest - Royal Jade (Last *½* **82**
Tycoon) Cl up, led 1f out, rdn & collared cl home: well bckd: cost 16,6500 gns: dam 7f wnr: win sn.
1906 **ORIENTAL MIST 9** [5] Miss L A Perratt 2-9-0 C Lowther 11/4: 5433: 2 gr c Balla Cove - Donna Katrina *2* **77**
(King's Lake) Cl up, led 2f out till 1f out, no extra: consistent: see 1906.
-- **COCCOLONA** [6] D Haydn Jones 2-8-9 Dale Gibson 20/1: 4: Sn rdn bhd, late gains: op 12/1: *2½* **65**
Mar foal, cost 8,500IR gns: half sister to useful sprinter Tiler: dam won at up to 9f: will enjoy 7f.
1823 **SHEER FOCUS 14** [3] 2-9-0 G Duffield 14/1: 05: Led till 2f out, wknd: op 8/1: see 1823. *2½* **63**
1835 **SENSIMELIA 13** [2] 2-8-9 C Teague 10/1: -536: Cl up, wknd over 1f out: op 6/1: btr 1835 (5f). *2* **52**
6 ran Time 1m 14.37 (5.07) (Peter G Ward) M L W Bell Newmarket

2138 **3.30 BEN CLASSIFIED STKS 3YO+ 0-80 (D) 1m rnd Good 44 -15 Slow**
£3731 £1148 £574 £287

1483 **PEARTREE HOUSE 29** [3] D Nicholls 6-9-6 J Fanning 5/2 FAV: 006031: 6 b g Simply Majestic - Fashion **83**
Front (Habitat) In tch, hdwy over 2f out, led on bit ins last, pushed out, cosily: slow run race: rnr-up in '99 for W Muir (rtd 94): eff at 7.5f/1m on firm & gd/soft, any trk: best without a visor: h'capped to win again.
1445 **COURT EXPRESS 31** [1] W W Haigh 6-9-8 F Lynch 5/1: 00-162: 6 b g Then Again - Moon Risk (Risk Me) *1* **81**

AYR   FRIDAY JUNE 23RD   Lefthand, Galloping Track

Keen cl up, ev ch over 1f out, kept on same pace: shld do better off a stronger pace: see 1445.
1879 **ZULU DAWN** 11 [5] J W Hills 4-9-6 S Whitworth 7/2: 164-33: 4 b g El Gran Senor - Celtic Loot (Irish   ½   78
River) Set slow pace, rdn over 1f out, hdd & no extra ins last: gd run: see 1879.
1851 **NOMORE MR NICEGUY** 13 [2] E J Alston 6-9-6 G Duffield 3/1: 000204: Keen, chsd ldr, wknd 2f out.   1½   75
1490 **TOM DOUGAL** 28 [4] 5-9-6 M Fenton 6/1: 00-005: Prom, wknd over 1f out: see 1490.   2   71
5 ran   Time 1m 41.3 (4.7)   (G Vettraino & Fayzad Throughbreds Ltd)   D Nicholls Sessay, N Yorks

2139   4.05 SPONSORSHIP HCAP 3YO+ 0-60 (E)   1m2f192y Good 44 +03 Fast   [60]
£3900   £1200   £600   £300   3 yo rec 13lb

1814 **PENNYS FROM HEAVEN** 14 [2] D Nicholls 6-9-7 (53) Clare Roche (7) 7/1: 030241: 6 gr g Generous -   58
Heavenly Cause (Grey Dawn) Chsd ldrs, hdwy over 1f out, led ins last, rdn out: gd time, op 7/2: unplcd over hdls
for Miss V Williams last winter: unplcd for L Cumani on the Flat in '98 (rtd 75): eff at 12/13f on firm,
gd/soft: has run well in blnks: on a handy mark.
1816 **MELODY LADY** 14 [13] F Murphy 4-9-2 (48) K Dalgleish (7) 10/1: 02-002: 4 b f Dilum - Ansellady   ½   51
(Absalom) Handy, led appr fnl 1f till ins last, not btn far: op 6/1: gd run but still a mdn: see 1496.
1769 **CAMARADERIE** 16 [10] Mrs M Reveley 4-9-2 (48) T Eaves (7) 3/1 JT FAV: 034-33: 4 b g Most Welcome - 1¾   48
Secret Valentine (Wollow) In tch, outpcd 3f out, kept on late: mdn, has ability & worth a try over further.
2048 **OCEAN DRIVE** 4 [9] Miss L A Perratt 4-8-11 (43) Dale Gibson 10/1: -05654: Chsd ldrs, eff 2f out, onepace.¾   42
1563 **PARABLE** 25 [8] 4-10-0 (60)(BL) F Lynch 20/1: 130005: In tch, eff 3f out, wknd appr fnl 1f: blnks.   3½   54
*1908 **SPREE VISION** 9 [5] 4-9-7 (53)(6ex) D Sweeney 3/1 JT FAV: 004516: Hld up, eff 3f out, sn btn.   1½   45
1259 **RENDITA** 42 [6] 4-9-3 (49) M Fenton 12/1: 000-07: Nvr a factor: longer trip, abs, see 1259.   5   34
1494 **SPIRIT OF KHAMBANI** 28 [7] 3-8-7 (52) J Fanning 16/1: 03-008: Al bhd: see 1159 (7f).   shd   37
1661 **BLAIR** 21 [3] 3-8-6 (51)(20w) C Lowther 14/1: 0-0049: Prom, wknd 4f out: op 8/1, flattered 1661.   ½   35
1432 **AMRON** 32 [12] 13-8-9 (41) P Bradley 15/1: -00600: Al bhd: fin 10th, 13yo.   1   23
1907 **SOCIETY TIMES** 9 [11] 7-7-12 (30) J Bramhill 9/1: 606/50: Led halfway till well over 1f out: 11th.   1½   10
1644 **WONDERLAND** 21 [4] 3-7-13 (44) P Hanagan (7) 20/1: -00500: Led till halfway, wknd: fin last, see 1365. 6   15
12 ran   Time 2m 19.4 (3.4)   (T Cooper, P Kent & R Stephenson)   D Nicholls Sessay, N Yorks

2140   4.40 CORPORATE BOXES MDN 3YO+ (D)   7f rnd   Good 44 -07 Slow
£3867   £1190   £595   £297   3 yo rec 9 lb

1537 **CAPRICHO** 27 [2] W J Haggas 3-8-12 G Duffield 5/6 FAV: 21: 3 gr g Lake Coniston - Star Spectacle   84
(Spectacular Bid) Cl up, hdwy to lead over 1f out, pushed out: stays 7f well, further will suit: acts on
gd & gd/soft: can rate higher & win again.
1708 **BARNIE RUBBLE** 19 [6] A Bailey 4-9-7 J Bramhill 12/1: 0-642: 4 ch g Pharly - Sharp Fairy (Sharpo)   2½   76
Led till halfway, led again 2f out till over 1f out, not pace of wnr: stays 7f: lightly raced 4yo.
1694 **TAKE FLITE** 20 [7] W R Muir 3-8-12 D Sweeney 6/4: 4-2003: 3 b c Cadeaux Genereux - Green Seed   hd   75
(Lead On Time) In tch, eff over 2f out, onepace: worth a try in headgear: see 1470, 1072.
-- **SIGN OF THE DRAGON** [4] I Semple 3-8-12 F Lynch 25/1: 4: Led halfway to 2f out: Sri Pekan gelding.   10   60
-- **FIZZLE** [1] 3-8-12 J Fanning 10/1: 5: Nvr a factor: half brother to a 7f wnr: Efisio colt.   3½   53
1818 **HOWABOYS QUEST** 14 [5] 3-8-12 K Dalgleish (7) 16/1: 40-006: Al bhd.   7   41
1655 **LITTLE LES** 21 [3] 4-9-7 P Hanagan (7) 66/1: 67: Al bhd: see 1655 (10f).   6   31
3085) **HELLO SAILOR** 326 [8] 3-8-7 P Bradley (7) 100/1: 00-8: In tch, btn over 4f out: poor.   8   12
8 ran   Time 1m 27.4 (3.6)   (M Tabor)   W J Haggas Newmarket

2141   5.15 FENWICK APPR MDN HCAP 3YO+ 0-70 (E)   1m5f   Good 44 -120 Slow   [56]
£2786   £796   £398   3 yo rec 15lb

1633 **LOVE BITTEN** 26 [6] M Johnston 3-9-10 (67) K Dalgleish 10/11 FAV: 004521: 3 b g Darshaan - Kentmere   67
(Galetto) Set v slow pace, kept on for press over 1f out: well bckd: eff over 13/14f on gd & fast grnd.
1722 **WILLIAM THE LION** 18 [4] A Berry 3-8-9 (52) P Bradley 12/1: 0-0552: 3 b g Puissance - Last Note   ½   52
(Welsh Pageant) Prom, eff over 3f out, kept on ins last, not btn far: op 7/1: enjoyed step up to 13f on gd grnd.
1707 **BROUGHTONS MILL** 19 [5] W J Musson 5-9-0 (42) P Shea (3) 11/4: -00423: 4 b g Saddlers' Hall -   ½   41
Pennine Pink (Pennine Walk) Cl up, chall fnl 1f, slightly short of room but held cl home: stays 13f: see 1707.
1633 **GARGOYLE GIRL** 22 [2] J S Goldie 3-8-5 (48) Dawn Rankin 5/1: 00-064: Keen, chsd wnr till over 3f   ½   46
out, rallied ins last: eff at 13f on gd, worth a try over further: see 1633.
1575 **TOTALLY SCOTTISH** 24 [3] 4-9-7 (49) T Eaves (5) 12/1: 004-05: Hld up, rdn 3f out, no impress: op 8/1. 3½   43
940   **PINMOOR HILL** 67 [1] 4-9-3 (45) Clare Roche (3) 12/1: 00/006: Nvr a factor: abs, see 940.   ½   38
6 ran   Time 3m 06.0 (21.4)   (M Doyle)   M Johnston Middleham, N Yorks

REDCAR   FRIDAY JUNE 23RD   Lefthand, Flat, Galloping Track

Official Going   FIRM. Stalls: Str Crse - Stands' Side; 1m6f - Centre; Rem - Inside.

2142   2.10 INGS MDN 2YO (D)   5f str Good/Firm 29 -11 Slow
£2860   £880   £440   £220

1943 **PARKSIDE PURSUIT** 8 [4] M R Channon 2-9-0 P Fessey 11/4: -001: 2 b c Pursuit Of Love - Ivory Bride   77
(Domynsky) Front rank, went on dist, held on well, drvn out: Mar foal, sire a high-class
6f/1m performer: eff at 5f on fast grnd, 6f suit: handles a gall trk: can rate more highly.
1782 **BACCURA** 15 [8] A P Jarvis 2-9-0 D Mernagh (3) 9/4 FAV: -02: 2 b c Dolphin Street - Luzzara (Tate   ½   76
Gallery) Dwelt & ran green, stayed on strongly fnl 1f, just failed: well bckd tho' op 1/1: eff at 5f on fast
grnd: handles a gall trk: much better effort & shld sn win similar: see 1782.
1954 **RED RYDING HOOD** 8 [5] C A Dwyer 2-8-9 O Pears 8/1: -63: 2 ch f Wolfhound - Downeaster Alexa   shd   71
(Red Ryder) Tried to make all, hdd dist, rallied & only just btn: op 5/1: eff at 5f on fast grnd: see 1955.
989   **HUMES LAW** 62 [6] A Berry 2-9-0 T E Durcan 12/1: -04: Stdd start, recovered to chase ldrs, kept on   ½   75
under press & only btn 1L: op 8/1, 9 wk abs: imprvd on this faster grnd: see 989 (hvy).
1864 **MISS BEADY** 11 [7] 2-8-9 R Winston 16/1: -005: Mid-div, styd on under press fnl 1f: btn under 2L.   ½   69
1906 **KELETI** 9 [3] 2-9-0 Dean McKeown 4/1: -56: Chsd ldrs, rdn & onepcd fnl 1f: see 1906.   2   68

688

1823	**THE LOOSE SCREW** 14 [9] 2-9-0 R Cody Boutcher (7) 12/1: -67: Chsd ldrs till outpcd fnl 2f: op 8/1.		6	50
1759	**ASTER FIELDS** 16 [1] 2-8-9 A Clark 16/1: -068: Front rank 3½f, wknd: see 1759.		nk	44
1823	**EAGLET** 14 [2] 2-9-0 G Hills 33/1: -09: Slowly away & al bhnd: see 1823.		1¾	44

9 ran   Time 58.5 (2.0)   (John Livock & Mrs Jean Keegan)   M R Channon West Isley, Berks.

2143   2.45 NEWTON CLAIMER 3YO+ (F)   1m2f   Good/Firm 29   -12 Slow
£2373   £678   £339   3yo rec 12lb

1936 **GUNBOAT DIPLOMACY GB** 8 [7] Mrs M Reveley 5-8-13 T E Durcan 12/1: 00-001: 5 br g Mtoto - Pepper **42**
Star (Salt Dome) In tch, gd prog to lead ins last, rdn out: lightly rcd & no form in '99: trained by M Fetherston
Godley in '98 & no form: eff at 10f on fast grnd: handles a gall trk: amazing effort at today's weights.
1880 **NIGHT CITY** 11 [8] K R Burke 9-9-9 M Tebbutt 10/11 FAV: 644152: 9 b g Kris - Night Secret (Nijinsky) ½ **52**
Led after 2f till ins last, rallied & only just btn: well bckd, 5L clr rem: not allowed to dominate today.
1689 **ACE OF TRUMPS** 20 [2] J Hetherton 4-9-1 (t) N Kennedy 7/2: 001203: 4 ch g First Trump - Elle Reef 5 **36**
(Shareef Dancer) Chsd ldrs, outpcd by front pair fnl 2f: much btr 1195.
1660 **RAYWARE BOY** 21 [3] D Shaw 4-9-3 (bl) A Clark 9/1: -00054: Chsd ldrs till outpcd 2f out. 2½ **35**
3344} **MITHRAIC** 315 [1] 8-9-1 P Goode(3) 7/1: 3313-5: Mid-div, eff over 3f out, sn btn: reapp: '99 wnr 3 **29**
at Newcastle (appr sell, rtd 44): missed 98: 97/98 wnr over hdles at Newcastle & Southwell (sell h'cap, eff at
2m/2½m on fast & hvy): '96 wnr at Hamilton (clmr) & Musselburgh (ltd stks, rtd 61): eff at 11/14f on firm &
hvy: handles any trk: eff with/without blnks.
2046 **JUST GOOD FRIENDS** 4 [9] 3-8-1 D Mernagh (3) 12/1: -0066: Mid-div, btn over 2f out: qck reapp. 4 **21**
1788 **RED ROSES** 15 [4] 4-8-12 Kim Tinkler 14/1: -00007: Chsd ldrs till outpcd 3f out: flattered 1788. 4 **14**
1681 **BRIGMOUR** 20 [5] 4-8-10 R Winston 33/1: -00008: Set pace 2f, dsptd lead till wknd 3f out, t.o. 24 **0**
1655 **MABSHUSH** 21 [6] 4-9-9 O Pears 33/1: -09: Al rear, t.o. in last: seems modest. 11 **0**

9 ran   Time 2m 06.4 (4.1)   (A Sharratt)   Mrs M Reveley Lingdale, N Yorks.

2144   3.20 STAITHES MDN 3YO+ (D)   1m6f   Good/Firm 29   -03 Slow
£2730   £840   £420   £210   3yo rec 17lb

1770 **FULL AHEAD** 16 [1] M H Tompkins 3-8-4 A Clark 4/9 FAV: -33221: 3 b c Slip Anchor - Foulard (Sadler's **85**
Wells) In tch, prog to chall fnl 2f, led nr line, rdn out: hvly bckd from 4/6: deserved win, plcd on prev 4 starts
this term: eff at 10/12f, apprec this step up to 14f: acts on gd & firm grnd: likes a stiff trk.
1824 **JARDINES LOOKOUT** 14 [4] A P Jarvis 3-8-4 D Mernagh (3) 2/1: -5362: 3 b g Fourstars Allstar - Foolish nk **84**
Flight (Fool's Holme) Chsd ldrs, led 3f out, prsd fnl 2f, worn down cl home: op 11/8, well clr of rem, rider
reportedly given a 1-day whip ban: handles fast & gd/soft: see 1369 (gd/soft).
1386 **ULSHAW** 34 [2] J D Bethell 3-8-4 R Lappin 33/1: 05-03: 3 ch g Salse - Kintail (Kris) 23 **54$**
In tch till outpcd by front 2 fnl 2f: longer 14f trip & faced a v stiff task: see 1386.
1975 **GLOW 7** [3] M J Polglase 4-9-2 Dean McKeown 14/1: -03524: Led till over 3f out, wknd: see 1975. 1¾ **47**

4 ran   Time 3m 02.3 (4.5)   (J H Ellis)   M H Tompkins Newmarket

---

2145   3.55 96.6 TFM BIRTHDAY HCAP 3YO 0-80 (D)   7f str   Good/Firm 29   +01 Fast   [82]
£5278   £1624   £812   £406

1768 **GOLDEN MIRACLE** 16 [2] M Johnston 3-9-7 (75) R Winston 10/1: 5-0001: 3 b g Cadeaux Genereux - Cheeky **79**
Charm (Nureyev) Made all, clr after 2f out, held on well, pushed out: top-weight, fair time: '99 wnr at Hamilton
(2, nurs, rtd 84): eff at 5/6f, stays 7f well: acts on firm & gd/soft grnd: handles a stiff trk, likes Hamilton:
gd weight carrier who can force the pace: has tried blnks, better without: fairly h'capped & cld win again.
857 **SOBA JONES** 74 [9] T D Easterby 3-7-11 (51) P Fessey 12/1: 3-6602: 3 b c Emperor Jones - Soba ¾ **53**
(Most Secret) Rear, prog halfway, fin fast but too late: 10 wk abs: eff at 7f on fast grnd, 1m will suit: see 558.
1826 **I PROMISE YOU** 14 [6] C E Brittain 3-9-2 (70) T E Durcan 7/2: -10003: 3 b g Shareef Dancer - Abuzz shd **72**
(Absalom) Chsd ldrs, onepcd 2f out, rallied well cl home: 4L clr 3rd: fair run on more suitable fast grnd: see 792.
*1793 **ANTHEMION** 15 [3] P C Haslam 3-9-3 (71) Dean McKeown 7/4 FAV: -03114: Trkd ldrs, ch dist, 4 **65**
fdd ins 1f: bckd from 11/4: not disgraced on hat-trick attempt: see 1793.
*1745 **ATYLAN BOY** 17 [7] 3-8-13 (67) D R McCabe 7/2: -00315: Chsd ldrs, eff 2f out, wknd & eased 1¼ **58**
fnl 1f: well clr of rem: much improved on the a/w in 1745 (equitrack).
1891 **BEBE DE CHAM** 10 [8] 3-8-9 (63) R Cody Boutcher 16/1: 060006: Rdn in rear, btn 2f out: see 617. 9 **36**
2063 **ENTITY** 3 [5] 3-8-10 (64)(bl) M Tebbutt 10/1: 003007: Prom 3f, wknd qckly: qck reapp. 5 **27**
1723 **RED MITTENS** 18 [1] 3-7-11 (50)(2oh)(1ow) N Kennedy 33/1: 600-08: Al rear, t.o.: see 1723 (6f). 5 **4**
1789 **CELEBRE BLU** 15 [4] 3-9-4 (72) D Mernagh 9/2: 7-: -63339: Nvr dngrs, t.o.: btr 1789, 1562 (gd/soft). 1¼ **22**

9 ran   Time 1m 23.8 (2.0)   (Gainsborough Stud)   M Johnston Middleham, N Yorks.

2146   4.30 RATING RELATED MDN 3YO 0-65 (F)   1m3f   Good/Firm 29   -11 Slow
£2268   £648   £324

1812 **PROTECTOR** 14 [5] J W Hills 3-9-0 M Tebbutt 9/2: 0-0401: 3 b g Be My Chief - Clicquot (Bold Lad) **66**
Trkd ldrs, pushed 4f out, chall 2f out, styd on well to lead cl home: lightly rcd in '99, rtd 77 in mdns: apprec
this step up to 11f, 12f will suit: acts on fast grnd, handles gd/soft & a stiff trk.
1770 **NOBLE CALLING** 16 [1] N A Graham 3-9-0 (BL) A Clark 9/2: 00-302: 3 b c Caller I D - Specificity ½ **64**
(Alleged) Tried to make all, worn down cl home: clr 3rd: gd eff in 1st time blnks: acts on gd & fast, stays 11f.
1895 **ABLE SEAMAN** 10 [2] C E Brittain 3-9-0 T E Durcan 4/7 FAV: -04533: 3 br g Northern Flagship - Love 6 **55**
At Dawn (Grey Dawn II) Trkd ldrs, ch 3f out, sn rdn & onepcd: well bckd: btr 1895 (gd).
1387 **DALYAN** 34 [3] T D Easterby 3-9-0 R Winston 15/2: 45-004: Rear, drvn & plugged on fnl 3f: see 1104. nk **54**
939 **ROYAL PASTIMES** 67 [4] 3-8-11 R Lappin 33/1: 00-605: Waited with, t.o. fnl 3f: 10 wk abs: see 783. *dist* **0**

5 ran   Time 2m 20.0 (4.5)   (Highclere Thoroughbred Racing Ltd)   J W Hills Lambourn, Berks.

2147   5.05 LADY AMAT MDN HCAP 3YO+ 0-70 (G)   1m str   Good/Firm 29   +01 Fast   [37]
£1848   £528   £264   3yo rec 10lb

1858 **TOEJAM** 12 [11] R E Barr 7-9-7 (30)(VIS) Miss P Robson 12/1: 40-001: 7 ch g Move Off - Cheeky **39**
Pigeon (Brave Invader) Chsd ldrs, led over 2f out, rnd clr fnl 1f: first time visor: mainly modest form in '00,
flattered when 5th in a mdn (rtd 63$): eff at 1m on fast grnd: handles a gall trk: set alight by a visor today.

REDCAR **FRIDAY JUNE 23RD** Lefthand, Flat, Galloping Track

1803 **CUTE CAROLINE** 14 [4] A Berry 4-10-10 (47)(BL) Miss E J Jones 8/1: -35062: 4 ch f First Trump - Hissma (Midyan) Prom, ev ch 2f out, outpcd by wnr fnl 1f: 6L clr 3rd, blnks first time: see 1190.   8   46

2060 **BEWILDERED** 3 [6] D W Chapman 3-9-7 (40)(bl) Miss A Deniel 20/1: 000603: 3 br f Prince Sabo - Collage (Ela Mana Mou) Mid-div, outpcd 2f out, no ch with ldrs after: qck reapp: mod form.   6   29

795 **FAS 85** [8] J D Bethell 4-9-3 (26)(VIS)(4oh) Miss A Armitage (5) 33/1: -60504: Led 3f, remained in tch till outpcd fnl 2f: 12 wk abs: tried a visor, has worn blnks prev: modest.   nk   14

1658 **KUWAIT THUNDER** 21 [1] 4-10-0 (37)(vis) Miss Diana Jones 6/1: 406005: Chsd ldrs till outpcd dist.   nk   24

1729 **BAHRAIN** 18 [5] A 4-11-7 (58)(t) Miss E Ramsden 11/4 FAV: -40006: Prom till saddle slipped over 1f out, eased consid ins fnl 1f: wld have fin at least 3rd & worth another chance in similar: see 961.   hd   45

1921 **ROYAL REPRIMAND** 9 [9] 5-9-10 (33)(vis) Miss S Samworth 11/1: 5-0007: Trkd ldrs, led after 3f till over 2f out, wknd: big drop in trip, prev tried over 10/14f: see 1009 (reapp).   1½   17

4312) **MA VIE** 256 [12] 3-11-5 (66) Mrs C Williams 3/1: 600-8: Rdn in rear, bhnd fnl 3f: nicely bckd on reapp: lightly rcd & some promise in mdn company in '99 (rtd 73): 40,000gns half sister to 1 7f juv wnr.   3½   44

643 **THE FOSSICK** 109 [7] 4-9-6 (29) Mrs S Eddery (5) 20/1: 5-609: Al rear, nvr in it: abs, new stable.   hd   7

1905 **THE CASTIGATOR** 9 [2] 3-11-0 (61) Miss R Bastiman 20/1: 004-60: Bhnd from halfway: see 1905 (6f).   13   19

1907 **SWYNFORD ELEGANCE** 9 [13] 3-9-13 (46) Mrs S Bosley 7/1: 0-0200: Chsd ldrs 3f, sn bhnd: fin 11th.   5   0

2060 Mount Park 3 [10] 3-9-9 (47)(bl) Miss R Clark 20/1:

1858 Otterington Girl 12 [3] 4-9-7 (30) Mrs D Wilkinson(7) 16/1:

13 ran   Time 1m 37.1 (2.3)   (Mrs R E Barr)   R E Barr Seamer, N Yorks.

ROYAL ASCOT **FRIDAY JUNE 23RD** Righthand, Stiff, Galloping Track

Official Going   GOOD TO FIRM (GOOD Places). Stalls: Straight Course - Stands side, Round Course - Inside.
A class adjustment of +20 was added to the pace figure of each race to compensate for the high-class of runners

2148 2.30 GR 2 KING EDWARD VII STKS 3YO (A) 1m4f Good 56 -22 Slow
£81000 £31050 £15525 £7425

1854 **SUBTLE POWER** 12 [5] H R A Cecil 3-8-8 T Quinn 7/4 FAV: 121: 3 b c Sadler's Wells - Mosaique Bleue (Shirley Heights) Trkd ldrs, led 2f out, pshd clr, cmftbly: hvly bckd: prev rnr-up in List company & earlier won debut at Newbury (mdn): eff at 10f, relished the step up to 12f, shld get further: acts on firm & gd grnd, stiff/gall tracks: smart & v progressive, Irish Derby and/or the St Leger look the logical path.   114

4292 **ZAFONIUM** 258 [1] P F I Cole 3-8-8 Pat Eddery 6/1: 31-2: 3 ch c Zafonic - Bint Pasha (Affirmed) Held up, eff ent straight, no impress till styd on appr fnl 1f & went 2nd towards fin, no ch wnr: bckd from 9/1: v useful reapp: '99 wnr at Ayr (mdn, rtd 95): dam a high-class mid-class performer: clearly suited by the step up to 12f, will get further: acts on gd & gd/soft grnd, stiff/gall tracks: should win a Group race before long.   3   108

1752 **ROSCIUS** 19 [2] Saeed bin Suroor 3-8-8 J Velazquez 7/1: 2-103: 3 b c Sadler's Wells - Rosefinch (Blushing Groom) Sn reluctant ldr, increased pace halfway, ev ch till fdd entering fnl 1f: op 5/1: not disgraced, stays a stiff 12f: rcd too keenly today: drop back to Listed/Gr 3 company will suit: see 1451.   ½   107

*1582 **TRAHERN** 24 [3] J H M Gosden 3-8-8 K Darley 12/1: -4214: Held up, rdn 3f out, no impression till styd on inside last: big step up in grade & improved over this longer 12f trip: useful, see 1582 (mdn).   1   105

*1193 **BANIYAR** 47 [7] 3-8-8 G Mosse 7/1: 0-415: Trckd ldrs, outpcd appr fnl 2f & flashed tail: 7 week abs: stiff task & poss flattered after winning a Hamilton mdn in 1193   ¾   104

1848 **GOING GLOBAL** 13 [4] 3-8-8 J Reid 10/1: -13206: Prom, eff ent fnl 3f, sn btn: op 7/1: easier grnd suits.   1½   102

1848 **HATHA ANNA** 13 [6] 3-8-8 J Bailey 5/1: 567: Prom till wknd quickly entering final 3f: stablemate 3rd, drifter from 3/1: reportedly has a breathing problem: cld do with a confidence booster, see 1848 (Derby), 1340.   11   92

7 ran   Time 2m 35.92 (6.92)   (The Thoroughbred Corporation)   H R A Cecil Newmarket

2149 3.05 GR 2 HARDWICKE STKS 4YO+ (A) 1m4f Good 56 +18 Fast
£81000 £31050 £15525 £7425

123 **FRUITS OF LOVE** 208 [11] M Johnston 5-8-12 (vis) O Peslier 9/2: 1320-1: 5 b c Hansel - Vallee Secrete (Secretariat) Trkd ldr, shkn up to lead dist, readily: reapp, nicely bckd tho' op 7/2, fast time: '99 wnr in Dubai (stks) & here at R Ascot (this Gr 2, rtd 123): '98 wnr at Newmarket (Gr 2, rtd 117): v eff at 12f: acts on firm & gd grnd, prob handles hvy: runs v well fresh & best in a visor coming late off a strong pace: loves Ascot, top-class.   122

1456 **YAVANAS PACE** 33 [3] M Johnston 8-8-9 D Holland 25/1: 010432: 8 ch g Accordion - Lady In Pace (Burslem) Set gd clip & qcknd ent str, hdd 1f out, styd on gamely: stablemate of wnr: ran to best in defeat & is smart when allowed to dominate: v tough, deserves a Group 2: see 987.   1½   114

*1152 **BLUEPRINT** 49 [10] Sir Michael Stoute 5-8-12 Pat Eddery 11/4 FAV: 142-13: 5 b h Generous - Highbrow (Shirley Heights) Keen, chsd ldrs, outpcd ent straight, kept on for press appr fnl 1f: 7 wk abs, hvly bckd: improved, most consistent & now v smart: shld win more Group races: see 1152 (bt this 2nd).   hd   117

*1474 **MUTAMAM** 30 [2] A C Stewart 5-8-9 W Supple 16/1: /0-214: Keen, prom, lost place appr fnl 2f, late hdwy under press: gd run from this smart entire, clearly gets a stiff 12f: keep an eye on: see 1474.   1¾   112

1625 **GREEK DANCE** 26 [1] 5-8-9 J Murtagh 9/2: 65-225: Held up, mid-div appr straight, chsd ldrs 2f out, same pace: nicely bckd: stays 12f, best at 10f: see 1115.   ¾   111

1057 **GOLD ACADEMY** 55 [7] 4-8-9 Dane O'Neill 16/1: 134-66: Mid div, chsd ldrs 3f out, soon rdn & one pace: 8 weeks abs, nicely bckd: longer trip, return to 10f will suit: see 1057.   1½   109

1625 **MUTAFAWEQ** 26 [8] 4-9-0 R Hills 4/1: 541-37: Held up, gd hdwy to track ldrs 5f out, fdd 2f out: well bckd.   2½   111

4239) **STATE SHINTO** 265 [9] 4-8-12 (VIS) J Velazquez 12/1: 1211-8: Held up, hmpd & lost grnd halfway, nvr dngrs after: visored: '99 wnr at M Laffitte (List) & Longchamp (2, Gr 3 & Gr 2, rtd 119, A Fabre): stays 11f, best at 10f: acts on gd & hvy grnd: can go well fresh: v smart at best & is worth another chance.   10   99

1625 **URBAN OCEAN** 26 [5] 4-8-9 M J Kinane 25/1: 16-159: Prom till wknd qkly 3f out: btr 1121 (Listed, 10f).   1¼   95

9 ran   Time 2m 31.10 (2.10)   (M Doyle)   M Johnston Middleham, N Yorks

2150 3.45 GR 1 CORONATION STKS 3YO (A) 1m rnd Good 56 -02 Slow
£156000 £59400 £29700 £13500

*1626 **CRIMPLENE** 26 [6] C E Brittain 3-9-0 P Robinson 4/1 JT FAV: 633111: 3 ch f Lion Cavern - Crimson Conquest (Diesis) Led, qcknd clr 2f out, rdn out, unchall: well bckd: superb hat-trick landed after wins in the German & Irish 1,000 Guineas: '99 wnr at Redcar (auct mdn) & Salisbury (stks, Gr 1 3rd, rtd 106): v eff forcing the pace at 1m, 10f still suit: acts on firm, suited by gd & hvy grnd, handles any trk: high-class, still   121

improving filly: credit to connections & will be aimed at the Breeders Cup Distaff.
1626 **PRINCESS ELLEN 26** [3] G A Butler 3-9-0 K Darley 6/1: 5-0252: 3 br f Tirol - Celt Song (Unfuwain) *2½* **115**
Mid div, niggled halfway, styd on fnl 2f, nvr nr wnr: clr rem & showed running in Irish Guineas to be all wrong (in season) tho' does show a preference for gd or faster grnd: v smart, deserves a Group race, see 1185.
*1319 **BLUEMAMBA 40** [5] P Bary 3-9-0 O Peslier 7/1: 31-313: 3 b f Kingmambo - Black Penny (Private *4* **107**
Account) Tkd ldr, eff 2f out, no impress: 6 wk abs: French raider, eff on gd but rtd higher on soft in 1319.
*1754 **ZARKIYA 19** [2] A de Royer Dupre 3-9-0 G Mosse 4/1 JT FAV: 1-2414: Held up, prog ent fnl 3f, sn rdn/no *1* **105**
further hdwy: well bckd to reverse placings with this 3rd on running in French Guineas: see 1754, 1319 (testing).
1733 **TOTAL LOVE 18** [1] 3-9-0 T Quinn 14/1: 33-025: Held up, mod hdwy appr fnl 2f, nvr dngrs: tchd 25/1. *2½* **100$**
1319 **IFTIRAAS 40** [7] 3-9-0 Pat Eddery 8/1: 42-156: Towards rear, no response when pace quickened appr *3* **94**
fnl 2f: 6 week abs, hvly bckd: closer to this 3rd & 4th in the French Guineas in 1319, see 913 (soft).
1485 **DECISION MAID 29** [8] 3-9-0 D Holland 12/1: 51-047: Held up, wide eff appr fnl 2f, soon btn: *nk* **93**
nicely bckd from 16/1: stiff task tho' stable has a fine record in this race, see 1485, 953.
1626 **SEAZUN 26** [9] 3-9-0 S Drowne 8/1: 1-2448: Cl up till wknd quickly entering straight: tchd 10/1: broke *3½* **86**
a blood vessel & best forgotten: much closer to this wnr in 1626, see 1185, 953.
1626 **AMETHYST 26** [4] 3-9-0 M J Kinane 15/2: 3-1029: Prom till drpd out quickly appr fnl 2f: surely *2½* **81**
something amiss, less than 2L bhd this wnr in 1626 (gd/soft), see 948.
9 ran Time 1m 41.55 (3.05) (Sheikh Marwan Al Maktoum) C E Brittain Newmarket

2151

4.20 WOKINGHAM HCAP 3YO+ 0-110 (B) 6f Good 56 -04 Slow [110]
£58000 £22000 £11000 £5000 3 yo rec 7 lb 2 Groups, stands side soon struggling

1337 **HARMONIC WAY 36** [28] R Charlton 5-9-6 (102) R Hughes 12/1: 0-6421: 5 ch h Lion Cavern - Pineapple **112**
(Superlative) Confidently held up far side, crept clsr after halfway, burst thro' dist & qcknd smartly to lead towards fin, v readily: '99 wnr at Goodwood (Stewards Cup h'cap), plcd in sev h'caps (rtd 103): rtd 97 in '98: v eff at 6f, stays 7f: likes firm & gd, acts on soft: best coming v late: smart & progressive, Group class.
1533 **TUSSLE 27** [17] M L W Bell 5-8-7 (89) T Quinn 14/1: 040-02: 5 b g Salse - Crime Ofthecentury *1* **95**
(Pharly) Chsd ldrs far side, qcknd to lead ent fnl 1f, ran on but unable to repel wnrs burst nr fin: nicely bckd: best effort when 5th in this v h'cap last term (won race on unfav'd side, rtd 97): rtd 100 in '98 (List): sole win came in a '97 Newmarket mdn (rtd 96): eff at 6f on firm & gd: runs v well fresh & can force the pace: fine run.
1470 **STRAHAN 30** [26] J H M Gosden 3-8-10 (99) K Darley 11/2 FAV: 1-1223: 3 b c Catrail - Soreze *1¼* **102**
(Gallic League) Towards rear far side, pshd along & hdwy halfway, ran on under press & went 3rd ins last, not pace of front pair: hvly bckd: fine performance from this 3yo (poor record in this race): useful, return to 7f will suit.
1674 **DEEP SPACE 20** [29] E A L Dunlop 5-9-9 (105) J Reid 16/1: 0-6354: Waited with far side, imprvd going *1½* **104**
well 2f out, rdn dist, styd on: ran to best tho' found less than expected: won this in '99 of 17lbs lower mark.
3628} **NICE ONE CLARE 300** [21] 4-8-7 (89) J P Spencer 12/1: 3211-5: Trkd ldrs far side, chall 2f out & ev ch *nk* **87**
till no extra ins last: gd reapp, bckd from 16/1: '99 wnr at Folkestone, (auct mdn, debut), Kempton & Newmarket (h'caps, rtd 92): eff at 6f, suited by 7f: acts on firm & gd grnd, any track: progressive, lightly raced & has a fine turn of foot, type to land a valuable h'cap this term.
1851 **ROYAL RESULT 13** [16] 7-8-5 (87) A Nicholls (3) 12/1: -00036: Towards rear far side, eff ent fnl 2f, *nk* **84**
styd on for press inside last, never near to chall: running into form, see 728.
2115 **CRETAN GIFT 1** [6] 9-9-12 (108)(vis) Dane O Neill 50/1: 146507: Well bhd stands side till gd hdwy *1¼* **101**
towards centre fnl 2f, nvr a ch with far side: ran yesterday: came out best of those drawn low, excellent run.
+1983 **INDIAN SPARK 7** [30] 6-9-11 (99)(8ex) A Culhane 14/1: 150118: Outpcd far side till hdwy appr fnl *¾* **98**
1f, nvr nr ldrs: well bckd from 33/1: prob ran near to best under an 8lbs penalty: see 1983.
*1728 **ALEGRIA 18** [19] 4-8-9 (91)(BL)(5ex) J Tate 25/1: 30-019: Cl up, led halfway, soon rdn & edged *hd* **82**
right, hdd dist & btn: a bold attempt in blinkers, similar tactics over a sharper 6f/5f will pay dividends: see 1728.
1983 **JUWWI 7** [7] 6-9-0 (96) Darren Williams (7) 33/1: 415050: Bhd stands side till gd hdwy & drifted *1* **84**
towards centre appr fnl 1f, no extra & eased towards fin: 10th, qk reapp: decent run from a poor draw, see 1337.
1173 **EMERGING MARKET 48** [4] 8-8-4 (86) J Bailey 33/1: 66-000: Bhd stands side, late hdwy, never a *1* **71**
threat: 11th, nicely bckd: last tasted victory in this very race 4 years ago: see 728.
1829 **TAYSEER 14** [27] 6-8-4 (86) F Norton 10/1: -00530: Mid-div far side, chsd ldrs 2f out, sn onepce: 12th. *½* **70**
*1531 **DANIELLES LAD 27** [25] 4-9-0 (96) Pat Eddery 25/1: 040110: Chsd ldrs far side, feeling pace halfway, *hd* **80**
not much room bef dist, no impresssion: 13th: easier grnd suits, see 1531.
1337 **RED LION GB 36** [9] 4-8-9 (91) M Roberts 33/1: 000-00: Outpcd stands side till kept on fnl 1f: 14th. *½* **74**
1622 **SOCIAL HARMONY 27** [10] 6-9-13 (109) P J Smullen 25/1: 24-020: Front rank stands side till appr *hd* **92**
fnl 1f: 15th: unfavoured side & grnd faster than ideal for this Irish raider under top-weight: won h'caps in '99 at The Curragh & Galway (rtd 108): eff at 6f, stays 7f on fast grnd, suited by gd/soft & hvy: with D Weld.
1533 **SHEER VIKING 27** [15] 4-9-3 (99) N Pollard 25/1: -22320: Chsd ldrs far side, no extra appr fnl 1f: 16th. *½* **81**
1702 **PIPS SONG 19** [5] 5-8-3 (85) J Lowe 66/1: 401030: Never a factor stands side: 17th: see 941. *nk* **66**
1324 **SUNLEY SENSE 37** [22] 4-8-4 (86) Craig Williams 33/1: -00220: Dsptd lead far side till 2f out, *nk* **66**
fdd: 18th, return to 5f will suit, see 1324, 1245, 926.
1529 **HALMAHERA 27** [12] 5-9-12 (108) J Murtagh 25/1: 520560: Nvr dngrs stands side: 2nd in this in '99. *nk* **87**
2035 **ROSE OF MOONCOIN 4** [24] 4-8-3 (85)(bl) L Newman (3) 100/1: 0-6660: Al bhd far side: 20th. *nk* **63**
*1952 **NIGRASINE 8** [20] 6-9-8 (104)(bl)(5ex) J F Egan 40/1: 304510: Prom far side till wknd appr fnl 1f: 21st. *1¼* **79**
1757 **PEPPERDINE 18** [1] 4-8-13 (95) G Carter 9/1: 02-350: In tch stands side till halfway, eased fnl 1f: 26th, **0**
no chance from poor draw: shorter priced stablemate of 6th: see 1173.
1338 **DOCTOR SPIN 36** [18] 4-9-9 (105) R Hills 12/1: 40-150: Keen & well plcd far side till wknd ent fnl 2f, **0**
eased: 27th, awash with sweat & rcd much too freely: 4th in this in '99, see 1338, 1182.
1983 **Bon Ami 7** [2] 4-8-4 (86) J Carroll 66/1:
1016 **Al Muallim 60** [3] 6-8-13 (95) D Holland 33/1:
1471 **Gracious Gift 30** [11] 4-8-3 (85) D Harrison 40/1:
1674 **Easy Dollar 20** [13] 8-8-7 (89)(bl) C Rutter 50/1:
-1946 **Delegate 8** [14] 7-8-10 (92) J Mackay (7) 20/1:
1980 **Speedy James 7** [23] 4-8-6 (88) W Supple 66/1:
29 ran Time 1m 15.49 (2.39) (Mrs Alexandra J Chandris) R Charlton Beckhampton, Wilts

2152

4.55 WINDSOR CASTLE CONDITIONS STKS 2YO (B) 5f Godd 56 -41 Slow
£20300 £7700 £3850 £1750

*1835 **AUTUMNAL 13** [4] B J Meehan 2-8-8 Pat Eddery 4/1: -311: 2 b f Indian Ridge - Please Believe Me **98**
(Try My Best) Prom, outpcd & rdn appr fnl 1f, reponded well for press inside last & got on top cl home: well bckd: recent Haydock wnr (mdn): sister to a sprint juv wnr: dam & sire both sprinters: eff at 5f, shapes like 6f will suit: acts on gd & gd/soft grnd, stiff/gall tracks: useful & progressive.
1809 **GIVE BACK CALAIS 14** [6] P J Makin 2-8-11 S Sanders 13/2: 32: 2 b c Brief Truce - Nichodoula *nk* **100**
(Doulab) In tch, rdn & qcknd to lead dist, kept on but collared cl home: bckd from 8/1: much improved & clr rem

on only 2nd ever start: eff at 5/6f on gd & gd/soft grnd: nailed on for a mdn, useful: see 1809.

1538	**ZIETUNZEEN** 27 [7] A Berry 2-8-6 J Carroll 20/1: 233: 2 b f Zieten - Hawksbill Special (Taufan) Cl up, qcknd to lead after halfway, rdn dist & hdd, hung on for 3rd: bckd at big odds, should win a fillies mdn.		3	86
--	**DIETRICH** [9] A P O'Brien 2-8-6 M J Kinane 5/1: 24: Keen in rear, not much room 2f out, kept on fnl 1f, unable to chall: clr rem, bckd: Irish raider, recent debut rnr-up: $2,000,000 Storm Cat Feb foal, half-sister got 1m as a juv: dam smart French juv, sire top class dirt sprinter: eff at 5f, 6f+ will suit: goes on gd & soft.		hd	86
1691	**PAGLIACCI** 20 [3] 2-8-11 O Peslier 11/2: -45: Chsd ldrs, kept on same pace appr fnl 1f: clrly unsuited by drop bck to 5f after looking in need of 7f on debut: see 1691.		3½	82
*1698	**FALCON GOA** 19 [11] 2-8-6 W Supple 33/1: -0416: Prom, ch 2f out, onepace: stiff task/not disgraced.		nk	76
1924	**MOONLIGHT DANCER** 9 [1] 2-8-11 Dane O'Neill 20/1: -4227: Rear, struggling 2f out, mod late rally.		1	78
*1437	**KACHINA DOLL** 32 [8] 2-8-8 T Quinn 7/2 FAV: 300118: Bhd ldrs, wknd quickly appr fnl 1f: well bckd, surely something amiss: progressive on fast grnd previously: see 1437.		nk	74
1691	**JOHNNY REB** 20 [5] 2-8-11 R Hughes 12/1: -269: Led till halfway, fdd, eased: bckd: see 1691, 1426.		5	65
1221	**BANJO BAY** 44 [2] 2-8-11 K Darley 50/1: 530: In tch till 2f out: 10th, 6 week abs, highly tried.		nk	64
1691	**CAUSTIC WIT** 20 [10] 2-8-11 J Reid 8/1: -50: Handy till lost place & action 2f out: 11th, see 1691 (6f).		3	57
11 ran	Time 1m 02.86 (3.86)	(Paul & Jenny Green)	B J Meehan Upper Lambourn, Berks	

2153   5.30 QUEEN ALEXANDRA COND STKS 4YO+ (B)   2m6f34y   Good 56 -10 Slow
£20300   £7700   £3850   £1750   4 yo rec 2 lb

*1329	**DOMINANT DUCHESS** 37 [4] J W Hills 6-8-9 T Quinn 7/1: P22-11: 6 b m Old Vic - Andy's Find (Buckfinder) Waited wth, eff appr straight, gd progress ent fnl 2f, ran on strgly to lead towards fin, cleverly: nicely bckd: earlier won reapp at York (h'cap): '99 Kempton wnr (reapp), rnr-up in the Cesarewitch (rtd 85): eff at 14f suited by 2m2f/2m6f: acts on firm & gd, any track: runs v well fresh: fast improving stayer.			99
*1897	**THREE CHEERS** 14 [1] J H M Gosden 6-9-5 (vis) S Guillot 9/4 FAV: 262-12: 6 b g Slip Anchor - Three Tails (Blakeney) Held up, imprvd ent str, rdn & chall dist, outstayed by wnr: hvly bckd: in gd form but remains a tricky ride, needs to hit the front as late as possible: eff between 14f & 2m6f: see 1897.		¾	108
1565	**SPIRIT OF LOVE** 25 [3] M Johnston 5-9-5 D Holland 8/1: 001-03: 5 ch g Trempolino - Dream Mary (Marfa) Cl up, shkn up to chall 2f out, lead briefly ins last, one pace: ran to best over this marathon 2m6f trip.		1½	106
1565	**EILEAN SHONA** 25 [8] J R Fanshawe 4-8-7 Pat Eddery 5/1: 11-054: Towards rear, rdn 2f out, styd on but no impression on ldrs: stiffish task but clearly styd this longer 2m6f trip: see 1222 (h'cap).		¾	95
--	**WINGED HUSSAR** [9] 7-9-0 J Murtagh 9/2: 00-315: Chsd ldrs, prog 2f out, rdn bef dist, one pace & flashed tail: nicely bckd Irish raider: earlier won at The Curragh (h'cap): '99 wnr at Leopardstown (h'cap): eff at 12f/2m, stays 2m6f: goes on fast & gd/soft grnd: useful: with J Oxx.		½	100
1339	**KAHTAN** 36 [7] 5-9-5 R Hills 4/1: 01-446: Tried to make all hdd dist, no extra: well bckd tho' op 3/1: big step up in trip, return to 12f/2m2f will suit: see 1152.		shd	105
1484	**TENSILE** 29 [11] M Johnston 25/1: 30-607: Held up, eff appr fnl 2f, btn bef dist: stiff task, flattered.		6	91S
1187	**KNOCKHOLT** 27 [5] 4-8-12 J Reid 16/1: 01-008: Chsd ldrs, wknd v qckly ent str: lkd a non-stayer over this longer 2m6f trip: '99 wnr at Salisbury (mdn), Goodwood (rtd h'cap) & Doncaster (h'cap, rtd 100): eff at 14f+ suited racing with/forcing the pace on firm or gd grnd, any trk: with S Woods.		24	71
8 ran	Time 4m 56.57 (10.07)	(Mrs Diana Patterson)	J W Hills Upper Lambourn, Berks	

REDCAR   SATURDAY JUNE 24TH   Lefthand, Flat, Galloping Track

Official Going   FIRM.   Stalls: Str Crse - Stands side; 1m6f - Centre; rem - Inside.

2154   2.15 RACING WELFARE MDN 3YO+ (D)   6f str   Good/Firm 28 -10 Slow
£2814   £804   £402

1783	**DESAMO** 16 [4] J Noseda 3-9-0 J Weaver 2/7 FAV: 331: 3 br c Chief's Crown - Green Heights (Miswaki) Easily made all: well bckd to land short odds: similar level of form all 3 starts, unrcd juvenile, cost $70,000: eff at 6/7f on fast & gd/sft grnd, sharp or gall trks: v simple task here, h'caps next.			77
2096	**PACIFIC PLACE** 3 [3] M Quinn 3-9-0 M Tebbutt 7/1: 024232: 3 gr c College Chapel - Kaitlin (Salmon Leap) Prom, outpcd by wnr appr fnl 2f: stiff task for this plater up in trip: see 2096, 1334.		6	56
1444	**CITY BANK DUDLEY** 32 [2] N Wilson 3-9-0 C Teague 100/1: 03: 3 b g Noble Patriarch - Derry's Delight (Mufrij) Never going pace: jockey given 3 day whip ban: no form yet from this stoutly bred gldg.		7	36
1516	**KIND EMPEROR** 28 [5] M J Polglase 3-9-0 Dean McKeown 11/2: 530004: Reared, prom 3f: see 731.		hd	35
4 ran	Time 1m 11.2 (2.3)	(K Y Lim)	J Noseda Newmarket, Suffolk	

2155   2.45 THEHORSESMOUTH.CO.UK SELLER 2YO (G)   7f str   Good/Firm 28 -39 Slow
£1841   £526   £263

2059	**BULA ROSE** 4 [1] W G M Turner 2-8-6 A Daly 3/1: -5231: 2 ch f Alphabatim - Titled Dancer (Where To Dance) Led, rdn clr appr fnl 1f, cmftbly: sold to E Tuer for 8,500 gns: deserved first win: Ir2,500 gns Apr foal, apprec return to 7f (dam mid-dist wnr): acts on fast & gd, gall trks: suited by forcing the pace.			59
1864	**EASTERN RED** 12 [2] K A Ryan 2-8-6 F Lynch 7/2: -0562: 2 b f Contract Law - Gargajulu (Al Hareb) Prom, ch ent fnl 2f, sn onepace: bckd from 5/1: prob handles fast grnd: 6f sell nurseries will suit.		5	53
1883	**BEAUTIFUL BUSINESS** 11 [6] M Quinn 2-8-6 R Fitzpatrick (3) 25/1: 03: 2 b f Deploy - Jade Mistress (Damister) Outpcd till moderate late hdwy: already in need of 1m, see 1883.		1¼	50
1704	**BANNINGHAM BLIZ** 20 [3] D Shaw 2-8-6 T Williams 13/2: -00654: Rear, wide prog appr fnl 2f, no extra.		nk	49
1950	**SEL** 9 [9] G Duffield 2/1 FAV: 35: Prom till outpcd fnl 2f: nicely bckd: needs more time.		3	43
1890	**IMPISH LAD** 11 [7] 2-8-11 Joanna Badger (7) 9/1: 05236: Handy till 2f out: op 7/1, btr 1890 (blnks).		nk	47
1420	**CITRUS** 33 [4] 2-8-6 Dean McKeown 12/1: -047: Chsd ldrs, wknd qckly ent fnl 2f: see 1420.		11	26
1890	**DOCKLANDS ROLLER** 11 [5] 2-8-11 Kim Tinkler 33/1: 058: Bhd from halfway: see 1890.		2	27
1916	**CROSS FINGERS** 10 [8] 2-8-6 A Clark 12/1: -69: Sn struggling: turf bow, see 1916.		10	6
9 ran	Time 1m 26.5 (4.7)	(Ray Gallop)	W G M Turner Corton Denham, Somerset	

2156	3.20 TEES COMPONENTS HCAP 3YO+ 0-60 (F)	1m6f	Good/Firm 28	-02 Slow	[60]
	£2884 £824 £412 3 yo rec 17lb				

*2123 **XELLANCE** 2 [3] M Johnston 3-7-11 (46)(6ex) K Dalgleish (7) 13/8 FAV: 1U0111: 3 b g Be My Guest - **52**
Excellent Alibi (Exceller) Well plcd, led going well 3f out & just had to be kept up to his work: nicely bckd,
qk-fire hat-trick: earlier won at Southwell (2), W'hampton (rtd 53a) & Musselburgh (h'caps): eff at 11/14f:
acts on firm/fast grnd & fibresand: runs well fresh on sharp or gall trks, likes Southwell: progressive.
1677 **WESTERN COMMAND** 21 [9] Mrs N Macauley 4-8-12 (44) R Fitzpatrick (3) 33/1: 451062: 4 b g Saddlers 1½ **46**
Hall - Western Friend (Gone West) Nvr far away, led appr fnl 3f, sn hdd, styd on: ran to turf best, btr 1501 (AW).
*1874 **ZINCALO** 12 [7] C E Brittain 4-9-13 (59)(t) T E Durcan 9/2: -04013: 4 gr g Zilzal - Silver Glitz ¾ **60**
(Grey Dawn II) Rear, rdn to go 3rd 3f out, styd on but no impress front 2: ran to best under a big weight.
1874 **KING FOR A DAY** 12 [4] Bob Jones 4-8-7 (39) A Daly 33/1: 00-004: Hld up, drvn ent strt, not pace to chall.1¾ **38**
1816 **SIMPLE IDEALS** 15 [2] Kim Tinkler 10/1: 3-0205: Bhd, late hdwy, no threat: shade btr 1563. nk **41**
*1909 **ROOFTOP PROTEST** 10 [5] 3-8-6 (55) D Holland 6/1: 5-0316: Mid-div, nvr any impress on ldrs: 4 **49**
unsuited by step up in trip/return to h'cap company: rtd much higher when winning a claimer in 1909 (11f).
2050 **WINSOME GEORGE** 5 [6] 5-8-11 (43)(vis) N Kennedy 16/1: 330047: Chsd ldrs till ent fnl 3f: qk reapp. 10 **27**
1894 **STOLEN MUSIC** 11 [10] 7-8-3 (35) G Duffield 4/1: 0-0328: Chsd ldrs far 1m: fin lame, won this in '99. 8 **11**
1996 **ZOLA** 7 [1] 4-7-12 (30)(bl) T Williams 25/1: 0-0509: Led till bef 3f out, sn lost pl: qk reapp, see 649. 1 **5**
1353 **BACKEND CHARLIE** 36 [8] 6-7-12 (30) J McAuley (5) 50/1: 65-00: Handy 9f: h'cap bow, nds sellers. dist **0**
10 ran   Time 3m 02.0 (4.2)   (T T Bloodstocks)   M Johnston Middleham, N Yorks

2157	3.55 TETLEY'S BITTER HCAP 3YO+ 0-90 (C)	1m2f	Good/Firm 28	+05 Fast	[82]
	£8697 £2676 £1338 £669 3 yo rec 12lb				

2001 **GRALMANO** 7 [4] K A Ryan 5-9-4 (72) F Lynch 7/1: 145251: 5 b g Scenic - Llangollen (Caerleon) **77**
Trkd ldrs, qcknd to lead 2f out, rdn out: gd time, qk reapp: gd runs in defeat since Feb W'hampton win (h'cap,
rtd 90a): '99 wnr here at Redcar (class stks) & Pontefract (h'cap, rtd 72 & 92a, earlier win N Littmoden): '98
Lingfield wnr (stks, rtd 99a & 82): eff at 1m/10f, stays 11f: acts on both AWs, firm & gd/sft grnd: suited by
sharp or gall trks: well w/without blnks/visor: gd weight carrier, can force the pace: tough, useful on sand.
*2102 **COLWAY RITZ** 3 [6] W Storey 6-10-2 (84)(6ex) T Williams 9/4 FAV: 036112: 6 b g Rudimentary - 1¼ **86**
Million Heiress (Auction Ring) Rear, prog 3f out to chse wnr fnl 2f, al being held: well bckd, qk reapp: hat-trick
foiled but lost no caste in winner glory under a mammoth weight: won this race in '99 off a 6lbs lower mark: see 2102.
1958 **BAILEYS PRIZE** 8 [2] M Johnston 3-8-13 (79) K Dalgleish (7) 10/3: 462223: 3 ch c Mister Baileys - Mar ¾ **79**
Mar (Forever Casting) Prom, led 3f out till 2f out, styd on same pace ins last: due another win: see 1735, 1299.
1452 **BALI BATIK** 32 [3] G Wragg 3-9-2 (82) D Holland 11/2: -43104: Trkd ldrs, eff 2f out, unable to qckn. 1¼ **80**
2001 **THE WIFE** 7 [5] 3-9-0 (80) J Weaver 7/2: 0-0035: Pld hard, rear, eff appr fnl 2f, no impress: well ½ **77**
bckd, qk reapp: in front of this wnr last time, see 2001, 1598.
1929 **MINGLING** 10 [1] 3-8-13 (79) G Duffield 8/1: -35236: Led till 3f out, no extra: btr 1929, 1439. ½ **75**
6 ran   Time 2m 04.6 (2.3)   (Coleorton Moor Racing)   K A Ryan Hambleton, N Yorks

2158	4.25 TOTE SCOOP6 HCAP 3YO+ 0-90 (C)	6f str	Good/Firm 28	-05 Slow	[86]
	£7182 £2210 £1105 £552 Those drawn stands side (high no's) probably had a slight edge				

2000 **EURO VENTURE** 7 [7] D Nicholls 5-8-8 (66) D Holland 6/1: 006001: 5 b g Prince Sabo - Brave **71**
Advance (Bold Laddie) Mid-div, prog to lead below dist, pshd out: nicely bckd: '99 wnr at Southwell (rtd 73a),
Thirsk & Carlisle (h'caps, rtd 79): '98 W'hampton wnr (mdn, rtd 78a & 59): eff at 6/7f on fast, soft grnd &
fibresand: can force the pace, any trk: h'capped to follow up.
2107 **COOL PROSPECT** 2 [10] K A Ryan 5-7-10 (54) Iona Wands (5) 7/1: 104232: 5 b g Mon Tresor - I Ran ¾ **57**
Lovely (Persian Bold) In tch, imprvd ent fnl 2f & went 2nd near fin: nicely bckd, ran 48 hrs ago: consistent.
2000 **FRANCPORT** 7 [12] A Berry 4-9-2 (74) J Weaver 11/1: 510003: 4 b c Efisio - Elkie Brooks (Relkino) ½ **75**
Bhd till strong burst/weaved thro' fnl 1f, nvr nrr: qk reapp: return to form, see 824.
1887 **POINT OF DISPUTE** 11 [5] P J Makin 5-9-8 (80)(vis) A Clark 2/1 FAV: 001-44: In tch, prog to chall 2f hd **81**
out, onepce ins last: hvly bckd from 3/1: ran to best, shld recoup losses before long: see 1887.
1979 **YOUNG BIGWIG** 8 [13] 6-7-11 (55) K Dalgleish (7) 6/1: 060345: Well plcd, led 2f out till below dist, 1¼ **52**
no extra: ran well enough, won this race in '99 off a 7lbs higher mark: see 425.
1861 **OCKER** 13 [4] 6-10-0 (86) R Fitzpatrick (3) 12/1: 0-0006: Chsd ldrs, ch 2f out, sn onepce: see 47. ½ **82**
1441 **PRINCE PROSPECT** 33 [1] 4-9-8 (80) T E Durcan 16/1: 102207: Wide, in tch till appr fnl 1f: op 12/1. 3 **67**
1980 **MISS FIT** 8 [8] 4-8-13 (71) G Duffield 12/1: -05008: Nvr nr ldrs tho' keeping on fin: see 926. nk **57**
2000 **BOLLIN RITA** 7 [2] 4-8-6 (64) G Parkin 20/1: 0-0009: Prom till ent fnl 2f: op 14/1: '99 wnr at 1¾ **45**
Thirsk (reapp, auct mdn, rtd 79 in h'cap): 86 rtd juv: eff at 6f on firm & gd/sft grnd, without blinkers.
2118 **MARENGO** 2 [3] 6-8-5 (63) R Price 20/1: 402400: Slow away, nvr in it: 10th, see 1073 (clmr). nk **43**
1869 **MOTHER CORRIGAN** 12 [11] 4-7-11 (55)(vis) T Williams 25/1: 010000: Led till 2f out, sn btn: last, see 1297. **0**
2000 **Venika Vitesse** 7 [6] 4-8-3 (61) P Fessey 20/1:   2000 **Green Ginger** 7 [9] 4-8-12 (70) A Daly 20/1:
13 ran   Time 1m 10.9 (2)   (W G Swiers)   D Nicholls Sessay N Yorks

2159	5.00 ROMFORDS MDN 3YO+ (D)	1m str	Good/Firm 28	+00 Fast	
	£2769 £852 £426 £213 3 yo rec 10lb				

1922 **GOLDEN CHANCE** 10 [4] M Johnston 3-8-11 D Holland 5/4: 3221: 3 b c Unfuwain - Golden Digger **81**
(Mr Prospector) Dsptd lead, led 2f out, rdn clr despite flashing tail: nicely bckd, fair time: deserved, unraced
juvenile: eff at 1m, 10f may suit: acts on firm & gd/sft grnd, stiff/gall trks: suited forcing the pace.
1771 **CABALLE** 17 [5] S P C Woods 3-8-6 G Duffield 1/1 FAV: 2-2332: 3 ch f Opening Verse - Attirance 3½ **69**
(Crowned Prince) Wide, prom, rdn & ch 2f out, onepce: nicely bckd: plcd all starts, worth a try in headgear.
-- **IL CAVALIERE** 2 Mrs M Reveley 5-9-7 T Eaves (7) 14/1: 3: 5 b g Mtoto - Kalmia (Miller's ¾ **72**
Mate) Outpcd till kept on well appr fnl 1f: Flatbow, 11 wk NH abs, jockey given 7 day ban for ill-judged
ride: '99 bmpr wnr at M Rasen & Sedgefield (2m): acts on fast: improve over mid-dists with a stronger ride.
4001} **MOON GLOW** 279 [1] Miss S E Hall 4-9-7 J Weaver 14/1: 3400-4: Narrow lead till 2f out, no extra: '99 1¼ **69$**
hdles wnr at Wetherby (2m juv nov, firm, rtd 108h): Flat plcd last term (mdn, rtd 76): eff arnd 1m on firm & gd.
1682 **ANNESPRIDE** 21 [3] 3-8-6 F Lynch 33/1: 0-55: Prom 4f: stablemate 3rd, see 1682. 23 **34**
5 ran   Time 1m 37.0 (2.2)   (Maktoum Al Maktoum)   M Johnston Middleham, N Yorks

2160 5.30 THEHORSESMOUTH HCAP 3YO 0-75 (E) 1m1f Good/Firm 28 -22 Slow [77]
£2968 £848 £424

1708 **STALLONE** 20 [10] J Noseda 3-9-7 (70) J Weaver 11/8 FAV: -4551: 3 ch g Brief Truce - Bering Honneur 75
(Bering) Waited with, gd prog on bit 3f out, led appr fnl 1f, sn hung left, shkn up, shade rdly: well bckd, h'cap
bow, referred to Jockey Club for imprvd performance: unrcd juv: apprec step up to 9f, stay further: acts on fast.
2094 **CLASSIC LORD** 3 [6] M Johnston 3-8-4 (50) K Dalgleish (7) 15/2: 0003U2: 3 b g Wolfhound - Janaat 1¼ 51
(Kris) Bhd ldrs, eff appr fnl 2f, no impress till styd on nicely ins last: styd lngr 9f trip, shld win a race. see 1907.
1895 **STEPASTRAY** 11 [2] R E Barr 3-7-11 (46) N Kennedy 50/1: 00-003: 3 gr g Alhijaz - Wandering Stranger shd 47
(Petong) Bhd, styd on well for press fnl 2f, nrst fin: clr rem: first form, stays 9f on fast: win a seall h'cap.
1436 **EREBUS 33** [4] M H Tompkins 3-9-4 (67) G Duffield 6/1: 0634: Led till appr fnl 1f, no extra: h'cap bow. 3 62
*1907 **STORMSWELL** 10 [7] 3-8-2 (51) R Mullen 4/1: -00315: In tch, prog & ev ch 2f out, onepace dist: ½ 45
stepped up another furlong in trip, return to 1m likely to suit: see 1907 (mdn h'cap).
1920 **QUIDS INN** 10 [3] 3-8-3 (52) P Fessey 8/1: 0-2006: Prom, not much room, onepace ent fnl 2f: see 1296. nk 45
1892 **FISHER ISLAND** 11 [5] 3-8-2 (51) P M Quinn (3) 10/1: 344047: Nvr a factor: softer grnd suits, see 1142. ¾ 42
1104 **STORMVILLE 52** [8] 3-9-1 (64) T Williams 25/1: 5-6408: Handy 6f: 7 wk abs: see 902, 736. 7 43
1689 **SEDONA** 21 [1] 3-8-7 (56) P Fitzsimons (5) 12/1: U30109: Al bhd: see 1365 (seller, gd/sft). ¾ 34
9 ran Time 1m 53.3 (4.5) (Lucayan Stud) J Noseda Newmarket, Suffolk

Official Going GOOD (GOOD/FIRM in places) Stalls: Straight course - Stands side; Round course - Inside.

2161 2.05 EBF MDN 2YO (D) 7f rnd Good 45 -17 Slow
£3562 £1096 £548 £274

1943 **TORTUGUERO** 9 [5] B W Hills 2-9-0 J Carroll 9/4: -061: 2 br c Highest Honor - Rahaam (Secreto) 82
Mde all, pressed over 1f out, styd on well, rdn out: 110,000gns Apr foal, brother to Irish 2,000 Guineas wnr
Verglas: apprec this step up to a gall 7f, 1m will suit: acts on fast & gd grnd: likes to dominate: improving.
-- **TAKE TO TASK** [4] M Johnston 2-9-0 J Fanning 11/10 FAV: 2: 2 b c Conquistador Cielo - Tash 1 80
(Never Bend) Trkd wnr, hdwy to chall appr fnl 1f, held ins last: half-brother to classy 2yo Mukadamah:
eff at 7f, 1m shld suit: acts on gd grnd & a gall trk: good debut, go one better soon.
2005 **PAY THE SILVER** 7 [3] A P Jarvis 2-9-0 D Mernagh (3) 7/2: 043: 2 gr c Petong - Marjorie's Memory 2½ 75
(Fairy King) In tch, rdn & not pace of front 2 over 1f out: qck reapp: stays 7f on gd: see 2005.
1161 **THEBAN 49** [2] D Nicholls 2-9-0 F Norton 20/1: 54: Prom, rdn/no extra fnl 2f: mkt drifter: 6 65
7 wk abs, big step up in trip: bred to get this 7f trip in time: see 1161.
1513 **TIP THE SCALES** 28 [1] 2-9-0 V Halliday 25/1: 05: Handy, lost tch after halfway: see 1513. 2½ 61
5 ran Time 1m 28.18 (4.38) (Trevor C Stewart) B W Hills Lambourn, Berks

2162 2.35 MELVILLE CRAIG NOV AUCT STKS 2YO (E) 5f str Good 45 -32 Slow
£2828 £808 £404

1813 **NIFTY ALICE** 15 [1] A Berry 2-8-4 F Norton 5/2 FAV: -12441: 2 ch f First Trump - Nifty Fifty 79
(Runnett) Made all, hung left when pressed ins fnl 1f, drvn out: earlier scored on debut at Musselburgh (mdn auct):
half-sister to juv wnr Nifty Major: eff over 5f, 6f may suit in time: runs well fresh on gd, gd/soft & a sharp
or gall trk: tough, genuine & speedy filly who can win more races.
1759 **FRANICA** 17 [3] A Bailey 2-8-4 P Hanagan (7) 3/1: 220152: 2 b f Inzar - Comfrey Glen (Glenstal) ½ 77
Chsd wnr, chall appr fnl 1f, styd on, not btn far: v consistent: see 1429.
1359 **SHATIN DOLLYBIRD** 36 [5] Miss L A Perratt 2-8-0 D Mernagh (3) 11/4: 223: 2 ch f Up And At 'Em - hd 73
Pumpona (Sharpen Up) Cl-up, rdn to chall dist, held cl-home: acts on firm & gd grnd: deserves a win: see 1359.
*1937 **LAST IMPRESSION** 9 [4] J S Goldie 2-8-6 A Culhane 3/1: 14: Chsd ldrs, rdn & ev ch appr ¾ 77
fnl 1f, onepcd well ins last: new stable, prev with A P Jarvis: worth a try at 6f now: see 1937.
1538 **PILGRIM PRINCESS** 28 [2] 2-8-3 J Bramhill 14/1: 005: Prom, well outpcd fnl 2f: tchd 25/1: see 1359. 10 54
5 ran Time 1m 00.46 (3.86) (Mrs Norma Peebles) A Berry Cockerham, Lancs

2163 3.10 BONUSPRINT HCAP 3YO+ 0-90 (C) 7f rnd Good 45 +10 Fast [84]
£10400 £3200 £1600 £800 3 yo rec 9 lb

*1826 **PEACOCK ALLEY** 15 [2] W J Haggas 3-9-4 (83) A Culhane 5/2 FAV: 3-5111: 3 gr f Salse - Tagaki 88
(Doyoun) Held up going well, sltly short of room 2f out, burst through to lead ins last, rdn out: fast time:
hat-trick landed after scoring at Warwick (mdn, comfortably) & Epsom (val h'cap): v eff at 7f/1m, bred to
apprec further: acts on fast, hvy & any trk: v progressive this term, wng run may not yet be over.
*2138 **PEARTREE HOUSE 1** [8] D Nicholls 4-9-2 (86)(6ex) F Norton 7/2: 060312: 6 b g Simply Majestic - ¾ 88+
Fashion Front (Habitat) Held up, eff when no room 2f out, switched right & flew home, not reach wnr: nicely
bkcd: unlucky in running on this bid to follow up yesterday's success: shld regain wng ways sn: see 2138.
2000 **REDOUBTABLE 7** [3] D W Chapman 9-9-3 (73) R Ffrench 25/1: 000003: 9 b h Grey Dawn II - Seattle shd 75
Rockette (Seattle Slew) Trkd ldr, led dist, hdd ins last, held nr fin: qck reapp: gd run: see 1060 (stks).
1920 **RYMERS RASCAL** 10 [7] E J Alston 8-8-2 (58) J Bramhill 10/1: 0-5634: Slow to break, keen in rear, nk 59
rdn & ran on well from 2f out, no extra cl-home: gd eff: on a fair mark & stable right back to form: see 1920.
1654 **PEPPIATT** 22 [4] 6-8-4 (60) J Fanning 16/1: 034035: Sn bhd, short of room 2f out, ran on well 1 59
fnl 1f, not reach ldrs: shade unlucky in running: enjoys soft grnd & most wng form at 6f: see 1654.
2000 **JEFFREY ANOTHERRED** 7 [6] 6-9-0 (70) D Sweeney 25/1: 3-0006: Held up, eff/short of room 2f out, 1½ 66
no ch after: unlucky in running: qck reapp: '99 wnr here at Ayr (2 h'caps, incl this race, rtd 78): '98 wnr
at Carlisle (stks) & again here at Ayr (h'cap, rtd 84 at best): eff at 6/7f on firm, loves gd/soft & hvy: handles
any trk, likes a stiff/gall one, esp Ayr: gd run here & on a fair mark: keep in mind, esp if the rain arrives.
1810 **GIFT OF GOLD** 15 [9] 5-10-0 (84) O Pears 10/1: 500137: Mid-div, rdn to imprv 2f out, not pace shd 80
of ldrs insl last: op 7/1: shade btr 1483 (gd/soft, sharp trk).
*2000 **FRIAR TUCK** 7 [13] 5-8-13 (69) Dale Gibson 7/1: 0-0218: Keen cl-up, fdd fnl 2f: best at 6f, see 2000. 1¼ 63
2000 **LUANSHYA** 7 [11] 4-8-12 (68) V Halliday 20/1: -45409: Prom, outpcd by ldrs over 1f out: qck reapp. 1¼ 60

AYR SATURDAY JUNE 24TH Lefthand, Galloping Track

2101 **ABLE AYR** 3 [5] 3-8-7 (72) P Goode (3) 33/1: 000500: Dwelt, nvr a threat, fin 10th: qck reapp. *shd* **64**
*1631 **PERSIAN FAYRE** 23 [12] 8-8-8 (64) J Carroll 7/1: 00-010: Set fast pace, hdd dist: 11th, btr 1631. 2 **52**
1631 **NORTHERN SVENGALI** 23 [10] 4-8-10 (66) Craig Williams 16/1: 000060: Cl-up, wknd qckly 1f out, 12th. 1¼ **52**
1920 **MELODIAN** 10 [1] 5-8-12 (68)(bl) D Mernagh (3) 25/1: 041000: Mid-div, lost tch halfway: 13th. 3 **49**
13 ran Time 1m 26.24 (2.44) (Mr & Mrs G Middlebrook) W J Haggas Newmarket

2164 3.40 DOUBLEPRINT HCAP 3YO+ 0-90 (C) 1m7f Good 45 -10 Slow [85]
£6825 £2100 £1050 £525

2002 **FIORI** 7 [5] P C Haslam 4-9-6 (77) P Goode (3) 6/1: 006441: 4 b g Anshan - Fen Princess **82**
(Trojan Fen) Made all & sn clr, increased tempo 3f out, styd on well, rdn out: fine tactical ride: qck reapp:
rnr-up over hdles in 99/00 (juv nov, rtd 112h): '99 wnr at Hamilton (auct mdn), Beverley & York (h'caps, rtd 89):
eff between 10f & 2m: acts on fast, soft & fibresand, handles firm grnd: acts on any trk: fairly h'capped.
*1959 **URGENT SWIFT** 8 [4] A P Jarvis 7-8-11 (68) D Mernagh (3) 3/1: 401012: 7 ch g Beveled - Good 3½ **68**
Natured (Troy) Raced in 3rd, went 2nd after 4f , rdn & not pace of wnr fnl 2f: in gd heart, eff at 12/15f.
1536 **PLEASANT MOUNT** 28 [1] Miss J A Camacho 4-8-6 (63) F Norton 6/1: -01503: 4 b g First Trump - Alo nk **63**
Ez (Alzao) Trkd ldr, rdn/outpcd 3f out, kept on again ins last, no dngr: see 1356, 918.
1791 **TURNPOLE** 16 [2] Mrs M Reveley 9-9-4 (75) A Culhane 11/2: 04/064: Raced in 4th, drvn 4f out, 1 **73**
sn onepcd: well h'capped on old form, but below best so far this term: see 1052.
1686 **STAR RAGE** 21 [3] 10-9-10 (81) J Fanning 11/8 FAV: 60F225: Settled last, drvn 4f out, sn btn: ½ **78**
top-weight: unsuited by race tactics, better with a stronger pace: see 1686, 714.
5 ran Time 3m 18.04 (8.24) (I Wilson) P C Haslam Middleham, N Yorks

2165 4.10 TRIPLEPRINT HCAP 3YO 0-85 (D) 5f str Good 45 -02 Slow [89]
£7072 £2176 £1088 £544

2060 **COLLEGE MAID** 4 [6] J S Goldie 3-8-4 (65) D Sweeney 12/1: 112501: 3 b f College Chapel - Maid Of **67**
Mourne (Fairy King) In tch, ran on strongly to lead well ins last, drvn out: qck reapp: earlier landed h'caps
at Ripon & Catterick: '99 Musselburgh wnr (mdn auct): eff at 5/6f on firm, soft & any trk: tough filly.
1600 **ELVINGTON BOY** 24 [3] M W Easterby 3-8-7 (68) T Lucas 4/1: 0-0032: 3 ch g Emarati - Catherines Well nk **69**
(Junius) Cl-up, rdn to chall appr fnl 1f, held nr fin: gd run, win sn: see 1600.
*1609 **ROZEL** 24 [10] R Guest 3-9-2 (77) R Ffrench 7/2 FAV: 013: 3 ch f Wolfhound - Noirmant shd **78**
(Dominion) Led, rdn & hdd ins last, not btn far: gd run on h'cap bow, acts on gd & gd/soft: see 1609.
1220 **RYTHM N TIME** 45 [11] E J Alston 3-8-13 (74) A Culhane 10/1: 430-04: Rear, ran on well for press ins 1¼ **72**
last, not reach ldrs: 6 wk abs: return to 6f shld suit: see 1220.
1817 **SHALARISE** 15 [11] 3-7-11 (58)(bl)(1ow)(2oh) Dale Gibson 33/1: 0-0005: Led early, with ldrs till nk **55**
no extra appr fnl 1f: '99 wnr at Newcastle (nov stks, 1st time blnks, rtd 73 at best): eff at 5f, just gets a
sharp 6f: acts on firm & gd, poss fibresand: likes a stiff/gall trk: back to something near best here.
1098 **CD FLYER** 53 [7] 3-8-13 (74) Craig Williams 4/1: -06446: Dwelt, late hdwy, nvr nrr: 8 wk abs. 1½ **67**
*2047 **POP THE CORK** 5 [8] 3-8-5 (66)(6ex) P Goode (3) 10/1: 030017: Prom, fdd fnl 2f: btr 2047. 2 **53**
*1712 **GDANSK** 20 [4] J Carroll 6/1: -40218: Nvr a dngr: btr 1712 (gd/soft). 1½ **60**
1687 **NIFTY MAJOR** 21 [9] 3-9-7 (82) F Norton 10/1: -02009: Handy, wknd 2f out: top-weight: see 1219. 1¾ **62**
1780 **BRANSTON PICKLE** 17 [1] 3-8-11 (72)(BL) J Fanning 33/1: 200000: Wide, al rear, fin 10th: blnks. 1¾ **48**
1219 **LOST IN HOOK** 46 [2] 3-9-2 (77) D Mernagh (3) 8/1: 2-3000: Al rear, fin last: 6 wk abs. ½ **52**
11 ran Time 58.97 (2.37) (S Bruce) J S Goldie Uplawmoor, E Renfrews

2166 4.40 BONUSPHOTO HCAP 3YO 0-80 (D) 1m1f20y Good 45 -08 Slow [83]
£3848 £1184 £592 £296

1452 **SOLLER BAY** 32 [1] K R Burke 3-9-7 (76) D Sweeney 6/4 FAV: -13101: 3 b g Contract Law - Bichette **82**
(Lidham) Settled last, smooth hdwy to lead 2f out, sn clr, rdn out, cosily: nicely bckd: earlier won at
W'hampton (AW mdn, rtd 66a) & Windsor (h'cap): rtd 76 when rnr-up sole '99 start: eff at 8.4/9.3f on gd, hvy
& fibresand: acts on a gall or sharp trk: goes well when fresh: genuine & progressive.
1560 **YENALED** 26 [4] J S Goldie 3-8-10 (65) A Culhane 13/8: 3-3162: 3 gr g Rambo Dancer - Fancy Flight 3½ **65**
(Arctic Tern) Keen in tch, led 3f out, hdd 2f out, sn not pace of wnr: clr rem: nicely bckd: see 1560, 1434.
2049 **ARIZONA LADY** 5 [3] J Semple 3-8-13 (68) O Pears 6/1: 0-1003: 3 ch f Lion Cavern - Unfuwaanah 5 **62**
(Unfuwain) Chsd ldr, rdn & no impress when flashed tail repeatedly ins last: qck reapp: see 902.
1895 **COSMIC SONG** 11 [2] R M Whitaker 3-7-12 (53) D Mernagh (3) 11/2: 635144: Bolted to post, raced 21 **22**
keenly & sn led, bit slipped thro' mouth & hdd 3f out, sn btn/eased: op 3/1: see 1722.
4 ran Time 1m 55.11 (4.81) (Mrs Melba Bryce) K R Burke Newmarket

ASCOT SATURDAY JUNE 24TH Righthand, Stiff, Galloping Track

Official Going GOOD TO FIRM (GOOD places)

2167 2.00 LISTED RTD HCAP 3YO 0-105 (A) 1m str Good 42 -10 Slow [106]
£15915 £6036 £3018 £1372 Field raced towards centre

*1771 **PAPABILE** 17 [3] W Jarvis 3-8-11 (89) Pat Eddery 5/1: 2-2411: 3 b f Chief's Crown - La Papagena **101**
(Habitat) Rear/in tch, prog over 2f out & led over 1f out, held on gamely ins last, drvn out: hvly bckd: recent
Yarmouth wnr (mdn, readily): juv rnr-up at Newmarket (fill mdn, rtd 92): eff at 1m, 10f may yet suit: acts on fast
& soft grnd, any trk: tough/progressive & useful filly, a typically strong Pat Eddery finish.
1485 **MYSTIFY** 30 [5] J H M Gosden 3-8-12 (90) R Hills 14/1: 55-152: 3 b f Batshoof - Santa Linda (Sir hd **101**
Ivor) Mid-div, briefly no room 2f out, prog to press wnr ins last, just held: shade unlucky: stays 1m, progressive.
1733 **COCO** 19 [6] Sir Michael Stoute 3-9-3 (95) J Reid 20/1: 0-143: 3 ch f Storm Bird - Fondromance 1½ **103**
(Fappiano) Prom, rdn/led over 2f out till over 1f out, kept on onepace ins last: op 12/1: h'cap bow: handles
firm & gd/soft grnd: likes a stiff/gall trk: see 1268.
1694 **ARABESQUE** 21 [2] H R A Cecil 3-9-1 (93) T Quinn 9/1: -31404: Bhd ldrs, ev ch over 1f out, edged 1¼ **98**
right/no extra ins last: hvly bckd, op 10/1: stays a stiff 1m, poss just best at 6/7f: see 1175 (mdn, 6f).
*1951 **ROSSE** 9 [9] 3-8-9 (87) M Roberts 6/4 FAV: 0-415: Keen/prom, rdn/ch 2f out, held fnl 1f: reportedly ¾ **90**

695

fin stiff bhd, hvly bckd: see 1951 (7f).

1853	RED LETTER 13 [11] 3-8-8 (86) R Hughes 7/1: 40-326: Rear, hdwy fnl 3f, no prog fnl 1f: bckd.				2½	84
1826	IYAVAYA 15 [10] 3-8-10 (88) S Drowne 40/1: 55-007: Keen/held up rear, mod gains fnl 3f: see 829 (6f).				1	84
*1811	MISS KIRSTY 15 [7] 3-8-8 (86)(t) G Mosse 14/1: 3-6018: Bhd, eff 3f out, no prog fnl 1f: op 10/1, clr rem.				1	80
1374	BROADWAY LEGEND 36 [13] 3-8-9 (87) M Henry 20/1: 30-109: Led after 2f till 2f out, fdd: see 1165.				7	67
1535	TWEED MILL 28 [8] 3-8-8 (86) Martin Dwyer 20/1: 3-2100: Rdn/twds rear, btn 2f out: 10th: btr 1032.				¾	64
1630	EBBA 23 [14] 3-8-10 (88) M Fenton 50/1: 05-040: Rear, eff 2f out, no prog: 11th: see 1630, 1384.				5	56
1825	PLEASURE CENTER 15 [1] 3-9-7 (99) K Darley 14/1: 4-140: Cl-up, ch 2f out, wknd qckly & eased				3½	60
	over 1f out: 12th: stablemate of rnr-up: jockey reported that saddle slipped, this is best forgotten: see 1825, 1269.					
1374	CREAM TEASE 36 [4] 3-8-9 (87)(BL) S Whitworth 66/1: 600-00: Prom 4f: 13th: blnks: see 1374.				3	42
1186	LOVE YOU TOO 48 [12] 3-8-10 (88) P Robinson 50/1: 40-040: Led 2f, prom till 3 out: 14th: 7 wk abs.				3½	36
14 ran	Time 1m 42.87 (4.17) (Exors of the late Lord Howard de Walden) W Jarvis Newmarket.					

2168   2.30 PALAN HCAP 3YO 0-105 (B)   5f   Good 42 -14 Slow   [107]
£17680   £5440   £2720   £1360 Mid- high no's favoured

1636	COMPTON BANKER 23 [11] G A Butler 3-7-12 (77) P Doe 16/1: 05 051: 3 br c Distinctly North - Mary					84
	Hinge (Dowsing) Rear, rdn & stdy prog from over 1f out to lead well in last, cosily: well bckd: unplcd in '99					
	(rtd 84): apprec this drop to 5f, 6f will suit: acts on gd & a stiff trk: open to further improvement.					
1098	LICENCE TO THRILL 53 [13] D W P Arbuthnot 3-7-10 (75)(3oh) M Henry 33/1: 5-1102: 3 ch f Wolfhound				½	79
	- Crime Of Passion (Dragonara Palace) Led, rdn/strongly pressed fnl 1f, hdd nr fin: abs: acts on equitrack & gd.					
1728	ARGENT FACILE 19 [16] D J S Cosgrove 3-8-10 (89)(t) J Reid 9/1: 220223: 3 b c Midhish - Rosinish				¾	91
	(Lomond) Cl-up, rdn & strong chall fnl 1f, just held nr fin: running well in defeat: see 1047, 959.					
1980	CONNECT 8 [6] M H Tompkins 3-7-13 (78)(VIS) A Beech (3) 8/1: -00004: Chsd ldrs, rdn & kept on				2½	74
	onepace from over 1f out: 2nd time visor: see 1186.					
1285	QUEEN OF THE MAY 42 [12] S Drowne 12/1: 13-165: Twds rear, kept on fnl 1f, no threat: abs.				nk	76
1285	BANDANNA 42 [7] 3-8-5 (84) M Roberts 16/1: 50-006: Held up, briefly no room 2f out, rdn/mod late				1¾	75
	gains: 6 wk abs: '99 debut wnr at Chepstow (seller, subs rnr-up in a list contest, rtd 95): eff over a stiff 5f/6f:					
	acts on fast & gd: likes a stiff/undul or gall trk: clearly retains ability, 6f & similar company shld suit.					
1285	ANSELLAD 42 [17] 3-8-7 (86) G Carter 25/1: 330-07: Cl-up, fdd over 1f out: 6 wk abs: see 1285.				shd	77
2003	CORRIDOR CREEPER 7 [18] 3-8-7 (86) Pat Eddery 11/2: 1-0308: Dwelt, sn prom, btn over 1f out.				nk	76
2003	DORCHESTER 7 [2] 3-8-13 (92) S Sanders 14/1: 04-009: Rear, mod gains 2f out, held/no room 1f				1¾	78
	out: '99 wnr at Nottingham (auct mdn), Southwell (nurs, rtd 92a) & Doncaster (nov stks, rtd 93 at best):					
	eff at 5f, tried 6f, may yet suit: acts on firm, gd & fibresand, sharp or gall trk: shld be plcd to effect.					
1427	SMOKIN BEAU 33 [10] 3-7-10 (75)(1oh) R Brisland (5) 33/1: 002000: Cl-up 4f: 10th: see 1285, 994.				½	60
*1795	BLUE HOLLY 16 [8] 3-8-6 (84)(1ow) R Hughes 10/1: -52010: Rear, prog fnl 2f, no impress fnl 1f &				shd	69
	eased in last: 11th: btr 1795 (gd/soft).					
1768	MOLLY BROWN 17 [14] 3-8-3 (82) K Darley 14/1: 5-0400: Trkd ldrs, hmpd/lost pl bef halfway: 12th.				1	64
2065	TRAVESTY OF LAW 4 [4] 3-9-7 (100) D R McCabe 33/1: 50-000: Rear, nvr factor: 13th: qck reapp.				¾	80
2003	JAILHOUSE ROCKET 7 [15] 3-8-5 (84) C Nutter 20/1: 33-000: Rear, nvr factor: 14th: stablemate of				nk	63
	9th: '99 wnr at Carlisle (auct mdn) & Beverley (nov stks, rtd 96 at best): suited by a stiff 5f on firm & soft.					
1987	SEE YOU LATER 7 [9] 3-9-3 (96) W Supple 10/1: 3-6330: Cl-up 3f: 15th: bckd: btr 1987, 1529.				nk	74
1871	HONESTY FAIR 12 [3] 3-8-5 (84) P Robinson 12/1: 411000: Held up, hmpd 3f out, sn btn: 16th.				½	60
1694	KATHOLOGY 21 [5] 3-9-1 (94) N Pollard 9/2 FAV: -21140: Chsd ldrs, rdn/struggling halfway: 17th.				13	44
17 ran	Time 1m 01.81 (2.81) (E Penser) G A Butler Blewbury, Oxon.					

2169   3.00 LISTED MILCARS STKS 3YO (A)   1m2f   Good 42 +09 Fast
£21157   £6510   £3255   £1627

1854	PORT VILA 13 [9] J H M Gosden 3-8-11 R Hills 5/2: 114-31: 3 b c Barathea - Girouette (Nodouble)					109
	Dwelt, settled rear, short of room 3f out, strong run fnl 2f, drvn out to lead well in last: fast time: won 1st					
	2 starts in '99, at Newbury (mdn) & Kempton (stks), subs 4th of 5 in a Gr 1 Dewhurst (rtd 108): eff at 7f, stays 10f,					
	further cld suit: acts on firm & gd, gall trk: v useful colt who remains on the up-grade, shld win in Gr company.					
*1697	RASM 21 [4] A C Stewart 3-8-11 W Supple 7/1: 3-12: 3 b c Darshaan - Northshiel (Northfields)				½	107
	Cl-up, rdn to lead appr fnl 1f, kept on but hdd well ins last: nicely bckd, clr rem: v progressive, win a Listed.					
980	CHINATOWN 65 [7] Sir Michael Stoute 3-8-11 Pat Eddery 7/1: 314-53: 3 b r c Marju - Sunley Saint				3	102
	(Artaius) Cl-up, outpcd 4 out, short of room 2f out, styd on late for press, no threat to front 2: 9 wk					
	abs: stays 10f & open to improvement: see 980.					
1857	SHAMAIEL 13 [2] C E Brittain 3-8-6 S Sanders 33/1: 44: In tch, rdn to improve 4f out, kept on				nk	96
	but not pace of ldrs: may apprec a step up to 12f: showed imprvd form here: see 1857.					
1451	MERRY MERLIN 32 [6] 3-9-2 J Reid 8/1: 5-0105: Sn clr ldr, hdd appr fnl 1f, wknd ins last: not				nk	106
	disgraced conceding weight to some v useful rivals: see 1246 (Listed).					
1108	FUNNY GIRL 52 [3] 3-8-6 Martin Dwyer 50/1: 45-56: Waited with, rdn/prog over 2f out, drvn/wknd				4	90
	ins last: 7 wk abs, up in trip: see 1108.					
1945	BEZZAAF 9 [5] 3-8-6 P Robinson 14/1: -15P7: Front rank, wknd 2f out, eased when btn: see 1469.				7	80
1825	HIGH WALDEN 15 [1] 3-8-6 T Quinn 13/8 FAV: 2-532W: Refused to enter stalls & withdrawn:					0
	reportedly found to be lame in season: see 1825.					
8 ran	Time 2m 07.27 (3.27) (Hamdan Al Maktoum) J H M Gosden Manton, Wilts.					

2170   3.35 LADBROKE HCAP 4YO+ 0-105 (B)   1m2f   Good 42 +06 Fast   [103]
£26000   £8000   £4000

1695	BLUE 21 [6] Mrs A J Perrett 4-9-1 (90) Pat Eddery 7/1: 22/151: 4 b c Bluebird - Watership					95
	(Foolish Pleasure) Cl-up, led 2f out & rousted 3L clr appr dist, ran on well: gd time, fine ride: earlier					
	overcame a 2 yr abs to win a Doncaster (mdn): rnr-up twice in '98 (mdn, rtd 86): eff at 1m/10f, tried 12f:					
	acts on fast & soft grnd, any trk: runs well fresh: gd weight carrier: progressive & useful.					
2001	SHARP PLAY 7 [7] M Johnston 5-9-3 (92) R Hills 3/1: 31042: 5 b g Robellino - Child's Play				½	96+
	(Sharpen Up) Bhd, plenty to do ent str, kept on strgly fnl 2f, post came too soon: clr rem, qck reapp: imprvd					
	in defeat but set an awful lot to do, usually races up with the pace: eff at 1m/10f: useful & imprvg, 1498.					
1450	POLISH SPIRIT 32 [3] B R Millman 5-8-6 (81) S Drowne 15/2: 111103: 5 b g Emarati - Gentle Star				2½	81
	(Comedy Star) Chsd ldrs, rdn appr fnl 2f, kept on till no extra towards fin: back to form, stays 10f, 1m					
	suits, as does softer grnd: v tough, see 1113 (here).					
1797	PRAIRIE WOLF 16 [4] M L W Bell 4-9-1 (90) M Fenton 12/1: 210-34: Chsd ldrs, rdn appr fnl 2f, not				¾	89

pace to chall: ran to best in this competitive race: see 1797.

1965 **MAKE WAY 8** [12] 4-8-7 (82) K Darley 9/1: 603225: Towards rear, briefly short of room appr fnl ½ 80
2f, unable to qckn once clr: well bckd, see 1528, 986.

*1762 **LITTLE AMIN 17** [2] 4-8-0 (75) Martin Dwyer 16/1: -00016: Held up, shkn up 3f out, not much room nk 72
but lkd onepace appr fnl 1f, nvr dngrs: nibbled each-way from 22/1: best clsr to the pace on softer grnd: see 1762.

1031 **IPLEDGEALLEGIANCE 59** [13] 4-9-6 (95) J Reid 12/1: 05-307: Mid-div, wide into str, onepace: see 757.shd 92

1797 **KOMISTAR 16** [10] 5-8-13 (88) M Roberts 10/1: 10-028: Set gd clip, hdd 2f out, no extra & eased nk 84
below clr: op 8/1: shapes like a drop back to 1m will suit: see 1797, 1031.

1327 **BRILLIANT RED 38** [8] 7-9-11 (100)(t) D Harrison 10/1: 21-009: Trkd ldrs, bmpd 3f, outpcd ent str, no ¾ 95
impress: jockey given 10 day ban for intentional interference: won this in '99 off 5lbs lower.

1850 **HUDOOD 14** [5] 5-9-2 (91) J Mackay (7) 5/1 FAV: -13350: Slow away & bhd, imprvd halfway, wide ¾ 84
into str & hard rdn, no further progress: 10th, well bckd from 8/1: better expected, see 1850.

1965 **DASHIBA 8** [11] 4-9-3 (92) P Robinson 6/1: 110-30: Pld hard, al towards rear: 11th, op 5/1, see 1965. nk 84

1821} **PROVOSKY 386** [9] 4-9-5 (94)(bl) D M Oliver 10/1: 0-4110: Trkd ldrs, hmpd after 3f, wknd under ½ 85
press fnl 3f: 12th: Irish raider, going for a hat-trick after wins at Killarney (ddht) & Leopardstown (h'caps):
well btn in a Gr 3 last term (rtd 85): eff at 1m/9f on fast & gd/soft grnd: with Miss Oakes.

1982 **HERITAGE 8** [14] 6-8-0 (75) A Nicholls (3) 33/1: 00/460: Al bhd: 13th, see 1982. 1 64

1113 **HADLEIGH 52** [1] 4-7-12 (73)(2ow)(4oh) L Newman (0) 33/1: 050-00: Nvr a factor: 14th, 7 wk abs: 4 56
unplcd in '99 for R Armstrong (h'caps, rtd 76): '98 Kempton wnr (mdn auct, rtd 88): eff at 6f, stays 7f on fast grnd.

14 ran   Time 2m 07.56 (3.56)   (K J Buchanan)   Mrs A J Perrett Pulborough, W.Sussex.

2171	4.10 DE BOER EBF CLASSIFIED STKS 3YO 0-95 (B 1m rnd Good 42 -05 Slow
	£8462 £3209 £1604 £729

*1584 **HYMN 25** [2] J H M Gosden 3-8-13 K Darley 11/8 FAV: -211: 3 b c Fairy King - Handsewn (Sir Ivor) 101
Handy, shkn up & qckn to lead appr fnl 1f, held on well: hvly bckd: recent Sandown wnr (mdn): eff at 1m, shld
get further: acts on firm & soft grnd, stiff/gall trks: useful, genuine & improving, well worth a try in Listed.

*1638 **MODERN BRITISH 23** [1] G L Moore 3-8-13 R Hughes 11/2: 12: 3 ch g Indian Ridge - Touraya (Tap On ½ 99
Wood) Waited with, imprvd 2f out, ran on well for press ins last, not btn far: nicely bckd from 7/1: imprvd
in defeat on only 2nd start, stays 1m: useful gelding.

3843} **COURTING 289** [5] W J Haggas 3-8-8 J P Spencer 3/1: 1100-3: 3 gr f Pursuit Of Love - Doctor's Glory nk 93
(Elmaamul) Led till appr fnl 1f, kept on for press: well bckd, clr rem, reapp: won first 4 juv starts for Sir M
Prescott at Catterick (2, auct mdn & auct stks), Thirsk & Newmarket (stks, rtd 100): eff at 7f/1m (related to a 2m
wnr): goes well fresh on firm & gd grnd, any trk: likes to force the pace: useful, return to faster surface will suit.

4201} **VIA CAMP 266** [6] E A L Dunlop 3-8-6 G Carter 8/1: 310-4: Prom & ch till fdd appr fnl 1f: reapp. 4 83
'99 Beverley wnr (fill mdn, rtd 95): eff at 7/7.5f on firm & gd grnd, stiff trks: useful at best, stable not firing.

955 **MOON EMPEROR 67** [4] J Stack 10/1: 45-105: Well plcd till wknd 2f out: 10 wk abs, best 826 (sft) nk 91

1872 **CEDAR MASTER 12** [3] P Doe 16/1: 4-0556: Al bhd: stiffish task, op 12/1, see 1029, 955. 4 78

6 ran   Time 1m 42.25 (3.75)   (Mrs B V Sangster)   J H M Gosden Manton, Wilts.

2172	4.45 BRUNSWICK NOV FILLIES STKS 2YO (D) 6f Good 42 -28 Slow
	£6841 £2104 £1052 £526

1759 **HEJAZIAH 17** [2] P F I Cole 2-8-9 K Darley 7/4 FAV: 231: 2 b f Gone West - Toptrestle (Nijinsky) 98
With ldr, kept on for press to lead just ins fnl 1f, drvn to assert: hvly bckd: Mar foal: dam 1m scorer:
apprec return to 6f & acts on gd & gd/soft grnd: useful & genuine, shld win again.

*1856 **MILLENIUM PRINCESS 13** [4] J M Bradley 2-8-9-2 R Hughes 7/2: 12: 2 b f Eagle Eyed - Sopran Marida 1¼ 100
(Darshaan) Led, rdn & hdd just ins fnl 1f, not pace of wnr: useful run conceding weight & acts on firm & gd.

1957 **CYCLONE CONNIE 8** [1] C A Cyzer 2-8-9 R Hills 7/1: 23: 2 ch f Dr Devious - Cutpurse Moll (Green 2 87
Desert) Kept waited with, eff & switched right over 1f out, kept on late: acts on gd/firm & gd: apprec 7f.

1986 **FOODBROKER FANCY 7** [6] D R C Elsworth 2-8-9 T Quinn 7/2: 24: Bhd, outpcd over 1f out, onepace 2½ 80
fnl 1f: apprec mdns on minor trks: see 1986.

1957 **MIN MIRRI 8** [3] 2-8-9 S Drowne 7/1: 45: Slow away, sn cl-up, wknd over 1f out: see 1957. nk 79

-- **ZAHEEMAH** [5] 2-8-9 P Robinson 8/1: 6: Al bhd: debut: Apr foal, cost $75,000: apprec 7f+ in time. 6 63

6 ran   Time 1m 17.32 (4.22)   (HRH Prince Fahd Salman)   P F I Cole Whatcombe, Oxon.

2173	5.15 BETTERWARE HCAP 3YO+ 0-80 (D) 2m45y Good 42 -01 Slow	[79]
	£7085 £2180 £1090 £545 3 yo rec 20lb	

1478 **GENEROUS WAYS 30** [15] E J Alston 5-8-1 (52) W Supple 8/1: 405401: 5 ch g Generous - Clara Bow 59
(Coastal) Keen in tch, gd hdwy over 4f out, styd on well to lead dist, drvn clr ins last: well bckd: in '99 won this
race (h'cap, rtd 65, 5lb higher mark): '98 wnr at Redcar (with E Dunlop, h'cap, rtd 72): eff at 14f, suited by 2m on
fm/fast, gd & any trk, loves Ascot: best without blnkrs: on a handy mark & his capable stable is right back to form.

1180 **TEMPLE WAY 48** [16] R Charlton 4-10-0 (79) R Hughes 13/2: 20-022: 4 b g Shirley Heights - Abbey 2 82
Strand (Shadeed) Cl-up, hdwy to lead over 1f out, edged left & collared dist, not pace of wnr: nicely bckd:
fine run under a big weight after a 7 wk abs: see 1180.

1852 **FLETCHER 13** [7] H Morrison 6-8-4 (55) L Newman (3) 10/1: 000223: 6 b g Salse - Ballet Classique ½ 57
(Sadler's Wells) Prom, eff over 3f out, no impress till kept on well ins last: nicely bckd: 2 wins in 43 starts.

1594 **KING OF MOMMUR 24** [13] B R Millman 5-7-10 (47)(1oh) A Nicholls (0) 14/1: 060-34: Made most till 1½ 47
over 5f out, led again over 4f out till over 1f out, no extra: clr of rem & poss just stays a stiff 2m, 14f suit: mdn.

2092 **TREASURE CHEST 3** [10] 5-8-12 (63)(vis) D M Oliver 16/1: 000405: In tch, rdn & no impress fnl 2f. 6 57

*1928 **BARCELONA 12** [2] 3-8-8 (79) Pat Eddery 3/1 FAV: 3-3116: In tch, eff over 2f out, sn no impress: shd 73
well bckd & better expected on hat-trick bid stepped up to 2m: see 1928 (14f).

1597 **OUR MONOGRAM 24** [9] 4-7-10 (47)(2oh) G Bardwell 25/1: 40-007: Cl-up, wknd over 2f out: see 1128. 1¼ 40

1524 **DUTCH DYANE 28** [6] 7-7-10 (47)(3oh) D Kinsella (2) 16/1: 03-538: Keen, prom, led over 5f out till 6 34
over 4f out, sn wknd: nicely bckd: btr 1524 (hvy, 14f), 1394.

*1996 **SHERIFF 7** [8] 4-9-4 (58) M Henry 10/1: 020219: In tch, btn over 2f out: btr 1996. ¾ 36

1635} **MOTET 392** [12] 6-9-12 (77)(bl) J P Spencer 33/1: 30/0-0: Waited with btn 3f out: 10th, recently refused 4 59
in a novice chase, in 99/00 won at Plumpton (h'cap hdle, rtd 104h), stays 2m5f on firm & gd/soft): well btn
sole Flat start in '99: rtd 91 for G Wragg in '98: stays 2m2f on fast & gd/soft grnd: best without blnks/vis.

1996 **DANEGOLD 7** [4] 8-8-7 (58) S Drowne 4/1: -04540: Held up, rdn over 3f out, no impression: hvly 2 38
bckd & capable of much better: see 1996.

2092 **SHARAZAN 3** [14] 7-8-4 (55)(VIS) Claire Bryan (5) 16/1: 0-0300: In tch, wknd qckly over 2f out: 12th, vis. 2½ 32

ASCOT SATURDAY JUNE 24TH Righthand, Stiff, Galloping Track

2037 **SECRET DROP 5** [8] 4-8-9 (60) J Reid 33/1: -00000: Keen, wide, handy till btn over 3f out: 13th. 1¾ 35
1867 **SALSKA 12** [5] 9-8-12 (63) R Havlin 33/1: 000-00: Slow away & al bhd: 14th. 2½ 35
1711 **SHARAF 20** [1] 7-8-0 (51) Sophie Mitchell 14/1: -P4230: In tch, wknd over 3f out: 15th, btr 1711. 3½ 19
1633 **ASTON MARA 23** [3] 3-7-13 (70)(bl) J Mackay (7) 14/1: 4-0000: Keen bhd, btn over 3f out: last. 1 37
16 ran Time 3m 32.86 (6.86) (Honest Traders) E J Alston Longton, Lancs.

PONTEFRACT SUNDAY JUNE 25TH Lefthand, Undulating Track, Stiff Uphill Finish

Official Going GOOD TO FIRM. Stalls: Inside, except 2m2f - Centre.

2174

2.15 EBF FILLIES MDN 2YO (D) 6f rnd Firm 18 -30 Slow
£5141 £1582 £791 £395

-- **DORA CARRINGTON** [5] P W Harris 2-8-11 Pat Eddery 3/1: 1: 2 b f Sri Pekan - Dorothea Brooke 78
(Dancing Brave) Made all, rdn & held on well fnl 1f: bckd tho' op 5/2: Mar foal, half-sister to top-class sprint juv Primo Valentino, dam a 1m wnr: eff over a stiff 6f, shld get further: acts on firm grnd & runs well fresh: improve.
1197 **NUN LEFT 48** [2] R M Beckett 2-8-11 W Supple 8/1: 32: 2 b f Bishop of Cashel - Salsita (Salse) nk 77
Chsd ldrs, prog & rdn/ev ch over 1f out, kept on well, just held: abs: acts on firm,fast: apprec step up to 6f.
1568 **EARLY WISH 27** [10] B Hanbury 2-8-11 W Ryan 11/1: -63: 2 ch f Rahy - Heaven's Nook (Great Above) nk 76
Chsd ldrs, kept on well for press fnl 2f, al held: apprec step up to 6f & firm: going the right way: see 1568.
1924 **ROOFER 11** [7] M R Channon 2-8-11 Craig Williams 5/2 FAV: 54: Mid-div, prog/chsd ldrs over 1f 2½ 69
out, held ins last: well bckd: handles firm/fast grnd: see 1924.
-- **PERFECT PLUM** [11] 2-8-11 G Duffield 10/1: 5: Rdn/bhd, styd on well under minimal press fnl 2f: 3½ 60+
Darshaan filly, Apr foal, half-sister to a Irish 7f juv wnr: sire a French Derby wnr: looks sure to relish 7f+: ran green, sure to leave this bhd & rate more highly over further for Sir Mark Prescott.
1538 **EFFERVESCE 29** [9] 2-8-11 J Carroll 10/1: 46: Cl-up, rdn/hung right & held 2f out: op 7/1: btr 1538. ½ 58
1659 **ALIS IMAGES 23** [12] 2-8-11 O Pears 40/1: -667: Cl-up 4f: see 1659, 1236. hd 57
-- **LE MERIDIEN** [1] 2-8-11 J McAuley (5) 50/1: 8: Mid-div, eff halfway, no hdwy: Magical Wonder filly, ¾ 55
Apr foal, sister to a juv wnr abroad: dam a mdn, sire high-class 1m/10f performer: with J S Wainwright.
-- **BAILEYS CREAM** [6] 2-8-11 D Holland 4/1: 9: Bhd/outpcd, mod late gains: Mister Bailey filly, shd 55
May foal, cost 26,000gns: half-sister to 2 juv wnrs: sire a miler: apprec 7f+ in time for M Johnston.
-- **BOWFELL** [8] 2-8-11 R Fitzpatrick (3) 40/1: 0: Dwelt, al bhd: 10th: Alflora filly, Apr first foal: 3½ 46
dam a 10f wnr, sire high-class 1m/12f performer: bred to apprec further for C Smith.
-- **Vincentia** [3] 2-8-11 M Fenton 50/1: 1864 **Light Of Aragon 13** [4] 2-8-11 A Culhane 40/1:
12 ran Time 1m 17.00 (2.9) (Mrs P W Harris) P W Harris Aldbury, Herts.

2175

2.45 SNICKERS HCAP 3YO 0-75 (E) 1m2f Firm 18 -08 Slow [82]
£4563 £1404 £754

1725 **JOCKO GLASSES 20** [2] C F Wall 3-8-13 (67) R Mullen 7/1: 5-051: 3 ch g Inchinor - Corinthia (Empery) 75
Trkd ldrs trav well, rdn/led 1f out, styd on strongly & in command nr fin: h'cap bow: eff at 10f, shld stay 12f: acts on firm & gd grnd, sharp/stiff trk: lightly rcd, shld improvement further in similar contests.
1812 **AMRITSAR 16** [7] Sir Michael Stoute 3-9-4 (72) Pat Eddery 5/4 FAV: -05432: 3 ch c Indian Ridge - 2½ 75
Trying For Gold (Northern Baby) Trkd ldrs, prog/led 3f out & clr 2f out, rdn/hdd 1f out, kept on tho' held: hvly bckd, rest well covered: handles firm & gd/soft grnd & is knocking at the door: see 1812.
1866 **RHODAMINE 13** [6] J L Eyre 3-9-0 (68) K Darley 4/1: 426143: 3 b c Mukaddamah - Persian Empress 3½ 66
(Persian Bold) In tch, eff 3f out, kept on onepace for press: op 5/1: see 1560 (11f).
1480 **CLEAR PROSPECT 31** [1] M A Buckley 3-9-7 (75) A Culhane 16/1: 43-004: Rear, hdwy 3f out, no 3 68
prog ins last: op 10/1: prob handles firm & gd/soft grnd: see 1480 (mdn).
1958 **HALHOO LAMMTARRA 9** [3] 3-9-2 (70) Craig Williams 13/2: 2-0055: Held up, eff 3f out, no impress. nk 63
1765 **INDY CARR 18** [4] 3-8-12 (66) F Lynch 20/1: 1-6046: Rear, eff 3f out, no threat: longer 10f trip. 2½ 55
1758 **SORRENTO KING 18** [5] 3-7-10 (50)(bl)(4oh) P M Quinn (3) 50/1: 00-007: Led 7f, fdd: see 1758. 1¾ 37
1738 **ROMNEY 20** [9] 3-8-4 (58) G Parkin 33/1: 00-58: Prom 7f, sn struggling: h'cap bow. nk 44
1967 **JOELY GREEN 9** [10] 3-8-3 (57) C Cogan (5) 14/1: 450009: Chsd ldrs 1m: op 10/1: btr 266 (1m). 1¾ 41
1819 **MR COSPECTOR 16** [8] 3-8-13 (67) J Carroll 14/1: -10040: Al bhd: 10th: btr 1819, 992 (soft/hvy). 10 40
10 ran Time 2m 10.7 (2.6) (Jocko Partnership) C F Wall Newmarket.

2176

3.15 TOTE HCAP 4YO+ 0-80 (D) 2m2f Firm 18 -22 Slow [78]
£7345 £2260 £1130 £565 4 yo rec 1 lb

1052 **BUSTLING RIO 57** [3] P C Haslam 4-8-4 (55) P Goode (3) 14/1: -15001: 4 b g Up And At 'Em - Une 63
Venitienne (Green Dancer) Mid-div, rdn/prog & bhd ldrs when hmpd ins last, switched & drvn to lead nr line: abs: earlier won at Southwell (h'cap, rtd 68a): '99 wnr at Southwell (2, rtd 61a) & here at Pontefract (h'caps, rtd 61): eff at 11/12f, suited by 2m/2m2f on firm, gd & fibresand, loves Southwell/Pontefract: runs well fresh.
*1867 **KAGOSHIMA 13** [14] J Norton 5-8-3 (53)(vis) O Pears 9/1: -02312: 5 b g Shirley Heights - Kashteh nk 59
(Green Desert) Held up, smooth prog to lead over 1f out, rdn/hung left ins last, hdd nr line: cl rem, in gd heart.
1867 **KEEP IKIS 13** [2] Mrs M Reveley 6-7-10 (46)(1oh) D Mernagh (1) 7/2 FAV: 23-143: 6 ch m Anshan - ¾ 51
Santee Sioux (Dancing Brave) Prom, led over 2f out, rdn/hdd over 1f out, kept on well for press, just held: acts on firm & gd: not btn far and lks fairly h'capped, win another styg h'cap: had 8lb pull with rnr-up for 1867.
1867 **BAISSE DARGENT 13** [7] D J S Cosgrove 4-8-2 (53) W Supple 7/1: -32324: Settled towards rear, 3½ 54
prog/chsd ldrs 2f out, onepace ins last: see 424, 317.
1701 **JAMAICAN FLIGHT 21** [12] 7-9-6 (70) D Holland 14/1: 040065: Led 15f, onepace fnl 2f: see 253. ½ 71
*2016 **GOLDEN CHIMES 7** [6] 5-9-3 (67) A Culhane 11/2: 030-16: Rear, hdwy 4f out, no prog fnl 1f: op 9/2. 1½ 67
1867 **LEDGENDRY LINE 13** [11] 7-8-7 (57) K Darley 10/1: 564157: Towards rear, eff over 2f out, no prog. 2½ 55
1894 **SALVAGE 12** [1] 5-7-10 (46)(3oh) P Fessey 20/1: 030048: Chsd ldrs, held over 2f out: see 779. ¾ 43
1928 **ROYAL CASTLE 11** [9] 6-9-10 (74) G Duffield 9/1: 30-659: Mid-div, lost pl 3f out, held after: see 1329. 1 70
760 **ONEFOURSEVEN 89** [13] 7-7-10 (46)(5oh) K Dalgleish (7) 20/1: /00030: Al towards rear: 10th: abs. 1¾ 40
1928 **AMEZOLA 11** [4] 4-9-5 (70)(t) Pat Eddery 11/1: 6-0660: Briefly led 3f out, wknd qckly fnl 2f: 13th. 0
-- **Velmez** [8] 7-8-10 (60)(bl) R Havlin 12/1: 2372} **The Gamboller 360** [10] 5-8-10 (60) M Fenton 50/1:
13 ran Time 3m 59.2 (7.2) (Rio Stainless Engineering Ltd) P C Haslam Middleham, N.Yorks.

2177   3.45 DE LACY CLASSIFIED STKS 3YO 0-80 (D)   6f rnd   Firm 18   -02 Slow
£5772   £1776   £888   £444

1285 **NISR 43** [6] J W Payne 3-8-11 J P Spencer 10/1: 02-601: 3 b g Grand Lodge - Tharwa (Last Tycoon)   79
Trkd ldrs, rdn fnl 2f, styd on gamely ins last to lead nr line: all out, op 7/1, 6 wk abs: rnr-up fnl of 3 '99 starts
(mdn, rtd 87): eff over a stiff 6f, further shld suit: acts on firm & gd & runs well fresh: likes a stiff track.
982 **SUMTHINELSE 66** [5] N P Littmoden 3-8-11 D Holland 16/1: 0-5402: 3 ch g Magic Ring - Minnie Love *shd*   78
(Homeric) Cl-up, rdn/led narrowly ins last, hdd line: op 14/1, 2 mth abs: handles firm & gd/soft: see 837, 731.
*1605 **NAJEYBA 25** [4] A C Stewart 3-8-11 W Supple 4/1: 13: 3 ch f Indian Ridge - Innocence (Unfuwain)   *nk*   77
Led, rdn over 1f out, hdd well ins last, just held: op 3/1: acts on firm & soft grnd: see 1605.
1925 **LABRETT 11** [1] B J Meehan 3-8-11 (bl) Pat Eddery 5/2: 000044: Held up, prog to chall fnl 1f,   *hd*   76
kept on well, just held: btn less than 1L into 4th: nicely bckd tho' op 2/1: see 1925, 988 (list).
1925 **BUDELLI 11** [2] 3-9-0 Craig Williams 13/8 FAV: 623125: Led/dsptd lead 1f, remained cl-up, no room   1   77+
on heels of leaders fnl 1f: hvly bckd, op 2/1: no luck in running, would have gone v close here: see 1339.
1795 **SUSIES FLYER 17** [3] 3-8-8 J Carroll 8/1: 5-5006: Chsd ldrs, outpcd 2f: see 988 (Listed).   7   58
6 ran   Time 1m 15.3 (1.2)   (C Cotran)   J W Payne Newmarket.

2178   4.15 CLASSIFIED STKS 3YO+ 0-90 (C)   1m2f   Firm 18   +12 Fast
£8190   £2520   £1260   £630   3 yo rec 12lb

1982 **ARABIAN MOON 9** [6] C E Brittain 4-9-5 P Robinson 13/2: 0-0351: 4 ch c Barathea - Excellent Alibi   89
(Exceller) Trkd ldrs, prog fnl 2f, drvn/led well ins last, all out: op 8/1, fast time: '99 scorer at Ripon &
Windsor (h'caps, rtd 89): rtd 74 in '98: eff at 10/12f, stays 2m: loves a fast run race on firm, acts on gd, any trk.
*1857 **MYNAH 14** [4] A C Stewart 4-9-5 P Robinson 7/1: 012: 3 b f Selkirk - Reyah (Young Generation)   *nk*   89
Held up rear, rdn & styd on strongly fnl 2f, just held: op 7/1: confirmed improv of latest: see 1857 (mdn).
1845 **JUST IN TIME 15** [1] T G Mills 5-9-9 A Clark 9/1: 141403: 5 b g Night Shift - Future Past (Super   *hd*   91
Concorde) Trkd ldr, rdn/led 2f out, hdd well ins last, just held: see 874 (C/D).
+2001 **ICE 8** [2] M Johnston 4-9-11 (vis) D Holland 11/2: -51614: Led, rdn/hdd 2f out, kept on well for   *nk*   92
press ins last: btn less than 1L: fine run giving weight away: stays 10f: see 2001.
*1493 **RIYAFA 30** [3] 3-8-8 F Lynch 7/2: 215: Trkd ldrs, rdn/wknd over 1f out: well bckd: handles firm & sft.   2½   83
*1668 **RHYTHMICALL 23** [5] 3-8-11 Pat Eddery 9/4 FAV: 016: Held up, eff 3f out, btn/eased fnl 1f: hvly bckd.   4   80
1845 **GOLCONDA 15** [7] 4-9-2 M Fenton 7/1: 0-3007: Rear, eff 3f out, no prog: see 1170.   2½   69
7 ran   Time 2m 08.7 (0.6)   (Salem Suhail)   C E Brittain Newmarket.

2179   4.45 POPPIN LANE MDN 3YO (D)   1m4f   Firm 18   -04 Slow
£2860   £880   £440   £220

1284 **BID FOR FAME 43** [6] T G Mills 3-9-0 A Clark 7/2: 5301: 3 b c Quest For Fame - Shroud (Vaguely   85
Noble) Led over 4f out, rdn/hdd over 1f out, styd on again ins last, held on gamely, all out: nicely bckd, op 4/1:
6 wk abs: eff over a stiff/gall 12f on firm & gd grnd: lightly raced, should improve again.
1956 **SENSE OF FREEDOM 9** [7] M Johnston 3-8-9 D Holland 2/1: 222: 3 ch f Grand Lodge - Greatest   *nk*   79
Pleasure (Be My Guest) Trkd ldrs, prog to lead over 1f out, rdn/swished tail & hdd ins last, kept on, just held:
well bckd from op 9/2: clr rem: acts on firm & gd grnd: lks a tricky ride, worth a try in headgear: see 1956, 1599.
1493 **CLEPSYDRA 30** [1] H R A Cecil 3-8-9 W Ryan 5/4 FAV: 223: 3 b f Sadler's Wells - Quandary (Blushing   4   73
Groom) Held up, prog/ch 2f out, wknd over 1f out: hvly bckd: handles firm & soft: clr rem: see 1493, 1051.
1386 **DOCTOR JOHN 36** [8] Andrew Turnell 3-9-0 P Fessey 50/1: 004: Mid-div, btn 3f out: apprec h'caps.   12   65
1697 **BURNING DAYLIGHT 22** [2] 3-9-0 G Duffield 25/1: -05: Keen/held up, held fnl 3f: longer 12f trip.   5   58
1857 **BEAU DUCHESS 14** [3] 3-8-9 A Culhane 16/1: 06: Held up, keen, btn 3f out: op 14/1, longer 12f trip.   *nk*   52
--   **BENVOLIO** [10] 3-9-0 N Carlisle 50/1: 7: Al bhd: Cidrax newcomer, with C Kellett.   *dist*   0
--   **PHANTOM FOOTSTEPS** [5] 3-9-0 T Williams 50/1: 8: Led till over 4f out, sn bhd: Komaite gldg.   *dist*   0
8 ran   Time 2m 36.7 (2.6)   (T G Mills)   T G Mills Headley, Surrey.

2180   5.15 PORTERS FILLIES HCAP 3YO+ 0-75 (E)   1m rnd   Firm 18   -08 Slow   **[65]**
£4251   £1308   £654   £327   3 yo rec 10lb

1892 **THORNTOUN GOLD 12** [5] J S Goldie 4-8-7 (44) A Culhane 11/2: 00-401: 4 ch f Lycius - Gold Braisim   46
(Jareer) Held up, rdn & prog over 1f out, styd on gamely ins last to lead nr fin: well bckd from 7/1:
'99 Thirsk wnr (sell h'cap, rtd 51 at best): rtd 57 in '98: suited by 7f/1m, tried 10f: acts on firm & soft.
2094 **SWYNNFORD PLEASURE 4** [8] J Hetherton 4-8-4 (41) J Fanning 7/1: 440132: 4 b f Reprimand -   *nk*   42
Pleasuring (Good Times) Chsd ldrs, prog to lead over 1f out, rdn/hdd well ins last: acts on firm & gd grnd.
1842 **TURTLES RISING 15** [6] M Mullineaux 4-9-13 (64) P Hanagan (7) 25/1: 000-03: 4 b f Turtle Island -   1¾   63
Zabeta (Diesis) Trkd ldrs, ev ch fnl 1f, held over 1f out: '99 Lingfield wnr (h'cap, rtd 72, B J Meehan): '98 Sandown
wnr (auct mdn, rtd 83): eff at 7f, stays 1m: acts on firm & gd, without blnks: likes to race with/force the pace.
2013 **ANGEL LANE 8** [4] A W Carroll 3-7-13 (46) D Mernagh (3) 14/1: 00-004: Held up, hdwy 3f out, no   3   42
prog fnl 1f: op 10/1: stays a stiff 1m, handles firm grnd: see 1448.
*1892 **TEMPRAMENTAL 12** [11] 4-9-4 (55) K Darley 9/4 FAV: 331415: Led, rdn/hdd 2f out, btn/eased nr fin: 1¼   50
hvly bckd, op 3/1: tough performer who has been busy: see 1892.
4257} **HELLO HOLLY 264** [2] 3-8-11 (58) G Duffield 20/1: 000-6: Chsd ldr, ch 3f out, sn held: op 14/1:   ¾   52
reapp/h'cap bow: unplcd last term (rtd 73, flattered): bred to apprec this 1m trip.
*1803 **SHADY POINT 16** [10] 3-9-9 (70)(vis) P Robinson 5/2: 056217: Trkd ldrs, rdn/btn 2f out: well bckd   1   63
tho' op 2/1: btr 1803 (AW mdn h'cap, 1st time visor), 1610 (gd/sft).
1920 **CHAMPAGNE N DREAMS 11** [3] 8-9-2 (53) Kim Tinkler 9/1: 0-U608: Held up, eff 3f out, btn 2f out.   4   42
--   **THE BOXER** [9] 4-8-8 (45)(t) K Dalgleish (7) 16/1: 0000-9: Dwelt, al rear: op 14/1, reapp, jumps   ½   33
fit (no form): ex-Irish, '99 Galway wnr (h'cap): eff at 1m on fast grnd: with K Morgan.
4584} **SAVOIR FAIRE 236** [12] 4-8-11 (48) D Holland 33/1: 00/0-0: Bhd halfway: 10th, h'cap bow, modest.   7   29
10 ran   Time 1m 43.9 (2.1)   (Tough Construction Ltd)   J S Goldie Uplawmoor, E.Renfrewshire.

LINGFIELD (Mixed)   SUNDAY JUNE 25TH   Lefthand, Sharp, Undulating Track

Official Going   TURF - GOOD TO FIRM; AW - STANDARD. Stalls: AW - Inside; Turf - Stands Side.

2181   2.25 VICTORIA MASSEY SELLER 3YO+ (G)   **1m4f aw   Standard   Inapplicable**
£1981   £566   £283   3 yo rec 14lb

1852 **FULL EGALITE** 14 [12] B R Johnson 4-9-7 (BL) C Rutter 14/1: 0-0001: 4 gr g Ezzoud - Milva (Jellaby)   **44a**
Chsd ldrs, wide into str, ran on strongly under press to lead fnl strides: no bid, woken by blnks on AW bow.
unplcd last term for W Haggas (rtd 63): '98 wnr at Brighton (mdn, rtd 70, R Simpson): prev eff at 6f, now
suited by 12f: goes on soft grnd & equitrack, sharp/undul trks, in blinkers, not visor.

2008 **LATIN BAY 8** [2] P G Murphy 5-9-7 S Drowne 9/1: 00-002: 5 b g Superlative - Hugging (Beveled)   shd **43a**
Led, hard rdn ent str, styd on but worn down line: clr rem, a bold attempt & ran to best, see 2008, .

3241} **DASHING CHIEF** 321 [10] W J Musson 5-9-7 (t) R Hughes 4/1 FAV: 0365-3: 5 b g Darshaan - Calaloo 3½ **39a**
Sioux (Our Native) Mid-div, eff 4f out, styd on but unable to chall: well clr rem, op 5/2, AW bow. reapp:
plcd in '99 (clmr, rtd 78): plcd in a Gr 3 in '98 (rtd 102, M Jarvis): '97 Pontefract wnr (mdn): eff at 1m/11.5f
on firm, gd, poss soft & equitrack: wore a t-strap, clrly prem this time, sole nr one of these.

1852 **BILLICHANG** 14 [6] P Howling 4-9-12 F Norton 8/1: 261004: Chsd ldrs, onepace 4f out: see 775 (10f).   13 **32a**
1540 **ALBINONA** 29 [5] 3-8-2 A Beech (5) 5/1: 00-625: Handy for 1m: tchd 8/1, stiff task, btr 1540 (AW bow).   3½ **19a**
1331 **SASEEDO** 35 [5] 10-9-7 (bl) G Bardwell 6/1: 040006: Dwelt, nvr better than mid-div: 6 wk abs.   3 **21a**
835 **APPYABO** 79 [9] 5-9-12 (BL) M Henry 33/1: 136507: Chsd ldrs till str: blnks, hdles rnr 4 days ago.   16 **14a**
1933 **FOOLS PARADISE** 10 [14] 3-8-7 T G McLaughlin 25/1: 0-6608: Nvr a factor: see 1502.   ¾ **8a**
-- **EXECUTIVE PROFILES** [7] 5-9-2 J Tate 25/1: 9: Al towards rear: Flat bow, hdles fit, moderate.   ¾ **2a**
1720 **LOST SPIRIT 20** [4] 4-9-12 Darren Williams (7) 5/1: 350640: Chsd ldrs till 5f out: 10th, tchd 7/1.   7 **7a**
1465 **FROZEN SEA 32** [11] 9-9-7 (t) I Mongan(5) 7/1: 022-00: Prom halfway, wknd qckly 4f out: 11th, hdles rnr.¾ **1a**
-- **FOR LOVE** [3] 4-9-12 Paul Smith 8/1: 11200: Sn struggling: 15th, Belgian raider, dual 12f sand wnr.   **0a**
1933 Scenic Lady 10 [8] 4-9-2 S Whitworth 33/1:   1647 Ki Chi Saga 23 [1] 8-9-7 (tvi) P McCabe 20/1:
3851} Raglan Accolade 290 [13] 3-8-2 S Righton 33/1:
15 ran   Time 2m 34.88 (5.68)   (Mrs P J Sheen)   B R Johnson Epsom, Surrey

---

2182   2.55 TAUBER MDN AUCT 2YO (E)   **7f str   Good/Firm 20   -19 Slow**
£3136   £965   £482   £241

1883 **MUSIC MAID** 12 [12] H S Howe 2-8-2 A Nicholls (3) 25/1: 61: 2 b f Inzar - Richardstown Lass   **84**
(Muscatite) Front rank, led after halfway, pshd out ins last: op 16/1: 2,800 gns Apr foal, half-sister to 2 wnrs:
clrly apprec step up to 7f, will get further: acts on fast grnd & a sharp trk, forcing the pace.

1691 **TRUSTTHUNDER** 22 [2] N P Littmoden 2-8-2 J Tate 4/1: -02: 2 ch f Selkirk - Royal Cat (Royal   1 **80**
Academy) Dwelt, imprvd 3f out, chsd wnr ins last, al held: tchd 5/1: earlier hghly tried on debut, gets
7f on fast grnd & could win similar.

1706 **ISLAND QUEEN** 21 [14] R Hannon 2-8-7(1ow) R Hughes 7/4 FAV: 43: 2 b f Turtle Island - Holy   2½ **79**
Devotion (Commanche Run) Mid-div, prog 2f out, onepace below dist, eased nr fin: well bckd: better run &
styd longer 7f trip on fast grnd tho' drop back to 6f may suit for now: see 1706.

1882 **FAZZANI** 12 [3] M R Channon 2-8-6 S Drowne 13/2: -0444: Chsd ldrs till no extra appr fnl 1f: op 5/1. 1¾ **73**
1954 **PATHAN** 10 [9] 2-8-8 I Mongan (5) 25/1: 05: In tch, wide, nvr any impress on ldrs: tchd 50/1.   1¾ **70**
1589 **POLISH PADDY** 25 [11] 2-8-8 A Daly 25/1: 06: Chsd ldrs, fdd appr fnl 1f: stablemate 3rd, longer trip.   1 **67**
1882 **EMMA CLARE** 12 [16] 2-8-3 C Rutter 40/1: 007: Same place thr'out: see 1673.   ½ **61**
1876 **MISSING YOU TOO 13** [5] 2-8-6 D Sweeney 7/1: 0-6608: Nvr a factor: see 1876.   nk **63**
-- **ELA DARLIN MOU** [8] 2-8-4 D O'Donohoe 25/1: 9: Dwelt & outpcd, late hdwy: debut: 6,600gns   nk **60**
Mtoto Feb foal, half-sister to sev wnrs, notably useful sprinter Night Flight: sire a 10/12f performer.
1924 **CIRCLE OF WOLVES 11** [7] 2-8-10 P McCabe 8/1: 00: Nvr a factor: 10th: see 1924.   1¼ **63**
1916 **PERTEMPS GILL 11** [13] 2-8-1 G Sparkes (7) 50/1: -0030: Led till halfway, grad wknd: 14th, see 1916 (5f).   **0**
-- **MUCHO GUSTO** [10] 2-8-9 G Carter 7/1: 0: Dwelt, al bhd: 16th, op 4/1: Casteddu Feb foal with J Dunlop.   **0**
849 Benjamin 76 [4] 2-8-11 S Sanders 50/1:   1838 By Definition 15 [17] 2-8-6 N Pollard 14/1:
1798 No Name City 17 [15] 2-8-11 S Whitworth 33/1:   1798 Sawbo Lad 17 [18] 2-8-6 L Newman (3) 25/1:
1236 Mer Made 45 [2] 2-8-2 M Henry 40/1:   970 Pelli 67 [6] 2-8-2 F Norton 33/1:
18 ran   Time 1m 23.16 (2.76)   (R J Parish)   H S Howe Oakford, Devon

---

2183   3.25 VERITAS DGC MDN 3YO+ (D)   **6f   Good/Firm 20   -07 Slow**
£3818   £1175   £587   £293   3 yo rec 7 lb

1783 **MISTER SUPERB** 17 [4] V Soane 3-8-12 S Sanders 11/4: 0-3021: 3 ch c Superlative - Kiveton Komet   **84**
(Precocious) Mid-div, imprvd 2f out, drvn dist & ran on to lead fnl 100y: nicely bckd: plcd in similar prev,
4th of 15 in '99 (mdn, rtd 83): eff at 6f, may get 7f: acts on firm/fast grnd, any trk & best held up.

1354 **STAR PRINCESS** 37 [2] K T Ivory 3-8-7 C Catlin (7) 10/1: 4-6422: 3 b f Up And At 'Em - Princess   1¼ **75**
Sharpenup (Lochnager) Trkd ldrs, shkn up to lead appr fnl 1f, sn hard rdn, hdd ins last: ran to best, see 1021.

1333 **STILL IN LOVE** 39 [16] H R A Cecil 3-8-7 A McGlone 7/2: 3-253: 3 b f Emarati - In Love Again   ¾ **73**
(Prince Rupert) Front rank & ev ch till onepace ins last: tchd 5/1, 6 wk abs: handles fast, suited by give?

-- **HONEST WARNING** [5] B Smart 3-8-12 S Drowne 12/1: 4: Bhd, styg on/run was blocked appr fnl   shd **78**
1f, ran on, ch had gone: op 6/1: Mtoto first foal, dam a mdn: handles fast grnd & is sure to apprec 7f+.
982 **PORT ST CHARLES 66** [18] 3-8-12 R Hughes 2/1 FAV: 33-245: Well plcd & ev ch till held below   nk **77**
dist: nicely bckd from 11/4, 9 wk abs: see 982 (hot Newmarket h'cap).
1971 **KEE RING 9** [6] 4-9-5 (bl) S Whitworth 25/1: -60606: Led till appr fnl 1f, no extra: stiff task, flattered.   2 **71$**
-- **MISS MARPLE** [10] 3-8-7 O Urbina 8/1: 7: Mid-div, styd on fnl 2f but not given a hard time: op 6/1:   nk **65+**
Puissance half-sister to a couple of wnrs, notably decent sprinter Glowing: handles fast grnd, expect improvement.
1811 **PSALMIST 16** [13] 3-8-7 Martin Dwyer 25/1: 308: Outpcd, late hdwy: now quai for h'caps, see 1525.   2 **59**
1811 **MOLLY MALONE 16** [8] 3-8-7 C Rutter 33/1: 609: Dwelt, al around mid-div: see 1468.   shd **59**
127 **BOLD EMMA 208** [11] 3-8-7 P McCabe 33/1: 0-0: Nvr a factor: 10th, reapp, no worthwhile form.   hd **58**
1605 **SAPPHIRE MILL 25** [11] 3-8-7 G Bardwell 9/1: Sn bhd: 15th: see 1605.   **0**
5 Azira 230 [9] 3-8-7 S Righton 25/1:   1012 Royal Tarragon 62 [3] 4-9-0 J Stack 50/1:
1428 Ejder 34 [1] 4-9-0 S Carson 50/1:   1783 Polished Up 17 [15] 3-8-7 G Carter 20/1:
1638 Lady Jeannie 24 [12] 3-8-7 L Newman (3) 20/1:
16 ran   Time 1m 10.44 (1.64)   (Gordon L Western)   V Soane East Garston, Berks

2184
3.55 SIMON & ANGELA HCAP 3YO+ 0-70 (E)   5f   Good/Firm 20   +08 Fast   [70]
£3721   £1145   £572   £286   3 yo rec 6 lb   High no's favoured on fast grnd here

1650 **FORGOTTEN TIMES 23** [17] K T Ivory 6-9-13 (69)(vis) A Nicholls (3) 5/1 FAV: 206221: 6 ch m Nabeel **73**
Dancer - Etoile d'Amore (The Minstrel) In tch, gd hdwy to chall appr fnl 1f, shkn up to assert nr fin, snugly:
op 6/1, fast time: '99 wnr at Goodwood (2), Folkestone, Brighton, Salisbury & Windsor (h'caps, rtd 66): '98 wnr
at Lingfield (AW h'cap, rtd 71a & 51): stays 7f, 5f specialist: acts on firm, suited by soft/hvy & equitrack:
goes on any trk but loves sharp ones: wears blnks or visor: hard as nails mare.
2124 **SIHAFI 2** [13] D Nicholls 7-8-11 (53) T Hamilton (7) 11/2: -04302: 7 ch g Elmaamul - Kit's Double ½ **55**
(Spring Double) Mid-div, prog ent fnl 2f & ev ch till held towards fin: ran 48 hrs ago, apprec drop back to 5f.
1932 **QUITE HAPPY 10** [20] M H Tompkins 5-8-11 (53) S Sanders 12/1: 033353: 5 b m Statoblest - Four hd **54**
Legged Friend (Aragon) Towards rear, gd prog appr fnl 1f, hard rdn & ch dist, kept on, not btn far: clr rem &
took good advantage of rails draw: see 1662, 897.
506 **BOLDLY CLIFF 134** [12] E C Denderland 6-9-0 (56)(bl) L Newman (3) 11/2: 01-204: Led till below 2½ **51**
dist, no extra: op 4/1, 7 wk abs: Belgian raider, handles fast, suited by soft grnd & equitrack: see 166.
2022 **GOLDEN POUND 7** [2] 8-8-4 (46) G Baker (7) 14/1: 056-45: In tch wide, styd on appr fnl 1f, no ½ **40**
impress on ldrs: quick reapp & gd work from low draw: spot on next time at 6f? see 2022.
*1932 **SUNSET HARBOUR 10** [10] 7-8-5 (47) Claire Bryan (5) 8/1: 0-2416: Mid-div, prog ent fnl 2f till dist. shd **41**
1512 **ARCADIAN CHIEF 30** [19] 3-7-10 (44)(3oh) C Catlin (5) 25/1: 4-0557: Bhd, edged left 2f out, late prog. 1¼ **35**
2047 **MARSHALL ST CYR 6** [18] 3-8-9 (57)(BL) T G McLaughlin 8/1: 056428: Prom 2f, mid-div after: blnkd. nk **47**
+2022 **THAT MAN AGAIN 7** [11] 8-10-2 (72)(bl) G Faulkner (3) 11/2: 000019: Prom till no extra appr fnl nk **61**
1f, eased: quick reapp, top-weight, still well h'capped: see 2022.
1971 **BREW 9** [7] 4-8-12 (54) R Hughes (1) 6/1: 60-060: Mid-div, hdwy under press & hung left 2f out: 10th. shd **43**
1961 **AROGANT PRINCE 9** [1] 3-8-12 (60) R Brisland (5) 16/1: 431600: Well plcd till dist: 11th, tricky draw. hd **48**
1264 **MANGUS 44** [5] 6-9-2 (58) N Pollard 12/1: -65000: Chsd ldrs, wknd qckly appr fnl 1f: 12th, 6 wk abs. nk **45**
-- **Clan Chief** [4] 7-9-9 (65) I Mongan (5) 16/1:   2095 **Arab Gold 4** [8] 5-7-10 (38)(2oh) M Henry 25/1:
1953 **Malaah 10** [16] 4-8-4 (46)(bl) A Daly 25/1:   1742 **Bangled 19** [15] 3-8-5 (53) D O'Donohoe 25/1:
3855} **Windrush Boy 290** [14] 10-7-13 (41) S Righton 25/1:   1817 **Princess Aurora 16** [6] 3-8-0 (48) F Norton 25/1:
398 **Mister Raider 151** [9] 8-7-10 (38)(bl) (1oh) D Kinsella (7) 25/1:
1913 **Glastonbury 11** [3] 4-7-10 (38) G Bardwell 25/1:
20 ran   Time 57.47 (0.62)   (John Crook)   K T Ivory Radlett, Herts

2185
4.25 MAIL ON SUNDAY HCAP 3YO+ 0-90 (C)   7f140y str   Good/Firm 20   -08 Slow   [84]
£7572   £2330   £1165   £582   3 yo rec 10lb

1113 **HONEST BORDERER 53** [5] J L Dunlop 5-9-7 (77) G Carter 9/2 CO FAV: 036-61: 5 b g Selkirk - Tell No **82**
Lies (High Line) Waited with, stdy hdwy from halfway, pshd into lead below dist, rdly: 8 wk abs: plcd twice in
'99 (h'cap, rtd 83): '98 Ripon wnr (h'cap, rtd 83): eff at 7.5f/10f: acts on fast & soft grnd, any trk, likes
sharp ones: best without blnks, goes well fresh: something in hand here & is on a fair mark.
1283 **RICH IN LOVE 43** [2] C A Cyzer 6-9-10 (80) I Mongan (5) 16/1: 00-002: 6 b m Alzao - Chief's 1 **82**
Quest (Chief's Crown) Chsd ldrs wide, rdn, prog & ev ch appr fnl 1f, outpcd by win nr fin: 6 wk abs, gd run.
1799 **MUTABASSIR 17** [12] G L Moore 6-8-4 (60) L Newman (3) 5/1: 0-6543: 6 ch g Soviet Star - Anghaam ½ **61**
(Diesis) Mid-div, prog & narrow lead appr fnl 1f, sn hard prsd/rdn, hdd below dist & onepace: back to best.
1810 **SALTY JACK 16** [9] V Soane 6-9-9 (79) S Sanders 9/2 CO FAV: 300054: Held up, styd on appr fnl 1f, nk **79**
nvr nrr: clr rem: well h'capped, usually comes with a late run: see 485.
2001 **CUSIN 8** [1] 4-9-2 (72) F Norton 9/2 CO FAV: -00305: Wide, in tch, eff & no impress appr fnl 1f: tchd 7/1. 3 **66**
1744 **CEDAR PRINCE 19** [4] 3-8-4 (70)(bl) P Doe 25/1: 0-0006: Well plcd, led appr fnl 2f till bef nk **63**
dist, no extra: apprec drop back to 7.5f, see 1744.
1836 **SILKEN DALLIANCE 15** [10] 5-9-11 (81) A Nicholls (3) 5/1: -00027: Held up, imprvg when short of 1½ **71**
room appr fnl 1f, ch had basically gone & not persevered with: forget this, see 1936, 601.
2124 **SCISSOR RIDGE 2** [8] 8-7-10 (52)(5oh) R Brisland (5) 16/1: 023068: Chsd ldrs till 2f out: ran 48 hrs ago. ½ **41**
1969 **LUCKY ARCHER 9** [6] 7-9-0 (70) P Fitzsimons (5) 16/1: 5W0-09: Bhd ldrs till wknd qckly appr fnl 1f. 1¼ **56**
1110 **SMOOTH SAILING 53** [11] 5-9-13 (83) S Drowne 10/1: 0-0400: Led till appr fnl 2f, sn btn: 10th, abs. 11 **53**
3296} **ALAZAN 318** [3] 5-7-10 (52)(12oh) S Righton 66/1: /00P-0: Al bhd: 11th, impossible task: plater. 23 **0**
11 ran   Time 1m 29.89 (2.09)   (Mrs A Johnstone)   J L Dunlop Arundel, W Sussex

2186
4.55 RODEO HCAP 3YO+ 0-70 (E)   1m2f aw   Standard   Inapplicable   [65]
£2912   £832   £416   3 yo rec 12lb

*1544 **RICH VEIN 29** [5] S P C Woods 3-9-7 (70)(VIS) S Drowne 10/3: 0-4211: 3 b g Up And At 'Em - **79a**
Timissara (Shahrastani) Mid-div, al going well, trkd ldrs halfway, led dist, sn clr, easily: earlier won here
at Lingfield (AW bow, h'cap): lightly rcd juv (mdn, rtd 71): eff at 1m/10f, shld get further: acts on gd grnd,
a revelation on equitrack & goes well with/without visor, likes Lingfield: progressive, more wins to come.
1915 **QUEEN OF THE KEYS 11** [3] S Dow 4-8-3 (40) A Nicholls (3) 10/1: 000032: 4 b f Royal Academy 6 **40a**
- Piano Belle (Fappano) Rear, prog halfway, rdn ent str, styd on same pace for 2nd: poss stays 10f, best at 1m?
1608 **PAPERWEIGHT 25** [7] Miss K M George 4-10-0 (65) J Tate 10/1: -42303: 4 b f In The Wings - Crystal 1 **63a**
Reay (Sovereign Dancer) Held up, drvn appr str, some late hdwy, nvr a factor: prob nr to best under top-weight.
2007 **MUST BE MAGIC 8** [9] H J Collingridge 3-8-12 (61) R Perham 9/1: 0-0634: Cl-up, led over 3f out ¾ **58a**
till dist, wknd: AW bow, return to 1m may suit: see 2007, 1569.
*1807 **BARBASON 16** [14] 8-9-6 (57) I Mongan (5) 2/1 FAV: -25515: Sn prom, eff 3f out, wknd: bckd from 3/1. 9 **42a**
*2049 **AGIOTAGE 6** [12] 4-9-0 (51)(6ex) G Faulkner (3) 5/1: -00016: Led till fnl 4f, btn 2f out: qk reapp/pen. nk **35a**
1743 **TEST THE WATER 19** [8] 6-8-13 (50) C Catlin (7) 20/1: 2-0007: Nvr a factor: see 1395. 4 **28a**
650 **RUSHED 109** [6] 5-7-10 (33)(2oh) D Kinsella (7) 25/1: 00-408: Dwelt, al towards rear: hdles fit, see 457. 6 **5a**
224 **TRIBAL PEACE 186** [11] 8-8-7 (44) T G McLaughlin 50/1: 5000-9: Nvr on terms: jmps abs, new stable. hd **16a**
2027 **QUEENS STROLLER 2** [2] 9-7-10 (33)(3oh) Clare Bryan (5) 50/1: 050/00: Sn struggling: 10th, quick 5 **0a**
reapp: missed '99, '97 Southwell wnr (fill h'cap, rtd 39a): eff at 7f/1m, stays 9.4f on fast, hvy, best on fibresand.
1785 **READING RHONDA 17** [13] 4-9-2 (53) S Sanders 16/1: 5/5000: Chsd ldrs till halfway: 11th, see 920. 5 **11a**
11 ran   Time 2m 06.5 (3.7)   (Arashan Ali)   S P C Woods Newmarket, Suffolk

NOTTINGHAM   MONDAY JUNE 26TH   Lefthand, Galloping Track

Official Going   GOOD TO FIRM. Stalls: Inside, except 6f - Stands Side.

2187
2.15 WELCOME SELL HCAP 3YO 0-60 (G)   1m54y rnd   Good/Firm 39   -41 Slow   [65]
£2094   £598   £299

1865 **MOUNTRATH ROCK 14** [7] N Tinkler 3-8-10 (47)(vis) T Quinn 8/1: 004401: 3 b f Rock Hopper - Point **51**
Of Law (Law Society) Towards rear, prog fnl 3f & rdn/led 1f out, in command/pushed out cl-home: op 13/2: no bid:
slow time: visor reapplied: dual '99 rnr-up (seller, rtd 62): suited by 1m on firm & gd/soft grnd, likes a gall trk:
seems best in a visor, has tried blnks.
2136 **RED SONNY 3** [9] A Berry 3-8-9 (46) G Carter 9/2 JT FAV: 002362: 3 ch g Foxhound - Olivia's Pride   1 **47**
(Digamist) Held up, rdn/prog to chall 1f out, kept on, not pace of wnr: op 7/2, qck reapp: acts on fast & fibresand.
1884 **WOODWIND DOWN 13** [6] M R Channon 3-8-11 (48) Craig Williams 10/1: 200003: 3 b f Piccolo - Bint   ½ **48**
El Oumara (Al Nasr) Held up, prog/switched over 2f out, no room & switched again over 1f out, styd on strongly
for press nr fin: no luck in running, closer with a clr run: acts on fast grnd & equitrack: shld win similar.
1572 **COLLEGE ROCK 27** [11] R Brotherton 3-8-11 (48)(vis) I Mongan (5) 9/1: 263064: Slowly away, rdn/   1¾ **45**
rapid prog to chase ldr after 1f, drvn & kept on onepace fnl 2f: visor reapplied: see 1572, 1331 & 806.
1772 **TIMELESS CHICK 19** [1] 3-8-10 (47)(bl) M Henry 8/1: 004305: Twds rear, rdn/late gains, no threat.   hd **43**
80 **DAKISI ROYALE 219** [2] 3-8-10 (47) F Norton 33/1: 0650-6: Mid-div, nvr pace to chall: 7 month abs,   1 **41**
now with L J Barratt: rnr-up in '99 (rtd 58, seller, R Whitaker): eff at 7f on firm & gd: has run well in a visor.
1930 **ANNS MILL 17** [17] 3-8-11 (48) R Hughes 20/1: -04007: Led, rdn fnl 3f, hdd/wknd 1f out: see 1212 (7f).   1¾ **39**
1979 **CUIGIU 10** [5] 3-9-7 (58) J Weaver 16/1: 205408: Held up, eff 3f out, no impress: op 14/1: see 930.   1¾ **46**
959 **JUST MAC 69** [8] 3-8-12 (49) Pat Eddery 16/1: 060609: Prom 6f: op 14/1, 10 wk abs: see 221 (6f).   ¾ **36**
1891 **CAPACOOSTIC 13** [14] 3-8-7 (44) S Finnamore (4) 40/1: 000-00: Chsd ldrs 6f: 10th: mod form.   3 **25**
1303 **CYBER BABE 42** [10] 3-9-5 (56) L Newnan (3) 14/1: -02100: Mid-div, nvr threat: 11th: abs: btr 1141 (AW).   1 **35**
1889 **ALABAMA WURLEY 13** [16] 3-8-12 (49) J Tate 9/2 JT FAV: 000000: Chsd ldrs 3f out, sn held: 12th.   1 **26**
1593 **BEDOUIN QUEEN 26** [4] 3-9-7 (58) S Carson (5) 12/1: -00000: Wide/chsd ldrs 3f out, sn held: 13th.   ½ **34**
1972 **PONTIKONISI 10** [4] 3-8-13 (50) T E Durcan 10/1: 45-050: Nvr threat: 14th: op 12/1: flattered 1972 (7f).   1 **24**
1914 **Walter The Whistle 12** [3] 3-8-8 (44)(low) D Griffiths (2) 11/1:
1572 **Kings Ginger 27** [13] 3-8-12 (49)(vis) R Fitzpatrick (3) 16/1:
1085 **Sweet Haven 55** [15] 3-8-10 (47)(VIS) S Sanders 33/1:
17 ran   Time 1m 46.00 (6.6)   (Racingclub.co.uk)   N Tinkler Langton, N.Yorks.

2188
2.45 HORSESMOUTH.CO.UK MDN 3YO+ (D)   1m54y rnd   Good/Firm 39   -27 Slow
£3672   £1130   £565   £282   3 yo rec 10lb

1763 **INCREDULOUS 19** [7] J R Fanshawe 3-8-6 Pat Eddery 9/4: 0-241: 3 ch f Indian Ridge - Fetlar (Pharly)   **87**
Made all, rdn/pressed 2f out, sn rdn clr, eased down nr fin, cmftbly: val for 10L+: nicely bckd: reportedly
found to have a sore mouth after pulling v hard latest: apprec this step up to 1m, further suit: acts on fast &
any trk: can force the pace: plenty in hand here, potentially useful filly, shld win more races.
3828} **ANGIES QUEST 292** [8] H R A Cecil 3-8-6 T Quinn 11/8 FAV: 630-2: 3 b f Inchinor - Chanson d'Avril   8 **72**
(Chief Singer) Chsd wnr, rdn to chall 2f out, sn outpcd: bckd: plcd in '99 for K R Burke (rtd 79, fill mdn): eff
around 1m: acts on gd grnd & a sharp/turning trk: caught a tartar here, h'caps shld suit.
1886 **TEE CEE 13** [11] R Guest 3-8-6 S Sanders 3/1: 533: 3 b f Lion Cavern - Hawayah (Shareef Dancer)   3 **66**
Prom, rdn/onepace fnl 2f: see 1886, 1084.
-- **SHARP BELLINE** [5] M Johnston 3-8-11 J Fanning 14/1: 4: Held up, rdn/mod gains, no threat: op   2 **67**
10/1, debut: 31,000gns purchase, brother to a French med-dist wnr: sure to apprec 10f- on this evidence, improve.
1922 **REDHILL 12** [9] P M Quinn (3) 66/1: 065: Rear, mod gains fnl 2f: better off in h'caps.   ¾ **61**
2012 **ZABIONIC 9** [6] 3-8-11 N Pollard 25/1: 400006: Chsd ldrs 6f: flattered, see 1521, 717.   nk **65$**
1725 **BROMEIGAN 21** [12] J Mackay 50/1: 07: Rear, mod late gains: dropped to 1m: see 1725.   1½ **57$**
1519 **MOON DREAM 30** [3] 4-9-2 R Perham 100/1: 000-08: Chsd ldrs halfway, btn 2f out: longer 1m trip.   ½ **56$**
1819 **AVERHAM STAR 17** [4] 5-9-7 L Vickers 40/1: 050-09: Prom till halfway: no form.   ¾ **60$**
-- **SWEET ENVIRONMENT** [10] 3-8-6 S Righton 50/1: 0: Al bhd: 10th: debut, with Mrs M Bridgwater.   8 **43**
-- **Supreme Silence** [1] 3-8-11 J Weaver 14/1:   3083} **Country Bumpkin 329** [2] 4-9-7 R Havlin 100/1:
12 ran   Time 1m 44.9 (5.5)   (Dr Cathering Wills)   J R Fanshawe Newmarket.

2189
3.15 EBF MDN 2YO (D)   6f   Good/Firm 39   -06 Slow
£3575   £1100   £550   £275

1943 **CEEPIO 11** [4] T G Mills 2-9-0 A Clark 10/11 FAV: -31: 2 b c Pennekamp - Boranwood (Exhibitioner)   **101+**
Sn cl-up, went on halfway & rdn clr over 1f out, styd on strongly & eased nr fin: hvly bckd, op 11/8: confirmed
promise of debut: eff at 6f, 7f will suit: acts on fast grnd & a gall trk: potentially smart, keep on his side.
1774 **PALATIAL 19** [6] J R Fanshawe 2-8-9 Pat Eddery 6/4: 22: 2 b f Green Desert - White Palace (Shirley   4 **84**
Heights) Trkd ldrs, rdn/chall 2f out, sn outpcd by wnr: clr rem: hvly bckd: acts on fast & gd: shld find a mdn.
-- **CELOTTI** [3] R Hollinshead 2-8-10(1ow) J F Egan 25/1: 3: 2 b f Celtic Swing - Zalotti (Polish Patriot)   6 **73**
Led, rdn/hdd halfway, no impress fnl 2f: op 10/1: Feb first foal: dam a 5f juv wnr, sire outstanding 2yo & subs
French Derby wnr: likely to apprec 7f+ later: clr of rem.
-- **STORMY VOYAGE** [5] E A L Dunlop 2-9-0 G Carter 12/1: 4: Chsd ldrs, outpcd from halfway: op   4 **67**
5/1: Storm Bird colt, Apr foal: dam a juv US wnr: sire Champion juv: shld improve in time.
-- **CHARENTE** [2] 2-9-0 K Darley 12/1: 5: Sn outpcd/bhd: op 5/1: Hennessy colt, Feb foal, cost   12 **44**
Ffr 350,000, a first foal: dam a mdn abroad: likely to appr further in time for M C Pipe.
-- **HALLIANA** [1] 2-8-9 Dean McKeown 25/1: 6: In tch, rdn/hung badly right from halfway, sn bhd: op 10/1: 7 **26**
Turtle Island filly, May foal, cost 450,000gns: half-sister to 2 wnrs abroad & a 6f juv wnr here: dam plcd as a juv.
6 ran   Time 1m 13.5 (2.7)   (Mrs C Stephens)   T G Mills Headley, Surrey.

2190
3.45 TOTE HCAP STKS 3YO+ 0-85 (D)   1m2f   Good/Firm 39   -07 Slow   [82]
£7475   £2300   £1150   £575   3 yo rec 10lb

*1912 **NEW ASSEMBLY 12** [2] Sir Michael Stoute 3-9-2 (82) Pat Eddery 9/4 FAV: 00-211: 3 b f Machiavellian   **88**
- Abbey Strand (Shadeed) Trkd ldr, rdn/prog to lead over 1f out, styd on well & in command nr fin: pushed out:
nicely bckd: recent Lingfield wnr (mdn): unplcd in '99 (rtd 85, mdn): suited by step up to 10f, 12f shld suit:
enjoys fast/firm grnd, any trk: a step ahead of the h'capper & shld go in again.

702

1921 **YOUNG UN 12** [8] M J Ryan 5-8-9 (63) J Mackay (5) 8/1: 604202: 5 b h Efisio - Stardyn (Star Appeal) *3½* **63**
Settled rear, rdn/styd on fnl 2f, not pace of wnr: caught a progressive sort: see 786 (C/D).
1965 **PINCHINCHA 10** [4] D Morris 6-9-9 (77) J Tate 7/2: 402343: 6 b g Priolo - Western Heights (Shirley *nk* **76**
Heights) Held up, rdn/prog to chall 2f out, sn outpcd by wnr: op 4/1: consistent, but on long losing run: see 1288.
*1288 **TONIGHTS PRIZE 43** [7] C F Wall 6-9-10 (78) S Sanders 11/2: 035-14: Bhd ldrs, eff when badly hmpd *2* **73**
2f out, switched & kept on fnl 1f, no threat: op 5/1, 6 wk abs: no luck in running, poss plcd with a clr run.
1788 **COSMO JACK 18** [1] 4-9-0 (68)(vis) M Roberts 20/1: 01-025: Chsd ldrs, onepace fnl 2f: see 1788, 1462. *nk* **63**
1445 **CALLDAT SEVENTEEN 34** [6] 4-9-9 (77) K Darley 6/1: 0-0246: Held up, prog to briefly lead 2f out, fdd. *nk* **71**
1998 **DINAR 9** [5] 5-7-12 (52)(2ow)(6oh) F Norton 11/1: 302027: Chsd ldr, fdd fnl 2f: see 1646. *nk* **45**
1635 **CRYSTAL CREEK 25** [3] 4-10-0 (82) R Hughes 7/1: 50-068: Led 1m, sn btn: op 5/1: see 1635 (1m). *1½* **73**
8 ran Time 2m 06.9 (4.6) (The Queen) Sir Michael Stoute Newmarket.

2191

4.15 E-MAIL CLAIMER 4YO+ (F) 2m Good/Firm 39 -29 Slow
£2383 £681 £340

1996 **FUJIYAMA CREST 9** [5] R Curtis 8-9-0 J Lowe 12/1: 3-0001: 8 b g Roi Danzig - Snoozy Time (Cavo Doro) **62**
Chsd ldr, went on 4f out, drvn & held on well from over 1f out, gamely: op 8/1: 3rd of 7 fnl '99 start (h'cap, rtd 75): 97/98 Stratford hdle wnr (nov, rtd 108h, 3m, firm & gd): lightly rcd on the level since '96 Ascot win (h'cap, rtd 90, Sir Michael Stoute): eff at 14f/2m on firm & gd: likes to race with/force the pace: eff with/without a vis.
3521} **PRINCESS TOPAZ 309** [2] G M McCourt 6-8-9 D O'Donohoe 100/30: 0035-2: 6 b m Midyan - Diamond *1* **55**
Princess (Horage) Trkd ldrs, prog to press wnr fnl 2f, ev ch ins last, held nr fin: op 3/1: tried hdles in 99/00 (rnr-up, rtd 88h, mdn hdle): unplcd last term (rtd 72, h'cap): '98 Newmarket wnr (h'cap, rtd 77 & 60, C Cyzer): suited by 12/14f, stays 2m well: acts on firm & gd, dislikes softer: likes a stiff/gall trk, handles any: gd reapp.
1894 **MONDRAGON 13** [8] Mrs M Reveley 10-8-8 T E Durcan 10/1: 04-253: 10 b g Niniski - La Lutine (My *1* **53$**
Swallow) Settled rear, rdn & styd on fnl 3f, not pace to chall: prob flattered but well h'capped on best form.
*1660 **HULLBANK 24** [7] W W Haigh 10-9-3 G Carter 11/2: 255-14: Rear, prog/chsd ldrs 1f out, held nr fin. *3* **59**
1251 **PIPED ABOARD 46** [4] 5-9-9 (vis) R Hughes 11/8 FAV: /00-35: Towards rear, switched/effort over 2f *3* **62**
out, sn btn: 6 wk abs: well bckd: btr 1251 (12f).
1597 **EUROLINK APACHE 26** [6] 5-9-6 (BL) K Darley 5/1: /24056: Held up, eff 3f out, al held: see 1597, 565. *1½* **58$**
4578} **STAR MANAGER 238** [1] 10-8-2 J Mackay (5) 50/1: 0000-7: Led till 4f out, sn btn: Flat reapp, jumps *1½* **39$**
fit (rnr-up, sell h'cap, rtd 69h): unplcd last term (rtd 48, h'cap & 43a): '98 Epsom wnr (clmr, rtd 79, P Cole): eff at 1m/10f on firm & soft grnd: runs well fresh & handles any track.
1707 **CALIFORNIA SON 22** [3] 4-8-2 N Pollard 50/1: 520-U8: Chsd ldrs halfway, btn 2f out: mod form. *4* **35**
-- **FAIR FINNISH** [9] 6-9-9 L Vickers (7) 50/1: 5/9: Struggling halfway: jumps fit, May wnr at Huntingdon *13* **46**
(nov h'cap, rtd 69h, 3m2f): only mod form on the level previously.
9 ran Time 3m 35.00 (10.8) (Glazer, Harris & Swaden) R Curtis Lambourn, Berks.

2192

4.45 RACING HCAP DIV 1 3YO+ 0-60 (F) 6f Good/Firm 39 -09 Slow **[58]**
£2593 £741 £370 3 yo rec 7 lb Raced across track, first 3 home on stands side

2124 **FAIRY PRINCE 3** [19] Mrs A L M King 7-9-12 (56) P M Quinn (3) 9/2: 0-0451: 7 b g Fairy King - Danger **62**
Ahead (Mill Reef) Chsd ldr stands side, rdn/prog to lead over 1f out, styd on strongly, rdn out: qck reapp: rnr-up 4 times last term (rtd 62, h'cap, incl in a visor): '98 Beverley wnr (stks, rtd 74 in a h'cap): suited by 5/6f on firm & gd/soft grnd, any trk, likes an uphill finish: on a handy mark, could win again.
1953 **BE MY WISH 11** [7] W A O'Gorman 5-9-12 (56) M Roberts 11/2: 45-322: 5 b m Be My Chief - Spinner *½* **58**
(Blue Cashmere) Rcd stands side after 1f, rdn/bhd halfway, styd on strongly from over 1f out, nrst fin: win at 7f.
2158 **YOUNG BIGWIG 2** [15] D W Chapman 6-9-11 (55) N Pollard 8/1: 603453: 6 b g Anita's Prince - Humble *1* **55**
Mission (Shack) Chsd ldrs stands side, ch 1f out, kept on onepace: qck reapp: on a fair mark: see 425 (AW).
1887 **ZEPPO 13** [3] B R Millman 5-9-13 (57) G Hind 12/1: -04064: Cl-up far side, ch ins last, held nr fin. *nk* **56**
2032 **MUJAS MAGIC 8** [11] 5-9-4 (48)(vis) R Fitzpatrick (3) 25/1: 205005: Chsd ldrs towards centre, briefly *½* **45**
no room/rdn over 1f out, kept on onepace: see 187 (AW).
1910 **EASTERN RAINBOW 12** [17] 4-8-8 (38)(bl) Iona Wands (5) 4/1 FAV: -00236: Nvr pace to chall stds side. *nk* **34**
2015 **EASTERN PROPHETS 8** [14] 7-9-10 (54)(bl) A Clark 20/1: 0-3007: Held up stands side, kept on fnl *nk* **49**
2f, nrst fin: blnks reapplied: op 14/1: see 1258.
1971 **ANOTHER VICTIM 10** [5] 6-8-9 (39) I Mongan (5) 20/1: 003008: Led far side group, btn 1f out. *shd* **34**
1681 **PRIX STAR 23** [1] 5-10-0 (58) J Fanning 12/1: 5-0329: Cl-up far side 5f: op 10/1: see 82 (AW). *hd* **52**
1794 **CORN DOLLY 18** [8] 4-8-13 (43) S Carson (5) 20/1: -25000: Chsd ldr, onepace fnl 2f: 10th: see 225. *nk* **36**
1358 **SOUNDS LUCKY 27** [10] 4-9-9 (53)(vis) C Cogan (5) 16/1: 416050: Chsd ldrs 5f: 11th: btr 563 (AW, 5f). *3½* **37**
2101} **ANGUS THE BOLD 373** [4] 4-9-1 (45) J Tate 33/1: 2/00-0: Bhd far side fnl 2f: 12th: reapp: mod form *1½* **25**
last term for J L Eyre: rnr-up sole '98 start (mdn seller, rtd 68, J Berry): eff at 5f & handles gd/soft grnd.
674 **JACK TO A KING 104** [12] 5-9-2 (46)(bl) J Weaver 8/1: 202120: Led overall in centre & sn clr, rdn/ *hd* **25**
hdd over 1f out & wknd: 13th: op 12/1: abs, prev with J Balding: will apprec drop to 5f: see 609 (AW, 5f).
2015 **Sammal 8** [6] 4-9-2 (46) O Pears 12/1: 1843 **Tawn Again 16** [13] 4-8-5 (35) T E Durcan 20/1:
896 **Rowlandsons Stud 74** [16] 7-8-3 (33)(t) D O'Donohoe 40/1712 **Eltars 22** [2] 3-8-8 (45) S Righton 33/1:
1818 **Belle Of Hearts 17** [9] 4-8-3 (33) N Carlisle 50/1: 1818 **Little Chapel 17** [20] 4-9-6 (50) Jonjo Fowle (7) 20/1:
1731 **Charlie Sillett 21** [18] 8-9-7 (51)(VIS) J D Smith 33/1:
20 ran Time 1m 13.7 (2.9) (All The Kings Horses) Mrs A L M King Wilmcote, Warwicks.

2193

5.15 RACING HCAP DIV 2 3YO+ 0-60 (F) 6f Good/Firm 39 +06 Fast **[58]**
£2593 £741 £370 3 yo rec 7 lb Raced across track, no advantage

1923 **MARINO STREET 12** [11] B A McMahon 7-9-4 (48) T E Durcan 10/1: 560-21: 7 b m Totem - Demerger **55**
(Dominion) Chsd ldrs centre, rdn/led over 1f out, styd on well ins last, drvn out: best time of day: op 8/1: '99 wnr at Warwick (fill h'cap) & Haydock (h'cap, rtd 50 at best): plcd in '98 (h'caps, rtd 44 & 29a, P Evans): eff at 5/6f, stays 7.5f: acts on firm, gd & fibresand: eff with/without blnks: has run well fresh & handles any trk.
1629 **GARNOCK VALLEY 25** [14] A Berry 10-9-4 (48) G Carter 20/1: 400362: 10 b g Dowsing - Sunley Sinner *1½* **49**
(Try My Best) Rear stands side, styd on well fnl 2f, not reach wnr: v tough (13 wins from 97 runs): see 47 (AW).
1923 **PREMIUM PRINCESS 12** [8] J J Quinn 5-9-6 (50) J Stack 14/1: 000553: 5 b m Distant Relative - Solemn *1* **49**
Occasion (Secreto) Mid-div, towards centre, kept on fnl 2f, not pace to chall: op 12/1: on a fair mark: see 802.
*1913 **AUBRIETA 12** [4] D Haydn Jones 4-9-9 (53)(bl) Dean McKeown 8/1: 450114: Chsd ldrs far side, kept *2* **47**
on onepace inside last: encouraging return to turf, remains in gd heart: see 1913 (AW clmr).
2097 **GRAND ESTATE 5** [12] 5-9-11 (55) N Pollard 8/1: 300545: In tch centre, onepace fnl 1f: qck reapp. *shd* **49**
2124 **CALANDRELLA 3** [7] 7-8-8 (38) G Sparkes (7) 33/1: -00006: Led overall far side for 2f, held fnl 1f. *½* **30**

NOTTINGHAM MONDAY JUNE 26TH Lefthand, Galloping Track

1953 **WISHBONE ALLEY** 11 [6] 5-9-1 (45)(bl) A Clark 25/1: 300007: Chsd ldrs centre 5f: blnks reapp. ¾ 35
1923 **SKYERS FLYER** 12 [10] 6-8-9 (39) R Fitzpatrick (3) 33/1: -00008: Towards centre, nvr pace to chall. ¾ 27
1806 **KOMASEPH** 17 [16] 8-8-3 (33) S Righton 33/1: 606409: Hmpd start, nvr on terms stds side: see 602 (AW)1¼ 18
2107 **PRESS AHEAD** 4 [18] 5-9-11 (55) S Finnamore (5) 16/1: 016000: Cl-up centre, led after 2f till over 1f ½ 38
out, fdd: 10th: op 14/1: qck reapp: see 1068 (clmr).
1842 **HEAVENLY MISS** 16 [19] 6-9-12 (56)(bl) I Mongan (5) 12/1: 414000: Cl-up stds side 4f: 11th: see 1244. nk 38
1913 **TROJAN HERO** 12 [17] 9-8-5 (35) J Tate 33/1: 006060: In tch stands side 4f: 12th: see 201 (AW, seller). 1½ 13
2054 **SIR JACK** 7 [2] 4-9-12 (56) J Weaver 5/2 FAV: 002440: Al twds rear far side, 13th: bckd, op 7/2: btr 2054. ½ 32
*2031 **OARE KITE** 8 [20] 5-9-8 (52)(bl) J Mackay (5) 7/2: 632010: Prom stands side 4f: 17th: bckd, op 4/1. 0
2184 **Malaah** 1 [15] 4-9-2 (46)(bl) A Daly 20/1:   1815 **Sound The Trumpet** 17 [3] 8-8-8 (38)(t) A Mackay 33/1:
1910 **Bataleur** 12 [13] 7-8-12 (42) R Lappin 25/1:   1868 **Defiance** 14 [9] 5-8-2 (32) C Rutter 25/1:
*1681 **Mybotye** 23 [1] 7-10-0 (58)(t) G Faulkner (3) 12/1:   3744} **Upper Chamber** 297 [5] 4-8-13 (43) J Fanning 33/1:
20 ran   Time 1m 12.8 (2.0)   (Roy Penton)   B A McMahon Hopwas, Staffs.

YARMOUTH MONDAY JUNE 26TH Lefthand, Flat, Fair Track

Official Going   GOOD/FIRM. Stalls: Str Course - Far Side; 14f - Stands Side; Rem - Inside.

2194   6.40 MILLS & REEVE MDN 3YO+ (D)   1m6f   Good/Firm 25   -01 Slow
£3068   £944   £472   £236   3 yo rec 17lb

1982 **MAJESTIC BAY** 10 [3] P W Harris 4-9-11 D Holland 7/4: 23-301: 4 b g Unfuwain - That'll Be The Day 77
(Thatching) Made all, styd on well fnl 2f, drvn out: op 6/4: dual '99 rnr-up (mdn, rtd 90): eff at 10f, stays 14f
v well: acts on firm, gd, poss hvy: acts on any trk & likes to force the pace: best without blnks.
957 **CARNBREA DANCER** 69 [1] W J Haggas 3-8-3 J F Egan 5/6 FAV: 52: 3 b f Suave Dancer - Cambrea ½ 72
Belle (Kefaah) Settled rear, hdwy & edged left 2f out, styd on well ins last, just held: nicely bckd, 10 wk abs:
styd this longer 14f trip well & shld win sn at this dist, handles fast grnd: see 957.
1949 **TUFTY HOPPER** 11 [2] P Howling 3-8-8 R Mullen 9/2: 422433: 3 b g Rock Hopper - Melancolia (Legend 2 74$
Of France) Chsd ldr, ev ch until rdn & not qckn ins last: clr rem: stays 14f on fast: gd run at the weights &
would go close in a h'cap if running to this form again: see 1949.
483 **HAMERKOP** 138 [4] John Berry 5-9-6 P Doe 50/1: 605-04: Trkd ldrs, wknd qckly 3f: long abs: 23 44$
impossible task at the weights (offic only 20): see 483.
1369 **TRUE ROMANCE** 38 [5] 4-9-11 D McGaffin (5) 50/1: /00005: In tch, wknd rapidly fnl 3f: no form. 5 45$
5 ran   Time 3m 01.5 (3.7)   (The Quiet Ones)   P W Harris Aldbury, Herts

2195   7.10 AEROPAK HCAP STKS 3YO 0-75 (E)   1m6f   Good/Firm 25   -20 Slow   [75]
£2821   £868   £434   £217

1758 **TYPHOON TILLY** 19 [1] C F Wall 3-8-4 (51) R Mullen 6/1: 000-31: 3 b g Hernando - Meavy (Kalaglow) 61
Settled rear, swtchd/hdwy 2f out, rdn to lead well ins last, drvn out: unplcd at up to 1m in '99 (rtd 60, mdn):
apprec recent step up in trip to 12/14f, further shld suit: acts on fast & gd/soft: rate more highly, win again.
*1911 **PENSHIEL** 12 [3] J L Dunlop 3-9-7 (68) T Quinn 11/8 FAV: 00-112: 3 b g Mtoto - Highland Ceilidh ¾ 77
(Scottish Reel) Cl-up, rdn to lead over 2f out, hdd ins last, rallied, not btn far: nicely bckd & well clr rem:
eff at 12/14f: remains on the up-grade & shld regain wng ways sn: see 1911.
*2141 **LOVE BITTEN** 3 [2] M Johnston 3-9-6 (67) R Ffrench 7/2: 045213: 3 b g Darshaan - Kentmere (Galetto) 6 70
Set stdy pace, hdd over 2f out, sn not pace of front 2: nicely bckd, qck reapp: longer 14f trip: see 2141.
1911 **HARD DAYS NIGHT** 12 [5] M Blanshard 3-7-10 (43)(7oh) G Bardwell 50/1: -00064: Rcd keenly cl-up, 1¾ 44$
fdd fnl 2f: stiffish task & not disgraced at these wng: see 1911.
1967 **THREE WHITE SOX** 10 [7] 3-9-4 (65) D Holland 7/1: 0-0325: Handy, rdn/eff 3f out, sn btn: up in trip. 2 64
1967 **DANDES RAMBO** 10 [4] 3-8-7 (54) P Doe 12/1: 0-5636: Rear, hung left/fdd 3f out: op 8/1, longer 14f trip. 7 46
1967 **PERCUSSION** 10 [6] 3-8-7 (54) S Whitworth 8/1: -00647: Bhd, eff 4f out, sn held/wknd: op 6/1, up in trip. 2 44
7 ran   Time 3m 04.1 (6.3)   (M Tilbrook)   C F Wall Newmarket

2196   7.40 SUTTON SELLER 2YO (G)   5f43y str   Good/Firm 25   -41 Slow
£1834   £524   £262

1916 **SOME DUST** 12 [4] W G M Turner 2-8-11 A Daly 6/4 FAV: -U021: 2 ch c King's Signet - Some Dream 61
(Vitiges) Made all, rdn clr fnl 1f: nicely bckd, no bid: cheaply bought May foal, dam a juv hdle wnr, sire
a sprinter: likes to force the pace over an easy or sharp 5f on fast & equitrack.
1950 **HARRY JUNIOR** 11 [5] C A Dwyer 2-8-7 (VIS) D Holland 9/2: 6052: 2 b c River Falls - Badger Bay 3 52
(Salt Dome) Prom, rdn, hung left & not pace of wnr appr fnl 1f: bckd from 7/1 & an imprvd eff in 1st time
visor here: poss stays an easy 5f on fast grnd: see 712.
2052 **DIAMOND MILLENNIUM** 7 [3] P D Evans 2-8-6 J F Egan 2/1: 505333: 2 ch f Clantime - Innocent 1½ 43
Abroad (Viking) Trkd wnr, rdn/btn fnl 2f: qck reapp: clr rem: see 2052, 849.
2009 **LITTLE MOUSE** 9 [1] G G Margarson 2-8-6 M Baird 10/1: 400: Prom, rdn/lost tch fnl 2f: op 8/1. 8 27
1937 **HOLBECK** 11 [2] 2-8-6 G Carter 9/1: 655: Dwelt, al last: no sign of ability. 7 12
5 ran   Time 1m 03.4 (3.3)   (Tocs Ltd)   W G M Turner Corton Denham, Somerset

2197   8.10 HEMBLINGTON EBF CLASS STKS 3YO 0-95 (B)   6f str   Good/Firm 25   +03 Fast
£8479   £3216   £1608   £731

1733 **DANDY NIGHT** 21 [6] B Hanbury 3-8-7 A Beech 13/2: 402-01: 3 b f Lion Cavern - Desert Venus (Green 99
Desert) Sltly hmpd start, sn led, styd on strongly fnl 1f, drvn out: best time of day: '99 debut scorer at
Newmarket (mdn, rtd 101 at best): eff at 5/6f, has tried 7f: acts on firm, gd/soft & a gall or easy trk:
loves to force the pace: genuine & useful filly who could win in Listed company sn.
955 **ABDERIAN** 69 [4] J Noseda 3-8-11 D Holland 5/1: 42-502: 3 b c Machiavellian - Aminata (Glenstal) 1 99
Trkd wnr thr'out, drvn & styd on ins last, not pace of wnr: 10 wk abs & a better effort here dropped back to 6f.
1694 **BAILEYS WHIRLWIND** 23 [3] M L W Bell 3-8-6 R Mullen 3/2: 10-503: 3 b f Mister Baileys - Tornado ¾ 92
Cat (Storm Cat) Front rank, rdn/no extra ins fnl 1f: sound run: see 1186.
1694 **FLOWINGTON** 23 [2] N P Littmoden 3-8-6 J F Egan 12/1: 00-504: Handy, wknd appr fnl 1f: btr 1371. 3½ 84

704

YARMOUTH MONDAY JUNE 26TH Lefthand, Flat, Fair Track

1987 **ALFIE LEE** 9 [1] 3-8-9 W Ryan 20/1: 00-005: Waited with, hdwy 2f out, nvr with ldrs: '99 Goodwood 1¼ 84
wnr (mdn, rtd 86 at best): eff at 5f on fast & gd grnd: handles a sharp/undul trk: h'cap company will suit.
1830 **TEODORA** 17 [7] 3-8-6 P Doe 8/1: 3-5006: Hmpd start, nvr a factor: drop in trip: btr 995. 3 74
*1843 **SHINBONE ALLEY** 16 [5] 3-8-13 G Carter 11/4 FAV: 05-517: Veered right start, sn prom, lost tch ½ 80
fnl 2f: better expected after a gd performance in 1843 (5f mdn).
1534 **SUDRA** 30 [8] 3-8-9 T Quinn 7/2: 310-08: Sn rdn in rear, al bhd: see 1534. 8 60
8 ran   Time 1m 11.7 (1.3)   (Abdullah Ali)   B Hanbury Newmarket

2198   8.40 BAZUKA FILLIES MDN 3YO (D)   1m str   Good/Firm 25   -108 Slow
£3558   £1095   £547   £273

1185 **MOSELLE** 50 [6] W J Haggas 3-8-11 T Quinn 4/7 FAV: 3-201: 3 b f Mtoto - Miquette (Fabulous Dancer) 90
Chsd ldr, led on bit 5f out, easily went clr fnl 2f, eased ins last, hard held: val 8/10L: recently down the
field in the 1,000 Guineas: showed promise sole '99 start (plcd, rtd 93, Listed): eff at 1m/10f on fast &
soft grnd: handles any trk & runs well fresh: useful filly, simple task here.
-- **LITIGIOUS** [3] K R Burke 3-8-11 J F Egan 20/1: 2: 3 b f Mtoto - Kiomi (Niniski) 4 70
Chsd ldr, rdn & not pace of easy wnr fnl 2f: came up against a useful rival today: poss stays 1m on fast.
2024 **ALZITA** 8 [2] J A R Toller 3-8-11 S Whitworth 16/1: 0-03: 3 b f Alzao - Tiavanita (J O Tobin) 1½ 67
Pulled hard cl-up, drvn & outpcd fnl 3f: low grade h'caps shld now suit: see 2024.
1811 **MUSALLIAH** 17 [4] J L Dunlop 3-8-11 R Hills 7/4: 04: Dwelt, hdwy from rear 4f out, hung left & ½ 66
btn over 2f out: poss not handle this fast grnd: shade better on gd/soft in 1811.
1548 **HANOI** 28 [1] 3-8-11 (bl) J Lowe 50/1: 05: Set ridiculously slow pace, hdd 5f out, wknd fnl 2f. 2½ 61
5 ran   Time 1m 45.8 (10.7)   (Mr & Mrs G Middlebrook/Mr & Mrs P Brain)   W J Haggas Newmarket

2199   9.10 HAPPINOSE HCAP 3YO+ 0-75 (E)   1m2f21y   Good/Firm 25   +02 Fast   [73]
£2951   £908   £454   £227   3 yo rec 12lb

1852 **SWINGING THE BLUES** 15 [5] C A Dwyer 6-8-9 (54)(vis) J F Egan 7/1: 12-001: 6 b g Bluebird - Winsong 55
Melody (Music Maestro) Waited with, hdwy to lead appr fnl 1f, styd on strongly & drvn out to hold on: '99 Redcar
wnr (h'caps, rtd 56): rtd 93h over hdles in 98/99: '98 wnr at Nottingham & again at Redcar (h'caps, rtd 68 at
best): eff at 1m/10f, has tried 12f: acts on firm, gd/soft & any trk, likes Redcar: eff with/without a visor.
1807 **ROGUE SPIRIT** 17 [1] P W Harris 4-9-8 (67) D Holland 12/1: 004002: 4 b g Petong - Quick Profit hd 68
(Formidable) Set gd pace, drvn/hdd dist, rallied ins last, just held: up in trip & stys 10f well: win similar.
1442 **LYCIAN** 35 [6] J A R Toller 5-8-11 (56) S Whitworth 6/1: 00-603: 5 b g Lycius - Perfect Time shd 57
(Dance Of Life) Rcd keenly in rear, hdwy halfway, styd on well ins last, nvr btn far: up in trip: eff at 1m/10f.
1921 **STROMSHOLM** 12 [7] J R Fanshawe 4-9-8 (67) T Quinn 7/4 FAV: 406324: Pulled hard in rear, short of 1½ 65
room 3f out, swtchd/ran on well ins last, nvr nrr: another sound run, lks capable of wng similar: see 1921.
4540} **EDIFICE** 242 [3] 4-9-11 (70) R Mullen 12/1: 0400-5: Trkd ldrs, rdn & kept on onepace ins last: shd 68
reapp: 4th at best in '99 (mdn, rtd 78 at best): eff around 10f on firm grnd.
1785 **ELMS SCHOOLGIRL** 18 [10] 4-9-8 (67) J Tate 14/1: 53-206: Waited with, outpcd 3f out, rallied & nk 64
hdwy 2f out, no extra well ins last: see 1332 (fills h'cap, firm).
1150 **HERR TRIGGER** 52 [4] 9-8-3 (48)(bl) J Lowe 16/1: 405-07: Cl-up, chall 3f out, btn dist: abs. 2½ 41
705 **GOLD BLADE** 95 [9] 11-8-0 (45) G Bardwell 20/1: 25-408: Nvr a threat after 3 month abs: see 412 (A/W). 1¾ 35
1615 **EN GRISAILLE** 26 [12] 4-7-13 (44) P Doe 11/1: 0-009: Prom, hung left & wknd fnl 3f: see 1265. 5 26
1921 **ZAHA** 12 [11] 5-9-2 (61) Dean McKeown 5/1: 600140: Waited with, drvn & fdd fnl 2f, fin last: btr 1370. 1¼ 40
10 ran   Time 2m 06.5 (2.3)   (S B Components (International) Ltd)   C A Dwyer Newmarket

MUSSELBURGH   MONDAY JUNE 26TH   Righthand, Sharp Track

Official Going   FIRM. Stalls: Inside, Except 5f & 2m - Stands Side.

2200   2.00 FLAMING JUNE SELLER 2YO (F)   5f   Good/Firm 33   -19 Slow
£2604   £744   £372

1918 **TOMMY SMITH** 12 [5] J S Wainwright 2-8-11 J Carroll 3/1: 0041: 2 ch g Timeless Times - Superstream 68
(Superpower) Sn bhd & hung right, hdwy over 1f out, styd on to lead cl-home, drvn out: no bid: Mar foal,
dam unrcd: apprec drop into sell grade & eff at 5f on gd/firm.
1906 **ITALIAN AFFAIR** 12 [6] A Bailey 2-8-6 G Duffield 5/4 FAV: 0202: 2 ch f Fumo Di Londra - Sergentti hd 62
(Common Grounds) Led over 2f out, kept on for press till collared cl-home, just btn: clr of rem, well bckd.
1628 **ANGELAS HUSBAND** 25 [2] A Dickman 2-8-11 (BL) D Mernagh (3) 7/1: 6003: 2 b c Up And At 'Em - 3 58
Lake Poopo (Persian Heights) Cl-up, rdn over 2f out, held when hmpd dist: op 9/2, tried blnks: see 1161.
2014 **PAT PINKNEY** 8 [1] E J Alston 2-8-6 W Supple 4/1: -054: Prom, rdn & onepace over 1f out: see 1776. hd 52
1916 **ROYLE FAMILY** 12 [3] 2-8-11 P Bradley (5) 14/1: -4545: Led till over 2f out, sn btn & hung left 1½ 53
appr fnl 1f: op 10/1: jockey received a 3 day careless riding ban: see 1206 (AW), 856.
2045 **MONICA** 7 [4] 2-8-6 R Winston 100/1: 00456: In tch, btn 2f out: wknd. 4 36
6 ran   Time 1m 0.1 (2.6)   (T W Heseltine)   J S Wainwright Kennythorpe, N Yorks

2201   2.30 ROYAL BANK NOV AUCT STKS 2YO (F)   7f30y rnd   Good/Firm 33   -14 Slow
£2730   £840   £420   £210

*1950 **SAND BANKES** 11 [4] W G M Turner 2-9-1 (vis) Darren Williams (7) 8/1: 061211: 2 ch c Efisio - 79
Isabella Sharp (Sharpo) Made all, kept on well fnl 1f, rdn out: big drifter from 7/2 despite earlier wins at
Chepstow & Yarmouth (sells): Jan foal, dam sprinter: eff over 6/7f on fast, hvy & fibresand: handles any trk
& best in a visor now: loves to dominate, proving tough & progressive.
1844 **MUJALINA** 16 [2] E J O'Neill 2-9-1 J Carroll 7/1: 02: 2 b c Mujadil - Talina's Law (Law Society) 2½ 67
Prom, eff to chase wnr over 1f out, onepace: bckd from 16/1 & imprvd for debut stepped up to 7f: handles gd/fm.
*1602 **CO DOT UK** 26 [1] K A Ryan 2-9-3 F Lynch 7/2: 53013: 2 b g Distant Relative - Cubist (Tate Gallery) 3 69
Handy, rdn & no impress over 1f out: better expected after 1602 (6f, soft grnd).
*2057 **PERSIAN CAT** 6 [5] Sir Mark Prescott 2-8-11 G Duffield 2/5 FAV: 514: Keen, chsd wnr till btn over 1 61
1f out: hvly bckd at odds-on & disapp: reportedly unsuited by this officially firm grnd, handled fast in 2057.

1429 **WHARFEDALE GHOST 35** [3] 2-8-6 R Winston 100/1: 005: Al bhd: see 1206.   *21* **20**
5 ran   Time 1m 28.3 (3.4)   (T Lightbowne)   W G M Turner Corton Denham, Somerset

---

2202   **3.00 ROYAL BANK FILLIES HCAP 3YO+ 0-65 (F)**   **1m4f**   **Good/Firm 33   +06 Fast**   **[47]**
£2808   £864   £432   £216   3 yo rec 14lb

*1955 **ALEXANDRINE 11** [8] Sir Mark Prescott 3-9-11 (58) G Duffield 2/5 FAV: 060-11: 3 b f Nashwan - **65**
Alruccaba (Crystal Palace) Trkd ldr, led over 1f out, kept on well: well bckd, best time of day,
top-weight: recently won at Yarmouth (fills h'cap): unplcd in 3 back-end mdns in '99 (rtd 56): eff at 10f,
enjoyed this step up to 12f & acts on fast: runs well fresh: improving as she steps up in trip, land hat-trick.
2048 **COSMIC CASE 7** [5] J S Goldie 5-9-0 (33) A McGlone 12/1: 040042: 5 b m Casteddu - La Fontainova   2½   **33**
(Lafontaine) In tch, hdwy to chase wnr appr fnl 1f, onepace: well h'capped, but only 1 win from 44 starts.
1939 **ASHLEIGH BAKER 11** [7] M Johnston 5-9-10 (43) K Dalgleish (7) 8/1: 3-6403: 5 b m Don't Forget Me -   2½   **39**
Gayla Orchestra (Lord Gayle) Cl-up, rdn & sltly outpcd over 2f out, rallied over 1f out, no impress: op 6/1.
2109 **PICCADILLY 4** [3] Miss Kate Milligan 5-9-4 (37) R Winston 12/1: 0-2004: Led till over 1f out, no   *hd*   **33**
extra: op 8/1, clr of rem, quick reapp: best 1432.
1658 **BONDI BAY 24** [6] 3-9-6 (53) F Lynch 25/1: 201005: Handy, btn 2f out: thrice below 1274 (sell, 10f).   6   **41**
1908 **ROMA 12** [2] 5-9-2 (35) (bl) W Supple 25/1: 0-0006: Slow away, wll in rr, wknd 3f out.   5   **16**
2007 **MILL AFRIQUE 9** [4] 4-9-9 (42) A Culhane 20/1: 000-07: Al bhd: see 2007 (10f).   6   **15**
1496 **AN SMEARDUBH 31** [9] 4-9-3 (36) P McCabe 7/1: 0-0068: Handy, wknd over 3f out: see 603.   16   **0**
8 ran   Time 2m 33.8 (3.2)   (Miss K Rausing)   Sir Mark Prescott Newmarket

---

2203   **3.30 RBS STAYERS HCAP 3YO+ 0-70 (E)**   **2m**   **Good/Firm 33   -18 Slow**   **[59]**
£5538   £1704   £852   £426   3 yo rec 20lb

2048 **SANDABAR 7** [7] Mrs M Reveley 7-10-0 (59)(t) A Culhane 13/2: -00321: 7 b g Green Desert -   **65**
Children's Corner (Top Ville) Trkd ldrs, imprvd to lead ent fnl 1f, ran on well, rdn out: top weight, op 7/2: '99
Ripon h'cap (h'cap, rtd 63): 98/99 wnr 4 times over hdles (rtd 124h, eff at 2m1f on fast): eff arnd 10/12f, apprec
this step up to 2m: acts on gd, loves fast & firm grnd: handles any trk, wears a t-strap: gd weight carrier: tough.
*2156 **XELLERON 2** [4] M Johnston 3-7-10 (47)(6ex)(1oh) K Dalgleish(7) 4/5 FAV: U01112: 3 b g Be My Guest   *nk*   **52**
- Excellent Alibi (Exceller) Tried to make all, collared ent fnl 1f, rallied & only just btn: clr rem, fine run.
2050 **NORTHERN MOTTO 7** [8] J S Goldie 7-9-6 (51) A McGlone 5/1: 000333: 7 b g Mtoto - Soulful (Zino)   5   **51**
Prom, rdn & onepcd fnl 2f: op 7/2: loves Chester/Musselburgh: see 2050 (14f here).
2016 **BATOUTOFTHEBLUE 8** [5] W W Haigh 3-7-9-1 (46) F Lynch 15/2: 43-134: Rear, rdn to improve 2f out,   *1*   **45**
not pace to chall: op 5/1: lightly rcd this term: see 797 (reapp, gd/soft grnd).
2037 **DANGER BABY 7** [3] 10-9-3 (48) Claire Bryan (5) 11/1: 40-625: Chsd ldrs till outpcd fnl 2f: op 8/1.   6   **41**
2037 **URGENT REPLY 7** [2] 7-7-10 (27) P Fessey 13/2: -00066: Front rank, wknd over 3f out: see 1614 (12f).   3   **17**
1867 **HIGHFIELD FIZZ 14** [6] 8-8-10 (41) T Williams 12/1: P00167: Slowly away, eff 3f out, sn btn & fin last.   8   **23**
7 ran   Time 3m 30.7 (8.2)   (W Williams)   Mrs M Reveley Lingdale, N Yorks

---

2204   **4.00 WAVERLEY MDN 3YO+ (D)**   **5f**   **Good/Firm 33   -01 Slow**
£2744   £784   £392   3 yo rec 6 lb

2047 **PARADISE YANGSHUO 7** [4] E J Alston 3-8-9 W Supple 9/2: 0-0041: 3 b f Whittingham - Poly Static   **49**
(Statoblest) Nvr far away, went on ins fnl 1f, held on well, drvn out: rnr-up thrice in '99 (sell/clmrs for M
Channon, rtd 63 at best): suited by 5f: handles gd/soft, loves fast/firm grnd: fine run at today's weights.
1578 **TARTAN ISLAND 27** [1] I Semple 3-9-0 (VIS) R Winston 33/1: 00-002: 3 b g Turtle Island - Welsh Harp   ¾   **52**
(Mtoto) Trkd ldrs, switched dist, styd on under press & not btn far: imprvd eff in 1st time visor: eff at 5f on fast.
1688 **POLAR HAZE 23** [2] Miss S E Hall 3-9-0 G Duffield 30/100 FAV: 026-23: 3 ch g Polar Falcon - Sky Music   ¾   **50**
(Absalom) Set pace till collared ins last, no extra: hvly bckd: would have met today's rivals on much worse
terms in h'cap company, had the form to win this: see 1688 (C/D).
2096 **CONSIDERATION 5** [5] A Berry 3-8-9 P Bradley (5) 9/2: 44-024: In tch, onepcd ins fnl 1f: qck reapp.   1¾   **40**
813} **MITCHELLS MAYHEM 444** [6] 3-8-9 Darren Williams (7) 20/1: 6-5: Dsptd lead 3f, grad fdd: reapp: 5   **28**
6th at Lingfield (AW mdn, rtd 42a) on sole '99 start: sire a smart sprinter: with W Turner.
2140 **LITTLE LES 3** [3] 4-9-6 D Mernagh (3) 66/1: 606: Slowly away, nvr a factor: quick reapp.   3½   **23**
6 ran   Time 59.2 (1.7)   (Valley Paddocks Racing Ltd)   E J Alston Longton, Lancs

---

2205   **4.30 BALMY DAYS HCAP 3YO 0-65 (F)**   **1m rnd**   **Good/Firm 33   -04 Slow**   **[72]**
£2744   £784   £392

1939 **PHILAGAIN 11** [2] Miss L A Peratt 3-7-10 (40) (3oh) N Kennedy 20/1: 00-401: 3 b f Ardkinglass -   **42**
Andalucia (Rheingold) Prom, forged ahead ins fnl 1f, ran on well, shade cosily: mainly mod form prev: half
sister to a couple of mid-dist wnrs, sire high-class at 7f: eff at 1m on fast grnd, handles a sharp trk.
1494 **ABSINTHER 31** [9] E J Alston 3-9-2 (60) G Duffield 10/1: 300-02: 3 b g Presidium - Heavenly Queen   ½   **61**
(Scottish Reel) Tried to make all, hdd ins fnl 1f, kept on well & only just btn: eff over an easy 1m on fast grnd.
*2036 **RIOS DIAMOND 7** [5] M J Ryan 3-8-9 (53)(6ex) Darren Williams (7) 2/1 FAV: -20513: 3 b f Formidable -   ¾   **52**
Rio Piedras (Kala Shikari) Prom, kept on fnl 1f, btn arnd 1L: bckd: stays 1m, 14lbs higher than 2036 (6.8f).
1939 **BLUE LEGEND 11** [4] B Mactaggart 3-8-0 (44) D Mernagh (3) 12/1: 000-04: Chsd ldr, ev ch dist, no   *hd*   **42**
extra cl-home: btn just over 1L: see 1939.
2047 **SPEEDFIT FREE 7** [7] 3-9-7 (65) A Culhane 20/1: 04-005: In tch till outpcd halfway, kept on again fnl   ¾   **61**
1f: mkt drifter, top weight: btn arnd 2L over this longer 1m trip: see 2047 (5f here).
1477 **HAIKAL 32** [1] 3-9-6 (64)(BL) W Supple 3/1: 0-0046: Rcd keenly in tch, not qckn ins last: tried blnks.   ½   **59**
2046 **GRANITE CITY 7** [3] 3-7-10 (40)(1oh) K Dalgleish (7) 10/1: -00007: Rear, eff 2f out, no impress fnl 1f.   *nk*   **34**
2017 **ALPATHAR 8** [8] 3-8-11 (55) T Williams 7/2: -16648: Slowly away, nvr a factor: see 2017.   1¾   **45**
1804 **MIST OVER MEUGHER 17** [6] 3-7-10 (40)(11oh) J McAuley (4) 50/1: 00-009: Prom 4f, sn bhd & fin last.   11   **10**
9 ran   Time 1m 40.5 (3)   (C D Barber-Lomax)   Miss L A Perratt Ayr, Strathclyde

Official Going   GOOD/FIRM (GOOD in straight). Stalls: Inside.

2206
6.30 QUEEN FILLIES HCAP 3YO 0-70 (E)   **1m2f**   **Good/Firm 38   -05 Slow**   **[75]**
£2982   £852   £4267

1537 **SUMMER SONG** 30 [7]   E A L Dunlop 3-9-7 (42) R Hughes 4/1: 1-4531: 3 b f Green Desert - High Standard   **73**
(Kris) Chsd ldrs, went 2nd appr fnl 3f, led bef dist, just pshd out: bckd from 11/2: landed a private stks event
at Newmarket on sole '99 start (rtd 79): eff at 1m, suited by step up to 10f: acts on fast & gd/soft grnd.
1955 **IMARI** 11 [8]   N P Littmoden 3-9-2 (63) M Tebbutt 5/2 FAV: 250132: 3 b f Rock City - Misty Goddess   ½ **65**
(Godswalk) In tch, hdwy und press 3f out, ev ch till held towards fin: nicely bckd: progressive, see 1955, 1772.
1911 **BLESS** 12 [4]   M Madgwick 3-7-11 (44)(VIS)(1ow)(6oh) A Nicholls (0) 25/1: 006003: 3 ch f Beveled -   ¾ **45**
Ballystake (Ballacashtal) Led, clr 4f out, hdd bef fnl 1f, styd on: imprvd in visor: stays 10f on fast grnd.
1955 **SWEET ANGELINE** 11 [12]   G G Margarson 3-9-0 (61) P Robinson 6/1: 0-0054: Waited with, imprvd   nk **61**
3f out, chsd ldrs fnl 1f, unable to chall: bckd from 8/1: stays 10f: acts on firm/fast grnd, see 1345.
1607 **CHEZ BONITO** 26 [6]   3-7-10 (43)(8oh) G Baker (7) 16/1: -5205: In tch, prog & ev ch 2f out, sn onepace.   2 **40**
1793 **CUMBRIAN PRINCESS** 18 [4]   3-8-6 (53) D Sweeney 25/1: 0-0006: Rear, hdwy 2f out, sn same pace: 1½ **48**
clr rem, longer trip: '99 wnr at Pontefract (6f nurs, rtd 61): shld get at least 1m: acts on gd/soft grnd.
1914 **SADLERS SONG** 12 [5]   3-8-2 (49) Craig Williams 8/1: 05-507: Nvr a factor: see 1758.   4 **38**
1948 **ALPHA HEIGHTS** 11 [13]   3-8-8 (55) L Newman (3) 25/1: 0-0058: Chsd ldrs till 2f out: see 1521.   nk **43**
2051 **WILEMMGEO** 7 [3]   3-8-3 (50) Joanna Badger (7) 33/1: 505009: Al bhd: qck reapp, longer trip.   1¾ **36**
1796 **CAPPELLINA** 18 [1]   3-8-11 (58) S Drowne 20/1: 00-00: Chsd ldrs till 3f out: 10th on h'cap bow.   1¼ **42**
1446 **MAGIC SUNSET** 34 [9]   3-8-13 (60)(VIS) K Darley 12/1: 00-000: Prom 7f: 11th, visored.   5 **39**
1414 **PASADENA** 37 [2]   3-9-2 (63) Martin Dwyer 14/1: 04000: Slow away, al bhd: 12th, up in trip, see 934.   3½ **39**
1803 **SALIENT POINT** 17 [11]   3-9-5 (66) Pat Eddery 9/1: -50040: Handy till lost pl 3f out: 13th, up in trip.   1½ **39**
13 ran   Time 2m 09.0 (4.3)   (Maktoum Al Maktoum)   E A L Dunlop Newmarket.

2207
6.55 NAISMITHS HCAP 3YO+ 0-80 (D)   **6f**   **Good/Firm 38   -05 Slow**   **[80]**
£4218   £1298   £649   £324   3 yo rec 7 lb   A high draw is favoured

1887 **BEYOND CALCULATION** 13 [10]   J M Bradley 6-8-12 (64) P Fitzsimons (5) 14/1: -51501: 6 ch g Geiger   **70**
Counter - Placer Queen (Habitat) Bhd ldrs, led appr fnl 1f, rdn out: earlier won at Nottingham (class stks): '99
wnr here at Windsor, Bath, Thirsk & Brighton (h'caps, rtd 70): eff at 5f, suited by 6f, stays 7f: acts on firm, gd/
soft, handles fibresand, any trk, best on sharp ones, likes Windsor: suited up with/forcing the pace: tough.
*1953 **THATCHAM** 11 [5]   R W Armstrong 4-8-6 (58)(bl) G Hall 7/1: 200412: 4 ch g Thatching - Calaloo   ¾ **61**
Sioux (Our Native) Front rank & ev ch till held fnl 100y: bckd from 9/1: much imprvd back at 6f: see 1953.
2184 **SIHAFI** 1 [15]   D Nicholls 7-8-8 (53) A Nicholls (3) 4/1 FAV: 043023: 7 ch g Elmaamul - Kit's Double   hd **55**
(Spring Double) In tch, eff ent fnl 2f, kept on & edged left: well bckd from 13/2, ran yesterday, in gd heart.
2054 **FULL SPATE** 7 [16]   J M Bradley 5-8-11 (63) Pat Eddery 11/2: 360354: Bhd, eff & not clr run 2f   1¾ **60**
out, kept on for press: nicely bckd from 7/1, stablemate wnr, qck reapp: on a handy mark: see 1028.
2054 **STYLISH WAYS** 7 [7]   8-8-11 (63) T G McLaughlin 8/1: 0-0625: V slow away, late hdwy, nvr a factor.   1 **57**
1636 **DIAMOND GEEZER** 25 [12]   4-8-11 (63) R Smith (5) 10/1: 244306: Towards rear, eff 2f out, nvr dngrs.   ¾ **55**
2042 **DOCTOR DENNIS** 7 [9]   3-8-1 (60) D Glennon (7) 16/1: 002127: Cl-up till dist: see 1508 (seller).   ½ **51**
*1887 **BOLD EFFORT** 13 [14]   8-10-0 (80)(bl) R Hughes 9/1: 005218: Bhd, not clr run ent fnl 2f, some   nk **70**
hdwy but nvr a threat: top-weight, beat this wnr in 1887.
1196 **BALANITA** 49 [2]   5-9-2 (68) D Sweeney 33/1: 000-09: Led till 1½f out, no extra: 7 wk abs: '99 rnr-up   1 **55**
(h'cap, rtd 74): '98 wnr here at Windsor (h'cap, rtd 77): eff at 6/7f on fast & gd/soft grnd, sharp/undul trks.
2054 **RED DELIRIUM** 7 [1]   4-8-12 (64)(tbl) K Darley 25/1: 000000: Wide, cl-up till wknd appr fnl 1f: 1¼ **48**
10th, qck reapp, tricky low draw, t-strap & blnks reapplied, see 746.
1781 **RETALIATOR** 19 [4]   4-8-12 (64) S Sanders 10/1: 0-0020: Nvr dngrs: 14th, tchd 14/1: see 1781, 780.   0
*1545 **AT LARGE** 28 [11]   6-9-10 (76) L Newton 8/1: 061010: Al towards rear: 15th, op 5/1, much btr 1545.   0
2000 **LA PIAZZA** 9 [6]   4-9-13 (79) F Norton 9/1: 0-0000: Nvr in it: 16th, op 7/1, see 1391.   0
1877 **Endymion** 14 [13]   3-8-9 (68) L Newman (3) 33/1:   1851 **Wax Lyrical** 16 [8] 4-9-12 (78) P Robinson 20/1:
1961 **Hunting Tiger** 10 [3]   3-9-0 (73) S Drowne 25/1:
16 ran   Time 1m 12.9 (2.6)   (E A Hayward)   J M Bradley Sedbury, Glos.

2208
7.25 R & J WISEMAN COND STKS 3YO (C)   **1m3f135y**   **Good/Firm 38   +03 Fast**
£7566   £2134

*1738 **MARIENBARD** 21 [1]   M A Jarvis 3-9-1 P Robinson 4/7 FAV: 11: 3 b c Caerleon - Marienbad (Dashaan)   **96**
Sat in bhd other rnr till pld out & qcknd to lead dist, v cmftbly: well bckd, fair time: unbtn after winning debut
at Leicester (mdn): eff at 11.5f, shld stay further: acts on fast & gd/soft grnd, sharp or stiff trk: runs well
fresh: hard to know what he achieved here but looks a colt of some potential.
1627 **PROMISING LADY** 29 [2]   M R Channon 3-8-10 S Drowne 11/8: 1-0602: 3 b f Thunder Gulch - Sovinista   2 **86**
(Soviet Star) Led, eff 2f out, hdd dist & sn outpcd: well bckd: longer 11.5f trip & new tactics poss against her:
handles fast & gd/soft grnd: see 1108.
2 ran   Time 2m 29.8 (4)   (Saif Ali)   M A Jarvis Newmarket.

2209
7.55 EDWARD SYMMONS MED AUCT MDN 2YO (E)   **6f**   **Good/Firm 38   -17 Slow**
£3802   £1170   £585   £292   A high draw is favoured

-- **CHAGUARAMAS** [10]   R Hannon 2-8-9 R Hughes 6/1: 1: 2 b f Mujadil - Sabaniya (Lashkari)   **85+**
Trkd ldrs, led 2f out, shkn up, easily: stylish debut: first known foal, dam Irish bmpr wnr, sire a sprinter:
eff over a sharp 6f on fast grnd, get further in time: runs well fresh & shld hold her own in better company.
1634 **MYHAT** 25 [2]   K T Ivory 2-8-9 M Roberts 12/1: 22: 2 ch f Factual - Rose Elegance (Bairn)   3 **73**
Dwelt & in rear till gd wide prog 2f out, styd on for 2nd, no ch with wnr & eased towards fin: improved for new
connections: handles fast & gd/soft grnd, 7f is going to suit: win a fillies mdn, see 1634.
-- **MADRASEE** [17]   M Blanshard 2-8-9 D Sweeney 20/1: 3: 2 b f Bevelled - Pendona (Blue Cashmere)   ½ **72**
Bhd ldrs, tried to chase wnr ent fnl 2f, kept on onepace: Apr foal, sister to sprinter Mon Bruce, sire usually
gets sprinters: eff at 6f on fast grnd: shld improve & cld go close next time.
1486 **MAROMA** 32 [9]   J L Dunlop 2-8-9 P Robinson 13/2: 54: In tch, chsd ldrs 2f out, switched bef dist,   ½ **71**
no impress till styd on towards fin: prob handles fast grnd, see 1486.

1864 **MERIDEN MIST** 14 [18] 2-8-9 Pat Eddery 13/8 FAV: 525: Front rank, no extra appr fnl 1f: btr 1864.   ¾   69
-- **PENNY LASS** [6] 2-8-9 O Urbina 16/1: 6: Mid-div, rdn 2f out, no prog till styd on towards fin: shd   69
debut: 5,000gns Feb foal: half-sister to a 6f juv wnr: dam a sprinter, sire a miler.
1737 **LADY KINVARRAH** 21 [7] 2-8-9 Martin Dwyer 20/1: 067: Chsd ldrs, short of room 2f out, onepace.   nk   68$
-- **LOOKING FOR LOVE** [3] 2-8-9 N Pollard 20/1: 8: Mid-div thr'out tho' staying on fin when short of   1   65+
room/eased ins last: IR 1,800gns Apr foal, half-sister to a wnr abroad, sire 6/7f performer: likely improver.
1876 **CHAUNTRY GOLD** 14 [1] 2-9-0 D R McCabe 20/1: 09: Dwelt, switched & towards rear till shkn up &   2½   64
drifted left into mid-div fnl 1f: IR 6,000gns Desert Style Apr gelding, needs 7f+: with B Meehan.
-- **FIRST DEGREE** [5] 2-8-9 T G McLaughlin 33/1: 0: Nvr a factor: 10th: Sabrehill first foal, dam 1m wnr.   2½   53
2055 **MISSING DRINK** 7 [15] 2-9-0 Joanna Badger (7) 33/1: 050: Led till appr fnl 2f, no extra/hung left: 11th.   1¼   54
-- **MUTAMADEE** [14] 2-9-0 M Tebbutt 12/1: 0: Nvr in it: 13th: 57,000gns Beau Genius Feb foal,   0
half-brother to a wnr in the States: with E Dunlop.
-- **Certainly So** [11] 2-8-9 S Drowne 33/1:   -- **Hammock** [8] 2-9-0 S Sanders 16/1:
1844 **Hidden Lake** 16 [4] 2-9-0 S Carson (5) 20/1:   1541 **One Beloved** 30 [13] 2-8-9 Craig Williams 25/1:
-- **Magic Gem** [16] 2-9-0 F Norton 16/1:
17 ran   Time 1m 13.6 (3.3)   (Dr A Haloute)   R Hannon East Everley, Wilts.

2210   8.25 EDGE ELLISON HCAP 3YO 0-75 (E)   1m3f135y   Good/Firm 38   +03 Fast   [82]
£2940   £840   £420

1446 **SECOND PAIGE** 34 [6] N A Graham 3-8-9 (62)(1ow) J Weaver 4/1: -40221: 3 b g Nicolotte - My First   72
Paige (Runnett) Mid-div, closed on bit 4f out, led bef 2f out, hard prsd & rdn appr fnl 1f, drvn out nr fin: 1st
win, unplcd in '99 (auct mdn, rtd 71): eff at 10f/12f on fast & gd/soft, prob any trk: imprvg, capable of wng again.
1967 **FANFARE** 10 [2] G A Butler 3-9-7 (75) K Darley 7/4 FAV: -01102: 3 b f Deploy - Tashinsky (Nijinsky)   1   83
Waited with, gd hdwy 3f out, chall appr fnl 1f, rider sn dropped whip, not pace of wnr towards fin: clr rem.
1270 **FLIQUET BAY** 45 [5] Mrs A J Perrett 3-8-2 (56)(bl) M Roberts 10/1: 0-4203: 3 b g Namaqualand -   4   59
Thatcherite (Final Straw) Prom, outpcd by front pair appr fnl 1f tho' held on for 3rd: 6 wk abs, apprec drop
back to trip, acts on fast & gd/soft, see 1096 (C/D).
1949 **SHRIVAR** 11 [3] M R Channon 3-8-11 (65) S Drowne 10/1: 552464: Rear, short of room bef halfway,   ½   67
prog under press 3f out, nvr able to chall: back in trip & apprec return to waiting tactics, see 1270.
1509 **LENNY THE LION** 31 [4] 3-8-0 (54) F Norton 12/1: 65-055: Hld up, hmpd 5f, chsd ldrs 3f out till 2f out.   hd   56
1736 **MUCHANA YETU** 21 [10] 3-8-7 (61) L Newman (3) 20/1: 5-0606: Led till appr fnl 2f, no extra: see 1177.   5   57
2012 **RONNI PANCAKE** 9 [7] 3-8-4 (58) N Pollard 12/1: 6-0157: Al rear: Ingr trip again, see 1752 (clmr).   1½   52
1425 **BLESS THE BRIDE** 35 [8] 3-9-6 (74) Pat Eddery 6/1: 66-108: Chsd ldrs, wknd appr fnl 2f: best 1094 (10f).   ¾   67
1878 **KATHAKALI** 14 [9] 3-8-6 (60) Martin Dwyer 20/1: 100009: Mid-div when hmpd halfway, struggling after.   3   49
1967 **JEUNE PREMIER** 10 [1] 3-8-8 (62) D R McCabe 25/1: 500500: Prom 1m: 10th, see 1967, 1485.   5   45
10 ran   Time 2m 29.8 (4)   (Coronation Partnership)   N A Graham Newmarket.

2211   8.55 DELOITTE MDN 3YO (D)   1m67y rnd   Good/Firm 38   -15 Slow
£4179   £1286   £643   £321

2019 **EAST CAPE** 8 [6] L M Cumani 3-9-0 G Sparkes (7) 3/1 JT FAV: -5421: 3 b c Bering - Reine de Danse   81
(Nureyev) Held up, switched left & gd prog 2f out, kept on well to lead towards fin, pshd out: unrcd juv:
eff at 10f, suited by drop back to extended 1m: goes on firm/fast grnd, stiff or sharp trk: consistent.
1532 **EVE** 30 [12] M L W Bell 3-8-9 M Fenton 3/1 JT FAV: 42: 3 b f Rainbow Quest - Fade (Persepolis)   nk   74
Pulled hard bhd ldrs, led appr fnl 2f, hard rdn ins last & worn down towards fin: clr rem, imprvd in defeat:
acts on fast, handles soft: win a fillies maiden.
1886 **CAPRICCIO** 13 [8] C G Cox 3-9-0 S Drowne 7/2: 43: 3 gr g Robellino - Yamamah (Siberian Express)   2   75
Chsd ldrs, rdn appr fnl 1f, edged left, not pace to chall: stays 1m, ran to level of debut in 1886.
1922 **EL EMPERADOR** 12 [3] J R Fanshawe 3-9-0 O Urbina 7/1: 6-54: Front rank, led appr fnl 3f till   hd   75
bef 2f out, no extra: clr rem: prob stays 1m: 'h'caps will now suit: see 1922.
1080 **JIMAL** 56 [9] 3-9-0 G Hind 33/1: 05: Dwelt, styd on fnl 2f, nvr nr ldrs: 8 wk abs: Reprimand   3   69
colt, will apprec 10f+ h'caps: with V Soane.
1532 **DICKIE DEADEYE** 30 [2] S Carson (5) 14/1: 056: Restrained, mod late hdwy: h'caps next.   2½   64
1912 **OPTION** 12 [5] F Norton 16/1: -57: Nvr better than mid-div: see 1912.   1¼   55
1697 **ONLY WORDS** 23 [10] 3-9-0 (t) M Roberts 16/1: -608: Left in lead bef halfway, hdd bef 3f out,   ¾   58
no extra & eased 2f out: tried a t-strap, see 1466.
1811 **KOINCIDENTAL** 17 [1] 3-8-9 S Sanders 20/1: 009: Nvr troubled ldrs: see 1268.   ½   55
-- **PAGAN PRINCE** [4] 3-9-0 J Weaver 8/1: 0: Al bhd: 10th: 48,000gns Primo Dominie newcomer.   1   55
1787 **TARCOOLA** 18 [11] 3-9-0 Craig Williams 20/1: 4-0F00: Early ldr, lost pl 3f out: 11th, plater.   nk   54
1669 **MAIDEN AUNT** 24 [7] 3-8-9 Martin Dwyer 25/1: 500: Prom 5f: 12th, see 1436.   3½   43
1811 **APLESTEDE** 17 [13] 3-8-9 D Sweeney 20/1: 00: Keen, led after & sn went v wide/hdd & btn: 13th.   4   37
13 ran   Time 1m 46.7 (4.4)   (Mrs M Schulthness)   L M Cumani Newmarket.

Official Going   Turf: GOOD/FIRM, AW - Standard. Stalls: Far Side; A/W - Inside.

2212   2.00 LOYALTY APPR HCAP 3YO+ 0-60 (G)   1m2f aw   Going 45   -10 Slow   [58]
£2002   £572   £286   3 yo rec 12lb

1934 **BECKON** 12 [11] B R Johnson 4-9-3 (47) J Mackay 11/4 FAV: -54501: 4 ch f Beveled - Carolynchristensen   52a
(Sweet Revenge) Held up wide early, prog/chsd ldrs halfway, rdn & reeled in ldr fnl 1f, led near fin, rdn out: bckd:
'99 Lingfield scorer (C/D sell, rtd 53a, flattered on turf, rtd 62): eff at 10f, tried 12f: loves eqtrk/Lingfield.
1921 **APPROACHABLE** 13 [2] K A Morgan 5-8-13 (43) L Branch (7) 13/2: 543202: 5 b h Known Fact -   1   46a
Western Approach (Gone West) Trckd ldrs halfway, led going well over 3f out, rdn/hdd inside last, no extra:
clr rem: op 10/1: see 1415, 710 & 45 (seller, 1m).
596 **KINNINO** 122 [13] G L Moore 6-8-11 (41)(bl) J Bosley 11/1: -13403: 6 b g Polish Precedent - On   7   34a
Tiptoes (Shareef Dancer) Chsd ldrs, ch over 2f out, held over 1f out: 4 month abs: see 405, 254.
1875 **RAKE HEY** 15 [7] D G Bridgwater 6-9-7 (51)(tvi) A Hawkins (5) 25/1: 026/64: Mid-div halfway, no threat.   1½   42a
1731 **THOMAS HENRY** 22 [12] 4-8-11 (41) N Farmer (7) 7/1: 550035: Towards rear, mod gains: op 5/1.   6   23a

1852 **COUNT FREDERICK** 16 [4] 4-8-12 (42) D Glennon (3) 20/1: 20-006: Rdn/twds rear halfway, no impress. *hd*   **23a**
1949 **CHILLI** 12 [1] 3-8-7 (49)(vis) N Esler (3) 6/1: 330357: Led after 3f till over 3f out: tchd 9/1, vis reapp.   *shd*   **30a**
2033 **MYSTERIUM** 8 [5] 6-9-7 (51) L Paddock (5) 5/1: 124008: Rear, wide/al bhd: tchd 15/2: btr 393 (fbrsnd).   ½   **31a**
2032 **LEVEL HEADED** 9 [8] 5-8-9 (39) Darren Williams 10/1: 0-0359: Towards rear, never factor: tchd 14/1.   ¾   **18a**
84} **BON GUEST** 580 [14] 6-10-0 (58) Leanne Masterton (3) 12/1: 10501/0: Al rear: 10th: op 10/1: long   3½   **32a**
abs: missed '99: '98 wnr twice at Lingfield (h,cap & claimer, rtd 63a, Miss B Sanders): eff at 1m/12f on fast & gd,
both AWs: handles any track: best without blinks & has run well fresh: with C Egerton.
1335 **SABOT** 41 [3] 7-9-10 (54) C Catlin (3) 10/1: 54-040: Rdn/led early, hdd after 3f & soon btn: 14th: abs.   **0a**
2186 **Tribal Peace** 2 [9] 8-9-0 (44)(BL) G Baker (3)   586} **Gee Bee Boy** 483 [10] 6-9-6 (50) Joanna Badger (3) 16/1:
-- **Another Beveled** [6] 5-9-1 (45) S Clancy (5) 25/1:
14 ran   Time 2m 08.27 (5.47)   (B A Whittaker)   B R Johnson Epsom, Surrey

---

2213   2.30 H STREETER MDN 3YO+ (D)   **1m2f aw   Going 45   +06 Fast**
£2782   £856   £428   £214   3 yo rec 12lb

2080 **SWINGING TRIO** 6 [1] T G Mills 3-8-11 L Carter 16/1: 0-0041: 3 b c Woodman - Las Meninas (Glenstal)   **76a**
Made all, rdn clr 3f out, always holding rivals after, rdn out inside last: gd time: op 12/1: eff forcing the pace
over a sharp 10f: acts on equitrack: open to improvement, win again on sand.
-- **SATARAX** [6] H R A Cecil 3-8-11 W Ryan 3/1: 2: 3 ch c Lammtarra - Gemaasheh (Habitat)   3½   **70a**
Dwelt, rear, rdn/prog to chase wnr 2f out, kept on tho' al held: well bckd tho' op 2/1, debut: 240,000gns yearling
purchase: sire a Derby wnr, 12f+ should suit: acts on equitrack: clr rem, could find similar when tackling further.
1779 **PRINCIPLE** 20 [4] Sir Mark Prescott 3-8-11 G Duffield 3/1: 624-43: 3 b c Caerleon - Point Of Honour   9   **60a**
(Kris) Chsd wnr halfway, hard rdn/held fnl 3f: tchd 9/2: see 1779.
1997 **QUIET READING** 10 [3] C A Cyzer 3-8-11 S Sanders 25/1: 00364: Chsd ldrs, held 3f out: AW bow.   *shd*   **60a**
1640 **SPEED VENTURE** 26 [2] 3-8-11 N Callan 6/4 FAV: 4225: Cl up 5f, btn 3f out: hvly bckd: AW bow.   14   **45a**
2044 **LEGENDAIRE** 8 [7] 3-8-11 S Whitworth 20/1: 224366: Struggling 3f out: btr 1333 (firm, mdn, 7f).   9   **35a**
1725 **NINNOLO** 22 [5] 3-8-11 R Morse 11/2: 537: Held up, wide/bhd 4f out: AW bow: btr 1725, 1386.   6   **26a**
7 ran   Time 2m 06.7 (3.9)   (T G Mills)   T G Mills Headley, Surrey

---

2214   3.00 TATTERSALLS AUCT MDN 2YO (E)   **5f   Good/Firm   Inapplicable**
£3640   £1120   £560   £280   Raced centre - stands side

1641 **FACE D FACTS** 25 [13] C F Wall 2-8-0 R Mullen 7/2: 51: 2 b f So Factual - Water Well (Sadler's Wells)   **77**
Rdn/in tch halfway, prog to chall fnl 1f & styd on well for press to lead near line: nicely bckd, tchd 8/1: eff at 5f,
dam a 7f wnr, 6f+ should suit: acts on fast grnd, handles gd/soft: likes a sharp/undul trk: going the right way.
1924 **LAI SEE** 13 [9] A P Jarvis 2-8-4(1ow) D Sweeney 7/1: 0002: 2 b c Tagula - Sevens Are Wild (Petorius)   *nk*   **80**
Handy, rdn/led over 1f out, duelled with wnr inside last, just hdd nr line: op 6/1: acts on fast grnd, eff at 5/6f.
1993 **MISTY BELLE** 10 [20] B R Millman 2-8-0 L Newman (3) 5/2 FAV: 0323: 2 gr f Petong - La Belle   2½   **69**
Dominique (Dominion) Soon handy, kept on tho' not pace of front pair: well bckd: acts on firm & good/sft grnd.
849 **GAME MAGIC** 78 [1] R Hannon 2-8-7 R Hughes 5/1: 44: Held up, kept on fnl 2f, not pace to chall: *nk*   **75**
11 week abs, tchd 13/2: handles fast & gd grnd, 6f+ should suit: see 849.
-- **CEDAR RANGERS** [19] 2-8-7 J F Egan 33/1: 5: Towards rear, styd on well under a kind ride fnl 2f, no   ½   **73+**
threat: Anabaa colt, March foal, 12,000gns first foal: dam a 4yo French wnr: encouraging, keep in mind.
2039 **TIMELESS FARRIER** 8 [14] 2-8-5 J Stack 14/1: 66: Prom, onepace fnl 2f: tchd 25/1: see 2039.   *hd*   **70**
2039 **LONDON EYE** 8 [17] 2-7-12 (bl) C Catlin (7) 20/1: 603327: Prom 4f: op 14/1: see 2039.   ¾   **61**
1993 **BARON CROCODILE** 10 [11] 2-8-5 G Carter 10/1: 22458: Prom 4f: op 7/1: btr 1001 (hvy).   ½   **66**
1798 **WATTNO ELJOHN** 19 [3] 2-8-7 S Whitworth 25/1: 009: Chsd ldrs, no impress over 1f out: see 1789.   *nk*   **67**
1993 **COUNT CALYPSO** 10 [12] 2-8-3 D R McCabe 50/1: 000: Led till over 1f out, wknd: 10th: see 1993.   ½   **61**
1924 **VENDOME** 13 [2] 2-8-5 F Norton 20/1: 000: Chsd ldrs halfway, soon held: 11th: see 1429.   ½   **61**
1962 **BEE J GEE** 11 [10] 2-8-5 S Sanders 25/1: 60: Mid div, never on terms: 12th: see 1962.   1   **59**
-- **SUPREME TEAM** [6] 2-8-3 G Bardwell 20/1: 0: Dwelt, bhd, mod late gains: 13th: Piccolo colt,   *nk*   **56**
March foal, cost 3,000gns: dam a mdn, sire tough/prog & high class sprinter: with J Pearce.
2029 **SHOLTO** 9 [15] 2-8-5 G Duffield 25/1: -00: Prom 3f: 14th: bhd on debut prev: Feb first foal, cost   *nk*   **57**
8,000gns: sire a 12f wnr: dam unraced: with B J Meehan.
1454 **Chispa** 35 [7] 2-8-0 C Rutter 16/1:   2009 **Rachel Green** 10 [4] 2-8-0 J Mackay (5) 20/1:
1782 **Agile Dancer** 19 [16] 2-8-0 Dale Gibson 14/1:   1882 **Violent** 14 [18] 2-7-12 M Henry 25/1:
1876 **Bosra Badger** 15 [5] 2-8-3 A Nicholls (3) 50/1:   1924 **Halcyon Magic** 13 [8] 2-8-4(1ow) R Perham 25/1:
20 ran   Time 58.04 (1.24)   (The Boardroom Syndicate)   C F Wall Newmarket, Suffolk

---

2215   3.30 FITZPATRICK CLASS STKS 3YO+ 0-70 (E)   **7f140y str   Good/Firm   Inapplicable**
£2884   £824   £412   3 yo rec 10lb   Raced towards centre

1926 **YEAST** 13 [7] W J Haggas 8-9-5 J F Egan 3/1 FAV: 0-0201: 8 b g Salse - Orient (Bay Express)   **75**
Made all, rdn/strongly pressed fnl 1f, styd on well & asserted near fin, rdn out: hvly bckd: op 3/1: '99 wnr at
Chepstow (class stks), Salisbury (h,cap) & Ripon (clmr, rtd 89 at best): plcd in '98 (rtd 80): loves to force the
pace at 7.5f/1m, prob stys 12f: acts on firm & fast grnd: handles soft grnd: handles any track.
2128 **SONG OF SKYE** 4 [6] T J Naughton 6-9-2 S Sanders 7/1: 360002: 6 b m Warning - Song Of Hope   1½   **68**
(Chief Singer) Chsd ldrs, rdn/prog to chall over 1f out, held near fin: op 6/1, quick reapp: see 169, 78.
1590 **COMPRADORE** 27 [10] M Blanshard 5-9-6 D Sweeney 8/1: 321103: 5 b m Mujtahid - Deswa (King's   2½   **67**
Lake) Towards rear, prog to press ldrs over 1f out, soon held: op 5/1: see 1467 (0-65 stakes).
1125 **APLOY** 54 [2] R F Johnson Houghton 3-8-4 D Holland 5/1: 530-64: In tch, rdn/onepace fnl 2f: abs.   ¾   **62**
1652 **AMBER FORT** 25 [9] 7-9-5 (vis) P Fitzsimons (5) 100/30: 254055: Chsd ldrs 7f: bckd, vis reapp.   1½   **62**
1829 **EASTERN CHAMP** 18 [3] 4-9-5 (t) G Duffield 9/2: 0-0206: Rear, mod gains, no threat: btr 1259 (AW).   3½   **55**
1799 **LOUGH SWILLY** 19 [1] 4-9-5 G Hind 20/1: 0-0007: Keen/prom 6f: op 14/1: see 854.   2½   **50$**
538 **GREEN PURSUIT** 130 [5] 4-9-5 F Norton 20/1: 106-08: Rear, no threat: abs: see 538 (AW, 6f).   *hd*   **49**
1933 **WESTMINSTER CITY** 12 [8] 4-9-5 (bl) L Branch (7) 16/1: 044049: Chsd ldrs 4f: see 1570, 748.   1½   **46**
1807 **KAFIL** 18 [4] 6-9-5 J Weaver 20/1: 260000: Prom 5f: 10th: see 254, 1 (AW).   3   **40**
10 ran   Time 1m 29.92 (2.12)   (The Not Over Big Partnership)   W J Haggas Newmarket, Suffolk

2216 | 4.00 TOTALBET.COM HCAP 3YO 0-85 (D)   6f   Good/Firm   Inapplicable   [92]
£7540   £2320   £1160   £290 Raced towards centre

2101 **CORUNNA** 6 [7] A Berry 3-8-12 (76) G Duffield 6/1: -33131: 3 b g Puissance - Kind Of Shy (Kind Of   78
Hush) Towards rear early, rdn/prog from halfway & narrow lead fnl 1f, held on gamely, all out: op 7/1, quick reapp:
earlier scored at Musselburgh (mdn): rnr up several times last term (rtd 84): eff at 5/6f on firm & gd, disapp on
soft: likes to race with/force the pace on a sharp or gall track: tough & consistent gelding, can win more races.
1409 **MELANZANA** 38 [5] E A L Dunlop 3-9-7 (85) G Carter 7/1: 31-42: 3 b f Alzao - Melody Park   nk   86
(Music Boy) Keen, held up, prog to chall fnl 1f, drvn & just held: fine h'cap bow: see 1409.
1891 **FEAST OF ROMANCE** 14 [4] Miss Gay Kelleway 3-7-11 (61)(BL) J Mackay (5) 20/1: 560603: 3 b c   ¾   60
Pursuit Of Love - June Fayre (Sagaro) Led 4f, held near fin: gd run in first time blinks: acts on fibresand & fast.
1826 **ZIETZIG** 18 [6] K R Burke 3-8-12 (76) N Callan 7/2: 550064: Chsd ldrs, ch fnl 1f, onepace nr fin.   shd   74
1694 **BANAFSAJYH** 24 [11] R Hills 2/1 FAV: 23-104: Handy, drvn/led 2f out till 1f out, just   dht   75
held near line: deadheated for fourth, only beaten around 1L: see 1694, 1266.
1406 **MIND THE SILVER** 38 [1] R Brisland (5) 33/1: 56-006: Bhd, late gains, no threat: unplcd   1½   55
last term (rtd 69): not given hard time on h'cap bow: handles fast grnd, 7f + in similar company could suit.
1887 **WAFFLES OF AMIN** 14 [8] 3-8-9 (73) L Newman (3) 9/1: -00407: In tch, outpcd fnl 2f: see 77 (AW, 5f).   1¾   63
2177 **LABRETT** 2 [9] 3-8-13 (77)(bl) J Weaver 6/1: 000448: In tch, outpcd fnl 2f: op 5/1, quick reapp.   nk   66
1742 **ITSGOTTABDUN** 21 [3] 3-7-10 (60)(bl) (3oh) C Catlin (5) 16/1: 366439: Drvn/rear, never on terms.   1¼   46
1708 **TERRA NOVA** 23 [2] 3-8-6 (70) R Price 12/1: 246-30: Keen, prom till over 1f out: 10th: btr 1708 (mdn).   2   51
1961 **DACCORD** 11 [10] 3-9-1 (79) S Sanders 10/1: 1-5350: Keen, in tch, rdn/btn 2f out: 11th: op 8/1.   ½   58
11 ran   Time 1m 10.32 (1.52)   (Chris & Antonia Deuters)   A Berry Cockerham, Lancs

2217 | 4.30 JACQUART FILLIES HCAP 3YO 0-70 (E)   1m4f aw   Going 45   -07 Slow   [72]
£2821   £868   £434   £217

1649 **ABLE NATIVE** 25 [5] R W Armstrong 3-9-7 (65) R Price 2/1 FAV: 25-021: 3 b f Thatching - Native Joy   70a
(Be My Native) Chsd ldrs wide halfway, rdn/chsd ldr fnl 2f, drvn to reel in ldr near fin, all out:
nicely bckd: first win: fillies mdn rnr up last term (rtd 78): eff at 10f, apprec step up to 12f, should
get further: acts on equitrack, gd & hvy grnd: likes a sharp track: op to further improvement in similar.
1544 **THE GIRLS FILLY** 31 [3] Miss B Sanders 3-8-8 (52) S Carson (5) 16/1: 230002: 3 b f Emperor Jones -   nk   56a
Sioux City (Simply Great)Led/dsptd lead, rdn clr over 1f out, hard rdn inside last, hdd near line:
clr rem: op 12/1: improved eff with blinks ommitted: styd longer 12f trip: see 570 (mdn).
1914 **BEE GEE** 13 [4] M Blanshard 3-7-11 (41)(1ow)(2oh) Dale Gibson 4/1: 0-0143: 3 b f Beveled -   5   38a
Bunny Gee (Last Tycoon) Chsd ldrs, rdn/held fnl 2f: op 7/2: see 1914, 1540. (C/D, seller).
2123 **ODYN DANCER** 5 [6] M D I Usher 3-8-2 (46) G Baker 7/1: 620604: Bhd, mod late gains: op   1¾   41a
12/1: quick reapp: see 537.
2041 **ESTABELLA** 8 [2] 3-9-2 (60) G Duffield 5/1: 130555: Chsd ldrs, btn 3f out: op 6/1: visor   9   45a
omitted: btr 1142, 978.
1742 **WHITE SANDS** 21 [10] 3-8-1 (45) F Norton 25/1: 0-0006: Rdn/rear, al bhd: longer 12f trip.   20   8a
*1914 **ADRIANA** 13 [1] 3-7-13 (43) A Nicholls (3) 100/30: 000017: Led after 3f till 7f out, soon btn: nk   5a
op 4/1: AW bow: btr 1914 (firm).
1917 **BUXTEDS FIRST** 13 [9] 3-8-7 (51) I Mongan (5) 7/1: 0-0338: Rdn/struggling halfway: op 6/1: AW bow   3   9a
longer 12f trip: btr 1917, 1511.
1873 **DOROTHEA SHARP** 15 [7] 3-7-11 (41)(vis) J Mackay 25/1: 050009: Bhd halfway: see 1035   15   0a
(aution mdn, 7f).
1804 **HAVENT MADE IT YET** 18 [8] 3-7-10 (40)(12oh) D Glennon (2) 50/1: 00-000: Bhd halfway: 10th: 12   0a
longer 12f trip, mod form.
10 ran   Time 2m 35.45 (6.25)   (Dr Cornel Li)   R W Armstrong Newmarket, Suffolk

---

Official Going   GOOD/FIRM. Stalls: Inside.

2218 | 2.15 ERNST YOUNG FILL AUCT MDN 2YO (E)   7f100y rnd   Firm 18   -17 Slow
£2835   £810   £405

1798 **MONTANA MISS** 19 [5] B Palling 2-8-0 D Mernagh (3) 4/6 FAV: 41: 2 b f Earl Of Barking - Cupid Miss   76
(Anita's Prince) Made all, pshd out, unchall: well bckd, val 6L: 2,800gns March foal, half-sister to 4 wnrs,
dam a juv wnr: clearly appr step up to 7f100y: acts on firm & gd/soft grnd, forcing the pace, stiff track.
-- **FIRST MEETING** [1] M Dods 2-8-0 T Williams 33/1: 2: 2 b f Contract Law - Sunday News'n'echo   3   67
(Trempolino) Held up, hdwy to go 2nd appr fnl 2f, styd on but never any impression on wnr: op 12/1, well
clr rem: 900gns Feb first foal, dam mid dist wnr, sire a sprinter: eff at 7f on firm grnd.
1864 **SOMETHINGABOUTMARY** 15 [8] J S Wainwright 2-8-3 J Tate 33/1: 0003: 2 b f Fayruz - Cut It Fine   8   54
(Big Spruce) Rear, went past btn horses to go 3rd dist, never dangerous: up in trip, needs sellers.
1304 **TENERIFE FLYER** 43 [9] J Norton 2-8-1(1ow) O Pears 33/1: 604: Struggling, moderate hdwy when   7   38
not much room 2f out: op 20/1, 6 week abs, longer trip: see 974.
1938 **BOMBAY BINNY** 12 [6] 2-8-4(1ow) K Darley 8/1: 0205: Handy 4f: longer trip, beat 1764 (5f, hvy).   1¾   37
1864 **SLIPPER ROSE** 15 [2] 2-8-0 P M Quinn (3) 9/1: -4306: Wide, prom till not handle bend/stumbled/   2   29
nearly u.r. rider halfway, bhd after: op 6/1, see 974.
1595 **KEEP DREAMING** 27 [7] 2-8-3 A Beech (5) 14/1: 007: In tch till halfway: tchd 20/1, needs sellers.   1½   29
1864 **PICTURE MEE** 15 [4] 2-8-1(1ow) J Fanning 8/1: 08: Keen, chsd ldrs till 3f out: see 1864.   6   17
1859 **PERTEMPS THATCHER** 16 [3] 2-8-3 N Pollard 6/1: -49: Not settle, pressed ldrs till ran v wide   dist   0
halfway, soon btn, t.o.: tchd 10/1: see 1859.
9 ran   Time 1m 33.4 (2.6)   (Mrs A L Stacey)   B Palling Cowbridge, Vale Of Glamorgan

2219   **2.45 BOYD LINE CLAIMER 4YO + (F)**   **1m4f**   **Firm 18 -25 Slow**
£2296   £656   £328

1816 **SKYERS A KITE 18** [6] Ronald Thompson 5-8-7 T Williams 15/2: 206531: 5 b m Deploy - Milady   47
Jade (Drumalis) Soon led & clr, over 5L up appr fnl 1f, kept on well, pushed out: op 6/1, fine ride: '99 wnr
here at Beverley (h'cap, rtd 45): '98 wnr again at Beverley & Catterick (sell h'cap, rtd 50): eff at 10/12f: acts
on firm & gd, soft grnd suits: Beverley specialist, right back to form from the front here.
*2139 **PENNYS FROM HEAVEN 4** [3] D Nicholls 6-8-12 Clare Roche (7) 3/1: 302412: 6 gr g Generous -   2   50
Heavenly Cause (Grey Dawn II) Rear, prog to go after wnr 2f out, styd on, never on terms: bckd tho'
drifted from 13/8: quick reapp, btr 2139 (gd grnd h'cap).
2109 **I CANT REMEMBER 5** [8] S R Bowring 6-8-6 (t) K Darley 5/2 JT FAV: 050603: 6 gr g Petong -   3   40
Glenfield Portion (Mummy's Pet) Prom, eff 4f out, same pace: qck reapp, op 5/1, tried a t strap, see 428.
723 **AMBIDEXTROUS 94** [7] M E Sowersby 8-8-5 O Pears 20/1: 045054: Chsd ldrs 3f out till 2f out: new stable.1   38
2098 **FIELD OF VISION 6** [4] 10-8-6 A Beech (5) 5/2 JT FAV: 432145: Nvr troubled ldrs: quick reapp.   1   38
1978 **ALL ON MY OWN 11** [1] 5-8-6 J McAuley 33/1: -306: Prom till 3f out: op 20/1: see 1660.   3   35
1816 **PHASE EIGHT GIRL 18** [9] 4-8-6 N Kennedy 14/1: 313-07: Early ldr, lost place 3f out: '99 wnr here   5   30
at Beverley (sell h'cap, rtd 38): eff between 12f & 2m on firm & gd/soft grnd, prob any track.
2011 **PARISIENNE HILL 10** [5] 4-7-11 P Hanagan (7) 33/1: 000-08: Struggling halfway: v stiff task.   7   14
707 **ROYAL DOLPHIN 96** [2] 4-9-2 K Hodgson 40/1: 043369: Al bhd: 3 mnth abs, new stable, flattered 686.   14   19
9 ran   Time 2m 36.4 (5.1)   (G A W Racing Partnership)   Ronald Thompson Stainforth, S Yorks

2220   **3.15 ARCO NSPCC HCAP 3YO+ 0-80 (D)**   **1m2f**   **Firm 18 -02 Slow**   [71]
£5564   £1712   £856   £428   3 yo rec 12lb

1940 **CYBERTECHNOLOGY 12** [6] M Dods 6-8-10 (53) A Culhane 9/1: 000031: 6 b g Environment Friend -   60
Verchinina (Star Appeal) Waited with, gd progress on ins rail fnl 3f, led dist, pshd out: '99 Doncaster wnr
(h'cap, rtd 74): '98 Redcar wnr (h'cap, rtd 82, Mrs Cecil): eff at 1m/10f, stays 12f: acts on firm, gd/soft grnd,
stiff or gall tracks: best without blinks/visor: well h'capped & cld follow up.
1921 **BACCHUS 13** [7] Miss J A Camacho 6-9-10 (67) K Darley 3/1: 15-232: 6 b g Prince Sabo - Bonica   1   72
(Rousillon) Rear, hdwy & not clr run appr fnl 2f, styd on ins last, nvr nrr: bckd from 4/1: shld go one better.
1852 **RARE TALENT 16** [9] S Gollings 6-8-10 (53) A Beech (5) 16/1: 00-003: 6 b g Mtoto - Bold As Love   1¼   56
(Lomond) Prom, led appr fnl 1f, soon hdd, one pace under press: ran to best, see 1272.
1860 **KHUCHN 16** [10] M Brittain 4-8-8 (49) D Mernagh (3) 10/1: 052654: Led till appr fnl 1f, onepace.   ½   51
1860 **FREEDOM QUEST 16** [3] 5-9-2 (59) M Fenton 8/1: 346425: Chsd ldrs, fdd fnl 2f: btr 1860, 793 (gd).   7   52
*2028 **SEA SQUIRT 9** [2] 3-9-7 (76) J Fanning 9/1: 230416: Well plcd till 3f out: btr 2108 (1m class stks).   1½   67
*1575 **ANNADAWI 28** [5] 5-8-7 (50) K Dalgleish (7) 10/1: 322217: Never dngrs: tchd 14/1, needs softer grnd.   ¾   40
2102 **ROUSING THUNDER 6** [1] 3-9-8 (77) J Reid 9/4 FAV: 36-028: Wide, prom till lost place 3f out: 2½   64
nicely bckd from 7/2, quick reapp: stable not really firing, see 2102,1177.
2061 **ILE DISTINCT 7** [8] 6-9-3 (60) N Pollard 9/1: 403-29: Bhd ldrs, wknd under press appr fnl 2f: qk reapp.   2½   44
1921 **LOKOMOTIV 12** [4] 4-8-11 (54) Claire Bryan (5) 16/1: 300-60: Al bhd: 10th, see 1921.   2   35
10 ran   Time 2m 04.3 (2)   (Exors Of The Late Mrs H M Carr)   M Dods Piercebridge, Co Durham

2221   **3.45 TANKCLEAN HCAP 3YO+ 0-75 (E)**   **7f100y**   **Firm 18 +02 Fast**   [71]
£3818   £1195   £587   £293   3 yo rec 9 lb

1658 **NORTHGATE 25** [5] M Brittain 4-8-3 (46)(bl) D Mernagh (3) 10/1: -05421: 4 b c Thatching - Tender   50
Time (Tender King) Trkd ldrs, rdn 2f out, hung left & right under press but ran on to lead towards fin: nicely
bckd, best time of day, first win: rnr up in '99 (mdn h'cap, rtd 49): eff at 7f/1m: acts on firm/fast grnd,
stiff/gall tracks: wears blinkers & can force the pace.
1920 **KASS ALHAWA 13** [10] D W Chapman 7-9-10 (67) A Culhane 4/1: 240542: 7 b g Shirley Heights -   hd   70
Silver Braid (Miswaki) Rear, imprvd 2f out, chall ins last, held when carried right cl home: op 7/1: see 908, 38.
2062 **PERFECT PEACH 7** [9] C W Fairhurst 5-9-8 (65) J Fanning 10/1: 000043: 5 b m Lycius - Perfect   ¾   66
Timing (Comedy Star) Waited with, not clr run 2f out, styd on, nrst fin: qck reapp: nicely h'capped, see 1250.
1438 **CRUSTY LILY 36** [13] J M Bradley 4-7-13 (42) T Williams 20/1: 100-04: Well plcd, led appr fnl 1f, sn   ½   42
hdd, one pace towards fin: '99 Yarmouth win (fill h'cap, rtd 44): eff at 6/6.7f, stys a stiff 7f100y: acts on
firm & gd grnd: return to sharper trkk or 6/7f likely to suit.
1892 **TAYOVULLIN 14** [4] 6-8-3 (46) Iona Wands (5) 10/1: 065225: Rear, shaken up & short of room appr   hd   46
fnl 2f, keeping on when short of room well in last: op 6/1: wld have made the frame: remains in gd heart, see 550.
1930 **FLYING PENNANT 12** [16] 7-7-10 (39)(bl)(3oh) Claire Bryan (5) 10/1: -55306: Mid div, styd on   nk   38
entering fnl 2f, never nearer: ran to best 3lbs 'wrong', see 896.
*2027 **SOUHAITE 9** [12] 4-8-0 (43) P Doe 7/1: 3-0017: Cl up, led appr fnl 2f till bef dist, no extra: btr 2027.   nk   41
1148 **BOLLIN ROBERTA 53** [2] 4-9-4 (61) K Darley 11/4 FAV: 00-528: Mid div, shaken up 2f out, styd   1½   56
on ins last but no impression on ldrs: nicely bckd from 4/1, 8 week abs: sharper next time, see 908.
4034} **CELANDINE 280** [11] 7-8-3 (46) A Daly 20/1: 0000-9: Nvr better than mid div: reapp: unplcd in   hd   41
'99 (h'cap, rtd 63): '98 Warwick & Catterick wnr (h'caps, rtd 63): eff at 6f, both wins at 7f: acts on firm &
gd/soft grnd, likes sharp/turning trks, handles any, without blinks/visor: well h'capped: with A Turnell.
1840 **ORIOLE 17** [15] 7-8-1 (44) Kim Tinkler 16/1: 5-0000: Nvr a factor: 10th: '99 rnr up (h'cap, rtd 51 at best):   1½   36
'98 wnr at Carlise & Redcar (h'caps, rtd 49): eff at 7f/1m on firm & soft grnd, with/without visor, likes Redcar.
247 **FOURTH TIME LUCKY 176** [14] 4-7-10 (39)(13oh) J McAuley (3) 66/1: 060-00: Led till ent fnl 3f, fdd: 11th.   2½   26
2027 **COMPATRIOT 9** [6] 4-9-7 (64) S Finnamore (5) 12/1: 4-2460: Al rear: 12th, see 1414 (mdn h'cap).   hd   51
2063 **MEHMAAS 7** [3] 4-9-5 (62)(vis) J Reid 10/1: 034100: Sn bhd: 16th, op 7/1, see 1920 (C/D, bt this rnr-up).   0
723 **Laa Jadeed 94** [1] 5-7-10 (39)(BL) J McAuley 50/1:   1979 **Mutabari 11** [7] 6-7-11 (40) K Dalgleish (7) 20/1:
637 **Dim Ofan 115** [8] 4-9-5 (62) M Fenton 20/1:
16 ran   Time 1m 32.0 (1.2)   (Mel Brittain)   M Brittain Warthill, N Yorks

2222   **4.15 NSPCC MDN 3YO (D)**   **1m100y**   **Firm 18 -35 Slow**
£3850   £1100   £550

1717 **ADAMAS 22** [3] Andrew Turnell 3-8-9 K Darley 4/6 FAV: 2-041: 3 b f Fairy King - Corynida (Alleged)   71 +
Trkd ldr, led going well appr fnl 1f, just nudged out, easily: nicely bckd: rnr up sole '99 start (fill mdn, rtd
80): eff at 1m, tried 10f: acts on firm, poss not gd/soft, stiff/gall tracks: better than the bare form.

1582 **EMPIRE DREAM** 28 [1] M Johnston 3-9-0 J Reid 11/8: 42: 2 b c Alzao - Triste Oeil (Raise A Cup)   nk   73
Pld hard, prom, led 3f out till appr fnl 1f, toyed with by wnr: flattered by margin of defeat, handles firm grnd.
4570} **WORTH THE RISK** 239 [2] Don Enrico Incisa 3-8-9 Kim Tinkler 20/1: 0050-3: 3 b f Chaddleworth - Bay   7   53
Risk (Risk Me) Led till 3f out, left bhd: reapp, flattered 5th of 7 in '99 (fill auct mdn, rtd 64$): flattered today?
3 ran   Time 1m 48.3 (4.5)   (Mrs Claire Hollowood)   Andrew Turnell Sandhutton, N Yorks

| 2223 | 4.45 E YORKS APPR MDN HCAP 3YO+ 0-70 (F)   5f   Firm 18   -22 Slow   [58] |
| | £2194   £627   £313   3 yo rec 6 lb   High numbers have an edge in sprints here |

2124 **INDIAN BAZAAR** 4 [20] J M Bradley 4-8-12 (42) D Watson 3/1 JT FAV: -03201: 4 ch g Indian Ridge -   46
Bazaar Promise (Native Bazaar) Made just about all, pushed out: nicely bckd, quick reapp: '99 rnr up
(h'cap, rtd 40, Sir M Prescott): well btn juv: eff at 6f, tried 12f, suited by drop back to 5f, forcing the pace:
handles firm & gd/soft grnd, a stiff finish: took advantage of far rail draw.
1994 **SHADY DEAL** 10 [14] M D I Usher 4-9-2 (46) G Sparkes 3/1 JT FAV: 300022: 4 b g No Big Deal -   1¼   46
Taskalady (Touching Wood) Rear, hdwy appr fnl 2f, switched dist, styd on, nvr nrr: nicely bckd from 5/1: see 1994.
2122 **NOW IS THE HOUR** 5 [11] P S Felgate 4-8-0 (30) G Gibbons 20/1: 662003: 4 ch g Timeless Times -   hd   29
Macs Maharanee (Indian King) Well plcd, rdn 2f out, one pace in last: qck reapp: acts on firm grnd & fibresand.
2122 **NOBLE PATRIOT** 5 [1] R Hollinshead 5-8-3 (33) Stephanie Hollinshead 25/1: 025534: Wide, handy,   shd   32
styd on fnl 1f, not pace to chall: quick reapp, back on turf: gd run from stall 1, return to 6f+ will suit: see 61.
2044 **BEST BOND** 8 [18] 3-10-0 (64) D Young 10/1: 030005: Bhd, styd on fnl 2f, never near to chall: 1¼   60
top-weight, handles firm & gd/soft grnd, see 1098.
1923 **TWICKERS** 13 [15] 4-9-5 (49)(bl) R Naylor 12/1: 000006: Trckd ldrs, no extra ent fnl 1f: see 1036.   hd   45
1994 **DON QUIXOTE** 10 [2] 4-8-8 (38) T Hamilton 11/1: -06007: Wide, towards rear, fnl 1f prog: return to 6f?   1   31
1971 **BLAKEY** 11 [17] 4-8-5 (35)(BL) D Egan (4) 25/1: 0-0008: Outpcd till ran on appr fnl 1f, blinkered,   shd   28
stablemate wnr, back in trip: '99 rnr up (auct mdn, rtd 60, J Berry): eff at 5/6f on fast grnd.
2006 **SEAHORSE BOY** 10 [19] 3-9-7 (57) R Farmer 14/1: -00049: Prom till 2f out: op 20/1.   nk   49
1516 **LAYAN** 31 [5] 3-9-3 (53) R Thomas 16/1: 6-5660: Hmpd start, never on terms: 10th: see 777.   1½   41
1036 **CARMARTHEN** 60 [12] 4-9-4 (48) D Kinsella 25/1: 4-0000: Al same place: 11th, 9 week abs, new stable.   nk   35
1843 **LAMMOSKI** 17 [8] 3-9-2 (52) L Gueller 25/1: 050050: Never troubled ldrs: 12th, see 217.   ½   38
1818 **EMLEY** 18 [13] 4-9-6 (50) D Allan (4) 10/1: 563-60: Struggling halfway: 13th, back on trip, h'cap bow.   ½   35
1817 **SWING CITY** 18 [16] 3-9-6 (56) T Eaves 12/1: -00300: Chsd ldrs 3f: 14th, btr 1605 (6f, soft).   ½   40
2015 **Colonel Sam** 9 [10] 4-8-12 (42)(tbl) N Mitchell (4) 14/12193 **Upper Chamber** 1 [4] 4-8-13 (43) Michael Doyle 33/1:
1780 **Bluegrass Mountain** 20 [7] 3-9-5 (55)(bl) M Worrell 14/1:
1105 **Lucky Uno** 55 [3] 4-8-10 (40) P Mundy 33/1:   783 **Martin 90** [9] 3-9-0 (50) L Vickers 40/1:
2047 **Power And Demand** 8 [6] 3-8-8 (44)(bl) L Swift 25/1:
20 ran   Time 1m 03.3 (2)   (Leeway Wholesale Meats Ltd)   J M Bradley Sedbury, Glous

Official Going   GOOD

| 2224 | 2.20 GR 2 PRIX DE MALLERET 3YO FILLIES   1m4f   Good |
| | £28818   £11527   £5764 |

1457 **AMERICA** 35 [2] Mme C Head 3-8-9 O Doleuze 2/5 JT FAVcp: 1-1161: 3 ch f Arazi - Green Rosy   112
(Green Dancer) Front rank, hdwy to lead over 1f out, kept on well, rdn out: landed 1st 2 starts this term,
incl a Gr 3 here at Longchamp: eff at 9f, stays 12f v well: acts on gd & hvy grnd: tough & progressive filly.
*1748 **SADLERS FLAG** 22 [5] Mme C Head 3-8-9 T Gillet 2/5 JT FAVcp: 132112: 3 b f Sadler's Wells -   1½   108
Animatrice (Alleged) Reared up leaving stalls, bhd, rdn to chall dist, sn held: acts on gd & gd/soft: see 1748.
1459 **POLAR CHARGE** 35 [1] B Grizzetti 3-8-9 G Bietolini 34/10: -13023: 3 b f Polar Falcon - Take Charge   ½   107
(Last Tycoon) Help up, drvn/prog appr fnl 1f, swtchd dist, sn onepcd: Italian raider, eff at 11/12f: see 1459.
5 ran   Time 2m 32.7   (Wertheimer Et Frere)   Mme C Head France

| 2225 | 2.50 GR 1 GRAND PRIX DE PARIS 3YO   1m2f   Good |
| | £115274   £46120   £23055   £11527 |

1848 **BEAT HOLLOW** 15 [6] H R A Cecil 3-9-2 T Quinn 7/5 FAV: 1-131: 3 b c Sadler's Wells - Wemyss Bight   120
(Dancing Brave) Trckd ldrs, rdn into lead 2f out, styd on well, drvn out: earlier won on reapp at Newmarket
(List), subs a fine 6L 3rd in the Epsom Derby: landed sole juv start, at Yarmouth (mdn, rtd 98): eff at 10f,
stays 12f: runs v well fresh on fast & gd grnd: high-class & lightly raced colt, open to further improvement & can land more Group races.
1025 **PREMIER PAS** 63 [7] Mme C Head 3-9-2 (BL) O Doleuze 18/1: 13-262: 3 b c Sillery - Passionnee   1   118
(Woodman) Settled rear, rdn/hdwy 2f out, ran on well ins last, al held by wnr: smart effort here in 1st time
blnks: eff at 1m/10f on gd & hvy: shld win a Group 2/3 at least.
1317 **RHENIUM** 42 [5] J C Rouget 3-9-2 T Jarnet 71/10: 1-1133: 3 ch c Rainbows For Life - Miss Mulaz   3   113
(Luthier) Mid-div, rdn/prog appr fnl 1f, sn not pace of front 2: 6 wk abs: see 1317, 1026.
1379 **BOUTRON** 38 [4] P Costes 3-9-2 D Bonilla 118/10: -33224: Rear, late gains for press, no dngr.   2   110
1848 **BEST OF THE BESTS** 15 [2] 3-9-2 S Guillot 17/2: 12-344: Led, rdn/hdd 2f out, wknd fnl 1f, ddhtd   dht   110
for 4th: will reportedly be given a break now & will apprec a drop to Group 2/3 company: see 1848, 1326.
-- **GUILLAMOU CITY** [1] 3-9-2 J R Dubosc 78/1: 0-1116: Trkd ldrs, drvn/no extra front 2f.   1½   107
1231 **CRIMSON QUEST** 48 [3] 3-9-2 O Peslier 6/4: 1-127: Cl-up, rdn/fdd appr fnl 2f: 7 wk abs: btr 1231.   2   104
7 ran   Time 2m 03.7   (K Abdulla)   H R A Cecil Newmarket

| 2226 | 3.20 GR 3 PRIX DE LA PORTE MAILLOT 3YO+   7f   Good |
| | £21134   £7685   £3842   £2305   3 yo rec 9 lb |

4396} **JOSR ALGARHOUD** 253 [8] Saeed bin Suroor 4-9-2 S Guillot 27/10: /123-1: 4 b c Darshaan - Pont Aven   116
(Try My Best) Settled in tch, rdn to chall 2f out, drvn out: reapp: '99 listed scorer at Newcastle (Gr 3,
rtd 117): lightly raced in '98, won at York (Gr 2 Gimcrack, rtd 114, M Channon): suited by 7f on firm & gd grnd:
runs esp well fresh on a stiff/gall trk: tough, lightly raced & v smart colt, win more Gr races.

LONGCHAMP
SUNDAY JUNE 25TH **Righthand, Stiff, Galloping Track**

3700} **CAP COZ 301** [2] R Collet 3-8-4 (BL) T Jarnet 135/10: 120-02: 3 b f Indian Ridge - Pont Aven (Try ½ **112**
My Best) Chsd ldrs, rdn & ran on strongly appr fnl 1f, just held: tried blnks: won twice in '99, subs 2nd in a
Gr 3 (rtd 105): half-sister to this wnr: eff at 7f, 1m shld suit: acts on gd grnd & in blnks: v useful.

*2070 **TUMBLEWEED RIDGE 11** [4] B J Meehan 7-9-5 M Tebbutt 21/10 FAV: 0-2313: 7 ch h Indian Ridge - ¾ **116**
Billie Blue (Ballad Rock) Led early, remnd cl-up, led again over 2f out, hdd dist, not btn far: v tough, see 2070.

2660} **DIABLENEYEV 348** [6] Mme C Head 5-9-2 (bl) O Doleuze 22/1: 04-244: Sn led, hdd appr fnl 1f, snk **112**
rall & styd on ins last: rtd 103 when 4th in a Gr 3 in '99: stays 6/7f on gd grnd.

-- **NO MATTER WHAT** [3] 3-8-4 O Peslier 28/10: 45-115: Held up, nvr with ldrs: unbtn prev this term. snk **109**

*1674 **MOUNT ABU 22** [7] 3-8-7 G Mosse 48/10: 6-4116: Settled rear, plenty to do over 2f out, gd hdwy ½ **111**
appr fnl 1f, sn btn: shade disapp on this step up to Group class, may apprec a drop back to 6f: see 1674 (List).

9 ran   Time 1m 19.4   (Goldolphin)   Saeed bin Suroor Newmarket

SALISBURY
WEDNESDAY JUNE 28TH **Righthand, Galloping Track, Stiff Finish**

Official Going   GOOD TO FIRM. Stalls: Str Crse - Far Side; 12f - Stands Side.

2227
2.10 EBF WEYHILL FILLIES MDN 2YO (D)   5f   Good/Firm 28 -11 Slow
£3354   £1032   £516   £258

1943 **STRUMPET 13** [2] R F Johnson Houghton 2-8-11 J Reid 7/2: -201: 2 b f Tragic Role - Fee (Mandamus): **79**
Chsd ldrs, rdn/prog final 2f & styd on strongly for press to lead ins last, going away: op 3/1: eff at 5f,
6f shld suit: acts on fast & gd/soft grnd, sharp/undul or stiff trk: clearly going the right way.

1454 **LADY EBERSPACHER 36** [8] Mrs P N Dutfield 2-8-11 L Newman (3) 4/1: 042: 2 b f Royal Abjar - Samriah 1¼ **75**
(Wassl): Led/dsptd lead till 2f out, rdn/led again 1f out, hdd ins last, held nr fin: op 7/2: handles fast & gd/soft.

1986 **CAYMAN EXPRESSO 11** [5] R Hannon 2-8-11 R Hughes 3/1 FAV: 63: 2 b f Fayruz - Cappuchino (Roi 1½ **71**
Danzig): Led/dsptd lead till went on over 2f out, hdd 1f out & no extra nr fin: bckd: clr rem, acts on fast.

-- **LADY IN THE NIGHT** [9] I A Balding 2-8-11 K Darley 10/1: 4: Dwelt/towards rear, mod gains final 2f, 4 **61+**
no threat: op 6/1: Royal Academy filly, May foal, 20,000 gns purchase: half-sister to a 10/12f wnr: dam related to
high class mid-dist performer Peintre Celebre: sure to relish much further in time & improve.

-- **ROXANNE MILL** [1] 2-8-11 R Perham 50/1: 5: Dwelt/rear, some hdwy over 2f out, no impress: op 1 **59**
6/1: Cyrano de Bergerac filly, Mar foal, cost 14,000 gns: dam a dual 5f 3yo wnr: with M D I Usher.

-- **MOMENTS IN TIME** [6] 2-8-11 S Drowne 15/2: 6: Dwelt, rdn/bhd halfway, late gains, nrst fin: op hd **58**
5/1: Emperor Jones filly, Apr foal: half-sister to a dual 7f juv wnr: do better over 6f+.

-- **MAGICAL FLUTE** [3] 2-8-11 Craig Williams 10/1: 7: Dwelt & rdn/bhd halfway, late gains: op 6/1: ¾ **56**
stablemate of 6th: Piccolo filly, Feb foal: half-sister to a 10f 3yo wnr: dam a 5/7f juv wnr.

-- **TURBO BLUE** [10] 2-8-11 S Sanders 6/1: 8: Dwelt, sn chsg ldrs, btn 2f out: bckd: op 12/1: Dolphin 1¼ **53**
Street filly, May foal, cost IR£9,000: dam lightly rcd, a half-sister to high class miler Teleprompter.

-- **ELLENDUNE GIRL** [11] 2-8-11 R Studholme (5) 25/1: 9: Bhd halfway: Mistertopogigo filly, Mar foal, 1¼ **50**
cheaply bought: dam modest: with D J S ffrench Davis.

2009 **RED FANFARE 11** [4] 2-8-11 J P Spencer 20/1: 00: Al outpcd rear: 10th: see 2009. nk **49**

2057 **MARY HAYDEN 8** [7] 2-8-11 D Sweeney 40/1: 00: Bhd halfway: 11th: see 2057. ½ **47**

11 ran   Time 1m 01.74 (1.94)   (Lady Rothschild)   R F Johnson Houghton Blewbury, Oxon.

2228
2.40 SOUTHAMPTON COND STKS 3YO (C)   7f str   Good/Firm 28 -05 Slow
£6138   £2178   £1089   £495

1830 **HOPEFUL LIGHT 19** [2] J H M Gosden 3-9-4 K Darley 6/4: 1-401: 3 b c Warning - Hope (Dancing Brave): **101**
Made all, hard rdn in duel with rnr-up fnl 2f, narrowly prevailed, all-out: hvly bckd tho' op 5/4: won sole juv
start at Doncaster (mdn, rtd 92): eff at 6/7f, 1m should suit: acts on fast & hvy, stiff/gall trk: has run well fresh.

1171 **MANA MOU BAY 53** [4] R Hannon 3-9-8 R Hughes 11/10 FAV: 21-02: 3 b c Ela-Mana-Mou - Summerhill hd **104**
(Habitat) With wnr all trav best, jockey only asked for effort fnl 100y, not qckn as expected: hvly bckd: reportedly
has had a lung infection: over-confident tactic to ask mount to qckn instantly cl home, disapp for backers.

*1556 **DIXIELAKE 30** [1] H Candy 3-8-13 C Rutter 5/1: 0-13: 3 b f Lake Coniston - Rathvindon (Realm): 8 **80**
Held up in tch, outpcd by front pair final 2f: op 7/1: see 1556.

996 **JAMADYAN 67** [3] H Akbary 3-9-6 A Whelan 14/1: 1-64: Trkd ldrs, outpcd final 3f: 2 mth abs: see 996. 1¾ **83**

4 ran   Time 1m 27.8 (2.3)   (K Abdullah)   J H M Gosden Manton, Wilts.

2229
3.10 NOEL CANNON HCAP 3YO+ 0-100 (C)   1m str   Good/Firm 28 -03 Slow   [98]
£6695   £2060   £1030   £515   3 yo rec 10lb Field raced towards centre

2090 **SPEEDFIT TOO 7** [6] C E Brittain 5-10-0 (98)(vis) T E Durcan 3/1 FAV: 150401: 5 b h Scenic - Safka **105**
(Irish River): Waited with rear, prog from halfway & rdn/led 1f out, drvn out to maintain advantage cl home: op 5/2:
confirmed promise of recent British reapp: has been racing in Dubai, earlier won over 7.5f: in '98 trained by
G Margarson to win at Kempton (Listed, rtd 104): eff at 6f, suited by 1m: acts on firm, prob soft, dirt & any trk:
gd weight carrier & suited by a visor: looks best held up for a late run & could win again.

1965 **PUNISHMENT 12** [7] K O Cunningham Brown 9-8-1 (71)(t) L Newman (3) 16/1: 500062: 9 b h Midyan - In ½ **75**
The Shade (Bustino): Cl-up, led after 2f, rdn/hdd 1f out, kept on well: apprec drop to 1m, nicely h'capped: see 157.

1853 **EL CURIOSO 17** [10] P W Harris 3-8-12 (92) J Reid 7/1: -01603: 3 b c El Gran Senor - Curious (Rare 2 **92**
Performer): Rear, rdn halfway, styd on final 2f, no threat to front pair: op 6/1: see 1262.

1872 **TAMMAM 16** [8] Mrs L Stubbs 4-9-3 (87) K Darley 100/30: 005344: Chsd ldr 3f out till 2f out, sn held. 2½ **82**

1160 **VIRTUAL REALITY 53** [9] 9-9-2 (86) M Roberts 5/1: 230-05: Led, hdd after 2f, btn 2f out: op 8/1, 4bs. 4 **73**

*1836 **SILK ST JOHN 18** [3] 6-9-9 (93) P McCabe 9/2: 651316: Keen/rear, efft 3f out, no prog: op 7/2. 1 **78**

1547 **PARKSIDE 30** [5] 4-8-5 (75) Martin Dwyer 12/1: 05-037: In tch, btn 2f out: op 8/1: see 1042. nk **59**

1598 **MISS RIMEX 28** [1] 4-8-5 (75) N Pollard 12/1: 01-508: Rear, effort 3f out, no prog: op 8/1: see 1473. 1¾ **56**

4616} **LOCH INCH 235** [4] 3-8-10 (90) D R McCabe 33/1: 0010-9: Chsd ldrs 6f: reapp: '99 wnr at Nottingham 1½ **68**
(auct mdn) & Windsor (nursery h'cap, rtd 90): suited by 6f, poss stys 7f: acts on fast & soft, not fibresand:
handles a sharp or gall trk, gd weight carrier: eff with/without blnks: useful at best, will appec a drop in trip.

9 ran   Time 1m 41.54 (2.44)   (H E Sheikh Rashid Al Maktoum)   C E Brittain Newmarket, Suffolk.

SALISBURY
WEDNESDAY JUNE 28TH   Righthand, Galloping Track, Stiff Finish

---

2230   3.40 DOWNTON FILLIES HCAP 3YO+ 0-70 (E)   6f   Good/Firm 28   -08 Slow   [63]
£2977   £916   £458   £229   3 yo rec 7 lb

1542 **CONTRARY MARY** 32 [1] J Akehurst 5-9-4 (53) T Quinn 7/1: 5-0051: 5 b m Mujadil - Love Street   60
(Mummy's Pet): Swtchd to race far rail from start, bhd, stdy prog from halfway & rdn/led inside last, styd on well:
'99 wnr at Folkestone (class stks, rtd 67): '98 wnr at Lingfield (turf h'cap) & Pontefract (clmr, subs disq, rtd 74
& 59a): suited by 6/7f on firm & soft, handles any trk: v well h'capped & given a typically astute T Quinn ride.
1741 **MAGIQUE ETOILE** 22 [16] M P Muggeridge 4-9-1 (50) K Darley 9/1: -00622: 4 b f Magical Wonder -   ¾   54
She's A Dancer (Alzao): Chsd ldrs, rdn/led 1f out, hdd inside last, kept on well: op 10/1: mdn after 26: see 114.
1545 **WAFFS FOLLY** 30 [2] D J S ffrench Davis 5-9-4 (53) R Studholme (5) 20/1: 34-003: 5 b m Handsome   3½   48
Sailor - Shirl (Shirley Heights): Cl-up till went on 2f out, hdd 1f out & no extra: see 1082.
1932 **ABSOLUTE FANTASY** 13 [8] E A Wheeler 4-8-13 (48)(bl) S Carson (5) 12/1: 014034: Rear, effort 2f out,   ½   41
kept on, no threat to front pair: in good heart, likes Brighton: see 1464, 1211.
1712 **SKYLARK** 24 [3] 3-9-11 (67) R Hughes 12/1: 00-465: Rear, drifted right & drvn/styd on fnl 2f, no threat.   ½   58
2022 **JONATHANS GIRL** 10 [14] 5-7-10 (31)(1oh) R Brisland (5) 33/1: 040006: Chsd ldrs, onepace final 2f.   ¾   20
*1971 **BAYONET** 12 [7] 4-9-7 (56) J P Spencer 11/4FAV: 0-0217: Rear, wknd over 2f out, no impress: bckd.   hd   44
2031 **BRAMBLE BEAR** 10 [9] 6-9-1 (50) D Sweeney 10/1: 001048: Held up, efft 2f out, mod gains: see 1464.   ½   36
1676 **AMBER BROWN** 25 [15] 4-9-13 (62)(bl) S Sanders 9/1: 100149: Led 4f: op 6/1: btr 1676, 1542 (sft, 7f).   ½   46
1799 **STRIDHANA** 20 [12] 4-9-12 (61) N Pollard 10/1: 000-00: Trkd ldrs, btn 2f out: 10th: op 8/1: '99   ½   43
Lingfield wnr (mdn, rtd 71): eff at 6f, tried 1m: acts on firm & fast, prob handles gd: prob handles any track.
2124 **SEREN TEG** 5 [11] 4-9-3 (52) C Rutter 20/1: 144000: Nvr on terms: 11th: op 14/1, sdk reapp: see 440.   ½   32
1345 **OARE PINTAIL** 41 [6] 3-9-7 (63) S Drowne 15/2: 060-00: Chsd ldrs 4f: 15th: 6 wk abs: see 1345.   0
2463} Tilia 359 [13] 4-9-0 (49) R Smith (5) 20/1:   *1670 Diamond Promise 26 [4] 3-9-3 (59) L Newman (3) 14/1:
2043 Satwa Boulevard 9 [5] 5-7-10 (31)(t)(4oh) M Henry 12/1:
2044 Emerald Imp 9 [10] 3-8-13 (55) Craig Williams 33/1:
1211 Fairytime 50 [17] 4-8-0 (35)(bl) Martin Dwyer 33/1:
17 ran   Time 1m 14.25 (2.15)   (Flisher Foods)   J Akehurst Epsom, Surrey.

2231   4.10 BIBURY CUP HCAP 3YO 0-95 (C)   1m4f   Good/Firm 28   +11 Fast   [97]
£6857   £2110   £1055   £527

*1948 **FIRECREST** 13 [4] J L Dunlop 3-9-7 (90) T Quinn 4/7 FAV: -01111: 3 b f Darshaan - Trefoil (Blakeney):   100
Made all, in command over 1f out, rdn out inside last, al holding rivals: fast time: hvly bckd at odds-on,
completed a four-timer: earlier won h'caps at Leicester (2) & Newbury: suited by 12f, 14f+ shd suit: acts on
fast & gd/soft grnd, loves a stiff/gall trk: has run well fresh: can force the pace: tough/progressive & useful.
1637 **DUCHAMP** 27 [3] I A Balding 3-9-0 (83) K Darley 7/2: 1-5402: 3 b c Pine Bluff - Higher Learning   2½   87
(Fappiano): Chsd wnr thro'out, rdn/ch 3f out, kept on final 2f, al held: pulled clr: stays a stiff 12f: see 1177.
1885 **REFLEX BLUE** 15 [1] J W Hills 3-9-2 (85) R Hills 6/1: 5-4423: 3 b g Ezzoud - Briggsmaid (Elegant Air):   8   80
Held up in tch, rdn/btn over 2f out & eased inside last: op 5/1: btr 1885, 1400.
1796 **POWERLINE** 20 [2] R Hannon 3-8-6 (75) R Hughes 6/1: 0-0634: Held up, btn 3f out & eased fnl 1f.   17   52
4 ran   Time 2m 34.42 (2.02)   (Sir Thomas Pilkington)   J L Dunlop Arundel, West Sussex.

2232   4.40 SHREWTON FILLIES MDN 3YO (D)   7f str   Good/Firm 28   -02 Slow
£3672   £1130   £565   £282

1708 **GWENDOLINE** 24 [14] J R Fanshawe 3-8-11 R Hills 5/2 FAV: 21: 3 b f Polar Falcon - Merlins Charm   80
(Bold Bidder): Trkd ldrs, rdn/led over 1f out, in command/pushed out cl-home: confirmed promise of debut:
eff at 7f, 1m should suit: acts on fast & gd/soft grnd, sharp/turning or stiff trk: op to further improvement.
1886 **HARMONIC** 15 [15] D R C Elsworth 3-8-11 N Pollard 7/2: 4-6022: 3 b f Shadeed - Running Melody   3½   72
(Rheingold): Chsd ldrs, ev ch 2f out, held by wnr final 1f: clr rem: worth a try in headgear: see 1886.
1725 **SPOT** 23 [11] Andrew Reid 3-8-11 M Henry 50/1: 03: 3 gr f Inchinor - Billie Grey (Chilibang):   3   66
Led, rdn/hdd over 1f out, no extra: apprec drop to 7f & left debut bhd: handles fast grnd: see 1725.
1500 **EFFERVESCENT** 33 [1] I A Balding 3-8-11 K Darley 5/1: 0234: Chsd ldrs, rdn/onepace over 1f out.   1   64
1857 **HATHEETHAH** 17 [2] 3-8-11 G Sparkes (7) 13/2: 055: Dwelt/rear, sn in tch, no threat: op 5/1.   2   60
-- **COLLISION** [9] 3-8-11 C Rutter 9/1: 6: Rear, drvn 3f out, mod gains: op 8/1, debut: with H Candy.   3   54
4310} **TURQUOISE GEM** 261 [8] 3-8-11 R Brisland (5) 33/1: 0006-7: Chsd ldrs 5f: reapp: unplcd last term   ½   53
(rtd 64, fillies mdn): h'cap company should suit.
-- **SUN SILK** [4] 3-8-11 R Havlin 8/1: 8: Rear, mod late gains, nvr a factor: op 9/2, debut: dam a   nk   52
smart 1m performer: market told story today: with J Gosden.
-- **APRIL STAR** [5] 3-8-11 S Sanders 16/1: 9: Mid-div, btn 3f out: op 10/1, debut: with G G Margarson   4   44
1947 **PING ALONG** 13 [10] 3-8-11 Martin Dwyer 20/1: -60: Al bhd: 10th: see 1947.   3½   37
-- Red White And Blue [3] 3-8-11 L Newman (3) 50/1:   2024 No Tomorrow 16 [6] 3-8-11 (t) Sophie Mitchell 25/1:
1972 Chiaro 12 [13] 3-8-11 J P Spencer 50/1:   -- Kerrich [12] 3-8-11 S Carson (5) 50/1:
14 ran   Time 1m 27.62 (2.12)   (Mrs M Slater)   J R Fanshawe Newmarket, Suffolk.

HAMILTON
WEDNESDAY JUNE 28TH   Righthand, Undulating Track, Stiff Uphill Finish

Official Going   GOOD/FIRM. Stalls: Stands Side, Except 1m/9f - Inside

---

2233   7.00 HAMILTON AMAT RDRS HCAP 3YO+ 0-60 (F)   5f   Good/Firm 25   -24 Slow   [27]
£2938   £904   £452   £226   3 yo rec 6 lb   Raced across track, winner raced far side

1358 **KALAR** 40 [9] D W Chapman 11-10-12 (39)(bl) Miss R Clark 11/2: 050041: 11 b g Kabour - Wind And   45
Reign (Tumble Wind) Made all, clr halfway, styd on strongly, pushed out: 6 wk abs: '99 wnr at Ripon (sell h'cap,
rtd 43): best dominating at 5f, stays 6f: acts on soft, likes firm, gd & both AWs: suited by blnks, runs well fresh.
1910 **BIFF EM** 14 [7] Miss L A Perratt 6-10-10 (37) Miss Diana Jones 7/4 FAV: 503042: 6 ch g Durgam - Flash   2   37
The Gold (Ahonoora) Prom, kept on fnl 2f, al held: hvly bckd: see 1143.
1766 **PALACEGATE JACK** 21 [4] A Berry 9-11-0 (41) Mr F Giuliani (7) 10/1: 323003: 9 gr g Neshad - Pasadena   3   33
Lady (Captain James) Prom, rdn/hung left 2f out, kept on tho' held fnl 1f: op 6/1: see 191 (AW).

2097 **JOHAYRO** 7 [2] J S Goldie 7-12-0 (55) Mr J Goldie (7) 3/1: 000024: Chsd ldrs, hung right/held 1f out. 1½ 43
1559 **BAYARD LADY** 30 [1] 4-10-0 (27) Miss K Smith (7) 66/1: 000005: Outpcd, styd on fnl 2f, nrst fin: see 973. nk 14
1907 **TAKE NOTICE** 14 [8] 7-9-12 (25) Mr J McSnane (7) 66/1: 000/06: Prom, onepace fnl 2f: no form. nk 11
2078 **SWEET MAGIC** 7 [5] 9-11-11 (52)(t) Miss L Vollaro (5) 8/1: 414007: Rear, nvr on terms: op 6/1. ¾ 36
1941 **ABSTRACT** 13 [6] 4-10-7 (34)(bl) Miss Rachel Clark (7) 33/1: 6-0008: Prom 3f: blnks reapp: unplcd hd 17
last term (rtd 42, vis, mdn, rtd 37a on sand): rtd 54 at best in '98 (D Cosgrove, tried blnks): eff at 5f & handles gd.
1941 **TIME FOR THE CLAN** 13 [10] 3-10-13 (46) Miss R Bastiman (7) 14/1: 400-09: Dwelt, al bhd: op 10/1: 3½ 20
unplcd last term (rtd 65, sell, J J O'Neill): mod form prev, incl in blnks: eff over a stiff grnd on firm grnd.
2095 **PALLIUM** 7 [11] 12-10-8 (28)(t)(7ow) Mr M G Williams (0) 33/1: 0-0000: In tch till halfway: 10th. 1¼ 5
1979 **TIME IS MONEY** 12 [3] 8-11-1 (42) Mr M Jenkins (0) 20/1: 205-00: Al outpcd: 11th: rnr-up last 2½ 5
term (rtd 63, prob flattered, 7 rnr clmr): stays 7f, handles firm & fast grnd.
11 ran   Time 1m 0.5 (2.4)   (David W Chapman)   D W Chapman Stillington, N Yorks

---

2234   7.25 EBF MDN 2YO (D)   6f   Good/Firm 24 -33 Slow
£3789 £1166 £583 £291

-- **BLUE PLANET** [2] Sir Mark Prescott 2-9-0 G Duffield 4/6 FAV: 1: 2 b c Bluebird - Miller Musique 85
(Miller's Mate) Chsd ldrs, led over 1f out, styd on well fnl 1f, rdly: well bckd at odds-on: May foal, cost
52,000gns: half brother to a smart 5f juv wnr: dam once rcd, sire a top-class sprinter: eff at 6f, shld get
further: acts on fast & a stiff trk: runs well fresh: open to improvement.
1595 **WALLY MCARTHUR** 28 [4] A Berry 2-9-0 J Carroll 4/1: -032: 2 b c Puissance - Giddy (Polar Falcon) 1¾ 76
Cl-up, rdn/edged right & outpcd by wnr fnl 1f: op 7/2: handles fast & gd grnd: see 1595.
-- **KILBARCHAN** [3] Miss L A Perratt 2-8-9 Dale Gibson 10/1: 3: 2 ch f Selkirk - Haitienne (Green ¾ 69
Dancer) Led till over 1f out, sn held: op 7/1: Selkirk filly, Apr foal, cost 36,000 gns: half sister to 3 juv wnrs,
dam a French 1m 3yo wnr: apprec 7f+ in time.
-- **AMEN CORNER** [1] M Johnston 2-9-0 J Fanning 7/2: 4: Cl-up, outpcd over 1f out: op 3/1: Mt ½ 72
Livermore colt, Feb foal: cost $75,000: dam a US sprint wnr.
4 ran   Time 1m 13.2 (3.4)   (Meg Dennis, Michael Blackburn, John Brown)   Sir Mark Prescott Newmarket

---

2235   7.55 OH! DE MOSCHINO HCAP 3YO 0-80 (D)   1m65y rnd Good/Firm 24 +04 Fast   [80]
£5408 £1664 £832 £416

2084 **GRANTED** 7 [1] M L W Bell 3-9-7 (73) M Fenton 5/4 JT FAV: 4-3321: 3 b f Cadeaux Genereux - Germane 76
(Distant Relative) Chsd ldrs, drvn fnl 2f, styd on gamely to lead nr line, all out: well bckd: 1st win: rtd 82 at
best in '99 (mdn): eff at 1m, tried 10f, shld suit: acts on fast & gd/soft, likes a stiff/gall trk: best without visor.
2166 **ARIZONA LADY** 4 [5] J Semple 3-9-2 (68) R Winston 12/1: -10032: 3 ch f Lion Cavern - Unfuwaanah hd 70
(Unfuwain) Led, rdn/strongly prsd ins last, kept on well, just hdd cl-home: op 8/1, quick reapp: see 902.
1895 **MARVEL** 15 [3] Don Enrico Incisa 3-8-6 (58) Kim Tinkler 20/1: 000203: 3 b f Rudimentary - Maravilla ¾ 58
(Mandrake Major) In tch, rdn & styd on well ins last, not reach front pair: eff at 1m/stiff 9.3f on fast & hvy grnd.
*2025 **GRUINART** 10 [2] H Morrison 3-9-6 (72) J Carroll 5/4 JT FAV: 004314: Trkd ldr, rdn & kept on onepace nk 71
from over 1f out: hvly bckd, op 13/8: only btn around 1L: see 2025.
2006 **HIGHLAND GOLD** 11 [4] 3-9-4 (70) G Duffield 10/1: 65-35: Dwelt, sn chsd ldrs, btn over 1f out. 5 59
5 ran   Time 1m 45.5 (1.7)   (E D Kessly)   M L W Bell Newmarket

---

2236   8.25 4 ELEMENTS SELLER 3YO+ (E)   1m1f36y Good/Firm 24 -07 Slow
£2847 £876 £438 £219   3 yo rec 11lb

3949} **PEGASUS BAY** 286 [10] D E Cantillon 9-9-4 A Beech (5) 11/10 FAV: 1162-1: 9 b g Tina's Pet - Mossberry 53
Fair (Mossberry) In tch, hdwy appr fnl 1f, sn led, rdn clr ins last, eased cl-home: nicely bckd: reapp (has had
a suspensory prob), no bid: '99 wnr at Newmarket (sell, rtd 66) & here at Hamilton (2, clmr & h'cap), subs won
over fences at Huntingdon (nov h'cap, rtd 88c, eff at 2m on fast): eff at 7/11.5f on firm, gd/soft & equitrack:
handles any trk, loves Hamilton: runs well fresh, likes sells/clmrs: fine reapp, follow up.
1939 **BAY OF BENGAL** 13 [5] J S Wainwright 4-8-13 J McAuley (5) 7/2: 40-032: 4 ch f Persian Bold - 2½ 43
Adjamiya (Shahrastani) Dwelt, rear, hdwy for press 2f out, styd on despite flashing tail ins last, al held
by wnr, clr rem: in gd form & could win a sell h'cap: see 1939, 1353.
2046 **UNMASKED** 9 [9] J S Goldie 4-8-13 A Culhane 16/1: 000033: 4 ch f Safawan - Unveiled (Sayf El Arab) 2½ 38$
Mid-div, prog/short of room over 2f out, late hdwy, no dngr: up in trip, not disgraced at the weights: stays 7f/9f.
2136 **SECONDS AWAY** 5 [11] J S Goldie 9-9-4 Dawn Rankin (7) 12/1: -60424: Hdwy from rear fnl 2f, nvr nrr. nk 42$
846 **WESTERN GENERAL** 81 [3] 9-9-4 R Winston 4/1: /42-05: Bhd, eff halfway, held fnl 2f: op 5/1: 1 40
4th over hdles (2m1f sell h'cap, rtd 76h) since 846.
2040 **BODFARI SIGNET** 9 [1] M Fenton 4-9-4 (bl) 33/1: 000006: Rcd keenly cl-up, rdn/btn fnl 2f: see 1190. ¾ 38$
1858 **FOUR MEN** 17 [4] 3-8-7 J Carroll 20/1: 40-007: Led, hdd appr fnl 1f, wknd qckly. ¾ 36
4078} **MEN OF WICKENBY** 278 [2] 6-9-4 C Teague 33/1: 0050-8: Front rank, drvn/lost tch fnl 2f: reapp: 8 20
'99 wnr here at Hamilton (sell, rtd 53): missed '98, prev term rtd 53 for R McKeller: eff at 9/11f on gd & soft.
1101 **SPECIAL K** 56 [7] 8-8-13 G Duffield 6/1: 4U0-09: Handy, rdn/wknd fnl 2f: btr 1101 (h'cap). 4 7
2046 **PRIESTRIG BRAE** 9 [6] 4-8-13 J Fanning 50/1: 00: Sn struggling, fin 10th. 16 0
1596 **BANK BUSTER** 28 [8] 3-8-7 (BL) Dale Gibson 50/1: 000: Prom, wknd qckly fnl 4f,fin last: blnkd. 1¾ 0
11 ran   Time 1m 57.0 (2.9)   (Don Cantillon)   D E Cantillon Carlton, Cambs

---

2237   8.55 PRETTY HAT NOV AUCT STKS 2YO (F)   6f str Good/Firm 25 -48 Slow
£2769 £852 £426 £213

1497 **WILSON BLYTH** 33 [5] A Berry 2-8-7 J Carroll 4/6 FAV: 221: 2 b c Puissance - Pearls (Mon Tresor) 83
Sn led, drvn clr fnl 1f, rdly: rnr-up both prev starts: Feb 1st foal, dam unrcd: eff at 6f on fast &
gd/soft grnd: acts on a gall or stiff/undul trk: going the right way, could win again.
2162 **LAST IMPRESSION** 4 [2] J S Goldie 2-8-8 A Culhane 11/4: 142: 2 b f Imp Society - Figment (Posse) 2 77
Prom, rdn/not pace of wnr ins last: quick reapp: up in trip, poss stays 6f: see 2162, 1937.
2162 **SHATIN DOLLYBIRD** 4 [4] Miss L A Perratt 2-8-0 Dale Gibson 3/1: 2233: 2 ch f Up And At 'Em - hd 68
Pumpona (Sharpen Up) Trkd wnr, drvn & no extra for press ins last: op 2/1, quick reapp: shade btr 2162 (5f).
1962 **LAW BREAKER** 12 [1] J Cullinan 2-8-7 J Fanning 16/1: 04: Led early, rem in tch, fdd fnl 2f: see 1962. 7 55
4 ran   Time 1m 14.1 (4.3)   (Dennis Blyth & Owen Wilson)   A Berry Cockerham, Lancs

2238 9.25 GREENOAKHILL HCAP 3YO+ 0-75 (E) 1m5f Good/Firm 24 +03 Fast [67]
£3493 £1075 £537 £268 3 yo rec 15lb

1821 **FORUM CHRIS 19** [3] M Johnston 3-8-12 (66) J Fanning 9/2: 04331: 3 ch g Trempolino - Memory Green 73
(Green Forest) Dsptd lead, went on over 4f out, sn clr, rdn out: gd time, 1st win: eff at 12/13f, has tried 14f:
acts on fast, handles gd/soft & soft & a stiff & gall trk: likes to race up with/force the pace: shld follow up.
*2098 **ONCE MORE FOR LUCK 7** [6] Mrs M Reveley 9-9-10 (63) T Eaves (7) 11/8 FAV: 060312: 9 b g Petorius - 3½ 65
Mrs Lucky (Royal Match) Waited on, smooth hdwy 3f out, styd on but not pace of wnr fnl 1f: quick reapp:
met a progressive rival here & remains in gd form: see 2098.
2110 **RED CANYON 6** [4] M L W Bell 3-8-9 (63) M Fenton 5/2: 244123: 3 b g Zieten - Bayazida (Bustino) 1¼ 63
Led, hdd over 4f out, drvn & not pace of wnr fnl 2f: quick reapp: poss not quite get 13f?: see 2110, 1633.
1909 **PAPI SPECIAL 14** [5] I Semple 3-8-2 (54)(vis)(2ow) R Winston 10/1: 2-0024: Front rank, dropped rear 1 55
4f out, rallied & styd on fnl 2f, no threat: longer 13f trip: see 1909 (11f).
2139 **SPREE VISION 5** [7] 4-9-1 (54) A Culhane 7/1: 045165: Rear, eff when hung right 3f out, held 1¼ 51
appr fnl 1f: quick reapp: twice below 1908.
2061 **BOLT FROM THE BLUE 8** [2] 4-8-5 (44) Kim Tinkler 20/1: 0-0056: Rcd keenly cl-up, no extra fnl 3f. 5 34
2119 **TEN PAST SIX 6** [1] 8-8-8 (47)(vis) J Carroll 33/1: 0-0567: Prom, rdn/btn fnl 3f: qck turf return. 10 23
7 ran Time 2m 48.2 (2.7) (Mrs Jacqueline Conroy) M Johnston Middleham, N Yorks

Official Going GOOD TO FIRM Stalls: Inside.

2239 2.00 EBF THWAITES MDN 2YO (D) 6f rnd Good/Firm 20 -28 Slow
£4030 £1240 £620 £310

1906 **MON SECRET 14** [7] J L Eyre 2-9-0 J F Egan 15/2: 03241: 2 b c General Monash - ron's Secret (Efisio) 80
Cl-up, rdn to lead over 1f out, edged right & drvn clr ins last: op 5/1: Mar 1st foal, dam won over 1m/9f:
eff at 5f, clrly apprec this step up to a stiff 6f, 7f will suit: acts on fast & gd/soft grnd: improved today.
1883 **EAU ROUGE 15** [5] M A Jarvis 2-8-9 P Robinson 5/4 FAV: 022: 2 ch f Grand Lodge - Tarsa (Ballad Rock) 2 70
Trkd ldrs, led over 1f out, sn hdd, keeping on but not pace of wnr when sltly hmpd ins last: bckd, clr rem.
-- **LITTLE TASK** [6] A Berry 2-9-0 A Culhane 20/1: 3: 2 b c Environment Friend - Lucky Thing (Green 3 67
Desert) In tch, rdn & styd on well fnl 1f, no threat to front 2: op 10/1: 2,600 gns Apr foal, sire high-class
at 10f: pleasing debut, shld improve & enjoy 7f.
2106 **LOVE LADY 6** [8] M Johnston 2-8-9 J Fanning 11/4: 44: Led, hdd appr fnl 1f, wknd, qck reapp: btr 2106. 1¼ 59
1893 **CYNARA 15** [4] 2-8-9 Dale Gibson 50/1: 05: Sn rdn in rear, late gains for press, no threat: see 1893. ¾ 57
-- **LENNEL** [10] 2-9-0 R Winston 14/1: 6: Dwelt, rear, prog when short of room appr fnl 2f, styd on, hd 62
no dngr: May 1st foal, dam scored over 1m as a 2yo: apprec 7f.
1838 **NISAN BIR 18** [3] 2-9-0 P Fessey 10/1: 047: Mid-div, gd hdwy appr fnl 1f, lost tch ins last: op 7/1. shd 62
1838 **BEE KING 18** [9] 2-9-0 M Tebbutt 33/1: -008: Trkd ldrs, fdd fnl 2f: see 1838. nk 61
1893 **THEWHIRLINGDERVISH 15** [2] 2-9-0 W Supple 33/1: 09: Al in rear: see 1893. 1¼ 58
2034 **UTMOST 9** [1] 2-8-9 Joanna Badger (7) 33/1: 00: Sn well bhd, fin last. 11 33
10 ran Time 1m 15.0 (2.9) (Pinnacle Monash Partnership) J L Eyre Sutton Bank, N Yorks

2240 2.30 C.G. FORD SELLER 3YO+ (F) 6f rnd Good/Firm 20 -18 Slow
£2446 £699 £349 3 yo rec 6 lb

2078 **TREASURE TOUCH 7** [4] D Nicholls 6-9-10 Iona Wands (5) 7/4 FAV: 011301: 6 b g Treasure Kay - Bally 60
Pourri (Law Society) Trkd ldrs, went on 2f out, sn clr, rdn out to hold on: nicely bckd tho' op 5/4, sold
for 7,000 gns: earlier won twice at Catterick (clmr & h'cap): rnr-up in '99 (stks, rtd 60), back in '97
scored at Southwell, Nottingham (2), Newmarket & Thirsk (rtd 71a & 89): suited by 6f on any trk: acts on
firm, gd/soft & fibresand, without blnks: likes sell/clmrs: tough, 8 wins from 38 starts.
1869 **SHARP EDGE BOY 16** [1] E J Alston 4-9-5 W Supple 14/1: 000002: 4 gr g Mystiko - Leap Castle 1 51
(Never So Bold) Prom, drvn & styd on well ins last: fine eff from a poor draw here, win a sell h'cap: see 622.
2097 **TANCRED ARMS 7** [8] D W Barker 4-9-0 F Lynch 16/1: 230003: 4 b f Clantime - Mischievous Miss ¾ 44
(Niniski) In tch, rdn & ran on well from 2f out, nrst fin: quick reapp: apprec a sell h'cap: see 698.
2015 **SEALED BY FATE 10** [6] J S Wainwright 5-9-5 (vis) J F Egan 6/1: 066044: Sn bhd, ran on nk 49
strongly for press fnl 1f, nrst fin: tchd 8/1: left himself with too much to do here: see 2015, 697.
1734 **JAYPEECEE 23** [10] 4-9-5 (vis) J F Egan 12/1: 0-0045: Trkd ldrs, chall 2f out, held appr fnl 1f. 1 46
2097 **SOUPERFICIAL 7** [11] 9-9-5 Kim Tinkler 9/1: -00206: Bhd, late hdwy, no threat: qck reapp. shd 46
2095 **FACILE TIGRE 7** [16] 5-9-5 R Winston 16/1: 005067: Rcd keenly in mid-div, eff 3f out, drvn & ¾ 44
btn appr fnl 1f: quick reapp: see 146.
2122 **GAD YAKOUN 6** [15] 7-9-5 Angela Hartley (7) 50/1: 0-0008: Mid-div at best: quick reapp. 2½ 38$
1972 **PLAYINAROUND 12** [5] 3-8-7 K Dalgleish (7) 16/1: 30-009: Handy, rdn/fdd fnl 2f: see 1972. hd 32
1994 **JUST DISSIDENT 11** [17] 8-9-5 Dean McKeown 7/1: 000550: Rcd keenly cl-up, wknd qckly over 1 35
1f out, fin 10th: bckd from 14/1: see 91.
1298 **BLUE SAPPHIRE 44** [7] 3-8-7 Kimberley Hart 33/1: 00-600: Al rear, fin 11th, 6 wk abs: see 1081. 4 19
1664 **APPLES AND PEARS 26** [9] 4-9-0 G Duffield 20/1: 500000: Set pace, hdd 2f out, sn lost tch, fin 12th. 2½ 14
2095 Palacegate Touch 7 [3] 10-9-10 (bl) P Bradley (5) 14/12136 **Double Entry 5** [14] 3-8-12 A Culhane 33/1:
1508 Johnny Staccato 33 [13] 6-9-5 (VIS) M Tebbutt 33/1: 2046 **Detroit City 9** [12] 5-9-5 M Fenton 14/1:
16 ran Time 1m 14.4 (2.3) (J P Honeyman) D Nicholls Sessay, N Yorks

2241 3.00 CROWTHER HOMES HCAP 3YO+ 0-80 (D) 7f rnd Good/Firm 20 -01 Slow [72]
£4231 £1302 £651 £325 3 yo rec 9 lb

2063 **INTRICATE WEB 8** [2] E J Alston 4-9-8 (66) W Supple 6/1: -60061: 4 b g Warning - In Anticipation 71
(Sadler's Wells) Trkd ldrs, went on 2f out, styd on well, readily: at Redcar (h'cap, rtd 68): unpicd in Irish mdns for D Weld (blnkd) prev: suited by a stiff/gall 7f on fast & soft grnd: quick follow up?.
2063 **ONLY FOR GOLD 8** [1] A Berry 5-8-13 (57) J Carroll 8/1: 662302: 5 b h Presidium - Calvanne Miss 2 57

(Martinmas) Prom, styd on fnl 1f but al held by wnr: consistent form but has not won since '97: see 780.

2017	**LADY OF WINDSOR** 10 [4] I Semple 3-9-3 (70)(vis) R Winston 8/1: -51023: 3 ch f Woods Of Windsor - North Lady (Northfields) Led, hdd appr fnl 1f, not pace of front 2 ins last: sound run: see 2017.	1½	67
1631	**DAY BOY** 27 [8] Denys Smith 4-9-10 (68) A Beech (5) 6/1: 0-3044: Prom, rdn & no impress appr fnl 1f.	½	64
2097	**NAISSANT** 7 [7] 7-8-3 (47) K Dalgleish (7) 9/2: 042535: Trkd ldrs, rdn to chall halfway, wknd fnl 1f.	¾	41
1998	**ITALIAN SYMPHONY** 11 [3] 6-8-11 (55)(vis) F Lynch 11/1: 455056: Waited with, nvr a factor: see 1330.	shd	49
1926	**SAMARA SONG** 14 [6] 7-9-0 (58) P Robinson 3/1 FAV: 052607: Dwelt, rear, hdwy when short of room over 1f out, no chafter: nicely bckd: on a far mark: see 1690, 1003.	1½	49
2133	**THREE ANGELS** 5 [9] 5-9-12 (70) G Duffield 10/1: 0-2508: Nvr a threat: op 8/1: see 1431.	nk	60
1869	**SWINO** 16 [5] 6-8-7 (51)(bl) J F Egan 14/1: 004469: Pulled hard in mid-div, rdn, hung right & wknd fnl 2f: best over a strong-run 6f but is not one to trust: see 1869.	5	33

9 ran   Time 1m 27.0 (1.5)   (Morris, Oliver, Pierce)   E J Alston Longton, Lancs

---

2242   3.30 CARLISLE BELL HCAP 3YO+ 0-80 (D)   1m rnd   Good/Firm 20   +22 Fast   [80]
£14950   £4600   £2300   £1150   3 yo rec 10lb

1964	**KIROVSKI** 12 [9] P W Harris 3-8-8 (70) J F Egan 10/1: 060-21: 3 b c Common Grounds - Nordic Doll (Royal Academy) Chsd ldrs, hdwy to lead appr fnl 2f, qcknd well ins last, rdn out: v fast time, 1st win: rtd 71 when unplcd on 3 juv starts: suited by a stiff/gall 1m on fast & gd grnd: lightly rcd & progressive, win again.		80
1964	**POLAR CHALLENGE** 12 [14] Sir Michael Stoute 3-9-2 (78) F Lynch 5/1 FAV: -03352: 3 b c Polar Falcon - Warning Light (High Top) Handy, short of room & switched over 2f out, ran on well for press ins last, nvr nrr: must have gone v close with clear run (wnr gpt first run) & shld find compensation: see 1964.	1½	84
2051	**LEGAL SET** 9 [4] K R Burke 4-9-4 (70) Darren Williams (7) 14/1: -20033: 4 gr g Second Set - Tiffany's Case (Thatching) Dwelt, sn in tch, hdwy appr fnl 1f, rdn & onepcd ins last: sound run, could shed mdn tag.	½	75
*2063	**TORNADO PRINCE** 8 [5] E J Alston 5-8-13 (65)(5ex) W Supple 9/1: 00-014: Waited with, hdwy going well over 2f out, rdn & found less than expected: worth another chance when seeing less daylight.	2	66
2111	**PENTAGON LAD** 6 [6] 4-9-1 (67) A Culhane 10/1: 140625: Handy, rdn to chall 4f out, drvn & not pace of ldrs fnl 2f: op 8/1, quick reapp: see 2111 (10f stks).	hd	68
1920	**TIPPERARY SUNSET** 14 [13] 6-8-8 (60) J Fanning 16/1: 002366: Dwelt, rear, late gains for press, nrst fin: handles fast but best on gd/soft or softer: see 1007.	hd	61
2027	**STYLE DANCER** 10 [3] 6-8-8 (60) G Duffield 16/1: -54047: Prom, onepace over 1f out: see 1300, 1007.	½	60
2032	**SOPHOMORE** 10 [12] 6-8-12 (64) K Dalgleish (7) 25/1: 060168: Mid-div at best: btr 1731 (clmr, gd/soft).	1	62
2126	**SKY DOME** 5 [2] 7-9-9 (75) A Beech (5) 12/1: 060239: Rear, late hdwy for press, no threat: qck reapp.	hd	54
2138	**COURT EXPRESS** 5 [1] 6-9-13 (79) M Fenton 12/1: 0-1620: Settled rear, nvr a dngr, fin 10th: qck reapp.	1	75
*1721	**ARC** 3 [7] 6-9-1 (67) R Winston 12/1: 412010: In tch, eff over 2f out, sn fdd: fin 11th, btr 1721.	hd	63
2063	**ACID TEST** 8 [15] 5-8-10 (62) Dean McKeown 16/1: 300030: Nvr a factor, fin 12th: btr 2063.	3½	52
2063	**HAKEEM** 8 [18] 5-8-9 (61) D Mernagh (3) 11/1: 0-0220: Set fast pace, hdd over 2f out, sn btn, 13th.	1	49
*1477	**SIGN OF THE TIGER** 34 [17] 3-8-11 (73) M Tebbutt 10/1: 442310: Prom 6f, fin 14th: btr 1477 (gd/soft).	½	60
1829	**FALLACHAN** 19 [11] 4-10-0 (80) P Robinson 6/1: 0-0440: Nvr dangerous, fin 15th: top weight, op 5/1.	4	60
1905	**PETERS IMP** 14 [8] 5-8-13 (65) J Carroll 20/1: 502530: Al rear, fin 16th: op 14/1.	2	42
975	**EL SALIDA** 70 [10] 4-9-4 (70) P Fessey 33/1: 44-000: Sn struggling, fin last: jumps rnr.	1¾	44

17 ran   Time 1m 38.6 (u0.2)   (Batten, Bowstead, Gregory & Manning)   P W Harris Aldbury, Herts

---

2243   4.00 THWAITES HCAP 3YO 0-70 (E)   6f rnd   Good/Firm 20   -20 Slow   [69]
£3656   £1125   £562   £281

1793	**CRYFIELD** 20 [6] N Tinkler 3-9-3 (58) J Fanning 11/4 FAV: 020131: 3 b g Efisio - Ciboure (Norwick) Hmpd early on, bhd, gd hdwy 2f out, ran on strongly ins last, drvn out to lead fnl stride: well bckd: earlier won at Redcar (amat mdn h'cap): eff over 6f on any trk: acts on fast, gd/soft & fibresand.		62
2154	**PACIFIC PLACE** 4 [10] M Quinn 3-9-1 (56) M Tebbutt 10/1: 242322: 3 gr c College Chapel - Kaitlin (Salmon Leap) Mid-div, led appr fnl 1f, styd on well, collared nr fin: qk reapp: eff at 5/6f on firm/fast.	shd	59
2060	**DESRAYA** 8 [3] K A Ryan 3-8-13 (54)(bl) F Lynch 5/1: -06023: 3 b g Desert Style - Madaraya (Shahrastani) Prom, went on 4f out, hdd over 1f out, not pace of front 2: sound run, see 2060.	2	51
2060	**UNFORTUNATE** 8 [9] Miss J F Craze 3-8-10 (51)(bl) V Halliday 15/2: 600144: Dwelt, sn rdn in rear, ran on well for press ins last, nrst fin: lost ch with slow start here: win another sell h'cap: see 2060.	1½	44
2097	**HOWARDS LAD** 7 [7] 3-9-7 (62)(vis) Dale Gibson 25/1: 00-005: Mid-div, eff 3f out, sn onepce: qck reapp.	½	54
*1891	**DANCE LITTLE LADY** 15 [8] 3-9-1 (56) G Parkin 5/1: 64-016: Prom, rdn to chall 2f out, fdd ins last: op 4/1: may appear a sltly easier surface: see 1891.	½	47
1578	**GENERAL DOMINION** 29 [2] 3-9-2 (57) R Winston 12/1: 00547: Led early, remnd with ldrs, btn fnl 1f.	3	41
2060	**PRIDE OF PERU** 8 [1] 3-8-11 (52) T Williams 33/1: 00-000: Front rank, rdn/fdd over 2f out: see 2060.	½	35
1891	**PRETENDING** 15 [5] 3-8-12 (53) G Duffield 10/1: 065369: Al in rear: btr 1723 (C/D, gd/soft).	nk	36
1665	**NATSMAGIRL** 26 [11] 3-8-7 (48) J Carroll 10/1: 050-50: Chsd ldrs, lost tch fnl 2f, fin 10th: tchd 14/1 & better expected after a promising reapp in 1665.	3½	23
1868	**COLLISION TIME** 16 [4] 3-8-11 (52) S Finnamore (5) 20/1: 30-000: Hmpd early, sn mid-div, rdn & slightly short of room over 2f out, wknd fin 11th: see 1795.	nk	27

11 ran   Time 1m 14.6 (2.5)   (Mr & Mrs G Middlebrook)   N Tinkler Langton, N Yorks

---

2244   4.30 CROWTHER MDN HCAP 3YO+ 0-60 (F)   2m1f52y   Good/Firm 20   -25 Slow   [60]
£2320   £663   £331   3 yo rec 20lb

2123	**WINDMILL LANE** 6 [12] B S Rothwell 3-8-1 (53) P Hanagan (7) 11/2: 263021: 3 b f Saddler's Hall - Alpi Dora (Valiyar) Mid-div, rdn to chall over 3f out, sn led, rdn clr: op 9/2, quick reapp: unplcd over 7f/1m in '99 (nov stks, rtd 70, A Jarvis): eff at 12f, clrly suited by this step up to 2m1f: acts on firm, hvy & fibresand: handles a stiff/gall or sharp trk: has tried a visor, best without.		57
1767	**LASTMAN** 21 [1] J J O'Neill 5-9-10 (56) A Culhane 7/2 FAV: /5-522: 5 b g Fabulous Dancer - Rivala (Riverman) Settled rear, hdwy after halfway, styd on well fnl 2f, held well ins last: tchd 5/1: rnr-up over fences (2m nov, rtd 95c, acts on firm & gd/soft) since 1767.	2½	57
1949	**HERSELF** 13 [8] R Guest 3-7-10 (48)(5oh) P Fessey 16/1: 00-0603: 3 b f Hernando - Kirsten (Kris) Prom, rdn/dropped rear after halfway, hung right & styd on well for press fnl 2f, no threat: stays 2m2f on fast.	3	46
1894	**ICE PACK** 15 [10] Don Enrico Incisa 4-8-0 (32) Kim Tinkler 6/1: 600034: Mid-div, hdwy halfway, rdn into lead 4f out, sn btn: op 10/1, well clr rem: see 1894.	shd	30
1936	**SEATTLE ART** 13 [13] 6-8-13 (45) R Winston 10/1: 66-605: Nvr a factor: recently plcd over hdles.	9	34
468	**SONICOS** 144 [5] 4-7-11 (29) J McAuley (4) 33/1: 0-006: Rear, late gains, no dngr: long abs, h'cap bow.	½	17

CARLISLE   WEDNESDAY JUNE 28TH   Righthand, Stiff, Uphill Finish

1596 **COLOMBE DOR 28** [4] 3-8-2 (54) Dale Gibson 14/1: -22607: Bhd, eff 4f out, sn btn: up in trip. — shd 42
2008 **TOP OF THE CHARTS 11** [11] 4-8-3 (35) P Robinson 4/1: 044-58: Prom, rdn/lost tch fnl 3f: btr 2008. — 3 20
2109 **CAMAIR CRUSADER 6** [7] 6-8-2 (33) (1ow) J Fanning 10/1: 435359: Rear, hdwy halfway, rdn & — 4 15
wknd qckly fnl 3f: quick reapp: see 1241, 822.
1975 **MAGENKO 12** [3] 3-7-12 (50) (2ow) (4oh) A Beech (0) 8/1: 00-260: Handy, rdn/wknd fnl 4f, fin 10th. — 3½ 28
-- **EVENING CHORUS** [2] 5-10-0 (60) (tvi) P Goode (3) 14/1: 4000/0: Al well in rear, fin 11th: recent — 12 28
4th at best on the Flat in '98 (rtd 70 at best), mdn, R Simpson): prev eff arnd 7f (1m on firm & hvy: with R Ford.
4253] **BERTY BOY 267** [6] 4-8-10 (42) G Duffield 20/1: 0640-0: Led, hdd bef halfway, qckly dropped thro' — 14 0
field, fin 12th: reapp: sole form when a well btn 4th in a '99 Ripon auct mdn (rtd 56$).
2109 **ROOFTOP 6** [9] 4-9-8 (54) (vis) T Williams 25/1: 500000: Prom, led bef halfway to 4f out, wknd: 13th. — 4 8
13 ran   Time 3m 49.7 (7.8)   (B Valentine)   B S Rothwell Musley Bank, N Yorks

---

CHESTER   WEDNESDAY JUNE 28TH   Lefthand, V Tight Track

Official Going   GOOD TO FIRM. Stalls: 10f - Stands Side; Rem - Inside.

2245   6.45 ASTBURY WREN CLAIMER 3YO+ (E)   1m2f75y   Good/Firm 30   -15 Slow
£3601   £1108   £554   £277   3 yo rec 12lb

4199] **PEKAN HEIGHTS 270** [11] P D Evans 4-9-12 (vis) J F Egan 7/4 FAV: 0400-1: 4 br g Green Dancer - Battle — 55
Drum (Alydar) In tch, imprvd 3f out, drvn to lead fnl 100y: well bckd: 7 days ago won over hdles at Worcester (2m
nov clm, firm, gd, rtd 100h, C Egerton, blnkd): '99 Nottingham reapp wnr for E Dunlop (h'cap, rtd 84): plcd in '98
(mdn, rtd 79): eff at 10f, tried 12f: acts on fast & gd/soft, tight/galn trks: goes well fresh with/without visor.
1933 **SPONTANEITY 13** [3] P D Evans 4-8-11 C Lowther 20/1: 00-062: 4 ch f Shalford - Mariyda — ¾ 37
(Vayrann), Prom, led after halfway, under press fnl, worn down in last: stays 10.5f: see 1933.
1819 **KNAVES ASH 19** [2] M Todhunter 9-9-4 Dean McKeown 16/1: -00003: 9 ch g Miswaki - Quiet — hd 44
Rendezvous (Nureyev) Pld hard towards rear, gd prog 3f out, rdn & ch ins last, held towards fin: ran to best.
1707 **ROCK SCENE 24** [8] A Streeter 8-9-3 P Dobbs (5) 16/1: 206554: Bhd, styd on final 2f, nvr nrr: handles — ¾ 41
fast & hvy grnd & is consistent in sellers & claimers: see 889.
684 **TUFAMORE 103** [1] 4-9-3 (vis) N Callan 10/1: 105335: Mid-div, hdwy & ev ch dist, onepace: abs. — 1½ 39
464 **PREMIERE FOULEE 144** [4] 5-8-11 R Perham 33/1: 0-0606: Bhd, late hdwy, nvr a threat: stiff task, abs. — 1 31
2094 **PRIDEWAY 7** [13] 4-9-0 P Bradley (5) 4/1: 306567: In tch, chsd ldrs appr final 2f, held when bmpd dist. — ¾ 33
1936 **MAJOR ATTRACTION 13** [6] 5-9-1 G Baker (7) 16/1: 001008: Nvr better than mid-div: see 1361. — ¾ 32
1519 **THREE LEADERS 32** [7] 4-9-6 W Supple 20/1: 000409: Held up, effort 3f out, nvr any impress: Ingr trip. — 1 35
1819 **VANBOROUGH LAD 19** [5] 11-8-13 A Nicholls (3) 9/1: 002100: Mid-div, eff 3f out, fdd fnl 2f: 10th. — shd 27
2033 **THE IMPOSTER 9** [10] 5-9-4 (VIS) M Tebbutt 14/1: 000050: Led, ran wide 3f, hdd halfway: 15th, visor. — 0
1685 Maydoro 25 [12] 7-8-8 D Mernagh (3) 25/1:   1865 Skelton Monarch 16 [9] 3-8-2 P M Quinn (3) 33/1:
1292 Bolder Alexander 44 [15] 3-8-7 K Dalgleish(7) 33/1:   2122 Ra Ra Rasputin 6 [14] 5-9-1 (VIS) Iona Wands(5) 50/1:
15 ran   Time 2m 13.14 (4.64)   (Mrs Claire Massey)   P D Evans Pandy, Gwent.

2246   7.15 CHRONICLE FILLIES HCAP 3YO 0-85 (D)   1m4f66y   Good/Firm 30   +08 Fast   [86]
£3731   £1148   £574   £287

2111 **JULIUS 6** [2] M Johnston 3-9-8 (80) (6ex) K Dalgleish (7) 4/9 FAV: -12111: 3 b f Persian Bold - Babushka — 88
(Dance Of Life) Held up, smooth prog 4f out, led 2f out, rdly pshd clr: hvly bckd to land the odds, gd time, qck
reapp: hat-trick landed, earlier won at Nottingham (stks), Musselburgh (h'cap) & Ripon (class stks): ex-Irish,
plcd in mdns last term: eff at 10/12f on firm & gd grnd, sharp or gall trk: improving at a rate of knots.
1177 **CRYSTAL FLITE 52** [4] W R Muir 3-8-8 (66) D Holland 8/1: 63-002: 3 b f Darshaan - Crystal City (Kris) — 3 67
Led, incrsd pace 4f out, hdd 2f out, sn no ch with wnr: op 6/1, 7 wk abs, clr rem: caught a tartar over longer
trip but clearly stays 12f: acts on fast & hvy grnd, any trk.
1939 **PIPS WAY 13** [1] K R Burke 3-9-7 (79) N Callan 7/1: 604143: 3 ch f Pips Pride - Algonquin Park — 7 70
(High Line) Pulled hard, chsd ldr, effort 3f out, no impression: Ingr trip, see 1765 (1m, hvy).
2033 **UNIMPEACHABLE 9** [5] J M Bradley 3-7-10 (54) G Baker (7) 7/1: 052644: Chsd ldrs till 3f out: op 5/1. — 3½ 40
1071 **TARA HALL 58** [3] 3-7-10 (54) (4oh) P M Quinn (3) 33/1: 050-05: Al bhd: op 20/1, 8 wk abs, stiff task. — 5 33
5 ran   Time 2m 39.12 (2.72)   (Mrs J E Daley)   M Johnston Middleham, Nth Yorks.

2247   7.45 HALLIWELL JONES HCAP 3YO+ 0-95 (C)   5f rnd   Good/Firm 30   +06 Fast   [93]
£11017   £3390   £1695   £847   3 yo rec 6 lb   Low numbers have a significant advantage

1849 **DAMALIS 18** [3] E J Alston 4-10-0 (93) W Supple 6/1 FAV: 461001: 4 b f Mukaddamah - Art Age (Artaius) — 98
Led early, trkd ldr till drvn to lead dist, ran on gamely, drvn out: gd time, top-weight: earlier won here at
Chester (clm h'cap): '99 Sandown wnr (rtd h'cap, rtd 96): '98 wnr again here at Chester (fill mdn) & Ripon (stks,
rtd 98): all 5 wins at 5f, tried 6f: acts on firm & soft grnd, any trk, Chester specialist: useful, plumb draw.
1871 **THE GAY FOX 16** [7] B A Mcmahon 6-8-3 (68) (tbl) K Dalgleish (7) 14/1: 0-5302: 6 gr g Never So Bold - — ½ 71
School Concert (Music Boy) Mid-div, ran on appr fnl 1f, kept on strongly & not btn far: back to form with blnks
reapplied & poss best in headgear nowadays: goes on any grnd but suited by gd/soft & hvy: see 1074.
2003 **BABY BARRY 11** [4] Mrs G S Rees 3-8-12 (83) Dean McKeown 7/1: -00343: 3 b c Komaite - Malcesine — nk 85
(Auction Ring) Chsd ldrs, rdn appr final 1f, kept on: fine effort from this 3yo back at 5f: see 954.
1999 **JACKIES BABY 11** [10] W G M Turner 4-9-3 (82) Darren Williams (7) 12/1: 454004: Sn swtchd to ins — 1½ 80
rail & led, hdd ent final 1f & onepace: tchd 16/1: gd run from poor high draw: see 1324, 394.
2000 **WILLIAMS WELL 11** [8] 6-8-3 (68) (bl) G Parkin 9/1: 014365: Way off the pace till strong run appr fnl 1f: — 1¼ 63
remains one to keep an eye on over 6f/stiff 5f: see 2000.
1983 **ACE OF PARKES 12** [2] 4-9-3 (82) O Pears 10/1: 06-506: Chsd ldrs, unable to qckn appr final 1f. — nk 76
2207 **RETALIATOR 2** [6] 4-7-13 (64) A Mackay 16/1: -00207: Struggled to go pace, late hdwy: op 12/1. — hd 57
2022 **EASTERN TRUMPETER 10** [14] 4-8-8 (73) P Fitzsimons (5) 12/1: 111138: Held up, imprvd 2f out, no — 1 63
extra dist: no ch from a poor high draw: see 1861.
*1868 **PIERPOINT 16** [11] 5-8-1 (66) A Nicholls (3) 10/1: -00010: Al same place: op 7/1, see 1868 (stks). — ¾ 54
1398 **PURE COINCIDENCE 39** [9] 5-8-11 (76) F Norton 16/1: -30000: Chsd ldrs wide, no extra appr fnl 1f: 10th. ¾ 62
2138 **NOMORE MR NICEGUY 5** [15] 6-9-0 (79) F Lynch 20/1: 002040: Bhd, some late hdwy: 11th, — 1¾ 61
stablemate wnr, qck reapp: won this in '99 (off 4lbs higher mark), no ch from high draw today: needs further.

718

2035 **CLASSY CLEO** 9 [5] 5-8-11 (76) J F Egan 13/2: 004640: Prom, outpcd ent fnl 2f & eased down: 12th. *hd* 57
1781 **ZIGGYS DANCER** 21 [13] 9-8-12 (77) D Holland 20/1: 340400: Wide, al towards rear: 13th, op 14/1, *shd* 58
stablemate wnr: tenderly rdn & Stewards asked about running/riding: jockey reported his instructions were to
come late on the inside rail but unfortunately the horse broke too freely: well h'capped, see 518, 223.
1966 **BLUNDELL LANE** 12 [12] 5-8-7 (72) D Mernagh (3) 16/1: -10060: Prom, wide halfway, lost pl fnl 2f: 14th. 1½ 49
1164 **LOOK HERE NOW** 53 [1] 3-8-10 (81) C Lowther 14/1: -150: Dwelt & nvr got in it: 15th, stablemate 2nd. ½ 56
2168 **LICENCE TO THRILL** 4 [16] 3-8-1 (72) P M Quinn (3) 11/1: -11020: In tch till went wide halfway: 16th. 2½ 40
16 ran Time 1m 01.01 (1.21) (Liam & Tony Ferguson) E J Alston Longton, lancs.

2248 8.15 EPICHEM NOV STKS 2YO (D) 5f rnd Good/Firm 30 -08 Slow
£3542 £1090 £545 £272

1813 **PRINCESS OF GARDA** 19 [5] Mrs G S Rees 2-8-11 Dean McKeown 11/4 FAV: U43121: 2 b f Komaite - 91
Malcesine (Auction Ring) Made ev yd, rdn clr appr final 1f, unchall: nicely bckd: earlier won at Haydock (auct
mdn): 14,500 gns sister to 2 5f juv wnrs, dam 1m wnr: eff forcing the pace at 5f on fast & gd/soft grnd, any trk.
*1740 **LAUREL DAWN** 22 [6] A Berry 2-9-0 P Bradley (5) 15/2: 4012: 2 gr c Paris House - Madrina (Waajib) 5 79
Unruly start, towards rear, drvn 2f out, kept on for 2nd, no ch wnr: handles fast, gd/soft grnd & equitrack, nds 6f.
1673 **OPEN WARFARE** 25 [3] M Quinn 2-9-0 F Norton 8/1: 413533: 2 b f General Monash - Pipe Opener ½ 77
(Prince Sabo) Chsd ldrs, effort & no impress appr final 1f: back in trip, see 1166.
-- **TALBOT AVENUE** [7] R F Johnson Houghton 2-8-8 D Holland 6/1: 4: Held up, effort & not clr run ¾ 69+
ent fnl 2f & again below plcd, position accepted: debut: Puissance Apr foal: half-brother to sev wnrs: dam
13f wnr, sire a sprinter: poor high draw, highly tried & will rate higher.
*2100 **BYO** 7 [1] 2-9-2 Joanna Badger (7) 13/2: -015: Outpcd, rdn 2f out, some hdwy but no threat ½ 76
when short of room cl-home: qck reapp, 6f will suit: see 2100.
-- **SMIRFYS PARTY** [9] 2-8-8 C Lowther 14/1: 6: Detached till kept on appr final 1f: Clantime Apr 1st *shd* 68
foal, dam unrcd, sire a sprinter: poor high draw on debut: with B McMahon.
2113 **TIME N TIME AGAIN** 6 [8] 2-9-5 W Supple 3/1: 1007: Wide, prom, flashed tail ent final 2f, fdd: well 3 71
bckd: first try on fast grnd today & al struggling from poor high draw: see 2113, 843.
1776 **GEMTASTIC** 21 [4] 2-8-7 J F Egan 14/1: -68: Chsd ldrs til 2f out: highly tried. *shd* 59
8 ran Time 1m 01.7 (1.9) (North West Racing Club - Owners Group) Mrs G S Rees Sollom, Lancs.

2249 8.45 FARNDON MDN 3YO (D) 1m5f89y Good/Firm 30 -04 Slow
£3750 £1154 £577 £288

1808 **DARARIYNA** 19 [2] Sir Michael Stoute 3-8-9 F Lynch 1/1 FAV: 221: 3 b f Shirley Heights - Dararita 83
(Halo) Rcd in 3rd, hdwy to lead ent final 2f, drvn out, cosy: nicely bckd: deserved, frn-up prev 2 starts,
unraced juvenile: eff at 12/13.5f on fast & gd/soft grnd, sharp/undul trk.
-- **MARLATARA** [3] P F I Cole 3-8-9 D Griffiths 11/2: 2: 3 br f Marju - Khalatara (Kalaglow) 1½ 79
Held up 4th, imprvd & ev ch 2f out, styd on but not pace of wnr: op 7/2, clr rem, debut: 38,000 gns foal,
dam unrcd: eff over a sharp 13f on fast grnd: shld improve & find a maiden.
1935 **TYCOONS LAST** 13 [4] W M Brisbourne 3-8-9 T G McLaughlin 25/1: 350043: 3 b f Nalchik - Royal 7 70$
Tycoon (Tycoon II) Led, under press 4f out, hdd before final 1f, fdd: v stiff task, flattered.
1064 **GUARD DUTY** 58 [1] M P Tregoning 3-9-0 (BL) R Perham 7/4: 33-624: Rcd in 2nd till 4f out, sn btn: blnks 6 67
4 ran Time 2m 54.33 (4.53) (H H Aga Khan) Sir Michael Stoute Newmarket

---

2250 9.15 MIDSUMMER HCAP 3YO 0-80 (D) 7f rnd Good/Firm 30 -07 Slow [81]
£4101 £1262 £631 £315

2177 **SUMTHINELSE** 3 [1] N P Littmoden 3-9-6 (73) D Holland 6/4 FAV: -54021: 3 ch g Magic Ring - Minne Love 75
(Homeric) Well plcd, led appr final 1f, rdn & edged right then left, just held on: qck reapp, 1st win: plcd in
'99 (nov, rtd 81): eff at 6/7f on firm & gd, handles gd/soft, sharp or gall trk: best without visor.
1866 **ROYAL CAVALIER** 16 [6] R Hollinshead 3-9-6 (73) N Callan 10/1: 100062: 3 b g Prince Of Birds - Gold *hd* 74
Belt (Bellypha) Mid-div, effort 2f out, no impress till ran on final 1f, post came too sn: apprec drop back
to 7f, acts on fast, hvy grnd & fibresand: see 720.
1793 **OSTARA** 20 [4] K A Ryan 3-8-1 (54) Iona Wands (5) 16/1: 240-03: 3 b g Petorious - Onde de Choc *nk* 54
(L'Enjoleur): Led till appr final 1f, kept on: ran to best, eff at 6/7f on fast grnd.
1333 **LAHAAY** 42 [5] M P Tregoning 3-9-3 (70) W Supple 10/1: 05-004: Held up, ran on appr final 1f, 1 68
nvr nrr: 6 wk abs, h'cap bow: eff at 7f, should get 1m: handles fast grnd, see 1333.
1569 **ALJAZIR** 30 [11] 3-8-5 (57)(1ow) F Lynch 10/1: 020505: Bmpd start, rear, short of room 2f out till 1¼ 54+
dist, kept on for press, ch had gone: gd run in the circumstances: handles fast & hvy grnd, keep in mind.
1889 **BLACKPOOL MAMMAS** 15 [3] 3-8-10 (63) P Fitzsimons (5) 13/2: 200606: Chsd ldrs, rdn & unable to *hd* 57
qckn final 1f: drop back in trip may suit: see 813.
1289 **POP SHOP** 44 [7] 3-9-5 (72) M Tebbutt 6/1: 2-0007: In tch, effort 2f out, unable to chall: clr rem, 1¼ 64
6 wk abs, signs of return to form, stays 7f, see 905.
1504 **AIR MAIL** 33 [10] 3-9-7 (74)(BL) T G McLaughlin 12/1: 210508: Nvr a factor: blnkd, see 651 (AW mdn). 6 54
1605 **LANDICAN LAD** 28 [2] 3-8-9 (62) A Nicholls (3) 8/1: 0059: Pulled hard in tch till 3f out: h'cap bow. 4 34
2093 **NO REGRETS** 7 [9] 3-8-4 (57)(BL) F Norton 25/1: 500050: Chsd ldrs till halfway: 10th: blnkd, qk reapp. 3½ 22
1780 **PEGGYS ROSE** 21 [8] 3-8-7 (60) J F Egan 7/1: 140020: Bhd final 3f: 11th, btr 1780 (6f, gd/soft). 3 19
11 ran Time 1m 27.62 (2.62) (Hanibel Racing Partnership) N P Littmoden Newmarket.

WARWICK WEDNESDAY JUNE 28TH Lefthand, Sharp, Turning Track

Official Going GOOD TO FIRM. Stalls: Inside.

2251 2.20 RAYNSFORD NOV AUCT STKS 2YO (E) 6f168y rnd Good/Firm Inapplicable
£2917 £833 £416

*2010 **SILK LAW** 11 [3] A Berry 2-8-10 G Carter 15/8 JT FAV: 11: 2 ch f Barathea - Jural (Kris) 80
Dwelt, imprvd after halfway, qcknd to lead fnl 100y: nicely bckd: unbtn, recent debut wnr at Nottingham (fill
auct mdn): 6,200gns first foal, dam a Gr 3 1m juv wnr: eff at 6f, apprec step up to 7f, sure to get further:

acts on fast & gd grnd, sharp or gall trk: runs well fresh, progressive filly with a turn of foot.
-1974 **JAMILA 12** [4] E J O'Neill 2-8-7 W Ryan 15/8 JT FAV: -022: 2 b f Green Desert - Virelai (Kris) 1¾ 72
Chsd ldr, rdn & ev ch appr fnl 1f, kept on but outpcd by wnr towards fin: well bckd: gd run back on turf, eff at 6/6.8f on fast grnd & fibresand: should find a fillies maiden.
1673 **QUANTUM LADY 25** [1] B R Millman 2-8-7 G Hind 13/2: -41223: 2 b f Mujadil - Folly Finnesse ½ 71
(Joligeneration) Sn in clr lead, under press appr fnl 1f, hdd & onepace fnl 100y: clr rem, v consistent, stays 6.8f but a return to 5/6f will suit this speedy filly: acts on fast & gd grnd.
*1864 **SHINNER 16** [8] T D Easterby 2-8-7 A Clark 7/2: 4214: In tch till appr fnl 1f: btr 1864 (fill auct mdn). 9 55
-- **IMPERO** [2] 2-8-12 J Stack 12/1: 5: Speed till 2f out: debut: 11,500gns Emperor Jones Mar foal, 1¼ 57
half-brother to 2 wnrs abroad & dam wnr in France: sire 1m/10f performer: highly tried, know more next time.
-- **DATIN STAR** [5] 2-8-1 P Doe 33/1: 6: Chsd ldrs 4f: highly tried on debut: 3,200gns Inchinor 1¾ 42
Apr foal, half-sister to a sprint wnr, dam a 9f wnr, sire 7f performer: with D Coakley.
6 ran Time 1m 23.8 (Kangaroo Courtiers) A Berry Cockerham, Lancs.

2252

2.50 COURTYARD FILLIES HCAP 3YO+ 0-70 (E) 5f rnd Good/Firm Inapplicable [66]
£2980 £851 £425 3 yo rec 6 lb

*2193 **MARINO STREET 2** [11] B A McMahon 7-9-2 (54)(6ex) D Holland 7/2: 60-211: 7 b m Totem - Demerger 59
(Dominion) Chsd ldrs, rdn ent fnl 1f, ran on to lead fnl 100y: bckd from 9/2, qck brace landed, 48hrs ago scored at Nottingham (h'cap): '99 wnr here at Warwick (this fill h'cap) & Haydock (h'cap, rtd 50): eff at 5/6f, stays 7.5f: acts on firm, gd grnd & fibresand, with/without blnks/visor: goes well fresh, likes Warwick.
1427 **POPPYS SONG 37** [14] H Candy 3-9-11 (69) S Whitworth 10/1: 41-002: 3 b f Owington - Pretty Poppy ¾ 71
(Song) Led till 2f out & briefly below dist, kept on: back to form on this quicker grnd: see 1098.
2184 **SUNSET HARBOUR 3** [6] J M Bradley 7-8-9 (47) Claire Bryan (5) 8/1: -24163: 7 br m Prince Sabo - nk 48
City Link Pet (Tina's Pet) Towards rear, imprvd ent str, chsd wnr ins last, no impress nr fin: gd run, see 1932.
1877 **ZOENA 16** [19] J G Portman 3-9-0 (58) A Nicholls (3) 33/1: 040-04: Prom, styd on appr fnl 1f, nvr ¾ 57
pace to chall: plcd fnl '99 start (auct mdn, rtd 62): eff at 5f, prob stays 6f: handles firm & gd/soft grnd.
1687 **ZARAGOSSA 25** [13] 4-9-8 (60) G Carter 10/1: 0-5005: Well plcd & ev ch till no extra ent fnl 1f. shd 59
2122 **SING FOR ME 6** [18] 5-7-11 (35) N Carter (7) 33/1: 506006: Dwelt, chsd ldrs 3f out till dist. ¾ 32
1923 **SOUNDS ACE 14** [1] 4-8-11 (49)(bl) O Pears 11/4 FAV: -06037: Cl-up, led appr fnl 1f, hdd & onepace shd 46
fnl 100y: nicely bckd from 6/1: also bhd this wnr in 1923.
2107 **ORIEL STAR 6** [9] 4-8-10 (48)(vis) R Mullen 11/1: 630068: Al same place: op 8/1, qck reapp, vis reapp. ¾ 43
1910 **TICK TOCK 14** [3] 3-8-10 (54) T G McLaughlin 12/1: 002209: Nvr a factor: op 8/1, see 1512. shd 49
1923 **DOMINELLE 14** [15] 8-8-11 (49) J Weaver 8/1: -00040: Sn well plcd, outpcd appr fnl 1f: 10th, op 6/1. hd 43
1925 **CORBLETS 14** [2] 3-9-8 (66) P Doe 16/1: 322500: Dwelt, ran on in the str: 11th, unsuited by return to 5f? nk 59
1877 **AUNT DORIS 16** [16] 3-9-0 (58) J Stack 20/1: 30-600: Prom, no extra appr fnl 1f: 12th, back in trip. nk 50
2122 **E B PEARL 6** [17] 4-7-13 (36)(1ow) A Daly 25/1: 605500: Nvr dngrs tho' staying on fin: 13th, see 751. nk 28
*1966 **KNOCKEMBACK NELLIE 12** [7] 4-10-0 (66)(bl) Pat Eddery 9/2: 001210: Chsd ldrs, rdn & no impress 0
ent fnl 2f, sn eased: 16th, tchd 7/1, top-weight, new stable: now with P Harris, see 1966.
1886 **Time Bomb 15** [8] 3-8-12 (56) G Hind 16/1:
1994 **Tinas Royale 11** [20] 4-7-11 (35) G Bardwell 50/1:
1971 **Bodfari Times 12** [4] 4-7-12 (36) J Lowe 50/1:
4172} **Pink Mosaic 272** [12] 4-9-7 (59) F Norton 25/1:
77 **Kerridge Chapel 221** [5] 3-8-5 (49) N Carlisle 50/1:
1670 **Sunrise Girl 26** [10] 3-7-12 (42)(2ow)(7oh) C Cogan(0) 66/1:
20 ran Time 1m 00.0 (Roy Penton) B A McMahon Hopwas, Staffs.

2253

3.20 GAVESTON SELLER 3YO (G) 1m2f110y Good/Firm Inapplicable
£1951 £557 £278

1770 **HOME FORCE 21** [8] C F Wall 3-8-13 R Mullen 13/8 FAV: 0-0061: 3 b g Chaddleworth - Breed Reference 58
(Reference Point) Made all, pshd clr appr fnl 1f, rdly: nicely bckd, sold for 7,600gns to Mrs V Ward: 4th in a '99 mdn (rtd 72): apprec this drop back to 10.5f in selling grade: acts on fast grnd & an easy trk, forcing the pace.
1142 **ROOM TO ROOM MAGIC 55** [11] B Palling 3-8-8 D O'Donohoe 16/1: 45602: 3 ch f Casteddu - Bellatrix 6 43
(Persian Bold) Chsd wnr thr'out, onepace appr fnl 1f: tchd 20/1, turf bow, 8 wk abs: prob stays 10.5f on fast.
1933 **LADY VIENNA 13** [9] W G M Turner 3-8-8 (VIS) A Daly 9/1: 05-503: 3 ch f Weldnaas - Fresh Lady 3½ 38
(Fresh Breeze) Chsd ldrs, no extra 2f out: op 7/1, visored, stiff task, see 1644.
2012 **CROOKFORD WATER 11** [3] J A Glover 3-8-13 J Weaver 4/1: 000-04: Rr, imprvd 4f out, fdd 2f out. 1 41
2008 **KNIGHTS RETURN 11** [7] 3-8-13 G Hind 33/1: 00-005: Prom till appr fnl 2f: stiff task, no form. 10 27
1919 **ROCK ON ROBIN 14** [4] 3-8-13 F Norton 7/1: -02606: Nvr a factor: see 1274. 3 22
1997 **WELCOME SHADE 11** [1] 3-8-13 W Ryan 6/1: -20007: In tch till 3f out: see 1212. 1¾ 20
242 **EMMAS HOPE 178** [5] 3-8-8 T G McLaughlin 16/1: 005-08: Handy till 4f out: 6 month abs, new stable. 2½ 12
1734 **JENSENS TALE 23** [10] 3-8-13 P M Quinn (3) 20/1: 0-0009: Al bhd: up in trip, see 830. ¾ 16
1972 **CALEBS BOY 12** [6] 3-8-13 S Whitworth 25/1: 00-00: Sn struggling: 10th, stiff task, no form. 25 0
10 ran Time 2m 17.2 (Induna Racing Partners) C F Wall Newmarket.

2254

3.50 CASTLE MDN HCAP DIV 1 3YO+ 0-60 (F) 1m4f56y Good/Firm Inapplicable [60]
£2415 £690 £345 3 yo rec 14lb

1758 **WETHAAB 21** [1] B W Hills 3-8-4 (50)(BL) G Carter 9/2: 0-0401: 3 b c Pleasant Colony - Binntastic 58
(Lyphard's Wish) Nvr far away, led appr fnl 2f, sn clr, easily: tchd 11/2, woken up by blnks: unplcd sole juv start: eff over a sharp 12f on fast grnd: at right end of handicap.
1874 **LUNAR LORD 16** [8] J S Moore 4-8-5 (37) G Hind 9/1: 004202: 4 b g Elmaamul - Cache (Bustino) 4 37
Rear, imprvd 3f out & tried to go after wnr appr fnl 1f, same pace: op 6/1, back in trip: acts on fast & soft grnd.
1997 **DANCING MARY 11** [9] B Smart 3-8-9 (55) F Norton 4/1 FAV: 035043: 3 gr f Sri Pekan - Fontenoy 3 51
(Lyphard's Wish) Towards rear, styd on thr' btn horses in the str: tchd 6/1: btr 1997 (class stks), see 500.
2033 **PURSUIVANT 9** [12] Mrs N Macauley 6-9-1 (47)(bl) R Fitzpatrick (3) 6/1: 603204: Chsd ldrs, 1½ 41
no extra 2f out: longer trip, see 2011 (10f, gd).
1775 **PARKERS PEACE 21** [5] 3-8-7 (53) J Mackay (5) 12/1: 00-005: Keen, handy till wknd 2f out: stays 12f? 4 43
1608 **TIGER GRASS 28** [7] 4-9-10 (56) D Holland 7/1: 240-06: In tch till 3f out: longer trip, see 1608. 2½ 43
1292 **LEES FIRST STEP 44** [3] 3-9-0 (60) P Doe 6/1: 020-07: Led till hung left & hdd appr fnl 2f, fdd. hd 47
1521 **DARCY DANCER 32** [11] 3-8-12 (58)(BL) J Weaver 16/1: 350-08: Nvr a factor: blnkd, see 1521. ¾ 44
1934 **WELDUNFRANK 13** [13] 7-10-0 (60) T G McLaughlin 11/1: 00569: Held up, brief eff 4f out: top-weight. 1½ 45
1758 **HORTON DANCER 21** [4] 3-8-3 (49)(vis) N Carlisle 12/1: 600400: Front rank till halfway: 10th, tchd 16/1. 7 27
1796 **CROSS LUGANA 20** [6] 4-9-4 (50) R Mullen 20/1: 0/000: Nvr in it: 11th on h'cap bow, op 14/1. 12 18

WARWICK WEDNESDAY JUNE 28TH Lefthand, Sharp, Turning Track

11 ran Time 2m 04.3 (Hamdan Al Maktoum) B W Hills Lambourn, Berks.

2255 **4.20 CASTLE MDN HCAP DIV 2 3YO+ 0-60 (F) 1m4f56y Good/Firm Inapplicable [60]**
£2404 £687 £343 3 yo rec 14lb

1942 **GOLD MILLENIUM 13** [4] C A Horgan 6-8-8 (40) I Mongan (5) 10/1: 40-041: 6 gr g Kenmare - Gold Necklace (Golden Fleece) Bhd ldrs, led ent str, pushed out: plcd once last term (h'cap, rtd 43): eff at 12f, tried 14f: acts on fast grnd & a sharp track. **46**
1878 **REDOUBLE 16** [11] J Akehurst 4-9-10 (56) S Whitworth 5/1: 550-02: 4 b g First Trump - Sunflower Seed (Mummy's Pet) Held up, hdwy 3f out, styd on und press, not trble wnr: tchd 12/1, top-weight, back to form. *2½* **58**
1956 **NIGHT MUSIC 12** [5] Major D N Chappell 3-9-0 (60) R Mullen 16/1: 00-053: 3 b f Piccolo - Oribi (Top Ville) Bhd, imprvd ent str, styd on for press without threatening: stays 12f on fast grnd. *1½* **60**
1784 **BONDS GULLY 20** [3] R W Armstrong 4-9-4 (50) A Clark 8/1: 204404: Cl-up, led 4f out till 2f out, same pace: clr of rem: handles fast grnd, drop back to 10f is going to suit, see 620, 547. *¾* **49**
2007 **COCO LOCO 11** [12] 3-8-10 (56) R Price 12/1: -60065: Mid-div, chsd ldrs 3f out till 2f out: lngr trip. *5* **50**
2007 **KAFI 11** [1] 4-9-3 (49)(vis) A Daly 20/1: 00-006: Mid-div thr'out: op 14/1, longer trip, see 2007. *3½* **39**
1914 **LOMOND DANCER 14** [7] 3-8-12 (58) Pat Eddery 3/1 FAV: 06-057: Led 1m, lost pl 2f out: btr 1914. *1½* **46**
1775 **TRY PARIS 21** [2] 4-8-3 (35)(vis) G Carter 10/1: 000448: Held up, eff 4f out, no impress, eased fnl 1f. *3½* **19**
1666 **ALMINSTAR 26** [6] 4-8-5 (37) G Hind 33/1: 550-09: Al towards rear: flattered 6th of 8 in '99 (rtd 60). *½* **20**
1710 **SILVER ARROW 24** [10] 3-9-0 (60) D Holland 12/1: -04000: Al bhd: 10th, big step up in trip, see 1035. *4* **39**
1914 **CROWN MINT 14** [9] 3-8-6 (52) D O'Donohoe 7/2: 000-20: Chsd ldrs till halfway: 11th, op 5/2: unsuited by change of tactics according to trainer, see 1914 (held up). *16* **16**
1998 **BERBERIS 11** [8] 4-8-3 (35) Claire Bryan (5) 33/1: 0-0000: Nvr dngrs: 12th. *12* **0**
12 ran Time 2m 40.5 (Mrs L M Horgan) C A Horgan Pulborough, W.Sussex.

2256 **4.50 THEHORSESMOUTH HCAP 3YO 0-80 (D) 1m7f181y Good/Firm Inapplicable [80]**
£3883 £1195 £597 £298 3 yo rec 19lb

*2037 **RENAISSANCE LADY 9** [3] T R Watson 4-7-11 (48)(1ow)(6ex) F Norton 11/4 FAV: 0-0011: 4 ch f Imp Society - Easter Morning (Nice Havrais) Trkd ldrs, led going well appr fnl 1f, not extended: val 5L+, tchd 7/2: 9 days ago won in similar fashion over C/D here at Warwick (h'cap): '99 Brighton wnr (auct mdn, rtd 55): eff at 12f, revelation since stepped up to 2m: loves fast grnd & this sharp/undul Warwick trk: shld make it 3. **55**
1784 **BID ME WELCOME 20** [1] Miss D A McHale 4-9-8 (74) D McGaffin (5) 6/1: 1-0052: 4 b g Alzao - Blushing Barada (Blushing Groom) In tch, bmpd when improving 2f out, kept on to chase wnr fnl 1f, easily held: tchd 8/1, clr rem: styd this longer 2m trip, is in gd heart & is well h'capped: see 1411. *1¾* **76**
1996 **VERSATILITY 11** [4] Dr J R J Naylor 7-7-10 (48) G Bardwell 9/1: 310563: 7 b m Teenoso - Gay Criselle (Decoy Boy) Led till appr fnl 1f, no extra: op 7/1: handles fast grnd but is suited by softer: see 963. *3* **47**
1874 **YATTARNA 16** [7] Ian Williams 4-8-1 (53) R Mullen 9/2: 100544: Held up, chsd ldrs 4f out till bef dist. *1½* **50**
*1874 **PRASLIN ISLAND 16** [6] 4-7-12 (50) P Doe 10/3: 3001D5: Prom till 2f out: return to 14f?, see 1874, 182. *4* **43**
1982 **JASEUR 12** [5] 7-10-0 (80)(vis) L Vickers (7) 14/1: 6-0006: Held up, in tch after 1m till wknd 2f out. *nk* **73**
1711 **DOUBLE RUSH 24** [8] 8-7-10 (48)(t)(4oh) J Lowe 9/1: 612347: Al bhd: op 7/1: see 1023. *3½* **38**
706} **MARSH MARIGOLD 457** [2] 6-7-12 (50)(2ow)(5oh) N Carlisle 8/1: 00/0-8: Nvr dngrs: op 12/1, jumps fit, May hat-trick scorer at Towcester, Worcester & Hexham (h'caps, 2m, firm & gd/soft, rtd 84h): lightly rcd, no Flat form since '97 Pontefract win (appr h'cap, rtd 64, J Hetherton): eff at 10f on fast & soft grnd. *6* **35**
8 ran Time 3m 27.6 (Alan A Wright) T R Watson Pinnock, Glos.

2257 **5.20 WWW.WARWICK HCAP 3YO+ 0-80 (D) 7f164y rnd Good/Firm Inapplicable [73]**
£3948 £1215 £607 £303 3 yo rec 10lb

1799 **MYTTONS MISTAKE 20** [2] R J Baker 7-8-6 (51) G Carter 10/3 FAV: 022421: 7 b g Rambo Dancer - Hi Hunsley (Swing Easy) Prom, shkn up to lead appr fnl 1f, rdn out: '99 Brighton wnr (sell, rtd 53, unplcd on sand, rtd 43a): '98 Bath & Kempton wnr (h'caps, rtd 71): eff at 6/7.7f, stays 1m: acts on firm & gd/soft, both AWs: best without blnks, any trk: well h'capped. **57**
1794 **WHITE EMIR 20** [1] L G Cottrell 7-8-12 (57) A Clark 6/1: 000-32: 7 b g Emarati - White African (Carwhite) Held up, prog to go 2nd appr fnl 1f, styd on but al held: well clr rem: eff at 5/6f, stays 7.7f. *1½* **60**
2099 **PHILISTAR 7** [6] D Shaw 7-8-2 (47)(bl) F Norton 16/1: 600503: 7 ch h Bairn - Philgwyn (Milford) Struggled to go pace till kept on fnl 1½f, nvr on terms: qck reapp, unsuited by drop back in trip, see 93. *6* **40**
1473 **WELODY 35** [10] K Mahdi 4-9-5 (64)(bl) R Mullen 9/1: 421004: Sn led, hdd bef dist, fdd: tchd 12/1. *3* **51**
1889 **BISHOPSTONE MAN 15** [3] 3-8-9 (64) P Doe 6/1: -40035: Nvr going pace: see 1889, 1061. *3* **45**
2031 **VIOLET 10** [5] 4-8-3 (48)(vis) J Mackay (5) 20/1: 00-006: Chsd ldrs till hung right appr str: op 14/1. *1½* **27**
2015 **ARCHELLO 10** [4] 6-8-4 (49) N Carlisle 16/1: -10007: Prom 4f: best 1258 (6f, reapp). *nk* **27**
1973 **HORMUZ 12** [9] 4-9-3 (62) D O'Donohoe 9/1: -00008: Handy till wknd 2f out: tchd 20/1, well h'capped. *1¾* **37**
2051 **NO MERCY 9** [7] 4-9-10 (69)(t) S Whitworth 4/1: 334-59: Al towards rear: top-weight, see 2051. *1* **42**
1794 **DAPHNES DOLL 20** [8] 5-8-3 (48) G Bardwell 10/1: -00000: Bhd from halfway: 10th, see 209. *2½* **16**
10 ran Time 1m 34.9 (P Slade) R J Baker Stoodleigh, Devon.

KEMPTON WEDNESDAY JUNE 28TH Righthand, Flat, Fair Track

Official Going GOOD/FIRM. Stalls: Inside, except 1m2f - Outside.

2258 **6.35 PIPES & DRUMS FILLIES MDN 3YO (D) 1m2f jub Firm 10 -06 Slow**
£4329 £1332 £666 £333

-- **TRUE CRYSTAL** [7] H R A Cecil 3-8-11 T Quinn 5/1: -1: 3 b f Sadler's Wells - State Crystal (High Estate) Dwelt, sn recovered to trk ldrs, led 2f out, styd on well despite drifting left: nicely bckd tho' op 3/1: dam smart over mid-dists: eff at 10f, will stay 12f: runs well fresh on firm: ran v green today, improve. **85+**
-- **AMNERIS** [6] R Charlton 3-8-11 S Drowne 12/1: -2: 3 b f Alzao - Top Lady (Shirley Heights) Rcd keenly in rear, imprvd to chase wnr fnl 1f, hmpd ins last & not recover: drifted from 6/1 on debut: dam a 12/14f wnr: eff at 10f on firm grnd, 12f will suit: done no favours by wnr today, sure to learn from this & win. *1½* **80**
1811 **DELAMERE 19** [4] J H M Gosden 3-8-11 R Hughes 2/1 FAV: 0-643: 3 b f Brocco - Shelia Dacre *2½* **77**

(Nureyev) Trkd ldrs, onepace when short of room & swtchd right dist, no impress after: well bckd: styd this longer 10f trip, further shld suit: acts on firm & gd/soft grnd: see 1811, 1261.

1811 **WHITGIFT ROSE** 19 [5] Lady Herries 3-8-11 W Ryan 14/1: -04: Rear, kept on steadily final 1f, nrst fin: tchd 20/1: encouraging effort: bred to stay 10f+: needs one more run to qual for h'caps, see 1811.   1   75

1697 **POLI KNIGHT** 25 [9] 3-8-11 R Hills 11/4: -55: Set pace 1m, fdd: op 9/4: stable back in form now.   ½   74

-- **GREEN WILDERNESS** [3] 3-8-11 Pat Eddery 12/1: -6: Slowly away & ran green, late prog, nvr a factor on debut: bred to apprec middle dists: with J Fanshawe & sure to learn from this.   nk   73

1970 **MASRORA** 12 [8] 3-8-11 Craig Williams 12/1: -4537: Chsd ldr till lost place after 4f, no ch after.   2½   70

1811 **MAGIC SYMBOL** 19 [2] 3-8-11 J Reid 25/1: -08: Prom 1m, fdd into last: mkt drifter: rcd too keenly for own gd here, longer prcd stablemate of 4th: should be capable of better.   ¾   69

8 ran   Time 2m 03.99 (1.69)   (Michael Poland)   H R A Cecil Newmarket.

2259   7.05 EBF FILLIES MDN 2YO (D)   7f jub rnd   Firm 10   -22 Slow
£4270   £1314   £657   £328

1798 **PEACEFUL PARADISE** 20 [2] J W Hills 2-8-11 R Hills 2/1 FAV: -31: 2 b f Turtle Island - Megdale (Waajib) In tch, imprvd to lead 2f out, styd on strongly, drvn out: well bckd tho' op 5/4: made most of prev experience: apprec this step up to 7f, 1m will suit: handles gd/soft, acts on firm grnd: improve further.   86

-- **CARIBBEANDRIFTWOOD** [5] P F I Cole 2-8-11 D Sweeney 4/1: -2: 2 ch f Woodman - Drifting (Lyphard) 1½   82
Led till 2f out, kept on well fnl 1f but not pace of wnr: 4L clr 3rd: Feb foal, cost $65,000: dam unrcd, related to a smart miler: sire a high class juv: eff at 7f on firm, 1m will suit: encouraging debut, should find similar.

-- **TOUCHY FEELINGS** [1] R Hannon 2-8-11 R Hughes 3/1: -3: 2 b f Ashkalani - Adjalisa (Darshaan)   4   74+
Dwelt, imprvd from rear halfway, kept on under a kind ride: IR 6,000gns Mar foal: half-sister to useful Irish 2yo wnr Access All Areas: eff at 7f, will stay 1m given time: handles firm: encouraging, learn from this, keep in mind.

-- **MISS TRESS** [6] P W Harris 2-8-11 K Darley 7/1: -4: Reared start & ran green, some hdwy but nvr   3   68
dngrs on debut: 32,000gns purchase: Mar foal: dam a 10f wnr in Ireland: sure to learn plenty from this.

-- **AWAY WIN** [7] 2-8-11 J Reid 12/1: -5: Chsd ldrs, jmpd path after 3f, wknd final 1f on debut: 2   60
48,000gns Mar foal: sire a high class miler: B Palling filly, should apprec 7f/1m.

-- **DIVAS ROBE** [4] 2-8-11 J Weaver 16/1: -6: Chsd ldr till wknd qckly final 2f: Feb foal, cost 13,500   2   60
gns: first foal, sire a high class 2yo wnr: likely to apprec 1m+ given time: with N Graham.

-- **IM A CHARACTER** [3] 2-8-11 C Rutter 12/1: -7: Prom till halfway, fdd into last: mkt drifter: Mar   ½   59
foal, dam unrcd: sire a middle dist scorer: M Blanshard filly.

7 ran   Time 1m 26.36 (2.26)   (Karen Scott Barrett (Abbott Racing Ptnrs))   J W Hills Upper Lambourn, Berks.

2260   7.35 LISTED MOWLEM GALA STKS 3YO+ (A)   1m2f jub   Firm 10   +11 Fast
£14235   £4380   £2190   £1095   3yo rec 12lb

*1482 **ISLAND HOUSE** 34 [1] G Wragg 4-9-8 M Roberts 5/2: 12-111: 4 ch c Grand Lodge - Fortitude (Last   114
Tycoon) In tch, strong run to lead well ins fnl 1f, cosily: well bckd, best time of day: unbtn this term after wins at Newmarket (stks) & Goodwood (List): '99 Pontefract (class stks) & Ayr wnr (stks, rtd 102 at best): eff at 1m/10f, may stay further: acts on firm & hvy grnd, handles any trk: runs well fresh: fast imprvg, smart colt who can force the pace or come from bhd: cosy wnr today, has shwn enough to win in Gr company.

*1340 **HATAAB** 41 [4] E A L Dunlop 3-8-10 R Hills 2/1 FAV: 121-12: 3 ch c Woodman - Miss Mistletoes   ¾   111
(The Minstrel) Trkd ldr till went on 2f out, not pace to repel wnr cl-home: nicely bckd, 6 wk abs: met a smart & progressive rival here: acts on gd & firm grnd: shld win another Listed race: see 1340.

2028 **ZINDABAD** 10 [2] B Hanbury 4-9-11 J Reid 11/2: 115-33: 4 b h Shirley Heights - Miznah (Sadler's   ¾   112
Wells) Set pace 1m, ev ch ent fnl 1f, no extra cl-home: not disgrcd conceding weight all round: see 2028.

1850 **AMALIA** 18 [3] P W Harris 4-9-0 K Darley 9/4: -04134: Waited with, effort 2f out, sn no impress till styd   ½   100
on cl-home: well bckd: not disgrcd on step up from h'cap company, a return to 12f should suit: see 1850, 1342.

4 ran   Time 2m 02.16 (0.14)   (Mollers Racing)   G Wragg Newmarket.

2261   8.05 NEWTON HCAP 3YO+ 0-85 (D)   7f jub rnd   Firm 10   +01 Fast   [84]
£4407   £1356   £678   £339   3yo rec 9lb

1018 **SHADOW PRINCE** 65 [5] R Charlton 3-8-7 (72) S Drowne 14/1: 6-501: 3 ch g Machiavellian - Shadywood   79+
(Habitat) Waited with, imprvg when short of room 2f out & again dist, qcknd well to lead cl-home, going away: op 10/1, 9 wk abs: gd time: much imprvd on h'cap debut: eff at 7f on firm grnd, 1m will suit: shwd a decent turn of foot here, looks well h'capped & one to keep on your side.

1590 **CARLTON** 28 [13] D R C Elsworth 6-9-5 (75) N Pollard 10/1: -42002: 6 ch g Thatching - Hooray Lady   1¼   76
(Ahonoora) Trkd ldrs, imprvd to lead 2f out, kept on well but not pace to repel wnr cl-home: bckd, gd run.

1989 **TEMERAIRE** 11 [14] D J S Cosgrove 5-9-13 (83) J Reid 7/2 FAV: 200423: 5 b h Dayjur - Key Dancer   1   82
(Nijinsky) Prom, rdn & lost pl halfway, rallied fnl 1f, not btn far: bckd from 9/2: unable to get to the front.

1450 **PARISIEN STAR** 36 [12] N Hamilton 4-9-10 (80) L Newman (3) 10/1: 00-404: Rear, imprvd 2f out, short   nk   78+
of room & swtchd dist, fin well: op 6/1: not much luck & eye-catching: well h'capped & primed to win sn.

1925 **ARETINO** 14 [1] J Weaver 25/1: 3-0505: Led till 2f out, kept on: op 14/1: front runner.   shd   78

*1884 **MY EMILY** 15 [8] 4-9-2 (72) I Mongan (5) 9/1: 00-216: Trkd ldrs, ev ch 2f out, not qckn ins last.   nk   69

1694 **KAMAREYAH** 25 [2] 3-9-1 (80) R Hills 20/1: 310-07: Waited with, effort 2f out, no impress till ran on   shd   77
again cl-home: mkt drifter: '99 Yarmouth wnr (fill mdn, rtd 90): sister to a useful 7f wnr: eff at 6f, prob stays 7f: acts on fast & gd/soft, runs well fresh: stable returning to form, shld be plcd to win.

1989 **DILKUSHA** 11 [3] 5-9-6 (76) T Quinn 10/1: 066-08: Rear, effort 2f out, styd on well cl-home: hd   73
won this race from a 3lb lower mark last term: see 1989.

1483 **COLD CLIMATE** 34 [11] 5-8-1 (57) A Daly 14/1: 0-5009: Rcd keenly in rear, no impress final 1f.   nk   53

2133 **TEOFILIO** 5 [6] 6-9-0 (70)(bl) K Darley 8/1: 160000: Waited with, imprvg when short of room briefly   1¼   62
dist, sn onepcd: fin 10th: qck reapp: see 2133.

1676 **BRAVE EDGE** 25 [7] 9-10-0 (84) Pat Eddery 5/1: 330230: Prom till wknd & eased final 1f: fin   hd   76
11th, bckd from 8/1, top weight: all wins over 5/6f: see 1676, 1590.

1810 **CHAMPAGNE RIDER** 19 [10] 4-9-12 (82) T E Durcan 25/1: 0-0000: Rear, prog 2f out, onepace &   ¾   72
eased inside last: fin 12th: best at 6f: see 1173.

1989 **THREAT** 11 [9] 4-9-2 (72) G Faulkner (3) 10/1: 000060: Dwelt, chase ldr, ev ch till wknd fnl 1f.   7   48

1467 **COMMANDER** 35 [4] 4-8-4 (60)(tVI) S Sanders 20/1: 5-5030: Prom 5f, wknd into last: tried a visor.   13   11

14 ran   Time 1m 24.76 (0.66)   (Hippodrome Racing)   R Charlton Beckhampton, Wilts.

722

2262

8.35 1812 OVERTURE FILL HCAP 3YO+ 0-80 (D)   1m1f rnd   Firm 10 -06 Slow   [80]
£4290   £1320   £660   £330   3yo rec 11lb

2085 **FREDORA** 7 [1] M Blanshard 5-10-0 (80) D Sweeney 11/2: 500241: 5 ch m Inchinor - Ophrys   85
(Nonoalco) Nvr far away, went on 4f out, held on gamely, drvn out: op 7/2, top weight: '99 Salisbury wnr (class
stks, rtd 87): '98 wnr here at Kempton (2, mdn & h'cap, rtd 91): eff at 7/10f on gd & firm grnd, handles gd/soft:
handles any trk, likes Kempton: gd weight carrier who is back on a fair mark.
1926 **FLIGHT SEQUENCE** 14 [6] Lady Herries 4-9-9 (75) W Ryan 4/1: 24-602: 4 b f Polar Falcon - Doubles   ¾   78
(Damister) Trkd ldrs, ev ch 2f out, just btn in a driving fin: nicely bckd: imprvd with more enterprising tactics.
1785 **AEGEAN DREAM** 20 [4] R Hannon 4-9-12 (78) R Hughes 11/4 FAV: 234433: 4 b f Royal Academy -   ½   80
L'Ideale (Alysheba) Trkd ldrs, travelling strongly 2f out, eff & not qckn cl-home: well bckd: often finds less
than expected under press: see 1785 (10f).
1873 **PHEISTY** 16 [2] R F Johnson Houghton 3-8-9 (72) J Reid 12/1: 600-54: Mid-div, styd on fnl 1f, nrst   ½   73
fin: fair run, btn under 2L: stays 9f, acts on firm & soft grnd: suggested another step up in trip is in order.
1973 **OSCIETRA** 12 [3] 4-8-1 (53) L Newman (3) 8/1: 0-0555: Rear, effort 2f out, onepace inside last: 1   52
grnd faster than ideal today: see 1096.
1807 **LITTLE TUMBLER** 19 [7] 5-7-10 (48)(1oh) R Brisland(5) 14/1: 000-56: Dwelt, eff 2f out, nvr nr ldrs.   ½   46
1930 **GRANDMA ULLA** 13 [8] 3-7-10 (59)(5oh) M Henry 33/1: -00007: Nvr a factor: stiffish task: see 888.   3½   50
2075 **DIZZY TILLY** 7 [5] 6-7-13 (51)(3ow)(7oh) C Cogan(0) 11/1: 004338: Prsd ldr till wknd 3f out: see 2023.   8   27
2086 **BLINDING MISSION** 7 [9] 3-8-7 (70) Pat Eddery 4/1: 50-039: Set pace 5f, wknd qckly into last: 5   36
well bckd: much better expected, needs to learn some restraint: see 2086 (C/D).
9 ran   Time 1m 51.50 (1.50)   (Peter Goldring)   M Blanshard Upper Lambourn, Berks.

2263

9.05 FIREWORKS FINALE HCAP 3YO+ 0-85 (D)   1m4f   Firm 10 -45 Slow   [85]
£4153   £1278   £639   £319   3yo rec 14lb   Slow run race

1927 **MY PLEDGE** 14 [3] C A Horgan 5-7-13 (56) N Pollard 3/1 FAV: 450-21: 5 b g Waajib - Pollys Glow   60
(Glow) Dwelt, prog from rear & in tch 2f out, forged ahead fnl 75yds, drvn out: well bckd, slow time: caught
the eye on reappearance here at Kempton 2 wks ago: 4th at best in '99 (h'caps, rtd 59): '98 Windsor wnr (h'cap,
rtd 71): eff at 10/12f on firm & gd/soft grnd: has slipped to a v handy mark & should win again.
2748} **FIRST IMPRESSION** 347 [1] Mrs A J Perrett 5-8-12 (69) Pat Eddery 4/1: /245-2: 5 b g Saddlers' Hall -   nk   71
First Sapphire (Simply Great) Set stdy pace till qcknd 4f out, overhauled by wnr cl-home: nicely bckd rcd when trained
by Lady Herries in '99, rnr-up at Leicester (mdn, rtd 71, reapp): eff at 12f on firm & hvy: runs well fresh.
1831 **MUWAKALL** 19 [5] R W Armstrong 3-8-9 (80) R Hills 9/1: 534553: 3 b c Doyoun - Sabayik (Unfuwain)   ½   81
Hld up, styd on fnl 1f, just btn: stays 12f: first 2 pinched first run (holding up off a slow pace is poor tactics).
1927 **FINAL SETTLEMENT** 14 [4] J R Jenkins 5-8-8 (65) L Newman (3) 4/1: -16534: Chsd ldrs, onepcd 2f out,   1½   64
rallied cl-home: see 1927 (C/D).
4176} **BE THANKFULL** 271 [6] 4-10-0 (85) T Quinn 9/2: 1621-5: Rcd keenly in bhd ldrs, no impress when   1¾   82
short of room 1f out: op 7/2, reapp, top weight: '99 Ascot (mdn, reapp) & Newmarket wnr (h'cap, rtd 86): eff
at 1m/10f, shld stay further: acts on gd/fast grnd, suited by stiff/gall trks: can run well fresh & best held up
for a late run: sharper next time & a drop back to 10f could suit.
1874 **RARE GENIUS** 16 [2] 4-8-8 (65) J Weaver 5/1: -23506: Rcd keenly in bhd ldr, wknd fnl 1f: see 1180.   1¼   60
6 ran   Time 2m 36.65 (6.65)   (Mrs B Sumner)   C A Horgan Pulborough, West Sussex.

Official Going   GOOD TO FIRM. Stalls: 12f - Stands Side, Str Crse - Far Side.

2264

2.10 AXMINSTER APPR HCAP 3YO 0-70 (F)   1m str   Good/Firm 25 -19 Slow   [77]
£2716   £776   £388

2044 **COLNE VALLEY AMY** 10 [12] G L Moore 3-8-3 (50)(2ow) I Mongan 6/1: 000-21: 3 b f Mizoram - Panchellita   56
(Pancho Villa) Trkd ldrs, went on over 3f out, strongly prsd final 1f, drvn & held on well: op 5/1: first win: unplcd
in '99 (rtd 58, mdn): eff at 7f/1m on firm & fast grnd, sharp or stiff/undul trk: open to further improvement.
2013 **MISTY MAGIC** 18 [2] P W Harris 3-8-4 (53) A Beech 11/4 FAV: -00432: 3 b f Distinctly North - Meadmore ½   55
Magic (Mansingh) Chsd ldrs, rdn & strong chall from over 1f out, held cl-home: nicely bckd, op 7/2: see 2013.
1964 **SPIRIT OF TENBY** 13 [5] S Dow 3-9-1 (64) M Howard (7) 7/1: 603033: 3 b g Tenby - Asturiana (Julio   ¾   65
Mariner) Towards rear, rdn & styd on well final 2f, not reach front pair: op 6/1: handles firm & gd, stays stiff 1m.
2025 **COWBOYS AND ANGELS** 11 [17] W G M Turner 3-9-7 (70) P Fitzsimons 3/1: 601024: Trkd ldrs, ev ch 2f   nk   70
out, rdn/no extra ins last: nicely bckd tho' op 5/2: stays 1m well, spot-on in similar back at 7f: see 2025, 1349.
2025 **ORLANDO SUNRISE** 11 [2] 3-8-11 (60) R Cody Boutcher (3) 20/1: -06045: Chsd ldrs, kept on for press   nk   59
final 2f: stays a stiff 1m, handles fast & prob firm grnd.
1972 **LEEN** 13 [15] 3-8-4 (53) Jonjo Fowle (3) 25/1: 000006: In tch, nvr pace to chall: lngr 1m trip: see 275.   3   46
1671 **CHRISS LITTLE LAD** 27 [3] 3-9-2 (65) R Brisland 16/1: 40-207: Rear, rdn/hdwy 3f out, no prog final 1f.   ½   57
2013 **HAZY HEIGHTS** 12 [13] 3-8-3 (52) D Glennon (5) 25/1: 60008: Led 5f, sn fdd: see 1080, 915.   1   42
*1977 **BELINDA** 13 [10] 3-8-13 (62) J Bosley (3) 20/1: 04019: Rear, mod prog 3f out, held 1f out: op 14/1.   ½   51
1886 **AEGEAN FLOWER** 16 [14] 3-8-8 (57)(bl) R Studholme 25/1: 0400: Mid-div, nvr threat: 10th: see 1886.   1   44
4557} **JOHN STEED** 243 [11] 3-8-3 (52) Claire Bryan (1) 25/1: 600-0: Sn rdn in rear, mod hdwy: 11th: op   1½   36
14/1, reapp: unplcd from 3 '99 starts (rtd 60, sell): h'cap bow today.
2043 Coral Shells 10 [1] 3-8-3 (52) S Carson 25/1:   1710 Flying Run 25 [16] 3-8-1 (50)(BL) D Watson (1) 33/1:
1889 Brompton Barrage 16 [4] 3-8-11 (60)(BL) P Dobbs 25/1: 164   Ring My Mate 202 [6] 3-8-13 (62) G Sparkes (5) 20/1:
2013 Count Tirol 12 [9] 3-8-11 (60) G Hannon (3) 33/1:   1205 Phoebus 52 [7] 3-8-11 (60)(t) D McGaffin (3) 33/1:
17 ran   Time 1m 42.59 (3.49)   (Colne Valley Golf (Deluxeward Ltd)   G L Moore Woodingdean, E Sussex

---

2265   **2.40 GOADSBY MDN 3YO+ (D)**   **1m1f198y**   Good/Firm 25   -05 Slow
£3688   £1135   £567   £283   3 yo rec 12lb

784   **EXPLODE** 92 [11] R Charlton 3-8-10 R Hughes 2/1 FAV: 31: 3 b c Zafonic - Didicoy (Danzig): **91+**
Led/dsptd lead, shkn up & asserted readily fnl 1f, eased nr line: value for 8L+, hvly bckd, 3 mth abs: apprec
this step up to 10f, 12f may suit: acts on fast grnd & a stiff/undul trk: looks potentially useful.
1692   **CLASSY IRISH** 26 [12] L M Cumani 3-8-10 J P Spencer 7/2: -62: 3 ch c Irish River - Stealthethunder   5   **79**
(Lyphard): Mid-div, prog/rdn to press ldr 2f out, outpcd over 1f out: nicely bckd, op 4/1: apprec step up
to 10f, handles fast grnd: caught a tartar here, could find similar: see 1692.
2056   **BOLD PRECEDENT** 10 [7] P W Harris 3-8-10 J Weaver 10/1: 0-43: 3 b c Polish Precedent - Shining   1   **78**
Water (Riverman): Keen/chsd ldrs, kept on onepace final 2f: handles fast grnd, h'cap company should suit.
1738   **BOULDER** 24 [2] L M Cumani 3-8-10 G Sparkes (7) 33/1: 64: Towards rear, rdn & styd on final 3f,   ½   **77**
nvr reach ldrs: lngr prcd stablemate of rnr-up: return to 11f+ should suit: see 1738.
1428   **BAMBOOZLE** 38 [13] 4-9-3 P Doe 33/1: 05: Chsd ldrs 4f out, onepace: improved over lngr 10f trip.   1½   **70**
1912   **CALDIZ** 15 [9] 3-8-10 (t) Pat Eddery 6/1: -66: Mid-div, no hdwy final 3f: op 5/1, lngr 10f trip.   ¾   **74**
--   **ALRISHA** [1] 3-8-5 N Pollard 20/1: 7: Rear, hmpd 3f out, rdn/mod late gains: debut: 12,000 gns   3   **65**
purchase, dam a Irish bmpr wnr: with D R C Elsworth.
2056   **WESTERN BAY** 10 [4] 4-9-8 S Whitworth 66/1: 0-68: Rear, nvr a factor: see 2056.   1¼   **68**
1929   **AEGEAN WIND** 15 [5] 3-8-10 S Sanders 20/1: 0-59: Rear, nvr threat: op 10/1: needs h'caps: see 1929.   2   **65**
1032   **RASMALAI** 64 [6] 3-8-5 L Newman (3) 12/1: 030: Chsd ldrs, btn 2f out: 10th: op 7/1, 2 mth abs.   nk   **59**
--   **DIAMOND** [8] 4-9-3 T Quinn 3/1: 0: Cl-up 5f out, rdn/fdd over 2f out: 11th: nicely bckd, debut: 2½   **55**
half-sister to a couple of wnrs in USA: belated first run for this 4yo, with H Cecil.
1556   **TASSO DANCER** 31 [10] 4-9-3 R Havlin 100/1: 0/000: Al bhd: 12th: lngr 10f trip, no form.   5   **48$**
2056   **SHERVANA** 10 [3] 4-9-3 R Studholme (5) 100/1: 00: Led after 2f till 5f out, sn bhd: 13th: no form.   dist   **0**
13 ran   Time 2m 07.51 (3.01)   (K Abdulla)   R Charlton Beckhampton, Wilts.

2266   **3.10 TOTE EXACTA HCAP 3YO+ 0-85 (D)**   **5f**   Good/Firm 25   +12 Fast   **[80]**
£7150   £2200   £1100   £550   3 yo rec 6 lb   Raced across track, wnr raced far side

2022   **DANCING MYSTERY** 11 [10] E A Wheeler 6-9-7 (73) S Carson (5) 10/1: 003351: 6 b g Beveled - Batchworth   **80**
Dancer (Ballacashtal): Handy, went on dist, drvn clr ins last: fast time: '99 wnr at Lingfield, Southwell (rtd
82a), Warwick (h'caps) & Redcar (stks, rtd 78): '98 Windsor & Goodwood wnr (h'cap, rtd 57 & 74a): stays 6f, suited
by 5f on fast, gd/soft & both AWs: acts on any trk, runs well fresh: eff in blnks, best without: tough & genuine.
1966   **CROWDED AVENUE** 13 [3] P J Makin 8-10-0 (80)(VIS) S Sanders 16/1: 40-032: 8 b g Sizzling Melody -   2½   **80**
Lady Bequick (Sharpen Up): Towards rear, drvn & kept on final 1f, not pace of wnr: op 14/1, 1st time visor.
1999   **CAUDA EQUINA** 12 [5] M R Channon 6-9-9 (75) T Quinn 13/2: 056043: 6 gr g Statoblest - Sea Fret   hd   **74**
(Habat): Rear, rdn halfway, fin fast but too late: on a fair mark, likes Bath: see 905.
2158   **PRINCE PROSPECT** 5 [2] Mrs L Stubbs 4-10-0 (80) J P Spencer 14/1: 022004: Rcd towards stands rail,   ½   **77**
rdn/bhd, kept on final 1f for press, no threat: op 12/1, qck reapp: see 376 (6f, AW, stks).
2124   **PERIGEUX** 6 [11] 4-8-7 (59)(bl) C Carver (3) 20/1: -55005: Chsd ldrs, held final 1f: blnks reapp.   shd   **56**
1887   **SAILING SHOES** 16 [1] 4-9-13 (79)(bl) R Hughes 16/1: 0-0006: Cl-up, led 3f out, hdd over 1f out,   shd   **75**
no extra nr fin: op 14/1: pacey type who is slipping to a handy mark, posted an imprvd effort here: see 1810.
*1881   **PALAWAN** 17 [7] 4-9-8 (74) N Chalmers (7) 7/1: 203017: Cl-up, briefly led over 3f out, no extra fnl 1f.   2   **65**
1999   **SEA HAZE** 12 [4] 3-9-0 (72) Pat Eddery 16/1: 0-0208: Outpcd bef halfway, nvr a threat: see 1795.   ½   **61**
-2022   **MUNGO PARK** 11 [12] 6-9-8 (74) J Weaver 100/30 FAV: 0-2029: Held up, hdwy over 2f out, sn no prog.   ½   **61**
1871   **SPEED ON** 17 [9] 7-9-13 (79) C Rutter 6/1: 0-0630: Chsd ldrs 4f: 10th: op 9/2: see 1871, 1013.   nk   **65**
2022   **RIVER TERN** 11 [6] 7-9-0 (66) P Fitzsimons (5) 10/1: 606000: Chsd ldrs till over 1f out: 11th: see 1357.   nk   **51**
2022   **RITAS ROCK APE** 11 [8] 5-9-7 (73) T G McLaughlin 9/1: 0-0060: Led till over 3f out, btn 2f out: 12th.   ¾   **56**
12 ran   Time 1m 0.47 (0.67)   (Austin Stroud & Co Ltd)   E A Wheeler Whitchurch On Thames, Oxon.

2267   **3.40 ELITE FILLIES COND STKS 2YO 0-80 (B)**   **7f str**   Good/Firm 25   -54 Slow
£10401   £3415   £1707

2091   **CELTIC ISLAND** 8 [1] W G M Turner 2-8-9 A Daly 7/2: 212201: 2 b f Celtic Swing - Chief Island (Be My   **93**
Chief): Trkd ldr, drvn & narrow lead over 2f out, just hdd ins last, rallied gamely to lead again cl-home: op
4/1, slow time: earlier scored at Pontefract (auct fill mdn): eff at 7f, 1m+ will suit: acts on firm & hvy,
loves a stiff/gall trk: tough, genuine & useful filly: can be plcd to win again.
2091   **SHE ROCKS** 8 [2] R Hannon 2-8-9 R Hughes 30/100 FAV: 142: 2 b f Spectrum - Liberty Song (Last   hd   **92**
Tycoon): Led, just hdd 2f out, drvn/led again inside last, hdd & just held cl-home: bckd at odds-on.
2182   **FAZZANI** 4 [3] M R Channon 2-8-9 T Quinn 10/1: -04443: 2 b f Shareef Dancer - Taj Victory (Final   5   **82$**
Straw): Trkd ldrs, drvn/chall over 2f out, sn held by front pair: op 8/1: qck reapp: needs a drop in grade: see 1568.
3 ran   Time 1m 30.95 (5.45)   (Bill Brown)   W G M Turner (Corton Denham, Somerset).

2268   **4.10 KING'S HEAD HCP STKS 3YO+ 0-80 (D)**   **1m6f**   Good/Firm 25   -36 Slow   **[78]**
£4290   £1320   £660   £330   3 yo rec 17lb

2033   **ALNAJASHEE** 10 [10] M R Bosley 4-8-8 (58)(t) D Sweeney 33/1: 146001: 4 b g Generous - Tahdid (Mtoto):   **61**
Chsd ldrs, briefly outpcd 3f out, styd on gamely to lead well ins last: op 16/1: earlier scored at Southwell
(appr mdn h'cap, rtd 63a): rnr-up on turf in '99 (mdn, P T Walwyn): rtd 72 in '98: eff at 12/14f, tried 2m:
acts on firm, fast & fibresand: handles a stiff/sharp trk & has run well fresh: eff in a t-strap.
1852   **HERBSHAN DANCER** 18 [8] V Soane 6-7-10 (46)(13oh) R Brisland (5) 50/1: 0/5602: 6 b g Warrshan -   ½   **47**
Herbary (Herbager): Keen, led after 2f till over 4f out, rdn to lead again ins last, just hdd cl-home: fine
effort from 13lbs o/h: eff at 12/14f: see 1287 (mdn).
2023   **HAPPY GO LUCKY** 11 [3] M J Weeden 6-9-0 (64) S Drowne 10/1: 1/0623: 6 ch m Teamster - Meritsu   1¼   **63**
(Lyphard's Special): Led 2f, remnd handy, outpcd 3f out, kept on for press inside last: op 6/1: eff at 10/14f.
1928   **TOTOM** 15 [7] J R Fanshawe 5-9-9 (73) W Ryan 7/4 FAV: 5-4344: Cl-up, led going well over 4f out, rdn   1¼   **70**
final 2f & hdd/wknd inside last: nicely bckd: stays 14f, prefers 10/14f h'caps should suit: see 1288 (10f).
1959   **NORTHERN FLEET** 13 [5] 7-9-2 (66) Pat Eddery 9/2: 100-45: Rear halfway, drvn/kept on final 2f, nvr   1   **62**
a threat: on a fair mark, crying out for a return to 2m: see 1959.
*1536   **ENFILADE** 33 [4] 4-10-0 (78)(t) R Hills 2/1: 4-5016: Settled towards rear, no prog: bckd.   5   **67**

SALISBURY THURSDAY JUNE 29TH Righthand, Galloping Track, Stiff Finish

1087 **RUBY LASER** 58 [1] 4-7-10 (46)(8oh) G Bardwell 25/1: 03-067: Keen/twds rear, nvr factor: op 14/1, abs. **7** | | **25**
-- **JUST GRAND** [9] 6-9-10 (74) J Weaver 33/1: 3415/8: Al bhd: long Flat abs, 12 wk hdles abs (mod **10** | | **42**
form): last rcd on the level in '97 for M Johnston, scored at Carlisle (h'cap, rtd 82): eff at 10/12f on fast ground. | |
168 **HENRIETTA HOLMES** 202 [6] 4-8-10 (60) R Hughes 20/1: 1465-9: Bhd, eased/no ch fnl 2f: jmps fit. *dist* | | **0**
9 ran Time 3m 06.5 (8.5) (Mrs Jean M O'Connor) M R Bosley Kingston Lisle, Oxon. | |

2269 4.40 H & G BLAGRAVE MDN 2YO (D) 7f str Good/Firm 25 -12 Slow
£3640 £1120 £560 £280

-- **PRIORS LODGE** [3] R Hannon 2-8-11 R Hughes 3⅛1 FAV: 1: 2 br c Grand Lodge - Addaya (Persian Bold): **90+**
Rear, prog 3f out, styd on strongly to lead ins last, rdn out: bckd from 7/1: Feb foal, cost 82,000gns: sire
top class 1m/10f performer: eff at 7f, 1m+ will suit: acts on fast grnd, runs well fresh: open to improvement.
-- **CLEARING** [5] J H M Gosden 2-8-11 W Ryan 8/1: 2: 2 b c Zafonic - Bright Spells (Alleged): ½ **87**
Dwelt, prog to lead over 1f out, hdd & no extra well ins last: op 6/1: Feb foal, a first fowl: dam a French 12f
wnr, sire top class juv/miler: eff over a stiff 7f, 1m+ will suit: acts on fast: will sn go one better.
1943 **POTARO** 14 [1] B J Meehan 2-8-11 D R McCabe ⅛00/30: -53: 2 b c Catrail - Bianca Cappello (Glenstal): 1¼ **84**
Trkd ldrs, drvn/chall over 1f out, kept on onepace: op 3/1: styd lngr 1f trip well: acts on fast: see 1943.
1943 **TUDOR PRINCE** 14 [9] M R Channon 2-8-11 S Drowne 14/1: -04: Led, hdd over 1f out, no extra inside 1¾ **81**
last: stays 7f: also bhd todays 3rd in 1943.
-- **PRIME TRUMP** [10] 2-8-11 Pat Eddery 5/1: 5: Chsd ldrs, outpcd final 2f: op 4/1: First Trump colt, 1¼ **78**
Feb foal, cost 23,000gns: dam a 7f juv wnr: 7f+ sure to suit, encouraging intro for P W Harris.
1943 **AINTNECESSARILYSO** 14 [6] 2-8-11 T Quinn 16/1: -006: Chsd ldr, drvn/ch 2f out, held when hmpd 1f out. 1 **76**
-- **GOLD STATUETTE** [8] 2-8-11 S Whitworth 14/1: 7: Dwelt, rear, rdn/mod late gains, no threat: op 12/1: ¾ **75**
Caerleon colt, May foal, cost IR95,000gns: dam a 10f wnr, sire top class 10/12f performer: sure to relish 1m+.
-- **ELMONJED** [4] 2-8-11 R Hills 7/2: 8: Chsd ldrs, btn 2f out: op 11/4: Gulch colt, Jan foal, a first 1 **73**
foal: dam a top class 1m performer: with J Dunlop & will improve.
-- **WAINAK** [2] 2-8-11 S Sanders 20/1: 9: Dwelt, sn rdn & al bhd: op 14/1, lngr prcd stablemate of 8th: 5 **63**
Silver Hawk colt, Mar foal, cost 110,000 gns: a first foal: dam 7f/1m 3yo wnr.
-- **DENNIS OUR MENACE** [7] 2-8-11 P Doe 66/1: 0: Dwelt, an outpcd: 10th: Mar foal, dam plcd at 6f/1m. 5 **53**
10 ran Time 1m 28.09 (2.59) (Lady Tennant) R Hannon East Everleigh, Wilts.

2270 5.10 LEVY BOARD HCAP 3YO+ 0-80 (D) 1m1f198y Good/Firm 25 -06 Slow [80]
£4004 £1232 £616 £308 3 yo rec 12lb

1853 **ABUZAID** 18 [10] J L Dunlop 3-9-0 (78) R Hills 8/1: 1-0001: 3 br c Nureyev - Elle Seule (Exclusive **82**
Native): Chsd ldrs, swtchd & prog to lead 1f out, styd on well ins last, drvn clr: op 5/1: '99 Newcastle wnr (mdn,
rtd 90): apprec step up to 10f, could get further: acts on firm & gd/soft, likes a stiff/gall trk: has run well fresh.
1973 **CLARENDON** 13 [4] V Soane 4-10-0 (80) G Hind 7/2: -00622: 4 ch g Forest Wind - Sparkish (Persian 2½ **79**
Bold): Chsd ldr 4f out, led over 2f out, sn hdd & hung right, kept on final 1f: gd run under topweight: see 968.
1785 **BONNIE FLORA** 21 [3] K Bishop 4-8-11 (63) R Perham 33/1: 00-003: 4 b f Then Again - My Minnie ½ **61**
(Kind Of Hush): Prog/rear, kept on well final 2f, not reach front pair: worth a try at 12f: handles fast: see 1343.
1927 **WADI** 15 [9] Dr J R J Naylor 5-8-0 (52) C Rutter 7/1: 0-0604: Chsd ldrs 6f, kept on onepace fnl 2f. shd **50**
2051 **BIRTH OF THE BLUES** 10 [1] 4-8-8 (60)(VIS) N Pollard 20/1: -00005: Rear, prog to lead over 1f out, ½ **57**
edged right/hdd 1f out & no extra: vis, imprvd efft: stays stiff 10f, return to 1m will suit: acts on fast & soft/hvy.
1812 **IN A TWINKLING** 20 [8] 3-7-10 (60)(1oh) G Sparkes (4) 20/1: 40-006: Rear, modest hdwy 3f out. nk **56**
1375 **CAPRIOLO** 41 [2] 4-9-5 (71) R Hughes 2/1 FAV: 001-67: Led over 2f out, hdd over 1f out, fdd: abs. 3½ **62**
1878 **DIRECT DEAL** 17 [5] 4-8-6 (58)(BL) D O'Donohoe 20/1: 000008: Led 7f, btn/eased fnl 1f: blnks. 3 **45**
1852 **BRIERY MEC** 18 [6] 5-7-10 (48)(1oh) G Bardwell 100/30: 3-0159: Rear, hdwy 3f out, sn held: op 4/1: ½ **34**
3644} **MAGICAL BAILIWICK** 305 [7] 4-9-4 (70) S Drowne 14/1: 4530-0: 10th: op 12/1: reapp: 3 **52**
plcd last term (rtd 75, mdn): stays a stiff 1m, mid-dists may yet suit.
10 ran Time 2m 07.56 (3.06) (Hamdan Al Maktoum) J L Dunlop Arundel, West Sussex.

NEWCASTLE THURSDAY JUNE 29TH Lefthand, Galloping Track

Official Going: FIRM (GOOD TO FIRM IN PLACES). Stalls: Straight Course/2m - Stands side: Round Course - Inside .

2271 2.20 NEWCASTLE UTD FC MDN 2YO (D) 7f str Good/Firm 32 -16 Slow
£3575 £1100 £550 £275

1876 **CAUVERY** 17 [3] S P C Woods 2-9-0 G Duffield 6/4 FAV: 21: 2 ch c Exit To Nowhere - Triple Zee **87**
(Zilzal) Bhd ldrs, led halfway, pushed out, easily: nicely bckd: 13,000gns Apr first foal: apprec step up to
7f & will stay 1m: acts on fast grnd, galloping track: improving, win again.
-- **DOUBLE HONOUR** [5] M Johnston 2-9-0 D Holland 4/1: 2: 2 gr c Highest Honor - Silver Cobra 4 **77**
(Silver Hawk) Led till appr fnl 3f, styd on for 2nd but no ch wnr: op 3/1 on debut: 150,000 Ffr Feb foal,
brother to a gd juv wnr in France, dam wnr abroad: sire 7f/10f performer: handles fast grnd, 1m suit: win a race.
1924 **MAGIC BOX** 15 [4] A P Jarvis 2-9-0 D Mernagh (3) 9/4: 6443: 2 b c Magic Ring - Princess Poquito ¾ **75**
(Hard Fought) Well plcd, rdn & no extra 2f out: clr rem, poss unsuited by step up to 7f, btr 1924 (6f).
-- **JOHN OGROATS** [2] T D Easterby 2-9-0 K Darley 4/1: 4: In tch till halfway: debut: 19,000lr gns 10 **57**
Distinctly North March first foal, sire a sprinter.
-- **SAVE THE POUND** [1] 2-9-0 J Reid 11/1: 5: Slow away, chsd ldrs 3f: op 8/1, stablemate 4th: 11 **37**
40,000 gns Northern Flagship April foal, brother & dam wnrs in the States.
5 ran Time 1m 27.46 (3.36) (W J P Jackson) S P C Woods Newmarket, Suffolk

2272 2.50 MAGPIES HCAP STKS 3YO 0-85 (D) 1m4f93y Good/Firm 32 -10 Slow [88]
£5398 £1661 £830 £415

*1735 **ORIGINAL SPIN** 24 [1] J L Dunlop 3-9-7 (81) K Darley 1/1 FAV: 42-211: 3 b f Machiavellian - Not **86**
Before Time (Polish Precedent) Rcd in 2nd, led 2f out, rdn & ran on well tho' was being reeled in cl home: well
bckd: earlier won at Leicester (h'cap bow): rnr up fnl of 2 '99 starts (mdn, rtd 83): eff at 10f, stys a gall
12.5f: acts on fast & hvy grnd, stiff/gall tracks: runs well fresh: lightly raced & progressive.

NEWCASTLE THURSDAY JUNE 29TH Lefthand, Galloping Track

*2012 **AFTER THE BLUE** 12 [2] M R Channon 3-8-2 (62) P Fessey 5/2: 006412: 3 b c Last Tycoon - Sudden nk 65
Interest (Highest Honor) Pld hrd held up, imprvg when denied room 2f out till fnl 100y, just failed: nicely
bckd, prob unlucky: suited by step up to 12.5f, goes on fast & gd grnd: improve further with an end to end gallop.
2110 **MICKLEY** 7 [4] J D Bethell 3-8-12 (72)(bl) J Reid 4/1: -25453: 3 b g Ezzoud - Dawsha (Slip Anchor) hd 74
Pld hard in tch, improved entering straight, rdn 2f out, styd on but never looked like getting to wnr:
quick reapp: hard to win with this term (stable without a winner for a long time): see 1225.
1758 **ONE DOMINO** 22 [3] M Dods 3-8-2 (60)(vis)(2ow) G Carter 5/1: 300324: Led till 2f out, sn btn & eased. 21 49
4 ran   Time 2m 43.07 (5.17)   (R Barnett)   J L Dunlop Arundel, W Sussex

2273 3.20 TOON ARMY STAYERS HCAP 3YO+ 0-70 (E)   2m   Good/Firm 32 -56 Slow   [67]
£3640   £1120   £560   £280   3 yo rec 20lb

1292 **BARROW** 45 [6] J L Dunlop 3-8-6 (65) G Carter 7/4 FAV: 34-001: 3 br c Caerleon - Bestow 72
(Shirley Heights) In tch, outpcd briefly appr straight, styd on strgly entering fnl 2f & led below dist, pshd clr:
well bckd, slow time, 6 week abs, first win: plcd in '99 (mdn, rtd 74): out & out stayer, been crying out for this
longer 2m trip: acts on fast grnd & stiff/gall tracks suit: goes well fresh: win more staying handicaps.
1919 **LITTLE DOCKER** 15 [1] T D Easterby 3-8-10 (69) K Darley 9/4: 4-3542: 3 b g Vettori - Fair Maid 3 71
Of Kent (Diesis) Set slow pace, increased tempo appr straight, under press & hdd entering fnl 1f, one pace:
nicely bckd: canny ride, stays a slow run/galloping 2m: see 1919, 1295.
2098 **ELSIE BAMFORD** 3 [3] M Johnston 4-8-12 (51) R Ffrench 7/2: 123333: 4 b f Tragic Role - Sara 1¾ 51
Sprint (Formidable) Trckd ldr, chall appr fnl 2f, soon rdn, same pace: consistent, easier grnd suits: see 1936, 1683.
1852 **ACEBO LYONS** 18 [5] A P Jarvis 5-9-4 (57) D Mernagh (3) 4/1: 166504: Held up, prog to chase front 1¼ 56
pair appr fnl 2f, kept on onepace: op 3/1: big step up in trip, poss stays a slow run 2m, btr 705 (10f).
2173 **SALSKA** 5 [4] 9-9-10 (63) L Newton 10/1: 00-005: Held up, rdn 3f out, no impression: op 7/1, top- 5 57
weight: '99 Redcar wnr (h,cap, rtd 73, A Streeter): '98 wnr at Nottingham (appr h'cap) & Newcastle (this
h'cap, rtd 77 at best): eff at 14f/2m on firm & gd/soft grnd, sharp or gall trks, likes Redcar: with D Clinton.
1824 **MILL EMERALD** 20 [2] 3-8-6 (65) D Duffield 16/1: 0-646: Chsd ldrs till wknd 3f out: h'cap bow, lngr trip. 6 50
6 ran   Time 3m 36.16 (10.66)   (Mrs S Egloff)   J L Dunlop Arundel, W Sussex

2274 3.50 EBF COND STKS 3YO+ (B)   1m str   Good/Firm 32 +11 Fast
£16120   £5720   £2860   £1300

1309 **MY HANSEL** 44 [4] B Hanbury 3-8-7(1ow) J Reid 4/1: 13-01: 3 b f Hansel - My Shafy (Rousilion) 98
Set gd pace, rdn appr fnl 1f, drifted left but held on for press: fast time, abs: failed to settle on reapp (10f
Gr 3): '99 debut wnr at Newmarket (fill mdn, rtd 102), subs 3rd of 6 in a Gr 1: apprec drop back to 1m tho' shld
get further: acts on firm & soft grnd, stiff/gall tracks: settled much better out in front today: useful filly.
1825 **HYPNOTIZE** 20 [2] Sir Michael Stoute 3-9-2 F Lynch 13/2: 15-602: 3 b f Machiavellian - Belle ¾ 105
Et Deluree (The Minstrel) Held up, prog under press appr fnl 1f, kept on but al held: op 5/1:
clearly apprec return to fast grnd and possibly flattered conceding weight: eff at 7f/1m: see 1184.
2150 **TOTAL LOVE** 6 [1] E A L Dunlop 3-8-3 G Carter 4/5 FAV: 3-0253: 3 ch f Cadeaux Genereux - 1¾ 89
Favourable Exchange (Excellor) Cl up, rdn appr fnl 1f, unable to quicken: well bckd, quick reapp: can do better.
1457 **BLUSIENKA** 39 [3] G A Butler 3-8-3 K Darley 3/1: 1-4354: Well plcd till appr fnl 2f, sn btn/eased. 15 69
6 week abs: reportedly made this fast grnd, see 1457, 995, 735.
4 ran   Time 1m 38.64 (1.64)   (Hilal Salem)   B Hanbury Newmarket, Suffolk

2275 4.20 NEWCASTLE FC HCAP 3YO+ 0-75 (E)   6f   Good/Firm 32 -03 Slow   [73]
£3916   £1205   £602   £301

1842 **ANGEL HILL** 19 [10] R A Fahey 5-8-7 (52) G Duffield 4/1 CO FAV: 000061: 5 ch m King's Signet - Tawny 55
(Grey Ghost) Prom, eff appr fnl 1f, ran on gamely & drvn to prevail in a blanket fin: nicely bckd: 1st time here
at Newcastle (h'cap, 1st time blnks, rtd 76): bck in '97 won again here at Newcastle (mdn, rtd 76, T Barron):
eff at 5f, 6f suits: acts on firm & soft grnd: eff with/without blinks: well h'capped & loves Newcastle.
2193 **GRAND ESTATE** 3 [3] D W Chapman 5-8-10 (55) D Holland 8/1: 005452: 5 b g Prince Sabo - shd 57
Ultimate Dream (Kafu) Held up centre, not much room going well appr fnl 1f, strong burst under hands & heels
inside last, just failed: quick reapp: back to form: h'capped to win & likes Hamilton: see 614.
2193 **WISHBONE ALLEY** 3 [9] M Dods 5-8-0 (45) Dale Gibson 7/1: 000003: 5 b g Common Grounds - Dul shd 47
Dul (Shadeed) In tch, hdwy under press appr fnl 1f, kept on well, just failed: quick reapp: back to form,
won this race in '99 (off 6lbs higher mark): on a handy mark: see 312.
2000 **MALLIA** 12 [12] T D Barron 7-9-8 (67)(bl) K Darley 4/1 CO FAV: 404444: Prom stands rail, rdn ½ 67
to lead bef fnl 1f, hdd cl home: remains in gd form, see 719.
1980 **REFERENDUM** 13 [1] 6-9-10 (69) Clare Roche 12/1: 000005: Well plcd centre & ev ch till fnl 100y. ¾ 67
2207 **SIHAFI** 3 [4] 7-8-8 (53) T Hamilton 7/1 CO FAV: 430236: Held up centre, keen, feeling pace nk 50
2f out, kept on inside last: op 3/1, quick reapp: see 1487.
2241 **SWINO** 1 [5] 8-6-6 (51)(vis) J Reid 14/1: 044607: Slowly into stride, never on terms: ran yesterday. 2½ 42
2158 **MOTHER CORRIGAN** 5 [11] 4-8-10 (55)(vis) D Mernagh (2) 20/1: 100008: Led stands side till bef fnl shd 46
1f no extra: quick reapp, reportedly finished lame on Saturday: see 1073 (1st time visor, claimer).
2015 **ALBERT THE BEAR** 11 [6] 7-8-12 (57)(vis) G Carter 6/1: 060039: In tch centre, rdn appr fnl 1f, ½ 47
no impression, eased inside last: better going around a bend: see 1438.
2095 **IMPALDI** 8 [8] 5-7-11 (42)(1ow)(8oh) Kimberley Hart 25/1: 0-0050: Well plcd centre till ent fnl 2f: 10th. 2½ 26
1559 **CHILLIAN** 31 [7] 4-7-10 (41)(16oh) P Fessey 50/1: 0-0500: In tch till halfway: 11th, v stiff task, see 674. 8 9
2097 **MISTER WESTSOUND** 8 [2] 8-8-11 (56)(bl) N Kennedy 16/1: 0-4000: Dwelt, al detached: 12th, see 1654. 4 16
12 ran   Time 1m 13.42 (2.12)   (Keith Taylor)   R A Fahey Butterwick, N Yorks

2276 4.50 BLACK & WHITE HCAP 3YO 0-75 (E)   1m1f   Good/Firm 32 -44 Slow   [73]
£3607   £1110   £555   £277

1495 **EYELETS ECHO** 34 [3] D Morris 3-9-7 (66) K Darley 7/2: 6-0001: 3 b g Inchinor - Kinkajoo 69
(Precocious) Bhd ldrs, eased fnl 2f, drifted left, rdn out: slow time, tchd 9/2, 1st win/time in the frame:
6th sole '99 start (mdn, rtd 66): half-brother to a 6f wnr tho' clrly apprec step up to a gall 9f: acts on fast grnd.
1909 **FRENCH MASTER** 15 [1] J L Eyre 3-8-8 (53)(vis) Iona Wands (5) 6/1: 310332: 3 b g Petardia - 1½ 53
Reasonably French (Reasonable) Held up, drvn & hdwy 2f out, styd on but not trouble wnr: see 806.
2093 **SAANEN** 8 [4] Mrs A Duffield 3-9-4 (63) G Duffield 11/8 FAV: 0-3223: 3 b g Port Lucaya - Ziffany 1 61

726

(Taufan) Set mod pace, hdd 3f out, styd on same pace: nicely bckd, ran to best: hard to win with, see 2093, 1722.
1758 **SUAVE PERFORMER** 22 [2] S C Williams 3-8-7 (52) G Faulner (3) 11/4: 454244: Cl up, led 3f out till   **3   45**
2f out, no extra: well bckd: probably needs softer grnd: see 1571.
2093 **JIMGAREEN** 8 [5] 3-9-1 (60)(BL) J Reid 9/1: 0-0645: Al bhd: blinkered, btr 2093, 1939.   **9   39**
5 ran   Time 1m 58.96 (6.86)   (Mrs G M Peel)   D Morris Newmarket, Suffolk

Official Going   GOOD TO FIRM. Stalls: Inside, except 12f - Outside.

2277	**2.00 THEHORSESMOUTH MED AUCT MDN 2YO (E) 5f rnd Firm 17 -43 Slow** £2977 £916 £458 £229

1844 **BIJAN** 19 [2] R Hollinshead 2-8-9 P M Quinn (3) 7/1: 531: 2 b f Mukaddamah - Alkariyh (Alydar)   **75**
Led 4f out, styd on strongly for press, rdn out: op 5/1: April foal, dam a 6f juv wnr: eff at 5f, 6f will
suit in time: acts on firm grnd & a stiff/undulating track: op to further improvement.
2029 **EXTRA GUEST** 11 [15] M R Channon 2-8-9 Craig Williams 2/1 FAV: 432622: 2 b f Fraam - Gibaltarik   **¾   72**
(Jareer) Trkd ldrs, chall appr fnl 1f, not pace of wnr ins last: bckd: consistent, worth a try in headgear.
1938 **KATIES DOLPHIN** 14 [11] J L Eyre 2-8-9 A Culhane 12/1: 623: 2 ch f Dolphin Street - Kuwah   **1¼   69**
(Be My Guest) In tch, slightly hmpd halfway, styd on late, no danger: eff at 5f, return to 6f shld suit.
-- **SO DIVINE** [3] M Johnston 2-8-9 J Fanning 8/1: 4: Rear, rdn/hdwy 2f out, styd on well ins last: **hd   69+**
op 11/2, debut: 4,700gns Mar foal, dam a 6f 2yo scorer: will improve & enjoy 6f.
1844 **CUMBRIAN HARMONY** 19 [8] 2-8-9 R Winston 10/1: 02305: Dwelt, settled rear, prog over 2f out,   **¾   67**
drvn & styd on late, nearest fin: see 1577.
-- **WHITE MARVEL** [7] 2-8-9 J F Egan 3/1: 6: Sn bhd, ran on well under hands & heels fnl 1f, nrst   **¾   65+**
fin: bckd: 29,000gns Jan foal, half sister to a 5f juv wnr: v encouraging debut, keep an eye on, 6f sure to suit.
-- **MR BOUNTIFUL** [4] 2-9-0 G Parkin 25/1: 7: Dwelt, rear, gd hdwy halfway, no extra appr fnl 1f: **½   69**
IR12,500gns half-brother to a juv 6/7f scorer: with A Turnell.
1776 **TUSCAN FLYER** 22 [6] 2-9-0 J Carroll 20/1: -058: Prom, wknd quickly over 1f out: see 1260.   **1¼   66**
-- **BRAITHWELL** [1] 2-9-0 O Pears 25/1: 9: Nvr a factor: Mujadil colt, dam scored over 6f as a 2yo.   **2½   60**
1595 **CLOONDESH** 29 [13] 2-9-0 P Hanagan (7) 14/1: 50: Soon rdn in rear, al bhd, fin 10th.   **1½   56**
1166 **BLOOM** 54 [5] 2-8-9 T Williams 20/1: 50: Al rear, fin 11th.   **nk   50**
2057 **LATE AT NIGHT** 9 [10] 2-9-0 C Lowther 20/1: 00: Led early, remaind prom, wknd appr fnl 2f, fin 12th.   **shd   55**
2162 **Pilgrim Princess** 5 [9] 2-8-9 (BL) W Supple 33/1:   2120 **High Society Lady** 7 [12] 2-8-9 F Norton 33/1:
2057 **Rising Passion** 9 [14] 2-9-0 A Nicholls (3) 25/1:
15 ran   Time 1m 02.5 (3.0)   (Geoff Lloyd)   R Hollinshead Upper Longdon, Staffs

2278	**2.30 CAT EGREMONT MED AUCT MDN 3-4YO (E) 6f rnd Firm 17 -44 Slow** £2743 £844 £422 £211 3 yo rec 7 lb

1266 **BILLY BATHWICK** 48 [4] E J O'Neill 3-9-0 J Carroll 11/2: 555201: 3 ch c Fayruz - Cut It Fine   **68**
(Big Spruce) Trkd ldrs, went on 3f out, strongly pressed fnl 1f, drvn clr inside last: op 9/2: 7 wk abs,
new stable: prev with B Smart, plcd in '99 (rtd 71, nursery h'cap): eff at 6f, stays a sharp 7f & has tried
1m: acts on firm, soft & a sharp or stiff/undulating track: goes well fresh: enjoying new stable.
-- **DAVEYS PANACEA** [3] R D Wylie 3-8-9 R Winston 40/1: 2: 2 ch f Paris House - Pampoushka   **3½   54**
(Pampabird) Dwelt, rear, hdwy to chall 2f out, rdn & no pace of wnr inside last: bred to be a sprinter:
encouraging debut by this rank outsider: stys 6f on firm grnd.
1723 **NORTHERN ECHO** 24 [7] M Dods 3-9-0 (bl) A Culhane 16/1: -00053: 3 b g Pursuit Of Love - Stop   **1½   56**
Press (Sharpen Up) Mid div, rdn/styd on fnl 1f, no threat to front 2: needs h'caps: see 909.
2204 **CONSIDERATION** 3 [6] A Berry 3-8-9 P Bradley (5) 10/1: 4-0244: Cl up, rdn/held fnl 2f: qck reapp.   **hd   51**
3948} **PRIMA** 287 [2] 3-8-9 J F Egan 1/3 FAV: 023-5: Prom, drvn & no impress appr fnl 1f, not given a hard   **1¼   48**
time after: well bckd on reapp: plcd on 2 of 3 '99 starts (mdns, rtd 82): eff at 5/6f on firm & fast grnd:
surely capable of much better than this, something amiss?.
2154 **CITY BANK DUDLEY** 5 [5] 3-9-0 C Teague 100/1: 036: Front rank, lost tch fnl 3f: qck reapp: see 2154.   **6   41**
2099 **FIRST LEGACY** 8 [8] 4-9-2 T Williams 50/1: /0-007: Led, hdd 3f out, wknd quickly: poor form.   **5   26**
7 ran   Time 1m 15.8 (3.7)   (W Clifford)   E J O'Neill Newmarket, Suffolk

2279	**3.00 CUMBERLAND PLATE HCAP 3YO+ 0-80 (D) 1m4f Firm 17 +16 Fast** £14820 £4560 £2280 £1140 3 yo rec 14lb	**[78]**

*2127 **COURT SHAREEF** 6 [1] R J Price 5-9-3 (67)(5ex) M Fenton 9/2 FAV: 5-1311: 5 b g Shareef Dancer -   **78**
Fairfields Cone (Celtic Cone) Settled rear, gd hdwy over 3f out, led appr fnl 1f, rdn clr, readily: fast time,
quick reapp: earlier won at Windsor (reapp) & Goodwood (h'caps): rnr up in a nov hdle in Nov '99 (rtd 103h):
bck in '98 won at Windsor & Leicester (h'caps, rtd 74 at best, R Dickin): suited by 12/14f on fast, gd & any
trk, likes Windsor: runs well fresh: v progressive this term, hat-trick awaits.
2048 **OCTANE** 10 [7] W M Brisbourne 4-8-4 (54) G Baker (7) 9/1: 313202: 4 b g Cryptoclearance -   **3   60**
Something True (Sir Ivor) Bhd, gd hdwy to chall appr fnl 1f, not pace of wnr inside last: excellent run, clr rem.
2048 **WARNING REEF** 10 [11] E J Alston 7-8-7 (57) W Supple 11/2: 456533: 7 b g Warning - Horseshoe   **5   56**
Reef (Mill Reef) Mid div, gd hdwy over 3f out, drvn & no impress appr fnl 1f: nicely bckd: see 2048, 1217.
2195 **LOVE BITTEN** 3 [5] M Johnston 3-8-3 (67) K Dalgleish (7) 14/1: 452134: Trckd ldrs, hmpd after 4f,   **nk   66**
hdwy to lead over 3f out, hdd appr fnl 1f, wknd: op 10/1, qck reapp: shade better 2141 (13f).
*2061 **FATEHALKHAIR** 9 [10] 8-9-3 (67)(52x) F Norton 9/1: 402315: Mid div, rdn to improve 2f out, not   **2   63**
pace of ldrs soon after: op 7/1: all wins have come on a left-handed track: see 2061.
1050 **MANZONI** 61 [14] 4-8-0 (50) G Parkin 12/1: 22-006: Handy, rdn & kept on one pace fnl 3f: 9 wk abs: **¾   45**
'99 scorer at Southwell (AW h'caps, rtd 54a), subs rnr up on turf (rtd 56): likes to force the pace around
a sharp 12f: acts on fast, gd & fibresand: eff with/without blinks.
2008 **BEST PORT** 12 [15] 4-7-10 (46)(14oh) P M Quinn (3) 50/1: 003437: Waited with, rdn/late gains,   **1   39$**
no threat: not disgraced from 14lbs o/ht.
2176 **GOLDEN CHIMES** 4 [12] 5-9-3 (67) A Nicholls (3) 11/1: 30-168: Never better than mid div: qck reapp.   **1   59**
2002 **BHUTAN** 12 [8] 5-9-4 (68) A Culhane 8/1: 44-169: Rear, hdwy when slightly hmpd by lose horse   **3½   55**
3f out, no extra appr fnl 1f: twice below 1194.

*1866 **WASEEM 17** [6] 3-8-11 (75) J Fanning 9/1: 100210: Chsd ldrs when hmpd after 4f, rdn/fdd fnl 2f. 1½ 60
2002 **ELVIS REIGNS 12** [13] 4-8-10 (60) P Robinson 20/1: -00000: Al rear, fin 11th: see 2002. ½ 44
2002 **NOUKARI 12** [3] 7-10-0 (78) J F Egan 14/1: 010200: Never a factor, fin 12th: top weight. 2 59
1940 **KIDZ PLAY 14** [9] 4-8-7 (57) Dean McKeown 16/1: 4-0140: Led, left clr after 4f, wknd/hdd 3f out, 1½ 36
soon lost tch, fin 13th: up in trip: not stay 12f, best at 1m/10f: see 1689.
1363 **LAWNETT 41** [4] 4-7-11 (47) J McAuley (5) 33/1: 560050: Handy, lost tch 4f out, t.o., 14th: 6 wk abs. 28 0
1965 **HIBERNATE 13** [2] 6-9-9 (73) N Callan 9/1: 00420S: Cl up when slipped & u.r. after 4f: 0
op 7/1: won this race last year off the same mark as today.
15 ran Time 2m 30.9 (0.1) (Derek & Cheryl Holder) R J Price Ullingswick, H'ford

2280

3.30 CLAYTON ARMS HCAP 3YO 0-75 (E) 5f rnd Firm 17 -17 Slow [78]
£3721 £1145 £572 £286

1877 **CUPIDS CHARM 17** [8] R Guest 3-9-7 (71) P Robinson 10/3: -00101: 3 b f Cadeaux Genereux - Chapka 77
(Green Desert) In tch, gd hdwy to lead appr fnl 1f, strongly pressed inside last, all out & just prevailed:
nicely bckd: earlier won at Brighton (h'cap, 1st win): 4th for P Chapple Hyam sole juv start (rtd 76):
eff at 5/6f on firm, poss not soft: acts on a sharp/undul or stiff trk: improving, could win again.
2060 **MARON 9** [1] A Berry 3-8-5 (55) J Carroll 9/1: 0-0032: 3 b g Puissance - Will Be Bold (Bold Lad) shd 60
Rear, smooth hdwy to chall ins fnl 1f, ran on well, just held: clr rem: eff at 5/6f on firm & gd: win similar.
1780 **FRAMPANT 22** [3] M Quinn 3-8-10 (60) F Norton 20/1: 000443: 3 ch f Fraam - Potent (Posen) 2½ 59
Handy, rdn/drpd rear after 2f, drvn & styd on late, no dngr to ldrs: apprec a return to 6f on an easier surface.
2118 **CHRISTOPHERSSISTER 7** [11] N Bycroft 3-9-0 (64) J Fanning 25/1: -10004: Dwelt, rear, styd on well ½ 62
for press fnl 2f, no danger: quick reapp & an improved eff on this turf return: see 479,426.
2047 **CAUTIOUS JOE 10** [9] 3-9-2 (66) P Hanagan (7) 5/2 FAV: -00035: Trckd ldrs, drvn/onepce fnl 1f. shd 64
1843 **THORNCLIFF FOX 19** [6] 3-8-11 (61)(vis) O Pears 14/1: -04036: Prom, went on 2f out, hdd dist, fdd. 1½ 55
1891 **WELCHS DREAM 16** [10] 3-9-3 (67) W Supple 9/1: 4-5607: Handy, eff appr fnl 1f, soon btn: op 7/1. ¾ 59
1891 **FANTASY ADVENTURER 16** [7] 3-8-3 (53) A Nicholls (3) 9/1: -00048: Nvr a factor: op 7/1: see 1891. 2 40
2101 **UNCLE EXACT 8** [4] 3-9-4 (68) A Culhane 12/1: 000059: Prom, short of room & wknd appr fnl 1f. 1 52
1665 **DANCING RIDGE 27** [5] 3-7-13 (49) S Righton 25/1: 60-000: In tch, fdd appr fnl 2f, 10th: see 1494. 1 30
2047 **PAPE DIOUF 10** [2] 3-7-11 (47) T Williams 33/1: 106000: Al in rear, fin 11th: btr 619 (AW). ¾ 26
2165 **SHALARISE 5** [12] 3-8-6 (56)(bl) J F Egan 11/2: -00050: Led, hdd 2f out, wknd qckly, 12th: qck reapp. 1½ 32
12 ran Time 1m 01.2 (1.7) (I Allan, Ming Yi Chen & Hung Chao-Hong) R Guest Newmarket, Suffolk

2281

4.00 RAYOPHANE HCAP 3YO 0-70 (E) 1m rnd Firm 17 -04 Slow [72]
£3705 £1140 £570 £285

*1682 **HAND CHIME 26** [6] W J Haggas 3-9-4 (62) J F Egan 9/2: 011: 3 ch g Clantime - Warning Bell 70
(Bustino) Settled rear, smooth hdwy to lead appr fnl 1f, rdn clr inside last, eased near fin: val 2/3L:
h'cap bow: earlier won at Catterick (auction mdn): eff at 7f/1m & will stay further: acts on soft & firm grnd,
sharp/turning or stiff track: runs v well fresh: progressive & one to keep on your side.
1940 **JUMBOS FLYER 14** [8] J L Eyre 3-9-1 (59) J Fanning 11/1: 052462: 3 ch c Jumbo Hirt - Fragrant ¾ 62
Princess (Germont) Waited with, hdwy to chall appr fnl 1f, soon outpcd by ldr: gd eff against a prog rival.
2145 **SOBA JONES 6** [3] T D Easterby 3-8-7 (51) J Carroll 4/1 JT FAV: -66023: 3 b c Emperor Jones - ¾ 52
Soba (Most Secret) Front rank, went on over 2f out, hdd appr fnl 1f, not pace of wnr: nicely bckd,
well clr rem: quick reapp: in gd heart, eff at 7f/1m on firm & fast: see 2145.
1477 **GLEN VALE WALK 35** [11] Mrs G S Rees 3-8-4 (47)(1ow) Dean McKeown 20/1: -00004: Rear, 6 39
late gains for press, no threat to ldrs: see 887.
1726 **LION GUEST 24** [7] 3-9-5 (63) P Robinson 8/1: 06-405: Mid div, rdn to improve over 2f out, 2½ 50
soon held: bred to apprec mid-dists: btr 1293 (reapp, 10f).
*1972 **BINT HABIBI 13** [9] 3-8-13 (57) Craig Williams 13/2: 00-016: Led, hdd appr fnl 2f, wknd: btr 1972. ¾ 43
2205 **SPEEDFIT FREE 3** [12] 3-9-7 (65) A Culhane 20/1: 4-0057: Never a factor: qck reapp: top-weight. nk 51
1678 **FOXY ALPHA 26** [2] 3-7-10 (40)(5oh) G Baker (7) 25/1: 0-058: Prom 6f, sn btn: up in trip on h'cap bow. 3½ 20
2160 **CLASSIC LORD 5** [10] 3-8-6 (50) K Dalgleish (7) 4/1 JT FAV: 003U29: Soon rdn in rear, no 1½ 28
impression from halfway: nicely bckd, quick reapp: better expected after an encouraging run in 2160.
2134 **DOLFINESSE 6** [13] 3-8-5 (49)(vis) T Williams 14/1: 052340: Prom, rdn/lost tch fnl 2f, 10th: qck reapp. nk 27
2017 **SEND IT TO PENNY 11** [1] 3-8-7 (51)(bl) G Parkin 9/1: 020150: Front rank, fdd fnl 3f, fin 11th. 8 15
2099 **BLUE LINE LADY 8** [4] 3-8-4 (48)(bl) R Winston 20/1: 005000: Handy, rdn/wknd rapidly fnl 3f, 12th. 13 0
12 ran Time 1m 40.5 (1.7) (Mrs M M Haggas) W J Haggas Newmarket, Suffolk

2282

4.30 AMAT LADY RIDERS HCAP 3YO+ 0-65 (F) 7f rnd Firm 17 -30 Slow [38]
£2878 £822 £411 3 yo rec 9 lb

2136 **SHAMWARI SONG 6** [2] K A Ryan 5-10-2 (40)(vis) Miss P Robson 10/1: 004031: 5 b g Sizzling Melody - 46
Spark Out (Sparkler) Mid div, gd hdwy to lead appr fnl 1f, rdn out: op 8/1, quick reapp: failed to make the frame
in '99 (rtd 41a & 41, h'caps, Miss L Jewell): '98 wnr at Beverley (claimer) & Newcastle (h'cap, rtd 75 & 71a, J
Glover): suited by 7f/1m on firm, gd, poss soft: eff with/without a visor & likes a stiff track: well h'capped.
*2136 **DOVEBRACE 6** [5] A Bailey 7-10-5 (43)(5ex) Miss Bridget Gatehouse (3) 5/2 FAV: 6-3212: 7 b g ¾ 47
Dowsing - Naufrage (Main Reef) Handy, rdn to chall appr fnl 1f, kept on, no extra cl home: bckd, clr rem.
*1672 **ROBELLION 26** [9] Miss E C Lavelle 9-11-7 (59) Miss S Newby Vincent (5) 10/1: 00-513: 9 b g 7 51
Robellilno - Tickled Trout (Red Alert) Handy, rdn/eff 2f out, sn not pace of ldrs: btr 1672 (gd, sharp track).
1941 **ZIBAK 14** [4] J S Goldie 6-9-11 (35) Mrs C Williams 7/1: 0-0654: Soon led, hdd appr fnl 1f, soon btn. 1 25
2193 **GARNOCK VALLEY 3** [13] 10-10-10 (48) Miss E J Jones 6/1: 003625: Handy, rdn/hdwy over 1f out, ½ 37
hung right & wknd inside last: quick reapp: stays 7f but best over 6f: see 2193.
1239 **THWAAB 49** [11] 8-10-7 (45)(bl) Miss A Deniel 20/1: 000-06: Prom, rdn/no impress fnl 2f: 7 wk abs. 4 28
1907 **PENG 15** [12] 3-10-10 (57) Miss R Bastiman (7) 33/1: 000007: Led early, remnd with ldrs, lost tch 2f out. 2 37
1760 **BODFARI ANNA 22** [15] 4-10-13 (51)(vis) Miss Diana Jones 7/1: 450108: Mid div, wknd fnl 2f. shd 31
1296 **PIPIJI 45** [1] 5-9-9 (33) Miss L J Harwood (7) 20/1: 02-009: Reared leaving stalls, never a threat: abs. ¾ 12
1137 **FIRST GOLD 56** [10] 11-9-3 (27)(2oh) Miss J Ellis (7) 50/1: 000-00: In tch, wknd over 3f out, 1½ 3
fin 10th: 8 week abs, mod recent form.
*2097 **JACMAR 8** [14] 5-11-4 (56)(5ex) Mrs S Bosley 6/1: 105210: Missed break & al bhd: 14th, btr 2097. 0
op 5/1: much btr 2097 (6f, Hamilton).
1254 **ADULATION 48** [8] 6-11-3 (55) Mrs C Ford 10/1: 05-000: Handy, bhd halfway, fin last: op 7/1, jumps fit. 0
1941 **Distant King 14** [6] 7-9-7 (31) Miss L Bradburne (5) 33/1:

CARLISLE

THURSDAY JUNE 29TH Righthand, Stiff Track, Uphill Finish

-- **Simand** [3] 8-9-6 (30) Miss S Brotherton (5) 33/1:
2147 **Fas 6** [7] 4-9-3 (27) (vis) (5oh) Miss A Armitage (5) 50/1:
15 ran   Time 1m 28.8 (3.3)   (Gallagher Equine Ltd)   K A Ryan Hambleton, N Yorks

2283

5.00 BLACK HORSE CLASS STKS 3YO+ 0-60 (F) 1m rnd Firm 17 -15 Slow
£2383 £681 £340 3 yo rec 10lb

2049 **BOWCLIFFE 10** [6] E J Alston 9-9-5 W Supple 2/1 FAV: 360221: 9 b g Petoski - Gwiffina (Welsh Saint) 62
Mid div, gd hdwy to lead appr fnl 1f, styd on well for press, rdn out: plcd over hdles in 99/00 (nov h'cap, rtd
78h): '99 Musselburgh (class stks, rtd 67), prev term won at W'hampton & Doncaster (h'caps, rtd 77a & 68):
suited by 1m/9f, stys 10f on firm, soft & fibresand: runs well fresh & best without blinks: in fine heart.
2049 **SPARKY 10** [2] M W Easterby 6-9-5 (bl) G Parkin 11/2: 0-2032: 6 b g Warrshan - Pebble Creek   1 60
(Reference Point) Front rank, chall ldr appr fnl 1f, hung left & no impression inside last: clr rem, in gd form.
2241 **ITALIAN SYMPHONY 1** [4] P D Evans 6-9-5 R Fitzpatrick (3) 6/1: 550563: 6 b g Royal Academy -   5 52
Terracotta Hut (Habitat) Mid div, rdn to improve halfway, nvr pace of ldrs appr fnl 1f: op 5/1, ran 24hrs ago.
2241 **SAMARA SONG 1** [1] Ian Williams 7-9-5 Darren Williams (5) 5/1: 526004: Dwelt, bhd, btn 2f out.   3 47
1355} **EUROLINK MOUSSAKA 410** [3] 5-9-5 J F Egan 10/1: 0100-5: Stumbled start but soon led, hdd   5 39
appr fnl 1f, fdd: bckd from 20/1 on reapp: '99 scorer at Southwell (h'cap, rtd 77a), well btn both turf starts:
late '98 scorer at W'hampton (mdn, rtd 68a), earlier rtd 66 on turf (C Wall): eff at 7f/1m on fibresand & a
sharp track: gd weight carrier: showed up well for a long way here & should be sharper next time.
2013 **BIRDSAND 12** [7] 3-8-6 P Robinson 6/1: 0-6066: Led early, remained with ldrs, lost tch fnl 2f.   3 31
1699} **TERRAZZO 393** [5] 5-9-5 J Carroll 10/1: 5514-7: Front rank, rdn/wknd quickly fnl 3f: op 8/1   5 26
on reapp: '99 scorer at Musselburgh (h'cap, rtd 61), earlier rtd 64a when plcd on sand: eff at 9f, stays
12f: acts on firm, both AW & easy track.
7 ran   Time 1m 41.4 (2.6)   (Philip Davies)   E J Alston Longton, Lancs

---

NEWMARKET (July)

FRIDAY JUNE 30TH Righthand, Stiff, Galloping Track

Official Going GOOD/FIRM. Stalls: Stands' Side.

2284

2.00 LARK CLAIMER 3YO (E) 1m2f Good/Firm 37 -35 Slow
£3581 £1102 £551 £275

1610 **LULLABY 30** [9] J R Fanshawe 3-8-8 M Hills 10/3: 0-3401: 3 b f Unfuwain - Heart's Harmony (Blushing 65
Groom) Chsd ldrs, went on 4f out, styd on strongly, pushed out: nicely bckd: apprec drop to claim grade, earlier
plcd at Windsor (fill mdn): half sister to a 10f wnr: eff at 1m, stays 10f on fast, handles hvy grnd & a gall trk.
2119 **FINERY 8** [5] C A Dwyer 3-8-11 (VIS) D Holland 9/1: 401400: 3 ch g Barathea - Micky's Pleasure   1¾ 63
(Foolish Pleasure) Trkd ldrs, eff 3f out & sn outpcd, fin well but too late despite drifting left: tried a visor: acts
on fast grnd: fine effort at today's weights, wld meet this wnr on 21lbs better terms in a h'cap.
1967 **BORDER RUN 14** [2] B J Meehan 3-8-13 R Hughes 7/2: 003603: 3 b g Missed Flight - Edraianthus   2½ 63
(Windjammer) Dwelt, prog & ch 2f out, onepcd ins last: top-weight: eff at 10f, return to 12f will suit: see 1292.
2013 **FOXS IDEA 13** [4] D Haydn Jones 3-8-2 F Norton 11/4 FAV: 305054: Chsd ldrs, chall 2f out, wknd fnl   3 47
1f: drifted from 7/4: not stay this longer 10f trip on drop to claim company: see 1405 (7f).
2134 **RUNAWAY STAR 7** [2] 3-8-4 L Newton 8/1: -665: Rear, mod late hdwy, nvr in it: clr of rem: now   2 46
qual for h'caps: promise in 2134 (1m longer).
2134 **WHO DA LEADER 7** [3] 3-8-13 G Carter 12/1: 6-0506: Rear, prog 4f out, btn 2f out: mkt drifter.   7 45
1274 **NEEDWOOD TRIDENT 48** [8] 3-8-4 G Bardwell 20/1: 0-0507: Rear, nvr in it: 7 wk abs, new stable.   2½ 33
1141 **WROTHAM ARMS 57** [1] 3-7-12 (BL) J Lowe 33/1: 0-008: Led till 4f out, wknd qckly, t.o.: qck reapp.   11 12
8 ran   Time 2m 09.10 (7.20)   (Mrs Denis Haynes)   J R Fanshawe Newmarket

2285

2.30 EBF FILLIES MDN 2YO (D) 6f str Good/Firm 37 -08 Slow
£4914 £1512 £756 £378

-- **ENTHUSED** [2] Sir Michael Stoute 2-8-11 M Hills 6/5 FAV: -1: 2 b f Seeking The Gold - Magic Of   91
Life (Seattle Slew) In tch, prog to lead 1½f out, drvn & just held on: hvly bckd tho' op 4/5 on debut: Mar
foal, half sister to sev wnrs, incl mid-dist wnr From Beyond: dam a smart miler: eff at 6f, 7f+ will suit: acts on
fast grnd & on a gall trk: runs well fresh: holds big race entries & will improve further & win again.
-- **ASHLINN** [4] S Dow 2-8-11 P Doe 33/1: -2: 2 ch f Ashkalani - Always Far (Alydar)   shd 90
Rear, prog 2f out, chall ins last, just btn in a driving fin: clr of rem: Ffr 400,000 Apr foal: dam unrcd tho'
well bred: sire a top-class miler: eff at 6f on fast, handles a gall trk: runs well fresh: will sn, esp at 7f.
1943 **MAINE LOBSTER 15** [6] J L Dunlop 2-8-11 K Darley 6/1: -03: 2 ch f Woodman - Capades (Overskate)   3½ 80
Chsd ldrs, outpcd 3f out, rdn & ran on again last, no ch with first 2: bckd from 8/1: Jan foal, cost 80,000gns:
dam multiple wnr in the States: already needs 7f+: handles fast grnd: interesting in nursery h'caps later on.
1856 **BOIS DE CITRON 19** [5] R Hannon 2-8-11 R Hughes 5/2: -34: Led till 1½f out, no extra & eased.   2½ 73
2034 **RENEE 11** [3] 2-8-11 M Fenton 10/1: -35: Trkd ldr, ch 2f out, sn wknd: see 2034 (5f).   2½ 66
-- **TAKESMYBREATHAWAY** [8] 2-8-11 G Carter 12/1: -6: Reared start, nvr a factor & bhnd fnl 1½f: 4 54
stablemate of 3rd: Jan foal, half sister to 1m wnr Mutakddim: dam a winning sprinter in the US.
-- **BONELLA** [1] 2-8-11 G Bardwell 33/1: -7: Al bhnd, no ch fnl 2f: Apr foal, cost 7,000gns: dam 9f wnr.   1½ 50
-- **AILINCALA** [7] 2-8-11 R Mullen 16/1: -U: Swerved badly left & u.r start: op 12/1: Feb foal, dam   0
a 1m wnr: sire a high-class f/1m performer: with C Wall & an unfortunate debut.
8 ran   Time 1m 13.72 (2.72)   (Niarchos Family)   Sir Michael Stoute Newmarket

2286

3.00 H & K HCAP 3YO+ 0-80 (D) 1m4f Good/Firm 37 -68 Slow   [73]
£4862 £1496 £748 £374

*2081 **MAY KING MAYHEM 9** [6] Mrs A L M King 7-8-2 (47) (bl) P M Quinn (3) 1/1 FAV: 651111: 7 ch g   50
Great Commotion - Queen Ranavalona (Sure Blade) Rear, prog 4f out, forged ahd ins last, drvn out: well bckd, v
slow time: completed 4-timer after wins at Lingfield, here at Newmarket & Kempton (h'caps): '99 wnr at Leicester
(appr h'cap) & Newmarket (amat h'cap, rtd 43): '98 Haydock & Pontefract wnr (h'caps, rtd 43): all wins at 12f,
stays 15f: acts on firm, gd/soft & handles f/sand: likes Newmarket: tried a visor, suited by blnks: in fine form.

2131 **JUST GIFTED** 7 [1] R M Whitaker 4-9-6 (65) D Holland 7/2: -20622: 4 b g Rudimentary - Parfait Amour nk **67**
(Clantime) Set slow pace, qcknd 3f out, collared ins last, rallied & just btn: gd front running eff: see 2131 (C/D).
2131 **NORCROFT JOY** 7 [3] N A Callaghan 5-9-10 (69) R Hughes 4/1: -50333: 5 b m Rock Hopper - Greenhills nk **70**
Joy (Radetzky) Chsd ldrs, switched to stands rail 1f out, ran on: tchd 5/1: on a handy mark: see 2131.
*2075 **MONO LADY** 9 [4] D Haydn Jones 7-10-0 (73)(bl) (5ex) Dean McKeown 8/1: 204514: Trkd ldrs, ev ch ½ **73**
2f out, no extra cl home: top-weight: see 2075 (AW).
2131 **LANCER** 7 [2] 8-9-6 (65) G Bardwell 16/1: 166065: Rear, outpcd fnl 3f: see 2131 (C/D). 7 **55**
5 ran   Time 2m 40.88 (12.68)   (S J Harrison)   Mrs A L M King Wilmcote, Warwicks.

2287   **3.30 ORWELL RTD HCAP 3YO+ 0-90 (C)**   **1m2f**   **Good/Firm 37** **-04 Slow**   **[88]**
            £6356   £2411   £1205   £548   3yo rec 12lb

1878 **CULZEAN** 18 [4] R Hannon 4-9-4 (78) R Hughes 8/1: 360041: 4 b g Machiavellian - Eileen Jenny (Kris) **86**
Rear, prog 2f out, switched stands rail, fin fast to lead cl home, won going away: plcd sev times in '99 (h'caps,
rtd 88): '98 Leicester wnr (mdn, debut, rtd 87): eff at 1m, stays 10f well: handles fast & soft grnd: can force
the pace, did well from bhnd today: well h'capped & can follow up.
+2183 **SECOND WIND** 7 [6] C A Dwyer 5-9-5 (79)(t) J Mackay(5) 9/1: 150012: 5 ch g Kris - Rimosa's 1¾ **82**
Pet (Petong) Rear, prog 2f out, led ins last, not pace to repel wnr cl home: qck reapp: stays 10f: in form.
1942 **WASP RANGER** 15 [8] G L Moore 6-9-1 (75) K Darley 4/1: -0-0223: 6 b g Red Ransom - Lady Climber ½ **77**
(Mount Hagen) Chsd ldrs, chall ent fnl 1f, no extra cl home: well bckd: see 1942, 1743.
*1984 **CAPTAINS LOG** 14 [9] M L W Bell 5-9-6 (80) M Fenton 7/2 FAV: 425114: Mid-div, prog 2f out, ch nk **81**
ent fnl 1f, no extra cl home: continues in gd form: see 1984.
1831 **BOLD EWAR** 21 [1] 3-8-4 (76)(bl) F Norton 9/1: 532505: Trkd ldr, went on 2f out, hdd ins last & no 1¾ **75**
extra: clr of rem: see 979 (C/D).
1825 **KUWAIT DAWN** 21 [10] 4-9-8 (82) G Carter 25/1: 0-0006: Rear, not pace to chall: see 1825 (1m, List). 5 **73**
1832 **NORTON** 20 [2] 3-9-4 (90) L Carter 11/2: 01-037: Chsd ldrs, rdn & ch 2f out, sn btn: bckd from shd **81**
7/1: better on softer grnd prev: see 1832 (gd/soft).
*1532 **COURT OF APPEAL** 34 [7] 3-9-4 (90) M Hills 8/1: 0-018: Chsd ldrs, wknd over 2f out: btr 1532 (1m, soft). 11 **66**
3953} **BRIGHT HOPE** 288 [3] 4-9-8 (82) D Holland 16/1: 0/31-9: Chsd ldrs till wknd over 3f out, eased on 12 **40**
reapp: top-weight: '99 Pontefract wnr on fnl of 2 starts (mdn, rtd 83): eff at 10f, further will suit: acts on fast/
firm grnd: can run well fresh: reportedly 'lost action' today.
633 **MODUS OPERANDI** 118 [5] 4-9-6 (80) N Callan 16/1: 15-640: Led till 2f out, wknd qckly: long abs. 1½ **36**
10 ran   Time 2m 06.02 (4.12)   (Stonethorn Stud Farms Ltd)   R Hannon East Everleigh, Wilts.

2288   **4.00 THEHORSESMOUTH HCAP 3YO 0-85 (D)**   **5f str**   **Good/Firm 37** **+07 Fast**   **[85]**
            £4966   £1528   £764   £382

*1961 **BOANERGES** 14 [3] R Guest 3-9-6 (77) D Holland 6/1: -00011: 3 br c Caerleon - Sea Siren **81**
(Slip Anchor) Chsd ldrs, strong run to lead fnl 20y, cosily: nicely bckd, best time of day: recent Goodwood wnr
(h'cap): plcd twice in '99 (mdn, rtd 83, with J Noseda, 1st time visor): eff at 5/7f: acts on fast & soft grnd:
handles a stiff/gall or sharp/undul trk: eff with/without a visor: fast improving & cld complete hat-trick.
1925 **LA CAPRICE** 16 [1] A Berry 3-9-4 (75) R Hughes 10/1: -03202: 3 ch f Housebuster - Shicklah (The nk **76**
Minstrel) Trkd ldr till went on halfway, drvn & collared cl home, only just btn: deserves to go one better.
2168 **CONNECT** 6 [8] M H Tompkins 3-9-7 (78)(vis) S Sanders 7/2: 000043: 3 b c Petong - Natchez Trace shd **79**
(Commanche Run) Chsd ldrs, chall strongly fnl 1f, just btn in a cl fin: nicely bckd, qck reapp: primed to win sn.
1961 **JAMES STARK** 14 [6] N P Littmoden 3-9-3 (74)(vis) R Mullen 9/1: 002034: Stumbled & nearly u.r. ½ **74**
leaving stalls, ran on strongly fnl 1f, nvr nrr: op 7/1: prob unfortunate: shld pinch a 6f h'cap: see 1961.
1891 **JUDIAM** 17 [5] 3-8-7 (64) F Norton 16/1: 450005: Mid-div going well, some late hdwy under a kind 1½ **60**
ride: slipping down the weights & hinted at a return to form: see 652 (AW, reapp).
1712 **DAWN** 26 [7] 3-8-9 (66) J Mackay 16/1: -36036: Rear, nvr a factor: btr 1712. nk **61**
1881 **JODEEKA** 18 [2] 3-9-3 (74) N Callan 10/1: -5157: Chsd ldrs, ev ch 2f out, fdd ins last: see 1516. hd **69**
2003 **RED REVOLUTION** 13 [4] 3-9-7 (78) K Darley 7/4 FAV: 32-168: Led till halfway, wknd fnl 1f: well 1¼ **69**
bckd, top-weight: much better expected after 2003 (6f).
8 ran   Time 1m 00.04 (1.54)   (P A & D G Sakal)   R Guest Newmarket

---

2289   **4.30 BURE FILLIES COND STKS 3YO+ (C)**   **6f str**   **Good/Firm 37** **-05 Slow**
            £6182   £2345   £1172   £533   3yo rec 7lb

2003 **BOAST** 13 [6] R F Johnson Houghton 3-8-1 R Mullen 11/4 JT FAV: 6-6351: 3 ch f Most Welcome - Bay **98**
Bay (Bay Express) Rear, pushed 2f out, flew ins fnl 1f to lead cl home, won going away: jock rec 2-day careless
riding ban: '99 Nottingham (nov med auct) & here at Newmarket wnr (nov, rtd 99 at best): eff at 6f, stays 7f:
acts on firm & gd/soft: handles any trk: useful & has a gd turn of foot: can follow up.
2197 **FLOWINGTON** 4 [7] N P Littmoden 3-7-12 P M Quinn(3) 14/1: 0-5042: 3 b f Owington - Persian Flower ½ **92**
(Persian Heights) Dwelt, hdwy to lead 1f out till collared cl home: op 10/1, qck reapp: met a useful, in-form rival.
*2197 **DANDY NIGHT** 4 [5] B Hanbury 3-8-11 A Beech (5) 11/2: 02-013: 3 b f Lion Cavern - Desert 1¼ **101**
Venus (Green Desert) Prom, styd on well fnl 1f, not pace of front 2: top-weight: qck reapp: jock rec a 3-day
ban for irresponsible riding: improved in defeat conceding plenty of weight: see 2197.
1283 **JEED** 48 [4] E A L Dunlop 3-7-12 F Norton 11/2: 1-04: Set pace till 1f out: abs, sharper for this. 1¼ **84**
1283 **SCARLETT RIBBON** 48 [8] 3-8-1 J Lowe 11/4 JT FAV: 10-25: Chsd ldrs till lost place & hmpd dist, 1¾ **82**
rallied ins last: 7 wk abs: not disgraced & a return to fit will suit: handles fast, bred on gd/soft prev: see 1283.
1987 **PRESENTATION** 13 [1] 3-7-12 P Doe 6/1: -23266: Chsd ldrs, ev ch 2f out, grad fdd: btr 1534. nk **78**
1987 **IMPERIALIST** 13 [3] 3-7-12 G Bardwell 20/1: 0-5007: Chsd ldrs, wk ch ent fnl 1f, fdd: see 1078. ½ **77**
1427 **SHANNON DORE** 39 [2] 3-8-1 J Mackay 33/1: 10-408: Rear, eff on outside halfway, sn btn & eased. 6 **65**
8 ran   Time 1m 13.56 (2.56)   (Lady Rothschild)   R F Johnson Houghton Newmarket

FOLKESTONE FRIDAY JUNE 30TH Righthand, Sharpish, Undulating Track

Official Going FIRM (GOOD/FIRM places) Stalls: Rnd Crse - Outside, Str Crse - Stands Side

2290

1.50 FAMILY FUN MED AUCT MDN 2YO (F) **7f str** **Good/Firm 34 -17 Slow**
£2488   £711   £355 Raced two groups, winner well clr stands side

1988 **BLACK KNIGHT** 13 [1] S P C Woods 2-9-0 J Reid 1/1 FAV: 31: 2 b c Contract Law - Another More 87
(Farm Walk) Made most stands side, led 2f out, rdn clr fnl 1f, easily: val 8L+, well bckd: eff at 7f on fast
grnd, 1m will suit: handles a stiff or sharp/undul trk: clearly going the right way, can rate more highly.
1856 **FADHAH** 19 [7] L M Cumani 2-8-9 J P Spencer 7/2: 52: 2 b f Mukaddamah - Ishtiyak (Green Desert) 6 70
Al prom centre, rdn/outpcd by wnr over 1f out: stays 7f, acts on firm & fast grnd: see 1856.
1876 **BOLSHOI BALLET** 18 [6] J L Dunlop 2-9-0 D Harrison 7/1: 03: 2 b c Dancing Spree - Broom Isle nk 74
(Damister) In tch stands side, rdn/outpcd 2f out, styd on well ins last, no threat: op 8/1: apprec this step up
to 7f, 1m looks sure to suit: acts on fast grnd & a sharp/undul trk: going the right way: see 1876.
-- **FLUTED** [4] M R Channon 2-9-0 S Drowne 12/1: 4: Chsd ldrs stands side halfway, rdn/no extra hd 73
over 1f out: Piccolo colt, April foal, half brother to a 5f juv wnr: sire a smart miler: handles fast grnd.
1463 **APRIL LEE** 37 [3] 2-8-9 (e) O Urbina 33/1: 6055: Chsd wnr stds side 2f out, sn held: eyeshield. 3½ 61
-- **FIGURA** [12] 2-8-9 T E Durcan 20/1: 6: In tch centre, held over 2f out: Rudimentary filly, Apr foal, ½ 60
cost 25,000gns 2yo: sire a smart/progressive miler: with K McAuliffe.
-- **RASSENDYLL** [11] 2-9-0 Pat Eddery 11/2: 7: Cl up centre 6f, btn/eased fnl 1f: op 7/2: Rudimentary 3½ 58
colt, May foal, half-brother to sev wnrs: dam a multiple 5/10f winner: sire a smart & progressive miler.
-- **SASHA STAR** [10] 2-9-0 J Bosley (7) 33/1: 8: In tch centre 5f: Namaqualand colt, Feb foal, 10 43
10,000 gns 2yo: half brother to an Irish 1m juv wnr: with G Brown.
1740 **OPERATION ENVY** 24 [9] 2-9-0 C Rutter 25/1: 46049: Bhd fnl 2f: btr 1260 (5f, g/s). 1¼ 40
1882 **KIRIWINA** 17 [2] 2-8-9 A Clark 50/1: 060: Bhd fnl 2f: 10th: mod form. 1 33
-- **Make A Wish** [5] 2-9-0 R Price 25/1:   891 **Hurlingham Star** 78 [8] 2-9-0 (VIS) W Ryan 33/1:
12 ran Time 1m 27.8 (3.6) (Rex Norton) S P C Woods Newmarket

2291

2.20 SPONSOR CLAIMER DIV 1 3YO+ (F) **6f** **Good/Firm 34 -04 Slow**
£1939   £554   £277 3 yo rec 7 lb Raced stands side

2124 **CHAKRA** 7 [6] J M Bradley 6-8-10 Pat Eddery 11/8 FAV: 000021: 6 gr g Mystiko - Maracuja (Riverman) 48
Trkd ldrs, led over 1f out, styd on well, drvn out: bckd: claimed for £4000: earlier scored at Lingfield (AW
h'cap, rtd 37a): rnr-up in '99 (h'cap, rtd 45): '98 wnr at Warwick (2, h'caps, rtd 54): eff at 5/6f on firm, gd &
equitrack: handles any trk, likes a sharp/turning one: appreciated this drop to claiming grade.
2099 **MR CUBE** 9 [5] J M Bradley 10-8-8 (bl) D Watson (7) 10/1: 043552: 10 ch g Tate Gallery - Truly Thankful 2 39
(Graustark) Settled rear/in tch, rdn/styd on well from over 1f out, no threat: eff at 6f, suited by 7f/1m: see 1336 (7f).
1971 **PETRIE** 14 [2] M R Channon 3-8-3 S Drowne 3/1: -03503: 3 ch g Fraam - Canadian Capers (Ballacashtal) ¾ 39
Prom, drifted right/no extra in last: acts on fast, soft & fibresand: see 42.
1971 **JUST FOR YOU JANE** 14 [7] T J Naughton 4-8-7 (bl) A McGlone 10/1: 3-0004: Chall 2f out, sn held. ½ 34
2040 **UBITOO** 11 [8] 3-8-7 (BL) C Rutter 20/1: 00-005: Trkd ldr, held over 1f out: blnks: mod form. ¾ 39$
504 **CLARA BLUE** 139 [9] 4-8-5 N Pollard 16/1: 000-06: Led till over 1f out, sn held: abs: see 504 (AW). 8 15
378 **SAMEEAH** 160 [3] 4-9-1 M Cotton (3) 12/1: 5-67: In tch, btn over 1f out: 5 mth abs: see 378 (AW). 3 18
2036 **SONTIME** 11 [4] 3-8-2 D O'Donohoe 3/1: 00-00W: Unseated rider & ran loose bef start, withdrawn. 0
8 ran Time 1m 13.30 (2.3) (Clifton Hunt) J M Bradley Sedbury, Gwent

2292

2.50 SPONSOR CLAIMER DIV 2 3YO+ (F) **6f** **Good/Firm 34 +11 Fast**
£1939   £554   £277 3 yo rec 7 lb Raced stands side

1884 **SHUDDER** 17 [4] R J Hodges 5-8-12 S Drowne 1/1 FAV: -43031: 5 b g Distant Relative - Oublier L'Ennui 58
(Bellman) Trkd ldrs, smooth prog to lead over 1f out, rdn clr ins last: bckd, tho' op 4/7: best time of day: '99
Haydock wnr (clmr, W Haggas, rtd 81, 1st time vis): eff at 6/7f on fast & gd, prob any trk: eff with/without visor.
2207 **BALANITA** 4 [2] B Palling 5-9-2 (BL) D Sweeney 5/1: 00-002: 5 b g Anita's Prince - Ballybannon 4 53
(Ballymore) Led, rdn/hdd over 1f out, no extra: op 4/1, tried blnks: qck reapp: see 2207.
2099 **CAVERSFIELD** 9 [8] J M Bradley 5-8-10 P Fitzsimons (5) 10/1: 000603: 5 ch h Tina's Pet - Canoodle 3½ 38
(Warpath) Chsd ldrs, kept on fnl 2f & took 3rd nr fin, no threat: return to 7f+ shld suit: see 1330, 336.
2040 **BONNIE DUNDEE** 11 [3] E A Wheeler 4-8-7 (bl) S Carson 9/1: 050004: Chsd ldrs 4f: op 12/1. ¾ 33
-- **NIGHT PEOPLE** [6] 5-9-2 Paul Smith 7/1: 0/4505: Al outpcd/bhd: op 10/1: mod Belgian form. 8 27
1664 **BEVERLEY MONKEY** 28 [1] 4-8-3 D O'Donohoe 33/1: -00006: Sn outpcd/bhd: see 1664, 436 (AW). 6 3
1438 **EARLEY SESSION** 39 [5] 3-8-13 C Rutter 14/1: 000-07: Outpcd/sn strugg: see 1438. nk 19
2134 **STOP THE TRAFFIC** 7 [9] 3-8-8 (VIS) W Ryan 7/1: 055008: Soon bhd: tried vis: see 397 (AW). 27 0
1884 **STRIDING KING** 17 [7] 5-8-12 (VIS) N Pollard 33/1: 00-00F: Bhd/fell 2f out, sadly died. 0
9 ran Time 1m 12.4 (1.4) (Footsteps Flyers) R J Hodges Charlton Adam, Somerset

2293

3.20 THEHORSESMOUTH MDN 3YO+ (D) **7f str** **Good/Firm 34 -23 Slow**
£2996   £856   £428 3 yo rec 9 lb Field raced stands side

1985 **THUNDER SKY** 14 [2] C E Brittain 4-9-7 (VIS) P Robinson 4/1: 0/0451: 4 b c Zafonic - Overcast (Caerleon) 75
Made all, asserted fnl 1f: op 9/4, first time visor: has been racing in Dubai: highly tried juv back in '98 (rtd
106, Gr 2): apprec this drop to 1m, tried 10f: acts on firm/fast & a sharp/undul trk: likes to force the pace.
1960 **HAIL THE CHIEF** 14 [3] R Hannon 3-8-12 R Smith (5) 12/1: 0-42: 3 b c Be My Chief - Jade Pet (Petong) 2½ 69
Chsd wnr till lost pl halfway, rallied & badly hmpd dist, kept on well: op 10/1: closer to this wnr without
interference: handles fast grnd, return to 1m & h'cap company shld now suit: see 1960.
-- **YAZAIN** [5] K Mahdi 4-9-7 S Drowne 16/1: 3: 4 b c Pips Pride - Trust Sally (Sallust) ½ 68
Held up, rdn to chase wnr over 1f out, al held: op 10/1, debut: stays 7f and handles fast ground.
1261 **KUWAIT ROSE** 49 [4] K Mahdi 4-9-7 J Reid 9/1: 26-454: Trkd ldrs, rdn/onepace fnl 2f: 7 wk abs. 2 64
1773 **EMANS JOY** 23 [8] 3-8-7 D Harrison 4/5 FAV: 35: Prom, rdn/jinked over 1f out, wknd ins last: hd 58
hvly bckd from 6/4: more expected over longer 7f trip: btr 1773 (6f, debut, gd).
1951 **TAFFETA** 15 [6] 3-8-7 Pat Eddery 9/2: 506: In tch, eff/no impress fnl 2f: needs h'caps. ¾ 57
-- **SILVER TONIC** [1] 4-9-7 M Cotton (7) 16/1: 7: Rear/outpcd early, mod prog: op 12/1, debut. 2 58
2086 **DIZZIE LIZZIE** 9 [7] 3-8-7 A McGlone 33/1: -08: Held up in tch, nvr threat: dropped in trip. 2½ 48
8 ran Time 1m 28.20 (4.0) (Ali Saeed) C E Brittain Newmarket

731

2294 3.50 ARENA LEISURE MDN 3YO+ (D)   5f   Good/Firm 34 -06 Slow
£2884   £824   £412   3 yo rec 6 lb   Majority raced stands side

808 **ANNETTE VALLON** 90 [9] P W Harris 3-8-9 Pat Eddery 15/8 FAV: 21: 3 b f Efisio - Christine Daae   79
(Sadler's Wells) Sn cl up, drvn/led ins last, gamely prevailed, all out: op 1/1, 3 mth abs: eff at 5f, 6f shld
suit: acts on fast & gd/sft grnd: handles a sharp/undul or gall trk: runs well fresh: can rate more highly.
4542↑ **MUKAABED** 245 [6] M P Tregoning 3-9-0 R Hills 5/2: 30-2: 3 ch c Phone Trick - Slick Delivery   ¾ 81
(Topsider) Led near side, drvn/narrowly hdd ent last, styd on gamely, just held: op 4/1, reapp: plcd on first
of 2 '99 starts (mdn, rtd 87): eff at 5/6f on gd & fast grnd, stiff/gall or sharp trk: can find similar.
1516 **FLY LIKE THE WIND** 34 [8] M A Jarvis 3-8-9 P Robinson 5/2: 5-223: 3 br f Cyrano De Bergerac -   hd 75
Thulium (Mansingh) Al prom/dsptd lead, rcd alone far side from halfway, styd on well, just held: op 3/1.
1961 **SUSSEX LAD** 14 [3] R Hannon 3-9-0 D Harrison 8/1: -04064: Prom 4f: op 4/1: btr 1175.   3 73
1334 **BORN TO RULE** 44 [1] 3-9-0 K Dalgleish (7) 50/1: 4-0005: Held up, nvr pace to chall: abs.   1½ 69$
1266 **ALMASHROUK** 49 [7] 3-9-0 J Reid 8/1: -66406: Chsd ldrs till over 1f out: op 12/1, abs: flattered 956.   1¼ 66
1712 **MAVIS** 26 [2] 3-8-9 D Sweeney 50/1: 07: Dwelt, nvr on terms: no form.   5 52
1175 **MARWELL MAGNUS** 54 [4] 3-9-0 A Eddery (5) 50/1: 0-08: Bhd halfway: 8 wk abs, no form.   5 48
8 ran   Time 1m 0.4 (2.0)   (Mrs P W Harris)   P W Harris Aldbury, Herts

2295 4.20 CARIBBEAN HCAP 3YO+ 0-65 (F)   1m4f   Good/Firm 34 -40 Slow   [56]
£2604   £744   £372   3 yo rec 14lb

2270 **WADI** 1 [6] Dr J R J Naylor 5-9-10 (52) C Rutter 14/1: -06041: 5 b g Green Desert - Eternal (Kris)   61
Chsd ldrs 3f out, rdn/led 2f out, held on gamely ins last, all out: op 12/1, 4th in a Salisbury h'cap yesterday:
'99 wnr for G McCourt at Warwick (sell h'cap) & Salisbury (clmr, rtd 70): '98 Pontefract wnr for H Cecil (mdn,
rtd 81): eff at 10/12f on firm, soft & equitrack, any trk: best without blnks/tongue strap: gd weight carrier.
2203 **XELLANCE** 4 [8] M Johnston 3-8-4 (46)(6ex) K Dalgleish (7) 11/8 FAV: 011122: 3 b g Be My Guest -   ½ 53
Excellent Alibi (Exceller) Trkd ldrs, drvn to chall dist, just held nr fin: hvly bckd, qck reapp: see 2203.
2081 **NORTH OF KALA** 9 [7] G L Moore 7-9-0 (42) P Dobbs (5) 7/2: 00-133: 7 b g Distinctly North - Hi Kala   3 45
(Kampala) Held up, prog/chsd leading pair over 1f out, kept on tho' al held: op 3/1: see 2081, 1888.
2032 **SACREMENTUM** 12 [10] J A Osborne 5-9-7 (49) Pat Eddery 10/1: 064024: Twds rear, rdn/late gains, no 2½
threat to leading pair: op 8/1: styd longer 12f trip, also eff at 1m: acts on firm, gd/sft & fibresand: see 381.   48
1935 **ESTABLISHED** 15 [2] 3-7-10 (38) (1oh) Claire Bryan (5) 25/1: 050355: Chsd ldrs, held fnl 2f: btr 1914.   1 36
2008 **CASHIKI** 13 [4] 4-8-7 (35) D O'Donohoe 14/1: 602026: Rear/bhd, late gains, no threat: op 12/1.   nk 32
*2007 **FIFE AND DRUM** 13 [9] 3-9-2 (58)(bl) J Reid 6/1: -00017: Led 10f, sn btn: btr 2007 (10f, mdn h'cap).   1½ 53
-- **OUT ON A PROMISE** [5] 8-9-2 (44) P Robinson 4/1: 0364/8: Rear/bhd, no impress: Flat reapp, jmps   1¼ 37
fit: '99/00 h'cap hdle wnr at Stratford, Bangor & Sandown (rtd 132h, eff at 2m/2m8f): last rcd on the level in
'98 (clmr, rtd 55, L Lungo): '95 Doncaster stks wnr: eff at 10/12f on firm & gd/sft, any trk.
1209 **WAR BABY** 52 [3] 4-8-2 (30) Sophie Mitchell 50/1: 0-0009: Al twds rear: abs: mod form: see 314.   10 12
1933 **ARAGANT** 15 [1] 4-8-12 (40) D Sweeney 33/1: 0-0000: Chsd ldrs 9f: 10th: longer 12f trip: see 1210 (sell)30 0
10 ran   Time 2m 40.4 (8.9)   (Mrs S P Elphick)   Dr J R J Naylor Shrewton, Wiltshire

2296 4.50 LOOKOUT FILLIES HCAP 3YO+ 0-70 (E)   1m1f149y Good/Firm 34 -43 Slow   [62]
£2954   £844   £422   3 yo rec 12lb

2041 **COMMON CONSENT** 11 [7] S Woodman 4-9-4 (52) Pat Eddery 9/1: 03-061: 4 b f Common Grounds -   56
Santella Bell (Ballad Rock) Trkd ldrs, rdn/styd on gamely fnl 1f, narrowly prevail nr fin, all out: 1st win: plcd
twice last term (h'cap, rtd 62): eff at 9.7/12f on fast & gd/sft grnd: likes a sharp/undul trk.
1892 **SILVER QUEEN** 17 [3] C E Brittain 3-9-3 (63) P Robinson 12/1: 0-0002: 3 ch f Arazi - Love Of Silver   nk 66
(Arctic Tern) Trkd ldr, rdn/chall fnl 2f, styd on well, just held: op 10/1: eff arnd 10f on fast & firm: see 1649.
2206 **BLESS** 4 [9] M Madgwick 3-7-10 (42)(vis)(4oh) D Kinsella 9/1: 060033: 3 ch f Beveled - Ballystate   ¾ 44
(Ballacashtal) Led, hdd well ins last, just held cl home: qck reapp: confirmed improvement of 2206.
2206 **CHEZ BONITO** 4 [13] J M Bradley 3-7-10 (42)(7oh) Claire Bryan (5) 9/2: -52054: Mid-div, no room/   ½ 43
dropped rear over 3f out, styd on well fnl 2f, not reach ldrs: op 10/1: no luck in running, qck reapp: see 2206.
2041 **SHARP SPICE** 11 [8] 4-9-10 (58)(VIS) J Reid 4/1 JT FAV: 444525: Rear, onepace fnl 2f: vis, op 7/1.   1½ 56
2032 **MAY QUEEN MEGAN** 12 [12] 7-8-5 (39) D Sweeney 11/2: 504-46: Rear, hdwy 4f out, no prog over 1f out.2½ 33
1942 **MELLOW MISS** 15 [4] 4-9-1 (49)(bl) C Rutter 14/1: 033007: Chsd ldrs over 2f out, sn held: op 12/1.   shd 34
*2011 **DION DEE** 13 [6] 4-8-12 (46) D O'Donohoe 11/2: 003618: Rear, drvn/no impress: op 4/1: btr 2011 (gd).   5 33
2186 **READING RHONDA** 5 [11] 4-9-5 (53) W Ryan 33/1: /50009: Rear, nvr a factor: qck reapp: mod form.   hd 39
1265 **AHOUOD** 49 [2] 4-8-10 (44) A McGlone 20/1: 256040: Chsd ldrs 1m: 10th: abs: see 446 (AW mdn).   3½ 25
2033 **INDIAN NECTAR** 11 [5] 7-9-5 (53) K Dalgleish (7) 4/1 JT FAV: 0-0420: Mid-div, btn 3f out: 12th: btr 2033.   0
233 Black Rocket 186 [1] 4-9-5 (53) T E Durcan 14/1:
2043 Heiress Of Meath 11 [10] 5-7-13 (33) (3ow)(10oh) A Whelan 33/1:
13 ran   Time 2m 06.4 (8.4)   (Mrs Fiona Gordon & Mrs Jenny Carter)   S Woodman East Lavant, W Sussex

SOUTHWELL (Fibresand)   FRIDAY JUNE 30TH   Lefthand, Sharp, Oval Track

Official Going   STANDARD. Stalls: Inside.

2297 2.10 ASH HCAP 3YO+ 0-65 (F)   6f aw rnd   Going 41 -04 Slow   [57]
£2296   £656   £328   3 yo rec 7 lb

1861 **NIFTY NORMAN** 19 [11] D Nicholls 6-9-9 (52) O Pears 11/4 FAV: 463061: 6 b g Rock City - Nifty Fifty   63a
(Runnett) Dsptd lead till went on 4f out, rdn clr fnl 2f, cmftbly: earlier won at Southwell (clmr): '99 wnr again at
Southwell (2, rtd 73a) & Chester (h'caps, rtd 69): '98 wnr again at Southwell (h'cap, rtd 58a): eff at 5/6f,
tried 7f: acts on fast, gd/soft, hvy & any trk, loves fibresand/Southwell: eff with/without blnks: tough.
2031 **PETITE DANSEUSE** 12 [13] D W Chapman 4-9-6 (48) D Mernagh (3) 6/1: 116052: 6 b m Aragon - Let   5 47a
Her Dance (Sovereign Dancer) Prom, rdn & not pace of wnr appr fnl 1f: see 1422 (C/D).
1559 **CZAR WARS** 32 [12] P T Dalton 5-8-12 (41)(bl) Martin Dwyer 25/1: 4-0003: 5 b g Warrshan - Dutch   hd 40a
Czarina (Prince Sabo) Front rank, rdn to improve 2f out, sn outpcd: clr rem: see 212, 199.

1913 **PALO BLANCO** 16 [4] Andrew Reid 9-9-7 (50) M Henry 10/1: 223324: Hmpd early, in tch, rdn & `3  42a`
not pace of ldrs fnl 2f: see 1913.
1422 **GRASSLANDIK** 39 [7] 4-9-4 (47)(BL) S Whitworth 9/1: 350045: Dwelt, hdwy from rear fnl 2f, nrst `1½  36a`
fin: first time blnks: btr 746 (h'cap, fast).
2118 **FEATHERSTONE LANE** 8 [3] 9-9-10 (53) J Weaver 9/1: 316336: Sn rdn in mid-div, no dgnr: btr 2118. `1¾  38a`
1578 **NADDER** 31 [6] 5-9-0 (43) C Cogan (5) 9/1: 030207: Led, hdd 4f out, wknd 2f out: twice below 1422. `½  18a`
1941 **RIVER BLEST** 15 [8] 4-9-10 (53) G Duffield 20/1: 36-508: Trkd ldrs, drvn/lost tch fnl 2f: jt top-weight. `4  25a`
2193 **SKYERS FLYER** 4 [14] 6-8-13 (42) T Williams 20/1: 000009: Sn rdn, nvr a threat: qck reapp. `1  10a`
4319] **HEATHER VALLEY** 263 [2] 4-9-1 (44) J F Egan 5/1: 000-0: Mid-div, wknd qckly fnl 2f, fin 10th: `1¾  6a`
bckd from 12/1, new stable: unplcd in 3 mdn starts for C F Wall in '99 (rtd 46): better expected on this
h'cap debut for W Haggas & could be capable of better.
2107 **KOSEVO** 8 [5] 6-9-7 (50)(vis) Darren Williams (5) 12/1: 005200: Handy, wknd from halfway, fin 11th. `2½  0a`
2017 Laund View Lady 12 [1] 3-8-11 (47) P Fessey 25/1:   1910 Miss Grapette 16 [10] 4-8-7 (36) A Daly 14/1:
1806 **Bally Cyrano** 21 [15] 3-9-1 (51)(VIS) W Supple 33/1: -- **Eastwell Minstrel** [16] 5-8-11 (40) J McAuley (5) 33/1:
15 ran   Time 1m 16.0 (2.7)   (The David Nicholls Racing Club)   D Nicholls Sessay, N.Yorks.

2298	**2.40 POPLAR CLAIMER 4YO+ (F) 1m4f aw Going 41 -08 Slow**
	£2219 £634 £317

2119 **ALS ALIBI** 8 [10] W R Muir 7-9-4 Martin Dwyer 15/8 FAV: /00021: 7 b g Alzao - Lady Kris (Kris) `71a`
Trkd ldrs, led appr fnl 3f, sn clr, easily: tchd 9/2: missed '99, prev term won at Newbury & Bath (h'caps, rtd 75):
eff at 11/12f on firm, gd/soft & f/sand: runs well fresh on any trk, likes Newbury: well h'capped on old form.
*1975 **STEAMROLLER STANLY** 14 [8] D W Chapman 7-8-10 D Mernagh (3) 6/1: 000412: 7 b g Shirley `15  43a`
Heights - Miss Demure (Shy Groom) Sn rdn in tch, imprvd 3f out, edged left & kept on fnl 2f, not pace of easy wnr.
1978 **STATE APPROVAL** 14 [4] D Shaw 7-8-6 Darren Williams (5) 16/1: 050603: 7 b g Pharly - Tabeeba `4  33a`
(Diesis) Trkd ldrs, rdn/outpcd 3f out, late gains for press, no threat: see 512, 270.
*2119 **CANADIAN APPROVAL** 8 [3] I A Wood 4-8-7 A Daly 11/4: 002114: Led, hdd over 3f out, wknd qckly `nk  34a`
for press: big mkt drifter on hat-trick bid: much btr 2119.
2049 **BRANDON MAGIC** 11 [2] 7-8-6 O Pears 8/1: 003055: In tch, wknd qckly fnl 3f, t.o.: up in trip: see 2049. `13  18a`
-- **ROUTE ONE** [1] 7-9-6 M Henry 20/1: 6: Dsptd lead, lost tch fnl 3f: op 14/1, Flat debut: back in `4  26a`
98/99 won over hdles at Hereford & Towcester (mdn/nov, rtd 109h, 2m, fast & gd/soft, S Sherwood): with A Reid.
2076 **MISALLIANCE** 9 [5] 5-7-13 P Fessey 12/1: -00337: Al well bhd: op 8/1: btr 2076. `5  0a`
1975 **SIPOWITZ** 14 [9] 6-10-0 G Duffield 20/1: 103/58: Sn lost tch, t.o.: see 1975. `12  13a`
1816 **NEEDWOOD MAESTRO** 21 [6] 4-8-8 (VIS) S Whitworth 25/1: 40-509: Handy, bhd halfway, t.o.: visor. `1¾  0a`
206} **DANZINO** 549 [7] 5-10-0 (vis) N Fitzpatrick (3) 9/1: 3135/0: Al well bhd, t.o. in 10th: mkt `dist  0a`
drifter on reapp: missed '99, '98 Southwell (auct mdn), Lingfield (2) & W'hampton wnr (2, h'caps, rtd 95a & 55):
eff at 1m/10f & loves both AWs: likes to force the pace in a visor: runs well fresh: better than this.
10 ran   Time 2m 40.2 (5.9)   (J Haim)   W R Muir Lambourn, Berks.

2299	**3.10 ELM MDN 3YO+ (D) 6f aw rnd Going 41 -21 Slow**
	£2821 £806 £403

1922 **ZIG ZIG** 16 [6] Mrs A Duffield 3-9-0 G Duffield 4/1: 0-31: 3 b g Perugino - Queen Of Erin (King Of `74a`
Clubs) With ldrs, rdn to led appr fnl 1f, styd on well, drvn out: op 3/1, AW bow: well btn sole '99 juv start
(6f mdn, soft): eff at 6/7.5f on firm grnd & fibresand: handles a stiff/undul or sharp track.
77 **GERONIMO** 223 [9] C W Thornton 3-9-0 O Pears 20/1: 0-2: 3 b c Efisio - Apache Squaw (Be My Guest) `1½  70a`
Dwelt, sn well in rear, plenty to do over 2f out, rdn & ran on strongly ins last, likes home: long abs: eff at
6f, sure to apprec 7f+ now: handles fibresand: eye-catching effort & one to keep in mind: see 77.
1877 **CHORUS** 18 [2] B R Millman 3-8-9 G Hind 9/4 FAV: 006323: 3 b f Bandmaster - Name That Tune (Fayruz) `½  64a`
Dsptd lead, hung right & onepcd fnl 1f: consistent but still a mdn after 17 starts: handles firm, hvy & f/sand.
1481 **SPORTING LADDER** 36 [5] P F I Cole 3-8-9 J F Egan 5/2: 404: Trkd ldrs, drvn/held appr fnl 1f: `nk  64a`
shld apprec a return to 7f+ in h'caps: see 1269.
1643 **RESILIENT** 28 [8] 3-9-0 K W Marks 12/1: 065: Rear, ran on strongly for press appr fnl 2f, nrst fin: `shd  69a`
well clr of rem: now quals for h'caps & shld apprec 7f/1m in that sphere: one to keep in mind: see 1643, 1532.
1578 **PRINCE NICO** 31 [10] 3-9-0 S Whitworth 25/1: -00006: Led, hdd appr fnl 1f, wknd qckly: dubious rating. `10  49$`
-- **EXECUTIVE WISH** [1] 3-8-9 M Henry 20/1: 7: Sn outpcd: Executive Man filly, with D Sasse. `12  22a`
-- **OVERSLEPT** [4] 3-9-0 J Weaver 5/1: 8: V slow to start & al in rear: op 7/2: 7,500gns Missed Flight `3  21a`
colt, v sleepy in the stalls here shld know more next time: with C F Wall.
1365 **COLLEGE GALLERY** 42 [3] 3-9-0 (BL) W Supple 33/1: 00-009: Prom, hmpd 3f out, sn btn, blnkd. `1¾  17a`
1103 **TINKERS CLOUGH** 58 [7] 3-9-0 Martin Dwyer 33/1: 00: Al well in rear, t.o. in last: 8 wk abs. `4  9a`
10 ran   Time 1m 17.0 (3.7)   (Mrs Betty Duxbury)   Mrs A Duffield Constable Burton, N.Yorks.

2300	**3.40 SILVER BIRCH HCAP 3YO 0-85 (D) 7f aw rnd Going 41 +08 Fast**	**[89]**
	£3851 £1185 £592 £296	

1310 **RUSHMORE** 45 [6] P F I Cole 3-8-13 (74) F Lynch 13/2: 3-1001: 3 ch c Mt Livermore - Crafty Nan `84a`
(Crafty Prospector) Led 5f out, rdn clr fnl 2f, cmftbly: op 4/1, best time of day, 6 wk abs: earlier won on
reapp at Doncaster (mdn): rtd 76 sole '99 start: brother to a smart 7f wnr: seems suited by 7f, has tried up
to 10f: acts on gd grnd & fibresand: runs well fresh: win again.
2145 **ATYLAN BOY** 7 [9] B J Meehan 3-8-11 (76) S Clancy (7) 10/1: 003152: 3 b g Efisio - Gold Flair (Tap On `6  77a`
Wood) Dwelt, sn rdn & chsd ldrs, onepcd fnl 2f: op 7/1, qck reapp: acts on both AWs: see 1745 (stks).
2025 **SOFISIO** 12 [8] W R Muir 3-8-12 (73) Martin Dwyer 14/1: 144-03: 3 ch g Efisio - Legal Embrace `2  70a`
(Legal Bid) Sn outpcd, ran on strongly for press fnl 2f, nvr nrr: shld apprec a return to 1m: see 94.
1735 **INVER GOLD** 25 [4] A G Newcombe 3-8-13 (74) S Whitworth 13/2: -13004: Sn well bhd, gd late hdwy, `hd  71a`
nrst fin: op 5/1: unsuited by this drop in trip & will apprec a return to 1m+: see 278.
1399 **TOYON** 41 [2] 3-8-6 (67) G Duffield 8/11 FAV: 6065: Prom, rdn 2f out, sn wknd: well bckd after 6 `nk  63a`
wk abs on h'cap bow: clearly though capable of much better by shrewd connections: see 1399, 1105.
1797 **GIRLS BEST FRIEND** 22 [7] 3-9-7 (82) W Supple 14/1: 40-056: Cl-up, rdn/lost tch fnl 3f: top-weight. `11  61a`
1390 **NODS NEPHEW** 41 [5] 3-7-13 (60) M Henry 14/1: -41047: Prom, wknd rapidly fnl 2f: op 10/1, 6 wk abs. `5  31a`
*1651 **LORD YASMIN** 28 [1] 3-9-0 (75) J Weaver 11/2: -10318: Led early, lost tch after halfway: op 7/2: `3  41a`
up in trip, much better on turf in 1651 (stks, 6f, gd).
1891 **NITE OWL MATE** 17 [3] 3-8-4 (65) R Fitzpatrick (0) 20/1: -33009: Al last: see 472. `shd  31a`
9 ran   Time 1m 28.9 (2.3)   (J S Gutkin)   P F I Cole Whatcombe, Oxon.

SOUTHWELL (Fibresand)   FRIDAY JUNE 30TH   Lefthand, Sharp, Oval Track

2301   4.10 BEECH SELLLER 2YO (G)   7f aw rn   Going 41   -30 Slow
£1869   £534   £267

1950 **CEDAR TSAR** 15 [3] Andrew Reid 2-8-11 M Henry 5/2: 62021: 2 b c Inzar - The Aspecto Girl (Alzao) 69a
Dsptd lead, led over 3f out, rdn clr fnl 2f: 1st win, sold to D Chapman for 6,800gns: Mar foal, sire high-class
at 6/7f: eff at 6/7f on fast, gd, fibresand & a sharp or easy trk: likes sells, win again in this grade.
2077 **JOHN FOLEY** 9 [7] W G M Turner 2-8-11 A Daly 9/4 FAV: 025242: 2 b c Petardia - Fast Bay (Bay   5   58a
Express) Trkd ldrs, rdn/not pace of wnr appr fnl 1f: up in trip, just stays 7f: see 1740, 1136.
2155 **IMPISH LAD** 6 [5] B S Rothwell 2-8-11 (bl) W Supple 7/2: 052363: 2 b g Imp Society - Madonna Da   shd   58a
Rossi (Mtoto) Cl-up, drvn/no extra over 1f out: op 3/1, 10L clr rem: qck reapp: blnks reapplied: see 1890.
2077 **SOBER HILL** 9 [8] D Shaw 2-8-11 R Fitzpatrick (3) 25/1: 04: Prom, rdn/lost tch halfway: see 2077. 10   41a
1890 **MASTER COOL** 17 [6] 2-8-11 O Pears 8/1: 445: Al outpcd: op 5/1: apprec 1m+ in time: see 1679.   ½   40a
*2079 **DECEIVES THE EYE** 9 [1] 2-9-3 J Weaver 7/1: 345016: Set pace, hdd over 3f out, sn btn: btr 2079 (6f). ½   45a
2120 **OLYS GILL** 8 [4] 2-8-6 S Whitworth 14/1: 407: Prom, wknd halfway, t.o.: op 8/1: up in trip.   23   0a
2132 **MISTY DIAMOND** 7 [2] 2-8-6 G Faulkner (0) 9/1: 008: Dwelt, al well bhd, t.o.: qck reapp.   27   0a
8 ran   Time 1m 31.6 (5.0)   (A S Reid)   Andrew Reid Mill Hill, London NW7.

2302   4.40 CYPRESS AMAT HCAP 4YO+ 0-70 (G)   1m aw rn   Going 41   -20 Slow   [46]
£1918   £546   £274

*2121 **GUILSBOROUGH** 8 [9] J G Smyth Osbourne 5-11-11 (71)(6ex) Mr M Baldock (7) 7/2: 060-11: 5 br g   78a
Northern Score - Super Sistes (Call Report) Trkd ldrs, went on dist, styd on strongly, rdn out: op 3/1, top-weight:
recent Southwell winner (h'cap): '99 scorer again here at Southwell (h'cap, rtd 68a & 57, D Morris): suited by 7f/1m
on fibresand/Southwell, handles fast & gd/soft: runs v well fresh: eff weight carrier: in fine form.
1690 **HOH GEM** 27 [4] B R Millman 4-10-3 (49) Mr G Richards (5) 3/1: 014102: 4 b g Be My Chief - Jennies'   ¾   54a
Gem (Sayf El Arab) Sn well in rear, ran on well for press fnl 2f, not quite rch wnr: back to nr best on fibresand.
*1741 **TAKHLID** 24 [2] D W Chapman 9-11-7 (67) Miss R Clark 4/1: 013313: 9 b h Nureyev - Savonnerie   4   65a
(Irish River) Led, drvn/hdd over 1f out, not pace of front 2: reportedly fin lame: op 7/2: v tough & consistent
but best in clmg grade these days: see 1741.
2118 **ELTON LEDGER** 8 [6] Mrs N Macauley 11-10-11 (57)(vis) Mrs M Morris (3) 14/1: 350064: Trkd ldrs,   7   45a
drvn/onepcd fnl 2f: veteran 11yo: see 389.
1979 **MIDNIGHT WATCH** 14 [1] 6-10-1 (47) Miss C Hannaford (5) 11/4 FAV: 220225: Prom, rdn/lost tch fnl 2f. nk   35a
2121 **TROJAN WOLF** 8 [5] 5-11-7 (67) Miss S Pocock (5) 16/1: 000006: Dwelt, nvr a threat: see 255 (8.5f).   4   50a
2139 **SOCIETY TIMES** 7 [5] 7-9-3 (35)(5oh) Miss Bridget Gatehouse (5) 9/1: 06/507: Handy, rdn/wknd   5   12a
fnl 3f: qck reapp: see 1907.
1979 **MARTON MERE** 14 [7] 4-9-4 (36) Miss A Deniel 33/1: 056-08: Dwelt, sn in tch, fdd fnl 2f: see 1979.   shd 13a
1979 **DREAM CARRIER** 14 [3] 12-9-4 (36)(bl)(1ow)(11oh) Mrs C Peacock (0) 40/1: 000009: Al well bhd.   7   0a
9 ran   Time 1m 44.3 (4.9)   (Mason Racing Ltd)   J G Smyth Osbourne Adstone, Northants.

GOODWOOD   FRIDAY JUNE 30TH   Righthand, Sharpish, Undulating Track

Official Going   Str - GOOD; Rnd - GOOD/FIRM. Stalls: Str - Stands Side; Rnd - Inside, 1m4f - Outside.

2303   6.40 DAILY ECHO APPR HCAP 4YO+ 0-80 (E)   7f rnd   Good 53   -04 Slow   [80]
£3623   £1115   £557   £278

1926 **TWIN TIME** 16 [9] J S King 6-8-12 (64) J Bosley (5) 5/1: 0-4231: 6 b m Syrtos - Carramba (Tumble   69
Wind) Made all, kept on for press fnl 2f, all out: '99 scorer at Bath (appr mdn h'cap): stays 10f well, apprec drop back to 7f: acts on firm, gd/soft & handles any
trk, loves Bath: has run well fresh, with/without a t-strap & loves to dominate: game.
2133 **JUST NICK** 7 [6] W R Muir 4-8-11 (63) R Brisland 11/2: 0-3652: 6 b g Nicholas - Just Never Know   shd 67
(Riverman) Handy, eff to chall over 1f out, al just held in last: knocking on the door & 1m could suit best.
+2126 **ADOBE** 7 [5] W M Brisbourne 5-9-6 (72)(6ex) G Baker (3) 7/4 FAV: 211113: 5 b g Green Desert -   2   72
Shamshir (Kris) Bhd, hdwy well over 2f out, kept on same pace in last: well bckd to 5-timer bid, best at 1m.
2130 **TOBLERSONG** 7 [2] Mrs L Stubbs 5-7-10 (48)(t)(2oh) Kristin Stubbs (5) 14/1: 400644: Handy,   1   46
onepce fnl 2f: see 2130, 958.
2185 **SCISSOR RIDGE** 5 [8] 8-7-10 (48)(1oh) Jonjo Fowle (0) 10/1: 230605: In tch, eff & not clr run over   1¾   42
2f out, some late gains: qck reapp: see 1542, 29.
1969 **FLASHFEET** 14 [10] 10-7-10 (48)(12oh) Joanna Badger (5) 33/1: 600406: Handy, btn 2f out: 1 win in 54.   ½   41
1807 **ALHUWBILL** 21 [4] 5-7-10 (48)(BL)(16oh) G Sparkes (5) 50/1: 00-607: Chsd wnr till wknd & hung   5   31
right over 1f out: blnks, stiff task: see 1672.
2124 **MOUTON** 7 [3] 4-7-10 (48)(16oh) D Cosgrave (4) 50/1: 006008: Al bhd: see 314.   1   29
2122 **DARK MENACE** 8 [1] 8-7-13 (51)(bl) S Carson 16/1: 601009: Al bhd: best 1462.   2½   28
1810 **CHEWIT** 21 [7] 8-9-10 (76) I Mongan 3/1: -6040R: Unruly bef start & refused to race: see 137.   0
10 ran   Time 1m 28.5 (4)   (Dajam Ltd)   J S King Broad Hinton, Wiltshire.

2304   7.10 WILEY EUROPE HCAP 3YO+ 0-90 (C)   1m1f   Good 53   -02 Slow   [87]
£8463   £2604   £1302   £651   3 yo rec 11lb

*1926 **MUYASSIR** 16 [9] P J Makin 5-9-6 (79) S Sanders 9/2: 40-011: 5 b h Brief Truce - Twine (Thatching)   84
Cl-up, rdn over 2f out, styd on for hard driving to get up close home: recently scored at Kempton (h'cap):
'99 wnr at Newmarket (h'cap, rtd 76 & 65a): '98 scorer at Lingfield (h'cap, rtd 72a & 72): eff over 1m/sharp
10f on firm/fast & equitrack: handles any trk: proving tough & game, given a typically strong S Sanders ride.
1765 **KATHIR** 23 [4] A C Stewart 3-8-13 (83) R Hughes 6/1: 21-032: 3 ch c Woodman - Alcando (Alzao)   ½   87
Set pace, kept on over 1f out, just collared cl-home: stays 9f & deserves another win: see 1765.
2170 **LITTLE AMIN** 8 [6] W R Muir 4-9-2 (75) J Reid 12/1: 000163: 4 b g Unfuwain - Ghassanah (Pas de Seul)   hd   78
Handy, trav well 2f out, chall 1f out, onepace for press: not btn far: qk reapp: handles fast, likes gd & soft.
-2163 **PEARTREE HOUSE** 6 [7] D Nicholls 6-9-13 (86)(6ex) F Norton 6/4 FAV: 603124: Keen bhd, hdwy & not   1¾   86
clr run 2f out, not qckn fnl 1f: well bckd, qck reapp: prob stays 9f: see 2163, 2138.

734

FRIDAY JUNE 30TH   Righthand, Sharpish, Undulating Track

2170	**MAKE WAY** 6 [6] 4-9-9 (82)(bl) Pat Eddery 11/2: 032255: Waited with, eff over 1f out, sn onepace.	½	81
*2157	**GRALMANO** 6 [3] 5-9-5 (78)(6ex) J Carroll 9/1: 452516: Prom, btn well over 1f out: just too soon?	2	74
1915	**SUPER MONARCH** 16 [10] 6-8-6 (63)(2ow) S Drowne 33/1: 0-0047: Keen, bhd, rdn & btn 2f out.	3½	56
2085	**NO EXTRAS** 9 [1] 10-9-0 (73) D Harrison 11/1: 0-1168: Al bhd: can do better, see 1690.	1	63
1878	**DIVORCE ACTION** 18 [5] 4-8-4 (63) P Doe 14/1: 0-0259: Prom, wknd well over 2f out: see 1878.	dist	0

9 ran   Time 1m 55.5 (5)   (William Otley)   P J Makin Newmarket

2305   7.40 ADENSTAR HCAP 3YO+ 0-90 (C)   1m6f   Good 53   +06 Fast   [86]
£6857   £2110   £1055   £527   3 yo rec 17lb

*2021	**FAIT LE JOJO** 12 [1] S P C Woods 3-8-5 (80) D Harrison 9/4 JT FAV: -45411: 3 b g Pistolet Bleu - Pretty Davis (Trempolino) Waited with, rdn over 3f out, kept on for press fnl 1f to get up cl-home: gd time: recently scored at Salisbury (rtd h'cap): '99 wnr at W'hampton (mdn, rtd 83a): eff at 10f, suited by 14f now & 2m shld suit: acts on firm, gd & fibresand, any trk: lightly rcd & improving, game.		82
*1991	**TOTAL DELIGHT** 13 [3] Lady Herries 4-9-10 (82)(t) P Doe 9/4 JT FAV: 100412: 4 b g Mtoto - Shesadelight (Shirley Heights) Set pace, kept on for press fnl 2f, worn down cl-home: fine run under top-weight.	½	82
1959	**AMANCIO** 14 [4] Mrs A J Perrett 9-8-11 (69) Pat Eddery 5/2: 130/23: 9 b g Manila - Kerry Ring (Ack Ack) Chsd ldr till 3f out, no extra well over 1f out: 9yo, see 1959.	7	62
1800	**STORMY SKYE** 22 [2] G L Moore 4-9-5 (77)(tbl) R Hughes 4/1: 42-324: Bhd over 4f out: btr 1800.	dist	0

4 ran   Time 3m 05.38 (6.58)   (G A Roberts)   S P C Woods Newmarket.

2306   8.10 CELER ET AUDAX FILLIES MDN 2YO (D)   7f rnd   Good 53   -47 Slow
£4231   £1302   £651   £325

--	**RIZERIE** [3] L M Cumani 2-8-11 J P Spencer 8/1: 1: 2 gr f Highest Honor - Riziere (Groom Dancer) Handy, eff to chall fnl 1f, styd on well for press, rdn out: debut, Jan foal, cost Ffr 600,000: dam won in France: eff over a sharp/undul 7f, 1m sure to suit: acts on gd grnd: looks game & open to improvement.		76
--	**IT GIRL** [6] I A Balding 2-8-11 R Hughes 8/1: 2: 2 b f Robellino - On The Tiles (Thatch) Set pace, kept on for press over 1f out, collared nr fin, just btn on debut: Apr foal, half-sister to a smart 10f wnr: dam 10f scorer: eff at 7f, sure to relish 1m+ in time: shaped with promise & shld win races.	shd	75
2029	**FASTINA** 12 [2] R Guest 2-8-11 D Harrison 11/2: -43: 2 b f Dunphy - Farandole (Gay Baron) Waited with, short of room 3f out, eff & ran again ins last, kept on cl-home, not btn far: stays 7f, improve.	½	74
--	**RAMBAGH** [1] J L Dunlop 2-8-11 Pat Eddery 5/4 FAV: 4: Waited with, eff & ran green over 1f out, kept on same pace: well bckd, Feb foal, cost 29,000gns: bred to apprec 1m in time: with J Dunlop, learn from this.	¾	72
--	**SPAIN** [5] 2-8-11 D Sweeney 9/4: 5: Chsd ldr till outpcd over 2f out, some late gains on debut: Apr foal, half-sister to some useful sprint wnrs: dam 7f juv wnr: bred to apprec 7f, with P Cole.	½	71
--	**LITTLE CALLIAN** [4] 2-8-11 R Price 33/1: 6: Sn rdn & btn halfway: debut, Feb foal: dam styd 7f.	14	47

6 ran   Time 1m 31.5 (7)   (Robert H Smith)   L M Cumani Newmarket.

2307   8.40 SUPERIOR NOV STKS 2YO (D)   6f   Good Inapplicable
£6890   £2120   £1060   £530

1943	**LOGIC LANE** 15 [2] R Charlton 2-8-12 S Sanders 3/1: -01: 2 ch c Lahib - Reflection (Mill Reef) Waited with, eff for press over 1f out, styd on well ins last to get up cl-home, drvn out: Feb foal, cost IR£45,000: half-brother to wnrs over 7f/2m: dam 5/7f juv scorer: eff at 6f, 7f sure to suit: useful & game.		89
*1823	**WHERES JASPER** 21 [3] K A Ryan 2-9-5 J Carroll 100/30: 212: 2 ch g Common Grounds - Stifen (Burslem) Handy, hdwy to lead appr fnl 1f, kept on till collared cl-home, just btn: acts on gd & soft: useful.	nk	94
1759	**INNIT** 23 [4] M R Channon 2-9-0 J Reid 7/2: 213543: 2 b f Distinctly North - Tidal Reach (Kris) Set pace till over 1f out, ev ch till no extra cl-home, only btn 1L: useful & stays 6f: see 1759.	1	86
*1876	**PICCOLO PLAYER** 18 [1] R Hannon 2-9-2 R Hughes 5/4 FAV: -214: Reared & lost 4L start, sn in tch till btn 2f out: shld do better, see 1876.	6	70

4 ran   Time 1m 14.41 (4.41)   (Michael Pescod)   R Charlton Beckhampton, Wilts.

2308   9.10 RACINGPOST MED AUCT MDN 3YO (E)   1m1f192y   Good 53   -16 Slow
£4114   £1266   £633   £315

1643	**FOREST HEATH** 28 [4] H J Collingridge 3-9-0 J Reid 9/4: 00-21: 3 gr g Common Grounds - Caroline Lady (Caro) Waited with, eff 2f out, kept on for press fnl 1f to get up cl-home: unplcd both '99 starts (mdns, rtd 82, with J Banks): eff at 1m, apprec this step up to 10f & acts on gd & soft grnd: improve again at this trip.		77
2129	**DIAMOND ROAD** 7 [3] C A Horgan 3-9-0 S Sanders 7/2: 0-332: 3 b c Dolphin Street - Tiffany's Case (Thatching) Set pace, hard rdn & kept on for press fnl 1f till collared nr fin: stays 10f & shld find a race: see 2129.	hd	76
1992	**JOHNNY OSCAR** 13 [2] J R Fanshawe 3-9-0 D Harrison 13/8 FAV: 43: 3 b g Belmez - Short Rations (Lorenzaccio) Chsd wnr, kept on same pace for hands-and-heels riding ins last, not btn far: will do better over 12f+.	½	75
1640	**LILLAN** 29 [5] G A Butler 3-8-11 (t)(2ow) R Hughes 7/2: 644: Held up, rdn & btn 2f out: see 1640.	21	40

4 ran   Time 2m 11.11 (6.91)   (Forest Heath Partnership)   H J Collingridge Newmarket.

FRIDAY JUNE 30TH   Lefthand, Galloping Track

Official Going   FIRM (GOOD/FIRM In Places). Stalls: Str Course - Stands Side; Round Course - Inside; 1m2f - Outside.

2309   7.00 BOLLINGER AMAT HCAP 4YO+ 0-75 (E)   1m2f32y   Good/Firm 25   -13 Slow   [40]
£3640   £1120   £560   £280

*2130	**MISSILE TOE** 7 [13] D Morris 7-10-5 (45) Mr Paul J Morris (5) 7/2 FAV: -55411: 7 b g Exactly Sharp - Debach Dust (Indian King) Dwelt, imprvd after halfway, led bef dist & ran on strongly: last week won at Newmarket (appr h'cap): '99 wnr again at Newmarket (h'cap, rtd 46): plcd in '98 (rtd 55$): eff at 1m/10f on fast, hvy grnd & fibresand, stiff/gall trks, likes Newmarket: gd mount for an inexp rider: in good heart.		51
2139	**MELODY LADY** 7 [10] F Murphy 4-10-8 (48) Mr T Doyle 6/1: 2-0022: 4 ch f Dilum - Ansellady (Absalom) Prom, led 2½f out till bef fnl 1f, outpcd by wnr: back in trip, eff btwn 10f & 12f: see 1496.	3	49

735

2139 **OCEAN DRIVE 7** [2] Miss L A Perratt 4-10-3 (43) Mr M Bradburne 8/1: 056543: 4 b g Dolphin Street - Blonde Goddess (Godswalk) Chsd ldrs, chall ent fnl 2f, same pace: eff at 10f, suited by 12/13f, see 846. ½ **43**
2219 **PENNYS FROM HEAVEN 3** [5] D Nicholls 6-11-4 (58)(5ex) Mr L Richardson (7) 7/1: 024124: Held up, imprvd 4f out, kept on but nvr nr to chall under a kind ride: qck reapp: will apprec a return to 11f+ & stronger handling: can win again: beat today's 2nd & 3rd in 2139. ¾ **57+**
*2147 **TOEJAM 7** [4] 7-9-10 (36)(5ex)(1oh) Mr R Walford 11/2: 0-0015: Mid-div, prog to chase ldrs 2f out, onepace: qk reapp, clr rem: stays 10f, will apprec a drop back to 1m as in 2147 (visored, not worn here). 1½ **33**
2081 **BACHELORS PAD 9** [7] 6-11-4 (58) Mr T Best (5) 14/1: 142346: Nvr a factor: see 855. 6 **47**
1921 **A DAY ON THE DUB 16** [6] 7-10-10 (50) Mr S Dobson (5) 16/1: 401407: Mid-div at best: gone off the boil. 6 **31**
1921 **EDMO HEIGHTS 16** [9] 4-10-12 (52) Mr Nicky Tinkler (5) 16/1: 00-008: In tch till 3f out: '99 wnr at Redcar (h'cap) & Beverley (class stks, rtd 70): '98 wnr again at Beverley (auct mdn, rtd 74): eff at 1m/10f, likes firm/fast grnd & forcing the pace on stiff trks, esp Beverley: with T Easterby. 6 **25**
1965 **BRAZILIAN MOOD 14** [8] 4-12-0 (68) H E Rasheed Al Maktoum 5/1: 210-59: Al towards rear. nk **40**
975 **RUTLAND CHANTRY 72** [12] 6-11-13 (67) Mr M Murphy (5) 14/1: -25660: Nvr on terms: 10th, 10 wk abs. 2½ **36**
441 **METEOR STRIKE 149** [3] 6-11-2 (56) Mr W Beasley (7) 20/1: -62160: Led till appr fnl 2f, sn lost pl: 11th. 5 **18**
2099 **ALAMEIN 9** [1] 7-10-6 (46)(t) Mr P Aspell (5) 33/1: 0-0000: Well plcd & ch till wknd 3f out: 12th, best at 7f. ¾ **7**
12 ran Time 2m 10.3 (3.8) (Stag & Huntsman) D Morris Newmarket

2310 **7.30 GOSFORTH PK HCAP 3YO+ 0-105 (B) 5f Good/Firm 25 +11 Fast [105]**
£17875 £5500 £2750 £1375 3 yo rec 6 lb 2 Groups, low numbers best

*1980 **HENRY HALL 14** [2] N Tinkler 4-8-13 (90) Kim Tinkler 9/1: 600311: 4 b c Common Grounds - Sovereign Grace (Standaan) Nvr far away far side, rdn to lead dist, pushed out: fast time: recent York wnr (h'cap): rnr-up 4 times in '99 (h'caps, rtd 100): '98 Beverley (nov), Thirsk (clmr) & Doncaster wnr (stks, rtd 98): eff at 6f, suited by a stiff/gall 5f: acts on firm & soft grnd: returned with a cut hoof but is at the top of his game. **97**
2151 **INDIAN SPARK 7** [6] J S Goldie 6-9-9 (100) A Culhane 10/1: 501102: 6 ch g Indian Ridge - Annes Gift (Ballymoss) Rear of far side group & sn shaken up, not clr run 2f out, strong run fnl 1f, post came too sn: cracking run back at the minimum tho' will apprec a return to 6f: useful, improving: see 1983. nk **105**
1980 **ANTONIAS DOUBLE 14** [4] A Berry 5-7-10 (73)(3oh) P Fessey 16/1: -50003: 5 ch m Primo Dominie - Mainly Sunset (Red Sunset) Cl-up far side, led appr fnl 1f till dist, onepace towards fin: morning gamble from 40/1: right back to form at favourite track, see 751. ¾ **75**
*1976 **AMBITIOUS 14** [11] K T Ivory 5-8-6 (83) C Catlin (7) 25/1: 104014: Prom stands side, ran on well & drifted left fnl 1½f, al playing catch up with far side: fine run from unfavoured side: see 1976. hd **84**
2107 **SHIRLEY NOT 8** [8] 4-7-11 (74)(bl)(1ow)(3oh) T Williams 25/1: 104055: Mid-div far side, shaken up & hdwy appr fnl 1f, kept on but unable to chall: consistent, see 1278. ½ **73**
1324 **BLESSINGINDISGUISE 44** [10] 7-7-13 (76)(bl) G Parkin 10/1: -50206: Well plcd stands side, led that group after 2f, grad drifted left & styd on, no ch far side: 6 wk abs: gd run, on the wrong side, see 758. hd **74**
1980 **ATLANTIC VIKING 14** [1] 5-8-9 (86)(bl) J Fanning 14/1: 41-007: Led far side till 1½f out, no extra. 1½ **80**
1980 **NIGHT FLIGHT 14** [3] 6-8-11 (88) K Darley 11/1: 200608: Prom far side, onepce fnl 1f: prefers softer. nk **81**
2000 **ELLENS ACADEMY 13** [14] 5-8-3 (80)(bl) J F Egan 7/2 FAV: 043039: Rear stands side, late hdwy, nvr a threat: hvly bckd: poorly drawn tho' will apprec a return to 6f: stable in fine form, see 1074. nk **72**
1983 **MIZHAR 14** [9] 4-8-3 (80) O Pears 16/1: 6-0000: Chsd ldrs far side, no extra appr fnl 1f: 10th, see 1173. nk **71**
2128 **SHAROURA 7** [12] 4-8-3 (80) A Nicholls (3) 20/1: 100-00: Prom stands side, onepace fnl 2f: 11th. nk **70**
*1871 **COASTAL BLUFF 18** [20] 8-8-5 (82) Craig Williams 10/1: -50210: Led stands side till bef halfway: 12th. 1 **69**
1980 **IVORYS JOY 14** [13] 5-8-9 (86) G Duffield 14/1: 603160: Nvr dangerous stands side: 13th, see 1650. hd **72**
2986} **TADEO 338** [18] 7-9-11 (102) D Holland 10/1: 6064-0: Rcd stands side, bhd from halfway: 16th, top-weight, reapp: '99 reapp rnr-up for B Meehan (h'cap, rtd 111): with current trainer in '98, won at Haydock (h'cap) & Fairyhouse (List, rtd 106): eff at 5/6f on firm & soft grnd, any trk, likes to force the pace: v useful at best. **0**
1952 **AFAAN 15** [16] 7-9-3 (94)(bl) T G McLaughlin 12/1: 064020: Prom stands side till 2f out: 18th, poor draw. **0**
1887 **Central Coast 17** [19] 4-8-4 (81) J Tate 16/1: 1871 **Gay Breeze 18** [17] 7-7-12 (75) D Mernagh (3) 16/1:
2003 **Taras Girl 13** [5] 3-8-10 (93) R Ffrench 33/1:
18 ran Time 58.91 (0.71) (Mike Goss) N Tinkler Langton, N Yorks

2311 **8.00 PERTEMPS HCAP 3YO+ 0-90 (C) 1m rnd Good/Firm 25 -10 Slow [88]**
£7020 £2160 £1080 £540 3 yo rec 10lb

4494} **LINDEN GRACE 251** [5] M Johnston 3-8-10 (80) J Fanning 20/1: 1250-1: 3 b f Mister Baileys - Gracefully Bold (Nasty And Bold) Prom going well, shaken up to lead appr fnl 2f, shade rdly: '99 Epsom wnr (auct mdn, debut, rtd 86 at best): eff at 7f/1m on firm/fast grnd, sharp/undul or gall trk: runs particularly well fresh: unexposed. **85**
2001 **TONY TIE 13** [1] J S Goldie 4-9-11 (85) A Culhane 9/2: 223102: 4 b g Ardkinglass - Queen Of The Quorn (Governor General) Prom, rdn 2f out, held on for 2nd but no ch wnr: ran to best back in trip: tough, see 1656 1½ **86**
*1922 **ADAWAR 16** [4] Sir Michael Stoute 3-8-9 (79) F Lynch 4/1: 56213: 3 b c Perugino - Adalya (Darshaan) Held up, imprvd to dspt 2nd 2f out, onepace nr fin: sound h'cap bow: see 1922. hd **80**
*1680 **DURAID 27** [6] Denys Smith 8-9-8 (82) A Nicholls (3) 10/1: 1-4214: Held up, going easily but short of room appr fnl 2f, clr bef dist & shaken up, unable to qckn: not far off best, see 1680. 1½ **80**
1598 **DONNAS DOUBLE 30** [7] 5-8-4 (64) R Winston 16/1: -05635: Held up, styd on fnl 1f, nvr dngrs: see 1011. nk **61**
1490 **TAFFS WELL 35** [2] 7-9-1 (75) D Holland 11/10 FAV: -40426: Held up, eff 2f out, onepace: well bckd: more expected, won this race last term off 2lbs higher mark, see 715. 1¾ **68**
2094 **FLOORSOTHEFOREST 9** [3] 4-7-10 (56)(1oh) Dale Gibson 8/1: 526527: Led till appr fnl 2f, fdd: more comfortable giving weight to lesser rivals, see 2094, 1689, 847. 6 **39**
7 ran Time 1m 41.8 (2.8) (R C Moules) M Johnston Middleham, N Yorks

2312 **8.30 NORTHERN RACING SELLER 2YO (E) 6f Good/Firm 25 -37 Slow**
£7280 £2240 £1120 £560

*1890 **WINDCHILL 17** [11] T D Easterby 2-8-6 K Darley 4/1: 002211: 2 ch f Handsome Sailor - Baroness Gymcrak (Pharly) Nvr far away trav well, went on appr fnl 1f, v cmftbly: bght in for 10,500 gns: recent Redcar wnr (sell): eff at 6/7f on fast & gd/soft grnd: goes on sharp or gall trks: progressive, may prove better than a plater. **61**
*1805 **ORCHARD RAIDER 21** [4] C A Dwyer 2-8-11 P Clarke (7) 10/1: -02412: 2 b c Mujadil - Apple Brandy (Cox's Ridge) Front rank, chall 2f out, sn outpcd by wnr: ran well back on turf, acts on fast grnd & fibresand. 3 **58**
*2039 **DECEITFUL 11** [2] Sir Mark Prescott 2-9-2 G Duffield 7/2: 13: 3 ch g Most Welcome - Sure Care (Caerleon) Sltly hmpd start, prom, ev ch 2f out, onepace dist: up in trip, eff at 5/6f on firm/fast grnd. nk **62**
1981 **CHORUS GIRL 14** [5] K A Ryan 2-8-7(1ow) A Culhane 20/1: -54304: Sn outpcd, kept on well for 2½ **47$**

NEWCASTLE FRIDAY JUNE 30TH Lefthand, Galloping Track

hands & heels fnl 2f, nvr dangerous: step up to 7f is going to suit.
1844 **FAST BUCK 20** [6] 2-8-11 R Winston 33/1: 0005: Nvr a factor tho' styg on fin: blnks omitted. ½ 50
*2059 **MILLTIDE 10** [1] 2-8-6 J F Egan 3/1: 416: Prom till 2f out: new stable, btr 2059. ½ 43
928 **BEACON OF LIGHT 76** [10] 2-8-6 Dean McKeown 33/1: -07: Nvr a factor: no form. ½ 42
1981 **JOINT INSTRUCTION 14** [7] 2-9-2 Craig Williams 5/2 FAV: 521528: Led till 2f out, fdd: see 1981, 1507. 1½ 48
1476 **BOBANVI 36** [8] 2-8-6 J McAuley (5) 20/1: -5409: Al bhd: see 1019, 856. ¾ 36
2155 **EASTERN RED 6** [12] 2-8-6 (BL) F Lynch 14/1: -05620: Cl-up till wknd qckly 2f out: 10th, blinkered. nk 35
938 **Wannabe Bold 74** [9] 2-8-6 P Goode (3) 16/1: 1443 **Poppys Choice 38** [3] 2-8-6 G Parkin 33/1:
12 ran Time 1m 15.0 (3.7) (Mrs Bridget Tranmer) T D Easterby Great Habton, N Yorks

2313 9.00 NEWCASTLE FILLIES MDN 3YO (D) 6f Good/Firm 25 -20 Slow
£5102 £1570 £785 £392

1697 **BIRDSONG 27** [4] R Guest 3-8-11 G Duffield 10/1: -001: 3 b f Dolphin Street - Gay France (Sir Gaylord) 66
Well plcd, went on after halfway, rdn out: left prev effs well bhd: unrcd juv, related to sev wnrs: apprec drop back to 6f & forcing tactics on fast grnd/gall trk.
1868 **DAYLILY 18** [6] T D Easterby 3-8-11 K Darley 10/11 FAV: 060332: 3 ch f Pips Pride - Leaping Water 1½ 62
(Sure Blade) In tch, chsd ldr after halfway, al being held: clr of rem, well bckd: acts on fast & hvy, see 1768.
1354 **BRITTAS BLUES 42** [2] M Johnston 3-8-11 D Holland 3/1: 03: 3 b f Blues Traveller - Missish 5 47
(Mummy's Pet) Led till halfway, outpcd: 6 wk abs, needs further & sellers, see 1354.
2976} **HARMONIZE 339** [1] Martyn Wane 3-8-11 C Teague 40/1: -066-4: In tch till 2f out, eased fnl 1f: *dist* 17
reapp: plating class last term over 5/6f (rtd 56).
2140 **HELLO SAILOR 7** [3] 3-8-11 P Bradley (5) 50/1: 00-05: Sn struggling: quick reapp, no form. 1½ 14
5 ran Time 1m 14.0 (2.7) (Matthews Breeding & Racing) R Guest Newmarket, Suffolk

2314 9.30 ST CLASSIFIED STKS 3YO+ 0-75 (D) 1m2f32y Good/Firm 25 -31 Slow
£5617 £1605 £802 3 yo rec 12lb

*2246 **JULIUS 2** [3] M Johnston 3-8-12 R Ffrench 4/6 FAV: 121111: 3 b f Persian Bold - Babuskha (Dance 82
Of Life) Set mod pace, qcknd 3f out, drvn out ins last: quick 4 timer landed, earlier won at Nottingham (stks), Musselburgh (h'cap), Ripon (class stks) & Chester (fill h'cap): ex-Irish, plcd in mdns last term: eff at 10/12f: acts on firm, gd grnd, sharp or gall trk: ran well from the front here tho' poss best held up: in fine form.
1729 **LUCKY GITANO 25** [2] J L Dunlop 4-9-7 K Darley 2/1: 32-002: 4 b g Lucky Guest - April Wind 1 76
(Windjammer) Third, in tch, imprvd to chase wnr ent fnl 2f, styd on but being held: ran to best against an improver.
1984 **ACHILLES SKY 14** [1] K R Burke 4-9-9 G Duffield 9/2: -10023: 4 b c Hadeer - Diva Madonna (Chief 2 75
Singer) Chsd wnr, eff 3f out, same pace: top-weight, prob a fair effort in a muddling race, see 805 (reapp).
3 ran Time 2m 12.1 (5.6) (Mirs K E Daley) M Johnston Middleham, N Yorks

DONCASTER SATURDAY JULY 1ST Lefthand, Flat, Galloping Track

Official Going GOOD/FIRM (FIRM places). Stalls: Str - Stands Side; Rnd - Ins, except 1m - Outside.

2315 6.55 FUTURE APP MDN HCAP 3YO+ 0-70 (E) 6f Good/Firm 25 -11 Slow [58]
£3068 £472 £236 3 yo rec 6 lb

2223 **NOBLE PATRIOT 4** [13] R Hollinshead 5-8-3 (33) Stephanie Hollinshead (4) 9/2: 255341: 5 b g Polish 41
Patriot - Noble Form (Double Form) Led bef halfway, rdn/styd on well fnl 1f: qck reapp: op 4/1: plcd form in 99 (mdn h'caps, rtd 39a & 33): eff btwn 5/7f, tried further: acts on firm, gd/soft & both AWs, sharp/gall trk.
1818 **FOUND AT LAST 22** [11] J Balding 4-9-6 (50) D Mernagh 5/2 FAV: 035022: 4 b g Aragon - Girton 1½ 52
(Balidar) Held up, prog/chsd wnr fnl 2f, onepace/held nr fin: op 9/2: see 1818, 781.
1889 **WILFRAM 18** [7] J M Bradley 3-9-3 (53) P Fitzsimons 14/1: 0-0003: 3 b g Fraam - Ming Blue (Primo ½ 53
Dominie) Held up, styd on well fnl 2f, nrst at fin: op 12/1: mod form prev: eff at 6f on fast, return to 7f shld suit.
2223 **COLONEL SAM 4** [15] S R Bowring 4-8-12 (42)(tbl) R Cody Boutcher (3) 16/1: 005004: Mid-div, kept ¾ 40
on fnl 2f, not pace to chall: qck reapp: has shown ability but is inconsistent: see 1412.
1814 **SUSY WELLS 22** [9] 5-8-2 (32) P M Quinn 20/1: 0-0055: Rear, styd on fnl 2f, nrst fin: see 1559 (7f). 1 28
1907 **LIONS DOMANE 17** [17] 3-8-8 (44) P Goode 6/1: 0-2606: In tch, outpcd fnl 2f: btr 257 (7f, AW). ½ 38
2223 **EMLEY 4** [1] 4-9-6 (50) D Allan (7) 16/1: 63-607: Mid-div at best: qck reapp: bhd runner-up in 1818. ¾ 42
1930 **SILVER TONGUED 16** [14] 4-8-2 (32) Claire Bryan (3) 15/2: -00068: Chsd ldrs 4f: op 6/1: see 1275. ½ 22
2192 **TAWN AGAIN 5** [12] 4-8-5 (35) Lynsey Hanna (5) 25/1: 6-0009: Saddle slipped start, led 2f: no form prev. 1¾ 21
2223 **LAMMOSKI 4** [16] 3-9-2 (52)(tbl) Joanna Badger (5) 25/1: 500500: Chsd ldrs 4f: 10th: see 426, 217. ¾ 36
1211 **NIGHT ADVENTURE 53** [10] 4-8-11 (41) D Watson (5) 8/1: 0-0000: Rear/efft halfway, no impress: 11th: abs. 0
2223 **Seahorse Boy 4** [5] 3-9-7 (57) S Finnamore (3) 16/1: 909 **Two Jacks 78** [4] 3-9-10 (60) P Hanagan (3) 50/1:
1500 **Abco Boy 36** [6] 3-8-12 (48) C Carver 33/1: 1082 **Sounds Special 60** [8] 3-9-6 (56) J Bosley (3) 25/1:
1787 **Distant Flame 23** [2] 3-9-0 (50)(bl) C Halliwell (7) 33/1:
16 ran Time 1m 12.97 (2.17) (The Four Dreamers) R Hollinshead Upper Longdon, Staffs

2316 7.25 EBF JULY FILLIES MDN 2YO (D) 7f str Good/Firm 25 -41 Slow
£3575 £1100 £550 £275

1988 **CASPIAN 14** [2] B W Hills 2-8-11 A Culhane 4/7 FAV: 21: 2 b f Spectrum - Sinking Sun (Danehill) 70
Made all, rdn/strongly pressed 2f out, drvn/holding rival nr fin, styd on well: well bckd at odds on: slow time: confirmed promise of debut: eff at 7f, bred to appreciate 1m+: acts on fast grnd & a stiff/gall trk.
-- **ST FLORENT** [3] J H M Gosden 2-8-11 K Darley 2/1: 2: 2 b f Thunder Gulch - Honfleur (Sadler's Wells) ½ 68
Dwelt/bhd, prog/handy halfway, rdn/ev ch fnl 2f, kept on tho' al just held ins last: op 6/4: Mar foal: dam a 14f wnr abroad: eff at 7f, shld relish 1m this term and will get further: acts on fast grnd: shld find a race.
1463 **JUSTINIA 38** [4] E J O'Neill 2-8-11 W Ryan 20/1: 03: 2 b f Inchinor - Just Julia (Natroun) nk 67$
Cl up, rdn/ev ch ins last, no extra nr fin: well held on debut previously: acts on fast grnd & stays 7f: see 1463.
-- **SOLO DANCE** [1] T D Easterby 2-8-11 W Supple 10/1: 4: Cl up, outpcd fnl 2f: op 8/1: Tragic Role 6 58
filly: half-sister to a 7f/1m wnr: dam a 10f wnr: sire a 12f wnr: will need 1m+.
4 ran Time 1m 27.81 (4.61) (K Abdulla) B W Hills Lambourn, Berks

DONCASTER SATURDAY JULY 1ST Lefthand, Flat, Galloping Track

2317 **7.55 MICHELOB MDN 3YO+ (D) 1m2f60y Good/Firm 25 +11 Fast**
£4387 £1350 £675 £337 3 yo rec 11lb

1912 **TOUGH MEN 17** [3] H R A Cecil 3-8-11 W Ryan 11/10 FAV: -521: 3 b c Woodman - Rhumba Rage (Nureyev) **95**
Made all, rdn fnl 3f, styd on strongly ins last: fast time: well bckd, op 2/1: confirmed improvement of latest: eff at 9/10.5f on firm & fast grnd, could get further: handles a sharp or gall trk & can force the pace: useful.
1282 **BANCO SUIVI 49** [6] B W Hills 3-8-6 A Culhane 4/1: 5-202: 3 b f Nashwan - Pay The Bank (High Top) ½ **88**
Chsd wnr 4f out, drvn/strong chall ins last, just held nr fin: op 7/2: abs: acts on fast & soft: well clr rem.
2086 **ORANGEVILLE 10** [1] J H M Gosden 3-8-11 K Darley 7/2: 2-43: 3 b c Dynaformer - Orange Sickle (Rich *14* **78**
Cream) Trkd ldrs, rdn/outpcd by front pair fnl 3f: op 3/1: see 2086 (9f).
2219 **ROYAL DOLPHIN 4** [7] A Smith 4-9-8 K Hodgson 100/1: 433604: Bhd halfway: see 584, 553 (AW). *17* **59**
-- **KARINS LAD** [2] 3-8-11 P M Quinn (3) 50/1: 5: Bhd halfway: debut, with R Hollinshead. *dist* **0**
2080 **ESPERE DOR 10** [5] 3-8-11 N Pollard 100/1: 050006: Cl up 6f, sn bhd: mod form. *dist* **0**
6 ran Time 2m 07.85 (1.45) (The Thoroughbred Corporation) H R A Cecil Newmarket, Suffolk

2318 **8.25 REGIONAL COND STKS 2YO (C) 5f Good/Firm 25 +07 Fast**
£6142 £1890 £945 £472 Raced stands side

-1759 **RED MILLENNIUM 24** [2] A Berry 2-8-6 F Norton 6/5 FAV: 12121: 2 b f Tagula - Lovely Me (Vision) **97**
Made all, readily asserted ins last, pushed out cl home: heavily bckd, op 7/4: earlier scored at Musselburgh (auct mdn) & Nottingham (auct stks): eff at 5f, 6f shld suit: acts on fast & gd/sft, poss handles firm, sharp/gall trk: has run well fresh & loves to force the pace: pacey/useful juvenile who deserves a crack at Listed/Group company.
1761 **UP TEMPO 24** [4] T D Easterby 2-8-11 K Darley 7/2: 2132: 2 b c Flying Spur - Musical Essence (Song) *4* **89**
Chsd ldrs, rdn/kept on fnl 1f, took second but no chance with wnr: op 3/1: useful, see 1761 & 1146.
2100 **DIVINE WIND 10** [3] B A McMahon 2-8-8 W Supple 20/1: -14033: 2 ch f Clantime - Breezy Day (Day Is *nk* **85**
Done) Held up, prog/chall 2f out, sn outpcd by easy wnr: improved run: see 2100, 730.
2088 **OH SO DUSTY 10** [5] B J Meehan 2-8-10 D R McCabe 7/2: 6104: Rdn/in tch, nvr pace to chall: op 5/2. ½ **85**
2152 **KACHINA DOLL 8** [7] 2-8-12 Craig Williams 13/2: 001105: Held up, outpcd over 2f out: see 1437. ¾ **85**
+2082 **IDLE POWER 10** [6] 2-9-1 A Culhane 6/1: -2516: Sn rdn/rear, al outpcd: see 2082. *4* **78**
-- **TALISKER BAY** [1] 2-8-11 R Fitzpatrick (3) 50/1: 7: Cl up till halfway: Clantime colt, May foal, half- *3½* **65**
brother to a multiple 1m wnr: dam a mid-dist wnr abroad: highly tried on debut for C Smith.
7 ran Time 59.08 (0.88) (The Red Shirt Brigade) A Berry Cockerham, Lancs

2319 **8.55 CASTLE HCAP 4YO+ 0-80 (D) 1m6f132y Good/Firm 25 -08 Slow** **[80]**
£4212 £1296 £648 £324 3 yo rec 17lb

1536 **WEET FOR ME 35** [2] R Hollinshead 4-9-9 (75) J F Egan 12/1: -00301: 4 b c Warning - Naswara (Al Nasr) **78**
Trkd ldrs, prog/lead 3f out, pressed fnl 2f, styd on gamely ins last, drvn out: op 10/1: prev sole win in '99 at Haydock (mdn, rtd 82): eff at 10.5f, now best around 14f, tried 2m+: acts on hvy, loves fast/firm & a gall trk.
2069 **SHARP STEPPER 11** [6] J H M Gosden 4-9-12 (78) K Darley 4/5 FAV: 21-362: 4 b f Selkirk - Awtaar *1½* **79**
(Lyphard) Held up, prog 5f out, drvn to press wnr 1f out, kept on, al held: bckd: stays 14.6f: see 1784, 84.
*2164 **FIORI 7** [4] P C Haslam 4-10-2 (82) P Goode (3) 6/1: 064413: 4 b g Anshan - Fen Princess (Trojan Fen) *shd* **83**
Trkd ldrs, rdn/kept on fnl 3f, not pace of wnr: see 2164 (made all, 5 rnr h'cap, gd).
2109 **MR FORTYWINKS 9** [8] J L Eyre 6-8-8 (60) R Cody Boutcher (7) 8/1: 204134: Led 11f, onepace after. ½ **60**
2156 **SIMPLE IDEALS 7** [5] 6-7-10 (48)(7oh) Kim Tinkler 20/1: -02055: Held up, efft fnl 3f, al held: see 1563. *1½* **46$**
2127 **LEGAL LUNCH 8** [7] 5-9-5 (71)(vis) A Culhane 6/1: 531356: Rear, hdwy 3f out, rdn/no prog fnl 1f. *3½* **64**
1736 **MURCHAN TYNE 26** [1] 7-7-11 (49) (3ow)N Pollard 7/1: 050437: Chsd ldr, rdn/btn 3f out: op 6/1. *20* **22**
1784 **IL PRINCIPE 23** [3] 6-8-13 (65) M Fenton 16/1: 000008: Held up, bhd 3f out: op 10/1, needs soft. *1¾* **33**
8 ran Time 3m 07.77 (4.77) (Ed Weetman Haulage & Storage Ltd) R Hollinshead Upper Longdon, Staffs

2320 **9.25 FILLIES HCAP 3YO+ 0-70 (E) 7f str Good/Firm 25 -16 Slow** **[66]**
£2411 £2411 £567 £283 3 yo rec 8 lb

2063 **UNCHAIN MY HEART 11** [10] B J Meehan 4-8-12 (50)(bl) D R McCabe 12/1: 163001: 4 b f Pursuit Of Love - **55**
Addicted To Love (Touching Wood) Prom, drvn/narrow lead ins last, styd on well, joined on line: op 16/1: earlier won at Lingfield (AW clmr, rtd 63a): '99 Lingfield mdn wnr, plcd on turf (h'caps, rtd 70): eff at 7f/1m, stays a sharp 10f: acts on firm & soft, likes equitrack/Lingfield, handles any trk: suited by blnks & has run well fresh.
2033 **LADYWELL BLAISE 12** [11] M L W Bell 3-8-7 (53) M Fenton 33/1: 640601: 3 b f Turtle Island - Duly *dht* **58**
Elected (Persian Bold) Led rdn/hdd ins last, battled on gamely to join leader on line: deadheated for 1st: earlier scored at Lingfield (AW mdn, rtd 73a): eff at 6/7f on both AWs & gd grnd: likes a sharp/gall trk.
1923 **PATSY CULSYTH 17** [15] Don Enrico Incisa 5-8-6 (44) Kim Tinkler 16/1: 003603: 5 b m Tragic Role - *1½* **46**
Regal Salute (Dara Monarch) Chsd ldrs, kept on fnl 2f, not pace of front pair: op 14/1: see 756 (reapp, sell).
4472} **CALCAVELLA 253** [5] M Kettle 4-9-10 (62) S Sanders 16/1: /000-4: Bhd, rdn/styd on fnl 2f, nrst *nk* **63**
fin: reapp: unplcd last term (rtd 63, h'cap): plcd form in '98 (rtd 75, h'cap): eff at 6/7f on firm & gd/sft grnd.
1892 **CRYSTAL LASS 18** [7] 4-8-4 (42) Dale Gibson 33/1: -05005: Rear, rdn/styd on fnl 2f, nrst fin. *nk* **42**
2124 **GRACE 8** [14] 6-8-4 (42) Claire Bryan (5) 11/2: 406646: Chsd ldrs, held ins last: see 802. ¾ **41**
1892 **FOSTON FOX 18** [9] 3-7-12 (44)(bl) K Dalgleish (7) 14/1: 050067: Cl up 5f, fdd: mod form prev. *4* **35**
2026 **SILK ST BRIDGET 13** [3] 3-7-13 (45)(BL) M Baird 20/1: -00008: Rear, mod gains fnl 2f: blnks. *1½* **33**
3957} **LADY HELEN 288** [1] 3-9-6 (66) J Carroll 14/1: 0100-9: Held up, efft 3f out, no impress: reapp: *nk* **53**
'99 Beverley wnr (5 rnr mdn, made all, rtd 74): eff over a stiff 7.5f on firm grnd.
2221 **TAYOVULLIN 4** [13] 6-8-8 (46) Iona Wands (5) 2/1 FAV: 652250: Slowly away, sn in tch, rdn/btn 2f out: *1½* **30**
10th: qck reapp: op 5/2: disapp after 2221, see 1892.
1794 **MISS MONEY SPIDER 23** [6] 5-8-7 (45) P Fitzsimons (5) 14/1: 06-000: Cl up over 2f out, sn fdd: 11th. ½ **28**
2192 **MUJAS MAGIC 5** [4] 5-8-10 (48)(vis) R Fitzpatrick (3) 7/1: 050050: In tch, btn over 1f out: 12th. ¾ **30**
2221 **CELANDINE 4** [8] 7-8-8 (46) A Daly 10/1: 000-00: Prom 5f: 13th: qck reapp: see 2221 (reapp). *2* **24**
1892 **OAKWELL ACE 18** [2] 4-8-3 (41) D Mernagh (3) 8/1: 005250: Mid-div, btn 2f out: 14th: btr 1892, 1559. *14* **0**
14 ran Time 1m 26.09 (2.89) (Lady G Parker) M L W Bell Newmarket

LINGFIELD   SATURDAY JULY 1ST   Lefthand, Sharp, Undulating Track

Official Going Turf - GOOD/FIRM; AW - STANDARD. Stalls: Str - Stands Side; Rnd 9f - Inside; Rnd 11f - Outside

2321 **6.35 NEVA HCAP 3YO 0-75 (E) 1m3f106y Firm 16 -22 Slow [78]**
£2842 £812 £406

2175 **JOELY GREEN 6** [2] N P Littmoden 3-8-7 (57)(BL) J Tate 20/1: 500001: 3 b g Binary Star - Comedy Lady (Comedy Star) Dwelt, switched & gd prog to lead 2f out, held on well, drvn out: op 14/1, first time blnks, qck reapp: '99 wnr at W'hampton (AW mdn, rtd 75a): stays 11.5f well: acts on firm grnd & f/sand: has tried a visor: can run well fresh: well h'capped on old form, woken up by blnks today. **61**
4185} **EXILE 274** [6] R T Phillips 3-9-2 (66) A Beech (5) 20/1: 0400-2: 3 b g Emperor Jones - Silver Venture (Silver Hawk) Rear, prog to chase wnr over 1f out, styd on well & only just btn: reapp: some mdn promise in '99 (trained by G Lewis, rtd 82): apprec this step up to 11.5f, acts on fast & firm: has tried blnks: runs well fresh. *nk* **69**
1821 **RAINBOW SPIRIT 22** [4] A P Jarvis 3-9-7 (71) D Harrison 11/1: -50343: 3 b g Rainbows For Life - Merrie Moment (Taufan) Trkd ldrs, eff 2f out, sn onepcd till styd on cl home: op 8/1: eff at 11.5f on firm grnd: see 1821. *1½* **72**
*2202 **ALEXANDRINE 5** [1] Sir Mark Prescott 3-9-0 (64)(6ex) G Duffield 4/7 FAV: 60-114: Set pace, ran wide, hdd over 2f out, no extra: hvly bckd: qck reapp & 5lbs pen for 2202, this came too sn? *3* **60**
*1935 **ESTABLISHMENT 16** [3] 3-9-6 (70) N Callan 5/1: 640215: Chsd ldrs, carried wide halfway, ev ch 2f out, sn btn: did not get the best of runs: btr 1935. *¾* **65**
*457 **DONT WORRY BOUT ME 147** [7] 3-8-12 (62) K Lavelle(7) 7/1: 00-016: Trkd ldrs, btn 2f out: abs. *¾* **56**
1730 **TWOS BETTER 26** [5] 3-8-5 (55) P Doe 11/1: -03607: In tch, rdn & btn 2f out: tchd 16/1. *3½* **44**
7 ran Time 2m 27.80 (4.40) (Paul J Dixon) N P Littmoden Newmarket

2322 **7.05 MOOR ENVELOPES MED AUCT MDN 3YO (F) 1m1f Firm 16 -40 Slow**
£2324 £664 £332

1911 **LAGO DI COMO 17** [3] T J Naughton 3-9-0 M Henry 8/1: 0-3041: 3 b c Piccolo - Farmer's Pet (Sharrood) Made all, clr over 3f out, just held on cl home, all-out: slow time: just stays 11.5f, apprec this drop back to 9f: acts on firm grnd & equitrack: likes a sharp/undul trk: enterprisingly rdn by M Henry today. **69**
1977 **GUARDED SECRET 15** [6] P J Makin 3-9-0 A Clark 3/1 JT FAV: 3-022: 3 ro c Mystiko - Fen Dance (Trojan Fen) Rcd keenly in rear, eff 2f out, fin v fast & only just failed: acts on firm & f/sand: 10f will suit. *nk* **69**
1532 **ORIENT EXPRESS 35** [1] B J Meehan 3-9-0 J D Smith 9/2: 0003: 3 b g Blues Traveller - Oriental Splendour (Runnett) Rcd keenly in tch, went in pursuit of wnr 2f out, no impress cl home: op 7/2: eff at 9f on firm. *1½* **66**
1204 **SHATHER 54** [5] J W Hills 3-9-0 S Whitworth 3/1 JT FAV: -034: Slowly away, kept on under press fnl 2f: nicely bckd, 8 wk abs: looks in need of 10f: see 1204 (f/sand). *½* **65**
-- **SASH** [7] 3-8-9 P Doe 20/1: -5: Dwelt, prog 2f out, no impress fnl 1f on debut: op 14/1: first foal: eff at 9f on firm grnd: with S Dow, sure to learn from this: sellers may suit. *1¾* **57**
2105 **MILLENNIUM SUMMIT 9** [2] 3-9-0 D Harrison 9/2: 46: Chsd wnr till 2f out, wknd: see 2105. *2½* **58**
-- **DARCY ROAD DANCER** [4] 3-9-0 A Beech(5) 8/1: -7: Rdn in rear, nvr a factor on debut: related to 10f wnr & smart hdler Mersey Beat: with G L Moore. *1½* **55**
1204 **SWALDO 54** [9] 3-9-0 R Brisland (5) 20/1: 023-08: Chsd ldrs 7f, fdd into last: 8 wk abs: see 1204. *8* **40**
8 ran Time 1m 55.61 (5.11) (Exors Of The Late E J Fenaroli) T J Naughton Epsom, Surrey

2323 **7.35 NORCAL SELLER 3YO+ (G) 1m5f aw Standard Inapplicable**
£1844 £527 £263 3yo rec 14lb

2008 **RIDGEWOOD BAY 14** [5] J C Fox 3-8-3 L Newman (3) 20/1: -00001: 3 b f Ridgewood Ben - Another Baileys (Deploy) Front rank, went on 5f out, styd on well fnl 2f, rdn out: op 16/1, no bid: only mod from, prev: eff at 13f on equitrack: handles a sharp trk. **35a**
*2181 **FULL EGALITE 6** [1] B R Johnson 4-9-13 (bl) C Rutter 2/1 FAV: -00012: 4 gr g Ezzoud - Milva (Jellaby) In tch, prog to chall 4f out, edged right & no extra ins last: well bckd, 13L clr 3rd, qck reapp: see 2181. *2½* **41a**
2181 **KI CHI SAGA 6** [8] P Burgoyne 8-9-8 (tbl) P McCabe 16/1: 400603: 8 ch g Miswaki - Cedilla (Caro) Dwelt, prog to chall 5f out, sn outpcd fnl 2f: clr of rem, qck reapp: again bhnd this 2nd in 2181, see 115. *13* **18a**
2037 **GROOMS GOLD 12** [3] J Pearce 8-9-8 (vis) G Bardwell 6/1: 000204: Nvr nr ldrs: op 4/1: see 1465. *10* **3a**
1975 **AQUAVITA 15** [2] 6-9-3 J Tate 11/1: 05/035: In tch 1m: tch 20/1: jumps rnr since 1975. *7* **0a**
2008 **MISCHIEF 14** [7] 4-9-8 N Callan 7/1: 000506: Rdn in rear, bhnd fnl 4f, t.o.: see 815. *12* **0a**
649 **COCO GIRL 115** [4] 4-9-3 P Doe 3/1: 04-207: Led 1m, wknd qckly, t.o.: jmps rnr since 649, see 483. *2½* **0a**
2181 **ALBINONA 6** [6] 3-8-3 A Whelan 7/1: 0-6258: Prom till 1m out, wknd & t.o.: op 4/1, qck reapp. *dist* **0a**
8 ran Time 2m 50.39 (8.09) (Lord Mutton Racing Partnership) J C Fox Collingbourne Ducis, Wilts.

2324 **8.05 EBF MARK PIGGOTT MDN 2YO (D) 5f str Firm 16 -14 Slow**
£3477 £1070 £535 £267

886 **ANTONIAS DILEMMA 80** [4] A Berry 2-8-9 R Mullen 5/2: -01: 2 ch f Primo Dominie - Antonia's Folly (Music Boy) Dwelt, sn recovered to press ldrs, went on dist, styd on well, drvn out: well bckd, 12 wk abs: 8,000 gns half sister to a 5f 2yo wnr: eff at 5f on firm grnd: handles a sharp/undul trk: improving. **77**
2082 **WARLINGHAM 10** [2] Miss Gay Kelleway 2-9-0 Dane O'Neill 13/8 FAV: -46362: 2 b c Catrail - Tadjnama (Exceller) Front rank, went on halfway, collared dist, kept on but not pace of wnr: well bckd: acts on gd & firm. *1½* **77**
-- **SUMMER SHADES** [1] C A Cyzer 2-8-9 N Callan 4/1: -3: 2 b f Green Desert - Sally Slade (Dowsing) Outpcd & ran green in rear, ran on well fnl 1f, not rch ldrs on debut: April foal, dam a multiple sprint wnr/miler: bred to apprec 6/7f in time: handles firm grnd: got going too late today, will know more next time. *1¾* **67**
1513 **RAMESES 35** [3] Mrs L Stubbs 2-9-0 (VIS) D Harrison 16/1: -04: Rcd keenly & led till halfway, btn fnl 1f: rcd keenly in first time visor: see 1513 (debut). *¾* **69**
1993 **RAMBLIN MAN 14** [6] 2-9-0 G Hind 12/1: -05: Front rank 3f, wknd: tchd 20/1: see 1993. *4* **57**
1943 **AMARONE 16** [5] 2-9-0 P McCabe 6/1: -06: Al outpcd, fin last: op 10/1: Apr foal, dam a 10f wnr. *8* **37**
6 ran Time 58.32 (1.52) (Slatch Farm Stud) A Berry Cockerham, Lancs.

LINGFIELD SATURDAY JULY 1ST Lefthand, Sharp, Undulating Track

2325
8.35 MER CAR POLISH HCAP 3YO 0-85 (D) 7f str Firm 16 -04 Slow [90]
£4251 £1308 £654 £327

1786 **BIG FUTURE** 23 [1] Mrs A J Perrett 3-9-3 (79) Dane O'Neill 2/1 FAV: -141: 3 b c Bigstone - Star **90**
Of The Future (El Gran Senor) Trkd ldrs going best, imprvd to lead dist, sn clr, easily: well bckd: debut Kempton
wnr (mdn): eff at 7f, stays 1m: acts on firm & soft grnd: has a gd turn of foot: useful, can win again.
2128 **ROYAL IVY** 8 [8] J Akehurst 3-8-4 (66) P Doe 5/1: 100542: 3 ch f Mujtahid - Royal Climber (King's **3 69**
Lake) Rear, prog when short of room 2f out, styd on well to take 2nd, but wnr in another parish: met a fast
improving & smart rival: stable back to form now & one to keep in mind: see 421 (AW mdn).
2031 **SANTIBURI GIRL** 13 [5] J R Best 3-8-5 (67) R Mullen 7/1: 610023: 3 b f Casteddu - Lake Mistassiu **2½ 65**
(Tina's Pet) Dwelt, prog to chase ldrs 2f out, styd on & nrst fin: not disgraced back over 7f: see 2031.
1964 **INSIGHTFUL** 15 [10] R Hannon 3-8-13 (75) (BL) P Dobbs (5) 7/1: 502644: Front rank till fdd ins fnl **hd 73**
1f: gd run in first time blnks: another consistent effort: see 1569, 108 (AW).
2145 **I PROMISE YOU** 8 [6] 3-8-10 (72) A Nicholls (3) 8/1: 100035: Rear, eff 2f out, keeping on when short **nk 69**
of room dist, nvr nrr: did not get the best of runs & worth another chance: see 2145.
2115 **INNKEEPER** 9 [2] 3-8-13 (75) D Harrison 10/1: -52006: Set pace till dist, grad fdd: btr 1263. **1 70**
2044 **DAWNS DANCER** 12 [9] 3-8-0 (62) M Henry 10/1: 2-0037: Chsd ldrs, dn & wknd fnl 1f: btr 2044. **1¾ 53**
1912 **WINDFALL** 17 [3] 3-8-13 (75) A Clark 14/1: 0-038: Prom, wknd fnl 2f: h'cap bow: see 1912 (9f here). **8 51**
1853 **RISK FREE** 20 [7] 3-9-7 (83) (BL) T G McLaughlin 16/1: 421409: Rcd keenly & prom 4f, sn wknd: top- **1¼ 56**
weight: much too free in first time blnks: see 921 (fibreaand).
2044 **GROVE LODGE** 12 [11] 3-7-10 (58) (14oh) R Brisland (5) 33/1: 000000: Rdn in rear, no ch from halfway. **3 25**
534 **TYCANDO** 135 [4] 3-8-10 (72) N Callan 20/1: 2-0500: Dwelt, eff 3f out, sn btn & fin last: abs. **9 24**
11 ran Time 1m 21.82 (1.42) (K Abdulla) Mrs A J Perrett Pulborough, W Sussex

2326
9.05 BARRIER REEF H'CAP 3YO+ 0-75 (E) 5f str Firm 16 +17 Fast [74]
£2786 £796 £398 3yo rec 5lb

2275 **SIHAFI** 2 [5] D Nicholls 7-8-10 (56) A Nicholls (3) 7/2: 302361: 7 ch g Elmaamul - Kit's Double **60**
(Spring Double) Nvr far away, chall halfway, led cl home, rdn out: well bckd from 9/2, best time of day, qck reapp:
deserved win, has been busy of late: plcd twice in '99 (h'caps, rtd 71): won 9 times in '98, at Lingfield (2),
Windsor, Bath, Folkestone, Salisbury, Sandown, Haydock & W'hampton (h'caps, rtd 71 & 81a): stays 6f, best at
5f: acts on both AW's, handles gd/soft, prefers gd & firm grnd: tough, well h'capped sprinter, cld win again.
*2107 **TUSCAN DREAM** 9 [8] A Berry 5-9-13 (73) P Bradley (5) 5/2 FAV: -00512: 5 b g Clantime - **nk 76**
Excavator Lady (Most Secret) Tried to make all, not pace to repel wnr cl home: bckd from 7/2: gd front running
effort, won this race from a 14lbs lower mark last year: in gd form, see 2107.
1881 **FAUTE DE MIEUX** 19 [9] M Kettle 5-10-0 (74) R Mullen 10/1: 601033: 5 ch g Beveled - Supreme Rose **¾ 74**
(Frimley Park) Prom, sl outpcd 2f out, rallied fnl 1f & not btn far: op 7/1, top-weight: see 1881.
1871 **AURIGNY** 19 [1] S Dow 5-9-11 (71) (VIS) O Urbina 14/1: 006404: Trkd ldrs, rdn onepcd in last: visor. **1¼ 67**
1650 **CHARGE** 29 [6] 4-9-4 (64) (t) N Callan 20/1: 215005: Prom, onepcd fnl 1f: mkt drifter: see 1196. **1 57**
2184 **QUITE HAPPY** 6 [2] A Beech 5-8-9 (55) A Beech 7/1: 333536: Dwelt, outpcd till late hdwy, nvr dngrs. **nk 47**
2184 **BREW** 6 [3] 4-8-5 (51) L Newman (3) 14/1: 0-0607: Chsd ldrs till fdd fnl 1f: qck reapp. **1 40**
4450} **POETRY IN MOTION** 255 [11] 5-9-4 (64) R Price 14/1: 2020-8: Dwelt, recovered & in tch 3f, sn struggling **hd 53**
on reapp: tchd 20/1: trained by E Alston to win at Musselburgh in '99 (mdn, rtd 72), also 2nd in h'caps: eff at
5f on firm & soft grnd, has tried 1m: handles any trk: has tried blnks: now with R Guest.
2035 **SYLVA PARADISE** 12 [7] 7-9-10 (70) (vis) G Bardwell 5/1: 0-0459: Al outpcd: btr 1871. **hd 59**
1999 **KILCULLEN LAD** 14 [4] 6-9-12 (72) (vis) T G McLaughlin 5/1: -05230: Slowly away, nvr a factor in last. **shd 61**
10 ran Time 56.72 (u0.08) (John Gilbertson) D Nicholls Sessay, N Yorks.

BATH SATURDAY JULY 1ST Lefthand, Turning Track With Uphill Finish

Official Going FIRM Stalls: Str Crse - Far Side, Rnd Crse - Inside.

2327
1.45 ST JOHN MDN 3YO+ (D) 1m3f144y Firm 07 -39 Slow
£3770 £1160 £580 £290 3 yo rec 13lb

2135 **TORRID KENTAVR** 8 [3] T G Mills 3-8-11 A Clark 1/3 FAV: 4-331: 3 b c Trempolino - Torrid Tango **84**
(Green Dancer) Led 5f out, rdn fnl 2f, always holding rivals in last, pushed out cl home: hvly bckd at odds on:
well btn 4th in Italy sole juv start (8.5f, hvy): eff at 10/12f, 14f+ may suit: acts on firm & fast grnd.
1404 **BAYSWATER** 42 [4] B W Hills 3-8-6 R Mullen 9/1: 02: 3 b f Caerleon - Shining Water (Kalaglow) **2 72**
Dwelt, held up, rdn/out 4f out, kept on fnl 2f, no threat to wnr: op 5/1, 6 wk abs: clr rem: improved over this
longer 12f trip: acts on firm grnd: keep in mind for mdn over 12f+: see khan.
2056 **SHAREEF KHAN** 12 [7] N A Graham 3-8-11 D Harrison 11/2: 0-033: 3 b g Alzao - Sharenara (Vaguely **5 70**
Noble) Chsd ldrs, outpcd by wnr fnl 2f: op 7/2: stays 12f, h'caps shld suit: see 2056, 1200.
2056 **QUEEN OF FASHION** 12 [5] J J Sheehan 4-9-5 A Daly 25/1: 04: Led till 5f out, hung left/no extra **2½ 61**
over 1f out: longer 12f trip: likely to appreciate mid-dist h'caps in time.
2129 **NAJMAT JUMAIRAH** 8 [6] 3-8-6 R Havlin 11/1: 65: In tch, outpcd 3f out: longer 12f trip: see 2129. **1 60**
1455 **PREMIERE VALENTINO** 39 [8] 3-8-11 S Whitworth 33/1: 0-56: Prom, struggling 3f out: see 1455. **8 56$**
1510 **LARAS DELIGHT** 36 [9] 5-9-5 F Norton 100/1: 07: Keen/rear, btn 4f out: no form. **nk 50**
1540 **NOVELLINI STAR** 35 [1] 3-8-11 S Righton 100/1: -08: Keen, in tch, struggling halfway: no form. **9 45**
8 ran Time 2m 30.4 (5.4) (Kentavr UK Ltd) T G Mills Headley, Surrey.

2328
2.15 WESTON AUCT MDN 2YO (E) 5f161y rnd Firm 07 -22 Slow
£2926 £836 £418

1882 **SIBLA** 18 [9] Mrs P N Dutfield 2-8-1 L Newman (3) 5/1: 521: 2 b f Piccolo - Malibasta (Auction Ring) **73**
Held up, rdn fnl 2f, styd on well for press to lead nr line: eff at 6f, 7f+ shld suit: acts on firm & fast grnd & a
stiff/gall trk: open to further improvement.
2010 **YETTI** 14 [5] H Candy 2-7-13 C Rutter 2/1 FAV: 22: 2 ch f Aragon - Willyet (Nicholas Bill) **hd 70**
Led, hard rdn & styd on well ins last: bckd, tho' op 7/4: acts on firm & gd: clr rem, make amends.

appr fnl 1f & no extra, eased: 10th, lkd well: beat this wnr on more fav'able terms in 2035 (class stks).

2275	**MALLIA 2** [5] 7-8-0 (67)(bl) P Fessey 12/1: 044440: Nvr a factor: 11th, ran 48hrs ago: see 719.	nk	53
1861	**UNSHAKEN 20** [10] 6-8-2 (69) W Supple 14/1: 240000: Nvr better than mid-div: 12th, lifeless in	nk	54

padd: won this race last year (off 6lbs higher mark): stable in form & worth another chance, prob on easier grnd.

2151	**JUWWI 8** [1] 6-10-0 (95) P Fitzsimons(5) 13/2 FAV: 150500: Stdd start, nvr on terms: 13th, bckd from 11/1. ¾	79
1989	**REDSWAN 14** [7] 5-8-3 (70)(t) N Pollard 25/1: 1-0000: Al towards rear: 14th, see 1810. 2	51
2151	**RED LION GB 8** [19] 4-9-8 (89) D Holland 10/1: 00-000: Al bhd: 15th, nicely bckd, see 1337.	64
1983	**PRINCELY DREAM 15** [2] 4-9-1 (82) K Darley 10/1: 20-000: Mid-div till halfway: 19th, see 1533.	0
1694	**Eastways 28** [8] 3-9-0 (87) R Ffrench 25/1: 2151 **Al Muallim 8** [9] 6-9-12 (93) Alex Greaves 25/1:	
1905	**Distinctive Dream 17** [16] 6-8-0 (67) C McCavish (7) 33/1:	

19 ran   Time 1m 11.37 (0.07)   (Anne Lady Scott)   M L W Bell Newmarket.

2335   3.10 LISTED CHIPCHASE STKS 3YO+ (A)   6f   Firm -01   +10 Fast
£21576   £8184   £4092   £1860   3 yo rec 6 lb

1338 **TEDBURROW 44** [6] E J Alston 8-9-5 W Supple 12/1: -00001: 8 b g Dowsing - Gwiffina (Welsh Saint)   116
In tch, imprvd 2f out, qcknd to lead & drifted left dist, ran on strongly, readily: crse record, lkd well, 6 wk
abs: '99 wnr at Doncaster (List), Chester (2, incl List) & Leopardstown (Gr 3, rtd 115): '98 wnr at Newmarket,
Chester (List) & Leopardstown (Gr 3, rtd 112): eff at 5/6f on firm & soft grnd, any trk, loves Chester & a strong
pace: v smart, goes for a 4th consecutive win in a Chester Listed race & will be hard to beat.

2151 **CRETAN GIFT 8** [4] N P Littmoden 9-9-1 (vis) J F Egan 10/1: 465002: 9 ch g Cadeaux Genereux -   1¼   108
Caro's Neice (Caro) Chsd ldrs, rdn & hdwy to lead briefly dist, not pace of wnr: ran to best, poor draw latest.

2151 **DEEP SPACE 8** [5] E A L Dunlop 9-9-1 G Carter 5/1: -63543: 5 br g Green Desert - Dream Season   1¼   104
(Mr Prospector) Mid-div, drvn & hdwy appr fnl 1f, onepace towards fin: not far off best: see 952.

2065 **TRINCULO 11** [2] N P Littmoden 3-8-9 J Quinn 25/1: 003404: Rcd in 2nd, led bef dist till ent fnl   nk   103
1f, onepace: tchd 50/1: back up in trip, acts on firm & gd/soft, fair run against elders: see 696.

4286} **LITTLEFEATHER 266** [9] 3-8-4 S Sanders 6/1: 1135-5: Held up, kept on well fnl 1f, nvr dngrs: hd   98+
fit for reapp: '99 hat-trick scorer at Ripon (mdn), Newcastle (nurs) & Chester (fill cond, Gr 1 3rd, rtd 107):
eff at 6f, stays 7f & that trip shld suit this term: acts on firm & gd/soft grnd, any trk: v useful, lengthy
nurs: has a good turn of foot, spot on next time at 7f.

*2151 **HARMONIC WAY 8** [7] 5-9-1 R Hughes 2/1 FAV: -64216: Waited with, shkn up appr fnl 1f, kept on   ¾   100
but nvr threatened: well bckd: up in grade after lifetime best in 2151 (Wokingham h'cap).

-2310 **INDIAN SPARK 1** [10] 6-9-1 A Culhane 12/1: 011027: In tch, unable to qckn appr fnl 1f: ran   nk   99
yesterday, up in grade & not disgraced: see 1983.

2087 **SCARTEEN FOX 10** [3] 3-8-9 N Pollard 16/1: -40508: Prom, no extra appr fnl 1f: dull in coat, see 950.   nk   98
1674 **WINNING VENTURE 28** [11] 3-8-9 K Darley 10/1: -30239: Al bhd: easier grnd suits?: see 1674, 950.   2   92
1090 **ROWAASI 60** [1] 3-8-4 Craig Williams 20/1: 124-00: Pulled hard & sn in clr lead, hdd bef dist &   ½   86
& wknd: 10th, 9 wk abs, set off too fast & is better at 5f: see 1090.

2115 **GAELIC STORM 9** [8] 6-9-1 D Holland 11/2: 6-0650: Sn struggling: 11th: this is not his form.   8   71
11 ran   Time 1m 10.64 (u0.66)   (Philip Davies)   E J Alston Longton, Lancs.

2336   3.45 NORTHUMB'D PLATE HCAP 3YO+ (B)   2m   Firm -01 -05 Slow   [114]
£75400   £28600   £14300   £6500   19yo rec lb

1982 **BAY OF ISLANDS 15** [4] D Morris 8-8-4 (90)(vis) K Darley 7/1: 3-0031: 8 b g Jupiter Island - Lawyer's   97
Wave (Advocator) Mid-div, stdly imprvd after halfway, led 2f out, drvn out: nicely bckd: '99 Nottingham wnr
(h'cap, rtd 93 when 3rd in this race): '98 Doncaster wnr (h'cap, rtd 89): eff at 12f/2m: acts on firm & gd/soft
grnd, any trk, likes gall ones: eff with/without visor: tough & useful stayer, at the top of his form.

2173 **TEMPLE WAY 7** [5] R Charlton 4-7-10 (82)(3oh) Dale Gibson 16/1: 0-0222: 4 b g Shirley Heights -   nk   88
Abbey Strand (Shadeed) In tch, hdwy ent str, ran on under press fnl 2f, post came too soon: qck reapp,
cracking run off a feather weight: looks tailor-made for the Cesarewitch later on: see 1180.

-2028 **RAINBOW WAYS 13** [13] B W Hills 5-9-11 (111) R Hughes 16/1: 5-1223: 5 b h Rainbow Quest - Siwaayib   2   115
(Green Desert) Early ldr, mid-div, prog over 3f out & chsd ldrs appr fnl 1f, no extra towards fin: padd pick,
cracking weight carrying performance from this rangy entire: shld win a Listed/Gr 3, rated 114, see 1187.

1222 **FANTASY HILL 52** [2] J L Dunlop 4-8-7 (93) G Carter 5/1: 02-534: Towards rear, short of room 5f   2½   94
out, kept on strongly fnl 2f, nvr nrr: not much luck in running but got going too late, 7 wk abs: see 917.

1565 **BIENNALE 33** [15] 4-9-4 (104) F Lynch 11/1: 13-445: Chsd ldrs, slipped ent str, same pace for   ¾   104
press 2f out: op 9/1: strong colt, shld better for race: return to 12f may suit, see 987.

1307 **INIGO JONES 46** [11] 4-8-7 (93) A Culhane 20/1: 3-1456: Bhd, not much room 4f out, kept on in   nk   93+
the str, nvr dngrs: lkd well, 7 wk abs: given too much to do over longer 2m trip? keep in mind, see 809.

*1686 **CHRISTIANSTED 28** [1] 5-7-10 (82)(1oh) K Dalgleish (7) 9/1: 52-617: Al arnd same place: nicely bckd.   2   80
*1478 **VIRGIN SOLDIER 37** [6] 4-7-12 (84) R Ffrench 9/2 FAV: 112-18: Cl-up, led & kicked clr ent str,   nk   82
no extra & hdd 2f out: well bckd from 8/1, lkd well: raced a shade too freely, see 1478.

2092 **ALHAWA 10** [12] 7-7-11 (83) J Quinn 20/1: 65-2B9: Nvr nr ldrs: do better with a positive ride.   1¾   79
1222 **ANSAR 52** [10] 4-8-5 (91) D M Oliver 8/1: 23-020: Prom till ent fnl 3f: 10th, Irish raider, lkd well, 7 wk abs.   1¼   86
1715 **KUMATOUR 26** [17] 5-9-0 (100) T E Durcan 25/1: 163-30: In tch, no impress 3f out: 11th: see 1715 (12f).   3   92
2069 **FIRST BALLOT 11** [8] 4-8-4 (90) J F Egan 25/1: 10-000: Al towards rear: 12th, see 1222.   1   81
2092 **HEROS FATAL 10** [18] 6-7-10 (82) J Mackay (5) 6/1: 453-30: Nvr a factor, btn 3f out: 13th, lkd well   4   69
& was bckd from 9/1: stocky gelding, this may have come too soon after 2092 (2½m).

2069 **AFTERJACKO 11** [19] 4-8-5 (91) N Pollard 20/1: -51200: Al bhd: 14th, longer trip, see 1180.   ½   77
4397} **LIFE OF RILEY 259** [16] 6-9-0 (100)(t) S Sanders 25/1: 3010-0: Sn led, hdd ent str & wknd qckly: 18th: 0
jumps fit, unbtn in 2 starts at Uttoxeter & N Abbot (nov hdles, 2½m/2m6f, firm/fast, rtd 115h, t-strap): '99 wnr
at Goodwood & Newmarket (h'caps, rtd 101, B Meehan): '98 wnr at Kempton & Sandown (h'caps, rtd 92): eff at 14f/
2m on firm & gd, handles gd/soft, any trk: eff with/without blnks & can carry big weights: wears a t-strap.

1791 **Karowna 23** [14] 4-7-10 (82)(15oh) J McAuley(5) 100/1: 2001 **Suplizi 14** [3] 9-7-10 (82)(8oh) Claire Bryan(5) 100/1:
2153 **Spirit Of Love 8** [9] 5-9-8 (108) D Holland 20/1:
18 ran   Time 3m 26.09 (0.59)   (Bloomsbury Stud)   D Morris Newmarket.

2337   **4.20 KRONENBOURG MDN 3YO+ (D)**   **1m rnd**   **Firm -01 -10 Slow**
£6743   £2075   £1037   £518   3 yo rec 9 lb

-- **TRUE THUNDER** [7] H R A Cecil 3-8-12 A McGlone 2/1 FAV: 1: 3 b c Bigstone - Puget Dancer (Seattle   88
Dancer) Nvr far away, rdn to lead dist, kept on well: well bckd from 3/1, fit for debut: dam 12f wnr: eff at 1m,
10f shld suit: acts on firm grnd & a gall trk, runs well fresh: leggy colt, useful debut.
1127 **TOLSTOY** 58 [5] Sir Michael Stoute 3-8-12 F Lynch 11/4: 22-52: 3 b c Nashwan - Milazure (Dayjur)   ¾ 85
Well plcd, led ent str till dist, styd on: nicely bckd, clr rem, 8 wk abs: rangy colt, acts on firm & gd/soft.
2129 **FLYING TREATY** 8 [8] J H M Gosden 3-8-12 K Darley 3/1: 523: 3 br c You And I - Cherie's Hope   6 73
(Flying Paster) Slow away, mid-div, styd on to chase front pair 2f out, no impress & not persevered with in
last: well bckd, clr rem: poss unsuited by drop back in trip & may appreciate an easier surface: see 2129.
4250} **CHAMPFIS** 270 [3] M Johnston 3-8-12 D Holland 16/1: 03-4: Bhd, late hdwy: reapp, trainer/jockey/   5 63
horse reportedly fined/banned/suspended under non-triers Rule, connections reported horse was lame & they will
appeal: plcd fnl 2 '99 starts (5f mdn on soft, rtd 75): half-brother to smart sprinter Superpower: shld
apprec 1m with a more positive ride: scopey & now qual for h'caps.
1135 **SHALBEBLUE** 58 [1] 3-8-12 Dean McKeown 20/1: 35: In tch fnl halfway: just better after 8 wk abs.   ½ 62
1678 **DAKOTA SIOUX** 28 [4] 3-8-7 R Winston 33/1: 3-36: Al towards rear: lengthy, unfurnished, fit.   2 53
2140 **FIZZLE** 8 [6] 3-8-12 R Ffrench 50/1: 57: Prom till hung left ent str: stablemate 4th, v fit, see 2140.   1¼ 56
2117 **PYTHAGORAS** 9 [2] 3-8-12 Martin Dwyer 12/2: 40-608: Led, slipped & hdd ent str, sn lost pl: sturdy.   1¾ 53
8 ran   Time 1m 39.73 (0.73)   (Buckram Oak Holdings)   H R A Cecil Newmarket.

2338   **4.55 JOURNAL HCAP 3YO+ 0-100 (C)**   **7f str**   **Firm -01 +01 Fast**   [96]
£14170   £4360   £2180   £1090   3 yo rec 8 lb 3 raced stands side, struggling after halfway

2133 **KAYO** 8 [1] M Johnston 5-9-12 (94) K Darley 11/4 FAV: 000231: 5 b g Superpower - Shiny Kay (Star   103
Appeal) Made all in centre, kept on strongly, pushed out: gd time, bckd from 5/1: '99 hat-trick scorer at Redcar,
Newmarket & here at Newcastle (h'caps, rtd 95): '98 wnr at Southwell (2, rtd 81a), Newbury & Warwick (h'caps, rtd
95, T Etherington): eff at 6f, suited by 7f, stays a sharp 1m on firm, hvy, both AWs, any trk, likes gall ones:
can carry big weights: tried blnks, better without: useful effort from the front today.
2001 **ROYAL ARTIST** 14 [2] W J Haggas 4-8-6 (74) J F Egan 7/1: -21262: 4 b g Royal Academy - Council   1½ 79
Rock (General Assembly) Chsd wnr thr'out, styd on but nvr any impression: lkd well, nicely bckd: apprec
drop back to 7f, acts on firm, gd/soft, both AWs, see 1037.
2151 **TAYSEER** 8 [3] D Nicholls 6-9-3 (85) D Holland 7/2: 005303: 6 ch g Sheikh Albadou - Milfit (Blushing   hd 90
Groom) Waited with centre, kept on strongly fnl 1f, no extra: bckd 9/2: tchd 9/2: uninspired ride: see 733.
2003 **PERUVIAN CHIEF** 14 [5] N P Littmoden 3-8-12 (88) J Quinn 8/1: -05204: Early ldr centre, prom,   1¾ 89
onepace appr fnl 1f: padd pick, clr rem: gd run up in trip against elders, return to 6f will suit: see 1694, 112.
2151 **EMERGING MARKET** 8 [4] 4-9-2 (84) G Carter 5/1: 6-0005: Held up centre, shkn up 2f out, no impress.   3½ 78
2163 **REDOUBTABLE** 7 [11] 9-8-6 (74) R Ffrench 11/1: 000036: Chsd ldrs stands side, led that group bef   1½ 65
dist, no chance with centre group: lkd well, won this 2 yrs ago: see 1060.
2090 **LATALOMNE** 10 [10] 6-9-4 (86) A Culhane 25/1: -00507: Led stands side group till ent fnl 2f, no extra.   ¾ 75
2117 **KAREEB** 9 [7] 3-8-4 (80) Martin Dwyer 20/1: 4-6508: In tch centre fnl 2f out: lkd well, stocky, see 1183.   ½ 68
2133 **MANTLES PRIDE** 8 [8] 5-9-3 (85)(bl) O Pears 11/1: 041069: Al bhd centre: can do better, see 1514.   nk 72
2090 **JO MELL** 10 [9] 7-10-0 (96) J Carroll 8/1: 101200: In tch stands side till 2f out, drifted left, eased: 10th.   14 63
10 ran   Time 1m 23.95 (u0.15)   (J David Abell)   M Johnston Middleham, N.Yorks.

2339   **5.25 LISTED EBF HOPPINGS STKS 3YO+ (A)**   **1m2f32y**   **Firm -01 -02 Slow**
£18444   £6996   £3498   £1590   3 yo rec 11lb

2260 **AMAL!A** 23 [2] P W Harris 4-9-3 W Supple 9/4: 041341: 4 b g Danehill - Cheviot Amble (Pennine Walk)   106
Prom, led 2f out, hard rdn ins last, just held on, gamely: well bckd, qck reapp: earlier won at York (rtd h'cap):
'99 wnr at Redcar (mdn), Chester & Doncaster (h'caps, rtd 99): eff at 1m/10f, stays 12f: acts on firm & gd/soft,
handles hvy: goes on a sharp or gall trk, can force the pace: small but v tough & v useful filly.
1747} **CLAXON** 393 [8] J L Dunlop 4-9-3 G Carter 6/4 FAV: -/115-2: 4 b f Caerleon - Bulaxie (Bustino)   shd 105
Early ldr, rechall 2f out, briefly outpcd dist, strong rally nr fin, just failed: hvly bckd: '99 wnr at Kempton &
Goodwood (List, rtd 109, 5th in Epsom Oaks): '98 Ayr wnr (fill mdn, rtd 93): eff at 10f, may get 12f this term
(bred to do so): acts on firm & hvy grnd, any trk, runs v well fresh: likes to force the pace: big, scopey, v useful.
*2198 **MOSELLE** 5 [3] W J Haggas 3-8-6 A Culhane 8/1: 3-2013: 3 b f Mtoto - Miquette (Fabulous Dancer)   1¼ 103
Chsd ldrs, hard rdn 2f out, kept on till no extra fnl 100y: qck reapp & imprvd up in grade: acts on firm & soft.
1945 **CHEZ CHERIE** 16 [1] L M Cumani 3-8-6 D Holland 6/1: 45-044: Prom, feeling pace 3f out, kept on   1½ 101
nicely towards fin: still better for race, gets 10f & is one to keep in mind: see 1185.
1965 **FIRST FANTASY** 15 [9] 4-9-3 R Hughes 14/1: -05105: Waited with, imprvd appr str, rdn & flashed   1½ 99$
tail 2f out, no impress: highly tried, surely flattered, see 1709 (3 runners).
2170 **DASHIBA** 7 [6] 4-9-3 J F Egan 4/1: 10-306: Al towards rear: qck reapp, lkd well, highly tried, flattered.   ½ 98$
1987 **YORBA LINDA** 14 [5] 5-9-3 J Carroll 50/1: -40507: Nvr a factor: flattered, outclassed, big leap in trip.   6 89$
2112 **ABSCOND** 9 [7] 3-8-6 F Lynch 9/1: 2-5108: Led after 3f & clr ent str, hdd/wknd 2f out: op 7/1, too free.   4 83
8 ran   Time 2m 06.6 (0.1)   (Mrs P W Harris)   P W Harris Aldbury, Herts.

2340   **5.55 CANTORINDEX HCAP 3YO+ 0-70 (E)**   **5f**   **Firm -01 -25 Slow**   [70]
£3640   £1120   £560   £280   3 yo rec 5 lb

1980 **DOUBLE OSCAR** 15 [2] D Nicholls 7-10-0 (70) Alex Greaves 5/2 FAV: 056321: 7 ch g Royal Academy -   74
Broadway Rosie (Absalom) Held up, prog ent fnl 2f, ran on strongly to pip stablemate on line: bckd from 4/1: '99
Ayr wnr (h'cap, rtd 82): '98 Lingfield, W'hampton & Ascot wnr (h'caps, rtd 89 & 89a): eff at 6f, best at 5f, stays
7f: handles gd/soft & hvy, likes firm & gd, both AWs: off weight carrier, h'capped to follow up.
2275 **REFERENDUM** 2 [10] D Nicholls 6-9-13 (69) S Sanders 8/1: 000052: 6 b g Common Grounds - Final   hd 72
Decision (Tap On Wood) Front rank, led below dist, drifted left & collared fnl stride: ran 48hrs ago,
stablemate wnr: in form, well h'capped, eff btwn 5f & 7f, see 941.
2107 **BOLLIN ANN** 9 [8] T D Easterby 5-9-10 (66) J Carroll 4/1: -01023: 5 b m Anshan - Bollin Zola   ½ 67
(Alzao) Handy, kept on strongly for press fnl 1f, not btn far: bckd from 8/1: in gd form, acts on firm & gd/soft.
2063 **MUKARRAB** 11 [9] D W Chapman 6-8-10 (52) A Culhane 12/1: 601004: Well plcd, led 1½f out till   ½ 52
dist, held nr fin: a bold attempt on grnd faster than ideal tho' clrly handles firm, see 1714.

NEWCASTLE SATURDAY JULY 1ST Lefthand, Galloping Track

2240	**SEALED BY FATE 3** [14] 5-8-6 (48)(vis) J McAuley (5) 14/1: 660445: Held up, styd on fnl 1½f, nvr dngrs.	½	46
2233	**BIFF EM 3** [7] 6-7-11 (39)(1ow)(2oh) Dale Gibson 8/1: 030426: Prom, onepace dist: qk reapp, see 1143.	nk	36
2275	**IMPALDI 2** [1] 5-7-10 (38)(6oh) J Mackay (5) 33/1: -00507: Mid-div, hdwy appr fnl 1f, no extra ins last.	1½	31
*2165	**COLLEGE MAID 7** [3] 3-9-8 (69) D Sweeney 8/1: 125018: Same place thr'out: qck reapp, btr 2165 (gd).	2	56
1999	**MALADERIE 14** [6] 6-9-1 (57)(vis) T Williams 14/1: 002009: Outpcd, mod late hdwy: see 908.	1	41
1815	**FRILLY FRONT 22** [16] 4-9-0 (56) P Fessey 16/1: 000500: Nvr going pace: 10th, see 631 (equitrack).	nk	39
2192	**JACK TO A KING 5** [12] 5-8-4 (46)(tbl) R Ffrench 16/1: 021200: Led till appr fnl 1f, fdd: 11th, qk reapp.	nk	28
2097	**ANSELLMAN 10** [17] 10-9-4 (60)(bl) G Carter 14/1: 025400: Mid-div, outpcd fnl 2f: 12th, shorter trip.	½	41
2078	**RING OF LOVE 10** [11] 4-9-10 (66) J F Egan 11/1: 653030: Al bhd: 14th, see 372.		0
787	**Time To Fly 94** [5] 7-8-0 (42)(bl) K Dalgleish(7) 16/1: 696 **Pips Star 103** [15] 3-8-13 (60) Dawn Rankin(7) 50/1:		
15 ran	Time 59.39 (1.19) (Trilby Racing) D Nicholls Sessay, N.Yorks.		

NEWMARKET (July) SATURDAY JULY 1ST Righthand, Stiff, Galloping Track.

Official Going GOOD TO FIRM. Stalls: Far Side, except 2.55 race - Stands Side.

2341 2.25 LISTED FRED ARCHER STKS 4YO+ (A) 1m4f Firm 18 +02 Fast
£13764 £4884 £2442 £1110

+2028 **MURGHEM 13** [4] M Johnston 5-9-0 R Hills 11/8: 242111: 5 b h Commons Grounds - Fabulous Pet **113**
(Somethingfabulous): Made all, styd on strongly when prsd ins last, drvn out: nicely bckd: hat-trick landed
after scoring at Epsom (rtd h'cap) & Leicester (List): '99 Sandown wnr (h'cap, rtd 100, B Hanbury), prev term
won at Kempton (mdn, rtd 105): stays 14f/2m, suited by 12f on firm, soft & fibresand: likes to race up with/force
the pace on any trk & runs well fresh, without blnks: eff weight carrier: smart, genuine & progressive.

-- **DOUBLE ECLIPSE** [1] M Johnston 4-8-11 J Weaver 14/1: 1225/2: 8 b h Ela Mana Mou - Solac nk **109**
(Gay Lussac): Chsd wnr tho'out, drvn & chall wnr ins last, just held: stablemate of wnr & an excellent run after
3yr abs (has been to stud): back in '97 won at York (Gr 3, rtd 117): unbtn in '96, at Haydock (reapp) & Longchamp
(2, Gr 2 & Gr 3, crse record, rtd 115): eff at 12f, suited by 15f/2m: acts on firm, soft & runs well fresh:
admirably tough & smart, fine comeback & looks capable of winning more valuable races over further.

2028 **MAYLANE 13** [2] A C Stewart 6-9-0 J P Spencer 10/1: 1-0463: 6 b g Mtoto - Possessive Dancer 1½ **109**
(Shareef Dancer): Dwelt, settled rear, swtchd/imprvd appr final 1f, hung right & no extra well ins last:
poss better on an easier surface these days & sometimes looks less than keen under pressure: see 987.

2069 **NATIONAL ANTHEM 11** [3] Sir Michael Stoute 4-8-11 Pat Eddery 11/10 FAV: 14-144: Cl-up, rdn, hd **95**
edged left & btn appr final 1f: well bckd: stays 12f but may be suited by a drop back to 10f: see 1170.

4 ran Time 2m 30.14 (1.94) (A Al-Rostamani) M Johnston Middleham, Nth Yorks.

2342 2.55 SOVEREIGN FILLIES HCAP 3YO+ 0-90 (C) 1m str Firm 18 -17 Slow [82]
£7020 £2160 £1080 £540 3 yo rec 9 lb

*1886 **SHALIMAR 18** [2] J H M Gosden 3-9-5 (82) R Hills 6/1: 26-311: 3 b f Indian Ridge - Athens Belle **89**
(Groom Dancer): Waited with & rcd keenly, short of room 2f out, sn found gap & strong run to lead well inside
last, drvn out, despite carrying head high: up in tbf: earlier won at Salisbury (mdn): rnr-up to subs 1,000
Guineas wnr Lahan on '99 debut (fillies mdn, rtd 95, P Chapple Hyam), subs trained by A G Foster: eff at 7f/1m
on firm & gd/soft: acts on a sharp or stiff/gall trk & best coming late: prog filly, could complete hat-trick.

2062 **PICTURE PUZZLE 11** [4] W J Haggas 4-9-4 (72) J P Spencer 11/2: 616-32: 4 b f Royal Academy - ¾ **76**
Cloudslea (Chief's Crown): Led, qcknd clr appr final 1f, hdd well inside last, not btn far: clr rem, good run.

*1879 **MADAM ALISON 19** [3] R Hannon 4-9-12 (80) Dane O'Neill 5/1: 26-313: 4 b f Puissance - Copper Burn 3 **78**
(Electric): Cl-up, drvn/not pace of front 2 final 1f: won this race last year (8lbs higher today): see 1879 (stks).

1915 **FEATHER N LACE 17** [6] C A Cyzer 4-8-10 (64) N Callan 10/1: 30-224: Prom, rdn/held appr final 1f. ½ **61**

*2128 **SILK DAISY 8** [8] 4-8-8 (62) W Ryan 9/2: 3-4515: Rear, strong run for press final 2f, nvr nrr: nk **59**
possibly worth a try over further now: see 2128.

1926 **MAGIC FLUTE 17** [1] 4-9-0 (68) P Doe 12/1: 20-206: Mid-div, no room 2f out, sn btn: btr 1407 (stks). nk **64**

1958 **SIPSI FAWR 15** [5] 3-9-1 (78) M Fenton 7/2 FAV: -0137: Dwelt, sn in tch, rdn/fdd appr final 1f: 1¼ **72**
reportedly fin lame: well bckd on h'cap bow: see 1958, 1084.

2056 **SPELLBINDER 12** [7] 4-9-4 (72) Pat Eddery 10/1: 0-3228: Chsd ldrs, qckly lost tch final 2f, 25 **36**
reportedly lost action: op 8/1: apprec an easier surface: see 2056.

8 ran Time 1m 40.02 (2.82) (Lady Bamford) J H M Gosden Manton, Wilts.

2343 3.25 GR 3 VAN GEEST CRITERION STKS 3YO+ (A) 7f str Firm 18 +15 Fast
£20300 £7700 £3850 £1750 3 yo rec 8 lb

1338 **ARKADIAN HERO 44** [6] L M Cumani 5-9-1 J P Spencer 10/3 FAV: 0-4041: 5 ch h Trempolino - Careless **115**
Kitten (Caro): Settled in tch, short of room & swtchd 2f out, ran on well to lead ins last, qcknd up, readily:
bckd, fast time, abs: '99 wnr at Newbury & Newmarket (Listed), also fine 2L 3rd in Gr 1 Sprint Cup (rtd 119):
rtd 118 in '98: eff at 6/7f on firm & gd, handles soft: acts on any trk, likes a stiff one, esp Newmarket: runs
well fresh: high-class, his turn of foot can see further Group race wins, but the Gr 1 Sussex looks too ambitious.

4476} **CHAGALL 253** [8] Bruce Hellier 3-8-7 W Ryan 33/1: -26612: 3 ch c Fraam - Pooka (Dominion): 2 **109**
Rear, last 2f out, strong run for press ins last, no ch with wnr: fine run by this German outsider, recent wnr in
native country (List): dual '99 wnr in Germany (stks & List), subs won at Doncaster (val 2yo stks, rtd 95): eff at
5/6f, stays 7f well: acts on firm, gd, likes soft & a gall trk: smart, win a Gr 3/Listed.

2064 **SHOWBOAT 11** [1] B W Hills 6-9-1 G Duffield 12/1: -06303: 6 b h Warning - Boathouse (Habitat): ½ **108**
Prom, drvn & not pace of wnr final 1f: back to nr best here, v useful & will apprec a return to 1m: see 657.

1171 **MISRAAH 56** [3] Sir Michael Stoute 3-8-7 R Hills 5/1: 41-104: Keen & sn led, rdn/hdd dist, sn held: shd **108**
8 wk abs: bounced back here after a disapp run in the 2,000 Guineas (1m), handles firm & gd/soft: see 955.

1825 **ICICLE 22** [2] 3-8-4 Pat Eddery 6/1: 14-035: Waited with, effort when short of room 2f out, kept ½ **104**
on appr final 1f, no threat to ldrs: not disgrcd here & should relish a return to 1m+: see 1825, 1185.

1834 **HOT TIN ROOF 21** [5] 4-8-12 M Fenton 11/2: 211236: Bhd, rdn/hdwy appr final 1f, edged left ½ **103**
inside last & sn btn: handles firm grnd but best form has come on gd or softer: see 1834, 1410.

2226 **TUMBLEWEED RIDGE 6** [7] 7-9-6 (tbl) M Tebbutt 5/1: -23137: Reached dsptd lead, drvn/fdd appr final 3½ **105**
1f: qck reapp: tough & smart at best, sheds below par here: see 2226 (gd), 2070.

2115 **LOTS OF MAGIC 9** [9] 4-9-6 Dane O'Neill 8/1: 40-608: Handy, rdn & lost tch over 1f out: yet to 1¼ **103**

745

find form so far this term, v smart at best: see 734.
967 **DESARU 73** [4] 4-9-1 J Weaver 33/1: /00-09: Waited with, al bhd: 10 wk abs: see 967. 1¼ **96**
9 ran Time 1m 24.14 (0.24) (Lindy Regis & Mrs Sean Kelly) L M Cumani Newmarket.

2344 **4.00 LISTED EMPRESS STKS 2YO (A) 6f str Firm 18 -18 Slow**
£12852 £4875 £2437 £1108

*1882 **IN THE WOODS 18** [2] D J S Cosgrove 2-8-8 G Duffield 14/1: 11: 2 br f You And I - Silent Indulgence (Woodman): Made all, ran on well when prsd inside last, drvn out: earlier won on debut at Salisbury (mdn auct, impressively): 11,000 gns Feb foal: eff at 6f, 7f should suit: runs well fresh on firm/fast & a stiff/gall trk: tough, useful & progressive filly, win more races. **95**
*2029 **SANTOLINA 13** [6] J H M Gosden 2-8-8 R Hills 5/2: -12: 2 b f Boundary - Alamosa (Alydar): Settled rear, short of room 2f out, strong run final 1f, closing at fin, just held: nicely bckd: excellent effort & unlucky in running here, will regain wng ways sn & sure to apprec 7f: see 2029. *nk* **94+**
*2137 **ALINGA 8** [1] M L W Bell 2-8-8 M Fenton 33/1: 513: 2 b f King's Theatre - Cheyenne Spirit (Indian Ridge): Front rank, rdn/kept on fnl 1f, not pace of wnr: fine run, imprvd in defeat, acts on firm & gd: see 2137. ½ **92**
1944 **GOODIE TWOSUES 16** [4] R Hannon 2-8-11 Dane O'Neill 12/1: -134: Dwelt, sn rdn, hdwy when swtchd appr final 1f, styd on well, no dngr: shade unlucky in running: acts on firm & gd/soft: useful, see 1944. ½ **94**
2132 **JELBA 8** [8] 2-8-8 O Urbina 33/1: 535: Handy, rdn to impr appr fnl 1f, sn held: apprec 7f next time. 1¼ **87**
2088 **DANCE ON 10** [10] 2-8-11 J Weaver 6/1: 106: Mid-div, rdn & not pace of wnrs appr final 1f: better expected after a decent run in Gr 3 company on most recent start in 2088 (5f). 1¼ **86**
*1954 **SILVER JORDEN 16** [5] 2-8-11 Pat Eddery 15/8 FAV: -117: Prom, rdn/fdd appr final 1f: hvly bckd & much better expected on this hat-trick bid: btr 1954 (gd/fm, auct stks). ¾ **84**
2088 **MIDNIGHT ARROW 10** [7] 2-8-11 W Ryan 12/1: -1508: Rear, nvr a threat: up in trip: see 1586, 1169. *hd* **84**
*2014 **ASH MOON 13** [3] 2-8-11 N Callan 12/1: -119: Keen in tch, rdn/wknd over 1f out: btr 2014, 1538. 1¾ **80**
1846 **DRESS CODE 21** [9] 2-8-11 M Tebbutt 16/1: 3100: Rcd keenly, al bhd, 10th: needs a drop in grade. 1½ **77**
10 ran Time 1m 13.14 (2.14) (Global Racing Club) D J S Cosgrove Newmarket.

2345 **4.30 PAPWORTH TRUST CLAIMER 3YO (E) 1m str Firm 18 -45 Slow**
£3601 £1108 £554 £277

2053 **PINHEIROS DREAM 12** [6] B J Meehan 3-8-11 (bl) Pat Eddery 9/4 FAV: 505031: 3 ch f Grand Lodge - Nikki's Groom (Shy Groom): Mid-div, rcd keenly, led after 4f, rdn clr appr final 2f, styd on well for press: nicely bckd, first win: plcd once in '99 (auct mdn, rtd 81 at best, possibly flattered): eff at 1m/10f on firm/fast grnd: eff in blnks & on a stiff/gall trk: apprec drop to clmrs, yet another fine Pat Eddery ride. **64**
4278} **EMALI 267** [1] C E Brittain 3-8-12 N Esler (6) 9/1: 06-2: 3 b g Emarati - Princess Poquito (Hard Fought): Set stdy pace, hdd 4f out, hard rdn & styd on fnl 2f but wnr had flown: reapp: unplcd in 2 mdns in '99 (rtd 69): stays 1m on firm grnd: encouraging reapp. 2 **62**
1955 **WINTZIG 16** [4] M L W Bell 3-8-9 M Fenton 10/3: 052503: 3 b f Piccolo - Wrangbrook (Shirley Heights): Chsd ldrs, rdn/no extra final 2f: nicely bckd tho' op 5/2: acts on firm & gd/soft: see 1495, 924. ¾ **57**
2080 **CLAUDIUS TERTIUS 10** [8] M A Jarvis 3-8-8 M Tebbutt 12/1: -00034: Settled rear, rdn & styd on appr final 1f, nvr nrr: drop in trip, treat rating with caution (offic only 42): see 2080. *hd* **56$**
1775 **DISTINCTLY EAST 24** [5] 3-9-2 (VIS) R Hills 6/1: 0-0405: Keen in tch, rdn/btn appr final 1f: visor. ½ **63**
1955 **SUPER KIM 16** [2] 3-7-13 A Polli (3) 20/1: 00-006: Dsptd lead, rdn/lost tch final 2f: mod prev form. 2 **42**
2134 **HTTP FLYER 8** [3] 3-8-7 L Newton 20/1: 07: Rear, lost tch halfway, late gains for press, no dngr. ½ **49$**
2093 **WISHFUL THINKER 10** [9] 3-8-8 Kim Tinkler 8/1: -00038: Nvr a factor: see 2093. ½ **49**
-- **GAYE CHARM** [7] 3-8-8 G Faulkner (3) 25/1: 9: Dwelt, al bhd on debut: with P S McEntee. ¾ **47**
9 ran Time 1m 42.25 (5.05) (The Chantilly Partnership) B J Meehan Upper Lambourn, Berks.

2346 **5.05 PAPWORTH ELECTRONICS MDN 2YO (D) 7f str Firm 18 -29 Slow**
£5148 £1584 £792 £396

1943 **KINGS IRONBRIDGE 16** [4] R Hannon 2-9-0 Dane O'Neill 1/1 FAV: -21: 2 b c King's Theatre - Dream Chaser (Record Token): Made all, rdn & qcknd up well inside last, rdn out: nicely bckd: Mar foal, half-brother to sprint & 1m wnrs, dam a 6f scorer: eff at 6f, apprec step up to 7f & 1m will suit: acts on fast: runs well fresh & likes forcing the pace on a stiff/gall trk: useful performance here, rate more highly & win again. **100+**
-- **SIXTY SECONDS** [3] J H M Gosden 2-9-0 J Weaver 11/4: 2: 2 b c Definite Article - Damemill (Damehill): In tch, rdn & ran on well final 1f, no impress on wnr: nicely bckd, clr rem: IR 50,000 gns Feb foal, dam an Irish 7f scorer: eff over a stiff/gall 7f on firm grnd: v promising debut, go one better sn. 2 **94**
-- **GRYFFINDOR** [7] B J Meehan 2-9-0 M Tebbutt 25/1: 3: 2 b c Marju - Hard Task (Formidable): Waited with, dropped rear over 3f out, strong run for press fnl 1f, no dngr: op 14/1 on debut: 32,000 gns Feb foal, dam 12f wnr: stoutly bred: fine debut, will apprec a step up to 1m & can win a race. 2½ **89**
1774 **DUSTY CARPET 24** [1] C A Dwyer 2-9-0 G Faulkner (3) 50/1: 64: Chsd ldrs, rdn/outpcd over 1f out: up in trip, possibly stays a stiff/gall 7f: see 1774. 1 **87**
2132 **NOBLE DOBLE 8** [8] 2-9-0 M Fenton 12/1: 45: Handy, rdn/no extra appr final 1f: see 2132. *shd* **87**
-- **VICIOUS KNIGHT** [9] 2-9-0 J P Spencer 16/1: 6: Cl-up, rdn/held fnl 2f: 160,000gns Night Shift colt, brother to a v useful 10f/2m scorer, half-brother to sev other wnrs: apprec 1m+ in time, with L Cumani. 1 **85**
-- **ASH HAB** [6] 2-9-0 R Hills 15/2: 7: Ran green in rear, hung left/no impress fnl 2f: op 6/1: Apr foal, half-brother to a number of wnrs, incl Derby wnr Erhaab: dam French 10f scorer: can improve, apprec 1m+. 2½ **81**
-- **SMYSLOV** [5] 2-9-0 Pat Eddery 8/1: 8: Waited with, effort 2f out, sn held: 170,000 gns Rainbow Quest colt who is bred to need mid-dists next term: with J L Dunlop. ½ **80**
984 **WALDOR 72** [2] 2-9-0 O Urbina 50/1: 09: Keen/rear, nvr dngrs: 10 wk abs. 1½ **77**
9 ran Time 1m 27.2 (3.3) (T A Johnsey) R Hannon East Everleigh, Wilts.

2347 **5.35 BOLLINGER AMAT HCAP 3YO+ 0-70 (E) 7f str Firm 18 -35 Slow** **[40]**
£3737 £1150 £575 £287 3 yo rec 8 lb

1501 **QUALITAIR PRIDE 36** [6] C A Dwyer 8-9-10 (36)(13oh) Mr M D'Arcy (7) 50/1: 000/01: 8 b m Siberian Express - Qualitairess (Kampala): Chsd ldrs, rdn to lead appr final 1f, styd on well, drvn out for a shock win: tchd 100/1, big drop in trip: recently well btn over hdles & on sole prev Flat start this term: 3 yr abs prev, '97 wnr at Southwell (amat h'cap, rtd 40a, J Bottomley), plater over hdles (rtd 76h): eff at 12f, suited by this drop to 7f: acts on firm, gd/soft & likes to race up with/force the pace: remarkable effort here from 13lbs o/h. **39**

NEWMARKET (July) SATURDAY JULY 1ST Righthand, Stiff, Galloping Track.

1942 **PADHAMS GREEN** 16 [9] B W Hills 4-11-9 (63) Mr C B Hills (3) 7/1: 00-362: 4 b g Aragon - Double ½ 65
Dutch (Nicholas Bill): Front rank, chall appr final 1f, kept on, held cl-home: gd run, will apprec a return to 1m.
1364 **SYLVA LEGEND** 43 [2] C E Brittain 4-12-0 (68)(tvi) HE Sheikh Rashid Al Maktoum (7) 14/1: -56033: 4 b g 1 68
Lear Fan - Likeashot (Gun Shot): Chsd ldrs, slightly outpcd over 3f out, styd on for press despite hanging
right final 1f: clr rem: drop in trip: 6 wk abs & a gd run under top weight: see 1364, 353.
*2122 **IMBACKAGAIN** 9 [12] N P Littmoden 5-10-8 (48) Mr Nicky Tinkler (5) 10/1: 020214: Chsd ldrs, 2½ 43
rdn/onepcd final 1f: nicely bckd: see 2122 (AW appr sell h'cap).
*2124 **MY BROTHER** 8 [5] 6-10-0 (40) Mr Ray Barrett (5) 10/1: 000-15: Dwelt, hdwy from rear final 2f, nrst fin. 1 33
1933 **TWOFORTEN** 8 [11] 5-10-0 (40)(vis) Mr R Lucey Butler (7) 33/1: 600036: Rear, effort when short of ¾ 31
room over 1f out, styd on, no threat: prev with M Madgwick, now with P Butler, flattered 1933 (10f sell).
2027 **DARYABAD** 13 [7] 8-10-7 (47)(bl) Mr K Santana (5) 9/2 FAV: 116-07: Prom, hdwy to lead over 2f 2 34
out, swerved right & hdd over 1f out, sn held: nicely bckd: see 28.
2124 **HALF TONE** 8 [19] 8-10-1 (41)(bl) Mr J J Best (4) 16/1: 053038: Nvr better than mid-div: best at 5/6f. shd 28
*1930 **NERONIAN** 16 [14] 6-9-10 (36)(1oh) Mr S Rees (7) 12/1: 050019: Nvr a factor: btr 1930. shd 22
2054 **BREVITY** 12 [18] 5-11-3 (57)(t) Mr S Walker (5) 14/1: 60-000: Rear, eff over 3f out, sn no extra, 10th. 1 41
*571 **APOLLO RED** 129 [10] 11-10-12 (52) Mr R L Moore (5) 11/2: 126110: Led, hdd 3f out, grad wknd, ¾ 34
fin 11th: shade disapp on hat-trick bid after a 4 mth abs: btr 571 (clmr, equitrack).
1969 **ERUPT** 15 [17] 7-11-5 (59) Mr T Best (5) 12/1: 211300: Trkd ldrs, lost tch final 2f, fin 12th. hd 41
1590 **MAGIC POWERS** 31 [15] 5-11-2 (56) Mr L Jefford (5) 1: 3/0-00: Al bhd, 15th: nicely bckd: see 1590. 0
-- **Zaola** [1] 4-11-13 (67) Mr J A Nolan (2) 14/1:
126} **Toujours Riviera** 572 [3] 10-11-11 (65) Mr A Page (4) 33/1:
929 **Novelty** 77 [4] 5-9-10 (36)(11oh) Mr A Quinn (5) 50/1:
1930 **Fox Star** 16 [13] 3-9-10 (44)(bl) (1oh) Mr H Poulton (7) 16/1:
1790 **Marching Orders** 23 [16] 4-12-0 (68)(VIS) Mr B Wharfe (7) 33/1:
1930 **Landican Lane** 16 [8] 4-9-10 (10oh) Mr T Radford (7) 50/1:
19 ran   Time 1m 27.64 (3.74)   (D Farrow)   C A Dwyer Newmarket.

DONCASTER SUNDAY JULY 2ND Lefthand, Flat, Galloping Track

Official Going GOOD. Stalls: Str Course - Stands Side, Round Course - Inside (Except 1m - Outside)

2348 2.30 SPRINT RATED HCAP 3YO+ 0-100 (B)   5f   Good/Firm 31 +10 Fast   [103]
£10764 £3312 £1656 £828   3 yo rec 5 lb Raced centre - stands side

1980 **ELLENS LAD** 1 [1] W J Musson 6-9-7 (96) L Newton 10/1: 501501: 6 b g Polish Patriot - Lady Ellen 102
(Horage) Led/dsptd lead, drvn ahead ins last, held on well: fast time, op 8/1: earlier scored at York (h'cap):
'99 wnr at Newbury, Haydock & Newmarket (h'caps, rtd 95): '98 Newmarket wnr (h'cap, rtd 86, E Alston): stays 6f,
suited by 5f: acts on firm, soft & any trk, likes a stiff one, esp Newmarket: best without blnks: gd weight carrier.
1687 **CRYHAVOC** 29 [14] D Nicholls 6-8-10 (85) D Holland 7/1: 303202: 6 b g Polar Falcon - Sarabah nk 90
(Ela Mana Mou) In tch, briefly outpcd 2f out, drvn & styd on well ins last, post came too soon: win soon: see 716.
1849 **SINGSONG** 22 [13] A Berry 3-8-9 (89) J Carroll 10/1: 0-4303: 3 b g Paris House - Miss Whittingham ½ 92
(Fayruz) Al handy & ev ch over 1f out, kept on well for press: see 1047.
2310 **IVORYS JOY** 2 [3] K T Ivory 5-8-11 (86) D O'Donohoe 10/1: 031604: Trkd ldrs, rdn/prog to chall ins nk 89
last, just held nr fin: op 12/1, quick reapp: see 1650.
1980 **LAGO DI VARANO** 16 [7] 8-8-7 (82)(bl)(1oh) Dean McKeown 16/1: 531505: Cl-up, ch 2f out, onepace. ¾ 82
2151 **ALEGRIA** 9 [2] 4-9-1 (90)(bl) J Tate 10/1: 0-0106: Mid-div, rdn & kept on fnl 1f, not pace to chall. nk 89
2334 **JUWWI** 1 [6] 6-9-6 (95) P Fitzsimons (5) 11/1: 505007: Dwelt/rear, mod late gains: unplcd yesterday. ½ 92
2247 **ZIGGYS DANCER** 4 [12] 9-8-7 (82)(5oh) T E Durcan 3/1: 404008: Bhd ldrs, nvr on terms: qck reapp. ½ 77
+2310 **HENRY HALL** 2 [15] 4-9-1 (90)(3ex) Kim Tinkler 100/30 FAV: 003119: Chsd ldrs, held 2f out: hvly nk 84
bckd under a 3lb pen: quick reapp: see 2310.
2151 **SUNLEY SENSE** 9 [9] 4-8-10 (85) Dane O'Neill 10/1: 002200: Chsd ldrs, fdd 1f out: 10th: op 9/1. ¾ 77
2003 **JEMIMA** 15 [8] 3-9-5 (99) K Darley 16/1: 5-0000: Cl-up 3f: 11th: see 953. 1¾ 86
2310 **NIGHT FLIGHT** 2 [11] 6-8-13 (88) A Culhane 12/1: 006000: Trkd ldrs, drvn 2f out: 12th: qck reapp. hd 75
2158 **Ocker** 8 [4] 6-8-10 (85)(BL) R Fitzpatrick (3) 16/1: 2168 **Dorchester** 8 [10] 3-8-9 (89) S Sanders 14/1:
14 ran   Time 59.25 (1.05)   (Mrs Rita Brown)   W J Musson Newmarket, Suffolk

2349 3.00 MAIL ON SUNDAY HCAP 3YO+ 0-80 (D)   1m rnd Good/Firm 31 -10 Slow   [80]
£7767 £2390 £1195 £597   3 yo rec 9 lb

2242 **STYLE DANCER** 8 [8] R M Whitaker 6-8-8 (60)(vis) D Holland 14/1: 540401: 6 b g Dancing Dissident - 71
Showing Style (Pas de Seul) Towards rear, stdy prog fnl 3f, rdn to lead ins last, styd on well: visor reapp: '99
Haydock wnr (h'cap, rtd 68 at best): '98 York wnr (h'cap, rtd 74): eff at 7f/1m, acts on firm, gd/soft & fibresand:
handles any trk, likes a gall one: nicely h'capped, well suited by the return of headgear today.
2126 **HARMONY HALL** 9 [1] J M Bradley 6-8-7 (59) P Fitzsimons (5) 9/1: 40-442: 6 ch g Music Boy - 1½ 65
Fleeting Affair (Hotfoot) Trkd ldrs travelling well, smooth prog to lead over 1f out, rdn/hdd ins last, not pace
of wnr: bckd, rest well covered: can find compensation in similar: see 1973.
2242 **HAKEEM** 4 [2] M Brittain 5-8-10 (62) T Williams 16/1: -02203: 5 ch g Kefaah - Masarrah (Formidable) 3 62
Chsd ldrs, prog/led 2f out, hdd over 1f out, kept on: op 14/1, qck reapp: back to form, deserves a race: see 1598.
2051 **PATSY STONE** 13 [4] M Kettle 4-9-3 (69) S Sanders 11/1: 501144: Mid-div, prog/rdn & chsd ldrs 1¾ 66
2f out, onepace/held ins last: see 1794 (7f).
2018 **KALA SUNRISE** 14 [19] 7-9-8 (74) K Darley 10/1: -00335: Held up, prog 3f out & drvn/prsd ldrs ¾ 70
over 1f out, sn held: gd run from a tricky high draw: nicely h'capped but not easy to win with: see 875.
2051 **COLONEL NORTH** 13 [12] 4-8-13 (65) M Henry 25/1: -00066: Chsd ldrs, rdn fnl 3f, kept on onepace. 1 59
1840 **OUT OF SIGHT** 22 [5] 6-8-3 (55) K Dalgleish (7) 10/1: 030007: Prom, eff fnl 3f, kept on onepace. nk 48
2018 **WEETMANS WEIGH** 14 [15] 7-9-4 (70) N Callan 16/1: 004648: Rear, rdn/late gains, no threat: see 49. shd 63
2062 **FALLS OMONESS** 12 [14] 6-7-11 (49) Dale Gibson 8/1: -20029: Rear, mod prog fnl 3f: op 7/1. ½ 41
1836 **ROLLER** 22 [17] 4-9-10 (76) T G McLaughlin 7/1: 122040: Held up, eff 3f out, sn held: 10th: op 6/1. ½ 67
2257 **VIOLET** 4 [6] 4-7-10 (48)(BL) A Mackay 50/1: 0-0060: Led/sn clr, hdd 2f out, wknd qckly: 11th. shd 39
2138 **TOM DOUGAL** 9 [3] 5-9-8 (74) J Tate 12/1: 0-0050: Towards rear, nvr a factor: 12th: see 1490. ½ 64
2257 **WELODY** 4 [9] 4-8-12 (64)(vis) Dane O'Neill 25/1: 210040: Rear, mod prog: 13th: quick reapp. 2½ 49
*2283 **BOWCLIFFE** 3 [20] 9-8-11 (63)(6ex) T E Durcan 11/2 FAV: 602210: Rear, eff 2f out, no prog: 15th: 0

747

DONCASTER   SUNDAY JULY 2ND   Lefthand, Flat, Galloping Track

nicely bckd under a 6lb pen, quick reapp: tricky high draw here, prob best forgotten: see 2283.
2242 **Acid Test** 4 [10] 5-8-13 (65) R Fitzpatrick (3) 33/1:   2027 **Derryquin** 14 [18] 5-8-8 (60) D O'Donohoe 14/1:
1872 **Sergeant York** 20 [13] 4-10-0 (80) G Faulkner (3) 25/1:2221 **Mehmaas** 5 [16] 4-8-10 (62) Dean McKeown 20/1:
2130 **Badrinath** 9 [11] 6-7-13 (51) R Ffrench 16/1:   1926 **Arterxerxes** 18 [7] 7-9-9 (75) A Daly 16/1:
20 ran   Time 1m 39.38 (3.28)   (Mrs C A Hodgetts)   R M Whitaker Scarcroft, W Yorks

---

2350

3.35 L.J. MONKS HCAP 3YO+ 0-105 (B)   1m2f60y   Good/Firm 31 -25 Slow   [98]
£10481   £3225   £1612   £806   3 yo rec 11lb

1984 **MCGILLYCUDDY REEKS** 16 [1] Don Enrico Incisa 9-8-1 (71) Kim Tinkler 9/2: 325231: 9 b m Kefaah -   73
Kilvaret (Furry Glen) Trkd ldrs, outpcd 3f out, chsd clr ldr 2f out, rdn & styd on well to overhaul eased down wnr
nr fin: '99 wnr at Beverley & here at Doncaster (h'caps, rtd 76): '98 wnr at Newcastle & Thirsk (h'caps, rtd 77):
eff at 1m, suited by 10/12f on firm & soft, any trk, likes Doncaster: eff with/without a t-strap: tough/genuine mare,
deserved to find a race but was a most fortunate wnr today.
2003 **HAPPY DIAMOND** 15 [3] M Johnston 3-8-0 (81) R Ffrench 8/1: 21-302: 3 b c Diesis - Urus (Kris S)   ½ 87+
Cl-up, rdn & went on 3f out, clr & in command 2f out, 5L ahd when hvly eased well ins last & caught nr line: op 6/1:
joc given 14 day ban for misjudged ride: apprec this step up to 10f: can be rtd a 5L+ wnr here, most unfortunate.
2085 **FORZA FIGLIO** 11 [5] M Kettle 7-8-5 (75) R Mullen 8/1: 40/033: 7 b g Warning - Wish You Well   5   70
(Sadler's Wells) Led, rdn/hdd 3f out, sn outpcd by front pair: op 6/1: see 1729.
*1790 **MANTUSIS** 24 [6] P W Harris 5-9-5 (89) K Darley 13/8 FAV: 1-3214: Held up rear, in tch, eff 3f out,   2   81
sn held: well bckd: ahd of this wnr in 1790 (gd/soft).
1170 **EX GRATIA** 57 [4] 4-9-4 (88) A Culhane 7/2: 214-05: Dwelt, rear/in tch, eff 3f out, no impression: abs.   1   79
1561 **J R STEVENSON** 34 [2] 4-9-11 (95) Alex Greaves 8/1: 0-0006: Chsd ldrs till 2f out: see 1770.   1¼ 84
6 ran   Time 2m 12.2 (5.8)   (Don Enrico Incisa)   Don Enrico Incisa Coverham, N.Yorks.

2351

4.15 CARBON LINK COND STKS 3YO+ (C)   1m2f60y   Good/Firm 31 -02 Slow
£6955   £2140   £1070   £535   3 yo rec 11lb

2004 **VINTAGE PREMIUM** 15 [1] R A Fahey 3-8-5 R Winston 4/1: 140221: 3 b c Forzando - Julia Domna   101
(Dominion) Prom, went on 2f out, pshd clr, rdly: nicely bckd: earlier won at Newbury (rtd h'cap): juv scorer at
Beverley (mdn auct, rtd 89): eff at 1m/10.3f: acts on firm & soft grnd, gall trks: useful, progressive colt.
*1965 **BLUE GOLD** 16 [5] R Hannon 3-8-8 Dane O'Neill 4/1: -42012: 3 b c Rainbow Quest - Relatively Special   3½ 98
(Alzao) Well plcd & ev ch till outpcd by wnr appr fnl 1f: prob ran to best, see 1965 (h'cap).
*1808 **TALAASH** 23 [4] M R Channon 3-8-8 S Drowne 5/2 FAV: 13: 3 b c Darshaan - Royal Ballet (Sadler's   ½ 97
Wells) Waited with, closed appr fnl 2f & ch till onepace bef dist: well bckd, clr rem: only 2nd ever start: eff
at 10f, return to 12f will suit: acts on gd/soft grnd: useful.
2178 **ICE** 7 [6] M Johnston 4-9-2 (vis) D Holland 3/1: 516144: Slow away, prom, led 3f out till 2f out,   5   87
no extra: nicely bckd, qck reapp: return to 1m/9f likely to suit, see 2001.
1847 **YAKAREEM** 22 [3] 4-9-2 J Tate 10/1: 000-45: Led till 3f out, fdd: longer trip, flattered 1847.   9   75
-- **ELA ARISTOKRATI** [2] 8-9-2 O Urbina 14/1: 5436/6: Handy till 3f out: over 2 yr Flat abs, 14 wk jmps   nk 74
abs (well btn sole start): '97 rnr-up for M Tompkins (Gr 3, rtd 112): '96 wnr at Epsom (h'cap, Gr 3 plcd, rtd 113,
L Cumani): eff at 10/12f on firm & gd grnd, any trk, likes Epsom: gd weight carrier but prob not the force of old.
6 ran   Time 2m 09.92 (3.52)   (J C Parsons)   R A Fahey Butterwick, N.Yorks.

2352

4.50 FAMILY DAY NOV STKS 2YO (D)   6f   Good/Firm 31 -13 Slow
£3762   £1075   £537

*2077 **BRAVADO** 11 [1] Sir Mark Prescott 2-9-5 S Sanders 5/6 FAV: 11: 2 b c Zafonic - Brave Revival   102
(Dancing Brave) Made all, shkn up, v cmftbly: hvly bckd: unbtn, earlier won debut at W'hampton (mdn): half-
brother to a 7f juv wnr, dam a miler: eff at 6f, 7f is going to suit: acts on fast grnd & fibresand, sharp or gall
trks: runs well fresh, from the front: looks useful, earned a step up in grade.
2318 **KACHINA DOLL** 1 [2] M R Channon 2-9-4 A Culhane 4/1: 011052: 2 b f Mujadil - Betelgeuse (Kalaglow)   4   89
Rcd in 3rd in tch, went after wnr appr fnl 1f, no impression: ran yesterday, prob gets 6f, see 1437.
*1995 **NEARLY A FOOL** 15 [3] B A McMahon 2-9-12 K Dalgleish (7) 15/8: 143313: 2 b g Komaite - Greenway   5   82
Lady (Prince Daniel) Prsd wnr till wknd qckly bef fnl 1f: nicely bckd: unsuited by step up in trip?: see 1995.
3 ran   Time 1m 13.43 (2.63)   (Cheveley Park Stud)   Sir Mark Prescott Newmarket.

2353

5.20 SUNDAY RACING MDN 3YO (D)   1m4f   Good/Firm 31 -43 Slow
£4134   £1272   £636   £318

2019 **MOUNTAIN DANCER** 14 [1] M Johnston 3-8-9 D Holland 8/11 FAV: -631: 3 b f Rainbow Quest - Jammaayil   74
(Lomond) Prom, led 3f out, 2½L up 1f out, pushed out, narrowly: hvly bckd, slow time: unrcd juv: apprec
step up to 12f on fast grnd: still green, should improve further.
4556} **FIVE OF WANDS** 246 [2] W Jarvis 3-8-9 D McGaffin (5) 11/2: 0-2: 3 b f Caerleon - Overact (Law Society)   nk 72
Trkd ldrs, eff 3f out, no impress till kept on well ins last, just btn: op 4/1, clr rem: reapp: unplcd for J
Dunlop sole '99 start: half-sister to a 12f wnr: eff at 12f, looks a thoro' stayer: acts on fast grnd.
1725 **MEMPHIS TEENS** 27 [4] J R Jenkins 3-9-0 S Sanders 11/4: 303: 3 b c Rock City - Minteen (Teenoso)   6   68
Held up, chsd ldrs 3f out till ent fnl 2f: nicely bckd: longer trip, see 1293.
2019 **KELBURNE** 14 [3] J M Jefferson 3-9-0 A Culhane 8/1: -544: Set slow pace, hdd 3f out & lost place.   dist 38
4 ran   Time 2m 38.71 (8.91)   (Maktoum Al Maktoum)   M Johnston Middleham, N.Yorks.

Official Going   Str - GOOD; Rnd - GOOD/FIRM. Stalls: Str - Stands Side; Round - Inside, except 1m4f - Outside.

2354

2.10 RON EDE FILLIES MDN 3YO (D)   1m4f   Good/Firm 22   -75 Slow
£4056   £1248   £624   £312 V Slow run race

--	**SOLO PERFORMANCE** [1] J H M Gosden 3-8-11 R Havlin 7/2: 1: 3 b f Sadler's Wells - Royal Heroine (Lypheor) Dwelt, waited with, rdn over 2f out, kept on well fnl 2f to lead ins last, pushed out to hold on: op 9/4 on debut, slow run race: dam high-class miler in the USA: stays a sharp/undul 1m4f on gd/firm: rate higher.		77
4537	**BATHWICK BABE** 248 [7] E J O'Neill 3-8-11 J F Egan 33/1: 00-2: 3 b f Sri Pekan - Olean (Sadler's Wells) Sn bhd, hdwy 3f out, sn outpcd till rallied fnl 1f to take 2nd cl-home: just btn: in '99 unplcd on 2 starts for B Smart: half sister to wnrs over 7f/10f: stays a slowly run 12f, further cld suit: pleasing h'cap qual run.	nk	75
2135	**PRECIOUS POPPY** 9 [2] Sir Michael Stoute 3-8-11 J Reid 5/6 FAV: 43: 3 b f Polish Precedent - Benazir (High Top) Led after 2f at stdy pace till 1m out, chall when sltly hmpd over 3f out, sn led, kept on for press ins last till collared fnl 100y, not btn far: bckd: ran to form of 2135 (12f on fast grnd).	nk	74
1992	**BLOSSOM WHISPERS** 15 [4] C A Cyzer 3-8-11 G Carter 14/1: 064: Led 2f, prom till outpcd over 3f out, late gains: op 20/1: stays 12f, better off in h'caps now.	3	69
1992	**VETORITY** 15 [3] 3-8-11 J Stack 6/1: 35: Handy, btn over 2f out: showed more in 192 (debut, 10f).	6	60
1796	**CELTIC BAY** 24 [5] 3-8-11 R Hills 5/1: 66: Keen, bhd, pulled into lead 1m out, edged left over 3f out, wknd: warm & on toes: showed more on debut in 1796 (gd/soft).	7	50

6 ran   Time 2m 42.41 (11.61)   (R E Sangster)   J H M Gosden Manton, Wilts

2355

2.40 VODAFONE HCAP 3YO+ 0-90 (C)   6f   Good   Inapplicable   [87]
£14267   £4390   £2195   £1097   3 yo rec 6 lb   2 Groups - no advantage

*1925	**BLUE MOUNTAIN** 18 [6] R F Johnson Houghton 3-9-9 (88) R Hills 10/1: -52211: 3 ch c Elmaamul - Glenfinlass (Lomond) Sltly hmpd start, bhd stands side, gd hdwy over 1f out, styd on strongly to get up cl-home, going away: recently scored at Kempton (h'cap): plcd on 2 of 3 juv starts (mdns, rtd 89): eff over 5/7f, well suited by 6f on firm, gd/soft & any trk: useful, progressive & has a turn of foot, a fill h'cap.		95
2054	**GLOWING** 13 [17] J R Fanshawe 5-9-1 (74) D Harrison 12/1: 10-202: 5 ro m Chilibang - Juliet Bravo (Glow) Cl-up centre, overall ldr over 2f out, kept on ins last till collared cl-home: fine run, win a fill h'cap.	½	79
2151	**BON AMI** 9 [5] A Berry 4-9-9 (82) P Bradley (5) 25/1: 400003: 4 b c Paris House - Felin Special (Lyphard's Special) In tch stands side, eff well over 1f out, styd on strongly ins last, not btn far: well h'capped.	hd	86
2151	**ROYAL RESULT** 9 [3] D Nicholls 7-10-0 (87) A Nicholls (3) 9/2 FAV: 000364: Chsd ldrs stands side, kept on for press over 1f out, only btn 1L: bckd tho' op 3/1: another gd run under 10-0: see 2151.	½	89
2124	**MR STYLISH** 9 [22] 4-8-11 (70)(VIS) J F Egan 20/1: 023305: In tch centre, edged left & sltly outpcd 2f out, kept on ins last: jockey received a 1 day careless riding ban: gd run in 1st time visor but a mdn.	½	71
1794	**HALMANERROR** 24 [19] 10-7-12 (57) F Norton 20/1: 533246: Chsd ldrs centre, onepace fnl 2f.	hd	57
+2266	**DANCING MYSTERY** 3 [21] 8-9-7 (80)(7ex) S Carson (5) 11/1: 033517: With ldrs centre, oncpd over 1f out: quick reapp under a pen after 2266 (7f).	hd	79
2266	**CAUDA EQUINA** 3 [10] 6-9-2 (75) Craig Williams 14/1: 560438: Sn bhd, some late gains, no impress.	½	72
*2168	**COMPTON BANKER** 8 [9] 3-9-3 (82) R Hughes 7/1: 5-0519: Chsd ldrs, eff over 1f out, held when hmpd & snatched up cl-home: btr 2168 (5f).	½	78
2054	**IVORY DAWN** 13 [8] 4-9-0 (73) C Carver (3) 14/1: 224030: In tch, carried right over 1f out, btn: 10th.	½	67
*2054	**NINEACRES** 13 [4] 9-8-10 (69)(bl) G Baker (7) 10/1: 210110: Unruly stalls, led after 1f till over 2f out, no extra: 11th: in fine form earlier, see 2054.	½	62
*2192	**FAIRY PRINCE** 6 [1] 7-8-5 (64)(7ex) P M Quinn (3) 16/1: -04510: Handy, wknd fnl 1f: 12th, btr 2192.	hd	56
2054	**LOCH LAIRD** 13 [14] 5-9-3 (76)(VIS) S Whitworth 33/1: -50000: In tch, btn 2f out: 13th, visor.	1¾	64
2261	**CHAMPAGNE RIDER** 4 [15] 4-9-9 (82) W Supple (5) -: In tch, btn 2f out: 14th, quick reapp.	¾	68
2163	**PEPPIATT** 8 [13] 6-8-1 (60) Martin Dwyer 16/1: 340350: Sn bhd, eff when not clr run over 2f out, no impress: 15th, likes soft: see 2163, 1654.	1	43
*2145	**Golden Miracle** 9 [2] 3-9-0 (79) J Reid 11/1: 1520 **Frederick James** 36 [11] 6-8-3 (57)(5ow) N Carlisle 33/1:		
1963	**Sarena Special** 16 [20] 3-8-9 (74)(bl) P Doe 33/1: 1676 **Sarson** 29 [16] 4-9-8 (81) R Smith (5) 20/1:		
2168	**Jailhouse Rocket** 8 [12] 3-9-0 (79) N Pollard 20/1: 1887 **Astrac** 19 [18] 9-8-8 (67) T Ashley 33/1:		
1126	**Mister Tricky** 29 [7] 5-8-8 (67) J Quinn 12/1:		

22 ran   Time 1m 12.85 (2.85)   (Mrs C J Hue Williams)   R F Johnson Houghton Blewbury, Oxon

2356

3.10 MAIL ON SUNDAY HCAP 3YO+ 0-90 (C)   1m rnd   Good/Firm 22   -03 Slow   [90]
£14495   £4460   £2230   £1115   3 yo rec 9 lb

2303	**JUST NICK** 2 [10] W R Muir 6-8-0 (62) P Doe 8/1: -36521: 6 b g Nicholas - Just Never Know (Riverman) Waited with, gd hdwy to lead over 1f out, rdn clr ins last: rnr-up here over 7f 2 days ago: plcd in '99 (rtd 75): missed '98, sole win back in '96 at Folkestone (auct mdn): eff at 7f, suited by 1m on a sharp & undul trk, handles any: best on firm & hvy grnd: in fine form.		71
1989	**VOLONTIERS** 15 [8] P W Harris 5-9-6 (82) M Fenton 14/1: 041602: 5 b g Common Grounds - Senlis (Sensitive Prince) Hld up, eff on outer over 2f out, kept on to chase wnr ins last, no impress: op 10/1, see 1160.	2½	85
2303	**ADOBE** 2 [11] W M Brisbourne 5-8-4 (66) G Baker (7) 6/1: 111133: 5 b g Green Desert - Shamshir (Kris) Handy, eff 2f out, kept on same pace for press: op 8/1, quick reapp, prob best at 1m: see 2303, 2126.	shd	69
2304	**PEARTREE HOUSE** 2 [5] D Nicholls 6-9-12 (88) F Norton 3/1 FAV: 031244: Keen in tch, eff & short of room when edged left over 2f out, onepace ins last: well bckd, jockey rec 3-day irresponsible riding ban.	½	90
1729	**TARAWAN** 27 [3] 4-9-3 (79) S Whitworth 25/1: -00005: Bhd, eff 2f out, kept on same pace, saddle slipped cl-home: back to form & shld win similar off this mark: see 580.	1½	78
2126	**NAVIASKY** 9 [6] 5-9-3 (79) Martin Dwyer 7/1: 040466: Bhd, eff & switched left well over 1f out, onepace.	½	77
*1598	**INDIAN PLUME** 32 [15] 4-9-0 (82) W Supple 10/1: 010017: Set pace till 1m out, no extra: see 1598.	1	78
2185	**MUTABASSIR** 7 [12] 6-7-13 (60)(1ow) J Quinn 7/1: -65438: Sn in tch, rdn & btn over 1f out: btr 2185.	1¾	52
*1829	**PRINCE SLAYER** 23 [7] 4-9-6 (82) L Newman (3) 8/1: -02019: Chsd ldrs, eff & short of room over 2f out, sn wknd: op 6/1: sole win in 1829 (gd/soft).	6	64
1829	**CHINA RED** 23 [14] 6-9-8 (84) R Hills 8/1: 00-000: Cl-up, wknd well over 1f out: 10th, see 1829.	2½	61
2185	**SILKEN DALLIANCE** 7 [4] 4-9-0 (76)(bl) J F Egan 10/1: 000200: In tch, wkng when hmpd over 2f out: 11th.	7	45
1810	**COMPTON ARROW** 23 [5] 4-9-8 (84)(t) R Hughes 20/1: 0-0000: Keen bhd, brief eff over 2f out, sn hmpd & no impress: 12th: see 1810 (blnks, 1450).	3	44
2304	**SUPER MONARCH** 2 [2] 6-8-1 (63) G Bardwell 25/1: -00400: In tch, eff 3f out, sn btn: 13th, qk reapp.	½	22

13 ran   Time 1m 39.43 (2.03)   (D G Clarke)   W R Muir Lambourn, Berks

GOODWOOD

SUNDAY JULY 2ND   Righthand, Sharpish, Undulating Track

2357   **3.45 CAPITAL GOLD MDN 2YO (D)**   6f   **Good**   Inapplicable
£4407   £1356   £678   £339

1957 **EUROLINK SUNDANCE** 16 [8] J L Dunlop 2-8-9 G Carter 8/1: 01: 2 ch f Night Shift - Eurolink   **79**
Mischief (Be My Chief) Prom, styd on to lead appr fnl 1f, kept on well, shade cosily: op 6/1: Mar foal,
dam useful 6/7f juv scorer: eff at 6f on gd grnd: type to rate higher & win again.
-2083 **DOUBLE BREW** 11 [7] R Hannon 2-9-0 P Eddery (5) 3/1 FAV: -3422: 2 ch c Primo Dominie - Boozy   ¾ **81**
(Absalom) Led 1f, cl-up & ev ch 2f out, kept on ins last, just held: shld find a minor trk mdn: see 2083.
-- **SILKEN WINGS** [2] I A Balding 2-8-9 J F Egan 8/1: 3: 2 b f Brief Truce - Winged Victory (Dancing   1½ **72+**
Brave) Bhd, eff over 1f out, kept on nicely ins last under a kind ride on debut: op 6/1: May foal, cost 11,000
gns: full sister to a 7f juv wnr: dam 7f wnr: eff at 6f, 7f suit: sure to improve for this & win races.
-- **TUSCAN** [10] M R Channon 2-8-9 Craig Williams 11/2: 4: Led after 1f till over 1f out, no extra: 2½ **65**
Apr foal, cost 17,000 gns: half sister to a smart sprinter: dam 5/6f juv wnr: bred for speed & showed some here.
-- **WESTERN FLAME** [9] 2-8-9 J Reid 10/1: 5: Bhd, kept on nicely over 1f out, kind ride: debut: May   hd **64**
foal, cost 18,000 gns: half sister to a 12f wnr: looks sure to relish a step up to 7f+, plenty to like about this.
1612 **HARD TO CATCH** 32 [5] 2-9-0 C Carver (3) 12/1: -5346: In tch, eff to chall 2f out, no extra fnl 1f.   1¾ **65**
-- **PHARMACYS PET** [1] 2-8-9 A Nicholls (3) 20/1: 5: Bhd, rdn & no impress well over 1f out on   ½ **59**
debut: Mar 1st foal, cost 4,000 gns: dam 6/7f wnr: speedily bred.
-- **RYANS GOLD** [12] 2-9-0 R Hughes 7/2: 8: Sn handy, wknd fnl 1f: debut: Apr foal, cost 21,000   1¼ **60**
gns: Distant View colt: with Mrs A Perratt.
-- **BRENDAS DELIGHT** [6] 2-8-9 D Sweeney 33/1: 9: Slowly away & al bhd on debut: Apr foal,   3 **47**
cheaply bought: half sister to 2 wnrs: dam 1m/10f scorer: bred to need 7f+.
-- **DONNA DOUGHNUT** [3] 2-8-9 G Baker (7) 33/1: 0: In tch, wknd over 2f out: 10th on debut: 3 **39**
Mar 1st foal, dam 6/7f wnr: speedily bred, with M Usher.
1673 **Father Seamus** 29 [14] 2-9-0 M Fenton 33/1:   2083 **Captain Gibson** 11 [11] 2-9-0 (VIS) J Quinn 33/1:
-- **Cearnach** [13] 2-9-0 D R McCabe 12/1:
13 ran   Time 1m 14.12 (4.12)   (Eurolink Group Plc)   J L Dunlop Arundel, W Sussex

---

2358   **4.20 TRIUMVIATE RTD HCAP 3YO 0-95 (C)**   1m2f   **Good/Firm 22   +03 Fast**   **[99]**
£9262   £3513   £1756   £798

2117 **NOOSHMAN** 10 [12] Sir Michael Stoute 3-9-0 (85) L Newman (3) 3/1: 2-1501: 3 ch g Woodman - Knoosh   **99**
(Storm Bird) In tch, hdwy to lead 2f out, pushed clr fnl 1f, readily: gd time: ealier scored at Thirsk (reapp,
h'cap): plcd twice in '99 (rtd 85, mdn): eff at 7f, clearly relished this step up to 10f & acts on gd/firm, hvy
& on any trk: has run well fresh: useful, unexposed at this trip & shld go in again.
*1885 **STARLYTE GIRL** 19 [10] R Hannon 3-8-13 (84) J Reid 6/1: 0-6012: 3 b f Fairy King - Blushing   7 **87**
Storm (Blushing Groom) Led till 3f out, kept on same pace for press: in gd form: see 1885.
2300 **INVER GOLD** 2 [6] A G Newcombe 3-8-4 (75)(1oh) S Whitworth 20/1: 130043: 3 ch c Arazi - Mary   ½ **77**
Martin (Be My Guest) Bhd, rdn over 2f out, kept on over 1f out, nrst fin: stays 10f on gd/firm, gd/soft & AWs.
2117 **KINGDOM OF GOLD** 10 [5] Sir Mark Prescott 3-8-10 (81) N Pollard 3/1: 416-04: Chsd ldrs, kept on   hd **82**
same pace fnl 2f: well bckd: stays 10f: see 2117.
1452 **SCOTTISH SPICE** 40 [1] 3-8-12 (83) Martin Dwyer 16/1: 1-6005: Sn bhd, eff & hung right over   ¾ **83**
1f out, onepace: 6 wk abs: see 912.
2117 **TUMBLEWEED TOR** [7] 3-9-7 (92) D R McCabe 12/1: -03106: Handy, led 3f out, hdd & no extra well   hd **91**
over 1f out: top weight, twice below 1366 (1m, gd/soft, made all).
2004 **MAKASSEB** 15 [8] 3-8-8 (79) Craig Williams 16/1: 5-0067: Bhd, rdn 2f out, onepace: see 1366.   hd **78**
*1480 **MUSALLY** 38 [11] 3-9-0 (85) R Hills 5/2 FAV: 418: In tch, btn over 2f out: well bckd: much better   11 **70**
expected tho' this was much faster grnd than 1480 (med act mdn, gd/soft).
1990 **MARAH** 15 [9] 3-9-2 (87)(BL) W Supple 14/1: 06-669: Chsd ldr, wknd 3f out: no improvement in blnks.   17 **50**
*1669 **LET ALONE** 84 [4] 3-8-10 (81) F Norton 10/1: 010: Bhd, btn well over 3f out: not enjoy gd/firm?   1¼ **42**
10 ran   Time 2m 06.15 (1.95)   (Maktoum Al Maktoum)   Sir Michael Stoute Newmarket

---

2359   **4.55 LISTED ON THE HOUSE STKS 3YO+ (A)**   1m rnd   **Good/Firm 22   -16 Slow**
£24687   £6963   3 yo rec 9 lb

2064 **SWALLOW FLIGHT** 12 [1] G Wragg 4-9-5 R Hughes 1/3 FAV: -21131: 4 b c Bluebird - Mirage (Red Sunset)   **119**
Made virtually all, rdn 2f out, 2½L eased ins last: val 3L: earlier scored at Windsor
(List) & Sandown (rtd h'cap), also btn under 1L in Gr 2 Queen Anne: '99 wnr at York (h'cap) & Doncaster (stks,
rtd 106): v eff at 1m, stays 10f: acts on firm & soft, any trk: best up with/forcing the pace & can carry big
weights: tough & high-class now, shld win a Gr race.
1847 **DUCK ROW** 22 [2] J A R Toller 5-9-2 S Whitworth 9/4: 60-122: 5 ch g Diesis - Sunny Moment (Roberto)   4 **109**
With wnr, rdn 3f out, switched right over 1f out, 2½L down when eased well ins last: caught a smart sort.
2 ran   Time 1m 40.42 (3.02)   (Mollers Racing)   G Wragg Newmarket

---

PONTEFRACT

MONDAY JULY 3RD   Lefthand, Undulating Track, Stiff Uphill Finish

Official Going   GOOD (GOOD TO SOFT places) Stalls: Inside.

2360   **2.15 TATTS AUCT MDN DIV I 2YO (E)**   5f rnd   **Good 53   -07 Slow**
£2925   £900   £450   £225

-- **SAMADILLA** [8] T D Easterby 2-8-0 P Fessey 20/1: 1: 2 b f Mujadil - Samnaun (Stop The Music)   **80**
Chsd ldrs, rdn/led ins last, styd on well, pushed out cl-home: op 14/1: Mar foal, cost 5,500gns: half-sister to a
10f 3yo wnr: dam uncrd: eff at 5f, 6f will suit: acts on gd & a stiff/undul trk: runs well fresh: scopey, improve.
2214 **LAI SEE** 6 [3] A P Jarvis 2-8-3 D Sweeney 6/4 FAV: 00022: 2 b c Tagula - Sevens Are Wild (Petorius)   1¼ **78**
Led, rdn/hdd well ins last & no extra: hvly bckd: eff at 5f on fast & gd: shld win a race: see 2214.
-- **MR PIANO MAN** [9] J L Eyre 2-8-7 J F Egan 20/1: 3: 2 gr g Paris House - Winter March (Ballad   2½ **75+**
Rock) Rdn chasing ldrs early, styd on fnl 2f, not pace of front pair: fit: Paris House gelding, Mar foal, cost
IR 12,000gns: dam a 6f juv Irish wnr: eff at 5f, 6f shld suit: acts on gd: improve plenty & win a race.

--   **PAID UP** [5] M W Easterby 2-8-3 G Parkin 25/1: 4: Dwelt, sn mid-div, rdn/outpcd over 2f out, kept   nk   70
on ins last, no threat: ndd this: Mind Games gelding, May foal: half-brother to 3 juv wnrs, dam a wnr abroad.
2100 **FLYING ROMANCE** 12 [2] 2-7-12 Kimberley Hart 20/1: -05: Towards rear, styd on fnl 2f under   2   60
hands-and-heels riding, no threat: 6f+ & h'cap company likely to suit in time: can improve: see 2100.
--   **WONDERGREEN** [10] 2-8-3 W Supple 14/1: 6: Rdn/towards rear, mod late gains: op 12/1, much   1½   61
sharper for this: stablemate of wnr: Wolfhound colt, May foal, cost 1,000gns: half-brother to a juv 1m wnr,
dam 6f/1m juv wnr: strong colt, looks sure to apprec further
1698 **TOMTHEVIC** 29 [7] 2-8-6(1ow) S Sanders 4/1: 47: Cl-up, wknd fnl 1f: lkd well, op 5/1: see 1698.   1   62
1418 **FRENCH BRAMBLE** 42 [6] 2-7-12 D Mernagh (3) 20/1: 608: Chsd ldrs, outpcd over 2f out: 6 wk abs.   1¼   51
--   **WESTERNMOST** [4] 2-8-5 J Carroll 16/1: 9: Slowly away, al towards rear: ndd this: Most Welcome   1½   54
gelding, Feb foal, cost 9,500gns: dam a 2m wnr, sire top-class at 1m/12f: sure to apprec further for T D Barron.
--   **MRS PERTEMPS** [1] 2-8-4 W Ryan 9/2: 0: Slowly away & sn well bhd, nvr factor: 10th: op 11/4:   ¾   51
lkd fit & well: op 11/4: Ashkalani filly, Mar foal, cost 18,000gns: half-sister to an Irish 5f juv wnr.
1864 **ROYAL MUSICAL** 21 [11] 2-8-0 T Williams 20/1: 500: Prom 3f: 11th: btr 1577.   2   42
11 ran   Time 1m 04.3 (3.0)   (W T Whittle)   T D Easterby Great Habton, N.Yorks.

2361   **2.45 TATTS AUCT MDN DIV II 2YO (E)**   **5f rnd**   **Good 53**   **-19 Slow**
          £2925   £450   £225

1924 **CANDOTHAT** [10] P W Harris 2-8-7 Pat Eddery 7/2: 061: 2 b c Thatching - Yo Cando (Cyrano de   80
Bergerac) Chsd ldrs, rdn & styd on well from over 1f out to lead nr fin, going away: op 3/1, lkd superb: apprec drop
to stiff 5f (dam a 6f juv wnr), return to that trip suit: acts on gd & a stiff trk: interesting in nursery h'caps.
2100 **AMAMACKEMMUSH** 12 [8] K A Ryan 2-8-8 F Lynch 5/1: -022: 2 b g General Monash - Paganina (Galetto)1¼   73
Led, rdn over 1f out & hdd well in last, no extra: acts on fast & gd grnd: see 2100.
--   **FAIRGAME MAN** [7] A Berry 2-8-5 J Carroll 11/2: 3: 2 ch c Clantime - Thalya (Crofthall)   nk   72
Prom, rdn/ev ch ins last, just held cl-home: Clantime colt, Feb foal, cost 6,800gns: dam unrcd: eff at 5f on gd.
2010 **ALQUID NOVI** 16 [2] J S Moore 2-8-2 J F Egan 3/1 FAV: 34: Chsd ldrs, kept on, not pace to chall.   1¾   65
1704 **FLINT** 29 [9] A Berry 2-8-3 G Parkin 20/1: 05: Dwelt, sn chsd ldrs wide, keen, held over 1f out: see 1704.   2   61
1294 **MISTER SANDERS** 49 [6] 2-8-9 M Tebbutt 20/1: 06: Mid-div, nvr on terms: abs, ndd this: see 1294.   nk   66
1864 **HARD TO LAY** 21 [3] 2-8-0 F Norton 6/1: 257: Rdn/twds rear, mod late gains: btr 1698 (debut, sft).   hd   56
1906 **KANDYMAL** 19 [5] 2-8-0 P Hanagan (7) 16/1: -068: In tch, outpcd bef halfway: op 14/1: see 730.   1½   52
1981 **CHRISTMAS MORNING** 17 [1] 2-8-3 Dale Gibson 20/1: -09: Dwelt, al outpcd: still ndd this.   shd   55
1698 **HARRIER** 24 [4] 2-8-5 (2ow) K Darley 6/1: 330: In tch 3f: 10th: op 5/1: btr 1698, 1102.   nk   56
--   **BROCKHALL LAD** [11] 2-8-9 S Sanders 14/1: 0: Sn bhd: 11th: op 12/1: Apr foal, dam a 6f juv wnr.   dist   0
11 ran   Time 1m 04.9 (3.6)   (The Thatchers)   P W Harris Aldbury, Herts.

2362   **3.15 SMEATON SELL HCAP 3YO 0-60 (F)**   **1m4f**   **Good 53**   **-14 Slow**   **[65]**
          £2269   £654   £327

1911 **IRISH DANCER** 19 [5] Miss Gay Kelleway 3-8-8 (45) J F Egan 5/1: 4-0031: 3 ch f Lahib - Mazarine Blue   56
(Chief's Crown) Held up, smooth prog 3f out, rdn/led over 1f out & rdn clr ins last, easily: sold for 10,800gns:
op 4/1: first win: unplcd in '99 (rtd 67, auct mdn): eff at 11.5f/12f, could get further: acts on firm & gd grnd,
sharp or stiff/undul trk: apprec this drop to sell grade: plenty in hand here, useful seller.
1758 **UNICORN STAR** 26 [4] J S Wainwright 3-8-11 (48) Pat Eddery 4/1 JT FAV: 0-4362: 3 b g Persian Bold -   9   49
Highland Warning (Warning) Prom, rdn & kept on fnl 3f, nvr ch with wnr: op 3/1: stays 12f: see 1274.
1955 **FLOATING EMBER** 18 [10] J L Eyre 3-8-1 (38) D Mernagh (3) 8/1: -00103: 3 b f Rambo Dancer - Spark   1¼   37
(Flash Of Steel) Led, rdn/hdd over 1f out & sn held: swtg: see 1699 (10f, soft).
2141 **GARGOYLE GIRL** 10 [9] J S Goldie 3-8-10 (47) A Culhane 4/1 JT FAV: 0-0644: Held up, rdn 6f out,   shd   46
kept on fnl 2f, no threat: op 5/1, paddock pick: see 2141 (mdn h'cap).
2253 **ROOM TO ROOM MAGIC** 5 [3] 3-8-10 (47) J Reid 8/1: 456025: Chsd ldrs 3f out, held 1f out: op 6/1.   3   42
2210 **RONNI PANCAKE** 7 [7] 3-9-7 (58) J Carroll 9/1: -01506: Mid-div, held 2f out: op 8/1: see 1572 (1m).   hd   52
2139 **BLAIR** 10 [12] 3-8-4 (45) W Supple 11/2: -00407: Held up, mod hdwy fnl 2f: see 1661, 328.   5   32
1758 **HIGHCAL** 26 [1] 3-8-5 (42) T Williams 25/1: 00-008: Cl-up 5f out, fdd fnl 2f: unplcd last term (rtd 64).   2   26
2011 **HIGH BEAUTY** 16 [6] 3-8-1 (38) J Mackay (5) 25/1: 040409: Rear, nvr factor: mod form.   3   18
1865 **DINKY** 21 [14] 3-7-10 (33)(13oh) M Baird 50/1: 00-000: Prom 10f: 10th: see 1865 (1m).   5   6
1907 **WAY OUT WEST** 19 [2] 3-8-0 (37) A Nicholls (3) 33/1: 00000: Cl-up halfway, btn/eased over 1f out: 11th.   ½   9
2160 **QUIDS INN** 9 [13] 3-8-13 (50) K Darley 7/1: -20060: Mid-div, bhd 3f out: 12th: op 6/1: btr 1296 (1m).   1¾   19
1758 **Bitty Mary** 26 [11] 3-8-9 (46)(VIS) S Sanders 33/1:
1911 **New Earth Maiden** 19 [8] 3-7-12 (35)(2ow)(10oh) F Norton 50/1:
14 ran   Time 2m 42.1 (8.0)   (Inside Track Racing Club)   Miss Gay Kelleway Lingfield, Surrey.

2363   **3.45 SPINDRIFTER COND STKS 2YO (C)**   **6f rnd**   **Good 53**   **-12 Slow**
          £6119   £2321   £1160   £527

2088 **SIPTITZ HEIGHTS** 12 [1] G C Bravery 2-8-5 A Culhane 4/1: 501: 2 b f Zieten - The Multiyorker   81
(Digamist) Prom, narrow lead 2f out, rdn/duelled with rnr-up fnl 1f, narrowly prevailed, all out: nicely bckd tho'
op 3/1, lkd well: apprec step up to 6f (dam a 7f juv wnr), further shld suit: acts on gd & a stiff trk: well regarded.
2083 **DAYGLOW DANCER** 12 [5] M R Channon 2-9-2 J Reid 9/1: -132: 2 b c Fraam - Fading (Pharly)   hd   91
Led, rdn/hdd 2f out, kept on well for press, just held: clr rem: op 8/1: game, improved today: see 2083.
--   **TIME TO REMEMBER** [4] T D Easterby 2-8-7 K Darley 11/10 FAV: 3: 2 b c Pennekamp - Bequeath   7   66+
(Lyphard) Chsd ldrs, rcd keenly, rdn over 1f out, held ins last & position accepted: hvly bckd: paddock pick: Feb
foal, half-brother to tough/v smart 7f/1m wnr Decorated Hero: dam a 9f French wnr: well grown, rangy colt, improve.
2201 **CO DOT UK** 7 [6] K A Ryan 2-9-2 F Lynch 10/1: 530134: Prom, ch 2f out, wknd: op 9/1: see 1602 (soft).   1   73
1954 **SYLVAN GIRL** 18 [3] 2-8-6(1ow) Pat Eddery 11/2: 325: Held up, bhd over 1f out: btr 1954, 1612.   16   33
2142 **HUMES LAW** 10 [2] 2-8-10 J Carroll 9/1: -046: Keen, in tch, wknd 2f out: op 7/1: btr 2142 (fast, 5f).   3   30
6 ran   Time 1m 18.00 (3.9)   (The TT Partnership)   G C Bravery Newmarket.

PONTEFRACT

2364   **4.15 TOTE EBF FILLIES HCAP 3YO+ 0-85 (D)**   6f rnd   Good 53   +11 Fast   [79]
£6955   £2140   £802   £802   3 yo rec 6 lb

2015 **CARRIE POOTER** 15 [6]   T D Barron 4-8-6 (57)(bl) D Mernagh (3) 20/1: 000001: 4 b f Tragic Role -   69
Ginny Binny (Ahonoora) Trkd ldrs trav well, went on 1f out, styd on well ins last, drvn out: best time of day:
earlier scored at Southwell (reapp, h'cap, rtd 75a): '99 scorer at Southwell & Hamilton (h'caps, rtd 72a & 72 at
best): '98 Redcar wnr (auct mdn, rtd 69): suited by 6/7f, stays 1m: acts on fast, hvy & fibresand: handles
any trk, eff with/without blnks: has run well fresh & is a gd weight carrier: back to form in blnks.
*1500 **CLOTTED CREAM** 38 [8]   P J Makin 3-9-4 (75) S Sanders 2/1 FAV. 03-012: 3 gr f Eagle Eyed - Seattle   2   81
Victory (Seattle Song) Chsd ldrs, rdn & kept on from over 1f out, al held by wnr: nicely bckd: h'cap bow: see 1500.
2241 **NAISSANT** 5 [5]   J S Goldie 7-7-12 (49) J Mackay (5) 15/2: 425353: 7 b m Shaadi - Nophe (Super   3   48
Concorde) Cl-up, led over 1f out, hdd 1f out & no extra: qck reapp: continues in form: see 844.
2257 **ARCHELLO** 5 [9]   M Brittain 6-7-12 (49) T Williams 25/1: 100003: Prom, rdn/outpcd & lost pl   dht   48
halfway, kept on ins last, no threat to wnr: qck reapp: worth another try at 7f on this evidence: see 1258 (fm).
2101 **ITS ALLOWED** 12 [10]   J-9-8 (79) K Darley 12/1: 02-005: Trkd ldrs, outpcd fnl 2f: op 10/1: ndd this.   3½   69
2026 **PAGEANT** 15 [3]   3-9-4 (75) M Tebbutt 11/4: 3-5126: Mid-div, nvr pace to chall: well bckd, op 7/2.   hd   64
1710 **FOOTPRINTS** 29 [7]   3-9-4 (75) D Holland 6/1: -10027: Slowly away, sn rdn/twds rear, nvr factor.   shd   64
2310 **SHAROURA** 3 [4]   4-9-13 (78) A Nicholls (3) 5/1: 00-008: Led till over 1f out, fdd: well bckd, op 6/1.   ¾   65
2941‡ **CAUTIONARY** 343 [2]   3-9-10 (81) D Allan (7) 33/1: 120-9: Rear, nvr on terms: reapp: '99 Hamilton   ½   66
wnr (mdn, J Berry, rtd 86): eff over a stiff 5f, tried 7f: acts on fast grnd, prob handles soft.
1341 **ZAGALETA** 46 [1]   3-9-1 (72)(t) W Supple 33/1: 22-000: Bhd halfway: 10th: abs: t-strap: see 931 (1m).   12   34
10 ran   Time 1m 16.6 (2.5)   (Stephen Woodall)   T D Barron Maunby, N.Yorks.

2365   **4.45 WRAGBY FILLIES MDN 3YO (D)**   1m2f   Good 53 -41 Slow
£3542   £1090   £575   £272

4561} **VALENTINE BAND** 247 [3]   R Charlton Pat Eddery 4/6 FAV: 6-1: 3 b f Dixieland Band - Shirley   96
Valentine (Shirley Heights) Dictated pace, rdn over 2f out & styd on well, in command fnl 1f: hvly bckd, slow time:
reapp: confirmed promise of sole '99 start (rtd 92, list): apprec step up to 10f, related to a smart 14f wnr & 12f+
will suit: acts on a stiff/undul trk & runs well fresh: strong, attractive filly, looks useful & can rate more highly.
-- **DRAMA CLASS** [1]   Sir Michael Stoute 3-8-11 F Lynch 11/1: 2: 3 ch f Careleon - Stage Struck   3½   90
(Sadler's Wells) Dwelt, settled rear, in tch, switched & rdn to chase wnr 1f out, kept on, al held: just sharper
for this on debut, op 5/1: dam a 12f wnr: eff at 10f, further will suit: acts on gd: can find a similar contest.
1990 **BURNING SUNSET** 16 [2]   H R A Cecil 3-8-11 W Ryan 15/8: -30223: 3 ch f Caerleon - Lingerie (Shirley   1   88
Heights) Trkd ldrs, rdn over 2f out & no extra ins last: hvly bckd tho' op 11/8: consistent mdn: see 1990.
1224 **TRIPLE WOOD** 54 [4]   B Hanbury 3-8-11 J Reid 16/1: 52-54: Trkd ldrs, keen, outpcd fnl 2f: 8 wk abs.   6   77
4 ran   Time 2m 17.5 (9.4)   (K Abdulla)   R Charlton Beckhampton, Wilts.

2366   **5.15 PONTEFRACT APPR HCAP 3YO+ 0-70 (F)**   1m2f   Good 53 -04 Slow   [62]
£2173   £621   £310   3 yo rec 11lb

1852 **WHISTLING DIXIE** 22 [8]   D Nicholls 4-8-6 (40) J Mackay 7/1: 0-2601: 4 ch g Forest Wind - Camdens   46
Gift (Camden Town) Held up, prog fnl 3f & styd on well for press to lead well ins last: bckd: first win: rnr-up in
'99 (rtd 50, h'cap, T J Etherington): eff around 10/14f, tried 2m: acts on fast, gd & fibresand: best without blnks.
2220 **ANNADAWI** 6 [14]   C N Kellett 5-9-2 (50) G Gibbons 10/1: 222102: 5 b g Sadler's Wells - Prayers' n   1¾   53
Promises (Foolish Pleasure) Chsd ldr, went on over 2f out & clr 1f out, rdn/hdd & no extra well ins last: clr rem.
*2094 **WESTGATE RUN** 12 [1]   R A Fahey 3-9-0 (59) P Hanagan 7/4 FAV: 0-0113: 3 b f Emperor Jones -   5   55
Glowing Reference (Reference Point) Handy, outpcd/held over 1f out: hvly bckd on hat-trick bid: see 2094 (fm).
*2099 **KIERCHEM** 12 [5]   C Grant 9-8-4 (38) T Hamilton (5) 10/1: /26014: Held up, kept on fnl 2f, no threat.   2½   30
2081 **SMARTER CHARTER** 12 [7]   7-9-10 (58) Kristin Stubbs (5) 7/2: 322325: Chsd ldrs 5f out, btn 2f out: bckd.1½   48
2136 **UP IN FLAMES** 10 [3]   9-8-6 (40)(t) Angela Hartley 16/1: 020356: Chsd ldrs halfway, wknd fnl 2f.   ¾   29
2202 **ASHLEIGH BAKER** 7 [2]   5-8-9 (43) R Naylor (5) 8/1: -64037: Chsd ldrs 1m: op 7/1: btr 2202 (fast).   3½   27
2220 **RARE TALENT** 6 [10]   6-9-5 (53) M Worrell (5) 8/1: 0-0038: In tch, btn 3f out: op 6/1: btr 2220.   2½   33
2141 **PINMOOR HILL** 10 [9]   4-8-5 (39) Clare Roche 25/1: 0/0069: Handy 7f: see 940.   6   10
2231} **SUCH BOLDNESS** 374 [6]   6-9-7 (55) M Pattinson (7) 25/1: 2035-0: Led till over 2f out, sn btn: 10th: 12   13
reapp: '99 wnr at Southwell (appr mdn h'cap) & Lingfield (stks, rtd 72a, plcd on turf, rtd 58, stks): plcd in '98 (rtd
58a & 57): eff at 10f, suited by front running at 12f, prob stays 14f & tried 2m+: likes both AWs, handles firm & gd/soft.
10 ran   Time 2m 13.8 (5.7)   (Mrs P D Savill)   D Nicholls Sessay, N.Yorks.

WINDSOR

WINDSOR   MONDAY JULY 3RD   Sharp, Fig 8 Track

Official Going   GOOD. Stalls: Inside.

2367   **6.40 INDEPENDENT HCAP STKS 3YO+ 0-70 (E)**   1m67y rnd   Good   Inapplicable   [70]
£3045   £870   £435   3yo rec 9lb

2190 **DINAR** 7 [12]   R Brotherton 5-8-4 (46) G Carter 9/1: 020201: 5 b h Dixieland Band - Bold Jessie   55
(Never So Bold) Nvr far away, chall dist, pushed into lead cl-home, won a shade cosily: nicely bckd: deserved
win, plcd sev times earlier: '99 Kempton wnr (h'cap, rtd 46, with P Bowen): eff at 1m/12f, has tried 2m: acts
on firm & hvy grnd, likes a sharp/easy trk: could win again.
1100 **SILVERTOWN** 62 [15]   B J Curley 5-8-11 (53) J P Spencer 8/1: -11002: 5 b g Danehill - Docklands   ½   60
(Theatrical) Tried to make all, flashed tail & not pace to repel wnr cl-home: drifted from 11/2, 9 wk abs:
front rnr, gd eff after abs: remains well h'capped, see 618 (sand).
*1646 **ADMIRALS FLAME** 31 [17]   C F Wall 9-9-4 (60) R Mullen 7/1: 00-013: 9 b g Doulab - Fan The Flame   2½   62
(Grundy) Trkd ldrs, switched & imprvd dist, drifted left ins last & not rch front pair: usually runs well at Windsor.
1407 **QUEENS PAGEANT** 44 [5]   J L Spearing 6-9-10 (66) M Roberts 16/1: 50-044: Rear, switched outside &   1½   65
prog 2f out, onepcd fnl 1f: 6 wk abs: well h'capped & one to keep an eye on when given a more enterprising ride.
1579 **MALARKEY** 34 [18]   3-9-2 (67) Dane O'Neill 6/1: 05545: Rear, ran wide into str, onepcd fnl 1f: hd   66
consistent, not disgraced against his elders: worth a try at 10f: see 1399 (6f mdn).

2032 **THIHN 15** [11] 5-8-11 (53) R Brisland (5) 9/1: 2-2036: Chsd ldrs, onepcd fnl 1½f: nicely bckd.   1¾ 48
1895} **GALI 388** [4] 4-8-6 (48) T Ashley 33/1: 3000-7: Dwelt, eff 2f out, not reach ldrs on reapp: lightly   nk 42
rcd in '99, plcd at Folkestone (mdn auct, reapp, rtd 56), disapp subs: with C Horgan.
1926 **ANEMOS 19** [10] 5-10-0 (70) P Robinson 5/1: 426348: Prom till wknd dist: top weight: btr 1201.   3½ 57
*2331 **ENTROPY 2** [8] 4-8-7 (49)(6ex) L Newman(3) 7/1: 230519: Prom 6½f, fdd: qck reapp & 6lb pen for 2331.   1¾ 32
1588 **BETCHWORTH SAND 34** [9] 4-8-7 (49) C Rutter 20/1: 0-000: Nvr a factor in 10th: no form.   2 28
4385} **MY MAN FRIDAY 261** [2] 4-8-5 (47) Sophie Mitchell 33/1: 3400-0: Rear, eff 2f out, sn btn & fin 11th: nk 25
reapp: plcd at Newmarket (clmr, rtd 60S) in '99: eff at 7f on firm grnd: with W Muir.
*2051 **FUEGIAN 14** [6] 5-9-3 (59) S Whitworth 9/2 FAV: 0-2010: Front rank & sn rdn, wknd qckly over 1f out: 2½ 32
fin 12th: usually runs well here at Windsor, but unable to dictate the pace today: see 2051 (C/D).
1926 **Mullaghmore 19** [13] 4-8-12 (54)(VIS) M Hills 25/1:   4035} **Susans Dowry 286** [3] 4-9-6 (62) D R McCabe 40/1:
1731 **Countess Parker 28** [16] 4-9-4 (60) P Fitzsimons(5) 20/11998 **Hard Lines 16** [7] 4-9-9 (65) R Hughes 14/1:
16 ran   Time 1m 42.4   (J Rees)   R Brotherton Elmley Castle, Worcs

2368   7.10 HUGH FITZROY NOV AUCT STKS 2YO (E)   5f str Good Inapplicable
    £3474 £1069 £534 £267

2113 **MISTY EYED 11** [8] Mrs P N Dutfield 2-8-7 L Newman (3) 4/5 FAV: -5101: 2 gr f Paris House - Bold   95
As Love (Lomond) Nvr far away, went on halfway, rdn clr fnl 1f, readily: hvly bckd: earlier won here at Windsor
(nov), poorly drawn when unplcd at R Ascot: half sister to a dual 5f wnr: eff at 5f on gd grnd, 6f will suit:
handles a sharp trk, likes Windsor: v useful juvenile, should win more races in thif form.
2088 **GOLD AIR 12** [11] B J Meehan 2-8-7 Pat Eddery 11/1: -0102: 2 b f Sri Pekan - Peggledash (Great   6 80
Commotion) Led till halfway, kept on fnl 1f but no ch with impress wnr: op 7/1: handles gd & soft: see 1568.
*2214 **FACE D FACTS 6** [2] C F Wall 2-8-5 R Mullen 5/1: -513: 2 b f So Factual - Water Well (Sadler's   shd 78
Wells) Prsd ldrs but rcd wide, onepcd fnl 1f: qck reapp: not disgraced in the circumstances, had a poor low draw.
2082 **FOCUSED ATTRACTION 12** [10] R Hannon 2-8-7 R Hughes 8/1: -654: Front rank, ev ch till fdd fnl   nk 79
1f: nicely bckd: not disgraced in an above average race, has shown enough to win a mdn: see 2082, 1290.
1876 **QUEENS COLLEGE 21** [7] 2-8-2 C Rutter 50/1: -05: Chsd ldrs till outpcd fnl 1f: will find easier tasks: 1½ 70
11,500 gns Feb foal: half sister to a wnr abroad, dam a 1m Irish scorer: sire high-class 6/7f: with M Bell.
--   **APPELLATION** [4] 2-8-10 Dane O'Neill 20/1: -6: Dwelt, imprvd halfway, no impress fnl 1f: mkt   1½ 74
drifter, debut: Mar foal, cost 27,000gns: brother to a 6/7f wnr: sire a smart sprinter: learn from this.
1558 **BEVERLEY MACCA 35** [6] 2-8-7 G Carter 10/1: 221147: Front rank, wknd qckly dist: drifted from 5/1.   5 56
1208 **TUMBLEWEED TENOR 55** [9] 2-8-7 D R McCabe 20/1: -528: Nvr a factor: op 10/1, 8 wk abs: btr 1208.   1¾ 51
--   **ROCK AND SKIP** [3] 2-8-4 G Hind 50/1: -9: Dwelt, ran green & al bhd on debut: cheaply bought   3½ 38
May foal: dam a wng stayer: V Soane colt.
--   **BROUGHTON STORM** [5] 2-8-4 L Newton 50/1: -0: Dwelt, al bhd, fin last on race-course bow: 6 23
2,800 gns purchase: Mar 1st foal: with W Musson.
10 ran   Time 59.5   (Mrs Jan Fuller)   Mrs P N Dutfield Axmouth, Devon

2369   7.40 SILENTNIGHT FILL COND STKS 2YO (C)   6f str Good Inapplicable
    £5196 £1971 £985 £448

+1759 **FREEFOURRACING 26** [4] B J Meehan 2-9-3 Pat Eddery 2/5 FAV: -11: 2 b f French Deputy - Gerri N Jo   100
Go (Top Command) Made all, kept on strongly fnl 1f, rdn out: hvly bckd: Beverley debut wnr (val stks, fast time):
half sister to 6/7f h'cap wnr Al Muallim: dam a 6/7f wnr: eff at 5/6f, acts on gd & gd/soft grnd: handles a
sharp or stiff trk: runs v well fresh: smart juv filly who looks sure to win more races.
*1893 **MAKBOOLA 20** [6] J L Dunlop 2-8-11 R Hills 3/1: -312: 2 b f Mujtahid - Haddeyah (Dayjur)   ¾ 90
In tch, not clr run 2f out, ev ch ent fnl 1f, kept on but not pace of wnr cl-home: nicely bckd, 5L clr 3rd: fine run.
2209 **MYHAT 7** [2] K T Ivory 2-8-8 M Roberts 10/1: -223: 2 ch f Factual - Rose Elegance (Bairn)   5 72
In tch, chsd wnr over 1f out, sn outpcd: drifted from 11/2: not disgraced bhd a couple of above average rivals.
--   **CARPET PRINCESS** [3] Mrs P N Dutfield 2-8-5 L Newman (3) 25/1: -4: Rcd keenly in bhd wnr, wknd   nk 68
fnl 1f: IR 20,000gns Feb foal: half sister to a 6f juv wnr in Ireland: dam a dual sprint wnr in Ireland, sire a
high-class miler: fair 1st run against some useful rivals: will face easier tasks.
--   **PIC OF THE FIELD** [1] 2-8-5 S Whitworth 40/1: -5: In tch till halfway, sn btn: mkt drifter on debut: 26 18
Mar foal, dam a wng stayer: sire a high-class sprinter: with D Arbuthnot.
5 ran   Time 1m 14.4   (Roldvale Ltd)   B J Meehan Upper Lambour, Berks

2370   8.10 G MIDDLETON FILL HCAP 3YO+ 0-75 (E)   1m3f135y Good Inapplicable   [61]
    £2842 £812 £406 3 yo rec 13lb

2262 **DIZZY TILLY 5** [6] A J McNae 6-8-11 (44) T G McLaughlin 9/2: 043301: 6 b m Anshan - Nadema   49
(Artaius) Handy, hdwy to lead 2f out, hung left but kept on, drvn to assert ins last: quick reapp: poor jumps
form last winter: '99 wnr of this race here at Windsor (h'cap, rtd 53): '97 wnr again at Windsor (2, ltd stks &
h'cap, rtd 66, with T Naughton): eff at 10/12f on firm & gd/soft, prob soft & fibresand: real Windsor specialist.
1212} **MISCONDUCT 23** [5] J G Portman 6-9-1 (48) N Pollard 12/1: 4/20-2: 6 gr m Risk Me - Grey Cree   2½ 49
(Creetown) Sn rdn in tch, hdwy over 3f out, kept on over 1f out to take 2nd ins last: recently unplcd in two
hdles, 99/00 wnr at Ascot (h'cap, rtd 111h, 2m, gd/soft & hvy): rnr-up on 1st of only 2 '99 Flat starts for Mrs
M Jones (rtd 49): 3 time hdle wnr in 98/99: '98 Flat wnr at Salisbury, Bath & Lingfield (fills h'caps, rtd 51 &
53a, with G L Moore): eff over 10/11.5f on fast, soft & equitrack: handles any trk: tough.
1785 **SURE QUEST 25** [1] D W P Arbuthnot 5-10-0 (61) S Carson (5) 5/2 FAV: 111223: 5 b m Sure Blade -   ¾ 61
Eagle's Quest (Leagle Eagle) In tch, eff to chall 2f out, no extra ins last: well bckd: v tough & consistent.
*2105 **LADY LUCHA 11** [2] B W Hills 3-9-12 (72) M Hills 100/30: -0214: Led 4f out till over 3f out,   2 69
onepace over 1f out: poss stays 11.5f: see 2105 (med auct mdn).
1914 **DEE DIAMOND 19** [4] 3-7-12 (44)(1ow) F Norton 20/1: 0-0005: Led over 3f out till over 2f out, no extra: see 873.   ½ 39
1440 **STREET WALKER 42** [8] 4-9-2 (49)(VIS) M Roberts 20/1: 3-4006: Slow away, btn 3f out: visor.   6 36
2033 **FOREST DREAM 14** [7] 5-8-13 (46) J Tate 10/1: 002307: Slow away, btn over 3f out: btr 1775 (10f).   20 3
1955 **LA FAY 18** [3] 3-9-8 (68) Pat Eddery 7/2: 24-008: Led to 4f out, sn wknd & eased: reportedly choked.   26 0
8 ran   Time 2m 29.0   (L R Gotch)   A J McNae Newmarket

WINDSOR   MONDAY JULY 3RD   Sharp, Fig 8 Track

2371 8.40 CHAMPS ELYSEES HCAP 3YO+ 0-80 (D)   6f   **Good Inapplicable**   [80]
£4140   £1274   £637   £318   3 yo rec 6 lb

2207 **DIAMOND GEEZER** 7 [8] R Hannon 4-8-11 (63) Dane O'Neill 12/1: 443061: 4 br c Tenby - Unaria   68
(Prince Tenderfoot) Prom, led 2f out, kept on well for press ins last to hold on: in '99 won at Lingfield (2) &
Windsor (2, h'caps, rtd 67 & 61a): '98 Sandown wnr (clmr, rtd 69): suited by 6f at Lingfield or Windsor, stays 7f.
*2230 **CONTRARY MARY** 5 [10] J Akehurst 5-8-7 (59)(6ex) S Sanders 7/2 FAV: -00512: 5 b m Mujadil - Love   nk 63
Street (Mummy's Pet) In tch, eff over 1f out, kept on ins last, just btn: in fine heart, see 2230.
2207 **STYLISH WAYS** 7 [11] J Pearce 8-9-0 (66) T G McLaughlin 7/1: -06253: 8 b g Thatching - Style Of Life shd 70
(The Minstrel) Handy, eff over 1f out, kept on for press ins last, just btn in a tight fin: on a handy mark: see 2054.
1714 **ARPEGGIO** 28 [5] D Nicholls 5-8-12 (64) A Nicholls (3) 7/1: 0-0004: Handy, eff to chall appr fnl 1f,   hd 67
just held in a tight fin: see 780.
4541} **MADMUN** 249 [12] 6-9-8 (74) R Hills 13/2: 5521-5: Sn niggled bhd, hdwy & short of room 2f out, kept   1¼ 74+
on & sltly short of room again ins last, nrst fin: reapp: won last of 5 '99 starts, at Windsor (mdn, rtd 76):
v eff at 6f, stays 7f on fast & soft/hvy, prob any trk: encouraging reapp, stable showing signs of a return to form.
2054 **SLUMBERING** 14 [1] 4-9-4 (70)(bl) Pat Eddery 14/1: 000006: Cl-up centre, rdn & onepace over 1f out.   nk 69
1636 **KHALIK** 32 [6] 6-9-3 (69)(t) J Stack 12/1: -31407: Dwelt, bhd, some late gains, no danger: btr 1264.   ½ 66
958} **CLEF OF SILVER** 439 [13] 5-10-0 (80) M Tebbutt 25/1: 01/0-8: Waited with, short of room over 2f   ¾ 75
out, switched left & kept on late: well btn sole '99 start: '98 wnr at Catterick (appr class stks, rtd 87):
eff over 5/6f on firm & gd, prob handles soft: likes Catterick: encouraging come-back.
1969 **BINTANG TIMOR** 17 [15] 6-9-6 (72) L Newton 15/2: 346259: Slow away, bhd, some late gains: see 1969. nk 66
1877 **FLEETING FANCY** 21 [9] 3-7-13 (57) N Pollard 20/1: 00-030: Dwelt, al bhd: 10th, btr 1877.   4 41
1861 **SUPREME ANGEL** 22 [7] 5-9-0 (66) F Norton 16/1: 013500: Handy, wkng when stumbled over 1f out,   ¾ 48
eased: 11th: see 1398, 1264.
2230 **AMBER BROWN** 5 [2] 4-8-10 (62)(bl) M Roberts 14/1: 001400: Handy, wknd 2f out: 12th, btr 1676.   hd 43
1966 **KING OF PERU** 17 [16] 7-9-5 (71)(vis) R Hughes 10/1: 644220: Prom trav well, wknd 2f out: 13th.   ¾ 50
1636 **OGGI** 32 [3] 9-9-8 (74) A Clark 33/1: 040/00: Al bhd: 14th: veteran, see 1636.   5 41
2124 **KILMEENA LAD** 10 [14] 4-8-10 (62)(BL) S Carson (5) 12/1: 000500: Sn clr ldr till hdd & wknd qckly   ¾ 27
2f out: fin last: too free in 1st time blnks: btr 1999, 462.
15 ran   Time 1m 13.3   (J B R Leisure)   R Hannon East Everleigh, Wilts

2372 9.10 FINANCIAL TIMES CLASS STKS 3YO+ 0-65 (E)   1m2f   **Good Inapplicable**
£2912   £832   £416   3 yo rec 11lb

1646 **WITH A WILL** 31 [5] H Candy 6-9-4 C Rutter 11/1: 40-331: 6 b g Rambo Dancer - Henceforth (Full Of   64
Hope) Waited with, hdwy to chall over 1f out, led ins last, drvn out: 4th at best in '99 (rtd 62): back in '98
won at Kempton (appr h'cap) & Lingfield (h'cap, rtd 62): prev term won at Chepstow (h'cap, rtd 64): suited by
10f on fast, gd/soft & poss soft: likes an easy trk: on a handy mark.
2085 **KENNET** 12 [1] P D Cundell 5-9-4 S Sanders 6/1: 600002: 5 b g Kylian - Marwell Mitzi (Interrex)   ¾ 63
Cl-up, led over 1f out, hdd & no extra ins last: blnks discarded & a better run: loves a sharp trk: see 2085.
1593 **SKYE BLUE** 33 [10] M R Channon 3-8-7 Craig Williams 7/1: -53023: 3 b g Blues Traveller - Hitopah   1¼ 61
(Bustino) Hld up, eff 2f out, not clr run over 1f out till ins last, fin well: shade unlucky, shown enough to win.
2007 **EIGHT** 16 [4] C G Cox 4-9-4 (VIS) A Clark 14/1: 0-0354: Handy, eff over 1f out, sn onepace: visor.   1½ 58
1955 **SHAM SHARIF** 18 [9] 3-8-6 M Hills 7/1: 0-5105: Left in lead halfway till over 1f out, wknd: btr 1632.   ¾ 55
2332 **AFRICAN PETE** 2 [8] 3-8-7 G Hind 7/1: 6-6026: Held up, eff over 3f out, wknd fnl 1f: btr 2332.   hd 55
1875 **FLAG FEN** 21 [13] 9-9-4 D McGaffin (5) 4/1 JT FAV: 50-0627: Handy, rdn & lost place 3f out: btr 1875. 3 50
1697 **HIGH DRAMA** 30 [11] 3-8-7 Martin Dwyer 12/1: -0008: Held up, rdn 3f out, no impress: see 1200.   3 45
1977 **AIWIN** 17 [2] 3-8-7 (t) O Urbina 14/1: -04539: Bhd, nvr a factor: see 1977.   4 39
*2213 **SWINGING TRIO** 6 [12] 3-8-9 L Carter 4/1 JT FAV: -00410: Prom, wknd 2f out: 10th, btr 2213 (aw).   4 35
1998 **PERUVIAN STAR** 16 [6] 4-9-4 J Tate 33/1: 005060: Led till ran wide bend halfway, wknd 3f out: 11th. 2½ 29
1481 **NUNKIE GIRL** 39 [3] 3-8-4 (BL) L Newman (3) 33/1: 0060: Prom, btn over 2f out: blnks.   10 10
12 ran   Time 2m 08.4   (Henry Candy)   H Candy Newmarket

MUSSELBURGH   MONDAY JULY 3RD   Righthand, Sharp Track

Official Going   FIRM (GOOD/FIRM in places). Stalls: Inside, except 5f/2m - Stands Side.

2373 6.55 STATE APPR HCAP 3YO+ 0-60 (F)   2m   **Firm 19 -106 Slow**   [45]
£2194   £627   £313   3 yo rec 19lb

2202 **COSMIC CASE** 7 [4] J S Goldie 5-9-6 (37) Dawn Rankin 11/4: 400421: 5 b m Casteddu - La Fontainova   38
(Lafontaine) Well plcd, narrow lead appr fnl 1f, edged left, al holding rnr-up: v slow time, tchd 4/1, qck reapp:
Feb '00 wnr over hdles at Catterick (nov h'cap, 2m, gd, visor, rtd 81h): last won on the Flat in '98 here at
Musselburgh (h'cap, rtd 65): eff at 12f/slow run 2m: acts on firm & gd/soft grnd, with/without visor.
2203 **URGENT REPLY** 7 [1] C A Dwyer 7-8-7 (24) N Carter (5) 4/1: 000662: 7 b g Green Dancer - Bowl   hd 24
Of Honey (Lyphard) Set funereal pace, hdd appr fnl 1f, still ev ch, held fnl 50y: clr rem, acts on firm & soft.
2123 **ALPHA ROSE** 11 [3] M L W Bell 3-9-10 (60) Gemma Sliz (5) 2/1 FAV: 411253: 3 ch f Inchinor - Philgwyn 7 53
(Milford) Held up, prog to chall appr fnl 2f, onepace bef dist: nicely bckd: not stay 2m?: see 1657 (13f).
1911 **ST GEORGES BOY** 19 [2] H Morrison 3-8-1 (37) G Sparkes 5/2: -60024: Well plcd/ev ch, wknd bef dist. 1½ 29
4 ran   Time 3m 42.5 (20)   (J S Goldie)   J S Goldie Uplawmoor, E Renfrews.

2374 7.25 STATE STREET SELL HCAP 3YO 0-60 (F)   5f   **Firm 19 -07 Slow**   [62]
£2310   £660   £330   Winner came from stands side tho' most pace in centre

2047 **GREY FLYER** 14 [1] Mrs L Stubbs 3-9-7 (55) C Lowther 8/1: 050301: 3 gr g Factual - Faraway Grey   59
(Absalom) Prom stands side, drvn appr fnl 1f, led dist, kept on well: no bid: earlier won at Lingfield (h'cap, rtd
66a): '99 wnr here at Musselburgh (clmr, rtd 66 & 35a): eff at 5/6f on firm, gd grnd & equitrack: likes sharp trks.
2047 **BRANSTON LUCY** 14 [8] T J Etherington 3-9-7 (55) R Ffrench 9/1: 1-0002: 3 b f Prince Sabo - Softly nk 57
Spoken (Mummy's Pet) Front rank centre, led halfway till ins fnl 1f, just btnd: op 7/1: back to best, blnks omitted.

754

2223 **LAYAN** 6 [9] J Balding 3-9-5 (53) O Pears 8/1: -56603: 3 b f Puissance - Most Uppitty (Absalom) ¾ 53
Chsd ldrs centre, eff appr fnl 1f, styd on but unable to chall: op 6/1, qck reapp: acts on firm & gd/soft grnd.
2095 **LUNALUX** 12 [13] C Smith 3-9-7 (55) J Fanning 8/1: 50-024: Led in centre, hdd over 2f out, no extra ½ 54
ins last: jt top-weight, not far off best, see 2095, 1773.
2204 **TARTAN ISLAND** 7 [11] 3-8-9 (43)(vis) R Winston 3/1 FAV: 0-0025: Slow away, in tch centre, edged hd 42
left appr fnl 1f, styd on: nicely bckd from 9/2, qck reapp: down in grade, acts on firm/fast, worth another try at 6f.
2047 **APRILS COMAIT** 14 [3] 3-8-13 (47)(bl) V Halliday 8/1: 300056: Chsd ldrs stands side, kept on ½ 44
but nvr pace to chall: op 6/1: handles firm grnd & fibresand, see 217.
2046 **THEOS LAD** 14 [2] 3-9-4 (52) Dale Gibson 8/1: 060-57: In tch stands side but nvr trbld ldrs: op 5/1. nk 48
2243 **COLLISION TIME** 5 [7] 3-9-4 (52)(vis) Dean McKeown 7/1: 0-0008: Well plcd centre till no extra 1f out. ¾ 46
2240 **BLUE SAPPHIRE** 5 [10] 3-8-5 (39) Kimberley Hart 20/1: 0-6009: Nvr dngrs: qck reapp, back in trip. 1 30
2280 **PAPE DIOUF** 4 [12] 3-8-8 (42) N Carter (7) 33/1: 060000: Stumbled start, prom centre till 2f out: 10th. 1 30
1817 **ELLPEEDEE** 24 [6] 3-9-0 (48) Kim Tinkler 12/1: 656000: Al towards rear: 11th, see 909. 1¼ 32
1932 **BOXBERRY** 18 [5] 3-8-5 (39) G Sparkes (7) 5/1: 000-40: Prom stands side till halfway: 12th, see 1932. 2½ 17
2036 **Jenin** 14 [4] 3-7-10 (30) Nicola Cole (0) 50/1: 　　　1562 **Sharp Smoke** 35 [14] 3-8-1 (35) J Bramhill 50/1:
14 ran　　Time 58.8 (1.3)　　(D M Smith)　　Mrs L Stubbs Newmarket.

2375　7.55 STATE STREET HCAP 3YO+ 0-75 (E)　1m6f　Firm 19　00 Slow　[64]
£4095　£1260　£630　£315　3 yo rec 15lb

*2238 **FORUM CHRIS** 5 [4] M Johnston 3-9-7 (72)(6ex) J Fanning 5/4 FAV: 043311: 3 ch g Trempolino - 81
Memory Green (Green Forest) Led, clr by halfway, readily: bckd: 5 days ago won at Hamilton (h'cap): eff at 12/14f:
acts on firm/fast, handles soft, any trk: best up with/forcing the pace: progressive gldg, shld land the hat-trick.
2173 **FLETCHER** 9 [3] H Morrison 6-9-6 (56) K Darley 5/2: 002232: 6 b g Salse - Ballet Classique 8 57
(Sadler's Wells) Mid-div, styd on appr 2f out, nvr nr wnr: consistent but hard to win with, see 182.
2236 **SECONDS AWAY** 5 [6] J S Goldie 9-8-1 (37)(5ow)(8oh) Dawn Rankin (0) 33/1: 604243: 9 b g Hard 2½ 36$
Fought - Keep Mum (Mummy's Pet) Rcd in 2nd, lost pl halfway, moderate late rally: qck reapp, flattered
2203 **NORTHERN MOTTO** 7 [2] J S Goldie 7-9-1 (51) A McGlone 7/1: 003334: Held up, imprvd after 7f, 3 47
fdd 3f out: qck reapp, stablemate 3rd, btr 2203, 2050.
*2203 **SANDABAR** 7 [5] 7-10-2 (66)(t)(6ex) A Culhane 11/4: 003215: Prom till ent str: qck reapp, big weight/pen. 3 60
1243 **PERSIAN POINT** 53 [1] 4-8-0 (36) Dale Gibson 50/1: 00-006: Nvr in it: 8 wk abs, longer trip, no form. 5 26
6 ran　　Time 2m 59.1 (2.6)　　(Mrs Jacqueline Conroy)　　M Johnston Middleham, N.Yorks.

2376　8.25 CLASSIFIED STAKES 3YO+ (E)　1m1f　Firm 19　+01 Fast
£3094　£952　£476　£238　3 yo rec 10lb

1778 **MASTER HENRY** 26 [4] M Johnston 6-9-6 R Ffrench 7/2: /66601: 6 b g Mille Balles - Maribelle 68
(Windwurf) Early ldr & again 3f out, pshd out cl-home: best time of night, 1st win: ex-German Flat rnr-up: has
tried hdles: eff at 1m/10f: acts on firm & soft grnd, sharp trk: has faced some stiff tasks, apprec drop in grade.
1892 **WOORE LASS** 14 [4] Don Enrico Incisa 4-9-3 Kim Tinkler 25/1: 4-0002: 4 ch f Persian Bold - Miss 3 56$
Ballylea (Junius) Rear, styd on appr fnl 1f & wnt 2nd nr fin, no wnr: prob flattered tho' did rate 70 last year.
1908 **LITTLE JOHN** 9 [1] Miss L A Perratt 4-9-6 C Lowther 6/1: 46-343: 4 b g Warrshan - Silver Venture hd 59
(Silver Hawk) Chsd ldrs, eff ent str, nvr any impression: prob ran to best back in trip, acts on firm & soft.
2015 **QUIET VENTURE** 15 [5] I Semple 6-9-6 (t) R Winston 7/2: -00004: Sn led, hdd 3f out, fdd: 5 49
out of sorts this term, t-strap reapplied, see 1158.
2094 **FUTURE PROSPECT** 12 [3] 6-9-6 A Culhane 3/1 JT FAV: 00-255: Chsd ldrs till wknd ent fnl 3f. shd 49
2053 **EASTWOOD DRIFTER** 14 [6] 3-8-10 (BL) O Pears 3/1 JT FAV: 303626: Prom 6f: blnkd, btr 2053. 1 47
6 ran　　Time 1m 52.3 (1.6)　　(The Winning Line)　　M Johnston Middleham, N.Yorks.

2377　8.55 C MACLEOD AUCT MDN 2YO (F)　7f30y rnd　Firm 19　-68 Slow

-- **MAGIC OF YOU** [4] M L W Bell 2-8-9 A Culhane 3/1: 1: 2 b f Magic Ring - Daarat Alayaam (Reference 69
Point) Outpcd & green till ran on ent fnl 2f, led dist, pshd out: slow time: 12,000gns Mar foal, dam unrcd,
sire a sprinter: eff at 7f, shld get 1m (stoutly bred on dam's side): acts on firm grnd & runs well fresh.
2014 **TEFI** 15 [2] T D Easterby 2-8-10 K Darley 1/1 FAV: -532: 2 ch c Efisio - Masuri Kabisa (Ascot Knight) nk 68
Chsd ldrs, rdn appr fnl 1f, kept on ins last but not pace of wnr: apprec step up to 7f.
2174 **ALIS IMAGES** 8 [3] A Berry 2-8-3 O Pears 11/2: -6603: 2 ch g Mind Games - Question Ali (Petoski) hd 60
Prom, led 2f out, under press & hdd dist, kept on: clr rem & best run yet, stays 7f on firm grnd.
1704 **ECKSCLUSIVE STORY** 29 [7] J J Quinn 2-8-9 R Ffrench 5/1: -044: Chsd ldrs, chall 3f out, 3 57
outpcd appr fnl 1f: bred to apprec this longer 7f trip, see 1704, 1252.
1418 **INZACURE** 42 [5] 2-8-10 R Winston 11/2: 005: Led, wide into str, rdn & hdd 2f out, fdd: 6 wk abs. 2½ 56
-- **COMEUPPANCE** [6] 2-8-5 Dean McKeown 7/1: 6: Al detached: debut: IR 3,600gns General Monash 7 37
May first foal, dam a mdn, sire a sprinter: with T Barron.
6 ran　　Time 1m 31.0 (6.1)　　(Mrs Maureen Buckley)　　M L W Bell Newmarket.

2378　9.25 EDINBURGH HCAP 3YO+ 0-70 (E)　1m rnd　Firm 19　-16 Slow　[61]
£2782　£856　£428　£214　3 yo rec 9 lb

2186 **AGIOTAGE** 8 [3] S C Williams 3-9-7 (54) G Faulkner (3) 5/2: 000161: 4 br g Zafonic - Rakli (Warning) 57
Trkd ldr, eff appr fnl 1f, kept on to lead cl-home: earlier won here at Musselburgh (h'cap): 4th at best in
'99 for H Cecil (h'cap, rtd 79, tried blnks): '98 Redcar wnr (mdn, rtd 93): eff at 7f/9f, tried 2m: best up
with/forcing the pace on firm, gd/soft grnd, sharp or gall trk: runs well fresh & is h'capped.
675 **DOBERMAN** 109 [2] P D Evans 5-8-9 (42)(vis) N Callan 12/1: 031002: 5 b g Dilum - Switch Blade hd 44
(Robellino) Led till ent fnl 2f, rdn & kept on well ins last, just btn, 16 wk abs, turf return, visor reapplied
(usually blnkd): acts on firm/fast grnd, both AWs: see 550.
2147 **CUTE CAROLINE** 10 [1] A Berry 4-8-13 (46)(bl) K Darley 4/1: 350623: 4 ch f First Trump - Hissma 1 46
(Midyan) Prom, wide prog to lead ent fnl 2f, hung left, hdd dist & no extra: clr rem, imprvd since blnkd.
2166 **YENALED** 9 [6] J S Goldie 3-9-9 (65) A McGlone 11/8 FAV: -31624: Chsd ldrs, kept on onepace fnl 2f. 3 59
2145 **ENTITY** 10 [5] 3-9-5 (61) Dean McKeown 14/1: 030005: Nvr in it: see 1053, 967. 3 49
1257 **KESTRAL** 52 [4] 4-8-7 (40)(t) R Winston 12/1: -50606: Prom till 3f out: 7 wk abs, up in trip, see 635. ½ 27
2311 **FLOORSOTHEFOREST** 3 [7] 4-9-11 (58) C Lowther 7/1: 265207: Sn struggling: ran Friday, btr 2094. 12 25

MUSSELBURGH MONDAY JULY 3RD **Righthand, Sharp Track**

7 ran   Time 1m 40.3 (2.8)   (Stuart C Williams)   S C Williams Newmarket.

SOUTHWELL (Fibresand)   MONDAY JULY 3RD   **Lefthand, Sharp, Oval Track**

Official Going   STANDARD. Stalls: Inside, Except 5f - Outside.

2379   2.00 BET DIRECT HCAP DIV I 3YO+ 0-60 (F)   1m aw rnd Going 41 -09 Slow   [60]
£1806   £516   £258   3 yo rec 9 lb

1421 **THE THIRD CURATE** 42 [15] B J Curley 5-8-7 (39)(bl) J P Spencer 6/1: 00-001: 5 b g Fairy King -   43a
Lassalia (Sallust) Settled rear, gd hdwy over 4f out, ran on well to lead cl-home, drvn out: bckd from 12/1,
6 wk abs: mod prev form in Britain, in June '99 won in native Ireland at The Curragh (7f h'cap, gd): eff at
7f/1m on gd grnd & fibresand: runs well fresh on a sharp trk, eff in blnks.
2220 **FREEDOM QUEST** 6 [4] B S Rothwell 5-9-7 (53) M Fenton 13/2: 464252: 5 b g Polish Patriot -   hd 56a
Recherchee (Rainbow Quest) Dwelt, bhd till prog over 3f out, styd on to lead ins last, hdd cl-home: quick
reapp: poss wnr with a level start, deserves to go one better: see 793.
2121 **SHAANXI ROMANCE** 11 [9] M J Polglase 5-8-13 (45)(vis) D Holland 6/1: 005543: 5 b g Darshaan - Easy 1¾ 45a
Romance (Northern Jove) Cl-up, led halfway, sn clr, wknd/hdd ins last, sn btn: clr rem: consistent: see 869, 778.
*1858 **GODMERSHAM PARK** 22 [16] P S Felgate 8-9-1 (47) Dean McKeown 7/1: 140014: Chsd ldrs,   6 37a
hung left & fdd appr fnl 1f: op 6/1: btr 1858 (sell, gd grnd).
2122 **KILLARNEY JAZZ** 11 [11] 5-9-13 (59)(vis) O Urbina 13/2: 015025: In tch, eff when hmpd over 1f out,   1½ 46a
kept on, no danger: top-weight: btr 2122 (7f sell h'cap).
1393 **C HARRY** 44 [13] 6-9-0 (46) P M Quinn (3) 16/1: 505006: Handy, mod late gains, no dngr: 6 wk abs.   5 25a
2122 **ABTAAL** 11 [10] 10-9-7 (53)(vis) R Fitzpatrick (3) 20/1: 360067: Dwelt, late hdwy: btr 1305 (sell, 7f).   shd 32a
2121 **AREISH** 11 [5] 7-9-11 (57) J Edmunds 14/1: 213568: Prom, rdn/lost tch fnl 2f: op 10/1: see 2121.   1½ 34a
2217 **WHITE SANDS** 6 [14] 3-8-4 (45) A Clark 40/1: -00069: Trkd ldrs, fdd fnl 3f: qck reapp: mod form.   2 19a
2187 **RED SONNY** 7 [12] 3-8-5 (46) P Bradley (5) 10/1: 023620: Dwelt, al bhd, 10th: qck reapp: btr 2187.   6 11a
1365 **DOVES DOMINION** 45 [8] 3-8-12 (53) K Dalgleish 25/1: 0-5000: Chsd ldrs, wknd qckly fnl 3f,   5 11a
11th: 6 wk abs: prev with M Channon, now with D Burchell.
2221 **SOUHAITE** 6 [7] 4-8-10 (42) Martin Dwyer 7/2 FAV: -00100: Missed break, al bhd, 12th: nicely bckd,   ½ 0a
quick reapp: much btr 2027 (firm grnd).
2027 **PRIORS MOOR** 15 [3] 5-7-12 (33) R Brisland (5) 40/1: -00000: Handy, wknd rapidly fnl 3f, 13th.   3½ 0a
647 **BROUGHTON MAGIC** 119 [1] 5-8-9 (41) L Newton 16/1: /51000: Nvr a threat, fin 14th: long abs.   1¾ 0a
1976 **JUST ON THE MARKET** 17 [6] 3-9-2 (57) T G McLaughlin 20/1: 00-000: Led early, lost tch halfway, 15th.   9 0a
2121 **KOCAL** 11 [2] 4-8-8 (40)(BL) J Quinn 20/1: 500000: Led after 2f to halfway, wknd, t.o., 16th: blnkd.   23 0a
16 ran   Time 1m 43.5 (4.1)   (P Byrne)   B J Curley Newmarket

---

2380   2.30 BET DIRECT HCAP DIV II 3YO+ 0-60 (F)   1m aw rnd Going 41 -05 Slow   [60]
£1799   £514   £257   3 yo rec 9 lb

1335 **ROBBIES DREAM** 47 [14] R M H Cowell 4-8-6 (38)(t) K Dalgleish (7) 16/1: 0-5001: 4 ch g Balla Cove -   47a
Royal Golden (Digamist) Trkd ldrs, went on fnl 2f, sn hung left, styd on well when prsd ins last, drvn out:
jockey received a 2 day careless riding ban, 7 wk abs: lightly rcd & unplcd for D Morris in '99 (rtd 51, stks):
unplcd in '98 (mdn, rtd 75): eff arnd 1m on fibresand and a sharp trk: goes well when fresh.
1689 **STITCH IN TIME** 30 [7] G C Bravery 4-8-12 (44) G Baker 10/1: 223302: 4 ch g Inchinor - Late   ½ 52a
Matinee (Red Sunset) Cl-up, rdn to chall appr fnl 1f, kept on, not btn far: op 8/1, clr rem: acts on firm,
soft & fibresand: often placed this term but remains a mdn: see 871.
2212 **APPROACHABLE** 6 [3] A Morgan 5-8-11 (43) L Newman (3) 6/1: 432023: 5 b h Known Fact - Western   5 43a
Approach (Gone West) Prom, went on after halfway, hdd 2f out & sltly hmpd sn after, sn held: op 8/1, quick
reapp: best form over further these days, see 2212 (10f).
2027 **FUTURE COUP** 15 [11] J Norton 4-9-7 (53) J Weaver 20/1: D-0004: Dwelt, rear, late hdwy for press   1¾ 50a
appr fnl 1f, no threat to ldrs: see 1254.
2121 **MAI TAI** 11 [5] 5-9-12 (58) A Clark 6/1: 401025: Settled rear, rdn/prog after halfway, no extra fnl 2f.   1¼ 53a
2119 **OVER THE MOON** 11 [8] 6-8-9 (41)(vis) R Fitzpatrick (3) 10/1: 000436: Outpcd early, late gains   2 32a
for press, no danger: drop in trip, btr 2119 (11f clmr).
1505 **SPRING BEACON** 38 [16] 5-7-10 (28) P M Quinn (5) 14/1: /60007: Rear, prog after halfway, fdd fnl 2f.   hd 19a
*2347 **QUALITAIR PRIDE** 2 [12] 8-7-12 (29)(1ow)(6ex) J Quinn 9/4 FAV: 00/018: Trkd ldrs, dropped rear   ¾ 20a
after halfway sn btn: shock 50/1 scorer on turf 48hrs ago in 2347 (fast grnd).
922 **HEATHYARDS JAKE** 79 [15] 4-8-13 (45) Dean McKeown 16/1: 066509: Nvr a factor after 11 wk abs.   3½ 29a
2122 **LEOFRIC** 11 [6] 5-8-5 (37) J Tate 14/1: 063000: Prom, rdn/fdd fnl 3f, fin 10th: op 10/1.   3 16a
1815 **LANDING CRAFT** 24 [1] 6-9-8 (54) R Lappin 12/1: 032000: Al bhd: 11th: see 1066.   ½ 32a
2011 **PROUD CAVALIER** 16 [10] 4-7-11 (29) R Brisland (5) 25/1: 00-050: Led to halfway, sn lost tch, 12th.   shd 7a
1594 **MALAKAL** 33 [4] 4-8-1 (33) D O'Donohoe 9/2: 000000: Handy, fdd fnl 3f, fin 13th: drop in trip.   5 0a
1771 **GOLDFINCH** 26 [13] 3-9-5 (60) R Mullen 10/1: 0-000: In tch, wknd halfway, fin 14th: op 6/1, h'cap bow.   4 24a
4548↓Time To Wyn 248 [9] 4-9-2 (48) J P Spencer 25/1:   2828↓ Arabella Girl 348 [2] 3-9-0 (55) R Perham 40/1:
16 ran   Time 1m 43.2 (3.8)   (James Brown)   R M H Cowell Six Mile Bottom, Cambs

---

2381   3.00 HAMPSTEAD APPR CLAIMER 3YO+ (G)   1m3f aw Going 41 -32 Slow
£1827   £522   £261   3 yo rec 12lb

2033 **PIPS BRAVE** 14 [11] M J Polglase 4-9-10 A Beech 20/1: 240001: 4 b g Be My Chief - Pipistrelle   45a
(Shareef Dancer) Settled rear, rdn/prog halfway, ran on well to lead out, drvn out: op 14/1: '99 wnr here
at Southwell (mdn) & Warwick (h'cap, rtd 61a & 55), prev term rtd 72 & 49a (mdn): eff at 1m/11f: acts on fast,
hvy & fibresand: eff with/without blnks & likes a sharp trk: apprec drop to claimers.
2080 **THE WALRUS** 12 [9] N P Littmoden 3-8-6 D Young (4) 10/1: 300552: 3 b g Sri Pekan - Cathy Garcia   ¾ 37a
(Be My Guest) Waited with, rdn to improve halfway, styd on to chall well ins last, just held: op 8/1: claimed
by R Cowell for £5,000: eff at 11f on gd grnd & fibresand.
1731 **MARIANA** 28 [5] T T Clement 5-9-8 D McGaffin (3) 66/1: 050003: 5 ch m Anshan - Maria Cappuccini   2 25a
(Siberian Express) Trkd ldr, rdn to lead dist, sn hdd & no extra: stays 1m/11f on fast, soft & both AWs: see 367.
*2298 **ALS ALIBI** 3 [6] W R Muir 7-9-12 R Brisland 1/5 FAV: 000214: Cl-up, went on after 4f, drvn/hdd ins   1¼ 40a
last, wknd: qck reapp: well bckd at long odds-on & much better expected, but poss hit the front too soon.

756

2143 **RAYWARE BOY** 10 [2] 4-9-4 (bl) S Finnamore (3) 14/1: 000545: Led early, remained with ldrs, wknd qckly fnl 3f: op 8/1: see 1660. — 11 18a

1615 **CAPERCAILLIE** 33 [7] 5-9-3 D Glennon (5) 25/1: 022-06: Nvr a factor: recently p.u. on hdles bow: rnr-up fnl 2 '99 starts (appr h'cap, rtd 37): plcd thrice in '98 (amat h'cap, rtd 55a & 43, D Morris): eff at 12/14f, stays 2m: handles fast grnd & both AWs, with/without blnks: with D Cantillon. — 2 14a

2007 **TALECA SON** 16 [3] 5-9-0 K Dalgleish (3) 20/1: 006547: Outpcd early, eff 4f out, sn btn: see 2007. — 7 2a

2121 **NICE BALANCE** 11 [1] 5-9-6 L Gueller (5) 33/1: 300008: Al well outpcd. — nk 8a

1788 **JATO DANCER** 25 [4] 5-8-9 Stephanie Hollinshead (5) 50/1: 054069: Prom, lost tch fnl 4f: see 1353. — 2 0a

1888 **SLAPY DAM** 20 [10] 8-9-4 C Cogan 25/1: 050-00: Cl-up, lost tch halfway, fin 10th: see 1888. — 3 0a

1977 Thewayshewalks 17 [8] 3-7-11 Claire Bryan (3) 100/1:1843 **Newryman** 23 [12] 5-9-12 M Cotton (7) 100/1:
12 ran   Time 2m 29.3 (8.0)   (Pastern Partnership)   M J Polglase Southwell, Notts

---

2382   3.30 0800 211222 HCAP 3YO 0-75 (E)   1m4f aw   Going 41   -18 Slow   [80]
£2775   £854   £427   £213

2103 **GIMCO** 12 [1] G C H Chung 3-9-7 (73) O Urbina 11/2: -43221: 3 b c Pelder - Valetta (Faustus) 77a
Trkd ldrs, rdn to chall 2f out, styd on well & drvn out to lead cl-home: 1st win: trained by A Kelleway & 5th at Sandown (mdn, rtd 79+) sole juv start: eff at 10/12f on gd, hvy, fibresand & a sharp trk: tough/consistent.

2123 **NICIARA** 11 [7] M C Chapman 3-7-10 (48)(bl) (7oh) Joanna Badger (7) 20/1: 040332: 3 b g Soviet Lad -shd 51$
Verusa (Petorius) Dwelt, sn with ldrs, led when hmpd over 2f out, styd on despite hanging left ins last, hdd cl-home: clr rem, op 10/1: excellent run from 7lbs o/h: eff at 7/12f on fibresand: mdn after 23 starts.

2012 **BAHAMAS** 16 [3] Sir Mark Prescott 3-8-11 (63) G Duffield 2/5 FAV: 00-123: 3 b g Barathea - Rum Cay 6 58a
(Our Native) Cl-up till went on 4f out, hung right/hdd 2f out, fdd fnl 1f: well bckd at odds-on & much better expected on this step up to 12f on AW bow: btr 2012, 1895 (10f, gd grnd).

1862 **SMUDGER SMITH** 22 [5] B S Rothwell 3-8-7 (59) M Fenton 10/1: -03464: Waited with, eff halfway, 5 47a
lost tch fnl 2f: AW bow: see 1581, 1446.

1939 **WITH RESPECT** 18 [2] 3-8-1 (53) G Baker (7) 33/1: 00-005: Bhd, rdn/prog halfway, wknd qckly fnl 2f; 9 29a
op 16/1: big step up in trip on this A/W bow: see 1939.

1919 **RAINWORTH LADY** 19 [6] 3-7-12 (50)(BL)(2ow)(12oh) Martin Dwyer 66/1: -50006: Led, hdd 4f out, dist 0a
wknd rapidly, u/p: blnkd: v stiff task, mod form.

2173 **ASTON MARA** 9 [8] 3-8-8 (60)(bl) K Dalgleish (7) 15/2: -00007: Prom early, bhd from halfway, sn t.o. 8 0a

934 **ISLA** 77 [4] 3-7-10 (48)(3oh) M Henry 50/1: 0-008: Al struggling, sn well t.o.: 11 wk abs, AW bow. dist 0a
8 ran   Time 2m 41.4 (7.1)   (Osvaldo Pedroni)   G C H Chung Newmarket

---

2383   4.00 PUTNEY MDN 2YO (D)   7f aw rnd   Going 41   -29 Slow
£2775   £854   £427   £213

2201 **MUJALINA** 7 [4] E J O'Neill 2-9-0 M Fenton 13/2: 021: 2 b c Mujadil - Talina's Law (Law Society) 72a
Dsptd lead, went on appr fnl 2f, rdn clr ins last: tchd 8/1, quick reapp: AW bow: dam a 2m/hdles wnr: eff at 7f, 1m & further is stepping up in trip later: acts on fast, fibresand & a sharp trk: going the right way.

1602 **BLUSHING SPUR** 33 [9] D Shaw 2-9-0 T G McLaughlin 50/1: 502: 2 b g Flying Spur - Bogus John 3½ 65a
(Blushing John) Prom, chall appr fnl 1f, sn not pace of wnr: imprvd form on AW bow, stays 7f on fibresand.

1864 **LADY BEAR** 21 [7] R A Fahey 2-9-0 N Pollard 7/4: 633: 2 b f Grand Lodge - Boristova (Royal Academy) 1¼ 58a
Chsg ldrs till hung left/fdd fnl 1f: nicely bckd tho' op 11/10: AW bow: handles fibresand, see 1864.

1488 **DENNIS EL MENACE** 38 [6] W R Muir 2-9-0 Martin Dwyer 11/1: -0464: Cl-up, rdn & grad wknd appr fnl 1f: 5 55a
op 8/1: up in trip & poss not quite get 7f: sells shld suit: see 730.

1589 **BORDER EDGE** 33 [1] 2-9-0 T E Durcan 20/1: 0405: Handy, drvn/fdd fnl 2f: up in trip: see 1236. nk 55a

2120 **MONICA GELLER** 11 [3] 2-8-9 K Dalgleish (7) 33/1: 06: Led, hdd 2f out, wknd: up in trip: see 2120. 3½ 44a

-- **ORANGERIE** [2] 2-9-0 G Duffield 5/4 FAV: 7: Sn outpcd, rdn/prog over 3f out, no impress fnl 2f: ½ 48a
hvly bckd on debut & clrly thought capable of better: IR115,000 gns Darshaan colt, dam a French juv wnr: shld learn from the experience & improve for Sir M Prescott.

2029 **ESSENCE** 15 [5] 2-8-9 R Fitzpatrick (3) 40/1: -08: Al outpcd: looks modest. 7 33a

-- **MIND OVER MATTER** [10] 2-9-0 A Clark 14/1: 9: Al well bhd on debut: op 10/1: Mar foal, half 2 34a
brother to a Swedish 3yo wnr, dam unrcd: with C A Cyzer.

1943 **JUNIOR BRIEF** 18 [8] 2-9-0 J Tate 16/1: -00: Chsd ldrs, lost tch halfway, fin 10th: op 10/1. 1¾ 31a
10 ran   Time 1m 31.5 (4.9)   (M Donovan)   E J O'Neill Newmarket

---

2384   4.30 DOCKLANDS SELLER 2YO (G)   5f aw str   Going 41   -35 Slow
£1827   £522   £261

2034 **SIMAS GOLD** 14 [6] W R Muir 2-8-6 Martin Dwyer 7/2: 61: 2 b f Goldmark - Mujadil Princess (Mujadil) 54a
Dsptd lead, chall appr fnl 1f, styd on strongly & drvn out to lead cl-home: mkt drifter, bought in for 9,400gns: 10,000 gns 1st foal, dam unrcd: eff at 5f, 6f will suit: acts on fibresand & a sharp trk: apprec drop to sells.

*2196 **SOME DUST** 7 [8] W G M Turner 2-8-4 A Daly 7/4 FAV: -U0212: 2 ch c King's Signet - Some Dream ¾ 61a
(Vitiges) Led, styd on well for press ins last, collared fnl strides: nicely bckd, quick reapp: fine run conceding weight all round, acts on fast & both AWs: see 2196.

2079 **BELLS BEACH** 12 [5] A Berry 2-8-6 T E Durcan 16/1: 033: 2 ch f General Monash - Clifton Beach 2 45a
(Auction Ring) Front rank, rdn/no extra fnl 1f: drop in trip: see 1713.

2214 **HALCYON MAGIC** 6 [1] Pat Mitchell 2-8-11 R Perham 7/1: 004: Swerved left start & sn well bhd, hd 50a
styd on well fnl 1f, nvr nrr: well bckd from 25/1, quick reapp: imprvd form on A/W bow.

2079 **RUNNING FOR ME** 12 [2] 2-8-11 A Hawkins (3) 7/2: 610225: Prom, rdn/fdd appr fnl 1f: btr 2079 (6f). 2 44a

1713 **MISS TOPOGINO** 28 [3] 2-8-6 K Dalgleish (7) 25/1: 056: Dwelt, nvr a danger: see 1136. 1 36a

2214 **LONDON EYE** 6 [4] 2-8-6 (bl) G Duffield 4/1: 033207: Chsd ldrs, rdn/btn fnl 2f: qck reapp: btr 2039. 1 33a

2079 **MACKEM BEAT** 12 [7] 2-8-6 J Tate 25/1: 0558: Sn rdn, al bhd, t.o.: see 1463. 23 0a
8 ran   Time 1m 01.6 (3.8)   (D J Kerwood)   W R Muir Lambourn, Berks

---

2385   5.00 BEST BETS HCAP 3YO+ 0-60 (F)   6f aw rnd   Going 41   +09 Fast   [60]
£2338   £668   £334   3 yo rec 6 lb

*1257 **BAHAMIAN PIRATE** 52 [15] D Nicholls 5-9-12 (58) Alex Greaves 6/4 FAV: 21-011: 9 ch g Housebuster - 75a
Shining Through (Deputy Minister) Nvr far away, led over 3f out, sn clr, readily: well bckd after 7 wk abs, best time of day: earlier won at Carlisle (h'cap): '99 Ripon wnr (mdn, rtd 72): suited by 5/6f, stays 7f: acts on gd,

SOUTHWELL (Fibresand)   MONDAY JULY 3RD   Lefthand, Sharp, Oval Track

firm, fibresand & a sharp or stiff trk: runs well fresh: looks well h'capped on AW, shld make a quick follow up.

1760 **FOIST** 26 [11] M W Easterby 8-9-0 (46) G Duffield 9/1: 006502: 8 b g Efisio - When The Saints   8   45a
(Bay Express) Waited with, rdn/prog appr fnl 2f, styd on but wnr had flown: gd run: see 587.

1658 **PUPS PRIDE** 31 [4] R A Fahey 3-8-9 (47)(VIS) J Weaver 14/1: -50003: 3 b g Efisio - Moogie   ¾   44a
(Young Generation) Dwelt, bhd until ran on well for press fnl 1f, nrst fin: 1st time visor, drop in trip:
will apprec a return to 1m+: handles gd/soft & fibresand: see 800.

2118 **SUPERFRILLS** 11 [2] Miss L C Siddall 7-8-6 (38) G Bardwell 14/1: 020004: In tch, eff over 2f out,   hd   35a
rdn/btn fnl 1f: op 12/1: see 923.

2297 **PETITE DANSEUSE** 3 [10] 6-9-2 (48) Claire Bryan (5) 7/1: 160525: Waited with, late gains, no threat.   3   38a

2297 **PALO BLANCO** 3 [12] 9-9-4 (50) M Henry 12/1: 233246: Nvr btr than mid-div: quick reapp: see 1913.   nk   40a

2302 **ELTON LEDGER** 3 [6] 11-9-8 (54)(vis) R Fitzpatrick (3) 16/1: 500647: Dwelt, sn outpcd, drvn/late prog.   ½   43a

2027 **DOUBLE DESTINY** 15 [9] 4-9-2 (48)(bl) C Carver (3) 20/1: 0-0008: Nvr a factor: AW bow, drop in trip.   nk   37a

602 **REAL TING** 126 [3] 4-7-10 (28)(vis) Joanna Badger (7) 33/1: 005-09: Prom, rdn/fdd fnl 2f: long abs.   1¼   14a

2124 **GOLD EDGE** 10 [8] 6-7-12 (30)(2ow)(5oh) J Quinn 20/1: 060000: Handy, lost tch fnl 2f, 10th: see 148.   1¾   12a

2063 **SAFFRON** 13 [5] 4-9-3 (49) A Clark 10/1: 00-000: Nvr dangerous, fin 11th: see 1842.   1¾   27a

2122 **DESERT INVADER** 11 [14] 9-7-11 (29) K Dalgleish (7) 33/1: 000050: Dwelt, al bhd, fin 12th: see 1305.   shd   7a

*543 **RUDE AWAKENING** 135 [16] 6-10-0 (60) P Goode (3) 12/1: 130310: Prom 3f, sn bhd, fin 13th: ½   37a
4 month abs, top weight: btr 543 (equitrack).

2015 **SEVEN SPRINGS** 15 [1] 4-8-3 (35) P M Quinn (3) 12/1: 030000: Led to 4f out, wknd rapidly fnl 2f, 14th.   3½   4a

2193 **Trojan Hero** 7 [13] 9-8-12 (44)(t) T G McLaughlin 20/1:

1794 **Marjory Polley** 25 [7] 3-8-10 (48) J Tate 33/1:

16 ran   Time 1m 15.2 (1.9)   (H E Lhendup Dorji)   D Nicholls Sessay, N Yorks

YARMOUTH   TUESDAY JULY 4TH   Lefthand, Flat, Fair Track

Official Going: FIRM. Stalls: Straight Course - Stand Side, Remainder - Inside

2386   2.00 ACLE MDN 3YO+ (D)   1m3f101y Firm 17 -23 Slow
£3848   £1184   £592   £296   3 yo rec 12lb

1056 **ZAFONICS SONG** 66 [1] Sir Michael Stoute 3-8-12 Pat Eddery 1/6 FAV: 4-351: 3 br c Zafonic -   78+
Savoureuse Lady (Caerleon) In tch, cruised into lead 2f out, maintained 1L advantage, canter: won with any amount
in hand, hvly bckd, 2 month abs: 4th in a Doncaster mdn on sole '99 start (rtd 85+): eff at 10/11.5f, shld get
further: acts on firm & hvy, stiff/gall trk: runs well fresh: straightforward task, can rate much higher.

2194 **TUFTY HOPPER** 8 [2] P Howling 3-8-12 J Quinn 10/1: 224332: 3 b g Rock Hopper - Melancolia   1¼   63
(Legend Of France) Chsd wnr, rdn & kept on fnl 3f, flatted by margin of defeat: caught a tartar: see 2194.

2135 **JAMAIEL** 11 [4] C E Brittain 3-8-7 P Robinson 15/2: 0-363: 3 b f Polish Precedent - Avice Caro (Caro)   17   36
Cl up, led 4f out, rdn/hdd over 2f out & soon btn: op 6/1: trainer reported that filly was in season.

1466 **VICTORIAN LADY** 41 [3] R M H Cowell 3-8-7 M Hills 50/1: 004: Led till 4f out, soon bhnd: 6 wk abs.   12   21

4 ran   Time 2m 27.4 (4.6)   (Satish K Sanan)   Sir Michael Stoute Newmarket

2387   2.30 LADIES AMAT HCAP 3YO+ 0-75 (F)   1m2f21y Firm 17 -51 Slow   [52]
£2100   £600   £300   3 yo rec 11lb

2262 **PHEISTY** 6 [4] R F Johnson Houghton 3-10-9 (72) Miss E Johnson Houghton 4/1: 00-541: 3 b f Faustus -   74
Phlirty (Pharly) Chsd ldrs, led dist, styd on well to narrowly prevail: op 7/2: '99 Leciester debut wnr (auct
mdn, rtd 75): apprec this step up to 10f: acts on firm & soft, stiff/gall trk: runs well for an amateur.

2002 **SILENT SOUND** 17 [7] Mrs A J Perrett 4-10-0 (52) Miss L J Harwood (7) 7/1: -04002: 4 b g Be My   hd   53
Guest - Whist Awhile (Caerleon) Rear, prog to chall ins last, kept on well, just held: eff with/without blinks.

2033 **JOIN THE PARADE** 15 [1] H J Collingridge 4-10-4 (56) Miss A L Hutchinson (7) 7/1: 100-03: 4 b f   nk   56
Elmaamul - Summer Pageant (Chief's Crown) Unruly paddock & start, raced mid div, prog to chall fnl 2f, every ch
inside last, just held nr line: op 6/1: see 2033.

2126 **COPPLESTONE** 11 [2] P W Harris 4-11-7 (73) Mrs A Hammond (7) 10/1: 024404: Chsd clr ldr, led 2f   2½   69
out, hdd over 1f out & no extra inside last: see 1744, 1070.

1930 **BELLAS GATE BOY** 19 [2] 8-9-13 (51) Mrs L Pearce 7/1: 000305: Rear, rdn/mod prog fnl 3f: op 8/1.   1¼   45

*1819 **SILVER SECRET** 25 [9] 6-9-9 (47) Mrs C Williams 7/2 FAV: 3-0516: Settled rear, no impress fnl 4f.   1   40

*2109 **TAJAR** 12 [6] 8-9-3 (41)(4oh) Mrs H Keddy (5) 6/1: 000317: Chsd ldrs, prog to chall, soon outpcd.   nk   33

1880 **YAHESKA** 22 [8] 3-9-3 (52)(BL) (26oh) Mrs S Owen (5) 40/1: 00-508: Raced keenly & sn well clr,   shd   44$
wide on bend 4f out, hdd 2f out, held after: raced freely in 1st time blinks: only mod form prev: see 1544.

1689 **MINJARA** 31 [10] 5-9-3 (41)(4oh) Miss S Samworth 9/1: 40-559: Al bhd: see 1331.   3½   28

9 ran   Time 2m 11.1 (6.9)   (Mrs R F Johnson Houghton)   R F Johnson Houghton Blewbury, Oxon

2388   3.00 DUNSTON SELLER 2YO (G)   6f   Firm 17 -38 Slow
£1897   £542   £271   Raced stands side

2200 **ITALIAN AFFAIR** 8 [5] A Bailey 2-8-6 S Sanders 9/4 FAV: 02021: 2 ch f Fumo Di Londra - Sergentti   64
(Common Grounds) Chsd ldrs, drvn ahead ins last, forged clr cl home: no bid: well bckd, first win: apprec
step up to 6f, 7f+ cld suit: acts on firm & fast, sharp/fair track: enjoys selling grade.

2301 **JOHN FOLEY** 4 [2] W G M Turner 2-8-11 (VIS) A Daly 3/1: 252422: 2 b c Petardia - Fast Bay (Bay   2   62
Express) Led, clr after 2f, rdn/hdd inside last & no extra: ran freely in 1st time visor: can find one
of these, this style of racing is well suited to sand: handles firm grnd & both AWs: see 2301, 1740.

2155 **BANNINGHAM BLIZ** 10 [4] D Shaw 2-8-6 T Williams 7/2: 006543: 2 ch f Inchinor - Mary From Dunlow   2½   50
(Nicholas Bill) Chsd ldrs, rdn/outpcd over 1f out: only mod form prev.

1667 **BLUEBEL** 32 [7] J S Moore 2-8-6 A Clark 7/1: 504: Held up, never pace to chall: bckd at long odds.   2   45

2079 **RIVER ALN** 13 [1] 2-8-6 (BL) G Duffield 11/2: 05: Raced alone centre, chsd ldr, btn 2f out: blnks.   2½   38

1916 **SOOTY TIME** 20 [3] 2-8-11 G Hind 16/1: -6306: Prom, struggling halfway: see 1206.   1   41

1443 **JEANNIES GIRL** 42 [8] 2-8-6 (BL) A Mackay 16/1: 007: Soon rdn/t.o.: blinks: stablemate of wnr, abs.   9   20

2196 **HARRY JUNIOR** 8 [6] 2-8-11 (BL) Pat Eddery 8/1: 6052W: Unseated rider & bolted bef start: withdrawn.   0

8 ran   Time 1m 13.7 (3.3)   (John A Duffy)   A Bailey Little Budworth, Cheshire

YARMOUTH

TUESDAY JULY 4TH   Lefthand, Flat, Fair Track

2389

3.30 TRETT COND STKS 3YO+ (C)   7f str   Firm 17 +10 Fast
£6380   £2420   £1210   £550   3 yo rec 8 lb Raced stands side

1410 **FLAVIAN** 45 [4] H Candy 4-8-6 C Rutter 20/1: /0-001: 4 b f Catrail - Fatah Flare (Alydar) **96**
Al handy, led going well 2f out, rdn clr fnl 1f, readily: fast time: op 14/1: 6 week abs: unplcd sole '99 start: '98 Newmarket wnr (mdn, rtd 95): eff at 6/7f on firm & fast grnd: likes a fair/gall track: runs well fresh: plenty in hand here & won in a good time, looks ready for step up to Listed company.

1693 **JARN** 31 [5] B Hanbury 3-8-13 (t) W Supple 9/2: 10-102: 3 b c Green Desert - Alkariyh (Alydar) **3 104**
Held up, rdn/prog to chase fnl 1f, al held: op 5/1: eff at 6f, stays 7f: useful, see 1371.

1291 **IFTITAH** 50 [1] Saeed bin Suroor 4-8-11 R Hills 2/1 FAV: 1/5-243: 4 ch c Gone West - Mur Taasha (Riverman) Mid div, rdn/pressed wnr over 1f out, held inside last: hvly bckd: 7 week abs: see 1291, 764 (1m). **½ 93**

*1643 **PRINCE CASPIAN** 32 [7] C E Brittain 3-8-6 P Robinson 20/1: 14: Led 5f, held fnl 1f: highly tried **1¼ 93**
after 1643 but not disgraced on this drop back to 7f: handles firm and soft grnd: see 1643 (mdn, soft).

969 **TROUBLE MOUNTAIN** 76 [6] 3-8-3 G Duffield 5/1: 132-65: Chsd ldrs, nvr pace to chall: abs, op 7/2. **hd 89**

*1574 **GRANNYS PET** 35 [3] Pat Eddery 3/1: 21-316: Towards rear, rdn halfway, never any impression **1 95**
on ldrs: hvly bckd: op 7/2: acts on firm, poss best on an easier surface nowadays: see 1574 (stks, gd/sft).

1946 **KUMAIT** 19 [2] 6-8-11 J Reid 7/1: 221-47: Raced alone centre, prom 5f: op 6/1: see 1946. **4 79**
7 ran   Time 1m 23.1 (0.5)   (Major M G Wyatt)   H Candy Wantage, Oxon

2390

4.00 HAPPISBURGH FILLIES MDN 2YO (D)   7f str   Firm 17 -09 Slow
£3750   £1154   £577   £288   Raced stands side

1312 **LILS JESSY** 49 [8] J Noseda 2-8-11 Pat Eddery 5/2 FAV: 51: 2 b f Kris - Lobmille (Mill Reef) **87**
Keen, rcd mid div, rdn/prog to lead over 1f out, styd on strongly, rdn out: hvly bckd, 7 wk abs: confirmed promise of debut: apprec this step up to 7f, 1m+ will suit: acts on firm grnd & a fair track: runs well fresh.

2174 **PERFECT PLUM** 9 [5] Sir Mark Prescott 2-8-11 G Duffield 7/2: 52: 2 b f Darshaan - Damascene **¾ 85**
(Scenic) Led after 1f, rdn/hld over 1f out, kept on for press: op 4/1: apprec step up to 7f, acts on firm grnd.

-- **CANDICE** [4] E A L Dunlop 2-8-11 J Reid 4/1: 3: 2 br f Caerleon - Criquette (Shirley Heights) **2½ 80+**
Slowly into stride, soon cl up, rdn/outpcd fnl 2f: nicely bckd tho' op 3/1, clr of rem: May foal, dam a 7f juv wnr: half sister to top class miler Markofdistinction: sire top class 10f/12f performer: stays 7f, sure to finish 1m+ in time: acts on firm grnd: encouraging intro & likely to rate more highly in time.

-- **EXOTIC FAN** [7] R Guest 2-8-11 S Sanders 12/1: 4: Rear, rdn/mod gains fnl 3f: op 10/1: Lear **5 70**
Fan filly, May foal, cost 21,000gns: half sister to an Irish 12f wnr, dam a wnr in France: apprec 1m+ in time.

2316 **JUSTINIA 3** [2] 2-8-11 W Ryan 14/1: 035: Led 1f, btn 2f out: op 16/1, qck reapp: btr 2316 (4 rnr mdn). **2 66**

-- **PRIMO VENTURE** [3] 2-8-11 N Callan 11/1: 6: Slowly away, al towards rear: op 8/1: Primo **1¾ 63**
Dominie filly, May foal: dam plcd at 1m/10f: should apprec 1m+ in time for S P C Woods.

2034 **CHOCOLATE FOG** 15 [1] 2-8-11 M Hills 25/1: 057: Keen/prom till halfway: btr 2034 (5f). **3 57**

-- **LIZZEY LETTI** [6] 2-8-11 A Clark 4/1: 8: In tch, drvn/struggling over 2f out: op 9/2: Grand Lodge **7 46**
filly, April foal, cost 45,000gns: sire top class 1m/10f performer: with T G Mills.
8 ran   Time 1m 26.4 (1.8)   (Razza Pallorsi)   J Noseda Newmarket

2391

4.30 LODDON FILLIES HCAP 3YO+ 0-80 (D)   7f str   Firm 17 -20 Slow **[80]**
£4251   £1308   £654   £327   3 yo rec 8 lb Raced towards centre

1564 **NIGHT EMPRESS** 36 [2] J R Fanshawe 3-9-1 (75) Pat Eddery 7/2: 0-2451: 3 br f Emperor Jones - **80**
Night Trader (Melyno) Made all, rdn fnl 2f, styd on well inside last, al holding rivals: op 3/1: first win: plcd on 2 of 4 juv starts (rtd 84): eff at 6/7f on firm & soft grnd, prob handles any track: effective forcing the pace.

*2320 **LADYWELL BLAISE** 3 [1] M L W Bell 3-7-13 (59)(6ex) J Mackay 15/2: 406012: 3 b f Turtle Island - **1¼ 60**
Duly Elected (Persian Bold) Cl up, rdn & kept on well fnl 2f, al just held inside last: quick reapp under pen: acts on both AWs & fast grnd: ran to form of 2320.

2185 **RICH IN LOVE** 9 [4] C A Cyzer 6-10-0 (80) I Mongan (5) 3/1: 0-0023: 5 b m Alzao - Chief's Quest **nk 80**
(Chief's Crown) Prom, drvn & onepcd fnl 2f: well bckd: slipping to a handy mark, likes Yarmouth: see 1283.

1869 **CAUTION** 22 [8] S Gollings 6-8-0 (52) J Quinn 16/1: 060004: Keen/in tch, rdn/outpcd over 2f out, **nk 51**
kept on after, no threat: well h'capped at present: stays 7.5f, 5/6f prob suits best: see 645.

2192 **BE MY WISH** 8 [6] 5-8-4 (56) M Roberts 2/1 FAV: 5-3225: Dwelt, held up, rdn/no impress fnl 2f: bckd. **nk 54**

1676 **SHAFAQ** 31 [3] 3-9-6 (80) R Hills 12/1: 13-06: Keen/cl up, held over 1f out: see 1676 (6f). **¾ 77**

2112 **SILK STOCKINGS** 12 [7] 3-8-13 (73) P Robinson 14/1: 0-0307: In tch till halfway, t.o. **23 36**
7 ran   Time 1m 25.2 (2.6)   (The Woodman Racing Syndicate)   J R Fanshawe Newmarket

HAMILTON

TUESDAY JULY 4TH   Righthand, Undulating Track, Stiff Uphill Finish

Official Going   GOOD TO FIRM. Stalls: Stands side, except 1m/1m1f - inside.

2392

2.15 HANDS AND HEELS APPR HCAP 3YO+ 0-70 (E)   1m4f   Firm 15 -110 Slow **[66]**
£2658   £818   £409   £204   3 yo rec 13lb

*2373 **COSMIC CASE** 1 [1] J S Goldie 5-7-13 (37)(6ex) Dawn Rankin (3) 13/2: 004211: 5 b m Casteddu - La **39**
Fontainova (Lafontaine) In tch, shkn up fnl 2f, kept on strgly: v slow time: defied a 6lbs pen for yesterday's win at Musselburgh (appr h'cap): Feb '00 hdles wnr at Catterick (nov h'cap, 2m, gd, vis, rtd 81h): last won on the Flat in '98 at Musselburgh (h'cap, rtd 65): eff at 12f/2m: acts on firm & gd/soft grnd, with/without visor.

2376 **LITTLE JOHN** 1 [4] Miss L A Perratt 4-9-6 (58) M Scott (6) 7/1: 6-3432: 4 b g Warrshan - Silver **1½ 59**
Venture (Silver Hawk) Waited with, imprvd ent fnl 3f, chsd wnr after, al held: ran yesterday, in form: see 1656.

2366 **WESTGATE RUN** 1 [6] R A Fahey 3-8-8 (59) B McHugh (6) 3/1: -01133: 3 b f Emperor Jones - **½ 59**
Glowing Reference (Reference Point) Set funereal pace, hdd after 6f, drpd rear till kept on well inside last: ran yesterday, back to form: eff at 9/10.5f, stays a slow run 12f: see 2094 (here).

2309 **OCEAN DRIVE** 4 [5] Miss L A Perratt 4-8-3 (41) D Watson 9/4: 565434: Well plcd & every ch till no **½ 40**
extra ins last: well bckd, quick reapp, stablemate of 2nd: won this last time off 17lbs higher mark.

2238 **ONCE MORE FOR LUCK** 6 [2] 9-10-0 (66) G Sparkes 2/1 FAV: 603125: Led after halfway till bef dist, **1½ 63**
fdd: bckd tho' op 6/4, qk reapp, top-weight: race worked out all wrong for this hold-up horse: see 2098.

HAMILTON TUESDAY JULY 4TH Righthand, Undulating Track, Stiff Uphill Finish

5 ran Time 2m 46.8 (15) (J S Goldie) J S Goldie Uplawmoor, E Renfrews

---

2393 2.45 CLASSIFIED CLAIMER 3YO+ 0-60 (F) 1m3f Firm 15 -27 Slow
£2240 £640 £320 3 yo rec 12lb

1867 **SANTA LUCIA 22** [5] M Dods 4-9-7 A Culhane 7/2: -02601: 4 b f Namaqualand - Villasanta 50
(Corvaro) Made all, pshd clr appr fnl 1f: first win: '99 rnr up (h'cap, rtd 65): eff at 11/12f, prob not stay 2m1f
last time: acts on firm & gd/soft grnd, stiff/gall track: ran well from the front here.
2156 **ROOFTOP PROTEST 10** [3] Mrs M Reveley 3-8-12 K Darley 4/5 FAV: -03162: 3 b g Thatching - 4 46
Seattle Siren (Seattle Slew) Held up in tch, prog to chse wnr ent fnl 2f, soon wandered, no impression: nicely
bckd: apprec drop back in trip though still below 1909 (C/D claimer).
2375 **SECONDS AWAY 1** [1] J S Goldie 9-8-12 Dawn Rankin (7) 11/2: 042433: 9 b g Hard Fought - Keep 1½ 32$
Mum (Mummy's Pet) Held up, prog to dispute 2nd 2f out, sn onepace: tchd 7/1, clr rem: flattered, like yesterday.
2143 **RED ROSES 11** [4] Don Enrico Incisa 4-8-13 Kim Tinkler 14/1: 000004: Prom till 3f out: stiff task. 7 23
2236 **WESTERN GENERAL 6** [2] 9-8-12 R Winston 8/1: 42-055: Raced in 2nd till lost pl 3f out: quick reapp. 2 19
5 ran Time 2m 23.4 (4.6) (J A Wynn-Williams) M Dods Piercebridge, Co Durham

---

2394 3.15 YANKEE DOODLE SELLER 2YO (F) 6f Firm 15 -47 Slow
£2163 £618 £309

*2200 **TOMMY SMITH 8** [3] J S Wainwright 2-9-3 J Carroll 6/4: 00411: 2 ch g Timeless Times - Superstream 70
(Superpower) Cl up, began hanging right/chall halfway, neck & neck, won on the nod: nicely bckd, slow time,
no bid: recent Musselburgh wnr (sell): eff at 5/6f on firm/fast, sharp or stiff track: improving in sellers.
2059 **MISS EQUINOX 14** [2] N Tinkler 2-8-6 Kim Tinkler 4/5 FAV: 5022: 2 b f Presidium - Miss Nelski shd 58
(Most Secret) Keen & led, hard pressed from halfway, hung sharply right fnl 1f, just btn: well bckd, clr
of 3rd: acts on firm/fast grnd, shld find a seller, see 2059.
1937 **DAVEYSFIRE 19** [1] Miss L A Perratt 2-8-6 C Lowther 20/1: 63: 2 b f Gildoran - Doubtfire (Jalmood) 9 28
Prom till entering fnl 2f: up in trip, no worthwhile form yet.
2059 **CONSPIRACY THEORY 14** [4] A Berry 2-8-6 O Pears 8/1: 63464: Struggling after 3f: tch 10/1, see 476. 3 19
4 ran Time 1m 13.5 (3.7) (T W Heseltine) J S Wainwright Kennythorpe, N Yorks

---

2395 3.45 TOTE HCAP 3YO+ 0-80 (D) 5f Firm 15 +03 Fast [79]
£6857 £2110 £1055 £527 3 yo rec 5 lb

*2095 **TANCRED TIMES 13** [2] D W Barker 5-7-10 (47)(1oh) Kimberley Hart 10/1: 532411: 5 ch m Clantime - 53
Mischievous Miss (Niniski) Made just about all, rdn & edged right appr fnl 1f, pshd out cl home: op 7/1, best time
of day: recent wnr here at Hamilton (clmr): rnr up in '99 (rtd 48 & 40a): '98 wnr at Carlisle (h'cap, rtd 65 & 47a):
eff at 5/6f, acts on firm, soft & fibresand, prob e/track: likes Hamilton/stiff finishes, without blnks.
824 **RIBERAC 90** [5] M Johnston 4-9-8 (73) J Fanning 3/1: 60-002: 4 b f Efisio - Ciboure (Norwick) 1½ 74+
Rear, kept on nicely fnl 1f, nvr nrr: bckd from 5/1, 3 month abs: highly tried in '99 for W Haggas (stks, rtd
91): '98 Windsor wnr (mdn, List 3rd, rtd 98): eff at 5/6f on firm/fast, any trk: h'capped to win at 6f soon.
2233 **JOHAYRO 6** [3] J S Goldie 7-8-5 (56) A McGlone 13/2: 000243: 7 ch g Clantime - Arroganza ½ 55
(Crofthall) Prsd ldr 2f, outpcd till ran on strgly towards fin: op 5/1, qk reapp: return to 6f will suit: see 798.
2334 **GET STUCK IN 3** [4] Miss L A Perratt 4-10-0 (79) K Darley 5/2 FAV: 060544: Well plcd & every ch hd 77
till one pace fnl 1f: well bckd, quick reapp: back in trip after 2334, see 844.
2240 **FACILE TIGRE 6** [1] 5-7-10 (47)(3oh) K Dalgleish (3) 33/1: 050605: Rear, keeping on fin but nvr dngrs. ½ 44
2118 **SHARP HAT 12** [6] 6-8-6 (57) A Culhane 11/2: 002526: In tch, shaken up 2f out, unable to quicken. ¾ 52
2192 **EASTERN PROPHETS 8** [7] 7-8-4 (54)(vis)(1ow) F Lynch 9/1: -30007: In tch till halfway: vis reapp. 2 44
1768 **GARTH POOL 27** [8] 3-9-3 J Carroll 4/1: -51108: Wide, prom till 2f out: see 1205 (f/sand, rtd 88a). 2½ 56
8 ran Time 58.7 (0.6) (D W Barker) D W Barker Scorton, N Yorks

---

2396 4.15 CLASSIFIED STKS 3YO+ 0-60 (F) 6f Firm 15 -02 Slow
£2240 £640 £320 3 yo rec 6 lb 2 Groups - far side (high no's) had the edge.

2243 **HOWARDS LAD 6** [8] I Semple 3-8-11 (bl) V Halliday 10/1: 000051: 3 b g Reprimand - Port Isaac 58
(Seattle Song) Made all far side, drvn out, just lasted: tchd 14/1, qk reapp: '99 Ayr (mdn, rtd 86 at best):
eff at 6f, tried 7f: acts on firm & gd/soft trks, stiff/gall trks: eff with/without blnks, not visor, forcing the pace.
*2015 **TECHNICIAN 16** [5] E J Alston 5-9-6 (bl) F Lynch 6/1: 520012: 5 ch g Archway - How It Works shd 60
(Commanche Run) In tch far side, drvn to go after wnr appr fnl 1f, just failed: plcd sev times in '99 (h'caps,
rtd 67 & 54a): eff at 6f/1m: acts on firm, soft & fibresand: wears blnks or visor: in gd form, can win again.
2275 **GRAND ESTATE 5** [3] D W Chapman 5-9-3 A Culhane 2/1 FAV: 054523: 5 b g Prince Sabo - 1 54
Ultimate Dream (Kafu) Held up far side, kept on appr fnl 1f, unable to chall: nicely bckd, qck reapp: in better
form now tha' can rate higher: won this last term (rtd 63): see 2275, 614.
2097 **SQUARE DANCER 13** [1] M Dods 4-9-3 G Parkin 4/1: 000054: Prom stands side, veered right from 3 45+
halfway & chsd wnr far side 2f out, no extra dist: likely winner if not conceding so much grnd: see 941.
*1941 **BOWLERS BOY 19** [4] 7-9-6 P Hanagan (7) 5/1: 241215: In tch far side, one pace 2f out: see 1941. 3½ 38
2036 **PRINTSMITH 15** [6] 3-8-11 O Pears 16/1: 0-0106: Al bhd far side: op 10/1: see 1710 (gd/sft). 1½ 30
2275 **ALBERT THE BEAR 5** [7] 7-9-3 (vis) J Carroll 5/1: 600307: Speed far side till halfway, saddle slipped. 4 20
2046 **POWER GAME 15** [2] 7-9-3 P Fessey 50/1: 00-048: Never in it stands side: v stiff task, see 2046, 1685. 8 3
8 ran Time 1m 10.8 (1) (Gordon McDowall) I Semple Carluke, S Lanarks

---

2397 4.45 STARS & STRIPES HCAP 3YO+ 0-75 (E) 1m1f36y Firm 15 -11 Slow [62]
£3607 £1110 £555 £277 3 yo rec 10lb

2235 **ARIZONA LADY 6** [7] I Semple 3-9-5 (63) R Winston 9/2: 100321: 3 ch f Lion Cavern - Unfuwaanah 67
(Unfuwain) Trck ldr, led 2f out, kept on well, pshd out: quick reapp: earlier won at Musselburgh (mdn): some juv
promise (rtd 62): suited by 9f: acts on firm, gd/soft grnd, any track: runs well fresh, up with/forcing the pace.
2094 **NOBBY BARNES 13** [5] Don Enrico Incisa 11-8-0 (34) Kim Tinkler 25/1: -02302: 11 b g Nordance - 1 35
Loving Doll (Godswalk) Rear, rdn appr fnl 2f, styd on up the far rail, nrst fin: typical effort, goes on any grnd.
2049 **LINCOLN DEAN 15** [9] J S Goldie 4-8-6 (40) A McGlone 10/1: 0-0003: 4 b g Mtoto - Play With Me hd 40
(Alzao) Chsd ldrs, prsd wnr dist, sn onepace: tchd 12/1: eff at 1m/9f, handles firm grnd & equitrack, see 1243.

760

HAMILTON   TUESDAY JULY 4TH   Righthand, Undulating Track, Stiff Uphill Finish

2245 **THREE LEADERS** 6 [4] E J Alston 4-8-6 (40) J Bramhill 12/1: 004004: Mid-div, chsd ldrs appr fnl   *hd*   **39**
1f, unable to quicken: qck reapp: stays 9f, handles firm & soft grnd, see 648.
2180 **SWYNFORD PLEASURE** 9 [2] 4-8-11 (45) J Fanning 6/1: 401325: Rear, prog 2f out, not pace to chall.   *¾*   **42**
2245 **KNAVES ASH** 6 [6] 9-8-9 (43) K Darley 4/1: 000036: In tch, outpcd appr fnl 1f: qk reapp, back in trip. *3½*   **34**
2378 **FLOORSOTHEFOREST** 1 [1] 4-9-10 (58) C Lowther 12/1: 652007: Led till 2f out, fdd: op 8/1, tchd 16/1.   *4*   **42**
2094 **PERCHANCER** 13 [8] 4-9-8 (56) P Goode (3) 7/2 FAV: 013448: Dwelt, closed by halfway, wknd   *6*   **30**
qckly appr fnl 3f: nicely bckd, see 846 (C/D).
*2180 **THORNTOUN GOLD** 9 [3] 4-9-1 (49) A Culhane 4/1: 0-4019: Never in it: bckd: something amiss?   *17*   **0**
9 ran   Time 1m 56.5 (2.4)   (Ian Crawford)   I Semple Carluke,S Lanarks

CHANTILLY   WEDNESDAY JUNE 28TH   Righthand, Galloping Track

Official Going   GOOD

2398	2.10 GR 3 PRIX DU LYS 3YO 1m5f Good
	£21134 £7685 £3842

-- **LYCITUS** F Doumen 3-8-11 (bl) G Mosse 37/10: -1211: 3 b c Lycius - Royal Lorna (Val De L'Orne)   **114**
Waited with, hdwy to lead over 2f out, styd on well & pshd out ins last: dual wnr prev this term: eff over
a gall 13f on gd grnd: eff in blnks: tough/consistent, v useful colt.
1317 **EPITRE** 45 A Fabre 3-8-11 O Peslier 9/10 FAV: -1242: 3 b c Common Grounds - Epistolienne   *1½* **111**
(Law Society) Settled last, rdn/hdwy 2f out, no extra fnl 1f: up in trip, stays 10/13f: Gr 1 4th in 1317.
-- **BOURGEOIS** Mme C Head 3-8-11 O Doleuze 29/10: -24123: 3 ch c Sanglamore - Bourbon Girl (Ile De   *2* **108$**
Bourbon) Led to 9f out, ev ch till no extra for press appr fnl 1f: stays 13f on gd grnd.
5 ran   Time 2m 48.6   (J D Martin)   F Doumen France

LEOPARDSTOWN   WEDNESDAY JUNE 28TH   Lefthand, Galloping Track

Official Going   GOOD TO FIRM

2399	7.15 LISTED SILVER FLASH STKS 2YO 6f Good/Firm
	£16250 £4750 £2250

-- **FRESHWATER PEARL** A P O'Brien 2-8-10 M J Kinane 5/4 FAV: 1: 2 b f Alzao - Sister Golden Hair   **97**
(Glint Of Gold) Front rank, rdn to imprv over 1f out, styd on well to lead well ins last, drvn out: fine debut
against some more experienced rivals here: eff over a gall 6f on fast, will reportedly be even better on soft:
another potentially v useful filly from the powerful A P O'Brien string.
-- **LA VIDA LOCA** A P O'Brien 2-8-10 P J Scallen 9/1: -52: 2 ch f Caerleon - Sharata (Darshaan)   *½*   **95**
Waited with, hdwy/no room over 1f out, styd on well, not btn far: gd run, stablemate of wnr: eff at 6f on fast.
1750 **MARSEILLE EXPRESS** 25 M J Grassick 2-8-10 E Ahern 5/1: 33: 2 ch f Caerleon - Sweet Soul Dream   *shd* **95**
(Conquistador Cielo) Prom, went on 2f out, hdd ins last, no extra cl-home: eff at 6f on fast: see 1750 (mdn).
6 ran   Time 1m 13.4   (Mrs John Magnier)   A P O'Brien Ballydolye, Co Tipperary

CURRAGH   FRIDAY JUNE 30TH   Righthand, Stiff, Galloping Track

Official Going   GOOD

2400	7.35 GOFFS 100,000 CHALLENGE 2YO 6f63y Good
	£59000 £19000 £9000 £4000

-- **BERLIN** E Lynam 2-9-0 E Ahern 10/1: 1: 2 b c Common Grounds - Carranza (Lead On Time)   **104**
Prom, cruised into lead 2f out, sn rdn clr, eased nr fin: v eff at 6.3f, further shld suit: runs well fresh
on gd grnd & a stiff/gall trk: impressive debut, looks smart & can win in Listed/Group class.
-- **MOWASSEL** K Prendergast 2-9-0 D M Oliver 6/1: -162: 2 b c General Monash - Dublah (Private   *2*   **97**
Account) Cl-up, styd on well fnl 2f, not pace of wnr: earlier won on debut at Cork (5f mdn, gd/soft): eff at
5/6.3f on gd & gd/soft grnd: 7L clr rem here & should win more races.
-- **ELBADER** D K Weld 2-9-0 P J Smullen 9/1: -533: 2 b c Machiavellian - Moon Drop (Dominion)   *7*   **81**
Waited with, rdn & stdy hdwy fnl 3f, no threat to front 2.
1988 **POUNCE** 13 J A Osborne 2-8-9 M J Kinane 7/1: 44: Bhd, swtchd/hdwy over 1f out, sn btn: fin best   *1½* **72**
of the 3 Brit runners, will apprec a return to 7f: stiff task, will appreciate a return to maidens.
*1413 **PHAROAHS GOLD** 41 2-9-0 M Tebbutt 5/1: -4417: Prom, rdn/fdd fnl 2f: btr 1413 (auct mdn).   **0**
1667 **SPIRIT OF SONG** 28 2-8-9 J Murtagh 10/3 FAV: 440: Led, hdd appr fnl 2f, sn lost tch, fin last: **0**
disappointing here but was later found to have breathing difficulties: see 1667, 1372.
11 ran   Time 1m 17.2   (R P Behan)   E Lynam Clonsilla, Co Dublin

CHANTILLY   FRIDAY JUNE 30TH   Righthand, Galloping Track

Official Going   GOOD

FRIDAY JUNE 30TH **Righthand, Galloping Track**

2401 2.25 GR 3 PRIX CHLOE 3YO FILLIES 1m1f Good
£21134 £7685 £3842

-- **DI MOI OUI** P Bary 3-8-9 S Guillot 122/10: -34101: 3 b f Warning - Biosphere (Pharly)   **110**
Waited with, strong run to lead dist, drvn out: winner two starts ago, also down the field in the French Oaks:
eff over a stiff/gall 9f, has tried 10.5f: acts on gd grnd & runs well fresh: tough/useful filly.
-- **PREMIERE CREATION** J De Roualle 3-8-9 T Thulliez 9/2: -12: 3 ch f Green Tune - Allwaki (Miswaki)   ¾ **108**
Mid-div, rdn/hdwy 2f out, ran on well ins last, held cl-home: clr rem: recent debut wnr: eff at 9f on gd.
-- **LA GANDILIE** R Gibson 3-8-9 G Mosse 353/10: 121-63: 3 gr f Highest Honor - Prospector's Star   3 **103**
(Mr Prospector) Settled rear, rdn to imprv 2f out, styd on fnl 1f but no threat to front 2.
11 ran   Time 1m 49.8   (Grundy Bloodstock Ltd)   P Bary France

2402 3.25 LISTED PRIX LA MOSKOWA 4YO+ 1m7f Good
£13449 £4611 £3458

1902 **LUCKY DREAM** 19 H A Pantall 6-8-11 T Jarnet : 15-551: 6 b h Homme De Loi - Lady Of The House   **108**
(Habitat) -:
*1484 **PAIRUMANI STAR** 36 J L Dunlop 5-8-11 G Mosse : 00-012: 5 ch h Caeleon - Dawn Star   snk **107**
(High Line) Front rank, led 1m out, hdd appr fnl 1f, rall well ins last & not btn far: fine run on this step
up to Listed class: tough & genuine: form of race 1484 (rtd h'cap) is working out well.
2323} **WAJINA** 369 A Fabre 4-8-8 T Gillet : -15-3: 4 b f Rainbow Quest - Wajd (Northern Dancer)   3 **100**
7 ran   Time 3m 13.7   (Mme C Dutertre-Hallope)   H A Pantall France

HAMBURG **SATURDAY JULY 1ST** **Righthand, Flat Track**

Official Going SOFT

2403 4.45 GR 3 HOLSTEN TROPHY 3YO+ 6f Soft
£38710 £13548 £6452

2981} **AREION** 343 A Wohler 5-9-1 A Starke : 1/3-1: 5 b h Big Shuffle - Aerleona (Caerleon)   **114**
Made all, drvn out ins last: eff arnd 6f on soft grnd: smart German-trained entire.
1622 **GORSE** 35 H Candy 5-9-5 T Mundry : 25-362: 5 b h Sharpo - Pervenche (Latest Model)   1 **115**
Nvr far away, drvn & not pace of wnr fnl 1f: won this race last year (rtd 115): smart, loves soft: see 952.
1746 **TERTULLIAN** 29 P Schiergen 5-9-5 T Hellier : 132-33: 5 ch h Miswaki - Turbaine (Trempolino)   ¾ **113**
Mid-div, hdwy over 1f out, no extra well ins last: see 1746.
11 ran   Time 1m 12.69   (Frau M Haller)   A Wohler Germany

CURRAGH **SATURDAY JULY 1ST** **Righthand, Stiff, Galloping Track**

Official Going YIELDING

2404 3.45 GR 2 PRETTY POLLY STKS 3YO+ FILLIES 1m2f Yielding
£48000 £15200 £7200 £2400 3 yo rec 11lb

1828 **LADY UPSTAGE** 22 B W Hills 3-8-8 M Hills 9/2: 4-1251: 3 b f Alzao - She's The Tops (Shernazar)   **111**
Prom, went on 2f out, clr dist, drvn out ins last, hld on nr fin: op 3/1: recent 5th in the Oaks, earlier won on
reapp at Kempton (List): '99 Brighton mdn wnr, also 4th in Listed company (rtd 98): eff at 1m, suited by 10f:
acts on gd & hvy, handles fast & any trk: tough & smart, reportedly heads for the Gr 1 Nassau Stks at Goodwood.
1626 **PRESELI** 34 M J Grassick 3-8-13 E Ahern 6/1: 11-102: 3 b f Caerleon - Hill Of Snow (Reference   shd **115**
Point) Mid-div, rdn/prog over 2f out, ran on strongly ins last, just held: clr rem: looks sure to be suited
by a step up to 12f now & deserves to take her chance in the Irish Oaks: see 1626.
1626 **ALLURING** 34 A P O'Brien 3-8-8 C O'Donoghue 20/1: 4-1503: 3 b f Lure - Shelbiana (Chieftain II)   2½ **106**
Waited with, eff when no room 2f out, styd on well fnl 1f: eff at 10f on gd, win soon over 12f.
1152 **ELA ATHENA** 57 M A Jarvis 4-9-5 P Robinson 8/1: 212-04: In tch, rdn & styd on appr fnl 1f,   ½ **105**
no threat to ldrs: 8 wk abs: smart at best, poss still needed this: see 1152.
1587 **LADY IN WAITING** 32 5-9-8 J Murtagh 8/1: 015-55: Led to 2f out, sn fdd: see 1587.   ¾ **106**
1626 **YARA** 34 3-8-8 D P McDonogh 12/1: -22016: Mid-div at best: recent Curragh wnr (9f mdn, gd/soft).   2 **99**
1469 **SPINNING TOP** 38 3-8-8 M J Kinane 11/8 FAV: 120: Trkd ldrs, smooth hdwy 3f out, rdn/wknd over   **0**
1f out, eased when btn: reportedly fin slightly lame: see 1469.
1378 **CAPE GRACE** 45 4-9-5 N G McCullagh 10/1: 4-6158: Handy, lost tch fnl 2f: 6 wk abs: btr 1378.   **0**
10 ran   Time 2m 07.7   (Mrs E Roberts)   B W Hills Lambourn, Berks

2405 4.45 GR 3 IAWS CURRAGH CUP 3YO+ 1m6f Yielding
£25200 £7980 £3780 £1260 3 yo rec 15lb

14   **QUALITY TEAM** 237 D K Weld 3-8-9 (bl) P J Smullen 7/2: -21011: 3 b c Diesis - Ready For Action   **113**
(Riverman) Mid-div, gd hdwy 3f out, hmpd dist but sn led, pshd out, readily: recent wnr at Gowran Park &
Leopardstown (stks): eff at 12/14f on gd, 2m suit: acts on a gall trk & eff in blnks: v useful & progressive.
*1620 **ROYAL REBEL** 38 M Johnston 4-9-10 (bl) J Murtagh 5/1: 10-012: 4 b g Robelino - Greenvera   2½ **108**
(Riverman) Front rank, led 3f out, hdd over 1f out, not pace of wnr fnl 1f: tough & useful: see 1620.
1565 **CHURLISH CHARM** 33 R Hannon 5-9-10 J Reid 5/4 FAV: 0-0323: 5 b h Niniski - Blushing Storm   ¾ **107**
(Blushing Groom) Prom, prog to lead over 2f out, hdd ins last, sn btn: below-par here, best at 2m: see 1565.
2068 **DUTCH HARRIER** 11 K Prendergast 3-8-9 D P McDonogh 7/1: 031224: Handy, btn fnl 2f: see 2068.   4½ **103**
1339 **SINON** 44 5-9-10 J Fanning 9/1: /01-65: Led to 3f out, lost tch fnl 2f: see 1339.   ¾ **102**
7 ran   Time 3m 05.6   (Moyglare Stud Farm)   D K Weld Curragh, Co Kildare

SAINT CLOUD
SUNDAY JULY 2ND   Lefthand, Galloping Track

Official Going   GOOD

2406	**3.00 GR 1 GRAND PRIX DE SAINT-CLOUD 3YO+** **1m4f** **Good**
	£119527 £46110 £23055 £11527

*1625 **MONTJEU** 35 J E Hammond 4-9-8 C Asmussen 1/5 JT FAVcp: 114-11: 4 b c Sadler's Wells - Floripedes **130**
(Top Ville) Rear, cruised into lead appr fnl 1f, easily qcknd clr, hard held: earlier won at The Curragh (Gr1):
'99 wnr at Longchamp (2 Gr 2's), Chantilly (Gr 1 French Derby), The Curragh (Gr1 Irish Derby, 5L) & notably the
Gr 1 Arc at Longchamp (rtd 136): juv wnr at Longchamp & Chantilly: eff at 10/12f on gd & hvy grnd, handles firm
& likes a gall trk: top class colt with a devastating turn of foot, will prove v hard to beat in the King George.

*1902 **DARING MISS** 21 A Fabre 4-9-5 O Peslier 26/10: 2-4112: 4 b f Sadler's Wells - Bourbon Girl **5** **116**
(Ile de Bourbon) Chsd ldrs, rdn & styd on fnl 2f but not pace of easy wnr: not disgraced bhd top-class rival.

1827 **SAGAMIX** 23 Saeed bin Suroor 5-9-8 S Guillot 38/10: 44-043: 5 b h Linamix - Saganeca (Sagace) **1** **117**
Cl-up, led appr fnl 2f, hdd appr fnl 1f, sn outpcd: former Arc wnr, much better on soft/hvy grnd: see 1827.

-- **STOP BY** J E Hammond 5-9-8 O Thirion 1/5 JT FAVcp: 5150-4: Led, hdd over 2f out, fdd: pacemaker. **6** **109**
4 ran   Time 2m 31.4   (M Tabor)   J E Hammond France

CURRAGH
SUNDAY JULY 2ND   Righthand, Stiff, Galloping Track

Official Going   GOOD

2407	**1.35 ANHEUSER EBF MDN 2YO** **7f** **Good**
	£6900 £1600 £700

-- **MOZART** A P O'Brien 2-9-2 J A Heffernan 2/9 FAV: 1: 2 b c Danehill - Victoria Cross (Spectacular **101**
Bid) Trkd ldrs, went on over 3f out, easily went clr fnl 2f: debut: v eff over a stiff/gall 7f & 1m will suit
in time: runs well fresh on gd: impressive & looks potentially smart, sure-fire Listed/Gr 3 wnr.

-- **SPEIRBHEAN** J S Bolger 2-8-11 K J Manning 10/1: 2: 2 b f Danehill - Saviour (Majestic Light) **8** **79**

-- **KHAYSAR** J Oxx 2-9-2 J Murtagh 9/2: 3: 2 b c Pennekamp - Khaytada (Doyoun) **2½** **80**
5 ran   Time 1m 27.5   (Michael Tabor)   A P O'Brien Ballydoyle, Co Tipperary

2408	**2.10 GR 3 RAILWAY STKS 2YO** **6f** **Good**
	£29450 £9025 £4275 £1425

*1896 **HONOURS LIST** 25 A P O'Brien 2-8-5h D M Oliver 1/4 FAV: 11: 2 b c Danehill - Gold Script (Script Ohio) **111**
Chsd ldrs going well, went on 3f out, pushed clr ins last, cmftbly: earlier won on debut at Gowran Park (mdn):
eff at 6/7f, further suit: acts on gd, gd/soft & a stiff trk: progressive & smart, win again in Gr company.

-- **SURE MARK** M Halford 2-8-10 F M Berry 10/1: -2142: 2 b c Goldmark - Sure Flyer (Sure Blade) **2** **102**
Prom, hdwy 2f out, chall wnr appr fnl 1f, sn outpcd: earlier scored here at The Curragh (5f auct mdn, gd/soft).

-- **SEQUOYAH** A P O'Brien 2-8-7 J A Heffernan 12/1: 3: 2 b f Sadler's Wells - Brigid (Irish River) **3½** **92**
Settled rear, rdn/eff 2f out, sn btn: debut, stablemate of wnr: bred to apprec 7f+ in time.
5 ran   Time 1m 14.5   (Mrs John Magnier)   A P O'Brien Ballydoyle, Co Tipperary

2409	**4.00 GR 1 BUDWEISER IRISH DERBY 3YO** **1m4f** **Good**
	£482400 £164400 £79400 £28400

+1848 **SINNDAR** 22 J Oxx 3-9-0 (t) J Murtagh 11/10 FAV: 1-2111: 3 b c Grand Lodge - Sinntara (Lashkari) **130**
Cl-up, rdn into lead appr fnl 1f, powered clear for a most impressive success: well bckd: earlier won at
Leopardstown (Gr 3) & notably Epsom (Gr 1 Derby, by 1L): '99 wnr at The Curragh (2, incl Gr 1, rtd 107): eff
at 1m, suited by 12f now & further sould suit: acts on fast, soft & any trk: wears a t-strap: most tough,
genuine, progressive & high-class colt, will now reportedly be given a break before an Arc bid.

*1899 **GLYNDEBOURNE** 22 A P O'Brien 3-9-0 J A Heffernan 16/1: -2112: 3 b c Sadler's Wells - Heaven Only **9** **118**
Knows (High Top) Settled in tch, hdwy halfway, styd on well fnl 2f but no ch with impressive wnr: fine run by
this lightly rcd colt: acts on gd & soft grnd: shld certainly win again in Gr 2/3 company: see 1899.

1752 **CIRO** 22 A P O'Brien 3-9-0 G Duffield 20/1: 1-3163: 3 ch c Woodman - Gioconda (Nijinsky) **1½** **116**
Mid-div, eff over 3f out, drvn & late hdwy ins last, no danger: stablemate of rnr-up: stays 12f well, 14f
shld now suit: smart run here, should win another Gr race: see 1317.

-- **RAYPOUR** J Oxx 3-9-0 N G McCullagh 200/1: -22624: Set fast pace, hdd appr fnl 1f, no extra fnl 1f: **½** **115**
mdn, put in as pacemaker for wnr but an excellent run in his own right to hold on for 4th: stays 12f on good.

1899 **TAKALI** 22 3-9-0 S W Kelly 200/1: -21445: Cl-up, rdn/held appr fnl 1f: stablemate of wnr: **1½** **113**
highly tried & not disgraced: handles gd & soft grnd: see 1899 (Gr3).

*1752 **HOLDING COURT** 28 3-9-0 P Robinson 9/4: 0-1116: Handy, rdn & ev ch appr 2f out, no extra over **shd** **112**
over 1f out: impressive French Derby wnr when able to dominate on soft in 1752, do better given those conditions.

1899 **MEDIA PUZZLE** 22 3-9-0 P J Smullen 66/1: 3-1137: Waited with, eff over 3f out, sn held: see 1899. **4** **104**

*1898 **SHAKESPEARE** 23 3-9-0 D M Oliver 33/1: 1-418: Al mid-div: stablemate of rnr-up & 3rd: see 1898 (10f). **½** **103**

-- **SHOAL CREEK** 3-9-0 C O'Donoghue 200/1: 2-5319: Prom, rdn/fdd fnl 3f: 10 wk abs: earlier this **2** **100**
term won a mdn at Cork (1m, gd/soft): v highly tried here.

1627 **KORASOUN** 35 3-9-0 K J Manning 66/1: -1250: Al rear, fin 10th: see 1627. **6** **92**

+1171 **KINGS BEST** 57 3-9-0 Pat Eddery 9/2: 15-21P: Bhd when p.u. lame bef halfway: sadly fractured a **0**
cannon bone & his racing career is almost certainly over: 3½L Newmarket 2000 Guineas winner in 1171.
11 ran   Time 2m 33.9   (H H Aga Khan)   J Oxx Currabeg, Co Kildare

2410	**5.20 GR 2 BUDWEISER INTERNATIONAL STKS 3YO+** **1m1f** **Good**
	£56000 £15200 £7200 £2400 3 yo rec 10lb

1460 **ALRASSAAM** 42 M A Jarvis 4-9-5 P Robinson 6/1: 12-041: 4 b h Zafonic - Lady Blackfoot (Prince **116**
Tenderfoot) Made all, rdn clr over 2f out, drvn to maintain advantage fnl 1f: jockey received a 1 day whip ban:
'99 wnr at Newbury (mdn, reapp), Haydock (stks) & Chantilly (Gr 3, rtd 116 at best): eff at 9/10f on firm &

CURRAGH SUNDAY JULY 2ND **Righthand, Stiff, Galloping Track**

v soft grnd: likes a stiff/gall trk: right back to best & a v smart run here, shld win another Group race.
*1627 **JAMMAAL** 35 D K Weld 3-8-9 (bl) P J Smullen 7/2: -21212: 3 b c Robellino - Navajo Love Song — 8 104
(Dancing Brave) Cl-up, rdn & not pace of wnr fnl 2f: v consistent this term: see 1627 (List, 1st time blnks).
2066 **SARAFAN** 12 Sir Mark Prescott 3-8-9 G Duffield 6/4 FAV: 221-53: 3 b c Lear Fan - Saraa Ree (Caro) — 3 99
Settled last, eff btwn 2f out, sn held: disapp here & can do much better, see 2066 (1m Gr 1).
2089 **KING ADAM** 11 Sir Michael Stoute 4-9-5 Pat Eddery 9/4: 16-154: Chsd ldrs, drvn/btn fnl 2f: well — hd 99
below par here, much better on reapp in 1841 (stks).
4 ran   Time 1m 52.9   (Sheikh Ahmed Al Maktoum)   M A Jarvis Newmarket

YARMOUTH WEDNESDAY JULY 5TH **Lefthand, Flat, Fair Track**

Official Going GOOD/FIRM. Stalls: Inside, Except Str Course - Stands Side

2411

6.15 CATFIELD CLAIMER 3YO+ (F) **1m str Good/Firm 31 +03 Fast**
£2373 £508 £508   3 yo rec 9 lb Raced towards centre

1998 **HUGWITY** 18 [4] G C Bravery 8-9-6 J Weaver 11/8 FAV: 621401: 8 ch g Cadeaux Genereux - Nuit d'Ete — 52
(Super Concorde) Rear, drvn 3f out, prog to chall over 1f out, styd on gamely to lead ins last: well bckd tho' op
4/5: earlier scored at Lingfield (2, AW clmrs, rtd 83a) & Nottingham (stks): '99 scorer again at Lingfield (h'cap,
rtd 86a): eff btwn 7/10f on fast, gd/soft & both AWs: handles any trk, loves Lingfield: tough.
2303 **TOBLERSONG** 5 [11] Mrs L Stubbs 5-9-1 (tvi) Pat Eddery 7/1: 006442: 5 b g Tirol - Winsong Melody — ¾ 44
(Music Maestro) Held up, smooth prog to lead halfway, rdn/hdd ins last: qck reapp: eff at 6f/1m: see 958.
2345 **CLAUDIUS TERTIUS** 4 [10] M A Jarvis 3-8-7 P Robinson 16/1: 000342: 3 b g Rudimentary - Sanctuary dht 45
Cove (Habitat) Prom, ev ch fnl 2f, drvn/just held well ins last: ddhtd for 2nd, qck reapp: eff at 1m/9f.
1935 **WENSUM DANCER** 20 [7] R Guest 3-8-4 M Roberts 33/1: -04064: Led 1f, drvn/no extra fnl 1f: dropped — 3 36
in trip: eff at 1m on fast grnd, only mod form prev.
2349 **COLONEL NORTH** 3 [2] 4-9-6 J Reid 5/1: Cl-up,drvn/held fnl 1f: op 7/1, quick reapp. shd 43
2345 **DISTINCTLY EAST** 4 [13] 3-8-9 (vis) Dale Gibson 11/1: -04056: Rcd stands rail, chsd ldrs, btn 1f out. 9 27
1772 **CAERDYDD FACH** 28 [1] 4-8-7 A Mackay 25/1: 50-047: Prom till halfway: see 1772 (sell h'cap). ¾ 15
1611 **SAIFAN** 35 [9] 11-9-4 (vis) D McGaffin (5) 9/1: 060-08: Cl-up 6f: op 8/1: '99 wnr at Yarmouth (2, — 4 14
clmr & h'cap, rtd 64): eff at 7f, suited by 1m: handles soft, likes gd & firm, any trk: loves Lingfield: tough.
2134 **REGARDEZ MOI** 12 [12] 3-8-4 A Beech (5) 7/1: 00-0639: Led after 1f till halfway, sn btn: btr 2134. 2½ 8
2118 **SWISS ALPS** 13 [6] 3-8-5 (bl) R Price 20/1: 0-0000: Bhd fnl 3f: 10th: mod form. shd 9
1335 **Mitie Access** 49 [5] 4-8-6 (VIS) P Clarke (6) 50/1:   408 **Sky City** 160 [8] 4-8-9 R Winston 66/1:
12 ran   Time 1m 37.4 (2.3)   (Sawyer Whatley Partnership)   G C Bravery Newmarket

2412

6.50 BBC LOOK EAST HCAP 3YO+ 0-80 (D) **1m str Good/Firm 31 +05 Fast** [80]
£5164 £1589 £794 £397   3 yo rec 9 lb Raced towards centre

2391 **RICH IN LOVE** 1 [7] C A Cyzer 6-10-0 (80) A Beech (5) 10/1: -00231: 6 b m Alzao - Chief's Quest — 86
(Chief's Crown) Chsd ldr, went on over 2f out, rdn & styd on strongly fnl 1f, al holding rivals: op 8/1, best time
of night: fin 3rd over 7f here yesterday (h'cap): rnr-up in '99 (rtd 98, flattered): '98 Ascot wnr (ladies h'cap)
& Yarmouth (h'cap, rtd 83 at best): suited by 7f/1m on firm, gd & any trk: loves Yarmouth.
2133 **TOPTON** 12 [1] P Howling 6-9-4 (70)(bl) R Winston 13/2: 005002: 6 b g Royal Academy - Circo 1½ 71
(High Top) Chsd ldrs, chsd wnr over 1f out, rdn/kept on, al held: tough & consistent gldg: see 463 (AW).
*1964 **TRICCOLO** 19 [3] A C Stewart 3-9-2 (77) M Roberts 9/4 FAV: -01513: 3 b c Piccolo - Tribal Lady 1½ 75
(Absalom) Rdn/towards rear, styd on fnl 2f, no threat: hvly bckd: see 1964.
1926 **PROSPECTORS COVE** 21 [11] J Pearce 7-9-4 (70) J Reid 8/1: 000104: Rear, no room 3f out, kept on fnl ½ 67
2f under hands & heels riding, no threat: no room at a crucial stage, keep in mind: see 1611 (C/D).
2133 **PETRUS** 12 [6] 4-9-8 (74)(t) P Robinson 16/1: -00005: Cl-up, onepace over 2f out: see 1286. 1½ 68
*2309 **MISSILE TOE** 5 [9] 7-8-5 (57)(6ex) Jonjo Fowle 7/1 100/30: 554116: Keen/rear, eff 3f out, mod prog. 2 47
1676 **SHARP GOSSIP** 32 [10] 4-8-6 (58) S Whitworth 25/1: -00007: Keen/rear, drvn, nvr threat: see 1676 (6f). 2 44
2085 **DILSAA** 14 [5] 3-8-11 (72)(BL) Pat Eddery 11/1: 5-5008: Keen, sn clr ldr, hdd over 2f out, fdd: 3½ 51
not settle tonight in 1st time blnks: see 810.
3859] **LIONARDO** 299 [2] 4-9-9 (75) Paul Smith 16/1: -00119: Rdn/towards rear, btn 3f out: op 14/1: recent nk 53
wnr of 2 races in native Belgium (stks h'cap): eff at 1m/9f on firm & soft grnd.
2349 **WELODY** 3 [2] 4-8-12 (64)(bl) Dale Gibson 33/1: 100400: Cl-up till halfway, wknd qckly 2f out: 10th. 3½ 35
2130 **ETISALAT** 14 [4] 5-8-7 (59) G Bardwell 14/1: 113000: Struggling halfway: 11th: btr 1254. 5 20
11 ran   Time 1m 37.2 (2.1)   (R M Cyzer)   C A Cyzer Maplehurst, W Sussex

2413

7.15 WHEATACRE SELLER 3YO (G) **7f str Good/Firm 31 -18 Slow**
£1939 £554 £277 Raced towards centre

2187 **ALABAMA WURLEY** 9 [10] D Morris 3-8-9 (vis) D McGaffin (5) 8/1: 006001: 3 b f Environment Friend - — 47
Logarithm (King Of Spain) Trkd ldrs, drvn to lead over 1f out, styd on well, drvn out: no bid, visor reapp: '99
Newmarket scorer (sell, rtd 65, rnr-up on sand, rtd 69a): eff at 7f, stays 1m: acts on firm, soft & fibresand:
handles any trk: suited by a visor: enjoys seil grade.
2042 **TERM OF ENDEARMENT** 16 [4] J Pearce 3-8-9 J Reid 9/2: 056052: 3 b f First Trump - Twilight Secret 1¼ 43
(Vaigly Great) Mid-div, prog/ev ch over 1f out, held by wnr nr fin: stays 1m, tried 10f: handles fast & gd/soft grnd.
2134 **SOBER AS A JUDGE** 12 [8] J Pearce 3-9-0 G Bardwell 20/1: 0-0003: 3 b g Mon Tresor - Flicker Toa nk 47$
Flame (Empery) Cl-up, drvn/led 2f out till over 1f out, no extra nr fin: eff at 1m on fast: prev with C Dwyer.
1972 **OUTSTANDING TALENT** 19 [2] A W Carroll 3-8-9 A Beech (5) 4/1 FAV: -60024: Rear, rdn/prog & ch 2f 2½ 37
out, sn outpcd: op 3/1: see 1972.
2134 **CUPIDS DART** 12 [5] 3-9-0 (bl) R Winston 11/1: 230005: Prom, led 3f out till 2f out, fdd: blnks reapp. 5 32
-- **LETTRE PERSANNE** [1] 3-8-9 Paul Smith 9/1: 213-66: Mid-div, btn 2f out: recently unplcd in 1¼ 24
native Belgium: '99 wnr at Ostend (6f, stks): eff at 6f on firm & gd grnd.
2187 **JUST MAC** 9 [6] 3-9-0 M Roberts 16/1: 606007: Keen/towards rear, nvr on terms: see 221. nk 28
2187 **ANNS MILL** 9 [9] 3-8-9 Dale Gibson 11/1: 040008: Led till halfway, sn btn: see 1212. ½ 22
2026 **SILCA FANTASY** 17 [7] 3-8-9 Pat Eddery 8/1: 444609: Briefly led halfway, sn btn: see 278 (AW mdn). 2 18
2036 **LADY CYRANO** 16 [3] 3-8-9 R Fitzpatrick (3) 11/2: 206020: Sn drvn/bhd: 10th: btr 2036. ½ 17
2240 **PLAYINAROUND** 7 [11] 3-8-9 Darren Williams (5) 14/1: 0-0000: Dwelt/bhd, al rear: 11th: op 12/1. 2 13

YARMOUTH   WEDNESDAY JULY 5TH   Lefthand, Flat, Fair Track

11 ran   Time 1m 26.00 (3.4)   (Wacky Racing)   D Morris Newmarket, Suffolk

2414   7.45 EBF HEMSBY MDN 2YO (D)   6f   Good/Firm 31 -54 Slow
£3510   £1080   £540   £270

-- QUINK [2] Sir Mark Prescott 2-9-0 M Worrell (7) 16/1: 1: 2 ch g Selkirk - Ink Pot (Green Dancer)   **84**
Trkd ldrs, chall over 1f out & rdn/led ins last, pushed clr cl-home: op 10/1: Feb foal, a 1st foal: dam plcd at 1m
as a juv: eff at 6f, 7f+ will suit: acts on fast grnd & a fair trk: runs well fresh: open to further improvement.

-- RED CARPET [1] M L W Bell 2-9-0 M Fenton 10/11 FAV: 2: 2 ch c Pivotal - Fleur Rouge (Pharly)   1½ **78**
Cl-up & went on halfway, rdn/hdd ins last, no extra under minimal press: hvly bckd, same ownership as wnr: Feb
foal, half-brother to numerous wnrs: dam a juv wnr: eff at 6f, may get further: acts on fast grnd & a fair trk.

-- WHERE THE HEART IS [6] M H Tompkins 2-9-0 Dale Gibson 16/1: 3: 2 ch c Efisio - Luminary (Kalaglow) 2½ **71**
Chsd ldrs, drvn/no impress on front final 1f: op 8/1: Efisio colt, Apr foal, cost 32,000 gns, a first foal:
dam uncrd: sire progressive 6f/1m performer: should improve for this intro.

2106 **IRON DRAGON 13** [3] J Noseda 2-9-0 (t) Pat Eddery 11/2: 64: Led 2f, held over 1f out: op 9/2.   ¾ **69**

-- MYTHICAL JINKS [5] 2-9-0 J Reid 10/1: 5: Dwelt, led after 2f till halfway, sn held: op 11/2: Miswaki   nk **68**
colt, Mar foal, cost 60,000 gns: half-brother to a wnr in US: sire a top class 2yo: with E A L Dunlop.

-- DEFINITE GUEST [4] 2-9-0 P Robinson 7/2: 6: Rear, rdn/outpcd final 2f: Definite Article colt, Mar   1¾ **64**
foal, cost 85,000 gns: half-brother to a 7f juv wnr: dam a 7f juv wnr: sire proved best at 10/12f.
6 ran   Time 1m 15.5 (5.1)   (Cheveley Park Stud)   Sir Mark Prescott Newmarket

2415   8.15 FRED ARMSTRONG HCAP 3YO+ 0-70 (E)   6f   Good/Firm 31 -09 Slow   [67]
£3526   £1085   £542   £271   3 yo rec 6 lb

2320 **MUJAS MAGIC 4** [10] Mrs N Macauley 5-8-9 (48)(vis) R Fitzpatrick (3) 16/1: 500501: 5 b m Mujadil -   **52**
Grave Error (Northern Treat) Sn rdn in tch, prog to chall over 1f out, styd on well to lead nr line: op 12/1: qck
reapp: rnr-up on sand earlier (rtd 63a, h'cap): '99 h'cap wnr at Beverley (K Ivory, h'cap, rtd 51) & W'hampton (rtd
64a): '98 Brighton wnr (h'cap, rtd 59): eff at 5/7f on firm, soft & fibresand, any trk: best in vis/blnks.

2221 **CRUSTY LILY 8** [11] J M Bradley 4-8-3 (42) R Mullen 11/2: 00-042: 4 gr f Whittingham - Miss   nk **45**
Crusty (Belfort) Bhd ldrs, prog to chall fnl 2f, ev ch ins last, outpcd: confirmed improvement of 2221.

2207 **THATCHAM 9** [7] R W Armstrong 4-9-5 (58)(bl) Pat Eddery 5/4 FAV: 004123: 4 ch g Thatching -   hd **60**
Calaloo Sioux (Our Native) Cl-up, drvn/led 2f out, strongly prsd & hdd/just held nr fin: hvly bckd: see 2207.

2340 **FRILLY FRONT 4** [9] T D Barron 4-9-3 (56) M Roberts 11/1: 005004: Mid-div, outpcd by front trio fnl   2½ **51**
2f: op 7/1, quick reapp: see 631 (AW, 5f).

2334 **DISTINCTIVE DREAM 4** [3] 6-10-0 (67) J Reid 12/1: 000405: Rear, rdn halfway, mod gains: op 8/1.   hd **61**

1395 **INDIAN WARRIOR 46** [2] 4-8-10 (49) L Newton 14/1: 600006: Dwelt, rear, prog under minimal press   2½ **36+**
fnl 2f: op 12/1, 6 wk abs: not given a hard time, one to note for similar contests at 7f: see 364.

2183 **KEE RING 10** [8] 4-9-3 (56)(bl) S Whitworth 16/1: 606067: Cl-up, wknd qckly fnl 2f: see 1464, 1213.   shd **43**

2184 **GLASTONBURY 10** [4] 4-7-10 (35) G Bardwell 33/1: 050308: Keen/led 4f, wknd qckly: see 1913, 425.   7 **9**

2293 **KUWAIT ROSE 5** [5] 4-9-12 (65) D McGaffin (5) 14/1: 6-4549: Rdn/al bhd: op 12/1, quick reapp.   3 **32**

1910 **HARVEYS FUTURE 21** [6] 6-8-7 (46) A Polli (3) 6/1: 20-32W: Refused to enter stalls, withdrawn.   **0**
10 ran   Time 1m 12.8 (2.4)   (T J Bird)   Mrs N Macauley Sproxton, Leics

2416   8.45 BREYDON WATER HCAP 3YO+ 0-75 (E)   1m6f   Good/Firm 31 -14 Slow   [64]
£3591   £1105   £552   £276   3 yo rec 15lb

*2195 **TYPHOON TILLY 9** [5] C F Wall 3-8-6 (57)(6ex) R Mullen 5/4 FAV: 00-311: 3 b g Hernando - Meavy   **65**
(Kalaglow) Trkd ldrs, smooth prog to lead 2f out, rdn/styd on well fnl 1f, al holding rival: hvly bckd under a 6lb
pen: earlier scored here at Yarmouth (C/D h'cap, 1st win): rtd 60 in '99 (mdn): eff at 12f, suited by 14f, may get
further: acts on fast & gd/soft, likes a stiff/fair trk, esp Yarmouth: progressive gelding.

2386 **TUFTY HOPPER 1** [2] P Howling 3-8-12 (63) R Winston 6/1: 243322: 3 b g Rock Hopper - Melancolia   ¾ **67**
(Legend Of France) Keen/prom, chsd ldr & ev ch 2f out, kept on tho' held nr fin: op 5/1: rnr-up in a mdn here
yesterday: clr of rem: see 2194 (C/D mdn).

2156 **ZINCALO 11** [3] C E Brittain 4-9-10 (60)(t) P Robinson 11/4: 040133: 4 gr g Zilzal - Silver Glitz   7 **54**
(Grey Dawn II) Briefly led halfway, led again 4f out till 2f out, sn held: bckd, op 4/1: btr 2156, 1874.

1927 **PRINCE DARKHAN 21** [1] P W Harris 4-9-0 (50) M Fenton 25/1: 0-0004: Led 12f, sn btn: see 1927 (12f).   6 **35**

1991 **CHEEK TO CHEEK 18** [4] 6-9-9 (59) M Roberts 7/2: 5-5525: Held up, rcd centre 4f out, btn 3f out.   nk **43**
5 ran   Time 3m 40.3 (42.5)   (M Tilbrook)   C F Wall Newmarket

CATTERICK   WEDNESDAY JULY 5TH   Lefthand, Undulating, V Tight Track

Official Going   GOOD/FIRM. Stalls: Inside.

2417   2.15 ZETLAND MED AUCT MDN 2YO (E)   7f rnd   Good/Firm 20 -38 Slow
£2828   £808   £404

1823 **PEREGIAN 26** [4] M Johnston 2-9-0 R Ffrench 9/4: -5301: 2 b c Eagle Eyed - Mo Pheata (Petorius)   **80**
Prom, hdwy over 2f out to lead just ins last, hung left but kept on well, rdn out: well bckd: Apr foal, cost
IR 35,000gns: dam 6f juv wnr: apprec step up to 7f & acts on gd/firm & gd, disapp on soft.

2057 **MAID OF ARC 15** [7] M L W Bell 2-8-9 (t) R Mullen 13/8 FAV: 022: 2 b f Patton - Holy Speed   3 **68**
(Afleet) Cl-up, hdwy to lead appr fnl 1f, sn hdd, onepace: well bckd: shld find a modest race, see 2057.

2161 **THEBAN 11** [2] D Nicholls 2-9-0 A Nicholls (3) 16/1: 543: 2 b g Inzar - Phoenix Forli (Forli)   1 **71**
Led till appr fnl 1f, no extra: prob stays a sharp 7f on fast grnd: see 2161, 1161.

1974 **IZZET MUZZY 19** [1] C N Kellett 2-9-0 T Williams 20/1: 50554: Handy, ev ch well over 1f out, no extra.   1¼ **69**

2209 **MISSING DRINK 9** [3] 2-9-0 Joanna Badger (7) 33/1: 0505: In tch, rdn & sltly outpcd over 2f out,   1¼ **67$**
some late gains: sell nurs will suit in time: see 2055.

1577 **DANCE QUEEN 36** [9] 2-8-9 J Bramhill 50/1: 6006: Bhd, eff & not clr run over 2f out, no impress fnl 1f.   nk **61**

2106 **MULLING IT OVER 13** [8] 2-8-9 G Parkin 9/1: 307: Slow away & al bhd: best 1737 (debut, gd/soft).   7 **47**

-- LIVE THE DREAM [6] 2-8-9 Dean McKeown 25/1: 8: Slow away & al bhd: debut: Mar foal, cost   1¼ **45**
5,000gns: half-sister to a 10f wnr: bred to need 7f+ in time.

765

2328 **THAILAND** 4 [10] 2-8-9 K Darley 10/1: 009: Handy, carried wide bend 4f out, wknd: see 1782.   12   21
1700 **NOT JUST A DREAM** 31 [5] 2-8-9 J Carroll 6/1: 430: V slowly away & al bhd: btr 1700.   9   5
10 ran   Time 1m 27.1 (4.1)   (J David Abell)   M Johnston Middleham, Nth Yorks.

2418   2.45 HORNBY HCAP 3YO+ 0-75 (E)   5f rnd   Good/Firm 20   +16 Fast   [73]
     £3298   £1015   £507   £253   3 yo rec 5 lb

1815 **ANTHONY MON AMOUR** 26 [8] D Nicholls 5-8-11 (56)(t) A Nicholls (3) 8/1: 0-0041: 5 b g Nicholas -   66
Reine De La Ciel (Conquistador Cielo) Prom, led 2f out, sn rdn well clr: op 6/1, fast time: rnr-up in '99 (rtd
66 & 68a): '98 scorer at Chepstow (mdn h'cap) & Southwell (class stks, rtd 69): wng form over 5/6f, just stays
7f: acts on fast, soft & fibresand: best in a t-strap: likes a sharp trk: took advantage of a handy mark.
1629 **SWYNFORD DREAM** 34 [5] J Hetherton 7-8-13 (58) R Ffrench 8/1: -52042: 7 b g Statoblest - Qualitair   5   59
Dream (Dreams To Reality) Cl-up, led over 2f out, sn hdd & not pace of wnr: picks up a 5f h'cap most seasons.
2252 **SOUNDS ACE** 7 [16] D Shaw 4-8-4 (49)(bl) J Fanning 12/1: 060303: 4 ch f Savahra Sound - Ace Girl   ½   49
(Stanford) In tch, effort over 2f out, kept on, no threat: knocking on the door: see 1923, 1133.
2107 **TORRENT** 13 [14] D W Chapman 5-9-1 (60)(bl) D Mernagh (3) 8/1: 04444: Chsd ldrs, onepace fnl 2f.   hd   59
1687 **SIR SANDROVITCH** 32 [11] 4-10-0 (73) P Hanagan (7) 3/1 FAV: 004105: Waited with, effort over 1f   ¾   70
out, sn no impress: well bckd under a big weight: reportedly pulled muscles in 1687: best 1629.
1869 **BENZOE** 23 [10] 10-8-8 (53) Iona Wands 20/1: 00-506: Bhd, kept on late, nvr a threat: still   ½   49
retains ability, keep an eye on him at Thirsk: see 1714.
1871 **PLEASURE TIME** 23 [4] 7-9-10 (69)(vis) K Darley 9/1: 00-067: Led till over 2f out, wknd over 1f out.   ¾   63
2223 **TWICKERS** 8 [12] 4-8-4 (49)(VIS) A Culhane 14/1: 000068: Waited with, effort & not clr run over   hd   42
2f out, some late gains: tried a visor: see 2223.
2340 **RING OF LOVE** 4 [6] 4-9-7 (66) R Cody Boutcher (7) 25/1: 530309: In tch, wknd over 2f out: see 2078.   1¾   54
2297 **KOSEVO** 5 [9] 6-8-2 (47)(vis) T Williams 14/1: 052000: Nvr a factor: 10th: btr 1976 (fibresand).   1¾   30
1923 **MISS BANANAS** 21 [13] 5-7-11 (42) D Meah (0) 33/1: 004000: In tch, wknd 2f out: 11th, best 872.   nk   24
2252 **ZARAGOSSA** 7 [15] 4-9-1 (60) W Supple 10/1: -50050: Al bhd: 12th: see 2252.   4   30
*2233 **KALAR** 7 [3] 11-8-0 (45)(bl) (6ex) Claire Bryan (5) 8/1: 500410: Handy, wknd 2f out: 13th, too soon.   ½   13
1298 **TANGERINE** 51 [2] 3-8-10 (60) T Lucas 50/1: 0-0000: Slow away & al bhd: 14th, 7 wk abs: in '99 won   10   8
at Bath (mdn, rtd 75): eff arnd 5/7f on gd/soft: prev with B Hills, now with M W Easterby.
870 **ALUSTAR** 85 [1] 3-9-2 (66) R Parkin 12/1: 000-PU: Sat down in stalls & u/r: 12 wk abs: form figures   0
resemble a nov chaser: '99 Pontefract wnr (mdn, rtd 78 at best): eff at 5f on firm/gd soft, f/sand & any trk.
15 ran   Time 57.5 (0.2)   (Tony Fawcett)   D Nicholls Sessay, Nth Yorks.

2419   3.15 RIPLEY FILLIES MDN 2YO (D)   6f rnd   Good/Firm 20   -18 Slow
     £2782   £856   £428   £214

-- **OLENKA** [6] J G Given 2-8-11 Dean McKeown 8/1: 1: 2 gr f Grand Lodge - Sarouel (Kendor)   82
Waited with, hdwy to lead dist, pushed clr inside last: debut: Feb foal, cost 3,600 gns: dam mdn:
eff at 6f, 7f looks sure to suit: runs well fresh on gd/firm grnd: pleasing debut, should win again.
2125 **QUEEN SPAIN** 12 [3] M R Channon 2-8-11 A Culhane 9/4: -02222: 2 b f Mister Baileys - Excellus   3   73
(Exceller) Prom, eff to chall over 1f out, not pace of wnr: well bckd tho' op 7/4: deserves a race, see 2125.
2239 **LOVE LADY** 7 [1] M Johnston 2-8-11 R Ffrench 9/1: 443: 2 b f Woodman - Franziska (Sadler's Wells)   1¼   70
Prom, rdn & kept on same pace over 1f out: op 6/1: will apprec 7f in nursery h'caps: see 2239.
1957 **ANDROMEDAS WAY** 19 [4] R Charlton 2-8-11 K Darley 1/1 FAV: 64: Slow away, sn chsd ldr, led appr   ½   68
final 1f, sn hdd & no extra: hvly bckd but only marginal improvement from debut in 1957.
2142 **MISS BEADY** 12 [5] 2-8-11 G Parkin 8/1: -0055: Led, hung right bend after 2f, hdd appr final 1f, wknd.   2   62
2039 **CARUSOS** 16 [7] 2-8-11 W Supple 16/1: 0036: Chsd ldrs till wknd over 2f out: btr 2039 (5f).   7   44
6 ran   Time 1m 12.6 (2.3)   (Nigel Munton)   J G Given Willoughton, Lincs.

2420   3.45 DARLINGTON HCAP 4YO+ 0-80 (D)   7f rnd   Good/Firm 20   -01 Slow   [71]
     £4192   £1290   £645   £322

2282 **DOVEBRACE** 6 [4] A Bailey 7-8-5 (48) J Bramhill 6/1: -32121: 7 b g Dowsing - Naufrage (Main Reef)   54
Waited with, prog 2f out, strong run to lead ins fnl 1f, won going away: nicely bckd: recent Ayr wnr (sell h'cap):
plcd in '99 (rtd 43), last won back in '95, at Haydock, York & Chester (mdn/stks, rtd 100): eff at 6f, suited by
7f/1m: acts on firm & gd/soft: eff with/without blnks/visor: in fine form & cld strike again quickly.
2163 **RYMERS RASCAL** 11 [1] E J Alston 8-9-1 (58) W Supple 3/1 FAV: -56342: 8 b g Rymer - City Sound   ¾   61
(On Your Mark) Trkd ldrs, rdn to lead dist, not pace to repel wnr cl-home: well bckd: met an in form rival.
2215 **SONG OF SKYE** 8 [6] T J Naughton 6-9-9 (66) K Darley 5/1: 600023: 6 b m Warning - Song Of Hope   1   67
(Chief Singer) Rear, prog 2f out, styd on fnl 1f & nrst fin: sound run, shld win another 7f h'cap.
2192 **PRIX STAR** 9 [10] C W Fairhurst 5-9-1 (58) J Fanning 16/1: -03204: Prom, ev ch ent fnl 1f, no extra.   ½   58
1685 **ENCOUNTER** 32 [8] 4-8-0 (43) R Ffrench 40/1: 040005: Prom, ev ch 2f out, onepcd inside last: not   ½   42
disgrcd from a poor high draw: see 1685.
1149 **LUNCH PARTY** 61 [9] 8-8-13 (56) Iona Wands(5) 17/2: 60-406: Set pace till dist, no extra: 9 wk abs.   ½   54
2349 **ACID TEST** 3 [5] 5-9-8 (65) P Hanagan (7) 16/1: 000307: Rear, late hdwy, nvr a factor: qck reapp.   hd   53
*1658 **ALMAZAR** 33 [2] 5-8-13 (56)(vis) A Culhane 7/1: 354218: Trkd ldrs 2f, rallied 2f out, sn btn.   ½   49
2163 **NORTHERN SVENGALI** 11 [3] 4-9-7 (64) D Mernagh (3) 6/1: 00609: In tch till btn dist: nicely bckd.   1   59
2185 **CUSIN** 10 [7] 4-10-0 (71) A Nicholls (3) 5/1: 003050: Rcd keenly rear & rcd wide, prom after 2f till   8   53
wknd 2f out, fin last: tchd 7/1, top weight: reportedly lost his action & this is not his form: see 1840.
10 ran   Time 1m 24.5 (1.5)   (Dovebrace Ltd Air-Conditioning-Projects)   A Bailey Little Budworth, Cheshire

---

2421   4.15 NORTHALLERTON MDN 3YO+ (D)   6f rnd   Good/Firm 20   -10 Slow
     £2730   £780   £390   3yo rec 6lb

2232 **EFFERVESCENT** 7 [3] I A Balding 3-8-9 K Darley 8/13 FAV: -02341: 3 b f Efisio - Sharp Chief (Chief   55
Singer) Prom, went on over 1f out, styd on well, pushed out: well bckd, won a shade cosily: consistent in mdns
earlier (rtd 75): eff at 6/7f, acts on firm & gd grnd: handles a sharp or gall trk: can rate much more highly.
2315 **FOUND AT LAST** 4 [5] J Balding 4-9-6 T G McLaughlin 5/1: 350222: 4 b g Aragon - Girton (Balidar)   2   52
Rear, prog 2f out, styd on fnl 1f but not rch wnr: qck reapp, op 7/2: consistent, needs sells or sell h'caps.
2099 **INDIAN DANCE** 14 [2] M C Chapman 4-9-6 (t) L Gueller (7) 50/1: 000003: 4 ch g Indian Ridge -   nk   51§
Petronella (Nureyev) Trkd ldrs, styd on under press fnl 1f: offic rating just 36, treat this rating with caution.

CATTERICK WEDNESDAY JULY 5TH Lefthand, Undulating, V Tight Track

2313 **BRITTAS BLUES** 5 [1] M Johnston 3-8-9 J Fanning 5/1: -034: Led till dist, no extra: qck reapp. — 1 — 43
-- **HERMITS HIDEAWAY** [6] 3-9-0 D Mernagh(3) 16/1: -5: Nvr a factor on debut: bred to apprec 7f/1m. — 2½ — 41
-- **CHASE THE BLUES** [8] 3-9-0 J Stack 9/2: -6: Dwelt, al bhd: half-brother to wnrs over 6/7f. — 3½ — 31
-- **SILOGUE** [4] 3-9-0 A Culhane 25/1: -7: Dwelt, al bhd on debut: sprint bred: with O Brennan. — nk — 30
2223 **CARMARTHEN** 8 [7] 4-9-6 K Hodgson 33/1: -00008: Chsd ldrs 4f, wknd & fin last: see 2223. — nk — 29
8 ran   Time 1m 12.1 (1.8)   (J C Smith)   I A Balding Kingsclere, Hants.

2422 4.45 STOCKTON HCAP 3YO+ 0-75 (E)   1m4f   Good/Firm 20 -04 Slow   [65]
£3185 £980 £490 £245   3yo rec 13lb

1852 **NEEDWOOD MYSTIC** 24 [2] B C Morgan 5-8-5 (42) A Nicholls (3) 16/1: 0-4001: 5 b m Rolfe - Enchanting — 48
Kate (Enchantment) Waited with, imprvd after 1m, drvn into lead 2f out, rdn clr fnl 1f, cmftbly: bckd at long
odds: reportedly had the virus last year: '99 Warwick wnr (2, h'caps, rtd 51): eff arnd 2m on gd & firm grnd,
handles any trk, likes a sharp one, esp Warwick: fairly h'capped, could follow up qckly.
2381 **RAYWARE BOY** 2 [1] D Shaw 4-8-3 (40) (bl) T Williams 20/1: 005452: 4 b c Scenic - Amata (Nodouble) — 7 — 38
Waited with, rdn to impr 2f out, no impress on wnr fnl 1f: op 12/1, qck reapp: met a back to form rival here.
2061 **HASTA LA VISTA** 15 [7] M W Easterby 10-8-13 (50) (vis) T Lucas 7/2: 102143: 10 b g Superlative - Falcon1¾ — 46
Berry (Bustino) Prom, led briefly 3f out, onepcd fnl 1½f: nicely bckd: see 1816.
2110 **HIGH TOPPER** 13 [5] M Johnston 3-9-10 (74) J Fanning 3/1: -25244: Prom, led halfway till 3f out, — shd — 70
no extra: top weight: see 1919.
1921 **GENUINE JOHN** 21 [4] 7-7-11 (34) D Mernagh(2) 25/1: 324505: In tch, onepcd final 2f: mkt drifter. — 1¼ — 28
*2254 **WETHAAB** 7 [6] 3-8-6 (56) (bl) (6ex) W Supple 5/4 FAV: -04016: In tch, eff 2f out, sn btn: too sn after 2254? 4 — 44
1499 **INDIGO BAY** 40 [3] 4-8-11 (48) (vis) Dean McKeown 8/1: 100007: Led till halfway, sn btn & fin last: abs. — 7 — 26
7 ran   Time 2m 34.1 (2.9)   (Needwood Racing Ltd)   B C Morgan Barton-under-Needwood, Staffs.

BRIGHTON WEDNESDAY JULY 5TH Lefthand, V Sharp, Undulating Track

Official Going   Race 1 to 3 - GOOD TO SOFT; Race 4 to 6 - SOFT. Stalls: 10/12f - Outside; Rem - Inside.

2423 2.00 ALEXANDERS CLAIMER 3YO+ (F)   1m2f   Good/Soft Inapplicable
£2278 £651 £325   3 yo rec 11lb   Field raced far side

2069 **WILLIE CONQUER** 15 [6] Andrew Reid 8-9-12 M Henry 7/4 FAV: 0-1001: 8 ch g Master Willie - Maryland — 64
Cookie (Bold Hour) Mid-div, rdn into lead appr fnl 1f, drvn out: nicely bckd tho' op 5/4: earlier won on
reapp here at Brighton (seller, D Elsworth): '99 reapp wnr again here at Brighton (h'cap, rtd 88, t-strap):
suited by 10/12f on firm, gd/soft & any trk, loves Brighton: runs well fresh: likes sells/clmrs.
2187 **CYBER BABE** 9 [3] A G Newcombe 3-8-0 L Newman (4) 8/1: 021002: 3 ch f Persian Bold - Ervedya — ¾ — 48
(Doyoun) Prom, outpcd 5f out, drvn/styd on well fnl 2f, not btn far: stays 10f well, acts on firm, gd/soft & f/sand.
2041 **SHEER FACE** 16 [2] W R Muir 6-9-10 Martin Dwyer 5/2: 540133: 6 b g Midyan - Rock Face (Ballad — 2½ — 57
Rock) Rcd keenly & sn led, hdd appr fnl 1f, sn btn: nicely bckd: see 2041, 1331.
3730 **PARTE PRIMA** 307 [5] C L Popham 4-8-12 (bl) D R McCabe 33/1: 6030-4: Rcd keenly in rear, — 5 — 38
drvn/late gains fnl 2f, no dngr: long abs, new stable: plcd thrice in '99 (mdns & seller, rtd 56a & 43,
S Kettlewell), subs unplcd over timber: stays 7f/1m on fast & both AWs.
2212 **CHILLI** 8 [4] 3-8-9 (vis) T E Durcan 11/2: 303505: In tch, hdwy appr fnl 3f, fdd: tchd 10/1: see 1804. — 1¾ — 44
*1933 **NAKED OAT** 20 [1] 5-9-12 J Bosley 9/1: 000016: V keen cl-up, wknd fnl 2f: tchd 9/2 (C/D, fast). — 1¾ — 48
1911 **COOL LOCATION** 21 [7] F Norton 50/1: 000-07: Led early, wknd rapidly fnl 4f, t.o. — dist — 0
7 ran   Time 2m 05.2 (7.4)   (A S Reid)   Andrew Reid Mill Hill, London NW7.

2424 2.30 CAPITAL RADIO SELLER 2YO (G)   7f rnd   Good/Soft Inapplicable
£1834 £524 £262   Field came stands side in home straight.

2155 **SEL** 11 [1] Sir Mark Prescott 2-8-6 (BL) S Sanders 15/8 FAV: 351: 2 b f Salse - Frog (Akarad) — 62
Sn led, styd on well despite hanging left fnl 2f, rdn out: nicely bckd: sold for 7,200gns: Apr 1st foal, dam 9/12f
wnr: apprec this step up to 7f, apprec further in time: acts on gd/soft & a sharp/undul trk: sharpened up by blnks.
-- **LOOK FIRST** [5] A P Jarvis 2-8-11 J Fortune 7/2: 2: 2 b c Namaqualand - Be Prepared (Be My — 3 — 63
Guest) Slow to break, sn prom, chall briefly 2f out, sn not pace of wnr: clr rem on debut: 5,500gns colt,
sire decent Jap 1m scorer: stays 7f on gd/soft: ran green here & shld improve for experience.
1931 **PRESENTOFAROSE** 20 [3] J S Moore 2-8-6 J F Egan 3/1: 55023: 2 b f Presenting - Little Red Rose — 3 — 53
(Precocious) Rcd keenly cl-up, fdd fnl 2f: tchd 9/2: up in trip: see 1931.
2052 **OUR LITTLE CRACKER** 16 [4] M Quinn 2-8-6 F Norton 5/1: 044: Sn outpcd, nvr a factor: op 4/1. — 5 — 46
2227 **MARY HAYDEN** 7 [2] 2-8-6 A Daly 13/2: 005: In tch, wknd qckly fnl 3f: qck reapp. — 9 — 34
5 ran   Time 1m 25.4 (5.6)   (B Haggas)   Sir Mark Prescott Newmarket.

2425 3.00 JOHN BLOOR MDN HCAP 3YO+ 0-75 (E)   1m4f   Good/Soft Inapplicable   [61]
£3542 £1090 £545 £272   3 yo rec 13lb   Field came stands side in home straight.

1949 **SPECTROMETER** 20 [6] Sir Mark Prescott 3-9-5 (65) S Sanders 7/2 FAV: 506-41: 3 ch c Rainbow Quest - — 74
Selection Board (Welsh Pageant) Prom, led 4f out, grabbed stands rail 2f out & sn clr, rdn out: nicely bckd:
showed promise up to 1m as a juv (mdn, rtd 72): eff around 12f, has tried 14f & that trip shld suit in time:
acts on gd/soft grnd & a sharp/undul track: can rate more highly for shrewd stable.
1951 **BAILEYS ON LINE** 20 [3] M Johnston 3-8-5 (51) F Norton 5/1: -0002: 3 b f Shareef Dancer - Three — 4 — 54
Stars (Star Appeal) Bhd, rdn to improve 5f out, chsd wnr fnl 2f, styd on but no impress: clr rem: stays 11.8f.
2146 **ABLE SEAMAN** 12 [1] C E Brittain 4-9-4 (64) T E Durcan 6/1: 045333: 3 b g Northern Flagship - — 5 — 60
Love At Dawn (Grey Dawn II) Cl-up, drvn & not pace of front 2 fnl 2f: consistent plcd form: see 2146, 1895.
1936 **ARTHURS KINGDOM** 20 [2] A P Jarvis 4-9-11 (58) N Callan 7/1: -03044: Mid-div, eff 3f out, no extra. — 5 — 48
2012 **COUNT ON THUNDER** 18 [5] 3-8-10 (56) G Carter 15/2: 00-565: Handy, rdn/fdd fnl 2f: see 1560. — 5 — 40
2011 **SUMMER CHERRY** 18 [8] 3-9-1 (61) J Fortune 9/2: 00-446: With ldrs, wknd qckly fnl 2f: up in trip. — 2½ — 42
1782] **SIEGFRIED** 396 [4] 4-9-8 (55) J P Spencer 11/1: 005-7: Rcd keenly in rear, lost tch halfway — 14 — 22
op 8/1 on reapp for new stable: unplcd in 7f/1m mdns for B Hills in '99 (rtd 69 & 54a).
2332 **LENNY THE LION** 4 [10] 3-8-8 (54) (bl) R Hughes 9/2: -05538: Led, hdd 4f out, wknd: no ch — 21 — 0

767

when saddle slipped final 2f, eased, t.o.: see 2332.

3939) ELMS SCHOOLPREFECT 293 [7] 3-8-4 (50) J Tate 20/1: 0000-9: Al bhd, t.o: up in trip on reapp: **14**   **0**
unplcd in 4 juv starts (rtd 55 at best, mdn auct): with J Eustace.
9 ran   Time 2m 34.6 (6.4)   (Lord Derby)   Sir Mark Prescott Newmarket.

2426   3.30 WEATHERBYS FILLIES MDN 3YO+ (D)   1m rnd   Soft   Inapplicable
£3883   £1195   £597   £298   Heavy shower before race. Field came stands side in home straight.

1405 FAIR IMPRESSION 46 [5] E A L Dunlop 3-8-12 G Carter 4/1: 02-001: 3 ch f Arazi - Al Najah   **82**
(Topsider): Mid-div, came stands side & hdwy 3f out, sn led, rdn clr appr final 1f, eased cl-home: nicely
bckd tho' op 5/2: rtd 86 when rnr-up on 2nd of only 2 juv starts: stays 7f, apprec this step up to 1m &
further could suit: acts on gd/soft & soft grnd & acts on a sharp/undul trk: won well here, could follow up.
2104 DEVIL LEADER 14 [6] B W Hills 3-8-12 R Hughes 7/2: -0532: 3 ch f Diesis - Shihama (Shadeed):   **6**   **72**
Slow to break, hdwy from rear appr final 2f, styd on, no ch with wnr: h'caps should now suit: see 2104.
2211 EVE 9 [1] M L W Bell 3-8-12 M Fenton 1/1 FAV: 423: 3 b f Rainbow Quest - Fade (Persepolis):   **nk**   **72**
Keen/waited with, rdn/prog 2f out, btn final 1f: well bckd: see 2211, 1532.
2086 VERDURA 14 [4] G A Butler 3-8-12 J Fortune 13/2: 0-64: Led, hdd appr fnl 2f, fdd: op 4/1: see 2086.   **1**   **70**
1808 BOGUS MIX 26 [3] 3-8-12 N Callan 20/1: 055: Dwelt, sn prom, wknd qckly fnl 2f: drop in trip: see 1404.   **6**   **62**
1886 PICCALILLI 22 [2] 3-8-12 (BL) L Newman (3) 50/1: 0606: With ldr, lost tch halfway, eased/t.o: blnkd: **dist**   **0**
6 ran   Time 1m 37.6 (5.6)   (Maktoum Al Maktoum)   E A L Dunlop Newmarket.

2427   4.00 COLLINS STEWART HCAP 3YO+ 0-70 (E)   7f rnd   Soft   Inapplicable   [67]
£5255   £1617   £808   £404   3 yo rec 8 lb   Field came stands side in home straight.

2221 FLYING PENNANT 8 [2] J M Bradley 7-7-11 (36)(bl) F Norton 9/2: 553061: 7 gr g Waajib - Flying   **41**
Beckee (Godswalk): Held up, gd hdwy 2f out, ran on well to lead inside last, drvn out: plcd over hdles in
99/00 (h'cap, rtd 71h, blnks): plcd on the Flat in '99 (h'cap, rtd 43): prev term scored at Chepstow
(h'cap, rtd 56): eff at 7f/1m on firm, soft & any trk: runs well fresh & eff in blnks/visor: fairly h'capped.
2054 RAINBOW RAIN 16 [16] S Dow 6-9-7 (60) O Urbina 9/1: 220002: 6 b g Capote - Grana (Miswaki):   **1¼**   **62**
In tch, hdwy to chall 2f out, styd on but not pace of wnr well inside last: op 5/1: handles soft, best on fast.
2347 NERONIAN 4 [15] Miss D A McHale 6-7-10 (35) Kin Tinkler 12/1: 500103: 6 ch g Mujtahid - Nimieza   **1½**   **34**
(Nijinsky): Mid-div, dropped rear 3f out, rallied & styd on well final 1f: qck reapp: acts on fast & soft grnd.
*2303 TWIN TIME 5 [6] J S King 6-9-11 (64) I Mongan (5) 15/8 FAV: -42314: Front rank, led appr final 1f,   **shd**   **63**
sn hdd, onepcd inside last: nicely bckd, top weight: qck reapp: in gd heart: handles firm & soft: see 2303.
2347 HALF TONE 4 [10] 8-8-2 (41)(bl) Craig Williams 10/1: 530305: Bhd, rdn/kept on final 2f, no threat.   **2½**   **36**
2347 IMBACKAGAIN 4 [5] 5-8-9 (48) J Quinn 11/2: 202146: Cl-up, no extra final 2f: op 4/1, qck reapp.   **hd**   **43**
2063 MILADY LILLIE 15 [7] 4-9-0 (53) D O'Donohoe 15/2: 002047: Sn outpcd, rdn/prog 2f out, held fnl 1f.   **nk**   **47**
1335 MUJKARI 49 [11] 4-8-0 (39)(vis) G Baker (7) 20/1: -00008: Sn well bhd, styd on well final 2f but   **shd**   **33**
no ch with ldrs: op 12/1, 7 wk abs: see 323.
2031 WHO GOES THERE 17 [13] 4-8-5 (44) J Tate 10/1: 000209: Dwelt, sn cl-up, went on appr final 3f,   **1¼**   **36**
hdd/wknd over 1f out: btr 1794 (gd trk, gall trk).
391 COURTNEY GYM 162 [14] 5-7-10 (35)(bl) (5oh) D Kinsella (7) 33/1: 00-000: Led to halfway, sn bhd, 10th. **12**   **12**
10 ran   Time 1m 24.0 (4.2)   (E A Hayward)   J M Bradley Sedbury, Gloucs.

2428   4.30 LADBROKES HCAP 3YO+ 0-60 (F)   5f59y rnd   Soft   Inapplicable   [60]
£2383   £681   £340   3 yo rec 5 lb   All bar one came stands side in home straight.

2266 PERIGEUX 6 [7] K T Ivory 4-9-13 (59)(bl) R Hughes 4/1: 550051: 4 b g Perugino - Rock On (Ballad   **63**
Rock): Dsptd lead, rdn/ev ch appr final 1f, ran on well to lead cl-home, all-out: nicely bckd from 8/1, qck reapp:
rnr-up thrice in '00 (rtd 69 & 74a, clmrs, J Berry), prev term won at Southwell (AW mdn), Ayr (nursery) & W'hampton
(stks, rtd 85 & 89a): eff at 5.3/7f on firm, soft, fibresand & any trk: eff with/without blnks: tough/genuine.
2230 ABSOLUTE FANTASY 7 [15] E A Wheeler 4-9-2 (48)(bl) S Carson (5) 7/1: 140342: 4 b f Beveled -   **shd**   **51**
Sharp Venita (Sharp Edge): Dwelt, sn prom, rdn to lead 2f out, styd on well for press, hdd nr fin: acts on
firm, soft & equitrack, likes Brighton: back to form here: see 1211.
2193 CALANDRELLA 9 [1] A G Newcombe 7-8-4 (36) G Sparkes (7) 10/1: 000063: 7 b m Sizzling Melody -   **hd**   **39**
Maravilla (Mandrake Major): U.r. & bolted to post, sn led, hdd over 2f out & remnd far side: sigpd on well
final 1f, not btn far: fine run considering pre-race exertions but only one win in 39 starts: likes soft grnd.
2042 WILLOW MAGIC 16 [2] S Dow 3-9-9 (60) J F Egan 13/2: 043034: Mid-div, effort when short of room   **1**   **60**
2f out, styd on well final 1f, nrst fin: shade unlucky in running here, see 2042, 1512.
2184 MANGUS 10 [5] 6-9-9 (55) S Sanders 10/1: 650005: Hmpd leaving stalls, sn outpcd, late hdwy, no dngr.   **2**   **50**
2252 SUNSET HARBOUR 7 [8] 7-9-1 (47) P Fitzsimons (5) 13/2: 241636: Prom, rdn/btn 2f out: qck reapp.   **nk**   **41**
*2223 INDIAN BAZAAR 8 [4] 4-8-9 (41) F Norton 5/2 FAV: 032017: Mid-div, rdn/held fnl 2f: btr 2223 (firm).   **nk**   **35**
1333 COMMONBIRD 49 [3] 3-8-3 (40) M Henry 33/1: 0-0508: Reluctant to enter stalls, nvr a threat: 7 wk abs.   **1**   **31**
2124 FRENCH FANCY 12 [14] 3-8-5 (42)(bl) P M Quinn (3) 16/1: 041009: Dwelt, al bhd: see 1742 (6f, AW).   **shd**   **33**
2192 SOUNDS LUCKY 9 [13] 4-9-7 (53)(vis) J Quinn 10/1: 160500: Handy, drvn/wknd appr final 1f, 10th.   **¾**   **43**
2230 TILIA 7 [10] 4-9-3 (49) R Smith (5) 20/1: 060-00: Prom, wknd qckly final 2f, fin last: qck reapp: **3**   **32**
4th at best in '99 (fillies h'cap, first time blnks, rtd 53): rtd 62 at best in '98: stays 6f, handles gd grnd.
11 ran   Time 1m 03.2 (3.2)   (Mrs Valerie Hubbard)   K T Ivory Radlett, Herts.

Official Going   GOOD TO SOFT (SOFT In Places). Stalls: Inside, Except 6f - Outside, 1m4f - Centre.

2429   6.30 TEAM DANDELION HCAP 3YO+ 0-70 (E)   1m4f   Good/Soft 64   -04 Slow   [70]
£4426   £1362   £681   £340   3 yo rec 13lb

2041 CHATER FLAIR 16 [12] A P Jarvis 3-8-0 (55) J Quinn 10/1: 00-041: 3 b g Efisio - Native Flair (Be My   **60**
Native): Towards rear, imprvd but still a lot to do appr fnl 1f, drvn, flashed tail, but ran on strgly ins last &
got up fnl strides: op 8/1, first win on h'cap bow: unplcd juv (rtd 66): apprec return to 12f on gd/soft, further
suit: handles a sharp/undul trk: jockey given a 1-day whip ban but would not have won but for jockeys strength.

1807 **HALF TIDE 26** [5] P Mitchell 6-7-11 (39) J Mackay (5) 8/1: 33-062: 6 ch g Nashwan - Double River *shd* 43
(Irish River) Rear, gd prog appr fnl 2f, led fnl 20y, collared by wnr's late burst: tchd 10/1: back to
best, acts on gd/soft grnd, likes equitrack: shld find a race on turf off this lowly mark: see 220.

*1934 **COPYFORCE GIRL 20** [4] Miss B Sanders 4-9-2 (58)(t) S Carson (5) 10/1: 040-13: 4 b f Elmaamul - *hd* 62
Sabaya (Seattle Dancer) Well plcd, hdwy to lead below dist, hdd cl-home, op 7/1: acts on firm & gd/soft.

3104} **MAGIC COMBINATION 342** [6] B J Curley 7-9-8 (64) J P Spencer 11/8 FAV: 00/1-4: Led, 3L clr *nk* 67
turning in, and press appr fnl 1f, hdd & no extra: reapp, well clr rem: Mar '00 hdles wnr
at Sandown (val Imperial Cup h'cap, 2m/2½m, gd & hvy, rtd 123h): landed sole '99 Flat start at Galway
(h'cap, rtd 55): back in '97 won at Sandown (h'cap, rtd 74): eff at 12f/2m on fast & soft grnd, up with/forcing
the pace: appeared ill at ease on the firmer ground in the home straight, recoup losses on a more conventional track.

2330 **FIELD MASTER 4** [2] 3-8-13 (68) S Sanders 12/1: 210005: Bhd, styd on in the str to lead home *11* 61
trailing pack, nvr dangerous: quick reapp, longer trip, new tactics: see 771 (AW mdn, made all).

1915 **MARMADUKE 21** [1] 4-10-0 (70) Dane O'Neill 20/1: 0-0366: Nvr better than mid-div: op 14/1, top- *1¼* 62
weight, visor omitted: not bred to appreciate 12f: see 1259.

2199 **ELMS SCHOOLGIRL 9** [8] 4-9-11 (67) J Tate 12/1: 3-2067: Held up, imprvd 4f out, sn no extra: op 7/1. *1¼* 57
2092 **SPOSA 14** [10] 4-8-5 (47) D Poe 9/1: 6305P8: Prom till lost pl 3f out: op 7/1, back in trip, see 644, 301. *½* 36
1394 **JOLI SADDLERS 46** [7] 4-7-10 (38)(VIS) R Brisland (5) 20/1: 0-0009: Chsd ldrs, wknd appr fnl 2f: visor. *¾* 26
1209 **QUAKERESS 57** [9] 5-7-10 (38)(13oh) K Dalgleish (7) 33/1: 453200: At bhd: 10th, v stiff task, 8 wk abs. *4* 22
1852 **SEA DANZIG 24** [3] 7-8-7 (49) D Holland 16/1: 100000: In tch till 5f out: 11th, see 772. *¾* 32
1934 **KEZ 20** [11] 4-9-2 (58)(VIS) N Callan 9/1: 0-0020: Bhd fnl 4f: 12th, visored, see 842. *4* 37
12 ran   Time 2m 43.0 (8.2)   (Hong Kong Cricket Club)   A P Jarvis Aston Upthorpe, Oxon

---

2430   7.00 CROWN MED AUCT MDN 2YO (E)   7f rnd   Good/Soft 64   -39 Slow
£4212   £1296   £648   £324

1798 **SMITH AND WESTERN 27** [3] R Hannon 2-9-0 Dane O'Neill 11/2: 501: 2 b c Factual - Temple Heights 82
(Shirley Heights) Early ldr & again appr fnl 2f, drew clr under press fnl 1f: imprvd, upset in stalls latest: half-brother
to a hdles wnr & dam got 2m: apprec step up to 7f, sure to get further: acts on gd/soft grnd, sharp/undul trk.

2346 **NOBLE DOBLE 4** [7] B W Hills 2-9-0 M Hills 2/1 FAV: 452: 2 b c Shareef Dancer - Kshessinskaya *2½* 75
(Hadeer) Well plcd & ev ch till outpcd by wnr below dist: nicely bckd, quick reapp: prob handles gd/soft.

2091 **MEDIA BUYER 14** [4] B J Meehan 2-9-0 (BL) D R McCabe 14/1: 0003: 2 b c Green Dancer - California *½* 74
Rush (Forty Niner) Sn led, hdd bef 2f out, hmpd appr fnl 1f, not qckn: tchd 20/1, ran well blnkd, handles gd/sft.

2227 **MOMENTS IN TIME 7** [1] M R Channon 2-8-9 Craig Williams 7/2: 64: Handy, onepace appr fnl 1f. *1½* 66
1968 **RORKES DRIFT 19** [6] 2-8-9 A McGlone 8/1: 35: Bhd, styd on fnl 2f, nvr nrr: lks capable of better. *hd* 65
--   **ORIGINAL SINNER** [8] 2-9-0 J P Spencer 6/1: 6: In tch & hung left 2f out, no extra: debut: *1½* 67
9,800 gns Rudimentary gelding, dam a mdn, sire a miler: with W Haggas.
1798 **VISLINK 27** [2] 2-9-0 J Fortune 33/1: 07: Al bhd: 4,000 gns Shalford brother to a 1m juv wnr. *7* 53
--   **PRINCESS EMERALD** [5] 2-8-9 D Holland 20/1: 8: Sn detached: half-sister to sev wnrs, dam 12f wnr. *14* 28
8 ran   Time 1m 27.33 (7.23)   (Paul Jubert)   R Hannon East Everleigh, Wilts

---

2431   7.30 FURLONG HCAP 3YO+ 0-85 (D)   7f rnd   Good/Soft 64   -06 Slow   [84]
£7247   £2230   £1115   £557   3 yo rec 8 lb

2133 **KINAN 12** [3] G C Bravery 4-9-11 (81) M Hills 10/1: 050-01: 4 b c Dixieland Band - Alsharta (Mr 87
Prospector) In tch, imprvd 3f out, drvn to lead below dist, sn on strgly: unplcd in '99 (h'caps, rtd 85, R
Armstrong): '98 Nottingham wnr (mdn, rtd 91): eff at 6/7f, tried 1m: acts on fast, gd/soft grnd, prob any trk.

2371 **CONTRARY MARY 2** [4] J Akehurst 5-8-2 (58)(5ex) J Quinn 4/1 FAV: 005122: 5 b m Mujadil - Love *1½* 60
Street (Mummy's Pet) Well plcd, kept on well fnl 2f, nvr nrr: well bckd, given a fair amount to do,
ran 48hrs ago: back up trip, remains in cracking form, see 2230.

2097 **MANA DARGENT 14** [1] M Johnston 3-8-7 (71) K Dalgleish (7) 9/2: 204563: 3 b c Ela Mana Mou - Petite *nk* 72
D'Argent (Noalto) Trkd ldr, led appr fnl 2f, rdn & hdd ins last, no extra: nicely bckd & ran to best back up in trip.

2261 **COLD CLIMATE 7** [5] Bob Jones 5-8-1 (57) A Daly 12/1: -50004: Patiently rdn, gd prog 2f out & *¾* 56
chance plat, onepace for press: clr rem, quick reapp: handles soft grnd, poss best on faster nowadays: see 1028.

2261 **PARISIEN STAR 7** [7] 4-9-10 (80) S Sanders 11/2: 0-4045: Chsd ldrs, prog to chall 2f out, no *3* 73
extra fnl 1f: nicely bckd, quick reapp: handles self grnd, quick reapp, poss best on faster: see 2261, 1286.

2355 **CHAMPAGNE RIDER 3** [10] 4-9-12 (82) T E Durcan 25/1: 000006: Bhd, imprvg but well off the *hd* 75
pace when no room 2f out till below dist, nvr a factor: quick reapp, top-weight: see 1173.

1989 **ELMHURST BOY 18** [13] 4-9-8 (78) D Poe 33/2: 601037: In tch, onepace ent fnl 2f: btr 1989, 1652. *1* 69
1794 **MYSTIC RIDGE 27** [9] 6-8-11 (67) J P Spencer 7/1: 100408: Led till 2½f out, fdd: see 476 (fibresand). *3* 52
2158 **MARENGO 11** [2] 6-8-6 (62) A Clark 33/1: 024009: Nvr troubled ldrs: op 20/1, see 1073 (6f clmr). *½* 46
1961 **MAGELTA 19** [12] 3-8-11 (75) Dane O'Neill 8/1: 3-0020: Chsd ldrs till wknd appr fnl 2f: 10th, see 1961. *1¼* 57
*1994 **ONES ENOUGH 18** [11] 4-7-11 (52)(1ow) F Norton 14/1: -00010: In tch till lost place 2f out: 11th. *2½* 30
1427 **MINT LEAF 44** [6] 3-8-2 (66) M Henry 33/1: 20-000: Unruly start, nvr in it: 12th, 6 wk abs, new stable: *3* 38
ex-Irish, dual '99 rnr-up (5f, fast grnd): with J Poulton.
12 ran   Time 1m 24.98 (4.88)   (Sawyer Whatley Partnership)   G C Bravery Newmarket, Suffolk

---

2432   8.00 R.O.A. HCAP STKS 3YO+ 0-90 (C)   6f rnd   Good/Soft 64   +08 Fast   [88]
£6487   £1996   £998   £499   3 yo rec 6 lb

-2348 **CRYHAVOC 7** [7] D Nicholls 6-9-11 (85) Alex Greaves 2/1 FAV: 032021: 6 b g Polar Falcon - Sarabah 94
(Ela Mana Mou) Mid-div, grabbed stands rail ent str & qcknd to lead appr fnl 1f, rdly: well bckd, gd time, qk
reapp: '99 wnr at Yarmouth, Goodwood (appr), Windsor, Catterick & Beverley (h'caps, rtd 89): unplcd in '98
J Arnold in '98 (tried blnks): eff btwn 5f & 7f: acts on firm & gd/soft grnd, any trk: tough, quick follow-up?

2355 **CAUDA EQUINA 3** [6] M R Channon 6-9-1 (75) Craig Williams 6/1: 604302: 6 gr g Statoblest - Sea *2½* 77
Fret (Habat) Held up, kept on nicely fnl 2f & went 2nd towards fin, nvr nrr: qck reapp, gd run, likes Bath.

1851 **THE FUGATIVE 25** [9] P Mitchell 7-10-0 (88) M Tebbutt 7/2: -04563: 7 b m Nicholas - Miss Runaway *1¼* 87
(Runnett) Well plcd, rdn & ch appr fnl 1f, hung left, onepace: nicely bckd: won this race off 6lb lower in '99.

1851 **ALASTAIR SMELLIE 25** [2] B W Hills 4-9-6 (80) M Hills 11/2: -00504: Handy, hdwy to chall 1f out, *1¾* 75
sn rdn, flashed tail & no extra: tchd 13/2: unreliable: see 1173.

2266 **SPEED ON 6** [4] 7-9-5 (79) C Rutter 10/1: -06305: Held up, staying on fin but nvr dngrs: qk reapp. *½* 73
1383 **SELHURSTPARK FLYER 46** [3] 9-8-12 (72) T E Durcan 12/1: 00-006: Led till fnl 1f: stalwart retires. *½* 65
2288 **LA CAPRICE 5** [8] 3-8-9 (75) R Hughes 6/1: 032027: Settled bhd, nvr got in it: stablemate 6th: *shd* 68
stewards asked about running/riding, noted explanations that she failed to handle trk/easier grnd: see 1517, 1219.

EPSOM WEDNESDAY JULY 5TH Lefthand, Sharp, Undulating Track

2060 **PARDY PET** 15 [5] 3-7-10 (62)(22oh) J Mackay (5) 66/1: 06-008: Pulled hard & chsd ldrs till ent str: | 1 | 52
v stiff task & prob flattered: '99 Leicester wnr (sell, rtd 57): eff at 5f on fast grnd: needs a return to sells.
8 ran   Time 1m 11.14 (3.34)   (John Gilbertson)   D Nicholls Sessay, N YOrks

2433 8.30 ST JOHN CLAIMER 3YO+ (E)   1m114y rnd   Good/Soft 64   -22 Slow
£2782   £856   £428   £214   3 yo rec 10lb

2030 **LAKE SUNBEAM** 17 [2] W R Muir 4-9-2 Martin Dwyer 3/1: 45-561: 4 b g Nashwan - Moon Drop | | 70
(Dominion) Sn led, grabbed stands rail in str & fought off rnr-up under press fnl 1f: nicely bckd, front 2 clear:
'99 Salisbury wnr (stks, rtd 92, R Hannon): rtd 93+ sole juv start: eff at 7f/1m, tried 12f: acts on firm, gd/soft
grnd, any trk: can run well fresh & likes to force the pace: better than a plater.
2126 **STOPPES BROW** 12 [5] G L Moore 8-9-10 (bl) I Mongan (5) 8/13 FAV: 400652: 8 b g Primo Dominie | ¾ | 76
- So Bold (Never So Bold) Waited with, prog on bit 2f out, strong chall dist, sn onepace: hvly bckd, clr rem.
1707 **MAX** 31 [8] J J Bridger 5-8-11 (t) A Daly 25/1: 600003: 5 gr g L'Emigrant - Miss Mendez (Bellypha) | 7 | 43$
Front rank & ev ch till outpcd appr fnl 1f: surely flattered, see 256.
1677 **FULHAM** 32 [1] M J Haynes 4-8-11 (bl) F Norton 25/1: -42004: In tch till ent fnl 2f: turf return, see 771. | 1¼ | 40
1930 **ANNIE APPLE** 20 [3] 4-8-11 (vis) S Sanders 6/1: 005045: Nvr a factor: op 8/1, stiff task, see 594. | 3½ | 34
2032 **WATER LOUP** 17 [7] 4-8-6 (VIS) P Doe 25/1: 600006: Chsd ldrs till appr fnl 2f: visored, stablemate wnr. | 3 | 23
2380 **LEOFRIC** 2 [4] 5-9-0 (bl) A Clark 25/1: 630007: Al last: ran 48hrs ago, stiff task, see 973. | 1¾ | 28
7 ran   Time 1m 49.21 (7.31)   (Percipacious Punters Racing Club)   W R Muir Lambourn, Berks

2434 9.00 CASTLEFIELDS MDN 3YO+ (D)   1m2f   Good/Soft 64   -18 Slow
£4389   £1254   £627

1960 **KRANTOR** 19 [1] H R A Cecil 3-8-12 W Ryan 3/1: 621: 3 ch c Arazi - Epagris (Zalazi) | | 94
Rcd in 3rd in tch, ran on to lead appr fnl 1f, rdn out: tchd 4/1: apprec step up to 10f & shld get further:
acts on gd/soft & prob fast grnd, sharp/undul trk: potentially useful.
1828 **CLOG DANCE** 26 [3] M Hills 3-8-7 M Hills 2/5 FAV: 2-2202: 3 b f Pursuit Of Love - Discomatic | 1½ | 86
(Roberto) Led till appr fnl 1f, rdn & same pace: well bckd: becoming disappointing, see 1184 (Listed, firm).
2263 **MUWAKALL** 7 [2] R W Armstrong 3-8-12 A Clark 13/2: 345533: 3 b c Doyoun - Sabayik (Unfuwain) | 18 | 71
Rcd in 2nd till ent str, eased dist: quick reapp, capable of better: see 2263, 606.
3 ran   Time 2m 12.03 (8.23)   (L Marinopoulos)   H R A Cecil Newmarket, Suffolk

CATTERICK THURSDAY JULY 6TH Lefthand, Undulating, Very Tight Track

Official Going   GOOD/FIRM. Stalls: Inside.

2435 2.20 MALTON SUITE SELLER 2YO (G)   5f rnd   Good/Firm 39   -47 Slow
£1890   £540   £270

1381 **DANCING PENNEY** 47 [3] K A Ryan 2-8-6 (bl) F Lynch 9/2: -5001: 2 b f General Monash - Penultimate | | 60
Cress (My Generation): Sn led, made rest, rdn out: 7 wk abs: cheaply bought Feb foal: dam uncrd, sire a
juv wnr: apprec forcing tactics over a sharp 5f on fast grnd: runs well fresh in blnks: apprec drop to sells.
-- **FAIR STEP** [2] W W Haigh 2-8-6 J Stack 16/1: 2: 2 ch f King's Signet - Miss Hocroft (Dominion): | 1 | 57
Slow to start, ran green in rear till rdn & ran on well inside last, clsg at fin: cheaply bought May foal, half-
sister to a 3yo sprint wnr: promising debut, can win a seller.
1981 **GAZETTE IT TONIGHT** 20 [7] A Berry 2-8-6 J Carroll 9/2: -5563: 2 b f Merdon Melody - Balidilemma | ¾ | 55
(Balidar): Led early, remnd with ldrs, rdn/onepcd final 1f: will apprec a return to 6f: see 1359.
1918 **FAYZ SLIPPER** 22 [4] T D Easterby 2-8-6 K Darley 2/1 FAV: 000424: Prom, rdn/no extra final 1f: | shd | 55
consistent free-going type, handles firm/fast grnd: see 1918.
2200 **PAT PINKNEY** 10 [5] 2-8-6 T E Durcan 9/2: -0545: Mid-div, btn fnl 2f: tchd 13/2: rtd higher 2200. | 5 | 44
2059 **NETTLES** 16 [6] 2-8-11 R Winston 25/1: 00006: Mid-div, btn when hung right final 2f: modest form. | ½ | 43
1937 **CARTMEL PRINCE** 21 [8] 2-8-11 T Williams 9/2: -60027: Trkd ldrs, rdn/wknd 2f out: btr 1937. | 2 | 42
-- **APORTO** [1] 2-8-11 A Mackay 16/1: 8: Missed break, al bhd: 5,000gns brother to 5/6f 2yo scorer. | 3½ | 35
8 ran   Time 1m 01.6 (4.3)   (Robert Chambers)   K A Ryan Hambleton, Nth Yorks.

2436 2.50 TURMERIC HCAP 3YO+ 0-75 (E)   1m7f177y   Good/Firm 39   -02 Slow   [65]
£3493   £1075   £537   £268

2176 **KEEP IKIS** 11 [2] Mrs M Reveley 6-8-13 (50) D Mernagh (3) 5/2 JT FAV: 3-1431: 6 ch m Anshan - Santee | | 56
Sioux (Dancing Brave): Front rank, rdn to lead dist, drvn out: consistent form this term, won on reapp at Ripon
(h'cap), plcd fnl 2 '99 starts (rtd 41, h'cap), formerly a bmpr rnr-up for S Gollings: eff at 15f/2m2f: acts on
fast, gd & any trk: runs well fresh: tough, thorough stayer, in fine form.
3242} **CRUZ SANTA** 332 [5] Mrs M Reveley 7-7-10 (33)(7oh) P Fessey 10/1: /0P4-2: 7 b m Lord Bud - Linpac | 3½ | 35
Mapleleaf (Dominion): Bhd, hdwy to lead appr fnl 1f, sn hdd, kept on, not pace of wnr: jumps fit, recent Cartmel
wnr (mares nov sell, rtd 79h, 2m1f/3m, firm & soft): well btn in 3 '99 Flat starts, prev term won at Southwell
(appr mdn auct, rtd 31a & 42, M Chapman): eff at 11f/2m on fast, gd/soft & fibresand: fine run from 7lbs o/h.
2273 **ELSIE BAMFORD** 7 [4] M Johnston 4-9-0 (51) R Ffrench 3/1: 233333: 4 b f Tragic Role - Sara Sprint | 4 | 49
(Formidable): Prom, drvn & not pace of ldrs final 2f: qck reapp & 6th consecutive plcd run: see 2273, 1683.
1597 **RIGADOON** 36 [3] R W Easterby 4-9-4 (55)(bl) T Lucas 5/2 JT FAV: 1-4504: Led, hdd appr final 1f, | 2½ | 51
wknd: nicely bckd & fin well clr rem: btr 797.
2191 **HULLBANK** 10 [7] 10-10-0 (65) P McCabe 10/1: 55-145: Rear, eff 3f out, sn btn: op btr 1660 (sell). | 19 | 46
2176 **THE GAMBOLLER** 11 [8] 5-9-2 (53)(VIS) R Winston 40/1: -00-06: Chsd ldrs, wknd qckly final 5f: | 5 | 30
visored: 98/99 hdles wnr at Sedgefield (nov, rtd 88h): '98 wnr on the level at Leicester (auct mdn, Mrs A
Perrett, rtd 73): eff over a gall 10f, stays 2m over timber: acts on fast/firm & can go well when fresh.
141 **BLACK WEASEL** 215 [1] 5-8-3 (40) A Mackay 8/1: 0524-7: Al bhd, t.o: 7 mth abs: see 141. | 6 | 12
7 ran   Time 3m 27.3 (6.5)   (T McGoran)   Mrs M Reveley Lingdale, Nth Yorks.

CATTERICK THURSDAY JULY 6TH Lefthand, Undulating, Very Tight Track

2437

3.20 MIDDLEHAM CLASS STKS 3YO+ 0-65 (F) 7f rnd Good/Firm 39 +08 Fast
£2769 £852 £426 £213 3 yo rec 8 lb

2371 **ARPEGGIO 3** [12] D Nicholls 5-9-3 A Nicholls (3) 5/1: -00041: 5 b g Polar Falcon - Hilly (Town Crier): **67**
Mid-div, hdwy to lead appr fnl 1f, styd on strongly when prsd ins last, drvn out: qck reapp: lightly rcd in '99, scored at Thirsk (reapp, mdn, rtd 84): suited by 6/7f on fast, soft & a gall or sharp trk: goes well when fresh.
1224 **BEADING 57** [7] J W Hills 3-8-6 (t) M Henry 10/1: 0-002: 3 b f Polish Precent - Silver Braid (Miswaki) *nk* **63**
Handy, rdn/ran on well fnl 1f, not btn far: 8 wk abs, fine run by this lightly rcd filly, eff at 7f on fast, win sn.
2126 **ANALYTICAL 13** [5] R Charlton 4-9-3 K Darley 4/1 JT FAV: 0-0003: 4 b g Pursuit Of Love - Risha *2* **62**
Flower (Kris): With ldrs, rdn/no extra well inside last: nicely bckd & will apprec a return to 1m: see 1113.
2221 **PERFECT PEACH 9** [9] C W Fairhurst 5-9-0 F Lynch 4/1 JT FAV: 000434: Dwelt, held up, short *nk* **58**
of room appr final 1f, kept on inside last, no dngr: shade btr 2221 (7.5f, stiff trk).
2420 **ACID TEST 1** [1] 5-9-3 R Fitzpatrick (3) 12/1: 030005: Prom, rdn/btn appr final 1f: ran yesterday. *1½* **59**
*2376 **MASTER HENRY 3** [11] 6-9-6 R Ffrench 7/1: 666016: Chsd ldrs, drvn/fdd ins last: op 5/1, qck *1¾* **59**
reapp & poss too soon after 2376 (9f, firm): had a poor high draw today.
2049 **THATCHED 17** [8] 10-9-3 P Fessey 33/1: 6-5067: Rear, nvr a dngr: stiff task. *1½* **53$**
2163 **PERSIAN FAYRE 12** [3] 8-9-6 J Carroll 7/1: 0-0108: Set fast pace, hdd appr final 1f, fdd: op 6/1. *1½* **54**
2136 **DILETTO 13** [2] 4-9-0 T E Durcan 20/1: 610609: Dwelt, al rear: v stiff task: see 778. *¾* **46$**
1103 **HAITHEM 64** [4] 3-8-9 J Fanning 12/1: 20-060: Rcd keenly & al in rear: 9 wk abs. *1½* **47**
2247 **RETALIATOR 8** [10] 4-9-0 P McCabe 8/1: 002000: In tch, wknd qckly final 2f, fin last: btr 1781 (5f). *1¾* **41**
11 ran Time 1m 25.3 (2.3) (H E Lhendup Dorji) D Nicholls Sessay, Nth Yorks.

2438

3.50 PADDOCK SUITE HCAP 3YO 0-75 (E) 7f rnd Good/Firm 39 -09 Slow [79]
£3445 £1060 £530 £265

*2017 **DESERT SAFARI 18** [8] E J Alston 3-9-6 (71) T E Durcan 4/1: 540011: 3 b f Desert Style - Dublah **75**
(Private Account): Mid-div, rdn/hdwy 2f out, ran on to lead nr fin, drvn out: recent Carlisle wnr (fill h'cap): won fnl juv start, at Musselburgh (fill med auct mdn, rtd 74): stays a sharp or stiff 7f, 1m shld suit: handles hvy, likes firm/fast: has tried blnks, best without: in fine form, could complete a hat-trick.
1255 **DIHATJUM 55** [6] T D Easterby 3-8-12 (63) J Carroll 8/1: 026-32: 3 b g Mujtahid - Rosie Potts *nk* **66**
(Shareef Dancer): Trkd ldrs, led dist, styd on ins last, hdd nr fin: fine run after 8 wk abs, go one better sn.
2205 **GRANITE CITY 10** [10] J S Goldie 3-7-11 (48)(1ow)(12oh) Kimberley Hart 25/1: 000003: 3 ro g Clantime - *1* **49$**
Alhargah (Be My Guest): Bhd, ran on well for press appr final 1f, nrst fin: much imprvd here, tho' rating is best treated with caution: eff at 7f on fast, probably worth a try at 1m+ in a mdn h'cap: see 1358.
2205 **RIOS DIAMOND 10** [5] M J Ryan 3-7-10 (47) J Mackay (5) 3/1 FAV: 205134: Mid-div, rdn to chall *¾* **46**
appr final 1f, held inside last: see 2205.
1930 **NOBLE PASAO 21** [4] 3-9-1 (66) P Fessey 10/1: 003055: Front rank, onepcd inside last: see 1275. *½* **64**
2101 **ZESTRIL 15** [1] 3-9-7 (72) R Winston 14/1: 4-0066: Led, hdd dist, sn btn: op 10/1: see 1215. *1½* **68**
2250 **POP SHOP 8** [2] 3-9-7 (72) K Darley 9/2: -00007: With ldr, drvn/fdd appr fnl 1f: top weight: see 2250. *1½* **65**
1818 **CLEAR MOON 27** [3] 3-7-12 (49) N Kennedy 20/1: 3-5058: Dwelt, nvr a dngr: see 929. *2½* **38**
689 **OSCAR PEPPER 111** [7] 3-9-1 (66) D Mernagh (3) 6/1: -11229: Rear, rdn/effort 2f out, no dngr: *2* **51**
4 mth abs & in fine form on the sand prev, just sharper for this: see 365.
1780 **MYTTONS AGAIN 29** [9] 3-8-13 (64) A Mackay 8/1: 026650: Al rear, fin last: see 1780. *3* **44**
10 ran Time 1m 26.4 (3.4) (The Burlington Partnership) E J Alston Longton, Lancs.

2439

4.20 SUITE MED AUCT MDN 3YO (F) 1m5f175y Good/Firm 39 -62 Slow
£2205 £630 £315

1447 **WINDMILL 44** [2] T D Easterby 3-8-9 K Darley 2/11 FAV: 41: 3 b f Ezzoud - Bempton (Blakeney): **53**
Trkd ldr, rdn from halfway, styd on to lead appr final 2f, kept on well, drvn out: slow time, 6 wk abs: half-sister to sev wnrs: eff at 10f, apprec this step up to 14f & 2m could suit: runs well fresh on fast, gd & a stiff or sharp trk: goes well fresh: can rate more highly (rtd 82 on recent debut).
2105 **SANDROS BOY 14** [1] P D Evans 3-9-0 P McCabe 4/1: 32: 3 b g Alhijaz - Bearnaise (Cyrano De *3* **53$**
Bergerac) Keen, rcd in 3rd, hdwy to chall appr final 2f, not pace of wnr inside last: op 3/1: stays 14f on fast.
2254 **HORTON DANCER 8** [3] M Brittain 3-9-0 D Mernagh (3) 25/1: 004003: 3 b g Rambo Dancer - Horton *hd* **52$**
Lady (Midyan): Set stdy pace, hdd 2f out, sn onepcd: offic rtd only 46 & probably flattered here.
3 ran Time 3m 09.3 (13.9) (Lord Halifax) T D Easterby Great Habton, Nth Yorks.

2440

4.50 SCOTCH CORNER HCAP 3YO 0-70 (E) 6f rnd Good/Firm 39 -19 Slow [74]
£3347 £1030 £515 £257

2280 **MARON 7** [7] A Berry 3-8-10 (56) J Carroll 7/4 FAV: -00321: 3 b g Puissance - Will Be Bold (Bold Lad) **61**
Rear, prog to chall appr fnl 1f, ran on to lead cl-home, drvn out: nicely bckd, qck reapp: '99 wnr at Hamilton (auct stks, rtd 73): eff at 5/6f on firm, gd & a stiff/undul or sharp trk: tough & in fine form, deserved this.
2060 **DISTINCTLY BLU 16** [2] K A Ryan 3-9-5 (65) F Lynch 9/2: 616252: 3 b f Distinctly North - Stifen *½* **68**
(Burslem): Led, kept on well fnl 1f, hdd nr fin: in gd heart, win again sn: handles fast & gd/soft: see 901.
2060 **WELCOME TO UNOS 16** [8] M Dods 3-9-6 (66) T Williams 11/1: 02-063: 3 ch g Exit To Nowhere - *1½* **66**
Royal Loft (Homing): Front rank, dropped rear after 3f, rallied & styd on well final 1f: looks in need of 7f+: stable in form & could win with a step up in trip: see 1768.
2047 **BENNOCHY 17** [3] A Berry 3-8-9 (55) O Pears 10/1: -10504: Trkd ldrs, rdn/onepcd final 1f: up in trip. *hd* **55**
2047 **LIZZIE SIMMONDS 17** [5] 3-8-11 (57) N Kennedy 7/1: 550165: Nvr dngrs: shade btr 1817 (5f, gd/soft). *2* **52**
*2042 **KINSMAN 17** [4] 3-9-7 (67)(vis) K Darley 5/2: 062316: Chsd ldrs, fdd fnl 2f: btr 2042 (firm, Brighton). *5* **51**
4582} **PLEASURE PRINCESS 247** [6] 3-7-10 (42)(2oh) D Mernagh (0) 33/1: 000-7: Al bhd: no form in '99. *6* **14**
515 **SKI FREE 143** [1] 3-8-0 (46) A Nicholls (3) 25/1: 05-608: Mid-div, hmpd halfway & sn lost tch: long abs. *4* **9**
8 ran Time 1m 13.8 (3.5) (A S Kelvin) A Berry Cockerham, Lancs.

HAYDOCK   THURSDAY JULY 6TH   Lefthand, Flat, Galloping Track

Official Going: GOOD TO FIRM. Stalls: 6f/14f - Centre, 7f - Inside, 12f - Outside

2441   2.10 SUMMER MDN CLAIMER 2YO (F)   6f   Good/Firm 21   -29 Slow
£2464   £704   £352   Raced towards centre

2039 **FOLEY MILLENNIUM** 17 [8] M Quinn 2-9-0 J Fortune 10/1: 551: 2 ch c Tagula - Inshirah (Caro)   **80**
Led after 2f, eased near fin, comfortably: val for 5L+: dam 5/7f wnr: apprec this step up to 6f, 7f shld
suit: acts on fast & a gall track: apprec drop to claiming grade & going the right way.

2057 **PETIT TOR** 16 [4] J Norton 2-8-4 O Pears 11/4 FAV: -04252: 2 b f Rock City - Kinoora (Kind Of Hush)   3   60
Handy, rdn/kept on fnl 2f, ev ch wnr: op 9/4: acts on fast & gd/soft grnd: see 1476.

2120 **TUPGILL TIPPLE** 14 [3] S E Kettlewell 2-8-6 A Beech (5) 7/2: 23: 2 b f Emperor Jones - Highest   4   52
Baby (Highest Honor) Rdn/chsd ldrs over 2f out, held 1f out: op 3/1: btn 2120 (5f, AW, debut).

-- **SPORTS EXPRESS** [5] W W Haigh 2-8-4 W Supple 33/1: 4: Dwelt/rear, rdn & some late gains: 1¾   46
Then Again filly, April foal, cost 2,500gns: half sister to a 6/7f juv wnr, dam a 12f wnr: apprec 7f+.

2218 **BOMBAY BINNY** 9 [7] 2-8-4 (BL) R Mullen 15/2: 02055: In tch till halfway: blinks: btr 1764 (hvy).   nk   45

2214 **SHOLTO** 9 [1] 2-8-4 (BL) J Quinn 10/1: -006: Keen, led 2f, btn over 1f out: op 8/1, blinks.   6   33

-- **ABERFOLLY** [6] 2-8-0 Joanna Badger (7) 25/1: 7: Soon rdn/al bhd: Minshaanshu Amad filly,   1¼   26
April foal: half sister to a 6f juv wnr abroad, dam a mdn: with P D Evans.

-- **LAND GIRL** [9] 2-8-2 Dale Gibson 25/1: 8: Dwelt, al outpcd rear: General Monash filly, Feb foal,   ½   26
cheaply bought, a first foal: dam a 3yo French wnr: with Miss S E Hall.

2077 **FORTUNA** 15 [2] 2-8-4 S Sanders 3/1: 059: Chsd ldrs, rdn/hung left & btn over 1f out: btr 2077 (AW).   1½   24

9 ran   Time 1m 14.27 (2.97)   (Mrs S G Davies)   M Quinn Sparsholt, Oxon

2442   2.40 HARRY HAYDOCK HCAP 3YO+ 0-70 (E)   7f130y rnd   Good/Firm 21   -01 Slow   [69]
£3276   £936   £468   3 yo rec 8 lb

2130 **SWYNFORD WELCOME** 13 [3] J Hetherton 4-8-2 (43) O Pears 33/1: 000000: 4 b f Most Welcome -   46
Qualitair Dream (Dreams To Reality) Made all, rdn & strongly pressed from 2f out, styd on, drvn out: mod form
this term, trainer reported filly improved for front running tactics today: '99 Brighton wnr (rtd 57, h'cap,
J Pearce, mod form prev): '98 Redcar wnr (fillies medium aution mdn, rtd 79, current connections): eff at
6/7f, tried further: acts on fast & gd/soft: likes to dominate & has run well fresh: unpredictable.

2126 **PENGAMON** 13 [8] M Wigham 8-8-13 (54) J Quinn 8/1: 12-302: 8 gr g Efisio - Dolly Bevan (Another   nk   57
Realm) Trkd ldr, smooth prog to chall over 1f out, rdn/held near line: has looked genuine previously: see 1037.

2282 **BODFARI ANNA** 7 [11] J L Eyre 4-8-10 (51)(vis) D Holland 16/1: 501003: 4 br f Casteddu - Lowrianna   ½   53
(Cyrano de Bergerac) Twds rear/wide, kept on over 1f out, nrst fin: op 14/1: back to form here: see 1606.

1869 **ON TILL MORNING** 24 [2] M Dods 4-9-0 (55) A Culhane 14/1: -00004: Rear, prog fnl 3f, drvn & styd   ¾   56
on ins last, not reach ldrs: improved effort, looks nicely h'capped & now coming to hand: see 910.

2221 **BOLLIN ROBERTA** 9 [13] 4-9-6 (61) Pat Eddery 9/1: 0-5205: Trckd ldrs, onepace fnl 2f: see 908.   nk   61

*2420 **DOVEBRACE** 1 [1] 7-8-7 (48) J Bramhill 100/30 FAV: 321216: Dwelt, rear, eff wide 3f out, mod   1   46
headway: hvly bckd after h'cap win at Catterick yesterday: see 2420.

4459} **IVORS INVESTMENT** 259 [7] P M Quinn (3) 33/1: D050-7: Mid div, one pace/held fnl 2f: 2   42
reapp: '99 wnr at Chepstow & Epsom (clmrs, for D R C Elsworth, rtd 72, h'cap): eff at 6/8.5f on firm & gd/soft.

*2282 **SHAMWARI SONG** 7 [14] 5-8-4 (45)(vis)(6ex) S Sanders 9/2: 040318: Trck ldr, fdd fnl 2f: bckd.   1   37

1875 **RAMBO WALTZER** 24 [10] 8-9-0 (55) T G McLaughlin 12/1: 113209: Mid div, rdn/btn 2f out: op 10/1.   1½   44

1275 **LYNTON LAD** 54 [5] 8-9-4 (59) W Supple 16/1: 5-6600: Chsd ldrs, outpcd fnl 2f: 10th: 8 week abs.   ¾   47

4522} **DESERT VALENTINE** 254 [6] 5-8-4 (45) S Carson 33/1: 0050-0: Rear, never any impresssion: 3   27
11th: reapp: unplcd last term (rtd 47, h'cap): '98 Goodwood wnr (h'cap, rtd 59): suited by a sharp/undulating
1m on gd/soft grnd: has run well fresh.

2241 **ONLY FOR GOLD** 8 [16] 5-9-1 (56) J Fortune 15/2: 623020: Chsd ldrs wide 5f: 13th: poor high draw.   0

2193 **AUBRIETA** 10 [12] 4-8-12 (53)(bl) Dean McKeown 10/1: 501140: Chsd ldrs 5f: 14th: btr 1913 (AW).   0

2221 Oriole 9 [9] 7-8-3 (44) Kim Tinkler 25/1:   2180 Turtles Rising 11 [15] 4-9-10 (65) P Hanagan (7) 20/1:

2275 Mister Westsound 7 [4] 8-8-13 (54)(bl) C Lowther 33/1:

16 ran   Time 1m 28.67 (1.57)   (Qualitar Holdings Ltd)   J Hetherton Malton, N Yorks

2443   3.10 HEUBACH MDN 3YO (D)   7f130y rnd   Good/Firm 21   +08 Fast
£4101   £1262   £631   £315

1532 **MAHFOOTH** 40 [1] Saeed bin Suroor 3-9-0 R Hills 11/10: 3-021: 3 ch c Diesis - I Certainly Am (Affirmed)   102
Made all, rdn & clr fnl 2f, eased down as was rnr-up when 8L clr: fast time, hvly bckd, abs: well btn in UAE
Derby (12f) earlier this year: ex French, cost sole '99 start at Deauville (Listed): eff at 7f/1m on fast
& soft, likes a gall track: runs well fresh: clearly useful, win more races.

2117 **ALL THE GEARS** 14 [4] Sir Michael Stoute 3-9-0 Pat Eddery 5/6 FAV: 3-5302: 3 b c Gone West -   13   84
Buckeye Gal (Good Counsel) Chsd wnr bef halfway, rdn & held 2f out, poss accepted fnl 1f when 8L bhd: see 1341.

2058 **SUPER DOMINION** 16 [3] R Hollinshead 3-9-0 P M Quinn (3) 33/1: 43: 3 ch c Superpower - Smartie   1¾   66
Lee (Dominion) Chsd wnr 3f, soon outpcd by front pair: flattered by proximity to rnr up: see 2058.

1669 **WHITEGATE WAY** 34 [5] A Bailey 3-8-9 J Bramhill 66/1: 004: Rear, never on terms: mod form prev.   1¾   58$

1218 **BREAKIN GLASS** 58 [2] 3-8-9 S Sanders 50/1: 55: Unruly stalls, dwelt/rear, no impress: abs.   7   44

3138} **YOUNG ROOSTER** 337 [6] 3-9-0 J Weaver 50/1: 00-6: Keen, in tch, btn 4f out: reapp: rtd 52 in '99.   2½   44

6 ran   Time 1m 28.01 (.91)   (Godolphin)   Saeed bin Suroor Newmarket, Suffolk

2444   3.40 TOTE HCAP 3YO+ 0-80 (D)   6f   Good/Firm 21   +02 Fast   [80]
£7962   £2450   £1225   £612   3 yo rec 6 lb   Raced centre to stands side

2207 **FULL SPATE** 10 [2] J M Bradley 5-8-11 (63) Pat Eddery 15/2: 603541: 5 ch h Unfuwain - Double   69
River (Irish River) Soon chsd ldrs, prog/rdn to chall over 1f out, led inside last, styd on well, rdn out: good time:
'99 Thirsk wnr (h'cap, sole win, rtd 79): '98 debut rnr up (rtd 80, with R Charlton): suited by 6/7f, stays 1m:
acts on fast & hvy grnd, any track: nicely h'capped, shld win again.

2158 **COOL PROSPECT** 12 [19] K A Ryan 5-8-4 (59) S Sanders 9/1: 042322: 5 b g Mon Tresor - I Ran Lovely   1   58
(Persian Bold) Chsd ldrs, rdn & kept on well fnl 1f, not pace of wnr: tough/consistent at 5/6f: see 2158, 1143.

2396 **TECHNICIAN** 2 [3] E J Alston 5-8-2 (54)(bl) N Pollard 6/1 FAV: 200123: 5 ch g Archway - How It   shd   56
Works (Commanche Run) Bhd ldr, rdn/prog to take narrow lead over 1f out, hdd inside last & no extra cl home.

772

HAYDOCK THURSDAY JULY 6TH Lefthand, Flat, Galloping Track

2247 **THE GAY FOX 8** [16] B A McMahon 6-9-2 (68)(tbl) R Hughes 9/1: -53024: Chsd ldrs, rdn/kept on fnl 1f. *1* **68**
2396 **GRAND ESTATE 2** [4] 5-8-3 (55) A Beech (5) 9/1: 545235: Held up, kept on fnl 2f, not rch ldrs. *nk* **54**
2015 **DOUBLE ACTION 18** [1] 6-8-12 (64)(bl) J Fortune 14/1: 053266: Held up, rdn/kept on onepace fnl 2f. *½* **61**
2334 **UNSHAKEN 5** [7] 6-9-3 (69) W Supple 10/1: 400007: Mid div, never pace to chall: op 8/1: see 716. *nk* **65**
2275 **SWINO 7** [9] 6-7-13 (51) Joanna Badger (7) 33/1: 446008: Mid div, rdn/never pace to chall: see 177. *1* **45**
1471 **HILL MAGIC 43** [6] 5-9-13 (79) S Carson (5) 14/1: 5-0009: Prom, fdd fnl 1f: 6 week abs: see 935. *nk* **72**
*1687 **XANADU 33** [13] 4-9-2 (68) Iona Wands (5) 10/1: 112010: Prom 4f, fdd: 10th: btr 1687 (5f). *nk* **60**
*2046 **MAMMAS BOY 17** [10] 5-8-2 (54) R Mullen 14/1: 041110: Chs d ldrs till halfway, sn held: 11th, btr 2046. *1* **44**
2163 **ABLE AYR 12** [17] 3-8-11 (69) Dawn Rankin (7) 33/1: 005000: Held up, mod prog, no threat: 12th. *¾* **57**
2395 **JOHAYRO 2** [15] 7-8-4 (56) A McGlone 14/1: 002430: Led till over 1f out: 13th: op 12/1, qck reapp. *¾* **42**
2334 **MALLIA 5** [11] 7-9-1 (67)(bl) D Holland 8/1: 444400: Held up, al towards rear: 17th: quick reapp, won this last term off a 3lb higher mark: see 719. **0**
2158 **Miss Fit 12** [18] 4-9-3 (69) Dean McKeown 20/1:
1869 **Sugar Cube Treat 24** [14] 4-8-2 (54) J Bramhill 25/1:
2338 **Redoubtable 5** [12] 9-9-8 (74) A Culhane 16/1:
1654 **Lady Boxer 34** [8] 4-9-4 (70) J Weaver 25/1:
716 **Rififi 104** [20] 7-9-4 (70) P Shea (7) 33/1:
19 ran Time 1m 12.46 (1.16) (E A Hayward) J M Bradley Sedbury, Gloucs

2445 — 4.10 GOOSE GREEN HCAP 3YO 0-80 (D) 1m6f Good/Firm 21 -07 Slow [87]
£4199 £1292 £646 £323

*1949 **GIVE NOTICE 21** [6] J L Dunlop 3-8-13 (72) Pat Eddery 1/1 FAV: 0-0611: 3 b c Warning - Princess Genista (Ile de Bourbon) Led after 1f, shaken up fnl 3f & rdn clr over 1f out, easily: val for 10L+: hvly bckd: recent wnr at Yarmouth, (h'cap, readily): rtd 69 in '99 (mdn): eff at 14f, 2m will suit: acts on fast grnd & a gall/fair track: can force the pace: v progressive colt, keep on your side. **86+**
1948 **PRINCE AMONG MEN 21** [7] M C Pipe 3-9-6 (79) R Hughes 7/1: -33332: 3 b g Robellino - Forelino (Trempolino) Held up, hdwy 3f out, soon outpcd by easy wnr, kept on to take 2nd 1f out: stays 14f, see 1948. *7* **79**
1919 **KISTY 22** [4] H Candy 3-8-12 (71) C Rutter 6/1: 4-0333: 3 b f Kris - Pine Ridge (High Top) Chsd wnr 3f out, soon outpcd & no extra/lost 2nd 1f out: op 5/1: prob stays 14f: see 1919, 1571 & 1094. *¾* **70**
2110 **MAZAARR 14** [3] M R Channon 3-8-11 (70) W Supple 6/1: 600014: Prom, rdn/btn over 2f out: op 5/1. *1* **68**
2110 **KAIAPOI 14** [2] 3-9-7 (80) P M Quinn (3) 15/2: -11U35: Held up, rdn/btn over 2f out: btr 1225. *1¼* **76**
1743 **GOLDEN ROD 30** [1] 3-8-5 (64) A Culhane 12/1: -00346: Led 1f, handy 12f: op 9/1: btr 1743, 1608. *nk* **59**
2144 **ULSHAW 13** [5] 3-7-11 (56) G Bardwell 33/1: 05-037: Held up, rdn/bhd 3f out: see 2144 (mdn). *8* **42**
7 ran Time 3m 02.08 (4.08) (I H Stewart-Brown) J L Dunlop Arundel, W Sussex

2446 — 4.40 VICTORIA FILL HCAP 3YO+ 0-80 (D) 1m3f200y Good/Firm 21 -22 Slow [76]
£3867 £1190 £595 £297 3 yo rec 13lb

*825 **CASHMERE LADY 92** [4] J L Eyre 8-8-13 (61) D Holland 7/1: 65-011: 8 b m Hubbly Bubbly - Choir (High Top) Held up, drvn/prog over 1f out, styd on strongly ins last for press, led near line: op 6/1: 3 month abs: earlier won at Ripon (h'cap): unplcd over jumps last winter, (rtd 84h): '99 Haydock scorer (amat h'cap, rtd 62): '98 wnr at Southwell & Thirsk (rtd 92a): eff at 1m, best at 12f on fast, hvy & fibresand: runs well fresh. **63**
1812 **INTRUM MORSHAAN 27** [9] J L Dunlop 3-8-9 (70) Pat Eddery 6/1: 063-02: 3 b f Darshaan - Auntie Maureeen (Roi Danzig) Handy, rdn/briefly outpcd 3f out, drvn/took narrow lead inside last, hdd near line: op 5/1: acts on fast & soft grnd: apprec step up to 12f: see 1812 (10f). *hd* **70**
2179 **SENSE OF FREEDOM 11** [1] M Johnston 3-9-4 (79) J Weaver 5/1: 2223: 3 ch f Grand Lodge - Greatest Pleasure (Be My Guest) Dwelt, rear, prog & every ch fnl 1f, swished tail/just held near line: well bckd. *hd* **78**
2286 **MONO LADY 6** [7] D Haydn Jones 7-9-6 (68)(bl) Dean McKeown 6/1: 045144: Held up, rdn/outpcd over 2f out, styd on inside last, not pace to chall: quick reapp: op 5/1: remains in gd heart: see 2075 (AW). *1¼* **65**
2362 **GARGOYLE GIRL 3** [10] 3-7-10 (57)(10oh)(1ow) J Quinn 16/1: -06445: Chsd ldrs, prog/led over 2f out, hdd inside last & no extra: quick reapp: see 2141, 1633. *hd* **54$**
4200} **LINEA G 278** [6] 6-9-2 (64) A Culhane 9/1: 5120-6: Cl up 3f out, soon outpcd: qck reapp, 5 month jumps abs, won 3 times over timber in 99/00 (rtd 108h): '99 Flat scorer at Southwell (AW mdn, rtd 53a), subs won at Newcastle (h'cap) & Beverley (stakes, rtd 67 at best): eff over a gall 12f, stays a sharp 2m on gd & fast. *5* **53**
2069 **MOLE CREEK 16** [8] 5-9-10 (72) R Hughes 16/1: 05-007: Cl up 10f: mod form this term: rtd 83 in '99 (unplcd, rtd h'cap): '98 Warwick wnr (class stks, rtd 86): eff at 10/12f on firm & soft grnd, sharp/gall trk: suited by a tongue strap, not worn here. *hd* **60**
*2023 **WATER FLOWER 18** [5] 6-9-8 (70) J Fortune 3/1 FAV: 00-018: Held up, rdn/btn 2f out: bckd. *nk* **57**
2023 **SEEKING UTOPIA 18** [2] 3-8-10 (71) R Mullen 15/2: 5-5049: Led till over 2f out, fdd: see 2023, 727. *shd* **58**
1683 **YANKEE DANCER 33** [3] 5-7-11 (45) P M Quinn (3) 40/1: 32/000: Keen/prom 1m: 10th: see 1496. *5* **25**
10 ran Time 2m 32.94 (5.14) (Mrs Sybil Howe) J L Eyre Sutton Bank, N Yorks

CHEPSTOW THURSDAY JULY 6TH Lefthand, Undulating, Galloping Track

Official Going GOOD TO FIRM. Stalls: Str Crse - Stands Side: Rnd Crse - Inside.

2447 — 2.00 TINTERN CLAIMER 2YO (F) 6f Good/Firm 38 -30 Slow
£2226 £636 £318

*1931 **YOUNG ALEX 21** [1] K R Burke 2-9-0 N Callan 9/2: -011: 2 ch g Midhish - Snipe Hunt (Stalker) Trkd ldrs, rdn to lead ent final 1f, held on well: op 7/2: 3 wks ago scored at Brighton (clmr, cmftbly): eff at 6f, should get 7f: acts on fast grnd, sharp/undul trks: runs well fresh: imprvg & looks better than a claimer. **74**
2312 **JOINT INSTRUCTION 6** [2] M R Channon 2-8-11 Craig Williams 6/1: 215202: 2 b c Forzando - Edge Of Darkness (Vaigly Great) Cl-up, led halfway till ent final 1f, drifted left, al held: op 4/1, qck reapp, ran to best. *½* **70**
2277 **WHITE MARVEL 7** [6] W J Haggas 2-9-0 J F Egan 1/1 FAV: 63: 2 b f Polar Falcon - Million Heiress (Auction Ring) Chsd ldrs, feeling pace 2f out, rdn & strong run fnl 150y, too late: hvly bckd, wnr in another 50y, qck reapp, clmd by R Hannon Jnr for £20,000: still found lngr 6f trip insufficient: goes on fast grnd, win at 7f. *hd* **72**
2312 **DECEITFUL 6** [3] Sir Mark Prescott 2-8-8 G Duffield 4/1: 134: Unruly start & led till halfway, no extra before dist: qck reapp: keen sort, do better back at 5f?: see 2312, 2039. *3½* **57**
2182 **MUCHO GUSTO 11** [4] 2-8-9 T Quinn 10/1: 05: Al outpcd: op 7/1, back in trip & grade. *4* **48**
-- **CHINA FAIN** [5] 2-8-2 J Tate 25/1: 6: Sn struggling: op 14/1, half-sister to sprinter Eastern Trumpeter. *26* **1**
6 ran Time 1m 12.9 (4.1) (D G & D J Robinson) K R Burke Newmarket, Suffolk.

2448   2.30 YPSL CYCLE SELLER 3YO (F)   1m str   Good/Firm 38 -10 Slow
£2303   £658   £329

2187 **COLLEGE ROCK** 10 [4] R Brotherton 3-9-0 (vis) G Carter 12/1: 630641: 3 ch g Rock Hopper - Sea Aura   57
(Roi Soleil) Mid-div, gd prog 2f out, led dist, rdn out: no bid, first win: plcd juv (sell, rtd 63, S Williams):
eff at 1m, stays 10f: acts on firm & soft grnd, any trk: tried blnks, best visored: at home in sellers.
2187 **BEDOUIN QUEEN** 10 [10] R F Johnson Houghton 3-8-9 J Bosley (7) 10/1: 006002: 3 ch f Aragon -   2   47
Petra's Star (Rock City) Outpcd & drvn, imprvd halfway, chsd wnr dist, sn onepace: eff at 6f, stays 1m.
1972 **LE LOUP** 20 [1] Miss E C Lavelle 3-9-0 Dane O'Neill 10/1: 0-0043: 3 b g Wolfhound - Chandni   1¾   48
(Ahonoora) Trkd ldrs, effort 2f out, not pace to chall: prob styd lngr 1m trip: handles fast & soft grnd.
1973 **CASTLEBRIDGE** 20 [11] M C Pipe 3-9-5 (vis) J Reid 1/1 FAV: 615304: Dwelt, recovered to lead by   1   51
halfway, wandered under press dist & sn hdd, no extra: well bckd: suited by softer, see 1002 (hvy grnd h'cap).
2040 **TALENTS LITTLE GEM** 17 [5] 3-8-9 M Roberts 12/1: 0-4505: Dwelt, late hdwy, nvr a threat: see 1336.   1   39
2281 **BINT HABIBI** 7 [16] 3-9-0 Craig Williams 9/1: 0-0166: Chsd ldrs, fdd appr final 1f: btr 1972 (7f).   1   42
1972 **SHAW VENTURE** 20 [12] 3-9-0 (bl) P Fitzsimons (5) 12/1: 0-6067: Al same pl: lngr trip, blnks reapp.   1¾   38
2284 **WHO DA LEADER** 6 [2] 3-9-0 L Newman (3) 10/1: -05068: Prom till ent final 2f: qck reapp, see 2025.   1   36
2206 **PASADENA** 10 [6] 3-8-9 (BL) M Tebbutt 3-9-0: 040009: Dwelt, nvr in it: blnkd, op 7/1, see 934 (hvy).   ¾   29
2250 **NO REGRETS** 8 [7] 3-9-0 F Norton 33/1: 000500: Handy 4f: 10th, stiff task, blnks omitted.   5   24
2187 **PONTIKONISI** 10 [9] 3-9-0 (bl) J Tate 16/1: 5-0500: Led till after halfway, fdd: 12th, blnks reapplied.   0
2187 **Walter The Whistle** 10 [15] 3-9-0 (bl) N Callan 25/1:   1972 **Rosetta** 20 [13] 3-8-9 R Havlin 16/1:
-- **Sigy Point** [14] 3-8-9 R Perham 25/1:   3562} **Swan Prince** 316 [3] 3-9-0 A Daly 33/1:
2080 **Research Master** 15 [8] 3-9-0 (BL) S Righton 25/1:
16 ran   Time 1m 35.7 (3.8)   (Miss Geradine P O'Reilly)   R Brotherton Elmsley Castle, Worcs.

2449   3.00 MONMOUTH FILLIES MDN 3YO (D)   1m2f36y   Good/Firm 38 -44 Slow
£3913   £1204   £602   £301

1951 **LAND AHEAD** 21 [5] H R A Cecil 3-8-11 T Quinn 1/3 FAV: 5-31: 3 ch f Distant View - Nimble Folly   87
(Cyane) Trkd ldr, led 4f out, rdn & narrowly hdd appr final 1f, rallied despite edging right, regained lead line:
well bckd from 8/15, slow time, front 2 clr: 5th of 19 sole '99 start (mdn, rtd 73): half-sister to smart 10f
performer Skimble: apprec step up to 10f: acts on fast grnd, sharp/undul trk: going the right way.
4601} **SABREON** 245 [3] J L Dunlop 3-8-11 G Carter 3/1: 2220-2: 3 b f Caerleon - Sabria (Miswaki)   shd   86
Trkd front pair, shkn up & slight advantage dist, sn carried right by wnr, hdd line (not tchd with whip): reapp,
clr of 3rd: 3 time rnr-up in '99 (fill mdn, rtd 89): eff at 1m/10f: acts on fast & soft grnd, must win soon.
-- **CAVANIA** [2] W R Muir 3-8-11 Martin Dwyer 10/1: 3: 3 ch f Lion Cavern - Ma Pavlova (Irish River)   10   71
Dwelt, imprvd to chase ldrs briefly 3f out, no extra: tchd 14/1 on debut: bred/rcd like apprec a drop back to 1m.
-- **STAR ATTRACTION** [4] M Quinn 3-8-11 G Hannon (7) 25/1: 4: Nvr in it: debut, Rambo Dancer filly.   22   41
2024 **ABERNANT LADY** 18 [1] F Norton 40/1: 05: Sn led, hdd 4f out, sn btn: see 2024.   13   21
5 ran   Time 2m 12.3 (8.2)   (K Abdulla)   H R A Cecil Newmarket, Suffolk.

2450   3.30 ST ARVANS HCAP 3YO 0-80 (D)   1m2f36y   Good/Firm 38 -21 Slow   [85]
£3900   £1200   £600   £300

2004 **ZIBELINE** 19 [9] C E Brittain 3-9-7 (78) P Robinson 10/3: -02441: 3 b c Cadaux Genereux - Zia   82
(Shareef Dancer) Handy, prog to lead 3f out, just held on under press: tchd 9/2, first win: 4th in a mdn here
in '99 (rtd 82): eff at 1m/10f: acts on firm & gd grnd, any track: genuine & improving.
*1388 **ASTRONAUT** 47 [7] W J Haggas 3-9-4 (75) J F Egan 5/1: 0412: 3 b g Sri Pekan - Wild Abandon   shd   78
(Graustark) Rear, plenty to do 2f out, kept on well bef dist, ran on strongly just failed: 7 week abs, h'cap bow:
gd run, eff at 9/10f on fast grnd & fibresand: type to win again soon.
761 **PEDRO PETE** 100 [6] M R Channon 3-8-11 (68) Craig Williams 8/1: -41433: 3 ch g Fraam - Stride   nk   70
Home (Absalom) Held up, prog 2f out, rdn & styd on fnl 1f, never nearer: not beaten far after 14 week abs:
apprec return to 10f, goes on fast, gd grnd & equitrack: see 597.
*2159 **GOLDEN CHANCE** 12 [3] M Johnston 3-9-7 (78) J Reid 3/1 FAV: 32213: Bhd ldrs, chall appr fnl   dht   80
2f, onepace till kept on well towards fin: got lngr 10f trip on h'cap bow, shapes like 12f will suit: see 2159.
2210 **KATHAKALI** 10 [2] R Brisland (5) 16/1: 000005: Pulled hard in mid div, rdn & short of   ½   61
room over 2f out, taken wide & kept on nicely fnl 1f: ran to best back in trip, see 880 (equitrack).
*467 **FAIR LADY** 152 [8] M Roberts 3-9-7 (78) 10/1: 026-16: Keen, bhd, gd progress to chall 3f out till dist,   ½   78
no extra: op 8/1, 5 mnth abs, h'cap bow: fair run, drop back in trip?: see 467 (9.4f fibresand).
1645 **MENTIGA** 34 [4] G Hind 14/1: -05067: Led till 3f out, fdd fnl 1f: lngr trip for this 7f mudlark.   3½   70
1866 **TOP HAND** 24 [1] G Carter 14/1: 1-4008: Never in it: stablemate 6th, see 999.   7   51
1669 **THERMAL SPRING** 34 [10] 3-9-7 (78) T Quinn 5/1: 5-249: Pulled hard in tch, prog 4f out, wknd   nk   69
quickly 2f out: op 4/1, h'cap bow: unsuited by step up in trip & faster grnd?: see 1669.
2250 **AIR MAIL** 8 [5] 3-9-3 (74)(VIS) J Tate 25/1: 105000: Keen, well plcd till lost place 3f out: 10th: 7   47
visored, longer trip, tried blinks last time, see 651 (7f equitrack mdn).
10 ran   Time 2m 10.0 (5.9)   (Sheikh Marwan Al Maktoum)   C E Brittain Newmarket

2451   4.00 WELSH SCURRY HCAP 3YO+ 0-100 (C)   5f   Good/Firm 38 -06 Slow   [96]
£6727   £2070   £1035   £517   3 yo rec 5 lb

1861 **WHIZZ KID** 25 [4] J M Bradley 6-7-13 (67) Claire Bryan (5) 11/1: 312601: 6 b m Puissance - Panienka   75
(Dom Racine) Prom, rdn to lead dist, ran on strongly: prev won at Warwick (h'cap) & W'hampton (fill h'cap,
rtd 42a): '99 wnr at Ripon, Redcar, here at Chepstow, Ayr & Newcastle (h'caps, rtd 62): eff at 5f/sharp 6f: acts
on firm, hvy, both AW's: goes on any track, likes Chepstow: v tough mare, credit to v competent connections.
2247 **EASTERN TRUMPETER** 8 [8] J M Bradley 4-8-5 (73) P Fitzsimons (5) 5/1: 111302: 4 b c First Trump -   1½   77
Oriental Air (Taufan) Front rank, led appr fnl 1f, sn hdd, kept on: s/mate wnr, back to form, poor draw in 2247.
1534 **AWAKE** 40 [3] M Johnston 3-9-7 (97) G Carter 6/1: -04203: 3 ch c First Trump - Pluvial (Habat)   1½   97
Prom till outpcd by front pair fnl1f: 6 wk abs: back in trip, stiffer track will suit at this trip: see 988.
2151 **DANIELLES LAD** 13 [6] B Palling 4-10-0 (96) D McGaffin (5) 11/2: 401104: Early ldr, cl up, drvn 2f out,   ½   95
onepace fnl 1f: op 4/1, top-weight: suited by 6f & softer grnd: see 1531.
2168 **BANDANNA** 2 [2] 3-8-8 (81) M Roberts 9/2 JT FAV: 0-0065: Wide, chsd ldrs, rdn appr fnl 1f, no   ¾   78
impression: nicely bckd from 7/1: prob not the best of draws, see 2168.

CHEPSTOW

THURSDAY JULY 6TH   Lefthand, Undulating, Galloping Track

2168 **CORRIDOR CREEPER 12** [7] 3-8-13 (86)(BL) J Reid 11/2: -03006: Chsd ldrs, fdd inside last: blinkd.   ½   82
2348 **JUWWI 4** [5] 6-9-13 (95) Darren Williams (5) 9/2 JT FAV: 050007: Dwelt, nvr in it: broke blood vessel: nk   90
stablemate of 1st & 2nd, been very busy, see 1337.
2326 **AURIGNY 5** [10] 5-8-3 (71)(vis) G Duffield 10/1: 064048: Soon led, hdd appr fnl 1f, grad wknd: see 191.   2½   60
1952 **LONE PIPER 21** [1] 5-9-5 (87)(VIS) P Robinson 16/1: -40009: Nvr a factor: vis, poor draw, t-strap off.   1½   72
1884 **ANNO DOMINI 23** [11] 4-8-12 (80) D Griffiths 251: 152/00: Al bhd: 10th, see 1884.   1¼   62
10 ran   Time 59.0 (2.2)   (B Paling)   J M Bradley Sedbury, Gloucs

---

2452   4.30 LIONS LODGE HCAP STKS 3YO+ 0-70 (E)   2m2f   Good/Firm 38   +06 Fast   [60]
       £2795   £860   £430   £215   3 yo rec 21lb

2295 **XELLANCE 6** [8] M Johnston 3-7-13 (52) K Dalgleish (5) 2/1 FAV: 111221: 3 b g Be My Guest -   66
Excellent Alibi (Exceller) Confidently held up, clsd on bit 6f out, led 4f out & sn settled matters: nicely bckd,
best time of day, qk reapp: earlier won at Southwell (2), W'hampton (rtd 53a) Musselburgh & Redcar (h'caps):
eff at 14f/2m2f on firm/fast grnd & fibresand: runs well fresh on sharp or gall trks: tough, progressive stayer.
2203 **DANGER BABY 10** [2] P Bowen 10-9-3 (49)(bl) Claire Bryan (5) 9/2: 0-6252: 10 ch g Bairn -   8   49
Swordlestown Miss (Apalachee) Soon led, hdd halfway, plodded on for 2nd: softer grnds suits: see 1800.
1852 **ZIGGY STARDUST 25** [1] Mrs A J Bowlby 5-8-1 (33) Craig Williams 11/2: 44-343: 5 b g Roi Danzig -   shd   33
Si Princess (Coquelin) Prom, chsd wnr appr fnl 3f till 2f out: big step up in trip: needs mdn h'caps.
2173 **SHARAF 12** [4] W R Muir 7-9-4 (50) Martin Dwyer 8/1: P42304: In tch, eff appr fnl 3f, kept on onepce.   shd   49
1167 **LITTLE BRAVE 61** [10] 5-9-10 (56) J Tate 9/1: 4-4605: Mid div, prog 6f out, wknd 3f out: top-weight, abs.   2   53
2092 **WILD COLONIAL BOY 15** [7] 5-8-4 (35)(1ow) M Roberts 16/1: 440006: Early ldr, wide into straight   9   26
& wknd: unproven beyond 13f but reportedly suffered a breathing problem: see 548.
2123 **BLUE CAVALIER 14** [11] 3-7-12 (51)(2ow)(12oh) N Carlisle 12/1: 0-0047: Bhd from halfway: v stiff task.   2½   39
4382} **CIROS PEARL 264** [9] 6-8-4 (36) S Righton 25/1: 0000-8: Never a factor: reapp: lightly raced &   2½   22
little worthwhile form (incl over timber) since plcd in '98 (h'cap, rtd 72 M Tompkins): '97 wnr at Lingfield &
Goodwood (plcd at R Ascot, h'cap, rtd 80): eff at 10/12f on fast & gd grnd, forcing the pace, without visor.
2256 **VERSATILITY 8** [12] 7-9-2 (48) G Duffield 4/1: 105639: Led haflway till entering straight, lost place.   2½   32
2011 **COURT CHAMPAGNE 19** [5] 4-7-10 (28) G Baker(7) 12/1: 006000: Rear, carried wide ent str & btn: 10th.   shd   12
--   **Shadirwan** [6] 9-8-8 (40) J Reid 33/1:   2156 **Zola 12** [3] 4-7-10 (28)(8oh) R Brisland (5) 25/1:
12 ran   Time 3m 57.6 (5.8)   (T T Bloodstocks)   M Johnston Middleham, N Yorks

---

HAYDOCK

FRIDAY JULY 7TH   Lefthand, Flat, Galloping Track

Official Going   GOOD TO FIRM. Stalls: 6f & 14f - Centre; 10f & 12f - Outside; Rem - Inside.

2453   7.00 RADIO CITY APPR HCAP 3YO+ 0-75 (E)   1m2f120y   Good/Firm 28   -10 Slow   [69]
       £3136   £896   £448   3 yo rec 11lb

2279 **OCTANE 8** [6] W M Brisbourne 4-8-13 (54) G Baker (3) 11/8 FAV: 132021: 4 b g Cryptoclearance -   61
Something True (Sir Ivor): Waited with, smooth hdwy to lead appr final 1f, styd on well, cmftbly: hvly bckd:
earlier won at Musselburgh (h'cap, first win): with H Cecil in '99 (rtd 80, debut, prob flattered): eff at
10/12f on firm/fast grnd: handles a sharp or gall trk: in fine form, win more races.
1705 **KATIE KOMAITE 33** [1] Mrs G S Rees 7-7-10 (37)(2oh) Angela Hartley (4) 25/1: -40002: 7 b m Komaite   3½   37
- City To City (Windjammer): Rear, gd hdwy to press ldrs 2f out, ev ch till not pace of wnr final 1f: acts
on firm/fast, prefers gd/soft & soft grnd: gd run: see 890.
1066 **PAARL ROCK 67** [13] G Barnett 5-8-0 (41)(vis) Graham Gibbons (0) 50/1: 0-0003: 5 ch g Common   ¾   40
Grounds - Markievicz (Doyoun): Set fast pace, hdd appr final 1f, onepcd inside last: abs: stays 10f on fast.
1299 **SEA EMPEROR 53** [3] Mrs G S Rees 3-7-11 (49) Claire Roche (5) 25/1: 0-0304: Cl-up, rdn/no extra   1¼   46
appr final 1f: 4L clr rem: see 1085.
2309 **A DAY ON THE DUB 7** [4] P Hanagan (3) 7-8-9 (50) P Hanagan (3) 14/1: 014005: Dwelt, rear, late gains: qck reapp.   4   41
2366 **SMARTER CHARTER 4** [12] 7-9-3 (58) Kristin Stubbs (5) 13/2: 223256: Dwelt, late prog: qck reapp.   1¼   47
2397 **KNAVES ASH 3** [5] 9-8-2 (43) K Dalgleish (5) 10/1: 000367: Slow to start, late gains from rear.   shd   32
2130 **GABLESEA 14** [14] 6-8-8 (49) J Bosley (3) 8/1: 505008: Mid-div at best: btr 890 (hvy).   4   32
2027 **KUSTOM KIT KEVIN 19** [2] 4-8-1 (42)(t) R Thomas (5) 10/1: 000039: Al in rear: btr 2027 (1m).   shd   25
1633 **MANSTAR 36** [7] 3-8-2 (54)(VIS) Iona Wands 25/1: 005000: Cl-up, wknd from halfway, fin 10th: visor.   3   33
2404} **DEAD AIM 371** [8] 6-9-5 (60) J McAuley 50/1: 00-0-0: Dwelt, nvr a factor: well btn sole '99 Flat start,   4   33
subs 4th over hdles (nov, rtd 74h, 2m3f, fast, Mrs J Brown): '97 Windsor wnr h'cap, rtd 77, I Balding):
eff at 12/13f, has tried further: acts on firm, soft, sharp/undul trks: without visor: now with J J Quinn.
2188 **AVERHAM STAR 11** [10] 5-7-10 (37)(2oh) D Kinsella (5) 66/1: 50-000: Prom, wknd qckly fnl 3f, 12th.   shd   10
2108 **IT CAN BE DONE 15** [9] 3-9-0 (66) Stephanie Hollinshead (5) 10/1: 032160: Dwelt, al rear, fin 13th.   8   30
2051 **TIGER TALK 18** [11] 4-9-10 (65)(VIS) D Allan (7) 40/1: 0-0000: Cl-up, wknd qckly fnl 2f, fin last: visor.   14   18
14 ran   Time 2m 14.04 (4.04)   (Christopher Chell)   W M Brisbourne Great Ness, Shropshire.

2454   7.30 WEATHERBYS AUCT MDN 2YO (E)   6f   Good/Firm 28   -56 Slow
       £3038   £868   £434

2029 **OUR DESTINY 19** [9] A P Jarvis 2-8-8 N Callan 6/1: -01: 2 b c Mujadil - Superspring (Superlative):   83
Trkd ldrs, went on 3rd out, styd on well, rdn out: gamble from 14/1: 22,000 gns first foal, dam unrcd:
eff over a gall 6f, 7f shld suit: acts on fast grnd: going the right way.
1924 **TOTALLY COMMITTED 23** [11] R Hannon 2-8-6 J F Egan 6/4 FAV: 032: 2 b c Turtle Island - Persian   1   77
Light (Persian Heights) Prom, rdn to chall appr fnl 1f, kept on inside last, not pace of wnr: btr 890 at 7f.
--   **SARATOV** [15] M Johnston 2-8-8 K Dalgleish (3) 5/1: 3: 2 b c Rudimentary - Sarabah (Ela Mana Mou):   ¾   77+
Slow away, bhd, styd on ins last, nrst fin: 17,000gns half-brother to useful sprinter Cryhavoc & 1m/9f
wnr Ice: dam 10f wnr: fine run despite running green throughout: learn plenty from this & win at 7f soon.
1385 **BEREZINA 48** [14] T D Easterby 2-8-1 P Fessey 16/1: 564: Handy, rdn/kept on inside last, not pace   1¼   67
of ldrs: up in trip, prob stays 6f: see 938.
--   **SHIRAZI** [7] 2-8-6 K Darley 14/1: 5: Trkd ldrs, drvn/no extra inside last: 55,000 gns Mtoto   1¼   69
colt, dam wng miler: gd debut & will appreciate 7f+ in time for J W Hills.
1838 **EAGLES CACHE 27** [2] 2-8-6 C Cogan (5) 9/1: 436: Chsd ldrs, outpcd appr final 1f: shade btr 1838.   nk   68
--   **BABY MAYBE** [12] 2-8-3 Dale Gibson 25/1: 7: Dwelt, sn mid-div, onepcd final 2f: 19,000 gns Mar   1¼   62

foal, half-sister to sev wnrs in the USA: with T H Caldwell.

2388	**JEANNIES GIRL 3** [8] 2-7-13 C McCavish (7) 50/1: 0008: Nvr a threat: qck reapp.	1¾	54$
--	**YOUNG TERN** [1] 2-8-7(1ow) J Reid 25/1: 9: Sn rdn, nvr dngrs: 6,000 gns Mar foal: dam a mdn.	nk	61
2218	**SLIPPER ROSE 10** [13] 2-7-13 P M Quinn (3) 20/1: -43060: Nvr better than mid-div, fin 10th: see 2218.	1¾	49
--	**TONY** [4] 2-8-6 T Lucas 33/1: 0: Al outpcd: Marju first foal, with M Easterby.	½	54
2106	**MEA CULPA 15** [5] 2-8-1 P Hanagan (7) 16/1: 50: Led, hdd 3f out, wknd qckly, fin 12th.	1¾	45
1924	**CAREFULLY 23** [3] 2-8-6 A Culhane 20/1: 00: Handy, lost tch halfway, fin 13th.	1¼	47
--	**POUR NOUS** [10] 2-8-4 D O'Donohoe 33/1: 0: Dwelt, al bhd, fin last: Petong gelding.	2	40

14 ran   Time 1m 16.31 (5.01)   (Quadrillian Partnership)   A P Jarvis Aston Upthorpe, Oxon.

2455   8.00 CHEAP AND CHIC HCAP 4YO+ 0-85 (D)   1m6f   Good/Firm 28   +07 Fast   [82]
£3828   £1178   £589   £294

1791	**FOUNDRY LANE 29** [2] Mrs M Reveley 9-9-6 (74) A Culhane 7/2: 40-421: 9 b g Mtoto - Eider (Niniski): **77**

Trkd ldr, led appr fnl 1f, kept on well, drvn out: gd time: 98/99 jumps wnr at Aintree (h'cap hdle, rtd 142h),
Catterick & Huntingdon (h'cap chases, rtd 128c, 2½m, gd & hvy): plcd on the Flat in '99 (rtd 78), prev term
won at York (h'cap, rtd 74): eff at 12f/2m on firm, soft & a gall trk: runs well fresh: v game & tough.

2002	**SANDBAGGEDAGAIN 20** [1] M W Easterby 6-9-1 (69) J Reid 4/1: 0-0552: 6 b g Prince Daniel - Paircullis ½ **70**

(Tower Walk): Waited with, eff when no room 2f out, trav well & led briefly appr fnl 1f, held when hung left
well ins last: gd run: jockey rec a 3-day careless riding ban: outbattled today: see 2002.

2256	**BID ME WELCOME 9** [4] Miss D A McHale 4-9-6 (74) J Quinn 5/2: -00523: 4 b g Alzao - Blushing Barada	2	**72**

(Blushing Groom): Cl-up, went on 3f out, hdd appr final 1f, held when hmpd inside last: sound run.

2092	**SON OF SNURGE 16** [3] P F I Cole 4-9-10 (78)(bl) K Darley 11/8 FAV: 3-0404: Led, hdd 3f out,	3½	**71**

rallied briefly 2f out, no extra when hmpd final 1f: bckd, top weight: blnks refitted, better without in 1329.

4 ran   Time 3m 0.96 (2.96)   (A Sharratt)   Mrs M Reveley Lingdale, Nth Yorks.

2456   8.30 NEWSTEAD RATED HCAP 3YO+ 0-95 (C)   7f130y   Good/Firm 28   +10 Fast   [102]
£6246   £2369   £1184   £538   3 yo rec 8 lb

*1820	**WAHJ 28** [2] C A Dwyer 5-9-0 (88) J F Egan 5/1: 40-011: 5 ch g Indian Ridge - Sabaah (Nureyev):		**96**

Made all, rdn out, unchall: earlier won here at Haydock (C/D class stks): plcd in '99 (Listed, rtd 100, Sir
M Stoute): '98 wnr at Windsor (mdn) & Chepstow (stks, rtd 109): eff at 7f/1m on fast & soft grnd, any trk,
likes Haydock: goes well fresh & likes to force the pace: useful, shld land another nice prize.

*2338	**KAYO 6** [5] M Johnston 5-9-9 (97)(3ex) K Darley 7/2 FAV: 002312: 5 b g Superpower - Shiny Kay	1¾	**100**

(Star Appeal): Dwelt, mid-div, styd on under press appr final 1f, not trouble wnr: qck reapp: bckd, v tough.

r2090	**FREE OPTION 16** [9] B Hanbury 5-9-6 (94) J Reid 5/1: 10-303: 5 ch g Indian Ridge - Saneena (Kris)	shd	**97**

Waited with, kept on final 1f, nvr nrr: ran well but a return to 1m will suit: see 1327.

1983	**FIRST MAITE 21** [1] S R Bowring 7-9-7 (95)(vis) Dean McKeown 8/1: 650034: Bhd ldrs, rdn appr	shd	**97**

final 1f, unable to qckn: best over a stiff 5/6f or sharp 7f: see 35.

2117	**COTE SOLEIL 16** [4] 3-8-2 Dale Gibson 16/1: 330005: Rear, gd prog 2f out, no extra final 100y.	nk	85
2128	**BOOMERANG BLADE 14** [8] 4-8-7 (81) D Holland 12/1: 662266: Chsd wnr, rdn 2f out, onepace: see 935.	½	81
2117	**CAIR PARAVEL 15** [3] 3-8-2 (84)(BL) J Quinn 11/1: -53007: Trkd ldrs, feeling pace 2f out, no	¾	83

threat after: tried blnks: won both juv starts: see 1153 (solid form), 994.

2090	**RIVER TIMES 16** [7] 4-9-3 (91) A Culhane 4/1: -20408: Nvr got in it: unsuited by drop in trip, see 663.	2½	85
1836	**CLEVER GIRL 27** [6] 3-8-4 (86) P Fessey 16/1: 401D09: Al towards rear: stablemate 8th, see 1645, 823.	¾	79
1836	**THE EXHIBITION FOX 27** [10] 4-8-7 (86)(5oh) K Dalgleish (5) 16/1: 00-030: Handy till 2f out: 10th.	10	59

10 ran   Time 1m 28.41 (1.31)   (S B Components (International) Ltd)   C A Dwyer Newmarket.

2457   9.00 MTB CLASSIFIED CLAIMER 3YO+ 0-70 (E)   1m4f   Good/Firm 28   -25 Slow
£2856   £816   £408   3 yo rec 13lb

2245	**MAJOR ATTRACTION 9** [1] W M Brisbourne 5-9-0 G Baker (7) 14/1: 010001: 5 gr g Major Jacko - My		48

Friend Melody (Sizzling Melody): Dwelt, rear, stdy wide prog 3f out to lead 2f out, drvn out: clmd for £3,000:
earlier won at Hamilton (sell h'cap): plcd in '99 for P Eccles (AW sell, rtd 50a, prob flattered): eff at
11f/12f, tried 2m: acts on fast grnd, without blnks/visor: at home in sellers & claimers.

1816	**DESERT FIGHTER 28** [3] Mrs M Reveley 9-9-10 A Culhane 4/1: -00102: 9 b g Green Desert - Jungle	nk	57

Rose (Shirley Heights): Held up, prog 3f out, prsd wnr appr final 1f, held nr fin: back to form, won this in '99.

1888	**DUELLO 24** [4] M C Pipe 9-9-2 (vis) K Darley 3/1 FAV: 21-333: 9 b g Sure Blade - Royal Loft	1½	47

(Homing): Bhd, imprvg & not much room bef dist, kept on for press: bckd: hdles rnr since 1888, see 1465.

2219	**I CANT REMEMBER 10** [9] S R Bowring 6-9-4 (t) J F Egan 5/1: 506034: Prom, rdn 2f out, same pace.	1½	47
1880	**MUTADARRA 25** [8] 7-9-4 D O'Donohoe 9/2: 000025: Held up, bmpd 2f out, no impress on ldrs.	1½	45
3323}	**KEEN DANCER 329** [6] 6-9-6 (tbl) J P Spencer 14/1: 0/60-6: Towards rear when badly hmpd 2f out,	hd	46

late rally: reapp, stablemate 3rd: lightly rcd last term (rtd 52): rtd 59 in '98 (h'cap): eff at 10f, poss
stays 12f, tried 2m: acts on gd/soft grnd, prob firm: mdn, tried visor, wearing t-strap & blnks today.

1860	**KEWARRA 26** [5] 6-9-10 L Vickers (7) 16/1: 050-07: Prom, hung 2f out, onepace: better at 10f.	shd	50
1919	**PORTIA LADY 23** [7] 3-8-4 (bl) P Fessey 8/1: 0-0058: Led till 2f out, wknd: see 1024.	2	40
2119	**SYRAH 15** [2] 4-8-13 N Callan 33/1: 00-609: Well plcd till wknd appr final 2f: see 1880.	5	29$
2703	**GRAY PASTEL 358** [10] 6-9-6 (vis) W Supple 14/1: 10/6-0: Cl-up, chall appr final 2f, sn btn:	17	17

10th, stablemate 2nd, hdles fit: ran once on the level last term, '98 wnr at Leicester (clmr, rtd 53):
former hdles wnr: eff arnd 12f on fast grnd: can go well fresh.

10 ran   Time 2m 34.21 (6.41)   (Positive Partners)   W M Brisbourne Great Ness, Shropshire.

2458   9.30 PENNY LANE COND STKS 3YO+ (C)   6f   Good/Firm 28   -09 Slow
£6177   £2343   £1171   £532   3 yo rec 6 lb

1987	**YORKIES BOY 20** [4] A Berry 5-8-10 D Holland 7/1: 522041: 5 ro h Clantime - Slipperose (Persepolis)		105

Made just about all, drew clr towards fin: plcd twice in '99 for B McMahon (incl Gr 3, rtd 110): '98 Newmarket
wnr (2, List & Gr 3, rtd 114): eff at 5/6f on fast gd/soft grnd, suited forcing the pace: v useful & back to form.

2115	**NOW LOOK HERE 15** [1] B A McMahon 4-8-10 K Darley 100/30 FAV: 334502: 4 b g Reprimand - Where's	2	99

Carol (Anfield) Trkd ldr, rdn to chase wnr below dist, no impress: ran to best but keeps something for himself.

2310	**TADEO 7** [2] M Johnston 7-8-10 K Dalgleish (5) 4/1: 064-03: 7 ch g Primo Dominie - Royal Passion	1	97

(Ahonoora) Prsd wnr, no extra dist: qck reapp: better run: see 2310.

776

HAYDOCK FRIDAY JULY 7TH Lefthand, Flat, Galloping Track

2115 **BOLSHOI GB 15** [9] A Berry 8-8-10 J F Egan 9/2: /00004: Prom, effort appr final 1f, unable to qckn: nk   96
all 9 wins at 5f: see 2115.

3875} **DIFFERENTIAL 300** [10] 3-8-4 J Quinn 12/1: 1340-5: Not settle rear, late prog but nvr dngrs: no easy   1¾   92
task against elders: won juv debut at Windsor (mdn, rtd 99): eff at 5f on firm, shld get 6f: fitter for this.

2389 **KUMAIT 3** [8] 6-9-1 J P Spencer 7/1: 21-406: Al bhd: back in trip: see 1946.   2   92

4286} **ALFAILAK 272** [3] 3-8-4 A Culhane 7/1: 3200-7: Chsd ldrs till 2f out: reapp: '99 debut wnr at   2½   80
Newmarket (mdn, Gr 3 3rd, rtd 100): eff at 5/6f on firm/fast grnd, any trk: useful at best, with M Channon.

4440} **HEATHYARDSBLESSING 261** [5] 3-8-4 Dean McKeown 8/1: 6521-8: In tch till appr final 1f: '99 wnr at   ½   78
Haydock (mdn auct), Chester (nurs) & Nottingham (nov stks, rtd 105): eff at 5/6f on firm/fast grnd, any trk: tough.

8 ran   Time 1m 13.49 (2.19)   (Mrs M Beddie)   A Berry Cockerham, Lancs.

WARWICK FRIDAY JULY 7TH Lefthand, Sharp, Turning Track

Official Going   GOOD. Stalls: Inside.

2459   1.50 TATTS AUCTION MDN 2YO (E)   6f168y   Good   Inapplicable
£3568   £1098   £549   £274

1844 **LUNAR LEO 27** [7] S C Williams 2-8-3 J Tate 9/4: -41: 2 b g Muhtarram - Moon Mistress (Storm   87
Cat) Broke well & made virtually all, clr over 2f out, unchal: hvly bckd from 5/1: 6,000gns first foal: dam a
miler: eff over an easy 6.8f, will stay 1m: acts on gd & fast grnd: fast improving, given a gd positive ride.

2290 **APRIL LEE 7** [2] K McAuliffe 2-8-0 (e)(2ow) R Ffrench 33/1: -60552: 2 b f Superpower - Petitesse   4   74
(Petong) Chsd wnr thro'out, no impress fnl 1f: an improving rival: eff at 6.8f on gd grnd: see 2290, 865 (AW).

1876 **TRUMPINGTON 25** [6] I A Balding 2-7-12 Martin Dwyer 14/1: -03: 2 ch f First Trump - Brockton   3   65
Flame (Emarati) Swerved at start, recovered to chase ldrs, onepcd fnl 2f: prob needs sellers: op 10/1, see 1876.

1876 **PASO DOBLE 25** [8] B R Millman 2-8-7 G Hind 6/1: -034: Rcd keenly & prom, came stands rail home   2½   69
str, no impress: poor high draw, op 7/2: much better expected after 1876 (6f, fast grnd).

1876 **DAWN ROMANCE 25** [4] 2-7-12 A Nicholls(1) 14/1: -005: Rcd keenly in rear, mod late prog, nvr dngrs.   1   58

2014 **GALAXY RETURNS 19** [5] 2-8-5 J Carroll 6/1: -026: Hmpd start, recovered to race in tch 3f, sn   nk   64
outpcd: clr of rem: btr 2014 (firm grnd).

2020 **ROYAL ASSAY 19** [10] 2-8-0 L Newman(2) 7/4 FAV: -37: Rcd keenly in rear, nvr nr ldrs: btr 2020.   5   49

-- **BANITA** [12] 2-7-12 J Quinn 33/1: -0: Chsd ldrs till halfway, sn bhd on debut: cheaply bought   nk   46
Mar first foal: dam a 1m juv wnr: sire a 9/10f wnr: bred to apprec 7f/1m+ given time: poor high draw.

1864 **STRATH FILLAN 25** [11] 2-7-12 J Lowe 25/1: -09: Rcd keenly & prom 4f, fdd: reportedly lost action.   1½   43

1883 **JARV 24** [3] 2-7-12 R Brisland (5) 20/1: -000: In tch till halfway, sn btn & fin 10th: see 1883.   1   41

-- **HETRA REEF** [1] 2-8-5 L Newton 33/1: -0: Dwelt, never a factor on deout, fin 11th: 6,500gns   hd   48
April foal: dam a 7/10f wnr: sire a top class juv: with W Musson.

2214 **SUPREME TRAVEL 10** [9] 2-8-3 C Rutter 16/1: -00: Slowly away & al rear, fin last: see 2214.   1   44

12 ran   Time 1m 23.2   (Bruce W Wyatt)   S C Williams Newmarket

2460   2.25 SOLIHULL SELL HCAP 3YO+ 0-60 (G)   7f164y rnd   Good   Inapplicable   [58]
£2144   £612   £306   3yo rec 9lb

2187 **TIMELESS CHICK 11** [3] Andrew Reid 3-8-8 (47)(vis) S Whitworth 8/1: 043051: 3 ch f Timeless   57
Times - Be My Bird (Be My Chief) Nvr far away, went on dist, drvn clr fnl 1f for a decisive victory: sold to P
Evans for 6,500gns: first success: eff at 7f, prob stys 10f: acts on gd, hndls fast grnd: wears blinks/visor.

2040 **RED CAFE 18** [8] P D Evans 4-8-10 (40)(bl) J P Spencer 7/1: 600042: 4 ch f Perugino - Test Case   5   40
(Busted) Rcd keenly in tch, prog 2f out, fin well but too late: met a much imprvd rival: see 2040 (1m).

2033 **ERTLON 18** [2] C E Brittain 10-8-12 (42) W Supple 10/1: 000603: 10 b g Shareef Dancer - Sharpina   hd   42
(Sharpen Up) In tch, ev ch over 1f out, soon onepace: 10yo, not disgraced: likes Brighton/Lingfield: see 1775.

2291 **MR CUBE 7** [16] J M Bradley 4-8-10 (40)(bl) D Watson (7) 7/1: 435524: Rear, styd on fnl 2f,   nk   39
nrst fin: bckd from 10/1: fair eff form a poor high draw: see 2291 (6f).

2099 **DANZAS 16** [6] 6-9-3 (47)(bl) Claire Bryan (5) 9/2 FAV: 032625: Prom, every ch dist, one pace.   ¾   44

2257 **PHILISTAR 9** [10] 7-8-13 (43)(bl) L Newton 7/1: 005036: Mid div, some late hdwy, not pace to chall.   ½   39

2245 **THE IMPOSTER 9** [7] 5-8-13 (43) M Tebbutt 12/1: 000507: Prom, led briefly 2f out, fdd dist: see 2245.   2   35

2180 **SAVOIR FAIRE 12** [5] 4-8-8 (38) Dean McKeown 33/1: 0/0-08: Chsd ldrs 5f, soon outpcd: little form.   1   28

2295 **ARAGANT 7** [15] 4-8-10 (40) J Quinn 25/1: -00009: Rear, some late prog, nvr dngrs: poor draw.   shd   32

1998 **BALLYKISSANN 20** [14] 5-8-6 (36) C Rutter 25/1: 30/000: Never a factor in 10th: mod, see 1666.   2½   21

*2040 **MUSTANG 18** [12] 7-9-1 (45)(vis) T G McLaughlin 15/2: 030610: In tch till halfway, soon bhd &   0
fin 13th: poor high draw: better expected after 2040 (seller).

2099 Victoire 16 [13] 4-9-10 (54)(VIS) J Stack 33/1:   1546 Kelling Hall 39 [11] 3-8-6 (45) V Halliday 40/1:

2303 Flashfeet 7 [18] 10-8-6 (36) Joanna Badger (7) 20/1:   2187 Dakisi Royale 11 [17] 3-8-8 (47) S Sanders 20/1:

2193 Sound The Trumpet 11 [9] 8-8-8 (38)(t) W Ryan 20/1:   1414 Kalahari Ferrari 48 [1] 4-9-1 (45) M Hills 14/1:

896 Titan 85 [4] 5-8-11 (41) R Brisland (5) 16/1:   1998 Clifton Wood 20 [20] 5-8-13 (43) G Sparkes (7) 20/1:

19 ran   Time 1m 37.1   (A S Reid)   Andrew Reid Mill Hill, London NW7

2461   3.0 SUOMI HCAP 3YO+ 0-70 (E)   1m6f135y   Good   Inapplicable   [70]
£3172   £976   £488   £244   3yo rec 17lb

*2256 **RENAISSANCE LADY 9** [6] T R Watson 4-8-12 (54)(5ex) Dean McKeown 7/4 FAV: -00111: 4 ch f Imp   56
Society - Easter Morning (Nice Havrais) Chsd ldrs, imprvd to lead 2f out, kept on strongly, drvn out: well bckd:
completed hat-trick after 2 wins here at Warwick (h'caps): '99 Brighton wnr (mdn auct, rtd 55): eff at 12f, suited
by 14f/2m: loves gd & fast grnd & this sharp/undul Warwick trk: in fine form & winning run may not be at an end.

1867 **YES KEEMO SABEE 25** [9] D Shaw 5-8-8 (50) L Newton 20/1: 000002: 5 b g Arazi - Nazeera   1   50
(Lashkari) Mid div, gd prog to chall fnl 1f, kept on but not pace of wnr: op 12/1: well h'capped gelding, met
an in form rival here: eff at 14f, a return to 2m+ will suit: acts on gd, soft grnd & fibresand: see 627 (AW).

*2255 **GOLD MILLENIUM 9** [2] C A Horgan 6-8-4 (45)(1ow)(5ex) J Carroll 13/2: 0-0413: 6 gr g Kenmare -   1   45
Gold Necklace (Golden Fleece) Chsd ldrs, rdn & onepcd fnl 1f: fine run under a 5lb pen, styas 14.6f well.

2008 **ORDAINED 20** [4] Miss Gay Kelleway 7-7-12 (40) Martin Dwyer 20/1: 423004: Rear, improved to chase   hd   39
ldrs fnl 1.5f, no extra: see 1332 (12f).

2176 **JAMAICAN FLIGHT 12** [7] 7-9-11 (67) J Quinn 12/1: 400655: Chsd ldr, one pace fnl 2f: top weight.   3½   62

2319 **MURCHAN TYNE 6** [12] 7-8-7 (49) W Supple 12/1: 504306: Rear, imprvng when hmpd entr str, no ch 4 38
after: quick reapp: no luck in running, foget this: slipped down the weights: see 1736.
1730 **FIERY WATERS 32** [5] 4-8-13 (55) S Whitworth 14/1: 000-07: Rdn in mid div, no impression fnl 2f: 1 42
op 10/1: unproven beyond 10f: see 1730.
2016 **TOTEM DANCER 19** [14] 7-9-4 (60) M Hills 11/2: 102428: Al towards rear, bhd fnl 2f: much 2016. 10 32
1743 **SIRINNDI 31** [11] 6-8-10 (52) J P Spencer 9/2: 65/059: Set pace 12f, wknd quickly: better expected ½ 23
with change of tactics, op 3/1: see 1416 (AW).
1821 **ELEGIA PRIMA 28** [8] 3-8-1 (60) L Newman(3) 11/1: 0-0420: Chsd ldrs 1m, soon btn: fin 10th. 8 19
428 **ROBELLITA 158** [13] 6-9-4 (60) S Sanders 25/1: 26-000: Al rear, t.o. in last: abs: better on AW. dist 0
11 ran Time 3m 15.9 (Alan A Wright) T R Watson Pinnock, Glous

---

2462	**3.35 G EVE MDN 3YO+ (D)**		**6f rnd**	**Good Inapplicable**
	£3672 £1130 £565 £282		3yo rec 6lb	

2293 **EMANS JOY 7** [2] J R Fanshawe 3-8-8 M Hills 7/2: -351: 3 b f Lion Cavern - Carolside (Music 62
Maestro) Made all, held on well fnl 1f, rdn out: nicely bckd: half sister to sev wnrs, cost 10,000gns: apprec
this drop back to 6f, 7f shld suit in time: acts on gd grnd & on a sharp/undul trk: can set the pace.
2415 **KUWAIT ROSE 2** [3] K Mahdi 4-9-5 J Tate 7/1: -45402: 4 b c Inchinor - Black Ivor (Sir Ivor) nk 66
Nvr far away, chall strongly fnl 2f, not go past cl home: bckd from 11/1: acts on gd, soft grnd & fibresand.
2183 **MISS MARPLE 12** [1] J R Fanshawe 3-8-8 O Urbina 9/2: -03: 3 b f Puissance - Juliet Bravo (Glow) ¾ 58
Chsd ldrs, ev ch dist, kept on & only btn arnd 1L: tchd 7/1: stablemate of wnr: eff at 6f on gd & fast.
2188 **TEE CEE 11** [4] R Guest 3-8-8 S Sanders 3/1 FAV: -5334: Chsd ldrs till outpcd 1.5f out, rallied cl home. 2 52
1886 **FLY MORE 24** [6] 3-8-13 J Quinn 13/2: -455: Very badly kicked in stalls & then ran loose bef start, ¾ 54
al bhd & came into str, some late hdwy but nvr dngrs: op 4/1: not disgraced in the circumstances.
2058 **CONDOR HERO 17** [5] 3-8-13 H Ffrench 10/3: -36: Slowly away, recovered to ch ldrs & raced keenly, nk 53
btn over 1f out: raced too keenly for own good here: much btr 2058 (7f, fast grnd, debut).
-- **POLAR BEAUTY** [7] 3-8-8 W Supple 20/1: -W: Reared over in stalls, withdrawn from intended 0
debut: sister to a 1m juv wnr in Ireland: with B McMahon & an unfortunate experience.
7 ran Time 1m 15.8 (Arashan Ali) J R Fanshawe Newmarket Suffolk

---

2463	**4.05 PADDOCK MDN HCAP 3YO+ 0-65 (F)**		**1m2f110y**	**Good Inapplicable**	**[63]**
	£2751 £786 £393		3yo rec 12lb		

2210 **SHRIVAR 11** [8] M R Channon 3-9-4 (65) W Supple 10/1: 524641: 3 b g Sri Pekan - Kriva (Reference 73
Point) Mid div, gd prog to lead dist, rdn clr fnl 1f for a decisive success: derserved win: eff at 10f, stays
14f on fast & gd/soft, hndls a gall or sharp/undul trk: much improved & cld win again with confidence on a high.
2147 **MA VIE 14** [7] J R Fanshawe 3-9-1 (62) M Hills 14/1: 600-02: 3 b f Salse - One Life (L'Emigrant) 4 62
Chsd ldrs, qcknd into lead 2f out, collered dist, soon outpcd by wnr: stys an easy 10f well on gd grnd.
1917 **RUSSIAN SILVER 23** [20] C E Brittain 3-9-2 (63) N Esler (7) 12/1: 40-043: 3 ch f Red Bishop - Russian 1½ 61
Maid (Cadeaux Genereux) Dwelt, switched & gd hdwy 1½f out, ran on: gd run from a poor draw, stays 10f.
2186 **PAPERWEIGHT 12** [6] Miss K M George 4-9-13 (62) J Tate 16/1: 423034: Chsd ldrs, onepace fnl 2f. 2 57
1671 **PILLAGER 35** [17] 3-9-1 (62) P McCabe 12/1: 602645: In tch, outpcd entering straight, styd on hd 57
again cl home: not disgraced from a poor high draw: btr 1085 (1m,/soft).
2141 **BROUGHTONS MILL 14** [13] 5-8-7 (42) L Newton 7/1: 004236: Mid div, kept on fnl 2f: see 2141. 1 35
2254 **PURSUIVANT 9** [3] 6-8-12 (47)(bl) R Fitzpatrick (3) 16/1: 032047: Chsd ldrs 1m, fdd: see 2011. nk 39
2296 **AHOUOD 7** [2] 4-8-9 (44) S Whitworth 33/1: 560408: Chsd ldrs 1m, grad fdd: see 490, 446 (AW). 1¼ 34
1575 **BITTER SWEET 38** [9] 4-9-0 (49) W Ryan 8/1: 403549: Bhd, mod late gains, nvr dngrs: see 1575. ¾ 38
1730 **DR COOL 32** [10] 3-8-9 (56)(VIS) J Quinn 8/1: 3-0540: Never better than mid div, 10th: tried a visor. nk 44
1907 **KING TUT 23** [5] 4-9-0 (49) Dean McKeown 4/1 FAV: 00-220: Rcd keenly mid div, eff 2f out, soon ½ 36
btn: fin 11th: disappointing run over this longer 10f trip, rcd too freely & not stay? much btr 1907, 1603.
3788↓ **SUMITRA 305** [18] 4-9-2 (51) A McGlone 20/1: 2530-0: Never a factor in 10th on reapp: plcd on ¾ 37
a couple of '99 starts (mdn auct, rtd 57): eff at 10f, poss stys 2m: acts on gd/soft & soft grnd.
1708 **BLUE STREET 33** [14] 4-9-11 (60) N Pollard 8/1: -0060: Chsd ldrs 1m, wknd qckly: fin 14th on h'cap 0
bow: much better expected: big step up in trip: see 1708, 1525.
1803 **STARBOARD TACK 28** [15] 4-10-0 (63) G Carter 6/1: 4-0030: V slowly away, no ch after & fin 17th. 0
1539 Save The Planet 41 [1] 3-8-11 (58) T G McLaughlin 33/1:2372 High Drama 4 [4] 3-9-4 (65) Martin Dwyer 16/1:
2033 City Guild 18 [16] 4-8-9 (44) R Havlin 33/1: 2024 Town Gossip 19 [19] 3-9-4 (65) S Sanders 14/1:
3560) Bosscat 317 [11] 3-9-4 (65) O Urbina 33/1:
19 ran Time 2m 15.6 (P D Savill) M R Channon West Isley, Berks

---

2464	**4.40 BREEDERS MDN DIV 1 3YO+ (D)**		**7f164y rnd**	**Good Inapplicable**
	£3006 £925 £462 £231		3yo rec 9lb	

1377 **MORNINGS MINION 49** [1] R Charlton 3-8-12 R Perham 6/4 FAV: -441: 3 b g Polar Falcon - Fair 84
Dominion (Dominion) Rcd keenly & chsd ldrs, forged ahead inside fnl 1f, just prevailed in a driving finish:
7 wk abs, well bckd: half brother to 1m wnr Dom Shadeed: dam a 1m/10f wnr: eff arnd 1m on gd grnd, will
stay further: hndls a sharp/undul trk, runs well fresh: can rate more highly.
1771 **SINCERITY 30** [6] J R Fanshawe 3-8-7 M Hills 13/2: -02: 3 b f Selkirk - Integrity (Reform) shd 78
Waited on, gd hdwy to lead dist, collered inside last, rallied well & just btn in a driving finish: tchd 10/1:
eff at 7.7f on gd grnd, will stay 1m+: has shown enough to find similar: see 1771.
2117 **EJTITHAAB 15** [9] R W Armstrong 3-8-12 W Supple 5/1: -44003: 3 ch c Arazi - Cunning (Bustino) 3 77
Chsd ldr, led halfway till hdd dist, kept on but not pace of front 2: well clr of rem: eff arnd 1m, prob stays 12f.
1072 **GINGKO 67** [4] J G Smyth Osbourne 3-8-12 W Ryan 9/1: -44: Rcd keenly in bhd ldrs, left bhd fnl 10 57
1½f: 10 wk abs: will find easier races: see 1072.
1771 **SATZUMA 30** [7] 3-8-12 (t) S Sanders 50/1: 0-05: Raced keenly in rear, some late hdwy, nvr dngrs ½ 56
on h'cap qualifying run: unplcd in a Doncaster mdn on a juv start: bred to apprec 1m+ given time.
1977 **REEMATNA 21** [12] 3-8-7 M Tebbutt 8/1: 0-4246: Prom 5f, fdd: op 6/1, btr 1675. 1½ 48
2265 **WESTERN BAY 8** [3] 4-9-7 S Whitworth 50/1: 0-607: Dwelt, outpcd till late hdwy: see 2056 (10f). ½ 52
1725 **AL AWAALAH 32** [5] 3-8-7 C Rutter 66/1: 008: Rear, eff to improve 2f out, never near ldrs: see 1436. 1¼ 44
3964) **BRIGHT QUESTION 294** [3] 3-8-12 G Carter 11/2: -50-9: Early ldr, remained in tch till btn dist: 2½ 44
reapp: promise in 2 juv events (rtd 78 at best): half brother to wnrs over 1m/10f: dam smart juv.
1977 **SATIRE 21** [8] 3-8-7 L Newton 66/1: 0-50: Chsd ldrs till outpcd halfway, no ch after: 10th. 1 37
2293 **YAZAIN 7** [2] 4-9-7 J Tate 11/1: -30: Dwelt, recovered to chase ldrs racing keenly, btn 3f out: fin 0

778

12th: raced too freely for own gd here: much btr 2293.
3785} **Macs Dream 305** [10] 5-9-7 (t) S Righton 50/1:   -- **Woodlands Lad Too** [11] 8-9-7 J Lowe 66/1:
13 ran   Time 1m 36.5   (Exors of the late D A Shirley)   R Charlton Beckhampton, Wilts

---

2465   5.10 BREEDERS MDN DIV 2 3YO+ (D)   7f164y rnd Good Inapplicable
       £2990   £920   £460   £230   3yo rec 9lb

2104 **WOODLAND RIVER 16** [4] J R Fanshawe 3-8-12 M Hills 6/4 FAV: -0021: 3 ch c Irish River -   **90**
Weiner Wald (Woodman) Slowly away, recovered & sn prom, rdn into lead dist, cmftbly: well bckd: eff arnd 1m
on gd & fast grnd, further shld suit: hndls a sharp/undul trk: improving & could win again, useful.
1404 **SHAAN MADARY 48** [3] B W Hills 3-8-7 G Carter 25/1: 0-02: 3 br f Darshaan - Madary (Green   3½ 77
Desert) Tried to make all, collered dist, not pace of cmftble wnr: 7 wk abs: little prev form: dam a 7f/1m wnr:
eff at 7.7f on gd grnd, 1m+ shld suit: runs well fresh: has shown enough to win a minor event.
1951 **SEA DRIFT 22** [5] L M Cumani 3-8-7 J P Spencer 7/2: 0-53: 3 gr f Warning - Night At Sea (Night   1¼ 74
Shift) Nvr far away rdn & onepcd fnl 2f: now qualified for h'caps & could improve in that sphere: handles gd.
--   **BEDEY** [2] A C Stewart 3-8-12 W Ryan 7/1: -4: Dwelt, bhd till styd on steadly fnl 2f, nvr plcd to chall   ½ 78+
on debut: half brother to a 1m h'cap wnr: bred to apprec 1m/10f given time: eye catching debut.
1922 **AMJAD 23** [10] 3-8-12 C Rutter 9/1: -5045: Chsd ldrs 5f, fdd: see 1922.   5 68
2293 **SILVER TONIC 7** [8] 4-9-7 J Tate 20/1: -06: Chsd ldrs, going nowhere when short of room 2f out.   3 62
--   **DENARIUS SECUNDUS** [12] 3-8-12 R Perham 12/1: -7: Dwelt, mid div on outside, btn 2f out: debut,   ½ 61
poor high draw: dam a smart 1m/10f wnr: sire a top class miler: with M Tregoning & shld be capable of better.
3830} **FORMAL BID 303** [9] 3-8-12 S Sanders 7/2: -35-8: Prom 5f, fdd on reapp: tchd 11/2: trained by P   1 59
Chapple Hyam & plcd at Newbury in '99 (mdn, debut, rtd 88): dam a 1m wnr in France, sire a high class 9/10f
performer in the USA: eff at 7f on fast grnd, 1m+ shld suit: now with P Makin & capable of much better.
--   **ATTO** [11] 6-9-8(1ow) F Keniry (5) 50/1: -9: Never near to chall on Flat debut: recent jumps rnr   5 50
& mod nov chase form: with J King.
1947 **FLAMEBIRD 22** [1] 3-8-7 M Tebbutt 50/1: -00: Never better than mid div, fin 10th: see 1947.   1¾ 40
1951 **SAHAYB 22** [6] 3-8-7 W Supple 20/1: 02-00: Al bhd, fin 11th: see 1951.   13 15
4155} **RATHER DIZZY 282** [7] 5-9-7 (VIS) R Fitzpatrick (3) 66/1: 00-0: Slowly away, al outpcd, fin last: vis.   7 6
12 ran   Time 1m 36.1   (Car Colston Hall Stud)   J R Fanshawe Newmarket

---

2466   5.40 BOLLINGER AMAT HCAP 4YO+ 0-75 (E)   1m4f56y Good Inapplicable   **[45]**
       £2847   £876   £438   £219

1888 **CLASSIC CONKERS 24** [3] Pat Mitchell 6-9-10 (41)(11oh) Mr S Rees (7) 33/1: 460-01: 6 b g Conquering   42
Hero - Erck (Sun Prince) Dwelt, imprvd from rear 3f out, styd on strongly to lead cl home, rdn out: fine run
from 11lbs o/h: mod jumps form: '98 Yarmouth wnr (sell h'cap, rtd 58): eff at 11/14f on fast & soft grnd.
*2286 **MAY KING MAYHEM 7** [5] Mrs A L M King 7-10-9 (54)(bl)(5ex) Mr T Best (5) 7/4 FAV: 511112: 7 ch g   1¾ 52
Great Commotion - Queen Ranavalona (Sure Blade) Mid div, smooth hdwy to lead 2f out, collared ins last & not
pace to repel wnr: op 5/4: 5 timer foiled but far from disgraced: see 2286.
4228} **MONACLE 277** [8] John Berry 6-9-10 (41)(2oh) Mr M Murphy (5) 16/1: 003F-3: 6 b g Saddlers' Hall -   1 37
Endless Joy (Law Society) Mid div, drvn to improve 2f out, kept on under press on reapp: '99 wnr at Yarmouth
& Lingfield (sub disqual, amat h'cap, rtd 44): eff at 11f, stays 2m+: acts on firm & fibresand: tried blnks.
1874 **PROTOCOL 25** [9] Mrs S Lamyman 6-9-11 (42)(t) Mr S Dobson (5) 11/2: 235504: Chsd ldr till went on   ¾ 37
halfway: hdd over 2f out, one pace: bckd from 10/1: see 1087.
2347 **TWOFORTEN 6** [2] 5-9-10 (41)(1oh) Mr R Lucey Butler(7) 20/1: 000365: Rdn in rear, mod late hdway.   shd 36
1730 **IN THE STOCKS 32** [7] 6-10-5 (50) Mr L Jefford 5/1: 61-006: Chsd ldrs till outpcd fnl 2f: see 1100.   ½ 44
441 **FAHS 156** [6] 8-12-0 (73) Mr G Rothwell (5) 8/1: 31-257: Chsd ldrs, grad outpcd: long abs.   1¾ 65
1888 **IL DESTINO 24** [1] 5-11-4 (60) Mr C B Hills (3) 11/2: 62-658: Led till halfway, grad fdd: see 1666.   3 47
2033 **MICE IDEAS 18** [4] 4-10-0 (45) Mr Ray Barrett (5) 13/2: 236169: Raced keenly rear, stumbled   11 17
leaving back straight, lost tch fnl 3f: much btr 2917 (10f, firm grnd).
9 ran   Time 2m 43.1   (Steven Rees)   Pat Mitchell Newmarket

---

Official Going   GOOD (GOOD TO SOFT PLACES) Stalls: Standside.

2467   6.40 CHANTILLY APP HCAP 3YO+ 0-70 (F)   1m str   Good/Soft 73 -06 Slow   **[70]**
       £2793   £798   £399   3 yo rec 9 lb   Field split into 2 groups - far side held advantage.

*2264 **COLNE VALLEY AMY 8** [16] G L Moore 3-8-7 (58)(6ex) I Mongan (3) 8/1: 00-211: 3 b f Mizoram -   66
Panchellita (Pancho Villa) Made all far side, ran on well inside last, rdn out: earlier won here at Salisbury
(appr h'cap, first win): unplcd in '99 (rtd 58, mdn): eff at 7f/1m on firm/fast & gd/soft grnd: handles a
sharp or stiff/undul track, likes Salisbury: progressing fast this term, shld complete a hat-trick.
*2281 **HAND CHIME 8** [18] W J Haggas 3-9-3 (68)(6ex) J Mackay (3) 6/5 FAV: 00112: 3 ch g Clantime -   2 71
Warning Bell (Bustino) Trckd wnr, kept on but not pace of wnr fnl 2f: hvly bckd: continues in fine form.
2257 **DAPHNES DOLL 9** [17] Dr J R J Naylor 5-8-6 (48) A Nicholls 25/1: 000003: 5 b m Polish Patriot -   1¾ 48
Helitta (Tyrnavos) Mid div far side, rdn/prog 3f out, not pace of front 2 fnl 2 out: ddhtd for 3rd: gd run.
2033 **CAPTAIN MCCLOY 18** [10] N E Berry 5-8-1 (43)(bl) R Brisland (3) 16/1: 50-633: Led stands side,   dht 44
rdn & styd on fnl 2f, no ch with far side: clr on unfavoured stands side: gd run but only 1 win in 32 starts.
1690 **COUGHLANS GIFT 34** [6] 4-8-11 (53) P Dobbs (3) 20/1: 000U05: Rear, rdn & styd on late, no threat.   1½ 50
2032 **CABARET QUEST 19** [11] 4-8-3 (45) P Fitzsimons (3) 20/1: -00006: Prom stands side, edged right to   2½ 37
join far side group after halfway, no extra fnl 2f: see 1003.
457 **SPRINGTIME LADY 153** [3] 4-9-4 (60) R Smith (3) 16/1: 0-2237: Dwelt, mid div at best: 5 month abs.   nk 52
2212 **THOMAS HENRY 10** [12] 4-8-7 (49) N Farmer (10) 25/1: 500358: Prom, fdd fnl 2f: btr 1731 (clmr).   2½ 36
1799 **FIONN DE COOL 29** [5] 9-8-6 (48) D McGaffin (3) 16/1: 053-09: Rear, mod late hdwy: plcd fnl '99   ½ 34
start (h'cap, rtd 55 at best): '98 Chepstow wnr (h'cap, rtd 63): eff at 7f/1m on fast & gd/soft grnd: fairly h'capped.
2264 **SPIRIT OF TENBY 8** [8] 3-8-13 (64) M Howard (7) 8/1: 030330: Never a threat, 10th: btr 2264 (C/D, fast).   7 40
1633 **DIVINE PROSPECT 36** [8] 3-9-4 (69) Lisa Jones (10) 11/1: -65640: Prom early, wknd from halfway, 11th.   1¼ 44
2270 **BIRTH OF THE BLUES 8** [4] 4-9-1 (57)(vis) L Branch (10) 14/1: 000050: Al bhd, 12th: btr 2270 (10f, fast).   hd 31
2347 **MAGIC POWERS 6** [13] 5-9-0 (56)(VIS) S Carson 12/1: /0-000: Prom 4f, fin 15th: quick reapp, visored: 0

jockey rec a 5-day irresponsible riding ban.
1873 **Evergreen** 25 [14] 3-9-5 (70) L Newman (3) 14/1:   2367 **Susans Dowry** 4 [2] 4-9-6 (62) Darren Williams (3) 25/1:
-- **Henry Heald** [9] 5-10-0 (70) O Kozak (10) 25/1:   1998 **Lucayan Beach** 20 [15] 6-8-8 (50) Jonjo Fowle (3) 33/1:
17 ran   Time 1m 45.41 (6.31)   (Colne Valley Golf)   G L Moore Woodingdean, E Sussex

2468   7.10 CLARE BEAHAN NURSERY HCAP 2YO (E)   7f str   Good/Soft 73   -10 Slow   [91]
£2873   £884   £442   £221

*2161 **TORTUGUERO** 13 [1] B W Hills 2-9-4 (81) J Fortune 13/8 FAV: -0611: 2 b c Highest Honor - Rahaam   85
(Secreto) Cl up, rdn to lead 2f out, styd on well, drvn out: well bckd: recent Ayr wnr (mdn): 110,000gns Apr
foal, brother to Irish 2,000 Guineas wnr Verglas: eff over a stiff 7f on fast & gd/soft, 1m suit: improving.
2091 **ZELOSO** 16 [7] J L Dunlop 2-9-7 (84) Pat Eddery 3/1: -0302: 2 b g Alzao -Silk Petal (Petorius)   nk 87
Slow into stride, hdwy 2f out, switched & ran on strongly for press ins last, not btn far: eff at 6/7f on fast &
gd/soft, 1m suit: fine run under top weight & would prob have won with a level break, keep in mind for similar.
2383 **DENNIS EL MENACE** 4 [4] W R Muir 2-8-7 (70) P Doe 20/1: -04643: 2 b c College Chapel -   1 71
Spanish Craft (Jareer) Cl up, rdn to lead appr 2f out, hdd over 1f out, no extra well inside last: quick reapp:
eff at 7f on gd/soft: gd run on this h'cap bow: see 2383.
1974 **TRUSTED MOLE** 21 [3] J A Osborne 2-8-4 (67) A Beech (5) 20/1: -66304: Rear, late hdwy for press,   ¾ 67
nvr nrr: up in trip: stays 7f on gd/soft: clr rem & should win a race, poss at 1m: see 1648, 1189.
2057 **YOUNG JACK** 17 [2] 2-8-9 (72) D McGaffin (5) 9/1: 5235: Rear, hdwy halfway, wknd fnl 1f: see 2057.   5 64
*2201 **SAND BANKES** 11 [5] 2-9-0 (77)(vis)(6ex) P Fitzsimons (5) 5/1: 612116: Led, hdd over 2f out,   10 54
wknd quickly: disappointing run on this hat-trick bid: much btr 2201 (nov auction, fast, sharp track).
1993 **BLUE ORLEANS** 20 [8] 2-8-2 (65) A Nicholls (3) 16/1: 3007: Soon rdn in rear, no danger: see 1136.   1¾ 39
1883 **THERESA GREEN** 24 [10] 2-8-6 (69) L Newman (3) 15/2: 0038: Handy, fdd halfway: btr 1883 (6f, fast).   1 41
1704 **GOLDEN WHISPER** 33 [9] 2-8-3 (66) N Pollard 8/1: -4039: Cl up, wknd qckly fnl 2f: longer 7f trip.   nk 38
9 ran   Time 1m 31.34 (5.84)   (Trevor C Stewart)   B W Hills Lambourn, Berks

2469   7.40 ANDERSON & CO AUCT STKS 2YO (C)   6f str   Good/Soft 73   +07 Fast
£6583   £2497   £1248   £567

*1403 **PATSYS DOUBLE** 48 [1] M Blanshard 2-8-7 T Quinn 5/2: 11: 2 b c Emarati - Jungle Rose (Shirley   97+
Heights) Mid div, qcknd into lead dist, rdn out, going away: 7 wk abs, best time of day: earlier won at debut
at Newbury (mdn, comfortably): 10,000gns half brother to 4 wnrs: dam a 10f wnr: eff at 6f, 7f will suit: acts
on fast, gd/soft & a stiff track: runs well fresh: v useful, won in a fast time, one to follow.
2088 **AZIZ PRESENTING** 16 [6] M R Channon 2-8-6 Craig Williams 13/2: 20102: 2 b r f Charnwood Forest -   1½ 91
Khalatara (Kalaglow) Set fast pace, rdn/hdd dist, not pace of wnr: best run to date, eff at 5/6f: jockey rec
a 3-day irresponsible riding ban: see 2088, 2020.
*2182 **MUSIC MAID** 12 [2] H S Howe 2-7-13 A Nicholls (3) 11/1: 613: 2 b f Inzar - Richardstown Lass   2 78
(Muscatite) Rear, rdn/ran on appr fnl 1f, held well ins last: will apprec a return to 7f, acts on fast & gd/soft.
2088 **SECRET INDEX** 16 [3] Mrs P N Dutfield 2-8-7 L Newman (3) 1/1 FAV: 1154: Cl up, chall ldrs 2f out,   nk 86
fdd inside last: well bckd: longer 6f trip: well ahead of today's rnr-up in 2088 (5f, Gd, Gr 3).
*1095 **IMPERIAL MEASURE** 66 [7] 2-8-11 J Fortune 10/1: 15: Handy, hung right & wknd fnl 2f: 9 wk abs.   12 70
1088 **EVERMOORE** 66 [5] 2-7-13 J Mackay (5) 50/1: -046: In tch, fdd fnl 2f, fin last: longer 6f trip.   1¼ 55
6 ran   Time 1m 16.09 (3.99)   (Mrs P Buckley)   M Blanshard Upper Lambourn, Berks

2470   8.10 CONDOR FERRIES HCAP 3YO 0-85 (D)   1m4f   Good/Soft 73   -03 Slow   [92]
£4062   £1250   £625   £312

*1967 **ROMANTIC AFFAIR** 21 [6] J L Dunlop 3-9-4 (82) Pat Eddery 5/4 FAV: 3-0211: 3 ch g Persian Bold -   94+
Broken Romance (Ela Mana Mou) Raced keenly cl up, hdway on bit appr fnl 2f, led dist, rdn out, readily: hvly
bckd: recent Sandown wnr (h'cap): '99 scorer at Newcastle (auction mdn, rtd 74): eff at 7f, suited by 11/12f,
further cld suit: acts on a gd, soft & a stiff track: v progressive, win a val prize, keep on your side.
2272 **AFTER THE BLUE** 8 [5] M R Channon 3-7-12 (62) Craig Williams 5/1: 064122: 3 b c Last Tycoon -   2½ 67
Sudden Interest (Highest Honor) Waited with, hdwy when raced wide halfway, styd on to lead appr fnl 2f, hdd
dist, not pace of wnr: another sound eff: acts on fast & gd/soft grnd: see 2272, 2012.
*1637 **STAR CAST** 36 [3] Major D N Chappell 3-8-13 (77) T Quinn 3/1: 00-113: 3 ch f In The Wings - Thank   2½ 79
One's Stars (Alzao) Settled rear, hdwy, short of room when switched over 2f out, chall appr fnl 1f, no extra
inside last: remains in gd heart: wide mkt move: see 1637.
1571 **DISTANT PROSPECT** 38 [4] J R Arnold 3-8-7 (71) S Sanders 14/1: 0-2354: Rear, switched/prog   ¾ 72
over 1f out, hdd well inside last: clr rem: see 1425.
1345 **TE DEUM** 50 [2] 3-7-13 (63) C Rutter 50/1: 030-05: Cl up, rdn/fdd inside last: 9 week abs: 3 59
plcd on 2nd of three '99 starts (mdn, rtd 73): stays 1m on soft grnd.
1832 **COLONIAL RULE** 21 [1] 3-9-2 (80)(BL) J Fortune 12/1: 1-0006: Led to over 2f out, fdd fnl 1f: blnkd.   3 72
*2131 **YOU DA MAN** 14 [7] 3-8-11 (75) Dane O'Neill 10/1: 412517: Mid div, eff 2f out, sn btn: btr 2131 (fast).   4 62
1404 **TOORAK** 48 [10] 3-8-11 (75) R Hughes 14/1: 6-008: Cl up, every ch until wknd quickly fnl 2f: 8 52
7 week abs: up in trip on h'cap bow: see 1099.
1696 **CEDAR GROVE** 34 [9] 3-7-12 (62) G Bardwell 25/1: -0049: Keen in tch, wknd quickly fnl 3f, fin last.   nk 39
9 ran   Time 2m 41.59 (9.19)   (The Earl Cadogan)   J L Dunlop Arundel, W Sussex

2471   8.40 EBF CLASSIFIED STKS 3YO+ 0-95 (B)   1m2f   Good/Soft 73   -19 Slow
£9045   £3209   £1604   £729   3 yo rec 11lb

*1958 **FORBEARING** 21 [3] Sir Mark Prescott 3-9-2 S Sanders 13/8: -00111: 3 b c Bearing - For Example   108
(Northern Baby) Raced keenly & settled last, gd hdwy to lead 3f out, rdn well clr inside last, eased cl-home:
nicely bckd: hat-trick completed after wng at Epsom & Goodwood (val h'caps): '99 wnr at Lingfield (mdn) &
W'hampton (nov, rtd 95a): eff at 1m, suited by 10f & further shld suit: acts on both AW, fast & hvy, any
trk: fast improving & a v useful performance here, shld hold his own in Listed/Group 3 class.
1014 **TURAATH** 74 [2] B W Hills 4-9-3 J Fortune 8/1: /1-002: 4 b c Sadler's Wells - Diamond Field   5 88
(Mr Prospector) Led, hdd appr fnl 3f, sn not pace of easy wnr: op 6/1, abs: sound run against a smart rival.
1982 **LOCOMBE HILL** 21 [1] M Blanshard 4-9-3 D Sweeney 20/1: 10-303: 4 b c Barathea - Roberts Pride   3½ 83
(Roberto) Chsd ldrs, rdn/fdd fnl 2f: prob unsuited by drop in trip, btr 1474.
2228 **MANA MOU BAY** 9 [4] R Hannon 3-8-10 R Hughes 4/6 FAV: 21-024: Raced keenly cl up, rdn & wknd   5 81

SALISBURY   FRIDAY JULY 7TH   Righthand, Galloping Track, Stiff Finish

qckly fnl 2f, fin last: hvly bckd: better expected but prob not stay 10f: unfortunate over 7f in 2228.
4 ran   Time 2m 13.78 (9.28)   (Eclipse Thoroughbreds - Osborne House)   Sir Mark Prescott Newmarket

2472	9.10 SOIR DE FRANCE FILLIES MDN 3YO (D) 6f str Good/Soft 73 -49 Slow
	£3575 £1100 £550 £275

--	**STEPPIN OUT** [7] W Jarvis 3-8-11 P Doe 9/1: 1: 3 ch f First Trump - Mo Stopher (Sharpo)		73

Cl up, went on appr fnl 1f, hdd inside last, rallied for strong press to get up near fin: slow time: debut:
dam a mdn: eff at 6f on gd/soft, 7f could suit: fine debut run, can rate more highly.
1783 **ULYSSES DAUGHTER 29** [9] G A Butler 3-8-11 (t) T Quinn 4/7 FAV: 42: 3 ch f College Chapel - hd 72
Trysinger (Try My Best) Settled rear, smoooth hdwy to chall over 1f out, led ins last, styd on well
but hdd cl-home, hands & heels riding: hvly bckd: acts on fast & gd/soft: can go one better soon.
1972 **TOPLESS IN TUSCANY 21** [2] P W Hiatt 3-8-11 Darren Williams (5) 33/1: 03: 3 b f Lugana Beach - 2½ 66
Little Scarlett (Mazilier) Set steady pace, hdd over 1f out, held well inside last: eff at 6f on gd/soft.
-- **ASHLEEN** [4] V Soane 3-8-11 G Hind 20/1: 4: Dwelt, soon with ldrs, rdn/fdd inside last: 3 58
Chilibang filly, glimmer of ability here & sellers should suit.
2232 **APRIL STAR 9** [8] S Sanders 14/1: 05: Rear, plenty to do 2f out, styd on well, no threat. 1¼ 55
221 **ANGELAS PET 198** [1] 3-8-11 R Smith (5) 50/1: 0066-6: Raced keenly cl up, lost tch fnl 2f: hd 55$
6 month abs: mod prev form & treat rating with caution (offic only 46).
-- **LE FOLLIE** [3] 3-8-11 N Pollard 7/2: 7: Mid div, wknd fnl 2f: Chilean bred B Hills newcomer. 1 52
1886 **PRIM N PROPER 24** [6] 3-8-11 Dane O'Neill 12/1: 008: Race keenly in tch, fdd halfway, fin last. 3 45
8 ran   Time 1m 19.45 (7.35)   (Canisbay Bloodstock Ltd)   W Jarvis Newmarket

SANDOWN   FRIDAY JULY 7TH   Righthand, Galloping Track, Stiff Finish.

Official Going   GOOD (GOOD/SOFT in places on rnd crse). Stalls: 5f - Far Side; 14f - Outside, rem - Inside.

2473	2.05 CARNIVAL HCAP 3YO+ 0-95 (C) 5f Good/Firm 24 +02 Fast	[90]
	£10822 £3330 £1665 £832 3 yo rec 5 lb	

2310 **AMBITIOUS 7** [5] K T Ivory 5-9-7 (83) C Catlin (7) 9/1: 040141: 5 b m Ardkinglass - Ayodhya (Astronef): 89
Prom, hdwy to chall dist, kept on to get up cl-home, drvn out: fair time: earlier won at Thirsk (class stks) &
Southwell (h'cap, rtd 75a): '99 wnr at Southwell (fillies h'cap, with J Fanshawe), Sandown (2, h'cap & clmr),
Redcar (class stks) & York (h'cap, rtd 79): eff at 6f, 7 most recent wins at 5f: acts on firm & fibresand, likes
gd & soft & any trk, esp Sandown: runs well for an appr: v tough & progressive, at the top of her form.
2326 **FAUTE DE MIEUX 6** [11] M Kettle 5-8-12 (74) N Callan 7/1: 010332: 5 ch g Beveled - Supreme Rose hd 79
(Frimley Park) With ldr, led 2f out, kept on for press till collared cl-home, just btn: rnr-up in this last term.
2348 **LAGO DI VARANO 5** [9] R M Whitaker 8-9-5 (81)(bl) K Darley 7/1: 315053: 8 b g Clantime - On The ¾ 84
Record (Record Token) Handy, short of room & lost place over 3f out, kept on well 1f out, nrst fin: 5f specialist.
2261 **BRAVE EDGE 9** [10] R Hannon 9-9-8 (84) Dane O'Neill 12/1: 302304: In tch, lost place over 2f 1 84
out, kept on appr final 1f, nrst fin: slipped down weights but winless for 2 years: see 2261, 1676.
2326 **POETRY IN MOTION 6** [7] 5-8-2 (64) P Doe 33/1: 020-05: Handy, rdn & onepcd over 1f out: qck reapp.shd 64
1676 **MIDNIGHT ESCAPE 34** [8] 7-9-6 (82) R Mullen 10/1: -00456: Dwelt, bhd, late gains, no threat. nk 81
2371 **SUPREME ANGEL 4** [12] 5-8-4 (66) T Quinn 9/1: 135007: Sn rdn bhd, late gains: qck reapp. 1½ 61
2184 **THAT MAN AGAIN 12** [14] 8-8-10 (72)(bl) J Reid 8/1: 000108: Led till 2f out, no extra: best 2022. hd 67
2310 **ANTONIAS DOUBLE 7** [6] 5-8-8 (70) P Fessey 8/1: 500039: Dwelt, sn handy, wknd over 1f out. 1¼ 61
2326 **KILCULLEN LAD 6** [4] 6-8-10 (72)(vis) J F Egan 20/1: 052300: Stumbled start, sn in tch, no impress 1¼ 60
final 2f: qck reapp: 10th, btr 1999.
1980 **STORYTELLER 21** [1] 6-9-4 (80)(vis) Dale Gibson 10/1: 000430: Nvr a factor on outer: 11th, poor draw. hd 67
2395 **RIBERAC 3** [2] 4-8-11 (73) J Fanning 16/1: 0-0020: Nvr a factor in 12th: poor draw, qck reapp. nk 59
2168 **TRAVESTY OF LAW 13** [3] 3-9-12 (93) D R McCabe 50/1: 0-0000: Bhd, no hdwy over 2f out: 13th. ½ 78
1728 **LIVELY LADY 32** [13] 4-10-0 (90)(vis) Pat Eddery 11/2 FAV: 410330: In tch, btn 1f out: bckd, btr 1728. 1 72
14 ran   Time 1m 0.7 (1.1)   (Dean Ivory)   K T Ivory Radlett, Herts.

2474	2.35 CARIBBEAN NOV STKS 2YO (D) 7f rnd Good Slow
	£6955 £2140 £1070 £535

-- **HOTELGENIE DOT COM** [2] M R Channon 2-8-3 Craig Williams 8/2: 1: 2 b f Selkirk - Birch Creek 85
(Carwhite) Dwelt, waited with, gd hdwy over 2f out, squeezed thro' to lead ins last, pushed out, shade cosily:
op 6/1, debut: Mar foal, cost 180,000 gns: half-sister to smart Lowther (6f) wnr Bianca Nera: eff at 7f,
further suit: runs well fresh on gd: plenty to like about this, should go on & win races in better grade.
1944 **BLUEBERRY FOREST 22** [4] J L Dunlop 2-9-5 Pat Eddery 5/4 FAV: -122: 2 br c Charnwood Forest - ¾ 98
Abstraction (Rainbow Quest) Prom, hdwy for press to lead over 1f out, edged right & collared inside last,
not pace of wnr: hvly bckd: jockey received a 4-day careless riding ban: hvly bckd: v useful run conceding
lumps of weight to this wnr & stays 7f: should land another nice prize: see 1944.
*2234 **BLUE PLANET 9** [6] Sir Mark Prescott 2-9-5 G Duffield 3/1: 13: 2 b c Bluebird - Millie Musique 4 89
(Miller's Mate) Slow away, bhd, eff to chall over 1f out, no extra ins last: prob improved & stays 7f: see 2234.
*2125 **NIGHT FALL 14** [5] R Hannon 2-9-0 P Fitzsimons (5) 10/1: 5614: Handy, effort & short of room but 1½ 81
probably held over 1f out, no impress: op 7/1: mdn wnr in 2125.
-- **THUNDERMILL** [1] 2-8-8 A Clark 25/1: 5: With ldr, wkng when hmpd 2f out, no extra: debut: 4 67
op 10/1: Mar foal, cost $20,000: bred to apprec 6/7f: with T Mills & has some ability.
*1988 **ADJOURNMENT 20** [3] 2-9-5 J Fortune 7/2: 016: Made most till hdd & badly hmpd over 1f out, no nk 77
extra: can rate more highly: pleasing mdn wnr in 1988.
6 ran   Time 1m 30.88 (4.48)   (Mr Derek D & Mrs Jean P Clee)   M R Channon Upper Lambourn, Berks.

2475   3.10 TOTE EXACTA HCAP 3YO+ (B)   1m2f   Good Fair   [111]
£58000   £22000   £11000   £5000   3 yo rec 11lb

*2030 **LADY ANGHARAD** 19 [9] J R Fanshawe 4-8-1 (84)(4ex) R Mullen 14/1: 00-111: 4 b f Tenby - Lavezzola **90**
(Salmon Leap) Handy, gd hdwy to lead appr fnl 1f, styd on well, drvn out to land a fine hat-trick: earlier won
at Nottingham & Leicester (class stks): rnr-up for A Jarvis in '99 (rtd 82): juv wnr at Epsom (Listed) &
Salisbury (stks, rtd 100): suited by 10f now on fast, gd & any trk: ran well once in a visor, prob best
without: runs well fresh: in fine heart, useful & has relished the move to this useful stable.

4559} **ALBARAHIN** 251 [6] M P Tregoning 5-9-10 (107) R Hills 25/1: 1612-2: 5 b h Silver Hawk - My Dear Lady hd **112**
(Mister Prospector) Waited with in tch, gd hdwy over 1f out to chase wnr inside last, styd on well but hung
slightly right & just held off: reapp: in '99 scored at Leicester (reapp), Sandown & Newbury (h'caps, rtd
105): rtd 76 for Godolphin in '98: eff at 1m, stays a stiff 10f well: acts on fast & hvy & likes a gall/stiff
trk: runs well fresh & can carry big weights: tremendous reapp under a big weight & this was a Gr class
performance: one to keep in mind, as is his stable, who are returning to form following a viral problem.

2170 **BRILLIANT RED** 13 [10] Mrs L Richards 7-9-3 (100)(t) I Mongan (5) 33/1: 1-0003: 7 b g Royal Academy 1 **103**
- Red Comes Up (Blushing Groom) Prom, led over 2f out, hdd over 1f out, kept on same pace: back to best.

2190 **PINCHINCHA** 11 [4] D Morris 6-7-11 (79)(1ow) Dale Gibson 40/1: 023434: Bhd, hdwy over 2f out, kept nk **81**
on late, nrst fin: fine run, often plcd: see 2190, 1288.

2116 **KINGS MILL** 15 [15] 3-8-4 (98) P Robinson 8/1: -11105: Prom, effort well over 1f out, kept on ½ **99**
same pace for press: back to best at 10f: see 2116, 1310.

2117 **ATLANTIC RHAPSODY** 15 [14] 3-8-1 (95) J Fanning 9/1: 441256: Held up rear, plenty to do 3f out, 2 **93+**
kept on well final 2f, again plenty of promise stepped up to 10f: no surprise to see another win.

1989 **TRIPLE DASH** 20 [8] 4-8-6 (89) G Duffield 7/1: 500007: Handy, hard rdn over 3f out, sn lkd held but hd **87**
kept on same pace final 2f: bckd: signs of a return to form & is well h'capped when doing so: prob stays 10f.

2069 **ULUNDI** 17 [5] 5-8-7 (90) P Doe 25/1: 113308: In tch, hdwy & not clr run over 2f out till dist, kept shd **88+**
on well, too late: encouraging: see 1342.

2170 **IPLEDGEALLEGIANCE** 13 [13] 4-8-12 (95) J Reid 33/1: 5-3009: In tch, rdn & onepace final 2f. 1 **91**

*1592 **DEHOUSH** 37 [3] 4-9-10 (107) M Roberts 20/1: 204-10: Led after 1f till over 2f out, wknd final 1f: ½ **102**
10th: stiff task under a big weight: see 1592 (stks).

2170 **HUDOOD** 13 [12] 5-8-8 (91) T E Durcan 20/1: 133500: Bhd, held when short of room over 1f out: 11th. 2 **83**

2170 **SHARP PLAY** 13 [11] 5-8-9 (92) R Hughes 7/1: /10420: Prom, btn over 1f out, eased ins last: 12th. hd **84**

*2170 **BLUE 13** [7] 4-8-11 (94)(4ex) Pat Eddery 8/1: 2/1510: In tch, btn 2f out: 13th, btr 2170. 5 **79**

2178 **JUST IN TIME** 12 [20] 5-8-7 (90) A Clark 16/1: 414030: Led 1f, chsd ldr till 3f out, no extra: 14th. 2 **72**

1452 **SECRET AGENT** 45 [1] 3-8-5 (99) K Darley 9/1: -14230: Dwelt, bhd, effort over 2f out, held when 1¾ **79**
hmpd over 1f out: 15th, op 6/1: much btr 1452, 1310.

1850 **NIGHT VENTURE** 27 [18] 4-8-4 (87) T Quinn 20/1: 6-1000: Dwelt, al bhd: 16th, best 1031 (hvy). ½ **66**

1451 **FERZAO** 45 [17] 3-8-1 (95) G Bardwell 20/1: 1-3150: Keen in tch, btn 2f out: 17th: btr 1198. 2½ **70**

2148 **TRAHERN** 14 [16] 3-7-12 (92) F Norton 5/1 FAV: -42140: Prom, rdn & wknd 2f out, reportedly lame: 1¾ **65**
18th, well bckd: lkd well in here after 4th in a Gr 2 in 2148 (12).

2085 **INDIUM** 16 [2] 6-7-10 (79) M Henry 33/1: 401050: V slow away & al bhd: 19th, see 2085. 1½ **50**

2004 **CAROUSING** 20 [19] 3-7-13 (93) J Mackay (5) 14/1: 11-150: Al bhd: fin last: btr 2004, 1703. 5 **57**

20 ran   Time 2m 07.57 (3.47)   (Ian M Deane)   J R Fanshawe Newmarket.

2476   3.45 BRITANNIC COND STKS 3YO (C)   1m rnd   Good Fair
£6380   £2420   £1210   £550

2066 **FANAAR** 17 [6] J Noseda 3-9-1 Pat Eddery 7/4 FAV: -101: 3 ch c Unfuwain - Catalonda (African Sky): **111**
Waited with, plenty to do over 3f out, styd on strongly over 1f out to get up cl-home: hvly bckd: earlier won
at Newmarket (stks, debut): related to wnrs over 1m/10f: v eff at 1m, further looks sure to suit: acts on
gd, gd/soft & on a stiff trk: runs well fresh & comes from bhd: has a turn of foot, win a List/Gr race.

2117 **CORNELIUS** 15 [3] P F I Cole 3-9-1 D Sweeney 20/1: 6-2502: 3 b c Barathea - Rainbow Mountain nk **109$**
(Rainbow Quest) Chsd clr ldr, went on over 2f out, kept on till cl-home, just btn: fine run: v useful.

1945 **CIRCLE OF LIGHT** 22 [5] P W D'Arcy 3-8-7 K Darley 5/1: 0-3233: 3 b f Anshan - Cockatoo Island 2½ **96**
(High Top) Set gd pace & sn clr till over 2f out, kept on same pace over 1f out: unsuited by drop back to 1m.

1171 **SUMMONER** 62 [2] R Charlton 3-9-3 R Hughes 3/1: 61-104: Waited with, effort over 2f out, onepace 2½ **101**
over 1f out: 2 mth abs & better expected: see 1171, looked smart in 735.

2171 **MODERN BRITISH** 13 [4] 3-9-1 T Quinn 15/2: 125: Chsd ldrs till no extra over 2f out: stiff task. 1¼ **97**

*1449 **REACH THE TOP** 45 [7] 3-9-1 J Fortune 1/1: 16: Sn rdn bhd, btn over 3f out: btr 1449 (debut, mdn). 13 **73**

1733 **FAIRY GEM** 32 [1] 3-8-12 Dane O'Neill 20/1: 0-0466: In tch, wknd over 3f out: stiff task, see 1733. 10 **50**

7 ran   Time 1m 42.15 (3.15)   (Saleh Al Homeizi)   J Noseda Newmarket.

2477   4.15 STEEL DRUM MDN 3YO+ (D)   1m6f   Good Slow
£4173   £1284   £642   £321   3 yo rec 15lb

1311 **BOX BUILDER** 52 [5] M R Channon 3-8-11 Craig Williams 100/30: 3351: 3 ch c Fraam - Ena Olley **85**
(Le Moss) In tch, eff to chall 2f out, led appr final 1f, kept on, rdn out: 7 wk abs: plcd twice prev: stays
14f well on gd, handles firm grnd & a stiff trk: runs well fresh: unexposed at this trip.

1696 **TAKWIN** 34 [4] B Hanbury 3-8-11 (t) R Hills 5/4 FAV: -0322: 3 b c Alzao - Gale Warning (Last Tycoon) ¾ **84**
Led over 7f out till over 1f out, not pace of wnr: not btn far, clr of rem, bckd: stays 14f, deserves similar.

2021 **GOLD QUEST** 19 [1] Sir Michael Stoute 3-8-11 (t) Pat Eddery 3/1: 0-5233: 3 ch c Rainbow Quest - 7 **76**
My Potters (Irish River) Hld up, eff over 2f out, sn onepace: op 6/4: probably stays 14f: see 2021, 1510.

2298 **ROUTE ONE** 7 [6] Andrew Reid 7-9-12 D Sweeney 40/1: 64: Cl-up, no extra appr 2f out: top weight. 1 **75$**

1824 **POT LUCK** 28 [3] 3-8-11 R Hughes 8/1: 35: Bhd, eff to chase ldr over 4f out till over 2f out, wknd. 4 **70**

782 **TUMBLEWEED WIZARD** 100 [8] 3-8-11 D R McCabe 20/1: 000-06: In tch, wknd over 3f out: abs. 11 **58**

1588 **KING OF THE WEST** 38 [7] 4-9-12 A Daly 33/1: 07: Sn led, hdd over 7f out, no extra over 4f out. dist **0**

7 ran   Time 3m 05.84 (10.84)   (M Hutchinson)   M R Channon Upper Lambourn, Berks.

SANDOWN FRIDAY JULY 7TH Righthand, Galloping Track, Stiff Finish.

2478 **4.50 CALYPSO HCAP 3YO 0-80 (D) 5f Good/Firm 24 -01 Slow [87]**
£5073 £1561 £780 £390

2003 **BLUE VELVET 20** [11] K T Ivory 3-9-6 (79) C Carver (3) 5/1: 600001: 3 gr f Formidable - Sweet Whisper (Pertong) Cl-up, gd hdwy to lead over 1f out, sn clr, readily: nicely bckd: in '99 won at Southwell (fill auct mdn, rtd 80a) & Newmarket (nursery h'cap, rtd 86): stays 6f, all 3 wins over 5f: handles any trk & grnd. **86**
2288 **JAMES STARK 7** [9] N P Littmoden 3-9-1 (74)(vis) Pat Eddery 4/1: 020342: 3 b g Up And At 'Em - June Maid (Junius) Dwelt, bhd, hdwy over 1f out, kept on ins last, nrst fin: looks crying out for 6f: see 2288. *1½* **76**
2168 **SMOKIN BEAU 13** [2] J Cullinan 3-8-13 (72) D Sweeney 33/1: 020003: 3 b g Cigar - Beau Dada (Pine Circle) Hld up, hdwy over 1f out, kept on same pace: gd run with visor discarded & should apprec a return to 6f as in 994: acts on fast, soft/hvy & both A/Ws. *¾* **72**
2168 **QUEEN OF THE MAY 13** [4] M R Channon 3-9-8 (80) Craig Williams 15/2: 3-1654: Bhd, kept on late. *¾* **78**
2252 **ZOENA 9** [3] 3-7-13 (58) Dale Gibson 20/1: 40-045: Cl-up, no extra appr final 1f: see 2252. *½* **55**
2216 **DACCORD 10** [12] 3-9-6 (79) N Callan 12/1: -53506: Handy, rdn & no impress over 1f out: best 444. *1½* **72**
2165 **GDANSK 13** [10] 3-9-2 (75) R Hughes 5/1: 402107: Bhd, no impress over 1f out: twice below 1712. *2½* **62**
2252 **CORBLETS 9** [14] 3-8-7 (66) P Doe 10/1: 225008: Led halfway till over 1f out, no extra. *nk* **52**
1562 **OUR FRED 39** [7] 3-9-2 (75) K Lavelle (7) 12/1: 33-449: Handy, btn 2f out: btr 1562, 1427 (gd/soft). *½* **59**
2184 **AROGANT PRINCE 12** [6] 3-8-0 (59) A Daly 16/1: 316000: Led till over 2f out, no extra: 10th, see 1175. *nk* **42**
2294 **BORN TO RULE 7** [1] 3-8-3 (62) D R McCabe 33/1: -00050: Al bhd: 11th: flattered 2294. *½* **43**
2216 **FEAST OF ROMANCE 10** [8] 3-8-2 (61)(bl) R Mullen 9/1: 606030: With ldr till wknd 2f out: 12th. *hd* **41**
1783 **KINSAILE 29** [13] 3-7-10 (55)(1oh) A Polli (3) 16/1: 0-000: Al bhd: 13th: see 1399. *¾* **33**
2280 **FRAMPANT 8** [5] 3-8-2 (60)(1ow) J Fanning 16/1: 004430: In tch, btn 2f out: fin last, btr 2280. *1* **35**
14 ran Time 1m 00.87 (1.27) (K T Ivory) K T Ivory Radlett, Herts.

BEVERLEY FRIDAY JULY 7TH Righthand, Oval Track with Stiff Uphill Finish

Official Going GOOD. Stalls: Inside.

2479 **6.50 FERGUSON SELL HCAP 3YO+ 0-60 (F) 7f100y rnd Good/Firm 29 00 Slow [55]**
£2576 £736 £368 3 yo rec 8 lb High numbers favoured here

2302 **MARTON MERE 7** [16] A J Lockwood 4-9-6 (47) O Pears 25/1: 56-001: 4 ch g Cadeaux Genereux - Hyatti (Habitat) Dwelt, imprvd appr final 2f, kept on well & got up towards fin, pshd out: first win, no bid: rtd 58 & 43a in '99 (mdn, rtd 58 & 43a, T Easterby): eff over a stiff 7.5f on fast grnd. **52**
2046 **BERNARDO BELLOTTO 18** [14] D Nicholls 5-8-13 (40) K Hodgson 7/1: 000002: 5 b g High Estate - Naivity (Auction Ring) Prom, led ent fnl 2f, rdn & worn down well ins last: apprec drop in grade, eff at 6/7.5f. *½* **43**
2099 **PIPPAS PRIDE 16** [9] S R Bowring 5-8-12 (39)(t) S Finnamore (5) 12/1: 435003: 5 ch g Pips Pride - Al Shany (Burslem) Handy, effort & hung left 2f out, kept on but unable to chall: t-strap: all wins on a/w. *2½* **37**
2240 **DETROIT CITY 9** [10] B S Rothwell 5-9-0 (41) M Fenton 5/1: 420204: Mid-div, late prog but nvr dngrs. *½* **37**
2130 **MEZZORAMIO 14** [15] 8-9-5 (46)(tvi) R Winston 9/2 FAV: 0-0035: Led till ent fnl 2f, no extra: vis reapp. *nk* **41**
1941 **SYCAMORE LODGE 22** [1] 9-9-7 (48) Alex Greaves 8/1: 003406: Late hdwy, nvr a threat: poor low draw. *½* **42**
1360 **TAKER CHANCE 49** [8] 4-9-0 (41) J Bramhill 14/1: 000007: Al same place: 6 wk jumps abs. *1* **33**
329 **RED WOLF 175** [13] 4-9-1 (42) V Halliday 9/1: 000-08: Chsd ldrs, fdd appr fnl 1f: over 5 mth abs, see 329. *1* **31**
1920 **ZECHARIAH 23** [6] 4-9-0 (41) R Cody Boutcher (7) 10/1: 656409: Mid-div thro'out: see 1760, 907. *¾* **28**
2099 **THREE CHERRIES 16** [7] 4-8-13 (40) P Goode (3) 20/1: 400000: Al towards rear: 10th, see 1191. *¾* **25**
2143 **ACE OF TRUMPS 14** [3] 4-9-8 (49)(t) N Kennedy 8/1: 012030: Nvr in it: 12th, poor draw, see 1361, 1195. **0**
1794 **Cedar Wells 29** [11] 4-9-7 (48) T Williams 20/1: 2180 **Champagne N Dreams 12** [2] 8-9-9 (50) Kim Tinkler 12/1:
806 **Portrack Junction 98** [12] 3-8-13 (48) C Lowther 33/1:2147 **Mount Park 14** [4] 3-9-1 (50) D Mernagh (3) 25/1:
2282 **Adulation 8** [5] 6-10-0 (55)(BL) F Lynch 20/1:
16 ran Time 1m 33.0 (2.2) (A J Lockwood) A J Lockwood Malton, N Yorks.

2480 **7.20 CHISHOLMS MDN 2YO (D) 5f Good/Firm 29 -13 Slow**
£3864 £1189 £594 £297 High numbers favoured

2234 **WALLY MCARTHUR 9** [16] A Berry 2-9-0 J Carroll 7/2: -0321: 2 b c Puissance - Giddy (Polar Falcon) Early ldr, rdn to regain lead below dist, ran on well: eff at 5f, stays 6f: acts on fast & gd, stiff/gall trks. **80**
2277 **EXTRA GUEST 8** [7] M R Channon 2-8-9 R Havlin 3/1 FAV: 326222: 2 b f Fraam - Gibaltarik (Jareer) Bhd ldrs, prog & drifted right appr final 1f, ev ch inside last, held nr fin: needs to try headgear, see 2029. *½* **72**
2077 **FIENNES 16** [14] M L W Bell 2-9-0 (t) M Fenton 7/1: 5063: 2 b c Dayjur - Artic Strech (Arctic Tern) Sn led, under press & hdd ent final 1f, onepace: t-strap: eff forcing the pace over a stiff 5f on fast grnd. *1¾* **72**
2100 **ALBANECK 16** [2] T D Easterby 2-9-0 D Mernagh (3) 14/1: -064: Chsd ldrs till dist: handles fast. *1½* **68**
1595 **PASITHEA 37** [6] 2-8-9 G Parkin 20/1: 45: Rear, late hdwy, nvr a threat: stablemate 4th, 6f will suit. *1½* **62**
-- **RUBY BABE** [13] 2-8-9 R Winston 16/1: 6: Struggling till kept on nicely inside last: debut: 500 gns Aragon half-sister to decent sprint juv Bolero Boy, dam 7f/9f wnr: improve for this at 6f: with J Quinn. *½* **60**
2277 **BRAITHWELL 8** [17] 2-9-0 O Pears 5/1: 07: In tch, effort appr final 1f, not pace to chall: op 9/1. *½* **64**
-- **SEDUCTIVE** [11] 2-9-0 M Worrell (7) 9/1: 8: Veered left start, nvr going pace: green on debut: 36,000 gns Pursuit Of Love Apr foal, half-brother to sev wnrs, notably 6f/9f scorer Rudimental, dam 10f wnr. *3* **55**
2057 **PENTAGON LADY 17** [4] 2-8-9 R Cody Boutcher (7) 33/1: -009: Nvr dngrs: 5,700 gns Secret Appeal May sister to a 1m wnr, sire a miler: with J Eyre. *3* **41**
1764 **SIAMO DISPERATI 30** [8] 2-9-0 K Hodgson 16/1: 30: Prom till lost place 2f out: 10th, btr 1764 (hvy). *2* **40**
1823 **THE FANCY MAN 28** [5] 2-9-0 Kim Tinkler 8/1: 40: Sn struggling: 12th, btr 1823 (6f, soft). **0**
2100 **Komaluna 16** [15] 2-9-0 S Finnamore (5) 25/1: -- **Flying Tackle** [10] 2-9-0 C Lowther 25/1:
13 ran Time 1m 03.4 (2.1) (T Herbert-Jackson) A Berry Cockerham, Lancs.

BEVERLEY   FRIDAY JULY 7TH   Righthand, Oval Track with Stiff Uphill Finish

2481
7.50 AUNT BESSIE'S HCAP 4YO+ 0-85 (D)   1m100y rnd   Good/Firm 29   +07 Fast   [75]
£6851   £2108   £1054   £527

*2349 **STYLE DANCER** 5 [4] R M Whitaker 6-9-5 (66)(vis)(6ex) G Duffield 5/1: 404011: 6 b g Dancing Dissident - 72
Showing Style (Pas de Seul) V keen in rear, pulled out & gd prog 2f out, led below dist, rdn clr: fair time,
qck reapp: defied a pen for Sunday's win at Doncaster (h'cap): '99 Haydock wnr (h'cap, rtd 68 at best): '98
York wnr (h'cap, rtd 74): eff at 7f/8.5f: acts on firm, gd/soft grnd & fibresand: goes on any trk, likes
stiff/gall ones: revitalised by reapplication of visor last twice, qck northern hat-trick beckons.
2220 **BACCHUS** 10 [6] Miss J A Camacho 6-9-6 (67) F Norton 2/1 FAV: 5-2322: 6 b g Prince Sabo - Bonica   1½   70
(Rousillon) Keen, bhd ldrs, strong chall appr final 1f, not pace of wnr final 100y: plcd all starts this term.
2397 **SWYNFORD PLEASURE** 3 [5] J Hetherton 4-7-12 (45) T Williams 9/1: 013253: 4 b f Reprimand -   nk   47
Pleasuring (Good Times) Held up, prog & narrow lead ent final 2f till below dist, onepace: qck reapp, clr rem.
2221 **KASS ALHAWA** 10 [3] D W Chapman 7-9-6 (67) D Mernagh (3) 7/2: 405424: Held up, chsd ldrs briefly   8   54
2f out, no extra: better than this, see 38.
2437 **MASTER HENRY** 1 [1] 6-9-10 (71)(6ex) R Ffrench 12/1: 660165: Pulled hard, prom, led 3f out till   ½   57
ent final 2f, fdd: ran yesterday, see 2376 (class stks).
2379 **SHAANXI ROMANCE** 4 [2] 5-7-12 (45)(vis) J Bramhill 12/1: 055436: Well plcd till wknd 2f out: qk reapp.   1¼   29
2018 **SUPREME SALUTATION** 19 [8] 4-10-0 (75) R Winston 7/1: -60627: Not settle & led till 3f out, lost   5   49
place: way too free under top weight, see 1011.
4475} **MINI LODGE** 259 [7] 4-9-4 (65)(VIS) F Lynch 6/1: 0600-8: Chsd ldrs & ch till wknd qckly 2f out: ¾   37
visored on reapp & bckd: well btn in '99 (h'cap, rtd 76): '98 debut wnr at Newcastle (mdn, rtd 89 at best):
eff at 7f, bred for further: acts on gd & hvy grnd: stable having a wretched time: with J Fitzgerald.
8 ran   Time 1m 45.7 (1.9)   (Mrs C A Hodgetts)   R M Whitaker Scarcroft, West Yorks.

2482
8.20 JOHN HAS RETIRED HCAP 3YO+ 0-70 (E)   1m4f   Good/Firm 29   -07 Slow   [69]
£4550   £1400   £700   £350   3 yo rec 13lb

2286 **NORCROFT JOY** 7 [8] N A Callaghan 5-10-0 (69) C Lowther 3/1 JT FAV: 503331: 5 b m Rock Hopper - 75
Greenhills Joy (Radetzky) Waited with, imprvd 3f out, gd wide prog to lead before dist, readily: qck reapp, top-
weight: '99 Warwick & Doncaster wnr (h'caps, rtd 77, M Ryan): '98 wnr at Yarmouth, Hamilton & here at Beverley
(h'caps, rtd 71): eff at 12/14f on fast & soft grnd, any trk, likes Beverley: can go well fresh, nicely h'capped.
1867 **SPA LANE** 25 [3] Mrs S Lamyman 7-8-2 (43) F Norton 8/1: 514332: 7 ch g Presidium - Sleekit   2½   45
(Blakeney) Held up, styd on for press final 2f, no ch wnr: back in trip, eff btwn 12f & 2m2f: tough.
1895 **ALTAY** 24 [2] R A Fahey 3-8-1 (55) G Duffield 10/1: 6-0363: 3 b g Erin's Isle - Aliuska (Fijar Tango)   ½   56
Keen, bhd, plenty to do appr final 2f, kept on well for press, no extra nr fin: acts on fast & gd/soft.
2109 **ACQUITTAL** 15 [5] P L Clinton 8-7-10 (37)(vis)(6oh) J Bramhill 14/1: 0-0044: Rear, mod late gains.   3   34
*2219 **SKYERS A KITE** 10 [11] 5-8-6 (47)(6ex) T Williams 8/1: 065315: Led & clr 4f out, hard rdn 2f   1   43
out, sn hdd & no extra: found this tougher than 2219 (clmr over C/D).
2382 **SMUDGER SMITH** 4 [7] 3-8-5 (59)(VIS) M Fenton 14/1: 034646: Chsd ldrs, same pace final 2f: vis.   2   53
2146 **DALYAN** 14 [6] 3-8-6 (60) J Carroll 14/1: 5-0047: Nvr a threat: op 10/1, see 1104.   hd   54
2272 **ONE DOMINO** 8 [9] 3-8-6 (60)(vis) F Lynch 12/1: 003248: Prom, fdd/hung left fnl 2f: see 1758 (3yo's).   1¼   52
2238 **BOLT FROM THE BLUE** 9 [12] 4-8-1 (42) Kim Tinkler 14/1: -00569: Prom till 3f out: see 1683.   nk   33
2309 **EDMO HEIGHTS** 7 [10] 4-8-11 (52)(BL) R Winston 14/1: 0-0000: Well plcd till 4f out: 10th, blnkd.   shd   43
2279 **LOVE BITTEN** 8 [1] 3-9-1 (69) R Ffrench 3/1 JT FAV: 521340: Mid-div till appr final 2f: 11th, see 2141.   3½   56
1919 **OLD FEATHERS** 23 [4] 3-8-2 (52) D Mernagh (3) 16/1: 6-0060: Dwelt, prog after 6f, lost pl 4f out: 12th.   24   23
12 ran   Time 2m 35.6 (4.3)   (Norcroft Park Stud)   N A Callaghan Newmarket.

2483
8.50 WELLBEING NOV STKS 2YO (D)   5f   Good/Firm 29   -11 Slow
£3412   £1050   £525   £262

2248 **BYO** 9 [5] M C Chapman 2-9-2 L Gueller (7) 7/1: -0151: 2 gr c Paris House - Navan Royal (Dominion   93
Royale) Prom, drvn to lead below dist, hung left, ran on well: earlier won at Ripon (nov auct stks):
cheaply bought first foal: eff at 5f, should get 6f: acts on fast grnd, prob any trk: improving.
2318 **UP TEMPO** 6 [1] T D Easterby 2-9-0 R Winston 1/1 FAV: 21322: 2 b c Flying Spur - Musical Essence   ¾   87
(Song) Outpcd early, chsd ldrs 2f out, onepcd till kept on towards fin: qck reapp, well bckd, below best.
2248 **OPEN WARFARE** 9 [2] M Quinn 2-9-0 F Norton 10/1: 135333: 2 b f General Monash - Pipe Opener   ¾   84$
(Prince Sabo) Chsd ldrs, unable to qckn appr final 1f: ran to best, see 1166.
*2237 **WILSON BLYTH** 9 [3] A Berry 2-9-0 J Carroll 9/4: 2214: Led till dist, no extra: btr 2237 (6f).   ½   82
*1236 **SANDLES** 57 [6] 2-9-0 F Lynch 8/1: 15: Went left start & lost many lengths, nvr in it: 8 wk abs, turf bow.   2½   76$
2218 **KEEP DREAMING** 10 [4] 2-8-7 D Mernagh (3) 20/1: 0006: Bhd from halfway: stiff task for this plater   17   34
6 ran   Time 1m 03.3 (2)   (Jalons Partnership)   M C Chapman Market Rasen, Lincs.

2484
9.20 W JACKSON FILLIES HCAP 3YO 0-70 (E)   1m2f   Good/Firm 29   -22 Slow   [72]
£3126   £962   £481   £240

2080 **DIVA** 16 [11] Sir Mark Prescott 3-9-6 (64) G Duffield 15/8 FAV: 605221: 3 b f Exit To Nowhere - Opera   69
Lover (Sadler's Wells) Keen, prom, pld out & rdn 2f out, kept on well to lead below dist: bckd, first win:
progressive on sand prev (rtd 64a): eff at 7f, suited by 10f: acts on fast grnd, fibresand, prob equitrack.
1255 **CARELESS** 56 [9] T D Easterby 3-8-11 (55)(BL) J Carroll 13/2: 0-4042: 3 b f Robellino - Life's Too   1½   57
Short (Astronef) Well plcd & ev ch, kept on inside last but not as well as wnr: 8 wk abs: gd run in first
time blnks & suited by step up to 10f, 12f may suit: see 976.
2183 **POLISHED UP** 12 [10] R M Beckett 3-8-3 (47) F Norton 12/1: 0-603: 3 b f Polish Precedent - Smarten Up   ½   48
(Sharpen Up) Led till 1f out, no extra under press: solid h'cap bow, new tactics: apprec step up to 10f on fast.
1955 **MOST STYLISH** 22 [7] C G Cox 3-9-7 (65) M Fenton 9/2: 52344: Chsd ldrs, feeling pace turning for   1   64
home, ran on late: top-weight, see 1955.
2222 **WORTH THE RISK** 10 [6] 3-7-11 (41) Kim Tinkler 14/1: 050-35: Held up, prog to chase ldrs 3f   shd   40
out, hard rdn 2f out, onepace: maiden h'cap: mdn h'caps will suit.
2007 **KUUIPO** 20 [1] 3-8-2 (46)(t) J Bramhill 8/1: 006026: Prom till fdd before final 1f: see 2007 (gd).   1   43
1837 **SISTER KATE** 27 [8] 3-8-3 (47) O Pears 33/1: 6-067: Nvr better than mid-div: h'cap bow, back up in trip.   1¾   42
2296 **CHEZ BONITO** 7 [4] 3-7-10 (40)(5oh) Claire Bryan (5) 7/2: 520548: Mid-div, outpcd 2f out: qck   ½   34
reapp, stiffish task, unlucky in running in 2296, see 1195.

784

BEVERLEY FRIDAY JULY 7TH Righthand, Oval Track with Stiff Uphill Finish

1865 **PIX ME UP 25** [2] 3-8-12 (56) Iona Wands (5) 10/1: 001249: Al bhd: see 1596 (1m). 5 42
1644 **SECRETARIO 35** [5] 3-8-0 (44) N Kennedy 33/1: 0-6600: Nvr a threat: 10th, now wth J Hetherton. 9 16
2123 **CHARLEM 15** [3] 3-7-12 (42)(vis) D Mernagh (3) 25/1: 0-6660: No ch from halfway: 11th, turf return. 3½ 9
11 ran Time 2m 07.4 (5.1) (Cheveley Park Stud) Sir Mark Prescott Newmarket.

CHANTILLY TUESDAY JULY 4TH Righthand, Galloping Track

Official Going HOLDING

2485 **1.55 GR 3 PRIX DU BOIS 2YO** 5f Holding
£21134 £7685 £3842

-- **OZONE LAYER** A Fabre 2-8-11 O Peslier 21/10: -131: 2 b c Zafonic - Ozone Friendly (Green Forest) 106
Waited with, rdn to chall ldrs appr fnl 1f, ran on to lead nr fin, drvn out: earlier won on debut: eff at 5f,
6f will suit: acts on hvy grnd & a gall trk: v useful juv who shld win more races.
-- **IRON MASK** Mme C Head 2-8-11 O Doleuze 7/10 FAV: -122: 2 b c Danzig - Raise A Beauty (Alydar) nk 105
Slow to stride, sn with ldrs, styd on well fnl 1f, not btn far: eff at 5f on hvy grnd: useful 2yo.
-- **DISTINCTLY DANCER** A Peraino 2-8-11 G Mosse 59/10: -41313: 2 b c Distinctly North - Shadow Casting 1½ 101
(Warning) Cl-up, went on appr halfway, hdd well ins last, no extra nr fin: stays 5f well on hvy.
5 ran Time 1m 02.0 (Maktoum Al Maktoum) A Fabre France

SAN SIRO THURSDAY JULY 6TH Righthand, Stiff, Galloping Track

Official Going GOOD TO FIRM

2486 **2.55 LISTED PREMIO GINO 2YO FILLIES** 7f110y Good/Firm
£22772 £10020 £5465

*2172 **HEJAZIAH 12** P F I Cole 2-8-11 F Jovine : 2311: 2 b f Gone West - Toptrestle (Nijinsky) 101
Made all, rdn & went clr fnl 2f, rdly: earlier won at Ascot (nov fillies stks): dam a 1m scorer: eff at 6f,
apprec this step up to a stiff/gall 7.5f: acts on fast, gd/soft & likes to dominate: useful, tough & consistent.
-- **SECRET VALLEY** Italy 2-8-11 M Planard : 2: 2 b f Valanour - Fabulous Secret (Fabulous Dancer) 3½ 92
-- **GULFSTREAM PARK** Italy 2-8-11 D Vargiu : 3: 2 b f Barathea - Off The Blocks (Salse) nk 91
7 ran Time 1m 34.6 (H R H Prince Fahd Salman) P F I Cole Whatcombe, Oxon

BORDEAUX - LA TESTE DE BUCH THURSDAY JULY 6TH --

Official Going GOOD

2487 **3.25 LISTED PRIX LA SORELLINA 2YO FILLIES** 1m Good
£12488 £4227 £3170

2171 **COURTING 12** W J Haggas 3-8-7 J P Spencer : 100-31: 3 gr f Pursuit Of Love - Doctor's Glory 100
(Elmaamul) Sn led, styd on strongly for press fnl 2f, drvn out: won 1st 4 in '99, at Catterick (2, auct mdn
& auct stks), Thirsk & Newmarket (stks, rtd 100, Sir M Prescott): eff at 7f/1m, further shld suit (related to
a 2m wnr): runs well fresh on firm, gd & any trk: loves to force the pace: v useful & genuine.
-- **TADORNE** J C Rouget 3-8-7 O Peslier : 2: 3 gr f Inchinor - Tambura (Kaldoun) 3 93
-- **GARDEN IN THE RAIN** France 3-8-7 G Mosse : 3: 3 b f Dolphin Street - Marcotte (Nebos) 2 89
7 ran Time 1m 36.7 (Cheveley Park Stud) W J Haggas Newmarket

CHEPSTOW SATURDAY JULY 8TH Lefthand, Undulating, Galloping Track

Official Going GOOD/FIRM (FIRM places). Stalls - Ins, except Str Crse - Stands Side.

2488 **2.25 WALES DAY MED AUCT MDN 2YO (E)** 6f Good/Firm 28 -12 Slow
£2788 £858 £429 £214

2082 **FACTUAL LAD 17** [9] B R Millman 2-9-0 Jonjo Fowle (7) 8/1: 233231: 2 b c So Factual - Surprise 88
Surprise (Robellino) Made virtually all, styd on well over 1f out, pushed out, cosily: deserved win after sev plcd
runs: Apr foal: half brother to a 7f wnr: dam 7f scorer: eff at 5/6f on fast, gd/soft & prob hvy, any trk: tough.
-- **FLIT ABOUT** [13] I A Balding 2-8-9 A Nicholls (3) 16/1: 2: 2 ch f Fly So Free - Oxava (Antheus) 1½ 79+
In tch, eff to chase wnr ins last, styd on: debut: Jan foal: dam 1m/10.5f wnr: eff at 6f, sure to relish 7f+:
acts on fast grnd: learn plenty from this pleasing debut & will win races, esp over further.
1986 **UPSTREAM 21** [5] Major D N Chappell 2-8-9 R Havlin 4/1 FAV: 443: 2 b f Prince Sabo - Rivers Rhapsody 2 73
(Dominion) Handy, eff to chall over 1f out, sn onepace: stays 6f on fast & gd/soft: shld find a race, see 1424.
2174 **NUN LEFT 13** [10] R M Beckett 2-8-9 M Worrell (7) 5/1: 324: In tch, outpcd 2f out, kept on late: hd 72
interesting in nursery h'caps over 7f: see 2174.
2189 **CELOTTI 12** [11] 2-8-9 Martin Dwyer 16/1: 35: Cl up, wknd fnl 1f: fair run, see 2189. ¾ 70
2209 **MADRASEE 12** [6] 2-8-9 D Sweeney 10/1: 36: Keen in tch, eff 2f out, sn no extra: too free, see 2209. nk 69
1798 **BALI ROYAL 30** [4] 2-8-9 P Fitzsimons (5) 14/1: 207: Handy, wknd over 1f out: best 1641 (debut). 3 61
1472 **FLOOT 45** [1] 2-9-0 A McGlone 10/1: 08: Sn bhd, no impress: abs, op 7/1, see 1472. 2 60
-- **MINUSCOLO** [3] 2-8-9 R Perham 33/1: 9: Slow away, bhd: Apr foal, cost 8,000gns: sister to a 1m wnr. hd 56
2290 **FLUTED 8** [2] 2-9-0 A Mackay 6/1: 40: Al bhd: 10th, btr 2290 (7f, debut). nk 58

-- **VISITATION** [7] 2-8-9 M Fenton 9/1: 0: Slow away, al bhd: 11th, op 6/1: Jan foal: bred for 7f/1m. *2½* **46**
1513 **SANDAL 42** [12] 2-8-9 (BL) L Newman (3) 9/1: 3450: Cl up, wknd 2f out: 12th, abs, blnks not work. *1¾* **41**
2082 **FIRE BELLE 17** [8] 2-8-9 I Mongan (5) 50/1: -00: Al bhd: 13th, see 2082. *10* **11**
13 ran Time 1m 11.2 (2.4) (Tarka Racing) B R Millman Kentisbeare, Devon

2489 **2.55 MONMOUTH MDN HCAP 3YO 0-70 (E) 6f Good/Firm 28 -04 Slow [75]**
£2860 £880 £440 £220

2315 **WILFRAM 7** [19] J M Bradley 3-8-6 (53) P Fitzsimons (5) 13/2: -00031: 3 b g Fraam - Ming Blue (Primo Dominie) Chsd ldrs, hdwy to lead over 1f out, kept on well, pushed out: plcd once prev: stays 6f on fast grnd. **60**
1971 **MARNIE 22** [3] J Akehurst 3-7-13 (46) C Catlin (5) 20/1: -00602: 3 ch f First Trump - Miss Aboyne (Lochnager) Handy, eff over 1f out, kept on, not btn far: op 14/1: cld pinch one of these modest races. *¾* **50**
2207 **ENDYMION 12** [9] Mrs P N Dutfield 3-9-2 (63) L Newman (3) 20/1: 0-0003: 3 ch f Paris House - Vaguely Jade (Corvaro) Led till over 1f out, onepace: better run: see 1178. *2* **61**
1787 **MUFFIN MAN 30** [16] M D I Usher 3-8-6 (53) G Sparkes (7) 12/1: 0-0004: In tch, kept on late, nrst fin: rnr-up in '99 (nusery h'cap, rtd 75): stays 7f on firm & soft, stiff trks: apprec 7f in this company. *1½* **48**
1971 **LUSONG 22** [2] 3-8-12 (59) P Dobbs (5) 10/1: 634055: Sn bhd, kept on late, no danger: see 852, 785. *shd* **53**
2252 **TIME BOMB 10** [14] 3-8-6 (53) R Havlin 25/1: 0-4006: In tch, eff 2f out, wknd fnl 1f: see 1525. *shd* **47**
1994 **ORLANDO SUNSHINE 21** [15] 3-8-7 (54) I Mongan (4) 20/1: 000-07: Handy, no impress over 1f out. *1½* **44**
2243 **PACIFIC PLACE 10** [4] 3-8-13 (60) Martin Dwyer 11/2: 423228: In tch, wknd appr fnl 1f: btr 2243. *1½* **46**
1712 **ABSENT FRIENDS 34** [1] 3-9-4 (65) A McGlone 20/1: 00-049: Nvr a factor: see 1712. *hd* **50**
2291 **PETRIE 8** [6] 3-8-0 (47) A Nicholls (3) 10/1: 035030: Bhd, some late gains: 10th, btr 2291. *shd* **32**
2216 **MIND THE SILVER 11** [12] 3-8-12 (59) R Brisland (5) 5/1 FAV: 6-0060: Sn bhd, mod late gains: 11th, reportedly 'lost a front shoe': worth another chance in this grade after 2216. *hd* **43**
1643 **SLIEVE BLOOM 36** [10] 3-9-1 (62) L Carter 8/1: 6050: Al bhd: fin 17th, see 1643. *¾* **0**
2184 **Bangled 13** [18] 3-8-1 (48) C Cogan (3) 33/1:
1795 **Dancemma 30** [11] 3-9-5 (66) R Perham 12/1:
2105 **Burcot Girl 16** [17] 3-7-10 (43)(13oh) D Kinsella (7) 66/1:
4430} **White Summit 263** [8] 3-8-6 (53) M Fenton 33/1:
2154 **Kind Emperor 14** [13] 3-9-7 (68)(VIS) L Newton 20/1: R
2036 **Lively Millie 19** [5] 3-8-1 (48)(VIS) A Mackay 14/1:
1742 **St Ives 32** [20] 3-7-12 (45) Jonjo Fowle (2) 33/1:
19 ran Time 1m 10.7 (1.9) (R D Willis) J M Bradley Sedbury, Gloucs

2490 **3.30 TEAM WALES MDN HCAP 3YO+ 0-70 (E) 2m2f Good/Firm 28 +03 Fast [70]**
£2749 £846 £423 £211 3 yo rec 21lb

-- **LAFFAH** [15] G L Moore 5-8-12 (54)(t) I Mongan (5) 11/2: 6440/1: 5 b g Silver Hawk - Sakiyah (Secretariat) Hld up, eff over 4f out, led 2f out, rdn clr: fair time: recent h'cap hdle wnr at Folkestone (rtd 93h, stays 2m6.5f on gd & hvy): 98/99 wnr at Taunton & Exeter (h'caps, rtd 106, with M Pipe): wears a t-strap: last rcd on the Flat in '98 (rtd 58, visor, with J Gosden): stays 2m2f well on gd/fm, undul/gall trk. **60**
-- **OUT RANKING** [5] M C Pipe 8-9-9 (65) A McGlone 15/2: 0/2: 8 b m Le Glorieux - Restless Nell (Northern Baby) Prom, led over 4f out till 2f out, onepace: op 5/1: fit from hdlg, in 99/00 won at Fontwell (clmr), Ascot (h'cap), Folkestone (2, mares h'cap & clmr, rtd 131h, stays 3m on any grnd & trk, runs well fresh under big weights): won 5 hdls in 98/99: stays 2m2f on gd/fm: v tough over hdls, only second Flat start here. *5* **65**
-- **SADLERS SECRET** [6] M C Pipe 5-10-0 (70)(vis) P Dobbs (5) 9/1: 0603/3: 5 b g Sadler's Wells - Athyka (Secretariat) Hld up, eff over 3f out, kept on too late: stablemate of rnr-up, op 6/1: hdle rnr 10 wks ago, won at Taunton (h'cap, rtd 112h, 2m1f, gd/soft & hvy, blnks): stays 2m2f on gd/fm & soft: over-confident ride. *hd* **70**
2008 **FANDANGO DREAM 21** [8] M D I Usher 4-7-10 (38)(vis)(11oh) Jonjo Fowle (0) 20/1: 045044: In tch, onepace over 2f out: prob flattered, see 2008. *2½* **36$**
2244 **HERSELF 10** [1] 3-7-11 (60)(1ow)(12oh) A Mackay 12/1: 006035: In tch, no impress fnl 2f: flattered. *1¾* **56$**
1996 **MU TADIL 21** [12] 8-7-10 (38)(6oh) G Sparkes (3) 25/1: -00006: Bhd, late gains, nrst fin: see 1394. *2½* **31**
1888 **ROYAL AXMINSTER 25** [13] 5-8-0 (42) L Newman (2) 10/1: 6-0047: Bhd, eff over 3f out, no impress. *nk* **34**
2173 **TREASURE CHEST 14** [2] 5-9-4 (60)(vis) Martin Dwyer 4/1 FAV: 004058: Led 10f out till over 4f out, wknd. *¾* **51**
2144 **GLOW 15** [7] 4-8-9 (51) L Newton 14/1: 035249: Led till 10f out, wknd over 4f out: see 2144. *5* **37**
1991 **ANGE DHONOR 21** [4] 5-8-13 (55) D Sweeney 13/2: 0-6040: Al bhd: 10th, see 1991. *2½* **38**
3355} **AGENT LE BLANC 329** [3] 5-10-0 (70) A Nicholls (3) 7/1: 5200-P: In tch, saddle slipped & p.u. after 5f: reapp: in '99 trained by T Etherington, rnr-up (rtd 72): eff at 10f/14.5f on fast grnd. **0**
3509} **Formidable Flame 321** [10] 7-7-12 (40)(2ow)(8oh) P Fitzsimons (0) 33/1:
3571} **Southampton 318** [9] 10-7-10 (38)(vis)(13oh) R Brisland (5) 33/1:
2255 **Kafi 10** [11] 4-8-5 (46)(vis)(1ow) R Havlin 33/1:
14 ran Time 3m 56.3 (4.5) (Richard Green Fine Paintings) G L Moore Woodingdean, E Sussex

2491 **4.00 CHEPSTOW FILLIES MDN 3YO (D) 7f rnd Good/Firm 28 -18 Slow**
£4104 £1263 £631 £315

1468 **DANIYSHA 45** [2] Sir Michael Stoute 3-8-11 L Newman (3) 1/1 FAV: 4-431: 3 b f Doyoun -Danishara (Slew O'Gold) Keen, trkd ldr, led over 2f out, clr fnl 1f, easily: val 6L+, bckd, 6 wk abs: rtd 82 sole juv start: stays 7f well, 1m will suit: acts on fast & gd/soft, any trk: runs well fresh: good confidence booster. **76**
2024 **PRINISHA 20** [5] H Candy 3-8-11 A McGlone 13/2: 0202: 3 gr f Prince Sabo - Nisha (Nishapour) Led till over 2f out, toyed with by wnr: eff at 7f/1m on fast & gd/soft: see 1548. *3½* **67**
1468 **BREAKWATER 45** [4] L M Cumani 3-8-11 M Fenton 9/4: 40-453: 3 b f Boundary - Flippers (Coastal) In tch, rdn & onepace fnl 2f: 6 wk abs: see 1468. *1½* **64**
-- **ALTARA** [3] W R Muir 3-8-11 Martin Dwyer 8/1: 4: In tch, no impress fnl 2f: dam smart juv: enjoy 1m. *½* **63**
2232 **PING ALONG 10** [1] 3-8-11 P Dobbs (5) 16/1: -605: Went left start, bhd, no danger: see 1947. *3½* **56$**
5 ran Time 1m 23.0 (3.2) (H H Aga Khan) Sir Michael Stoute Newmarket

2492 **4.30 COME RACING HCAP 3YO+ 0-85 (D) 1m rnd Good/Firm 28 +07 Fast [82]**
£4114 £1266 £633 £316 3 yo rec 9 lb

*1969 **GOODENOUGH MOVER 22** [5] J S King 4-8-10 (64) R Havlin 13/8 FAV: 0-0111: 4 ch g Beveled - Rekindled Flame (King's Lake) Made all, clr 2f out, rdn out to hold on ins last: gd time, nicely bckd: hat-trick after 2 wins here at Chepstow (h'caps): with G Charles Jones in '99 (mdn, rtd 64): loves to dominate over 7f/1m here at Chepstow: acts on fast & gd/soft grnd: improving fast & given a good positive ride. **70**

CHEPSTOW
SATURDAY JULY 8TH Lefthand, Undulating, Galloping Track

2349 **HARMONY HALL** 6 [3] J M Bradley 6-8-9 (63) P Fitzsimons (5) 3/1: 0-4422: 6 ch g Music Boy - Fleeting Affair (Hotfoot) Hld up, 5L bhd wnr & trav well 2f out, kept on fnl 1f, too late: tricky ride, 1 win in 37 starts. **1 67**

*2257 **MYTTONS MISTAKE** 10 [4] R J Baker 7-8-2 (56) G Sparkes (7) 100/30: 224213: 7 b g Rambo Dancer - Hi Hunsley (Swing Easy) In tch, eff over 2f out, sn btn: clr rem: btr 2257. **4 52**

2126 **KANZ RUN** 15 [2] W R Muir 4-8-12 (66) Martin Dwyer 12/1: 0-1004: Hld up, btn over 2f out: best 1473. **6 51**

2185 **SMOOTH SAILING** 13 [6] 5-9-12 (80) A Nicholls (3) 9/1: -04005: Keen, handy, wknd over 2f out. **nk 65**

1583 **BLUE ACE** 39 [1] 7-8-1 (55) L Newman (3) 12/1: 500066: Keen, al bhd: see 927. **3½ 34**

6 ran   Time 1m 33.6 (1.7)   (D Goodenough Removals & Transport)   J S King Broad Hinton, Wilts

---

2493   5.00 FISHGUARD FILLIES HCAP 3YO+ 0-80 (D)   1m2f36y Good/Firm 28 -07 Slow   [72]
£4182   £1287   £643   £321   3 yo rec 11lb

*2085 **THE WILD WIDOW** 17 [2] M C Pipe 6-9-10 (68)(vis) Martin Dwyer 6/4 FAV: 221111: 6 gr m Saddler's Hall - No Cards (No Mercy) Made all, v cmftbly: top-weight: 4-timer after wins at Newbury, Leicester & Kempton (h'caps), prev with Miss S Wilton: '99 wnr at W'hampton (slr, with H Collingridge, rtd 59a) & Warwick (seller): loves to dominate at 1m/11f on firm, soft, fibresand & any trk: eff with/without headgear: v tough & progressive. **79**

1998 **PARISIAN LADY** 21 [5] A G Newcombe 5-8-5 (49) A Nicholls (3) 7/2: -63442: 5 b m Paris House - Mia Gigi (Hard Fought) Hld up, eff to chase wnr over 2f out, no impress: nicely bckd: caught a fast improving sort. **7 48**

1666 **KINGFISHERS BONNET** 36 [3] S G Knight 4-8-6 (50) L Newman (3) 14/1: 135403: 4 b f Hamas - Mainmast (Bustino) Chsd wnr, eff over 3f out, sn btn: see 1350, best 889 (heavy grnd). **6 40**

1866 **ALLEGRESSE** 26 [4] J L Dunlop 3-9-2 (71)(BL) M Fenton 11/2: 6-3504: Al bhd: tried blnks to no avail. **7 52**

2179 **CLEPSYDRA** 13 [1] 3-9-7 (76) A McGlone 11/4: 2235: Handy, wknd over 3f out, eased: something amiss? **3 53**

5 ran   Time 2m 07.6 (3.5)   (Mrs Pam Pengelly & Mrs Helen Stoneham)   M C Pipe Nicholashayne, Devon

---

SANDOWN
SATURDAY JULY 8TH Righthand, Galloping Track, Stiff Finish

Official Going   GOOD. Stalls: 5f - Far Side; Rem - Inside.

2494   2.15 EBF MDN 2YO (D)   7f rnd Good/Firm 25 -38 Slow
£7280   £2240   £1120   £560

-- **NO EXCUSE NEEDED** [8] Sir Michael Stoute 2-9-0 Pat Eddery 4/1: 1: 2 ch c Machiavellian - Nawaiet (Zilzal) In tch, gd hdwy to lead over 1f out, styd on well, drvn out: well bckd, scope: Feb foal: dam 6f scorer: stays a stiff 7f, 1m will suit: runs well fresh on gd/firm: useful, should go on from here. **82**

-- **STEINITZ** [10] J L Dunlop 2-9-0 T Quinn 8/1: 2: 2 ch c Nashwan - Circe's Isle (Be My Guest) Bhd, hdwy well over 1f out, kept on nicely ins last, only heads-and-heels on debut: op 5/1: Feb foal, cost 175,000gns: half-brother to wnrs over 6f/10f: eff over a stiff 7f, 1m+ sure to suit in time: acts on gd/firm: will learn plenty from this kind & useful debut, looks one to follow. **½ 81+**

1798 **MONSIEUR LE BLANC** 30 [12] I A Balding 2-9-0 M Roberts 9/1: 63: 2 b c Alzao - Dedara (Head For Heights) Set pace till over 1f out, kept on for press, not btn far: improved at 7f on gd/firm: win sn. **½ 79**

2125 **PERSUADE** 15 [7] J H Baker 2-9-0 (t) N Forton 11/1: 44: Bhd, gd hdwy over 1f out, no extra cl-home: op 8/1: stays 7f on gd/firm: shld win a race: see 2125. **1 78**

-- **SPECIFIC SORCEROR** [3] S G Knight 2-9-0 N Callan 16/1: 5: Sn rdn in tch, outpcd over 2f out, rallied over 1f out, onepace: Feb first foal, cost 15,000gns: nicely bckd: eff at 7f on gd/firm: relish a minor track mdn. **1 76**

1472 **HAWKES RUN** 45 [6] 2-9-0 G Duffield 12/1: 66: Prom, rdn & outpcd over 1f out: scope, abs. **2 72**

-- **NORTHFIELDS DANCER** [5] 2-9-0 S Sanders 16/1: 7: Nvr a factor: well grown, ndd race on debut: Mar foal, cost IR 62,000gns: half-brother to sev useful wnrs: bred to relish 1m+ in time: with R Hannon. **5 62**

-- **SANNAAN** [4] 2-9-0 A Daly 16/1: 8: In tch, wknd 2f out: ndd race on debut: Feb foal, cost 62,000gns: half-brother to a 6/7f wnr: bred to need mid-dists next term: with M Tregoning. **hd 61**

-- **ALFASEL** [2] 2-9-0 R Hills 7/1: 9: In tch, wkng when short of room over 2f out: ndd race, op 7/2 on debut: Feb foal, cost 280,000gns: half-brother to a 10f wnr: dam 10.5f scorer: will relish mid-dists in time. **¾ 59**

-- **BOUND** [9] 2-9-0 J Reid 14/1: 0: In tch, wknd 2f out: 10th: scope, on toes: Apr foal, half-brother to wnrs over 1m/10f: bred to need mid-dists next term: with B Hills. **6 47**

-- **REVERIE** [1] 2-9-0 Dane O'Neill 7/2 FAV: 0: Prom, trav well till rdn & wknd qckly over 1f out: well bckd: 11th on debut: Apr foal, cost 50,000gns: half-brother to a useful 5f juv wnr: relish a drop back to 6f. **shd 47**

-- **ACHILLES SUN** [11] 2-9-0 Darren Williams (5) 33/1: U: Keen, waited with, u.r. soon after start. **0**

12 ran   Time 1m 30.82 (4.42)   (Maktoum Al Maktoum)   Sir Michael Stoute Newmarket.

2495   2.50 RIO DE JANEIRO HCAP 3YO 0-100 (C)   7f rnd Good/Firm 25 -01 Slow   [105]
£23200   £8800   £4400   £2000

*2300 **RUSHMORE** 8 [14] P F I Cole 3-7-11 (74) P Doe 12/1: -10011: 3 ch c Mt Livermore - Crafty Nan (Crafty Prospector) Prom, led over 1f out, wandered but kept on for press ins last: recent scorer at Southwell (h'cap, rtd 84a) & earlier at Doncaster (mdn): rtd 76 in '99: full brother to a smart 7f wnr: all 3 wins at 7f, tried further: acts on fast, gd & fibresand, any trk: runs well fresh: took advantage of gd draw & handy mark. **81**

2087 **SMART RIDGE** 17 [10] K R Burke 3-9-7 (98) N Callan 33/1: -50202: 3 ch c Indian Ridge - Guanhumara (Caerleon) Chsd ldrs, eff to chase wnr over 1f out, kept on, not btn far: v useful effort under a big weight. **1¼ 102**

+2163 **PEACOCK ALLEY** 14 [15] W J Haggas 3-8-9 (86) T Quinn 4/1 JT FAV: -51113: 3 gr f Salse - Tagiki (Doyoun) Sltly hmpd start, keen, short of room over 2f out till over 1f out, kept on well fnl 1f: hvly bckd & a shade unlucky on 4-timer bid: clearly thriving & could well go in again: see 2163. **nk 90+**

+1946 **DUKE OF MODENA** 23 [3] G B Balding 3-9-3 (94) S Carson (5) 10/1: -11514: Bhd, eff & switched outside over 1f out, styd on strongly: fine run from poor draw & eating up the grnd at finish: progressing well, see 1946. **½ 97**

*2325 **BIG FUTURE** 7 [13] 3-8-12 (89) Pat Eddery 15/1: -1415: Waited with, eff 2f out, sn onepace: gd run. **1½ 89**

*1569 **CELEBRATION TOWN** 40 [6] 3-7-13 (76) M Henry 11: 5-1016: Bhd, eff well over 1f out, sn onepace. **shd 76**

1470 **LAGOON** 45 [11] 3-9-4 (95) J Reid 7/1: 35-047: Handy, rdn & onepcd for press over 1f out: 6 wk abs. **nk 93**

2035 **SILVA SILCA** 19 [4] 3-8-2 (79) Craig Williams 25/1: 2138: Cl-up, led 2f out till over 1f out, no extra. **2 74**

1694 **NORFOLK REED** 35 [12] 3-8-9 (86) Dane O'Neill 20/1: 0-4509: Bhd, modest late gains: shld stay 7f. **½ 80**

2003 **SHATIN VENTURE** 21 [8] 3-9-4 (95) R Mills 20/1: 24-300: Handy, btn 2f out: 10th: see 1308. **3½ 82**

2117 **PRETRAIL** 16 [7] 3-7-13 (76) N Carlisle 33/1: -02100: In tch, rdn & hmpd 2f out, not recover: 11th, carries condition: twice below 1675 (mdn). **hd 62**

*2117 **EL GRAN PAPA** 16 [9] 3-9-3 (94) F Norton 4/1 JT FAV: 3-2110: Waited with, hdwy & not clr run **nk 80**

787

over 1f out, staying on when badly hmpd ins last, not recover: hvly bckd, fin 12th: best to ignore this
(no luck in running) & sure to relish a return to a stiff 1m as in 2117 (val h'cap).

1826	**KNOCKTOPHER ABBEY 29** [2] 3-8-5 (82) M Roberts 20/1: 600-50: Led briefly over 2f out, sn no extra: 13th: showed more in 1826.		2	64
*2108	**NOBLE PURSUIT 16** [16] 3-8-13 (90) A Clark 20/1: -40410: Led till over 2f out: 14th: btr 2108 (1m).		3½	65
1262	**TAP 57** [1] 3-8-10 (87) S Whitworth 33/1: 2-160: Al bhd, 15th: see 1262.		1¾	58
2261	**ARETINO 10** [5] 3-8-2 (79) G Bardwell 33/1: -05050: In tch, wknd over 2f out: fin last, see 2261.		25	10

16 ran   Time 1m 28.2 (1.8)   (J S Gutkin)   P F I Cole Whatcombe, Oxon.

2496   3.25 LISTED SPRINT STKS 3YO+ (A)   5f   Good/Firm   Inapplicable
£19500   £6000   £3000   £1500   3 yo rec 5 lb

2065	**WATCHING 18** [7] R Hannon 3-9-2 Dane O'Neill 9/2: 212201: 3 ch c Indian Ridge - Sweeping (Indian King) Cl-up, led over 1f out, styd on well, rdn out: earlier scored at Haydock (List): '99 wnr at Chester (mdn, rtd 100): stays 6f, better up with/forcing the pace at 5f on gd/firm & hvy, any trk: proving v tough & smart.			114
2065	**LORD KINTYRE 18** [8] B R Millman 5-9-3M Roberts 10/1: -24402: 5 b g Highland Rowena (Royben) Prom, eff to chase wnr ins last, kept on well, only btn ½L: fine run & deserves a Listed race.		½	108
-1987	**REPERTORY 21** [4] M S Saunders R Price 11/1: -00323: 7 b g Anshan - Susie's Baby (Balidar) Set gd pace till appr fnl 1f, onepace: useful run from poor draw & will take some catching at Chester next Sat.		1½	104
*1849	**ASTONISHED 28** [1] J E Hammond 4-9-7 J Reid 7/4 FAV: 10-114: Waited with, eff over 1f out, kept on same pace ins last: lkd well, hvy bckd under top-weight: poor draw (unable to get enough cover), can rate higher.		hd	107
*2003	**COTTON HOUSE 21** [6] 3-8-7 Craig Williams 9/1: 4-1515: Sn outpcd bhd, styd on nicely over 1f out: totally unsuited by drop back to 5f & sure to go closer next time with a return to 6f as in 2003 (val h'cap).		¾	96+
1324	**DASHING BLUE 52** [9] 7-9-3 Pat Eddery 8/1: 600-06: Waited with, brief eff over 1f out, no impress: 7 wk abs: in '99 scored at Sandown (stks) & plcd in Gr 3 company (rtd rtd 110): in '98 plcd at York (Gr 1, rtd 112): stays 6f, suited by a stiff 5f: acts on firm, handles easy grnd & any trk: has run well fresh: v useful.		1½	97
2065	**RAMBLING BEAR 18** [2] 7-9-3 T Quinn 10/1: 0-3307: In tch, btn over 1f out: best fresh: see 1566.		5	83
1849	**VITA SPERICOLATA 28** [10] 3-8-11 G Bardwell 10/1: 60-248: In tch, btn 2f out: btr 1849.		hd	80
2473	**POETRY IN MOTION 1** [5] 5-8-12 P Doe 100/1: 20-059: Al bhd: impossible task, see 2473.		1½	73$
--	**DANCING MAESTRO** [3] 4-9-3 G Duffield 40/1: 135-00: Cl-up, wknd over 1f out: fin last: French import, won over 6f at M-Laffitte in Apr '99 (soft grnd).		1¼	74

10 ran   Time 1m 0.21 (0.61)   (Mrs Dare Wigan)   R Hannon East Everleigh, Wilts.

2497   4.05 GR 1 CORAL-ECLIPSE STKS 3YO+ (A)   1m2f   Good/Firm 25   +13 Fast
£216000   £82800   £41400   £19800   3 yo rec 11lb

*2066	**GIANTS CAUSEWAY 18** [4] A P O'Brien 3-8-10 G Duffield 8/1: -12211: 3 ch c Storm Cat - Mariah's Storm (Rahy) Cl-up, led 2f out till edged slightly left & hdd ins last, styd on strongly & rallied most gamely for hard driving to get up again nr line: nicely bckd, fast time: jockey of this wnr & rnr-up referred to JC over misuse of whip - again displaying the ineffective & unfair current whip Rules: in fine form this term, earlier won at The Curragh (Gr 3), R Ascot (Gr 1 St James, 1m) & rnr-up in both English & Irish 2000 Guineas: juv wnr at Naas, The Curragh (Gr 3) & Longchamp, Gr 1, rtd 118): v eff at 1m, imprvd over this 10f: acts on fast, soft & on any trk, likes a stiff one: runs well fresh: best up with the pace: high-class, thoroughly tough & genuine.			126
+2064	**KALANISI 18** [2] Sir Michael Stoute 4-9-7 Pat Eddery 7/2: 11-212: 4 b c Doyoun - Kalamba (Green Dancer) In tch, rdn over 3f out, hdwy 2f out, styd on well for press to take narrow lead ins last, edged silty right & collared last strides: well bckd, jockey referred to JC over whip use: clearly stays 10f & lost nothing in defeat: top-class & lightly rcd 4yo who shld gain Gr 1 success this summer: see 2064.		hd	125
+1587	**SHIVA 33** [3] H R A Cecil 4-9-4 T Quinn 4/1: 02-013: 5 ch m Hector Protector - Lingerie (Shirley Heights) Keen, handy, hdwy when short or room over 1f out, close 3rd & hard rdn when squeezed out ins last: hvly bckd: would have gone closer with a clr run & can find comp, prob on an easier surface: see 1587 (Gr 3, soft).		2½	118
-1848	**SAKHEE 28** [5] J L Dunlop 3-8-10 R Hills 7/4: 1-1124: Led 2f, led again briefly over 2f out, onepace for press: hvly bckd: poss unsuited by drop back to 10f, but did not fire today: rnr-up in Epsom Derby in 1848 (wnr & 3rd impressive Gr 1 wnrs since) & could have to forgive him this.		1½	119
1827	**FANTASTIC LIGHT 29** [1] 4-9-7 J Reid 5/1: 10-125: Handy, hard rdn 2f out, no extra: nicely bckd: 3rd in this race last term but prob best around 12f as in 1827.		2	116
2149	**GOLD ACADEMY 15** [7] 4-9-7 Dane O'Neill 33/1: 34-666: Held up, rdn over 2f out, no impress: swtg, needs stks/List company: see 2149, 1057.		3	112$
1827	**BORDER ARROW 29** [8] 5-9-7 S Sanders 16/1: 3-6237: Waited with, outpcd over 3f out, brief eff over 2f out, sn btn, fin tired: swtg & boiled over in prelims: worth forgiving this, promising in 1827.		14	92
1530	**SUN CHARM 42** [6] 3-8-10 (VIS) D O'Donohoe 150/1: 15-38: Slow away, hdwy to lead after 2f, hdd & wknd qckly over 2f out: on wk abs, visor, intended pacemaker: see 1530.		8	80

8 ran   Time 2m 05.32 (1.22)   (Mrs John Magnier & Mr M Tabor)   A P O'Brien Ballydoyle, Co.Tipperary.

2498   4.40 THEODORE GODDARD HCAP 3YO+ 0-90 (C)   2m78y   Good/Firm 25   -19 Slow   [87]
£14105   £4340   £2170   £1085

2092	**RENZO 17** [7] J L Harris 7-8-12 (71) S Sanders 14/1: -11301: 7 b g Alzao - Watership (Foolish Pleasure) In tch, gd hdwy 2f out, styd on to lead ins last, pushed out: earlier scored here at Sandown & Thirsk (h'caps): back in 98/99 won over timber at Ascot (debut, nov, rtd 132h): unplcd on the Level in '99 (rtd 80): '98 wnr at Doncaster (h'cap, rtd 84): eff 14f, suited by 2m on any trk, loves Sandown: acts on firm, hvy & best without blnks: revitalised by hobday operation last winter & still on a fair mark.			78
2336	**VIRGIN SOLDIER 7** [11] M Johnston 4-9-10 (83) M Roberts 11/4 FAV: 12-102: 4 ch g Waajib - Never Been Chaste (Posse) Cl-up, went on 3f out till ins last, no extra: poor run of wnr: hvly bckd: back to form: tough.		2	87
1800	**BRAVE TORNADO 30** [9] G B Balding 9-9-5 (78) S Carson 12/1: 122453: 9 ch g Dominion - Accuracy (Gunner B) Prom, eff to chall over 1f out, onepace: gd run on grnd faster than ideal: see 1527.		1¾	80
2153	**TENSILE 15** [10] J R Fanshawe 5-9-11 (84) Pat Eddery 10/1: 6-0004: Chsd ldrs, badly hmpd & dropped rear over 1f out, styd on strongly ins last, too late: sure to have gone close with a clr run, keep tabs on.		¾	85+
2336	**CHRISTIANSTED 7** [4] 3-9-8 (81) A Daly 13/2: 2-6105: Handy, slightly short of room over 1f out but appeared held anyway: see 2336, 1686.		1¼	81
2092	**MANE FRAME 17** [6] 5-8-10 (69) D O'Donohoe 6/1: 002106: Handy, rdn & onepace fnl 2f: best 1711.		nk	68
2173	**DANEGOLD 14** [2] 8-7-13 (57)(1ow) Craig Williams 9/1: 045407: Bhd, eff over 2f out, kept on late: signs of a return to form & has slipped to a v handy mark: see 1996.		¾	55
*1440	**PULAU PINANG 47** [5] 4-9-7 (80)(t) T Quinn 9/1: 0-2218: Waited with, gd hdwy over 2f out, wknd		shd	78

over 1f out: 7 wk abs: poss not see out this stiff 2m, interesting back at around 13f as in 1440.
2092 **PRAIRIE FALCON 17** [3] 6-10-0 (87) J Reid 10/1: -604F9: Al bhd: top weight, see 2092. *3* **82**
1791 **NICELY 30** [1] 4-9-6 (79) R Hills 12/1: 10-050: Al bhd: 10th: btr 1791, 1527 (soft). *6* **68**
2176 **AMEZOLA 13** [8] 4-8-6 (65)(tBL) Dane O'Neill 33/1: -06600: Chsd ldr till wknd well over 2f out: *3* **51**
11th, tried blnks to no avail: see 1928, 1527.
2305 **TOTAL DELIGHT 8** [12] 4-9-12 (85)(t) P Doe 12/1: 004120: Led till 3f out, wknd qckly: 12th, *dist* **0**
surely better than this: see 2305, 1991 (14f).
12 ran Time 3m 36.95 (7.15) (Cleartherm Ltd) J L Harris Eastwell, Leics

2499 **5.15 COPACABANA HCAP 3YO 0-85 (D) 1m2f Good/Firm 25 -12 Slow [90]**
£7507 £2310 £1155 £577

1697 **THUNDERING SURF 35** [1] J R Jenkins 3-8-13 (75) S Whitworth 14/1: 5-001: 3 b c Lugana Beach - **84**
Thunder Bug (Secreto) Bhd, eff over 2f out, switched right & squeezed through to lead appr fnl 1f, styd on,
drvn out: lkd superb: promise in 3 mdns, eye-catching on latest start: rtd 81 sole unplcd juv start: stays
a stiff 10f well, further shld suit: acts on gd/firm grnd: lightly rcd & open to improvement.
*2186 **RICH VEIN 13** [8] S P C Woods 3-8-8 (70)(vis) S Sanders 7/2 FAV: -42112: 3 b g Up And At'Em - *¾* **77**
Timissara (Shahrastani) In tch, hdwy & not clr run 2f out, switched right & styd on well ins last, held by wnr:
hvly bckd & must have gone v close with clr run: acts on gd, gd/firm & equitrack: progressing well, see 2186.
1885 **POLAR RED 25** [6] M J Ryan 3-9-7 (83) P McCabe 13/2: -31243: 3 ch g Polar Falcon - Sharp Top *1½* **88**
(Sharpo) Bhd, hdwy & not clr run 2f out, kept on same pace fnl 1f: gd run: see 1637, 1491.
2358 **KINGDOM OF GOLD 6** [12] Sir Mark Prescott 3-9-5 (81) G Duffield 5/1: 16-044: Led 1f, cl-up, *3* **82**
onepace over 1f out: qck reapp, see 2358.
2321 **EXILE 7** [3] 3-8-6 (68) T Quinn 10/1: 400-25: In tch, outpcd over 3f out, styd on strongly over 1f *hd* **69+**
out, nrst fin: totally unsuited by drop back to 10f, shown enough to win a race with a return to 12f.
2030 **MANDOOB 20** [11] 3-8-13 (75) R Hills 16/1: 5-0456: Bhd, eff & edged right over 1f out, no dngr. *1½* **74**
*2053 **MUSCHANA 19** [14] 3-9-7 (83) Pat Eddery 9/2: 32-317: Led after 1f till wknd over 1f out: btr 2053. *½* **81**
*2019 **FAYRWAY RHYTHM 20** [9] 3-9-4 (80) M Roberts 14/1: -44518: In tch, eff 2f out, wknd over 1f out. *2½* **74**
*2166 **SOLLER BAY 14** [4] 3-9-6 (82) N Callan 8/1: 131019: In tch, wknd over 1f out: nicely bckd: btr 2166. *¾* **75**
2213 **NINNOLO 11** [13] 3-8-8 (70)(t) Dane O'Neill 33/1: 5300: Handy, btn when short of room over 1f out. *hd* **62**
4599} **THREE LIONS 247** [10] 3-8-6 (68) S Carson (5) 20/1: 040-0: Handy, wknd 2f out: reapp, 11th: 3 *1½* **57**
unplcd but pleasing juv starts (rtd 67, inadequate sprint trips): full brother to useful stayer Spunky: dam
plater over hdles: will need 10f+, stable in fine heart & shld be much sharper for this.
2235 **GRUINART 10** [15] 3-8-10 (72) D O'Donohoe 12/1: 043140: Keen bhd, no impress over 2f out: 12th: *2½* **57**
not stay 10f?: btr 2235, 2025 (1m).
2322 **ORIENT EXPRESS 7** [2] 3-8-6 (68) J D Smith 33/1: 00030: Keen in tch, btn over 2f out: 13th. *6* **44**
1637 **BOX CAR 37** [7] 3-8-5 (67) F Norton 20/1: 532200: In tch, wknd over 2f out: fin last, op 10/1, see 1199. *¾* **42**
14 ran Time 2m 07.86 (3.76) (Mr C N & Mrs J C Wright) J R Jenkins Royston, Herts.

HAYDOCK SATURDAY JULY 8TH Lefthand, Flat, Galloping Track

Official Going GOOD TO FIRM. Stalls: 5f & 6f - Centre, 1m & 4f - Outside.

2500 **2.35 EBF FILLIES NOV STKS 2YO (D) 6f Good/Firm 33 -64 Slow**
£3841 £1182 £591 £295

-- **GREEN TAMBOURINE** [2] R Charlton 2-8-5 K Darley 10/11 FAV: 1: 2 b f Green Desert - Maid For The **86**
Hills (Indian Ridge) Dsptd lead, went on halfway, pshd clr ins last: hvly bckd on debut: 250,000gns Mar first
foal, dam useful 6f juv: eff at 6f on fast, will get 7f: runs well fresh: shld improve & win again.
2088 **PROUD BOAST 17** [3] Mrs G S Rees 2-9-2 J F Egan 20/1: -102: 2 b f Komaite - Red Rosein (Red *2½* **87**
Sunset) Mid-div, imprvd 2f out, styd on for press but no ch with wnr: apprec step up to 6f, acts on fast & gd/soft.
-- **FOREVER TIMES** [7] T D Easterby 2-8-5 T E Durcan 14/1: 3: 2 b f So Factual - Simply Times *hd* **76+**
(Dodge) Slow start & last, gd progress to chase wnr appr fnl 1f, no extra & hung left inside last: clr rem:
Feb first foal, sire a sprinter: stays 6f on fast grnd: will find a maiden.
2318 **DIVINE WIND 7** [8] B A McMahon 2-8-13 D Holland 8/1: 140334: In tch, feeling pace 2f out, no threat. *2½* **77**
-- **TROYS GUEST** [5] 2-8-5 W Supple 50/1: 5: Rear, not much room appr fnl 1f, switched & some hdwy: *nk* **68+**
Be My Guest Feb foal, half-sister to a couple of mid dist/stayers: improve & will relish 7f+.
*1312 **BARATHIKI 28** [6] 2-9-2 J Fortune 3/1: -146: Narrow lead till halfway, fdd bef dist: bckd from *1½* **75**
9/2: 4th of 10 in an Italian Listed event since winning debut in 1312.
-- **ESPANA** [1] 2-8-5 M Hills 7/1: 7: Wide, in tch till dist: 32,000gns Hernando Feb foal: half-sister *shd* **64**
to juv sprinters Marl & Rowaasi: dam a sprinter, sire a 12f performer: with B Hills.
2174 **EFFERVESCE 13** [4] 2-8-9 J Quinn 20/1: 468: Bhd ldrs till wknd appr fnl 1f: tchd 33/1: stiff task. *2* **62**
8 ran Time 1m 17.14 (5.84) (Mountgrange Stud) R Charlton Beckhampton, Wilts

2501 **3.05 GR 3 LANCASHIRE OAKS STKS 3YO+ (A) 1m4f Good/Firm 33 +11 Fast**
£24000 £9200 £4600 £2200 3 yo rec 13lb

2404 **ELA ATHENA 7** [7] M A Jarvis 4-9-3 P Robinson 5/1: 12-041: 4 gr f Ezzoud - Crodelle (Formidable) **110**
Chsd ldrs, brght centre in str & sn led, kept on well despite edging left, rdn out: fast time, qk reapp: '99 wnr
at Newbury (fill mdn) & Chepstow (List, Gr 1 rnr up, rtd 114): eff at 12f on firm/fast grnd, handles gd/soft &
likes gall tracks: goes well fresh: smart filly, attempts to go one better in Yorshire Oaks next time.
1828 **SOLAIA 29** [4] P F I Cole 3-8-4 J F Egan 16/1: 5-4102: 3 ch f Miswaki - Indian Fashion (General *1½* **105**
Holme) Mid div, boxed in 4f out till 3f out, styd on well once clr but wnr got first run: improved effort &
appreciated return to fast grnd: suited by 11/12f & is v useful, win another Listed race: see 1223.
2339 **CHEZ CHERIE 7** [3] L M Cumani 3-8-4 W Supple 16/1: 5-0443: 3 ch f Wolfhound - Gerante *1½* **103**
(Private Account) Rear, prog to go 3rd 3f out, same pace dist: qk reapp: ran to best, stays a gall 12f, see 1185.
2112 **INTERLUDE 16** [8] Sir Michael Stoute 3 8-5(1ow) R Hughes 5/2 FAV: 1-34: Waited with, not clr run *½* **103**
ent str till 2f out, styd on for press, nvr nr to chall: well bckd: would have made the frame: goes on fast & soft
grnd: also found plenty of trouble in 2112 & worth another chance with more positive tactics: see 2112 (Gr 2).
1325 **LIMELIGHTING 52** [6] 4-9-3 J Fortune 12/1: 212-45: Rear, prog to chase wnr 3f out, kept on onepce. *¾* **101**
2116 **FILM SCRIPT 16** [9] 3-8-4 K Darley 3/1: 61136: Mid div, under press appr fnl 3f, never any *½* **100**

impression on ldrs: well bckd from 4/1: prob ran to best back on quicker grnd, see 2116 (h'cap, 1282).
1223 **FAME AT LAST** 59 [1] 3-8-4 M Hills 12/1: 1-47: Led till over 3f out, btn bef dist & eased: 8 wk abs. 8 90
2114 **ENDORSEMENT** 16 [11] 4-9-6 W Ryan 8/1: 116-08: Pld hard, mid div, outpcd 3f out: big drop in trip. 2 90
1828 **DOLLAR BIRD** 29 [5] 3-8-4 G Carter 12/1: 0-3209: Rear, chsd ldrs bef halfway till wknd 3f out. ½ 86
2169 **SHAMAIEL** 14 [2] 3-8-4 B Marcus 25/1: -440: Chsd ldrs till wknd qckly 3f out: 10th, highly tried mdn. 1 85
1828 **SO PRECIOUS** 29 [10] 3-8-4 J Quinn 50/1: 1-4000: Never in it: 11th, highly tried, see 1108. 3 82
11 ran　Time 2m 30.42 (2.62)　(Andreas Michael)　M A Jarvis Newmarket Suffolk

---

2502　**3.40 OLD NEWTON CUP HCAP 3YO+ 0-110 (B)**　**1m4f**　**Good/Firm 33**　**+04 Fast**　[108]
£36887　£11350　£5675　£2837　3 yo rec 13lb

2069 **RADAS DAUGHTER** 18 [8] I A Balding 4-8-11 (91) K Darley 11/1: 0-0001: 4 br f Robellino - Drama 98
School (Young Generation) Patiently rdn, steady prog ent straight, styd on to lead below dist, drvn out: fair time:
'99 wnr at Bath, Windsor, Ascot & Newmarket (h'caps, rtd 92): rtd 74 in '98: eff at 12f, shld stay further:
acts on firm, soft & any track, suited by stiff/gall ones: useful & back to form.
*2004 **ALVA GLEN** 21 [14] Sir Michael Stoute 3-8-7 (100) R Hughes 6/1: 1-6012: 3 b c Gulch - Domludge 1½ 104
(Lyphard) Prom, rdn to lead appr fnl 2f, hdd bef dist, styd on but not as well as wnr: fine run from this
progressive, useful 3yo: eff at 10/12f: shld win again: see 2004.
+2178 **ARABIAN MOON** 13 [15] C E Brittain 4-8-9 (89) P Robinson 7/1: -03513: 4 ch c Barathea - Excellent 1 91
Alibi (Exceller) Held up, prog 3f out & led bef dist till fnl 150y, no extra: gd run back up in trip, see 2178.
2127 **HANNIBAL LAD** 15 [13] W M Brisbourne 4-7-10 (76)(1oh) G Baker (7) 25/1: 421144: Held up, wide into ½ 77
straight & improved, ended up on stands side rail dist, same pace: tough, see 1839.
1845 **GENTLEMAN VENTURE** 28 [6] 4-7-12 (78) D Glennon (7) 12/1: -36425: Mid div, prog to track ldrs 1½ 77
going well 3f out, soon rdn & edged left, no extra 1f out: stays 12f, may apprec a drop bck to 10f: see 1845, 1968.
2069 **AKBAR** 18 [12] 4-9-5 (99) M Hills 16/1: 0-1106: Cl up, led ent str till bef 2f out, wknd fnl 1f: see 1903. 1 97
1247 **ELMUTABAKI** 58 [7] 4-10-0 (108) W Supple 14/1: 150-57: In tch, chsd ldrs 2f out, soon onepace. hd 76
2069 **RAIN IN SPAIN** 18 [3] 4-9-10 (104) D Holland 8/1: -32408: Waited with, prog into mid div 3f nk 101
out, sn no further impression: becoming hard to place, see 732.
+2279 **COURT SHAREEF** 9 [4] 5-7-11 (77) J Quinn 4/1 FAV: -13119: Same pl thr'out: bckd, progressive prev. 1 72
2738} **STRATEGIC CHOICE** 358 [5] 9-9-5 (99) J Fortune 33/1: 0/46-0: Prom till 3f out: 10th: ran twice in '99 4 89
(rtd 85): last won in '97 in Turkey (rtd 118): former Gr 1 wnr: eff at 12/14f on firm & gd grnd, with/without blinks.
2191 **PIPED ABOARD** 12 [9] 5-7-13 (79)(bl) A Polli (3) 33/1: 00-350: Al towards rear: 11th, now wth T Barron. ½ 68
2002 **CELESTIAL WELCOME** 21 [11] 5-7-13 (79) N Kennedy 10/1: 610000: Al bhd & came stands side in 1¼ 66
the straight: 12th: won this last term on favoured easy grnd (rtd 91): see 986 (here, hvy).
2279 **HIBERNATE** 9 [10] 6-7-10 (76)(3oh) P M Quinn (3) 25/1: 0420S0: Sn led, hdd appr str & lost pl: 13th. 5 57
*1929 **TOTAL CARE** 24 [1] 3-7-10 (89) J Lowe 5/1: 22210: Cl up, led bef straight till appr fnl 3f, btn & 6 64
hung right: 14th on h'cap bow: some of stable's runners below par: see 1929 (made all).
14 ran　Time 2m 31.24 (3.44)　(Mrs Richard Plummer)　I A Balding Kingsclere, Hants

---

2503　**4.15 LISTED JULY TROPHY STKS 3YO (A)**　**1m4f**　**Good/Firm 33**　**-15 Slow**
£15015　£4620　£2310　£1155

*2208 **MARIENBARD** 12 [4] M A Jarvis 3-8-10 P Robinson 9/1: 111: 3 b c Caerleon - Marienbad (Darshaan) 111
Hld up, prog 2f out, rdn bef dist, ran on strgly for hard driving to get up fnl strides: unbtn, earlier won
debut at Leicester (mdn) & Windsor (match, stks): unrcd juv: eff at 12f on fast & gd/soft, any trk: runs well
fresh: smart & v progressive colt, shade more improvement shld see him go close in the Great Voltigeur.
4483} **AIR MARSHALL** 259 [3] Sir Michael Stoute 3-8-10 R Hughes 7/2: -214-2: 3 ch c The Wings - Troyanna hd 110
(Troy) Rcd in 2nd, led 2f out, kept on well but collared line, winning jockeys strength the decisive factor: bckd
from 5/1, reapp: '99 Goodwood wnr (mdn, Gr 1 4th, rtd 104): eff at 1m last term, suited by longer 12f trip: acts
on firm/fast grnd, any trk: best up with/forcing the pace: v useful & shld find similar soon (St Leger entry).
1848 **ST EXPEDIT** 28 [2] G Wragg 3-8-10 D Holland 11/4: 201203: 3 b c Sadler's Wells - Miss Rinjani 1¼ 108
(Shirley Heights) In tch, prog & every ch appr fnl 1f, no extra 100y: clr rem: ran well & stays 12f but
looks sure to apprec a drop bck to 10f: acts on fast & gd/soft: see 1103.
2148 **ZAFONIUM** 15 [1] P F I Cole 3-8-10 J Fortune 5/4 FAV: 31-24: Led till 2f out, fdd: well bckd: 8 98
unsuited forcing the pace & prob prefers easier grnd tho' reapp was a big improvement on juv form: see 2148.
2068 **OPTIMAITE** 15 [5] D Hind 3-8-10 G Hind 7/1: 0-3105: Bhd, eff 3f out, soon btn, eased dist: tchd 10/1. 5 93
5 ran　Time 2m 33.63 (5.83)　(Saif Ali)　M A Jarvis Newmarket, Suffolk

---

2504　**4.50 AWARD WINNER HCAP 3YO 0-100 (C)**　**6f**　**Good/Firm 33**　**-26 Slow**　[98]
£7085　£2180　£1090　£545

2117 **PAYS DAMOUR** 16 [12] R Hannon 3-8-5 (75) J Quinn 15/2: -02001: 3 b c Pursuit Of Love - Lady Of 80
The Land (Wollow) Prom going well, led appr fnl 1f & rdn, held on well: '99 Epsom wnr (4 rnr nursery, rtd 76):
apprec drop back to 6f after trying 1m: suited by firm/fast grnd & being up with/forcing the pace on any track.
2101 **ROO** 17 [7] R F Johnson Houghton 3-9-7 (91) M Hills 11/2: 065322: 3 b f Rudimentary - Shall We ½ 94
Run (Hotfoot) In tch, prog to chase wnr appr fnl 2f, kept on for press, held nr fin: bckd, jt top-weight, useful.
*2288 **BOANERGES** 8 [14] R Guest 3-8-9 (79) D Holland 4/1: 000113: 3 br c Caerleon - Sea Siren ¾ 79
(Slip Anchor) Dwelt, improved going well 2f out, rousted bef dist, kept on but found less than expected:
well bckd: gd run but a sharper 6f or return to 5f likely to suit this speedy, improving colt: see 2288.
2168 **HONESTY FAIR** 14 [8] J A Glover 3-8-12 (82) S Finnamore (5) 25/1: 110004: Slow away, held up, 1½ 77
going well but shorn of room/lost pl 2f out, kept on fnl 1f, never dngrs: unlucky in running last trace, keep an eye on.
2101 **INDIAN MUSIC** 17 [10] 3-8-2 (70)(2ow) G Carter 14/1: 0-0045: Towards rear, drvn & hdwy appr fnl ½ 65
1f, onepace inside last: nvr far off best: prob handles fast grnd, sole win on hvy: try 7f next: see 1654.
*2216 **CORUNNA** 11 [2] 3-8-9 (79) T E Durcan 9/1: 331316: Held up, wide prog appr fnl 1f, no extra fnl 1f. ½ 71
2334 **EASTWAYS** 7 [5] 3-9-0 (84) R Hughes 12/1: 300007: Pulled hard bhd, came stands rail & improved 1 73
halfway, styd on but never troubled ldrs: tchd 14/1, quick reapp: return to 7f will suit: see 982.
2101 **PIPADASH** 17 [6] 3-9-7 (91) J Fortune 16/1: -20008: Restrained, nvr nr to chall & eased below dist. 2½ 74
1308 **CARD GAMES** 53 [11] 3-8-13 (83) K Darley 10/3 FAV: 000129: Well plcd, fdd bef fnl 1f: nicely bckd. ¾ 64
2165 **RYTHM N TIME** 14 [9] 3-8-3 (73) W Supple 11/1: 30-040: Prom, lost pl appr fnl 1f: 10th, see 2165, 1220. 2½ 48
2101 **FINE MELODY** 17 [13] 3-8-7 (77) W Ryan 16/1: 311400: Led till appr fnl 1f, eased: 11th, see 773. 3½ 42
2101 **KILBRANNAN SOUND** 17 [1] 3-8-3 (73) P Robinson 20/1: 0-4500: Prom, wide & ch till wknd appr fnl 1½ 34
1f: 12th, prob not the best of draws in stall 1: see 1219.
2003 **SAFRANINE** 21 [3] 3-9-1 (85) J F Egan 25/1: 0-0000: Al towards rear: 13th, see 630. ½ 45

HAYDOCK   SATURDAY JULY 8TH   Lefthand, Flat, Galloping Track

1384 **SABRE LADY 49** [4] 3-8-13 (83) C Lowther 20/1: 30-340: In tch, wide, under press/hmpd 2f out: 14th.   ½   42
14 ran   Time 1m 14.81 (3.51)   (Mrs M W Bird)   R Hannon East Everleigh, Wilts

---

2505   5.25 VALE (UK) HCAP 3YO+ 0-70 (E)   5f   Good/Firm 33   -19 Slow   [70]
£3122   £892   £446   3 yo rec 5 lb

2444 **XANADU 2** [2] Miss L A Perratt 4-9-12 (68) C Lowther 7/1: 120101: 4 ch g Casteddu - Bellatrix (Persian   77
Bold) Nvr far away, led ent fnl 2f, rdn & ran on strongly: ran 48hrs ago: earlier won at Hamilton (2f, incl
class stks) & Musselburgh (h'caps): '99 wnr again at Hamilton (sell) & Carlisle (h'cap, rtd 56): eff at 5/6f
on firm/fast grnd, any track, likes stiff ones, likeable customer: suited forcing the pace: tough, still imprvg.
2158 **BOLLIN RITA 14** [14] T D Easterby 4-9-3 (59) J Fortune 12/1: -00002: 4 b f Rambo Dancer - Bollin   2   62
Harriet (Lochnager) Held up, gd prog appr fnl 1f & went 2nd below dist, no impression wnr: coped with
drop back to 5f, sole win at 6f: h'capped to go in soon: see 2158.
2240 **PALACEGATE TOUCH 10** [5] A Berry 10-8-2 (44)(bl) G Carter 25/1: 300303: 10 gr g Petong - Dancing   1   44
Chimes (London Bells) Held up, kept on well appr fnl 1f, never nearer: op 16/1: 10yo, ran to best, see 1139.
2340 **MUKARRAB 7** [13] D W Chapman 6-8-10 (52) K Darley 6/1: 010044: Handy, rdn/not qckn appr fnl 1f.   nk   51
*2204 **PARADISE YANGSHUO 12** [17] 3-8-2 (49) W Supple 12/1: -00415: Well plcd, rdn appr fnl 1f, hung left.   1¼   44
1806 **LORD HIGH ADMIRAL 29** [16] 12-8-10 (52)(vis) W Ryan 14/1: 140046: Led till bef dist, no extra: see 673.   1   44
2240 **GAD YAKOUN 10** [8] 7-7-10 (38)(8oh) Angela Hartley (4) 40/1: -00007: Al arnd same pl, edged left fnl 1f.   nk   29
+2326 **SIHAFI 7** [9] 7-9-3 (59) P Goode (3) 4/1: 023618: Slow away, nvr better than mid div: too sn after 2326?   1   47
2418 **RING OF LOVE 3** [11] 4-9-7 (63)(vis) R Cody Boutcher (7) 16/1: 303009: Never dangerous: quick reapp.   ½   49
1877 **RED TYPHOON 26** [4] 3-9-8 (69) M Hills 20/1: 0-0000: Hmpd start, nvr in it & forced to race wide: 10th.   ½   54
2252 **KNOCKEMBACK NELLIE 10** [12] 4-9-10 (66)(bl) J F Egan 10/1: 012100: Chsd ldrs till 2f out: 11th.   ¾   44
1781 **RED CHARGER 31** [3] 4-9-7 (63) R Hughes 10/1: 01-000: Mid-div, not much room 2f out, btn after: 12th.   1¼   41
2252 **MARINO STREET 10** [7] 7-9-2 (58) D Holland 7/2 FAV: 0-2111W: Withdrawn bef start: won this in '99.
2252 **Tick Tock 10** [15] 3-8-5 (52) P Robinson 16/1:   2252 **Bodfari Times 10** [1] 4-7-10 (38)(2oh) J Lowe 50/1:
2252 **Kerridge Chapel 10** [10] 3-7-11 (44) N Kennedy 50/1:
16 ran   Time 1m 01.39 (2.59)   (David Sutherland - Ian Hay)   Miss L A Perratt Ayr, Strathclyde

---

LEICESTER   SATURDAY JULY 8TH   Righthand, Stiff, Galloping Track

Official Going   GOOD TO FIRM Stalls: Stands Side

2506   2.05 GARY & SARAH'S HCAP DIV 1 3YO 0-70 (E)   1m str   Good/Firm 29   -11 Slow   [74]
£3168   £975   £487   £243

2012 **DATURA 21** [3] M L W Bell 3-8-10 (56) J Mackay (5) 11/2: 0-0641: 3 b f Darshaan - Realize (Al Nasr)   60
Settled gd hdwy 2f out, ran on well for press ins last to lead cl-home, drvn out: op 7/1, 1st win: plcd
in '99 for J Gosden (rtd 86, rnr-up, fill mdn): eff at 6f/1m, has tried 10f: acts on fast & gd, stiff/gall trk.
2187 **CAPACOOSTIC 12** [5] S R Bowring 4-7-10 (46)(3oh) Claire Bryan (5) 50/1: 00-002: 3 ch f Savahra   shd   45
Sound - Cocked Hat Girl (Ballacashtal) Cl-up, led dist, drvn out, hdd line: mod form prev: eff at 1m on fast grnd.
2332 **LOUP CERVIER 7** [9] S Dow 3-8-0 (46) R Ffrench 25/1: 000003: 3 b g Wolfhound - Luth d'Or   ¾   47
(Noir Et Or) Cl-up, outpcd 4f out, rdn/ran on late, nrst fin: quick reapp & 1st time in the frame: eff at 1m on fast.
1726 **PRINCE OMID 33** [13] J R Fanshawe 3-9-7 (67) O Urbina 10/1: -34004: Cl-up, went on after halfway,   ½   67
hung left & hdd dist, no extra for press: clr rem, top weight: visor omitted: see 1726.
1793 **HEATHYARDS LAD 30** [1] J Carroll 3-9-1 (61) J Carroll 10/1: 325655: Dwelt, hdwy from rear when hung right   4   54
appr fnl 1f, no danger: op 8/1, one win in 25: see 976.
2166 **COSMIC SONG 14** [8] 3-8-7 (53) Dean McKeown 13/2: 351446: Dwelt, rear, late hdwy, no threat: ½   45
drop in trip & will apprec a return to 9f+: see 1722.
1292 **WOODBASTWICK CHARM 54** [15] 3-8-3 (49) J Tate 33/1: 0-0007: Mid-div at best: 8 wk abs, new stable. nk   41
2243 **PRETENDING 10** [10] 3-8-4 (50) A Beech 8/1: 653608: Nvr a factor: op 6/1: see 1723.   1   40
1399 **OZAWA 49** [6] 3-8-5 (51) R Mullen 20/1: 0-009: Front rank, wknd fnl 2f: 7 wk abs: mod 6f mdn form.   ½   40
1997 **LUCKY STAR 21** [7] 3-9-8 (55) J D Smith 12/1: 131400: Led, hdd after 4f, sn fdd: 10th: see 1997.   nk   44
*2345 **PINHEIROS DREAM 7** [11] 3-9-5 (65)(bl) D R McCabe 5/1 JT FAV: 050310: Prom, rdn/lost tch   1   51
fnl 2f, eased, fin 11th: quick reapp: btr 2345 (clear, firm).
2331 **CALDEY ISLAND 7** [2] 3-8-4 (50) J Stack 14/1: -00000: Al rear, fin 12th: quick reapp.   3½   31
2025 **COMMONWOOD 20** [14] 3-9-4 (64) N Pollard 5/1 JT FAV: 06-400: Waited with, lost tch halfway, 13th.   3½   40
1877 **Silver Auriole 26** [12] 3-7-10 (42)(bl) (7oh) S Righton 66/1:
2026 **The Diddler 20** [4] 3-7-11 (43) M Baird 7/1:
15 ran   Time 1m 37.6 (3.2)   (Lord Hartington)   M L W Bell Newmarket

---

2507   2.40 CENTURY 106 SELLER 2YO (G)   5f str   Good/Firm 29   -25 Slow
£1876   £536   £268

812 **ACORN CATCHER 96** [6] B Palling 2-8-6 D McGaffin (4) 33/1: 01: 2 b f Emarati - Anytime Baby (Bairn)   64
Dwelt, sn in tch, hdwy/stumbled 3f out, led 2f out, drvn out: bt in for 4,500 gns: long abs & t.o. sole prev
start: 2,000 gns 1st foal, dam 5f scorer: eff on 5f on fast, poss not soft: runs well fresh in selling grade.
1381 **SCREAMIN GEORGINA 49** [1] S C Williams 2-8-6 (t) J Tate 6/5 FAV: 02: 2 b f Muhtarram - Carrie   1   62
Kool (Prince Sabo) Front rank, eff/hung right appr fnl 1f, kept on ins last, no pace of wnr: nicely bckd,
7 wk abs: wore a t-strap: shade better expected on this drop to sells: stays 5f on fast: see 1381.
2394 **MISS EQUINOX 4** [3] N Tinkler 2-8-6 Kim Tinkler 5/2: 50223: 2 b f Presidium - Miss Nelski (Most   ½   61
Secret) Prom, rdn & hung right dist, no extra well ins last: quick reapp: v consistent, eff at 5/6f: see 2394.
1679 **BAYRAMI 35** [4] S E Kettlewell 2-8-6 A Beech (5) 66/1: 050004: Led 2f out, sn held: mod prev form.   1½   57
1918 **CAPTAINS FOLLY 24** [5] 2-8-6 V Halliday 50/1: -005: Handy, rdn/btn fnl 2f: see 1918.   1½   54
2196 **DIAMOND MILLENNIUM 12** [6] 2-8-6 (VIS) J Mackay (5) 7/1: 053336: Al in rear: visored: see 2052.   5   44
2120 **GOLGOTHA 16** [7] 2-8-6 P Bradley (5) 8/1: 057: Dwelt, al bhd: op 5/1: see 1906.   ¾   43
--   **SHARP VISION** [8] 2-8-6 Dean McKeown 9/1: 8: Rear, lost tch halfway: op 5/1, debut: 3,500 gns   14   18
half-sister to a decent 1m scorer: dam unrcd: with J S Moore.
8 ran   Time 1m 01.0 (2.7)   (N C Phillips & T Davies)   B Palling Cowbridge, Vale Of Glamorgan

LEICESTER   SATURDAY JULY 8TH   Righthand, Stiff, Galloping Track

2508   3.10 A ALLEN CLASSIFIED STKS 3YO+ 0-70 (E)   7f str   Good/Firm 29   +09 Fast
£3705   £1140   £570   £285   3 yo rec 8 lb

*2215 **YEAST 11** [13] W J Haggas 8-9-5 J P Spencer 2/1 FAV: -02011: 8 b g Salse - Orient (Bay Express)   **79**
Made all, styd on well fnl 1f, rdn out: nicely bckd, fast time: earlier won at Lingfield (stks): '99 wnr at
Chepstow (stks), Salisbury (h'cap) & Ripon (clmr, rtd 89 at best): plcd in '98 (rtd 80): loves to force the
pace at 7f/1m, poss stays 12f: likes firm/fast, handles soft grnd & any trk: v tough & in-form front-runner.
2261 **TEOFILIO 10** [5] A J McNae 6-9-2 (bl) T G McLaughlin 8/1: 600002: 6 ch h Night Shift - Rivoltade   ¾ **74**
(Sir Ivor) Waited with, hdwy fnl 2f, styd on well ins last, not btn far: clr rem: back to form here, on a fair mark.
*2241 **INTRICATE WEB 10** [3] E J Alston 4-9-5 J Mackay (5) 11/2: 600613: 4 b g Warning - In Anticipation   4 **70**
(Sadler's Wells) Sn rdn in rear, gd hdwy appr fnl 1f, kept on, no threat to front 2: shade btr 2241 (h'cap).
2121 **AIR OF ESTEEM 16** [12] P C Haslam 4-9-2 A Beech (5) 16/1: 0-35004: Front rank, rdn/fdd over 1f out.   1 **65**
2215 **AMBER FORT 11** [10] 7-9-2 (vis) R Mullen 12/1: 540555: In tch, eff over 3f out, sn held: tchd 16/1.   1½ **62**
2349 **WEETMANS WEIGH 6** [1] 7-9-2 Dean McKeown 14/1: 046406: Cl-up, fdd fnl 2f: quick reapp: see 49.   ½ **61**
*2278 **BILLY BATHWICK 9** [4] 3-8-11 J Carroll 9/1: 552017: Chsd ldrs, drvn/wknd appr fnl 1f: longer 7f   3 **59**
trip: rated higher when scoring in 2278 (auct mdn, 6f, firm).
2342 **MAGIC FLUTE 7** [7] 4-8-13 N Pollard 10/1: 0-2068: Cl-up, rdn & wknd qckly fnl 2f: quick reapp.   7 **43**
2355 **MR STYLISH 6** [6] 4-9-2 (vis) J Stack 7/1: 233059: Stumbled start, nvr a factor: see 2355.   1 **44**
2442 **TURTLES RISING 2** [11] 4-8-13 (bl) R Lappin 25/1: 0-0300: Prom 5f, fin 10th: ran 48hrs ago.   1 **39**
2330 **Cinnamon Court 7** [2] 3-8-5 C Rutter 25/1:   2317 **Espere Dor 7** [9] 3-8-8 D Griffiths 100/1:
2236 **Four Men 10** [14] 3-8-8 P Bradley (5) 66/1:   2239/ **Jampet 378** [8] 4-9-2 S Righton 100/1:
14 ran   Time 1m 23.4 (1.4)   (The Not Over Big Partnership)   W J Haggas Newmarket

2509   3.45 EBF ADMIRAL HCAP 3YO+ 0-85 (D)   1m3f183y   Good/Firm 29   +01 Fast   [85]
£7182   £2210   £1105   £552   3 yo rec 13lb

1970 **METRONOME 22** [7] L M Cumani 3-8-12 (82) J P Spencer 6/1: 0221: 3 b g Salse - Rapid Repeat   **85**
(Exactly Sharp) Trkd ldrs, hdwy when hmpd appr fnl 1f, switched & styd on well ins last, led cl-home, drvn
out: gd time, h'cap bow: half-sister to a 7f juv wnr: eff at 12f, further could suit: acts on fast,
gd & a stiff/gall trk: progressive & lightly raced filly who shld win again.
*2103 **RED EMPRESS 17** [3] Sir Michael Stoute 3-9-0 (84) J Mackay (5) 2/1 FAV: -2612: 3 b f Nashwan -   ¾ **85**
Nearctic Flame (Sadler's Wells) Dwelt, rear, hdwy to chall 2f out, led appr fnl 1f, hdd cl-home: bckd, gd run.
1958 **MARAHA 22** [8] J L Dunlop 3-8-8 (78) J Carroll 4/1: 610-43: 3 ch f Lammtarra - Taroob (Roberto)   ½ **78**
Settled rear, outpcd 4f out, ran on well for press ins last, not btn far: acts on fast & can win a race at 12f+.
2370 **SURE QUEST 5** [5] D W P Arbuthnot 5-8-4 (61) R Ffrench 7/1: 112234: Trkd ldrs, outpcd 3f out,   hd **61**
rallied & styd on well ins last: quick reapp: tough & consistent: see 1555.
2023 **COMMON CAUSE 20** [2] 4-9-4 (75) R Mullen 8/1: 0-4455: Waited with, rdn & kept on fnl 1f, nrst   1 **73**
fin: op 6/1, clr rem: see 1271.
1959 **FOREST FIRE 22** [11] 5-9-12 (83) N Pollard 15/2: -20036: Pulled hard & sn in clr lead, wknd/hdd   9 **68**
appr fnl 1f, sn lost tch: rcd too keenly for own gd here, needs to learn to settle: see 1959.
-- **SEASONAL 6** [6] 4-9-5 (76) C Rutter 14/1: 1-7: Prom, wknd qckly fnl 2f: reapp/Brit bow: 9 **48**
ex-French, won 3 out of 5 starts in '99 (12f, incl h'cap, v soft): with P R Webber.
2287 **KUWAIT DAWN 8** [9] 4-9-6 (77) J Tate 20/1: -00068: Al bhnd: see 1825.   ½ **48**
2270 **BONNIE FLORA 9** [4] 4-8-5 (62) Dean McKeown 20/1: 0-003U: Keen, saddle slipped/u.r. after 6f.   **0**
9 ran   Time 2m 31.7 (3.4)   (Lord Hartington)   L M Cumani Newmarket

2510   4.20 RACEGOERS CLAIMER 3YO (F)   1m2f   Good/Firm 29   -28 Slow
£2341   £669   £334

1895 **PRESTO 25** [6] W J Haggas 3-9-1 (tbl) J P Spencer 4/1: -05101: 3 b g Namaqualand - Polish Dancer   **62**
(Malinowski) Bhd, gd hdwy 2f out, led appr fnl 1f, pshd clr, readily: earlier won at Newbury (clmr, 1st win):
suited by 10f on fast, gd/soft & a stiff/gall trk: well in in blnks/t-strap & clmrs: win again in this grade.
2246 **UNIMPEACHABLE 10** [5] J M Bradley 3-8-10 Claire Bryan (5) 3/1 JT FAV: 526442: 3 b f Namaqualand -   5 **47**
Bourbon Topsy (Ile de Bourbon) Settled rear, rdn/prog 3f out, styd on but not pace of wnr: see 2033, 1644.
2134 **SPARK OF LIFE 15** [1] P R Chamings 3-8-8 (bl) S Whitworth 3/1 JT FAV: 0-0323: 3 b f Rainbows For   1¾ **42**
Life - Sparkly Girl (Danehill) Rcd keenly in rear, styd on well fnl 2f, no threat to wnr: drifted from
9/4 & a shade better expected on this return to 10f: btr 2134 (1m clmr).
2105 **SNATCH 16** [7] M L W Bell 3-9-0 J Mackay (5) 12/1: 64: Chsd ldrs, hdwy to lead 3f out, hdd appr   1 **46**
fnl 1f, wknd: showed some promise here on only 2nd start, stays 10f on fast: see 2105.
2362 **HIGH BEAUTY 5** [15] 3-8-8 A Beech (5) 40/1: 404005: Waited with, rdn/prog 2f out, sn no extra.   hd **40$**
2013 **HEATHYARDS MATE 21** [8] 3-9-3 Dean McKeown 12/1: 421006: Dwelt, rear, late hdwy: up in trip.   1½ **47**
2141 **WILLIAM THE LION 15** [4] 3-9-5 J Carroll 5/1: -05527: Mid-div at best: op 7/1: btr 2141 (13f h'cap).   5 **42**
2253 **LADY VIENNA 10** [11] 3-8-6 (vis) N Pollard 20/1: 5-5038: Cl-up, wknd qckly appr fnl 1f: btr 2253 (sell).   hd **29**
1803 **THIRTY SIX CEE 29** [9] 3-9-2 J Tate 25/1: -05059: Led to 3f out, sn wknd, eased: see 171.   1¼ **37**
1772 **COULD BE EXPENSIVE 31** [12] 3-9-1 (bl) A Whelan 33/1: -66400: Handy, rdn/lost tch fnl 2f: fin 10th.   shd **36**
2315 **Lammoski 7** [13] 3-8-11 T G McLaughlin 40/1:   2253 **Emmas Hope 10** [14] 3-8-2 R Ffrench 50/1:
2362 **Dinky 5** [2] 3-8-2 M Baird 50/1:
13 ran   Time 2m 08.2 (5.7)   (Mr & Mrs Peter Lumley)   W J Haggas Newmarket

2511   4.55 S JORDAN FILLIES HCAP 3YO 0-70 (E)   6f str   Good/Firm 29   -04 Slow   [73]
£3997   £1230   £615   £307

1877 **WATER BABE 26** [1] J W Payne 3-9-0 (59) N Pollard 11/2: 050-41: 3 b f Lake Coniston - Isabella Sharp   **64**
(Sharpo) Waited with, rdn/prog appr fnl 1f, ran on well ins last, led cl-home, all out: 1st win: rtd 64 when
unplcd in '99 (mdns): eff over a stiff/gall 6f on fast: lightly rcd & speedily bred, op to further improvement.
2044 **MUFFLED 19** [7] J L Dunlop 3-9-0 (60) R Ffrench 11/1: 40-002: 3 ch f Mizaaya - Sound It (Believe It)   shd **64**
Led, hung right appr fnl 1f, styd on for press, hdd nr fin: apprec this drop back to 6f on fast: win similar.
2036 **KIRSCH 19** [8] C A Dwyer 3-8-11 (56)(vis) T G McLaughlin 9/1: 560053: 3 ch f Wolfhound - Pondicherry   1½ **56**
(Sir Wimborne) Cl-up, eff when hmpd appr fnl 1f, no extra ins last: sound run: see 361.
2252 **AUNT DORIS 10** [9] R F Johnson Houghton 3-8-9 (54) J Stack 10/1: 0-6004: Chsd ldrs, drvn & held   shd **54**
well ins last: best run to date this term: see 1467.

LEICESTER   SATURDAY JULY 8TH   Righthand, Stiff, Galloping Track

2280 **CAUTIOUS JOE 9** [6] 3-9-7 (66) R Mullen 9/2: 000355: Cl-up, rdn/outpcd 2f out, rallied & ran on   1   63
well ins last, no threat: top weight: crying out for a step up to 7f: see 2047.
105 **SIMBATU 227** [10] 3-9-3 (62) J Mackay (5) 16/1: 5300-6: With ldr, wknd qckly well ins last: 8 month   ½   58
abs: plcd on 2nd of 3 juv starts (fills auct mdn, rtd 74): eff at 5f, has tried 7f: handles gd grnd.
1390 **DIAMOND RACHAEL 49** [3] 3-9-3 (62)(vis) R Fitzpatrick (3) 14/1: 123667: Chsd ldrs, rdn/fdd appr   2½   52
fnl 1f: 7 wk abs: turf return: better on fibresand in 549.
1787 **SIRENE 30** [2] 3-8-7 (52) A Beech (5) 25/1: 020008: Nvr a threat: see 300 (fibresand).   3½   35
1723 **MADAME GENEREUX 33** [12] 3-8-12 (57) J Carroll 12/1: 0-4569: Front rank, wknd fnl 2f: see 992.   1½   37
514 **WISHEDHADGONEHOME 145** [13] 3-8-6 (51) C Rutter 33/1: -30560: Dwelt, al bhd, 10th: abs, new stable.1½   28
2479 **MOUNT PARK 1** [11] 3-8-5 (50)(bl) Claire Bryan (5) 33/1: 600000: Dwelt, al rear, 11th: ran yesterday.   2   22
2243 **UNFORTUNATE 10** [14] 3-8-7 (52)(bl) V Halliday 7/2 FAV: 001440: Missed break, al well bhd, 12th.   ¾   22
2036 **BALLETS RUSSES 19** [5] 3-8-5 (50) Dean McKeown 10/1: 00-430: Reared & veered right start, al last.   7   6
13 ran   Time 1m 11.8 (2.0)   (Raymond Tooth)   J W Payne Newmarket

---

2512	5.25 GARY & SARAH'S HCAP DIV 2 3YO 0-70 (E) 1m str Good/Firm 29 -08 Slow	[73]
	£3168 £975 £487 £243	

2257 **BISHOPSTONE MAN 10** [10] S Mellor 3-9-5 (64) C Rutter 14/1: 400351: 3 b g Piccolo - Auntie   68
Gladys (Great Nephew) Trkd ldrs, went on 2f out, styd on strongly, rdn out: 1st win: plcd in '99 (mdn,
rtd 71): eff at 6f/1m on fast & soft grnd: handles a stiff/gall trk & likes to races up with/force the pace.
1985 **BAJAN SUNSET 22** [3] J D Bethell 3-8-4 (49) J Tate 25/1: 0-062: 3 ch c Mujtahid - Dubai Lady (Kris)   ½   52
Settled rear, hdwy appr fnl 1f, styd on well ins last, not btn far: eff at 1m on fast: fine h'cap bow, win similar.
2160 **STORMSWELL 14** [12] R A Fahey 3-8-6 (51) R Mullen 5/1: 003153: 3 ch f Persian Bold - Stormswept   ½   53
(Storm Bird) Dwelt, rear, hdwy appr fnl 1f, styd on, nvr nrr: may have won with a level break: in gd form.
2215 **APLOY 11** [15] R F Johnson Houghton 3-9-7 (66) N Pollard 6/1: 30-644: Waited with, rdn to improve   1   66
2f out, no extra well ins last: see 1125.
2330 **TWIST 7** [13] J P Spencer 3-9-4 (63) R Price 10/1: 4-0505: Bhd, prog 2f out, rdn/held ins last: qck reapp.   hd   63
2264 **MISTY MAGIC 9** [1] 3-8-10 (55) R Lappin 10/3 FAV: 004326: Prom, dropped rear halfway, late gains.   2   51
1889 **VICTORIET 25** [8] 3-8-5 (50) Dean McKeown 16/1: 00-557: Dwelt, nvr a factor: see 1435.   shd   46
2320 **SILK ST BRIDGET 7** [11] 3-7-10 (41)(bl) J Mackay (5) 7/1: 000008: Rcd keenly cl-up, wknd   1¼   35
qckly fnl 2f: quick reapp: see 1610.
2080 **PYJAMA GIRL 17** [9] 3-8-9 (54)(BL) S Righton 25/1: -30009: Dwelt, eff halfway, no dngr: blnkd.   1¼   45
2264 **FLYING RUN 9** [6] 3-8-2 (47)(bl) A Whelan 33/1: -00000: Led, hdd over 2f out, sn lost tch, 10th.   nk   38
2147 **BEWILDERED 15** [5] 3-7-10 (41)(bl) Claire Bryan (5) 40/1: 006030: Handy, wknd 2f out, 11th.   7   22
2250 **ALJAZIR 10** [7] 3-8-12 (57) J Carroll 11/2: 205050: Al bhd, fin 12th: tchd 15/2: much btr 2250.   2½   34
2013 **MIDNIGHT MAX 21** [2] 3-7-10 (41)(4oh) J Bramhill 50/1: 50-000: Prom, fdd fnl 2f, fin 13th.   nk   18
2105 **LUCKYS SON 16** [4] 3-8-4 (49) R Ffrench 12/1: 0000: Front rank, lost tch fnl 2f, 14th: h'cap bow.   1¼   24
14 ran   Time 1m 37.4 (3.0)   (The Bishopstone Ducks)   S Mellor Wanborough, Wilts

---

BEVERLEY   SATURDAY JULY 8TH   Righthand, Oval Track With Stiff, Uphill Finish

Official Going   GOOD (GOOD/FIRM Places) Stalls: Inside

2513	2.00 CAPTAIN SELLER 2YO (F) 7f100y rnd Good/Firm 25 -24 Slow	
	£2268 £648 £324	

2388 **RIVER ALN 4** [9] Sir Mark Prescott 2-8-6 (bl) J Fanning 11/1: 051: 2 b f Inchinor - Play With Me (Alzao)   72
Made all, styd on well fnl 2f, rdn out: bght in for 7,200gns: qck reapp: apprec step up to 7.5f & front running
tactics, shld stay 1m+: acts on fast grnd: suited by blnks & drop to sell grade.
2301 **IMPISH LAD 8** [2] B S Rothwell 2-8-11 (bl) J Bramhill 9/2: 523632: 2 b g Imp Society - Madonna Da   6   63
Rossi (Mtoto) Handy, ev ch 2f out, sn held by wnr: op 7/2: met a much imprvd rival: see 2301, 1890.
2155 **BEAUTIFUL BUSINESS 14** [4] M Quinn 2-8-6 R Fitzpatrick (3) 3/1: 033: 2 b f Deploy - Jade Mistress   3   52
(Damister) Rear/bhd, late gains fnl 2f, no threat: op 11/4: see 2155, 1883.
2424 **PRESENTOFAROSE 3** [1] J S Moore 2-8-6 K Dalgleish (5) 14/1: 550234: Cl-up, drvn/wknd over 1f out.   ¾   51
2301 **MASTER COOL 8** [3] 2-8-11 Dale Gibson 12/1: 4455: In tch, btn 2f out: op 7/1: see 2301, 1679.   1¼   53
2312 **CHORUS GIRL 8** [6] 2-8-6 A Culhane 5/2 FAV: 543046: Badly hmpd start & dropped rear, carried wide   ¾   47+
on bend halfway, late gains under minimal press: op 3/1, no luck in running tackling longer 7.5f trip, ignore this.
2059 **PROPERTY ZONE 18** [8] 2-8-11 T Lucas 33/1: 007: Rear, ran wide halfway, nvr factor: longer 7.5f trip.   ¾   51
2312 **BEACON OF LIGHT 8** [7] 2-8-6 M Tebbutt 7/1: -008: In tch, rdn/no impress fnl 3f: op 11/2:   2   42
2059 **SILK SOUK 18** [5] 2-8-6 (VIS) R Winston 25/1: 09: Went left/hmpd start, chsd ldrs 4f: visor.   dist   0
9 ran   Time 1m 34.5 (3.7)   (Cyril Humphris)   Sir Mark Prescott Newmarket

---

2514	2.30 BELLA NOV STKS 2YO (D) 7f100y rnd Good/Firm 25 -03 Slow	
	£4342 £1336 £668 £334	

*2290 **BLACK KNIGHT 8** [1] S P C Woods 2-9-0 M Tebbutt 4/9 FAV: 311: 2 b c Contract Law - Another Move   88
(Farm Walk) Trkd front rank, rdn fnl 3f, led 1f out, styd on well, drvn out: nicely bckd at odds-on: earlier won
easily at Folkestone (auct mdn): eff at 7/7.5f, 1m+ will suit: acts on fast & a stiff or sharp/undul trk: useful.
-- **SPIRIT HOUSE 5** [5] M Johnston 2-8-8 J Fanning 4/1: 2: 2 b c Hansel - Ashwood Angel (Well Decorated)   2   77
Sn cl-up, led 3f out, rdn/hdd 1f out, kept on well: op 5/1: Feb foal, cost $15,000, a 1st foal: dam a US wnr:
stays 7.5f, 1m+ shld suit: acts on fast grnd: encouraging intro, shld find a race.
2057 **SIENA STAR 18** [2] J L Eyre 2-8-12 A Culhane 25/1: -00443: 2 b g Brief Truce - Gooseberry Pie   3   75
(Green Desert) Rdn/rear early, kept on fnl 2f, nvr pace to chall: prob stays 7.5f, h'caps shld suit: see 2057.
*1838 **WITNEY ROYALE 28** [4] J S Moore 2-9-2 Dale Gibson 9/1: 14: Rdn/rear halfway, hdwy over 2f out,   2½   74
no prog over 1f: op 7/1: this longer 7.5f trip shld suit: see 1838.
2363 **CO DOT UK 5** [3] 2-9-5 F Lynch 10/1: 301345: Led, wide on bend halfway, hdd 3f out & fdd fnl 2f.   6   68
5 ran   Time 1m 32.9 (2.1)   (Rex Norton)   S P C Woods Newmarket, Suffolk

793

2515

3.00 MILLERS MILE HCAP 3YO 0-85 (D) 1m100y rnd Good/Firm 25 +04 Fast [91]
£6077 £1870 £935 £467

1477 **FLYING CARPET 44** [7] T D Easterby 3-7-10 (59)(1oh) P Fessey 15/2: -60031: 3 b f Barathea - Flying Squaw (Be My Chief) Dwelt, prog 2f out, drvn & styd on well ins last, won going away: best time of day, 1st win, 6 wk abs: unplcd at York in '99 (rtd 57): eff at 1m, further shld suit: acts on fast & gd/soft, reportedly suited by some cut: handles a stiff trk: runs well fresh: on a fair mark, has a turn of foot & worth following. **68+**

2287 **BOLD EWAR 8** [9] C E Brittain 3-8-11 (74)(bl) M Tebbutt 9/2: 325052: 3 ch c Persian Bold - Hot Curry (Sharpen Up) Tried to make all, edged left & ins last, no extra: eff at 1m/10f: see 979, 125. *1¼* **77**

2117 **CHAPEL ROYALE 16** [10] K Mahdi 3-9-1 (78) Dale Gibson 14/1: 500203: 3 gr c College Chapel - Merci Royale (Fairy King) Held up, rdn & styd on fnl 2f, not pace of wnr: worth another try at 10f+: see 1879 (stks). *½* **80**

2108 **MASTERPIECE USA 16** [11] Sir Michael Stoute 3-9-3 (80) F Lynch 11/2: 01-044: Chsd ldrs, rdn/onepace over 1f out: op 7/1: eff at 7f/8.5f on fast & soft grnd: see 2108, 1826. *1¼* **79**

2157 **MINGLING 14** [1] 3-9-0 (77)(VIS) O Pears 12/1: 352365: Cl-up, fdd 1f out: op 10/1: vis: see 1310. *3½* **69**

*1444 **WILLOUGHBYS BOY 46** [3] 3-9-3 (80) A Culhane 7/2 JT FAV: 0316: In tch, btn over 1f out: 6 wk abs. *2* **68**

2062 **BELLA BELLISIMO 18** [2] 3-8-13 (76) R Winston 14/1: 5-0067: Al towards rear: see 874. *¾* **63**

2145 **CELEBRE BLU 15** [5] 3-8-7 (70) Iona Wands (5) 20/1: 633308: Al bhd: see 1562 (6f). *½* **56**

2060 **BENBYAS 18** [6] 3-7-10 (59)(vis) K Dalgleish (5) 20/1: -06109: Chsd ldrs, btn 2f out: btr 1723 (6f). *2½* **40**

2300 **NODS NEPHEW 8** [8] 3-8-1 (64) T Williams 20/1: 410400: Chsd ldrs 2f out, sn btn: 10th: see 976. *1* **43**

*2311 **LINDEN GRACE 8** [4] 3-9-7 (84) J Fanning 7/2 JT FAV: 250-1P: Mid-div, p.u. lame after 2f: op 3/1. **0**

11 ran Time 1m 45.6 (1.8) (Burton Agnes Bloodstock) T D Easterby Great Habton, N Yorks

2516

3.35 BRAMBLEBERRY HCAP 3YO+ 0-70 (E) 2m35y Good/Firm 25 -18 Slow [67]
£4628 £1424 £712 £356 3 yo rec 19lb

*2176 **BUSTLING RIO 13** [7] P C Haslam 4-9-7 (60) M Tebbutt 7/1: 150011: 4 b g Up And At 'Em - Une Ventitienne (Green Dancer) Rear, prog 5f out, switched & rdn/led 1f out, styd on well, drvn out: earlier scored at Southwell (rtd 68a) & Pontefract (h'caps): '99 wnr at Southwell (2, rtd 61a) & Pontefract (h'caps, rtd 61): eff at 11/12f, suited by 2m/2m2f on firm, gd & fibresand, loves Southwell/Pontefract: runs well fresh: in gd form. **69**

1563 **MENTAL PRESSURE 40** [4] Mrs M Reveley 7-8-13 (52) A Culhane 11/1: 0/3252: 7 ch g Polar Falcon - Hysterical (High Top) Rear, rdn & styd on well fnl 2f, not reach wnr: clr rem: abs: eff at 12f/2m: see 788. *1½* **59**

1411 **SUDEST 49** [9] J L Harris 6-9-7 (60)(BL) R Winston 40/1: 000-03: 6 b g Taufan - Frill (Henbit) Led, rdn/hdd 1f out, no extra: blnks, 7 wk abs: '99 scorer at W'hampton (3, h'caps, rtd 85a at best): plcd on the level in '98 (rtd 66): Dec '98 hdles wnr at Doncaster (rtd 98h): suited by 14f/2m1f on firm, handles gd/soft, fibresand/W'hampton specialist: gd weight carrier. *5* **62**

*2452 **XELLANCE 2** [13] M Johnston 3-8-0 (58)(6ex) K Dalgleish (5) 1/1 FAV: 112214: Held up, prog halfway, rdn/chall 2f out, no extra ins last: hvly bckd under a 6lb pen, op 6/4: see 2452. *nk* **60**

2482 **SPA LANE 1** [8] 7-8-4 (43) J Fanning 10/1: 143325: Chsd ldrs, onepace/held fnl 2f: op 7/1, qck reapp. *2* **43**

2203 **HIGHFIELD FIZZ 12** [12] 8-8-1 (40) T Williams 33/1: 001606: Rear, prog halfway, held fnl 2f. *2* **38**

*2244 **WINDMILL LANE 10** [1] 3-8-2 (60) P Hanagan (7) 10/1: 630217: Chsd ldrs, held over 2f out: op 7/1. *hd* **58**

1711 **IRELANDS EYE 34** [10] 5-9-0 (53) O Pears 13/2: 0-3328: Trkd ldrs 4f out, wknd fnl 2f: op 8/1: btr 1276. *4* **47**

-- **THE LAD** [6] 11-7-10 (35)(5oh) P Fessey 66/1: 6000/9: Chsd ldrs till halfway: long abs: missed '99: mod form in '98 (rtd 23, Mrs L Stubbs, h'cap): back in '96 trained by L Montague Hall to win at Lingfield (AW h'cap), Folkestone & Chepstow (h'caps, rtd 47): eff at 12f/2m on firm grnd & equitrack, has disapp on fibresand: has run well fresh & for an appr: now with J M Bradley, probably ndd this. *2* **27**

2244 **LASTMAN 10** [2] 5-9-6 (59) F Lynch 16/1: 5-5220: Chsd ldrs 3f out, sn btn: 10th: op 14/1: btr 2244. *2½* **49**

1867 **OLD HUSH WING 26** [11] 7-8-2 (41) D Mernagh (3) 16/1: 600000: Al rear: 11th: see 714. *1½* **29**

2164 **PLEASANT MOUNT 14** [3] 4-9-10 (63) T Lucas 9/1: 015030: Cl-up, rdn/wknd fnl 3f: 12th: op 16/1. *1½* **49**

2080 **THE LAST RAMBO 17** [5] 3-7-10 (54)(12oh) Iona Wands (5) 100/1: 0-0000: Bhd 5f out: 13th: mod form. *15* **29**

13 ran Time 3m 37.3 (7.0) (Rio Stainless Engineering Ltd) P C Haslam Middleham, N Yorks

2517

4.10 HYPAC HCAP 3YO+ 0-80 (D) 5f Good/Firm 25 -01 Slow [80]
£6110 £1880 £940 £470 3 yo rec 5 lb

2334 **EURO VENTURE 7** [7] D Nicholls 5-9-4 (70) Iona Wands (5) 4/1 FAV: 600161: 5 b g Prince Sabo - Brave Advance (Bold Laddie) Trkd ldrs, prog/led over 1f out, rdn & styd on strongly ins last, rdn out: op 7/2: earlier won at Redcar (h'cap): '99 wnr at Southwell (rtd 73a), Thirsk & Carlisle (h'caps, rtd 79): '98 W'hampton wnr (mdn, rtd 78a & 59): eff at 5/7f on fast, soft & fibresand: can force the pace & handles any trk. **77**

2266 **MUNGO PARK 9** [3] M Dods 6-9-7 (73)(bl) A Culhane 6/1: -20202: 6 b g Selkirk - River Dove (Riverman) Held up, prog fnl 2f & squeezed thro' gap to chase wnr fnl 1f, al held: op 9/1: see 758. *2* **74**

2266 **RIVER TERN 9** [5] J M Bradley 7-8-12 (64) K Dalgleish (5) 12/1: 060003: 7 b g Puissance - Millaine (Formidable) Rear, styd on from over 1f out, no threat to wnr: see 1357. *¾* **63**

2252 **DOMINELLE 10** [2] T D Easterby 8-7-10 (48) P Fessey 14/1: 000404: Trkd ldrs, switched/rdn & not much room 1f out, onepace ins last: well h'capped, gd run here: see 1842. *hd* **46**

2078 **SOTONIAN 17** [6] 7-8-8 (60) D Mernagh (3) 14/1: 066345: Cl-up, no extra fnl 1f: see 394. *½* **56**

*1768 **ROYAL ROMEO 31** [4] 3-9-5 (76) R Winston 7/1: 31-016: Rear, switched & prog 2f out, onepace. *½* **70**

2340 **SEALED BY FATE 7** [10] 5-7-10 (48)(vis) J McAuley (3) 11/2: 604457: Led 2f out till over 1f out, fdd. *½* **40**

2310 **MIZHAR 8** [8] 4-9-11 (77) Alex Greaves 6/1: -00008: Led/dsptd lead 3f: stablemate of wnr: see 1173. *2½* **62**

2266 **PRINCE PROSPECT 9** [9] 4-9-13 (79) F Lynch 6/1: 220049: Briefly led halfway, btn/hmpd 1f out. *¾* **62**

2310 **SHIRLEY NOT 8** [1] 4-9-7 (73)(VIS) T Williams 12/1: 040550: Chsd ldrs, wknd over 1f out: vis, op 10/1. *1* **54**

10 ran Time 1m 02.6 (1.3) (W G Swiers) D Nicholls Sessay, N Yorks

2518

4.45 MITSUBISHI HCAP 3YO+ 0-75 (E) 1m2f Good/Firm 25 -11 Slow [69]
£3146 £968 £484 £242 3 yo rec 11lb

2048 **BOLD AMUSEMENT 19** [4] W S Cunningham 10-9-5 (60) O Pears 12/1: 0-2001: 10 ch g Never So Bold - Hysterical (High Top) Rear, prog 2f out, led ins last, rdn out: '99 Newcastle wnr (2, h'caps, rtd 67): '98 Redcar wnr (h'cap, rtd 60): stays 12f, suited by 10f on firm & gd/soft, with/without blnks: handles any trk. **64**

2220 **KHUCHN 11** [3] M Brittain 4-8-7 (48) D Mernagh (3) 9/1: 526542: 4 b c Unfuwain - Stay Sharpe (Sharpen Up) Cl-up, rdn/ev ch fnl 2f, kept on well: see 1575, 871. *1¼* **50**

2366 **RARE TALENT 5** [1] S Gollings 6-8-12 (53) Clare Roche (7) 10/1: -00303: 6 b g Mtoto - Bold As Love *hd* **54**

BEVERLEY SATURDAY JULY 8TH Righthand, Oval Track With Stiff, Uphill Finish

(Lomond) Rear, switched & styd on well fnl 2f, not pace of wnr: op 8/1: quick reapp: see 1272.
2048 **RINGSIDE JACK** 19 [6] C W Fairhurst 4-9-10 (65) J Fanning 25/1: -10604: Mid-div, prog/ev ch over   hd 65
1f out, drvn/onepace nr fin: see 975 (C/D, hvy).
2061 **BUTTERSCOTCH** 18 [14] 4-8-6 (47) T Williams 8/1: -00335: Trkd ldrs, rdn/briefly led over 1f out,   ½ 46
just held nr fin: 5th but only btn around 2L in a bunched fin: see 1705, 248.
*2220 **CYBERTECHNOLOGY** 11 [13] 6-9-3 (58) A Culhane 11/4 FAV: 000316: Rear, prog to press ldrs over   ½ 56
1f out, kept on onepace despite little room fnl 1f: op 4/1: see 2220 (C/D).
2257 **HORMUZ** 10 [8] 4-9-2 (57) F Lynch 20/1: 000007: Cl-up, led going well over 2f out, rdn/hdd & wknd   1¼ 53
over 1f out: posted a much imprvd effort, looks well h'capped & a return to 1m could suit: see 1860.
2412 **WELODY** 3 [10] 4-9-5 (60) Dale Gibson 33/1: 004008: Led till over 2f out, fdd: qck reapp: see 658.   2 53
2221 **LAA JADEED** 11 [11] 5-7-10 (37)(bl)(7oh) Joanna Badger (7) 66/1: 050609: Chsd ldrs 3f out, sn held.   3 26
1767 **ALBARDEN** 31 [5] 3-8-2 (54) P Fessey 40/1: 40-550: Al bhd: 10th: see 1295 (mdn).   hd 42
2309 **MELODY LADY** 8 [12] 4-8-9 (50) K Dalgleish (5) 3/1: -00220: Chsd ldrs 1m: 11th: btr 2309, 2139.   hd 37
1735 **XIBALBA** 33 [2] 3-9-3 (69) M Tebbutt 11/2: 00-140: Bhd, no ch fnl 2f: 14th: btr 1735, 1414.   0
2296 Black Rocket 8 [9] 4-8-9 (50) G Parkin 33/1:   2242 Sophomore 10 [7] 6-9-8 (63) R Winston 16/1:
14 ran   Time 2m 05.9 (3.6)   (Mrs Ann Bell)   W S Cunningham Hutton Rudby, N Yorks

2519
5.20 FLORADORA MDN 3YO+ (D) 5f Good/Firm 25 -19 Slow
£3809 £1172 £586 £293 3 yo rec 5 lb

808 **BOND BOY** 98 [5] B Smart 3-9-0 M Tebbutt 11/10 FAV: 62-451: 3 b c Piccolo - Arabellajill (Aragon)   71
Led 1f, remained handy & drvn/narrow led again ins last, just held on, all out: 3 month abs: plcd twice in
'99 (rtd 91): eff at 5/6f on firm & soft, sharp or stiff trk: runs fresh well.
2315 **TAWN AGAIN** 7 [4] T D Barron 4-9-5 D Mernagh (3) 33/1: -00002: 4 b g Then Again - Tawny (Grey   shd 70$
Ghost) Trkd ldrs, rdn/prog to chall over 1f out, styd on well, just held: only mod form prev, eff at 5f on fast grnd.
2313 **DAYLILY** 8 [2] T D Easterby 3-8-9 R Winston 11/8: 603323: 3 ch f Pips Pride - Leaping Water   1½ 61$
(Sure Blade) Led after 1f till over 1f out, rdn/no extra nr fin: nicely bckd tho' op 5/4: see 2313, 1768 (hvy).
3948} **SASHA** 296 [6] J Balding 3-9-0 J Edmunds 14/1: 0-4: Cl-up, no extra over 1f out: reapp: rtd 53 in   2 61
'99 for J L Eyre (sole start): now with J Balding.
2299 **PRINCE NICO** 8 [1] 3-9-0 A Culhane 8/1: 000065: In tch, onepace fnl 2f: op 14/1: offic rtd 36.   1½ 57$
2047 **MIMANDI** 19 [3] 3-8-9 O Pears 40/1: 0-0606: Sn bhd: mod form.   9 36
6 ran   Time 1m 03.5 (2.2)   (R C Bond)   B Smart Lambourn, Berks

NEWCASTLE SUNDAY JULY 9TH Lefthand, Galloping, Stiff Track

Official Going   GOOD TO FIRM (GOOD Places) Stalls : Str Course - Stands side: Rnd course - Inside: 10f - Outside.

2520
2.25 SUNDAY MDN 3YO (D) 1m str Good 48 -37 Slow
£5187 £1596 £798 £399

1643 **RIPARIAN** 37 [3] Sir Michael Stoute 3-9-0 F Lynch 2/11 FAV: -5-31: 3 b g Last Tycoon - La Riveraine   72
(Riverman) Cl up, rdn to lead dist, drvn out to hold on: well bckd at long odds-on: promising 5th on sole '99
juv start (7f mdn, rtd 79): dam dual 12f wnr: eff at 7f/1m, further suit: acts on firm, soft & a stiff/gall track.
2337 **FIZZLE** 8 [1] M Johnston 3-9-0 J Fanning 7/1: -502: 3 ch c Efisio - Altaia (Sicyos)   nk 72
Prom, went on at 4f out, hdd dist, rall, not btn far: much improved form, eff at 1m on gd grnd: win a mdn soon.
-- **LA SYLPHIDE GB** Mrs A Duffield 3-8-9 G Duffield 14/1: -3: 3 ch f Rudimentary - Primitive Gift   2½ 62
(Primitive Rising) Chsd ldrs, rdn & styd on fnl 2f, not pace of front 2: stys 1m on gd grnd: promising debut.
-- **GRACILIS** [4] W W Haigh 3-9-0 W Supple 14/1: -4: Dwelt, bhd, rdn/prog 3f out, flashed tail for   1 65
press 2f out, no extra inside last: clr rem on debut: bred to apprec mid dists, imprv over further.
2026 **NINETEENNINETYNINE** 21 [2] 3-9-0 R Fitzpatrick (3) 50/1: 06-005: Led, hdd 4f out, sn fdd: see 694.   11 45
1766 **REDS DESIRE** 32 [6] 3-9-0 V Halliday 66/1: -006: Al well bhd, t.o.: no form.   29 0
6 ran   Time 1m 43.80 (6.80)   (J H Richmond-Watson)   Sir Michael Stoute Newmarket

2521
2.55 EBF FAMILY WEEKEND MDN 2YO (D) 7f str Good 48 -25 Slow
£5239 £1612 £806 £403

-- **CRAZY LARRYS** [7] J Noseda 2-9-0 D Holland 5/1: -1: 2 ch c Mutakddim - No Fear Of Flying (Super   83
Concorde) Chsd ldrs, led appr fnl 1f, kept on well, drvn out: 22,000gns Apr foal: dam a dual wnr in the States:
eff at 7f, 1m will suit: runs well fresh on gd & a stiff/gall track: excellent debut, should progress & win again.
2161 **TAKE TO TASK** 15 [13] M Johnston 2-9-0 J Fanning 10/11 FAV: -22: 2 b c Conquistador Cielo -   1 80
Tash (Never Bend) Led, hdd appr fnl 1f, kept on well inside last but not pace of wnr: nicely bckd:
clr rem & should do even better soon: see 2161.
2239 **THEWHIRLINGDERVISH** 11 [12] T D Easterby 2-9-0 W Supple 50/1: -003: 2 ch c Definite Article -   3½ 73
Normadic Dancer (Nabeel Dancer) Cl up, rdn & ran on well appr fnl 1f, never nearer: much improved on
this step up to 7f & further should suit: acts on fast grnd: see 1893.
2005 **SNOWEY MOUNTAIN** 22 [3] N A Callaghan 2-9-0 J P Spencer 4/1: -64: Waited with, rdn & ran on   nk 72
fnl 2f, nrst fin: prob styd this longer 7f trip, handles gd grnd: see 2005.
2333 **EAGLET** 8 [14] 2-9-0 G Hills 66/1: -0005: Rear, eff when short of room 2f out, late hdwy, no dngr.   2 68
-- **BARNINGHAM** [11] 2-9-0 R Lappin 66/1: -6: Dwelt, soon rdn in rear, mod late gains: 22,000gns   6 56
Jan first foal: dam French wnr, sire high class at 1m/10f: with J D Bethell.
2277 **KATIES DOLPHIN** 10 [4] 2-8-9 R Cody Boutcher (7) 10/1: -6237: Trckd ldrs, fdd fnl 2f: see 2277.   2½ 46
2239 **LITTLE TASK** 11 [2] 2-9-0 J Carroll 12/1: -38: Handy, eff 3f out, sn held, eased when btn: up in trip.   10 31
1503 **MR PERTEMPS** 44 [8] 2-9-0 Kim Tinkler 66/1: -069: Front rank, lost tch fnl 2f: 6 wk abs.   ¾ 29
1475 **SMART DANCER** 45 [5] 2-9-0 G Parkin 25/1: -50: Mid div, fdd fnl 2f, 10th: 6 wk abs: see 1475.   2½ 24
2014 **SIR EDWARD BURROW** 21 [6] 2-9-0 R Winston 50/1: -040: Al rear, 11th: see 2014.   2 20
1859 **TOBYTOO** 28 [1] 2-9-0 (BL) R Fitzpatrick (3) 66/1: -000: Veered badly left leaving stalls, pulled   dist 0
v hard & al t.o., 12th: looked virtually unrideable in first time blinks.
-- **WORTHY** [9] 2-9-0 A Culhane 12/1: -0: Missed break, virtually p.u. after 2f, came home in own time,   2½ 0
fin last: 20,000gns March foal: dam wnr in the States: with M R Channon, something clearly amiss.
13 ran   Time 1m 29.24 (5.14)   (Crazy Radio Ltd)   J Noseda Newmarket Suffolk

2522 **3.30 WEST INDIES HCAP 3YO+ 0-90 (C) 1m2f32y Good 48 +07 Fast** **[90]**
£6909 £2126 £1063 £531 3yo rec 11lb

2379 **FREEDOM QUEST 6** [5] B S Rothwell 5-7-10 (58) J Bramhill 6/1: 642521: 5 b g Polish Patriot - Recherchee (Rainbow Quest) Mid div, rdn to lead appr fnl 2f, styd on strongly inside last, drvn out: qck reapp, gd time: plcd prev this term: '99 Beverley & Musselburgh wnr (h'caps, plcd sev times, rtd 64): rtd 76 in '98: eff at 1m/10f, stys 12f, acts on firm, gd/soft, fibresand & any trk: eff without a visor: v tough, deserved this. **63**
2350 **HAPPY DIAMOND 7** [2] M Johnston 3-9-2 (89) R Winston 1/1 FAV: -3022D: 3 b c Diesis - Urus (Kris S) Trkd ldrs, no room when swtchd & squeezed thro' gap 2f out, every ch fnl 1f, just held: fin 2nd, disqual & plcd 4th: jockey received a 5 day irresponsible riding ban: no luck recently: most unfortunate in 2350. *nk* **94**
2311 **DONNAS DOUBLE 9** [1] D Eddy 5-8-2 (64) P Fessey 12/1: 056352: 5 ch g Weldnaas - Shadha (Shirley Heights) Waited with, rdn/prog 2f out, styd on well fnl 1f, nrst fin: clr rem: fin 3rd, plcd 2nd: see 1011. *1¼* **67**
1582 **DARK SHADOWS 40** [7] W Storey 5-8-0 (62) T Williams 7/1: -5363: Trck ldrs, cl up when hmpd over 2f out, no impress after: fin 4th, plcd 3rd: 6 week abs, h'cap bow: see 1193. *6* **56**
2242 **COURT EXPRESS 11** [3] 6-9-4 (80) F Lynch 13/2: -16205: Nvr a dngr: up in trip: twice below 2138. *2½* **70**
2090 **YAROB 18** [6] 7-10-0 (90) Alex Greaves 13/2: 102606: Pulled hard & led at fast pace, hdd 2f out, wknd quickly: top weight: capable of better, see 1217. *5* **72**
2001 **INITIATIVE 22** [4] 4-8-12 (74) J McAuley(5) 33/1: 15-007: Trck ldrs, wknd rapidly fnl 3f, t.o.: raced twice in '99, won at Thisk (reapp, mdn, rtd 88, H Cecil): rtd 89 on sole '98 start (3rd bhd Auction House & Beat All): eff at 7f/1m, further shld suit: acts on fast: yet to come to hand this term for B W Murray. *17* **31**
7 ran Time 2m 10.60 (4.10) (B Valentine) B S Rothwell Musley Bank, N Yorks

2523 **4.05 FUNDAY CLASS STKS 3YO+ 0-80 (D) 1m4f93y Good 48 +08 Fast**
£5018 £1544 £772 £386 3yo rec 13lb

2287 **CAPTAINS LOG 9** [4] M L W Bell 5-9-7 K Dalgleish(5) 10/11 FAV: 251141: 5 b g Slip Anchor - Cradle Of Love (Roberto) Mid div, hdwy appr fnl 4f, led appr fnl 1f, drvn out: nicely bckd, best time of day: earlier won at Windsor (h'cap) & York (stakes): rnr up in '99 (rtd 80 at best), prev term scored at Warwick (mdn) & here at Newcastle (h'cap, rtd 82): eff at 10/12.4f on any grnd/trk: runs well fresh: tough/consistent, in fine form. **80**
1518 **HUNTERS TWEED 43** [2] J D Bethell 4-9-3 D Holland 6/1: 5-0202: 4 ch c Nashwan - Zorette (Zilzal) Cl up, drvn & styd on well fnl 2f, not pace of wnr inside last: ran to near best: see 1194. *1¼* **72**
997 **ROMAN KING 78** [6] M Johnston 5-9-3 J Fanning 7/2: 41-603: 5 b g Sadler's Wells - Romantic Feeling (Shirley Heights) Mid div, hdwy to lead 4f out, hdd dist, sn held: 11 wk abs: prev with M Hammond. *1½* **70**
2358 **MAKASSEB 7** [7] M R Channon 3-8-4 W Supple 4/1: -00604: Settled rear, rdn & styd on fnl 2f, no threat to ldrs: dist clr rem: quick reapp: up in trip, poss gets 12f: see 1366. *1¼* **68**
1936 **LOYAL TOAST 24** [5] 5-9-3 Kim Tinkler 50/1: 030505: Hdd 4f out, wknd quickly, t.o.: hopeless task at level weights against rivals officially rated almost 60lbs higher. *dist* **0**
2016 **STAMFORD HILL 21** [1] 5-9-3 D Allan (7) 66/1: 000056: Chsd ldrs, lost tch halfway, t.o.: poor. *21* **0**
3955} **FASTWAN 296** [3] 4-9-3 A Culhane 40/1: 5600-7: Keen, al bhd, t.o.: modest in '99 (rtd 38$). *1½* **0**
7 ran Time 2m 42.95 (5.05) (Christopher Wright) M L W Bell Newmarket, Suffolk

2524 **4.40 RAMSIDE HCAP 3YO 0-75 (E) 1m rnd Good 48 -17 Slow** **[82]**
£5343 £1644 £822 £411

*2160 **STALLONE 15** [5] J Noseda 3-9-7 (75) D Holland 2/1 FAV: -45511: 3 ch g Brief Truce - Bering Honneur (Bering) Mid div, hdwy to lead well ins last, drvn out: nicely bckd: prev won at Redcar (h'cap, 1st win): eff at 1m/9f, further could suit: acts on fast, gd & stiff/gall track: on the upgrade & could complete a hat-trick. **81**
*2058 **HADATH 19** [2] M A Buckley 3-9-7 (75) Dean McKeown 7/1: 005612: 3 br g Mujtahid - Al Sylah (Nureyev) Led, hdd well inside last, kept on, not btn far: eff at 7f/1m: in gd heart: see 2058 (mdn). *¾* **78**
2111 **NOBLE SPLENDOUR 17** [7] L M Cumani 3-8-11 (65) J P Spencer 5/1: -50233: 3 ch c Grand Lodge - Haskeir (Final Straw) Handy, rdn/hdwy 2f out, ran on well fnl 1f: op 8/1: eff at 1m/9f: v consistent, deserves to win. *½* **67**
2099 **CALLING THE SHOTS 18** [3] W Storey 3-7-10 (50)(10oh) J Bramhill 50/1: -00004: Chsd ldrs, chall appr fnl 1f, soon held: fine run from 10lbs o/h but treat rating with caution: see 1477. *1* **50$**
2320 **LADY HELEN 8** [8] 3-8-8 (62) J Carroll 16/1: 100-05: Settled rear, prog 3f out, styd on, no impress. *shd* **62**
2235 **MARVEL 11** [9] 3-8-4 (58) Kim Tinkler 16/1: 002036: Front rank, rdn/btn appr fnl 1f: see 2235. *1* **56**
2205 **ABSINTHER 13** [6] 3-8-7 (61) W Supple 10/1: 00-027: Cl up, rdn /fdd fnl 2f: btr 2205. *1¾* **55**
2281 **JUMBOS FLYER 10** [12] 3-8-7 (61) R Cody Boutcher (7) 12/1: 524628: Never dngrs: btr 2281 (firm). *nk* **54**
1726 **TAKE MANHATTAN 34** [14] 3-9-2 (70) A Culhane 10/1: 611009: Mid div at best: much btr 1255. *2* **59**
1387 **WINGED ANGEL 50** [13] 3-8-5 (59) K Hodgson 16/1: 40000: Never a factor after 7 week abs. *2* **44**
1822 **NOWT FLASH 30** [1] 3-8-6 (60) Joanna Badger (7) 16/1: 522500: Al rear, fin 11th: see 1477. *½* **44**
2242 **SIGN OF THE TIGER 11** [4] 3-9-5 (73) S Finnamore (5) 12/1: 423100: Al bhd, 12th: btr 1477 (gd/soft). *1¾* **54**
1448 **City Flyer 47** [10] 3-8-2 (55)(1ow) R Lappin 33/1:
2159 **Annespride 15** [11] 3-7-11 (51)(t)(1ow)(21oh) Dale Gibson 40/1:
14 ran Time 1m 44.20 (5.20) (Lucayan Stud) J Noseda Newmarket

2525 **5.10 NORTH EAST HCAP 3YO+ 0-75 (E) 5f str Good 48 -28 Slow** **[73]**
£7202 £2216 £1108 £554 3yo rec 5lb

2395 **SHARP HAT 5** [10] D W Chapman 6-8-12 (57) A Culhane 16/1: 205261: 6 b g Shavian - Madam Trilby (Grundy) Front rank, went on appr fnl 1f, rdn clr ins last: qck reapp: late '99 wnr at Lingfield (h'cap, rtd 62a): unplcd earlier in '99 for T Etherington (rtd 74 & 39a): plcd in '98 (rtd 87, stks, R Hannon), prev term won at Newbury (h'cap, rtd 93): eff at 5/6f, stys 7f: acts on firm, soft, equitrack & any trk: best without blinks. **67**
2517 **MUNGO PARK 1** [2] M Dods 6-10-0 (73) J Fanning 11/2: 202022: 6 b g Selkirk - River Dove (Riverman) Strong run from rear fnl 1f, no threat to wnr: top weight: ran 24 hrs ago & another sound run. *2½* **76**
2193 **PREMIUM PRINCESS 13** [1] J J Quinn 5-8-7 (52) D Mernagh (3) 8/1: 005533: 5 b m Distant Relative - Solemn Occasion (Secreto) In tch, eff over 2f out, kept on inside last, no threat to wnr: see 2193. *½* **54**
*1910 **BEYOND THE CLOUDS 25** [12] J S Wainwright 4-8-11 (56) R Winston 11/1: 002614: Hmpd start, sn in mid div, ran on inside last, no danger: remains in gd heart: see 1910. *nk* **57**
2340 **TIME TO FLY 8** [8] 7-7-10 (41)(bl)(2oh) P Hanagan(3) 33/1: 30-005: Dwelt, rear, switched & hdwy 2f out, & styd on well ins last: '99 scorer at Lingfield (h'cap, rtd 71a, subs rnr-up on turf, rtd 48): '98 wnr at W'hampton (2, h'caps) & Lingfield (h'cap, rtd 82a at best): eff at 5/6f on both AW & firm grnd: wears blinks & *¾* **39**

likes racing up with the pace: well h'capped & signs of a return to form here.

2418 **TORRENT** 4 [19] 5-9-1 (60)(bl) D Holland 14/1: 444446: Rear, hdwy when short of room & switched appr fnl 1f, ran on well inside last: quick reapp: tricky ride: see 2107, 205.   nk   57

2329 **KEEN HANDS** 8 [3] 4-9-5 (64)(vis) R Fitzpatrick (3) 14/1: 551047: Mid div, mod late hdwy, no threat.   2   55

2517 **DOMINELLE 1** [16] 8-8-3 (48) W Supple 16/1: 004048: In tch, late hdwy, no threat: ran yesterday.   1   36

2340 **COLLEGE MAID** 8 [5] 3-9-5 (69) F Lynch 14/1: 250109: Mid div at best: twice below 2165.   nk   56

*1923 **DAZZLING QUINTET** 25 [4] 4-8-4 (49) J McAuley (5) 7/1: -60210: Front rank, wknd appr fnl 1f, 10th.   ½   35

*2275 **ANGEL HILL** 10 [14] 5-8-10 (55)(VIS) G Duffield 5/1 FAV: 000610: In tch, eff when hmpd over 1f out, soon btn: 11th: nicely bckd & better expected in first time visor: btr 2275 (6f).   shd   41

1334 **SERGEANT SLIPPER** 53 [20] 3-8-3 (53)(vis) K Dalgleish(5) 25/1: -00100: Dwelt, al bhd, 12th: 8 wk abs.   ½   38

2280 **CHRISTOPHERSSISTER** 10 [15] 3-8-12 (62) J Bramhill 25/1: 100040: Missed break, al rear, 13th.   ¾   44

3440} **PURE ELEGANCIA** 326 [9] 4-9-13 (72) Alex Greaves 7/1: 1516-0: Prom, led over 2f out, hdd appr fnl 1f, wknd quickly, fin 14th: reapp: '99 wnr at Catterick & Goodwood (h'caps, rtd 72): eff up with/forcing the pace at 5f, poss stys 6f: acts on gd, firm & likes a sharp track: can go well when fresh.   hd   54

2233 **PALACEGATE JACK** 11 [7] 9-7-10 (41)(10h) P Fessey 20/1: 230030: Mid div, lost tch appr fnl 1f, 15th.   ¾   20

2418 **KALAR** 4 [6] 11-8-2 (47)(bl) Claire Bryan (5) 14/1: 004100: Led, hdd over 2f out, wknd rapidly fin last: quick reapp: twice below 2233 (amat h'cap).   0

1714 **Precision** 34 [18] 5-8-2 (47) O Pears 40/1:   2340 **Pips Star** 8 [11] 3-8-4 (54) Dawn Rankin(3) 25/1:

2340 **Jack To A King** 8 [17] 5-7-12 (43)(tbl) Dale Gibson 20/1:2418 **Kosevo** 4 [13] 6-8-2 (47)(vis) T Williams 20/1:

20 ran   Time 1m 02.00 (3.80)   (Miss N F Thesiger)   D W Chapman Stillington, N Yorks

---

Official Going   1st 5 races - GOOD; GOOD TO SOFT last race. Stalls: Inside, except 5f - Stands Side.

2526   2.00 EBF FILLIES MDN 2YO (D)   5f str   Good/Firm   Inapplicable
£4290   £1320   £660   £330

1986 **SILLA** 22 [8] ! A Balding 2-8-11 K Darley 4/1 JT FAV: -031: 2 b f Gone West - Silver Fling (The Minstrel) Front rank, led after halfway, rdn out: nicely bckd tho' op 5/2, imprvd with every run: Jan foal, bred in the purple, dam a top sprinter: eff at 5f, get 6f in time: acts on fast grnd, stiff track: progressing.   86

1424 **PRIYA** 48 [9] C E Brittain 2-8-11 B Marcus 11/2: -462: 2 b f Primo Dominie - Promissory (Caerleon) Wide, chsd ldrs, kept on ins last but not pace of wnr: 7 wk abs, imprvd run: eff at 5f on fast, 6f suit.   1¼   81

2227 **MAGICAL FLUTE** 11 [6] M R Channon 2-8-11 Craig Williams 10/1: -03: 2 ch f Piccolo - Stride Home (Absalom) In tch, niggled halfway, kept on towards fin but nvr dngrs: handles fast grnd, needs 6f +.   1¼   77

-- **SHEPPARDS WATCH** [2] M P Tregoning 2-8-11 Martin Dwyer 4/1 JT FAV: -4: Prom, ch 2f out, same pace below dist: Night Shift Feb foal: dam 7f wnr: sire gets sprinters: handles fast grnd.   shd   77

2227 **CAYMAN EXPRESSO** 11 [5] 2-8-11 R Hughes 11/2: -635: Led till appr fnl 2f, onepace ins last: op 4/1: sown enough to find similar on a minor track: see 1986.   hd   77

-- **PETALITE** [1] 2-8-11 P Robinson 5/1: -6: Hmpd early, in tch, outpcd & not given a hard time appr fnl 1f: bckd on debut: 6,000gns Petong Jan first foal, sire/dam sprinters: expect improvement: with M Jarvis.   3½   67+

1883 **MISS INFORM** 26 [7] 2-8-11 T Quinn 10/1: -357: Speed 3f: op 7/1, see 1639 (gd/soft).   ½   66

-- **SONG N DANCE** [3] 2-8-11 G Baker(7) 33/1: -8: Dwelt, nvr in it: debut: 1,850gns Dancing Spree Apr foal: half-sister to a mdn, dam 6/9f wnr, sire a sprinter: with M Usher.   shd   66

-- **CLASSIC MILLENNIUM** [4] 2-8-11 R Perham 33/1: -9: Sn bhd: 9,200gns Midyan Mar foal.   hd   66

9 ran   Time 1m 02.96 (3.36)   (George Strawbridge)   I A Balding Kingsclere, Hants.

2527   2.35 UTRAVEL.CO.UK HCAP 4YO+ 0-80 (D)   1m2f   Good/Firm 37   -06 Slow   [78]
£7085   £2180   £1090   £545

*2453 **OCTANE** 2 [14] W M Brisbourne 4-8-9 (59) Martin Dwyer 5/1 CO FAV: 320211: 4 b g Cryptoclearance - Something True (Sir Ivor) Mid-div, hdwy under press appr fnl 2f, led below dist, going away: bckd, won 48hrs ago at Haydock (appr h'cap) & earlier at Musselburgh (h'cap): with H Cecil when fav for 1st 2 in '99 (rtd 80): eff at 10f/12f on firm/fast grnd: goes on any trk: progressive, at right end of h'cap, win again.   70

2199 **STROMSHOLM** 13 [15] J R Fanshawe 4-9-3 (67) Pat Eddery 5/1 CO FAV: 063242: 4 ch g Indian Ridge - Upward Trend (Salmon Leap) Prom, hdwy to lead ent fnl 2f till ent fnl 1f, sn outpcd by wnr: nicely bckd, in-form.   5   68

2127 **SWEET REWARD** 16 [7] J G Smyth Osbourne 5-9-3 (67) F Norton 8/1: 0-4403: 5 ch g Beveled - Sweet Revival (Claude Monet) Held up, briefly not clr run 4f out, kept on ins fnl 2f, nvr dngrs: suited by drop back to 10f.   hd   68

*1973 **AMRAK AJEEB** 23 [6] R J Baker 8-9-10 (74) G Sparkes (7) 11/1: 0-0314: Way off the pace till styd on strongly up the straight, nvr nrr: op 8/1, top-weight: given a lot to do, suited by slightly easier grnd.   1   73

2190 **YOUNG UN** 13 [3] 5-9-0 (64) S Carson (3) 9/1: 042025: In tch, short of room/outpcd turning in, late hdwy.   nk   62

2262 **OSCIETRA** 11 [8] 4-8-1 (51)(VIS) L Newman(3) 10/1: -05556: Chsd ldrs, onepace appr fnl 1f: visored.   nk   48

2130 **ASCARI** 16 [4] 4-9-0 (64) D McGaffin (5) 10/1: 31-027: Handy till 2f out: op 8/1, see 2130, 1973.   nk   60

2085 **JUNIKAY** 18 [11] 6-9-2 (66) T Quinn 5/1 CO FAV: 211328: Held up, rdn 2f out, no impress: see 1395.   ¾   60

2270 **CAPRIOLO** 10 [1] 4-9-6 (70) R Hughes 12/1: 01-609: Nvr dngrs: op 11/1, see 2190, 1973.   nk   63

2372 **KENNET** 6 [12] 5-8-10 (60)(VIS) S Sanders 12/1: 000020: Led & clr after 5f, no extra 2f out, sn hdd, fdd: 10th, op 9/1, way too free in first time visor, qck reapp: see 512.   1½   51

1888 **FAMOUS** 26 [5] 7-7-10 (46)(11oh) R Brisland(5) 50/1: 050000: Al towards rear: 11th: see 90.   6   28

2181 **Saseedo** 14 [13] 10-7-10 (46)(16oh) G Bardwell 66/1:   2212 **Sabot** 12 [16] 7-7-10 (46) C Catlin(3) 33/1:

2185 **Alazan** 14 [10] 5-7-10 (46)(10oh) S Righton 66/1:

-- **Tudor Romance** [9] 15-7-10 (46)(t)(16oh) D Kinsella(7) 100/1:

15 ran   Time 2m 08.43 (4.33)   (Christopher Chell)   W M Brisbourne Great Ness, Shropshire.

2528   3.10 VICTOR CHANDLER HCAP 3YO+ 0-105 (B)   1m rnd   Good/Firm 37   +06 Fast   [105]
£29000   £11000   £5500   £2500   3yo rec 9lb

*2090 **CARIBBEAN MONARCH** 18 [8] Sir Michael Stoute 5-9-11 (102) Pat Eddery 5/2 FAV: -43211: 5 b g Fairy King - Whos The Blonde (Cure The Blues) Confidently held up, gd prog ent fnl 2f, led below dist, idled & had to be rdn out: hvly bckd from 7/2, gd time: recent R Ascot wnr (Hunt Cup h'cap): rtd 84 when 4th in '99: '98 wnr at Newmarket (mdn) & Windsor (h'cap, rtd 99): eff at 7f/1m: acts on firm, soft grnd, any trk: runs well fresh, best coming late: smart & improving, has a fine turn of foot & looks well up to winning in List/Gr 3.   110

*2229 **SPEEDFIT TOO 11** [4] C E Brittain 5-9-12 (103)(vis) T E Durcan 12/1: 504012: 2 b h Scenic - Safka (Irish River) Off the pace, gd wide prog 2f out, chsd wnr below dist, kept on well: fine weight-carrying performance from this progressive entire: v useful, shld win again: see 2229. ½ **108**
2001 **REGAL PHILOSOPHER 22** [18] J W Hills 4-8-13 (90) R Hills 8/1: 622403: 4 b g Faustus - Princess Lucy (Local Suitor) Chsd ldrs, going well when briefly short of room 3f out, kept on fnl 1f, not get to front pair: tchd 10/1: ran to v best against a pair of Listed/Group class performers: see 851. 1¼ **92**
2229 **SILK ST JOHN 11** [11] M J Ryan 6-9-1 (92) P McCabe 14/1: 513164: Waited with, sltly short of room appr fnl 2f, styd on, nvr dngrs: not far off best, tough sort: see 1836. ½ **93**
2117 **SOBRIETY 17** [7] 3-9-0 (100) R Hughes 11/1: 4-1065: Mid-div, drvn 2f out, no impress but kept on well towards fin: gd run from this lightly raced & useful 3yo, can land a valuable prize, prob at 10f. *hd* **101**
2090 **CALCUTTA 18** [16] 4-9-4 (95) M Hills 12/1: 6-0006: Well plcd, led appr fnl 1f, sn rdn, flashed tail & hdd, onepace & eased towards fin: better effort, see 1829. *1* **94**
1851 **DEBBIES WARNING 29** [17] 4-9-0 (91) Dane O'Neill 33/1: -06407: Led till ent fnl 2f, btn below dist. *shd* **90**
*2262 **FREDORA 11** [6] 5-8-6 (83) D Sweeney 16/1: 002418: Chsd ldrs, fdd fnl 1f: better giving weight. 1½ **79**
2090 **ESPADA 18** [14] 4-9-0 (91) S Sanders 10/1: -62109: Mid-div thr'out: op 8/1, see 1077 (solid form). *nk* **86**
2170 **PRAIRIE WOLF 15** [13] 4-8-13 (90) M Fenton 12/1: 10-340: In tch feeling pace turning for home, staying on when briefly hmpd bef fnl 1f, no threat: 10th, nicely bckd: unsuited by drop back to 1m, see 1797. *1* **83**
2171 **CEDAR MASTER 15** [10] 3-7-13 (85)(bl) P Doe 40/1: -05560: Reared & bhd till kept on fnl 2f: 11th. *nk* **77**
2138 **ZULU DAWN 16** [9] 4-8-1 (78) M Henry 16/1: 64-330: Pld hard, towards rear, bmpd appr fnl 2f & btn: 12th 3½ **63**
2170 **POLISH SPIRIT 15** [2] 5-8-4 (81) K Darley 8/1: 111030: Handy, fdd fnl 2f: 13th, bckd: softer grnd suits. 2½ **61**
2351 **ICE 7** [12] 4-9-4 (95)(vis) R Ffrench 14/1: 161440: Chsd ldrs till 3f out: 14th, bckd from 20/1, qk reapp. *1* **73**
2356 **PRINCE SLAYER 7** [15] 4-8-5 (82) L Newman (3) 20/1: 020100: Well plcd till appr fnl 2f, eased fnl 1f: 16th. **0**
1042 **The Whistling Teal 72** [5] 4-8-5 (82) F Norton 16/1: 2001 **Weet A Minute 22** [3] 7-8-12 (89)(BL) J Quinn 40/1:
2133 **Gudlage 16** [1] 4-8-11 (88)(t) N Pollard 33/1:
18 ran Time 1m 41.55 (2.55) (Pierpoint Scott & C H Scott) Sir Michael Stoute Newmarket.

2529

3.45 LISTED DRAGON STKS 2YO (A) 5f str Good/Firm Fast
£13910 £4280 £2140 £1070

*2368 **MISTY EYED 6** [6] Mrs P N Dutfield 2-8-7 L Newman 3/1: -51011: 2 gr f Paris House - Bold As Love (Lomond) Sn cl-up, pushed into lead appr fnl 2f, readily: well bckd, gd time, qck reapp: earlier won at Windsor (2, nov stks): eff at 5f on fast & gd grnd, sharp or stiff trk: v useful, progressive, speedy filly. **100**
2067 **TRIPLE BLUE 19** [5] R Hannon 2-9-1 Dane O'Neill 7/1: -11352: 2 ch c Bluebird - Persian Tapestry (Tap On Wood) Well plcd till outpcd appr fnl 1f, rallied under press to grab 2nd nr line: v useful effort back in trip but return to 6f sure to suit: acts on fast & soft grnd, see 1526. 2½ **100**
2152 **GIVE BACK CALAIS 16** [7] P J Makin 2-8-12 S Sanders 2/1 FAV: -323: 2 b c Brief Truce - Nichodoula (Doulab) Bhd ldrs, imprvd to go 2nd dist, sn rdn & onepace: hvly bckd, useful but could do with a confidence boosting mdn win: handles fast & gd/soft grnd: see 2152, 1809. *nk* **96**
2113 **MAMMAS TONIGHT 17** [2] A Berry 2-9-3 G Carter 11/1: 333154: Struggling & well off the pace till kept on strgly & wide appr fnl 1f: ran to best giving weight away, needs a return to 6f now: see 1761. ¾ **98**
1944 **ANIMAL CRACKER 24** [4] 2-8-7 D Sweeney 40/1: -05155: Bhd, some late hdwy: stiff task, ran well. 1¼ **84**
2172 **MILLENIUM PRINCESS 15** [1] 2-8-7 R Hughes 4/1: -126: Led till appr fnl 2f, no extra: nicely bckd, shorter-priced stablemate of rnr-up: much btr 2172 (6f). *nk* **83**
*1962 **SPEEDY GEE 23** [3] 2-8-12 Craig Williams 10/1: -3617: Front rank & ev ch till fdd appr fnl 1f: stiff task. ¾ **85**
2020 **MILLENNIUM MAGIC 21** [8] 2-8-7 T Quinn 33/1: -13428: Wide, in tch for 3f: stiffish task, see 1762. ½ **79**
8 ran Time 1m 01.38 (1.78) (Mrs Jan Fuller) Mrs P N Dutfield Axmouth, Devon.

2530

4.15 STANLEY HCAP 3YO+ 0-85 (D) 1m3f91y Good Inapplicable [82]
£7312 £2250 £1125 £562

2287 **WASP RANGER 9** [2] G L Moore 6-9-7 (75)(bl) I Mongan (5) 6/1: -02231: 6 b g Red Ransom - Lady Climber (Mount Hagen) Waited with, hard rdn 2f out, kept on well ins last to lead cl-home: op 4/1, headgear reapplied for first time in 3 years: '99 wnr at Kempton (h'cap, rtd 75): missed '98, '97 wnr at Goodwood (mdn, P Cole, rtd 93): eff at 10/11.5f on firm & gd/soft grnd, any trk: apprec reapplication of blnks. **80**
2286 **JUST GIFTED 9** [4] R M Whitaker 4-8-12 (66) K Darley 9/2 JT FAV: 206222: 4 b g Rudimentary - Parfait Amour (Clantime) Chsd ldrs, rdn fnl 1f, ran on to lead well ins last, hdd fnl strides: bckd, consistent. ¾ **68**
2002 **KIRISNIPPA 22** [13] Derrick Morris 5-7-12 (52) P Doe 16/1: 320403: 5 b g Beveled - Kiri Te (Liboi) Led, under press & hdd well ins last, onepace: ran to best, see 1784, 1128. 1½ **52**
1991 **WHO CARES WINS 22** [12] C E Brittain 4-9-7 (75) P Robinson 7/1: -00034: Prom, hdwy & ev ch appr fnl 2f, onepce below dist: nicely bckd from 9/1: drop in trip, reportedly wears blnks next time, see 1991, 1329. ¾ **74**
1984 **GREYFIELD 23** [8] 4-9-5 (73) Craig Williams 8/1: 306-45: Waited with, imprvd up ins rail 2f out till short of room ins last: nicely bckd from 10/1, prob have made the frame with a clr run: worth another ch. *shd* **72**
1860 **SHAFFISHAYES 28** [3] 8-8-3 (57) F Norton 5/1: -06546: Keen bhd, styd on well for press ins last, nvr nrr. ½ **55**
*2295 **WADI 9** [10] 5-8-5 (59) C Rutter 6/1: 060417: Chsd ldrs rdn 2f out, same pace & eased towards fin. 1¾ **55**
1729 **FANTAIL 34** [9] 6-9-10 (78) S Sanders 20/1: 000/08: Handy till appr fnl 1f: missed '99, '98 wnr at Beverley (h'cap, rtd 91 at best): eff at 12f, stays 14f: acts on firm & soft, any trk, likes Redcar. ¾ **73**
*2263 **MY PLEDGE 11** [7] 5-8-4 (58) N Pollard 9/2 JT FAV: 50-219: Al rear: well bckd, too sn after 2263? 2½ **49**
2336 **SUPLIZI 8** [6] 9-8-11 (65) G Carter 20/1: P-4000: Chsd ldrs till 3f out: 10th: see 1788. 1¾ **54**
2031 **ARANA 21** [1] 5-7-10 (50)(bl)(22oh) S Righton 66/1: 00-000: Dwelt, al bhd: 11th, blnks reapp, no form. *dist* **0**
11 ran Time 2m 29.39 (7.39) (R Sargent) G L Moore Woodingdean, E.Sussex.

2531

4.50 HAZEL ADAIR MDN 3YO (D) 1m2f Good Inapplicable
£4426 £1362 £681 £340

1697 **KIFTSGATE 36** [13] Sir Michael Stoute 3-9-0 G Carter 4/1: -61: 3 ch c Kris - Blush Rambler (Blushing Groom) In tch, imprvd 2f out, sn rdn, no impress till qcknd to lead ins last, pushed out: nicely bckd tho' op 9/4: eye-catching in a hot race last time, unrcd juv: half-brother to smart mid-dist wnr Rambling Rose: eff at 10f, 12f will suit: acts on gd grnd, stiff/gall trk: progressive, win again, poss over 12f. **88**
1668 **DE TRAMUNTANA 37** [14] W Jarvis 3-8-9 Dane O'Neill 10/1: 00-242: 3 b f Alzao - Glamour Game (Nashwan) Sn led, under press appr fnl 1f, worn down ins last: op 6/1: better run, see 1218. *nk* **80**
1269 **SHATTERED SILENCE 58** [5] R Charlton 3-8-9 K Darley 7/2: -03: 3 b f Cozzene - Sunday Bazaar (Nureyev) Towards rear, struggling & under press ent str, kept on strongly ins last, nvr nrr: bckd from 11/2: better effort & apprec step up to 10f on gd grnd, 12f will suit even more & can find a race. 1¼ **78**

SANDOWN
SUNDAY JULY 9TH   Righthand, Galloping Track, Stiff Finish

2135 **EXECUTIVE ORDER** 16 [6] Sir Michael Stoute 3-9-0 Pat Eddery 7/4 FAV: -424: Well plcd, ch 2f out,   2½   79
sn rdn, onepce: hvly bckd stablemate of wnr: clrly well thought of, sharper 10f or drop back to 1m may suit.
1725 **JOONDEY** 34 [9] 3-9-0 P Robinson 8/1: -0325: In tch, wide, hdwy 3f out till 2f out: win a northern mdn.   2   76
-- **MYSTICAL STAR** [10] 3-9-0 D R McCabe 33/1: -6: Held up, gd prog to chase ldrs 2f out, sn wknd: 1   74
debut: Nicolotte first foal: sire a sprinter, drop back to 1m likely to suit this gelding: with J Sheehan.
2179 **BEAU DUCHESS** 14 [11] 3-8-9 M Fenton 33/1: -067: Prom & trav well till wknd 2f out: 1m h'cap?   1¾   67
1912 **CITRUS MAGIC** 25 [7] 3-9-0 C Rutter 25/1: -48: Nvr a factor: one more run for h'cap mark.   5   64
2188 **SUPREME SILENCE** 13 [12] 3-9-0 G Bardwell 20/1: -09: Sn cl-up, lost pl 3f out: Bluebird colt.   3   59$
1947 **GENERAL JACKSON** 24 [8] 3-9-0 N Pollard 12/1: -0430: In tch till 3f out: 10th, unsuited by longer trip?   ½   58
2056 **HERRING GREEN** 20 [3] 3-9-0 S Carson (5) 33/1: -00: U.r. bef start, early ldr, btn 4f out: 15th.   0
-- **Travellers Rest** [4] 3-9-0 F Norton 33/1:   1708 **Dawn Traveller** 35 [15] 3-8-9 D McGaffin (5) 33/1:
-- **Batwink** [2] 3-8-9 S Sanders 33/1:   2198 **Hanoi** 13 [1] 3-8-9 J Lowe 33/1:
15 ran   Time 2m 12.33 (8.23)   (Sir Evelyn de Rothschild)   Sir Michael Stoute Newmarket.

MUSSELBURGH
MONDAY JULY 10TH   Righthand, Sharp Track

Official Going: GOOD TO SOFT (SOFT Places) Stalls: Inside, except 5f/2m - Stand Side

2532
2.15 MCEWANS EBF MED AUCT MDN 2YO (E)   5f   **Good/Soft 75**   -07 Slow
£2808   £864   £432   £216 Raced stands side

2055 **FANTASY BELIEVER** 21 [8] J J Quinn 2-9-0 K Darley 1/1 FAV: 324221: 2 b g Sure Blade - Delicious   79
(Dominion) Dwelt, soon trckd ldrs, rdn & styd on well to lead near fin: hvly bckd: eff at 5f, 6f should suit: acts
on firm & hvy grnd, sharp/gall track: deserved this first success.
2214 **BARON CROCODILE** 13 [4] A Berry 2-9-0 C Lowther 14/1: 224502: 2 b g Puissance - Glow Again (The   ½   76
Brianstan) Led, rdn/hdd well inside last, no extra: op 8/1: acts on gd/sft & hvy, poss handles firm: see 1001.
2132 **TOP NOLANS** 17 [1] M H Tompkins 2-9-0 G Duffield 7/2: 03: 2 ch c Topanoora - Lauretta Blue   2   71
(Bluebird) Cl up, outpcd over 1f out: bckd, op 9/2: dropped in trip: see 2132 (mdn).
1776 **PERTEMPS JARDINE** 33 [2] R A Fahey 2-9-0 P Hanagan (7) 7/2: -34: Keen/held up, outpcd fnl 2f.   2½   65
1429 **NOWT BUT TROUBLE** 49 [3] 2-9-0 N Kennedy 8/1: 635: Cl up, outpcd over 1f out: op 5/1: 7 week abs.   ½   63
1189 **BOLD MCLAUGHLAN** 64 [6] 2-9-0 A Culhane 25/1: -0006: Bhd halfway: abs: rtd higher 700 (debut).   6   52
2009 **SAVANNA MISS** 23 [5] 2-8-9 J F Egan 14/1: 57: Bhd halfway: op 8/1: btr 2009 (gd).   3½   39
755 **MANX GYPSY** 104 [7] 2-8-9 Dean McKeown 33/1: 408: Soon t.o.: 4 month abs: see 712.   dist   0
8 ran   Time 1m 01.6 (4.1)   (The Fantasy Fellowship)   J J Quinn Settrington, N Yorks

2533
2.45 MILLER SELL HCAP 3YO+ 0-60 (F)   1m rnd   Good/Soft 75   -25 Slow   [49]
£2660   £760   £380   3 yo rec 9 lb   Remained far side straight

2099 **JAMMIE DODGER** 19 [5] R M Whitaker 4-9-0 (35) V Halliday 8/1: 000201: 4 b g Ardkinglass - Ling Lane   40
(Slip Anchor) Made all, rdn & styd on well fnl 2f, in command/eased down near line: no bid: op 7/1: first win:
eff at 1m, tried 12f: acts on gd & gd/soft grnd, sharp track: eff forcing the pace in selling grade.
2297 **MISS GRAPETTE** 10 [1] A Berry 4-9-1 (36) P A Darley 25/1: 000502: 4 b f Brief Truce - Grapette   1½   37
(Nebbiolo) Cl up, every ch over 3f out, outpcd by wnr fnl 2f: styd this longer 1m trip: see 1734 (6f).
2236 **UNMASKED** 12 [7] J S Goldie 4-8-6 (27) A Culhane 8/1: 000333: 4 ch f Safawan - Unveiled (Sayf   ¾   27
El Arab) Chsd ldrs, outpcd 3f out, kept on inside last, no threat: handles firm & gd/soft: see 2236, 798.
2460 **RED CAFE** 3 [3] P D Evans 4-9-0 (40)(bl) C Lowther 5/1: 000424: Chsd ldrs wide halfway, held fnl 2f.   ¾   39
1699 **SITTING PRETTY** 36 [6] 4-8-3 (24) D Mernagh (3) 33/1: 00-P05: Chsd ldrs, held fnl 2f: see 1353.   shd   23
2479 **TAKER CHANCE** 3 [4] 4-9-6 (41) G Duffield 8/1: 000006: Held up, never on terms: quick reapp.   ¾   39
2298 **BRANDON MAGIC** 10 [10] 7-9-10 (45)(bl) O Pears 7/2 FAV: 030557: Chsd ldrs 6f: op 2/1: see 497.   ¾   42
2453 **KNAVES ASH** 3 [11] 9-9-8 (43) Dean McKeown 6/1: 003608: Held up, eff 3f out, no prog: quick reapp.   nk   39
2147 **KUWAIT THUNDER** 17 [9] 4-9-0 (35)(vis) J F Egan 7/1: 060059: Rear, never dangerous: op 6/1.   ½   30
1296 **MY TYSON** 56 [8] 5-9-3 (38) F Lynch 16/1: 136000: Al bhd: 10th: op 14/1: 8 week abs: see 676.   1   31
3498} **CLAIM GEBAL CLAIM** 324 [2] 4-9-3 (38) K Dalgleish (5) 20/1: 0546-0: Bolted bef start, chsd ldrs 5f: 5   21
11th: reapp: rnr up on reapp in '99 (rtd 52, Mrs G Duffield, seller): rtd 68 at best in '98: eff between 5/7f, tried
10f: acts on fast & gd/soft grnd: best without blinks: now with P Monteith.
11 ran   Time 1m 45.5 (8.0)   (R M Whitaker)   R M Whitaker Scarcroft, W Yorks

2534
3.15 MCEWANS HCAP 3YO 0-70 (E)   1m1f rnd   Good/Soft 75   +04 Fast   [74]
£4270   £1314   £657   £328 Raced stands side fnl 3f

4222} **TWILIGHT WORLD** 280 [4] Sir Mark Prescott 3-8-2 (47)(1ow) G Duffield 10/11 FAV: 006-1: 3 b g Night Shift   52
- Masskana (Darshaan) Chsd ldrs, rdn/led 2f out, held on well fnl 1f, rdn out: hvly bckd, best time of day: reapp/
h'cap bow: mod form at up to 6f last term (rtd 54, 3 starts, mdns): apprec step up to 9f, 10f + could suit: acts on
gd/soft & a sharp track: runs well fresh: typical Sir M Prescott improver when sent over further once h'capped.
*2093 **BOLD STATE** 19 [2] M H Tompkins 3-9-6 (66) K Darley 7/2: 000112: 3 b g Never So Bold - Multi Sofft   1   67
(Northern State) Rdn/chsd wnr over 1f out, kept on, al just held: op 5/2: clr rem: acts on firm & gd/soft.
2284 **FINERY** 10 [3] C A Dwyer 3-9-0 (60)(vis) O Pears 8/1: 010023: 3 ch g Barathea - Micky's Pleasure   4   53
(Foolish Pleasure) Led, rdn/hdd 2f out, & soon held: prob handles gd/soft, btr in 2284 (fast, claimer).
2175 **RHODAMINE** 15 [5] J L Eyre 3-9-7 (67) A Culhane 7/2: 261434: In tch 7f: op 5/2: btr 1560 (11f).   3½   53
2205 **BLUE LEGEND** 14 [7] 3-7-10 (42) D Mernagh (3) 14/1: 00-045: In tch, btn 3f out: op 12/1: see 1939.   7   17
*2205 **PHILAGAIN** 14 [1] N Kennedy 3-7-10 (42) N Kennedy 12/1: 0-4016: Chsd ldrs 6f: op 8/1: btr 2205 (1m, fast).   11   1
6 ran   Time 1m 57.1 (6.4)   (J Fishpool - Osborne House)   Sir Mark Prescott Newmarket, Suffolk

2535
3.45 KRONENBOURG HCAP 3YO+ 0-60 (F)   5f   Good/Soft 75   -03 Slow   [59]
£2576   £736   £368   3 yo rec 5 lb   Majority raced stands side - centre

2374 **BRANSTON LUCY** 7 [6] T J Etherington 3-9-5 (55) R Ffrench 8/1: -00021: 3 b f Prince Sabo - Softly   60
Spoken (Mummy's Pet) Chsd ldrs, rdn/led over 1f out, edged right & just held on for press: op 6/1: '99 Redcar
wnr (nursery, rtd 62 & 57a): eff at 5f on firm & gd/soft grnd, any track.
2282 **GARNOCK VALLEY** 11 [10] A Berry 10-9-7 (52) F Lynch 11/2: 036252: 10 b g Dowsing - Sunley Sinner shd   56

799

MUSSELBURGH   MONDAY JULY 10TH   Righthand, Sharp Track

(Try My Best) Rear, rdn & styd on well inside last, post came too soon: op 5/1: eff at 5/7f: see 47 (AW).

*2297	**NIFTY NORMAN** 10 [7] D Nicholls 6-10-0 (59) O Pears 7/4 FAV: 630613: 6 b g Rock City - Nifty Fifty	1¾	59	

(Runnett) Chsd ldrs, rdn/one pace & held inside last: well bckd: btr 2297 (AW, 6f, made most).

2326 **QUITE HAPPY** 9 [12] M H Tompkins 5-9-10 (55) G Duffield 10/1: 335364: Trckd ldrs, onepace fnl 1f.	nk 54
2395 **FACILE TIGRE** 6 [14] 5-8-13 (44) R Winston 11/1: 506055: Dwelt, late gains, never threat: qck reapp.	1 41
1806 **BOWCLIFFE GRANGE** 31 [3] 8-8-5 (36) Kimberley Hart 20/1: 003006: Led till over 1f out, fdd: see 798.	2 28
2282 **ZIBAK** 11 [11] 6-8-2 (33) K Dalgleish (5) 12/1: -06547: Prom, outpcd fnl 2f: see 1685.	nk 24
2315 **TWO JACKS** 9 [16] 3-9-2 (52) A Culhane 25/1: 00-008: Never on terms far side: mod form.	1¾ 39
2252 **ORIEL STAR** 12 [8] 4-9-0 (45)(bl) C Lowther 9/1: 300609: Prom 3f: op 8/1: blinks reapplied: see 312.	nk 31
2233 **PALLIUM** 12 [5] 12-7-11 (28)(tbl) J Bramhill 50/1: -00000: Dwelt, never on terms: 10th: see 1358.	¾ 12
1910 **PISCES LAD** 26 [13] 4-9-10 (55) K Darley 5/1: 102000: Dwelt, eased halfway, saddled slipped: 13th.	0
2240 **Just Dissident** 12 [4] 8-8-7 (38) Dean McKeown 16/1:	
1430 **Six For Luck** 49 [15] 8-8-7 (38)(t)(11ow)(14oh) V Halliday 66/1:	
2784} **Johs Brother** 359 [9] 4-8-1 (31)(1ow) Dawn Rankin (0) 33/1:	

14 ran   Time 1m 01.4 (3.9)   (J David Abell)   T J Etherington Norton, N Yorks

---

2536   4.15 MCEWANS CLAIMER 4YO+ (E)   2m   Good/Soft 75 -18 Slow
£2743   £844   £422   £211

2295 **CASHIKI** 10 [9] B Palling 4-8-6 J F Egan 3/1: 020261: 4 ch f Case Law - Nishiki (Brogan)		35

Led 6f out, styd on strongly & in command fnl 1f, pushed out cl home: op 2/1: plcd twice in '99 (rtd 66, h'cap): '98 wnr at Lingfield (seller), Chepstow (claimer) & Pontefract (nursery, rtd 73): eff at 14f/2m on firm & gd/soft, prob handles any track: apprec this drop to claiming grade.

2219 **ALL ON MY OWN** 13 [6] J S Wainwright 5-8-9 J McAuley (5) 11/2: -3062: 5 ch g Unbridled - Someforall	4	34

(One For All) Held up, prog to chase wnr over 1f out, kept on, al held: op 4/1: stays 2m, handles gd & gd/soft grnd.

-- **PRIDDY FAIR** [5] B Mactaggart -K Dalgleish (5) 10/1: 0000/3: 7 b m North Briton - Rainbow Ring	2½	32

(Rainbow Quest) Cl up 14f: op 8/1: long flat abs, jumps fit, May '2000 Hexham wnr (sell, rtd 87h, eff at 2m/2m4f).

1689 **NOTATION** 37 [4] D W Chapman 6-8-5 Claire Bryan (5) 16/1: 400004: Held up, mod late gains: op 12/1.	4	23$
2176 **SALVAGE** 15 [3] 5-9-3 F Lynch 4/1: 300405: Chsd ldrs halfway, btn 2f out: see 779.	3	32
2373 **URGENT REPLY** 7 [8] 7-8-3 J Bramhill 12/1: 006626: Led 7f out till 6f out, btn 4f out: well bckd.	11	12
-- **S AND O P** [2] 6-8-7 C Lowther 7-: Led 9f, soon btn: op 12/1, flat debut, mod jumps form.	dist	0
-- **INHERIT THE EARTH** [7] 6-9-0 R Winston 10/1: 8: Bhd 4f out: op 20/1, debut: no points form.	7	0

8 ran   Time 3m 37.4 (14.9)   (The Valley Commandos)   B Palling Cowbridge, Vale Of Glamorgan

---

2537   4.45 SPA FILLIES HCAP 3YO+ 0-65 (F)   1m4f   Good/Soft 75 -32 Slow   [50]
£2702   £772   £386   3 yo rec 13lb   Raced stands side 3f

2366 **ASHLEIGH BAKER** 7 [4] M Johnston 5-9-7 (43) R Winston 3/1 JT FAV: 640301: 5 b m Don't Forget Me -		48

Gayla Orchestra (Lord Gayle) Chsd ldrs, went on over 3f out, styd on strongly fnl 2f, rdn out: op 2/1: plcd in '99 (rtd 54 at best): '98 Ayr wnr (h'cap, win A Bailey, rtd 65 at best): suited by 12f, tried 2m: acts on firm & soft.

1501 **AMSARA** 45 [7] D W Chapman 4-8-3 (25) Claire Bryan (5) 20/1: 600002: 4 b f Taufan - Legend Of Spain	2½	26

(Alleged) In tch, rdn & kept on fnl 2f, no impression on wnr: 6 week abs: apprec sell h'caps: see 412.

1772 **SILKEN LADY** 33 [5] M J Ryan 4-8-3 (25) Kimberley Hart 25/1: 0-0003: 4 b f Rock Hopper - Silk St	shd	26

James (Pas de Seul) Rear, rdn & styd on fnl 2f, no threat: prob styd this longer 12f trip: only mod form prev.

2139 **SPIRIT OF KHAMBANI** 17 [8] M Johnston 3-8-11 (46) K Dalgleish (5) 11/1: 3-0004: Chsd wnr 3f out,	¾	46

rdn/no extra fnl 1f: op 8/1, stablemate of wnr: prob stays a sharp 12f, 10f could prove ideal on this evidence.

2245 **SPONTANEITY** 12 [1] 4-9-6 (42) C Lowther 4/1: 0-0625: Keen/cl up, btn 2f out: see 2245, 1933 (sell).	3½	37
1955 **NUTMEG** 25 [10] 3-9-6 (55) K Darley 9/2: -40066: Held up, never any impress: op 7/2: btr 894 (1m).	14	35
2219 **PHASE EIGHT GIRL** 13 [2] 4-8-8 (30) N Kennedy 10/1: 13-007: Bhd 4f out: see 2219.	4	16
2236 **BAY OF BENGAL** 12 [9] 4-9-7 (43) J McAuley (5) 3/1 JT FAV: 0-0328: Reared start & rider lost iron,	nk	16

keen/chsd ldrs, btn 2f out: bckd: proved a difficult ride for jockey in circumstances, best forgotten: see 2236, 1939.

1560 **MANX SHADOW** 42 [3] 3-8-10 (45) J F Egan 33/1: 050-09: Led 9f, soon bhd: 6 week abs: see 1560.	12	5

9 ran   Time 2m 43.4 (12.8)   (The David James Partnership)   M Johnston Middleham, N Yorks

---

RIPON   MONDAY JULY 10TH   Righthand, Sharpish Track

Official Going   GOOD/SOFT. Stalls: Str Course - Stands Side; Round Course - Inside.

2538   6.55 CLARO SELLER 3YO+ (F)   1m2f   Soft 103 +05 Fast
£2275   £650   £325   3 yo rec 11lb

2245 **ROCK SCENE** 12 [17] A Streeter 8-9-7 P Dobbs (5) 11/2: 065541: 8 b g Scenic - Rockeater (Roan Rocket)		49

Held up, prog 3f out, led ent fnl 1f, styd on well, drvn out: no bid, fair time: missed '99, '98 Warwick wnr (mdn h'cap, rtd 48): eff at 10/11f on fast & hvy grnd: consistent in sellers/claimers.

2062 **TIME TEMPTRESS** 20 [4] G M Moore 4-9-2 P Hanagan (7) 13/2: 6-0002: 4 b f Timeless Times -	1	43

Tangalooma (Hotfoot) Front rank, went on 3f out till collared ent last, styd on & not btn far: op 4/1, 6L clr 3rd: stays an easy 10f on fast & soft: shld win similar, see 1303 (AW).

2422 **GENUINE JOHN** 5 [12] J Parkes 7-9-7 T Quinn 10/1: 245053: 7 b g High Estate - Fiscal Folly (Foolish	6	40$

Pleasure) In tch, onepace fnl 2f: qck reapp: offic rtd just 34, so treat this rating with caution: see 561 (AW h'cap).

2212 **LEVEL HEADED** 13 [10] P W Hiatt 5-9-2 P Goode (3) 16/1: -03504: Led till 3f out, no extra: see 2011.	1½	33
2362 **BLAIR** 7 [6] 3-8-10 W Supple 16/1: 004005: Rear, imprvg when short of room 2f out, switched, kept	3	34

on but ch had gone: no luck in running today: see 1661 (flattered, 12f mdn).

2221 **MUTABARI** 13 [2] 6-9-7 (vis) J Parkes 16/1: 565006: Chsd ldrs, onepcd over 2f out: see 255 (AW).	nk	33
38 **MARGARETS DANCER** 240 [15] 5-9-7 (t) R Cody Boutcher (7) 16/1: 6550-7: Mid-div, prog when short	4	28

of room over 2f out, nvr nr to chall: long abs: rnr-up at Hamilton in '99 (class stks, rtd 61): '98 Pontefract, Thirsk (sells) & Beverley wnr (h'cap, rtd 61): eff arnd 1m on fast & hvy, trk: wears a t-strap: tried blnks.

2245 **TUFAMORE** 12 [20] 4-9-12 (bl) Darren Williams (5) 12/1: 053358: In tch, rdn & btn 2f out: see 684.	1	32
2457 **I CANT REMEMBER** 3 [18] 6-9-7 (t) S Finnamore (5) 100/30 FAV: 060349: Slowly away, mod late prog,	½	26

nvr dngrs: nicely bckd, qck reapp: much btr 2457, 2219 (12f, fast grnd).

2393 **RED ROSES** 6 [1] 4-9-2 (BL) Kim Tinkler 25/1: 000040: Dwelt, mod late prog, nvr dngrs in 10th: blnks.	3	17
*1546 **ESPERTO** 42 [11] 7-9-12 G Bardwell 10/1: 000610: Held up ent 1m, wknd & eased considerably, fin 15th:		0

6 wk abs, top weight: much btr 1546.

2282 **Simand 11** [22] 8-9-2 P Fessey 33/1:		1353 **Wrangel 52** [8] 6-9-7 J Carroll 16/1:
2278 **First Legacy 11** [14] 4-9-2 D Mernagh (3) 33/1:		2119 **Sakharov 18** [16] 11-9-7 P Bradley (5) 50/1:
2147 **The Fossick 17** [3] 4-9-7 G Parkin 33/1:		2331 **Artful Dane 9** [19] 8-9-7 (bl) G Hannon (7) 11/1:
2136 **Silver Bullet 17** [5] 4-9-7 (vis) J Bosley (7) 25/1:		1699 **Ferny Factors 36** [7] 4-9-7 T Williams 20/1:
2236 **Bodfari Signet 12** [9] 4-9-7 (bl) M Fenton 50/1:		2317 **Royal Dolphin 9** [13] 4-9-7 K Hodgson 50/1:
21 ran Time 2m 13.1 (9.8) (Mrs J Hughes)		A Streeter Uttoxeter, Staffs

---

2539   7.20 THWAITES FILL MDN AUCT 2YO (F)   5f   Soft 103 -33 Slow
£2824   £869   £434   £217

2277 **SO DIVINE 11** [9] M Johnston 2-8-2 J Fanning 3/1: 41: 2 br f So Factual - Divina Mia (Dowsing)   **77**
Prom, went on 1½f out, rdn clr ins last: nicely bckd: 4,700gns purchase, dam a 6f juv wnr: eff over an easy
5f, 6f will suit: handles firm, acts on soft grnd: imprvg filly who can rate more highly & win again.

1893 **NEW WONDER 27** [11] J G Given 2-8-4(2ow) Dean McKeown 4/1: 3042: 2 b f Presidium - Miss Tri Colour 4   **70**
(Shavian) Rcd keenly rear, prog halfway, styd on fnl 1f, but no ch with wnr: eff at 5f, will apprec a return
to 6f: acts on gd, soft grnd & fibresand: see 1893.

2045 **CHARTLEYS PRINCESS 21** [1] K R Burke 2-8-2 W Supple 11/4 FAV: -533: 2 b f Prince Sabo - Ethel   nk   **67**
Knight (Thatch) Set pace till collared last, no extra: nicely bckd: handles firm & soft grnd: see 2045.

-- **MADIES PRIDE** [10] J J Quinn 2-8-5 J Carroll 10/1: 4: Dwelt, imprvd halfway, no impress ins last under   1   **68**
a kind ride: bckd from 14/1, debut: May foal, cost IR 6,500gns: dam 5f juv scorer: pleasing debut, improve.

1294 **ALPHACALL 56** [7] 2-8-2 P Fessey 9/1: 45: In tch, kept on without pace to chall: 8 wk abs, op   shd   **65**
6/1: looks in need of 6f+: will improve over further: see 1294.

-- **MARE OF WETWANG** [4] 2-8-2 R Lappin 33/1: 6: Pushed along in rear, styd on well fnl 1f, nvr nrr   shd   **64$**
on debut: ran green: cheaply bt Apr foal: looks sure to relish 6f+.

-- **EMMA THOMAS** [8] 2-8-2 O Pears 10/1: 7: Dwelt, eff halfway, switched & late hdwy, nvr dngrs on   1   **62**
debut: Jan foal, dam a minor 5f juv wnr: A Berry filly who will learn from this.

1304 **WHITE STAR LADY 56** [3] 2-8-2 G Bardwell 20/1: 58: Prom 3½f, grad fdd: 8 wk abs: see 1304 (5f sand).   hd   **61**

-- **JUST AS YOU ARE** [5] 2-8-8 (t) G Parkin 14/1: 9: Chsd ldrs till wknd halfway: op 10/1, debut: 4   **59**
Apr foal, cost IR 11,000gns: dam a 1m wnr in Ireland: with T Easterby.

-- **PETRAIL** [2] 2-8-6(1ow) A Culhane 10/1: 0: Speed 3f, fdd into 10th: tchd 14/1, debut: IR 8,200gns   ¾   **55**
purchase: Apr foal, dam a 5f juv wnr: sire a high-class 6/7f performer: D Nicholls filly.

1267 **YUKA SAN 59** [6] 2-8-2 A Nicholls (3) 20/1: 60: Speed till halfway, sn wknd & fin last: 8 wk abs.   3½   **44**
11 ran   Time 1m 04.6 (6.8)   (The 5th Middleham Partnership)   M Johnston Middleham, N Yorks

---

2540   7.50 LAND ROVER HCAP 3YO 0-80 (D)   1m4f60y   Soft 103 -08 Slow   [83]
£4920   £1514   £757   £378

*2362 **IRISH DANCER 7** [4] Ronald Thompson 3-7-10 (51)(6ex) J Bramhill 9/4 FAV: -00311: 3 ch f Lahib -   **56**
Mazarine Blue (Chief's Crown) Waited with, short of room 2f out, switched & fin well to lead cl-home, rdn out, won
a shade cosily: well bckd: recent Pontefract wnr when trained by Miss G Kelleway (sell h'cap): unplcd in '99
(rtd 67, mdn auct): eff at 11/12f, shld stay further: acts on firm & soft grnd, handles a sharp or stiff/undul
trk: imprvg filly who seems suited by waiting tactics: could complete hat-trick.

1411 **SUDDEN FLIGHT 51** [7] E A L Dunlop 3-9-7 (76) T Quinn 3/1: 0-1302: 3 b c In The Wings - Ma Petite   ¾   **79**
Cherie (Caro) Nvr far away, qcknd into lead 1½f out, not pace to repel wnr cl-home: nicely bckd, top weight,
7 wk abs: sound eff, eff at 12f, worth another try at 14f: see 924.

1919 **MIDDLETHORPE 26** [6] M W Easterby 3-8-0 (55) Dale Gibson 4/1: -05103: 3 b g Noble Patriarch -   1   **57**
Prime Property (Tirol) Chsd ldrs, rdn & ev ch dist, kept on under press: acts on gd & soft grnd: see 1758.

2238 **RED CANYON 12** [3] M L W Bell 3-8-10 (65) M Fenton 3/1: 441234: Led till 1½f out, fdd: well bckd.   3½   **62**

2482 **DALYAN 3** [5] P Fessey 10/1: -00405: Slowly away, prog from rear & ev ch 2f out,   5   **47**
fdd ins last: quick reapp: see 1104 (10f).

2145 **BEBE DE CHAM 17** [2] T Williams 16/1: 600066: Dwelt, recovered & in tch, wknd 2f out,   dist   **0**
eased considerably, t.o. in last: slipping down the h'cap: see 617 (AW).

6 ran   Time 2m 47.0 (13.5)   (B Bruce)   Ronald Thompson Stainforth, S Yorks

---

2541   8.20 TAYLOR WOODROW HCAP 3YO 0-80 (D)   6f   Soft 103 -34 Slow   [85]
£5723   £1761   £880   £440

2243 **DESRAYA 12** [6] K A Ryan 3-7-13 (56)(bl) Iona Wands (5) 11/2: 060231: 3 b g Desert Style - Madaraya   **61**
(Shahrastani) Prom, short of room over 2f out, styd on over 1f out to lead ins last, edged left for press, drvn
out: jockey rode out of careless riding: first win: rtd 73 in '99: stays 6f on fast, likes soft: wears blnks.

2355 **GOLDEN MIRACLE 8** [4] M Johnston 3-9-7 (78) R Winston 11/2: 000102: 3 b g Cadeaux Genereux -   1   **80**
Cheeky Charm (Nureyev) Made most till collared ins last, only btn 1L: topweight: acts on firm & soft: see 2355.

2517 **ROYAL ROMEO 2** [2] T D Easterby 3-9-5 (76) W Supple 3/1: 1-0163: 3 ch c Timeless Times - Farinara   ½   **76**
(Dragonara Palace) In tch, eff to chall dist, held by wnr when sltly hmpd cl-home: in gd form: see 1768.

2280 **FANTASY ADVENTURER 11** [1] J J Quinn 3-7-10 (53)(10h) P Fessey 12/1: 000404: In tch, eff 2f out,   hd   **52**
kept on ins last, btn less than 2L: acts on fast & soft: mdn h'caps will suit, see 1891.

1891 **LORDOFENCHANTMENT 27** [3] 3-8-5 (62) Kim Tinkler 6/1: 052205: Prom wknd over 1f out: btr 1768.   7   **47**

2165 **ELVINGTON BOY 16** [7] 3-9-0 (71) T Lucas 11/4 FAV: -00325: Prom, wknd over 1f out: see 2165 (gd).   1¾   **52**

*2440 **MARON 4** [5] 3-8-9 (66)(6ex) J Carroll 6/1: 003217: In tch, wknd well over 1f out: not handle soft?   8   **31**
7 ran   Time 1m 18.2 (8.2)   (Pendle Inn Partnership)   K A Ryan Newmarket

---

2542   8.50 WESTGATE HCAP 3YO+ 0-70 (E)   1m rnd   Soft 103 +03 Fast   [66]
£3653   £1124   £562   £281   3 yo rec 9 lb

907 **REQUESTOR 87** [7] J G FitzGerald 5-9-8 (60) J Carroll 16/1: 663-01: 5 br g Distinctly North -   **65**
Bebe Altesse (Alpenkonig) Hld up, hdwy over 2f out, led ins last, drvn out: gd time, 3 month abs, first win:
plcd once in '99 (rtd 82 back in '97: stays 1m on firm & soft: has tried blnks: runs well fresh.

2063 **LOVE KISS 20** [6] W Storey 5-8-6 (44) T Williams 25/1: 00-002: 5 b g Brief Truce - Pendulina   1   **47**
(Prince Tenderfoot) Handy, hdwy to lead over 1f out, collared cl-home, only btn 1L: handles soft: see 2063.

1431 **YOUNG ROSEIN 49** [2] Mrs G S Rees 4-9-1 (53) S Whitworth 14/1: 20-003: 4 b f Distant Relative - Red   1½   **53**
Rosein (Red Sunset) Handy, eff over 1f out, kept on same pace: 7 wk abs: stays 1m on fast & soft: see 1243.

RIPON MONDAY JULY 10TH Righthand, Sharpish Track

*2221 **NORTHGATE 13** [20] M Brittain 4-8-11 (49)(bl) D Mernagh (3) 3/1 FAV: 054214: Led till over 1f out, onepace: acts on firm & soft: see 2221. *nk* **48**
1920 **HIGH SUN 26** [15] 4-8-12 (50) A Nicholls (3) 7/1: 000005: Chsd ldrs, no impress over 1f out: see 942. *3* **44**
2380 **MAI TAI 7** [13] 5-8-4 (42) F Lynch 11/2: 010256: Hld up, eff 2f out, sn no impress: btr 2121. *1* **35**
2221 **DIM OFAN 13** [17] 4-9-6 (58)(bl) M Fenton 20/1: 106007: In tch, wknd well over 1f out: see 326 (a/w). *¾* **50**
2033 **TROPICAL BEACH 21** [10] 7-8-4 (42)(vis) G Bardwell 14/1: -06608: Slow away, bhd, some late gains. *shd* **33**
2484 **PIX ME UP 3** [16] 3-8-9 (56) Iona Wands (5) 9/1: 012409: Bhd, mod late gains: qk reapp: btr 1822. *1¾* **45**
125 **JUST BREMNER 223** [12] 3-9-1 (62) W Supple 12/1: 1004-0: Al bhd: 10th on reapp: see 125. *6* **41**
1843 **TRYSOR 30** [14] 4-9-2 (54) T Quinn 8/1: 0000: In tch, wknd over 2f out: 11th, appears flattered 1525. *3* **29**
1760 **PLEADING 33** [4] 7-9-6 (58)(bl) A Culhane 10/1: 300500: Hld up, eff 3f out, wknd 2f out: 12th. *7* **23**
2147 **The Castigator 17** [8] 3-8-6 (53) O Pears 25/1: 2315 **Colonel Sam 9** [18] 4-8-2 (40)(tbl) Dale Gibson 12/1:
2283 **Eurolink Moussaka 11** [3] 5-9-3 (55) R Winston 14/1:
15 ran Time 1m 45.7 (8) (Marquesa de Moratalla) J G FitzGerald Norton, N Yorks

2543

9.20 KIRKGATE MDN 3YO+ (D) 1m rnd Soft 103 -27 Slow
£3367 £1036 £518 £259 3 yo rec 9 lb

4217} **VARIETY SHOP 282** [4] H R A Cecil 4-9-2 T Quinn 1/2 FAV: -2-1: 4 b f Mr Prospector - Nimble Feet (Danzig) Made all at slow pace, qcknd appr 3f out, 3L ahead dist, pushed out, val 4L (rnr-up eased): well bckd: rnr-up sole juv start (rtd 79): eff at 1m/10f on soft & hvy: runs well fresh: open to further improvement. **85**
1669 **LATOUR 38** [5] J W Hills 3-8-7 S Whitworth 9/4: 45-232: 3 b f Sri Pekan - Fenny Rough (Home Guard) Trkd ldr, rdn 3f out, kept on same pace, 4L bhd wnr when eased ins last: nicely bckd: acts on firm & soft. *5* **77**
1643 **HAZIRAAN 38** [2] Sir Michael Stoute 3-8-12 F Lynch 9/1: 03: 3 b c Primo Dominie - Hazaradjat (Darshaan) Keen, waited with in tch, rdn 3f out, no impress over 1f out: see 1643. *3* **77$**
1539 **BUTTERWICK CHIEF 44** [3] R A Fahey 3-8-12 P Hanagan (7) 50/1: 04: Handy till rdn & outpcd 3f out. *5* **68**
-- **FACT OR FICTION** [1] 3-8-7 A Culhane 33/1: 5: Sn well bhd on debut: half sister to a 7f/12f wnr. *29* **23**
5 ran Time 1m 47.9 (10.4) (K Abdullah) H R A Cecil Newmarket

WINDSOR MONDAY JULY 10TH Sharp Fig 8 Track

Official Going SOFT. Stalls: Inside.

2544

6.40 WISTERIA HCAP 3YO+ 0-70 (E) 1m2f Soft Inapplicable [70]
£3570 £1020 £510 3 yo rec 11lb

2457 **MUTADARRA 3** [10] G M McCourt 7-8-10 (52) D O'Donohoe 10/1: 000251: 7 ch g Mujtahid - Silver Echo (Caerleon) Bhd, stdy prog ent fnl 4f, rdn to lead below dist, styd on well: op 8/1, qck reapp: earlier won a Huntingdon mdn hdle (2m, firm, rtd 101h): '99 wnr at Sandown (h'cap, rtd 69, W Musson): dual rnr-up in '98 (rtd 65): suited by 10f, stays 11.5f: acts on firm & soft grnd, poss hvy: goes on any trk & is well h'capped. **53**
2143 **NIGHT CITY 17** [22] K R Burke 9-8-7 (49) N Callan 13/2: 441522: 9 b g Kris - Night Secret (Nijinsky) Led, clr halfway, und press appr fnl 2f, worn down ent last, kept on: tchd 8/1, well clr rem: v tough. *¾* **53**
1807 **SAMMYS SHUFFLE 31** [12] Jamie Poulton 5-7-13 (41)(bl) M Henry 10/1: 640223: 5 b h Touch Of Grey - Cabinet Shuffle (Thatching) Held up, imprvd 4f out, kept on best of the rest but no ch front pair: best on e/trk. *10* **35**
*2372 **WITH A WILL 7** [4] H Candy 6-9-4 (60)(6ex) C Rutter 6/1: 0-3314: Prom till no extra appr fnl 2f: op 4/1, qck reapp with a penalty, much btr 2372 (gd grnd). *3* **51**
2186 **BARBASON 15** [16] 8-10-0 (70) I Mongan (5) 16/1: 255155: Chsd ldrs, same pace fnl 3f: op 10/1. *1½* **59**
2492 **BLUE ACE 2** [2] 7-8-13 (55) M Tebbutt 20/1: 000666: Held up, wide hdwy 3f out, onepace 2f out. *1½* **42**
2220 **LOKOMOTIV 13** [6] 4-8-7 (49)(bl) P Fitzsimons (5) 33/1: 00-607: Handy till fnl 2f: best at 7f/1m on faster. *3* **33**
*2370 **DIZZY TILLY 7** [13] 6-8-8 (50)(6ex) T G McLaughlin 5/1 FAV: 433018: Prom, fdd ent fnl 3f: too sn after 2370? *2* **32**
1978 **ULTRA CALM 24** [17] 4-8-5 (47) J Tate 12/1: 600229: Cl-up till wknd qckly over 2f out: new stable. *1½* **27**
2429 **FIELD MASTER 5** [20] 3-8-12 (65) S Sanders 20/1: 100050: Nvr a factor: 10th, op 14/1, qck reapp. *2½* **42**
2199 **ZAHA 14** [8] 5-9-5 (61) R Price 12/1: 001400: Al towards rear: 11th: capable of better, see 1370. *2½* **35**
633 **RAYIK 128** [11] 5-9-4 (60) W Ryan 11/1: 214120: Al bhd: 14th, abs, equitrack specialist, see 621. **0**
*1389 **DESERT SPA 51** [5] 5-8-3 (45) A Clark 10/1: -11010: Sn bhd: 16th, abs, progressive at W'hampton. **0**
2799} **Merry Prince 357** [14] 5-8-6 (48) Dane O'Neill 25/1: 2366 **Such Boldness 7** [7] 6-8-13 (55) D Sweeney 20/1:
2453 **Tiger Talk 3** [1] 4-9-9 (65)(vis) J Quinn 20/1:
16 ran Time 2m 11.6 (McCourt Fine Meats Ltd) G M McCourt Letcombe Regis, Oxon.

2545

7.05 CLEMATIS MDN 2YO (D) 5f Soft Inapplicable
£2938 £904 £452 £226

-- **SING A SONG** [13] R Hannon 2-8-9 Dane O'Neill 8/1: 1: 2 b f Blues Traveller - Raja Moulana (Raja Baba) Held up, imprvd/went far side after halfway, led bef dist & rdn, ran on strgly, shade rdly in the end: op 5/1 on debut: Ir2,800gns Apr foal, later made 24,000gns: half-sister to 2 wnrs, incl 6/9f juv Futurballa, dam 7f wnr: sire styd 12f: eff at 5f, further will suit: acts on soft grnd & a sharp trk: runs well fresh, type to improve. **81**
2082 **SO SOBER 19** [7] C F Wall 2-9-0 S Sanders 11/2: -542: 2 b c Common Grounds - Femme Savante (Glenstal) Towards rear, prog to chall appr fnl 1f, kept on but held: op 4/1: imprvd: goes on fast & soft grnd. *1* **82**
1667 **JETHAME 38** [6] B J Meehan 2-8-9 Pat Eddery 10/1: 003: 2 ch f Definite Article - Victorian Flower (Tate Gallery) Chsd ldrs, rdn 2f out, kept on onepace: op 6/1: apprec nurseries now: prob handles soft grnd. *2½* **70**
1962 **VALDESCO 24** [5] M A Jarvis 2-9-0 P Robinson 11/4: 34: Prom, unable to qckn appr fnl 1f: nicely bckd from 4/1: more expected after promising gd grnd debut in 1962. *¾* **73**
1924 **SHARP ACT 26** [2] 2-9-0 R Hills 14/1: -005: Front rank, led after 2f till bef dist, no extra: op 8/1. *shd* **73**
2088 **FAIR PRINCESS 19** [12] 2-8-9 M Hills 13/8 FAV: 2206: Chsd ldrs, eff 2f out, no impression: well bckd, tho' op evens: more expected after running in a Gr 3 last time: see 1538 (gd/soft). *1* **65**
1486 **VINE COURT 46** [8] 2-8-9 A Clark 16/1: 067: Led 2f, fdd appr fnl 1f: 7 wk abs, nurseries or sellers next. *¾* **63**
-- **RISQUE SERMON** [11] 2-9-0 N Pollard 20/1: 8: Nvr a factor: debut, op 8/1: 12,000gns Risk Me Apr gldg, brother to sev wnrs, incl useful sprint juv Signs: dam 9f wnr, sire 1m/10f performer: with Miss Sanders. *1¾* **64**
-- **BATCHWORTH BREEZE** [10] 2-8-9 S Carson (5) 33/1: 9: Dwelt, nvr in it: debut: Beveled Mar sister to 3 winning sprinters (none as juveniles), dam 7f wnr: with E Wheeler. *6* **47**
-- **PICKETT POINT** [4] 2-9-0 A Daly 33/1: 0: Dwelt, sn struggling: 10th, debut: Magic Ring gelding. *13* **32**
10 ran Time 1m 03.9 (Lady Davis) R Hannon East Everleigh, Wilts.

2546
7.35 TOM SMITH HCAP 3YO+ 0-70 (E)   1m67y   Soft   Inapplicable   [70]
£3307   £945   £472   3 yo rec 9 lb

*2367 **DINAR 7** [13] R Brotherton 5-8-12 (54)(6ex) G Carter 6/1: 202011: 5 b h Dixieland Band - Bold Jessie **62**
(Never So Bold) Led thr'out, well in command when eased considerably towards fin, v cmftbly: val 6L+:
last week won over C/D here at Windsor (h'cap): '99 Kempton wnr (h'cap, rtd 46, P Bowen): eff at 12f, tried
2m, suited by 1m on firm & hvy, likes sharp/easy trks: revelation from the front today, land a qk hat-trick.

2221 **COMPATRIOT 13** [2] P S Felgate 4-9-6 (62) W Ryan 20/1: -24602: 4 b g Bigstone - Campestral   2½ **63**
(Alleged) Prom in chsg pack, styd on under press for 2nd but no ch with wnr: gd run, remains a mdn: see 1414.

2367 **ADMIRALS FLAME 7** [12] C F Wall 9-9-4 (60) Pat Eddery 7/2 FAV: 0-0133: 9 b g Doulab - Fan The   1½ **58**
Flame (Grundy) Mid-div, hdwy under press appr fnl 2f, chsd wnr briefly bef dist, onepace: clr remn qk reapp.

2121 **CHAMPAGNE GB 18** [7] Andrew Reid 4-8-11 (53)(bl) M Henry 25/1: 301004: Mid-div, staying on   5 **43**
fin but nvr nr ldrs: return to 10f may suit, see 1393 (fibresand).

2349 **PATSY STONE 8** [18] 4-9-13 (69) S Sanders 11/2: 011445: Held up, prog fnl 2f, nvr dngrs: see 1794.   1 **54**

2293 **HAIL THE CHIEF 10** [8] 4-9-5 (70) R Smith (5) 8/1: 0-426: Handy in the pack till no extra appr fnl 2f: 4 **51**
h'cap bow, back up in trip: promising on fast grnd in 2293.

1978 **INDIAN SWINGER 24** [14] 4-8-4 (46) J Quinn 33/1: 003307: Nvr troubled ldrs: turf return, see 582.   ½ **26**

2467 **CABARET QUEST 3** [3] 4-8-3 (45) P Fitzsimons (5) 33/1: 000068: Prom in the pack till fdd appr fnl 2f.   ½ **24**

1370 **DR MARTENS 52** [11] 6-8-3 (45)(BL) L Newton 16/1: 06-009: Al towards rear: 7 wk abs, blnkd, see 965.   hd **24**

1606 **GUEST ENVOY 40** [17] 5-8-6 (48) L Newman 33/1: 605550: Nvr on terms: 10th, 6 wk abs, see 811.   3½ **22**

2380 **STITCH IN TIME 7** [6] 4-8-2 (44) G Baker (7) 8/1: 233020: Mid-div till ent fnl 3f: 11th, qck reapp.   2½ **14**

2302 **HOH GEM 10** [9] 4-8-7 (49) G Hind 6/1: 141400: Al bhd: 12th: see 1520.   1¾ **16**

2129 Glendale Ridge 17 [16] 5-9-10 (66) O Urbina 12/1:   2170 **Hadleigh 16** [10] 4-9-12 (68) R Hills 33/1:
2329 **Bandbox 9** [5] 5-9-5 (61) J Weaver 16/1:
15 ran   Time 1m 46.8   (J Rees)   R Brotherton Elmley Castle, Worcs.

2547
8.05 EBF CLASSIFIED STKS 3YO+ 0-90 (C)   1m3f135y   Soft   Inapplicable
£5562   £2109   £1054   £479   3 yo rec 13lb

1831 **COOL INVESTMENT 22** [5] M Johnston 3-8-5 R Hills 10/3: 206441: 3 b c Prince Of Birds - Superb   **92**
Investment (Hatim) Trkd ldrs, went on 3f out, held on well, drvn out: won sole juv start at Musselburgh (auct mdn,
rtd 78): eff at 10f, suited by soft & fast grnd, sharp trk: progressive colt.

*1970 **LUCKY LADY 24** [4] Sir Michael Stoute 3-8-6 Pat Eddery 5/2: 212: 3 ch f Nashwan - Jet Ski Lady   1¼ **90**
(Vaguely Noble) In tch, prog 3f out, drvn to press wnr appr fnl 1f, held nr fin: clr rem: acts on fast & soft.

2068 **WAFFIGG 20** [6] M A Jarvis 3-8-9 P Robinson 6/5 FAV: 5103: 3 b c Rainbow Quest - Celtic Ring   7 **87**
(Welsh Pageant) Chsd ldrs, eff appr fnl 2f, outpcd fnl 1f: similar level of form as 2068 & 1554 (hvy grnd mdn).

2090 **GREEN CARD 19** [2] S P C Woods 6-9-4 (vis) J Reid 12/1: -46304: Led till 3f out, fdd: visors   1 **82**
in place of blnks: unsuited by step up in trip on ground softer than preferred: see 1112.

2002 **BASMAN 23** [1] 6-9-4 M Tebbutt 25/1: /5-605: Held up, lost tch 2f out: see 1841.   23 **67**

2530 **ARANA 1** [3] 5-9-4 (bl) I Mongan (5) 150/1: 0-0006: Prom 7f: ran yesterday.   dist **0**
6 ran   Time 2m 37.7   (Markus Graff)   M Johnston Middleham, N.Yorks.

2548
8.35 SUCKLE FILLIES MDN 3YO (D)   1m67y rnd   Soft   Inapplicable
£4257   £1310   £655   £327

2086 **TANGO TWO THOUSAND 19** [12] J H M Gosden 3-8-11 R Havlin 7/2: -521: 3 b f Sri Pekan - Run Bonnie   **83**
(Runnett) Nvr far away, led halfway, drifted left fnl 2f but still won easily: unrcd juv: eff at 1m/9f: handles
fast, imprvd considerably on this soft grnd: goes on sharp trks: progressive filly.

1268 **BERZOUD 59** [14] J Noseda 3-8-11 J Weaver 25/1: 02: 3 b f Ezzoud - Bertie's Girl (Another Realm)   4 **75**
Pld hard, led till halfway, kept on for 2nd but no ch with wnr: 8 wk abs: imprvd on soft, may apprec 10f.

2365 **TRIPLE WOOD 7** [2] B Hanbury 3-8-11 J Reid 9/2: 52-543: 3 b f Woodman - Triple Kiss (Shareef   ½ **74**
Dancer) Rcd in 2nd till halfway, styd on till no extra dist: qck reapp: poss handles soft, see 2365, 1224 (fast & gd).

-- **SOLO BID** [7] B R Millman 3-8-11 G Hind 20/1: 4: In tch, eff 3f out, onepace appr fnl 1f: fair debut.   3½ **69**

1481 **EUROLINK ARTEMIS 46** [1] Pat Eddery 5/2 FAV: 435: Chsd ldrs, rdn appr fnl 2f, sn onepace: 3 **64**
7 wk abs, surely something amiss after 1481 & 915.

4202} **GOLDEN WAY 282** [9] 3-8-11 G Carter 12/1: 0-6: Held up, moderate late hdwy: reapp: unplcd sole   nk **63**
'99 start (fill mdn, rtd 68): half-sister to sev wnrs, dam 10f wnr: one more run for h'cap mark: with E Dunlop.

2322 **SASH 9** [10] 3-8-11 P Doe 12/1: -57: Held up, gd hdwy 3f out, rdn 2f out, flashed tail, fdd: see 2322.   ½ **62**

1428 **BRIONEY 49** [4] 3-8-11 (t) M Tebbutt 12/1: 08: Nvr a factor: 7 wk abs, stablemate wnr.   2 **59**

1912 **MISS MANETTE 26** [11] 3-8-11 J Lowe 33/1: 609: Al bhd: see 1460.   1¾ **56$**

2232 **COLLISION 12** [3] 3-8-11 C Rutter 8/1: 60: In tch till 3f out: 10th, see 2232.   3½ **51**

2024 **Ffynnon Gold 22** [13] 3-8-11 N Pollard 33/1:   2232 **Red White And Blue 12** [5] 3-8-11 S Sanders 33/1:
2381 **Thewayshewalks 7** [6] 3-8-11 ( ) D Sweeney 33/1:   1863 **Exhibition Girl 29** [8] 3-8-11 M Hills 25/1:
14 ran   Time 1m 49.6   (Mrs C A Waters & Ms Rachel Hood)   J H M Gosden Manton, Wilts.

2549
9.05 CREEPER HCAP 3YO 0-70 (E)   6f   Soft   Inapplicable   [76]
£3237   £925   £462   3 stayed stands side & filled first 3 places.

2207 **DOCTOR DENNIS 14** [13] B J Meehan 3-8-12 (60) Pat Eddery 2/1 FAV: 021201: 3 b g Last Tycoon -   **69**
Noble Lustre (Lyphard's Wish) Prom stands side, led 2f out, rdn out: earlier won at Brighton (seller): '99
rnr-up (nurs, rtd 69): eff at 6f/sharp 7f on firm, soft grnd, likes sharp trks: eff with/without blnks.

1732 **CARNAGE 35** [11] Mrs P N Dutfield 3-7-12 (45)(1ow) P Fitzimons (0) 33/1: 00-002: 3 b g Catrail -   2 **48**
Caranina (Caro) Trkd other 2 stands side, feeling pace 2f out & rdn, kept on well ins last, no trouble wnr.

2284 **FOXS IDEA 10** [12] T D Barron 3-9-2 (64) N Callan 10/1: 050543: 3 b f Magic Ring - Lindy Belle   2½ **61**
(Alleging) Led stands side till 2f out, fdd below dist: clr of rest over on far side: suited by drop back
in trip for new connections tho' clrly much fav'd by racing stands side: acts on fibresand, fast & soft, see 294.

1925 **NIGHT DIAMOND 26** [8] I A Balding 3-9-7 (69)(tVIS) M Hills 8/1: 0-0004: Prom far side, led that grp   5 **56**
2f out, kept on, no ch with stands side trio: top-weight & visored, handles firm, gd/soft & prob soft: gd run.

1591 **LADY NOOR 40** [2] 3-8-7 (55) L Newman (3) 13/2: -00005: Front rank far side, onepace appr fnl 1f: 2 **37**
6 wk abs: plcd twice in '99 (nurs, rtd 71): eff at 5/6f, likes soft/hvy grnd: with Mrs Dutfield.

2223 **BEST BOND 13** [6] 3-9-0 (62) J Quinn 7/1: 300056: Slow away far side, late hdwy: best forgotten.   1 **42**

WINDSOR   MONDAY JULY 10TH   Sharp Fig 8 Track

2371 **FLEETING FANCY** 7 [10] 3-8-9 (57) N Pollard 14/1: 0-0307: Dwelt, rcd far side, nvr a factor: see 1877 (fast).½   36
2054 **PERLE DE SAGESSE** 21 [7] 3-8-11 (59) A Daly 11/1: 302108: Prom far side till 2f out: see 1877 (fast).   1   36
1971 **GOLD RIDER** 24 [3] 3-7-12 (46) G Baker (7) 25/1: 00009: Chsd ldrs far side till 2f out: no form.   ¾   21
2216 **ITSGOTTABDUN** 13 [9] 3-8-9 (57)(bl) S Sanders 8/1: 664300: Cl-up far side, wknd qckly fnl 2f: 10th.   nk   31
2292 **STOP THE TRAFFIC** 10 [4] 3-8-4 (52) Martin Dwyer 25/1: 550000: Nvr in it: 11th, vis omitted, see 397.   17   6
1675 **COST AUDITING** 37 [1] 3-8-9 (57) M Henry 14/1: 000-50: Led far side group till halfway, sn btn: 12th.   24   0
12 ran   Time 1m 16.1   (Mrs Judith Mendonca)   B J Meehan Upper Lambourn, Beks.

BATH   MONDAY JULY 10TH   Lefthand, Turning Track With Uphill Finish

Official Going   GOOD TO SOFT. Stalls: Str Crse - Far Side; Rnd Crse - Inside.

2550   2.00 EBF EVERSHOT MDN 2YO (D)   5f161y   Good/Soft 82   -16 Slow
£3493   £1075   £537   £268

-- **SHAARD** [9] B W Hills 2-9-0 (BL) R Hills 11/2: 1: 2 b c Anabaa - Braari (Gulch)   95
Dwelt, bhd, hdwy over 2f out, led dist, rdn clr: Feb foal, dam a 6f 2yo scorer: eff at 5.7f, further will suit:
acts on gd/soft & a sharp/turning trk: runs well fresh: blinkered for debut but this was a promising first run.
1208 **WESTERN HERO** 62 [10] R Hannon 2-9-0 Dane O'Neill 4/1: 332: 2 ch c Lake Coniston - Miss Pickpocket 5   83
(Petorius) Led, hdd appr fnl 1f, sn not pace of wnr: clr rem: op 3/1, 9 wk abs: eff at 5/5.7f on gd/soft: win sn.
993 **THE TRADER** 79 [11] M Blanshard 2-9-0 D Sweeney 13/2: 33: 2 ch c Selkirk - Snowing (Tate Gallery)   3   76
In tch, gd hdwy appr fnl 2f, no extra ins last: 11 wk abs, acts on gd/soft & soft: see 993.
-- **RUN ON** [7] B J Meehan 2-9-0 J Weaver 20/1: 4: Trkd ldrs, rdn/fdd appr fnl 1f: op 12/1: Feb   2½   70
foal, brother to a 9f wnr, also a successful hdler: dam won over 6f as a 2yo: improve at 6f+.
-- **SALSA** [1] 2-9-0 Martin Dwyer 12/1: 5: Dwelt, sn mid-div, wknd fnl 2f: tchd 20/1: 18,000gns   ½   69
Salse colt, dam a hdles scorer: shld apprec further in time for W R Muir.
-- **PARKSIDE PROPHECY** [13] 2-9-0 Craig Williams 8/1: 6: Dwelt, rear, late hdwy: op 6/1: May   2   64
first foal, dam won over 12f: sure to apprec 6f+ in time for M R Channon.
-- **AMPULLA** [3] 2-9-0 S Carson (5) 33/1: 7: Mid-div at best: 12,500gns 1st foal: dam a French juv wnr.   1   61
-- **POMFRET LAD** [4] 2-9-0 S Sanders 11/4 FAV: 8: Missed break, rear, eff halfway, sn btn: well bckd: hd   61
10,000gns Feb foal: half-brother to a juv 5/6f scorer: dam 1m wnr: shld be capable of better for P J Makin.
-- **WINFIELD** [2] 2-9-0 J Reid 14/1: 9: Dwelt, al rear: Feb foal, dam a 6f 2yo scorer: with C Cox.   7   47
1968 **REPEAT PERFORMANCE** 24 [2] 2-9-0 (t) A Daly 9/2: 424440: Prom, wknd qckly halfway, fin 10th.   hd   47
2357 **CEARNACH** 8 [14] 2-9-0 Pat Eddery 12/1: 00: Sn prom, lost tch fnl 3f, fin 11th.   2½   42
2052 **Immaculate Charlie** 21 [6] 2-8-9 N Pollard 20/1:   -- **Truth Be Known** [8] 2-9-0 S Whitworth 25/1:
-- **Dancing Milly** [5] 2-8-9 J Fortune 16/1: U
14 ran   Time 1m 14.7 (5.6)   (Hamdan Al Maktoum)   B W Hills Lambourn, Berks.

2551   2.30 KNOCKDOWN SELLER 2YO (F)   5f rnd   Good/Soft 82   -44 Slow
£2163   £618   £309

2214 **WATTNO ELJOHN** 13 [1] D W P Arbuthnot 2-8-12 J Weaver 7/4 FAV: 0001: 2 b c Namaqualand - Caroline   65
Connors (Fairy King) Trkd ldrs, went on over 1f out, drvn out: nicely bckd, no bid: dam a prolific wnr
abroad: eff around a sharp/turning 5f on gd/soft grnd: apprec drop to selling grade.
2328 **ONE BELOVED** 9 [4] M R Channon 2-8-7 Craig Williams 2/1: -0032: 2 b f Piccolo - Eternal Flame   1¼   56
(Primo Dominie) Rear, hdwy to chall 2f out, no pace of wnr well in last: nicely bckd: acts on firm & gd/soft.
1916 **QUEENS SONG** 26 [2] R J Hodges 2-8-7 F Norton 20/1: -03: 2 ch f King's Signet - Darakah (Doulab)   shd   56
Led, hdd appr fnl 1f, no extra well in last: clr rem: imprvd eff on this turf debut, stays 5f on gd/soft: see 1916.
2052 **BILLYJO** 21 [6] B J Meehan 2-8-12 Pat Eddery 8/1: 664: Rear, prog halfway, btn appr fnl 1f: see 1740.   3   54
2182 **PERTEMPS GILL** 15 [5] 2-8-7 S Whitworth 25/1: -00305: Cl-up, ev ch till wknd appr fnl 1f: see 1916.   4   41
2388 **JOHN FOLEY** 6 [3] 2-8-12 (BL) A Daly 3/1: 524226: Veered right start, sn in tch, hung right &   ¾   45
wknd fnl 2f: qck reapp: tried blnks & looks one to avoid: btr 2388 (firm grnd).
6 ran   Time 1m 06.6 (6.3)   (Essandess Partners)   D W P Arbuthnot Upper Lambourn, Berks.

2552   3.00 TOTE HCAP 3YO+ 0-80 (D)   1m2f46y   Good/Soft 82   +07 Fast   [74]
£6938   £2135   £1067   £533   3 yo rec 11lb

1845 **CHIEF CASHIER** 30 [7] G B Balding 5-10-0 (74) A Daly 8/1: -50001: 5 b g Persian Bold - Kentfield   82
(Busted) Dsptd lead, went on appr fnl 2f, qcknd up well & rdn clr ins last: best time of day, top-weight:
'99 wnr at Epsom (val h'cap, rtd 83), earlier unplcd over hdles (rtd 101h): '98 wnr again at Epsom (2, h'caps,
rtd 78): suited by 10f, stays a sharp 12.5f: acts on firm, loves gd/soft & soft grnd: eff weight carrier:
loves a sharp/turning trk, esp Epsom: back on a wng mark & could follow up if grnd remains in his favour.
1973 **REAL ESTATE** 24 [5] J S King 4-9-10 (70) I Mongan 6/1: 10/3: 113/32: 6 b g High Estate - Haitienne   6   70
(Green Dancer) Mid-div, rdn to chall appr fnl 1f, sn outpcd by wnr: nicely bckd: shld apprec a step up to 12f.
1942 **TARSKI** 25 [13] L G Cottrell 6-8-2 (48) S Carson (3) 9/2: 0-0033: 6 ch g Polish Precedent - Illusory   nk   48
(King's Lake) Prom, hdwy 3f out, drvn & not pace of wnr fnl 2f: op 3/1: plcd in this race last term (6lb
lower today): acts on fast & gd/soft: on a fair mark & could get his head in front soon: see 1395.
2429 **SEA DANZIG** 5 [3] J J Bridger 7-8-3 (49) L Newman (3) 20/1: 000004: Rear, late gains ins last,   1½   46
no dngr: qck reapp: best when able to dominate: see 772.
2423 **SHEER FACE** 5 [9] 6-8-11 (57) Martin Dwyer 7/1: 401335: Rear, eff halfway, rdn/kept on ins   1½   52
last, no dngr: op 5/1, qck reapp: btr 1331 (clmr, grnd).
2311 **ADAWAR** 10 [11] 3-9-9 (80) Pat Eddery 3/1 FAV: 562136: Rcd keenly in rear, prog appr fnl 2f,   shd   75
sn btn: longer trip & softer grnd: op 9/4: btr 1922 (7.5f mdn).
1575 **THE SHADOW** 41 [4] 4-8-4 (50)(VIS) J Quinn 14/1: 5-0057: Rear, nvr a dngr: 6 wk abs, visor.   1   43
1853 **SHOTACROSS THE BOW** 29 [1] 3-9-2 (73) M Hills 14/1: 41-008: Led, hdd appr fnl 1f, fdd: 3   61
longer 10f trip: landed 3rd of 3 '99 starts, at Epsom (mdn, rtd 81): eff around 6f on firm, handles gd/soft.
894 **RAPID DEPLOYMENT** 88 [12] 3-8-10 (67) F Norton 25/1: 030-09: Handy, lost tch fnl 4f: 12 wk   7   46
abs: up in trip: plcd once in '99 (auct mdn, 6.7f, gd grnd, rtd 75).
1912} **RISING SPRAY** 395 [8] 9-9-7 (67) N Pollard 20/1: 0206-0: Hdwy from rear halfway, wknd fnl 3f, 10th: 3   41
rnr-up once in '99 (h'cap, rtd 70, C Horgan, subs blnkd): '97 wnr at Salisbury & Folkestone (h'caps, rtd 70):
stays 12f, best at 12f on firm, gd/soft & any trk, likes Folkestone, without visor/blnks: now with Dr J Naylor.

BATH

2199 **ROGUE SPIRIT 14** [2] 4-9-8 (68) Carol Packer (7) 10/1: 040020: Front rank, wknd qckly fnl 3f, 11th. 1¼ 40
11 ran   Time 2m 13.7 (7.7)   (Surgical Spirits)   G B Balding Fyfield, Hants.

2553   3.30 LIMPLEY STOKE MDN 3YO (D)   1m2f46y   Good/Soft 82   -20 Slow
£3760   £1157   £578   £289

2365 **DRAMA CLASS 7** [6] Sir Michael Stoute 3-8-9 Pat Eddery 1/1 FAV: 21: 3 ch f Caerleon - Stage Stuck 94+
(Sadler's Wells) Sn led, qcknd clr appr fnl 1f, cmftbly: well bckd tho' op 4/6, qck reapp: dam 12f wnr: eff at
10f, 12f will suit: acts on gd, gd/soft & any trk: useful filly, win more races, prob over further.
957 **PHANTOM RAIN 83** [9] B W Hills 3-8-9 M Hills 5/1: 02: 3 b f Rainbow Quest - Illusory (King's Lake) 3½ 85
Cl-up, rdn/styd on fnl 2f, no impress on wnr: 8 wk abs: stays 10f on gd/soft: shown enough to land a mdn.
1584 **HIGHLAND REEL 41** [4] D R C Elsworth 3-9-0 N Pollard 5/2: -3033: 3 ch c Selkirk - Taj Victory (Final ¾ 89
Straw) Waited with, prog 2f out, styd on, no threat: 6 wk abs: stays 1m/10f on gd/soft & hvy: see 1584, 1041.
-- **HIGH TOWER** [5] Mrs A J Perrett 3-9-0 Dane O'Neill 10/1: 4: Mid-div, rdn/no extra appr fnl 1¾ 86
1f: on 7/1: full brother to a decent 10f scorer: showed promise here, shld improve.
2211 **CAPRICCIO 14** [1] D J Reid 5/1: 435: Cl-up, rdn/btn fnl 2f, 8L clr rem: up in trip, poss stays 10f. 1 84
1863 **FREE WILL 29** [2] 3-9-0 J P Spencer 25/1: -56: Nvr a factor: see 1863. 8 74
2211 **OPTION 14** [7] R Norton 33/1: -507: Al rear: needs low-grade h'caps: see 1912. 4 63$
1796 **DAJAM VU 32** [3] 3-8-9 R Havlin 100/1: 008: Handy, lost tch halfway: modest form. 4 57$
2129 **CIRCUS PARADE 17** [8] 3-9-0 J Fortune 8/1: 59: Led early, prom til wknd qckly fnl 3f: bckd from 20/1. 5 56
9 ran   Time 2m 16.4 (10.4)   (Lord Weinstock)   Sir Michael Stoute Newmarket.

2554   4.00 MIDSOMER MDN HCAP 3YO 0-75 (E)   1m3f144y   Good/Soft 82   -04 Slow   [81]
£2886   £888   £444   £222

1866 **BRISBANE ROAD 28** [10] I A Balding 3-8-7 (60)(t) M Hills 8/1: 00-451: 3 b g Blues Traveller - Eva Fay 66
(Fayruz) Rear, prog halfway, chall dist, drvn out to lead nr fin: op 12/1: up in trip: unplcd in '99 (rtd 60):
styd this longer 11.6f trip, further shld suit: acts on gd/soft & a sharp/turning trk: could follow up.
4256] **LANZLO 279** [14] P J Hobbs 3-8-8 (61) A McGlone 25/1: 0500-2: 3 br g Le Balafre - L'Eternite nk 66
(Cariellor) In tch, hdwy to chall appr fnl 1f, led dist, styd on, hdd cl-home: clr rem: 5th at best in '99
(rtd 74, mdn): half-brother to a useful juv hdler: stays 11.6f well on gd/soft: win a mid-dist mdn h'cap.
2175 **AMRITSAR 15** [4] Sir Michael Stoute 3-9-7 (74) Pat Eddery 9/4 FAV: 054323: 3 ch c Indian Ridge - 5 72
Trying For Gold (Northern Baby) Cl-up, led appr fnl 2f, hdd dist, onepcd: bckd: up in trip & plcd yet again.
2264 **JOHN STEED 11** [19] C A Horgan 3-7-10 (49)(1oh) G Baker (7) 16/1: 600-04: Rear, rdn/prog 3f 2 44
out, hung left & no extra ins last: up in trip: see 2264.
2210 **MUCHANA YETU 14** [3] 3-8-6 (59) L Newman (3) 25/1: -06065: Handy, rdn/held appr fnl 2f: see 1177. 2 51
1909 **STAFFORD KING 26** [13] R Brisland (5) 25/1: 420006: Rear, rdn/late hdwy: see 1002. hd 43
2463 **PILLAGER 3** [7] 3-8-9 (62) J Reid 11/1: 026457: Mid-div at best: op 9/1, qck reapp: see 2463 (10.5f). hd 54
2255 **NIGHT MUSIC 12** [9] 3-8-7 (60) C Rutter 12/1: 0-0538: Dwelt, nvr a factor: tchd 16/1: btr 2255. 1¼ 50
2146 **NOBLE CALLING 17** [1] 3-8-11 (64)(bl) J Weaver 12/1: 0-3029: Cl-up, led after 4f out, hdd 5 47
2f out, wknd qckly: op 9/1: btr 2146 (fast grnd mdn).
2254 **LEES FIRST STEP 12** [15] 3-8-2 (55) P Doe 20/1: 20-000: Rear, eff halfway, no dngr, fin 10th. nk 38
2116 **PROPER SQUIRE 18** [12] 3-8-6 (73) J Fortune 4/1: 2-6200: Dwelt, al rear, fin 11th: tchd 11/2 5 49
& much better expected on this big drop in grade: see 2116 (val h'cap), 1668.
1668 **LORD ALASKA 38** [6] 3-8-7 (60) S Whitworth 12/1: 0050: Al rear, fin 12th: see 1668. 1½ 34
2195 **DANDES RAMBO 14** [16] 3-8-0 (53) J Quinn 25/1: -56360: Handy, fdd fnl 3f, 13th: op 10/1: see 2195. 2½ 23
2258 **MASRORA 12** [8] 3-9-7 (74) Craig Williams 14/1: -45300: Dwelt, rear, eff 3f out, sn btn, 14th: op 10/1. 20 24
2477 **TUMBLEWEED WIZARD 3** [18] 3-8-12 (65)(BL) R Perham 25/1: 00-060: Led, hdd after 4f, wknd hd 15
qckly appr fnl 3f, 15th: qck reapp, blnkd: see 2477.
2041 Arctic High 21 [2] 3-7-11 (50) A Mackay 33/1:   1793 Taxmere 32 [17] 3-7-10 (49)(9oh) R Thomas (1) 33/1:
723 Stafford Prince 107 [11] 3-7-10 (49) D Sweeney (7) 33/1:
18 ran   Time 2m 35.0 (10.0)   (Lord Lloyd-Webber)   I A Balding Kingsclere, Hants.

2555   4.30 PRETENDERS H/H APPR HCAP 3YO+ 0-65 (F)   5f rnd   Good/Soft 82   -04 Slow   [59]
£2215   £633   £316   3 yo rec 5 lb

2223 **SHADY DEAL 13** [10] M D I Usher 4-9-2 (47) G Sparkes (3) 11/2: 000221: 4 b g No Big Deal - Taskalady 51
(Touching Wood) Rear, gd hdwy 2f out, led ins last, hung left & rdn out: plcd thrice prev this term: plcd
in '99 (rtd 57a & 68): eff btwn 5f & 7f on fast, gd/soft & equitrack: belated first win on 29th career start.
2192 **ANOTHER VICTIM 14** [5] M R Bosley 6-8-6 (37) R Naylor (5) 14/1: 030002: 6 ch g Beveled - Ragtime ½ 40
Rose (Ragstone) Rear, hdwy appr fnl 2f, ev ch ins last, no extra nr fin: apprec drop back to 5f: see 1508 (sell).
2428 **CALANDRELLA 5** [9] A G Newcombe 7-8-5 (36) G Gibbons (5) 5/1 FAV: 000633: 7 b m Sizzling Melody - 2 34
Maravilla (Mandrake Major) Led, hdd well ins last, sn btn: qck reapp & remains in gd heart: see 2428.
2385 **GOLD EDGE 7** [13] A G Newcombe 6-7-13 (30) D Glennon 25/1: 600004: Rear, rdn & taken wide 2f out, ½ 27
styd on well appr fnl 1f, nrst fin: qck reapp, stablemate of 3rd: see 148.
2207 **RED DELIRIUM 14** [20] 4-10-0 (59)(t) Michael Doyle (8) 12/1: 000005: Dwelt, rear, rdn & ran on ½ 55
well ins last, no threat to ldrs: top-weight, apprec return to 6f+: see 746.
2230 **SEREN TEG 12** [12] 4-9-2 (47) R Thomas (3) 8/1: 400006: Cl-up, rdn/held ins last: see 440 (AW). hd 43
2240 **JOHNNY STACCATO 12** [11] 6-7-11 (28)(vis) G Oliver (0) 33/1: -00007: Handy, rdn/no extra fnl 1f. shd 24
2184 **WINDRUSH BOY 15** [17] 10-8-7 (38) Joanna Badger 25/1: 054-08: Front rank, rdn/fdd appr fnl ½ 33
1f: '99 scorer here at Bath (clmr, rtd 53): '98 Lingfield wnr (h'cap, rtd 40): eff at 5f on firm, gd &
equitrack: runs well fresh on a sharp/turning track: 10yo.
73 **GO SALLY GO 234** [7] 4-7-13 (30) Angela Hartley (3) 20/1: 0000-9: Prom, rdn/fdd fnl 2f: long abs, nk 23
new stable: unplcd in 4 starts for F Murphy in '99 (rtd 38): modest prev for R Craggs: now with Mrs G Rees.
2478 **BORN TO RULE 3** [6] 3-9-12 (62) P Mundy (5) 25/1: 000500: Hmpd start, sn in tch, stumbled over ½ 54
3f out & sn held: fin 10th: qck reapp: see 2478.
2427 **HALF TONE 5** [1] 8-8-10 (41)(bl) M Worrell (5) 14/1: 303050: Rear, switched 2f out, no dngr: 11th. ½ 32
1994 **SUNPOINT 13** [3] 4-8-9 (40) Cheryl Nosworthy (7) 12/1: 60-030: Cl-up, rdn/wknd & hmpd fnl 1f: 12th. 1 28
2428 **INDIAN BAZAAR 5** [8] 4-9-2 (47) D Watson (3) 13/2: 320100: Prom, wknd/hmpd dist: btr 2223 (firm). ½ 34
2428 **SUNSET HARBOUR 5** [2] 7-9-3 (48) N Esler 7/1: 416360: Mid-div, hmpd halfway, wknd qckly ¾ 33
ins last: fin 14th: on 5/1, qck reapp: btr 2252 (fast grnd).
1799 Addition 32 [19] 4-9-11 (56) P Shea 16/1:

805

BATH MONDAY JULY 10TH Lefthand, Turning Track With Uphill Finish

2230 **Diamond Promise 12** [4] 3-9-8 (58) Kathleen McDermott (10) 12/1:
2223 **Blakey 13** [14] 4-8-2 (33)(bl) S Clancy (3) 20/1: 2184 **Arab Gold 15** [16] 5-8-5 (36)(bl) D Meah (5) 25/1:
2184 **Arcadian Chief 15** [15] 3-8-5 (41) C Catlin (3) 20/1:
19 ran Time 1m 04.6 (4.3) (G A Summers) M D I Usher Kingston Lisle, Oxon.

PONTEFRACT TUESDAY JULY 11TH Lefthand, Undulating Track, Stiff Uphill Finish

Official Going: GOOD. Stalls: Inside

2556 2.20 LADY RIDERS HCAP 3YO+ 0-60 (F) 1m2f Good/Firm 27 -28 Slow [39]
£3120 £960 £480 £240 3 yo rec 11lb

1807 **WERE NOT STOPPIN 32** [2] R Bastiman 5-11-0 (53) Miss R Bastiman (7) 7/1: 511141: 5 b g Mystiko - Power Take Off (Aragon) Chsd ldrs, prog to lead over 1f out, styd on well, rdn out: op 6/1: earlier scored at Beverley (seller) & Redcar (2, h'caps): suited by 1m/10f, tried further: acts on firm & hvy grnd, stiff/gall tracks: progressive type, could win again in this grade. **61**
2366 **ANNADAWI 8** [4] C N Kellett 5-10-8 (47) Mrs S Bosley 7/2: 221022: 5 b g Sadler's Wells - Prayers' n Promises (Foolish Pleasure) Trkd ldrs, rdn/pressed wnr fnl 1f, al just held: hvly bckd: acts on fast & hvy grnd. *1¾* **52**
2387 **TAJAR 7** [14] T Keddy 8-9-12 (37) Mrs H Keddy (5) 16/1: 003103: 8 b g Slew O' Gold - Mashaarif (Mr Prospector) Held up, prog to press ldrs over 1f out, rdn/no extra inside last: see 2109. *2½* **38**
*2366 **WHISTLING DIXIE 8** [16] D Nicholls 4-10-1 (40) Miss J Allison 100/30 FAV: -26014: Towards rear, styd on fnl 2f, not reach front trio: bckd, tho' op 9/4: see 2366 (C/D). *1¼* **39**
2199 **GOLD BLADE 15** [11] 11-10-4 (43) Mrs L Pearce 10/1: 5-4005: Mid div, rdn & kept on onepace fnl 3f. *2* **39**
2366 **KIERCHEM 8** [5] 9-9-13 (38) Mrs F Needham 16/1: 260146: Mid div, never pace to chall: see 2099 (1m). *¾* **33**
2244 **COLOMBE DOR 13** [13] 3-10-1 (51) Miss A Armitage (5) 33/1: 226007: Twds rear, mod hdwy 3f out. *3* **42**
2387 **SILVER SECRET 7** [18] 6-10-8 (47) Mrs C Williams 10/1: -05168: Prom 1m: btr 1819 (soft). *½* **37**
2397 **THREE LEADERS 7** [7] 4-9-13 (38) Miss E J Jones 16/1: 040049: In tch, rdn/btn 2f out: see 2397, 648. *1¼* **26**
2309 **TOEJAM 11** [15] 7-10-3 (42)(vis) Miss P Robson 10/1: -00150: Mid div, eff 3f out, sn held: 10th. *1¼* **28**
2331 **ALCOVE 10** [1] 9-10-7 (46)(bl) Miss E Johnson Houghton 20/1: 0/0000: Cl up 9f: 11th: see 2331. *1¾* **30**
2255 **LOMOND DANCER 13** [6] 3-10-7 (57) Miss A Elsey 14/1: 6-0500: Chsd ldrs 9f: 12th: op 10/1: see 1914. *½* **40**
2276 **French Master 12** [17] 3-10-4 (54) Miss A Deniel 11/1:
4179} **Mazeed 284** [10] 7-11-4 (57)(vis) Mrs S Moore (5) 40/1:
2032 **Burning 23** [9] 8-9-9 (34)(bl) Miss E Folkes (5) 50/1:
562 **Myttons Moment 140** [8] 4-10-12 (51)(bl) Miss S Hatton (7) 25/1:
-- **Tapatch** [19] 12-10-5 (44) Miss S Brotherton (5 25/1:
17 ran Time 2m 13.6 (5.5) (I B Barker) R Bastiman Cowthorpe, N Yorks

2557 2.50 DIANNE NURSERY H'CAP 2YO (D) 6f rnd Good/Firm 27 +04 Fast [93]
£3753 £1155 £577 £288

*1503 **DIM SUMS 46** [9] T D Barron 2-9-0 (79) K Darley 5/1 CO FAV: 211: 2 b g Repriced - Regal Baby (Northern Baby) Trckd ldrs, rdn/prog to lead 1f out, styd on strongly inside last, pushed clr near fin: gd time: op 4/1, abs, h'cap bow: earler scored at Southwell (AW mdn, rtd 72a): eff at 6f, 7f+ shld suit: acts on fast grnd & fibresand: handles a sharp or stiff trk, runs well fresh: impressive turf bow, can win again under a penalty. **95**
2162 **FRANICA 17** [6] A Bailey 2-8-9 (74) P Hanagan (7) 8/1: 201522: 2 b f Inzar - Comfrey Glen (Glenstal) Chsd ldrs, rdn/chsd wnr fnl 1f, kept on, al held: op 10/1: styd 6f well, 7f suit: consistent performer. *3* **79**
*2301 **CEDAR TSAR 11** [12] D W Chapman 2-7-11 (62) G Bardwell 10/1: 620213: 2 b c Inzar - The Aspecto Girl (Alzao) Led halfway till 1f out, no extra: op 8/1: prev with A Reid, gd run on first start in h'caps: see 2301. *1* **65**
2055 **FLUMMOX 22** [8] M Johnston 2-9-7 (86) J Carroll 14/1: 1344: Chsd ldrs, rdn fnl 3f, al held: op 12/1. *4* **79**
*1938 **FLOWING RIO 26** [2] 2-8-13 (78) M Tebbutt 14/1: 015: Trkd ldrs, onepace fnl 2f: op 10/1. *shd* **71**
2106 **CIRCUIT LIFE 19** [1] 2-7-12 (63) D Mernagh (3) 20/1: -05306: Towards rear, rdn/mod gains fnl 2f. *½* **54**
1761 **AFFARATI 34** [7] 2-9-1 (80) A Culhane 11/2: 2167: In tch, btn 2f out: see 1497 (stakes). *1¾* **67**
2388 **BANNINGHAM BLIZ 7** [10] 2-7-12 (63)(BL)(2ow)(10oh) T Williams 40/1: 065438: Al rear: blnks. *½* **48**
1835 **EMISSARY 31** [11] 2-8-3 (68) K Dalgleish (5) 5/1 CO FAV: -6649: Led 3f: op 9/2: btr 1835 (5f). *shd* **53**
*1628 **WATERPARK 40** [3] 2-8-12 (77) F Lynch 5/1 CO FAV: 632110: Al bhd: 10th, abs, btr 1628. *nk* **61**
*1679 **HAMASKING 38** [4] 2-7-10 (61)(4oh) P Fessey 5/1 CO FAV: 6610: Mid div, btn 2f out: 11th: op 4/1. *3½* **36**
11 ran Time 1m 15.5 (1.4) (Harrowgate Bloodstock Ltd) T D Barron Maunby, N Yorks

2558 3.20 BRADLEY MDN 3YO+ (D) 1m2f Good/Firm 27 -21 Slow
£3672 £1130 £565 £282 3 yo rec 11lb

2102 **KRISPIN 20** [4] G Wragg 3-8-10 K Darley 3/1: -60331: 3 ch c Kris - Mariakova (The Minstrel) Made all, rdn fnl 3f, held on gamely inside last: well bckd: eff at 1m, suited by 10f, 12f sure to suit: acts on fast & gd/soft grnd, sharp or stiff/undulating track: well suited by forcing tactics today, game. **80**
2258 **GREEN WILDERNESS 13** [1] J R Fanshawe 3-8-5 J Carroll 4/1: -62: 3 b f Green Dancer - Wild Vintage (Alysheba) Held up in tch, rdn/prog to press wnr fnl 1f, drvn & kept on, al just held: bckd: eff at 10f, 12f could suit. *½* **73**
1992 **KATIYPOUR 24** [2] Sir Michael Stoute 3-8-10 F Lynch 3/1: -023: 3 ch c Be My Guest - Katiyfa (Auction Ring) Trkd ldrs, rdn over 1f out & no extra inside last: bckd: see 1992. *4* **72**
2265 **CLASSY IRISH 12** [3] L M Cumani 3-8-10 J P Spencer 11/4 FAV: -624: Trckd ldrs, rdn to press wnr over 1f out, soon no extra: well bckd tho' op 9/4: h'cap company could now suit: see 2265. *3* **68**
-- **KALEMAAT** [5] 3-8-6(1ow) R Price 16/1: 5: Held up, rdn & kept on one pace fnl 2f, flashed tail: op 10/1, debut: half sister to smart mid dist/staying performer Kutta: will apprec 12f+. *¾* **63**
1863 **PIES AR US 30** [8] 3-8-10 P Goode (3) 50/1: -46: Rear, mod gains fnl 2f: longer 10f trip: see 1863. *6* **58**
1717 **DOUBLE BID 36** [6] 3-8-10 T Lucas 14/1: 27: Keen, in tch 1m: op 8/1: longer 1m trip: btr 1717 (g/s). *15* **42**
1921 **TAKING 27** [7] 4-9-7 T Williams 50/1: 508: Cl up, btn/hmpd 2f out: stiff task: ex French, mod Brit form over hurdles & on the level so far. *5* **35**
8 ran Time 2m 12.9 (4.8) (John Pearce Racing Ltd) G Wragg Newmarket, Suffolk

2559   3.55 ST. GILES HCAP 3YO+ 0-80 (D)   6f rnd   Good/Firm 27   +07 Fast   [78]
£7702   £2370   £1185   £592   3 yo rec 6 lb

*1869 **BUNDY** 29 [16] M Dods 4-9-0 (64) A Clark 12/1: -15311: 4 b g Ezzoud - Sanctuary Cove (Habitat)   67
Made most, held on gamely near line, all out: best time of day: earlier won at Nottingham & here at Pontefract
(h'caps): plcd in '99 (h'cap, rtd 71): '98 wnr at Newcastle (sell) & Warwick (h'cap, rtd 73): stays 7f, suited by
6f on fast & hvy, sharp or gall trk, likes Pontefract: best without blnks, has run well fresh: tough & genuine.
2396 **ALBERT THE BEAR** 7 [12] A Berry 7-8-7 (57)(vis) C Lowther 14/1: 003002: 7 b g Puissance -   hd   59
Florentynna Bay (Aragon) Trkd ldrs, rdn to chall & every ch fnl 1f, kept on well, just held: op 1438.
2000 **ZUHAIR** 24 [11] D Nicholls 7-9-7 (71) Alex Greaves 20/1: 000003: 7 ch c Mujtahid - Ghzaalh   nk   72
(Northern Dancer) Trkd ldrs, rdn/prog wide to chall fnl 1f, ev ch inside last, just held near line: returned to
form, looks well h'capped: stable in form & shld be winning sn, one to keep in mind at Goodwood: see 716.
2396 **BOWLERS BOY** 7 [6] J J Quinn 7-8-7 (57) J Carroll 7/1: 412154: Towards rear, rdn & styd on fnl   nk   57
2f, nrst fin: remains in gd heart & loves Pontefract: see 1941.
2118 **PRESENT CHANCE** 19 [7] 6-8-8 (58)(bl) J P Spencer 25/1: 000505: Chsd ldrs, prog to chall 1f out,   hd   57
just held near fin: not btn far in a bunched finish, looks nicely h'capd for similar contests: see 674.
+2292 **SHUDDER** 11 [15] 5-8-10 (60) R Havlin 12/1: 430316: Chsd ldrs, ch over 1f out, no extra nr fin.   hd   58
2247 **PIERPOINT** 13 [17] 5-9-2 (66) Iona Wands (5) 9/1: 000107: Cl up, onepace fnl 2f: op 7/1: btr 1868 (5f).   1¼   62
2355 **PEPPIATT** 9 [10] 6-8-9 (59) F Lynch 8/1: 403508: Held up, drvn/not pace to chall fnl 2f: see 2163.   2½   47
2247 **NOMORE MR NICEGUY** 13 [8] 6-9-13 (77) T E Durcan 14/1: 020409: In tch, hmpd 2f out, no impress.   ½   63
2420 **PRIX STAR** 6 [5] 5-8-6 (56) G Bardwell 14/1: 032040: Cl up 4f: 10th: op 10/1, quick reapp.   hd   41
2444 **ABLE AYR** 5 [9] 3-8-13 (69) A Culhane 20/1: 050000: At rear: 11th: quick reapp: see 1768, 1074.   ½   52
2444 **DOUBLE ACTION** 5 [4] 6-9-0 (64)(bl) K Darley 3/1 FAV: 532660: In tch 4f: 12th: well bckd, op 4/1.   1½   43
2355 **FAIRY PRINCE** 9 [1] 7-8-10 (60) P M Quinn (3) 10/1: 045100: Al bhd: 14th: btr 2192.   0
1590 **The Downtown Fox** 41 [13] 5-9-7 (71) N Pollard 16/1: 2158 **Green Ginger** 17 [2] 4-9-1 (65)(VIS) A Daly 20/1:
15 ran   Time 1m 15.3 (1.2)   (A J Henderson)   M Dods Piercebridge, Co Durham

2560   4.25 J WRAFTER MDN 3YO+ (D)   1m4f   Good/Firm 27   -33 Slow
£3493   £1075   £537   £268   3 yo rec 13lb

1857 **ZIBILENE** 30 [1] L M Cumani 3-8-3 K Darley 2/9 FAV: 21: 3 b f Rainbow Quest - Brocade (Habitat)   74
Trckd ldrs, rdn fnl 2f, styd on well to lead ins last & going away near line: hvly bckd at long odds on: apprec
step up to 12f, further could suit: acts on firm & fast, stiff/undul or gall trk: simple task here.
2222 **EMPIRE DREAM** 14 [3] M Johnston 3-8-8 J Carroll 5/1: 422: 3 b c Alzao - Triste Oeil (Raise A Cup)   1½   73
Led, rdn fnl 2f, hdd & no extra inside last: op 7/2: styd longer 12f trip well: acts on firm & fast grnd.
1582 **PERPETUO** 42 [2] R A Fahey 3-8-3 P Hanagan (7) 14/1: 33: 3 b f Mtoto -Persian Fountain   2   65
(Persian Heights) Keen/held up, rdn & kept on onepace fnl 2f: op 12/1, 6 wk abs: longer 12f trip: see 1582.
-- **BETTER MOMENT** 5 [5] J G FitzGerald 3-8-8 J P Spencer 16/1: 4: Held up, rdn/btn 2f out: op 14/1,   4   64
debut: 35,000gns foal, dam a 7f Irish wnr.
1661 **DESERT MUSIC** 39 [4] 4-9-2 G Hind 50/1: -055: Cl up, rdn/btn over 2f out: needs low grade h'caps.   13   45
5 ran   Time 2m 41.3 (7.2)   (Gerald Leigh)   L M Cumani Newmarket, Suffolk

2561   5.00 RICHARD III FILL HCAP 3YO+ 0-70 (E)   1m rnd   Good/Firm 27   -12 Slow   [59]
£3068   £944   £472   £236   3 yo rec 9 lb

1907 **PUPPET PLAY** 27 [10] E J Alston 5-9-2 (47) T E Durcan 10/1: 203041: 5 ch m Broken Hearted -   51
Fantoccine (Taufan) Made all, clr over 2f out, rdn & held on well ins last: first win: rnr-up on turf in native
Ireland & on sand in '99 (rtd 52a, AW mdn): eff forcing the pace at 1m, stays a stiff 9f & has tried further: acts
on firm, fast & both AWs: handles any track: has run well in blnks, best without: suited by forcing tactics.
2391 **CAUTION** 7 [8] S Gollings 6-9-7 (52) D Mernagh (3) 14/1: 600042: 6 b m Warning - Fairy Flax   nk   54
(Dancing Brave) Held up, prog over 2f out, drvn & styd on well inside last, post came too soon: op 12/1: well
h'capped mare, eff between 5f/1m, can find a race: see 2391, 645.
2481 **SWYNFORD PLEASURE** 4 [19] J Hetherton 4-9-0 (45) O Pears 9/1: 132533: 4 b f Reprimand -   1   45
Pleasuring (Good Times) Towards rear, rdn & styd on well fnl 2f, nrst fin: op 8/1, quick reapp: see 2180, 1939.
2376 **WOORE LASS** 8 [3] Don Enrico Incisa 4-8-13 (44) Kim Tinkler 7/1: -00024: Chsd ldrs, onepace fnl 2f.   3   38
2296 **MAY QUEEN MEGAN** 11 [18] 7-8-5 (36) A Daly 14/1: 04-465: Mid div, rdn & styd on onepace fnl 2f.   1   28
2206 **IMARI** 15 [13] 3-9-9 (63) M Tebbutt 4/1 FAV: 501326: Mid div, onepace fnl 2f: well bckd: see 1955.   1   53
2180 **TEMPRAMENTAL** 16 [9] 4-9-10 (55) S Finnamore (5) 11/1: 314157: Chsd wnr, fdd fnl 2f: op 9/1.   ½   44
2479 **THREE CHERRIES** 4 [20] 4-8-9 (40) P Goode (3) 33/1: 000008: Rear, mod late gains: quick reapp.   3½   22
2027 **GYMCRAK FLYER** 23 [6] 9-9-2 (47) G Hind 25/1: 0-0009: Towards rear, mod gains late on: '99   shd   29
h'cap wnr at Carlisle & Musselburgh (rtd 57): '98 Beverley wnr (amat h'cap, rtd 61): suited by 7f/1m on
firm & gd/soft, best in a visor, tried blinks: handles any track.
2364 **ARCHELLO** 8 [17] 6-9-2 (47) T Williams 16/1: 000030: Chsd ldrs 6f: 10th: op 12/1: see 2364, 1258.   ½   28
2397 **THORNTOUN GOLD** 7 [15] 4-9-4 (49) A Culhane 14/1: -40100: Rear, rdn/mod gains: 11th: op 12/1.   ½   29
2130 **BROWNS FLIGHT** 18 [2] 4-9-0 (45)(t) J P Spencer 14/1: 0-0000: Chsd ldrs, btn 2f out: 12th.   1   23
2192 **CORN DOLLY** 15 [16] 4-8-10 (41)(BL) N Pollard 16/1: 250000: Keen, wide/mid div 6f: 13th: blinks.   ½   18
2315 **EMLEY** 10 [7] 4-9-1 (46) J Carroll 12/1: 3-6000: Chsd ldrs, btn 1f out: 14th: op 16/1: see 1818.   ¾   22
2099 **Isit Izzy** 20 [14] 8-8-6 (37) C Lowther 14/1:   2192 **Little Chapel** 15 [1] 4-9-0 (45) S Whitworth 33/1:
2337 **Dakota Sioux** 10 [11] 3-9-2 (56) T Lucas 12/1:   -- **Charlton Imp** [4] 7-8-4 (35) R Havlin 33/1:
-- **Hard To Follow** [12] 5-7-10 (27)(2oh) D Kinsella (7) 50/1:
19 ran   Time 1m 44.9 (3.1)   (Mrs F D McAuley)   E J Alston Longton, Lancs

2562   5.30 MONKHILL CLASS STKS 3YO+ 0-75 (D)   1m2f   Good/Firm 27   -27 Slow
£3851   £1185   £592   £296   3 yo rec 11lb

1816 **ARCHIE BABE** 32 [1] J J Quinn 4-9-11 J P Spencer 6/1: 010101: 4 ch g Archway - Frensham Manor   79
(Le Johnstan) Made all, clr over 2f out, styd on strongly inside last, rdn out: op 5/1: earlier scored here at
Pontefract & Newcastle (h'caps): '99 scorer again at Potefract & Redcar (2, h'caps, rtd 70): '98 Thirsk scorer
(auct mdn, rtd 75): suited by 10/12f on firm or hvy, any track, likes a stiff/gall one, esp Redcar or Pontefract:
gd weight carrier: tough & genuine gelding, well suited by front running tactics today.
2450 **ASTRONAUT** 5 [2] W J Haggas 3-8-12 A Culhane 13/8 FAV: 04122: 3 b g Sri Pekan - Wild Abandon   2   74

807

PONTEFRACT TUESDAY JULY 11TH Lefthand, Undulating Track, Stiff Uphill Finish

(Graustark) Chsd wnr, drvn & kept on fnl 2f, al held: rest well covered: hvly bckd, quick reapp: see 2450, 1388.
1341 **NIAGARA 54** [4] M H Tompkins 3-8-10 J Carroll 7/1: 60-003: 3 b c Rainbows For Life - Highbrook 4 **66**
(Alphabatim) Rear, rdn & styd on onepace fnl 2f: op 6/1, 8 week abs: see 1153 (7f).
2314 **LUCKY GITANO 11** [5] J L Dunlop 4-9-7 K Darley 9/4: 2-0024: Keen/trkd ldrs, eff over 2f out, sn held. ½ **65**
2211 **EL EMPERADOR 15** [6] 3-8-10 M Tebbutt 7/1: 6-545: Held up, hdwy 3f out, no prog over 1f out: op 6/1. 9 **52**
2508 **FOUR MEN 3** [3] 3-8-10 P Bradley (5) 50/1: -00006: Keen/chsd ldrs 7f, sn btn: qck reapp: mod form. 5 **45$**
6 ran Time 2m 13.5 (5.4) (Mrs K Mapp) J J Quinn Settrington, N Yorks

NEWMARKET (JULY) TUESDAY JULY 11TH Righthand, Stiff, Galloping Track

Official Going GOOD/SOFT. Stalls: Far side, except 1m4f - Stands side. Last 3 wnrs rcd on a fresh strip under stands rail.

2563

2.05 STRUTT & PARKER MDN 2YO (D) 7f str Good 40 -34 Slow
£6207 £1910 £955 £477

-- **LONDONER** [8] H R A Cecil 2-9-0 T Quinn 11/4 JT FAV: 1: 2 ch c Sky Classic - Love And Affection **94+**
(Exclusive Era) Nvr far away, led ent fnl 3f, held on well under hands & heels: nicely bckd, debut: Mar foal, half brother to sev wnrs in the States, dam 5f/1m wnr: sire 9/12f performer: eff at 7f, sure to apprec 1m+ in time: acts on gd & a stiff track: useful debut, from a powerful stable, sure to rate higher & hold his own in Gr class.
-- **ROSIS BOY** [9] J L Dunlop 2-9-0 Pat Eddery 9/1: 2: 2 b c Caerleon - Come On Rosi (Valiyar) ½ **92**
Sn well plcd, dsptd lead appr fnl 1f, rdn dist, kept on, held nr fin: Apr foal, brother to useful 7f/1m juv Aunty Rose: dam 6f wnr, sire 10/12f performer: eff at 7f, bred for further: acts on gd grnd & a mdn is a formality.
-- **COSI FAN TUTTE** [3] B Hanbury 2-9-0 Dane O'Neill 14/1: 3: 2 b c Inchinor - Bumpkin (Free State) *nk* **91**
Towards rear, feeling pace halfway, styd on appr fnl 1f, fin well: 32,000gns Jan foal, half-brother to wnrs at 6f & 10f: dam a sprinter, sire 7f performer: eff at 7f on gd grnd, 1m will suit next time: looks a promising type.
-- **CANADA** [4] B W Hills 2-9-0 G Duffield 33/1: 4: Dwelt, improved halfway, chsd ldrs dist, onepce: ½ **90+**
clr rem: Mar foal, half-brother to a 6f wnr: eff at 7f but has a mid-dist pedigree: improve bundles over further.
-- **DON ALFRED** [2] 2-9-0 J Fortune 12/1: 5: Narrow lead till appr fnl 2f, no extra: op 8/1: 32,000gns *6* **78**
Mark Of Esteem Feb first foal, dam 7f juv wnr, sire a miler: ran well for a long way, improve plenty for this.
-- **MAWHOOB** [1] 2-9-0 R Hills 11/4 JT FAV: 6: Chsd ldrs, fdd ent fnl 2f: well bckd tho' op 7/4, stablemate ½ **77**
of 2nd: Dayjur Apr foal: half-brother to a smart 12f wnr: dam 7f/12f wnr: clearly shown plenty at home.
-- **MR COMBUSTIBLE** [11] 2-9-0 M Hills 10/1: 7: Slow away, nvr got near ldrs under a kind ride: *shd* **77+**
shorter-priced stablemate of 4th: IR£30,000 Hernando Feb foal, half-brother to smart 12f wnr Miletrian & a 6f juv wnr: dam unraced, sire 12f performer: mid-dists are going to suit but expect plenty of improvement next time.
-- **WOODFIELD** [10] 2-9-0 P Robinson 9/1: 8: Trckd ldrs, outpcd 2f out: op 12/1: 30,000gns Zafonic *hd* **76**
Feb foal, half brother to 2 7f juv wnrs, dam unraced, sire a miler: will find much easier mdns: with C Brittain.
-- **SENOR MIRO** [6] 2-9-0 J Reid 25/1: 9: Front rank till wknd entering fnl 2f: 11,000gns Be My *4* **68**
Guest Feb first foal, dam unraced (sprint/mile pedigree): may apprec a drop back to 6f for now.
-- **PORT MORESBY** [12] 2-9-0 W Ryan 25/1: 0: Dwelt, al bhd: 10th: 25,000gns Tagula March foal, *3* **62**
dam 1m/12f h'capper, sire 6/7f performer: with N Callaghan.
-- **CHARLATAN** [5] 2-9-0 T G McLaughlin 33/1: 0: Slow away, al bhd: 11th: 15,000Ir gns Charnwood *12* **42**
Forest Feb foal, dam & sire milers: with C Dwyer.
11 ran Time 1m 29.05 (5.15) (H R H Prince Fahd Salman) H R A Cecil Newmarket, Suffolk

2564

2.35 H&K COMMISSIONS HCAP 3YO+ 0-80 (D) 1m str Good 40 -04 Slow [80]
£9776 £3008 £1504 £752 3 yo rec 9 lb

2001 **IRON MOUNTAIN 24** [15] N A Callaghan 5-9-2 (68) J Mackay (5) 5/1 FAV: 353401: 5 b g Scenic - **73**
Merlannah (Shy Groom) Held up, gd prog ent fnl 2f, drftd left & led below dist, drvn out, narrowly: well bckd: '99 Goodwood wnr (amat h'cap, rtd 75), 2nd in this race: '98 wnr at Yarmouth, Brighton, Beverley & Leicester (h'caps, rtd 73): eff at 1m/11f on firm & gd/soft, poss not soft: goes on any track, without blnks: tough.
*1840 **I CRIED FOR YOU 31** [17] J G Given 5-9-13 (79) Dean McKeown 8/1: -13212: 5 b g Statoblest - Fall Of *nk* **82**
The Hammer (Auction Ring) Mid div, trav strgly ent fnl 2f, sn improved & rdn to chall 1f out, edged left, held nr fin: cracking run under top-weight: clearly gets 1m tho' last 2 wins at 7f: can score again: see 1840.
2412 **TOPTON 6** [16] P Howling 6-9-4 (70)(bl) R Winston 10/1: 050023: 6 b g Royal Academy - Circo ¾ **71+**
(High Top) Waited with, improved going well & not clr run over 1f & dist, kept on strongly towards fin, unlucky: op 8/1, quick reapp: tough: stays 1m, most wins at 7f: unlucky here, h'capped to win, keep on your side.
2242 **TIPPERARY SUNSET 13** [8] D Shaw 6-8-8 (60) N Callan 12/1: 023664D: In tch, hdwy to lead & hung *hd* **61**
left appr fnl 1f, hdd below dist, styd on: bckd, fin 4th plcd 5th: gd run, likes rain softened grnd: see 1007.
2242 **TORNADO PRINCE 13** [18] 5-8-13 (65) W Supple 14/1: -0144: Waited with, gd progress 2f out, hmpd *nk* **65**
& carr left dist, hard rdn, onepace cl-home: op 10/1: fin 5th, plcd 4th: needs plenty of cover, in form.
-2126 **BARABASCHI 18** [11] 4-9-9 (75) J Fortune 8/1: 22-226: Keen, trckd ldrs, ch appr fnl 1f, onepace *1* **73**
inside last: nicely bckd: suited by 7f/sharper 1m: mdn after 13 starts & finds less than expected off the bit.
2190 **CALLDAT SEVENTEEN 15** [2] 4-9-8 (74) W Ryan 10/1: -02467: Towards rear, prog & rdn to chall ¾ **70**
appr fnl 1f, soon no impression: back in trip: likes cut in the grnd & all 3 wins on sharp/undul trks: see 1271.
2330 **EASTERN SPICE 10** [12] 3-9-2 (77) J Reid 14/1: -02138: Prom, feeling pace over 2f out, short of *shd* **73**
room bef fnl 1f, late rally under press: gd run against elders & clr of rem: see 2330, 2129.
2062 **MINETTA 21** [3] 5-9-7 (73) M Fenton 2o/1: 10-659: Led till appr fnl 1f, fdd: faster grnd suits, see 1879. 3½ **62**
1925 **STEALTHY TIMES 27** [9] 3-9-4 (79) G Baker (7) 50/1: 1-0000: Well plcd till rdn & wknd appr fnl 1f *1* **66**
10th: signs of returns to form, drop back to 6/7f will suit: see 1138.
2380 **QUALITAIR PRIDE 8** [1] 8-7-10 (48)(9oh) Claire Bryan (5) 40/1: 0/0100: Raced alone on far rail, *hd* **35**
in with every ch till wknd qkly bef fnl 1f: 11th, stiff task, see 2347.
2412 **ETISALAT 6** [13] 5-8-7 (59) D Watson (7) 40/1: 130000: Chsd ldrs till 2f out: 12th, see 1524. ¾ **44**
1907 **BURNING TRUTH 27** [5] 6-8-10 (62) G Duffield 20/1: 044-60: Al towards rear: 13th, see 1907. *hd* **46**
1729 **FINAL LAP 36** [7] 4-9-4 (70) T Quinn 20/1: 245-00: Chsd ldrs, lost pl 2f out: 14th: see 56. *shd* **53**
1926 **DOLPHINELLE 27** [14] 4-8-12 (64) O Urbina 12/1: 403160: Al bhd: 15th, can do better, see 1926, 1590. ½ **47**
169 **MAWINGO 214** [19] 7-8-10 (62) Y Take 16/1: 0354-0: Never a factor on reapp: 16th, see 169. 1½ **42**
2229 **PARKSIDE 13** [4] 4-9-7 (73) Martin Dwyer 14/1: 050300: Dwelt, chsd ldrs halfway till appr fnl 1f: 17th. 1½ **50**
2475 **INDIUM 4** [6] 6-9-12 (78) Pat Eddery 9/1: 010500: Al bhd: 18th, bckd, quick reapp, see 1375 (10f). 3½ **49**
18 ran Time 1m 40.73 (3.53) (Gallagher Equine Ltd) N A Callaghan Newmarket, Suffolk

2565　3.05 GR 2 CHERRY HINTON STKS 2YO (A)　6f　Good 40　+02 Fast
£29000　£11000　£5500　£2500

*2174　**DORA CARRINGTON** 16 [11]　P W Harris　2-8-9　T Quinn　12/1: 11: 2 b f Sri Pekan - Dorothea Brooke　108
(Dancing Brave) Prom rdn to chall appr fnl 1f, edged in front inside last, drvn out: gd time: ealier won debut at
Pontefract (fill mdn): half-sister to top-class sprint juv Primo Valentino, dam a miler: eff over a stiff 6f,
7f will suit: acts on firm & gd grnd & runs well fresh: smart, unbtn & progressive filly with a good attitude.

*2285　**ENTHUSED** 11 [9]　Sir Michael Stoute　2-8-9　M Hills　4/1: -12: 2 b f Seeking The Gold - Magic Of　½　106
Life (Seattle Slew) Well plcd, led going best of all ent fnl 2f, edged left & rdn dist, soon hdd, kept on: well
bckd: v useful, acts on fast & gd: has a high cruising speed, will apprec a longer lead, shld find a Group race.

*1968　**LADY LAHAR** 25 [10]　M R Channon　2-8-9　Craig Williams　12/1: 13: 2 b f Fraam - Brigadiers Bird　1¾　101
(Mujadil) Waited wth, shaken up 2f out, slightly outpcd over 1f out, styd on again ins last: fine run from
this useful filly who can regain winning ways over 7f: see 1968.

2172　**ZAHEEMAH** 17 [1]　C E Brittain　2-8-9　P Robinson　25/1: 64: Led till 2f out, no extra & hung left:　2　95
highly tried, eff at 6f on gd: maiden a formality on this evidence: see 2172.

2344　**GOODIE TWOSUES** 10 [8]　2-8-9　Dane O'Neill　11/2: -1345: Well plcd & ch till one pace appr fnl 1f:　1　92
bckd: consistent filly, will apprec a drop back to Listed company as in 2344 (C/D).

2088　**STRANGE DESTINY** 20 [7]　2-8-9　G Carter　7/2 JT FAV: 3146: Handy, eff 2f out, soon same pace:　shd　92
nicely bckd: not disgraced up in trip, see 2088 (Queen Mary).

2344　**ALINGA** 10 [5]　2-8-9　M Fenton　9/1: 5137: In tch, rdn 2f out, no impression, short of room ins last.　1½　87

*2369　**FREEFOURRACING** 8 [4]　2-8-9　Pat Eddery　7/2 JT FAV: -118: Well plcd till fdd appr fnl 1f:　1　84
well bckd, lost unbeaten record, surely something amiss: see 2369 (made all).

2251　**JAMILA** 13 [2]　2-8-9　W Ryan　33/1: -0229: Front rank & every ch till wknd quickly appr fnl 1f:　7　64
highly tried, win a minor track mdn, see 2251, 1974 (fast time on AW).

9 ran　Time 1m 13.3 (2.3)　(Mrs P W Harris)　P W Harris Aldbury, Herts

2566　3.40 GR 2 PRINCESS OF WALES'S STKS 3YO+ (A)　1m4f　Good 40　-03 Slow
£34800　£13200　£6600　£3000

1902　**LITTLE ROCK** 30 [4]　Sir Michael Stoute　4-9-2　Pat Eddery　10/3: 01-161: 4 b h Warning - Much Too　116
Risky (Bustino) Handy, rdn appr fnl 1f, grabbed stands rail dist & ran on strongly to lead cl home: well bckd:
unluckly in running in France since reapp wnr at Sandown (Gr 3): '99 wnr at Sandown (stks) & here at Newmarket
(List, rtd 113): juv wnr at Leicester (mdn): eff at 10/12f: acts on fast, likes soft/hvy: goes on any track,
likes stiff/gall ones: runs well fresh: v smart & progressive entire, win a Group 1 abroad.

2149　**YAVANAS PACE** 18 [2]　M Johnston　8-9-2　J Fanning　3/1 FAV: 104322: 8 ch g Accordion - Lady In Pace　1　114
(Burslem) Led after 2f & lkd set to make rest untill began hanging appr fnl 1f, soon rdn, collared cl-home:
hvly bckd: another fine run from this ultra-tough & smart gldg, hard to beat in Irish St Leger.

1057　**COMMANDER COLLINS** 73 [3]　J H M Gosden　4-9-2　J Fortune　7/1: /04-43: 4 b h Sadler's Wells -　2½　111
Kanmary (Kenmare) Held up, hdwy 2f out, rdn bef dist, styd on but no impression on front pair: 10 wk
abs: v useful effort: up in trip, stays 12f: apprec a drop into Group 3 company: see 1057 (also bhd this wnr).

2336　**RAINBOW WAYS** 10 [6]　B W Hills　5-9-2　J Reid　7/1: -12234: Early ldr, prom, rdn, hung left & no extra　4　106
fnl 1f: op 11/2, unsuited by drop back in trip: prefers fast grnd: see 2336, 1187 (h'cap).

*1401　**SEA WAVE** 52 [1]　5-9-2　(t)　R Hills　7/2: 43-015: Well plcd & every ch till wknd quickly appr fnl 1f:　¾　105
nicely bckd, 7 week abs: see 1401 (form looks dubious).

1902　**LUCIDO** 30 [5]　4-9-2　T Quinn　13/2: 03-546: Al bhd, lost tch 2f out, eased: something amiss, see 1152. *dist*　75

6 ran　Time 2m 33.3 (5.1)　(J M Greetham)　Sir Michael Stoute Newmarket, Suffolk

2567　4.10 FILLIES RATED HCAP 3YO 0-100 (B)　7f str　Good 40　-02 Slow　[111]
£9488　£3599　£1799　£818　High numbers had an edge

1630　**OUT OF REACH** 40 [7]　B W Hills　3-8-7 (90)　M Hills　3/1 JT FAV: 1-521: 3 b f Warning - Well Beyond　98
(Don't Foget Me) Grabbed stands rail, made all, rdn clr dist, readily: well bckd, 6 wk abs since running into
v smart Medicean: won sole '99 start at Newbury (mdn, rtd 86): eff at 7f/1m: acts on fast & hvy grnd, stiff/
gall tracks: best up with/forcing the pace now: runs well fresh & is a useful & progressive filly.

2197　**TEODORA** 15 [4]　S Dow　3-8-4 (87)　M Roberts　12/1: -50062: 3 b f Fairy King - Pinta (Ahonoora)　2½　88
Held up, gd progress appr fnl 1f & went 2nd dist, soon rdn & no impress on wnr: back to form, see 995.

2167　**EBBA** 17 [9]　M L W Bell　3-8-2 (85)　R Mullen　25/1: 5-0403: 3 ch f Elmaamul - Strawberry Song　hd　86
(Final Straw) In tch, lost place & short of room appr fnl 1f, switched & kept on inside last, never near to
chall: good run back at 7f though again shaped like 1m would suit: see 1630, 1384.

1186　**PERUGIA** 65 [10]　B W Hills　3-8-9 (92)　J Fortune　25/1: 200-04: Pld hard, trkd wnr, unable to qckn appr　3　87
fnl 1f: stablemate of wnr, 9 wk abs: stable beginning to find its feet again, keep in mind: see 1186.

1308　**QUEENS BENCH** 56 [6]　3-8-3 (86)　W Supple　5/1: 11-405: Prom, no extra fnl 1f: 8 wk abs, see 954.　¾　79

2171　**VIA CAMP** 17 [8]　3-8-7 (90)　G Carter　11/1: 310-46: Cl-up, one pace appr fnl 1f: see 2171.　shd　83

*2188　**INCREDULOUS** 15 [2]　3-8-4 (85) (2ow)　Pat Eddery　7/2: 0-2417: Taken to race alone far side, in tch　3　74
till appr fnl 1f, eased ins last: well bckd: jockey took wrong option on h'cap bow: see 2188.

*2342　**SHALIMAR** 10 [3]　3-8-5 (88)　R Hills　3/1 JT FAV: 6-3118: Dwelt, al rr: hvly bckd, too sn after 2342 (1m)?　1　73

8 ran　Time 1m 26.82 (2.92)　(K Abdulla)　B W Hills Lambourn, Berks

2568　4.45 HAMILTON RATED HCAP 3YO 0-100 (B)　6f　Good 40　00 Slow　[106]
£10092　£3828　£1914　£870　High numbers had considerable advantage

*2478　**BLUE VELVET** 4 [13]　K T Ivory　3-8-7 (85) (3ex)(3oh)　C Carver (3)　8/1: 000011: 3 gr f Formidable - Sweet　91
Whisper (Petong) Bhd ldrs, eff appr fnl 1f, burst thro' to lead dist, pshd out: well bckd, fair time, qk reapp:
on Friday scored at Sandown (h'cap): '99 wnr at Southwell (fill auct mdn, rtd 80a) & here at Newmarket (nurs, rtd
86): 3 prev wins at 5f, clrly eff at 6f: goes on any trk/grnd, likes Newmarket: progressive, tough filly.

2003　**GLENROCK** 24 [17]　A Berry　3-8-9 (87)　A McGlone　12/1: -06502: 3 ch c Muhtarram - Elkie Brooks　¾　89
(Relkino) Grabbed stands rail, tried to make all, rdn bef dist, hdd ins last, kept on: ran to best from fav'ble draw.

2338　**PERUVIAN CHIEF** 10 [10]　N P Littmoden　3-8-9 (87)　J Quinn　9/1: 052043: 3 b c Foxhound - John's Ballad　½　87
(Ballad Rock) Mid-div, not much room 2f out, switched left & then carried even further left dist, kept on for press,
unable to chall: nicely bckd: likely to have gone v close with a clr passage: acts on fast, gd & both AWs: see 112.

2197　**BAILEYS WHIRLWIND** 15 [4]　M L W Bell　3-9-0 (92)　R Mullen　20/1: 0-5034: Well plcd & ev ch, edged　½　91

left ent fnl 1f & drvn, held fnl 100y: ran to best, in form: see 1186.
2216 **MELANZANA 14** [15] 3-8-9 (87) G Carter 12/1: 31-425: Trkd ldrs, keen, chall & hung badly left dist, 1½ **82**
sn no extra: nicely bckd: lightly rcd, unexposed filly, keep in mind when stable returns to form: see 1409.
2348 **JEMIMA 9** [7] 3-9-4 (96) W Supple 20/1: -00006: Bhd, rdn appr fnl 1f, no impress till kept on fnl 150y. *hd* **91**
1111 **RUDIK 69** [5] 3-9-7 (99) J Reid 8/1: 313-57: Held up in tch, shaken up appr fnl 1f, lkd onepaced *nk* **93**
when carried badly left dist, no extra: 10 wk abs: top-weight on h'cap bow & not disgraced, see 1111.
2289 **PRESENTATION 11** [8] 3-9-2 (94) Dane O'Neill 12/1: 232668: Rear, niggld halfway, kept on ins last. *nk* **87**
2310 **TARAS GIRL 11** [9] 3-8-10 (88) R Winston 16/1: 350009: Held up, shaken up 2f out, no impress: ¾ **79**
op 25/1: well h'capped if getting favoured soft/hvy grnd, see 988.
2168 **ARGENT FACILE 17** [12] 3-8-12 (90)(t) J Fortune 12/1: 202230: Front rank & ev ch till edged left & 2½ **75**
wknd dist: 10th, nicely bckd: best at 5f, see 959.
2247 **BABY BARRY 13** [6] 3-8-7 (85) G Duffield 10/1: 003430: Chsd ldrs wide till appr fnl 1f: 11th, poor draw. ½ **69**
*2101 **ALJAWF 20** [2] 3-9-0 (92) R Hills 11/2 JT FAV: 1-0610: Well plcd till fdd appr fnl 1f, eased ins last: 1½ **72**
12th, nicely bckd: poor low draw: stablemate of 5th, faster grnd suits: see 2101.
1534 **DONT SURRENDER 45** [1] 3-9-2 (94) Pat Eddery 11/2 JT FAV: 1-0230: Chsd ldrs wide till 2f out: *1* **71**
13th, well bckd after 6 wk abs but this is prob best forgotten from stall 1: see 1534, 1178.
1078 **KELSO MAGIC 71** [11] 3-9-1 (93) J Weaver 25/1: 46-000: Bolted bef start, sn detached: 14th, 10 wk abs. *21* **40**
14 ran Time 1m 13.31 (2.31) (K T Ivory) K T Ivory Radlett, Herts

2569 **5.15 NGK SOHAM HCAP 3YO+ 0-85 (D) 5f Good 40 +12 Fast** **[83]**
£6142 £1890 £945 £472 3 yo rec 5 lb High numbers had considerable advantage

1479 **RECORD TIME 47** [11] E J Alston 4-8-0 (54)(1ow) W Supple 8/1: -00401: 4 ch f Clantime - On The Record **63**
(Record Token) Grabbed stands rail, made all, rdn out ins last: bckd from 10/1, fast time, 7 wk abs: '99 wnr
here at Newmarket (h'cap, rtd 63): sister to sprint h'capper Lago Di Varano: tried 6f, suited by 5f: acts on
firm & gd/soft grnd, likes Newmarket: best up with/forcing the pace: well ridden by very capable jockey.
*2385 **BAHAMIAN PIRATE 8** [7] D Nicholls 5-9-5 (74)(7ex) A Nicholls (3) 4/1: 1-0112: 5 ch g Housebuster - *1* **78**
Shining Through (Deputy Minister) Prom, ch appr fnl 1f, styd on but not pace of wnr: nicely bckd: gd run
back in trip: in cracking form, likely to go in again, see 2385.
*2294 **ANNETTE VALLON 11** [10] P W Harris 3-9-9 (83) T Quinn 7/1: 213: 3 b f Efisio - Christine Daae *hd* **86**
(Sadler's Wells) Cl-up & ev ch, held fnl 100y: nicely bckd on h'cap bow: gd run, win more races, see 2294.
2348 **OCKER 9** [8] Mrs N Macauley 6-10-0 (83) R Fitzpatrick (3) 20/1: 000604: Bhd ldrs, drvn 2f out, ¾ **83**
kept on but not pace to chall: better run, top-weight, see 47.
2107 **STATOYORK 19** [1] 7-8-3 (58) R Winston 20/1: 00-005: Rear & had to be switched from stall 1, hdwy *hd* **57+**
appr fnl 1f, nvr nr ldrs: had it all to do from worst draw: h'capped to win & one to keep in mind: see 2107.
2340 **REFERENDUM 10** [4] 6-9-2 (71) S Sanders 7/1: 000526: Front rank tho' wide, fdd fnl 1f: stablemate 1½ **66**
2nd: not done any favours having to race 5 horses deep, see 2340, 941.
2207 **AT LARGE 15** [3] 6-9-7 (76) L Newton 12/1: 610107: Bhd, staying on cl-home: ignore this from stall 3. *nk* **70**
2418 **SOUNDS ACE 6** [2] 4-7-10 (51)(bl)(2oh) J Mackay (5) 16/1: 603038: Dwelt, racd widest of all, *shd* **45**
nvr in it: quick reapp, best forgotten: see 1923.
2451 **AURIGNY 5** [13] 5-9-0 (69) O Urbina 20/1: 640409: Al towards rear: qck reapp, vis omitted: see 191. 1½ **59**
2329 **FORGOTTEN TIMES 10** [6] 6-9-5 (74)(vis) M Roberts 9/1: 622120: In tch wide till 1f out, eased: 10th. *shd* **64**
*1591 **FEARBY CROSS 41** [9] 4-9-11 (80) Pat Eddery 3/1 FAV: -13410: Al bhd: 11th, well bckd, 6 wk abs. *nk* **69**
11 ran Time 59.91 (1.41) (Peter Onslow) E J Alston Longton, Lancs

LEOPARDSTOWN SATURDAY JULY 8TH Lefthand, Galloping Track

Official Going GOOD TO FIRM

2570 **3.55 LISTED BROWNSTOWN STKS 3YO+ 1m Good/Firm**
£19500 £5700 £2700

-- **KERMIYANA** J Oxx 3-8-10 J Murtagh 7/2: -11: 3 b f Green Desert - Keraka (Storm Bird) **103**
Front rank, went on appr fnl 1f, rdn clr, eased nr fin: market drifter: recent Gowran Park debut winner
(maiden, made all): eff at 7f/1m, further will suit: runs well fresh on fast & gd/sft grnd: v useful filly
who was reportedly in season here, open to further improvement in Gr 3 company next time.
1751 **SAND PARTRIDGE 35** K Prendergast 3-8-10 D P McDonogh 14/1: 10-022: 3 b f Desert Style - Pipe 2½ **95**
Opener (Prince Sabo) Waited with, hdwy over 2f out, styd on but not pace of wnr: acts on fast & gd/soft: see 1751.
-- **TOPSY MORNING** P Prendergast 3-8-10 S Craine 14/1: 41-03: 3 b f Lahib - Grand Morning (King Of *hd* **94**
Clubs) Settled rear, switched/hdwy over 1f out, styd on well: 8 wk abs: eff at 1m on fast.
10 ran Time 1n 41.2 (H H Aga Khan) J Oxx Currabeg, Co Kildare

DEAUVILLE SATURDAY JULY 8TH Righthand, Galloping Track

Official Going VERY SOFT

2571 **1.50 GR 3 PRIX MESSIDOR 3YO+ 1m V Soft**
£21134 £7685 £3842 £2305

-- **FABERGER** Frau E Mader 4-9-2 L Hammer Hansen 617/10: -26341: 4 b c Dashing Blade - Friedrichslust **116**
(Caerleon) Mid-div, rdn/prog over 1f out, styd on strongly to lead nr fin, all out for a shock 61/1 success:
German raider, only one win in 15 starts prev (maiden): eff arnd a gall 1m on soft grnd: smart colt.
1458 **CHELSEA MANOR 48** P Bary 4-9-2 T Thulliez 47/10: -02332: 4 b c Grand Lodge - Docklands (Theatrical) *hd* **115**
Trkd ldrs, chall ldr over 1f out, led well ins last, hdd nr fin, just btn: v consistent, win similar: see 1458 (Gr 1).
*1619 **KINGSALSA 39** A Fabre 4-9-6 O Peslier 39/10: -13213: 4 b c Kingmambo - Caretta (Caro) ¾ **117**
Settled rear, gd hdwy to chall over 1f out, ev ch till no extra cl-home: v tough, win another Gr 3, see 1619.
*1847 **TRANS ISLAND 28** I A Balding 5-9-6 G Mosse 7/5 FAV: 3-2214: Led, hung left after 2f, ¾ **116**
rdn/hdd dist, drvn/no extra well ins last: reportedly never travelling, but ran to near best: tough, see 1847.
9 ran Time 1m 39.5 (Gestut Etzean) Frau E Mader Germany

DEAUVILLE   SUNDAY JULY 9TH   Righthand, Galloping Track

Official Going   HOLDING

2572   3.10 GR 3 PRIX MINERVE 3YO FILLIES   1m4f110y Holding
£21134   £7685   £3842

1901 **FOLIE DANSE** 28 Y de Nicolay 3-8-9 D Bonilla 27/10: -15251: 3 b f Petit Loup - Folle Envie   **110**
(Un Desperado) Rear, gd hdwy to lead 1f out, rdn out: earlier won on reapp, also a fine 5th in the Gr 1 French
Oaks: eff at 10/12.5f on gd/soft and hvy grnd: runs well fresh on a gall trk: useful/consistent filly.
1313 **PLAYACT** 58 N Clement 3-8-9 G Mosse 42/10: -51422: 3 ch f Hernando - Play Or Pay (Play Fellow)   **1** **108**
Settled last, strong run to chall dist, not pace of wnr well ins last: eff at 12.5f on hvy grnd.
1748 **FLAWLY** 36 E Lellouche 3-8-9 C Soumillon 3/1: 6-5123: 3 b f Old Vic - Flawlessly (Rainbow Quest)   **3** **103**
Cl-up, went on 2f out, hdd dist, not pace of front 2: acts on gd/soft & hvy: stoutly bred filly.
7 ran   Time 2m 46.5   (C Thulliez)   Y de Nicolay France

HOPPEGARTEN   SUNDAY JULY 9TH   -

Official Going   GOOD

2573   3.50 GR 2 BERLIN BRANDENBURG TROPHY 3YO+   1m   Good
£38710 £12903 £6452

2090 **SLIP STREAM** 18 Saeed bin Suroor 4-9-6 Paul Eddery : -54001: 4 ch c Irish River - Sous Entendu   **118**
(Shadeed) Made all, shaken up & went clr fnl 2f, readily: recently down the field under top-weight in the Hunt Cup:
'99 wnr at Goodwood (List, rtd 118), also just btn in a Chantilly Gr 1: '98 Leicester winner (mdn, D Loder):
eff at 10f, suited by forcing the pace over 1m on firm & soft grnd: runs well fresh: smart, front-running colt.
-- **UP AND AWAY** Frau E Mader 6-9-6 L Hammer Hansen : 2: 6 b g Le Glorieux - Ultima Ratio (Vice Regal)   **4** **109**
Chsd ldr, dropped rear halfway, styd on well fnl 1f but no ch with wnr: stays 1m on gd grnd.
-- **BERNARDON** P Schiergen 4-9-6 T Hellier : 3: 4 b c Suave Dancer - Bejaria (Konigsstuhl)   **nk** **108**
Prom, drvn & not pace of wnr fnl 2f, lost 2nd place nr fin: stays 1m on gd grnd.
5 ran   Time 1m 38.0   (Godolphin)   Saeed bin Suroor Newmarket

DEAUVILLE   TUESDAY JULY 11TH   Righthand, Galloping Track

Official Going   VERY SOFT

2574   3.35 GR 3 PRIX DE RIS-ORANGIS 3YO+   6f   V Soft
£21134   £7685   £3842   £2305   3 yo rec 6 lb

2403 **GORSE** 10 H Candy 5-9-4 G Mosse 53/10: 5-3621: 5 b h Sharpo - Pervenche (Latest Model)   **114**
Cl-up, went on over 2f out, styd on gamely when pressed ins last, drvn out: '99 wnr at Hamburg & Leopardstown
(Gr 3's, rtd 115): '98 scorer at Salisbury (mdn), Newmarket (stks), & Doncaster (List, rtd 108): all wins at 6f,
handles firm, loves gd or softer grnd: acts on a stiff trk: v tough & smart mud-loving entire.
*945 **DANGER OVER** 88 P Bary 3-8-8 T Thulliez 29/10: 25-112: 3 b c Warning - Danilova (Lyphard)   **snk** **109**
Mid-div going well, hdwy over 1f out, ran on well for press, not btn far: fine run, will apprec a return to 7f.
1746 **TOMBA** 39 M A Jarvis 6-9-4 O Peslier 36/10: 10-203: 6 ch h Efisio - Indian Love Song (Be My Guest)   **3** **105**
Rdn/rear, rdn to imprv over 1f out, kept on, no ch with front 2: twice below par in Gr company, btr 1453 (stks).
820 **TERROIR** 98 Mlle I Turc 5-9-0 (bl) C Soumillon 74/10: 334424: Cl-up, rdn/held dist, lost 3rd nr fin.   **shd** **101**
7 ran   Time 1m 12.6   (Girsonfield Ltd)   H Candy Wantage, Oxon

DONCASTER   WEDNESDAY JULY 12TH   Lefthand, Flat, Galloping Track

Official Going: GOOD Stalls: Straight Course - Stands Side, Round Course - Inside, Round Mile - Outside

2575   2.15 THEHORSESMOUTH NURSERY HCAP 2YO (D)   5f   Good/Firm 36 -21 Slow   **[87]**
£3510   £1080   £540   £270

1642 **ONLY ONE LEGEND** 40 [3] T D Easterby 2-9-3 (76) R Winston 6/1: -0331: 2 b g Eagle Eyed - Afifah   **80**
(Nashwan) Made all, styd on well, pushed out nr fin: 6 wk abs, first win: eff at 5f, 6f will suit: acts on firm
& fast grnd, prob handles gd/soft: likes a stiff/gall track: runs well fresh: open to further improvement.
1131 **FENWICKS PRIDE** 69 [8] B S Rothwell 2-9-2 (75) M Fenton 11/2: -5332: 2 b g Imperial Frontier -   **nk** **78**
Stunt Girl (Thatching) Trckd ldrs, rdn to chall fnl 1f, styd on well, al just held: abs: handles fast & soft grnd.
*1549 **NAUGHTY KNIGHT** 44 [4] G B Balding 2-8-4 (63) D Mernagh (3) 9/4 FAV: 050113: 2 ch c King's Signet - 3½ **57**
Maid Of Mischief (Be My Chief) Chsd ldrs, rdn & kept on fnl 1f, not pace to chall: abs: see 1549 (clmr, soft).
*2045 **EASTERN PROMISE** 23 [7] A Berry 2-9-1 (74) J Carroll 4/1: 2414: Close up 4f: see 2045 (firm).   **1½** **65**
1995 **DENSIM BLUE** 25 [2] 2-9-7 (80) G Bardwell 11/2: 024145: Prom till over 1f out: op 9/2: btr 1995, 1463.   **1** **69**
*2394 **TOMMY SMITH** 8 [5] 2-8-12 (71)(6ex) J Weaver 10/1: 004116: In tch rear, soon rdn, no hdwy.   **hd** **59**
1870 **ORANGE TREE LAD** 30 [6] 2-9-3 (76) P Goode (3) 12/1: 023207: Dwelt/bhd, never on terms: see 1302. **nk** **63**
7 ran   Time 1m 01.06 (2.86)   (The Four Ball Partnership)   T D Easterby Great Habton, N Yorks

811

2576	**2.45 FLYING SCOTSMAN COND STKS 2YO (C)** 7f str Good/Firm 36 -13 Slow
	£6201 £1908 £954 £477

+2083 **ECOLOGY** 21 [3] J L Dunlop 2-9-3 W Ryan 10/11 FAV: -2111: 2 b c Sri Pekan - Ecco Mi (Priolo)   **102**
Made all, styd on strongly & rdn clr ins last: hvly bckd: earlier scored at Ripon (mdn) & Kempton (nov stks):
apprec step up to 7f, 1m shld suit: acts on fast & gd, gall or sharpish track: useful colt.
2067 **IMPERIAL DANCER** 22 [5] M R Channon 2-9-0 A Culhane 7/2: 421302: 2 b c Primo Dominie - Gorgeous 4   **89**
Dancer (Nordico) Trkd wnr, rdn fnl 2f, outpcd fnl 1f: op 11/4: longer 7f trip: prob handles fast & hvy.
*2414 **QUINK** 7 [2] Sir Mark Prescott 2-8-11 R Winston 9/4: 13: 2 ch g Selkirk - Ink Pot (Green Dancer)   shd   **89**
Prom, ch 2f out, soon rdn/outpcd: bckd: longer 7f trip: see 2414.
2106 **SOME WILL DO** 41 [4] T D Easterby 2-8-11 R Winston 100/1: 04: In tch, btn over 2f out: highly tried.   12   **68**
2333 **FORMULA VENETTA** 11 [1] J Carroll 50/1: 05: Dwelt/bhd halfway: highly tried: see 2333.   12   **50**
5 ran   Time 1m 26.66 (3.46)   (Hesmonds Stud)   J L Dunlop Arundel, W Sussex

---

2577	**3.20 TRANSPENNINE HCAP 3YO 0-85 (D)** 6f Good/Firm 36 -06 Slow	**[90]**
	£4407 £1356 £678 £339	

2168 **MOLLY BROWN** 18 [6] R Hannon 3-9-4 (80) J Carroll 14/1: -04001: 3 b f Rudimentary - Sinking (Midyan)   **86**
Cl up, went on 2f out, rdn fnl 1f, just held on: op 12/1: '99 Haydock debut wnr (mdn): eff at 5/6f on fast & good
grnd, suited up with/forcing the pace: likes a gall track.
1826 **LORD PACAL** 33 [7] N A Callaghan 3-9-3 (79) W Ryan 8/1: -00002: 3 b g Indian Ridge - Please Believe shd   **84**
Me (Try My Best) Trckd ldrs, drvn & styd on well inside last, just held: op 10/1: eff at 5/6f: see 1471.
2165 **CD FLYER** 18 [1] M R Channon 3-8-11 (73) W Supple 10/1: 064463: 3 ch g Grand Lodge - Pretext   hd   **78**
(Polish Precedent) Towards rear, no room over 1f out, switched & styd on stronly near fin, post came too soon:
no luck in running, probable wnr with a clr run: can find compensation in similar: see 852.
2177 **NAJEYBA** 17 [12] A C Stewart 3-9-1 (77) M Roberts 4/1 FAV: 134: Led till 2f out, onepace inside last: ½   **80**
hvly bckd tho op 3/1: h'cap bow: see 2177,1605.
2504 **INDIAN MUSIC** 4 [9] (BL) F Lynch 13/2: -00455: Prom, no extra inside last: qck reapp, blnks.   ½   **71**
2078 **DANCING EMPRESS** 21 [8] 3-9-1 (77) Dean McKeown 8/1: 012406: Held up, never pace to chall.   1   **76**
2325 **SANTIBURI GIRL** 11 [3] 3-8-5 (67) R Mullen 12/1: 100237: Mid div, outpcd fnl 2f: see 2031, 1397 (7f).   ½   **64**
*2183 **MISTER SUPERB** 17 [11] 3-9-7 (83) M Fenton 8/1: -30218: Bhd ldrs, outpcd over 1f out: see 2183 (mdn). ¾   **78**
1441 **WILDFLOWER** 51 [4] 3-8-12 (74) J Weaver 7/1: 109: Mid div, held 2f out: 7 wk abs: see 1012 (7f, mdn). hd   **68**
2111 **DIANEME** 20 [10] 3-7-12 (60) P Fessey 20/1: -30450: Prom 4f: 10th: see 826.   ¾   **51**
2315 **SEAHORSE BOY** 11 [2] 3-7-10 (58) (60h) G Bardwell 33/1: 004000: Soon outpcd/bhd: 11th: mod form.   ¾   **47**
2431 **MANA DARGENT** 7 [5] 3-8-9 (71) J Fanning 9/2: 045630: Prom 4f: 12th: well bckd: see 1387, 717.   4   **50**
12 ran   Time 1m 13.34 (2.54)   (The Sinking Fast Partnership)   R Hannon East Everleigh, Wilts

---

2578	**3.50 SPONSORSHIP COND STKS 3YO+ (C)** 1m rnd Good/Firm 36 -04 Slow
	£7117 £2190 £1095 £547 3 yo rec 9 lb

1171 **FRENCH FELLOW** 67 [4] T D Easterby 3-8-5 J Carroll 8/15 FAV: 11-201: 3 b c Suave Dancer -   **110**
Mademoiselle Chloe (Night Shift) Chsd ldr, drvn 3f out, led inside last, styd on well, rdn out: hvly bckd at odds on,
2 mth abs: most progressive in '99, won at Ayr (auct mdn), Redcar, York, Doncaster (h'caps) & Ascot (List, rtd 105):
eff at 1m, further may suit: acts on firm & soft, reportedly prefers cut: likes a stiff/gall trck: tough & v useful.
1693 **MEADAAAR** 39 [1] J L Dunlop 3-8-2 W Supple 7/2: 213-02: 3 ch c Diesis - Katiba (Gulch)   1   **103**
Led, increased tempo halfway, rdn/hung right & hdd inside last, no extra: styd longer 1m trip: see 1693.
3581↓ **DYNAMIC DREAM** 321 [5] P W Harris 3-7-11 G Bardwell 10/1: 1-3: 3 b f Dynaformer - Hip Hip Hur Rahy 1½   **95**
(Rahy) Chsd ldrs, drvn/outpcd by front pair fnl 2f: reapp: won sole start in '99, at Folkestone (fillies mdn, rtd
82): eff at 7f, 1m+ should suit this term: acts on gd grnd & a sharp/undul track: has run well fresh.
2349 **SERGEANT YORK** 10 [3] C Smith 4-8-11 G Faulkner (3) 50/1: 533604: In tch, outpcd fnl 3f: see 1291.   ¾   **99$**
1574 **ON TIME** 43 [2] 3-8-5 O Urbina 6/1: 113-35: In tch, btn 3f out: op 9/2, 6 week abs: flattered 1574.   7   **91**
5 ran   Time 1m 39.32 (3.22)   (T H Bennett)   T D Easterby Great Habton, N Yorks

---

2579	**4.25 CHARNWOOD HCAP 3YO 0-80 (D)** 1m str Good/Firm 36 -00 Slow	**[85]**
	£4023 £1238 £619 £309	

*2235 **GRANTED** 14 [5] M L W Bell 3-9-5 (76) M Fenton 5/1: -33211: 3 b f Cadeaux Genereux - Germane   **82**
(Distant Relative) Confidently rdn bhd ldrs, prog under hands & heels riding to lead 1f out, al holding rival after,
pushed out: op 9/2: earlier recorded first win at Hamilton (h'cap): rtd 82 in '99: suited by 1m, tried 10f: acts
on fast & gd/soft grnd, stiff/gall track: best without a visor: prog filly, three-timer looks very possible.
1853 **MAMZUG** 31 [1] B Hanbury 3-9-7 (78) G Faulkner (3) 11/2: 0-4142: 3 b c Hamas - Bellissi (Bluebird)   ½   **81**
Led till 1f out, rdn & kept on, al held by wnr: rest well covered: op 9/2: see 1435 (mdn).
2186 **MUST BE MAGIC** 17 [2] H J Collingridge 3-8-4 (61) M Roberts 5/1: -06343: 3 b c Magic Ring -   3   **58**
Sequin Lady (Star Appeal) Rear, styd on for press fnl 2f, no threat to front pair: bckd: handles fast & soft grnd.
1793 **ALAWAR** 34 [9] C G Cox 3-8-4 (61)(t) J Carroll 9/1: -00044: Chsd ldrs, held over 1f out: see 1793.   4   **50**
2250 **LAHAAY** 16 [4] 3-8-13 (70) W Supple 7/1: 5-0045: Held up in tch, eff over 2f out, no impresssion.   1½   **50**
2211 **ONLY WORDS** 16 [3] 3-8-2 (59)(t) R Mullen 20/1: -6006: In tch, btn 2f out: see 2211.   1½   **42**
1552 **MONDURU** 44 [7] 3-9-1 (72) O Pears 25/1: 0-0357: In tch, outpcd over 2f out: 6 week abs: btr 1012.   shd   **55**
1495 **IN THE ARENA** 47 [8] 3-9-1 (72) W Ryan 11/4 FAV: 0-4348: Held up, eff 2f out, sn btn: hvly bckd, abs.   1½   **52**
1973 **HUTOON** 26 [4] 3-8-13 (70) J Weaver 12/1: 43-609: Prom 6f: op 9/1: see 1362.   4   **42**
9 ran   Time 1m 39.35 (2.85)   (E D Kessly)   M L W Bell Newmarket, Suffolk

---

2580	**5.00 CLASSIFIED STKS 3YO+ 0-75 (D)** 6f Good/Firm 36 +10 Fast
	£4023 £1238 £619 £309 3 yo rec 6 lb

2334 **PIPS MAGIC** 11 [2] J S Goldie 4-9-1 F Lynch 16/1: 00W001: 4 b g Pips Pride - Kentucky Starlet (Cox's   **79**
Ridge) Handy, led over 2f out, held on well near fin, rdn out: fast time: '99 Ascot wnr, (val h'cap, rtd 93):
'98 Ripon & Ayr wnr (nov, rtd 92): eff at 5/6f on firm & soft, handles any trk: v well h'capped.
*2504 **PAYS DAMOUR** 4 [7] R Hannon 3-8-12 J Carroll 9/2 JT FAV: 020012: 3 b c Pursuit Of Love - Lady Of   nk   **82**
The Land (Wollow) Led till over 2f out, rdn & styd on well ins last, just held: bckd tho' op 7/2: qck reapp.

DONCASTER   WEDNESDAY JULY 12TH   Lefthand, Flat, Galloping Track

2000 **ZIRCONI 25** [10] D Nicholls 4-9-1 J Fanning 5/1: 40-403: 4 b g Zieten - Muirfield (Crystal Glitters)   ¾   77
Trkd ldrs, rdn & kept on fnl 1f: bckd from 7/1: looks fairly h'capped, shld win sn: see 1517.
1842 **ALMASI 32** [11] C F Wall 8-8-12 R Mullen 9/2 JT FAV: 30-534: Twds rear, rdn/hung left & late gains.   ½   72
2371 **MADMUN 9** [4] 6-9-1 W Supple 6/1: 521-55: Held up, outpcd/little room halfway, switched & kept on   1   73
well fnl 1f, no threat: often fin fast & shapes as if a return to 7f will suit: see 2371.
2334 **FRANCPORT 11** [6] 4-9-1 J Weaver 15/2: 000306: Mid div, not pace to chall: see 824 (soft).   nk   72
2432 **CAUDA EQUINA 7** [9] 6-9-1 R Perham 13/2: 043027: Chsd ldrs, rdn/held 1f out: op 11/2: see 905.   2   67
2133 **SURVEYOR 19** [14] 5-9-1 R Morse 50/1: 00-008: Rear, mod late gains, no threat: see 1851.   shd   67
2000 **TOM TUN 25** [1] 5-9-1 T Lucas 11/1: 300509: Chsd ldrs 4f: op 10/1: see 47.   ¾   65
2133 **SEA DEER 19** [8] 11-9-1 G Bardwell 25/1: 00-000: Prom 3f: 10th: now with J Pearce: see 1952.   hd   64
2444 Redoubtable 6 [5] 9-9-4 G Parkin 25/1:   1074 Mister Mal 72 [3] 4-9-1 O Pears 16/1:
2151 Rose Of Mooncoin 19 [13] 4-8-12 (bl) D Mernagh (3) 20/1:
2282 Distant King 13 [12] 7-9-1 Suzanne France (7) 100/1:
14 ran   Time 1m 12.33 (1.53)   (Frank Brady)   J S Goldie Uplawmoor, E Renfrews

KEMPTON   WEDNESDAY JULY 12TH   Righthand, Flat, Fair Track

Official Going   GOOD/SOFT (GOOD places). Stalls: Inside, except Straight Course - Far Side.

2581   6.30 PUSSY GALORE FILLIES HCAP 3YO+ 0-80 (D)   1m1f rnd Good/Soft 65   -10 Slow   [77]
£4348   £1338   £669   £334   3 yo rec 10lb

2246 **PIPS WAY 14** [7] K R Burke 3-9-4 (77) N Callan 9/1: 041431: 3 ch f Pips Pride - Algonquin Park   82
(High Line) Nvr far away, drvn to lead cl home, all out: earler won at Newcastle (h'cap): '99 Ripon wnr (mdn,
debut, rtd 84): eff at 1m/9f, poss stays 12f: hndles fast, best on gd/soft & hvy grnd: hndles any trk, has tried
a visor, better without: can run well fresh: tough & geniune filly.
2467 **DIVINE PROSPECT 5** [4] A P Jarvis 3-8-10 (69) J Fortune 16/1: 656402: 3 br f Namaqualand -   1   71
Kayu (Tap On Wood) Dwelt, recovered & sn in tch, led briefly fnl 1f, not pace of wnr cl home: qck reapp: on a
handy mark, can find similar poss over 10f: see 701 (reapp).
2228 **DIXIELAKE 14** [11] H Candy 3-9-7 (80) C Rutter 10/1: 0-133: 3 b f Lake Coniston - Rathvindon   shd   82+
(Realm) Rear, imprvd 2f out, short of room & switched ins fnl 1f, nrst fin under hands & heels riding: eff at
1m/9f, shld sty 10f: promising run, sure to find a h'cap when more enterprisingly rdn: see 2228, 1556.
931 **NATALIE JAY 88** [10] M R Channon 4-8-13 (62) A Daly 16/1: 25-304: Prom, led dist till inside last,   nk   63
no extra: 12 week abs: bck on a winning mark, won off 63 last term: see 831.
2084 **SAFARI BLUES 21** [8] 3-9-3 (76) P Dobbs (5) 16/1: 11-505: Rear, improved 2f out, no impression   2   73
inside last: see 1855, 54 (AW).
2041 **LADY JO 23** [6] 4-8-7 (56) R Smith (5) 10/1: -66606: Rear, prog over 1f out, nvr nrr: best form   hd   52
prev over 10f & a return to further will suit: see 290 (12f, saand).
2183 **PSALMIST 17** [12] 3-8-4 (63) Martin Dwyer 25/1: 3007: Never better than mid div: not given a hard time   2   55
on h'cap bow: shown promise over sprint trips: see 2183, 1525.
*2493 **THE WILD WIDOW 4** [9] 6-9-11 (74)(vis)(6ex) J Mackay (5) 7/4 FAV: 211118: Led after 1f till 1f out,   ½   65
wknd: hvly bckd: quick reapp & going for a 5 timer: much btr 2493 (fast grnd).
2262 **FLIGHT SEQUENCE 14** [14] 4-9-13 (76) J Quinn 4/1: 4-6029: Prom 7f, grad fdd: btr 2262 (firm).   3½   60
2130 **DENS JOY 19** [13] 4-9-2 (65) D Sweeney 16/1: 001200: Dwelt, prog 2f out, sn btn: 10th: btr 2051.   1¼   46
1547 **UMBRIAN GOLD 44** [3] 4-9-13 (76) S Whitworth 12/1: 0-2000: Never a factor, fin 11th: 6 week abs.   6   48
1785 Daniella Ridge 34 [5] 4-9-0 (63) Dane O'Neill 16/1:   1733 Aura Of Grace 37 [2] 3-9-2 (75) A Clark 16/1:
2509 Kuwait Dawn 4 [1] 4-10-0 (77)(VIS) I Mongan (5) 20/1:
14 ran   Time 1m 56.72 (6.72)   (Paul James McCaughey)   K R Burke Newmarket

2582   7.00 BLOFELD MDN 3YO (D)   6f   Good/Soft 65   +07 Fast
£4368   £1248   £624

2042 **CRISS CROSS 23** [1] R Hannon 3-9-0 P Dobbs (5) 15/8: 224541: 3 b c Lahib - La Belle Katherine   76
(Lyphard) Nvr far away, went on 2f out, asserted for press ins last: well bckd: gd time: deserves win,
rnr-up thrice prev: eff at 6/7.7f, seems best on gd/soft & hvy, handles fast: acts on a sharp or gall trk.
3322} **WHISTLER 334** [3] R Hannon 3-9-0 Dane O'Neill 15/8: 4203-2: 3 ch g Selkirk - French Gift   2½   70
(Cadeaux Genereux) Set pace till over 2f out, left bhd by wnr ins fnl 1f: nicely bckd & stablemate of wnr:
rnr-up at Windsor in '99 (stks, rtd 80): eff at 5/6f, hndls gd/soft, prob prefers fast grnd: sharper next time.
2216 **TERRA NOVA 15** [2] R W Armstrong 3-8-9 R Price 7/4 FAV: 46-303: 3 ch f Polar Falcon - Tarsa   11   46
(Ballad Rock) Rcd keenly & prom, wknd 2f out, eased: nicely bckd: raced too keenly for own gd today.
3 ran   Time 1m 14.58 (3.48)   (Michael Pescod)   R Hannon East Everleigh, Wilts

2583   7.30 HELICAL BAR FILLIES MDN 2YO (D)   7f rnd   Good/Soft 65   -20 Slow
£4348   £1338   £669   £334

2259 **CARIBBEANDRIFTWOOD 14** [4] P F I Cole 2-8-11 J Fortune 15/8 FAV: -21: 2 ch f Woodman - Drifting   84
(Lyphard) Made all, hrd on fnl 1f, drvn out: well bckd from 5/2: $65,000 purchase: eff at 7f on firm &
gd/soft grnd, 1m will suit: can force the pace: looks game & useful.
1957 **AKER WOOD 26** [8] A P Jarvis 2-8-11 B Marcus 20/1: 02: 2 b f Bin Ajwaad - Wannaplantatree   1   80
(Niniski) Rcd keenly & nvr far away, styd on fnl 1f but not pace of wnr: pulled clr of 3rd: clearly stys 7f &
acts on gd/soft grnd: much improved here & should find a mdn judged on this: see 1957.
2174 **EARLY WISH 17** [10] B Hanbury 2-8-11 J Reid 9/4: -633: 2 ch f Rahy - Heaven's Nook (Great Above)   3½   73
Prom, rdn & onepaced fnl 1f: tchd 7/2: prob stys 7f: hndles gd/soft tho' just better in 2174 (firm grnd).
-- **DODONA** [5] T D McCarthy 2-8-11 P Doe 33/1: 4: Rear, styd on fnl 2f, nrst fin on debut: April   ½   72+
foal, half sister to a wnr abroad: dam won at 10f, sire a top class miler: plenty to like about this, 1m suit.
-- **HUREYA** [7] 2-8-11 R Hills 6/1: 5: Bhd, hdwy & ev ch dist, no extra ins last: tchd 8/1, debut: nk   71
Jan first foal: dam unrcd, but from a gd family: ran well for a long way & will improve.
-- **MISS PITZ** [13] 2-8-11 A Culhane 20/1: 6: Dwelt, improving when hmpd when 2f out, styd on   1½   69+
nicely fnl 1f under a kind ride: mkt drifter: April foal, cost 18,000gns: sister to mid-dist h'capper Remaadi:
eye catching debut, open to plenty of improvement & stable is just beginning to hit form.
-- **LA VITA E BELLA** [3] 2-8-11 S Sanders 25/1: 7: Rear, kept on fnl 2f, nrst fin on debut: Jan foal,   hd   68

813

cost 19,000gns: half sister to 5f 2yo scorer Light The Rocket: dam stayed mid-dists: bred to apprec 1m+.

2390	**PRIMO VENTURE 8** [9] 2-8-11 N Callan 25/1: 68: Never a factor: see 2390.		11	52
1883	**SHIMLA 29** [12] 2-8-11 Dane O'Neill 25/1: 09: Al towards rear: see 1883.		¾	51
1876	**GOLDEN BEACH 30** [11] 2-8-11 L Newman (3) 25/1: 00: Rcd keenly mid div, btn after halfway: 10th.		2½	46
1986	**EAGALITY 25** [2] 2-8-11 S Clancy (7) 25/1: 00: Rcd keenly & front rank 5f, fdd into 11th: see 1986.		2½	41
2125	**UNDERCOVER GIRL 19** [1] 2-8-11 Martin Dwyer 25/1: 50: Speed till halfway, fdd into 12th.		2½	36
2357	**PHARMACYS PET 10** [6] 2-8-11 Pat Eddery 8/1: 00: Al badly outpcd, t.o.in last: bckd from 20/1: better clearly expected & something amiss? see 2357.		21	6

13 ran Time 1m 30.02 (5.92) (Christopher Wright) P F I Cole Whatcombe, Oxon

---

2584 8.00 CASINO ROYALE HCAP 3YO+ 0-90 (C) 1m6f92y Good/Soft 65 -04 Slow [81]
£6922 £2130 £1065 £532 3 yo rec 15lb

*2445 **GIVE NOTICE 6** [3] J L Dunlop 3-8-9 (77)(5ex) Pat Eddery 4/6 FAV: -06111: 3 b c Warning - Princess **86**
Genista (Ile de Bourbon) Cl up, led on bit over 2f out, shaken up fnl 1f, shade readily: hvly bckd under a pen
to land a hat-trick after wins at Yarmouth & Haydock (h'caps, easily): rtd 69 in '99: much improved since step
up to 14f, 2m will suit: acts on fast, gd/soft & on a gall or easy track: can force the pace: v progressive.
1637 **BUSY LIZZIE 41** [4] J L Dunlop 3-8-5 (73) G Carter 14/1: 0-2062: 3 b f Sadler's Wells - Impatiente ½ **78**
(Vaguely Noble) Waited with, slightly outpcd 3f out, eff to chase wnr over 1f out, al held: back to form
on favoured gd/soft grnd & clr of rem: stays 14.4f: see 964.
*2194 **MAJESTIC BAY 16** [1] P W Harris 4-9-8 (75) A Culhane 8/1: 3-3013: 4 b g Unfuwain - That'll Be 6 **74**
The Day (Thatching) Led, qckd over 3f out, hdd over 2f out, no extra & flashed tail: btr 2194 (mdn, gd/firm).
2164 **URGENT SWIFT 18** [2] A P Jarvis 7-9-1 (68) J Fortune 6/1: 010124: Waited with, eff 3f out, wknd. 7 **60**
2268 **ENFILADE 13** [5] 4-9-10 (77)(t) R Hills 9/2: -50165: Cl up, wknd quickly 3f out: nicely bckd: 26 **43**
something amiss? twice below 1536 (similar race).
5 ran Time 3m 12.76 (9.96) (I H Stewart-Brown) J L Dunlop Arundel, W Sussex

---

2585 8.30 SCARAMANGA MDN 3YO (D) 7f rnd Good/Soft 65 -32 Slow
£4134 £1272 £636 £318

-- **CAYMAN SUNSET** [3] E A L Dunlop 3-8-9 J Fortune 6/4 FAV: 1: 3 ch f Night Shift - Robinia **80**
(Roberto) In tch, eff 2f out, flashed tail but qckd readily when led ins last, going away: hvly bckd on
debut: half sister to a useful 7f scorer: dam 7f wnr: stays an easy 7f well, 1m shld suit: runs well
fresh on gd/soft: looks potentially useful & a promising first run.
2058 **NIGHT SIGHT 22** [1] G Wragg 3-9-0 M Roberts 2/1: 022322: 3 b c Eagle Eyed - El Hamo (Search For 3 **78**
Gold) Cl up, led over 2f out till just ins last, not pace of wnr: bckd: consistent but lacks a finishing kick.
2230 **SKYLARK 14** [1] R Hannon 3-8-9 Dane O'Neill 7/1: 0-4653: 3 ch f Polar Falcon - Boozy (Absalom) 1½ **71$**
Led till over 2f out, onepace: op 5/1: better with forcing tactics on this gd/soft, handles firm & stays 7f.
1947 **FLYING BACK 27** [4] R Hannon 3-9-0 L Newman (3) 11/1: -44: Handy, btn 2f out: op 6/1, see 1947. 2½ **72**
3613j **SLAM BID 319** [2] 3-9-0 S Sanders 14/1: 00-5: Keen, cl up till wknd over 2f out: op 8/1: rtd 62 2 **69**
on two unplcd juv starts: bred to apprec 1m+.
2211 **JIMAL 16** [5] 3-9-0 Pat Eddery 14/1: 056: Al bhd: see 2211 (1m). 3 **65**
-- **BOP** [6] 3-8-9 N Pollard 12/1: 7: Al bhd on debut: dam 1m scorer: op 6/1: with D Elsworth. hd **60**
7 ran Time 1m 30.89 (6.79) (M P Burke) E A L Dunlop Newmarket, Suffolk

---

2586 9.00 SHAKEN HCAP 3YO 0-75 (E) 5f Good/Soft 65 +03 Fast [76]
£4329 £1332 £666 £333

2288 **JUDIAM 12** [1] C A Dwyer 3-9-0 (62) J Fortune 3/1 FAV: 500051: 3 b f Primo Dominie - Hoist **65**
(Bluebird) Waited with, gd hdwy appr fnl 1f, styd on well for press to get up cl home: fair time: '99 wnr at
Yarmouth (nursery h'cap, rtd 71): suited by 5f on fast, prefers gd/soft & soft: hndles any track.
2505 **RED TYPHOON 4** [5] M Kettle 3-9-0 N Callan 12/1: -00002: 3 ro f Belfort - Dash Cascade hd **71**
(Absalom) Cl up, led dist, kept on for press till collared cl home: op 8/1: clr of rem & enjoyed this easy surface.
2478 **CORBLETS 8** [8] S Dow 3-9-2 (64) P Doe 5/1: 250003: 3 b f Timeless Times - Dear Glenda 3 **60**
(Gold Song) Chsd ldrs, onepace appr fnl 1f: quick reapp: btr 1427, 883.
2478 **AROGANT PRINCE 5** [4] J J Bridger 3-8-11 (59) A Daly 10/1: 160004: Handy, short of room & switched 1¼ **53**
left over 1f out, kept on same pace: quick reapp, enjoyed return to easy grnd: best 1427.
2207 **HUNTING TIGER 16** [7] 3-9-6 (68) Craig Williams 9/1: 000005: Bhd, some late gains: see 1427. nk **61**
2078 **CAROLS CHOICE 21** [2] 3-8-13 (61) Pat Eddery 5/1: 332356: In tch, wknd 1f out: see 1795. 2 **50**
1817 **PRIME RECREATION 33** [6] 3-9-0 (62) Dale Gibson 4/1: -00037: Led till over 1f out, wknd: bckd. nk **50**
2183 **AZIRA 17** [3] 3-8-12 (60) S Righton 8/1: 56-08: Trckd ldr, led briefly over 1f out, soon wknd: ½ **47**
rtd 52 on sole juv start: dam 1m wnr.
8 ran Time 1m 01.42 (3.12) (R West) C A Dwyer Newmarket, Suffolk

---

Official Going Turf - GOOD; AW - STANDARD. Stalls: AW - Inside; Turf - Far Side.

2587 1.55 BAR SELLER 3YO+ (G) 1m2f aw Standard Inapplicable
£1928 £551 £275 3 yo rec 11lb

1331 **OCEAN LINE 56** [7] G M McCourt 5-9-6 G Baker (7) 10/1: 204001: 5 b g Kefaah - Tropic Sea (Sure Blade) **42a**
Cl-up, went on appr fnl 2f, rdn out: no bid: recently plcd over hdles (2m nov, gd, rtd 73h): '99 wnr at Windsor
(sell h'cap, first win) & Brighton (clmr, rtd 47): eff btwn 1m & 11.5f on fast, gd & both AWs: likes to race up
with/force the pace on a sharp trk: likes sellers/clmrs.
2136 **SAINT GEORGE 19** [5] K R Burke 4-9-6 N Callan 13/2: 0-0042: 4 b g Unblest - Jumana (Windjammer) 2 **38a**
Front rank, rdn to chall appr fnl 2f, no extra fnl ins last: op 5/1: clr rem: up in trip, eff at 10f on equitrack.
2467 **THOMAS HENRY 5** [6] J S Moore 4-9-6 A Clark 8/1: 003503: 4 br g Petardia - Hitopah (Bustino) 6 **30a**
Prom, rdn/outpcd halfway, drvn/late gains fnl 2f: qck reapp: see 786.
2181 **BILLICHANG 17** [1] P Howling 4-9-12 J Quinn 7/1: 610044: Led, hdd appr fnl 2f, sn btn: btr 775. 3 **32a**

2460 **MUSTANG 5** [10] 7-9-12 (vis) T G McLaughlin 14/1: 306105: Prom, drpd rear after halfway,   *shd* **32a**
late hdwy, no dgnr: qck reapp: btr 2040 (1m, firm).
2181 **FROZEN SEA 17** [11] 9-9-6 (t) S Whitworth 12/1: 22-006: Handy, rdn/no extra fnl 3f: see 1465.   *hd* **26a**
2411 **CAERDYDD FACH 7** [8] 4-9-1 A Beech (5) 20/1: 0-0407: Prom, bhd halfway, late gains: qck reapp.   *¾* **20a**
1933 **EI EI 27** [3] 5-9-6 I Mongan (5) 9/1: 624058: Rcd keenly in tch, wknd fnl 3f: op 7/1: see 893, 404.   *1* **23a**
2199 **HERR TRIGGER 16** [13] 9-9-6 (ebl) J Lowe 13/8 FAV: 05-009: Dsptd lead, wknd qckly fnl 3f: *1* **21a**
nicely bckd & better expected at these weights, reportedly resented the kickback: see 22.
2380 **PROUD CAVALIER 9** [9] 4-9-6 M Baird 33/1: 0-0500: Dwelt, rcd keenly in rear, nvr a threat.   *4* **15a**
2323 **KI CHI SAGA 11** [14] 8-9-6 (t) P McCabe 25/1: 006030: Al rear, fin 11th: see 2323.   *3½* **10a**
2119 **NORTH ARDAR 20** [12] 10-9-6 G Carter 12/1: 003350: Dwelt, sn struggling, fin 12th: flattered 2119.   *2½* **6a**
1972 Little Tara 26 [4] 3-8-4 J Mackay (5) 33/1:   1741 Tucson 36 [2] 3-8-9 C Rutter 25/1:
14 ran   Time 2m 07.0 (4.2)   (Christopher Shankland)   G M McCourt Letcombe Regis, Oxon.

2588   **2.25 CHAMPAGNE AUCT MDN 2YO (E)**   **6f str**   **Good 40**   **00 Slow**
        £3185   £910   £455

1962 **PAIRING 26** [18] H Morrison 2-8-7 G Carter 14/1: 41: 2 ch g Rudimentary - Splicing (Sharpo)   **82**
Prom, hdwy to lead appr fnl 1f, rdn out despite hanging left ins last: 5,500gns Mar foal, dam a 5/6f scorer:
apprec this step up to 6f: acts on gd & a sharp/undul trk: on the up-grade & could improve further.
1641 **THATS JAZZ 40** [11] M L W Bell 2-7-13 J Mackay (5) 12/1: 02: 2 b f Cool Jazz - Miss Mercy (Law   *1¾* **68**
Society) Settled bhd, hdwy 3f out, rdn & ran on well appr fnl 1f, no ch with wnr: 6 wk abs: stays 6f on gd
& shld appre a step up to 7f now: see 1641.
2209 **LOOKING FOR LOVE 16** [4] J G Portman 2-7-13 N Pollard 14/1: 03: 2 b f Tagula - Mousseux (Jareer)   *¾* **66**
Front rank, dsptd lead over 2f out, rdn/held well ins last: may apprec 7f next time: see 2209.
2459 **ROYAL ASSAY 5** [6] Mrs P N Dutfield 2-8-5 F Fitzsimons (5) 10/1: -304: Cl-up, went on appr   *½* **71**
fnl 2f, hdd over 1f out, swished tail & no extra ins last: qck reapp: see 2020.
2459 **APRIL LEE 5** [8] 2-8-2 (e) J Tate 16/1: 60525: Handy, ev ch till no extra appr fnl 1f: qck reapp.   *1¾* **64**
-- **ROSELYN** [9] 2-8-5 D Sweeney 14/1: 6: Bhd, rdn/prog 2f out, kept on but no threat to ldrs: will improve.   *1½* **63+**
9,500gns Mar foal, sister to a decent 5f/2yo wnr: dam won over 6f: promising debut for I Balding, will improve.
2005 **LOST AT SEA 25** [7] 2-8-10 N Callan 4/7 FAV: -027: Cl-up, rdn/fdd fnl 2f: nicely bckd, btr 2005 (firm).   *1* **65**
-- **CARNOT** [12] 2-8-7 I Mongan (5) 14/1: 2: Prom, ev ch till wknd appr fnl 1f: bckd from 25/1:   *½* **61**
6,500gns Apr foal, dam 7/9f wnr abroad: with G Bravery.
-- **TICKLE** [3] 2-7-13 J Quinn 16/1: 9: Ran green in rear, nvr with ldrs: op 10/1: cheaply bght   *2* **47**
Primo Dominie filly, dam scored at up to 15f: shld learn for experience & improve, poss over 7f.
2306 **LITTLE CALLIAN 12** [1] 2-7-13 P M Quinn (3) 50/1: 60: Rcd alone on far rail, wknd from halfway, 10th.   *2* **42**
2285 **BONELLA 12** [13] 2-8-5 C Rutter 25/1: -00: Nvr a factor, fin 11th: see 2285.   *1¾* **44**
1981 **UNLIKELY 26** [10] 2-8-4 G Baker (7) 20/1: -30: Led, hdd appr fnl 2f, wknd qckly, 15th: btr 1981 (sell).   **0**
-- **TYPE ONE** [2] 2-8-10 A Clark 14/1: 0: Dwelt, sn in tch, fdd fnl 2f, fin 16th: 10,000gns Apr foal,   **0**
half-brother to a 6f/1m 2yo scorer: with T G Mills.
2237 Law Breaker 14 [16] 2-8-7 D O'Donohoe 33/1:   1924 Jacks Birthday 28 [5] 2-8-10 S Whitworth 33/1:
2368 Rock And Skip 9 [17] 2-8-4 G Hind 50/1:   -- Susie The Floosie [15] 2-8-5 R Havlin 33/1:
-- Highland Flight [14] 2-7-13 A Daly 33/1:
18 ran   Time 1m 11.2 (2.4)   (The Beach Club)   H Morrison East Isley, Berks.

2589   **3.00 BEST BETS NURSERY HCAP 2YO (D)**   **6f str**   **Good 40**   **-12 Slow**   **[91]**
        £3679   £1132   £566   £283

1944 **NORCROFT LADY 27** [5] N A Callaghan 2-9-7 (84) J Quinn 6/1: -141: 2 b f Mujtahid - Polytess   **89**
(Polish Patriot) Cl-up, rdn to lead ins last, drvn out: earlier won at Yarmouth (debut, mdn): Feb 1st foal, dam
styd 10f, sire a sprinter: eff at 6f, 7f will suit: runs well fresh on gd & a sharp/undul or easy trk: progressive.
*1883 **EBULLIENCE 29** [6] R Charlton 2-8-12 (75) C Rutter 13/2: 012: 2 b f Makbul - Steadfast Elite   *½* **78**
(Glenstal) Front rank, gd hdwy appr fnl 1f, ev ch ins last, no extra cl-home: op 5/1: acts on fast & gd grnd.
*2357 **EUROLINK SUNDANCE 10** [10] J L Dunlop 2-9-2 (79) G Carter 7/4 FAV: 013: 2 ch f Night Shift -   *1* **79**
Eurolink Mishcief (Be My Chief) Rcd keenly cl-up, led 4f out, rdn/hung left & hdd ins last, sn held: nicely bckd.
2209 **MERIDEN MIST 16** [9] P W Harris 2-8-10 (73) I Mongan (5) 11/2: 5254: Mid-div, rdn to improve   *nk* **73**
appr fnl 1f, kept on well ins last, no threat to ldrs: consistent form: see 1864, 1413.
*1550 **CHURCH MICE 44** [7] 2-8-11 (74)(vis) J Mackay (5) 10/1: 24215: Dwelt, rear till ran on for press   *nk* **73**
ins last, no dngr: 6 wk abs & shld apprec a step up to 7f now: see 1550.
1673 **BROUGHTONS MOTTO 39** [3] 2-8-1 (64) L Newton 11/2: 0146: Led early, remained prom till no   *nk* **63**
extra ins last: op 9/2: shade btr 1304 (fibresand).
1993 **ONCE REMOVED 25** [4] 2-8-7 (70) A Clark 11/1: 0447: Prom, rdn/wknd over 1f out: btr 1993 (5f, firm).   *2½* **63**
2009 **TROUBLESHOOTER 25** [2] 2-8-9 (72) Martin Dwyer 9/1: 6028: Bhd, eff 2f out, no threat: btr 2009.   *shd* **65**
2290 **OPERATION ENVY 12** [8] 2-7-10 (59)(4oh) D Kinsella (7) 33/1: 460409: Al in rear: stiffish task.   *1* **49**
1497 **BLAKESHALL BOY 47** [1] 2-9-4 (81) R Havlin 8/1: 34140: Front rank, wknd fnl 2f, 10th: 7 wk abs.   *1* **68**
10 ran   Time 1m 11.95 (3.15)   (Norcroft Park Stud)   N A Callaghan Newmarket.

2590   **3.30 VENNER MED AUCT MDN 3-4YO (F)**   **5f str**   **Good 40**   **+07 Fast**
        £2247   £642   £321

2294 **FLY LIKE THE WIND 12** [7] M A Jarvis 3-8-9 N Callan 8/13 FAV: 5-2231: 3 br f Cryrano de Bergerac -   **73**
Thulium (Mansigh) Reared leaving stalls, sn with ldrs, went on 2f out, pushed clr appr fnl 1f, cmftbly: best
time of day: plcd all 3 prev starts this term: rtd 66 when 5th on sole juv start: eff around 5f on firm &
gd grnd: handles any trk: tough, could follow up in h'cap company.
2478 **OUR FRED 5** [5] T G Mills 3-9-0 (BL) A Clark 5/2: 3-4402: 3 ch g Prince Sabo - Sheila's Secret   *3½* **69**
(Bluebird) Led, hdd 2f out, not pace of easy wnr: qck reapp & back to best in first time blnks: see 1427 (h'cap).
4306} **WORSTED 275** [6] Major D N Chappell 3-8-9 R Havlin 10/1: 00-3: 3 ch f Whittingham - Calamanco   *3* **56**
(Clantime) Dwelt, outpcd, styd on fnl 2f, no ch with ldrs: unplcd as a juv (rtd 65): speedily bred, stays 5f on gd.
1670 **QUEENSMEAD 40** [2] D Burchell 3-8-9 (t) R Price 20/1: -00004: Front rank, rdn/wknd fnl 2f: *3½* **48**
6 wk abs: stiff task, needs low-grade h'caps: see 1266.
2421 **CHASE THE BLUES 7** [1] 3-9-0 J Stack 20/1: -65: Dwelt, nvr with ldrs: qck reapp: see 2421.   *hd* **53**
-- **TOPOSHEES** [3] 3-9-0 J Quinn 10/1: 6: Al outpcd on debut: speedily bred colt, with B Smart.   *shd* **53**
-- **MASTER LUKE** [4] 3-9-0 S Whitworth 10/1: 7: Slow to start, al rear: half-brother to a 7f scorer.   *2* **47**
1280 **RAPIDASH 60** [8] 3-9-0 (vis) R Fitzpatrick (3) 33/1: 00-008: Veered right start, al bhd: 8 wk abs.   *1¼* **43$**

8 ran   Time 58.45 (1.65)   (Cosmic Greyhound Racing Partnership III)   M A Jarvis Newmarket.

2591	4.05 BET DIRECT HCAP DIV 1 3YO 0-65 (F) 7f str Good 40 -05 Slow		[72]
	£1893 £541 £270		

1643 **ANYHOW** 40 [14] Andrew Reid 3-9-4 (62) M Henry 4/1: 3-041: 3 b f Distant Relative - Fast Chick **67**
(Henbit) Trkd ldrs, led dist, rdn out: gamble from 12/1, 6 wk abs, h'cap bow: rtd 65a when plcd sole '99 start:
eff at 7f on gd & both AWs: runs well fresh on a sharp/undul trk: lightly rcd & improving, can follow up.

2300 **TOYON** 12 [12] Sir Mark Prescott 3-9-7 (65) D Sweeney 6/1: 60652: 3 b g Catrail - Princess Toy   1¼   **67**
(Prince Tenderfoot) Trkd ldrs, went on over 3f out, rdn/hdd dist, not pace of wnr: op 4/1: eff at 7f on
gd: gd effort under top-weight, should find similar: see 2300.

2025 **ANNIJAZ** 24 [6] J G Portman 3-8-4 (48) D O'Donohoe 12/1: 004633: 3 b f Alhijaz - Figment (Posse)   1¾   **47**
Hmpd early, hdwy from rear halfway, ev ch till no extra over 1f out: in gd heart, acts on firm & gd: see 2025

*2467 **COLNE VALLEY AMY** 5 [3] G L Moore 3-8-11 (55) I Mongan (5) 5/4 FAV: 0-2114: Front rank, rdn & not   2   **50**
pace of ldrs appr fnl 1f: qck reapp & not disgraced on this hat-trick bid: shade btr 2467 (1m, gd/soft).

2428 **FRENCH FANCY** 7 [10] P M Quinn (3) 25/1: 410005: Led, hdd over 3f out, wknd fnl 2f.   5   **29**
2489 **MUFFIN MAN** 4 [2] 3-8-9 (53) G Baker (7) 10/1: -00046: Rear, rdn/prog 2f out, kept on but no dngr.   3   **35**
2026 **CHILWORTH** 24 [7] 3-8-12 (56)(vis) R Price 9/1: 560427: Chsd ldrs, fdd fnl 2f: nicely bckd: btr 2026.   1¼   **36**
2043 **BROWNS DELIGHT** 23 [9] 3-8-4 (48) A Clark 20/1: 400658: In tch to halfway, sn btn: see 287.   nk   **28**
1971 **MOBO BACO** 26 [4] 3-8-11 (55) R Havlin 25/1: 406009: Nvr a factor: see 1397.   shd   **35**
1972 **NORTHERN LIFE** 26 [13] 3-7-11 (41)(1ow)(4oh) A Mackay 25/1: -00600: Prom to halfway, wknd, 10th.   2½   **17**
2211 **KOINCIDENTAL** 16 [8] 3-9-0 (58) N Callan 20/1: 0000: Prom 4f, fin 11th: h'cap bow.   1½   **31**
1423 **Cappucino Lady** 51 [5] 3-7-13 (43)(3ow)(8oh) A Daly 33/1:
2026 **Jenko** 24 [11] 3-8-2 (46)(BL) Dale Gibson 25/1:
1783 **Blue Dove** 34 [1] 3-8-10 (54) N Pollard 25/1:

14 ran   Time 1m 23.59 (3.19)   (A S Reid)   Andrew Reid Mill Hill, London NW7

2592	4.35 BET DIRECTHCAP DIV II 3YO 0-65 (F) 7f str Good 40 -33 Slow		[69]
	£1883 £538 £269		

1085 **STARLIGHT** 71 [7] E A L Dunlop 3-9-7 (62) G Carter 5/2 FAV: 45-101: 3 br f King's Signet - Petinata   **70**
(Petong) Mid-div going well, swtchd/hdwy 2f out, sn led, rdn clr despite wandering fnl 1f: nicely bckd, 10 wk abs,
top-weight: earlier won at Thirsk (reapp, rtd mdn): 4th in a nurs in '99 (rtd 68): eff over 7f on gd, soft & a
sharp/undul or gall trk: runs well fresh, eff weight carrier: op to further improvement & could follow up.

1877 **DANCING LILY** 30 [8] J J Bridger 3-8-2 (43) A Daly 20/1: -00002: 3 ch f Clantime - Sun Follower   3½   **43**
(Relkino) Mid-div, rdn/hdwy over 2f out, not pace of wnr well in last: imprvd form on this step up to 7f on gd.

2291 **UBITOO** 12 [11] R M Flower 3-7-10 (37)(b)(7oh) D Kinsella (7) 20/1: 0-0053: 3 b g Puissance -   nk   **37$**
Cassiar (Connaught) Led, hdd appr fnl 1f, no extra ins last: fine run from 7lb o/h: stays 7f on gd: mod prev.

2264 **HAZY HEIGHTS** 13 [3] B J Meehan 3-8-7 (48) C Rutter 8/1: 600004: Sn rdn in tch, hdwy 2f out,   1   **46**
no extra for press ins last: see 1080.

929 **SUNLEYS PICC** 88 [1] J Tate 11/1: 6-0605: Prom, switched/hdwy halfway, led 2f out,   1½   **55**
rdn/hdd appr fnl 1f, wknd: 12 wk abs: previously with M Channon, now with C Weedon: see 729.

2026 **LATINO BAY** 24 [13] 3-9-1 (56) J Quinn 3/1: 000-06: Trkd ldrs, rdn/btn fnl 2f: nicely bckd: see 2026.   7   **41**
2264 **RING MY MATE** 13 [5] 3-9-2 (57) Martin Dwyer 14/1: 634-07: Sn rdn in rear, nvr dangerous: btr 48.   1¼   **40**
4476} **WERE NOT JOKEN** 264 [2] 3-9-0 (55) R Fitzpatrick (3) 25/1: 6600-8: Nvr better than mid-div on reapp: 1½   **35**
unplcd in mdn company in '99 (rtd 59 & 67$).

2512 **PYJAMA GIRL** 4 [10] 3-8-13 (54)(bl) S Righton 20/1: 300009: Dwelt, sn prom, wknd qckly fnl 3f.   1¾   **31**
1368 **BOND DIAMOND** 54 [6] 3-8-12 (53) N Callan 7/1: 050000: Reared start, sn in tch, fdd fnl 2f, 10th.   nk   **30**
2374 **BOXBERRY** 9 [9] 3-7-12 (39) J Mackay 6/1: 00-400: Rcd ldrs, lost tch fnl 3f, t.o. in 11th.   14   **0**
1376 **LITE A CANDLE** 54 [12] 3-8-9 (50) A Beech 20/1: 0000: Handy, qckly lost tch halfway, 12th: abs.   12   **0**

12 ran   Time 1m 25.56 (5.16)   (Mrs Mollie Cooper Webster)   E A L Dunlop Newmarket.

2593	5.10 FILLIES HCAP 3YO+ 0-70 (E) 1m4f aw Standard Inapplicable		[59]
	£2695 £770 £385 3 yo rec 13lb		

2373 **ALPHA ROSE** 9 [3] M L W Bell 3-8-9 (53) J Mackay (5) 2/1 FAV: 112531: 3 ch f Inchinor - Philgwyn   **61a**
(Milford) Rcd keenly in mid-div, hdwy to lead 4f out, clr fnl 2f, rdn out: earlier won at Musselburgh & Ayr
(class stks): unplcd for R Williams in '99 (rtd 65): eff at 10/14f, has tried 2m: acts on firm/fast & equitrack:
handles a sharp or gall trk: in fine form, win again.

2186 **QUEEN OF THE KEYS** 17 [3] S Dow 4-8-10 (41) A Clark 8/1: 000322: 4 b f Royal Academy - Piano   5   **41a**
Belle (Fappiano) Waited with, hdwy halfway, not pace of wnr appr fnl 1f: op 7/1: up in trip, stays 12f on equitrack.

2296 **READING RHONDA** 12 [5] P Mitchell 4-9-2 (47) I Mongan (5) 16/1: 500003: 4 b f Eastern Echo - Higher   1¾   **44a**
Learning (Fappiano) Held up, rdn/prog 3f out, edn fnl 1f: clr rem: up in trip & first time in the frame.

2217 **ESTABELLA** 15 [7] S P C Woods 3-8-13 (57)(BL) N Callan 7/1: 305554: Front rank, ev ch till wknd   3½   **49a**
qckly 2f out: first time blnks (prev worn visor): see 2041, 1142.

*2212 **BECKON** 15 [2] 4-9-8 (53) P Shea (7) 7/2: 545015: Prom, rdn/wknd appr fnl 3f: op 5/2: btr 2212 (10f).   2   **42a**
2217 **THE GIRLS FILLY** 15 [8] 3-9-0 (58) A Beech (5) 4/1: 300026: Sn led, hdd 4f out, sn btn: btr 2217.   6   **39a**
*2323 **RIDGEWOOD BAY** 11 [4] 3-7-10 (40)(4oh) M Baird 9/1: 000017: Led early, wknd from halfway.   5   **14a**
2032 **PURPLE DAWN** 24 [9] 4-8-1 (32) G Baker 25/1: 000-08: Front rank, bhd halfway, fin last: hdles rnr.   11   **0a**

8 ran   Time 2m 32.33 (3.13)   (Richard I Morris Jnr)   M L W Bell Newmarket.

NEWMARKET (JULY)   WEDNESDAY JULY 12TH   Righthand, Stiff, Galloping Track

Official Going   GOOD. Stalls: Far Side, Except 2.05, 3.10, 5.20 - Stands Side.
All 7 winners at this meeting had the advantage of a faster strip of ground on the stands rail - an unfortunate situation

2594

2.05 LISTED BAHRAIN TROPHY 3YO (A)   1m6f175y Good/Firm 33 -04 Slow
£14355   £5445   £2722   £1237

1832 **CEPHALONIA 32** [3] J L Dunlop 3-8-5 Pat Eddery 8/1: 4-1161: 3 b f Slip Anchor - Cephira (Abdos)   99
Made just about all on ins rail, hard prsd fnl 2f, drvn out & edged left cl home, gamely: earlier won at Pontefract
& Newbury (rtd h'cap): promise fnl '99 start (mdn, rtd 80): eff at 12f/14.8f: acts on gd/soft, suited by fast &
stiff trks: can come late/force the pace: runs well fresh: progressive, useful & game.
2068 **SAMSAAM 22** [6] J L Dunlop 3-8-10 R Hills 7/4 FAV: -11132: 3 b c Sadler's Wells - Azyaa (Kris)   nk   103
Nvr far away, chall appr fnl 2f, kept on for press, held nr fin: hvly bckd: ran to best in defeat, acts on
fast & hvy grnd: useful, tough & progressive just like his winning stablemate: see 1821.
*1956 **SHUWAIB 26** [2] M R Channon 3-8-10 Craig Williams 16/1: 13: 3 b c Polish Precident - Ajab Alzaman   2   100
(Rainbow Quest) Bhd ldrs rdn 2f out, onepace till kept on fnl 100y: op 12/1: big step up in grade & improved
for step up to 14.8f but did have advantage of stands rail strip: see 1956.
2210 **FANFARE 16** [4] G A Butler 3-8-5 K Darley 25/1: 011024: Waited with, rdn 2f out, kept on same pace: 3   91$
stiff task, prob flattered tho' improved for step up to 14.8f: see 1585.
1885 **CANFORD 29** [8] 3-8-10 M Tebbutt 16/1: 4-135: Keen, cl-up, hung left halfway, drvn 3f out, fdd bef   1   94
dist: not disgraced over much longer trip/in grade: 12f could prove ideal: see 1885, 1588 (soft grnd mdn).
*2144 **FULL AHEAD 19** [9] 3-8-10 S Sanders 33/1: 332216: Held up, feeling pace 4f out, nvr dangerous.   1   92$
*2038 **ANDROMEDES 23** [5] 3-8-10 T Quinn 5/1: 3-4317: Held up, prog to trk ldrs 6f out, wide eff appr fnl 2f,   1½   90$
sn btn: nicely bckd from 7/1: up in grade & trip after wng 4 rnr mdn: see 2038 (12f).
1347 **ROYAL EAGLE 55** [7] 3-8-10 J Fortune 12/1: 2-0038: Held up, wide, shaken up 2f out, wknd: 8 wk abs.   hd   89
1451 **TANTALUS 50** [1] 3-8-10 M Hills 7/2: 2-1349: Mid-div, carried wide halfway, lost place ent fnl 3f: 9   79
nicely bckd, longer trip, 7 wk abs: better judged 1216 (12f).
9 ran   Time 3m 11.04 (5.54)   (Exors Of The Late Lord Howard de Walden)   J L Dunlop Arundel, W Sussex

2595

2.35 GR 3 TNT JULY STKS 2YO (A)   6f   Good/Firm 33   -01 Slow
£20300   £7700   £3850   £1750

--   **NOVERRE** [4] D R Loder 2-8-13 J Fortune 5/2 FAV: -111: 2 b c Rahy - Danseur Fabuleux (Northern   109
Dancer) Trkd ldr, went on appr fnl 1f, sn rdn, joined/hung left ins last, all-out to hold on: hvly bckd French raider:
earlier won at Chantilly & M-Laffitte (List): half-brother to sev wnrs, notably Champ 2yo Arazi: dam stayed 12f,
sire a miler: eff at 5/6f, will get further: acts on fast & soft grnd, any trk: progressive, unbtn, smart colt.
*1475 **MEDIA MOGUL 48** [6] T D Barron 2-8-10 K Darley 16/1: 1312: 2 b g First Trump - White Heat (Last   shd   105
Tycoon) Held up, qcknd to chall below dist, hard rdn, just lost out in a bobbing finish: up in grade & much
improved after 7 wk abs: apprec step up to 6f: acts on fast & hvy grnd: very useful, win a Gr race in this form.
2067 **BRAM STOKER 22** [1] R Hannon 2-8-10 Dane O'Neill 10/3: 21123: 2 ch g General Monash - Taniokey   2   99
(Grundy) In tch, wide, rdn & ch dist, edged left, sn onepace: nicely bckd: prob ran to best despite racing
wide: acts on fast & gd/soft grnd: v useful, shld win a Listed race: see 1367.
*2352 **BRAVADO 10** [3] Sir Mark Prescott 2-8-10 G Duffield 7/2: 114: Led on stands rail, hdd appr fnl 1f,   ½   97
no extra: hvly bckd: lost unbtn record but prob imprvd in defeat in this higher grade: useful, see 2352 (3 rnrs).
*1944 **MARINE 27** [7] 2-8-10 Pat Eddery 11/4: -5115: Held up, taken wide & rdn appr fnl 1f, no impress: nk   96
well bckd: gd effort racing on the slowest grnd for final 2f, keep an eye on: see 1944.
2333 **PRINCE OF BLUES 11** [5] 2-8-10 J F Egan 50/1: -526: Trkd ldr, beginning to feel pace when hmpd   2   90
appr fnl 1f: highly tried mdn & not disgraced: see 2333, 2029.
6 ran   Time 1m 13.06 (2.06)   (Goldophin)   D R Loder Evry, France

2596

3.10 BONUSPRINT HCAP 3YO 0-105 (B)   1m2f   Good/Firm 33   +05 Fast   [108]
£26000   £8000   £4000   £2000

2117 **MOON SOLITAIRE 20** [1] E A L Dunlop 3-8-11 (91) T Quinn 12/1: 131301: 3 b g Night Shift - Gay   99
Fantastic (Ela Mana Mou) Sn grabbed stands rail, made all, pushed out ins last, unchall: nicely bckd, best
time of day: earlier won at Folkestone (mdn) & impress at Goodwood (val h'cap): promise sole juv start (mdn,
rtd 75): eff at 9/10f on firm, soft & any trk: back to form from the front today, does not have to lead: tried
a visor last time: improving & useful colt, jockey out-witted rivals by grabbing stands rails from outside draw.
*2471 **FORBEARING 5** [10] Sir Mark Prescott 3-9-11 (105)(6ex) S Sanders 9/2 FAV: 001112: 3 b c Bering - For   1¼   111
Example (Northern Baby) Trkd wnr thr'out, eff 2f out, kept on but al held: well bckd, quick reapp: v useful
weight carrying performance & looks Listed/Gr 3 class: see 2471, 1838 (beat this wnr more than 3L).
2004 **FATHER JUNINHO 25** [13] A P Jarvis 3-8-10 (90) K Darley 10/1: 065233: 3 b c Distinctly North -   shd   96
Shane's Girl (Marktingo) Held up, shaken up over 2f out, short of room bef dist & switched to centre, ran on well,
nrst fin: nicely bckd: v encouraging, overdue a win: eff at 1m/10f: see 1831 (in front of this wnr).
2117 **KOOKABURRA 20** [12] B J Meehan 3-9-2 (96) M Tebbutt 14/1: 104634: Mid-div, against stands rail,   1   100
eff appr fnl 1f, kept on but not pace to chall: eff at 1m/10f: useful, see 704.
*2450 **ZIBELINE 6** [2] 3-8-4 (84)(6ex) B Marcus 25/1: 024415: Cl-up, rdn appr fnl 2f, onepace: qk reapp/pen.   1   86
*2351 **VINTAGE PREMIUM 10** [6] 3-9-7 (101) G Duffield 8/1: 402216: Trkd ldrs, feeling pace & lost place   hd   103
2f out, no threat: another sound effort from this useful/consistent colt, see 2351.
2476 **CORNELIUS 5** [8] 3-9-6 (100) J Fortune 9/1: -25027: Mid-div, shaken up 2f out, no impression: 1   100
quick reapp: back up in trip, due to go up 9lbs for fin 2nd in a Sandown stks in 2476 & this poss came too soon.
1812 **FREDDY FLINTSTONE 33** [3] 3-7-11 (76)(1ow) P Doe 25/1: 5-0408: Held up, wide, prog under press   ½   76
appr fnl 1f, sn no extra: decent effort from this mdn considering rcd widest of all in fnl 2f, see 1183.
*1218 **AIR DEFENCE 64** [9] 3-9-2 (96) M Hills 11/2: 2-219: Held up, wide, hdwy 2f out, fdd dist: nicely   1   93
bckd on h'cap bow, probably worth another chance: see 1218.
2351 **BLUE GOLD 10** [4] 3-9-4 (98) J Reid 14/1: 420120: Wide, mid-div, chsd ldrs 3f out till bef dist: 10th.   1   93
2475 **ATLANTIC RHAPSODY 5** [7] 3-9-1 (95)(bl) R Hills 11/2: 412560: Chsd ldrs wide, rdn 2f out, held   ½   89
when bmpd dist: 11th, bckd from 7/1, qck reapp: blnks reapplied: can do better (rcd away form stands rail).
1459 **NAVAL AFFAIR 52** [5] 3-9-7 (101) Pat Eddery 12/1: 31-400: Al bhd: 12th, 7 wk abs, h'cap bow, see 1184.   6   86
1452 **PETIT MARQUIS 50** [11] 3-8-10 (90) J P Spencer 40/1: 2-1200: Al towards rear: 13th, 7 wk abs, see 977.   5   67
13 ran   Time 2m 04.68 (2.78)   (Maktoum Al Maktoum)   E A L Dunlop Newmarket

2597   3.40 GR 2 FALMOUTH STKS 3YO+ (B)   1m str   Good/Firm 33   +02 Fast
£34800   £13200   £6600   £3000   3 yo rec 9 lb

1319 **ALSHAKR** 59 [1] B Hanbury 3-8-6 R Hills 9/2: 64-131: 3 b f Bahri - Give Thanks (Relko)   **109**
Managed to tack over & grab the all important stands rail, made all, rdn out: nicely bckd, fair time, 8 wk abs:
earlier won at Newmarket (fill mdn, plcd in the French Guineas): 4th fnl '99 start for P Walwyn (mdn, rtd 76):
eff at 7f/1m: acts on fast & soft grnd, stiff/gall trks: runs v well fresh: imprvd from the front: smart filly.
2112 **CROESO CARIAD** 20 [6] M L W Bell 3-8-6 T Quinn 12/1: 0-5042: 3 b f Most Welcome - Colorsnap   1¼ **107**
(Shirley Heights) Mid-div, 3 off the rail, drvn appr fnl 1f, ran on well ins last, not trouble wnr: apprec
drop back in trip, 10f could prove ideal: v useful filly, shld certainly win another Listed race: see 2112.
2087 **DANCEABOUT** 21 [8] G Wragg 3-8-6 K Darley 9/2: 153: 3 b f Shareef Dancer - Putupon (Mummy's Pet)   ½ **106**
Held up, 4 off the rail, hdwy & rdn appr fnl 1f, kept on, unable to chall: nicely bckd: v useful run from
this lightly rcd, progressive filly: acts on fast & gd/soft grnd & stays 1m: interesting in Gr 3/Listed.
*1733 **BEDAZZLING** 37 [7] J R Fanshawe 3-8-6 M Tebbutt 14/1: 20-014: Held up, wide, prog appr fnl 1f,   hd **105**
no extra nr fin: excellent run on unfavoured part of the trk: eff at 7f/1m: improving fast, see 1733.
2064 **GOLDEN SILCA** 22 [3] 4-9-1 Craig Williams 4/1 FAV: -04105: Pulled hard, in tch but widest of all,   1¼ **103**
edged further into centre appr fnl 1f, unable to qckn: well bckd, prob best forgotten: see 1825.
2180 **SHADY POINT** 17 [9] 3-8-6 B Marcus 100/1: 562106: Chsd ldrs, onepace fnl 2f: 70 rtd h'capper,   1¼ **100$**
surely flattered with visor omitted: see 1803.
1485 **LAST RESORT** 48 [2] 3-8-6 M Hills 20/1: -4136: Prom, rcd 3 deep, prog to chall ent fnl 2f, sn   dht **100**
rdn/fdd: 7 wk abs: needs a drop in grade: see 1224.
913 **GLEN ROSIE** 56 [4] 3-8-7(1ow) J Reid 20/1: 63-248: Well plcd & ev ch till wknd appr fnl 1f: nk **100**
8 wk abs: 4th of 7 in a French Listed since 913: drop in trip required.
2150 **IFTIRAAS** 19 [10] 3-8-6 Pat Eddery 13/2: 2-1569: Bhd, rdn 2f out, staying on when short of room   shd **99**
appr fnl 1f, no danger: checked at a crucial stage, worth another chance: see 913.
1309 **EMBRACED** 57 [5] 3-8-6 J P Spencer 9/2: 1-160: In tch wide, eff & btn appr fnl 1f: 10th, not   nk **98**
persevered with after 8 wk abs, see 1108.
10 ran   Time 1m 39.7 (2.5)   (Hamdan Al Maktoum)   B Hanbury Newmarket, Suffolk

2598   4.15 SWAYTHLING NOV STKS 2YO (D)   6f   Good/Firm 33   -39 Slow
£6012   £1850   £925   £462

1107 **DOMINUS** 70 [4] R Hannon 2-8-12 Dane O'Neill 15/8 FAV: 221: 2 b c Primo Dominie - Howlin' (Alleged)   **97**
Got the stands rail, made just about all, hard prsd & rdn appr fnl 1f, edged left, held on well: hvly bckd,
slow time, deserved, rnr-up both prev starts: Ir33,000 gns Apr foal, dam wnr abroad: sire a sprinter: eff
at 5f, apprec step up to 6f: acts on fast & soft: runs well fresh on stiff trks, from the front: useful.
-- **RED MAGIC** [5] R Hannon 2-8-8 L Newman (3) 7/1: 2: 2 b c Grand Lodge - Ma Priere (Highest Honor)   ¾ **91**
Dwelt, prom, 3 deep, strong chall fnl 1f, drifted left, held cl-home: bckd from 16/1, stablemate wnr: 700,000 Ffr Mar
foal, dam wnr in France, sire 1m/10f performer: eff at 6f on fast, 7f+ will suit: fine debut, must win sn.
-- **LOYAL TYCOON** [2] S Dow 2-8-8 P Doe 33/1: 3: 2 br c Royal Abjar - Rosy Lydgate (Last Tycoon)   1 **88**
Held up wide, qcknd up well in centre appr fnl 1f & then veered left, same pace nr fin: 11,500Ir gns Apr
first foal, dam sprinter: eff at 6f on fast grnd, get further in time: promising.
2067 **ARMAGNAC** 22 [7] D Sasse 2-8-12 T Quinn 16/1: 6404: Trkd wnr stands rail, switched bef dist, kept on shd **92$**
but not pace to chall: gd run, has ability tho' poss flattered racing on the fresh strip of grnd: see 1846.
-- **CLOUDY** [6] 2-8-3 S Carson (5) 25/1: 5: Prsd wnr & ev ch till outpcd below dist: promising debut: ¾ **81**
Ashkalani Apr half-sister to a 2m wnr, sire a miler: shld apprc 7f/1m, handles fast grnd: improvement likely.
2346 **DUSTY CARPET** 11 [3] 2-8-12 J F Egan 33/1: 646: Bmpd start, wide, mid-div, nvr any impress.   1 **87$**
-- **SPY MASTER** [1] 2-8-8 Pat Eddery 6/1: 7: Dwelt, chsd ldrs widest of all till fdd appr fnl 1f: op 4/1, stiff 2½ **76**
task from stall 1: Green Desert first foal, dam useful juv sprinter, sire sprinter/miler: will leave this behind.
-- **LONER** [2] 2-8-8 G Duffield 33/1: 8: Keen, nvr dangerous: Magic Ring Apr foal: dam stayer.   1 **73**
-- **STYLISH FELLA** [8] 2-8-8 J Fortune 8/1: 9: In tch till 3f out: Irish River half-brother to a 7f juv.   6 **58**
-- **PUTRA PEKAN** [10] 2-8-8 M Tebbutt 4/1: 0: Held up, short of room bef halfway, sn struggling: 5 **48**
10th, nicely bckd tho' op 11/4: 42,000 gns Grand Lodge half-brother to 3 juv wnrs, one of them smart, dam sprinter.
10 ran   Time 1m 15.3 (4.33)   (Noodles Racing)   R Hannon East Everleigh, Wilts

2599   4.45 MONDI SELLER 2YO (E)   7f str   Good/Firm 33   -27 Slow
£5096   £1568   £784   £392

1798 **FOREVER MY LORD** 34 [11] R F Johnson Houghton 2-8-11 J Reid 9/2: 601: 2 b c Be My Chief - In Love   **76**
Again (Prince Rupert) Cl-up on stands rail, went on 2f out, rdn bef dist, drew clr towards fin: bckd tho' op
3/1, bght in for 19,000 gns: 11,000 gns Feb foal, dam a sprinter, sire a 7f/1m performer: apprec step up to
7f, will get 1m: acts on fast grnd, stiff trk: advantage of stands rail here & enjoyed drop in grade.
2214 **VIOLENT** 15 [8] Andrew Reid 2-8-6 (VIS) M Hills 33/1: -0002: 2 b f Deploy - Gentle Irony (Mazilier)   3 **65**
Led, 2 off the rail, hdd 2f out, outpcd by wnr: suited by drop in grade & step up to 7f in a visor: win similar.
2209 **CHAUNTRY GOLD** 16[14] B J Meehan 2-9-7 Pat Eddery 5/1: -003: 2 b g Desert Style - Ervedya (Doyoun) ¾ **78**
Trkd wnr stands rail, switched & hdwy 2f out, onepace und press: hvly bckd from 7/1: apprec step up to 7f on fast.
-- **DUCS DREAM** [5] D Morris 2-8-11 D McGaffin (5) 16/1: 4: Held up wide, styd on fnl 1½f, nvr nrr: 2 **64**
nicely bckd on debut: Bay Tern half-brother & dam sprinters, sire a decent hdler: looks sure to apprec 1m+.
2010 **THE CHOCOLATIER** 25 [2] 2-8-6 A Polli (3) 20/1: 65: Prom, wide, rdn & ch 2f out, fdd: this is his grade. 4 **51**
1988 **HOMELIFE** 25 [9] 2-9-7 K Darley 8/1: 6406: Prom till 2f out: nicely bckd: btr 1413 (6f).   2 **62**
1304 **BILLIE H** 58 [7] 2-9-2 Y Take 14/1: 007: Wide, nvr better than mid-div: up in trip, see 1197.   nk **56**
1048 **SKITTLES** 74 [12] 2-8-11 S Sanders 8/1: 08: Nvr a factor: 11 wk abs, up in trip.   1¼ **49**
2312 **ORCHARD RAIDER** 12 [4] 2-8-11 G Duffield 5/1: 024129: Keen, front rank till lost place 2f out.   hd **49**
-- **STAR BRIEF** [3] 2-9-2 K W Marks 25/1: 0: Al towards rear: 10th: 2,000gns Cosmonaut first foal.   1 **52**
2368 **BROUGHTON STORM** 9 [6] 2-8-11 M Tebbutt 25/1: -00: Chsd ldrs 4f: 11th, longer trip.   2 **43**
2447 **JOINT INSTRUCTION** 6 [1] 2-9-7 T Quinn 7/2 FAV: 152020: Chsd ldrs till wknd qckly ent fnl 2f,   hd **53**
eased: 12th, hvly bckd, quick reapp, longer trip: btr 2447, 1981 (6f).
2312 **FAST BUCK** 12 [1] 2-8-11 J Fortune 40/1: 00050: Al bhd: 13th, modest.   6 **33**
13 ran   Time 1m 28.11 (4.21)   (W H Ponsonby)   R F Johnson Houghton Blewbury, Oxon

NEWMARKET (JULY) WEDNESDAY JULY 12TH Righthand, Stiff, Galloping Track

2600 5.20 REG DAY HCAP 3YO+ 0-95 (C) 2m24y Good/Firm 33 -37 Slow [90]
£7046 £2168 £1084 £542 3 yo rec 19lb

2164 **TURNPOLE 18** [7] Mrs M Reveley 9-8-12 (74) T Quinn 6/1: 4/0641: 9 br g Satco - Mountain Chase (Mount Hagen) Trkd ldrs eff 2f out, styd on well up the stands rail to lead below dist, pushed out cl-home: slow time: 98/99 wnr over fences at Catterick & Sedgefield (novs, rtd 112c): missed '99 Flat season, prev term won at Doncaster (h'cap, rtd 88): eff at 12f, suited by 2m, stays extreme dists: acts on fast & gd/soft: likes stiff trks & can run well fresh: well h'capped, former Cesarewitch wnr & being aimed for that again. **78**
2319 **FIORI 11** [5] P C Haslam 4-9-6 (82) M Tebbutt 4/1: 644132: 4 b g Anshan - Fen Princess (Trojan Fen) Set slow pace, rcd up the stands rail till edged left ent fnl 2f & rdn, hdd ins last, kept on: well bckd, in gd form. 1½ **83**
*2305 **FAIT LE JOJO 12** [4] S P C Woods 3-8-3 (84) G Duffield 3/1: 454113: 3 b g Pistolet Bleu - Pretty Davis (Trempolino) Pld hard, held up, taken wide & imprvd going well appr fnl 2f, ev ch, carr left dist, unable to qckn: well bckd: lost little in defeat over longer trip: stays 2m, return to 14f/sharper 2m will suit. 1½ **83**
1832 **THE WOODSTOCK LADY 32** [6] B W Hills 3-8-10 (91) M Hills 9/2: 1-0024: Held up, shaken up appr fnl 2f, not much room, nvr a factor: poss worth another try over longer 2m trip, handles fast & gd/soft grnd. 2½ **87**
1715 **MONTECRISTO 37** [2] 7-10-0 (90) K Darley 7/1: 00-355: Held up, wide, nvr dngrs: bckd, longer trip. 1 **85**
*2319 **WEET FOR ME 11** [3] 4-9-1 (77) J F Egan 9/2: 003016: Handy, 3 off the rail, rdn 2f out & sn btn: bckd. 4 **68**
2176 **ROYAL CASTLE 17** [1] 6-8-10 (72)(VIS) Pat Eddery 11/1: 0-6507: Trkd ldr, ch appr fnl 2f, sn wknd: visor. ¾ **62**
7 ran Time 3m 32.03 (9.53) (Mr & Mrs W J Williams) Mrs M Reveley Lingdale, N Yorks

WOLVERHAMPTON (Fibresand) THURSDAY JULY 13TH Lefthand, Sharp Track

Official Going: STANDARD Stalls: Inside

2601 2.15 BET FILL MDN HCAP 3YO+ 0-65 (F) 1m100y aw rnd Going 21 -28 Slow [54]
£2275 £650 £325 3 yo rec 9 lb

2512 **BEWILDERED 5** [2] D W Chapman 3-8-1 (36)(bl) Claire Bryan (5) 16/1: 060301: 3 br f Prince Sabo - Collage (Ela Mana Mou) Led after 2f, rdn clr over 1f out, styd on well: quick reapp: only mod form previously, first win today: eff at 8.5f, tried further: acts on fibresand & a sharp track: suited by blinks. **41a**
2484 **CHARLEM 6** [6] D Shaw 3-8-5 (40)(vis) D Mernagh (3) 20/1: -66602: 3 br f Petardia - La Neva (Arctic Tern) Chsd ldrs, rdn & kept on fnl 1f, no threat: qck reapp: eff arnd 8.5f on fibresand: see 920 (C/D). 1¼ **41a**
2233 **ABSTRACT 15** [9] J S Wainwright 4-8-10 (36) R Winston 20/1: -00003: 4 b f Perugino - Kalapa (Mouktar) Led 2f, chsd wnr, no extra inside last: op 14/1: styd longer 8.5f trip: handles fibresand & gd grnd. ½ **36a**
2282 **PIPIJI 14** [3] Mrs G S Rees 5-8-4 (30) Dean McKeown 16/1: 2-0004: Chsd ldrs, never pace to chall. nk **29a**
2297 **HEATHER VALLEY 13** [1] 4-8-13 (39) A Culhane 5/1: 000-05: Cl up 5f: op 3/1: see 2297 (6f). 3 **32a**
2463 **AHOUOD 6** [11] 4-8-12 (38) C Lowther 10/1: 604006: Rdn/bhd halfway, mod gains wide: quick reapp. 4 **23a**
2134 **ERIN ANAM CARA 20** [13] 3-9-4 (53) R Mullen 9/1: 43-007: In tch 5f: op 5/1: see 1572. ½ **37a**
2378 **CUTE CAROLINE 10** [5] 4-9-5 (45)(VIS) J Carroll 7/2 JT FAV: 506238: Trckd ldrs 6f: op 5/2: visor. 5 **19a**
2446 **YANKEE DANCER 7** [4] 5-9-5 (45) P M Quinn (3) 33/1: 2/0009: Al rear: see 1496. 1 **17a**
2136 **KATIES VALENTINE 20** [7] 3-9-5 (54)(vis) F Lynch 8/1: -32000: Al bhd: 10th: op 7/1: see 1723 (6f). ½ **25a**
2146 **ROYAL PASTIMES 20** [10] 3-7-13 (34) P Fessey 33/1: 0-6050: Al rear: 11th: AW bow: see 783. 1 **3a**
2308 **LILLAN 13** [12] 3-9-13 (62)(BL) P Doe 7/2 JT FAV: 644W: Refused to enter stall, withdrawn: blnks. **0a**
12 ran Time 1m 50.4 (4.2) (T S Redman) D W Chapman Stillington, N Yorks

2602 2.45 PRICEWATERHOUSE CLAIMER 3YO (F) 1m1f79y aw Going 21 -00 Slow
£2198 £628 £314

2206 **MAGIC SUNSET 17** [1] I A Balding 3-8-2 (vis) J Fanning 6/1: 0-0001: 3 b f Magic Ring - Run To The Sun (Run The Gantlet) Made all, rdn fnl 2f, styd on well, rdn out: op 4/1: first win: unplcd in '99 (rtd 62): eff at 9.4f, tried further, may yet suit: acts on fibresand & a sharp track: suited by a vis: suited by claiming grade. **47a**
2025 **RIDE THE TIGER 25** [2] M D I Usher 3-9-3 G Baker (7) 13/2: 0-1362: 3 ch g Imp Society - Krisdaline (Kris S) Chsd wnr, rdn & kept on fnl 1f, al held: op 5/1: see 1234 (C/D). 1¼ **58a**
2345 **WINTZIG 12** [8] M L W Bell 3-8-10 R Mullen 5/2 FAV: 525033: 3 b f Piccolo - Wrangbrook (Shirley Heights) Held up, rdn/prog to chase wnr 2f out, soon no extra: op 2/1: AW bow: btr 2345, 924. 2½ **46a**
*2448 **COLLEGE ROCK 7** [6] R Brotherton 3-8-13 (vis) A Culhane 7/1: 306414: Chsd ldrs, held over 2f out. 2½ **44a**
1502 **SHARP RISK 48** [5] 3-8-13 R Winston 6/1: 530025: Bhd ldrs, btn 3f out: op 7/2, abs: see 1502, 373. 11 **28a**
2510 **HEATHYARDS MATE 5** [3] 3-8-13 P M Quinn (3) 9/2: 210066: Rear, no impress: see 741 (7f, sell). 1¼ **25a**
2253 **WELCOME SHADE 15** [9] 3-8-7 (BL) K Dalgleish (5) 10/1: 200007: In tch, btn 3f out: op 7/1, blnks. 19 **0a**
1970 **STRECCIA 27** [7] 3-8-10 Dale Gibson 33/1: 648: Prom till halfway: AW bow: see 1970, 1668. 7 **0a**
2299 **TINKERS CLOUGH 13** [4] 3-9-7 Dean McKeown 33/1: 009: Soon t.o.: no form. 26 **0a**
9 ran Time 2m 0.2 (2.0) (M E Wates) I A Balding Kingsclere, Hants

2603 3.15 HAMILTONS HCAP 3YO 0-70 (E) 6f aw rnd Going 21 +08 Fast [72]
£2785 £857 £428 £214

2300 **NITE OWL MATE 13** [6] G Woodward 3-9-4 (62)(t) T G McLaughlin 14/1: 330001: 3 b c Komaite - Nite Owl Dancer (Robelino) Made all, rdn clr over 2f out, styd on strongly, rdn out: gd time: op 16/1: first win: eff at 6f, tried 7f: acts on fibresand & a sharp track: suited by application of t strap today. **75a**
*2549 **DOCTOR DENNIS 3** [8] B J Meehan 3-9-8 (66)(6ex) D Glennon (7) 100/30: 212012: 2 b g Last Tycoon - Noble Lustre (Lyphard's Wish) Rdn/chsd wnr fnl 2f, al held: op 7/4, 6lb pen: AW bow: acts on firm, soft & fbrsnd. 3 **67a**
2489 **BANGLED 5** [3] D J Coakley 3-8-6 (50) P Doe 25/1: -00003: 3 ch g Beveled - Bangles (Chilibang) Prom, slightly hmpd/lost place over 2f out, kept on fnl 2f, no threat: quick reapp: see 1494. 1¾ **47a**
2385 **PUPS PRIDE 10** [1] R A Fahey 3-8-3 (47)(vis) J Fanning 6/4 FAV: 500034: Never pace to chall: bckd. ¾ **42a**
2243 **NATSMAGIRL 15** [5] 3-8-1 (45) P Fessey 14/1: 50-505: Al outpcd: op 10/1: see 1665, 74 (seller). 5 **31a**
1994 **JEPAJE 26** [4] 3-8-9 (53)(bl) R Mullen 14/1: 0-0006: Dwelt, al bhd: see 105. 1¾ **35a**
2489 **ABSENT FRIENDS 5** [7] 3-9-7 (65) Dean McKeown 12/1: 0-0407: Chsd wnr, btn over 2f out: quick reapp: op 10/1: AW bow: see 1712 (mdn). 6 **36a**
1891 **PADDYWACK 30** [2] 3-9-6 (64)(bl) Claire Bryan (5) 9/2: 20020U: Rdn chasing ldrs when saddle **0a**

WOLVERHAMPTON (Fibresand)
THURSDAY JULY 13TH   Lefthand, Sharp Track

slipped & u.r halfway: op 7/2: see 1742, 654.
8 ran   Time 1m 13.60 (0.8)   (Burntwood Sports Ltd)   G Woodward Brierley, S Yorks

2604
3.50 THORPE THOMPSON MDN 3YO (D)   6f aw rnd   Going 21   -07 Slow
£2765   £851   £425   £212

2299 **GERONIMO 13** [3] C W Thornton 3-9-0 O Pears 5/2 JT FAV: 0-21: 3 b c Efisio - Apache Squaw **71a**
(Be My Guest) Chsd ldrs, prog & rdn to chall inside last, narrow lead near fin, just prevailed in a blanket fin:
op 7/4: eff at 6f, further may suit: acts on fibresand & a sharp track: op to further improvement in h'caps.
2299 **RESILIENT 13** [7] W J Haggas 3-9-0 K W Marks 9/2: 0652: 3 b c Last Tycoon - Alilisa (Alydar)   hd **70a**
Held up, prog from over 2f out, styd on strongly for press inside last, post came too soon, just held: op 7/2: eff
at 6f, crying out for return to 7f/1m: acts on fibresand: h'cap company over further will now suit.
4072J **TOP OF THE PARKES 293** [5] N P Littmoden 3-8-9 C Cogan (5) 8/1: 350-3: 3 b f Mistertopogigo - Bella nk **64a**
Parkes (Tina's Pet) Led, hdd over 1f out, styd on well for press inside last, just held near fin: op 7/1: reapp:
AW bow: plcd on debut in '99 (auct fill mdn, rtd 69, N P Littmoden): eff at 5/6f, handles firm & fibresand.
2232 **SPOT 15** [6] Andrew Reid 3-8-9 M Henry 5/2 JT FAV: 034: Cl up, led over 1f out, rdn/hdd inside last,   ½ **62a**
not btn far: op; 2/1: AW bow: handles fast grnd & fibresand, eff at 6/7f: clr of rem here: see 2232.
2549 **STOP THE TRAFFIC 3** [8] 3-8-9 C Lowther 12/1: 500005: Outpcd from halfway: op 7/1, quick reapp.   12 **40a**
2472 **TOPLESS IN TUSCANY 6** [4] 3-8-9 G Baker (7) 8/1: 036: Cl up, wknd quickly over 1f out: AW bow.   1¾ **36a**
2299 **EXECUTIVE WISH 13** [2] 3-8-9 P Doe 25/1: 07: Al outpcd rear: no form.   4 **26a**
2299 **OVERSLEPT 3** [1] 3-9-0 R Mullen 9/1: 08: Dwelt, al bhd: op 12/1: no form.   3 **24a**
8 ran   Time 1m 14.5 (1.7)   (Guy Reed)   C W Thornton Coverham, N Yorks

2605
4.20 0800211222 SELLER 2YO (G)   5f aw rnd   Going 21   -42 Slow
£1820   £520   £260

2384 **RUNNING FOR ME 10** [2] R Hollinshead 2-8-11 G Gibbons (7) 9/2: 102251: 2 ch f Eagle Eyed - Running **64a**
For You (Pampabird) Went on halfway, styd on strongly to assert under hands & heels riding fnl 1f: no bid: earlier
scored at Southwell (seller, mod turf form): eff at 5/6f on fibresand & a sharp track: relishes selling grade.
*2435 **DANCING PENNEY 7** [5] K A Ryan 2-8-11 (bl) F Lynch 6/5 FAV: -50012: 2 b f General Monash -   1¾ **58a**
Penultimate Cress (My Generation) Prom, chsd wnr 2f out, held fnl 1f: clr rem, bckd: acts on fast & fibresand.
2435 **GAZETTE IT TONIGHT 7** [4] A Berry 2-8-6 C Lowther 7/2: -55633: 2 b f Merdon Melody -   4 **43a**
Balidilemma (Balidar) Chsd ldrs, never on terms: op 9/4: AW bow: btr 2435.
2200 **ROYLE FAMILY 17** [1] A Berry 2-8-11 O Pears 14/1: -45454: Led till halfway, soon held: op 12/1.   3 **41a**
2357 **DONNA DOUGHNUT 11** [3] 2-8-6 G Baker (7) 5/1: 05: Al outpcd: op 4/1, AW bow: see 2357.   5 **27a**
2388 **SOOTY TIME 9** [6] 2-8-11 R Mullen 16/1: -63066: Soon outpcd, saddle slipped & eased down fnl 1f.   17 **0a**
6 ran   Time 1m 03.33 (3.13)   (R Hollingshed)   R Hollinshead Upper Longdon, Staffs

2606
4.55 BEST BETS HCAP STKS 3YO+ (0-65)   2m46y aw   Going 21   -46 Slow   [65]
£2303   £658   £329   3 yo rec 19lb

1711 **VINCENT 39** [6] J L Harris 5-9-0 (51) K Dalgleish (5) 11/2: 44-101: 5 b g Anshan - Top Anna (Ela **56a**
Mana Mou) Trkd ldrs, lost place 5f out, rdn & styd on strongly for 2f to lead near line: op 4/1: earlier scored at
Southwell (h'cap): '99 wnr at Southwell & Wolverhampton (h'caps, rtd 52a, unplcd on turf, rtd 48, h'cap): plcd in
'98 (rtd 55a, tried vis): suited by 2m on fast, fibresand/sharp track specialist, handles eqtrk: has run well fresh.
2298 **STEAMROLLER STANLY 13** [10] D W Chapman 7-9-4 (55) R Studholme (5) 4/1 FAV: 004122: 7 b g   ½ **58a**
Shirley Heights - Miss Demure (Shy Groom) Handy, rdn/led 2f out, styd on well, just hdd cl home: bckd, op 6/1:
fine return to h'caps, in gd heart: see 1975 (claimer, 14f).
1852 **TIME CAN TELL 32** [9] A G Juckes 6-8-10 (47) Dean McKeown 6/1: 134203: 6 ch g Sylvan Express -   ¾ **49a**
Stellaris (Star Appeal) Held up, prog chsd ldrs 2f out, hard rdn/onepace fnl 1f: op 4/1: see 737.
2323 **AQUAVITA 12** [12] Miss K M George 6-7-10 (33) (12oh) P M Quinn (3) 33/1: 5/0354: Trkd ldrs halfway,   1¾ **33$**
led over 4f out till 2f out, soon held: see 1501.
2436 **BLACK WEASEL 7** [7] 5-8-3 (40) J Bramhill 9/1: 524-05: Mid div, lost place halfway, mod late gains.   3½ **37a**
2380 **OVER THE MOON 10** [4] 6-8-4 (41) (vis) R Fitzpatrick (1) 12/1: 004366: Rear, mod prog fnl 2f: op 10/1.   ½ **37a**
2217 **ODYN DANCER 16** [11] 3-7-10 (52) (11oh) G Baker (7) 33/1: 206047: Mid div at best: see 537 (11f).   1¾ **46$**
1874 **TOPAZ 31** [5] 5-7-11 (34) Claire Bryan (5) 12/1: 0-0408: 1th halfway, wkn 2f out: see 1608.   2 **26a**
2075 **FLY LIKE A BIRD 22** [8] 4-8-3 (40) Dale Gibson 10/1: 60-049: Chsd ldrs 13f: op 6/1: see 2075.   6 **26a**
2203 **BATOUTOFTHEBLUE 17** [3] 7-10-0 (65) F Lynch 6/1: 3-1340: 1n 5th hlf halfway, soon bhd: 10th: op 4/1 3½ **48a**
2298 **STATE APPROVAL 13** [2] 7-7-10 (33) (1oh) D Mernagh (0) 12/1: 506030: Led, rdn clr with over a   8 **8a**
circuit to go, hdd over 4f out, btn: 11th: jockey only given 12 day ban for riding a finish too early, despite
this being his third offence of that nature (bizarrely given a 14-day ban last time!): ignore this farcical run.
940 **MEDELAI 87** [1] 4-8-6 (43) P Doe 11/1: -01040: Al rear: 12th: 12 week abs: btr 318.   5 **13a**
2429 **QUAKERESS 8** [5] 5-7-10 (33) (6oh) M Henry 6/1: 53200P: Strugg 6f out, p.u. 3f out, dismounted: see 577.   **0a**
13 ran   Time 3m 40.1 (10.9)   (P Caplan)   J L Harris Eastwell, Leics

---

DONCASTER
THURSDAY JULY 13TH   Lefthand, Flat, Galloping Track

Official Going   GOOD (GOOD/FIRM Places) Stalls: Str Course - Stands Side, Rnd Course - Inside, Round 1m - Outside

2607
6.45 DUNNINGTON AMAT HCAP 3YO+ 0-80 (F)   2m110y   Good/Firm 36   -48 Slow   [49]
£2247   £642   £321   3yo rec 19lb

*2516 **BUSTLING RIO 5** [5] P C Haslam 4-11-2 (65) (5ex) Miss A Armitage (5) 11/8 FAV: 500111: 4 b g Up And At 'Em **67**
- Une Venitienne (Green Dancer) Held up, stdy prog fnl 4f & rdn/led over 1f out, styd on well: hvly bckd: slow
time: quick reapp under a pen: earlier scored at Southwell (rtd 68a), Pontefract & Beverley (h'caps): '99 wnr
at Southwell (2, rtd 61a) & Pontefract (h'cap, rtd 61): suited by 2m/2f on firm, gd & fibresand, loves
Southwell/Pontefract: has run well fresh: in great form at present.
2466 **PROTOCOL 6** [1] Mrs S Lamyman 6-9-7 (42) (t) Mr S Dobson (5) 5/1: 355042: 6 b g Taufan - Ukraine's   1½ **41**
Affair (The Minstrel) Prom in chasing group, rdn & prog to chall over 1f out, not pace of wnr ins last: op 6/1.
2382 **NICIARA 10** [8] M C Chapman 3-9-3 (57) (bl) (16oh) Mrs S Bosley 16/1: 403323: 3 b g Soviet Lad - Verusa   7 **49$**

(Petorius) Led & sn clr, rdn/hdd over 1f out & no extra: op 12/1: stiff task & a bold effort: longer 2m trip.

2109 **NOSEY NATIVE 21** [2] J Pearce 7-9-10 (45) Mrs L Pearce 6/1: 322624: Held up, eff 3f out, no prog.   6 **31**

1647 **RAWI 41** [6] 7-9-3 (38)(8oh) Miss L J Harwood (7) 12/1: 060025: Prom in chasing group, btn 3f out.   10 **14**

*2466 **CLASSIC CONKERS 6** [3] 6-9-3 (38)(5ex)(3oh) Mr S Rees (5) 13/2: 60-015: Held up, eff 4f out, no   dht **14**
prog: ddhtd for 5th: op 5/1, 5lb pen for latest: see 2466 (12f).

*2245 **PEKAN HEIGHTS 15** [4] 4-11-7 (70)(vis) Mr A Evans 7/1: 400-17: In tch in chasing group, btn 4f out: 9 **36**
much longer trip: see 2245.

7 ran   Time 3m 42.72 (13.92)   (Rio Stainless Engineering Ltd)   P C Haslam Middleham, N Yorks

---

2608	**7.15 ALLERTHORPE MDN 2YO (D)** **6f str** **Good/Firm 36** **-08 Slow**

£3753   £1155   £577   £288

2152 **CAUSTIC WIT 20** [9] E A L Dunlop 2-9-0 P Robinson 15/2: -501: 2 b c Cadeaux Genereux - Baldemosa   **101**+
(Lead On Time) Made all, rdn & qknd to draw clr from over 1f out, impressive: op 6/1: eff at 6f, dam a 1m wnr:
7f+ shld suit: acts on fast grnd & a gall trk: plenty to like about this, looks one to follow in higher grade.

--   **RIDGE RUNNER** [10] J L Dunlop 2-9-0 K Darley 7/1: -2: 2 b c Indian Ridge - By Charter (Shirley   5 **86**
Heights) Held up, rdn & styd on fnl 2f, no ch with easy wnr: op 5/1: Feb foal, cost 185,000 gns: half brother to
two 7f juv wnrs, also a 2f wnr: dam a 7f juv wnr: acts on fast: will find a race.

--   **RUSSIAN WHISPERS** [6] B J Meehan 2-9-0 Pat Eddery 7/2 JT FAV: -3: 2 b c Red Ransom - Idle Gossip   1 **83**
(Lyphard) Chsd ldrs, ev ch over 1f out, sn outpcd: hvly bckd tho' op 3/1: 12b foal, half brother to an Irish
9f wnr: dam US 6f/9f wnr: will know more next time: shld improve.

--   **MASTERFUL** [1] J H M Gosden 2-9-0 R Havlin 6/1: -4: Dwelt, settled towards rear, styd on well fnl   hd **83**+
2f, nrst at fin: op 5/1: Danzig colt, Apr foal, cost $250,000: dam a French 12f 3yo wnr: looks sure to relish
further in time, educational intro, will leave this bhd over 7f+.

--   **GRANDERA** [5] 2-9-0 D Harrison 7/2 JT FAV: -5: Dwelt, bmpd start, prog/chsd ldrs 2f out, sn held: hd **83**
nicely bckd, op 6/1: Grand Lodge colt, Apr foal, dam a French 13f wnr, sire top class at 1m/10f: will apprec further.

--   **RINGWOOD** [3] 2-9-0 R Mullen 13/2: -6: Held up, rdn/outpcd fnl 2f: op 11/2: Foxhound colt, Feb   2 **77**
foal, cost 35,000 gns: dam a US wnr: likely to apprec 7f+ in time for C Wall.

2333 **QUEENS MUSICIAN 12** [12] 2-9-0 A Culhane 10/1: -337: Keen/held up, nvr on terms: op 8/1.   2 **71**

2333 **MY AMERICAN BEAUTY 12** [4] 2-8-9 W Supple 25/1: -68: Cl-up till over 1f out: see 2333.   hd **66**

2360 **MR PIANO MAN 10** [7] 2-9-0 J F Egan 25/1: -39: Chsd ldrs till over 1f out: btr 2360 (5f).   2½ **64**

--   **WEET A WHILE** [2] 2-9-0 J P Spencer 33/1: -0: Nvr on terms: 10th: Lahib colt, Mar foal, cost   2½ **57**
13000 gns: dam a lightly rcd mdn: with R Hollinshead.

--   **KAURI** [13] 2-8-9 J Carroll 14/1: -0: Chsd ldrs 4f: 11th: op 12/1: Woodman filly, May foal, cost   2½ **45**
$50,000, a first foal: dam a US sprint wnr: with M Johnston.

2361 **BROCKHALL LAD 10** [11] 2-9-0 R Winston 66/1: -00: Bhd halfway, virtually p.u.: 12th: no form.   dist **0**

12 ran   Time 1m 13.44 (2.64)   (Maktoum Al Maktoum)   E A L Dunlop Newmarket, Suffolk

---

2609	**7.45 NEWPORT MDN 3YO+ (D)** **1m4f** **Good/Firm 36** **-01 Slow**

£3883   £1195   £597   £298   3yo rec 13lb

1554 **FRANGY 45** [3] L M Cumani 3-8-6 K Darley 7/2: -31: 3 b f Sadler's Well - Fern (Shirley Heights)   **79**
Trkd ldrs, went on appr fnl 3f, kept on well, drvn out: half sister to sev mid-dist wnrs: eff at 12f,
further could suit: acts on fast, hvy & a gall trk: runs well fresh: open to further improvement.

1956 **TROILUS 27** [1] J H M Gosden 3-8-11 J Fortune 3/1 JT FAV: 50-032: 3 ch c Bien Bien - Nakterjal   1 **80**
(Vitiges) Led, hdd appr fnl 3f, kept on, not pace of wnr in last: stays 12f: btr 1m: worth a try in headgear.

2308 **JOHNNY OSCAR 13** [6] J R Fanshawe 3-8-11 D Harrison 3/1 JT FAV: -433: 3 b g Belmez - Short Ration   ¾ **78**
(Lorenzaccio) Front rank, ev ch till not pace of front 2 fnl 1f: poss stays 12f: h'caps should now suit.

1929 **KADOUN 29** [5] L M Cumani 3-8-11 J P Spencer 9/2: -244: Ran in snatches in rear, wandered &   nk **77**
styd on well fnl 2f, no threat: stable-mate of wnr & looks a tricky ride: see 1554.

1956 **POLLSTER 27** [4] 3-8-11 (VIS) Pat Eddery 11/2: -0045: Waited with, rdn/eff over 2f out, no dngr: visor.   6 **68**

1588 **VICTORY ROLL 44** [2] 4-9-10 R Havlin 16/1: -026: Prom, wknd qckly fnl 3f, t.o.: btr 1588.   dist **0**

6 ran   Time 2m 34.27 (4.47)   (Fittocks Stud)   L M Cumani Newmarket

---

2610	**8.15 RANSKILL HCAP 3YO 0-95 (C)** **1m2f60y** **Good/Firm 36** **+03 Fast** **[99]**

£7215   £2220   £1110   £555

2522 **HAPPY DIAMOND 4** [7] M Johnston 3-9-4 (89) J Carroll 9/1: 3022D1: 3 b c Diesis - Urus (Kris S)   **96**
Made all, increased pace appr fnl 3f, styd on well, rdn out: deserved this after being unlucky both recent
starts (prematurely eased & just btn 2 runs ago, disqual from 1st last time): '99 wnr on 2nd of 2 starts, at
Thirsk, rated btr 87): suited by 10f on fast, gd & a gall trk: in fine form & a much deserved victory today.

2167 **BROADWAY LEGEND 19** [1] J W Hills 3-9-0 (85) M Henry 20/1: 0-1002: 3 b f Caerleon - Tetradonna   2½ **87**
(Teenoso) Waited with, short of room & hmpd halfway, ran on well for press fnl 2f, no threat to wnr: unlucky
in running, may apprec a step up to 12f now: see 1165.

1837 **PARAGON OF VIRTUE 33** [9] Sir Michael Stoute 3-8-12 (83) Pat Eddery 8/1: -0233: 3 ch c Cadeaux   shd **85**
Genereux - Madam Dubois (Legend Of France) Settled rear, gd hdwy 4f out, ev ch until not pace of wnr appr
fnl 1f: h'cap bow, styd this longer 10f trip & further shld suit: see 1352.

1310 **FLITWICK 43** [11] B Hanbury 3-8-9 (92) W Supple 9/1: 20-064: Rear, late hdwy for press, no dngr: abs.   ½ **93**

1853 **KELTIC BARD 32** [10] 3-8-1 (71)(1ow) R Mullen 20/1: -0005: Settled bhd, rdn/late hdwy, no threat   3½ **68**
to ldrs: longer 10f trip: see 1183.

*1599 **FLITWICK 43** [11] 3-9-0 (85) T Quinn 13/2: -016: Trkd ldr, rdn & wknd appr fnl 2f: 6 wk abs.   1¼ **79**

810 **MAC BE LUCKY 103** [4] 3-8-2 (73) G Duffield 9/1: 320-07: Front rank, rdn & wknd fnl 3f: up in trip: 5 **59**
plcd on 1st 2 '99 runs (mdns, once unlucky at long odds-on, rtd 81): eff at 7f on soft/hvy grnd, 10f shld suit.

1866 **JUDICIOUS 31** [3] 3-7-13 (70) J Quinn 4/1: 00-038: Mid-div, lost tch fnl 2f: btr 1866.   3½ **51**

1183 **AZUR 67** [5] 3-8-11 (82) P Robinson 14/1: 01-09: Prom, rdn/fdd appr fnl 3f: 9 wk abs: landed fnl   ¾ **62**
of just 2 '99 starts at Lingfield (auct mdn, rtd 82): eff at 7f, 10f shld suit: acts on gd grnd & a sharp trk.

1225 **OSOOD 64** [6] 3-9-2 (85) Dale Gibson 16/1: 61-660: Dwelt, nvr a danger, 10th: abs: btr 1225 (12f).   1¾ **65**

2116 **BALDAQUIN 21** [8] 3-9-0 (85) J Fortune 7/4 FAV: -04150: Mid-div, wknd qckly fnl 3f, eased, t.o. in   dist **0**
11th: much better expected, something amiss?: much btr 2116, 1640.

11 ran   Time 2m 09.82 (3.42)   (Jaber Abdullah)   M Johnston Middleham, N Yorks

2611
8.45 GREAT LEGER MDN 3YO+ (D) 1m str Good/Firm 36 -03 Slow
£3883 £1195 £597 £298   3yo rec 9lb

2117 **ARGENTAN 21** [3] J H M Gosden 3-8-12 J Fortune 11/8 FAV: 3-2201: 3 b c Gulch - Honfleur (Sadler's 86
Wells) Made all, drvn out, held on gamely: plcd both juv starts for A Foster (mdns, rtd 94): eff at 7f/1m
on fast & gd/soft grnd, any trk: tough sort, best up with/forcing the pace.
2001 **INVADER 26** [13] C E Brittain 4-9-7 (VIS) P Robinson 6/1: -55002: 4 b c Danehill - Donya (Mill Reef) hd 85
Chsd ldrs, rdn to chall below dist, held nr fin: back to best in a visor: eff at 1m/9f, shld shed mdn tag soon.
1093 **ALWAYS VIGILANT 72** [5] R Charlton 3-8-7 M Tebbutt 14/1: -03: 3 b f Lear Fan - Crowning Ambition 2 76
(Chief's Crown) Mid-div, prog to go 3rd dist, not trouble front pair: w'ever abs: apprec drop back to 1m
tho' is bred to get further: handles fast grnd, do better once h'capped?
4338} **GOTHIC REVIVAL 275** [11] J L Dunlop 3-8-12 K Darley 13/2: 40-4: Dwelt, imprvd appr fnl 1f, styd ¾ 79+
on for hands & heels, nvr dangerous: reapp, well clr rem: 4th of 5 on debut last term (stks, rtd 86): half brother
to a 2m wnr: one to note in mid-dist h'caps.
2135 **SHARP LIFE 20** [8] 3-8-12 T Quinn 15/2: -055: Chsd ldrs till fdd appr fnl 1f: see 1539. 6 67
1539 **LADY TWO K 47** [4] 3-8-7 J Quinn 20/1: -046: Cl-up till 2 out: 7 wk abs, see 1539. 4 54
2159 **IL CAVALIERE 19** [12] 5-9-7 A Culhane 10/1: -37: Nvr a factor under a kind ride: mid-dist h'cap type. ½ 58
34 **ARANUI 244** [10] 3-8-12 (t) J Carroll 8/1: 0-8: In tch till 2f out: reapp, t-strap: no worthwhile form. 2 54
2337 **SHALBEBLUE 12** [9] 3-8-12 Dean McKeown 20/1: 359: Chsd ldrs till outpcd appr fnl 2f: see 2337, 1135.shd 54
1692 **CHOCSTAW 40** [1] 3-8-12 Pat Eddery 8/1: -00: Prom till lost place appr fnl 2f: 10th. 2 50
1599 **VENTO DEL ORENO 43** [2] 3-8-7 J P Spencer 20/1: -6560: Nvr a factor, 11th, 6 wk abs, btr 1344. hd 45
115} **NIP IN SHARP 589** [7] 7-9-7 J F Egan 50/1: 45/0: Al bhd: 12th: long abs, rtd 74 & 52a back in '98. 2 46
-- **Stardreamer** [14] 3-8-12 W Supple 14/1: -- **Victor Power** [6] 5-9-7 Claire Bryan (5) 50/1:
14 ran   Time 1m 39.69 (3.19)   (Mr R E Sangster & Mr A K Collins)   J H M Gosden Manton, Wilts

2612
9.15 BEACHCOMBER HCAP 3YO+ 0-75 (E) 7f str Good/Firm 36 +03 Fast [68]
£3916 £1205 £602 £301   3yo rec 8lb Raced stands side, high numbers favoured.

2442 **PENGAMON 7** [18] M Wigham 8-9-0 (54) J Quinn 4/1 FAV: 2-3021: 8 gr g Efisio - Dolly Bevan 64
(Another Realm) Trkd ldrs going well on stands rail, shaken up to lead bef dist, sn clr, easily: '99 wnr at
Lingfield (AW h'cap, rtd 57a, D Thom): missed '98, '97 wnr again at Lingfield (h'cap, rtd 77a & 76): eff at
7f/1m: acts on fast, gd/soft grnd, likes equitrack/Lingfield: has a turn of foot in this grade, well h'capped.
2542 **NORTHGATE 3** [22] M Brittain 4-8-9 (49)(bl) D Mernagh (3) 12/1: 542142: 4 b c Thatching - Tender 4 50
Time (Tender King) Led on stands rail, hdd bef fnl 1f, easily outpcd by wnr: quick reapp, in gd form, see 2221.
2347 **DARYABAD 12** [9] N A Graham 8-8-5 (45)(bl) Dale Gibson (3) 12/1: 16-003: 8 b g Thatching - Dayanata ½ 45
(Shirley Heights) Chsd ldrs, drvn appr fnl 1f, kept on for 3rd: signs of a return to form, see 28.
2281 **SOBA JONES 14** [14] T D Easterby 3-8-4 (52) K Darley 10/1: 600234: Mid-div, eff appr fnl 1f, styd ¾ 50
on, not pace to chall: ran to best tho' may apprec a return to 1m: see 2281.
2084 **TIME VALLY 22** [12] 3-9-9 (71) P Doe 16/1: 6-0105: Dwelt, rear, short of room ent fnl 2f till below ¾ 67
dist, ran on wide, nvr dangerous: acts on firm/fast grnd, worth another try at 1m, see 1855.
2420 **SONG OF SKYE 8** [20] 6-9-13 (67) J Fortune 12/1: 000236: Bhd, nowhere to go 2f out, staying on fin. ¾ 61
2320 **CALCAVELLA 12** [10] 4-9-8 (62) G Duffield 11/1: 000-47: Chsd ldrs, no extra appr fnl 1f: see 2320. hd 56
2240 **JAYPEECEE 15** [8] 4-8-8 (48)(vis) J P Spencer 25/1: 000458: Rear, late hdwy: btr 1734 (1st time vis). nk 41
2320 **CELANDINE 12** [4] 7-8-3 (43) P Fessey 20/1: 00-009: Chsd ldrs till 2f out: see 2221. 1 34
2396 **SQUARE DANCER 9** [15] 4-9-6 (60) A Culhane 16/1: 000540: Prom, fdd appr fnl 1f: 10th, return to 6f? nk 50
2340 **MALADERIE 12** [11] 6-9-1 (55)(vis) T Williams 20/1: 020000: Handy till appr fnl 1f: 11th, see 908. ½ 44
2347 **ERUPT 12** [16] 7-9-3 (57) P Dobbs 5/1: 113000: Nvr a factor: 12th, see 2601. hd 46
2320 **CRYSTAL LASS 12** [17] 4-8-1 (41) O Pears 16/1: 050050: Al towards rear: 13th, see 513. ½ 29
2334 **REDSWAN 12** [5] 5-10-0 (68)(t) G Bardwell 3/1 J2: -00000: Mid-div, wknd appr fnl 1f: 14th, poor draw. ¾ 54
2453 **KUSTOM KIT KEVIN 6** [13] 4-8-4 (42)(t)(2ow) Dean McKeown 16/1: 000300: Slow away, al bhd: 15th. nk 29
*2437 **ARPEGGIO 7** [7] 5-10-2 (70)(6ex) Alex Greaves 9/1: 000410: Prom 5f: 18th, top weight & pen, poor draw. 0
*2427 **FLYING PENNANT 8** [2] 7-8-4 (44)(bl)(6ex) W Supple 14/1: 530610: Nvr better than mid-div: pen, poor draw. 0
2415 **CRUSTY LILY 8** [1] 4-8-2 (42) R Mullen 12/1: 0-0420: Mid-div till 2f out: poor draw, see 2415. 0
2320 **Patsy Culsyth 12** [6] 5-8-4 (44) Kim Tinkler 14/1:   2126 **Green God 20** [21] 4-9-9 (63) J Carroll 25/1:
2464 **Macs Dream 6** [3] 5-8-6 (44)(t)(2ow) M Tebbutt 25/1:
21 ran   Time 1m 25.54 (2.34)   (Miss Arabella Smallman)   M Wigham Newmarket

Official Going GOOD TO SOFT. Stalls: Far Side, except 4.10 - Stands Side.
The advantageous stands rail strip of ground, greatly favoured yesterday's winners, mysteriously held no advantage today.

2613
2.05 LISTED SUPERLATIVE STKS 2YO (A) 7f str Good/Firm 33 -11 Slow
£12818 £4862 £2431 £1105

-- **VACAMONTE** [8] H R A Cecil 2-8-11 T Quinn 7/4 FAV: 1: 2 ch c Caerleon - Bahamian (Mill Reef) 113+
Dwelt, trckd ldr, qcknd to lead when gap appeared appr fnl 1f, sn clr, impressive: hvly bckd, stable 11 out of
11 in this race: Apr foal, half-brother to several mid-dist wnrs, incl Irish Oaks heroine Wemyss Bight: eff at
7f on fast, shld take high-rank over mid-dists next term: runs well fresh: v impressive, must be followed.
2067 **SHADOWLESS 23** [4] C E Brittain 2-8-11 P Robinson 12/1: 402: 2 b c Alzao - Warning Shadows 3½ 101
(Cadeaux Genereux) Prom, under press ent fnl 2f & tried to bite Dane O'Neill, kept on for 2nd but no ch with wnr:
op 8/1: caught a tartar though was suited by step up to 7f on fast & will apprec 1m: nailed on for a mdn.
-- **BONNARD** [3] A P O'Brien 2-9-0 G Duffield 11/2: 13: 2 b c Nureyev - Utr (Mr Prospector) hd 104
Well plcd, rdn to chall appr fnl 1f, sn same pace: nicely bckd tho' op 4/1, 6 wk abs: Irish raider, earlier won
Fairyhouse debut (mdn): 265,000gns Mar foal, brother to 12f wnr Andromedes: eff at 6/7f on fast & gd/soft grnd.
2067 **STREGONE 23** [2] B J Meehan 2-9-0 G Mosse 25/1: 652204: Held up, wide, progress 2f out, rdn 1½ 101
bef dist, nvr hdwy: ran to best over longer trip, sharper 7f or drop bck 6f likely to suit: see 1214, 743.
*2346 **KINGS IRONBRIDGE 12** [5] 2-9-0 Dane O'Neill 3/1: -215: Got the stands rail & led, rdn appr fnl 1f, sn ½ 100
edged left & hdd, no extra: hvly bckd: not disgraced tho' more expected after impressive C/D wnr in 2346 (firm).

2067 **EARL GREY 23** [1] 2-9-0 M Tebbutt 13/2: 146: Chsd ldrs, wide, eff & not much room entering fnl 2f, outpcd: worth another ch at 7f, see 2067 (Coventry stakes, in front of this 2nd & 4th). ¾ **98**
2346 **GRYFFINDOR 12** [6] 2-8-11 Pat Eddery 14/1: 37: In tch till 2f out: highly tried, see 2346. ½ **94**
*2383 **MUJALINA 10** [7] 2-9-0 M Fenton 50/1: 0218: Al bhd: highly tried, see 2383 (fibresand mdn). 1¾ **92$**
8 ran Time 1m 26.95 (3.05) (K Abdulla) H R A Cecil Newmarket, Suffolk

2614

2.35 MONDI HCAP 3YO 0-95 (C) 1m str Good/Firm 33 -04 Slow [99]
£7709 £2372 £1186 £593 Raced stands side

2515 **CHAPEL ROYALE 5** [8] K Mahdi 3-8-7 (78) G Duffield 16/1: 002031: 3 gr c College Chapel - Merci Royale (Fairy King) Trckd ldrs, rdn appr fnl 1f, ran on well to lead inside last: quick reapp: '99 Newcastle wnr (auct mdn, rtd 85, A Turnell): eff at 7f/1m on fast & soft grnd, any track: well h'capped, quick follow-up? **82**
1873 **RESOUNDING 31** [15] A C Stewart 3-8-8 (79) M Roberts 3/1 FAV: 51-32: 3 b f Elmaamul - Echoing (Formidable) Mid-div, pshd along halfway, kept on strgly appr fnl 1f & went 2nd near fin, not trble wnr: well bckd: clrly suited by step up to 1m & shld get further: goes on fast & soft, handles firm: progressive, win again. 1¼ **80**
2358 **TUMBLEWEED TOR 11** [1] B J Meehan 3-9-6 (91) G Mosse 16/1: 031063: 3 b g Rudimentary - Hilly (Town Crier) Led/dsptd lead till 150y out, no extra und press: apprec drop bck to 1m, acts on fast & hvy grnd. *nk* **91**
2330 **SOVEREIGN STATE 12** [6] M A Jarvis 3-8-5 (76) P Robinson 12/1: -01054: Led/dsptd lead on stands rail, hdd dist, one pace: ran to best, see 1387. ¾ **74**
1853 **SPIN A YARN 32** [14] 3-8-10 (81) J Reid 5/1: 1-0055: Chsd ldrs, feeling pace 2f out, brief rally dist. 1½ **76**
2117 **KINGSDON 21** [7] 3-9-7 (92)(t) Dane O'Neill 7/1: -63006: Wide, in tch, rdn 2f out, no impress: clr rem. ¾ **85**
*2084 **MOSSY MOOR 22** [13] 3-9-4 (89) Pat Eddery 11/2: 4-5317: Rear, eff & boxed in 2f out, soon no chance: not given a hard time & this is prob best forgotton: see 2084. 3 **76**
2456 **CLEVER GIRL 6** [5] 3-9-1 (86) J Fortune 16/1: 01D008: Chsd ldrs, fdd fnl 1f: btr 1645, 823. 1¼ **70**
*2211 **EAST CAPE 17** [2] 3-8-8 (79) J P Spencer 10/1: -54219: Wide, al bhd: h'cap bow, see 2211. 1 **61**
2003 **LOCHARATI 26** [16] 3-9-0 (85) J Tate 20/1: -10200: Keen, nvr got in it: 10th, up in trip, see 1409, 837. 1 **65**
4376} **PHOEBE BUFFAY 272** [4] 3-8-6 (77) D O'Donohoe 25/1: 1200-0: Al wide & bhd: 11th on reapp: '99 Southwell wnr (auction mdn, rtd 75a, nursery rnr up, rtd 79): eff at 6f, stys 7f: acts on firm grnd & fibresand, handles soft, any track, without blinkers: with C Allen. 2 **53**
*2222 **ADAMAS 16** [10] 3-9-1 (86) K Darley 20/1: 2-0410: Dwelt, mid div till 2f out: 12th, h'cap bow, btr 2222. 2 **58**
12 ran Time 1m 40.17 (2.97) (Prospect Estates Ltd) K Mahdi Newmarket, Suffolk

2615

3.05 GR 1 DARLEY JULY CUP STKS 3YO+ (A) 6f Good/Firm 33 -03 Slow
£95700 £36300 £18150 £8250 3 yo rec 6 lb Raced stands side

2065 **AGNES WORLD 23** [6] Hideyuki Mori 5-9-5 Y Take 4/1 FAV: 12-321: 5 b h Danzig - Mysteries (Seattle Slew) Well plcd, rdn appr fnl 1f, narrow lead below dist, just held on: hvly bckd Japanese raider: won 4 last term, notably at Longchamp (Gr 1 Prix de l'Abbaye, rtd 120): 6 time winner in native land: eff at 5/6f on firm & hvy grnd, any track: ultra-tough & smart globe-trotting entire, the first Japanese trained horse to win in this country. **120**
*1534 **LINCOLN DANCER 47** [10] M A Jarvis 3-8-13 M Roberts 9/2: 0-4012: 3 b c Turtle Island - Double Grange (Double Schwartz) Shkn up to keep prom, rdn/hung left/bmpd & lost hind legs briefly appr fnl 1f, soon led, hdd fnl 150y, rallied, just failed: nicely bckd, 7 wk abs: cracking run from this much improved colt, acts on fast & gd/soft grnd: now a smart performer, must win a Group race: see 1534 (Listed rtd h'cap). *shd* **119**
2115 **PIPALONG 21** [5] T D Easterby 4-9-2 K Darley 10/1: 112103: 4 b f Pips Pride - Limpopo (Green Desert) In tch stand side, drvn appr fnl 1f, kept on well ins last: v useful, shwd last run to be all wrong, see 133. *shd* **116**
1746 **PRIMO VALENTINO 41** [9] P W Harris 3-8-13 Pat Eddery 5/1: 11-064: Led till dist, no extra: nicely bckd, 6 week abs: back to near smart juv form: a real speedster who can win again when dropped back to 5f. 1½ **114**
2115 **LEND A HAND 21** [2] 5-9-5 J Reid 6/1: 4-6135: Switched & held up, imprvg & tried to squeeze btwn horses appr fnl 1f, gap sn clsd & hmpd, kept on: op 9/2: may have been involved in the finish with a clr run. *nk* **113**
2065 **BERTOLINI 23** [1] 4-9-5 (vis) R Hills 8/1: 20-236: Switched from low draw, in tch, prog going well when barged into Lend A Hand appr fnl 1f, no extra: op 6/1, best ignored: 3rd in this last year (rtd 118): see 766. 2 **107**
2335 **WINNING VENTURE 12** [11] 3-8-13 K Take 33/1: 302307: Soon struggling, went past btn horses fnl 1f: op 66/1, highly tried: needs a drop back to Listed company, see 1674, 950. *hd* **106**
2335 **TRINCULO 12** [4] 3-8-13 J Quinn 66/1: 034048: Handy till fdd appr fnl 1f: stiff task, see 2335, 969. 1¾ **101**
2087 **MONASHEE MOUNTAIN 22** [3] 3-8-13 (VIS) G Duffield 13/2: -11509: Prom, wide, rdn appr fnl 1f, soon btn: well bckd from 8/1: visored Irish raider, has lost his way & was unsuited by drop to sprinting, see 1120 (soft). 3½ **91**
4100} **MUNJIZ 291** [8] 4-9-5 W Supple 20/1: 6262-0: Chsd ldrs till lost pl 2f out: 10th , highly tried on reapp: plcd in Dubai in March: '99 reapp wnr here at Newmarket (h'cap, Gr 2 rnr up, rtd 115): '98 Goodwood wnr (mdn, rtd 100 at best): eff at 6f: acts on firm & soft grnd, likes stiff/straight tracks: with B Hills. 5 **76**
10 ran Time 1m 13.18 (2.18) (Takashi Watanabe) Hideyuki Mori Japan

2616

3.40 BUNBURY CUP HCAP 3YO+ 0-105 (A) 7f str Good/Firm 33 +13 Fast [105]
£26000 £8000 £4000 £2000 3 yo rec 8 lb 2 went far side, beaten 2f out.

2338 **TAYSEER 12** [8] D Nicholls 6-8-9 (86) G Mosse 9/1: 053031: 6 ch g Sheikh Albaadou - Millifit (Blushing Groom) Held up stands side, gd wide hdwy ent fnl 2f, led below dist, edged right, ran on strgly, pshd out: op 7/1, fast time: poorly rdn last time: ended '99 with wins at Brighton (clmr, W Muir), Ayr & here at Newmarket (val h'cap, rtd 87): '98 Southwell wnr (clmr, rtd 86a): eff at 6f, suited by 7f/1m: acts on firm, soft & fibresand, likes stiff trks: well treated, shld go close under a pen in the Tote International at Ascot later this month. **97**
2090 **PERSIANO 22** [18] J R Fanshawe 5-9-5 (96) D Harrison 7/1: -03132: 5 ch g Efisio - Persiandale (Persian Bold) Prom stands side, rdn appr fnl 1f, kept on & edged left, not trouble wnr: most consistent in these val h'caps, 5th in this race last term: progressive, useful gelding: see 2090, 1450. 1 **104**
2151 **NICE ONE CLARE 20** [20] J W Payne 4-8-12 (89) J P Spencer 11/2: 211-53: 4 b f Mukaaddamah - Sarah Clare (Reach) Held up stands side, gd progress appr fnl 1f, kept on well under press, never nearer: well bckd, given a lot to do: ran well, looks sure to land a valuable prize before long: see 2151. 1¾ **94**
2287 **SECOND WIND 13** [6] C A Dwyer 5-8-6 (83)(t) J Mackay (5) 20/1: 500124: Front rank stands side, led 2f out till below dist, slightly hmpd, onepace: apprec the drop bck to 7f, tough: see 2287, 2133. *shd* **88**
2185 **SALTY JACK 18** [1] 6-8-2 (79) J F Egan 20/1: 000545: Held up stands side, hdwy under press in centre appr fnl 1f, kept on, nrst fin: typical late flourish, rnr up in this last term (off 6lbs higher): see 485. *nk* **83**
2528 **DEBBIES WARNING 4** [11] 4-9-0 (91) Dane O'Neill 25/1: 064006: Got stands rail & led till 2f out, rdn & hung left dist, onepace: qk reapp: apprec drop bck to 7f & may do even better at 6f: see 703. *nk* **94**
2090 **OMAHA CITY 22** [12] 6-9-1 (92) J Reid 25/1: 06-007: Held up stands side, shaken up 2f out, kept on, never dangerous: being primed for a big run at Glorious Goodwood early next month?: see 1450. ½ **94**

2356 **PEARTREE HOUSE 11** [7] 6-8-11 (88) A Nicholls (3) 16/1: 312448: Chsd ldrs stands side, rdn 2f out, **nk 89**
no impression on ldrs when hmpd & snatched up briefly below dist: stablemate of wnr, apprec a return to 1m?
2163 **GIFT OF GOLD 19** [5] 5-8-7 (84) G Duffield 20/1: 001309: Chsd ldrs stands side, rdn appr fnl 1f, **shd 85**
soon onepace: fair run, suited by softer grnd, see 1483.
2151 **STRAHAN 20** [19] 3-9-2 (101) K Darley 4/1 JT FAV: -12230: Towards rear stands side, feeling pace **¾ 100**
ent fnl 2f, no threat: 10th, hvly bckd 3yo: progressive in val h'caps prev, may be better off in Listed company now.
2090 **TILLERMAN 22** [13] 4-9-12 (103) Pat Eddery 4/1 JT FAV: 11-350: Waited with stands side, rdn 2f out, **½ 101**
keeping on but no ch with ldrs when hmpd & eased ins last: 11th, nicely bckd: worth another chance back at 1m.
2133 **JUNO MARLOWE 20** [15] 4-9-4 (95) T Quinn 12/1: -00020: Bhd ldrs stands side, outpcd appr fnl **nk 92**
1f & not perservered with: 12th, capable of better: usually runs well here at Newmarket, see 2133, 1077.
1983 **POLES APART 27** [4] 4-8-3 (80) J Quinn 40/1: 0-0000: Front rank stands side till 2f out: 13th, best at 6f. **1 75**
*1989 **CHOTO MATE 26** [3] 4-8-13 (90) P Dobbs (5) 25/1: /W0410: Never a factor stands side: 14th, btr 1989. **¾ 83**
*2431 **KINAN 8** [2] 4-8-9 (86)(5ex) M Hills 25/1: 50-010: In tch far side till appr fnl 2f: 19th, foget this, see 2431. **0**
2133 Tayit 20 [16] 4-9-1 (92) A McGlone 33/1:   2090 Exeat 22 [10] 4-9-12 (103)(vis) J Fortune 25/1:
2151 Pips Song 20 [14] 5-8-6 (83) J Lowe 50/1:   *2293 Thunder Sky 13 [4] 4-8-3 (80)(vis) P Robinson 50/1:
19 ran   Time 1m 25.33 (1.43)   (Sammy Doo Racing)   D Nicholls Sessay, N Yorks

---

2617   4.10 BEDFORD LODGE MDN 3YO (D)   1m2f   Good/Firm 33   -23 Slow
     £5655   £1740   £870   £435

--   **INAAQ** [7] Saeed bin Suroor 3-8-9 R Hills 6/4 FAV: 1: 3 ch f Lammtarra - Elfaslah (Green Desert) **90**
Prom, briefly outpcd 3f out, kept on well & edged left bef fnl 1f, soon led, rdn out: hvly bckd: half-sister to
high-class 10f performer Almutawekel: eff over a stiff 10f on fast, sure to apprec 12f: runs well fresh: Gr 1 entry.
--   **ROYAL TRYST** [1] Sir Michael Stoute 3-9-0 Pat Eddery 5/2: 2: 3 ch c Kingmambo - In On The Secret **2 91**
(Secretariat) Never far away, rdn to chall appr fnl 1f, outpcd by wnr & eased near fin: well bckd on debut:
$400,000gns half-brother to several decent wnrs: eff at 10f on fast grnd: go one better soon.
1242 **WHITE HOUSE 63** [6] W Jarvis 3-8-9 M Tebbutt 25/1: 0-443: 3 b f Pursuit Of Love - Much Too Risky **½ 85**
(Bustino) Set steady pace, under press & hdd appr fnl 1f, onepace: apprec return to 10f, acts on fast & hvy.
--   **SHAIR** [3] J H M Gosden 3-9-0 J Fortune 16/1: 4: Waited with, wide, styd on nicely to go 4th ins **2½ 86**
last: op 11/1: Warning half-brother to St Leger wnr Shantou: eff at 10f, 12f+ is going to suit: hndles fast grnd.
--   **ROSE ADAGIO** [5] 3-8-9 W Ryan 16/1: 5: Pulled hard, cl up, chald 2f out, fdd dist: op 12/1: **1 79**
Sadler's Wells half-sister to a 10f h'capper: improvement likely when settling better: with H Cecil.
--   **CLOUD HOPPING** [2] 3-9-0 T Quinn 11/2: 6: Held up, chsd ldrs after 6f till 2f out: better fancied **2½ 80**
stablemate of 5th: Mr Prospector half-brother to a fair miler & may do better at that trip himself.
4379} **KARAJAN 272** [8] 3-9-0 M Hills 15/2: 3-7: Al bhd: plcd sole '99 start in a hot mdn here (1m, gd, rtd 94). **3 75**
--   **ELLWAY QUEEN** [4] 3-8-9 J Reid 25/1: 8: In tch till 3f out: Bahri half sister to a wnr in the States. **3½ 65**
2104 **BIGGLES 22** [9] 3-9-0 K Darley 33/1: -49: Never a factor: highly tried: see 2104. **1½ 68**
9 ran   Time 2m 07.52 (5.62)   (Godolphin)   Saeed bin Suroor Newmarket, Suffolk

---

2618   4.45 PRINCESS FILLIES MDN 2YO (D)   6f   Good/Firm 33   -07 Slow
     £5785   £1780   £890   £445

--   **KHULAN** [4] J L Dunlop 2-8-11 R Hills 8/11 FAV: 1: 2 b f Bahri - Jawlaat (Dayjur) **106**
Trkd ldr, pshd into lead appr fnl 1f, qcknd clr: hvly bckd, impressive debut: Jan first foal, dam 6f wnr:
eff at 6f, will get further: acts on fast grnd & a stiff track: runs well fresh: v highly regarded by
powerful stable & a potentially high-class filly, won here in a fast juv time, keep on your side.
--   **MUJADO** [7] B J Meehan 2-8-11 Pat Eddery 8/1: 2: 2 b f Mujadil - Unaria (Prince Tenderfoot) **3½ 93**
Chsd ldrs, eff appr fnl 1f, styd on for 2nd but no ch with wnr & not given a hard time: nicely bckd from 10/1:
30,000gns Feb foal, half-sister to a wng sprinter: eff at 6f on fast: will not al meet one this useful, win similar.
--   **SEVEN SING** [1] B W Hills 2-8-11 M Hills 7/1: 3: 2 b f Machiavellian - Seven Springs (Irish River) **1 90**
Led till ent fnl 2f, onepace: op 5/1: April half-sister to top class miler Distant View, dam high-class sprint
juv, sire a miler: bred to be very good indeed: handles fast grnd, expect improvement, will win a maiden.
1568 **ECSTATIC 45** [6] R Hannon 2-8-11 Dane O'Neill 8/1: -24: Chsd ldrs, outpcd appr fnl 1f, styg on fin. **½ 88**
--   **LADY MILETRIAN** [2] 2-8-11 M Roberts 8/1: 5: Dwelt, in tch, wide, no extra appr fnl 1f, eased: **4 76**
tchd 10/1: 75,000gns Barathea April foal, half-sister to decent 6f juv Bergen, sire a miler: with M Channon.
--   **SAUCE TARTAR** [5] 2-8-11 K Darley 12/1: 6: Al towards rear: tchd 16/1: Salse foal, bred for 10f+. **5 61**
1943 **RICHENDA 28** [9] 2-8-11 G Duffield 33/1: -07: Al bhd/hung left: stablemate 4th: Mister Baileys filly. **shd 61**
2285 **AILINCALA 13** [8] 2-8-11 M Tebbutt 33/1: -U8: Al bhd: see 2285. **1¼ 57**
--   **BENEVOLENCE** [3] 2-8-11 J Reid 25/1: 9: Chsd ldrs till halfway: IR£11,500 Lahib first foal. **3 49**
9 ran   Time 1m 13.43 (2.43)   (Hamdan Al Maktoum)   J L Dunlop Arundel, West Sussex

---

FOLKESTONE   THURSDAY JULY 13TH   Righthand, Sharpish, Undulating Track

Official Going   GOOD Stalls: Str Course - Stands Side; Round Course - Outside.

2619   1.55 MED AUCT MDN DIV 1 2YO (F)   7f str   Good 57   -13 Slow
     £1778   £508   £254

2290 **FIGURA 13** [7] K McAuliffe 2-8-9 T E Durcan 6/1: 61: 2 b f Rudimentary - Dream Baby (Master Willie) **82**
Dwelt, sn mid-div, hdwy to lead over 2f out, rdn clr appr fnl 1f: impv: 25,000 gns Apr foal, half sister to a couple
of 2yo scorers: eff at 7f, 1m shld suit: runs well fresh on gd & a sharpish/undl trk: impvg, should win again.
1648 **KALUKI 41** [6] W R Muir 2-9-0 Martin Dwyer 6/1: -63342: 2 ch c First Trump - Wild Humour (Fayruz) **6 75**
Led, hdd 2f out, kept on but no pace of cmftble wnr: op 8/1, 6 wk abs: stays 5/7f on gd & gd/soft: h'caps suit.
2209 **LADY KINVARRAH 17** [9] J R Arnold 2-8-9 C Rutter 7/1: 0603: 2 b f Brief Truce - Al Corniche **1 68**
(Bluebird) Front rank, drvn & no extra when hung right over 1f out: op 5/1: up in trip, poss stays 7f: see 1424.
--   **MISTER BUCKET** [2] P W Harris 2-9-0 J Weaver 7/2: 4: Waited with, eff 2f out, kept on under hands **¾ 72**
& heels: half brother to a 12/14f scorer, dam 2yo 6f wnr: promising debut & not given a hard time, will improve.
2209 **HAMMOCK 17**.[4] 2-9-0 S Sanders 20/1: 05: Prom, rdn/btn fnl 2f: Hamas colt, dam 6f/1m scorer. **2½ 67**
2430 **MOMENTS IN TIME 8** [3] 2-8-9 Craig Williams 9/4 FAV: 646: Handy, edged right 2f out & sn held. **½ 62**
2251 **IMPERO 15** [5] 2-9-0 N Callan 25/1: 57: Prom, fdd fnl 2f: op 14/1: needs sells: see 2251. **2 63**
--   **ALLTHEDOTCOMS** [1] 2-9-0 S Whitworth 10/1: 8: Al bhd: 8,200gns Elmaamul half brother to a **9 50**

1m scorer, dam won over 11f: with N A Callaghan.

--   **EXPLOSIVE** [8] 2-9-0 I Mongan (5) 16/1: 9: In tch, hung badly right & saddle slipped 3f out,   3½   45
sn lost tch: Mar 1st foal: dam scored over 6f as a juv: forget this: with C A Cyzer.
9 ran   Time 1m 29.1 (4.9)   (Alex Fraser)   K McAuliffe Lambourn, Berks

---

2620   **2.25 MED AUCT MDN DIV 2 2YO (F)**   **7f str**   **Good 57**   **-16 Slow**
     £1778   £508   £254

1993   **EL MAXIMO** 26 [1] M G Quinlan 2-9-0 T E Durcan 7/1: 63261: 2 b c First Trump - Kentucky Starlet   75
(Cox's Ridge) Cl-up, sltly outpcd 2f out, rallied & ran on well for press to lead cl-home, drvn out: Apr foal,
half brother to useful sprinter Pips Magic, dam 7f wnr: apprec this step up to 7f, acts on gd, fast grnd & a
sharpish/undul trk: tough & consistent colt.
2218   **PERTEMPS THATCHER** 16 [4] S C Williams 2-8-9 G Faulkner (3) 25/1: -402: 2 b f Petong - Nadema   ¾   68
(Artaius) Led, clr appr fnl 1f, wknd well ins last & hdd nr fin: best run to date, stays 7f on gd: see 1859.
--   **SIMPATICH** [2] L M Cumani 2-9-0 G Sparkes (7) 8/1: -43: 2 ch c First Trump - Arc Empress Jane   nk   72
(Rainbow Quest) Sn well outpcd, drvn & ran on strongly fnl 2f, nvr nrr: well clr rem: recent 4th in a minor event
in Italy: 38,000 gns colt, half brother to a 12f scorer: eff at 7f on gd, sure to apprec 1m+ in time.
1079   **COUNTRYWIDE PRIDE** 73 [7] K R Burke 2-9-0 N Callan 12/1: 04: Prom, rdn/btn fnl 2f: 10 wk abs.   5   62
1988   **SOONA** 26 [5] 2-8-9 D Sweeney 3/1: 0555: Trkd ldrs, rdn/fdd fnl 2f: see 1988.   1¼   55
2125   **TRAVELLERS DREAM** 20 [3] 2-9-0 G Hind 11/2: 036: Bhd, eff halfway, late hdwy: tchd 9/1: btr 2125.   nk   60
2132   **HOSSRUM** 20 [9] 2-9-0 G Carter 5/2 FAV: 67: Mid-div, rdn to improve 3f out, sn wknd: nicely bckd   4   53
tho' op 6/4: surely capable of better, see 2132.
2259   **IM A CHARACTER** 15 [6] 2-8-9 C Rutter 16/1: -08: Chsd ldrs, lost tch halfway: see 2259.   13   30
2029   **BISHOPS SECRET** 25 [8] 2-9-0 S Sanders 8/1: -09: Handy, wknd rapidly fnl 3f, t.o.: tchd 14/1:   5   28
18,000 gns 1st foal, sire high-class 7f/1m: with M H Tompkins.
9 ran   Time 1m 29.3 (5.1)   (Mario Lanfranchi)   M G Quinlan Newmarket

---

2621   **2.55 MCCABE FORD MDN 3YO (D)**   **7f str**   **Good 57**   **-04 Slow**
     £2769   £852   £426   £213

2140   **TAKE FLITE** 20 [2] W R Muir 3-9-0 Martin Dwyer 4/1: -20031: 3 b g Cadeaux Genereux - Green Seed   77
(Lead On Time) Cl-up, went on appr fnl 1f, drvn out well ins last, op 5/2: plcd once as a juv (mdn, rtd
89): eff around 7f, bred to sprint: acts on firm, gd/soft & a sharp/undul or gall trk.
2232   **HARMONIC** 15 [8] D R C Elsworth 3-8-9 N Pollard 13/8 FAV: -60222: 3 b f Shadeed - Running Melody   2   68
(Rheingold) Rcd wide & prom, rdn to chall appr fnl 1f, no extra ins last: well bckd: worth a try in headgear.
1969   **PARKER** 27 [3] B Palling 3-9-0 D Sweeney 6/1: 4-2463: 3 b c Magic Ring - Miss Loving (Northfields)   shd   73
Dsptd lead until no extra for press fnl 1f: see 1266.
2355   **SARENA SPECIAL** 11 [1] R J O'Sullivan 3-9-0 (bl) I Mongan (5) 7/1: 250304: Led, rdn/hdd appr fnl   1¾   70
1f out, sn held: clr rem: needs h'caps: see 1532, 1018.
2463   **BOSSCAT** 6 [9] 3-9-0 T E Durcan 25/1: 600-05: Sn outpcd, late hdwy: unplcd juv (5f/7.6f mdns, rtd 70).   7   60
2183   **BOLD EMMA** 18 [6] 3-8-9 P McCabe 33/1: 0-06: Al in rear: mod form.   shd   55
1012   **LEEROY** 80 [5] 3-9-0 L Newman (3) 6/1: 24-207: Trkd ldrs, wknd qckly halfway, eased: btr 840.   11   45
--   **ENDEAVOUR TO DO** [4] 3-9-0 N Callan 14/1: 8: Dwelt, struggling on debut: Eff with/without blnks.   11   30
2160   **EREBUS** 19 [7] 3-9-0 S Sanders 10/1: 06349: Prom to halfway, sn lost tch: op 6/1: drop in trip.   1¼   28
9 ran   Time 1m 28.5 (4.3)   (The Wheet Partnership)   W R Muir Lambourn, Berks

---

2622   **3.25 BEST BETS HCAP 3YO+ 0-60 (F)**   **2m9y**   **Good 57**   **-24 Slow**   **[60]**
     £2593   £741   £370   3 yo rec 19lb

2452   **DANGER BABY** 7 [12] P Bowen 10-9-0 (46)(bl) S Sanders 4/1: -62521: 10 ch g Bairn - Swordlestown   49
Miss (Apalachee) Held up, switched/hdwy over 2f out, ran on strongly to lead cl-home, drvn out: quick reapp:
unreliable chaser (often refuses): '99 Bath wnr (h'cap, rtd 52): chase wnr in 98/99, at Sedgefield (h'cap, 2½m,
any grnd, rtd 128c): eff at 2m/2m2f on gd & gd/soft, handles fast: likes a sharpish trk & with blnkrs.
2452   **ZIGGY STARDUST** 7 [2] Mrs A J Bowlby 5-8-1 (33) Craig Williams 11/2: 4-3432: 5 b g Roi Danzig -   nk   35
Si Princess (Coquelin) In tch, hdwy 4f out, ran on well to lead well ins last, styd on, hdd cl-home: quick
reapp, stays 2m: also just bhd this wnr in 2452.
*2490   **LAFFAH** 5 [9] G L Moore 5-10-0 (60)(t)(6ex) I Mongan (5) 3/1 FAV: 440/13: 5 b g Silver Hawk - Sakiyah   1¼   61
(Secretariat) Cl-up, rdn to chall over 2f out, short of room & no extra well ins last: nicely bckd, qck reapp:
remains in gd heart & a fine eff under top weight: see 2490 (2m2f, gall trk).
2416   **CHEEK TO CHEEK** 8 [7] C A Cyzer 6-9-13 (59) G Carter 9/1: -55254: Prom, led 3f out & sn clr,   nk   60
drvn & flashed tail appr fnl 1f, hdd well ins last, sn held: up in trip, poss stays 2m: see 1991.
1867   **HETRA HEIGHTS** 31 [5] 5-7-12 (30) Martin Dwyer 14/1: 110305: Bhd, gd hdwy when hmpd 3f out,   hd   31
rallied & ran on strongly appr fnl 1f, closing at fin: op 10/1, unfortunate not to fin closer: see 644.
2212   **GEE BEE BOY** 16 [14] 6-8-13 (45) P Fitzsimons (5) 25/1: 406-06: Prom, outpcd 4f out, eff 2f out,   3½   43
sn held: 4th best in '99 (AW h'cap, rtd 46a): plcd numerous times in '98 (rtd 62), '97 wnr at Redcar (rtd mdn,
rtd 70, A P Jarvis): eff arnd 11/12f, tried further: acts on fast, gd & a sharp or gall trk: can go well fresh.
649   **BEAUCHAMP MAGIC** 127 [4] 5-7-11 (29) R Brisland (5) 14/1: 405437: Waited with, outpcd 4f out,   1½   25
mod late hdwy: 4 month abs: see 649.
2176   **BAISSE DARGENT** 18 [11] 4-9-6 (52) C Rutter 6/1: 323248: Prom, wknd appr fnl 1f, eased: tchd 9/1.   1½   47
1819   **BLOWING AWAY** 34 [8] 6-7-10 (28)(2oh) G Bardwell 20/1: -00059: Keen, al bhd: big step up in trip.   3   20
2323   **GROOMS GOLD** 12 [13] 8-7-12 (30) (vis)(2ow)(4oh) A Daly 20/1: 002040: Led to 3f out, wknd qckly, 10th.   3   19
2256   **PRASLIN ISLAND** 15 [10] 4-9-3 (49) N Callan 5/1: 001D50: Prom, lost tch fnl 3f, fin 11th: btr 1874.   2   36
1614   Classic Eagle 43 [6] 7-9-4 (50) A Clark 25/1:
2388†   Lajadhal 377 [1] 11-7-10 (28)(14oh) Joanna Badger (7) 100/1:
13 ran   Time 3m 44.6 (13.3)   (Shark Racing)   P Bowen Letterston, Pembrokes

---

2623   **4.00 BURSTIN HCAP 3YO+ 0-70 (E)**   **5f str**   **Good 57**   **+15 Fast**   **[69]**
     £2791   £797   £398   3 yo rec 5 lb

2535   **NIFTY NORMAN** 3 [5] D Nicholls 6-9-4 (59) Alex Greaves 9/4 FAV: 306131: 6 b g Rock City - Nifty   67
Fifty (Runnett) Front rank, went on over 2f out, rdn clr appr fnl 1f: nicely bckd, fast time, qck reapp: earlier
won at W'hampton (clmr, rtd 75a) & Southwell (h'cap): '99 wnr again at Southwell (2, rtd 73a) & Chester (h'caps,

rtd 69): prev term scored again at Southwell (h'cap, rtd 58a): suited by 5/6f, has tried 7f: acts on fast, hvy
& any trk, loves fibresand/Southwell: eff with/without blnks: tough & in fine form.

2184 **CLAN CHIEF** 18 [2] J R Arnold 7-9-5 (60) A Clark 12/1: 000/02: 7 b g Clantime - Mrs Meyrick (Owen Dudley) Led, hdd over 2f out, ev ch until not pace of wnr dist: op 8/1: missed '99, prev term plcd thrice (stks & h'caps, rtd 74 at best, subs tried blnks): won 4 times back in '96 (rtd 82): eff at 5/6f on firm, gd & any trk, likes Sandown & Goodwood: weighted to win again sn.		2½	61
2428 **WILLOW MAGIC** 8 [3] S Dow 3-9-0 (60) B Marcus 11/2: 430343: 3 b f Petong - Love Street (Mummy's Pet) Waited with, rdn to improve 2f out, ran on fnl 1f, not pace of wnr: op 4/1: consistent: see 2428.		¾	60
2192 **ZEPPO** 17 [7] B R Millman 5-9-2 (57) G Hind 6/1: 040644: Cl-up, outpcd 2f out, late gains: op 5/1.		3	50
2555 **SUNSET HARBOUR** 3 [9] 7-8-7 (48) P Fitzsimons (5) 11/1: 163605: Rcd wide cl-up, rdn & fdd well ins fnl 1f: quick reapp: see 2252.		1	38
2478 **ZOENA** 6 [11] 3-8-11 (57) N Pollard 8/1: 0-0456: Chsd ldrs to halfway, sn wknd: qck reapp: btr 2252.		½	46
2555 **WINDRUSH BOY** 3 [1] 10-7-11 (38) S Righton 14/1: 54-007: Sn bhd, nvr a factor: quick reapp.		¾	25
2555 **HALF TONE** 3 [8] 8-8-0 (41)(bl) C Rutter 14/1: 030508: Sn badly outpcd, late hdwy: quick reapp.		shd	28
*2428 **PERIGEUX** 8 [6] 4-9-9 (64)(bl) (6ex) C Carver (3) 7/2: 500519: Prom 3f, sn btn: btr 2428 (soft).		2½	45
9 ran Time 1m 00.5 (2.1) (The David Nicholls Racing Club) D Nicholls Sessay, N Yorks			

4.30 0800 HCAP 3YO 0-70 (E)   1m4f   Good 57   -51 Slow   [73]
£2905   £830   £415

2051 **GOT ONE TOO** 24 [2] D Sasse 3-8-1 (46)(t) Martin Dwyer 33/1: 0-0001: 3 ch g Green Tune - Gloria Mundi (Saint Cyrien) Sn led & set slow pace, qcknd 4f out, styd on well, drvn out: 1st win: unplcd as a juv (rtd 62 at best, demoting arnd 12f on gd): best dominating arnd 12f on gd: wears a t-strap, handles a sharpish/undul trk.			51
*1997 **PINCHANINCH** 26 [7] J G Portman 3-9-7 (66) L Newman (3) 3/1: 004212: 3 ch g Inchinor - Wollow Maid (Wollow) Chsd ldrs, rdn/prog 2f out, kept on ins last, no threat to wnr: see 1997 (stks, firm).		1¾	68
2382 **BAHAMAS** 10 [6] Sir Mark Prescott 3-9-4 (63)(BL) S Sanders 15/8 FAV: 0-1233: 3 b g Barathea - Rum Cay (Our Native) Handy, rdn/prog 3f out, drvn/not pace of wnr fnl 1f: nicely bckd in 1st time blnks: see 2382.		½	64
*2463 **SHRIVAR** 6 [11] M R Channon 3-9-10 (69)(6ex) Craig Williams 3/1: 246414: Keen/rear, hmpd over 3f out, switched/hdwy fnl 2f, not reach ldrs: tchd 9/2, qck reapp: top weight, apprec a stronger pace: see 2463.		nk	70
2276 **SUAVE PERFORMER** 14 [3] 3-8-5 (50) N Pollard 9/2: 542445: Keen in rear, ran wide after 3f, hdwy over 2f out, wknd appr fnl 1f: tchd 7/1: see 2276, 1571.		1¼	49
2195 **HARD DAYS NIGHT** 17 [4] 3-7-10 (41)(2oh) G Bardwell 12/1: 000646: Mid-div at best: see 2195 (14f).		5	33
1270 **DURLSTON BAY** 62 [8] 3-9-1 (60) A Daly 25/1: 0-3007: Led early, rem prom, wknd qckly fnl 3f: abs.		hd	52
206 **GOLD KRIEK** 208 [10] 3-8-1 (46) R Brisland 20/1: 000-8: Rcd keenly at bhd: 7 month abs, modest.		13	23
2332 **STREAK OF DAWN** 12 [9] 3-7-10 (41)(9oh) M Baird 33/1: 00-009: V slow to start & lost 15L+, recovered by halfway, lost tch fnl 4f: h'cap bow, modest mdn form.		shd	18
2264 **AEGEAN FLOWER** 14 [1] 3-8-7 (52)(bl) C Rutter 20/1: 04000: Prom, wknd fnl 4f, t.o., 10th: op 12/1.		13	14
10 ran Time 2m 44.5 (13.0) (Christopher P Ranson) D Sasse Newmarket			

5.05 BET DIRECT HCAP 3YO+ 0-70 (E)   1m1f149y Good 57   -60 Slow   [64]
£2867   £819   £409   3 yo rec 11lb

*2206 **SUMMER SONG** 17 [9] E A L Dunlop 3-9-9 (70) G Carter 1/1 FAV: -45311: 3 b f Green Desert - High Standard (Kris) Prom, eff 2f out, pushed into lead cl-home, cheekily: nicely bckd, val for more than wng dist: recent Windsor scorer (fill h'cap): landed a private stks event at Newmarket on sole '99 start (rtd 79): eff btwn 1m & 10f: acts on fast, gd/soft & a sharp/undul or turning trk: on the up grade & can complete a hat-trick.			76
2296 **DION DEE** 13 [10] Dr J R J Naylor 4-8-10 (46) N Pollard 12/1: 036102: 4 ch f Anshan - Jade Mistress (Damister) Set v slow pace, qcknd appr fnl 2f, clr dist, hdd cl-home: gd eff against a prog rival, see 2011.		nk	48
2467 **SPRINGTIME LADY** 6 [6] S Dow 4-9-10 (60) R Smith 12/1: -22303: 4 ch f Desert Dirham - Affaire de Coeur (Imperial Fling) Dwelt, sn prom, outpcd 2f out, rallied & ran on ins last, no threat to wnr: see 457		2½	57
2296 **SILVER QUEEN** 13 [2] C E Brittain 3-9-4 (65)(VIS) B Marcus 5/1: -00024: With ldr, ev ch until outpcd appr fnl 1f: op 7/2, 1st time visor: see 2296.		¾	61
2296 **SHARP SPICE** 13 [8] 4-9-5 (55) S Sanders 5/1: 445255: Pulled hard & waited with, rdn/sltly outpcd 2f out, late hdwy, no threat: needs a stronger pace to be seen to best effect (often held up): see 2041.		½	50
2296 **MELLOW MISS** 13 [5] 4-8-10 (46)(bl) C Rutter 16/1: 330006: Rcd keenly in tch, rdn/no extra fnl 2f.		¾	39
1921 **SWING BAR** 29 [4] 7-8-5 (41) P Fitzsimons (5) 12/1: 00-007: Dwelt, bhd, no impress fnl 2f: see 965.		5	26
859 **SEWARDS FOLLY** 94 [1] 4-8-6 (42) N Callan 11/1: 05-008: Front rank, ev ch until wknd qckly fnl 2f: op 7/1: plcd twice over hdles (nov h'caps, rtd 80h, eff at 2m on firm & gd) since last Flat start: unplcd on the level in '99 (rtd 70 at best, auct mdn): poss stays 7f on fast.		6	18
-- **GINNY WOSSERNAME** [7] 6-7-10 (32)(4oh) S Righton 33/1: 9: Al last: 3 year abs, plcd once back in '97 (h'cap, rtd 30 at best, N Meade): subs trained briefly by W G M Turner: '96 Warwick wnr (clmr, rtd 52): eff around 7f on firm, gd & best in blnks: now with Dr J Naylor.		1¼	
9 ran Time 2m 09.4 (11.4) (Maktoum Al Maktoum) E A L Dunlop Newmarket			

Official Going   GOOD/SOFT. Stalls: Inside, except 6f - Outside; 12f - Centre.

6.30 BANSTEAD APPR HCAP 3YO+ 0-75 (E)   1m4f   Good/Soft 86   +01 Fast   [75]
£3425   £1054   £527   £263   3 yo rec 13lb

2429 **HALF TIDE** 8 [9] P Mitchell 6-7-10 (43)(4oh) J Mackay (5) 2/1 FAV: 3-0621: 6 ch g Nashwan - Double River (Irish Rake) Waited with, hdwy to lead over 2f out, styd on well, pushed out: deserved win: in '99 won at Lingfield (h'cap, rtd 52a): rtd 43a & 54 when rnr-up in '98: suited by 12f on equitrack or gd/soft.			48
2429 **COPYFORCE GIRL** 8 [1] Miss B Sanders 4-8-11 (58)(t) S Carson (3) 9/2: 40-132: 4 b f Elmaamul - Sabaya (Seattle Dancer) Cl-up, eff & sltly short of room appr fnl 1f, kept on for press, not btn far: see 2429.		1½	60
1878 **PRODIGAL SON** 31 [3] Mrs V C Ward 5-9-8 (69) A Beech (3) 11/1: 0-3603: 5 b g Waajib - Nouveau Lady (Taufan) Waited with, hdwy to lead over 2f out, sn hdd & onepace: stays 12f, winning form around 1m: acts on fast, gd/soft & both AWs: see 1878.		1¼	69
2295 **SACREMENTUM** 13 [2] J A Osborne 5-8-1 (48) G Sparkes (5) 12/1: 640244: Dwelt, sn in tch, eff to chall 2f out, no extra appr fnl 1f: see 2295, 381.		½	47

2309	**PENNYS FROM HEAVEN** 13 [6] 6-8-9 (56) Clare Roche (5) 9/2: 241245: Waited with, eff over 2f out, sn no extra: better expected after 2309, see 2138.	2½	51
2127	**GOODBYE GOLDSTONE** 20 [7] 4-9-9 (70) L Newman 7/1: 0-0506: Handy, wknd over 2f out: see 2127.	5	58
2033	**CEDAR FLAG** 24 [8] 6-7-10 (43)(3oh) Jonjo Fowle (0) 25/1: 100407: Al bhd: see 1707, 682.	9	19
2314	**ACHILLES SKY** 13 [4] 4-10-0 (75) Darren Williams (5) 10/1: 100238: Prom, wknd 2f out: btr 2314.	3	47
1707	**GOLD LANCE** 39 [5] 7-7-10 (43) (5oh) A Polli 33/1: 0-5609: Led, styd alone far side str, hdd over 2f out.	8	3
9 ran	Time 2m 44.97 (10.17)　　(The Fruit Cake Partnership)　　P Mitchell Epsom, Surrey.		

2627　　7.00 CHANTILLY FILL MDN 3YO+ (D)　　**1m2f**　　Good/Soft 86　　-10 Slow
£4114　£1266　£633　£316　3 yo rec 11lb

1796	**TWIN LOGIC** 35 [1] J H M Gosden 3-8-10 J Reid 11/10 FAV: 54321: 3 ch f Diesis - Indigenous (Lyphard) Cl-up trav well, led over 2f out, v readily: well bckd: promise earlier: stays 10f well on gd, gd/soft & prob any trk: gd confidence booster.		83
1343	**HAVANA** 56 [3] Mrs A J Perrett 4-9-7 Dane O'Neill 7/2: -33-42: 4 b f Dolphin Street - Royaltess (Royal And Regal) Led after 1f till after 2f out, sn outpcd by wnr: abs & ran to form of 1343: handles gd/soft.	8	73
2258	**POLI KNIGHT** 15 [6] J W Hills 3-8-10 (t) S Whitworth 9/4: -553: 3 b f Polish Precedent - River Spey (Mill Reef) Keen, waited with, rdn over 2f out, no impress: op 13/8: rtd higher 2258 & 1697 (gd/firm).	2½	69
--	**TACHOMETER** [5] H S Howe 6-9-7 A Nicholls (3) 33/1: 4: Waited with, btn 3f out on debut: plcd in a couple of recent h'cap hdles (rtd 72h, 2m1f on gd/soft, poss firm).	2½	65
2258	**MAGIC SYMBOL** 15 [4] 3-8-10 W Ryan 16/1: -005: Waited with, btn over 3f out: poss flattered 2258.	10	51
2188	**BROMEIGAN** 17 [2] 3-8-10 S Sanders 40/1: 006: Led 1f, with ldr till wknd 3f out: see 1725.	5	44
6 ran	Time 2m 13.44 (9.64)　　(K Abdulla)　　J H M Gosden Manton, Wilts.		

2628　　7.30 NABS MED AUCT MDN 2YO (E)　　**6f rnd**　　Good/Soft 86　　-15 Slow
£4153　£1278　£639　£319

1876	**ACHILLES SPIRIT** 31 [6] K R Burke 2-9-0 J Weaver 5/1: 01: 2 b c Deploy - Scenic Spirit (Scenic) Prom, eff 2f out, styd on well to lead ins last, rdn out: Apr first foal, cost 18,000gns: imprvd for debut & eff at 6f (stoutly bred), 7f+ sure to suit: acts on gd/soft & a sharp/undul trk: progress as he steps up in trip.		80
2480	**SEDUCTIVE** 9 [9] Sir Mark Prescott 2-9-0 S Sanders 5/12: 02: 2 b c Pursuit Of Love - Full Orchestra (Shirley Heights) Cl-up, ev ch over 3f out, sltly outpcd dist, kept on again cl-home: ran green but with promise over this sharp/undul 6f on gd/soft: sure to relish 7f & interesting next time on a more conventional trk.	¾	78
878	**MAMORE GAP** 92 [4] R Hannon 2-9-0 Dane O'Neill 11/4 FAV: 223: 2 b c General Monash - Ravensdale Rose (Henbit) Cl-up, led over 3f out, collared ins last, hard rdn, not btn far: 3 month abs & stays 6f on gd/soft & gd/firm.	½	77
--	**FLY BOY FLY** [7] M Johnston 2-9-0 J Fanning 4/1: 4: Dwelt, bhd, eff over 2f out, onepace: op 5/2: debut: Mar foal: bred to apprec 7f+ in time & showed promise here: improve.	¾	75
1893	**INVESTMENT FORCE** 30 [8] 2-9-0 M Roberts 25/1: 005: Waited with, rdn & no impress over 2f out.	3½	68
2029	**FORMAL PARTY** 25 [3] 2-8-9 J Reid 7/2: -66: Dwelt, waited with, brief eff over 2f out, sn btn: nicely bckd & better expected after 2029 (fine grnd, debut).	2½	58
886	**MARGARITA** 92 [1] 2-8-9 T Ashley 25/1: 07: Al bhd: now with C Weedon, see 886.	2	54
1924	**SPIRIT OF TEXAS** 29 [2] 2-9-0 T E Durcan 25/1: 008: Al bhd: see 932.	shd	59
--	**MONTEV LADY** [5] 2-8-9 A Daly 14/1: 9: Led till over 3f out, wknd: Apr first foal, dam 6f wnr.	10	34
9 ran	Time 1m 13.86 (6.06)　　(Achillies International)　　K R Burke Newmarket.		

2629　　8.00 SCOTS EQUITABLE HCAP 3YO+ 0-85 (D)　　**1m114y**　　Good/Soft 86　　+00 Fast　　[83]
£4914　£1512　£756　£378　3 yo rec 10lb

2528	**FREDORA** 4 [7] M Blanshard 5-10-0 (83) D Sweeney 13/2: 024101: 5 ch m Inchinor - Ophrys (Nonoalco) Nvr far away, led dist, kept on strongly, drvn out: qck reapp, fair time, top-weight: earlier won at Kempton (fill h'cap): '99 Salisbury wnr (class stks, rtd 87): '98 wnr again at Kempton (2, mdn & h'cap, rtd 91): eff at 7/10f on firm & gd/soft grnd, handles any trk, likes Kempton: gd weight carrier who remains in fine form.		86
1366	**KIND REGARDS** 55 [2] M Johnston 3-9-3 (82) J Reid 7/1: 14-052: 3 b f Unfuwain - Barari (Blushing Groom) Waited with, hdwy & ev ch dist, kept on but not pace of wnr cl-home: 8 wk abs: shld sn be winning.	1¼	84
2242	**SKY DOME** 15 [5] M H Tompkins 7-9-4 (73) S Sanders 7/1: 602303: 7 ch g Bluebird - God Speed Her (Pas de Seul) Waited with, prog 2f out, kept on under press & nrst fin: won this last term: comes late.	½	74
2229	**PUNISHMENT** 15 [11] K O Cunningham Brown 9-9-5 (74)(t) M Roberts 11/2: 000624: Set pace till collared dist, no extra: see 2229 (fast grnd).	¾	73
2433	**STOPPES BROW** 8 [8] 8-9-8 (77)(bl) I Mongan (5) 7/2 JT FAV: 006525: Dwelt, imprvd from rear 2f out, no qckn ins fnl 1f: see 2433.	1	75
2242	**LEGAL SET** 15 [9] 4-9-3 (72)(VIS) Darren Williams (5) 7/1: 200336: Mid-div, trav well & no room 2f out, kept on ins fnl 1f: had been off the track (coded?) after 12 starts: see 2242.	2½	66
2167	**RED LETTER** 19 [6] 3-9-6 (85) Dane O'Neill 7/2 JT FAV: 0-3267: Mid-div, rdn & btn over 1f out: see 1853.	1¾	76
2054	**MIDHISH TWO** 24 [10] 4-9-0 (69) J Fanning 12/1: 000008: Nvr nr ldrs: out of form.	4	53
4615¹	**SHANGHAI LADY** 250 [4] 4-9-1 (70)(t) W Ryan 20/1: 4100-9: Prom till halfway, wknd qckly & t.o. on reapp: trained by J Gosden to win at Brighton in '99 (mdn, rtd 74, little form subs): eff at 1m on soft grnd, handles a sharp/undul trk: wears a t-strap: now with P D'Arcy & equitrack clrly amiss.	dist	0
9 ran	Time 1m 49.16 (7.36)　　(P Goldring)　　M Blanshard Upper Lambourn, Berks.		

2630　　8.30 WOOTTON COND STKS 3YO+ (C)　　**1m2f**　　Good/Soft 86　　-55 Slow
£6572　£2332　£1166　£530　3 yo rec 11lb

*2265	**EXPLODE** 14 [2] R Charlton 3-8-7 W Ryan 13/8: 311: 3 b c Zafonic - Didicoy (Danzig) Made all at slow pace, qcknd 2f out, held on under hands-&-heels riding: prev Salisbury wnr (mdn): eff at 10f, will stay 12f: acts on fast & gd/soft, handles a stiff or sharp/undul trk: smart, fast improving, potentially Gr class.		108
967	**BRANCASTER** 85 [3] Sir Michael Stoute 4-8-13 J Reid 4/7 FAV: 400-52: 4 br c Riverman - Aseltine's Angels (Fappiano) Chsd wnr thr'out, kept on well: not btn far after 12 wk abs: prob not suited to this tactical race: smart performer at best & will prove sharper for this: see 967.	nk	102
1528	**PHILATELIC LADY** 47 [1] M J Haynes 4-8-8 S Carson (5) 14/1: -53303: 4 ch f Pips Pride - Gold Stamp (Golden Act) Chsd ldrs till outpcd fnl 2f: 7 wk abs: offic rtd 77 & flattered bhd 2 smart performers here.	2½	93$
--	**RIVERTOWN** [4] Mrs A J Perrett 6-8-13 T Ashley 25/1: 1/4: Waited with, no impress on ldrs fnl 3f:	4	91$

missed '99, won sole start in native NZ in '98 (1m, soft, mdn): almost certainly flattered bhnd some smart rivals.
4 ran   Time 2m 17.93 (14.13)   (K Abdulla)   R Charlton Beckhampton, Wilts.

2631	**9.00 JOHN CANN HCAP 3YO+ 0-80 (D) 6f rnd Good/Soft 86 +04 Fast**	**[80]**
	£4426 £1362 £681 £340 3 yo rec 6 lb	

2349 **VIOLET 11** [5] R C Spicer 4-7-10 (48)(bl) (4oh) J Mackay (5) 25/1: -00601: 4 b f Mukaddamah - Scanno's   **50**
Choice (Pennine Walk) Dwelt, gd hdwy dist, fin strongly to lead on line, rdn out: gd time: '99 W'hampton wnr
(mdn, rtd 78a): prev eff at 7f/1m, suited by this drop to 6f: acts on gd/soft, soft grnd & on both AWs, likes
sharp trks: eff with/without blnks/visor: prev rcd up with the pace, suited by switch to waiting tactics.
1792 **BODFARI PRIDE 35** [8] D Nicholls 5-9-10 (76) A Nicholls (3) 7/4 FAV: 001162: 5 b g Pips Pride -   shd **77**
Renata's Ring (Auction Ring) Tried to make all, caught on line: fine front-running effort, remains in fine form.
2371 **SLUMBERING 10** [6] B J Meehan 4-9-4 (70)(bl) J Reid 14/1: 000063: 4 b g Thatching - Bedspread   ¾ **69**
(Seattle Dancer) In tch, styd far side, ev ch ins fnl 1f, just btn in a close fin: bold tactics nearly paid off.
2184 **GOLDEN POUND 18** [9] Miss Gay Kelleway 8-7-10 (48)(3oh) G Baker (7) 10/1: 56-454: Waited with,   1¼ **44**
imprvd 2f out, not qckn ins last: see 2184.
2207 **BOLD EFFORT 17** [3] 8-10-0 (80)(bl) M Roberts 5/1: 052105: Rear, kept on fnl 2f, nrst fin: see 1887.   3½ **67**
*2207 **BEYOND CALCULATION 17** [2] 6-9-3 (69) P Fitzsimons (5) 9/2: 515016: Trkd ldrs, styd far side,   1 **54**
wknd fnl 1f: prob best to ignore this: much btr 2207 (fast grnd).
2261 **MY EMILY 15** [4] 4-9-4 (70) I Mongan (5) 8/1: 0-2167: Rear, imprvd over 1f out, no impress ins last.   nk **54**
2431 **COLD CLIMATE 8** [11] 5-8-3 (55)(vis) A Daly 9/2: 500048: Chsd ldrs till wknd dist: see 2431 (7f).   nk **38**
499   **SWEET AS A NUT 153** [7] 4-8-3 (55) L Newman (3) 25/1: 50-009: Nvr a factor: long abs: prev   1 **36**
trained by D Carroll, now with G L Moore: see 425 (AW).
2473 **RIBERAC 6** [10] 4-9-7 (73) J Fanning 10/1: -00200: Speed to halfway, fdd & fin last: qck reapp.   7 **40**
10 ran   Time 1m 12.71 (4.91)   (John Purcell)   R C Spicer West Pinchbeck, Lincs.

SOUTHWELL (Fibresand)   FRIDAY JULY 14TH   Lefthand, Sharp, Oval Track

Official Going   STANDARD   Stalls: 5f - Outside, Remainder - Inside

---

2632	**2.00 BET DIRECT FILL HCAP 3YO+ 0-65 (F) 5f aw str Going 28 +10 Fast**	**[62]**
	£2261 £646 £323 3 yo rec 5 lb Raced across the track	

1464 **TWO STEP 51** [12] R M H Cowell 4-7-10 (30)(t)(2oh) G Sparkes (3) 33/1: 60-001: 4 b f Mujtahid - Polka   **34a**
Dancer (Dancing Brave) Chsd ldrs halfway, rdn/led over 1f out, styd on well ins last: 7 wk abs: best time of day:
mod form prev, has broken blood vessels: eff at 5f on a sharp trk: acts on fibresand & runs well fresh in a t-strap.
2121 **MUJAGEM 22** [6] M W Easterby 4-8-12 (46)(bl) O Pears 14/1: 014602: 4 b f Mujadil - Lili Bengam   nk **49a**
(Welsh Saint) Prom, rdn/pressed wnr 1f out, kept on, al just held: clr rem: eff with/without blnks: see 1303 (1m).
2511 **SIRENE 6** [4] M J Polglase 3-9-5 (58) T G McLaughlin 14/1: 200003: 3 ch f Mystiko - Breakaway (Song)   4 **51a**
Driven chasing leaders halfway, kept on for press, no threat: op 8/1, qck reapp: see 300, 88 (7f).
2252 **E B PEARL 16** [2] A Dickman 4-8-6 (40) N Pollard 8/1: 055004: Chsd ldrs, not pace to chall: new stable.   nk **32a**
2252 **SING FOR ME 16** [11] 5-8-1 (35) N Carter (7) 10/1: 060065: Rdn/bhd ldrs 2f out, sn no extra: see 272.   nk **26a**
1976 **UNITED PASSION 28** [8] 3-9-1 (54)(t) S Finnamore (5) 6/1: -20036: Went right start, led till over 1f out.   nk **44a**
2505 **RING OF LOVE 6** [13] 4-9-10 (58) R Cody Boutcher (3) 12/1: 030007: Nvr going pace to threaten: op 8/1. ¾ **46a**
2078 **YABINT EL SHAM 23** [10] 4-10-0 (62)(t) L Newman (3) 10/1: 000008: Sn rdn, nvr pace of ldrs: op 8/1.   1 **48a**
2418 **TWICKERS 9** [17] 4-9-9 (57)(bl) G Parkin 14/1: 000609: Rdn chasing ldrs, btn 2f out: op 10/1.   1¼ **40a**
2058 **ANNAKAYE 24** [7] 3-7-11 (36) J Mackay 10/1: 0050: Nvr on terms: 10th: op 8/1: h'cap/AW bow.   2½ **12a**
2340 **IMPALDI 13** [1] 5-7-12 (32) P M Quinn (3) 10/1: 005000: Strugg halfway: AW bow: 11th: see 1143.   ½ **6a**
1910 **DUBAI NURSE 30** [5] 6-8-1 (35) P Hanagan (7) 20/1: -04600: In tch till halfway: 12th: see 901.   nk **8a**
2525 **CHRISTOPHERSSISTER 5** [9] 3-9-2 (55)(BL) W Supple 5/1 FAV: 000400: Hampered start & v slowly   1 **26a**
away, al bhd: op 8/1, tried blnks: lost chance at start: see 426.
1734 **SNAP CRACKER 39** [16] 4-8-11 (45) R Lappin 33/1: Bhd halfway: 14th: op 10/1: see 751, 235.   **0a**
2379 **JUST ON THE MARKET 11** [3] 3-9-4 (57) Claire Bryan (5) 16/1: 0-0000: Strugg halfway: 15th: see 1976.   **0a**
15 ran   Time 58.7 (0.9)   (J B Robinson)   R M H Cowell Six Mile Bottom, Cambs

---

2633	**2.30 CHATTANOOGA CLAIMER 3YO (F) 7f aw rnd Going 28 -28 Slow**	
	£2247 £642 £321	

2031 **MOONLIGHT SONG 26** [12] W Jarvis 3-8-8 M Tebbutt 5/1: 0-0001: 3 b f Mujadil - Model Show (Dominion)   **62a**
Trkd ldrs, drvn to lead ins last, going away nr line: AW bow: ex-German mdn wnr, unplcd/mod form on turf in
Britain: acts on fibresand & a sharp trk: apprec drop to claiming grade.
934   **PRESIDENTS LADY 88** [11] J G Smyth Osbourne 3-7-12 J Mackay (5) 33/1: 0-002: 3 b f Superpower -   2½ **46a**
Flirty Lady (Never So Bold) Led, rdn fnl 3f, hdd ins last & sn held: AW bow, abs: eff at 7f on fibresand: mod prev.
2264 **PHOEBUS 15** [6] W R Muir 3-8-11 (t) O Pears 15/2: 5-0003: 3 b c Piccolo - Slava (Diesis)   1¾ **56a**
Cl up/dsptd lead, rdn & no extra 1f out: op 6/1: imprvd effort: see 31 (C/D).
2017 **AFRICA 26** [10] T D Barron 3-8-8 W Supple 11/4: 0-1604: Rdn mid-div, nvr able to chall: see 1202.   3 **47a**
1663 **GYPSY SONG 42** [4] 3-8-13 N Whitworth 20/1: -005: Chsd ldrs, btn 3f out: abs, topweight: AW bow.   4 **44a**
2017 **GABIDIA 26** [2] 3-8-8 N Pollard 5/2 FAV: 3-6406: In tch 4f, sn btn: AW bow: see 1063.   nk **38a**
1665 **MAJOR BART 42** [8] 3-8-9 P Hanagan (7) 33/1: -05007: Mid-div, btn 3f out: abs: mod form prev.   4 **31a**
2134 **LOUS WISH 21** [7] 3-8-12 F Norton 14/1: 600008: Twds rear, no impress: blnks omitted: see 346.   5 **24a**
1858 **MINSTREL GEM 33** [13] 3-8-11 P M Quinn (3) 33/1: -009: Al bhd: AW bow, no form.   shd **23a**
2134 **MISS SPRINGFIELD 21** [5] 3-8-8 (vis) D McGaffin (5) 14/1: -30450: Dwelt, al rear: 10th: see 2036.   2½ **15a**
2387 **Yaheska 10** [1] 3-8-6 (bl) G Hind 33/1:   48   **Mikes Wife 242** [9] 3-8-8 D O'Donohoe 50/1:
2413 **Term Of Endearment 9** [3] 3-8-7 T G McLaughlin 14/1:
13 ran   Time 1m 30.5 (3.9)   (Rams Racing Club)   W Jarvis Newmarket

2634

3.00 0800 211222 HCAP STKS 3YO+ 0-75 (E) 1m aw rnd Going 28 -22 Slow [75]
£2873 £884 £442 £221 3 yo rec 9 lb

*2302 **GUILSBOROUGH 14** [6] J G Smyth Osbourne 5-10-0 (75) J Mackay (5) 3/1 FAV: 60-111: 5 br g Northern Score - Super Sisters (Call Report) Chsd ldrs halfway, rdn/led over 1f out, duelled with rnr-up fnl 1f, just prevailed in a bobbing heads finish: earlier won twice here at Southwell (h'caps): '99 Southwell scorer (h'cap, rtd 68a & 57, D Morris): suited by 7f/1m on fibresand/Southwell, handles fast & gd/soft: gd weight carrier: on top of his form. **81a**
*2380 **ROBBIES DREAM 11** [11] R M H Cowell 4-7-11 (44)(t)(6ex) P M Quinn (3) 9/2: -50012: 4 ch g Balla Cove - Royal Golden (Digamist) Cl up h'way, rdn/led over 2f out, hdd over 1f out, styd on well for press, just held: 6lb pen, in great heart at present & can win again here: see 2380 (C/D). *shd* **49a**
2380 **APPROACHABLE 11** [12] K A Morgan 5-8-0 (47) P Hanagan (7) 14/1: 320233: 5 b h Known Fact - Western Approach (Gone West) Prom wide halfway, drvn/kept on fnl 2f, not pace of front pair: see 710, 45. *2* **47a**
1250 **NOMINATOR LAD 64** [8] B A McMahon 6-9-11 (72) W Supple 20/1: 0-0004: Chsd ldrs, held fnl 2f: abs. *2½* **65a**
1840 **COOL TEMPER 34** [2] 4-9-13 (74)(t) T G McLaughlin 11/1: -55505: Trkd ldr, btn 2f out: AW bow. *2* **62a**
2542 **MAI TAI 4** [5] 5-8-11 (58)(vis) R Cody Boutcher (7) 10/1: 102566: Dwelt, twds rear, nvr on terms: qk reapp. *½* **44a**
1690 **THE BARGATE FOX 41** [14] 4-8-8 (55) M Tebbutt 16/1: 403007: Rear, mod gains for press: abs: see 260. *4* **31a**
2518 **WELODY 6** [10] 4-9-8 (69) D McGaffin 20/1: 040008: Led till over 2f out, fdd: qck reapp: see 658. *¾* **43a**
2479 **PIPPAS PRIDE 7** [3] 5-9-3 (64)(t) S Finnamore (5) 8/1: 350039: Rdn chsng ldrs halfway, wknd: see 2479. *1¼* **35a**
2264 **BELINDA 15** [9] 3-8-10 (66) J Bosley (7) 20/1: 040100: Al bhd: 10th: btr 1977 (C/D, mdn). *5* **28a**
921 **THE STAGER 90** [4] 8-10-0 (75)(tvi) S Whitworth 9/1: 145100: Dwelt, nvr on terms: 11th: 2 mth jmps abs. *1¾* **33a**
2460 **Philistar 7** [13] 7-8-13 (60)(bl) F Norton 16/1: 2380 **Future Coup 11** [1] 4-8-6 (53) O Pears 16/1:
13 ran Time 1m 43.4 (4.0) (Mason Racing Limited) J G Smyth Osbourne Adstone, Northants

2635

3.30 BEST BETS MED AUCT MDN 2YO (F) 6f aw rnd Going 28 -39 Slow
£2254 £644 £322

2077 **SEBULBA 23** [7] J G Given 2-9-0 S Finnamore (5) 15/8 FAV: 21: 2 b g Dolphin Street - Twilight Calm (Hatim) Cl up, led over 2f out, drvn clr 1f out, styd on strongly: op 13/8: confirmed promise of debut: eff at 6f, 7f shld suit: acts on fibresand & a sharp trk: open to further improvement. **77a**
-- **SPREE LOVE** [4] A G Newcombe 2-8-9 S Whitworth 20/1: 2: 2 b f Dancing Spree - Locorotondo (Broken Hearted) Chsd ldrs, drvn/chsd wnr 2f out, kept on, al held: Mar foal, 15,500gns 2yo: dam unraced: sire high-class juv & subsequent miler: stays 6f well, will get further: acts on fibresand & a sharp trk: gd debut. *1¾* **65a**
2383 **MONICA GELLER 11** [12] C N Allen 2-8-9 D O'Donohoe 33/1: 063: 2 b f Komaite - Rion River (Taufan) Twds rear, prog wide halfway, kept on fnl 2f for press, nvr threat: eff at 6f, return to 7f may suit: acts on fibresand. *2½* **58a**
2417 **MAID OF ARC 9** [3] M L W Bell 2-8-9 (t) J Mackay (5) 9/4: 0224: Dwelt, twds rear, late gains wide: Aw bow, op 6/4: return to 7f will suit: rtd higher 2417, 2057 (fast). *3½* **49a**
1488 **PRINCE NOR 49** [10] 2-9-0 G Hind 11/1: 05: Chsd ldrs 4f: abs: op 8/1: see 1488 (5f). *4* **44a**
1628 **MR SQUIGGLE 43** [2] 2-9-0 G Parkin 12/1: 06: Narrow lead till over 2f out: abs: op 10/1: see 1628. *1¾* **40a**
2383 **JUNIOR BRIEF 11** [1] 2-9-0 T G McLaughlin 40/1: -007: Cl up, fdd over 2f out: mod form prev. *4* **30a**
2277 **LATE AT NIGHT 15** [8] 2-9-0 M Tebbutt 10/1: 008: Chsd ldrs, btn over 2f out: AW bow: btr 2057. *nk* **29a**
2120 **DANITY FAIR 22** [6] 2-8-9 O Pears 16/1: 49: Cl up till over 2f out: op 14/1: btr 2120 (5f). *1* **22a**
2277 **HIGH SOCIETY LADY 15** [9] 2-8-9 N Pollard 33/1: 000: Twds rear, no impress: 10th: longer 6f trip. *2* **17a**
-- **TONY DANCER** [11] 2-9-0 J Bosley (7) 20/1: 0: Slowly away, wide/sn well bhd: 11th: Apr first foal, related to a 7f juvenile wnr, dam modest: showed little on debut here for K Bell. *¾* **20a**
11 ran Time 1m 17.60 (A Clarke) J G Given Willoughton, Lincs

2636

4.00 CONFEDERATES SELLER 3-5YO (G) 1m4f aw Going 28 -72 Slow
£1806 £516 £258 3 yo rec 13lb

2429 **SPOSA 9** [6] M J Polglase 4-9-0 T G McLaughlin 4/6 FAV: 305P01: 4 b f St Jovite - Barelyabride (Blushing Groom) Cl up going well over 5f out, led over 4f out & rdn clr fnl 2f, easily: val for 20L+, no bid, well bckd: ex-Irish, '99 Tramore wnr (mdn): eff at 12, stays 2m on fast & fibresand: apprec drop to sell grade. **49a**
2433 **WATER LOUP 9** [3] W R Muir 4-9-0 O Pears 14/1: 000062: 4 b f Wolfhound - Heavenly Waters (Celestial Storm) Held up, drvn/kept on fnl 3f, no threat: op 12/1: vis omitted, longer 12f trip: see 692. *15* **31a**
2253 **CROOKFORD WATER 16** [1] J A Glover 3-8-6 (tVIS) J Mackay (5) 5/2: 00-043: 3 b g Rock City - Blue Nile (Bluebird) Prom 3f out, sn btn: op 4/1: wore vis & t-strap, no improvement: AW bow: see 2253. *3½* **32a**
2381 **CAPERCAILLIE 11** [4] D E Cantillon 5-9-5 N Pollard 14/1: 22-064: Chsd ldr 5f, sn btn: see 2381. *4* **26a**
2381 **TALECA SON 11** [7] 5-9-5 (vis) R Lappin 14/1: 065405: Led & sn clr, hdd over 4f out, sn btn: vis reapp. *14* **11a**
2423 **PARTE PRIMA 9** [2] 4-9-5 (bl) J Bosley (7) 8/1: 030-46: Keen/prom 4f, sn bhd: op 6/1: see 2423. *4* **5a**
6 ran Time 2m 45.3 (12.0) (The Lovatt Partnership) M J Polglase Southwell, Notts

2637

4.30 GETTYSBURGH H/H APPR HCAP 3YO+ 0-65 (F) 7f aw rnd Going 28 -09 Slow [62]
£2324 £664 £332 3 yo rec 8 lb

1101 **GENERAL KLAIRE 72** [12] D Morris 5-10-0 (62) D McGaffin (3) 8/1: 364001: 5 b m Presidium - Klairover (Smackover) Mid-div, prog to lead over 1f out, styd on well under hands & heels riding: op 6/1: abs, prev with R Fahey: earlier won here at Southwell (C/D, sell): '99 wnr here at Southwell (fill h'cap, rtd 77a, B McMahon, rtd 52 at best on turf): '99 Wolverhampton wnr (auct mdn, rtd 67a, unplcd on turf, rtd 65): eff at 6f/1m, suited by 7f on gd, soft & loves fibresand/Southwell: runs well fresh: well h'capped for new connections. **69a**
*2118 **MY ALIBI 22** [4] K R Burke 4-9-13 (61) Darren Williams (3) 4/1 JT FAV: -12612: 4 b f Sheikh Albadou - Fellwaati (Alydar) Mid-div, smooth prog to trk ldrs when momentum checked over 1f out, styd on well ins last, wnr had got first run: op 7/1: travelled like a wnr, finished clr of rem & one to keep on the right side: see 2118. *¾* **66a**
*1979 **STILL WATERS 28** [9] I A Wood 5-9-3 (51) S Finnamore (3) 4/1 JT FAV: 600313: 5 b g Rainbow Quest - Krill (Kris) Cl up, led over 2f out till over 1f out, sn held by front pair: op 7/1: see 1979 (C/D). *9* **43a**
2297 **CZAR WARS 14** [8] P T Dalton 5-8-7 (41)(bl) J Bosley (3) 14/1: -00034: Cl up 6f: op 10/1: see 212, 199. *3* **27a**
2546 **GUEST ENVOY 4** [2] 5-9-4 (52) J Mackay (3) 15/2: 055505: Rear, mod late gains, no threat: qck reapp. *shd* **38a**
2481 **SHAANXI ROMANCE 7** [6] 5-8-11 (45)(vis) Hayley Turner (5) 9/1: 554366: Led till over 2f out, fdd. *1¾* **28a**
2130 **MUDDY WATER 21** [1] 4-9-0 (48) R Naylor (5) 16/1: 032507: Sn rdn, nvr factor: op 10/1: see 1303. *2½* **26a**
2379 **KILLARNEY JAZZ 11** [5] 5-9-11 (59)(vis) Dean Williams (7) 10/1: 150258: Twds rear, nvr factor: see 869. *3* **31a**
2281 **SEND IT TO PENNY 15** [3] 3-8-11 (53)(bl) P Hanagan (3) 16/1: 201509: Cl up 4f: op 10/1: btr 1804 (1m). *3* **19a**
1941 **SAN MICHEL 29** [13] 8-8-0 (34)(vis) G Sparkes (5) 6/1: 005430: Al bhd: 10th: op 5/1: see 148. *3* **0a**

SOUTHWELL (Fibresand) FRIDAY JULY 14TH Lefthand, Sharp, Oval Track

2032 **Druridge Bay 26** [7] 4-7-10 (30)(BL)(2oh) R Cody Boutcher (3) 33/1:
1806 **Tong Road 35** [10] 4-8-1 (35) T Hamilton (5) 33/1:
12 ran   Time 1m 29.2 (2.6)   (D Morris)   D Morris Newmarket

---

HAMILTON FRIDAY JULY 14TH Righthand, Undulating Track, Stiff Uphill Finish

Official Going: GOOD Stalls: 1m/9f - Inside, Remainder - Stands Side

2638 6.50 LADY RIDERS AMAT HCAP 3YO+ 0-70 (F) 1m3f Good/Firm 36 -05 Slow [34]
£2341 £669 £334 3 yo rec 12lb

1720 **WAFIR 39** [3] T A K Cuthbert 8-10-9 (43) Miss H Cuthbert (7) 6/1: 326421: 8 b g Scenic - Tanokey 49
(Grundy) Held up, stdy run under hands & heels riding fnl 3f & led well inside last: earlier claimed for £3,000:
'99 Redcar wnr (claimer, rtd 66): '98 Newcastle wnr (class, rtd 83, P Calver): eff at 10/12f on fast, hvy & any trk.
2392 **OCEAN DRIVE 10** [7] Miss L A Perratt 4-10-8 (42) Miss S Brotherton (5) 11/2: 654342: 4 b g Dolphin ½ 47
Street - Blonde Goddess (Gods Walk) Trkd ldrs, led 3f out, rdn inside last & hdd near fin: clr rem, see 2309.
2556 **ANNADAWI 3** [8] C N Kellett 5-10-13 (47) Mrs S Bosley 5/2 FAV: 210223: 5 b g Sadler's Wells - 12 37
Prayers' n Promises (Foolish Pleasure) Prom, rdn & onepace fnl 2f: quick reapp: see 1575 (g/s).
2556 **GOLD BLADE 3** [9] J Pearce 11-10-9 (43) Mrs L Pearce 13/2: -40054: Rear, mod gains fnl 4f: qck reapp. ¾ 32
2446 **GARGOYLE GIRL 8** [5] 3-10-1 (47) Mrs C Williams 7/2: 064455: Led 5f out till 3f out, fdd: see 2446. ¾ 35
2016 **HOMBRE 26** [4] 5-11-3 (51) Mrs A Hammond (7) 20/1: 550/46: Chsd ldrs, btn 3f out: see 2016. nk 39
2538 **BLAIR 4** [6] 3-9-13 (45) Miss Helen Bedford (7) 20/1: 040057: Cl up 9f: quick reapp: mdn, see 1661, 328. ¾ 32
2254 **WELDUNFRANK 16** [1] 7-11-7 (55) Miss K Rockey (5) 16/1: 005608: Bhd 4f out: mdn, see 848. 2½ 38
2238 **TEN PAST SIX 16** [2] 8-10-3 (37)(vis) Miss A Deniel (5) 33/1: -05609: Led till 5f out, wknd: see 1417. ½ 19
2276 **JIMGAREEN 15** [10] 3-10-10 (56)(bl) Miss E Folkes (5) 14/1: -06450: Bhd halfway: 10th: see 1632. 29 0
10 ran   Time 2m 23.3 (4.5)   (T A K Cuthbert)   T A K Cuthbert Little Corby, Cumbria

2639 7.20 EBF QUAL MDN 2YO (D) 5f Good/Firm 36 -12 Slow
£3493 £1075 £537 £268

1893 **RIVER RAVEN 31** [5] Sir Mark Prescott 2-9-0 G Duffield 1/3 FAV: 21: 2 b c Efisio - River Spey 84
(Mill Reef) Cl up, led 2f out, shaken up & styd on well inside last: confirmed promise of debut, bckd: April foal,
half brother to sev wnrs, including useful mid dist/styer Jahafil: eff at 5f, return to 6f+ sure to suit: acts on
fast & gd grnd, stiff/gall track: should win more races, particulary when tackling further.
-- **CHOOKIE HEITON** [4] I Semple 2-9-0 R Winston 20/1: 2: 2 br g Fumo Di Londra - Royal Wolff 1¾ 77
(Prince Tenderfoot) Chsd ldrs, every ch over 1f out, not pace of wnr inside last: April foal, cost IR£3,200: dam
an Irish sprint wnr: eff at 5f on fast grnd: encouraging intro & shld win a race on this form.
1835 **KIRKBYS TREASURE 34** [6] A Berry 2-9-0 C Lowther 10/1: -03: 2 br c Mind Games - Gem Of Gold 1½ 73
(Jellaby) Cl up, rdn & onepace from over 1f out: left debut bhd: eff at 5f on fast grnd: see 1835.
2009 **SEANS HONOR 27** [2] C N Kellett 2-9-0 R Winston 8/1: 544: Cl up, held fnl 2f: see 1706. 1 65
2234 **KILBARCHAN 16** [3] 2-8-9 Dale Gibson 4/1: 35: Led 3f, soon held: btr 2234. 4 55
1719 **NEENUAM STAR 39** [7] 2-9-0 J Bramhill 20/1: 3P: Pulled up lame after 2f: see 1719. 0
6 ran   Time 1m 00.5 (2.4)   (Hesmonds Stud)   Sir Mark Prescott Newmarket, Suffolk

2640 7.50 QUIGLEY MDN STKS 3YO+ (D) 6f Good/Firm 36 -17 Slow
£3445 £1060 £530 £265 3 yo rec 6 lb

1548 **MI AMIGO 46** [4] L M Cumani 3-9-0 J P Spencer 2/5 FAV: 0-2431: 3 b c Prince Dominie - Third 65
Movement (Music Boy) Held up, prog to lead over 1f out, shaken up & asserted inside last, styd on well: 6 week abs:
unplcd sole juv start: eff at 6f, stays a stiff/gall 1m well: acts on firm & soft grnd: runs well fresh.
2278 **CONSIDERATION 15** [7] A Berry 3-8-9 P Bradley (5) 20/1: -02442: 3 ch f Perugino - Reflection 3 61$
Time (Fayruz) Handy, rdn & kept on fnl 2f, not pace of wnr: eff at 5/6f: needs mdn h'caps: see 2096.
2421 **HERMITS HIDEAWAY 9** [3] T D Barron 3-9-0 G Duffield 9/1: -53: 3 b g Rock City - Adriya (Vayrann) 2 51
Al handy, rdn/every ch over 1f out, soon outpcd: only mod form on debut prev.
2374 **TARTAN ISLAND 11** [1] I Semple 3-9-0 (vis) R Winston 10/1: -00254: Chsd ldrs, held fnl 1f. shd 51$
2278 **DAVEYS PANACEA 15** [5] 3-8-9 C Lowther 5/1: 25: Dwelt, led after 1f till over 1f out, fdd. nk 45
2233 **TAKE NOTICE 16** [6] 7-9-6 C Teague 66/1: 00/066: Led 1f, cl up 4f: mod form. 9 32
6 ran   Time 1m 13.0 (3.2)   (M J Dawson)   L M Cumani Newmarket, Suffolk

2641 8.20 CHARD HCAP 3YO+ 0-75 (E) 6f Good/Firm 36 +01 Fast [68]
£3786 £1165 £582 £291 3 yo rec 6 lb

2364 **NAISSANT 11** [11] J S Goldie 7-8-8 (48) A Beech (5) 6/1: 253531: 7 b m Shaadi - Nophe (Super 54
Concorde) Nvr far away, led appr fnl 1f, kept on strongly: '99 wnr here at Hamilton (appr h'cap) & Carlisle
(class stks, rtd 67): '98 wnr again at Hamilton (2, h'caps, rtd 65, M Wane): eff btwn 5f & 7f on firm & hvy
grnd, any trk, Hamilton specialist: v tough & on a handy mark, reportedly in foal.
2420 **ENCOUNTER 9** [2] J Hetherton 4-8-3 (43) G Duffield 20/1: 400052: 4 br g Primo Dominie - Dancing 2 43
Spirit (Ahonoora) Outpcd in centre till ran on strongly appr fnl 1f, nvr nrr: likes Hamilton & well h'capped.
2282 **JACMAR 15** [13] Miss L A Perratt 5-8-11 (51) Dale Gibson 5/1: 052103: 5 br g High Estate - Inseyab nk 50
(Persian Bold) Rear, ran on ins last, nvr dangerous: back to best at fav trk (all 6 wins here): see 2097 (C/D).
2240 **SOUPERFICIAL 16** [14] Don Enrico Incisa 9-8-8 (48) Kim Tinkler (7) 14/1: 002064: Mid-div, rdn 2f out, ½ 46
styd on but nvr pace to chall: gd run, win another seller on softer grnd: see 1073.
*2395 **TANCRED TIMES 10** [6] 5-8-12 (52)(6ex) Kimberley Hart 6/1: 324115: Led after 2f till bef dist, no extra: ½ 49
prev 2 wins here, but over the minimum trip: see 2395 (5f).
2385 **FOIST 11** [8] 8-8-4 (44) T Lucas 10/1: 065026: Towards centre, mid-div, hung right halfway, nvr dngrs. 1 38
2535 **FACILE TIGRE 4** [8] 5-8-4 (44) J Bramhill 12/1: 060557: In tch, no extra appr fnl 1f, quick reapp. ¾ 36
2442 **MISTER WESTSOUND 8** [7] 8-8-12 (52)(bl) N Kennedy 20/1: 400008: Slow away, al bhd, hmpd dist. nk 44
2444 **GRAND ESTATE 8** [12] 5-9-3 (57) A Culhane 11/4 FAV: 452359: Nvr a factor: nicely bckd from 4/1. 1 46
2415 **DISTINCTIVE DREAM 9** [3] 6-9-10 (64) K Hodgson 4/1: 004050: Slow away, al towards rear: 10th. ½ 52
2418 **MISS BANANAS 9** [5] 5-8-2 (42) D Meah (5) 33/1: 040000: Prom till halfway: 11th, back up in trip. 3 23

830

HAMILTON FRIDAY JULY 14TH Righthand, Undulating Track, Stiff Uphill Finish

*2396 **HOWARDS LAD 10** [10] 3-9-4 (64)(bl)(6ex) V Halliday 9/1: 000510: Handy in centre till 2f out: 12th. ½ **44**
2444 **JOHAYRO 8** [9] 7-9-2 (56) R Winston 7/1: 024300: Early ldr, btn appr fnl 2f: 13th, see 798. *hd* **36**
13 ran Time 1m 11.9 (2.1) (William Graham) J S Goldie Uplawmoor, East Renfrew

2642 **8.50 CLASSIFIED CLAIMER 3YO+ 0-60 (F) 1m1f36y Good/Firm 36 -04 Slow**
£2383 £681 £340 3 yo rec 10lb

*2236 **PEGASUS BAY 16** [4] D E Cantillon 9-9-9 A Beech (5) 8/11 FAV: 162-11: 9 b g Tina's Pet - Mossberry Fair (Mossberry) Rear, wide prog 3f out, drifted right, led below dist, pushed out, just held on: well bckd: prev won here at Hamilton (sell): '99 wnr at Newmarket (sell, rtd 66) & again here at Hamilton (2, clmr/h'cap), also won over fences at Huntingdon (nov h'cap, rtd 88c, 2m, fast): eff at 1m/11.5f on firm, gd/soft grnd & equitrack, any trk, loves Hamilton: runs well fresh: has a fine runs to wins ratio for one so lowly rtd (7 out of 23). **55**
2309 **ALAMEIN 14** [1] W Storey 7-8-9 (t) T Williams 16/1: -00002: 7 ch g Roi Danzig - Pollination (Pentotal) Rear, imprvg when short of room & lost grnd appr fnl 2f, ran on strongly ins last, just failed: unlucky not to land this & is clrly eff at 9f in this grade: deserves compensation: see 1254. *shd* **40**
2393 **SECONDS AWAY 10** [2] J S Goldie 9-8-9 Dawn Rankin (7) 12/1: 424333: 9 b g Hard Fought - Keep Mum (Mummy's Pet) Mid-div, short of room appr fnl 2f till bef dist, wide prog & ch ins last, no extra: prob flattered. ½ **39$**
2244 **ROOFTOP 16** [12] C W Fairhurst 4-9-9 (vis) A Culhane 25/1: 000004: Chsd ldrs, hung right ent fnl 3f, onepace till kept on towards fin: massive drop in trip, stays 9f, see 453. *1¾* **50**
2392 **LITTLE JOHN 10** [9] 4-9-13 C Lowther 5/1: -34325: Front rank, no extra appr fnl 1f: btr 2392 (12f) ½ **53**
2397 **NOBBY BARNES 10** [7] 11-9-1 Kim Tinkler 10/1: 023026: Mid-div, feeling pace 3f out, late rally. *nk* **40$**
2479 **ACE OF TRUMPS 7** [6] 4-8-13 (t) N Kennedy 5/1: 120307: Cl-up & ev ch till fdd fnl 1f: longer trip. *hd* **38**
2533 **CLAIM GEBAL CLAIM 4** [8] 4-8-11 J Bramhill 16/1: 546-08: Led till dist, wknd: stiff task, quick reapp. *1½* **33**
2046 **MONACO 25** [3] 6-8-11 R Winston 33/1: -00009: In tch, onepace fnl 3f: stiff task. ¾ **32**
2245 **MAYDORO 16** [10] 7-8-6 J Fanning 14/1: 062400: Al towards rear: 10th, stiff task, see 1601. *hd* **27**
1940 **IRANOO 29** [5] 3-8-3 (t) J McAuley (5) 25/1: 002-00: Nvr a factor: 11th, see 1940. ¾ **32**
2533 **UNMASKED 4** [11] 4-8-10 N Carlisle 9/1: 003330: Prom till ent fnl 2f: 12th, stiff task, stablemate 2nd. *hd* **29$**
12 ran Time 1m 57.7 (3.6) (Don Cantillon) D E Cantillon Carlton, Cambs

2643 **9.20 PARLIAMO GLASGOW HCAP 3YO+ 0-65 (F) 1m5f Good/Firm 36 +08 Fast [55]**
£2894 £827 £413 3 yo rec 14lb

*2425 **SPECTROMETER 9** [8] Sir Mark Prescott 3-10-2 (71)(6ex) G Duffield 13/8 FAV: 06-411: 3 ch c Rainbow Quest - Selection Board (Welsh Pageant) Trkd ldrs, rdn to lead & edged right below dist, held on well: gd time, fine weight-carrying performance: 9 days ago won at Brighton (mdn h'cap): juv promise (mdn, rtd 72): eff at 12/13f on fast & gd/soft grnd, prob any trk: shrewd stable have this one ahead of the H'capper. **76**
2098 **HAPPY DAYS 23** [1] D Moffatt 5-8-11 (38) J Bramhill 9/1: 426252: 5 b g Primitive Rising - Miami Dolphin (Derrylin) Prom, chsd wnr fnl 1f, kept on but al being held: sound run against a leniently h'capped 3yo. ½ **41**
*2392 **COSMIC CASE 10** [7] J S Goldie 5-8-10 (37) Dawn Rankin (7) 7/1: 042113: 5 b m Casteddu - Le Fontainova (Lafontaine) In tch, wide into str, imprvd 2f out, styd on, nrst fin: remains in fine form, see 2392. *nk* **40**
2436 **ELSIE BAMFORD 8** [6] M Johnston 4-9-9 (50) J Fanning 4/1: 333334: Cl-up, led bef str till ent fnl 1f, no extra: prob ran to best, consistent, see 1683. *1¼* **51**
2422 **HASTA LA VISTA 9** [5] 10-9-9 (50)(bl) T Lucas 6/1: 021435: Led till appr str, rechall 2f out, onepce dist. *2* **48**
2319 **SIMPLE IDEALS 13** [10] 6-9-3 (44) Kim Tinkler 16/1: 020556: Bhd, late hdwy, nvr a threat: see 1563. *1½* **40**
2279 **BEST PORT 15** [2] 4-8-5 (32) P Goode (3) 8/1: 034307: Rear, wide into str, nvr a factor: see 2008. ½ **27**
*2422 **NEEDWOOD MYSTIC 9** [12] 5-9-7 (48)(6ex) A Culhane 6/1: -40018: Mid-div, same pace appr fnl 2f. *shd* **43**
2238 **PAPI SPECIAL 16** [9] 3-8-13 (54)(vis) R Winston 12/1: -00249: Well plcd, fdd ent fnl 2f: see 1909 (11f). ½ **48**
1936 **DIAMOND CROWN 29** [3] 9-8-5 (32) J McAuley (5) 25/1: 0-0200: Rear, brief eff 3f out, btn 2f out: 10th, won this last year off 7lbs higher mark, recent jumps rnr: see 1814. *5* **19**
2536 **NOTATION 4** [4] 6-7-12 (25)(2ow)(7oh) N Kennedy 33/1: 000040: Al bhd, saddle slipped, eased: 13th. *17* **0**
11 ran Time 2m 49.1 (3.6) (Lord Derby) Sir Mark Prescott Newmarket

YORK FRIDAY JULY 14TH Lefthand, Flat, Galloping Track

Official Going GOOD. Stalls: 5f & 6f Stands Side; 7f & Round - Inside.

2644 **2.10 MR KIPLING HCAP 3YO+ 0-95 (C) 5f Good/Firm 27 -21 Slow [85]**
£9061 £2788 £1394 £697 3 yo rec 5 lb

2451 **EASTERN TRUMPETER 8** [7] J M Bradley 4-9-2 (73) K Darley 8/1: 113021: 4 b c First Trump - Oriental Air (Taufan) Al cl-up, styd on well to lead ins last, rdn out: poorly drawn of late, earlier scored at W'hampton (2, h'caps, rtd 72a), Carlisle (class stks), Lingfield, Redcar & Ripon (h'caps): '99 wnr at Folkestone (clmr) & Ayr (h'cap): all wins at 5f, stays 6f: acts on firm, soft, fibresand & any trk: most tough & prog (9 wins from 34). **80**
2310 **BLESSINGINDISGUISE 14** [4] M W Easterby 7-9-5 (76)(bl) T Lucas 11/2: 502062: 7 b g Kala Shikari - Blowing Bubbles (Native Admiral) Led after 1f, styd on well till collared ins last, not btn far: tough 5f specialist. *1¼* **79**
2559 **ZUHAIR 3** [3] D Nicholls 7-9-0 (71) Pat Eddery 6/1: 000033: 7 ch g Mujahid - Ghzaalh (Northern Dancer) Missed break, bhd, styd on strongly & switched right over 1f out, nrst fin: quick reapp: h'capped to win sn, one to be on at Goodwood over 6f next time: see 2559. ¾ **74+**
*2517 **EURO VENTURE 6** [10] D Nicholls 5-9-6 (77)(7ex) Iona Wands (5) 10/1: 001614: Handy stands side, hard rdn 2f out, kept on: stable-mate of 3rd: fine run under a pen for landing 2517 (stiff). *shd* **78**
2473 **STORYTELLER 7** [1] 6-9-9 (80)(vis) Dale Gibson 10/1: 004305: Handy, rdn 2f out, rallied cl-home: slipping down the weights & prefers a stiffer 5f: see 1980. *1¼* **77**
2517 **RIVER TERN 6** [6] 7-8-7 (64) P Fitzsimons (5) 12/1: 600036: Slow away, bhd, eff over 1f out, nrst fin: qk reapp, stable-mate of wnr & landed this race last term off a 1lb higher mark: shld be plcd to win another h'cap. *1¼* **57**
+2418 **ANTHONY MON AMOUR 9** [8] 5-8-6 (63)(7ex) J F Egan 4/1 FAV: -00417: Cl-up, wknd over 1f out: stable-mate of 3rd & 4th: normal t-strap not declared here & it could pay to ignore this run: see 2418. *nk* **55**
1980 **POLLY GOLIGHTLY 28** [13] 7-8-11 (68)(bl) M Roberts 12/1: 220648: Sn bhd, mod late gains: usually shows plenty of pace, mulish today: see 1980, 1398. *1* **57**
2340 **BOLLIN ANN 13** [9] 5-8-10 (67) J Fortune 14/1: 010239: In tch, no impress over 1f out: btr 2340. *shd* **56**
2473 **LAGO DI VARANO 7** [2] 8-9-10 (81)(bl) Dean McKeown 12/1: 150530: Al bhd: 10th, btr 2473. *nk* **69**
1980 **WESTCOURT MAGIC 28** [12] 7-9-4 (75) A Culhane 16/1: 100-00: Handy stands side, wknd 1f out: 11th. *1¾* **59**

YORK FRIDAY JULY 14TH Lefthand, Flat, Galloping Track

2000 **BRECONGILL LAD 27** [14] 8-9-6 (77) Alex Greaves 14/1: 032200: In tch stands side, no impress over 1f out, 12th: stablemate of 3rd & 4th: twice below 1861, see 1580. *hd* **60**
2473 **ANTONIAS DOUBLE 7** [11] 5-9-2 (73) P Fessey 16/1: 000300: Jockey slow in removing hood when stalls opened & subs dwelt, al bhd: 13th: much btr 2310 & another example of some poor recent jockeyship: see 751. ¾ **54**
2548} **MAROMITO 371** [5] 3-9-9 (85) T Quinn 33/1: 10-0: Free to post, led 1f, wknd 2f out on reapp: won 1st of 2 juv starts, at Lingfield (auct mdn, rtd 84): eff at 5f on fast grnd, has run well fresh. 2½ **59**
14 ran Time 59.23 (2.43) (R G G Racing) J M Bradley Sedbury, Glos

2645 — 2.40 HEARTHSTEAD HCAP 3YO+ 0-85 (D) 1m rnd Good/Firm 27 -30 Slow [83]
£11017 £3390 £1695 £847 3 yo rec 9 lb

1760 **SPORTING GESTURE 37** [8] M W Easterby 3-8-1 (65) J Fanning 16/1: 0-0001: 3 ch g Safawan - Polly Packer (Reform) Set slow pace till 4f out, sn led again & qckned over 1f out, kept on well, rdn out: slow run race: '99 wnr at Catterick (nurs h'cap, rtd 77): eff at 7f, suited by setting the pace over this 1m: acts on gd/firm & a sharp or gall trk: well rdn by dictating matters at a modest pace: wore a sliding bit today. **70**
2492 **HARMONY HALL 6** [4] J M Bradley 6-8-8 (63) P Fitzsimons (5) 11/2 FAV: -44222: 6 ch g Music Boy - Fleeting Affair (Hotfoot) In tch, gd hdwy trav well 2f out, sltly short of room over 1f out, styd on late: qk reapp: confident ride, but often finds little under press (1 win in 38 starts): see 2492, 2349. *1* **66**
2349 **HAKEEM 12** [1] M Brittain 5-8-7 (62) D Mernagh (3) 10/1: 022033: 5 ch g Kefaah - Masarrah (Formidable) Handy, eff & sltly short of room over 2f out, kept on same pace ins last: gd run: see 2349, 1598. ¾ **63**
2356 **ADOBE 12** [3] W M Brisbourne 5-8-13 (68) R Mullen 7/1: 1133 4: Handy, rdn & onepace over 1f out. 1¼ **67**
2157 **THE WIFE 20** [2] 3-9-2 (80) Pat Eddery 13/2: -00355: Cl-up, led 4f out, sn hdd & no extra when short of room ins last: slipped back to a handy mark: see 2001, 1341. ¾ **77**
2367 **QUEENS PAGEANT 11** [9] 6-8-11 (66) M Roberts 12/1: 0-0446: Held up rear, hdwy & short of room 2f out, nvr plcd to chall: poor tactics held up off the pace in a slow run race: well h'capped/interesting. ¾ **63**
*2481 **STYLE DANCER 7** [7] 6-9-4 (73)(vis)(6ex) G Duffield 7/1: 040117: Keen, waited with, eff over 2f out, no impress: will do better off a stronger pace: in fine heart, see 2481. *nk* **69**
2216 **ZIETZIG 17** [5] 3-8-12 (76) J P Spencer 16/1: 500648: Keen in tch, btn over 1f out: see 1826, 689. 1¾ **68**
2349 **KALA SUNRISE 12** [11] 7-9-4 (73) J Stack 8/1: 003359: In tch, no impress over 1f out: op 16/1. *nk* **64**
2311 **TAFFS WELL 14** [12] 7-9-6 (75) J Fortune 6/1: 404260: Bhd, no danger: bckd: wants a stronger pace. *3* **60**
1860 **ROBZELDA 33** [10] 4-9-4 (73)(bl) Iona Wands (5) 16/1: 564400: In tch, btn over 2f out: 11th, see 1790. 3½ **51**
2356 **TARAWAN 12** [6] 4-9-10 (79) K Darley 9/1: 000050: Slow away, bhd: better in a strong run race. 1½ **54**
12 ran Time 1m 40.37 (4.57) (Steve Hull) M W Easterby Sheriff Hutton, N Yorks

2646 — 3.10 LISTED SUMMER STKS 3YO+ (A) 6f Good/Firm 27 -20 Slow
£17468 £5375 £2687 £1343 3 yo rec 6 lb

2343 **HOT TIN ROOF 13** [9] T D Easterby 4-9-4 K Darley 11/2: 112361: 4 b f Thatching - No Reservations (Commanche Run) Switched to race centre, slow away, hdwy 2f out, strong run fnl 1f to get up ins last, rdn out: earlier scored at Lingfield & Nottingham (List fills): '99 scorer at Newcastle (fills mdn, with J Banks, rtd 103): stays 7f, poss just best at 6f on firm, soft & any trk: v tough & useful with a turn of foot. **111**
2065 **CASSANDRA GO 24** [4] G Wragg 4-9-4 M Roberts 3/1 JT FAV: 0-1262: 4 gr f Indian Ridge - Rahaam (Secreto) Waited with, gd hdwy to load over 1f out, trav well & jockey only asked his mount for extra when wnr came along side, kept on, not btn far: bckd: another below par M Roberts ride & deserves another listed win. ¾ **109**
1410 **JEZEBEL 55** [1] C F Wall 3-8-8 R Mullen 14/1: 11-253: 3 b f Owington - Just Ice (Polar Falcon) Held up, hdwy over 1f out, kept on same pace: 8 wk abs & ran to best: lightly rcd: see 2078. 1½ **101**
2115 **MAGIC OF LOVE 22** [5] M L W Bell 3-8-8 M Fenton 14/1: 1-3304: In tch, eff 2f out, no extra ins last. *nk* **100**
1626 **MEIOSIS 47** [2] 3-8-8 (t) T E Durcan 3/1 JT FAV: -105: Led till over 1f out, no extra: abs, btr 1155. 1¼ **97**
2496 **COTTON HOUSE 6** [6] 3-8-8 Craig Williams 6/1: -15156: Sn bhd, eff over 1f out, sn btn: too sn? *2* **91**
2289 **FLOWINGTON 14** [3] 3-8-8 T Quinn 25/1: -50426: With ldr, wknd 1f out: stiff task, see 2289 *dht* **91**
2289 **DANDY NIGHT 14** [8] 3-8-8 J Reid 15/2: 2-0138: With ldrs, wknd over 1f out: btr 2289. 1¼ **87**
-1410 **HALLAND PARK GIRL 55** [7] 3-8-12 R Hughes 9/1: 1-6029: Handy, wknd over 1f out: abs, btr 1410. 1¾ **87**
9 ran Time 1m 12.21 (2.81) (Giles W Pritchard-Gordon) T D Easterby Great Habton, N Yorks

2647 — 3.40 CUISINE RTD HCAP 3YO+ 0-100 (A) 1m3f195y Good/Firm 27 +07 Fast [104]
£10869 £4123 £2061 £937 3 yo rec 13lb

-- **BOREAS** [6] L M Cumani 5-8-6 (82) J P Spencer 9/2: 5143/1: 5 b g In The Wings - Reamur (Top Ville) Cl-up, led over 1f out, qknd ins last, eased cl-home: fair time: missed '99, in '98 scored at Ripon (mdn, rtd 87): eff at 12f, further suit: acts on fast & gd: runs well fresh: fine training performance, the Ebor is the plan. **89**
1850 **LIGNE GAGNANTE 34** [4] W J Haggas 4-9-2 (92) J F Egan 2/1 FAV: 2-6022: 4 b g Turtle Island - Lightino (Bustino) Cl-up, hdwy & short of room over 2f out till over 1f out, kept on: shade unfortunate here & hvly bckd. *3* **94**
1850 **THREE GREEN LEAVES 34** [9] M Johnston 4-8-13 (89) J Fanning 11/2: 000103: 4 ch f Environment Friend - Kick The Habit (Habitat) With ldr, hard rdn over 2f out, kept on same pace: useful: see 1695. *1* **89**
1695 **FLOSSY 41** [7] C W Thornton 4-8-9 (85) Pat Eddery 4/1: 21-044: Waited with, eff & stly short of room over 2f out, kept on ins last: 6 wk abs: tough (6 wins from 17 starts), see 1170. *2* **82**
2350 **J R STEVENSON 12** [1] 4-9-2 (92) Alex Greaves 16/1: -00065: Set pace till over 1f out, no extra. *hd* **89**
1832 **FIRST OFFICER 34** [3] 3-8-0 (87)(2ow) Craig Williams 10/1: -02106: In tch, outpcd over 3f out, brief eff over 2f out, no impress: twice below 1539 (gd/soft). ¾ **83**
2502 **STRATEGIC CHOICE 6** [2] 9-9-11 (99)(bl) J Fortune 25/1: /46-07: Hld up, rdn & btn over 2f out. 1½ **93**
991 **LOOP THE LOUP 83** [8] 4-9-5 (95) A Culhane 16/1: 22-508: Bhd, nvr a factor: 3 month abs, see 732. *3* **85**
1216 **GALLEON BEACH 66** [5] 3-8-6 (95) M Hills 12/1: 32-30P: Lost tch over 6f out, t.o. & p.u. in home str: 2 month abs & clearly something amiss, returned distressed: see 1029. **0**
9 ran Time 2m 29.17 (2.37) (Aston House Stud) L M Cumani Newmarket

2648 — 4.10 JOHN WEST TUNA RTD HCAP 3YO+ 0-100 (B) 1m rnd Good/Firm 27 +11 Fast [103]
£9483 £3597 £1798 £408 3 yo rec 9 lb

2311 **DURAID 14** [3] Denys Smith 8-8-7 (82) D Mernagh (3) 10/1: -42141: 8 ch g Irish River - Fateful Princess (Vaguely Noble) Waited with, hdwy over 2f out, styd on to chall ins last, got up cl-home, drvn out: gd time: earlier scored at Catterick (h'cap): '99 wnr at Beverley, Ripon & Catterick (h'caps, rtd 79): eff at 7f/1m on firm, soft & any trk: likes Catterick: in the form of his life at 8yo, credit to his trainer. **88**

YORK FRIDAY JULY 14TH   Lefthand, Flat, Galloping Track

1068} **SWAN KNIGHT** 441 [1] J L Dunlop 4-9-1 (90) Pat Eddery 13/2: 10-2: 4 b c Sadler's Wells - Shannkara (Akarab) Led over 2f out, fine duel to the line & collared cl-home: reapp: won 1st of 2 3yo starts, at Newmarket (stks, rtd 89): eff at 1m on fast & a gall trk: runs well fresh & clr of rem here: useful, can improve. — hd 95

1851 **SILCA BLANKA** 34 [7] A G Newcombe 8-9-4 (93) J Reid 8/1: -11103: 8 b h Law Society - Reality (Known Fact) Waited with, eff over 2f out, sn onepace: not disgraced, best on a sharp trk: see 1778 (7f). — 3½ 92

2475 **SHARP PLAY** 7 [5] M Johnston 5-9-7 (96) J Fanning 6/1: 104204: In tch, rdn over 2f out, no extra. — hd 94

2528 **REGAL PHILOSOPHER** 5 [4] 4-9-1 (90) M Hills 11/4 FAV: 224035: Led early, hdwy & short of room over 2f out, no extra: well bckd: quick reapp, see 2528, 851. — 1 86

2003 **DESERT FURY** 27 [6] 3-8-6 (90) F Lynch 16/1: -30006: Bhd, eff over 2f out, wknd over 1f out. — 1¾ 82

2528 **ICE 5** [2] 4-9-6 (95)(vis) K Darley 7/2: 614407: Slow away, sn recovered to lead till over 2f out, no extra: quick reapp, 4 wins here prev: see 2351. — nk 86

2229 **EL CURIOSO** 16 [8] 3-8-8 (92)(BL) T Quinn 13/2: 016038: In tch, rdn & wknd over 2f out: blnks. — 4 75

8 ran   Time 1m 37.08 (1.28)   (A Suddes)   Denys Smith Bishop Auckland, Co Durham

---

2649	4.40 RAMESYS MDN 2YO (D) 7f rnd Good/Firm 27 -37 Slow

£7085   £2180   £1090   £545

2454 **SARATOV** 7 [4] M Johnston 2-9-0 K Darley 11/2: 31: 2 b c Rudimentary - Sarabah (Ela Mana Mou) Trkd ldr, led after 2f till over 1f out, rallied gamely to get up again cl-home, rdn out: 17,000 gns half brother to useful sprinter Cryhavoc & 1m/9f York specialist Ice: dam 10f wnr: stays 7f well on gd/firm, 1m sure to suit in time: useful & typically game M Johnston charge, should go in again. — 91

— **HURRICANE FLOYD** [8] J Noseda 2-9-0 J Reid 15/8 FAV: 2: 2 b f Pennekamp - Mood Swings (Shirley Heights) Hld up trav well, gd hdwy to lead over 1f out, rdn & collared ins last, no extra: well bckd: Feb first foal, cost 60,000 gns: dam 6f juv scorer: stays 7f on gd/firm: worried out of it here, but shaped with promise. — ½ 90+

985 **EMMS** 85 [12] P F l Cole 2-9-0 J Fortune 4/1: 23: 2 gr c Fastness - Carnation (Carwhite) Jinked right start, sn handy, rdn & kept on ins last: 3 month abs & stays 7f on fast, handles soft: win a mdn. — ½ 89

— **OLDEN TIMES** [1] J L Dunlop 2-9-0 Pat Eddery 7/2: 4: Waited with, eff & short of room over 2f out, styd on well under a kind ride ins last: well bckd: Apr foal, dam smart 6f wnr: bred to relish 1m+ in time & shaped with bundles of promise here: one to keep in mind. — nk 89+

2414 **RED CARPET** 9 [5] 2-9-0 M Fenton 13/2: 25: Handy, rdn over 2f out, onepace: stays 7f. — 3 83

2269 **GOLD STATUETTE** 15 [2] 2-9-0 M Hills 14/1: 06: Bhd, eff & short of room over 2f out, onepace: some promise & will relish 1m+: see 2269. — ¾ 81

2132 **CEZZARO** 21 [9] 2-9-0 M Roberts 10/1: 57: Sn bhd, eff over 2f out, no impress: op 7/1: see 2132. — ¾ 79

— **QUI WARRANTO** [10] 2-9-0 T Quinn 25/1: 8: In tch, hmpd when wkng over 2f out: debut: Apr foal, cost 350,000 Ff: half brother to a 1m/12f wnr: dam 12f scorer: will need mid-dists next term: with J Fitzgerald. — 1½ 76

— **PRINCESS CLAUDIA** [3] 2-8-9 T E Durcan 33/1: 9: Al bhd on debut: Feb 1st foal: need 10f+. — 2 67

— **CONGENIALITY** [7] 2-8-9 D Mernagh (3) 33/1: 0: Led 2f, handy till wknd over 2f out: 10th on debut: Jan foal: half sister to sev wnrs: with T Easterby. — 2 63

2005 **COTTONTAIL** 27 [11] 2-9-0 J Stack 50/1: 00: Al bhd: see 2005. — 7 54

11 ran   Time 1m 25.78 (4.48)   (J David Abell)   M Johnston Middleham, N Yorks

---

LINGFIELD (MIXED)   FRIDAY JULY 14TH   Lefthand, Sharp, Undulating Track

Official Going   AW - STANDARD; Turf - GOOD. Stalls: AW - Outside. Turf: Str - Stands side, 1m2f - Ins, 1m3f106y - Outside

2650	2.20 0800 211 222 CLAIMER 3YO+ (F) 5f aw rnd Standard Inapplicable

£2236   £639   £319   3 yo rec 5 lb

*354 **KRYSTAL MAX** 177 [5] T G Mills 7-8-12 L Carter 2/1: 0-2511: 7 b g Classic Music - Lake Isle (Caerleon) Narrow Lead, pshd 2L up ent str, ran on strly: 6 month abs: back in Jan won here at Lingfield (clmr): '99 wnr here at Lingfield (3) & W'hampton (clmrs, rtd 79a): '98 Lingfield (2) & Southwell (h'caps, rtd 80a): eff at 5/6f on fast, poss gd/soft, AW/sharp trk specialist, loves Lingfield: can force the pace: hard to beat in claimers. — 70a

2415 **FRILLY FRONT** 9 [1] T D Barron 4-9-5 N Callan 6/4 FAV: 050042: 4 ch f Aargon - So So (Then Again) Well plcd, unable to qckn with wnr ent str, kept on: well bckd: can do better, see 631 (made all, h'cap here). — 1 72a

2078 **SAMWAR** 23 [7] Mrs N Macauley 8-8-10 (vis) R Fitzpatrick (3) 9/2: 122563: 8 b g Warning - Samaza (Arctic Tern) Outpcd till kept on well fnl 2f, never nearer: ran to best at the weights, prefers fibresand, see 1237. — 1½ 58a

2519 **PRINCE NICO** 6 [4] R Guest 3-8-5 P Doe 25/1: 000654: With wnr till appr fnl 2f, same pace: qk reapp: treat rating with caution, eff rtd just 38: well clr of rem here: handles equitrack. — ½ 56$

2525 **PALACEGATE JACK** 5 [10] 9-9-0 (bl) G Carter 12/1: 300305: Raced wide, never in it: stiff task, op 8/1. — 4 48a

2415 **GLASTONBURY** 9 [9] 4-8-6 G Bardwell 25/1: 503006: Al bhd: stiff task, inadequate trip, see 425. — 6 25a

1932 **MINIMUS TIME** 29 [2] 3-7-10 (VIS) M Baird 10/1: 464067: Slow away, badly hmpd & snatched up bef 2f out, no ch after: tried a visor: this is best ignored, see 357 (seller). — 1¾ 15a

2204 **MITCHELLS MAYHEM** 18 [8] 3-7-10 A Polli 33/1: 6-58: Soon struggling: no worthwhile form. — 7 0a

8 ran   Time 59.47 (1.67)   (Shipman Racing Ltd)   T G Mills Headley, Surrey

---

2651	2.50 CARE FUND HCAP 3YO 0-70 (E) 1m4f aw Standard Inapplicable	[76]

£2990   £920   £460   £230

1593 **VANISHING DANCER** 44 [5] K R Burke 3-8-11 (59) N Callan 10/1: 3W0331: 3 ch g Llandaff - Vanishing Prairie (Alysheba) Mid-div, rdn briefly halfway, kept on to lead appr fnl 2f, drew clr: op 7/1, 6 wk abs, first win: unplcd in '99 (auct mdn, rtd 59): apprec return to 12f: acts on equitrack & gd/soft grnd, without visor. — 71a

2321 **DONT WORRY BOUT ME** 13 [2] T G Mills 3-9-0 (62)(vis) A Clark 9/1: 0-0162: 3 b g Brief Truce - Coggle (Kind Of Hush) Cl up, led halfway hdd & slightly hmpd turning for home, no extra: prob ran to best & well clr rem with visor reapplied: stable in gd form: see 457 (12f mdn, here). — 7 64a

*2041 **SHAMAN** 25 [6] G L Moore 3-9-7 (69) J Mongan (5) 7/2: -21013: 3 b g Fraam - Magic Maggie (Beveled) Rear, closed halfway, fdd entering fnl 3f: tchd 5/1, return to 1m/10f will suit: see 2041. — 5 64a

*2484 **DIVA** 7 [4] Sir Mark Prescott 3-9-7 (69)(5ex) S Sanders 7/2: 4AV: 052214: Well plcd till wknd appr fnl 3f: qck reapp, well bckd: switched to sand with a pen: rcd too freely & unsuited by step up to 12f?: see 2484. — 6 55a

2373 **ST GEORGES BOY** 11 [1] 3-7-12 (46)(1ow)(8oh) J Lowe 14/1: 600245: Led till halfway, bhd after. — 7 21a

2321 **ESTABLISHMENT** 13 [8] 3-9-5 (67) G Carter 7/2: 402156: Cl up 4f, soon lost place: better than this. — 6 34a

1644 **TE ANAU** 42 [3] 3-7-10 (44) M Henry 14/1: 0-0007: Al bhd: 6 week abs, longer trip, nds sells, see 300. — 1 10a

LINGFIELD (MIXED)   FRIDAY JULY 14TH   Lefthand, Sharp, Undulating Track

2332 **TITUS BRAMBLE 13** [7] 3-7-13 (47) P Doe 25/1: -00068: Bhd from halfway: AW bow, lngr trip, see 748. ½ 12a
8 ran   Time 2m 34.18 (4.98)   (Mrs Elaine M Burke)   K R Burke Newmarket, Suffolk

2652   3.20 RYDON GROUP MDN 2YO (D)   6f   Good 54   -42 Slow
£4023   £1238   £619   £309

2214 **CEDAR RANGERS 17** [6] R J O'Sullivan 2-9-0 P Doe 11/2: 51: 2 b c Anabaa - Chelsea (Miswaki)   80
With ldr, slight lead appr fnl 2f, held on well, drvn out: slow time, imprvd for eye-catching debut: 12,000gns
first foal, dam a French wnr: apprec step up to 6f, will stay further: acts on gd grnd, sharp trk: improving.
898 **MIDNIGHT VENTURE 92** [2] Mrs L Stubbs 2-9-0 D Sweeney 12/1: 0302: 2 b c Night Shift - Front Line   nk 78
Romance (Caerleon) Led till appr fnl 2f, kept on: op 8/1: back to form, apprec step up to 6f, goes on gd & soft.
-- **FOREST DANCER** [4] R Hannon 2-9-0 Dane O'Neill 6/4 FAV: 3: 2 b c Charnwood Forest - Forest   ¾ 75
Berries (Thatching) Chsd ldrs, hdwy & every ch dist, no extra fnl 100y: bckd from 5/2: 20,000gns Feb foal,
half-brother to a cple of wng juv sprinters, sire a miler: eff at 6f on gd grnd, shld improve & win similar.
-- **TAR FIH** [3] J L Dunlop 2-9-0 R Hills 10/3: 4: Dwelt, handy tho' rcd wide, rdn & ch appr fnl 1f,   2 64
sn btn: March first foal, dam smart 6f juv, sire a miler: stable juvs usually improve for their first run.
2383 **ORANGERIE 11** [1] J Dunlop 2-9-0 S Sanders 7/1: 05: Slow away, detached from front 4 till moderate late hdwy.   ¾ 67
2414 **IRON DRAGON 9** [5] 2-9-0 (t) J Weaver 6/1: 646: Dwelt, closed halfway, wknd fnl 1½f: lost   4 57
all chance at the start, not given a hard time after: now qual for nurseries & one to keep in mind: see 2414.
2189 **STORMY VOYAGE 18** [7] 2-9-0 G Carter 10/1: 47: Reared/banged head stalls, completed t.o..   27 27
7 ran   Time 1m 14.57 (5.77)   (We Are QPR Racing Partnership)   R J O'Sullivan Epsom, Surrey

2653   3.50 BET DIRECT AUCT MDN 2YO (F)   7f str   Good 54   -14 Slow
£2534   £724   £362

2182 **PATHAN 19** [1] S P C Woods 2-8-5 B Marcus 9/1: 051: 2 b c Pyramus - Langton Herring (Nearly A Hand)   76
Made all, pshd clr inside last, readily: half-brother to 5 wnrs, incl fair sprinter Sylvan Breeze: eff at 7f,
shld get 1m: acts on gd grnd & a sharp trk, forcing the pace: improved with every run.
2454 **EAGLES CACHE 7** [7] A Berry 2-8-9 G Carter 10/1: 4362: 2 b c Eagle Eyed - Cache (Bustino)   3 72
With wnr till no extra below dist: tchd 14/1: ran to best over longer 7f trip though return to 6f may suit: see 1838.
1924 **BROWSER 30** [8] K R Burke 2-8-9 N Callan 6/1: 03: 2 b c Rubiano - Just Looking (Marju)   1¾ 68
Chsd ldrs, rdn & flashed tail appr fnl 1f, not pace to chall: apprec step up to 7f & will get further.
-- **CASHNEEM** [14] P W Harris 2-8-9 J Mongan (5) 14/1: 4: Rear, wide, improved 2f out, soon same pace: 1¼ 65
op 10/1, not given a hard time: IR 7,000gns Case Law Mar foal, half-brother & dam wnrs abroad, sire a sprinter:
handles gd grnd: promising debut, sure to improve & one to keep in mind.
1424 **SHIRLEY OAKS 53** [9] 2-8-7 D Sweeney 12/1: 05: Waited wth, hdwy 2f out, no extra bef dist: 8 wk   1½ 60
abs: 14,000gns Sri Pekan May foal, half-sister to 4 wnrs, sire a sprinter: with Miss G Kelleway.
2182 **POLISH PADDY 19** [2] 2-8-5 R Smith (5) 12/1: 06: Wide, al around same place: tricky low draw.   1½ 55
1876 **ALAGAZAM 32** [4] 2-8-9 W Ryan 20/1: 07: Slow away, bhd, shkn up into mid-div fnl 1f. nrst fin: hd 58+
given a v kind ride & showed plenty of promise here: prob already need 1m: see 1876.
-- **PILGRIM GOOSE** [13] 2-8-9 S Sanders 14/1: 8: Outpcd till kept on fnl 1f: green debut: ¾ 50
IR£3,800 Rainbows For Life April foal, needed this: with M Tompkins.
2010 **STARRY MARY 27** [10] 2-8-9 G Duckwell 4/1 FAV: 049: Chsd ldrs, outpcd 2f out: more expected.   nk 46
-- **MERRY DANCE** [6] 2-8-0 M Henry 8/1: 0: Wide never a factor: 10th, tchd 20/1: 1,300gns Suave   4 38
Dancer March foal, dam & half-sisters won abroad, sire 12f performer: with A Jarvis.
2251 **DATIN STAR 16** [3] 2-8-0 A Polli (3) 33/1: 60: Mid div, no ch from 2f out: 11th.   shd 38
1876 **CRIPSEY BROOK 32** [11] 2-8-12 P Doe 9/2: 450: Never a factor, eased fnl 1f: fin 12th, tchd 6/1:   shd 50
shwd considerably better than this prev, keep in mind for a small nursery: see 1472.
843 **VISCOUNT BANKES 97** [12] 2-8-9 A Daly 10/1: 400: Chsd ldrs till halfway: 13th, 3 month abs.   ¾ 45
2137 **COCCOLONA 21** [5] 2-8-4 A Clark 10/1: 40: Wide, bhd from halfway: 14th, btr 2137 (6f).   ½ 39
14 ran   Time 1m 25.19 (4.79)   (S P C Woods)   S P C Woods Newmarket, Suffolk

2654   4.20 NICHOLSON FILLIES HCAP 3YO+ 0-70 (E)   6f   Good 54   +04 Fast   [68]
£3097   £865   £442   3 yo rec 6 lb

1842 **EVENTUALITY 34** [3] R F Johnson Houghton 4-9-7 (61) S Carson (5) 11/2: 6-5001: 4 b f Petoski -   68
Queen's Tickle (Tickled Pink) In tch, imprvd appr fnl 2f, led dist, pushed out, just lasted: op 8/1: '99 wnr at
Salisbury (fill h'cap) & Epsom (h'cap, rtd 69): plcd in '98 (rtd 66): eff at 6/7f, tried 10f: acts on firm, gd
grnd, sharp/undul or gall tracks: nicely h'capped & back to form.
2385 **PALO BLANCO 11** [8] Andrew Reid 9-9-10 (50) M Henry 15/2: 332462: 9 b m Precocious - Linpac   shd 56
Mapleleaf (Dominion) Led till appr fnl 1f, rallied under press & almost got back up: clr rem, op 11/2: consistent.
2230 **BRAMBLE BEAR 16** [2] M Blanshard 6-8-9 (49) D Sweeney 12/1: 010403: 6 b m Beveled - Supreme   2½ 48
Rose (Frimley Park) Prom, rdn & ch entering fnl 2f, not pace of front pair: better run tho' still below 1464.
2230 **STRIDHANA 16** [13] D R C Elsworth 4-9-3 (57) O Urbina 12/1: 00-004: Towards rear, hdwy & switched   ¾ 53
appr fnl 1f, styd on for press but unable to chall: found this sharp 6f inadequate, see 2230.
2031 **TALARIA 26** [5] 4-9-10 (64)(VIS) G Faulkner (3) 11/1: 100405: U.r. in stalls bef start, keen, bhd ldrs,   ¾ 58
rdn & edged left appr fnl 1f, not qckn: op 8/1: unsuited by visor? see 1082.
2230 **MAGIQUE ETOILE 16** [12] 4-9-1 (55) P Doe 3/1 FAV: 006226: Chsd ldrs, no extra appr fnl 1f: bckd, mdn.   ½ 47
*2415 **MUJAS MAGIC 9** [6] 5-8-13 (53)(vis)(6ex) R Fitzpatrick (3) 6/1: 005017: Dwelt, soon in tch, wide   shd 45
hdwy 2f out, soon onepace: better than this, 6lbs penalty for 2415.
2230 **JONATHANS GIRL 16** [10] 5-7-10 (36)(6oh) A Polli (3) 25/1: 400068: Mid-div thro'out: see 358.   ½ 26
1889 **TEA FOR TEXAS 31** [11] 3-8-4 (50) G Carter 9/1: 201609: Cl up till 2f out: btr 1212 (7f firm, clmr).   nk 39
1211 **BETTINA BLUE 66** [9] 3-9-0 (60) J Weaver 14/1: 65-660: Dwelt, keen, never got in it: 10th, 9 wk abs.   hd 49
2385 **Saffron 11** [7] 4-8-9 (49) A Clark 16/1:   939 **Flight Of Dreams 88** [1] 3-7-10 (42)(5oh) G Bardwell 33/1:
2252 **Pink Mosaic 16** [4] 4-9-1 (55) S Sanders 20/1:
13 ran   Time 1m 11.84 (3.04)   (Anthony Harrison)   R F Johnson Houghton Blewbery, Oxon

LINGFIELD (MIXED)   FRIDAY JULY 14TH   Lefthand, Sharp, Undulating Track

2655
4.50 C BREWER HCAP 3YO+ 0-70 (E)   1m2f   Good 54   -03 Slow
£3027   £865   £432   3 yo rec 11lb   **[70]**

2556 **WHISTLING DIXIE** 3 [2] D Nicholls 4-7-12 (40) M Henry 6/4 FAV: 260141: 4 ch g Forest Wind - Camdens **47**
Gift (Camden Town) Slow away, imprvd bef halfway, switched appr fnl 2f & ran on to lead dist, styd on well: qck
reapp, well bckd: earlier won at Pontefract (appr h'cap): '99 rnr up (h'cap, rtd 50, T Etherington): stays 14f,
tried 2m, best at 10f: acts on fast, gd grnd & fibresand, without blnks: in fine form & cld win again.
2212 **MYSTERIUM** 17 [5] N P Littmoden 6-8-0 (42) R Brisland (5) 11/1: 240002: 6 gr g Mystiko - Way To Go 1½ **47**
(Troy) Pld hard, prom, led appr fnl 2f, und press/hdd bef fnl 1f, styd on: clr rem, gd run despite leading too sn.
2270 **BRIERY MEC** 15 [10] H J Collingridge 5-8-4 (46) G Bardwell 13/2: -01503: 5 b g Ron's Victory - Briery 6 **42**
Fille (Sayyaf) Well plcd & every ch till no extra 2f out: capable of better, see 1509 (gd/soft).
2538 **LEVEL HEADED** 4 [3] P W Hiatt 5-7-11 (39)(2oh)(1ow) A Mackay 16/1: 035044: Led till appr fnl 2f, onepce. ½ **34**
2527 **YOUNG UN** 5 [6] 5-9-8 (64) S Carson (5) 3/1: 420255: Handy till outpcd appr fnl 2f: quick reapp. 2 **56**
2425 **ARTHURS KINGDOM** 9 [1] 4-9-2 (58) D Sweeney 8/1: 030446: Chsd ldrs, outpcd 5f out & no threat. shd **50**
2429 **MARMADUKE** 9 [8] 4-10-0 (70) W Ryan 14/1: -03667: Al towards rear: op 10/1, top-weight. 6 **53**
2245 **VANBOROUGH LAD** 16 [7] 11-7-10 (38)(1oh) S Righton 16/1: 021008: In tch till 3f out: gone off the boil. 2 **18**
1969 **REACHFORYOURPOCKET** 28 [9] 5-8-0 (42) P Doe 16/1: 366009: Never a factor: longer trip, vis omitted. ¾ **21**
2433 **MAX** 9 [4] 5-7-10 (38)(12oh)(t) A Polli 3) 20/1: 000030: Mid div till 5f out: 10th, stiff task, flattered latest. nk **16**
2139 **RENDITA** 21 [11] 4-8-3 (45)(2ow)(BL) A Clark 20/1: 00-000: Pulled hard bhd ldrs till wknd quickly appr 1¾ **21**
fnl 3f: too free in blinkers & is unproven beyond 1m: see 1259.
11 ran   Time 2m 09.97 (5.77)   (Mrs P D Saville)   D Nicholls Sessay, N Yorks

CHEPSTOW   FRIDAY JULY 14TH   Lefthand, Undulating, Galloping Track

Official Going   GOOD/FIRM.   Stalls: Str Course - Stands Side; Round Course - Inside.

2656
6.40 EVENING APPR HCAP 3YO+ 0-70 (F)   1m4f   Good/Firm 26   -24 Slow
£2268   £648   £324   3 yo rec 13lb   **[68]**

2490 **FANDANGO DREAM** 6 [12] M D I Usher 4-7-10 (36)(9oh) G Baker 11/1: 450441: 4 ch g Magic Wonder - **39**
Fandikos (Taufan) Rear, hdwy when ran wide 4f out, went on over 2f out, drvn out ins last: gd reapp, first
win: unplcd in '99 (rtd 76, prob flattered, mdn), subs disapp in blnks/visor: eff at 12/14f, has tried 2m2f:
acts on firm, gd & a gall/undul trk: fine run from 9lbs o/h here.
2254 **LUNAR LORD** 16 [2] J S Moore 4-7-11 (37) C Catlin (3) 9/2: 042022: 4 b g Elmaamul - Cache (Bustino) ¾ **38**
Cl-up, led on bit over 3f out, sn hdd, not pace of wnr well ins last: clr rem: consistent: see 2254.
2457 **KEWARRA** 7 [7] A Streeter 6-10-0 (68) L Vickers (5) 14/1: 50-003: 6 b g Distant Relative - Shalati 2½ **65**
(High Line) Rear, hdwy halfway, chall ldrs 3f out, no extra appr fnl 1f: back to nr best off top weight: see 1860.
2554 **STAFFORD KING** 4 [10] J G M O'Shea 3-7-13 (51)(1ow) D Watson (0) 16/1: 200064: Hdwy from rear nk **49**
halfway, styd on well fnl 2f, no threat to ldrs: see 1002.
2296 **INDIAN NECTAR** 14 [9] 7-9-1 (55) S Clancy (5) 7/1: -04205: Handy, hdwy halfway, rdn/no extra fnl 2f. 1 **51**
2245 **PREMIERE FOULEE** 16 [4] 5-7-10 (36)(6oh) R Thomas (0) 20/1: -06066: Rcd keenly in mid-div, rdn & ¾ **31**
dropped rear 2f out, late gains, no threat: see 260.
2273 **ACEBO LYONS** 15 [3] 5-9-1 (55) Lisa Jones (7) 13/2: 665047: Prom, drvn/fdd fnl 2f: see 2273 (2m). 1¾ **47**
2007 **CLASSIC COLOURS** 27 [5] 7-7-10 (36)(4oh) D Kinsella (5) 20/1: 00-008: Keen in mid-div, gd hdwy to 5 **22**
lead halfway, hdd over 3f out, sn lost tch: see 1523.
1880 **MONUMENT** 32 [13] 8-8-11 (51) Jonjo Fowle 11/4 FAV: 450-39: Waited with, nvr dngrs: btr 1880 (clmr). 1¾ **34**
2255 **CROWN MINT** 16 [11] 3-7-13 (52) Claire Bryan 9/1: 00-200: Dwelt, al rear, fin 10th: twice below 2255. 4 **30**
109 **BRIGHT BLADE** 231 [8] 4-8-0 (40) D Glennon (3) 14/1: 000-0: Prom, lost tch after halfway, fin 11th: 10 **5**
reapp/h'cap bow: mod mdn form in '99 (rtd 34a at best).
2245 **BOLDER ALEXANDER** 16 [1] 3-7-10 (49)(b)(7oh) Clare Roche(3) 20/1: 0-0000: Led 7f out-5f out, fdd, 12th. 8 **4**
2464 **WOODLANDS LAD TOO** 7 [6] 8-7-10 (36)(10oh) D Cosgrave (2) 50/1: 000/00: Led, to 7f out, sn bhd, 13th 29 **0**
13 ran   Time 2m 37.1 (6.0)   (Mid Week Racing)   M D I Usher Wantage, Oxon

2657
7.10 EBF NOV STKS 2YO (D)   5f str   Good/Firm 26   -32 Slow
£3376   £1039   £519   £259

2055 **JACK SPRATT** 25 [2] R Hannon 2-8-12 Dane O'Neill 9/4 JT FAV: 0331: 2 b c So Factual - Raindancing **78**
(Tirol) Made all, rdn & strongly prsd well ins last, drvn out: 1st win: plcd twice prev: Apr foal, dam a useful
6f juv wnr: eff at 5f, 6f shld suit: acts on fast, gd/soft & a gall/undul trk: deserved this.
1176 **MILLYS LASS** 68 [5] M R Channon 2-8-11 R Havlin 9/4 JT FAV: 312132: 2 b f Mind Games - Millie's nk **76**
Lady (Common Grounds) Waited with, short of room 2f out, switched wide appr fnl 1f, styd on strongly well
ins last, just held: 10 wk abs: unlucky in running & sure to regain wng ways sn: see 1176, 1083.
2083 **SHINING OASIS** 23 [1] P F I Cole 2-8-9(2ow) D Griffiths 7/2: -43: 2 b f Mujtahid - Desert Maiden 1¼ **70**
(Green Desert) Cl-up, chsd 2f out, no extra ins last: imprvd, tho' will apprec a return to 6f: handles fast.
2227 **LADY EBERSPACHER** 16 [4] Mrs P N Dutfield 2-8-7 L Newman (3) 3/1: 0424: Reared leaving stalls, ¾ **66**
rcd keenly in rear, hdwy to chall wnr over 2f out, no extra fnl 1f: see 2227.
4 ran   Time 59.7 (2.9)   (Lady Davis)   R Hannon East Everleigh, Wilts

2658
7.40 SUNSET SELL HCAP 3YO+ 0-60 (F)   1m str   Good/Firm 26   -03 Slow
£2422   £692   £346   3 yo rec 9 lb   **[54]**

2099 **PRIORY GARDENS** 23 [20] J M Bradley 6-8-12 (38) P Fitzsimons (5) 7/1: 035461: 6 b g Broken Hearted - **42**
Rosy O'Leary (Majetta) Made all, strongly prsd fnl 2f, styd on well, drvn out: no bid: '99 Leicester wnr (h'cap,
rtd 42), prev term scored at Goodwood & Carlise (h'caps, rtd 36): eff btwn 6f & 1m on firm, gd & equitrack:
handles any trk & goes well for an amat/appr: enjoys sell grade.
2331 **ARBENIG** 13 [11] B Palling 5-9-8 (48) D Harrison 4/1 JT FAV: 031052: 5 b m Anita's Prince - Out On ½ **50**
Her Own (Superlative) Cl-up, hdwy to chall over 2f out, styd on ins last, just held: gd eff: see 1732.
2427 **WHO GOES THERE** 9 [17] T M Jones 4-9-4 (44) R Price 14/1: 002003: 4 ch f Wolfhound - Challanging hd **46**
(Mill Reef) Dwelt, rear, rdn & styd on strongly appr fnl 1f, nvr nrr: back to nr best: see 1794, 265.

2427 **MUJKARI** 9 [12] J M Bradley 4-8-13 (39)(vis) G Baker (7) 16/1: 000004: Cl-up, rdn/no extra appr fnl 1f. — 5 — 32
2215 **WESTMINSTER CITY** 17 [2] 4-9-9 (49)(bl) L Branch (7) 14/1: 440405: Rear, gd hdwy appr fnl 2f, — ½ — 41
styd on, no danger: will apprec a return to further: see 748.
1889 **DIAMOND KISS** 31 [15] 3-9-3 (52) L Newman (3) 25/1: 0-0006: Prom, rdn/btn fnl 2f: see 850 (mdn). — 1¼ — 41
2460 **DANZAS** 7 [18] 6-9-7 (47)(bl) Claire Bryan (5) 8/1: 326257: Dwelt, rear, mod late gains: btr 2099. — ½ — 35
2448 **LE LOUP** 8 [3] 3-9-7 (56) C Catlin (7) 8/1: -00438: In tch, brief eff 3f out, sn fdd: see 2448. — 1 — 42
2561 **ISIT IZZY** 3 [1] 8-8-11 (37)(VIS) S Clancy (7) 16/1: 0/0309: Cl-up, rdn/lost tch appr fnl 2f: visor. — ½ — 22
2331 **DEMOCRACY** 13 [14] 4-9-10 (50) R Havlin 4/1 JT FAV: 005340: Handy, eff 3f out, fdd, 10th: top-weight. — ½ — 34
2460 **BALLYKISSANN** 7 [6] 5-8-10 (36)(VIS) C Rutter 25/1: 0/0000: Rear, mod gains, 11th: visor, qck reapp. — ¾ — 18
2264 **LEEN** 15 [4] 3-9-1 (50)(VIS) A Daly 11/1: 000060: Prom, wknd halfway, find 14th: visored: see 275. — 0
2331 **ARIUS** 13 [19] 4-9-5 (45)(t) J Tate 10/1: -00060: Dwelt, al rear, fin 16th: see 1068. — 0
3163} Velvet Jones 344 [16] 7-8-10 (36) D Kinsella (7) 33/1: 2448 **Who Da Leader** 8 [7] 3-9-4 (53) Dane O'Neill 14/1:
159   Lady Caroline 219 [10] 4-9-2 (42) A McGlone 33/1:   1423 Rose Of Hymus 53 [13] 3-9-1 (50) M Tebbutt 12/1:
1933 Lioness 29 [9] 4-8-12 (38) Jonjo Fowle (5) 25/1:   2460 Clifton Wood 7 [8] 5-9-3 (43) D Griffiths 40/1:
19 ran   Time 1m 34.2 (2.3)   (Gwilym Fry)   J M Bradley Sedbury, Glos

---

2659   8.10 JACK BROWN HCAP 3YO 0-75 (E)   2m49y   Good/Firm 26   -22 Slow   [79]
£3425   £1054   £527   £263

2332 **JACK DAWSON** 13 [8] John Berry 3-8-3 (54) G Baker (7) 8/1: 0W2501: 3 b g Persian Bold - Dream Of — 64
Jenny (Caerleon) Rear, hdwy to chall appr fnl 4f, sn led, pushed clr appr fnl 1f, cmftbly: unplcd in 3 '99 starts
for J Noseda (7f/1m mdns, rtd 75): relished this step up to a gall/undul 2m: acts on fast grnd: shld follow up.
*2273 **BARROW** 15 [6] J L Dunlop 3-9-7 (72) T Quinn 4/5 FAV: 4-0012: 3 br c Caerleon - Bestow (Shirley — 6 — 72
Heights) Rcd keenly, ran wide after 2f, led after halfway, rdn/hdd 3f out, not pace of wnr fnl 2f: clr of rem:
not disgraced conceding weight all round, ran to form of 2273 & could win again sn.
2354 **BLOSSOM WHISPERS** 12 [2] C A Cyzer 3-9-5 (70) I Mongan (5) 10/1: 0643: 3 b f Ezzoud - Springs — 5 — 67
Welcome (Blakeney) Mid-div, hdwy halfway, ev ch till not pace of front 2 fnl 3f: h'cap bow, poss stays 2m.
2321 **RAINBOW SPIRIT** 13 [3] A P Jarvis 3-9-6 (71) N Callan 10/1: 503434: Prom, dropped rear after — 2½ — 66
halfway, late gains, no threat: up in trip: see 2321 (11.5f).
2206 **SADLERS SONG** 18 [9] 3-7-12 (49)(2ow)(3oh) L Newman (0) 14/1: 5-5005: Rear, prog appr fnl 5f, — 2½ — 42
rdn/fdd fnl 3f: longer 2m trip: see 1758.
*2321 **JOELY GREEN** 13 [4] 3-8-10 (61)(bl) J Tate 7/1: 000016: Dwelt, rear, eff when hmpd 6f out, no — 1¼ — 53
threat after: up in trip: see 2321 (11.5f, firm).
1707 **COSMIC BUZZ** 40 [5] 3-7-10 (47)(2oh) Claire Bryan (5) 25/1: -00007: Led, ran wide & hdd after — 5 — 34
2f, ev ch till lost tch fnl 4f: 16 wk abs: see 1064.
2217 **BEE GEE** 17 [1] 3-7-10 (47)(8oh) Jonjo Fowle (0) 25/1: -01438: Led after 2f, hdd halfway, wknd 4f out. — ¾ — 33
2210 **FLIQUET BAY** 18 [7] 3-8-4 (55)(bl) T Ashley 10/1: -42039: Rear, eff halfway, no threat: btr 2210. — 19 — 26
9 ran   Time 3m 35.6 (7.8)   (The Premier Cru)   John Berry Newmarket

---

2660   8.40 EBF CLASSIFIED STKS 3YO+ (C)   6f str   Good/Firm 26   +08 Fast
£7313   £2774   £1387   £630   3 yo rec 6 lb

1983 **UNDETERRED** 20 [2] C F Wall 4-8-11 J Quinn 7/4 FAV: -03641: 4 ch c Zafonic - Mint Crisp (Green Desert) — 88
Settled rear, smooth hdwy appr fnl 1f, led well ins last, pushed out, cmftbly: val for more than wng margin:
best time of day: unplcd in '99 (rtd 109, Listed): '98 wnr at Yarmouth (mdn, ddht) & York (Listed, rtd 110):
eff at 6/7f on firm, soft & any trk: useful colt who is well h'capped on old form, could win again.
2473 **BRAVE EDGE** 7 [5] R Hannon 9-8-11 Dane O'Neill 7/2: 023042: 9 b g Beveled - Daring Ditty (Daring — nk — 85
March) Cl-up, went on over 2f out, rdn/hdd ins last, kept on but not ch with wnr: quick reapp: v consistent
& on a fair mark, but has not won for nearly 2 years: see 725.
1694 **PUNCTUATE** 41 [1] W J Haggas 3-8-5 D Harrison 15/8: -00003: 3 b g Distant Relative - Niggle (Night — 1¼ — 81
Shift) Chsd ldr, rdn/outpcd over 1f out, rallied ins last, no threat to ldrs: 16 wk abs, has been gelded since 1694.
2432 **THE FUGATIVE** 9 [6] P Mitchell 7-8-8 M Tebbutt 4/1: 045634: Set fast pace, hdd over 2f out, sn held. — hd — 77
4 ran   Time 1m 09.9 (1.1)   (S Fustok)   C F Wall Newmarket

2661   9.10 STRAIGHT MILE HCAP 3YO 0-80 (D)   1m str   Good/Firm 26   -05 Slow   [87]
£3822   £1176   £588   £294

2084 **YOUR THE LADY** 23 [1] M R Channon 3-8-11 (70) R Havlin 7/1: 0-0851: 3 b f Indian Ridge - Edwina — 77
(Caerleon) Rcd keenly cl-up, chall ldr over 3f out, went on appr fnl 2f, drvn out ins last: 1st win: ex-Irish,
unplcd in 3 starts in native country: eff around an easy or gall/undul 1m, further could suit: acts on fast grnd.
2300 **SOFISIO** 14 [2] W R Muir 3-8-4 (63) P Doe 10/1: 44-032: 3 ch g Efisio - Legal Embrace (Legal Bid) — 1 — 67
Sn led, rdn/hdd over 2f out, ev ch until no extra well ins last: acts on fast & both AWs: consistent, see 2300.
2108 **ARANYI** 22 [3] J L Dunlop 3-9-7 (80) T Quinn 3/1: -54133: 3 gr c El Gran Senor - Heather's It — ½ — 83
(Believe It) Front rank, rdn to improve appr fnl 2f, no extra ins last: top weight: proving tough: see 1863.
2330 **AMORAS** 13 [6] M J Wills 3-8-9 (68) B Marcus 7/1: 4-4004: Rear, rdn/prog 2f out, sltly outpcd appr — hd — 71
fnl 1f, rallied & styd on well ins last, no threat: worth a try over 10f now: see 1125.
*1671 **KELTECH GOLD** 42 [5] 3-8-12 (71) D Harrison 11/8 FAV: 0-0215: Rcd keenly in mid-dist, rdn/held — 1 — 72
appr fnl 1f: 6 wk abs, failed to settle today: see 1671 (gd/soft).
1967 **GOOD FRIDAY** 28 [7] 3-8-4 (63) L Newman 16/1: -656U6: Prom, rdn/btn appr fnl 2f: drop in trip. — nk — 63
2330 **OCEAN RAIN** 13 [8] 3-8-13 (72)(vis) A Daly 9/1: 050047: Waited wth, hdwy to chall 2f out, fdd fnl 1f. — ¾ — 70
4194} **SHERATON HEIGHTS** 286 [4] 3-7-10 (55)(1oh) Jonjo Fowle 20/1: 560-8: Led early, with ldrs till wknd — 22 — 31
qckly fnl 3f: reapp/h'cap bow: unplcd in 3 '99 mdns for K Burke (6/8.4f, rtd 56 & 34a): now with B R Millman.
8 ran   Time 1m 34.4 (2.5)   (John McKay)   M R Channon Upper Lambourn, Berks

Official Going   SOFT (GOOD/SOFT places). Stalls: Inside, except 10f - Stands' Side.

2662

6.30 RUINART FILLIES MDN 3YO+ (D)   7f122y rnd   Good 43   -26 Slow
£4396   £1256   £628   3yo rec 9lb

1811 **MISS DORDOGNE** 35 [2] G Wragg 3-8-12 R Hughes 1/7 FAV: -2521: 3 br f Brief Truce - Miss Bergerac   82
(Bold Lad) Made all, clr over 1f out, v easily: hvly bckd: earlier rnr-up twice, incl Newmarket mdn (rtd 94):
half sister to wnrs over 7f/1m: eff at 7.5f/1m on gd & gd/soft grnd: can run well fresh: simple task today.
2198 **LITIGIOUS** 18 [4] K R Burke 3-8-12 Dean McKeown 6/1: -22: 3 b f Mtoto - Kiomi (Niniski)   5 64$
Chsd wnr thro'out, no ch fnl 2f: again came up againts a useful rival: see 2198.
2347 **NOVELTY** 13 [1] N P Littmoden 5-9-7 C Cogan (5) 50/1: 00-003: 5 b m Primo Dominie - Nophe (Super   3 58$
Concorde) Rdn in rear, no ch from halfay: highly tried, off rtd just 25: no prev form.
466 **MEGS PEARL** 160 [3] W M Brisbourne 4-9-7 R Mullen 33/1: 000-0R: long abs: see 466.   0
4 ran   Time 1m 37.59 (5.19)   (J L C Pearce)   G Wragg Newmarket

2663

7.00 KPMG HCAP STKS 3YO 0-95 (C)   5f rnd   Good 42   +19 Fast   [98]
£8580   £2640   £1320   £660 Low draw a huge advantage.

2440 **DISTINCTLY BLU** 8 [3] K A Ryan 3-7-10 (66)(2oh) Iona Wands (5) 9/4 FAV: 162521: 3 b f Distinctly   73
North - Stifen (Burslem) Made all, ran on strongly rdn out: well bckd, fast time, made most of v fav low draw:
earlier won at Musselburgh (mdn h'cap): eff at 5/6f on fast & gd/soft: likes to force the pace on a sharp trk.
2289 **IMPERIALIST** 14 [1] R Hannon 3-8-12 (82)(BL) P Dobbs (5) 7/1: -50002: 3 b f Imperial Frontier -   2 83
Petrine (Petorius) Chsd ldrs, styd on fnl 1f, not rch wnr: back to form in first time blnks & with fav low draw.
2348 **SINGSONG** 12 [11] A Berry 3-9-7 (91) D Allan (7) 8/1: -43033: 3 b g Paris House - Miss Whittingham   1 89
(Fayruz) Broke well & chsd ldrs, eff dist, no qckn cl home: fine run from poor high draw: shld be winning sn.
2478 **GDANSK** 7 [12] A Berry 3-8-5 (75) J Carroll 12/1: 021004: Prom till no extra fnl 1f: longer priced   3 64
stablemate of 3rd & a fine effort from a poor high draw: one to keep in mind when better drawn: see 1712.
2525 **COLLEGE MAID** 5 [6] 3-7-13 (69) F Norton 5/1: 501005: Chsd ldrs, kept on but no ch to chall.   shd 58
2280 **WELCHS DREAM** 15 [10] P M Quinn (3) 25/1: -56006: Mid-div, nvr a factor: poor high   nk 54
draw & this is best forgiven: stable in fine form: see 1219.
2165 **NIFTY MAJOR** 20 [13] 3-8-10 (80) R Hughes 16/1: 020007: In tch till fdd fnl 1f: poor high draw.   1½ 64
2541 **ROYAL ROMEO** 4 [7] 3-8-6 (76) P Fessey 11/2: -01638: Chsd ldrs, hmpd 2f out, no ch after: qck reapp: hd 60
did not get this run of the race & no ch once hmpd: forget this: see 2541, 1768 (6f).
1384 **COCO DE MER** 55 [9] 3-8-5 (75) K Darley 16/1: 0-0009: Slowly away, no ch after: 8 wk abs, poor high   6 44
draw: usually a front runner, lost all ch at the start today: prev Chester wnr: see 1047.
2504 **KILBRANNAN SOUND** 6 [8] 3-8-3 (73) W Supple 20/1: -45000: Hmpd after st, al bhnd: forget this.   ¾ 39
2355 **JAILHOUSE ROCKET** 12 [4] 3-8-4 (74) C Nutter 7/1: -00000: Slowlt away, al bhnd: fin last.   nk 39
11 ran   Time 1m 01.01 (1.21)   (The Gloria Darley Racing Partnership)   K A Ryan Newmarket

2664

7.30 CORBETT COND STKS 2YO (B)   5f rnd   Good 43   -00 Slow
£9135   £3465   £1732   £787

+2318 **RED MILLENNIUM** 13 [3] A Berry 2-8-11 F Norton 4/6 FAV: 121211: 2 b f Tagula - Lovely Me   100
(Vision) Nvr far away, went on halfway, kept on strongly, rdn out: hvly bckd, gd juv time: earlier scored at
Musselburgh (mdn), Nottingham & Doncaster (stks): eff at 5f, will stay 6f: acts on fast & gd/soft grnd, handles a
sharp or gall trk: can run well fresh, loves to force the pace: cost just 2,000gns, deserves her ch in Gr 3 Molecomb.
*2483 **BYO** 7 [4] M C Chapman 2-9-0 R Hughes 12/1: -01512: 2 gr c Paris House - Navan Royal   1 99
(Dominion Royale) Prom, ev ch 2f out, onepcd till ran on well cl home: acts on gd & fast grnd: useful, see 2483.
-2469 **AZIZ PRESENTING** 7 [6] M R Channon 2-8-9 Craig Williams 7/1: 201023: 2 br f Charnwood   ¾ 91
Forest - Khalatara (Kalaglow) In tch, styd on fnl 1f, not pace of wnr: op 9/2: ran to best, poor draw: see 2469 (6f).
*2248 **PRINCESS OF GARDA** 16 [2] Mrs G S Rees 2-8-9 Dean McKeown 10/3: 431214: Led till halfway,   2 85
grad fdd: well bckd: front runner, not disgraced against some useful rivals: see 2248 (C/D).
*1764 **RUMORE CASTAGNA** 37 [5] 2-9-0 K Darley 16/1: -15: Slowly away, late hdwy but nvr dngrs: shd 90
big step up in grade, lost all ch at the start: 6f will now suit: see 1764 (debut, hvy grnd).
-- **ANTHONY ROYLE** [1] 2-8-8 J Carroll 20/1: 6: Dwelt, al bhnd on debut: stablemate of wnr & highly   14 54
tried: April foal, cost 6,000gns: sire a useful sprinter: shld be capable of better.
6 ran   Time 1m 01.97 (2.17)   (The Red Shirt Brigade)   A Berry Cockerham, Lancs.

2665

8.00 CAPEL CURE NURSERY HCAP 2YO (D)   5f rnd   Good 43   -06 Slow   [87]
£5586   £1719   £859   £429

1995 **MY LUCY LOCKET** 27 [1] R Hannon 2-9-7 (80) R Hughes 6/4 FAV: -3321: 2 b f Mujadil - First Nadia   85
(Auction Ring) Stumbled stalls, recovered to chase ldrs, imprvd to lead ins last, ran on strongly, rdn out: well
bckd: eff at 5f, will stay 6f: acts on firm & hvy grnd: handles a sharp trk: fine run in the circumstances,
reportedly well regarded & can win again in nursery h'caps.
1938 **LOVE TUNE** 29 [4] K R Burke 2-8-3 (62) J F Egan 9/1: -5362: 2 b f Alhijaz - Heights Of Love   1¾ 63
(Persian Heights) Tried to make all, collared ins last, not pace to repel wnr: fine run under a positive ride &
nearly made the most of fav low draw: met a useful rival & shld win similar: see 1304 (AW).
*1918 **CLANSINGE** 30 [7] A Berry 2-8-11 (70) J Carroll 9/1: -5313: 2 ch f Clantime - North Pine (Import)   1¾ 65
Chsd ldrs, short of room dist, kept on but ch had gone: not much luck & had a poor high draw: see 1918.
*1019 **DIAMOND MAX** 81 [8] P D Evans 2-8-7 (66) Joanna Badger (7) 8/1: -0414: Rear, late hdwy & nrst   1 58
fin: 12 wk abs: promising run from a poor high draw: fitter next time & one to keep in mind for similar.
2435 **FAYZ SLIPPER** 8 [3] 2-7-11 (56) P Fessey 9/1: 004245: Nvr better than mid-div: see 1918.   ½ 47
*1916 **COZZIE** 30 [5] 2-8-4 (63) F Norton 9/2: 305116: Front rank, wide ent str, grad fdd: speedy sort, not   ¾ 51
handle sharp home turn? dual selling wnr prev: see 1916 (AW).
*2388 **ITALIAN AFFAIR** 10 [6] 2-8-7 (66)(6ex) R Mullen 8/1: 020217: In tch 3½f, wknd: see 2388.   2 48
1641 **TICCATOO** 42 [2] 2-8-11 (70) P M Quinn (3) 14/1: -1008: Struggling in rear, eased when btn: 6 wk abs.   3 43
8 ran   Time 1m 02.29 (2.49)   (Mrs H F Prendergast)   R Hannon East Everleigh, Wilts.

CHESTER   FRIDAY JULY 14TH   Lefthand, Very Tight Track

2666   8.30 PINNACL HCAP 3YO 0-85 (D)   1m2f75y   Good 43 -14 Slow   [90]
£8736   £2688   £1344   £672

2450 **PEDRO PETE** 8 [7] M R Channon 3-8-6 (68) Craig Williams 8/1: 414331: 3 ch g Fraam - Stride Home **73**
(Absalom) Trkd ldrs, imprvd to lead cl home, rdn out: earlier won at Lingfield (AW h'cap): eff at 10f, 12f
will suit: acts on gd, firm & equitrack: handles a sharp trk: had the run of the race today.
2030 **MYTHICAL KING** 26 [3] B Palling 3-9-5 (81) K Darley 7/1: -33142: 3 b c Fairy King - Whatcombe 1½ **83**
(Alleged) In tch till hmpd & lost place after 2f, no room 2f out, switched & flew cl home, not rch wnr: no luck
& prob unlucky: best up with the pace prev: must be given another chance: see 2030, 1812.
2116 **EL ZITO** 22 [10] M G Quinlan 3-9-7 (83) J F Egan 5/1: 021103: 3 b g Mukaddamah - Samite (Tennyson) ½ **84**
In tch, went on over 2f out, wandered ins last, caught cl home: back to form, went off too fast in 2116: see 1919.
2157 **BALI BATIK** 20 [1] G Wragg 3-9-5 (81) R Hughes 13/2: 431044: Rear, prog to chase ldrs dist, not 2 **79**
qckn cl home: seems to stay 10f: see1261 (mdn).
*2581 **PIPS WAY** 2 [2] 3-9-7 (83)(6ex) R Mullen 13/2: 414315: Mid-div & going well when short of ½ **80**
room 2f out, ran on late but ch had gone: qck reapp, 5L clr rem: no luck today: 6lbs pen for 2581.
2272 **MICKLEY** 15 [11] 3-8-9 (71)(VIS) W Supple 10/1: 254536: Rear, improving when hmpd ent str, fin well: 5 **60**
first time visor: another hard luck story, a return to 12f shld suit: eye-catching here, see 2272.
2484 **CARELESS** 7 [8] 3-7-10 (58)(bl)(3oh) P Fessey 12/1: -40427: Prom till fdd dist: see 2484. 2½ **44**
2450 **GOLDEN CHANCE** 8 [4] 3-9-2 (78) J Reid 4/1 FAV: 322138: Mid-div, prog to chall ent str, sn wknd: shd **64**
well bckd from 6/1: a big run clearly expected, prob finds less than expected under press: see 2159.
2445 **KAIAPOI** 8 [12] 3-9-4 (80) P M Quinn (3) 10/1: 11U359: Rear, eff 3f out, btn dist: btr 2110 (12f). 2 **63**
2358 **INVER GOLD** 12 [9] 3-8-13 (75) S Whitworth 16/1: 300430: Nvr nr ldrs: fin 10th: btr 2358. 1½ **56**
2534 **RHODAMINE** 4 [5] 3-8-5 (67) Dean McKeown 12/1: 614340: Dwelt, prog when short of room 2f out, sn 6 **39**
btn: fin 11th, qck reapp: see 2284 (claimer).
*2322 **LAGO DI COMO** 13 [6] 3-8-9 (71) F Norton 20/1: -30410: Led till 2f out, wknd into last. 3½ **38**
12 ran   Time 2m 14.46 (5.96)   (Peter Taplin)   M R Channon West Isley, Berks.

2667   9.00 CHESHIRE CLASS STKS 3YO+ 0-70 (E)   1m4f66y   Good 43 -13 Slow
£3961   £1219   £609   £304   3yo rec 13lb

2527 **CAPRIOLO** 5 [5] R Hannon 4-9-6 (bl) R Hughes 11/2: 1-6001: 4 ch g Priolo - Carroll's Canyon (Hatim) **69**
Broke well & made all, styd on strongly fnl 1f, rdn out: qck reapp: '99 wnr at Salisbury (mdn h'cap) & Leicester
(h'cap, rtd 73): eff at 10/12f, acts on firm & gd/soft grnd: tried a visor, better in blnks: handles a sharp or
stiff trk: can set the pace: well bckd from the front by R Hughes today.
*2284 **LULLABY** 14 [7] J O'Keeffe 3-8-6 K Darley 11/4: -34012: 3 b f Unfuwain - Heart's Harmony 2½ **63**
(Blushing Groom) Waited with, prog 2f out, took 2nd ins last, not rch wnr: well bckd: prev trained by J Fanshawe:
eff at 10/12f on gd & fast, handles hvy: see 2284 (claimer).
1594 **GEMINI GUEST** 44 [9] G G Margarson 4-9-6 J Carroll 12/1: 0-0503: 4 ch g Waajib - Aldhabyih 1½ **62**
(General Assembly) Rear, prog 4f out, ev ch dist, sn onepcd: 5L clr rem, 6 wk abs: see 1271 (10f).
2461 **JAMAICAN FLIGHT** 7 [2] Mrs S Lamyman 7-9-6 J F Egan 11/2: 006554: Prom, outpcd 4f out, no ch after. 5 **54**
2482 **ACQUITTAL** 7 [8] 8-9-6 F Norton 40/1: -00445: Rdn in rear, nvr nr ldrs: off rtd just 31. 1 **52$**
2246 **CRYSTAL FLITE** 16 [6] 3-8-4 O Pears 9/4 FAV: 3-002b: Prom till wknd fnl 1½f: btr 2246. 13 **29**
1777 **ANGIE MARINIE** 37 [4] 4-9-3 W Supple 7/1: 05-067: Prom 10f, wknd: unplcd in a h'cap hdle since 1777. 6 **20**
2510 **EMMAS HOPE** 6 [3] 3-8-4 P Fessey 66/1: 5-0008: In tch 1m, sn wknd & fin last: qck reapp. ¾ **19**
8 ran   Time 2m 43.34 (6.94)   (Taylor Homer Racing)   R Hannon East Everleigh, Wilts.

CHESTER   SATURDAY JULY 15TH   Lefthand, Very Tight Track

Official Going   GOOD/SOFT (GOOD PLACES) Stalls: Inside, except 10f - Stands Side

2668   2.20 EBF ARTHUR MDN 2YO (D)   5f rnd   Good/Firm 23 -35 Slow
£4212   £1296   £648   £324

1870 **KARITSA** 33 [2] M R Channon 2-8-9 Craig Williams 6/4: 251: 2 b f Rudimentary - Desert Ditty (Green **72**
Desert) Made all, holding rivals fnl 1f, styd on well, pushed out: op 5/4: eff forcing the pace over a sharp 5f,
will get further: dam a 6f wnr: acts on fast grnd: speedy filly, can improve further.
2248 **SMIRFYS PARTY** 17 [3] B A McMahon 2-9-0 T G McLaughlin 5/1: 62: 2 ch c Clantime - Party Scenes 1½ **72**
(Most Welcome) Dwelt, sn chsd ldrs, chsd wnr over 1f out, kept on, always held: acts on fast grnd: see 2248.
2361 **AMAMACKEMMUSH** 12 [4] K A Ryan 2-9-0 A Culhane 11/8 FAV: -0223: 2 b g General Monash - Paganina 5 **60**
(Galetto) Cl up 3f, held over 1f out: hvly bckd: just btr 2361, 2100.
2435 **PAT PINKNEY** 9 [1] E J Alston 2-8-9 E Ahern 25/1: -05454: Chsd ldrs, held fnl 2f: mod form prev. ¾ **53**
-- **HEATHYARDS SIGNET** [5] 2-9-0 R Winston 25/1: 5: Sn outpcd/held: May foal, dam a 5f juv wnr. 12 **36**
5 ran   Time 1m 02.7 (2.9)   (Colin Brown Racing III)   M R Channon West Isley, Berks

2669   2.50 LISTED JANI CITY WALL STKS 3YO+ (A)   5f rnd   Good/Firm 23 +05 Fast
£20300   £7700   £3850   £1750   3 yo rec 5 lb   Low draw imperative over 5/6f.

2335 **INDIAN SPARK** 14 [1] J S Goldie 6-9-0 A Culhane 5/1: 110201: 6 ch g Indian Ridge - Annes Gift (Ballymoss) **110**
Rear, swtchd & prog to chall fnl 2f, styd on strongly fnl 1f, gd time, best draw: earlier won at
Newcastle, Haydock & York (h'caps): '99 York wnr (rtd h'cap, rtd 91): '98 wnr at Thirsk & Doncaster (2):
suited by 5/6f on any grnd or trk, loves York & Doncaster: gd weight carrier: most progressive & smart.
2065 **ROSSELLI** 25 [2] A Berry 4-9-0 J Carroll 16/1: -46002: 4 b h Puissance - Miss Rossi (Artaius) 1½ **105**
Led/dsptd lead, rdn/hdd ins last, held by wnr near fin: back to form from fav low draw: see 1172, 927.
+2335 **TEDBURROW** 14 [5] E J Alston 8-9-4 J Bramhill 9/4 FAV: 000013: 8 b g Dowsing - Gwiffina (Welsh 2½ **102**
Saint) Twds rear, rdn & styd on fnl 2f, nvr threat: hvly bckd: reportedly returned with a cut on near fore & had
the worst of the draw today: won this race prev 3 seasons: worth forgiving this, see 2669 (this wnr bhd).
2335 **ROWAASI** 14 [4] M R Channon 3-8-4 Craig Williams 14/1: 24-004: Chsd ldrs, nvr pace to chall: see 1090. 1 **91**
2496 **REPERTORY** 7 [6] 7-9-0 R Price 10/1: 003235: Led/dsptd lead wide 4f: v speedy, poor high draw. hd **95**
2065 **PROUD NATIVE** 25 [7] 6-9-0 Alex Greaves 5/1: 002206: Rear, nvr threat to ldrs: op 4/1: see 1172. 2½ **88**

838

2065 **FLANDERS** 25 [3] 4-8-9 E Ahern 100/30: 16-107: Led/dsptd lead till over 1f out, btn/eased fnl 1f.   6   72
4170} **TO THE ROOF** 289 [9] 8-9-0 M Tebbutt 16/1: 0000-8: Bhd fnl 2f: sadly died after the race.   9   61
8 ran   Time 1m 0.7 (0.9)   (Frank Brady)   J S Goldie Uplawmoor, E Renfrews

---

2670	3.25 OCTEL O'HARE COND STKS 3YO+ (B) 7f rnd Good/Firm 23 +13 Fast
	£9570 £3630 £1815 £825 3 yo rec 8 lb

764   **LATE NIGHT OUT** 112 [5] W Jarvis 5-8-13 M Tebbutt 4/1: 524-01: 5 b g Lahib - Chain Dance (Shareef   105
Dancer) Handy, led over 2f out till ins last, rallied gamely to prevail in a thrilling fin: fast time, 4 mth abs:
'99 Haydock wnr (List h'cap, rtd 106 at best): '98 Redcar stks wnr (rtd 100): eff at 6f, suited by 7f on firm &
soft grnd, any trk: runs well fresh & likes to race up with the pace: v useful gelding.
2648 **SILCA BLANKA** 1 [2] A G Newcombe 8-8-13 A Culhane 3/1: 111032: 8 b h Law Society - Reality (Known *shd* 104$
Fact) Dwelt, rear, smooth prog to trk ldrs 1f out, rdn to narrowly lead ins last, just hdd on line: op 5/1: qck
reapp, 3rd in a York h'cap yesterday: loves Chester & remains in great heart: see 1778 (h'cap).
2003 **BALLY PRIDE** 28 [1] T D Easterby 3-8-5 E Ahern 4/1: 62-403: 3 ch g Pips Pride - Ballysnip (Ballymore)   hd   103
Chsd ldrs, rdn to chall dist, styd on strongly, just btn in a v cl fin: pulled clr with first 2 in a pulsating
finish: eff at 6f/sharp 7f: fine effort, useful gelding who can be plcd to effect: see 1534 (6f).
2335 **GAELIC STORM** 14 [3] M Johnston 6-9-2 R Winston 7/4 FAV: -06504: Bhd ldrs, held over 1f out: bckd.   4   98
2247 **ACE OF PARKES** 17 [4] 4-8-13 J Carroll 16/1: 6-5065: Led till over 2f out, sn held: see 1245 (5f).   2   91$
2437 **RETALIATOR** 9 [6] 4-8-8 J Bramhill 40/1: 020006: Cl up 3f: highly tried: see 1781, 780.   dist   0
6 ran   Time 1m 25.7 (0.7)   (J M Greetham)   W Jarvis Newmarket

---

2671	3.55 BBA O'HARE HCAP 4YO+ 0-80 (D) 1m2f75y Good/Firm 23 -10 Slow	[80]
	£5798 £1784 £892 £446 3 yo rec 11lb	

2481 **BACCHUS** 8 [2] Miss J A Camacho 6-9-3 (69)(VIS) J Carroll 4/1 JT FAV: -23221: 6 b g Prince Sabo - Bonica   76
(Rousillon) Mid-div, prog to lead over 2f out, sn rdn clr, rdn out: op 7/2, first time visor: deserved win, plcd
on all 4 prev starts this term: '99 Beverley wnr (h'caps, rtd 64): suited by 7.5/10f on firm & gd/sft grnd, any
trk, likes Beverley: tough & most consistent gelding, woken up by visor today.
2453 **PAARL ROCK** 8 [3] G Barnett 5-7-10 (48)(vis)(4oh) J McAuley (3) 14/1: -00032: 5 ch g Common   2½   50
Grounds - Markievicz (Doyoun) Led, rdn/hdd over 2f out, kept on, always held: op 10/1: see 2453.
2279 **WARNING REEF** 16 [11] E J Alston 7-8-3 (55) E Ahern 5/1: 565333: 7 b g Warning - Horseshoe Reef (Mill ½   56
Reef) Held up, no room 3f out, styd on fnl 2f despite no room dist, no threat: no luck, deserves similar.
*2522 **FREEDOM QUEST** 6 [9] B S Rothwell 5-8-8 (60) J Bramhill 4/1 JT FAV: 425214: Late gains from rear.   nk   60
2279 **NOUKARI** 16 [5] 7-9-10 (76) A Culhane 9/1: 102005: Mid-div, onepace fnl 2f: see 1217 (C/D).   1¼   74
*2537 **ASHLEIGH BAKER** 5 [7] 5-7-10 (48)(6ex) K Dalgleish (5) 5/1: 403016: Prom till over 1f out.   nk   45
2518 **BUTTERSCOTCH** 7 [4] 4-7-10 (48)(1oh) G Baker (7) 12/1: 003357: Held up, hdwy over 2f out, sn no prog. 4   39
2493 **KINGFISHERS BONNET** 7 [6] 4-7-10 (48)(2oh) Jonjo Fowle (1) 16/1: 354038: Prom, grad fdd fnl 2f.   2¾   35
2502 **PIPED ABOARD** 7 [10] 5-9-9 (75) M Tebbutt (1) 0-3509: Al bhd: op 10/1: see 1251.   1¼   60
2537 **SPONTANEITY** 5 [8] 4-7-10 (48)(6oh) Joanna Badger (7) 20/1: -06250: Chsd ldrs 7f: 10th: btr 2245.   nk   32
4410} **HADEQA** 271 [6] 4-8-11 (63) R Winston 20/1: 1100-0: In tch 7f: 11th: reapp: '99 Catterick (h'cap),   6   38
Pontefract (sell) & Carlisle wnr (clmr, for P D Evans): '98 Redcar wnr (nurs, rtd 73 & 55a): suited by 7f/1m on firm
& soft grnd, any trk: best blnkd/visored, neither worn here for F Jordan.
11 ran   Time 2m 11.9 (3.4)   (L A Bolingbroke)   Miss J A Camacho Norton, N Yorks

---

2672	4.30 CHLOR CHEMICALS HCAP 3YO+ 0-80 (D) 2m Good/Firm 23 -43 Slow	[77]
	£14235 £4380 £2190 £1095 3 yo rec 19lb	

2422 **HIGH TOPPER** 10 [1] M Johnston 3-8-5 (73) J Carroll 5/1: 252441: 3 b c Wolfhound - Blushing Barada   78
(Blushing Groom) Made all, rdn/styd on well fnl 2f, drvn out: op 4/1: 1st win: unplcd sole juvenile start last
term: eff at 12f, apprec step up to 2m: acts on firm & fast grnd, prob handles soft: handles a sharp/gall trk.
*2498 **RENZO** 7 [4] J L Harris 7-10-0 (77) A Culhane 9/4 FAV: 113012: 7 b g Alzao - Watership (Foolish   1½   80
Pleasure) Bhd ldrs, rdn to press wnr fnl 1f, kept on, always just held: hvly bckd: in fine form: see 2498.
2516 **WINDMILL LANE** 7 [3] B S Rothwell 3-7-10 (64)(8oh) P Hanagan (3) 14/1: 302103: 3 b f Saddlers Hall -   1   66$
Alpi Dora (Valiyar) Prom, rdn & ch 1f out, kept on onepace: clr rem: stiff task: see 2244 (mdn h'cap).
2375 **NORTHERN MOTTO** 12 [5] J S Goldie 7-8-1 (50) Craig Williams (7) 2: 033344: Bhd ldrs, held fnl 2f: op   5   47
9/2: won this race last time off a 3lb higher mark but has yet to hit best form this term: likes Musselburgh: see 797.
2461 **YES KEEMO SABEE** 8 [6] 5-8-1 (50) O Pears 7/2: 000025: Held up, eff 3f out, no hdwy: see 2461, 627.   ½   46
2606 **BLACK WEASEL** 2 [2] 5-7-10 (45)(10oh) J Bramhill 25/1: 24-056: Trkd ldrs, btn 2f out: qck reapp.   5   36
2498 **NICELY** 7 [7] 4-9-12 (75) Jonjo Fowle (5) 10/1: 0-0507: Rear/in tch, eff 3f out, no prog: see 1527.   1½   65
7 ran   Time 3m 33.1 (10.5)   (Maktoum Al Maktoum)   M Johnston Middleham, N Yorks

---

2673	5.05 EVC O'HARE APPR HCAP 3YO+ 0-70 (E) 7f122y rnd Good/Firm 23 -10 Slow	[66]
	£2951 £908 £454 £227 3 yo rec 9 lb	

2442 **BODFARI ANNA** 9 [17] J L Eyre 4-9-0 (52)(vis) R Cody Boutcher (5) 9/1: 010031: 4 br f Casteddu - Lowrianna   57
(Cyrano de Bergerac) Mid-div, hdwy/swtchd to rail & led dist, styd on well, rdn out: op 7/1: earlier won at
Southwell (h'cap): '99 Haydock wnr (sell h'cap, rtd 50): '98 Nottingham wnr (sell, rtd 66, M Easterby): eff at 6f,
suited by 7f on firm, soft & f/sand, any trk: suited by blnks/visor: in great form & fine eff to overcome high draw.
2561 **CAUTION** 4 [10] S Gollings 6-9-0 (52) K Dalgleish (3) 4/1 FAV: 000422: 6 b w Warning - Fairy Flax   1¾   53
(Dancing Brave) Held up, drvn/prog wide fnl 3f, styd on, not pace of wnr: bckd: op 7/1: see 2561, 645.
*2240 **TREASURE TOUCH** 17 [11] P D Evans 6-9-12 (64) Joanna Badger (5) 11/1: 113013: 6 b g Treasure Kay - 1½   62
Bally Pourri (Law Society) Prom, led over 2f out till over 1f out, no extra: stays 7.5f, winning form at 6f.
2453 **GABLESEA** 8 [3] B P J Baugh 6-8-7 (45)(VIS) J Bosley (5) 16/1: 050004: Trkd ldrs, onepace fnl 2f.   ½   42
2027 **KNOBBLEENEEZE** 287 [15] 10-8-3 (41)(vis) M Mathers (7) 16/1: 003005: Mid-div, kept on onepace ins last. ¾   37
2442 **DOVEBRACE** 9 [5] 7-9-1 (53) Jonjo Fowle (3) 9/2: 212166: Reared start & missed break, styd on fnl 2f,   2   45
no threat to ldrs: often costly to miss the break on this ultra sharp trk, fair run in circumstances: see 2420.
2438 **MYTTONS AGAIN** 9 [16] 3-8-13 (60)(bl) P Dobbs (3) 16/1: 266507: Trkd ldrs 3f out, onepace fnl 2f.   1½   50
2250 **OSTARA** 17 [7] 3-8-8 (55) Iona Wands 12/1: 40-038: Led 5f, fdd: op 10/1: btr 2250.   1½   42
2411 **TOBLERSONG** 10 [18] 5-8-7 (45)(f) Kristin Stubbs (7) 14/1: 064429: Dwelt/rear, mod gains: see 2411.   ½   31
2641 **DISTINCTIVE DREAM** 1 [6] 6-9-12 (64) C McCavish (7) 10/1: 040500: Chsd ldrs 5f: 10th: qck reapp.   1¾   47
2331 **PRIDEWAY** 14 [14] 4-9-4 (56) G Baker (3) 16/1: 656000: Dwelt, sn rdn rear, no impress: 11th: see 1778. nk   38

*2442　**SWYNFORD WELCOME** 9 [12] 4-8-8 (46) A Polli 10/1: 000010: Prom 4f: 16th: op 8/1: btr 2442.　　**0**
2453　**It Can Be Done** 8 [8] 3-9-4 (65) A Hawkins (7) 16/1:　2192　**Angus The Bold** 19 [1] 4-8-2 (40) R Naylor (7) 50/1:
2442　**Only For Gold** 9 [13] 5-9-4 (56) D Allan (7) 12/1:　2444　**Rififi** 9 [4] 7-9-11 (63)(VIS) P Shea (5) 33/1:
2444　**Lady Boxer** 9 [2] 4-9-11 (63) P Hanagan (5) 16/1:
17 ran　　Time 1m 34.90 (2.5)　　(The Haydock Badgeholders)　　J L Eyre Sutton Bank, N Yorks

Official Going　GOOD. Stalls: Straight Course - Stands Side: Round Course: Inside: Round Mile - Centre.

2674	**2.00 BONUSPRINT HCAP 3YO+ 0-90 (C)**　　1m4f　　Good 46　-01 Slow	[90]

£13682　£4210　£2105　£1052　3 yo rec 13lb

2502　**HANNIBAL LAD** 7 [12] W M Brisbourne 4-9-0 (76) B Marcus 8/1: 211441: 4 ch g Rock City -　　**82**
Appealing (Star Appeal) In tch, prog appr fnl 3f, burst through to lead well in las, drvn out: quick reapp:
proving tough this term, winning at W'hampton, Southwell (2 AW & turf h'cap, rtd 80a) & Doncaster (h'cap):
'99 wnr again at W'hampton (seller, rtd 66a, P Evans): suited by 11/12f on firm, gd & fibresand: acts on any
track, likes Southwell: runs well fresh: admirably tough & progressive.
2030　**ST HELENSFIELD** 27 [4] M Johnston 5-9-3 (79) J Weaver 12/1: 030322: 5 ch g Kris - On Credit　　1　**83**
(No Pass No Sale) Settled rear, smooth hdwy over 3f out, drvn & ran on strongly inside last, nearest fin:
visor ommitted: consistent placed form, deserves a win: see 2030, 1518.
*1788　**RAPIER** 37 [9] M D Hammond 6-9-2 (78) D R McCabe 20/1: 0-4013: 6 b g Sharpo - Sahara Breeze　　nk　**81**
(Ela Mana Mou) Prom, slightly outpcd over 4f out, rdn/prog over 2f out, ran on well for press fnl 1f, closing
at fin: excellent run, shld win again soon: see 1788.
*2527　**OCTANE** 6 [13] W M Brisbourne 4-8-5 (67) S Sanders 10/3 FAV: 202114: Waited with, hdwy when　　nk　**70**
short of room over 2f out, found gap & ran on well fnl 1f: nicely bckd & unluckly in running bhd wng stablemate.
*2523　**CAPTAINS LOG** 6 [11] 5-9-4 (80) M Fenton 6/1: 511445: Cl up, every ch over 2f out, no extra well　　nk　**83**
inside last: quick reapp: sound effort, remains in fine form: see 2523.
809　**EVANDER** 105 [6] 5-9-8 (84) J Fortune 20/1: 524-06: Handy, smooth hdwy over 4f out, soon chall　　nk　**86**
ldrs, rdn/wknd well inside last: op 14/1, gd run after near 4 month abs: see 809.
*2314　**JULIUS** 15 [5] 3-8-12 (87) M Hills 6/1: 211117: Cl up, went on over 4f out, hdd/btn well inside　　shd　**89**
last: not disgraced on this 5-timer bid: see 2314.
*2327　**TORRID KENTAVR** 14 [7] A Clark 10/1: 4-3318: Racd keenly in rear, hdwy 2f out, onepace　　1½　**86**
when short of room well inside last: op 8/1: h'cap bow: worth another chance: see 2327.
1484　**QUEDEX** 51 [14] 4-9-6 (82) S Whitworth 10/1: 020149: Rear, prog 4f out, staying on well when　　shd　**81**
checked ins last, not recover: 7 wk abs: ran better than fin position suggests, apprec a return to 14f: see 1167.
*2446　**CASHMERE LADY** 9 [3] 8-8-1 (63) A Nicholls (3) 9/1: 5-0110: Rear, switched/hdwy over 3f out,　　½　**61**
late hdwy, no threat to ldrs, fin 10th: shade below best on hat-trick bid: btr 2446.
2069　**CARLYS QUEST** 25 [15] 6-10-0 (90)(tvi) W Ryan 20/1: -31300: Rear, rdn/prog over 2f out,　　1¼　**86**
keeping but no threat to ldrs when hmpd inside last, eased, 11th: top weight: see 1373.
997　**SEREN HILL** 84 [10] 4-9-9 (85) Dane O'Neill 14/1: 130-00: Dwelt, rear, mod late gains: 12 wk abs.　　1¾　**79**
--　　**VHIN** [1] 5-9-4 (80) G Sparkes (7) 16/1: 01/0. Prom, rdn/fdd fnl 3f: reapp after over 2 year abs:　　1¾　**71**
rcd just twice bck in '99, scoring at York (auct mdn, rtd 76): eff over a gall 12f on gd/soft: sharper for this.
2530　**WHO CARES WINS** 6 [8] 4-8-12 (74)(BL) P Robinson 14/1: 000340: Led to 4f out, sn btn/eased: blnks.　　9　**55**
14 ran　　Time 2m 34.69 (5.69)　　(John Pugh)　　W M Brisbourne Great Ness, Shropshire

2675	**2.30 LISTED SILVER TROPHY STKS 3YO+ (A)**　　1m rnd　　Good 46　+10 Fast	

£33800　£10400　£5200　£2600　3 yo rec 9 lb

2064　**SUGARFOOT** 25 [8] N Tinkler 6-9-7 W Ryan 7/2 FAV: 5-1551: 6 ch h Thatching - Norpella (Northfields)　　**115**
Prom, sltly outpcd over 3f out, rall & gd hdwy over 2f out, led dist, styd on gamely, drvn out: nicely bckd,
fast time: earlier won at Doncaster (reapp, Gr 3): now in fine form in '99, won at York (2, List rtd h'cap & h'cap)
& Doncaster (Gr 3, rtd 115): '98 Ascot & York wnr (2, val h'caps, rtd 104): eff at 7f, suited by a gall 1m on
firm & hvy, loves York/Doncaster: runs well fresh: most tough & smart, win more Gr 3/Listed races.
1834　**PULAU TIOMAN** 35 [5] M A Jarvis 4-9-2 P Robinson 4/1: 212422: 4 b c Robellino - Ella Mon Amour　　½　**108**
(Ela Mana Mou) Rear, rdn & improved appr fnl 1f, ran on strongly for press inside last, not btn far: progressive.
2359　**DUCK ROW** 13 [3] J A R Toller 5-9-2 S Whitworth 9/2: 0-1223: 5 ch g Diesis - Sunny Moment　　shd　**108**
(Roberto) Cl up, led after 3f, clr 2f out, hdd ins last, kept on: proving v tough this term: see 2359, 1847.
*1186　**SPENCERS WOOD** 69 [7] P J Makin 3-8-7 S Sanders 12/1: 1-14: Dwelt, soon mid div, outpcd 3f out,　　nk　**107**
ran on well for press fnl 1f, nrst fin: 10 wk abs & a fine run up in grade: stays 1m: lightly raced, win a Listed.
2087　**NICOBAR** 24 [6] 3-8-10 J Weaver 13/2: 316105: Rcd keenly in rear, prog over 1f out, styd on　　¾　**108**
inside last, no threat to ldrs: shade btr 1830 (sharp/undulating 7f, gd/soft).
4239/　**SURE DANCER** 287 [2] 5-9-2 J Fortune 6/1: 110-6: Prom, hdwy to chall over 2f out, soon no extra:　　nk　**104**
op 4/1 on reapp: won first 2 of 3 '99 starts, at Leicester (debut, mdn), & Doncaster (stakes, rtd 111): eff
at 1m/10f on firm, gd & stiff/gall tracks: runs well fresh: smart at best, poss just sharper for this.
-2274　**HYPNOTIZE** 16 [4] 3-8-5 B Marcus 14/1: 5-6027: Rear, late hdwy for press, no threat: see 2274.　　3　**96**
--　　**ASAKIR** [9] 5-9-2 R Hills 12/1: 112/8: Led, hdd after 3f, every ch until wknd fnl 2f: reapp after　　1¾　**95**
3 year abs: smart 2yo for Saeed bin Suroor in '97, won at Nottingham (mdn), Leicester (stakes), subs rnr-up in a
Gr 1 in France (rtd 109): eff at 10f, don't stay mid-dists: acts on fast & soft grnd: likes to force the pace:
runs well fresh but entitled to need this: now with M Tregoning, sharper next time over further.
2343　**SHOWBOAT** 14 [1] 6-9-2 M Hills 9/1: 063039: Rcd keenly in tch, rdn/wknd over 2f out: can do better.　　hd　**95**
9 ran　　Time 1m 41.43 (2.93)　　(Mrs D Wright)　　N Tinkler Langton, N Yorks

2676	**3.05 MAXIMS HCAP 3YO+ 0-100 (C)**　　5f　　Good 46　-01 Slow	[100]

£24700　£7600　£3800　£1900　3 yo rec 5 lb　Low numbers favoured

+2348　**ELLENS LAD** 13 [2] W J Musson 6-10-0 (100) L Newton 9/1: 015011: 6 b g Polish Patriot - Lady Ellen　　**106**
(Horage) Mid div, edged right & hdwy over 2f out, led dist, rdn clr: op 7/1, top weight: earlier won at York
(h'cap) & Doncaster (rtd h'cap): '99 Newbury, Haydock & Newmarket wnr (h'caps, rtd 95) prev term won again at
Newmarket (h'cap, rtd 86, E Alston): stays 6f, suited by a stiff/gall 5f: acts on firm, soft & any trk, likes
Newmarket: best without blnks: very useful run conceding weight all round on favoured stands rail.

2348 **SUNLEY SENSE 13** [6] M R Channon 4-8-11 (83) J Weaver 14/1: 022002: 4 b g Komaite - Brown Velvet (Mansingh) Dsptd lead, went on over 1f out, hdd ins last, not pace of wnr: op 10/1: ran to best: see 1324. *1½* **85**
2451 **CORRIDOR CREEPER 9** [1] P W Harris 3-8-7 (84)(t) J Fortune 14/1: 030063: 3 ch c Polish Precedent - Sonia Rose (Superbity) Rear, rdn & styd on well over 1f out, ran on strongly inside last, nvr nrr: fine run in a t-strap, blinks omitted: will apprec a return to 6f & should win at that trip: see 1285. *hd* **86**
2355 **BON AMI 13** [3] A Berry 4-8-12 (84) P Bradley (5) 8/1: 000034: Dwelt, rear, rdn/prog over 1f out, styd on well inside last: not disgraced after a slow start here: see 2355. *1* **83**
2348 **IVORYS JOY 13** [7] 5-9-1 (87) C Carver (3) 11/1: 316045: Prom, rdn/not pace of wnr fnl 1f: see 1650. *¾* **84**
1983 **MAGIC RAINBOW 29** [10] 5-8-9 (81) M Fenton 20/1: 106006: Held up, swtchd wide & prog over 1f out, ran on ins last, no threat to ldrs: gd run from a unfavoured wide draw: back on a wng mark, keep in mind at 6f. *shd* **78+**
*2473 **AMBITIOUS 8** [13] 5-9-2 (88) C Catlin (7) 7/1: 401417: Handy, rdn/no extra over 1f out: op 6/1. *1½* **81**
2458 **TADEO 8** [8] 7-9-12 (98) R Hills 7/1: 64-038: Front rank, rdn/fdd fnl 1f: btr 2458 (6f). *¾* **89**
2451 **LONE PIPER 9** [11] 5-8-10 (82)(tvi) B Marcus 20/1: 400009: Speed early, bhd halfway: needs further. *¾* **72**
*2432 **CRYHAVOC 10** [15] 6-9-7 (93) A Nicholls (3) 5/1 FAV: 320210: Prom, rdn/no extra appr fnl 1f, 10th: ignore this run, had the worst of the draw here: see 2432. *nk* **83**
2473 **LIVELY LADY 8** [4] 4-9-2 (88)(BL) S Whitworth 16/1: 103300: Rcd keenly in mid div, rdn/no extra fnl 2f: tried in blinks: btr 1728 (6f, stakes). *2* **73**
2473 **TRAVESTY OF LAW 8** [9] 3-8-8 (85)(BL) D R McCabe 40/1: -00000: Prom 3f, btn dist, 12th: blnks. *shd* **70**
1531 **PARADISE LANE 49** [12] 4-8-9 (81) Cheryl Nosworthy (7) 33/1: 0-2000: Led over 3f, wknd: 13th: abs. *¾* **64**
2473 **FAUTE DE MIEUX 8** [5] 5-8-6 (78) S Sanders 10/1: 103320: In tch 3f, wknd, 14th: see 2473. *1½* **58**
2151 **SHEER VIKING 22** [14] 4-9-13 (99) M Hills 8/1: 223200: Prom till halfway, fin last: tchd 10/1. *1* **76**
15 ran Time 1m 01.37 (2.37) (Mrs Rita Brown) W J Musson Newmarket, Suffolk

2677 — 3.40 M. PAGE NOV STKS 2YO (D) 7f str Good 46 -16 Slow
£6646 £2045 £1022 £511

*1943 **FORWOOD 30** [1] M A Jarvis 2-9-5 P Robinson 1/3 FAV: -11: 2 b c Charnwood Forest - Silver Hut (Silver Hawk) Front rank, swtchd/hdwy over 2f out, led appr fnl 1f, rdn out, readily: hvly bckd at odds-on: earlier won at Newbury (debut, mdn): 58,000gns Mar foal, half-brother to a useful 1m scorer, dam won over 1m: eff at 6/7f, 1m will suit: acts on fast, gd & stiff or gall trk: useful/progressive juv, one to keep on your side. **99**
*2430 **SMITH AND WESTERN 10** [2] R Hannon 2-9-2 Dane O'Neill 9/2: 5012: 2 b c Factual - Temple Heights (Shirley Heights) Dsptd lead, went on over 2f out, hdd over 1f out, styd on but not pace of wnr: op 3/1 clr rem: not disgraced against a useful rival: acts on gd & gd/soft grnd: see 2430. *2* **87**
-- **TAKAROA** [4] I A Balding 2-8-8 M Hills 7/1: 3: 2 b c Tagula - Mountain Havest (Shirley Heights) Led, hdd appr 2f out, fdd fnl 1f: tchd 10/1 on debut: 36,000gns half brother to a wnr abroad: sire high class 6f juv wnr: encouraging debut & will find easier opportunities. *4* **72**
2494 **ACHILLES SUN 7** [3] K R Burke 2-8-12 J Weaver 20/1: U4: Veered right, start, hung right & no extra fnl 2f: quick reapp: looks a tricky ride, u.r. on debut in 2494. *5* **68**
4 ran Time 1m 30.33 (4.33) (Mr & Mrs Raymond Anderson Green) M A Jarvis Newmarket

2678 — 4.15 ILPH NURSERY HCAP 2YO (C) 6f Good 46 -06 Slow [89]
£6825 £2100 £1050 £525

*1870 **PREFERRED 33** [1] R Hannon 2-9-3 (78) Dane O'Neill 11/4 FAV: 011: 2 b c Distant Relative - Fruhingserwachen (Irish River) Led early, rem cl-up, led again appr fnl 1f, qcknd & went clr ins last, rdn out, eased nr fin: well bckd: recent Nottingham wnr (mdn): IR9,000gns half-brother to a wnr abroad, sire a miler: eff at 5/6f on gd: acts on a stiff or gall trk: impressive h'cap bow on favoured stands rail, qk follow-up? **91+**
*2251 **SILK LAW 17** [3] A Berry 2-9-7 (82) J Fortune 7/2: 112: 2 ch f Barathea - Jural (Kris) Prom, hdwy to chall over 1f out, styd on but soon not pace of easy wnr: nicely bckd, met a prog rival. *4* **84**
2328 **FAST FOIL 14** [5] M R Channon 2-9-1 (76) A Nicholls (3) 9/1: -3263: 2 b f Layhib - Fast Chick (Henbit) Rear, rdn/prog 2f out, styd on well inside last, no impress: op 6/1: worth a try over 7f: see 1844. *¾* **76**
*2239 **MON SECRET 17** [4] J L Eyre 2-9-4 (79) W Ryan 7/1: 032414: Rear, switch/prog over 2f out, stying on when hung right over 1f out, held inside last: 7L clr rem: see 2239. *nk* **79**
2383 **BLUSHING SPUR 12** [2] 2-8-7 (68) A Clark 33/1: 5025: Prom, rdn/fdd appr fnl 1f: btr 2383 (7f, AW). *7* **53**
2251 **QUANTUM LADY 17** [8] 2-8-13 (74) M Fenton 7/1: 412236: Led 5f out, hdd appr fnl 1f, sn btn: op 5/1. *3* **52**
1761 **SOLDIER ON 38** [6] 2-9-5 (80) S Whitworth 20/1: 021557: Mid div, improved over 2f out, wknd quickly over 1f out: longer 6f trip: btr 1208 (5f, firm). *shd* **58**
2368 **GOLD AIR 12** [9] 2-9-7 (82) J Weaver 10/1: -01028: Mid div, eff when badly hmpd appr fnl 1f, not recover: op 6/1 & ran better than finishing position suggests: see 2368. *2* **55**
*1981 **SOMERS HEATH 29** [7] 2-8-8 (69) B Marcus 13/2: -0019: Rear, eff 2f out, no dngr: btr 1981 (sell). *1½* **39**
9 ran Time 1m 16.27 (3.17) (R J Brennan & N J Hemmington) R Hannon East Everleigh, Wilts

2679 — 4.50 SILWOOD PARK MDN 3YO (D) 1m str Good 46 -03 Slow
£5382 £1656 £828 £414

1985 **MAY BALL 29** [2] J H M Gosden 3-8-9 J Fortune 13/2: -1241: 3 b f Cadeaux Genereux - Minute Waltz (Sadler's Wells) Made all, qcknd & went clr over 2f out, styd on well, rdn out, eased cl-home: op 9/2: won a meaningless 2-rnr chall race on debut earlier this term: half-sister to a 1m/9f scorer: stays a gall 9f on fast & gd/soft: loves to dominate: can rate more highly. **84**
2465 **BEDEY 8** [5] A C Stewart 3-9-0 W Ryan 9/2: -42: 3 b c Red Ransom - Mount Helena (Danzig) Rear, soon mid div, outpcd 3f out, rdn & ran on strongly inside last, no ch with wnr: gd run & looks sure to relish a step up to 10f next time: acts on gd grnd: see 2465. *1½* **84+**
-- **ELJOHAR** [6] Saeed bin Suroor 3-9-0 (t) R Hills 4/6 FAV: 3: 3 ch c Nashwan - Methhaaf (Nureyev) Keen in rear, rdn/hdwy appr fnl 1f, ev ch till no extra ins last: hvly bckd on debut tho' op 1/2: superbly bred, sire won the Derby, dam won the Irish 1,000 Guineas: should learn from this & do better next time. *shd* **84**
-- **AYMARA** [4] J H M Gosden 3-8-9 J Weaver 20/1: 4: Dwelt, soon rdn in tch, drpd rear over 3f out, late gains: stablemate of wnr: Darshaan filly who will find easier opportunities. *3½* **73**
4358} **ALQAWAASER 275** [7] 3-9-0 S Whitworth 33/1: 30-5: Rear, late hdwy, no threat: reapp: plcd on 1st of 2 '99 starts (mdn, rtd 70, E Dunlop): half-brother to a 1m Gr 3 wnr: now with Major D Chappell. *2½* **74**
2024 **SEEKING SUCCESS 27** [8] 3-8-9 Dane O'Neill 6/1: -00226: Front rank, rdn/wknd appr fnl 1f: op 9/2 & much better expected after 2024 (firm grnd). *nk* **69**
1333 **MADURESE 59** [3] 3-9-0 B Marcus 16/1: 47: Trkd ldrs, rdn & wknd/qckly fnl 2f: op 10/1, 8 wk abs. *1¾* **71$**
7 ran Time 1m 42.63 (3.93) (Lord Hartington) J H M Gosden Manton, Wilts

Official Going   GOOD TO FIRM. Stalls: Inside, except 5/6f - Stands Side.

2680   **2.15 EVENING POST SELLER 3YO + (G)**   **6f str**   **Good/Firm 37   -13 Slow**
£2052   £586   £293   3 yo rec 6 lb

1368 **SUPERBIT** 57 [20] B A McMahon 8-9-4 G Faulkner (3) 5/1: 31-061: 8 b g Superpower - On A Bit   **54**
(Mummy's Pet) Prom, rdn/led over 1f out, styd on well, rdn out: no bid: op 6/1, 8 wk abs: landed fnl '99 start here
at Nottingham (class stks, rtd 61 & 51a): '98 Ripon wnr (sell h'cap, rtd 59 at best): eff at 5/6f on firm, soft &
fibresand, any trk, likes Nottingham: best without blnks/vis: runs well fresh & apprec this drop to sell grade.
2517 **SEALED BY FATE** 7 [18] J S Wainwright 5-9-4 (vis) D Harrison 11/1: 044502: 5 b g Mac's Imp - Fairy   1¼   49
Don (Don) Held up, rdn/prog to chase wnr fnl 1f, kept on tho' al held: eff at 6/7f, suited by a stiff 5f: see 697.
2505 **PALACEGATE TOUCH** 7 [19] A Berry 10-9-10 (hbl) G Carter 10/1: 003033: 10 gr g Petong - Dancing   2½   48$
Chimes (London Bells) Chsd ldrs, rdn & styd on from over 1f out: op 20/1: see 1139.
2329 **BALANITA** 14 [12] B Palling 5-9-4 (bl) D Sweeney 11/1: -00254: Chsd ldrs, hung left/onepace fnl 2f.   ½   40
1412 **BLACK ARMY** 56 [4] 5-9-4 R Mullen 6/1: 030-05: Prom, rdn/hmpd over 1f out, no impress after: abs.   ½   38
2193 **SIR JACK** 19 [9] 4-9-4 F Norton 9/1 FAV: 024406: Rdn/bhd early, mod gains: op 3/1: btr 2054, 905.   ½   36
2489 **ORLANDO SUNSHINE** 7 [10] 3-8-12 (BL) R Cody Boutcher (7) 14/1: 00-007: Led 5f: blnks, op 12/1.   ½   34
2374 **APRILS COMAIT** 12 [17] 3-8-7 (bl) V Halliday 12/1: 000568: Prom 5f: op 8/1: see 2374, 217.   1½   25
2054 **DELTA SOLEIL** 26 [16] 8-9-4 R Brisland (5) 12/1: 000009: Chsd ldrs 4f: op 8/1: vis omitted.   2   25
585 **FRANKLIN LAKES** 141 [13] 5-9-4 S Righton 66/1: 305460: Outpcd early, mod gains: 10th: 5 mth abs.   nk   24
2385 **ELTON LEDGER** 12 [8] 11-9-10 (vis) R Fitzpatrick (3) 33/1: 006400: Dwelt, sn rdn, nvr on terms: 11th.   1   28
790 **Castrato** 107 [1] 4-9-4 J Lowe 66/1:   4252 **Petra Nova** 284 [3] 4-8-13 S Finnamore (5) 40/1:
2183 **Royal Tarragon** 20 [5] 4-8-13 Sophie Mitchell 40/1:   2421 **Silogue** 10 [2] 3-8-12 Dale Gibson 40/1:
2612 **Erupt** 2 [11] 7-9-10 (vis) R Studholme (5) 16/1:   2252 **Tinas Royale** 17 [6] 4-8-13 D Watson (7) 66/1:
2118 **Ballina Lad** 23 [14] 4-9-4 D O'Donohoe 25/1:   2122 **Picassos Heritage** 23 [15] 4-9-4 L Vickers (1) 66/1:
1801 **Bold Aristocrat** 36 [7] 9-9-4 P M Quinn (3) 33/1:
20 ran   Time 1m 13.8 (3.0)   (Neville H Smith)   B A McMahon Hopwas, Staffs.

2681   **2.45 E MIDLANDS HCAP 3YO + 0-75 (E)**   **1m6f**   **Good/Firm 37   -09 Slow**   **[67]**
£2955   £844   £422   3 yo rec 15lb

*2416 **TYPHOON TILLY** 10 [6] C F Wall 3-8-9 (63) R Mullen 5/4 FAV: 0-3111: 3 b g Hernando - Meavy   **72**
(Kalaglow) Held up, no room over 2f out, prog to lead ins last & asserted under hands & heels riding: hvly bckd, op
7/4: completed hat-trick after 2 wins at Yarmouth (h'caps): rtd 60 in 99 (mdn): eff at 12f, suited by 14f, shld
stay 2m: acts on fast & gd/soft grnd, likes a stiff/gall or fair trk, esp Yarmouth: progressive gelding.
1928 **HAMBLEDEN** 31 [1] M A Jarvis 3-9-6 (74) G Carter 7/2: 031032: 3 b g Vettori - Dalu (Dancing Brave)   ¾   81
Prom, rdn/led over 1f out, hdd ins last, kept on well for press: pulled clr of rem: op 4/1: eff at 12/14f on firm,
hvy & fibresand: caught an improving rival, can find a similar contest: see 1238 (AW).
1927 **CUPBOARD LOVER** 31 [2] D Haydn Jones 4-8-13 (52) D Harrison 6/1: -65663: 4 ch g Risk Me - Galejade   7   49
(Sharrood) Held up, keen, rdn/prog & ev ch over 1f out, no extra ins last: op 9/2: see 1411, 788.
2370 **STREET WALKER** 12 [7] S Mellor 4-8-5 (44) F Norton 16/1: -40064: Held up, prog/hmpd 3f out,   nk   40
held fnl 2f: op 20/1: visor omitted: see 853 (12f).
*2191 **FUJIYAMA CREST** 19 [8] 8-9-6 (59) J Lowe 7/1: -00015: Led till over 1f out, fdd: op 5/1: see 2191 (clmr).   ¾   52
2191 **PRINCESS TOPAZ** 19 [4] 6-9-10 (63) D O'Donohoe 12/1: 035-26: Held up, btn 2f out: op 8/1, topweight.   11   45
*2268 **ALNAJASHEE** 16 [9] 4-9-8 (61)(t) D Sweeney 8/1: 460017: Chsd ldr, wknd over 1f out: op 10/1.   1   42
3707) **ALLOTROPE** 318 [5] 5-9-7 (60) T Eaves (7) 14/1: 0460-8: Al bhd: op 10/1, reapp, 8 month jumps abs   13   26
(rnr-up, nov, rtd 84h, eff at 2½m/2m6f on firm & gd grnd): unplcd on the level in '99 (rtd 65, h'cap, tried blnks):
ex-Irish, '98 Tralee wnr (14f, mdn): eff at 14f/2m on firm & gd grnd.
2076 **WHITE WILLOW** 24 [3] 11-8-1 (40)(bl) Dale Gibson 66/1: 440/49: Prom, btn over 3f out: see 2076.   8   0
9 ran   Time 3m 04.8 (6.5)   (M Tilbrook)   C F Wall Newmarket.

2682   **3.20 PAULINE CLASS STKS 3YO + 0-70 (E)**   **1m54y**   **Good/Firm 37   -26 Slow**
£2879   £822   £411   3 yo rec 9 lb

2349 **OUT OF SIGHT** 13 [1] B A McMahon 6-9-5 G Faulkner (3) 16/1: 300001: 6 ch g Salse - Starr Danias   **67**
(Sensitive Prince) Prom, led 2f out, held on gamely fnl 1f, all out: earlier scored at Southwell (AW h'cap, rtd
75a): '99 wnr again at Southwell (h'cap, rtd 67a, rtd 72 on turf, h'cap): rtd 75 in '98: eff at 7f/1m on firm,
gd & fibresand, handles hvy & gd trk, likes Southwell: gd weight carrier.
1496 **INCHINNAN** 50 [10] C Weedon 3-8-9 D Sweeney 7/2: 2-2132: 3 b f Inchinor - Westering (Auction Ring) shd   66
Al prom, drvn/strong chall fnl 2f, styd on well, just held: op 3/1, 7 wk abs: remains in gd heart: see 1496, 1033.
2467 **HAND CHIME** 8 [2] W J Haggas 3-9-0 F Norton 2/1: 01123: 3 ch g Clantime - Warning Bell (Bustino)   2   67
Held up, keen, prog to press ldrs over 1f out, held ins last: well bckd, clr rem: see 2281.
*2564 **IRON MOUNTAIN** 4 [5] N A Callaghan 5-9-7 R Mullen 13/8 FAV: 534014: Held up, eff over 2f out,   5   55
hung left/btn 1f out: hvly bckd: qck reapp, poss too soon after 2564 (h'cap).
2130 **ASSURED PHYSIQUE** 22 [3] 3-8-10 (tvi) D Harrison 8/1: 053665: Trkd ldrs, held over 1f out: op 6/1.   1   51
2562 **FOUR MEN** 4 [4] 3-8-10 Angela Hartley (7) 100/1: 000066: Keen, led/dsptd lead 6f, fdd: qck reapp: 2½   46$
rtd 53 in '99 (J Berry, auct mdn): needs a drop in grade.
2282 **FAS** 16 [7] 4-9-5 (vis) L Gueller (7) 100/1: 050407: Led/dsptd lead after 2f till over 2f out, wknd.   ½   45$
2193 **DEFIANCE** 19 [9] 5-9-5 Sophie Mitchell 100/1: -00008: Held up, nvr factor: see 1578.   7   34$
254 **KARAKUL** 193 [6] 4-9-2 G Carter 20/1: 000-09: Dwelt, al rear: op 10/1, 6 month abs: '99 h'cap wnr   7   20
at Windsor, Leicester & Beverley (M J Fetherson Godley, rtd 68): '98 Brighton scorer (clmr, rtd 65): eff at 10f,
may get further: acts on firm & gd grnd: best with waiting tactics on any track.
2508 **ESPERE DOR** 7 [6] 3-8-10 Dale Gibson 100/1: 000600: Chsd ldrs 7f: see 2317 (mdn).   ¾   22
10 ran   Time 1m 44.6 (5.2)   (D J Allen)   B A McMahon Hopwas, Staffs.

2683   **3.50 EBF FAMILY DAY FILLIES MDN 2YO (D)**   **6f str**   **Good/Firm 37   -13 Slow**
£3623   £1115   £557   £278

1986 **MAURI MOON** 28 [5] G Wragg 2-8-11 F Norton 5/2: 51: 2 b f Green Desert - Dazzling Heights (Shirley   **92**
Heights) Cl-up, led over 3f out, styd on well & asserted well ins last, rdn out: apprec step up to 6f, sure to
relish 7f+: dam a 7/11f wnr: acts on fast grnd & a gall trk: well regarded filly, shld win in better company.

NOTTINGHAM SATURDAY JULY 15TH Lefthand, Galloping Track

2189 **PALATIAL 19** [7] J R Fanshawe 2-8-11 D Harrison 11/10 FAV: 222: 2 b f Green Desert - White Palace (Shirely Heights) Trkd wnr 2f out, rdn/chall 1f out, held well ins last: rest well covered: well bckd: see 2189. ¾ 89
-- **SUNSHINE NSHOWERS** [2] A Berry 2-8-11 G Carter 6/1: 3: 2 b f Spectrum - Maily Dry (The Brianstan) Chsd ldrs, not pace of front pair fnl 2f: op 5/1: May foal, half-sister to high-class sprinter Bolshoi: dam unrcd, sire top-class at 1m/10f: eff at 6f, 7f+ will suit: handles fast grnd & a gall trk, encouraging intro. 3½ 80
-- **PRINCESS TITANIA** [3] N A Callaghan 2-8-11 R Mullen 6/1: 4: Slowly away, styd on fnl 2f, no threat: Fairy King filly, Apr foal, dam a List wnr abroad: 7f+ shld suit on this evidence: improve. 2½ 73
-- **MAID TO DANCE** [6] 2-8-11 G Parkin 20/1: 5: Dwelt, sn handy, btn over 1f out: Pyramus filly, Apr foal, cost 7,800gns: dam a wnr abroad: with T D Easterby. 1 71
2174 **BOWFELL 20** [9] 2-8-11 R Fitzpatrick (3) 50/1: 06: Led 3f, sn btn: see 2174. 1¾ 67
-- **CELTS DAWN** [4] 2-8-11 D O'Donohoe 25/1: 7: Dwelt, keen/hung left towards rear, hdwy over 2f out, btn & eased fnl 1f: op 12/1: Celtic Swing Apr foal: half-sister to pacey 5f sprinter Repertory: sire outstanding juv & subs French Derby wnr: green on debut, shld improve for J G Smyth Osbourne. hd 66
-- **LADY WARD** [1] 2-8-11 Dale Gibson 20/1: 8: Al bhd: op 10/1: Mujadil filly, Jan foal, cost IR£16,000: half-sister to a wnr abroad, dam a 7f Irish wnr: stable quiet at present, with M H Tompkins. 2½ 59
-- **TWILIGHT MISTRESS** [8] 2-8-11 J D Smith 25/1: 9: Prom 4f, sn btn: Mar foal, dam a 6f 3yo wnr. 1½ 56
9 ran Time 1m 13.8 (3.0) (Peter R Pritchard) G Wragg Newmarket.

2684 **4.25 E MIDS FILLIES HCAP 3YO+ 0-85 (D) 5f str Good/Firm 37 +09 Fast [76]**
£3900 £1200 £600 £300 3 yo rec 5 lb

2252 **POPPYS SONG 17** [2] H Candy 3-9-4 (71) D Sweeney 5/1: 1-0021: 3 b f Owington - Pretty Poppy (Song) Cl-up & went on bef halfway, rdn & held on gamely ins last: best time of day: '99 Catterick wnr (mdn, rtd 74): eff at 5f on firm & soft grnd, sharp/gall track. 75
2364 **SHAROURA 12** [6] D Nicholls 4-9-12 (74) F Norton 6/1: 0-0002: 4 ch f Inchinor - Kinkajoo (Precocious) Led till bef halfway, remained cl-up & styd on well ins last, just held: back to form: see 2128. nk 77
2525 **PREMIUM PRINCESS 6** [4] J J Quinn 5-8-3 (51) R Mullen 8/1: 055333: 5 b m Distant Relative - Solemn Occasion (Secreto) Dwelt, held up in tch, swtchd & styd for press nr line, not btn far: op 6/1, qck reapp: no luck in running today, on a fair mark, can find similar: see 802. nk 53
2355 **GLOWING 13** [5] J R Fanshawe 5-10-0 (76) D Harrison 2/1 FAV: 0-2024: Cl-up, onepace fnl 1f. ½ 76
2505 **MARINO STREET 7** [1] 7-8-10 (58) G Faulkner (3) 4/1: -211W5: Cl-up, no extra fnl 1f: op 3/1: see 2252. ½ 56
2504 **HONESTY FAIR 7** [8] 3-10-0 (81) S Finnamore(5) 8/1: 100046: Held up, nvr pace to chall: see 2504, 1384. 1½ 76
2418 **ZARAGOSSA 10** [7] 4-8-10 (58) G Carter 7/1: 500507: Prom till over 1f out: op 6/1: see 1687. 2 48
7 ran Time 59.9 (1.4) (Thomas Frost & Partners) H Candy Wantage, Oxon.

2685 **5.00 NEXT MEETING HCAP 3YO 0-70 (E) 1m2f Good/Firm 37 -26 Slow [76]**
£3005 £858 £429

2160 **FISHER ISLAND 21** [6] R Hollinshead 3-8-1 (49) P M Quinn (3) 16/1: 440401: 3 b f Sri Pekan - Liberty Song (Last Tycoon) Led/dsptd lead, asserted over 1f out, pushed out: first win: plcd once in '99 (nurs, rtd 59): eff at 10f, tried 12f, shld suit: acts on fast, soft & fibresand, sharp/gall trk. 54
2345 **EMALI 14** [10] C E Brittain 3-9-1 (63) D Harrison 8/1: 06-22: 3 b g Emarati - Princess Poquito (Hard Fought) Chsd wnr, led over 2f out till over 1f out, held by wnr ins last: op 6/1: styd longer 10f trip on h'cap bow: acts on firm & fast grnd: see 2345 (clmr). 1¾ 65
*2332 **CHAKA ZULU 14** [1] W J Haggas 3-7-10 (44) F Norton 11/10 FAV: 000-13: 3 b g Muhtarram - African Dance (El Gran Senor) Held up, briefly no room over 2f out, prog over 1f out, held ins last: well bckd, clr rem. nk 45
623 **KARA SEA 135** [4] D J G Murray Smith 3-9-2 (64) D O'Donohoe 20/1: 104: Prom, keen, outpcd fnl 2f: op 14/1, 4 mth abs: prob styd longer 10f trip: see 500 (AW mdn, 1m). 4 59
192 **SAMARARDO 213** [11] 3-8-10 (58) D Sweeney 33/1: 1203-5: Chsd ldrs till over 1f out: 7 month abs. nk 52
2086 **CHELONIA 24** [2] 3-9-7 (69) G Carter 10/1: 3-056: Held up, briefly no room over 2f out, sn held: op 6/1. ½ 62
2013 **NATURAL 28** [3] 3-9-2 (64) Dale Gibson 11/2: 0-0627: Prom till over 1f out: btr 2013 (1m, h'cap). 1 56
2281 **GLEN VALE WALK 16** [7] 3-7-11 (45) J Lowe 7/1: 000048: Held up, keen, eff 3f out, sn held: op 10/1. ½ 36
2450 **KATHAKALI 9** [5] 3-8-11 (59) R Brisland (5) 9/1: 000059: Keen/prom, btn 2f out: op 10/1: btr 2450. ½ 49
2111 **BAJAN BROKER 23** [9] 3-9-7 (69) R Mullen 20/1: 43-040: Held up, eff 2f out, no hdwy: 10th: op 14/1. 2½ 55
10 ran Time 2m 08.6 (6.3) (The CHF Partnership) R Hollinshead Upper Longdon, Staffs.

SALISBURY SATURDAY JULY 15TH Righthand, Galloping Track, Stiff Finish

Official Going GOOD. Stalls: Stands Side.

2686 **2.10 EBF QUEENPOT MDN 2YO (D) 7f str Good 40 -15 Slow**
£3913 £1204 £602 £301

-- **ELNAHAAR** [5] E A L Dunlop 2-9-0 W Supple 6/1: 1: 2 b c Silver Hawk - Futuh (Diesis) Held up, eff ent fnl 2f, ran on strongly ins last to get up cl-home, going away: op 4/1: Apr foal, half-brother to a useful sprint/10f wnr: dam 6f wnr, sire a miler: eff at 7f on gd, 1m suit: runs well fresh: rate higher. 86+
2269 **WAINAK 16** [9] J L Dunlop 2-9-0 P Doe 20/1: 02: 2 b c Silver Hawk - Cask (Be My Chief) Chsd ldrs, rdn appr fnl 1f, ran on to lead fnl 100y, sn hdd, kept on: eff at 7f, 1m will suit: win a race. ½ 84
-- **BREAKFAST BAY** [7] R Charlton 2-8-9 R Perham 7/1: 3: 2 b f Charnwood Forest - Diavolina (Lear Fan) Front rank, led appr fnl 2f till below dist, onepace: op 3/1: 80,000 gns Feb foal, half-sister to sev wnrs, notably a smart French mid-dist performer: dam 10f wnr, sire a miler: eff at 7f, shld improve. 1½ 76
2269 **PRIME TRUMP 16** [2] P W Harris 2-9-0 N Callan 3/1: 54: In tch, drvn after halfway, styd on: stays 7f. ¾ 79
-- **MURRENDI** [1] 2-9-0 R Havlin 14/1: 5: In tch, wide, unable to qckn appr fnl 1f: op 10/1, fair effort from widest draw: 55,000 gnslr gns Ashkalani Feb 1st foal, dam 5f wnr, sire a miler: with M Channon. hd 79
-- **COSMIC MILLENNIUM** [4] 2-9-0 C Rutter 33/1: 6: Bhd, late hdwy, nvr a threat: 9,500 gns In The Wings May half-brother to 3 wnrs: bred to apprec 10f+: with R Guest. ½ 78
-- **PRIZE DANCER** [8] 2-9-0 N Pollard 6/4 FAV: 7: Mid-div, eff & btn 2f out: nicely bckd: Suave Dancer Mar half-brother to 7f juv Premier Prize, dam 5f wnr, later styd mid-dists: needs 1m+ already: with D Elsworth. 2 74
-- **LAGGAN MINSTREL** [11] 2-9-0 R Smith (5) 16/1: 8: Keen & led till appr fnl 2f, wknd dist: op 12/1: 28,000 gns Mark Of Esteem Apr foal, half-brother to a 5f juv wnr, dam 9f wnr, sire a miler: with R Hannon. 1 72
-- **RED DEER** [3] 2-9-0 A McGlone 16/1: 9: Slow away, wide, nvr in it: op 12/1, stablemate wnr: ¾ 70

110,000 Cadeaux Genereux Feb half brother to a 10f wnr, dam a miler, sire a sprinter.

--	**KELLS** [6] 2-9-0 G Hind 10/1: 0: Prom till appr fnl 2f: 10th: Dilum first foal, dam a miler.	3½ 63
2383	**MIND OVER MATTER** 12 [10] 2-9-0 I Mongan (5) 66/1: 00: Mid-div till halfway: 11th.	7 49

11 ran   Time 1m 29.36 (3.86)   (Hamdam Al Maktoum)   E A L Dunlop Newmarket, Suffolk

---

2687   2.40 MYROBELLA NOV AUCT STKS 2YO (F)   6f str   Good 40 -15 Slow
£2394   £684   £342

*1906 **BECKY SIMMONS** 31 [5] A P Jarvis 2-8-10 N Callan 5/1: 11: 2 b f Mujadil - Jolies Eaux (Shirley   84
Heights) Trkd ldrs, under press appr fnl 1f, no response till strong burst well ins last led fnl strides: earlier
won debut at Hamilton (auct mdn): 6,000 gns half sister to 2 juv wnrs: apprec step up to 6f & looks sure to
improve further at 7f: acts on fast & gd grnd, stiff/undul trks: goes well fresh & is a progressive filly.

*2328 **SIBLA** 14 [6] Mrs P N Dutfield 2-8-10 P Doe 7/2: 5212: 2 b f Piccolo - Malibasta (Auction Ring)   hd 82
Held up, gd prog appr fnl 1f, kept on well ins last, just btn: op 11/4: acts on firm & gd: consistent.

*2441 **FOLEY MILLENNIUM** 9 [4] M Quinn 2-8-13 G Hind 12/1: 5513: 2 ch c Tagula - Inshirah (Caro)   ½ 83
Led, rdn appr fnl 1f, worn down cl-home: a bold attempt, acts on fast & gd grnd, see 2441 (clmr).

2307 **INNIT** 15 [1] M R Channon 2-9-1 W Supple 11/4 FAV: 135434: Well plcd & ev ch till onepace fnl 50y: shd 85
clr of rem but is capable of better: sharper 6f or return to 5f may suit: see 1189.

*2361 **CANDOTHAT** 12 [8] 2-9-4 I Mongan (5) 5/1: 0615: Dwelt, rear, rdn 2f out, edged left, nvr trbld ldrs.   2½ 81

*1396 **CHAWENG BEACH** 56 [2] 2-8-3 C Rutter 10/1: 016: Held up, nvr a factor: 8 wk abs, see 1396 (sell).   3½ 56

-- **LAY DOWN SALLY** [9] 2-8-7 S Carson (5) 12/1: 7: V slow away, nvr on terms with ldrs: highly tried,   1¼ 56
debut: cost Ir3,600gns: General Monash Apr foal: half-sister to 2 wnrs, dam & sire sprinters: with J Portman.

1798 **PHYSICAL FORCE** 37 [7] 2-8-9 A Daly 50/1: 008: Chsd ldrs till halfway: stiff task, needs sells.   4 48

-- **CAMBIADO** [3] 2-8-12 O Urbina 11/2: 9: Slow away, nvr dngrs: op 4/1: 20,000 gns Ashkalani colt.   ½ 50

2182 **BENJAMIN** 20 [10] 2-8-12 N Pollard 33/1: 000: Mid-div till halfway: 10th, no form.   9 30

10 ran   Time 1m 15.42 (3.32)   (Mrs D B Brazier)   A P Jarvis Aston Upthorpe, Oxon

---

2688   3.10 FAIR TRIAL HCAP 3YO 0-85 (D)   1m str   Good 40 -04 Slow   [90]
£5681   £1748   £874   £437

2456 **CAIR PARAVEL** 8 [5] R Hannon 3-9-6 (82) A Daly 8/1: 530001: 3 b c Dolphin Street - Queen's Ransom   88
(Last Tycoon) Made ev yard, rdn appr fnl 1f, kept on strongly: won both juv starts at Leicester (auct mdn) &
Doncaster (stks, match, rtd 89): eff at 7f/1m on fast & gd/soft, without blnks: improved for forcing tactics.

2495 **PRETRAIL** 7 [10] A C Stewart 3-8-12 (74) C Rutter 6/1: 021002: 3 b c Catrail - Pretty Lady (High Top)   1 77
Mid-div, prog appr fnl 2f, ch bef dist, styd on but held: clr rem, quick reapp: back to form at 7f/1m.

2117 **CHEMS TRUCE** 23 [8] W R Muir 3-9-7 (83) N Callan 12/1: -30003: 3 b c Brief Truce - In The Rigging   3 80
(Topsider) Pulled hard in tch, eff ent fnl 3f, same pace bef dist: signs of a return to form, see 912.

2084 **OGILIA** 24 [1] I A Balding 3-9-4 (80) Leanne Masterton (7) 10/1: 03-004: Held up, wide, went past   3 71
btn horses appr fnl 1f, nvr dangerous: yet to convince at this 1m trip, see 1826.

2211 **DICKIE DEADEYE** 19 [9] 3-8-10 (72) S Carson (5) 8/1: 0565: Held up, sn pushed along, nvr going pace   1¾ 59
of ldrs: tchd 14/1 on h'cap bow, step up in trip may suit, see 884.

2450 **MENTIGA** 9 [2] 3-8-12 (74) G Hind 7/1: 050606: Al towards rear: op 11/2, see 2450, 810.   3 55

2084 **LARITA** 24 [7] 3-9-7 (83) R Havlin 7/2: 0-2D47: Chsd ldrs, bmpd appr fnl 2f, fdd: see 2084, 1855.   ½ 63

1297 **DIVERS PEARL** 61 [3] 3-9-1 (77) O Urbina 10/3 FAV: 3-2138: Mid-div, wknd ent fnl 2f: longer trip.   shd 57

1726 **SPIRIT OF LIGHT** 40 [6] 3-8-6 (68) P Doe 12/1: 023009: Well plcd, no extra when lost action 2f out.   2½ 43

2524 **TAKE MANHATTAN** 6 [4] 3-8-6 (68) W Supple 7/1: 110000: Handy till ent fnl 3f: 10th, quick reapp.   9 23

10 ran   Time 1m 42.65 (3.55)   (Mrs Caroline Parker)   R Hannon East Everleigh, Wilts

---

2689   3.45 AMAT RDRS HCAP 3YO+ 0-75 (F)   1m4f   Good 40 -01 Slow   [54]
£2590   £740   £370   3 yo rec 13lb

2375 **FLETCHER** 12 [20] H Morrison 6-10-1 (55) Mrs S Bosley 6/1: 022321: 6 b g Salse - Ballet Classique   59
(Sadler's Wells) Nvr far away, hdwy appr fnl 2f, rdn bef dist, ran on to lead fnl 150y: plcd in '99 (stks, rtd 73):
'98 Ascot wnr (amat h'cap, rtd 79): eff at 12f/2m: acts on firm & gd, likes soft: needs to come late on any trk,
likes a stiff finish: responds well to kinder urgings of an amateur & in fine form.

1852 **MEILLEUR** 34 [13] Lady Herries 6-10-12 (56) Miss R Woodman (7) 14/1: 606302: 6 b g Nordico - Lucy   1¼ 58
Limelight (Hot Spark) Rear, imprvd 4f out, pushed into lead below dist, hdd fnl 150y: ran to best, see 68.

2370 **MISCONDUCT** 12 [1] J G Portman 6-9-9 (49) Mr T Best (7) 8/1: -/20-23: 6 gr m Risk Me - Grey Cree   1½ 49
(Creetown) Chsd ldrs, feeling pace 3f out, styd on well fnl 1f: tchd 14/1: gets 12f, worth a try over further.

2212 **ANOTHER BEVELED** 18 [16] G L Moore 5-9-3 (43)(5oh) M A Quinn (5) 40/1: 550/04: Chsd ldrs,   nk 42
onepace fnl 2f: stiff task, first glimmer of ability: stays 12f on good grnd.

2387 **SILENT SOUND** 11 [8] 4-9-13 (53) Miss L J Harwood (7) 12/1: 040025: Prom, rdn & ev ch appr fnl 1f,   hd 52
sn onpace: will apprec a return to 10f: see 1100.

*2387 **PHEISTY** 11 [19] 3-10-7 (74) Miss E Johnson Hough 8/1: 0-5416: In tch, imprvd 3f out, sn same pace.   hd 72

*2482 **NORCROFT JOY** 8 [5] 5-11-7 (75) Mr S Callaghan (7) 9/1: 033317: Rear, late hdwy, nvr a threat.   1 71

2466 **MAY KING MAYHEM** 8 [15] 7-9-9 (49)(bl) Mrs C Williams 5/1 FAV: 111128: Rear, prog to chase ldrs   hd 45
appr fnl 2f, sn no extra: in gd form under stronger jockey previously, worth another chance: see 2286.

2490 **ROYAL AXMINSTER** 7 [6] 5-9-3 (43)(3oh) Miss C Stretton (5) 20/1: -00409: Cl-up, led 4f out-dist, eased.   nk 38

2081 **ADMIRALS SECRET** 24 [10] 11-9-9 (49) Miss H Webster (5) 14/1: 501060: Chsd ldrs till 2f out: 10th.   1¾ 42

2607 **CLASSIC CONKERS** 2 [17] 6-9-3 (43)(1oh) Mr S Rees (5) 14/1: 0-0150: Nvr better than mid-div: 11th.   ¾ 35

2446 **WATER FLOWER** 9 [2] 6-11-2 (70) Mr L Jefford 10/1: 0-0100: Al towards rear: 14th, see 2023 (firm)   0

2190 **COSMO JACK** 19 [12] 4-10-11 (65)(vis) Mr T Scudamore 8/1: 1-2000: Nvr threatened ldrs: 15th.   0

4228J **PAY HOMAGE** 285 [3] 12-9-5 (45) Mr J Gee (5) 25/1: 3046-0: V keen & sn in clr lead, hdd 4f out & btn: 0
18th: '99 rnr-up (h'cap, rtd 58): '98 Warwick wnr (h'cap, rtd 67): eff at 10/12f on hvy, suited by gd or fm.

2463 **Bitter Sweet** 8 [14] 4-9-4 (44)(VIS) Miss T Spearing (4) 20/1:

1997 **Hoteliers Pride** 28 [9] 9-9-7 (60) Miss S Rowe (5) 25/1:

1594 **Pekay** 45 [7] 7-10-2 (56) Mrs V Smart (5) 14/1:   --   **Rainbow Star** [11] 6-10-11 (65) Mr K Ford (7) 50/1:

2270 **Magical Bailiwick** 16 [18] 4-10-13 (67) Mr G Shenkin (5) 25/1:

2466 **Twoforten** 8 [4] 5-9-3 (43)(vis)(5oh) Mr R Lucey Butler (7 25/1:

20 ran   Time 2m 37.31 (4.91)   (Lady Margadale)   H Morrison East Ilsley, Berks

2690	4.20 OWEN TUDOR HCAP 3YO+ 0-70 (E) 6f str Good 40 +05 Fast	[70]

£3198 £984 £492 £246 3 yo rec 6 lb

*2492 **GOODENOUGH MOVER** 7 [6] J S King 4-10-0 (70) R Havlin 3/1 JT FAV: -01111: 4 ch g Beveled - Rekindled **78**
Flame (King's Lake) Made all, clr appr fnl 1f, unchall: best time of day, quick reapp: 4 timer landed after
3 wins at Chepstow in '99 (h'caps): with G Charles Jones in '99 (mdn, rtd 64): eff forcing the pace at 6f/1m: acts
on fast & gd/soft grnd, any trk, likes Chepstow: can carry big weights: progressive, shld make it 5 on the bounce.
1971 **BALI STAR** 29 [5] M J Weeden 5-8-4 (46) A McGlone 20/1: 200002: 5 b g Alnasr Alwasheek - Baligay 2½ **47**
(Balidar) Chsd wnr thr'out, nvr any impress: caught a tad imprvg sort, shwn enough to land a mdn h'cap.
2559 **SHUDDER** 4 [7] R J Hodges 5-9-4 (60) S Carson (5) 6/1: 303163: 5 b g Distant Relative - Oublier nk **60**
L'Ennui (Bellman) Dwelt, bhd, wide prog to go 3rd below dist, nvr nr ldrs: tchd 15/2, qk reapp: consistent.
2303 **ALHUWBILL** 15 [3] J J Bridger 5-7-10 (38)(6oh) D Kinsella (7) 40/1: 0-6004: Well off the pace till ½ **36**
gd late wide hdwy: stiff task, blnks omitted: first sign of form: eff at 6f on gd: interesting in a sell h'cap?
1799 **DAYS OF GRACE** 37 [1] 5-8-13 (55) C Rutter 16/1: 322005: Well plcd, onepace ent fnl 2f: see 466. 1 **50**
889 **WOOLLY WINSOME** 94 [8] 4-8-1 (43) A Daly 40/1: -30006: Mid-div, feeling pace after halfway, switched nk **37**
& late rally: over 3 month abs, now with Dr J Naylor: suited by 7f/1m: see 225.
2431 **CONTRARY MARY** 10 [10] P Doe 3/1 JT FAV: 051227: Nvr dangerous: btr 2371, 2230. ½ **55**
2133 **HYPERACTIVE** 22 [2] 4-10-0 (70) N Pollard 9/2: 1-0208: Wide, no ch appr fnl 1f, shorter trip, see 1483. 1½ **58**
2431 **ONES ENOUGH** 10 [12] 4-8-10 (52)(t) W Supple 12/1: 000109: Chsd ldrs till 2f out: see 1994 (sell h'cap) 1½ **37**
2444 **SWINO** 9 [13] 6-8-6 (48)(vis) N Callan 12/1: 460000: In tch till 3f out: 10th, op 9/1. 2 **27**
2489 **Dancemma** 7 [9] 3-9-4 (66) R Perham 25/1: 2266 **Sea Haze** 16 [4] 3-9-8 (70) O Urbina 16/1:
2215 **Lough Swilly** 18 [11] 4-8-4 (46) G Hind 16/1:
13 ran Time 1m 14.17 (2.07) (D Goodenough Removals & Transport) J S King Broad Hinton, Wilts

2691	4.55 ODSTOCK MDN 3YO+ (D) 1m6f Good 40 +03 Fast	

£3718 £1144 £572 £286 3 yo rec 15lb

2144 **JARDINES LOOKOUT** 22 [2] A P Jarvis 3-8-8 N Callan 11/2: -53621: 3 b g Fourstars Allstar - Foolish **92**
Flight (Fool's Holme) Mid-div, not much room ent fnl 4 out till 2f out, sn qcknd into lead & went well clr:
drifted from 7/2, fair time: unrcd juv: eff at 14, shld get 2m: acts on fast & gd/soft grnd, any trk: improving.
1929 **ARMEN** 31 [6] M C Pipe 3-8-8 W Supple 9/4 FAV: 0-22: 3 b c Kaldoun - Anna Edes (Fabulous Dancer) 10 **82**
Cl-up, led appr fnl 2f, sn hdd & no ch with wnr: caught a decent sort, may apprec a drop back to 12f, as in 1929.
2353 **FIVE OF WANDS** 13 [4] W Jarvis 3-8-3 D McGaffin (1) 6/1: 0-23: 3 b f Caerleon - Overact (Law Society) 6 **71**
Chsd ldrs, ch appr fnl 2f, sn onepace: this longer 14f trip lkd likely to suit after 2353 (4 rnrs).
1929 **ARTHUR K** 31 [14] H Morrison 3-8-8 A Daly 50/1: 64: Rear, chsd ldrs 4f out till 2f out. 6 **70**
2477 **ROUTE ONE** 8 [5] 7-9-9 R Perham 12/1: 645: Keen in lead till hdd appr fnl 2f, wknd: op 8/1, btr 2477. 3½ **67**
2477 **POT LUCK** 8 [11] 3-8-8 G Hind 20/1: 356: Dwelt, nvr a factor: stablemate 4th, now qual for h'caps 3 **64**
-- **LOST THE PLOT** [12] 5-9-4 S Carson (5) 11/2: 7: Nvr a factor: Flat bow, near 4 month hdles abs, 1½ **58**
back in 98/99 won bmprs at Fontwell & Cheltenham (gd & gd/soft grnd): with D Arbuthnot.
1179 **ICE CRYSTAL** 69 [13] 3-8-8 C Rutter 7/1: 0048: Chsd ldrs till 3f out: 10 wk abs, much btr 1179 (12f, firm). 5 **58**
3173} **WILDERNESS** 344 [1] 3-8-4(1ow) R Havlin 33/1: -0-9: Nvr dangerous: reapp, new stable, no form. nk **53**
4442} **CHIEF WALLAH** 269 [10] 4-9-9 N Pollard 16/1: 6-0: Dwelt, al towards rear: 10th: rtd 58 sole '99 start. ½ **56**
2265 **BAMBOOZLE** 16 [9] 4-9-4 P Doe 8/1: 050: Al bhd: 11th, longer trip, btr 2265 (10f). 2 **49**
2135 **Betachance Dot Com** 22 [3] 3-8-4(1ow) A McGlone 50/1: -- **Mister Ermyn** [1] 7-9-9 (bl) I Mongan (5) 33/1:
588} **Spinner Toy** 501 [8] 5-9-9 R Smith (5) 66/1:
14 ran Time 3m 03.15 (5.15) (Ambrose Turnbull) A P Jarvis Aston Upthorpe, Oxon

Official Going GOOD. Stalls: Sprint - Stands Side; 7f & Rnd - Inside.

2692	1.55 E. SMITHSON MED AUCT MDN 2YO (E) 6f Good 43 -45 Slow	

£7507 £2310 £1155 £577

-- **PRIZEMAN** [3] R Hannon 2-9-0 R Hughes 6/1: 1: 2 b c Prized - Shuttle (Coquistador Cielo) **102+**
Cl-up trav slightly well, styd on well led over fnl 1f, qcknd clr, v readily: well bckd on debut: Feb foal, cost 30,000
gns: dam won in the US: eff at 6f, 7f looks sure to suit: runs well fresh: looks v useful, one to follow.
-- **PETONGSKI** [8] D W Barker 2-9-0 F Lynch 50/1: 2: 2 b g Petong - Madam Petoski (Petoski) 4 **89**
Prom, led over 2f out, hdd appr fnl 1f, not pace of wnr & flashed tail under press: debut: Jan foal, full
brother to a 6f wnr: speedily bred & eff at 6f: win similar on this form, encouraging.
2480 **PASITHEA** 8 [15] T D Easterby 2-8-9 T E Durcan 20/1: 453: 2 b f Celtic Swing - Midnight's Reward 2 **78**
(Night Shift) Keen, hld up, eff over 1f out, kept on ins last, no dngr: looks a nursery h'cap type, poss at 7f.
2480 **EXTRA GUEST** 8 [12] M R Channon 2-8-9 T Quinn 9/2: 262224: Handy, rdn & onepace over 1f out. 1½ **74**
2100 **NAMLLAMS** 24 [17] 2-9-0 A Beech (5) 33/1: -005: Handy, rdn & no impress fnl 1f: better run at 6f. 1¼ **75**
2500 **FOREVER TIMES** 7 [11] 2-8-9 K Darley 100/30 FAV: 36: Slow away, bhd, late gains: rate higher. nk **69**
-- **SANDORRA** [10] 2-8-9 J Reid 50/1: 7: In tch, rdn & no extra appr fnl 1f on debut: Feb foal, ½ **67**
cost 3,800gns: bred to apprec 7f in time: with M Brittain.
-- **SAFINAZ** [9] 2-8-9 P McCabe 50/1: 8: Slow away, bhd, some late gains on debut: Mar foal: 1½ **63**
half-sister to sev wnrs: dam 1m scorer: bred to apprec 7f/1m in time & showed some promise here.
-- **ZENDIUM** [2] 2-9-0 J P Spencer 25/1: 9: In tch, brief eff over 1f out, nvr dngrs on debut: Apr nk **67**
foal, cost IR 6,500gns: half-brother to 2 wnrs: dam 10f scorer: sure to relish 7f & improve: with T D Easterby.
2057 **DARWIN TOWER** 25 [5] 2-9-0 K Hodgson 50/1: 000: Bhd, eff over 2f out, sn no impress: 10th: Mar ½ **65**
foal, cost 3,600gns: bred to apprec 7f: with B Murray.
2331 **MISTER SANDERS** 12 [6] 2-9-0 Dean McKeown 33/1: 060: In tch, wknd 2f out: 11th: see 2361. nk **64**
2333 **SQUIRE TAT** 14 [14] 2-9-0 G Duffield 25/1: 50: Nvr a factor: 12th: see 2333. ½ **63**
-- **MAULD SEGOISHA** [4] 2-8-9 M Roberts 25/1: 0: In tch, btn 2f out: 13th on debut: Apr foal, ½ **56**
cost IR 21,000: bred for 6/7f: with J FitzGerald.
-- **INJAAZ** [18] 2-8-9 Pat Eddery 11/2: 0: In tch, wknd 3f out: 14th: Mar foal, cost 32,000gns: 4 **44**
half-sister to 2 wnrs: bred to apprec 7f+ in time.

1893 **Amy Dee 32** [1] 2-8-9 Kim Tinkler 25/1: 2277 **Mr Bountiful 16** [4] 2-9-0 P Fessey 25/1:
1938 **Classy Act 30** [7] 2-8-9 C Lowther 12/1: 1823 **Kimoe Warrior 36** [16] 2-9-0 J F Egan 33/1:
18 ran Time 1m 14.71 (5.31) (Highclere Thoroughbred Racing Ltd) R Hannon Everleigh, Wilts.

2693 **2.25 THEAKSTON COND STKS 2YO (B) 7f str Good 43 -48 Slow**
£10622 £3481 £1740

*2005 **CHIANTI 28** [1] J L Dunlop 2-9-0 Pat Eddery 30/100 FAV: 11: 2 b c Danehill - Sabaah (Nureyev) **100**
Made all, styd on well over 1f out, pushed out, cmftbly: hvly bckd to land the odds: debut wnr here at York (mdn): Mar foal, cost IR£500,000: full brother to Irish 2,000 Guineas/Derby wnr Desert King: eff at 6/7f, 1m looks sure to suit: acts on firm & gd, runs well fresh: potentially smart, keep on the right side.
*2306 **RIZERIE 15** [4] L M Cumani 2-8-9 J P Spencer 7/2: 12: 2 gr f Highest Honor - Riziere (Groom Dancer) *5* **83**
Chsd wnr, edged left over 2f out, no impress fnl 1f: prob ran to form of 2306 (wng debut) bhd a useful sort.
-- **TUPGILL TURBO** [3] S E Kettlewell 2-8-8 K Darley 12/1: 3: 2 ch g Rudimentary - Persian Alexandra *27* **32**
(Persian Bold) Chsd ldrs, wknd qckly over 2f out, eased: debut: Mar foal, cost 16,000gns: half-brother to 3 wnrs, dam juv 7f scorer: bred to apprec 7f+ in time.
3 ran Time 1m 27.77 (6.47) (Wafic Said) J L Dunlop Arundel, W.Sussex.

2694 **3.00 KRONENBOURG HCAP 3YO+ 0-90 (C) 7f str Good 43 -20 Slow [85]**
£9724 £2992 £1496 £748 3 yo rec 8 lb

2522 **DONNAS DOUBLE 6** [16] D Eddy 5-8-6 (63) A Beech (5) 14/1: 563521: 5 ch g Weldnaas - Shadha (Shirley **69**
Heights) In tch, switched right & hdwy well over 1f out, styd on well for press to get up cl-home: qck reapp: '99 wnr at Catterick & Redcar (h'caps, rtd 67): '98 scorer at Musselburgh & Hamilton (mdn h'cap & h'cap, rtd 57): suited by 7f/8.5f on gd & soft, does stay 12f & handles firm: acts on any trk: tough & game.
1840 **KARAMEG 35** [14] P W Harris 4-9-7 (78) T Quinn 15/2: 15-042: 4 b f Danehill - House Of Queens (King *nk* **83**
Of Clubs) In tch, hdwy over 3f out to lead over 1f out, kept on well for press ins last, just collared cl-home: deserves a win, but likely to go up in the weights again for this fine run: see 1840, 1483.
2508 **AMBER FORT 7** [15] J M Bradley 7-8-9 (66)(bl) P Fitzsimons (5) 25/1: 405553: 7 gr g Indian Ridge - *1* **69**
Lammastide (Martinmas) Chsd ldrs, eff to chall well over 1f out, onepace for press ins last: best eff for a while & slipping down the weights: blnks reapplied here, see 1483.
1820 **PREMIER BARON 36** [20] P S McEntee 5-9-6 (77) L Newman (3) 20/1: 006444: Waited with, hdwy *2* **76**
over 2f out, kept on fnl 1f, no extra cl-home: fine run from high draw on slower grnd & slipped back to a fair mark.
2559 **PRESENT CHANCE 4** [18] 6-8-1 (58)(bl) J Fanning 25/1: 005055: Waited with, eff well over 1f *hd* **57**
out, kept on ins last: qck reapp, another fair run: see 2559, 674.
2481 **SUPREME SALUTATION 8** [8] 4-9-2 (73) K Darley 12/1: 606206: In tch, eff to chall over 1f out, wknd. *1¾* **68**
2444 **COOL PROSPECT 9** [10] 5-8-3 (60) J F Egan 10/1: 423227: In tch, rdn & no extra over 1f out. *hd* **54**
2511 **CAUTIOUS JOE 7** [1] 3-8-0 (65) P Fessey 20/1: 003558: Cl-up, led briefly 2f out, no extra fnl 1f. *¾* **57**
2364 **ITS ALLOWED 12** [22] 3-8-10 (75) T E Durcan 20/1: 2-0059: Bhd, late gains, nr dngrs: see 1308. *nk* **66**
2325 **ROYAL IVY 14** [9] 3-8-3 (68) J Quinn 14/1: 005420: In tch, wknd 2f out: 10th: btr 2325, 421. *½* **58**
2054 **ANTONIO CANOVA 26** [19] 4-9-2 (73) J Reid 16/1: 23-300: Waited with wide, btn over 1f out: 11th. *½* **62**
2215 **COMPRADORE 18** [21] 5-8-11 (68) M Roberts 16/1: 211030: Waited with, rdn & btn 2f out: 12th. *hd* **56**
2338 **MANTLES PRIDE 14** [11] 5-9-13 (84)(bl) G Duffield 16/1: 410600: Waited with, brief eff over 2f *nk* **71**
out, sn btn: 13th: been busy, btr 2133, best 1514.
2645 **HAKEEM 1** [2] 5-8-5 (62) D Mernagh (3) 12/1: 220330: Handy, rdn & wknd over 1f out: 14th, qk reapp. *¾* **47**
2420 **CUSIN 10** [12] 4-8-13 (70) K Hodgson 14/1: 030500: Waited with, eff & barged through 2f out, *¾* **53**
no impress: 15th, jockey received a 7-day irresponsible riding ban: see 2185, 1840.
2371 **BINTANG TIMOR 12** [7] 6-9-1 (72) Pat Eddery 11/2 FAV: 462500: Al bhd: 16th, bckd, better expected. *1¾* **51**
2247 **LOOK HERE NOW 17** [6] 3-8-13 (78) C Lowther 25/1: -1500: Prom, edged right & wknd 2f out: 17th. *3½* **50**
2163 **JEFFREY ANOTHERRED 21** [17] 6-8-12 (69) F Lynch 14/1: -00060: Chsd ldrs, rdn & hmpd over 1f out, *1½* **39**
sn btn: 18th, prefers soft grnd: see 2163.
2163 **MELODIAN 21** [5] 5-8-9 (66)(bl) T Williams 20/1: 410000: Led halfway till over 2f out, wknd: 19th. *6* **24**
2356 **INDIAN PLUME 13** [4] 4-9-10 (81) Dean McKeown 12/1: 100100: Led till halfway, no extra: 20th. *1½* **37**
1853 **SORBETT 34** [3] 3-9-8 (87) J P Spencer 33/1: -60400: In tch, wknd 3f out: fin last: see 1164, 1069. *3* **37**
21 ran Time 1m 25.73 (4.43) (James R Adams) D Eddy Ingoe, Northumberland.

2695 **3.35 LISTED SILVER CUP RATED HCAP 4YO+ 0-105 (A) 1m6f Good 43 +04 Fast [109]**
£18913 £7174 £3587 £1630

1982 **EMINENCE GRISE 29** [2] H R A Cecil 5-9-0 (95) T Quinn 100/30 FAV: 64-021: 5 b g Sadler's Wells - **97**
Impatiente (Vaguely Noble) Cl-up, hdwy to lead 2f out, hdd over 1f out, rallied for press in a thrilling duel to the line, just got up: good time: sole prev win in '99, at Kempton (h'cap, rtd 96 at best): eff over 14f/2m, tried 2m6f: acts on firm, gd/soft & on a gall or easy trk: has run well fresh & in blnks: useful, 4th in Ebor last term.
1187 **MUSICIAN 69** [8] J R Fanshawe 4-8-13 (94) R Hughes 10/1: 115-02: 4 b f Shirley Heights - Rose *shd* **95**
Alto (Adonijah) In tch, hdwy over 3f out, styd on to lead over 1f out, kept on for hands-&-heels riding ins last, just tchd off in a thrilling fin: fine run after a 10 wk abs & stays 14f well: most progressive & useful.
*2336 **BAY OF ISLANDS 14** [6] D Morris 8-9-2 (97)(vis) K Darley 13/2: -00313: 8 b f Jupiter Island - Lawyer's *shd* **98**
Wave (Advocator) Waited with, hdwy & sltly short of room over 1f out, switched left & styd on well ins last, tchd off in a stirring fin: another fine run from this tough & useful stayer: shade unlucky & apprec a return to 2m.
2069 **MOWBRAY 25** [4] P F I Cole 5-9-2 (97) L Newman 11/1: 5-5604: Waited with, hdwy over 2f out, strong *hd* **98**
run fnl 1f, just failed in a 4-way photo: excellent run: fin 2L 3rd in Ebor h'cap last term off a 1lb lower mark than this & must have strong each-way claims again in this form: see 1401.
874 **SEEK 95** [9] 4-8-7 (88)(2oh) J P Spencer 7/2: 21-25: Cl-up, ev ch over 2f out, wknd over 1f out: *3* **86**
nicely bckd: 3 month abs & far from disgraced: stays 14f & open to improvement: see 874.
2498 **PRAIRIE FALCON 7** [1] 6-8-7 (88)(3oh) J Reid 14/1: 604F06: Set pace till over 2f out, onepace. *hd* **85**
2405 **SINON 14** [7] 5-9-7 (102) J Fanning 12/1: 01-657: Cl-up, wknd 2f out: top-weight: see 1339. *1* **98**
2336 **FANTASY HILL 14** [5] 4-9-1 (96) Pat Eddery 4/1: 2-5348: Waited with, eff 3f out, sn btn: btr 2336. *¾* **91**
1850 **RAISE A PRINCE 35** [3] 7-8-11 (92)(t) G Duffield 25/1: -56609: Al bhd: needs soft grnd: see 1109. *2½* **84**
9 ran Time 2m 58.8 (5.4) (Wafic Said) H R A Cecil Newmarket.

2696	**4.10 JOHN SMITHS CUP HCAP 3YO+ 0-110 (B)** **1m2f85y** **Good 43** **+17 Fast**		**[109]**
	£87750 £27000 £13500 £6750 3 yo rec 11lb		

2528 **SOBRIETY** 6 [8] R F Johnson Houghton 3-8-8 (100) J Reid 20/1: -10651: 3 b c Namaqualand - Scanno's **109**
Choice (Pennine Walk) In tch, hdwy over 2f out, strong run appr fnl 1f to get up cl-home, drvn out: fast time, qk
reapp: been catching the eye over 1m earlier & scored on reapp at Doncaster (stks): in '99 won at Salisbury
(mdn auct, rtd 95): eff over a stiff 1m, relished this 10.4f: acts on firm, gd/soft & likes a gall trk: runs well
fresh: gets on well with J Reid: smart & has a turn of foot, unexposed at this trip & shld land another val prize.
2117 **MAN OMYSTERY** 23 [3] J Noseda 3-8-2 (94) J F Egan 11/2: 0-1242: 3 b c Diesis - Eurostorm hd **102**
(Storm Bird) Waited with, gd hdwy over 3f out, styd on to lead over 1f out, kept on well till collared nr line,
just btn: well bckd & a tremendous run in this val h'cap stepped up to 10f: lightly rcd, keep on the right side.
*2358 **NOOSHMAN** 13 [11] Sir Michael Stoute 3-8-1 (93) L Newman (3) 9/1: -15013: 3 ch g Woodman - Knoosh 1 **99**
(Storm Bird) In tch, eff & switched right over 2f out, kept on ins last, only btn 1L: op 7/1: v progressive
& shld land another val h'cap: see 2358.
2475 **TRIPLE DASH** 8 [5] Sir Mark Prescott 4-8-3 (84) G Duffield 8/1: 000004: Cl-up, led 3f out till over 1f 1 **88**
out, onepace: bckd tho' op 6/1: excellent effort (fully 6L clr of rem) & shld land a less competetive h'cap.
2090 **CARDIFF ARMS** 24 [9] Dean McKeown 6-9-0 (95) 40/1: 200505: Bhd, hdwy 3f out, switched left 6 **90**
2f out, nvr dngrs: in h'capper's grip at present: see 1829, 1112.
2190 **TONIGHTS PRIZE** 7 [4] Mrs J Ramsden 4-8-10 (91) J Fanning 33/1: 35-146: Cl-up, wknd appr 2f out: btr 1288. nk **72**
2069 **WESTENDER** 25 [2] J P Spencer 9/1: 3-2257: Slow away, bhd, eff & switched right ½ **84**
2f out, no impress: op 7/1: see 2069, best 1695.
*2350 **MCGILLYCUDDY REEKS** 13 [1] 9-7-12 (79)(8ex) Kim Tinkler 50/1: 252318: In tch, eff 3f out, no impress. ½ **71**
2090 **TISSIFER** 24 [13] 4-9-12 (107) J Fanning 50/1: 0-2209: Bhd, some late gains, nvr dngrs: see 1841, ¾ **98**
2178 **GOLCONDA** 20 [12] 4-8-5 (86)(VIS) A Beech (5) 40/1: -30000: Waited with, btn 2f out: 10th, visor. hd **76**
2170 **KOMISTAR** 21 [18] 5-8-7 (88) J Stack 66/1: 0-0200: Set pace till 3f out, wknd: 11th: see 2170. 2 **75**
1845 **NOBELIST** 35 [6] 5-9-8 (103) T E Durcan 40/1: 4/6100: Bhd, modest late gains, 12th: twice 1561. 1½ **88**
2339 **FIRST FANTASY** 14 [15] 4-8-6 (86)(1ow) R Hughes 20/1: 051050: Hld up, eff 3f out, wknd: 13th. 1¾ **68**
2066 **MEDICEAN** 25 [21] 3-8-10 (102) Pat Eddery 5/2 FAV: -31130: Waited with, well bhd 4f out, sn rdn ¾ **83**
& no impress: 14th, hvly bckd: lkd a h'cap snip after being btn less than 1L in a Gr 1 over 1m last time (rtd
117) but nvr got competitive from a poor high draw here: expect much better next time, see 2066.
2311 **TONY TIE** 15 [14] 4-8-4 (85) F Lynch 40/1: 231020: Chsd ldrs, rdn & wknd well over 2f out: 15th. ½ **65**
*757 **MILLIGAN** 109 [20] 5-8-4 (85) M Roberts 14/1: 000-10: In tch, brief eff over 4f out, sn btn: 16th: 1 **63**
with D Nicholls on the Flat earlier: plcd in a 2m h'cap hdle 5 wks ago after impressing in 757.
2157 **COLWAY RITZ** 21 [19] 6-8-2 (83)(5ex) T Williams 33/1: 361120: Al bhd: 17th: btr 2157, 2102. 2½ **57**
-2001 **JEDI KNIGHT** 28 [10] 6-8-8 (89) T Lucas 20/1: 40-020: Handy, wknd over 3f out: 18th: btr 2001. ¾ **62**
2001 **PENSION FUND** 28 [16] 6-8-0 (81) J Quinn 25/1: 06-300: Al bhd: 19th, btr 1217. 1½ **52**
2350 **MANTUSIS** 13 [7] 5-8-8 (89) T Quinn 25/1: -32140: Waited with, brief eff over 3f out, sn wknd: 20th. 2 **57**
*1982 **INCH PERFECT** 29 [22] 5-8-6 (87) K Darley 8/1: 131310: Keen, sn cl-up, wknd over 3f out: 21st, 1¼ **53**
gamble from 20/1: rare below-par run: progressive earlier & shld prove better when settling/having more cover.
2616 **DEBBIES WARNING** 2 [17] 4-8-10 (91) J Mackay (5) 50/1: 640060: Al bhd, t.o.: too soon? 27 **17**
22 ran   Time 2m 10.0 (2.7)   (Anthony Pye-Jeary)   R F Johnson Houghton Blewbury, Oxon.

2697	**4.45 BECK'S BIER HCAP 3YO+ 0-90 (C)** **6f** **Good 43** **-32 Slow**		**[86]**
	£11895 £3660 £1830 £915 3 yo rec 6 lb		

2444 **THE GAY FOX** 9 [16] B A McMahon 6-8-13 (71)(tbl) T E Durcan 20/1: 530241: 6 gr g Never So Bold - **75**
School Concert (Music Boy) Sn bhd, not clr run & plenty to do 2f out, strong run appr fnl 1f to get up cl home:
plcd in '99 (rtd 71): '98 wnr at Sandown (h'cap, rtd 94): suited by 5/6f, stays 7f on any trk: handles fm, likes
gd or hvy: gd weight carrier who has run well fresh in a t-strap: eff with/without blnks: well h'capped.
2559 **PEPPIATT** 4 [1] N Bycroft 6-8-1 (59) J Quinn 25/1: 035002: 6 ch g Efisio - Fleur Du Val (Valiyar) hd **62**
In tch, hdwy over 1f out to lead ins last, kept on till collared last strides: qck reapp, jockey rec a 2 day
whip ban: enjoyed this easier surface & on a winning mark: see 2163, 1654.
2355 **NINEACRES** 13 [2] J M Bradley 9-8-10 (68)(bl) P Fitzsimons (5) 20/1: 101103: 9 b g Sayf El Arab - hd **70**
Mayor (Laxton) Prom, eff to lead briefly ins last, kept on for press, just btn in a 3-way photo: most tough.
2580 **CAUDA EQUINA** 3 [19] M R Channon 6-9-3 (75) T Quinn 20/1: 430204: Sn well bhd, fin fast fnl 1f: 1 **75**
qck reapp: on a long losing sequence, but this was encouraging & has won 6 times at Bath: see 2432, 905.
1861 **DAAWE** 34 [10] 9-9-0 (72)(bl) Clare Roche (7) 25/1: 100505: Set gd pace centre, edged left for hd **71**
press fnl 1f but kept on till collared well ins last, not btn far: gd effort: best 1074.
2559 **DOUBLE ACTION** 4 [6] 6-8-6 (64)(bl) K Darley 20/1: 326606: In tch, kept for press fnl 1f: qck reapp. ½ **61**
2644 **LAGO DI VARANO** 1 [17] 8-9-11 (83)(bl) Dean McKeown 20/1: 505307: Handy, kept on same pace for ½ **79**
press fnl 1f: unplcd here yesterday & all 10 wins at 5f: see 2473.
1887 **CADEAUX CHER** 32 [18] 6-9-8 (80) J Reid 16/1: -22008: Sn bhd, late gains: likes Doncaster. 2½ **70**
+2580 **PIPS MAGIC** 3 [5] 4-9-7 (79)(6ex) F Lynch 12/1: 0W0019: Handy, btn appr fnl 1f: too soon? ½ **67**
2334 **FRIAR TUCK** 14 [15] 5-8-12 (70) J Mackay (5) 4/1 FAV: 021030: In tch, eff over 1f out, no impress: 1 **55**
10th: hvly bckd from 7/1: likes this trk: btr 2334 & 2000.
1471 **DOWNLAND** 52 [4] 4-9-8 (80) M Roberts 6/1: 20-060: In tch, rdn & btn over 1f out: 11th, bckd, abs. 1½ **61**
*2444 **FULL SPATE** 9 [11] 5-8-12 (70) Pat Eddery 20/1: 035410: In tch, rdn & no impress over 1f out: 12th. ½ **50**
2631 **BODFARI PRIDE** 2 [3] 5-9-4 (76) K Hodgson 14/1: 011620: Cl-up, rdn & wknd over 1f out: 13th. ½ **54**
2334 **BOLDLY GOES** 14 [14] 4-9-10 (82)(bl) J Fanning 16/1: 043100: In tch, wknd over 1f out: 14th. hd **59**
2310 **CENTRAL COAST** 15 [12] 4-9-7 (79) J Tate 20/1: 20-000: Al bhd: 15th: in '99 scored at Newbury nk **55**
(h'cap, rtd 85 at best): '98 wnr at Nottingham (auct mdn, rtd 83): suited by 6f on firm/fast grnd & a gall
trk: shld do better if stable returns to form.
2569 **At Large** 4 [22] 6-9-4 (76) R Hughes 20/1:   2371 **Stylish Ways** 12 [7] 8-8-12 (70) T G McLaughlin 16/1:
2334 **Smart Predator** 14 [20] 4-9-4 (76) J Stack 12/1:   2505 **Red Charger** 7 [13] 4-8-5 (63) G Duffield 25/1:
2288 **Red Revolution** 15 [8] 3-8-13 (77) J F Egan 16/1:   2431 **Marengo** 10 [21] 6-8-2 (60) L Newman (3) 33/1:
2275 **Mother Corrigan** 16 [9] 4-9-10 (54)(vis)(1oh) D Mernagh (1) 50/1:
2395 **Get Stuck In** 11 [23] 4-9-7 (79) C Lowther 16/1:
23 ran   Time 1m 13.92 (4.52)   (Mrs J McMahon)   B A McMahon Hopwas, Staffs.

YORK SATURDAY JULY 15TH Lefthand, Flat, Galloping Track

2698 | 5.15 MILLER NURSERY HCAP 2YO (C) 5f Good 43 -74 Slow [94]
£8827   £2716   £1358   £679

2248 **LAUREL DAWN** 17 [3] A Berry 2-8-10 (76) R Hughes 4/1: 40121: 2 gr c Paris House - Madrina (Waajib) **81**
Made all, clr when jinked right ins fnl 1f, kept on, pushed out: earlier scored at Lingfield (mdn auct mdn):
Apr first foal, dam 6f wnr: eff at 5f on fast, gd/soft & equitrack, 6f shld suit: proving tough & progressive.
*2333 **SILCA LEGEND** 14 [4] M R Channon 2-9-7 (87) T Quinn 11/8 FAV: 242212: 2 ch c Efisio - Silca Cisa **½ 90**
(Hallgate) Chsd wnr, rdn & outpcd over 1f out, rallied ins last, not btn far: hvly bckd & another useful
run: v tough & consistent, shld relish a return to 6f as in 2333.
1981 **TIME MAITE** 29 [1] M W Easterby 2-7-13 (65) D Mernagh (3) 8/1: 431353: 2 b g Komaite - Martini Time **1 65**
(Ardoon) Handy, rdn over 1f out, kept on same pace: see 1549, 1476.
1761 **HAMBLETON HIGHLITE** 38 [2] K A Ryan 2-9-5 (85)(BL) F Lynch 8/1: 1304: Slow away, bhd, eff over 2f **hd 84**
out, no extra ins last: fine run in the circumstances in first time blnks: see 1475.
2277 **CUMBRIAN HARMONY** 16 [6] J A Glover 2-8-1 (67) P Fessey 7/1: 023055: Sn rdn in tch, no impress over 1f out. **3 57**
2480 **FIENNES** 8 [5] J Mackay (5) 4/1: 50636: Handy, wknd 2f out: btr 1480. **4 47**
6 ran Time 1m 02.68 (5.88) (Laurel Leisure Ltd) A Berry Cockerham, Lancs.

HAYDOCK SUNDAY JULY 16TH Lefthand, Flat, Galloping Track

Official Going GOOD/FIRM. Stalls: 5/6f - Centre, 7f/1m - Inside, 10/12f - Outside

2699 | 2.20 METRO NEWS FILLIES HCAP 3YO 0-80 (D) 1m30y rnd Good/Firm 21 -04 Slow [82]
£4426   £1362   £681   £340

2524 **LADY HELEN** 7 [4] T D Easterby 3-8-8 (62) J Carroll 3/1 FAV: 00-051: 3 b f Salse - Old Domesday Book **71 +**
(High Top) Trkd ldrs, led over 2f out & sn rdn clr, eased down nr fin, rdly: hvly bckd, op 7/2: '99 Beverley wnr
(mdn, made all, rtd 74): eff at 1m, may get further: acts on firm & fast, stiff/gall trk: op to further improvement.
2044 **CIBENZE** 27 [1] M R Channon 3-8-12 (66) A Culhane 7/1: 642602: 3 b f Owington - Maria Cappuccini **3 67**
(Siberian Express) Held up, rdn/prog to chase wnr 1f out, al held: op 6/1: styd longer 1m trip well: see 1405.
*2438 **DESERT SAFARI** 10 [2] E J Alston 3-9-7 (75) T E Durcan 4/1: 400113: 3 b f Desert Style - Dublah **1 74**
(Private Account) Keen, chsd ldrs, kept on onepace fnl 2f: op 7/2: stays 1m, in fine form at 7f recently: see 2438.
2512 **VICTORIET** 8 [6] A T Murphy 3-7-10 (50)(2oh) K Dalgleish (5) 16/1: 0-5504: Keen/prom, led over 3f **½ 48**
out till over 2f out, no extra: op 14/1: see 1435.
2542 **PIX ME UP** 6 [8] 3-7-13 (53) Iona Wands (5) 11/1: 124005: Rear, switched/mod gains fnl 3f: op 9/1. **3 45**
2175 **INDY CARR** 21 [9] 3-8-8 (62) F Lynch 14/1: -60466: Chsd ldrs 6f: op 12/1: see 900. **2½ 49**
2418 **TANGERINE** 11 [5] Dale Gibson 20/1: -00007: Mid-div, btn 3f out: blnks, lngr 1m trip. **shd 42**
2241 **LADY OF WINDSOR** 18 [3] 3-9-1 (69)(vis) R Winston 5/1: 510238: Led till over 3f out, fdd: op 4/1. **1¼ 53**
2043 **LADY JONES** 27 [7] 3-8-4 (58) G Bardwell 6/1: 0-0139: Rear, nvr factor: op 5/1: see 2043, 1822 (C/D). **2 38**
9 ran Time 1m 42.55 (2.05) (M P Burke) T D Easterby Great Habton, N Yorks

2700 | 2.50 CHANNEL M MDN 2YO (D) 6f str Good/Firm 21 -48 Slow
£3753   £1155   £577   £288

2029 **XIPE TOTEC** 28 [11] R A Fahey 2-9-0 S Sanders 20/1: -01: 2 ch c Pivotal - Northern Bird (Interrex) **87**
Made virtually all, rdn/strongly prsd fnl 2f, held on gamely nr fin: op 14/1: left debut bhd: eff at 6f, 7f + shld
suit: acts on fast grnd & a gall trk: clearly going the right way, can raise more highly.
2137 **XALOC BAY** 23 [6] K R Burke 2-9-0 N Callan 1/2 FAV: -22: 2 br c Charnwood Forest - Royal Jade **nk 87$**
(Last Tycoon) Cl-up, joined wnr going best 2f out, styd on press fnl 1f, just held nr line: hvly bckd at odds-on:
acts on fast & gall grnd, can find one of these: see 2137.
2360 **TOMTHEVIC** 13 [2] J J Quinn 2-9-0 R Mullen 16/1: -403: 2 ch g Emarati - Madame Bovary (Ile de **1½ 82**
Bourbon) Held up towards rear, keen, styd on from over 1f out, no threat to front pair: op 12/1: styd longer 6f
trip, handles fast grnd, al apprec 7f +: see 1698.
2174 **LE MERIDIEN** 21 [7] J S Wainwright 2-8-9 J McAuley (5) 20/1: -04: Chsd ldrs, outpcd over 1f out. **¾ 75$**
2333 **STORM KING** 15 [1] 2-9-0 J Carroll 10/1: -005: Prom till over 1f out: op 8/1: see 2333, 1513. **4 68**
2480 **THE FANCY MAN** 9 [4] 2-9-0 Kim Tinkler 10/1: -406: Chsd ldrs till over 2f out: op 8/1: see 1823. **3½ 58**
2417 **LIVE THE DREAM** 11 [9] 2-8-9 M Tebbutt 33/1: -07: Dwelt, rear, no impress fnl 3f: see 2417. **1½ 49**
-- **LONGCHAMP DU LAC** [10] 2-9-0 O Pears 11/1: -8: In tch 3f: Lake Coniston colt, Mar foal, cost **5 39**
6,000 gns: dam a juv wnr abroad: sire prog/top class sprinter: with A Berry.
2521 **TOBYTOO** 7 [8] 2-9-0 R Fitzpatrick (3) 66/1: -009: Dwelt, bmpd start, al bhd: mod form. **1¾ 34**
9 ran Time 1m 15.45 (4.15) (Mrs Brigitte Pollard) R A Fahey Butterwick, N Yorks

2701 | 3.20 EVENING NEWS HCAP 3YO+ 0-80 (D) 5f str Good/Firm 21 -02 Slow [77]
£7507   £2310   £1155   £577   3yo rec 4lb

2418 **BENZOE** 11 [5] D Nicholls 10-8-3 (52) Iona Wands(5) 16/1: 0-5061: 10 b g Taufan - Saintly Guest **58**
(What A Guest) Chsd ldrs, rdn & styd on well to lead well ins last: op 14/1: '99 Leicester wnr (h'cap, A Turnell,
rtd 66): '98 wnr at Thirsk & Redcar (h'caps, Mrs Ramsden, rtd 76): eff at 5/6f on soft & hvy grnd, suited by gd &
firm, best without blnks: handles any trk & loves Thirsk: well h'capped, could win again.
2525 **MUNGO PARK** 7 [11] M Dods 6-9-10 (73)(bl) A Culhane 15/2: 020222: 6 b g Selkirk - River Dove **¾ 76**
(Riverman) Dwelt, rdn & styd on well fnl 2f, not rch wnr: a tricky ride but on a fair mark for similar: see 758.
2247 **PURE COINCIDENCE** 18 [3] K R Burke 5-9-10 (73) F Norton 20/1: 300003: 5 b g Lugana Beach - **hd 76**
Esilam (Henny Park) Handy, led over 1f out till well ins last, no extra: nicely h'capped, back to form.
2505 **MUKARRAB** 8 [12] D W Chapman 6-8-2 (51) K Dalgleish (5) 10/1: 100444: Chsd ldrs, rdn/ch fnl 1f, **¾ 51**
just held cl-home: op 8/1: see 2340, 1714.
2444 **MISS FIT** 10 [9] 4-9-0 (63) M Tebbutt 12/1: 500005: Chsd ldrs, onepace fnl 1f: op 14/1: see 926. **1 60**
2310 **GAY BREEZE** 16 [14] 7-9-10 (73) J Weaver 12/1: 035006: Prom, fdd fnl 1f: op 10/1: see 905 (stks). **nk 69**
1664 **BEDEVILLED** 44 [10] 5-9-6 (69) Lynsey Hanna (7) 16/1: 1OW027: Dwelt, mid-div, not pace to chall: abs. **nk 64**
2690 **SWINO** 1 [2] 6-7-13 (48) (vis) Joanna Badger 25/1: 600008: Rdn/outpcd, kept on fnl 1f, nrst fin: **nk 42**
unplcd at Salisbury yesterday: see 177.

848

2444 **SUGAR CUBE TREAT 10** [13] 4-8-3 (52) J Bramhill 25/1: 003509: Rdn/twds rear, late gains, no threat. ¾ **43**
2569 **STATOYORK 5** [8] 7-8-9 (58) R Winston 7/1: 0-0050: Unruly stalls, held up, steady prog & just in bhnd ldrs when badly hmpd ins last, eased: 10th: prob unlucky, wld have gone v close with a clear run: best held up & needs luck in running but is v well h'capped & well worth another chance: see 2569, 2107. *shd* **49+**
2266 **RITAS ROCK APE 17** [1] 5-9-7 (70) N Callan 20/1: -00600: Led till over 1f out, btn/eased nr fin: 11th. *hd* **61**
1074 **TRINITY 76** [4] 4-9-9 (72) D Mernagh (3) 33/1: 000-00: Chsd ldrs, btn/eased ins last: 12th: 11 wk abs: '99 reapp wnr at Doncaster (auct mdn, subs unplcd in h'caps, rtd 88 at best, tried a t-strap): rnr-up at York in '98 (List, rtd 98$): eff at 5/6f on firm & gd grnd: likes to race with/force the pace: has run well fresh. *hd* **63**
2525 **KOSEVO 7** [7] 6-7-10 (45)(vis)(3oh) P M Quinn(3) 25/1: 200000: Al outpcd: 13th: won this last term off a 13lb higher mark: see 673. ¾ **33**
1976 **HIGH ESTEEM 30** [6] 4-8-4 (53) Dale Gibson 20/1: 0-1000: Prom 4f: 14th: btr 1421 (AW, 6f). *nk* **40**
*2451 **WHIZZ KID 10** [15] 6-9-10 (73) Claire Bryan (5) 7/1: 126010: Mid-div, outpcd fnl 2f: 15th: well bckd. ½ **59**
2505 **BOLLIN RITA 8** [20] 4-8-10 (59) J Carroll 7/2 FAV: 000020: Mid-div, btn 2f out: 17th: bckd: btr 2505. **0**
1999 **Moocha Cha Man 29** [19] 4-9-4 (67)(bl) S Sanders 33/1:
2505 **Gad Yakoun 8** [16] 7-7-10 (45)(14oh) Angela Hartley(4) 50/1:
2525 **Pips Star 7** [17] 3-7-13 (52) P Fessey 25/1:
19 ran Time 59.99 (1.19) (Tony Fawcett) D Nicholls Sessay, N Yorks

2702 3.50 MEN SPORT HCAP 3YO 0-95 (C) 1m4f Good/Firm 21 +19 Fast [99]
£7280 £2240 £1120 £560

2213 **PRINCIPLE 19** [1] Sir Mark Prescott 3-8-3 (74) S Sanders 6/1: 24-431: 3 b c Caerleon - Point Of Honour (Kris) Keen & led 2f, remained cl-up till went on again over 3f out, styd on gamely ins last, drvn out: fast time: 1st win: '99 rnr-up (med auct, rtd 79 at best): prev eff at 1m/10f, apprec step up to 12f, could get further: acts on fast & gd grnd, poss handles gd/soft: likes a gall trk & forcing tactics: can be plcd to win more races. **80**
2116 **BONAGUIL 24** [5] C F Wall 3-9-2 (87) R Mullen 9/4 JT FAV: 111342: 3 b g Septieme Ciel - Chateaubrook (Alleged) Held up, rdn/prog to chase wnr 2f out, styd on well, not reach wnr: see 2116, 1310 & 1075. 1¼ **90**
1948 **MORNING LOVER 31** [2] K R Burke 3-8-4 (74)(t)(1ow) N Callan 20/1: 0-5143: 3 b c Ela Mana Mou - The Dawn Trader (Naskra) Trkd ldrs, rdn/onepace fnl 2f: t-strap: see 1661 (mdn). 1¾ **76**
1225 **UNAWARE 67** [4] R Charlton 3-9-7 (92) F Lynch 9/4 JT FAV: 04-534: Held up, rdn & kept on fnl 2f, not pace to chall: hvly bckd, 10 wk abs: topweight: see 990. 1½ **91**
*2270 **ABUZAID 17** [6] 3-8-13 (84) J Weaver 7/2: -00015: Handy till over 1f out: bckd: btr 2270 (10f). 2½ **79**
2116 **BUCKMINSTER 24** [3] 3-9-2 (87) J Carroll 8/1: 4-3106: Led/dsptd lead 9f, fdd: op 6/1: btr 1295 (mdn). *8* **70**
6 ran Time 2m 28.10 (0.30) (Sir Edmund Loder) Sir Mark Prescott Newmarket, Suffolk

2703 4.20 MANCHESTERONLINE MDN 3YO+ (D) 1m2f120y Good/Firm 21 -19 Slow
£3945 £1214 £607 £303 3yo rec 11lb

1697 **STAGE DIRECTION 43** [5] J H M Gosden 3-8-12 (t) J Carroll 2/1: -441: 3 b c Theatrical - Carya (Northern Dancer) Handy, rdn/led 2f out, clr ins last, held on well, rdn out: hvly bckd, 6 wk abs: wore a t-strap: eff at 10f, 12f+ shld suit: acts on fast grnd & a stiff/gall trk: lightly rcd, op to further improvement. **92**
1985 **HELENS DAY 30** [2] W Jarvis 4-9-4 M Tebbutt 15/8 FAV: -22: 4 ch f Grand Lodge - Swordlestown Miss (Apalachee) Handy, rdn/no room over 1f out, styd on ins last, not reach wnr: hvly bckd: eff at 10/10.5f, will get further: no luck in running at a crucial stage, can find a similar contest: see 1985. ¾ **82**
-2317 **BANCO SUIVI 15** [3] B W Hills 3-8-7 A Culhane 9/4: 5-2023: 3 b f Nashwan - Pay The Bank (High Top) Led, rdn/hdd 2f out, kept on well for press: see 2317, 1017. 1¼ **80**
1661 **HERACLES 44** [4] A Berry 4-9-9 O Pears 33/1: -634: Keen/prom, kept on onepace fnl 2f: 6 wk abs: eff at 10/12f, may get further & shld apprec h'cap company: see 1661. ½ **84$**
-- **TAW PARK** [8] 6-9-9 T Williams 50/1: -5: Held up, eff 3f out, not pace to chall: debut. 2½ **81$**
2160 **STEPASTRAY 22** [9] 3-8-12 P Fessey 66/1: 0-0036: Keen/held up, nvr pace to chall: offic rtd 47. ¾ **80$**
2102 **GRAND AMBITION 25** [6] 4-9-9 J Weaver 33/1: 0-5057: In tch 1m: see 1352. *6* **71$**
2520 **GRACILIS 7** [7] 3-8-12 T E Durcan 33/1: -48: Rear, nvr factor: see 2520 (1m). *1* **69$**
2327 **NAJMAT JUMAIRAH 15** [1] 3-8-7 R Mullen 16/1: -659: Dwelt/held up, brief eff 3f out: see 2327, 2129. 1¾ **62**
9 ran Time 2m 14.26 (4.26) (K Abdulla) J H M Gosden Manton, Wilts

2704 4.55 MEN PINK CLASSIFIED STKS 3YO+ 0-75 (D) 7f30y rnd Good/Firm 21 -14 Slow
£4043 £1244 £622 £311 3yo rec 7lb

*2426 **FAIR IMPRESSION 11** [5] E A L Dunlop 3-8-11 M Tebbutt 13/8 FAV: 2-0011: 3 ch f Arazim - Al Najah (Topsider) Chsd ldrs, rdn & led ins last, styd on well to assert nr fin: hvly bckd: earlier won at Brighton (fill mdn): rtd 86 when rnr-up in '99: eff at 7f/1m: acts on fast & soft, sharp/undul or gall trk: shld win in h'caps. **78**
2559 **THE DOWNTOWN FOX 5** [1] B A McMahon 5-9-4 (bl) S Sanders 10/1: 060002: 5 br g Primo Dominie - Sara Sprint (Formidable) Bhd ldrs, rdn/led over 2f out till ins last, held cl-home: quick reapp: see 320 (AW, 6f). 1¾ **70**
2580 **ZIRCONI 4** [13] D Nicholls 4-9-4 Alex Greaves 5/2: 0-4033: 4 b g Zieten - Muirfield (Crystal Glitters) Cl-up, led over 3f out till over 2f out, onepace ins last: hvly bckd: quick reapp: acts on fast & hvy: see 1517. ¾ **68**
2580 **REDOUBTABLE 4** [8] D W Chapman 9-9-7 A Culhane 12/1: 036004: Rear, rdn/prog 3f out, held fnl 1f. ½ **70**
2437 **THATCHED 10** [6] 10-9-4 P Fessey 50/1: -50605: Mid-div, onepace fnl 2f: needs h'caps: see 1254. *2* **63$**
2026 **JAMESTOWN 28** [14] 3-8-11 R Fitzpatrick (3) 7/1: 16-046: Prom till over 1f out: see 2026. 3½ **56**
2000 **DOUBLE SPLENDOUR 29** [10] 10-9-4 J Weaver 8/1: 0-0007: Rear, hdwy 3f out, no prog fnl 2f: op 7/1. ½ **55**
2533 **TAKER CHANCE 6** [3] 4-9-4 A Robertson (7) 66/1: 000068: Towards rear, mod late gains: qck reapp. *2* **51$**
1559 **BY THE GLASS 48** [11] 4-9-4 Kim Tinkler 100/1: 00-609: Rdn/twds rear, nvr factor: abs: see 1132. 2½ **46$**
2580 **DISTANT KING 4** [7] 7-9-4 Suzanne France (7) 100/1: 000000: Bhd halfway: 10th: qck reapp: see 1256. ¾ **44$**
2682 **FOUR MEN 1** [9] 3-8-11 P Bradley(5) 100/1: 000660: Led till over 3f out, fdd: 11th: unplcd yesterday. 1¼ **41$**
2523 **Fastwan 7** [2] 4-9-4 V Halliday 100/1: 2682 **Espere Dor 1** [4] 3-8-11 Dale Gibson 100/1:
2349 **Mehmaas 14** [12] 4-9-7 J Carroll 33/1:
14 ran Time 1m 29.61 (2.51) (Maktoum Al Maktoum) E A L Dunlop Newmarket

Official Going   GOOD/FIRM (GOOD In Places). Stalls: Str Crse & 2m - Stands Side: Rnd Crse - Centre

2705

2.00 SAVERNAKE HCAP 3YO+ 0-105 (B)   **2m**   **Firm 07**   **-05 Slow**   **[105]**
£10156   £3125   £1562   £781

2153 **KNOCKHOLT** 23 [1]   S P C Woods   4-9-4 (95)   R Hughes   9/4 **FAV**: 1-0001: 4 b g Be My Chief - Saffron   **98**
Crocus (Shareef Dancer) Trkd ldrs, eff & feeling pace appr fnl 3f, rallied to chall/narrow lead dist, held on well:
nicely bckd: '99 wnr at Salisbury (mdn), Goodwood (rtd h'cap) & Doncaster (h'cap, rtd 100): eff at 14f/2m,
tried 2m6f last time: eff up with/forcing the pace on gd grnd, loves firm: handles any track: useful.
1800 **KINNESCASH** 38 [4]   P Bowen   7-7-13 (76)   J Quinn   9/2: 01-002: 7 ch g Persian Heights - Gayla   nk   **78**
Orchestra (Lord Gayle) Held up, prog to lead appr fnl 2f, soon hard rdn, hdd ent fnl 1f, kept on:
recent hdles rnr up: back to form today: eff at 12f/2m: see 1030.
2336 **SPIRIT OF LOVE** 15 [5]   M Johnston   5-10-0 (105)(BL)   J Fanning   11/4: 1-0303: 5 ch g Trempolino -   1¼   **106**
Dream Mary (Marfa) Led, hung left ent fnl 3f, soon hdd, styd on till no extra towards fin: blnkd, bckd, gd run.
2114 **ASHGAR** 24 [3]   C E Brittain   4-9-9 (100)(vis)   P Robinson   3/1: 056404: Rcd in 2nd till appr str, t.o.   dist   **71**
4 ran   Time 3m 27.86 (1.86)   (Crawley Racing)   S P C Woods Newmarket, Suffolk

2706

2.30 ROBINSON KEANE RTD HCAP 3YO+ 0-105 (B)   **6f**   **Firm 07**   **+01 Fast**   **[112]**
£8914   £3381   £1690   £768   3 yo rec 5 lb

2451 **AWAKE** 10 [3]   M Johnston   3-8-8 (97)   P Robinson   6/1: 042031: 3 ch c First Trump - Pluvial (Habat)   **100**
Pld hard, handy, led appr fnl 1f, hard rdn, just held on: '99 wnr at Epsom (mdn) & Newbury (nurs, rtd 98):
eff at 5f, suited by 6f: goes on firm & hvy grnd, any trk, likes Newbury: can run well fresh: progressive & useful.
-2456 **KAYO** 9 [6]   M Johnston   5-9-1 (99)   J Fanning   4/1: 023122: 5 b g Superpower - Shiny Kay (Star   shd   **101**
Appeal) Cl up, led 2f out till dist, rallied & almost got bck up: nicely bckd tho' op 3/1, stablemate of wnr:
handled drop back to 6f: tough & consistent: see 2338.
1327 **HO LENG** 60 [8]   Miss L A Perratt   5-9-6 (104)   G Carter   7/2 FAV: 53-303: 5 ch g Statoblest - Indigo   nk   **105+**
Blue (Bluebird) Waited with, not clr run 2f out, ran on strongly appr fnl 1f, fin fast: abs, most unlucky.
1674 **ANDREYEV** 43 [4]   R Hannon   6-9-7 (105)   R Hughes   14/1: 100504: Held up, smooth wide prog 2f out,   nk   **105**
ch dist, onepace: 6 wk abs: back to form on grnd faster than ideal: yet to win in h'cap company: see 734 (List).
1952 **CUBISM** 31 [4]   4-9-5 (103)(t)   B Marcus   8/1: 64-035: Bhd ldrs, drvn appr fnl 1f, unable to qckn.   shd   **103**
*2458 **YORKIES BOY** 9 [1]   5-9-7 (105)   J Fortune   9/1: 220416: Set decent clip, hdd 2f out, fdd below dist.   3   **96**
1983 **FIRE DOME** 30 [9]   8-8-7 (91)(4oh)   M Henry   9/1: 111107: Chsd ldrs, outpcd & edged left appr fnl 1f.   ¾   **80**
1182 **BLACKHEATH** 70 [2]   4-8-8 (92)(BL)   S Whitworth   20/1: 30-008: Chsd ldrs till 2f out, eased: blnkd, abs.   5   **69**
2496 **DASHING BLUE** 8 [7]   7-9-2 (100)   T Quinn   9/2: 00-069: Al bhd: nicely bckd, better at 5f, see 2496.   10   **57**
9 ran   Time 1m 11.96 (0.36)   (Lord Hartington)   M Johnston Middleham, N Yorks

2707

3.00 MAIL ON SUNDAY MILE HCAP 3YO+ 0-100 (C)   **1m str**   **Firm 07**   **-04 Slow**   **[99]**
£2150   £1075   £537   3 yo rec 8 lb

*2356 **JUST NICK** 14 [7]   W R Muir   6-7-11 (68)   P Doe   7/4 FAV: 365211: 6 b g Nicholas - Just Never Know   **74**
(Riverman) Waited with, gd hdwy appr fnl 2f, led dist, ran on strongly: well bckd: recent Goodwood wnr (h'cap):
plcd in '99 (rtd 75): missed '98: eff at 7f, suited by 1m: acts on firm & hvy grnd, any track: in terrific
form, could land a decent prize whilst in this form.
1750} **BOUND FOR PLEASURE** 408 [2]   M R Gosden   4-8-4 (75)(t)   R Havlin   16/1: 0600-2: 4 gr c Barathea -   1¾   **77**
Dazzlingly Radiant (Try My Best) Dwelt, rear, wide prog 2f out, styd on for 2nd but no trouble wnr: solid reapp:
lightly raced in '99 (h'cap, rtd 80, G L Moore): '98 Lingfield wnr (mdn, rtd 81): eff at 7f, stays 1m: acts on
firm & hvy grnd, gall or sharp/undul trk, without blnks: wore a t-strap, go close next time.
2090 **MAYARO BAY** 25 [3]   R Hannon   4-10-0 (99)   R Hughes   7/2: 001603: 4 b f Robellino - Down The Valley   hd   **100**
(Kampala) In tch, hdwy 2f out, styd on for press but no ch with wnr: nicely bckd, & a gd weight-carrying
performance (conceded 31lbs to wnr): see 1327 (solid form).
2431 **ELMHURST BOY** 11 [4]   S Dow   4-8-7 (78)(vis)   B Marcus   8/1: 010304: Led chsg pack, same pace appr   1¼   **76**
fnl 1f: stays 1m, will apprec a return to sharp/undulating 7f: see 1652.
2133 **WILD SKY** 23 [8]   6-8-3 (74)(tvi)   J Quinn   8/1: 0-0005: Steadied in rear, not much room appr   2   **68**
fnl 2f, never a threat: not given a hard time: nicely h'capped, see 1150.
3028} **ZUCCHERO** 352 [5]   4-8-5 (76)(VIS)   M Henry   11/1: 1126-6: Pld hard & bolted into a clr lead, und   1¼   **67**
press 2f out, sn hdd, fdd: visored & way too free on reapp: ran up a hat-trick in '99 at Chepstow (mdn h'cap),
Lingfield & Newmarket (h'caps, rtd 79): unplcd juv: will apprec a drop back to 6/7f: acts on firm/fast grnd,
any track, in blnks: best up with/forcing the pace: should leave this behind: with D Arbuthnot.
2964} **ORMELIE** 355 [9]   5-9-8 (93)   J Fortune   8/1: 6551-7: Held up, eff & not much room 2f out, nvr a factor: ¾   **82**
reapp, stablemate rnr-up: won fnl '99 start at Goodwood (val h'cap, rtd 97, P C Hyam): '98 wnr Ayr (mdn) & here
at Newbury (h'cap, rtd 89): stays 1m, suited by 10f: acts on firm & gd/soft: best forgotten, sharper at 10f.
2528 **ZULU DAWN** 7 [6]   4-8-5 (76)   T Quinn   9/2: 4-3308: Prom till wknd 2f out: qk reapp, tchd 6/1, see 1879.   5   **55**
8 ran   Time 1m 37.69 (0.89)   (D G Clarke)   W R Muir Lambourn, Berks

2708

3.30 NEWBURY EBF MDN 2YO (D)   **7f str**   **Firm 07**   **-21 Slow**
£5356   £1648   £824   £412

--   **SWING BAND** [16]   G B Balding   2-9-0 A Daly   12/1: 1: 2 b c Celtic Swing - Inchkeith (Reference   **88+**
Point) Sn led, made rest, pshd out, unchall: tchd 33/1 on debut: 5,000gns April foal, dam 10f wnr: eff at 7f but
is bred to apprec 10f+: acts on firm grnd & a gall track: runs well fresh, forcing the pace: type to improve.
2494 **NORTHFIELDS DANCER** 8 [3]   R Hannon   2-9-0 Dane O'Neill   10/1: 02: 2 ch c Dr Devious - Heartland   2   **83**
(Northfields) Prom, chsd wnr appr fnl 1f, no impress & eased near fin: improved, eff at 7f on firm grnd.
2269 **DENNIS OUR MENACE** 17 [9]   S Dow   2-9-0 P Doe   50/1: 03: 2 pb c Piccolo - Free On Board (Free   1½   **80+**
State) Rear, shkn up 2f out, styd on strgly ins last, nvr nrr: eye-catching, eff at 7f on firm, 1m will suit.
2346 **SMYSLOV** 15 [1]   J L Dunlop   2-9-0 A McGlone   13/2: 04: Prom, eff appr fnl 1f, outpcd by ldrs: shd   **80**
do better in 1m nurserys after next start.
--   **AQUARIUS** [6]   2-9-0 T Quinn   11/4 FAV: 5: Rear, late wide prog, nvr dngrs: bckd from 4/1, stablemate   ¾   **78**
4th: Royal Academy half-brother to v useful 1m/12f performer Sadian: dam high-class at 12f: likely improver.
--   **FOLLOW YOUR STAR** [5]   2-9-0 J Fortune   5/1: 6: In tch wide, one pace appr fnl 1f: 72,000gns   hd   **78**
Pursuit Of Love Jan foal: dam 11f wnr, sire 6f/1m performer: pleasing debut: with P Harris.

NEWBURY   SUNDAY JULY 16TH   Lefthand, Flat, Galloping Track

-- **BUY A VOWEL** [10] 2-9-0 L Newman (3) 15/2: 7: Same pl thro'out: Capote colt, dam 6f juv wnr. *hd* **77**
-- **EASY ENIGMA** [14] 2-9-0 W Supple 12/1: 8: Al mid-div: Selkirk first foal, dam 7f wnr, sire a miler. *1½* **74**
-- **ARC EN CIEL** [12] 2-9-0 D Harrison 16/1: 9: Prom till 2f out: stablemate 4th: 60,000gns *4* **66**
Rainbow Quest half-brother to several wnrs, dam 6f wnr: bred to apprec 1m+.
-- **RECIPROCAL** [2] 2-8-9 N Pollard 16/1: 0: Dwelt, al bhd, not much room 2f out: 10th: 21,000gns *4* **53**
Night Shift April half sister to 4 wnrs abroad: with D Elsworth.
2357 **FATHER SEAMUS 14** [8] 2-9-0 I Mongan (5) 66/1: 000: Slow away but chsd ldrs till 2f out: 11th. *½* **57**
-- **TRILLIONAIRE** [4] 2-9-0 R Hughes 7/1: 0: Speed 4f: 12th: Dilum half-brother to sprinter Sharp Hat. *nk* **56**
-- **ALBASHOOSH** [18] 2-9-0 G Carter 7/1: 0: Dwelt, never in it: 14th, tch 14/1: Cadeaux Genereux Mar foal. **0**
2494 **Bound 8** [13] 2-9-0 A Eddery (5) 25/1: -- **Hellofabundle** [15] 2-9-0 R Smith (5) 33/1:
2357 **Brendas Delight 14** [17] 2-8-9 D Sweeney 66/1: -- **Freecom Net** [7] 2-9-0 B Marcus 16/1: U
17 ran   Time 1m 26.26 (1.96)   (The Swingers)   G B Balding Fyfield, Hants

2709   4.00 SHOW 2000 COND STKS 3YO+ (C)   1m2f   Firm 07   +03 Fast
£6235 £2365 £1182 £537   3 yo rec 10lb

1318 **EKRAAR 63** [8] M P Tregoning 3-8-8 W Supple 9/4: 43-341: 3 b c Red Ransom - Sacahuista (Raja **116**
Baba) Led, rdn clr appr fnl 1f, easing down: best time of day, 9 week abs, nicely bckd: '99 wnr at Goodwood (Gr 3), subs 3rd in Gr 1 R Post Trophy (1st time blinks, rtd 114): eff at 1m, has been crying out for this step up to 10f: acts on firm, soft grnd, any track: eff with/without blnks, forcing the pace: runs well fresh: smart colt.
4139} **PEACOCK JEWEL 292** [2] E A L Dunlop 3-8-5 G Carter 6/1: 21-2: 3 ch c Rainbow Quest - Dafrah *5* **102**
(Danzig) Held up, keen, improved appr fnl 3f, went 2nd dist, no ch with wnr, not given a hard time: won fnl of 2 '99 starts at Newmarket (mdn, rtd 97): eff at 1m, stays 10f: acts on firm & soft grnd: useful, type to win again.
*957 **BIEN ENTENDU 89** [6] H R A Cecil 3-8-8 T Quinn 1/2 FAV: 13: 3 b c Hernando - Entente Cordiale *2½* **101**
(Affirmed) Prom, went 2nd halfway, chance 3f out sn no extra: well bckd, 3 month abs, clr rem: not disgraced on this much quicker ground & is well worth another chance to improve on impressive debut effort in 957 (mdn).
2028 **HELVETIUS 28** [1] P C Ritchens 4-9-1 Dane O'Neill 40/1: 560-54: Handy till appr fnl 3f: stiff task. *22* **68**
2379 **DOVES DOMINION 13** [3] 3-8-5 A Daly 100/1: -50005: Prom till halfway: impossible task. *4* **61$**
-- **MOORLANDS AGAIN** [5] 5-9-1 R Price 100/1: 6: Dwelt, never in it: Flat bow, modest bumper form. *6* **51**
2527 **ALAZAN 7** [4] 5-9-1 I Mongan (5) 100/1: 0P-007: Soon bhd: quick reapp, would struggle in a seller. **0**
7 ran   Time 2m 03.23 (0.43)   (Hamdan Al Maktoum)   M P Tregoning Lambourn, Berks

2710   4.30 PORTMAN SQUARE MDN 3YO (D)   1m4f   Firm 07   -30 Slow
£4134 £1272 £636 £318

-- **TALK TO MOJO** [5] J H M Gosden 3-9-0 R Havlin 14/1: 1: 3 ch c Deploy - Balnaha (Lomond) **74**
Waited with, gd progress appr fnl 3f, led 2f out & edged left, rdn out: unrcd juv: 50,000gns yearling half brother to high class miler Balisada: eff at 12f, shld cope with 10f: acts on firm grnd & runs well fresh.
2416 **TUFTY HOPPER 11** [3] P Howling 3-9-0 J Quinn 7/1: 433222: 3 b g Rock Hopper - Melancolia (Legend *¾* **72$**
Of France) Rear, prog to chase ldrs 3f out, one pace till kept on well dist: not btn far: op 10/1: prob flattered here tho' is consistent & eff at 12/14f: acts of firm, gd/soft & fibresand.
2258 **AMNERIS 18** [4] R Charlton 3-8-9 T Quinn 1/1 FAV: -23: 3 b f Alzao - Top Lady (Shirley Heights) *½* **66$**
Cl up, led halfway till 4f out, sn rdn, switched bef fnl 1f, same pace: nicely bckd tho' op 1/2: drop back to 10f?
-- **QUARRELL** [7] J H M Gosden 3-8-9 J Fortune 2/1: 4: Soon prom, ch 3f out, no extra appr fnl 1f: *3* **62**
debut, better fancied stablemate of wnr, bckd from 5/1: Nashwan filly out of a stoutly bred mare.
2465 **AMJAD 9** [8] 3-9-0 P Robinson 14/1: -50455: Well plcd, led 4f out till 2f out, fdd: stiff task, lngr trip. *4* **62**
1808 **ZERO GRAVITY 37** [1] 3-9-0 R Studholme (5) 16/1: 636: Mid-div, wknd 3f out: see 1808 (gd/soft). *4* **57**
2086 **WINGS AS EAGLES 25** [2] 3-9-0 G Hind 25/1: -07: Led till halfway, lost place: stiff task, up in trip. *12* **45**
2531 **BATWINK 7** [6] 3-8-9 N Pollard 50/1: -08: Al rear: quick reapp, no form. *13* **27**
8 ran   Time 2m 34.77 (4.43)   (Owen Promotions Ltd)   J H M Gosden Manton, Wilts

WINDSOR   MONDAY JULY 17TH   Sharp, Fig 8 Track

Official Going GOOD (GOOD TO FIRM In Places). Stalls: Inside.

2711   6.30 GREAT ORMOND ST MED AUCT MDN 2YO (E)   5f   Good   Inapplicable
£2951 £908 £454 £227

2550 **WESTERN HERO 7** [5] R Hannon 2-9-0 Dane O'Neill 5/1: 3321: 2 ch c Lake Coniston - Miss Pickpocket **79**
(Petorius) Prom, hdwy/carried left appr fnl 1f, ran on strongly to lead cl-home, drvn out: nicely bckd, qck reapp: 26,000gns Mar 1st foal, dam 5f juv wnr: eff around 5f on firm & gd/soft: tough/improving, deserved this.
1782 **AVERY RING 39** [12] A P Jarvis 2-9-0 B Marcus 5/2 FAV: 62: 2 b c Magic Ring - Thatcherella (Thatching) *hd* **77**
Sn rdn in tch, hdwy to lead when hung left ins last, hdd cl-home: eff at 5f on gd: shld win a race, see 1782.
2488 **MADRASEE 9** [4] M Blanshard 2-8-9 D Sweeney 15/2: 363: 2 b f Beveled - Pendona (Blue Cashmere) *hd* **71**
Dsptd lead, went on 2f out, edged left & hdd dist, rall, not btn far: op 6/1: eff at 5/6f on fast & gd: win similar.
-- **KOMENA** [11] J W Payne 2-8-9 A McGlone 14/1: 4: Dwelt, sn outpcd, rdn/hdwy 2f out, styd on well *1¾* **66+**
fnl 1f, nvr nrr: Mar 1st foal, dam plcd as a juv: pleasing debut, improve plenty & relish 6f.
2227 **ELLENDUNE GIRL 19** [7] 2-8-9 J Mackay (5) 33/1: 05: Sn outpcd, hdwy when hung right over 1f out, *2* **60**
styd on ins last: shld apprec 7f next time: see 2227.
-- **BE MY TINKER** [13] 2-8-9 M Fenton 25/1: 6: Dsptd lead, rdn & grad wknd over 1f out: May foal, *½* **59**
half-sister to 1m scorer Scolding: dam scored over 5/6f: with G Brown.
-- **MISHKA** [10] 2-9-0 A Daly 33/1: 7: Led, hdd 2f out, grad wknd ins last: op 16/1 on debut: 8,800gns *½* **62**
Apr foal, half-brother to a 2yo 5f scorer: showed some speed today.
1782 **BATCHWORTH LOCK 39** [6] 2-9-0 D Kinsella (7) 33/1: 08: Outpcd early, late hdwy, no danger: Mar *2½* **55**
foal, half brother to a couple of prolific sprint wnrs: with E Wheeler.
2324 **RAMBLIN MAN 16** [3] 2-9-0 G Hind 20/1: -059: Rcd wide, nvr a danger: see 2324. *3½* **46**
-- **FLAPDOODLE** [9] 2-8-9 C Rutter 25/1: 0: Chsd ldrs to halfway, fdd, 10th: Superpower May foal, *½* **40**
dam scored over 1m: apprec 6f next time for A W Carroll.
1962 **RUSHBY 31** [8] 2-9-0 L Newman (3) 7/2: -63620: Boiled over bef start, chsd ldrs to halfway, wknd: *shd* **44**
11th: well bckd, lost all chance with unruly display in preliminaries: much btr 1962.
2209 **FIRST DEGREE 21** [2] 2-8-9 G Faulkner (3) 16/1: 00: Al rear, fin 12th: see 2209. *3½* **30**

2539 **MARE OF WETWANG** 7 [1] 2-8-9 R Lappin 14/1: 60: Sn bhd, 13th: qck reapp, poor draw: btr 2539. 2 24
13 ran   Time 1m 0.7   (Michael Pescod)   R Hannon East Everleigh, Wilts

---

2712   6.55 LADBROKES HCAP 3YO 0-85 (D)   1m3f135y Good Inapplicable   [86]
        £3887   £1196   £598   £299

*2210 **SECOND PAIGE** 21 [11] N A Graham 3-8-11 (69) J Weaver 3/1-FAV: 402211: 3 b g Nicolotte - My First   74
Paige (Runnett) Settled rear, hdwy when sltly short of room over 2f out, styd on strongly to lead cl-home,
drvn out: nicely bckd: recent wnr here at Windsor (h'cap, 1st win): unplcd in '99 (auct mdn, rtd 71):
eff at 10/12f on fast, gd/soft & any trk, likes Windsor: progressive & in fine form.
2372 **SKYE BLUE** 14 [2] M R Channon 3-8-7 (65) R Havlin 11/2: 530232: 3 b g Blues Traveller - Hitopah   ½ 69
(Bustino) Bhd, gd hdwy 4f out, led over 2f out, veered badly left under a strong right-hand drive well ins fnl 1f,
hdd nr fin: shade unlucky here, would prob have won if holding a straight course: see 2372.
2030 **INCHING CLOSER** 29 [8] N A Callaghan 3-8-9 R Hughes 9/2: -00133: 3 b g Inchinor - Maiyaasah   nk 83
(Kris) In tch, hdwy/short of room over 3f out, rdn & ran on strongly appr fnl 1f, not btn far: stays 11.5f.
1093 **SHAPOUR** 76 [5] Sir Michael Stoute 3-9-4 (76) D Harrison 11/2: 02-04: Led, hdd 2f out, rallied ins   hd 79
last, held cl-home: eff at 10/11.5f on gd: stays 11.5f: see 1093.
2554 **LANZLO** 7 [9] 3-8-3 (61) A McGlone 6/1: 500-25: Trkd ldrs, wknd over 1f out: nicely bckd, qck reapp.   6 56
2499 **BOX CAR** 9 [10] 3-8-6 (64) F Norton 16/1: 322006: Front rank, rdn/fdd fnl 2f: see 1199.   1¼ 57
*2217 **ABLE NATIVE** 20 [6] 3-8-12 (70)(BL) R Price 10/1: 5-0217: Rcd keenly in rear, hdwy to chall 5f   3½ 58
out, wknd for press fnl 2f: op 6/1: below best in 1st time blnks: abt 2217 (12f fills h'cap, equitrack).
2053 **SPANISH STAR** 28 [7] 3-8-11 (69) M Tebbutt 16/1: -51368: Bhd, rdn to improve 3f out, sn btn.   6 49
2254 **DARCY DANCER** 19 [4] 3-7-10 (54)(10h) J Quinn 33/1: 50-009: Trkd ldrs, dropped rear after halfway.   6 26
2213 **QUIET READING** 20 [3] 3-8-2 (60) P Doe 33/1: 003640: In tch, hdwy qckly fnl 3f, fin 10th: btr 1997.   13 14
10 ran   Time 2m 27.3   (Coronation Partnership)   N A Graham Newmarket

---

2713   7.25 TOTE FILLIES HCAP 3YO+ 0-85 (D)   1m67y rnd Good Inapplicable   [81]
        £3861   £1188   £594   £297   3 yo rec 8 lb

2358 **STARLYTE GIRL** 15 [9] R Hannon 3-9-10 (85) R Hughes 11/4: -60121: 3 b f Fairy King - Blushing Storm   90
(Blushing Groom) Keen, led/dsptd lead thr'out, styd on strongly fnl 2f, rdn out: earlier made all at Salisbury
(5 rnr class stks): '99 Warwick wnr (fills mdn, rtd 86): eff at 1m/10f on firm & gd grnd, disapp on gd/soft:
handles any trk: gd weight carrier & loves to force the pace: useful when allowed to dominate.
2084 **MIDNIGHT ALLURE** 26 [3] C F Wall 3-8-13 (74)(t) R Mullen 6/1: -21162: 3 b f Aragon - Executive Lady   1¼ 76
(Night Shift) Held up, drvn/prog to chall 1f out, held by wnr nr fin: op 5/1: back to best with t-strap: see 1873.
2546 **PATSY STONE** 7 [8] M Kettle 4-9-2 (69) S Sanders 7/1: 114453: 4 b f Jester - Third Dam (Slip   1¾ 67
Anchor) Trkd ldrs, rdn to press ldr over 1f out, kept on onepace for press: see 1794 (gd/soft, 7f).
*2579 **GRANTED** 5 [7] M L W Bell 3-9-7 (82)(6ex) M Fenton 7/4-FAV: 332114: Chsd ldrs, ev ch over 1f out,   nk 79
sn no extra: hvly bckd, clr rem: quick reapp under a pen: just btr 2579.
1812 **FAHAN** 38 [4] 3-8-5 (66) J Mackay (5) 16/1: 430-05: Trkd ldrs, rdn/ev ch over 2f out, wknd over 1f out.   5 55
*398 **ROUGE** 173 [1] 5-7-11 (1ow) (50) J Quinn 10/1: 4-1316: Keen, rear, prog/trkd ldrs 2f out, sn no extra: op   ¾ 37
8/1, 6 month abs: now with K R Burke: all 3 wins on gd: see 398 (AW, 7f, clmr).
1877 **NIGHT SHIFTER** 35 [2] 3-8-2 (63) M Henry 33/1: 63-007: Keen, held up rear, no hdwy fnl 2f: '00   1¾ 46
Lingfield wnr (h'cap, M R Channon, rtd 75 at best): eff at 5/6f on firm & gd, shld get further: likes a sharp/easy trk.
2298 **CANADIAN APPROVAL** 17 [5] 4-7-12 (51) F Norton 12/1: 021148: Cl-up till over 2f out: op 8/1.   13 8
8 ran   Time 1m 42.7   (Mohamed Suhail)   R Hannon East Everleigh, Wilts

---

2714   7.55 J ROWE FILLIES COND STKS 2YO (C)   6f   Good Inapplicable
        £5185   £1966   £983   £447

*1798 **BLUE GODDESS** 39 [6] R Hannon 2-8-11 Dane O'Neill 8/13-FAV: 11: 2 b f Blues Traveller - Classic   96
Goddess (Classic Secret) Cl-up, rdn/went on over 2f out, styd on strongly & rdn clr fnl 1f, cmftbly: earlier scored
at Chepstow (auct mdn, debut): eff at 6f, further will suit: acts on gd & gd/soft, sharp/undul trk: has run
well fresh: potentially useful, again impressed & can rate more highly in stronger company.
2369 **MYHAT** 14 [5] K T Ivory 2-8-9 R Hughes 14/1: -2232: 2 ch f Factual - Rose Elegance (Bairn)   3½ 82
Dwelt, held up in tch, rdn/prog to chase wnr over 1f out, kept on, al held: shld find a modest race.
-- **CARPET LADY** [7] Mrs P N Dutfield 2-8-6 L Newman (3) 7/1: 3: 2 b f Night Shift - Lucky Fountain   3½ 70
(Lafontaine) Rdn/rear halfway, styd on fnl 2f, no threat: Feb foal, cost IR19,000gns: half sister to a 6f juv wnr:
dam unraced: shld apprec 7f+ & improve for this.
2318 **OH SO DUSTY** 16 [4] B J Meehan 2-8-13 D R McCabe 11/2: 61044: Led till over 2f out, sn held.   ¾ 75
2483 **OPEN WARFARE** 10 [3] 2-8-13 F Norton 20/1: 353335: Cl-up till over 1f out: btr 2483, 2248 (5f).   4 63
2324 **SUMMER SHADES** 16 [2] 2-8-9 S Sanders 16/1: -36: Cl-up till over 1f out, wknd qckly: btr 2324 (5f).   5 46
1893 **PIVOTABLE** 34 [1] 2-8-9 M Fenton 10/1: -3257: Dwelt, sn handy, btn 2f out, virtually p.u. ins last: 11 16
jockey reported filly lost action: btr 1706, 1541.
7 ran   Time 1m 12.3   (David Mort)   R Hannon East Everleigh, Wilts

---

2715   8.25 PERTEMPS SELL STKS 3-4YO (G)   1m3f135y Good Inapplicable
        £1907   £545   £272   3 yo rec 12lb

2270 **DIRECT DEAL** 18 [3] G M McCourt 4-9-8 (t) D O'Donohoe 100/30-FAV: 000001: 4 b g Rainbow Quest -   53
Al Najah (Topsider) Made all, rdn out: bght in for 4,800 gns, blnks omitted: '99 Bath wnr (mdn, rtd 85, E Dunlop):
promise in '98 (mdn, rtd 80): eff at 10/11.5f on firm & gd/soft: likes forcing the pace on a sharp trk in a t-strap.
2362 **ROOM TO ROOM MAGIC** 14 [2] B Palling 3-8-5 D McGaffin (3) 4/1: 560252: 3 ch f Casteddu - Bellatrix   3½ 43
(Persian Bold) Well plcd, chsd wnr appr fnl 1f, same pace under press: prob stays 11.5f: handles fast & gd grnd.
1707 **WEST END DANCER** 43 [10] G N Crichton 3-8-5 O Urbina 6/1: -00503: 3 b f West By West - Chateau   1 41
Dancer (Giacometti) Hld up, prog to chase ldrs 3f out, plugged on for 3rd: abs, ran to best, clr rem, stays 11.5f.
2587 **SAINT GEORGE** 5 [5] K R Burke 4-9-8 N Callan (7) -2: -00424: Pld hard mid-div, clsd on bit & ch appr fnl   6 37
2f, sn rdn, hung left & btn: qk reapp: failed to see out longer 11.5f trip, shown enough to win similar back at 10f.
1087 **MALIAN** 76 [8] 4-9-8 (BL) D Sweeney 7/1: 0-0005: Prom till 3f out: jumps fit, blnkd, new stable.   6 28
2423 **COOL LOCATION** 12 [1] 3-8-5 G Hannon (5) 20/1: 00-006: Al bhd: v stiff task, no form.   10 8
1972 **TITAN LAD** 31 [4] 3-8-10 I Mongan (5) 25/1: 00-007: Nvr on terms: stiff task, flattered when rtd 60 as a juv.   6 4
2411 **SKY CITY** 12 [7] 4-9-3 J Quinn 33/1: 560008: Sn bhd: v stiff task.   18 0

WINDSOR   MONDAY JULY 17TH   Sharp, Fig 8 Track

1804 **LEA VALLEY EXPRESS 38** [9] 3-8-5 P Doe 8/1: -00009: Bhd from halfway: unproven beyond 5f.   **5   0**
2433 **FULHAM 12** [6] 4-9-8 (bl) F Norton 20/1: 420040: Chsd ldrs 4f, lost pl, virt p.u.: 10th, struck into.   *dist*   **0**
10 ran   Time 2m 29.0   (Mrs B Taylor)   G M McCourt Letcombe Regis, Oxon

| **2716** | 8.55 CADOGAN HCAP 3YO+ 0-70 (E)   5f   Good   Inapplicable | [70] |
| | £2870   £820   £410   3 yo rec 4 lb | |

2525 **BEYOND THE CLOUDS 8** [7] J S Wainwright 4-8-13 (55) R Winston 7/1: 026141: 4 b g Midhish - Tongabezi   **62**
(Shernazar) Chsd ldrs, eff & edged left appr fnl 1f, ran on well to lead fnl 50y, pshd out, narrowly: earlier won
at Hamilton (h'cap): plcd last term (h'cap), rtd 54): eff at 5f, stays 6f on fast & gd: best without visor now.
2022 **MOUSEHOLE 29** [8] R Guest 8-9-10 (66) S Sanders 5/1: 000202: 8 b g Statoblest - Alo Ez (Alzao)   *hd*   **72**
Held up, niggled halfway, ran on to chall dist, hard drvn & just failed: game effort, won this last term.
*2555 **SHADY DEAL 7** [11] M D I Usher 4-8-5 (47) G Baker (7) 9/2: 002213: 4 b g No Big Deal - Taskalady   *¾*   **51**
(Touching Wood) Well plcd, rdn to lead 1f out, hdd fnl 50y, qk reapp, remains in gd form, clr rem, see 2555.
*2371 **DIAMOND GEEZER 14** [10] R Hannon 4-9-13 (69) P Fitzsimons (5) 7/1: 430614: Cl-up, led ent fnl 1f,   *2½*   **67**
rdn & hdd dist, no extra: not disgraced under top-weight back in trip: eff at 5f, suited by 6f, stays 7f.
+2623 **NIFTY NORMAN 4** [6] 6-9-9 (65)(6ex) Alex Greaves 3/1 FAV: 061315: Front rank/ev ch till no extra 1f out.   *½*   **61**
2586 **CORBLETS 5** [3] 3-9-2 (62) P Doe 16/1: 500036: Held up, imprvd & in tch 2f out, sn onepace: qk reapp.   *1¼*   **54**
2233 **SWEET MAGIC 19** [13] 9-8-7 (49)(t) A Daly 33/1: 140007: Sn led, hdd ent fnl 2f, no extra: see 1392.   *1*   **38**
2428 **ABSOLUTE FANTASY 12** [4] 4-8-9 (51)(bl) D Kinsella (7) 12/1: 403428: Al towards rear: see 2428, 1211.   *½*   **38**
2489 **ENDYMION 9** [1] 3-9-2 (62) L Newman (3) 14/1: -00039: In tch till 2f out: back in trip, usually forces it.   *3*   **41**
2623 **PERIGEUX 4** [5] 4-9-9 (63)(bl) (2ow) R Hughes 10/1: 005100: Al bhd: 10th, qk reapp, see 2428 (soft grnd).   *½*   **42**
2291 **Clara Blue 17** [12] 4-7-11 (39)(1ow)(11oh) F Norton 33/1: 432   **Bicton Park 167** [9] 6-7-10 (38)(14oh) J Tate 66/1:
2385 **Trojan Hero 14** [2] 9-7-10 (38)(vis)(7oh) R Brisland (5) 50/1:
13 ran   Time 59.1   (Peter Charalambous)   J S Wainwright Pennythorpe, N Yorks

AYR   MONDAY JULY 17TH   Lefthand, Galloping Track

Official Going   GOOD TO FIRM (FIRM In Places). Stalls: Round Course - Inside; Str Course - Stands Side.

| **2717** | 2.15 EBF MDN 2YO (D)   6f str   Good/Firm 22   -38 Slow | |
| | £3679   £1132   £566   £283 | |

2234 **AMEN CORNER 19** [7] M Johnston 2-9-0 D Holland 4/6 FAV: 41: 2 ch c Mt Livermore - For All Seasons   **80**
(Crafty Prospector) Led, rdn clr appr fnl 1f, eased cl-home, cmftbly: nicely bckd: $75,000 Feb foal, dam a US
sprint wnr: eff at 6f, 7f shld suit: acts on fast grnd & a gall trk: going the right way, could win again.
2521 **LITTLE TASK 8** [6] A Berry 2-9-0 O Pears 12/1: -302: 2 b c Environment Friend - Lucky Thing (Green   *2*   **70**
Desert) Chsd wnr, eff appr fnl 1f, styd on, not pace of wnr: op 8/1: handles fast: shld apprec 7f nurseries now.
2239 **LENNEL 19** [2] Denys Smith 2-9-0 M Roberts 10/1: 63: 2 b g Presidium - Ladykirk (Slip Anchor)   *nk*   **70**
Waited with, rdn to improve 2f out, styd on but no threat to wnr: op 7/1: 7f will now suit: see 2239.
-- **SHATIN PLAYBOY** [3] Miss L A Perratt 2-9-0 K Darley 14/1: 4: Prom, hung right & fdd appr fnl 1f: *1¾*   **66**
op 8/1: IR17,000gns half brother to 3 wnrs, incl a 9f scorer, dam 2yo scorer abroad: shld improve for experience.
1252 **THORNTON DANCER 66** [8] 2-8-9 Dean McKeown 33/1: -005: Nvr a dngr after 9 wk abs: up in trip.   *3*   **54**
1475 **BALL GAMES 53** [4] 2-9-0 G Duffield 10/1: 646: Front rank, edged left & wknd appr fnl 1f: 8 wk abs: *nk*   **59**
below-par run on this faster grnd, btr 1475 (gd), 821 (soft).
-- **HO PANG YAU** [1] 2-9-0 G Carter 9/1: 7: Slow away, sn bhd, eased fnl 1f: op 4/1: 16,000gns   *15*   **39**
colt, half-brother to smart hdler Teaatral (won the Flat over 12/15f), dam juv sprint wnr.
7 ran   Time 1m 12.94 (3.64)   (M Doyle)   M Johnston Middleham, N Yorks

| **2718** | 2.45 G OWEN NURSERY HCAP 2YO (E)   7f rnd   Good/Firm 22   -17 Slow | [93] |
| | £2811   £865   £432   £216 | |

*2417 **PEREGIAN 12** [3] M Johnston 2-8-9 (74) D Holland 2/1 FAV: -53011: 2 b c Eagle Eyed - Mo Pheata   **87**
(Petorius) Cl-up, hdwy when switched appr fnl 2f, chall ldr dist, ran on strongly to lead wll ins last, drvn out:
nicely bckd: recent Catterick scorer (auct mdn): Apr foal, dam a 6f juv wnr: eff around a sharp or gall 7f,
1m could suit in time: acts on fast, gd, has disappointed on soft grnd: tough & improving.
*2468 **TORTUGUERO 10** [2] B W Hills 2-9-7 (86) M Hills 5/2: -06112: 2 br c Highest Honor - Rahaam   *nk*   **98**
(Secreto) Led, rdn clr over 2f out, drvn/hdd well ins last, held cl-home: nicely bckd tho' op 6/4: remains
in fine form: 5L clr rem & an excellent run under top-weight: useful & shld regain winning ways soon.
2557 **CEDAR TSAR 6** [7] D W Chapman 2-8-0 (65) D Mernagh (3) 10/1: 202133: 2 b c Inzar - The Aspecto Girl   *5*   **68**
(Alzao) Chsd ldrs, eff over 3f out, rdn/no extra over 1f out: tchd 14/1, quick reapp: see 2301 (sell, AW).
2383 **LADY BEAN 14** [6] R A Fahey 2-8-2 (67) G Duffield 8/1: 6334: Settled rear, rdn/prog over 3f out,   *½*   **69**
drvn/held appr fnl 1f: see 2383, 1864.
2239 **NISAN BIR 19** [4] 2-7-12 (63) P Fessey 7/1: 0405: Mid-div, rdn/held over 2f out: op 6/1: up in trip.   *¾*   **63**
1507 **CARRABAN 52** [1] 2-8-8 (73) K Darley 10/1: -5W336: Pulled hard in mid-div, rdn/no response fnl 2f: *¾*   **72**
op 8/1, 7 wk abs: worth a try in headgear: see 1507.
2435 **CARTMEL PRINCE 1** [5] 2-7-7 (58)(1oh) J Bramhill 33/1: 600207: Sn outpcd, eff 2f out, nvr   *2½*   **53**
dangerous: op 16/1: longer 7f trip: needs sells/clmrs: see 1937 (5f).
7 ran   Time 1m 26.54 (2.74)   (J David Abell)   M Johnston Middleham, N Yorks

| **2719** | 3.15 ROCK STEADY HCAP 3YO 0-70 (E)   7f rnd   Good/Firm 22   -16 Slow | [77] |
| | £2973   £915   £457   £228 | |

2264 **COWBOYS AND ANGELS 18** [5] W G M Turner 3-9-7 (70) Darren Williams (5) 9/4 FAV: 010241: 3 b c   **74**
Bin Ajwaad - Halimah (Be My Guest) Trkd ldrs, chall 2f out, went on dist, styd on well & just held on, drvn out:
nicely bckd: earlier won at Salisbury (clmr, 1st win): plcd twice in '99 (auct mdns, rtd 79): eff at 7f/1m,
stays 9.4f: acts on fast, hvy & fibresand: acts on a gall trk, gd weight carrier: tough, in fine form
2524 **CALLING THE SHOTS 8** [3] W Storey 3-8-0 (49)(VIS) J Bramhill 10/1: 000042: 3 b c Democratic -   *hd*   **52**
Two Shots (Dom Racine) Led, chall 2f out, hdd dist, rall well ins last & just held: visor: eff at 7f on fast:
showed imprvd form in 1st time headgear, looks capable of wng a 1m mdn h'cap.

2534 **PHILAGAIN 7** [2] Miss L A Perratt 3-7-10 (45)(4oh) N Kennedy 25/1: -40163: 3 b f Ardkinglass - Andalucia 2   44
(Rheingold) Prom, rdn/hdwy over 2f out, no extra appr fnl 1f: qck reapp & a gd run from 4lbs o/h: see 2205 (1m).
2524 **NOWT FLASH 8** [8] B S Rothwell 3-8-9 (58) M Roberts 12/1: 225004: Settled rear, rdn/prog over 2f   ¾   55
out, styd on for press ins last, nvr nrr: will apprec a return to 1m & sell/claiming grade: see 1477.
2577 **INDIAN MUSIC 5** [1] 3-9-7 (70)(bl) G Carter 8/1: 004555: Rear, rdn/hdwy 2f out, no extra fnl 1f.   ¾   66
2673 **MYTTONS AGAIN 2** [4] 3-8-11 (60)(bl) J Fortune 7/1: 665006: Handy, rdn 2f out, sn fdd: qck reapp.   hd   56
1723 **ROBIN HOOD 42** [10] Dale Gibson 12/1: 004447: Front rank, rdn/wknd appr fnl 1f: 6 wk abs.   ¾   43
1855 **BAJAN BELLE 36** [9] D Holland 5/1: 004038: Mid-div, eff after halfway, fdd fnl 2f: see 1855.   ½   63
2438 **GRANITE CITY 11** [7] 3-8-0 (66) Kimberley Hart 10/1: 000039: Rear, prog halfway, rdn/lost tch fnl 2f.   1   40
2440 **WELCOME TO UNOS 11** [6] 3-9-3 (66) F Lynch 5/1: 2-0630: Cl-up, rdn/btn appr fnl 2f, 10th: btr 2440.   shd   57
10 ran   Time 1m 26.48 (2.68)   (Mascalls Stud)   W G M Turner Corton Denham, Somerset

2720   3.45 GR 3 SCOTS CLASSIC STKS 3YO+ (A)   1m2f   Good/Firm 22   +25 Fast
£20300   £7700   £3850   £1750   3 yo rec 10lb

*2074 **ENDLESS HALL 29** [6] L M Cumani 4-9-9 J P Spencer 7/1: 1-5011: 4 b c Saddlers' Hall - Endless Joy   121
(Law Society) Sn led, set fast pace, strongly prsd appr fnl 1f, narrowly hdd ins last, rallied gamely for press
to nose ahead nr fin, all out: course rec time: earlier won at San Siro (Gr1, by 5½L): won again at San Siro
in '99 (Listed, rtd 110), prev in Italy: loves to force the pace at 10/12f & likes fast, handles hvy & stiff
trks: tough, genuine & v progressive, this was a high-class run conceding weight all round, win more Gr races.
2089 **BEAT ALL 26** [3] Sir Michael Stoute 4-9-2 K Darley 11/4: 4-W432: 4 b h Dynaformer - Spirited Missus   shd   114
(Distinctive) Prom, chall appr fnl 1f, styd on strongly to lead well ins last, drvn out, hdd fnl stride: nicely bckd
tho' op 2/1, clr rem: v smart, apprec this return to Gr 3 company & can win similar this year: see 2089, 1248.
*2169 **PORT VILA 23** [2] J H M Gosden 3-8-6 R Hills 10/3: 14-313: 3 b c Barathea - Girouette (Nodouble)   3½   109
Waited on, rdn/hdwy over 2f out, styd on but not pace of front 2 fnl 1f: nicely bckd & worth a try over
12f now: not disgraced against elders & will apprec a return to 3yo List/Gr 3 company: see 2169.
*2339 **AMALIA 16** [4] P W Harris 4-8-13 J Fortune 9/1: 413414: Cl-up, eff when short of room over 2f out,   ½   105
sn held: op 7/1: shade btr 2339 (Listed, firm).
+2260 **ISLAND HOUSE 19** [7] 4-9-2 M Roberts 9/4 FAV: 2-1115: Settled rear, switched wide & eff over 3f out,   nk   108
rdn/onepace fnl 2f: nicely bckd on four-timer bid: v progressive prev, something slightly amiss?: btr 2260 (firm).
2169 **MERRY MERLIN 23** [1] 3-8-6 G Duffield 14/1: -01056: Rcd keenly cl-up, drvn/wknd over 1f out: 1¼   106
lost all chance here by refusing to settle, btr 1246.
1618 **NIGHT STYLE 50** [5] 3-8-6 G Carter 16/1: -60407: Led early on, remained with ldrs, rdn & lost tch   1½   103
fnl 2f: 7 wk abs: needs a drop in grade: see 1216, 656.
7 ran   Time 2m 04.02 (u0.38) Course Record   (Il Paralupo)   L M Cumani Newmarket

2721   4.15 TOTE HCAP 3YO+ 0-90 (C)   5f str   Good/Firm 22   -15 Slow   [84]
£7020   £2160   £1080   £540   3 yo rec 4 lb

*2525 **SHARP HAT 8** [4] D W Chapman 6-8-9 (65) A Culhane 11/2: 052611: 6 b g Shavian - Madam Trilby   69
(Grundy) Front rank, rdn to chall dist, styd on strongly to lead cl-home, drvn out: recent Newcastle scorer
(h'cap): late '99 wnr at Lingfield (h'cap, rtd 62a), unplcd prev that term for T Etherington (rtd 74 & 39a):
plcd in '98 (rtd 87, stks, R Hannon), prev term won at Newbury (h'cap, rtd 93): stays 7f, suited by 5/6f:
acts on firm, soft, equitrack & any trk: best without blnks: tough & remains in gd heart.
*2505 **XANADU 9** [6] Miss L A Perratt 4-9-5 (75) K Dalgleish (7) 5/2 FAV: 201012: 4 ch g Casteddu -   nk   78
Bellatrix (Persian Bold) Reared leaving stalls & lost grnd, hdwy from near halfway, led 2f out, clr dist, drvn/hdd
cl-home: well bckd: shade unlucky, would prob have won with a level break, v progressive: see 2505.
2641 **FACILE TIGRE 3** [9] P Monteith 5-7-10 (52)(6oh) J Bramhill 25/1: 605503: 5 gr g Efisio - Dancing   1¼   52$
Diana (Raga Navarro) Sn outpcd, rdn/prog 2f out, switched & styd on well ins last, no impress on front 2.
2310 **ATLANTIC VIKING 17** [3] D Nicholls 5-10-0 (84)(bl) K Hodgson 3/1: 1-0004: Trkd ldr, chall over 2f   ¾   82
out, rdn/no extra appr fnl 1f: nicely bckd: top weight: back on a winning mark & is slowly returning to form.
1143 **LEGS BE FRIENDLY 73** [5] 5-8-10 (66)(bl) K Darley 3/1: 00-W035: Dwelt, rear, prog 2f out, kept on   shd   64
fnl 1f, no threat: 10 wk abs: stable-mate of 4th: see 1143.
2418 **SWYNFORD DREAM 12** [10] 7-8-2 (58) T Williams 6/1: 520426: Led to halfway, fdd appr fnl 1f: tchd 8/1.   1   53
2641 **JOHAYRO 3** [2] 7-8-0 (56)(bl) J McAuley (5) 10/1: 243007: Front rank, chall ldr appr fnl 2f,   ½   49
fdd over 1f out: quick reapp, blnks reapplied: not firing this term, unlike many of his stablemates: see 2395.
+2078 **CARTMEL PARK 26** [8] 4-9-8 (78) O Pears 10/1: 050018: Prom, hdwy appr fnl 2f, rdn/lost tch over   ½   70
1f out: needs to dominate to be seen at best: btr 2078 (made all, fibresand).
8 ran   Time 58.49 (1.89)   (Miss N F Thesiger)   D W Chapman Stillington, N Yorks

2722   4.45 ROCK STEADY MDN 3YO+ (D)   1m2f   Good/Firm 22   -13 Slow
£3848   £1184   £592   £296   3 yo rec 10lb

2258 **DELAMERE 19** [3] J H M Gosden 3-8-7(1ow) J Fortune 9/4: 0-6431: 3 b f Brocco - Shelia Dacre (Nureyev)   81
Prom, sltly outpcd after halfway, rall & styd on to chall over 2f out, led dist, hung left for press ins last,
drvn out: op 3/1: unplcd sole '99 start (mdn, rtd 68, A G Foster): dam a 9f wnr: stays 10f, 12f shld suit:
acts on firm, gd/soft & a gall trk.
1831 **TIGRE 38** [5] B W Hills 3-8-11 M Hills 11/2: 2-4002: 3 b c Mujtahid - Vice Vixen (Vice Regent)   1   83
Led, qcknd halfway, pressed appr fnl 2f, hdd dist, held well ins last: op 7/10f, win similar: see 1159.
-2242 **POLAR CHALLENGE 19** [4] Sir Michael Stoute 3-8-11 F Lynch 8/11 FAV: 033523: 3 b c Polar Falcon -   hd   83
Warning Light (High Top) Prom, chall ldr appr fnl 2f, ev ch over 1f out, looked just held when sltly hmpd ins
last, no extra: well bckd at odds-on & better expected: up in trip & stays 10f: see 2242.
2611 **IL CAVALIERE 4** [1] Mrs M Reveley 5-9-7 A Culhane 10/1: -304: Settled last, rdn & kept on fnl   1   81$
2f, nvr nrr: op 7/1, quick reapp: stays 10f but 12f+ is sure to suit for this former bmpr wnr in h'caps.
-- **SPIRIT OF PARK** [2] 3-8-11 Dale Gibson 33/1: 5: Chsd ldrs, rdn & lost tch over 3f: debut, half   20   54
brother to a couple of NH wnrs: shld apprec further in time for L Lungo.
5 ran   Time 2m 07.94 (3.54)   (R E Sangster, H Lester & R Clifton)   J H M Gosden Manton, Wilts

Official Going: FIRM (GOOD TO FIRM PLACES) Stalls: Inside, except 10/12f - outside

2723   2.30 GUINNESS CLAIMER 2YO (F)   7f rnd Good/Firm 26 -21 Slow
£2236   £639   £319

2599 **VIOLENT 6** [7] Andrew Reid 2-8-4 (vis) M Henry 11/4: -00021: 2 b f Deploy - Gentle Irony (Mazilier) 62
Chsd ldr, rdn/led over 2f out, held on well fnl 1f, drvn out: eff at 7f, 1m+ should suit: acts on fast grnd, stiff/
gall or sharp track: sharpened up by visor last twice & suited by selling/claiming grade.
*2424 **SEL 13** [3] G L Moore 2-8-8 (bl) J Mongan (5) 5/1: 3512: 2 b f Salse - Frog (Akarad) 1½ 62
Chsd ldr, drvn/chsd wnr over 1f out, kept on, al held: acts on fast & gd/soft: prev with Sir Mark Prescott.
2424 **LOOK FIRST 13** [5] A P Jarvis 2-8-13 J Quinn 8/1: 23: 2 b c Namaqualand - Be Prepared (Be My 2½ 62
Guest) Held up, rdn fnl 2f, kept on, not pace to chall: handles fast & gd/soft grnd, 1m should suit in time.
2551 **ONE BELOVED 8** [1] M R Channon 2-8-6 G Carter 5/1: -00324: Bhd ldrs, outpcd fnl 2f: see 2551. nk 54
2468 **SAND BANKES 11** [4] 2-9-3 A Daly 5/2 FAV: 121165: Led till over 2f out, fdd, fin lame: vis omitted. 1¾ 62
1553 **DISTANT DAWN 50** [2] 2-8-9 D Harrison 12/1: 4026: Dwelt, rear, in tch, outpcd over 2f out: op 7/1: 8 42
7 week abs: this longer 7f trip should suit in time: see 1553, 1000.
2599 **SKITTLES 6** [6] 2-8-6 S Sanders 16/1: 007: Held up, btn over 2f out: quick reapp: see 1048. ¾ 38
7 ran   Time 1m 23.1 (3.3)   (A S Reid)   Andrew Reid Mill Hill, London NW7

2724   3.00 EBF BACARDI BREEZER MDN 2YO (D)   6f rnd Good/Firm 26 -22 Slow
£3380   £1040   £520   £260

2545 **VALDESCO 8** [4] M A Jarvis 2-9-0 P Robinson 11/4: 341: 2 ch c Bluebird - Allegheny River (Lear 76
Fan) Cl up, rdn/narrow lead 1f out, held on well for press inside last: tchd 7/2: apprec step up to 6f, should get
further (dam a 7f wnr): acts on fast & gd, handles soft: handles a stiff/gall or sharp trk: op to further improvement.
2152 **MOONLIGHT DANCER 25** [1] R Hannon 2-9-0 Dane O'Neill 2/5 FAV: -42202: 2 b c Polar Falcon - ¾ 73
Guanhumara (Caerleon) Led, drvn/hdd 1f out, kept on well for press fnl 1f: hvly bckd at odds on: see 1924, 1776.
2532 **TOP NOLANS 8** [2] M H Tompkins 2-9-0 S Sanders 8/1: 033: 2 ch c Topanoooora - Lauretta Blue shd 73
(Bluebird) Bhd ldrs, switched for eff over 1f out, styd on well near fin, not reach wnr: op 6/1: appreciated return
to 6f, 7f will suit: handles fast grnd: h'cap company may suit best: see 2132.
2214 **RACHEL GREEN 21** [3] C N Allen 2-8-9 Martin Dwyer 33/1: 604: In tch, outpcd fnl 2f: see 2009 (5f). 4 58
4 ran   Time 1m 10.70 (2.9)   (D Fisher)   M A Jarvis Newmarket, Suffolk

2725   3.30 BOLCHOVER CLASS STKS 3YO+ 0-60 (F)   1m3f196y Good/Firm 26 +07 Fast
£2310   £660   £330   3 yo rec 12lb

2392 **WESTGATE RUN 14** [5] R A Fahey 3-8-7 G Carter 9/4 FAV: 011331: 3 b f Emperor Jones - Glowing 65
Reference (Reference Point) Led/dsptd lead till went on over 2f out, drvn & held on well inside last: best time of
day: well bckd: earlier scored at Warwick (appr h'cap) & Hamilton (h'cap): '99 rnr up (claimer, rtd 75): suited
by 9/12f, may get further: relishes firm/fast grnd, handles gd, any track: likes to race with/force the pace.
1874 **KING FLYER 36** [3] H J Collingridge 4-9-6 (t) J Quinn 11/4: 0-6052: 4 b g Ezzoud - Al Guswa 1 64
(Shernazar) Held up in tch, prog/chsd ldrs 3f out, kept on, al just held: well bckd: see 835.
2012 **NOBLE REEF 31** [1] Mrs G S Rees 3-8-8 S Sanders 4/1: 60-033: 3 b c Deploy - Penny Mint (Mummy's 1¼ 62
Game) Held up, prog/chsd ldrs 3f out, kept on onepace under hands & heels riding fnl 2f: stays a sharp 12f: see 2012 (10f).
2429 **KEZ 13** [7] S P C Woods 4-9-6 N Callan 12/1: -00204: Rear, switched & smooth prog to press ldrs 8 53
3f out, soon btn: vis omitted: did not find as much as looked likely here, drop to 10f could suit: see 1934, 842.
2530 **KIRISNIPPA 9** [2] S P C Woods 6-9-2 R Price 6/1: 204035: Chsd ldrs 9f: needs low grade h'caps: see 1784, 1128. 3 49
2651 **DONT WORRY BOUT ME 4** [6] 3-8-8 (vis) K Lavelle (7) 6/1: -01626: Led, clr halfway, hdd/btn over 2f out. 1 48
6 ran   Time 2m 30.5 (2.3)   (Mark A Leatham)   R A Fahey Butterwick, N Yorks.

2726   4.00 FOSTER'S HCAP 3YO+ 0-80 (D)   1m rnd Good/Firm 26 -03 Slow   [76]
£3835   £1180   £590   £295   3 yo rec 8 lb

*1915 **TAPAGE 34** [5] Andrew Reid 4-8-7 (55) M Henry 9/4: 0-11111: 4 b g Great Commotion - Irena (Bold Lad) 62
Made all, strgly pressed fnl 2f, styd on gamely to assert inside last: well bckd: earlier won at Lingfield (2
AW h'caps, rtd 53a) & Bath (h'cap): dual '99 rnr up (claimer, rtd 69, W Muir): '98 Lingfield wnr (auct mdn,
rtd 78a, D Gillespie): eff at 7f, suited by 1m: acts on firm, fast, loves equitrack/Lingfield: prob handles
any trk, loves a sharp one: best without blnks: trainer reports forcing tactics essential: tough & in great form.
2356 **MUTABASSIR 16** [9] G L Moore 6-8-11 (59) J Mongan (5) 2/1 FAV: 654302: 6 ch g Soviet Star - Anghaam 1 63
(Diesis) Trckd ldrs, chall fnl 2f, kept on well, just held nr fin: hvly bckd, clr rem: loves Brighton, win sn.
2387 **COPPLESTONE 14** [4] P W Harris 4-9-10 (72) Carol Packer (7) 11/1: 244043: 4 b g Second Set - 3½ 69
Queen Of The Brush (Averof) Bhd ldrs, styd on onepace under hands & heels riding fnl 2f: mdn, see 1774.
1651 **DUSKY VIRGIN 46** [1] S Woodman 3-7-13 (55) A Nicholls (3) 20/1: 51-004: Mid-div, never on terms: abs. ¾ 51
*2378 **AGIOTAGE 15** [7] 4-8-9 (57) G Carter 5/1: 001615: Chsd ldrs, never on terms: op 9/2: see 2378. shd 53
574 **FORT KNOX 146** [3] 9-7-12 (46)(bl)(2ow)(18oh) A Daly 66/1: 000-66: Bhd, never factor: 5 mth abs. 13 22
1127 **CEDAR LORD 75** [6] 3-8-2 (58) N Pollard 33/1: 0-607: Soon bhd: 11 week abs, h'cap bow: see 936. 12 16
2040 **LAGO DI LEVICO 29** [2] 3-7-12 (54) P Doe 14/1: -15468: Slowly away & al bhd: see 2040, 783 (gd). dist 0
2367 **FUEGIAN 15** [8] 5-8-11 (59)(vis) M Fenton 8/1: -2010P: Prom 5f, p.u. lame over 1f out: vis reapp. 0
9 ran   Time 1m 34.3 (2.3)   (A S Reid)   Andrew Reid Mill Hill, London NW7

2727   4.30 COURAGE BEST HCAP 3YO+ 0-60 (F)   1m2f Good/Firm 26 -16 Slow   [59]
£3861   £1188   £594   £297   3 yo rec 10lb

2423 **CYBER BABE 13** [10] A G Newcombe 3-8-11 (52) L Newman (3) 16/1: 210021: 3 ch f Persian Bold - 56
Ervedya (Doyoun) Al prom, rdn/led 2f out, held on gamely inside last, drvn out: op 12/1: earlier scored at
W'hampton (AW sell, A Reid, rtd 51a): rnr up twice in '99 for M Tompkins (rtd 58): eff at 1m/10f on firm, gd/sft
& fibresand: likes to race with/force the pace on a sharp/undul track: best without a visor.
2544 **SAMMYS SHUFFLE 8** [4] Jamie Poulton 5-8-10 (41)(bl) O Urbina 8/1: 402232: 5 b h Touch Of Grey - ½ 43
Cabinet Shuffle (Thatching) Mid-div, switched & rdn/styd on well from over 1f out, nrst fin: likes fast grnd.
2592 **BOND DIAMOND 6** [6] B Smart 3-8-12 (53) M Tebbutt 33/1: 500003: 3 gr g Prince Sabo - Alsiba nk 54

(Northfields) Dwelt/towards rear, rdn & styd on well fnl 3f, nearest fin: quick reapp: return to form: winning
form at 7f, clearly stys a sharp 10f, may get further: acts on fast & fibresand: see 427 (AW auct mdn).

2199 LYCIAN 22 [9] J A R Toller 5-9-12 (57) S Whitworth 4/1 FAV: 0-6034: Chsd ldrs 2f out, onepace nr fin.	½	57
2262 LITTLE TUMBLER 20 [3] 5-9-1 (46) J P Spencer 8/1: 00-565: Held up, prog/chall 2f out, no extra nr fin.	hd	45
1209 HURGILL DANCER 70 [1] 6-8-5 (36) (BL) S Sanders 14/1: -34066: Led, rdn/hdd 2f out, kept on	hd	34

well tho' no extra nr fin: op 16/1, gd run in first time blinks: recently unplcd over jumps: see 100.

2295 OUT ON A PROMISE 18 [5] 8-8-10 (41) J Weaver 11/1: 364/07: Held up well off the pace, styd on strgly	1¾	37+

fnl 1f under hands & heels, nrst fin: op 8/1, most eye-catching: useful over timber: looks v well h'capped
on the Flat & worthy of the closest inspection next time, particularly at 12f with a more positive ride.

2387 MINJARA 14 [14] 5-8-4 (35) P Doe 16/1: 0-5508: Rear, styd on fnl 2f, no threat: see 1331.	nk	30
*2544 MUTADARRA 8 [13] 7-9-9 (54) (6ex) D O'Donohoe 5/1: 002519: Twds rear, eff 2f out, sn held: bckd.	nk	48
1364 CITY GAMBLER 6 [18] 6-9-3 (48) A Nicholls (3) 10/1: 540-50: Mid div, prog/chsd ldrs over 2f out,	hd	41

sn no extra: 10th: 2 mth abs, op 12/1: nicely h'capped, likes Leicester: see 1364.

2591 BROWNS DELIGHT 6 [2] 3-8-7 (48) A Clark 33/1: 006500: Rear, mod gains fnl 3f: 11th: qck reapp.	2½	37
2367 MULLAGHMORE 15 [11] 4-9-6 (51) (bl) N Callan (3) 33/1: 155000: Cl up till over 1f out, eased: 12th.	1¾	38
2527 FAMOUS 9 [8] 7-8-4 (35) (bl) J Quinn 33/1: 500000: Chsd ldrs 5f: 13th: blnks reapplied: see 90.	nk	21
2689 Twoforten 3 [16] 5-8-7 (38)(vis) M Henry 33/1:	2367 Gali 15 [12] 4-9-0 (45) I Mongan (5) 16/1:		
2552 Sea Danzig 8 [15] 7-8-13 (44) A Daly 14/1:	2423 Naked Oat 13 [20] 5-9-7 (52) D Harrison 25/1:		
2296 Bless 18 [17] 3-8-4 (45)(vis) D Kinsella (7) 14/1:	2425 Elms Schoolprefect 13 [7] 3-8-4 (45) J Tate 33/1:		
19 ran Time 2m 02.00 (4.2) (Advanced Marketing Services Ltd) A G Newcombe Huntshaw, Devon			

2728   5.0 SAFFIE JOSEPH HCAP DIV 1 3YO+ 0-60 (F)   7f rnd Good/Firm 26 -05 Slow   [60]
£1925   £550   £275   3 yo rec 7 lb

2655 REACHFORYOURPOCKET 4 [5] M D I Usher 5-8-10 (42) Martin Dwyer 20/1: 660001: 5 b g Royal Academy -		46

Gemaasheh (Habitat) Al prom, rdn/led over 2f out, styd on well fnl 1f, drvn out: quick reapp: earlier scored at
Lingfield (AW mdn h,cap, rtd 47a at best) unplcd for K Mahdi in '99 (rtd 64, tried t strap, suffered breathing probs,
had a soft palate op): suited by 7f on firm, fast & equitrack: likes a sharp/undul trk: best without blinks/vis.

1926 BUTRINTO 34 [11] B R Johnson 6-9-13 (59) I Mongan (5) 3/1 FAV: 611402: 6 ch c Anshan - Bay Bay	1¼	59

(Bay Express) Chsd ldrs, hard rdn & kept on fnl 1f, not pace of wnr: bckd: see 1462, 1335.

2612 FLYING PENNANT 5 [4] J M Bradley 7-8-9 (41) (bl) P Fitzsimons (5) 8/1: 306103: 7 gr g Waajib -	2½	36

Flying Beckee (Godswalk) Outpcd, switched 2f out & styd on well fnl 1f, not much extra fnl frat pair: qck reapp: see 2427.

2673 TOBLERSONG 3 [1] Mrs L Stubbs 5-8-13 (45) (tvi) D Harrison 100/30: 644204: Bhd ldrs, ch 2f out,	2	36

soon no extra: well bckd, tchd 9/2: quick reapp: see 2411, 958.

2561 CORN DOLLY 7 [10] 4-8-9 (41) (bl) N Pollard 14/1: 500005: Rear, drvn & styd on fnl 2f, no threat.	3	26
2479 CEDAR WELLS 11 [13] 4-8-12 (44) L Newman (3) 20/1: 006006: Prom, held fnl 2f: see 681.	1¼	26
2433 ANNIE APPLE 13 [15] 4-9-1 (47) (vis) S Sanders 10/1: 050457: Rear, mod gains over 6/1, poor draw.	3	24
1953 ALFAHAAL 33 [6] 7-8-4 (36) G Bardwell 12/1: 000000: In tch, jumped path after 1f, btn 2f out: new stble.	nk	11
2592 UBITOO 6 [3] 3-7-10 (35) (bl) (5oh) D Kinsella (7) 10/1: -00539: Mid div at best: op 8/1, qck reapp.	¾	9
2612 CRUSTY LILY 5 [14] 4-8-13 (45) P Doe 12/1: -04200: Keen/chsd ldrs 5f: 10th: poor draw: see 2221.	½	18
1915 FRANKLIN D 34 [8] 4-8-13 (45) (vis) S Whitworth 20/1: 340600: Led till over 2f out: 11th: see 58.	5	8
2549 Gold Rider 8 [12] 4-8-7 (46) (BL) D O'Donohoe 25/1:	2654 Jonathans Girl 4 [9] 5-7-12 (30) J Quinn 33/1:		
4019} Flying Memory 302 [7] 4-8-5 (37) Claire Bryan (5) 20/1:			
14 ran Time 1m 22.00 (2.2) (Bryan Fry) M D I Usher Kingston Lisle, Oxon			

2729   5.30 SAFFIE JOSEPH HCAP DIV 2 3YO+ 0-60 (F)   7f rnd Good/Firm 26 -15 Slow   [59]
£1914   £547   £273   3 yo rec 7 lb

*2379 THE THIRD CURATE 15 [3] B J Curley 5-9-0 (45) J P Spencer 7/4 FAV: 0-0011: 5 b g Fairy King -		49

Lassalia (Sallust) Towards rear early, rdn & prog fnl 2f, led inside last, drvn out: hvly bckd from 7/2: recent
Southwell wnr (AW h'cap, rtd 43a): June '99 wnr in native Ireland at The Curragh (7f h'cap): suited by 7f/1m on fast,
gd & fibresand: has run well fresh & likes a sharp/undul trk: eff with/without blinks: needs strong handling.

2673 KNOBBLEENEEZE 3 [10] M R Channon 10-8-10 (41) (vis) M Mathers 14/1: 030052: 10 ch g Aragon	1	43

- Proud Miss (Semi Pro) Chsd ldrs, drvn to chall fnl 1f, kept on well: op 10/1: quick reapp: nicely h'capped
& signalled a return to form here, keep in mind for a small h'cap, particularly on softer grnd: see 1462.

*2291 CHAKRA 18 [5] M S Saunders 6-9-2 (47) J Weaver 13/2: 000213: 6 gr g Mystiko - Maracuja (Riverman)	1	47

Led, rdn/hdd inside last & no extra: op 7/1: stays a sharp 7f, suited by 5/6f: see 2291 (claimer, J Bradley).

2658 DEMOCRACY 4 [9] P G Murphy 4-9-5 (50) D Harrison 12/1: 053404: Rear, rdn/hdwy to chase ldrs 1f	¾	49

out, onepace ins last: op 10/1, quick reapp: 2 gd runs here at Brighton this term: 1 win in 28 starts.

2315 NIGHT ADVENTURE 17 [14] 4-8-5 (36) L Newman (3) 12/1: -00005: Chall 2f out, held in last: op 8/1.	1¼	32
2427 MILADY LILLIE 13 [13] 4-9-7 (52) C Carver (3) 14/1: 020406: Rear, styd on fnl 2f, nrst fin: poor draw.	¾	47
2658 MUJKARI 6 [12] 4-8-5 (36) Claire Bryan (5) 14/1: 000047: Prom 6f: op 10/1: qck reapp: see 323.	2	47
2631 SWEET AS A NUT 5 [4] 4-9-10 (55) I Mongan (5) 12/1: 0-0008: Chsd ldrs 5f: op 14/1, quick reapp.	nk	45
2427 NERONIAN 13 [11] 6-8-5 (35) (1ow) M Henry 14/1: 001039: Wide/chsd ldrs 5f: poor draw, op 12/1.	¾	45
*2658 PRIORY GARDENS 4 [2] 6-8-13 (44) (6ex) P Fitzsimons (5) 15/2: 354610: Trkd ldrs 5f: 10th: btr 2658.	1¼	30
2292 CAVERSFIELD 18 [1] 5-8-7 (38) S Sanders 10/1: 006030: Chsd ldrs 5f: 11th: op 8/1: see 336.	½	23
2591 ANNIJAZ 6 [8] 3-8-10 (48) D O'Donohoe 13/2: 046330: Rear, eff/hmpd twice over 1f out, no ch after	7	22

& position accepted: 12th: quick reapp, likely to have gone much closer here, thus best forgotten: see 2591.

1742 Parkside Prospect 42 [12] 3-9-0 (52) P Dobbs (5) 25/1:			
2542 Tropical Beach 8 [15] 7-8-11 (42) (vis) G Bardwell 16/1:			
14 ran Time 1m 22.7 (2.9) (P Byrne) B J Curley Newmarket, Suffolk			

Official Going   GOOD TO FIRM (FIRM In Places) Stalls: Inside.

2730   2.15 TURNSTILE MDN AUCT 2YO (E)   5f   Firm 06 -18 Slow
£3107   £956   £478   £239   High numbers favoured

2363 **HUMES LAW** 15 [18] A Berry 2-8-4(1ow) J Carroll 11/4: -0461: 2 b c Puissance - Will Be Bold   76
(Bold Lad) Handy, eff entering fnl 2f, ran on to lead below dist, held on well: nicely bckd, plum far-rail
draw: 4,000gns May foal: eff at 5f, stay 6f in time: suited by firm/fast grnd, stiff/gall tracks.
2589 **ONCE REMOVED** 6 [3] S Dow 2-7-13(1ow) F Norton 14/1: 04402: 2 b f Distant Relative - Hakone   nk 70
(Alzao) Towards rear, kept on appr fnl 1f, pressed wnr fnl 150y, al held: clr rem & gd run from poor draw.
1918 **AMELIA** 34 [13] J Cullinan 2-7-12 T Williams 10/1: 4233: 2 b g General Monash - Rose Tint   2½ 62
(Salse) Led till entering fnl 1f, no extra: genuine filly: best off in sell nurseries: see 1918.
2361 **FLINT** 15 [10] M W Easterby 2-8-4(1ow) T Lucas 16/1: 054: Chsd ldrs, eff 2f out, not pace to chall.   nk 67
2328 **YETTI** 17 [5] C Rutter 9/4 FAV: 225: Prom, wide, rdn & one pace appr fnl 1f: well bckd   1 58
from 7/2: not the best of draws but still appeared to have every chance: see 2328 (6f), 2010.
2360 **PAID UP** 15 [9] G Parkin 9/1: 46: Al mid-div: not given a hard time, stablemate 4th: needs 6f +.   1¼ 59
2539 **PETRAIL** 8 [12] N Kennedy 16/1: 07: Chsd ldrs, no extra appr fnl 1f: quick reapp, see 2539.   nk 53
2454 **SLIPPER ROSE** 11 [4] 2-7-12 P M Quinn (3) 40/1: 430608: Never on terms from low draw: back in trip.   1¼ 49
2417 **MISSING DRINK** 13 [16] 2-8-3 Joanna Badger (7) 20/1: 05059: Prom till 2f out: btr 2417 (7f).   nk 53
2360 **WONDERGREEN** 15 [11] 2-8-4(1ow) K Darley 12/1: 60: Never in it: 10th, see 2360.   hd 53
1938 **RUNAWAY BRIDE** 33 [17] 2-7-12 K Dalgleish (5) 10/1: 550: In tch till halfway: 15th, op 8/1: see 1981.   0
2361 **Christmas Morning** 15 [7] 2-8-3 Dale Gibson 33/1:   2435 **Aporto** 12 [6] 2-8-3 A Mackay 66/1:
-- **Charmed** [1] 2-8-3 G Baker (7) 66/1:   -- **The Generals Lady** [2] 2-7-12 D Mernagh (3) 50/1:
-- **Got Alot On** [14] 2-8-3 P Fessey 25/1:   1704 **Fathers Footsteps** 44 [8] 2-8-3 J McAuley (5) 50/1:
17 ran   Time 1m 02.5 (1.2)   (T Herbert-Jackson)   A Berry Cockerham, Lancs

2731   2.45 CATTLE LINES CLAIMER 3YO (E)   7f100y rnd   Firm 06 -02 Slow
£2852   £815   £407

2633 **AFRICA** 4 [9] T D Barron 3-8-2 D Mernagh (3) 9/2: -16041: 3 b f Namaqualand - Tannerrun (Runnett)   52
Bhd ldrs, shaken up to lead appr fnl 1f cmftbly: op 7/2, qk reapp: earlier won at Southwell (fill h'cap, rtd 61a):
'99 Catterick wnr (sell, rtd 61 at best): eff at 7f/7.5f on firm, gd, fibresand & any trk: best without blinks.
2278 **NORTHERN ECHO** 19 [7] M Dods 3-8-9 (bl) A Culhane 5/1: 000532: 3 b g Pursuit Of Love - Stop   1½ 56
Press (Sharpen Up) Towards rear, not handle bend 3f out, kept on ent fnl 2f & chsd wnr ins last, no impression:
suited by step up to 7.5f on firm, handles soft: wears blnks & will apprec mod/selling h'caps.
2245 **SKELTON MONARCH** 20 [5] R Hollinshead 3-8-3 P M Quinn (3) 25/1: 630003: 3 ch c Prince Of Birds   2 46$
- Toda (Absalom) Bhd, styd on fnl 2f, never near to chall: surely flattered back in trip: handles firm grnd.
2281 **SPEEDFIT FIVE** 19 [3] M A Buckley 3-8-7 Dean McKeown 4/1: -00504: Waited with, mod late hdwy.   2 46
2243 **PRIDE OF PERU** 20 [2] 3-8-1 T Williams 10/1: 00-005: Led till bef fnl 1f, no extra: stiff task, lngr trip.   ½ 39
2524 **CITY FLYER** 9 [1] 3-8-11 (t) K Darley 9/1: -50006: In tch till 2f out: stiff task, down in trip.   4 41
1865 **THREEFORTYCASH** 36 [8] 3-8-5 P Fessey 25/1: 500607: Handy till appr fnl 2f: stiff task, see 427.   nk 34
*2413 **ALABAMA WURLEY** 13 [4] 3-8-8 (vis) D McGaffin (5) 10/3 FAV: 060018: Prom till lost pl appr fnl 2f: ¾ 35
nicely bckd but had it to do on official ratings (offic rtd 46): see 2413 (seller).
1865 **SOLOIST** 36 [6] 3-7-12 K Dalgleish (5) 33/1: -00009: Al bhd: v difficult task.   5 15
9 ran   Time 1m 31.4 (0.6)   (Laurence O'Kane)   T D Barron Maunby, N Yorks

2732   3.15 STRUTHERS HCAP 3YO+ 0-60 (F)   5f   Firm 06 -08 Slow   [56]
£3302   £1016   £508   £254   3 yo rec 4 lb   High numbers favoured

2118 **OFF HIRE** 26 [14] C Smith 4-9-9 (51)(vis) R Fitzpatrick (3) 16/1: 060441: 4 b g Clantime - Lady   55
Pennington (Blue Cashmere) Chsd ldr, ran on und press ins last, led cl-home: fav'bly drawn: earlier won at
W'hampton (2, clmr & h'cap, rtd 59a): '99 rnr-up (rtd 58 & 57a): '98 Musselburgh wnr (sell nurs, rtd 42 & 63a):
stays 6f, suited by 5f: acts on firm, soft & fibresand, any track, likes W'hampton: eff with/without vis, forcing it.
2124 **POLAR MIST** 25 [18] M Wigham 3-9-13 (55)(tbl) Dean McKeown 16/1: 010602: 5 b g Polar Falcon -   hd 58
Post Mistress (Cyrano de Bergerac) Tried to make all, worn down nr fin: op 12/1: well drawn, back to form.
2440 **LIZZIE SIMMONDS** 12 [11] N Tinkler 3-9-11 (57) Iona Wands (5) 14/1: 501653: 3 b f Common Grounds - ½ 58
Able Susan (Formidable) Chsd ldrs, ran on inside last but never got to front pair: back to best:
acts on firm & gd/soft grnd & goes on any track: see 1258.
2395 **EASTERN PROPHETS** 14 [13] M Dods 7-9-9 (51)(vis) A Culhane 14/1: 300004: Rear, rdn entering fnl   nk 51
2f, ran on well, never nearer: well h'capped, interesting one 6f next time: see 1258.
2555 **INDIAN BAZAAR** 8 [16] 4-9-5 (47) G Baker (7) 9/2: 201005: Chsd ldrs, short of rm appr fnl 2f, rdn   ¾ 45
appr fnl 1f, unable to qckn: better run, likes firm grnd: see 2223.
2525 **DOMINELLE** 9 [20] 8-9-4 (46) J Carroll 4/1 FAV: 040406: Handy, hmpd briefly bef fnl 2f, same pace.   shd 44
2680 **SEALED BY FATE** 3 [12] 5-9-5 (47)(vis) K Darley 11/2: 445027: Bhd till kept on nicely fnl 1f, nvr dngrs.   nk 44
2015 **AMERICAN COUSIN** 30 [15] 5-9-6 (48) Alex Greaves 7/1: 000008: Mid div thro'out: likes Doncaster.   ¾ 43
2280 **THORNCLIFF FOX** 19 [8] 3-9-12 (58)(vis) O Pears 25/1: 400369: Rear, improved into mid 2f out,   1 50
rdn dist & no further hdwy: softer grnd suits: mdn, see 1061.
2535 **GARNOCK VALLEY** 8 [17] 10-9-10 (52) F Lynch 7/1: 362520: Slow away, nvr in it: 10th, 100th race today. ½ 42
2243 **DANCE LITTLE LADY** 20 [19] 3-9-9 (55) G Parkin 7/1: 4-0160: Chsd ldrs 2f: 13th, see 2243, 1891 (gd).   0
2193 **Press Ahead** 22 [6] 5-9-9 (51)(vis) Dale Gibson 50/1:   1256 **Dunkellin House** 67 [7] 3-9-8 (54) P Fessey 25/1:
3205} **L A Touch** 346 [9] 7-9-7 (49) D Mernagh (3) 20/1:   2577 **Seahorse Boy** 6 [1] 3-9-6 (52) T G McLaughlin 33/1:
2525 **Dazzling Quintet** 9 [4] 4-9-6 (48) J McAuley (5) 20/1: 4121}   **Going Home** 295 [3] 3-9-7 (53) T Lucas 33/1:
17 ran   Time 1m 02.0 (0.7)   (John Martin-Hoyes)   C Smith Temple Bruer, Lincs

2733   3.45 TOTE HCAP STKS 3YO 0-85 (D)   7f100y rnd   Firm 06 +03 Fast   [85]
£7475   £2300   £1150   £575

2524 **HADATH** 9 [4] M A Buckley 3-9-6 (77) Dean McKeown 7/1: 056121: 3 br g Mujtahid - Al Sylah   82
(Nureyev) Made every yard, drifted left appr fnl 1f, rdn out: op 11/2, best time of day: earlier won at
Thirsk (mdn): '99 rnr up (nov stakes, rtd 91, T Mregoning): eff at 7f/1m on firm & soft, any track:
best up with/forcing the pace: can go well fresh: best without a visor & is on the upgrade.
2160 **STORMVILLE** 24 [9] M Brittain 3-8-2 (59) D Mernagh (3) 12/1: -64002: 3 b g Catrail - Haut Volee   1 61
(Top Ville) Chsd wnr, ch appr fnl 1f, held below dist: op 8/1: eff at 6/7.5f on firm & gd grnd: still a mdn.

BEVERLEY TUESDAY JULY 18TH Righthand, Oval Track with Stiff Uphill Finish

2579 **MAMZUG 6** [6] B Hanbury 3-9-7 (78) G Faulkner (3) 7/4 FAV: -41423: 3 b c Hamas - Bellissi (Bluebird) Trckd ldrs, rdn ent fnl 2f, styd on but never able to chall: well bckd from 5/2, top-weight, qk reapp: ran well tho' a return to 1m will suit: acts on firm/fast grnd, see 1435 (made all in an auction mdn). *hd* **79**
2438 **DIHATJUM 12** [1] T D Easterby 3-8-9 (66) J Carroll 9/1: 26-324: Towards rear, wide eff appr fnl 2f, never pace to chall: op 7/1: mdn, btr 2438, see 1255. *1¾* **63**
*2060 **LORD OMNI 28** [8] 3-9-0 (71)(t) K Darley 4/1: 04-615: Mid-div, rdn 2f out, onepace: bckd tho' op 3/1. *¾* **66**
*2489 **WILFRAM 10** [5] 3-8-3 (60) G Baker (7) 7/1: 000316: Dwelt, off the pace, ran on well fnl 150y: op 11/1: waiting tactics overdone trying longer 7.5f trip?: worth another chance: see 2489 (6f). *hd* **54**
2515 **CELEBRE BLU 10** [7] 3-8-9 (66) F Lynch 25/1: 333007: Al towards rear: see 1562. *nk* **59**
2060 **COMEX FLYER 28** [3] 3-7-13 (56) T Hamilton (7) 25/1: 600108: Chsd ldrs till 2f out: see 1818 (g/s). *1½* **46**
2524 **JUMBOS FLYER 9** [2] 3-8-4 (61) K Dalgleish (5) 12/1: 246209: Dwelt, nvr dngrs & ran wide fnl 2f. *1* **49**
9 ran Time 1m 31.0 (0.2) (Mrs D J Buckley) M A Buckley Upper Helmsley, N Yorks

2734 4.15 WATT MEMORIAL HCAP 3YO+ 0-70 (E) 2m35y Firm 06 -50 Slow [58]
£3523 £1084 £542 £271 3 yo rec 17lb V Slow Pace

2176 **KAGOSHIMA 23** [3] J Norton 5-10-0 (58)(vis) O Pears 7/2: 023121: 5 b g Shirley Heights - Kashteh (Green Desert) Well plcd, drvn entering fnl 2f, led below dist, styd on grimly: slow time, jt top-weight: earlier won at Pontefract (h'cap): unplcd in '99 (rtd 53): ran once in '98 for L Cumani (mdn, rtd 78): eff at 2m/2m1.5f: acts on firm & gd/soft grnd, suited by stiff/gall tracks & wears a visor: can carry big weights. **61**
2607 **NICIARA 5** [2] M C Chapman 3-7-10 (43) K Dalgleish (5) 8/1: 033232: 3 b g Soviet Lad - Verusa (Petorius) Led, hdd 6f out, rallied under press appr fnl 1f, nearly got back up: op 6/1, mdn, stays 2m. *1¼* **45**
2244 **ICE PACK 20** [8] Don Enrico Incisa 4-8-0 (30) Kim Tinkler 14/1: 000343: 3 gr f Mukaddamah - Mrs Gray (Red Sunset) Chsd ldrs, feeling pace 3f out, styd on ins last, not btn far: op 10/1: handles firm & fibresand. *½* **31**
2273 **SALSKA 19** [4] P L Clinton 9-10-0 (58) L Newton 12/1: 0-0054: Waited with, struggling 3f out, ran on appr fnl 1f, never nearer: tchd 16/1: coming hand, see 2273. *nk* **59**
*2436 **KEEP IKIS 12** [7] 6-9-12 (56) D Mernagh (3) 7/4 FAV: -14315: Chsd ldrs, feeling pace 5f out, wide prog 2f out, same pace below dist: nicely bckd: in form, see 2436. *½* **56**
2141 **TOTALLY SCOTTISH 25** [5] 4-9-0 (44) K Darley 9/1: 04-056: Well off the pace, plenty to do & not handle bend 4f out, no impress till strong burst ins last, nvr nrr: clearly gets 2m, flatter trk & faster pace will suit. *nk* **43**
2516 **SPA LANE 10** [1] 7-9-0 (44) F Norton 7/2: 433257: Chsd ldrs, no extra appr fnl 1f: see2482, 1276. *nk* **41**
2643 **NOTATION 4** [6] 6-7-10 (26)(8oh) P Fessey 50/1: 000408: Chsd ldrs, led 6f out till below dist, wknd. *½* **22$**
8 ran Time 3m 39.3 (9) (Keep On Running) J Norton High Hoyland, S Yorks

2735 4.45 COLLECTING APPR HCAP 3YO 0-65 (F) 1m100y rnd Firm 06 -01 Slow [72]
£2478 £708 £354

2206 **WILEMMGEO 22** [10] M C Chapman 3-8-1 (45) Joanna Badger (5) 16/1: 050001: 3 b f Emarati - Floral Spark (Forzando) Towards rear, wide progress ent fnl 3f, kept on well to lead ins last, pshd out: earlier won at W'hampton (2, sells, rtd 55a): '99 wnr again at W'hampton (seller, rtd 55a & 62): eff at 1m/9.4f: acts on firm, gd/soft grnd, loves fibresand/W'hampton: eff with/without visor, any track: well ridden. **49**
2537 **SPIRIT OF KHAMBANI 8** [7] M Johnston 3-8-2 (46) K Dalgleish (5) 9/2: -00042: 3 ch f Indian Ridge - Khambani (Royal Academy) Held up, improved appr fnl 2f, rdn bef dist, kept on but not pace of wnr: gd run back at 1m, 10f looks like it may be the optimum: handles firm & soft grnd. *¾* **48**
2438 **NOBLE PASAO 12** [13] Andrew Turnell 3-9-7 (65) P M Quinn 7/1: 030553: 3 b g Alzao - Belle Passe (Be My Guest) Led, clr after 4f, und press 2f out, worn down well ins last: tchd 9/1, bold attempt, top-weight. *½* **66**
2506 **LOUP CERVIER 10** [12] S Dow 3-8-3 (47) R Smith (5) 7/1: 000034: Mid div, rdn 2f out, styd on without threatening: improved last twice, handles firm/fast grnd: see 2506. *¾* **46**
1581 **WELCOME BACK 49** [8] 3-7-10 (40) Iona Wands (3) 12/1: 6-0055: Rear, gd wide prog appr fnl 2f rdn bef dist & no extra: tchd 16/1, 7 week abs: suited by drop in trip, sharper track might help. *nk* **38**
2281 **DOLFINESSE 19** [11] 3-8-2 (46)(vis) D Mernagh 11/1: 523406: Led chasing pack, fdd appr fnl 1f: op 8/1: found this stiff 8.5f too far: see 2017. *1½* **41**
2506 **CAPACOOSTIC 10** [9] 3-8-1 (45) R Brisland (1) 12/1: 0-0027: Prom till 2f out: op 8/1, btr 2506. *3* **34**
939 **JONLOZ 92** [2] 3-7-10 (40)(3oh) J McAuley (2) 33/1: 545668: Never on terms with ldrs: 3 month abs. *nk* **28**
2506 **HEATHYARDS LAD 10** [4] 3-9-1 (59) G Gibbons (5) 14/1: 256559: Held up, eff 3f out, soon btn. *3½* **41**
2379 **WHITE SANDS 15** [5] 3-7-13 (43) A Beech (3) 25/1: 000600: Dwelt, al towards rear: 10th, nds sells. *2½* **20**
2281 **FOXY ALPHA 19** [3] 3-7-10 (40)(7oh) G Baker (5) 33/1: 0-0500: In tch till halfway: 11th, stiffish task. *½* **16**
2534 **FINERY 8** [6] 3-9-2 (60)(vis) P Clarke (5) 10/1: 100230: Dwelt, nvr dngrs: 12th, op 8/1: see 2534, 2284. *5* **26**
1921 **BEST EVER 34** [1] 3-8-9 (53) P Goode 5/2 FAV: 000250: Chsd ldrs wide till 3f out: 13th, well bckd. *2* **15**
13 ran Time 1m 44.4 (0.6) (R J Hayward) M C Chapman Market Rasen, Lincs

DEAUVILLE FRIDAY JULY 14TH Righthand, Galloping Track

Official Going VERY SOFT

2736 2.15 GR 2 PRIX EUGENE ADAM 3YO 1m2f V Soft
£28818 £11527 £5764 £2882

-- **SOBIESKI** [3] A Fabre 3-8-11 O Peslier 26/10: -11611: 3 b c Polish Precedent - Game Plan (Darshaan) Waited with, smooth hdwy to lead over 2f out, went on & edged left appr fnl 1f, pshd clr, comfortably: won 3 of his 4 prev starts this term: eff at 10f, shld stay further: acts on soft: v smart, win again. **116**
2225 **PREMIER PAS 19** [2] Mme C Head 3-8-11 (bl) O Doleuze 1/1 FAV: 3-2622: 3 b c Sillery - Passionnee (Woodman) Bhd, hdwy over 2f out, rdn/not pace of wnr appr fnl 1f: rated higher in 2225 (gd grnd). *5* **107**
1752 **HESIODE 40** [5] J C Rouget 3-8-11 (BL) T Thulliez 34/10: -11303: 3 gr c Highest Honor - Elite Guest (Be My Guest) Cl-up, went on 2f out, hdd appr fnl 1f, sn outpcd by wnr: 6 wk abs: blnkd: see 1752, 1231. *snk* **107**
2066 **COMPTON BOLTER 24** [4] G A Butler 3-8-11 G Mosse 68/10: -40504: Chsd ldrs, slightly outpcd when short of room over 1f out, sn no extra: prob stays 10f on soft: would enjoy Listed class: see 2066 (1m). *shd* **107**
-- **BLEU DALTAIR** [1] 3-8-11 D Boeuf 52/10: -31415: Led, hdd 2f out, fdd. *2* **103**
5 ran Time 2m 10.2 (Sheikh Mohammed) A Fabre France

MAISONS LAFFITTE SUNDAY JULY 16TH Left & Righthand, Sharpish Track

Official Going SOFT

2737 3.25 GR 2 PRIX MAURICE DE NIEUIL 3YO+ 1m4f110y Soft
£28818 £11527 £5764 £2882 3 yo rec 13lb

1378 **WAR GAME** 60 [2] A Fabre 4-9-1 O Peslier 19/10 FAV: 1-121: 4 b f Caerleon - Walensee (Troy) **111**
Chsd clr ldr, hdwy to lead appr fnl 1f, rdn out: eff at 12.5f on soft grnd: smart & lightly raced.
1380 **HERCULANO** 59 [4] Mme M Bollack Badel 3-8-5 D Boeuf 52/10: 123352: 3 b c Subotica - Hokey Pokey 1 **112**
(Lead On Time) Sn well bhd, gd hdwy to chall over 1f out, not pace of wnr: handles gd & soft: see 1380.
*2402 **LUCKY DREAM** 16 [3] H A Pantall 6-9-8 T Thulliez 32/10: 5-5513: 6 b h Homme De Loi - 3 **111**
Lady Of The House (Habitat) Trkd ldrs, went on over 2f out, rdn/hdd over 1f out, sn no extra: see 2402 (15f).
-- **MAYARO** [5] Mme C Head 4-9-4 T Gillet 26/10: 2-0164: Sn clr ldr, wknd/hdd 2f out, sn lost tch. 6 **100**
1902 **BEN EWAR** 35 [1] 6-9-4 D Bonilla 32/10: -1423P: Bhd when p.u halfway: broke blood vessel. **0**
5 ran Time 2m 38.4 (D Wildenstein) A Fabre France

CURRAGH SUNDAY JULY 16TH Righthand, Stiff, Galloping Track

Official Going Round course - GOOD/FIRM; Straight course - GOOD

2738 3.10 GR 3 ANGLESEY STKS 2YO 6f63y Good
£27300 £7980 £3780

2113 **PAN JAMMER** 24 [5] M R Channon 2-8-12 J Murtagh 5/1: 41231: 2 b c Piccolo - Ingerence (Akarad) **104**
Cl-up, led appr fnl 1f, rdn clr fnl 1f: op 7/2: earlier won at Salisbury (mdn), also close 3rd in the Gr 3 Norfolk
at R Ascot: half-brother to a 10f/hdles wnr: eff at 5f, stays 6f well & 7f shld suit: acts on fast, gd & likes
a stiff/gall trk: tough, fast improving & v useful juvenile who looks one to follow in Gr company this term.
*1756 **PIRATE OF PENZANCE** 41 [4] A P O'Brien 2-8-12 J A Heffernan 8/11 FAV: 12: 2 b c Southern 2 **99**
Halo - Stolen Pleasures (Marfa) Trkd ldr, went on 3f out, hdd over 1f out, sn not pace of wnr: acts on fast &
gd/soft grnd: better expected after beating this winner in 1756 (yldg grnd).
*2400 **BERLIN** 16 [2] E Lynam 2-8-12 E Ahern 7/2: 13: 2 b c Common Grounds - Carranza (Lead 1½ **95**
On Time) Prom, swtchd/eff appr fnl 1f, sn no extra: rtd higher on debut in 2400 (C/D, gd).
5 ran Time 1m 17.5 (Ms Lynn Bell) M R Channon West Isley, Berks

2739 4.15 GR 1 IRISH OAKS 3YO FILLIES 1m4f Good/Firm
£112425 £38425 £18425 £6425

1828 **PETRUSHKA** 37 [10] Sir Michael Stoute 3-9-0 J Murtagh 11/2: 1-1341: 3 ch f Unfuwain - Ballet Shoes **122**
(Ela Mana Mou) Cl-up going well, smooth hdwy to lead appr fnl 1f, rdn well clr ins last, eased nr fin: reversed
English Oaks form with rnr-up & 5th: earlier won on reapp at Newmarket (Gr 3, readily) & 3rd in the 1,000 Guineas:
won sole juv start at Leicester (mdn, rtd 100+): eff at 1m, suited by 12f: acts on firm & gd/soft: improved for
this more gall trk: top-class filly with a turn of foot, will prove hard to beat in the Yorkshire Oaks.
1828 **MELIKAH** 37 [5] Saeed bin Suroor 3-9-0 K Darley 2/1 FAV: -132: 3 ch f Lammtarra - Urban Sea 5½ **114**
(Miswaki) Prom, rdn over 5f out, styd on well for press fnl 1f but no ch with impress wnr: smart/lightly rcd filly
who fin clr of rem here: met a top-class rival today but did fin in front of her in the Epsom Oaks (sharp trk).
1945 **INFORAPENNY** 31 [9] R A Fahey 3-9-0 K J Manning 100/1: -12353: 3 b f Deploy - Morina (Lyphard) 3 **109**
Waited with, hdwy over 2f out, styd on, no threat: remarkable effort by this rank outsider: stays 12f: well btn
in List company prev & would relish a return to Listed company: see 1945.
*1945 **LITTLEPACEPADDOCKS** 31 [1] M Johnston 3-9-0 M Hills 16/1: 1-314: Led, rdn/hdd appr fnl ¾ **108**
1f, sn btn: not disgraced on this step up in grade & would relish a return to Listed company: see 1945.
1828 **KALYPSO KATIE** 37 [3] 3-9-0 G Duffield 5/2: 1-125: Prom, smooth hdwy appr fnl 3f, rdn 2f out ¾ **107**
& sn btn: below-par run & was later found to be suffering from a 'physical problem': much btr 1828 (gd/soft).
*2112 **MILETRIAN** 24 [7] 3-9-0 M Roberts 9/1: -04016: Waited with, rdn/eff over 2 out, onepace: ½ **106**
reportedly unsuited by the slow galloping track today: btr 2112 (Gr 2 Ribblesdale).
2150 **AMETHYST** 23 [6] 3-9-0 J A Heffernan 20/1: -10207: Nvr dangrs: lngr trip, btr 1626. **0**
1626 **THEORETICALLY** 49 [2] 3-9-0 P J Smullen 25/1: 11-368: Mid-div, lost tch fnl 2f: abs, lngr trip. **0**
2404 **PRESELI** 15 [4] 3-9-0 E Ahern 13/2: 1-1029: Handy, rdn/wknd fnl 2f: btr 2404 (10f, gd/soft). **0**
2112 **TEGGIANO** 24 [8] 3-9-0 R Hills 11/1: 111-20: Chsd ldrs, hdwy to chall ldrs 3f out, rdn & wknd **0**
qckly fnl 2f, fin last: most disappointing here, something amiss?: much btr 2112 (Gr 2).
10 ran Time 2m 31.2 (Highclere Thoroughbred Racing Ltd) Sir Michael Stoute Newmarket

2740 5.45 GR 3 MINSTREL STKS 3YO+ 1m Good/Firm
£22750 £6650 £3150 £1050 3 yo rec 8 lb

-- **SHIBL** [6] K Prendergast 3-8-10 S Craine 5/1: 212211: 3 b c Arazi - Mahasin (Danzig) **111**
Prom, hdwy to lead appr fnl 1f, edged right & drvn out: dual wnr prev this term, most recently here at The
Curragh (stks): suited by a stiff/gall 1m, further could suit: acts on gd/soft & fast grnd: v useful.
3111} **MCDAB** 349 [1] D Hanley 3-8-10 (t) J Murtagh 14/1: 223412: 3 b c Mr Greeley - Country Queen 2 **107**
(Unknown) Led, rdn/hdd over 1f out, hmpd dist, sn no extra: recent Leopardstown mdn wnr (7f, gd, placed several
times prev): fine run but surely flattered here (offic rated a meagre 88): stays 7f/1m on fast/gd.
3405} **SAFFRON WALDEN** 334 [2] A P O'Brien 4-9-4 J A Heffernan 5/2: 1020-3: 4 b h Sadler's Wells - Or 2 **103**
Vision (Irish River) Bhd, eff over 3f out, kept on but no threat to front 2: reapp: high-class form in early '99,
wng at Leopardstown (List) & The Curragh (incl Gr 1 Irish Derby, rtd 123), form subs dropped away (tried visor
on fnl start): eff at 1m/10f on gd & soft: high-class at best but seems to be out of love with the game at present.
2071 **FREE TO SPEAK** 32 [5] D K Weld 8-9-4 P J Smullen 7/1: -02204: Held up, hdwy 4f out, rdn/btn fnl 2f. shd **103**
*2570 **KERMIYANA** 8 [4] 3-8-7 N G McCullagh 4/6 FAV: -115: Prom, drvn/fdd fnl 2f: reportedly 6 **90**
came home lame with a breathing problem: much btr 2570 (Listed).
6 ran Time 1m 36.9 (Hamdan Al Maktoum) K Prendergast Kildare, Co Kildare

CATTERICK WEDNESDAY JULY 19TH Lefthand, Undulating, Very Tight Track

Official Going GOOD/FIRM (FIRM places). Stalls: Inside

2741

2.20 SWALE NOV MED AUCT STKS 2YO (F) 7f rnd Good/Firm 36 -10 Slow
£2289 £654 £327

*2218 **MONTANA MISS 22** [5] B Palling 2-8-13 K Darley 3/1: 411: 2 b f Earl Of Barking - Cupid Miss (Anita's Prince) Led after 2f, styd on well fnl 2f, drvn out: earlier scored at Beverley (fill auct mdn): eff at 7/7.5f, shld get further: acts on firm & gd/soft grnd, likes to force the pace & handles a stiff/sharp track. **81**

*1408 **PARVENUE 60** [6] E A L Dunlop 2-8-13 J Carroll 4/7 FAV: 12: 2 b f Ezzoud - Patria (Mr Prospector) Rdn rear, styd on for press to chase wnr over 1f out, kept on, al held: well bckd at odds on, 2 mth abs: stays 7f, shld get further: acts on fast & gd grnd: see 1408. *1¼* **78**

*2377 **MAGIC OF YOU 16** [4] M L W Bell 2-8-11 A Culhane 6/1: 13: 2 b f Magic Ring - Daarat Alayaam (Reference Point) Rear, kept on from halfway, no impression on front pair: see 2377. *3½* **69**

2521 **EAGLET 10** [2] A Scott 2-8-12 F Norton 20/1: -00054: Led 2f, btn over 2f out: needs sellers. *4* **62**

1252 **LADY AMBITION 68** [1] 2-8-7 T Lucas 50/1: -05: Drvn/bhd halfway: 10 week abs, longer 7f trip. *1* **55**

2417 **IZZET MUZZY 14** [3] 2-8-12 T Williams 33/1: 505546: Cl up, btn 2f out: btr 2417 (C/D). *1¼* **57**

6 ran Time 1m 26.2 (3.2) (Mrs A L Stacey) B Palling Cowbridge, Vale Of Glamorgan

2742

2.50 DRAGON TROOP CLAIMER 3YO+ (F) 1m4f Good/Firm 36 -04 Slow
£2268 £648 £324 3 yo rec 12lb

2457 **DESERT FIGHTER 12** [3] Mrs M Reveley 9-9-12 A Culhane 1/1 FAV: 001021: 9 b g Green Desert - Jungle Rose (Shirley Heights) Trkd ldrs, rdn fnl 2f, styd on gamely ins last to lead near line, drvn out: hvly bckd: earlier scored at Thirsk (clmr): '99 wnr at Thirsk, Haydock, Hamilton & Catterick (this race, all clmrs, rtd 66): plcd in '98 (h'caps, rtd 71): suited by 10/12f on firm & gd/soft, handles soft & any trk: loves claimers. **61**

2538 **TIME TEMPTRESS 9** [8] G M Moore 4-9-1 P Hanagan (7) 9/2: -00022: 4 b f Timeless Times - Tangalooma (Hotfoot) Led/dsptd lead, rdn/hdd 2f out, rallied gamely for press to lead again 1f out, hdd/no extra nr line: op 7/2: claimed for £5,000: stays a sharp 12f: acts on fast & soft grnd: see 2538, 1303. *½* **48**

2309 **METEOR STRIKE 19** [7] D Nicholls 6-9-6 (t) Alex Greaves 8/1: 621603: 6 ch g Lomond - Meteoric (High Line) Led till dsptd lead halfway, led 2f out till 1f out, no extra: clr rem: op 6/1: t-strap: see 369. *2½* **49**

2561 **THREE CHERRIES 8** [6] R E Barr 4-8-11 P Goode (3) 25/1: 000004: Rear, mod gains for press fnl 4f. *7* **30**

2156 **WINSOME GEORGE 25** [2] 5-9-0 (vis) N Kennedy 12/1: 300405: In tch, outpcd halfway, held after. *½* **32**

2143 **MITHRAIC 26** [4] 8-9-4 O Pears 8/1: 313-56: Chsd ldrs 2f out, soon wknd: op 7/1: see 2143. *¾* **35**

3892} **GO WITH THE WIND 310** [9] 7-9-6 W Supple 6/1: 2203-7: Chsd ldrs 5f out, drvn/fdd fnl 3f: reapp: '99 Beverley wnr (h'cap, J S Goldie, rtd 54 at best): rtd 50 in '98 (h'cap): eff at 12/14f, stays 2m on firm & fast. *2½* **33**

2638 **TEN PAST SIX 5** [5] 8-9-4 (vis) J Carroll 14/1: 056008: Struggling 4f out: quick reapp: see 1417. *12* **18**

651} **SHARP MONKEY 488** [1] 5-9-0 (bl) K Dalgleish (5) 50/1: 3050-9: Rdn/bhd halfway, t.o.: Flat reapp, jmps fit (unplcd, rtd 69h): plcd last term for Mrs N Macauley (rtd 41a, AW h'cap): '98 Southwell wnr (2, sell h'cap & clmr, rtd 63a): suited by 7f/1m, likes fibresand/Southwell, best in a visor up with/forcing the pace. *dist* **0**

9 ran Time 2m 36.00 (4.8) (A Frame) Mrs M Reveley Lingdale, N Yorks

2743

3.20 5TH REGIMENT HCAP 3YO+ 0-75 (E) 5f rnd Good/Firm 36 -04 Slow [75]
£3512 £1090 £545 £272 3 yo rec 1 lb

2385 **RUDE AWAKENING 16** [4] C W Fairhurst 6-7-11 (43)(1ow) T Williams 16/1: 303101: 6 b g Rudimentary - Final Call (Town Crier) Chsd ldrs, chall fnl 1f & drvn ahead nr fin: tchd 33/1: fine return to turf: earlier won at Lingfield (2, AW h'caps, rtd 62a): plcd in '99 (rtd 49a & 47, h'caps): '98 Southwell scorer (h'cap, rtd 55a & 53): stays 1m, suited by 5/6f on firm, gd/soft & both AWs: eff with/without bl/vis: loves to front run on a sharp trk. **48**

2334 **WILLIAMS WELL 18** [9] M W Easterby 6-9-6 (67)(bl) T Lucas 9/2: 436552: 6 ch g Superpower - Catherines Well (Junius) Held up, styd on well for press fnl 2f, not reach wnr: won this in '99 of 10lb lower mark. *½* **68**

2517 **SOTONIAN 11** [3] P S Felgate 7-8-11 (58) D Mernagh (3) 8/1: 663453: 7 br g Statoblest - Visage (Vision) Al handy, rdn/every ch over 1f out, no extra nr fin: see 394. *nk* **58**

-2326 **TUSCAN DREAM 18** [6] A Berry 5-10-0 (75) P Bradley (5) 7/2: 005124: Led, rdn over 1f out, rdn/hdd nr fin: bckd: in good form & can find one of these soon: see 2326, 2107. *shd* **75**

2701 **MUKARRAB 3** [5] 6-8-4 (51) K Darley 4/1: 004445: Chsd ldrs, not pace to chall: op 7/2, quick reapp. *1¾* **47**

2569 **REFERENDUM 8** [2] 6-9-10 (71) Alex Greaves 3/1 FAV: 005266: Soon hndy, wknd over 1f out: bckd. *1½* **63**

2721 **SWYNFORD DREAM 2** [8] 7-8-11 (58) O Pears 17/2: 204267: Unruly stalls, dwelt, al rear: qck reapp. *1* **48**

1133 **PIGGY BANK 76** [1] 4-8-9 (56) G Parkin 25/1: 46-008: Cl up 3f: 11 week abs: '99 Ripon wnr (h'cap, rtd 65): '98 Haydock wnr (nurs, rtd 72 at best): eff at 5f/sharp 6f, tried 1m: acts on fast & soft, any track. *6* **35**

1877 **LADY STALKER 37** [7] 3-8-3 (54) F Norton 16/1: 660-09: Bhd halfway: op 14/1: see 1877. *1½* **29**

9 ran Time 59.3 (2.0) (William Hill) C W Fairhurst Middleham, N Yorks

2744

3.50 HONDEGHEM SELLER 3YO+ (G) 6f rnd Good/Firm 36 +08 Fast
£1911 £546 £273 3 yo rec 5 lb

2680 **BLACK ARMY 4** [10] J M P Eustace 5-9-0 J Carroll 3/1: 30-051: 5 b g Aragon - Morgannwg (Simply Great) Trkd ldrs, rdn to lead 1f out, styd on well, rdn out: sold to K Ryan for 8,600gns: quick reapp: '99 Beverley scorer (h'cap, rtd 72 & 74a): rtd 74 in '98 (mdn): eff at 5/6f on fast, hvy & fibresand, any track: suited by sells. **55**

2632 **IMPALDI 5** [1] B Ellison 5-8-9 F Norton 12/1: 050002: 5 b m Imp Society - Jaldi (Nordico) Cl up, rdn/led over 2f out till 1f out, kept on for press: op 10/1, quick reapp: off rtd 30: see 1143. *¾* **47$**

2680 **SIR JACK 4** [5] D Nicholls 4-9-0 (bl) A Culhane 11/4 FAV: 244063: 4 b g Distant Relative - Frasquita (Song) Chsd ldrs, rdn/kept on onepace from over 1f out: qck reapp: blinks reapp: see 2054, 905. *1½* **49**

2535 **JUST DISSIDENT 9** [4] R M Whitaker 8-9-0 C Lowther 14/1: 055004: Led till over 2f out, fdd: see 91. *2* **44$**

2680 **BALLINA LAD 4** [2] 4-9-0 D Mernagh (3) 20/1: 00-005: Chsd ldrs, not pace to chall: qck reapp: see 2118. *hd* **43**

2680 **PALACEGATE TOUCH 4** [9] 10-9-6 (bl) P Bradley (5) 5/1: 030336: Chsd ldrs, held 1f out: qck reapp. *nk* **48**

2136 **CAIRN DHU 26** [3] 6-9-0 Kimberley Hart 50/1: -00007: Rear, switched & mod gains fnl 2f: see 159. *2½* **35$**

2535 **PISCES LAD 9** [7] 4-9-6 K Darley 3/1: 020008: Chsd ldrs, stumbled/rdn halfway, soon held: well bckd. *2½* **34**

1663 **GET A LIFE 47** [6] 7-8-9 R Lappin 16/1: -05059: Al rear: 7 week abs: see 930 (mdn). *¾* **21**

2533 **MY TYSON 9** [12] 5-9-6 (BL) F Lynch 20/1: 360000: Bhd halfway: 10th: blinks: see 676. *1½* **28**

2297 **NADDER 19** [11] 5-9-0 (vis) C Cogan (5) 16/1: 302000: Chsd ldrs 4f: op 12/1: 11th: vis reapp. *½* **20**

2680 **PICASSOS HERITAGE 4** [8] 4-9-0 (VIS) O Pears 50/1: 300000: Dwelt, al bhd: 12th: visor, no improv. *¾* **18**

CATTERICK
WEDNESDAY JULY 19TH   Lefthand, Undulating, Very Tight Track

12 ran   Time 1m 12.00 (1.7)   (Usk Valley Stud)   J M P Eustace Newmarket, Suffolk

2745
4.20 PALLETT MED AUCT FILLIES MDN 3YO (F)   7f rnd   Good/Firm 36   -01 Slow
£2184   £624   £312

1468 **JAWLA** 56 [2]   J H M Gosden 3-8-11 W Supple 1/5 FAV: 0-321: 3 ch f Wolfhound - Majmu (Al Nasr)   **80**
Chsd ldr, led 2f out & rdn clr over 1f out, in command & eased nr fin: hvly bckd at long odds on: abs: well btn
sole '99 start: eff at 7f, 1m should suit: acts on fast & gd/soft grnd, likes a sharp track: runs well fresh.
2491 **PRINISHA** 11 [1]   H Candy 3-8-11 K Darley 4/1: 02022: 3 gr f Prince Sabo - Nisha (Nishapour)   3½   **71$**
Led, rdn 3f out, hdd 2f out & soon held, eased nr line: see 2491, 1548.
2374 **BLUE SAPPHIRE** 16 [4]   D W Barker 3-8-11 Kimberley Hart 50/1: -60003: 3 b f Blues Traveller - Era   4   **63$**
(Dalsaan) Rear, never on terms with front pair: eff rtd jusr 36, treat this rating with caution: see 1081.
1818 **LADY TILLY** 40 [3]   B Ellison 3-8-11 J Carroll 20/1: 0-0544: Chsd leading pair, btn halfway: 6 wk abs.   5   **53$**
4 ran   Time 1m 25.60 (2.6)   (Hamdan Al Maktoum)   J H M Gosden Manton, Wilts

2746
4.50 BECKSIDE HCAP 3YO 0-70 (E)   1m4f   Good/Firm 36   -15 Slow   [69]
£3672   £1130   £565   £282

2685 **CHAKA ZULU** 4 [3]   W J Haggas 3-8-3 (44) F Norton 6/4 FAV: 00-131: 3 b g Muhtarram - African Dance   **52**
(El Gran Senor) Trckd ldrs, smooth prog to lead 2f out, qcknd clr, easily: val for 5L+: hvly bckd: quick reapp:
earlier scored at Bath (h'cap bow): mod form in '99 (rtd 38): eff at 10f, apprec step up to 12f, should get
further: acts on firm & fast grnd & runs well fresh: plenty in hand here, type to win under a pen.
2175 **SORRENTO KING** 24 [6]   M W Easterby 3-8-2 (43)(bl) J Dale Gibson 20/1: 0-0002: 3 ch g First Trump -   1½   **42**
Star Face (African Sky) Keen/chsd ldrs, rdn & styd to fnl 2f, no ch with wnr: stays 12f & handles fast: see 1758.
2332 **TYCOONS LAST** 18 [2]   W M Brisbourne 3-7-10 (37)(20h) K Dalgleish (5) 5/1: 004353: 3 b f Nalchik -   shd   **36**
Royal Tycoon (Tycoon II) Rear, prog 4f out, rdn & styd on fnl 2f, never a threat: op 4/1: stays a sharp 12f: see 799.
2510 **WILLIAM THE LION** 11 [12]   A Berry 3-8-11 (52) P Bradley (5) 12/1: 055204: Held up, eff 4f out, kept   1¼   **49**
on onepace: op 9/1: see 2141 (mdn h'cap).
2362 **UNICORN STAR** 16 [10]   O Pears 3-8-9 (50)(VIS) O Pears 9/1: -43625: Trckd ldrs, one pace/held fnl 2f: visor: 2   **44**
op 10/1: jockey reported gelding hung badly from before halfway: see 2362, 1274.
1909 **LUCKY JUDGE** 35 [9]   F Lynch 3-9-5 (60) F Lynch 14/1: 0-5046: Chsd ldr, btn 2f out: see 1909, 902.   shd   **54**
1758 **FIRST BACK** 42 [4]   3-9-11 (56) P Goode (3) 14/1: 06-407: In tch, btn 2f out: 6 week abs: see 1480.   ½   **49**
2372 **SHAM SHARIF** 16 [8]   3-9-7 (62) J Carroll 5/1: -51058: Led till 2f out, wknd: see 1632 (mdn, 9f).   shd   **55**
1202 **GYMCRAK FIREBIRD** 72 [13]   3-8-9 (50) Dean McKeown 33/1: 46-009: Rear, mod late gains: 10 wk abs.   2   **40**
1907 **PHARAOHS HOUSE** 35 [5]   3-8-5 (46) P Fessey 25/1: 90-000: Never factor: 10th: blinks omitted.   ¾   **35**
2464 Satire 12 [7] 3-8-3 (44) P Hanagan (2) 16/1:   2273 **Mill Emerald** 20 [11] 3-9-3 (58) W Supple 20/1:
1581 **Amber Go Go** 50 [1] 3-7-13 (40) J Bramhill 66/1:
13 ran   Time 2m 37.3 (6.1)   (J D Ashenheim)   W J Haggas Newmarket, Suffolk

KEMPTON
WEDNESDAY JULY 19TH   Righthand, Flat, Fair Track

Official Going   GOOD TO FIRM.   Stalls: Str Crse - Stands Side; 1m2f - Outside; Rem - Inside.

2747
6.20 LADIES NIGHT CLAIMER 3YO+ (E)   6f   Good/Firm 22   -02 Slow
£2795   £860   £430   £215   3 yo rec 5 lb

2216 **LABRETT** 22 [1]   B J Meehan 3-8-4 (bl) L Newman (3) 11/4: 004401: 3 b g Tragic Role - Play The Game   **78**
(Mummy's Game) Chsd ldr, rdn to lead appr fnl 1f, pushed out in last: '99 wnr at Redcar & Chester (nov stks,
rtd 98): eff at 5/6f on fast & gd/soft, any trk, wears blnks: relished drop to claiming grade.
2207 **LA PIAZZA** 23 [3]   W J Haggas 4-8-11 J P Spencer 11/8 FAV: -00002: 4 ch f Polish Patriot - Blazing   2   **76**
Glory (Glow) Held up, kept on appr fnl 1f, no impress on wnr: clr rem, well bckd: gd run, see 1391.
1884 **SHARP SHUFFLE** 36 [5]   Ian Williams 7-8-7 A Nicholls (3) 12/1: 240023: 7 ch g Exactly Sharp - Style   3   **63**
(Traffic Judge) Towards rear, eff appr fnl 1f, styd on for 3rd, nvr nr ldrs: stiff task back in trip, see 138.
2247 **BLUNDELL LANE** 21 [4]   A P Jarvis 5-8-11 (vis) N Callan 8/1: 100604: Led till appr fnl 1f, no extra.   ¾   **65**
2462 **KUWAIT ROSE** 12 [2]   4-9-7 R Hills 12/1: 454025: Handy till 2f out: tchd 20/1, softer grnd suits.   2   **69$**
2542 **PLEADING** 9 [6]   7-8-11 (bl) J Fortune 10/1: 005006: Slow away, nvr trbld ldrs: stiff task, see 454.   shd   **59**
2042 **TINSEL WHISTLE** 30 [7]   3-8-6 M Tebbutt 12/1: 6-0667: Chsd ldrs till appr fnl 2f: better than this, see 1289. 7   **39**
2467 **LUCAYAN BEACH** 12 [8]   6-8-6 S Sanders 50/1: 3-0008: Dwelt, hung badly left, nvr in it: stiff task, see 92. 5   **19**
8 ran   Time 1m 12.56 (1.46)   (T G Holdcroft)   B J Meehan Upper Lambourn, Berks

2748
6.50 SISTERS MED AUCT FILLIES MDN 2YO (E)   6f   Good/Firm 22   -18 Slow
£3591   £1105   £552   £276

1691 **SWEET PROSPECT** 46 [8]   C F Wall 2-8-11 R Mullen 5/1: -01: 2 b f Shareef Dancer - Vayavaig (Damister)   **82**
Held up, prog to trck ldrs on bit halfway, drvn appr fnl 1f, ran on to lead towards fin: tchd 7/1, 7 wk abs:
30,000 gns half-sister to 2 sprinters: eff at 6f, shld stay further: acts on fast grnd, easy trk: runs well fresh.
2526 **PRIYA** 10 [6]   C E Brittain 2-8-11 B Marcus 9/2: -4622: 2 b f Primo Dominie - Promissory (Caerleon)   hd   **81**
Front rank, led 2f out, hard rdn dist, worn down fnl 50y: clr rem, op 3/1: improving, stays 6f, win a race.
2500 **ESPANA** 11 [5]   B W Hills 2-8-11 R Hills 6/1: 03: 2 gr f Hernando - Pamela Peach (Habitat)   4   **70**
Slow away, towards rear, not much room 3f out, switched v wide & styd on for 3rd lns dist, nvr dangerous:
tchd 8/1: looks capable of better, step up to 7f will suit: see 2500.
2306 **IT GIRL** 19 [7]   I A Balding 2-8-11 W Ryan 4/1 FAV: 24: Well plcd & ev ch till no extra appr fnl 1f.   1½   **66**
2029 **MAYTIME** 31 [14]   J P Spencer 20/1: -005: Restrained rear, kept on nicely fnl 2f, nvr   ½   **65+**
plcd to chall: op 14/1, eye-catching nursery qualifying run & looks sure to better: keep in mind.
2357 **TUSCAN** 17 [2]   2-8-11 Craig Williams 5/1: 46: Prom, onepace appr fnl 1f: op 7/2: see 2357.   shd   **64**
-- **PRECIOUS PENNY** [3]   2-8-11 N Callan 20/1: 0: In tch till outpcd appr fnl 1f: Persian Bold Mar   1¾   **60**
1st foal, dam unrcd, sire a miler: with A Jarvis.
2526 **PETALITE** 10 [10]   2-8-11 M Tebbutt 8/1: -68: Chsd ldrs wide till appr fnl 1f: up in trip, see 2526.   nk   **59**
2526 **CLASSIC MILLENNIUM** 10 [1]   2-8-11 R Perham 33/1: -09: Prom till after halfway: see 2526.   1   **56**
-- **AUNT RUBY** [9]   2-8-11 S Sanders 20/1: 0: Slow away, al bhd tho' staying on fin: 10th, stablemate   hd   **55**

5th, debut: 20,000 gns 2yo: Rubiano Mar foal, dam wnr abroad, sire 6f/1m dirt performer: with M Bell.
-- **QUATREDIL** [4] 2-8-11 L Newman (3) 20/1: 0: Led till 2½f out, fdd: 11th, mkr drifter on debut: **5** **41**
2,500 gns Mujadil Apr foal, half-sister to a 7f wnr, dam & sire sprinters: with R Hannon.
2583 **EAGALITY** 7 [11] 2-8-11 D R McCabe 33/1: 000: Hung left, in tch till halfway: 12th.   **3** **33**
-- **RAINBOW PRINCESS** [13] 2-8-11 O Urbina 20/1: P: Dwelt, t.o./p.u. after 2f: 36,000 gns   **0**
Spectrum Feb foal, half-sister to sev wnrs, sire 1m/10f performer: with P d'Arcy.
13 ran   Time 1m 13.5 (2.4)   (The Silver & Blue Horse Racing Club)   C F Wall Newmarket, Suffolk

---

2749   **7.20 CITY INDEX 4 OVER 7 HCAP 3YO+ 0-70 (E)**   **7f rnd**   **Good/Firm 22 -03 Slow**   **[69]**
£4836   £1488   £744   £372   3 yo rec 7 lb .

2257 **WHITE EMIR** 21 [1] L G Cottrell 7-9-4 (59) A Clark 16/1: 00-321: 7 b g Emarati - White African   **64**
(Carwhite) Well plcd, shaken up to take narrow lead ent fnl 2f, held on well, rdn out: plcd in '99 for B
Millman (h'cap, rtd 72): last won in '97, at Sandown (clmr) & Salisbury (h'cap, rtd 83, B Meehan): eff at 5/6f,
suited by 7f: acts on firm & hvy grnd, with/without blnks, any trk: well h'capped.
*2612 **PENGAMON** 6 [3] M Wigham 8-9-7 (62)(6ex) J Quinn 2/1 FAV: -30212: 8 gr g Efisio - Dolly Bevan   **hd** **66**
(Another Realm) Bhd ldrs, qcknd up to chall appr fnl 2f, hard drvn, al being held: hvly bckd, ran well, see 2612.
2385 **DOUBLE DESTINY** 16 [11] K T Ivory 4-8-7 (48)(bl) C Carver (3) 33/1: -00003: 4 b g Anshaan - Double   **1¼** **49**
Gift (Cragador) Held up, wide prog ent str, drvn to chase ldrs dist, no extra cl-home: ran to best, eff at
7f, handles fast grnd, wears blnks & is at right end of h'cap: see 1611.
*2329 **LAW COMMISSION** 18 [9] D R C Elsworth 10-9-10 (65) R Thomas (7) 8/1: 0-6014: Bhd, wide prog appr   **½** **65**
fnl 1f, kept on well, nvr dangerous: clr form, remains in form: see 2329.
2612 **CALCAVELLA** 6 [10] 4-9-7 (62) S Sanders 20/1: 00-405: Bhd, prog to chase ldrs appr fnl 1f, sn onepace.   **2** **58**
2492 **MYTTONS MISTAKE** 11 [8] 7-9-1 (56) G Sparkes (7) 14/1: 242136: Held up & rcd widest of all,   **nk** **51**
prog 2f out, rdn dist, same pace: not get run of race, better judged 2257 (beat this wnr).
*2631 **VIOLET** 6 [6] 4-8-9 (50)(bl) (6ex) W Ryan 9/1: 006017: Keen in tch, prog & ev ch 2f out, sn no   **¾** **43**
extra: unsuited by return to 7f on much quicker grnd: see 2631 (6f, gd/soft).
2658 **WHO GOES THERE** 5 [7] 4-8-1 (42) A Nicholls (3) 14/1: 020038: Rear, prog 3f out till ent fnl 2f.   **nk** **34**
2415 **INDIAN WARRIOR** 14 [13] 4-8-6 (47) L Newton 10/1: 000069: Last, late hdwy, nvr a threat: see 364.   **1¾** **35**
2044 **WORK OF FICTION** 30 [2] 3-8-13 (61) Dane O'Neill 16/1: -04440: Cl-up, led 3f out, sn hdd, fdd: 10th.   **3** **43**
2185 **CEDAR PRINCE** 24 [16] 3-9-4 (66)(bl) J Fortune 15/2: -00060: Held up, boxed in 3f out till 2f out,   **0**
position accepted: 12th, ignore this, see 2185, 1744.
2391 **LADYWELL BLAISE** 15 [4] 3-8-12 (60) A Daly 16/1: 060120: Led till 3f out, sn btn: 14th: new stable.   **0**
1676 **Kayo Gee** 46 [5] 4-9-5 (60)(vis) C Rutter 33/1:   2427 **Rainbow Rain** 14 [12] 6-9-7 (62) O Urbina 11/1:
195 **Ok Babe** 215 [15] 5-7-10 (37) P Doe 20/1:   2508 **Magic Flute** 11 [14] 4-9-10 (65)(t) P Doe 16/1:
16 ran   Time   (Miss D M Stafford)   L G Cottrell Cullompton, Devon

---

2750   **7.50 TOTE HCAP 3YO+ 0-90 (C)**   **1m2f**   **Good/Firm 22 -03 Slow**   **[83]**
£7182   £2210   £1105   £552   3 yo rec 10lb

2499 **POLAR RED** 11 [2] M J Ryan 3-9-6 (85) P McCabe 6/1: 312431: 3 ch g Polar Falcon - Sharp Top (Sharpo)   **91**
Trkd ldrs, led appr fnl 2f, sn hard rdn, drvn clr ins last despite edging left: earlier won at Haydock (rtd h'cap):
juv wnr at Windsor (nurs, rtd 73): eff dwn 1m & 12f: acts on fast & soft grnd, any trk: progressive & tough.
1831 **IMPERIAL ROCKET** 40 [11] R Hannon 3-9-5 (84) Dane O'Neill 8/1: -46002: 3 b c Northern Flagship -   **3** **85**
Starsawhirl (Star de Naskra) Cl-up, led ent str till bef 2f out, styd on for 2nd but no ch with wnr: 6 wk abs,
not disgraced, caught an improver: eff at 1m/10f on fast & gd/soft grnd: see 912.
2527 **AMRAK AJEEB** 10 [7] R J Baker 8-9-5 (74) G Sparkes (7) 6/1: -03143: 8 b h Danehill - Noble Dust   **shd** **75**
(Dust Commander) Bhd, wide hdwy ent str, kept on to go 3rd near fin, nvr nrr: took the scenic route, see 2527.
*2552 **CHIEF CASHIER** 9 [5] G B Balding 5-9-10 (79)(5ex) A Daly 6/1: 500014: Led/dsptd lead till 3f   **nk** **79**
out, no extra dist: suited by softer grnd, as in 2552.
1927 **PUZZLEMENT** 35 [12] 6-9-1 (70) B Marcus 9/1: 310055: Rear, prog to chase ldrs 2f out, same pace.   **½** **69**
2530 **SUPLIZI** 10 [8] 9-8-5 (60) G Baker (7) 16/1: -40006: Bhd, late wide prog: bckd, on handy mark.   **½** **58**
1969 **LOVERS LEAP** 33 [9] 4-9-6 (75) C Rutter 12/1: -00607: Nvr a factor: visor omitted, much longer trip.   **2½** **70**
2287 **MODUS OPERANDI** 19 [6] 4-9-6 (75) N Callan 25/1: 5-6408: Keen, chsd ldrs till appr fnl 1f: see 593   **½** **69**
4494} **IGNITE** 270 [3] R Pollard 33/1: 4340-9: Pld hard, al bhd: reapp: plcd sev times for M Bell   **2½** **63**
as a juv (mdn, rtd 84, nurs, rtd 77, 1st time blnks): eff at 5/6f, not bred for 10f: acts on firm & soft grnd.
2674 **ST HELENSFIELD** 4 [10] 5-9-10 (79) J Fanning 100/30 FAV: 303220: Sn led, hdd 3f out & btn: 10th: **¾** **68**
joint top-weight: consistent previously, possibly came too soon after 2674, see 1518.
1990 **DARE HUNTER** 32 [1] 3-9-4 (83) J Reid 14/1: 6-0240: Chsd ldrs till appr fnl 2f: 11th, longer trip.   **4** **66**
2190 **CRYSTAL CREEK** 23 [4] 4-9-9 (78) J Fortune 12/1: 0-0600: 1n tch till 2f out: 12th, nds a drop back to 1m.   **½** **60**
12 ran   Time 2m 04.8 (2.5)   (M Byron)   M J Ryan Newmarket

2751   **8.20 LADY IN RED MDN 3YO (D)**   **1m4f**   **Good/Firm 22 +08 Fast**
£4095   £1260   £630   £315

2477 **TAKWIN** 12 [3] B Hanbury 3-9-0 (t) R Hills 9/4: -03221: 3 b c Alzao - Gale Warning (Last Tycoon)   **91**
Made all, unchall, easily: earlier rnr-up to subsequent Gr 3 wnr Dalampour: unrcd juv: eff at 12f/14f: acts on
fast & gd, not softer?: goes on any trk & wears a t-strap: can force the pace/come from bhd: progressive.
2265 **ALRISHA** 20 [8] D R C Elsworth 3-8-9 N Pollard 33/1: 02: 3 b f Persian Bold - Rifaya (Lashkari)   **5** **78**
Held up, feeling pace ent str, styd on well to grab 2nd nr fin, no ch wnr: apprec step up to 12f & handles fast.
2531 **SHATTERED SILENCE** 10 [7] R Charlton 3-8-9 J Fortune 7/4 FAV: -033: 3 b f Cozzene - Sunday   **shd** **78**
Bazaar (Nureyev) Trkd ldrs, chsd wnr 2f out, sn hard rdn, onepace: lkd ready for this step up to 12f, see 2531 (10f).
2213 **SATARRA** 22 [6] H R A Cecil 3-9-0 W Ryan 5/1: 24: Chsd wnr till 2f out: drifted late, see 2531   **5** **76**
2265 **BOULDER** 20 [1] 3-9-0 J P Spencer 16/1: 645: 1n tch, shaken up & outpcd appr fnl 2f: h'cap qual run.   **1½** **74**
2308 **DIAMOND ROAD** 19 [5] 3-9-0 I Mongan (5) 12/1: 0-3326: Outpcd & detached, late prog: see 2308, 2129.   **1¾** **71**
1343 **SALZGITTER** 62 [9] 3-8-9 C Rutter 12/1: 5-337: Chsd ldrs, fdd fnl 2f: unsuited by step up to 12f.   **1** **64**
2322 **DARCY ROAD DANCER** 18 [2] 3-9-0 S Whitworth 50/1: -08: Sn struggling: see 2322.   **dist** **0**
1588 **PENNY MUIR** 50 [4] 3-8-9 J Lowe 50/1: 09: Al out the back: 7 wk abs, see 1588.   **dist** **0**
9 ran   Time 2m 31.64 (1.64)   (Hamdan Al Maktoum)   B Hanbury Newmarket, Suffolk

KEMPTON WEDNESDAY JULY 19TH Righthand, Flat, Fair Track

2752 8.50 DRESS TO IMPRESS HCAP 3YO+ 0-75 (E) 1m rnd Good/Firm 22 +00 Fast [75]
£4368 £1344 £672 £336 3 yo rec 8 lb

2231} **DOM SHADEED** 390 [1] R J Baker 5-8-3 (50) G Sparkes (7) 33/1: 0000-1: 5 b g Shadeed - Fair Dominion 53
(Dominion) Waited with, plenty to do 2f out, switched & rapid hdwy appr fnl 1f, 'flew home' & got up fnl stride,
pshd out: reapp: unplcd in '99 (rtd 53a & 53, tried blnks on fnl start, R Charlton): subs joined current
connections & unplcd over hdles: '98 W'hampton wnr (AW mdn, rtd 66a): rtd 77 in '98: eff arnd 1m, 10f shld
suit: acts on fast, fibresand & a sharp or easy trk: runs esp well when fresh: win again in this form.
1300 **ELLWAY PRINCE** 65 [14] M Wigham 5-8-2 (49) J Quinn 11/4 FAV: 011432: 5 b g Prince Sabo - Star shd 51
Arrangement (Star Appeal) Mid-div, gd hdwy to lead appr fnl 1f, clr ins last, kept on, caught cl-home: abs.
1007 **ONE DINAR** 86 [4] K Mahdi 5-9-3 (64) J Lowe 11/1: 120503: 5 b h Generous - Lypharitissima (Lightning) 2½ 61
Trkd ldrs, chall appr fnl 2f, no extra over 1f out: 12 wk abs & not disgraced: see 1007.
2130 **PIPE DREAM** 26 [2] P Burgoyne 4-7-10 (43)(3oh) G Baker (7) 33/1: 600504: Settled rear, switched & hd 39
hdwy 3f out, styd on, nvr nrr: stays 1m on fast, ran to nr best: see 353.
2331 **CLONOE** 18 [6] 6-7-10 (43)(t) (2oh) D Kinsella (7) 10/1: 410005: Front rank, chall 2f out, held fnl 1f. ½ 38
2580 **SEA DEER** 7 [10] 11-10-0 (75) D Watson (7) 33/1: 0-0006: Bhd, rdn/hdd 2f out, kept on but not pace 2 66
of ldrs: quick reapp, top weight: 1st try at 1m, best at 6/7f: see 1952.
2085 **THE GREEN GREY** 28 [12] 6-9-5 (66) N Pollard 9/1: 006107: Dwelt, waited with, ran on for press hd 56
appr fnl 1f, no threat: drop in trip: twice below 1878 (10f).
2512 **TWIST** 11 [5] 3-8-7 (62)(BL) Martin Dwyer 14/1: -05058: Prom, rdn to improve 2f out, sn btn: blnkd. ¾ 50
1915 **SALORY** 35 [7] 4-8-8 (55)(t) L Newman (3) 20/1: 0-3009: Dsptd lead to halfway, btn over 2f out. shd 42
*2296 **COMMON CONSENT** 19 [11] 4-8-8 (55) S Whitworth 6/1: 3-0610: Front rank, wknd appr fnl 1f, 10th. 2½ 37
2304 **DIVORCE ACTION** 19 [13] 4-9-0 (61) D Sweeney 14/1: -02500: Bhd, hmpd over 2f out, no dngr, 11th. nk 42
4035} **FIFTH EDITION** 302 [8] 4-8-12 (59) R Mullen 13/2: 0405-0: Dwelt, nvr dangerous, fin 12th: 4th at ½ 39
best in '99 (mdn, rtd 66): bred to apprec mid-dists.
2512 **BISHOPSTONE MAN** 11 [3] 3-8-12 (67) C Rutter 9/1: 003510: Led, hdd appr fnl 1f, wknd rapidly, 13th. 1¾ 43
2085 **GIKO** 28 [9] 6-8-6 (53)(bl) M Henry 14/1: 065600: Sn rdn in mid-div, lost tch fnl 2f, fin last: choked. 6 17
14 ran Time 1m 38.78 (1.78) (Graham Brown) R J Baker Stoodleigh, Devon

DONCASTER WEDNESDAY JULY 19TH Lefthand, Flat, Galloping Track

Official Going GOOD/FIRM (FIRM Places). Stalls: Str Crse - Stands Side; Rnd Crse - Inside; Rnd 1m - Outside.

2753 6.40 HORSESMOUTH APPR HCAP 3YO+ 0-65 (F) 5f str Good/Firm 21 -03 Slow [65]
£2457 £702 £351

*2315 **NOBLE PATRIOT** 18 [10] R Hollinshead 5-8-2 (39) Stephanie Hollinshead(5) 13/2: 553411: 5 b g Polish 48
Patriot - Noble Form (Double Form) Early ldr, remained prom till regained lead halfway, just held on cl-home
under a quiet ride: recent wnr here at Doncaster (appr mdn h'cap): plcd in '99 (mdn h'cap, rtd 39a & 33): eff
btwn 5/7f, acts on firm, gd/soft & both AWs: handles a sharp or gall trk: likes to run-up with or force the pace.
1778 **FLAK JACKET** 42 [12] D Nicholls 5-9-11 (62)(t) A Eddery 10/1: -00002: 5 b g Magic Ring - Vaula shd 70
(Henbit) In tch, ran on strongly under press fnl 1f, just failed in a v close fin: 6 wk abs: fine eff conceding
23lbs to this wnr: eff at 5f, a return to 6f will suit: v well h'capped: & back to form wearing a t-strap here.
2525 **TORRENT** 1 [1] D W Chapman 5-9-7 (58)(bl) Lynsey Hanna(5) 4/1: 444463: 5 ch g Prince Sabo - 1½ 62
Maiden Pool (Sharpen Up) Al chasing ldrs, styd on under press fnl 1f: consistent, usually finds a couple too gd.
2505 **SIHAFI** 11 [4] D Nicholls 7-9-8 (59) T Hamilton 5/1: 236104: Mid-div, kept on fnl 1f, nrst fin. shd 63
2192 **EASTERN RAINBOW** 23 [7] 4-8-1 (38)(bl) Iona Wands 10/1: 002365: Rear, prog halfway, nrst fin. nk 41
2623 **SUNSET HARBOUR** 6 [5] 7-8-10 (47) Claire Bryan 12/1: 636056: Chsd ldrs, onepcd fnl 1f: qck reapp. 2 44
2569 **SOUNDS ACE** 8 [8] 4-8-11 (48)(bl) P Bradley 10/1: 030307: Dwelt, late hdwy, nvr dngrs: btr 2418. 2½ 38
2418 **PLEASURE TIME** 14 [13] 7-10-0 (65)(vis) J McAuley 9/2 FAV: 0-0608: Dwelt, recovered to lead after 1f 3 46
till halfway, wknd & eased: nbd from 6/1, top weight: burnt himself out overcoming slow start, forgive this.
2421 **CARMARTHEN** 14 [11] 4-8-7 (44)(t) D Meah (5) 33/1: 000009: Speed 3f, fdd: see 2223. shd 25
2555 **ANOTHER VICTIM** 9 [3] 6-8-0 (37) R Naylor (5) 10/1: 300020: In tch, wandered under press 1½f out, shd 18
sn btn: fin 10th: btr 2555 (gd/soft).
2496 **POETRY IN MOTION** 11 [14] 5-9-13 (64) D McGaffin (3) 11/1: 0-0500: Mid-div, btn fnl 2f: fin 11th. ¾ 42
2525 **TIME TO FLY** 10 [2] 7-8-5 (42)(bl) P Hanagan (3) 11/1: 0-0050: In tch 3f, fdd into 12th: see 2525. 2 14
628 Baritone 137 [6] 6-8-2 (39)(vis) D Glennon(5) 20/1: 1868 Lucky Cove 37 [9] 4-8-13 (50) Giorgia Lamberti(5) 33/1:
14 ran Time 59.42 (1.22) (The Four Dreamers) R Hollinshead Upper Longdon, Staffs

2754 7.10 GRESLEY COND STKS 2YO (C) 6f str Good/Firm 21 -29 Slow
£6201 £1908 £954 £477

*2480 **WALLY MCARTHUR** 12 [3] A Berry 2-9-1 J Carroll 6/1: -03211: 2 b c Puissance - Giddy (Polar Falcon) 87
In tch, rdn to lead ins fnl 1f, held on well, drvn out: op 4/1: recent Beverley wnr (mdn): eff at 5/6f on gd
& fast grnd: handles a stiff/gall trk: imprvg, useful colt who looks tough.
*2307 **LOGIC LANE** 19 [5] R Charlton 2-9-1 R Hughes 4/9 FAV: -012: 2 ch c Lahib - Reflection (Mill Reef) ½ 87
Slowly away, no room from 2f out, switched ins over 1f out & no room till ins last, ran on well but not rch wnr:
hvly bckd: jockey again less than inspired, finding plenty of trouble in this 5 rnr race! find compensation.
2664 **RUMORE CASTAGNA** 5 [2] S E Kettlewell 2-9-1 K Darley 8/1: -153: 2 ch g Great Commotion - False 1 84
Spring (Petorius) Tried to make all, collared ins last, short of room when held cl-home: op 5/1, qck reapp:
acts on fast & hvy grnd, stays 6f: see 2664, 1764.
-- **MATADI** [1] C E Brittain 2-8-8 W Supple 8/1: -4: Rdn in rear, some late hdwy, nvr dngrs on debut: 4 65
drifted from 4/1: Mar foal, half brother to 12f wnr Liefling: dam a useful 7f wnr, sire a smart 9/10f performer.
2575 **TOMMY SMITH** 7 [4] 2-8-11 T G McLaughlin 50/1: 041165: Dsptd lead 4f, wknd into last: see 2394. 3 59
5 ran Time 1m 13.85 (3.05) (T Herbert-Jackson) A Berry Cockerham, Lancs

863

2755   7.40 SASHA LYONS HCAP 3YO+ 0-80 (D)   1m4f   Good/Firm 21   -33 Slow   [76]
£4270   £1314   £657   £328   3yo rec 12lb

1167 **DOUBLE BLADE** 74 [2] Mrs M Reveley 5-8-12 (60) A Culhane 5/1: 40-201: 5 b g Kris - Sesame (Verrylin)   67
Waited with, stdy prog over 2f out, styd on under hands & heels riding to lead in shadow of post: 10 wk abs:
won 4 times over hdles in 99/00 (novs, rtd 123h, eff arnd 2m on gd & firm): 1st Flat win here, plcd in '98 (h'cap,
rtd 82, with M Johnston): eff at 12/14f on fast & gd/soft grnd: tried blnks: runs well fresh: well h'capped.
*2308 **FOREST HEATH** 19 [5] H J Collingridge 3-9-1 (75) T Quinn 4/1: 00-212: 3 gr g Common Grounds -   nk   80
Caroline Lady (Caro) Led 4f, remained prom & regained lead 3f out, kept on gamely but worn down cl-home:
eff at 1m, stays a gall 12f well: acts on fast & soft grnd: lightly rcd gldg who can win again: see 2308.
*2674 **HANNIBAL LAD** 4 [1] W M Brisbourne 4-10-6 (82)(6ex) T G McLaughlin 13/8 FAV: 114413: 4 ch g Rock   1½   85
City - Appealing (Star Appeal) Hld up, hdwy to chall 2f out, ev ch till no extra cl-home: clr of rem, qck reapp.
1997 **FLITE OF ARABY** 32 [4] W R Muir 3-8-4 (64) K Darley 8/1: 000-34: Rear, imprvd 2f out, nrst fin: eff   3   62
at 12f, will stay further: handles fast & firm grnd: see 1997.
2643 **SIMPLE IDEALS** 5 [6] 6-7-10 (44) Kim Tinkler 8/1: 205565: Led after 4f till 3f out, grad fdd: op 12/1.   ½   41
2170 **HERITAGE** 25 [7] 6-9-8 (70) Alex Greves 10/1: 0/4606: Trkd ldrs, ev ch 3f out, wknd fnl 2f: see 1982.   1¼   65
2422 **RAYWARE BOY** 14 [3] 4-7-10 (44)(bl)(3oh) K Dalgleish (5) 16/1: 054527: Chsd ldrs, eff 3f out, wknd.   3½   34
7 ran   Time 2m 36.31 (6.51)   (The Mary Reveley Racing Club)   Mrs M Reveley Lingdale, Cleveland

2756   8.10 EBF VYNER FILLIES NOV STKS 2YO (D)   5f str   Good/Firm 21   -24 Slow
£3510   £1080   £540   £270

-- **COLUMBINE** [4] A Berry 2-8-5 J Carroll 9/1: -1: 2 b f Pivotal - Heart Of India (Try My Best)   82+
Waited with, repeatedly short of room 2f out till 1f out, showed a smart turn of foot to lead cl-home, won going
away: op 7/1, debut: Mar foal, cost 45,000gns: half sister to a 6f 2yo wnr in Ireland: dam unrcd tho' related
to sev useful wnrs, sire a high-class sprinter: eff at 5f, will stay 6f judged on this: acts on fast grnd & on
a gall trk, runs well fresh: showed a decent turn of foot to win this, holds some big race entries & one to follow.
2692 **EXTRA GUEST** 4 [7] M R Channon 2-8-9 T Quinn 5/1: 622242: 2 b f Fraam - Gibaltarik (Jareer)   ¾   78
Tried to make all, not pace to repel wnr ins fnl 1f: qck reapp: most consistent, deserves a change of luck.
2500 **PROUD BOAST** 11 [2] Mrs G S Rees 2-9-2 Dean McKeown 9/2: -1023: 2 b f Komaite - Red Rosein   hd   85
(Red Sunset) Prom with, prog to chall dist, no extra cl-home: eff at 5f, will apprec a return to 6f: see 2500.
*2360 **SAMADILLA** 16 [6] T D Easterby 2-8-13 K Darley 5/2: -14: Prom, ev ch dist, no extra & eased ins   1½   78
last: tchd 4/1: see 2360 (gd).
*2539 **SO DIVINE** 9 [3] 2-8-11 D Holland 9/4 FAV: -415: Prom till grad wknd fnl 1f: btr 2539 (soft).   shd   76
2009 **CRIMSON RIDGE** 32 [5] 2-8-9 P M Quinn (3) 20/1: -36: Rear, nvr nr ldrs under a quiet ride: see 2009.   2½   67
2539 **JUST AS YOU ARE** 9 [1] 2-8-9 W Supple (3) 5/1: -07: Waited with, nvr nr ldrs: s/mate of 4th.   1¾   62
7 ran   Time 1m 00.46 (2.26)   (Miss Lilo Blum)   A Berry Cockerham, Lancs

2757   8.40 ARKSEY COND STKS 3YO+ (C)   1m str   Good/Firm 21   +18 Fast
£7215   £2220   £1110   £555   3yo rec 8lb

2476 **SUMMONER** 12 [2] R Charlton 3-9-2 R Hughes 7/1: 1-1041: 3 b c Inchinor - Sumoto (Mtoto)   115
Trkd ldrs, qcknd into lead 2f out, ran on strongly, rdn out: fast time: reapp wnr here at Doncaster (stks), subs
9th in 2,000 Guineas: '99 wnr again at Doncaster (mdn auct, rtd 97+): half brother to a high-class 10f wnr: eff
at 1m, will stay 10f: acts on fast & hvy, runs well fresh on a gall trk, esp Doncaster: smart run at these weights.
2090 **PYTHIOS** 28 [1] H R A Cecil 4-9-1 (t) T Quinn 1/2 FAV: 31-042: 4 b c Danehill - Pithara (Never So   2   102
Bold) Pushed along in rear, imprvd 2f out, styd on into 2nd but no impress on wnr: hvly bckd: not disgraced.
2675 **SHOWBOAT** 4 [3] B W Hills 6-9-4 D Holland 8/1: 630303: 6 b h Warning - Boathouse (Habitat)   1¼   102
In tch, sltly short of room over 2f out, switched & no impress fnl 1f: qck reapp, dngr: btr 2343.
*1960 **DIVULGE** 33 [4] J H M Gosden 3-8-11 K Darley 9/2: -514: Trkd ldr till wknd fnl 2f: see 1960 (mdn).   7   85
2578 **SERGEANT YORK** 7 [5] 4-9-1 (VIS) G Faulkner (3) 50/1: 336045: Set v fast pace, wknd over 2f   4   77
out: highly tried: first time visor: flattered 2578.
5 ran   Time 1m 36.81 (0.31)   (Michael Pescod)   R Charlton Beckhampton, wilts

2758   9.10 THEHORSESMOUTH HCAP 3YO+ 0-85 (D)   1m rnd   Good/Firm 21   -17 Slow   [82]
£4290   £1320   £660   £330

2645 **ADOBE** 5 [6] W M Brisbourne 5-9-0 (68) T G McLaughlin 9/2: 113341: 5 b g Green Desert - Shamshir   71
(Kris) Slowly away, hdwy on outside 2f out, styd on strongly to lead cl home, drvn out: qck reapp: earlier won at
W'hampton, Hamilton (2), Bath & Goodwood (h'caps): '99 wnr at Bath & Nottingham (h'caps, rtd 55 & 49a): eff at
7f/1m on gd, firm & f/sand, handles soft: likes Hamilton & Bath: eff with/without a t-strap: v tough & genuine.
2356 **VOLONTIERS** 17 [3] P W Harris 5-10-0 (82) A Culhane 11/4 FAV: 416022: 5 b g Common Grounds -   hd   84
Senlis (Sensitive Prince) Rcd keenly in mid-div, short of room 2f out, qcknd to lead dist, worn down cl-home: well
bckd, too weight: showed a gd turn of speed, but prob hit the front too sn: beat this wnr in 2356, see 1160.
2508 **INTRICATE WEB** 11 [4] E J Alston 4-9-3 (71) W Supple 10/3: 006133: 4 b g Warning - In Anticipation   1¾   69
(Sadler's Wells) Early ldr, remained prom, ev ch till no extra ins fnl 1f: remains in gd form, stays a gall 1m.
2304 **GRALMANO** 19 [7] K A Ryan 5-9-7 (75) F Lynch 9/2: 525164: Prom, led 3f out till dist, onepcd after.   1   71
2561 **WOORE LASS** 8 [5] 4-7-10 (50) Kim Tinkler 14/1: 000245: In tch, outpcd 2f out, kept on again ins fnl 1f.   ½   45
875 **ITS MAGIC** 99 [9] 4-9-3 (71) K Darley 11/2: 116-06: Rear, nvr a factor after long abs: '99   5   56
wnr at Newcastle & Leicester (2, h'caps, rtd 75): eff at 1m, has tried 12f: acts on gd & firm grnd, likes a gall
trk, loves Leicester: best in blnks, not worn today: slipping down the weights & one to keep in mind back in blnks.
2634 **PHILISTAR** 5 [2] 7-7-10 (50)(bl)(8oh) K Dalgleish (5) 33/1: 503607: Rcd keenly rear, no ch fnl 4f.   9   17
1445 **HARLEQUIN DANCER** 57 [1] 4-9-5 (73) J Carroll 16/1: 00-008: Led after 1f till 3f out, fdd: abs.   2½   35
8 ran   Time 1m 39.21 (3.11)   (P R Kirk)   W M Brisbourne Great Ness, Shropshire

LINGFIELD

WEDNESDAY JULY 19TH   AW - Lefthand, Very Sharp; TURF - Lefthand, Sharp, Undulating

Official Going   TURF - GOOD/FIRM (FIRM Places). AW - STANDARD Stalls: Str Crs - Far Side; Rnd Crs - Outside, AW - Ins.

2759

2.10 BEST BETS CLAIMER 3YO+ (F)   7f aw   Standard Inapplicable
£2299   £657   £328   3 yo rec 7 lb

*2650 **KRYSTAL MAX** 5 [4] T G Mills 7-9-3 L Carter 2/1 JT FAV: -25111: 7 b g Classic Music - Lake Isle (Caerleon) Led early, led again appr fnl 2f, rdn clr appr fnl 1f: nicely bckd, qck reapp: claimed for £6,000: hat-trick landed after wng twice here at Lingfield (clmrs): '99 wnr here at Lingfield (3) & W'hampton (clmrs, rtd 79a): '98 Lingfield (2) & Southwell wnr (h'caps, rtd 80a): eff at 5/7f on fast & gd/soft, loves both AWs, esp equitrack/Lingfield: loves a sharp trk & likes to force the pace: loves claimers & is most tough (16 wins from 48).   **74a**

2549 **ITSGOTTABDUN** 9 [1] B A Pearce 3-8-6 G Baker (7) 8/1: 643002: 3 b g Foxhound - Lady Ingrid (Taufan) Sn outpcd, late gains for press appr fnl 1f, nrst fin: bckd from 16/1: prev wnr K T Ivory: claimed for £4,000 here & will now join this wnr at the A Reid stable: sole win in a seller: see 527.   8   **55a**

1913 **GAELIC FORAY** 35 [11] R P C Hoad 4-8-10 L Newman (3) 25/1: -00353: 4 b f Unblest - Rich Heiress (Last Tycoon) Sn well bhd, ran on for press fnl 2f, no dngr: fine eff at the weights, dubious rating: see 1741.   ¾   **51$**

2347 **APOLLO RED** 18 [6] G L Moore 11-9-5 A Clark 2/1 JT FAV: 261104: Prom, rdn/fdd fnl 3f: can do better.   ½   **59a**

2291 **SONTIME** 19 [3] D Daly 12/1: 0-00W5: Led over 5f out, hdd appr fnl 2f, wknd: op 8/1: see 2036.   6   **44a**

2325 **TYCANDO** 18 [5] N Callan 9/1: -05006: Dwelt, sn mid-div, rdn/no extra over 2f out: op 6/1.   hd   **55a**

2356 **SUPER MONARCH** 17 [7] 6-9-3 G Bardwell 16/1: 004007: Al outpcd: see 1542.   1   **45a**

2590 **MASTER LUKE** 7 [1] 3-9-0 S Whitworth 25/1: 08: Dwelt, al rear: quick reapp, up in trip.   10   **33a**

2467 **HENRY HEALD** 12 [8] 5-9-1 S Sanders 14/1: 221/09: Al well outpcd: op 10/1: well btn over timber in 99/00 (rtd 85h at best): missed '99 on the rvel, back in '98 scored a wnr at Brighton (mdn, rtd 78 at best, P J Makin): eff at 7f/1m, has tried 10f: acts on firm/fast & a sharp or gall trk: with J Old.   3½   **21a**

4430 **SHEBEG** 274 [3] 3-7-13 R Brisland (5) 25/1: 0-0: In tch, wknd qckly halfway, fin 10th: mod form.   1   **10a**

1734 **GREEN TURTLE CAY** 44 [10] 4-9-1 I Mongan (5) 33/1: 6-0000: Al well bhd, t.o. in 11th: 6 wk abs.   30   **0a**

11 ran   Time 1m 25.02 (2.22)   (Shipman Racing Ltd)   T G Mills Headley, Surrey

2760

2.40 EBF MDN 2YO (D)   6f str   Firm 18 -21 Slow
£3601   £1108   £554   £277

2545 **RISQUE SERMON** 9 [10] Miss B Sanders 2-9-0 A Nicholls (3) 25/1: 01: 2 b g Risk Me - Sunday Sport Star (Star Appeal) Made all, styd on well despite veering right for press appr fnl 1f, drvn out: showed little on soft grnd debut prev: dam 9f wnr: eff at 6f on firm & a sharp/undul trk: going the right way.   **79**

2550 **THE TRADER** 9 [8] M Blanshard 2-9-0 D Sweeney 7/2: 332: 2 ch c Selkirk - Snowing (Tate Gallery) Rcd keenly cl-up, hdwy to chall appr fnl 2f, styd on, just held: clr rem: eff at 5/6f on firm & soft: consistent.   ¾   **77**

-- **SCARTEEN SISTER** [1] D R C Elsworth 2-8-9 N Pollard 4/1: 3: 2 ch f Eagle Eyed - Best Swinger (Ela Mana Mou) Prom, rdn & not pace of ldrs fnl 2f: nicely bckd on debut: IR 32,000 gns filly, half sister to high-class 7f juv Scarteen Fox, dam scored over 7f: sharper for this.   5   **60**

-- **HARD TO KNOW** [6] D J S Cosgrove 2-9-0 N Callan 11/2: 4: Mid-div, rdn/prog 2f out, sn held: op 9/2: 31,000 gns Mar foal, dam related to a high-class US juv: shld improve, prob over further.   1   **62**

-- **ACT OF REFORM** [2] 2-9-0 J Fortune 5/2 FAV: 5: Chsd ldrs, rdn/dropped rear fnl 2f: Apr foal, dam scored over 1m in the States: sire 6f/1m wnr abroad: with R Charlton.   hd   **62**

-- **WELL MAKE IT** [9] 2-9-0 I Mongan 14/1: 6: Front rank, rdn/fdd fnl 2f: tchd 20/1: 37,000 gns Spectrum colt, half brother to a juv scorer abroad: with G L Moore.   hd   **62**

2652 **ORANGERIE 5** [5] 2-9-0 S Sanders (3) 10/1: 057: Nvr better than mid-div: op 7/2, quick reapp: btr 2652.   7   **48**

-- **JOLLANDS** [4] 2-9-0 D O'Donohoe 12/1: 8: Dwelt, al outpcd: 8,800 gns Apr foal, half brother to a sprint wnr, dam 6f juv scorer: with D Marks.   1¼   **45**

-- **BASE LINE** [3] 2-9-0 C Rutter 20/1: 9: Al bhd: cheaply bought Apr foal, dam 7f wnr: with R M Flower.   8   **29**

9 ran   Time 1m 11.14 (2.34)   (R Lamb)   Miss B Sanders Epsom, Surrey

2761

3.10 ARENA LEISURE HCAP 3YO+ 0-80 (D)   6f str   Firm 18 +09 Fast
£3984   £1226   £613   £306   3 yo rec 5 lb   **[77]**

2355 **IVORY DAWN** 17 [1] K T Ivory 6-9-9 (72) C Carver (3) 8/1: 240301: 6 b m Batshoof - Cradle Of Love (Roberto) Bhd, rdn to improve 2f out, strong run to lead nr fin, drvn out: best time of day: '99 wnr at Brighton & here at Lingfield (h'caps, rtd 77): '98 wnr again at Brighton & Lingfield (h'caps, rtd 74): suited by 6f, stays a sharp 7f: acts on firm, gd/soft grnd: suited by sharp/undul trks, Brighton/Lingfield specialist.   **78**

-2569 **BAHAMIAN PIRATE** 8 [5] D Nicholls 5-9-7 (70) A Nicholls (3) 4/5 FAV: -01122: 5 ch g Housebuster - Shining Through (Deputy Minister) Cl-up, rdn to lead appr fnl 1f, drvn/hdd nr fin: well bckd, in gd form.   shd   **75**

2371 **KHALIK** 16 [4] Miss Gay Kelleway 6-9-5 (68) S Sanders 12/1: 314003: 6 b g Lear Fan - Silver Dollar (Shirley Heights) Waited with, rdn to improve 3f out, chall appr fnl 1f, sn no extra: see 1264, 1092.   1¾   **68**

2261 **CARLTON** 21 [2] D R C Elsworth 6-10-0 (77) N Pollard 9/1: 420024: Sn outpcd, gd hdwy appr fnl 2f, ev ch until outpcd fnl 1f: op 6/1: in gd heart & not disgraced under top weight: clr rem: see 2261.   hd   **77**

1038 **BORDER GLEN** 82 [8] 4-8-4 (53)(bl) L Newman (3) 16/1: 626005: Set fast pace, hdd appr fnl 1f, sn btn: tchd 25/1 after 12 wk abs: see 292 (9f).   3½   **45**

2431 **MYSTIC RIDGE** 14 [7] 6-9-2 (65) J P Spencer 9/1: 004006: Prom, rdn/outpcd appr fnl 2f: btr 476.   3½   **49**

2473 **KILCULLEN LAD** 12 [3] 6-9-6 (69)(vis) J Fortune 12/1: In tch, rdn/held fnl 2f, ddthd for 6th.   dht   **53**

-2623 **CLAN CHIEF** 6 [10] 7-8-11 (60) A Clark 11/1: 00/028: Al in rear: quick reapp: btr 2623 (5f).   nk   **44**

2525 **KEEN HANDS** 10 [9] 4-8-13 (62)(vis) R Fitzpatrick (3) 16/1: 510409: Sn outpcd: btr 1504.   2   **40**

1915 **SUPERCHIEF** 35 [6] 5-7-10 (45)(tbl)(3oh) G Bardwell 25/1: 115500: Front rank, wknd qckly fnl 2f, 10th.   3   **16**

2326 **CHARGE** 18 [11] 4-8-12 (61)(t) N Callan 20/1: 150050: Handy, lost tch fnl 2f, fin last.   5   **21**

11 ran   Time 1m 09.28 (0.48)   (Dean Ivory)   K T Ivory Radlett, Herts

2762

3.40 EBF CLASS STKS 3YO+ 0-90 (C)   7f140y   Firm 18 00 Slow
£5863   £2224   £1112   £505   3 yo rec 8 lb

2117 **RED N SOCKS** 27 [4] J L Dunlop 3-8-7 J Fortune 4/4 JT FAV: 0-2001: 3 ch c Devil's Bag - Racing Blue (Reference Point) Rcd keenly in mid-div, hdwy to lead appr fnl 1f, strongly prsd ins last, drvn out: hvly bckd: rnr-up in a val Newmarket h'cap on reapp this term: '99 Yarmouth scorer (nurs, rtd 84): eff at 7f/1m, has tried 10f: acts on firm/fast & a stiff/gall or sharp trk: runs well fresh: useful & game colt.   **94**

2616 **NICE ONE CLARE** 6 [1] J W Payne 4-8-12 J P Spencer 6/4 JT FAV: 11-532: 4 b f Mukaddamah - Sarah   hd   **90**

865

Clare (Reach) Waited with, smooth hdwy to chall ldr ins last, styd on strongly, just failed: nicely bckd, quick reapp: clr rem here & deserves similar: eff at 7/7.6f: see 2151.

2495 **NOBLE PURSUIT 11** [3] T G Mills 3-8-13 L Carter 7/1: 404103: 3 b c Pursuit Of Love - Noble Peregrine *4* **91**
(Lomond) Rcd keenly cl-up, drvn & not pace of front 2 ins last: op 6/1: prob ran to best: see 2108.

3629} **FLAMENCO RED 326** [7] R Charlton 3-8-4 C Rutter 12/1: 1235-4: Pulled hard in mid-div, rdn/no *1* **80**
extra appr fnl 1f: op 8/1 on reapp: '99 Nottingham scorer (mdn, rtd 90+), tried visor on fnl start: eff at 6f, 7f shld suit in time: acts on fast, gd & a stiff/gall trk: just sharper for this.

1330 **GULF SHAADI 63** [2] 8-9-1 N Callan 25/1: 405405: Rcd keenly, chsd ldrs, rdn/fdd appr fnl 1f: *¾* **81$**
9 wk abs: poorly placed here (all rivals offic rated around 20lbs higher), needs h'caps: see 1213, 169.

1826 **SHOUF AL BADOU 40** [5] 3-8-7 S Sanders 14/1: 1-0006: Trkd ldrs, went on appr fnl 2f, hdd over *shd* **81**
1f out, wknd: 6 wk abs: useful at best, but yet to hit form this term: see 765.

2567 **TEODORA 8** [6] 3-8-4 B Marcus 11/1: 500627: Rcd keenly, led, hdd appr fnl 2f, hmpd over 1f out *5* **70**
& sn btn: op 8/1: much btr 2567 (7f fill h'cap, gd).

7 ran Time 1m 29.08 (1.26) (Mrs H Focke) J L Dunlop Arundel, W Sussex

2763

4.10 BET DIRECT HCAP 3YO+ 0-70 (E) 2m Firm 18 -15 Slow [65]
£2922 £835 £417 3 yo rec 17lb

2452 **LITTLE BRAVE 13** [2] J M P Eustace 5-9-3 (54) J Tate 5/1: -46051: 5 b g Kahyasi - Littlemisstrouble **64**
(My Gallant) Bhd, hdwy 1m out, went on 4f out, clr fnl 2f, pushed out: '99 wnr at Lingfield (class stks, rtd 70a), Warwick & Yarmouth (h'caps, rtd 51): prev term scored at Southwell (mdn, rtd 69a & 62): suited by 2m/2m2f on fast, soft & both AWs: runs well fresh on any trk, likes Lingfield.

211 **MARTHA REILLY 211** [6] Mrs Barbara Waring 4-7-10 (33)(2oh) A Mackay 25/1: 0346-2: 4 ch f *10* **33**
Rainbows For Life - Debach Delight (Great Nephew) Settled rear, gd hdwy 5f out, styd on well fnl 2f but no ch with wnr: fin 13L clr rem: not disgraced after a 7 month abs, needs sells: see 70.

2622 **CHEEK TO CHEEK 6** [4] C A Cyzer 6-9-7 (58) S Sanders 9/2: 552543: 6 b m Shavian - Intoxication *13* **48**
(Great Nephew) In tch, rdn/wknd fnl 3f: quick reapp: see 2622.

2606 **AQUAVITA 6** [10] Miss K M George 6-7-10 (33)(12oh) G Bardwell 25/1: /03544: Dwelt, bhd, mod *nk* **23**
late gains: quick reapp, stiff task from 12lbs o/h.

2544 **NIGHT CITY 9** [3] 9-8-12 (49) N Callan 9/2: 415225: Led till 10f out, drvn/lost tch fnl 4f: *4* **35**
up in trip, unproven beyond 12f, prob not get 2m?: see 2544.

2416 **PRINCE DARKHAN 14** [7] 4-8-8 (45) J Fortune 11/1: -00046: Prom, fdd from halfway: see 1927. *nk* **31**

*2536 **CASHIKI 9** [5] 4-8-3 (40)(5ex) A Daly 9/2: 202617: Handy, rdn/wknd fnl 3f: op 4/1: btr 2536. *hd* **26**

2156 **WESTERN COMMAND 25** [11] 4-8-9 (46) R Fitzpatrick (3) 4/1: 510628: Mid-div, went on over 6f out, *1¼* **31**
hdd 4f out, qckly lost tch: see 2156 (14f).

2461 **SIRINNDI 12** [8] 6-8-12 (49) J P Spencer 7/2 FAV: 5/0509: Prom, went on 10f out, hdd 6f out, *19* **19**
wknd rapidly & sn t.o.: nicely bckd, something amiss?: see 1416.

9 ran Time 3m 30.73 (5.53) (Brave Maple Partnership) J M P Eustace Newmarket

2764

4.40 CLASSIFIED STKS 3YO+ 0-65 (E) 1m2f aw Standard Inapplicable
£2765 £790 £395 3 yo rec 10lb

2593 **QUEEN OF THE KEYS 7** [2] S Dow 4-9-1 A Nicholls (3) 8/1: 003221: 4 b f Royal Academy - Piano Belle **50a**
(Fappiano) Settled rear, gd hdwy after halfway, went on appr fnl 1f, styd on well, rdn out: quick reapp: 1st win on 18th career start: plcd sev times prev: unplcd in '99 (rtd 33 & 28a), well btn as a juv: eff at 1m/10f, poss stays 12f: acts on both AWs & a sharp/undul trk: deserved this.

2527 **KENNET 10** [3] P D Cundell 5-9-4 (vis) S Sanders 3/1: 000202: 5 b g Kylian - Marwell Mitzi *3* **48a**
(Interrex) Trkd ldr, rdn/eff over 1f out, sn held: better expected at these weights: see 2527, 2372.

2215 **KAFIL 22** [4] J J Bridger 6-9-4 (bl) I Mongan (5) 25/1: 600003: 6 b g Housebuster - Alchaasibiyeh *1* **46a**
(Seattle Slew) Set stdy pace, drvn/hdd appr fnl 1f, sn held: not disgraced at these weights: see 254, 1.

2463 **PAPERWEIGHT 12** [6] Miss K M George 4-9-1 J Tate 9/4 FAV: 230344: Front rank, drvn/no extra *1¾* **41a**
fnl 2f: capable of better, see 2186 (h'cap).

2411 **COLONEL NORTH 14** [7] 4-9-4 M Henry 9/2: 006655: Rcd wide in mid-div, drvn/btn fnl 3f: see 90. *4* **38a**

1807 **WAIKIKI BEACH 40** [8] 9-9-4 (bl) P Cheng 16/1: 004006: Dwelt, nvr dangerous, 6 wk abs: up in trip. *1½* **36a**

2032 **MASSEY 31** [1] 4-9-4 J Fortune 11/2: 160007: Al bhd: see 752. *nk* **36a**

2544 **SUCH BOLDNESS 9** [5] 6-9-4 N Callan 8/1: 35-008: In tch, wknd from halfway, fin last: see 2366. *10* **22a**

8 ran Time 2m 07.46 (4.66) (Mrs A M Upsdell) S Dow Epsom, Surrey

YARMOUTH WEDNESDAY JULY 19TH Lefthand, Flat, Fair Track

Official Going GOOD. Stalls: Str Crse - Far Side; Rem - Inside.

2765

2.00 BRITANNIA PIER SELLER 3YO+ (G) 1m2f Firm 13 -25 Slow
£1886 £539 £269 3 yo rec 10lb

2651 **TITUS BRAMBLE 5** [2] B R Millman 3-8-9 J F Egan 16/1: 000601: 3 b g Puissance - Norska (Northfields) **40**
Rear, prog appr fnl 2f, led below dist, held on well: bght in for 3,750gns, qck reapp: unplcd & tried blnks once in '99 (mdn, rtd 74, prob flattered): appreciated the ease in grade & drop back to 10f on firm grnd.

*2587 **OCEAN LINE 7** [6] G M McCourt 5-9-11 R Studholme (5) 9/1: 040012: 5 b g Kefaah - Tropic Sea (Sure *½* **44**
Blade) Made most till ent fnl 1f, rallied: clr rem, qck reapp, mixing turf & AW: acts on firm, gd, both AWs.

2188 **SHARP BELLINE 23** [11] M Johnston 3-8-9 M Hills 2/1 FAV: 43: 3 b g Robellino - Moon Watch (Night *3* **34**
Shift) Chsd ldrs, eff appr fnl 2f, unable to qckn: nicely bckd: lkd a gd thing after debut (1m mdn): shld get 10f.

2538 **ESPERTO 9** [1] J Pearce 7-9-11 T Quinn 14/1: 006104: Mid-div, late hdwy, nvr pace to chall: op 10/1. *½* **39**

2460 **ERTLON 12** [3] 10-9-5 P Robinson 8/1: 006035: Early ldr, prom till no extra 2f out: op 6/1: see 2460. *¾* **32**

2587 **THOMAS HENRY 7** [5] 4-9-5 J Reid 10/1: 035036: Dwelt, prog into mid-div 3f out, no further hdwy. *1¼* **30**

2544 **LOKOMOTIV 9** [8] 4-9-5 P Fitzsimons (5) 10/1: 0-6007: Mid-div, outpcd appr fnl 2f: see 2544, 1921 *5* **23**

2715 **SAINT GEORGE 2** [10] 4-9-5 D Harrison 9/1: 004248: Cl-up, led 4f out till bef 2f out, btn/eased dist. *¾* **22**

2510 **HIGH BEAUTY 11** [9] 3-8-4 A Beech (5) 20/1: 040059: In tch till 3f out: op 14/1: flattered last time. *3* **12**

2587 **EI EI 7** [7] 5-9-5 D Holland 14/1: 240500: Keen, rear, brief eff ent str: 10th, qck reapp, see 404. *¾* **15**

2546 **INDIAN SWINGER 9** [4] 4-9-5 J Quinn 14/1: 033000: Al bhd: 11th, op 10/1, reportedly lost a shoe. *1¼* **13**

11 ran Time 2m 08.0 (3.8) (Henry Rix) B R Millman Kentisbeare, Devon.

2766   2.30 BRITANNIA PIER MDN 2YO (D)   5f43y   Firm 13 -27 Slow
£3428   £1055   £527   £263

2324 **WARLINGHAM** 18 [2] Miss Gay Kelleway 2-9-0 T Quinn 9/1: 463621: 2 b c Catrail - Tadjnama (Exceller)   80
Prom, led ent fnl 1f, rdn & ran on strongly: op 7/1: imprvd today after a string of consistent efforts: eff
at 5f on firm & gd, handles gd/soft, sharp or gall tracks: game colt.
-- **RACINA** [1] W J Haggas 2-8-9 M Hills 5/2 FAV: 2: 2 ch f Bluebird - Swellegant (Midyan)   ½   74
Dwelt, towards rear, imprvd appr fnl 1f & kept on well, post came too soon: Mar half-sister to sprinter Dil, dam
& sire sprinters: bred for speed tho' shaped like a step up to 6f would suit: handles firm grnd, go one better soon.
1782 **HOT PANTS** 41 [3] K T Ivory 2-8-9 C Catlin (7) 9/1: 053: 2 ch f Rudimentary - True Precision   nk   73
(Presidium) Led till ent fnl 1f, kept on: op 7/1, 6 wk abs: suited forcing the pace at 5f on firm grnd.
2142 **RED RYDING HOOD** 26 [8] C A Dwyer 2-8-9 J F Egan 7/1: -634: Handy, eff appr fnl 1f, kept on: 1   70
clr rem, tchd 9/1: improved on this v quick ground.
2285 **RENEE** 19 [7] 2-8-9 M Fenton 5/1: -355: Prom, rdn & outpcd appr fnl 1f: see 2285.   3   61
-- **NORDIC SABRE** [4] 2-8-9 D Harrison 11/1: 6: Chsd ldrs till appr fnl 1f: tchd 25/1 on debut: ¾   59
8,000gns Sabrehill May foal, half-sister to a winning sprint juv, dam 6f juv wnr, sire got 10f: with Mrs Stubbs.
2545 **SO SOBER** 9 [6] 2-9-0 R Mullen 11/4: -5427: Well plcd till lost pl ent fnl 2f: bckd: much qcker   4   54
grnd today, worth another chance after 2545 (soft).
2039 **PAT THE BUILDER** 30 [5] 2-9-0 P Robinson 33/1: 548: Bhd from halfway: btr 2039.   13   29
8 ran   Time 1m 02.1 (2)   (Martin Butler)   Miss Gay Kelleway Lingfield, Surrey.

2767   3.00 DOVERCOURT FILLIES HCAP 3YO+ 0-70 (E)   1m str   Firm 13 -28 Slow   [64]
£3071   £945   £472   £236   3 yo rec 8 lb

2013 **SADAKA** 32 [1] E A L Dunlop 3-9-8 (66) G Carter 4/1 FAV: 0-0341: 3 ch f Kingmambo - Basma (Grey   71
Dawn II) Prom, led below dist, rdn out: first wn: plcd in '99 (mdn, fill mdn, rtd 74): eff at 7f/1m:
goes on firm & gd grnd, flat tracks: stable in cracking form now, could follow up.
1666 **JESSINCA** 47 [6] A P Jones 4-8-7 (43) J F Egan 6/1: 000142: 4 b f Minshaanshu Amad - Noble Soul   1   44
(Sayf El Arab) Held up, eff 2f out, no impress till styd on fnl 1f, nrst fin: 7 wk abs, gd run for new stable:
acts on firm, soft grnd & fibresand, see 1511.
1113 **BOBBYDAZZLE** 77 [10] C A Dwyer 5-9-2 (52) J Quinn 16/1: -24403: 5 ch m Rock Hopper - Billie Blue   hd   52
(Ballad Rock) Mid-div, rdn fnl 2f, onepace till ran on ins last, nvr nrr: abs, well h'capped for new stable.
2320 **OAKWELL ACE** 18 [11] J A Glover 4-8-3 (39) J Mackay (5) 12/1: 052504: Front rank & ev ch till held   shd   39
towards fin: handles firm, acts on gd & soft, see 1892, 872.
2380 **GOLDFINCH** 16 [4] 3-9-0 (58) M Hills 10/1: 0-0005: Handy, feeling pace 3f out, late hdwy: turf bow.   ½   57
2512 **SILK ST BRIDGET** 11 [14] 3-7-11 (41)(bl) (1ow)(3oh) A Beech (0) 14/1: 000006: Led after 2f till   1¼   37
ent fnl 1f, onepace: stiffish task & jockey putting up 6lbs o/wt: see 1610.
2625 **SWING BAR** 6 [8] 7-8-5 (41) P Fitzsimons (5) 20/1: 0-0007: Early ldr, onepce appr fnl 1f: op 14/1, qk reapp. 1   35
2180 **ANGEL LANE** 24 [12] 3-7-13 (43) S Righton 7/1: 0-0048: Unruly start, nvr better than mid-div: see 2180.   1¾   33
2128 **LADY BREANNE** 26 [2] 4-9-0 (50) D Holland 16/1: 36-009: Chsd ldrs till wknd appr fnl 1f: see 109.   ¾   38
2342 **FEATHER N LACE** 18 [9] 4-10-0 (64) T Quinn 5/1: 0-2240: Outpcd: 10th, top-weight, see 1915, 1348.   5   42
1730 Wickham 44 [7] 4-8-7 (43) G Hind 25/1:   2531 Hanoi 10 [13] 3-8-5 (49)(bl) J Lowe 33/1:
2460 Victoire 12 [3] 4-8-12 (48)(vis) J Stack 20/1:   2027 Elba Magic 31 [5] 5-9-1 (51) D Harrison 20/1:
14 ran   Time 1m 38.4 (3.3)   (Hamdan Al Maktoum)   E A L Dunlop Newmarket.

2768   3.30 S THREADWELL HCAP 3YO+ 0-95 (C)   7f str   Firm 13 +06 Fast   [95]
£6922   £2130   £1065   £532   3 yo rec 7 lb

2515 **WILLOUGHBYS BOY** 11 [13] B Hanbury 3-8-5 (78)(1ow) D Harrison 12/1: 03161: 3 b c Night Shift - Andbell   84
(Trojan Fen) Made just about all & rcd alone stands side, held on well, rdn out: gd time, tchd 16/1: prev
won at Beverley (mdn): eff at 7/7.5f on firm & gd: lightly rcd, jockey used his initiative to out-fox rivals.
+2456 **WAHJ** 12 [5] C A Dwyer 4-9-11 (92) J F Egan 7/2 FAV: 0-0112: 5 ch g Indian Ridge - Sabaah   ¾   96
(Nureyev) Led centre, under press appr fnl 1f, kept on but being held by wnr: bckd from 5/1, clr rem: lost
nothing in defeat against unexposed wnr, acts on firm & soft grnd: useful: see 2456.
2242 **FALLACHAN** 21 [8] M A Jarvis 4-8-11 (78) P Robinson 9/1: -04403: 4 ch g Diesis - Afaff (Nijinsky)   3   76
Handy centre, eff appr fnl 1f, unable to qckn: prob ran near to best: see 1490.
*2185 **HONEST BORDERER** 24 [11] J L Dunlop 5-8-13 (80) G Carter 9/2: 36-614: Held up centre, imprvd   shd   78
appr fnl 1f, nvr nr to chall: ran well, handles firm, acts on fast & soft, return to further will suit: see 2185.
2564 **TOPTON** 8 [6] 6-8-5 (72)(bl) J Quinn 13/2: 500235: In tch centre, niggled after halfway, nvr a threat.   1   68
2412 **PROSPECTORS COVE** 14 [9] 7-8-3 (70) J Mackay (5) 14/1: 001046: Slow away, rear centre, went past   3   60
btn horses appr fnl 1f: return to 1m well suit: see 1611 (gd/soft).
2261 **TEMERAIRE** 21 [10] 5-9-2 (83) J Reid 10/1: 004237: Prom in centre till fdd appr fnl 1f: see 834.   1¾   69
*2412 **RICH IN LOVE** 14 [12] 6-9-4 (85) A Beech (5) 8/1: 002318: Chsd ldrs centre, outpcd appr fnl 1f: ½   70
unsuited by drop in trip?: use 2412 (1m, here, in front of 5th & 6th).
2495 **ARETINO** 11 [4] 3-8-3 (77) J Lowe 20/1: 050509: Nvr a factor in centre: inconsistent but nds to lead.   1   60
2616 **TAYIF** 6 [7] 4-9-11 (92) A McGlone 20/1: -00000: In tch centre till 2f out: 10th, jt top-weight, see 1110.   ½   74
2412 **PETRUS** 14 [3] 4-8-6 (72)(t) (1ow) D Holland 10/1: 000050: Dwelt, nvr on terms: 11th, won this in '99.   1¼   52
2391 **SHAFAQ** 15 [1] 3-8-4 (78) R Price 20/1: 13-060: Speed centre till 2f out: 12th, drop back to 6f?   nk   56
2334 **RED LION GB** 18 [2] 4-9-5 (86) M Roberts 14/1: 0-0000: Al bhd centre: 13th: better at 6f.   ½   63
13 ran   Time 1m 23.1 (0.5)   (Mrs G E M Brown)   B Hanbury Newmarket.

2769   4.00 EBF FILLIES COND STKS 3YO (C)   7f str   Firm 13 +02 Fast
£6090   £2310   £1155   £525

2167 **ROSSE** 25 [2] G Wragg 3-8-13 M Roberts 13/8 FAV: 0-4151: 3 ch f Kris - Nuryana (Nureyev)   98
Held up, trkd ldrs 3f out, rdn appr fnl 1f & ran on to lead below dist, kept on well: bckd from 5/2, fair time:
prev won here at Yarmouth (fill mdn): unplcd sole '99 start (mdn, rtd 68): half-sister to high-class miler Rebecca
Sharp: apprec drop back to 7f: acts on firm/fast, likes this easy Yarmouth trk: useful effort today.
1069 **VEIL OF AVALON** 79 [1] R Charlton 3-8-9 Pat Eddery 3/1: 116-62: 3 b f Thunder Gulch - Wind In Her   nk   93
Hair (Alzao) Keen, nvr far away, chall appr fnl 1f, held towards fin: 11 wk abs: gd run back in trip, see 1069.
1952 **MISS ORAH** 34 [5] J Noseda 3-8-9 J Weaver 14/1: 24-003: 3 b f Unfuwain - Massorah (Habitat)   ½   91

Led till worn down fnl 150y: op 10/1: ran to best: see 1283.

2568 **BAILEYS WHIRLWIND** 8 [3] M L W Bell 3-8-9 J Mackay (5) 6/1: -50344: Held up, not much room appr   1¾   87$
fnl 1f, styd on without threatening: tchd 8/1: worth another try at this longer 7f trip: see 1186.

*2391 **NIGHT EMPRESS** 15 [6] 3-8-9 D Harrison 9/1: -24515: Prom till kept on onepace appr fnl 1f: ½   85
stiffish task & poss flattered tho' is definitely on the upgrade: see 2391 (C/D fill h'cap).

3453} **JOURNALIST** 335 [4] 3-8-9 J Reid 4/1: -120-6: Well plcd till ent fnl 2f: reapp: '99 debut wnr at   6   75
Newmarket (fill mdn, subs rnr-up in Gr 3 at R Ascot, rtd 102, B Hills): half-sister to useful sprinter Sheer
Viking: eff at 6f on firm/fast grnd: return to sprinting likely: now with Godolphin.

6 ran   Time 1m 23.4 (0.8)   (A E Oppenheimer)   G Wragg Newmarket.

2770   4.30 BURKE FORD MDN 3YO (D)   7f str   Firm 13   -06 Slow
      £3737   £1150   £575   £287

1963 **DANCE WEST** 33 [8] H R A Cecil 3-9-0 T Quinn 10/3: -00421: 3 b c Gone West - Danzante (Danzig)   85
Pulled hard rear, imprvd appr fnl 2f, ran on to lead ins last, shkn up: front 2 clear: eff at 7f, tried 1m, shld
stay on this evidence: acts on firm & gd grnd, easy track: suited by more patient tactics today, useful.

1377 **SHADOWBLASTER** 61 [5] B Hanbury 3-9-0 Dane O'Neill 13/8 FAV: 52: 3 b c Wolfhound - Swame (Jade   1   82
Hunter) Prom, led ent fnl 2f till ins last, not pace of wnr: bckd, clr rem, abs: trip: eff at 7f/1m on firm & gd.

2464 **SINCERITY** 12 [3] J R Fanshawe 3-8-9 M Hills 11/4: -023: 3 b f Selkirk - Integrity (Reform)   6   65
Prom, outpcd by front appr fnl 1f: onepace: not this much faster grnd: worth another ch after 2464 (gd).

2211 **APLESTEDE** 23 [7] I A Wood 3-8-9 J F Egan 50/1: 004: Led till appr fnl 1f, fdd: stiff task, Thowra filly.   7   51

--   **ASSURANCE** [4] 3-9-0 P Robinson 14/1: 5: Handy till ent fnl 2f: op 10/1 on debut: Green   3   50
Desert colt out of a useful mare: with C Brittain.

--   **FLAVIA** [2] 3-8-9 R Price 25/1: 6: Speed till lost place appr fnl 2f: debut: Lahib filly out of a 1m wnr.   shd   45

2472 **APRIL STAR** 12 [1] 3-8-9 M Fenton 40/1: 057: Dwelt, al bhd: needs sell h'caps.   ¾   43

--   **SUBSTANTIVE** [6] 3-8-9 A McGlone 9/1: 8: Dwelt, keen, nvr in it, fin lame: op 6/1, stablemate   7   33
wnr, debut: Distant View half-sister to the useful Moratorium.

8 ran   Time 1m 23.9 (1.3)   (K Abdulla)   H R A Cecil Newmarket.

2771   5.00 SOUTH PIER HCAP 3YO+ 0-70 (E)   1m3f101y   Firm 13   -32 Slow   [69]
      £2482   £812   £406   3 yo rec 11lb

2466 **FAHS** 12 [3] N Hamilton 8-10-0 (69) T Quinn 15/2: 1-2501: 8 b g Riverman - Tanwi (Vision)   74
Nvr far away, led appr fnl 1f, pshd clr, readily: conceded 13lbs+ to rivals: '99 wnr here at Yarmouth (rtd 77)
& Lingfield (h'cap, rtd 79a): '98 wnr again at Lingfield (amat h'cap, rtd 80a & 81): eff at 10/12f, stays 14f
on firm, gd & equitrack: handles soft: likes Yarmouth: suited by coming late/giving weight to lesser rivals.

2518 **RARE TALENT** 11 [7] S Gollings 6-8-12 (53) Clare Roche (7) 13/2: 003032: 6 b g Mtoto - Bold As Love   2½   54
(Lomond) Led halfway till appr fnl 1f, onepace: ran to best from the front off a steady pace: see 1272.

2206 **SWEET ANGELINE** 23 [2] G G Margarson 3-8-8 (60) M Roberts 7/1: -00543: 3 b f Deploy - Fivefivefive   hd   61
(Fairy King) Rear, imprvd 4f out, not much room 2f out, styd on, nvr dngrs: stays 12f, improving: see 2206.

826 **KINGS VIEW** 105 [9] E A L Dunlop 3-8-12 (64) G Carter (7) 50-04: Led till halfway, no extra appr fnl   ½   64
1f: op 7/1, 15 wk abs, lngr trip, h'cap bow: 5th on juv debut (mdn, rtd 78): stays 11.5f on firm, drop to 10f may suit.

2655 **MYSTERIUM** 5 [8] 6-8-1 (42) J Quinn 4/1: 400025: Held up, late hdwy, nvr a threat: won this in '99.   ¾   40

2537 **SILKEN LADY** 9 [1] 4-7-10 (37)(12oh) A Polli (3) 25/1: -00036: Chsd ldrs till drifted right & outpcd   ½   34
appr fnl 1f: stiff task, prob handles firm & gd/soft grnd: shown enough to find a sell h'cap.

2710 **TUFTY HOPPER** 3 [4] 3-8-13 (65) P Robinson 7/2 FAV: 332227: Rear, short of room throughout fnl 2f,   1¾   59
eased inside last: qck reapp: remains a maiden but this should be forgotten: see 2710.

*2199 **SWINGING THE BLUES** 23 [5] 6-9-1 (56)(vis) J F Egan 7/1: 2-0018: Al towards rear: up in trip.   4   45

613 **THE SHEIKH** 141 [6] 3-8-4 (56) J Mackay (5) 20/1: 00-259: Held up, eff 3f out, sn btn: op 14/1, abs.   11   33

9 ran   Time 2m 28.0 (5.2)   (City Industrial Supplies Ltd)   N Hamilton Epsom, Surrey.

LEICESTER   THURSDAY JULY 20TH   Righthand, Stiff, Galloping Track

Official Going   GOOD TO FIRM (GOOD In Places). Stalls: Stands Side.

2772   2.20 HIGH SHERIFF'S SELLER 2YO (G)   5f   Good/Firm 27   -23 Slow
      £1907   £545   £272

2507 **SCREAMIN GEORGINA** 12 [2] S C Williams 2-8-6 (t) G Faulkner (1) 5/2 FAV: 021: 2 b f Muhtarram -   63
Carrie Kool (Prince Sabo) Prom, led appr fnl 2f, drew clr ins last: nicely bckd, bght in for 3,300 gns: half-
sister to a useful 6f juv wnr: eff at 5f, 6f shld suit: acts on fast grnd & a stiff/gall trk: wears a t-strap.

2605 **SOOTY TIME** 7 [3] J S Moore 2-8-11 P M Quinn (3) 50/1: 630662: 2 ch g Timeless Times - Gymcrak   3½   58
Gem (Don't Forget Me) Dwelt & rear till styd on appr fnl 1f, went 2nd nr fin: qk reapp, 1st form: handles fast.

2435 **FAIR STEP** 14 [4] W W Haigh 2-8-6 J Stack 7/2: 23: 2 ch f King's Signet - Miss Hocroft (Dominion)   nk   52
Bhd, late hdwy, nvr a threat: nicely bckd: prob ran to form off debut: handles fast grnd, 6f will suit now.

2507 **BAYRAMI** 12 [7] S E Kettlewell 2-8-6 A Beech (5) 10/1: 500044: Led till after halfway, no extra: op 16/1.   nk   51$

--   **BONNYELLA** [9] 2-8-6 D Mernagh (3) 16/1: 5: Dwelt, chsd ldrs till appr fnl 1f: 1,200 gns   nk   50
Phountzi Mar foal, sister to multiple wng 5f juv Fonzy, sire a maiden: with B Palling.

2551 **QUEENS SONG** 10 [8] 2-8-6 T Quinn 9/2: -036: Chsd ldrs till wknd appr fnl 1f: btr 2551 (gd/soft).   4   38

2384 **MISS TOPOGINO** 17 [5] 2-8-6 P Robinson 25/1: 0567: In tch, stumbled halfway, onepace: modest.   2   32

--   **FLOWLINE RIVER** [6] 2-8-6 R Price 33/1: 8: Dwelt, nvr in it: debut: May first foal.   4   22

2532 **SAVANNA MISS** 10 [1] 2-8-6 D McGaffin (4) 9/2: 509: Dwelt, handy till halfway: op 3/1, see 2009.   2   17

9 ran   Time 1m 00.8 (2.5)   (The Lager Khan)   S C Williams Newmarket, Suffolk

---

2773   2.50 QUILTER & CO NURSERY HCAP 2YO (E)   6f   Good/Firm 27   -11 Slow   [96]
      £3698   £1138   £569   £284

2091 **SHUSH** 29 [9] C E Brittain 2-9-7 (89) P Robinson 3/1 FAV: 15601: 2 b c Shambo - Abuzz (Absalom)   92
Nvr far away, led appr fnl 1f, rdn clr: earlier won debut at Kempton (mdn): half-brother to useful juv World
Premier: eff at 5/6f, bred for further: acts on fast & hvy, any trk: useful, apprec the drop in grade & trip.

LEICESTER THURSDAY JULY 20TH Righthand, Stiff, Galloping Track

2589 **TROUBLESHOOTER 8** [7] W R Muir 2-8-4 (72) Martin Dwyer 7/2: 60202: 2 b c Ezzoud - Oublier **2 70**
L'Ennui (Bellman) Prom, rdn appr fnl 1f, styd on for 2nd but not pace of wnr: op 5/1: gd run, acts on
fast & gd grnd: eff at 6f, step up to 7f will suit.
*2507 **ACORN CATCHER 12** [8] B Palling 2-7-10 (64) (5oh) D Mernagh (1) 11/2: 013: 2 b f Emarati - Anytime **¾ 60**
Baby (Bairn) Unruly start, led till appr fnl 1f, edged right & onepace: tchd 20/1, clr rem: stays 6f: see 2507.
2469 **EVERMOORE 13** [6] J S Moore 2-7-10 (64) (4oh) P M Quinn (3) 10/1: -0464: In tch, outpcd appr fnl 1f. **3½ 50**
2575 **NAUGHTY KNIGHT 8** [3] 2-7-10 (64) (2oh) R Brisland (5) 10/3: 501135: Nvr going pace: longer 6f trip **1 47**
shld suit, much better over 5f prev: may need softer grnd: see 1549.
1463 **UNVEIL 57** [2] 2-7-10 (64) (4oh) D Kinsella (7) 9/1: 4466: Dwelt, al bhd: 8 wk abs, see 1136. **shd 47**
2377 **ECKSCLUSIVE STORY 17** [5] 2-7-10 (64) (5oh) J McAuley (3) 16/1: -0447: Prom till halfway: stiff task. **5 32**
1823 **MAYSBOYO 41** [4] 2-7-10 (64) (19oh) C Catlin (4) 50/1: -3008: Nvr in it: 6 wk abs: needs sells. **10 2**
8 ran Time 1m 12.1 (2.3) (Mrs C E Brittain) C E Brittain Newmarket, Suffolk

2774 3.20 CHOICE MED AUCT MDN 3-4YO (F) 1m2f Good/Firm 27 -21 Slow
£2520 £720 £360 3 yo rec 10lb

2548 **EUROLINK ARTEMIS 10** [15] J L Dunlop 3-8-5 T Quinn 5/2 FAV: 4351: 3 b f Common Grounds - Taiga **72**
(Northfields) Held up, prog 3f out, styd on to lead dist, ran on well: nicely bckd: unrcd juv, apprec step up
to 10f: acts on fast & soft grnd, latter may suit better: goes on stiff/gall or undul trks: can rate higher.
1796 **MARENKA 42** [1] H Candy 3-8-5 C Rutter 11/4: 42: 3 b f Mtoto - Sliprail (Our Native **¾ 69**
Tried to make all, hdd ent fnl 1f, styd on: 6 wk abs: handles fast & prob soft grnd, knocking at the door.
2354 **VETORITY 18** [5] B Smart 3-8-5 M Tebbutt 11/1: 353: 3 b f Vettori - Celerite (Riverman) **1¾ 66+**
Bhd, imprvng when short of room appr fnl 2f, switched & kept on well, nvr nrr: op 8/1: eye-catching h'cap qual
run: eff at 10f, 12f h'caps will suit: handles fast grnd: one to keep in mind: see 2354, 1992.
2322 **MILLENNIUM SUMMIT 19** [2] J R Fanshawe 3-8-10 D Harrison 14/1: 464: Chsd ldrs, eff/onepace fnl 2f. **2 68**
-- **BREEZE HOME** [8] 4-9-6 R Mullen 66/1: 5: Handy, eff & hung left appr fnl 2f, unable to qckn: **½ 67**
debut: half-brother to a bmpr wnr, prob handles fast grnd.
2560 **PERPETUO 9** [7] 3-8-5 G Carter 6/1: 336: Rear, eff over 2f out, onepace: op 4/1, h'caps next. **2½ 58**
1725 **PRINCE ELMAR 45** [12] 3-8-10 (t) Martin Dwyer 25/1: 0-0007: Nvr better than mid-div: 6 wk abs: **1½ 61$**
plcd on debut last term (mdn, rtd 81): half-brother to a useful 6/7f juv: bred for 1m+, handles gd/soft grnd.
1352 **BLUE HAWK 62** [14] 3-8-10 J Weaver 25/1: 300-08: Rear, imprvd str, fdd 2f out: 9 wk abs, lngr trip. **1½ 59$**
-- **PLAIN CHANT** [11] 3-8-10 W Supple 6/1: 9: Rcd in 2nd till 2f out, wknd qckly: debut: Doyoun **hd 58**
colt out of a useful mid-dist mare, related to smart stayer Top Cees: shld come on for this: with P Harris.
2621 **BOSSCAT 7** [9] 3-8-10 T E Durcan 33/1: 00-050: Al towards rear: 10th, quick reappr. **½ 57$**
4614} Sail With The Wind 257 [13] 3-8-5 P Doe 33/1: 1796 **Lady Abai 42** [10] 3-8-5 J Tate 25/1:
-- **Shannons Dream** [4] 4-9-1 G Hind 33/1: 2265 **Shervana 21** [6] 4-9-1 R Studholme (5) 66/1:
2811} Wilby Willie 366 [3] 4-9-6 F Keniry (5) 66/1:
15 ran Time 2m 07.3 (4.8) (Eurolink Group Plc) J L Dunlop Arundel, W Sussex

2775 3.50 ALLIANCE HCAP 3YO+ 0-80 (D) 7f str Good/Firm 27 +11 Fast [79]
£7514 £2312 £1156 £578 3 yo rec 7 lb

2338 **ROYAL ARTIST 19** [4] W J Haggas 4-9-10 (75) T Quinn 11/10 FAV: 212621: 4 b g Royal Academy - Council **87**
Rock (General Assembly) Front rank, led appr fnl 2f, easily qcknd clr, eased fnl 100y: fast time, well bckd,
impressive: prev won at W'hampton (AW h'cap, rtd 78a): '99 wnr at Lingfield (mdn, rtd 69a & 73): eff at 8.5f,
suited by 7f: acts on firm, gd/soft grnd, both AWs, any trk: can carry big weights: progressive, qk follow up?
2612 **REDSWAN 7** [10] S C Williams 5-9-3 (68)(t) G Hind 8/1: 000002: 5 ch g Risk Me - Bocas Rose **6 68**
(Jalmood) Keen, in tch, rdn appr fnl 1f, styd on for 2nd but no ch with wnr: tchd 10/1: quick reappr & back
to form tho' caught a tartar: won this race last term (off 2lbs lower mark): see 1810.
1611 **SAGUARO 50** [5] K A Morgan 6-7-10 (47)(2oh) P M Quinn (3) 16/1: 0-2103: 6 b g Green Desert - **shd 47**
Badawi (Diesis) In tch, feeling pace & rdn 2f out, styd on towards fin: 7 wk abs: acts on fast, soft & fibresand.
2063 **DANDY REGENT 30** [9] J L Harris 6-8-7 (58) P Doe 20/1: 101004: Led till appr fnl 2f, onepace: see 1351. **¾ 56**
2512 **APLOY 12** [1] 3-8-7 (65) R Mullen 12/1: 0-6445: Bhd, late hdwy, nvr nr ldrs: struggling to find a trip. **nk 62**
2412 **DILSAA 15** [11] 3-8-11 (69) A Beech 25/1: -50006: Prom, same pace fnl 2f: back in trip, blnks off. **hd 66**
1969 **SUSANS PRIDE 34** [8] 4-9-11 (76) P Mulrennan (7) 11/1: 030347: Al same place: op 8/1, see 780. **1 71**
2431 **CHAMPAGNE RIDER 15** [3] 4-9-13 (78) T E Durcan 8/1: 000068: Chsd ldrs till appr fnl 1f: tchd 12/1. **hd 72**
2163 **LUANSHYA 26** [12] 4-9-1 (66) M Tebbutt 16/1: 454009: Chsd ldrs till wknd 2f out: softer grnd needed. **½ 59**
2283 **SAMARA SONG 21** [5] 7-8-5 (56) Darren Williams (3) 6/1: 260040: Al towards rear: 10th, see 1003. **shd 49**
2367 Countess Parker 17 [7] 4-8-1 (52) Claire Bryan (5) 25/1: 2546 **Hadleigh 10** [6] 4-9-3 (68) G Carter 40/1:
12 ran Time 1m 23.1 (1.1) (Tony Hirschfeld) W J Haggas Newmarket, Suffolk

2776 4.20 NEXT CLAIMER 3YO+ (F) 1m3f183y Good/Firm 27 -28 Slow
£2394 £684 £342 3 yo rec 12lb

*2636 **SPOSA 6** [7] M J Polglase 4-9-3 G Carter 7/4: 05P011: 4 b f St Jovite - Barelyabride (Blushing Groom) **52**
Trkd ldrs, led appr fnl 1f, rdn out: nicely bckd: 6 days ago won at Southwell (sell, v easily, rtd 49a): ex-Irish,
'99 Tramore wnr (mdn): eff at 12f, stays 2m on fast grnd & fibresand, sharp or stiff/gall trk.
2510 **UNIMPEACHABLE 12** [2] J M Bradley 3-8-1 Claire Bryan (5) 5/4 FAV: 264422: 3 b f Namaqualand - **½ 47**
Bourbon Topsy (Ile de Bourbon) Rear, prog to press wnr fnl 1f, held nr fin: nicely bckd, claimed for £8,000.
-- **CLASSIC DEFENCE** [4] B J Llewellyn 7-9-0 Sophie Mitchell 20/1: 20B0/3: 7 b g Cyrano de Bergerac **1½ 46**
- My Alanna (Dalsaan) Held up, styd on appr fnl 1f, nvr nr to chall: long abs, back in 96/97 scored over
timber at Kempton (hdles bow, rtd 105h, J Hills): '96 wnr on the Flat at Musselburgh (mdn) & Goodwood
(h'cap, rtd 74): eff at 10f on firm & gd grnd & shld be much sharper for this.
2736} LUDERE 370 [3] B J Llewellyn 5-9-0 R Havlin 16/1: 2400-4: Sn led, hdd ent str, kept on onepace: **nk 45$**
reappr: 99/00 hdles wnr at Sedgefield (2m1f nov, rtd 72h, rtd 88h, P Monteith): dual '99 rnr-up (h'cap, rtd 40):
'98 wnr at Musselburgh (clmr, rtd 62): eff at 12f, stays 2m: acts on firm & gd/soft grnd.
2709 DOVES DOMINION 4 [6] 3-8-10 (VIS) J Weaver 11/1: 500055: Not settle, early ldr, again ent str **1¾ 51**
till bef dist, no extra & eased: quick reappr, too free in visor: flattered 2709.
2038 **REPUBLICAN LADY 31** [5] 8-9-7 D McGaffin (5) 20/1: -046: Dwelt, chsd ldrs till appr fnl 2f: see 2038. **16 35**
4548} LENNOX 265 [1] 4-9-8 J Tate 8/1: 3400-7: Trkd ldrs till appr fnl 1f, wknd: reappr last term (h'cap, rtd **29 11**
59 & 72$, P Cole): flattered in '98 (auct mdn, rtd 80$): stays 7f, bred to get further: handles gd grnd.
7 ran Time 2m 36.6 (6.3) (The Lovatt Partnership) M J Polglase Southwell, Notts

LEICESTER THURSDAY JULY 20TH Righthand, Stiff, Galloping Track

2777 **4.50 CRIMEBEAT HCAP 3YO+ 0-70 (E) 6f Good/Firm 27 00 Slow [69]**
£3266 £1005 £502 £251 3 yo rec 5 lb A small group raced stands side, never got in it

2673 **TREASURE TOUCH 5** [6] P D Evans 6-9-9 (64) Joanna Badger (7) 11/2 FAV: 130131: 6 b g Treasure Kay - **70**
Bally Pourri (Law Society) Front rank, led appr fnl 1f, pshd out, shade rdly: op 4/1, fair time, quick reapp: earlier won at Catterick (2, clmr & h'cap, D Nicholls): '99 rnr-up (stks, rtd 60): won 5 times in '97 (rtd 71a & 89): stays 7.5f, suited by 6f: acts on firm, gd/soft grnd & fibresand, without blnks: tough & well h'capped.
2511 **AUNT DORIS 12** [15] R F Johnson Houghton 3-8-8 (54) R Mullen 11/1: -60042: 3 b f Distant Relative - *1¾* **55**
Nevis (Connaught) Waited with, kept on fnl 1½f, nvr nr to chall: grad coming to hand, likes Leicester: see 1467.
2326 **SYLVA PARADISE 19** [16] C E Brittain 7-9-13 (68)(vis) P Robinson 14/1: -04503: 7 b g Dancing *nk* **68**
Dissident - Brentsville (Arctic Tern) Well plcd, going well 2f out, shkn up bef dist, unable to qckn: well h'capped.
2420 **NORTHERN SVENGALI 15** [10] T D Barron 4-9-6 (61) D Mernagh (3) 12/1: 006004: Bhd ldrs, prog to *½* **59**
chall appr fnl 1f, kept on onepace ins last: ran well back in trip, see 631.
2623 **ZEPPO 7** [7] 5-9-2 (57)(bl) G Hind 10/1: 406445: In tch, styd on for press appr fnl 1f, unable to chall. *½* **54**
2546 **BANDBOX 10** [3] 5-9-6 (61) J Weaver 14/1: 060306: Held up stands side, late hdwy, nvr a factor. *¾* **56**
2631 **GOLDEN POUND 7** [8] 8-8-4 (45) W Supple 6/1: 6-4547: Rear, styd on fnl 1f, nvr on terms: tchd 9/1. *¾* **38**
2192 **SAMMAL 24** [14] 4-8-5 (46) D Harrison 16/1: 046208: Waited with, shaken up 2f out, nvr dangerous. *1* **36**
2654 **MUJAS MAGIC 6** [17] 5-8-11 (52)(vis) C Catlin (7) 16/1: 050109: Slow away, nvr trbled ldrs: see 2415. *nk* **41**
2701 **KOSEVO 4** [1] 6-8-1 (42)(bl) J Tate 25/1: 000000: Led stands side, hung right appr fnl 1f & wknd: 10th. *1* **28**
2525 **ANGEL HILL 11** [5] 5-9-0 (55)(vis) G Carter 8/1: 006100: Rcd stands side, switched halfway, al bhd: 11th. *1½* **38**
2230 **BAYONET 22** [4] 4-9-1 (56) G Hannon (7) 11/1: -02100: Chsd ldrs stands side till halfway: 15th, tchd 14/1. **0**
2193 **OARE KITE 24** [9] 5-8-11 (52)(bl) Dale Gibson 7/1: 320100: V slow away, al struggling: 16th, ignore see 2031. **0**
1971 **Fastrack Time 34** [13] 3-9-3 (63) C Rutter 33/1: 439 **Amaro 169** [18] 4-8-1 (42) P Doe 33/1:
2591 **French Fancy 8** [12] 3-7-10 (42)(3oh) P M Quinn (3) 33/1: 2320 **Grace 19** [2] 6-8-1 (42) Claire Bryan (5) 16/1:
1349 **Sonbelle 63** [11] 3-9-5 (65) D McGaffin (5) 20/1:
18 ran Time 1m 11.4 (1.6) (David Oxley & James Mitchell) P D Evans Pandy, Gwent

HAMILTON THURSDAY JULY 20TH Righthand, Undulating Track, Stiff Uphill Finish

Official Going: GOOD/FIRM (FIRM places). Stalls: Stands Side, except 9f/1m Inside.

2778 **2.10 FAIR MDN AUCT 2YO (E) 6f rnd Good/Firm 27 -28 Slow**
£2808 £864 £432 £216 Raced stands side

1628 **MILLIKEN PARK 49** [5] Miss L A Perratt 2-8-3 J Mackay(5) 9/2: -61: 2 ch f Fumo Di Londra - Miss **71**
Ironwood (Junius) Made all, styd on well fnl 2f, rdn out: op 3/1, 7 wk abs: eff at 6f, 7f+ shld suit: acts on fast & a stiff/undul track: runs well fresh: eff forcing the pace: open to further improvement.
865 **SHARP SECRET 100** [6] M Johnston 2-8-3 J Fanning 4/1: -52: 2 b f College Chapel - State Treasure *1¼* **66**
(Secretariat) Cl up, rdn & not pace of wnr ins last: op 3/1, 3 month abs: stays 6f on fast grnd: see 865 (AW).
2377 **ALIS IMAGES 17** [7] A Berry 2-8-1 O Pears 3/1 FAV: -66033: 2 b f Mind Games - Question Ali *½* **63**
(Petoski) Chsd ldrs kept on onepace fnl 2f: op 5/2: return to 7f could suit: see 2377.
1704 **JEZADIL 46** [4] M Dods 2-8-2 T Williams 50/1: -064: Prom, rdn/held over 1f out: 6 week abs. *1* **61**
2360 **FLYING ROMANCE 17** [1] 2-7-13 Kimberley Hart 6/1: -055: Cl up, struggling 2f out: op 11/4. *4* **46**
2361 **KANDYMAL 17** [3] 2-8-2 P Fessey 9/2: -0606: Cl up 4f: btr 1906 (5f). *1¾* **44**
-- **MULSANNE** [2] 2-8-6 J Carroll 12/1: -7: Chsd ldrs 3f, soon btn: op 8/1: Clantime colt, March *12* **18**
foal, cost 6,000gns, a first foal: dam a mdn: with M Quinn.
7 ran Time 1m 13.1 (3.3) (Dr J Walker) Miss L A Perratt Ayr, Strathclyde

2779 **2.40 FUN OF THE FAIR HCAP 3YO 0-70 (E) 6f rnd Good/Firm 27 -04 Slow [76]**
£2938 £904 £452 £226 Raced centre/stands side

*2541 **DESRAYA 10** [9] K A Ryan 3-9-1 (63)(bl)(7ex) F Lynch 9/2: 602311: 3 b g Desert Style - Madaraya **76**
(Shahrastani) Bhd ldrs, rdn/led over 1f out, styd on strongly, eased nr line: nicely bckd: 7lb pen for recent Ripon success (h'cap, first win): rtd 73 in '99: suited by 6f on fast & soft grnd: wears blinks: progressive gelding.
2641 **HOWARDS LAD 6** [3] I Semple 3-8-12 (60)(bl) V Halliday 12/1: 005102: 3 b g Reprimand - Port *3* **61**
Isaac (Seattle Song) Led till 1f out, kept on onepace: op 10/1, qck reapp: see 2396 (C/D, stks).
2505 **PARADISE YANGSHUO 12** [5] E J Alston 3-7-13 (47) J Bramhill 15/2: 004153: 3 b f Whittingham - Poly *hd* **48**
Static (Statoblest) Handy, every ch 2f out, no extra fnl 1f: stys 6f, return to 5f could prove ideal: see 2204 (mdn).
2603 **JEPAJE 7** [7] A Bailey 3-8-2 (50)(bl) P Fessey 14/1: -00064: Chsd ldrs, styd on fnl 2f, not pace *hd* **51**
to chall: op 10/1: handles fast, gd/soft & equitrack: worth another try at 7f: see 105.
2440 **BENNOCHY 14** [12] 3-8-7 (55) O Pears 7/1: 105045: Bhd ldrs centre, held fnl 1f: see 777 (5f). *¾* **53**
2719 **ROBIN HOOD 3** [10] 3-8-1 (49) Iona Wands(5) 7/1: 044406: Chsd ldrs, held over 1f out: qck reapp. *1¼* **43**
2374 **PAPE DIOUF 17** [1] 3-7-10 (44)(6oh) K Dalgleish (5) 50/1: 600007: Dwelt, never on terms: see 619. *3½* **28**
2438 **CLEAR MOON 14** [4] 3-7-12 (46)(BL) N Kennedy 20/1: -50508: Dwelt, never on terms: blinks. *2* **24**
2541 **FANTASY ADVENTURER 10** [2] 3-8-4 (52) T Lucas 10/1: 004049: Chsd ldrs till over 1f out: op 7/1. *shd* **30**
2438 **ZESTRIL 14** [11] 3-9-7 (69) J Mackay (5) 4/1 FAV: -00660: In tch 4f: 10th: op 3/1: see 1215. *2½* **40**
2489 **PACIFIC PLACE 12** [8] 3-8-12 (60) J Carroll 7/1: 232200: Chsd ldrs 4f: 11th: op 6/1: see 2243, 1334. *½* **30**
11 ran Time 1m 11.7 (1.9) (Pendle Inn Partnership) K A Ryan Hambleton, N Yorks

2780 **3.10 EARLYBIRD CLASS CLAIMER 4YO+ 0-65 (F) 1m1f36y Good/Firm 27 -05 Slow**
£2772 £792 £396

2642 **CLAIM GEBAL CLAIM 6** [7] P Monteith 4-7-13 P Hanagan(6) 16/1: 46-001: 4 b g Ardkinglass - Infra **39**
Blue (Bluebird) Made all, drvn appr fnl 1f, styd on strongly & held on well: op 10/1, first win, qck reapp: rnr-up on '99 reapp (rtd 52, Mrs A Duffield, seller): rtd 68 at best in '98: eff at 5f, now suited by 7/9f, has tried 10f: acts on fast & gd/soft grnd: has tried blinks, best without: loves to dominate.
2642 **ACE OF TRUMPS 6** [6] J Hetherton 4-8-3 (t) N Kennedy 4/1: 203002: 4 ch g First Trump - Elle *1¼* **40**
Reef (Shareef Dancer) Trckd wnr, every ch until hung right & no extra appr fnl 1f: see 1195.
2642 **ALAMEIN 6** [2] W Storey 7-7-13 (t) T Williams 13/8 FAV: 000023: 7 ch g Roi Danzig - Pollination *1¾* **33**

(Pentotal) Settled rear, eff when hung right over 2f out, drvn/btn fnl 1f: well bckd, qck reapp: fin ahead of several of todays rivals over C/D in 2462.

2642 **SECONDS AWAY 6** [5] J S Goldie 9-7-13 K Dalgleish (5) 5/1: 243334: Mid div, eff when short of room 2f out, switched wide & kept on inside last, no threat: quick reapp: flatted 2642 (C/D).	hd	33
2556 **THREE LEADERS 9** [3] 4-8-7 J Bramhill 5/1: 400405: Prom, rdn to improve 2f out, soon held.	nk	40
2642 **ROOFTOP 6** [1] 4-9-1 (vis) J Fanning 11/1: 000046: Trckd ldrs, eff over 4f out, wknd fnl 2f: op 7/1, quick reapp: btr 2642 (C/D, flattered).	8	33
2642 **UNMASKED 6** [4] 4-7-10 Iona Wands (5) 12/1: 033307: Prom, outpcd 4f out, no dngr after: qck reapp.	2½	10

7 ran   Time 1m 57.0 (2.9)   (Stan M Moffat)   P Monteith Rosewell, Midlothian

---

2781 3.40 PANORAMA CLASSIFIED STKS 3YO+ 0-60 (F)   1m65y rnd   Good/Firm 27   +01 Fast
£2716   £776   £388   3yo rec 8lb

*2542 **REQUESTOR 10** [1] J G FitzGerald 5-9-9 J Carroll 10/3: 63-011: 5 br g Distincly North - Bebe Altesse (Alpenkonig) Settled mid-div, smooth hdwy to lead appr fnl 1f, pushed clr, readily: op 5/2: recent Ripon scorer (h'cap, 1st win): plcd once in '99 (rtd 63): rtd 82 bck in '97: stys 1m on firm & soft grnd: has tried blnks, best without: goes well when fresh: in fine form.		71
1892 **LEGACY OF LOVE 37** [4] Miss S E Hall 4-9-4 J Fanning 7/2: 044-02: 4 b f Distant Relative - May Hills Legacy (Be My Guest) Led, hdd appr fnl 1f, kept on, not pace of wnr: nicely bckd & ran to near best: see 1892.	3	58
*2506 **DATURA 12** [5] M L W Bell 3-8-12 J Bramhill 5/2/1 FAV: -06413: 3 b f Darshaan - Realize (Al Nasr) Cl up, chall ldr appr fnl 3f, no extra well inside last: well bckd, clr rem: see 2506.	shd	60
2279 **KIDZ PLAY 21** [2] J S Goldie 4-9-9 Dean McKeown 3/1: -01404: Trck ldr, rdn/fdd fnl 2f: see 2279, 1689.	6	51
2397 **FLOORSOTHEFOREST 16** [3] 4-9-7 K Dalgleish (5) 16/1: 520005: Prom, rdn to chall halfway, hung right & lost tch fnl 2f: drifted from 8/1: see 2094.	5	39

5 ran   Time 1m 46.0 (2.2)   (Marquesa de Moratalla)   J G FitzGerald Norton, N Yorks

---

2782 4.10 DUKES HCAP 3YO+ 0-70 (E)   1m3f   Good/Firm 27   +08 Fast   [64]
£3510   £1080   £540   £270   3yo rec 11lb

2530 **WADI 11** [6] Dr J R J Naylor 5-9-8 (58) Dean McKeown 5/2: 604101: 5 b g Green Desert - Eternal (Kris) Led chsg grp, imprvd to lead appr fnl 3f, rdn clr: crse rec, tchd 5/1: earlier won at Folkestone (h'cap): '99 wnr at Warwick (sell h'cap) & Salisbury (clmr, rtd 70, G McCourt): '98 Pontefract wnr (mdn, rtd 81, H Cecil): eff at 10/12f on firm, soft grnd & equitrack, any trk: best without blnks/t-strap: gd weight carrier & well h'capped.		66
2638 **OCEAN DRIVE 6** [1] Miss L A Perratt 4-8-6 (42) J Mackay (5) 7/4 FAV: 543422: 4 b g Dolphin Street - Blonde Goddess (Godswalk) Chsd ldrs, chsd wnr fnl 3f, no impression: well bckd from 11/4, in-form.	3	44
2453 **KATIE KOMAITE 13** [7] Mrs G S Rees 7-8-2 (38) Angela Hartley (7) 7/1: 400023: 7 b m Komaite - City To City (Windjammer) Held up, eff 3f out, kept on same pace: ran well & clr of rem, , see 2453, 890.	3½	35
2220 **ILE DISTINCT 23** [4] Mrs A Duffield 6-9-10 (60) J Carroll 33/1: 03-204: Held up, prog to press ldrs 3f out, grad wknd: op 7/1, top-weight: much btr 2061 (reapp).	8	45
2735 **SPIRIT OF KHAMBANI 2** [5] 3-7-13 (46) K Dalgleish (5) 7/2: 000425: Prom, ch 3f out, soon wknd.	½	30
1822 **RUDETSKI 41** [3] 3-8-6 (53) T Williams 33/1: -00656: Held up, chsd ldrs 4f out till 3f out: op 16/1, abs.	½	36
2422 **INDIGO BAY 15** [2] 4-8-8 (44)(tbl) O Pears 12/1: 000007: Soon in a clr lead, hdd appr fnl 3f & btn.	1¼	25

7 ran   Time 2m 20.9 (2.1) Crse Record   (Mrs S P Elphick)   Dr J R J Naylor Shrewton, Wiltshire

---

2783 4.40 HASTE YE BACK HCAP 3YO+ 0-60 (F)   1m4f   Good/Firm 27   -17 Slow   [60]
£2814   £804   £402   3yo rec 12lb

2671 **ASHLEIGH BAKER 5** [3] M Johnston 5-9-2 (48)(6ex) J Fanning 4/1: 030161: 5 b m Don't Forget Me - Gayla Orchestra (Lord Gayle) Led till appr fnl 3f, onepace till rallied grimly dist to get up again nr fin: op 5/2: earlier won at Musselburgh (fill h'cap): plcd in '99 (rtd 54): '98 Ayr wnr (h'cap, rtd 65, A Bailey): best at 12f, tried 2m: acts on firm & soft grnd, any track: showed a gd attitude here.		52
2642 **LITTLE JOHN 6** [2] Miss L A Perratt 4-9-13 (59)(VIS) J Mackay (5) 10/1: 343252: 2 b g Warrshan - Silver Venture (Silver Hawk) Cl up, led appr fnl 3f, rdn bef dist & worn down towards fin: op 6/1, quick reapp, top-weight, visored: v difficult to win with, see 1656.	nk	62
2523 **LOYAL TOAST 11** [6] N Tinkler 5-7-10 (28)(20h) Kim Tinkler 10/1: 305053: 5 b g Lyphard - Lisieux (Steady Growth) Chsd ldrs, drpd rear halfway, late rally: ran to best: stays 12f, see 670.	1¼	29
1190 **HAYSTACKS 74** [4] D Moffatt 4-9-7 (53)(vis) J Bramhill 10/1: 056-04: Held up, under press 4f out, late hdwy: op 6/1:n 7 weeks ago won over timber at Cartmel (2m6f, fast grnd, rtd 102h): see 1190.	hd	54
2482 **ALTAY 13** [1] 3-8-11 (55) J Carroll 5/4 FAV: -03635: Chsd ldrs, ev ch 3f out till fdd below dist: nicely bckd.	½	55
2202 **PICCADILLY 24** [5] 5-8-4 (36) O Pears 11/2: -20046: Prom till 3f out: see 1432.	8	24

6 ran   Time 2m 37.1 (5.3)   (The David James Partnership)   M Johnston Middleham, N Yorks

---

BATH THURSDAY JULY 20TH Lefthand, Turning Track with Uphill Finish

Official Going: FIRM   Stalls: Straight Course - Far Side, Round Course - Inside

2784 2.00 7 DAYS A WEEK MED AUCT MDN 2YO (F)   5f161y rnd   Firm 15   -14 Slow
£2464   £704   £352

2526 **MAGICAL FLUTE 11** [3] M R Channon 2-8-9 Craig Williams 2/1: -031: 2 ch f Piccolo - Stride Home (Absalom) Chsd ldrs, drvn & styd on well from over 1f out to lead nr line, won going away: jockey given a 2-day whip ban: bckd, op 9/4: apprec step up to 5.8f (half sister to a 10f wnr) & further is sure to suit: acts on firm/fast ground: needed every yard of this trip, could prove intersting in nursery company over 6f+.		77
2357 **SILKEN WINGS 18** [5] I A Balding 2-8-9 J F Egan 15/8 FAV: 32: 2 b f Brief Truce - Winged Victory (Dancing Brave) Chsd ldr, rdn/led over 1f out, hdd nr line: nicely bckd: acts on firm & gd grnd: see 2357.	nk	74
-- **AUCTIONEERS CO UK** [1] B Palling 2-9-0 D Sweeney 14/1: 3: 2 br c Anita's Prince - Carmelina (Habitat) Led, rdn/hdd over 1f out, kept on onepace: clr rem: op 10/1: April foal, 4,500gns 2yo: half-brother to a 1m-11f 3/4yo wnr: dam a 7f/1m wnr abroad: looks sure to apprec 6f+, can improve.	1¾	75
2034 **ITS SMEE AGAIN 31** [2] B W Hills 2-8-9 M Hills 6/1: 444: Keen/chsd ldrs, btn over 1f out: op 9/2.	4	60
-- **YNYSMON** [4] 2-9-0 J Fortune 6/1: 5: Rear, al outpcd: op 4/1: Mind Games colt, Jan foal, cost	1	63

10,000gns: dam a 5f juv wnr: half brother to multiple sprint h'cap wnr Albert The Bear: with A Berry.
-- **TINY TIM** [6] 2-9-0 A Nicholls (3) 16/1: 6: Al bhd: op 8/1: Brief Truce gelding, May foal, cost *5* **54**
14,000gns: dam a 6f 3yo wnr: longer priced stablemate of rnr-up.
6 ran Time 1m 10.8 (1.7) (Peter Taplin) M R Channon West Isley, Berks

2785

2.30 DIGITAL SELLER 4YO+ (F) 1m3f144y Firm 14 -15 Slow
£2317 £662 £331

2457 **DUELLO 13** [13] M C Pipe 9-9-2 (vis) M Roberts 7/4 FAV: 1-3331: 9 b g Sure Blade - Royal Loft **54**
(Homing) Rear, rdn & stdy prog fnl 3f to lead inside last, rdn out: well bckd: no bid: plcd over jumps last winter (rtd 96h, h'cap): '99 Leicester wnr (clmr, rtd 58, M Blanshard): '98 Nottingham wnr (h'cap, rtd 59): eff at 12/14f on any grnd, fibresand & any track: enjoys selling grade.
2727 **MUTADARRA 2** [7] G M McCourt 7-9-7 D O'Donohoe 4/1: 025102: 7 ch g Mujtahid - Silver Echo *1¼* **56**
(Caerleon) Dwelt, rear, drvn/prog to lead ins last, soon hdd & no extra close home: op 5/2, qk reapp: see 2544.
2655 **MARMADUKE 6** [15] Miss Gay Kelleway 4-9-2 (vis) Dane O'Neill 7/1: 036603: 4 ch g Perugino - *1¾* **49**
Sympathy (Precocious) Chsd ldrs 2f out, kept on onepace: op 6/1: visor reapp: stays 11.5f on fm & soft.
2587 **PROUD CAVALIER 8** [10] K Bell 4-9-2 D Sweeney 50/1: -05004: Led, rdn/hdd inside last & no extra. *½* **48$**
2463 **SUMITRA 13** [9] 4-8-11 A McGlone 9/1: 530-05: Chsd ldrs 3f out, soon held: see 2463. *1¾* **41**
2327 **LARAS DELIGHT 19** [8] 5-8-11 N Callan 25/1: 006: Chsd ldr 3f out, wknd over 1f out: see 2327. *4* **35**
2467 **BIRTH OF THE BLUES 13** [5] 4-9-2 (vis) N Pollard 6/1: 000507: Rear, effort 4f out, no prog fnl 2f. *½* **39**
-- **VILLEGGIATURA** [6] 7-9-2 A Daly 12/1: /6228: Chsd ldrs 9f: Flat reapp, 9 month jumps abs (mod *3½* **34**
form): rnr up twice in France in '99: '95 Salisbury wnr (mdn): sole win at 7f, stays 2m: acts on firm & gd/soft.
2561 **HARD TO FOLLOW 9** [12] 5-8-11 J F Egan 33/1: 000/09: Bhd, mod gains: mod form. *10* **18**
2122 **COLONEL CUSTER 28** [4] 5-9-7 (vis) L Newman (3) 20/1: 065040: Chsd ldr, btn over 2f out: 10th. *hd* **27**
2331 **Castle Beau 19** [2] 5-9-2 F Norton 20/1: 2186 **Queens Stroller 25** [11] 9-8-11 G Baker (7) 50/1:
2611 **Victor Power 7** [3] 5-9-2 S Sanders 20/1: 43} **Magni Momenti 611** [1] 5-8-11 P Fitzsimons (5) 33/1:
-- **Springfieldsupreme** [14] 5-9-2 G Oliver (7) 50/1:
15 ran Time 2m 28.4 (3.4) (T M Hely-Hutchinson) M C Pipe Nicholashayne, Devon

2786

3.00 ON CABLE CLASSIFIED STKS 3YO+ 0-75 (D) 1m rnd Firm 14 -01 Slow
£4049 £1157 £578 3 yo rec 8 lb

2342 **PICTURE PUZZLE 19** [3] W J Haggas 4-9-0 J P Spencer 1/6 FAV: 16-321: 4 b f Royal Academy - **73**
Cloudslea (Chief's Crown) Made all, shaken up & readily pulled clr over 1f out: val for 8L+: hvly bckd at long odds on: '99 wnr at Thirsk (mdn), Yarmouth (fillies h'cap) & Newcastle (h'cap, rtd 74): suited by 7f/1m on firm & fast.
1786 **MAJOR REBUKE 42** [2] S P C Woods 3-8-9 N Callan 6/1: 0-0002: 3 b g Reprimand - Ackcontent *5* **60**
(Key To Content) Held up bhd front pair, rdn/chsd wnr 2f out, soon held: op 4/1, 6 week abs: see 1786.
2367 **ENTROPY 17** [4] B A Pearce 4-9-2 G Baker (7) 9/1: 305103: 4 b f Brief Truce - Distant Isle (Bluebird) *4* **51$**
Trkd ldr, rdn/no extra fnl 2f: op 8/1: see 2331 (c.j. claiming h'cap).
3 ran Time 1m 39.5 (1.2) (M H Wilson) W J Haggas Newmarket, Suffolk

2787

3.30 WILLIE CARSON HCAP 3YO 0-90 (C) 5f rnd Firm 14 +04 Fast [89]
£6922 £2130 £1065 £532

2451 **BANDANNA 14** [6] R J Hodges 3-9-4 (79) M Roberts 6/1: -00651: 3 gr f Bandmaster - Gratclo (Belfort) **84**
Held up, rdn/switched over 2f out & styd on well for press to lead well inside last: best time of day: op 5/1: '99 debut wnr at Chepstow (sell, subs rnr up in a listed contest, rtd 95): suited by a stiff/undul 5/6f on firm & gd grnd: has run well fresh: looks on a handy mark & could win again.
2168 **ANSELLAD 26** [9] A Berry 3-9-7 (82) R Hughes 10/1: 30-002: 3 b g Dancing Dissident - Dutch Queen *1* **84**
(Ahonoora) Chsd ldr, drvn/led halfway till well inside last, no extra: op 7/1: see 1285.
1925 **ILLUSIVE 36** [4] M Wigham 3-8-9 (70)(bl) F Norton 8/1: 203553: 3 b c Night Shift - Mirage (Red *½* **70**
Sunset) Rdn/towards rear, styd on fnl 2f, not pace to chall: acts on firm & gd/soft, both AWs: see 592 (AW, 6f).
2478 **JAMES STARK 13** [8] N P Littmoden 3-8-13 (74)(vis) J F Egan 11/2: 203424: Dwelt, soon trkd ldrs, *1¼* **71**
drvn/no extra fnl 1f: op 4/1: acts on firm, gd/soft & both AWs: see 1961, 105.
1925 **PEDRO JACK 36** [7] 3-9-5 (80)(BL) D R McCabe 8/1: 106035: Chsd ldrs, held fnl 1f: blinks, op 6/1. *hd* **76**
2504 **CORUNNA 12** [1] 3-9-4 (79) J Fortune 11/2: 313166: Held up, not pace to chall : see 2216. *nk* **74**
2478 **QUEEN OF THE MAY 13** [10] 3-9-4 (79) Craig Williams 9/1: -16547: Never on terms: op 6/1. *hd* **73**
-2663 **IMPERIALIST 6** [3] 3-9-7 (82)(bl) P Dobbs (5) 6/1: 500028: Chsd ldrs 4f: btr 2663 (gd). *5* **67**
2288 **CONNECT 20** [2] 3-9-4 (79)(BL) S Sanders 5/1 FAV: 000439: Led till halfway, fdd: blinks: btr 2288. *2* **59**
2663 **KILBRANNAN SOUND 6** [5] 3-8-9 (70) N Pollard 16/1: 450000: Al rear: 10th: op 14/1: see 1219. *½* **48**
10 ran Time 1m 0.8 (0.5) (Miss R Dobson) R J Hodges Charlton Adam, Somerset

2788

4.00 IN PUBS AND CLUBS CLAIMER 3YO+ (F) 5f rnd Firm 14 -02 Slow
£2401 £686 £343 3 yo rec 4 lb

2340 **ANSELLMAN 19** [1] A Berry 10-9-5 (bl) R Hughes 11/4: 254001: 10 gr g Absalom - Grace Poole **63**
(Sallust) Made all, held on well fnl 2f, rdn out: '99 Bath wnr (h'cap, rtd 75): '98 Redcar wnr (clmr, rtd 87 & 67 at best): eff at 6f, just best at 5f: acts on any ground/track: has run well fresh: suited by blinks/visor & relishes claiming grade nowadays: genuine & tough 10yo.
2535 **QUITE HAPPY 10** [2] M H Tompkins 5-8-12 S Sanders 5/2 FAV: 353642: 5 b m Statoblest - *¾* **53**
Four Legged Friend (Aragon) Held up in tch, rdn/prog to ch wnr fnl 1f, kept on, al held: well bckd: see 897.
2555 **ARAB GOLD 10** [10] M Quinn 5-8-9 J F Egan 50/1: 034003: 5 b g Presidum - Parklands Belle *2½* **43$**
(Stanford) Rcd mid div, kept on for press fnl 2f, no threat to wnr: acts on firm & equitrack: see 634 (AW).
2623 **WINDRUSH BOY 7** [4] M R Bosley 10-8-9 S Righton 14/1: 4-0004: Held up, rdn/late gains, no threat. *¾* **41$**
2505 **KNOCKEMBACK NELLIE 12** [11] 4-9-6 (bl) J Fortune 11/2: 121005: Chsd wnr, no extra over 1f out. *nk* **51**
1092 **NICKLES 79** [12] 5-8-13 A Daly 12/1: 000-06: Chsd ldrs 3f: op 10/1: 11 week abs: '99 Lingfield *1¾* **40**
wnr (6 rnr clmr, rtd 63): plcd twice in '98 (mdn, rtd 73): eff at 5f on gd & soft: eff forcing the pace.
2632 **SING FOR ME 6** [6] 5-8-4 N Carter (7) 33/1: 600657: Never on terms: quick reapp: see 272. *2½* **24**
1092 **LADYCAKE 79** [5] 4-8-4 F Norton 10/1: 006-08: Chsd ldrs till over 1f out: op 8/1: 11 week abs. *½* **22**
1994 **WILLRACK TIMES 33** [3] 3-8-4 N Pollard 10/1: -50009: Chsd ldrs 4f: op 8/1: see 706 (AW). *2½* **19**
2555 **SANDPOINT 10** [9] 4-8-10 A Clark 12/1: 0-0300: Dwelt & al outpcd: 10th: see 1994 (seller). *1¾* **17**
1994 **SPLIT THE ACES 33** [8] 4-8-9 M Roberts 10/1: 005500: Al outpcd rear: 11th: see 1734, 1092. *nk* **15**

BATH THURSDAY JULY 20TH Lefthand, Turning Track with Uphill Finish

2294 **MAVIS** 20 [7] 3-8-1(1ow) Craig Williams 50/1: 000: Al outpcd rear: 12th: no form. ¾ 9
12 ran Time 1m 01.10 (0.8) (Ansells Of Watford) A Berry Cockerham, Lancs

2789 4.30 DIGITAL FILLIES HCAP 3YO+ 0-70 (E) 1m2146y Firm 14 -06 Slow [64]
£3620 £1114 £557 £278 3 yo rec 10lb

2655 **LEVEL HEADED** 6 [1] P W Hiatt 5-8-0 (36) A Mackay 10/1: 350441: 5 b m Beveled - Snowline (Bay 41
Express) Led after 3f & rdn clr over 2f out, styd on well, rdn out: op 8/1, qk reapp, first win: unplcd for E
Wheeler in '99 (mdn, rtd 40): rtd 40 on h'cap bow in '98: eff up with/forcing the pace at 10f on firm & hvy.
2656 **INDIAN NECTAR** 6 [6] R Brotherton 7-9-5 (55) L Newman (3) 7/2: 042052: 7 b m Indian Ridge - Sheer 2½ 55
Nectar (Piaffer) Keen/ch ldrs, drvn/chsd wnr 3f out, held over 1f out: op 4/1, quick reapp: see 1332.
2625 **SHARP SPICE** 7 [8] D J Coakley 4-9-5 (55) S Sanders 5/2 FAV: 452553: 4 b f Lugana Beach - Ewar nk 54
Empress (Persian Bold) Rear, rdn & styd on fnl 2f, never threat to wnr: see 2041, 943.
1951 **SEEKING SANCTUARY** 35 [7] Dr J D Scargill 3-7-13 (45) J Lowe 12/1: 0-004: Chsd ldrs, lost plc bef nk 43
halfway, styd on fnl 2f, no threat: stays longer 10f trip, 12f+ could suit: handles firm grnd.
2265 **TASSO DANCER** 21 [3] 4-8-11 (47) M Roberts 16/1: 0/0005: Rear, mod late prog: see 2265 (mdn). 7 35
2544 **DIZZY TILLY** 10 [9] 6-9-0 (50) T G McLaughlin 6/1: 330106: Held up, eff 3f out, sn held: see 2370. 2 35
2296 **HEIRESS OF MEATH** 20 [1] 5-7-12 (34)(2ow)(7oh) A Daly 25/1: 300407: Led 3f, btn 3f out: see 2043. ¾ 18
2581 **DANIELLA RIDGE** 8 [2] 4-9-13 (63)(BL) P Dobbs (5) 7/1: 30-008: Keen/chsd ldrs 6f: plcd twice 24 20
last term (rtd 76, mdn): rtd 86 in '98 (debut, mdn): off at 1m on firm & gd, stiff track: tried blnks.
2625 **SEWARDS FOLLY** 7 [4] 4-8-6 (42) N Pollard 20/1: 5-0009: Held up in tch, btn 4f out: see 2625. 11 0
2446 **SEEKING UTOPIA** 14 [10] 3-9-7 (67) N Callan 1/2: -5040P: Chsd ldrs, wide on bend 4f out & soon 0
p.u.: op 7/2: jockey reported saddle slipped, this is best forgotten: see 2023 & 727.
10 ran Time 2m 08.00 (2.0) (Anthony Harrison) P W Hiatt Hook Norton, Oxon

EPSOM THURSDAY JULY 20TH Lefthand, V Sharp, Undulating Track

Official Going GOOD (GOOD/FIRM in places). Stalls: Inside, except 1m4f - Centre.

2790 6.20 MICKLEHAM APPR HCAP 3YO+ 0-75 (E) 1m2f Good 48 -11 Slow [70]
£3474 £1069 £534 £267 3 yo rec 10lb

2727 **SAMMYS SHUFFLE** 2 [5] Jamie Poulton 5-7-13 (41)(bl) D Kinsella (5) 5/1: 022321: 5 b h Touch Of 46
Grey - Cabinet Shuffle (Thatching) Waited with, hdwy over 2f out, kept on well, pushed out: deserved win
after 4 plcd runs, last Feb scored at Lingfield (h'cap, rtd 61a): '99 wnr again at Lingfield (h'cap, rtd 59a & 37):
in '98 won twice at Brighton (rtd 48, h'caps) & once at Lingfield (h'cap): all wins at 10f, stays 12f: acts on
firm, soft & equitrack: loves a sharp/undul trk & best in blnks: in top form at present, tough.
2212 **KINNINO** 23 [10] G L Moore 6-7-10 (38)(5oh) P Cheng (3) 33/1: 134032: 6 b g Polish Precedent - On 1½ 40
Tiptoes (Shareef Dancer) Keen, cl-up, led over 3f out till over 2f out, not pace of wnr: stays 10f.
2467 **CAPTAIN MCCLOY** 13 [2] P Mitchell 5-8-0 (42)(bl) R Brisland 10/1: 0-6333: 5 ch g Lively One - Fly ¾ 43
Me First (Herbager) In tch, eff 2f out, kept on onepace: prev with N Berry & yet another plcd run: see 2467.
2527 **JUNIKAY** 11 [4] R Ingram 6-9-10 (66) J Mongan 7/2 FAV: 113204: Waited with, eff over 2f out, no ½ 66
extra fnl 1f: well bckd: better expected: see 1743, 1395.
2625 **DION DEE** 7 [6] 4-8-4 (46) K Lavelle (0) 13/2: 361025: Bhd, eff over 2f out, onepace: see 2625. ¾ 45
2771 **RARE TALENT** 1 [1] 6-8-11 (53) Karen Peippo (7) 13/2: 030326: Bhd, some late gains, nvr dngrs: ½ 51
rnr-up at Yarmouth yesterday, see 2771.
2544 **ZAHA** 10 [5] 9-9-5 (61) D Watson (5) 16/1: 014007: Sn bhd, kept on late, no too much to do: op 10/1. nk 58
2493 **PARISIAN LADY** 12 [8] 5-8-7 (49) A Nicholls 6/1: 634428: Cl-up, wknd over 1f out: btr 2493, 1998. 1¾ 43
2544 **FIELD MASTER** 10 [7] 3-8-11 (63) R Smith (3) 14/1: 000509: Cl-up, wknd 3f out: see 2429, 771. 1½ 55
2655 **MAX** 6 [11] 5-7-10 (38)(t) (4oh) G Baker (3) 50/1: 000300: Led bit over 3f out: 10th, flattered 2433. 1¾ 27
1442 **ARDENT** 59 [3] 6-8-4 (46) P Fitzsimons 10/1: 6-6400: Al bhd: hrd last, 2 month abs, see 23. 4 29
11 ran Time 2m 09.71 (5.91) (Mrs G M Temmerman) Jamie Poulton Telscombe, E.Sussex.

2791 6.50 EBF MED AUCT MDN 2YO (E) 7f rnd Good 48 -32 Slow
£4173 £1284 £642 £321

-- **ATLANTIS PRINCE** [3] S P C Woods 2-9-0 J Reid 9/2: 1: 2 ch c Tagula - Zoom Lens (Caerleon) 82
Cl-up, hdwy to lead appr fnl 1f, kept on well under hands-and-heels on debut: Mar foal, cost 75,000gns:
half-brother to juv wnrs over 5f/1m: stays a sharp/undul 7f well, 1m sure to suit: runs well fresh: improve
again for this kind debut & shld win in better company.
2430 **MEDIA BUYER** 15 [4] B J Meehan 2-9-0 (bl) D R McCabe 4/1: 00032: 2 b c Green Dancer - California ½ 77
Rush (Forty Niner) Keen, waited with, gd hdwy to lead over 2f out till appr fnl 1f, kept on for press but
al held: shown enough to win similar: clr of rem, see 2430.
2454 **TOTALLY COMMITTED** 13 [8] R Hannon 2-9-0 P Fitzsimons (5) 8/11 FAV: 0323: 2 b c Turtle Island - 3 73
Persian Light (Persian Heights) Cl-up, rdn & sltly outpcd 2f out, no impress over 1f out: hvly bckd & better
expected, tho' did not look at ease on this unconventional trk: shld stay 7f on a more gall trk: see 2454.
2619 **ALLTHEDOTCOMS** 7 [1] N A Callaghan 2-9-0 J P Spencer 20/1: 04: Set pace till over 2f out, no 3 67
extra: better run from the front, see 2619.
2619 **HAMMOCK** 7 [6] 2-9-0 W Ryan 16/1: 055: Prom, wknd 2f out: see 2619. ½ 66
2290 **SASHA STAR** 20 [7] 2-9-0 M Fenton 33/1: 06: Nvr a factor: see 2290. 10 46
2545 **PICKETT POINT** 10 [5] 2-9-0 Dane O'Neill 33/1: 07: Al bhd: see 2545. 1¾ 42
7 ran Time 1m 25.71 (5.61) (Lucayan Stud) S P C Woods Newmarket

2792 7.20 SODEXHO CLASSIFIED STKS 3YO+ 0-80 (D) 7f rnd Good 48 -07 Slow
£7020 £2160 £1080 £540 3 yo rec 7 lb

-2580 **PAYS DAMOUR** 8 [5] R Hannon 3-8-11 Dane O'Neill 11/2: 200121: 3 b c Pursuit Of Love - Lady Of The 84
Land (Wollow) Set pace, hdd briefly over 1f out, rallied gamely, all out: earlier scored at Haydock (h'cap):
'99 Epsom wnr (4 rnr nurs, rtd 76): eff over 6/7f on firm/fast, gd & on any trk: likes Epsom: best up
with/forcing the pace: in fine heart & is very game.

EPSOM THURSDAY JULY 20TH Lefthand, V Sharp, Undulating Track

2577 **LORD PACAL 8** [4] N A Callaghan 3-8-9 W Ryan 13/2: 000022: 3 b g Indian Ridge - Please Believe Me (Try My Best) With wnr, eff to lead briefly over 1f out, just held in a driving fin: well h'capped & stays 7f. ***shd*** **81**
2356 **NAVIASKY 18** [2] W R Muir 5-9-2 Martin Dwyer 6/1: 404663: 5 b g Scenic - Black Molly (High Top) Bhd, eff over 2f out, kept on same pace over 1f out: on a fair mark & best at 1m: see 2126, 733. ***1¾*** **77**
2261 **DILKUSHA 22** [3] B J Meehan 5-9-2 D Holland 6/1: 66-004: Waited with, rdn 2f out, kept on late. ***nk*** **76**
2495 **KNOCKTOPHER ABBEY 12** [7] 3-8-9 K Darley 11/2: 00-505: Prom, wknd over 2f out: nicely bckd. ***6*** **65**
*2495 **RUSHMORE 12** [6] 3-8-13 J Fortune 15/8 FAV: 100116: Handy, rdn & wknd 2f out: hvly bckd tho' op 6/4: reportedly not handle this sharp/undul trk, but did not fire today: see 2495. ***2½*** **65**
438 **ROTHERHITHE 169** [1] 4-9-2 F Norton 100/1: 6-0007: Keen, bhd, btn 3f out: abs, poorly plcd. ***13*** **41**
7 ran Time 1m 23.95 (3.85) (Mrs M W Bird) R Hannon East Everleigh, Wilts.

2793

7.50 SPECIAL PIPING HCAP 3YO+ 0-70 (E) 1m4f Good 48 +10 Fast [69]
£5232 £1610 £805 £402 3 yo rec 12lb

2319 **LEGAL LUNCH 19** [6] P W Harris 5-10-0 (69)(bl) J Fortune 8/1: 313561: 5 b g Alleged - Dinner Surprise (Lyphard) Hld up, eff over 2f out, edged left for press ins last but kept on to lead cl-home, drvn out under top-weight: best time of day: earlier scored at Doncaster (h'cap, first time blnks): plcd in '99 (rtd 86): '98 Haydock wnr (mdn, rtd 91): stays 2m, suited by 10.5f/12f on firm, soft or equitrack: eff with/without a visor, best in blnks now on any trk: can carry big weights: best with a strong jockey. **72**
2255 **REDOUBLE 22** [3] J Akehurst 4-9-3 (58) T Quinn 9/2: 50-022: 4 b g First Trump - Sunflower Seed (Mummy's Pet) Cl-up, kept on to lead ins fnl 1f, hdd & sltly bmpd cl-home, just btn: shade unfortunate. ***hd*** **60**
*2656 **FANDANGO DREAM 6** [2] M D I Usher 4-7-10 (37)(10oh) G Baker (7) 5/1: 504413: 4 ch g Magical Wonder - Fandikos (Taufan) Waited with, hdwy 2f out, short of room dist, kept on cl-home, only btn 1L: qck reapp & a fine run from 10oh: improving, see 2656. ***¾*** **38**
2425 **ABLE SEAMAN 15** [1] C E Brittain 3-8-9 (62) B Marcus 8/1: 453334: Led 3f out, hdd & no extra ins last: see 2425. ***1*** **61**
4503} **TULSA 269** [9] 6-7-12 (39)(2ow)(7oh) F Norton 33/1: 3100-5: In tch, sltly outpcd over 3f out, late gains: 6 wk jumps abs, plcd in a nov hdle (2m, fast grnd, rdn 94h): in '99 won on the Flat at Lingfield (AW mdn h'cap, rtd 42a): stays 10f on fast, soft, equitrack, likes a sharp trk & has tried a visor. ***2*** **35**
160 **IMPREVUE 225** [7] 6-9-8 (63) S Sanders 12/1: 3114-6: Held up, rdn & onepace over 2f out: unplcd over hdles back in Feb: sharper for this: see 1 (AW). ***hd*** **59**
*2510 **PRESTO 12** [5] 3-9-1 (68)(tbl) J P Spencer 15/2: 051017: Dwelt, waited with, eff 2f out, no dngr: prev with W Haggas, now with Mrs M Jones: see 2510 (clmr). ***nk*** **63**
2286 **LANCER 20** [4] 8-9-7 (62)(vis) G Bardwell 14/1: 660658: Dwelt, sn in tch, wknd 2f out: see 2002. ***7*** **47**
*2626 **HALF TIDE 7** [10] 6-8-1 (42) M Henry 3/1 FAV: -06219: In tch, wkng when not clr run over 1f out: better expected after 2626 (gd/soft, C/D). ***1½*** **25**
2081 **TOMMY CARSON 29** [8] 5-8-12 (53)(bl) O Urbina 20/1: 2-6250: Led, clr over 4f out, hdd 3f out, wknd. ***6*** **28**
10 ran Time 2m 39.38 (4.58) (The Alleged Partnership) P W Harris Tring, Berks.

2794

8.20 PLC SECURITY HCAP 3YO 0-70 (E) 7f rnd Good 48 -01 Slow [77]
£5255 £1617 £808 £404

2729 **ANNIJAZ 2** [1] J G Portman 3-7-13 (48) G Baker (7) 8/1: 463301: 3 b f Alhijaz - Figment (Posse) Rear, gd hdwy to lead dist, ran on strongly, rdn out: qck reapp: first win: rnr-up twice in '99 (trained by A Jarvis, rtd 70): eff at 7f/1m on gd & firm grnd: handles a sharp/undul trk: could make a qck follow-up. **57**
2489 **MARNIE 12** [6] J Akehurst 3-8-3 (52) F Norton 6/1: 006022: 3 ch f First Trump - Miss Aboyne (Lochnager) Nvr far away, ev ch 2f out, not pace of wnr fnl 1f: stays a sharp 7f, acts on gd & fast grnd. ***2½*** **56**
2448 **BINT HABIBI 14** [8] M R Channon 3-8-1 (50) Craig Williams 16/1: -01663: 3 b f Bin Ajwaad - High Stepping (Taufan) Mid-div, kept on under press fnl 1f, not pace to chall: not disgraced: see 1972 (claimer). ***2*** **50**
2300 **ATYLAN BOY 20** [16] B J Meehan 3-9-4 (67) K Darley 12/1: 031524: Mid-div, kept on under press fnl 1f, not pace of chall: ddhtd for 4th: rtd higher on the AW in 2300 & 1745. ***¾*** **67**
2128 **MAGIC BABE 27** [2] 3-8-10 (59) O Urbina 4/1 FAV: 024124: Trkd ldrs till outpcd fnl 2f: ddhtd for 4th. ***dht*** **59**
1202 **DIAMOND OLIVIA 73** [14] 3-8-6 (55) J F Egan 20/1: 0-3406: Rcd keenly in rear, nvr nr ldrs: abs. ***½*** **53**
2026 **MISTER CLINTON 32** [10] 3-8-13 (62) D O'Donohoe 9/1: 103167: Dwelt, late hdwy, nvr dngrs: lost all ch at the start here: btr 1889. ***hd*** **58**
*2044 **ANDYS ELECTIVE 31** [13] 3-9-2 (65)(vis) S Whitworth 12/1: 360518: In tch, led after 2f till 2f out, fdd. ***½*** **60**
2654 **TEA FOR TEXAS 6** [7] 3-8-1 (50) P Doe 20/1: 016009: Al mid-div: qck reapp, stablemate of rnr-up. ***3½*** **38**
2440 **KINSMAN 14** [15] 3-9-4 (67)(vis) M Roberts 14/1: 623160: Prom 5f, fdd into 10th: twice below 2042. ***¾*** **53**
2489 **TIME BOMB 12** [5] 3-8-3 (52) G Hind 16/1: -40060: Slowly away, nvr got into race: fin 11th. ***hd*** **37**
2546 **HAIL THE CHIEF 10** [3] 3-9-7 (70) R Hughes 9/1: 0-4260: Led 2f, remained prom & regained lead 2f out till dist, wknd into 12th: top-weight: much btr 2293. ***1¾*** **51**
2026 **OTIME 32** [17] 3-9-4 (67)(bl) Dean McKeown 9/1: 066250: Trkd ldrs 5f, wknd: fin 15th: btr 1889. **0**
2585 **Skylark 8** [9] 3-9-2 (65) Dane O'Neill 12/1: 2591 **Chilworth 8** [4] 3-8-7 (56) R Price 14/1:
2654 **Bettina Blue 6** [12] 3-8-11 (60) I Mongan(5) 20/1: 2489 **Mind The Silver 12** [11] 3-8-10 (59)(VIS) S Sanders 33/1:
17 ran Time 1m 23.52 (3.42) (Christopher Shankland) J G Portman Compton, Berks.

2795

8.50 RUBBING HOUSE MDN HCAP 3YO 0-70 (E) 1m114y rnd Good 48 -05 Slow [77]
£3656 £1125 £562 £281

2579 **MUST BE MAGIC 8** [4] H J Collingridge 3-8-12 (61)(VIS) M Roberts 7/1: 063431: 3 b c Magic Ring - Sequin Lady (Star Appeal) Mid-div, short of room & switched 2f out, imprvd to lead dist, ran on, rdn out: vis: plcd in '99 (mdn, rtd 80): eff at 1m, prob stays 10f on fast & soft, sharp/undul trk: woken up by visor. **66**
2467 **EVERGREEN 13** [9] R Hannon 3-9-4 (67)(t) R Hughes 9/1: 504002: 3 ch f Lammtarra - Nettle (Kris) Bhd, switched wide & imprvd 2f out, ev ch dist, kept on & not btn far: eff at 1m, does stay 10f: wears a t-strap. ***1½*** **69**
2499 **ORIENT EXPRESS 12** [10] B J Meehan 3-9-1 (64) D Holland 8/1: 000303: 3 b g Blues Traveller - Oriental Splendour (Runnett) Waited with, eff 2f out, styd on late but not reach front 2: eff at 1m, a return to 9f+ suit. ***3*** **60**
2467 **SPIRIT OF TENBY 13** [3] S Dow 3-9-2 (65) P Doe 6/1: 303304: Rear, eff 2f out, not pace to chall. ***1¾*** **57**
1855 **SANGRA 39** [2] 3-9-1 (64) K Darley 4/1: 56-425: In tch, led briefly dist, sn no extra: btr 1855 (7f). ***shd*** **56**
2699 **CIBENZE 4** [5] 3-9-3 (66) T Quinn 3/1 FAV: 426026: Slowly away, imprvd from rear 2f out, wknd fnl 1f. ***3½*** **51**
2332 **DOM MIGUEL 19** [6] 3-7-13 (48) G Bardwell 14/1: 5-0007: Rcd keenly in tch, led 2f out till dist, fdd. ***4*** **25**
2332 **AROB PETE 19** [1] 3-8-8 (57) T G McLaughlin 16/1: -00608: Set pace 6f, wknd: flattered 1725 (10f). ***1*** **32**
2601 **CHARLEM 7** [11] 3-7-10 (45)(vis)(8oh) F Norton 33/1: 666029: Nvr a factor: stiff task: see 2601 (AW). ***nk*** **19**
2325 **WINDFALL 19** [12] 3-9-7 (70) I Mongan (5) 14/1: 0-0300: Rear, eff 3f out, sn btn & fin 10th: btr 1912. ***3½*** **37**

EPSOM THURSDAY JULY 20TH Lefthand, V Sharp, Undulating Track

2426 **Piccalilli** 15 [13] 3-7-10 (45)(6oh) R Brisland (5) 40/1: 4406} **So Dainty** 276 [7] 3-8-13 (62) A Clark 20/1:
2624 **Aegean Flower** 7 [8] 3-8-3 (52)(bl) C Rutter 16/1:
13 ran   Time 1m 46.33 (4.53)   (The Headquarters Partnership III)   H J Collingridge Newmarket.

HAMILTON   FRIDAY JULY 21ST   Righthand, Undulating Track, Stiff Uphill Finish

Official Going   GOOD/FIRM (FIRM Places). Stalls - Stands Side, Except 1m/9f - Inside

2796	6.50 SPRINT AMAT RDRS HCAP 3YO+ 0-70 (E) 6f Good/Firm 24 -06 Slow	[41]
	£2899 £892 £446 £223 3 yo rec 5 lb Raced stands side	

2641 **ENCOUNTER** 7 [2] J Hetherton 4-10-0 (41) Mrs S Bosley 9/2: 000521: 4 br g Primo Dominie - Dancing   **49**
Spirit (Ahonoora) Chsd ldrs, prog to lead 1f out, rdn & styd on well: op 7/2: landed a 24hr brace in '99 at Ayr
(sell) & Hamilton (h'cap) rtd 58 at best): flattered in '98 for C Brittain (mdn, rtd 77$): eff at 6/7f, tried 1m:
acts on fast grnd & a stiff/gall trk: runs well for an amateur
*2641 **NAISSANT** 7 [6] J S Goldie 7-10-11 (52)(5ex) Mr D Boyd (7) 5/1: 535312: 7 b m Shaadi - Nophe   1½   **54**
(Super Concorde) Chsd ldrs, chall fnl 2f & ev ch till nr fin: op 7/2: 5lb pen, in gd heart: see 2641 (C/D).
2192 **YOUNG BIGWIG** 25 [3] D W Chapman 6-11-0 (55) Miss R Clark 6/1: 034533: 6 b g Anita's Prince -   ½   **55**
Humble Mission (Shack) Held up, prog to chall 1f out, onepace nr fin: on a fair mark & a likely type for similar.
2732 **EASTERN PROPHETS** 3 [9] M Dods 7-10-10 (51)(vis) Miss A Deniel 13/2: 000044: Held up, styd on   1¾   **47**
fnl 2f, not pace to chall: spot reapp: see 1258.
*1905 **SURPRISED** 37 [4] 5-12-0 (69) Miss S Brotherton (5) 5/1: 0-0015: Chsd ldrs, held 1f out: op 4/1.   nk   **64**
2535 **ZIBAK** 11 [5] 6-9-10 (37)(4oh) Mrs C Williams 12/1: 065406: Handy, led 2f out till 1f out, fdd: op 10/1.   ½   **30**
2641 **JACMAR** 7 [7] 5-10-10 (51) Miss Diana Jones 4/1 FAV: 521037: Twds rear, nvr able to chall: op 7/2.   hd   **43**
2673 **DISTINCTIVE DREAM** 6 [8] 6-11-9 (64)(vis) Mrs S Moore (5) 12/1: 405008: Dwelt, rear, nvr on terms: 1   **47**
op 10/1, quick reapp: visor reapplied: see 1250, 598 (AW).
2233 **BAYARD LADY** 23 [1] 4-9-10 (37)(12oh) Miss K Smith (7) 66/1: 000059: Led till halfway, wknd: see 973.   1   **25**
2535 **SIX FOR LUCK** 11 [10] 8-9-10 (37)(t)(13oh) Mr Ashlee Price (7) 100/1: -00000: Cl-up 3f: 10th: rtd   15   **0**
48 in '99 (flattered, stks): last scored in '94 at Musselburgh (auct mdn, rtd 72): wears a t-strap, has worn blnks.
10 ran   Time 1m 11.6 (1.8)   (C D Barber-Lomax)   J Hetherton Malton, N Yorks

2797	7.15 JOE PUNTER NOV AUCT STKS 2YO (F) 5f Good/Firm 24 -04 Slow	
	£2843 £875 £437 £218 Raced stands side	

2237 **SHATIN DOLLYBIRD** 23 [1] Miss L A Perratt 2-8-1 A Beech (4) 7/2: 22331: 2 ch f Up And At 'Em -   **73**
Pumpona (Sharpen Up) Led/dsptd lead, went on fnl 1f, hung right but forged clr nr fin: eff at 5f, tried 6f, shld
suit in time: acts on firm & fast grnd, stiff/undul trk: can force the pace.
*2120 **MISS VERITY** 29 [4] H Akbary 2-8-4 J Stack 3/1: -6212: 2 ch f Factual - Ansellady (Absalom)   1¾   **70**
Cl-up, ev ch over 1f out, kept on to chall in last: acts on fast, gd/soft & fibresand: see 2120 (AW).
2483 **WILSON BLYTH** 14 [3] A Berry 2-8-12 P Bradley (5) 5/2: 22143: 2 b c Puissance - Pearls (Mon Tresor)   hd   **77**
Dwelt, sn led/dsptd lead, rdn/hdd 1f out & no extra: see 2237 (6f).
2698 **HAMBLETON HIGHLITE** 6 [2] A K Ryan 2-8-13 (bl) Iona Wands (5) 9/4 FAV: 13044: Cl-up, rdn halfway,   9   **61**
btn/eased fnl 1f: qck reapp: btr 2698, 1240 (C/D).
4 ran   Time 59.5 (1.4)   (Shatin Racing Group)   Miss L A Perratt, Ayr

2798	7.45 SUNDAY MAIL SELLER 3YO+ (E) 6f Good/Firm 24 -03 Slow	
	£2973 £915 £457 £228 3 yo rec 5 lb Majority racing stands side favoured	

2374 **THEOS LAD** 18 [1] R Allan 3-8-12 J McAuley (5) 9/1: 60-501: 3 b g Shareef Dancer - Inshirah (Caro)   **54**
Al prom stands side, rdn/led 1f out, styd on well, drvn out: no bid: '99 debut Catterick wnr (sell, rtd 68, R Guest):
eff over a sharp/stiff 6f, mid-dist bred: acts on firm & fast grnd: best without blnks & enjoys sell grade.
1994 **HENRY THE HAWK** 34 [2] M Dods 9-9-3 K Dalgleish (5) 16/1: 400502: 9 b g Doulab - Plum Blossom   1¼   **49$**
(Gallant Romeo) Chsd ldrs stands side, rdn/led over 1f out, hdd in last & no extra: see 756 (sell, soft).
1132 **BIRCHWOOD SUN** 78 [11] M Dods 10-9-3 J Fanning 12/1: -33403: 10 b g Bluebird - Shapely Test   1   **47**
(Elocutionist) Dwelt/rear, rdn & styd on fnl 2f, not reach front pair: 11 wk abs: see 756.
2779 **JEPAJE** 1 [6] A Bailey 3-8-12 (bl) A Beech (5) 8/1: 000644: Chsd ldrs stands side, onepace over   shd   **47**
1f out: fin 4th here yesterday (C/D): see 105 (AW).
2744 **PALACEGATE TOUCH** 2 [8] 10-9-9 P Bradley (5) 12/1: 303365: Chsd ldrs, held 1f out: quick reapp.   ½   **51**
2641 **SOUPERFICIAL** 7 [5] 9-9-3 Kim Tinkler 8/1: 020646: In tch stds side, not pace to chall: see 1073.   shd   **45**
2640 **TARTAN ISLAND** 7 [7] 3-8-12 (BL) O Pears 14/1: 002547: In tch stands side, held 1f out: blnks.   3   **38**
2721 **FACILE TIGRE** 4 [12] 5-9-3 J Bramhill 5/1: 055038: Carried badly right after 1f, led far side bef   2½   **31**
halfway, hdd over 2f out & wknd: quick reapp: see 146.
88   **LANDFALL LIL** 242 [4] 3-8-7 P Hanagan (7) 50/1: 6000-9: Nvr on terms: 6 month abs: rnr-up in '99   ½   **24**
(rtd 61, sell): eff over a stiff/undul 5f, handles fast grnd.
2744 **SIR JACK** 2 [3] 4-9-3 (bl) Iona Wands (5) 4/1 FAV: 440630: Led stands side 3f, fdd: 10th, qck reapp.   1   **27**
2641 **MISTER WESTSOUND** 7 [10] 8-9-3 (bl) N Kennedy 8/1: 000000: Rcd alone centre, al bhd: see 1654.   5   **18**
2535 **JOHS BROTHER** 11 [9] 4-9-3 Dawn Rankin (7) 66/1: /00-00: Rcd far side, overall ldr till bef halfway.   1½   **14**
12 ran   Time 1m 11.4 (1.6)   (London Gold Ltd)   R Allan Cornhill On Tweed, Northd

2799	8.15 SERIES FINAL HCAP 3YO+ (B) 1m1f36y Good/Firm 24 +16 Fast	[68]
	£10773 £3315 £1657 £828 3 yo rec 9 lb	

2242 **PENTAGON LAD** 23 [12] J L Eyre 4-9-13 (67) R Cody Boutcher (7) 13/2: 406251: 4 ch g Secret Appeal -   **74**
Gilboa (Shirley Heights) Handy, rdn/chsd ldr 2f out, led ins last, styd on strongly, drvn out: fast time: earlier
scored here at Hamilton (h'cap): '99 h'cap scorer at Carlisle, Thirsk, Ripon & Chester (rtd 75): eff btwn 1m/10.3f
on firm, gd/soft & any trk, likes Hamilton: gd weight carrier: tough gldg.
2397 **LINCOLN DEAN** 17 [4] J S Goldie 4-8-0 (40) K Dalgleish (5) 10/1: -00032: 4 b g Mtoto - Play With Me   2   **42**
(Alzao) Sn led, rdn/hdd ins last, no extra nr fin: bold front running eff, handles firm, fast & eqtrk: see 2397.
2397 **PERCHANCER** 17 [5] P C Haslam 4-9-0 (54) G Baker (7) 8/1: 134403: 4 ch g Perugino - Irish Hope   3½   **49**
(Nishapour) Rear, stdy prog fnl 3f, held ins last: see 846.

HAMILTON FRIDAY JULY 21ST Righthand, Undulating Track, Stiff Uphill Finish

2561 **SWYNFORD PLEASURE 10** [2] J Hetherton 4-8-5 (45) T Williams 6/1: 325334: Chsd ldrs 2f out, held fnl 1f. *hd* **39**
*2397 **ARIZONA LADY 17** [16] 3-9-5 (68) A Beech (5) 5/1 FAV: 003215: Chsd ldrs over 2f out, sn held. *nk* **61**
2537 **BAY OF BENGAL 11** [10] 4-8-3 (43) J McAuley (5) 14/1: -03206: Chsd ldrs 3f out, sn onepace: see 1939. *¾* **35**
2642 **NOBBY BARNES 7** [11] 11-7-10 (36)(2oh) Kim Tinkler 25/1: 230267: Dwelt/rear, late gains for press. *1* **26**
1598 **IMPULSIVE AIR 51** [1] 8-8-4 (44) J Fanning 20/1: 500208: Mid-div at best: 7 wk abs: see 569. *½* **33**
2601 **CUTE CAROLINE 8** [14] 4-8-6 (46)(vis) P Bradley (5) 14/1: 062309: Chsd ldr, btn 2f out: see 2601. *hd* **34**
2349 **FALLS OMONESS 19** [7] 6-8-9 (49) J Bramhill 14/1: 200200: Chsd ldrs 3f out, sn held: 10th: see 2062. *shd* **37**
2463 **PURSUIVANT 14** [9] 6-8-4 (44)(bl) J Stack 25/1: 320400: Rear, nvr any impress: 11th: see 2011, 446. *1¾* **29**
2719 **PHILAGAIN 4** [8] 3-7-11 (46)(1ow)(5oh) N Kennedy 25/1: 401630: Al bhd: 12th, qck reapp: see 2205. *1* **29**
2376 **FUTURE PROSPECT 18** [3] 6-9-8 (62) Dale Gibson 16/1: 0-2550: Chsd ldrs, btn over 2f out: 13th. *hd* **44**
2781 **Floorsotheforest 1** [15] 4-9-2 (56) V Halliday 33/1: 2638 **Jimgareen 7** [6] 3-8-7 (56) Iona Wands (5) 33/1:
15 ran Time 1m 54.8 (0.7) (Creskeld Racing) J L Eyre Sutton Bank, N Yorks

2800 8.45 FIELD CLASSIFIED CLAIMER 3YO+ 0-65 (F) 1m3f Good/Firm 24 -04 Slow
£2712 £775 £387 3 yo rec 11lb

*2393 **SANTA LUCIA 17** [1] M Dods 4-9-6 J Fanning 5/4 FAV: 026011: 4 b f Namaqualand - Villasanta (Corvaro) **50**
Made all, styd on well fnl 2f, drvn out: earlier scored at Hamilton (C/D clmr): suited by front running tactics at 11/12f, tried 2m1f: acts on firm & gd/soft, stiff/gall trk: enjoys clmg grade & Hamilton.
2219 **FIELD OF VISION 24** [8] Mrs A Duffield 10-9-5 A Beech (5) 4/1: 321452: 10 b g Vision - Bold Meadows *¾* **47**
(Persian Bold) Chsd ldrs, rdn to press wnr over 1f out, no extra ins last: gd run: see 1720 (gd/soft).
2780 **SECONDS AWAY 1** [6] J S Goldie 9-9-2 Dawn Rankin (7) 14/1: 433343: 9 b g Hard Fought - Keep Mum *3½* **39$**
(Mummy's Pet) Held up, prog to chall 2f out, sn no extra: ran yesterday, off rtd just 29: see 1191.
2783 **LITTLE JOHN 1** [7] Miss L A Perratt 4-9-10 (vis) K Dalgleish (5) 5/2: 432524: Held up, prog to chall *¾* **46**
2f out, sn btn: rnr-up over 12f here yesterday: see 1656.
2782 **INDIGO BAY 1** [4] 4-9-11 (tbl) O Pears 25/1: 000005: Nvr on terms: unplcd over 11f here yesterday. *7* **37**
1699 **NAVAN PROJECT 47** [5] 6-9-5 P Hanagan (7) 50/1: 50-006: Al bhd: 7 wk abs: see 1699. *½* **30$**
2538 **RED ROSES 11** [3] 4-9-1 (bl) Kim Tinkler 25/1: 000407: Al rear: see 825. *6* **17**
7 ran Time 2m 21.9 (3.1) (J A Wynn-Williams) M Dods Piercebridge, Co Durham

2801 9.15 SCOTTISHPOWER HCAP 3YO+ 0-75 (E) 1m5f Good/Firm 24 -25 Slow [65]
£3087 £950 £475 £237 3 yo rec 13lb

2643 **PAPI SPECIAL 7** [2] I Semple 3-8-4 (54) O Pears 10/1: 002401: 3 b f Tragic Role - Practical (Ballymore) **58**
Held up, rdn/prog to lead over 1f out, held on well nr fin, drvn out: 1st win: rnr-up fnl 2 '99 starts (rtd 74, auct mdn): eff at 13f on fast & soft grnd: eff with/without a visor: likes a stiff/undul trk, handles any.
2392 **ONCE MORE FOR LUCK 17** [3] Mrs M Reveley 9-10-0 (65) T Eaves (7) 7/4 FAV: 031252: 9 b g Petorius - *nk* **67**
Mrs Lucky (Royal Match) Rear, smooth prog to chall over 1f out, rdn/ev ch ins last, just held: see 2098 (C/D).
2643 **ELSIE BAMFORD 7** [1] M Johnston 4-8-13 (50) K Dalgleish (5) 5/2: 333343: 4 b f Tragic Role - Sara *¾* **51**
Sprint (Formidable) Chsd ldrs, rdn/ev ch 2f out, kept on onepace: has been v busy, a return to 14f+ could suit.
2536 **PRIDDY FAIR 11** [6] B Mactaggart 7-7-10 (33) G Baker (7) 10/1: 000/34: Led over 4f out, rdn/hdd *hd* **33**
over 1f out, kept on onepace: see 2536.
1432 **SING AND DANCE 60** [4] 7-9-1 (52) A Beech (4) 100/30: 02-255: Trkd ldrs, outpcd fnl 2f: abs: see 1147. *1¾* **50**
2098 **LORD ADVOCATE 30** [5] 12-7-10 (33)(vis)(10oh) Iona Wands (4) 20/1: 006066: Led, rdn/hdd over 4f out, *1½* **29$**
ch over 1f out, wknd: stiff task: see 1689.
6 ran Time 2m 51.9 (6.4) (Mrs E Chung) I Semple Carluke, S Lanarks

NEWMARKET (July) FRIDAY JULY 21ST Righthand, Stiff, Galloping Track

Official Going GOOD/FIRM. Stalls: Far Side; 10f+ - Stands Side.

2802 6.30 BOLLINGER AMAT HCAP 4YO+ 0-75 (E) 1m str Good/Firm 38 -16 Slow [46]
£3679 £1132 £566 £283 2 Groups - no apparent advantage

2347 **PADHAMS GREEN 20** [3] B W Hills 4-11-5 (65) Mr C B Hills (3) 13/2: 0-3621: 4 b g Aragon - Double **69**
Dutch (Nicholas Bill) Chsd ldr far side, overall ldr over 1f out, drifted badly right fnl 1f but styd on, pushed out: in '99 trained by M Tompkins to win at Salisbury (appr h'cap, rtd 69): suited by 1m on gd, fm & a stiff trk.
*2508 **YEAST 13** [13] W J Haggas 8-12-0 (74) Mr O Jennings (7) 9/2 JT FAV: 020112: 8 b g Salse - *¾* **77**
Orient (Bay Express) Led stands side group, hdd over 1f out, kept on: nicely bckd: in fine form, see 2508.
2682 **IRON MOUNTAIN 6** [14] N A Callaghan 5-11-13 (73)(5ex) Mr S Callaghan (7) 7/1: 340143: 5 b g Scenic *1* **74**
- Merlannah (Shy Groom) Chsd ldr stands side, onepace over 1f out: qk reapp: back to form, see 2564.
2349 **DERRYQUIN 19** [17] P L Gilligan 5-11-0 (60)(bl) Mr J Best (7) 14/1: 010204: Handy stands side, *1½* **59**
onepace over 1f out: not disgraced: see 2027, 1296.
2412 **MISSILE TOE 16** [15] 7-10-5 (51) Mr Paul J Morris (5) 9/2 JT FAV: 541165: Bhd stands side, late gains. *shd* **50**
2556 **SILVER SECRET 10** [16] 6-10-0 (46) Mr T Best (5) 9/1: 051606: Prom stands side, outpcd over 1f out, *½* **44**
late gains: best at 10f now as in 1819.
2727 **TWOFORTEN 3** [11] 5-9-10 (42)(4oh) Mr R Lucey Butler (7) 40/1: 365007: Bhd stands side, late gains. *nk* **39**
2612 **DARYABAD 8** [6] 8-9-13 (45)(bl) Mr K Santana (5) 10/1: 6-0038: Nvr a factor on stands side, see 2612. *¾* **40**
2564 **QUALITAIR PRIDE 10** [1] 8-9-10 (42)(3oh) Mr Nicky Tinkler (5) 14/1: /01009: Led far side over 4f. *6* **25**
2622 **CLASSIC EAGLE 8** [5] 7-10-4 (50) Mr S Rees (5) 40/1: 4-0000: In tch far side, wknd over 2f out: 10th. *1¾* **29**
2347 **TOUJOURS RIVIERA 20** [9] 10-11-5 (62)(3ow) Mr A Page (0) 33/1: 002/00: Prom stands side, wknd over **0**
2f out: well btn sole '99 start: in '98 won at Lingfield (h'cap, 80a & 76): eff over 1m/12f on firm, soft & both a/w's.
2049 **Qualitair Survivor 32** [4] 5-9-10 (42)(7oh) Mr V Lukaniuk (3) 33/1:
2556 **Alcove 10** [7] 9-10-7 (46)(bl)(7ow) Dr M Allingham (0) 50/1:
2542 **High Sun 11** [10] 4-10-4 (50)(bl) Mr B Hitchcott 14/1:
2011 **Crungh Express 34** [2] 4-10-5 (51)(bl) Mr R Barrett (5) 20/1:
1772 **Beguile 44** [8] 6-10-2 (48)(t) Mr M Regan (7) 25/1:
16 ran Time 1m 41.55 (4.35) (Mrs B W Hills) B W Hills Lambourn, Berks

2803

6.55 R.G. CARTER COND STKS 3YO+ (C)   1m4f   Good/Firm 38   +20 Fast
£6572   £2332   £1166   £530   3 yo rec 12lb

2028 **LIGHTNING ARROW** 33 [4] J L Dunlop 4-8-13 T Quinn 3/1: 0-0241: 4 br g Silver Hawk - Strait Lane 109
(Chieftain II) Led over 3f out, pushed clr to assert ins last: fast time: dual '99 rnr-up (Gr 3, rtd 105):
'98 Newmarket scorer (stks, rtd 103+): eff btwn 10/13.3f on firm & gd/soft, not hvy: handles any trk: best
without blnks: best up with/forcing the pace: v useful, apprec drop into stks class.
2502 **RAIN IN SPAIN** 13 [2] J Noseda 4-8-13 R Hughes 3/1: 324002: 4 b c Unfuwain - Maria Isabella (Young 4 102
Generation) In tch, keen, ev ch chase wnr over 1f out, sn outpcd: ran to best: see 2502, 732.
2169 **RASM** 27 [1] A C Stewart 3-8-4 R Hills 5/6 FAV: 3-123: 3 b c Darshaan - Northshiel (Northfields) 4 99
Cl up, ev ch over 2f out till wknd fnl 1f: well bckd: is bred to stay this trip: btr 2169 (10f).
2351 **ELA ARISTOKRATI** 19 [3] M A Jarvis 8-8-13 P Robinson 16/1: 436/64: Led till over 3f out, wknd, eased. 23 56
4 ran   Time 2m 30.34 (2.14)   (Wafic Said)   J L Dunlop Arundel, West Sussex

2804

7.25 FILLIES HCAP 3YO+ 0-80 (D)   6f   Good/Firm 38   -05 Slow   [78]
£4348   £1338   £669   £334   3 yo rec 5 lb

2684 **GLOWING** 6 [7] J R Fanshawe 5-9-12 (76) R Cochrane 7/4 FAV: -20241: 5 ro m Chilibang - Juliet Bravo 80
(Glow) Hld up, not clr run 2f out, hdwy over 1f out, styd on well to lead ins last, drvn out: fast time: in '99
won at Nottingham & Doncaster (h'caps, rtd 76): '98 wnr at Folkestone (auct mdn, rtd 72): eff at 5/6f on firm &
gd/soft: runs well fresh: R Cochrane has clearly lost none of his strength following injuries sustained in an air-crash.
1892 **CARINTHIA** 38 [1] C F Wall 5-8-10 (60) R Mullen 6/1: -00202: 5 br m Tirol - Hot Lavender (Shadeed) ½ 62
Led till ins last, not pace of wnr: not btn far: shld win a fill h'cap off this mark: see 1511.
2747 **LA PIAZZA** 2 [4] W J Haggas 4-10-0 (78) J P Spencer 9/2: 000023: 4 ch f Polish Patriot - Blazing Glory 1½ 76
(Glow) Hld up, hdwy to chase wnr over 1f out, no extra ins last: qk reappr: see 2747.
2637 **GUEST ENVOY** 7 [2] C N Allen 5-7-12 (48) M Henry 16/1: 555054: Chsd ldr, onepace over 1f out. 1¾ 42
2549 **FLEETING FANCY** 11 [8] 3-8-1 (56) N Pollard 14/1: -03005: Went right start, bhd, eff & short of room 1 47
over 1f out, no impress: mdn, see 2371.
*2280 **CUPIDS CHARM** 22 [5] 3-9-9 (78) J Mackay (5) 5/1: 001016: Prom, hampd when held over 1f out. ½ 67
2207 **WAX LYRICAL** 25 [6] 4-9-10 (74) P Robinson 7/1: 0-0007: Keen cl up, wkng when hmpd over 1f out. 3½ 53
2673 **SWYNFORD WELCOME** 6 [3] 4-7-10 (46) G Bardwell 14/1: 000108: Handy, wknd 2f out: inconsistent. ½ 23
8 ran   Time 1m 13.57 (2.57)   (Peters Friends)   J R Fanshawe Newmarket

2805

7.55 ANT HCAP 3YO+ 0-95 (C)   1m2f   Good/Firm 38   -05 Slow   [89]
£7241   £2228   £1114   £557   3 yo rec 10lb

2157 **BAILEYS PRIZE** 27 [8] M Johnston 3-8-8 (79) M Hills 6/1: 622231: 3 ch c Mister Baileys - Mar Mar 1 83
(Forever Casting) Hld up hdwy over 4f out, chall over 1f out, kept on, fin 2nd btn 1L, awarded race: earlier won
at Redcar (h'cap) & plcd sev times: suited by 10f on firm, gd/soft, fibresand & a gall trk: tough & consistent.
2475 **HUDOOD** 14 [3] C E Brittain 5-10-0 (89) T E Durcan 7/1: 35001D: 5 ch h Gone West - Fife (Lomond) 95
Hld up, hdwy & barged through over 2f out, led over 1f out, kept on, rdn out: subs disq & plcd last, jockey rec a
5-day irresponsible riding ban: top-weight: acts on fast, soft & dirt: deserves similar, see 1850.
-2178 **MYNAH** 26 [5] A C Stewart 3-9-4 (89) R Hills 6/1: 0122: 4 gr f Linamix - Thank One's Stars 2½ 89
(Alzao) Hld up, short of room over 2f out, hdwy over 1f out, onepace: fin 3rd, plcd 2nd: consistent, see 2178.
2263 **BE THANKFULL** 302 [2] Major D N Chappell 4-9-10 (85) J Reid 12/1: 621-53: Led till over 1f out. 3½ 80
4060} **INDUCEMENT** 302 [4] 4-9-8 (83) R Hughes 8/1: 6400-4: In tch, lost plc 4f out, late gains: in '99 1¾ 75
won at Sandown (h'cap, rtd 88, with B Hills): stays 10f on fast, soft & on a gall trk.
2614 **KINGSDON** 8 [6] 3-9-7 (92)(t) Dane O'Neill 12/1: 630065: Slow away, bhd, hmpd over 2f out, no dngr. nk 83
2372 **FLAG FEN** 18 [7] 9-8-2 (63) C Cogan (5) 20/1: -06206: Chsd ldr, wknd over 1f out: btr 1875. 4 48
*2423 **WILLIE CONQUER** 16 [1] 8-9-0 (75) M Henry 9/4 FAV: -10017: Hld up, btn over 2f out: best ¾ 59
in claimers/sellers around Brighton as in 2423.
*2135 **LUXOR** 28 [9] 3-9-7 (92) T Quinn 14/1: 4218: In tch, hmpd & wknd over 2f out: bckd, btr 2135. dist 0
9 ran   Time 2m 06.16 (4.26)   (Mrs Val Armstrong)   M Johnston Middleham, N Yorks

2806

8.25 BUPA FILLIES MDN 2YO (D)   7f str   Good/Firm 38   -13 Slow
£4264   £1312   £656   £328

-- **CRYSTAL MUSIC** [5] J H M Gosden 2-8-11 J Fortune 5/4 FAV: 1: 2 b f Nureyev - Crystal Spray 105
(Beldale Flutter) Slow away, hdwy to lead over 2f out, kept on well, pushed out: well bckd: Feb foal: half
sister to wnrs over 7f & an Irish Derby 3rd: dam 14f wnr: eff at 7f, will relish 1m+ in time: acts on fast
grnd & runs well fresh on a stiff trk: looks useful, win in better company.
-- **ELREHAAN** [3] J L Dunlop 2-8-11 R Hills 5/2: 2: 2 b f Sadler's Wells - Moss (Woodman) 5 93
Chsd ldr, led over 3f out till over 2f out, not pace of wnr: Mar foal: cost 190,000 gns: bred to need 1m+.
-- **DUCHCOV** [4] L M Cumani 2-8-11 J P Spencer 2/1: 3: 2 ch f Caerleon - Amandine (Darshaan) hd 93
Cl up, outpcd 2f out, some late gains: 65,000 gns May foal: sister to a 1m wnr: dam 1m scorer: needs 1m.
2174 **VINCENTIA** 26 [6] C Smith 2-8-11 M Roberts 14/1: 04: Led till over 3f out: Apr foal, cost 2,300 14 71
gns: half sister to a 12f wnr: bred to apprec 7f+.
4 ran   Time 1m 27.5 (3.6)   (Lord Lloyd-Webber)   J H M Gosden Manton, Wilts

2807

8.55 INJURED JOCKEYS MDN 3YO+ (D)   6f   Good/Firm 38   -25 Slow
£4160   £1280   £640   £320   3 yo rec 5 lb   Slow run race

4607} **STRONG PRESENCE** 259 [2] T P Tate 3-9-0 T Lucas 4/1: 5-1: 3 b c Anshan - Lazybird Blue (Bluebird) 82
Led till over 1f out, rallied v gamely to get up again cl home, drvn out: reapp, bckd: rtd 80 when 5th sole '99
start in a back-end mdn: stays 6f on fast & hvy: acts on a stiff trk.
1951 **DOUBLE PLATINUM** 36 [4] J H M Gosden 3-8-9 J Fortune 2/1: 00-362: 3 ch f Seeking The Gold - Band hd 76
(Northern Dancer) In tch, eff over 1f out, kept on ins last, just held: see 1951, 1609.
2294 **MUKAABED** 21 [1] M P Tregoning 3-9-0 R Hills 6/4 FAV: 30-23: 3 ch c Phone Trick - Slick Delivery ¾ 79
(Topsider) Keen cl up, hdwy to lead over 1f out, collared cl home, not btn far: bckd: ran to form of 2294.
2582 **WHISTLER** 9 [3] R Hannon 3-9-0 Dane O'Neill 4/1: 203-24: Chsd ldr, chall ins last, no extra cl home. nk 78

NEWMARKET (July)
FRIDAY JULY 21ST   Righthand, Stiff, Galloping Track

4 ran   Time 1m 14.8 (3.8)   (T P Tate)   T P Tate Tadcaster, N Yorks

NEWBURY
FRIDAY JULY 21ST   Lefthand, Flat Galloping Track

Official Going   GOOD/FIRM. Stalls: Str Crse - Stands' Side; 10f - Inside; Rem - Outside.

2808   2.00 EBF ECCHINSWELL NOV STKS 2YO (D)   6f str   Firm -06   -06 Slow
£4992   £1536   £768   £394

-- **ENDLESS SUMMER** [7] J H M Gosden 2-8-8 J Fortune 4/6 FAV: -1: 2 b c Zafonic - Well Away (Sadler's **96+**
Wells) Trkd ldrs going well, imprvd to lead 1½f out, pushed clr under hands-&-heels: hvly bckd, impressive,
gd juv time: Jan foal, dam a 1m 2yo wnr in France, from a v gd family: sire a top-class miler: eff at 6f, 7f will
suit: acts on firm grnd & on a gall trk: runs well fresh: potentially smart colt who holds a Gr 1 entry.

*1924 **MAN OF DISTINCTION** 37 [8] D R C Elsworth 2-9-2 T Quinn 5/1: -512: 2 b c Spectrum - Air Of   2½ **90**
Distinction (Distinctly North) Prom, ev ch dist, kept on well, but not pace of impressive wnr: op 4/1: met an
above average rival & shld sn be winning again: 7f will now suit: see 1924.

*2454 **OUR DESTINY** 14 [10] A P Jarvis 2-9-2 N Callan 9/1: -013: 2 b c Mujadil - Superspring   1½ **86**
(Superlative) In tch, kept on nicely under hands-&-heels riding: mkt drifter: gd effort in this better company.

-- **FAITHFUL WARRIOR** [9] B W Hills 2-8-8 J Reid 11/2: -4: Rcd freely & set pace till 1½f out, grad fdd   ¾ **75**
on debut: tchd 7/1: Apr foal, half brother to sev decent performers: dam a smart miler: shld apprec 7f, but
needs to learn some restraint: will prove better than this.

2529 **SPEEDY GEE** 12 [6] 2-9-5 Craig Williams 14/1: -36105: Rear, slightly short of room 2f out, no   ½ **85**
impress in last: op 8/1: not quite stay 6f? see 2529 (5f).

1221 **PRINCE MILLENNIUM** 72 [9] 2-8-12 Dane O'Neill 12/1: -56: Mid-div, rdn & no impress fnl 1f: 10 wk abs.   hd **78**

2563 **PORT MORESBY** 10 [2] 2-8-12 J F Egan 40/1: -07: Pushed in rear, btn over 1f out: see 2563.   hd **78**

2189 **CHARENTE** 25 [5] 2-8-12 M Roberts 33/1: -58: Rdn in rear, al outpcd: will find easier races.   1 **75**

*2488 **FACTUAL LAD** 13 [1] 2-9-2 Jonjo Fowle 11/1: 332319: Rcd centre & prom 4f, wknd & eased: 6 **64**
prob not suited by racing away from rivals: much better than this, see 2488 (mdn auct).

9 ran   Time 1m 11.65 (0.05)   (K Abdulla)   J H M Gosden Manton, Wilts

---

2809   2.30 ANAC COND STKS 3YO+ (B)   7f str   Firm -06   +34 Fast
£9674   £3669   £1834   £834   3yo rec 7lb

2087 **THREE POINTS** 30 [8] J L Dunlop 3-8-4 T Quinn 2/1 FAV: -32441: 3 b c Bering - Trazl (Zalazl)   **113**
Made all, qcknd clr fnl 1f, v easily: well bckd, impressive, broke trk rec by 2secs!: gd 4th in Gr 3 Jersey at R
Ascot prev: Kempton (mdn) & Nottingham (nov, rtd 103) wnr in '99: stays 10f, suited by 7f: acts on gd & firm grnd:
handles a stiff or easy trk: can run well fresh: front runner, who has a smart turn of foot: smart colt who shld
win in List or Gr company & hds to Glorious Goodwood in top form.

1623 **GLAD MASTER** 55 [4] Saeed bin Suroor 3-8-7 D O'Donohoe 11/1: 11-002: 3b c Big Shuffle - Glady   4 **107**
Star (Star Appeal) In tch, eff 2f out, kept on but no ch with impressive wnr: 8 wk abs: back to form, acts on
firm & soft grnd: stiff task conceding weight to a smart rival: see 1623.

2528 **SPEEDFIT TOO 12** [3] C E Brittain 5-9-0 (vis) T E Durcan 9/4: 040123: 5 b h Scenic - Safka (Irish   2½ **102**
River) Mid-div, eff 2f out, kept on without troubling ldrs: bckd from 7/2: return to 1m will suit: see 2528, 2229.

1830 **CATCHY WORD** 42 [9] E A L Dunlop 3-8-4 G Carter 11/1: 1-2054: In tch, eff 2f out, onepcd fnl 1f: shd **99**
6 wk abs: needs 1m now & worth another chance when stable back in form: see 1830 (List).

2616 **OMAHA CITY** 8 [5] 6-8-11 C Rutter 25/1: 6-0005: Rear, outpcd 2f out, mod late prog under a kind   1¾ **95+**
ride: bckd at long adds: stiff task at today's weights, likes Goodwood & one to keep in mind for a h'cap there.

1834 **ADJUTANT** 41 [1] 5-9-0 P Robinson 20/1: 031206: Rear, mod late prog, nvr dngrs: stiffish task at   hd **98**
these weights, 6 wk abs: see 1514, 1286.

2343 **LOTS OF MAGIC** 20 [6] 4-8-11 Dane O'Neill 10/1: 0-6007: Prom, drvn & wknd 2f out: see 2343, 734.   1¼ **92**

2389 **GRANNYS PET** 17 [10] 6-9-3 J Fortune 12/1: 1-3168: Chsd ldrs, wknd 1½f out: top-weight: see 1574.   1 **96**

2389 **TROUBLE MOUNTAIN** 17 [7] 3-8-7 J Reid 12/1: 32-659: Mid-div, improving when hmpd 2f out, sn btn: shd **93**
not much luck & better than this: see 969.

9 ran   Time 1m 21.50 (u2.80) Crse Record   (Hesmonds Stud)   J L Dunlop Arundel, W Sussex

---

2810   3.00 TATTERSALLS FILLIES AUCT MDN 2YO (E)   7f str   Firm -06   -27 Slow
£4446   £1368   £684   £342

2459 **TRUMPINGTON** 14 [9] I A Balding 2-8-0 A Nicholls (3) 7/1: -031: 2 ch f First Trump - Brockton Flame   **76**
(Emarati) Set pace till 2f out, rallied gamely to reagin lead cl home, rdn out: dam a 6f wnr: eff at 7f on firm
grnd, handles gd: handles a stiff, gall trk: likes to run up with or force the pace: game effort here.

2182 **TRUSTTHUNDER** 26 [10] N P Littmoden 2-8-0 J Tate 15/8 FAV: -022: 2 ch f Selkirk - Royal Cat (Royal   hd **75**
Academy) Trkd ldrs going v well, led 2f out, rdn & caught cl home: well bckd: acts on fast & firm grnd: lkd all
over the wnr today, reportedly saw much to much daylight: prob worth another chance: see 2182.

1589 **TEMPLES TIME** 51 [11] R Hannon 2-8-2 J F Egan 10/3: -43: 2 b f Distinctly North - Midnight Patrol   3 **71**
(Ashmore) Chsd ldrs, rdn & kept on but no pace of first 2: 7 wk abs: longer 7f trip, prob needs further.

1924 **KWAHERI** 36 [6] Mrs P N Dutfield 2-8-6 L Newman (3) 14/1: -R04: Rdn in rear, fin well into 4th,   hd **75**
no ch with ldrs: better effort over this more suitable trip, 1m will suit: see 762.

2545 **JETHAME** 11 [2] 2-8-2 D R McCabe 9/2: -0035: Rcd keenly in rear, short of room 2f out, no impress   nk **70**
till ran on cl home: tchd 11/2: handles firm & soft: see 2545.

2259 **DIVAS ROBE** 23 [5] 2-8-4 P Robinson 25/1: -66: In tch, eff 2f out, fdd ins last: see 2259.   hd **72**

2459 **DAWN ROMANCE** 14 [7] 2-8-0 Craig Williams 12/1: -0057: Rear, switched centre 2f out, kept on under   ½ **67+**
a kind ride: nursery h'caps shld suit & one to keep in mind: see 2459, 1876.

-- **PERSIAN SPIRIT** [3] 2-8-2 P Fitzsimons (5) 14/1: -8: In tch centre, ch 2f out, grad fdd: mkt   nk **68**
drifter, stablemate of 3rd: 8,800gns Feb foal: half sister to a 6f juv wnr: sire a high-class miler: with R Hannon.

2459 **STRATH FILLAN** 14 [1] 2-8-0 A Daly 33/1: -009: Prom till wknd 2f out: see 2459, 1864.   ¾ **64**

-- **GOLDEN WINGS** [4] 2-8-5(1ow) Dane O'Neill 10/1: -0: Chsd ldrs 3f, sn wknd & bhnd: debut: Feb   6 **57**
foal, cost 13,000gns: dam a 6/7f juv wnr: with B Smart.

-- **POCKET VENUS** [8] 2-8-2 P Doe 40/1: -0: Bmpd leaving stalls & nearly u.r., al well bhnd: unfortunate   23 **4**
debut: Feb foal cost 5,500gns: first foal, dam a 12f wnr: with M Salaman, forget this.

11 ran   Time 1m 25.83 (1.53)   (Park House Partnership)   I A Balding Kingsclere, Berks

878

2811
3.30 P JONES FILL HCAP 3YO 0-80 (D)   1m2f   Firm -06 -78 Slow   **[83]**
£4368   £1344   £672   £336

2330 **ROSHANI** 20 [3] M R Channon 3-9-5 (74) Craig Williams 6/1: -21061: 3 b f Kris - Maratona (Be My Guest) Prom, eff 2f out, styd on well to lead line under hands-&-heels riding: slow time: earlier won at Newcastle (fill mdn): eff at 1m/10f on firm & hvy: handles a stiff, gall trk or sharp trk: well rdn by C Williams here. **77**

2581 **SAFARI BLUES** 9 [1] R Hannon 3-9-7 (76) R Hughes 9/2: 1-5052: 3 b f Blues Traveller - North Hut (Northfields) Tried to make all, drvn & caught on line: bckd from 6/1, top-weight: game front running eff, deserves to go one better: stays a stiff 10f well: see 54 (AW). **shd 78**

2581 **DIVINE PROSPECT** 9 [7] A P Jarvis 3-8-12 (67) N Callan 9/4 FAV: 564023: 3 br f Namaqualand - Kayu (Tap On Wood) Rear & rcd wide, prog & ch 2f out, onepcd ins fnl 1f: well bckd: stays 10f: bt this 2nd in 2581 (9f). **3 64**

1697 **MOUJEEDA** 48 [4] W Jarvis 3-9-0 (69) T Quinn 11/4: 0-504: Mid-div, rdn 3f out, kept on for press till onepcd ins fnl 1f: well bckd, 7 wk abs: h'cap bow: see 1281 (mdn). **nk 65**

2025 **RIBBON LAKE** 33 [5] 3-8-5 (60) L Newman (3) 25/1: 0-0005: Pushed in mid-div, outpcd fnl 1½f. **3 51**

2036 **CLEAR CRYSTAL** 32 [8] 3-7-10 (51)(t)(3oh) D Glennon (2) 12/1: -60066: Trkd ldr till wknd 1½f out. **nk 41**

2426 **VERDURA** 16 [6] 3-9-1 (70) P Doe 12/1: 0-647: Rear, bhnd fnl 2f: h'cap bow: see 2426. **2½ 56**

2206 **CUMBRIAN PRINCESS** 25 [3] 3-7-10 (51)(3oh) Jonjo Fowle(1) 14/1: -00068: Chsd ldrs, wknd over 2f out. **5 29**

8 ran   Time 2m 10.07 (7.27)   (Sheikh Ahmed Al Maktoum)   M R Channon West Ilsley, Berks

2812
4.00 NEWBURY HCAP 3YO+ 0-85 (D)   2m   Firm -06 -25 Slow   **[82]**
£4342   £1336   £668   £334   3yo rec 17lb

2455 **BID ME WELCOME** 14 [3] Miss D A McHale 4-9-7 (75) J Reid 11/1: 005231: 4 b g Alzao - Blushing Barada (Blushing Groom) Mid-div, prog to lead 1½f out, sn clr, rdn out: stays 2m well: acts on gd & firm grnd, handles soft: handles any trk, runs well fresh: gd weight carrier who can force the pace: well h'capped, won well here & could follow up. **80**

*2461 **RENAISSANCE LADY** 14 [2] T R Watson 4-8-2 (56) Craig Williams 9/2: 001112: 4 ch f Society - Easter Morning (Nice Havrais) Early ldr, chsd ldrs & ev ch 2f out, kept on well, but no ch with wnr: met a well h'capped rival & not disgraced on bid for 4-timer: see 2461. **1½ 58**

2195 **PENSHIEL** 25 [6] J L Dunlop 3-8-4 (75) T Quinn 1/1 FAV: 0-1123: 3 b g Mtoto - Highland Ceilidh (Scottish Reel) Led after 3f till 1½f out, no extra: hvly bckd: has won on firm grnd prev, but did not look totally at home on it here: prob stayed this longer 2m trip: see 2195 (14f), 1911 (12f). **hd 77**

*2763 **LITTLE BRAVE** 2 [5] J M P Eustace 5-8-6 (60)(6ex) J Tate 7/2: 460514: Trkd ldrs, ev ch 2f out, onepcd fnl 1f: qck reappb & 6lb pen since 2763. **1½ 60**

2164 **STAR RAGE** 27 [5] 10-9-13 (81) M Roberts 10/1: 0F2255: Chsd ldrs, rdn & ch 2f out, onepcd: tchd 14/1. **¾ 80**

2131 **WOODYS BOY** 28 [1] 6-8-9 (63) A Daly 11/1: 231/56: Rear, eff 3f out, nvr nr ldrs: op 14/1. **3½ 58**

2584 **URGENT SWIFT** 9 [4] 7-9-0 (68) D Harrison 16/1: 101247: Rear, prog on outer 3f out, sn held & eased. **4 59**

-- **NAVARRE SAMSON** [7] 5-9-1 (69) L Newman(3) 33/1: 3002/8: Mid-div, bhnd fnl 2f, t.o.: missed '99: prev term trained in France (plcd over 10f): 99/00 nov h'cap hdle wnr at Stratford (rtd 117h, eff at 2m/2m6f on firm & soft): 5 times wnr in 98/99 (tried blnks): with P Hobbs. **24 35**

8 ran   Time 3m 29.13 (3.13)   (P Burban)   Miss D A McHale

2813
4.30 TOTE JACKPOT HCAP 3YO+ 0-95 (C)   6f str   Firm -06 +03 Fast   **[94]**
£7052   £2170   £1085   £542   3yo rec 5lb

2334 **ALPEN WOLF** 20 [9] W R Muir 5-9-5 (85) T Quinn 5/1: 102101: 5 ch g Wolfhound - Oatfield (Great Nephew) Trkd ldrs, strong run to lead ins fnl 1f, rdn out: earlier won at Bath & Warwick (class stks): '99 wnr at Brighton & Bath (h'caps, rtd 79): '98 wnr at Brighton (3) & Folkestone (class stks, rtd 71): eff at 5/7f, acts on firm & fast grnd: handles any trk, loves Brighton: gd weight carrier, can force the pace: tough & genuine. **89**

2586 **HUNTING TIGER** 9 [7] M R Channon 3-7-13 (68)(2ow) Craig Williams 10/1: 000052: 3 ch g Pursuit Of Love - Pernilla (Tate Gallery) Rear, prog to lead dist, collared ins last, just btn: 2lbs over weight proved v costly: back to form & v well h'capped: win sn: see 792. **nk 73**

2660 **BRAVE EDGE** 7 [3] R Hannon 9-9-4 (84) R Hughes 9/2: 230423: 9 b g Beveled - Daring Ditty (Daring March) Rear, short of room 2f out, ran on well, nvr nrr: op 7/2: another sound run but tricky to win with. **¾ 84**

2631 **SLUMBERING** 8 [4] B J Meehan 4-8-4 (70)(bl) D R McCabe 8/1: 000634: Set pace till collared dist, kept on: gd run, deserves similar: see 2631. **nk 69**

2504 **ROO** 13 [5] 3-9-7 (92) J Reid 9/4 FAV: 653225: Dwelt, prog 2f out, no impress ins last: well bckd: lost all chance at the start today: see 2504, 2101. **2 85**

2577 **MISTER SUPERB** 9 [2] 3-8-12 (83) G Hind 12/1: 302106: Chsd ldrs, ch 2f out, fdd ins last: btr 2183 (mdn). **nk 75**

2151 **EASY DOLLAR** 28 [8] 8-9-9 (89)(bl) C Rutter 9/1: 06-607: Dwelt, sn prom, wknd 2f out: see 1674. **nk 80**

1999 **PETARGA** 34 [6] 5-8-8 (74) S Whitworth 11/1: 300-08: Waited with, nvr in it: see 1999. **nk 64**

2451 **JUWWI** 15 [1] 6-10-0 (94) P Fitzsimons(5) 9/1: 500009: Speed on outside, onepcd fnl 1f: op 13/2. **nk 83**

9 ran   Time 1m 11.01 (u0.59)   (R Haim)   W R Muir Lambourn, Berks

2814
5.00 LEVY BOARD HCAP 3YO+ 0-85 (D)   7f64y rnd   Firm -06 -03 Slow   **[80]**
£4030   £1240   £620   £310   3yo rec 7lb

2707 **ZUCCHERO** 5 [3] D W P Arbuthnot 4-9-10 (76)(bl) J Weaver 7/2: 126-61: 4 br g Dilum - Legal Sound (Legal Eagle) Broke well & made all, styd on strongly fnl 1f, drvn out: qck reappb, gamble from 7/1: '99 wnr at Chepstow (mdn h'cap), Lingfield & Newmarket (h'caps, rtd 79): eff at 6/7f, will stay 1m: acts on fast & firm grnd & on any trk: tried a visor, best in blnks: loves to force the pace: useful h'capper. **82**

2133 **SURPRISE ENCOUNTER** 28 [5] E A L Dunlop 4-9-12 (78) J Reid 1/1 FAV: -00542: 4 ch g Cadeaux Genereux - Scandalette (Niniski) Waited with, prog to chase wnr dist, kept on but nvr lkd like getting there: well bckd, top-weight: stable back in form & one to keep in mind back over 1m: eye-catching in 2133. **1 81**

2508 **TEOFILIO** 13 [2] A J McNae 6-9-3 (69)(bl) T G McLaughlin 9/2: 000023: 6 ch h Night Shift - Rivoltade (Sir Ivor) Rcd keenly in tch, rdn & onepcd fnl 1f: knocking on the door: see 2508. **1½ 69**

2504 **EASTWAYS** 13 [4] M Johnston 3-9-8 (81) M Roberts 15/2: 000004: Chsd ldrs, onepcd fnl 2f: clr rem. **1 79**

2775 **SUSANS PRIDE** 1 [7] 4-9-10 (76) S Clancy 12/1: 303405: Rdn in rear, late hdwy but nvr dngrs: unplcd at Leicester 24hrs prev: see 792. **3½ 67**

1631 **TRAJAN** 50 [1] 3-9-2 (75) N Callan 16/1: 55-406: Trkd ldr 4f, grad fdd: 7 wk abs: see 651 (AW). **8 51**

2546 **GLENDALE RIDGE** 11 [8] 5-9-0 (66) J F Egan 33/1: -44407: Chsd ldrs till wknd 2f out: btr 2129 (9f). **shd 42**

NEWBURY FRIDAY JULY 21ST Lefthand, Flat Galloping Track

2431 MINT LEAF 16 [6] 3-8-1 (60)(t) P Doe 50/1: 0-0008: Nvr a factor, t.o. fnl 1f: see 2431. 15 6
8 ran Time 1m 27.58 (u0.22) (Philip Banfield) D W P Arbuthnot Compton, Berks

SOUTHWELL (Fibresand) FRIDAY JULY 21ST Lefthand, Sharp, Oval Track

Official Going STANDARD. Stalls: 5f - Outside, Rem - Inside.

2815 2.20 BET DIRECT HCAP 3YO 0-65 (F) 1m4f aw Going 42 -34 Slow [67]
£2261 £646 £323

2624 BAHAMAS 8 [3] Sir Mark Prescott 3-9-7 (60)(bl) S Sanders 2/1 FAV: -12331: 3 b g Barathea - Rum 70a
Cay (Our Native) Outpcd early, clsd on bit halfway, led 4f out, bckd, front 2 clr: prev won at Redcar
(h'cap): only beat 4 horses home in 4 '99 starts (mdn, rtd 61): half-brother to smart stayer Persian Punch:
eff at 10/12f, shld get further: acts on gd grnd & fibresand: eff with/without blnks, sharp or gall trks: improving.
4613} FURNESS 258 [8] J G Smyth Osbourne 3-9-1 (54) F Norton 20/1: -000-2: 3 b g Emarati - Thelma 1¾ 60a
(Blakeney) Led till 4f out, styd on for press but being held by wnr: clr of 3rd on reapp/turf/h'cap bow: unplcd in
3 '99 starts (auct mdn, rtd 59): apprec step up to 12f on fibresand: suited by forcing the pace.
2012 OCEAN SONG 34 [7] S R Bowring 3-9-4 (57) Dean McKeown 20/1: 003003: 3 b f Savahra Sound - Marina 7 56a
Plata (Julio Mariner) Sn feeling pace & rdn rear, plodded on for 3rd, nvr nr ldrs: worth another try at 12f, see 794.
2179 DOCTOR JOHN 26 [6] Andrew Turnell 3-9-7 (60) P Fessey 25/1: 0044: Nvr dngrs tho' staying on fin. ¾ 58a
2672 WINDMILL LANE 6 [2] 3-9-3 (56) M Fenton 9/4: 021035: Nvr a factor: down in trip, flattered 6 days ago. 1¼ 52a
409 SUBADAR MAJOR 176 [4] 3-7-10 (35)(5oh) Angela Hartley (5) 66/1: 0-006: Chsd ldrs till halfway: abs. 5 26a
2540 MIDDLETHORPE 11 [5] 3-9-2 (55) T Lucas 7/2: 051037: In tch, went 3rd 4f out, sn wknd: AW bow. 6 40a
2520 NINETEENNINETYNINE 12 [9] 3-8-13 (52) I Mongan (5) 25/1: 6-0058: Prom till halfway: much lngr trip. 21 17a
2295 ESTABLISHED 21 [10] 3-7-10 (35)(bl)(1oh) Claire Bryan (5) 12/1: 503559: Pressed ldr 6f: blnks reapplied.6 0a
1767 LOBLITE LEADER 44 [11] 3-8-1 (40) G Bardwell 33/1: -00040: In tch 6f out: 10th, 6 wk abs, AW bow. 10 0a
10 ran Time 2m 43.4 (9.1) (Eclipse Thoro'breds - Osborne House III) Sir Mark Prescott Newmarket.

2816 2.50 UNIVERSAL CLAIMER 3YO+ 0-65 (F) 1m aw rnd Going 42 -29 Slow
£2254 £644 £322 3yo rec 8 lb

2302 TROJAN WOLF 21 [10] P Howling 5-9-8 D Holland 7/1: 000061: 5 ch g Wolfhound - Trojan Lady (Irish 69a
River) Cl-up, rdn to lead 2f out, drvn out: back in Jan won at W'hampton (amat h'cap): late '99 wnr here
at Southwell (2, h'caps, rtd 58 & 56a): rtd 76 in '98 for M Tompkins: eff at 1m/11f: best up with/forcing
the pace on firm, gd grnd, equitrack, loves fibresand/Southwell: best without t-strap on sharp tracks.
2634 PIPPAS PRIDE 7 [8] S R Bowring 5-9-5 S Finnamore (5) 11/4 FAV: 500302: 5 ch g Pips Pride - Al Shany 1½ 62a
(Burslem) Chsd ldrs, ev ch ent fnl 2f, held nr fin: clr of 3rd, qck reapp, t-strap omitted: btr 473 (C/D h'cap).
2080 STANDIFORD GIRL 30 [4] J G Given 3-7-13 M Henry 10/1: 620003: 3 b f Standiford - Pennine Girl 5 40a
(Pennine Walk) Outpcd wide, styd on late for 3rd, nvr nr ldrs: acts on fibresand, return to 10f shld suit.
2130 JIBEREEN 28 [11] P Howling 8-9-8 F Norton 7/2: 310004: Rear, mod late prog: stablemate of wnr. 4 47a
2634 FUTURE COUP 7 [1] 4-9-8 D Sweeney 25/1: 000405: Outpcd, late hdwy into mid-div: qck reapp. 2 43a
2379 ABTAAL 18 [12] 10-9-0 (vis) P McCabe 20/1: 600606: Wide, prom till 3f out: see 1305 (7f sell, here). 1¾ 32a
384 THE BARNSLEY BELLE 179 [3] 7-8-11 J Edmunds 33/1: 56-457: Sn bhd: 6 month abs, new stable. 5 19a
1732 ALABAMY SOUND 46 [2] 4-9-5 Darren Williams (5) 14/1: 1-4048: Led till 2f out, wknd: abs, AW bow. 1½ 24a
2118 EVER REVIE 29 [9] 3-8-9 (bl) I Mongan (5) 12/1: 001409: Nvr going pace: up in trip, see 1603 (7f, sft). 1¾ 18a
1721 WELLCOME INN 46 [5] 6-8-12 (t) L Newton 11/1: 334140: Chsd ldrs till wknd qckly ent str: 10th, abs. 6 0a
273} RIPSNORTER 559 [7] 11-8-10 Joanna Badger (7) 66/1: 0-00: Al bhd: 11th: reapp, lightly rcd & no 5 0a
form since early '98 Lingfield wnr (sell h'cap, rtd 33a): eff at 1m on fast, gd/soft grnd, both AWs.
2264 CHRISS LITTLE LAD 22 [6] 3-9-0 Martin Dwyer 13/2: 0-2000: Al bhd, eased considerably fnl 2f: 12th. 5 0a
12 ran Time 1m 44.3 (4.9) (Max Pocock) P Howling Newmarket.

2817 3.20 0800 211222 HCAP 3YO+ 0-85 (D) 1m aw rnd Going 42 -03 Slow [79]
£3731 £1148 £574 £287 3 yo rec 8 lb

2637 SHAANXI ROMANCE 7 [8] M J Polglase 5-7-11 (48)(1ow)(vis) F Norton 11/1: 543661: 5 b g Darshaan - 55a
Easy Romance (Northern Jove) Wide, in tch, prog to lead appr fnl 2f, pshd out: op 7/1, qck reapp: '99 wnr at
Carlisle (class stks, rtd 60, I Semple): '98 W'hampton wnr (mdn, rtd 73a & 79, M Bell): eff at 7f/1m, tried
further: acts on firm, soft & f/sand: runs well fresh, can force the pace: nicely h'capped.
2591 TOYON 9 [7] Sir Mark Prescott 3-8-4 (63) S Sanders 9/4 FAV: 606522: 3 b g Catrail - Princess Toy 1½ 66a
(Prince Tenderfoot) Trkd ldrs, led going well ent str, hdd 2f out, rallied for strong press but held: nicely
bckd: eff at 7f/1m on gd grnd & fibresand: shld win soon.
2215 EASTERN CHAMP 24 [3] S P C Woods 4-9-9 (72)(t) M Tebbutt 15/2: -02063: 4 ch c Star de Naskra 1¼ 72a
- Dance Troupe (Native Charger) Rear, prog after halfway, chsd ldrs fnl 2f, no impress: suited by return to AW.
2634 NOMINATOR LAD 7 [5] B A McMahon 6-9-7 (72) W Supple 10/3: -00044: Sn outpcd, late hdwy. 2 68a
2546 COMPATRIOT 11 [4] 4-8-11 (62) M Ryan 9/1: 246025: Cl-up till fdd appr fnl 2f: AW bow, op 13/2. 3½ 52a
1953 RAIN RAIN GO AWAY 36 [1] 4-10-0 (79) D Holland 8/1: 431106: Led till ent str, sn lost pl: top-weight, ½ 68a
mkt drifter: may have just hld this & will apprec a return to 7f: see 879.
2634 THE STAGER 7 [6] 8-9-0 (75)(tvi) A Clark 8/1: 451007: Wide, outpcd thr'out: tchd 12/1, qck reapp. 2 60a
2121 ONE QUICK LION 29 [2] 4-8-6 (57) R Price 14/1: 5-0408: Chsd ldrs till halfway, sn btn, lame: see 271. 26 12a
8 ran Time 1m 43.0 (3.6) (Mark Lewis) M J Polglase Southwell, Notts.

2818 3.50 UNIVERSAL MED AUCT MDN 2YO (F) 5f aw Going 42 -36 Slow
£2205 £630 £323

2488 CELOTTI 13 [8] R Hollinshead 2-8-9 J P Spencer 13/8: 351: 2 b f Celtic Swing - Zalotti (Polish Patriot) 73a
Trkd ldr, led dist, drvn out: well bckd: eff at 5/6f on fast & fibresand, bred to stay much further.
-- CLARION 1 [3] Sir Mark Prescott 2-9-0 S Sanders 6/4 FAV: 2: 2 ch c First Trump - Area Girl (Jareer) 1 74a
In tch, prog to chase wnr 1f out, kept on: well bckd on debut, clr rem: half-brother to 3 wnrs, notably 6f
juv Flying Officer, dam & sire sprinters: eff at 5f on fibresand, shld improve & find similar.
2214 COUNT CALYPSO 24 [7] D J Coakley 2-9-0 D Holland 25/1: 0003: 2 ch c King's Signet - Atlantic 3 65a

SOUTHWELL (Fibresand)   FRIDAY JULY 21ST   Lefthand, Sharp, Oval Track

Air (Air Trooper) Led till 1f out, no extra: imprvd forcing the pace on fibresand & was clr of rem.
2441 **TUPGILL TIPPLE 15** [5] S E Kettlewell 2-8-9 F Norton 12/1: 234: Chsd ldrs till 2f out: btr 2120 (C/D).   5 45a
-- **SUN BIRD** [6] 2-9-0 M Worrell (7) 16/1: 5: Struggled, moderate late hdwy: stablemate 2nd: Ir55,000gns 2½ 44+
half-brother to v useful 10f wnr Salford Express & v smart 10/12f peformer Definite Article: improve over further.
-- **KING OF TRUTH** [2] 2-9-0 Dean McKeown 33/1: 6: Chsd ldrs 3f: 1,000gns King's Signet gelding.   ½ 43a
2328 **TROUBADOUR GIRL 20** [3] 2-8-9 M Henry 16/1: 007: Al bhd: needs sellers.   4 28a
2480 **RUBY BABE 14** [4] 2-8-9 T Lucas 7/2: 68: Chsd ldrs 3f: AW bow, see 2480.   10 0a
8 ran   Time 1m 01.7 (3.9)   (P D Savill)   R Hollinshead Upper Longdon, Staffs.

2819   4.20 BEST BETS SELLER 3YO+ (G)   6f aw rnd   Going 42   -13 Slow
£1869 £534 £267   3 yo rec 5 lb

2732 **GARNOCK VALLEY 3** [5] A Berry 10-9-10 D Holland 4/6 FAV: 625201: 10 b g Dowsing - Sunley Sinner   66a
(Try My Best) Trkd ldr, led 2f out, rdly: bckd, no bid: '99 wnr at W'hampton, Lingfield (clmr), here at Southwell
(2, class stks & h'cap), Newbury (h'cap, rtd 52 & 68a): '98 Musselburgh wnr (h'cap, rtd 57 & 57a): eff at 5/7f on
fast, soft, both AWs, with/without blnks: goes well fresh & can carry big weights, any trk: tough.
1273 **PURPLE FLING 70** [4] A J McNae 9-9-5 S Sanders 7/2: 16-002: 9 ch g Music Boy - Divine Fling   2½ 53a
(Imperial Fling) Led till 2f out, kept on for 2nd: 10 wk abs: signs of return to form, can do better: see 82.
2297 **FEATHERSTONE LANE 21** [10] Miss L C Siddall 9-9-10 Dean McKeown 6/1: 163363: 9 b g Siberian   ½ 56a
Express - Try Gloria (Try By Best) Chsd ldrs, eff & onepace 2f out, styd on late: gd run at the weights, see 1235.
2680 **BOLD ARISTOCRAT 6** [2] R Hollinshead 9-9-5 D Sweeney 12/1: 13-004: Chsd ldrs, onepace ent fnl   2 45a
2f: qck reapp, stiffish task: '99 wnr at Southwell (2, clmr & seller, rtd 57a): '98 wnr again at Southwell (3,
sells, rtd 69a): eff at 6/7f, stays 1m: acts on fast, fibresand/Southwell specialist: goes well for an apprentice.
2642 **MAYDORO 7** [6] 7-9-0 Martin Dwyer 14/1: 624005: Nvr a factor: qck reapp: see 1601, 1137.   5 25a
2680 **TINAS ROYALE 6** [9] 4-9-0 F Norton 50/1: 000006: In tch till halfway: qck reapp, AW bow.   1½ 21a
752 **HONEY HOUSE 115** [7] 4-9-0 S Righton 33/1: 00-07: Al bhd: 4 month absence.   3½ 11a
2833} **HANAS PRIDE 366** [3] 4-9-0 N Pollard 50/1: 6/60-8: Sn struggling: reapp, no form.   dist 0a
8 ran   Time 1m 16.6 (3.3)   (Robert Aird)   A Berry Cockerham, Lancs.

2820   4.50 UNIVERSAL HCAP 3YO+ 0-70 (E)   6f aw rnd   Going 42   +04 Fast   [69]
£2783 £795 £397   3 yo rec 5 lb

2637 **MY ALIBI 7** [10] K R Burke 4-9-6 (61) Darren Williams (5) 2/1 FAV: 126121: 4 b f Sheikh Albadou -   69a
Fellwaati (Alydar) Mid-div, going well, clsd ent fnl 2f, rdn to lead ins last, shade rdly: best time of day, bckd:
earlier won here at Southwell (2, fillh'cap & class stks): formerly with E Dunlop, unplcd in '99 (h'cap, rtd 57):
eff btwn 6f & 1m on gd & soft, becoming a fibresand/Southwell specialist: runs well fresh & can carry big weights.
1868 **RUSSIAN ROMEO 39** [13] B A McMahon 5-9-10 (65)(bl) D Holland 16/1: 322002: 5 b g Soviet Lad -   2 66a
Aotearoa (Flash Of Steel) Chsd ldrs, wide, ch & rdn appr fnl 1f, kept on for 2nd but not pace of wnr: ran
to best against an improving filly, see 1257, 40.
2716 **NIFTY NORMAN 4** [12] D Nicholls 6-10-1 (70)(6ex) Alex Greaves 5/1: 613153: 6 b g Rock City - Nifty   hd 71a
Fifty (Runnett) Cl-up, led halfway, going well ins str, rdn bef dist, hdd & no extra ins last: well clr rem, qck
reapp with a penalty: gd weight-carrying performance: see 2623.
2385 **PETITE DANSEUSE 18** [7] D W Chapman 6-8-6 (47) Claire Bryan (5) 12/1: 605254: Chsd ldrs 4f.   5 36a
2121 **ROCK ISLAND LINE 29** [11] 6-9-11 (66) L Newton 16/1: 202655: Cl-up, ch ent str, sn no extra: btr 738.   nk 54a
2297 **GRASSLANDIK 21** [2] 4-8-3 (44)(bl) N Pollard 11/1: 500456: Outpcd, late hdwy: see 175.   2 26a
2641 **FOIST 7** [8] 8-8-5 (46) G Parkin 8/1: 650267: Towards rear, wide into str & ended up on stands   1¾ 23a
rail, nvr a factor: qck reapp: prob something amiss (hung right last twice): see 587.
2690 **DANCEMMA 6** [1] 3-9-6 (66) D Sweeney 40/1: 025008: Led 3f, sn lost pl: qk reapp, AW bow, drop to 5f? 1½ 39a
2489 **KIND EMPEROR 13** [5] 3-9-8 (68) Dean McKeown 33/1: 0004R9: Al bhd, wide into str: vis omitted, see 34. 2½ 35a
1202 **LYDIAS LOOK 74** [14] 3-8-12 (58) W Ryan 33/1: 541000: Wide, nvr trbld ldrs: 10th, 11 wk abs, poor draw. ½ 24a
1580 **RIOJA 52** [4] 5-9-8 (63) T Lucas 6/1: 000/00: Prom, wknd qckly ent str: 11th, AW bow, 2nd start after abs. 1 26a
*2632 **TWO STEP 7** [3] 4-7-10 (37)(t)(6ex)(3oh) G Sparkes (3) 8/1: 0-0010: Outpcd from halfway: 13th, see 2362.   0a
2385 **Superfrills 18** [9] 7-7-10 (37) G Bardwell 20/1:   687 **Sand Hawk 126** [6] 5-10-0 (69)(bl) F Norton 16/1:   26a
14 ran   Time 1m 15.6 (2.3)   (L F S Associtates)   K R Burke Newmarket.

CARLISLE   FRIDAY JULY 21ST   Righthand, Stiff Track, Uphill Finish

Official Going   FIRM Stalls: Inside, Except 12f & 14f - Outside.

2821   2.10 CUMBRIAN AUCT MDN 2YO (E)   5f rnd   Firm 07   -11 Slow
£2795 £860 £430 £215

2361 **FAIRGAME MAN 18** [1] A Berry 2-8-7 J Carroll 9/4 FAV: 31: 2 ch c Clantime - Thalya (Crofthall)   79
Trkd ldrs, went on appr fnl 2f, styd on well, rdn out: 6,800 gns Feb foal, dam unrcd: eff around 5f, 6f
will suit: acts on firm, gd & a stiff/undul trk: clearly going the right way.
2698 **CUMBRIAN HARMONY 6** [7] T D Easterby 2-7-13 T Williams 11/2: 230552: 2 b f Distinctly North -   1¼ 67
Sawaki (Song) Prom, drvn & not pace of wnr well ins last: op 4/1, qck reapp: handles firm & gd/soft.
2360 **MRS PERTEMPS 18** [5] J R Fanshawe 2-8-5 K Darley 11/2: 03: 2 ch f Ashkalani - Allepolina (Trempolino) 2½ 67
Handy, rdn/styd on fnl 1f, not pace of front 2: well bckd, shld relish a step up to 6f now: see 2360.
2521 **SMART DANCER 12** [4] T D Easterby 2-8-10 A Culhane 25/1: -504: Rear, late hdwy for press, no threat. 1¼ 69
2539 **WHITE STAR LADY 11** [6] 2-7-13 G Baker (7) 14/1: 505: Led, hdd appr fnl 2f, sn fdd: see 2539 (soft). 1½ 54
-- **SHES GRAND** [2] 2-7-13 D Mernagh (3) 7/1: 6: Dwelt, nvr dangerous on debut: cheaply bought filly,   2 49
half sister to a 5f juv wnr: dam related to a smart sprinter: with T D Barron.
2539 **MADIES PRIDE 11** [3] 2-8-2 J Fanning 4/1: 47: Trkd ldrs, wknd rapidly fnl 2f: better on soft in 2539. 6 39
7 ran   Time 1m 00.4 (0.9)   (Robert Ogden)   A Berry Cockerham, Lancs

CARLISLE   FRIDAY JULY 21ST   Righthand, Stiff Track, Uphill Finish

---

2822   **2.40 INDUSTRIAL CLASSIFIED STKS 3YO+ 0-70 (E)   5f rnd   Firm 07   +09 Fast**
£2756   £848   £424   £212   3 yo rec 4 lb

2697 **FRIAR TUCK** 6 [5] Miss L A Perratt 5-9-3 K Dalgleish (5) 11/8 FAV: 210301: 5 ch g Inchinor - Jay Gee Ell   77
(Vaigly Great) Bhd, rdn to improve over 2f out, ran on strongly to lead well ins last, drvn out: nicely bckd,
crse rec time: qck reapp: earlier ddhtd for 1st at York (h'cap): rnr-up in '99 (rtd 87, h'cap), prev term won
again at York (val h'cap, rtd 101): suited by 5/6f on firm & soft: acts on any trk, loves York: runs well fresh
& likes to come late off a strong pace: has prev suffered breathing probs: useful at best, now well h'capped.
2525 **PURE ELEGANCIA** 12 [1] D Nicholls 4-8-11 K Darley 9/4: 516-02: 4 b f Lugana Beach - Esilam   1½   67
(Frimley Park) Mid-div, gd hdwy to lead appr fnl 1f, drvn/hdd well ins last, sn held: op 2/1: see 2525 (h'cap).
2719 **INDIAN MUSIC** 4 [4] A Berry 3-8-10 (bl) F Lynch 7/2: 045553: 3 b g Indian Ridge - Dagny Juel   1½   66
(Danzig) Chsd ldrs, chall appr fnl 2f, sn btn: qck reapp: gd run back to 5f on grnd faster than ideal: see 2504.
2650 **PALACEGATE JACK** 7 [3] A Berry 9-9-0 P Bradley (5) 25/1: 003054: Front rank, rdn/fdd fnl 1f: 2   59$
quick reapp & not disgraced at these weights, tho' treat rating with caution: see 2233, 191.
1665 **DANAKIM** 49 [10] 3-8-10 J Fanning 14/1: 002405: Prom, wknd qckly fnl 1f: abs, see 1021 (hvy).   ½   57
2704 **DISTANT KING** 5 [9] 7-9-0 Kim Tinkler 100/1: 000006: Sn rdn in rear, mod gains: qck reapp, stiff task.   2   50$
1910 **BANDIDA** 37 [2] 6-8-11 O Pears 100/1: 0607: Al in rear: prob flattered, see 1244.   2   40$
1976 **SOAKED** 35 [7] 7-9-0 A Culhane 14/1: 000008: Led 4f out, hdd over 1f out, wknd qckly, eased when btn.   ½   42
1239 **YOUNG BEN** 71 [8] 8-9-0 J McAuley (5) 66/1: 0-0509: In tch, rdn/wknd appr fnl 1f: 10 wk abs.   shd   41$
2275 **CHILLIAN** 22 [6] 4-9-0 D Mernagh (3) 100/1: -05000: Led early, remnd prom till wknd from halfway, 10th.   5   29
10 ran   Time 59.4 (u0.1)   (Cree Lodge Racing Club)   Miss L A Perratt Ayr, Strathclyde

---

2823   **3.10 H & H GROUP HCAP 3YO+ 0-70 (E)   7f rnd   Firm 07   -02 Slow**   [61]
£3042   £936   £468   £234   3 yo rec 7 lb

2282 **THWAAB** 22 [6] F Watson 8-8-8 (41) P Goode (3) 14/1: 00-061: 8 b g Dominion - Velvet Habit   49
(Habitat) Twrds rear, gd hdwy over 2f out, ran on well to lead ins last, drvn out: well btn in 4 '99 starts,
prev term scored at Doncaster (h'cap, rtd 62): back in '96 won at Redcar & Ayr (h'caps, rtd 63): eff at 6/7f
on firm, gd/soft & any trk: eff with/without a visor: well h'capped & could follow up.
1658 **RYEFIELD** 49 [3] Miss L A Perratt 5-9-9 (56) K Darley 14/1: 60-0R2: 5 b g Petong - Octavia (Sallust)   1   62
Dwelt, rear, eff when hmpd/stumbled 2f out, switched wide & ran on strongly fnl 1f, despite carrying head high,
no threat to wnr: 7 wk abs & ran to best: h'capped to win similar at 1m: see 1243.
*2561 **PUPPET PLAY** 10 [1] E J Alston 5-9-6 (53)(6ex) F Lynch 7/1: 030413: 5 ch m Broken Hearted -   1½   56
Fantoccini (Taufan) Led early, remained with ldr till went on again 3f out, hdd ins last, sn held: back in trip.
*2673 **BODFARI ANNA** 6 [7] J L Eyre 4-9-5 (52)(vis) R Cody Boutcher (7) 5/1: 100314: In tch, sltly short   ½   54
of room 2f out, kept on, no threat to ldrs: quick reapp: remains in gd heart: unpenalised for win in 2673.
2063 **SANTANDRE** 31 [5] 4-9-0 (47) P M Quinn 3) 16/1: 500005: Prom, rdn/prog over 2f out, fdd ins last.   1   47
2704 **THATCHED** 5 [15] 10-8-8 (41) K Dalgleish (5) 8/1: 506056: Dwelt, bhd, fin well: needs 1m+.   nk   41
2559 **PRIX STAR** 10 [12] 3-9-10 (57) J Fanning 20/1: 320407: Trkd ldrs, rdn/fdd over 1f out: top weight.   shd   57
2479 **SYCAMORE LODGE** 14 [10] 9-9-0 (47) O Pears 10/1: 034068: Mid-div, short of room 2f out, no dngr.   2   43
2561 **GYMCRAK FLYER** 10 [14] 9-9-0 (47)(vis) A Culhane 11/1: -00009: Bhd, mod late gains: see 2561.   ½   42
2444 **MAMMAS BOY** 15 [4] 5-9-6 (53) P Bradley (5) 10/1: 411000: In tch, drvn/btn over 2f out, fin 10th.   ¾   46
2240 **TANCRED ARMS** 23 [8] 4-9-1 (48) Kimberley Hart 12/1: 300030: Wide/prom 5f, wknd, 11th: see 2240.   3½   35
2612 **NORTHGATE** 8 [9] 4-9-2 (49)(bl) D Mernagh (3) 9/2 FAV: 421420: Sn led, hdd 3f out, wkng when   hd   36
hmpd fnl 1f, 12th: nicely bckd: below par here, capable of much better, see 2612.
2632 **CHRISTOPHERSSISTER** 7 [2] 3-9-6 (60) J McAuley 25/1: 004000: Slow start, al bhd, 13th, qck reapp.   2   43
2479 **DETROIT CITY** 14 [11] 5-8-8 (41) J Bramhill 12/1: 202040: Missed break, al in rear, 14th: op 8/1.   4   43
2542 **LOVE KISS** 11 [13] 5-8-11 (44) T Williams 9/1: 0-0020: Handy, rdn & wknd qckly fnl 2f, eased ins   2½   18
last, fin 15th: reportedly swallowed tongue: btr 2542 (1m, soft).
15 ran   Time 1m 26.1 (0.6)   (F Watson)   F Watson Sedgefield, Co Durham

---

2824   **3.40 KIER NORTHERN MDN 3YO+ (D)   7f rnd   Firm 07   -15 Slow**
£4075   £1254   £627   £313   3 yo rec 7 lb

2548 **TRIPLE WOOD** 11 [5] B Hanbury 3-8-9 K Darley 4/7 FAV: 2-5431: 3 b f Woodman - Triple Kiss (Shareef   71
Dancer) Trkd ldr, went on 3f out, clr dist, rdn out, cmftbly: nicely bckd at odds-on: rnr-up on fnl of 2
'99 starts (fills mdn, rtd 80): eff at 7f, will apprec 1m: acts on firm & gd, poss handles soft:
handles a stiff/undul trk: plenty in hand here & could rate more highly.
2159 **MOON GLOW** 27 [1] Miss S E Hall 4-9-7 Paul Eddery 2/1: 400-42: 4 b g Fayruz - Jarmar Moon   5   62
(Unfuwain) Held up, rdn & ran on late, no threat to wnr: will apprec a return to 1m in h'caps: see 2159.
2443 **SUPER DOMINION** 15 [2] R Hollinshead 4-9-7 P M Quinn (3) 9/1: 433: 3 ch c Superpower - Smartie   1½   59$
Lee (Dominion) Chsd ldr, rdn/onepcd fnl 2f: low grade h'caps will now suit: see 2443, 2058.
2601 **ABSTRACT** 8 [3] J S Wainwright 4-9-2 (vis) J McAuley (5) 25/1: 000034: Pulled hard in rear,   1¾   50$
nvr nr ldr: treat rating with caution (offic rtd only 31): see 2601 (mdn h'cap).
2538 **SILVER BULLET** 11 [4] 4-9-7 (BL) F Lynch 50/1: -00005: Led, rdn/hdd 3f out, sn btn, eased: blnks.   18   35$
5 ran   Time 1m 27.1 (1.6)   (Hilal Salem)   B Hanbury Newmarket

---

2825   **4.10 TARMAC HCAP 3YO 0-70 (E)   1m1f61y   Firm 07   +05 Fast**   [63]
£2977   £916   £458   £229

2080 **INVISIBLE FORCE** 30 [8] M Johnston 3-8-3 (38)(BL) K Dalgleish (5) 12/1: 604661: 3 b c Imperial   48
Frontier - Virginia Cottage (Lomond) Trkd ldr, went on 3f out, sn clr, rdn out, eased nr fin: gd time: 1st time
blnks: trained by B Rothwell in '99 & fin last on both starts (rtd 71, flattered): has apprec this recent step
up to 9f & even further could suit: acts on firm grnd & a stiff/undul trk: sharpened up by blnks today.
2187 **WOODWIND DOWN** 25 [5] M Todhunter 3-8-13 (48) J McAuley (5) 10/1: 000032: 3 b f Piccolo - Bint El   6   48
Oumara (Al Nasr) Settled rear, rdn/prog 4f out, styd on fnl 2f but no th with wnr: fair run for new stable,
prev with M Channon: up in trip & poss stays 9.4f: see 2187 (sell h'cap).
*2534 **TWILIGHT WORLD** 11 [2] Sir Mark Prescott 3-9-4 (53)(6ex) K Darley 1/2 FAV: 006-13: 3 b g Night Shift -   3   48
Masskana (Darshaan) Mid-div, eff 2f out, sn held: nicely bckd: reportedly not handle this v firm grnd.
2453 **SEA EMPEROR** 14 [6] Mrs G S Rees 3-8-13 (48) J Fanning 7/1: -03044: Prom, rdn/fdd appr fnl 1f.   nk   43
2362 **BITTY MARY** 18 [4] 3-8-3 (38)(vis) G Baker (7) 20/1: -00005: Rear, late gains, no impress: see 807.   2½   29

882

CARLISLE   FRIDAY JULY 21ST   Righthand, Stiff Track, Uphill Finish

2540 **BEBE DE CHAM** 11 [7] 3-9-7 (56) T Williams 16/1: 000666: Led, hdd 3f out, sn lost tch: top weight. 4 **41**
2484 **WORTH THE RISK** 14 [3] 3-8-5 (40) Kim Tinkler 16/1: 50-357: Mid-div, no extra fnl 3f: see 2484, 2222. 1¼ **23**
1895 **BOLLIN NELLIE** 38 [1] 3-9-3 (52) A Culhane 15/2: -45058: Rear, nvr dangerous: btr 782 (12f). shd **35**
8 ran   Time 1m 55.6 (0.2)   (Jim Browne)   M Johnston Middleham, N Yorks

---

2826   4.40 CLASSIFIED STKS 3YO+ 0-70 (E)   1m4f   Firm 07 -34 Slow
£2795   £860   £430   £215   3 yo rec 12lb

2321 **ALEXANDRINE** 20 [3] Sir Mark Prescott 3-8-9 K Darley 2/9 FAV: 0-1141: 3 b f Nashwan - Alruccaba **59**
(Crystal Palace) In tch, cruised into lead on bit ins last, not extended/hard held: won with any amount in hand:
earlier won at Yarmouth & Musselburgh (fills h'cap): unplcd in 3 mdns in late '99 (rtd 56): eff at 10f, suited by
12f & further shld suit: acts on firm/fast & a sharp or stiff/undul trk: won with ridiculous ease, win more races.
1936 **RIGHTY HO** 36 [4] W H Tinning 6-9-6 K Hodgson 20/1: 3-0002: 6 b g Reprimand - Challanging (Mill Reef) 1 **44**
Led & sn clr, rdn/hdd ins last, kept on but no ch with easy wnr: stiff task, will apprec a return to h'caps.
2783 **LOYAL TOAST** 1 [1] N Tinkler 5-9-6 Kim Tinkler 16/1: 050533: 5 b g Lyphard - Lisieux (Steady Growth) ¾ **42$**
Prom, rdn/kept on fnl 2f, no ch with wnr: treat rating with caution (offic only 26): ran yesterday: see 2783 (h'cap).
3860} **GRAND SLAM GB** 315 [6] L Lungo 5-9-6 J McAuley (5) 9/2: 2042-4: Settled last, rdn/prog over 2f out, nk **42**
onepace but no threat to ldrs: Flat reapp: 8 wk hdles abs, plcd once in that sphere (2m1.5f nov, gd, rtd 79h):
with R Hannon on the Flat in '99, rnr-up twice (h'caps, rtd 69, also tried blnks): '98 wnr at Warwick (med auct
mdn, rtd 77, plcd numerous times): eff over 1m, poss styd this longer 12f trip: acts on firm, gd/soft & any trk.
2742 **THREE CHERRIES** 2 [5] 4-9-3 P Goode 20/1: 000045: Dwelt, rdn/mod late gains: ran 48hrs ago. ½ **38$**
2538 **FIRST LEGACY** 11 [2] 4-9-3 R Farmer (7) 50/1: -00006: Mid-div, rdn/lost tch fnl 2f: up in trip. 9 **25**
6 ran   Time 2m 35.8 (5.0)   (Miss K Rausing)   Sir Mark Prescott Newmarket

---

2827   5.10 BURGH BARONY AMAT HCAP 3YO+ 0-70 (E)   1m6f   Firm 07 -44 Slow   [35]
£2758   £788   £394

2323 **MISCHIEF** 20 [1] M Quinn 4-9-10 (31)(vis)(1oh) Miss J Ellis (7) 14/1: 005061: 4 ch g Generous - Knight's **35**
Baroness (Rainbow Quest) Led, sn hdd, rallied to lead again appr fnl 2f, styd on strongly, drvn out: 1st
win: plcd fnl of just 4 '99 starts (h'cap, rtd 66, P Cole): eff at 12/14f on firm & soft/hvy, in a vis.
2607 **PROTOCOL** 8 [7] Mrs S Lamyman 6-10-4 (39)(t) Mr S Dobson (5) 7/2: 550422: 6 b g Taufan - Ukraine's ¾ **41**
Affair (The Minstrel) Settled mid-div, gd hdwy over 3f out, rdn/chall 2f out, held cl-home: in gd heart: see 2607.
*2638 **WAFIR** 7 [6] T A K Cuthbert 8-10-13 (48)(5ex) Miss H Cuthbert (5) 7/2: 264213: 8 b g Scenic - Taniokey 2 **47**
(Grundy) Settled rear, rdn/hdwy over 2f out, ev ch until no extra ins last: qck reapp: eff at 10/12f, just stays 14f.
2466 **MONACLE** 14 [3] John Berry 6-10-4 (39) Mr M Murphy (5) 5/2: 03F-34: Dwelt, rear, rdn/prog 3f out, 2 **35**
no extra appr last: nicely bckd: see 2466 (12f).
2109 **SWANDALE FLYER** 29 [2] 8-9-10 (31)(9oh) Mr W Fearon (7) 33/1: 50-005: Cl-up, rdn/wknd appr fnl 2f. 6 **19$**
2279 **GOLDEN CHIMES** 22 [5] 5-12-0 (63) Mr G Tuer (5) 2/1 FAV: 0-1606: Front rank, led over 4f out, 12 **38**
hdd 2f out & wknd rapidly: nicely bckd, top weight: capable of much better: see 2016.
1363 **CRESSET** 63 [4] 4-11-1 (50) Miss P Robson 14/1: 122007: Rear, lost tch fnl 3f: sn t.o., 9 wk abs. dist **0**
7 ran   Time 3m 08.2 (8.4)   (Mrs Angela Ellis)   M Quinn Sparsholt, Oxon

---

PONTEFRACT   FRIDAY JULY 21ST   Lefthand, Undulating Track With Stiff Uphill Finish

Official Going   GOOD TO FIRM (watered). Stalls: Inside.

2828   6.40 RED SHIRT AUCTION MDN 2YO (E)   6f rnd   Good/Firm 29 -31 Slow
£3302   £1016   £508   £254

2142 **BACCURA** 28 [3] A P Jarvis 2-8-3 D Mernagh (3) 5/2 FAV: -021: 2 b c Dolphin Street - Luzzara **84**
(Tate Gallery) Front rank, went on appr fnl 1f, styd on well, drvn out: nicely bckd: 6,000gns May foal, half-brother
to a juv wnr abroad: dam an Italian juv wnr: eff at 5f, apprec 6f on fast & a stiff trk: improving.
2598 **ARMAGNAC** 9 [13] D Sasse 2-8-7 Martin Dwyer 9/2: 64042: 2 b c Young Ern - Arianaa Aldini (Habitat) 2½ **80**
Prom, hdwy when edged left over 1f out, styd on but not pace of wnr: handles fast & gd: shld win a race.
2333 **BORDERS BELLE** 20 [10] J D Bethell 2-8-5 K Darley 7/1: 43: 2 b f Pursuit Of Love - Sheryl Lynn ¾ **76**
(Miller's Mate) Cl-up, rdn to chall 2f out, short of room last, onepace: op 5/1: improved at 6f on fast, 7f suit.
-- **GARDOR** [4] J G FitzGerald 2-8-4(1ow) L Newton 33/1: 4: Dwelt, rdn/prog 3f out, styd on well fnl 2½ **68**
1f, nvr nrr: 5,000gns Mar 1st foal: dam a 2yo scorer in France: sharper for this & 7f+ will suit.
-- **PEACE BAND** [14] 2-8-5 S Sanders 16/1: 5: Led, hdd appr fnl 1f, sn held: IR 9,400gns colt, 1 **67**
half-brother to a 2yo 5f scorer: dam related to sev wnrs: with M H Tompkins, showed plenty of speed here.
2653 **EAGLES CACHE** 7 [15] 2-8-5 J Carroll 7/1: 43626: Dsptd lead, wknd over 1f out: op 5/1, qk reapp. 3½ **58**
2454 **POUR NOUS** 14 [2] 2-8-3 W Supple 40/1: 07: Dwelt, late hdwy from rear, no threat: see 2454. 1½ **52**
2454 **BEREZINA** 14 [16] 2-8-0 P Fessey 9/1: 5648: Sn rdn in rear, modest late hdwy: op 5/1: btr 2454. ¾ **47**
2360 **FRENCH BRAMBLE** 18 [7] 2-7-12 S Righton 33/1: 6009: Cl-up to halfway, grad wknd: see 1304. nk **44**
-- **EVERY HINT** [12] 2-8-10 D Holland 14/1: 0: Dwelt, nvr dngrs, fin 10th: 29,000gns Mar foal: 1 **54**
dam 2yo wnr abroad: sire high-class juv/miler: with T D Easterby.
2360 **WESTERNMOST** 18 [8] 2-8-5 M Fenton 33/1: 00: Missed break, al bhd, 11th. ½ **40**
1659 **MADAME ROUX** 49 [9] 2-8-0 F Norton 12/1: -40: Prom 4f, wknd qckly, 12th: 7 wk abs: see 1659. 2½ **35**
-- **The Merry Widow** [6] 2-7-12 Joanna Badger (7) 33/1:-- **Kathann** [11] 2-7-12 A Mackay 25/1:
14 ran   Time 1m 17.7 (3.6)   (Jalal Harake)   A P Jarvis Aston Upthorpe, Oxon.

2829   7.05 V CHANDLER FILLIES HCAP 3YO+ 0-70 (E)   1m4f   Good/Firm 29 +02 Fast   [63]
£3159   £972   £486   £243   3 yo rec 12lb

2461 **ORDAINED** 14 [4] Miss Gay Kelleway 7-8-3 (38) Martin Dwyer 6/1: 230041: 7 b m Mtoto - In The Habit **46**
(Lyphard) Mid-div, gd hdwy over 3f out, led 2f out, rdn clr: gd time: unplcd in '99 for E Alston (rtd 55, h'cap):
plcd twice in '98 (h'caps, rtd 61): eff at 12/14f on firm & gd: likes a stiff trk: v well h'capped, qk follow up?
2674 **CASHMERE LADY** 6 [2] J L Eyre 8-10-0 (63) D Holland 5/1 CO FAV: -01102: 8 b m Hubbly Bubbly - 5 **63**
Choir (Hightop) Settled rear, hdwy over 3f out, styd on but not pace of wnr: ran to best under top-weight.
2656 **ACEBO LYONS** 7 [5] A P Jarvis 5-9-6 (55) D Mernagh (3) 12/1: 650403: 5 b m Waajib - Etage (Ile ½ **54**

883

De Bourbon) Held up, smooth hdwy over 3f out, rdn/held fnl 1f: qck reapp: see 2273.

*2776 **SPOSA 1** [3] M J Polglase 4-9-0 (49) (6ex) L Newton 9/1: 5P0114: Front rank, rdn/outpcd appr fnl 1f: 1½   46
ran 24hrs ago, poss too soon after 2776.

2484 **KUUIPO 14** [1] 3-7-13 (46) (t) Joanna Badger (7) 14/1: 060265: Rcd keenly in lead, qc'nd pace   ¾   42
3f out, hdd 2f out, grad wknd: mdn after 16 starts: see 2007 (10f).

2254 **DANCING MARY 23** [6] 3-8-7 (54) M Tebbutt 9/1: 350436: Dwelt, sn mid-div, drvn/fdd fnl 2f: see 2254.   3½   45

4256} **MARJEUNE 290** [10] 3-9-6 (67) A Culhane 9/1: 0041-7: Front rank, drvn/lost tch fnl 2f: up in trip: nk   57
won fnl '99 start, at Nottingham (nurs, rtd 67): sire top-class over 1m/12f: eff at 7f/10f on soft & a gall trk.

1002 **CALICO 88** [5] 3-9-3 (64) F Norton 33/1: 550-08: With ldr, drvn/drpd rear after halfway, sn bhd: abs.   15   38

*2540 **IRISH DANCER 11** [7] 3-9-7 (68) (6ex) S Sanders 5/1 CO FAV: 003119: Settled mid-div, eff 5f out,   1½   40
wknd rapidly fnl 3f: hat-trick bid & v disapp here, much btr 2540 (soft grnd).

2667 **LULLABY 7** [8] 3-9-6 (67) K Darley 5/1 CO FAV: 340120: Handy, rdn/lost tch fnl 3f, t.o. in   7   29
10th: qck reapp & capable of much better, see 2667 (stks).

10 ran   Time 2m 37.3 (3.2)   (Peter Ebdon Racing)   Miss Gay Kelleway Lingfield, Surrey.

2830   7.35 A. DEUTERS HCAP 3YO+ 0-80 (D)   5f rnd   Good/Firm 29   +01 Fast   [80]
£7345   £2260   £1130   £565   3 yo rec 4 lb

2644 **ANTHONY MON AMOUR 7** [7] D Nicholls 5-9-0 (66) (t) D Holland 4/1 FAV: 004101: 5 b g Nicholas - Reine   74
De La Ciel (Conquistador Cielo) Dsptd lead, led over 3f out, rdn clr ins last: qck reapp: recent Catterick wnr
(h'cap): '99 rnr-up (rtd 66 & 68a), '98 Chepstow (mdn h'cap) & Southwell (stks, rtd 69): all wins at 5/6f, just
stays 7f: acts on fast, soft, f/sand & any trk: best in a t-strap: best up with/forcing the pace: in fine form.

2612 **SQUARE DANCER 8** [4] M Dods 4-8-7 (59) A Culhane 20/1: 005402: 4 b g Then Again - Cubist (Tate   1½   61
Gallery) Prom, rdn/prog over 2f out, kept on but not pace of wnr: up again & ran to nr best: both wins at 6f.

2644 **BRECONGILL LAD 7** [1] D Nicholls 8-9-11 (77) F Norton 12/1: 322003: 8 b g Clantime - Chikala   1   77
(Pitskelly) Held up, switched/hdwy over 1f out, ran on well ins last: stablemate of wnr, top-weight: sound run.

2721 **XANADU 4** [11] Miss L A Perratt 4-9-9 (75) C Lowther 9/2: 010124: Trkd ldrs, ev ch till not   shd   75
pace of ldrs fnl 1f: qck reapp: remains in gd heart: tough: see 2721, 2505.

2749 **VIOLET 2** [5] 4-7-13 (51) (bl) (7ex) R Brisland (5) 20/1: 060105: Totally missed break, strong run   1¼   48
fnl 2f, closing at fin: ran 48hrs ago: would surely have gone close with a level break, wn again sn at 6f.

2684 **PREMIUM PRINCESS 6** [2] 5-7-13 (51) D Mernagh (3) 13/2: 553356: Mid-div, late hdwy, no threat.   ½   46

*2340 **DOUBLE OSCAR 20** [12] 7-9-7 (73) (bl) Alex Greaves 9/2: 563217: Cl-up, rdn/btn appr fnl 2f: btr 2340.   ½   66

2504 **RYTHM N TIME 13** [10] 3-9-2 (72) W Supple 20/1: 0-0408: Led early, remnd cl-up till fdd over 1f out.   1½   61

2517 **SHIRLEY NOT 13** [9] 4-9-6 (72) (bl) S Sanders 11/1: 405509: Front rank, wknd halfway: see 2310, 1278.   ¾   59

787 **RUM LAD 114** [8] 6-8-9 (61) M Fenton 20/1: 500-00: Prom 3f, sn btn, 10th: 4 month abs: see 787.   2   43

2644 **RIVER TERN 7** [3] 7-8-11 (63) K Darley 13/2: 000360: Sn rdn, nvr dngrs, 11th, qck reapp: see 2644.   5   36

2663 **GDANSK 7** [6] 3-9-2 (72) J Carroll 20/1: 210040: Unruly start, wknd qckly halfway, 12th: qck reapp.   3½   36

12 ran   Time 1m 02.7 (1.4)   (Tony Fawcett)   D Nicholls Sessay, N.Yorks.

2831   8.05 COUNTRYWIDE HCAP 3YO+ 0-70 (E)   1m rnd   Good/Firm 29   +05 Fast   [66]
£3341   £1028   £514   £257   3 yo rec 8 lb

2442 **LYNTON LAD 15** [11] E J Alston 8-9-3 (55) W Supple 10/1: -66001: 8 b g Superpower - House Maid   60
(Habitat) Made ev gd, ran on strongly, pushed out: '99 Ayr wnr (h'cap, rtd 67), unplcd on sand (rtd 42a):
eff at 1m on fast & soft grnd, with/without blnks: back to form forcing the pace & back on a good mark.

2378 **KESTRAL 18** [12] T J Etherington 4-7-12 (36) F Norton 25/1: 506062: 4 ch g Ardkinglass - Shiny Kay   1¼   37
(Star Appeal) In tch, prog appr fnl 2f: rdn & styd on, unable to chall: t-strap omitted: stays 1m: mdn after 21.

2442 **BOLLIN ROBERTA 15** [9] T D Easterby 4-9-8 (60) J Carroll 8/1: -52053: 4 b f Bob's Return - Bollin   shd   61
Emily (Lochnager) Prom, ch 2f out, unable to qckn dist: stayed this longer/stiff 1m trip, wnk bhd.

2524 **NOBLE SPLENDOUR 12** [3] J D Bethell 3-9-6 (66) K Darley 4/1: 502334: Mid-div, kept on appr   1   65
fnl 1f, not pace to chall: clr rem, new stable: consistent but hard to win with (mdn after 11): see 2524.

2673 **CAUTION 6** [6] 6-9-0 (52) D Mernagh (3) 11/4 FAV: 004225: Chsd ldrs, onepace appr fnl 1f: qck reapp.   4   43

2094 **OLLIES CHUCKLE 30** [10] 5-7-13 (37) Martin Dwyer 25/1: 006606: Chsd ldrs, fdd ent fnl 2f: see 908.   hd   27

2538 **MARGARETS DANCER 11** [4] 5-8-10 (48) (t) D Holland 12/1: 550-07: Handy, no extra 2f out.   nk   37

2542 **YOUNG ROSEIN 11** [5] 4-9-1 (53) Dean McKeown 9/1: 0-0038: Front rank till wknd ent fnl 2f: see 1243.   hd   41

1157 **RIMATARA 76** [2] 4-8-12 (50) G Parkin 25/1: 6-009: Nvr a factor: 11 wk abs, h'cap bow, new stable.   2½   33

2511 **WISHEDHADGONEHOME 13** [7] 3-7-12 (44) (vis) S Righton 40/1: 305600: Keen, mid-div, hmpd halfway   ¾   26
& bhd: 10th, back up in trip, see 236, 192.

2602 **WINTZIG 8** [1] 3-9-2 (62) M Fenton 9/1: 250330: In tch till 3f out: 11th, qck reapp, see 2345.   5   34

2297 **LAUND VIEW LADY 21** [13] 3-7-13 (45) P Fessey 50/1: -06000: Chsd ldrs halfway: 12th, see 1351.   4   9

1690 **ITS OUR SECRET 48** [8] 4-9-13 (65) S Sanders 9/1: 0-2400: Speed 4f: 13th, top-weight, 7 wk abs.   13   9

13 ran   Time 1m 43.7 (1.9)   (Miss Kim E Jones)   E J Alston Preston, Lancs.

2832   8.35 ST JOHN MDN 3YO (D)   1m2f   Good/Firm 29   -10 Slow
£3721   £1145   £572   £286

2220 **ROUSING THUNDER 24** [1] E A L Dunlop 3-9-0 G Carter 1/1 FAV: 6-0201: 3 b c Theatrical - Moss   76
(Woodman) Led, hdd appr fnl 2f, regained lead bef dist, held on gamely: well bckd: plcd in '99 (mdn, rtd 83):
eff at 10f on firm/fast grnd, any track: stable back in top form.

1697 **NEW IBERIA 48** [3] Sir Michael Stoute 3-9-0 F Lynch 11/2: -002: 3 gr c Tabasco Cat - Carolina Saga   nk   75
(Caro) Cl-up, led 2½f out, hdd bef fnl 1f, held nr fin: 7 wk abs: $300,000 yearling, eff at 10f on fast grnd.

2553 **FREE WILL 11** [7] L M Cumani 3-9-0 G Sparkes (7) 8/1: -563: 3 ch c Indian Ridge - Free Guest   1   74
(Be My Guest) Held up, prog to press ldrs appr fnl 1f, onepace in last: stays 10f on fast grnd, h'caps next.

2265 **BOLD PRECEDENT 22** [2] P W Harris 3-9-0 A Culhane 5/2: 0-434: Dwelt, handy till outpcd appr fnl 1f.   2½   70

-- **LETS REFLECT** [6] 3-8-9 M Fenton 50/1: 5: Held up, chsd ldrs 3f out till bef fnl 1f: clr rem, debut: ¾   64
3,000gns Mtoto filly out of a winning sprinter, related to wnrs btwn 5f & 1m: with J Turner.

3813} **JOSEPH VERNET 318** [4] 3-9-0 M Tebbutt 50/1: 56-6: Bhd fnl 2f: unplcd in '99 for P Cole (rtd 59).   6   60

2362 **HIGHCAL 18** [5] 3-9-0 S Sanders 66/1: 0-0007: Handy till 3f out: impossible task.   16   43

7 ran   Time 2m 12.00 (3.9)   (Abdullah Ali)   E A L Dunlop Newmarket.

PONTEFRACT FRIDAY JULY 21ST Lefthand, Undulating Track With Stiff Uphill Finish

2833

9.05 CLASSIFIED STKS 3YO+ 0-65 (E)   6f rnd   Good/Firm 29 -01 Slow
£3198   £984   £492   £246   3 yo rec 5 lb

2753 **FLAK JACKET** 2 [6] D Nicholls 5-9-0 (t) D Holland 5/4 FAV: 000021: 5 b g Magic Ring - Vaula   **74**
(Henbit) Prom, led ent fnl 1f, qcknd clr, easily: ran 48hrs ago, well bckd: rnr-up in '99 (rtd 82, B Meehan):
'98 wnr at Kempton & Haydock (rtd 86): suited by 6f on firm & soft, without blnks: wears a t-strap: well h'capped.
2444 **TECHNICIAN** 15 [2] E J Alston 5-9-3 (bl) W Supple 5/1: 001232: 5 ch g Archway - How It Works   4   **65**
(Commanche Run) Cl-up, led after 3f till below dist, outpcd by wnr: not disgraced, clr of rem: see 2396.
2438 **OSCAR PEPPER** 15 [5] T D Barron 3-8-9 K Darley 8/1: 112203: 3 b g Brunswick - Princess Baja   6   **51**
(Conquistador Cielo) Dwelt, grad recovered, chsd ldrs 2f out, sn onepace: clr of 4th, see 365.
1884 **CAPE COAST** 38 [1] R M Beckett 3-8-12 M Tebbutt 10/1: 016304: Narrow lead till 3f out, grad wknd.   5   **45**
4362} **DETECTIVE** 281 [7] 4-9-0 J Lowe 12/1: 5200-5: Chsd ldrs till 2f out: reapp: '99 rnr-up (h'cap,   8   **27**
rtd 67): no form earlier for J Gosden: eff at 6f on firm grnd: with Dr Scargill.
2559 **ALBERT THE BEAR** 10 [4] 7-9-0 (vis) C Lowther 7/2: 030026: Prsd ldrs till wknd 2f out: much btr 2559.   1¾ **23**
*2603 **NITE OWL MATE** 8 [3] 3-8-12 (t) L Newton 9/1: 300017: Chsd ldrs 3f: much btr 2603 (AW).   12   **0**
7 ran   Time 1m 15.9 (1.8)   (The Knavesmire Alliance)   D Nicholls Sessay, N.Yorks.

RIPON SATURDAY JULY 22ND Righthand, Sharpish Track

Official Going   GOOD/FIRM. Stalls: Str Crse - Stands Side; Rnd Crse - Inside.

2834

2.20 CENTAUR SELLER 3YO+ (E)   1m rnd   Good/Firm 40 -05 Slow
£2600   £800   £400   £200   3yo rec 8lb

2518 **HORMUZ** 14 [10] J M Bradley 4-9-7 J Fanning 5/2: 000001: 4 b g Hamas - Balqis (Advocator)   **57**
Made all, clr fnl 2f, eased down: bt in for 4,000gns: '99 wnr at Lingfield (2, rtd 83a), Ripon (stks) & Beverley
(h'cap, rtd 90, with M Johnston): eff at 1m/10f: acts on firm, gd/soft grnd & equitrack: handles any trk, runs
well fresh: likes to force the pace: well h'capped on old form, sure to win again in this grade.
2747 **SHARP SHUFFLE** 3 [8] Ian Williams 7-9-7 L Newman (3) 5/4 FAV: 400232: 7 ch g Exactly Sharp -   4   **47**
Style (Traffic Judge) Dwelt, hmpd ent str, styd on well fnl 1f, no ch with wnr: well bckd, qck reapp: see 2747.
2479 **RED WOLF** 15 [2] J G Given 4-9-2 Dean McKeown 20/1: 00-003: 4 ch g Timeless Times - Stealthy   shd **42**
(Kind Of Hush) Prom till onepcd fnl 2f: mkt drifter, 4L clr rem: handles fast & soft grnd: see 329 (AW).
2744 **GET A LIFE** 3 [7] G Woodward 7-8-11 R Lappin 14/1: 050504: Prom till outpcd fnl 2½f: op 25/1.   4   **29**
2380 **HEATHYARDS JAKE** 19 [1] 4-9-7 M Tebbutt 16/1: 665005: Rear, hmpd ent str, styd on late, nvr dngrs: 1   **37**
drifted from 10/1: had it to do at these weights: see 229 (AW mdn).
2221 **FOURTH TIME LUCKY** 25 [4] 4-9-2 K Hodgson 66/1: 60-006: Chsd ldrs, left bhnd fnl 2f: see 2221 (h'cap). 2   **28**
2704 **BY THE GLASS** 6 [6] 4-9-7 Kim Tinkler 40/1: 0-6007: Rear, hmpd ent str, nvr a factor: stiff task.   ¾   **31**
1596 **DISPOL JAZZ** 52 [12] 3-8-8 O Pears 10/1: -30008: Rear, nvr a factor: op 6/1, 7 wk abs: see 900.   1¼ **23**
2460 **SAVOIR FAIRE** 15 [13] 4-8-11 (VIS) A Culhane 33/1: /0-009: Prom 4f, wknd: op 16/1, tried a visor.   ½   **17**
1858 **THE REPUBLICAN** 41 [11] 3-8-8 (vis) T Williams 100/1: -00000: In tch 4f, fin 10th: 6 wk abs.   4   **14**
*2533 **JAMMIE DODGER** 3 [3] 4-9-7 V Halliday 4/1: 00201U: In tch when slipped & u.r. enter str: **0**
bckd from 8/1: forget this, better off in sell h'caps: see 2533.
2143 **Just Good Friends** 29 [9] 3-8-8 G Parkin 50/1:   2143 **Brigmour** 29 [5] 4-8-11 J McAuley (5) 66/1:
13 ran   Time 1m 41.1 (3.6)   (E A Hayward)   J M Bradley Sedbury, Gloucs.

2835

2.55 LEEDS HOSPICES MDN 2YO (D)   5f str   Good/Firm 40 -36 Slow
£3367   £1036   £518   £259

1870 **MAJESTIC QUEST** 40 [1] J Neville 2-9-0 A Culhane 5/6 FAV: -421: 2 b c Piccolo - Teanarco (Kafu)   **71**
Chsd ldrs, styd on strongly to lead cl home, drvn out: well bckd, 6 wk abs: dam a 6f 2yo wnr: eff at 5f on gd
& fast grnd, 6f will suit: handles a gall or sharpish trk: can rate more highly.
2480 **ALBANECK** 15 [6] T D Easterby 2-9-0 G Parkin 5/1: -0642: 2 gr g Timeless Times - Strawberry Pink   shd **70**
(Absalom) Trckd far away, led ins last till caught nr line: op 7/2: sound run, eff at 5f on fast grnd: see 2480.
2608 **MY AMERICAN BEAUTY** 9 [5] T D Easterby 2-8-9 T E Durcan 8/1: -603: 2 ch f Wolfhound - Horray Lady   ½   **64**
(Ahonoora) Chsd ldrs, styd on well fnl 1f, just btn in a cl fin: op 12/1, longer priced stablemate of 2nd: see 2333.
1906 **LADY ROCK** 38 [4] R Bastiman 2-8-9 O Pears 25/1: -004: Led till ins last: only btn arnd 1L.   ½   **63**
2532 **PERTEMPS JARDINE** 12 [3] 2-9-0 P Hanagan (7) 7/1: -345: Outpcd till last gains, nvr dngrs: btr 1776. 3   **59**
2639 **KIRKBYS TREASURE** 8 [2] 2-9-0 C Lowther 11/2: -036: Slowly away, nvr in it: btr 2639.   7   **39**
6 ran   Time 1m 01.6 (3.8)   (Brian K Symonds)   J Neville Coedkernew, Monmouths.

2836

3.25 LEEDS HCAP 3YO+ 0-80 (D)   1m2f   Good/Firm 40 +03 Fast
£4875   £1500   £750   £375   3yo rec 10lb   **[78]**

2481 **MINI LODGE** 15 [2] J G FitzGerald 4-8-10 (60) A Culhane 6/1: 600-01: 4 ch g Grand Lodge - Mirea   **67**
(The Minstrel) Waited with, hdwy to lead ins fnl 1f, won going away: bckd from 12/1: gd time: well btn in '99
(rtd 76, h'cap): '98 Newcastle wnr (debut, mdn, rtd 89): eff at 7f, apprec this step up to 10f & shld stay 12f:
acts on fast & hvy, handles a gall or sharpish trk: tried a visor, better without: on a fair mark & can win again.
2463 **BLUE STREET** 15 [7] S C Williams 4-8-8 (58) G Faulkner 9/2: -00602: 4 b c Deploy - Kumzar   1¼   **60**
(Hotfoot) Chsd ldrs, prog to lead dist, styd on despite edging right, not pace to repel wnr cl home: mkt drifter:
sound run, clearly stays 10f on fast grnd: met a well h'capped rival: see 2463.
2522 **COURT EXPRESS** 15 [8] W W Haigh 4-10-0 (78) T E Durcan 13/2: 162053: 6 b g Then Again - Moon   shd **80**
Risk (Risk Me) Rear, prog 2f out, switched dist, ran on & not btn far: op 5/1: see 2138.
2523 **ROMAN KING** 13 [4] M Johnston 5-9-13 (77) J Fanning 11/8 FAV: 1-6034: Trckd ldrs, went on 3f out   1¾   **77**
till hdd dist, no extra: well bckd from 2/1, 6l clr rem: back in trip on faster grnd: see 2523 (12f, gd).
2213 **SPEED VENTURE** 25 [3] 3-9-0 (74) L Newman (3) 9/2: 42255: Dsptd lead till wknd dist: op 3/1.   6   **65**
2199 **EDIFICE** 26 [5] 4-9-5 (69) N Carlisle 9/2: 400-56: Led till 3f out, wknd: btr 2199.   ¾   **53**
4587} **ALDWYCH ARROW** 263 [1] 5-8-10 (60) Dean McKeown 25/1: 0000-7: In tch 1m, outpcd: reapp: '99 wnr   nk   **49**
at Catterick (h'cap, rtd 68), also plcd sev times: '98 Ayr & Musselburgh wnr (h'caps, rtd 67): eff at 12f/2m on fast,
soft grnd & on both AW's: tried blnks, best without: can force the pace: tough & back on a winning mark.

RIPON   SATURDAY JULY 22ND   Righthand, Sharpish Track

4365} **FALCON SPIRIT 282** [6] 4-8-12 (62) Dale Gibson 16/1: 5320-8: In tch 1m, sn rdn & btn on reapp: *nk*   50
failed to complete on 2 99/00 hdle starts: trained by W Haggas in '99, plcd sev times (rtd 66 & 68a, h'caps): eff
at 7/12f on firm, fast & on both AW's: eff in blnks, left off today: now with G M Moore.
8 ran   Time 2m 07.0 (3.7)   (Marquesa de Moratalla)   J G FitzGerald Norton, N Yorks.

2837   **3.55 L'ANSON HCAP 3YO+ 0-85 (D)**   **1m4f60y**   **Good/Firm 40**   **-29 Slow**   **[81]**
     £6786   £2088   £1044   £522   3yo rec 12lb

2750 **ST HELENSFIELD 3** [3] M Johnston 5-10-0 (81) J Fanning 3/1: 032201: 5 ch g Kris - On Credit (No   87
Pas No Sale) Made all, held on well fnl 1f, drvn out: qck reapp, top-weight: deserved win, plcd sev times this
term: '99 wnr at Newcastle (h'cap, rtd 88): '97 Bath scorer (mdn, debut), also plcd in List company (rtd 90):
eff at 10/12f, will stay further: acts on firm & soft grnd: gd weight carrier, can run well fresh: eff with/
without a visor: handles a stiff/gall or sharpish trk: can set the pace: tough & consistent.
*2272 **ORIGINAL SPIN** [1] J L Dunlop 3-9-5 (84) M Tebbutt 5/2 FAV: 2-2112: 3 b f Machiavellian - Not   *1¾*   86
Before Time (Polish Precedent) Dsptd lead, not pace of wnr ins last: op 7/4: sound run, in gd form: see 2272.
2666 **MICKLEY 8** [6] J D Bethell 3-8-5 (70)(vis) L Newman (3) 4/1: 545363: 3 b g Ezzoud - Dawsha (Slip   *2*   69
Anchor) Chsd ldrs, rdn & onepcd fnl 1½f: 5L clr rem: caught the eye in 2666 (sharp trk).
*2439 **WINDMILL 16** [4] T D Easterby 3-8-10 (75) T E Durcan 6/1: -414: Rear, nvr nr to chall: op 4/1:   *5*   66
prob not apprec this drop back in trip: see 2439 (14f).
2530 **SHAFFISHAYES 13** [5] 8-8-3 (56) Dean McKeown 3/1: 065465: Dwelt, rcd keenly & sn chsd ldrs, wknd   *hd*   47
2f out: bckd from 5/1: rcd too freely for own gd today: see see 1860.
5 ran   Time 2m 42.1 (8.6)   (Paul Dean)   M Johnston Middleham, N Yorks.

2838   **4.25 POSTHOUSE MED AUCT MDN 3YO (E)**   **1m1f**   **Good/Firm 40**   **-33 Slow**
     £3500   £1000   £500

1282 **KARALIYFA 70** [1] Sir Michael Stoute 3-8-9 L Newman (3) 1/5 FAV: 3-61: 3 gr f Kahyasi - Karliyka   75
(Last Tycoon) Made all, styd on well fnl 1f, drvn out: well bckd, 10 wk abs: earlier 6th in a List event: eff
at 9f, bred for mid-dists & prob stays 12f: handles fast & firm grnd: runs well fresh: can rate more highly.
2531 **JOONDEY 13** [3] M A Jarvis 3-9-0 M Tebbutt 4/1: -03252: 3 b c Pursuit Of Love - Blueberry Walk   *½*   78
(Green Desert) Trkd wnr tho'out, drifted right fnl 1f, kept on well & only just btn: op 5/2: acts on fast & hvy.
2611 **ARANUI 9** [2] R Hollinshead 3-9-0 (t) Dean McKeown 16/1: 0-03: 3 b c Pursuit Of Love - Petite   *11*   56
Rosanna (Ile de Bourbon) Chsd ldrs, rdn & no impress fnl 2f: bckd at long odds: stiff task: see 2611.
3 ran   Time 1m 56.6 (6.6)   (H H Aga Khan)   Sir Michael Stoute Newmarket

---

2839   **5.00 EUREST MDN HCAP 3YO+ 0-70 (E)**   **6f str**   **Good/Firm 40**   **-18 Slow**   **[64]**
     £3250   £1000   £500   £250   3yo rec 5lb

2462 **FLY MORE 15** [20] J M Bradley 3-9-9 (64) T Williams 9/1: -4551: 3 ch g Lycius - Double River   71
(Irish River) Chsd ldrs far side, went on 2f out, ran on strongly, rdn out: h'cap bow: clearly not affected by
nasty experience at Warwick last time (mdn): eff at 6f on fast grnd: handles a sharpish trk: cost connections
14,000gns, half brother to useful sprint h'capper So Intrepid: reportedly still v green, can progress further.
2519 **TAWN AGAIN 14** [19] T D Barron 4-8-6 (42) J Fanning 4/1 FAV: 000002: 4 b g Then Again - Tawny   *1½*   44
(Grey Ghost) Nvr far away far side, chall fnl 1f, not pace of wnr ins fnl 1f: well bckd: flattered 2519 (mdn).
2612 **SOBA JONES 9** [6] T D Easterby 3-9-0 (51)(BL) T E Durcan 13/2: 602343: 3 b c Emperor Jones - Soba   *1*   50
(Most Secret) Led after 2f stands side, edged right & kept on well, no ch with far side: gd run in first time blnks.
2421 **FOUND AT LAST 17** [2] J Balding 4-9-1 (51) C Lowther 6/1: 502224: Rear stands side, styd on fnl 2f.   *2½*   43
2555 **BLAKEY 12** [17] 4-7-10 (32)(bl)(2oh) Jonjo Fowle(1) 25/1: 000005: Hmpd start, styd on fnl 2f far   *4*   12
side, nvr nrr: stablemate of wnr: lost ch at the start: see 2223.
2223 **NOW IS THE HOUR 25** [7] 4-7-11 (33)(1ow)(3oh) Dale Gibson 12/1: 620036: Prom 4f stands side.   *¾*   10
2690 **WOOLLY WINSOME 7** [16] 4-8-4 (40) Dean McKeown 8/1: 300067: Rear far side, mod late prog.   *nk*   16
2525 **PRECISION 13** [9] 5-8-7 (43) A Culhane 14/1: 000608: Front rank 4f stands side: see 1714.   *1*   16
1858 **RUDCROFT 41** [14] 4-7-10 (32)(12oh) J McAuley(3) 100/1: 0:0009: Set pace 2f stands side, wknd: abs.   *hd*   5
2577 **DIANEME 10** [18] 3-9-1 (56) G Parkin 20/1: 304500: Prom 4f far side, fin 10th: see 826.   *shd*   29
2673 **OSTARA 7** [15] 3-9-0 (55) M Tebbutt 11/1: 0-0300: Prom 3f far side, sn btn: fin 11th, tchd 14/1.   *1*   25
2680 **APRILS COMAIT 7** [12] 3-8-4 (45)(bl) V Halliday 25/1: 005600: Nvr a factor on far side: 12th.   *¾*   12
2315 **SUSY WELLS 21** [5] 5-7-10 (32)(2oh) P Hanagan(3) 14/1: -00550: Rcd stands side & al bhnd: fin 13th.   *hd*   0
1280 **RUM LASS 70** [3] 3-8-12 (53) T Lucas 33/1: 50-000: Led 4f far side, wknd into 15th: 10 wk abs.   0
2511 **MUFFLED 14** [11] 3-9-10 (64) L Newman (3) 13/2: 0-0020: Reared start & nvr dngrs stands side: fin   0
18th, top-weight: lost al ch at the start: btr 2511.
2680 Petra Nova 7 [8] 4-8-0 (36) N Carlisle 50/1:   2511 Mount Park 14 [4] 3-8-3 (44) O Pears 33/1:
2640 Consideration 8 [10] 3-8-10 (51) P Bradley (5) 14/1:   2753 Lucky Cove 3 [13] 4-9-0 (50) Kim Tinkler 100/1:
19 ran   Time 1m 13.5 (3.5)   (E A HAyward)   J M Bradley Sedbury, Gloucs.

WARWICK   SATURDAY JULY 22ND   Lefthand, Sharp, Turning Track

Official Going   GOOD TO FIRM   Stalls: Inside

2840   **2.15 GRANDSTAND APPR HCAP 3YO+ 0-70 (G)**   **7f rnd**   **Good/Firm Inapplicable**   **[65]**
     £1886   £539   £269   3 yo rec 7 lb

2242 **PETERS IMP 24** [5] A Berry 5-9-13 (64) D Allan (10) 7/1: 025301: 5 b g Imp Society - Catherine Clare (Sallust) 67
Rear, rdn/prog wide over 1f out to lead ins last, styd on well: op 5/1: '99 scorer at Hamilton & Redcar (class
stks, rtd 82, J Berry): '98 Haydock wnr (class stks, rtd 75): eff at 6/7.5f on soft & fibresand, suited by firm &
fast: handles any trk: eff with/without blnks: can go well fresh: runs well for an apprentice.
2378 **DOBERMAN 19** [13] P D Evans 5-8-7 (44)(vis) Joanna Badger (3) 7/1: 310022: 5 br g Dilum - Switch   *nk*   46
Blade (Robellino) Chsd ldr, led over 1f out till ins last, kept on for press: op 6/1: eff at 7f/1m: see 2378.
2732 **L A TOUCH 4** [6] C A Dwyer 7-8-12 (49) T Eaves (3) 10/1: 300-03: 7 b m Tina's Pet - Silvers Era (Balidar)   *hd*   50
Chsd ldrs, styd on onepace from over 1f out: op 8/1: '99 h'cap wnr at Yarmouth & Chester (h'caps, rtd 52): '98
Yarmouth wnr (fill h'cap, J Quinn, rtd 38): suited by 6f, stays 7.5f well: handles gd/soft, likes gd or firm grnd:

WARWICK   SATURDAY JULY 22ND   Lefthand, Sharp, Turning Track

likes a sharp or fair track, loves Yarmouth & is one to note in similar events at that track.
2544 **BLUE ACE** 12 [1] A W Carroll 7-8-12 (49) A Hall (10) 20/1: 006664: Dwelt, rear, styd on fnl 2f, nrst fin.   1¼ 47
2601 **HEATHER VALLEY** 9 [3] 4-8-7 (44) M Worrell (4) 14/1: 00-055: Mid-div, onepace fnl 2f: see 2297.   hd 41
2612 **CELANDINE** 9 [14] 7-8-4 (41) R Thomas (3) 7/1: 0-0006: Held up, late gains: op 7/1: see 2221.   nk 37
2682 **DEFIANCE** 7 [7] 5-7-10 (33)(1oh) Michael Doyle (5) 25/1: 000007: Prom, btn over 1f out: see 1578.   1¾ 25
*2728 **REACHFORYOURPOCKET** 4 [10] 5-8-6 (43)(6ex) G Sparkes 9/2 FAV: 600018: Chsd ldrs 6f: bckd.   ¾ 33
1799 **JAMES DEE** 44 [11] 4-9-12 (63) Lisa Jones (10) 10/1: 226209: Mid-div, nvr on terms: op 7/1: abs.   nk 52
2729 **MUJKARI** 4 [12] 4-7-13 (36)(vis) D Kinsella (5) 33/1: 000400: Mid-div, no impress: 10th: see 323.   ¾ 23
1913 **ECUDAMAH** 38 [16] 4-9-7 (58) S Clancy (3) 20/1: 000640: Held up, nvr factor: 11th: see 40 (AW, 5f).   2½ 38
2320 **MISS MONEY SPIDER** 21 [4] 5-8-5 (42) D Glennon 7/1: 6-0000: Led, clr halfway, hdd & wknd qckly over   nk 21
1f out: 12th: '99 wnr at Folkestone (2, clmrs) & Lingfield (Fillies h'cap, rtd 54, unplcd on sand, rtd 44a): '98
Yarmouth wnr (sell, N Callaghan, rtd 59): loves to dominate over 7f, stays 1m on firm & gd, best without blnks.
1971 **ARZILLO** 36 [15] 4-8-12 (49) D Watson (3) 13/2: 034040: Prom 6f: op 5/1: see 1211.   nk 27
2680 **Franklin Lakes** 7 [8] 5-7-10 (33)(bl) (1oh) R Naylor (4) 20/1:
2489 **Burcot Girl** 14 [2] 3-7-10 (40)(BL)(10oh) Clare Roche 50/1:
2542 **Colonel Sam** 32 [9] 4-8-3 (40)(tbl) M Mathers (3) 20/1: R
16 ran   Time 1m 28.40   (Mr & Mrs Peter Foden)   A Berry Cockerham, Lancs

2841 2.50 E.C. HARRIS AUCT MDN 2YO (E)   7f rnd   Good/Firm   Inapplicable
£2884   £824   £472

2494 **SPECIFIC SORCEROR** 14 [1] A P Jarvis 2-8-10 N Callan 10/11 FAV: 51: 2 ch c Definite Article - Mystic   73
Dispute (Magical Strike) Chsd ldr, led over 2f out, drvn & strongly pressed ins last, held on well: well bckd:
confirmed promise of debut: eff at 7f, 1m will suit: acts on fast ground & a stiff/sharp trk.
-- **DILLY** [11] P R Chamings 2-8-1 S Righton 50/1: 2: 2 br f Dilum - Princess Rosananti (Shareef Dancer)   1¼ 60
Twds rear, swtchd wide fnl 2f & styd on well for press, not reach wnr: April foal, cost 1400gns: half sister to a
7f juvenile wnr: dam unraced: stays 7f, will appreciate 1m+ in time: acts on fast grnd: encouraging intro.
2620 **COUNTRYWIDE PRIDE** 9 [3] K R Burke 2-8-12 Darren Williams (5) 20/1: 043: 2 ch c Eagle Eyed -   hd 70
Lady's Dream (Mazilier) Mid-div, prog to press wnr 1f out, just held nr fin: stays 7f, handles fast: improving.
2430 **ORIGINAL SINNER** 17 [2] W J Haggas 2-8-12 Paul Eddery 4/1: 64: Trkd ldrs, ch 2f out, no extra.   1½ 67
-- **OCEAN LOVE** [6] 2-8-3 A Beech (5) 12/1: 5: Held up, eff 2f out, kept on onepace, no threat to   1¾ 55
wnr: Apr foal, cost 9000gns: dam a 1m wnr abroad: likely to appreciate 1m in time for M Bell.
2653 **DATIN STAR** 8 [9] 2-8-1 M Henry 50/1: 606: Mid-div, rdn/pressed wnr over 1f out, sn no extra.   ½ 52
1943 **LIMBURG** 17 [10] 2-8-6 Martin Dwyer 12/1: -07: Chsd ldrs, btn/eased ins last: longer 7f trip.   6 48
2361 **HARD TO LAY** 19 [5] 2-8-3 L Newton 12/1: 2508: Dwelt, nvr on terms: longer 7f trip: see 1698.   nk 44
2430 **VISLINK** 17 [7] 2-8-10 Lisa Jones (7) 50/1: 009: Led till over 2f out, fdd: see 2430.   1 49
-- **POLWHELE** [8] 2-8-12 R Mullen 33/1: 0: Prom till over 1f out: 10th: op 12/1: Mujtahid colt,   4 43
8200gns May foal: dam a 7f Irish wnr: sire a high-class juvenile: with R M H Cowell.
2052 **ONLY WHEN PROVOKED** 33 [4] 2-8-6 (vis) R Havlin 50/1: 000: Al twds rear: 11th: see 2052 (6f).   9 24
11 ran   Time 1m 29.60   (The Aston Partnership)   A P Jarvis Aston Upthorpe, Oxon

2842 3.20 BANK OF IRELAND HCAP 3YO 0-80 (D)   1m2f188y   Good/Firm   Inapplicable   [85]
£3883   £1195   £597   £298

*2175 **JOCKO GLASSES** 27 [7] C F Wall 3-9-3 (74) R Mullen 5/4 FAV: 5-0511: 3 ch g Inchinor - Corinthia (Empery)   84
Chsd ldrs, led 1f out, rdn clr ins last, readily: heavily bckd: earlier scored at Pontefract (h'cap): eff at 10/11f
on firm & gd grnd, sharp/stiff trk: lightly raced, plenty in hand here, hat-trick beckons in similar company.
2552 **RAPID DEPLOYMENT** 12 [9] J G Smyth Osbourne 3-8-5 (62) S Carson (3) 25/1: 30-002: 3 b g Deploy -   6 63
City Times (Last Tycoon) Chsd ldrs, rdn/led over 1f out, hdd 1f out, sn held: stays 10f: caught a tartar: see 2552.
2552 **SHOTACROSS THE BOW** 12 [4] B W Hills 3-8-11 (68) Paul Eddery 10/1: 1-0003: 3 b c Warning - Nordica   1 68
(Northfields) Trkd ldrs, drvn/ch over 1f out, sn held: see 2552.
2685 **SAMARARDO** 7 [8] N P Littmoden 3-7-13 (56) G Baker (7) 11/1: 203-54: Prom till over 1f out: see 2685.   3 52
4305} **BANDLER CHING** 285 [1] R Morse 16/1: 2533-5: Led 9f, fdd: op 12/1: reapp: plcd twice   1 66
in '99 (h'caps, rtd 72, Pat Mitchell): eff at 1m, shld stay 10f: acts on firm & gd, sharp/gall trk.
1341 **KNIGHTS EMPEROR** 65 [3] I Mongan (5) 20/1: 0-4006: Al rear, abs, new stable, Ingr trip.   6 57
2624 **SHRIVAR** 9 [6] 3-9-2 (73) R Havlin 100/30: 464147: Al twds rear: btr 2463 (C/D).   6 50
2795 **WINDFALL** 2 [5] 3-8-13 (70) N Callan 14/1: -03008: Prom 1m, eased fnl 1f: op 10/1: qck reapp.   9 38
2543 **LATOUR** 12 [2] 3-9-7 (78) M Henry 11/1: 5-2329: Al bhd, eased fnl 1f: op 8/1: btr 2543 (sft, 1m).   5 39
9 ran   Time 2m 20.20   (Jocko Partnership)   C F Wall Newmarket, Suffolk

2843 3.50 J. HOWLETT SELL HCAP 3YO+ 0-60 (G)   1m4f134y   Good/Firm   Inapplicable   [56]
£2027   £579   £289   3 yo rec 13lb

2181 **LOST SPIRIT** 13 [13] P W Hiatt 4-8-2 (30) G Baker (7) 15/2: 506401: 4 b g Strolling Along - Shoag (Affirmed)   33
Made all, rdn/strongly pressed over 3f out, shook off rivals over 1f out, rdn/just held on nr line despite drifting
right: op 6/1: bought in for 5,450gns: earlier won at Lingfield (AW h'cap, rtd 49a): '99 wnr at Southwell (clmr)
& Wolverhampton (h'cap, rtd 66a, plcd on turf, rtd 49): rnr-up in '98 (sell, rtd 55, B Hanbury): best dominating at
12f on firm, gd/sft & both AWs on a sharp trk: eff with/without blnks: enjoys sell grade.
2636 **WATER LOUP** 8 [9] W R Muir 4-8-1 (29) Martin Dwyer 12/1: 000622: 4 b f Wolfhound - Heavenly Waters   nk 31
(Celestial Storm) Held up, rdn & styd on well fnl 2f, just held: op 10/1: stays 12f: mdn after 17: see 692.
2655 **ARTHURS KINGDOM** 8 [2] A P Jarvis 4-10-0 (56) N Callan 100/30 FAV: 304463: 4 b g Roi Danzig -   ½ 57
Merrie Moment (Taufan) Drvn along/clr with wnr over 3f out, just held by wnr over 1f out: bckd, top-weight, mdn.
2656 **PREMIERE FOULEE** 8 [10] F Jordan 5-8-2 (30) S Carson (3) 8/1: 060664: Held up, nvr on terms.   2½ 27
737 **ACTION JACKSON** 117 [11] 8-8-5 (33) A Beech (5) 16/1: 604-05: Chsd ldrs, held fnl 2f: op 12/1: abs: ¾ 29
rnr-up in '99 (h'cap, rtd 39a, plcd on turf, rtd 32, sell h'cap): rnr-up twice in '98 (rtd 46): eff at 10f, stays 14f,
tried 2m: acts on firm, gd/sft & fibresand: handles any trk.
2130 **ITALIAN ROSE** 29 [5] 5-8-7 (35) S Righton 25/1: 006-06: Twds rear, nvr a threat: unplcd in '99   4 25
(h'caps, rtd 28a & 48, sell): dual turf rnr-up in '98 (rtd mdn, rtd 55): eff at 6/7f on firm & soft, without blnks.
2606 **FLY LIKE A BIRD** 9 [3] 4-8-9 (37) R Mullen 8/1: 0-0407: Bhd, mod gains: op 7/1: see 2075.   2½ 23
2191 **CALIFORNIA SON** 26 [6] 4-8-4 (32) G Sparkes 20/1: 20-U08: Dwelt/bhd, nvr factor: mod form.   ½ 17
2362 **RONNI PANCAKE** 19 [8] 3-9-1 (56) I Mongan (5) 8/1: 015069: Chsd ldrs 9f: btr 1572 (1m, clmr).   hd 40
1852 **RONQUISTA DOR** 41 [4] 6-9-3 (45)(bl) Paul Eddery 4/1: -60400: Held up, btn 3f out: 10th: abs.   19 8
2033 **HAYA YA KEFAAH** 33 [12] 8-9-5 (47) M Henry 10/1: 010000: Bhd 4f out: 11th: btr 822 (sft).   15 0
887

889   **Dancing Dervish 101** [1] 5-9-8 (50) (vis) R Havlin 25/1: --   **Chocolate Ice** [7] 7-9-4 (46) M Fenton 40/1:
13 ran   Time 2m 46.20   (Red Lion Partnership)   P W Hiatt Hook Norton, Oxon

2844

4.20 EBF CLASSIFIED STKS 3YO+ 0-85 (C)   1m   Good/Firm Inapplicable
£7070 £2681 £1340 £609   3 yo rec 8 lb

2304 **KATHIR 22** [4] A C Stewart 3-8-8 R Mullen 5/4 FAV: 1-0321: 3 ch c Woodman - Alcando (Alzao)   **88**
Made all, readily asserted under hands & heels riding from over 1f out: val for 5L: heavily bckd: '99 Nottingham
mdn wnr (rtd 84): suited by 1m, stays 9f: acts on fast & hvy grnd, sharp/gall trk: eff forcing the pace.
*2287 **CULZEAN 22** [5] R Hannon 4-9-6 Martin Dwyer 4/1: 600412: 4 b g Machiavellian - Eileen Jenny   3½ **83**
(Kris) Held up, rdn/chsd wnr over 1f out, no impress: op 3/1: eff at 1m, return to 10f could suit: see 2287 (h'cap).
2528 **CEDAR MASTER 13** [2] R J O'Sullivan 3-8-8 (bl) F Norton 12/1: 055603: 3 b c Soviet Lad - Samriah   1½ **76**
(Wassl) Prom, hung left/held over 1f out: op 8/1: see 1029.
2699 **VICTORIET 6** [1] A T Murphy 3-8-5 K Dalgleish (5) 66/1: -55044: Cl up till over 3f out: flattered.   2½ **68**
2567 **EBBA 11** [6] 3-8-5 M Fenton 7/2: -04035: Chsd ldrs, rdn/btn 2f out: op 11/4: see 2567, 1384.   8 **56**
2704 **FOUR MEN 6** [7] 3-8-8 D Allan 7/1: 006606: Struggling 3f out: offic rated 30, flattered: see 2682.   4 **51**
2167 **IYAVAYA 28** [3] F Norton 3-8-5 R Havlin 6/1: 5-000R: Refused to race: see 829.   **0**
7 ran   Time 1m 39.70   (Hamdan Al Maktoum)   A C Stewart Newmarket

2845

4.50 PEARCE HCAP STKS 3YO+ 0-85 (D)   6f   Good/Firm Inapplicable   **[83]**
£10790 £3320 £1660 £830   3 yo rec 5 lb

2697 **CADEAUX CHER 7** [8] B W Hills 6-9-9 (78) F Norton 6/1: 220001: 6 ch g Cadeaux Genereux - Home Truth   **84**
(Known Fact) Chsd ldrs, rdn to lead over 1f out, drvn out to hold on: unplcd last term (rtd 88 at best): '98 wnr
at Doncaster, Leicester (class stks), Ripon & Doncaster (val h'caps, rtd 96): suited by 5.5f/6f on firm & gd grnd:
runs well fresh: best without blnks: handles any trk, likes Doncaster: well h'capped, could win again.
*2654 **EVENTUALITY 8** [7] R F Johnson Houghton 4-8-12 (67) S Carson (3) 8/1: -50012: 4 b f Petoski -   hd **72**
Queen's Tickle (Tickled Pink) Dwelt, twds rear, rdn/styd on well form over 1f out, post came too soon: op 6/1.
*2777 **TREASURE TOUCH 2** [10] P D Evans 6-9-1 (70) (6ex) Joanna Badger (7) 3/1 FAV: 301313: 6 b g   1¼ **72**
Treasure Kay - Bally Pourri (Law Society) Handy, rdn/ch fnl 2f, just held cl home: hvly bckd: qck reapp.
2631 **BEYOND CALCULATION 9** [1] J M Bradley 6-9-0 (69) Martin Dwyer 7/1: 150164: Trkd ldrs, rdn,   1 **69**
onepace fnl 1f: op 6/1: back to form, could pinch another one of these races on the prevailing fast grnd.
2569 **OCKER 11** [5] 6-10-0 (83) N Callan 11/1: 006045: Led over 4f out till over 1f out, fdd: op 6/1: see 47.   4 **73**
2701 **TRINITY 6** [2] 4-9-0 (69) Paul Eddery 14/1: 00-006: Pressed ldrs 3f: op 8/1: qck reapp: see 2701.   1½ **55**
2701 **STATOYORK 6** [3] 7-8-3 (58) R Mullen 14/1: -00507: Twds rear, rdn/btn over 1f out: eyecatching 2701 (5f).   5 **35**
2697 **NINEACRES 7** [4] 9-9-1 (70)(bl) P Fitzsimons (5) 7/2: 011038: Reared start, no chance after: forget this.   1 **45**
2670 **ACE OF PARKES 7** [9] 4-9-11 (80) I Mongan (5) 14/1: -50659: Led till over 4f out, sn btn: see 1245.   shd **55**
9 ran   Time 1m 15.00   (N N Browne)   B W Hills Lambourn, Berks

2846

5.25 GROSVENOR MDN 3YO (D)   1m   Good/Firm Inapplicable
£4290 £1320 £660 £330

2426 **DEVIL LEADER 17** [1] B W Hills 3-8-9 F Norton 11/10 FAV: -05321: 3 ch f Diesis - Shihama (Shadeed)   **72**
Made all, rdly asserted under hands & heels riding over 1f out: val for 7L+: bckd: suited by 1m on fast grnd, tried
10f, may yet suit: eff forcing the pace on a sharp trk: untested here, could make her mark in h'caps.
661 **ATALYA 133** [4] G A Ham 3-9-0 Paul Eddery 10/1: 0-2452: 3 ch g Afzal - Sandy Looks (Music Boy)   5 **65**
Chsd wnr, rdn/btn over 1f out: op 8/1: 4 mth abs: see 319.
4091‡ **NEGRONI 301** [5] J W Hills 3-8-9 M Henry 4/1: 6-3: 3 br f Mtoto - Carousel Music (On Your Mark)   1¾ **57**
Chsd ldrs, outpcd fnl 2f: op 3/1: reapp: unplcd sole '99 start (mdn, rtd 76): sire a high-class mid-dist performer.
2135 **TALENT STAR 29** [3] A W Carroll 3-9-0 S Righton 33/1: 04: Nvr on terms: no form.   6 **53**
2554 **MASRORA 12** [2] 3-8-9 P Fessey 5/2: 453005: Dwelt, twds rear, rdn/btn 2f out: btr 1970 (12f).   nk **47**
5 ran   Time 1m 41.90   (Mohamed Obaida)   B W Hills Lambourn, Berks

NEWBURY   SATURDAY JULY 22ND   Lefthand, Flat, Galloping Track

Official Going   GOOD/FIRM. Stalls: Str - Centre; Rnd - Inside.

2847

1.30 LISTED HACKWOOD STKS 3YO+ (A)   6f str   Firm -18 +12 Fast
£15795 £4860 £2430 £1215   3 yo rec 5 lb

3794‡ **AUENKLANG 323** [9] Saeed bin Suroor 3-8-12 (VIS) J Reid 9/2: 2121-1: 3 ch c Big Shuffle -   **119**
Auenglocke (Surumu) Made all, qcknd over 1f out, sn clr, impressive: crse rec time: in '99 trained in Germany by
H Hiller, won at Baden-Baden (Gr 2, rtd 108) & Hamburg (List): loves to force the pace over 6f on gd & firm: has
run well in blinks & here in a visor: smart, high-class young sprinter, win Group races.
2335 **HARMONIC WAY 21** [4] R Charlton 5-9-3 R Hughes 11/4 FAV: 642162: 5 ch h Lion Cavern - Pineapple   6 **105**
(Superlative) Steady start, held up, plenty to do & jockey sat motionless till dist, styd on strongly when asked
for eff but wnr had flown: well bckd: must come late but set too much to do today: can win a Listed: see 2151.
-2335 **CRETAN GIFT 21** [6] N P Littmoden 9-9-7 (vis) J F Egan 13/2: 650023: 9 ch g Cadeaux Genereux -   hd **108**
Caro's Niece (Caro) Handy, eff to chase wnr over 1f out, kept on same pace: most tough: see 2335, 2151 & 952.
2151 **HALMAHERA 29** [8] I A Balding 5-9-3 M Hills 9/1: 205604: Chsd ldrs, rdn & onepace over 1f out.   1 **101**
2458 **ALFAILAK 15** [5] 3-8-12 Craig Williams 33/1: 200-05: Waited with, eff 2f out, onepace: gd run.   1¼ **98**
2670 **GAELIC STORM 7** [11] 6-9-3 D Holland 9/1: 065046: In tch, eff over 1f out, no impress: needs cut.   shd **97**
2458 **NOW LOOK HERE 15** [10] 4-9-3 J P Spencer 10/1: 345027: Chsd ldrs, wknd over 1f out: btr 2458.   1 **94**
2646 **HALLAND PARK GIRL 8** [2] 3-8-7 (BL) Dane O'Neill 12/1: -60208: Bhd, brief eff 2f out, soon wknd: ¾ **87**
tried blinks & twice well below 1410, 953.
2065 **TABHEEJ 32** [1] 3-8-7 W Supple 14/1: 13-609: Never a factor: see 2065 (h'cap), 1338.   1 **84**
1987 **DON PUCCINI 35** [7] 3-8-12 J Carroll 8/1: 161-50: Chsd wnr, wknd over 1f out: 10th, btr 1987.   1 **86**
2343 **DESARU 21** [3] 4-9-3 M Roberts 33/1: 00-000: Al bhd: 11th: see 967 (9f).   nk **85**
11 ran   Time 1m 09.81 (Crse Rec Time)   (Godolphin)   Saeed bin Suroor Newmarket

NEWBURY SATURDAY JULY 22ND Lefthand, Flat, Galloping Track

2848

2.00 MTOTO COND STKS 2YO (B) 7f str Firm -18 -18 Slow
£11245 £4158 £2079 £945

+2469 **PATSYS DOUBLE 15** [1] M Blanshard 2-9-4 D Sweeney 3/1: 111: 2 b c Emarati - Jungle Rose (Shirley Heights) Keen, waited with, hdwy to lead 2f out, styd on well ins last, rdn out: joint top weight: unbtn after wins at Newbury (mdn) & Salisbury (auction): 10,000gns half brother to 4 wnrs: dam 10f scorer: eff at 6f, stays 7f well & 1m shld suit: acts on firm, gd/soft & stiff tracks: has run well fresh: v progressive, genuine & smart. **103**
2474 **BLUEBERRY FOREST 15** [5] J L Dunlop 2-8-13 G Carter 7/4 FAV: -1222: 2 br c Charnwood Forest - Abstraction (Rainbow Quest) Set pace till 2f out, edged left for press inside last but kept on: hvly bckd, gd run. *1¼* **95**
*2678 **PREFERRED 7** [2] R Hannon 2-8-13 Dane O'Neill 11/4: 0113: 2 b c Distant Relative - Fruhlingserwachen (Irish River) Chsd ldr till 3f out, slightly outpcd 2f out, kept on again close home: bckd: imprvd at 7f on fm. *2* **91**
2576 **IMPERIAL DANCER 10** [3] M R Channon 2-8-13 Craig Williams 20/1: 213024: Handy, eff to chase ldr over 3f out till 2f out, onepace: gd run if not flattered: see 2576, 1995. *nk* **90**
2595 **MARINE 10** [4] 2-9-4 J Reid 7/2: -51155: Waited with, brief eff 2f out, no impression: joint top weight but shade better expected after 2595 (6f), see 1944: should stay this trip. *¾* **93**
5 ran Time 1m 24.31 (0.01) (Mrs Patricia Buckley) M Blanshard Upper Lambourn, Berks

2849

2.35 WEATHERBYS SUPER SPRINT STKS 2YO (B) 5f34y str Firm -18 +04 Fast
£72500 £27500 £13750 £6250

*2113 **SUPERSTAR LEO 30** [18] W J Haggas 2-8-6 M Hills 9/2: -21111: 2 b f College Chapel - Council Rock (General Assembly) Cl up, hdwy to lead over 1f out, soon qckd clr, impressive: gd time: 4-timer landed after wins at Catterick (2, stks) & R Ascot (Gr 3 Norfolk): v eff at 5f, 6f will suit: acts on firm, soft & on any track: v smart & progressive juv with a turn of foot, must win another Group race in this form. **109**
1586 **ELSIE PLUNKETT 53** [3] R Hannon 2-7-12 A Daly 13/2: 511132: 2 b f Mind Games - Snow Eagle (Polar Falcon) With ldrs, kept on over 1f out, not pace of wnr: 7 week abs & an excellent run from this prob disadvantageous low draw: deserves another nice prize: see 1586, 1372. *3½* **90**
2113 **THREEZEDZZ 30** [21] J G Portman 2-8-3 J F Egan 12/1: 1263: 2 ch c Emarati - Exotic Forest (Dominion) Handy, eff over 1f out, kept on: v useful, should be placed to win again: see 2113, 1290. *shd* **95**
2483 **UP TEMPO 15** [22] T D Easterby 2-8-6 M Roberts 33/1: 213223: Chsd ldrs, hdwy over 1f out, kept on well ins last: fine run in this competitive event & looks one to keep on your side at 6f: handles firm & hvy. *dht* **98+**
2152 **ZIETUNZEEN 29** [13] 2-8-3(1ow) G Carter 20/1: 2335: In tch, hdwy over 1f out, kept on fnl 1f, nvr dngrs: acts on firm & gd/soft: must win a mdn: see 1538, 1166. *1¼* **90$**
*2088 **ROMANTIC MYTH 31** [17] 2-8-11 J Carroll 10/11 FAV: 1116: In tch, eff well over 1f out, onepace: hvly bckd & clearly better expected: reportedly returned with cuts on hind legs & got upset in the stalls: impressive Gr 3 wnr in 2088 & could pay to forgive this. *½* **97**
2352 **KACHINA DOLL 20** [20] 2-8-1 Craig Williams 33/1: 110527: Bhd, eff over 1f out, kept on late: see 2352. *nk* **86**
*2162 **NIFTY ALICE 28** [9] 2-7-12 J Bramhill 33/1: 124418: Led over 3f out till over 1f out, no extra: speedy. *nk* **82**
2687 **INNIT 7** [8] 2-8-1 P Fessey 33/1: 354349: Bhd, some late gains, never dangerous: needs 6f. *shd* **84**
2307 **WHERES JASPER 22** [4] 2-8-9 F Lynch 33/1: 2120: In tch, rdn & onepace over 1f out: 10th, see 2307. *nk* **91**
2113 **SHOESHINE BOY 30** [1] 2-8-8 (BL) D Holland 16/1: 211100: Rcd alone far side, led till over 3f out, wknd fnl 1f: fin 11th: poor draw, this run is best ignored: tried blinks, best 1107. *1¼* **86**
2526 **CAYMAN EXPRESSO 13** [5] 2-8-6 C Rutter 50/1: -6350: In tch, rdn over 2f out, no impression: 12th. *1¾* **79**
1472 **REEL BUDDY 59** [16] 2-8-11 R Hughes 25/1: 620: Cl up till wknd fnl 1f: 13th: 2 month abs, see 1472. *¾* **82**
2529 **MILLENNIUM MAGIC 13** [11] 2-7-11 J Lowe 25/1: 134200: Never a factor: 14th: twice below 2020. *¾* **66**
2657 **MILLYS LASS 8** [19] 2-7-12 A Nicholls 25/1: 121320: Al bhd: 15th: btr 2657, 1176. *½* **65**
*1986 **MISE EN SCENE 35** [15] 2-7-13 F Norton 14/1: -010: Slow away, al bhd: 16th: see 1986 (fillies mdn). *nk* **65**
1418 **Regal Air 61** [10] 2-8-0 P M Quinn 100/1:
1550 **Cyrazy 54** [12] 2-7-12 A Mackay 66/1:
2500 **Divine Wind 14** [14] 2-8-0 W Supple 33/1:
2469 **Imperial Measure 15** [2] 2-8-6 G Hind 50/1:
2619 **Kaluki 9** [7] 2-8-4 R Brisland 66/1:
2708 **Reciprocal 6** [6] 2-8-5 N Pollard 100/1:
22 ran Time 59.19 (u1.11) (Juv Crse Rec Time) (Lael Stable) W J Haggas Newmarket, Suffolk

2850

3.10 LISTED ROSE BOWL STKS 2YO (A) 6f str Firm -18 -15 Slow
£12636 £3888 £1944 £972

-- **ASCENSION** [1] M R Channon 2-8-6 Craig Williams 5/2: -11: 2 ch f Night Shift - Outeniqua (Bold Lad) Waited with, gd hdwy over 1f out to lead ins last, styd on strongly, rdn out: gamble from 6/1: earlier won a Leopardstown mdn for D Wachmann: Mar foal, cost IR£22,000: stays 6f on gd & firm grnd: v useful filly with a turn of foot, should win a Group race. **102**
2613 **STREGONE 9** [5] B J Meehan 2-8-11 D Holland 13/2: 522042: 2 b g Namaqualand - Sabonis (The Ministrel) Handy, hdwy to lead over 1f out, collared just inside last, not pace of wnr: imprvd for drop back to 6f on this very firm grnd: see 2613. *1¼* **102**
2595 **BRAVADO 10** [3] Sir Mark Prescott 2-8-11 N Pollard 13/8 FAV: 1143: 2 b c Zafonic - Brave Revival (Dancing Brave) Stumbled start, soon recovered to press ldr, no extra fnl 1f: hvly bckd: shade btr 2595 (fast). *1¾* **97**
2529 **TRIPLE BLUE 13** [6] R Hannon 2-9-0 R Hughes 9/2: 113524: In tch, wknd fnl 1f: handles fm & soft. *½* **98**
2595 **PRINCE OF BLUES 10** [4] 2-8-11 J F Egan 9/1: -5265: Led till over 1f out, no extra: must win a mdn. *shd* **95**
*2589 **NORCROFT LADY 10** [2] 2-8-6 J P Spencer 10/1: -1416: Bhd, eff over 2f out, wknd well over 1f out: stiff task, see 2589 (nursery h'cap). *3* **81**
6 ran Time 1m 11.43 (u0.17) (Juv Crse Rec Time) (Norman Cheng) M R Channon West Isley, Berks

2851

3.40 LISTED STEVENTON STKS 3YO+ (A) 1m2f Firm -18 -24 Slow
£14690 £4520 £2260 £1130 3 yo rec 10lb

2339 **CLAXON 21** [1] J L Dunlop 4-8-12 G Carter 7/4 FAV: 115-21: 4 b f Caerleon - Bulaxie (Bustino) Made virtually all, kept on well for press over 1f out, drvn out, gamely: well bckd: '99 wnr at Kempton & Goodwood (List, rtd 109), also 5th in Epsom Oaks: '98 Ayr wnr (fillies h'cap, rtd 93): suited by 10f on firm, hvy & any track: runs well fresh: loves to dominate: scopey, v useful & game filly. **104**
1854 **TRUMPET SOUND 41** [5] L M Cumani 3-8-7 J P Spencer 7/2: 4-1042: 3 b c Theatrical - Free At Last (Shirley Heights) Waited with, hdwy to chase wnr over 1f out, chall inside last, flicked tail & no extra cl home: bckd: 6 week abs & confirmed improved form of 1854: smart, see 1127. *1¼* **107**
2475 **DEHOUSH 15** [2] A C Stewart 4-9-3 M Roberts 5/1: 04-103: 4 ch c Diesis - Dream Play (Blushing *shd* **107**

Groom) Keen, handy, eff to go 2nd over 2f out, onepace: well clr of rem & ran to form of 1592 (stakes).
2696 **TISSIFER** 7 [4] M Johnston 4-9-3 D Holland 15/2: -22004: Chsd wnr, wknd 2f out: see 2696.   6 98
2404 **CAPE GRACE** 21 [6] 4-9-1 R Hughes 12/1: -61505: Waited with, eff over 2f out, wknd over 1f out.   1¾ 93
2502 **ELMUTABAKI** 14 [3] 4-9-3 W Supple 7/2: 50-506: Al bhd: btr 1247.   9 81
6 ran   Time 2m 03.38 (0.58)   (Hesmonds Stud)   J L Dunlop Arundel, W Sussex

---

2852   **4.10 LADBROKE HCAP 3YO+ 0-90 (C)**   **1m5f61y** **Firm -18** **-47 Slow**   **[90]**
    £7052   £2170   £1085   £542   3 yo rec 13lb Falsely run race

-2231 **DUCHAMP** 24 [7] I A Balding 3-8-8 (83) J F Egan 11/4 FAV: -54021: 3 b c Pine Bluff - Higher   87
Learning (Fappiano) Waited with, not clr run over 2f out, switched right & styd on well to lead cl home, rdn
out: hvly bckd: slow run race: '99 scorer at York (nursery h'cap, rtd 84): eff at 1m, enjoyed this step
up to 13.3f & acts on firm & gd/soft, gall tracks.
-- **MASAMADAS** [9] N J Henderson 5-9-6 (82) M Roberts 7/1: 6330/2: 5 ch g Elmaamul - Beau's Delight nk 85
(Lypheor) Waited with, hdwy over 2f out, led dist, collared cl home, just btn: recent hdles rnr, earlier won
at Stratford (h'cap hdle, stays 2m3f, rtd 131h, firm & hvy): last raced on the Flat back in '98, scored at Windsor (h'cap, rtd 84 at best): stays
13.3f on fast, soft & fibresand: handles any track: fine return to the Flat.
*2179 **BID FOR FAME** 27 [2] T G Mills 3-8-10 (85) L Carter 11/1: 53013: 3 b c Quest For Fame - Shroud ½ 87
(Vaguely Noble) Led over 5f out till over 1f out, kept on same pace, not btn far: stys 13.3f: lightly raced.
2674 **CARLYS QUEST** 7 [5] J Neville 6-9-13 (89) (tvi) J Carroll 14/1: 313004: Bhd, hdwy & switched right 1¼ 89
over 2f out, kept on late: stays a slow run 13.3f: see 1373.
2268 **TOTOM** 23 [8] 5-8-11 (73) O Urbina 6/1: -43445: Waited with, gd hdwy to lead over 1f out, hdd & 1 72
no extra inside last: see 2268, 1288.
2647 **THREE GREEN LEAVES** 8 [4] 4-9-13 (89) D Holland 5/1: 001036: Waited with, brief eff 2f out, ½ 87
no impression: nicely bckd, joint top weight, longer trip: see 2647, 1695.
2530 **GREYFIELD** 13 [1] 4-8-11 (73) Craig Williams 5/1: 06-457: In tch, wknd well over 1f out: btr 2530 (12f). ½ 70
2674 **SEREN HILL** 7 [10] 4-9-7 (83) J P Spencer 16/1: 30-008: In tch, wknd 2f out: see 997. 2½ 76
2263 **FIRST IMPRESSION** 24 [6] 5-8-8 (70) R Hughes 5/1: 245-29: Led till 10f out, wknd over 2f out. 6 55
2475 **NIGHT VENTURE** 15 [3] 4-9-9 (85) J Reid 12/1: -10000: Led 10f out till 5f out, wkng when short of hd 70
room 2f out: 10th: best 1031 (10f, hvy).
10 ran   Time 2m 49.02 (3.92)   (Mrs Paul Mellon)   I A Balding Kingsclere, Hants

---

2853   **4.40 GETTING MARRIED HCAP 3YO+ 0-90 (C)**   **1m1f** **Firm -18** **-50 Slow**   **[90]**
    £6760   £2080   £1040   £520   3 yo rec 9 lb

2262 **AEGEAN DREAM** 24 [2] R Hannon 4-9-2 (78) R Hughes 4/1: 344331: 4 b f Royal Academy - L'Ideale   82
(Alysheba) Waited with, keen, eff & short of room over 1f out, styd on to lead ins last, rdn out: well bckd:
plcd several times prev, sole success came in '99, at Epsom (mdn, rtd 79): suited by 1m/9f, stays 10f: handles
hvy, prefers firm/fast & any track: needs to be produced late & kidded to the front today.
3506} **SIR EFFENDI** 335 [6] M P Tregoning 4-10-0 (90) W Supple 9/2: 012-2: 4 ch c Nashwan - Jeema ½ 92
(Thatch) Led 1f, chsd ldr till led again over 2f out, hard rdn & collared cl home, not btn far: fine reapp
under top-weight: plcd 3 times in '99, scored at Lingfield (mdn, rtd 93): stys 9f well on firm & any trk:
runs well fresh: lightly raced, useful & should find compensation.
*2304 **MUYASSIR** 22 [5] P J Makin 5-9-6 (82) A Clark 9/4 FAV: 0-0113: 5 b h Brief Truce - Twine (Thatching) shd 84
Bhd, hdwy to chall over 1f out, kept on for press, not btn far: well bckd: in fine heart: see 2304.
*2629 **FREDORA** 9 [8] M Blanshard 5-9-10 (86) D Sweeney 6/1: 241014: Handy, eff to chall 2f out, no extra 2½ 84
fnl 1f: not disgraced, just btr 2629.
2528 **WEET A MINUTE** 13 [1] 7-9-10 (86) J F Egan 20/1: 256005: Handy, wknd over 1f out: blnks discarded. 2 81
2564 **CALLDAT SEVENTEEN** 11 [4] 4-8-10 (72) J Reid 11/2: 024606: Al bhd: see 2564 (needs gd grnd), 1271. 5 59
2581 **LADY JO** 10 [3] 4-7-10 (58) (4oh) P M Quinn (3) 7/1: 666067: Al bhd: see 2581, 290. 2 41
1630 **AL GHABRAA** 51 [3] 3-9-3 (88) J P Spencer 12/1: 1-658: Led after 1f till over 2f out, wknd: abs, see 1630. ½ 70
8 ran   Time 1m 51.91 (2.91)   (Theobalds Stud)   R Hannon East Everleigh, Wilts

---

Official Going   GOOD/FIRM. Stalls: Far Side; except 10f+ - Stands Side.

2854   **2.10 GLOYSTARNE MDN 2YO (D)**   **6f str** **Good/Firm 20** **-14 Slow**
    £4290   £1320   £660   £330

2172 **FOODBROKER FANCY** 28 [3] D R C Elsworth 2-8-9 T Quinn 9/2: -241: 2 ch f Halling - Red Rita (Kefaah):   81
In tch, strong run to lead cl-home, hands & heels: well bckd: IR 75,000gns half-sister to a useful 6f juv scorer:
dam raced eff at 6f, will stay 7f: acts on fast grnd & a gall trk: improving.
2618 **LADY MILETRIAN** 9 [10] M R Channon 2-8-9 J Fortune 3/1: -52: 2 b f Barathea - Local Custom hd 80
(Be My Native): Trkd ldrs, imprvd to lead ent fnl 1f, not pace to repel wnr cl-home: bckd from 9/2, clr of rem:
eff over a gall 6f on fast grnd, will stay 7f: has shwn enough to find a mdn, see 2618 (C/D).
-- **BULLSEFIA** [5] B W Hills 2-9-0 R Cochrane 12/1: -3: 2 gr c Holy Bull - Yousefia (Danzig): 3½ 75+
Rear, imprvd 2f out, badly hmpd dist, fin well but ch had gone: mkt drifter, debut: Jan foal, half-brother to
a smart 6f juv wnr: eff over a stiff 6f, will stay 7f/1m: acts on fast: eye-catching, keep a close eye on.
993 **ZHITOMIR** 91 [11] S Dow 2-9-0 B Marcus 33/1: -64: Prom till onepcd final 1f: 3 mth abs, 7f suit. 1 72
2563 **SENOR MIRO** 11 [2] 2-9-0 J Weaver 20/1: -05: Tried to make al, collared inside final 1f: may ½ 71
benefit from a drop back to 5f: see 2563 (7f here).
-- **ALNAHAAM** [1] 2-9-0 R Hills 5/2 FAV: -6: Trkd ldrs, rdn & btn over 1f out: hvly bckd, debut: Feb 2 65
first foal, dam styd 7f: B Hanbury colt who has clearly been shwg plenty at home.
-- **LONG WEEKEND** [9] 2-9-0 D Harrison 16/1: -7: Rear, nvr a factor on debut: mkt drifter: 20,000gns shd 65
Mar foal: dam lightly rcd, from a stay family: J Dunlop colt who is sure to do better over further given time.
-- **MODRIK** [8] 2-9-0 R Price 20/1: -8: Slowly away, no ch after on debut: drifted from 14/1: Feb 1 62
foal, cost £30,000: half brother to two wnrs in the States, incl a smart 6f performer: with R Armstrong.
-- **FLASH BACK** [4] 2-9-0 W Ryan 8/1: -9: Nvr a factor on debut: drifted from 5/1, needed race: Feb 1¼ 58
foal, dam a multiple 12/14f wnr: sire a top class sprinter: Sir M Stoute colt who is sure to benefit from this.

1426 **SAVING LIVES ATSEA 61** [7] 2-9-0 A Whelan 40/1: -60: Chsd ldrs 4½f, wknd into 10th: 9 wk abs. *3* **49**
1424 **ARMIDA 61** [6] 2-8-9 P Robinson 33/1: -00: Rcd keenly & prom 4f, sn wknd & fin last: 9 wk abs: *5* **29**
prev trained by W Muir: Apr foal, related to sev wnrs both here & abroad: dam a 10f wnr in France.
11 ran Time 1m 13.08 (2.08) (Food Brokers Ltd) D R C Elsworth Whitsbury, Hants.

2855

2.40 INVESCO HCAP 3YO 0-80 (D) 7f str Good/Firm 20 +02 Fast [87]
£4862 £1492 £748 £374

*2140 **CAPRICHO 29** [3] W J Haggas 3-9-1 (74) T Quinn 13/8 FAV: -211: 3 gr g Lake Coniston - Star Spectacle **85+**
(Spectacular Bid): Trkd ldrs going well, smooth prog to lead 2f out, sn clr, readily: hvly bckd from 9/4, gd time: recent Ayr wnr (mdn): eff over a stiff 7f, will stay 1m: acts on fast & gd/soft grnd, likes a gall trk: has a decent turn of foot: lightly rcd, imprvg gelding who looks sure to win more races.
2364 **PAGEANT 19** [9] W Jarvis 3-9-2 (75) R Cochrane 12/1: -51262: 3 br f Inchinor - Positive Attitude (Red *3* **78**
Sunset): Rear, short of room when imprvg over 1f out, fin well but wnr had flown: caught a progressive rival here.
2322 **SHATHER 21** [4] J W Hills 3-8-7 (66) S Whitworth 16/1: -0343: 3 br c Goofilik - Western Pride (Priamos): *¾* **67**
Trkd ldrs racing keenly, drifted left & onepcd final 1f: bckd at long odds: fair h'cap bow over this inadequate 7f trip: one to keep in mind over 1m/10f: see 2322 (mdn auct).
*2250 **SUMTHINELSE 24** [6] N P Littmoden 3-9-4 (77) J Mackay (5) 10/1: 540214: Slowly away, effort 2f out, *1½* **75**
fin well but too late: change of tactics today, al well plcd when successful in 2250 (sharp trk).
2612 **TIME VALLY 9** [10] 3-8-11 (70) P Doe 10/1: -01055: Dwelt, prog halfway, onepcd fnl 1f: tchd 14/1. *nk* **67**
1205 **SHOWING 75** [2] 3-8-1 (60)(t) J Tate 33/1: 00-006: Trkd ldrs, short of room dist, ch had gone: 11 wk *¾* **55**
abs: in the process of running a gd race in first time t-strap: worth another ch, see 839.
2167 **CREAM TEASE 28** [11] 3-9-7 (80) R Studholme (5) 50/1: 00-007: Front rank, ev ch 2f out, gradually *shd* **75**
fdd final 1f: hinted at a return to form: tried blnks in 2167, see 1374.
2216 **BANAFSAJYH 25** [12] 3-9-4 (77) R Hills 10/1: 3-1048: Rear, hdwy & ev ch 2f out, btn 1f out: see 2216. *nk* **71**
2438 **POP SHOP 16** [8] 3-8-10 (69) A McGlone 16/1: 000009: Imprvd from rear halfway, wkng when hmpd dist. *¾* **61**
*2699 **LADY HELEN 6** [1] 3-8-11 (70) J Fortune 6/1: 0-0510: Chsd ldrs, hmpd over 1f out, no ch after: *1½* **59**
fin 10th, qck reapp: forget this: see 2699 (1m).
2465 **FORMAL BID 15** [13] 3-9-1 (74) D Harrison 8/1: 35-00: Chsd ldrs 5f, fdd into 11th: see 2465. *shd* **63**
2794 **OTIME 2** [7] 3-8-8 (67)(bl) J Weaver 20/1: 662500: Prom, ev ch 2f out, short of room when wkng *2* **52**
final 1f: fin 12th, qck reapp: see 1889.
2614 **PHOEBE BUFFAY 9** [5] 3-9-2 (75) D O'Donohoe 25/1: 200-00: Set pace 5f, wknd into last: see 2614. *5* **50**
13 ran Time 1m 25.20 (1.30) (M Tabor) W J Haggas Newmarket.

2856

3.15 PAYNES HCAP 4YO+ 0-85 (D) 1m6f175y Good/Firm 20 -15 Slow [83]
£7085 £2180 £1090 £545

2263 **FINAL SETTLEMENT 24** [2] J R Jenkins 5-8-10 (65) S Whitworth 7/1: 165341: 5 b g Soviet Lad - Tender **69**
Time (Tender King): In tch, rdn & styd on well to lead ins fnl 1f, forged clr: nicely bckd: reapp wnr at Kempton (h'cap): Kempton hdle wnr in 99/00 (nov, rtd 113h, eff at 2m on gd): plcd on 2 of 4 '99 Flat starts (rtd 63): '98 Windsor & Lingfield wnr (h'caps, rtd 64): suited by 14/15f & will get 2m+ on firm & soft, any trk: tough.
2600 **FIORI 10** [8] P C Haslam 4-9-13 (82) P Goode (3) 4/1: 441322: 4 b g Anshan - Fen Princess (Trojan Fen) *2½* **84**
Set pace & sn clr, collared ins fnl 1f, no extra: bold front running tactics under top weight nearly paid off.
2622 **PRASLIN ISLAND 9** [6] Miss Gay Kelleway 4-7-10 (51)(4oh) J Mackay (5) 16/1: 01D503: 4 ch c Be My *½* **52**
Chief - Hence (Mr Prospector): Chsd ldr till lost place 5f out, swtchd & rallied well fnl 1f: ran to best.
2622 **LAFFAH 9** [4] G L Moore 5-8-5 (60)(t) Dane O'Neill 15/2: 40/134: Prom, onepcd final 2f: see 2622. *1½* **59**
2429 **MAGIC COMBINATION 17** [1] 7-8-11 (66) J Stack 2/1 FAV: 0/1-45: Rear, imprvd 5f out, no impress *¾* **64**
final 1f: hvly bckd: see 2429.
2416 **ZINCALO 17** [7] 4-8-4 (59)(t) P Robinson 10/1: 401336: Prom till wknd 3f out: see 1874. *9* **47**
2523 **HUNTERS TWEED 13** [3] 4-9-4 (73) J Weaver 11/1: -02027: Imprvd from rear halfway, btn 3f out, t.o. *16* **46**
2509 **COMMON CAUSE 14** [5] 4-9-4 (73) T Quinn 8/1: -44558: Slowly away, effort halfway, sn btn & fin *9* **36**
last: nicely bckd: puzzling effort despite step up in trip: stable in form: see 1785 (10f).
8 ran Time 3m 10.76 (5.26) (The Meek partnership) J R Jenkins Royston, Herts.

2857

3.45 LISTED APHRODITE STKS 3YO+ (A) 1m4f Good/Firm 20 -04 Slow
£14703 £5577 £2788 £1267 3yo rec 12lb

-- **ABITARA** [2] A Wohler 4-9-2 J Weaver 20/1: 411111: 4 ch f Rainbow Quest - Arastou (Surumu): **106**
Rear, prog to lead over 2f out, held on well cl-home, drvn out: German raider, completed a 5-timer here after wins at Bremen (3, h'caps) & M Laffitte: eff at 10/12f, wng form on fast & soft: handles a gall trk: useful filly.
2501 **CHEZ CHERIE 14** [9] L M Cumani 3-8-4 D Harrison 5/1: -04432: 3 ch g Wolfhound - Gerante (Private *½* **105**
Account): Rear, imprvd to chall dist, kept on well & not btn far: stays 12f well: useful filly, deserves a win.
1545} **EVIL EMPIRE 55** [11] Saeed bin Suroor 4-9-2 R Hills 7/1: 33-13: 4 ch f Acatenango - Elea (Dschingis *shd* **105**
Khan): Trkd ldrs, short of room 2f out, fin well & just btn in a v cl-fin: 8 wk abs: 4th in a Gr 2 at Capanelle 8 wk ago (12f fast): '99 wnr at Cologne & Hanover (Gr 3): eff at 12f on fast & hvy grnd: spot-on next time.
+2231 **FIRECREST 24** [10] J L Dunlop 3-8-4 Dane O'Neill 9/1: 011114: In tch till short of room & *3* **100+**
outpcd over 2f out, styd on ins last but not reach ldrs: can rate higher & further will suit: keep on your side.
1325 **FANTAZIA 66** [1] 4-9-2 R Cochrane 8/1: 111-25: Rear, kept on final 1½f, nvr nrr: 10 wk abs: *1¾* **98**
prob stays 12f: gd effort in this better company & spot-on next time: see 1325.
2501 **ENDORSEMENT 14** [6] 4-9-2 T Quinn 7/1: 16-006: Trkd ldr till wknd dist: bckd from 10/1: yet to *3½* **93**
sparkle this term, probably better over 2m: see 2114 (Gr 1).
*2073 **SAILING 34** [8] 3-8-9 J Fortune 10/1: -21417: In tch till lost pl after 5f, rallied 3f out, btn fnl 1f. *hd* **98**
2114 **LIFE IS LIFE 30** [7] 4-9-2 P Robinson 5/2 FAV: 2-3258: Led till 2f out, grad fdd: well bckd: better *1½* **91**
expected with this drop in class: big drop back in trip after 2114 (2½m): see 1247.
*2258 **TRUE CRYSTAL 24** [3] 3-8-4 A McGlone 14/1: -19: Dwelt, imprvd after 4f, btn 2f out: only 2nd start. *4* **85**
2597 **SHADY POINT 10** [5] 3-8-4 (vis) B Marcus 50/1: 621060: Prom 10f, wknd & fin last: highly tried. *6* **76**
10 ran Time 2m 31.10 (2.90) (Gestut Ittingen) A Wohler Germany.

2858   4.15 FOODBROKERS RTD HCAP 3YO 0-100 (B)   1m str   Good/Firm 20   -05 Slow   [100]
£17400   £6600   £3300   £1500

2087 **JATHAABEH** 31 [5] M A Jarvis 3-9-3 (89) P Robinson 10/1: 0-101: 3 ch f Nashwan - Pastorale (Nureyev): **94+**
Trkd ldrs till lost pl 3f out, imprvg when hmpd dist, swtchd & strong run to lead cl-home, going away: earlier
won here at Newmarket (mdn, reapp): dam scored over 7f: eff over a stiff 1m, will stay further: acts on fast
grnd & on a gall trk, runs well fresh: improving, useful & her turn of foot can see further success.

1820 **BLUE SUGAR** 43 [3] J R Fanshawe 3-8-13 (85) D Harrison 9/2 JT FAV: 1-422: 3 ch c Shuailaan - Chelsea nk **88**
My Love (Opening Verse): Prom, went on inside final 1f, not pace to repel wnr cl-home: well bckd, 6 wk abs:
eff at 7f/1m, has tried further: acts on fast & soft grnd: met a potentially useful rival here: see 1820, 998.

1452 **ATAVUS** 60 [12] G G Margarson 3-8-13 (85) J Mackay 5/1: 9/2 JT FAV: 4-103: 3 b c Distant Relative - 1 **86**
Elysian (Northfields): Dwelt, recovered & sn prom, ev ch inside final 1f, not btn far: well bckd, 9 wk abs:
prev trained by W Muir: sound effort, spot-on next time, possibly over 10f: see 1183.

*2611 **ARGENTAN** 9 [6] J H M Gosden 3-9-0 (86)(BL) J Fortune 9/1: -22014: Rear, prog 2f out, fin well but shd **87**
too late: nicely bckd, first time blnks: change of tactics, made all in 2611 (mdn).

2629 **KIND REGARDS** 9 [5] 3-8-10 (82) R Hills 10/1: 4-0525: Trkd ldrs till lost place 2f out, short of nk **82**
room dist, fin well: not much luck here: see 2629.

2614 **TUMBLEWEED TOR** 9 [10] 3-9-6 (92) D R McCabe 12/1: 310636: Led after 3f till ins last, no extra. 1 **90**
2515 **BOLD EWAR** 14 [7] 3-8-7 (79)(bl) B Marcus 16/1: 250527: Chsd ldrs, onepcd when short of room ¾ **75**
inside final 1f: one win in 17 starts: see 2515.

2648 **DESERT FURY** 8 [2] 3-9-1 (87) W Ryan 25/1: 300068: Rear, imprvg when hmpd dist, no ch after: ½ **82**
ran better than fin position suggests & hinted at a return to form: prob stays 1m: looks handily weighted, see 1016.

*2688 **CAIR PARAVEL** 7 [13] 3-9-2 (88) Dane O'Neill 14/1: 300019: Led 3f, ev ch till no extra fnl 1f: btr 2688. nk **82**
*2614 **CHAPEL ROYALE** 9 [11] 3-8-11 (83) J Tate 12/1: 020310: Hdwy from rear 2f out, btn final 1f: 10th. 1¼ **74**
*1853 **SIR FERBET** 41 [4] 3-9-1 (87) M Hills 13/2: 210010: Nvr a factor in 11th: 6 wk abs: see 1853 (C/D). 1¼ **74**
2501 **SO PRECIOUS** 14 [9] 3-9-3 (89) J Weaver 33/1: -40000: Nvr a factor in 12th: see 1108 (Listed). ½ **75**
2475 **FERZAO** 15 [8] 3-9-7 (93) T Quinn 12/1: -31500: In tch, wkng when hmpd inside final 1f, eased 5 **69**
considerably: top weight: see 1198 (stks).

13 ran   Time 1m 39.23 (2.03)   (Sheikh Ahmed Al Maktoum)   M A Jarvis Newmarket.

2859   4.45 CHEMIST BROKERS HCAP 3YO+ 0-100 (C)   5f str   Good/Firm 20   +14 Fast   [97]
£7358   £2264   £1132   £566   3yo rec 4lb

1983 **GUINEA HUNTER** 36 [7] T D Easterby 4-9-13 (96) J Fortune 9/2: -01001: 4 b g Pips Pride - Prepoderance **101**
(Cyrano de Bergerac): Rear, imprvd 1½f out, strong run to force head in front on line: best time of day, top
weight: earlier won at Haydock (stks): '99 wnr again at Haydock (rtd 103, stks): '98 Carlisle wnr (mdn, rtd
92): eff at 5/6f on firm, soft grnd & on any trk, likes Haydock: useful gelding.

2569 **ANNETTE VALLON** 11 [2] P W Harris 3-8-12 (85) T Quinn 9/4 FAV: 2132: 3 b f Efisio - Christine Daae shd **89**
(Sadler's Wells): Chsd ldrs, rdn into lead inside final 1f, caught in shadow of post: well bckd: progressive.

2504 **PIPADASH** 14 [6] T D Easterby 3-9-0 (87) Dane O'Neill 9/1: 200003: 3 b f Pips Pride - Petite Maxine 1½ **87**
(Sharpo) Outpcd, ran on well fnl 1f, too late: stablemate of wnr: fairly h'capped & interesting on easier grnd.

2473 **THAT MAN AGAIN** 15 [5] S C Williams 3-8-2 (71)(bl) J Mackay (5) 11/4: 001004: Front rank, went on 1 **68**
halfway till inside last, no extra: well bckd: see 2022.

2458 **DIFFERENTIAL** 15 [1] 3-9-10 (97) M Hills 12/1: 340-55: Nvr pace to chall: see 2458. 3 **85**
3023} **HALF MOON BAY** 358 [4] 3-9-5 (92) J Weaver 13/2: 5511-6: Led till halfway, wknd: reapp: '99 wnr at 7 **60**
Thirsk (2) & Doncaster (nursery, rtd 96): half-brother to a 1m wnr, dam a wng sprinter: v eff at 5f, shld stay 6f:
acts on gd & firm grnd, runs well fresh: gd weight carrier who is capable of much better than this.

6 ran   Time 58.82 (0.32)   (M P Burke)   T D Easterby Great Habton, Nth Yorks.

2860   5.20 FOODBROKERS MDN 3YO (D)   7f str   Good/Firm 20   -18 Slow
£4420   £1360   £680   £340

2465 **SEA DRIFT** 15 [5] L M Cumani 3-8-9 B Marcus 9/2: 0-531: 3 gr f Warning - Night At Sea (Night Shift): **74**
Prom, effort & short of room dist, strong run to lead cl-home, drvn out: half-sister to wnrs over 7/10f, dam
a smart sprinter: eff over a stiff 7f, will stay 1m: acts on fast grnd: imprvg filly.

-- **GRAMPAS** [9] J H M Gosden 3-9-0 J Fortune 4/6 FAV: -2: 3 br c El Gran Senor - Let There Be Light hd **78**
(Sunny's Halo): Dwelt, imprvd 2f out, led ins fnl 1f despite edging left, caught cl-home: hvly bckd debut: IR
52,000 gns purchase: eff over a stiff 7f, 1m will suit: handles a gall trk & fast grnd: should win similar

-- **HANNAH BURDETT** [1] R M H Cowell 3-8-9 M Hills 33/1: -3: 3 ch f Kris - Polka Dancer (Dancing Brave): 1 **71**
Led after 1f till ins last: debut: dam a useful 1m/10f wnr: bred to apprec 1m/10f+ given time: handles fast grnd.

1886 **HAMLYN** 39 [6] D R C Elsworth 3-9-0 (BL) T Quinn 9/1: 0-6464: In tch, hmpd 1½f out, rallied final 1f ¾ **74**
but not quite get there: op 5/1, first time blnks: not much luck here: see 1886.

-- **NASHAAB** [2] 3-9-0 R Hills 11/1: -5: Dwelt, recovered to chase ldrs, no impress when hmpd ins fnl ½ **73**
1f: drifted from 6/1, debut: dam a 6/7f wnr, sire a top class miler: bred to apprec 7f/1m: with R Armstrong.

2617 **ELLWAY QUEEN** 9 [4] 3-8-9 Dane O'Neill 13/2: -06: Early ldr, prom till onepcd fnl 1f: bckd from 20/1. hd **68**
2590 **CHASE THE BLUES** 10 [3] 3-9-0 T Stack 33/1: -657: Slowly away, nvr dngrs under a kind ride: 1¼ **70$**
looks poised to do better in h'caps under a more positive ride: see 2421.

2213 **LEGENDAIRE** 25 [8] 3-9-0 S Whitworth 33/1: 243668: Hdwy from rear halfway, btn 2f out: see 1333 (mdn).6 **55**

8 ran   Time 1m 26.56 (2.66)   (Lady Juliet Tadgell)   L M Cumani Newmarket.

REDCAR   SUNDAY JULY 23RD   Lefthand, Flat, Galloping Track

Official Going   GOOD/FIRM (FIRM Places). Stalls: Str Course - Stands Side, 2m - Centre, Remainder - Inside

---

2861 **2.20 SUNDAY APPR HCAP 3YO+ 0-60 (G)** **1m str** **Good/Firm 39 -10 Slow** **[60]**
£2261 £646 £323 3yo rec 8lb

*2823 **THWAAB** 2 [22] F Watson 8-8-9 (41)(bl)(6ex) P Goode 7/1: 0-0611: 8 b g Dominion - Velvet Habit 48
(Habitat) Rear going well, stdy prog fnl 3f, led well ins last, pushed clr cl-home, rdly: op 6/1: recent Carlisle
wnr (h'cap): well btn in 4 '99 starts (h'cap, rtd 39): prev term scored at Doncaster (h'cap, rtd 62): suited by 6/
7f on firm, gd/soft & any trk: eff with/without a vis: taking advantage of fav h'cap mark, hat-trick on the cards.
2411 **SAIFAN** 18 [7] D Morris 11-9-0 (46)(vis) D McGaffin (5) 25/1: 60-002: 11 ch g Beveled - Superfrost 3 47
(Tickled Pink) Mid-div, prog to lead 2f out & kicked clr, rdn & edged left, hdd well in last: jockey given a
1-day whip ban: gd run from this 11yo: see 2411 (clmr).
2546 **CABARET QUEST** 13 [23] J M Bradley 4-8-9 (41) P Fitzsimons (3) 6/1 FAV: 000603: 4 ch g Pursuit Of shd 42
Love - Cabaret Artiste (Shareef Dancer) Mid-div, styd on well for press fnl 2f, not pace of wnr: see 1003.
2463 **KING TUT** 16 [26] J G Given 4-9-3 (49) G Baker (5) 7/1: 0-2204: In tch, styd on fnl 2f for press. ¾ 49
2533 **KUWAIT THUNDER** 13 [19] 4-8-0 (32)(vis) Joanna Badger (5) 14/1: 600505: Chsd ldrs, rdn & kept on nk 31
onepace fnl 2f: op 12/1: see 1360, 368.
2027 **HEVER GOLF GLORY** 35 [10] 6-8-0 (32)(VIS) D Meah (2) 25/1: 030056: Mid-div, styd on fnl 2f, no ½ 30
threat: tried a visor: recent jumps runner (mod form): see 383.
2147 **ROYAL REPRIMAND** 30 [24] 5-7-10 (28) Jonjo Fowle (1) 33/1: -0007: Led 6f, fdd: see 2147, 1009. ¾ 25
2297 **SKYERS FLYER** 23 [9] 6-8-3 (35) R Fitzpatrick 25/1: 000008: Mid-div, nvr on terms: see 1421. 1 30
2479 **MEZZORAMIO** 16 [20] 8-8-13 (45)(t) Darren Williams (5) 12/1: -00359: Chsd ldrs 6f: see 1920. ¾ 39
1658 **RAASED** 51 [14] 8-8-6 (38)(vis) K Dalgleish (5) 20/1: 00-000: Mid-div, btn 2f out: 10th: op 14/1: shd 32
7 wk abs: '99 Carlisle & Nottingham wnr (h'caps, rtd 46): '98 Southwell wnr (h'cap, rtd 46a & 41): eff btwn
7/10f on firm, gd/soft & fibresand: suited by a t-strap & visor: has run well fresh.
2704 **MEHMAAS** 7 [4] 4-10-0 (60)(vis) G Gibbons (2) 33/1: 100000: Cl-up 6f: 11th: visor reapp: see 1920. ½ 53
2556 **KIERCHEM** 12 [2] 9-8-5 (37) T Hamilton (7) 20/1: 601460: Chsd ldrs, 6f, 12th: see 2099 (sell h'cap). ¾ 29
2448 **TALENTS LITTLE GEM** 17 [3] 3-8-4 (44) D Watson (1) 20/1: -45050: Bhd, mod gains: 13th: see 1336. shd 36
2275 **WISHBONE ALLEY** 24 [13] 5-9-1 (47) J McAuley (3) 16/1: 000030: Cl-up 6f, 14th: btr 2275 (6f). shd 39
2728 **TOBLERSONG** 5 [1] 5-8-13 (45)(t) Kristin Stubbs (7) 12/1: 442040: Mid-div, no impress: 15th. 2 33
2442 **IVORS INVESTMENT** 17 [29] 4-9-0 (46) A Polli 11/1: 050-00: Chsd ldrs 5f: op 9/1: see 2442. 0
2099 Flashtalkin Flood 32 [21] 6-8-9 (41) R Cody Boutcher(5) 20/1: 2467 **Daphnes Doll** 16 [8] 5-9-1 (47) A Nicholls 12/1:
2479 Portrack Junction 16 [15] 3-8-2 (42) G Sparkes (5) 50/1:
*2479 Marton Mere 16 [17] 4-9-6 (52) P Bradley (3) 16/1:
2795 Charlem 3 [11] 3-7-11 (37)(vis) M Watters (2) 16/1:
2612 Kustom Kit Kevin 10 [30] 4-8-8 (40)(t) S Finnamore (5) 16/1:
2062 Hi Nicky 33 [28] 4-9-4 (50) R Farmer (7) 16/1: 2824 Abstract 2 [25] 4-7-13 (31)(vis) Claire Bryan (3) 20/1:
2538 Royal Dolphin 13 [5] 4-8-2 (34) N Carter (7) 50/1: 2745 Lady Tilly 4 [16] 3-8-6 (46) P Hanagan (7) 33/1:
2704 Fastwan 7 [27] 4-7-10 (28) A Robertson (7) 33/1:
2396 Power Game 19 [12] 7-7-10 (28) Clare Roche (5) 33/1:
28 ran Time 1m 38.7 (3.9) (F Watson) F Watson Sedgefield, Co Durham

---

2862 **2.55 EBF MDN 2YO (D)** **7f str** **Good/Firm 39 -31 Slow**
£3003 £924 £462 £231

-- **GULCHIE** [5] H R A Cecil 2-9-0 T Quinn 1/4 FAV: -1: 2 ch c Thunder Gulch - Asterita (Rainbow Quest) 80
Handy, led over 1f out, al holding rivals ins last, rdn out: nicely bckd at odds-on: Apr foal: dam a useful 12f
wnr: eff at 7f, 1m+ will suit: acts on fast grnd & a gall trk: runs well fresh: op to further improvement.
-- **EDDYS LAD** [1] R M H Cowell 2-9-0 K Darley 6/1: -2: 2 b c Lahib - Glamour Model (Last Tycoon) 1¼ 75
Sn handy, prog to chall over 1f out, kept on, not pace of wnr: op 5/1: Feb foal, cost 38,000 gns, a 1st foal:
dam a 7f Irish juv wnr: eff at 7f, 1m will suit: acts on fast grnd & a gall trk: pleasing intro.
-- **KINGS WELCOME** [7] C W Fairhurst 2-9-0 P Goode (3) 20/1: -3: 2 b c Most Welcome - Reine de 2½ 70
Thebes (Darshaan) Rdn/bhd early, styd on well fnl 3f, nrst fin: May foal, cost 6,000 gns: half brother to
useful sprinter Boldly Goes: dam a 1m/11f wnr, sire top-class at 1m/12f: stays 7f, sure to apprec 1m+.
2521 **BARNINGHAM** 14 [4] J D Bethell 2-9-0 G Carter 14/1: -64: Prom, onepace fnl 2f: op 12/1: see 2521. 3½ 63
2480 **PENTAGON LADY** 16 [3] 2-8-9 R Cody Boutcher (7) 66/1: -0005: Chsd ldrs 3f out, sn held: see 2480. ½ 57
2557 **CIRCUIT LIFE** 12 [2] 2-9-0 O Pears 16/1: 053066: Held up, eff halfway, no impress: longer 7f trip. 1¼ 53
2635 **HIGH SOCIETY LADY** 9 [6] 2-9-0 Dean McKeown 66/1: -0007: Led till over 1f out, wknd: longer 7f trip. ¾ 53
1130 **DISPOL LAIRD** 80 [10] 2-9-0 R Winston 25/1: -508: Bhd halfway: 11 wk abs: see 755 (5f). 4 50
2700 **TOBYTOO** 7 [9] 2-9-0 R Fitzpatrick (3) 66/1: -00009: Bhd halfway: mod form. 4 42
1844 **KUMAKAWA** 43 [8] 2-9-0 (VIS) V Halliday 33/1: -000: Chsd ldrs 4f: 10th: vis: abs, longer 7f trip. nk 41
10 ran Time 1m 26.7 (4.9) (The Thoroughbred Corporation) H R A Cecil Newmarket

---

2863 **3.30 PIRATE SHIP HCAP 3YO 0-80 (D)** **1m3f** **Good/Firm 39 -36 Slow** **[84]**
£7215 £2220 £832 £832

2524 **WINGED ANGEL** 14 [4] Miss J A Camacho 3-7-13 (55) F Norton 11/1: 400001: 3 ch g Prince Sabo - Silky 58
Heights (Head For Heights) Held up, prog to lead ins last, just prevailed, all out: 1st win: caught the eye in
mdns earlier: apprec this step up to 11f, shld get further: acts on fast grnd & a gall trk: can improve further.
2110 **FANTASTIC FANTASY** 31 [3] J L Dunlop 3-9-5 (75) K Darley 5/4 FAV: 0-1162: 3 b f Lahib - Gay Fantasy 77
(Troy) Led 3f out, rdn/hdd ins last, styd on well for press, just held: hvly bckd: acts on fast & gd grnd: see 1770.
2703 **STEPASTRAY** 7 [6] R E Barr 3-7-10 (52)(5oh) P Fessey 10/1: -00363: 3 gr g Alhijaz - Wandering ½ 53$
Stranger (Petong) Bhd, rdn/outpcd 3f out, styd on well from press 2f out, not reach front pair: styd longer 11f trip well.
2450 **FAIR LADY** 17 [5] B W Hills 3-9-7 (77) A Culhane (3) 7/2: 26-163: Trkd ldrs, no room 3f out till swtchd dht 78
& styd on strongly ins last, not reach front pair: no luck, would have gone v close here: stays 11f.
*2276 **EYELETS ECHO** 24 [2] 3-9-0 (70) D McGaffin (5) 7/2: -00015: Led till 3f out, wknd: btr 2276 (9f). 5 64
2378 **YENALED** 20 [1] 3-8-8 (64) F Lynch 9/1: 316246: Held up, outpcd fnl 2f: btr 2378, 2166 (9f/1m). 4 52
6 ran Time 2m 23.7 (8.2) (Bernard Bloom) Miss J A Camacho Norton, N Yorks

893

2864
4.00 FAMILY FUNDAY SELL HCAP 3YO 0-60 (F)   5f str   Good/Firm 39   -21 Slow   [65]
£2404   £687   £343

2839 **MOUNT PARK 1** [9] D W Chapman 3-8-7 (44)(bl) Claire Bryan (5) 25/1: 000001: 3 b f Colonel Collins   49
- Make Hay (Nomination) Chsd ldrs, rdn & styd on well fnl 2f to lead well ins last: no bid: unplcd in a mdn h'cap
at Ripon yesterday: 1st win: plcd for H Howe in '99 (rtd 70, mdn & h'cap): eff at 5/6f on fast & gd/soft
grnd, sharp or gall trk: suited by blnks & apprec this drop to sell grade.
2280 **SHALARISE 24** [1] Miss L A Perratt 3-9-4 (55)(bl) K Darley 6/1: 000502: 3 ch f Shalford - Orthorising   1¼ 55
(Aragon) Chsd ldrs, prog to chall fnl 1f, not pace of wnr nr fin: eff at 5/6f: see 2165.
2732 **THORNCLIFF FOX 5** [2] J A Glover 3-9-7 (58)(vis) O Pears 10/1: 403603: 3 ch g Foxhound - Godly Light nk 57
(Vayrann) Handy, led 2f out till ins last, no extra: quick reapp: handles fast, gd/soft & fibresand: see 1061.
2374 **LAYAN 20** [13] J Balding 3-9-3 (54) J Edmunds 6/1: 566034: Mid-div, kept on fnl 2f, not able to chall.   ½ 51
2632 **ANNAKAYE 9** [4] 3-7-12 (33)(2ow) Dale Gibson 33/1: 00505: In tch, styd on onepace: mod form.   nk 31
2315 **ABCO BOY 22** [7] 3-8-6 (43)(BL) P Goode 3) 25/1: 0-0006: Held up, nvr able to chall: tried in blnks: ½ 37
jockey given a 1-day whip ban: mod prev.
2374 **LUNALUX 20** [3] 3-9-3 (54) R Fitzpatrick 3) 6/1: 0-0247: Led 1f, cl-up 4f: see 2095, 1773.   nk 47
2590 **QUEENSMEAD 11** [6] 3-9-0 (51)(t) R Price 12/1: 000048: Chsd ldrs, held fnl 2f: see 1266.   shd 44
2281 **BLUE LINE LADY 24** [15] 3-8-4 (41) F Lynch 10/1: 050009: In tch 3f: now with K Ryan: see 1600.   ¾ 32
2592 **WERE NOT JOKEN 11** [10] 3-9-1 (52) P M Quinn 3) 12/1: 600-00: Rdn/bhd, nvr on terms: 10th.   ½ 41
2184 **MARSHALL ST CYR 28** [11] 3-9-7 (58) Dean McKeown 7/2 FAV: 564200: Chsd ldrs 4f: 11th: bckd, op 4/1½ 45
2233 **TIME FOR THE CLAN 25** [8] 3-8-4 (41)(VIS) P Fessey 9/1: 00-000: Led after 1f till 2f out, wknd: 13th: 0
tried in a visor, bckd from 14/1: see 2233.
2520 **Reds Desire 14** [14] 3-7-12 (35)(2ow)(13oh) A Mackay 33/1:
2650 **Mitchells Mayhem 9** [12] 3-7-12 (35) A Polli (3) 14/1:
2223 **Martin 26** [1] 3-8-9 (44)(2ow) C Teague (3) 25/1:
15 ran   Time 59.5 (3.0)   (David W Chapman)   D W Chapman Stillington, N Yorks

2865
4.35 CRICKET CLUB CLASS STKS 3YO+ 0-70 (E)   1m1f   Good/Firm 39   +06 Fast
£4111   £1265   £632   £316   3yo rec 9lb

*2625 **SUMMER SONG 10** [7] E A L Dunlop 3-9-0 G Carter 5/6 FAV: 453111: 3 b f Green Desert - High Standard   77
(Kris) Cl-up, rdn to lead 3f out, narrowly asserted nr line, all out: best time of day, hvly bckd: completed a
hat-trick after h'cap wins at Windsor & Folkestone: landed a prize stks event at Newmarket on sole '99 start
(rtd 79): eff btwn 1m & 10f on fast, gd/soft, prob handles any trk: tough, in form filly.
*2771 **FAHS 4** [10] N Hamilton 8-9-9 T Quinn 9/4: -25012: 8 b g Riverman - Tanwi (Vision)   nk 76
Chsd ldrs, rdn to lead over 1f out, styd on well, just held nr line: clr rem: well bckd, op 3/1: eff btwn 9/13f.
2823 **THATCHED 2** [4] R E Barr 10-9-6 P Fessey 12/1: 060563: 10 b g Thatching - Shadia (Naskra)   10 58$
Trkd ldrs, held by front pair fnl 2f: quick reapp: see 1254.
2481 **KASS ALHAWA 16** [9] D W Chapman 7-9-6 A Culhane 9/2: 054244: Held up, eff 3f out, no impress.   4 50
2844 **FOUR MEN 1** [2] 3-8-11 P Bradley (5) 66/1: 066065: Led 6f: unplcd at Warwick yesterday: see 2682.   8 38$
2704 **TAKER CHANCE 7** [3] 4-9-6 A Robertson (7) 50/1: 000606: Chsd ldrs, btn 4f out: see 907.   2 34
2682 **FAS 8** [11] 4-9-6 (vis) P Goode (3) 66/1: 504007: Al towards rear: off rtd 22: flattered 2682.   ½ 33$
2822 **DISTANT KING 2** [8] 7-9-6 Suzanne France (7) 66/1: 000068: Chsd ldrs 5f: quick reapp: see 1256.   ½ 32
2523 **STAMFORD HILL 14** [6] 5-9-6 D Allan (7) 100/1: 000569: Bhd 4f out: off rtd 20: mod form.   ½ 31$
1732 **LA CINECITTA 48** [1] 4-9-3 K Hodgson 100/1: 0-0060: Mid-div, btn 3f out: 10th: 7 wk abs: see 1415.   hd 27
2834 **BRIGMOUR 1** [5] 4-9-3 J McAuley (5) 100/1: 000000: Al rear: 11th: unplcd at Ripon yesterday.   1¼ 24
11 ran   Time 1m 51.8 (3.0)   (Maktoum Al Maktoum)   E A L Dunlop Newmarket, Suffolk

2866
5.10 2 FOR 1 HCAP STKS 3YO+ 0-75 (E)   2m   Good/Firm 39   -20 Slow   [70]
£4654   £1432   £716   £358   3yo rec 17lb

2516 **XELLANCE 15** [4] M Johnston 3-8-3 (62) K Dalgleish (5) 2/1 FAV: 122141: 3 b g Be My Guest -   66
Excellent Alibi (Exceller) Trkd ldrs, prog to lead 3f out, sn clr, held on well for press ins last: well bckd: earlier
won at Southwell (2), W'hampton (rtd 53a), Musselburgh, Redcar & Chepstow (h'caps): suited by 14f/2m2f on firm,
fast & f/sand, handles a sharp/gall trk: runs well fresh: tough & progressive stayer, a credit to connections.
2734 **SALSKA 5** [10] P L Clinton 9-9-2 (58) F Norton 4/1: -00542: 9 b m Salse - Anzeige (Soderini)   1 60
Chsd ldrs 6f out, drvn/chsd wnr over 1f out, kept on, al held: quick reapp: won this race last term off a 9lb
higher mark: met a progressive type, could find similar: see 2273.
2173 **OUR MONOGRAM 29** [5] A C Stewart 4-8-0 (42) G Bardwell 7/1: 0-0003: 4 b g Deploy - Darling Splodge nk 43
(Elegant Air) Keen/chsd ldrs, onepace/held fnl 2f: see 1128.
1991 **ROYAL PATRON 36** [3] J L Dunlop 4-10-0 (70) T Quinn 9/2: 2-2354: Led 5f out till 3f out, fdd: clr rem.   3 68
2292† **RUM BABA 391** [11] 6-8-0 (42) P Fessey 10/1: 4402-5: Bhd, nvr any impress: Flat reapp, 3 month   8 32
jumps abs, 99/00 wnr at Huntingdon & M Rasen (h'caps, rtd 88h, eff at 2½m2m5.5f on firm & gd/soft, best
blnkd): rnr-up on fnl Flat start in '99 (rtd 44, 5 rnr h'cap): back in '97 won in native Ireland at Tralee (12f mdn):
prob stays 2m, handles fast & hvy grnd: shld prove sharper for this & well h'capped on the level.
2375 **SANDABAR 20** [7] 7-9-8 (64)(t) A Culhane 9/2: 032156: Trkd ldrs, ev ch 3f out, sn rdn/btn: btr 2203.   nk 54
1683 **MINALCO 50** [1] 4-7-10 (38)(9oh) G Baker (7) 66/1: 000-07: Led till 5f out, fdd: abs, longer 2m trip.   4 24
-- **ARDARROCH PRINCE** [6] 9-8-13 (55) Dale Gibson 25/1: 5402/8: Al bhd: long abs: former bmpr wnr: 9 32
last rcd in '97 when rnr-up at Catterick (mdn h'cap, rtd 59): stays a sharp 2m & handles fast grnd.
-- **RUNNING FREE** [8] 6-8-9 (51) O Pears 33/1: 1145/9: Al bhd: 4 month pts abs (mod form): last rcd   14 17
on the level in '97 for M Fetherston Godley, scored at Nottingham (h'cap, rtd 53): eff at 12/14f
on fast grnd, enjoys gd/soft: best without blnks: likes a stiff/gall trk & can front run.
9 ran   Time 3m 34.2 (9.4)   (T T Bloodstocks)   M Johnston Middleham, N Yorks

Official Going   GOOD TO FIRM. Stalls: Str Crse - Far Side, Rem - Inside

---

2867   **2.00 PLATINUM MDN STKS 2YO (D)**   **7f jub rnd**   **Firm 09**   **-38 Slow**
£4553   £1395   £697   £348

1513 **DANCE ON THE TOP 57** [14] E A L Dunlop 2-9-0 J Reid 5/2 FAV: -61: 2 ch c Caerleon - Fern (Shirley Heights) Made most, styd on well & holding rivals ins last, pushed out: op 7/4, 8 wk abs: apprec step up to 7f, 1m+ lks sure to suit: acts on firm grnd & an easy trk: runs well fresh: clearly going the right way.   93+
-- **GLEAMING BLADE** [16] Mrs A J Perrett 2-9-0 R Hughes 10/1: -2: 2 ch c Diesis - Gleam Of Light (Danehill) Cl-up, rdn/ev ch over 1f out, kept on, not pace of wnr: op 8/1, Feb foal, a first foal: dam a 7f wnr: eff at 7f, 1m will suit: acts on firm grnd: encouraging intro, can find similar.   1¾   82
2474 **THUNDERMILL 16** [12] T G Mills 2-9-0 L Carter 14/1: -53: 2 ch c Thunder Gulch - Specifically (Sky Classic) Keen/cl-up, kept on onepace from over 1f out: op 10/1: acts on firm grnd: see 2474.   1¾   79
-- **SYLVA STORM** [15] C E Brittain 2-9-0 P Robinson 14/1: -4: Prom, onepace fnl 2f: op 10/1: Miswaki colt, Apr foal, cost 44,000gns: half-brother to a 7f juv wnr: eff at 7f on firm grnd.   shd   79
-- **LUCAYAN CHIEF** [6] 2-9-0 B Marcus 7/2: -5: Trkd ldrs, outpcd over 2f out, styd on well nr fin: well bckd, op 4/1: Apr foal, cost 23,000gns: dam unrcd, sire a top-class performer at 10/12f: really got the hang of things late on here, looks sure to relish 1m+, will rate more highly.   ¾   78+
2494 **ALFASEL 15** [9] 2-9-0 R Perham 14/1: -06: Cl-up, onepace fnl 2f: clr rem: op 10/1: see 2494.   ½   77
2708 **FATHER SEAMUS 7** [7] 2-9-0 J Fortune 50/1: -0007: Mid-div, btn 3f out: needs a drop in grade.   6   68
-- **KING OF INDIA** [5] 2-9-0 M Tebbutt 33/1: -8: Towards rear, mod gains: longer priced stablemate of wnr: Indian Ridge gelding, Apr foal, cost 90,000gns: dam a wnr in the USA.   3½   61
-- **STORMING HOME** [13] 2-9-0 M Hills 8/1: -9: Dwelt, pushed along early, late prog, nvr a threat: op 6/1: Machiavellian colt, Feb foal: half-brother to a 7f 2yo wnr: dam a 1m wnr abroad: will improve.   hd   60
-- **PERSIAN PRIDE** [4] 2-9-0 J Weaver 10/1: -0: Rear, nvr factor: 10th: op 8/1: Barathea colt, Mar foal, cost 95,000gns: dam a wnr abroad: sire a top-class miler: with P W Harris.   1¼   57
2346 **ASH HAB 22** [2] 2-9-0 T E Durcan 10/1: -00: Twds rear, no impress: 11th: mkt drifter, op 5/1.   shd   57
-- **LEGAL WORD** [8] 2-9-0 W Ryan 7/1: -0: Al bhd: 14th: mkt drifter, op 7/2: Nashwan colt, Feb foal: half-brother to a smart juv 1m performer: dam an Irish 6f juv wnr: bred to apprec 1m+ for Sir M Stoute.   0
1454 **Mujalia 61** [10] 2-9-0 Dane O'Neill 33/1:   1403 **Court One 64** [11] 2-9-0 L Newman (3) 50/1:
-- **Mad Habit** [17] 2-9-0 Martin Dwyer 33/1:
15 ran   Time 1m 27.38 (3.28)   (Khalifa Sultan)   E A L Dunlop Newmarket.

2868   **2.35 MARRIED NURSERY HCAP 2YO (D)**   **5f str**   **Firm 09**   **-15 Slow**   [96]
£5512   £1696   £848   £424

*2526 **SILLA 14** [5] I A Balding 2-8-13 (81) M Hills 11/8 FAV: -0311: 2 b f Gone West - Silver Fling (The Minstrel) Cl-up, went on going well over 3f out, styd on strongly fnl 1f, pushed out: hvly bckd: recent Sandown wnr (fill mdn): eff at 5f, 6f shld suit: acts on firm & fast grnd & a stiff/easy trk: progressive type.   86
2360 **LAI SEE 20** [8] A P Jarvis 2-8-11 (79) J Fortune 7/1: 000222: 2 b c Taguia - Sevens Are Wild (Petorius) Chsd ldrs, rdn/styd on fnl 2f, not pace of wnr: rnr-up last 3 starts, deserves a change of luck.   1¼   79
2589 **BLAKESHALL BOY 11** [4] M R Channon 2-8-10 (78) Craig Williams 9/1: 341403: 2 b g Piccolo - Giggleswick Girl (Full Extent) Bhd halfway, styd on well from over 1f out under hands-and-heels riding, nrst fin: op 7/1: eye-catching late hdwy, a stiffer trk or step up to 6f could bring success in similar: see 1124.   hd   77
2034 **FIAMMA ROYALE 34** [7] Mrs P N Dutfield 2-9-1 (83) L Newman (3) 8/1: 422524: Led till over 3f out, no extra fnl 1f: shown enough to find a mdn on a minor trk: see 1522.   ¾   80
2384 **HALCYON MAGIC 20** [1] 2-7-10 (64)(11oh) R Brisland 25/1: 40/1: -0045: Rdn bhd ldrs, fdd fnl 1f.   nk   60
*2532 **FANTASY BELIEVER 13** [3] 2-9-4 (86) J P Spencer 6/1: 242216: Held up, nvr pace to chall: see 2532.   1¼   79
*2665 **MY LUCY LOCKET 9** [6] 2-9-7 (89) R Hughes 7/2: -33217: Chsd ldrs, btn/eased ins last: nicely bckd, top-weight: not given a hard time once btn, useful eff in 2665 (nursery).   ½   68
1236 **IF BY CHANCE 73** [2] 2-8-3 (71) Martin Dwyer 14/1: -0428: Held up, rdn/btn 2f out: op 12/1, abs.   5   53
8 ran   Time 59.51 (1.21)   (George Strawbridge)   I A Balding Kingsclere, Hants.

2869   **3.10 SUNDAY CLASS STKS 3YO+ 0-80 (D)**   **6f str**   **Firm 09**   **+16 Fast**
£6909   £2126   £1063   £531   3yo rec 5lb

2473 **MIDNIGHT ESCAPE 16** [8] C F Wall 7-9-0 R Hughes 6/1: 004561: 7 b g Aragon - Executive Lady (Night Shift) Al cl-up trav well, went on over 2f out, held on well fnl 1f, drvn out: fast time: well bckd: rtd 99 at best in '99: '98 Kempton wnr (List, rtd 115): suited by 5f/easy 6f on firm & soft grnd, handles any trk & has run well fresh.   83
1961 **LAS RAMBLAS 37** [6] R F Johnson Houghton 3-8-9 J Reid 9/1: 000042: 3 b c Thatching - Raise A Warning (Warning) Chsd ldrs, rdn & chsd wnr in last, al just held: sound effort: see 982.   ½   80
*2792 **PAYS DAMOUR 3** [10] R Hannon 3-9-1 Dane O'Neill 4/1: 001213: 3 b c Pursuit Of Love - Lady Of The Land (Wollow) Led/dsptd lead till over 2f out, held ins last: qck reapp, bckd: see 2792 (7f).   hd   85
2310 **ELLENS ACADEMY 23** [5] E J Alston 5-9-0 T E Durcan 3/1 FAV: 430304: Dwelt, waited on with rear, hdwy over 1f out, no prog ins last: bckd, op 4/1: prefers a stiffer trk: see 1533, 1277, 1074.   1¼   76
2616 **POLES APART 10** [7] 4-9-0 J Fortune 20/1: -00005: Chsd ldrs till over 1f out: see 2616, 1337.   ½   74
*2787 **BANDANNA 3** [4] 3-8-9 M Roberts 4/1: 006516: Chsd ldrs, outpcd fnl 2f: op 7/2, lngr trip.   1¼   71
1999 **EASTER OGIL 36** [1] 5-9-3 (vis) Leanne Masterton (7) 14/1: 412507: Held up, nvr on terms: op 10/1.   nk   73
2697 **CAUDA EQUINA 8** [2] 6-9-0 Craig Williams 12/1: 302048: Rear, nvr on terms: op 10/1: see 2697.   3   63
2371 **CLEF OF SILVER 20** [3] 5-9-0 M Tebbutt 10/1: 1/0-09: Rear, rdn/btn over 1f out: see 2371.   nk   62
9 ran   Time 1m 10.69 (u.41)   (Mervyn Ayers)   C F Wall Newmarket.

2870   **3.40 MAIL ON SUNDAY RTD HCAP 3YO+ 0-95 (C)**   **1m rnd**   **Firm 09**   **-10 Slow**   [101]
£9382   £3558   £1779   £808   3yo rec 8lb

2456 **FREE OPTION 16** [9] B Hanbury 5-9-7 (94) J Reid 3/1 FAV: 0-3031: 5 ch g Indian Ridge - Saneena (Kris) Mid-div, hdwy when no room over 2f out till well ins last, rdn & qcknd to lead nr line: hvly bckd from 9/2: '99 wnr at Kempton (rtd h'cap), Chester (stks) & Newmarket (h'cap, rtd 96): '98 Lingfield (mdn) & Newbury wnr (h'cap, rtd 94 & 68a): suited by 7f/1m, stays 10f: acts on firm & gd, handles equitrack, any trk: best without t-strap.   97
2090 **PANTAR 32** [8] I A Balding 5-9-5 (92)(bl) J Fortune 12/1: 363002: 5 b g Shirley Heights - Spring Daffodil (Pharly) Keen, rear, prog over 1f out & ev ch ins last, just held in a thrilling fin: op 8/1: see 1015.   shd   95

895

2528 **CALCUTTA 14** [1] B W Hills 4-9-7 (94) M Hills 4/1: -00063: 4 b c Indian Ridge - Echoing (Formidable) *hd* **96**
Trkd ldrs, rdn to chall over 1f out, briefly lead nr fin, just btn in a 3-way photo: well bckd: see 1829.
2614 **MOSSY MOOR 10** [2] Mrs A J Perrett 3-8-8 (89) R Hughes 11/2: -53104: Keen/trkd ldr, rdn/led *nk* **90**
over 1f out, kept on well, just held nr line: 8/1: see 2084.
2707 **ELMHURST BOY 7** [4] 4-8-7 (83)(vis)(3oh) B Marcus 14/1: 103045: Rear, styd on fnl 1f, nrst fin. *¾* **80**
2528 **POLISH SPIRIT 14** [3] 5-8-8 (81) J F Egan 12/1: 110306: Cl-up, outpcd over 2f out, kept on fnl 1f. *nk* **80**
2616 **CHOTO MATE 10** [11] 4-9-3 (90) P Dobbs (5) 11/1: W04107: Chsd ldrs, outpcd fnl 3f: btr 1989 (7f). *¾* **88**
2616 **THUNDER SKY 10** [12] 4-8-7 (80)(vis) P Robinson 33/1: 045108: Led till over 1f out, fdd: see 2293. *½* **77**
2809 **OMAHA CITY 2** [6] 6-9-4 (91) C Rutter 12/1: -00059: Keen/rear, outpcd fnl 2f: op 10/1: qck reapp. *2* **84**
1341 **RESPLENDENT STAR 66** [7] 3-8-1 (82)(bl) L Newman (3) 7/1: 010-40: Al twds rear: 10th: abs. *1½* **72**
2564 **INDIUM 12** [10] 6-8-7 (83)(3oh) L Newton 16/1: 105000: Rear, nvr factor: 11th: see 1375 (10f). *nk* **69**
11 ran Time 1m 38.5 (1.5) (Ahmed Ali) B Hanbury Newmarket.

2871

4.15 CITY INDEX MDN 3YO (D) 1m jub rnd Firm 09 -05 Slow
£4306 £1325 £662 £331

-- **SUMMER VIEW** [8] R Charlton 3-9-0 R Hughes 10/11 FAV: -1: 3 ch c Distant View - Miss Summer **90+**
(Luthier) Led after 1f, readily asserted under hands-and-heels riding fnl 2f: val for 7L+: hvly bckd on belated debut, reportedly had a wind op & suffered sore shins: eff at 1m, may get further: acts on firm grnd & an easy trk: runs well fresh: plenty in hand here, looks potentially useful & one to follow in a higher grade.
2258 **WHITGIFT ROSE 25** [9] Lady Herries 3-8-9 W Ryan 9/2: -042: 3 b f Polar Falcon - Celtic Wing *4* **74**
(Midyan) Trkd ldrs, rdn & styd on fnl 2f, no ch with wnr: met a potentially useful rival, h'cap company shld suit.
1018 **SHAHED 90** [7] M P Tregoning 3-9-0 R Perham 6/1: 443-63: 3 ch g Arazi - Nafhaat (Roberto) *shd* **79**
Led early, sn chsd wnr, btn 2f out: op 5/1, 3 month abs: see 1018.
-- **MUSICAL HEATH** [2] P W Harris 3-9-0 (t) J Fortune 8/1: -4: Chsd ldrs, outpcd 2f out, kept on *nk* **78**
cl-home, no threat: debut, cost IR 26,000gns: full brother to 6f wnr: clr of rem, shaped as if mid-dists could suit.
2548 **SASH 13** [10] 3-8-9 P Doe 20/1: -505: Keen/trkd ldrs, btn over 1f out: op 12/1: see 2322. *10* **58**
2345 **GAYE CHARM 22** [5] 3-9-0 G Faulkner (3) 66/1: -06: Chsd ldrs, btn/eased ins last. *5* **53**
2531 **SUPREME SILENCE 14** [4] 3-9-0 J Weaver 16/1: -007: Bhd, no ch fnl 3f: mod form. *8* **41**
2710 **BATWINK 7** [1] 3-8-9 S Whitworth 33/1: -008: Prom till halfway, sn bhd: big drop in trip, no form. *2* **32**
-- **LORD GIZZMO** [3] 3-9-0 M Tebbutt 33/1: -9: Slowly away & sn well bhd: debut: with V Soane. *13* **17**
9 ran Time 1m 37.93 (1.13) (K Abdulla) R Charlton Beckhampton, Wilts.

2872

4.50 STANLEY RACING HCAP 3YO+ 0-80 (D) 1m4f Firm 09 -21 Slow [80]
£7182 £2210 £1105 £552 3yo rec 12lb

2671 **WARNING REEF 8** [8] E J Alston 7-8-3 (55) T E Durcan 13/2: 653331: 7 b g Warning - Horseshoe Reef **60**
(Mill Reef) Held up, stdy prog fnl 3f, narrow lead ins last, just held on in a bunched fin: plcd sev times in '99 (h'caps, rtd 65): '98 wnr at Carlisle, Sandown & Ascot (h'caps, rtd 65 at best): suited by 10/12f, stays 14f: acts on firm, gd/soft & fibresand, handles any trk: consistent & well h'capped gelding, deserved this.
2499 **EXILE 15** [11] R T Phillips 3-8-3 (67) A Beech (5) 5/1 JT FAV: 00-252: 3 b g Emperor Jones - Silver *nk* **70**
Venture (Silver Hawk) Towards rear, rdn/prog to chall over 1f out, ev ch ins last, just held: bckd: eff at 10/12f.
2116 **PALUA 31** [10] Mrs A J Bowlby 3-8-11 (75)(bl) J Reid 14/1: 343203: 3 b c Sri Pekan - Reticent *shd* **78**
Bride (Shy Groom) Cl-up, led 3f out, rdn/hung left & hdd ins last, just held: op 12/1: see 2116, 1094.
2470 **AFTER THE BLUE 16** [3] M R Channon 3-8-1 (65) Craig Williams 5/1 JT FAV: 641224: Slowly away, *½* **67+**
rdn/eff wide over 2f out, forced further wide over 1f out, styd on well nr fin, not reach wnr: no luck in running here, looks a likely type for similar & is one keep a close eye on: see 2470, 2272 & 2012.
2195 **THREE WHITE SOX 27** [6] 3-8-0 (64) L Newman (2) 12/1: -03255: Mid-div, rdn & kept on fnl 2f, not *nk* **65**
reach ldrs: op 10/1: stays 12f: see 1967, 1640.
*2530 **WASP RANGER 14** [1] 6-9-13 (79)(bl) I Mongan (5) 13/2: 022316: Slowly away, drvn to sn race *¾* **79**
mid-div, ev ch 2f out, hung left/no extra nr fin: bckd: topweight, chance not helped by tardy start: see 2530 (11f).
*2429 **CHATER FLAIR 18** [12] 3-7-11 (61)(1ow)(3oh) J Quinn 13/2: 0-0417: Trkd ldrs, ch over 1f out, rdn *¾* **60**
& swished tail/held ins last: see 2429.
2387 **JOIN THE PARADE 19** [4] 4-8-5 (57) C Cogan (5) 10/1: 00-038: Mid-div, eff wide over 2f out, sn held. *1½* **54**
4067} **POWDER RIVER 303** [15] 6-8-12 (64) S Whitworth 12/1: 1342-9: Rear, no room 2f out, mod late gains, *4* **55**
no impress on ldrs: op 7/1, reapp: '99 wnr at Lingfield (AW, h'cap, rtd 70a, K Burke) & subs at Redcar for current connections (h'cap, rtd 64 at best): suited by 10/11f on firm, soft & equitrack: likes a sharp trk & best LHd.
2446 **MOLE CREEK 17** [9] 5-9-1 (67) J Fortune 16/1: 5-0000: Prom till over 2f out: 10th: see 2446. *5* **51**
2750 **SUPLIZI 4** [13] 9-8-8 (60) J F Egan 10/1: 400060: Led till 3f out, btn/eased 2f out: 13th: op 8/1. **0**
2790 **Field Master 3** [16] 3-7-12 (62)(2ow)(3oh) P Doe 33/1:-- **Colour Key** [14] 6-7-10 (48)(3oh) R Brisland (5) 66/1:
13 ran Time 2m 33.62 (3.62) (Valley Paddocks Racing Ltd) E J Alston Longton, Lancs.

AYR MONDAY JULY 24TH Lefthand, Galloping Track

Official Going FIRM. Stalls: Rnd Crse - Inside, Str Crse - Centre.

2873

2.15 EBF MDN 2YO (D) 7f rnd Firm 19 -45 Slow
£3542 £1090 £545 £272

2091 **SNOWSTORM 33** [3] M L W Bell 2-9-0 M Fenton 1/3 FAV: 261: 2 gr c Environment Friend - Choral Sundown **89+**
(Night Shift) Trkd ldr, led 2f out, asserted under hands-and-heels riding fnl 1f: hvly bckd, slow time: eff at 7f, 1m+ will suit: acts on firm & gd, handles a stiff/gall trk: well regarded, holds a Racing Post Trophy entry.
2174 **BAILEYS CREAM 29** [5] M Johnston 2-8-9 K Darley 10/1: 02: 2 ch f Mister Baileys - Exclusive Life *3* **75**
(Exclusive Native) Trkd ldrs, rdn/chsd wnr ins last, kept on, al held: op 8/1: acts on firm, stays 7f, get further.
2628 **SEDUCTIVE 11** [1] Sir Mark Prescott 2-9-0 S Sanders 4/1: 023: 2 b c Pursuit Of Love - Full Orchestra *hd* **79**
(Shirley Heights) Led, rdn/hdd 2f out, fdd: op 5/2: this longer 7f trip will suit: handles firm & gd/soft: see 2628.
2717 **LITTLE TASK 7** [2] A Berry 2-9-0 J Carroll 20/1: -3024: Chsd ldrs, held 2f out: see 2717, 2239 (6f). *3½* **72**
2717 **HO PANG YAU 7** [6] 2-9-0 A Culhane 50/1: 05: Rear, in tch, outpcd fnl 3f: see 2717. *1½* **69**
2717 **THORNTOUN DANCER 7** [4] 2-8-9 Dean McKeown 50/1: -0056: Bhd halfway: longer 7f trip, needs sells. *3½* **57**
-- **SECOND VENTURE** [7] 2-9-0 J Fanning 100/1: 7: In tch 4f: Petardia colt, Apr foal, cheaply bght. *5* **52**
7 ran Time 1m 28.25 (4.45) (Lord Blyth) M L W Bell Newmarket.

2874

2.45 CAPEL CURE NURSERY HCAP 2YO (D)   6f   Firm 19   -32 Slow   [92]
£3464   £1066   £533   £266

2576 **QUINK 12** [4] Sir Mark Prescott 2-9-7 (85) S Sanders 2/1 FAV: 131: 2 ch g Selkirk - Ink Pot (Green   93
Dancer), Prom, led dist, styd on well, pushed out: hvly bckd: debut Yarmouth wnr (mdn): eff at 6f, tried 7f, shld
suit: acts on firm & fast: likes a gall/fair trk & runs well fresh: gd weight carrier: useful & progressive.
2557 **EMISSARY 13** [1] M Johnston 2-8-1 (65) K Dalgleish (5) 5/1: -66402: 2 gr c Primo Dominie - Misty   2½   66
Goddess (Godswalk), Prom, rdn/briefly led 2f out, kept on onepace for press: op 4/1: eff at 6f on firm grnd.
2718 **CEDAR TSAR 7** [5] D W Chapman 2-7-12 (62) Claire Bryan (5) 4/1: 021333: 2 b c Inzar - The Aspecto   ½   61
Girl (Alzao) Cl-up, ev ch halfway, outpcd by wnr fnl 2f: op 7/2: acts on firm, gd & fibresand: see 2301 (sell, 7f).
2665 **CLANSINGE 10** [3] A Berry 2-8-4 (68) J Carroll 9/4: -53134: Led 5f: op 3/1: btr 2665, 1918 (5f).   5   58
2665 **ITALIAN AFFAIR 10** [2] 2-7-10 (60) J Bramhill 8/1: 202105: Saddle slipped start, unrideable.   dist   0
5 ran   Time 1m 12.37 (3.07)   (Cheveley Park Stud)   Sir Mark Prescott Newmarket.

2875

3.15 CAMERON LODGE SELLER 3YO+ (F)   1m2f192y Firm 19   -11 Slow
£2282   £652   £326   3 yo rec 11lb

2765 **LOKOMOTIV 5** [3] J M Bradley 4-9-5 (bl) P Fitzsimons (5) 10/1: -60001: 4 b g Salse - Rainbow's End   42
(My Swallow), Rear, rdn & styd on well from 2f out to lead well in last: op 8/1: no bid: blnks reapplied, qck reapp:
rnr-up in '99 (h'cap, rtd 57, P D Evans): '98 Yarmouth wnr (7f seller, rtd 75 at best, M Channon): eff at 7f/1m prev,
now stays gall 11 well: acts on firm & gd/soft: tried visor: enjoys sell grade.
2561 **THORNTOUN GOLD 13** [2] J S Goldie 4-9-7 A Culhane 3/1: 401002: 4 ch f Lycius - Gold Braisim   ¾   43
(Jareer) Held up, rdn/prog to lead 1f out, hdd well ins last, no extra: bckd: stays 11f: see 2180 (h'cap, 1m).
2800 **SECONDS AWAY 3** [5] J S Goldie 9-9-5 Dawn Rankin (7) 7/1: 333433: 9 b g Hard Fought - Keep Mum   2½   37$
(Mummy's Pet), Rear, rdn & styd on fnl 2f, not reach front pair: qck reapp: keeping v busy: see 1191.
2765 **ESPERTO 5** [1] J Pearce 7-9-5 Dean McKeown 11/4 FAV: 061044: Chsd ldrs, onepace/held over 1f   ¾   36
out: hvly bckd, op 4/1, qck reapp: ahd of this wnr latest: see 1546 (soft, 10f).
2780 **ACE OF TRUMPS 4** [4] 4-9-12 (t) M Fenton 9/2: 030025: Led till 4f out, btn 1f out: qck reapp.   shd   43$
*2780 **CLAIM GEBAL CLAIM 4** [7] 4-9-12 P Hanagan (7) 6/1: 6-0016: Led 4f out, hdd 1f out, wknd: op 5/1.   nk   42$
2642 **MONACO 10** [8] 6-9-5 R Winston 20/1: 000007: Chsd ldrs, btn 3f out: op 10/1: see 1685.   7   25$
1904} **BRAMBLES WAY 409** [6] 11-9-5 Claire Bryan (5) 33/1: 50/0-8: Bhd 3f out: jumps fit (mod form): no   24   0
form sole '99 start on the level (sell, F Jordan): 98/99 hdles wnr at Cartmel, Warwick & Leicester (2m/2m1f clmrs,
gd/sft & hvy): rnr-up on the level in '98 for Mrs M Reveley (amat h'cap, rtd 44): last won in '97 at Newcastle
(h'cap): suited by 10f on firm & soft, any trk, likes a stiff/gall one, eff with/without blnks or visor.
8 ran   Time 2m 19.33 (3.33)   (Mrs Heather Raw)   J M Bradley Sedbury, Glos.

2876

3.45 FRESH AYR CLASSIFIED STKS 3YO+ 0-70 (E)   1m5f   Firm 19   -50 Slow
£2746   £845   £422   £211   3 yo rec 13lb

*2826 **ALEXANDRINE 3** [3] Sir Mark Prescott 3-8-12 S Sanders 1/4 FAV: -11411: 3 b f Nashwan - Alruccaba   72
(Crystal Palace) Trkd ldrs, stoked up from over 2f out, styd on for press to overhaul ldr well ins last: hvly bckd at
long odds on: qck reapp: earlier scored at Yarmouth, Musselburgh (h'caps) & Carlisle (class stks): unplcd in 3
back-end mdns in '99 (rtd 56): suited by 12/13f on firm/fast, any trk: has run well fresh: gd weight carrier:
well placed by his excellent trainer to land 4 races this term & is still improving.
2755 **HERITAGE 5** [1] D Nicholls 6-9-8 (VIS) Alex Greaves 9/2: /46062: 6 b g Danehill - Misty Halo (High   ¾   67
Top) Dictated pace, rdn clr over 3f out, rdn & strongly press fnl 2f, hdd well ins last & no extra: op 7/2, qck
reapp in a 1st time vis: creditable effort tho' had the run of the race: acts on firm & gd: can find similar.
2793 **LANCER 4** [4] J Pearce 8-9-8 (vis) Dean McKeown 9/1: 606503: 8 ch g Diesis - Last Bird (Sea Bird II)   5   60$
Held up in tch, rdn/outpcd by front pair fnl 2f: qck reapp: see 815 (soft).
2782 **OCEAN DRIVE 4** [2] Miss L A Perratt 4-9-8 K Dalgleish (5) 20/1: 434224: Bhd ldr, btn 2f out: see 2309. shd   60$
4 ran   Time 2m 53.63 (9.03)   (Miss K Rausing)   Sir Mark Prescott Newmarket.

2877

4.15 TOTALBET.COM HCAP 3YO+ 0-90 (C)   6f   Firm 19   +03 Fast   [84]
£7182   £2210   £1105   £552   3 yo rec 5 lb   Majority raced towards centre

*2822 **FRIAR TUCK 3** [10] Miss L A Perratt 5-9-5 (75)(6ex) K Dalgleish (5) 5/1: 103011: 5 ch g Inchinor - Jay   80
Gee Ell (Vaigly Great) Al prom, went on over 1f out, held on well, rdn out: best time of day: bckd under a pen:
earlier scored at York (h'cap) & Carlisle (class stks, broke course record): rnr-up in '99 (rtd 87, h'cap): '98
York wnr (val h'cap, rtd 101): suited by 5/6f, tried 7f: acts on firm & soft, any trk, loves York: has run well
fresh: wind problems seem well bhd him, remains attractively h'capped & shld win again.
2701 **MUNGO PARK 8** [6] M Dods 6-9-5 (75)(bl) A Culhane 6/1: 202222: 6 b g Selkirk - River Dove   ½   77
(Riverman) Held up, rdn & squeezed thr' to chase wnr ins last, styd on: well bckd, rnr-up on 6 of last 8 starts.
2697 **FULL SPATE 9** [1] J M Bradley 5-9-0 (70) K Darley 6/1: 354103: 5 ch h Unfuwain - Double River (Irish   1   70
River) Trkd ldrs, rdn to chall 2f out, not pace of wnr: acts on firm & hvy grnd: see 2444.
2796 **YOUNG BIGWIG 3** [12] D W Chapman 4-6-13 (55) Claire Bryan (5) 10/1: 345334: Chsd ldrs stands   1¼   52
rail, outpcd fnl 1f: qck reapp: well h'capped: see 425.
*2701 **BENZOE 8** [2] 10-8-1 (57) A Nicholls (3) 5/1: -50615: Handy, edged right/fdd fnl 1f: op 4/1, btr 2701.   nk   53
2676 **BON AMI 9** [4] 4-10-0 (84) P Bradley (5) 9/2 FAV: 000346: Trkd ldrs, wknd ins last: see 1337, 1004.   ¾   78
2631 **RIBERAC 11** [9] 4-9-3 (73) J Fanning 10/1: 002007: Prom, briefly led 2f out, wknd: see 2395.   1¼   64
2697 **PIPS MAGIC 9** [11] 4-9-8 (78) M Fenton 8/1: W00108: Chsd ldrs till over 1f out, wknd: see 2580 (stks).   1   67
2699 **LADY OF WINDSOR 8** [8] 3-8-6 (67)(vis) R Winston 20/1: 102309: Dwelt, nvr on terms: see 2017, 1144. 1¾   52
2777 **NORTHERN SVENGALI 4** [5] 4-8-5 (61) S Sanders 10/1: 060040: Led 4f: 10th: qck reapp: see 780.   nk   45
2798 **FACILE TIGRE 3** [7] 5-7-10 (52)(8oh) P Hanagan (3) 33/1: 550300: Chsd ldrs 4f: qck reapp: see 146.   7   23
11 ran   Time 1m 10.25 (0.95)   (Cree Lodge Racing Club)   Miss L A Perratt Ayr, Strathclyde.

2878   4.45 WESTERN HOUSE HCAP 3YO+ 0-95 (C)   7f rnd   Firm 19 -02 Slow   [89]
          £6987   £2150   £1075   £537   3 yo rec 7 lb

2823 **RYEFIELD** 3 [2] Miss L A Perratt 5-7-10 (57) (1oh) J McAuley (5) 9/2 JT FAV: 0-0R21: 5 b g Petong -   62
Octavia (Sallust) Rear, smooth prog to lead well ins last, held on well, drvn out: qck reapp: confirmed return to
form of latest: '99 Newcastle & Ayr wnr (h'cap, rtd 68): '98 Carlisle wnr (mdn, rtd 80): suited by 7f/1m on firm &
gd/soft, loves Ayr: runs well fresh & best without blnks: best held up: took advantage of a slip in the weights.
2696 **TONY TIE** 9 [1] J S Goldie 4-9-10 (85) A Culhane 12/1: 310202: 4 b g Ardkinglass - Queen Of The   nk 89
Quorn (Governor General) Trkd ldrs, drvn & styd on well for press ins last, just held: op 8/1: eff at 7f/10f.
2577 **MANA DARGENT** 12 [7] M Johnston 3-8-4 (72) (BL) K Dalgleish (5) 14/1: 456303: 3 b c Ela Mana Mou -   ¾ 74
Petite D Argent (Noalto) Held up, prog/chall 1f out, no extra ins last: op 8/1, gd run in first time blnks: acts
on firm & hvy grnd: mdn, see 1387 & 717.
2694 **AMBER FORT** 9 [3] J M Bradley 7-8-9 (70) (bl) P Fitzsimons (5) 9/2 JT FAV: 055534: Trkd ldrs, eff   nk 71
when hmpd 1f out, kept on ins last: shade unlucky, gone close without interference: likes Goodwood: see 1011.
2694 **MANTLES PRIDE** 9 [5] 5-9-8 (83) (bl) R Winston 10/1: 106005: Held up, prog/chall 1f out, sn held.   1 82
2673 **DOVEBRACE** 9 [10] 7-7-10 (57) (4oh) J Bramhill 8/1: 121666: Rear, styd on ins last: op 11/2.   nk 55
2694 **SUPREME SALUTATION** 9 [9] 4-8-11 (72) K Darley 5/1: 062067: Cl-up, rdn/led over 1f out, hdd   hd 69
ins last & no extra: worth a try over a stiff 6f: see 1011.
2437 **PERSIAN FAYRE** 18 [8] 8-8-4 (63) (2ow) J Carroll 7/1: -01008: Led till over 1f out, fdd: btr 1631 (C/D).   1¾ 59
2334 **AL MUALLIM** 23 [4] 6-10-0 (89) (t) Alex Greaves 7/1: 300009: Keen/held up, btn 2f out: t-strap.   nk 82
4512] **GLENDAMAM** 272 [6] 3-8-8 (76) J Fanning 33/1: 2033-0: Chsd ldrs, btn 2f out: 10th: reapp: 2½ 64
'99 wnr for E Weymes at Newcastle (auct mdn, rtd 79, subs plcd in h'cap company): eff at 6f, 7f/1m shld suit:
acts on firm & hvy grnd, stiff/gall trk: eff with/without a visor: likes to race with/force the pace.
10 ran   Time 1m 25.27 (1.47)   (Mrs Elaine Aird)   Miss L A Perratt Ayr, Strathclyde.

Official Going   GOOD TO FIRM. Stalls: Inside.

2879   6.30 DOROTHY MDN HCAP 3YO 0-65 (F)   2m35y   Good 50 -16 Slow   [67]
          £3107   £956   £478   £239

536 **TURNED OUT WELL** 157 [4] P C Haslam 3-8-1 (40) Dale Gibson 9/1: 00-551: 3 b g Robellino - In   41
The Shade (Bustino) Mid-div, rdn to improve over 3f out, styd on to lead ins last, rdn out: op 7/1, 5 month abs:
unplcd in '99 (rtd 41): apprec this step up to a stiff 2m on gd: runs well fresh: lightly raced.
2624 **HARD DAYS NIGHT** 11 [14] M Blanshard 3-7-13 (36) (2ow) F Norton 14/1: 006462: 3 b g Mujtahid - Oiche 2 37
Mhaith (Night Shift) Rcd keenly cl-up, hdwy to lead over 2f out, hdd dist, no extra, ddhtd for 2nd: stays 2m.
2734 **NICIARA** 6 [11] M C Chapman 3-8-7 (46) Joanna Badger (7) 7/2 FAV: 332322: 3 b g Soviet Lad -   dht 45
Verusa (Petorius) In tch, improved 1m out, wandered appr fnl 1f, onepace, ddhtd for 2nd: clr rem, hard ride.
2746 **LUCKY JUDGE** 5 [13] W W Haigh 3-9-7 (60) F Lynch 10/1: -50464: Rear, eff when short of room over   4 55
3f out, styd on fnl 2f, nvr nrr: qck reapp: jt top-weight: up in trip & seems to stay 2m: see 1909, 902.
2482 **ONE DOMINO** 17 [7] 3-9-5 (58) (vis) A Clark 12/1: 032405: Settled rear, hdwy over 5f out, btn 2f out.   3½ 50
1369 **SHARVIE** 66 [8] 3-8-13 (52) T G McLaughlin 50/1: 0-006: Hld up, eff 5f out, btn over 2f out: abs.   3 41
2518 **ALBARDEN** 16 [9] 3-8-10 (49) J P Spencer 16/1: 0-5507: In tch, short of room & dropped rear   2 36
5f out, late hdwy for press, no impress: up in trip: see 1255.
2482 **OLD FEATHERS** 17 [2] 3-8-11 (50) O Pears 7/1: -00608: Mid-div at best: up in trip: see 1448.   3 34
2445 **GOLDEN ROD** 18 [12] 3-9-7 (60) W Supple 11/1: 003469: Led, hdd appr fnl 2f, wknd: jt top-weight.   nk 44
2746 **TYCOONS LAST** 5 [1] 3-7-10 (35) G Baker (5) 5/1: 043530: Dwelt, al bhd, 10th: qck reapp, btr 2746 (12f).2½ 16
2659 **SADLERS SONG** 10 [15] 3-8-5 (44) P Fessey 7/1: -50050: Prom, wknd qckly over 4f out, 11th: see 1758. 1 24
2210 **Jeune Premier** 28 [5] 3-9-3 (56) M Tebbutt 16/1:   2445 **Ulshaw** 18 [10] 3-8-7 (46) J Stack 33/1:
2691 **Betachance Dot Com** 9 [16] 3-8-12 (51) C Lowther 33/1:
2624 **Streak Of Dawn** 11 [17] 3-7-10 (35) (3ow) M Baird 33/1:
2484 **Secretario** 17 [3] 3-8-0 (39) N Kennedy 33/1:   2439 **Horton Dancer** 18 [6] 3-8-7 (46) T Williams 33/1:
17 ran   Time 3m 41.0 (10.7)   (Middleham Park Racing XVIII)   P C Haslam Middleham, N.Yorks.

2880   7.00 SAILORS CLAIMER 2YO (F)   5f   Good 50   +00 Fast
          £2380   £680   £340

2730 **FLINT** 6 [12] M W Easterby 2-8-13 T Lucas 3/1 FAV: 0541: 2 b g Fayruz - Full Of Sprakle (Persian   70
Heights) Made all, styd on strongly ins last, pushed out: nicely bckd, qck reap: 2,000gns Apr foal, sire
a sprinter: eff around 5f on gd grnd & a stiff/undul trk: improved for forcing the pace today.
2120 **PATRICIAN FOX** 32 [8] J J Quinn 2-8-6 F Lynch 9/1: 003432: 2 b f Nicolotte - Peace Mission   1¾ 57
(Dunbeath) In tch, hdwy over 2f out, styd on ins last, no impress: clr rem: consistent, sell nurseries suit.
1236 **FLAMBE** 74 [11] P C Haslam 2-8-13 Dean McKeown 25/1: 03: 2 b c Whittingham - Uaeflame (Polish   4 54
Precedent) Handy, rdn/styd on onepce fnl 2f: 10 wk abs, imprvd on this turf bow: stays 5f on gd, 6f suit next time.
1864 **CATCH THE CHRON** 42 [7] N Tinkler 2-8-2 N Kennedy 13/2: 204: Rear, late hdwy, no dngr: op 9/2, abs. 3 34
2723 **ONE BELOVED** 6 [6] 2-8-1 P Fessey 8/1: 003245: Mid-div, rdn/held fnl 2f: qck reapp: see 2723, 2551. 2½ 26
2059 **PREMIER LASS** 34 [9] 2-8-1 W Supple 20/1: -0046: Dwelt, late gains, no dngr: op 14/1: btr 2059. ½ 25
2480 **BRAITHWELL** 17 [3] 2-8-11 O Pears 9/1: 007: Sn rdn in rear, nvr a factor: see 2277.   3 26
2635 **PRINCE NOR** 10 [5] 2-8-11 S Sanders 25/1: 058: Handy, rdn, edged left & wknd over 2f out: op 16/1. hd 26
2741 **LADY AMBITION** 5 [10] 2-8-4 G Parkin 20/1: -040: Al in rear: op 14/1, bckd away: see 2741.   2½ 12
--   **RED OCARINA** [2] 2-8-4 J Stack 11/1: 0: Slow to start, al bhd, fin 10th: op 8/1: 5,000gns   6 0
Piccolo foal, half-sister to a juv 5f scorer: dam won over 5f: with A Berry, shld be capable of better.
2419 **MISS BEADY** 19 [1] 2-8-6 (BL) K Darley 4/1: 00550: Prom, rdn/wknd qckly over 2f out, fin 11th: 4 0
bckd from 7/1 & v disappointing in first time blnks: btr 2419, 2142.
2324 **RAMESES** 23 [4] 2-8-11 (vis) C Lowther 16/1: -040: In tch, hung left & wknd rapidly fnl 2f, fin 12th. 10 0
12 ran   Time 1m 03.8 (2.5)   (Guy Reed)   M W Easterby Sheriff Hutton, N.Yorks.

2881

7.30 PRIORY PARK EBF NOV STKS 2YO (D)   7f100y rnd   Good 50   +03 Fast
£4134   £1272   £636   £318

2346 **VICIOUS KNIGHT 23** [5] L M Cumani 2-8-12 J P Spencer 6/4 JT FAV: 61: 2 b c Night Shift - Myth   86
(Troy) Dsptd lead, went on going well appr fnl 2f, styd on well, rdn out: well bckd: 160,000gns brother to
a v useful 10f/2m scorer: half-brother to several other wnrs: eff at 7.5f, further will suit in time: acts on
gd grnd & a stiff/undul trk: can rate more highly & win again.
2132 **SABANA 31** [1] N A Callaghan 2-8-12 J Mackay (5) 10/1: 02: 2 b c Sri Pekan - Atyaaf (Irish River)   3   79
Rear, rdn/hdwy over 3f out, ev ch over 1f out, sn not pace of wnr, not given hard time once btn: op 8/1:
styd this longer 7.5f trip on gd: shld be capable of winning a mdn: see 2132.
2390 **PERFECT PLUM 20** [4] Sir Mark Prescott 2-8-7 S Sanders 6/4 JT FAV: 523: 2 b f Darshaan - Damascene   4   66
(Scenic) Sn rdn in tch, drvn/onepcd appr fnl 1f: well bckd & better expected: btr 2390 (fm).
2271 **DOUBLE HONOUR 25** [3] M Johnston 2-8-12 K Darley 4/1: 24: Set gd pace, hdd appr fnl 1f, wknd   3   65
qckly over 1f out: rtd higher on debut in 2271 (fast).
4 ran   Time 1m 34.3 (3.5)   (D Metcalf & J Samuel)   L M Cumani Newmarket.

2882

8.00 SAILORS HCAP 3YO+ 0-70 (E)   7f100y rnd   Good 50   -01 Slow   [65]
£4524   £1392   £696   £348   3 yo rec 7 lb

*2735 **WILEMMGEO 6** [15] M C Chapman 3-8-1 (45) Joanna Badger (7) 12/1: 500011: 3 b f Emarati - Floral   52
Spark (Forzando) Chsd ldrs, prog to lead over 1f out, styd on well, pushed out: earlier won twice at W'hampton
(sellers, rtd 55a) & once here at Beverley (appr h'cap): '99 wnr again at W'hampton (seller, rtd 55a & 62):
suited by 7.5f/9.4f on firm, gd/soft, loves fibresand, W'hampton & Beverley: eff with/without visor.
4363} **JORROCKS 284** [10] M W Easterby 6-9-8 (59) T Lucas 4/1: 5010-2: 6 b g Rubiano - Perla Fina (Gallant   ¾   64
Man) Led till over 1f out, kept on well for press ins last: reapp: '99 wnr here at Beverley (h'cap, rtd 61): plcd
in '98 (list rtd h'cap, rtd 93, I Balding): eff at 7f/7.5f on fast, enjoys gd/soft & soft, any trk: fine reapp.
2831 **KESTRAL 3** [3] T J Etherington 4-7-13 (36) F Norton 16/1: 060623: 4 ch g Ardkinglass - Shiny Kay   1½   38
(Star Appeal) Rear, styd on well fnl 2f, not reach front pair: qck reapp: mdn, but a gd run from a poor draw.
2556 **TOEJAM 13** [14] R E Barr 7-8-3 (40) P Fessey 10/1: 001504: Rear, no room over 2f out, styd on for   2   38
press from over 1f out, not reach ldrs: no luck in running, suited by drop in trip, acts on fast & gd: see 2147.
2420 **RYMERS RASCAL 19** [11] 8-9-9 (60) W Supple 5/2 FAV: 563425: Keen/mid-div, al held by ldrs: see 942.1¾   54
2861 **SKYERS FLYER 1** [9] 6-7-12 (35) K Dalgleish (5) 33/1: 000006: Rear, late gains: unplcd yesterday.   1½   26
2733 **DIHATJUM 6** [8] K Darley 13/2: 6-3247: Mid-div, btn 2f out: qck reapp: see 2733, 1255.   2½   52
2437 **ACID TEST 18** [7] 5-9-11 (62) R Fitzpatrick (3) 25/1: 300058: Mid-div, btn 2f out: see 525 (AW).   hd   47
2442 **ON TILL MORNING 18** [12] 4-9-4 (55) A Clark 6/1: 000049: Keen/chsd ldrs, btn 2f out: see 910.   1¼   38
2823 **NORTHGATE 3** [2] 4-8-12 (49)(bl) T Williams 16/1: 214200: Chsd ldrs till 4f out: 10th: qck reapp.   1   30
2839 Susy Wells 2 [13] 5-7-12 (35)(2ow)(5oh) Dale Gibson 33/1:
2823 Santandre 3 [6] 4-8-10 (47) P M Quinn (3) 20/1:
2823 Detroit City 3 [4] 5-8-4 (41) F Lynch 25/1:   880   **Pacific Alliance 103** [1] 4-10-0 (65)(bl) Dean McKeown 25/1:
2512 Stormswell 16 [5] 3-8-8 (52) G Parkin 25/1:   2731 **City Flyer 6** [16] 3-8-6 (50)(t) S Sanders 33/1:
16 ran   Time 1m 34.6 (3.8)   (R J Hayward)   M C Chapman Market Rasen, Lincs.

2883

8.30 I J BLAKEY HCAP 3YO+ 0-70 (E)   1m2f   Good 50   -18 Slow   [67]
£5304   £1632   £816   £408   3 yo rec 10lb

2790 **RARE TALENT 4** [11] S Gollings 6-9-0 (53) J P Spencer 100/30: 303261: 6 b g Mtoto - Bold As Love   59
(Lomond) Held up, smooth prog to join ldr over 1f out, pushed ahd ins last, v cheekily: val for 4L+: '99 wnr at
Beverley (ladies h'cap) & Windsor (amat h'cap, rtd 61): '98 wnr at Doncaster (amat h'cap) & Chester (h'cap, rtd 65):
suited by 10/11.5f & handles gd/soft, enjoys gd & firm grnd: handles any trk: best without a visor: tough.
2518 **KHUCHN 16** [7] M Brittain 4-8-9 (48) T Williams 10/1: 265422: 4 b c Unfuwain - Stay Sharpe (Sharpen   1   49
Up) Led, rdn clr bef halfway, rdn fnl 3f & hdd ins last, no ch with wnr: acts on firm & gd/soft: brave run: see 2825.
*2825 **INVISIBLE FORCE 3** [4] M Johnston 3-7-10 (45)(bl)(6ex)(1oh) K Dalgleish (5) 9/4 FAV: 046613: 3 b c   ½   45
Imperial Frontier - Virginia Cottage (Lomond) Held up, prog 4f out, sn outpcd, styd on well from over 1f out,
no threat to wnr: qck reapp under a pen: acts on firm & gd/soft: stays 16f, shaped as if 12f will suit: see 2825.
965 **DIAMOND FLAME 97** [10] A B Mulholland 6-8-13 (52) S Sanders 16/1: 0-0004: Chsd ldrs, held fnl 2f: 2½   48
3 month abs: prev with P Harris, a tricky ride but slipped down the wights: see 681.
2546 **STITCH IN TIME 14** [6] 4-8-1 (40) G Baker 25/1: 330205: Held up, rdn/btn 2f out: see 2380, 871   2½   32
*2518 **BOLD AMUSEMENT 16** [3] 10-9-10 (63) O Pears 9/1: -20016: Held up, nvr on terms: see 2518 (C/D).   ¾   54
1432 **RAINBOW RAVER 63** [9] 4-7-12 (37) Joanna Badger (7) 33/1: 5-0007: Slowly away, nvr on terms: 9   14
2 month abs: rnr-up twice in '99 (rtd 48, h'cap): unplcd in '98 (rtd 69): eff at 10/12f on firm & fast grnd:
handles a sharpish or stiff/undul trk: best without a visor.
1908 **GREEN BOPPER 40** [8] 7-9-10 (63) T G McLaughlin 14/1: 210558: Held up, nvr any impress: 6 wk abs.   1   39
2538 **GENUINE JOHN 14** [5] 7-7-11 (36) P Fessey 10/1: 450539: Chsd ldr, btn 3f out: see 215, 131.   shd   12
2482 **EDMO HEIGHTS 17** [2] 4-8-4 (42)(bl)(1ow) K Darley 10/1: -00000: Chsd ldrs, strugg 3f out: 10th.   10   3
2160 **SEDONA 30** [1] 3-8-5 (54) F Norton 20/1: 30100R: Refused to race: see 1365 (1m, sell h'cap).   0
11 ran   Time 2m 09.1 (6.8)   (John King)   S Gollings Louth, Lincs

2884

9.00 PAUL CLASS STKS 3YO+ 0-65 (E)   1m2f   Good 50   -24 Slow
£2873   £884   £442   £221   3 yo rec 10lb   Slow run race

2499 **THREE LIONS 16** [2] R F Johnson Houghton 3-8-9 K Darley 7/4 FAV: 040-01: 3 ch g Jupiter Island -   67
Super Sol (Rolfe) Dictated pace, increased tempo over 1f out, held on well fnl 1f, drvn out: first win: unplcd in
'99 (rtd 67): eff at 10f, get further: acts on gd grnd & stiff trk: eff forcing the pace: likely raced.
2364 **ZAGALETA 21** [5] Andrew Turnell 3-8-6 F Norton 12/1: 0-0002: 3 b f Sir Pekan - Persian Song (Persian   1   63
Bold) Held up, prog to chase wnr 1f out, kept on, al just held: stays a slowly run 10f: see 931 (1m).
2527 **ASCARI 15** [1] W Jarvis 4-9-5 D McGaffin (5) 9/4: 1-0203: 4 b g Presidium - Ping Pong (Petong)   3½   61
Keen/cl-up, onepace over 1f out: clr rem: see 2130, 1973.
2278 **CITY BANK DUDLEY 25** [6] N Wilson 3-8-9 O Pears 50/1: 0364: Chsd ldrs, held fnl 3f: longer 10f trip.   5   54
2372 **AFRICAN PETE 21** [3] 3-8-9 S Sanders 100/30: -60265: Held up, chsd ldrs 3f out, sn held: see 2332.   1¾   51
2673 **IT CAN BE DONE 9** [4] 3-8-11 P M Quinn (3) 8/1: 216006: Chsd ldrs till over 2f out: btr 1645 (1m, sft).   ½   52
6 ran   Time 2m 09.7 (7.4)   (Jim Short)   R F Johnson Houghton Blewbury, Oxon.

Official Going   GOOD/FIRM. Stalls: Inside.

2885   6.20 READING HCAP 3YO 0-75 (E)   6f str   Good/Firm   Inapplicable   [82]
£3052   £872   £436

1963 **RAVINE** 38 [13] R Hannon 3-9-0 (68) R Hughes 10/1: 6-041: 3 ch f Indian Ridge - Cubby Hole (Town **71**
And Country) Nvr far away, chall strongly dist, styd on well to lead cl-home, rdn out: eff over a sharp 6f on
fast grnd, has tried 7f/1m: likes to run-up with the pace: lightly rcd & open to further improvement.

2603 **DOCTOR DENNIS** 11 [6] B J Meehan 3-8-13 (67) D R McCabe 11/2: 120122: 3 b g Last Tycoon - Noble nk **69**
Lustre (Lyphard's Wish) Chsd ldrs, ev ch over 1f out, just btn in a cl-fin: another sound run: see 2603, 2549.

2577 **CD FLYER** 12 [1] M R Channon 3-9-6 (74) Craig Williams 6/1: 644633: 3 ch g Grand Lodge - Pretext shd **76**
(Polish Precedent) Rdn in rear, imprvd 2f out, led dist till caught cl-home: deserves similar: see 2577.

2716 **ENDYMION** 7 [12] Mrs P N Dutfield 3-8-8 (62) L Newman (3) 14/1: 000304: Set pace till dist, kept 1 **61**
on & btn just over 1L: front rnr, rdn after 14 starts: see 2489.

1405 **KISSING TIME** 65 [2] J Fortune 12/1: 506-05: Rear, prog over 1f out, eased fnl 100y: 9 ¾ **71 +**
wk abs, top weight: not given a hard time, promising after abs & sharper next time: one to keep in mind.

2549 **CARNAGE** 14 [9] J Fortune 3-7-13 (53) G Bardwell 10/1: 0-0026: Chsd ldrs till outpcd halfway, rallied fnl 1f: hd **49**
shorter priced stable-mate of 4th: see 2549 (soft grnd).

*2511 **WATER BABE** 16 [14] J Hills 3-8-11 (65) N Pollard 7/2 FAV: 50-417: Prom, ev ch dist, no extra ins last: hd **61**
well bckd: not disgraced, only btn around 2L: see 2511.

2555 **BORN TO RULE** 14 [8] 3-8-3 (57) R Havlin 20/1: 005008: Dwelt, imprvd from rear 2f out, nrst fin. shd **53**

2478 **FEAST OF ROMANCE** 17 [5] 3-8-6 (60)(bl) S Whitworth 20/1: 060309: Switched start, kept on fnl 1f, hd **56**
nrst fin: btn just over 2L: see 2216.

2549 **NIGHT DIAMOND** 14 [7] 3-8-12 (66)(tvi) M Hills 6/1: -00040: Chsd ldrs, short of room & switched hd **61**
2f out, no extra cl-home: fin 10th, btn under 3L: see 2549 (C/D).

2105 **JUMBO JET** 32 [3] 3-9-5 (73) T E Durcan 10/1: 40550: Al towards rear, fin last: see 1099 (1m). **0**

1607 Barden Lady 54 [10] 3-8-6 (60) M Roberts 25/1:   2690 Sea Haze 9 [4] 3-8-13 (67) G Carter 20/1:
13 ran   Time 1m 13.4   (Lord Carnarvon)   R Hannon East Everleigh, Wilts

2886   6.45 EBF FILLIES MDN 2YO (D)   6f str   Good/Firm   Inapplicable
£3688   £1135   £567   £283

-- **GALAPAGOS GIRL** [9] B W Hills 2-8-11 M Hills 12/1: -1: 2 b f Turtle Island - Shabby Doll **78**
(Northfields) Chsd ldrs & ran green, imprvd to lead dist, ran on well, rdn out: gambled from 20/1 on debut:
Apr foal, cost 15,000gns: half sister to sev wnrs, dam a 10/11f scorer: sire a top-class miler: eff over a sharp
6f, will stay 7f: acts on fast grnd & runs well fresh: plenty to like about this, sure to prog & win more races.

2285 **MAINE LOBSTER** 24 [5] J L Dunlop 2-8-11 T Quinn 13/8 FAV: -032: 2 ch f Woodman - Capades ¾ **74**
(Overskate) Pushed along in rear, imprvd to chall dist, kept on but not the pace of wnr cl-home: hvly bckd from
9/4: now qual for run h'caps, crying out for 7f: see 2285 (stiff trk).

2588 **LOOKING FOR LOVE** 12 [1] J G Portman 2-8-11 N Pollard 16/1: -033: 2 b f Tagula - Mousseux (Jareer) ½ **73**
Prsd ldrs on outside, ev ch 1f out, kept on & not btn far: op 12/1: much imprvd form, shld find a mdn.

2588 **LITTLE CALLIAN** 12 [10] T M Jones 2-8-11 A Price 40/1: -604: Led dist, grad fdd: Feb foal, cost 2½ **66**
1,000 gns: half sister to sev wnr, incl sprinter Chalice: sire a smart miler, dam from a gd family: 5f suit?

-- **STARFLEET** [6] 2-8-11 J Fortune 9/2: 5: Trkd ldrs, not pace of front trio fnl 1f: drifted from 7/2, nk **65**
debut: Feb foal, related to sev wnrs, incl 7f/1m scorer Russian Musiac & decent 2yo scorer Pool Music.

2091 **ACADEMIC ACCURACY** 33 [7] 2-8-11 R Hughes 5/2: -06: Trkd ldr, onepcd fnl 1f: well bckd, btr 2091. 1½ **61**

2447 **WHITE MARVEL** 18 [3] 2-8-11 D Sweeney 40/1: -637: Trkd ldr travelling well, rdn & btn over 1f out: 3 **52**
prev trained by W Haggas, now with N Littmoden: found disapp little here, worth a try in blnks: see 2447.

2683 **TWILIGHT MISTRESS** 9 [8] 2-8-11 J D Smith 40/1: -08: Rcd keenly & in tch 4½f, fdd: see 2683. 1 **49**

2369 **CARPET PRINCESS** 21 [2] 2-8-11 L Newman (3) 16/1: -49: Slowly away, not recover: see 2369. 2 **43**

2419 **ANDROMEDAS WAY** 19 [11] 2-8-11 R Perham 11/1: -640: Well bhd, some late prog tho' nvr dngrs: 10th.1¾ **39**

2628 **MARGARITA** 11 [12] 2-8-11 J Tate 40/1: -00: Speed 3f, sn struggling & fin 11th: see 2628. ¾ **36**

2545 **BATCHWORTH BREEZE** 14 [4] 2-8-11 S Carson (3) 40/1: -00: Al outpcd, fin detached in last: see 2545. 8 **8**

12 ran   Time 1m 14.1   (Mrs Simon Polito)   B W Hills Lambourn, Berks

2887   7.15 B WALLACE SELL HCAP 3YO+ 0-60 (F)   1m3f135y   Good/Firm   Inapplicable   [56]
£2730   £780   £390   3yo rec 12lb

1039 **ARTIC COURIER** 87 [1] D J S Cosgrove 9-9-3 (45) J Fortune 8/1: -11441: 9 gr g Siberian Express - **48**
La Reine de France (Queens Hussar) Rear, stdy prog ent str, switched & strong run to lead cl-home, going away:
12 wk abs, no bid: earlier won at W'hampton (2, sells): plcd sev times in '99 (rtd 52 & 57a): '96 wnr at Epsom
& Kempton (h'caps, awdd race, rtd 83): eff at 12/14f, has tried blnks: acts on firm, soft grnd & on both AWs:
handles any trk, likes a sharp/undul one: has tried blnks, best without: gd weight carrier, runs v well fresh.

2466 **IN THE STOCKS** 7 [6] L G Cottrell 4-9-4 (46) S Carson (3) 5/1 JT FAV: 1-0062: 6 b m Reprimand - nk **48**
Stock Hill Lass (Air Trooper) Chsd ldrs, ev ch over 1f out, led briefly ins last, not pace to repel wnr cl-home:
nicely bckd: apprec this drop into sell company, shld win similar: see 1100 (10f here, reapp).

2622 **BLOWING AWAY** 11 [15] J Pearce 6-7-10 (24)(20h) G Bardwell 14/1: 000503: 6 b m Last Tycoon - 1 **24**
Taken By Force (Persian Bold) Chsd ldrs, hmpd home turn & lost place, switched & fin strongly fnl 1f, not
quite get there: poss a shade unlucky: see 1819.

2765 **THOMAS HENRY** 5 [7] J S Moore 4-9-3 (45) R Hughes 14/1: 350364: Tried to make all, kicked clr nk **44**
2f out, worn down cl-home: quick reapp: see 2587 (10f, sand).

*2381 **PIPS BRAVE** 21 [8] J Weaver 7/1: 400015: Prom till onepcd fnl 1f: now with L Dace. ¾ **42**

2622 **GROOMS GOLD** 11 [17] 8-7-10 (24)(vis) M Henry 16/1: 020406: Prom till lost pl ent str, rallied fnl 1f. ½ **21**

2771 **SILKEN LADY** 5 [11] 4-7-11 (25) A Polli (5) 5/1 JT FAV: 000367: Mid-div, wide into str, ev ch 1f out, shd **22**
sn no extra: quick reapp: see 2537.

2510 **DINKY** 16 [4] 3-7-10 (36)(16oh) D Kinsella (7) 33/1: -00008: Rcd keenly in rear, imprvd 2f out, no impress. ½ **32$**

2601 **ERIN ANAM CARA** 11 [20] 3-8-10 (50) C Rutter 20/1: 3-0009: Rcd keenly in rear, keeping on when 1¾ **44**
hmpd ent fnl 1f, no ch after: may have made the frame with a clr run: see 1572 (1m clmr).

1852 **ABLE PETE** 43 [10] 4-8-1 (29) D Glennon (7) 13/2: 146000: Chsd ldrs 10f, wknd: fin 10th, 6 wk abs. ¾ **22**

2765 **HIGH BEAUTY** 5 [19] 3-7-12 (38) A Beech (5) 16/1: 400500: Reared start, imprvg when short of room, nk **30**
2f out, no ch after: quick reapp: flattered 2510.

2547 **ARANA** 14 [18] 5-8-1 (28)(bl)(1ow) Sophie Mitchell 33/1: -00060: Front rank 10f, wknd into 12th. 3 **16**

900

2206 **Alpha Heights 28** [9] 3-8-10 (50) L Newman (3) 14/1: 2008 **Xylem 37** [14] 9-7-10 (24)(bl)(2oh) R Brisland (5) 14/1:
3718} **Regal Academy 327** [2] 6-8-11 (39)(bl) Paul Eddery 14/1:
2656 **Woodlands Lad Too 10** [16] 8-7-12 (26) S Righton 40/1:
1884 **Napper Blossom 41** [13] 3-8-3 (43) N Pollard 25/1:
2548 **Thewayshewalks 14** [3] 3-7-10 (36)(t)(11oh) Jonjo Fowle(0) 33/1:
18 ran   Time 2m 30.5   (D J S Cosgrove)   D J S Cosgrove Newmarket

---

2888	7.45 COTES DU RHONE HCAP 3YO+ 0-80 (D) 1m2f Good/Firm Inapplicable					**[71]**
	£4309 £1326 £663 £331 3yo rec 10lb					

2752 **THE GREEN GREY 5** [6] L Montague Hall 6-9-9 (66) N Pollard 9/2: 061001: 6 gr g Environment Friend - 70
Pea Green (Try My Best) Slow away, sn recovered to lead, made rest, held on gamely fnl 1f, drvn out: quick
reapp: earlier scored here at Windsor (h'cap): lightly rcd in '99 (rtd 66a & 54): '98 wnr at Yarmouth (h'cap),
Bath, Brighton (clmr, with W Muir), Kempton & Lingfield (h'caps, rtd 59a, with D Morris): eff over 7f/1m, suited
by 10f now & likes firm/fast, handles gd/soft & equitrack: acts on any trk, loves Windsor: best without a visor
& can carry big weights: loves to dominate, tough & game.
2257 **NO MERCY 26** [7] J W Hills 4-9-9 (66) M Hills 12/1: 34-502: 4 ch g Faustus - Nashville Blues   ½ 68
(Try My Best) Led 2f, chsd wnr, hard rdn 2f out, kept on ins last, not btn far: gd run: see 2051.
2527 **STROMSHOLM 15** [8] J R Fanshawe 4-9-10 (67) D Harrison 9/4 FAV: 632423: 4 ch g Indian Ridge -   1½ 67
Upward Trend (Salmon Leap) Keen cl-up, eff to chall over 1f out, no extra ins last: another gd run in defeat: mdn.
1785 **SUPERSONIC 46** [2] R F Johnson Houghton 4-9-9 (66) J Reid 12/1: 0-4604: In tch, brief eff 2f out,   nk 65
no impress till onepace ins last: 7 wk abs: see 679.
2552 **TARSKI 14** [5] 6-8-5 (48) J Lowe 7/1: -00335: Waited with, eff over 2f out, onepace: see 2552.   nk 46
2625 **SPRINGTIME LADY 11** [3] 4-9-3 (60) R Smith 14/1: 223036: Slow away, bhd, no impress: mdn.   1¾ 56
2655 **YOUNG UN 10** [9] 5-9-6 (63) T Quinn 6/1: 202557: Cl-up, wknd well over 1f out: btr 2190, 786.   nk 58
2367 **THIHN 21** [1] 5-8-9 (52) M Roberts 10/1: -20368: Keen cl-up, wknd 3f out: now with J Spearing.   15 25
1853 **MONKEY BUSINESS 43** [4] 3-9-2 (69) R Hughes 6/1: 34-069: Cl-up, wknd over 2f out: 6 wk abs.   nk 41
9 ran   Time 2m 08.0   (J Daniels)   L Montague Hall Tadworth, Surrey

---

2889	8.15 READING MDN 3YO (D) 1m2f Good/Firm Inapplicable			
	£3965 £1220 £610 £305			

-- **WELSH MAIN** [5] H R A Cecil 3-9-0 T Quinn 3/1: -1: 3 br c Zafonic - Welsh Daylight (Welsh Pageant)   92
In tch, hdwy to chase ldr over 1f out, kept on well to lead last strides, drvn out on debut: half brother to
a useful miler: stays 10f well, 12f suit: runs well fresh on gd/firm: looks useful & shld improve.
971 **MISS RIVIERA GOLF 96** [8] G Wragg 3-8-9 R Hughes 6/1: -02: 3 b f Hernando - Miss Beaulieu   shd 86
(Northfields) Cl-up, led 3f out, clr 2f out, kept on ins last till collared last strides: just btn & well clr
of rem after a 3 month abs: stays 10f on gd/firm: strip fitter for this & must win a mdn: see 971.
2553 **CIRCUS PARADE 14** [2] J H M Gosden 3-9-0 J Fortune 20/1: -503: 3 b c Night Shift - Circus Maid   5 83$
(High Top) Led till 3f out, onepace under hands & heels: better run over this sharp 10f on fast grnd: see 2129.
2501 **SHAMAIEL 16** [1] C E Brittain 3-8-9 P Robinson 6/5 FAV: -4404: Prom, rdn & btn over 1f out: well   hd 78
bckd & better expected after 2169 (Listed), 1857.
2531 **TRAVELLERS REST 15** [10] 3-9-0 Craig Williams 25/1: -05: Handy, btn 2f out: bred to stay 10f+.   3½ 78
2354 **CELTIC BAY 22** [4] 3-8-9 M Hills 16/1: -666: Bhd, eff over 4f out, btn over 2f out: see 2354.   2 70$
2531 **CITRUS MAGIC 15** [3] 3-9-0 C Rutter 33/1: -407: Waited with, no danger: see 1912.   4 69
4569} **MISS ASIA QUEST 266** [7] 3-8-9 D Holland 10/1: 035-8: Keen cl-up, btn over 3f out, eased on reapp: ½ 63
stable-mate of rnr-up, too keen: plcd in a mdn in '99 (rtd 79): eff at 7f, bred to stay mid-dists: handles gd/soft.
2465 **DENARIUS SECUNDUS 17** [9] 3-9-0 R Perham 20/1: -09: Al bhd: see 2465.   2½ 64$
-- **DUEMILA** [6] 3-9-0 J Reid 40/1: -0: Slow away, al bhd: 10th: with M Haynes.   2½ 60
10 ran   Time 2m 08.3   (K Abdulla)   H R A Cecil Newmarket

2890	8.45 CITY INDEX FILLIES HCAP 3YO+ 0-80 (D) 1m67y rnd Good/Firm Inapplicable					**[80]**
	£3867 £1190 £595 £297 3yo rec 8lb					

2342 **MADAM ALISON 23** [10] R Hannon 4-10-0 (80) Dane O'Neill 10/3 FAV: 6-3131: 4 b f Puissance - Copper   84
Burn (Electric) Made all, edged left over 1f out & hard prsd ins last but kept on for press: well bckd: earlier
won here at Windsor (class stks): '99 scorer at Newmarket (fills h'cap, rtd 83): '98 Leicester scorer (fills mdn
auct, rtd 77): eff around 8.3f on fast, handles hvy & any trk, likes Windsor: can run well fresh under big weights.
2713 **PATSY STONE 7** [4] M Kettle 4-9-2 (68) T Quinn 5/1: 144532: 4 b f Jester - Third Dam (Slip Anchor)   nk 71
Prom, eff to chall ins last, no extra cl-home, just held: in gd form: see 2713, 1794.
2581 **NATALIE JAY 12** [1] M R Channon 4-8-10 (62) Craig Williams 8/1: 5-3043: 4 b f Ballacashtal - Falls   ¾ 63
Of Lora (Scottish Rifle) Keen in tch, eff to chall over 1f out, onepace, not btn far: handles fast, hvy & equitrack.
2752 **COMMON CONSENT 5** [2] S Woodman 4-8-3 (55) S Whitworth 12/1: -06104: Waited with, eff to chall   hd 56
over 1f out, onepace: quick reapp, see 2296.
2645 **QUEENS PAGEANT 10** [3] 6-8-12 (64) M Roberts 4/1: -04465: Handy, rdn over 2f out, no extra till   ¾ 63
late gains: looks a tricky ride now: see 2645, 1407.
2625 **SILVER QUEEN 11** [8] 3-8-5 (65)(vis) P Robinson 10/1: 000246: With wnr till wknd fnl 1f: see 2625.   ¾ 62
2727 **CITY GAMBLER 6** [7] 6-7-10 (48) G Bardwell 8/1: 40-507: Keen bhd, brief eff over 2f out, sn   ¾ 43
btn: quick reapp, too keen: see 1364.
2564 **MINETTA 13** [4] 5-9-5 (71) M Fenton 11/2: 0-6508: Prom, wknd well over 1f out: see 2062, 1879.   3 60
-- **ISLAND ESCAPE** [5] 4-7-12 (50) R Brisland (5) 16/1: 5530-9: Irish import, last rcd in   10 19
Oct '99, plcd in a 9f h'cap on soft grnd.
2682 **KARAKUL 9** [6] 4-8-9 (61) G Carter 16/1: 00-000: Dwelt, al bhd: see 2682.   7 15
10 ran   Time 1m 45.0   (William J Kelly)   R Hannon East Everleigh, Wilts

Official Going   FIRM. Stalls: 10/12f - Outside; Rem - Inside.

2891   **2.30 DOWNS FILLIES MED AUCT MDN 2YO (F)**   **5f59y**   Firm 20   -14 Slow
£2236   £639   £319

2384 **LONDON EYE** 21 [5] K T Ivory 2-8-11 (bl) C Catlin (7) 4/1: 332001: 2 b f Distinctly North - Clonavon   **64**
Girl (Be My Guest) Dsptd lead till went on after halfway, drvn out: 1st win, plcd thrice prev: cheaply bought
Apr 1st foal, dam modest: eff at 5f, poss stays 6f: acts on firm & likes a sharp/undul trk: eff in blnks.
2368 **QUEENS COLLEGE** 21 [4] M L W Bell 2-8-11 T Quinn 1/3 FAV: -052: 2 b f College Chapel - Fairy Lore   1¼   **61**
(Fairy King) Front rank, rdn to chall over 1f out, ev ch when lkd to get unbalanced ins fnl 1f, sn held:
seems unsuited by this sharp/undul trk: rated higher in 2368 (flat trk).
2513 **PRESENTOFAROSE** 16 [1] J S Moore 2-8-11 B Marcus 16/1: 502343: 2 b f Presenting - Little Red Rose   3½   **53$**
(Precocious) Prom, rdn/no extra fnl 2f: tchd 25/1: drop in trip, plating class form prev: see 1396.
2551 **PERTEMPS GILL** 14 [3] A D Smith 2-8-11 S Whitworth 33/1: 003054: Led, hdd after halfway, sn lost tch. 2½   **47**
--   **GET IT SORTED** [2] 2-8-11 Hayley Turner (7) 20/1: 5: Slow to stride, lkd v reluctant & sn t.o.:   *dist*   **0**
1,350 gns Apr foal, half sister to a couple of wnrs: dam modest: with M Polglase, looks temperamental.
5 ran   Time 1m 01.8 (1.8)   (J B Waterfall)   K T Ivory Radlett, Herts

---

2892   **3.00 VIC MALTBY SELLER 3YO+ (G)**   **1m rnd**   Firm 20   -07 Slow
£1926   £550   £275   3 yo rec 8 lb

2510 **SPARK OF LIFE** 16 [5] P R Chamings 3-8-6 (bl) S Righton 11/8 FAV: -03231: 3 b f Rainbows For Life -   **49**
Sparkly Girl (Danehill) Dwelt, rear, flashed tail 3f out, hdwy & hung left 2f out, ran on well to lead ins last, rdn
clr: well bckd tho' op 5/4: 1st win: acts to T D McCarthy for 15,000gns: rtd 64 in 1st time blnks when unplcd as
a juv (1m): eff at 7f/1m, bred to get further: acts on fast/firm & a sharp/undul trk: enjoys sell/clmg grade.
2303 **DARK MENACE** 24 [3] E A Wheeler 8-9-10 (bl) S Carson (3) 2/1: 010002: 8 br g Beveled - Sweet And   4   **51**
Sure (Known Fact) Led, clr halfway, wknd appr fnl 1f, sn hdd & btn: likes Brighton: see 1462 (C/D, h'cap, gd/soft).
567 **PURNADAS ROAD** 153 [4] Dr J R J Naylor 5-9-0 N Pollard 50/1: 00-603: 5 ch m Petardia - Choral Park   2½   **36$**
(Music Boy) Keen in tch, rdn/held appr fnl 2f: 5 month abs: mod form & treat rating with caution (offic only 25).
2587 **MUSTANG** 12 [1] J Pearce 7-9-10 (vis) T Quinn 9/4: 061054: Rcd keenly cl-up, wknd qckly appr fnl   1¾   **42**
1f: op 7/4, top weight: see 2040 (C/D).
775 **MISS SCARLETT** 117 [2] 7-9-0 D Griffiths 100/1: 05: Lost tch halfway, t.o.: fin distressed, no form.   *dist*   **0**
5 ran   Time 1m 34.2 (2.2)   (Mrs V K Shaw)   P R Chamings Baughurst, Hants

---

2893   **3.30 FILLIES HCAP 3YO+ 0-75 (E)**   **1m3f196y** Firm 20   -08 Slow   **[67]**
£2925   £900   £450   £225   3 yo rec 12lb

*2593 **ALPHA ROSE** 12 [5] M L W Bell 3-8-9 (60) A Beech (5) 7/4 FAV: 125311: 3 ch f Inchinor - Philgwyn   **67**
(Milford) Nvr far away, went on after halfway, rdn clr fnl 1f: nicely bckd tho' op 5/4: earlier won at Musselburgh,
Ayr (stks) & Lingfield (fill h'cap): unplcd for R Williams in '99 (rtd 68): eff btwn 10f & 14f, has tried 2m:
suited by firm/fast & equitrack: handles a sharp or gall trk: tough filly who remains in fine form.
2790 **PARISIAN LADY** 4 [3] A G Newcombe 5-8-10 (49) S Whitworth 10/1: 344202: 5 b m Paris House - Mia   4   **48**
Gigi (Hard Fought) Dwelt, settled last, rdn/prog over 2f out, styd on, no impress: clr rem: styd longer 12f trip.
2793 **IMPREVUE** 4 [1] R J O'Sullivan 6-9-10 (63)(bl) J Reid 2/1: 114-63: 6 ch m Priolo - Las Bela   3   **57**
(Welsh Pageant) Mid-div, rdn to improve 2f out, sn btn: well bckd, quick reapp: see 2793, 1.
2173 **SECRET DROP** 30 [4] K McAuliffe 4-9-2 (55) O Urbina 12/1: 000004: Cl-up, rdn, hung left/fdd fnl 2f.   ¾   **48**
1936 **KELTECH STAR** 39 [6] 4-8-6 (45)(VIS) W Ryan 16/1: 3-6005: Led, hdd after halfway, wknd qckly   6   **30**
fnl 2f: tried in a visor to little effect: btr 1272.
2429 **ELMS SCHOOLGIRL** 19 [2] 4-9-12 (65) J Tate 10/3: -20606: Waited with, rdn to improve over 4f out,   23   **25**
wknd rapidly for press fnl 3f: op 5/2, top-weight: reportedly in season, forget this: see 1332.
6 ran   Time 2m 31.6 (3.4)   (Richard I Morris Jr)   M L W Bell Newmarket

---

2894   **4.00 CONCORDE 2 NURSERY HCAP 2YO (D)**   **7f rnd**   Firm 20   -07 Slow   **[87]**
£3523   £1084   £542   £271

2589 **MERIDEN MIST** 12 [7] P W Harris 2-8-13 (72) A Beech (5) 4/1: 52541: 2 b f Distinctly North - Bring   **74**
On The Choir (Chief Singer) Settled last, gd hdwy over 2f out, ran on strongly ins last, squeezed thro' gap
& got up nr fin, drvn out: up in trip, 1st win: 11,000 gns Mar 1st foal, dam a 5f juv wnr: eff at 6f, apprec
this step up to 7f: acts on firm, gd & a stiff or sharp/undul trk: genuine/consistent, deserved this.
*2723 **VIOLENT** 6 [5] Andrew Reid 2-8-5 (64)(vis)(6ex) M Henry 7/2: 000052: 2 b f Deploy - Gentle Irony   *shd*   **65**
(Mazilier) Front rank, rdn to chall ldr 2f out, duelled with rivals ins last, just held: quick reapp & another
sound run, acts on firm/fast grnd: can win again sn: see 2723.
1988 **BARAKANA** 37 [3] B J Meehan 2-9-7 (80)(BL) D R McCabe 10/1: 33263: 2 b c Barathea - Safkana   *hd*   **81**
(Doyoun) Led, strongly prsd appr fnl 2f, held narrow advantage until hdd cl-home: op 8/1: gd run under
top-weight in 1st time blnks, can find similar: eff at 7f on firm: see 1328, 911.
*2653 **PATHAN** 10 [4] S P C Woods 2-9-5 (78) B Marcus 9/4 FAV: 0514: Front rank, rdn & not pace of ldrs   1½   **76**
appr fnl 1f: nicely bckd: acts on gd, handles firm grnd: see 2653.
2550 **REPEAT PERFORMANCE** 14 [2] 2-8-12 (71)(t) A Daly 14/1: 244405: Rear, rdn to improve 2f out,   *shd*   **69**
styd on, nvr nrr: see 1463.
*2551 **WATTNO ELJOHN** 14 [6] 2-8-10 (69) J Weaver 10/1: 00016: Rcd keenly mid-div, drvn/btn appr fnl 1f: 3   **61**
up in trip, h'cap bow: btr 2551 (5f sell, gd/soft).
2267 **FAZZANI** 25 [1] 2-9-2 (75) T Quinn 5/1: 044437: Prom, wknd qckly appr fnl 2f, eased when btn: 8   **55**
reportedly unsuited by this sharp/undul trk: btr 2267 (stks, stiff/gall trk).
2589 **OPERATION ENVY** 12 [8] 2-7-10 (55)(4oh) D Kinsella (7) 33/1: 604008: Al in rear: see 1124.   3   **30**
8 ran   Time 1m 21.7 (1.9)   (Mr G E Williams & Mr B Lawrence)   P W Harris Aldbury, Herts

BRIGHTON

MONDAY JULY 24TH **Lefthand, Very Sharp, Undulating Track**

2895

4.30 HANNINGTONS CLASS STKS 3YO+ 0-70 (E) **1m rnd** **Firm 20** **-04 Slow**
£2716 £776 £388 3 yo rec 8 lb

*2661 **YOUR THE LADY** 10 [4] M R Channon 3-8-8 T Quinn 4/5 FAV: -08511: 3 b f Indian Ridge - Edwina (Caerleon) Trkd ldr, rdn/led dist, styd on well, rdn out: well bckd: earlier won at Chepstow (h'cap): ex-Irish, unplcd in 3 starts in native country: eff around 1m on any trk: acts on firm/fast grnd: can rate more highly. **68**

2534 **BOLD STATE** 14 [2] M H Tompkins 3-8-13 D Holland 7/2: 001122: 3 b g Never So Bold - Multi Soft (Northern State) Held up, rdn, switched & hdwy appr fnl 1f, ran on well, not btn far: op 3/1: gd run, see 2534, 2093. ½ **72$**

2544 **BARBASON** 14 [3] G L Moore 3-8-9-5 l Mongan (5) 9/2: 551553: 8 ch g Polish Precedent - Barada (Damascus) Rcd keenly cl-up, hdwy to lead briefly appr fnl 1f, no extra ins last: op 3/1: see 1807 (9f). 1½ **67**

2817 **EASTERN CHAMP** 3 [1] S P C Woods 4-9-3 (t) J Reid 9/2: 020634: Led, hdd appr fnl 1f, sn onepcd: quick reapp: shade btr 2817 (h'cap, fibresand). 1¼ **63**

4 ran Time 1m 34.0 (2.0) (John McKay) M R Channon West Isley, Berks

2896

5.00 LADBROKES MDN HCAP 3YO+ 0-60 (F) **6f rnd** **Firm 20** **+08 Fast** **[55]**
£2383 £681 £340 3 yo rec 5 lb

2794 **MARNIE** 4 [4] J Akehurst 3-9-6 (52) J Weaver 6/4 FAV: 060221: 3 ch f First Trump - Miss Aboyne (Lochnager) Made all, rdn clr appr fnl 1f, styd on strongly, pushed out: nicely bckd, best time of day, quick reapp: rnr-up twice prev: best juv run on debut when rtd 74 (plcd): eff over 6f, stays a sharp 7f: acts on firm & gd grnd & likes an undul, sharp or gall trk: loves to force the pace: could follow up. **59**

2512 **LUCKYS SON** 16 [3] J L Dunlop 3-8-10 (42) J Reid 8/1: 00002: 3 gr g Lucky Guest - April Wind (Windjammer) Chsd wnr, rdn & styd on appr fnl 1f, no impress when flashed tail for press ins last: clr rem: imprvd form here, stays 6f on firm: could win a mdn/sell h'cap: see 2105. 2½ **42**

1971 **CEDAR LIGHT** 38 [2] R J O'Sullivan 3-9-1 (47) P McCabe 33/1: -00003: 3 b g Dolphine Street - Maxencia (Tennyson) Outpcd early, late hdwy for press, nrst fin: worth another try over 7f/1m?: see 1742. 2½ **41**

2623 **WILLOW MAGIC** 11 [11] S Dow 3-9-13 (59) B Marcus 5/2: 303434: Prom, rdn/no extra appr fnl 1f: op 7/2: poor wide draw: btr 2623 (5f, gd). hd **53**

2193 **MALAAH** 28 [12] A Daly 14/1: 005005: Rcd wide in rear, rdn/styd on fnl 2f, no threat: suffered the worst of the draw here: see 1092. nk **35**

2654 **FLIGHT OF DREAMS** 10 [8] 3-8-3 (35)(BL) Paul Eddery 12/1: 00-006: Dwelt, sn well outpcd, ran on strongly fnl 2f, nvr nrr: glimmer of ability here in 1st time blnkrs. shd **28**

2728 **UBITOO** 6 [5] 3-8-4 (36)(bl) C Rutter 16/1: 005307: Sn rdn in mid-div, btn 2f out: quick reapp. 1¼ **26**

2427 **COURTNEY GYM** 19 [1] 5-8-1 (28)(bl) R Brisland (5) 33/1: 0-0008: Sn in tch, rdn/wknd appr fnl 1f: rnr-up once in '99 (mdn h'cap, rtd 36): stays 6f on firm/fast grnd. ¾ **16**

2415 **KEE RING** 19 [7] 4-9-7 (48)(bl) S Righton 7/1: 060609: In tch, wknd qckly over 2f out: see 1213. 1 **33**

2743 **LADY STALKER** 5 [9] 3-9-8 (54) M Henry 16/1: 60-000: Cl-up, qckly lost tch over 1f out, 10th: qck reapp. nk **39**

1349 **FOXDALE** 67 [6] 3-8-12 (44) Dane O'Neill 16/1: 0-5000: Handy, lost tch fnl 2f, 11th: 9 wk abs, h'cap bow. 3 **22**

11 ran Time 1m 08.5 (0.7) (The Grass Is Greener Partnership) J Akehurst Epsom, Surrey

YARMOUTH

TUESDAY JULY 25TH **Lefthand, Flat, Fair Track**

Official Going: GOOD/FIRM. Stalls: 14f - Stands Side, Straight Course - Far Side, Remainder - Inside

2897

2.15 MB CREDIT MDN 3YO+ (D) **1m3f101y** **Firm 18** **+01 Fast**
£3750 £1154 £577 £288 3 yo rec 11lb

2477 **GOLD QUEST** 18 [1] Sir Michael Stoute 3-8-12 W Ryan 3/1: -52331: 3 ch c Rainbow Quest - My Potters (Irish River) Prom, smooth prog to lead 3f out, soon rdn clr, readily: val for 5L+, gd time, nicely bckd: apprec drop to 11.5f, prob stays a stiff 14f: acts on firm & gd/soft grnd, stiff/gall or sharp track: has run well in a t-strap, not worn today: open to further improvement in this h'cap company. **88**

2609 **TROILUS** 12 [3] J H M Gosden 3-8-12 (VIS) J Fortune 5/4 FAV: 0-0322: 3 ch c Bien Bien - Nakterjal (Vitiges) Led, hdr & hdd 3f out, sn held by easy wnr: clr of rem, hvly bckd, first time visor: see 1956. 3½ **80**

-- **SEEKER** [2] H R A Cecil 3-8-7 T Quinn 11/4: 3: 3 ch f Rainbow Quest - Sarmata (Danzig) Trkd ldrs, ev ch 3f out, sn held by front pair: op 6/4, clr of rem: half sister to a 7f wnr: sire a high class mid dist performer: looks one of stable lesser lights on this evidence. 8 **63**

2771 **TUFTY HOPPER** 6 [8] P Howling 3-8-12 R Winston 14/1: 322204: Trckd ldrs, btn 2f out: quick reapp. 5 **61**

-- **DOUBLE ROCK** [4] 4-9-4 R Mullen 50/1: 5: Bhd 3f out: Flat debut, 7 wk jumps abs (mod bmpr form). 5 **49**

2611 **STARDREAMER** 12 [6] 3-8-12 G Faulkner (3) 20/1: -06: Rear, bhd 3f out: longer 11.5f trip, no form. 5 **47**

2179 **BURNING DAYLIGHT** 30 [7] 3-8-12 S Sanders 66/1: -057: Rear, bhd fnl 3f: needs low grade h'caps. nk **46**

7 ran Time 2m 24.7 (1.9) (Lady Clague) Sir Michael Stoute Newmarket

2898

2.45 MB DOUBLE RESULT SELLER 2YO (G) **7f str** **Firm 18** **-43 Slow**
£1865 £533 £266

1418 **RIVER OF FIRE** 64 [1] J M P Eustace 2-8-11 J Tate 5/1 CO FAV: 01: 2 ch g Dilum - Bracey Brook (Gay Fandango) Made all, styd on well ins last, rdn out: slow time, bt in for 5,500gns, 2 month abs: half brother to a 10f juv wnr: apprec step up to 7f, 1m+ shld suit: acts on firm grnd & a fair track: runs well fresh. **61**

2557 **BANNINGHAM BLIZ** 14 [2] D Shaw 2-8-6 (bl) T Williams 6/1: 654302: 2 ch f Inchinor - Mary From Dunlow (Nicholas Bill) Trckd ldrs, drvn to press wnr over 1f out, held inside last: had rest well covered: stays 7f, prob handles firm & fast grnd: eff in blnks: could find a similar contest. 1¼ **52**

2182 **PELLI** 30 [4] P Howling 2-8-6 R Winston 20/1: -003: 2 gr f Saddlers' Hall - Pellinora (King Pellinore) Cl up, rdn & kept on onepace fnl 2f: only mod form prev. 3½ **45**

2551 **BILLYJO** 15 [8] B J Meehan 2-8-11 (BL) D R McCabe 8/1: 6644: Prom/rdn halfway, held 1f out: blnks. ½ **49**

2513 **BEAUTIFUL BUSINESS** 17 [7] 2-8-6 (VIS) F Norton 5/1 CO FAV: 0335: Cl up 5f: first time visor. 2 **40**

-- **SUGAR ROLO** [6] 2-8-7(1ow) D McGaffin (5) 12/1: 6: Dwelt, never on terms: op 8/1: Bin Ajwaad filly, Jan foal, a first foal: sire a high class 7f/1m performer, dam a lightly raced mdn: with D Morris. 3 **35**

-- **HARD TO CASH** [5] 2-8-11 L Newton 8/1: 7: Soon rdn/bhd: op 6/1: Distinctly North colt, April foal, cost IR 2,700gns: dam a wnr abroad, sire a high class juv: with D Cosgrove. 5 **29**

2388 **HARRY JUNIOR** 21 [9] 2-8-11 (vis) D Holland 5/1 CO FAV: 6052W8: Raced alone stands side, sn   21   0
rdn in tch, btn & eased considerably over 1f out: rider prob took wrong option: btr 2196 (5f).
2723 **SKITTLES** 7 [3] 2-8-6 (BL) S Sanders 7/1: 000P: Pulled up after 1f: blinks, op 11/2: no form.   0
9 ran   Time 1m 26.3 (.7)   (J C Smith)   J M P Eustace Newmarket

---

2899   3.15 BERNSTEIN INTERNET HCAP 3YO+ 0-75 (E)   7f str   Firm 18   -05 Slow   [72]
          £2782   £856   £428   £214   3 yo rec 7 lb   Raced far side

2768 **TOPTON** 6 [2] P Howling 6-10-0 (72)(bl) R Winston 3/1 FAV: 002351: 6 b g Royal Academy - Circo   75
(High Top) Al prom, rdn from halfway, drvn into narrow lead inside last, held on gamely, all out: hvly bckd, qck
reapp: earlier scored at Lingfield (AW h'cap, rtd 93a): '99 wnr at Lingfield (h'cap, rtd 86a), Doncaster (2) &
Yarmouth (h'caps, rtd 80): '98 Doncaster (rtd 72), Southwell & Lingfield wnr (h,caps, rtd 75a): suited by 7f/1m on
firm, gd/soft & both AWs: hndles any trk: gd weight carrier: suited by blinks/visor: tough & genuine performer.
2861 **MEZZORAMIO** 2 [9] K A Morgan 8-8-1 (45)(tvi) P Hanagan (7) 10/1: 003502: 8 ch g Cadeaux Genereux   nk   47
- Hopeful Search (Vaguely Noble) Led, strongly pressed/hdd over 1f out, hdd inside last, kept on well, just
held: quick reapp, gd run with visor reapplied, likes Yarmouth: see 1920.
2107 **DON BOSCO** 33 [3] N A Callaghan 4-9-5 (63) R Hughes 14/1: -00003: 4 ch g Grand Lodge - Suyayeb   hd   64
(The Minstrel) Chsd ldrs, rdn/outpcd 2f out, rallied well for press in last, just held: gd run with blnks omitted.
*2320 **UNCHAIN MY HEART** 24 [6] B J Meehan 4-8-9 (53)(bl) D R McCabe 6/1: 630014: Prom, held fnl 1f.   2½   49
2654 **SAFFRON** 11 [5] 4-8-0 (44)(BL) F Norton 12/1: -00005: Prom, held over 1f out: blnks, op 10/1.   1¼   37
2729 **MILADY LILLIE** 7 [11] 4-8-8 (52)(BL) C Catlin (7) 8/1: 204066: Rdn/mid div, not pace to chall: blnks.   ½   44
2580 **SURVEYOR** 13 [7] 5-9-12 (70) R Morse 10/1: 0-0007: Keen/rear, mod gains: op 8/1: see 1851 (6f).   2   58
2538 **MUTABARI** 15 [4] 6-7-10 (40)(vis)(6oh) J Lowe 33/1: 650068: Rdn/rear, no impress: see 255.   1¼   25
2752 **SEA DEER** 6 [8] 11-10-0 (72) T Quinn 5/1: -00069: Prom 5f: bckd, op 6/1: quick reapp: see 2580.   1¼   54
2749 **RAINBOW RAIN** 6 [10] 6-9-4 (62) O Urbina 6/1: 000200: Bhd ldrs, keen, rdn/btn 2f out: op 5/1.   ¾   43
1201 **MY BOLD BOYO** 78 [12] 5-8-10 (54)(bl) R Mullen 12/1: 440500: Struggling 3f out, fin lame: 11th: op   8   23
10/1, 11 week abs: blinks reapplied: see 268 (AW).
11 ran   Time 1m 24.2 (1.6)   (Liam Sheridan)   P Howling Newmarket, Suffolk

---

2900   3.45 TOTE CREDIT CLUB HCAP 3YO 0-95 (C)   6f   Firm 18   +03 Fast   [99]
          £6955   £2140   £1070   £535   Raced far side

2792 **LORD PACAL** 5 [10] N A Callaghan 3-8-9 (80) R Hughes 5/1: 000221: 3 b g Indian Ridge - Please   85
Believe Me (Try My Best) Al prom, styd on gamely for press to lead well inside last, all out: gd time: qck reapp:
'99 debut wnr at Newbury (mdn, subs Gr 3 4th, rtd 100): eff at 5/6f, stays a sharp 7f well: acts on firm & fast
grnd, prob handles any track: looks on a fair mark, could win again in similar grade.
2787 **PEDRO JACK** 5 [2] B J Meehan 3-8-9 (80)(bl) D R McCabe 8/1: 060352: 3 b g Mujadil - Festival Of   hd   83
Light (High Top) Led, drvn/hdd well inside last, styd on well, just held: op 7/1, quick reapp: apprec this return to
6f, likes to dominate: effective in blinks: see 1289.
2787 **ILLUSIVE** 5 [7] M Wigham 3-7-13 (70)(bl) F Norton 8/1: 035533: 3 b c Night Shift - Mirage (Red   ¾   71
Sunset) Chsd ldrs, drvn & kept on fnl 1f, not pace of front pair: quick reapp: see 2787, 592.
2183 **STAR PRINCESS** 30 [3] K T Ivory 3-8-4 (75) C Catlin (7) 16/1: -64224: Cl up, rdn & kept on fnl 1f   nk   75
despite little room, not pace to chall: op 14/1: acts on firm & hvy grnd: see 1021 (mdn).
2787 **CONNECT** 5 [3] 3-8-8 (79) S Sanders 12/1: 004305: Towards rear, rdn/hdwy 2f out, no prog fnl 1f: 1   77
quick reapp: blinks omitted & a change to waiting tatics, improved effort: see 2168, 1186.
994 **CASTLE SEMPILL** 94 [4] 3-8-5 (76) R Mullen 20/1: 135106: Mid div, never pace of ldrs: 3 mth abs.   2½   67
2568 **ALJAWF** 14 [6] 3-9-7 (92)(VIS) R Hills 7/4 FAV: -06107: Soon rdn, never on terms: visor, hvly bckd.   1¼   80
2197 **ALFIE LEE** 29 [1] 3-9-4 (89) W Ryan 25/1: 0-0058: Cl up still over 1f out: see 2197.   3½   68
2495 **KING SILCA** 17 [8] 3-8-7 (78) T Quinn 4/1: 21309: Outpcd halfway: nicely bckd: btr 1708 (7f, g/s).   ¾   55
1645 **GRAND BAHAMIAN** 53 [9] 3-8-11 (82) J Weaver 20/1: 010P0: Sn bhd, eased fnl 1f: 10th: 8 wk abs.   1   57
10 ran   Time 1m 11.3 (0.9)   (Paul & Jenny Green)   N A Callaghan Newmarket

---

2901   4.15 EBF MANNY BERNSTEIN MDN 2YO (D)   5f43y   Firm 18   -07 Slow
          £3396   £1045   £522   £261   Raced far side

2818 **CLARION** 4 [6] Sir Mark Prescott 2-9-0 S Sanders 11/4: 21: 2 ch c First Trump - Area Girl (Jareer)   85
Rdn cl up early, went on 2f out, drvn to maintain advantage in last: well bckd, qck reapp: eff at 5f, 6f will
suit: acts on firm & f/sand, sharp/fair track: can improve further for shrewd trainer.
2766 **RED RYDING HOOD** 6 [5] C A Dwyer 2-8-9 D Holland 6/1: -6342: 2 ch f Wolfhound - Downeaster   ½   77
Alexa (Red Ryder) Cl up, led halfway till 2f out, just held ins last: op 3/1: quick reapp: acts on firm & fast grnd.
-- **FARHA** [7] B Hanbury 2-8-9 R Hills 8/11 FAV: 3: 2 b f Nureyev - Arutua (Riverman)   ½   75
Chsd ldrs, outpcd over 1f out, kept on ins last for press: hvly bckd, op 10/11: Feb foal, cost $375,000: half sister
to a juv Irish wnr: dam unraced tho' related to high class mid dist performers: looks sure to relish further.
2598 **LONER** 13 [3] N A Callaghan 2-9-0 R Hughes 12/1: 04: Cl up, outpcd fnl 1f: op 10/1: see 2598 (6f).   3   73
2318 **TALISKER BAY** 24 [4] 2-9-0 R Fitzpatrick (3) 33/1: 05: Keen/led till halfway, fdd: see 2318.   5   64
-- **CHALLENOR** [1] 2-9-0 T Quinn 16/1: 6: Well bhd early, mod late prog: op 10/1: Casteddu colt,   3   57
April foal: dam a 5f juv wnr, sire a 7f performer: will apprec 6f+ for J Pearce.
-- **NORTH BY NORTH** [2] 2-9-0 A Whelan 33/1: 7: Soon bhd: Distinctly North colt, April foal, cost   9   41
IR 2,700gns: dam unraced: with M H Tompkins.
7 ran   Time 1m 01.4 (1.3)   (Neil Greig)   Sir Mark Prescott Newmarket

---

2902   4.45 MANNY BERNSTEIN MDN HCAP 3YO+ 0-70 (E)   1m6f   Firm 18   -20 Slow   [64]
          0800 821821   £2873   £884   £442   £221   3 yo rec 14lb

2156 **KING FOR A DAY** 31 [4] Bob Jones 4-8-2 (38)(vis) F Norton 8/1: 0-0041: 4 b g Machiavellian - Dizzy   42
Heights (Danzig) Keen/held up, steady prog fnl 4f, styd on strongly to lead well ins last: visor reapplied: mod
sell hdle form prev (rtd 72): rtd 68 on the level in '99 (h,cap): eff at 14f, 2m could suit: acts on firm & hvy
grnd: suited by blinks/visor: likes a fair track.
1997 **SEND ME AN ANGEL** 38 [8] S P C Woods 3-8-11 (61) R Hughes 11/2: 0-4422: 3 ch f Lycius - Niamh   ¾   63
Cinn Oir (King Of Clubs) Led, drvn over 1f out, styd on well tho' hdd nr fin: nicely bckd: styd this longer
14f trip well: a likely type for a similar contest: see 1997, 1157.
2425 **BAILEYS ON LINE** 20 [1] M Johnston 3-8-5 (55) D Holland 13/8 FAV: -00023: 3 b f Shareef Dancer -   3   53

904

YARMOUTH TUESDAY JULY 25TH Lefthand, Flat, Fair Track

Three Stars (Star Appeal) Trckd ldrs, drvn to chall over 1f out, no extra inside last: hvly bckd, op 2/1: styd lngr
14f trip, return to 12f could suit: acts on firm & gd/soft grnd: see 2425.

2470 **CEDAR GROVE** 18 [9] A C Stewart 3-8-5 (55) R Mullen 20/1: -00404: Mid div, prog/chsd ldrs 2f out, 1 52
swished tail/hung left & no extra ins last: clr rem: stays 14f, return to 12f could prove ideal: handles firm grnd.
2499 **NINNOLO** 17 [2] 3-9-2 (66)(t) R Morse 8/1: 53005: Rear, rdn/mod gains fnl 3f: longer 14f trip. 4 57
2554 **NOBLE CALLING** 15 [5] 3-8-12 (62)(bl) J Weaver 6/1: -30206: Trkd ldrs 4f out, fdd fnl 2f: op 5/1. 1¼ 51
2265 **AEGEAN WIND** 26 [11] 3-9-3 (67) T Quinn 11/2: 0-507: Held up, eff 4f out, no impression: op 7/2. 8 47
2651 **ST GEORGES BOY** 11 [6] 3-7-11 (47)(1ow)(12oh) J Lowe 40/1: 002458: Prom, btn/eased 3f out: see 1911.10 16
937 **BLAYNEY DANCER** 99 [10] 3-7-10 (46)(10oh) D Kinsella (7) 40/1: 036509: Keen/prom 11f, eased: abs. ½ 14
2464 **WESTERN BAY** 18 [3] 4-10-0 (64) S Whitworth 20/1: 0-6000: Mid div, drvn/btn 3f out, eased: 10th. dist 0
2715 **SKY CITY** 8 [12] 4-7-12 (34)(BL)(2ow)(10oh) T Williams 40/1: 600000: Soon cl up, wknd quickly 4f 23 0
out, eased over 1f out: fin 11th, tried in blnks: longer 14f trip.
11 ran   Time 3m 03.1 (5.3)   (Mrs Joan Marioni)   Bob Jones Wickhambrook, Suffolk

BRIGHTON TUESDAY JULY 25TH Lefthand, Very Sharp, Undulating Track

Official Going FIRM. Stalls: 10/12f - Outside: Remainder - Inside.

2903	2.30 WORTHING HERALD MED AUCT MDN 2YO (F) 5f59y Firm 20 -12 Slow

£2703 £772 £386

2628 **MAMORE GAP** 12 [2] R Hannon 2-9-0 Dane O'Neill 1/1 FAV: 2231: 2 b c General Monash - Ravensdale 80
Rose (Henbit) Led early, remd with ldr, led again appr fnl 1f, pshd clr: well bckd: 22,000gns March foal,
half-brother to a wnr abroad: eff at 5f/7f on firm, gd/soft, equitrack & a sharp/undulating trk: v consistent.
2599 **CHAUNTRY GOLD** 13 [4] B J Meehan 2-9-0 (BL) M Tebbutt 5/2: 0032: 2 b g Desert Style - Ervedya 3 72
(Doyoun) Rcd keenly, led after 2f till appr fnl 1f, not pace of wnr: rcd too freely in first time blnks: see 2599.
2488 **FLUTED** 17 [3] M R Channon 2-9-0 Craig Williams 11/2: 403: 2 ch c Piccolo - Champagne Grandy 2 68
(Vaigly Great) Settled last, rdn to improve 2f out, kept on at one pace: op 7/2: better on debut on 2290.
2635 **MAID OF ARC** 11 [5] M L W Bell 2-8-9 (t) M Fenton 4/1: 02244: Prom, wknd qckly fnl 2f: btr 2417. 12 47
4 ran   Time 1m 22.1 (4.2)   (The South-Western Partnership II)   R Hannon East Everleigh, Wilts

2904	3.00 SUSSEX SELL HCAP 3YO+ 0-60 (G) 1m4f Firm 20 -09 Slow [53]

£2299 £657 £328 3 yo rec 12lb

2622 **BEAUCHAMP MAGIC** 12 [9] M D I Usher 5-8-0 (25) G Baker (5) 7/1: 054301: 5 b g Northern Park - 31
Beauchamp Buzz (High Top) Prom, drpd rear halfway, rallied to lead over 1f out, drvn clr fnl 1f: tchd 10/1, no
bid: '99 W'hampton wnr (AW h'cap, rtd 37a & 54, t-strap, tried blnks): plcd in '98 (rtd 69, h'cap): eff arnd
12f/2m: acts on fibresand & firm, handles gd grnd: acts on a sharp/undul trk: best form without a visor/blnks.
2181 **SCENIC LADY** 30 [6] L A Dace 4-7-10 (21)(BL)(10h) G Bardwell 20/1: 06-002: 4 b f Scenic - Tu Tu 2½ 23
Maori (King's Lake) Dwelt, hdwy to lead over 4f out, sn racing alone on stands rail, sn hdd, hung bdly left ins last,
no extra: blnkd: rnr-up once in '99 (class clmr, rtd 44 at best): stys 10/12f on firm/fast: sharpened up by blnks.
2037 **REMEMBER STAR** 36 [8] R J Baker 7-8-0 (25) G Sparkes (7) 9/2: /00-43: 7 ch m Don't Foget Me - ½ 26
Star Girl Gay (Lord Gayle) Cl up, drpd rear appr 3f, rall/styd on fnl 1f: recent 4th in a 2m nov h'cap chse (rtd 56c).
2656 **LUNAR LORD** 11 [4] J S Moore 4-8-13 (38) G Hind 4/1 FAV: 420224: Sn in tch, drvn/one pace fnl 2f. ½ 38
2742 **METEOR STRIKE** 6 [2] 6-9-11 (50)(t) Alex Greaves 9/2: 216035: Led, hdd 7f out, led again briefly 2½ 46
over 2f out, sn btn: top-weight, qck reapp: shade btr 2742 (clmr).
2460 **ARAGANT** 18 [10] 4-8-9 (34) S Carson (3) 14/1: 000006: Rcd keenly rear, hdwy appr fnl 2f, sn no extra. nk 30
2587 **FROZEN SEA** 13 [5] 9-8-7 (30)(t)(2ow) Dane O'Neill 11/1: 2-0067: Bhd, eff halfway, nvr dngrs: op 7/1. ½ 27
2134 **KATIE KING** 32 [3] 3-7-10 (33)(6oh) J Mackay 5/2: 6008: Trckd ldrs, lost tch fnl 5f: h'cap bow. 15 12
2843 **PREMIERE FOULEE** 3 [11] 5-8-5 (30)(bl) A Clark 7/1: 606649: Raced keenly, pulled into lead 4 4
7f out, hdd 4f out, wknd quickly: quick reapp: failed to settle today.
2008 **CHILDRENS CHOICE** 38 [7] 9-8-11 (36) T G McLaughlin 25/1: 134000: Mid div, rdn/lost tch fnl 3f, 10th. 4 5
10 ran   Time 2m 31.8 (3.6)   (The Music And Dance Partnership)   M D I Usher Kingston Lisle, Oxon

2905	3.30 CLASSIFIED STKS 3YO+ 0-60 (F) 5f59y Firm 20 +02 Fast

£2226 £636 £318 3 yo rec 4 lb

2118 **CITY REACH** 33 [4] P J Makin 4-9-2 (vis) D Sweeney 10/1: 413051: 4 b g Petong - Azola (Alzao) 54
Dwelt, rcd rear, prog appr fnl 1f, ran on well to lead nr fin, drvn out: op 7/1: earlier won at Southwell (AW auct
mdn, 1st time visor, rtd 63a): plcd in '99 (rtd 57a & 75): rtd 77 sole '98 start: eff at 5.3f, stays a sharp 7f well,
has tried 1m: acts on firm, hvy & both AW: handles a sharp/undul or gall trk: now eff in a visor.
2716 **ABSOLUTE FANTASY** 8 [5] E A Wheeler 4-9-2 (bl) S Carson (3) 6/1: 03402: 4 b f Beveled - Sharp ½ 52
Venita (Sharp Edge) Dwelt, hdwy from rear halfway, led appr fnl 1f, hdd cl home: likes Brighton: see 2428.
2753 **SIHAFI** 6 [2] D Nicholls 7-9-5 Alex Greaves 10/1 FAV: 361043: 7 ch g Elmaamul - Kit's Double 1¾ 51
(Spring Double) Led, hung right/hdd over 1f out, soon btn: quick reapp: shade btr 2326 (h'cap).
2788 **WINDRUSH BOY** 5 [1] M R Bosley 10-9-2 Joanna Badger (7) 20/1: -00044: Prom, rdn/no extra 2½ 42$
over 2f out: op 14/1: quick reapp: treat rating with caution (official only 38): see 2555.
2511 **SIMBATU** 17 [7] 3-8-9 J P Spencer 3/1: 300-65: Trkd ldrs, no room/wknd fnl 2f: btr 2511 (6f h'cap). 1½ 35
2586 **AZIRA** 13 [3] 3-8-9 S Righton 10/1: 56-006: Front rank, wknd quickly fnl 2f, fin last: see 2586. 4 26
6 ran   Time 1m 01.0 (1.0)   (T W Wellard Partnership)   P J Makin Ogbourne Maisey, Wilts

2906	4.00 T R BECKETT HCAP 3YO 0-80 (D) 1m rnd Firm 20 +05 Fast [87]

£3818 £1175 £587 £293

2688 **TAKE MANHATTAN** 10 [4] M R Channon 3-8-6 (65) Craig Williams 8/1: 100001: 3 b g Hamas - Arab 72
Scimetar (Sure Blade) Mid div, edged left/prog appr fnl 1f, ran on strongly to lead well inside last, drvn out:
best time of day: earlier this season scored at Nottingham & Carlisle (h'caps), form subs tailed off: eff at 1m
on firm, gd/soft & poss any track: likes to come late: back to best today.
2661 **ARANYI** 11 [3] J L Dunlop 3-9-7 (80) G Carter 5/2 FAV: 541333: 3 gr c El Gran Seno - Heather's ¾ 84
It (Believe It) Dwelt, rear, outpcd halfway, styd on strongly fnl 1f, never nearer: should apprec a return

to further or a more gall track: see 2661, 1863.

2591 **COLNE VALLEY AMY 13** [1] G L Moore 3-8-5 (64) P Doe 7/2: -21143: 3 b f Mizoram - Panchelita ½ 67
(Pancho Villa) Led, hdd appr halfway, remnd with ldrs until no extra well inside last: clr rem: see 2467.

2506 **PINHEIROS DREAM 17** [2] B J Meehan 3-8-4 (63)(bl) L Newman (3) 6/1: 503104: Cl up, went on 3 61
over 4f out, hdd inside last, wknd: btr 2345 (claimer, gall trk).

2330 **MY RETREAT 24** [7] 3-8-10 (69)(BL) Dane O'Neill 13/2: 100505: Mid div, rdn to improve 2f out, 6 58
soon lost tch: failed to sparkle in 1st time blinks here: see 884 (mdn, hvy).

2278 **PRIMA 26** [6] 3-9-1 (74) J P Spencer 5/1: 023-56: Dwelt, al bhd: op 4/1: reportedly in foal, up in trip. hd 63

2604 **SPOT 12** [5] 3-8-8 (67) M Henry 10/1: 0347: Raced keenly cl up, wknd quickly fnl 2f: h'cap bow. 2½ 52
7 ran   Time 1m 33.2 (1.2)   (M G St Quinton)   M R Channon West Isley, Berks

---

2907	4.30 EASTBOURNE CLAIMER 3YO+ (F) 7f rnd Firm 20 -12 Slow
	£2362 £675 £337 3 yo rec 7 lb

1237 **CELTIC VENTURE 75** [12] Julian Poulton 5-9-0 A Daly 14/1: 00-661: 5ch g Risk Me - Celtic River 48
(Caerleon) Trkd ldrs, went on appr fnl 1f, drvn clr ins last: op 10/1, 10 wk abs: '99 reapp wnr here at Brighton
(clmr, rtd 60, mod form subs): rnr-up bck in '97 (sell, rtd 62, M Channon): eff at 5f/7f on firm grnd: likes to
race up with/force the pace on a sharp/undul trk, runs well fresh: likes Brighton & claiming grade.

1601 **HI MUJTAHID 55** [5] J M Bradley 6-8-10 Claire Bryan (5) 20/1: 0-0002: 6 ch g Mujtahid - High Tern 2½ 39$
(High Line) Hdwy from rear appr fnl 2f, ran on inside last, no impression on wnr: gd eff at the weights
but treat rating with caution (offically only 25): see 1139.

2291 **JUST FOR YOU JANE 25** [3] T J Naughton 4-8-9 I Mongan (5) 7/1: -00043: 4 b f Petardia - Steffi 1 36
(Precocious) In tch, stying on when short of room & switched wide appr fnl 1f, ran on well inside last,
never nearer: unlucky not to fin closer & worth another ch in similar: see 1971.

2728 **CEDAR WELLS 7** [9] J M Bradley 4-8-10 (BL) L Newman (3) 13/2: 060064: Dsptd lead, rdn/no extra ¾ 36
over 1f out: reportedly broke blood vessel: quick reapp, first time blinks: see 681.

2292 **BONNIE DUNDEE 25** [10] 4-8-5 (bl) S Carson (3) 12/1: 500045: Led, drvn /hdd appr fnl 1f, sn btn. ½ 30

2591 **NORTHERN LIFE 13** [7] 3-7-12 (VIS) G Baker (5) 16/1: 006006: Dwelt, soon mid div, drpd rear ½ 29
halfway, late hdwy for press: first time visor: see 1572.

2460 **MR CUBE 18** [8] 10-8-10 (bl) D Watson (7) 11/4 FAV: 355247: Prom, eff when no room over 1f out, ¾ 32
not perservered with after: not much luck in running here: see 2460, 2291.

2489 **PETRIE 21** [11] 3-8-5 Craig Williams 15/2: 350308: Rear, late gains, no danger: see 2291. 2½ 30

2729 **NIGHT ADVENTURE 7** [2] 4-9-0 P Fitzsimons (5) 9/2: 000059: Settled rear, late gains: qck reapp. 3½ 26

2788 **SPLIT THE ACES 5** [6] 4-8-10 R Havlin (2) 12/1: 055000: Mid div, lost tch fnl 2f, fin 10th: qck reapp. ¾ 21

2792 **ROTHERHITHE 5** [4] 4-8-10 J P Spencer 14/1: -00000: Al bhd, fin last: quick reapp. 6 12
11 ran   Time 1m 22.1 (2.3)   (Gerald West)   Julian Poulton Lewes, E Sussex

---

2908	5.00 LADBROKES HCAP 3YO 0-60 (F) 1m2f Firm 20 -21 Slow [67]
	£2383 £681 £340

2217 **ADRIANA 28** [6] C E Brittain 3-8-3 (42) A Nicholls (3) 10/1: 000101: 3 b f Tragic Role - Beatle Song 46
(Song) Made all, styd on strongly when pressed ins last, drvn out & just held on: op 7/1: earlier won at
Lingfield (h'cap, 1st win): eff at 10/11.5f on firm: loves to force the pace on a sharp/undul trk.

2651 **SHAMAN 11** [2] G L Moore 3-9-7 (60) I Mongan (5) 4/1: 210132: 3 b g Fraam - Magic Maggie shd 63
(Beveled) Prom, rdn/prog over 1f out, styd on well ins last, just failed: tch 6/1: tough/consistent: see 2041.

94 **ARROGANT 245** [11] R M Flower 3-7-13 (37)(1ow) C Rutter 50/1: 4000-3: 3 b g Aragon - Miss Ark ½ 40
Royal (Broadsword) Rcd keenly in rear, drvn/prog over 2f out, styd on well inside last, not btn far: fine run
after an 8 month abs: 4th at best in '99 (stakes, rtd 52 at best), mod form otherwise: stys 10f on firm.

2735 **LOUP CERVIER 7** [7] S Dow 3-8-8 (47) B Marcus 14/1: 000344: Cl up, drpd rear after 5f, 1¼ 47
rallying when hmpd appr fnl 1f, styd on well: op 10/1, quick reapp: shade unlucky in running: see 2735.

2659 **BEE GEE 11** [5] 3-8-0 (39) Dale Gibson 33/1: 014305: Soon rdn in tch, drvn/late gains, no impress. shd 39

2602 **COLLEGE ROCK 12** [13] 3-9-2 (55)(vis) G Carter 10/1: 064146: Rcd keenly in mid div, hdwy to chall hd 55
over 2f out, no extra appr fnl 1f: shade btr 2448 (1m seller).

2624 **GOLD KRIEK 12** [8] 3-8-2 (41) J Mackay (5) 33/1: 000-07: Prom, drpd rear over 4f out, edged left nk 40
& styd on well fnl 1f: glimmer of abilility here, only mod form prev.

2484 **CHEZ BONITO 18** [10] 3-8-3 (42) P Fitzsimons (5) 6/1: 205408: Rear, mod late gains, no threat. 1¼ 39

2726 **DUSKY VIRGIN 7** [9] 3-9-2 (55) J P Spencer 12/1: 1-0049: Soon in tch, rdn/wknd quickly over 4 46
1f out: quick reapp, prob not stay this longer 10f trip: see 1651.

2593 **THE GIRLS FILLY 13** [4] 3-8-12 (51) S Carson (3) 10/1: 000260: Rcd keenly cl up, rdn/btn fnl 3f, 10th. 5 35

2556 **LOMOND DANCER 14** [3] 3-9-1 (54) A Beech (5) 8/1: -05000: Chsd ldrs, wknd quickly fnl 3f, fin 11th. 8 28

2727 **BOND DIAMOND 7** [1] 3-8-10 (49) M Tebbutt 3/1 FAV: 000030: Reared start, eff 3f out, al bhd, 1 21
fin 12th: well bckd, quick reapp: much better expected after 2727 (C/D).

2703 **NAJMAT JUMAIRAH 9** [12] 3-9-4 (57) Craig Williams 12/1: -6500: Prom to 2f out, wknd/eased, 13th. 1¼ 27
13 ran   Time 2m 01.9 (4.1)   (R A Pledger)   C E Brittain Newmarket, Suffolk

---

LEOPARDSTOWN   SATURDAY JULY 22ND   Lefthand, Galloping Track

Official Going   GOOD.

2909	3.00 LISTED CHALLENGE STKS 3YO+ 1m6f Good
	£16250 £4750 £2250 £750 3yo rec 14lb

2402 **PAIRUMANI STAR 22** [5] J L Dunlop 5-9-8 P Shanahan 4/1: 0-0121: 5 ch h Caerleon - Dawn Star (High 107
Line) Trkd ldrs, prog to chall dist, led cl home, all-out: earlier won at Goodwood (listed h'cap): '99 wnr at York
(rtd h'cap), Salisbury (stks) & Newbury (h'cap, rtd 96): eff at 12/15f, stays a slowly run 2m: acts on firm & soft
grnd & on any trk: can run well fresh: tried blnks, prob better without: tough & useful entire.

2405 **ROYAL REBEL 21** [10] M Johnston 4-9-12 (bl) K J Manning 11/4 FAV: 0-0122: 4 b g Robellino - hd 110
Greenvera (Riverman) Chsd ldrs, went on 1½f out, not pace to repel wnr cl home: fine run under top-weight:
runs well here at Leopardstown: stays & v useful stayer: see 1620 (C/D).

2405 **DUTCH HARRIER 21** [9] K Prendergast 3-8-8 D P McDonogh 8/1: 312243: 3 ch c Barathea - Fanny 3 101
Blankers (Persian Heights) in tch, prog 1f out, kept on but not pace of front 2: again bhnd this 2nd in 2405.

LEOPARDSTOWN   SATURDAY JULY 22ND   Lefthand, Galloping Track

1267} **MORNING BREEZE** 440 [6] T Doyle 4-9-5 J A Heffernan 33/1: -06264: Chsd ldrs, styd on under press.   2   **95**
--   **TOBARANAMA** [8] 3-8-5 P J Smullen 12/1: 3-145: Rear, not pace to chall: reapp mdn wnr.   2   **92**
11 ran   Time 3m 00.6   (Windflower Overseas Holdings Inc)   J L Dunlop Arundel, W Sussex

DUSSELDORF   SUNDAY JULY 23RD   Lefthand, Tight, Undulating Track

Official Going GOOD.

2910   3.13 LISTED PREIS DER WGZ 3YO+   7f110y   Good
£7742   £3097   £1581

2339 **YORBA LINDA** 22 [8] E J O'Neill 5-8-9 D Holland : 405001: 5 ch m Night Shift - Allepolina (Trempolino)   **90**
Rear, hdwy 2f out, led ins fnl 1f, drvn out: trained in Ireland in '99, won at The Curragh (h'cap): The Curragh
mdn wnr in '97: eff at 5/7.5f, has tried 10f: acts on fast & soft grnd: well placed to land some val prize money.
--   **SIGNATORY** [2] Germany 5-9-4 T Mundry : -2: 5 ch g King's Signet - Pearl Pet (Mummy's Pet)   nk   **98**
--   **LYMOND** [9] Germany 5-9-4 A Starke : -3: 5 b h Bakharoff - La Lyra (Slip Anchor)   1¼   **95**
10 ran   Time 1m 29.32   (T F Brennan)   E J O'Neill Newmarket

2911   3.50 GR 1 WGZ BANK-DEUTCHLAND-PREIS 3YO+   1m4f   Good
£64516   £25806   £12903   3yo rec 12lb

2149 **MUTAFAWEQ** 30 [3] Saeed bin Suroor 4-9-6 R Hills : 41-301: 4 b h Silver Hawk - The Caretaker   **122**
(Caerleon) In tch, styd on well to lead cl home, drvn out: '99 wnr at Doncaster (stks, reapp), R Ascot (Gr 2
King Edward) & again at Doncaster (Gr 1 St Leger, rtd 125): '98 Newmarket mdn wnr: eff at 12/14f on gd & firm
grnd, handles gd/soft: runs well fresh: high-class entire who shld take a deal of beating in the Irish St Leger.
--   **QUEZON CITY GER** [1] P Schiergen 3-8-2 F Minarik : 111202: 3 br f Law Society - Queen Of Love   ¾   **115**
(Nebos) Tried to make all, worn down by wnr cl home: eff at 14f on gd grnd: smart German filly.
2074 **CATELLA** 35 [5] P Schiergen 4-9-2 T Hellier : 1-1223: 4 ch f Generous - Crystal Ring (Kris)   ¾   **116**
Mid-div, prog ent str, styd on to take 3rd cl home: stablemate of rnr-up: smart filly, see 2074.
2566 **YAVANAS PACE** 12 [6] M Johnston 8-9-6 D Holland : 043226: Prom till onepcd fnl 1½f: just btr 2566.   **112**
8 ran   Time 2m 27.31   (Godolphin)   Saeed bin Suroor Newmarket

ARLINGTON   SUNDAY JULY 23RD   -

Official Going Firm

2912   10.47 GR 2 AMERICAN DERBY 3YO   1m1f110y   Firm
£73171   £24390   £13415

--   **PINE DANCE** [4] D K Weld 3-8-2 E Ahern 76/10: -01: 3 b c Pine Bluff - Dancing Affair (Dancing   **108**
Champ) Cl-up, went on over 1f out, styd on strongly: earlier won twice, tho' only 7th in a h'cap at The Curragh
last time: eff at 9.5f on firm grnd: useful colt who may remain in the US for a val prize here next month.
*2171 **HYMN** 29 [2] J H M Gosden 3-8-9 Y Take 24/10: -2112: 3 b c Fairy King - Handsewn (Sir Ivor)   1½   **105**
Set pace till collared cl home, kept on: fine run from this English raider: stays 9.5f: see 2171.
--   **DEL MAR SHOW** [5] America 3-8-2 M Guidry 18/10: -3: 3 b c Theatrical - Prankstress (Foolish   nk   **104**
Pleasure) -:
4 ran   Time 1m 55.46   (Highland Farms, P Wetzel & Five Star Racing)   D K Weld The Curragh, Co Kildare

CHANTILLY   TUESDAY JULY 25TH   Righthand, Galloping Track

Official Going SOFT.

2913   1.45 GR 3 PRIX DAPHNIS 3YO   1m1f   Soft
£21134   £7685   £3842

2225 **BOUTRON** 30 [?] P Costes 3-8-9 A Junk 48/10: 332241: 3 b c Exit To Nowhere - Vindelonde (No Lute)   **111**
Rcd keenly in bhnd ldr, went on dist, pushed out cl home: deserved win: eff at 9/10f on gd & hvy grnd: smart.
1900 **CRYSTAL DASS** 44 [?] T Clout 3-8-9 (bl) T Gillet 193/10: -14532: 3 b c Northern Crystal - Assiana (Al   ½   **109**
Nasr) Set pace till dist, not pace of wnr cl home: 6 wk abs: see 1900 (9f here).
--   **SPECIAL RING** [?] Mme C Head 3-8-9 O Doleuze 19/10 FAV: 23-113: 3 b c Nureyev - Ring Beaune (Bering)   ¾   **107**
Nvr far away, switched dist, no impress cl home: recent List wnr: eff at 9f on soft grnd: useful.
8 ran   Time 1m 54.5   (Gary A Tanaka)   P Costes France

LEICESTER   WEDNESDAY JULY 26TH   Righthand, Stiff, Galloping Track

Official Going GOOD TO FIRM (GOOD places) Stalls: Stands Side

2914   6.25 LOROS SELLER 3YO (G)   1m str   Good/Firm 24   -01 Slow
£2023   £578   £289 Raced towards centre

2794 **BINT HABIBI** 6 [12] M R Channon 3-8-12 Craig Williams 3/1 FAV: 016631: 3 b f Bin Ajwaad - High   **56**
Stepping (Taufan) Bhd ldrs, went on 2f out, rdn & hung left ins last, just held on: op 7/2: sold to J Pearce for
8,000 gns: earlier scored at Chepstow (clmr): rnr-up once in '99 (auct mdn, rtd 69): eff over 7f/1m on firm & gd.

2187 **CUIGIU** 30 [4] D Carroll 3-8-11 K Dalgleish (5) 12/1: 054002: 3 b c Persian Bold - Homosassa   *shd* 54
(Burslem) Al handy, rdn & ev ch fnl 2f, styd on well, just held: clr rem, mdn: stays 1m on fast & soft.
2731 **SKELTON MONARCH** 8 [9] R Hollinshead 3-8-11 P M Quinn (3) 14/1: 300033: 3 ch c Prince Of Birds -   4 46
Toda (Absalom) Held up, rdn/styd on fnl 2f, no threat: op 12/1: stays a stiff 1m, handles firm & fast grnd.
2731 **SPEEDFIT FREE** 8 [13] M A Buckley 3-8-11 Dean McKeown 7/1: 005044: Led over 3f out till 2f out, fdd.   1½ 43
2448 **SHAW VENTURE** 20 [1] 3-8-11 K Darley 16/1: -60605: Prom, kept on onepace fnl 2f: blnks omitted.   hd 42
2680 **SILOGUE** 11 [11] 3-8-11 G Gibbons 50/1: -006: Prom, held 1f out: see 2421 (6f).   1¾ 39
2510 **LADY VIENNA** 18 [2] 3-8-6 A Daly 25/1: -50307: Led 2f, btn over 1f out: stiff task, see 2253, 1644.   shd 34
2322 **SWALDO** 25 [7] 3-8-11 G Baker (5) 16/1: 23-008: Dwelt, nvr on terms: see 1204 (AW).   2 35
2510 **SNATCH** 18 [5] 3-8-6 J Mackay (5) 4/1: 649: Al towards rear: btr 2510 (10f).   ½ 29
2413 **SOBER AS A JUDGE** 21 [15] 3-8-11 G Bardwell 7/1: -00030: Held up, keen, no impress fnl 2f: 10th.   shd 34
2715 **LEA VALLEY EXPRESS** 9 [6] 3-8-6 (vis) K Pierrepont 33/1: 000000: Led 6f out till over 3f out, fdd: 15th.   0
2253 **Jensens Tale** 28 [3] 3-8-11 D Sweeney 40/1:   2413 **Cupids Dart** 21 [14] 3-8-11 (bl) J Quinn 16/1:
1434 **Wee Barney** 65 [8] 3-8-11 C Teague 50/1:   2413 **Lady Cyrano** 21 [10] 3-8-6 Claire Bryan (5) 12/1:
15 ran   Time 1m 36.4 (2.0)   (A Merza)   M R Channon West Isley, Berks

---

2915   6.55 BERKELEY BURKE NURSERY HCAP 2YO (E)   5f   Good/Firm 24   -08 Slow   [95]
£2925   £900   £450   £225   Raced stands side

1602 **HAMATARA** 56 [7] I A Balding 2-8-2 (69)(t) K Darley 7/2: 4041: 2 ch g Tagula - Arctic Poppy (Arctic   75
Tern) Prom, led over 1f out & rdn clr ins last, readily: 8 wk abs, h'cap bow: eff at 5f, 6f suit: acts on fast,
handles soft: likes a stiff/gall trk & suited by a t-strap: runs well fresh: looks worth following.
2665 **TICCATOO** 12 [1] R Hollinshead 2-7-11 (64) P M Quinn (3) 25/1: -10002: 2 br f Dolphin Street -   2½ 62
Accountancy Jewel (Pennine Walk) Prom, outpcd by wnr over 1f out: acts on fast & fibresand: see 865 (AW).
2352 **NEARLY A FOOL** 24 [5] B A McMahon 2-9-10 (91) G Faulkner (3) 5/2 FAV: 433133: 2 b g Komaite -   shd 89
Greenway Lady (Prince Daniel) Cl-up, ch over 1f out, sn outpcd by wnr: nicely bckd under topweight: see 1995.
2714 **OH SO DUSTY** 9 [6] B J Meehan 2-9-10 (91)(BL) S Clancy (7) 4/1: 610444: Chsd ldrs, not pace to   ½ 87
chall: tried blnks: see 1782 (mdn).
2665 **DIAMOND MAX** 12 [2] 2-7-12 (65) Joanna Badger (7) 6/1: -04145: Prom, held 1f out: op 5/1: see 2665. shd 61
1759 **QUIZZICAL LADY** 49 [4] 2-8-7 (74) J Mackay (5) 5/1: 160406: Cl-up, onepace fnl 2f: abs, op 4/1.   hd 69
2639 **SEANS HONOR** 12 [3] 2-7-13 (66) T Williams 9/1: 5447: Led 3f, sn btn: op 6/1: btr 2639, 2009.   3½ 52
7 ran   Time 59.9 (1.6)   (Robert Hitchins)   I A Balding Kingsclere, Hants

---

2916   7.25 SPEARING AUCT MDN 2YO (E)   7f str   Good/Firm 24   -10 Slow
£3055   £940   £470   £235   Raced towards centre

2598 **LOYAL TYCOON** 14 [7] S Dow 2-8-6 P Doe 8/11 FAV: 31: 2 br c Royal Abjar - Rosy Lydgate (Last Tycoon)   86
Trkd ldrs, led over 1f out, styd on strongly ins last under hands & heels riding: hvly bckd: confirmed promise
of debut: apprec step up to 7f, will get further: acts on fast & gall trk: going the right way.
2620 **SOONA** 13 [4] A P Jarvis 2-8-0 J Quinn 14/1: 05552: 2 ch f Royal Abjar - Presently (Cadeaux Genereux) 3½ 71
Led 5f, sn held by wnr tho' kept on ins last: rest well covered: see 1988, 849.
2077 **EL HAMRA** 35 [11] B A McMahon 2-8-2 W Supple 7/1: 5033: 2 gr c Royal Abjar - Cherlinoa (Crystal   2 69
Palace) Held up, keen, styd on well under hands & heels riding fnl 2f, no threat: handles fast grnd & fibresand,
ran to best over this longer 7f trip: should apprec h'caps: see 2077, 1136.
-- **ABBY GOA** [8] B Hanbury 2-8-4 J Mackay (5) 13/2: 4: Cl-up, wknd over 1f out: Dr Devious filly, Feb   3 65
foal, cost IRE20,000: half sister to 2 wnrs: dam well related, sire a high-class mid-dist performer: apprec 1m+.
2583 **SHIMLA** 14 [12] 2-8-0 A Daly 33/1: 005: Chsd ldrs 5f: see 1883.   2½ 56
-- **MARABAR** [2] 2-8-7 K Darley 10/1: 6: Prom 5f: Sri Pekan filly, Apr foal, cost 26,000 gns: half-   1¼ 60
sister to a wnr abroad: dam unrcd: with J Arnold.
-- **HEATHYARDS GUEST** [1] 2-8-11 J P Spencer 20/1: 7: Held up, nvr any impress: Be My Guest colt,   2½ 59
Apr foal, cost IR25,000gns: half brother to a 5/6f juv wnr: dam unrcd: with R Hollinshead.
-- **BLUE FALCON** [5] 2-8-7 Dean McKeown 25/1: 8: Chsd ldr halfway, btn 2f out: Eagle Eyed colt,   5 45
May foal: cost 11,000 gns as a 2yo: dam a mdn: with M A Buckley.
-- **TRICKSY** [3] 2-8-4 (2ow) P Robinson 6/1: 9: Al towards rear: Dr Devious filly, Apr foal, cost 16,000gns,   ½ 41
dam a mdn: sire a high-class mid-dist performer: bred to apprec 1m+ in time for M A Jarvis.
-- **ALJOHONCHA** [10] 2-8-2 T Williams 33/1: 0: Al bhd: 10th: Apr foal, dam a 7f Irish juv wnr.   14 19
10 ran   Time 1m 24.4 (2.4)   (Michael A J Hall & Miss M Shields)   S Dow Epsom, Surrey

---

2917   7.55 OWEN BROWN HCAP 3YO+ 0-95 (C)   1m3f183y   Good/Firm 24   +02 Fast   [92]
£7046   £2168   £1084   £542   3 yo rec 12lb

2696 **MANTUSIS** 11 [2] P W Harris 5-9-10 (88) A Culhane 4/1: 321401: 5 ch g Pursuit Of Love - Mana   92
(Windwurf) Held up, prog to lead 1f out, styd on well, rdn out: earlier scored at Haydock (h'cap): '99 Yarmouth
wnr (h'cap, rtd 85): rnr-up in '98 (rtd 94): eff at 10/12f on firm & hvy grnd: handles any trk & has run well fresh.
2502 **COURT SHAREEF** 18 [4] R J Price 5-8-13 (77) P Fitzsimons (5) 9/4: 131102: 5 b g Shareef Dancer -   ½ 78
Fairfields Cone (Celtic Cone) Dwelt/held up in tch, drvn & styd on well ins last, not reach wnr: gd run.
2131 **ANGELS VENTURE** 33 [3] J R Jenkins 4-8-10 (74)(tVIS) S Whitworth 13/2: -00043: 4 ch c Unfuwain -   3½ 70
City Of Angels (Woodman) Handy, led 2f out till 1f out, fdd: tried a visor: see 1180.
2610 **MINKASH** 13 [1] B Hanbury 3-9-2 (92) W Supple 2/1 FAV: 0-0644: Cl-up, led over 2f out, sn hdd/btn.   10 77
2547 **WAFFIGG** 16 [5] 3-9-0 (90) P Robinson 5/1: 51035: Led, increased tempo 4f out, hdd/btn over 2f out.   16 57
5 ran   Time 2m 30.9 (2.6)   (The Romantics)   P W Harris Aldbury, Herts

---

2918   8.25 LOROS FILLIES HCAP 3YO 0-80 (D)   7f str   Good/Firm 24   -02 Slow   [83]
£4121   £1268   £634   £317   Raced towards centre

2511 **DIAMOND RACHAEL** 18 [3] Mrs N Macauley 3-8-3 (58)(vis) Joanna Badger (7) 25/1: 236601: 3 b f Shalford   65
- Brown Foam (Horage) Led/dsptd lead till went on again over 1f out, drifted left ins last, rdn & styd on well:
earlier scored at W'hampton (mdn, rtd 63a): no form on turf in'99, plcd on sand (rtd 63a, mdn): eff at 6/7f on fast
grnd & fibresand, sharp or stiff/gall trk: eff in a visor.
*2633 **MOONLIGHT SONG** 12 [7] W Jarvis 3-8-5 (60) F Norton 12/1: -00012: 3 b f Mujadil - Model Show   1½ 63
(Dominion) Al handy & rdn/ev ch 1f out, no extra nr fin: acts on fast grnd & fibresand: see 2633 (AW clmr).
2128 **ALPHILDA** 33 [1] B W Hills 3-9-5 (74) R Cochrane 7/1: 003403: 3 gr f Ezzoud - Desert Delight   nk 76

(Green Desert) Dwelt & held up in tch, prog 2f out, no impress on wnr nr fin: stays 7f, return to 6f could suit.
2293 **TAFFETA 26** [8] J L Dunlop 3-8-11 (66) K Darley 4/1 FAV: 5064: Led/dsptd lead till over 1f out, no extra: h'cap bow: eff at 7f on fast grnd: see 1638. *1* **66**
2564 **STEALTHY TIMES 15** [4] 3-9-5 (74) G Baker (5) 12/1: -00005: Held up, eff 3f out, not able to chall. *hd* **73**
2699 **DESERT SAFARI 10** [6] 3-9-6 (75) W Supple 11/2: 001136: Handy, briefly led over 1f out, fdd. *¾* **73**
2511 **KIRSCH 18** [2] 3-8-1 (56)(vis) J Quinn 12/1: 600537: Held up, rdn/held 2f out: see 361 (5f, AW). *½* **53**
2795 **CIBENZE 6** [12] 3-8-11 (66) Craig Williams 5/1: 260268: Rdn/rear, late gains: qck reapp: needs 1m. *shd* **63**
2577 **SANTIBURI GIRL 14** [5] 3-8-11 (66) R Mullen 8/1: 002309: Chsd ldrs, held 1f out: btr 2031, 1397. *1½* **60**
*2460 **TIMELESS CHICK 19** [11] 3-8-2 (57)(vis) K Dalgleish (5) 11/1: 430510: Chsd ldrs 5f: 10th: btr 2460 (sell). *¾* **50**
2180 **HELLO HOLLY 31** [10] 3-7-11 (52) P M Quinn (3) 20/1: 000-60: Prom 5f: 11th: see 2180. *½* **44**
2128 **SARENA PRIDE 33** [9] 3-9-7 (76) P Doe 7/1: 024300: Dwelt & al rear: 12th: something amiss?. *16* **44**
12 ran Time 1m 23.8 (1.8) (Diamond Racing Ltd) Mrs N Macauley Sproxton, Leics

2919

8.55 LOROS MED AUCT MDN 3YO (F) 5f Good/Firm 24 +00 Fast
£2366 £676 £338 Raced towards centre

2590 **OUR FRED 14** [3] T G Mills 3-9-0 (bl) L Carter 5/1: -44021: 3 ch g Prince Sabo - Sheila's Secret (Bluebird) Made all, rdn/wandered ins last, held on well: plcd on 3 of 4 juv starts (nurs, rtd 79): eff at 5/6f on firm & soft grnd, sharp or stiff/gall trk: galvanised by blnks last twice: deserved this. **78**
2299 **CHORUS 26** [9] B R Millman 3-8-9 G Hind 7/2 JT FAV: 063232: 3 b f Bandmaster - Name That Tune (Fayruz) Prom, rdn/chsd wnr halfway, styd on well ins last, al just held: mdn after 19 starts: see 2299, 888. *½* **70**
2640 **DAVEYS PANACEA 12** [6] R D Wylie 3-8-9 P Bradley (5) 16/1: 253: 3 ch f Paris House - Pampoushka (Pampabird) Trkd ldrs, rdn/outpcd by front pair over 1f out: return to 6f could suit: needs low grade h'caps. *3½* **61**
4508} **AMAZED 274** [11] I A Balding 3-8-9 K Darley 7/2 JT FAV: 6-4: Dwelt, rdn/rear, styd on well from over 1f out, no threat: reapp: unplcd sole '99 start (auct mdn, rtd 59): looks sure to relish 6f+ & h'caps in time. *1* **59**
-- **RUSSIAN RHAPSODY** [8] 3-8-9 P Robinson 7/1: 5: Outpcd early, late gains, no threat: debut: half sister to a 6f 3yo wnr: looks sure to relish 6f+ for M Jarvis. *½* **57**
1266 **NEEDWOOD TRICKSTER 75** [2] 3-9-0 M Roberts 4/1: -0336: Dwelt/outpcd, late gains: 11 wk abs. *¾* **60**
3804} **IN SEQUENCE 323** [7] 3-8-9 S Whitworth 12/1: 40-7: Nvr on terms: reapp: unplcd both '99 starts (auct mdns): stays 5.5f & handles firm grnd, shld get further: now qual for h'caps. *½* **53**
2864 **WERE NOT JOKEN 3** [4] 3-8-9 R Fitzpatrick (3) 33/1: 00-008: Struggling fnl 2f: quick reapp. *shd* **53**
2489 **WHITE SUMMIT 18** [10] 3-9-0 D Sweeney 40/1: 600-09: Chsd wnr 3, sn btn: mod, incl in a visor. *1¾* **54**
2519 **SASHA 18** [1] 3-9-0 (BL) J Edmunds 16/1: 0-40: Chsd ldrs till halfway: 10th: blnks: btr 2519. *1½* **50**
2590 **RAPIDASH 14** [5] 3-9-0 (vis) Sarah Robinson (7) 50/1: 0-0000: Al outpcd rear: 11th: mod form. *7* **37**
11 ran Time 59.5 (1.2) (Sherwoods Transport Ltd) T G Mills Epsom, Surrey

SANDOWN WEDNESDAY JULY 26TH Righthand, Galloping Track, Stiff Finish

Official Going GOOD/FIRM (FIRM Places on Sprint Course). Stalls: Str Crse - Far Side; 14f - Outside; Rem - Inside.

2920

6.10 WESTLB PANMURE CLAIMER 3YO+ (E) 1m rnd Good/Firm 40 -15 Slow
£2795 £860 £430 £215 3yo rec 8lb

*2433 **LAKE SUNBEAM 21** [6] W R Muir 4-9-7 Martin Dwyer 2/1 JT FAV: 5-5611: 4 b g Nashwan - Moon Drop (Dominion) Trkd ldr till went on over 2f out, hdd dist, rallied gamely to regain lead ins last, held on well, all out: well bckd: recent Epsom wnr (clmr): '99 Salisbury wnr (stks, rtd 92, with R Hannon): eff at 7f/1m, has tried 12f: acts on firm, gd/soft & on any trk: likes to run up with or force the pace, can run well fresh: in fine form. **69**
2752 **SALORY 7** [9] Miss Jacqueline S Doyle 4-9-2 Dane O'Neill 14/1: -30002: 4 b c Salse - Mory Kante (Icecapade) Trkd ldrs, switched to inside & prog to chall fnl 1f, just btn in a close fin: improved, offic rtd 52. *¾* **62$**
2762 **GULF SHAADI 7** [4] Miss Gay Kelleway 8-9-10 S Sanders 3/1: 054053: 8 b g Shaadi - Ela Meem (Kris) Rear racing keenly, imprvd 2f out, onepcd ent fnl 1f till rallied cl-home: top weight: last won back in '98. *2* **66**
2206 **CAPPELLINA 30** [5] P G Murphy 3-8-4 R Havlin 33/1: 00-004: Trkd ldrs, imprvd to lead dist till ins last, no extra: 5L clr rem: ran well for a long way over this shorter 1m trip, a drop back to 7f shld suit. *nk* **53**
*2411 **HUGWITY 21** [3] 8-9-7 M Hills 2/1 JT FAV: 214015: Prom, ev ch dist, sn btn: better expected after 2411. *5* **52**
-- **LAKOTA BRAVE** [8] 6-9-7 R Morse 33/1: 0/6: Dwelt, eff 2f out, nvr nr ldrs: last rcd back in '97, unplcd at Leicester (mdn auct): with C Allen. *½* **51**
2345 **HTTP FLYER 25** [7] 3-8-6 L Newton 33/1: -007: Al rear, nvr a factor: seems mod: see 2134. *hd* **44**
2634 **WELODY 12** [1] 4-9-7 (bl) J Reid 25/1: 400008: Led till 2f out, fdd: see 658 (AW mdn). *1½* **48**
2056 **PRINCESS SENORITA 37** [2] 5-8-10 (t) M Fenton 50/1: 0/009: Al bhd, t.o. fnl 1f: poor. *15* **7**
9 ran Time 1m 43.41 (4.41) (Percipacious Punters Racing Club) W R Muir Lambourn, Berks

2921

6.40 EXPERTS EBF MDN 2YO (D) 7f rnd Good/Firm 40 -33 Slow
£4309 £1326 £663 £331

-- **MATLOCK** [9] P F I Cole 2-9-0 J Fortune 15/8 FAV: -1: 2 b c Barathea - Palio Flyer (Slip Anchor) Broke well & made all, ran on strongly fnl 1f, won a shade cosily: hvly bckd from 5/2 on racecourse debut: Feb foal, cost 28,000gns: 1st foal from an unrcd dam, sire a top class miler: eff at 7f, will stay 1m+: acts on fast grnd & on a gall trk, runs well fresh: highly regarded colt, well entered up & looks one to follow. **88+**
2708 **NORTHFIELDS DANCER 10** [4] R Hannon 2-9-0 Dane O'Neill 9/2: -022: 2 ch c Dr Devious - Heartland (Northfields) Chsd wnr thr'out, no impress fnl 1f till ran on cl-home: op 7/2: eff at 7f on fast & firm grnd: met a potentially decent rival here, shld win a mdn & apprec 1m: see 2708, 2494. *½* **85**
-- **MARK ONE** [6] B W Hills 2-8-9 R Hughes 14/1: -3: 2 b f Mark Of Esteem - One Wild Oat (Shareef Dancer) Rear, imprvg when short of room 2f out, switched & fin well, nvr nrr: drifted from 7/1 on debut: IR 36,000gns Mar foal: half sister to 7f 2yo wnr Common Place: dam successful in France, sire a top-class miler: eff over a stiff 7f on fast grnd, 1m will suit: little luck today, eye-catching eff & will sn make amends. *shd* **80+**
-- **REDUIT** [11] G A Butler 2-9-0 B Marcus 16/1: -4: Chsd ldrs, eff over 1f out, styd on well cl-home on debut: Feb foal, cost 19,500gns: sire a smart 6/7f performer: dam from a decent family: eff at 7f on fast grnd, 1m will suit: pleasing first eff, will learn plenty from this & win a mdn. *hd* **85+**
2269 **POTARO 27** [1] 2-9-0 D R McCabe 9/2: -535: Trkd ldrs, eff over 1f out, eased when held ins fnl 1f. *2½* **80**
2414 **MYTHICAL JINKS 21** [2] 2-9-0 J Reid 20/1: -56: Mid-div, onepcd fnl 1f: mkt drifter: see 2414. *nk* **79**
2269 **ELMONJED 27** [3] 2-9-0 R Hills 10/1: -07: Slowly away, late hdwy, not pace to chall: op 7/1: *shd* **79**

stable's juvs usually improve given time: likely to apprec mid-dist next term: see 2269.
2686 **MURRENDI 11** [5] 2-9-0 T Quinn 8/1: -58: Rcd keenly in bhd ldrs, btn fnl 1f: see 2686. *1¾* **75**
-- **BALLADEER** [8] 2-9-0 M Hills 33/1: -9: Pushed along in rear, nvr a factor on debut: Feb foal, *nk* **74**
cost IR 11,000gns: dam a mid-dist wnr in Ireland, sire a top-class mid-dist performer: will improve over further.
2708 **BOUND 10** [10] 2-9-0 A Eddery (5) 50/1: -000: Keen in rear, nvr a factor in 10th: stablemate 3rd. *½* **73**
1691 **TAMIAMI TRAIL 53** [7] 2-9-0 M Tebbutt 50/1: -00: Rcd keenly in tch, lost place after 2f, no ch after *½* **72**
& fin last: 8 wk abs: 55,000gns purchase: Mar foal, half brother to sev wnrs: dam a smart mid-dist/stayer.
11 ran Time 1m 31.56 (5.16) (W J Smith & M D Dudley) P F I Cole Whatcombe, Oxon

2922 **7.10 ENTREPRENEURS HCAP 3YO 0-90 (C) 7f rnd Good/Firm 40 -19 Slow [92]**
£7345 £2260 £1130 £565

2792 **RUSHMORE 6** [9] P F I Cole 3-9-1 (79) J Fortune 11/2: 001161: 3 ch c Livermore - Crafty Nan **87**
(Crafty Prospector) Held up, gd hdwy over 1f out, strong run to lead well ins fnl 1f, won going away: well bckd, qck reapp: earlier won at Doncaster (mdn), Southwell (AW, rtd 84a) & Sandown (h'cap): all 3 wins at 7f, tried further: acts on gd, fast, fibresand & any trk, likes Sandown: runs well fresh: prog, has a decent turn of foot.
*2330 **FALCONIDAE 25** [13] P J Makin 3-9-3 (81) S Sanders 5/1: 4-0512: 3 ch c Polar Falcon - Barbary *1½* **84**
Court (Grundy) Mid-div, drvn into lead ins fnl 1f, not pace to repel wnr cl-home: eff at 7f, stays 1m: in fine form.
*2261 **SHADOW PRINCE 28** [8] R Charlton 3-9-0 (78) T Quinn 3/1 FAV: 6-5013: 3 ch g Machiavellian - *1* **79+**
Shadywood (Habitat) Hld up, imprvd 2f out, badly hmpd ent fnl 1f, ran on well but ch had gone: hvly bckd: must have gone v close with a clr run, possesses a gd turn of foot & must be given another chance: see 2261.
2794 **MISTER CLINTON 6** [12] K T Ivory 3-7-12 (62) C Catlin(6) 9/1: 031604: Rear, gd hdwy over 1f out, *½* **62**
nrst fin: op 12/1, qck reapp: made gd late hdwy, one to keep in mind for similar: se 2794, 1889.
*1947 **HILLTOP WARNING 41** [11] 3-9-1 (79) J Reid 16/1: 23-015: Trkd ldrs till onepace fnl 1f: 6 wk abs. *shd* **79**
*2768 **WILLOUGHBYS BOY 7** [6] 3-9-6 (84)(6ex) I Mongan (5) 8/1: 031616: Front rank, ev ch ent fnl 1f, *¾* **82**
no extra cl-home: sound run under a 6lb pen: se 2768.
2431 **MAGELTA 21** [10] 3-8-11 (75) Dane O'Neill 20/1: -00207: Rear, eff 2f out, kept on fnl 1f: see 1961. *½* **72**
2495 **NORFOLK REED 18** [5] 3-9-7 (85) R Hughes 16/1: -45008: Set pace till ins fnl 1f, wknd: top weight: *nk* **81**
has been fin well over 6f, change to forcing tactics over this longer 7f trip: see 1694 (6f).
2456 **COTE SOLEIL 19** [7] 3-9-4 (82) M Fenton 7/1: 300059: Trkd ldrs, onepcd when short of room ent fnl 1f. *1½* **75**
2749 **CEDAR PRINCE 7** [4] 3-8-2 (66)(bl) A Nicholls(3) 33/1: 000600: Rear, eff 2f out, sn btn: fin 10th. *nk* **58**
2694 **ROYAL IVY 11** [3] 3-8-3 (67) N Pollard 16/1: 054200: Chsd ldrs, eff when hmpd 2f out, no ch after: *½* **58**
fin 11th, forget this: see 2325.
1826 **PROUD CHIEF 47** [1] 3-8-8 (72) D Harrison 33/1: 260000: Prom 5f, wknd & fin last: 7 wk abs. *3* **57**
12 ran Time 1m 30.55 (4.15) (J S Gutkin) P F I Cole Whatcombe, Oxon

2923 **7.40 GLOBAL EQUITY HCAP 4YO+ 0-80 (D) 1m6f Good/Firm 40 -19 Slow [75]**
£4192 £1290 £645 £322

*2689 **FLETCHER 11** [4] H Morrison 6-8-11 (58) R Hughes 3/1: 223211: 6 b g Salse - Ballet Classique **64**
(Sadler's Wells) Prom, al trav best, styd on to lead over 1f out, drvn out: well bckd: recently won at Salisbury (h'cap): plcd in '99 (rtd 73), '98 wnr at Ascot (amat h'cap, rtd 79): wng form over 12/14f, stays 2m on fm, gd & soft: best coming late & likes a stiff fin: slipped down the weights & has looked a tricky ride, but in fine form.
2626 **COPYFORCE GIRL 13** [2] Miss B Sanders 4-8-13 (60)(t) S Carson (3) 7/1: 0-1322: 4 b f Elmaamul - *1½* **64**
Sabaya (Seattle Dancer) Prom, eff to chall over 1f out, kept on same pace ins last: stays 14f on any trk.
2455 **SON OF SNURGE 19** [7] P F I Cole 4-10-0 (75)(bl) T Quinn 9/4 FAV: -04043: 4 b g Snurge - Swift *3* **74**
Spring (Bluebird) Led till over 2f out, onepace fnl 1f: well bckd: gd run under a big weight: see 1329, 1222.
2829 **SPOSA 5** [8] M J Polglase 4-8-2 (49)(6ex) L Newton 11/1: P01144: Chsd ldr, led over 2f out till *nk* **47**
over 1f out, no extra: quick reapp: longer trip, just btr 2776 (12f, clmr).
2812 **URGENT SWIFT 5** [3] 7-9-6 (67) D Harrison 8/1: 012405: Waited with, hmpd bend over 4f out, bhd, *hd* **65**
some late gains: quick reapp, see 2164, 1959.
2593 **READING RHONDA 14** [6] 4-7-12 (45) M Henry 20/1: 000036: Nvr a factor: mdn, see 2593 (12f, a/w). *6* **34**
2681 **PRINCESS TOPAZ 11** [5] 6-8-11 (58)(BL) D O'Donohoe 9/1: 35-267: Waited with, eff over 2f out, sn *7* **37**
wknd & eased ins last: tried blnks, btr 2191 (clmr, 2m).
2490 **AGENT LE BLANC 18** [1] 5-9-9 (70) A Nicholls (3) 8/1: 200-P8: Dsptd 2nd till wknd over 4f out, t.o. *dist* **0**
8 ran Time 3m 03.28 (8.28) (Lady Margadale) H Morrison East Isley, Berks

2924 **8.10 TRADERS MDN 3-4YO (D) 1m2f Good/Firm 40 -24 Slow**
£4329 £1332 £666 £333 3yo rec 10lb

2617 **CLOUD HOPPING 13** [1] H R A Cecil 3-8-11 T Quinn 6/4: -61: 3 ch c Mr Prospector - Skimble (Lyphard) **84**
Made all, styd on well over 2f out, pushed clr appr fnl 1f: half brother to a 1m wnr: stays 10f well, further shld suit: acts on gd/firm grnd: open to further improvement.
2770 **SHADOWBLASTER 7** [3] B Hanbury 3-8-11 Dane O'Neill 4/6 FAV: -522: 3 b c Wolfhound - Swame (Jade *3* **78**
Hunter) Trkd wnr, eff to chall well over 1f out, no extra fnl 1f: hvly bckd: better expected after 2770 (7f).
2327 **QUEEN OF FASHION 25** [4] J J Sheehan 4-9-2 D R McCabe 20/1: -043: 4 b f Barathea - Valuewise *3½* **68**
(Ahonoora) Stdy start, waited with, rdn & outpcd over 2f out, some late gains: see 2327.
2449 **CAVANIA 20** [2] W R Muir 3-8-6 Martin Dwyer 14/1: -34: Prom, wknd well over 1f out: see 2449. *shd* **68**
4 ran Time 2m 10.50 (6.40) (K Abdulla) H R A Cecil Newmarket

2925 **8.40 HIGH YIELD HCAP 4YO+ 0-80 (D) 5f str Good/Firm 40 +09 Fast [80]**
£4348 £1338 £669 £334

2716 **MOUSEHOLE 9** [11] R Guest 8-9-0 (66) S Sanders 5/2 FAV: 002021: 8 b g Statoblest - Alo Ez (Alzao) **71**
In tch, sn rdn, styd on well to lead ins last, drvn out: well bckd, gd time: '99 wnr at Nottingham (2, h'cap & stks) & Windsor (2, h'caps, rtd 76): '98 scorer at Carlisle & Bath (stks, rtd 73): stays 6f, last 10 wins at 5f: loves gd, firm & any trk, can carry big weights: v tough sprinter who comes into his own on fast grnd.
2716 **DIAMOND GEEZER 9** [2] R Hannon 4-9-1 (67) Dane O'Neill 8/1: 306142: 4 br c Tenby - Unaria *nk* **71**
(Prince Tenderfoot) Prom, eff to chall appr fnl 1f, kept on, just held: fine run: best form at 6f: see 2716.
2355 **DANCING MYSTERY 24** [7] E A Wheeler 6-10-0 (80) S Carson (3) 8/1: 335103: 6 b g Beveled - *¾* **81**
Batchworth Dancer (Ballacashtal) Hld up, eff over 1f out, kept on ins last, not btn far: gd run, in top form.
*2716 **BEYOND THE CLOUDS 9** [9] J S Wainwright 4-8-9 (61)(6ex) R Cody Boutcher(7) 9/2: 261414: Bhd, eff *hd* **62**

well over 1f out, kept on ins last, not btn far: in form, beat this wnr in 2716.
*2732 **OFF HIRE 8** [5] 4-8-5 (57)(vis)(6ex) M Fenton 12/1: 604415: Chsd ldr, btn when hmpd cl-home. ¾ 55
2266 **PALAWAN 27** [6] 4-9-7 (73) A Nicholls (3) 11/1: 030106: Set pace, rdn & collared ins last, no extra: all 3 wins on sharp trks: see 1881. *shd* 71
2732 **AMERICAN COUSIN 8** [8] 5-7-10 (48) J Bramhill 10/1: 000007: Slow away, hdwy far rail 2f out, sn short of room, kept on ins last: has slipped to a good mark & his shrewd trained can exploit: promise here. *shd* 46
2517 **PRINCE PROSPECT 18** [10] 4-9-12 (78) J Reid 9/1: 200408: Bhd, brief eff well over 1f out, onepace. ½ 74
268 **BRIMSTONE 203** [4] 5-8-6 (58) J Tate 66/1: 006-09: Sn bhd, btn over 1f out: now with P Gilligam. 1½ 51
2517 **MIZHAR 18** [12] 4-9-9 (75) J Fortune 7/1: 000000: Handy, wknd over 1f out, short of room & eased ins last, 10th: see 1173. ½ 67
1591 **DOUBLE MARCH 56** [1] 7-8-5 (57) C Catlin (7) 33/1: 0-0500: Prom, wknd over 1f out: abs, see 1591. ½ 48
2732 **SEALED BY FATE 8** [3] 5-7-12 (50)(vis) Martin Dwyer 20/1: 450200: Al bhd, fin last: see 2680 (sell). 3 32
12 ran Time 1m 01.19 (1.59) (Mrs Janet Linskey) R Guest Newmarket

CATTERICK WEDNESDAY JULY 26TH Lefthand, Undulating, V Tight Track

Official Going GOOD/FIRM. Stalls: Inside.

2926 2.00 LEVY BOARD MDN 2YO (D) 6f rnd Good/Firm 28 -30 Slow
£3591 £1105 £552 £276

1067 **TIMES SQUARE 86** [3] G C H Chung 2-9-0 O Urbina 5/1: -431: 2 b c Timeless Times - Alaskan Princess (Prince Rupert) Trkd ldrs, rdn & styd on well ins last to lead nr line: op 6/1, 12 wk abs: apprec step up to 6f, shld get further: dam a 7f scorer: acts on fast & gd/soft grnd, prob handles hvy: runs well fresh. 82
2700 **TOMTHEVIC 10** [7] J J Quinn 2-9-0 (t) R Mullen 5/1: -4032: 2 ch g Emarati - Madame Bovary (Ile de Bourbon) Cl-up, led over 2f out, rdn & hdd nr line: op 6/1: see 2700, 1698. *nk* 81
-- **EARLY MORNING MIST** [6] M Johnston 2-8-9 D Holland 11/2: 3: 2 b f Alzao - Welsh Mist (Damister) Chsd ldrs, rdn & styd on fnl 1f, not pace of wnr: op 9/2: Jan foal, cost 32,000gns, a first foal: dam a 5f juv wnr: eff at 6f, will stay further: acts on fast grnd & a sharp trk: encouraging intro. 1 73
-- **LAPWING** [1] B W Hills 2-9-0 K Darley 13/8 FAV: 4: Dwelt, sn chsd ldrs/rdn, held ins last: bckd: Tagula colt, Apr foal, cost 38,000gns: dam a 7f wnr: sire top-class 6f juv: eff over a sharp 6f on fast grnd. *hd* 77
2608 **MR PIANO MAN 13** [4] 2-9-0 A Culhane 14/1: -305: Led till over 2f out, held when no room nr fin: op 12/1: stays a sharp 6f, handles fast & gd grnd: see 2360. ½ 75
-- **CERALBI** [2] 2-9-0 J P Spencer 14/1: 6: Held up, rdn fnl 2f, not pace to chall: op 25/1: Goldmark colt, Apr foal, cost 7,500gns: dam a Irish sprint wnr: with R Hollinshead. *nk* 74
-- **BOLLIN THOMAS** [8] 2-9-0 R Winston 40/1: 7: Rear/bhd halfway, mod late gains: Alhijaz gelding, Apr foal, dam a mdn: sire a smart juv: will know more & shld improve next time for T D Easterby. 3 66
-- **PEGGYS SONG** [5] 2-8-9 J Carroll 10/1: 8: In tch 4f: op 5/1: Mind Games filly, Apr foal, cost 13,000gns: half-sister to a 5f juv wnr, dam a 5/6f wnr: market told story here: with A Berry. 10 36
-- **DI CANIO** [9] 2-9-0 M Tebbutt 20/1: 9: Bhd halfway: Piccolo colt, Feb foal, cost 16,000gns. 3½ 32
9 ran Time 1m 13.8 (3.5) (Ian Pattle) G C H Chung Newmarket.

2927 2.30 HUDDERSFIELD SELLER 2YO (G) 7f rnd Good/Firm 28 -41 Slow
£1890 £540 £270

2605 **GAZETTE IT TONIGHT 13** [10] A Berry 2-8-6 J Carroll 12/1: 556331: 2 b f Merdon Melody - Balidilemma (Balidar) Handy, led ins last, drvn & just held on nr line: no bid: first win: apprec step up to 7f, may get further: acts on fast grnd & a sharp trk: enjoys sell grade. 59
2239 **CYNARA 28** [7] G M Moore 2-8-6 Dale Gibson 4/1: 052: 2 b f Imp Society - Reina (Homeboy) Mid-div, rdn/chsd ldrs halfway, styd on well for press ins last, just held: op 7/2: styd longer 7f trip well on fast. *nk* 58
2513 **IMPISH LAD 18** [2] B S Rothwell 2-8-11 (bl) J P Spencer 6/1: 236323: 2 b g Imp Society - Madonna Da Rossi (Mtoto) Led, rdn/hdd ins last, kept on, just held: op 5/1: acts on fast, gd & fibresand, sharp/gall trk. *hd* 62
2441 **SPORTS EXPRESS 20** [9] W W Haigh 2-8-6 W Supple 4/1: 44: Held up, no room over 4f out & hmpd halfway, drvn & styd on well for press ins last, nrst fin: no luck in running, would have gone v close here with a clr run: styd longer 7f trip & handles fast grnd: fin clr of rem, one to note in similar. *shd* 57
2513 **CHORUS GIRL 18** [4] 2-8-6 A Culhane 6/1: 430465: Trkd ldrs, hmpd halfway, held 2f out: see 2513. 6 45
2441 **ABERFOLLY 20** [5] 2-8-6 Joanna Badger (7) 50/1: 06: Chsd ldrs 5f: longer 7f trip. 3 39
-- **BORDER TERRIER** [1] 2-8-11 K Darley 14/1: 7: Rear, mod gains fnl 3f: mkt drifter, op 7/1: Mar foal, cheaply bght: dam unrcd, sire a 9/10f wnr: 1m+ shld suit. 3½ 37
1577 **WHARFEDALE LADY 57** [11] 2-8-6 R Winston 12/1: -0008: Twds rear, nvr factor: abs: longer 7f trip. 1¾ 30
2599 **FAST BUCK 14** [13] 2-8-11 R Mullen 20/1: 000509: Mid-div at best: mod form. 5 25
2200 **MONICA 30** [14] 2-8-6 J McAuley (5) 100/1: 004560: Bhd halfway, 10th: no form. ½ 19
1653 **ARIES FIRECRACKER 54** [12] 2-8-11 O Pears 33/1: 0000: Al bhd: 11th: 8 wk abs: mod form. 1½ 22
1974 **LIMBO DANCER 40** [8] 2-8-6 Dean McKeown 66/1: 6000: Keen/mid-div, btn 2f out: 12th: 6 wk abs. 6 5
2874 **ITALIAN AFFAIR 2** [3] 2-8-12 A Beech (5) 11/4 FAV: 021050: Trkd ldrs, saddle slipped 3f out, soon eased: 13th: hvly bckd, op 4/1: twice saddle has slipped in the space of 3 days: see 2388 (6f). 12 0
13 ran Time 1m 27.8 (4.8) (The Gazetters) A Berry Cockerham, Lancs.

2928 3.00 LEEDS NURSERY HCAP 2YO (D) 7f rnd Good/Firm 28 -30 Slow [81]
£3510 £1080 £540 £270

*2718 **PEREGIAN 9** [5] M Johnston 2-9-13 (80)(6ex) D Holland 4/6 FAV: 530111: 2 b c Eagle Eyed - Mo Pheata (Petorius) Cl-up, led 2f out, al in command after, pushed out, easily: value for 4L+: hvly bckd under a 6lb pen: earlier scored here at Catterick (auct mdn) & Ayr (h'cap): eff around a sharp or gall 7f, 1m could suit: acts on fast & gd, has disapp on soft: gd weight carrier: plenty in hand here, shld win more races. 87
2514 **SIENA STAR 18** [4] J L Eyre 2-9-5 (72) J P Spencer 25/1: 004432: 2 b g Brief Truce - Gooseberry Pie (Green Desert) Chsd wnr 2f out, rdn & al held: acts on fast grnd: see 2514, 2057. 1¼ 76
*2312 **WINDCHILL 26** [1] T D Easterby 2-8-7 (60) K Darley 11/4: 022113: 2 ch f Handsome Sailor - Baroness Gymcrak (Pharly) Held up, drvn & styd on fnl 2f, no ch with wnr: bckd: see 2312. *hd* 63
*2447 **YOUNG ALEX 20** [3] K R Burke 2-9-6 (73) Darren Williams (5) 7/1: -0114: Held up, rcd wide & not handle bend into str, nvr nr ldrs: poss not stay 7f, a more gall trk will suit: forget this, see 2447. 3 70

2778 **ALIS IMAGES 6** [2] 2-8-9 (62) G Carter 14/1: 660335: Chsd ldrs 5f: qck reapp: see 2377. ¾ **57**
2441 **PETIT TOR 20** [6] 2-8-8 (61) O Pears 14/1: 042526: Led 5f, sn btn: btr 2441, 1476 (6f). ½ **55**
6 ran Time 1m 27.1 (4.7) (J David Abell) M Johnston Middleham, N.Yorks.

2929 **3.30 HALIFAX HCAP 3YO+ 0-85 (D) 5f rnd Good/Firm 28 +18 Fast [80]**
£3984 £1226 £613 £306 3 yo rec 4 lb

*2833 **FLAK JACKET 5** [5] D Nicholls 5-9-2 (68)(t)(6ex) D Holland 6/5 FAV: 000211: 5 b g Magic Ring - Vaula (Henbit) Prom, rdn to lead 1f out, pushed out, rdly: nicely bckd, qck reapp, fast time: earlier won at Pontefract (stks): rnr-up in '99 (rtd 82, B Meehan): '98 wnr at Kempton & Haydock (rtd 86): suited by 5/6f on firm & soft grnd: acts on any trk: eff without blnks, wears a t-strap: well h'capped: in tremendous form, will race off a 6lb lower mark at Goodwood next week & looks sure to run well. **74**
2743 **WILLIAMS WELL 7** [13] M W Easterby 6-9-1 (67)(bl) T Lucas 9/1: 365522: 6 ch g Superpower - Catherines Well (Junius) Rear, switched over 3f out, prog appr fnl 1f, ran on ins last, no impress on wnr: quick reapp & another gd run, shld go in again sn: see 2743. ½ **71**
2721 **CARTMEL PARK 9** [10] A Berry 4-9-12 (78)(vis) O Pears 16/1: 500103: 4 b g Skyliner - Oh My Oh My (Ballachashtal) Rcd alone stands side, prom, styd on/hung left ins last, no threat to wnr: gd run, likes dominating. 1¼ **78**
2822 **PURE ELEGANCIA 5** [12] D Nicholls 4-9-4 (70) Alex Greaves 10/1: 16-024: Cl-up, rdn to chall appr fnl 1f, hung right & no extra fnl 1f: quick reapp, stable-mate of wnr: see 2827 (stks). ½ **69**
2641 **TANCRED TIMES 12** [9] 5-8-0 (52) Kimberley Hart 20/1: 241155: Chsd ldrs, ev ch till no extra fnl 1f. *nk* **50**
2743 **SOTONIAN 7** [3] 7-8-6 (58) K Darley 10/1: 634536: Front rank, drvn/fdd fnl 1f: qck reapp: see 2743. ¾ **54**
2845 **TREASURE TOUCH 4** [6] 6-9-4 (70)(6ex) Joanna Badger (7) 12/1: 013137: Bhd, late hdwy, no threat: quick reapp: unsuited by this drop in trip, relish a return to 6f: see 2777. *1* **63**
+2663 **DISTINCTLY BLU 12** [2] 3-9-3 (73) F Lynch 9/1: 625218: Led early, remained with ldrs till went on again appr fnl 1f, hdd ins last, wknd qckly: btr 2663. *1* **63**
*2743 **RUDE AWAKENING 7** [1] 6-7-11 (49)(6ex) T Williams 7/1: 031019: Led 2f till over 1f out, fdd: qck reapp. ¾ **37**
2644 **WESTCOURT MAGIC 12** [8] 7-9-7 (73) A Culhane 25/1: 00-000: Went right start & al bhd: fin 10th: op 14/1: stablemate of 2nd: needs to dominate, likes Chester: see 1980. 1¼ **57**
2054 **DIAMOND DECORUM 37** [4] 4-9-4 (70) R Fitzpatrick (3) 10/1: -61060: Dwelt, nvr dngrs: see 1356 (6f). *hd* **53**
2568 **Taras Girl 15** [7] 3-10-0 (84) R Winston 33/1: 2822 **Soaked 5** [11] 7-8-4 (56) G Parkin 33/1: R
13 ran Time 57.8 (0.5) (The Knavesmire Alliance) D Nicholls Sessay, N Yorks

2930 **4.00 DEWSBURY MDN 3YO+ (D) 1m5f175y Good/Firm 28 -17 Slow**
£2769 £852 £426 £213 3 yo rec 14lb

2703 **HERACLES 10** [1] A Berry 4-9-9 G Carter 9/2: -6341: 4 b g Unfuwain - La Masse (High Top) Led early, led again 7f out, drvn & styd on strongly fnl 2f despite waving tail: op 7/2: dual bpmr rnr-up back in Feb '00 (gd & gd/soft): eff at 10/12f, apprec this step up to 13.8f: acts on fast grnd & a sharp trk. **78**
2327 **BAYSWATER 25** [4] B W Hills 3-8-4 K Darley 2/9 FAV: 022: 3 b f Caerleon - Shining Water (Kalaglow) Waited with, hdwy after 1m, drvn & kept on fnl 2f, no extra well ins last: nicely bckd at long odds-on & better expected: stays 13.8f on firm/fast, shld find a mdn: see 2327. 1¾ **70**
800 **CONCINO 118** [2] Miss A Stokell 3-8-9 P Fessey 100/1: 000-03: 3 b g Zafonic - Petronella (Nureyev) Reared leaving stalls, sn led, hdd 7f out, sn lost tch, t.o.: long abs: new stable, no form. *dist* **53$**
2558 **PIES AR US 15** [3] C W Fairhurst 3-8-9 P Goode (3) 14/1: -464: Waited with, lost tch fnl 5f, t.o. *3* **50**
-- **TODAYS MAN** [5] 3-8-9 O Pears 16/1: 5: Bhd, wknd rapidly after halfway, t.o.: speedily bred gldg. *dist* **0**
5 ran Time 3m 01.6 (6.2) (Exors Of The Late Lord Mostyn) A Berry Cockerham, Lancs

2931 **4.30 LEYBURN CLAIMER 3YO+ (F) 5f rnd Good/Firm 28 +00 Fast**
£2236 £639 £319 3 yo rec 4 lb

2371 **KING OF PERU 23** [2] D Nicholls 7-9-4 Alex Greaves 4/1: 442201: 7 b g Inca Chief - Julie's Star (Thatching) Mid-div, chall appr fnl 1f, led ins last, drvn out: new stable, on a long losing run for N Littmoden prev: '99 Brighton wnr (h'cap, plcd numerous times, rtd 71 & 81a): plcd in '98 (rtd 94a & 77, h'caps): suited by 5/6f, stays 7f: acts on firm, gd/soft & fibresand, poss soft: acts on any trk, likes a sharp/undul one, with or without a visor: new trainer is a master at revitalising this type of horse, can win more races. **74**
*2535 **BRANSTON LUCY 16** [5] T J Etherington 3-8-4 R Ffrench 4/1: 000212: 3 b f Prince Sabo - Softly Spoken (Mummy's Pet) Led, hdd just ins last, drvn, hung right & not pace of wnr cl-home: not disgraced at these weights. ½ **62**
2804 **LA PIAZZA 5** [6] W J Haggas 4-9-2 J P Spencer 10/11 FAV: 000233: 4 ch f Polish Patriot - Blazing Glory (Glow) Dwelt, rear, hdwy from rear over 2f out, hung left & no extra well ins last: well bckd, quick reapp: clr rem: will apprec at reurn to 6f, as in 2804 (h'cap). 1½ **66**
*2788 **ANSELLMAN 6** [1] A Berry 10-9-1 (bl) G Carter 6/1: 540014: Mid-div, rdn/no extra fnl 2f: quick reapp: shade btr 2788 (made all, firm grnd). 3½ **55**
2744 **JUST DISSIDENT 7** [3] 8-8-11 D Holland 25/1: 550045: Prom, rdn/wknd appr fnl 1f: quick reapp. *hd* **50$**
2505 **KERRIDGE CHAPEL 18** [7] 3-8-2 (bl) N Kennedy 200/1: 00-006: Chsd ldrs to halfway, sn bhd: stiff task. *6* **33**
2632 **DUBAI NURSE 12** [4] 6-8-6 (VIS) J Carroll 100/1: 046007: Dwelt, al outpcd: visored. 3½ **26**
7 ran Time 58.7 (1.4) (The Gardening Partnership) D Nicholls Sessay, N Yorks

2932 **5.00 W CARSON APPR HCAP 3YO+ 0-65 (F) 7f rnd Good/Firm 28 -26 Slow [57]**
£2233 £638 £319 3 yo rec 7 lb

*2796 **ENCOUNTER 5** [8] J Hetherton 4-9-7 (50)(6ex) A Robertson 3/1 JT FAV: 005211: 4 br g Primo Dominie - Dancing Spirit (Ahonoora) Mid-div, imprvd 2f out, ran on well to lead nr fin, drvn out: qck reapp: earlier won at Hamilton (amat h'cap): won 2 in 2 days in '99, at Ayr (sell) & Hamilton (h'cap, rtd 58 at best): flattered in '98 for C Brittain (mdn, rtd 77$): eff at 6/7f, tried 1m: acts on fast & a stiff/gall or sharp trk: in fine form. **52**
2297 **RIVER BLEST 26** [7] Mrs A Duffield 4-9-10 (53) L Enstone 20/1: 6-5002: 4 b g Unblest - Vaal Salmon (Salmon Leap) Led, clr after halfway, drvn & collared nr fin: bold eff trying to make all, win similar: see 1760. *nk* **54**
2823 **SYCAMORE LODGE 5** [3] D Nicholls 9-9-4 (47) P Mulrennan 3/1 JT FAV: 340603: 9 ch g Thatching - Bell Tower (Lyphard's Wish) Waited with, rdn to improve 2f out, styd on ins last, not reach ldrs: op 2/1, qck reapp. ¾ **46**
2823 **MAMMAS BOY 5** [5] A Berry 5-9-10 (53) D Egan 8/1: 111004: Rear, drvn/hdwy appr fnl 1f, styd on well ins last, no threat: quick reapp: see 2046. *1* **50**
2283 **ITALIAN SYMPHONY 27** [6] 6-9-10 (53)(vis) M Cotton 7/2: 505635: Mid-div, late hdwy: nicely bckd. ½ **49**
1680 **MR PERRY 53** [4] 4-9-7 (50) Claire Westerby 12/1: 230006: Cl-up, rdn/fdd appr fnl 1f: op 8/1, 8 wk abs. *4* **38**

CATTERICK WEDNESDAY JULY 26TH Lefthand, Undulating, V Tight Track

2443 **WHITEGATE WAY 20** [1] 3-9-2 (52) C McCavish 16/1: 0047: Dwelt/rear, nvr dangerous: h'cap bow. *shd* **40**
2381 **JATO DANCER 23** [2] 5-7-10 (25)(6oh) N Carter 10/1: 540608: Trkd ldrs, rdn/lost tch fnl 2f. *nk* **12**
2460 **THE IMPOSTER 19** [9] 5-9-0 (43) R Lake 25/1: 005009: Dwelt, sn prom, rdn & wknd qckly appr fnl 1f. *3½* **23**
9 ran Time 1m 26.8 (3.8) (C D Barber-Lomax) J Hetherton Malton, N Yorks

SANDOWN THURSDAY JULY 27TH Righthand, Galloping Track, Stiff Finish

Official Going GOOD/FIRM (FIRM in places). Stalls: Sprint Crse - Far Side; 14f - Outside; Rem - Inside

2933 2.10 TATTERSALLS MDN AUCT 2YO (E) 5f Good/Firm 32 -30 Slow
£3558 £1095 £547 £223

1522 **BLUE REIGNS 61** [9] N P Littmoden 2-8-5 J Quinn 5/2 JT FAV: 51: 2 b c Whittingham - Gold And Blue (Bluebird) Keen cl up, led & edged left over 1f out, kept on despite edging right ins last, drvn out: abs, well bckd tho' op 7/4: brother to a 6f scorer: eff at 5f & apprec this fast grnd: runs well fresh on a stiff track. **80**
2756 **EXTRA GUEST 8** [10] M R Channon 2-8-4 Craig Williams 5/2 JT FAV: 222422: 2 b f Fraam - Gibaltarik (Jareer) Cl up, ev ch over 1f out, not pace of wnr ins last but kept on: well bckd: consistent in defeat. *1¼* **75**
2588 **TYPE ONE 15** [8] T G Mills 2-8-5 L Carter 20/1: 03: 2 b c Bigstone - Isca (Caerleon) Keen, hld up, eff & short of room over 1f out, switched left ins last, kept on: handles fast: pleasing, win at 6f. *hd* **75**
2730 **AMELIA 9** [3] J Cullinan 2-7-12 P M Quinn (3) 20/1: 42334: Led till 1f out, onepace: op 12/1: better run, tho' poss flattered: see 2730, 1918. *nk* **67$**
2357 **DOUBLE BREW 25** [1] 2-8-5 Dane O'Neill 11/4: -34225: Cl up, btn over 1f out: needs headgear? *¾* **72**
1088 **MY FRIEND JACK 86** [6] 2-8-3 G Carter 16/1: -506: Keen, prom, wknd well over 1f out: 3 month abs. *2* **64**
2214 **TIMELESS FARRIER 30** [4] 2-8-5 M Tebbutt 14/1: 667: In tch, wknd 2f out: op 10/1: see 2039. *1½* **62**
-- **LADY LIFFEY** [2] 2-7-12 J Mackay (5) 16/1: 8: Slow away, al bhd on debut: op 10/1: March foal, cheaply bought: full sister to a 6f/1m scorer: bred to apprec 6f. *3½* **45**
-- **SALTAIRE** [5] 2-8-0 P Doe 20/1: 9: Slow away, soon in tch till wknd over 2f out: Feb foal, cost IR8,500 gns: half sister to a useful sprinter & mid dist scorer: dam 12f wnr: bred to need 7f+ & time. *6* **29**
9 ran Time 1m 02.71 (3.11) (J R Salter) N P Littmoden Newmarket, Suffolk

2934 2.45 FRED AND ADA HCAP 3YO 0-80 (D) 5f Good/Firm 32 +03 Fast [86]
£4270 £1314 £657 £328

2432 **LA CAPRICE 22** [6] A Berry 3-9-4 (76) G Carter 6/1: 320201: 3 ch f Housebuster - Shicklah (The Minstrel) Prom, hdwy to lead over 1f out, kept on gamely for press ins last: fair time: deserved win, reportedly not handle track/easier grnd in 2432: '99 scorer at Lingfield (mdn, rtd 81): eff over 5/6f & likes gd & firm grnd, handles soft & any track: best up with/forcing the pace. **81**
2900 **ILLUSIVE 2** [7] M Wigham 3-8-12 (70)(bl) R Cochrane 7/1: 355332: 3 b c Night Shift - Mirage (Red Sunset) In tch, eff to chall fnl 1f, kept on ins last, just held: deserves to go one better: quick reapp. *shd* **74**
2676 **TRAVESTY OF LAW 12** [4] B J Meehan 3-9-7 (79)(bl) D R McCabe 14/1: 000003: 3 ch g Case Law - Bold As Love (Lomond) Prom, hdwy appr fnl 1f, onepace ins last: bckd from 25/1: better run, well h'capped now. *1½* **79**
1891 **BALFOUR 44** [10] C E Brittain 3-8-2 (60) A Nicholls (3) 12/1: 156034: Waited with, eff 2f out, onepace inside last: 6 week abs, needs 6/7f: see 1891, 1787. *¾* **58**
2590 **WORSTED 15** [8] 3-8-2 (60) R Mullen 20/1: 00-35: Prom, rdn & wknd inside last: not disgraced. *shd* **58**
2478 **SMOKIN BEAU 20** [5] 3-8-13 (71) T Quinn 12/1: 200036: Led over 2f out till over 1f out, no extra. *2* **63**
2813 **HUNTING TIGER 6** [9] 3-8-6 (64) Craig Williams 6/4 FAV: 000527: Bhd, never in it: hvly bckd & much better expected racing off a 4lb lower mark than in 2813: should do better & will apprec a return to 6f+. *1* **53**
*2586 **JUDIAM 15** [3] 3-8-9 (67) J Fortune 10/1: 000518: In tch, wknd well over 1f out: much btr 2586. *¾* **54**
2549 **BEST BOND 17** [11] 3-8-2 (60) J Quinn 9/1: 000569: Bhd, no impression fnl 2f: see 1098. *2½* **40**
*2096 **SCAFELL 36** [2] 3-8-6 (64)(vis) R Winston 20/1: 205310: Led till over 2f out, wknd: 10th: btr 2096. *3* **35**
10 ran Time 1m 01.05 (1.45) (Slatch Farm Stud) A Berry Cockerham, Lancs

2935 3.15 LISTED MILCARS STKS 2YO (A) 7f rnd Good/Firm 32 -13 Slow
£14105 £4340 £2170 £1085

2344 **SILVER JORDEN 26** [2] J L Dunlop 2-8-12 T Quinn 8/1: -1101: 2 gr f Imp Society - Final Call (Town Crier) Cl up, hdwy to lead over 2f out, kicked clr dist, kept on for press ins last: op 6/1: cost 17,000 gns, half sister to sev wnrs: dam 5f juv scorer: earlier won at Lingfield (fill mdn, debut) & Yarmouth (nov auct): eff at 6f, stays 7f on fast, handles soft & any trk: runs well fresh: relished forcing tactics: useful & game. **98**
*2474 **HOTELGENIE DOT COM 20** [8] M R Channon 2-8-12 Craig Williams 5/2 FAV: 12: 2 b f Selkirk - Birch Creek (Carwhite) Dwelt, held up bhd, plenty to do 3f out, gd hdwy over 1f out, kept on: hvly bckd: handles gd & fast grnd: pleasing having been set too much to do & looks worth following: see 2474. *1¼* **95+**
*1957 **BRING PLENTY 41** [1] J H M Gosden 2-8-12 J Fortune 6/1: 013: 2 b f Southern Halo - Alcando (Alzao) Waited with, hdwy 2f out, kept on inside last, no danger: 6 week abs & a useful run stepped up to 7f. *nk* **94**
*2267 **CELTIC ISLAND 28** [10] W G M Turner 2-9-0 A Daly 16/1: 122014: Prom, eff to chase wnr over 1f out, no extra well inside last: useful, ran to form of 2267. *shd* **96$**
*2259 **PEACEFUL PARADISE 29** [4] 2-8-12 R Hills 10/1: -315: Waited with, eff 2f out, kept on inside last: gd run: looks sure to relish 1m: see 2259. *shd* **93**
*2619 **FIGURA 14** [3] 2-8-9 T E Durcan 16/1: 616: Slow away, hld up, eff 2f out, kept on: handles gd & fast. *¾* **88**
2693 **RIZERIE 12** [5] 2-8-12 J P Spencer 10/1: 127: Hld up, eff & not clr run 2f out, late gains: improve. *nk* **90**
1750 **LADY OF KILDARE 54** [9] 2-8-9 J Reid 11/2: -028: Handy, wknd fnl 1f: 8 week abs, see 1750. *3* **81**
*2583 **CARIBBEANDRIFTWOOD 15** [12] 2-8-12 K Darley 13/2: -219: Led till over 2f out, wknd over 1f out: raised in class after 2583 (fillies mdn, gd/soft). *2* **80**
*2390 **LILS JESSY 23** [6] 2-8-12 D Holland 8/1: 510: In tch, wknd well over 1f out: 10th, step up in class. *3½* **73**
2810 **TRUSTTHUNDER 6** [11] 2-8-9 J Quinn 25/1: -0220: Handy, wknd 2f out: 11th, qk reapp, see 2810. *2* **66**
2469 **MUSIC MAID 20** [7] 2-8-9 A Nicholls 33/1: 6130: Pressed wnr till wknd over 2f out: see 2469 (stks). *1* **64**
12 ran Time 1m 29.55 (3.15) (Mr & Mrs Gary Pinchen) J L Dunlop Arundel, W Sussex

SANDOWN   THURSDAY JULY 27TH   Righthand, Galloping Track, Stiff Finish

2936   3.50 SCOTS EQUITABLE HCAP 3YO 0-85 (D)   1m6f   Good/Firm 32   -30 Slow   [89]
£5027   £1547   £773   £386

*2751 **TAKWIN** 8 [2] B Hanbury 3-9-12 (87)(t)(5ex) R Hills 2/1 FAV: 032213: 3 b c Alzao - Gale Warning   91
(Last Tycoon) Made all, clr over 2f out, kept on strongly, readily: well bckd: recent Kempton wnr (mdn, easily):
eff at 12/14f on gd & fast grnd: goes on any track, wears a t-strap: likes to run up with/force the pace, can
come from behind: progressive, in form, useful colt.

*2681 **TYPHOON TILLY** 12 [5] C F Wall 3-8-11 (72) R Mullen 5/2: -31112: 3 b g Hernando - Meavy (Kalaglow) 3½ 71
Rear, prog to chse wnr fnl 2f, no impress ins last: well bckd: failed to complete 4 timer, but far from disgraced.

2793 **ABLE SEAMAN** 7 [1] C E Brittain 3-8-1 (62) A Nicholls (3) 11/2: 533343: 2 br g Northern Flagship - 1¾ 59
Love At Dawn (Grey Dawn II) Chsd wnr till onepace fnl 2f: op 9/2: seemed to stay this longer 14f trip: see 2793.

2523 **MAKASSEB** 18 [4] M R Channon 3-9-1 (76) Craig Williams 7/1: 006044: Rear, no impression fnl 2f. nk 73

*2249 **DARARIYNA** 29 [3] J Mackay (5) 4/1: 2215: Rcd keenly in bhd ldr, hmpd over 2f out, sn   3   75
btn: op 11/4: rcd too keenly today, lost all ch when hmpd: see 2249 (sharp track mdn).

5 ran   Time 3m 03.65 (8.65)   (Hamdan Al Maktoum)   B Hanbury Newmarket, Suffolk

2937   4.25 TOTE HCAP 3YO+ 0-90 (C)   1m2f   Good/Firm 32   +09 Fast   [90]
£6955   £2140   £1070   £535   3 yo rec 10lb

2499 **RICH VEIN** 19 [4] S P C Woods 3-8-2 (74)(vis) R Mullen 2/1 FAV: 421121: 3 b g Up And At 'Em -   83
Timissara (Shahrastani) Rear, smooth hdwy to lead 1½f out, sn clr, easily: hvly bckd, fast time: earlier
won at Lingfield (2, AW h'caps, visored first time): eff at 1m/10f, shld stay 12f: acts on gd, fast & equitrack:
eff in a visor, hndles a sharp/undul or stiff/gall trk: prog 3yo who apprec this fast run race.

2475 **ULUNDI** 20 [5] Lady Herries 5-10-0 (90) P Doe 3/1: 133002: 5 b g Rainbow Quest - Flit (Lyphard)   8   90
Track ldr till went on over 2f out, hdd 1½f out, easily outpcd by wnr: nicely bckd: joint top weight: met a
fast improving rival: unlucky in 2475 (C/D).

2270 **CLARENDON** 28 [2] V Soane 4-9-4 (80) R Cochrane 5/1: 006223: 4 ch c Forest Wind - Sparkish   2   77
(Persian Bold) Chsd ldrs, every ch 2f out, sn one pace: see 2270, 1973.

2502 **ARABIAN MOON** 19 [1] C E Brittain 4-10-0 (90) J Reid 9/4: 035134: Set decent pace till 2f out, wknd: 1½ 85
well bckd from 3/1, joint top weight: prob went off a shade too fast here: see 2502, 2178.

1570 **ALCAYDE** 59 [3] 5-8-1 (63) J Quinn 25/1: 25/005: Slowly away, rcd keenly in tch, wknd 3f out,   25 18
t.o.: 8 week abs: see 1373 (12f).

5 ran   Time 2m 06.45 (2.35)   (Arashan Ali)   S P C Woods Newmarket, Suffolk

2938   5.00 HEATHROW MDN 3YO+ (D)   1m rnd   Good/Firm 32   -17 Slow
£4231   £1302   £651   £325   3 yo rec 8 lb

2611 **INVADER** 14 [3] C E Brittain 4-9-7 (vis) P Robinson 11/2: 550021: 3 b c Danehill - Donya (Mill   83
Reef) Led till dist, rallied gamely to regain lead ins last, all out cl home: nicely bckd, top weight: deserved
win, 5th in List company earlier (rtd 99a): unplcd from 2 starts in '99 (rtd 102, Gr 3): eff at 1m/9f on fast
grnd & equitrack: wears a visor: apprec switch to forcing tactics today.

2596 **FREDDY FLINTSTONE** 15 [7] R Hannon 3-8-13 Dane O'Neill 5/1: -04002: 3 b c Bigstone - Daring Ditty nk 82
(Daring March) Dwelt, recovered to ch ldr, chall strongly fnl 1f, just btn: nicely bckd: deserves similar.

-- **WOOLFE** [2] J H M Gosden 3-8-8 J Fortune 10/1: 3: 3 ch f Wolfhound - Brosna (Irish River)   1¾ 75
Slowly away, prog from rear 2f out, ev ch 1f out, not qckn cl home: op 6/1, debut: dam styd mid dist: eff at
1m, 10f will suit: hndles fast grnd: sure to learn from this.

-- **DANZIG WITHWOLVES** [2] H R A Cecil 3-8-8 T Quinn 8/11 FAV: 4: Waited with, improved 2f out, shd 74
led dist till inside last, no extra: hvly bckd on debut: dam a smart juv wnr in the USA: clearly been working
well at home, but bandaged today & may have found this grnd too fast: prob worth another chance.

-- **CONWY CASTLE** [5] 3-8-13 R Havlin 25/1: 5: Slowly away & well bhd, kept on late, never plced to   7   66
chall: market drifter, longer priced stable mate of 3rd: half brother to a winning stayer in France: sure
to benefit from mid distances: will know more next time.

2491 **ALTARA** 19 [4] 3-8-8 Martin Dwyer 25/1: 46: Chsd ldrs till grad wknd fnl 2f: see 2491.   1¾ 59

2860 **HAMLYN** 5 [6] 3-8-13 (bl) K Darley 10/1: -64647: Chsd ldrs 6f, fdd: bckd from 16/1, qck reapp. 1¾ 61

2627 **TACHOMETER** 14 [8] 6-9-2 A Nicholls (3) 50/1: 48: Rcd keenly rear, btn over 2f out: see 2627.   5   48

8 ran   Time 1m 42.89 (3.89)   (R J Swinbourne)   C E Brittain Newmarket, Suffolk

BATH   THURSDAY JULY 27TH   Lefthand, Turning Track with Uphill Finish

Official Going: FIRM   Stalls: Straight Course - Far Side, Round Course - Inside

2939   2.00 MEADOW MED AUCT FILL MDN 2YO (E)   5f161y rnd   Firm 14   -03 Slow
£3474   £1069   £534

1882 **MISS DOMUCH** 44 [5] R Hannon 2-8-11 R Hughes 5/2: 231: 2 ch f Definite Article - Eliza Orzeszkowa 77
(Polish Patriot) Made all, rdn clr over 1f out, pushed out cl home: easily: bckd, 6 week abs: return
to 6f should suit: acts on firm & soft grnd: likes to force the pace & handles a stiff/gall trk: rate higher.

2711 **BE MY TINKER** 10 [7] G Brown 2-8-11 M Fenton 8/1: 62: 2 ch f Be My Chief - Tinkerbird (Music   3½ 64
Boy) Chsd ldrs, rdn/chsd wnr over 1f out, kept on, al held: op 6/1: eff at 5.8f, handles firm grnd: see 2711.

-- **HILL WELCOME** [3] B W Hills 2-8-11 M Hills 100/30: 3: 2 ch f Most Welcome - Tarvie (Swing   2½ 57
Easy) Dwelt/rear, late gains, no threat: op 7/4: May foal, dam a 6f wnr as a 2/3yo: will apprec 6f.

2214 **MISTY BELLE** 30 [6] B R Millman 2-8-11 L Newman (3) 7/4 FAV: 03234D: Chsd wnr, rdn/hung badly hd 56
right over 1f out, soon btn: fin 4th, disqualified & plcd last: btr 2214, 1993.

2539 **YUKA SAN** 17 [8] 2-8-11 G Hannon (7) 40/1: 604: Chsd ldrs, held when forced badly right 1f out. ½   54

-- **ZANDOS CHARM** [4] 2-8-11 R Smith (5) 14/1: 5: Dwelt, never on terms: Forzando filly, March foal, ¾   52
a first foal: dam unrcd: sire tough/progressive, stayed up to 9f: with R Hannon.

2550 **DANCING MILLY** 17 [2] 2-8-11 S Whitworth 20/1: U6: Chsd ldrs, btn 3f out: op 14/1: no form.   11 32

-- **PINK CHAMPAGNE** [1] 2-8-11 G Baker (5) 25/1: 7: Dwelt & al bhd: March foal, dam lightly rcd.   11 12

8 ran   Time 1m 10.1 (1.0)   (E K Cleveland)   R Hannon East Everleigh, Wilts

914

2940　　2.35 EBF NOV STKS 2YO (D)　　5f rnd　Firm 14　-04 Slow
　　£3406　£1048　£524　£262

*2209　**CHAGUARAMAS** 31 [4]　R Hannon 2-8-11 R Hughes 2/5 FAV: 11: 2 b f Mujadil - Sabaniya (Lashkari)　　　　87
Led, rdn/hdd over 1f out, drvn & rallied well to lead again well inside last, holding rivals/pushed out close home:
hvly bckd at odds on: earlier scored at Windsor (auction mdn): eff at 5f, return to 6f will suit: acts on firm &
fast grnd: open to improvement when returning to 6f+.
2760　**THE TRADER** 8 [1]　M Blanshard 2-8-12 D Sweeney 5/1: 3322: 2 ch c Selkirk - Snowing (Tate Gallery)　　½　85
Rdn to press wnr fnl 2f & led over 1f out, hdd well ins last & held nr fin: op 7/1, clr rem: acts on firm & soft.
2730　**ONCE REMOVED** 9 [2]　S Dow 2-8-7 F Norton 5/1: 044023: 2 b f Distant Relative - Hakone (Alzao)　　6　69
Keen, chsd wnr, rdn 2f out: op 7/2: too keen: btr 2730.
2915　**QUIZZICAL LADY** 1 [3]　M Quinn 2-8-11 G Hannon (7) 16/1: 604064: Bhd 2f out: unplcd last night.　　3½　64
4 ran　　Time 1m 01.2 (0.9)　　　(Dr A Haloute)　　　R Hannon East Everleigh, Wilts

---

2941　　3.05 CHUCKLESTONE HCAP 3YO+ 0-70 (E)　　2m1f34y　Firm 14　-10 Slow　　　[69]
　　£2749　£846　£423　£211　3 yo rec 17lb

2856　**LAFFAH** 5 [3]　L M Moore 5-9-5 (60)(t)　R Hughes 3/1 FAV: 0/1341: 5 b g Silver Hawk - Sakiyah　　　65
(Secretariat) Bhd ldrs, lost pl 5f out, drvn & prog to chall 1f out, led line, all out: well bckd: qck reappr: earlier
won at Chepstow (mdn h'cap): prev a wnr over hurdles: eff around 2m/2m2f on firm & fast: suited by a t-strap.
2801　**ELSIE BAMFORD** 6 [11]　M Johnston 4-8-8 (49) K Dalgleish (5) 5/1: 333432: 3 b f Tragic Role -　　shd　53
Sara Sprint (Formidable) Rear, rdn/prog to lead over 1f out, duelled with wnr inside last, just held: clr of rem.
2173　**SHERIFF** 33 [1]　J W Hills 9-8-8 (49) M Henry 11/2: 202103: 9 b g Midyan - Daisy Warwick (Ribot)　　6　47
Led 1f, drvn/led again 3f out, hdd over 1f out & no extra inside last: see 1996 (C/D).
2622　**ZIGGY STARDUST** 14 [2]　Mrs A J Bowlby 5-7-10 (37)(4oh) G Baker (5) 4/1: -34324: Held up, prog/bhd　　3　32
ldrs 3f out, held over 1f out: mdn after 34 starts: see 2622, 1647.
2490　**OUT RANKING** 19 [8]　8-9-10 (65) A McGlone 7/1: 0/25: Led after 1f till 3f out, sn held: btr 2490.　　½　59
2461　**ELEGIA PRIMA** 20 [9]　3-8-0 (58) N Pollard 10/1: -04206: Held up, eff 4f out, not pace to chall: op 7/1.　　1　51
2490　**MU TADIL** 19 [7]　8-7-10 (37)(10oh) G Sparkes (6) 25/1: 000067: Rear, mod gains: now with R Dickin.　　1　29
788　**FAITH AGAIN** 120 [6]　4-7-13 (40) C Rutter 8/1: 534-08: Al bhd: 4 mth abs: see 788 (14f).　　1¾　30
1996　**NOTEWORTHY** 40 [10]　4-8-0 (41) Claire Bryan (5) 16/1: -00009: Chsd ldrs, btn 3f out: 6 week abs.　　19　17
2452　**ZOLA** 21 [5]　4-7-12 (39)(2ow)(19oh) F Norton 50/1: 050000: Trkd ldrs halfway, bhd 3f out: 10th.　　11　7
2785　**VILLEGGIATURA** 7 [4]　7-9-5 (60) Darren Williams (5) 40/1: 00: Chsd ldrs 13f: 11th: see 2785 (sell).　　28　8
11 ran　　Time 3m 45.1 (4.2)　　　(Richard Green (Fine Paintings)　　　G L Moore Woodingdean, E Sussex

---

2942　　3.40 P WALWYN HCAP 3YO+ 0-80 (D)　　1m rnd　Firm 14　+08 Fast　　　[73]
　　£6792　£2090　£1045　£522　3 yo rec 8 lb

2564　**EASTERN SPICE** 16 [4]　R Hannon 3-9-10 (77) R Hughes 6/1: 021301: 3 b c Polish Precedent - Mithl　　　81
Al Hawa (Salse) Chsd ldrs, rdn 3f out, prog/no room over 1f out, rdn to lead well inside last, drvn out: best time
of day: op 5/1: earlier scored at Goodwood (mdn): plcd twice in '99 (rtd 82): suited by 1m/9f on firm & gd grnd,
sharp or stiff/gall track, good weight carrier: tough.
2878　**DOVEBRACE** 3 [3]　A Bailey 7-8-8 (53) A Culhane 10/1: 216662: 7 b g Dowsing - Naufrage (Main Reef)　　¾　55
Waited with rear, switched & styd on strongly fnl 1f, not pace of wnr cl home: remains in gd form: see 2420.
2427　**TWIN TIME** 22 [2]　J S King 6-9-6 (65) D Harrison 7/2 CO FAV: 423143: 5 b m Syrtos - Carramba　　½　66
(Tumble Wind) Led, hard rdn from 3f out, hdd inside last, kept on well: op 9/2: loves Bath: see 2427, 2303.
2614　**SPIN A YARN** 14 [5]　B W Hills 3-9-12 (79) M Hills 7/2 CO FAV: -00554: Chsd ldrs, rdn to briefly lead/　　nk　79
edged left inside last, held near fin: bckd: btn less than 2L in a blanket fin: eff around 1m on firm & fast grnd.
2467　**FIONN DE COOL** 20 [10]　9-8-0 (45) G Baker (5) 20/1: 53-005: Rear, prog when no room/switched 1f　　¾　44
out, switched again nr line, not reach ldrs: no luck in running & not btn far: on a fair mark, keep in mind: see 2467.
*2726　**TAPAGE** 9 [9]　4-9-3 (62)(7ex) M Henry 5/1: -11116: Cl up 6f: needs to dominate: see 2726.　　¾　60
2645　**HARMONY HALL** 13 [6]　9-9-6 (65) P Fitzsimons (5) 7/2 CO FAV: 442027: Chsd ldrs, onepace fnl 2f.　　1　61
2761　**SUPERCHIEF** 8 [7]　5-7-13 (42)(tbl)(2ow) C Rutter 33/1: 115008: Rear, never on terms: see 596 (AW).　　½　39
2729　**DEMOCRACY** 9 [6]　4-8-1 (46) F Norton 14/1: 534049: Al bhd: see 2729, 258.　　24　5
2463　**STARBOARD TACK** 20 [1]　4-9-1 (60) L Newman (3) 33/1: -00300: Virtually ref to race, t.o.: 10th.　　dist　0
10 ran　　Time 1m 38.8 (0.5)　　　(Mohamed Suhail)　　　R Hannon East Everleigh, Wilts

---

2943　　4.10 VALLEY CLASS STKS 3YO+ 0-80 (D)　　1m3f144y　Firm 14　-08 Slow
　　£3701　£1139　£569　£284　3 yo rec 12lb

*2609　**FRANGY** 14 [4]　L M Cumani 3-8-5 B Marcus 11/8 FAV: -311: 3 b f Sadler's Wells - Fern (Shirley Heights)　　79
Led/dsptd lead, rdn/strongly pressed over 1f out, narrowly asserted nr line, all out: nicely bckd: earlier scored
at Doncaster (mdn): eff at 11.5f/12f: acts on firm, hvy & a gall track: runs well fresh.
2872　**WASP RANGER** 4 [6]　G L Moore 6-9-6 (bl) R Hughes 6/4: 223162: 6 b g Red Ransom - Lady Climber　　nk　81
(Mount Hagen) Trckd ldrs travelling well, rdn to chall wnr over 1f out, just held nr line: clr rem: nicely bckd.
2627　**HAVANA** 14 [1]　Mrs A J Perrett 4-9-1 M Roberts 3/1: 33-423: 4 b f Dolphin Street - Royaltess (Royal　　6　67
And Regal) Led/dsptd lead till over 2f out, soon held by front pair: clr rem: op 4/1: btr 2627, 1343.
3509}　**ROYAL SIGNET** 340 [2]　M J Weeden 5-9-1 F Norton 66/1: 6500-4: In tch, btn 3f out: reappr:　　8　58$
unplcd last term (rtd 47, h'cap): rtd 65$ in '98 (mdn): has tried 2m+ prev.
--　　**AMITGE** [5]　6-9-1 Darren Williams (5) 25/1: 6303/5: Bhd 3f out: long Flat abs, 7 week jumps abs,　　½　57
earlier scored at Folkestone (sell hdle, rtd 90h), 99/00 wnr at Plumpton & Warwick (nov, rtd 119c), eff at 2m1f/2m4f
on fast & soft, eff with/without blinks: last raced on the level in native France in '97, plcd twice at 10f on soft.
2457　**KEEN DANCER** 20 [3]　6-9-4 (bl) O Pears 25/1: /60-66: Al bhd: see 2457.　　7　50
6 ran　　Time 2m 27.6 (2.6)　　　(Fittocks Stud)　　　L M Cumani Newmarket, Suffolk

2944   4.45 HILLSIDE HCAP 3YO+ 0-80 (D)   5f161y rnd   Firm 14   -02 Slow   [75]
£3818   £1175   £587   £293   3 yo rec 5 lb

2054 **RING DANCER** 38 [2] P J Makin 5-9-11 (72) A Clark 14/1: 0-0001: 5 b g Polar Falcon - Ring Cycle   75
(Auction Ring) Dwelt, sn tracking ldrs trav well, no room from 2f out till 1f out, switched/hard rdn to lead nr line:
op 10/1: unplcd in '99 (h'cap, rtd 83): plcd twice in '98 (rtd 88, h'cap): '97 Ripon wnr (auct mdn, rtd 94): suited
by 5.8f/6f, stays a sharp 7f: acts on firm & gd/soft grnd, sharp or gall track: nicely h'capped.
2701 **SWINO** 11 [8] P D Evans 6-7-13 (46)(vis) Joanna Badger (7) 9/1: 000002: 6 b g Forzando - St   shd 47
Helena (Monsanto) Prom, rdn/outpcd halfway, rallied well for press to chall inside last, just held: op 10/1:
return to form here & although not one to rely on is well h'capped & shld pinch another race: see 177.
*2830 **ANTHONY MON AMOUR** 6 [11] D Nicholls 5-9-11 (72)(t)(7ex) Darren Williams (5) 2/1 FAV: 041013:   ½ 71
5 b g Nicholas - Reine De La Ciel (Conquistador Cielo) Dwelt, held up in tch, smooth prog to lead 1f out, rdn/hdd
inside last & held nr line: well bckd: see 2830 (made most).
2555 **SEREN TEG** 17 [1] R M Flower 4-7-11 (44)(bl) D Kinsella (7) 20/1: 400064: Led/dsptd lead till 1f out,   ½ 41
kept on onepace nr line: see 440 (AW).
2508 **MR STYLISH** 17 [9] 4-9-9 (70)(t) M Hills 7/1: 330505: Rear, prog/not much room over 1f out, kept   hd 66
on, not pace to chall: needs 6f+: see 2355, 1438.
2830 **SQUARE DANCER** 6 [6] 4-8-11 (58) A Culhane 7/2: 054026: Led/dsptd lead till over 1f out, fdd.   1¼ 51
2555 **RED DELIRIUM** 17 [12] 4-8-9 (56)(t) Michael Doyle (7) 14/1: 000057: Chsd ldrs, not pace to chall.   3 42
2729 **CHAKRA** 9 [5] 6-8-0 (47) G Baker (5) 12/1: 002138: Cl up, fading/bmpd over 1f out: see 2729, 2291.   nk 32
2508 **BILLY BATHWICK** 19 [10] 3-9-2 (68) J Stack 12/1: 520109: Al outpcd: op 10/1: btr 2278 (6f).   2½ 46
2788 **ARAB GOLD** 7 [7] 5-7-10 (43)(10oh) K Dalgleish (5) 25/1: 340030: Cl up 3f: 10th: see 2788, 634.   nk 20
2830 **RIVER TERN** 6 [3] 7-9-1 (62) Claire Bryan (5) 10/1: 003600: Chsd ldrs 3f out, soon btn: 11th: op 7/1.   5 30
11 ran   Time 1m 10.00 (0.9)   (Mrs Tricia Mitchell)   P J Makin Ogbourne Maisey, Wilts

Official Going   STANDARD. Stalls: Inside.

2945   1.55 BET DIRECT HCAP 3YO 0-70 (E)   1m3f aw   Going 50   -20 Slow   [77]
£2863   £881   £440   £220

*2815 **BAHAMAS** 7 [1] Sir Mark Prescott 3-9-3 (66)(bl)(6ex) S Sanders 5/4 FAV: 123311: 3 b g Barathea -   71a
Rum Cay (Our Native) Rear, imprvd halfway, led 3f out, ran on strongly, rdn out: well bckd from 2/1, 6lb pen:
recent wnr here at Southwell, earlier scored at Redcar (h'caps): half-brother to smart stayer Persian Punch: eff
at 10/12f, shld stay further: acts on gd & fibresand, with/without blnks: handles any trip: improving.
2685 **KARA SEA** 13 [6] D J G Murray Smith 3-9-1 (64) C Lowther 10/1: 1042: 3 ch f River Special - Arctic   ½ 68a
Interlude (Woodman) Mid-div, styd on under press fnl 2f, rdn out: tchd 14/1, 6L clr 3rd: gd run back on
fibresand, stays a sharp 11f: shld go one better, see 500 (1m here).
2634 **BELINDA** 14 [8] K Bell 3-9-2 (65) D Sweeney 33/1: 401003: 3 ch f Mizoram - Mountain Dew (Pharly)   6 60a
Chsd ldrs, styd on under press fnl 2f, no ch with front 2: prob stays a sharp 11f: see 1977 (1m mdn auct, here).
2883 **INVISIBLE FORCE** 4 [7] M Johnston 3-7-10 (45)(bl)(6ex)(1oh) K Dalgleish (5) 4/1: 466134: Led till   8 28a
over 3f out, wknd: qck reapp & 6lb pen: well bckd 2883, 2825 (turf).
2372 **AIWIN** 25 [11] 3-9-6 (69) J Mackay 12/1: 045305: Bhd & ran wide, modest late gains: see 1977.   nk 51a
2484 **MOST STYLISH** 21 [2] A Daly 13/2: 523446: Chsd ldrs till lost pl halfway, rallied 2f out, sn btn.   5 38a
2463 **SAVE THE PLANET** 21 [1] 3-8-5 (54)(BL) Dean McKeown 50/1: -00007: Front rank till halfway, sn   3½ 23a
bhd: tried in blnks: modest form, see 794.
1804 **JUST THE JOB TOO** 49 [5] 3-8-3 (52) Dale Gibson 16/1: 410608: Front rank fnl halfway, sn btn: abs.   6 12a
1722 **RED SEPTEMBER** 53 [4] 3-7-12 (47)(BL) G Bardwell 33/1: 65-069: In tch, btn halfway: first time   9 0a
blnks, 8 wk abs: see 1722 (turf).
1705 **BOSS TWEED** 54 [10] 3-8-13 (62) A Clark 7/1: 431050: Al well bhd, fin 10th: op 11/2, 8 wk abs: nk 9a
reportedly lost his action: see 827 (soft grnd).
2735 **CAPACOOSTIC** 10 [9] 3-7-10 (45) Claire Bryan (5) 25/1: -00200: Early ldr, lost pl entr str, fin last.   2½ 0a
11 ran   Time 2m 29.0 (7.7)   (Eclipse Thoro'breds - Osborne House III)   Sir Mark Prescott Newmarket.

2946   2.25 CLAIMER DIV I 3YO+ (F)   1m aw rnd   Going 50   -22 Slow
£1736   £496   £248   3yo rec 8lb

2816 **THE BARNSLEY BELLE** 7 [4] J Balding 7-8-6 J Edmunds 33/1: 6-4501: 7 b m Distinctly North - La Tangue   54a
(Last Raise) Set pace till 3f out, regained led 2f out, styd on well, rdn out: earlier trained by G Woodward, '99
wnr here at Southwell (fill h'cap, rtd 41a): plcd in '98 (appr fill h'cap, rtd 51a): eff at 7f/1m: acts on gd
grnd, loves fibresand & Southwell: apprec this drop to claim company.
2816 **STANDIFORD GIRL** 7 [1] J G Given 3-7-10 too late: op 8/1: sound effort, see 2816 (C/D).   1 50a
2816 **PIPPAS PRIDE** 7 [5] S R Bowring 5-9-1 S Finnamore (5) 6/4 FAV: 003023: 5 ch g Pips Pride - Al Shany   nk 60a
(Burslem) Chsd ldrs, sltly outpcd halfway, kept on under press fnl 1f: well bckd: bt this 1st & 2nd in 2816 (C/D).
2699 **PIX ME UP** 12 [11] K A Ryan 3-7-12 Iona Wands 9/1: 240054: In tch, rcd wide, onepcd fnl 1½f.   1½ 48a
2508 **AIR OF ESTEEM** 20 [3] 4-9-9 (VIS) P Goode (3) 3/1: -35045: Dwelt, recovered to trk ldrs, led 3f   1½ 62a
out till 2f out, wknd: first time visor: ran well for a long way: see 1790.
2634 **MAI TAI** 14 [8] 5-9-2 (vis) F Lynch 5/1: 025666: Chsd ldrs & rcd wide, onepcd fnl 2f: see 2121 (C/D).   1½ 52a
2606 **OVER THE MOON** 15 [2] 6-8-8 (vis) R Fitzpatrick (3) 16/1: 043667: Dwelt, chsd ldrs, onepcd fnl 2f.   ¾ 42$
1772 **SHONTAINE** 51 [10] 7-8-13 C Lowther 20/1: 330008: Rear, nvr nr ldrs: 7 wk absence.   4 39a
2633 **LOUS WISH** 14 [6] 3-8-9 L Newton 12/1: 000009: Nvr better than mid-div: op 7/1: see 346.   nk 42a
2538 **SIMAND** 8 [8] 4-8-8 (BL) Dean McKeown 66/1: 43/000: Chsd ldrs till lost pl halfway, t.o. in 10th: 8 17a
tried in blnks: missed prev 3 seasons, back in '95 won at Thirsk & Carlisle (seller/clmr): eff at 7f/1m on gd & fm.
2819 **HONEY HOUSE** 7 [9] 4-8-10 S Righton 66/1: 00-000: Unruly start, al struggling & bhd from halfway.   6 7a
11 ran   Time 1m 45.2 (5.8)   (K Meynell)   J Balding Scrooby, Notts.

SOUTHWELL (Fibresand) FRIDAY JULY 28TH Lefthand, Sharp, Oval Track

2947

2.55 GOLF CLUB MED AUCT MDN 3YO (F) 6f aw rnd Going 50 +02 Fast
£2254 £644 £322

1280 **BRANSTON FIZZ 76** [6] M Johnston 3-8-9 J Fanning 6/1: 3-4001: 3 b f Efisio - Tuxford Hideaway (Cawston's Clown) Front rank, went on halfway, hdd briefly dist, kept on strongly, drvn out: drifted from 4/1, gd time, 11 wk abs: rnr-up twice in '99 (mdn, rtd 85): half-sister to sev wnrs, incl tough sprinter Branston Abbey: eff at 6f on gd, soft & f/sand, has disapp on equitrack: handles a sharp or stiff/undul trk, runs well fresh. **68a**
2864 **LAYAN 5** [10] J Balding 3-8-9 J Edmunds 14/1: 660342: 3 b f Puissance - Most Uppitty (Abslaom) *1¾* **62$**
Chsd ldrs, drvn to lead dist, not pace of wnr cl-home: tchd 20/1, qck reapp, 3L clr 3rd: offic rtd 54, so treat this rating with caution: acts on firm, gd/soft & fibresand: see 2374 (sell h'cap).
2817 **TOYON 7** [9] Sir Mark Prescott 3-9-0 S Sanders 13/8 FAV: 065223: 3 b g Catrail - Princess Toy *3* **58a**
(Prince Tenderfoot) Mid-div, kept on under press 2f out, no impress ins last: bckd from 2/1: rtd higher 2817.
2464 **GINGKO 21** [11] J G Smyth Osbourne 3-9-0 F Norton 7/1: -444: Chsd ldrs, kept on under press *nk* **57a**
cl home: op 10/1, clr of rem: AW debut: now qual for h'caps & 1m may suit: see 1072.
2604 **STOP THE TRAFFIC 15** [3] 3-8-9 C Lowther 16/1: 000055: Nvr better than mid-div: see 2604. *6* **37a**
2585 **SLAM BID 16** [7] 3-9-0 D Sweeney 7/1: 00-56: Front rank till wknd 2f out: op 5/1: see 2585 (turf). *hd* **42a**
2604 **TOP OF THE PARKES 15** [5] 3-8-9 C Cogan (5) 7/2: 350-37: Front rank 4f, sn lost pl: btr 2604. *1½* **34a**
4445} **LADY FEARLESS 282** [4] 3-8-9 R Lappin 40/1: 06-8: Front rank 4f, wknd: reapp: unplcd both '99 *6* **19a**
starts (rtd 61, turf mdn): half-sister to 6f 2yo wnr Lady Boxer: dam a 7f wnr.
2822 **DANAKIM 7** [2] 3-9-0 F Lynch 33/1: 024059: Prom 4f, wknd: see 1021 (turf). *3½* **15a**
1125 **GROESFAEN LAD 85** [1] 3-9-0 G Faulkner (3) 16/1: 0-0400: Led till halfway, wknd into 10th: abs. *1½* **11a**
1500 **JOEBERTEDY 63** [8] 3-9-0 A Clark 66/1: 0-0000: Al well bhd, t.o. in last: 9 wk abs: no form. *22* **0a**
11 ran Time 1m 16.2 (2.9) (J David Abell) M Johnston Middleham, N.Yorks.

2948

3.25 BET DIRECT NURSERY HCAP 2YO (E) 6f aw rnd Going 50 -03 Slow [83]
£2741 £783 £391

2874 **CEDAR TSAR 4** [9] D W Chapman 2-9-0 (69) S Finnamore(5) 4/1 FAV: 213331: 2 b c Inzar - The Aspecto Girl (Alzao) Made all, qcknd clr fnl 1f, easily: qck reapp, fair juv time: earlier trained by A Reid to win here at Southwell (sell): eff at 6/7f on gd, fast grnd & fibresand: likes a sharp/easy trk, esp Southwell: likes to force the pace & can win again if making a qck reapp. **82a**
2599 **ORCHARD RAIDER 16** [10] C A Dwyer 2-9-0 (69) A Beech (5) 9/1: 241202: 2 b c Mujadil - Apple Brandy *7* **68a**
(Cox's Ridge) Dwelt, well bhd halfway, fin well but no ch with facile wnr: ran to best against an improver.
2589 **CHURCH MICE 16** [2] M L W Bell 2-9-7 (76)(vis) J Mackay (5) 11/2: 242153: 2 br f Petardia - Negria *hd* **75a**
(Al Hareb) Dwelt & well bhd, styd on fnl 2f, nrst fin: top-weight: lost all ch at the start, will apprec 7f now.
2417 **THEBAN 23** [4] D Nicholls 2-9-0 (69) F Norton 5/1: -5434: Front rank till grad fdd fnl 1½f: op 3/1. *½* **67a**
2312 **EASTERN RED 28** [8] 2-7-13 (54) Iona Wands 16/1: 056205: Front rank 4f, grad fdd: btr 2155. *1½* **48a**
1648 **THOMAS SMYTHE 56** [1] 2-9-5 (74) N Callan 10/1: -0226: Prsd ldrs 4f, wknd: 8 wk abs: see 1648. *hd* **68a**
2635 **MONICA GELLER 14** [5] 2-8-12 (67) G Bardwell 11/1: -0637: Al outpcd: see 2635. *¾* **58a**
*2605 **RUNNING FOR ME 15** [6] 2-8-7 (62) G Gibbons (7) 12/1: 022518: With ldrs 4f, wknd: btr 2605 (seller). *½* **52a**
2251 **SHINNER 30** [3] 2-9-4 (73) A Clark 9/2: -42149: Slowly away, no ch after: lost all ch at the start. *1½* **59a**
2384 **BELLS BEACH 25** [7] 2-7-11 (52)(1ow)(2oh) Dale Gibson 16/1: -0330: Front rank 4f: 10th: see 2384. *7* **23a**
10 ran Time 1m 16.5 (3.2) (Michael Hill) D W Chapman Stillington, N.Yorks.

2949

4.00 NOTTS FILLIES SELLER 2YO (G) 7f aw rnd Going 50 -20 Slow
£1862 £532 £266

2488 **VISITATION 20** [3] M L W Bell 2-8-8 J Mackay (5) 3/1 FAV: -01: 2 b f Bishop Of Cashel - Golden Envoy (Dayjur) Slowly away, drvn to improve dist, strong run to lead cl-home: nicely bckd, bt by K Ryan for 7,600 gns: Jan foal, sire a high-class 7f/1m performer: eff over 7f on f/sand, 1m will suit: handles a sharp trk. **53a**
1938 **MISS PROGRESSIVE 43** [8] N Tinkler 2-8-8 J Fanning 8/1: 600002: 2 b f Common Grounds - Kaweah *hd* **52a**
Maid (General Assembly) Early ldr, remained prom & regained led over 2f out, worn down cl-home: 6 wk abs: imprvd form on the this step up to 7f: acts on fibresand & on a sharp trk: runs well fresh.
2312 **BOBANVI 28** [6] J S Wainwright 2-8-8 F Norton 7/1: -54003: 2 b f Timeless Times - Bobanlyn (Dance *¾* **50a**
Of Life) Outpcd, imprvd 2f out, fin well but too late: bckd from 12/1: longer 7f trip, again fin fast: see 1019.
1805 **SWEET VELETA 49** [9] R M Whitaker 2-8-8 A Beech (5) 12/1: -344: Well bhd, styd on strongly fnl *2½* **45a**
2f, nvr nrr: op 8/1, 7 wk abs: longer 7f trip & some promise here: 1m nurs h'caps cld suit: see 1420 (6f here).
2620 **IM A CHARACTER 15** [11] 2-8-8 Dale Gibson 9/1: -005: Front rank, onepcd fnl 1½f: see 2259. *1* **42a**
2383 **ESSENCE 25** [7] 2-8-8 R Fitzpatrick (3) 20/1: -006: Struggling early, some latge hdwy but nvr *1* **41a**
dngrs: mkt drifter: dropped into sellers: little prev form.
-- **RAGING TIMES** [2] 2-8-8 A Daly 9/2: -7: Dwelt, recovered to lead 5f, wknd: debut: Mar foal, *5* **31a**
cost 1,000gns: half-sister to 6/7f juv wnr Dovebrace: with W G M Turner.
2394 **CONSPIRACY THEORY 24** [5] 2-8-8 C Lowther 14/1: 634648: Front rank 5f, wknd: op 10/1. *6* **19a**
1890 **LASTOFTHEWHALLEYS 45** [4] 2-9-0 F Lynch 11/2: -00169: Dwelt, recovered to chase ldrs 5f, wknd *17* **0a**
qckly & t.o.: 6 wk abs: twice below 1713 (gd/soft grnd).
2312 **WANNABE BOLD 28** [10] 2-8-8 Dean McKeown 16/1: -000: Al struggling, t.o. in 10th: see 938. *3* **0a**
2772 **FLOWLINE RIVER 8** [1] 2-8-8 R Price 20/1: -00: Front rank till halfway, sn well bhd & t.o. in last. *6* **0a**
11 ran Time 1m 31.5 (4.9) (Cheveley Park Stud) M L W Bell Newmarket.

2950

4.35 CLAIMER DIV II 3YO+ (F) 1m aw rnd Going 50 +02 Fast
£1729 £494 £247 3yo rec 8lb

3197} **BARON DE PICHON 357** [9] K R Burke 4-9-9 N Callan 10/1: 06-051: 4 b g Perugino - Ariadne (Bustino) Trkd ldrs going well, smooth hdwy to lead 2f out, collared dist, regained lead gamely ins last, drvn out: fair time, long abs: well btn in a couple of runs in the USA since trained by N Littmoden to win at W'hampton (3), Southwell & Lingfield (AW h'caps, rtd 84a) in '99: eff 7f/1m on both AWs: likes sharp trks, esp W'hampton: apprec this drop to claim company, sure to win more races. **71a**
2442 **RAMBO WALTZER 22** [7] Miss S J Wilton 8-9-11 R Lake(7) 4/1: 132002: 8 b g Rambo Dancer - Vindictive *hd* **72a**
Lady (Foolish Pleasure) Mid-div, imprvd to lead dist, not pace to repel wnr cl-home & just btn in a close fin.
2633 **PHOEBUS 14** [6] W R Muir 3-8-11 (t) C Lowther 10/1: -00033: 3 b c Piccolo - Slava (Diesis) *1½* **63$**
Outpcd, kept on fnl 2f, nvr nrr: rider given a 3 day whip ban: met a couple of decent AW performers: see 2633.

SOUTHWELL (Fibresand)   FRIDAY JULY 28TH   Lefthand, Sharp, Oval Track

2834 **HEATHYARDS JAKE** 6 [3] R Hollinshead 4-8-13 P M Quinn (3) 33/1: 650054: Outpcd, styd on under   3½ 50$
press fnl 2f, nvr nrr: qck reapp: offic rtd 41, treat this rating with caution: 1 win in 48 starts: see 2834.
*2816 **TROJAN WOLF** 7 [11] 5-9-9 F Norton 7/2 FAV: 000615: Front rank, led 3f out till 2f out, no extra.   2½ 55a
2673 **PRIDEWAY** 13 [4] 4-8-8 C Cogan (5) 4/1: 560006: Dwelt, mid-div halfway, onepcd fnl 2f: op 11/4.   3 34a
2134 **CONCIERGE** 35 [1] 3-8-7 G Parkin 11/2: -07: Slowly away, no ch after: mkt drifter: prev trained   9 26a
by P Cole, now with D W Chapman: see 2134 (turf, debut).
2561 **TEMPRAMENTAL** 17 [2] 4-8-10 S Finnamore (5) 7/1: 141508: Led till 3f out, wknd: gamble from 16/1:   ½ 20a
stiff task at today's weights: see 1892 (turf h'cap).
2556 **BURNING** 17 [10] 8-8-9 J Fanning 40/1: 000009: Prom 5f, wknd: '99 wnr at W'hampton (AW seller,   6 7a
rtd 61a) & Doncaster (amat h'cap, rtd 56, with N Littmoden): '98 Brighton (clmr, rtd 63) & W'hampton wnr
(seller, rtd 61a): eff at 1m/12f on gd, firm grnd & fibresand: handles a sharp or gall trk: now with B Leavy.
2767 **WICKHAM** 9 [8] 4-8-8 (BL) A Clark 33/1: /00000: Al bhd, t.o. in 10th: first time blnks.   11 0a
2506 **THE DIDDLER** 20 [5] 3-8-1 J Mackay(5) 50/1: 000000: Al struggling in rear, t.o. in last: no form.   8 0a
11 ran   Time 1m 43.3 (3.9)   (DGH Partnership)   K R Burke Newmarket.

2951   5.05 SUMMER APPR HCAP 3YO+ 0-60 (G)   2m aw   Going 50 -72 Slow   [60]
£1862   £532   £266

2763 **AQUAVITA** 9 [6] Miss K M George 6-7-10 (28)(1oh) P M Quinn 12/1: 035441: 6 b m Kalaglow - Aigua   33a
Blava (Solford) Mid-div, hdwy to lead dist, kept on well, drvn out: slow time: missed '99, '98 Lingfield wnr
(clmr, rtd 52a, with J Moore): prev term won over hdles at Hereford (seller, rtd 95h): eff at 12f, suited by 2m:
acts on gd, firm grnd & on both AWs: likes a sharp trk: v well h'capped nowadays.
2098 **PIPE MUSIC** 37 [12] P C Haslam 5-9-11 (57)(bl) P Goode 10/1: 050022: 5 b g Mujadil - Sunset Cafe   ½ 61a
(Red Sunset) Rear, imprvd 3f out, chall fnl 1f, just btn in a driving fin: fine run conceding 29lb to this wnr.
*2606 **VINCENT** 15 [7] J L Harris 5-9-7 (53) A Beech 9/2 FAV: 4-1013: 5 b g Anshan - Top Anna (Ela   ½ 56a
Mana Mou) Rear, styd hdwy fnl 3f, nrst fin: bckd from 6/1, 4L clr rem, not btn far in a close fin: in gd form.
2452 **SHARAF** 22 [2] W R Muir 7-9-4 (50) R Brisland (3) 14/1: 423044: Prom, led over 2f out till dist, onepcd.   4 48a
— **MACHALINI** [13] 7-10-0 (60)(t) S Finnamore (5) 16/1: 0030/5: Hdwy from rear 3f out, no impress fnl   5 53a
2f: top-weight: p.u. in a h'cap chase 7 wk ago: back in 98/99 won thrice over fences (rtd 110c, eff at 2m2f/3m
on fast & soft): last won on the Flat in '97, at Listowel: winning form on gd/soft & soft grnd on the Flat, fast
over fences: wears a t-strap: with R Cowell.
1867 **BLACK ICE BOY** 46 [16] 9-7-10 (28)(vis) Michael Doyle(5) 14/1: 000406: Prom, led 5f out till   shd 21a
4f out, grad fdd: bckd at long odds, 7 wk abs: flattered 1701 (turf).
2381 **MARIANA** 25 [9] 5-8-0 (32)(4ow)(7oh) C Cogan(0) 20/1: 500037: In tch, ev ch 3f out, onepcd fnl 2f.   nk 24a
2606 **STATE APPROVAL** 15 [15] 7-8-0 (32) A Polli 20/1: 060308: Prom, led 4f out till 2f out, wknd.   3½ 20a
1701 **CHARMING ADMIRAL** 54 [14] 7-8-10 (42)(bl) L Enstone (7) 11/1: 120039: Nvr a factor: 8 wk abs.   7 23a
2606 **TIME CAN TELL** 15 [1] 6-9-1 (47) R Fitzpatrick 11/2: 342030: Rear, nvr nr ldrs, fin 10th: btr 2606.   ½ 27a
2606 **STEAMROLLER STANLY** 15 [5] 7-9-10 (56) R Studholme (3) 13/2: 041220: Front rank til wknd qckly   6 30a
ent str, fin 11th: much btr 2606, 1975.
2643 **HASTA LA VISTA** 14 [10] 10-8-6 (38)(vis) J Mackay (3) 5/1: 214350: Led till 5f out, wknd into 15th.   0a
1852 **Mister Pq** 47 [8] 4-7-11 (29) N Carter(7) 25/1:   2636 **Capercaillie** 14 [11] 5-7-12 (30) D Glennon (5) 33/1:
2536 **All On My Own** 18 [3] 5-8-3 (35)(VIS) P Hanagan(5) 16/1 /2861 **Royal Dolphin** 5 [4] 4-8-2 (34)(bl) S Clancy(0) 50/1:
16 ran   Time 3m 45.6 (19.6)   (Miss K George)   Miss K M George Princess Risborough, Bucks.

ASCOT   FRIDAY JULY 28TH   Righthand, Stiff, Galloping Track

Official Going   GOOD TO FIRM (GOOD places after 4th race). Stalls: Str crse - Stands Side; Rnd Crse - Inside.

2952   2.15 CAPEL CURE MDN 2YO (D)   6f   Good/Firm 35 -07 Slow
£8112   £2496   £1248   £624

— **REGAL ROSE** [2] Sir Michael Stoute 2-8-11 J Murtagh 10/11 FAV: 1: 2 b f Danehill - Ruthless Rose   99+
(Conquistador Cielo): Settled rear, hdwy over 2f out, ran green under press appr final 1f, styd on well to
lead cl-home, rdn out: hvly bckd on debut: Mar foal, half-sister to a couple of juv scorers: dam related
to a high-class miler at 6f, sure to relish 7f: acts on fast grnd & a stiff/gall trk: runs fresh:
ran v green here (reportedly in season), highly regarded & looks potentially very smart.
2618 **MUJADO** 15 [7] B J Meehan 2-8-11 D Holland 11/4: 22: 2 b f Mujadil - Unaria (Prince Tenderfoot):   ¾ 94
Led, drvn & prsd over 1f out, hdd cl-home: nicely bckd: imprvd from debut run & sure to win in mdn company sn.
— **VELVET GLADE** [5] I A Balding 2-8-11 R Cochrane 12/1: 3: 2 b f Kris S - Vailmont (Diesis):   1¼ 90
Front rank, rdn to chall over 2f out, no extra rem last: 6L clr rem: Feb foal, half-sister to 2 wnrs in the USA:
dam 5f juv wnr: stays a stiff/gall 6f on fast grnd: v promising debut, sure to win sn.
— **BIANCHI** [6] P F I Cole 2-8-11 J Fortune 10/1: 4: Bhd, rdn/late gains, no threat: Mar foal,   6 76
half-sister to a French 2yo wnr, dam high class over mid-dists: will improve & relish 7f/1m+ in time.
— **CANOPY** [4] 2-8-11 R Hughes 12/1: 5: Prom, rdn/fdd appr final 1f: May foal, half-sister to a   1 73
useful 7f wnr, dam scored over 8.5f: should learn from experience & apprec 7f+ in time.
2598 **CLOUDY** 16 [1] 2-8-11 J Reid 20/1: 56: Not far away, rdn/wknd appr final 2f: btr 2958 (debut).   3½ 65
— **MAMEHA** [8] 2-8-11 P Robinson 10/1: 7: Handy, wknd qckly final 2f: Feb 1st foal, dam won   2 60
between 7f & 12f: can improve over further for C E Brittain.
— **FOUR LEGS GOOD** [3] 2-8-11 J Tate 33/1: 8: Dwelt, al in rear: IR 25,000 gns Apr foal, half-   6 48
sister to 4 wnrs: stiff introduction: with G Bravery.
8 ran   Time 1m 15.63 (2.53)   (Cheveley Park Stud)   Sir Michael Stoute Newmarket.

2953   2.45 BROWN JACK HCAP 3YO+ 0-85 (D)   2m45y   Good/Firm 35 -12 Slow   [84]
£12155   £3740   £1870   £935   3 yo rec 17lb

1729 **SKI RUN** 53 [11] G A Butler 4-9-5 (75) J P Spencer 12/1: 001-01: 4 b f Petoski - Cut And Run (Slip   85+
Anchor): In tch, smooth hdwy over 3f out, qcknd lead well ins last, pushed out, cosily: 8 wk abs, up in trip:
lightly rcd in '99, trained by R Johnson Houghton to win at Bath (mdn, rtd 78): eff at 11.6f, relished this
step up to 2m, further will suit: acts on fast, gd/soft & a sharp/turning or stiff/gall trk: runs well fresh:
lightly raced & fast improving, has a turn of foot & looks one to follow.
4397) **SILENT WARNING** 286 [6] Sir Mark Prescott 5-9-12 (82) M Roberts 10/1: /030-2: 5 b g Ela-Mana-Mou -   ¾ 89

918

Buzzbomb (Bustino): Keen cl-up, rdn to lead over 2f out, clr dist, hdd well ins last, not btn far: 6L clr rem on reapp: plcd on 2nd of 2 '99 starts (h'cap, rtd 83): '99 Leicester (stks), Musselburgh (h'cap, rtd 80) & Southwell wnr (2 h'caps, rtd 88+): eff at 12f/2m on fast, soft & fibresand: eff weight carrier & goes v well when fresh: lightly raced & progressive, this was an excellent return & should go one better.

2812 **LITTLE BRAVE** 7 [8] J M P Eustace 5-8-2 (58)(4ex) J Tate 10/1: 605143: 5 b g Kahyasi - Littlemisstrouble 6   **59**
(My Gallant): Cl-up, rdn/no extra over 2f out, late hdwy: qck reapp: gd run bhd two progressive sorts.

2667 **JAMAICAN FLIGHT** 14 [10] Mrs S Lamyman 7-8-4 (60) J Quinn 14/1: 065544: Led, drvn/hdd over ¾ **60**
2f out, kept on but not pace of front 2: gd effort, v tough front runner: see 253.

2812 **RENAISSANCE LADY** 7 [7] 4-8-0 (56) L Newman (3) 8/1: 011125: Dsptd lead, ev ch until not qckn ¾ **55**
final 2f: qck reapp: remains in gd heart: see 2812, 2461.

2490 **TREASURE CHEST** 20 [1] 5-8-0 (56)(vis) Martin Dwyer 16/1: 040506: Waited with, rdn to impr over 2½ **53**
2f out, late gains, no threat to ldrs: maiden, rnr-up in this race off a 19lb higher mark last term: see 1800.

2672 **RENZO** 13 [4] 7-9-9 (79) D Holland 9/1: 130127: Nvr better than mid-div: btr 2672, 2498. 1¼ **75**

2498 **DANEGOLD** 20 [5] 8-8-0 (56) Craig Williams 8/1: 454008: Rear, well bhd 5f out, rdn/late hdwy, no dngr: 2 **50**
reportedly slipped on fnl bend: out of sorts this term, now 8lb lower than when wng this race last year: see 2498.

2455 **SANDBAGGEDAGAIN** 21 [12] 6-9-0 (70) J Reid 9/2 FAV: -05529: Prom, rdn/fdd final 2f: nicely bckd nk **64**
to follow up his '98 win in this race (6lb higher today): see 2455.

2490 **SADLERS SECRET** 20 [3] 5-9-0 (70)(vis) T Quinn 9/1: 603/30: Wide, bhd, halfway, no ch after, fin 10th. 3½ **61**

*2173 **GENEROUS WAYS** 9 [4] 5-8-2 (58) T E Durcan 11/2: 054010: Dwelt, waited with, nvr dngr: nk **49**
11th: can to a lot better, won over course & distance in 2173.

*2734 **KAGOSHIMA** 10 [2] 5-8-6 (62)(vis)(4ex) O Pears 9/1: 231210: Front rank, rdn & wknd qckly final 3f, 12th. 4 **49**
12 ran   Time 3m 33.8 (7.8)   (T D Holland-Martin)   G A Butler Blewbury, Oxon.

2954	3.15 CITY INDEX RTD HCAP 3YO+ 0-95 (C)	6f	Good/Firm 35 +18 Fast	[101]

£12261 £4650 £2325 £1057 3 yo rec 51b Those low drawn held narrow advantage.

+2775 **ROYAL ARTIST** 8 [3] W J Haggas 4-8-7 (80)(3ex)(2oh) T Quinn 11/4 FAV: 126211: 4 b g Royal Academy - 93+
Council Rock (General Assembly): Front rank, rdn to lead ins last, readily went clr, pshd out: hvly bckd: recent
Leicester wnr (h'cap, impressively by 6L): prev won at W'hampton (AW h'cap, rtd 78a): '99 wnr at Lingfield (mdn,
rtd 69a & 73): half-brother to leading juv Superstar Leo: eff at 8.5f, suited by 6/7f on firm, gd/soft & both AWs:
handles any trk: fast improving & developing into a v useful performer, can win more valuable races.

2676 **CRYHAVOC** 13 [9] D Nicholls 6-9-6 (93) Alex Greaves 9/1: 202102: 6 b g Polar Falcon - Sarabah 3 **96**
(Ela-Mana-Mou): Front rank, went on appr final 2f, hdd ins last, not pace of winr: tough-as-teak sprinter.

2568 **PERUVIAN CHIEF** 17 [4] N P Littmoden 3-8-10 (88) J Quinn 14/1: 520433: 3 b c Foxhound - John's 1 **88**
Ballad (Ballad Rock): Dwelt, rear, drvn/styd on strongly over 1f out, closing fin: shld win again, poss at 7f.

2878 **AL MUALLIM** 4 [2] D Nicholls 6-9-2 (89)(t) A Nicholls (3) 20/1: 000004: Waited with, rdn to impr over 1 **86**
2f out, swtchd & styd on well ins last: qck reapp: back to form here & is on a v handy mark now: see 2878, 728.

2676 **MAGIC RAINBOW** 13 [12] 5-8-7 (80) J Fortune 9/1: 060065: Prom, drvn & not qckn appr final 1f: shd **77**
rnr-up in this contest last year (race run over 5f) off a 5lb higher mark: stiff 5f shld prove ideal now.

*2814 **ZUCCHERO** 7 [1] 4-8-7 (80)(bl)(3ex)(1oh) M Roberts 7/1: 26-616: Set fast pace, hdd over 2f out, hd **77**
wknd inside last: qck reapp: shade btr 2814 (7f).

2813 **JUWWI** 7 [10] 6-9-7 (94) Darren Williams (5) 25/1: 000007: Well bhd, rdn & styd on late, no threat. nk **90**

2568 **GLENROCK** 17 [5] 3-8-11 (89) A McGlone 14/1: 065028: Handy, drvn/no extra over 1f out, eased. 1¼ **81**

2504 **BOANERGES** 20 [14] 3-8-2 (80) P Doe 10/1: 001139: In tch, rdn/eff over 2f out, fdd fnl 1f: btr 2504. ¾ **70**

2813 **EASY DOLLAR** 7 [11] 8-9-2 (89)(bl) R Hughes 25/1: 6-6000: Waited with, rdn/modest late gains, 1¼ **76**
no threat: fin 10th: qck reapp: see 1674.

2775 **CHAMPAGNE RIDER** 8 [15] 4-8-7 (80)(2oh) J Reid 33/1: 000600: Bhd, rdn/effort when short of room ½ **66**
over 1f out, no impress: fin 11th: see 2431, 1173.

2616 **KINAN** 15 [16] 4-8-13 (86) R Hills 20/1: 0-0100: Sn outpcd, 12th: twice below 2431 (7f, soft). ½ **71**

1534 **KASHRA** 62 [18] 3-9-3 (95) D Holland 25/1: 6-4000: Settled rear, swtchd/hdwy 2f out, sn fdd, 13th: abs. ½ **79**

*2660 **UNDETERRED** 14 [6] 4-9-3 (90) R Mullen 12/1: 036410: Nvr dngr, fin 14th: much btr 2660 (stks). ½ **73**

*2845 **CADEAUX CHER** 6 [8] 6-8-8 (81)(3ex) R Cochrane 8/1: 200010: V unruly & reared up in stalls, 0
bhd, short of room & btn 2f out, eased, 17th: boiled over in stalls & lost race there.

2676 **Lone Piper** 13 [17] 5-8-7 (80)(tvi)(2oh) P Robinson 33/1:
2660 **The Fugative** 14 [13] 7-8-11 (84) I Mongan (5) 20/1:
2697 **Central Coast** 13 [7] 4-8-7 (80)(3oh) J Tate 25/1:
18 ran   Time 1m 14.14 (1.04)   (Tony Hirschfeld)   W J Haggas Newmarket.

2955	3.50 OCTOBER CLUB HCAP 3YO 0-90 (C)	1m2f	Good/Firm 35 -33 Slow	[92]

£8307 £2556 £1278 £639

*2666 **PEDRO PETE** 14 [2] M R Channon 3-8-9 (73) Craig Williams 9/1: 143311: 3 ch g Fraam - Stride Home 77
(Absalom): In tch, hdwy to chall 4f out, led briefly 2f out, rdn to lead again well inside last, drvn out, gamely:
jockey received a 3-day whip ban: earlier won at Lingfield (AW h'cap, rtd 69a) & Chester (h'cap): suited by 10f,
12f should suit: acts on fast/firm & equitrack: handles sharp & genuine gelding.

2750 **IMPERIAL ROCKET** 9 [8] R Hannon 3-9-6 (84) Dane O'Neill 7/2 FAV: 460022: 3 br c Northern Flagship - 1 **87**
Starsawhirl (Star de Naskra): Waited with, gd hdwy to chall over 4f out, went on 2f out, hdd well inside
last, no extra: another gd run, deserves to get his head in front: see 2750, 912.

*2086 **TARABAYA** 37 [6] Sir Michael Stoute 3-9-7 (85) J Murtagh 4/1: -613: 3 b f Warning - Tarakana nk **88**
(Shahrastani): Rcd keenly in tch, imprvg when hung right 2f out, kept on final 1f, closing at fin: lightly
rcd & this was an imprvd run on h'cap bow, stays 10f: fine run under top-weight: see 2086.

2666 **GOLDEN CHANCE** 14 [9] M Johnston 3-9-0 (78) J Reid 10/1: 221304: Front rank, hmpd/dropped 2 **77**
rear over 4f out, eff & short of room again over 1f out, kept on ins last: rate higher: see 2159.

1779 **NEVER DISS MISS** 51 [7] 3-8-12 (76) R Hills 10/1: -51325: Waited with, ran on late, nvr shd **75**
dangrs: 7 wk abs: shld do better: see 1448.

*2645 **SPORTING GESTURE** 14 [10] 3-8-6 (70) M Roberts 8/1: -00016: Prom, lost plc 4f out, sn 2½ **65**
detached, late run under quiet ride: strange run, his jockey is not as strong as he used to be: made most in 2645.

2710 **AMJAD** 12 [5] 3-8-5 (69) P Robinson 20/1: 504557: Bhd, rdn/prog 4f out, held fnl 2f: see 1377, 789. ½ **63**

2567 **QUEENS BENCH** 17 [11] 3-9-5 (83) R Cochrane 16/1: 1-4058: Prom, went on over 4f out, hdd 2f 7 **67**
out, sn btn & eased: big step up in trip & probably not 10f: see 954.

2666 **MYTHICAL KING** 14 [4] 3-9-5 (83) T Quinn 6/1: 331429: Led, hdd 4f out, ev ch until wknd qckly fnl 2f. 6 **59**

2358 **LET ALONE** 26 [1] 3-9-1 (79) J Fortune 16/1: 0100: Bhd, nvr dngrs, 10th: again disapp on fast grnd. 1 **53**
10 ran   Time 2m 10.82 (6.82)   (Peter Taplin)   M R Channon West Isley, Berks.

2956   **4.25 EBF MDN 2YO (D)**   **7f str**   Good/Firm 35   -16 Slow
£6825   £2100   £1050   £525

2598 **RED MAGIC** 16 [1] R Hannon 2-9-0 R Hughes 9/4 FAV: 21: 2 b c Grand Lodge - Ma Priere (Highest Honor): **97+**
Front rank, smooth hdwy to lead over 1f out, rdn clr final 1f, readily: up in trip, well bckd: earlier rnr-up on
debut (stks): cost 700,000 Ffr: dam a wnr in France: sire 1m/10f performer: eff at 6f, relished this step up to
7f: acts on fast & a stiff/gall trk: smart run here & looks sure to win in List/Group company in time.

2613 **GRYFFINDOR** 15 [10] B J Meehan 2-9-0 M Tebbutt 8/1: 302: 2 b c Marjun - Hard Task (Formidable): 4 **87**
Cl-up, led appr final 2f, hdd over 1f out, kept on but not pace of cmftble wnr: op 6/1: caught a tartar, imprvd
yet again & will win in mdn company sn: eff at 7f on fast: see 2346.

2563 **WOODFIELD** 17 [5] C E Brittain 2-9-0 B Marcus 20/1: 03: 2 b c Zafonic - Top Society (High Top): 1 **85**
Led, hdd appr fnl 2f, held when no room fnl 1f: eff at 7f on fast: imprvd run here, win a mdn sn: see 2563.

-- **BORDER COMET** [9] Sir Michael Stoute 2-9-0 J Murtagh 13/2: 4: Dwelt, settled last: rdn/hdwy 2f out, ¾ **84+**
styd on under hands-&-heels appr final 1f: op 4/1 on debut: Jan foal, half-brother to useful 1m juv Interlude,
dam scored over 7f/1m: eye-catching debut & not given a hard time here, sure to win similar & apprec 1m.

-- **MORSHDI** [8] 2-9-0 P Robinson 20/1: 5: Front rank, rdn/not qckn final 2f: Mar foal, dam related 3 **80**
to a high-class sprinter, sire won Derby: should impr at 1m in time for M A Jarvis.

-- **WANNABE AROUND** [7] 2-9-0 T Quinn 20/1: 6: Trkd ldrs, drvn/outpcd final 2f: 70,000gns half- hd **79**
brother to smart 10f h'capper Nobelist, dam scored over 10f abroad: will need 1m+ in time: with T G Mills.

-- **TAABEER** [2] 2-9-0 R Hills 6/1: 7: Dwelt, rear, effort 2f out, no dngr: Caerleon Mar foal, half 1¼ **77**
-brother to a useful juv, dam scored over 6/7f: with E Dunlop, will improve in time.

-- **COMPTON COMMANDER** [6] 2-9-0 D Holland 9/1: 8: Waited with, no hdwy final 2f: 56,000gns 2 **73**
half-brother to sev wnrs: dam a 1m/10f wnr: with G A Butler.

-- **CHANGING SCENE** [3] 2-9-0 R Cochrane 10/1: 9: Front rank, rdn/wknd qckly final 2f: Jan foal, 2 **69**
half-brother to a 7f 2yo scorer, dam a 6f wnr: with I A Balding.

-- **HILL COUNTRY** [4] 2-9-0 J Fortune 9/2: 0: Veered left leaving stalls, nvr dngr: fin 10th: market ¾ **68**
drifter from 7/4: May foal, half-brother to Derby wnr Dr Devious: dam related to a high-class middle dist
rnr: with J H M Gosden & surely capable of better, should learn from this.

-- **ASTRAL PRINCE** [11] 2-9-0 D R McCabe 25/1: 0: Dwelt, al bhd, fin last: IR65,000 gns Efisio colt. ½ **67**

11 ran   Time 1m 29.58 (3.58)   (Terry Neill)   R Hannon East Everleigh, Wilts.

2957   **5.00 CITY INDEX MDN 3YO+ (D)**   **1m2f**   Good/Firm 35   -30 Slow
£6678   £2055   £1027   £513   3 yo rec 10lb

-- **SAVOIRE VIVRE** [1] J H M Gosden 3-8-11 J Fortune 8/11 FAV: 1: 3 b c Sadler's Well - Oh So Sharp **100+**
(Kris): Dwelt, settled rear, smooth hdwy to chall halfway, went on over 1f out, pushed clr despite running green
inside last, veered left cl-home: hvly bckd on debut: related to sev wnrs: eff at 10f, sure to apprec 12f+ in
time: acts on fast grnd & a stiff/gall trk: has plenty of scope & should improve bundles, potentially smart colt.

2116 **PURPLE HEATHER** 36 [2] R Hannon 3-8-6 (bl) Dane O'Neill 3/1: -25302: 3 b f Rahy - Clear Attraction 4 **85**
(Lear Fan): Front rank, went on over 2f out, hdd appr final 1f, not pace of cmftble wnr: shld win a mdn.

4477} **BADR RAINBOW 280** [5] M A Jarvis 3-8-11 P Robinson 9/1: 0042-3: 3 b c Rainbow Quest - Baaderah 2 **87**
(Cadeaux Genereux): Settled rear, rdn to impr 2f out, keeping on when no room over 1f out, no impress:
reapp: rnr-up on final '99 start (nursery, rtd 89 at best): eff at 1m, this 10f trip & further will suit
in time: acts on soft grnd, handles fast: just sharper for this.

1692 **POLAR STAR 55** [6] C F Wall 3-8-11 R Mullen 20/1: 02-04: Dwelt, bhd, rdn/hdwy appr final 1f, no ½ **86$**
threat to ldrs: rnr-up on 2nd of 2 '99 starts (mdn, 50/1, rtd 86): bred to apprec this 10f trip & further this term.

2553 **PHANTOM RAIN** 18 [4] R Hills 6/1: 025: Led, hdd appr fnl 2f, wknd tamely fnl 1f. 1¾ **78**

2703 **TAW PARK** 12 [3] 6-9-7 G Sparkes (7) 33/1: -56: Prom, wknd qckly final 2f: highly tried: btr 2703. 15 **63**

6 ran   Time 2m 10.48 (6.48)   (Sheikh Mohammed)   J H M Gosden Manton, Wilts.

NEWMARKET (July)   **FRIDAY JULY 28TH**   Righthand, Stiff, Galloping Track

Official Going   GOOD/FIRM (GOOD places). Stalls: 10f & 12f - Stands Side; Rem - Centre.

2958   **6.15 LADY RIDERS HCAP 3YO+ 0-75 (E)**   **1m2f**   Good/Firm 40   -42 Slow   **[47]**
£3893   £1198   £599   £299   3yo rec 10lb

2655 **BRIERY MEC** 14 [12] H J Collingridge 5-9-12 (45) Miss A L Hutchinson(7) 12/1: 015031: 5 b g Ron's **48**
Victory - Briery Fille (Sayyaf): Waited with, imprvd 4f out, styd on well to lead ins fnl 1f, pushed out: earlier
won at Brighton (h'cap): plcd in '99 (rtd 43): eff at 10f on fast & soft grnd: handles any trk & runs well fresh.

2118 **ROFFEY SPINNEY 36** [8] C Drew 6-9-13 (46) Miss Michelle Saunders(7) 50/1: 06-002: 6 ch g Masterclass nk **48**
- Crossed Line (Thatching): Set pace 6f, remnd prom, regained lead dist till ins last, just btn in a cl fin: stays
a stiff 10f well: likes to run-up with the pace & a fine effort here: see 1603.

2689 **SILENT SOUND** 13 [4] Mrs A J Perrett 4-10-6 (53) Miss L J Harwood (7) 9/1: 400253: 4 b g Be My Guest - ¾ **53**
Whilst Awhile (Caerleon): In tch, kept on under press fnl 1f, not btn far: consistent performer: see 2689, 2387.

2727 **MINJARA 10** [1] Derrick Morris 5-9-3 (36)(10h) Miss S Vickery 16/1: -55004: Rcd keenly & prom, ev ch ent ½ **35**
final 1f, not btn far in a cl fin: remains a mdn after 17 races: see 1331.

2689 **PHEISTY** 13 [16] Mrs E J Houghton 7/1: -54165: Chsd ldrs, onepace final 1f: just btr 2387. ¾ **71**

2638 **GOLD BLADE** 14 [11] 11-9-7 (40) Mrs L Pearce 16/1: 400546: Waited with, imprvd 2f out, nrst fin. ¾ **35**

2626 **PENNYS FROM HEAVEN** 15 [17] 6-10-8 (55) Miss J Ellis(5) 5/1 FAV: 412457: Waited with, short of room ½ **49**
2f out, swtchd & fin well, not much luck in running here: see 2309, 2139.

2802 **SILVER SECRET** 7 [3] 6-9-13 (46) Miss E J Jones 10/1: 516068: Chsd ldrs, outpcd 3f out, rallied fnl 1f. ¾ **38**

2347 **SYLVA LEGEND** 27 [10] 4-11-7 (68)(tvi) Mrs C Williams 8/1: 560339: Rcd keenly in bhd ldrs, led shd **60**
3f out till dist, no extra: top weight: see 2347, 1364.

2372 **EIGHT** 25 [15] 4-11-1 (62)(vis) Miss Joanna Rees (7) 16/1: -03540: Chsd ldrs, rdn & btn final 1f: 10th. nk **53**

2790 **CAPTAIN MCCLOY** 8 [5] 5-9-9 (42)(bl) Mrs S Bosley 12/1: -63330: Rear, eff 3f out, no impress: 11th. hd **33**

4020} **RAINSTORM 312** [9] 5-9-9 (42) Mrs S Owen (5) 40/1: 0000-0: Rcd keenly rear, imprvg & swtchd 2f nk **32**
out, btn final 1f: fin 12th, belated reapp: with E J O'Neill in '99, 4th in an AW h'cap (rtd 74): '98 Lingfield
wnr (AW mdn, with C Dwyer, rtd 69a): eff at 7f/1m on equitrack, handles a sharp trk, has tried a visor.

2540 **RED CANYON** 18 [6] 3-10-6 (63) Mrs G Bell (5) 7/1: 412340: Prom 1m, wknd into 14th: much btr 2238.   0
2552 **Sheer Face** 18 [2] 6-10-8 (55) Mrs C Dwyer(7) 14/1: 2323 **Full Egalite** 27 [14] 4-9-10 (43) Miss L Sheen(5) 14/1:
1647 **Roman Reel** 56 [7] 9-9-3 (36)(t)(3oh) Mrs J Moore 40/1:
562 **Love Diamonds** 157 [13] 4-10-2 (49) Miss L Johnston (5) 33/1:
17 ran   Time 2m 10.09 (8.19)   (N H Gardner)   H J Collingridge Exning, Suffolk.

2959   6.45 C HEIDSIECK EBF NOV STKS 2YO (D)   6f str   Good/Firm 40   -34 Slow
£4290   £1320   £660   £330   Slow run race

1774 **RASOUM** 51 [2] E A L Dunlop 2-8-12 T Quinn 1/1 FAV: -31: 2 gr c Miswaki - Bel Ray (Restivo)   88+
Rcd keenly rear, improving when hmpd dist, qcknd to lead ins fnl 1f, cmftbly: 7 wk abs, val for 4L+: $50,000
half-brother to 7f 2yo wnr Qamous: acts on gd & fast grnd, handles a stiff/gall trk:
showed a decent turn of foot today, runs well fresh: can progress further & win a more races.
1954 **KNOCK** 43 [4] R Hannon 2-9-2 J Fortune 7/1: -4152: 2 b c Mujadil - Beechwood (Blushing Groom)   1   80
Front rank, rdn to lead ins fnl 1f, not pace to repel wnr cl-home: 6 wk abs: met an above average rival here.
*2717 **AMEN CORNER** 11 [1] M Johnston 2-9-5 D Holland 9/4: -413: 2 ch c Mt Livermore - For All Seasons   nk   82
(Crafty Prospector) Trkd ldrs, ev ch ent fnl 1f, kept on well: 4L clr rem: sound run in this better grade: see 2717.
2687 **FOLEY MILLENNIUM** 13 [5] M Quinn 2-9-0 J Quinn 7/1: 55134: Led till ins fnl 1f, no extra.   4   65
-- **GAY CHALLENGER** [3] 2-8-8 W Ryan 20/1: -5: Waited with, outpcd by ldrs fnl 2f on debut: May foal,   7   39
brother to wnrs over 6f & 1m: sire a smart 7f performer: with N Callaghan.
5 ran   Time 1m 15.43 (4.43)   (Khalid Ali)   E A L Dunlop Newmarket.

2960   7.15 SAWSTON COND STKS 3YO+ (C)   5f str   Good/Firm 40   +11 Fast
£6426   £2437   £1218   £554   3yo rec 4lb

2496 **LORD KINTYRE** 20 [4] B R Millman 5-8-8 M Roberts 13/8 FAV: 244021: 5 b g Makbul - Highland Rowena   107
(Royben) Prom, led well ins fnl 1f, drvn out: gd time, first win for 3 yrs: unplcd dsch '99 starts, reportedly
broke blood vessels: plcd sev times in '98 (rtd 109 when 3rd in Gr 3 Kings Stand): '97 wnr at Windsor & Newbury
(val Super Sprint, rtd 112): prob best at 5f, stays 6f: acts on firm & hvy, any trk: runs well fresh: v useful.
2310 **COASTAL BLUFF** 28 [8] N P Littmoden 8-8-8 J Quinn 25/1: 502102: 8 gr g Standaan - Combattante   nk   106$
(Reform) Early ldr, remained prom, chall strongly fnl 1f & only just btn: v useful run but prob flattered.
2496 **VITA SPERICOLATA** 20 [6] J S Wainwright 3-7-13 G Bardwell 6/1: 0-2403: 3 b f Prince Sabo - Ahonita   nk   100
(Ahonoora) Waited with, prog over 1f out, short of room dist & again in last, fin well & only just btn: looked
most valuable, conserves: deserves compensation: see 1529 (Listed).
2310 **AFAAN** 28 [1] R F Marvin 7-8-8 (bl) P McCabe 16/1: 640204: Front rank, led halfway till ins last,   1   102$
no extra: offic rtd 93, so treat this rating with caution: see 1952.
2115 **SIR NICHOLAS** 36 [5] 3-9-1 J Weaver 9/4: 3-1265: Prom, outpcd dist, rallied cl-home: ran to best.   nk   112
2496 **DANCING MAESTRO** 20 [7] 4-8-8 J Fortune 16/1: 35-006: Rear, late prog, not pace to chall: see 2496. shd 101
2706 **YORKIES BOY** 12 [2] 5-9-5 D Holland 9/1: 204167: Led after 1f till halfway, fdd fnl 1f: top-weight.   3   103
1674 **SEVEN NO TRUMPS** 55 [3] 3-8-4 R Naylor (7) 3-0008: Chsd ldrs, fading when short of room   2   86
dist: 8 wk abs: tried blnks in 1674.
8 ran   Time 59.94 (1.44)   (M Calvert)   B R Millman Kentisbeare, Devon.

2961   7.45 Q103 FM HCAP 3YO+ 0-90 (C)   6f   Good/Firm 40   +00 Fast   [88]
£7670   £2360   £1180   £590   3 yo rec 5 lb

2694 **ANTONIO CANOVA** 13 [3] Bob Jones 4-8-10 (70) F Norton 14/1: 3-3001: 4 ch g Komaite - Joan's Venture   76
(Beldale Flutter) Prom, kept on to lead ins last, edged right but styd on, drvn out: in '99 plcd fnl 3 starts
(rtd 75, stks): eff at 5f, stays 6f well on fast & gd/soft: handles any track.
2761 **BAHAMIAN PIRATE** 9 [9] D Nicholls 4-9-2 (76) A Nicholls (3) 100/30 FAV: 011222: 5 ch g Housebuster 1¼   78
- Shining Through (Deputy Minister) Waited with, hdwy over 1f out, styd on well ins last, not reach wnr: in-form.
-2869 **LAS RAMBLAS** 5 [7] R F Johnson Houghton 3-9-1 (80)(VIS) D Holland 9/1: 000423: 3 b c Thatching   ½   81
- Raise A Warning (Warning) Hld up, hdwy over 1f out, kept on ins last: qck reapp & gd run in a visor.
2869 **POLES APART** 5 [4] M H Tompkins 4-9-4 (78)(t) J Fortune 20/1: 000054: Led, edged right over   1¾   74
1f out, collared ins last, no extra: qck reapp & gd run in first time visor: on a fair mark: see 2616, 1337.
*2761 **IVORY DAWN** 9 [5] 6-9-5 (79)(7ex) C Catlin (7) 10/1: 403015: Handy, onepace for press over 1f out. 1¼   71
2694 **PRESENT CHANCE** 13 [13] 6-7-12 (58)(bl) J Quinn 14/1: 050556: Waited with, eff over 1f out,   ½   49
no dngr: gd run from poor draw: see 2559, 674.
*2559 **BUNDY** 17 [10] 4-8-7 (67) A Clark 11/2: 153117: In tch, wknd fnl 1f: better expected after 2559.   1   55
2706 **BLACKHEATH** 21 [1] 4-10-0 (88) S Whitworth 20/1: 0-0008: Slow away, in tch, no impress fnl 2f.   1¾   71
*478 **CHAMELEON** 171 [12] 4-9-2 (76) T Quinn 11/2: 0/19: Dwelt, al bhd: long abs since 478 (7f, mdn).   shd   58
2934 **HUNTING TIGER** 1 [16] 3-7-13 (64) A Mackay 8/1: 005200: In tch, wknd 2f: 10th, unplcd yesterday.   2½   49
2777 **SYLVA PARADISE** 8 [6] 7-8-8 (68)(vis) P Robinson 14/1: 045030: Chsd ldr, wknd well over 1f out: 11th. hd   42
2629 **MIDHISH TWO** 15 [11] 4-8-7 (67)(t) D Harrison 16/1: 000000: In tch, btn over 2f out: 12th, out of sorts. ¾ 39
2694 **BINTANG TIMOR** 13 [18] 6-8-10 (70) L Newton 12/1: 625000: Slow away, al bhd: btr 1989 (7f), 1810.   ½   40
2944 **Billy Bathwick** 1 [14] 3-8-3 (68) J Stack 33/1:   2768 **Red Lion Gb** 9 [2] 4-9-12 (86)(BL) R Cochrane 20/1:
2347 **Brevity** 27 [17] 5-7-10 (56)(t)(3oh) J Lowe 20/1: 1953 **Ajnad** 43 [15] 6-7-10 (56)(bl)(1oh) Hayley Turner (7) 40/1:
17 ran   Time 1m 13.41 (2.41)   (The Antonio Canova Partnership)   Bob Jones Wickhambrook, Suffolk

---

2962   8.15 H&K COMMISSIONS NURSERY HCAP 2YO (D)   7f str   Good/Firm 40   -12 Slow   [96]
£5200   £1600   £800   £400

*2599 **FOREVER MY LORD** 16 [2] R F Johnson Houghton 2-8-1 (69) J Quinn 15/8 FAV: 6011: 2 b c Be My Chief -   76
In Love Again (Prince Rupert) Handy, eff for press to lead ins last, kept on, drvn out: recent wnr here at
Newmarket (seller, bt in for 19,000gns): dam sprinter: stays a stiff 7f well on fast & likes Newmarket: in form.
2468 **DENNIS EL MENACE** 21 [1] W R Muir 2-8-4 (72) D Harrison 10/1: 046432: 2 b c College Chapel -   hd   78
Spanish Craft (Jareer) Chsd ldr, eff & short of room over 1f out, styd on to chall ins last, kept on, just held
off in a driving fin: acts on fast & gd/soft & deserves a race: see 2468.
*2459 **LUNAR LEO** 21 [3] S C Williams 2-9-1 (83) G Faulkner (3) 11/4: -413: 2 b g Muhtarram - Moon Mistress 1¼   85
(Storm Cat) Set pace till collared well ins last, no extra: prob imprvd in defeat: convincing wnr in 2459 (auct mdn).
2598 **DUSTY CARPET** 16 [7] C A Dwyer 2-8-13 (81) D Holland 11/2: 6464: Cl-up, hung left 2f out,   3½   74
no extra ins last: shld stay 7f: see 2346, 1774.

NEWMARKET (July) FRIDAY JULY 28TH Righthand, Stiff, Galloping Track

*2620 **EL MAXIMO 15** [9] 2-8-9 (77) T E Durcan 9/1: 632615: Bhd, nvr a factor: rtd higher 2620 (mdn, gd). *2½* **63**
2791 **TOTALLY COMMITTED 8** [5] 2-8-12 (80) J Fortune 8/1: 03236: Sn rdn & al bhd: btr 2791. *2½* **59**
1809 **ANALYZE 49** [8] 2-8-4 (71)(1ow) T Quinn 10/1: 0357: Handy, wknd over 2f out, eased ins last: abs. *nk* **50**
1577 **IVANS BRIDE 59** [4] 2-7-10 (64)(1oh) M Baird 20/1: 0648: Slow away, al bhd: 8 wk abs: see 1577. *½* **40**
8 ran Time 1m 27.52 (3.62) (W H Ponsonby) R F Johnson Houghton Blewbury, Oxon

2963 **8.45 NGK SPARK PLUGS MDN 3YO (D) 1m4f Good/Firm 40 -56 Slow**
£4186 £1288 £644 £322

2024 **SHEER SPIRIT 40** [3] D R C Elsworth 3-8-9 (t) T Quinn 100/30: 31: 3 b f Caerleon - Sheer Audacity (Troy) Trkd ldr, hdwy to lead over 1f out, edged left but kept on ins last, drvn out: 6 wk abs: half-sister to Derby wnr Oath: relished this step up to 12f & acts on gd/firm grnd: open to plenty of further improvement. **80**
2617 **SHAIR 15** [1] J H M Gosden 3-9-0 J Fortune 10/11 FAV: 42: 3 b g Warning - Shaima (Shareef Dancer) In tch, hdwy to chall over 1f out, not pace of wnr cl-home: clr of rem & hvly bckd: ran to form of 2617 stepped up to 12f & shld find similar. *½* **84**
1404 **VARIETY 69** [5] J R Fanshawe 3-8-9 D Harrison 25/1: 03: 3 ch f Theatrical - Kamsi (Afleet) Swerved left start, bhd, eff over 2f out, sn btn: 10 wk abs: bred for mid-dists. *7* **69$**
1343 **ARDANZA 71** [2] B Hanbury 3-8-9 M Roberts 3/1: 24: Led till wknd & hdd over 1f out: 10 wk abs. *8* **57**
4 ran Time 2m 39.71 (11.51) (Mrs Max Morris) D R C Elsworth Whitsbury, Hants

THIRSK FRIDAY JULY 28TH Lefthand, Flat, Oval Track

Official Going FIRM. Stalls: Round - Inside: Straight - Stands Side.

2964 **2.05 COOPERS SELL HCAP 3YO 0-60 (F) 1m rnd Good/Firm 19 -16 Slow [59]**
£2632 £752 £376

2637 **SEND IT TO PENNY 14** [7] M W Easterby 3-9-4 (49)(bl) T Lucas 5/1: 015001: 3 b f Marju - Sparkish (Persian Bold) Keen, led after 1f, made rest, kept on inside last, driven out: no bid: earlier scored at Southwell (h'cap, rtd 54a): eff at 6f, suited by 1m on an easy track: acts on fast, fibresand & wears blinks: enjoyed forcing tactics & drop into the lowest grade. **54**
2719 **GRANITE CITY 11** [4] J S Goldie 3-9-4 (49) A Culhane 9/2 FAV: 000302: 3 ro g Clantime - Alhargah (Be My Guest) Chsd ldrs, eff to chall over 1f out, kept on ins last for press, just held: stays 1m: mdn after 17. *nk* **53**
2735 **WELCOME BACK 10** [11] K A Ryan 3-8-9 (40) P Fessey 13/2: -00553: 3 ch g Most Welcome - Villavina (Top Ville) In tch, eff & edged left over 1f out, kept on same pace: mdn: see 2735. *3½* **37**
2831 **WISHEDHADGONEHOME 7** [15] J Balding 3-8-13 (44)(vis) M Fenton 20/1: 056004: Led 1f, cl up, no impress fnl 1f: mdn after 18: see 2326, 192. *2½* **36**
2731 **PRIDE OF PERU 10** [8] 3-9-3 (48) T Williams 14/1: 0-0055: Handy, onepace over 1f out: see 3731. *nk* **39**
2884 **CITY BANK DUDLEY 4** [5] 3-9-0 (45) C Teague 12/1: 03646: Keen, handy, outpcd 3f out, late gains. *¾* **34**
2745 **BLUE SAPPHIRE 9** [9] 3-8-5 (36) Kimberley Hart 12/1: 600036: Never a factor: flattered 2745. *dht* **23**
2633 **TERM OF ENDEARMENT 14** [14] 3-8-12 (43) R Thomas (7) 16/1: 605208: Waited with, rdn & no impress over 2f out: twice below 2413 (7f). *1¾* **26**
2731 **THREEFORTYCASH 10** [2] 3-8-11 (42) K Darley 7/1: 006008: Al bhd: see 427. *shd* **25**
2932 **WHITEGATE WAY 2** [10] 3-9-7 (52) G Duffield 11/1: 00400: In tch, wknd over 2f out: 10th, quick reapp. *hd* **34**
2861 **Lady Tilly 5** [13] 3-9-1 (46) R Winston 14/1:
2839 **Aprils Comait 6** [16] 3-9-0 (45) V Halliday 16/1:
2834 **Just Good Friends 6** [6] 3-7-11 (28)(BL) J Bramhill 14/1:
2460 **Dakisi Royale 21** [3] 3-8-11 (42) G Carter 16/1:
2914 **Wee Barney 2** [12] 3-8-5 (36) P Bradley (5) 25/1:
2633 **Mikes Wife 14** [1] 3-8-0 (31) J McAuley 33/1:
16 ran Time 1m 38.2 (2.8) (Guy Reed) M W Easterby Sheriff Hutton, N Yorks

2965 **2.35 HORSESMOUTH MDN 3YO (D) 7f rnd Good/Firm 19 -01 Slow**
£3893 £1198 £599 £299

2465 **SHAAN MADARY 21** [6] B W Hills 3-8-9 M Hills 10/11 FAV: 0-021: 3 b f Darshaan - Madary (Green Desert) Made all, clr over 1f out, comfortably: val 8L+, well bckd, gd-bodied: dam 7f/1m wnr: eff over 7f/7.7f on fast & gd grnd, further should suit: has run well fresh on an easy track: going the right way. **78**
2183 **HONEST WARNING 33** [4] B Smart 3-9-0 K Darley 11/8: 42: 3 b c Mtoto - Peryllys (Warning) Soon handy, outpcd by wnr appr fnl 1f: bckd, clr rem, small, swtg: prob ran to form of 2183 & stays 7f. *5* **71**
2640 **HERMITS HIDEAWAY 14** [5] T D Barron 3-9-0 G Duffield 12/1: -533: 3 b g Rock City - Adriya (Vayrann) Prom till btn over 2f out: swtg: see 2640. *8* **57**
2443 **BREAKIN GLASS 22** [3] A Bailey 3-8-9 P Fessey 50/1: 554: Al bhd & hung right bend over 3f out. *2½* **47**
-- **BOLLIN ROCK** [1] 3-9-0 R Winston 14/1: 5: Slow away & al bhd: debut: bred to apprec 7f/1m. *2* **48**
5 ran Time 1m 24.3 (1.4) (Hilal Salem) B W Hills Lambourn, Berks

2966 **3.05 GROSVENOR STKS 2YO (C) 7f rnd Good/Firm 19 -07 Slow**
£5829 £2211 £1105 £502

2067 **BARKING MAD 22** [7] M L W Bell 2-9-2 M Fenton 11/8 FAV: 31621: 2 b c Dayjur - Avian Assembly (General Assembly) Made all, kept on well fnl 1f, pushed out: bckd tho' op 8/11: rnr-up in List contest in Italy since winning at York (mdn) & gd 6th in Group 3 Coventry: Jan foal, cost $32,000: dam smart up to 9f: stays 7f, 1m will suit: acts on firm, handles soft & a stiff or easy track: v useful, going the right way. **95**
2474 **ADJOURNMENT 21** [1] P F I Cole 2-9-2 M Hills 5/1: 0162: 2 b c Patton - Miss Cabell Co (Junction) Prom, eff over 1f out, onepace ins last: improved run on this fast grnd: should be plcd to win again, see 1988. *1½* **90**
*2784 **MAGICAL FLUTE 8** [4] M R Channon 2-8-6 K Darley 9/2: -0313: 2 ch f Piccolo - Stride Home (Absalom) Squeezed start, waited with, short of room 3f out, hdwy over 1f out, kept on ins last: padd pick, gd-bodied: stays 7f: shade unlucky & type to rate more highly: see 2784. *shd* **80**
*2639 **RIVER RAVEN 14** [5] Sir Mark Prescott 2-9-2 G Duffield 2/1: 214: Keen cl up, onepace over 1f out: well bckd, not disgraced on step up to 7f: clr rem, see 2639 (mdn). *½* **89**
2741 **EAGLET 9** [2] 2-8-11 P Bradley (5) 50/1: 000545: Prom, wknd well over 1f out: stiff task, see 2521. *5* **74**
2664 **ANTHONY ROYLE 14** [3] 2-8-11 D Allan (7) 66/1: 66: Al bhd: stiff task: see 2664. *5* **64**

2576 **FORMULA VENETTA** 16 [6] 2-8-11 R Winston 66/1: 057: Waited with, btn over 2f out: see 2333.   1   62
7 ran   Time 1m 24.7 (1.8)   (Christopher Wright)   M L W Bell Newmarket, Suffolk

2967	3.40 GROSVENOR HCAP 3YO 0-80 (D)	1m4f	Good/Firm 19	+05 Fast	[79]

£3893   £1198   £599   £299

2837 **MICKLEY** 6 [5] J D Bethell 3-9-5 (70)(vis) K Darley 15/3 FAV: 453631: 3 b g Ezzoud - Dawsha   76
(Slip Anchor) Made all, clr over 2f out, kept on, pushed out: qk reapp, gd time, bckd: '99 wnr at Musselburgh
(auct mdn) & Chester (nursery, rtd 86): eff at 1m, stys 12f well: acts on firm, soft & any trk: has run well
fresh in blnks & a visor: improved for forcing tactics & gd ride today, on a fair mark.
2752 **TWIST** 9 [3] W R Muir 3-8-11 (62) M Hills 4/1: 050502: 3 b c Suave Dancer - Reason To Dance   5   61
(Damister) Hld up, hdwy to chase wnr 2f out, no impress over 1f out: no blnks: stays 12f on gd/firm & gd/soft.
2733 **JUMBOS FLYER** 10 [4] J L Eyre 3-8-10 (61) R Winston 10/1: 462003: 3 ch c Jumbo Hirt - Fragrant   4   54
Princess (Germont) Slow away, bhd, eff over 3f out, onepace: much longer trip: see 2281.
2426 **EVE** 23 [2] M L W Bell 3-9-7 (72) M Fenton 3/1: 4234: Keen, in tch, hmpd after 3f, btn over 2f out: 5   58
big step up in trip after 2426 (1m).
2638 **GARGOYLE GIRL** 14 [1] 3-7-13 (50) J McAuley 8/1: 644555: Chsd wnr till wknd 4f out: mdn, see 2446.   9   22
2327 **SHAREEF KHAN** 27 [6] J Duffield 3-9-7 (72) G Duffield 6/1: 0-0336: Handy, wknd 4f out: btr 2327, 2056. 4   38
6 ran   Time 2m 31.5 (1.7)   (Wwwclarendon Racingcouk)   J D Bethell Middleham, N Yorks

2968	4.10 EBF RISEBOROUGH FILL MDN 2YO (D)	6f str	Good/Firm 19	-01 Slow

£3591   £1105   £552   £276

2618 **SEVEN SING** 15 [4] B W Hills 2-8-11 M Hills 1/2 FAV: 31: 2 b f Machiavellian - Seven Springs   88
(Irish River) Made all, kept on well ins last, pushed out: well bckd: Apr foal, half sister to a top-class miler:
dam high class sprint juv: eff at 6f, 7f should suit: handles gd/firm: open to plenty of further improvement.
2692 **FOREVER TIMES** 13 [3] T D Easterby 2-8-11 K Darley 9/4: 362: 2 b f So Factual - Simply Times   2   79
(Dodge) Prom, rdn & ev ch 2f out, not pace of wnr in last: op 5/1: caught a fair sort & should win a race.
--   **SUMMERHILL PARKES** [5] A Berry 2-8-11 G Carter 3/1: 3: 2 b f Zafonic - Summerhill Spruce   4   67
(Windjammer) Dwelt, sn in tch, outpcd over 2f out, mod late gains: debut, padd peck: April foal: half sister
to num winning sprinters: dam 6f wnr: bred to win races over sprint trips: with A Berry.
--   **FERNDOWN** [2] Denys Smith 2-8-11 R Winston 33/1: 4: Slowly away, al bhd on debut: April foal,   9   41
cost 15,000gns: half sister to a 6f juv wnr: dam 7f juv scorer: needed this race.
--   **LAS LLANADAS** [1] 2-8-11 G Duffield 16/1: 5: Slow away, al bhd: debut, swtg, boiled over   2   35
before race, cost 2,800gns: half sister to a useful 1m wnr: with T D Barron.
5 ran   Time 1m 10.7 (1.2)   (K Abdulla)   B W Hills Lambourn, Berks

2969	4.45 GROSVENOR FILL HCAP 3YO+ 0-80 (D)	6f str	Good/Firm 19	+01 Fast	[70]

£2694   £2694   £634   £317   3 yo rec 5 lb

+2364 **CARRIE POOTER** 25 [4] T D Barron 4-9-9 (65)(bl) G Duffield 5/1: 000011: 4 b f Tragic Role - Ginny   70
Binny (Ahonoora) Dsptd lead throughout, kept on well for press mistk late, dead-heated with Dominelle: op
7/1: recently won at Pontefract (fill h'cap) & Southwell (reapp, rtd 75a): '99 wnr at Southwell & Hamilton
(h'caps, rtd 72a & 72): '98 Redcar wnr: suited by 6/7f, stays 1m: acts on fast, hvy & fibresand: handles
any trk & eff with/without blnks: has run well fresh under big weights: tough & genuine.
2732 **DOMINELLE** 10 [7] T D Easterby 8-8-4 (46) P Fessey 10/1: 404061: 8 bm Domynsky - Gymcrak   dht   51
Lovebird (Taufan) With ldr throughout, kept on for press fnl 1f, dead-heated: '99 rnr up (rtd 66): in '98 won
at Doncaster (fill h'cap), Pontefract, Redcar & Ripon (h'caps, rtd 69): eff at 5/6f, just stays 7f: acts on
firm, gd/soft & any track: likes a stiff fin & best without blnks: well h'capped.
2775 **LUANSHYA** 8 [5] R M Whitaker 4-9-10 (66) G Carter 7/1: 540003: 4 b f First Trump - Blues Indigo   2½   64
(Music Boy) Slow away, soon in tch, eff over 1f out, not pace of front 2: good run under a big weight: see 1514.
2701 **BOLLIN RITA** 12 [8] T D Easterby 4-9-3 (59) K Darley 5/2 FAV: 000204: Prom, onepace over 1f out. ½   56
2612 **CRYSTAL LASS** 15 [1] 4-7-12 (40) J Bramhill 12/1: 500505: Bhd, eff over 1f out, btn when short of   hd   36
room inside last: op 14/1: btr 2320, 513.
2728 **CRUSTY LILY** 10 [10] 4-8-3 (45) Claire Bryan (5) 9/1: 042006: Nvr dngrs: op 7/1: see 2415.   1   38
2632 **MUJAGEM** 14 [9] 4-8-3 (45) T Lucas 10/1: 146027: Bhd, brief eff over 1f out, no extra: btr 2632.   ¾   36
*2796 **MOUNT PARK** 5 [3] 3-8-3 (50)(bl) (6ex) Kiberley Hart 10/1: 000018: With ldrs till wknd over 1f out. 1¼   38
2796 **NAISSANT** 7 [6] 7-8-12 (54) A Culhane 9/1: 353129: Wknd 2f out, short of room in last: btr 2796.   hd   40
2775 **COUNTESS PARKER** 8 [2] 4-8-10 (52) T Williams 20/1: 4-0000: Dwelt, sn in tch, wknd over 1f out: last. 3   30
10 ran   Time 1m 10.6 (1.1)   (Stephen Woodall)   T D Barron Maunby, N Yorks

2970	5.15 LEVY BOARD APPR HCAP 3YO+ 0-70 (E)	1m rnd	Good/Firm 19	-17 Slow	[61]

£2801   £862   £431   £215   3 yo rec 8 lb

2735 **NOBLE PASAO** 10 [3] Andrew Turnell 3-9-10 (65) R Thomas 4/1: 305531: 3 b g Alzao - Belle Passe   70
(Be My Guest) Made all, kept on well inside last, drvn out: plcd earlier this term: sole prev win in '99, at
Musselburgh (nursery, rtd 73): suited by 1m/8.5f on firm, gd & fibresand: best without blnks & handles
any track: can carry big weights: enjoyed dominating today & a fine run conceding weight to elders.
2865 **TAKER CHANCE** 5 [6] J Hetherton 4-8-6 (39) T Hamilton 12/1: 006062: 4 b g Puissance - Flower   2   40
Princess (Ahonoora) Chsd ldrs, eff to chase wnr 2f out, onepace ins last: stays 1m: see 907.
2875 **THORNTOUN GOLD** 4 [2] J S Goldie 4-9-2 (49) Dawn Rankin (3) 7/2 FAV: 010023: 4 ch f Lycius - Gold   1   48
Braisim (Jareer) Handy, hit rail after 3f, kept on same pace over 1f out: should rate higher: see 2875, 2180.
2658 **DANZAS** 14 [7] J M Bradley 6-8-12 (45)(bl) D Allan 7/1: 262504: Slow away, late gains: see 2099.   nk   43
1002 **SHAMSAN** 95 [9] 3-9-7 (62) Carrie Sanderson (8) 15/2: 103205: Chsd wnr, onepace over 1f out: ½   59
needed this race after 3 month abs: see 709 (AW).
2834 **BY THE GLASS** 6 [4] 4-7-11 (30) Giorgia Lamberti 25/1: -60006: Slow away, bhd, some late gains.   2   23
2861 **KUWAIT THUNDER** 5 [5] 4-7-13 (32)(vis) M Mathers 7/1: 005057: Slow away, nvr a factor: 1360.   1   23
2601 **PIPIJI** 15 [8] 5-7-11 (30) Stephanie Hollinshead 12/1: -00048: Never a factor: btr 2601.   1½   18
2907 **HI MUJTAHID** 3 [11] 6-7-11 (30)(5oh) D Watson 7/1: -00029: Al bhd: btr 2907.   13   0
2611 **NIP IN SHARP** 15 [10] 7-9-8 (55) L Gueller 25/1: 45/00: Slow away, al bhd: 10th: see 2611.   4   17
2753 **CARMARTHEN** 9 [1] 4-8-11 (44) M Worrell 33/1: 000000: In tch, wknd 2f out, last: see 2223 (5f).   11   0
11 ran   Time 1m 38.3 (2.9)   (Mrs Claire Hollowood)   Andrew Turnell Sandhutton, N Yorks

Official Going: FIRM (GOOD TO FIRM IN PLACES) Stalls: Str course - stands side, Rnd course - inside

---

2971	6.25 LYSAGHT AMAT HCAP 3YO+ 0-70 (F)	1m4f	Good/Firm 31	-38 Slow	[27]
	£2992 £855 £427	3 yo rec 12lb			

2727 **OUT ON A PROMISE** 10 [1] B J Meehan 8-11-0 (41) Miss J Allison 5/1: 64/001: 8 b g Night Shift - **46**
Lovers' Parlour (Beldale Flutter) Led after 1f & clr halfway, rdn & styd on well fnl 2f, al holding rivals: prev with
C Mann, 99/00 jumps wnr at Stratford, Bangor & Sandown (h'caps, rtd 132h, eff at 2m/2m3f): last rcd on the Flat
in '98 (rtd 55, clmr, L Lungo): stays 12f on firm & gd/soft, any track: given a good positive ride tonight.

2442 **DESERT VALENTINE** 22 [2] L G Cottrell 5-11-1 (42) Mr L Jefford 12/1: 050-02: 5 b g Midyan - Mo Ceri 1½ **44**
(Kampala), Rear, hard rdn/chsd wnr over 1f out, kept on: stays 12f: acts on fast & gd/soft: see 2442.

2689 **ROYAL AXMINSTER** 13 [13] Mrs P N Dutfield 5-10-13 (40) Miss C Stretton (5) 14/1: 004003: 5 b g 1 **41**
Alzao - Number One Spot (Reference Point) Led 1f, chsd wnr, rdn/held 1f out: clr rem: stays 12f, tried 2m+.

1 **HAYDN JAMES** 263 [5] P J Hobbs 6-11-10 (51) Mr A Bateman (7) 7/1: 2326-4: Rear, late gains, no 6 **43**
threat: jumps fit, earlier scored at Hereford (nov) & N'Abbot (h'cap, rtd 96h at best): plcd numerous times in '99
(rtd 63a & 53, h'caps, P Harris): '98 wnr at Nottingham, Windsor & W'hampton (h'caps, rtd 60a & 56): suited by 10f/
sharp 12f on firm, gd/soft & both AWs, any track: eff with/without (blinks or vis: has run well fresh: on a good mark.

2793 **FANDANGO DREAM** 8 [9] A 4-10-11 (38) Mrs A Usher 3/1 FAV: 444135: Rear, drvn/prog to chase ¾ **29**
ldrs 2f out, soon held: see 2793, 2656.

2516 **THE LAD** 20 [6] 11-10-1 (28) Miss Hayley Bryan (7) 25/1: 000/06: Chsd ldrs, held fnl 2f: see 2516. ½ **18**
2626 **GOLD LANCE** 15 [7] 7-10-7 (34) Mr G Lewars (7) 16/1: -56007: Rear, late gains, never on terms. 1½ **22**
2556 **TAJAR** 17 [11] 8-10-10 (37) Mrs H Keddy (5) 11/2: 031038: Rear, eff 3f out, no impress: see 2109. ¾ **24**
2742 **WINSOME GEORGE** 9 [8] 5-10-13 (40) Nr N Bertran De Balanda 14/1: 004059: Al rear: changed stable. 1¼ **25**
2544 **RAYIK** 18 [3] 5-12-0 (55) Mr H Poulton (7) 14/1: 141200: Keen/chsd ldrs 9f: 10th: see 621 (AW). 5 **33**
2587 **LITTLE TARA** 16 [12] 3-9-10 (35)(8oh) Miss Sarah Jane Durman (7) 50/1: -00000: In tch 1m: 11th. 16 **0**
2689 **ANOTHER BEVELED** 13 [10] A 5-11-2 (43) Mr A Quinn (5) 7/1: 50/04U: Bhd/saddled slipped & u.r ins last. **0**
1023 **JANE ANN** 95 [4] 4-11-1 (42) Miss S Arnold (7) 16/1: 200-0R: Unruly start, refused to race: jumps fit, **0**
mod form: '99 Lingfield wnr (auct mdn, rtd 52a, A P Jarvis, rnr up on turf, rtd 50): eff at 10/13f on firm, gd & both AWs.

13 ran   Time 2m 39.4 (8.3)   (Mrs Lynsey Le Cornu)   B J Meehan Upper Lambourn, Berks

---

2972	6.55 LUNDY ISLAND AUCT MDN 2YO (E)	6f str	Good/Firm 31	+04 Fast	
	£2824 £807 £403				

2649 **RED CARPET** 14 [7] M L W Bell 2-8-7 J P Spencer 11/10 FAV: 251: 2 ch c Pivotal - Fleur Rouge **82**
(Pharly) Cl up, went on over 2f out, readily asserted fnl 1f, pushed out: gd time: eff at 6f, stays 7f & return to
that trip could suit: acts on fast grnd & a gall/undul track: open to further improvement.

-- **SCOTISH LAW** [4] P R Chamings 2-8-5 S Righton 33/1: 2: 2 ch g Case Law - Scotia Rose (Tap 1¾ **74**
On Wood) Rdn/bhd, prog to chase wnr over 1f out, styd on, al held: March foal, cost 10,000gns: dam a
Irish 3yo 12f wnr: stays 6f, 7f sure to suit: acts on fast grnd & a gall/undul track: encouraging.

2808 **PRINCE MILLENNIUM** 7 [8] R Hannon 2-8-10 R Smith (5) 6/1: -563: 2 b c First Trump - Petit Point 1½ **75**
(Petorius) Chsd ldrs, rdn/held over 1f out: eff at 6f on fast grnd: see 1221.

2550 **WINFIELD** 18 [10] C G Cox 2-8-7 S Sanders 40/1: 04: Chsd ldrs, onepace 1f out: better run. ¾ **70**
2657 **SHINING OASIS** 14 [9] 2-8-5 D Sweeney 10/1: -435: Led till over 2f out, fdd: see 2657, 2083. shd **68**
2454 **SHIRAZI** 21 [2] 2-8-5 M Henry 6/1: 56: Dwelt, sn in tch, rdn/btn 2f out: see 2454. ½ **66**
2419 **QUEEN SPAIN** 23 [3] 2-8-2 Craig Williams 5/1: 022227: Chsd ldrs over 2f out, sn held: see 2125. 2 **58**
2361 **ALQUID NOVI** 25 [1] 2-8-0 G Baker (5) 7/1: 348: In tch, btn over 2f out: see 2010. 1¼ **53**
-- **BOISDALE** [6] 2-8-7 K Dalgleish (5) 20/1: 9: Chsd ldrs 4f: Common Grounds Colt, March foal, 6 **49**
cost IR22,000gns: dam a mdn, sire a high class juvenile: with G Bravery.

2635 **TONY DANCER** 14 [5] 2-8-5 D O'Donohoe 50/1: 00: Sn well bhd: no form. dist **0**

10 ran   Time 1m 10.4 (1.6)   (Cheveley Park Stud)   M L W Bell Newmarket, Suffolk

---

2973	7.25 GORDON RICHARDS HCAP 3YO 0-80 (D)	2m49y	Good/Firm 31	-16 Slow	[85]
	£5018 £1544 £772 £386				

*2672 **HIGH TOPPER** 13 [1] M Johnston 3-9-7 (78) K Dalgleish (5) 7/4: 524411: 3 b c Wolfhound - Blushing **82**
Barada (Blushing Groom) Led, hdd 3f out, led again 2f out, held on well inside last, drvn out: earlier scored at
Chester (made all, first win, h'cap): eff at 12f, a revelation stepped up to 2m: acts on firm & fast grnd, prob
handles soft ground: handles a sharp/undul track: loves to dominate: typically game & prog M Johnston stayer.

*2659 **JACK DAWSON** 14 [2] John Berry 3-8-5 (62) G Baker (5) 5/6 FAV: W25012: 3 b g Persian Bold - ½ **64**
Dream Of Jenny (Caerleon) In tch, rdn/prog to lead 3f out, hdd 2f out, kept on for press, no extra cl home.

2445 **MAZAARR** 22 [4] M R Channon 3-8-12 (69) Craig Williams 4/1: 000143: 3 ch c Woodman - River Missy 2 **69**
(Riverman) Chsd wnr, outpcd 4f out, kept on ins last, not pace to chall: prob stays 2m: see 2110 (12f).

2659 **COSMIC BUZZ** 14 [3] A T Murphy 3-7-10 (53)(13oh) M Henry 25/1: 000004: Bhd 4f out: see 1064. dist **0**

4 ran   Time 3m 35.4 (7.6)   (Maktoum Al Maktoum)   M Johnston Middleham, N Yorks

---

2974	7.55 TINTERN ABBEY HCAP 3YO+ 0-70 (E)	7f str	Good/Firm 31	+04 Fast	[64]
	£3055 £873 £436	3 yo rec 7 lb			

2749 **WHO GOES THERE** 9 [16] T M Jones 4-8-10 (46) R Price 10/1: 200301: 4 ch f Wolfhound - Challanging **52**
(Mill Reef) Dwelt/towards rear, prog from halfway & led over 1f out, styd on well, rdn out: gd time: first win:
rnr up thrice in '99 (rtd 53 & 29a): rtd 41 at best in '98: suited by 7f/9f on firm & soft grnd, handles any track.

2840 **MUJKARI** 6 [15] J M Bradley 4-8-0 (36)(vis) G Baker (5) 16/1: 004002: 4 ch g Mujtahid - Hot Curry 1½ **40**
(Sharpen Up) Rear, prog to chall 2f out, kept on inside last, al held by wnr: quick reapp: see 323.

2729 **PRIORY GARDENS** 10 [9] J M Bradley 6-8-8 (44) J P Spencer 8/1: 546103: 6 b g Broken Hearted 3 **41**
- Rosy O'Leary (Majetta) Dwelt, sn chsd ldrs & chance 2f out, kept on onepace: see 2658 (selling h'cap, 1m).

2729 **KNOBBLEENEEZE** 10 [13] M R Channon 10-8-3 (39)(vis) Craig Williams 9/2 FAV: 300524: Rear, styd on nk **35**
fnl 2f, not reach ldrs: well h'capped 10yo who relishes an easy surface: see 2729, 1462.

2437 **BEADING** 22 [6] 3-9-9 (66)(t) M Henry 13/2: 0-0025: Rear, rdn/kept on fnl 3f, no threat: see 2437. shd **62**
2728 **FLYING PENNANT** 10 [3] 7-8-5 (41)(bl) P Fitzsimons (5) 6/1: 061036: Rear, late gains, no threat. ½ **36**
2367 **MY MAN FRIDAY** 25 [1] 4-8-7 (43) O Pears 33/1: 400-07: Chsd ldrs 5f: needs mdn h'caps: see 2367. 1¼ **35**
2840 **MISS MONEY SPIDER** 6 [2] 5-8-6 (42) J P Spencer 7/1: -00008: Led over 3f out, hdd over 1f out, fdd. 2 **30**

924

CHEPSTOW FRIDAY JULY 28TH Lefthand, Undulating, Galloping Track

2749 **DOUBLE DESTINY 9** [7] 4-8-12 (48)(bl) C Carver (3) 6/1: 000039: Chsd ldrs 5f: see 2749, 1611. *nk* **35**
2689 **MAGICAL BAILIWICK 13** [12] 4-9-10 (60) Paul Eddery 20/1: 30-000: In tch 5f: 10th: topweight. *1½* **44**
2673 **ANGUS THE BOLD 13** [17] 4-7-10 (32)(VIS) Joanna Badger (7) 33/1: 00-000: Al bhd: 11th: vis. *shd* **16**
2612 **MACS DREAM 15** [8] 5-8-8 (44)(t) M Tebbutt 20/1: 05-000: Al bhd: 12th: plcd twice last term *shd* **27**
(rtd 46, sell h'cap): unplcd in '98 (rtd 55): eff around 1m on firm & fast grnd.
2489 **LUSONG 20** [19] 3-9-1 (58) R Smith (5) 9/1: 340550: Chsd ldrs 4f: 15th: see 785 (6f). **0**
1889 **Cruise 45** [11] 3-9-3 (60) Dane O'Neill 16/1: 2184 **Mister Raider 33** [14] 8-7-12 (34)(bl) D Kinsella (7) 25/1:
2255 **Berberis 30** [4] 4-7-10 (32)(BL)(4oh) K Dalgleish (5) 40/1: 1799 **Anstand 50** [5] 5-9-2 (52) F Lynch 25/1:
2704 **Espere Dor 12** [10] 3-8-0 (43)(4ow)(18oh) G Sparkes (7) 50/1:
18 ran Time 1m 21.7 (1.9) (The Rest Hill Partnership) T M Jones Albury, Surrey

2975 **8.25 LISTED DAFFODIL STKS 3YO+ (A) 1m2f36y Good/Firm 31 -03 Slow**
£12786 £4849 £2424 £1102 3 yo rec 10lb

2501 **FILM SCRIPT 20** [5] R Charlton 3-8-9 S Sanders 11/4: 611361: 3 b f Unfuwain - Success Story (Sharrood) **102**
Led, drvn/hdd over 1f out, rallied gamely for press to lead again well inside last, all out: earlier scored at Salisbury (mdn) & Lingfield (Listed Oaks Trial): suited by 10/12f on firm & gd/soft grnd, sharp or stiff track: most tough/genuine & v useful filly who loves to dominate.
2851 **CAPE GRACE 6** [3] R Hannon 4-9-5 Dane O'Neill 9/1: 615052: 4 b g Priolo - Saffron (Fabulous *nk* **101**
Dancer) Trckd ldrs, prog to chall over 2f out & drvn/narrow lead over 1f out, hdd ins last, just held: eff at 9/10f.
*2553 **DRAMA CLASS 18** [1] Sir Michael Stoute 3-8-5 F Lynch 9/2: 213: 3 ch f Caerleon - Stage Struck *3* **93**
(Sadlers Wells) Keen/chsd ldrs, rdn/wandered from over 2f out, kept on inside last, not pace of front pair: improved eff in a higher grade from this lightly raced filly, acts on fast & gd/soft: see 2553 (mdn).
1587 **DIAMOND WHITE 59** [8] M J Ryan 5-9-1 A Daly 5/2 FAV: 234564: Rear, drvn/prog over 2f out, no threat *1½* **91**
to ldrs: 2 month abs: btr 1057, 967.
*2024 **SECRET DESTINY 40** [7] 3-8-5 M Tebbutt 10/1: 33-515: Keen/held up rear, eff when no room 3f out, *nk* **90**
btn over 1f out: 6 week abs: big step up in class: see 2024 (1m, mdn).
4242} **EARLENE 300** [4] 3-8-5 (t) D O'Donohoe 4/1: -212-6: Rear, eff 3f out, sn btn: reapp: ex Irish, '99 *7* **80**
scorer at The Curragh (stks, subs rnr up in a Gr 3, rtd 101): eff at 7f/1m, mid dists shld suit: acts on soft & hvy.
2597 **GLEN ROSIE 16** [6] 3-8-5 Paul Eddery 16/1: 3-2407: Chsd ldr, btn 2f out: btr 913 (7f). *1* **79**
7 ran Time 2m 07.6 (3.5) (The Queen) R Charlton Beckhampton, Wilts

2976 **8.55 SAFFIE JOSEPH HCAP 3YO+ 0-70 (E) 5f str Good/Firm 31 -05 Slow [68]**
£3013 £861 £430 3 yo rec 4 lb

2701 **RITAS ROCK APE 12** [10] R Brotherton 5-10-0 (68) C Carver (3) 5/1: 006001: 5 b m Mon Tresor - **70**
Failand (Kala Shikari) Made all, hard rdn/strongly pressed fnl 2f, held on gamely, all out: progressive last term, won at Brighton (2, incl stakes), Bath, Lingfield & Salisbury (h'cap/appr h'caps, rtd 80): plcd in '98 (rtd 62 & 56a): best forcing the pace at 5f on firm & gd, handles gd/soft, fibresand & any trk: back on a wng mark.
2777 **BANDBOX 8** [7] M Salaman 5-9-6 (60) S Sanders 15/2: 603062: 5 ch g Imperial Frontier - Dublah *nk* **62**
(Private Account) Rear, drvn/prog from halfway, styd on well inside last, just held: gd run: best at 6f.
2840 **ECUDAMAH 6** [12] Miss Jacqueline S Doyle 4-9-4 (58)(bl) J Bosley (7) 20/1: 006403: 4 ch g *nk* **59**
Mukaddamah - Great Land (Friends Choice) Chsd ldrs, drvn fnl 2f, styd on well, just held nr fin: quick reapp.
2788 **NICKLES 8** [16] L G Cottrell 5-8-10 (50) A Daly 16/1: 00-064: Chsd ldrs, drvn/kept on onepace fnl 2f. *¾* **49**
2230 **WAFFS FOLLY 30** [11] 5-8-12 (52) R Studholme (5) 8/1: 4-0035: Chsd ldrs, one pace fnl 2f, see 1082. *nk* **50**
2732 **INDIAN BAZAAR 10** [14] 4-8-7 (47) P Fitzsimons (5) 5/1: 010056: Chsd ldrs, held fnl 1f: see 2223. *nk* **44**
2944 **SWINO 1** [9] 6-8-6 (46)(vis) Joanna Badger (7) 7/2 FAV: 000027: Dwelt/rear, rdn/styd on strongly *½* **41**
inside last, nrst fin: rnr up at Bath yesterday, gelding's performances not easy to predict: see 177.
2753 **SUNSET HARBOUR 9** [4] 7-8-6 (46) G Baker (5) 8/1: 360568: Chsd ldrs, wknd fnl 1f: see 1932. *½* **39**
1994 **MUTASAWWAR 41** [6] 6-8-1 (41) O Pears 14/1: 0-5009: Chsd ldrs 4f: 6 week abs: se 1508. *½* **32**
2432 **PARDY PET 23** [15] 3-7-10 (40)(bl) D Kinsella (7) 12/1: 6-0000: Dwelt, never a factor: see 2432. *shd* **31**
2885 **BORN TO RULE 4** [5] 3-8-13 (57) R Price 16/1: 050000: Dwelt, never a factor: unplcd last term *2* **43**
(rtd 73, mdn, prob flattered): only mod form this term.
2555 **CALANDRELLA 18** [3] 7-7-12 (38) G Sparkes (7) 7/1: 006330: Al outpcd: 12th: changed stable. *3½* **15**
2130 **Uzy 35** [8] 4-8-3 (43)(t) A Polli (3) 16/1: 2788 **Ladycake 8** [1] 4-8-0 (40) Paul Eddery 20/1:
14 ran Time 58.6 (1.8) (Mrs Janet Pearce) R Brotherton Elmley Castle, Worcs

SALISBURY FRIDAY JULY 28TH Righthand, Galloping Track, Stiff Finish

Official Going FIRM (GOOD TO FIRM places). Stalls: 10f - Inside, 12f - Stands Side, Rem - Far Side.

2977 **6.05 NEWNHAM MDN 3YO+ (D) 6f str Good/Firm 38 +03 Fast**
£3737 £1150 £575 £287 3 yo rec 5 lb

2807 **WHISTLER 7** [4] R Hannon 3-8-12 L Newman (3) 6/1: 03-241: 3 ch g Selkirk - French Gift (Cadeaux **83**
Genereux) Handy, rdn/led 2f out, held on well ins last, rdn out: rnr-up in '99 (stks, rtd 80): eff at 5/6f on fast grnd, handles gd/soft, sharp or stiff track.
1951 **MUNEEFA 43** [12] Saeed bin Suroor 3-8-7 (t) Sophie Mitchell 11/8 FAV: 22: 3 b f Storm Cat - By *¾* **75**
Land By Sea (Sauce Boat) Led 4f out till 2f out, onepace & jockey became unbalanced over 1f out: abs, do better.
2338 **KAREEB 27** [11] W R Muir 3-8-12 (BL) Martin Dwyer 8/1: -65003: 3 b g Green Desert - Braan (Gulch) *shd* **80**
Dwelt/rear, styd on from 2f out, not reach front pair: better run in first time blnks but a mdn after 10.
-- **TRUE NIGHT** [5] H Candy 3-8-12 C Rutter 4/1: 4: Keen/prom & led after 1f till 4f out, kept on *nk* **79**
onepace: debut: dam a smart juv: eff over a stiff 6f on fast grnd: gd intro.
1787 **CALLAS 50** [9] 3-8-7 S Carson (3) 25/1: 04-005: Mid-div, held over 1f out: abs, not hard time. *3* **67**
2325 **INNKEEPER 27** [10] 3-8-12 I Mongan (5) 16/1: 520066: Led 1f, cl-up till over 1f out: see 1263. *½* **70**
2472 **ASHLEEN 21** [2] 3-8-7 J Tate 33/1: 47: Chsd ldrs, held over 1f out: see 2472. *nk* **64**
961 **FARRIERS GAMBLE 101** [13] 4-8-12 D Cosgrave (7) 100/1: 0-58: Held up, nvr pace to threaten: abs. *5* **55**
-- **SECOND GENERATION** [1] 3-8-12 N Pollard 20/1: 9: Held up, nvr on terms: debut: with D Elsworth. *½* **58**
2759 **MASTER LUKE 9** [8] 3-8-12 P Cheng 66/1: 000: Mid-div, eff over 2f out, no prog: 10th: mod form. *12* **36**
1605 **AJYAAL 58** [3] 3-8-12 (BL) R Havlin 6/1: 00: Prom, fdd over 2f out: 11th: blnks, 8 wk abs: no form. *2* **31**
1886 **HARVY 45** [7] 3-8-12 A Eddery (5) 100/1: 000: Hmpd start, al rear: 12th: 6 wk abs: no form. *22* **0**

SALISBURY FRIDAY JULY 28TH Righthand, Galloping Track, Stiff Finish

12 ran   Time 1m 14.17 (2.07)   (Raymond Tooth)   R Hannon East Everleigh, Wilts.

2978
6.35 MAGDALENE FILLIES HCAP 3YO+ 0-75 (E)   7f str   Good/Firm 38 -12 Slow   [65]
£4582   £1410   £705   £352   3 yo rec 7 lb

2775 **APLOY** 8 [1] R F Johnson Houghton 3-9-7 (65) J Reid 11/2: -64451: 3 b f Deploy - Amidst (Midyan)   71
Held up, prog to lead ins last, styd on well, rdn out: first win: plcd twice last term (rtd 78 at best, mdns):
stays 1m, suited by 7f: acts on fast & gd grnd, likes a stiff/gall track.
2661 **AMORAS** 14 [3] J W Hills 3-9-10 (68) L Newman 4/1: -40042: 3 b f Hamas - Red Lory (Bay Express) nk 72
Prom, led 2f out, hdd ins last, ran on well for press, just held: gd run under top-weight: see 2661, 1125.
2690 **DAYS OF GRACE** 13 [8] L Montague Hall 5-9-2 (53) Martin Dwyer 5/1: 220053: 5 gr m Wolfhound - 1½ 54
Inshirah (Caro) Led till 2f out, no extra ins last: stays 7f well, poss just beat at 5/6f: see 466 (AW, 6f).
2555 **ADDITION** 18 [9] R J Hodges 4-9-2 (53) S Carson (3) 12/1: 60-004: Chsd ldrs, no room/switched 1f hd 53
out, kept on onepace ins last: see 1799.
2794 **MAGIC BABE** 8 [10] R J Hodges 3-9-1 (59) P Doe 3/1 FAV: 241245: Prom, fdd fnl 1f: fin lame: see 1787.   3   53
2654 **MAGIQUE ETOILE** 14 [5] R J Hodges 4-9-4 (55) J Tate 7/1: 062266: Chsd ldrs, btn over 1f out: btr 2230, 1741. 2½ 44
2804 **FLEETING FANCY** 7 [4] R J Hodges 3-8-11 (55) N Pollard 10/1: 030057: Keen/held up, nvr factor: see 2804, 1877. ½ 43
2625 **GINNY WOSSERNAME** 15 [7] R J Hodges 6-7-10 (33)(5oh) Jonjo Fowle (2) 50/1: 08: Dwelt, al bhd: see 2625. ½ 20
2680 **ROYAL TARRAGON** 13 [2] R J Hodges 4-8-5 (42) Sophie Mitchell 25/1: 09000: Trkd ldrs 5f: see 838. 2½ 24
--   **LADY JAZZ** [6] R J Hodges 5-9-2 (53)(t) I Mongan (5) 33/1: 0204/0: Held up, rdn/btn over 2f out: 10th: reapp,   4   27
long abs: missed '99: rnr-up twice in '98 (rtd 58a & 48, h'caps).
10 ran   Time 1m 29.00 (3.5)   (Mrs P Robeson)   R F Johnson Houghton Blewbury, Oxon.

2979
7.05 ST JOHN MDN 2YO (D)   6f str   Good/Firm 38 -41 Slow
£3874   £1192   £596   £298

--   **TRILLIE** [5] D R C Elsworth 2-8-9 N Pollard 11/10 FAV: 1: 2 b f Never So Bold - Trull (Lomond)   76
Cl-up, rdn/led over 1f out, held on well under hands & heels: Mar foal, cost 14,000gns: half-sister to 2 juv wnrs:
dam a mdn: eff over a stiff 6f, shld get further: acts on fast grnd & runs well fresh: op to further improvement.
--   **PROLETARIAT** [4] H Candy 2-9-0 C Rutter 5/4: 2: 2 gr c Petong - Primulette (Mummys Pet)   nk   80
Led, rdn/hdd over 1f out, kept on well, just held by wnr nr line: Mar foal, half-brother to numerous wnrs, incl
6 as a juv: dam a 5f juv wnr: eff over a stiff 6f, may get further: acts on fast grnd & a stiff track.
2708 **HELLOFABUNDLE** 12 [6] S Dow 2-9-0 P Doe 5/1: 03: 2 b g Phountzi - Hellebore (King Of Spain)   14   54
Prom till over 2f out: bhd on debut previously.
3 ran   Time 1m 16.83 (4.73)   (Sir Stanley & Lady Grinstead)   D R C Elsworth Whitsbury, Hants.

2980
7.35 WILTSHIRE SOUND HCAP 3YO 0-70 (E)   1m str   Good/Firm 38 -29 Slow   [77]
£3266   £1005   £502   £251

2795 **EVERGREEN** 8 [11] R Hannon 3-9-4 (67) R Hughes 3/1 FAV: 040021: 3 ch f Lammtarra - Nettle (Kris)   73
Settled in tch, short of room over 3f out, switched/hdwy appr fnl 1f, led well ins last, pshd out: first win:
plcd twice as a juv (rtd 85 at best), then styd 12f: eff at 7f/8.5f on fast, gd/soft & any trk.
2512 **BAJAN SUNSET** 20 [2] J D Bethell 3-8-2 (51) J Tate 9/2: 0-0622: 3 ch c Mujtahid - Dubai Lady 1¾ 52
(Kris) Waited with, rdn/gd hdwy over 2f out, kept on ins last, not pace of wnr: knocking at the door.
2795 **AEGEAN FLOWER** 8 [3] R M Flower 3-8-0 (49)(bl) P Doe 40/1: 400003: 3 b g Robellino - Bercheba hd   50
(Bellypha) Led, veered left for press over 2f out, hdd ins last, sn held: first time in the frame today, stays 1m.
2661 **SOFISIO** 12 [12] W R Muir 3-9-1 (64) Martin Dwyer 7/2: 4-0324: Waited with, rdn to chall over hd   65
1f out, no extra well ins last: see 2661.
2025 **FLYOVER** 40 [13] R Hannon 3-8-5 (54)(BL) G Hind 6/1: 00-005: Dwelt, rear, short of room when hdwy 2f ¾   54
out, styd on ins last, no threat: 6 wk abs & a better effort in first time blnks, 10f could suit: see 2025.
2679 **ALQAWAASER** 13 [5] R Havlin 12/1: 30-56: Mid-div, smooth hdwy to chall ldrs over 1f out, ¾   68
fdd ins last: h'cap bow under top-weight, see 2679 (mdn).
2661 **GOOD FRIDAY** 14 [14] L Newman 3-8-12 (61) L Newman 14/1: 656U67: Sn rdn in tch, no impress fnl 2f. ¾   58
2592 **DANCING LILY** 16 [9] R Hannon 3-7-12 (47)(2ow)(4oh) N Carlisle 12/1: 000028: Cl-up, hmpd 2f out, ev ch shd 42
till fdd ins last: up in trip & will apprec a drop back to 7f: see 2592.
2591 **MOBO BACO** 16 [8] R Hannon 3-8-2 (51) S Carson (3) 25/1: 060009: Front rank, rdn/wknd over 2f out. 2½ 46
2713 **NIGHT SHIFTER** 11 [7] W R Muir 3-9-0 (63) O Urbina 20/1: 3-0000: Mid-div at best, fin 10th: see 1397.   1   54
2025 **Golden Retriever** 40 [4] 3-8-13 (62) N Pollard 14/1:   1886 **Father Ted** 45 [6] 3-7-12 (47) C Adamson 33/1:
2294 **Marwell Magnus** 28 [10] 3-7-10 (45)(2oh) Jonjo Fowle (2) 40/1:
13 ran   Time 1m 44.51 (5.41)   (The Queen)   R Hannon East Everleigh, Wilts.

2981
8.05 DOWNING CLAIMER 3YO+ (F)   1m1f198y Good/Firm 38 +01 Fast
£2478   £708   £354   3 yo rec 10lb

2805 **WILLIE CONQUER** 7 [8] Andrew Reid 8-9-5 J Reid 5/2 JT FAV: 100101: 8 ch g Master Willie - Maryland   71
Cookie (Bold Hour) Settled rear, gd hdwy to lead appr fnl 1f, rdn out, just held on: qck reapp: earlier won
twice at Brighton (seller for D Elsworth & clmr): '99 reapp wnr again at Brighton (h'cap, rtd 88, t-stap):
suited by 10/12f on firm, gd/soft & any trk, loves Brighton: runs well fresh: tough, loves sellers/clmrs.
--   **IORANA** [12] M C Pipe 4-9-10 P Dobbs 16/1: 2: 4 ch g Marignan - Fareham (Fast Topaze)   nk   75
Dwelt/rear, rdn to lead over 2f out, styd on ins last, not btn far: Flat debut, useful hdler in 99/00, won
at Worcester & Fontwell (juv novs, rtd 120h), eff at 2m/2m2.5f on gd & soft, not hvy, sharp or gall trk):
ex-French, prev won at Auteuil (1m7f hdle, v soft): eff at 10f on fast grnd: win similar on this form.
*2920 **LAKE SUNBEAM** 2 [13] W R Muir 4-9-10 Martin Dwyer 5/2 JT FAV: -56113: 4 b g Nashwan - Moon   2   72
Drop (Dominion) Led, hdd 4f out, cl-up till not qckn well ins last: qck reapp, bold effort in hat-trick bid.
2607 **PEKAN HEIGHTS** 7 [5] P D Evans 4-9-10 (bl) R Hughes 4/1: 00-104: Front rank, rdn/fdd over   4   66
1f out: prob not stay 2m last time, see 2245.
2752 **DIVORCE ACTION** 9 [3] 4-8-13 L Newman 3) 11/2: 025005: Bhd, smooth hdwy to lead over 4f out,   4   49
edged left & hdd appr fnl 1f, wknd: see 1364 (h'cap).
2465 **ATTO** 21 [11] 6-9-7 I Mongan (5) 33/1: -06: Mid-div at best: see 2465.   9   45
2785 **HARD TO FOLLOW** 8 [10] 3-7-10 R Havlin 50/1: 00/007: Nvr dngrs: modest recent form.   ½ 30$
661   **PENALTA** 139 [9] 4-9-9 G Hind 66/1: 08: Rcd keenly cl-up, wknd qckly after halfway: long abs: turf bow.   4   33
1572 **ALBERGO** 59 [4] 3-8-9 C Rutter 25/1: 500209: Al in rear: 8 wk abs: see 1234 (AW clmr, flattered).   2   33

926

SALISBURY   FRIDAY JULY 28TH   Righthand, Galloping Track, Stiff Finish

2448 **SIGY POINT** 22 [14] 3-7-13 Jonjo Fowle (5) 66/1: 00: Prom, lost tch halfway, 10th: no form. 4 19
2689 **COSMO JACK** 13 [1] 4-9-1 (vis) Sophie Mitchell 6/1: -02500: Waited with, eff halfway, sn btn, 11th. 1½ 23
2508 **JAMPET** 20 [2] 4-8-12 (bl) N Carlisle 66/1: 000-00: Waited with, lost tch fnl 3f, t.o. in 12th: poor. 25 0
12 ran   Time 2m 08.21 (3.71)   (A S Reid)   Andrew Reid Mill Hill, London NW1.

2982	8.35 PEMBROKE HCAP 3YO+ 0-70 (E) 1m6f Good/Firm 38 -03 Slow	[70]
	£3380 £1040 £520 £260 3 yo rec 14lb	

2727 **SEA DANZIG** 10 [2] J J Bridger 7-8-3 (45) L Newman (1) 20/1: 000401: 7 ch g Roi Danzig - Tosaira (Main 51
Reef) Mid-div, drpd rear halfway, rall & ran on strongly to lead ins last, drvn out: first try at 14f: earlier
won on the AW at Lingfield (2, stks, rtd 71a): '99 wnr at Epsom (h'cap, rtd 59, unplcd on sand, rtd 68a): '98 wnr
at Lingfield (2, rtd 74a), Goodwood & Folkestone (h'caps, rtd 69): eff at 1m/10f, seems revitalised by this step
up to 14f: loves equitrack/Lingfield, eff on firm, soft, f/sand, without blnks: could win again at this trip.
*2829 **ORDAINED** 7 [8] Miss Gay Kelleway 7-8-2 (44)(6ex) Martin Dwyer 4/1: 300412: 7 b m Mtoto - In The 1 48
Habit (Lyphard) Settled rear, rdn to impr 3f out, went on over 1f out, hdd well ins last, held cl-home: clr
rem: remains in gd heart, rcd under a 6lb pen for scoring in 2829 (12f fill h'cap).
2554 **NIGHT MUSIC** 18 [9] Major D N Chappell 3-8-3 (58)(1ow) R Havlin 16/1: -05303: 3 b f Piccolo - 4 58
Oribi (Top Ville) Bhd, rdn & styd on fnl 2f, no threat to front 2: seemed to stay this longer 14f trip: see 2255.
1911 **CROSS DALL** 44 [14] Lady Herries 3-7-13 (54)(1ow) C Rutter 10/1: 100504: Rear, hdwy to chall ¾ 53
ldrs over 2f out, fdd fnl 1f: 6 wk abs: up in trip, poss gets 14f: see 1730, 1096.
2268 **HERBSHAN DANCER** 29 [10] 6-8-6 (48) G Hind 16/1: /56025: Led to over 1f out, sn wknd: btr 2268. 1 45
2461 **GOLD MILLENIUM** 21 [5] 6-8-4 (46) Sophie Mitchell 10/1: -04136: Prom, rdn/wknd fnl 2f: see 2255 (12f). 3 39
2624 **DURLSTON BAY** 15 [7] 3-7-13 (55) Jonjo Fowle (5) 16/1: -30007: Nvr btr than mdid-div: see 832. hd 48
2295 **NORTH OF KALA** 28 [6] 7-8-1 (43) P Doe 7/2 FAV: 0-1338: Rcd keenly & sn prom, ev ch till ½ 35
wknd qckly fnl 2f: longer 14f trip: see 2081, 1888.
2268 **NORTHERN FLEET** 29 [11] 7-9-7 (63) J Reid 11/2: 00-459: In tch, dropped rear after fnl 6f, no dngr after. 2 52
2552 **REAL ESTATE** 18 [4] 6-10-0 (70) I Mongan (3) 9/2: 13/320: Rear, eff 3f out, nvr dngrs: top-weight. 2 56
424 **HIGHLY PRIZED** 181 [3] 6-9-13 (69) S Carson (3) 14/1: 3-1600: Trkd ldrs, lost tch fnl 4f, 11th: long abs. 2 52
2656 **BRIGHT BLADE** 14 [1] 4-7-10 (38)(3oh) C Adamson 50/1: 000-00: Sn bhd, t.o. last: modest form. 27 0
12 ran   Time 3m 03.93 (5.83)   (P Cook)   J J Bridger Liphook, Hants.

NEWCASTLE   SATURDAY JULY 29TH   Lefthand, Galloping, Stiff Track

Official Going   GOOD/FIRM (FIRM on Rnd Crse) Stalls: Str Crse - Stands Side, Rnd Crse - Inside

2983	2.10 MORNING NEWS SELLER 2YO (G) 6f Good/Firm 33 -36 Slow	
	£1869 £534 £267 Majority raced towards centre	

2507 **MISS EQUINOX** 21 [7] N Tinkler 2-8-7 A Culhane 4/1 FAV: 502231: 2 b f Presidium - Miss Nelski (Most 61
Secret) Chsd ldrs, rdn/prog to lead 1f out, drvn out: op 7/2: no bid: 1st win: eff at 5f, suited by 6f, shld get
further: acts on firm & fast grnd: likes a stiff/galloping or undul trk: enjoys sell grade.
2605 **DANCING PENNEY** 16 [5] K A Ryan 2-8-11 J Carroll 11/2: 500122: 2 b f General Monash - Penultimate 1½ 60
Cress (My Generation) Held up, rdn/styd on fnl 2f, not get to wnr: stays 6f well: see 2605, 2435 (5f).
2730 **APORTO** 11 [4] D W Barker 2-8-12 T Williams 14/1: 003: 2 ch c Clantime - Portvally (Import) ¾ 59
Led till 1f out, onepace: op 16/1: eff at 6f on fast grnd: handles a stiff trk: only mod form at 5f prev.
2635 **LATE AT NIGHT** 15 [2] T D Barron 2-8-12 (BL) J Fanning 16/1: 0004: Rcd alone far side, cl up 5f. 1 57
2665 **FAYZ SLIPPER** 15 [6] 2-8-7 W Supple 5/1: 042455: Chsd ldrs 5f: btr 2435 (5f). 2½ 45
2773 **ECKSCLUSIVE STORY** 9 [9] 2-8-7 R Winston 7/1: -04406: Dwelt, rear/rdn, mod gains: btr 1704 (sft). ¾ 43
2218 **PICTURE MEE** 32 [10] 2-8-7 J Bramhill 11/1: 007: Cl up, btn 2f out: see 1864. ¾ 41
2772 **FAIR STEP** 9 [11] 2-8-7 J Stack 13/2: 238: Cl up, held over 1f out: op 11/2: btr 2772, 2435 (5f). 1 39
1981 **FIRST SIGHT** 43 [8] 2-8-12 (VIS) J P Spencer 14/1: -209: In tch 3f: tried a visor, 4 wk abs. 14 18
2841 **VISLINK** 7 [1] 2-8-12 N Callan 6/1: 0000: Chsd ldrs 3f: 10th: see 2430 (7f, gd/soft). 2 13
10 ran   Time 1m 15.45 (4.15)   (Contract Natural Gas Ltd)   N Tinkler Langton, N Yorks

2984	2.45 NORTHERN SPIRIT HCAP 3YO+ 0-85 (D) 1m6f97y Good/Firm 33 Inapplicable	[85]
	£4532 £1133 3 yo rec 14lb	

*2837 **ST HELENSFIELD** 7 [1] M Johnston 5-10-0 (85) J Fanning 4/5 FAV: 322011: 5 ch g Kris - On Credit (No 88
Pass No Sale) Made all, asserted dist, pushed out, readily: hvly bckd: recent Ripon wnr (h'cap): '99 wnr here
at Newcastle (h'cap, rtd 88): first try at 10/12f, now stays 14f: acts on firm & soft: gd weight carrier who can run
well fresh: eff with/without a visor: prob handles any trk: likes Newcastle: likes to force the pace.
2509 **MARAHA** 21 [2] J L Dunlop 3-8-7 (78) W Supple 10/11: 10-432: 3 ch f Lammtarra - Taroob (Roberto) 6 74
Cl up, rdn 3f out, held by wnr over 1f out & position accepted well ins last: bckd, longer 14f trip: see 2509, 1958.
2 ran   Time 3m 08.70   (Paul Dean)   M Johnston Middleham, N Yorks

2985	3.15 SLAG CEMENT MDN AUCT 2YO (E) 7f str Good/Firm 33 -08 Slow	
	£6955 £2140 £1070 £535	

-- **BRILLIANTRIO** [2] Miss J A Camacho 2-8-7 A Culhane 20/1: 1: 2 ch f Selkirk - Loucoum (Iron Duke) 80
Held up, prog to lead ins last, styd on gamely, drvn out: Feb foal, half-sister to sev mid-dist/staying wnrs: dam
a multiple US wnr: eff at 7f, sure to relish 1m+: acts on stiff/gall trk & fast grnd: open to improvement.
2588 **THATS JAZZ** 17 [9] M L W Bell 2-8-1 A Beech (5) 11/8 FAV: 022: 2 b f Cool Jazz - Miss Mercy (Law nk 73
Society) Led to ins last, battled on gamely for press, just held: hvly bckd: stays 7f well: acts on fast & gd grnd.
2290 **BOLSHOI BALLET** 29 [5] J L Dunlop 2-8-8 J Carroll 4/1: 033: 2 b c Dancing Spree - Broom Isle 3½ 73+
(Damister) Handy, outpcd 2f out, late gains: bckd, tho' op 3/1: will relish 1m nursery h'caps: see 2290.
2828 **GARDOR** 8 [1] J G FitzGerald 2-8-7 M Tebbutt 10/1: 44: Chsd ldrs 2f out, onepace: stays 7f. ½ 71
2161 **PAY THE SILVER** 35 [13] 2-8-11 N Callan 9/2: 0435: Prom, outpcd fnl 2f: bckd, op 6/1: see 2161. 3½ 68
2692 **SANDORRA** 14 [12] 2-8-2 T Williams 8/1: 06: Chsd ldrs 6f: see 2692 (6f). 4 51
-- **GHADIR** [7] 2-8-7 J Stack 20/1: 7: Dwelt, in tch 5f: Bering filly, Apr foal, cost 14000gns: a first 1½ 53
foal: dam a wnr abroad: sire top-class 12f performer: looks sure to relish 1m+ in time: with E O'Neill.

NEWCASTLE   SATURDAY JULY 29TH   Lefthand, Galloping, Stiff Track

755 CHEMICALATTRACTION 123 [8] 2-8-11 R Winston 33/1: 08: Cl up 5f: long abs, longer 7f trip.   nk 56
2718 NISAN BIR 12 [14] 2-8-8 R Ffrench 25/1: 04059: Prom, hung left/btn 2f out: see 1838 (6f).   ¾ 52
-- PRINCESS EMILY [4] 2-8-1 W Supple 25/1: 0: Outpcd early, nvr on terms: 10th: Dolphin Street   1¼ 42
filly, March foal: cost 1,500gns: with B Rothwell.
1838 Lady In Love 49 [10] 2-8-3 (BL) P Hanagan (7) 40/1: -- Premier Boy [6] 2-8-5 J Bramhill 40/1:
1704 Graceful Emperor 55 [11] 2-8-7 J Fanning 33/1:
13 ran   Time 1m 26.95 (2.85)   (Brian Nordan)   Miss J A Camacho Norton, N Yorks

2986   3.45 STANLEY HCAP 3YO+ 0-90 (C)   7f str   Good/Firm 33 +08 Fast   [87]
          £10400 £3200 £1600 £800   3 yo rec 7 lb   Raced across the track

2878 TONY TIE 5 [2] J S Goldie 4-9-12 (85) A Culhane 8/1: 102021: 4 b g Ardkinglass - Queen Of The Quorn   88
(Governor General) Rcd alone far side, al prom, drvn/led ins last, held on gamely, all out: best time of day:
earlier won at Ayr (h'cap): '99 Doncaster wnr (lady rdrs h'cap, rtd 74): '98 Salisbury (stks) & Chester wnr (nurs
h'cap, rtd 89, W Turner): eff btwn 7/10f on firm & hvy grnd, any trk: has runs well fresh: tough, well ridden.
2694 KARAMEG 14 [7] P W Harris 4-9-11 (84) A Beech (3) 7/2 JT FAV: 5-0422: 4 b f Danehill - House Of Queens nk 86
(King Of Clubs) Dwelt, held up, strong run for press fnl 2f, just held: well bckd: fine run, see 2694, 1483.
2878 SUPREME SALUTATION 5 [3] T D Barron 4-8-13 (72) J P Spencer 14/1: 620603: 4 ch g Most Welcome shd 74
- Cardinal Press (Sharood) Held up, not settle early, rdn & styd on well fnl 1f, just held: gd run with waiting tactics.
2858 KIND REGARDS 7 [1] M Johnston 3-9-2 (82) J Fanning 5/1: -05254: Al prom, rdn/onepace fnl 1f.   ½ 83
2697 PEPPIATT 14 [12] 6-8-3 (61)(1ow) R Winston 10/1: 350025: Trkd ldrs, onepace over 1f out: see 802.   ½ 62
2882 JORROCKS 5 [4] 6-8-0 (59) P Hanagan (7) 7/2 JT FAV: 010-26: Cl up, ch 1f out, no extra: hvly bckd,   ½ 58
qck reapp: btn under 2L: prob suited by easier grnd as in 2882 (reapp, gd).
2694 ITS ALLOWED 14 [10] 3-8-6 (72) W Supple 11/2: -00507: Prom, onepace/held fnl 1f: nicely bckd.   ½ 70
2704 ZIRCONI 13 [6] 4-9-3 (76) Alex Greaves 10/1: -40338: Keen/chsd ldrs 6f: see 2704, 1517.   4 66
2694 CUSIN 14 [9] 4-8-8 (67) O Pears 14/1: 305009: Held up, nvr land blow: op 20/1: see 926.   ¾ 56
2694 HAKEEM 14 [5] 5-8-4 (63) T Williams 14/1: 203300: Chsd ldrs 5f: 10th: btr 1598.   3½ 45
2645 ROBZELDA 15 [11] 4-8-11 (70) J Carroll 20/1: 644000: In tch till halfway: 11th: btr 715 (1m, gd).   ½ 51
11 ran   Time 1m 25.86 (1.76)   (Frank Brady)   J S Goldie Uplawmoor, E Renfrews

2987   4.15 UKBETTING.COM HCAP 3YO+ 0-90 (C)   5f   Good/Firm 33 +05 Fast   [82]
          £6906 £2125 £1062 £531   3 yo rec 4 lb   Raced towards stands side

2830 BRECONGILL LAD 8 [8] D Nicholls 8-9-9 (77) Alex Greaves 5/1: 220031: 8 b g Clantime - Chikala (Pitskelly)   85
Trkd ldr, rdn/led ins last, sn asserted & pushed out cl home: bckd: '99 wnr at Catterick, Pontefract, Yarmouth &
Goodwood (h'caps, rtd 75): dual rnr-up in '98 (rtd 68, M Hammond): eff at 5/6f on firm & soft, any trk: has run
well fresh: eff with/without blnks: prob best held up for a late run, this race went perfectly (got a good lead).
2644 ANTONIAS DOUBLE 15 [7] A Berry 5-9-3 (71) P Fessey 11/2: 003002: 5 ch m Primo Dominie - Mainly   1 75
Sunset (Red Sunset) Led to ins last, held by wnr after: op 9/2: back to form: on a fair mark for similar: see 2644
2830 XANADU 8 [3] Miss L A Perratt 4-9-9 (77) A Beech 5/1: 101243: 4 ch g Casteddu - Bellatrix (Persian   ½ 79
Bold) Chsd ldrs, rdn/kept on from over 1f out, not pace of wnr: see 2505.
2644 EURO VENTURE 15 [2] D Nicholls 5-9-9 (77) W Supple 5/1: 016144: Held up, not able to chall.   4 69
2701 MISS FIT 13 [6] 4-8-7 (61) M Tebbutt 9/1: 000055: Chsd ldrs, rdn/held over 1f out: see 926.   2 48
*2721 SHARP HAT 12 [1] 6-9-0 (68) A Culhane 5/1: 526116: Prom racing twds centre, held over 1f out.   ½ 53
2701 BEDEVILLED 13 [5] 5-8-13 (67) Lynsey Hanna (7) 12/1: 0W0207: Chsd ldrs 3f: op 10/1: btr 758 (sft).   3½ 43
2644 BLESSINGINDISGUISE 15 [4] 7-9-10 (78)(bl) T Lucas 11/4 FAV: 020628: Strugg halfway: hvly bckd: ½ 52
trainer unable to offer explanation for this below par effort: see 2644, 758.
8 ran   Time 59.6 (1.4)   (P Davidson Brown)   D Nicholls Sessay, N Yorks

2988   4.45 BELLWAY HOMES HCAP 3YO 0-85 (D)   1m1f   Good/Firm 33 -06 Slow   [89]
          £3770 £1160 £580 £290

2855 LADY HELEN 7 [4] T D Easterby 3-8-9 (70) J P Spencer 5/1: -05101: 3 b f Salse - Old Domesday Book   75
(High Top) Cl up, rdn/lead ins last, styd on well: earlier landed a Haydock fill h'cap: '99 Beverley mdn wnr (rtd
74): eff at 1m/9f on firm & fast grnd, stiff/gall trk: likes to race with/force the pace.
2220 SEA SQUIRT 32 [5] M Johnston 3-9-0 (75) J Fanning 5/1: 304162: 3 b g Fourstars Allstar - Polynesian   1 76
Goddess (Salmon Leap) Led, rdn/hdd ins last, kept on for press: see 2018 (1m).
2713 GRANTED 12 [1] M L W Bell 3-9-6 (81) A Beech (5) 7/2: 321143: 3 b f Cadeaux Genereux - Germane   2½ 77
(Distant Relative) Prom, ch 3f out, onepace/held over 1f out: stays 9f: see 2579 (1m).
2085 SALIM 38 [2] Sir Michael Stoute 3-9-6 (81) W Supple 5/1: 0-1404: In tch, held over 2f out: btr 1159 (7f). 2½ 72
2611 GOTHIC REVIVAL 16 [3] 3-9-7 (82) J Carroll 6/4 FAV: 40-45: Keen/cl up, rdn/outpcd fnl 3f: hvly bckd: 3½ 66
h'cap bow: longer 9f trip, breeding suggests 10f+ will suit: prob worth another look.
5 ran   Time 1m 55.6 (3.5)   (M P Burke)   T D Easterby Great Habton, N Yorks

REDCAR   SATURDAY JULY 29TH   Lefthand, Flat, Galloping Track

Official Going   GOOD/FIRM (FIRM in places). Stalls: Straight - Stands Side: 2m - Centre: Round - Inside .

2989   2.30 COMERACING MDN SELLER 3YO (G)   1m3f   Good/Firm   Slow
          £1904 £544 £272

2345 WISHFUL THINKER 28 [2] N Tinkler 3-9-0 O Pears 9/4 FAV: 000301: 3 b g Prince Sabo - Estonia   47
(King's Lake) Prom, gd hdwy to lead dist, kept on, rdn out: no bid: rnr up in '99 (rtd 82): apprec step
up to 11f & acts on firm & gd grnd, gall trk: this was a very poor race.
1699 MISS CASH 55 [1] J R Turner 3-8-9 F Lynch 12/1: 42: 3 b f Rock Hopper - Miss Cashtal   1¼ 40
(Ballacashtal) Cl up, led 3f out till dist, onepace: op 8/1: abs: stays 11f on gd/firm in modest company.
2715 WEST END DANCER 12 [8] G C H Chung 3-8-9 O Urbina 100/30: 005033: 3 b f West By West - Chateau 1¾ 37
Dancer (Giacometti) In tch, hdwy over 2f out, onepace over 1f out: needs selling h'caps: see 2715.
4408 FOSTON SECOND 285 [3] C B B Booth 3-8-9 K Dalgleish (5) 50/1: 00-4: Bhd, wandered when hdwy nk 37
2f out, nrst fin: poor juv form: stays 11f on gd/firm.

928

2746 **PHARAOHS HOUSE 10** [4] 3-9-0 (bl) G Parkin 7/1: 0-0005: In tch, rdn & btn over 2f out: op 12/1. 1¼ 40
2865 **FOUR MEN 6** [5] 3-9-0 P Bradley (5) 10/1: 660656: Led till 3f out, no extra: see 2865, 2682. 6 31$
2642 **IRANOO 15** [6] 3-9-0 (t) J McAuley 16/1: 02-007: Slow away, al bhd: op 10/1, see 1940. 5 24
2746 **MILL EMERALD 10** [7] 3-8-9 (VIS) S Sanders 100/30: -64608: Chsd ldr, wknd 3f out: vis, see 1386. 11 4
8 ran Time 2m 23.1 (7.6) (Mrs Marie Tinkler) N Tinkler Langton, N Yorks

---

2990 3.00 SUNDERLAND MED AUCT FILLIES MDN 2YO (E) 6f Good/Firm V Slow
£2779 £794 £397

2828 **BEREZINA 8** [1] T D Easterby 2-8-11 J Weaver 5/1: 56401: 2 b f Brief Truce - Lithe Spirit 67
(Dancing Dissident) Made all, kept on for press inside last, drvn out: Feb first foal, cost 13,000gns: stays
6f on gd/firm grnd & improved for forcing tactics today.
-- **MICKLOW MAGIC** [8] C Grant 2-8-11 L Newton 50/1: 2: 2 b f Farfelu - Scotto's Regret (Celtic ¾ 65
Cone) Prom, eff to chase wnr 3f out, kept on ins last, not btn far on debut: cheaply bought Apr foal: dam
mdn: stays 6f on gd/firm: gd first run: see 2029.
2628 **FORMAL PARTY 16** [4] J L Dunlop 2-8-11 A McGlone 5/1: -663: 2 ch f Fromidable - Tea Colony ¾ 63+
(Pleasant Colony) Sn outpcd, switched right & kept on over 1f out nrst fin: bred for & races as if 7f+ will suit:
sure to improve over further now she qualifies for nursery h'caps.
2417 **NOT JUST A DREAM 24** [7] A Berry 2-8-11 C Lowther 6/1: 4304: Chsd wnr, wknd well over 1f out. 1 60
2778 **SHARP SECRET 9** [9] 2-8-11 K Dalgleish (5) 9/4 FAV: -525: Chsd ldrs, outpcd over 2f out, late gains. nk 59
2828 **FRENCH BRAMBLE 8** [3] 2-8-11 J Edmunds 40/1: 60006: In tch, wknd well over 1f out, saddle slipped. ½ 58
-- **TANCRED WALK** [2] 2-8-11 F Lynch 40/1: 7: Went left start, sn in tch, wandered & wknd over 3 49
1f out: cheaply bought March foal: sister to a juv wnr over 6/7f: dam won up to 2m: with D Barker.
-- **AGO** [6] 2-8-11 G Parkin 25/1: 8: Slowly away, al bhd on debut: Feb foal, cost 3,400gns: 3 41
half sister to a 7f wnr: dam juv 6f scorer: with T D Easterby.
-- **SUNSET SHORE** [5] 2-8-11 S Sanders 5/2: P: In tch, p.u. lame over 3f out on debut: op 7/4: April 0
foal: half sister to wnrs over sprint trips: dam juv 5/7f scorer: with Sir M Prescott.
9 ran Time 1m 13.3 (4.4) (Chris & Antonia Deuters) T D Easterby Great Habton, N Yorks

---

2991 3.30 HERTEL NURSERY HCAP 2YO (D) 7f str Good/Firm Slow [82]
£4595 £1414 £707 £353

1704 **DOMINAITE 55** [4] M W Easterby 2-9-3 (71) J Weaver 9/4 FAV: -00321: 2 b g Komaite - Fairy Kingdom 75
(Prince Sabo) Hld up, gd hdwy to lead over 1f out, kept on ins last, drvn out: 8 week abs: Apr foal, cheaply bt:
first win: plcd over 5f earlier, apprec step up to 7f & acts on fast & soft grnd: runs well fresh.
2521 **THEWHIRLINGDERVISH 20** [1] T D Easterby 2-9-2 (70) S Sanders 100/30: -0032: 2 ch c Definite Artice ¾ 72
- Nomadic Dancer (Nabeel Dancer) Prom, rdn & slightly outpcd 2f out, kept on inside last, just held.
2557 **FLOWING RIO 18** [3] P C Haslam 2-9-6 (74) P Goode (3) 13/2: 0153: 2 b f First Trump - Deanta In ½ 75
Eirinn (Red Sunset) Dwelt, in tch, hdwy to lead briefly over 1f out, kept on samepace: stays 7f: see 1938.
2718 **LADY BEAR 12** [6] R A Fahey 2-8-10 (64)(VIS) F Lynch 9/2: 63344: Prom, onepace over 1f out: shd 65
fair run in a visor: stays 7f: see 2383, 1864.
2557 **AFFARATI 18** [2] 2-9-7 (75) R Cody Boutcher (7) 6/1: 21605: Led till over 1f out, no extra: prob hd 75
stys 7f on fast & gd/soft: see 1497.
2862 **CIRCUIT LIFE 6** [5] 2-8-4 (58)(BL) A McGlone 8/1: 530666: In tch, wknd well over 1f out: tried blnks. 3½ 51
6 ran Time 1m 26.5 (4.7) (B Bargh, T Beston, J Walsh & S Godber) M W Easterby Sheriff Hutton, N Yorks

---

2992 4.00 LITTLEWOODS HCAP 3YO 0-80 (D) 1m2f Good/Firm Slow [86]
£5027 £1547 £773 £386

*2524 **STALLONE 20** [1] J Noseda 3-9-7 (79) J Weaver 10/11 FAV: 455111: 3 ch g Brief Truce - Bering Honneur 84
(Bering) Cl up, led over 1f out, kept on for press ins last: nicely bckd to land hat-trick: top weight:
earlier scored at Redcar & Newcastle (h'caps): winning form over 1m/10f on fast, gd & stiff tracks, likes
Redcar: can carry big weights: geniune & progressive.
1600 **PETEURESQUE 59** [3] T D Barron 3-8-8 (66) S Sanders 14/1: -62002: 3 ch g Peteski - Miss Ultimo shd 70
(Screen King) Hld up, hdwy 2f out, kept on to chall fnl 1f, just held: fine run after 2 month abs: stays 10f.
2279 **WASEEM 30** [4] M Johnston 3-9-3 (75) K Dalgleish (5) 7/2: 002103: 3 ch c Polar Falcon - Astolat 1¾ 76
(Rusticaro) Trckd wnr, ev ch till no extra ins last: gd run: suited by 10f & hndles fast, gd/soft & fibresand.
*2520 **RIPARIAN 20** [2] Sir Michael Stoute 3-9-1 (73) F Lynch 3/1: 5-314: Cl up, rdn & onepace well over 2 71
1f out: should stay 10f: see 2520 (mdn, 1m, gd grnd).
2839 **OSTARA 7** [5] 3-7-10 (54) Iona Wands 14/1: -03005: Led till hdd & wknd over 1f out: longer trip. ½ 51
5 ran Time 2m 07.7 (5.4) (Lucayan Stud) J Noseda Newmarket, Suffolk

---

2993 4.30 BET DIRECT HCAP 3YO+ 0-85 (D) 2m Good/Firm Fair [82]
£4823 £1484 £742 £371 3 yo rec 17lb

2584 **MAJESTIC BAY 17** [4] P W Harris 4-9-7 (75) J Weaver 5/1: -30131: 4 b g Unfuwain - That'll Be The 81
Day (Thatching) Led, kept on over 1f out despite swishing tail, rdn out: earlier made all at Yarmouth (mdn):
dual '99 rnr up (rtd 90): eff at 10f, stays 2m well on firm & gd, poss hvy: hndles any track & likes to force
the pace: best without blinks: on the upgrade.
2516 **PLEASANT MOUNT 21** [1] Miss J A Camacho 4-8-8 (62) F Lynch 8/1: 150302: 4 b g First Trump - Alo 2½ 65
Ez (Alzao) Trckd wnr, kept on samepace over 1f out: gd run: see 2164, 918.
2812 **PENSHIEL 8** [2] J L Dunlop 3-8-6 (77) S Sanders 9/4 FAV: -11233: 3 b g Mtoto - Highland Ceilidh 3 77
(Scottish Reel) Prom, rdn & no impress fnl 1f: nicely bckd: consistent: see 2812, 2195.
2812 **STAR RAGE 8** [5] M Johnston 10-9-12 (80) K Dalgleish (5) 11/4: F22554: In tch, eff over 2f out, 1½ 78
sn btn: topweight, can do better: see 1686, 714.
2866 **SALSKA 6** [3] 9-8-6 (60) L Newton 11/4: 005425: Waited with, eff over 3f out, sn btn: much btr 2866. 5 53
5 ran Time 3m 31.5 (6.7) (The Quiet Ones) P W Harris Aldbury, Herts

REDCAR   SATURDAY JULY 29TH   Lefthand, Flat, Galloping Track

2994   5.05 HARTLEPOOL AMAT CLASS STKS 3YO+ 0-70 (G)   7f str   Good/Firm   Slow
£1974   £564   £282   3 yo rec 7 lb

2704 **REDOUBTABLE** 13 [12] D W Chapman 9-11-3 Miss R Clark 7/2: 360041: 9 b h Grey Dawn II - Seattle   70
Rockette (Seattle Slew) Chsd ldrs, hdwy over 1f out, kept on to lead ins last, pushed out: earlier scored at
Southwell, Lingfield (h'caps, rtd 84a) & Warwick (class stakes, rtd 84): '99 wnr at Thirsk (h'cap, rtd 81): '98
h'cap wnr at Lingfield, Ayr & Newcastle: suited by 6/7f, stays a sharp 1m: acts on firm, soft & both AW's:
tried blinks: handles any track: v tough 9yo, on handy mark now.
2865 **KASS ALHAWA** 6 [5] D W Chapman 7-11-0 Miss Diana Jones 4/1: 542442: 7 b f Shirley Heights -   shd   66
Silver Braid (Miswaki) Cl up, eff over 1f out, kept on ins last, just held: qk reapp: likes Beverley: see 908.
*2860 **SEA DRIFT** 7 [3] L M Cumani 3-10-7 Mr N Bertran de Balanda 15/8 FAV: 0-5313: 3 gr f Warning -   1   64
Night At Sea (Night Shift) Handy, hdwy to lead briefly appr fnl 1f, onepace: qk reapp: rtd 2860 (mdn).
2442 **ORIOLE** 23 [4] Don Enrico Incisa 7-11-0 Mrs R Howell (3) 33/1: 000004: In tch, hdwy over 1f out,   3   58$
kept on inside last: treat rating with caution (officially rtd 39) & mod h'caps will suit better: see 2221.
2861 **ROYAL REPRIMAND** 6 [8] 5-11-0 Mrs F Needham 33/1: 000005: Led till well over 1f out, no extra: nk   57$
quick reapp, treat rating with caution: btn in a h'cap off 28 in 2861, see 2147.
2882 **TOEJAM** 5 [1] 7-11-3 Miss P Robson 12/1: 015046: In tch, some late gains: quick reapp, see 2882.   3   54$
2861 **HI NICKY** 6 [17] 4-10-11 Mr S Dobson (5) 33/1: 000007: Slow away, eff 3f out, no impress fnl 1f.   1   46
2798 **PALACEGATE TOUCH** 8 [2] 10-11-3 (bl) Mr A Evans 20/1: 033658: Prom, wknd over 1f out: btr 2680.   nk   51
2970 **TAKER CHANCE** 1 [10] 4-11-0 Mr V Lukaniuk (3) 16/1: 060629: In tch, drvn & no impress over 1f out.   hd   47$
2865 **DISTANT KINGS** 6 [9] 7-11-0 Miss A Armitage (5) 50/1: 000600: Bhd, eff 2f out, no impress: 10th.   hd   46
2861 **KIERCHEM** 6 [16] 9-11-0 Mrs C Ford 20/1: 014600: Al bhd: 11th: qk reapp: best 2099 (sell h'cap).   ½   45$
2861 **Abstract** 6 [15] 4-10-11 (vis) Miss Rachel Clark (6) 50/1:2861 **Marton Mere** 6 [20] 4-11-3 Miss A Deniel 20/1:
2796 **Bayard Lady** 8 [22] 4-10-11 Miss K Smith (7) 66/1:   2823 **Love Kiss** 8 [18] 5-11-0 (t) Miss C Morgan (7) 14/1:
2822 **Chillian** 8 [14] 4-11-0 Mr W Fearon (7) 66/1:   2839 **Precision** 7 [21] 5-11-0 Mr T Scudamore 16/1:
2865 **Fas** 6 [19] 4-11-0 (vis) Mr W Worthington (7) 66/1:   2861 **Fastwan** 6 [13] 4-11-0 Mr J McShane (7) 66/1:
322 **Court House** 198 [23] 6-11-0 Miss V Price (6) 66/1:   4409] **St Pacokise** 285 [11] 3-10-4 Mr W Beasley (6) 33/1:
2233 **Time Is Money** 31 [24] 8-11-0 Mr M Jenkins (3) 33/1:   2798 **Johs Brother** 8 [7] 4-11-0 Mr D Boyd (7) 66/1:
23 ran   Time 1m 25.6 (3.8)   (David W Chapman)   D W Chapman Stillington, N Yorks.

ASCOT   SATURDAY JULY 29TH   Righthand, Stiff, Galloping Track

Official Going   GOOD TO FIRM. Stalls: Str Crse - Stands Side, Rnd Crse - Inside.

2995   1.45 MILLENNIUM RTD HCAP 3YO+ 0-105 (B)   1m2f   Good/Firm 30   -09 Slow   [112]
£15361   £5826   £2913   £1324   3 yo rec 10lb

*2610 **HAPPY DIAMOND** 16 [5] M Johnston 3-8-0 (94) P Doe 7/1: 022D11: 3 b c Diesis - Urus (Kris S)   100
Held up, prog over 2f out, rdn/led over 1f out, styd on well fnl 1f, drvn out: earlier scored at Doncaster (h'cap,
made all) & prev disql from 1st in a h'cap at Doncaster: '99 wnr on 2nd of 2 starts at Thirsk (mdn, rtd 87):
suited by 10f on fast, gd & a stiff/gall trk: v progressive & tough colt.
2696 **WESTENDER** 14 [1] W J Haggas 4-8-7 (92)(1oh) M Hills 5/1: -22502: 4 b g In The Wings - Trude   ½   95
(Windwurf) Trkd ldr 4f out, rdn/led over 2f out till over 1f out, styd on, held by wnr ins last: fine run.
1845 **HIMSELF** 49 [3] H R A Cecil 5-8-7 (92)(1oh) T Quinn 4/1 FAV: 014-43: 5 b h El Gran Senor - Celtic   1   94
Loot (Irish River) Rear, prog/rdn & chsd ldrs over 1f out, al held: nicely bckd after abs: worth a try at 11f+.
2696 **CARDIFF ARMS** 14 [4] M Johnston 6-8-10 (94) O Peslier 11/2: 005054: Held up, rdn & styd on fnl   2   94
2f, nvr pace to chall: op 9/2, shorter priced stablemate of wnr: see 1112.
2707 **ORMELIE** 13 [6] W J Musson 5-9-3 (93) J Fortune 5/1: 551-05: Held up, eff over 2f out, no impress: see 2707.   ½   92
2475 **BRILLIANT RED** 22 [8] 7-9-4 (102)(t) I Mongan (5) 8/1: -00036: Trkd ldrs, rdn/btn 2f out: btr 2475.   ½   100
1246 **SHABLAM** 79 [9] 3-8-11 (105) J Murtagh 9/1: 1-5447: Prom, rdn/btn 2f out: op 7/1, abs: see 1246, 955.   1¾   101
2696 **NOBELIST** 14 [2] 5-9-3 (101) M J Kinane 16/1: /61008: Mid-div, btn over 1f out: thrice below 1561.   2½   93
2675 **ASAKIR** 14 [7] 5-9-7 (105) Martin Dwyer 11/2: 112/09: Led till over 2f out, fdd: see 2675 (1m).   1   96
9 ran   Time 2m 07.85 (3.85)   (Jaber Abdullah)   M Johnston Middleham, N.Yorks.

2996   2.35 GR 3 PRINCESS MARGARET STKS 2YO (A)   6f str   Good/Firm 30   -17 Slow
£24000   £9200   £4600   £2200

-2565 **ENTHUSED** 18 [3] Sir Michael Stoute 2-8-9 J Murtagh 2/1 FAV: -121: 2 b f Seeking The Gold - Magic   110+
Of Life (Seattle Slew) Dwelt/held up rear, smooth prog from halfway, led 1f out & readily qcknd clr: hvly bckd:
earlier scored on debut at Newmarket (fill mdn): half sister to 3 mid-dists wnrs: dam high-class over 6f/1m: eff
at 6f, will apprec 7f/1m in time: acts on gd: plenty in hand, potentially high-class, keep on your side.
*2152 **AUTUMNAL** 36 [6] B J Meehan 2-8-9 J Fortune 4/1: -3112: 2 b f Indian Ridge - Please Believe Me   2½   101
(Try My Best) Led over 3f out, hard rdn/hdd over 1f out, kept on tho' held by impressive wnr ins last: acts on
fast & gd/soft grnd: handled step up to 6f well: progressive & tough, win a Listed/Gr 3: see 2152.
2849 **KACHINA DOLL** 7 [1] M R Channon 2-8-9 Craig Williams 40/1: 105203: 2 b f Mujadil - Betelgeuse   1   99
(Kalaglow) Trkd ldrs, rdn/briefly hmpd over 1f out, onepace/held ins last: stays a stiff 6f well: see 2352, 1437.
2344 **SANTOLINA** 28 [5] J H M Gosden 2-8-9 R Hills 4/1: -124: Reared start, rcd keenly, held up in tch,   2   94
not much room then/eff over 1f out, held/hung right ins last: hvly bckd: acts on firm/fast: up in class.
2565 **ZAHEEMAH** 18 [4] 2-8-9 P Robinson 12/1: 645: Led till over 3f out, outpcd fnl 2f: win a mdn.   ¾   92
*2500 **GREEN TAMBOURINE** 21 [7] 2-8-9 K Darley 4/1: 16: Dwelt, rcd keenly rear, rdn/btn 2f out: hvly   3½   83
bckd: needs to learn to settle in this higher grade: see 2500 (stks).
2088 **FLYING MILLIE** 38 [8] 2-8-9 R Hughes 40/1: 167: Cl-up 3f, wknd qckly fnl 1f: op 10/1: btr 2088 (5f).   nk   82
*2344 **IN THE WOODS** 28 [10] 2-8-12 G Duffield 12/1: 118: Prom 4f, wknd: ahd of today's 4th in 2344.   2   80
*2363 **SIPTITZ HEIGHTS** 26 [9] 2-8-9 M Hills 50/1: 5019: Held up, eff 2f out, sn btn/eased: stiff task.   ¾   75
9 ran   Time 1m 15.89 (2.79)   (Niarchos Family)   Sir Michael Stoute Newmarket.

930

2997   3.10 TOTE INTERNATIONAL HCAP 3YO+ (B)   7f str   Good/Firm 30   -00 Slow   [121]
£87000   £33000   £16500   £7500   3 yo rec 1 lb   Field raced centre - stands side

2616 **TILLERMAN** 16 [2] Mrs A J Perrett 4-8-10 (103) M J Kinane 10/1: 1-3501: 4 b c In The Wings - Autumn   112
Tint (Roberto) Hld up rear, rapid prog over 1f out, styd on strongly to lead ins last, drvn out: well bckd:
unbtn in '99, won at Lingfield (auct mdn) & Newmarket (class stks, rtd 101): eff btwn 7f/9f on fast & gd/soft
grnd: has run well fresh: smart & progressive colt, shld win in Listed/Gr 3 if reproducing this turn of foot.
2495 **EL GRAN PAPA** 21 [1] J H M Gosden 3-7-10 (96)(2oh) F Norton 8/1: -21102: 3 b c El Gran Senor -   nk 104
Banner Hit (Oh Say) Trkd ldrs, rdn to lead over 1f out, sn hdd, styd on well for press, just held: hvly bckd,
op 8/1: rest well covered: eff at 7f/1m: progressive/useful colt, keep on the right side: see 2117.
+2616 **TAYSEER** 16 [8] D Nicholls 6-8-0 (93)(3ex) J Quinn 8/1: 530313: 4 b g Sheikh Albadou - Millfit   2½ 96
(Blushing Groom) Rear, rdn/no room over 1f out, prog to chase ldrs ins last, kept on: op 7/1: ahead of this
wnr latest but no luck in running here: must go close in chosen Goodwood engagement next week: see 2616.
2495 **DUKE OF MODENA** 28 [18] G B Balding 3-7-10 (96)(2oh) P M Quinn (3) 20/1: 115144: Towards rear,   2½ 94
hdwy over 1f out, kept on samepace ins last: fine run from prob unfavoured outside draw: tough & progressive.
-2616 **PERSIANO** 16 [4] 5-8-3 (96) D Harrison 9/1: 031325: Trkd ldrs, rdn/no room over 1f out, styd on   ½ 93
ins last, no threat: no luck in running at a crucial stage but prob only fin 4th at best: tough, see 2616 & 1450.
2616 **PEARTREE HOUSE** 16 [21] 6-7-11 (90) A Nicholls (1) 25/1: 124406: Rear, prog to chall over 1f out,   ½ 86
sn onepace/held: longer priced stablemate of rnr-up, in gd form, return to 1m shld suit: see 2304, 2138.
2809 **SPEEDFIT TOO** 8 [13] 5-8-10 (103)(vis) T E Durcan 16/1: 401237: Rear, prog/no room 2f out, styd on   ¾ 98
ins last when gap appeared, no threat: no luck in running, would have bustled up plcd horses with clr run.
-- **EL GRAN LODE** [6] 5-8-7 (100) Fernando Diaz 50/1: -13118: Led till over 1f out, btn/eased ins last: 1 93
Swedish raider, thrice a wnr this year, incl in Germany: eff at 6f, return to that trip shld suit: acts on gd & hvy.
2757 **SHOWBOAT** 10 [5] 6-9-1 (108) M Hills 25/1: 303039: Cl-up, held fnl 2f: see 657.   ½ 100
*2870 **FREE OPTION** 6 [10] 5-8-2 (94)(1ow) P Robinson 20/1: -30310: Mid-div, rdn/onepace over 1f out   1¾ 84
when sltly hmpd, held/eased well ins last: 10th: qck reapp: see 2870 (1m).
2675 **NICOBAR** 14 [3] 3-8-10 (110)(t) K Darley 25/1: 161050: Prom 5f: 11th: btr 1830 (gd/soft).   ½ 98
*2528 **CARIBBEAN MONARCH** 20 [15] 5-8-12 (105)(3ex) J Murtagh 9/2 FAV: 432110: Keen/held up rear, no   hd 92
room repeatly fnl 2f: hvly bckd, 12th: forget this: saw no daylight in the closing stages: v progressive.
+2675 **SUGARFOOT** 14 [22] 6-9-10 (117)(3ex) R Cochrane 16/1: -15510: Held up, efft/held over 1f out: 1¼ 101
stiff task conceding lumps of weight to progressive rivals: 1m Listed winner here in 2675.
2090 **MUCHEA** 38 [14] 6-8-7 (100)(vis) Craig Williams 33/1: 205400: Mid-div, eff 2f out, held fnl 1f: 14th.   hd 83
2762 **NICE ONE CLARE** 10 [11] 4-7-11 (90) Martin Dwyer 10/1: 1-5320: Mid-div, bmpd/hmpd over 1f out, sn   ¾ 72
held: 15th: hvly bckd: had a troublesome passage but not likely to have troubled ldrs: see 2762, 2151.
*2289 **BOAST** 29 [17] 3-7-11 (97) P Doe 33/1: -63510: Prom, wknd over 1f out: 16th: btr 2289 (6f).   hd 78
1946 **Bold King** 44 [9] 5-8-0 (93) M Henry 16/1:   2847 **Now Look Here** 7 [7] 4-8-10 (103)(BL) J Fortune 40/1:
2616 **Juno Marlowe** 16 [24] 4-8-2 (95) G Duffield 50/1:   2809 **Catchy Word** 8 [26] 3-8-4 (104) G Carter 33/1:
2151 **Tussle** 36 [12] 5-8-1 (94) J Mackay (5) 20/1:   -- **Senador** [19] 7-7-13 (92) G Bardwell 50/1:
-- **Woven Roving** [16] 4-8-4 (97) T Quinn 50/1:   2768 **Wahj** 10 [23] 5-7-11 (90) Dale Gibson 11/1:
24 ran   Time 1m 28.1 (2.1)   (K Abdulla)   Mrs A J Perrett Pulborough, W.Sussex.

2998   3.50 GR 1 KING GEORGE V STKS 3YO+ (A)   1m4f   Good/Firm 30   +22 Fast
£435000   £165000   £82500   £37500   3 yo rec 12lb

*2406 **MONTJEU** 27 [5] J E Hammond 4-9-7 M J Kinane 1/3 FAV: 14-111: 4 b c Sadler's Wells - Floripedes   134+
(Top Ville) Waited with rear, smooth prog with rider simply steering over 2f out, led over 1f out & readily
asserted ins last on bit, most impressive: any amount in hand: fast time, hvly bckd: earlier won Gr 1 events
at The Curragh & St-Cloud: '99 wnr at Longchamp (3, incl Gr 1 Arc, rtd 136 & 2 Gr 2s), Chantilly (Gr 1, French
Derby) & The Curragh (Gr 1 Irish Derby, 5L): suited by 10/12f on fast & hvy, handles firm: loves a stiff/gall
trk: colt out of the very highest drawer: not to be opposed.
2497 **FANTASTIC LIGHT** 21 [7] Saeed bin Suroor 4-9-7 J Reid 12/1: 0-1252: 4 b c Rahy - Jood (Nijinsky)   1¾ 124
Held up rear, rdn & styd on fnl 2f for press, nvr any ch with wnr: op 10/1, pulled clr of rem: high-class colt
who appreciated this return to 12f, can find a similar event when avoiding this wnr: see 1827, 767.
*1827 **DALIAPOUR** 50 [3] Sir Michael Stoute 4-9-7 J Murtagh 13/2: 20-113: 4 b c Sadler's Wells - Dalara   3½ 119
(Doyoun) Trkd clr ldr, led over 3f out, rdn/hdd over 1f out & sn held: op 5/1, 7 wk abs: acts on firm
& fast but prob seen to best effect on easy grnd: ahead of this rnr-up in 1827 (sharp/undul trk, gd/soft).
-2720 **BEAT ALL** 12 [4] Sir Michael Stoute 4-9-7 K Darley 33/1: -W4324: Chsd ldrs, kept on onepace for   1 116
press fnl 2f: has a list/Gr success in him this term, but this is above his level: see 2720, 1248.
-- **AIR SHAKUR** [8] 5-8-9 Y Take 10/1: 1-2125: Held up, dropped to rear halfway, eff 3f out, little   2 103
headway: Japanese raider, 2 month abs: earlier won a 10f Gr 1 in contest in native land, subs rnr-up over 12f (Gr 1):
eff at 10/12f on firm & gd grnd: high-class colt who hmpd his chance today by becoming upset in preliminaries.
2409 **RAYPOUR** 27 [6] 3-8-9 J Fortune 100/1: 226246: Led & clr after 3f out, hdd over 3f out, sn btn: btr 2409.   8 106
2497 **SHIVA** 21 [1] 5-9-4 T Quinn 14/1: 2-0137: Chsd ldrs, rdn/btn over 2f out, eased over 1f out: op 10/1:   14 87
longer trip & best with cut in the grnd: btr 2497, 1587 (Gr 3, sft).
7 ran   Time 2m 29.99 (0.99)   (M Tabor)   J E Hammond France.

2999   4.25 LADY RIDERS HCAP 3YO+ 0-85 (D)   7f str   Good/Firm 30   -39 Slow   [71]
£8580   £2640   £1320   £660   3 yo rec 7 lb   Raced towards centre

*2840 **PETERS IMP** 7 [15] A Berry 5-9-10 (67) Miss E J Jones 14/1: 253011: 5 b g Imp Society - Catherine   75
Clare (Sallust) Mid-div, prog to lead over 1f out, strongly pressed ins last, drvn out/holding rival nr fin: recent
Warwick wnr (appr h'cap): '99 scorer at Hamilton & Redcar (class stks, rtd 82, J Berry): '98 Haydock wnr (class stks,
rtd 75): suited by 6/7.5f on soft/fibresand, loves firm & fast grnd: handles any trk: eff with/without blnks & can
go well fresh: tough & in fine form, given a strong ride by her accomplished lady rider.
2564 **TORNADO PRINCE** 18 [8] E J Alston 5-9-8 (65) Miss E Ramsden 5/1: -01442: 5 ch g Caerleon - Welsh   ¾ 71
Flame (Welsh Pageant) Towards rear, smooth prog from halfway, rdn to press wnr 1f out, styd on well, just
held nr fin: hvly bckd, clr of rem: remains in gd form, can find another h'cap: see 2242, 2063.
2728 **BUTRINTO** 11 [10] B R Johnson 6-9-5 (62) Mrs A Perrett 20/1: 114023: 6 ch g Anshan - Bay Bay   5 58
(Bay Express) Dwelt, towards rear, styd on fnl 2f, no threat to front pair: gd run, likes Brighton: see 1462.
2752 **ELLWAY PRINCE** 10 [26] M Wigham 5-8-10 (53)(2oh) Mrs A Hammond (3) 12/1: 114324: Sn prom, ev   ½ 48
ch 1f out, onepace: op 8/1: see 2752.

2581 **DENS JOY** 17 [6] 4-9-6 (63) Miss L Johnston (5) 25/1: 012005: Towards rear, styd on fnl 2f, nrst fin.   1   56
2437 **PERFECT PEACH** 23 [22] 5-9-9 (66) Mrs C Williams 25/1: 004346: Dwelt, keen/held up, prog to press   1½   56
ldrs over 1f out, no extra ins last: see 1250.
2761 **CARLTON** 10 [2] 6-10-6 (77) Mrs D Holley (7) 16/1: 200247: Chsd ldrs, onepace over 1f out: see 76.   shd   67
2580 **ALMASI** 17 [11] 8-10-2 (73) Miss H Webster (5) 20/1: 0-5348: Towards rear, no room over 1f out,   shd   62
mod late gains, no threat to ldrs: all wins at 6f: see 1531 (6f).
2749 **CALCAVELLA** 10 [14] 4-9-4 (61) Mrs C Kettle (5) 33/1: 0-4059: Rear, styd on fnl 2f, nvr factor: see 2320.   ½   49
1829 **MISTER RAMBO** 50 [20] 5-10-10 (81) Miss J Allison 12/1: 052060: Mid-div, btn over 1f out: 10th: 1   67
won this last term off a 1lb higher mark: 7 wk abs: best form this term has been on easy grnd: see 817 (soft).
*2491 **DANIYSHA** 21 [18] 3-9-12 (76) Miss C Preston (7) 4/1 FAV: 4-4310: Mid-div, smooth prog to trk ldrs   ½   61
2f out, sn btn: 11th: hvly bckd, op 6/1: h'cap bow: better expected after 2491 (fill mdn).
2845 **EVENTUALLY** 7 [25] 4-9-13 (70) Miss E Johnson Houghton 10/1: 500120: Twds rear, mod gains: 12th.   nk   54
2869 **EASTER OGIL** 6 [28] 5-10-7 (78)(vis) Miss S Samworth 20/1: 125000: Mid-div at best: 13th: qck reapp.   1½   59
2830 **VIOLET** 8 [7] 4-8-10 (53)(bl) (2oh) Mrs S Moore (5) 16/1: 601050: Prom 5f: 14th: btr 2631 (6f, g/s).   1½   31
2621 **HARMONIC** 16 [16] 3-9-7 (71) Miss L Sheen (5) 16/1: 602220: Prom 5f: 15th: btr 2621, 2232 (mdns).   ¾   48
1892 **ROUGE ETOILE** 46 [4] 4-8-10 (53)(2oh) Miss J Ellis (5) 33/1: 000600: Led till over 1f out, wknd qckly/   0
eased: 7th: stablemate of rnr-up, 6 wk abs: well h'capped if showing a return to form: see 811.
2869 **Cauda Equina** 6 [24] 6-10-4 (75) Ms T Dzieciolowska (7) 25/1:
2130 **Manxwood** 36 [3] 3-8-13 (63) Miss L McIntosh (7) 20/1:
2768 **Rich In Love** 10 [1] 6-11-0 (85) Mrs S Bosley 20/1:
2456 **The Exhibition Fox** 22 [19] 4-10-5 (76) Miss E Folkes (5) 14/1:
2697 **Stylish Ways** 14 [5] 8-9-11 (68) Mrs L Pearce 14/1:
2347 **Fox Star** 28 [23] 3-8-10 (60)(bl) (18oh) Ms D Goad (3) 100/1:
2282 **Robellion** 30 [9] 9-9-2 (59) Miss S Newby Vincent (0) 20/1:
2631 **My Emily** 16 [21] 4-9-11 (68) Mrs J Moore 33/1:
*2831 **Lynton Lad** 8 [12] 8-9-2 (59) Miss Kim Jones (0) 20/1: 2564 **Parkside** 18 [27] 4-9-13 (70) Mrs C Dwyer (7) 33/1:
3940} **Kissed By Moonlite** 317 [17] 4-8-10 (53)(9oh) Miss A Elsey 66/1:
1647 **Fourdaned** 57 [13] 7-8-10 (53)(bl) (29oh) Mrs K Hills (0) 100/1:
28 ran   Time 1m 30.81 (4.81)   (Mr & Mrs Peter Foden)   A Berry Cockerham, Lancs.

3000   5.00 EBF CROCKER BULTEEL MDN 2YO (D)   6f str   Good/Firm 30   -12 Slow
£6711   £2065   £1032   £516

--   **RUMPOLD** [4] P F I Cole 2-8-11 J Fortune 12/1: 1: 2 b c Mister Baileys - Southern Psychic (Alwasmi)   111+
Trkd ldr, led 2f out, readily asserted under hands-and-heels riding, styd on strongly: most impressive debut: clocked
a faster time than Gr 3 contest over same trip earlier: Mar foal, cost 30,000gns: dam a 4yo US wnr: sire high-class
juv & subs 2,000 Guineas wnr: acts on fast grnd & a stiff/gall trk: runs well fresh:
looks smart & open to any amount of improvement, the type to win in Group company.
--   **MINARDI** [8] A P O'Brien 2-8-11 M J Kinane 5/4 FAV: 2: 2 br c Boundary - Yarn (Mr Prospector)   5   96
Held up, rdn/prog to chase wnr over 1f out, ran but no impress: hvly bckd, op 7/4: Mar foal, cost
$1,650,000: dam a 3yo wnr: looks sure to relish 7f+ in time: useful intro, shld go on from here.
--   **MAGNUSSON** [3] J H M Gosden 2-8-11 K Darley 16/1: 3: 2 b c Primo Dominie - Nunsharpa (Sharpo)   2   91+
In tch, rdn fnl 3f, styd on ins last, no threat: bckd, op 20/1: Feb foal, cost 77,000gns, a first foal: dam
a 3yo 7f wnr: eff at 6f, 7f+ looks sure to suit: acts on fast & a stiff trk: improve plenty & win races.
--   **JENTZEN** [6] R Hannon 2-8-11 R Hughes 9/2: 4: Cl-up, outpcd fnl 3f: bckd, op 5/1: Miswaki   nk   90
colt, Jan foal, cost 19,000gns: brother to smart 6f wnr Abou Zous: dam a 6f list juv wnr: bred to be useful.
--   **STUTTER** [6] 2-8-11 M Hills 12/1: 5: Held up, rdn/onepace fnl 2f: op 10/1: Polish Precedent colt,   hd   89
Apr foal, cost 22,000gns: half-brother to a 7f juv wnr, dam a juv wnr at 6f: sire a top-class miler.
--   **GHAYTH** [5] 2-8-11 R Hills 5/1: 6: Trkd ldrs, hmpd over 2f out & again over 1f out, no impress after: 1   87
bckd: Sadlers Wells colt, Jan foal, cost 300,000gns: a first foal: dam a smart juv 6f wnr: sire top-class 1m/12f
performer: forget this run, had no luck in running: sure to leave this bhd over 7f+ for Sir M Stoute.
--   **DANE FLYER** [7] 2-8-11 Craig Williams 13/2: 7: Led 4f, fdd: op 10/1: Danehill colt, May foal,   nk   86
cost IR160,000gns: half-brother to top-class sprinter Owington, dam a 10f 3yo wnr: will apprec 7f in time.
--   **SEATTLE PRINCE** [1] 2-8-11 Dane O'Neill 33/1: 8: Dwelt & al rear: Cozzene colt, Apr foal,   1¾   82
74,000gns 2yo wnr: half-brother to a juv US wnr: longer priced stablemate of 4th.
--   **REAP** [2] 2-8-11 G Bardwell 66/1: 9: Dwelt, well bhd 2f out, flashed tail: Emperor Jones colt,   10   63
7,500gns 2yo: dam 6f wnr: highly tried on intro for J Pearce.
9 ran   Time 1m 15.60 (2.5)   (Anthoy Speelman)   P F I Cole Whatcombe, Oxon.

3001   5.35 BULTFONTEIN HCAP 3YO+ 0-95 (C)   1m4f   Good/Firm 30   -02 Slow   [94]
£8996   £2768   £1384   £692   3 yo rec 12lb

2127 **WAIT FOR THE WILL** 36 [1] G L Moore 4-9-0 (80)(bl) R Hughes 6/1: 012231: 4 ch g Seeking The Gold -   86
You'd Be Surprised (Blushing Groom) Rear, smooth prog to trk ldrs 3f out, drvn over 1f out & led ins last, al
holding rivals after, rdn out: hvly bckd, tchd 8/1: earlier scored at Salisbury (h'cap): '99 wnr again at Salisbury
(amat h'cap, rtd 82): suited by 12f, stays 14f well: acts on firm & gd/soft, loves a stiff/gall trk, esp Salisbury:
well suited by reapplication of blnks today: in good form and could well head for Goodwood next week.
2069 **GALLERY GOD** 39 [3] G Wragg 4-9-11 (91) Y Take 2/1 FAV: 063122: 4 ch c In The Wings - El   1¾   93
Fabulous (Fabulous Dancer) Chsd clr ldrs 9f, rdn & styd on onepace fnl 2f: hvly bckd: tough & useful.
*2547 **COOL INVESTMENT** 19 [5] M Johnston 3-8-13 (91) R Hills 5/1: 064413: 3 b c Prince Of Birds - Superb   ½   92
Investment (Hatim) Went clr with ldr, went on 3f out & rdn clr, wknd/hdd ins last, no extra: hvly bckd: ran to best
under an enterprising ride: stays a stiff 12f: see 2547 (form).
2069 **VERIDIAN** 39 [4] N J Henderson 7-9-2 (82) T Quinn 9/2: 62/134: Chsd ldrs 3f out, rdn/chsd ldr 2f out,   3   79
held fnl 1f: bckd: btr 2069, 1251.
2502 **GENTLEMAN VENTURE** 21 [6] 4-8-11 (77) O Peslier 7/1: 364255: Rear, rdn/mod late gains: see 2502.   nk   73
2339 **DASHIBA** 28 [7] 4-9-12 (92) K Darley 12/1: 0-3066: Rear, nvr any impression: bckd, op 14/1.   1¼   86
2852 **CARLYS QUEST** 7 [8] 6-9-8 (88)(vis) F Norton 12/1: 130047: Rear, no ch 3f out: see 2852, 1373.   1¼   80
2498 **TOTAL DELIGHT** 21 [2] 4-9-2 (82)(VIS) P Doe 12/1: 041208: Led, racing keenly, clr after 2f, hdd 3 out,   18   54
wknd qckly: bckd, op 14/1: rcd far too freely in first time visor: see 2305, 1991.
8 ran   Time 2m 32.80 (3.80)   (Richard Green Fine Paintings)   G L Moore Woodingdean, E.Sussex.

NOTTINGHAM   SATURDAY JULY 29TH   Lefthand, Flat, Galloping Track

Official Going   FIRM (GOOD/FIRM Places), Becoming GOOD/FIRM after 2-40. Stalls: Inside, Except 5/6f - Stands Side.

3002 2.05 CALVERTON SELL HCAP 3YO+ 0-60 (G)   1m6f   Good/Firm 37 -12 Slow   **[50]**
£2035   £581   £290   3 yo rec 14lb

2843 **ITALIAN ROSE** 7 [6] A W Carroll 5-8-6 (28) S Righton 16/1: 06-061: 5 ch m Aragon - Cayla (Tumble   29
Wind) In tch, imprvd 2 out, kept on well & led cl-home: no bid, qck reapp: 1st win, unplcd in '99 (h'cap, rtd 28a,
sell, rtd 48$): '98 rnr-up (rtd mdn, rtd 55): eff at 7f, suited by step to 14f: acts on firm & soft, without blnks.
2643 **BEST PORT** 15 [12] J Parkes 4-8-7 (29) M Roberts 3/1 FAV: 343002: 4 b g Be My Guest - Portree   ½ 29
(Slip Anchor) Mid-div, smooth prog appr str, led bef dist, hard rdn & hdd towards fin: acts on fast & gd grnd.
2667 **ACQUITTAL** 15 [8] P L Clinton 8-8-13 (35)(vis) P Dobbs (5) 7/1: 004453: 8 b g Danehill - Perfect   1¼ 33
Alibi (Law Society) Mid-div, rdn ent fnl 2f, styd on: not trouble ldrs: visor reapplied, stays 14f: see 1852.
1852 **STICKS AND STONES** 48 [10] J A Gilbert 8-8-12 (34) A Mackay 25/1: /02004: Dwelt, cl-up by   shd 32
halfway, led bef str till appr fnl 1f, onepace: 7 wk abs: styd longer 14f trip, see 581.
2843 **FLY LIKE A BIRD** 7 [4] 4-8-8 (30) R Mullen 12/1: -04005: In tch, chsd ldrs 3f out till same pace fnl 1f.   1   27
2887 **GROOMS GOLD** 5 [13] 8-8-2 (24)(bl) C Rutter 14/1: 204066: Al around same place: quick reapp.   1   19
1506 **SMARTS MEGAN** 64 [2] 4-8-3 (25) G Baker (5) 25/1: 0-0007: Dwelt, late hdwy: 9 wk abs, new stable.   ¾ 18
2843 **ACTION JACKSON** 7 [9] 8-8-7 (29) M Fenton 13/2: 04-058: Led till ent fnl 4f, no extra: quick reapp   ½ 21
2789 **TASSO DANCER** 9 [11] 4-9-6 (42) L Newman (3) 25/1: /00059: Front rank till fdd 2f out: longer trip   ¾ 33
2765 **OCEAN LINE** 10 [5] 5-9-10 (46) P Fitzsimons (5) 6/1: 400120: Mid-div till lost place 2f out: 10th, top-weight.3 33
2904 **CHILDRENS CHOICE** 4 [3] 9-9-0 (36)(vis) Dean McKeown 15/2: 340000: Nvr a factor: 11th, qck reapp.   2½ 20
460 **BARANN** 175 [1] 4-7-10 (18)(3oh) Claire Bryan (5) 100/1: 00-000: Well plcd, led 4f out, sn hdd/btn: 12th. 3   0
2656 Classic Colours 15 [16] 7-8-9 (31) Jonjo Fowle 25/1:
2518 Laa Jadeed 21 [14] 5-8-8 (30) Joanna Badger (7) 25/1:
490 Wee Jimmy 170 [7] 4-8-13 (35)(BL) S Finnamore (5) 25/1:
15 ran   Time 3m 05.2 (6.9)   (Serafino Agodino)   A W Carroll Alcester, Warwicks

---

3003 2.40 CHURCH WARSOP FILLIES MDN 2YO (D)   6f str   Good/Firm 37 -18 Slow
£4368   £1344   £672   £336

1957 **TEREED ELHAWA** 43 [1] E A L Dunlop 2-8-11 W Ryan 1/2 FAV: 631: 2 b f Cadeaux Genereux - Dimakya   84
(Dayjur) Easily made all: nicely bckd: 40,000 gns 1st foal, dam a wnr abroad: eff forcing the pace at 6f on fast grnd
-- **NIGHT HAVEN** [5] M L W Bell 2-8-11 M Fenton 9/2: 2: 2 gr f Night Shift - Noble Haven (Indian King)   6   67
Held up in tch, prog to chase wnr appr fnl 1f, sn onepace: op 3/1 on debut, clr rem rem: 18,500 gns Apr foal,
sister to a couple of wnrs, dam 6f juv wnr: bred to be a sprinter, shld improve in similar next time.
-- **DREAMIE BATTLE** [4] R Hollinshead 2-8-11 Paul Eddery 25/1: 3: 2 br f Makbul - Highland Rossie   6   52
(Pablond) Chsd ldrs till 2f out: debut: 3,800 gns Mar foal, half-sister to sev wnrs, dam juv wnr.
2618 **BENEVOLENCE** 16 [2] S P C Woods 2-8-11 R Mullen 7/1: 04: Dwelt, nvr troubled ldrs: tchd 9/1.   5   37
2390 **CHOCOLATE FOG** 25 [3] 2-8-11 N Pollard 20/1: 0505: Prom, lost pl after halfway: stiff task.   1¾ 33
5 ran   Time 1m 14.1 (3.3)   (Khalifa Sultan)   E A L Dunlop Newmarket, Suffolk

---

3004 3.10 NEWSTEAD CLAIMER 3YO (F)   1m54y   Good/Firm 37 -62 Slow
£2727   £779   £389

2914 **SPEEDFIT FREE** 3 [4] M A Buckley 3-9-1 Dean McKeown 4/1: 050441: 3 b g Night Shift - Dedicated Lady   57
(Pennine Walk) Led after 2f: nicely bckd: '99 Yarmouth wnr (nov stks, G Margarson, rtd 83): eff frnt rnk 6f & 1m: acts on fast grnd: goes on
any trk, up with/forcing the pace, without blnks: wears sheepskin cheek pieces.
2735 **DOLFINESSE** 11 [7] M Brittain 3-8-6 (vis) D Egan (7) 5/1: 234062: 3 ch f Dolphin Street - Gortadoo   1½ 44
(Sharpen Up) Prom, under press appr fnl 2f, styd on but not onepace of wnr: op 8/1: stays 1m in clmg grade.
2840 **BURCOT GIRL** 7 [5] J L Spearing 3-8-0 A Mackay 66/1: 0-0003: 3 b f Petardia - Phoenix Forli (Forli)   1   36$
Chsd ldrs, prog & ch 2f out, onepace dist: stiff task, qk reapp, prob flattered: blnks omitted, stays 1m on fast grnd.
2105 **CENTAUR SPIRIT** 37 [3] A Streeter 3-8-13 R Havlin 25/1: 0-04: Held up, prog to chase ldrs appr   ¾ 47
fnl 2f, no further impress: suited by drop back to 1m.
*2187 **MOUNTRATH ROCK** 33 [2] 3-8-6 (bl) W Ryan 13/8 FAV: 044015: Held up, wide, nvr nr ldrs: well bckd.   1   38
2250 **BLACKPOOL MAMMAS** 31 [6] 3-8-6 P Fitzsimons (5) 5/2: 006066: Nvr dngrs, btn 2f out: longer trip.   5   28
2448 **NO REGRETS** 23 [1] 3-8-13 Paul Eddery 25/1: 005007: Early ldr, no extra aftr, hdd & btn appr fnl 1f.   3½ 29
7 ran   Time 1m 47.3 (7.9)   (Mrs N W Buckley & Mr S N Buckley)   M A Buckley Upper Helmsley, N Yorks

---

3005 3.40 CLIFTON HCAP 3YO 0-85 (D)   1m54y rnd   Good/Firm 37 -33 Slow   **[89]**
£7475   £2300   £1150   £575

2412 **TRICCOLO** 24 [8] A C Stewart 3-9-2 (77) M Roberts 7/4 FAV: 015131: 3 b c Piccolo - Tribal Lady   82
(Absalom) Chsd ldrs, shaken up appr fnl 1f, led ins last, rdn out: nicely bckd from 11/4: earlier won at
Salisbury & Sandown (h'cap): rtd 77+ in '99: eff at 1m, could get further: handles soft grnd but needs gd or
faster: suited by stiff/gall trks & coming late: progressive colt.
*2733 **HADATH** 11 [4] M A Buckley 3-9-7 (82) Dean McKeown 6/1: 561212: 3 br g Mujtahid - Al Sylah (Nureyev)1¼ 83
Sn led, rdn appr fnl 1f, worn down ins last: op 9/2: stays 1m, tough & improving: see 2733.
2733 **WILFRAM** 11 [6] J M Bradley 3-7-13 (60) Claire Bryan (5) 10/1: 003163: 3 b g Fraam - Ming Blue   ½ 60
(Primo Dominie) Held up wide, styd on under hands & heels fnl 2f, not reach ldrs: tchd 14/1: styd longer
1m trip, go close with more positive tactics next time: see 2489.
2515 **MASTERPIECE USA** 21 [3] Sir Michael Stoute 3-9-4 (79) W Ryan 11/2: 1-0444: Waited with, not much   ½ 78
room ent fnl 2f, switched & short of room again dist, unable to qckn: op 9/2: worth another ch: see 2515.
2855 **PAGEANT** 7 [7] 3-9-1 (76) J Tate 6/1: 512625: Keen, held up, rdn appr fnl 1f, kept on, nvr dangerous.   nk 74
2614 **SOVEREIGN STATE** 16 [2] 3-9-1 (76) D Sweeney 7/1: 010546: Early ldr, no extra appr fnl 1f: see 1387.   1¾ 70
2250 **ROYAL CAVALIER** 31 [5] 3-9-0 (75) Paul Eddery 12/1: 000627: In tch, onepace when hmpd 2f out.   nk 68
2614 **ADAMAS** 16 [1] 3-9-7 (82) S Whitworth 25/1: -04108: Prom till appr fnl 2f: op 14/1, see 2222 (3 rnr mdn). 8 60
8 ran   Time 1m 45.0 (5.6)   (Bruce Corman)   A C Stewart Newmarket, Suffolk

933

NOTTINGHAM   SATURDAY JULY 29TH   Lefthand, Flat, Galloping Track

3006   4.10 RAINWORTH FILLIES MDN 3YO (D)   1m2f   Good/Firm 37 -03 Slow
£4771   £1468   £734   £367

-- **AMELLNAA** [7] Saeed bin Suroor 3-8-11 D O'Donohoe 11/10 FAV: 1: 3 gr f Sadler's Wells - Alydaress   85
(Alydar) Led, hard rdn/prsd appr fnl 1f, held on gamely: drifted from 4/6: prev unplcd in 2 Dubai trials: eff at
10f, shld stay 12f (Gr 1 entry): acts on fast grnd & runs well fresh: shld rate higher/hold her own in better company.
*2449 **LAND AHEAD** 23 [6] H R A Cecil 3-8-11 W Ryan 7/4: 5-31D2: 3 ch f Distant View - Nimble Folly (Cyane)   nk   84
Nvr far away, rdn to chall appr fnl 1f, held nr fin: clr of rem: lost nothing in defeat: see 2449.
2774 **MARENKA** 9 [8] H Candy 3-8-11 C Rutter 8/1: 423: 3 b f Mtoto - Sliprail (Our Native)   7   72
Chsd ldrs, shaken up 2f out, outpcd by front pair: will find easier fillies mdns, see 2774.
2548 **BRIONEY** 19 [1] J H M Gosden 3-8-11 (t) R Havlin 12/1: 004: Keen, rear, prog 3f out, sn no extra.   nk   71
2232 **SUN SILK** 31 [5] 3-8-11 G Hall 20/1: 05: Chsd ldrs, fdd appr fnl 1f: op 12/1, longer trip.   3   66
-- **SILKY FINISH** [2] 3-8-11 M Fenton 14/1: 6: In tch till 3f out: op 10/1 on debut: A P Indy filly,   10   52
dam a prolific wnr in the States: with B Hanbury.
1506 **NILOUPHAR** 64 [4] 3-8-11 Paul Eddery 100/1: 00-007: Al towards rear: 9 wk abs, new stable.   1½   50
2449 **STAR ATTRACTION** 23 [3] 3-8-11 G Hannon (7) 100/1: 48: Dwelt, al bhd: see 2449.   24   25
3189} **FASTBEAT RACING** 358 [9] 3-8-11 S Whitworth 100/1: 0-9: Unruly start, wide, struggling bef str, t.o.   dist   0
9 ran   Time 2m 06.3 (4)   (Godolphin)   Saeed bin Suroor Newmarket

3007   4.40 S JOSEPH HCAP 3YO+ 0-70 (E)   1m2f   Good/Firm 37 +04 Fast   [68]
£4192   £1290   £645   £322   3 yo rec 10lb

*2725 **WESTGATE RUN** 11 [2] R A Fahey 3-8-11 (61) W Ryan 3/1 FAV: 113311: 3 b f Emperor Jones - Glowing   69
Reference (Reference Point) In tch, prog to lead 2f out, pushed out, v cmftbly: best time of day: earlier won
at Warwick (appr h'cap), Hamilton (h'cap) & Brighton (class stks): '99 rnr-up (clmr, rtd 75): eff at 9/12f: likes
firm/fast grnd, handles gd, any trk: best up with/forcing the pace: progressive, in-form filly.
2626 **SACREMENTUM** 16 [12] J A Osborne 5-8-7 (47) G Sparkes (7) 11/1: 402442: 5 b g Night Shift - Tantum   2½   48
Ergo (Tanfirion) Bhd, styd on well fnl 2f, no ch with wnr: clr rem: apprec drop back to 10f: see 2295, 381.
2789 **INDIAN NECTAR** 9 [6] R Brotherton 7-9-1 (55) L Newman (3) 11/2: 420523: 7 b m Indian Ridge - Sheer   3½   51
Nectar (Piaffer) Prom, chall appr fnl 3f, onepace bef dist: clr rem but capable of better: see 1332.
2382 **WITH RESPECT** 26 [1] J G Given 3-7-13 (49) G Baker (5) 33/1: 0-0054: Waited with, mod late hdwy,   4   39
nvr dangerous: interesting in a sell h'cap with stronger handling: see 2382 (AW).
*2143 **GUNBOAT DIPLOMACY** GB 36 [11] 5-8-0 (40) C Rutter 6/1: 0-0015: Held up, prog 3f out, sn onepace.   ½   29
2453 **AVERHAM STAR** 22 [9] 5-7-10 (36) (14oh) N Carter (7) 66/1: 0-0006: Led till 2f out, fdd: stiff task.   ½   24
2861 **KING TUT** 6 [13] 4-8-9 (49) Dean McKeown 4/1: -22047: Keen, prom, wknd 2f out: op 7/1, st/mate 4th.   nk   37
2805 **FLAG FEN** 45 [5] 9-9-6 (60) R Studholme (5) 13/2: 062068: Mid-div, chsd ldrs halfway till 2f out: see 1150.   8   36
2552 **ROGUE SPIRIT** 19 [8] 4-10-0 (68) M Fenton 10/1: 400209: Well plcd till wknd qckly fnl 2f: see 2709, 746.   nk   43
*2764 **QUEEN OF THE KEYS** 10 [7] 4-8-0 (37)(3ow) N Pollard 15/2: 032210: Al towards rear: 10th, op 6/1.   ½   14
2764 **Massey** 10 [4] 4-9-1 (55) D O'Donohoe 25/1:
2802 **Qualitair Survivor** 8 [10] 5-7-12 (38)(vis) (2ow) (3oh) A Mackay 33/1:
12 ran   Time 2m 05.6 (3.3)   (Mark A Leatham)   R A Fahey Butterwick, N Yorks

RIPON   SUNDAY JULY 30TH   Righthand, Sharpish Track

Official Going: GOOD TO FIRM   Stalls: Straight Course - Stands side, Round Course - Inside

3008   2.25 WELFARE APPR SELL HCAP 3YO 0-60 (F)   1m2f   Good/Firm 24 -28 Slow   [61]
£2804   £863   £431   £215

2832 **HIGHCAL** 9 [7] Ronald Thompson 3-8-3 (36) T Hamilton (5) 25/1: -00001: 3 gr g King's Signet -   43
Guarded Expression (Siberian Express) Dwelt, sn prom, led over 1f out, rdn & styd on well, pushed out cl home:
no bid: 1st win: unplcd last term (rtd 64): eff at 10f, tried 12f, may suit: acts on fast & a sharpish trk.
2825 **BOLLIN NELLIE** 9 [5] T D Easterby 3-9-2 (49) M Worrall (5) 5/1: 450502: 3 ch f Rock Hopper - Bollin   1   53
Magdalene (Teenoso) Prom, prog to chall 2f out, ev ch dist, onepace ins last: eff at 1m, tried 12f: see 782.
2914 **CUIGIU** 4 [14] D Carroll 3-9-7 (54) Hayley Turner (5) 5/1: 540023: 3 b c Persian Bold - Homosassa   1   56
(Burslem) Led till over 1f out, onepace: lkd well, qck reapp: eff btwn 7/10f on fast & soft grnd: see 2914.
*2765 **TITUS BRAMBLE** 11 [9] B R Millman 3-8-8 (41) G Sparkes (7) 13/8 FAV: 006014: Rear, mod late gains.   4   37
2638 **BLAIR** 16 [8] 3-8-4 (37) C Catlin 8/1: 400505: In tch, held over 1f out: op 7/1: see 1661, 328.   1   31
2825 **BITTY MARY** 9 [10] 3-8-1 (34)(tvi) P Mundy (5) 12/1: 000056: Towards rear/rdn, mod gains: see 807.   1¾   26
2556 **FRENCH MASTER** 19 [6] 3-9-6 (53)(vis) L Gueller (3) 7/1: 033207: Cl up, held fnl 2f: jumps fit   nk   44
(unplcd, juv nov, rtd 73h): see 806 (seller).
2861 **PORTRACK JUNCTION** 7 [3] 3-8-7 (38)(2ow) R Farmer(0) 33/1: -00008: Struggling halfway: see 688.   5   23
2904 **KATIE KING** 5 [2] 3-7-10 (29)(BL)(2oh) Clare Roche 16/1: 60009: Held up, never a factor: blnks.   hd   12
2633 **MINSTREL GEM** 16 [12] 3-8-8 (41) Lynsey Hanna 33/1: -0000: Cl up 2f: 10th: h'cap bow.   2½   20
2656 **BOLDER ALEXANDER** 16 [11] 3-8-7 (40)(bl) S Clancy (3) 25/1: -0000F: In tch, slipped/fell on bend 5f out.   0
11 ran   Time 2m 08.5 (5.2)   (J Bradwell)   Ronald Thompson Stainforth, S Yorks

3009   2.55 HORSEFAIR MDN 2YO (D)   6f str   Good/Firm 24 -24 Slow
£3900   £1200   £600   £300

2608 **RIDGE RUNNER** 17 [2] J L Dunlop 2-9-0 K Darley 1/2 FAV: -21: 2 b c Indian Ridge - By Charter   86
(Shirley Heights) Chsd ldrs, led 2f out, styd on well inside last, rdn out: related to wnrs btwn 7/12f: eff at 6f,
looks sure to apprec further: acts on fast & a gall/sharpish track: open to improvement.
-- **ANNATTO** [8] I A Balding 2-8-9 F Lynch 11/2: -2: 2 b f Mister Baileys - Miss Rossi (Artaius)   ¾   77
Rear, hdwy 2f out, styd on well ins last, not rch wnr: strong filly, fit for debut: May foal, cost 54,000gns:
sire high class miler: eff at 6f, 7f+ looks sure to suit: acts on fast grnd: encouraging intro, win likely.
-- **LOVE EVERLASTING** [5] M Johnston 2-8-9 J Fanning 7/1: -3: 2 b f Pursuit Of Love - In Perpetuity   3   68+
(Great Nephew) Dwelt, sn chsd ldrs, outpcd by front pair fnl 1f: sharper for this: March foal, half sister to a
10f wnr, dam a 10f wnr: tall, scopey filly, highly encouraging intro & looks to relish further: win a mdn over 7f+.

RIPON   SUNDAY JULY 30TH   Righthand, Sharpish Track

-- **PRINCE PYRAMUS** [6] C Grant 2-9-0 A Culhane 33/1: -4: Led till inside last, not pace of ldrs: ndd 1½ 69
this debut: April foal, cheaply bought: dam unraced, sire a 7f wnr: ran well for a long way.
-- **RATHKENNY** [1] 2-9-0 S Finnamore (5) 66/1: -5: Rdn/bhd early, styd on well fnl 2f, nrst fin: sharper 3 60
for this: March foal, a first foal: dam a mdn wnr: sure to relish 7f+ & improve.
-- **GIBNEYS FLYER** [4] 2-8-9 C Lowther 16/1: -6: In tch, outpcd fnl 2f: ndd this: May foal, cost shd 55
IR 3,100gns: dam a sprint mdn: sire high class 1m/10f performer: with A Berry.
-- **VICIOUS DANCER** [3] 2-9-0 V Halliday 66/1: -7: In tch, btn 2f out: Timeless Times gelding, ½ 40
April foal, cost 3,800gns: dam a mdn: scopey gelding, with R M Whitaker.
1302 **CHILLI BOY 76** [14] 2-9-0 J McAuley 100/1: -08: In tch, btn 2f out: 11 week abs, mod form. 7 33
-- **ZIETING** [11] 2-9-0 N Callan 12/1: -9: U.r. bef start, in tch 3f: op 10/1: Zieten colt, Feb foal, 2½ 29
cost IR 13,000gns: a first foal: dam a wnr abroad: with K Burke.
2862 **HIGH SOCIETY LADY 7** [7] 2-8-9 T Williams 66/1: -00000: In tch 4f: 10th: mod form. 1¾ 15
2635 **DANITY FAIR 16** [10] 2-8-9 P Hanagan(7) 66/1: -400: Sn bhd: 11th: turf bow: see 2120 (5f, AW). 3 15
1558 **CATALAN BAY 62** [11] 2-8-9 O Pears 66/1: -00: Cl up 4f: 12th: 2 month abs: see 1558. hd 0
-- **College Star** [12] 2-9-0 T Lucas 66/1: **Bollin Toby** [15] 2-9-0 G Parkin 25/1:
14 ran   Time 1m 12.9 (2.9)   (Seymour Cohn)   J L Dunlop Arundel, W Sussex

---

3010   **3.25 MEREWOOD HCAP 3YO 0-80 (D)**   6f str Good/Firm 24 +13 Fast   [84]
£4875   £1500   £750   £375   Majority racing stands side favoured.

*2779 **DESRAYA 10** [3] K A Ryan 3-9-1 (71)(bl) F Lynch 4/1: 023111: 3 b g Desert Style - Madaraya 78
(Shahrastani) Trckd ldrs, rdn/prog to lead ins last, styd on well: fast time: earlier won h'caps at Ripon &
Hamilton: rtd 73 in '99: suited by 6f on fast & soft: suited by blnks: scopey, can continue to progress.
2541 **ELVINGTON BOY 20** [4] M W Easterby 3-9-0 (70) T Lucas 7/1: 003252: 3 ch g Emarati - Catherines ½ 75
Well (Junius) Led till ins last, styd on, but held by wnr: op 6/1: rest well covered: can find similar.
*2421 **EFFERVESCENT 25** [5] I A Balding 3-9-2 (72) K Darley 5/1: 023413: 3 b f Efisio - Sharp Chief 2½ 70
(Chief Singer) Prom, no extra fnl 1f: op 6/1: see 2421 (mdn).
2787 **JAMES STARK 10** [7] N P Littmoden 3-9-4 (74) J Fanning 11/1: 034244: In tch, styd on fnl 2f, never 1 69
able to chall: consistent sort, see 2787, 275 & 105.
*2839 **FLY MORE 8** [11] 3-9-1 (71) P Fitzsimons (5) 11/4 FAV: -45515: Chsd ldrs 5f: bckd: lkd well. hd 66
2364 **CAUTIONARY 27** [10] 3-9-7 (77) P Bradley (5) 33/1: 220-06: Chsd ldrs, held over 1f out: see 2364. 2½ 65
2855 **POP SHOP 8** [8] 3-8-11 (67) N Callan 12/1: 000007: Never on terms: paddock pick: see 2250, 905. 2½ 48
2663 **COLLEGE MAID 16** [13] 3-8-12 (68) A Culhane 16/1: 010058: Cl up far side, held fnl 2f: see 2165. nk 48
2779 **HOWARDS LAD 10** [6] 3-8-4 (60)(bl) V Halliday 14/1: 051029: Dwelt, nvr on terms: closer to wnr in 2779. nk 48
2396 **PRINTSMITH 26** [9] 3-8-1 (57) O Pears 25/1: -01060: Chsd ldrs, btn 2f out: 10th: btr 1710 (g/s). hd 36
2204 **POLAR HAZE 34** [12] 3-9-2 (72) Paul Eddery 14/1: 26-230: Prom far side 4f: 11th: see 2204, 1688. 1 48
2823 **CHRISTOPHERSSISTER 9** [1] 3-9-13 (55) J McAuley 33/1: 040000: Outpcd from halfway: 12th. nk 30
1840 **PERTEMPS FC 50** [14] 3-7-13 (55) T Williams 20/1: -00000: Led far side till dist, fdd: 13th: abs. shd 30
2603 **PADDYWACK 17** [2] 3-7-13 (55)(bl) Claire Bryan (5) 14/1: 0020U0: Dwelt, sn bhd: 14th: see 1742. dist 0
14 ran   Time 1m 10.7 (0.7)   (Pendle Inn Partnership)   K A Ryan Hambleton, N Yorks

---

3011   **4.00 CITY OF RIPON HCAP 3YO+ 0-80 (D)**   1m1f Good/Firm 24 -09 Slow   [79]
£7637   £2350   £1175   £587

2758 **GRALMANO 11** [2] K A Ryan 5-9-10 (75) F Lynch 11/1: 251641: 5 b g Scenic - Llangollen (Caerleon) 80
Handy, drvn/forged ahead over 1f out, held on gamely: lkd well: earlier scored at W'hampton (AW h'cap, rtd 98a)
& Redcar (h'cap): '99 wnr at Redcar (class stks) & Pontefract (h'cap, rtd 72 & 92a, earlier won h'caps with N Littmoden:
'98 Lingfield wnr (stks, rtd 99a & 82): eff btwn 1m/10f, stays 11f: acts on both AWs, firm & gd/soft, any trk:
likes Redcar: eff with/without blnks or vis, gd weight carrier: likes to race with/force the pace.
2564 **BURNING TRUTH 19** [11] Mrs A Duffield 6-8-9 (60) L Enstone(7) 25/1: 44-602: 6 ch g Known Fact - ½ 64
Galega (Sure Blade) Held up, prog & every ch 1f out, kept on inside last: can find similar: see 1907 (mdn h'cap).
2799 **SWYNFORD PLEASURE 9** [13] J L Eyre 4-7-11 (47)(10w) T Williams 10/1: 253343: 4 b f Reprimand - nk 51
Pleasuring (Good Times) Prom, rdn/chall over 1f out, styd on: btn less than 1L: consistent: see 2180, 1939.
+2799 **PENTAGON LAD 9** [10] J L Eyre 4-9-9 (74) R Cody Boutcher (7) 3/1 FAV: 062514: Held up, prog to 2½ 73
chall over 1f out, held inside last: well bckd, op 9/2: see 2799.
2726 **AGIOTAGE 12** [6] A Beech (5) 12/1: 016155: Chsd ldrs ldrs 2f out, held fnl 1f: lkd well. ¾ 54
*2781 **REQUESTOR 10** [1] 5-9-5 (70) T Lucas 4/1: 3-0116: Held up, late gains fnl 2f, no threat: see 2781. hd 67
2279 **BHUTAN 31** [5] 5-9-1 (66) A Culhane 10/1: 4-1607: Cl up, every ch going well 4f out, wknd qckly nk 62
1f out: poss saw too much daylight here, best held up for a late run: see 1194 (12f).
*2834 **HORMUZ 8** [3] 4-8-10 (61) K Darley 4/1: 000018: Led till over 1f out, fdd: op 7/2: see 2834 (sell, 1m). ¾ 55
895 **ROUTE SIXTY SIX 108** [15] 4-9-5 (70) O Pears 33/1: 00-009: Prom 3f, lost pl bef halfway, mod late 1¾ 61
gains: 3 month abs, prev with G L Moore, blnks omitted: '99 Newmarket wnr (val h'cap, rtd 84): '98 Brighton
wnr (nurs, rtd 77): suited by 7f/1m on firm & hvy grnd, any track: now with Jedd O Keeffe.
2780 **ALAMEIN 10** [14] 7-7-10 (47)(t)(10oh) J Bramhill 20/1: 000230: Held up, no room 3f out, never threat: 10th. ½ 37
2834 **JAMMIE DODGER 8** [17] 4-7-10 (47)(6oh) G Sparkes(3) 16/1: 0201U0: Cl up 6f: 11th: btr 2533 (g/s). ¾ 35
2865 **THATCHED 7** [16] 10-7-10 (47)(2oh) P M Quinn (3) 14/1: 605630: Al bhd: 12th: flatted 2865. nk 34
2831 **YOUNG ROSEIN 9** [8] 4-8-3 (53)(10w) Paul Eddery 16/1: -00300: Keen/chsd ldrs 6f: 13th: op 14/1. 2 37
2750 **MODUS OPERANDI 11** [12] 4-9-6 (71) N Callan 11/1: -64000: Pulled hard/chsd ldrs 7f: 14th: needs 1 52
to learn restraint & a drop to 7f/1m could suit: see 593.
2781 **LEGACY OF LOVE 10** [9] 4-8-9 (60) J Fanning 10/1: 44-020: Prom 5f: 15th: op 12/1: btr 2781. 6 31
2671 **HADEQA 15** [12] 4-8-9 (60) S Carson (3) 33/1: 100-00: Bhd halfway: 16th: see 2671. 5 21
16 ran   Time 1m 53.0 (3.0)   (Coleorton Moor Racing)   K A Ryan Hambleton, N Yorks

---

3012   **4.35 KNARESBOROUGH MDN 3YO (D)**   1m2f Good/Firm 24 -04 Slow
£3575   £1100   £550   £275

2722 **TIGRE 13** [12] B W Hills 3-9-0 K Darley 2/1 FAV: -40021: 3 b c Mujtahid - Vice Vixen (Vice Regent) 83
Made all, hard rdn from 3f out, held on gamely inside last, drvn out: hvly bckd, op 3/1, lkd well: rnr up on 4 of
5 '99 starts (rtd 89, mdn): eff at 7f/1m, suited by front running tactics at 10f: acts on fast & soft grnd, gall
or sharpish track: belated first win, could now find 7f class suit.
1808 **SCACHMATT 51** [3] L M Cumani 3-9-0 G Sparkes (7) 7/1: -50242: 3 b c Zafonic - Svanzega (Sharpen Up) ½ 82
Chsd ldrs, prog to chall over 1f out, styd on well, just held nr fin: padd pick, op 6/1, 7 wk abs, clr of rem:
eff at 10/12f on fast & gd: could find similar, particularly with stronger handling: see 1386, 1054.

935

RIPON

SUNDAY JULY 30TH **Righthand, Sharpish Track**

2354 **PRECIOUS POPPY** 28 [7] Sir Michael Stoute 3-8-9 (VIS) F Lynch 9/2: -433: 3 b f Polish Precedent - 5 69
Benazir (High Top) Handy, ev ch 2f out, sn held by front pair: visor: mid dist h'cap should now suit.
2832 **LETS REFLECT** 9 [8] J R Turner 3-8-9 A Beech (5) 33/1: -54: In tch, held fnl 2f: see 2832. 3 64
2531 **DE TRAMUNTANA** 21 [11] 3-8-9 N Callan 9/4: 0-2425: Chsd ldrs, btn 2f out: bckd: strong gelding. 6 55
2520 **LA SYLPHIDE GB** 21 [1] 3-8-9 T Williams 50/1: -36: Held up, never a threat: see 2520. 2½ 52
-- **WHAT A DANCER** [10] 3-9-0 J Fanning 50/1: -7: Cl up 7f: debut: needed this: with W Haigh. 1½ 55
2198 **MUSALLIAH** 34 [6] 3-8-9 Paul Eddery 7/1: -048: Chsd ldrs, btn 3f out: op 5/1: improve in h'caps. 2½ 47
2558 **DOUBLE BID** 19 [2] 3-9-0 T Lucas 33/1: -209: Bhd 4f out: btr 1717 (1m). 17 27
2703 **GRACILIS** 14 [4] 3-9-0 C Lowther 50/1: -400: Sn bhd: 10th: see 2520 (1m). ¾ 26
-- **MY LINE** [9] 3-9-0 A Culhane 33/1: -0: Sn bhd: 11th: debut: with Mrs M Reveley. 5 18
1670} **BLACK JACK GIRL** 425 [5] 3-8-9 O Pears 66/1: 0-0: Bhd halfway: 12th: reapp, no form. dist 0
12 ran   Time 2m 06.1 (2.8)   (Guy Reed & J Hanson)   B W Hills Lambourn, Berks

---

3013 5.10 SUNDAY RACING HCAP 3YO+ 0-85 (D)   1m4f60y   Good/Firm 24 -16 Slow   [76]
£5307 £1633 £816 £408   3yo rec 12lb

1862 **NAJJM** 49 [4] J L Dunlop 3-8-13 (73) Paul Eddery 8/1: 33-651: 3 br c Dynaformer - Azusa (Flying 82
Paster) Led/dsptd lead, went on over 2f out, rdn & styd on strongly, eased nr line: val for 4L+, 7 wk abs: plcd
all 4 '99 starts at 8f, could get further: acts on firm, soft & a sharpish or stiff/gall trk.
*3007 **WESTGATE RUN** 1 [9] R A Fahey 3-8-7 (67)(6ex) G Parkin 9/4 FAV: 133112: 3 b f Emperor Jones - 2 70
Glowing Reference (Reference Point) Chsd ldrs, led over 3f out till over 2f out, held by wnr ins last: rest
well covered, hvly bckd: continues to run well: won at Nottingham yesterday: see 3007 (10f).
2837 **SHAFFISHAYES** 8 [6] Mrs M Reveley 8-8-6 (54) A Culhane 11/2: 654653: 8 ch g Clantime - Mischievous 2½ 53
Miss (Niniski) Held up towards rear, rdn & styd on fnl 3f, no threat to front pair: op 9/2: running well enough
but would be served by a little cut in the ground to pinch one of these: see 943.
*2805 **BAILEYS PRIZE** 9 [3] M Johnston 3-9-9 (83) K Darley 3/1: 222314: Held up, rdn/hung right 3f out & 1½ 80
sn held: tough colt who has been busy: see 2805.
2876 **OCEAN DRIVE** 6 [7] 4-7-12 (46) A Beech(1) 12/1: 342245: Rear, late gains, no threat: quick reapp. 1¾ 41
2671 **PIPED ABOARD** 15 [8] 5-9-10 (72) N Callan 14/1: -35006: In tch, btn 3f out: op 12/1: topweight. ¾ 66
2829 **CASHMERE LADY** 9 [10] 8-9-1 (63) R Cody Boutcher 6/1: 011027: Held up, never a factor: btr 2446. ¾ 56
2836 **ALDWYCH ARROW** 8 [2] 5-8-10 (58) J Fanning 20/1: 000-08: Held up, rdn/btn 2f out: needed this. 8 39
2279 **ELVIS REIGNS** 31 [5] 4-8-6 (54) P Goode (3) 25/1: 000009: Led over 1f till over 3f out, fdd: see 2002. 8 23
9 ran   Time 3m 38.5 (5.0)   (Hamdan Al Maktoum)   J L Dunlop Arundel, W Sussex

---

ASCOT

SUNDAY JULY 30TH **Righthand, Stiff, Galloping Track**

Official Going   GOOD TO FIRM (GOOD in places). Stalls: Str Crse - Stands Side; Rnd Crse - Inside.

3014 2.15 SHA TIN HCAP 3YO 0-85 (D)   1m4f   Good/Firm 36 -00 Slow   [92]
£6890 £2120 £1060 £530

2878 **MANA DARGENT** 6 [8] M Johnston 3-8-8 (72) K Dalgleish (5) 14/1: 563031: 3 b c Ela Mana Mou - Petite 84
D Argent (Noalto) In tch, prog to lead appr fnl 2f, edged left & rdn, edged right & drew clr below dist: tchd 20/1,
qck reapp: 1st win, campaigned over inadequate trips prev, incl when plcd 2 of 3 juv starts (rtd 93): prev eff at
7f, relished this step up to 12f: acts on firm & hvy, any trk: open to further improvement over mid-dists.
2596 **ZIBELINE** 18 [2] C E Brittain 3-9-5 (83) B Marcus 11/1: 244152: 3 b c Cadeaux Genereux - Zia 3½ 87
(Shareef Dancer) Bhd till ran on strongly fnl 2f, went 2nd nr fin, nvr nrr: op 8/1, waiting tactics overdone
over longer trip, clrly stays 12f: progressive: see 2450.
2712 **INCHING CLOSER** 13 [10] N A Callaghan 3-9-3 (81) R Hughes 11/1: 001333: 3 b g Inchinor - nk 84
Maiyaasah (Kris) Mid-div, rdn ent str, styd on fnl 1f: op 9/1: eff at 10/12f: tough sort, see 1655.
+2702 **PRINCIPLE** 14 [15] Sir Mark Prescott 3-8-13 (77) G Duffield 5/2 FAV: 4-4314: Well plcd, no extra shd 80
appr fnl 1f: well bckd: gd run tho' shade btr 2702.
2872 **AFTER THE BLUE** 7 [12] 3-8-2 (66) P Fessey 6/1: 412245: Mid-div, prog to chase ldrs 2f out, ¾ 67
kept on same pace: qck reapp, not far off best & clr rem, see 2872, 2470, 2272.
2750 **IGNITE** 11 [1] 3-8-4 (68) J Carroll 20/1: 340-06: Rear, prog appr fnl 2f, nvr nr ldrs: tchd 33/1, lngr trip. 3 64
2836 **SPEED VENTURE** 8 [3] 3-8-8 (72) R Mullen 20/1: 422557: Held up, eff & short of room appr fnl 1 66
2f, not persevered with over longer 12f trip: see 1640.
*1725 **RAGDALE HALL** 55 [4] 3-9-7 (85) R Havlin 7/1: -518: Nvr threatened ldrs: tchd 10/1, jt top-weight nk 78
on h'cap bow after 8 wk abs: see 1725 (10f, gd grnd).
2685 **KATHAKALI** 15 [6] 3-7-10 (60)(10h) R Brisland (5) 33/1: 000509: Mid-div, rdn 3f out, onepace: struck into. 2 50
2560 **EMPIRE DREAM** 19 [9] 3-8-11 (75) J Reid 10/1: 4220: Held up, wide into str, nvr dngrs: 10th, st/mate wnr. nk 64
2509 **RED EMPRESS** 22 [13] 3-9-7 (85) R Hills 11/2: -26120: Led till 2f out, sn btn: 11th, bckd, jt top- 1¾ 72
weight: progressive earlier, surely something amiss: see 2103.
2712 **ABLE NATIVE** 13 [11] 3-8-3 (67)(bl) L Newman (3) 20/1: -02100: Mid div: 12th: see 2217 (AW). 1 53
2751 **DIAMOND ROAD** 11 [14] 3-8-10 (74) J Mongan (5) 25/1: -33260: Handy till 4f out: 13th, struck into. 13 40
13 ran   Time 2m 33.39 (4.39)   (Daniel A Couper)   M Johnston Middleham, N.Yorks.

3015 2.45 HONG KONG AUCT STKS 2YO (B)   7f str   Good/Firm 36 -12 Slow
£14495 £4460 £2235 £1115   Raced stands side

*2649 **SARATOV** 16 [13] M Johnston 2-8-5 R Hills 9/4 FAV: -311: 2 b c Rudimentary - Sarabah (Ela Mana Mou) 98
With ldr, narrow lead halfway, rdn ent dist, held on well for press: hvly bckd: recent York wnr (dam):
17,000gns half-brother to useful sprinter Cryhavoc & 1m/9f performer: dam 10f wnr: eff at 7f, 1m
suit: acts on fast grnd, stiff trks: game, progressive & useful colt, has earned a step up in grade.
*2708 **SWING BAND** 14 [6] G B Balding 2-8-2 A Daly 5/1: -12: 2 b c Celtic Swing - Inchkeith (Reference ½ 93
Point) Led till halfway, kept on well for press but wnr would not be denied: nicely bckd: clr rem: has plenty
of pace for one so stoutly bred: acts on firm/fast grnd: improving: see 2708.
2678 **SILK LAW** 15 [2] A Berry 2-7-12 G Bardwell 11/2: -1123: 2 c f Barathea - Jural (Kris) 2½ 84
Trkd ldrs, keen, not much room 3f out, rdn bef dist, kept on but not pace of front pair: styd longer 7f trip,
could have done with a faster pace: see 2251.
2935 **FIGURA** 3 [4] K McAuliffe 2-8-1 F Norton 10/1: -6164: Trkd ldrs, switched appr fnl 2f, unable to qckn: 3½ 80

936

op 7/1, qck reapp: possibly flattered in Listed company on Thursday: see 2619.
2494 **MONSIEUR LE BLANC** 22 [3] 2-8-4 J F Egan 9/1: -635: Held up, eff ent fnl 3f, nvr nr ldrs: 1½ 80
possibly unsuited by different tactics, btr 2494 (forced the pace).
*2514 **BLACK KNIGHT** 22 [10] 2-8-3 G Duffield 4/1: -3116: Prom, ch 3f out, rdn & edged left 2f out, fdd: hd 79
well bckd: something amiss? btr 2514.
2137 **ORIENTAL MIST** 37 [7] 2-8-5 B Marcus 20/1: -54337: Nvr a factor: mdn, up in trip, see 1906, 1653. hd 81
1876 **NELSONS FLAGSHIP** 48 [11] 2-8-3 P Doe 50/1: -08: Al bhd: 7 wk abs, highly tried Petong colt. 9 64
*2588 **PAIRING** 18 [9] 2-8-3 L Newman 20/1: -419: Held up, brief single effort appr fnl 2f: btr 2588 (6f, gd). 1¼ 62
2894 **VIOLENT** 6 [5] 2-7-11 (vis) M Henry 25/1: 002120: Prom till halfway: 10th, qck reapp: see 2723 (clmr). hd 56
2120 **THE WALL** 38 [1] 2-7-11 A Nicholls 100/1: -0500: Keen, struggling bef halfway: 11th: stiff task. 8 41
2748 **TUSCAN** 11 [12] 2-8-0 P Fessey 33/1: -460: Dwelt, al towards rear: 12th, stiff task. 5 34
12 ran   Time 1m 29.38 (3.38)   (J David Abell)   M Johnston Middleham, N.Yorks.

3016   3.15 HONG KONG HCAP 3YO+ (B)   5f str Good/Firm 36 -04 Slow   [114]
£46000 £17600 £8800 £4000   3yo rec 4lb All but one raced centre-stands side

2954 **MAGIC RAINBOW** 2 [6] M L W Bell 5-7-10 (82)(1oh) J Mackay (5) 8/1: 600651: 5 b g Magic Ring - Blues 87
Indigo (Music Boy) Prom, rdn to lead dist, drvn & ran on strgly: ran 48hrs ago: earlier won at Lingfield (stks,
rtd 90a): '99 wnr again at Lingfield (rtd 94a) & Kempton (h'caps, rtd 88): '98 Southwell & Newmarket wnr (h'caps,
rtd 86a & 84): v eff over a stiff 5f, stays 7f on firm, gd/soft, both AWs: goes well fresh: tough.
2355 **COMPTON BANKER** 28 [9] G A Butler 3-7-11 (87)(1ow)(5oh) P Doe 15/2: -05102: 3 br c Distinctly ¾ 89+
North - Mary Hinge (Dowsing) Last, nowhere to go appr fnl 2f till bef dist, strong run, too late: bckd from 9/1:
progressive 3yo, unlucky here: acts on fast & gd grnd: likes Ascot, can find compensation: see 2168 (C/D).
1980 **FURTHER OUTLOOK** 44 [5] D Nicholls 6-8-10 (96) Dane O'Neill 15/2: 053253: 6 gr g Zilzal - Future hd 98
Bright (Lyphard's Wish) Led till 1f out, kept on: bckd from 9/1, 6 wk abs: running well in defeat, see 1182.
2165 **ROZEL** 36 [2] R Guest 3-7-10 (86)(6oh) G Baker (5) 14/1: 0134: Chsd ldrs, kept on und press bef nk 87
fnl 1f, not btn far: fine run 6lbs o/h on only 4th ever start: acts on fast & gd/soft grnd: sure to win more races.
2348 **DORCHESTER** 28 [1] 3-7-10 (86)(BL)(2oh) F Norton 7/1 FAV: -00005: Front rank, outpcd fnl 1f: 1½ 83
hvly bckd from 9/1: more expected in first time blnks, lks well h'capped on juvenile form: see 2168.
2065 **EASTERN PURPLE** 40 [15] 5-9-12 (112) J Carroll 20/1: 030056: Mid-div in centre, carr right appr fnl hd 109
1f, kept on without threatening: 6 wk abs, top-weight: not the best of draws & will apprec a return to 6f: see 927.
2676 **IVORYS JOY** 15 [7] 5-8-2 (87)(1ow) G Duffield 20/1: 160457: Chsd ldrs, eff appr fnl 1f, came pace. nk 84
2954 **CRYHAVOC** 2 [10] 6-8-7 (93)(5ex) A Nicholls (3) 15/2: 021028: Rear, not much room appr fnl 2f, sn shd 89
rdn, kept on ins last: well bckd, stablemate 3rd: ran 48hrs ago, unsuited by drop back to 5f: see 2954, 2432.
2721 **ATLANTIC VIKING** 13 [14] 5-7-12 (84)(bl) M Henry 16/1: -00049: In tch, centre, prog & hung right hd 80
2f out, onepace for press: stablemate 3rd: see 2721, 1861.
2676 **SHEER VIKING** 15 [3] 4-8-13 (99) R Hills 16/1: 232000: Mid-div, not clr run appr fnl 2f, nvr dngrs: 10th. 1 92
2456 **FIRST MAITE** 23 [20] 7-8-9 (95)(vis) Dean McKeown 12/1: 500340: Alone far side, prom till fnl 1f: 11th. 1 85
2495 **SHATIN VENTURE** 22 [19] 3-8-5 (95) R Winston 33/1: 4-3000: Outpcd in centre, nvr dngrs: 12th. ½ 84
2877 **BON AMI** 6 [11] 4-7-12 (84) G Bardwell 12/1: 003460: Chsd ldrs towards centre till 2f out: 12th, see 1004. shd 73
2676 **SUNLEY SENSE** 15 [13] 4-7-11 (83) P Fessey 11/1: 220020: Dwelt, nvr got in it: 14th, better than this. shd 72
2168 **KATHOLOGY** 36 [18] 3-8-3 (93) N Pollard 20/1: 211400: Prom centre till after halfway: 15th, see 1219. ½ 81
2348 **HENRY HALL** 28 [12] 4-8-9 (95) J Reid 12/1: 031100: Prom towards centre till wknd ent fnl 2f: 16th. ¾ 80
2706 Dashing Blue 14 [16] 7-9-5 (105) J F Egan 25/1:   2065 Seraphina 40 [8] 3-8-10 (100)(BL) K Dalgleish(5) 40/1:
*2247 Damalis 14 [17] 4-8-12 (98) R Hughes 25/1:
19 ran   Time 1m 01.02 (2.02)   (P T Fenwick)   M L W Bell Newmarket.

3017   3.50 SINO GROUP CLASS STKS 3YO+ 0-95 (B)   1m2f Good/Firm 36 -13 Slow
£9893 £3044 £1522 £761   3yo rec 10lb

*2006 **ASLY** 43 [5] Sir Michael Stoute 3-8-11 R Hills 13/8 FAV: -211: 3 b c Riverman - La Pepite (Mr Prospector) 105
Trkd ldr halfway, led ent fnl 2f, sn drvn, kept on well, psh out fnl 1f: well bckd, 6 wk abs: earlier won at York
(mdn): unrcd juv, cost $440,000: eff at 1m/10f on firm/fast grnd: v useful/progressive try Listed/Group 3.
3843} **HIDDNAH** 325 [7] M Johnston 3-8-8 J Reid 11/2: 2315-2: 3 ch f Affirmed - L'Extra Honor (Hero's 1¾ 98
Honor) Rcd in 2nd till halfway, switched 2f out, kept on to regain 2nd bef dist: gd reapp by wnr: clr rem, reapp: '99 wnr
at Newcastle (mdn, rtd 94 at best): eff at 1m, suited by step up to 10f & shld stay 12f: acts on firm & gd grnd.
2090 **TACTFUL REMARK** 39 [4] J A Osborne 4-9-5 R Hughes 9/1: -05403: 4 ch c Lord At War - Right Word 4 93
(Verbatim) Clr ldr till halfway, hdd ent fnl 2f, no extra: op 12/1, 6 wk abs: caught 2 unexposed types: see 1015.
*1990 **COMMON PLACE** 43 [6] C F Wall 3-8-11 R Mullen 10/3: 113214: Held up, chsd ldrs appr str, fdd 2f 1½ 93
out: nicely bckd despite difficult task at the weights after 6 wk abs: continues career in Hong Kong, see 1990.
*2434 **KRANTOR** 25 [8] 3-8-13 A McGlone 10/3: -6215: Al bhd: hvly bckd: see 2434 (gd/soft grnd mdn). 21 65
5 ran   Time 2m 08.90 (4.90)   (Hamdan Al Maktoum)   Sir Michael Stoute Newmarket.

3018   4.25 HAPPY VALLEY HCAP 3YO+ 0-90 (C)   1m str Good/Firm 36 +02 Fast   [89]
£7085 £2180 £1090 £545   3yo rec 8lb Field came stands side

2616 **SALTY JACK** 17 [16] V Soane 6-9-4 (79) J F Egan 9/1: 005451: 6 b h Salt Dome - Play The Queen 85
(King Of Clubs) Held up, crept closer after halfway, led dist, drvn out: op 7/1, fair time: earlier won at
Lingfield (h'cap, rtd 87a): '99 wnr again at Lingfield (h'cap, rtd 81a & 89): '98 wnr at Doncaster, Folkestone
(ltd stks), Epsom & Newmarket (h'caps, rtd 89 & 75a): eff at 7f/1m: acts on firm, hvy grnd & equitrack: goes
on any trk, likes Lingfield: can run well fresh & carry big weights: tough & well h'capped entire.
2758 **ITS MAGIC** 11 [5] B Hanbury 4-8-8 (69)(bl) Dane O'Neill 8/1: 16-062: 4 b g Magic Ring - Ryewater ½ 73+
Dream (Touching Wood) Towards rear, keen, going well but no room 2f out, switched widest of all & ran on
ins last, too late: bckd from 10/1, prob unlucky: clrly apprec refitting of blnks: win soon, see 2758.
2117 **TRAVELLING LITE** 38 [17] B R Millman 3-8-11 (80) G Hind 16/1: -34203: 3 b c Blues Traveller - Lute ¾ 82
And Lyre (The Noble Player) Front rank, led after halfway till bef dist, onepcd towards fin: back to best.
2634 **COOL TEMPER** 16 [2] J M P Eustace 4-8-12 (73) J Tate 20/1: 555054: Mid-div, rdn 2f out, no 1¼ 72
impress till kept on fnl 150y: stays 1m & is likely to get further still on this evidence: see 1060.
2999 **RICH IN LOVE** 1 [7] 6-9-10 (85) I Mongan (5) 20/1: 231005: Chsd ldrs, hdwy & ev ch appr fnl ½ 83
1f, onepace dist: up in trip, unplcd over 7f here yesterday, see 2412.
2629 **PUNISHMENT** 17 [8] 9-8-12 (73)(t) J Reid 12/1: 006246: Well plcd, led briefly appr fnl 1f, fdd. hd 71
2758 **INTRICATE WEB** 11 [14] 4-8-10 (71) R Hughes 9/1: 061337: Trkd ldrs, rdn ent fnl 2f, unable to hd 69
qckn when short of room & snatched up below dist: op 7/1: prev in gd form: btr 2241 (7f).

937

ASCOT   SUNDAY JULY 30TH   Righthand, Stiff, Galloping Track

2768 **PETRUS** 11 [3] 4-8-8 (69)(t) B Marcus 20/1: 000508: Al around mid-div: well h'capped: see 1286. — 1 / 65
2645 **TAFFS WELL** 16 [15] 7-8-12 (73) J Carroll 6/1 FAV: 042609: Waited in tch, eff 2f out, onepace ¾ 67
& eased below dist: nicely bckd: better expected from this well h'capped gelding: see 715.
2890 **PATSY STONE** 6 [6] 4-8-7 (68) F Norton 9/1: 445320: Mid-div, eff & btn appr fnl 1f, eased: 10th: 3 56
op 7/1, qck reapp: better giving weight to lesser rivals as in 1794.
2704 **THE DOWNTOWN FOX** 14 [10] 5-8-9 (70)(bl) K Dalgleish(5) 12/1: 600020: Wide, nvr trbld ldrs: 11th. 3 52
2814 **TEOFILIO** 9 [11] 6-8-8 (69)(bl) R Winston 9/1: 000230: Bhd, shkn up 3f out, sn short of room & no 3½ 44
ch with ldrs: 12th, nicely bckd: probably worth forgetting: see 594.
2853 **CALLDAT SEVENTEEN** 8 [13] 4-8-9 (70) G Duffield 12/1: 246060: Towards rear, widest of all, btn 7 31
2f out: 13th: worth ignoring, see 2564, 1271.
2522 **YAROB** 21 [1] 7-9-13 (88) A Nicholls 3) 9/1: 026060: Led but hung, hdd after halfway, lost pl: 14th. hd 49
1327 **NIMELLO** 74 [9] 4-10-0 (89) D Sweeney 14/1: 0-0100: Prom till 3f out: 15th, top-weight, 11 wk abs. 4 42
15 ran   Time 1m 41.48 (2.78)   (Salts Of The Earth)   V Soane East Garston, Berks.

<table>
<tr><td>3019</td><td>5.00 DRAGON FILL MDN 3YO (D)   1m str   Good/Firm 36   -24 Slow
£6711   £2065   £1032   £516</td></tr>
</table>

1374 **VELVET LADY** 72 [3] P F I Cole 3-8-11 D Sweeney 13/8: -2651: 3 b f Nashwan - Velvet Moon (Shaadi) 106
Made all, held on well, rdn out: nicely bckd, 10 wk abs, highly tried earlier (fine 6th in 1,000 Guineas): unrcd
juv: eff at 7f/1m, tried further: acts on firm & soft grnd, stiff/gall trks: suited forcing the pace: useful.
2089] **FARRFESHEENA** 407 [1] Saeed bin Suroor 3-8-11 (t) J Reid 5/4 FAV: 5-2: 3 ch f Rahy - Bevel (Mr nk 105
Prospector) In tch, closed to press wnr 2f out, rdn & kept on, kpt hvly bckd, clr rem on reapp: disapp 11/8
shot sole juv start (rtd 64, D Loder): eff at 1m on fast grnd in a t-strap: useful reapp, similar a formality.
1901 **ARDUINE** 49 [4] J H M Gosden 3-8-11 R Havlin 7/2: 6-3303: 3 ch f Diesis - Ardisia (Affirmed) 15 80
In tch, outpcd appr fnl 2f: bckd, 7 wk abs, drop in trip & grade: see 1901, 1200.
1388 **ANASTASIA VENTURE** 71 [2] S P C Woods 3-8-11 G Duffield 16/1: -5324: Cl-up till ent str: 10 wk abs. 11 60
4 ran   Time 1m 43.33 (4.83)   (HRH Prince Fahd Salman)   P F I Cole Whatcombe, Oxon.

NEWMARKET (July)   SUNDAY JULY 30TH   Righthand, Stiff, Galloping Track

Official Going   GOOD. Stalls: Race 1 & 3 - Far Side; Rem - Stands Side.

<table>
<tr><td>3020</td><td>2.05 EBF FILL MDN 2YO (D)   7f str   Good 44   -09 Slow
£5164   £1589   £794   £397</td></tr>
</table>

-- **SUMMER SYMPHONY** [10] L M Cumani 2-8-11 J P Spencer 6/1: 1: 2 gr f Caerleon - Summer Sonnet 97
(Baillamont): Mid-div, gd hdwy to lead over 2f out, strongly pressed ins last, drvn out: Apr foal, full sister
to a 10f wnr abroad, dam scored over 12f: eff at 7f, will relish 1m + in time: runs well fresh on gd grnd & a
stiff/gall trk: fine debut run: looks genuine, can rate more highly & win again.
-- **FLIGHT OF FANCY** [7] Sir Michael Stoute 2-8-11 W Ryan 7/2: 2: 2 b f Sadler's Wells - Phantom Gold hd 96
(Machiavellian): Dwelt, settled rear, gd hdwy over 2f out, ran on well to chall ins last, just held: Mar foal,
dam a high class mid-dist 3yo performer: eff over a stiff/gall 7f on gd, 1m will suit: gd debut, go one better sn.
2390 **CANDICE** 26 [1] E A L Dunlop 2-8-11 T Quinn 6/1: 33: 2 b f Caerleon - Criquette (Shirley Heights): 2½ 91
Prom, slightly outpcd over 3f out, styd on but no threat to front 2: handles firm & gd: relish 1m next time.
-- **ZULFAA** [9] J L Dunlop 2-8-11 W Supple 10/1: 4: Rear, rdn/hdwy 2f out, kept on, no impress: 1 89
Feb foal, half-sister to 7f juv scorer Atwaar, dam scored over 12f: spot-on next time.
-- **FRUIT PUNCH** [2] M Roberts 16/1: 5: Dwelt, held up, badly hmpd & dropped last halfway, 1½ 86
swtchd wide, rdn & styd on inside last, no threat: op 12/1: Apr foal: Baratheea filly, half-brother to a 7f
wnr: did not have the run of the race here & can rate more highly: with T Easterby.
-- **BOIRA** [5] 2-8-11 R Cochrane 50/1: 6: Dwelt, rear, rdn/kept on onepace final 2f: Diesis filly, ½ 85
sire high class juv: will find easier opportunities, with D Morris.
2683 **PRINCESS TITANIA** 15 [6] 2-8-11 S Sanders 20/1: 47: Prom, rdn/outpcd 2f out, late hdwy: see 2683. hd 85
2316 **ST FLORENT** 29 [4] 2-8-11 J Fortune 9/2: 28: Led, hdd over 3f out, wknd qckly appr final 1f: 2 81
v disapp here, rated much higher on debut in 2316.
-- **BACK PASS** [11] M Hills 10/3 FAV: 9: Cl-up, went on over 3f out, hdd 2f out, sn fdd: ¾ 80
Feb foal, dam a wng miler abroad: sire Derby wnr: shld be capable of better, sharper next timer for B W Hills.
1236 **BLUE LADY** 80 [8] 2-8-11 J Quinn 33/1: -0650: In tch, wknd qckly final 2f, fin 10th: 11 wk abs. 10 65
-- **TALAT** [3] 2-8-11 P McCabe 66/1: 0: Prom to halfway, 11th: cheap May foal, dam plcd as a juv. ¾ 64
11 ran   Time 1m 27.62 (3.72)   (Gerald Leigh)   L M Cumani Newmarket.

<table>
<tr><td>3021</td><td>2.35 S CARTER CLAIMER 3YO (E)   1m2f   Good 44   -14 Slow
£7312   £2250   £1125   £562</td></tr>
</table>

2666 **CARELESS** 16 [5] T D Easterby 3-8-4 (bl) M Roberts 7/1: 404201: 3 b f Robellino - Life's Too Short 67
(Astronef): Settled near, hdwy to lead appr fnl 1f, rdn out: 1st win: 4th on debut in '99 for J Banks (auct mdn,
rtd 66): eff at 10f, 12f should suit: acts on fast, hvy & now eff in blnks: apprec this drop to clmg grade.
1703 **MISBEHAVE** 56 [2] M L W Bell 3-8-12 M Fenton 7/2: 0-0442: 3 b f Reprimand - Princess Moodyshoe ¾ 74
(Jalmood): Slow to start, rear, hdwy to chall appr final 1f, onepcd well inside last: nicely bckd, 8 wk abs:
better expected at the weights here (offic rtd 20lbs + ahead of all 13 rivals): see 990.
2633 **GABIDIA** 16 [8] M A Jarvis 3-7-13 J Quinn 8/1: -64063: 3 br f Bin Ajwaad - Diabaig (Precocious): 1½ 58
Bhd, rdn to impr 2f out, styd on, nvr nrr: up in trip & stays 10f well: see 1083.
2765 **SHARP BELLINE** 11 [10] J L Harris 3-8-9 S Sanders 16/1: 434: Front rank, went on appr final 2f, nk 68
sn hdd, held inside last: low grade h'caps will now suit: see 2765, 2188.
-- **DANGEROUS DEPLOY** [6] 3-8-11 L Branch (6) 16/1: 5: Waited with, rdn & kept on final 2f, not 2 67
pace of ldrs: tchd 25/1 on debut: dam a 10f wnr: should improve for this: with D Elsworth.
2712 **SPANISH STAR** 13 [1] 3-8-9 M Tebbutt 12/1: 513606: Handy, rdn & led briefly over 2f out, fdd fnl 1f. 1¼ 63
2887 **HIGH BEAUTY** 6 [12] 3-7-13 A Polli 33/1: 005007: Rear, eff/hung right 2f out, sn btn: flattered. 2 50$
2887 **DINKY** 6 [4] 3-7-13 D Kinsella 33/1: 000008: Nvr a factor: qck reapp: modest, dubious rating. 8 37$
2685 **EMALI** 15 [7] 3-8-9 W Supple 11/4 FAV: 06-229: Prom, went on 3f out, hdd over 2f out, wknd 4 41
qckly: capable of much better, as in 2685 (h'cap).
2871 **GAYE CHARM** 7 [9] 3-8-9 G Faulkner (3) 33/1: -060: Al in rear: 10th, qck reapp: see 2345. 1 39

NEWMARKET (July) SUNDAY JULY 30TH Righthand, Stiff, Galloping Track

--	**ROYAL EXPOSURE** [3] 3-8-6 L Newton 12/1: 0: Dwelt, al bhd, 11th: related to 3 wnrs: with W Musson.	¾	35
2735	**FINERY** 12 [13] 3-8-9 (vis) J Fortune 10/1: 002300: Prom, wknd qckly final 2f, 12th: twice below 2534.	7	28
2411	**REGARDEZ MOI** 25 [14] 3-8-4 J Stack 20/1: 006300: Keen in lead, hdd over 3f out, wknd rapidly, 13th.	1	22
2591	**JENKO** 18 [11] 3-8-7 Dale Gibson 50/1: 60-000: In tch, bhd after halfway, t.o. in last.	9	13
14 ran	Time 2m 07.71 (5.81) (Giles W Pritchard-Gordon) T D Easterby Great Habton, Nth Yorks.		

3022 3.05 MAIL ON SUNDAY HCAP 3YO 0-90 (C) 1m str Good 44 +04 Fast [97]
£11310 £3480 £1740 £870

+2242 **KIROVSKI** 32 [4] P W Harris 3-8-7 (76) J Fortune 9/2: 60-211: 3 b c Common Grounds - Nordic Doll **85**
(Royal Academy): Made all, rdn clr appr final 1f: nicely bckd, best time of day: earlier won at Carlisle
(h'cap, first win, fast time): rtd 71 when unplcd on 3 juv starts: suited by a stiff/gall 1m on fast & gd
grnd: lightly raced & v progressive, should complete a hat-trick.
2814 **EASTWAYS** 9 [1] M Johnston 3-8-12 (81) R Ffrench 14/1: 000042: 3 ch c Efisio - Helens Dreamgirl 1½ **86**
(Caerleon) Front rank, rdn to trk wnr appr fnl 1f, kept on, no impress: up in trip & stays 1m well: see 982.
*2515 **FLYING CARPET** 22 [9] T D Easterby 3-7-11 (66)(1ow)(2oh) J Quinn 13/2: 600313: 3 b f Barathea - shd **71+**
Flying Squaw (Be My Chief) Dwelt, rear, rdn/hdwy 2f out, sn short of room, styd on inside last, nvr nrr: 5L clr
rem, op 5/1: would have gone close but for interference & remains one to keep in mind: see 2515.
1879 **OMNIHEAT** 48 [10] M J Ryan 3-8-11 (80) P McCabe 33/1: 231654: Waited with, rdn to impr 2f out, 5 **77**
not pace of ldrs over 1f out: 7 wk abs: see 1649.
2858 **ATAVUS** 8 [11] 3-9-2 (85) M Fenton 11/2: -41035: Chsd ldrs, hung left/btn appr fnl 1f: btr 2858 (C/D). nk **82**
2688 **OGILIA** 15 [6] 3-8-8 (77) N Chalmers (7) 33/1: 3-0046: Rear, effort when short of room over 2f ¾ **73**
out, late hdwy, no impress on ldrs: see 1826.
*2104 **RAINBOW HILL** 39 [8] 3-9-2 (85) W Ryan 5/1: -217: Rcd keenly cl-up, outpcd after halfway, no ch nk **81**
after: nicely bckd & a disapp run on this h'cap bow, could improve with experience: see 2104.
2762 **NOBLE PURSUIT** 11 [5] 3-9-7 (90) L Carter 20/1: 041038: Mid-div at best: btr 2762 (stks). nk **85**
2858 **SIR FERBET** 8 [3] 3-9-3 (86) M Hills 11/1: 100109: Dsptd lead, rdn/fdd appr final 1f: twice below 1853. nk **81**
*2465 **WOODLAND RIVER** 23 [3] 3-9-3 (86) R Cochrane 7/2 FAV: -00210: Mid-div, wknd rapidly final 2f, 1¾ **78**
fin 10th: nicely bckd: much btr 2465 (sharp 7.7f).
*2824 **TRIPLE WOOD** 9 [5] 3-8-6 (75) W Supple 25/1: -54310: Rear, eff 4f out, sn btn, 11th: btr 2824 (7f, fm). 1 **65**
11 ran Time 1m 40.46 (3.26) (Batten, Bowstead, Gregory & Manning) P W Harris Aldbury, Herts.

3023 3.40 FARRAR MDN 3YO (D) 1m6f175y Good 44 00 Slow
£4036 £1242 £621 £310

2751 **ALRISHA** 11 [1] D R C Elsworth 3-8-9 S Sanders 13/8 FAV: 021: 3 b f Persian Bold - Rifaya (Lashkari): **77**
Front rank, went on appr final 1f, rdn clr, readily: well bckd: 12,000gns purchase, dam Irish bmpr wnr: eff at
12f, relished this step up to 14.7f: acts on fast, gd & an easy or stiff/gall trk: shld rate higher, win again.
2659 **BLOSSOM WHISPERS** 16 [3] C A Cyzer 3-8-9 M Hills 16/1: 06432: 3 b f Ezzoud - Springs Welcome 3 **72$**
(Blakeney): Mid-div, hdwy appr final 1f, kept on but not pace of wnr: op 10/1 & a gd run at the weights
(offic only 65), will apprec a return to h'cap company: see 2659.
2609 **KADOUN** 17 [5] L M Cumani 3-9-0 J P Spencer 5/2: -2443: 3 b c Doyoun - Kumta (Priolo): 3½ **74**
Led early, led again appr fnl 3f, hdd over 1f out, fdd: nicely bckd, prob not stay this lngr 14.7f trip.
2194 **CARNBREA DANCER** 34 [4] W J Haggas 3-8-9 T Quinn 5/2: 524: Led after 2f, hdd appr final 3f, 4 **65**
drvn & wknd sn after: h'caps should now suit: see 2194.
2897 **TUFTY HOPPER** 5 [2] 3-9-0 (BL) J Quinn 11/1: 222045: Dwelt, rcd keenly in rear, effort 2f out, ½ **69$**
sn btn: op 8/1, qck reapp: tried in blnks: lngr 14.7f trip: looks a tricky ride: see 2710.
5 ran Time 3m 10.24 (6.5) (N S P C C) D R C Elsworth Whitsbury, Hants.

3024 4.15 TOTE SUNDAY HCAP 3YO+ 0-95 (C) 1m2f Good 44 -04 Slow [91]
£17631 £5425 £2712 £1356 3 yo rec 10lb

3871} **PRINCE ALEX** 323 [6] Mrs A J Perrett 6-9-10 (87)(t) S Sanders 12/1: 1102-1: 6 b g Night Shift - **97**
Finalist (Star Appeal): Waited with, smooth hdwy to lead appr final 1f, edged right but rdn clr well inside last:
top weight on reapp: landed a hat-trick in '99, at Kempton (2) & Ascot (h'caps, rtd 88 at best): missed '98,
'97 Newmarket wnr (h'cap, rtd 58, A Stewart): suited by 10/12f, disapp sole try over further: acts on fast,
gd/soft & an easy or stiff trk, likes Kempton: eff in a t-strap: runs well fresh: tough/genuine, still improving.
2475 **PINCHINCHA** 23 [4] D Morris 6-9-0 (77) R Cochrane 11/2: 234342: 6 b g Priolo - Western Heights 1¾ **83**
(Shirley Heights): Waited with, rdn to impr halfway, ev ch appr final 1f, not pace of wnr: nicely bckd:
admirably consistent but has not won for 3 yrs: see 1288.
*2865 **SUMMER SONG** 7 [10] E A L Dunlop 3-8-3 (76) G Carter 5/1: 531113: 3 b f Green desert - High 1¼ **80**
Standard (Kris): Rear, hdwy when short of room over 3f out, rdn & styd on well appr final 1f, nvr nrr: qck
reapp & a shade unlucky in running here, remains in fine form: see 2865.
2674 **JULIUS** 15 [5] M Johnston 3-9-0 (87) M Hills 9/2: 111104: Front rank, went on appr final 3f, hdd 2½ **87**
appr final 1f, wknd: tough but looks in h'cappers grip now: see 2314.
*2671 **BACCHUS** 15 [8] 6-8-12 (75)(vis) J Weaver 7/1: 232215: Keen in mid-div, eff 2f out, sn btn: btr 2671. 2½ **71**
2594 **ANDROMEDES** 18 [9] 3-8-9 (82) T Quinn 3/1 FAV: -43106: Chsd ldrs, rdn to lead appr final 3f, sn 3½ **73**
hdd, lost tch fnl 2f: well bckd, better expected: poss flattered in List company last time (14.7f), see 2038.
2696 **KOMISTAR** 15 [2] 5-9-9 (86) W Supple 20/1: -02007: Led, hdd 4f out, gradually wknd: see 2170. nk **77**
*2562 **ARCHIE BABE** 19 [3] 4-9-2 (79) J Fortune 12/1: 101018: Prom 5f, drvn/fdd fnl 3f: btr 2562 (made all). 11 **56**
2674 **CAPTAINS LOG** 15 [1] 5-9-4 (81) M Fenton 9/1: 114159: Handy, wknd rapidly final 2f: btr 2674 (12f) 3 **53**
2169 **BEZZAAF** 36 [7] 3-9-0 (93) M Roberts 20/1: -15P00: Nvr dngr, fin 10th: out of form: see 1469, 1200. 6 **58**
10 ran Time 2m 06.67 (4.77) (M Dawson, K Mercer, A Jones) Mrs A J Perrett Pulborough, West Sussex.

3025 4.45 NSPCC FULL STOP HCAP 3YO+ 0-85 (D) 1m6f175y Good 44 +02 Fast [85]
£7020 £2160 £1080 £540 3 yo rec 15lb

2725 **KING FLYER** 12 [9] H J Collingridge 4-8-3 (60)(t) J Quinn 5/1: -60521: 4 b g Ezzoud - Al Guswa **65**
(Shernazar): Front rank, effort when short of room over 1f out, drvn to lead well inside last, styd on strongly
& went clr cl-home: '99 wnr here at Newmarket (clmr, rtd 70 & 59a): rtd 78 for B Hanbury in '98: eff at 10/14.7f
on firm, gd & e/track: handles any trk, likes a stiff/gall one, especially Newmarket: eff with/without a t-strap.
1996 **HILL FARM BLUES** 43 [6] Miss S E Baxter 7-8-3 (60) W Supple 20/1: 450002: 7 b m Mon Tresor - 2½ **62**

939

NEWMARKET (July)   SUNDAY JULY 30TH   Righthand, Stiff, Galloping Track

Loadplan Lass (Nicholas Bill): Settled rear, effort 7f out, went on appr final 4f, kept on well inside last,
sn btn: 6L clr rem, 6 wk abs: on a fair mark: see 991, 809.

2923 **SPOSA** 4 [8] M J Polglase 4-7-10 (53)(7oh) Joanna Badger (7) 16/1: 011443: 4 b f St Jovite - Barelyabride 6   49\$
(Blushing Groom): Cl-up, rdn/dropped rear 4f out, late hdwy, no dngr: qck reapp: see 2776.

2336 **ALHAWA** 29 [4] K R Burke 7-9-12 (83) J Weaver 3/1 FAV: -25B04: Mid-div, effort over 2f out, sn rdn/wknd. 2   77

2674 **EVANDER** 15 [3] 5-9-13 (84) P Dobbs (5) 7/1: 24-065: Led, hdd 6f out, lost tch appr final 1f: up in trip. nk   77

2231 **REFLEX BLUE** 32 [1] 3-8-11 (83) M Hills 4/1: -44236: Rcd keenly in rear, rdn to impr 4f out, no hd   76
extra final 2f: up in trip: see 1885 (12f).

2763 **CHEEK TO CHEEK** 11 [5] 6-7-10 (53) A Polli (3) 13/2: 525437: Prom, wknd qckly fnl 3f, t.o: btr 2763. dist   19

1852 **MELVELLA** 49 [7] 4-7-10 (53)(17oh) D Kinsella (7) 100/1: 600008: Al well in rear: 7 wk abs, v stiff task. ¾   18

2681 **HAMBLEDEN** 15 [2] 3-8-9 (81) M Tebbutt 7/2: 310329: In tch, wknd rapidly fnl 4f, t.o: much btr 2681. 6   41

9 ran   Time 3m 11.67 (6.17)   (In The Know)   H J Collingridge Exning, Suffolk.

YARMOUTH   MONDAY JULY 31ST   Lefthand, Flat, Fair Track

Official Going   GOOD. Stalls: Str Crse - Stands Side, Rem - Inside.

3026   6.00 EDP WHAT'S ON HCAP 3YO+ 0-70 (E)   2m   Good 50 -12 Slow   [54]
£3493   £1075   £537   £268   3 yo rec 17lb

2827 **MONACLE** 10 [1] John Berry 6-8-10 (36) P Mullen 10/1: 3F-341: 6 b g Saddlers' Hall - Endless Joy   41
(Law Society) Rear, rdn & prog to lead dist, rdn clr, eased in last: '99 wnr at Yarmouth & Lingfield (subs disq,
amat h'cap, rtd 44): eff at 11f/2m on firm, gd & f/sand: best without blnks: one-eyed gldg, won decisively here.

*2866 **XELLANCE** 8 [6] M Johnston 3-9-9 (66) K Dalgleish (5) 1/1 FAV: 221412: 3 b g Be My Guest - Excellent 3½   66
Alibi (Exceller) Led 4f out, rdn & hdd dist, held in last: clr of rem, hvly bckd: acts on firm, gd & fibresand.

2622 **BAISSE DARGENT** 18 [7] D J S Cosgrove 4-9-10 (50) G Carter 14/1: 232403: 3 b g Common Grounds - 5   45
Fabulous Pet (Somethingfabulous) Chsd ldrs, rdn fnl 4f, onepace/held 2f out: op 10/1: see 424, 317.

2879 **NICIARA** 7 [3] M C Chapman 3-8-1 (44)(bl) Joanna Badger (7) 6/1: 323224: Led 12f, btn 2f out. 2½   37

2037 **NUBILE** 42 [5] 6-8-8 (34)(tbl) L Newton 16/1: 600255: Held up, eff 4f out, no impress: op 12/1, abs. 1   26

2866 **RUM BABA** 8 [4] 6-8-13 (39)(bl) J Mackay (5) 9/2: 402-56: Cl-up 12f, btn 2f out, eased: btr 2866. 10   23

2755 **RAYWARE BOY** 12 [2] 4-8-13 (39)(bl) N Callan 33/1: 545207: In tch 4f out, sn hard rdn/btn: see 1660. 3½   20

7 ran   Time 3m 33.20 (9.9)   (Chris Benest)   John Berry Newmarket.

3027   6.25 EDP 7 DAY GUIDE COND STKS 2YO (C)   5f43y   Good 50 -18 Slow
£5510   £2090   £1045   £475

2344 **DANCE ON** 30 [2] Sir Michael Stoute 2-8-9 T Quinn 11/10 FAV: 1061: 2 ch f Caerleon - Dance   96
Sequence (Mr Prospector) Trkd ldrs, rdn/led 1f out, styd on well under hands-and-heels riding nr fin: hvly bckd,
op 13/8: earlier scored on debut at Leicester (2yo mdn, subs ran creditably in Gr 3/List company): eff at 5f,
tried 6f, will suit: acts on gd & gd/soft, prob handles firm: handles a stiff/gall or fair trk: useful filly.

-- **TISSALY** [5] C E Brittain 2-8-3 P Robinson 10/1: 2: 2 b f Pennekamp - Island Ruler (Ile de Bourbon) 1¼   86+
Dwelt, rdn & styd on strongly from over 1f out, not trouble wnr: op 7/1: Apr foal, cost 25,000gns: half-sister to
2 7f juv wnrs: dam a 12f French wnr: eff at 5f, looks sure to relish 6f+: acts on gd grnd: eye-catching intro,
merits consideration in a mdn over 6/7f next time.

*1642 **QUIESCENT** 59 [4] R Hannon 2-8-9 L Newman (3) 5/1: 013: 2 ch f Primo Dominie - Tranquility (Night 1½   88
Shift) Cl-up, led 2f out, hdd 1f out, kept on onepace: 2 month abs: acts on gd & gd/soft grnd: see 1642.

2664 **BYO** 17 [3] M C Chapman 2-9-0 L Gueller (7) 9/2: 015124: Cl-up, hard rdn halfway, sn held: btr 2664. 4   83

2849 **MISE EN SCENE** 9 [1] 2-8-9 J Quinn 11/2: -0105: Drvn/bhd, nvr factor: op 9/2: btr 1986. 1¼   75

2915 **OH SO DUSTY** 5 [6] 2-8-9 (bl) J Weaver 7/1: 104446: Led/dsptd lead 3f, sn btn: op 6/1: qck reapp. 1½   71

6 ran   Time 1m 03.5 (3.4)   (Cheveley Park Stud)   Sir Michael Stoute Newmarket.

3028   6.55 EDP JOBS SELLER 2YO (G)   6f   Good 50 -55 Slow
£1844   £527   £263

2891 **PRESENTOFAROSE** 7 [6] J S Moore 2-8-6 J Mackay (5) 7/1: 023431: 2 b f Presenting - Little Red Rose   53
(Precocious) Made virtually all, drvn out to hold on: slow time, bght in for 3,250gns, 1st win: eff at 6f, tried
7f & that trip shld suit: handles fast & gd, sharp/fair trk: enjoys sellers & battled on well today.

-2898 **BANNINGHAM BLIZ** 6 [3] D Shaw 2-8-6 (bl) J Quinn 11/4: 543022: 2 ch f Inchinor - Mary From Dunlow ½   50
(Nicholas Bill) Rear, rdn halfway, prog & briefly led ins last, not run on cl home: qck reapp: eff at 6/7f on firm
& gd grnd in sell grade: eff in blnks: lkd a tricky rider here: see 2898.

-- **TEENAWON** [5] K R Burke 2-8-6 N Callan 4/1: 3: 2 ch f Polar Falcon - Oasis (Valiyar) 3   43
Rdn in rear, hdwy over 1f out, no prog ins last: op 3/1: Feb foal, cost 4,500gns: half-sister to a 6/7f juv wnr:
dam a hdles wnr: looks sure to apprec 7f+ in time.

2898 **HARD TO CASH** 6 [4] D J S Cosgrove 2-8-11 L Newton 14/1: 04: Cl-up, held over 1f out: qck reapp. 1¾   44

2773 **UNVEIL** 11 [1] 2-8-6 D O'Donohoe 5/2 FAV: 44665: Prom, drvn/btn 2f out: btr 1136 (AW). 10   28

-- **MRS MITCHELL** [2] 2-8-6 G Bardwell 5/1: 6: Dwelt, sn trkd ldrs, drvn/btn 2f out: River Falls filly, 1¾   24
Mar foal, a first foal: dam a mdn: sire a high-class performer at 6/7f as a juv: with D Nicholls.

6 ran   Time 1m 16.7 (6.3)   (Chris Bradbury)   J S Moore East Garston, Berks.

3029   7.25 EDP SPORT AUCT MDN 2YO (E)   7f str   Good 50 -47 Slow
£2821   £868   £434   £217

2588 **LOST AT SEA** 19 [7] K R Burke 2-8-8 N Callan 9/4: -0201: 2 b c Exit To Nowhere - Night At Sea (Night   81
Shift) Handy, went on bef halfway, hard rdn fnl 3f & just held on ins last, all out: eff over longer 7f trip,
connections reported return to 6f is likely: acts on firm & gd grnd & a gall/fair trk: jockey reports colt requires
a t-strap: showed admirable resolution tonight & can win more races.

2588 **APRIL LEE** 19 [2] K McAuliffe 2-8-0 (e) K Dalgleish (5) 6/1: 055252: 2 b f Superpower - Petitesse nk   72
(Petong) Drvn/chsd wnr fnl 2f, styd on well for press, just held: rest well covered: eff around 7f on gd grnd.

2810 **JETHAME** 10 [10] B J Meehan 2-8-3 D Glennon (7) 8/1: -00353: 2 ch f Definite Article - Victorian 3   69
Flower (Tate Gallery) Narrow lead 3f, drvn/onepace fnl 2f: stays 7f, could apprec h'cap company now: see 2810.

YARMOUTH MONDAY JULY 31ST Lefthand, Flat, Fair Track

2653 **POLISH PADDY 17** [9] R Hannon 2-8-5 L Newman (5) 10/1: 0664: Rdn/mid-div, not pace to chall. 1½ **68**
-- **LUCKY CHRYSTAL** [6] 2-8-5 G Carter 9/1: 5: Dwelt, sn chsd ldrs, btn 2f out: Lucky Guest colt, Feb foal, cost 1,600gns: related to sev wnrs in US, dam a multiple US wnr: with E A L Dunlop. ½ **67**
2791 **ALLTHEDOTCOMS 11** [4] 2-8-8 J Mackay (5) 20/1: 046: Dwelt, rdn/chsd ldrs halfway, btn 2f out. 5 **60**
-- **ST NICHOLAS** [5] 2-8-5 J Quinn 25/1: 7: Dwelt, rdn/rear, little prog: cheaply bought Apr foal: half-brother to a 10f wnr: dam 12/15f wnr: bred to relish 1m in time: with D Shaw. 2½ **52**
2841 **POLWHELE 9** [8] 2-8-11 Dale Gibson 50/1: 08: Prom 3f: see 2841. 4 **50**
2730 **MISSING DRINK 13** [1] 2-8-5 Joanna Badger (7) 33/1: 050509: Prom, wknd qckly halfway: needs sellers. ¾ **43**
-- **ECCLESIASTICAL** [3] 2-8-11 R Cochrane 2/1 FAV: 0: Slowly away, sn rdn/bhd, no ch/eased fnl 1f: Bishop Of Cashel colt, May foal, cost 18,000gns: half-brother to 7f juv wnr Muharib: dam a mdn: with J Fanshawe. 1¾ **46**
10 ran Time 1m 29.4 (6.8) (David H Morgan) K R Burke Newmarket.

3030

7.55 EDP CLASSIFIEDS HCAP 3YO+ 0-70 (E) 7f str Good 50 -10 Slow [70]
£3984 £1226 £613 £306 3 yo rec 7 lb

2802 **DARYABAD 10** [12] N A Graham 8-8-2 (44)(bl) Dale Gibson 8/1: -00301: 8 b g Thatching - Dayanata (Shirley Heights) Chsd ldrs, drvn ahd over 1f out & al holding rivals after, rdn out: '99 scorer for R McGhin, at Lingfiled (2, class stks & h'cap, rtd 69a), no turf form: '98 Catterick wnr (stks, rtd 66): eff at 1m, suited by 7f on firm, gd/soft & fibresand, equitrack/Lingfield specialist: best in blnks & has run well fresh: nicely h'capped. **51**
2749 **INDIAN WARRIOR 12** [13] W J Musson 4-8-3 (45) L Newton 15/2: 000602: 4 b g Be My Chief - Wanton (Kris) Chsd ldrs, drvn/chsd wnr ins last, no impress: see 364. 2 **47**
2752 **CLONOE 12** [14] R Ingram 6-7-13 (41) D Kinsella (7) 12/1: 100053: 6 b g Syrtos - Anytime Anywhere (Daring March) Led till over 1f out, drvn/held ins last: see 574 (AW seller, made all). 1 **41**
*2462 **EMANS JOY 24** [9] J R Fanshawe 3-9-2 (65) R Cochrane 7/1: -3514: Towards rear, rdn/not much room halfway, held fnl 1f: h'cap bow: see 2462 (mdn). 1½ **62**
2682 **ASSURED PHYSIQUE 16** [6] 3-9-1 (64)(tvi) P Robinson 20/1: 536655: Chsd ldrs, held over 1f out. *nk* **60**
2802 **QUALITAIR PRIDE 10** [7] 8-7-11 (39) J Mackay (5) 16/1: 010006: Held up, nvr able to chall: see 2347. 1 **33**
*2794 **ANNIJAZ 11** [3] 3-8-7 (56) L Newman (3) 7/1: 633017: Cl-up till over 1f out: btr 2794 (Epsom). *hd* **49**
2899 **MEZZORAMIO 6** [1] 8-8-2 (44)(tvi) K Dalgleish (5) 11/2: 035028: Prom, drvn/ch 2f out, rdn/btn 1f out. ½ **36**
2511 **BALLETS RUSSES 23** [8] 3-8-4 (50)(3ow) G Carter 20/1: 0-4309: Al rear: see 2036, 1609. 5 **35**
2464 **SATZUMA 24** [10] 3-9-1 (64)(t) R Mullen 20/1: 0-050: Keen/rear, btn 2f out: 10th: see 2464 (mdn). 1½ **43**
2899 **DON BOSCO 6** [5] 4-9-7 (63) J Quinn 6/1: 000030: Twds rear, hmpd 3f out, sn btn: 11th: qck reapp. 4 **34**
2775 **REDSWAN 11** [2] 5-9-10 (66)(t) G Hind 5/1 FAV: 000020: Rear, struggling halfway: 13th: reportedly ran without declared t-strap: poss best forgotten: see 2775, 1810. **0**
889 **Bridal White 110** [11] 4-7-10 (38)(4oh) A Polli (3) 50/1:2281 **Lion Guest 32** [4] 3-8-11 (60)(BL) J Weaver 20/1:
14 ran Time 1m 26.8 (4.2) (The Three Amigos) N A Graham Newmarket.

3031

8.25 SATURDAY FILLIES HCAP 3YO+ 0-70 (E) 1m2f Good 50 +11 Fast [66]
£2925 £900 £450 £225 3 yo rec 10lb

2890 **CITY GAMBLER 7** [1] G C Bravery 6-8-8 (46) M Fenton 12/1: 0-5001: 6 b m Rock City - Sun Street (Ile de Bourbon) Trkd ldrs, al trav well, rdn/led over 1f out, styd on well: best time of night: plcd in '99 (h'cap, rtd 61): '98 Leicester wnr (h'cap, rtd 68 at best): eff over 10/12f on fast & gd/soft grnd, poss handles soft: likes a stiff/gall or fair trk, likes Leicester: on a handy mark, could well win again. **51**
2872 **JOIN THE PARADE 8** [7] H J Collingridge 4-9-4 (56) G Carter 5/1 JT FAV: 0-0302: 4 b f Elmaamul - Summer Pageant (Chiefs Crown) Mid-div, prog to trk ldrs over 2f out, rdn/chsd wnr ins last, kept on, al held: on a fair mark & could well find similar: see 2387, 2033. 1½ **58**
*2789 **LEVEL HEADED 11** [4] P W Hiatt 5-8-2 (40) A Mackay 8/1: 504413: 5 b m Beveled - Snowline (Bay Express) Led, rdn/hdd over 1f out, no extra: rest well covered: brave front running effort, remains in gd heart. 2½ **38**
2767 **BOBBYDAZZLE 12** [10] C A Dwyer 5-9-0 (52) J Quinn 13/2: 244034: Held up, late gains, no threat. 3 **46**
2853 **LADY JO 9** [9] 4-9-2 (54) R Smith (5) 11/1: 660605: Rear, mod gains fnl 3f: see 2581, 290. ½ **47**
4092} **LADY DONATELLA 310** [2] 3-8-12 (60) J Mackay (5) 14/1: 600-6: Rear, mod gains fnl 3f: reapp/h'cap bow: unplcd over 6f from 3 starts last term (rtd 63): half-sister to smart miler Right Wing, dam stoutly bred: likely to apprec 10f+, shld prove sharper next time. ½ **52**
2463 **MA VIE 24** [8] 3-9-1 (63) R Cochrane 5/1 FAV: 00-027: Cl-up halfway, rdn/btn over 2f out: btr 2463. 1½ **53**
2391 **SILK STOCKINGS 27** [3] 3-9-8 (70) P Robinson 20/1: -03008: Rear, mod gains: mod form at 7/12f. 4 **54**
2727 **BROWNS DELIGHT 13** [14] 3-7-11 (45) G Bardwell 33/1: 065009: Cl-up, rdn/fdd over 3f out: see 287. 1 **28**
2752 **FIFTH EDITION 12** [11] 4-9-5 (57) R Mullen 12/1: 405-00: Mid-div at best: see 2752 (1m). 1¾ **38**
2888 **SUPERSONIC 7** [15] 4-10-0 (66) M Tebbutt 10/1: -46040: Drvn/bhd 4f out: 15th: top-weight: see 679. **0**
2861 **Charlem 8** [12] 3-7-10 (44)(BL)(7oh) Joanna Badger (7) 50/1:
2611 **Vento Del Oreno 18** [5] 3-9-6 (68) D O'Donohoe 14/1:
2767 **Elba Magic 12** [6] 5-8-8 (46)(vis) L Newman(3) 25/1: 2799 **Bay Of Bengal 10** [13] 4-8-4 (42) K Dalgleish(5) 16/1:
15 ran Time 2m 08.1 (3.9) (J J May) G C Bravery Newmarket.

NEWCASTLE MONDAY JULY 31ST Lefthand, Galloping, Stiff Track

Official Going GOOD. Stalls: Str Course - Stands Side; Round Course - Inside

3032

2.15 TATTERSALLS AUCT MDN 2YO (E) 6f str Good 53 -11 Slow
£3445 £1060 £530 £265

2821 **CUMBRIAN HARMONY 10** [7] T D Easterby 2-7-12 T Williams 4/1: 305521: 2 b f Distinctly North - Sawaki (Song) Made all, styd on fnl 2f, pushed out: op 3/1: IR 5,500gns Apr foal: half sister to a wng 5f juv, dam scored over 7f: eff at 5/6f on firm & gd/soft grnd: handles a stiff/gall or sharp trk: deserved this. **72**
2926 **CERALBI 5** [8] R Hollinshead 2-8-5 P M Quinn (3) 9/4 FAV: 62: 2 b c Goldmark - Siwana (Dom Racine) Prom, kept on under hands/heels fnl 2f, not pace of wnr: clr rem: nicely bckd, qck reapp: stays 6f on gd: see 2926. 3 **72**
-- **ROYAL GLEN** [4] Martyn Wane 2-7-12 P Fessey 16/1: 3: 2 b f Royal Abjar - Sea Glen (Glenstal) In tch, rdn, ran green & no extra fnl 2f: Apr foal, dam unrcd: half sister to a 6f juv scorer: sire a high-class miler abroad: shld improve for the experience. 4 **55**
2821 **SMART DANCER 10** [1] T D Easterby 2-8-9 K Darley 11/2: -5044: Mid-div, drvn/held appr fnl 2f: op 4/1. *hd* **66**
2693 **TUPGILL TURBO 16** [6] 2-8-9 A Culhane 7/1: 35: Cl-up, lost tch fnl 2f: bckd from 20/1: see 2693. 3 **59**

--   **BAJAN BLUE** [3] 2-7-12 F Norton 4/1: 6: Dwelt, nvr dangerous: mkt drifter: 3,000 gns Lycius filly: 5   38
half-sister to a 6/7f juv scorer: dam won over mid-dists: with M Johnston, sharper next time & will apprec 7f.
--   **RIMFAXI** [5] 2-8-5 A Nicholls (3) 6/1: 7: Handy, drvn/wknd qckly fnl 2f: op 4/1: 6,500gns March   2   40
foal: brother to a 7f wnr, half brother to sev other wnrs: dam scored over 6f: with D Nicholls.
1221   **PRINCE GRIGORI** 82 [2] 2-8-7 P Lynch 5/1: 0408: Chsd ldrs, drvn/fdd halfway: 12 wk abs: up in trip.   3½   35
8 ran   Time 1m 15.15 (3.85)   (Cumbrian Industrials Ltd)   T D Easterby Great Habton, N Yorks

---

3033   2.45 NORTHERN HCAP 3YO 0-65 (F)   7f str   Good 53   +04 Fast   [71]
£2709   £774   £387

2561   **DAKOTA SIOUX** 20 [13] R A Fahey 3-8-8 (51)(BL) G Parkin 14/1: 3-3601: 3 ch f College Chapel -   60
Batilde (Victory Piper) Made all, switched left after 2f, clr 2f out, styd on well, rdn out: tchd 20/1, gd time:
1st win in first time blnks: plcd sole '99 start (med auct mdn, rtd 71): eff at 5f, clrly relished forcing the pace
over a stiff/gall 7f: handles fast & gd grnd, poss not soft: imprvd form in blnks today.
2794   **DIAMOND OLIVIA** 11 [14] John Berry 3-8-10 (53) O Pears 13/2: -34062: 3 b f Beveled - Queen Of The   2½   56
Quorn (Governor General) Mid-div, rdn/eff appr fnl 2f, styd on, no threat to wnr: stays 7f on gd, hvy & fibresand.
2964   **BLUE SAPPHIRE** 3 [3] D W Barker 3-7-10 (39) J Bramhill 25/1: 000303: 3 b f Blues Traveller - Era   3½   36
(Dalsaan) Prom, drvn/onepcd appr fnl 1f: quick reapp: see 2745, 1081.
2799   **PHILAGAIN** 10 [10] Miss L A Perratt 3-8-0 (43) J McAuley 12/1: 016304: Dwelt, rear, prog when short   shd   40
of room appr fnl 1f, swtchd/kept on fnl 1f, no impress: shade unlucky in running here: see 2205 (sharp 1m).
2632   **SIRENE** 17 [2] 3-8-5 (48) F Norton 20/1: 000035: Chsd ldrs, drvn/no extra fnl 2f: btr 2632 (5f, f'sand).   ½   44
2603   **NATSMAGIRL** 18 [1] 3-8-1 (44) P Fessey 20/1: 0-5056: Handy, rdn/btn over 1f out: see 1665.   nk   39
2833   **OSCAR PEPPER** 10 [8] 3-9-3 (60)(BL) K Darley 7/2 FAV: 122037: Veered left start, mid-div, brief   1¼   53
eff 2f out, sn held: well bckd in 1st time blnks: see 2833, 365.
2699   **INDY CARR** 15 [16] 3-9-2 (59) A Culhane 16/1: 604668: Waited with, eff/no room over 2f out, sn btn.   nk   52
1579   **LADY LOVE** 62 [9] 3-9-7 (64) R Winston 16/1: 0-5029: Prom, rdn/wknd appr fnl 1f: op 12/1, 9 wk   ¾   56
abs: headgear omitted: btr 1579 (stks, gd/soft), 1st time blnks.
2524   **ABSINTHER** 22 [6] 3-9-3 (60) F Lynch 8/1: 0-0200: Handy, rdn & wknd over 2f out, no ch when sltly   ¾   51
hmpd over 1f out: op 6/1: btr 2205 (sharp 1m).
2735   **HEATHYARDS LAD** 13 [15] 3-8-13 (56) P M Quinn (3) 16/1: 565500: Nvr dangerous, fin 11th: see 2506.   1½   44
2205   **ALPATHAR** 35 [17] 3-8-10 (53) J Fanning 12/1: 166400: Al in rear: fin 12th: see 2017.   1¾   38
2855   **SHOWING** 9 [4] 3-9-3 (60)(t) Dean McKeown 5/1: 0-0060: Keen in tch, hung/wknd over 2f, 13th: op 3/1.   ½   44
2719   **NOWT FLASH** 14 [11] 3-8-13 (56) R Lappin 10/1: 250040: In tch, wknd qckly fnl 2f, 16th: op 7/1.   0
2484   Sister Kate 24 [5] 3-8-0 (43) A Nicholls (2) 25/1:   2699   Tangerine 15 [18] 3-8-9 (52)(bl) T Lucas 20/1:
1192   Forest Queen 85 [7] 3-8-11 (54) C Lowther 25/1:   2974   Espere Dor 3 [12] 3-7-10 (39)(14oh) N Carter (7) 33/1:
18 ran   Time 1m 27.51 (3.41)   (Mrs Una Towell)   R A Fahey Butterwick, N Yorks

---

3034   3.15 EXPRESS MDN 3YO+ (D)   1m4f93y   Good 53   -08 Slow
£3376   £1099   £519   £259   3 yo rec 12lb

2703   **HELENS DAY** 15 [2] W Jarvis 4-9-3 K Darley 1/6 FAV: -221: 4 ch f Grand Lodge - Swordlestown Miss   85
(Apalachee) Trkd ldr going well, pushed into lead on bit 2f out, easily went clr, hard held: val any amount:
well bckd at long odds-on: rnr-up both prev starts: 35,000gns purchase: eff at 10f, suited by this step
up to 12.4f: acts on fast, gd & a gall/stiff trk: simple task here, could rate more highly.
1157   **ROVERETTO** 86 [3] Mrs M Reveley 5-9-8 A Culhane 16/1: 0/62: 5 b g Robellino - Spring Flyer (Waajib)   6   68
Settled rear, rdn/eff 2f out, styd on to take 2nd lns last, no impress on easy wnr: op 10/1: handles gd grnd:
now qual for h'caps & may do better over further in this sphere: see 1157.
2382   **RAINWORTH LADY** 28 [1] M J Polglase 3-8-5 F Norton 50/1: 500063: 3 b f Governor General -   6   53$
Monongelia (Welsh Pageant) Keen in tch, drvn/btn appr fnl 2f: treat this rating with caution: mod form prev.
951   **WILD RIVER** 104 [6] M Johnston 3-8-10 J Fanning 6/1: 04: Dsptd lead, went on 4f out, hdd over   3½   53
2f out, wknd qckly: op 3/1, long abs: bred to apprec this 12f trip in time: see 951.
--   **ANGEL DUST** [4] 4-9-3 R Studholme (5) 40/1: 5: Led, hdd over 4f out, sn lost tch: op 14/1:   6   41
recent hdles scorer at Perth (2m nov h'cap, hvy, rtd 79n, mod form otherwise): with G McCourt.
--   **CARELLA BOY** [5] 3-8-10 C Teague (5): 6: Handy, wknd rapidly from halfway, t.o.: debut.   dist   0
6 ran   Time 2m 45.5 (7.6)   (Mrs M Dearman)   W Jarvis Newmarket

---

3035   3.45 HIGH GOSFORTH MDN 3YO+ (D)   5f str   Good 53   -08 Slow
£3328   £1024   £512   £256   3 yo rec 4 lb

2839   **SOBA JONES** 9 [1] T D Easterby 3-9-0 (bl) K Darley 4/9 FAV: 023431: 3 b g Emperor Jones - Soba   62
(Most Secret) Led 4f out, rdn & cmftbly went clr over 1f out, eased cl-home, val 6/7L: well bckd: fin 3rd on
sole '99 start (rtd 72, mdn): eff btwn 5f & 1m on firm & gd: now eff in blnks: handles a stiff/gall or sharp trk.
2820   **KIND EMPEROR** 10 [6] M J Polglase 3-9-0 Dean McKeown 5/1: 004R02: 3 br g Emperor Jones - Kind   3   44
Lady (Kind Of Hush) Prom, rdn/hdwy over 2f out, kept on but no impress on cmftble wnr: op 3/1: see 2820, 34.
2744   **IMPALDI** 12 [3] B Ellison 5-8-13 R Winston 5/1: 500023: 5 b m Imp Society - Jaldi (Nordico)   1   36
Led early, remained in tch until hung left & wknd over 1f out: tchd 7/1: see 2744 (6f sell, flattered).
--   **ZILUTTE** [5] John Berry 3-9-0 O Pears 12/1: 4: Dwelt, al last: op 7/1 on debut: Zieten gelding.   6   29
4 ran   Time 1m 01.26 (3.06)   (Mrs M Hills)   T D Easterby Great Habton, N Yorks

---

3036   4.15 TYNE BRIDGE HCAP 3YO+ 0-70 (E)   1m4f93y   Good 53   -09 Slow   [57]
£2756   £848   £424   £212   3 yo rec 12lb

*2746   **CHAKA ZULU** 12 [1] W J Haggas 3-8-11 (52) F Norton 8/13 FAV: 0-1311: 3 b g Muhtarram - African Dance   61
(El Gran Senor) Trkd ldrs going well, cruised into lead over 1f out, effortless/any amnt in hand: well bckd:
earlier won at Bath (reapp) & Catterick (h'caps): mod in '99 (rtd 38): eff at 10f, suited by 12f on firm, gd
& a sharp/turning of stiff/gall trk: won v easily, shld have no trouble in completing hat-trick.
2783   **HAYSTACKS** 11 [5] D Moffatt 4-9-10 (53)(vis) J Bramhill 11/1: 56-042: 4 b g Contract Law - Florissa   1¾   53
(Persepolis) Waited with, rdn to improve 2f out, styd on but no ch with v easy wnr: flattered by proximity to wnr.
2518   **MELODY LADY** 23 [2] F Murphy 4-9-5 (48) C Lowther 8/1: 002203: 4 ch f Dilum - Ansellady (Absalom)   shd   48
Led, hdd appr fnl 1f, sn held: see 2309, 1496.
*2800   **SANTA LUCIA** 10 [6] M Dods 4-9-3 (46) A Culhane 9/2: 260114: Mid-div, kept on fnl 2f, no threat to   1   44
ldrs: well clr rem: op 7/2: shade disapp, btr 2800 (11f class clmr, made all).

NEWCASTLE   MONDAY JULY 31ST   Lefthand, Galloping, Stiff Track

2560 **DESERT MUSIC** 20 [7] 4-9-3 (46) F Lynch 25/1: -0555: Handy, rdn/lost tch fnl 2f: h'cap bow.   11   32
4447} **VANADIUM ORE** 285 [4] 7-8-12 (41) R Winston 9/1: 0500-6: Chsd ldrs, wknd qckly appr fnl 1f: bckd   2   24
from 16/1 on reapp for new stable: plcd once in '99 (apprec h'cap, rtd 50, W McKeown), plcd twice over hdles
(h'caps, rtd 89h, 2m1f, gd, eff in blnks): landed a hat-trick in '98, at Chester, Ayr & Newcastle (h'caps, rtd
60 at best): eff at 10/12.4f on fast & gd/soft grnd: likes Newcastle: just sharper next time, now with D Eddy.
2827 **SWANDALE FLYER** 10 [3] 8-7-10 (25) (3oh) J McAuley 50/1: 0-0057: Prom 1m, wknd: mod recent form.   2   5
7 ran   Time 2m 45.6 (7.7)   (J D Ashenheim)   W J Haggas Newmarket

---

3037   4.45 GT NORTH ROAD HCAP 3YO+ 0-85 (D)   6f str   Good 53   +07 Fast   [79]
£3848   £1184   £592   £296   3 yo rec 5 lb   Raced in 2 groups - stands side held advantage.

2877 **PIPS MAGIC** 7 [14] J S Goldie 4-9-13 (78) A Culhane 13/2: 001001: 4 b g Pips Pride - Kentucky Starlet   82
(Cox's Ridge) Prom stands side, rdn into lead appr fnl 1f, styd on well, drvn out: op 5/1, best time of day:
qck reapp: earlier won at Doncaster (stks): '99 Ascot wnr (val h'cap, rtd 89), '98 wnr at Ripon & Ayr (nov,
rtd 92): suited by 5/6f on firm, soft & any trk: well h'capped & took advantage of the favd stands rail today.
2833 **TECHNICIAN** 10 [11] E J Alston 5-8-11 (62) (bl) F Lynch 4/1 FAV: 012322: 5 ch g Archway - How It   ¾   64
Works (Commanche Run) Front rank stands side, hdwy to chall appr fnl 1f, kept on ins last, not btn far:
nicely bckd: v consistent & deserves to win again sn: see 2396, 2015.
2641 **GRAND ESTATE** 17 [13] D W Chapman 5-8-5 (56) O Pears 7/1: 523503: 5 b g Prince Sabo - Ultimate   ¾   56
Dream (Kafu) Mid-div stands side, rdn to improve 2f out, styd on ins last, nvr nrr: see 2396, 2275
2845 **TRINITY** 9 [5] M Brittain 4-9-1 (66) T Williams 20/1: 0-0064: Led far side, styd on well but no ch   ½   65
with stands side group: fin best of those on the unfav far side, well h'capped on old form: see 2701.
2861 **WISHBONE ALLEY** 8 [7] 5-7-10 (47) (2oh) P Fessey 12/1: 000305: Trkd ldrs far side, styd on well   nk   46
ins last, no danger: not disgraced on the unfavd far side: see 2275.
2697 **MARENGO** 16 [12] 6-8-5 (56) F Norton 20/1: 400006: Mid-div stands side, late hdwy: see 1073.   1   52
2823 **PRIX STAR** 10 [10] 5-8-3 (54) Dean McKeown 12/1: 204007: In tch stands side, drvn/onepace fnl   1½   46
2f: on a fair mark & may apprec softer grnd: see 82.
2779 **ZESTRIL** 11 [9] 3-8-10 (66) (VIS) R Winston 12/1: 006608: Prom stands side, btn fnl 2f: visor: see 1215.   ½   57
2158 **VENIKA VITESSE** 37 [8] 4-8-7 (58) K Darley 7/1: 000009: Led stands side, hdd appr fnl 1f, fdd.   3½   41
2796 **JACMAR** 10 [6] 5-8-0 (51) J McAuley 9/1: 210300: Sn outpcd far side, late gains, 10th: see 2641, 2097.   2½   27
2719 **BAJAN BELLE** 14 [2] 3-8-12 (68) J Fanning 8/1: 040300: Dwelt, sn prom far side, wknd qckly   ½   43
over 1f out, 11th: op 6/1: btr 1855 (7f, firm).
2697 **MOTHER CORRIGAN** 16 [1] 4-8-0 (51) (vis) P M Quinn (3) 25/1: 000000: V slow to start, al bhd, 12th.   2½   20
2612 **MALADERIE** 14 [4] 6-8-2 (53) (vis) G Parkin 10/1: 200000: Al outpcd, fin 13th: see 908.   hd   22
3502} **JACOBINA** 345 [3] 5-8-1 (52) A Nicholls (3) 10/1: 0600-0: Chsd ldrs, rdn/wknd qckly fnl 2f, fin last: 1½   18
op 8/1, reapp: unplcd for B Rothwell in '99 (rtd 50 at best): '98 Haydock wnr (h'cap, rtd 66): eff over a gall
7f, just stays 1m: acts on firm & gd, handles gd/soft: well h'capped & just sharper for this for D Nicholls.
14 ran   Time 1m 14.05 (2.75)   (Frank Brady)   J S Goldie Uplawmoor, E Renfrews

---

FOLKESTONE   MONDAY JULY 31ST   Righthand, Sharpish, Undulating Track

Official Going   GOOD TO FIRM.   Stalls: Round Course - Outside; Str Course - Stands Side.

3038   2.00 BEST BETS CLAIMER 2YO (F)   5f   Good/Firm 29   -23 Slow
£2194   £627   £313

*2772 **SCREAMIN GEORGINA** 11 [2] S C Williams 2-9-0 (t) G Faulkner (3) 15/8: 0211: 2 b f Muhtarram -   66
Carrie Kool (Prince Sabo) Narrow lead, rdn to assert below dist: nicely bckd from 3/1: recent Leicester wnr
(sell): half-sister to a useful 6f juv wnr: eff at 5f, shld get 6f: acts on fast grnd, prob any trk: wears
a t-strap & likes to force the pace: going the right way.
1995 **JUSTALORD** 44 [6] W G M Turner 2-9-5 Darren Williams (5) 4/5 FAV: 616152: 2 b g King's Signet -   1¼   68
Just Lady (Emarati) Prsd wnr & ev ch till outpcd ent fnl 1f: nicely bckd, 6 wk abs: acts on fast & good
grnd: may make fpres sltly flattered in a higher grade last time, ran to similar level as 1381.
2772 **SOOTY TIME** 11 [5] J S Moore 2-8-5 J F Egan 10/1: 306623: 2 ch g Timeless Times - Gymcrak Gem   2½   47
(Don't Forget Me) Held up, outpcd halfway, late prog to go 3rd: op 6/1: needs 6f now: see 2772.
2766 **PAT THE BUILDER** 12 [3] K R Burke 2-9-5 N Callan 10/1: 5404: Chsd ldrs, no extra appr fnl 1f.   nk   60
--   **DESIRE ME** [4] 2-8-4 S Whitworth 20/1: 5: Nvr in it: op 10/1: Silca Blanka (7f/1m) 1st foal.   1½   41
2290 **HURLINGHAM STAR** 31 [7] 2-8-9 J Quinn 33/1: 006: Sn bhd: no form.   13   16
6 ran   Time 1m 01.0 (2.6)   (The Lager Khan)   S C Williams Newmarket, Suffolk

---

3039   2.30 0800 211222 FILLIES MDN 2YO (D)   7f str   Good/Firm 29   -27 Slow
£4387   £1350   £675   £337

2618 **SAUCE TARTAR** 18 [3] N A Callaghan 2-8-11 R Hughes 8/1: 61: 2 ch f Salse - Filly Mignonne (Nashwan)   72
With ldrs, led appr fnl 1f, rdn out: tchd 10/1: found herself in a hot Newmarket fill mdn on debut: 1st foal of a
well related mare: apprec step up to 7f, shld get 10f+ next term: acts on fast grnd & a sharp/undul trk: improving.
2306 **RAMBAGH** 31 [4] J L Dunlop 2-8-11 T Quinn 1/1 FAV: 42: 2 b f Polish Precedent - My Preference   1½   68
(Reference Point) Narrow lead, hdd appr fnl 1f, sn rdn & flashed tail, onepace: nicely bckd again tho' op
4/6: handles fast grnd & gets 7f: not a straightforward filly but prob has the ability to win similar.
--   **MY PLACE** [7] B W Hills 2-8-11 M Hills 7/1: 3: 2 b f Environment Friend - Verchinina (Star Appeal)   1¾   64
Slow away, in tch, chsd front pair appr fnl 1f, sn no impress: op 5/1, tchd 10/1 on debut: Feb foal, half-sister
to sev wnrs, incl fair 7f/1m juv Cybertechnology, dam a miler: shld apprec a step up to 1m, prob handles fast grnd.
1957 **DANCING VENTURE** 45 [1] S P C Woods 2-8-11 J Reid 5/2: 54: Prom, ch 2f out, outpcd: tchd 7/2,   nk   63
6 wk abs, clr of rem: this longer 7f trip shld suit, see 1957.
--   **GREAT MANOEUVRE** [5] 2-8-11 C Rutter 16/1: 5: Chsd ldrs till appr fnl 2f: op 10/1 on debut: 4   55
v stoutly bred Deploy Mar foal: prob needs more time & a lot further: with H Candy.
--   **GRECIAN HALO** [6] 2-8-11 M Fenton 12/1: 6: Al bhd: op 10/1 on debut: $35,000 Southern Halo   nk   54
Dec foal, half-sister to sev wnrs in the States, sire high-class on dirt: with M Bell.
2384 **MACKEM BEAT** 28 [2] 2-8-11 T Ashley 100/1: 05507: U.r./bolted bef start, sn struggling, virt p.u..   dist   0
7 ran   Time 1m 28.1 (3.9)   (Wafic Said)   N A Callaghan Newmarket, Suffolk

943

3040   3.00 DRIVELINE HCAP 3YO+ 0-70 (E)   1m7f92y   Good/Firm 29   -32 Slow   [53]
     £2842   £812   £406

2622 **HETRA HEIGHTS** 18 [6] W J Musson 5-8-3 (28) Martin Dwyer 5/1: 103051: 5 b m Cox's Ridge - Top Hope   31
(High Top) Held up, shaken up appr str, sn imprvd to chall dist, drvn to get up towards fin: tchd 7/1, 1st
turf win: earlier won at W'hampton & Southwell (h'caps, rtd 52a): unplcd in '99 & had a wind op: '98
rnr-up (h'cap, rtd 51): eff at 12f but now suited by 2m: acts on fast, gd grnd & fibresand, best on sharp trks.

2904 **REMEMBER STAR** 6 [8] R J Baker 7-8-0 (25) J Quinn 11/1: 00-432: 7 ch m Don't Forget Me - Star Girl   ¾   26
Gay (Lord Gayle) Early ldr, recall 2f out, styd on but not as well as wnr: quick reapp: apprec return to 2m.

2037 **FAST FORWARD FRED** 42 [7] L Montague Hall 9-9-13 (52) A Clark 6/1: /0-003: 9 gr g Sharrood - Sun   nk   52
Street (Ile de Bourbon) Prom, led appr str, hard prsd 2f out, worn down ins last: 6 wk abs, top-weight.

--   **GOLDBRIDGE** [3] T P McGovern 5-9-1 (40) R Hughes 2/1 FAV: 0004/4: fit from hdles wins at M Rasen & Stratford (2m4f/2m6.5f h'caps, handles   2½   37
styd on but nvr nr ldrs: poor tactical ride: fit from hdles wins at M Rasen & Stratford (2m4f/2m6.5f h'caps, handles
gd/sft, best on firm, without blnks, rtd 104h): ex-Irish mdn, missed '99, prev unplcd: prob capable of better.

2941 **ELSIE BAMFORD** 4 [5] 4-9-11 (50) R Ffrench 11/4: 334325: Held up, prog 3f out, no extra bef   nk   46
dist, fin lame: quick reapp: see 1683.

*2622 **DANGER BABY** 18 [2] 10-9-10 (49)(bl) S Sanders 9/2: 625216: Al bhd: op 3/1: btr 2622 (C/D, gd).   5   40

2785 **SUMITRA** 11 [4] 4-9-4 (43) A McGlone 12/1: 30-057: Chsd ldrs till lost pl ent str: mdn, better at shorter.   6   29

2536 **URGENT REPLY** 21 [1] 7-8-3 (28) Paul Eddery 12/1: 066268: Sn led, hdd appr str & btn: see 2373, 1614.nk   13

8 ran   Time 3m 26.6 (9.4)   (K L West)   W J Musson Newmarket, Suffolk

---

3041   3.30 TOTE PLACEPOT HCAP 3YO+ 0-80 (D)   7f str   Good/Firm 29   -05 Slow   [80]
     £7124   £2192   £1096   £548   3 yo rec 7 lb

2794 **HAIL THE CHIEF** 11 [4] R Hannon 3-8-9 (68) S Sanders 10/1: -42601: 3 b c Be My Chief - Jade Pet   72
(Petong) Held up, switched & imprvd ent fnl 2f, led below dist, drvn out: tchd 16/1: 1st win: unplcd sole
'99 start (auct mdn, rtd 55): eff at 7f, tried 1m: acts on fast grnd, sharp/undul trk.

2768 **ARETINO** 2 [3] P W Harris 3-9-2 (75) A Beech (5) 8/1: 505002: 3 ch c Common Grounds - Inonder   ¾   76
(Belfort) Narrow lead till appr fnl 2f, sn pushed along & onepace till kept on well ins last, not btn far:
op 5/1: difficult ride but back to form here: see 1262.

2792 **DILKUSHA** 11 [1] B J Meehan 5-9-10 (76) T Quinn 3/1: 6-0043: 5 b g Indian Ridge - Crimson Glen   ¾   75
(Glenstal) Waited with, imprvd 2f out, styd on for 3rd but not pace of ldrs: tchd 4/1: back to form, see 1989.

*2690 **GOODENOUGH MOVER** 16 [7] J S King 4-9-11 (77) R Havlin 2/1 FAV: 011114: Cl-up, led & went 2L clr   1¼   73
2f out, sn rdn, hdd bef dist & no extra: back up in trip: unable to dominate but probably remains in form.

1470 **RULE OF THUMB** 68 [6] 3-9-2 (75) J F Egan 12/1: 6-0005: Chsd ldrs, eff & unable to qckn appr fnl 1f.   2½   66

2840 **L A TOUCH** 9 [5] 7-7-13 (51) J Quinn 7/1: 00-036: Hung right, al bhd: tchd 9/1: see 2840.   5   32

2690 **SHUDDER** 16 [8] 5-8-8 (60) S Carson 6/1: 031637: Chsd ldrs till wknd appr fnl 2f: up in trip, see 2292.   3½   35

2437 **ANALYTICAL** 25 [2] 4-8-13 (65)(VIS) R Hughes 6/1: -00038: Handy till wknd qckly 3f out: visored.   6   30

8 ran   Time 1m 26.6 (2.4)   (Peter M Crane)   R Hannon East Everleigh, Wilts

---

3042   4.00 EBF CLASSIFIED STKS 3YO+ 0-85 (C)   1m1f149y   Good/Firm 29   +05 Fast
     £6027   £2228   £1114   £506   3 yo rec 10lb

2696 **GOLCONDA** 16 [3] M L W Bell 4-9-1 A Beech (5) 3/1: 300001: 4 br f Lahib - David's Star (Welsh Saint)   85
Waited with, hugged ins rail thr'out, closed 2f out, burst thro' to lead below dist, v cmftbly: tchd 4/1, fair time,
vis omitted: '99 wnr at W'hampton (mdn, rtd 67a), Kempton & Lingfield (h'caps, rtd 90 at best): eff arnd 10f,
tried 12f: suited by firm/fast grnd & fibresand, poss handles soft, without visor: likes sharp trks: well ridden.

2337 **TOLSTOY** 30 [1] Sir Michael Stoute 4-9-8 T Quinn 1/1 FAV: 22-522: 3 b c Nashwan - Millazure (Dayjur)   2½   83
Held up, imprvd appr str, styd on to go 2nd towards fin, no ch with wnr: bckd: consistent, eff at 1m/9.5f.

2666 **EL ZITO** 17 [2] M G Quinlan 3-9-0 J F Egan 6/1: 211033: 3 b g Mukaddamah - Samite (Tennyson)   ½   88
Set decent clip, hdd ent fnl 1f, no extra: op 4/1: improved from the front, progressing well: see 1744.

1744 **CARENS HERO** 55 [4] Mrs A J Perrett 3-8-12 R Hughes 6/1: 0-3104: Pld hard, trkd ldr, shkn up 2f out,   2½   82
unable to qckn & squeezed for room in last: op 4/1, 8 wk abs: lngr trip/different tactics: see 1436 (made all).

4332} **DANCE IN TUNE** 293 [5] 3-8-8 G Duffield 5/1: 1430-5: Handy, rdn appr fnl 1f, sn hmpd/snatched up,   1¼   76
eased: drifted from 2/1 on reapp: '99 wnr at W'hampton (mdn, rtd 82a) & Musselburgh (nurs, rtd 91): half-
brother to useful 10f wnr Dancing Phantom: eff at 7f, stays 1m, shld get further this term: acts on firm/fast
grnd & fibresand, well btn on gd/soft & hvy: goes on sharp trks: can leave this bhd next time: with Sir M Prescott.

5 ran   Time 2m 00.3 (2.3)   (Innlaw Racing)   M L W Bell Newmarket, Suffolk

---

3043   4.30 EXPRESS HCAP 3YO 0-75 (E)   1m1f149y   Good/Firm 29   -12 Slow   [82]
     £2926   £836   £418

2610 **KELTIC BARD** 18 [7] S P C Woods 3-9-0 (68) G Duffield 2/1 FAV: -00051: 3 b g Emperor Jones -   74
Broughton Singer (Common Grounds) Led, rdn 2f out, kept on strgly, pshd out cl-home: '99 W'hampton wnr (nov
auct, rtd 88a & 80): eff at 1m/9.5f on firm/fast & fibresand: suited forcing the pace on sharp/undul trks.

2842 **BANDLER CHING** 9 [8] C N Allen 3-9-0 (68) Martin Dwyer 9/2: 533-52: 3 b c Sri Pekan - Stanerra's   ¾   72
Wish (Caerleon) Nvr far away, rdn appr fnl 1f, kept on but being held: op 3/1, tubed: styd lnger 9.5f trip.

2367 **MALARKEY** 28 [2] J A Osborne 3-8-11 (65) D Holland 6/1: 055453: 3 b g Mukaddamah - Malwiya   1   67
(Shahrastani) Waited with, prog appr str, ch but not qckn thro' flailing whips ins last: stays 9.5f on fast.

1604 **MURJAN** 61 [6] E A L Dunlop 3-9-2 (70) W Ryan 9/2: 34-504: In tch, shaken up 2f out, unable to qckn.   1   70

2713 **FAHAN** 14 [4] 3-8-8 (62) M Hills 9/1: 30-055: Al bhd: op 7/1: longer trip, see 1812.   11   47

*2382 **GIMCO** 28 [5] 3-9-7 (75) O Urbina 5/1: 432216: Prom till ent str: much btr 2382 (12f fibresand).   3   55

2811 **CLEAR CRYSTAL** 10 [3] 3-7-10 (50)(2oh) J Lowe 33/1: 600667: Well plcd till 3f out: op 14/1: see 930.   3   25

2726 **LAGO DI LEVICO** 13 [1] 3-7-10 (50)(1oh) R Brisland (5) 12/1: 154608: Sn prom, keen, wknd qckly 3f   4   19
out: tchd 20/1: too free back up in trip & easier grnd will suit, see 892, 783.

8 ran   Time 2m 01.9 (3.9)   (G A Roberts)   S P C Woods Newmarket, Suffolk

Official Going   GOOD/FIRM. Stalls: Inside.

3044
6.10 FEDORA MDN 2YO (D)   **5f**   **Good/Firm**   **Inapplicable**
£3737   £1150   £575   £287

1403 **BAD AS I WANNA BE 72** [8] B J Meehan 2-9-0 J Fortune 6/1: 01: 2 ch c Common Grounds - Song Of The   **109**
Glens (Horage) Made all, kept on well to go clr fnl 1f, cmftbly: abs, nicely bckd: 62,000gns Mar foal: brother
to a 7f juv wnr: eff at 5f, further suit: handles gd/firm: runs well fresh: looks useful, win in better company.
--   **SENIOR MINISTER** [16] J M P Eustace 2-9-0 J Tate 7/1: 2: 2 b c Lion Cavern - Crime Ofthecentury   3   **97**
(Pharly) Slow away, sn handy, eff over 1f out, not pace of wnr: Feb foal, cost 55,000gns: half-brother to
useful sprinter Tussle: dam 5f wnr: v pleasing first run: handles fast & sprint trips will suit: win races.
1454 **HAWK 69** [1] R Hannon 2-9-0 (t) R Hughes 11/4 JT FAV: 333: 2 b c A P Jet - Miss Enjoleur (L'Enjoleur) 1½   **93**
With wnr, rdn & onepace over 1f out: well bckd after a 10 wk absence, t-strap: similar form to 1454.
2368 **APPELLATION 28** [7] R Hannon 2-9-0 M Roberts 12/1: -64: Dwelt, sn in tch, kept on same pace over   2   **88**
1f out: stablemate of 3rd & showing some promise: 6f will suit: see 2368.
2808 **FAITHFUL WARRIOR 10** [6] 2-9-0 J Reid 11/4 JT FAV: -45: Prom, btn over 1f out: see 2808 (6f).   ½   **86**
2901 **LONER 6** [10] 2-9-0 S Whitworth 20/1: 046: Bhd, late gains: nvr dngrs: qck reapp & may do better 1¼   **82**
in nursery h'caps over further: see 2901.
2227 **ROXANNE MILL 33** [11] 2-8-9 G Baker (5) 20/1: 57: Waited with, brief effort over 1f out, no impress.   shd   **76**
2711 **MADRASEE 14** [4] 2-8-9 D Sweeney 16/1: 3638: Prom, wknd over 1f out: btr 2711. 1¼   **72**
2766 **HOT PANTS 12** [5] 2-8-9 C Catlin (7) 10/1: 0539: Prom, wknd over 1f out: much btr 2766.   2   **66**
2711 **BATCHWORTH LOCK 14** [13] 2-9-0 S Carson (3) 33/1: 000: In tch, wknd over 2f out: see 2711.   6   **55**
2034 Miss Damina 42 [15] 2-8-9 R Ffrench 33/1:   --   Bravura [9] 2-9-0 I Mongan (5) 33/1:
--   Leggit [12] 2-8-9 (t) R Havlin 20/1:   2894 Operation Envy 7 [14] 2-9-0 C Rutter 50/1:
--   Packin Em In [3] 2-9-0 S Sanders 33/1:   --   Atemme [2] 2-8-9 B Marcus 20/1:
16 ran   Time 58.9   (Joe L Allbritton)   B J Meehan Upper Lambourn, Berks.

3045
6.40 PANAMA HCAP 3YO+ 0-70 (E)   **1m2f**   [67]
£3318   £948   £474   3 yo rec 10lb

2890 **QUEENS PAGEANT 7** [21] J L Spearing 6-9-11 (64) M Roberts 5/1 FAV: 044651: 6 ch m Risk Me -   **70**
Mistral's Dancer (Shareef Dancer) Hld up, hdwy over 2f out, led over 1f out, kept on, rdn out: eye-catching earlier:
'99 wnr on reapp at Thirsk (h'cap, rtd 76): York scorer in '98 (h'cap, rtd 75 & 84a): prev eff at 1m, suited by
step up to 10f on fast, soft, fibresand & any trk: runs well fresh: well h'capped: cld go in again at this trip.
2554} **BARRETTSTOWN 388** [4] P R Chamings 5-9-12 (65) B Marcus 33/1: 3204-2: 5 ch g Cadeaux Genereux - 3   **66**
Sagar (Habitat) Waited with, hdwy 2f out, onepace over 1f out: reapp: plcd for M C Pipe in '99 (rtd 69):
modest jumps form prev: eff over 10/11.9f on fast, gd/soft grnd & on any trk: goes well fresh: gd reapp.
2817 **COMPATRIOT 10** [9] P S Felgate 4-9-9 (62) D Duffield 10/1: 460253: 4 b g Bigstone - Campestral   ½   **62**
(Alleged) Waited with, hdwy over 1f out, onepace: mdn after 20: stays 10f: see 2546, 1414.
2542 **DIM OFAN 21** [14] B Palling 4-9-1 (54) R Hughes 14/1: 060004: Waited with, eff 2f out, sn onepace.   ½   **53**
2689 **BITTER SWEET 16** [15] 4-8-1 (40)(vis) S Carson (3) 14/1: 354005: Handy, led over 3f out till   nk   **38**
over 1f out, no extra: see 2689, 1272.
2790 **DION DEE 11** [12] 4-8-11 (50) N Pollard 9/1: 610256: Bhd, some late gains: btr 2625, 2011 (gd grnd). 1½   **46**
2795 **SPIRIT OF TENBY 11** [17] 3-9-0 (63) P Doe 8/1: 033047: Waited with, keeping on when short of   nk   **58**
room over 1f out, onepace: see 2264, 1964.
1735 **WAVERLEY ROAD 56** [13] 3-8-11 (60) J Fortune 12/1: -50658: Nvr a factor: 8 wk abs: see 702.   1   **53**
2727 **GALI 13** [5] 4-8-2 (41)(VIS) T Ashley 20/1: 00-009: Dwelt, bhd, eff 2f out, sn no extra: tried visor.   1   **33**
2831 **OLLIES CHUCKLE 10** [10] 5-7-10 (35) Claire Byran (5) 33/1: 066060: Al bhd: 10th: see 908.   3½   **22**
2699 **LADY JONES 15** [18] 3-8-7 (56) J Reid 8/1: -01300: In tch, btn over 2f out: 11th: btr 2043 (1m).   ½   **42**
1062 **SALVA 91** [19] 4-9-10 (63)(t) D Sweeney 14/1: 30-460: In tch, btn over 2f out: 12th: abs, see 920. 1¾   **46**
--   **PADDYS RICE** [20] 9-8-2 (41) C Rutter 33/1: 0500/0: In tch, wknd over 3f out: 13th: last rcd back 1¾   **21**
in '98, won at Bath (claim h'cap, rtd 55, with M Blanshard): '97 wnr at Brighton (h'cap, rtd 58): eff over
7f/1m on firm, gd/soft & any track.
2262 **GRANDMA ULLA 33** [1] 3-8-3 (52) J F Egan 14/1: 000000: Led till over 4f out, wknd over 2f out: 14th. 2½   **28**
2920 **WELODY 5** [7] 4-9-3 (56) W Supple 25/1: 000000: Led over 4f out till over 3f out, wknd, eased: 17th.   **0**
2752 **GIKO 12** [6] 6-8-12 (51)(t) M Henry 10/1: 656000: Al bhd: 19th: see 1729, 1033.   **0**
2764 Kafil 12 [8] 6-7-10 (35)(bl)(3oh) R Brisland (5) 20/1:   2774 Shannons Dream 11 [3] 4-8-3 (42) A Clark 33/1:
2816 Ripsnorter 10 [11] 11-7-10 (35)(11oh) G Baker (5) 40/1:2726 Cedar Lord 13 [16] 3-8-3 (52) D R McCabe 33/1:
2890 Island Escape 7 [2] 4-8-11 (50)(bl) S Sanders 20/1:
21 ran   Time   (Mrs Robert Heathcote)   J L Spearing Kinnersley, Worcs.

3046
7.10 EXPRESS FILLIES HCAP 3YO+ 0-80 (D)   **6f**   **Good/Firm**   **Inapplicable**   [77]
£4140   £1274   £637   3 yo rec 5 lb

2713 **ROUGE 14** [13] K R Burke 5-7-10 (45) M Henry 14/1: -13161: 5 gr m Rudimentary - Couleur de Rose   **54**
(Kalaglow) Made all, kept on well over 1f out, rdn out: last winter scored at Southwell & Lingfield (clmrs,
rtd 80a, with J Leigh): '99 scorer at W'hampton (h'cap, rtd 71a): stays 1m, suited by 6/7f: acts on fast &
both AWs: likes a sharp trk: well h'capped on turf for shrewd new connections, shld be plcd to further effect
2830 **PREMIUM PRINCESS 10** [6] J J Quinn 5-8-3 (52) J F Egan 7/1: 533362: 5 b m Distant Relative · 1¾   **56**
Solemn Occasion (Secreto) Chsd ldrs, eff to chase wnr over 1f out, no impress ins last: consistent in defeat.
2654 **BRAMBLE BEAR 17** [10] M Blanshard 6-8-0 (49) P Doe 7/1: 104033: 6 b m Beveled - Supreme Rose 1¼   **49**
(Frimley Park) Waited with, hdwy over 1f out, nvr dngrs: fair run: see 2654, 1464.
2905 **ABSOLUTE FANTASY 6** [2] E A Wheeler 4-8-1 (50)(bl) S Carson (3) 9/1: 342024: In tch, eff to 2½   **44**
chase wnr over 2f out till over 1f out: qck reapp, btr 2905.
2820 **TWO STEP 10** [14] 4-7-10 (45)(t)(4oh) G Baker (5) 25/1: -00105: Prom, edged left & no extra   shd   **38**
over 1f out: twice below 2632 (fibresand, 5f).
2944 **SEREN TEG 4** [12] 4-7-10 (45)(bl)(1oh) G Sparkes (3) 8/1: 000646: Handy, sn lost pl, late gains.   hd   **37**
2961 **IVORY DAWN 3** [15] 6-10-0 (77) C Carver (3) 100/30 FAV: 030157: Handy, wknd over 1f out: qck 1½   **65**
reapp, nicely bckd: better expected after 2961 & 2761.
2592 **SUNLEYS PICC 19** [8] 3-8-4 (58) J Tate 14/1: -06058: In tch, wknd 2f out: see 2592, 729.   nk   **45**
1405 **BELIEVING 72** [9] 3-9-2 (70) R Hughes 14/1: 0-4609: Waited with, effort over 1f out, no impress: abs.   ¾   **55**
2701 **WHIZZ KID 15** [5] 6-9-10 (73) Claire Bryan (5) 12/1: 260100: Nvr a factor: 10th, btr 2451 (5f).   ¾   **56**

2124 **Nightingale Song** 38 [7] 6-7-12 (47) (2ow) (3oh) Martin Dwyer 16/1:
2777 **Oare Kite** 11 [4] 5-8-3 (51) (bl) (1ow) G Duffield 16/1:
2654 **Stridhana** 17 [11] 4-8-6 (55) N Pollard 12/1:   2768 **Shafaq** 12 [16] 3-9-9 (77) (BL) W Supple 16/1:
2749 **Kayo Gee** 12 [3] 4-8-10 (59) (vis) C Rutter 20/1:
15 ran   Time 1m 11.7   (Nigel Shields)   K R Burke Newmarket.

3047   7.40 BERET MDN 2YO   6f   Good/Firm   Inapplicable
£4049 £1246 £623   £311

-- **GREENWOOD** [8] J M P Eustace 2-9-0 J Tate 6/1: 1: 2 ch c Emarati - Charnwood Queen (Cadeaux **77**
Genereux) Nvr far away, went on 2f out, held on well, drvn out on debut: 13,000gns Jan foal: dam a dual
sprint wnr: eff at 6f on fast grnd on a sharp trk, 7f will suit: battled on well today & showed a gd attitude.
-- **UNPARALLELED** [16] I A Balding 2-8-9 J F Egan 20/1: 2: 2 b f Primo Dominie - Sharp Chief (Chief hd **71**
Singer) Chsd ldrs, eff 2f out, keeping on when drifted left ins last, only just btn in a tight fin: Mar foal, half-
sister to sprinter Effervescent: dam a 6f juv wnr: eff at 6f on fast grnd, runs well fresh: gd debut.
2711 **AVERY RING** 14 [5] A P Jarvis 2-9-0 J Fortune 9/2: 623: 2 b c Magic Ring - Thatcherella (Thatching) 1 **73**
Nvr far away, ev ch when bmpd ins last, kept on & not btn far: eff at 5/6f on gd & fast grnd: see 2711 (AW).
2521 **SNOWEY MOUNTAIN** 22 [6] N A Callaghan 2-9-0 W Supple 10/1: -644: Mid-div, styd on nicely fnl 1f, ½ **72+**
nrst fin: promising, will improve back over 7f now qual for nursery h'caps: see 2521.
-- **NOSY BE** [13] 2-9-0 S Sanders 12/1: 5: Slowly away, styd on well fnl 2f, nvr nrr on debut: Feb foal, 2 **66**
a first foal: sire a decent sprinter: P Makin colt, sure to learn from this & will improve.
1957 **SECURON DANCER** 45 [11] 2-8-9 P Doe 20/1: 406: Prom, ev ch 2f out, no extra fnl 1f: 6 wk abs: 1 **58**
fair effort, stable not known for its juvs: see 1176 (5f).
-- **PARTY PLOY** [7] 2-9-0 D Sweeney 25/1: 7: Slowly away, eff halfway, kept on but nvr nr to chall: ½ **61**
debut: Mar foal, sire a high-class mid-dist performer: likely to apprec 1m + given time: with K Burke.
2854 **ZHITOMIR** 9 [18] 2-9-0 B Marcus 5/1: -648: Front rank 5f, fdd: see 2854. nk **60**
-- **BEVEL BLUE** [9] 2-9-0 S Carson 20/1: 9: Dwelt, recovered to chase ldrs 4½f, grad wknd: 1½ **56**
debut: Apr foal, related to sprint wnrs Supreme Angel & Patsy Grimes: G Balding colt.
2494 **REVERIE** 23 [12] 2-9-0 R Hughes 7/2 FAV: 00: Set pace 4f, wknd into 10th: see 2494. nk **55**
-- **LUCKY BREAK** [17] 2-9-0 Paul Eddery 33/1: 0: Slowly away, late prog, nvr plcd to chall on debut: ½ **53**
fin 11th: Feb foal, dam a 5f winning juv: sire a top-class 1m/10f performer: with C Horgan, do better.
2818 **SUN BIRD** 10 [4] 2-9-0 G Duffield 14/1: 50: Nvr a factor in 12th: see 2818 (AW). 3 **45**
2598 **STYLISH FELLA** 19 [10] 2-9-0 D Griffiths 9/1: 00: Al towards rear, fin 13th: see 2598. hd **44**
-- **RESPLENDENT FLYER** [2] 2-9-0 D Holland 9/1: 0: Al rear, fin last on debut: 20,000gns Apr foal: **0**
first foal, sire a high-class miler: P Harris colt who shld be capable of better.
-- **Madame Butterfly** [3] 2-8-9 A Clark 33/1:   -- **Single Track Mind** [15] 2-9-0 J Reid 14/1:
-- **Girl Band** [1] 2-8-9 R Havlin 14/1:   -- **Ambassador Lady** [14] 2-8-9 S Whitworth 33/1:
18 ran   Time 1m 13.1   (J C Smith)   J M P Eustace Newmarket.

3048   8.10 CITY INDEX MDN 3YO (D)   1m67y rnd   Good/Firm   Inapplicable
£4218 £1298 £649   £324

2553 **HIGHLAND REEL** 21 [16] D R C Elsworth 3-9-0 N Pollard 7/1: -30331: 3 ch c Selkirk - Taj Victory **86**
(Final Straw) In tch, went on after 3f, clr fnl 1f, cmftbly: val for 6L+: half-brother to a 1m wnr: stays 10f, eff
over an easy 1m: acts on gd/soft & frm, impvd on today's fast grnd: a useful run, win again in this form.
2117 **MATERIAL WITNESS** 39 [15] W R Muir 3-9-0 Martin Dwyer 9/4 FAV: -22302: 3 b c Barathea - Dial Dream 4 **79**
(Gay Mecene) Prom, kept on fnl 1f but no ch with easy wnr: met a much imprvd rival here: see 1535.
1155 **ENTAIL** 87 [2] J H M Gosden 3-8-9 J Fortune 4/1: 3-53: 3 b f Riverman - Estala (Be My Guest) hd **74+**
Mid-div, eff 2f out, styd on under press cl-home: 3 month abs: some promise over an inadequate trip, bred to
like mid-dists: now qual for h'caps & one to keep in mind in that sphere over 10f+: see 1155.
-- **DIGITAL** [12] M R Channon 3-9-0 R Havlin 7/1: -4: Rear, imprvd 3f out, no impress fnl 1f on debut: 1¾ **75**
dam unrcd: eff at 1m on fast grnd, looks like 10f will suit: shld learn plenty from this.
2860 **NASHAAB** 9 [9] 3-9-0 W Supple 6/1: -55: Hdwy from rear halfway, btn fnl 1f: see 2860 (7f). 3 **69**
-- **SPRING GIFT** [13] 3-8-9 J Reid 20/1: -6: Waited wth, eff 2f out, btn fnl 1f: debut: first foal: bred 2 **60**
to apprec mid-dists: with K Mahdi.
-- **COOLING OFF** [7] 3-8-9 D Holland 9/1: -7: Rear, eff 3f out, no impress fnl 2f: racecourse bow: hd **60**
half-sister to mid-dist wnr Out On A Promise: will need 10f+: with G Wragg.
4473} **JULIA TITUS** 283 [5] 3-8-9 D Harrison 33/1: 00-8: Nvr better than mid-div: reapp: unplcd in 2 juv 1 **58**
starts (rtd 63 at best): half-sister to high-class sprinter Cadeaux Genereux: sire a top-class miler.
429 **PEPPERCORN** 182 [17] 3-8-9 G Baker 25/1: 40/1: 00-609: Nvr a factor: long abs: flattered. 1¼ **55$**
-- **COOL SPICE** [11] 3-8-9 D Sweeney 33/1: -0: Slowly away, nvr a factor in 10th on debut: half- shd **55**
sister to 6f/1m wnr: dam a mid-dist scorer: with B Palling.
4556} **MOON OF ALABAMA** 275 [14] 3-8-9 D R McCabe 16/1: 50-0: Effort from rear 3f out, btn fnl 2f: 11 **35**
fin 11th, reapp: trained by J Hills in '99, 5th at York (mdn, rtd 60, debut): sister to a mid-dist wnr in France.
2621 **SARENA SPECIAL** 18 [3] 3-9-0 (bl) J F Egan 16/1: 503040: Rcd keenly & led 3f, btn 2f out: 12th. nk **39**
4597} White Magic 270 [8] 3-8-9 S Carson 33/1:   -- Lively Felix [6] 3-9-0 C Rutter 25/1:
-- Joli Eclipse [10] 3-8-9 Paul Eddery 33/1:   2889 Duemila 7 [4] 3-9-0 G Duffield 40/1:
-- Culminate [1] 3-9-0 J Tate 40/1:
17 ran   Time 1m 43.4   (Sir Gordon Brunton)   D R C Elsworth Whitsbury, Hants.

3049   8.40 TRILBY HCAP 3YO+ 0-70 (E)   1m3f135y   Good/Firm   Inapplicable   [69]
£3192 £912 £456   3yo rec 12lb

2771 **MYSTERIUM** 12 [15] N P Littmoden 6-8-4 (45) R Brisland(5) 20/1: 000251: 6 gr g Mystiko - Way To Go **52**
(Troy) Rcd keenly in tch, imprvd to lead 3f out, ran on strongly, rdn out: earlier scored at W'hampton (AW h'cap,
rtd 54a): '99 wnr at Yarmouth (h'cap, rtd 44) & W'hampton (h'cap, rtd 53a): eff at 9/12f on gd, fast & f/sand,
loves W'hampton: has tried a visor, seems better without: ideally suited by waiting tactics & well h'capped now.
2764 **KENNET** 12 [4] P D Cundell 9-9-5 (60) S Sanders 12/1: 002022: 5 b g Kylian - Marwell Mitzi (Interrex) 1½ **64**
Rear, gd hdwy to chall dist, kept on ins last but not pace of wnr cl-home: sound run: see 2764, 2372.
2530 **MY PLEDGE** 22 [2] C A Horgan 5-9-3 (58) R Hughes 15/2: 0-2103: 5 b g Waajib - Pollys Glow (Glow) 1 **60**
Slowly away, imprvd from rear 3f out, ev ch dist, no extra cl-home: in gd form to form of 2263.
*2782 **WADI** 11 [10] Dr J R J Naylor 5-9-10 (65) C Rutter 3/1 FAV: 041014: Rear, prog to chall 2f out, nk **66**
not qckn ins fnl 1f: top-weight: in gd form, see 2782.

2793 **TULSA** 11 [5] 6-7-10 (37)(bl)(2oh) G Baker(5) 12/1: 100-55: Slowly away, imprvd 2f out, not qckn fnl 1f: lightly rcd this term & running into form: see 2793.   1   36
2872 **SUPLIZI** 8 [9] 9-9-3 (58) A Clark 12/1: 000606: Hdwy from rear 2f out, no impress fnl 1f: see 1788.   2½   53
*2971 **OUT ON A PROMISE** 3 [12] J S Wainwright 3-8-8-6 (47)(6ex) D R McCabe 5/1: 4/0017: Prom, ev ch 2f out, wknd ins last: qck reapp & too soon after 2971?   hd   42
2552 **THE SHADOW** 21 [7] 4-8-4 (45)(vis) M Henry 25/1: -00508: Mid-div till lost pl halfway, no ch after.   9   25
2725 **KIRISNIPPA** 13 [6] 5-8-9 (50) P Doe 14/1: 040359: Slowly away, nvr a factor: see 2725.   ¾   29
*2715 **DIRECT DEAL** 14 [20] 4-8-12 (53)(tt) D Harrison 10/1: 000010: Made most till 3fout, wknd into 10th.   shd   32
2667 **CRYSTAL FLITE** 17 [14] 3-8-12 (65) D Holland 10/1: -00260: Rear, rdn & btn 3f out: 11th: btr 2246.   1¾   42
2656 **MONUMENT** 17 [13] 8-8-5 (46) R Havlin 15/2: 50-300: Nvr better than mid-div, 12th: btr 1880 (reapp).   3½   18
2789 **DIZZY TILLY** 11 [19] 6-8-8 (49) T Ashley 9/1: 301060: In tch 1m, wknd: fin 17th: usually runs well here at Windsor: much btr 2370 (C/D).   0
*2624 **GOT ONE TOO** 18 [18] 3-7-13 (52)(t) N Pollard 12/1: -00010: Prom 1m, wknd & fin last: btr 2624.   0
2601 **Ahouod** 18 [17] 4-7-12 (39) N Carlisle 20/1:   2264 **Coral Shells** 32 [11] 3-7-10 (49)(4oh) G Sparkes(3) 33/1:
2727 **Famous** 13 [1] 7-7-10 (37)(bl)(6oh) Claire Bryan(5) 33/1:2872 **Colour Key** 8 [3] 6-8-1 (42) S Carson(3) 33/1:
830   **Northern Trio** 116 [16] 3-7-10 (49)(5oh) J Lowe 33/1:
19 ran   Time 2m 27.8   (Alcester Associates)   N P Littmoden Newmarket.

Official Going: GOOD (GOOD TO SOFT IN PLACES)   Stalls: Inside

3050   2.00 CIRCUS SELL HCAP 3YO 0-60 (F)   1m4f   Good/Soft 89 -16 Slow   [63]
            £2310   £660   £330

2735 **JONLOZ** 14 [6] G Woodward 3-8-2 (37) P Fessey 20/1: 456601: 3 ch c Presidium - Stratford Lady (Touching Wood) Held up, rdn/prog to lead over 2f out & rdn clr over 1f out, styd on strongly: bt in for 5,200 gns, first win: unplcd in '99 (mdn, rtd 57): eff at 12f on gd/soft grnd & fibresand, any trk.   44
2746 **UNICORN STAR** 13 [13] J S Wainwright 3-8-13 (48) R Winston 11/2: 436252: 3 b g Persian Bold - Highland Warning (Warning) Held up, drvn fnl 3f & styd on to take 2nd ins last, no impress: see 2362, 1274.   8   45
2556 **COLOMBE DOR** 21 [7] P C Haslam 3-8-12 (47) Dean McKeown 6/1: 260003: 3 br g Petong - Deep Divide (Nashwan) Prom, rdn/chsd wnr 2f out, al held: bckd, op 8/1: mdn: see 4311 & 213.   1½   43
2510 **LAMMOSKI** 24 [4] M C Chapman 3-8-5 (40) K Dalgleish (5) 33/1: 050004: Bhd, late gains: jmps fit.   ¾   35
2989 **PHARAOHS HOUSE** 3 [10] 3-8-7 (42)(bl) G Parkin 10/1: -00055: Chsd clr ldr, lost plce 4f out, sn held.   ½   36
2964 **WELCOME BACK** 4 [3] 3-8-5 (40) F Lynch 5/1 JT FAV: 005536: Held up, never a threat: quick reapp.   nk   33
2908 **GOLD KRIEK** 7 [14] 3-8-6 (41) J Mackay (5) 5/1 JT FAV: 00-007: Drvn/chsd ldrs over 3f out, sn btn.   2   31
2908 **BEE GEE** 7 [11] 3-8-4 (39) Dale Gibson 6/1: 143058: Held up, drvn/chsd ldrs over 3f out, btn: op 4/1.   ½   28
3021 **HIGH BEAUTY** 2 [9] 3-8-0 (35)(BL) G Bardwell 10/1: 050009: Al bhd: blnks: qck reapp: mod form.   3   20
2879 **JEUNE PREMIER** 8 [5] 3-9-7 (56)(BL) D R McCabe 16/1: 050000: Led after 1f & sn clr, hdd over 2f out, sn btn: 10th: rcd freely in first time blnks, op 12/1: mod form.   5   35
1195 **Comanche Queen** 86 [8] 3-8-7 (42) J Quinn 16/1:   3021 **Dinky** 2 [2] 3-7-10 (31)(11oh) D Kinsella (7) 20/1:
1914 **Indiana Springs** 48 [12] 3-8-10 (43)(vis)(2ow) J Weaver 14/1:
13 ran   Time 2m 43.9 (12.6)   (P Appleyard)   G Woodward Brierley, S Yorks

3051   2.30 MOORGATE MDN DIV I 2YO (D)   7f100y rnd   Good/Soft 89 -08 Slow
            £3285   £1011   £505   £252

2867 **LUCAYAN CHIEF** 9 [9] S P C Woods 2-9-0 G Duffield 7/4 FAV: -51: 2 b c With Approval - Littleladyleah (Shareef Dancer) Made all, rdn & asserted from over 1f out, styd on strongly: hvly bckd: eff over longer 7.5f trip, sure to relish further: enjoyed this gd/soft grnd & forcing tactics: useful, win again.   90
2686 **WAINAK** 17 [1] J L Dunlop 2-9-0 W Supple 7/2: 022: 2 b c Silver Hawk - Cask (Be My Chief) Prom, rdn/chsd wnr over 1f out, hung right & held inside last: rest well covered: acts on gd & gd/soft: see 2686.   3½   84
2620 **HOSSRUM** 19 [7] E A L Dunlop 2-9-0 G Carter 20/1: 603: 2 br c Definite Article - Petite Maxine (Sharpo) Rear, kept on fnl 3f, nvr nr to front pair: stays stiff 7.5f on gd/soft: cld improve in h'caps.   3½   77
2649 **GOLD STATUETTE** 18 [6] J W Hills 2-9-0 J Weaver 5/1: 064: Towards rear, mod hdwy fnl 2f, al held.   shd   77
2754 **MATADI** 13 [5] 2-9-0 J Quinn 12/1: -45: Prom, rdn/hung right & btn 1f out: op 8/1: longer 7.5f trip.   nk   76
2708 **BUY A VOWEL** 16 [3] 2-9-0 F Lynch 11/4: 06: Chsd wnr 4f out, rdn/btn 2f out: bckd: see 2708 (firm).   5   66
2271 **SAVE THE POUND** 33 [8] 2-9-0 R Winston 50/1: 57: Chsd wnr 3f, btn over 1f out: see 2271.   2   62
2653 **ALAGAZAM** 18 [4] 2-9-0 M Tebbutt 66/1: 008: Dwelt, nvr nr to chall: stewards enquired into run, jockey suspended gelding was unable to handle undul on softer grnd, explanations noted: kind ride also in 2653.   2   58
1809 **UNCLE FOLDING** 53 [2] 2-9-0 W Ryan 66/1: 69: Held up, eff 3f out, no hdwy: abs: longer 7.5f trip.   12   40
9 ran   Time 1m 38.1 (7.3)   (Lucayan Stud)   S P C Woods Newmarket, Suffolk

3052   3.05 D LAIRD LADY RIDERS HCAP 3YO+ 0-75 (F)   1m2f   Good/Soft 89 -31 Slow   [42]
            £3500   £1077   £538   £269   3 yo rec 9 lb

2958 **GOLD BLADE** 4 [10] J Pearce 11-9-12 (40) Mrs L Pearce 8/1: 005461: 11 ch g Rousillon - Sharp Girl (Sharpman) Led halfway, rdn fnl 2f & styd on strongly to assert inside last: op 7/1, quick reapp: '99 Lingfield & Pontefract wnr (amat/ladies h'cap, rtd 48): lightly rcd in '98, plcd in '97 (h'caps, rtd 62 & 57a): eff at 1m, suited by 10/13f on firm, soft, both AWs & any track: runs well fresh & for Mrs L Pearce: tough.   47
4037} **BUZZ THE AGENT** 315 [5] M W Easterby 5-9-8 (36)(tbl) Miss Brotherton (0) 12/1: 0453-2: 5 b g Prince Sabo - Chess Mistress (Run The Gantlet) Trckd ldrs, rdn/chsd wnr 4f out, al held: op 7/1, reapp: plcd on fnl start in '99 (rtd 36, h'cap): '98 wnr here at Beverley (h'cap, rtd 58): eff at 10f, suited by 12f: acts on firm & soft: prob handles any track, suited by t-strap & blnks.   5   36
2453 **SMARTER CHARTER** 25 [6] Mrs L Stubbs 7-11-0 (56) Kristin Stubbs (5) 7/1: 232563: 7 br g Master Willie - Irene's Charter (Persian Bold) Dwelt, waited with rear, styd on fnl 2f, no threat to wnr: see 2081, 871 (10f).   nk   55
2958 **PENNYS FROM HEAVEN** 3 [8] D Nicholls 6-10-13 (55) Alex Greaves 2/1 FAV: 124504: Chsd ldrs, eff over 2f out, onepace: bckd, op 5/2: quick reapp: see 2139.   1¼   53
*2883 **RARE TALENT** 8 [1] 6-11-2 (58)(5ex) Miss J Allison 3/1: 032615: Rear, mod gains fnl 2f, no threat.   5   56
2887 **THOMAS HENRY** 8 [2] 4-9-13 (41) Mrs S Moore (0) 7/1: 503646: Led till halfway, btn 2f out: new stble.   2   30
2188 **ZABIONIC** 36 [7] 3-10-3 (54) Miss P Robson 25/1: 000067: Chsd ldrs, btn 2f out: changed stable.   ¾   42

2799 **PURSUIVANT 11** [2] 6-10-0 (42)(VIS) Mrs M Morris 25/1: 204008: Chsd ldrs 7f: visor: btr 2011. 1¼ 29
2861 **HEVER GOLF GLORY 9** [4] 6-9-7 (35)(vis) Mrs C Williams 20/1: 300569: Rear, eff halfway, no hdwy. 1¼ 21
9 ran Time 2m 14.3 (12.0) (Arthur Old) J Pearce Newmarket, Suffolk

3053

3.35 EXPRESS HCAP 3YO+ 0-70 (E) 1m4f Good/Soft 89 -07 Slow [62]
£4121 £1268 £634 £317 3 yo rec 11lb

*2843 **LOST SPIRIT 10** [5] P W Hiatt 4-7-12 (32) G Baker (5) 7/1: 064011: 4 b g Strolling Along - Shoag (Affirmed) Made all, styd on well ins last, drvn out: op 6/1: earlier scored at Lingfield (AW h'cap, rtd 49a) & Warwick (sell h'cap): '99 wnr at Southwell (clmr) & W'hampton (h'cap, rtd 66a, plcd on turf, rtd 49): best dominating at 12f on firm, gd/soft & both AWs, sharp or stiff track: eff with/without blinks: in form. 36
2381 **ALS ALIBI 29** [8] W R Muir 7-9-10 (58) J Weaver 7/1: 002142: 7 b g Alzao - Lady Kris (Kris) Chsd wnr, rdn/ch over 1f out, held nr fin: on a fair mark: see 2298 (claimer, AW). 1¾ 59
2672 **YES KEEMO SABEE 17** [11] D Shaw 5-8-13 (47) J Fanning 10/1: 000253: 5 b g Arazi - Nazeera (Lashkari) Held up, styd on for press fnl 2f, not pace to chall front pair: op 7/1: enjoys easy grnd but needs 14f+. 2½ 46
3007 **SACREMENTUM 3** [13] J A Osborne 5-8-13 (47) G Sparkes (7) 4/1 FAV: 024424: Dwelt/held up, late gains fnl 2f, no threat: op 3/1, quick reapp: clr rem: see 2295. 1¼ 45
2544 **TIGER TALK 22** [12] 4-9-9 (57) O Pears 33/1: 000005: Held up, never a factor: now with M Sowersby. 14 41
2453 **DEAD AIM 25** [9] 6-9-7 (55) R Winston 20/1: 0/0-06: Held up, never land a blow: see 2453. ½ 38
2734 **SPA LANE 14** [3] 7-8-9 (43) J Quinn 8/1: 332507: Prom, btn 2f out: btr 2482 (C/D, fast). ¾ 25
1921 **NOIRIE 48** [1] 6-8-6 (40) W Ryan 20/1: 230208: Held up, never land blow: abs: see 1769, 1003 & 943. 5 17
2601 **YANKEE DANCER 19** [10] 5-8-2 (36) P M Quinn (3) 25/1: /00009: Al towards rear: see 1496. 2½ 11
1936 **INDIAN ROPE TRICK 47** [4] 4-8-10 (44)(t) Dean McKeown 25/1: 00-000: Keen/prom, btn 3f out: 10th: 7 week abs: t-strap: unplcd last term (rtd 57, mdn). 2½ 17
2279 **MANZONI 33** [2] 4-9-0 (48) T Lucas 9/2: 2-0060: Chsd ldrs, hmpd 4f out, sn btn: 11th: see 2279. 2½ 19
2883 **GENUINE JOHN 8** [7] 7-8-2 (36) G Duffield 10/1: 505300: Al bhd: 12th: op 8/1: flattered 2538. 7 0
2883 **KHUCHN 8** [6] 4-9-0 (48) T Williams 15/2: 65422P: Btn/p.u. over 1f out: has a breathing problem. 0
13 ran Time 2m 42.8 (11.5) (Red Lion (Chipping Norton) Partnership) P W Hiatt Hook Norton, Oxon

3054

4.10 TOUCH ABOVE HCAP 3YO+ 0-80 (D) 1m100y rnd Good/Soft 89 +02 Fast [79]
£4368 £1344 £672 £336 3 yo rec 7 lb

2831 **BOLLIN ROBERTA 11** [3] T D Easterby 4-8-9 (60) R Winston 5/1: 520531: 4 b f Bob's Return - Bollin Emily (Lochnager) Chsd ldr, drvn to chall fnl 2f, styd on gamely inside last to narrowly prevail in a thrilling 3 horse finish: best time of day: op 4/1: '99 Musselburgh wnr (auction mdn, rtd 68): rtd at 71 in '98: eff at 6/7.5f, now stays a stiff 8.5f well: acts on fast & gd/soft grnd, handles soft & prob any track. 64
2994 **KASS ALHAWA 3** [2] D W Chapman 7-9-2 (67) A Culhane 3/1 FAV: 424422: 7 b g Shirley Heights - Silver Braid (Miswaki) Held up, prog 3f out & drvn to chall from over 1f out, every ch inside last, just held: bckd, though op 5/2: quick reapp: typical gd run here at Beverley: see 908, 38. *shd* 70
2694 **INDIAN PLUME 17** [4] C W Thornton 4-10-0 (79) W Supple 9/2: 001003: 4 b c Efisio - Boo Hoo (Mummy's Pet) Led, rdn fnl 2f, styd on gamely & duelled with 2 rivals inside last, just hdd nr line: bckd, op 8/1: bold run under topweight: see 1598 (made all). *shd* 82
2564 **TIPPERARY SUNSET 21** [1] D Shaw 6-8-9 (60) J Quinn 9/2: 3664D4: Rear, styd on fnl 2f, no threat. 2 59
2861 **MEHMAAS 9** [5] 4-8-7 (58) P Fessey 25/1: 000005: Chsd ldrs 6f: vis omitted: btr 1920 (7.5f, firm). 4 49
2752 **ONE DINAR 13** [8] 5-8-13 (64) G Duffield 7/2: 205036: Held up, eff 3f out, no impress: see 580 (AW). ¾ 54
2547 **BASMAN 22** [7] 6-9-13 (78) M Tebbutt 20/1: 5-6057: Chsd ldrs 3f out, sn btn: see 1841. 9 55
554 **AL MABROOK 164** [6] 5-8-5 (56) F Lynch 33/1: 0-1008: Bhd halfway: 5 month abs: see 270 (AW). 2 29
8 ran Time 1m 51.2 (7.4) (Lady Westbrook) T D Easterby Great Habton, N Yorks

3055

4.45 FAMILY DAY FILLIES AUCT MDN 2YO (F) 5f Good/Soft 89 +01 Fast
£2408 £688 £344

938 **ERRACHT 106** [8] P C Haslam 2-8-3 Dean McKeown 6/1: 21: 2 gr f Emarati - Port Na Blath (On Your Mark) Made all, rdn & in command fnl 1f, styd on strongly: 3 month abs: confirmed promise of debut: eff over a stiff 5f (dam 6f wnr) & should get further: acts on gd/soft & hvy grnd: can force the pace: open to improvement. 82
2045 **PEYTO PRINCESS 43** [7] C W Fairhurst 2-8-1(1ow) J Fanning 7/1: 322: 2 b f Bold Arrangement - Bo Babbity (Strong Gale) Chsd wnr, rdn fnl 2f, kept on, al held: 6 week abs: see 2045, 1641. 3 70
2849 **REGAL AIR 10** [14] B I Case 2-8-3 W Supple 4/1: 35303: 2 b f Distincly North - Dignified Air (Wolver Hollow) Held up racing keenly, no room over 1f out, styd on inside last, no threat: well bckd, op 5/1. 1½ 68
2730 **PETRAIL 14** [15] D Nicholls 2-8-3 K Dalgleish (5) 14/1: 004: Chsd ldrs 4f: op 12/1: handles gd/sft. ¾ 66
1823 **GILLS DIAMOND 53** [13] 2-8-7 F Lynch 10/1: 35: Chsd ldrs till over 1f out: op 8/1, abs: see 1823. 3½ 62
2880 **PATRICIAN FOX 8** [10] 2-8-0 J Quinn 12/1: 034326: Prom 4f: op 10/1: btr 2880 (gd), 2120. 1¼ 52
2730 **SLIPPER ROSE 14** [4] 2-8-0 P M Quinn (3) 50/1: 306007: Held up, mod gains: disapp since 730. 2 48
1876 **ADWEB 50** [3] 2-8-0 T Williams 33/1: 08: Never a factor: abs: tricky low draw: no form prev. 1¼ 45
2539 **EMMA THOMAS 22** [16] 2-8-1(1ow) O Pears 6/1: 09: Chsd ldrs, btn over 1f out: op 5/1: btr 2539. ½ 44
2711 **ELLENDUNE GIRL 15** [11] 2-8-0 J Mackay (5) 12/1: 050: Prom 3f: 10th: op 10/1: see 2711, 2227. 1½ 39
2454 **MEA CULPA 25** [2] 2-8-3 R Winston 50/1: 500: Rcd alone stands side, never on terms: 11th. 2 38
1835 **LOVE THING 52** [5] 2-8-2(2ow) G Duffield 7/2 FAV: -60: Prom till halfway: 12th: well bckd, op 9/2, abs. 1¾ 33
2818 **Tupgill Tipple 11** [6] 2-8-0 A Beech (3) 25/1:
2419 **Carusos 27** [12] 2-8-3 J Stack 25/1: -- **Middlehamparkflyer** [9] 2-8-3 Dale Gibson 16/1:
16 ran Time 1m 05.7 (4.4) (Lord Bolton) P C Haslam Middleham, N Yorks

3056

5.15 CLASSIFIED STKS 3YO+ 0-70 (E) 5f Good/Soft 89 -05 Slow
£3009 £926 £463 £231 3 yo rec 3 lb

2830 **RYTHM N TIME 11** [11] E J Alston 3-8-10 W Supple 9/4 FAV: -04001: 3 b f Timeless Times - Primum Tempus (Primo Dominie) Chsd ldrs, rdn & styd on well from over 1f out to lead well inside last: nicely bckd: '99 wnr here at Beverley (fills nurs, rtd 85 at best, T Easterby): eff at 5/6f, tried 7f: acts on gd & gd/soft grnd, prob handles firm: handles a stiff/sharp track, likes Beverley. 70
2929 **SOAKED 6** [12] D W Chapman 7-9-2 (bl) A Culhane 25/1: 0000R2: 7 b g Dowsing - Water Well (Sadler's Wells) Chsd ldrs, prog to lead over 1f out, hdd well inside last & no extra: blnks reapp, prob flattered. 1 72$
2859 **THAT MAN AGAIN 10** [7] S C Williams 8-9-5 (bl) G Faulkner (3) 6/1: 010043: 8 ch g Prince Sabo - 3½ 67

BEVERLEY   TUESDAY AUGUST 1ST   Righthand, Oval Track With Stiff, Uphill Finish

Milne's Way (The Noble Player) Led, rdn/hdd & no extra 1f out: op 3/1: see 2022 (firm).

2753	**TIME TO FLY** 13 [14] B W Murray 7-9-2 (bl) K Hodgson 50/1: -00504: In tch, outpcd halfway, held after.	½	62$
2822	**PALACEGATE JACK** 11 [13] 9-9-2 P Bradley (5) 14/1: 030545: Cl up, btn 1f out: prob flattered.	1	60$
2644	**BOLLIN ANN** 18 [9] 5-9-2 R Winston 5/2: 102306: Cl up, wknd fnl 1f: bckd, op 3/1: see 2340, 2107.	2½	54
2839	**RUDCROFT** 10 [10] 4-9-2 J McAuley 100/1: /00007: In tch, held 2f out: mod form.	2	50
2994	**DISTANT KING** 3 [3] 7-9-2 Dean McKeown 66/1: 006008: Al outpcd/bhd: quick reapp: see 1256.	shd	50$
2994	**CHILLIAN** 3 [2] 4-9-2 D Egan (7) 100/1: 500009: Rdn/sn bhd: quick reapp: see 674.	¾	48$
2663	**COCO DE MER** 18 [1] 3-8-13 G Duffield 14/1: -00000: Bhd halfway, 10th: see 2663, 1047.	6	37
2721	**LEGS BE FRENDLY** 15 [4] 5-9-2 (bl) Alex Greaves 4/1: 0-W350: Slowly away, looked reluctant to race		0
	& sn t.o.: 13th: well bckd: showed worrying signs of temperment here (1 win in 23 starts): see 2721.		
2525	**Jack To A King** 23 [5] 5-9-2 (tbl) C Teague 66/1:		
2604	**Topless In Tuscany** 19 [8] 3-8-10 Darren Williams (5) 33/1:		
13 ran	Time 1m 06.00 (4.7) (Springs Equestrian) E J Alston Longton, Lancs		

3057   5.45 MOORGATE MDN DIV II 2YO (D)   7f100y rnd   Good/Soft 89   -26 Slow
£3263   £1004   £502   £251

2808	**PORT MORESBY** 11 [9] N A Callaghan 2-9-0 J Mackay (5) 11/10 FAV: -001: 2 b c Tagula - Santana Lady		75
	(Blakeney) Chsd ldrs halfway, rdn/edged right & pressed ldr over 1f out, styd on well for press to lead well ins		
	last: hvly bckd: eff at 7.5f (dam a 1m/12f h'capper), further looks sure to suit: acts on gd/soft & a stiff trk.		
2628	**INVESTMENT FORCE** 19 [6] M Johnston 2-9-0 J Fanning 7/1: 0052: 2 b c Imperial Frontier -	¾	73
	Superb Investment (Hatim) Led, rdn/drvn when strongly pressed fnl 1f, hdd well inside last & no extra: clr		
	rem: bold front running eff: styd longer 7.5f trip, should get further: acts on gd/soft grnd.		
2649	**PRINCESS CLAUDIA** 18 [7] T D Easterby 2-8-9 G Parkin 16/1: 03: 2 b f Kahyasi - Shamarra (Zayyani)	5	59
	Chsd ldr, one pace/mild over 1f out: longer 7.5f trip, further shld suit in time: see 2649.		
--	**DARDANUS** [2] E A L Dunlop 2-9-0 G Carter 7/1: 4: Held up, styd on fnl 3f, nrst fin: op 2/1:	shd	64
	Komaite colt, Feb foal, a first foal: dam a 7f juv wnr: market drifter here, will move more next time.		
2966	**EAGLET** 4 [8] 2-9-0 P Bradley (5) 25/1: 005405: Keen/chsd ldrs, btn 2f out.	2½	59
2620	**SIMPATICH** 19 [4] 2-9-0 G Sparkes (7) 3/1: -436: Rear, eff halfway, no impress: bckd: btr 2620 (gd).	¾	58
2390	**JUSTINIA** 28 [1] 2-8-9 W Ryan 20/1: 0357: Al bhd: op 12/1: btr 2316 (fast, 4 rnr mdn).	3	47
--	**CHICKASAW TRAIL** [5] 2-8-9 P M Quinn (3) 33/1: 8: Al bhd: April, a first foal: dam a mdn.	4	40
--	**THE BARNSLEY CHOP** [3] 2-9-0 O Pears 33/1: 9: Chsd ldrs halfway, sn btn: March foal, a first foal.	5	36
9 ran	Time 1m 39.4 (8.6) (Martin Moore) N A Callaghan Newmarket, Suffolk		

GOODWOOD   TUESDAY AUGUST 1ST   Righthand, Sharpish, Undulating Track

Official Going   GOOD TO FIRM. Stalls: Straight Course - Stands Side: Round Course - Inside, except 1m4f - outside.

3058   2.15 MONEYGURU HCAP 3YO+ 0-105 (B)   1m6f   Good/Firm 24   -01 Slow   [100]
£32500   £10000   £5000   £2500   3 yo rec 13lb

2336	**TEMPLE WAY** 31 [17] R Charlton 4-9-2 (88)(VIS) R Hughes 10/1: -02221: 4 b g Shirley Heights -		95
	Abbey Strand (Shadeed) Towards rear, imprvd ent str, qcknd to lead 2f out, rdn clr: op 8/1: deserved win after		
	3 consecutive 2nds: '99 Chepstow wnr (h'cap in 1st time blinks), rtd 76 at best): eff at 14f/2m on gd, suited by		
	firm/fast: just sharpened up by visor, eff in blnks: progressive & useful, claims in the Ebor despite 7lb pen.		
*2691	**JARDINES LOOKOUT** 17 [6] A P Jarvis 3-8-5 (90) N Callan 25/1: 536212: 3 b g Fourstars Allstar -	2½	93
	Foolish Flight (Fool's Holme) Mid-div, eff & hung right 3f out, drvn & kept on wide appr fnl 1f, went 2nd nr		
	fin: fine run from this improving 3yo, looks well worth a try at 2m now: can win again: see 2691.		
*3001	**WAIT FOR THE WILL** 3 [10] G L Moore 4-8-11 (83)(bl)(3ex) M J Kinane 13/2 JT FAV: 122313: 4 ch g	nk	86
	Seeking The Gold - You'd Be Surprised (Blushing Groom) Patiently rdn, last turning in, gd prog 3f out, chsd		
	wnr appr fnl 1f, onepace for press: hvly bckd, tchd 8/1, qck reapp: stays 14f, just best at 12f?: tough.		
2695	**MOWBRAY** 17 [14] P F l Cole 5-9-11 (97) D Sweeney 13/2 JT FAV: -56044: Not settle early, mid-div,	1	99
	rdn & sltly chckd 3f out, imprvg when not clr run 2f out, styd on, nvr dngrs: well bckd, op 8/1: no luck in running		
	going for a repeat win in this race under top weight (8lbs higher today): likely to go well in the Ebor (3rd last year).		
2336	**AFTERJACKO** 31 [9] 4-9-3 (89) N Pollard 11/1: 512005: Held up, improved 3f out, short of room 2f	1¼	89
	out, styd on well ins last: would have gone close with clr run, keep in mind: see 1180 (bt wnr).		
2852	**THREE GREEN LEAVES** 10 [5] 4-9-2 (88) R Hills 25/1: 010366: Handy, prog to dispute 3rd 2f out,	¾	87
	sn rdn, slightly hmpd & no extra: longer trip: not far off best though will apprec a return to 12f: see 1695.		
2674	**QUÉDEX** 17 [12] 4-8-10 (82) S Whitworth 16/1: 201407: Bhd, under press entering straight, onepace	1¾	79
	till styd on inside last: worth a try at 2m now: see 1167.		
*2984	**ST HELENSFIELD** 3 [13] 5-9-2 (88)(3ex) J Carroll 16/1: 220118: Led till 4f out, fdd appr fnl 1f: too sn?	½	84
2068	**RIDDLESDOWN** 42 [15] 3-9-3 (102) B Marcus 33/1: -22109: Chsd ldrs, eff 3f out, wknd 2f out: 6 wk abs.	½	97
1850	**MARDANI** 52 [9] 5-9-6 (92) D Holland 33/1: 0-0000: Prom, eff & lkd onepace when squeezed for	shd	87
	room & lost place 2f out, no threat after: 10th, stablemate 6th: all wins at 12f: see 633.		
*2695	**EMINENCE GRISE** 17 [16] 5-9-9 (95) T Quinn 8/1: 4-02010: Well plcd eff entering fnl 3f, unable to	shd	90
	quicken & slightly hmpd 2f out, samepace: 11th: capable of much better: see 2695 (beat this 4th).		
2068	**RAVENSWOOD** 42 [8] 3-8-8 (93)(t) M Roberts 10/1: -42140: Towards rear, rdn entering fnl 3f,	½	87
	never any impress: 12th: 6 week abs: back in trip, see 2068, 1784.		
*2584	**GIVE NOTICE** 20 [1] 3-8-3 (88) K Darley 7/1: 061110: Dwelt, rdn to go prom, sent on 4f out, hdd	hd	82
	2f out & lost place: 13th, backed: winning run ended, v positively rdn: btr 2584.		
2002	**BATSWING** 45 [11] 5-8-5 (77) F Norton 16/1: 020120: Never a factor: 14th, 6 week abs: best at 10f.	5	66
2917	**COURT SHAREEF** 6 [2] 5-8-5 (77) P Fitzsimons (5) 14/1: 311020: Never in it: 15th, lngr trip.	½	66
2647	**LOOP THE LOUP** 18 [7] 4-9-6 (92) D Harrison 33/1: 2-5000: Prom trail 3f out: 16th, lngr trip, see 732.	4	75
2695	**PRAIRIE FALCON** 17 [4] 6-8-12 (84) M Hills 14/1: 04F060: Mid div till 3f out: 17th: see 917.	3½	63
17 ran	Time 3m 02.26 (3.46) (The Queen) R Charlton Beckhampton, Wilts		

GOODWOOD TUESDAY AUGUST 1ST Righthand, Sharpish, Undulating Track

3059 **2.45 GR 3 KING GEORGE STKS 3YO+ (A) 5f Good/Firm 24 -02 Slow**
£30000 £11500 £5750 £2750 3 yo rec 3 lb Raced stands side

2646 **CASSANDRA GO 18** [1] G Wragg 4-8-10 M Roberts 11/2: -12621: 4 gr f Indian Ridge - Rahaam (Secreto) **110**
Prom stands rail switched & hdwy appr fnl 1f, rdn to lead towards fin, won all-out in a drving fin: jockey made no mistake today: nicely bckd tho' op 9/2: earlier won reapp at Bath (fill List): '99 wnr at Newmarket (2, mdn & stks, rtd 105): eff at 6f/1m, suited by 5f now on fast & gd/soft, any trk: runs well fresh, with/without t-strap: smart, tough & geniune.
3016 **EASTERN PURPLE 2** [8] K A Ryan 5-9-4 B Marcus 13/2: 300562: 5 b g Petorius - Broadway Rosie (Absalom) Rear, prog ent fnl 2f, drvn below dist, ran on strgly & just failed in a thrilling fin: well bckd from 16/1: qk reapp: v smart run & has improved for being gelded in June: win a Gr race, prob at 6f/stiffer 5f. *shd* **117**
2065 **RUDIS PET 42** [10] D Nicholls 6-9-4 (bl) S Sanders 7/2 FAV: 16-103: 6 ch g Don't Forget Me - Pink Fondant (Northfields) Slow away, imprvd to lead halfway, sn edged onto stands rail, hard rdn & worn down nr fin, just btn: hvly bckd: rtd 118 when landing this race last term & would have won but for sloppy start: v smart. *hd* **116**
*2496 **WATCHING 24** [14] R Hannon 3-8-10 R Hughes 7/1: 122014: Wide, in tch, pushed along halfway, improved 2f out, no extra below dist: poss unfavourably drawn: btr 2496 (Listed). *2* **105**
2496 **RAMBLING BEAR 24** [4] 7-9-4 D Sweeney 16/1: -33005: Rear, improving when checked 2f out, kept on, never dangerous: won this 4 years ago & far from disgraced today: has another good race in him: see 1566. *½* **108**
2669 **ROSSELLI 17** [6] 4-8-13 J Carroll 20/1: 460026: Chsd ldrs stands side, outpcd 2f out, keeping on fin. *nk* **102**
*2676 **ELLENS LAD 17** [2] 6-8-13 L Newton 8/1: 150117: Prom stands side till hmpd & lost grnd bef halfway, kept on inside last: up in grade: little luck in running & it could pay to ignore this: see 2676. *nk* **101**
1283 **MAY CONTESSA 80** [3] 3-8-7 N Pollard 14/1: 5-1138: V slow away, switched wide & improved 2f out, never nr ldrs: rusty after 11 week abs over an inadequate trip, interesting in a fills stks/List at 6f+. *1½* **94**
3875} **EMERALD PEACE 325** [12] 3-8-7 P Robinson 25/1: 2112-9: Dsptd lead in centre till halfway, fdd dist: reapp: '99 wnr at Lingfield (2, mdn & stakes, Gr 2 hd rnr up, rtd 101): eff at 5/6f on firm & gd/soft grnd, sharp or gall tracks: better for this: with M Jarvis. *1½* **89**
2168 **SEE YOU LATER 38** [7] 3-8-7 K Darley 50/1: -63300: Handy, shaken up & no impression when slightly short of room 2f out: 10th, highly tried, needs a return to h'caps: see 1371. *1* **86**
-- **INOURHEARTS** [13] 4-8-10 J Reid 50/1: -50210: Dsptd lead in centre till halfway, fdd: 11th, Irish Raider: last month scored at Curragh (List h'cap): '99 Cork wnr (mdn): eff at 5f on fast & gd grnd. *1¾* **81**
2960 **AFAAN 4** [11] 7-8-13 (bl) T G McLaughlin 50/1: 402040: Bhd from halfway: 12th, stiff task, see 113. *nk* **83**
2065 **WARRIOR QUEEN 42** [5] 3-8-7 (VIS) M J Kinane 13/2: 10-0020: In tch 2f: 13th, visored Irish raider. *5* **65**
13 ran Time 58.01 (1.31) (Trevor C Stewart) G Wragg Newmarket, Suffolk

3060 **3.20 BET DIRECT SUMMER HCAP 4YO+ (B) 1m1f192y Good/Firm 24 -02 Slow [101]**
£32500 £10000 £5000 £2500 3 yo rec 11lb

2648 **SHARP PLAY 18** [5] M Johnston 5-9-9 (96) D Holland 11/2: 042041: 5 b g Robellino - Child's Play (Sharpen Up) Waited with, still well off the pace turning in, gd prog bef fnl 2f, checked dist, qcknd well to lead cl home, cleverly: well bckd: earlier overcame a 2 yr abs to win at Pontefract (clmr): v useful in '98, won at Ripon (stks, reapp), Swiss 2,000 Guineas & Thirsk (stks, rtd 107): eff at 1m, suited by 10f, tried 12f: acts on fast & gd/soft, any track & runs well fresh: tough, progressive & v useful, likes to come late. **102**
2528 **PRAIRIE WOLF 23** [10] M L W Bell 4-9-2 (89) M Fenton 11/2: 0-3402: 4 ch g Wolfhound - Bay Queen (Damister) Bhd ldrs, pld out appr fnl 1f, rdn to lead dist, hdd nr fin: well bckd: fine run, suited by 10f. *shd* **92**
2870 **PANTAR 9** [7] I A Balding 5-9-5 (92) K Darley 6/1: 630023: 5 b g Shirley Heights - Spring Daffodil (Pharly) Held up, imprvg when not much room appr fnl 2f, kept on under press ins last, npt btn far: often plcd. *½* **94**
2502 **AKBAR 24** [3] M Johnston 4-9-10 (97) M Hills 12/1: -11064: Mid-div, widest into str, drvn & prog appr fnl 1f, styd on, unable to chall: nicely bckd stablemate of wnr, tchd 16/1, top-weight: back in trip. *nk* **98**
2937 **ULUNDI 5** [9] 5-9-3 (90) P Doe 10/1: 330025: Trckd ldrs, feeling pace 3f out, kept on same pace. *1½* **89**
2750 **CHIEF CASHIER 13** [11] 5-8-7 (80) S Carson (3) 12/1: 000146: Led till dist, no extra: likes cut. *hd* **79**
2853 **SIR EFFENDI 10** [1] 4-9-4 (91) R Hills 9/2 FAV: 012-27: Pressed ldr & every ch till fdd below dist: well bckd: possibly got this longer 10f trip: v lightly raced, stable only saddled 1 winner this term: see 2853. *nk* **89**
2870 **POLISH SPIRIT 9** [8] 5-8-7 (80) T Quinn 10/1: 103068: Held up, prog to chase ldrs 2f out, not much room dist, unable to chall: best at 1m & has gone up the wights: see 2870. *hd* **78**
*2805 **HUDOOD 11** [4] 5-9-7 (94) P Robinson 8/1: 5001D9: Waited with, shaken up 3f out, improving when short of room ent fnl 2f, switched wide & styd on, never dangerous: see 2805. *hd* **91**
2844 **CULZEAN 10** [2] 4-8-10 (83) R Hughes 9/1: 004120: Al towards rear: 10th, see 2287. *3½* **75**
2471 **LOCOMBE HILL 25** [6] 4-8-12 (85) D Sweeney 25/1: 0-3030: Handy till entering fnl 3f: 11th, see 1474. *10* **62**
11 ran Time 2m 06.78 (2.58) (Mrs I Bird) M Johnston Middleham, N Yorks

3061 **3.50 GR 3 GORDON STKS 3YO (A) 1m4f Good/Firm 24 -06 Slow**
£29000 £11000 £5500 £2500

1752 **MILLENARY 58** [4] J L Dunlop 3-8-13 T Quinn 9/1: 5-1101: 3 b c Rainbow Quest - Ballerina (Dancing Brave) Held up, arnd 10L last 4f out, imprvd ent fnl 3f, ran on strgly under hands & heel to put head in front on line: nicely bckd, 8 wk abs: not disgraced in the French Oaks last time, prev won at Newbury (mdn) & Chester (Gr 3): highly tried/ran well both '99 starts (stks, rtd 89): eff at 11/12f, sure to apprec the 14f: acts on soft, suited by firm/fast, any track: runs well fresh: smart & improving colt, to be trained for the St Leger. **112**
2503 **AIR MARSHALL 24** [1] Sir Michael Stoute 3-8-10 J Murtagh 7/2: 214-22: 3 ch c In The Wings - Troyanna (Troy) Prom, rdn to lead 2f out, styd on well for press, jockey put whip down & looked round shoulder cl home, collared line: well bckd: would almost certainly have won if jockey had been more forceful, deserves comp. *shd* **111**
+2696 **SOBRIETY 17** [3] R F Johnson Houghton 3-8-10 J Reid 6/1: 106513: 3 b c Namaqualand - Scanno's Choice (Pennine Walk) Mid-div, shkn up turning for home, styd on for press fnl 2f but never able to chall: another v useful run up in grade & trip: eff at 10f/12f: very game & progressive colt: win a Listed/Gr 3. *1* **109**
+2116 **GIVE THE SLIP 40** [7] Mrs A J Perrett 3-8-10 M J Kinane 4/1: -31214: Led till 2f out, kept on till held fnl 100y: well bckd, clr rem, 6 week abs: improved in this higher grade: v useful & game colt. *nk* **108**
2068 **KUWAIT TROOPER 42** [11] 3-8-10 J P Spencer 33/1: 103105: Rear, styd on fnl 2f without threatening. *2* **105$**
2351 **TALAASH 30** [9] 3-8-10 Craig Williams 20/1: 136: Towards rear, shaken up 3f out, never any impress on ldrs: not disgraced, only 3rd ever start: possibly worth a try over further: see 2351. *4* **100**
-2260 **HATAAB 34** [6] 3-8-10 R Hills 3/1 FAV: 21-127: Unruly in stalls, not handle first bend, trkd ldr till fdd appr fnl 2f: well bckd: shld get longer 12f trip but return to 10f/more gall track will prob suit. *hd* **100**

2503 **ST EXPEDIT** 24 [8] 3-8-10 D Holland 9/1: 012038: Pulled hard, prom, shaken up & hmpd by ldr appr 2½ 97
fnl 3f, btn 2f out, eased dist: yet to fully convince at 12f, see 1103 (10f).

2148 **GOING GLOBAL** 39 [5] 3-8-10 B Marcus 16/1: 132069: Never in it: prefers softer grnd, see 1284, 823. 2 94

2503 **OPTIMAITE** 24 [2] 3-8-10 G Hind 33/1: -31050: Mid div till 4f out, 10th: btr 1347 (class stks). 10 82

10 ran   Time 2m 35.42 (3.62)   (L Neil Jones)   J L Dunlop Arundel, W Sussex

---

3062   4.25 CAPEL CURE SHARP NURSERY HCAP 2YO (C)   6f   Good/Firm 25 -18 Slow   [95]
£11388   £3504   £1752   £876

2307 **PICCOLO PLAYER** 32 [8] R Hannon 2-9-4 (85) L Newman (3) 7/1: -2141: 2 b g Piccolo - The Frog Lady 97
((Al Hareb) Unruly stalls, prom, rdn to lead appr fnl 1f, pushed clr inside last: well bckd: earlier won at
Windor (auct mdn): 12,000gns half-brother to a 7f juv wnr: eff at 6f, 7f will suit: acts on fast grnd,
sharp/undulating tracks: can force the pace: gelded since last start & much improved for it, v useful.

*2828 **BACCURA** 11 [7] A P Jarvis 2-9-6 (87) N Callan 8/1: -0212: 2 b c Dolphin Street - Luzzara (Tate 3 89
Gallery) Held up in tch, hard rdn appr fnl 1f, switched & kept on for 2nd, no ch with wnr: op 6/1, gd run.

2677 **SMITH AND WESTERN** 17 [5] R Hannon 2-9-4 (85) Dane O'Neill 7/2 JT FAV: 50123: 2 b c Factual - shd 87
Temple Heights (Shirley Heights) Dwelt, chsd ldrs wide, chsd wnr appr fnl 1f, onepace for press: well
bckd though op 5/2: handles fast & gd/soft grnd, return to 7f likely to suit: see 2430.

2483 **SANDLES** 25 [6] S C Williams 2-8-7 (74) M J Kinane 5/1: 154: Led after 2f till bef dist, same pace 1¼ 72
for press: hvly bckd from 7/1: unsuited by step up to 6f?: see 1236.

2687 **SIBLA** 17 [1] 2-8-13 (80) T Quinn 9/1: 52125: Held up, brief eff appr fnl 1f: step up to 7f will suit now. 2½ 72

*2227 **STRUMPET** 34 [2] 2-8-12 (79) J Reid 7/2 JT FAV: -2016: Had a barging match in rear for most of race 6 56
with Wally McArthur & was nvr in it: well bckd: worth another eff, see 2227.

*2760 **RISQUE SERMON** 13 [4] 2-8-13 (80) A Nicholls (3) 11/1: 017: Led till halfway, lost pl: see 2760. 1 54

*2754 **WALLY MCARTHUR** 13 [3] 2-9-7 (88) J Carroll 13/2: 032118: Barged by Strumpet throughout, al 2½ 56
rear, lost action 2f out & btn: poss best to ignore this: see 2754.

8 ran   Time 1m 12.5 (2.5)   (Park Walk Racing)   R Hannon East Everleigh, Wilts

---

3063   5.00 BROOK ST HCAP 3YO+ 0-85 (D)   1m rnd   Good/Firm 24 +08 Fast   [85]
£11700   £3600   £1800   £900   3 yo rec 7 lb

2431 **PARISIEN STAR** 27 [5] N Hamilton 4-9-8 (79) T Quinn 10/1: -40451: 4 ch g Paris House - Auction Maid 86
(Auction Ring) Held up, closed entering straight, shaken up & qcknd to lead below dist, pushed out, readily:
gd time, op 7/1: dual '99 rnr up (class stakes), rtd 90, G Lewis): '98 wnr at Epsom & Newbury (h'cap, rtd 94):
eff at 7f/sharp 1m: acts on soft, suited by fast grnd: runs well fresh & will go one better soon.

2870 **ELMHURST BOY** 9 [10] S Dow 4-9-7 (78)(vis) B Marcus 14/1: 030452: 4 b c Merdon Melody - Young 1¾ 80
Whip (Bold Owl) Prom, led 3f out, under press & hdd entering fnl 1f, no ch with wnr: tchd 20/1: gd run
with more positive tactics: stays 1m tho' return to 7f with same tactics will suit: loves a sharp/undul trk.

*2026 **SOCIAL CONTRACT** 44 [6] R Hannon 3-9-1 (79) J F Egan 14/1: 0-0013: 3 b g Emarati - Just Buy Baileys 1 79
(Formidable) Trckd ldrs, rdn 2f out, kept on but unable to chall: op 10/1, 6 week abs: eff at 7f/1m, see 2026.

2792 **NAVIASKY** 12 [2] W R Muir 5-9-7 (78) Martin Dwyer 5/1: 046634: Mid div, imprvd on bit to dspt 2nd nk 77
ent str, unable to qckn appr fnl 1f: nicely bckd to repeat last year's success in this race (9lbs higher here).

2853 **MUYASSIR** 10 [3] S Sanders 5/1: -01135: Held up, imprvg when no room 3f out till ent fnl 1 80
2f, switched widest of all & styd on, nrst fin: bckd, forget this, progressive earlier & return to 9f will suit.

2629 **STOPPES BROW** 19 [1] 8-9-4 (75)(bl) I Mongan (5) 9/1: 065256: Held up, shaken up appr fnl 2f, rdn hd 72
bef dist, no impression on ldrs: op 7/1: see 662.

2758 **VOLONTIERS** 13 [11] 5-10-0 (85) M Fenton 9/2 FAV: 160227: Waited with, prog into mid-div 2f out, nk 81
sn rdn & onepace: big gamble from 4/1, top-weight: capable of better, see 2758, 1160.

1836 **DANGEROUS FORTUNE** 52 [4] 4-9-8 (79) M Hills 20/1: 15-608: Wide, al towards rear: 7 week abs. 1½ 72

2355 **LOCH LAIRD** 30 [9] 5-9-3 (74) P Doe 33/1: 500009: Al bhd: both wins at 6f, see 1471. 1 65

2694 **COMPRADOR** 17 [12] 5-8-9 (66) D Sweeney 16/1: 110300: Mid div & still travelling well when hd 57
hmpd & lost pl 3f out, not recover: 10th, forget this: see 1467.

*2558 **KRISPIN** 21 [7] 3-9-6 (84) D Holland 6/1: 603310: Cl up & every ch till wknd 2f out: 11th: tchd 8/1. 3 69

2325 **INSIGHTFUL** 31 [8] 3-8-10 (74)(bl) R Hughes 11/1: 026440: Led till 3f out, lost pl/hmpd/eased: 12th. 19 34

12 ran   Time 1m 38.65 (1.25)   (P Elliott)   N Hamilton Epsom, Surrey

---

3064   5.35 EVENING STANDARD MDN 2YO (D)   6f   Good/Firm 24 -24 Slow
£7182   £2210   £1105   £552

1943 **GOGGLES** 47 [6] H Candy 2-8-11 C Rutter 7/2: -41: 2 b c Eagle Eyed - Rock On (Ballard Rock) 98
With ldr, went on halfway & ran on strongly, pshd out: nicely bckd, 7 wk abs: imprvd plenty for debut: 20,000gns
half-brother to a 6f juv wnr: eff at 6f, will get 7f: acts on fast grnd & a sharp/undul trk: v useful, win again.

-- **MOOTAFAYILL** [5] B W Hills 2-8-11 R Hills 7/2: 2: 2 b c Danzig - Ruznama (Forty Niner) ¾ 95
Keen, trckd ldrs, chse wnr inside last, al held: useful debut: Jan first foal, dam smart 7f juv: eff
at 6f on fast grnd, 7f will suit: runs well fresh & will go one better soon.

-- **KAI ONE** [7] R Hannon 2-8-11 Dane O'Neill 25/1: 3: 2 b c Puissance - Kind Of Shy (Kind Of Hush) 1¼ 91$
Chsd ldrs wide, rdn appr fnl 1f, kept on same pace: bigger-priced stablemate of fav, debut: 21,000gns Feb
foal, brother to 2 5f juv wnrs, sire a sprinter: eff at 6f on fast grnd & should have no trouble finding a mdn.

-1782 **ZILCH** 54 [1] R Hannon 2-8-11 R Hughes 15/8 FAV: 24: Dwelt, rear, shaken up to improve appr fnl ¾ 88
1f, nvr trbled ldrs: hvly bckd, stablemate 3rd, 8 week abs: up in trip & looks in need of further again: see 1782.

-- **LILLEMAN** [3] 2-8-11 J P Spencer 6/1: 5: Held up, switched wide appr fnl 1f, no impress on ldrs: bckd hd 88
on debut tho' op 4/1: Distant Relative brother to wnrs at 6f & 1m, sire a miler: type to improve over 7f+.

2598 **PUTRA PEKAN** 20 [2] 2-8-11 P Robinson 7/1: 06: Chsd ldrs, not much room 2f out, onepace: bckd. 1¾ 83

2269 **AINTNECESSARILYSO** 33 [4] 2-8-11 N Pollard 9/1: -0067: Unruly start, narrow lead till halfway, fdd. 1 80

7 ran   Time 1m 12.88 (2.88)   (Mrs J K Powell)   H Candy Wantage, Oxon

---

951

CHANTILLY
FRIDAY JULY 28TH   **Righthand, Galloping Track**

Official Going   SOFT

3065   2.55 GR 3 PRIX BERTEUX 3YO   1m7f   Soft
£21134   £7685   £3842   £2305

2594 **SAMSAAM** 16 J L Dunlop 3-8-11 W Supple 8/5 FAV: 111321: 3 b c Sadler's Wells - Azyaa (Kris)   **109**
Front rank, went on after halfway, clr 4f out, eased ins last, val 5/6L: earlier landed a hat-trick of h'caps,
at Windsor, Doncaster & Haydock: promise as a juv (rtd 74): suited by 12/15f & even further shld suit, acts on
fast, hvy & any trk: runs well fresh: v useful & tough, has made rapid improvement this term, win more Gr races.
--   **MISTER KICK** A Fabre 3-8-11 A Junk 133/10: -43142: 3 gr c Linamix - Mrs Arkada (Akarad)   3   **103**
Led early, remnd prom, drvn & no impress on wnr fnl 2f: stays 15f on soft: useful.
--   **LE NOMADE** P Bary 3-8-11 S Guillot 46/10: 011113: 3 b c Nashwan - La Splendide (Slip Anchor)   2½   **100**
Waited with, styd on late, no dngr: progressive prev (winner of all 4 most recent starts).
2398 **BOURGEOIS** 30 Mme C Head 3-8-11 O Doleuze 53/10: 241234: Chsd ldrs, drvn/held fnl 2f.   1   **99**
9 ran   Time 3m 15.4   (Hamdan Al Maktoum)   J L Dunlop Arundel, W Sussex

MAISONS LAFFITTE
SATURDAY JULY 29TH   **Left & Righthand, Sharpish Track**

Official Going   VERY SOFT

3066   2.10 GR 2 PRIX ROBERT PAPIN 2YO   5f110y   V Soft
£33622   £13449   £6724   £3362

--   **ROLLY POLLY** B Grizzetti 2-8-12 M Demuro 52/10: -1111: 2 b f Mukaddamah - Rare Sound (Rarity)   **104**
Cl-up, hdwy to lead appr 1f out, rdn out: four-timer landed: eff around a sharpish 5.5f, 6f will suit: acts on
soft grnd: v useful & unbeaten Italian-trained filly, will reportedly step up to Gr 1 company next time.
2485 **IRON MASK** 25 Mme C Head 2-9-2 O Doleuze 42/10: -1222: 2 b c Danzig - Raise A Beauty (Alydar)   1   **105**
Trkd ldrs, went on over 2f out, hdd dist, not pace of wnr: acts on soft & hvy: tough & smart, see 2485.
2595 **BRAM STOKER** 17 R Hannon 2-9-2 D Bonilla 76/10: 211233: 2 ch c General Monash - Toniokey (Grundy) 2   **100**
Front rank, drvn/not qckn over 1f out: tough/useful & consistent colt, shld win in Listed class: see 2067.
--   **CUPERCOY** H Carlus 2-9-2 T Thulliez 35/1: -41144: Settled rear, eff 2f out, styd on, nrst fin.   shd   **100**
*2485 **OZONE LAYER** 25 2-9-2 A Junk 47/10: -1315: Sn rdn in rear, hdwy 2f out, sn btn: btr 2485.   2   **95**
--   **SHAMO** 2-8-12 S Guillot 6/5 FAV: -16: In tch, rdn/no extra 2f out: better expected, debut wnr prev.   ¾   **90**
8 ran   Time 1m 04.2   (Mac Ferrer)   B Grizzetti Italy

CURRAGH
SATURDAY JULY 29TH   **Righthand, Stiff, Galloping Track**

Official Going   GOOD TO FIRM

3067   3.00 LISTED TARA TYROS STKS 2YO   7f   Good/Firm
£16250   £4750   £2250   £750

--   **SOFTLY TREAD** C Collins 2-8-9 P Shanahan 8/1: -11: 2 b f Tirol - Second Guess (Ela Mana Mou)   **102**
Mid-div, gd hdwy to chall 2f out, sn led, all out to hold on: 12 wk abs: earlier won on debut at Cork (mdn):
eff at 6/7f on good & fast grnd: runs well fresh: tough, useful & improving filly.
--   **RESONATE** J S Bolger 2-8-12 K J Manning 12/1: -56142: 2 b c Erin's Isle - Petronelli (Sir Ivor)   shd   **104**
In tch, strong run to chall dist, just held: Navan mdn wnr prev: eff at 5/7f on fast & gd/soft: imprvd here.
--   **BLIXEN** J Oxx 2-8-9 N G McCullagh 5/2: -13: 2 b f Gone West - Danish (Danehill)   1½   **98**
Front rank, rdn & went on 2f out, sn hdd, not pace of ldrs well ins last: Curragh mdn wnr (debut, 6f, gd/soft).
2067 **MODIGLIANI** 39 A P O'Brien 2-8-12 J A Heffernan 5/2: FAV: 134: Chsd ldrs, rdn over 3f out, ev ch   1   **99**
till not quicken appr fnl 1f: capable of more than this: better expected after 2067 (Gr 3 Coventry Stks).
8 ran   Time 1m 25.7   (A Balzarini)   C Collins Curragh, Co Kildare

3068   4.35 GR 3 MELD STKS 3YO+   1m2f   Good/Firm
£22750   £6650   £3150   £1050   3 yo rec 10lb

2409 **TAKALI** 27 J Oxx 3-8-9 N G McCullagh 9/2: 214451: 3 ch c Kris - Takarouna (Green Dancer)   **113**
Prom, hdwy to lead dist, styd on strongly to get up nr fin, drvn out: Cork mdn wnr earlier this term, not
disgraced when 5th in the Irish Derby (at 200/1): eff at 10/12f on fast & soft: smart & tough colt.
2404 **YARA** 28 K Prendergast 3-8-6 D P McDonogh 9/1: 201632: 3 b f Sri Pekan - Your Village (Be My Guest)   nk   **109**
Cl-up, rdn to lead over 2f out, pressed ins last, caught cl-home: clr rem: eff at 10f on fast: fine run, see 2404.
--   **CHIMES AT MIDNIGHT** L Comer 3-8-9 W J Smith 33/1: -5413: 3 b c Danzig - Surely Georgies (Alleged)   5   **104**
With ldrs, drvn & not pace of front 2 fnl 2f: recent Leopardstown mdn wnr (10f, gd, with A P O'Brien).
2410 **JAMMAAL** 27 D K Weld 3-8-9 (bl) P J Smullen 7/4 FAV: 212124: In tch, rdn to imprv over 2f out, sn btn.   ½   **103**
2404 **ALLURING** 28 3-8-6 C O'Donoghue 5/1: -15035: Bhd, eff over 2f out, sn held: see 2404.   ¾   **99**
2149 **URBAN OCEAN** 36 4-9-5 J A Heffernan 7/2: -15006: Let to over 2f out, sn fdd: btr 1121 (List).   **0**
6 ran   Time 2m 04.1   (H H Aga Khan)   J Oxx Currabeg, Co Kildare

DEAUVILLE SUNDAY JULY 30TH Righthand, Galloping Track

Official Going GOOD/SOFT

3069
2.30 GR 2 PRIX D'ASTARTE 3YO+ 1m Good/Soft
£28818 £11527 £5764 £2882 3 yo rec 8 lb

1901 **LADY OF CHAD** 49 R Gibson 3-8-7 Y Take 15/2: 1-1001: 3 b f Last Tycoon - Sahara Breeze (Ela Mana Mou) 117
Made all, clr fnl 1f, rdn out: disapp since wng on reapp at Longchamp (Gr 3): dual Longchamp wnr in '99
(incl Gr 1, rtd 114): v eff over a stiff/gall 1m on gd & hvy, has tried 10f: v smart filly, win more Gr races.

*10 **DANZIGAWAY** 267 Mme C Head 4-9-1 O Doleuze 63/10: 1141-2: 4 b f Danehill - Blushing Away 4 111
(Blushing Groom) Cl-up, hmpd after 2f, held ev ch till not pace of wnr appr fnl 1f: not disgraced after a
near 9 month abs: eff at 1m on gd/soft & hvy grnd: shld be sharper next time & can win a Gr race this term.

2597 **IFTIRAAS** 18 J L Dunlop 3-8-7 D Bonilla 26/1: -15603: 3 b f Distant Relative - Ideal Home (Home Guard) 1 109
Raced v keenly in tch, short of room over 1f out, sn rdn/held: gd eff & ran to best, unlucky in running in 2597.

2401 **PREMIÈRE CREATION** 30 J De Roualle 3-8-7 T Thulliez 58/10: -124: Mid-div, late hdwy: see 2401. hd 108

1319 **PEONY** 77 3-8-7 C Asmussen 8/5 FAV: 1-1125: Hmpd/dropped rear after 2f, late gains, no threat. hd 108
13 ran Time 1m 38.9 (T Yoshida) R Gibson France

3070
3.30 GR 2 PRIX DE POMONE 3YO+ 1m5f110y Good/Soft
£28818 £11527 £5764 3 yo rec 13lb

2501 **INTERLUDE** 22 Sir Michael Stoute 3-8-5 T Jarnet 41/10: 1-341: 3 b f Sadler's Wells - Starlet 109
(Teenoso) Cl-up, rdn to lead over 2f out, styd on strongly & drvn out to hold on: landed sole '99 start, at
term: landed sole '99 start, at Doncaster (fill mdn, rtd 90+): eff at 1m, suited by 12/13.5f on gd, soft & a stiff
trk: runs well fresh: given a more sensible/positive ride by today's change of jockey: smart & lightly raced.

2224 **SADLERS FLAG** 35 Mme C Head 3-8-5 O Doleuze 7/5 FAV: 321122: 3 b f Sadler's Wells - Animatrice snk 109
(Alleged) Waited with, hdwy to chall over 1f out, styd on, just held: tough/consistent: see 2224, 1748.

873} **AUBERGADE** 473 Mme M Bollack Badel 4-9-4 A Badel 162/10: 0-6453: 4 gr f Kaldoun - Anna Edes 1½ 107
(Fabulous Dancer) Rear, gd hdwy appr fnl 1f, no extra well ins last: stays 13.5f on gd/soft.

2739 **INFORAPENNY** 14 R A Fahey 3-8-5 Y Take 51/10: 123537: Prom to halfway, rdn/wknd fnl 3f, fin 7th: 9 95
capable of better & poss not stay this longer 13.5f trip: see 2739.
8 ran Time 3m 03.5 (The Queen) Sir Michael Stoute Newmarket

MUNICH SUNDAY JULY 30TH Lefthand, Galloping Track

Official Going SOFT

3071
3.50 GR 1 GROSSER DALLMAYR-PREIS 3YO+ 1m2f Soft
£56452 £22581 £11290 £6452 3 yo rec 10lb

2149 **GREEK DANCE** 37 Sir Michael Stoute 5-9-6 J Murtagh : 5-2251: 5 b h Sadler's Wells - Hellenic 121
(Darshaan) Settled rear, rdn & ran on strongly to lead ins last, drvn clr: '99 wnr at Haydock (Gr 3), subs 8L
2nd to Royal Anthem in Gr 1 Juddmonte at York (rtd 121): '98 Newmarket (mdn) & York wnr (stks, rtd 119): best
at 10f, stays 12f: acts on fast, hvy & any trk: runs well fresh: high-class & tough.

2089 **SUMITAS** 39 P Schiergen 4-9-6 T Hellier : 4-3D22: 4 b c Lomitas - Subia (Konigsstuhl) 2¼ 117
Waited with, rdn/prog over 2f out, kept on, no ch with wnr: eff at 10f on gd & soft: v smart.

2149 **STATE SHINTO** 37 Saeed bin Suroor 4-9-6 (vis) D O'Donohoe : 211-03: 4 br c Pleasant Colony - Sha shd 117
Tha (Mr Prospector) Front rank, led over 1f out, hdd well ins last, sn held: back to best, win a Gr 2/3.

1587 **ELLE DANZIG** 61 A Schutz 5-9-2 A Starke : 1-0224: Mid-div, rdn to imprv 3f out, drvn & no extra ½ 112
appr fnl 1f: rtd 115 when landing this race 2 years ago: see 1587.

1848 **BARATHEA GUEST** 50 3-8-8 P Robinson : -13405: Trkd ldrs, rdn/hdwy over 2f out, chall appr fnl 1f, 1¼ 112
sn drvn & no impress: 7 wk abs: needs a drop in grade: see 1848.
8 ran Time 2m 12.4 (Lord Weinstock) Sir Michael Stoute Newmarket

GALWAY MONDAY JULY 31ST Righthand, Sharpish, Undulating, Uphill Finish

Official Going GOOD

3072
6.10 C & G EBF MDN 2YO 7f Good
£8280 £1920 £840 £480

-- **HEMINGWAY** A P O'Brien 2-9-0 M J Kinane 2/7 FAV: 1: 2 b c Spectrum - Welsh Love (Ela Mana Mou) 106+
Made all, rdn & qckly went clr over 2f out, v easily debut: eff at 7f, 1m will suit: runs well fresh on gd
grnd & a sharpish/undul trk: impressive debut, reportedly one of A P O'Brien's best juveniles: one to follow.

-- **AVORADO** J S Bolger 2-9-0 K J Manning 6/1: -0542: 2 b c Royal Academy - Voronova (Sadler's Wells) 7 85
In tch, rdn/hdwy over 2f out, kept on but no ch with easy wnr.

-- **SUMMER STOCK** D K Weld 2-9-0 (BL) P J Smullen 10/1: -603: 2 b c Theatrical - Lake Placid 5½ 77
(Royal Academy) Cl-up, drvn/oncpcd appr fnl 2f: 1st time blnks.
7 ran Time 1m 31.5 (Michael Tabor) A P O'Brien Ballydoyle, Co Tipperary

Official Going   GOOD TO FIRM (GOOD places) Stalls: Str Course - Stands Side, Rem - Inside

---

3073   6.00 IRELAND APPR HCAP 3YO+ 0-75 (E)   1m4f   Good/Firm 34 -31 Slow   [69]
£3415   £1051   £525   3 yo rec 11lb

2872 **EXILE** 10 [5] R T Phillips 3-9-3 (69) G Sparkes (5) 100/30: 0-2521: 3 b g Emperor Jones - Silver Venture   74
(Silver Hawk) Made all, rdn & held on well fnl 1f: op 4/1: 1st win: mdn promise last term (G Lewis, rtd 82): eff
at 10/12f on firm & fast: best without blnks, has run well fresh: handles a sharp or gall trk.
2829 **ACEBO LYONS** 12 [6] A P Jarvis 5-8-13 (54) Lisa Jones (7) 16/1: 504032: 5 b w Waajib - Etage   1   57
(Ile de Bourbon) Mid-div, rdn 4f out, styd on fnl 2f, nvr reached wnr: could rate higher: see 2273, 705.
*3014 **MANA DARGENT** 3 [8] M Johnston 3-9-12 (78)(6ex) K Dalgleish 10/11 FAV: 630313: 3 b c Ela Mana   hd   80
Mou - Petite D Argent (Noalto) Hld up, hdwy 2f out, ch 1f out, sn no extra: bckd: 6lb pen & just too sn after 3014?
2624 **PINCHANINCH** 20 [7] J G Portman 3-9-1 (67) L Newman 7/1: 042124: Prom, held over 1f out: see 1997. 3½   64
2689 **PAY HOMAGE** 18 [9] 12-7-13 (40) Michael Doyle (5) 33/1: 046-05: Rear, mod hdwy fnl 3f: see 2689.   1¾   35
2689 **MEILLEUR** 18 [2] 6-9-3 (58) D Wallace (7) 8/1: 063026: Cl-up, ch 2f out, sn held: op 6/1: see 68.   ¾   52
2552 **RISING SPRAY** 23 [1] 9-9-10 (65) C Carver 20/1: 206-07: Chsd ldrs, btn 3f out: see 2552.   1   58
3049 **SUPLIZI 2** [4] 9-9-3 (58)(VIS) Claire Bryan 10/1: 006068: Prom 10f: vis, op 8/1: qck reapp: see 1788.   ½   50
-- **HOBART JUNCTION** [3] 5-9-10 (65) G Baker (3) 40/1: 2013/9: Held up, nvr factor: Flat reapp after   2½   53
long abs, 7 wk jumps abs, mod form, plcd once in 99/00 (h'cap, rtd 77h): wnr on the Level in '98 at Hamilton (clmr,
rtd 73, S Williams, eff at 9/10f on fast/firm).
9 ran   Time 2m 37.8 (7.8)   (Ellangowan Racing Partners)   R T Phillips Temple Guiting, Glos

---

3074   6.30 IRISH NIGHT FILL MDN 2YO (D)   7f rnd   Good/Firm 34 -03 Slow
£4524   £1392   £696   £348

-- **WAKI MUSIC** [6] R Charlton 2-8-11 W Ryan 2/1 FAV: 1: 2 b f Miswaki - Light Music (Nijinsky)   95+
Chsd ldrs, led 2f out, sn rdn clr, styd on strongly, readily: val for 6L+: hvly bckd: Mar first foal: dam 1m
juv wnr: eff at 7f, 1m will suit: acts on fast grnd & a fair trk: runs well fresh: impressive, worth following.
-- **JOHNSONS POINT** [9] B W Hills 2-8-11 M Hills 12/1: 2: 2 ch f Sabrehill - Watership (Foolish Pleasure)   5   81
Dwelt, sn in tch, rdn & kept on fnl 3f, no ch with wnr: op 8/1: Apr foal, half sister to wng 10f h'capper Blue: dam
a mdn: eff at 7f, 1m+ looks sure to suit: acts on fast grnd: improve for this & looks the type to win races.
2488 **FLIT ABOUT** 25 [4] I A Balding 2-8-11 G Hind 7/2: 23: 2 ch f Fly So Free - Oxava (Antheus)   ½   80
Mid-div, rdn/outpcd over 2f out, onepace fnl 1f: nicely bckd tho' op 9/4: styd longer 7f trip, 1m will suit.
2583 **HUREYA** 21 [8] J L Dunlop 2-8-11 R Hills 5/1: 54: Led 5f, sn outpcd: bckd, tho' op 7/2: see 2583.   hd   79
-- **CAPE ROSE** [5] 2-8-11 J Quinn 16/1: 5: Dwelt, rdn early, late gains when no room well ins last,   ½   78
hands & heels: op 10/1, longer priced stablemate of 4th: Mar foal, cost $40,000: sure to apprec 1m, improve plenty.
-- **PANG VALLEY GIRL** [2] 2-8-11 G Duffield 33/1: 6: Sn rdn, nvr on terms: Rock Hopper filly, May   8   66
foal, a 1st foal: dam lightly rcd, sire high-class 10/12f performer: apprec further in time for H Morrison.
-- **NEXT CHAPTER** [3] 2-8-11 B Marcus 25/1: 7: Dwelt, al towards rear: cheaply bought Apr foal, half-   6   57
sister to wnrs over 1m/10f: dam unrcd: with A Charlton.
2760 **SCARTEEN SISTER** 14 [1] 2-8-11 N Pollard 6/1: 38: Chsd ldrs, btn 2f out: btr 2760 (6f, firm).   1¾   54
2583 **DODONA** 21 [7] 2-8-11 P Doe 10/1: 49: Loose bef start, cl-up 4f: op 5/1: this is best forgotten.   nk   53
9 ran   Time 1m 26.7 (2.6)   (K Abdulla)   R Charlton Beckhampton, Wilts

---

3075   7.00 CARA NURSERY HCAP 2YO (D)   6f   Good/Firm 34 -09 Slow   [92]
£4231   £1302   £651   £325

2468 **THERESA GREEN** 26 [3] Mrs P N Dutfield 2-8-0 (64) L Newman (2) 10/1: 00301: 2 b f Charnwood Forest -   71
In Your Dreams (Suave Dancer) Made all, rdn/clr over 1f out, held on gamely ins last, drvn out: 1st win:
eff at 6f, tried 7f, shld suit in time: acts on fast grnd & a stiff or fair trk: likes to force the pace.
2849 **IMPERIAL MEASURE** 11 [4] B R Millman 2-9-1 (79) G Hind 12/1: 1502: 2 b g Inchinor - Fair Eleanor   nk   85
(Saritamer) Cl-up, rdn/outpcd 2f out, styd on well ins last, just held: eff at 5/6f, now looks worth a try at 7f:
acts on fast & gd/soft grnd: see 1095.
*2874 **QUINK** 9 [9] Sir Mark Prescott 2-9-13 (91)(6ex) G Duffield 9/4 FAV: 1313: 2 ch g Selkirk - Ink Pot   ¾   95
(Green Dancer) Held up, drvn & styd on well from 2f out, not reach wnr: clr of rem under a big weight: see 2874.
2271 **MAGIC BOX** 34 [6] A P Jarvis 2-8-12 (76) J Fortune (5) 11/4: 64434: Trkd ldrs, outpcd halfway, no impress.   4   70
2868 **HALCYON MAGIC** 18 [8] 2-7-10 (60)(3oh) R Brisland (5) 14/1: -00455: In tch, rdn/btn over 1f out.   nk   53
2468 **GOLDEN WHISPER** 26 [5] 2-8-0 (64) R Ffrench 10/1: -40306: Rdn/mid-div, btn 2f out: see 1704, 1067.   2½   50
2526 **MISS INFORM** 24 [2] 2-8-5 (69) N Pollard 9/1: -3507: Rdn/mid-div, btn 2f out: btr 1639 (debut).   1   53
1673 **CHURCH BELLE** 60 [1] 2-7-12 (62) J Quinn 11/2: 0208: Prom 4f: 2 month abs: btr 1463 (5f, gd/soft).   2   41
2678 **GOLD AIR** 18 [7] 2-9-2 (80) D R McCabe 9/1: 010209: Trkd ldrs 4f: btr 2368 (5f).   5   50
9 ran   Time 1m 13.66 (2.56)   (M Bevan)   Mrs P N Dutfield Axmouth, Devon

---

3076   7.30 CITY INDEX HCAP 3YO 0-85 (D)   7f rnd   Good/Firm 34 -02 Slow   [91]
£7605   £2340   £1170   £585

2682 **HAND CHIME** 18 [7] W J Haggas 3-8-7 (70) M Hills 9/2: 011231: 3 ch g Clantime - Warning Bell   80
(Bustino) Held up, prog to lead over 1f out & sn rdn clr, v readily: earlier scored at Catterick (auct mdn)
& Carlisle (h'cap): eff at 7f/1m, may get further: acts on firm & soft grnd, sharp or stiff trk: runs well fresh:
progressive, in fine heart & shld go in again under a pen.
*2719 **COWBOYS AND ANGELS** 16 [5] W G M Turner 3-8-11 (74) Darren Williams (5) 7/1: 102412: 3 b c   3½   75
Bin Ajwaad - Halimah (Be My Guest) Led till over 1f out, no ch with wnr ins last: remains in gd form: see 2719.
2813 **MISTER SUPERB** 12 [11] V Soane 3-9-4 (81) G Hind 12/1: 021063: 3 ch c Superlative - Kiveton Komet   2½   77
(Precocious) Held up, rdn & styd on from over 1f out, no threat to front pair: eff at 6/7f: see 2183.
2858 **DESERT FURY** 11 [8] B Hanbury 3-9-7 (84) J Mackay (5) 11/4 FAV: 000604: Trkd ldrs, no room over 1f   1¾   77
out, sn held: see 2858, 1016.
2762 **SHOUF AL BADOU** 14 [9] 3-9-6 (83) J Reid 14/1: -00065: Mid-div, briefly no room over 2f out, nvr   nk   75
dngrs under a quiet ride: well h'capped if returning to form: rtd 97 in '99: see 2762.
2794 **ATYLAN BOY** 13 [4] 3-8-4 (67) D R McCabe 11/1: 315246: Trkd ldrs, btn 1f out: see 2300, 1745.   nk   58
2794 **ANDYS ELECTIVE** 13 [6] 3-8-4 (65)(vis)(2ow) S Whitworth 25/1: 605107: Chsd ldrs 5f: btr 2044.   1   56
852 **DANZIGEUSE** 114 [12] 3-7-12 (61) K Dalgleish (5) 33/1: 500-08: Rear, nvr on terms: abs: unplcd last   ½   49

term (rtd 63, auct mdn): bred to apprec 7f/1m this term.

2922 **MAGELTA** 7 [3] 3-8-12 (75) Dane O'Neill 9/1: 002009: Chsd ldrs till over 1f out: btr 1961.		½	62
2577 **WILDFLOWER** 21 [1] 3-8-9 (72) T Quinn 5/1: 1000: Mid-div, rdn/btn 2f out: 10th: jockey reported filly suffered interference in early stages, nvr travelling after: see 1012 (C/D mdn, soft).		2	55
1960 **JAZZY MILLENNIUM** 47 [10] 3-8-7 (70) A Clark 12/1: 0-0350: Held up, rdn/btn over 2f out: 11th: abs: prev with Miss G Kelleway, now with B R Millman: btr 1399, 1181.		6	44
2749 **LADYWELL BLAISE** 14 [2] 3-7-11 (60) G Bardwell 20/1: 601200: Dwelt, nvr on terms: 12th: btr 2391.		3	28
12 ran Time 1m 26.84 (2.54) (Mrs M M Haggas) W J Haggas Newmarket			

3077   8.00 IRISH POST CLAIMER 3YO+ (E)   5f   Good/Firm 34   +04 Fast
£2795   £860   £430   £215   3 yo rec 3 lb

*2931 **KING OF PERU** 7 [3] D Nicholls 7-9-4 Alex Greaves 2/1: 422011: 7 b g Inca Chief - Julie's Star (Thatching) Led till over 2f out, rdn & led again ins last, styd on well for press: recent Catterick wnr (clmr), earlier with N Littmoden: '99 Brighton wnr (h'cap, plcd num times, rtd 71 & 81a): plcd in '98 (rtd 94a & 77): stays 7f, suited by 5/6f on firm, gd/soft, fibresand & any trk, likes a sharp/undul one: eff with/without a visor.			69
2788 **QUITE HAPPY** 13 [1] W H Tompkins 5-8-6 G Duffield 7/1: 536422: 5 b m Statoblest - Four Legged Friend (Aragon) Prom, rdn/led over 2f out till ins last, just held nr fin: claimed for £7000: see 897.		½	54
3037 **MARENGO** 2 [5] M J Polglase 6-8-10 F Norton 16/1: 000063: 6 b g Never So Bold - Born To Dance (Dancing Brave) Waited on, switched & styd on ins last, not pace to chall: qck reapp: see 1073 (clmr, g/s).		hd	57
753 **LEGAL VENTURE** 127 [4] Julian Poulton 4-8-9 (bl) I Mongan (5) 25/1: 340204: Prom 4f: abs.		5	47
2568 **ARGENT FACILE** 22 [2] 3-9-4 (t) J Fortune 8/11 FAV: 022305: Held up, eff/hit rail & stumbled over 1f out, not recover & eased: jockey reported colt lost his action: prob best forgotten: see 959.		13	35
5 ran Time 59.8 (1.5) (the Gardening Partnership) D Nicholls Sessay, N Yorks			

3078   8.30 LONDON IRISH HCAP 3YO+ 0-75 (E)   1m rnd   Good/Firm 34   -12 Slow   [74]
£4485   £1380   £690   £345   3 yo rec 7 lb

*2817 **SHAANXI ROMANCE** 12 [13] M J Polglase 5-7-11 (43)(vis) F Norton 6/1: 436611: 5 b g Darshaan - Easy Romance (Northern Jove) Chsd ldrs, rdn/led 2f out, styd on well ins last, pushed out cl-home: recent Southwell wnr (AW h'cap, rtd 55a): '99 wnr at Carlisle (class stks, rtd 60, I Semple): '98 W'hampton wnr (mdn, rtd 73a & 79, M Bell): eff at 7f/1m, tried further: acts on firm, soft & fibresand, with/without visor: runs well fresh.			48
2629 **SKY DOME** 20 [6] M H Tompkins 7-9-12 (72) T Quinn 7/4 FAV: 023022: 7 ch g Bluebird - God Speed Her (Pas de Seul) Held up, prog/no room over 2f out, chsd ldr ins last, al held: on a fair mark & can find similar.		1¼	73
2752 **PIPE DREAM** 14 [11] P Burgoyne 4-7-10 (42)(2oh) G Baker (5) 12/1: 005043: 4 b g King's Signet - Rather Warm (Tribal Chief) Mid-div, styd on onepace for press fnl 2f: mdn after 21: see 2752, 353.		½	42
2349 **ARTERXERXES** 31 [12] C G Cox 7-9-13 (73) A Clark 11/1: 0-3004: Prom, onepace fnl 2f: see 1250.		nk	72
2707 **ZULU DAWN** 17 [2] 4-10-0 (74) M Hills 15/2: -33005: Held up, rdn fnl 2f, not pace to chall: topweight.		¾	72
3045 **KAFIL** 2 [7] 6-7-10 (42)(bl)(10oh) R Brisland (5) 40/1: 000306: Rear, eff 2f out, al held: qck reapp.		nk	39
2629 **LEGAL SET** 20 [1] 4-9-12 (72)(vis) Darren Williams (5) 6/1: 003367: Held up, not pace to chall.		hd	68
2974 **DOUBLE DESTINY** 5 [10] 4-8-2 (48)(bl) D O'Donohoe 14/1: 000308: Rear, hdwy over 1f out, sn held.		3	38
2790 **ARDENT** 13 [3] 6-7-12 (44) J Quinn 10/1: -64009: Mid-div, btn 1f out: see 23.		1¼	31
2920 **SALORY** 7 [4] 4-8-6 (52) I Mongan (5) 7/1: 300020: Prom 6f: 10th: flattered 2920.		6	30
2794 **CHILWORTH** 13 [8] 3-8-2 (55)(vis) A Nicholls (3) 25/1: 042000: Mid-div, btn 2f out: 11th: vis reapp.		nk	32
2795 **ORIENT EXPRESS** 13 [9] 3-8-10 (63) D R McCabe 14/1: 003030: Led, clr halfway, hdd 2f out/sn btn & eased ins last: 12th: jockey cautioned for allowing colt to ease down well before the line.		2	36
2460 **FLASHFEET** 26 [5] 10-7-10 (42)(8oh) G Bardwell 50/1: 040600: Al rear: 13th: see 398.		nk	14
13 ran Time 1m 40.64 (3.64) (Mark Lewis) M J Polglase Southwell, Notts.			

Official Going: FIRM. Changed to GOOD after RACE 3.   Stalls: Inside

---

3079   2.05 TATTERSALLS MDN AUCT 2YO (E)   6f   Good/Firm 30   -28 Slow
£3233   £995   £497   £248

2459 **GALAXY RETURNS** 26 [7] A Berry 2-8-5 J Carroll 6/1: -0261: 2 ch c Alhijaz - Naulakha (Bustino) Prom, rdn/outpcd over 2f out, rdn & styd on well inside last to lead nr line: eff at 6f, tried 7f, return to that trip should suit: acts on firm/fast grnd & a stiff track.			70
2377 **TEFI** 30 [8] T D Easterby 2-8-5 R Winston 11/2: -5322: 2 ch g Efisio - Masuri Kabisa (Ascot Knight) Trckd ldrs, short of room over 2f out, styd on well to press to briefly lead inside last, just held: eff at 6/7f.		hd	69
2724 **TOP NOLANS** 15 [6] M H Tompkins 2-8-7 S Sanders 3/1: 0333: 2 ch c Topanoora - Lauretta Blue (Bluebird) Dwelt, rdn & styd on well fnl 2f, not pace of front pair: op 7/2: eff at 6f, 7f & h'caps should suit.		1	68
2588 **ROSELYN** 21 [1] I A Balding 2-8-1(1ow) J F Egan 11/4 FAV: 64: Chsd ldrs, rdn/led over 2f out, hdd well inside last & no extra: eff at 6f, prob handles fast & gd grnd.		hd	61
2588 **CARNOT** 21 [3] 2-8-6(1ow) A Culhane 6/1: 05: Cl up, ch over 2f out, sn one pace/held: see 2588.		1¾	61
1719 **OLYS WHIT** 58 [4] 2-8-5 (VIS)(2ow) F Lynch 25/1: 46: Led till over 2f out, sn held: visor, 8 wk abs.		5	42
-- **GARRISON** [5] 2-7-12 J McAuley 16/1: 7: Rear, never on terms: May foal, cost 5,200gns as a 2yo, a first foal: dam unrcd: with Miss L A Perratt.		6	17
2377 **COMEUPPANCE** 30 [2] 2-8-4(1ow) Dean McKeown 25/1: 68: Slowly away, never on terms: see 2377.		1¼	19
8 ran Time 1m 15.6 (3.5) (Galaxy Moss Side Racing) A Berry Cockerham, Lancs			

3080   2.35 NORMAN BONHAM-CARTER CLMR 3YO+ (F)   6f   Good/Firm 30   -08 Slow
£2394   £684   £342   3 yo rec 4 lb

2929 **TREASURE TOUCH** 7 [7] P D Evans 6-9-13 Joanna Badger (7) 11/10 FAV: 131301: 6 b g Treasure Kay - Bally Pourri (Law Society) Cl up halfway, duelled with rnr up from over 1f out, styd on well for press to narrowly assert nr line: well bckd: earlier won twice at Catterick for D Nicholls (claimer & h'cap) & Leicester (current connections): '99 rnr up (stakes, rtd 60): stays 7.5f, suited by 6f on firm, gd/soft & fibresand, without blinks.			72
2823 **TANCRED ARMS** 12 [1] D W Barker 4-8-10 F Lynch 8/1: 000302: 4 b f Clantime - Mischievous Miss		hd	54

(Niniski) Chsd ldrs, rdn/duelled with wnr over 1f out, styd on well, just held: clr rem: op 6/1, gd run: see 698.
2637 **SAN MICHEL 19** [2] J L Eyre 8-8-9 (vis) R Winston 8/1: 054303: 8 b g Scenic - The Top Diesis 6 37
(Diesis) Led, rdn/hdd over 1f out & sn held: see 148.
2885 **NIGHT DIAMOND 9** [5] I A Balding 3-9-1 (tvi) J F Egan 3/1: 000404: Bhd ldrs, eff over 1f out, sn held. *nk* **46**
2744 **CAIRN DHU 14** [6] 6-8-8 Kimberley Hart 40/1: 000005: Dwelt, never on terms: see 159. *3½* **26**
2777 **SAMMAL 13** [8] 4-8-13 O Pears 8/1: 462006: In tch 4f: btr 2015 (C/D h'cap). *2* **25**
-- **GREMLIN ONE** [3] 3-8-5 T Williams 40/1: 7: Dwelt, never on terms: debut, with W Storey. *3* **12**
1012 **ROISTERER 100** [4] 4-8-13 A Culhane 66/1: 08: Rdn/rear, never on terms: abs, prev with M Tregoning. *1¼* **12**
8 ran Time 1m 14.4 (2.3) (David Oxley & James Mitchell) P D Evans Pandy, Gwent

3081

3.10 EXPRESS CLASS STKS 3YO+ 0-75 (D) 1m rnd Good/Firm 30 +06 Fast
£3957 £1217 £608 £304 3 yo rec 7 lb

2645 **KALA SUNRISE 19** [4] C Smith 7-9-2 R Fitzpatrick (3) 7/2: 033501: 7 ch h Kalaglow - Belle Of The **80**
Dawn (Bellypha) In tch, rdn fnl 3f & prog to lead inside last, styd on strongly: op 4/1: '99 Leicester wnr (h'cap, rtd 86): rtd 81 in '98: eff at 7f/1m on firm & gd/soft, likes a stiff/gall track: slipped down the weights.
*2786 **PICTURE PUZZLE 13** [8] W J Haggas 4-9-1 A Culhane 11/10 FAV: 6-3212: 4 b f Royal Academy - *3½* **73**
Cloudslea (Chief's Crown) Keen/led after 2f, hdd inside last & no extra: bckd: see 2786.
2988 **SEA SQUIRT 4** [1] M Johnston 3-8-11 J Fanning 100/30: 041623: 3 b g Fourstars Allstar - Polynesian *1¼* **74**
Goddess (Salmon Leap) Led 2f, cl up till outpcd fnl 1f: op 5/2, quick reapp: see 2018 (C/D class stks, 4 rnrs).
2994 **HI NICKY 4** [5] W Storey 4-8-13 T Williams 50/1: 000004: Chsd ldrs, outpcd fnl 2f: quick reapp. *1¾* **65$**
2989 **FOUR MEN 4** [6] 3-8-9 M Flynn (7) 66/1: 606565: Keen, held up, eff 2f out, no hdwy: quick reapp. *1¼* **66$**
3011 **JAMMIE DODGER 3** [10] 4-9-4 V Halliday 50/1: 201U06: Dwelt/rear, mod gains: quick reapp: see 2533. *4* **60$**
125 **VILLA ROMANA 246** [7] 3-8-6 J F Egan 14/1: 4150-7: Chsd ldrs 6f: op 10/1, 6 month abs: '99 *7* **43**
Brighton scorer for A Bailey (nurs h'cap, rtd 75): eff between 5f/sharp 7f on fast & soft, any track.
2994 **FAS 4** [2] 4-9-2 S Sanders 100/1: 400008: Struggling halfway: quick reapp: see 2147, 584 & 367. *½* **45$**
2703 **GRAND AMBITION 17** [11] 4-9-2 J Carroll 20/1: -50509: Al rear: gelding reportedly swallowed tongue. *2* **41**
1924} **EL KARIM 417** [9] 4-9-2 (t) R Winston 66/1: 3/00-0: Dwelt, never on terms: 10th: reapp: rtd 72 *10* **23**
on first of just 2 starts in '99 for J Dunlop (mdn): plcd as a juv in '98 (stakes, rtd 78): wore a t-strap today.
2865 **BRIGMOUR 10** [3] 4-8-13 O Pears 100/1: 000000: Bhd 3f out: 11th: mod form. *12* **0**
11 ran Time 1m 40.7 (1.9) (A E Needham) C Smith Temple Bruer, Lincs

3082

3.40 WORTHINGTON HCAP 3YO 0-60 (F) 1m rnd Good/Firm 30 -02 Slow [67]
£3029 £865 £432

2882 **CITY FLYER 9** [1] J D Bethell 3-8-6 (45) R Winston 33/1: 000601: 3 br c Night Shift - Al Guswa **54**
(Shernazar) Made all & rdn/clr over 1f out, styd on well inside last, pushed out, unchall: t-strap omitted today: 1st win: rtd 75 in '99 (unplcd, mdn): eff over a stiff 1m on fast grnd: well suited by forcing tactics today.
2685 **GLEN VALE WALK 18** [7] Mrs G S Rees 3-8-3 (42) W Supple 16/1: 000402: 3 ch g Balla Cove - Winter *4* **44**
Harvest (Grundy) Held up, prog to chase wnr ins last, kept on, al held: eff at 1m, tried 10f, handles fast & gd/sft.
2825 **SEA EMPEROR 12** [14] Mrs G S Rees 3-8-8 (47)(VIS) J Carroll 14/1: 030443: 3 br g Emperor Jones - *3½* **42**
Blumarin (Scenic) Chsd wnr, rdn/held over 1f out: tried visor: see 1085.
2964 **CITY BANK DUDLEY 5** [2] N Wilson 3-8-6 (45) R Lappin 33/1: 036464: Keen/cl up, held over 1f out. *hd* **39**
2825 **WOODWIND DOWN 12** [8] 3-8-9 (48) J McAuley 10/1: 000325: Mid div, held over 1f out: see 2825. *nk* **41**
*2731 **AFRICA 15** [9] 3-8-12 (51) C Lowther 7/1 CO FAV: 160416: Rear, mod gains fnl 2f: see 2731 (clmr). *2* **40**
2967 **JUMBOS FLYER 5** [3] 3-9-7 (60) J F Egan 7/1 CO FAV: 620037: Mid div, btn 2f out: quick reapp. *1¾* **46**
2506 **COSMIC SONG 25** [15] 3-8-12 (51) Dean McKeown 15/2: 514468: Dwelt/rear, mod gains: see 1722. *¾* **36**
2731 **NORTHERN ECHO 15** [10] 3-9-3 (56)(bl) A Culhane 11/1: 005329: Rear, never on terms: op 8/1. *nk* **39**
3004 **DOLFINESSE 4** [11] 3-8-7 (46)(vis) D Egan (7) 10/1: 340620: In tch, btn 1f out: 10th: quick reapp. *¾* **17**
3033 **BLUE SAPPHIRE 2** [6] 3-8-0 (39) J Bramhill 20/1: 003030: Rear, never a factor: 11th: quick reapp. *6* **9**
2411 **CLAUDIUS TERTIUS 28** [4] 3-8-7 (46) O Pears 10/1: 003420: Chsd ldrs 5f: 12th: new stable. *hd* **15**
*2964 **SEND IT TO PENNY 5** [12] 3-9-2 (55)(bl)(6ex) T Lucas 7/1 CO FAV: 150010: Keen/chsd ldrs 6f: 13th: *½* **0**
op 5/1: quick reapp: see 2964 (selling h'cap, made most).
3008 **Blair 3** [16] 3-7-12 (37) T Williams 14/1: 2732 **Going Home 15** [13] 3-8-9 (48)(bl) J Fanning 25/1:
1571 **Great Riches 64** [5] 3-8-0 (39) Dale Gibson 25/1:
16 ran Time 1m 41.4 (2.6) (N D Fisher) J D Bethell Middleham, N Yorks

3083

4.15 .CO.UK FILLIES HCAP 3YO+ 0-75 (E) 7f rnd Good/Firm 30 +06 Fast [72]
£2795 £860 £430 £215 3 yo rec 6 lb

2128 **CANTINA 40** [2] A Bailey 6-10-0 (72) J Carroll 5/1: -01431: 6 b m Tina's Pet - Real Claire (Dreams **82**
To Reality) Made all, rdn fnl 3f, styd on well ins last, rdn out: 6 week abs, op 4/1: earlier scored at Beverley (amat riders h'cap): '99 wnr at Redcar (amat stakes, rtd 73 & 72a): '98 Chester wnr (2, h'caps, disqualified once, rtd 80): loves to force the pace over 7/7.5f on firm, gd/soft & on any track: runs well fresh: gd weight carrier.
2823 **PUPPET PLAY 12** [9] E J Alston 5-8-9 (53) W Supple 7/2 FAV: 304132: 5 ch m Broken Hearted - *2½* **58**
Fantoccini (Taufan) Chsd wnr, rdn & styd on fnl 2f, al held by wnr: op 11/4: well clr of rem: produced a fine effort despite being unable to front run as in 2561.
2823 **BODFARI ANNA 12** [5] J L Eyre 4-9-1 (59)(vis) J F Egan 4/1: 003143: 4 br f Casteddu - Lowrianna *8* **52**
(Cyrano de Bergerac) Held up in tch, eff to chase ldrs 2f out, soon held: also bhd todays rnr up in 2823.
2899 **SAFFRON 8** [4] D Shaw 4-8-0 (44) J Bramhill 16/1: 000054: Rear, rdn/mod gains: blinks omitted. *nk* **36**
2767 **OAKWELL ACE 14** [6] 4-7-10 (40)(vis)(1oh) Dale Gibson 9/1: 525045: Chsd ldrs 5f: visor reapplied. *2½* **28**
2877 **LADY OF WINDSOR 9** [1] 3-9-3 (67)(vis) R Winston 11/1: 023006: Dwelt/sn rdn, btn 2f out: see 2017. *nk* **54**
2969 **NAISSANT 5** [7] 7-8-10 (54) P Goode (3) 9/2: 531207: Keen/chsd ldrs till over 1f out: quick reapp. *1¼* **39**
2882 **ON TILL MORNING 9** [3] 4-8-11 (55) J Fanning 8/1: 000408: In tch 5f: op 7/1: twice below 2442. *1* **38**
8 ran Time 1m 27.2 (1.7) (R Kinsey, Mrs M Kinsey & Miss B Roberts) A Bailey Little Budworth, Cheshire

3084

4.50 SAFFIE JOSEPH HCAP 3YO+ 0-60 (F) 1m6f32y Good/Firm 30 -39 Slow [54]
£2828 £808 £404 3 yo rec 13lb

2951 **PIPE MUSIC 5** [7] P C Haslam 5-8-11 (37)(bl) P Goode (3) 7/2 FAV: 500221: 5 b g Mujadil - Sunset **41**
Cafe (Red Sunset) Held up, prog to lead over 2f out, styd on well ins last, rdn out: op 4/1, quick reapp: '99 wnr at Southwell (h'cap, rtd 70a, unplcd on turf, rtd 54, h'cap): '98 wnr again at Southwell (h'cap, first time visor,

CARLISLE   WEDNESDAY AUGUST 2ND   Righthand, Stiff Track, Uphill Finish

rtd 66a & 69): suited by 14f/2m on fast, gd/soft & both AWs, prob handles firm: eff with/without visor or blinks.
2843 **WATER LOUP 11** [11] W R Muir 4-8-4 (30) J F Egan 11/2: 006222: 4 b f Wolfhound - Heavenly Waters   1¼   32
(Celestial Storm) Cl up 3f out, every ch 1f out, styd on, not pace of wnr: stays 14f well: see 2843, 692.
2827 **PROTOCOL 12** [8] Mrs S Lamyman 6-9-0 (40)(t) Sarah Thomas (7) 11/2: 504223: 6 b g Taufan -   3½   37
Ukraine's Affair (The Minstrel) Handy, bumped 3f out, kept on under v weak ride fnl 2f: do better with pro jockey.
2643 **HAPPY DAYS 19** [9] D Moffatt 5-8-13 (39) J Bramhill 6/1: 262524: In tch, lost pl halfway, held after.   1¼   34
-- **OPPORTUNE** [6] 5-9-0 (40) D Egan (7) 14/1: 0314/5: Led over 3f out till over 2f out, fdd: op 12/1,   2½   31
long abs: missed '99: '98 Beverley wnr (seller, C Smith, rtd 49, unplcd on sand, rtd 31a): eff at 10/12f on firm &
hvy, likes a stiff track: enjoys sell grade: now with W M Brisbourne, ran well for a long way, sharper next time.
672 **PILOTS HARBOUR 141** [1] 4-9-10 (50) S Finnamore (5) 9/1: 00-006: Chsd ldrs, held 3f out: jumps fit   8   31
(May wnr at Cartmel, nov hdle, rtd 97h, F P Murtagh): see 672.
2879 **ULSHAW 9** [4] 3-8-7 (46)(VIS) R Lappin 50/1: -03007: Keen/in tch, btn 3f out: visor: see 2144, 1386.   2   24
2801 **PRIDDY FAIR 12** [10] 7-8-7 (33) Dean McKeown 25/1: 00/348: Led after 2f till over 4f out, sn btn.   1¾   9
2638 **HOMBRE 19** [12] 5-9-4 (44) W Supple 25/1: 50/469: Led over 4f out till over 3f out, sn btn: see 2016.   nk   19
2866 **ARDARROCH PRINCE 10** [2] 9-9-10 (50) Dale Gibson 20/1: 402/00: Sn bhd: 10th: see 2866.   15   5
2866 **MINALCO 10** [5] 4-8-3 (29) Iona Wands 66/1: 00-000: Led 2f, cl up 10f: 11th: mod form.   nk   0
1084 **FLINTSTONE 92** [3] 3-9-4 (57)(VIS) R Fitzpatrick (3) 14/1: 03-00: Bhd 2f out: 12th: vis, op 25/1.   11   0
12 ran   Time 3m 09.5 (9.7)   (Lord Scarsdale)   P C Haslam Middleham, N Yorks

GOODWOOD   WEDNESDAY AUGUST 2ND   Righthand, Sharpish, Undulating Track

Official Going   GOOD/FIRM. Stalls: Str Crse - Stands Side; 12f - Outside; Rem - Inside.

3085   2.15 MARRIOTT HCAP 3YO+ 0-95 (C)   2m4f   Good/Firm 40   -13 Slow   [85]
£17225   £5300   £2650   £1325

*2941 **LAFFAH 6** [8] G L Moore 5-8-5 (61)(f)(1ow)(3ex) R Hughes 6/1: /13411: 5 b g Silver Hawk - Sakiyah   67
(Secretariat) Mid-div, eff ent str, no impress till styd on strongly fnl 1f to lead ins last, drvn out: well bckd, qck
reapp: recent Bath wnr, earlier scored at Chepstow (reapp, h'caps): prev hdles wnr: eff at 2m/2½m on firm &
fast grnd: suited by a t-strap, handles any trk, reportedly best going RH'd: sn rushed off account stayer, in fine form.
2092 **SELIANA 42** [7] G Wragg 4-9-5 (76) F Norton 3/1 FAV: 234022: 4 b f Unfuwain - Anafi (Slip Anchor)   1½   78
Trkd ldr going well, went on over 2f out, hdd ins last, ran on again cl-home: hvly bckd from 9/2, 6 wk abs:
idles in front, ran on again once hdd: talented but a tricky ride, see 2092.
2953 **RENAISSANCE LADY 5** [5] T R Watson 4-8-1 (58) Craig Williams 16/1: 111253: 4 ch f Imp Society -   1½   59
Easter Morning (Nice Havrais) Led till 2f out, rallied fnl 1f & not btn far: op 12/1, qk reapp, tough, stays 2m4f.
2498 **VIRGIN SOLDIER 25** [1] M Johnston 4-10-0 (85) K Darley 11/2: 2-1024: Trkd ldrs, ev ch 2f out,   nk   85
onepace fnl 1f: far from disgraced under top-weight: prob stays 2½m tho' may prove best at 2m: see 2498.
*2607 **BUSTLING RIO 20** [3] 4-8-10 (67) J Mackay 6/1: 001115: Rear, eff 2f out, kept on but no ch with   5   62
ldrs: op 9/2: attempting 4-timer over this longer 2½m trip: see 2607 (2m).
2953 **SILENT WARNING 5** [2] 5-9-11 (82) G Duffield 7/2: 030-26: Rear, imprvd halfway, rdn & btn 2f out: 1½   76
well bckd tho' op 5/2: this prob came too soon after fine reapp in 2953 (2m).
2498 **CHRISTIANSTED 25** [6] 5-9-10 (81) R Cochrane 9/1: -61057: Mid-div, rdn & btn over 1f out: prob   9   68
not stay this longer 2½m trip: see 1686 (2m).
1928 **JAWAH 49** [4] 6-8-8 (65) T Quinn 25/1: 0-0008: Al bhd, t.o. home straight: 7 wk abs: out of   dist   0
form this term, subs slipping down the h'cap: likes easy grnd: see 1527.
8 ran   Time 4m 27.40 (10.60)   (Richard Green, Fine Paintings)   G L Moore Woodingdean, E.Sussex.

3086   2.45 GR 3 LANSON VINTAGE STKS 2YO (A)   7f rnd   Good/Firm 40   -05 Slow
£30000   £11500   £6750   £2750

*2494 **NO EXCUSE NEEDED 25** [3] Sir Michael Stoute 2-8-11 J Murtagh 12/1: -11: 2 ch c Machiavellian -   108+
Nawaiet (Zilzal) Waited with, imprvd 2f out, led ent fnl 1f, ran on strongly, rdn out: debut Sandown wnr (mdn):
dam a 6f wnr: eff at 7f, 1m will suit: acts on fast grnd & on a sharp/undul or stiff/gall trk: progressive &
v smart juvenile with a turn of foot, one to keep on your side in Gr company.
2613 **BONNARD 20** [8] A P O'Brien 2-8-11 M J Kinane 9/1: -132: 2 b c Nureyev - Utr (Mr Prospector)   1¾   105
Mid-div, imprvd 2f out, ev ch ent fnl 1f, not pace of wnr cl-home: Irish raider, fine effort in the circumstances,
reared up badly in the stalls: smart colt who looks sure to win in List/Gr 3 company: see 2613.
*2550 **SHAARD 23** [7] B W Hills 2-8-11 (bl) R Hills 16/1: -13: 2 b c Anabaa - Braari (Gulch)   ½   103
Rear, improving when not much room 2f out, qcknd to lead briefly dist, no extra ins last: fine effort over this
longer 7f trip, will reportedly drop back to 6f: smart colt, could head for the Mill Reef Stks: see 2550 (debut).
2718 **TORTUGUERO 16** [2] B W Hills 2-8-11 M Hills 25/1: 061124: Rear, eff ent str, ran on well fnl 1f,   2   100
nrst fin: drifted from 12/1 & longer priced stablemate of 3rd: got going too late & will apprec a return to
a stiffer trk &/or 1m: useful colt see 2718 (nurs h'cap).
2091 **BAARIDD 42** [9] 2-8-11 P Robinson 3/1: -125: Trkd ldrs, eff 2f out, onepcd fnl 1f: 6 wk abs, hvly   1¼   97
bckd: slightly disapp after 2091 (Royal Ascot, stiff trk).
*2693 **CHIANTI 18** [10] 2-8-11 T Quinn 6/4 FAV: -116: Set pace till over 1f out, wknd: hvly bckd from 2/1:   1½   94
prob went off too fast for own gd here: clearly held in some regard, up in grade after 2693.
*2271 **CAUVERY 34** [6] 2-8-11 G Duffield 14/1: -217: Prom, ev ch 2f out, fdd ins fnl 1f: padd pick: 1   92
trav well for a long way, will apprec a drop back into List company: see 2271.
*2576 **ECOLOGY 21** [5] 2-8-11 K Darley 12/1: -21118: Chsd ldrs, switched 3f out, short of room 2f out,   ¾   90
rallied cl-home but ch had gone: longer price stablemate of 6th: not much luck in running: see 2576.
*2928 **PEREGIAN 7** [4] 2-8-11 D Holland 25/1: 301119: Mid-div, rdn & btn 2f out: see 2928 (nurs h'cap).   4   82
*1846 **ATMOSPHERIC 53** [1] 2-9-0 J Reid 12/1: -1210: Qckly away & pressed ldrs, wknd when hmpd 2f out,   9   67
eased & fin last: 8 wk abs, top-weight: much btr 1846 (6f, gd grnd).
10 ran   Time 1m 27.70 (3.20)   (Maktoum Al Maktoum)   Sir Michael Stoute Newmarket.

3087 3.20 GR 1 SUSSEX STKS 3YO+ (A) 1m rnd Good/Firm 40 +25 Fast
£159500 £60500 £30250 £13750 3yo rec 7lb

+2497 **GIANTS CAUSEWAY 25** [6] A P O'Brien 3-9-0 M J Kinane 3/1 JT FAV: 122111: 3 ch c Storm Cat - Mariah's Storm (Rahy) Trkd ldr, qcknd into lead dist, styd on strongly for press: hvly bckd, fast time: remarkable Gr 1 hat-trick in the space of 6 wks, won at R Ascot (Gr 1 St James Palace) & Sandown (Gr 1 Eclipse), earlier won on reapp at The Curragh (Gr 3) & rnr-up in both the English & Irish 2000 Guineas: juv wnr at Naas, The Curragh (Gr 3) & Longchamp (Gr 1, rtd 118): v eff at 1m/10f on fast, soft & on any trk: runs v well fresh & likes to run up with pace: remarkably tough, genuine & high-class performer who heads for the Juddmonte International at York. **126**

-2064 **DANSILI 43** [3] A Fabre 4-9-7 O Peslier 3/1 JT FAV: 3-1122: 4 b c Danehill - Hasili (Kahyasi) Rcd keenly in rear, smooth hdwy to chall 1f out, not pace of wnr ins last: hvly bckd, 6 wk abs: fine eff but met a top-class rival today who is reluctant to admit defeat: deserves to win a Gr 1: see 2064. *¾* **123**

2696 **MEDICEAN 18** [2] Sir Michael Stoute 3-9-0 J Murtagh 12/1: 311303: 3 ch c Machiavellian - Mystic Goddess (Storm Bird) Rcd keenly in rear, eff & no impress 2f out, ran on strongly to take 3rd cl-home: much better effort after disapp run in 2696 (h'cap, poor draw): high-class, win a Gr race at 10f: see 2066. *1½* **120**

2597 **GOLDEN SILCA 21** [9] M R Channon 4-9-4 Craig Williams 40/1: 041054: Trkd ldrs, onepcd fnl 1f: needs to be held up for a late chall & ran to v best here: see 1829 (List). *1½* **114**

2064 **ALJABR 43** [10] 4-9-7 R Hills 11/2: 14-145: Led till dist, no extra: op 9/2, 6 wk abs: first Goodwood defeat, won this race last year & the Champagne Stks in '98: capable of better than this, see 1402 (reapp). *1½* **114**

+2343 **ARKADIAN HERO 32** [8] 5-9-7 J P Spencer 8/1: -40416: Waited with, imprvd 3f out, no impress fnl 1f: well bckd, prob not quite stay 1m in today's company: 7f back at Newbury/Newmarket will suit. *hd* **114**

2066 **VALENTINO 43** [5] 3-9-0 (t) G Mosse 9/2: 14-327: Trkd ldrs, eff 2f out, wknd fnl 1f: well bckd, 6 wk abs: disapp run, much closer to today's wnr in 2066. *shd* **114**

*2226 **JOSR ALGARHOUD 38** [4] 4-9-7 J Reid 20/1: 123-18: Eff from rear 3f out, sn no impress: longer priced stablemate of Aljabr: needs Gr 3 company: see 2226 (7f, gd grnd). *1* **112**

1402 **ALMUSHTARAK 74** [1] 7-9-7 T Quinn 33/1: 20-369: Slowly away, nvr nr to chall: 10 wk abs: 3rd in this race last year: see 1043 (reapp). *1¾* **108**

-- **MANHATTAN** [7] 3-9-0 Paul Scallan 50/1: 1-10: Slowly away, sn drvn to press ldr, wknd 3f out, t.o. in last: reportedly pacemaker for today's wnr but completely missed the break: 9 wks ago won at Tipperary (stks), '99 Fairyhouse mdn wnr on sole start: eff at 6/9f & winning form on gd & soft grnd: highly tried here. *29* **78**

10 ran Time 1m 38.65 (1.25) (Mrs John Magnier & Mr M Tabor) A P O'Brien Ballydoyle, Co.Tipperary.

3088 3.50 TOTE GOLD TROPHY HCAP 3YO 0-105 (B) 1m4f Good/Firm 40 -16 Slow **[110]**
£45500 £14000 £7000 £3500

2596 **BLUE GOLD 21** [10] R Hannon 3-9-1 (97) J Reid 14/1: 201201: 3 b c Rainbow Quest - Relatively Special (Alzao) Waited with, imprvd 3f out, went on dist, held on gamely cl-home, all out: lkd superb: earlier won at Sandown (h'cap): '99 Sandown wnr again (mdn, rtd 92): eff at 10/12f on firm & gd/soft grnd: handles a sharp/undul or stiff/gall trk, likes Sandown: useful, v game & improving colt. **103**

*2386 **ZAFONICS SONG 29** [7] Sir Michael Stoute 3-9-0 (96) M J Kinane 11/2: 4-3512: 3 br c Zafonic - Savoureuse Lady (Caerleon) Trkd ldrs, imprvd to chall dist, ran on strongly & just btn in a driving fin: well bckd, tho' op 4/1: fine h'cap bow, stays 12f well: useful & lightly raced colt, see 2386 (mdn). *hd* **101**

2502 **ALVA GLEN 25** [5] Sir Michael Stoute 3-9-7 (103) J Murtagh 5/1: -60123: 3 b c Gulch - Domludge (Lyphard) Trkd ldr going well, imprvd to lead 2f out till dist, rallied well & only just btn in a v tight fin: stablemate of rnr-up: v useful weight carrying run: tough & improving colt: see 2502, 2004. *nk* **107**

*2470 **ROMANTIC AFFAIR 26** [6] J L Dunlop 3-8-9 (91) T Quinn 5/2 FAV: -02114: Waited with, improving till onepcd 2f out, rallied well cl-home & nrst fin: hvly bckd: prob unsuited by today's sharp trk, a return to a more gall one & or further will suit: likely type for the Tote Ebor at York: see 2470. *2* **92**

1848 **CRACOW 53** [9] 3-8-5 (87) M Hills 10/1: -43105: Held up, imprvd 2f out, onepace when bmpd 1f out: 8 wk abs: highly tried in 1848 (the Derby): see 1510 (mdn). *1¾* **86**

2208 **PROMISING LADY 37** [4] 3-8-6 (88) Craig Williams 25/1: -06026: Waited with, some late hdwy tho' not pace to chall: not given a hard ride: shld stay 12f, likely to benefit from a more gall trk: see 2208. *nk* **86**

2594 **ROYAL EAGLE 21** [1] 3-8-12 (94) D Sweeney 33/1: -00307: Sn in clr lead, hdd 3f out, wkng when hmpd 2f out, ran on again cl-home: lkd v well: ran a strange race: see 1347. *hd* **92**

2702 **UNAWARE 17** [2] 3-8-8 (90) R Hughes 9/2: 4-5348: Trkd ldr going well, went on 3f out till hdd 2f out, wknd & eased: well bckd from 11/1: better clrly expected, see 1225. *1¾* **86**

2674 **TORRID KENTAVR 18** [8] 3-8-5 (87) L Carter 16/1: -33109: Prom till wknd 2f out: see 2327. *¾* **82**

2068 **IL CAPITANO 43** [3] 3-8-13 (95) D Holland 20/1: 62-050: Al bhd, lost tch fnl 3f: fin last, 6 wk abs. *6* **81**

10 ran Time 2m 38.54 (6.74) (Mohamed Suhail) R Hannon East Everleigh, Wilts.

3089 4.25 WEATHERBYS FILL HCAP 3YO+ 0-90 (C) 1m1f Good/Firm 40 -23 Slow **[86]**
£11180 £3440 £1720 £860 3yo rec 8lb

*2853 **AEGEAN DREAM 11** [7] R Hannon 4-9-9 (81) R Hughes 5/1: 443311: 4 b f Royal Academy - L'Ideale (Alysheba) Waited with, smooth prog 2f out, qcknd to lead fnl 100yds, won going away: well bckd: recent Newbury wnr (h'cap): '99 Epsom wnr (mdn, rtd 79), also plcd sev times: eff at 1m/10f: handles hvy, much prefers fast or firm grnd: handles any trk: best produced for a late run, improving & at the top of her form. **88**

2890 **COMMON CONSENT 9** [2] S Woodman 4-7-11 (55) F Norton 14/1: 061042: 4 b f Common Grounds - Santella Bell (Ballad Rock) Waited with, imprvd 2f out, styd on well fnl 1f but not pace of wnr: looks sure to apprec a return to 10f: see 2296 (rcd up with the pace). *2* **56**

2499 **MUSCHANA 25** [1] J L Dunlop 3-9-1 (81) T Quinn 13/2: 2-3103: 3 ch f Deploy - Youthful (Green Dancer) Early ldr, remained prom till regained lead over 2f out & went for home, collared closing stages: fine eff, likes to run up with/force the pace: see 2053. *shd* **82**

2999 **DENS JOY 4** [5] Miss D A McHale 4-8-5 (63) K Darley 10/1: 120054: Rear, imprvd 2f out, went after ldr 1½f out, fdd ins last: quick reapp: see 2999, 1917. *1½* **62**

*2548 **TANGO TWO THOUSAND 23** [9] 3-9-5 (85) R Havlin 4/1 FAV: -5215: Trkd ldrs, rdn & onepcd fnl 1f: well bckd on h'cap debut: see 2548 (mdn, easily). *1¼* **82**

*2080 **PERFECT MOMENT 42** [3] 3-7-13 (65) J Mackay(5) 10/1: 421116: Led after 1f till 2f out, fdd: abs. *shd* **62**

2853 **FREDORA 11** [8] 5-10-0 (86) D Sweeney 9/1: 410147: Mid-div, no impress fnl 2f: top weight, op 6/1. *2½* **79**

2855 **PHOEBE BUFFAY 11** [10] 3-8-6 (72) Dane O'Neill 33/1: 00-008: Nvr better than mid-div, btn dist. *3½* **59**

*2704 **FAIR IMPRESSION 17** [6] 3-9-4 (84) J Reid 11/2: -00119: Trkd ldrs, wknd 2f out, well btn: well bckd: *14* **49**

GOODWOOD

GOODWOOD WEDNESDAY AUGUST 2ND Righthand, Sharpish, Undulating Track

much better than this: see 2704.
*2811 ROSHANI 12 [4] 3-8-13 (79) Craig Williams 9/1: 210610: Prom till wknd qckly 2f out, eased   9 29
considerably, t.o. in last: something amiss? see 2811 (10f, galloping).
10 ran   Time 1m 56.24 (5.74)   (Theobalds Stud)   R Hannon East Everleigh, Wilts

---

3090 5.00 LANSON FILLIES MDN 2YO (D) 6f str Good/Firm 40 -12 Slow
£7052 £2170 £1085 £542

2526 SHEPPARDS WATCH 24 [1] M P Tregoning 2-8-11 Martin Dwyer 7/2 JT FAV: -41: 2 b f Night Shift -   92
Sheppard's Cross (Soviet Star) Unruly stalls, trkd ldrs, switched & prog over 1f out, drvn into lead cl-home:
well bckd: Feb foal, dam a 7f wnr: eff over a sharp/undul 6f on fast grnd, shld stay 7f: improving filly.
--   TEMPTING FATE [4] J W Hills 2-8-11 K Darley 20/1: -2: 2 b f Persian Bold - West Of Eden (Crofter) ½ 91+
Dwelt, eff 2f out, fin fast but just too late: lkd v well for debut: 27,000 gns Mar foal: half sister to a couple
of juv wnrs: eff over a sharp/undul 6f on fast grnd: 7f sure to suit & will win soon.
--   NASMATT [5] M R Channon 2-8-11 Craig Williams 4/1: -3: 2 b f Danehill - Society Lady (Mr nk 90+
Prospector) Rear, imprvng when short of room dist, fin well but just btn in a close fin: well bckd, debut: Jan
foal, half sister to top class juv filly Bint Allayal: sire a top class miler: eff over a sharp/undul 6f on fast
grnd, 7f will suit: poss a shade unlucky, sure to improve & must win a mdn.
2088 BEE ONE 42 [7] D R C Elsworth 2-8-11 T Quinn 11/2: -5404: Nvr far away, led 2f out till dist, ev ch ½ 89
till no extra cl-home: 6 wk abs: stays a sharp 6f, may apprec a drop back to 5f: see 2088.
2849 ZIETUNZEEN 11 [9] 2-8-11 G Carter 7/2 JT FAV: -23355: Dwelt, recovered to chase ldrs, led dist shd 89
till ins last, no extra: hvly bckd: see 2849, 1252.
2618 RICHENDA 20 [2] 2-8-11 Dane O'Neill 33/1: -006: Led 4f, no extra: imprvd eff: 22,000gns Apr foal: 1½ 85
half sister to a 2yo wnr abroad: dam a smart 2yo in Italy, sire a top class miler: with R Hannon.
--   MILLENNIUM LADY [8] 2-8-11 J Reid 10/1: -7: Slowly away, some hdwy 2f out, sn btn & eased: 1¾ 80
not given a hard time on debut: Feb foal, cost $190,000: dam a 2yo wnr in the States.
--   HOW DO I KNOW [6] 2-8-11 J P Spencer 20/1: -8: Slowly away, ran green & nvr a factor on debut: 1¼ 76
Apr foal, sister to sev 2yo wnrs: dam a 5f wng juv: sire a decent sprinter: with G Butler & bred for speed.
2020 NEARCTIC LADY 45 [3] 2-8-11 R Hughes 7/1: -49: Trkd ldr till wknd dist: bckd from 10/1, abs. 1 73
9 ran   Time 1m 13.17 (3.17)   (Major & Mrs R B Kennard & Partners)   M P Tregoning Lambourn, Berks

---

3091 5.35 CHARLTON HCAP 4YO+ 0-80 (D) 5f str Good/Firm 40 +01 Fast [80]
£9555 £2940 £1470 £735

2644 ZUHAIR 19 [17] D Nicholls 7-9-6 (72) Alex Greaves 7/2 FAV: 000331: 7 ch g Mujahid - Ghzaalh 83
(Northern Dancer) Waited with, prog halfway, burst thro' to lead ent fnl 1f, sn clr, shade cmftbly: hvly bckd, gd
time: 1st win this term, laid out to win at this meeting: '99 wnr at Lingfield & York (h'caps), also twice in the
space of 3 days here at Goodwood (this race & Steward's Cup consolation, rtd 88): trained by D McCain in '98,
'97 W'hampton wnr (rtd 93 & 80a): best with waiting tactics over 5/6f, handles gd/soft & fibresand, loves fast &
firm grnd: has tried blnks, best without: handles any trk, loves Goodwood: remains on a fair mark & no surprise
to see him follow up in the Steward's Cup consolation here on Friday.
2905 SIHAFI 8 [8] D Nicholls 7-8-7 (59) G Bardwell 12/1: 610432: 7 ch g Elmaamul - Kit's Double 1¼ 62
(Spring Double) Held up, prog halfway, edged to fair side, fin strongly but no ch with stable-mate: well h'capped.
2929 PURE ELEGANCIA 7 [15] D Nicholls 4-9-2 (68) A Nicholls (3) 13/2: 6-0243: 4 b f Lugana Beach - Esilam 1½ 67
(Frimley Park) Front rank, went on halfway till collared ins last, no extra: completed a memorable 1-2-3 for
trainer D Nicholls: speedster who won at this meeting last year (3lb lower mark): see 2929, 2822.
2961 AJNAD 5 [13] R F Marvin 6-8-3 (55)(bl) Craig Williams 33/1: 506604: Outpcd & well bhd, weaved thro' nk 53+
fnl 1f & fin well, not quite get to ldrs: quick reapp: hugely eye-catching but has only one win from 33 starts.
2877 NORTHERN SVENGALI 9 [2] 4-8-9 (61) J P Spencer 25/1: 600405: Dwelt, styd on strongly fnl 1f nk 58+
against stands rail, nrst fin: op 16/1: fine eff from this well h'capped gelding, one to keep in mind: see 2777.
2569 FORGOTTEN TIMES 22 [7] 6-9-8 (74)(vis) C Catlin (7) 16/1: 221206: Rear, imprvd fin, nrst fin. hd 71
2761 BORDER GLEN 14 [14] 4-7-13 (51)(bl) Martin Dwyer 20/1: 260057: Chsd ldrs, styd on under press fnl 1f. shd 48
*2644 EASTERN TRUMPETER 19 [3] 4-9-13 (79) K Darley 5/1: 130218: Prom, onepcd fnl 1f: top-weight. nk 75
2644 POLLY GOLIGHTLY 19 [6] 7-9-1 (67)(bl) D Sweeney 25/1: 206409: Front rank 3f, grad fdd: see 2644. hd 63
2761 KILCULLEN LAD 14 [19] 6-9-1 (67)(vis) P Fitzsimons (5) 20/1: 230060: Front rank, drifted right ¾ 60
over 1f out, fdd into 10th: fairly h'capped now: see 1999.
2743 REFERENDUM 14 [11] 6-9-4 (70) F Norton 16/1: 052660: Chsd ldrs, held when short of room ins fnl 1f: ½ 62
fin 11th, stable-mate of 1st 3 home: see 2569.
2701 GAY BREEZE 17 [9] 7-9-5 (71) J Weaver 25/1: 350060: Chsd ldrs till fdd ins fnl 1f: fin 12th. shd 63
2788 KNOCKEMBACK NELLIE 13 [4] 4-8-11 (63)(bl) I Mongan (5) 25/1: 210050: Prom till fdd dist: fin 13th. 1 52
2753 SOUNDS ACE 14 [12] 4-7-10 (48)(bl)(2oh) J Mackay (5) 50/1: 303000: Unsettled stalls & slowly away, hd 37
no ch after: fin 14th: see 2418.
2743 TUSCAN DREAM 14 [5] 5-9-9 (75) P Bradley (5) 11/1: 051240: Front rank 3f, fdd: fin 15th: btr 2326. ¾ 61
1441 PRICE OF PASSION 72 [1] 4-9-4 (70)(bl) D Holland 25/1: 10-000: Al outpcd, fin 16th: 10 wk abs: hd 56
lightly rcd & out of form this term, quite slipping down the h'cap: see 1441.
2987 ANTONIAS DOUBLE 4 [20] 5-9-5 (71) G Carter 25/1: 030020: Slowly away, recovered to chase ldrs, 1 54
btn dist: fin 17th: lost all ch at the start today: quick reapp since 2987.
2845 STATOYORK 11 [18] 7-8-4 (56) A Clark 16/1: 005000: Unsettled stalls & lost 10/15L start, no ch 1½ 35
after: fin 18th: lost all ch at the start today, eye-catching 2 runs ago in 2701, broke a blood vessel last time.
2676 PARADISE LANE 18 [10] 4-9-12 (78) Cheryl Nosworthy (7) 33/1: -20000: Led till halfway, wknd qckly ½ 56
& fin last: see 1013 (reapp, soft grnd).
19 ran   Time 58.66 (1.96)   (The Gardening Partnership)   D Nicholls Sessay, N Yorks

959

Official Going   GOOD/FIRM. Stalls: Stands side.

3092   6.10 EBF MDN 2YO (D)   5f   Good/Firm 27 -01 Slow
£3601   £1108   £554   £277

2285 **BOIS DE CITRON** 33 [7] R Hannon 2-8-9 M Roberts 2/7 FAV: -341: 2 b f Woodman - Lemon Souffle   89
(Salse) Unruly start, easily made all, hard held: well bckd to land the odds: promise at Newmarket both prev
starts: Ffr4,400,000 half-sister to a useful 6f juv: dam 5/7f juv wnr: eff at 6f, apprec drop back to 5f: acts
on firm/fast grnd, stiff/undul trks: speedy, well regarded filly, likes to force the pace
2550 **RUN ON** 23 [3] B J Meehan 2-9-0 M Tebbutt 11/2: 42: 2 b c Runnett - Polar Storm (Law Society)   10 68
Prom, lost place after 2f, rallied for 2nd bef dist but no hope with wnr: caught a tartar, needs 6f+.
--   **EMPRESS OF AUSTRIA** [5] Miss Gay Kelleway 2-8-9 N Callan 7/1: 3: 2 ch f Foxhound - Falabella   11¾ 58
(Steel Heart) Prom, outpcd by wnr after halfway: op 4/1 on debut: April foal, half-sister to a couple of
juv wnrs (one Listed): sire a sprinter: should come on for this & apprec 6f.
2756 **CRIMSON RIDGE** 14 [1] R Hollinshead 2-8-9 P M Quinn (3) 25/1: -364: Never going pace: btr 2756.   2 52
--   **EAGER ANGEL** [2] 2-8-9 M Fenton 33/1: 5: Struggling from halfway: debut: 4,500gns Up And At'Em   5 37
May foal, sister to a 6f juv wnr, sire a sprinter: with D Carroll.
2668 **HEATHYARDS SIGNET** 18 [6] Paul Eddery 50/1: 56: Sn prom, wknd qckly fnl 2f: needs sellers.   1¾ 37
--   **ROZARY** [4] 2-8-9 J Tate 25/1: 7: Dwelt, al bhd: debut: Ezzoud Mar first foal, dam mid-dist/hdles wnr.   6 17
7 ran   Time 59.7 (1.4)   (Fieldspring Racing)   R Hannon East Everleigh, Wilts

3093   6.40 EXPRESS HCAP 3YO+ 0-80 (D)   1m2f   Good/Firm 27 -26 Slow   [69]
£3906   £1202   £601   £300   3 yo rec 9 lb

2671 **PAARL ROCK** 18 [5] G Barnett 5-8-9 (50)(vis) G Gibbons (3) 7/2 JT FAV: 000321: 5 ch g Common   54
Grounds - Markievicz (Doyoun) Led, hdd appr fnl 1f, rall gamely und press despite hanging left & regained
lead fnl strides: 1st win, plcd in '99 (h'cap, blnkd, rtd 52): now suited forcing the pace at 10f: acts on fast
& gd grnd, in a visor or blnks: goes on any track & has improved of late.
2970 **SHAMSAN** 5 [4] M Johnston 3-8-12 (62) M Roberts 4/1: 032052: 3 ch c Night Shift - Awayil   hd 65
(Woodman) Prom, hdwy to lead appr fnl 1f, rdn inside last & hdd fnl strides: looked sure to win at the
furlong pole: eff at 1m/10f on fast grnd & both AW's: shld win again soon.
2861 **CABARET QUEST** 10 [7] J M Bradley 4-8-1 (42) M Henry 4/1: 006033: 4 ch g Pursuit Of Love -   2½ 41
Cabaret Artiste (Shareef Dancer) Rear, closed 3f out, rdn bef dist, sn slightly hmpd & switched, no extra:
fair run, just about saw out this stiff 10f: see 1003.
2893 **ELMS SCHOOLGIRL** 9 [3] J M P Eustace 4-9-10 (65) J Tate 13/2: 206064: Held up, eff appr fnl 2f,   2½ 60
no impress on ldrs: op 5/1, top-weight: return to 12f likely to suit: see 1332.
2793 **PRESTO** 13 [2] 3-9-3 (67)(tbl) M Tebbutt 7/2 JT FAV: 510105: Nvr in it: op 5/1, both wins in clmrs.   3½ 57
2855 **FORMAL BID** 11 [6] 3-9-6 (70) D Harrison 12/1: 35-006: Prom, fdd appr fnl 2f: longer trip, see 2465.   6 51
2671 **KINGFISHERS BONNET** 18 [1] 4-8-5 (46) P M Quinn (3) 11/1: 540307: Keen, chsd ldrs till 3f out.   1½ 25
7 ran   Time 2m 07.8 (5.3)   (J C Bradbury)   G Barnett Stoke-On-Trent, Staffs

3094   7.10 LILIAN PRIME CLAIMER 3YO (F)   1m str   Good/Firm 27 -13 Slow
£2520   £720   £360

2908 **COLLEGE ROCK** 8 [11] R Brotherton 3-8-13 (vis) P M Quinn (3) 4/1 FAV: 641461: 3 ch g Rock Hopper   57
- Sea Aura (Roi Soleil) Dwelt, stdly imprvd, led bef fnl 1f, shkn up to repel rnr-up at home: front 2 clr:
earlier won at Chepstow (sell): plcd juv (sell, rtd 63, S Williams): eff at 1m, stays 10f: acts on firm & soft
grnd, any track: tried blnks, best visored: at home in sellers/claimers.
2187 **SWEET HAVEN** 37 [12] C G Cox 3-8-2 (vis) Joanna Badger (7) 33/1: -00002: 3 b f Lugana Beach -   hd 45
Sweet Enough (Caerleon) Never far away, led appr fnl 2f till bef dist, rallied but held: clr rem, best run
this term: sole win at 5f, clearly stays 1m: acts on fast grnd, with/without visor: see 976.
2602 **HEATHYARDS MATE** 20 [1] R Hollinshead 3-8-9 M Tebbutt 14/1: 100663: 3 b g Timeless Times -   5 42
Quenlyn (Welsh Pageant) Not go early pace, kept on appr fnl 1f, nvr nrr: back in trip, btr 2510, 741.
2658 **LE LOUP** 19 [2] Miss E C Lavelle 3-8-7 M Fenton 13/2: 004304: Bhd, kept on fnl 2f but unable to chall.   1 38
1884 **EDEIFF** 50 [5] 3-7-13 (t) (1ow) A Daly 12/1: -60505: Prom, led after halfway till bef 2f out, onepace: 1 28
recently p.u. over hdles, tried a t-strap today: see 1439.
3004 **MOUNTRATH ROCK** 4 [13] C Rutter 9/2: 440156: Towards rear, hdwy under press 2f out,   shd 29
onepace fnl 1f: quick reapp: much btr 2187 (sell h'cap).
2543 **HAZIRAAN** 23 [9] 3-9-7 P Hanagan (7) 10/1: 037: Cl up, led briefly over 2f out, fdd: now with R Fahey.   2 46
2776 **DOVES DOMINION** 13 [7] 3-8-13 (vis) M Roberts 12/1: 000558: Al mid-div: down in trip & grade.   ½ 37
2320 **FOSTON FOX** 32 [10] 3-8-5 (bl) (1ow) K Hodgson 9/1: 500609: Never troubled ldrs: stiffish task.   1¼ 27
--   **AQUADAM** [3] 3-8-5 D McGaffin (3) 16/1: 0: Al towards rear: 10th, debut: Namaqualand gelding.   1¼ 25
3004 **BURCOT GIRL** 4 [6] 3-7-12 A Mackay 10/1: -00030: Keen, chsd ldrs till 3f out: 11th, quick reapp.   4 10
2907 **NORTHERN LIFE** 8 [15] 3-7-12 (vis) A Polli 9/1: 060060: Keen, led briefly halfway, sn wknd: 12th.   14 0
2448 Pontikonisi 27 [14] 3-8-5 M Henry 25/1:   3713} Time To Skip 336 [8] 3-8-8 S Righton 33/1:
2950 Concierge 5 [4] 3-8-9 G Parkin 16/1:
15 ran   Time 1m 37.6 (3.2)   (Ms Gerardine P O'Reilly)   R Brotherton Elmsley Castle, Worcs.

3095   7.40 MALC HAINES HCAP 3YO 0-70 (E)   1m str   Good/Firm 27 -01 Slow   [77]
£3623   £1115   £557   £278

2610 **JUDICIOUS** 20 [13] G Wragg 3-9-7 (70) M Roberts 7/4 FAV: 0-0301: 3 b c Fairy King - Kama Tashoof   76
(Mtoto) Trkd ldrs, led 2f out, readily: top-weight, first win: well bckd both juv starts (rtd 74): cost
180,000gns: eff at 1m, stays 10f: acts on fast & gd grnd, stiff/undul trk: improving.
2752 **BISHOPSTONE MAN** 14 [8] S Mellor 3-9-4 (67) C Rutter 10/1: 035102: 3 b g Piccolo - Auntie Gladys   1¾ 68
(Great Nephew) Imprvd after 3f, chsd wnr appr fnl 1f, onepace below dist: back to form after tried forcing tactics.
*2970 **NOBLE PASAO** 5 [5] Andrew Turnell 3-9-2 (65) R Thomas (7) 10/3: 055313: 3 b g Alzao - Belle   ½ 65
Passe (Be My Guest) Chsd ldrs, eff 2f out, styd on onepace: fair run tho' rtd higher 2970 (appr h'cap, made all).
2794 **MIND THE SILVER** 13 [11] V Soane 3-8-7 (56) M Tebbutt 33/1: 006004: Towards rear, imprvd 2f out,   nk 55
kept on under press, nvr nrr: well clr rem & appr this step up to 1m: interesting in a mdn h'cap, see 2216.
153 **SKY HOOK** 240 [14] 3-8-9 (58) M Fenton 33/1: 0305-5: Prom, no extra appr fnl 1f: reapp: plcd in   5 47

'99 for N Littmoden (nursery, rtd 61 & 51a): eff at 6f on gd/soft grnd: now with J Osborne.
2947 **GROESFAEN LAD 5** [18] 3-9-5 (68) G Faulkner (3) 25/1: -04006: Mid div, eff 3f out, no impress on ldrs. *½* **56**
2861 **TALENTS LITTLE GEM 10** [17] 3-7-10 (45)(1oh) S Righton 25/1: 450507: Reared start, al same place. *nk* **32**
2745 **PRINISHA 14** [9] 3-9-2 (65) D Harrison 7/1: 020228: Chsd ldrs, fdd ent fnl 2f: back up in trip, h'cap bow. *1½* **49**
1021 **NICOLAI 100** [7] 3-8-1 (50) R Mullen 25/1: -0009: Al mid-div: big step up in trip, 14 wk abs, h'cap bow. *½* **33**
2843 **RONNI PANCAKE 11** [10] 3-8-4 (53) J Tate 9/1: 150600: Nvr a factor: 10th, back in trip, see 1572 (C/D). *1* **34**
2549 **COST AUDITING 23** [1] 3-8-1 (50) M Henry 33/1: 00-500: Al towards rear: 11th, up in trip, see 1675. *nk* **30**
2825 **BEBE DE CHAM 12** [2] 3-7-13 (48) Joanna Badger (7) 33/1: 006660: Chsd ldrs till halfway: 12th. *½* **27**
2884 **IT CAN BE DONE 9** [3] 3-9-1 (64) P M Quinn (3) 20/1: 160060: Nvr on terms: 13th: see 1645 (sft). *1¼* **40**
2879 **SECRETARIO 9** [6] 3-7-10 (45)(BL)(6oh) P Hanagan (3) 50/1: 660000: Led till after halfway, sn lost pl: 15th. **0**
2464 **Al Awaalah 26** [12] 3-8-1 (50) A Daly 25/1: 31 **Chiko 264** [19] 3-9-2 (65) V Halliday 25/1:
1345 **Storm Prince 76** [4] 3-9-5 (68) R Cody-Boutcher(7) 33/1:2794 **Time Bomb 13** [15] 3-8-0 (49) S Carson(0) 25/1:
4107} **Swallow Jaz 311** [16] 3-8-5 (54) G Parkin 33/1:
19 ran Time 1m 36.8 (2.2) (Mollers Racing) G Wragg Newmarket, Suffolk

3096

8.10 EBF FILL MED AUCT MDN 2YO (E) 6f Good/Firm 27 -28 Slow
£2925 £900 £450 £225

2692 **INJAAZ 18** [7] J L Dunlop 2-8-11 D Harrison 4/1: 01: 2 ch f Sheikh Albadou - Ferber's Follies **83**
(Saratoga Six) Keen, front rank, led appr fnl 1f, cmftbly pshd clr: poorly drawn/green on debut last month: 32,000gns half-sister to 2 wnrs: eff at 6f, shld get 7f: acts on fast grnd, stiff/undul track: better than bare form?
2711 **KOMENA 16** [8] J W Payne 2-8-11 A McGlone 7/4 FAV: 42: 2 b f Komaite - Mena (Blakney) *2½* **76**
Well plcd & every ch, not pace of wnr fnl 1f: well bckd: improved over lngr 6f trip on fast grnd.
-- **ARTIFACT** [3] R Hannon 2-8-11 M Roberts 4/1: 3: 2 b f So Factual - Ancient Secret (Warrshan) *2½* **70**
Slow away, detached, improved after halfway & went 3rd bef dist, nvr nr front pair: green debut, stablemate 4th: Feb foal, half-sister to a 6f juv wnr, dam stoutly bred, sire a sprinter: know more next time over 7f & improve.
2748 **QUATREDIL 14** [9] R Hannon 2-8-11 A Daly 20/1: 04: Led till 2f out, same pace: try 5f? *nk* **69$**
-- **TOPOS GUEST** [6] 2-8-11 V Halliday 20/1: 5: Cl up till appr fnl 2f, hung left: debut: 2,400gns *1¼* **65**
Mistertopogigo March foal: dam 7f wnr, sire a sprinter: with J Given.
2692 **SAFINAZ 18** [4] 2-8-11 M Fenton 5/1: 06: Prom 3f, btn & short of room bef dist: see 2692. *3* **56**
-- **ANNE SOPHIE** [1] 2-8-11 R Mullen 4/1: 7: Dwelt, nvr going pace: First Trump Mar first foal, with M Bell. *6* **41**
-- **LIFFORD LADY** [5] 2-8-11 C Rutter 33/1: 8: Chsd ldrs, hmpd 3f out, bhd after: debut: v stoutly bred. *3* **32**
8 ran Time 1m 13.1 (3.3) (Kuwait Racing Syndicate) J L Dunlop Arundel, W Sussex

3097

8.40 WIGSTON CLASSIFIED STKS 3YO+ 0-70 (E) 6f Good/Firm 27 +01 Fast
£2778 £855 £427 £213 3 yo rec 4 lb

2580 **TOM TUN 21** [8] Miss J F Craze 5-9-2 (t) T Lucas 9/4 FAV: 005001: 5 b g Bold Arrangement - B Grade **71**
(Lucky Wednesday) Chsd ldrs, led appr fnl 1f, held on well, rdn out: '99 wnr at Southwell (2, h'caps, rtd 75a), Newcastle (h'cap) & Doncaster (2, h'cap & stks, rtd 82): '98 wnr at Newcastle & Southwell (h'caps, rtd 62a & 65): eff at 5/6f on firm, soft & both AW's: likes Southwell & Doncaster: back to form in t-strap, eff without.
2822 **INDIAN MUSIC 12** [6] A Berry 3-8-12 (bl) M Roberts 5/1: 455532: 3 b g Indian Ridge - Dagny Juel *¾* **68**
(Danzig) Prom, chall appr fnl 1f, held nr fin: fine run, eff at 5/6f, tried 7f: goes on fast grnd, sole win on hvy.
2976 **BANDBOX 5** [7] M Salaman 5-9-2 S Carson (3) 7/2: 030623: 5 ach g Imperial Frontier - Dublah *shd* **68$**
(Private Account) Chsd ldrs, eff appr fnl 1f, onepace till kept on well towards fin: stiff task on offic. ratings.
*2994 **REDOUBTABLE 4** [5] D W Chapman 9-9-5 G Parkin 11/4: 600414: Well plcd, rdn 2f out, unable to *½* **69**
quicken: prob ran near to best & clr rem but is prob suited by 7f nowadays: see 2994.
1877 **KEBABS 51** [3] 3-8-9 D Harrison 10/1: 000305: Led till 2f out, fdd: 7 wk abs, blnks omitted, see 736. *8* **43**
2994 **BAYARD LADY 4** [4] 4-8-13 K Hodgson 50/1: 005006: Dwelt, nvr got in it: v stiff task, quick reapp. *3½* **34$**
2804 **WAX LYRICAL 12** [2] 4-8-13 (BL) M Tebbutt 6/1: -00007: Chsd ldrs till 3f out: unsuited by blinkers? *1¾* **30**
7 ran Time 1m 11.4 (1.6) (Mrs O Tunstall) Miss J F Craze Elvington, York

MUSSELBURGH WEDNESDAY AUGUST 2ND Righthand, Sharp Track

Official Going GOOD. Stalls: 5f/2m - Stands Side; Rem - Inside.

3098

6.20 FILLIES MED AUCT MDN 2YO (E) 5f Good 50 -08 Slow
£2795 £860 £430 £215

2766 **NORDIC SABRE 14** [4] Mrs L Stubbs 2-8-11 C Lowther 14/1: 61: 2 b f Sabrehill - Nordico Princess **79**
(Nordico) Sn led, styd on well despite hanging left fnl 1f, drvn out: left debut run bhd: half sister to a wng sprint juv, dam 6f juv wnr: eff at 5f, 6f shld suit: acts on gd, sharp trks, forcing the pace: going the right way.
2933 **EXTRA GUEST 6** [6] M R Channon 2-8-11 A Culhane 6/5 FAV: 224222: 2 b f Fraam - Gibaltarik (Jareer) *1¾* **73**
Mid-div, gd hdwy appr fnl 1f, drvn & not qckn well ins last: quick reapp: rnr-up for the 7th time in 11 starts.
-- **CREDIBILITY** [7] Sir Mark Prescott 2-8-11 S Sanders 11/4: 3: 2 ch f Komaite - Integrity (Reform) *1½* **69**
Dwelt, with ldrs halfway, drvn/no extra over 1f out: Apr foal, half sister to a Gr 3 7f 2yo scorer: dam Listed 6f wnr: v pleasing debut, will learn from this & win a mdn sn.
2700 **LE MERIDIEN 17** [5] J S Wainwright 2-8-11 P Fessey 8/1: -044: Prom, drvn over 2f out, btn appr dist. *1¾* **64**
2137 **SENSIMELIA 40** [8] 2-8-11 C Teague 10/1: -5365: Trkd ldrs, drvn/fdd fnl 2f: see 1835. *¾* **61**
2835 **LADY ROCK 11** [9] 2-8-11 O Pears 6/1: -0046: Chsd ldrs, hung left over 2f out & sn wknd: see 1659. *2½* **54**
2045 **WHARFEDALE CYGNET 44** [3] 2-8-11 J McAuley 66/1: 647: Slow start, sn in tch, rdn/btn over 2f out. *3½* **45**
898 **OLYS DREAM 111** [1] 2-8-11 F Lynch 12/1: 58: Al outpcd: 4 month abs: see 898. *¾* **42**
8 ran Time 1m 00.4 (2.9) (K F F Potatoes Ltd) Mrs L Stubbs Newmarket

3099

6.50 LE BISTRO SELL HCAP 3YO+ 0-60 (F) 2m Good 50 -22 Slow **[38]**
£3103 £955 £477 £238

2244 **TOP OF THE CHARTS 35** [2] Mrs M Reveley 4-9-8 (32)(bl) A Culhane 3/1: 44-501: 4 b g Salse - **39**
Celebrity (Troy) Rear, hdwy to lead dist, easily went clr: 1st win, bt in for 9,000gns: 4th at best in '99 for J Noseda (appr mdn h'cap, rtd 44, tried visor/blnks): eff at 14f/2m, half brother to a 2m wnr: acts on fast, gd

grnd & a sharp trk: likes sell grade & found an extremely poor contest today (top-weight offically rtd just 34).

| -- | **VICTOR LASZLO** 6 [3] R Allan 8-9-7 (31) R Winston 9/1: 0050/2: 8 b g Illum - Report 'Em (Staff Writer) | 6 | 31 |

Prom, led appr fnl 2f, hdd over 1f out, kept on but no ch with wnr: recently plcd over fences (nov, rtd 84c, 2m/2½m, gd & firm): unplcd '98 Flat rnr (tried blnks), last won way back in '96, at Hamilton (13f h'cap, fast).

2875 **SECONDS AWAY** 9 [3] J S Goldie 9-9-8 (32) Dawn Rankin(7) 9/2: 334333: 9 b g Hard Fought - Keep Mum 6 27
(Mummy's Pet) Outpcd, lost tch halfway, rdn/prog 3f out, styd on late, no threat: longer 2m trip: see 2875, 1191.

2643 **DIAMOND CROWN** 19 [1] Martyn Wane 9-9-4 (28) C Teague 7/1: -02004: Nvr a factor: see 2643, 1814. 8 17

2783 **PICCADILLY** 13 [7] 5-9-10 (34) F Lynch 9/1: 200465: Led, hdd appr fnl 2f, wknd qckly: up in trip. 5 18

2826 **LOYAL TOAST** 12 [4] 5-9-6 (30) O Pears 5/2 FAV: 505336: Waited with, nvr dangerous: flattered 2826. 6 9

2219 **PARISIENNE HILL** 36 [5] 4-8-10 (20) S Sanders 33/1: 00-007: In tch, rdn & wknd qckly fnl 4f: jmps rnr. ½ 0

7 ran Time 3m 34.0 (11.5) (P D Savill) Mrs M Reveley Lingdale, N Yorks

---

3100 7.20 LE BISTRO MDN AUCT 2YO (F) 7f30y rnd Good 50 -33 Slow
£2604 £744 £372

2653 **CASHNEEM** 19 [6] P W Harris 2-8-9 A Culhane 6/4 FAV: 41: 2 b c Case Law - Haanem (Mtoto) 77
Prom, rdn & went on dist, ran on well, drvn clr: half brother & dam wnrs abroad, sire a sprinter: eff at
7f, further could suit: handles gd grnd & a sharp trk: imprvg, qcknd up well here & could follow up.

2841 **OCEAN LOVE** 11 [2] M L W Bell 2-8-4 A Beech (5) 3/1: 52: 2 b f Dolphin Street - Scuba Diver 2½ 66
(King's Lake) Mid-div, rdn/dropped rear over 3f out, drvn/late hdwy, no impress on wnr: stays 7f on gd
grnd, likely to apprec further/more gall trk: see 2841.

2849 **KALUKI** 11 [1] W R Muir 2-8-9 S Sanders 5/1: 334203: 2 ch c First Trump - Wild Humour (Fayruz) ½ 70
Led, rdn/hdd dist, sn btn: see 2619.

2700 **LIVE THE DREAM** 17 [3] J Hetherton 2-8-2 O Pears 50/1: -004: Rear, rdn/prog fnl 2f, no impress: 3½ 56
bred to apprec mid-dists next term: see 2417.

2218 **FIRST MEETING** 36 [4] 2-8-0 T Williams 4/1: 25: Cl-up, chall 2f out, sn wknd: btr 2218 (stiff 7.5f). nk 53

2810 **DAWN ROMANCE** 12 [5] 2-8-2 P Fessey 7/1: -00506: In tch, wknd qckly 2f out: eyecatching in 2810. 3 49

6 ran Time 1m 30.7 (5.8) (Law Abiding Citizens) P W Harris Oldbury, Herts

---

3101 7.50 LE BISTRO NURSERY HCAP 2YO (E) 5f Good 50 +08 Fast [92]
£4290 £1320 £660 £330

2687 **CANDOTHAT** 18 [5] P W Harris 2-9-5 (80) A Culhane 6/1: 06151: 2 b c Thatching - Yo Cando (Cyrano 84
de Bergerac) Hmpd start, hdwy from rear over 2f out, short of room & switched over 1f out, styd on strongly to
lead nr fin, drvn out: best time of day: earlier won at Pontefract (auct mdn): dam a 6f juv wnr: eff arnd 5f,
6f shld suit: acts on gd & a sharp or stiff trk: fine eff after finding trouble in running, could follow up.

2868 **BLAKESHALL BOY** 10 [8] M R Channon 2-9-1 (76) J Carroll 9/2: 414032: 2 b g Piccolo - Gigglleswick hd 79
Girl (Full Extent) Prom, gd hdwy to lead ins last, rdn & hdd cl-home: gd run, deserves similar: see 2868, 1124.

2100 **ROUGH SHOOT** 42 [9] T D Barron 2-8-12 (73)(h) S Sanders 4/1: -153: 2 ch g King's Signet - Tawny hd 75
(Grey Ghost) Front rank, rdn to lead briefly ins last, kept on, not btn far: 6 wk abs: acts on fast, gd &
fibresand: v consistent, win again sn: see 2100, 1418.

2927 **ITALIAN AFFAIR** 7 [6] A Bailey 2-7-13 (60) P Fessey 20/1: 210504: Prom, ev ch until no extra ¾ 59
well ins last: drop in trip: see 2927.

*2880 **FLINT** 9 [3] 2-7-13 (74)(7ex) J Fanning 3/1 FAV: 05415: Trkd ldrs, hung right for press over 1f out, ¾ 70
sn held: 7lb pen for scoring in 2880 (forced the pace).

2665 **COZZIE** 19 [7] 2-7-13 (60) T Williams 12/1: 051166: Led early, went on again appr fnl 1f, hdd 2 50
dist, wknd: shld apprec a return to sell grade: see 2665, 1916.

1659 **MRS TIGGYWINKLE** 61 [2] 2-8-1 (62) O Pears 20/1: -6407: Dwelt, rear, late hdwy: see 1304, 1136. 2 46

*2797 **SHATIN DOLLYBIRD** 25 [1] 2-9-1 (76) A Beech (5) 6/1: 223318: Dwelt, al outpcd: btr 2797. 1¾ 55

2927 **MONICA** 7 [10] 2-7-10 (57)(17oh) J McAuley 66/1: 045609: Nvr dangerous: quick reapp, stiff task. 4 26

2849 **NIFTY ALICE** 11 [4] 2-9-7 (82) J Bramhill 5/1: 244100: Led over 3f out, hdd appr fnl 1f, wknd/eased. 3 42

10 ran Time 59.6 (2.1) (The Thatchers) P W Harris Oldbury, Herts

---

3102 8.20 EXPRESS HCAP 3YO+ 0-75 (E) 1m4f Good 50 -03 Slow [62]
£3412 £1050 £525 £262 3 yo rec 11lb

2800 **INDIGO BAY** 12 [2] R Bastiman 4-8-4 (38)(tbl) O Pears 10/1: 000051: 4 b g Royal Academy - Cape 42
Heights (Shirley Heights) Made all, styd on strongly despite hanging all way up the str, rdn out: earlier this
term scored at Lingfield (AW clmr, rtd 65a, S Dow): '99 at Brighton (sell h'cap) & Lingfield wnr (h'cap, rtd 72):
rtd 71 in '98 for A Stewart: suited by forcing the pace over 11/13f, has tried further: acts on firm, gd &
equitrack: eff with/without blnks/visor & likes a sharp/undul trk: well h'capped & back to form today.

*2783 **ASHLEIGH BAKER** 13 [3] M Johnston 3-9-3 (51) J Fanning 3/1: 301612: 5 b m Don't Forget Me - Gayla 2½ 51
Orchestra (Lord Gayle) Front rank, chall wnr over 2f out, drvn/held appr fnl 1f: in gd form: see 2783.

2801 **SING AND DANCE** 12 [5] J R Weymes 7-9-3 (51) R Winston 9/2: 2-2553: 7 b m Rambo Dancer - 1½ 49
Musical Princess (Cavo Doro) Dwelt, hdwy to chase ldrs over 2f out, no extra appr dist: see 1147 (C/D).

*2893 **ALPHA ROSE** 9 [4] M L W Bell 3-9-7 (66)(6ex) A Beech (5) 11/10 FAV: 253114: Handy, chall wnr appr 3½ 60
fnl 2f, hung left & wknd qckly over 1f out: shade disapp on this hat-trick bid, btr 2893 (firm).

2049 **TROIS** 44 [1] 4-9-10 (58) Dean McKeown 11/2: 005045: Settled last, rdn to improve over 2f out, 3 49
sn btn: top weight, 6 wk abs: longer 12f trip: see 1279.

5 ran Time 2m 37.0 (6.4) (Robin Bastiman) R Bastiman Cowthorpe, N Yorks

---

3103 8.50 CARBERRY MDN HCAP 3YO+ 0-60 (F) 7f30y rnd Good 50 -25 Slow [54]
£2562 £732 £366 3 yo rec 6 lb

2964 **GRANITE CITY** 5 [2] J S Goldie 3-9-2 (48) A Culhane 9/2: 003021: 3 ro g Clantime - Alhargah 53
(Be My Guest) Rcd keenly cl-up, hdwy to chall ldr appr fnl 1f, ran on well to lead ins last, drvn out: quick
reapp, 1st win: plcd once in '99 (nurs h'cap, rtd 60 at best): eff btwn 5f & 7f: acts on firm & gd, sharp trks.

2834 **RED WOLF** 11 [3] J G Given 4-8-13 (39) R Winston 8/1: 0-0032: 4 ch g Timeless Times - Stealthy ½ 42
(Kind Of Hush) Chsd ldrs, led appr fnl 1f, rdn/hdd well ins last, not btn far: gd run, go one better sn: see 2834.

2839 **FOUND AT LAST** 11 [10] J Balding 4-9-11 (51) Dean McKeown 11/4 FAV: 022243: 4 b g Aragon - 1¾ 50
Girton (Balidar) Dwelt, rear, gd hdwy halfway, ev ch until no extra well ins last: joint top weight: consistent
recent plcd form but remains a mdn after 17 starts: handles fast & gd/soft: see 2421.

MUSSELBURGH   WEDNESDAY AUGUST 2ND   Righthand, Sharp Track

3007 **QUALITAIR SURVIVOR 4** [8] J Hetherton 5-8-9 (35) T Williams 25/1: 600004: Front rank, led appr fnl nk 33
2f, hdd over 1f out, sn onepcd: quick reapp: drop in trip: see 1360.
2798 **JEPAJE 12** [11] 3-9-4 (50)(bl) P Fessey 6/1: 006445: Keen/prom, rdn to improve over 2f out, no ½ 47
extra appr dist: see 2798 (sell).
2145 **RED MITTENS 40** [4] 3-8-12 (44) C Teague 66/1: 00-006: Led, hdd over 2f out, wknd appr fnl 1f: abs. nk 40
2378 **ENTITY 30** [13] 3-9-11 (57) S Sanders 10/1: 300057: Dwelt/rear, prog appr fnl 2f, ev ch until 4 45
short of room & wknd qckly ins last: joint top weight: btr 1053.
1910 **CLOHAMON 49** [1] 5-8-8 (34) J Carroll 12/1: 000-68: Rear, drvn/late gains, no threat: 7 wk abs: 1 20
prev with M Peill, now with R A Fahey, see 1910.
2506 **WOODBASTWICK CHARM 25** [14] 3-8-12 (44) O Pears 5/1: -00009: Nvr dangerous: see 2506. 1½ 27
2505 **BODFARI TIMES 25** [5] 4-8-6 (32) F Lynch 50/1: 000000: Al well bhd, fin 10th. shd 15
2964 **Wee Barney 5** [6] 3-8-4 (36)(BL) J McAuley 66/1:   2779 **Clear Moon 13** [9] 3-8-10 (42)(bl) A Beech (5) 14/1:
4588} **Doubtless Risk 273** [12] 3-8-10 (42) C Lowther 20/1: 2864 **Abco Boy 10** [7] 3-8-9 (41)(bl) P Goode (3) 25/1:
14 ran   Time 1m 30.2 (5.3)   (Aberdeenshire Racing Club)   J S Goldie Uplawmoor, E Renfrews

GOODWOOD   THURSDAY AUGUST 3RD   Righthand, Sharpish, Undulating Track

Official Going: GOOD Stalls: Round Course - Inside, 12f - Outside

3104   2.15 LISTED OAK TREE STKS 3YO+ (A)   7f rnd Good 46 +01 Fast
£22750   £7000   £3500   £1675   3 yo rec 6 lb

2597 **DANCEABOUT 22** [11] G Wragg 3-8-7 K Darley 15/8 FAV: 1531: 3 b f Shareef Dancer - Putupon 105
(Mummy's Pet) Trckd ldrs, rdn/strong chall from over 1f out, styd on gamely for press to narrowly assert nr fin,
all out: hvly bckd: earlier scored here at Goodwood (C/D, fillies mdn, debut): stays stiff 1m well, suited by
7f on fast & gd/soft, any trk, likes Goodwood: lightly raced & smart, open to further improvement.
1830 **CLARANET 55** [10] K Mahdi 3-8-7 J Tate 66/1: 310002: 3 ch f Arazi - Carmita (Caerleon) hd 104
Led, rdn/strongly pressed fnl 2f, hdd inside last, styd on gamely, just held: 8 week abs: acts on good, hvy &
fibresand: improved run & should find more races if repeating this: see 934 (fillies mdn).
2597 **LAST RESORT 22** [9] B W Hills 3-8-7 R Hills 6/1: -31363: 3 ch f Lahib - Breadcrumb (Final Straw) ¾ 103
Chsd ldrs, prog to chall over 1f out, drvn/every ch ent last, no extra nr fin: stablemate of 3rd, useful.
*2567 **OUT OF REACH 23** [6] B W Hills 3-8-7 M Hills 6/1: 1-5214: Chsd ldr halfway, rdn/every ch over nk 102
1f out, no extra inside last: hvly bckd: fine run on step up from h'cap company: see 2567 (rtd h'cap).
2567 **INCREDULOUS 23** [1] 3-8-8(1ow) R Cochrane 33/1: -24104: Keen, held up rear, rdn & styd on fnl dht 103
2f, not able to chall: ddhtd for 4th: finishing stronger than any & shld win more races if learning to settle.
2339 **MOSELLE 33** [3] 3-8-7 T Quinn 9/1: -20136: Held up, kept on onepace 2f, nvr pace to chall: nk 101
op 6/1.
2167 **COCO 40** [7] 3-8-8(1ow) J Murtagh 14/1: 0-1437: Chsd ldrs, rdn/outpcd 3f out, keeping on inside 1½ 99
last though held when eased nr fin: op 10/1: abs: stays 1m well, a return to that trip will suit: see 2167, 1268.
+2389 **FLAVIAN 30** [5] 4-8-13 C Rutter 10/1: 0-0018: Prom, held fnl 2f: see 2389 (stakes). hd 97
1825 **VERBOSE 55** [2] 3-8-7 R Hughes 14/1: 5-1259: Rear, no hdwy late: op 12/1, abs: btr 1108, 745 (1m). 1¼ 94
2675 **HYPNOTIZE 19** [8] 3-8-7 M J Kinane 9/1: -60200: Held up rear, no hdwy: 10th: btr 2274 (1m). nk 93
+2274 **MY HANSEL 35** [4] 3-8-7 J Reid 8/1: 13-010: Mid div, rdn/btn 3f out: 11th: bckd: btr 2274 (fast). 1 91
11 ran   Time 1m 27.62 (3.12)   (Bloomsbury Stud)   G Wragg Newmarket, Suffolk

3105   2.45 GR 2 RICHMOND STKS 2YO (A)   6f   Good 46 -04 Slow
£29000   £11000   £5500   £2500

*2808 **ENDLESS SUMMER 13** [8] J H M Gosden 2-8-11 J Fortune 2/1 FAV: -11: 2 b c Zafonic - Well Away 113
(Sadler's Wells) Trckd ldr halfway, qcknd to lead over 1f out & in command under hands & heels riding fnl 1f: hvly
bckd: confirmed promise of winning debut at Newbury (nov stakes): eff at 6f (dam a 1m juv wnr) & 7f will suit:
acts on firm & gd grnd, any trk: has run well fresh: v smart & only twice raced, looks sure to win more Gr races.
*1621 **PYRUS 68** [6] A P O'Brien 2-8-11 M J Kinane 11/4: 1-012: 2 b c Mr Prospector - Most Precious 1 108
(Nureyev) Led, rdn/hdd over 1f out, styd on well inside last though held by nwr: hvly bckd: 10 week abs: styd
longer 6f trip well, 7f will suit: acts on gd & gd/soft: v useful, should find a Gr race: see 1621 (Listed).
*2189 **CEEPIO 38** [2] T G Mills 2-8-11 T Quinn 6/1: -313: 2 b c Pennekamp - Boranwood (Exhibitioner) 1¾ 104
Prom, hard rdn fnl 2f, kept on well though no threat to wnr: acts on fast & gd grnd: win a Listed/Gr 3 at 7f.
*2738 **PAN JAMMER 18** [4] M R Channon 2-9-0 J Murtagh 11/2: 412314: Dwelt & lost around 4L, held up 1½ 103
rear/in tch, rdn & kept on fnl 2f, no threat: bckd: would have finished closer with a clean break, rate higher.
2850 **TRIPLE BLUE 12** [1] 2-8-11 R Hughes 16/1: 135245: Held up in tch, outpcd fnl 2f: see 2850, 2529. nk 99
*2598 **DOMINUS 22** [5] 2-8-11 Dane O'Neill 10/1: 2216: Prom, hard rdn/fdd fnl 2f: see 2598 (stakes). ½ 97
2850 **STREGONE 12** [3] 2-8-11 D R McCabe 16/1: 220427: Held up, rdn/slightly hmpd over 1f out, sn held. ¾ 95
2529 **MAMMAS TONIGHT 25** [7] 2-8-11 G Carter 16/1: 331548: Bhd ldrs, btn 2f out: op 14/1: btr 2113 (5f). 1½ 91
8 ran   Time 1m 12.99 (2.99)   (K Abdulla)   J H M Gosden Manton, Wilts

3106   3.20 GR 2 GOODWOOD CUP STKS 3YO+ (A)   2m   Good 46 -00 Slow
£46400   £17600   £8800   £4000   3 yo rec 15lb

2909 **ROYAL REBEL 12** [2] M Johnston 4-9-2 (vis) M J Kinane 10/1: -01221: 4 b g Robellino - Greenvera 118
(Riverman) Trkd ldr, rdn/chall over 3f out, narrow lead fnl 2f & drvn/styd on gamely to narrowly assert close home:
1st time visor: earlier scored at Leopardstown (Listed): '99 wnr at Newcastle (mdn) & Leopardstown (stakes, rtd 108):
5th in a Grp 1 in '98 (rtd 102): eff at 14f, suited by step up to 2m: acts on firm & gd/soft, any track, likes
Leopardstown: eff with/without blinks, improved for application of visor today: runs best for strong handling:
high-class run today & open to improvement at this trip.
2114 **FAR CRY 42** [7] M C Pipe 5-9-2 K Darley 2/1 FAV: 115-22: 5 b g Pharly - Darabaka (Doyoun) ½ 118
Trckd ldr, drvn/led over 3f out, hdd over 2f out, styd on gamely inside last, just held nr fin: v hvly bckd, op 5/2:
6 week abs: tough & high-class, reportedly has the Melbourne Cup as main autumn target: see 2114.
2114 **SAN SEBASTIAN 42** [3] J L Dunlop 6-9-2 (bl) D M Oliver 9/1: 2-4643: 6 ch g Niniski - Top Of The 1 117
League (High Top) Chsd ldrs, rdn & styd on well fnl 2f for press: abs: shld be placed to win a Listed/Gr race.
1222 **RAINBOW HIGH 85** [1] B W Hills 5-9-2 M Hills 9/2: 321-54: Held up, smooth prog to chall 3f out, rdn/ 2 115
briefly led over 2f out, drvn/held 1f out: 12 wk abs: travelled like a wnr here, poss just in need of the run?
2114 **PERSIAN PUNCH 42** [5] 7-9-2 T Quinn 9/1: -20165: Led, rdn/hdd over 3f out, held fnl 2f: bckd, abs. 1¾ 113

963

2405 **CHURLISH CHARM 33** [6] 5-9-2 R Hughes 13/2: -03236: Keen early, chsd ldrs, held fnl 2f: see 2405. 2½ **111**
2153 **THREE CHEERS 41** [8] 6-9-2 (vis) J Fortune 10/1: 62-127: Held up rear, no ch 3f out: 6 week abs. 4 **107**
2566 **RAINBOW WAYS 23** [4] 5-9-2 J Reid 10/1: 122348: Held up rear, btn 3f out; op 7/1: see 2566, 2336. 6 **101**
8 ran Time 3m 31.71 (7.41) (P D Savill) M Johnston Middleham, N Yorks

3107 **3.50 WILLIAM HILL MILE HCAP 3YO+ (B) 1m rnd Good 46 +31 Fast [113]**
£65000 £20000 £10000 £5000 3 yo rec 7 lb High numbers have advantage on Rnd Crse

2997 **PERSIANO 5** [18] J R Fanshawe 5-8-12 (97) D Harrison 10/1: 313251: 5 ch g Efisio - Persiandale (Persian Bold) Trckd ldrs, shaken up to lead ent fnl 2f, styd on gamely for press ins last, just held on: op 8/1, v fast time, qck reapp: earlier won here at Goodwood (h'cap): plcd twice in '99 (h'cap, rtd 101): '98 wnr at Warwick, Salisbury & Doncaster (h'caps, rtd 100): eff at 7f/1m on firm & gd/soft, handles hvy: goes on any trk, likes Goodwood: best without visor: progressive & consistent in these valuable/big field h'caps, credit to trainer. **103**
*3063 **PARISIEN STAR 2** [12] N Hamilton 4-7-13 (84)(5ex) J Quinn 20/1: 404512: 4 ch g Paris House - Auction Maid (Auction Ring) Midfield, gd hdwy appr fnl 2f, kept on strongly for press inside last, post came too sn: fine run after winning here 48 hrs ago: tough & in-form, likes this trk: see 3063. *shd* **89**
2870 **OMAHA CITY 11** [21] B Gubby 6-8-8 (92)(1ow) R Cochrane 16/1: 000503: 6 b g Night Shift - Be Discreet (Junius) Mid-div, prog ent fnl 2f, drvn to press ldrs below dist, not btn far: loves Goodwood, see 1450. ½ **97**
2090 **JOHN FERNELEY 43** [22] P F I Cole 5-9-2 (101) J Fortune 5/1 FAV: 3-3124: Trckd ldrs, eff 2f out, kept on samepace ins last: hvly bckd from 7/1, 6 week abs: v useful & tough: loves these big field/val h'caps. *nk* **104**
2596 **ATLANTIC RHAPSODY 22** [14] 3-8-3 (95) J Fanning 14/1: 125605: Mid-div, tried to improve but short of room more than once fnl 2f, kept on: blnks omitted: wld have made the frame: tough, apprec return to 1m. ½ **97**
2997 **PEARTREE HOUSE 5** [16] 6-8-3 (88) A Nicholls (3) 14/1: 244066: Cl up, led 2f out, sn hdd, no extra inside last: quick reapp, prob ran to best & suited by return to 1m: see 2138. *1* **88**
*2762 **RED N SOCKS 15** [2] 3-7-12 (90) P Doe 16/1: -20017: U.r. rider/bolted bef start, bhd, kept on strgly from 2f out, nvr nrr: gd run in the circumstances & did much the best of those drawn low: keep in mind. 1¼ **87+**
2997 **CARIBBEAN MONARCH 5** [17] 5-9-10 (109) J Murtagh 6/1: 321108: Waited with, shkn up appr fnl 2f, styd on, nvr nr ldrs: well bckd, qk reapp, top-weight: stiffer trk needed, see 2528, 2090 (bt this wnr & 4th). *shd* **106**
2616 **SECOND WIND 21** [5] 5-7-12 (83)(t) J Mackay (5) 33/1: 001249: Cl-up, rdn ent fnl 2f, no impress & eased fnl 100y: awash with sweat: prob best at 7f but far from disgraced from poor low draw: see 2616, 2133. 1¾ **77**
2997 **EL GRAN PAPA 5** [3] 3-8-2 (94) F Norton 7/1: 211020: Switched from wide draw & bhd, niggled turning in, no impress till kept on well ins last: 10th, bckd, quick reapp: best to ignore this, see 2997. *shd* **88**
2696 **TRIPLE DASH 19** [9] 4-8-2 (87) G Duffield 12/1: 000040: In tch, not travel well, hdwy to chse ldrs 2f out, onepace under press: 11th, poss unsuited by drop back to a sharp 1m: see 2696, 1112. *nk* **80**
1308 **FULL FLOW 79** [10] 3-8-11 (103) J Reid 25/1: 20-440: In tch, eff & slightly checked 2f out, same pace: 12th, 11 week abs: see 969 (7f). 1¾ **93**
*3060 **SHARP PLAY 2** [8] 5-9-4 (103)(7ex) R Hills 16/1: 420410: Mid-div throughout: 13th, quick reapp & penalty for Tuesday's win here over 10f: clearly unsuited by drop back to 1m: see 3060. *shd* **93**
3063 **VOLONTIERS 2** [4] 5-7-11 (82) Dale Gibson 33/1: 602200: Slow away, nvr on terms: 14th, poor draw. ½ **71**
-2757 **PYTHIOS 15** [11] 4-9-7 (106)(t) T Quinn 8/1: 1-0420: Dwelt, v wide into straight, nvr nr ldrs: 15th, well bckd: best forgotten, only a neck bhd this wnr in 2090 (stiff track). ½ **94**
2696 **DEBBIES WARNING 19** [15] 4-8-5 (90) J Tate 40/1: 400600: Set furious gallop, hdd 2f out & lost pl: 16th. ¾ **77**
2528 **SILK ST JOHN 25** [19] 6-8-7 (92) P McCabe 25/1: 131640: Bhd, shkn up/short of room appr fnl 2f: 17th. ½ **78**
-2675 **PULAU TIOMAN 19** [7] 4-9-7 (106) P Robinson 20/1: 124220: Chsd ldrs, fdd appr fnl 1f: 18th, bckd. 1½ **89**
2870 **CALCUTTA 11** [6] 4-8-9 (94) M Hills 14/1: 000630: Al bhd & wide: 19th, tchd 20/1, poor draw, see 1829. 3 **71**
2090 **BOMB ALASKA 43** [20] 5-9-9 (108) J F Egan 25/1: 434000: Bhd, no impress/hmpd 2f out, eased: 20th. 7 **74**
2456 **RIVER TIMES 27** [13] 4-8-5 (90)(bl) K Darley 25/1: 204000: Prom till 3f out: 21st, see 663 (AW). 3 **50**
2707 **MAYARO BAY 18** [1] 4-9-0 (99) R Hughes 33/1: 016030: Switched start, al last, eased fnl 2f: 22nd, ignore. 8 **47**
22 ran Time 1m 38.58 (1.18) (Miss A Church) J R Fanshawe Newmarket, Suffolk

3108 **4.25 EBF NEW HAM FILLIES MDN 2YO (D) 7f rnd Good 46 -31 Slow**
£10920 £3360 £1680 £840

-- **AMEERAT** [6] M A Jarvis 2-8-11 P Robinson 3/1 FAV: 1: 2 b f Mark Of Esteem - Walimu (Top Ville) Press ldr, led appr fnl 2f, ran on strgly, pshd out, readily: well bckd, op 4/1: April foal, half-sister to a 7f/1m wnr, dam 1m/12f wnr, sire a miler: eff at 7f, step up to 1m will suit: acts on gd grnd, sharp/undul trk & runs well fresh: useful introduction, shld improve & develop into a Group performer. **99+**
-- **SAYEDAH** [9] M P Tregoning 2-8-11 W Supple 5/1: 2: 2 b f Darshaan - Balaabel (Sadler's Wells) Bhd ldrs, eff & slty checked ent fnl 3f, styd on nicely fnl 1f: well bckd: Jan foal, half-sister to a 7f wnr, dam miler: eff at 7f on gd, sure to apprec further: fine debut, not given a hard time & looks sure to win races. 2 **92+**
-- **PAGE NOUVELLE** [5] B W Hills 2-8-11 M Hills 5/1: 3: 2 b f Spectrum - Page Bleue (Sadler's Wells) Slow away & held up, kept on stdly fnl 2f, nvr trbled ldrs: well bckd from 7/1: Jan foal, half-sister to a German Gr 3 wnr, sire 1m/10f performer: step up to 1m lks sure to suit, should improve & find similar. 2 **88**
2635 **SPREE LOVE 20** [10] A G Newcombe 2-8-11 J Reid 25/1: 24: Led till appr fnl 2f, same pace: not disgraced, handles fibresand & gd grnd: this was much tougher than 2635 (AW auction mdn). 1½ **85$**
-- **ZANZIBAR** [7] 2-8-11 M Fenton 12/1: 5: Pulled hard, hdwy 2f out, sn no further prog: tchd 16/1: 40,000gns In The Wings Mar first foal, dam 10f wnr, sire 12f performer: bred to need 10f+ & improve with age. *hd* **84**
-- **IFFAH** [3] 2-8-11 R Hills 5/1: 6: Chsd ldrs, outpcd appr fnl 2f: bckd tho' op 5/2: Halling Feb foal, half-sister to a 1m wng juv, dam 9f juv wnr, sire got 10f: will leave this bhd over 1m+: with J Dunlop. 1¾ **81**
2583 **AKER WOOD 22** [8] 2-8-11 J Fortune 6/1: 027: Sn prom, no extra 2f out & eased: bckd tho' op 4/1. 1½ **78**
-- **ENGLISH HARBOUR** [2] 2-8-11 G Duffield 16/1: 8: Wide into str, nvr dngrs: stablemate 3rd, tchd 25/1: Sabrehill Jan foal, half-sister to sev wnrs, notably high-class 10f performer Enviroment Friend: will apprec 10f+. 1¾ **75**
-- **MAJOR REVIEW** [4] 2-8-11 J Mackay (5) 33/1: 9: Dwelt, v wide ent straight & btn: debut, stablemate of 5th: 14,000gns Definite Article Jan first foal, dam & sire mid-dist performers: will need mid-dists next term. 3 **69**
9 ran Time 1m 29.91 (5.41) (Sheikh Ahmed Al Maktoum) M A Jarvis Newmarket, Suffolk

3109 **5.00 LORAINE KIDD NURSERY HCAP 2YO (C) 5f Good 46 -29 Slow [89]**
£7670 £2360 £1180 £590

2678 **SOLDIER ON 19** [1] M R Channon 2-8-12 (73) Craig Williams 16/1: 215501: 2 b g General Monash - Golden Form (Formidable) Waited with, smooth prog on stands rail appr fnl 1f, qcknd to lead ins last, going away, cleverly: tchd 25/1: earlier won at Brighton (mdn): apprec drop back to 5f: acts on firm & gd/soft, sharp track. **79**
*2915 **HAMATARA 8** [3] I A Balding 2-8-13 (74)(t)(6ex) K Darley 7/2 JT FAV: 40412: 2 ch g Tagula - 1¼ **75**

GOODWOOD THURSDAY AUGUST 3RD Righthand, Sharpish, Undulating Track

Arctic Poppy (Arctic Tern) Shkn up towards rear, improved halfway, kept on und press & ch ins last, outpcd by wnr cl-home: nicely bckd under a pen: lost little in defeat, acts on fast & gd, handles soft: see 2915.
*2324 **ANTONIAS DILEMMA 33** [2] A Berry 2-9-2 (77) J Carroll 5/1: -013: 2 ch f Primo Dominie - Antonia's *nk* **77**
Folly (Music Boy) Cl up & every ch, no extra well inside last: solid h'cap bow, acts on firm & gd grnd.
2589 **EUROLINK SUNDANCE 22** [4] J L Dunlop 2-9-5 (80) T Quinn 7/2 JT FAV: 0134: Towards rear, eff & not *½* **78**
much room below dist, styd on, nvr dngrs: nicely bckd: prob in the frame with a clr run: worth another ch at 6f.
2868 **LAI SEE 11** [8] 2-9-3 (78) J Fortune 4/1: 002225: Held up, wide, switched wider still appr fnl 1f, *1* **74**
no impress on ldrs: well bckd: see 2868, 2360.
3044 **HOT PANTS 3** [7] 2-8-12 (73) G Duffield 20/1: 05306: Prom, wide, rdn appr fnl 1f, unable to qckn. *nk* **68**
*2818 **CELOTTI 13** [5] 2-9-3 (78) J P Spencer 9/1: 3517: Led till well inside last, fdd: op 6/1 on h'cap bow. *shd* **73**
*2657 **JACK SPRATT 20** [6] 2-9-7 (82) Dane O'Neill 8/1: 03318: Keen, pressed ldr till wknd fnl 150y: *shd* **76**
tchd 10/1, top-weight on h'cap bow: see 2657 (made all).
8 ran Time 1m 0.43 (3.73) (T S M Cunningham) M R Channon West Isley, Berks

3110

5.35 DRAWING ROOM HCAP 3YO+ 0-80 (D) 1m1f Good 46 -14 Slow [80]
£9789 £3012 £1506 £753 3 yo rec 8 lb High numbers have an edge on rnd course

2790 **JUNIKAY 14** [11] R Ingram 6-8-13 (65) M Roberts 12/1: 132041: 6 bg Treasure Kay - Junijo (Junius) **73**
Held up, gd wide prog 3f out to lead bef dist, rdn & ran on strongly: earlier won at Nottingham & Lingfield (h'caps): '99 wnr of same race at Nottingham (rtd 57), prev term scored at Brighton (h'cap, rtd 57): eff held up at 1m/10f: acts on firm, gd/soft grnd, any trk, likes Nottingham: tough, has a decent turn on foot for this level.
2836 **ROMAN KING 12** [22] M Johnston 5-9-10 (76) M Hills 6/1: -60342: 5 b g Sadler's Wells - Romantic *1½* **80**
Feeling (Shirely Heights) Off the pace, imprvd on ins rail appr fnl 2f, had to be switched bef dist, ran on, nvr nrr: well bckd from 8/1: not much luck in this big field: in grand formm, win again at 10f+: see 845.
2707 **BOUND FOR PLEASURE 18** [12] J H M Gosden 4-9-9 (75)(t) J Fortune 4/1 FAV: 600-23: 4 gr c *2* **75+**
Barathea - Dazzlingly Radiant (Try My Best) Last of all & pshd along halfway, widest of all str, kept on fnl 3f, nrst fin: hvly bckd from 11/2: eff at 7f, stays 9f: nicely h'capped, poised to strike with a more positive ride.
2350 **FORZA FIGLIO 32** [5] M Kettle 7-9-8 (74) T Quinn 25/1: 0/0334: In tch, prog to chall appr fnl 1f, *shd* **74**
kept on same pace: gd run from a poor low draw: likes it here at Goodwood, see 1729.
*2888 **THE GREEN GREY 10** [13] 6-9-5 (71)(6ex) G Duffield 12/1: 610015: Prom, slightly hmpd bef halfway *1¼* **68**
eff/ch when briefly sandwiched appr fnl 1f, onepace: had a rather bumpy passage & is worth another ch after 2888.
2682 **INCHINNAN 19** [15] 3-8-10 (70) J Tate 12/1: -21326: Chsd ldrs, eff & barged appr fnl 1f, unable to qckn. *nk* **66**
2658 **ARBENIG 20** [10] 5-7-12 (50) P Doe 20/1: 310527: Cl up, led 3f out, rdn & hdd bef dist, no extra. *½* **45**
2764 **SUCH BOLDNESS 15** [18] 6-7-10 (48) J Mackay (5) 40/1: 5-0008: Rear, v wide into straight, styd on *2½* **38**
into mid-div but nvr dangerous: well h'capped if returning to form: see 2366.
2356 **CHINA RED 32** [8] 6-10-0 (80) R Hills 20/1: 0-0009: Handy, chsd ldr ent fnl 2f, sn onepace & hmpd/eased. *1* **68**
2890 **NATALIE JAY 10** [14] 4-8-10 (62) Craig Williams 14/1: -30430: Towards rear, closing on inside rail *1* **48**
when not clr run appr fnl 2f, switched & onepace: 10th, worth another chance, see 2890, 831.
2712 **BOX CAR 17** [16] 3-8-1 (61) F Norton 33/1: 220060: Chsd ldrs, rdn & held when hmpd ent fnl 2f: 11th. *1¾* **44**
2502 **HIBERNATE 26** [2] 6-9-5 (71) N Callan 25/1: 420S00: Switched from low draw & led, hdd 3f out, *1¼* **51**
grad wknd: 12th: had to show plenty of pace to lead from stall 2 & subs paid for it: see 1829, 422.
2558 **KATIYPOUR 23** [21] 3-9-5 (79) J Murtagh 7/1: -0230: Nvr better than mid-div: 13th, h'cap bow, see 1992. *1* **57**
4008} **THATCHMASTER 318** [17] 9-9-0 (66)(t) Paul Eddery 20/1: 0144-0: Never troubled ldrs: 14th on reapp: *¾* **43**
'99 wnr here at Goodwood (amat h'cap, rtd 68): '98 wnr at Windsor (2, h'caps, rtd 71): eff at 9/12f on fast & gd, handles hvy, likes sharp trks, esp Goodwood: best without visor, wears a t-strap: well h'capped.
*2942 **EASTERN SPICE 7** [20] 3-9-9 (83)(6ex) J Reid 8/1: 213010: Al towards rear: 15th, bckd tho' op 6/1. *1* **58**
2645 **TARAWAN 20** [19] 4-9-10 (76)(vis) K Darley 10/1: 000500: Dwelt, nvr in it: 19th, bckd though op 8/1, see 580. **0**
2814 **Glendale Ridge 13** [3] 5-8-12 (64) R Mullen 50/1: 968 **Bay View 106** [7] 5-9-2 (68) J P Spencer 25/1:
2980 **Night Shifter 6** [6] 3-7-12 (58) J Quinn 40/1: 3045 **Giko 3** [1] 6-7-13 (51)(tbl) A Daly 50/1:
20 ran Time 1m 55.89 (5.39) (Ellangowan Racing Partners) R Ingram Epsom, Surrey

NOTTINGHAM FRIDAY AUGUST 4TH Lefthand, Galloping Track

Official Going: GOOD TO FIRM Stalls: 5/6f - Stands side, Remainder - Inside

3111

6.10 BOLLINGER AMAT HCAP 4YO+ 0-75 (E) 1m2f Good/Firm 39 -25 Slow [45]
£2938 £904 £452 £226

2790 **KINNINO 15** [2] G L Moore 6-9-10 (41)(2oh) Mr R L Moore (5) 8/1: 340321: 6 b g Polish Precedent **44**
- On Tiptoes (Shareef Dancer) Trkd ldrs, led going well over 2f out, strongly pressed fnl 1f, held on well under hands and heels riding: earlier scored at W'hampton (AW amat h'cap, rtd 45a): rnr up on sand in '99 (rtd 43a & 45): unplcd in '98 (rtd 57 & 57a): eff at 1m/10f on fast, gd & both AWs, any trk: best without blinks.
3052 **RARE TALENT 3** [11] S Gollings 6-11-0 (59)(6ex) Mr T Best (5) 9/2: 326152: 6 b g Mtoto - Bold As Love *½* **60**
(Lomond) Held up, prog to chall over 1f out, not pace of wnr inside last: qk reapp: tough (7 wins from 51).
2802 **MISSILE TOE 14** [1] D Morris 7-10-5 (50) Mr Paul J Morris (5) 7/2 FAV: 411653: 7 b g Exactly Sharp *¾* **50**
- Debach Dust (Indian King) Dwelt, held up, switched & prog to chall inside last, onepace/held close home.
2546 **HOH GEM 25** [4] B R Millman 4-10-2 (47) Mr G Richards (5) 10/1: 410204: Dwelt/held up, eff/hmpd *2½* **43**
over 2f out, styd on inside last, not able to chall: see 1520.
2958 **SILVER SECRET 7** [6] 6-9-13 (44) Mr B Hitchcott 7/1: 160605: Prom, onepace fnl 2f: see 1819 (soft). *nk* **39**
*1666 **SOVEREIGNS COURT 63** [12] 7-12-0 (73) Mr L Jefford 6/1: 0/3016: Held up, prog/ch 2f out, fdd: *5* **61**
op 9/2, 2 month abs: btr 1666 (gd/soft).
1394 **SURE FUTURE 76** [7] 4-10-4 (49)(bl) Mr J J Best (7) 33/1: 002-07: Chsd ldrs 1m: Jumps fit, plcd *¾* **36**
twice (rtd 91h, 2m1f, blnks): rnr-up fnl '99 start (rtd 55, mdn h'cap, A Stewart, also rtd 35a): stays 12f on soft.
2466 **IL DESTINO 28** [9] 5-10-10 (55)(BL) Mr C B Hills (3) 11/2: 2-6508: Chsd ldr after 3f, btn 2f out: blnks. *3½* **37**
-- **TIYE** [10] 5-10-5 (50)(vis) Mr Christian Williams (5) 50/1: 2306/9: Al rear: jumps fit (mod form): *3½* **27**
long Flat abs, plcd twice in '98 (rtd 60, R Hannon, clmr): prob stays 2m & handles firm & gd: best without blinks/vis.
2785 **PROUD CAVALIER 15** [5] 4-10-1 (46)(5ow)(8oh) Mr S J Edwards (0) 33/1: 050040: Led after 1f to 2f out. *1* **22**
516 **FRENCH CONNECTION 171** [8] 5-10-3 (48)(VIS) Mr S Morton (7) 25/1: -62000: Chsd ldrs 1m: 11th: *3* **20**
visor: jumps fit (mod form): tried a visor here: see 341, 298 (AW).
11 ran Time 2m 08.7 (6.4) (A Moore) G L Moore Woodingdean, E Sussex

3112
6.40 LADIES NIGHT HCAP 3YO 0-65 (F)   2m   Good/Firm 39 -02 Slow   [69]
£2815   £804   £402

2815 **ESTABLISHED** 14 [4] J R Best 3-7-10 (37)(3oh) A Polli (3) 16/1: 035501: 3 b g Not In Doubt - Copper   45
Trader (Faustus). Prom, rdn/lost plce 5f out, drvn & prog to lead over 2f out, styd on well inside last, drvn out:
blnks omitted: 1st win: unplcd in '99 (rtd 49, h'cap, earlier with H Candy): eff over a gall 2m on fast grnd.
2973 **JACK DAWSON** 7 [14] John Berry 3-9-7 (62) G Baker (5) 7/2 CO FAV: 250122: 3 b g Persian Bold -   1¾ 67
Dream Of Jenny (Caerleon) Held up, rdn/prog & every ch fnl 1f, held by wnr cl home: op 5/1: see 2973, 2659.
*2879 **TURNED OUT WELL** 11 [7] P C Haslam 3-8-4 (45)(5ex) P Goode (3) 7/2 CO FAV: 0-5513: 3 b g Robellino 3½ 47
- In The Shade (Bustino) Held up, prog 5f out, onepace & held fnl 2f: see 2879 (mdn h'cap).
2284 **NEEDWOOD TRIDENT** 35 [16] J Pearce 3-7-10 (37) P M Quinn (3) 20/1: -05004: Held up, late gains, no 2½ 37
threat to front trio: not disgraced over this longer 2m trip: see 2284, 1022.
2776 **UNIMPEACHABLE** 15 [6] 3-8-10 (51) P Dobbs (5) 10/1: 644225: Dwelt, held up, styd on fnl 2f, no threat   ¾ 50
to ldrs: op 9/1: prev with J M Bradley, now with G M McCourt: longer trip: see 2776, 2033 & 1002.
2902 **SEND ME AN ANGEL** 10 [9] 3-9-6 (61) N Callan 7/2 CO FAV: -44226: Led till over 2f out, wknd: lngr trip.   3 57
3026 **NICIARA** 4 [2] 3-8-3 (44)(bl) S Righton 10/1: 232247: Dwelt, nvr on terms: qck reapp: blnks reapp.   3½ 37
2370 **DEE DIAMOND** 32 [11] 3-7-13 (40) N Carlisle 25/1: -00058: Chsd ldrs 4f out, sn btn: longer 2m trip.   3 30
2902 **CEDAR GROVE** 10 [12] 3-9-0 (55) T E Durcan 10/1: 004049: Held up, eff 5f out, sn held: see 2902.   1¼ 44
2879 **SHARVIE** 11 [8] 3-8-11 (52) T G McLaughlin 20/1: 0-0060: Chsd ldrs 5f out, sn btn: 10th: see 1369.   5 36
2606 **ODYN DANCER** 22 [13] 3-7-12 (39) Jonjo Fowle (4) 20/1: 060400: Prom 1m: 11th: see 537 (11f).   ½ 22
2815 **OCEAN SONG** 14 [10] 3-8-11 (52) Dean McKeown 14/1: 030030: Prom, btn 3f out: 12th: btr 2815 (12f).   2 33
2879 **HARD DAYS NIGHT** 11 [5] 3-7-11 (38)(1ow)(2oh) Dale McKeown 9/1: 064620: Chsd ldr 5f out, wknd 2f out.   1¼ 18
2829 Calico 14 [17] 3-8-13 (54) Paul Eddery 33/1:   2715 **Cool Location** 18 [1] 3-7-10 (37)(20oh) D Kinsella (7) 66/1:
2386 Victorian Lady 31 [15] 3-8-8 (49) S Carson (2) 33/1:   2712 **Darcy Dancer** 18 [3] 3-8-8 (49) J Tate 33/1:
17 ran   Time 3m 30.8 (6.6)   (Teapot Lane Partnership)   J R Best Hucking, Kent

3113
7.10 EXPRESS CLASSIFEID STKS 3YO+ 0-65 (E)   5f   Good/Firm 39 +03 Fast
£3094   £952   £476   £238   3 yo rec 3 lb Field raced centre - stands side

2753 **PLEASURE TIME** 16 [1] C Smith 7-9-1 (vis) R Fitzpatrick (3) 5/1: -06001: 7 ch g Clantime - First   68
Experience (Le Johnstan) Broke well & sn 3L clr in centre, drvn 1f out, styd on strongly: '99 Bath wnr (class stakes,
rtd 80): '98 wnr here at Nottingham & also Thirsk (h'caps, rtd 71): loves to force the pace at 5/5.7f & likes
firm/fast, handles gd/sft grnd: likes a gall track, especially Nottingham: best visored, tried blnks.
2931 **BRANSTON LUCY** 9 [9] T J Etherington 3-8-12 Paul Eddery 9/2: 002122: 3 b f Prince Sabo - Softly   2½ 61
Spoken (Mummy's Pet) Chsd wnr, hung badly left over 2f out, kept on, al held: see 2535 (h'cap).
2976 **ECUDAMAH** 7 [6] Miss Jacqueline S Doyle 4-9-1 (bl) J Bosley (7) 10/1: 064033: 4 ch g Mukaddamah -   ½ 59
Great Land (Friend's Choice) Chsd ldrs, hmpd over 2f out, styd on inside last, no threat: 1 win in 29.
2559 **FAIRY PRINCE** 24 [2] Mrs A L M King 7-9-4 (BL) P M Quinn (3) 10/1: 451004: Chsd ldrs, nvr pace to   hd 61
chall: tried blnks, shld appreciate a return to a stiffer track or 6f: see 2192 (6f).
2559 **PIERPOINT** 24 [4] 5-9-4 N Callan 9/4 FAV: 001005: Chsd ldrs, hampered over 2f out, sn held: btr 1868. shd 61
2684 **MARINO STREET** 20 [3] 7-9-4 T E Durcan 6/1: 211W56: Chsd ldrs till over 1f out: see 2252.   nk 60
3091 **AJNAD** 2 [5] 6-9-1 (bl) T G McLaughlin 5/1: 066047: Nvr on terms: quick reapp: eyecatching 3091.   2½ 50
784 **NOBLE CHARGER** 128 [8] 5-9-1 (vis) P McCabe 40/1: 000-08: Al outpcd: abs, visor reapp: see 784.   6 39
1795 **PALMSTEAD BELLE** 57 [7] 3-8-9 M Fenton 16/1: 45-000: Al bhd: 8 wk abs: see 1219.   hd 35
9 ran   1m 0.3 (1.8)   (A E Needham)   C Smith, Temple Bruer, Lincs

3114
7.40 EBF AVANTI MDN STKS 2YO (D)   5f   Good/Firm 39 -23 Slow
£3835   £1180   £590   £295

2940 **THE TRADER** 8 [5] M Blanshard 2-9-0 Dale Gibson 2/5 FAV: 33221: 2 ch c Selkirk - Snowing   84
(Tate Gallery) Trckd ldrs, rdn/led over 1f out, rdn clr, styd on: eff at 5/6f on firm & soft grnd, any trk.
2939 **BE MY TINKER** 8 [4] G Brown 2-8-9 M Fenton 5/1: 622: 2 ch f Be My Chief - Tinkerbird (Music Boy)   6 64
Cl up, rdn/ch over 1f out, sn outpcd by wnr: bred to want further: see 2939, 2711.
3044 **ATEMME** 4 [2] Miss Jacqueline S Doyle 2-8-9 J Tate 33/1: 03: 2 b f Up And At 'Em - Petersford shd 64
Girl (Taufan) Rdn/outpcd early, mod late gains: quick reapp: 6f suit: bhd on debut previously.
2849 **CYRAZY** 13 [3] J G Given 2-8-9 Dean McKeown 4/1: 304: Led 3f, sn held: btr 1550 (debut, soft).   1 62
2891 **GET IT SORTED** 11 [1] 2-8-9 Hayley Turner (7) 25/1: 5U: Swerved left & u.r. start: see 2891.   0
5 ran   Time 1m 01.6 (3.1)   (Mrs C J Ward)   M Blanshard Upper Lambourn, Berks

3115
8.10 M PAGE HCAP 3YO+ 0-80 (D)   1m54y rnd Good/Firm 39 -41 Slow   [77]
£5307   £1633   £816   £408   3 yo rec 7 lb

2342 **SILK DAISY** 34 [7] H Candy 4-8-13 (62) A McGlone 100/30: -45151: 4 b f Barathea - Scene Galante   66
(Sicyos) Held up, prog fnl 2f & led 1f out, styd on well inside last, rdn out: slow time: earlier scored at
Goodwood (fillies h'cap, 1st win): plcd thrice in '99 (rtd 69): suited by 7f/1m on fast & gd/sft grnd, handles firm.
*2758 **ADOBE** 16 [2] W M Brisbourne 5-9-9 (72) T G McLaughlin 9/4 FAV: 133412: 5 b g Green Desert -   ¾ 73
Shamshir (Kris) Dwelt/held up, prog to chall over 1f out, not pace of wnr cl home: ran to best, tough & genuine.
3923} **MOST SAUCY** 324 [5] I A Wood 4-10-0 (77) J Bosley (7) 16/1: 1014-3: 4 br f Most Welcome - So Saucy hd 77
(To Know So) Prom, rdn/every ch over 1f out, just held well inside last: reapp: '99 wnr at Leicester (fillies h'cap)
& Lingfield (h'cap, rtd 78 at best, B Meehan): suited by 7f/1m, stays a sharp 10f: acts on firm & gd grnd, any track.
*2682 **OUT OF SIGHT** 20 [8] B A McMahon 6-8-13 (62) W Supple 9/2: 000014: Trkd ldrs, keen, went on 2f out 2½ 57
till 1f out, rdn inside last: see 2682 (C/D, class stakes).
2831 **ITS OUR SECRET** 14 [9] 4-9-1 (64) Dale Gibson 11/1: -24005: Held up, keen, kept on onepace fnl 2f.   nk 58
2840 **BLUE ACE** 13 [4] 4-9-1 (64) S Righton 10/1: 066646: Held up, keen, outpcd over 2f out: see 927 (stks).   2 39
1762 **OPEN ARMS** 58 [1] 4-9-5 (68) P M Quinn (3) 40/1: /3-007: Trckd ldrs, btn 1f out: abs: see 1762.   nk 57
2750 **DARE HUNTER** 16 [6] 3-9-10 (80) Paul Eddery 9/1: -02408: Dictated pace 6f, held 1f out: see 1366.   1¾ 66
2786 **MAJOR REBUKE** 15 [3] 3-8-10 (66)(VIS) N Callan 10/1: -00029: Chsd ldr, btn 1f out: vis: see 2786.   1½ 49
9 ran   Time 1m 46.00 (6.6)   (Mrs C M Poland)   H Candy Wantage, Oxon

966

NOTTINGHAM FRIDAY AUGUST 4TH Lefthand, Galloping Track

3116 **8.40 P FINN MED AUCT MDN 3YO (E) 1m54y rnd Good/Firm 39 -44 Slow**
£3055 £940 £470 £235

2860 **ELLWAY QUEEN 13** [2] B Hanbury 3-8-9 W Supple 3/1: -061: 3 b f Bahri - Queen Linear (Polish Navy) **77**
Dictated pace, rdn/qcknd clr over 1f out, always holding rivals after, rdn out: eff forcing the pace at 1m, tried 10f: acts on fast grnd & a gall track: given a fine tactical ride by W Supple.
2871 **MUSICAL HEATH 12** [5] P W Harris 3-9-0 (t) M Fenton 4/6 FAV: -42: 3 b c Common Grounds - Song Of The Glens (Horage) Keen/trkd wnr after 2f, rdn/outpcd over 1f out, held after: bckd: handles fast/firm. *1¾* **78**
2846 **NEGRONI 13** [3] J W Hills 3-8-9 Jonjo Fowle (5) 4/1: 6-33: 3 br f Mtoto - Carousel Music (On Your Mark) Trkd ldrs, keen, onepace/held over 1f out: bred for 10f+ & must learn to settle: see 2846. *1½* **70**
-- **DAZZLING DAISY** [7] Pat Mitchell 3-8-9 J Tate 25/1: 4: Held up, eff 3f out, sn held: bred for 1m+. *4* **62$**
2465 **FLAMEBIRD 28** [1] 3-8-9 P M Quinn (3) 40/1: -005: Dwelt/held up, no threat: mod form prev. *½* **61**
-- **CARRIE CAN CAN** [4] 3-8-9 Dean McKeown 20/1: 6: Dwelt/held up, al bhd: debut: dam a 10f wnr. *¾* **60**
2188 **REDHILL 39** [6] 3-8-9 A Hawkins (7) 20/1: 0657: Prom 6f: see 1922. *nk* **59**
7 ran Time 1m 46.3 (6.9) (Ellway Racing) B Hanbury Newmarket, Suffolk

NEWMARKET FRIDAY AUGUST 4TH Righthand, Stiff, Galloping Track

Official Going GOOD Stalls: Far side, Except Race 6 - Stands Side

3117 **6.00 BOOTLEG BEATLES SELLER 3YO+ (E) 1m str Good/Firm 32 -13 Slow**
£3913 £1204 £602 £301 3 yo rec 7 lb

2802 **TOUJOURS RIVIERA 14** [13] J Pearce 10-9-5 J F Egan 100/30: 02/001: 10 ch g Rainbow Quest - Miss Beaulieu (Northfields) Rcd alone stands side, led, hung badly left for press appr fnl 1f, styd on strongly, drvn out: no bid: well btn sole '99 start, in '98 won at Lingfield (h'cap, rtd 80a & 76): eff over 1m/12f on firm, soft & both AWs: acts on any trk: retains ability & apprec drop to sell grade. **52**
2964 **TERM OF ENDEARMENT 7** [6] J Pearce 3-8-7 J Quinn 12/1: 052002: 3 b f First Trump - Twilight Secret (Vaigly Great) Prom, rdn to improve over 2f out, ran on, no threat to wnr: quick reapp: ran to form of 2413 (7f). *1¼* **43**
2861 **SAIFAN 12** [9] D Morris 11-9-5 (vis) R Cochrane 2/1 FAV: 0-0023: 11 ch g Beveled - Superfrost (Tickled Pink) Rear, rdn/prog over 2f out, styd on ins last, nrst fin: 11yo, in gd heart: see 2861, 2411. *½* **47**
1335 **PRIVATE SEAL 79** [4] Julian Poulton 5-9-5 (t) G Faulkner (3) 25/1: 566004: Led far side, drvn & wknd fnl 1f: 11 wk abs: not disgraced at these weights tho' treat rating with caution: see 262. *1¼* **44$**
2315 **DISTANT FLAME 34** [3] 3-8-7 D Harrison 25/1: -00005: Mid-div, mod late gains, no threat: mod form. *1½* **36**
-- **MODEL GROOM** [7] 4-9-5 N Pollard 33/1: 6: Mid-div at best, Flat bow: t.o. bmpr rnr in April. *nk* **40**
2538 **ARTFUL DANE 25** [5] 8-9-5 (vis) G Duffield 8/1: 050307: Prom, rdn/fdd fnl 2f: op 7/1: see 2331, 1407. *6* **31**
1210 **GAME TUFTY 87** [12] 4-9-5 S Whitworth 10/1: 10-008: Nvr a factor: op 8/1, 12 wk abs: btr 1210 (10f). *2½* **26**
2194 **HAMERKOP 39** [10] 5-9-0 D Williamson (7) 33/1: 05-049: Al well in rear: see 2194. *5* **11**
2728 **ALFAHAAL 17** [2] 7-9-5 G Bardwell 20/1: 000000: Handy, wknd rapidly halfway, eased/t.o. fin 10th. *3½* **11**
2726 **FORT KNOX 17** [8] 9-9-5 (bl) O Urbina 25/1: 00-660: U.r. & bolted to post, sn t.o., 11th. *16* **0**
2758 **PHILISTAR 16** [11] 7-9-5 (bl) L Newton 16/1: 036000: Also u.r. & bolted to post, al well bhd, 12th. *12* **0**
12 ran Time 1m 40.8 (3.6) (The Fantasy Fellowship) J Pearce Newmarket

3118 **6.30 H&K COMMISSIONS HCAP 3YO+ 0-80 (D) 1m str Good/Firm 32 -03 Slow** **[79]**
£4582 £1410 £705 £352 3 yo rec 7 lb

2492 **SMOOTH SAILING 27** [2] K McAuliffe 5-9-12 (77) O Urbina 16/1: 040051: 5 gr g Beveled - Sea Farer Lake (Gairloch) Front rank, outpcd over 3f out, switched/hdwy appr fnl 1f, ran on strongly to lead cl-home, drvn out: jockey rec a 3-day careless riding ban: 99/00 hdle scorer at Leicester (nov, rtd 98h, 2m, soft): rnr-up on the Flat in '99 (rtd 90), prev term scored at Leicester (h'cap, rtd 88): eff around 1m on fast, soft & a stiff trk. **82**
*2232 **GWENDOLINE 37** [3] J R Fanshawe 3-9-8 (80) R Cochrane 6/1: 212: 3 b f Polar Falcon - Merlins Charm (Bold Bidder) Prom, hdwy to lead appr fnl 1f, sn clr, collared cl-home: stays 1m: lightly rcd, win again. *½* **83**
360 **KHALED 197** [10] K Mahdi 5-9-1 (66) D McGaffin (5) 40/1: /50-03: 5 b g Petorius - Felin Special (Lyphards Special) Led, hdd appr fnl 1f, ev ch until no extra well ins last: fine eff after a 6 month abs: see 360. *1¼* **66**
3063 **SOCIAL CONTRACT 3** [9] R Hannon 3-9-7 (79) J F Egan 13/2: -00134: In tch, rdn to improve 2f out, no extra fnl 1f: quick reapp: stays 1m, prev best at 7f: see 2026. *1¾* **76**
4456} **BYZANTIUM GB 288** [13] 6-9-3 (68) W Ryan 16/1: 2350-5: Prom, dropped rear over 2f out, ran on strongly ins last, no danger: recent rnr-up over hdles (mdn, rtd 87h, 2m, gd, H Daly): '99 Flat scorer at Windsor (h'cap, rtd 71 at best, M Fetherston Godley): late '98 Lingfield wnr (2, h'caps, rtd 72a): eff over 1m/10f & likes firm/fast & equitrack: best on a sharp trk: runs well fresh, tried a visor: now with W Jarvis. *hd* **64**
2768 **PROSPECTORS COVE 16** [5] 7-9-3 (68) D Harrison 12/1: 010466: Sltly hmpd after start, rear, gd hdwy to chall over 2f out, no extra when hmpd just ins last: nicely bckd: see 2768, 1611. *½* **63**
2727 **LYCIAN 17** [4] 5-8-6 (57) S Whitworth 10/1: -60347: Front rank, rdn/held over 2f out: see 2199 (10f). *nk* **51**
2802 **DERRYQUIN 14** [8] 5-8-7 (58)(bl) D O'Donohoe 12/1: 102048: Pulled v hard, nvr dngrs: btr 2802. *¾* **51**
3018 **ITS MAGIC 5** [15] 4-9-4 (69)(bl) Dane O'Neill 5/2 FAV: 6-0629: Rcd keenly in tch, rdn/fdd appr fnl 1f, eased when btn: well bckd: better expected after 2018 & this poss came too sn. *nk* **61**
2999 **ELLWAY PRINCE 6** [14] 5-8-0 (51) J Quinn 7/1: 143240: Nvr a factor, fin 10th: btr 2752. *2½* **38**
2958 **SYLVA LEGEND 7** [11] 4-9-3 (68)(tvi) B Marcus 20/1: 603300: Chsd ldrs, wknd qckly fnl 2f: qck reapp. *½* **54**
2542 **TRYSOR 25** [12] 4-8-1 (52) N Pollard 33/1: 00000: Dwelt, al bhd, 12th: mod form. *4* **30**
2768 **FALLACHAN 16** [7] 4-9-13 (78) P Robinson 12/1: 044030: In tch, wknd qckly fnl 2f, 13th: btr 2768 (7f). *5* **46**
2860 **CHASE THE BLUES 13** [1] 3-8-12 (70) J Stack 16/1: -6500: Prom 4f, wknd rapidly, fin last: h'cap bow. *2½* **33**
14 ran Time 1m 40.00 (2.8) (A R Parrish) K McAuliffe Lambourn, Berks

3119 **7.00 VARDY HCAP 3YO+ 0-90 (C) 6f Good/Firm 32 -03 Slow** **[88]**
£7553 £2324 £1162 £581 3 yo rec 4 lb

2158 **POINT OF DISPUTE 41** [8] P J Makin 5-9-6 (80)(vis) A Clark 9/2: 01-441: 5 b g Cyrano de Bergerac - Opuntia (Rousillon) Dwelt, settled rear, switched/hdwy over 1f out, styd on strongly to lead cl-home, hands & heels: 6 wk abs: '99 Lingfield & Nottingham wnr (h'caps, rtd 80), prev term won at Salisbury (mdn, rtd 86): **86**

suited by 6/7f on fast & gd, any trk: best in a visor: likes coming late: improving, win again in this form.
2925 **DIAMOND GEEZER 9** [7] R Hannon 4-8-7 (67) Dane O'Neill 3/1 FAV: 061422: 4 br c Tenby - Unaria (Prince Tenderfoot) Front rank, went on appr fnl 1f, rdn/hdd cl-home, not btn far: remains in gd form. 1¼ 68
2986 **PEPPIATT 6** [2] N Bycroft 6-8-1 (61) J Quinn 11/2: 500253: 6 ch g Efisio - Fleur Du Val (Valiyar) Prom, rdn to chall appr fnl 1f, ev ch until no extra cl-home: 6 wk abs: well h'capped: see 667. *shd* 62
2977 **KAREEB 7** [9] W R Muir 3-8-13 (77)(bl) J Reid 11/1: 650034: Rcd alone centre trk, cl-up, drvn/onepcd ins last: quick reapp: gd run again in blnks but still a mdn: see 2977 (mdn). *hd* 77
2845 **OCKER 13** [10] 6-9-8 (82) G Duffield 12/1: 060455: Sn rdn in rear, late hdwy, no threat: see 47. ¾ 80
2694 **PREMIER BARON 20** [6] 5-9-3 (77) L Newman (3) 7/1: 064446: Waited with, rdn/prog over 2f out, no extra fnl 1f: both wins at 7f: see 2694 (7f). *hd* 74
2833 **DETECTIVE 14** [1] 4-7-13 (59) J Lowe 33/1: 200-57: Rcd keenly & sn led, drvn/hdd appr fnl 1f, wknd. 1¼ 52
2961 **BLACKHEATH 7** [4] 4-10-0 (88) S Whitworth 12/1: -00008: Held up, drvn/not qckn appr fnl 1f, top weight: quick reapp: see 1016. 3 75
2961 **POLES APART 7** [5] 4-9-3 (77)(vis) J F Egan 7/1: 000549: Prom, lost tch fnl 2f: qck reapp: btr 2961. 2½ 57
2697 **AT LARGE 20** [3] 6-9-1 (75) L Newton 8/1: 010000: Lost tch halfway, fin last: much btr 1545 (soft). 9 38
10 ran Time 1m 13.11 (2.11) (Mrs B J Carrington) P J Makin Ogbourne Maisey, Wilts

3120

7.30 EGERTON STUD FILLIES COND STKS 3YO+ (C) 6f Good/Firm 32 +07 Fast
£6461 £2450 £1225 £557 3 yo rec 4 lb

2335 **LITTLEFEATHER 34** [7] Sir Mark Prescott 3-8-7 G Duffield 2/1 FAV: 135-51: 3 b f Indian Ridge - Marwell (Habitat) Prom, eff appr fnl 1f, qcknd smartly for press to lead ins last, going away: gd time, hvly bckd: '99 hat-trick scorer at Ripon (mdn), Newmarket (nurs) & Chester (fill cond, Gr 1 3rd, rtd 107): eff at 6f, stays 7f on firm, gd/soft & any trk, likes Newmarket: smart & prog, her turn of foot can secure a Gr win. 108
2646 **JEZEBEL 21** [1] C F Wall 3-8-2 R Mullen 100/30: 1-2532: 3 b f Owington - Just Ice (Polar Falcon) Held up, prog ent fnl 3f, rdn to lead dist, hdd & outpcd towards fin: bckd: ran to best, tough: see 1078. 1¼ 100
2646 **FLOWINGTON 21** [4] N P Littmoden 3-8-2 J Quinn 16/1: 504203: 3 b f Owington - Persian Flower (Persian Heights) Chsd ldrs, ch appr fnl 1f, kept on same pace: stiff task, ran v well, likes Newmarket. 1¾ 96
3989} **FEMME FATALE 321** [9] W Jarvis 3-8-7 R Cochrane 4/1: 4231-4: Pld hard, cl-up, led 2f out till dist, no extra: reapp: won fnl '99 start at Ayr (List, rtd 108): eff at 6f on fast & gd, gall trk: sharper for this. ½ 99
2568 **PRESENTATION 24** [8] 3-8-2 J F Egan 16/1: 326605: In tch, outpcd appr fnl 1f: stiffish task, see 1534. 2 89
2847 **TABHEEJ 13** [10] 3-8-7 R Hills 10/1: 3-6006: Trkd ldrs, fdd appr fnl 1f: see 1338. *hd* 93
2476 **FAIRY GEM 28** [3] 3-8-2 L Newman (3) 14/1: -04667: Dwelt, nvr in it: unsuited by drop in trip?: see 995. ½ 86
2567 **PERUGIA 24** [6] 3-8-2 J Lowe 25/1: 00-048: Keen, al towards rear: left B Hills for K McAuliffe. 2½ 79
2568 **JEMIMA 24** [2] 3-8-13 J Fortune 11/1: 000069: Bhd from halfway: see 953. ¾ 88
2669 **ROWAASI 20** [5] 3-8-2 Craig Williams 10/1: 4-0040: Led till 2f out, sn btn: 10th, better at 5f: see 1090. *nk* 76
10 ran Time 1m 12.5 (1.5) (Sir Edmund Loder) Sir Mark Prescott Newmarket

3121

8.00 EBF HUGO MDN 2YO (D) 7f str Good/Firm 32 -19 Slow
£4251 £1308 £654 £327

2867 **STORMING HOME 12** [10] B W Hills 2-9-0 J Reid 16/1: -01: 2 b c Machiavellian - Try To Catch Me (Shareef Dancer) In tch, wide, rdn 3f out, hdwy ent fnl 2f, pshd into lead below dist, shade cmftbly: Feb foal, half-brother to a 7f 2yo wnr: dam & sire milers: eff at 7f on fast grnd, 1m sure to suit: improve & win again. 100+
2563 **CANADA 24** [4] B W Hills 2-9-0 G Duffield 3/1: 42: 2 b c Ezzoud - Chancel (Al Nasr) Led till 2f out, not pace of wnr ins last: much shorter priced stablemate of wnr: rtd higher on debut but has shown more than enough to find a mdn: acts on fast & gd grnd. 2½ 92
2854 **MODRIK 13** [3] R W Armstrong 2-9-0 R Hills 14/1: -03: 2 ch g Dixieland Band - Seattle Summer (Seattle Slew) Chsd ldrs, eff appr fnl 1f, styd on but not pace to threaten: apprec step up to 7f, win at 1m. *shd* 92$
-- **TEMPEST** [5] Sir Michael Stoute 2-9-0 Pat Eddery 1/1 FAV: 4: Prom, chall appr fnl 1f, sn onepace, kind ride: well bckd newcomer: Zafonic Mar foal, dam & sire milers: handles fast grnd, improve. 1¼ 89
-- **NATIVE TITLE** [7] 2-9-0 R Cochrane 25/1: 5: Held up, imprvd 2f out, held when eased below dist: 15,000 gns Pivotal Feb foal, half-brother to sev wnrs, incl juvs, dam & sire sprinters: not given a hard time. 1½ 86
2708 **FOLLOW YOUR STAR 19** [9] 2-9-0 B Marcus 5/1: 66: Chsd ldrs till 2f out: see 2708. *hd* 85
-- **TEDSTALE** [2] 2-9-0 J P Spencer 9/1: 7: Handy till lost place 2f out: 65,000lr gns Irish River Feb foal, dam a wnr in the States, sire a miler: with L Cumani. 2½ 80
-- **MAY PRINCESS** [8] 2-8-9 D McGaffin (5) 33/1: 8: Al towards rear: 500 gns Prince Sabo 1st foal. 5 65
2686 **RED DEER 20** [6] 2-9-0 P Robinson 33/1: 09: Dwelt, chsd ldrs till halfway: see 2686. 5 60
2959 **GAY CHALLENGER 7** [1] 2-9-0 W Ryan 33/1: -50: Sn struggling: 10th. 12 42
10 ran Time 1m 27.5 (3.6) (Maktoum Al Maktoum) B W Hills Lambourn, Berks

3122

8.30 WICKEN FEN HCAP 3YO+ 0-80 (D) 1m4f Good/Firm 32 -20 Slow [75]
£4368 £1340 £672 £336 3 yo rec 11lb

2865 **FAHS 12** [7] N Hamilton 8-10-0 (75) Dane O'Neill 9/2: 250121: 8 b g Riverman - Tanwi (Vision) In tch, clsd 2f out, burst thro' & qcknd to lead dist, pushed clr, cmftbly: bckd: prev won at Yarmouth (h'cap): '99 wnr at Yarmouth (rtd 77) & Lingfield (h'cap, rtd 79a): '98 wnr at Lingfield (amat h'cap, rtd 80a & 81): eff at 10/12f, stays 14f on firm, gd & equitrack, handles soft, likes Yarmouth: suited coming late: qk follow-up? 82
2982 **ORDAINED 7** [5] Miss Gay Kelleway 7-7-12 (45) Martin Dwyer 4/1 FAV: 004122: 7 b m Mtoto - In The Habit (Lyphard) Patiently rdn, imprvd 3f out, switched dist, kept on, no ch wnr: nicely bckd, quick reapp. 3 46
2836 **BLUE STREET 13** [11] S C Williams 4-8-12 (59) G Faulkner (3) 9/1: 006023: 4 b c Deploy - Kumzar (Hotfoot) Led till 1f out, no extra: poss stays a stiff 12f, sharper trk or a drop back to 10f likely to suit: see 2836. *shd* 60
2689 **NORCROFT JOY 20** [6] N A Callaghan 5-9-13 (74) Pat Eddery 9/2: 333104: Held up, prog & not clr run appr fnl 1f, kept on, nvr dangerous: nicely bckd: gd run & worth another ch after 2482. ½ 74
2540 **SUDDEN FLIGHT 25** [3] 3-9-6 (78) J Reid 5/1: -13025: Pulled hard in tch, imprvg when hmpd, snatched up 2f out, nvr nr ldrs: worth another try at 14f: see 2540, 924. *nk* 77
2461 **FIERY WATERS 28** [8] 4-8-2 (49) J Quinn 12/1: 00-006: Prom & ev ch till fdd appr fnl 1f: drop back to 10f? 3 44
2832 **BOLD PRECEDENT 14** [10] 3-9-3 (75) J P Spencer 12/1: 0-4347: Well plcd till 2f out: lngr trip. *nk* 69
2530 **FANTAIL 26** [4] 6-10-0 (75) G Duffield 16/1: 00/008: In tch till 2f out: joint top weight, see 2530. ½ 68
2626 **PRODIGAL SON 22** [2] 5-9-8 (69)(bl) L Newman (3) 12/1: -36039: Chsd ldrs, wknd qckly appr fnl 2f. 5 55
2319 **IL PRINCIPE 34** [1] 6-9-1 (62) J F Egan 12/1: 000000: Al bhd: 10th, has been tubed. 12 35
10 ran Time 1m 34.42 (6.22) (City Industrial Supplies Ltd) N Hamilton Epsom, Surrey

Official Going GOOD (GOOD/SOFT places). Stalls: Round - Inside; Str - Stands Side.

3123 2.00 P BELL HCAP 3YO+ 0-80 (D) 6f str Good/Firm 20 +23 Fast [79]
£4624 £1423 £711 £355 3 yo rec 4 lb 2 Groups - Stands Side favoured

1082 **MILL END QUEST** 94 [10] M W Easterby 5-7-11 (48)(bl) Dale Gibson 16/1: 000-01: 5 b m King's Signet - 56
Milva (Jellaby) Made most stands side, kept on but drifted left ins last, drvn out: fast time, 3 month abs:
'99 scorer at Pontefract (fills h'cap, rtd 59): eff over 5/6f on fast, soft & any trk: has tried blnks: runs
well h'cap: improved for re-application of blnks today.

-2929 **WILLIAMS WELL** 9 [20] M W Easterby 6-9-3 (68)(bl) T Lucas 13/2 FAV: 655222: 6 ch g Superpower - 2 70
Catherines Well (Junius) With ldrs stands side, trav well over 1f out, onepace for press over 1f out: stablemate
of wnr: often plcd & all 5 wins over 5f: see 2929.

2877 **BENZOE** 11 [6] D Nicholls 10-8-6 (57) Iona Wands 9/1: 506153: 10 b g Taufan - Saintly Guest (What A 2½ 52
Guest) Slow away, made far side, kept on over 1f out, nvr dangerous: gd run from unfav trk: v tough, see 2701.

2969 **LUANSHYA** 7 [16] R M Whitaker 4-9-0 (65) Dean McKeown 14/1: 400034: Handy stands side, onepace nk 59
over 1f out: better off in fills h'cap: see 2969, 1514.

*2744 **BLACK ARMY** 16 [19] M W Easterby 5-8-12 (63) A Culhane 14/1: 0-0515: Handy stands side, onepace over 1f out: hd 56
now with K Ryan & ran to form of 2744 (sell).

2969 **CRUSTY LILY** 7 [18] 4-7-10 (47)(4oh) Claire Bryan (5) 16/1: 420066: In tch stands side, eff over 1½ 36
1f out, sn no impress: see 2415, 2221.

*2932 **ENCOUNTER** 9 [17] 4-7-10 (47)(1oh) J McAuley 13/2: 052117: Sn rdn stands side, some late gains: ½ 34
needs 7f or a stiffer trk: in fine form earlier, see 2932.

2987 **EURO VENTURE** 6 [12] 5-9-12 (77) W Supple 10/1: 161448: In tch stands side, no extra over 1f out. ½ 63

2877 **FULL SPATE** 11 [21] 5-9-5 (70) P Fitzsimons (5) 11/4: 541039: Handy stands side, sltly short of room hd 55
2f out, no impress: see 2877, best 2444.

1383 **BLAKESET** 76 [5] 5-8-11 (62) D Mernagh (3) 20/1: 000060: Led far side group till over 1f out: 10th. ½ 45

2694 **COOL PROSPECT** 20 [13] 5-8-9 (60)(vis) F Lynch 12/1: 232200: In tch stands, wknd over 1f out: 11th. hd 42

2976 **SWINO** 7 [7] 6-7-10 (47)(vis)(1oh) Joanna Badger (7) 10/1: 000200: Al bhd far side, fin last: untrustworthy. 0

2775 Dandy Regent 15 [1] 6-8-4 (55) K Dalgleish (5) 16/1: 2820 **Rioja** 14 [14] 5-8-12 (63) T Williams 14/1:
2969 Crystal Lass 7 [2] 4-7-10 (47)(7oh) S Righton 25/1: 2348 **Ziggys Dancer** 33 [8] 9-9-13 (78) L Swift (7) 16/1:
1250 Demolition Jo 85 [15] 5-9-7 (72)(BL) T G McLaughlin 16/1:
2247 Classy Cleo 37 [3] 5-9-8 (73) J Weaver 20/1:
2777 Kosevo 15 [9] 6-7-10 (47)(bl)(8oh) P Fessey 33/1: 2743 **Piggy Bank** 16 [11] 4-8-2 (53) G Parkin 25/1:
2830 Rum Lad 14 [4] 6-8-7 (58) R Winston 20/1:
21 ran Time 1m 09.3 (u0.2) (W T Allgood) M W Easterby Sheriff Hutton, N Yorks

3124 2.35 DUNNINGTON MDN HCAP 3YO+ 0-70 (E) 6f str Good/Firm 20 -03 Slow [59]
£4137 £1273 £636 £318 3 yo rec 4 lb 2 Groups - Stands Favoured

2896 **LUCKYS SON** 11 [13] J L Dunlop 3-8-7 (42) Paul Eddery 5/2 FAV: 000021: 3 gr g Lucky Guest - 47
April Wind (Windjammer) Handy stands side, led that group halfway, kept on ins last, hands & heels: poor race:
has flashed tail in the past: stays 6f on firm & fast grnd, easy trk.

2662 **MEGS PEARL** 21 [17] W M Brisbourne 4-8-10 (41)(BL) T G McLaughlin 20/1: 00-0R2: 4 grf Petong - ½ 43
Heaven Leigh Grey (Grey Desire) Handy stands side, eff over 1f out, kept on ins last: better run in first time
blnks but looks a v hard ride (refused to race last time) & best kept to this company: stays 6f on fast grnd.

2840 **COLONEL SAM** 13 [14] S R Bowring 4-8-9 (40)(bl) Dean McKeown 12/1: 0040R3: 4 b g Puissance - 2 36
Indian Summer (Young Generation) Slow away, hdwy halfway, late gains: like rnr-up also refused last time out.

2315 **SILVER TONGUED** 34 [18] J M Bradley 4-7-13 (30) Claire Bryan (5) 8/1: 000604: In tch stands side, 1½ 22
onepace over 1f out: see 1275.

2421 **BRITTAS BLUES** 30 [2] 3-9-1 (50) J Fanning 8/1: -0345: With ldrs far side, led that group over hd 41
1f out, onepace: see 2313.

3103 **RED JAMES** 2 [16] 3-8-9 (44) C Teague 16/1: 0-0066: Handy stands side, btn over 1f out. ½ 33

2047 **EMMA AMOUR** 46 [19] 3-8-9 (44) T Lucas 12/1: -00007: Led stands side group till halfway, no extra. hd 32

3035 **KIND EMPEROR** 4 [10] 3-10-0 (63) R Fitzpatrick (3) 12/1: 04R028: Sn rdn stands side, no impress. ½ 49

3056 **RUDCROFT** 3 [12] 4-7-10 (27)(7oh) J McAuley 33/1: 000009: Al bhd stands side: quick reapp. ½ 12

2779 **FANTASY ADVENTURER** 15 [15] 3-9-3 (52) R Winston 6/1: 040400: Slowly away, al bhd: 10th. ¾ 35

2555 Go Sally Go 25 [9] 4-7-11 (28) Angela Hartley (5) 16/1:2969 **Countess Parker** 7 [20] 4-9-3 (48) J Weaver 14/1:
2728 Flying Memory 17 [1] 4-8-2 (33) P Fitzsimons (3) 20/12621 **Bold Emma** 22 [11] 3-9-11 (60) R Studholme (5) 25/1:
2658 Lioness 21 [3] 4-8-3 (34)(BL) T Williams 25/1: 2511 **Madame Genereux** 27 [6] 3-9-4 (53) W Supple 20/1:
3103 Abco Boy 2 [5] 3-8-6 (41)(bl) P Goode (3) 25/1: 1600 **Silver Socks** 65 [4] 3-9-1 (50) G Parkin 20/1:
2315 Sounds Special 34 [7] 3-9-1 (50)(BL) S Finnamore (5) 16/1:
19 ran Time 1m 10.9 (1.4) (Anamoine Ltd) J L Dunlop Arundel, W Sussex

3125 3.05 BARKERS FILLIES HCAP 3YO-70 (E) 1m4f Good/Firm 20 -22 Slow [77]
£3373 £1038 £519 £259

2771 **SWEET ANGELINE** 16 [11] G G Margarson 3-8-11 (60) G Hind 100/30: 005431: 3 b f Deploy - Fiveofive 65
(Fairy King) Waited with, gd hdwy to lead over 1f out, rdn to assert ins last: first win, nicely bckd: rtd 82
at best in '99: stays 12f well on firm/fast grnd & on any trk: prob best without a t-strap: on the upgrade.

2829 **MARJEUNE** 14 [8] P W Harris 3-9-4 (67) A Culhane 4/1 FAV: 041-02: 3 b f Marju - Ann Veronica 1 70
(Sadler's Wells) In tch, eff over 1f out, sn short of room, kept on late: would have gone closer with clr
run & stays 12f on fast, soft & on any trk: open to improvement, see 2829.

2811 **MOUJEEDA** 14 [4] W Jarvis 3-9-5 (68) W Supple 5/1: 0-5043: 3 ch f Zafonic - Definah (Graustark) ¾ 69
Led till over 1f out, no extra: poss just stays 12f on fast grnd: see 1281.

2837 **WINDMILL** 13 [1] T D Easterby 3-9-7 (70) J Weaver 6/1: -4144: Handy, rdn & onepace over 1f out. 2½ 67

2553 **OPTION** 25 [10] 3-8-5 (54) M Fenton 12/1: -5005: In tch, btn 2f out: mod, see 1912. 4 45

4614J **WHAT A CRACKER** 272 [5] 3-7-12 (47) A Daly 12/1: 000-6: Keen, handy, wknd 2f out: op 8/1: 1½ 36
well btn all 3 juv starts: bred to stay mid-dist.

2946 **PIX ME UP** 7 [6] 3-8-1 (50) Iona Wands 12/1: 400547: Sn bhd, mod late gains: much longer trip. nk 38

2450 **TOP HAND** 29 [9] 3-9-0 (63) O Pears 20/1: -40008: With ldrs, wknd 2f out: now with E Tuer: see 999. 4 45

3008 **BITTY MARY** 5 [3] 3-7-10 (45)(tvi)(11oh) K Dalgleish (5) 33/1: 000569: Slow away & al bhd: qk reapp. 2½ 23

2746 **GYMCRAK FIREBIRD** 16 [2] 3-7-12 (46)(1ow) D Mernagh (3) 16/1: 6-0000: Al bhd: see 171. 5 17

2370 **LA FAY 32** [7] 3-9-5 (68)(t) Paul Eddery 10/1: 4-0000: With ldrs till wknd qckly over 3f out: last, op 7/1. ½ **38**
11 ran Time 2m 34.8 (5) (Mrs T A Forman) G G Margarson Newmarket

3126 **3.40 QUEEN MOTHER MDN 3YO+ (D) 1m rnd Good/Firm 20 -10 Slow**
£4319 £1234 £617 3 yo rec 7 lb

-- **MOO AZ** [2] M P Tregoning 3-9-0 R Hills 1/2 FAV: 1: 3 b c Red Ransom - Fappies Cosy Miss (Fappiano) Chsd ldr, went on over 2f out, cmftly drew clr: well bckd: stays 1m well, further will suit: runs well fresh on gd/firm: pleasing debut, shld win again. **90**
2159 **CABALLE 41** [1] S P C Woods 3-8-9 N Callan 7/4: -23322: 3 ch f Opening Verse - Attirance (Crowned Prince) Set pace till over 2f out, held when sltly hmpd ins last: bckd: plcd all 6 starts: see 2159. *3* **78**
-- **MAYBEE** [3] J G Given 4-9-2 Dean McKeown 20/1: 3: 4 b f Then Again - Miss Ritz (Robellino) Slow away, al bhd: dam 7f scorer: bred to stay 1m+. *11* **56**
3 ran Time 1m 37.8 (2.4) (Hamdan Al Maktoum) M P Tregoning East Ilsley, Wilts

3127 **4.15 SMEATON CLAIMER DIV I 2YO (E) 7f rnd Good/Firm 20 -29 Slow**
£2388 £735 £367 £183

2361 **HARRIER 32** [5] T D Easterby 2-8-9 J Weaver 9/2: 3301: 2 b g Prince Of Birds - Casaveha (Persian Bold) Dsptd lead, went on over 2f out, easily: val 7L+: Jan foal, cost 4,000: suited by step up to 7f on fast grnd, handles soft: best up with/forcing the pace & apprec drop into claiming grade. **77**
*2949 **VISITATION 7** [1] K A Ryan 2-8-4 F Lynch 17/2: -012: 2 b f Bishop Of Cashel - Golden Envoy (Dayjur) Handy, rdn & kept on same pace over 1f out: prev with M Bell: handles fibresand & fast: sell wnr in 2949. *3½* **62**
2991 **FLOWING RIO 6** [11] P C Haslam 2-8-8 Dean McKeown 5/2: 01533: 2 b f First Trump - Deanta In Erinn (Red Sunset) Prom, rdn & onepace over 1f out: quick reapp, nicely bckd: btr 2991. *1¼* **64**
2927 **BORDER TERRIER 9** [4] R A Fahey 2-8-6 G Hind 20/1: 04: In tch, eff 2f out, sn no extra: see 2927. *3* **56**
1981 **JUST MISSED 49** [3] 2-8-4 G Parkin 33/1: -005: Slow away, bhd, late gains: 7 wk abs, see 1698. *¾* **52**
2841 **ORIGINAL SINNER 13** [8] 2-9-0 Paul Eddery 9/4 FAV: 646: In tch, rdn & no impress over 1f out: bckd from 7/2: btr expected after 2841. *hd* **61**
2927 **ABERFOLLY 9** [6] 2-7-13 Joanna Badger (7) 40/1: 067: In tch, short of room 2f out, no impress: bckd. *shd* **45**
2711 **MARE OF WETWANG 18** [7] 2-7-12 D Mernagh (3) 10/1: 608: In tch, wide, btn 2f out: flattered 2539. *3½* **37**
2927 **IMPISH LAD 9** [2] 2-8-4 (bl) M Fenton 9/1: 363239: Dsptd lead till over 2f out, wknd: btr 2927. *¾* **41**
2174 **LIGHT OF ARAGON 40** [10] 2-8-0 P Fessey 40/1: 000: In tch, wknd 2f out: abs: Mar foal, cost 3,000 gns: half sister to wnrs over 5f/7f: dam 1m sell scorer. *1¾* **33**
2120 **Tomamie 43** [12] 2-8-2 O Pears 40/1: -- **Mud N Bert** [9] 2-8-0 T Williams 40/1:
12 ran Time 1m 26.3 (3.4) (The Rumpole Partnership) T D Easterby Great Habton, N Yorks

3128 **4.50 SMEATON CLAIMER DIV II 2YO (E) 7f rnd Good/Firm 20 -33 Slow**
£2388 £735 £367 £183

2894 **FAZZANI 11** [7] M R Channon 2-8-2 P Fessey 11/4: 444301: 2 b f Shareef Dancer - Taj Victory (Final Straw) Hmpd start, sn recovered to lead, made rest, rdn out: Mar foal: full sister to a 1m wnr: dam 10/13f scorer: stays 7f & handles fast & soft grnd: further will suit in time & relished this drop into claiming grade. **63**
2182 **EMMA CLARE 40** [8] J A Osborne 2-8-4 G Hind 12/1: 0002: 2 b f Namaqualand - Medicosma (The Minstrel) Hmpd start, in tch, chall over 1f out, not pace of wnr ins last: abs: better run over 7f on fast. *1* **63**
*2927 **GAZETTE IT TONIGHT 9** [3] A Berry 2-8-1 O Pears 7/1: 563313: 2 b f Merdon Melody - Balidilemma (Balidar) Handy, ev ch over 1f out, sn onepace: ran to form of 2927 (sell). *1* **58**
2778 **JEZADIL 15** [9] M Dods 2-8-4 T Williams 11/1: -0644: With ldr, rdn & onepace over 1f out: stays 7f. *¾* **59**
2678 **SOMERS HEATH 20** [2] 2-8-6 G Parkin 9/4 FAV: -00105: In tch, onepace over 1f out: bckd, btr 1981. *½* **60**
2668 **PAT PINKNEY 20** [5] 2-8-1 W Supple 12/1: 054546: Went right start, in tch will wknd 2f out: see 2668. *5* **45**
2161 **TIP THE SCALES 41** [6] 2-8-9 (VIS) V Halliday 14/1: 057: Hmpd start, nvr a factor: tried a visor. *½* **52**
2828 **THE MERRY WIDOW 14** [10] 2-8-4 Joanna Badger (7) 25/1: 08: Slow away, al bhd: May foal, cheaply bought: half sister to a 5f juv wnr: with B Rothwell. *1* **45**
-- **BODFARI MILLENNIUM** [1] 2-8-11 T Lucas 20/1: 9: Al bhd on debut: Feb foal, cost 4,500 gns: half brother to 2 wnrs: with M W Easterby. *nk* **51**
2927 **CHORUS GIRL 9** [11] 2-7-12 Iona Wands 20/1: 304650: Hmpd start, sn cl-up till wknd 2f out: 10th. *2½* **33**
3055 **MIDDLEHAMPARKFLYER 3** [4] 2-7-12 G Sparkes (4) 33/1: 00: Al bhd: fin last: Feb foal, cost 6,500 gns. *½* **32**
11 ran Time 1m 26.6 (3.7) (Denjen Racing) M R Channon Upper Lambourn, Berks

3129 **5.20 APPR MDN HCAP 3YO+ 0-70 (E) 7f rnd Good/Firm 20 -20 Slow** **[56]**
£2814 £866 £433 £216 3 yo rec 6 lb

2315 **LIONS DOMANE 34** [15] P C Haslam 3-8-7 (41) G Sparkes 6/1: -26061: 3 b g Lion Cavern - Vilany (Never So Bold) Handy, hdwy to lead over 2f out, pushed clr ins last: mod prev (rtd 50a at best): best up with/forcing the pace around 7f on gd/firm & fibresand: this was a v weak contest. **49**
2994 **ROYAL REPRIMAND 6** [13] R E Barr 5-8-1 (29) L Enstone (5) 5/1 FAV: 000052: 5 b g Reprimand - Lake Ormond (King's Lake) Handy, rdn & onepace over 1f out: quick reapp, flattered 2994: see 2147. *5* **28**
2840 **ARZILLO 13** [12] J M Bradley 4-9-6 (48) P Shea 11/1: 340403: 4 b g Forzando - Titania's Dance (Fairy King) In tch, onepace over 1f out: see 1211. *1¼* **45**
2840 **HEATHER VALLEY 13** [1] W J Haggas 4-9-2 (44) M Worrell (3) 6/1: 0-0554: In tch, onepace over 1f out. *½* **40**
2561 **EMLEY 24** [10] 4-9-1 (43) D Allan (3) 10/1: -60005: Led till over 2f out, wknd: see 1818. *1¼* **37**
2839 **PETRA NOVA 13** [7] 4-8-4 (32) R Thomas 33/1: 00-006: Handy, wknd 2f out: mod. *nk* **25**
3103 **ENTITY 2** [14] 3-9-9 (57) Lynsey Hanna 11/1: 000507: Waited with, wide & hung right into str, nvr dngrs. *½* **49**
2970 **PIPIJI 7** [2] 5-8-2 (30) Angela Hartley 16/1: 000408: Nvr a factor: best 2601. *½* **21**
2223 **DON QUIXOTE 38** [9] 4-8-8 (36) T Hamilton (3) 6/1: 060009: Slowly away, al bhd: see 1994. *2½* **22**
1326} **BLOOD ORANGE 447** [5] 6-8-7 (35) Kristin Stubbs (3) 33/1: 00/0-0: In tch, wknd 2f out: 10th, poor. *1* **19**
2147 **SWYNFORD ELEGANCE 42** [11] 3-8-10 (44) A Robertson (3) 10/1: -02000: In tch, wknd 2f out: 11th, abs *2½* **23**
2839 **BLAKEY 13** [4] 4-8-2 (30)(bl) Clare Roche 7/1: 000050: Al bhd: fin 14th: see 2839. **0**
2853} **Katie Hawk 378** [16] 6-7-10 (24)(1oh) R Naylor (3) 100/1:
4303} **Beau Chevalier 298** [6] 4-9-10 (52) M Mathers (3) 33/1:
1134 **Mr Stickywicket 92** [8] 3-7-12 (32) Hayley Turner (3) 33/1:
15 ran Time 1m 25.7 (2.8) (Mrs C Barclay) P C Haslam Middleham, N Yorks

Official Going   GOOD.   Stalls: Str Crse - Stands Side; Rnd Crse - Inside; 1m4f - Outside

---

3130   **2.15 BONUSPRINT HCAP 3YO 0-100 (C)   7f rnd   Good/Firm 20 -08 Slow**   [101]
£29250   £9000   £4500   £2250

2645 **ZIETZIG 21** [10] K R Burke 3-8-2 (75) J F Egan 33/1: 006401: 3 b c Zieten - Missing You (Ahonoora)   81
Switched to ins rail, made all, rdn out, unchall: well ridden: '99 York wnr (sell, rtd 84 at best): eff at
6/7f on firm/fast grnd, handles gd/soft: likes to be up with/forcing the pace on sharp trks: well ridden.

*2855 **CAPRICHO 13** [18] W J Haggas 3-8-11 (84) T Quinn 9/4 FAV: -2112: 3 gr g Lake Coniston - Star   1½ 87
Spectacle (Spectacular Bid) Mid-div, kept on ent fnl 2f, chsd wnr ins last, unable to chall: hvly bckd: lost
little in defeat, continues on the upgrade & can win again over further or on a stiffer trk: see 2855.

2922 **SHADOW PRINCE 9** [15] R Charlton 3-8-5 (78) S Sanders 11/2: -50133: 3 ch g Machiavellian -   nk 80
Shadywood (Habitat) Towards rear, rdn halfway, kept on appr fnl 1f, nvr nrr: hvly bckd: prob improved
again in this competitive race: can win again, prob when stepped up to 1m: see 2922, 2261.

3107 **ATLANTIC RHAPSODY 1** [7] M Johnston 3-9-7 (94) D Holland 12/1: 256054: Held up, not much room   nk 95
fnl 2f, kept on strongly once clr bef dist, nrst fin: ran a similar race to yesterday, drop back to 7f against him.

2986 **KIND REGARDS 6** [19] 3-8-8 (82) J Reid 12/1: 052545: Towards rear, hmpd bend, prog ent fnl 2f,   shd 83
kept on well: quick reapp, swtg, bckd from 16/1, stablemate 4th: return to 1m will suit, see 1366.

*2568 **BLUE VELVET 24** [1] 3-9-3 (90) C Carver (3) 33/1: 000116: Wide, in tch, prog to dspte 3rd 2f out,   ½ 90
same pace: hat-trick attempt: fine run from poor draw over longer 7f trip, 6f prob best trip: see 2568.

3410} **MERSEY MIRAGE 353** [4] R Hughes 50/1: 1302-7: Prom, rdn appr fnl 2f, fdd bef fnl 1f: ½ 85
reapp: '99 wnr at Brighton (mdn, rtd 87): eff at 6f & a return to that trip shld suit: acts on firm &
gd/soft grnd, sharp/undul trk: encouraging reapp from a poor draw.

2885 **CD FLYER 11** [17] 3-8-1 (74) A Nicholls (3) 14/1: 446338: Rear, hdwy & short of room over 2f   nk 72
out, kept on late, no danger: would have gone closer with clear run & interesting next time at this trip.

2762 **TEODORA 16** [8] 3-8-13 (86)(t) M Roberts 33/1: 006209: Last, switched & kept on fnl 1½f, nvr on terms: hd 84
caught the eye: see 2567.

2003 **RENDITION 48** [6] 3-9-2 (89) F Norton 14/1: 0-1130: Boxed in towards rear for most of the 1st   ¾ 85
5f, kept on late: 10th: forget this, stablemate of rnr-up: see 2003, 1308.

2813 **ROO 14** [2] 3-9-5 (92) S Carson (3) 33/1: 532250: Nvr better than mid-div: 11th, btr 1887, 912.   nk 87

839 **WIND CHIME 119** [9] 3-8-5 (78) P Robinson 33/1: 24-20: Chsd ldrs, lost place appr fnl 1f: 12th: 1¾ 69
4 month abs, h'cap bow, may apprec a drop back to 6f: see 839.

*1470 **CAMBERLEY 72** [13] 3-9-6 (93) K Darley 7/2: -32210: Mid-div, eff 3f out, no impress, hmpd bef   nk 83
dist: 13th, hvly bckd: reportedly broke a blood vessel: C/D wnr in 1470.

2954 **GLENROCK 7** [14] 3-9-2 (89) A McGlone 33/1: 650200: Well plcd till 2f out, sn btn & hmpd: 14th.   nk 78

2495 **Lagoon 27** [5] 3-9-7 (94) M Hills 20/1:   2177 **Budelli 40** [11] 3-8-7 (80) Craig Williams 20/1:

2922 **Norfolk Reed 9** [12] 3-8-12 (85)(BL) Dane O'Neill 33/1:   2900 **Castle Sempill 10** [3] 3-8-3 (76) R Mullen 50/1:

18 ran   Time 1m 26.45 (1.95)   (Nigel Shields)   K R Burke Newmarket

---

3131   **2.45 VOLVO TRUCK HCAP 3YO 0-110 (B)   1m2f   Good/Firm 20 +09 Fast**   [109]
£32500   £10000   £5000   £2500

*2995 **HAPPY DIAMOND 6** [9] M Johnston 3-9-6 (101)(7ex) J Reid 15/2: 22D111: 3 b c Diesis - Urus (Kris S)   109
Mid-div, kept on appr fnl 2f & grad reeled in ldr to get up towards fin, going away: gd time: hat-trick after wins
at Doncaster (h'cap) & Ascot (rtd h'cap), earlier disqual after wng at Doncaster: '99 Thirsk wnr (mdn, rtd 87):
suited by 10f, stay further: acts on fast & gd grnd, any trk: progressive, v useful & game, win a List/Gr race.

*2713 **STARLYTE GIRL 18** [7] R Hannon 3-8-9 (90) L Newman (3) 16/1: 601212: 3 b f Fairy King - Blushing   1¼ 95
Storm (Blushing Groom) Set gd clip & tried to make all, worn down well ins last: a game attempt & clr of rem.

-2116 **WATER JUMP 43** [2] J L Dunlop 3-9-0 (95) T Quinn 11/4 FAV: 21-123: 3 b c Suave Dancer - Jolies   3 95
Eaux (Shirley Heights) Towards rear, styd on fnl 2f, nvr nr ldrs: 6 wk abs, hvly bckd: ran well tho' appeared
unsuited by drop back to a sharp 10f: can regain winning thread at 12f: see 2116, 1177.

*2937 **RICH VEIN 8** [5] S P C Woods 3-8-0 (80)(1ow)(4ex) R Mullen 4/1: 211214: Bhd, kept on appr   1 79
fnl 2f, nvr nrr: poss shade too sn under a pen after 2937: see 2937.

2596 **FATHER JUNINHO 23** [13] K Darley 3-8-12 (93) 652335: Held up, prog halfway, onepace ent fnl 3f.   1 90

2594 **TANTALUS 23** [11] 3-9-3 (98)(t) M Hills 20/1: -13406: Bhd, nvr a factor: found things happening   3 91
much to qckly over this shorter 10f trip, see 1216, 713.

*3048 **HIGHLAND REEL 4** [3] 3-8-6 (87)(4ex) N Pollard 8/1: 303317: V keen, prsd ldr till wknd 3f out: qk reapp   nk 79
with a pen: paid the price for competing with searching gallop up in trip: worth another ch if containing keeness.

*2955 **PEDRO PETE 7** [1] 3-7-13 (77)(3ow)(4ex) Craig Williams 12/1: 433118: Keen, al bhd: quick reapp: 4 67
v progressive earlier: see 2955.

1853 **MICHELE MARIESCHI 54** [6] 3-8-6 (87) J F Egan 33/1: 2-5009: Chsd ldrs till 3f out, eased: 8 wk abs.   1 73

2116 **FOREIGN SECRETARY 43** [10] 3-8-13 (94) Pat Eddery 7/1: 4-1260: Chsd ldrs till btr: 10th.   hd 80

1830 **SIR NINJA 56** [8] 3-9-7 (102) R Hughes 33/1: -56260: Sn bhd: 11th: 8 wk abs, topp-weight, up in trip.   dist 0

11 ran   Time 2m 05.26 (1.06)   (Jaber Abdullah)   M Johnston Middleham, N Yorks

---

3132   **3.20 GR 3 LENNOX STKS 3YO+ (A)   7f rnd   Good/Firm 20 +03 Fast**
£30000   £11500   £5750   £2750   3 yo rec 6 lb

*2087 **OBSERVATORY 44** [6] J H M Gosden 3-8-12 K Darley 11/4: 41-211: 3 ch c Distant View - Stellaria   121
(Roberto) Handy, prog appr fnl 1f, rdn to lead below dist, going away: 6 wk abs, well bckd: earlier won at
R Ascot (Gr 3 Jersey stks): '99 Yarmouth wnr (2, mdn & stks, rtd 100): eff over a stiff or sharp/undul 7f, 1m
suit: acts on fast & gd, runs v well fresh: has a turn of foot & is high-class & progressive, shld follow up
here later this month in the Gr 2 Celebration Mile.

+2809 **THREE POINTS 14** [5] J L Dunlop 3-8-8 Pat Eddery 3/1: 324412: 3 b c Bering - Trazi (Zalai)   1½ 114
Trkd ldr, led 2f out, hdd ent fnl 1f & not pace of wnr: well bckd: had the rest well covered & lost little in defeat
against this v smart wnr: shld find a Group race: see 2809, 2087 (also bhd this wnr).

*2359 **SWALLOW FLIGHT 33** [7] G Wragg 4-9-0 M Roberts 11/8 FAV: 211313: 4 b c Bluebird - Mirage (Red   3½ 108
Sunset) Sn scrubbed along, in tch, eff over 2f out, styd on to take a moderate 3rd, no ch with front pair: hvly
bckd: ran into a couple of fast imprvg 3yos but is capable of much better/high-class form with a return to 1m.

2343 **TUMBLEWEED RIDGE 34** [8] B J Meehan 7-9-4 (tbl) M Tebbutt 12/1: 231304: Held up in tch, shkn up   2½ 107
over 2f out, no impress: this was a hot Gr 3 but can do better: prolific Gr 3 wnr abroad: see 2226.

3107 **DEBBIES WARNING 1** [3] 4-9-0 J Reid 66/1: 006005: In tch, prog to chase ldrs ent fnl 3f, sn no extra.   nk 102$

1834 **ARCTIC CHAR 55** [1] 4-8-11 D R McCabe 33/1: 2-0106: Al bhd: 8 wk abs, stablemate 4th, stiff task.   1½   96
2115 **MITCHAM 43** [4] 4-9-7 L Carter 33/1: 0-0407: Set strong pace, hdd 2f out, sn btn: 6 wk abs,   3   99
up in trip, better at sprinting, see 1172.
2351 **YAKAREEM 33** [9] 4-9-0 R Hughes 66/1: 00-458: Sn struggling: v stiff task, see 1847.   13   72
8 ran   Time 1m 25.67 (1.17)   (K Abdulla)   J H M Gosden Manton, Wilts

3133   3.50 GR 3 MOLECOMB STKS 2YO (A)   5f   Good/Firm 20   -16 Slow
£24000 £9200 £4600 £2200

*2529 **MISTY EYED 26** [6] Mrs P N Dutfield 2-8-10 L Newman 3/1 FAV: 510111: 2 gr f Paris House - Bold As   109
Love (Lomond) Held up in tch, switched & qcknd appr fnl 1f, kept on to lead below dist, pushed out: hvly bckd:
cheaply bred May foal: sprint bred: earlier won at Windsor (2, nov stks) & Sandown (listed): v eff at 5f on
fast & gd, any trk: v useful & progressive: proving tough & has the priceless ability to quicken.
2113 **BOUNCING BOWDLER 43** [5] M Johnston 2-8-12 D Holland 7/2: 221222: 2 b c Mujadil - Prima Volta   1¼   106
(Primo Dominie) Shaken up, prom, wide, prsd wnr ent fnl 1f, kept on but outpcd towards fin: nicely bckd,
swtg, 6 wk abs: lost little in defeat, v tough & useful: win a Listed/Gr 3 on a stiffer trk &/or over 6f.
*2664 **RED MILLENNIUM 21** [2] A Berry 2-8-7 F Norton 5/1: 212113: 2 b f Tagula - Lovely Me (Vision)   1¾   96
Front rank, led 2f out, under press & hdd below dist, no extra: nicely bckd: up in grade, proving very tough.
2849 **ELSIE PLUNKETT 13** [4] R Hannon 2-8-7 Dane O'Neill 9/2: 111324: Chsd ldrs, eff appr fnl 1f,   shd   96
onepace till kept on nr fin: nicely bckd: fine run: can land a nice prize at 6f: see 1586.
2067 **TARAS EMPEROR 45** [3] 2-9-1 K Darley 14/1: 414105: Bhd ldrs, rdn appr fnl 1f, onepace: ran   nk   103
to best conceding weight after 6 wk abs on grnd faster than ideal: see 1586.
2808 **SPEEDY GEE 14** [1] 2-8-12 Craig Williams 25/1: 361056: Held up, imprvd appr fnl 1f, not clr run   ½   98
thro' fnl 1f: poss flattered in this better grade but has ability: see 2808, 1962.
2849 **REEL BUDDY 13** [8] 2-8-12 R Hughes 25/1: 6207: Cl-up till fdd appr fnl 1f: highly tried, stablemate   nk   97
4th: must find a mdn on this evidence: see 1472.
2849 **SHOESHINE BOY 13** [7] 2-8-12 Pat Eddery 9/1: 111008: Led till 2f out, wknd ins last: see 1107.   shd   97
*1639 **PICCLED 64** [9] 2-8-12 T Quinn 14/1: 619: Bhd from halfway: stiff task, 9 wk abs: see 1639 (C/D).   12   72
9 ran   Time 58.48 (1.78)   (Mrs Jan Fuller)   Mrs P N Dutfield Axmouth, Devon

3134   4.25 LISTED RTD H'CAP 4YO+ 0-110 (A)   1m4f   Good/Firm 20   -09 Slow   [117]
£29000 £11000 £5500 £2500

*2341 **MURGHEM 34** [1] M Johnston 5-9-7 (110) D Holland 5/2 FAV: 421111: 5 b h Common Grounds - Fabulous   114
Pet (Somethingfabulous) Nvr far away, led ent fnl 4f, hard prsd 2f out, found extra for press: game: hvly bckd,
top-weight: 4 timer landed after wins at Epsom (rtd h'cap), Leicester & Newmarket (List): '99 Sandown wnr (h'cap,
rtd 100, B Hanbury): prev term won at Kempton (mdn, rtd 105): stays 2m, suited by 12f on firm, soft & fibresand,
up with/forcing the pace: runs well fresh, without blnks, can carry big weights: smart, progressive & most genuine.
+2803 **LIGHTNING ARROW 14** [6] J L Dunlop 4-9-5 (108) T Quinn 9/2: -02412: 4 br g Silver Hawk - Strait Lane   ½   110
(Chieftain II) Chsd ldrs, rdn appr fnl 1f, kept on to chase wnr ins last, being held: bckd tho' op 7/2:
imprvd in defeat against this tough wnr: v useful, see 2803.
2647 **LIGNE GAGNANTE 21** [5] W J Haggas 4-8-7 (96)(2oh) K Darley 7/2: -60223: 4 b g Turtle Island -   1¼   96§
Lightino (Bustino) Prom, chall 2f out, onepace under press ins last: well bckd, ran up to best, also bhd wnr in 1850.
4103] **VICIOUS CIRCLE 313** [7] L M Cumani 6-9-6 (109) J P Spencer 4/1: 1211-4: Waited with, shaken up   nk   108
3f out, no impress on ldrs till kept on towards fin: hvly bckd, reapp: '99 wnr at Newcastle, York (val Ebor h'cap)
& Ascot (h'cap, rtd 110): '98 Ayr wnr (mdn, rtd 89): eff at 12/14f, may get further: acts on fast & hvy grnd, likes
gall trks & goes well fresh: lightly rcd, smart & progressive, go close next time on a more gall trk over further.
2475 **JUST IN TIME 28** [3] 5-8-7 (96)(6oh) L Carter 14/1: 140305: Led till appr fnl 3f, no extra dist: nk   94§
tchd 20/1, stiffish task & prob a shade flattered back up in trip: see 874.
4359] **BALLADONIA 295** [4] 4-8-7 (96)(3oh) J Reid 9/1: 4024-6: Al bhd: reapp: '99 wnr here at Goodwood   5   88
(fill mdn, rtd 97 at best): rnr-up both '98 starts (mdn, rtd 85): eff at 9f/12f on firm & hvy grnd, any trk.
1307 **FAIR WARNING 80** [2] 4-8-7 (96)(4oh) M Hills 25/1: 12-507: Nvr a factor, btn 4f out: 11 wk abs, see 1030. 17   73
7 ran   Time 2m 35.22 (3.42)   (A Al Rostamani)   M Johnston Middleham, N Yorks

3135   5.00 EXPRESS HCAP 3YO 0-90 (C)   5f   Good/Firm 20   -08 Slow   [93]
£9262 £2850 £1425 £712   Raced centre to stands side, those in centre prob just favoured

2934 **SMOKIN BEAU 8** [17] J Cullinan 3-8-6 (71) R Mullen 16/1: 000361: 3 b g Cigar - Beau Dada (Pine   81
Circle) Cl-up centre, led bef halfway, drew clr despite edging right appr fnl 1f, styd on, drvn out: tchd 20/1:
'99 wnr at Southwell (mdn, rtd 81a & 76): eff at 5f, stays 6f: acts on fast, soft/hvy grnd & both AWs: suited
by a sharp trk & forcing the pace, without a visor.
2934 **TRAVESTY OF LAW 8** [3] B J Meehan 3-9-0 (79)(bl) D R McCabe 8/1: 000032: 3 ch g Case Law - Bold   1¼   85
As Love (Lomond) Held up stands side, strong run appr fnl 1f, nvr nrr: nicely bckd from 11/1: fine run from
prob unfavourable draw: back in form & well h'capped, keep on your side next time: see 1849.
2568 **BABY BARRY 24** [15] Mrs G S Rees 3-9-0 (85) J Carroll 20/1: 034303: 3 b c Komaite - Malcesine   2½   85
(Auction Ring) Hmpd after 1f, towards rear in centre, kept on for press fnl 1½f, took 3rd nr fin: back to
form, poorly drawn at Newmarket last time & apprec drop back to 5f: see 954.
*2684 **POPPYS SONG 20** [14] H Candy 3-8-8 (73) C Rutter 8/1: -00214: Cl-up centre, tried to go with   hd   73
wnr appr fnl 1f, kept on same pace: nicely bckd: in form tho' a shade better in 2684 (fill h'cap).
2787 **ANSELLAD 15** [8] 3-9-5 (84) R Hughes 10/1: 0-0025: Front rank kept on centre, unable to qckn appr fnl 1f.   1   81
2568 **MELANZANA 24** [5] 3-9-7 (86) G Carter 9/1: 1-4256: Towards rear stands side, imprvg but   1   80
unlikely to have made the frame when hmpd below dist: hvly bckd, top-weight: unsuited by drop back to 5f.
2247 **LICENCE TO THRILL 37** [9] 3-8-12 (77) M Henry 4/1: 110207: Chsd ldrs stands side, onepace appr   2   65
fnl 1f, eased ins last: both wins on equiutrack at Lingfield: bckd, see 2168, 652.
2504 **SABRE LADY 27** [6] 3-9-1 (80) L Newman 33/1: 0-3408: Prom stands side till 2f out: see 1219.   hd   68
1427 **NEEDWOOD TRUFFLE 74** [2] 3-8-10 (75) M Roberts 25/1: 100-09: Struggled to go pace stands side,   nk   62
late hdwy: 11 wk abs: '99 wnr here at Goodwood (nurs, rtd 78): eff forcing the pace at 5f, return to 6f lks
sure to suit: acts on firm & gd grnd, sharp/undul or gall trk: with B Morgan.
3526] **TIME FOR MUSIC 347** [11] 3-9-3 (82) L Carter 25/1: 2261-0: Al towards rear in centre: 10th, reapp: shd   69
won fnl '99 start at Nottingham (nurs, rtd 83): eff at 6f, stays 7f: acts on fast grnd & a sharp/gall trk.
2787 **QUEEN OF THE MAY 15** [16] 3-8-12 (77) Craig Williams 20/1: 165400: Switched towards stands side,   shd   64
nvr on terms: 11th, jockey made the wrong call: see 1098.
2586 **AROGANT PRINCE 23** [12] 3-7-10 (61)(6oh) R Brisland (5) 33/1: 600040: Speed centre 3f: 12th, stiff task.   ¾   45

2644 **MAROMITO** 21 [13] 3-9-1 (80) T Quinn 11/2 JT FAV: 10-00: Well plcd in centre till 2f out: 13th,   shd 64
bckd from 10/1: stable usually not far off when the money is down: see 2644.
2787 **IMPERIALIST** 15 [4] 3-9-4 (83)(bl) Dane O'Neill 20/1: 000200: Chsd ldrs stands side till halfway: 14th.   ¾ 64
2663 **NIFTY MAJOR** 21 [7] 3-8-12 (77) J Reid 25/1: 200000: Reared start, prom stands side 3f: 15th.   shd 58
2934 **ILLUSIVE** 8 [10] 3-8-6 (71)(bl) F Norton 10/1: 553320: Mid-div stands side, shaken up halfway,   1¾ 47
no impress & short of room bef dist: 16th, much btr 2934.
*2590 **FLY LIKE THE WIND** 23 [1] 3-8-8 (73) P Robinson 11/2 JT FAV: -22310: Led stands side till halfway,   ½ 48
sn btn: v hvly bckd: reportedly fin distressed & cld pay to forgive this: see 2590.
17 ran   Time 58.09 (1.39)   (Turf 2000 Ltd)   J Cullinan Quainton, Bucks

---

3136   5.35 STEWARDS' SPRINT HCAP 3YO+ (B)   6f   Good/Firm 20   +07 Fast   [83]
£17290   £5320   £2660   £1330   3 yo rec 4 lb Those racing in centre prob had edge

+2929 **FLAK JACKET** 9 [16] D Nicholls 5-8-8 (62)(t) D Holland 7/4 FAV: 002111: 5 b g Magic Ring - Vaula   71
(Henbit) Confidently held up in centre, imprvd on bit appr fnl 2f, qcknd below dist & drvn to lead towards fin:
hvly bckd, gd time: hat-trick landed after wins at Pontefract (stks) & Catterick (h'cap): rnr-up in '99
(rtd 82, B Meehan): '98 wnr at Kempton & Haydock (rtd 86): eff at 5/6f on firm & soft grnd: acts on
any trk, without blnks, wears a t-strap: well h'capped & wng run probably not at an end.
3091 **REFERENDUM** 2 [7] D Nicholls 6-9-3 (71) F Norton 25/1: 526602: 6 b g Common Ground - Final   1 76
Decision (Tap On Wood) Led stands side group, came clr of those rivals & ev ch dist, not pace of wnr in
centre: stablemate wnr: ran a cracking race on what was prob the unfav'd side: well h'capped, see 2340, 941.
2697 **SMART PREDATOR** 20 [12] J J Quinn 4-9-8 (76) J Fortune 20/1: 105203: 4 gr g Polar Falcon - She's   ½ 79
Smart (Absalom) Set gd pace in centre, drvn appr fnl 1f, worn down well ins last: clr rem & a bold attempt.
3016 **COMPTON BANKER** 5 [3] G A Butler 3-9-10 (82) P Doe 9/2: 051024: Held up stands side, ran on   2 79
strongly appr fnl 1f & went 4th bef fin, nvr nrr: well bckd, back up in trip: stays a sharp 6f, needs a stiffer trk.
*3091 **ZUHAIR** 2 [2] 7-9-8 (76)(5ex) Alex Greaves 5/1: 003315: Chsd ldrs stands side, unable to qckn   ¾ 70
appr fnl 1f: nicely bckd reminder of 1st & 2nd: won here 48hrs ago over 5f: won this race in '99.
2954 **BOANERGES** 7 [5] 3-9-7 (79) K Darley 16/1: 011306: Chsd ldrs stands side, nvr pace to chall.   ¾ 71
*897 **MISS HIT** 113 [14] 5-9-1 (69) J P Spencer 16/1: 000-17: Rear in centre, late hdwy, nvr a threat.   hd 60
3018 **PETRUS** 5 [10] 4-9-6 (74)(t) Pat Eddery 14/1: 005008: Prom centre onepace appr fnl 1f: tchd 25/1.   shd 65
2830 **DOUBLE OSCAR** 14 [8] 7-9-5 (73)(bl) A Nicholls 33 (3) 16/1: 632109: In tch stands side, prog to   2 58
dspt lead that side 2f out, sn onepace: stablemate of 1st 2, btr 2340 (5f).
2929 **DIAMOND DECORUM** 9 [9] 4-9-2 (70) M Roberts 33/1: 610600: Prsd ldr in centre till after halfway: 10th.   1 52
2787 **CORUNNA** 15 [15] 3-9-7 (79) G Carter 33/1: 131660: Prom in centre till appr fnl 2f: 11th: btr 2216.   ¾ 54
2580 **FRANCPORT** 23 [1] 4-9-7 (75) T Quinn 20/1: 003060: Nvr a factor stands side: 12th, op 14/1, see 824.   ½ 53
-2078 **TEYAAR** 44 [4] 4-9-8 (76) I Mongan (5) 20/1: 252220: Prom stands side, edged towards centre   hd 53
2f out, rdn & btn: 13th, 6 wk abs: back on turf, capable of better: see 2078. 923.
2684 **Sharoura** 20 [6] 4-9-9 (77) R Hughes 20/1:   3091 **Statoyork** 2 [13] 7-8-4 (58) D R McCabe 25/1:
2830 **Gdansk** 14 [11] 3-9-3 (75) J Carroll 33/1:
16 ran   Time 1m 10.75 (0.75)   (The Knavesmire Alliance)   D Nicholls Sessay, N Yorks

---

Official Going   GOOD TO FIRM. Stalls: Straight Course - Stands Side: Round Course - Outside

3137   6.20 EBF MDN 2YO (D)   6f   Good/Firm 38   -29 Slow
£3464   £1066   £533   £266

2926 **LAPWING** 9 [5] B W Hills 2-9-0 A Culhane 4/1: 41: 2 b c Tagula - Wasaif (Lomond)   75
Made all, drvn clr ins last: 38,000gns Apr foal, dam a 7f wnr: sire a top class 6f juv: eff over a sharp
or gall 6f on fast grnd, 7f should suit: likes to force the pace: uconv eff in fluent way.
2873 **LITTLE TASK** 11 [1] A Berry 2-9-0 R Winston 25/1: -30242: 2 b c Environment Friend - Lucky Thing   1¾ 70
(Green Desert) Trckd wnr, rdn/dropped rear after halfway, late hdwy, no impress on wnr: needs 7f in nurs h'caps.
-- **SMOOTHIE** 2 [7] P F I Cole 2-9-0 D Sweeney 2/7 FAV: 3: 2 gr c Definite Article - Limpopo   ¾ 68
(Green Desert) Front rank, rdn & outpcd appr fnl 1f: well bckd: 40,000gns Feb foal, half brother to smart
sprinter Pipalong: better expected on this debut but should improve for the experience.
-- **JOHNSTONS DIAMOND** 6 [3] E J Alston 2-9-0 J Bramhill 50/1: 4: In tch, rdn/fdd over 1f out: 3 61
IR 10,500gns gelding, half brother to a 1m juv wnr: dam 5f wnr.
-- **FINMAR** 4 [2] A Crowther 25/1: 5: Dwelt, al last: 39,000gns Efisio 1st foal, sire useful at 6f/1m.   6 49
5 ran   Time 1m 13.32 (4.02)   (The Hon Mrs J M Corbett & Mr C Wright)   B W Hills Lambourn, Berks

---

3138   6.50 ARRAN SELL HCAP 3YO+ 0-60 (F)   7f rnd   Good/Firm 38   -21 Slow   [55]
£2534   £724   £362   3 yo rec 6 lb

1858 **CODICIL** 54 [10] M Dods 4-8-9 (36) J Fanning 16/1: -00341: 4 ch f Then Again - Own Free Will   39
(Nicholas Bill) Front rank, prog to lead appr dist, styd on strongly, drvn out: no bid, op 8/1: unplcd in '99
(rtd 56, stakes), prev term scored at Redcar (auction mdn, rtd 68, Mrs J Ramsden): eff between 7f & 10f: acts
on fast, soft & a gall track: runs well fresh: apprec recent drop to selling grade.
2944 **CHAKRA** 8 [6] M S Saunders 6-9-6 (47) R Price 8/1: 021302: 6 gr g Mystiko - Maracuja (Riverman)   ½ 49
Prom, rdn to chall appr fnl 1f, not pace of wnr well inside last: gd run, see 2729, 2291.
2719 **MYTTONS AGAIN** 18 [3] A Bailey 3-9-10 (57)(bl) J Bramhill 14/1: 650063: 3 b g Rambo Dancer -   hd 59
Sigh (Highland Melady) Settled rear, rdn & ran on strongly appr fnl 1f, closing at fin: gd eff under top-weight.
2099 **BROCTUNE GOLD** 44 [11] Mrs M Reveley 9-8-13 (40) A Culhane 9/2: 60-504: Led, hdd appr fnl 1f,   3 36
sn drvn/held: 6 week abs: see 1658.
2994 **FASTWAN** 6 [12] 4-7-12 (25) K Dalgleish (5) 50/1: -00005: Rear, switched/hdwy over 2f out, kept   ¾ 20
on, never nrr: mod form prev year: see 2523.
2533 **KNAVES ASH** 25 [8] 9-8-13 (40) R Havlin 14/1: 036006: Rear, rdn/late gains, no dngr: drop in trip.   nk 34
2533 **MISS GRAPETTE** 25 [7] 4-8-10 (37) R Winston 6/1: 005027: Mid div, hdwy appr fnl 2f, wknd fnl 1f.   nk 31
2796 **ZIBAK** 14 [4] 6-8-4 (31) D Sweeney 5-2 FAV: 654068: Chsd ldrs, eff 3f out, sn drvn/fdd: bckd.   ¾ 24
2822 **BANDIDA** 14 [5] 6-8-4 (31) P Bradley (5) 66/1: 06009: Mid div at best: mod form this term: see 1244.   1¼ 22
2798 **MISTER WESTSOUND** 14 [2] 8-9-4 (45)(bl) C Lowther 20/1: 000000: Dwelt/rear, mod late gains, 10th.   1¼ 34

2994 **TAKER CHANCE** 6 [14] 4-8-12 (39) K Hodgson 8/1: 606200: Prom, rdn/lost tch fnl 2f, 11th: qck reapp.   hd   27
2780 **Unmasked** 15 [4] 4-8-0 (27) (BL) J McAuley 16/1:   2798 **Landfall Lil** 14 [9] 3-9-2 (49) P Hanagan (7) 50/1:
13 ran   Time 1m 27.97 (4.17)   (Harry Whitton)   M Dods Piercebridge, Co Durham

---

3139	7.20 WALKER MDN STKS 3YO+ (D) 1m rnd Good/Firm 38 -15 Slow
	£3412 £1050 3 yo rec 7 lb

2564 **BARABASCHI** 24 [2] J H M Gosden 4-9-7 R Havlin 4/7 FAV: 2-2261: 4 b g Elmaamul - Hills Presidium   68
(Presidium) Led, rdn & went clr appr fnl 1f, readily: well bckd, plcd num times prev: 4-time rnr-up in '99
for A Foster (rtd 78): rtd 82 in '98: eff at 7f/1m on fast & hvy: best without blinks: this was a poor mdn.
2800 **LITTLE JOHN** 14 [4] Miss L A Perratt 4-9-7 (vis) C Lowther 10/1: 325242: 4 b g Warrshan - Silver   3   60
Venture (Silver Hawk) Trkd wnr, drvn/no extra over 1f out: clr rem: mdn after 20 starts: see 2783.
-- **ELSAS PRIDE** [5] J M Jefferson 5-9-7 P Hanagan (7) 66/1: 3: 5 b g Mon Tresor - Elsa (Green Ruby)   10   44
Mid div, drvn/btn fnl 2f: Flat debut: 8 days ago a lucky wnr over hdles at Sedgefield (2m5.5f, fast, rtd 72h).
2204 **LITTLE LES** 39 [3] P Monteith 4-9-7 R Winston 100/1: 6064: Dwelt/rear, eff 2f out, kept on, no   2   40$
danger: treat rating with caution (offically only 40): see 1655.
1054 **RAMPART** 97 [6] 3-9-0 A Culhane 7/4: 03-05: Prom, wknd rapidly appr fnl 2f: very disappointing   5   32
again after a long abs, something amiss?: see 1054.
-- **JUST WHATEVER** [1] 3-8-9 J Fanning 33/1: 6: Dwelt, sn chasing ldrs, wknd quickly over 2f out,   17   4
eased when btn: debut: Major Jacko filly, with F P Murtagh.
6 ran   Time 1m 40.85 (4.25)   (Dr Ornella Carlilni Cozzi)   J H M Gosden Manton, Wilts

---

3140	7.50 TURN O' FOOT HCAP 3YO 0-70 (E) 1m3f Good/Firm 38 -08 Slow	[72]
	£2941 £905 £452 £226	

3013 **WESTGATE RUN** 5 [5] R A Fahey 3-9-9 (67) (6ex) S Sanders 10/11 FAV: 331121: 3 b f Emperor Jones -   70
Glowing Reference (Reference Point) Front rank, hdwy to lead appr 3f out, drvn out to hold on: well bckd: earlier
won at Warwick (appr h'cap), Hamilton (h'cap), Brighton (class stakes) & Nottingham (h'caps): '99 rnr up (clmr,
rtd 75): eff at 9/12f & likes firm/fast, hndles gd & any trk: best up with/forcing the pace: v tough & progressive.
2842 **SHOTACROSS THE BOW** 13 [6] B W Hills 3-9-7 (65) A Culhane 9/2: -00032: 3 b c Warning - Nordica   ½   67
(Northfields) Settled rear, gd hdwy to chall ldr over 2f out, no extra ins last: stays 11f on fast.
2746 **FIRST BACK** 16 [2] C W Fairhurst 3-8-8 (52) P Bradley 5/1: 6-4003: 3 b g Fourstars Allstar -   2½   50
Par Un Nez (Cyrano de Bergerac) Waited with, rdn/prog over 3f out, not pace of front 2 appr fnl 1f: see 1480.
2967 **GARGOYLE GIRL** 7 [1] J S Goldie 3-8-8 (50) J Fanning 16/1: 445554: Prom, drvn/no extra fnl 2f.   nk   48
*2863 **WINGED ANGEL** 12 [4] 3-9-0 (58) K Hodgson 7/2: 000015: Rear, hdwy to improve over 2f out, sn held.   2   53
2799 **JIMGAREEN** 14 [3] 3-8-6 (50) C Lowther 66/1: 645006: Led, hdd appr 3f out, wknd rapidly: see 1632.   22   20
6 ran   Time 2m 21.13 (5.13)   (Mark A Leatham)   R A Fahey Butterwick, N Yorks

---

3141	8.20 LADIES NIGHT HCAP 3YO+ 0-70 (E) 1m1f20y Good/Firm 38 -01 Slow	[65]
	£3006 £925 £462 £231 3 yo rec 8 lb	

2518 **CYBERTECHNOLOGY** 27 [7] M Dods 6-9-7 (58) J Fanning 11/2: 003161: 6 b g Enviroment Friend -   62
Verchinina (Star Appeal) Waited with, gd hdwy to lead dist, styd on strongly, drvn out: earlier scored at
Beverley (h'cap): '99 Doncaster wnr (h'cap, rtd 74), previous term won at Redcar (h'cap, rtd 82, Mrs J
Cecil): suited by 1m/10f, stys 12f: acts on firm & gd/soft grnd, stiff/gall tracks: best without blinks/
visor & needs to come late off a strong pace: in gd form & on a fair mark.
2882 **KESTRAL** 11 [8] T J Etherington 4-8-3 (37) (3ow) R Havlin 12/1: 606232: 4 ch g Ardkinglass - Shiny   1   42
Kay (Star Appeal) Settled rear, smooth hdwy appr fnl 2f, led briefly over 1f out, not pace of wnr cl-home: not
btn far & mdn tag would prob have been lost but for 3ow & backers shld feel v disappointed: stays 9f: see 2831.
2942 **DOVEBRACE** 8 [9] A Bailey 7-9-2 (53) J Bramhill 9/2 FAV: 166623: 7 b g Dowsing - Naufrage (Main   nk   54
Reef) Rear, hdwy to chall ldrs dist, drvn/no extra well ins last: remains in gd heart: stays 9f: see 2942.
2799 **IMPULSIVE AIR** 14 [4] J R Weymes 8-8-6 (43) R Winston 14/1: 002004: Rear, switched/hdwy over 2f   shd   44
out, kept on strongly, nrst fin: signs of a return to form here & is on a winning mark: see 569.
2970 **THORNTOUN GOLD** 7 [5] 4-8-12 (49) D Sweeney 8/1: 100235: Mid div, eff 2f out, btn fnl 1f.   2½   46
2875 **ACE OF TRUMPS** 11 [1] 4-8-4 (41) (t) J McAuley 12/1: 300256: Led to over 4f out, every ch till   ½   37
no extra over 1f out: flattered 2875, see 1195.
2875 **CLAIM GEBAL CLAIM** 11 [10] 4-8-2 (39) P Hanagan (7) 12/1: -00167: Front rank, went on over 4f out,   2   31
hdd over 1f out, wknd quickly: best in claiming grade these days, as in 2780.
2782 **SPIRIT OF KHAMBANI** 15 [6] 3-8-2 (47) K Dalgleish (5) 5/1: 004258: Prom, rdn/wknd fnl 2f.   nk   38
-2799 **LINCOLN DEAN** 14 [3] 4-8-6 (43) A Culhane 5/1: 000329: Handy, chall over 2f out, sn wknd qckly.   nk   34
2349 **BOWCLIFFE** 33 [11] 9-9-10 (61) S Sanders 7/1: 022100: Nvr dngrs, 10th: top weight: btr 2283.   1¾   49
2780 **ROOFTOP 15** [12] 4-8-6 (43) P Bradley 5/1: 000460: Trckd ldrs, rdn/lost tch over 2f out, 11th.   nk   30
2932 **MR PERRY** 9 [2] 4-8-13 (50) (vis) C Lowther 20/1: 300060: Keen/prom, rdn/wknd rapidly fnl 2f, 12th.   16   17
12 ran   Time 1m 53.9 (3.6)   (Exors Of The Late Mrs H M Carr)   M Dods Piercebridge, Co Durham

---

3142	8.50 CLASSIFIED STKS 3YO+ 0-80 (D) 1m2f Good/Firm 38 +09 Fast
	£4060 £1160 £580

2617 **WHITE HOUSE** 22 [2] W Jarvis 3-8-9 S Sanders 6/4: 0-4431: 3 b f Pursuit Of Love - Much Too Risky   80
(Bustino) Trckd clr ldr, rdn to lead over 3f out, styd on well to go clr inside last, rdn out: gd time:
first win: unplcd sole '99 start over 1m (rtd 58): half sister to wnrs between 7 & 13.5f: eff around 10f
on fast & hvy grnd: acts on a gall track: quickened well here.
2955 **GOLDEN CHANCE** 7 [3] M Johnston 3-9-1 J Fanning 1/2 FAV: 213042: 3 b c Unfuwain - Golden Digger   4   79
(Mr Prospector) Settled last, hdwy to chall appr fnl 2f, sn wknd: not pace of wnr: sweating: see 2955, 2159.
3081 **FOUR MEN** 2 [1] A Berry 3-8-12 Mark Flynn (7) 25/1: 065653: 3 b g Nicolotte - Sound Pet (Runnett)   22   40$
Sn clr ldr, hdd 3f out, sn lost tch: quick reapp, outclassed.
3 ran   Time 2m 07.27 (2.87)   (J M Greetham)   W Jarvis Newmarket, Suffolk

Official Going   GOOD TO FIRM. Stalls: Round Course - Inside; Straight Course - Stands Side.

3143   2.05 THOMAS LORD MDN 2YO (D)   5f   Good/Firm 20   -04 Slow
             £4179   £1286   £643   £321

2926 **TOMTHEVIC 10** [1] J J Quinn 2-9-0 (t) D Mernagh (3) 6/1: -40321: 2 ch g Emarati - Madame Bovary   79
(Ile de Bourbon) Trkd ldr, went on over 1f out, kept on strongly, rdn out: plcd twice prev: half-brother to a
7f juv wnr: dam scored over 1m/10f: eff at 5/6f on fast grnd, gall or easy trk: tough, a deserved win.
2968 **FOREVER TIMES 8** [2] T D Easterby 2-8-9 M Fenton 8/11 FAV: 3622: 2 b f So Factual - Simply Times   1   72
(Dodge) Prom, eff when short of room appr fnl 1f, ran on strongly ins last, no reach wnr: well bckd at odds-on:
shade unlucky in running, would have gone closer with a clr run: will apprec a return to 6f & shld win a race.
2214 **VENDOME 39** [6] J A Osborne 2-9-0 R Havlin 10/1: 0003: 2 b c General Monash - Kealbra Lady   hd   77
(Petong) Cl-up, chall over 1f out, not pace of wnr well ins last: improved run, eff at 5f on fast: see 1429.
2532 **BARON CROCODILE 26** [2] A Berry 2-9-0 C Lowther 9/2: 245024: Led, hdd appr fnl 1f, sn btn.   2   72
2532 **BOLD MCLAUGHLAN 26** [8] 2-9-0 A Culhane 16/1: -00065: Settled rear, rdn/late gains, no dngr: see 700. 3 65
2916 **BLUE FALCON 10** [10] 2-9-0 J Stack 33/1: 06: Nvr a factor: drop in trip: see 2916 (debut, 7f).   3½ 58
2880 **FLAMBE 12** [5] 2-9-0 Dean McKeown 20/1: 037: Mid-div, drvn/btn over 2f out: see 2880.   1   55
--   **GOGS GIFT** [3] 2-9-0 K Hodgson 12/1: 8: Handy, rdn/wknd from halfway: debut: Apr 1st foal,   1   53
dam scored over 5f as a 3yo, sire decent juv: with C B B Booth.
--   **CRYSTAL CHANDELIER** [9] 2-8-9 J McAuley 33/1: 9: Al outpcd: May foal, half-sister to a 6f wnr,   6   36
dam related to v smart sprinter Emerging Market: with B W Murray.
--   **ROGHAN JOSH** [4] 2-9-0 Dale Gibson 20/1: 0: Dwelt, al last, 10th: dam a winning sprinter.   5   29
10 ran   Time 58.2 (1.2)   (Derrick Bloy)   J J Quinn Settrington, N Yorks

3144   2.35 LADIES SELL HCAP 3YO+ 0-60 (F)   6f   Good/Firm 20   -15 Slow   [35]
             £3692   £1136   £568   £284   3 yo rec 4 lb

3123 **ENCOUNTER 1** [14] J Hetherton 4-11-2 (51) Mrs S Bosley 6/1 JT FAV: 521101: 4 br g Primo Dominie -   54
Dancing Spirit (Ahonoora) Handy, rdn/prog appr fnl 1f, ran on well to lead nr fin, drvn out: op 8/1: bought in
for 8,400gns: unplcd here yesterday: earlier scored at Hamilton (amat h'cap) & Catterick (appr h'cap): won 2
in 2 days in '99, at Ayr (sell) & Hamilton (h'cap, rtd 58 at best): rtd 77$ for C Brittain in '98: has tried 1m,
suited by 6/7f: acts on fast grnd & any trk, likes Hamilton: goes particularly well for an amat/appr: most tough.
2632 **E B PEARL 22** [22] A Dickman 4-9-13 (34) Miss K Smith (7) 14/1: 550042: 4 ch f Timeless Times -   ½   35
Petite Elite (Anfield) Led stands side, drvn ins last, hdd nr fin: gd run trying to make all: all wins at 5f.
3035 **IMPALDI 5** [23] B Ellison 5-10-5 (40) Miss A Armitage (5) 10/1: 000233: 5 b m Imp Society - Jaldi   shd 41
(Nordico) Chsd ldrs stands side, hung left & ran on well fnl 1f, nrst fin: qck reapp: in gd form, mdn after 30.
3037 **GRAND ESTATE 5** [6] D W Chapman 5-11-7 (56) Miss R Clark 6/1 JT FAV: 235034: Led far side 3f out,   shd 57
ev ch when hung badly left appr fnl 1f, not btn far: qck reapp: may well have won if holding a straight course.
2864 **BLUE LINE LADY 13** [21] 3-9-13 (38) Miss Diana Jones 7/1: 500005: Trkd ldr, edged left/no extra fnl 1f. 1½ 35
2637 **CZAR WARS 22** [13] 5-9-13 (34)(bl) Miss L Allan (5) 20/1: 000346: Mid-div, rdn/kept on fnl 2f.   hd   31
2223 **UPPER CHAMBER 39** [17] 4-10-2 (37) Miss J Foster (5) 25/1: 00-007: Prom, drvn/btn appr fnl 1f: ½   33
rnr-up on mdn (mdn, rtd 67, subs tried binks/visor): rtd 70 when '98 rnr-up: eff at 5f on firm & gd/soft.
2907 **MR CUBE 11** [20] 10-10-5 (40)(bl) Mrs S Moore (5) 14/1: 552408: Rear stands side, late hdwy.   ½   35
2994 **PALACEGATE TOUCH 7** [1] 10-11-0 (49)(bl) Miss E J Jones 20/1: 336509: Outpcd after 3f, late gains.   nk   43
2932 **SYCAMORE LODGE 10** [2] 9-10-10 (45) Miss J Ellis (5) 9/1: 406030: Sn outpcd, late gains: 10th.   hd   39
2798 **HENRY THE HAWK 15** [18] 9-10-10 (45) Miss E Folkes (5) 12/1: 005020: Sn rdn, mid-div at best, 11th.   nk   38
2637 **TONG ROAD 22** [24] 4-10-2 (37) Miss A Deniel 33/1: 00-000: Nvr dngrs, 12th: modest form.   shd 30
2798 **BIRCHWOOD SUN 15** [11] 10-10-12 (47)(vis) Miss C Johnston (7) 16/1: 334030: Well in rear till ran   ½   38
on well appr fnl 1f, not threat to ldrs, 13th: best on a stiff trk, see 756.
2744 **BALLINA LAD 17** [12] 4-10-12 (47) Miss S Brotherton 16/1: 0-0050: Handy, lost tch fnl 2f, 14th.   ¾   36
1941 **NAPIER STAR 51** [10] 7-9-12 (33)(t) Miss A Elsey 12/1: -26040: Al rear far side, 15th: 7 wk abs.   1½ 19
2641 **MISS BANANAS 22** [4] 5-10-4 (39) Miss S Phizacklea (5) 33/1: 400000: Led far side, hdd 2f out, 16th. 1½ 21
2864 **Time For The Clan 13** [8] 3-9-11 (36) Miss R Bastiman (0) 25/1:
2798 **Souperficial 15** [9] 9-10-12 (47) Mrs R Howell (4) 20/1:
3129 **Arzilli 1** [3] 4-10-13 (48) Miss C Williams 14/1:   2820 **Superfrills 15** [15] 7-10-3 (38) Mrs C Ford 25/1:
2744 **My Tyson 17** [7] 5-9-13 (34)(t) Miss H Cuthbert (5) 25/1:
3124 **Lioness 1** [19] 4-9-13 (34)(BL) Miss Hayley Bryan (7) 50/1:
2525 **Kalar 27** [16] 11-10-10 (45)(bl) Mrs F Needham 25/1:
2947} **Pips Tango 376** [5] 3-10-1 (40) Miss M Mullineaux (7) 50/1:
24 ran   Time 1m 11.6 (2.1)   (C D Barber-Lomax)   J Hetherton Malton, N Yorks

3145   3.05 HALIFAX NURSERY HCAP 2YO (C)   5f   Good/Firm 20   +14 Fast   [94]
             £7150   £2200   £1100   £550

2756 **PROUD BOAST 17** [10] Mrs G S Rees 2-9-7 (85) A Culhane 7/1: -10231: 2 b f Komaite - Red Rosein   93+
(Red Sunset) Waited with, smooth hdwy to lead ins last, pshd clr, going away: v fast juv time: earlier won on
debut at Chester (mdn): 9,500gns half-sister to a juv wnr, dam a decent sprinter: eff at 5/6f on fast, gd/soft
& any trk: can force the pace or come late: useful & progressive, has a turn of foot & can win again.
1776 **MISS BRIEF 59** [12] P D Evans 2-8-7 (71) Joanna Badger (7) 8/1: -02442: 2 b f Brief Truce -   1¾ 73
Preponderance (Cyrano de Bergerac) Prom, rdn appr fnl 1f, kept on but not pace of wnr: gd eff after an 8 wk abs.
*2698 **LAUREL DAWN 21** [11] A Berry 2-9-4 (82) D Allan (7) 6/1: 401213: 2 gr c Paris House - Madrina   ¾   82
(Waajib) Front rank, led appr fnl 1f, hdd ins last, not qckn: v consistent: see 2698.
2756 **SAMADILLA 17** [7] T D Easterby 2-9-0 (78) P Fessey 5/1: -144: Rear, rdn/ran on well appr fnl 1f,   nk   77
nvr nrr: lightly raced sort, shld relish a step up to 6f: see 2756.
2668 **AMAMACKEMMUSH 13** [13] J Stack 3/1 FAV: -00235: Led at a scorching gallop, hdd over   3   61
1f out, sn wknd: trailblazer, poss went off too fast for own good here: see 2361.
2575 **FENWICKS PRIDE 24** [2] 2-9-3 (81) M Fenton 10/1: -53326: Mid-div when forced wide by rival halfway,   ¾   72
no impress appr fnl 1f: op 7/1: shade btr 2575.
2539 **NEW WONDER 26** [4] 2-8-7 (71) Dean McKeown 20/1: 30427: Handy, rdn/mod late hdwy: btr 2539.   1¼ 59
2714 **OPEN WARFARE 19** [9] 2-8-13 (77) K Dalgleish 16/1: 533358: Prom, drvn/btn fnl 2f: btr 2483.   shd 65
2835 **PERTEMPS JARDINE 14** [1] 2-8-4 (68) P Hanagan (7) 12/1: -3459: Hanging thro'out, nvr a factor.   1¾ 52
2575 **EASTERN PROMISE 24** [8] 2-8-6 (70) C Lowther 9/1: 24140: Hung left over 2f out, sn wknd, 10th.   shd 54

975

1995 **DA VINCI** 49 [5] 2-8-11 (75) R Havlin 20/1: 100: Chsd ldrs, qckly lost tch fnl 2f, fin last: 7 wk abs.   4   49
11 ran   Time 57.2 (0.2) Juvenile Course Record   (J W Gittins)   Mrs G S Rees Sollom, Lancs

---

3146   **3.35 EXPRESS FILLIES MDN 3YO (D)**   **7f rnd   Good/Firm 20   -16 Slow**
£3997   £1230   £615   £307

2465 **SAHAYB** 29 [4] R W Armstrong 3-8-11 (bl) Dale Gibson 13/2: 02-001: 3 b f Green Desert - Matila   64
(Persian Bold) Front rank, went on 3f out, sn rdn, kept on strongly, drvn out: below-par prev this term:
rnr-up in France for D Loder in '99 (7f, v soft): eff over an easy 7f on fast grnd.
2839 **DIANEME** 14 [5] T D Easterby 3-8-11 M Fenton 12/1: 045002: 3 b f Primo Dominie - Aunt Jemima   1¼   61$
(Busted) Chsd ldr, rear over 3f out, rall & styd on strongly fnl 2f: handles fast, appr return to further.
2464 **REEMATNA** 29 [1] M A Jarvis 3-8-11 Dean McKeown 9/4: -42463: 3 b f Sabrehill - Reem Albaraani   1½   58
(Sadler's Wells) Handy, drvn/no extra appr fnl 1f: clr rem: btr 1675.
-- **REPLACEMENT PET** [3] A J McNae 3-8-11 R Havlin 10/1: 4: Bhd, rdn/prog 2f out, sn no impress: 2½   54
debut: cheaply bought Petardia filly.
2860 **HANNAH BURDETT** 14 [2] 3-8-11 A Culhane 11/10 FAV: -35: Led, hdd after halfway, sn fdd: well bckd: 2½   50
much better expected here after a v encouraging debut in 2860.
1354 **MAWDSLEY** 78 [6] 3-8-11 C Lowther 50/1: 0-06: Al last: 11 wk abs: no form.   20   25
6 ran   Time 1m 25.4 (2.5)   (Hamdan Al Maktoum)   R W Armstrong Newmarket

---

3147   **4.05 OWN A HORSE HCAP 3YO+ 0-95 (C)**   **1m rnd   Good/Firm 20   -15 Slow**   [88]
£6890   £2120   £1060   £530   3 yo rec 7 lb

3115 **ADOBE** 1 [5] W M Brisbourne 5-8-12 (72) K Dalgleish (5) 4/1: 334121: 5 b g Green Desert - Shamshir   77
(Kris) Mid-div, rdn, hdwy 2f out, led dist, qcknd well for press, readily: rnr-up at Nottingham just 24hrs ago
(1m h'cap), earlier won at W'hampton, Hamilton (2), Bath, Goodwood & Doncaster (h'caps): '99 wnr at Bath &
Nottingham (h'caps, rtd 55 & 49a): suited by 7f/1m: acts on firm, gd & fibresand, handles soft grnd: acts on
any trk, likes Hamilton/Bath: eff with/without a t-strap: admirably tough/genuine & progressive this term.
2696 **COLWAY RITZ** 21 [6] W Storey 6-9-10 (84) T Williams 7/1: 611202: 6 b g Rudimentary - Million Heiress   1¾   84
(Auction Ring) Cl-up, eff when short of room 2f out, swtchd/kept on, no threat to wnr: best at 10f: see 2157.
3005 **HADATH** 7 [2] M A Buckley 3-9-2 (83) Dean McKeown 11/2: 612123: 3 br g Mujtahid - Al Sylah   nk   83
(Nureyev) Led, hung left for press over 1f out, styd on: best at 1m: acts any trk: qck reapp: proving tough/consistent.
*2965 **SHAAN MADARY** 8 [3] B W Hills 3-8-10 (77) A Culhane 5/1: 0-0214: Prom, rdn to chall 2f   ½   76
out, sn drvn & not qckn: lightly raced & not disgraced on this h'cap bow: see 2965.
2986 **SUPREME SALUTATION** 7 [4] 4-8-13 (73) P Fessey 3/1 FAV: 206035: Slow to break, pulled hard in rear, nk   71
rdn/hdwy over 2f out, no dngr: qck reapp: nicely bckd & can do better when able to settle: see 2986.
+2648 **DURAID** 22 [1] 8-10-0 (88) D Mernagh (3) 6/1: 421416: Prom, chall 2f out, sn held: nk   86
top-weight: likes coming late off a strong pace: won in a fast time in 2648 (rtd h'cap).
2853 **AL GHABRAA** 14 [7] M Fenton 3-9-2 (83) A Culhane 10/1: 1-6507: In tch, rdn/fdd fnl 2f: see 1630.   3½   75
7 ran   Time 1m 38.2 (2.8)   (P R Kirk)   W M Brisbourne Great Ness, Shropshire

---

3148   **4.40 FILEY HCAP 3YO+ 0-80 (D)**   **1m4f   Good/Firm 20   -09 Slow**   [70]
£4127   £1270   £635   £317   3 yo rec 11lb

2992 **WASEEM** 7 [2] M Johnston 3-9-8 (75) K Dalgleish (5) 7/4: 021031: 3 ch c Polar Falcon - Astolat   78
(Rusticaro) Trkd ldr, went on 3f out, hung left 2f out & sn hdd, rall for strong press ins last, got up fnl stride,
all out: jockey received a 1 day careless riding ban: qck reapp: earlier won at W'hampton (AW mdn, rtd 68a) &
Pontefract (h'cap): now suited by 10/12f on fast, gd/soft & fibresand: prob handles any trk.
*2742 **DESERT FIGHTER** 17 [1] Mrs M Reveley 9-9-4 (60) A Culhane 5/2: 010212: 9 b g Green Desert -   shd   62
Jungle Rose (Shirley Heights) Settled last, gd hdwy to lead appr fnl 1f, sn rdn, idled in front & hdd shadow of
post: remains in fine form & deserves another win sn: see 2742 (claimer).
2872 **PALUA** 13 [4] Mrs A J Bowlby 3-9-10 (77)(bl) Dean McKeown 11/8 FAV: 432033: 3 b c Sri Pekan -   2½   75
Reticent Bride (Shy Groom) Led, rdn/hdd 3f out, sn hmpd & snatched up, drvn & not qckn appr fnl 1f.
3 ran   Time 2m 33.3 (3.5)   (A Al-Rostamani)   M Johnston Middleham, N Yorks

---

Official Going   GOOD (GOOD/FIRM in places). Stalls: Str - Stands Side; Rnd - Inside; 1m4f - Outside.

3149   **2.15 VODAFONE NURSERY HCAP 2YO (C)**   **7f rnd   Firm 14   -25 Slow**   [101]
£11375   £3500   £1750   £875

*2962 **FOREVER MY LORD** 8 [8] R F Johnson Houghton 2-8-2 (75) J Quinn 15/2: 60111: 2 b c Be My Chief - In   81
Love Again (Prince Rupert): With ldr, led over 2f out, kept on well for press over 1f out: nicely bckd: hat-trick
landed after 2 wins at Newmarket (sell, bt in for 19,000 gns & nursery h'cap): dam sprinter: stays 7f well, shld
get 1m: acts on firm/fast grnd & on any trk, likes Newmarket: in fine form & improving.
*2867 **DANCE ON THE TOP** 13 [5] E A L Dunlop 2-8-11 (84) J Reid 9/4 FAV: -612: 2 ch c Caerleon - Fern   ½   89
(Shirley Heights) Prom, edged right over 1f out, kept on for press ins last, not reach wnr: hvly bckd & ran
well: should regain winning ways over 1m &/or on a stiffer trk: see 2867.
*2628 **ACHILLES SPIRIT** 23 [11] K R Burke 2-8-6 (78)(low) S Sanders 7/1: 013: 2 b c Deploy - Scenic Spirit   1¼   82
(Scenic) Set pace till over 2f out, kept on same pace for press, short of room cl-home: stays 7f on fm & gd/soft.
*2894 **MERIDEN MIST** 12 [12] P W Harris 2-8-1 (74) A Beech (5) 12/1: 525414: Dwelt, sn in tch, effort   ¾   75
over 1f out, onepace when short of room inside last: gd run, see 2894.
2940 **ONCE REMOVED** 9 [3] 2-7-11 (70) P Doe 40/1: 440234: Waited with, effort 2f out, onepace inside   dht   71
last: stays 7f & should win a race on a minor trk on this form: see 2730.
2948 **CHURCH MICE** 8 [13] 2-8-0 (73)(vis) N Pollard 25/1: 421536: Keen, handy, short of room over   1½   71
1f out, onepcd inside last: stays 7f & will apprec a return to the minor trks: see 2589, 1550.
2903 **FLUTED** 11 [1] 2-7-13 (72)(3ow)(4oh) Craig Williams 40/1: 4037: Sn bhd, hdwy over 2f out, nvr dngrs-   ½   69
2754 **LOGIC LANE** 17 [6] 2-9-1 (88) R Hughes 7/1: -0128: Dwelt, in tch, eff 2f out, sn no extra: btr 2754.   1   83
*2724 **VALDESCO** 18 [9] 2-8-9 (82) P Robinson 14/1: 3419: Hld up, late gains, nvr dngrs: rate higher.   nk   76

2474 **NIGHT FALL 29** [4] 2-8-8 (81) P Fitzsimons (5) 14/1: 56140: Sn handy, wknd 2f out: 10th: btr 2474. ¾ 73

2962 **DENNIS EL MENACE 8** [7] 2-8-4 (77) Martin Dwyer 10/1: 464320: Prom, wkng when short of room over nk 68
1f out: 11th: just bhd this wnr in 2962 & capable of better.

2791 **MEDIA BUYER 16** [10] 2-8-7 (80) Pat Eddery 14/1: 000320: Al bhd: 12th: only form on prev 2 5 61
starts when wearing blnks (omitted today): see 2791.

*2773 **SHUSH 16** [2] 2-9-7 (94) A Nicholls (3) 20/1: 156010: Forced wide after 1f, handy, wknd over 2f ¾ 73
out: 13th: proving inconsistent: much btr 2773 (6f, stiff trk).

13 ran   Time 1m 27.66 (2.73)   (W H Ponsonby)   R F Johnson Houghton Blewbury, Oxon.

3150 2.45 LISTED THOROUGHBRED STKS 3YO (A) 1m rnd Firm 14 -03 Slow
£17269 £6385 £3192 £1451

981 **ADILABAD 107** [4] Sir Michael Stoute 3-8-12 Pat Eddery 100/30: 11-51: 3 b c Gulch - Adaiyka (Doyoun) 116
In tch, swtchd left & hdwy 2f out, styd on strongly ins last to get up cl-home under a strong Pat Eddery drive: 3
mth abs: won both juv starts, at Sandown & Newmarket (stks, rtd 96): eff over 7f/1m, cld get further (dam 9f
scorer): acts on firm, gd/soft & any trk: runs well fresh: lightly rcd, a reproduction of this cld see a Gr win.

+2757 **SUMMONER 17** [3] R Charlton 3-8-12 R Hughes 11/10 FAV: -10412: 3 b c Inchinor - Sumoto (Mtoto) nk 115
Trkd ldr, went on 2f out, kept on over 1f out till collared cl-home, just btn: hvly bckd: caught a smart sort.

2720 **MERRY MERLIN 5** [5] M L W Bell 3-9-2 T Quinn 11/1: 010563: 3 b c Polar Falcon - Bronzewing 2½ 114$
(Beldale Flutter) Set pace till 2f out, onepcd: better run, tho' prob a shade flattered by this rating back at 1m.

2596 **CORNELIUS 24** [1] P F I Cole 3-8-12 M Roberts 9/2: 250204: Waited with, bmpd & lost action 2f out, 6 98
sn wknd: shade frustrating, has not won since debut last season: twice below 2476.

2471 **MANA MOU BAY 29** [2] 3-9-2 K Darley 9/1: 1-0245: Handy, lost plc over 3f out, wknd 2f out: stiff task. ½ 101

5 ran   Time 1m 38.72 (1.34)   (H H Aga Khan)   Sir Michael Stoute Newmarket.

3151 3.20 GR 1 VODAFONE NASSAU STKS 3YO+ (A) 1m1f192y Firm 14 +03 Fast
£78300 £29700 £14850 £6750 3 yo rec 9 lb

*2150 **CRIMPLENE 43** [3] C E Brittain 3-8-6 P Robinson 7/4 FAV: 331111: 3 ch f Lion Cavern - Crimson Conquest 120
(Diesis) Cl-up till led 5f out, rdn 2f out, 6L in front bfr, kept on but drvn out to hold closing rnr-up: hvly bckd
tho' op 11/8, gd time, 6 wk abs: 4 timer after wins in German & Irish 1000 Guineas & at R Ascot (Gr 1 Coronation):
'99 Redcar (mdn) & Salisbury wnr (stks, rtd 106): loves to dominate over 1m, stays a sharp 10f: acts on firm & hvy:
runs well fresh: v tough, progressive & top class: can quicken from the front & shld win more top-class races.

+2501 **ELA ATHENA 28** [4] M A Jarvis 4-9-1 M Roberts 7/1: 2-0412: 4 grf Ezzoud - Crodelle (Formidable) 1¾ 116
Keen, made till 5f out, sn lost place & outpcd, styd on well final 1f, not reach wnr: v smart effort over
too sharp a trip: sure to go cl in the 12f Gr 1 Yorkshire Oaks later this month (1½L rnr-up last term).

2150 **PRINCESS ELLEN 43** [8] G A Butler 3-8-6 K Darley 7/2: -02523: 3 br f Tirol - Celt Song (Unfuwain) 2½ 112
Prom, hdwy to chase wnr 5f out till 3f out, sn outpcd, onepace over 1f out: nicely bckd: 6 wk abs & again bhd
this wnr on step up to 10f: deserves another win & should do so with a drop into Gr 3 company: see 2150.

2169 **HIGH WALDEN 42** [1] H R A Cecil 3-8-6 T Quinn 9/2: -532W4: Prom, effort to chase wnr 3f out, hung ¾ 111
right over 1f out, wknd: well bckd after 6 wk abs: ran to best & will enjoy a return to Listed company in 1825.

2975 **DIAMOND WHITE 8** [5] 5-9-1 J F Egan 25/1: 345645: Bhd, btn 3f out: see 1057, 967. 5 104

*2190 **NEW ASSEMBLY 40** [7] 3-8-6 J Reid 25/1: 0-2116: Waited with, rdn & outpcd over 3f out: 6 wk abs, 1½ 102$
massive step up in class after wng a h'cap off 82 in 2190 & will relish a return to that company.

*2404 **LADY UPSTAGE 35** [6] 3-8-6 M Hills 6/1: -12517: Waited with, rdn & outpcd 3f out, no impress: shd 102
not handle firm grnd? much btr 2404 (Gr 2, gd/soft).

7 ran   Time 2m 05.3 (1.1)   (Sheikh Marwan Al Maktoum)   C E Brittain Newmarket.

3152 3.50 VODAFONE STEWARDS CUP HCAP 3YO+ (B) 6f str Firm 14 +13 Fast [110]
£55250 £17000 £8500 £4250 3 yo rec 4 lb 2 Groups - Far Side held sowe advantage

2997 **TAYSEER 7** [28] D Nicholls 6-8-11 (93)(7ex) R Hughes 13/2: 303131: 6 ch g Sheikh Albadou - Millfit 103
(Blushing Groom) Hld up far side trav well, gd hdwy 2f out, swtchd right over 1f out & strong run to lead ins
last, sn clr, v cleverly: fast time: earlier scored at Newmarket (Bunbury Cup H'cap) & no luck in running at
Ascot last time: in '99 won at Brighton (clmr wth W Muir), Ayr & Newmarket (val h'cap, rtd 85): '98 Southwell
scorer (clmr, rtd 86a): eff btwn 6f/1m on firm, soft & fibresand: handles any trk: most progressive & useful,
has a turn of foot & a revelation since joining his excellent trainer.

3016 **BON AMI 6** [24] A Berry 4-8-2 (84) P Bradley (5) 40/1: 034602: 4 b c Paris House - Felin Special 1½ 87
(Lyphard's Special) Prom far side, overall ldr over 1f out, collared inside last, kept on: qck reapp & back
to form: well h'capped (rtd 101 last term): tried blnks in 1337, see 1004.

2706 **CUBISM 20** [4] J W Hills 4-9-7 (103)(t) M Hills 33/1: 4-0353: 4 b h Miswaki - Seattle Kat (Seattle 1½ 103
Song) Prom stands side, led that group over 1f out, styd on well inside last: clear wnr of unfav stands side group:
v useful & should land a nice prize this term: see 1952, 1338.

2355 **ROYAL RESULT 34** [19] D Nicholls 7-8-6 (88) A Nicholls (3) 10/1: 003644: In tch far side, eff & ½ 86
slightly short of room dist, styd on well inside last: stablemate of wnr: tough & likes this course: see 2355.

3107 **SECOND WIND 2** [30] 5-8-1 (83)(t) A Beech 25/1: 012405: Prom far side, onepace final 1f: ½ 80
qck reapp & ran well: 4 prev wins at 7f: see 2616.

3016 **FURTHER OUTLOOK 6** [29] 6-9-0 (96) K Darley 10/1: 532536: Chsd far side ldr, onepace final 1f: hd 92
nicely bckd: qck reapp, stablemate of wnr & 4th: v tough: see 3016, 1182.

2954 **CADEAUX CHER 6** [10] 6-8-3 (85)(5ex) N Pollard 33/1: 000107: Waited with stands side, hdwy over nk 80
1f out, kept on inside last: encouraging: see 2845.

*1173 **SARTORIAL 91** [15] 4-9-4 (100) S Sanders 9/1: 2-1418: Prom far side, ev ch 1f out, no extra: well nk 94
bckd: 3 mth abs & reportedly laid out for this race: lightly raced & could improve: see 1173.

2847 **HALMAHERA 14** [6] 5-9-10 (106) M Roberts 25/1: 056049: Held up stands side, hdwy over 1f out, nk 99
kept on inside last: gd run on unfav side under top weight: 1½L rnr-up in this race off a 1lb higher mark in '99.

2335 **DEEP SPACE 35** [7] 5-9-0 (105) J Reid 14/1: 635430: Waited with stands side, gd hdwy 2f out, 1¼ 94
rdn & btn final 1f: 10th: better expected after 2335 (Listed), 952.

2954 **AL MUALLIM 8** [16] 6-8-7 (89)(t) W Supple 25/1: 000040: Bhd far side, kept on late: 11th, fair run. shd 77

2568 **RUDIK 25** [17] 3-8-13 (99)(t) Pat Eddery 12/1: 13-500: In tch far side, btn final 1f, eased: 12th. nk 86

2669 **REPERTORY 21** [1] 7-9-9 (105) J Weaver 50/1: 032350: Overall ldr stands side till over 1f out, nk 91
no extra: 13th, big weight, all wins at 5f: see 2496.

2432 **ALASTAIR SMELLIE 31** [23] 4-7-12 (80) Iona Wands 33/1: 005040: In tch far side, onepace over 1f nk 65
out: 14th: stablemate of wnr, prev wins at 5f: see 2432, 1173.

*2355 BLUE MOUNTAIN 34 [26] 3-8-6 (92) J P Spencer 5/1 FAV: 522110: Dwelt, bhd far side, some late   hd 76
gains: 15th: hvly bckd, swtg: better expected after impressing here in 2355: shld put this below par run bhd him.
3016 CRYHAVÓC 6 [5] 6-8-9 (91)(3ex) G Bardwell 16/1: 210200: With ldrs stands side till over 1f out: 16th.   ¾ 73
2925 DANCING MYSTERY 10 [2] 6-7-12 (80) S Carson (1) 40/1: 351030: With ldrs, wknd 1f out: 17th.   nk 61
2451 DANIELLES LAD 30 [12] 4-9-0 (96) P Fitzsimons (5) 33/1: 011040: Handy, wknd over 1f out: 18th.   nk 76
2706 HO LENG 20 [14] 5-9-8 (104) G Duffield 12/1: 3-3030: In tch far side, hung right & wknd fnl 1f: 19th.   hd 83
2954 JUWWI 8 [25] 6-8-12 (94) Darren Williams (5) 33/1: 000000: Dwelt, bhd, nvr dngrs: 20th: see 1337.   1 70
2615 Trinculo 23 [3] 3-9-8 (108) J F Egan 50/1:   2348 Alegria 34 [27] 4-8-8 (90)(bl) T Quinn 33/1:
2697 Get Stuck In 21 [21] 4-7-11 (78)(1ow) P Doe 50/1:
1676 Return Of Amin 63 [20] 6-7-13 (81)(bl) Martin Dwyer 40/1:
-2960 Coastal Bluff 8 [9] 8-7-13 (81) J Quinn 25/1:   2631 Bold Effort 23 [22] 8-7-12 (80)(bl) D Glennon (7) 50/1:
2954 Lone Piper 8 [18] 5-8-5 (87)(tvi) P Robinson 66/1:   2813 Brave Edge 15 [8] 9-8-2 (84) A Daly 40/1:
2954 Champagne Rider 8 [11] 4-7-10 (78) J Lowe 66/1:   2847 Alfailak 14 [13] 3-9-1 (101) Craig Williams 40/1:
30 ran   Time 1m 10.08 (0.08)   (Sammy Doo Racing)   D Nicholls Sessay, Nth Yorks.

3153   4.25 TURF CLUB RTD HCAP 3YO 0-95 (C)   1m6f   Firm 14 -11 Slow   [102]
    £9512   £3608   £1804   £820

2594 FANFARE 24 [5] G A Butler 3-8-7 (81) K Darley 3/1 FAV: 110241: 3 b f Deploy - Tashinsky (Nijinsky)   84
Dwelt, hld up, hdwy 2f out, styd on for press to lead ins last, drvn out: hvly bckd: earlier won at Windsor &
Sandown (h'caps) & 4th in Listed company: eff at 10f, stays 14f well on firm, soft & any trk: tough & useful.
2501 DOLLAR BIRD 28 [2] J L Dunlop 3-9-7 (95) T Quinn 10/1: -32002: 3 b f Kris - High Spirited (Shirley   nk 97
Heights) Cl-up, hdwy to lead over 1f out, kept on, collared cl-home, just btn: back to form, dropped into h'cap
company (unplcd in Gr class earlier) & apprec this step up to 14f: handles firm & gd/soft, any trk: win again.
2116 COVER UP 44 [4] Sir Michael Stoute 3-8-4 (92) Pat Eddery 9/1: 32-103: 3 b g Machiavellian - Sought   ¾ 93
Out (Rainbow Quest) Waited with, hdwy over 2f out, kept on inside last, but probably just held when short of room
cl-home: 6 wk abs & stays 14f on firm, possibly handles hvy: useful, see 850.
*2477 BOX BUILDER 29 [7] M R Channon 3-8-11 (85) Craig Williams 13/2: 33514: Prom, hdwy to chall over   nk 86
1f out, slightly short of room but onepcd inside last: gd run: see 2477.
2600 FAIT LE JOJO 24 [3] 3-8-8 (82) G Duffield 9/2: 541135: Waited with, effort 2f out, kept on   1¾ 81
same pace final 1f: proving consistent: see 2600, 2305 (C/D).
*2973 HIGH TOPPER 8 [8] 3-8-7 (81) J Reid 9/2: 244116: Trkd ldr till over 2f out, lost place & hmpd   hd 79
over 1f out, no extra inside last: will apprec a return to 2m as in 2973.
2852 BID FOR FAME 14 [6] 3-8-12 (86) L Carter 7/1: 530137: Dwelt, sn bhd, brief effort 3f out, onepace.   2 82
2600 THE WOODSTOCK LADY 24 [1] 3-9-2 (90) M Hills 12/1: -00248: Led till over 1f out, no extra.   5 81
8 ran   Time 3m 02.26 (3.46)   (T D Holland-Martin)   G A Butler Blewbury, Oxon.

3154   5.00 EBF RICHARD BAERLEIN MDN 2YO (D)   7f rnd   Firm 14 -35 Slow
    £7020   £2160   £1080   £540

2091 ARCHDUKE FERDINAND 45 [6] P F I Cole 2-8-11 Pat Eddery 4/1: 01: 2 ch c Demier Empereur - Lady   95
Norcliffe (Norcliffe) Keen, held up, hdwy 2f out, styd on well ins last to get up fnl 75y, drvn out: well bckd,
6 wk abs since highly tried on debut: Jan foal, cost 56,000 gns: half-brother to sev juv wnrs: dam 11f wnr:
stays 7f well, 1m sure to suit: acts on firm & runs well fresh on a sharp/undul trk: v useful, improve.
-- TAMBURLAINE [3] R Hannon 2-8-11 R Hughes 15/2: 2: 2 b c Royal Academy - Well Bought (Auction   ¾ 93+
Ring) Trkd ldr, led over 1f out, kept on ins last till collared by wnr cl-home: debut: Feb foal, cost 110,000
gns: stays 7f, further will suit in time: handles firm: v useful debut, type to win races.
2677 TAKAROA 21 [11] I A Balding 2-8-11 K Darley 10/1: 33: 2 b c Tagula - Mountain Harvest (Shirley   3½ 86
Heights) Prom, eff 2f out, onepace: improved for debut & stays 7f on firm: sure to win a mdn & apprec further.
-- REPULSE BAY [4] M R Channon 2-8-11 Craig Williams 8/1: 4: Waited with, hdwy 2f out, ran green but   hd 85+
kept on nicely final 1f, nrst fin: op 5/1 on debut: Mar foal, cost IR60,000 gns: half-brother to a 1m juv
scorer: dam smart over mid-dists: sure to relish 1m+ in time: caught the eye here, sure-fire improver.
2921 MURRENDI 10 [7] 2-8-11 J Reid 33/1: -505: Set pace till over 1f out, onepace: stays 7f on firm grnd.   nk 84
1260 GILDED DANCER 85 [8] 2-8-11 Martin Dwyer 14/1: 36: Handy, lost pace over 2f out, late gains: 1 82
3 mth abs: already in need of 1m+ & the type to progress with racing: see 1260.
2494 STEINITZ 28 [10] 2-8-11 T Quinn 11/8 FAV: 27: Prom, rdn over 2f out, no extra final 1f: hvly   nk 81
bckd: better expected after catching the eye in 2494 (stiff task).
-- MOBTAKER [9] 2-8-11 W Supple 8/1: 8: Keen cl-up, wknd over 1f out: debut: Apr foal: full   1¼ 77
brother to a smart 6f juv wnr: dam 11f scorer: with B Hills.
2760 WELL MAKE IT 17 [5] 2-8-11 J Mongan (5) 50/1: 69: Keen, waited with, rdn & no impress 2f out.   ½ 76$
2677 ACHILLES SUN 21 [2] 2-8-11 J Weaver 50/1: U40: Dwelt, keen bhd, btn 2f out: 10th: see 2677.   1½ 73$
2867 MUJALIA 13 [1] 2-8-11 J F Egan 50/1: -000: Bhd, btn over 2f out: 11th: see 1454.   1½ 70
11 ran   Time 1m 27.9 (3.4)   (Mr C Wright & The Hon Mrs J M Corbett)   P F I Cole Whatcombe, Oxon.

3155   5.35 EBF RACEGOERS CLASS STKS 3YO+ 0-95 (B)   7f rnd   Firm 14 -14 Slow
    £8810   £3341   £1670   £759   3 yo rec 6 lb

2769 VEIL OF AVALON 17 [3] R Charlton 3-8-4 K Darley 100/30 JT FAV: 16-621: 3 b f Thunder Gulch - Wind   96
In Her Hair (Alzao) Cl-up, led over 2f out, styd on well over 1f out, drvn out: well bckd: '99 scorer at Lingfield
& Newbury (stks, rtd 95 at best): stays 7f well on gd & firm, handles gd/soft: fast imp here: has run well: useful.
2954 KASHRA 8 [5] M Johnston 3-8-4 M Hills 12/1: -40002: 3 b f Dancing Dissident - Tudor Loom (Sallust)   1 94
Hld up, gd hdwy over 2f out, not clr run & swtchd left over 1f out, styd on well inside last, not reach
wnr: back to form stepped up to 7f: looked a shade unlucky here & should win again: see 1090.
2495 SMART RIDGE 28 [1] K R Burke 3-8-12 J Weaver 4/1: 502023: 3 ch c Indian Ridge - Guahhumara   ½ 101
(Caerleon) Cl-up, hdwy to chase wnr over 1f out, kept on same pace: proving tough & useful: see 2495.
2997 MUCHEA 7 [6] M R Channon 6-9-2 (vis) Craig Williams 8/1: 054004: Prom, hdwy over 1f out, no extra.   1¾ 95
2954 EASY DOLLAR 8 [7] 3-8-13 (vis) T Quinn 14/1: -60005: Led till over 2f out, wknd inside last: 1 90
stiff task at the weights & ran well with visor applied: see 2954 (blnks), 1674.
-2648 SWAN KNIGHT 22 [2] 4-8-13 Pat Eddery 100/30 JT FAV: -40026: In tch, effort over 2f out, no extra   nk 89
over 1f out: well bckd: better expected after 2648 (1m).
2847 HALLAND PARK GIRL 14 [8] 3-8-9 R Hughes 8/1: 602007: Waited with, eff well over 1f out, no dngr.   ¾ 89
2809 ADJUTANT 15 [4] 5-9-7 P Robinson 16/1: 312068: Al bhd: better than this: see 1514, 1286.   2½ 90
2458 KUMAIT 29 [9] 6-9-0 J Reid 14/1: 1-4069: Keen cl-up, brief effort over 1f out, sn wknd: see 1946.   1¾ 79

GOODWOOD SATURDAY AUGUST 5TH Righthand, Sharpish, Undulating Track

9 ran   Time 1m 26.44 (1.94)   (Jeffen Racing)   R Charlton Beckhampton, Wilts.

DONCASTER SATURDAY AUGUST 5TH Lefthand, Flat, Galloping Track

Official Going   GOOD/FIRM. Stalls: Str Crse - Stands Side, Rnd Crse - Inside, Rnd Mile - Outside.

3156   2.25 STRAWBERRY MDN STKS 2YO (D)   7f str   Good/Firm 22   -19 Slow
£3770   £1160   £580   £290

--   **TARFSHI** [2] M A Jarvis 2-8-9 M Tebbutt 15/2: 1: 2 b f Mtoto - Pass The Peace (Alzao)   85
Chsd ldrs, prog/narrow lead ins last, styd on strongly to narrowly prevail: drifted from 4/1: Apr foal, half-sister to smart juv Embassy, dam a high-class French miler: sire top-class mid-dist performer: eff over a gall 7f, looks sure to apprec 1m+: acts on fast grnd & runs well fresh: fine intro.

2854   **ALNAHAAM 14** [1] B Hanbury 2-9-0 G Faulkner (3) 12/1: -62: 2ch c Hamas - Abir (Soviet Star)   hd   89
Mid-div, rdn & prog to lead 2f out, hdd ins last, rallied well, just held: longer 7f trip: acts on fast grnd: had the next well covered & can find a similar contest: see 2854.

--   **PERFECT SUNDAY** [6] B W Hills 2-9-0 J Carroll 3/1: 3: 2 b c Quest For Fame - Sunday Bazaar   3   82
(Nureyev) Trkd ldrs, rdn & kept on fnl 2f, not pace of front pair: bckd: Apr foal, half-brother to 2 wnrs abroad, dam a French 12f wnr: looks sure to relish 1m+: handles fast grnd.

2563   **MAWHOOB 25** [3] J L Dunlop 2-9-0 R Hills 11/4 FAV: 64: Cl-up, outpcd fnl 2f: bckd, op 7/2.   1   80

--   **REGENT COURT** [11] 2-8-9 T E Durcan 20/1: 5: Towards rear, rdn/switched & styd on fnl 2f, no   ½   73+
threat: Marju filly, Mar foal, cost IR 40,000gns: half-sister to an Irish juv wnr, dam 5f wnr: sire top-class 1m/12f performer: stays 7f, looks sure to relish 1m+ on this evidence: handles fast grnd.

2921   **MYTHICAL JINKS 10** [7] 2-9-0 J Fanning 16/1: -566: Mid-div, not much room 3f out, rdn/switched &   ½   76
styd on ins last, no threat: likely to apprec 1m+ & h'cap company: see 2921, 2414.

2563   **DON ALFRED 25** [13] 2-9-0 D Sweeney 8/1: 57: Chsd ldrs, rdn/no extra over 1f out: see 2563.   ½   74
2686   **PRIME TRUMP 21** [8] 2-9-0 R Mullen 8/1: 548: Held up, rdn over 2f out, no impress: see 2269.   nk   73

--   **REIMS** [10] 2-9-0 W Ryan 25/1: 9: Rear, some hdwy 2f out, sn held: stablemate of 5th: Topanoora   hd   72
colt, Mar foal, cost 38,000gns: dam a 6f Irish juv wnr, sire high-class 10/12f performer: will apprec further in time.

--   **CARDINAL VENTURE** [12] 2-9-0 F Lynch 11/2: 0: Led 5f: 10th: Apr foal, 22,000gns 2yo, dam a 7f wnr.   3   65
2828 **Kathann 15** [5] 2-8-9 O Pears 66/1:   --   **Miss Phantine** [9] 2-8-9 Graham Gibbons (7) 50/1:
1102 **Mount Royale 94** [4] 2-9-0 G Parkin 50/1:
13 ran   Time 1m 26.08 (2.88)   (Sheikh Ahmed Al Maktoum)   M A Jarvis Newmarket.

3157   2.55 EXPRESS FILLIES MDN 3YO+ (D)   1m4f   Good/Firm 22   -05 Slow
£4192   £1290   £645   £322   3 yo rec 11lb

2703   **BANCO SUIVI 20** [5] B W Hills 3-8-10 J Carroll 15/8: -20231: 3 b f Nashwan - Pay The Bank (High Top)   86
Made all, rdn when pressed over 1f out, styd on well & al holding rival ins last, rdn out: 5th on sole juv start (rtd 91+): apprec step up to 12f, could get further: acts on fast & soft, gall/easy trk: enjoyed front-running today.

1269   **SECOND AFFAIR 85** [4] C F Wall 3-8-10 R Mullen 1/1 FAV: 32: 3 b f Pursuit Of Love - Startino   ¾   84
(Bustino) Held up, prog 4f out, chsd wnr fnl 3f, kept on well for press tho' always just held: well clr of rem: hvly bckd from 6/4, 12 wk abs: styd longer 12f trip well: see 1269 (1m).

--   **VILLIAN** [2] J G Smyth Osbourne 5-9-7 D Sweeney 33/1: 3: 5 b m Kylian - Shotsville (Random Shot)   11   72
Chsd ldrs, outpcd by front pair fnl 3f: Flat debut, 10 wk jumps abs, earlier scored at Uttoxeter (nov hdle, rtd 83h, eff at 2m on fast & gd, with Mrs H Mobley).

2265   **DIAMOND 37** [3] H R A Cecil 4-9-7 W Ryan 5/1: 04: In tch, btn over 3f out: op 7/2: longer 12f trip.   1   71
814   **DOODLE BUG 124** [1] 3-8-10 A Polli (3) 12/1: 30-35: Chsd wnr halfway, btn 4f out: op 8/1: 4 mth abs.   9   61
1824   **DAME HATTIE 57** [6] 5-9-7 F Lynch 50/1: 556: Bhd 3f out: 8 wk abs: see 1824, 1599.   1½   59
6 ran   Time 2m 33.02 (3.22)   (Wafic Said)   B W Hills Lambourn, Berks.

3158   3.25 UKBETTING.COM STKS 3YO+ (C)   6f   Good/Firm 22   +08 Fast
£7540   £2320   £1160   £580   3 yo rec 4 lb

2087   **FATH 45** [4] Saeed bin Suroor 3-8-9 (t) R Hills 1/2 FAV: 12-061: 3 b c Danzig - Desirable (Lord Gayle)   111
Made all, rdn/qcknd over 2f out, styd on strongly ins last, pushed out cl-home: fast time: hvly bckd at odds on: earlier wnr of a Godolphin trial: '99 debut York wnr (mdn), rdn rnr-up to Primo Valentino on sole subs start (Gr 1, rtd 117, M Tregoning): well suited by this return to 6f, styd 1m in the Dubai Trial: acts on fast & gd grnd, stiff/gall tracks: eff in a t-strap & runs well fresh: this smart colt shld make his mark in Listed/Gr sprinting company.

2669   **PROUD NATIVE 21** [7] D Nicholls 6-9-7 Alex Greaves 4/1: 022062: 6 b g Imp Society - Karamana   2   110
(Habitat) Bhd ldrs, keen, rdn/chsd wnr 2f out, kept on tho' al held: clr of rem: op 3/1: met a smart rival.

2960   **SEVEN NO TRUMPS 8** [6] B W Hills 3-8-9 R Naylor (7) 20/1: -00003: 3 ch g Pips Pride - Classic Ring   4   90
(Auction Ring) Keen/held up in tch, rdn/switched left over 1f out, no threat to front pair: see 2960, 950.

2859   **DIFFERENTIAL 14** [3] B Smart 3-8-9 M Tebbutt 14/1: 40-554: Keen/prom, outpcd fnl 2f: op 12/1.   1   88
2997   **NOW LOOK HERE 7** [1] 4-8-13 L Newton 4/1: 502005: Bhd ldrs, outpcd fnl 2f: btr 2458, 1337 & 734.   nk   87
2228   **JAMADYAN 38** [5] 3-8-12 G Hind 25/1: 1-646: Rear, nvr on terms: see 996.   3½   81
2900   **ALFIE LEE 11** [2] 3-8-9 (t) W Ryan 25/1: -00507: Trkd ldrs, btn 2f out: t-strap: see 2197.   6   67
7 ran   Time 1m 11.66 (.86)   (Godolphin)   Saeed bin Suroor Newmarket.

3159   3.55 WEATHERBYS HCAP 3YO+ 0-85 (D)   1m2f60y   Good/Firm 22   -11 Slow   [83]
£15080   £4640   £2320   £1160   3 yo rec 9 lb

*3011   **GRALMANO 6** [3] K A Ryan 5-9-11 (80) F Lynch 8/1: 516411: 5 b g Scenic - Llangollen (Caerleon)   85
Cl-up, rdn/led over 1f out, styd on well ins last, rdn out: qck rapp: earlier scored at W'hampton (AW h'cap, rtd 98a), Redcar & Ripon (h'caps): '99 wnr at Redcar (class stks) & Pontefract (h'cap, rtd 72 & 92a, earlier with N Littmonden): '98 Lingfield wnr (stks, rtd 99a & 82): suited by 1m/10f, stays 11f well: acts on both AWs, firm & gd/soft, any trk: eff with/without blnks or vis, a gd weight carrier: in great heart at present, hat-trick possible.

*2872   **WARNING REEF 13** [8] E J Alston 7-8-3 (58) T E Durcan 9/1: 533312: 7 b g Warning - Horseshoe Reef   1¼   60
(Mill Reef) Held up, prog over 2f out & drvn/styd on well ins last, not reach wnr: consistent gelding: see 2872 (12f).

2702   **ABUZAID 20** [7] J L Dunlop 3-9-6 (84) R Hills 10/1: 000153: 3 br c Nureyev - Elle Seule (Exclusive   ½   85

DONCASTER SATURDAY AUGUST 5TH Lefthand, Flat, Galloping Track

Native) Mid-div, rdn & styd on fnl 2f for press, not pace of wnr: see 2270.

2853 **WEET A MINUTE** 14 [2] N P Littmoden 7-10-0 (83) D Sweeney 14/1: 560054: Led, rdn/hdd over 1f out, no extra: imprvd effort last twice with blnks discarded: has slipped to a handy turf mark: see 230.	hd	83
2674 **OCTANE** 21 [6] 4-9-1 (70) T G McLaughlin 5/2 FAV: 021145: Held up, rdn fnl 3f, onepace: well bckd.	shd	70
2638 **ANNADAWI** 22 [4] 5-7-10 (51)(1oh) G Baker (5) 25/1: 102236: Held up, eff 3f out, no threat: see 1575.	1¾	49
*2838 **KARALIYFA** 14 [5] 3-9-7 (85) L Newman (3) 9/2: 3-617: Chsd ldrs, fdd over 1f out: h'cap bow.	½	82
2671 **FREEDOM QUEST** 21 [9] 5-8-5 (60) J Bramhill 8/1: 252148: Chsd ldrs 1m: btr 2522.	3½	52
2937 **CLARENDON** 9 [12] 4-9-10 (79) G Hind 9/1: 062239: In tch 7f: see 968.	4	65
2888 **YOUNG UN** 12 [1] 5-8-7 (62) P McCabe 12/1: 025500: Chsd ldrs, btn 2f out, eased fnl 1f: 10th.	nk	47
2863 **FAIR LADY** 13 [11] 3-9-0 (78) J Carroll 8/1: 6-1630: Held up, rdn 3f out, no impress: 11th: btr 2863.	1¼	61
2836 **COURT EXPRESS** 14 [10] 6-9-10 (79) R Mullen 10/1: 620530: Pulled hard rear, al bhd, eased fnl 1f: 12th: needs a strong pace, poss best dropped back to 1m off a stronger gallop: see 1279 (8.5f).	1¾	60
12 ran Time 2m 09.80 (3.4) (Coleorton Moor Racing) K A Ryan Hambleton, N.Yorks.		

3160 4.30 SUMMER FILLIES HCAP 3YO 0-85 (D) 1m rnd Good/Firm 22 -24 Slow [87]
£4446   £1368   £684   £342

*2745 **JAWLA** 17 [9] J H M Gosden 3-9-7 (80) R Hills 7/4 FAV: 0-3211: 3 ch f Wolfhound - Majmu (Al Nasr) Cl-up, led going well over 2f out, drvn & styd on well ins last, narrowly: hvly bckd: recent Catterick wnr (fill auct mdn): well btn sole '99 start: eff at 7f, well suited by step up to 1m, could get further: acts on fast & gd/soft grnd, sharp or gall trk: has run well fresh: fine h'cap bow.		84
*2918 **DIAMOND RACHAEL** 10 [7] Mrs N Macauley 3-8-4 (63)(vis) R Fitzpatrick (3) 16/1: 366012: 3 b f Shalford - Brown Foam (Horage) Cl-up, drvn & strong chall fnl 1f, just held cl-home: op 14/1: eff at 6f/1m.	½	65
2713 **MIDNIGHT ALLURE** 19 [5] C F Wall 3-9-3 (76)(t) R Mullen 13/2: 211623: 3 b f Aragon - Executive Lady (Night Shift) Rear, prog over 2f out & drvn/strong chall 1f out, just held well ins last: clr of rem: see 2713.	1	76
*2846 **DEVIL LEADER** 14 [2] B W Hills 3-9-1 (74) J Carroll 13/2: 053214: Cl-up, hmpd/lost pl after 2f, outpcd fnl 2f: see 2846 (mdn).	5	64
2918 **STEALTHY TIMES** 10 [1] 3-8-13 (72) G Baker (5) 14/1: 000055: Held up, mod hdwy 3f out, sn held.	1¾	59
2955 **QUEENS BENCH** 8 [3] 3-9-6 (79)(t) W Ryan 4/1: -40506: Held up, drvn/btn over 2f out, eased: see 2955.	nk	65
*2988 **LADY HELEN** 7 [4] 3-9-2 (75) T E Durcan 9/2: 051017: Hmpd/drpd rear halfway, drvn/held after.	½	60
2504 **SAFRANINE** 28 [8] 3-9-7 (80) D Sweeney 25/1: -00008: Led till over 2f out, sn btn: see 630.	3	59
3022 **OMNIHEAT** 6 [3] 3-9-7 (80)(bl) P McCabe 12/1: 316549: Trkd ldrs after 3f, wknd qckly 2f out: op 8/1.	17	33
9 ran Time 1m 39.78 (3.68) (Hamdan Al Maktoum) J H M Gosden Manton, Wilts.		

3161 5.05 RACING WELFARE HCAP 3YO 0-70 (E) 5f Good/Firm 22 +07 Fast [77]
£3721   £1145   £572   £286

2701 **PIPS STAR** 20 [12] J S Goldie 3-7-11 (46) G Baker (5) 20/1: 240001: 3 b f Pips Pride - Kentucky Starlet (Cox's Ridge) Al prom, rdn & duelled with rnr-up fnl 1f, styd on well for press to lead nr fin: gd time: '99 wnr at W'hampton (seller, rtd 68a, earlier plcd on turf, rtd 77, auct mdn): suited by 5f on fast grnd & fibresand: handles a sharp or gall trk: looks well h'capped & can win again in this grade.		52
-3010 **ELVINGTON BOY** 6 [4] M W Easterby 3-9-11 (74) T Lucas 13/8 FAV: 032522: 3 ch g Emarati - Catherine's Well (Junius) Led, rdn/hdd well ins last & no extra: well bckd: clr of rem: qck reappr: deserves to find similar.	nk	79
2623 **ZOENA** 23 [8] J G Portman 3-8-6 (55) L Newman (3) 11/1: -04563: 3 ch f Emarati - Exotic Forest (Dominion) Prom, outpcd 2f out, kept on ins last for press, no threat: jockey given 1 day whip ban: see 2252.	3½	51
2779 **BENNOCHY** 16 [5] A Berry 3-8-5 (54) O Pears 10/1: 050454: Chsd ldrs, outpcd over 1f out: op 12/1.	nk	49
2969 **MOUNT PARK** 8 [6] 3-8-1 (50)(bl) Claire Bryan (5) 14/1: 000105: Bmpd start, held up, drvn/mod gains.	nk	44
2934 **BEST BOND** 9 [15] 3-8-7 (56)(VIS) D Sweeney 14/1: 005606: Towards rear, nvr pace to chall: visor.	1¼	47
1994 **CLANSMAN** 49 [11] 3-8-2 (51) A Polli (3) 25/1: 5-00007: Mid-div, outpcd fnl 2f: abs: see 1795.	shd	42
2919 **SASHA** 10 [14] 3-8-2 (50)(1ow) J Fanning 20/1: 0-408: Chsd ldrs 4f: h'cap wind.	shd	41
2947 **LAYAN** 8 [2] 3-8-5 (54) J Edmunds 11/1: 603429: Prom 3f: flattered 2947.	½	42
2864 **SHALARISE** 13 [7] 3-9-0 (75)(VIS) J Carroll 7/1: 005020: Bmpd start/rear, rdn/no impress when no room 1f out: 10th: tried visor: btr 2864.	nk	44
426 **LADY SANDROVITCH** 187 [10] 3-7-12 (47)(2ow)(3oh) N Carlisle 33/1: 43-060: Al rear: 11th: abs.	¾	32
2779 **PARADISE YANGSHUO** 16 [3] 3-7-12 (47) J Bramhill 7/1: 041530: Chsd ldrs 3f: 12th: btr 2779, 2204.	nk	31
1861 **SEVEN OF SPADES** 55 [13] 3-8-13 (62) F Lynch 8/1: 35-000: Struggling fnl 2f: 13th: op 14/1: abs.	½	44
2788 **WILLRACK TIMES** 16 [1] 3-7-12 (47) A Mackay 25/1: 500000: Chsd ldrs 3f: 14th: see 706.	¾	27
14 ran Time 58.97 (0.77) (Colin Barnfather & Frank Steele) J S Goldie Uplawmoor, E Renfrewshire		

NEWMARKET (July) SATURDAY AUGUST 5TH Righthand, Stiff, Galloping Track

Official Going   GOOD. Stalls: 1m4f - Stands Side; Rem - Far Side.

3162 2.10 EBF EXPRESS MDN 2YO (D) 6f Good/Firm 23 -17 Slow
£4426   £1362   £681   £340   Raced stands side, high numbers favoured

2649 **HURRICANE FLOYD** 22 [11] J Noseda 2-9-0 D Holland 10/11 FAV: 21: 2 b c Pennekamp - Mood Swings (Shirley Heights) Trkd ldrs going well, burst thro' to lead 1f out, shaken up & qcknd readily: hvly bckd from 9/4: 60,000 gns Feb 1st foal, dam 6f juv wnr: stays 7f, apprec the drop back to 6f: acts on fast grnd, stiff/gall trk: useful, improving colt with a fine turn of foot, expect a bold display in the Gr 2 Gimcrack later this month.		110
-1809 **BANNISTER** 57 [18] R Hannon 2-9-0 Dane O'Neill 5/1: 22: 2 ch c Inchinor - Shall We Run (Hotfoot) Well plcd, narrow lead appr fnl 1f, sn rdn, hdd dist & outpcd by wnr: nicely bckd: lost little in defeat against a potentially smart rival: acts on fast & gd/soft grnd & will go one better soon: see 1809.	1¾	100
-- **EMINENCE** 15 [9] Sir Michael Stoute 2-9-0 R Cochrane 3/1: 3: 2 b c Machiavellian - Divine Danse (Kris) Towards rear, hands & heels hdwy ent fnl 2f, not trouble front pair: well bckd, clr of rem: 140,000 gns Apr foal, half-brother to 6f juv & high-class miler Valentino, dam a top sprinter, sire a miler: eff at 6f, step up to 7f is going to suit: handles fast grnd: looks sure to find much more before going on to better things.	2	94+
2979 **PROLETARIAT** 8 [6] H Candy 2-9-0 C Rutter 20/1: 24: In tch, wide, prog to chase ldrs when bmpd & carried left appr fnl 1f, onepace under hands & heels: not disgraced in a fast race, win soon: see 2979.	3½	84
-- **STATUE GALLERY** 17 [17] 2-9-0 S Whitworth 20/1: 5: Mid-div, hdwy under press appr fnl 2f, no extra bef dist: op 14/1 on debut: 52,000 gns Cadeaux Genereux Apr 1st foal, dam 10f wnr, sire a sprinter: promise here.	1¼	80

-- **BRANDON WIZZARD** [14] 2-9-0 D O'Donohoe 25/1: 6: Led, rdn & hung left over 1f out, sn hdd & btn: debut: 27,000IR gns Tagula Jan foal, half-brother to a 6f juv wnr: ran well for a long way, improve. 1½ **76**
-- **WHALE BEACH** [7] 2-9-0 A Eddery (5) 33/1: 7: Slow away, wide, keen, imprvd appr fnl 2f, sn same pace: promising, unfav'ble draw: 60,000IR gns Known Fact Feb 1st foal, dam multiple wnr in the States. *shd* **76**
-- **SHEER PASSION** [13] 2-9-0 G Carter 20/1: 8: Slow away, styg on fin but nvr better than than mid-div: 13,000 gns Distant Relative Mar foal, half-brother to a juv wnr & a fair mid-dist performer, dam 7f juv, sire a miler. 1¼ **73**
-- **DOMINION PRINCE** [16] 2-9-0 R Smith (5) 25/1: 9: Keen, al towards rear: 11,500 gns First Trump Mar foal, brother to a mdn, half-brother to sev wnrs, sire & dam sprinters: stablemate of 2nd. *hd* **73**
-- **COSMIC RANGER** [5] 2-9-0 O Urbina 33/1: 0: Wide, nvr a factor & flashed tail under press bef dist: 10th: 5,000 gns Magic Ring Mar foal, half-brother to 2 wnrs, incl a juv: sire a sprinter: with N Littmoden. ¾ **70**
993 **THATS ALL JAZZ 105** [12] 2-8-9 M Henry 50/1: 00: Prsd ldr till fdd ent fnl 2f & hung left: 11th, abs. 3½ **56**
2106 **LEATHERBACK 44** [4] 2-9-0 J Mackay (5) 40/1: 00: Switched from low draw, nvr trbled ldrs: 12th. 1¼ **57**
-- **Saorsie** [9] 2-9-0 R Ffrench 33/1:
-- **Pentland** [2] 2-9-0 F Norton 20/1:
2760 **Hard To Know 17** [1] 2-9-0 N Callan 33/1:
2324 **Amarone 35** [8] 2-9-0 A Clark 66/1:
16 ran Time 1m 13.38 (2.38) (Lucayan Stud) J Noseda Newmarket, Suffolk

3163

2.40 TOTE HCAP 3YO 0-80 (D) 7f str Good/Firm 23 -04 Slow [85]
£4621 £1422 £711 £355

2495 **CELEBRATION TOWN 28** [12] D Morris 3-9-5 (76) R Cochrane 5/1 FAV: -10161: 3 b g Case Law - Battle Queen (Kind Of Hush) Waited with, gd prog ent fnl 2f, drvn below dist, ran on gamely to lead cl-home: nicely bckd: earlier won at Southwell & Sandown (h'caps): unplcd for J J O'Neill in '99 (rtd 73): eff at 7f, tried 1m: acts on fast & soft grnd, any trk: runs well fresh: progressive, lightly raced & genuine. **87**
2855 **SHATHER 14** [7] J W Hills 3-8-9 (66) S Whitworth 7/1: -03432: 3 b c Goofalik - Western Pride (Priamos) Chsd ldrs, rdn to lead appr fnl 1f, hung left ins last, collared towards fin: nicely bckd tho' op 11/2, well clr of 3rd: another fine run tho' is rising in the weights without wng: see 2855, 2322. ½ **75**
2661 **OCEAN RAIN 22** [11] C G Cox 3-9-0 (71) Dane O'Neill 16/1: 500403: 3 ch c Lake Coniston - Alicedale (Trempolino) In tch, rdn 2f out, kept on for 3rd but no ch front 2: back in trip, can do better, see 2330, 954. 5 **70**
2775 **DILSAA 16** [14] P W Harris 3-8-8 (65) J Mackay (5) 16/1: 500064: Dsptd lead & ev ch till onepace under press appr fnl 1f: mdn, see 810. ¾ **62**
*2592 **STARLIGHT 24** [4] 3-8-13 (70) G Carter 7/1: 5-1015: Rear, late hdwy, nvr a threat: qckr grnd today. *nk* **66**
2855 **SUMTHINELSE 14** [1] 3-9-6 (77) D Holland 9/1: 402146: Chsd ldrs, eff & no impress appr fnl 1f. *nk* **72**
2261 **KAMAREYAH 38** [10] 3-9-7 (78) G Hall 14/1: 10-007: Towards rear, drvn appr fnl 2f, dropped reins bef dist, nvr nr to chall: top-weight: poor ride from jockey reported to have ridden many wnrs in Australia. *hd* **73**
3076 **ATYLAN BOY 3** [3] 3-8-10 (67)(bl) S Clancy (7) 16/1: 152468: Prsd ldr, led 2½f out till bef dist, fdd. ½ **61**
2918 **ALPHILDA 10** [13] 3-9-3 (74) F Norton 14/1: 034039: Rear, hdwy into mid-div when sltly short of room ent fnl 2f & again dist, nvr a factor: tricky ride, see 2918, 1289. *nk* **67**
2604 **RESILIENT 23** [9] 3-8-12 (69) B Marcus 9/1: 06520: Al towards rear: 10th, h'cap bow, much btr 2604 (AW). 2½ **57**
3021 **REGARDEZ MOI 6** [6] 3-7-10 (53)(5oh) D Kinsella (7) 33/1: 063000: Led till 3f out, grad wknd: 11th. *shd* **41**
2577 **NAJEYBA 24** [5] 3-9-6 (77) D Harrison 15/2: 1340: Not settle, al bhd: 12th, lngr trip, different tactics/trip. 3½ **59**
2183 **PORT ST CHARLES 41** [2] 3-9-6 (77) A Clark 11/1: 3-2450: Unruly start, nvr dangerous: 13th, 6 wk abs. 5 **49**
*2591 **ANYHOW 24** [8] 3-8-12 (69) M Henry 11/2: 3-0410: Chsd ldrs, btn 3f out, eased: 14th: much btr 2591 3 **35**
14 ran Time 1m 25.76 (1.86) (Meadowcrest Ltd) D Morris Newmarket, Suffolk

3164

3.10 TOTE COND STKS 2YO (C) 7f str Good/Firm 23 -08 Slow
£6322 £2398 £1199 £545

*2791 **ATLANTIS PRINCE 16** [3] S P C Woods 2-8-11 L Dettori 11/4 JT FAV: 11: 2 ch c Tagula - Zoom Lens (Caerleon) Trkd ldr, shaken up to chall 2f out, rdn bef dist, ran on to lead fnl 100y: bckd tho' op 2/1: unbtn, landed debut at Epsom (auct mdn): 75,000 gns Mar foal, half-brother to juv wnrs at 5f/1m: eff at 7f, 1m likely to suit: acts on fast & gd grnd, prob any trk: progressive & well regarded colt. **101**
*2521 **CRAZY LARRYS 27** [5] J Noseda 2-9-1 D Holland 5/1: -12: 2 ch c Mutakddim - No Fear Of Flying (Super Concorde) Chsd ldrs, led ent fnl 2f, under press & hdd ins last: nicely bckd, clr rem: improved in defeat up in grade: acts on fast & gd grnd: progressive colt: see 2521. ¾ **102**
-- **FREEFOURINTERNET** [4] B J Meehan 2-8-8 Paul Eddery 13/2: 3: 2 b c Tabasco Cat - Dixie Chimes (Dixieland Band) Held up in tch, shaken up to chase front pair 2f out, onepace dist: promise: Apr foal, half-brother to a juv wnr, dam a dirt wnr, sire 1m/12f dirt performer: eff at 7f on fast, 1m will suit: shld improve. 2 **90**
2741 **PARVENUE 17** [1] E A L Dunlop 2-8-6 G Carter 7/1: 124: Held up, feeling pace 2f out, styd on late. ½ **87**
2881 **SABANA 12** [2] 2-8-11 J Mackay (5) 11/4 JT FAV: 025: Chsd ldrs wide, no extra appr fnl 1f: well bckd, op 4/1: will apprec a return to mdn company, see 2881. 3½ **85**
2088 **PARTY CHARMER 45** [6] 2-8-10 B Marcus 9/2: 1406: Led till 2f out, wknd: 6 wk abs: unsuited by step up to 7f & forcing tactics?: see 1059 (5f on soft). ¾ **82**
6 ran Time 1m 26.09 (2.19) (Lucayan Stud) S P C Woods Newmarket, Suffolk

3165

3.45 TOTE SCOOP6 NURSERY HCAP 2YO (B) 6f Good/Firm 23 -08 Slow [98]
£19500 £6000 £3000 £1500 Raced stands side

+2557 **DIM SUMS 25** [6] T D Barron 2-9-7 (91) L Dettori 2/1 FAV: 2111: 2 b g Repriced - Regal Baby (Northern Baby) Trkd ldrs, shkn up 2f out, ran on to lead dist, cmftbly: hvly bckd: hat-trick landed after wins at Southwell (mdn, rtd 72a) & Pontefract (nurs): eff at 6f, shld apprec 7f: acts on fast grnd & fibresand, sharp or stiff trk: runs well fresh: progressive & v useful, can quicken & looks Listed/Gr 3 class. **105**
*2608 **CAUSTIC WIT 23** [5] E A L Dunlop 2-9-5 (89) G Carter 3/1: -5012: 2 b c Cadeaux Genereux - Baldemosa (Lead On Time) Prom, wide, chall appr fnl 1f, always held by wnr: nicely bckd on h'cap bow: lost little in defeat against a v progressive rival: step up to 7f will suit now: see 2608. 1½ **95**
2363 **SYLVAN GIRL 33** [8] C N Allen 2-7-11 (67) P M Quinn (3) 20/1: 3253: 2 ch f Case Law - Nordic Living (Nordico) Bhd, gd prog appr fnl 1f, styd on under hands & heels, nvr nrr: sound h'cap bow, 7f will suit, see 1954. 1¼ **69**
2959 **KNOCK 8** [10] R Hannon 2-8-10 (80) D Harrison 12/1: -41524: Sn led, drvn 2f out, hdd 1f out, onepace: ran well on h'cap bow, sharper trk might suit: see 2959, 1648. ½ **80**
*2711 **WESTERN HERO 19** [9] 2-8-11 (81) Dane O'Neill 12/1: 33215: Bhd ldrs, eff & unable to qckn appr fnl 1f: op 8/1, stablemate 4th: up in trip on h'cap bow: prob capable of better at 5f: see 2711. 1½ **77**
2808 **OUR DESTINY 15** [7] 2-9-2 (86) N Callan 8/1: -0136: Prsd ldr till fdd ent fnl 2f: h'cap bow, btr 2808, 2454. 1½ **78**
*2854 **FOODBROKER FANCY 14** [11] 2-9-2 (86) R Cochrane 7/1: -2417: Waited with, not clr run & switched ent fnl 2f, not much room after, nvr dangerous: 7f will suit & this is worth forgiving: see 2854. *nk* **77**

NEWMARKET (July)   SATURDAY AUGUST 5TH   Righthand, Stiff, Galloping Track

3079 **TOP NOLANS 3** [3] 2-8-9 (79)(VIS) A Clark 25/1: 03338: Early ldr, wide, wknd appr fnl 1f: visored,   ½ 68
poss not the best of draws, quick reapp: see 3079, 2724.
*2575 **ONLY ONE LEGEND 24** [1] 2-8-13 (83) R Winston 16/1: -03319: Mid-div, wide, no impress 2f out: ½ 71
longer trip, possibly unfav'bly drawn over longer 6f trip: made all in 2575 (5f).
2985 **THATS JAZZ 7** [2] 2-8-5 (75) J Mackay (5) 8/1: 0220: Rear, not much room 2f out, sn btn: 10th,   1¾ 58
prob a poor draw, quick reapp, back in trip: much btr 2985 (7f).
*2730 **HUMES LAW 18** [4] 2-8-9 (79) D Holland 25/1: -04610: In tch wide 3f: 11th, tricky draw on h'cap bow.   2 56
2850 **NORCROFT LADY 14** [12] 2-9-6 (90) F Norton 14/1: -14160: Chsd ldrs, losing pl/hmpd 2f out: 12th.   hd 67
12 ran   Time 1m 12.87 (1.87)   (Executive Network Pertemps Group)   T D Barron Maunby, N Yorks

3166   4.15 TOTE SCOOP6 HCAP 3YO+ 0-90 (C)   1m2f   Good/Firm 23 +01 Fast   [82]
£8573   £2638   £1319   £659   3 yo rec 9 lb

3024 **PINCHINCHA 6** [2] D Morris 6-9-10 (78) R Cochrane 7/4 FAV: 343421: 6 b g Priolo - Western Heights   82
(Shirley Heights) Patiently rdn, imprvd 2f out, drvn dist, led fnl 100y, narrowly: well bckd from 5/2, fair time,
qk reapp: consistent in defeat, incl when '99 rnr-up (h'caps, rtd 78): last won in '97 at Folkestone, Doncaster
(ltd stks) & Pontefract (h'caps, rtd 85): suited by 10f on firm & gd/soft, any trk, without visor: v tough.
3022 **EASTWAYS 6** [5] M Johnston 3-9-6 (83) D Holland 7/2: 000422: 3 ch c Efisio - Helens Dreamgirl   shd 86
(Caerleon) Chsd ldrs, ran on to lead 1f out, hdd well ins last, rallied, just failed: nicely bckd, quick reapp:
imprvd again over this longer 10f trip but is creeping up the weights without reward: see 3022, 982.
2102 **ANOTHER TIME 45** [4] S P C Woods 3-8-9 (77) N Callan 8/1: -05043: 8 ch g Clantime - Another Move   hd 79
(Farm Walk) Towards rear, imprvd appr fnl 2f, sn drvn, styd on & not much room below dist, ran on well, just
failed: op 6/1, poss unlucky: worth another chance, see 1170.
2688 **CHEMS TRUCE 21** [3] W R Muir 3-9-5 (82) B Marcus 10/1: 300034: Held up, shaken up appr fnl 2f,   ¾ 83
styd on ins last, nvr nrr: op 7/1, longer trip, clrly stays 10f: interesting with more positive ride next time?
2527 **SWEET REWARD 27** [8] 5-8-13 (67) D Harrison 7/1: -44035: Early ldr, again 2f out till dist, no extra.   ½ 67
*2884 **THREE LIONS 12** [6] 3-8-5 (68) F Norton 6/1: 40-016: Sn led, hdd 2f out, onepce: see 2884 (class stks).   1¼ 66
2888 **NO MERCY 12** [1] 4-9-0 (68) M Henry 8/1: 4-5027: Chsd ldrs, eff 2f out, no impress, outpcd: btr 2888.   2 63
2750 **AMRAK AJEEB 17** [7] 3-9-6 (74) G Sparkes (7) 13/2: 031438: Al bhd: see 2750, 1973.   1¼ 67
8 ran   Time 2m 04.06 (2.16)   (T J Wells)   D Morris Newmarket, Suffolk

3167   4.50 GEORGE GILL HCAP 3YO 0-70 (E)   1m4f   Good/Firm 23 +08 Fast   [77]
£5408   £1664   £832   £416

4613} **WELSH DREAM 273** [8] A C Stewart 3-8-4 (53) S Whitworth 16/1: 000-1: 3 b c Mtoto - Morgannwg (Simply   61
Great) Waited with, hdwy & switched 2f out, kept on well to lead below dist, rdn out: gd time on reapp/h'cap bow:
outpcd in 3 '99 mdns (rtd 69): half-brother to a 7f wnr but relished this step up to 12f, likely to get further:
acts on fast grnd & a stiff/gall trk: goes well fresh: well plcd, at right end of h'cap to win again.
2902 **NINNOLO 11** [10] C N Allen 3-8-13 (62)(t) R Morse 25/1: 530052: 3 b c Perugino - Primo Stampari   1½ 67
(Primo Dominie) Held up, smooth prog over 3f out to lead bef 2f out, sn rdn, hdd ent fnl 1f, kept on: well clr of
rem: apprec drop back to 12f on fast grnd & can go one better when held up for a later challenge: see 1725.
*3036 **CHAKA ZULU 5** [13] W J Haggas 3-8-8 (57)(5ex) F Norton 4/6 FAV: -13113: 3 b g Muhtarram - African   5 57
Dance (El Gran Senor) Chsd ldrs, eff appr fnl 2f, styd on for 3rd but no ch with ldrs: hvly bckd, one bet
of £22,000: quick reapp with a pen: poss too many races in quick succession.
2945 **INVISIBLE FORCE 8** [14] M Johnston 3-7-13 (48)(bl) R Ffrench 10/1: 661344: Cl-up, led briefly   ¾ 47
appr fnl 2f, same pace bef dist: not quite see out this longer, stiff 12f trip? see 2883, 2825.
2815 **FURNESS 15** [1] 3-8-9 (58) D Harrison 16/1: 000-25: Prom, shaken up 2f out, no extra appr fnl 1f.   hd 57
2842 **SAMARARDO 14** [15] 3-8-3 (52) G Carter 16/1: 03-546: Led till 3f out, fdd bef dist: unsuited by   ½ 50
step up to 12f & forcing tactics? see 80.
2284 **RUNAWAY STAR 36** [9] 3-7-10 (45)(1oh) P M Quinn (3) 16/1: -6657: Bhd, late hdwy, nvr a threat: hd 43$
h'cap bow, looks worth another ch over 12f on a minor trk: see 2284.
2992 **PETEURESQUE 7** [4] 3-9-6 (69) N Callan 10/1: 620028: Waited with, not clr run 3f out, sn no extra.   nk 66
2691 **ICE CRYSTAL 21** [12] 3-9-7 (70) C Rutter 25/1: 00409: Mid-div, eff & hung badly left ent fnl 3f, no dngr.   2 64
2255 **COCO LOCO 38** [11] 3-8-4 (53) D O'Donohoe 25/1: 600650: Al towards rear: 10th, see 884.   nk 46
2863 **EYELETS ECHO 13** [5] 3-9-6 (69) R Cochrane 14/1: 000150: Nvr trbled ldrs: 11th, much btr 2276 (9f).   2½ 59
2712 **SKYE BLUE 19** [2] 3-9-5 (68) J Mackay (5) 5/1: 302320: Nvr better than mid-div: 12th, bckd from 9/1.   ¾ 57
2470 Te Deum 29 [6] 3-8-10 (59) Dane O'Neill 20/1:   2518 Xibalba 28 [16] 3-9-6 (69) B Marcus 33/1:
2463 Dr Cool 29 [3] 3-8-5 (54)(BL) Paul Eddery 25/1:   2746 Sham Sharif 17 [7] 3-8-11 (60)(BL) D Holland 20/1:
16 ran   Time 2m 29.99 (1.79)   (Mr K J Mercer & Mrs S Mercer)   A C Stewart Newmarket, Suffolk

CHESTER   SUNDAY AUGUST 6TH   Lefthand, V Tight Track

Official Going   GOOD. Stalls: 1m2f & 2m2f - Stands Side: Rem - Inside.

3168   2.20 SALTNEY NURSERY HCAP 2YO (D)   6f rnd   Firm 15 -18 Slow   [87]
£3640   £1120   £560   £280   Low draw a huge advantage here

*2821 **FAIRGAME MAN 16** [1] A Berry 2-9-2 (75) J Carroll 2/1 FAV: -311: 2 ch c Clantime - Thalya (Crofthall)   90
Led, clr appr fnl 1f, eased down: unchall from v advantageous draw, well bckd on h'cap bow: earlier won at Carlisle
(auct mdn): dam unrcd: eff at 5/6f on firm, gd grnd, stiff/undul or tight trk: suited being up with/forcing the pace.
2665 **LOVE TUNE 23** [4] K R Burke 2-8-5 (64) W Supple 9/1: -53622: 2 b f Alhijaz - Heights Of Love   4 65
(Persian Heights) Chsd ldrs, chsd wnr appr fnl 1f, sn onepce, just held on for 2nd: gd run, will prob
apprec a return to 5f: see 2665 (again well drawn here), 1304.
*1302 **UHOOMAGOC 83** [3] D Nicholls 2-9-1 (74) O Pears 11/2: -2113: 2 b c Namaqualand - Point Of Law   shd 75
(Law Society) Keen, handy, feeling pace & lost pl ent str, kept on ins last: 12 wk abs, not disgraced on
h'cap bow & this longer 6f trip looks likely to suit: see 1302 (fibresand clmr).
2557 **FRANICA 26** [8] A Bailey 2-9-5 (78) J Mackay (5) 6/1: 015224: Chsd ldrs wide, kept on late without   hd 79
threatening: consistent, poorly drawn today: see 2557 (wnr gone in again since), 1429.
2521 **KATIES DOLPHIN 26** [6] 2-8-8 (67) F Norton 11/1: -62305: Slow away mod late hdwy, nvr a threat: 2½ 61
h'cap bow: v little chance here after a slow start: see 1938.
3101 **ITALIAN AFFAIR 4** [9] 2-8-1 (60) A Beech (5) 20/1: 105046: Dwelt, nvr in it: qk reapp, worst of the draw.   2 48

982

CHESTER   SUNDAY AUGUST 6TH   Lefthand, V Tight Track

2797 **HAMBLETON HIGHLITE 16** [7] 2-9-7 (80) F Lynch 20/1: 130447: Rear, nvr on terms: see 2797.   *shd*   **68**
-3145 **MISS BRIEF 1** [5] 2-8-12 (71) J F Egan 11/2: 024428: Prsd wnr, lost pl ent fnl 2f: rnr-up   6   44
over 5f here yesterday, came too soon over longer 6f trip? see 3145.
2773 **NAUGHTY KNIGHT 17** [2] 2-8-1 (60) D Mernagh(3) 9/1: 011359: Sn struggling: see 2773, 1549.   4   21
9 ran   Time 1m 15.08 (1.98)   (Robert Ogden)   A Berry Cockerham, Lancs.

3169   2.50 HOPE HOUSE MDN 2YO (D)   7f rnd   Firm 15   -25 Slow
£3575   £1100   £550   £275

2686 **COSMIC MILLENNIUM 22** [5] R Guest 2-9-0 D Harrison 9/1: -61: 2 b c In The Wings - Windmill   **84**
Princess (Gorytus) Held up, hugged the ins rail, prog 2f out, led dist, drifted right, ran on strongly: op 7/1,
imprvd for debut: eff at 7f, further is going to suit: goes on firm grnd & a tight track.
2828 **BORDERS BELLE 16** [7] J D Bethell 2-8-9 Paul Eddery 7/1: -432: 2 b f Pursuit Of Love - Sheryl   1¼   75
Lynn (Miller's Mate) Mid-div, widest of all, prog ent str, ev ch, sn onepace, kept on nr fin: fair effort having
to race wide & clrly stays 7f: goes on firm/fast grnd, could find a fillies maiden.
2649 **CEZZARO 23** [1] A C Stewart 2-9-0 D Holland 9/2: -503: 2 ch c Ashkalani - Sept Roses (Septieme Ciel)   hd   80
Sn cl-up, led 2f out, sn hdd, held when sltly checked by wnr ins last: op 7/2: imprvd: stays 7f on firm grnd.
2708 **SMYSLOV 21** [8] J L Dunlop 2-9-0 Pat Eddery 10/3 FAV: -044: Bhd ldrs, improving when carr right   shd   80
ent str, sn ev ch, unable to qckn under press: bckd, not ideally drawn: see 2708, 2346.
2708 **EASY ENIGMA 21** [9] 2-9-0 F Norton 11/2: -05: Waited with, pld hard, chsd ldrs appr fnl 1f, sn onepce.   2   76
2269 **TUDOR REEF 38** [2] 2-9-0 A Culhane 7/2: -046: Led, hung badly right appr fnl 2f, sn hdd & btn: 4   68
bckd tho' op 9/4: bit reportedly slipped, this shld be forgotten: see 2269.
-- **ACADEMIC RECORD** [3] 2-9-0 N Callan 16/1: -7: Dwelt, nvr in it: debut, op 10/1, Royal Academy colt.   7   53
2635 **JUNIOR BRIEF 23** [4] 2-9-0 (BL) T E Durcan 50/1: -0008: Chsd ldrs till 2f out: blnkd, needs sellers.   4   45
989 **NAKWA 106** [6] 2-9-0 W Supple 20/1: -09: Dwelt, nvr travelling, sn btn: 15 wk abs, see 989.   6   33
9 ran   Time 1m 27.84 (2.84)   (Cosmic Greyhound Racing Partnership III)   R Guest Newmarket.

3170   3.25 MAIL ON SUNDAY HCAP 3YO+ 0-90 (C)   7f122y rnd   Firm 15   +15 Fast   [83]
£8892   £2736   £1368   £684   3yo rec 7lb

*3083 **CANTINA 4** [9] A Bailey 6-9-9 (78)(6ex) J Mackay (5) 5/1 FAV: 014311: 6 b m Tina's Pet - Reel Claire   **88**
(Dreams To Reality) Broke well to grab rail, made all, clr appr straight, easily: well bckd from 7/1, qck time,
quick repp with a pen: earlier won at Beverley (ladies amat h'cap) & Carlise (fill h'cap): '99 wnr at Redcar
(amat stks, rtd 73 & 72a): '98 wnr here at Chester (2, h'caps, disqual once, rtd 80): loves to force the pace
over 7/7.5f: acts on firm, gd/soft grnd, any track, likes Chester: in-form, genuine mare.
*3078 **SHAANXI ROMANCE 4** [17] M J Polglase 5-7-11 (52)(vis)(1ow)(6ex)(3oh) F Norton 20/1: 366112: 5 b g   3   54$
Darshaan - Easy Romance (Northern Jove) In tch, shaken up appr straight, kept on to grab 2nd fnl strides,
no hope with runaway wnr: quick reapp with a penalty: remains in grand form: see 3078.
2882 **RYMERS RASCAL 13** [15] E J Alston 8-8-5 (60) J Carroll 16/1: 634253: 8 b g Rymer - City Sound   shd   62
(On Your Mark) Held up, improving when much room 2f out, drvn appr fnl 1f, nvr nr to chall: back to form
despite difficult draw, won this in '99 (off same mark): see 942.
2694 **JEFFREY ANOTHERRED 22** [6] M Dods 6-8-11 (66) J F Egan 9/1: 000004: Handy, went a moderate   nk   67
2nd ent fnl 2f, onepace towards fin: ran to best from favourable draw, well h'capped on softer grnd: see 2163.
3018 **INTRICATE WEB 7** [12] 4-9-2 (71) W Supple 11/1: 613305: Mid div, late hdwy, nvr a threat: s/mate 3rd.   2   68
2559 **NOMORE MR NICEGUY 26** [1] 6-9-6 (75) A Culhane 10/1: 204006: Prom till onepace entering fnl 2f.   ½   71
2999 **TORNADO PRINCE 8** [3] 5-9-1 (70) T E Durcan 6/1: 014427: Rear, late wide hdwy, nvr nr ldrs: see 2063.   1¼   63
3141 **DOVEBRACE 2** [7] 7-8-1 (56) J Bramhill 12/1: 666238: Slow away, hmpd 2f, nvr nr ldrs: s/mate wnr.   1¼   46
2878 **MANTLES PRIDE 13** [2] 5-10-0 (83)(bl) Pat Eddery 12/1: 060059: Al around same place, eased dist.   ½   72
2564 **I CRIED FOR YOU 26** [10] 5-9-13 (82) Dean McKeown 8/1: 132120: Mid-div when bdly hmpd after 2f,   1½   68
no threat: 10th, tchd 10/1: much better than this, well worth another chance: see 1840.
*2697 **THE GAY FOX 22** [4] 6-9-5 (74)(tbl) K Dalgleish (5) 11/1: 302410: Prom, went 2nd 3f out till bef   shd   60
dist, wknd: 11th: better at sprinting: see 2697.
3018 **TAFFS WELL 7** [14] 7-9-4 (73) D Holland 10/1: 426000: In tch, under press & hmpd bef 2f out: 12th.   ½   58
2999 **LYNTON LAD 8** [5] 8-8-4 (59) L Newton 12/1: 600100: Nvr a factor: 13th, s/mate 3rd, see 2831 (made all). 5   34
*2694 **Donnas Double 22** [16] 5-9-1 (70) A Beech (5) 16/1:   3011 **Hadeqa 8** [8] 4-7-13 (54) T Williams 66/1:
2673 **Lady Boxer 22** [13] 4-8-8 (63) R Lappin 50/1:   852 **First Venture 118** [11] 3-8-10 (72) D O'Donohoe 33/1:
17 ran   Time 1m 32.37 (u0.03)   (R Kinsey, Mrs M Kinsey & Miss B Roberts)   A Bailey Little Budworth, Cheshire

3171   3.55 CURZON PARK RTD HCAP 4YO+ 0-105 (B)   2m2f147y   Firm 15   -58 Slow   [119]
£15051   £5709   £2854   £1297

2695 **FANTASY HILL 22** [4] J L Dunlop 4-8-5 (95)(BL)(1ow) Pat Eddery 2/1 FAV: -53401: 4 b g Danehill - Gay   **99**
Fantasy (Troy) Waited with, shkn up 3f out, imprvd bef dist, styd on to lead fnl 100y, drifted left, eased down:
well bckd, slow time, woken up by blnks: '99 wnr at Nottingham (h'cap, rtd 92): eff at 2m/2m2f: acts on firm &
hvy grnd, any track, with/without blinks: useful, out & out stayer, win more marathon races.
3085 **VIRGIN SOLDIER 4** [1] M Johnston 4-7-11 (88)(3oh) K Dalgleish (5) 10/3: -10242: 4 ch g Waajib -   1   87
Never Been Chaste (Posse) Nvr far away, led ent fnl 2f, edged left for press, hdd fnl 100y: nicely bckd, qk reapp,
jockey given 2 day ban for careless riding: tough sort, eff at 2m/2m2f, stays 2m4f: see 1478.
2498 **TENSILE 29** [5] M C Pipe 5-7-11 (88)(2oh) J Mackay (5) 10/3: -60043: 5 b g Tenby - Bonnie Isle   1   86
(Pitcairn) In tch, improved to press ldrs appr straight, onepace till styd on inside last: nicely bckd, new stable.
3058 **PRAIRIE FALCON 5** [2] B W Hills 6-7-11 (88)(4oh) F Norton 9/1: 4F0604: Set v slow pace, hdd appr   1¼   85
fnl 1f, onepace when hmpd ins last: op 6/1: qck reapp: stiffish task, prob ran to best, see 917.
-- **YORKSHIRE** [3] 6-9-0 (105) D Sweeney 8/1: 2655/5: Held up, prog to chase ldrs 3f out, kept   shd   102
on same pace: 2 season abs: won '98 reapp at Newbury (Listed, rtd 112): '97 rnr up (stakes rtd 106): eff
between 13f & 2m6f on firm & gd/soft grnd, any track: sharper next time: with P Cole.
-- **KHATANI** [5] 5-8-7 (98) D Harrison 7/1: /011-6: Chsd ldrs till 4f out: fit from notching a 4-timer over   9   85
hdles at Bangor & Worcester (3, h'caps, 2m/2m4f, firm, gd, rtd 121h): ex Irish, '99 Flat wnr at The Curragh &
Gowran (14f/2m h'caps, J Oxx): acts on fast & gd grnd: with D Gandolfo.
6 ran   Time 4m 12.72 (13.82)   (Windflower Overseas Holding Inc)   J L Dunlop Arundel, W Sussex

CHESTER SUNDAY AUGUST 6TH Lefthand, V Tight Track

3172

4.30 LISTED QUEENSFERRY STKS 3YO+ (A)   6f rnd   Firm 15   +03 Fast
£13572   £5148   £2574   £1170   3yo rec 4lb

2960 **YORKIES BOY 9** [7] A Berry 5-9-0 J Carroll 10/1: 041601: 5 ro h Clantime - Slipperose (Persepolis)   108
Broke well despite high draw, got the rail, made all, drvn out: fair time: plcd in '99 for B McMahon (Gr 3, rtd 110):
'98 Newmarket wnr (2, List & Gr 3, rtd 114): eff forcing the pace at 5/6f on firm & gd/soft grnd, any trk: v useful.
2087 **SELKING 46** [6] K R Burke 3-8-10 N Callan 6/1: -32402: 3 ch c Selkirk - Stay That Way (Be My   1½ 103
Guest) In tch, eff appr fnl 1f, kept on to gd 2nd fnl stride, not trouble wnr: bckd, 7 wk abs: prob ran to best
back in trip: eff at 6f, return to 7f will suit: acts on firm, gd grnd & fibresand, prob handles soft: see 955.
3016 **DAMALIS 7** [3] E J Alston 4-8-9 T E Durcan 10/1: 001003: 4 b f Mukaddamah - Art Age (Artaius)   shd 98
Pulled hard, trkd wnr, rdn appr fnl 1f, unable to qckn: op 7/1, quick reapp: ran to best at these weights over
longer trip, all wins at 5f: loves Chester, see 2247 (h'cap here).
2847 **CRETAN GIFT 15** [1] N P Littmoden 9-9-4 (vis) J F Egan 3/1: 500234: Chsd ldrs, niggled from halfway,   shd 107
slightly hmpd 2f out, not pace to chall wnr: nicely bckd, see 952.
1834 **MANORBIER 57** [4] 4-9-0 F Lynch 13/2: 041405: Rear, wide progress fnl 1f, nvr nrr: 8 week abs.   nk 102
3123 **DEMOLITION JO 2** [2] 5-8-9 (vis) T G McLaughlin 33/1: 060006: Held up, drvn appr fnl 1f, nvr a threat.   ¾ 94
2669 **TEDBURROW 22** [8] 8-9-4 W Supple 11/8 FAV: 000137: Keen, wide, handy, eff appr fnl 1f, sn btn: 1½ 99
hvly bckd to repeat last season's success in this race: favoured by these weights but now twice well below 2335.
7 ran   Time 1m 13.87 (0.77)   (Mrs M Beddis)   A Berry Cockerham, Lancs

3173

5.00 WATERGATE HCAP STKS 3YO+ 0-90 (C)   1m4f66y   Firm 15   -02 Slow   [89]
£7117   £2190   £1095   £547   3yo rec 11lb

2647 **FLOSSY 23** [5] C W Thornton 4-9-9 (84) W Supple 2/1 FAV: 1-0441: 4 b f Efisio - Sirene Bleu Marine   88
(Secreto) Mid-div, improved going well 3f out, switched dist, rdn to lead inside last: well bckd from 3/1: '99
wnr at Beverley, Musselburgh, Newbury, Ripon (subs disq), Newcastle, Haydock & Doncaster (November h'cap, rtd
88): suited by 12f: goes on any grnd/track & best coming with a late run: worth his place in the 14f Ebor.
2002 **MORGANS ORCHARD 50** [8] A G Newcombe 4-7-13 (60) G Baker (5) 16/1: 155202: 4 ch g Forest Wind -   ½ 63
Regina St Cyr (Doulab) Sn led, under press ent fnl 2f, worn down inside last, kept on: 7 week abs, a bold
attempt, acts on firm grnd & fibresand, see 607.
2852 **NIGHT VENTURE 15** [2] B W Hills 4-9-10 (85) F Norton 20/1: 100003: 4 b c Dynaformer - Charming   nk 87
Ballerina (Caerleon) Well plcd, eff 2f out, styd on under press inside last: drifted from 12/1: eff at 10/12f.
2852 **GREYFIELD 15** [1] M R Channon 4-8-10 (71) A Culhane 13/2: 6-4504: Waited wth, imprvd appr fnl 2f   ¾ 72
hard rdn bef dist, looked onepaced when short of room nr fin: op 5/1, 4s not btn far: see 1984.
2755 **HANNIBAL LAD 18** [10] T G McLaughlin 7/1: 144135: Patiently rdn, shaken up appr   ¾ 84
fnl 2f, onepace till styd on towards fin: op 5/1: unsuited by this sharper 12f?: see 2674 (Ascot).
*2667 **CAPRIOLO 23** [11] 4-8-11 (72)(bl) D Harrison 8/1: -60016: Bhd, late hdwy: btr 2667 (C/D stks, made all).   2 69
2530 **JUST GIFTED 28** [6] 4-8-7 (68) D Holland 8/1: 062227: Early ldr, chsd ldrs till fdd appr fnl 1f: see 1499.   ¾ 64
2712 **SHAPOUR 20** [7] 3-8-6 (78) Pat Eddery 4/1: 02-048: Nvr trbld ldrs, brief eff appr fnl 2f: bckd, btr 2712 (gd).hd 74
2981 **PEKAN HEIGHTS 9** [1] 4-8-3 (64)(bl) J F Egan 20/1: 0-1049: Prom till 3f out: best at 10f, see 2245.   3 55
3013 **PIPED ABOARD 7** [3] 5-8-8 (69) N Callan 20/1: 350060: Mid div, chsd ldrs wide 3f out, btn 2f out: 10th.   6 51
*2930 **HERACLES 11** [9] 4-9-0 (75) J Carroll 16/1: -63410: Chsd ldrs till 4f out, t.o., lost action: 11th, h'cap bow.27 17
11 ran   Time 2m 38.52 (2.12)   (Guy Reed)   C W Thornton Coverham, N Yorks

NEWBURY SUNDAY AUGUST 6TH Lefthand, Flat, Galloping Track

Official Going   GOOD TO FIRM Stalls: Straight Course - Far Side: Round Course - Inside

3174

2.00 CANTORINDEX NOV STKS 2YO (D)   5f34y str   Good/Firm 23   -22 Slow
£3718   £1144   £572   £286

2959 **FOLEY MILLENNIUM 9** [5] M Quinn 2-9-0 J Fortune 7/1: 551341: 2 ch c Tagula - Inshirah (Caro)   86
Trck ldr, went on over 2f out, hard pressed inside last, drvn out to hold on: earlier won at Haydock
(mdn claimer): dam 5/7f wnr: eff at 5/6f on fast, gd & a gall track: battled well here.
*2939 **MISS DOMUCH 10** [1] R Hannon 2-8-11 R Hughes 5/6 FAV: -2312: 2 ch f Definite Article - Eliza   nk 82
Orzeszkowa (Polish Patriot) Led, hdd appr fnl 2f, rallied well inside last, styd on, not btn far: hvly bckd.
2849 **MILLYS LASS 15** [4] M R Channon 2-8-11 T Quinn 9/4: 213203: 2 b f Mind Games - Millie's Lad   ¾ 79
(Common Grounds) Chsd ldrs, hdwy to chall appr fnl 1f, no extra under only hands & heels: nicely bckd: see 2657.
-- **DEIDAMIA** [2] P W Harris 2-8-4 R Mullen 6/1: -4: Dwelt, al last: op 4/1: Feb first foal, dam   4 60
related to sev wnrs in the USA: sire high class sprinter.
4 ran   Time 1m 02.56 (2.26)   (Mrs S G Davies)   M Quinn Sparsholt, Oxon

3175

2.30 CANTOR NURSERY HCAP 2YO (D)   7f str   Good/Firm 23   -10 Slow   [91]
£4368   £1344   £672   £336

*2903 **MAMORE GAP 12** [5] R Hannon 2-9-0 (77) R Hughes 9/4 FAV: -22311: 2 b c General Monash -   87
Ravensdale Rose (Henbit) Rcd keenly in rear, gd hdwy appr fnl 1f, led dist, pushed clr: nicely bckd: earlier
won at Brighton (auction mdn): 22,000gns Mar foal, half-brother to a wnr abroad: stays 7f well, 1m will suit:
acts on firm, gd/soft, equitrack & any trk: tough & progressing with every run.
2459 **PASO DOBLE 30** [9] B R Millman 2-8-7 (70) G Hind 14/1: -0342: 2 b c Dancing Spree - Delta Tempo   1 76
(Bluebird) Front rank, led appr fnl 2f, drvn/hdd dist, not pace of wnr: eff at 7f on fast: shld win a race.
2921 **POTARO 11** [7] B J Meehan 2-9-7 (84) J Fortune 13/2: -5353: 2 b c Catrail -Bianca Cappello   3 84
(Glenstal) Led, hdd appr fnl 2f, drvn & not pace of front 2 inside fnl 1f: bckd from 10/1, top-weight stays 7f.
2468 **TRUSTED MOLE 30** [10] J A Osborne 2-8-7 (69)(1ow) S Sanders 14/1: 663044: Rear, late hdwy.   1¼ 67
2915 **DIAMOND MAX 11** [11] 2-8-0 (63) Joanna Badger (7) 16/1: 041455: Mid div, hdwy halfway, fdd   2½ 55
appr fnl 1f: up in trip & prob not stay 7f: see 2665.
2714 **MYHAT 20** [1] 2-9-3 (80) C Catlin (7) 10/1: -22326: Dwelt, sn chasing ldrs, rdn/btn fnl 2f: up in trip.   ¾ 70
2773 **TROUBLESHOOTER 17** [6] 2-8-8 (71) Martin Dwyer 14/1: 602027: Mid div at best: op 10/1: btr 2773.   hd 61
3029 **APRIL LEE 6** [4] 2-8-7 (70)(e) L Newman (3) 8/1: 552528: Front rank, rdn & wknd quickly   3½ 53

fnl 2f: quick reapp: btr 3029 (auction mdn, gd).

2678 **FAST FOIL** 22 [8] 2-9-0 (77) T Quinn 5/1: -32639: Sn rdn, al rear, eased fnl 2f: up in trip, btr 2678. ½ 59

*2810 **TRUMPINGTON** 16 [2] 2-9-0 (77) A Nicholls (3) 7/1: -0310: Prom, rdn/wknd quickly over 2f out, hd 59
fin 10th: can do much better, fill mdn wnr over C/D in 2810 (firm).

2841 **COUNTRYWIDE PRIDE** 15 [3] 2-8-12 (75) Darren Williams (5) 14/1: -0430: Cl up, rdn & wknd rapidly 3 51
fnl 2f, fin 11th: bckd from 20/1: much btr 2841.

11 ran   Time 1m 26.67 (2.37)   (The South-Western Partnership II)   R Hannon East Everleigh, Wilts

---

3176   3.00 CANTOR INDEX HCAP 3YO+ 0-95 (C)   5f34y str   Good/Firm 23 +03 Fast   [87]
£7085   £2180   £1090   £545

2676 **AMBITIOUS** 22 [6] K T Ivory 5-10-0 (87) C Catlin (7) 15/2: 014101: 5 b m Ardkinglass - Ayodhya 91
(Astronef) Mid div, rdn to improve appr fnl 1f, ran on strongly inside last to get up fnl strides, drvn out:
gd time: earlier won at Thirsk (class stakes) Southwell (AW h'cap, rtd 75a) & Sandown (h'cap): '99 wnr at
Southwell (fillies h'cap, J Fanshawe), Sandown (2, h'cap & claimer), Redcar (class stakes) & York (h'cap,
rtd 79): eff at 6f, 8 most recent wins at 5f: acts on firm & fibresand, likes fast & soft grnd: acts on
any trk, likes Sandown: goes well for an appr & likes to come late: very tough & progressive this term.

*2987 **BRECONGILL LAD** 8 [10] D Nicholls 8-9-9 (82) Alex Greaves 9/2: 200312: 8 b g Clantime - Chikala shd 85
(Pitskelly) Waited with, gd hdwy to lead appr fnl 1f, drvn inside last, hdd nr fin: gd eff & remains in gd form.

3091 **EASTERN TRUMPETER** 4 [8] J M Bradley 4-9-6 (79) P Fitzsimons (5) 8/1: 302103: 4 b c First Trump - nk 81
Oriental Air (Taufan) Front rank, led over 2f out, hdd appr fnl 1f, rallied well ins last, not btn far: most tough.

2999 **CAUDA EQUINA** 8 [4] M R Channon 6-9-2 (75) T Quinn 14/1: 204004: Sn last, drvn & ran on strongly 1½ 73
fnl 1f, nrst fin: on a long losing run: likes Bath: see 2697, 905.

2944 **ANTHONY MON AMOUR** 10 [1] 5-9-0 (73)(t) A Nicholls (3) 7/2 JT FAV: 410135: With ldr, drvn/fdd 1¼ 67
appr fnl 1f: op 11/4: stablemate of rnr-up: btr 2944, 2830.

1264 **TIGER IMP** 86 [5] 4-8-11 (70) J Fortune 12/1: 223-06: Prom, drvn & grad fdd appr fnl 1f: op 16/1 ¾ 61
after 12 wk abs: lightly raced sort, shld be suited by this step up: should find easier opportunities & just sharper for this: see 1264.

+2869 **MIDNIGHT ESCAPE** 14 [3] 7-9-9 (82) R Mullen 7/2 JT FAV: 045617: Outpcd early, switched/eff hd 73
appr fnl 1f, late hdwy, no threat: well bckd & capable of much better: see 2869 (6f class stakes).

3046 **WHIZZ KID** 6 [7] 6-9-0 (73) J P Spencer 20/1: 601008: Sn rdn in rear, nvr dangerous: quick reapp. hd 64

2266 **SAILING SHOES** 38 [2] 4-9-5 (78)(bl) R Hughes 7/1: -00069: Broke well, sn led, hdd over 2f out, wknd. 1½ 65

3091 **POLLY GOLIGHTLY** 4 [9] 7-8-8 (67)(bl) Dale Gibson 20/1: 064000: Cl up wide, wknd qckly over 2f out. 1½ 50

10 ran   Time 1m 01.32 (1.02)   (Dean Ivory)   K T Ivory Radlett, Herts

---

3177   3.35 LISTED CHALICE STKS 3YO+ (A)   1m4f   Good/Firm 23 +07 Fast
£13166   £4994   £2497   £1135   3yo rec 11lb

2068 **MISS LORILAW** 47 [7] J W Hills 3-8-4 M Hills 16/1: -33601: 3 b f Homme de Loi - Miss Lorika (Bikala) 103
In tch, gd hdwy to lead over 4f out, hmpd/switched over 2f out, ran on well to lead appr last, drvn out:
7 wk abs, best time of day: outclassed in Gr company last 2 starts: won sole '99 start, at York (med auct mdn,
rtd 87): eff at 1m, suited by 12f, prob not stay 2m: acts on fast, gd/soft & a stiff/gall track: runs well
fresh: apprec this drop to Listed company & shld win again in this grade.

1325 **FARFALA** 81 [2] P F I Cole 4-9-1 J Fortune 11/1: 010-52: 4 gr f Linamix - Fragrant Hill 1¼ 100
(Shirley Heights) Waited with, switched & rapid hdwy to lead over 3f out, sn hung left, hdd appr fnl 1f, not pace
of wnr: op 8/1, jockey received a 2 day careless riding ban: fine run after a 12 wk abs: see 1325.

*2975 **FILM SCRIPT** 9 [6] R Charlton 3-8-7 R Hughes 7/4 FAV: 113613: 3 b f Unfuwain - Success Story 1 101
(Sharood) Rcd keenly & sn led, hdd after 3f, slightly outpcd over 3f out, drvn & kept on appr fnl 1f, no
threat to ldr: nicely bckd: ran to form of 2975 (10f).

2501 **LIMELIGHT** 29 [1] J H M Gosden 4-9-1 R Havlin 3/1: 12-454: Prom, eff when short of room shd 98
appr fnl 2f, drvn/held over 1f out: see 1325.

*2560 **ZIBILENE** 26 [8] 3-8-5(1ow) J P Spencer 6/1: -215: Mid div, drpd rear halfway, switched/eff 1½ 97
appr fnl 2f, no extra inside last: lightly rcd & showed marked improvement here: see 2560 (mdn).

2805 **BE THANKFULL** 16 [4] 4-9-1 S Sanders 33/1: 21-536: Handy, hdwy halfway, drpd rear 3f out, rallied shd 96$
/late hdwy, no threat: treat rating with caution (offic only 83): see 2502.

*2502 **RADAS DAUGHTER** 29 [3] 4-9-1 R Mullen 6/1: -00017: Waited with, nvr dngrs: nicely bckd. 1 94

2476 **CIRCLE OF LIGHT** 30 [5] 3-8-4 T Quinn 8/1: -32338: Rcd v keenly cl up, went on after 3f, hdd over dist 0
4f wknd rapidly, t.o.: up in trip, prob not stay 12f: see 2476.

8 ran   Time 2m 31.23 (1.93)   (David A Caruth)   J W Hills Upper Lambourn, Berks

---

3178   4.10 EXPRESS FILLIES HCAP 3YO 0-85 (D)   1m2f   Good/Firm 23 -25 Slow   [92]
£5005   £1540   £770   £385

2918 **SANTIBURI GIRL** 11 [9] J R Best 3-8-0 (64) L Newman(2) 20/1: 023001: 3 b f Casteddu - Lake Mistassiu 69
(Tina's Pet) Dwelt, rear, gd hdwy appr fnl 2f, led dist, drvn out: up 14/1: up in trip: earlier won at
Lingfield (class stks): '99 wnr at Salisbury (nov auct, rtd 87): eff at 7f, clearly relished this step up
to a gall 10f: acts on firm, gd & a sharp/undulating or gall track: could improve again at this trip.

*2722 **DELAMERE** 20 [8] J H M Gosden 3-9-4 (82) J Fortune 5/1: -64312: 3 b f Brocco - Sheila Dacre 1¼ 84
(Nureyev) Front rank, led appr fnl 2f, hdd dist, kept on but not pace of wnr: improved in defeat, win similar.

2685 **CHELONIA** 22 [3] B W Hills 3-8-2 (66) A Daly 14/1: 3-0563: 3 gr f Turtle Island - Whirl (Bellypha) 1 66
Rear, hdwy to chall ldrs over 2f out, short of room appr fnl 1f, rall/styd on fnl 1f: op 10/1: eff at 10f on fast.

2614 **RESOUNDING** 24 [2] A C Stewart 3-9-2 (80) R Mullen 2/1 FAV: 51-324: Waited with, hdwy when shd 80
short of room appr fnl 1f, nrst fin: well bckd: up in trip, stays 10f: see 2614 (1m).

2449 **SABREON** 31 [5] 3-9-7 (85) G Carter 8/1: 220-25: Rcd keenly/prom, switched & barged through 1½ 83
gap appr fnl 1f, sn onepcd: see 2449 (mdn).

2811 **SAFARI BLUES** 16 [4] 3-9-2 (80) R Hughes 7/1: -50526: Set steady pace, hdd over 2f out, wknd fnl 1f. 1¾ 75

*2895 **YOUR THE LADY** 13 [1] 3-8-10 (74) T Quinn 4/1: 085117: Handy, drvn, switched & short of room nk 68
over 1f out, sn btn: up in trip, hat-trick bid: poss not stay 1m: see 2895, 2661 (10f).

1785 **SWEET CICELY** 59 [6] 3-8-2 (66) D Cosgrave (7) 12/1: 00-358: Dwelt/rear, switched wide & hdwy 2 57
over 3f out, fdd fnl 2f: tchd 20/1, 8 week abs: just sharper for this: see 1287.

1045 **ISLAND PRINCESS** 100 [7] 3-9-1 (79) N Pollard 14/1: 020-59: Prom, chall ldr 3f out, wkng when 2 67
badly hmpd appr fnl 1f: op 8/1, 3 month abs: see 1045, (hvy).

2774 **VETORITY** 17 [10] 3-8-9 (73) M Tebbutt 20/1: -3530: Dwelt, al last, fin 10th: h'cap bow. 2½ 57

10 ran   Time 2m 07.69 (4.89)   (Alan Turner)   J R Best Hucking, Kent

NEWBURY

SUNDAY AUGUST 6TH   Lefthand, Flat, Galloping Track

3179   **4.40 ESPEED MDN 3YO (D)**   **1m1f**   **Good/Firm 23   -26 Slow**
£4387   £1350   £675   £337

2860 **GRAMPAS 15** [3] J H M Gosden 3-9-0 J Fortune 1/1 FAV: -21: 3 b c El Gran Senor - Let There Be Light   96
(Sunny's Halo) Prom, led appr fnl 2f, rdn/qcknd well fnl 1f, readily: well bckd: narrowly btn on recent debut
(7f): cost IR52,000gns: this step up to 9f & further could suit: acts on fast grnd & a gall track:
useful performance here & showed a decent turn of foot, should win more races.

2169 **FUNNY GIRL 43** [8] W R Muir 3-8-9 Martin Dwyer 4/1: 45-562: 3 b f Darshaan - Just For Fun   4   81
(Lead On Time) Prom, rdn to chall appr fnl 1f, kept on but well outpcd by wnr: drop in grade: nicely bckd:
6 wk abs: stays 9f on fast & gd: see 1108 (Listed).

2938 **FREDDY FLINTSTONE 10** [10] R Hannon 3-9-0 R Hughes 7/2: 040023: 3 b c Bigstone - Daring Ditty   3   80
(Daring March) Waited with, rdn/hdwy appr fnl 2f, no extra fnl 1f: will apprec h'cap company: see 2596, 1183.

--   **MARRAKECH** [5] P W Harris 3-8-9 T Quinn 9/1: -4: Prom, led appr fnl 3f, hdd over 2f out, sn btn   ¾   73
& not given a hard time: Barathea filly, half-sister to a number of wnrs: encouraging debut & should improve.

--   **SELVORINE** [7] 3-8-9 J P Spencer 8/1: -5: Waited with, rdn/prog appr fnl 3f, hung left & fdd   4   65
fnl 2f: Selkirk filly, with R Charlton & should improve for experience.

1349 **WOODYATES 80** [1] 3-8-9 N Pollard 33/1: -06: Settled rear, & nvr a factor: 11 wk abs, up in trip.   6   53

--   **ELLWAY HEIGHTS** [6] 3-9-0 L Newman(3) 14/1: -7: Sn rdn in rear, nvr dngrs: op 8/1: with I Balding.   1   56

--   **BISHOPS BLADE** [9] 3-9-0 R Havlin 33/1: -8: Al rear on debut: Sure Blade gelding.   2   52

3048 **CULMINATE 6** [2] 3-9-0 P McCabe 66/1: -09: Led, hdd appr fnl 3f, wknd rapidly, t.o.: qck reapp.   15   22

9 ran   Time 1m 53.45 (4.45)   (Thomas P Tatham)   J H M Gosden Manton, Wilts

---

RIPON

MONDAY AUGUST 7TH   Righthand, Sharpish Track

Official Going   GOOD (GOOD/FIRM In Places)   Stalls: Str Course - Stands Side; Round Course - Inside.

3180   **2.15 W. JENKYNS SELL HCAP 3YO+ 0-60 (F)**   **5f str**   **Good/Firm 22   -14 Slow**   [56]
£2338   £668   £334   3 yo rec 3 lb   Raced across track - low numbers held advantage.

1806 **YOUNG IBNR 59** [3] B A McMahon 5-9-5 (47) J Weaver 33/1: 443001: 5 b g Imperial Frontier - Zalatia   50
(Music Boy) Led stands side, rdn to lead overall dist, styd on strongly, drvn out: no bid: 9 wk abs, 1st turf
run for 2 years: earlier won at W'hampton (AW sell, rtd 56a at best): plcd in '99 (rtd 49a, h'cap): suited by
5f on fm, soft, firesand & a sharp trk: has tried blnks/visor, best without: apprec return to turf & selling grade.

2744 **PISCES LAD 19** [1] T D Barron 4-9-8 (50) D Mernagh (3) 12/1: 200002: 4 b g Cyrano de Bergerac -   1   50
Tarnside Rosal (Mummy's Game) Prom stands side, hdwy to chall dist, held cl-home, imprvd eff here: see 781.

2864 **THORNCLIFF FOX 15** [2] J A Glover 3-10-0 (59)(vis) O Pears 10/1: 036033: 3 ch g Foxhound - Godly   ½   58
Light (Vayrann) Cl-up stands side, drvn/no extra in last: padd pick: gd eff under top weight: see 2864, 1061.

2905 **WINDRUSH BOY 13** [12] M R Bosley 10-8-10 (38) S Righton 16/1: 000444: In tch centre, ran on fnl 1f.   ½   36

2839 **NOW IS THE HOUR 16** [11] 4-8-2 (30) Dale Gibson 14/1: 200365: Trkd ldrs, outpcd fnl 2f, late gains.   nk   27

2976 **SUNSET HARBOUR 10** [17] 7-9-2 (44) Claire Bryan (5) 11/2: 605606: In tch far side, styd on fnl 2f,   nk   41
no threat to nr side group: not disgraced racing on the unfavd far side: lkd well: see 1932.

3144 **IMPALDI 2** [18] 5-8-12 (40) F Norton 5/1: 002337: Prom, drvn/onepcd in last: see 3144.   ½   36

3144 **UPPER CHAMBER 2** [13] 4-8-9 (37) J Fanning 10/1: 0-0008: Front rank, chall over 1f out, rdn/btn fnl 1f.   1   30

2535 **BOWCLIFFE GRANGE 28** [14] 8-8-5 (33)(bl) A Culhane 12/1: 030069: Led, rdn/hdd over 1f out, wknd.   hd   26

2864 **LUNALUX 15** [19] 3-9-8 (53)(vis) R Fitzpatrick (3) 12/1: -02400: Cl-up, drvn/fdd over 1f out, fin 10th.   ½   45

3138 **ZIBAK 3** [15] 6-8-3 (31) A Beech (5) 12/1: 540600: Nvr a factor, 11th: qck reapp: see 1685.   ½   22

2970 **CARMARTHEN 10** [4] 4-8-12 (40)(tVI) Kimberley Hart 50/1: 000000: Mid-div at best, 12th, visored.   shd   31

2716 **SWEET MAGIC 21** [16] 9-9-4 (46)(t) K Darley 11/2: 400000: Dwelt, al bhd, 13th: op 7/1: see 1392 (AW).J½   33

2839 **Rum Lass 16** [7] 3-9-2 (47) T Lucas 20/1:   2732 **Press Ahead 20** [5] 5-9-4 (46)(vis) S Finnamore (5)   14/1:

3056 **Chillian 6** [6] 4-7-12 (25)(1ow) T Williams 33/1:   2819 **Bold Aristocrat 17** [20] 9-9-3 (45) P M Quinn (3)   25/1:

2798 **Tartan Island 17** [9] 3-9-2 (47)(bl) R Winston 33/1:   2994 **Johs Brother 9** [10] 4-8-0 (28) K Dalgleish (5)   66/1:

19 ran   Time 59.6 (1.8)   (Roy Preston)   B A McMahon Hopwas, Staffs

---

3181   **2.45 RADIO YORK HCAP 3YO+ 0-70 (E)**   **1m4f60y**   **Good/Firm 22   -15 Slow**   [70]
£2941   £905   £452   £226   3 yo rec 11lb

2522 **DARK SHADOWS 29** [8] W Storey 5-9-2 (58) T Williams 9/2: -53631: 5 b g Machiavellian - Instant   61
Desire (Northern Dancer) Settled rear, gd hdwy to lead appr fnl 1f, ran on strongly, drvn out: 1st win: up in
trip: bmpr plcd prev (stays 13.5f on firm grnd): related to wnrs on the Flat: acts on fast & a sharpish trk:
further will suit: acts on fast & gd/soft grnd: can rate more highly & cld win again over further.

*3050 **JONLOZ 6** [12] G Woodward 3-7-10 (49)(6ex)(6oh) K Dalgleish (5) 8/1: 566012: 3 ch c Presidium -   ¾   50
Stratford Lady (Touching Wood) Mid-div, rdn, switched & ran on well over 1f out, closing at fin: boiled over in
prelims: op 5/1: acts on fast & gd/soft grnd: gd eff from 6lbs o/h: improving, see 3050.

2634 **THE BARGATE FOX 24** [4] D J G Murray Smith 4-8-6 (48) T Quinn 16/1: 030003: 4 b g Magic Ring -   hd   49
Hithermoor Lass (Red Alert) Bhd, hdwy 2f, kept on same pace: apprec return to 12f: acts on fast & fibresand.

3102 **ASHLEIGH BAKER 5** [7] M Johnston 5-8-9 (51) J Fanning 4/1: 016124: Led, hdd 2f out, onepcd well   hd   52
ins last: nicely bckd, quick reapp: remains in gd heart: see 2783.

2782 **KATIE KOMAITE 18** [1] 7-7-11 (39)(1ow)(4oh) F Norton 12/1: 000235: Settled rear, rdn/hdwy appr fnl   5   33
2f, wknd over 1f out, eased well ins last: likes gd/soft or softer grnd: see 2453, 890.

2856 **HUNTERS TWEED 16** [11] 4-10-0 (70) K Darley 7/2 FAV: 020206: Prom, rdn/fdd appr fnl 1f: top weight.   ¾   63

3052 **BUZZ THE AGENT 6** [10] 5-7-10 (38)(bl)(2oh) Dale Gibson 5/1: 453-27: Handy, drvn/onepcd fnl 2f: 1½   28
quick reapp: padd pick: better on reapp in 3052 (ladies h'cap, gd/soft).

3053 **YANKEE DANCER 6** [2] 5-7-10 (38)(2oh) P M Quinn (3) 50/1: 000008: Rear, eff 2f out, no dngr: qk reapp. hd   28

2836 **FALCON SPIRIT 16** [5] 4-9-4 (60) J Weaver 20/1: 320-09: Keen/prom, rdn/fdd over 2f out: see 2836.   ¾   49

1501 **ST LAWRENCE 73** [6] 6-7-12 (40) J Bramhill 25/1: 300240: Al bhd, fin 10th: lkd v well: plcd over   3   24
timber (2m6f mdn, rtd 90h) since 1501, see 542.

2422 **WETHAAB 33** [3] 3-8-6 (59)(bl) F Lynch 20/1: 040160: Keen/front rank, rdn/lost tch fnl 3f, fin 11th: 6   35
lkd well: prev with B W Hills, now with G M Moore, see 2254.

2883 **SEDONA 14** [9] 3-8-1 (54)(BL) P Fessey 40/1: 0100RR: Again refused to race: blnkd: one to avoid.   0

986

12 ran   Time 2m 38.0 (4.5)   (D O Cremin)   W Storey Muggleswick, Co Durham

3182   3.15 T SHEDDEN HCAP 3YO 0-90 (C)   1m1f   Good/Firm 22   +05 Fast   [90]
£6617   £2036   £1018   £509

2906 **ARANYI** 13 [5] J L Dunlop 3-9-7 (83) T Quinn 10/3: 413331: 3 gr c El Gran Senor - Heather's lt   **91**
(Believe It) Led after 1f, rdn & went clr 2f out, ran on strongly, eased cl home: val 5L: sturdy: plcd thrice
since scoring here at Ripon (mdn): rtd 92 at best when 4th on 2nd of 3 juv starts: eff around 9/10f, further
cld suit: acts on fast, gd/soft & a sharpish or gall trk, likes Ripon: progressive, could rate higher.
3005 **WILFRAM** 9 [4] J M Bradley 3-7-12 (60) F Norton 6/1: 031602: 3 b g Fraam - Ming Blue (Primo Dominie) 3   **61**
Mid-div, rdn/prog over 2f out, styd on but no ch with wnr: clr rem: up in trip, stays a sharp 9f well: scope.
*2992 **STALLONE** 9 [1] J Noseda 3-9-7 (83) J Weaver 5/2 FAV: 551113: 3 ch g Brief Truce - Bering Honneur 2½   **80**
(Bering) Handy, drvn & not pace of ldrs appr fnl 1f: well bckd & a shade below par on this 4 timer bid: btr 2992.
2614 **CLEVER GIRL** 25 [8] T D Easterby 3-9-7 (83) K Darley 8/1: 1D0004: Led early, remained cl-up,   1½   **77**
rdn/wknd fnl 2f: lkd well: longer 9f trip: see 1645.
2942 **SPIN A YARN** 11 [2] 3-9-4 (80) J Reid 10/3: 005545: Front rank, rdn to chall over 2f out, wknd   ½   **73**
qckly over 1f out: nicely bckd: paddock pick: up in trip: see 2942.
*2604 **GERONIMO** 25 [3] 3-8-8 (70) D Holland 7/1: 0-216: Green/al bhd: turf bow: btr 2604 (6f).   22   **38**
6 ran   Time 1m 51.5 (1.5)   (Benny Andersson)   J L Dunlop Arundel, W Sussex

3183   3.45 ARMSTRONG RATED HCAP 3YO+ 0-95 (C)   6f str   Good/Firm 22   +10 Fast   [102]
£6370   £2416   £1208   £549   3 yo rec 4 lb

2697 **LAGO DI VARANO** 23 [9] R M Whitaker 8-8-8 (82)(bl) F Lynch 16/1: 053001: 8 b g Clantime - On The   **87**
Record (Record Token) Broke well, switched to stands rail & sn led, hdd 2f out, rallied well to lead ins last,
drvn out: jockey received a 2-day whip ban: first win at 6f: earlier won at Haydock (h'cap): '99 scorer at York
& Sandown (h'caps, rtd 87), prev term won at Ripon (h'cap, rtd 93), plcd in the Ayr Gold Cup: eff at 6f, prev 10
wins at 5f: acts on firm, soft & any trk: loves to dominate in blnkrs/visor: v tough & genuine, gd ride.
2338 **EMERGING MARKET** 37 [2] J L Dunlop 8-8-8 (82) T Quinn 13/2: -00052: 8 b g Emarati - Flitteriss Park nk   **86**
(Beldale Flutter) Mid-div stands side, rdn & ran on strongly fnl 1f, closing at fin under only hands & heels: best
run to date this season, well h'capped but has not won for over 4 years: see 728.
*2877 **FRIAR TUCK** 14 [1] Miss L A Perratt 5-8-7 (82)(1oh) K Dalgleish (5) 3/1 JT FAV: 030113: 5 ch g Inchinor - ¾   **83**
Jay Gee Ell (Vaigly Great) Front rank, rdn to chall 2f out, switched dist, no extra well ins last: bckd, in form.
3016 **ATLANTIC VIKING** 8 [10] D Nicholls 5-8-8 (82) A Nicholls (3) 13/2: 000404: Front rank, went   nk   **83**
on appr fnl 2f, hdd dist, no extra cl-home: quick reapp: gd run, on a fair mark: see 1861.
1983 **AMARANTH** 52 [8] 4-8-9 (83) D Holland 16/1: 001265: Dwelt/rear, rdn/prog over 2f out, running on   ½   **83**
when short of room ins last, nrst fin: 7 wk abs: see 1687, 1654.
2697 **BOLDLY GOES** 23 [4] 4-8-7 (81)(bl) J Fanning 10/1: 431006: Cl-up, drvn & lkd held when hmpd dist,   shd   **81**
sn btn: lkd superb & ran to nr best here: up 14/1: see 2000.
3152 **JUWWI** 2 [5] 6-9-4 (92) Claire Bryan (5) 16/1: 000007: Sn outpcd, ran on late, no danger: qck reapp.   2½   **86**
*3037 **PIPS MAGIC** 7 [3] 4-8-7 (81)(3ex) A Culhane (3) 3/1 JT FAV: 010018: Prom, drvn/fdd over 1f out: ½   **74**
well bckd, quick reapp: lkd well: better expected after 3037.
2997 **JUNO MARLOWE** 9 [13] 4-9-6 (94) A Beech (3) 25/1: 002009: Rcd wide, al rear: poor draw: see 2616.   2½   **81**
3119 **OCKER 3** [7] 6-8-8 (82) R Fitzpatrick (3) 20/1: 604550: Front rank, rdn/lost tch fnl 2f, 10th: qck reapp.   nk   **68**
2694 **LOOK HERE NOW** 23 [12] 3-8-3 (81)(6oh) F Norton 66/1: -15000: Rcd wide, al rear: 11th: see 731.   ¾   **65**
3016 **FIRST MAITE** 8 [6] 7-9-7 (95)(vis) J Weaver 16/1: 003400: Prom, rdn/wknd qckly over 2f out, 12th.   ¾   **78**
2859 **PIPADASH** 14 [11] 3-8-9 (87) K Darley 12/1: 000030: Wide, al bhd, 13th: op 10/1: poor draw.   hd   **70**
13 ran   Time 1m 10.7 (0.7)   (The Pbt Group)   R M Whitaker Scarcroft, W Yorks

3184   4.15 HORSESMOUTH NOV STKS 2YO (D)   6f str   Good/Firm 22   -28 Slow
£3484   £1072   £536   £268

-- **HEALEY** [5] J D Bethell 2-8-8 J Reid 20/1: 1: 2 ch c Dr Devious - Bean Siamsa (Solinus)   **83+**
Dwelt, sn mid-div, switched/hdwy over 1f out, ran on strongly to lead fnl strides, hands & heels: op 12/1:
IR30,000gns May foal: half brother to a useful 10f scorer: sire Derby wnr: eff at 6f, 7f+ sure to suit: runs
well fresh on fast & a sharpish trk: fine debut, should have plenty of improvement & win more races.
2849 **UP TEMPO** 16 [4] T D Easterby 2-9-0 K Darley 2/7 FAV: 132232: 2 b c Flying Spur - Musical Essence shd   **88**
(Song) Front rank, cruised into lead appr fnl 1f, drvn & collared fnl strides: v fit: well bckd at long
odds-on: stays 6f but poss needs to come late: rated higher 2849 (val stks).
*2700 **XIPE TOTEC** 22 [7] R A Fahey 2-9-5 G Duffield 6/1: -013: 2 ch c Pivotal - Northern Bird (Interrex)   1   **90$**
Trkd ldrs, went on 4f out, rdn/hdd appr fnl 1f, edged right & no extra well ins last: improved in defeat &
a fine run conceding weight all round, win again bt: see 2700.
-- **PURE SHORES** [8] M Johnston 2-8-8 D Holland 10/1: 4: Veered right start, sn prom, ev ch until   1¼   **75**
fdd appr fnl 1f: lkd well: mkt drifter: May foal, dam a smart wng miler in USA: stays 6f on fast: can improve.
-- **NO DISS GRACE** [2] 2-8-8 A Beech (5) 33/1: 5: Al outpcd on debut: swtg: Apr 1st foal, dam scored   9   **55**
over 1m abroad, sire mod: tall gelding, ex-French: fine eff for this: with P C Haslam.
2927 **WHARFEDALE LADY** 12 [6] 2-8-7 R Winston 100/1: -00006: Led early, wknd qckly fnl 2f: mod form.   3   **46**
-- **ROYAL WANDERER** [3] 2-8-8 J Fanning 33/1: 7: Al bhd: backward: 20,000gns colt, dam unrcd.   1½   **44**
2480 **KOMALUNA** 31 [1] 2-8-12 (t) J Weaver 66/1: -0008: Trkd ldrs, wknd rapidly over 2f out.   8   **30**
8 ran   Time 1m 13.0 (3.0)   (Www.Clarendon Racing.Com)   J D Bethell Middleham, N Yorks

3185   4.45 CHILDRENS DAY MDN 3YO+   1m2f   Good/Firm 22   -04 Slow
£3510   £1080   £540   £270   3 yo rec 9 lb

2957 **PHANTOM RAIN** 10 [1] B W Hills 3-8-7 J Reid 8/11 FAV: 0251: 3 b f Rainbow Quest - Illusory (King's   **80**
Lake) Front rank, chall over 2f out, styd on to lead ins last, drvn out: lkd fit: nicely bckd at odds-on:
eff at 10f, further cld suit: acts on fast, gd/soft & a sharpish or turning trk.
-- **SOUTH SEA PEARL** [6] M Johnston 3-8-7 D Holland 12/1: 0-6602: 3 b f Southern Halo - Naturalracer   ½   **80**
(Copelan) Led, clr halfway, drvn/hdd dist, rall cl-home, not btn far: 7L clr rem on Brit bow: ex-French,
unplcd btwn 7f & 10f prev: eff at 10f on fast: goes well fresh: fine eff for new connections, win similar.
1824 **SON OF A GUN** 59 [3] J Neville 6-9-7 J Weaver 11/4: 423: 6 b g Gunner B - Sola Mia (Tolemeo)   7   **71**
Prom, rdn/fdd appr fnl 2f: 8 wk abs: ex-bmpr rnr, a return to further in h'caps shld now suit: see 1824.

RIPON MONDAY AUGUST 7TH Righthand, Sharpish Track

1824 **BOURKAN 59** [2] A C Stewart 3-8-12 K Darley 13/2: 004: Mid-div, rdn/eff over 3f out, sn no extra: *shd* **71**
tchd 10/1: 8 wk abs: scope, could improve in h'caps now: see 1824, 1539.
2838 **ARANUI 16** [5] 3-8-12 (t) P M Quinn (3) 33/1: 0-035: Handy, wknd fnl 3f: carr cond: btr 2838. *9* **55**
-- **ALI OOP** [4] 3-8-12 R Winston 25/1: 6: Al last, t.o. halfway: debut, burly/backward. *dist* **0**
6 ran Time 2m 05.9 (2.6) (K Abdulla) B W Hills Lambourn, Berks

WINDSOR MONDAY AUGUST 7TH Sharp, Fig 8 Track

Official Going GOOD/FIRM - GOOD In Str (Watered Ground & Showers In The Morning). Stalls: Inside.

3186 **6.00 BOLLINGER AMAT HCAP 3YO+ 0-75 (E) 1m3f135y Good [42]**
£2828 £808 £404 3 yo rec 11lb Field raced on stands rail

2971 **RAYIK 10** [2] G L Moore 5-10-5 (47) Mr R L Moore (5) 5/1: 412001: 5 br g Marju - Matila (Persian **53**
Bold) Led after 2f, made rest, clr over 1f out, kept on for hands & heels riding: last winter scored 3 times
at Lingfield (h'caps, rtd 79a): rnr-up in '99 (rtd 81a): won again at Lingfield in '98 (mdn, with N Berry): eff
over 10/13f on gd & both AWs, loves Lingfield/equitrack & racing up with/forcing the pace : tough & genuine.
2689 **CLASSIC CONKERS 23** [11] Pat Mitchell 6-9-10 (38) Mr S Rees (5) 16/1: -01502: 6 b g Conquering Hero *½* **43**
Erck (Sun Prince) Slow away, held up, hdwy over 2f out, chall ins last, just held: clr of rem & back to form.
2982 **GOLD MILLENIUM 10** [4] C A Horgan 6-10-2 (44) Mr B Hitchcott 7/1: 041363: 6 gr g Kenmare - Gold *6* **41**
Necklace (Golden Fleece) In tch, eff over 2f out, sn onepace: see 2982, 2255.
2888 **TARSKI 14** [7] L G Cottrell 6-10-5 (47) Mr L Jefford 9/2: 003354: Sn handy, eff to chase wnr over *½* **43**
2f out, wknd over 1f out: nicely bckd: see 2552, 1395.
3111 **SILVER SECRET 3** [8] 6-10-2 (44)(BL) Mr T Best (5) 7/1: 606055: Prom, lost pl over 5f out, late gains. *1¾* **37**
2802 **TWOFORTEN 17** [1] 5-9-10 (38)(4oh) Mr R Lucey Butler (7) 20/1: 650006: Waited with, rdn & no *½* **30**
impress fnl 2f: visor discarded: see 2347 (7f), 1933.
3073 **PAY HOMAGE 5** [6] 12-9-12 (40) Mr J Gee (5) 12/1: 46-057: Sn bhd, no impress fnl 2f: qk reapp. *1¼* **30**
2501} **ELAANDO 397** [12] 5-12-0 (70) Mr Nicky Tinkler (5) 16/1: 13/0-8: Dwelt, sn in tch, wknd 3f out: recently *7* **51**
well btn in a h'cap hdle, in 99/00 won at M Rasen & Towcester (h'caps, rtd 111h): won at Folkestone & Exeter in
98/99 (stays 2m3f on firm, gd & handles hvy): Flat wnr in France back in '98: stays 11f on soft grnd.
*3031 **CITY GAMBLER 7** [9] 6-10-9 (51)(5ex) Mr T Scudamore 5/2 FAV: -50019: Prom, wknd 3f out: hvly *nk* **31**
bckd & better expected under a pen after 3031.
2802 **ALCOVE 17** [10] 9-10-6 (43)(bl)(5ow) Dr M Allingham (0) 33/1: 000000: Prom, wknd over 3f out: 10th. *3* **24**
3045 **PADDYS RICE 7** [5] 9-10-1 (41)(2ow) Mr S J Edwards (0) 33/1: 500/00: Led 2f, wknd over 2f out: 11th. *2* **16**
514 **ROYAL CZARINA 175** [3] 3-10-2 (55)(6ow)(16oh) Mr Ben Salaman (0) 50/1: 0-000: Al bhd: last: see 514. *6* **20**
12 ran Time 2m 33.6 (Lancing Racing Syndicate) G L Moore Woodingdean, E Sussex

3187 **6.30 SHANKLIN FILLIES MDN 2YO (D) 6f str Good**
£3854 £1186 £593 £296 Field raced in centre of Crse

2952 **MUJADO 10** [4] B J Meehan 2-8-11 Pat Eddery 8/13 FAV: 221: 2 b f Mujadil - Unaria (Prince Tenderfoot) **91**
Made all & allowed to dominate, sn clr, easily: hvly bckd: 30,000 gns Feb foal, half sister to a wng sprinter:
eff at 6f, 7f will suit: likes to force the pace on gd/firm, gd & any trk: useful.
2588 **TICKLE 26** [5] P J Makin 2-8-11 S Sanders 33/1: 02: 2 b f Primo Dominie - Funny Choice (Commanche *5* **73**
Run) Chsd wnr over 3f out, nvr a threat: caught a useful sort: shld improve again & win a race: see 2588.
2683 **LADY WARD 23** [12] M H Tompkins 2-8-11 A Clark 33/1: 03: 2 b f Mujadil - Sans Ceriph (Thatching) *¾* **72**
Sn rdn in tch, some late gains: better run: sure to apprec 7f & shld find a race: see 2683.
-- **POPPAEA** [10] R Hannon 2-8-11 Dane O'Neill 20/1: 4: Dwelt, bhd, some late gains: debut: Apr *2½* **64**
foal, cost IR 38,000gns: half sister to a juv 5/6f wnr: dam 7f juv scorer: with R Hannon, some promise here.
-- **MARIKA** [7] 2-8-11 M Hills 10/1: 5: Squeezed out start, bhd, mod late gains: debut, op 6/1: *6* **49**
Feb foal, half sister to a smart 7f wnr: dam 6f/1m scorer: with B Hills, shld improve.
3047 **GIRL BAND 7** [6] 2-8-11 R Havlin 33/1: 06: In tch, no impress fnl 2f: Apr 1st foal, cost IR 24,000gns: *1* **46**
dam 7f/1m scorer: bred to apprec 7f+ in time: with M Channon.
2748 **ESPANA 19** [1] 2-8-11 G Carter 16/1: 037: Dwelt, bhd, no impress fnl 2f: btr 2748. *nk* **45**
2854 **LADY MILETRIAN 16** [8] 2-8-11 J Fortune 5/1: -528: Chsd wnr till over 3f out, sn eased when held: *1* **42**
shld do better, poss on a faster surface: see 2854.
-- **CIRCLET** [11] 2-8-11 B Marcus 33/1: 9: Slow away, al bhd: debut: Apr 1st foal: bred to apprec 7f. *shd* **41**
-- **MANUKA TOO** [3] 2-8-11 R Mullen 33/1: 0: Dwelt, al bhd: 10th. *1¼* **38**
3096 **Artifact 5** [2] 2-8-11 R Hughes 16/1: -- **Arabian Waters** [14] 2-8-11 S Carson (3) 33/1:
1782 **Gone With The Wind 60** [16] 2-8-11 Paul Eddery 25/1: 2748 **Precious Penny 19** [9] 2-8-11 N Callan 33/1:
-- **Vitesse** [13] 2-8-11 R Ffrench 33/1: 2939 **Zandos Charm 11** [15] 2-8-11 A Daly 33/1:
2227 **Lady In The Night 40** [17] 2-8-11 R Cochrane 16/1:
17 ran Time 1m 13.7 (Total (Bloodstock) Ltd) B J Meehan Upper Lambourn, Berks

3188 **7.00 SOLENT HCAP 3YO+ 0-70 (E) 1m67y Good [69]**
£3066 £876 £438 3 yo rec 7 lb Field raced in the centre of the Crse

2544 **WITH A WILL 28** [16] H Candy 6-9-6 (61) C Rutter 13/2: -33141: 6 b g Rambo Dancer - Henceforth **68**
(Full Of Hope) In tch, hdwy to lead over 1f out, styd on well for press: earlier scored here at Windsor (class
stks): back in '98 won at Kempton (appr h'cap) & Lingfield (rtd 62): eff at 1m, stays 10f well: handles fast,
likes gd & gd/soft & an easy trk, esp Windsor: proving tough.
2831 **CAUTION 17** [13] S Gollings 6-8-13 (54) J Quinn 7/1: 042252: 6 b m Warning - Fairy Flax (Dancing *1¾* **57**
Brave) Handy, eff to chase wnr over 1f out, onepace: tough, but prefers to be placed than to win: see 2561.
1998 **WARRING 51** [9] M S Saunders 6-7-12 (39) N Carlisle 14/1: 503003: 6 b g Warrshan - Emerald Ring *1* **40**
(Auction Ring) Handy, hdwy to chall over 1f out, no extra ins last: gd run after abs: slipped down the weights.
3018 **THE DOWNTOWN FOX 8** [17] B A McMahon 5-9-13 (68)(bl) R Hughes 10/1: 000204: In tch, eff 2f *shd* **69**
out, onepace over 1f out: prob stays 8.3f: see 2704, 320.
2727 **MULLAGHMORE 20** [7] 4-8-6 (47) N Callan 20/1: 550005: Slow away, bhd, late gains, nvr dangerous. *1¼* **46**
*2974 **WHO GOES THERE 10** [14] 4-8-11 (52) P Doe 10/1: 003016: Slow away, bhd, some late gains: btr 2974. *1¾* **47**
2564 **MAWINGO 27** [3] 7-9-5 (60) Paul Eddery 14/1: 354-07: Bhd, brief eff over 2f out, no impress: see 169. *½* **54**
2593 **BECKON 26** [8] 4-7-11 (38) A Polli (3) 12/1: 450158: Nvr a factor: twice below 2212 (equitrack, 10f). *½* **31**

WINDSOR   MONDAY AUGUST 7TH   Sharp, Fig 8 Track

1998 **MOON AT NIGHT 51** [12] 5-10-0 (69) M Roberts 11/2 FAV: 0-1039: Set gd pace till wknd over 1f out: 1¼   60
7 wk abs, top weight, better expected after 1998, see 1129 (gd/firm).
3007 **MASSEY 9** [2] 4-8-10 (51) J Fortune 14/1: 000000: Chsd ldr till wknd 2f out: 10th: see 752.   ½   41
3045 **GALI 7** [11] 4-8-0 (41) T Ashley 16/1: 0-0000: In tch al bhd, not clr run over 1f out: 11th: see 1729.   1¾   27
1439 **SILENT NIGHT 77** [5] 3-9-8 (70)(BL) N Pollard 12/1: 50-050: Chsd ldrs till wknd over 2f out: 12th, blnks.   3⅓   49
598 **LILANITA 161** [10] 5-8-0 (40)(vis)(1ow) J Tate 25/1: 200000: Slow away, al bhd: 13th, long abs.   2   16
2726 **FUEGIAN 20** [1] 5-9-4 (59) D Harrison 10/1: 2010P0: Handy, weakend 2f out: 14th, something amiss?   2   30
2727 **LITTLE TUMBLER 20** [4] 5-8-5 (46) Pat Eddery 10/2: 0-5650: Al bhd, 15th: see 2262.   1   15
2958 Love Diamonds 10 [15] 4-8-4 (45)(VIS) M Fenton 25/12795 So Dainty 18 [18] 3-8-9 (57) A Clark 33/1:
2890 Karakul 14 [6] 4-9-3 (58) L Newman (3) 20/1:
18 ran   Time 1m 45.2   (Henry Candy)   H Candy Wantage, Oxon

---

3189   7.30 WEATHERBYS MDN 3YO+ (D)   1m2f   Good
£4082   £1256   £628   £314   3 yo rec 9 lb   Rcd across the course - strung out like sell hdlrs.

2957 **PURPLE HEATHER 10** [11] R Hannon 3-8-7 (bl) Dane O'Neill 15/8: 253021: 3 b f Rahy - Clear Attraction   85
(Lear Fan) Early ldr, remained prom till regained lead 3f out, kept on strongly, blnk out: hvly bckd from 3/1:
deserved win, plcd several times prev: 4th in a Gr 3 on 2nd of 3 '99 starts (rtd 95): eff at 1m/10f, has tried
12f & that trip shld suit: acts on gd & fast, handles a stiff/gall or sharp trk: suited by blnks: decisive wnr.
2679 **BEDEY 23** [2] A C Stewart 3-8-12 M Roberts 13/8 FAV: -422: 3 b c Red Ransom - Mount Helena (Danzig)   5   83
Trkd ldrs, chsd wnr fnl 3f, 4L 2nd when eased ins fnl 1f: hvly bckd tho' drifted from 4/5: clr 3rd: prob stays 10f.
3938} **SOPHALA 326** [4] C F Wall 3-8-7 R Mullen 33/1: 0-3: 3 b f Magical Wonder - Fujaiyrah (In Fijar)   8   68
Mid-div, prog to chase front pair 2f out, sn no impress: reapp: unplcd in a Yarmouth mdn on sole '99 start
(with D Morris, rtd 62): half sister to a 7f sell wnr, also related to wnr abroad: dam a 6f juv wnr.
2938 **TACHOMETER 11** [10] H S Howe 6-9-2 L Newman (3) 33/1: 404: Mid-div, late hdwy, no ch with ldrs.   2½   65
2974 **MACS DREAM 10** [8] 5-9-7 (t) M Tebbutt 33/1: 5-0005: Rear, imprvd 3f out, no impress fnl 2f: ¾   68$
top weight: offic rtd just 42, treat this rating with caution: see 2974.
2871 **LORD GIZZMO 15** [5] 3-8-12 G Hind 33/1: -06: Prom till wknd over 2f out: see 2871.   6   60$
-- **CARAMELLE** [6] 4-9-2 I Mongan (5) 25/1: 7: Slowly away, some late hdwy, nvr dangerous on debut: 4   49
related to a 1m/12f wnr: G L Moore filly, shld be capable of better.
-- **LEILA** [9] 5-9-2 R Havlin 40/1: 8: Slowly away, well bhd till mod late gains on Flat debut: well   1½   47
btn in bmprs/nov hdles in 1999/00, incl when tried in blnks: with J King.
2764 **PAPERWEIGHT 19** [3] 4-9-2 (BL) J Tate 20/1: 303449: Led after 1f till over 3f out, styd stands side   2½   43
& wknd qckly: rode keenly in 1st time blnks: rider picked the wrong side here: see 2764 (sand).
-- **SAND PEBBLES** [13] 3-8-7 J Fortune 9/2: 0: Slowly away, nvr a factor & t.o. in 10th on debut: 8   31
well bred filly, related to sev wnrs: bred to apprec mid-dists: with J Gosden & shld be capable of better.
2774 Plain Chant 18 [7] 3-8-12 Carol Packer (7) 16/1:   -- **Pampered Queen** [1] 6-9-2 A Polli (3) 33/1:
1261 Pembroke Star 87 [12] 4-9-2 G Bardwell 33/1:
13 ran   Time 2m 08.3   (The Queen)   R Hannon East Everleigh, Wilts

---

3190   8.00 CITY INDEX MDN 3YO (D)   1m67y   Good
£4062   £1250   £625   £312   Field raced far side

2722 **POLAR CHALLENGE 21** [7] Sir Michael Stoute 3-9-0 (t) Pat Eddery 6/4: 335231: 3 b c Polar Falcon -   81
Warning Light (High Top) Made all, in command fnl 1f, cmftbly: hvly bckd: deserved win, plcd sev times prev,
incl in h'caps: half brother to a 6/7f wng 2yo, dam mid-dist bred: acts on fast & gd/soft: stays 10f, seems best
arnd 1m: handles a stiff/gall or sharp trk: imprvd for switch to forcing tactics today & application of a t-strap.
1885 **FINISHED ARTICLE 55** [8] D R C Elsworth 3-9-0 N Pollard 8/1: -46352: 3 b c Indian Ridge - Summer   1   78
Fashion (Moorestyle) Trkd ldrs, imprvd to chall 2f out, onepcd 1f out till ran on well clr-home: 8 wk abs: eff
at 1m, will apprec a return to 10f: stable in gd form now, shld win similar: see 1885, 1599.
2938 **WOOLFE 11** [4] J H M Gosden 3-8-9 J Fortune 10/1 FAV: 33: 3 ch f Wolfhound - Brosna (Irish River)   ½   72
Chsd ldrs, ev ch 2f out, onepace ins fnl 1f: well bckd, 9L clr rem: acts on gd & fast grnd: see 2938.
2977 **INNKEEPER 10** [5] Miss Gay Kelleway 3-9-0 N Callan 25/1: 200664: Rcd keenly & chsd wnr 6f, fdd.   9   59
3021 **DANGEROUS DEPLOY 8** [2] 3-9-0 L Branch (7) 25/1: 55: Rear, some late hdwy, no ch with ldrs: nk   58
mkr drifter, longer priced s/mate of rnr-up: appeared unsuited by this drop back to 1m: see 3021 (10f clmr).
2472 **LE FOLLIE 31** [3] 3-8-9 M Hills 16/1: 06: In tch till btn 3f out, op 10/1: see 2472.   3   47
-- **REGAL VISION** [6] 3-9-0 S Sanders 33/1: 7: Slowly away & al bhd on debut: ran greeen: related   4   44
to sev wnrs, incl hdler Symonds Inn: with C Cox.
7 ran   Time 1m 45.0   (Cheveley Park Stud)   Sir Michael Stoute Newmarket

---

3191   8.30 ISLE OF WIGHT HCAP 3YO+ 0-70 (E)   5f str   Good   [70]
£2926   £836   £418   3 yo rec 3 lb   Field raced far side

3056 **SOAKED 6** [6] D W Chapman 7-8-8 (50)(bl) M Roberts 7/2: 000R21: 7 b g Dowsing - Water Well   56
(Sadler's Wells) In tch, drvn to lead ins fnl 1f, styd on well, drvn out: nicely bckd from 9/2, qck reapp: '99
Lingfield wnr (AW h'cap, rtd 87a): prolific wnr in '98, at Musselburgh (2), Hamilton, Southwell (3) & Lingfield
(2, h'caps, rtd 83a & 65): eff at 5/6f on fast, gd/soft & both AWs: off with/without blnks, handles any trk.
2925 **BEYOND THE CLOUDS 12** [10] J S Wainwright 4-9-5 (61) Pat Eddery 6/4 FAV: 614142: 4 b g Midhish -   ½   65
Tongabezi (Shernazar) Waited with, imprvd halfway, led briefly dist, not pace of wnr cl-home: bckd, tough.
3135 **AROGANT PRINCE 3** [1] J J Bridger 3-8-10 (55) R Brisland (3) 11/1: 000403: 3 ch c Aragon -   1½   55
Versaillesprincess (Legend Of France) Led till dist, kept on under press: qk reapp: likes gd & soft grnd.
3091 **PRICE OF PASSION 5** [11] D W P Arbuthnot 4-10-0 (70)(vis) R Cochrane 12/1: 0-0004: Rdn in rear,   nk   69
prog to chall dist, no extra cl-home: tchd 16/1, qck reapp, top weight: signalled a return to form here.
2929 **SOTONIAN 12** [8] 7-9-2 (58) W Ryan 6/1: 34535: Trkd ldrs, short of room 2f out, not pace to   2   52
chall after: not get the run of tonight's race: see 2743, 394.
2478 **FRAMPANT 31** [7] 3-8-13 (58) R Hughes 12/1: 044306: Front rank till onepace fnl 1f: mkt drifter.   ½   50
2632 **YABINT EL SHAM 24** [5] 4-9-4 (60)(t) J Fortune 16/1: 000007: Rear, no impress fnl 1½f: little   2   46
form since 466 & has subs slipped down the weights: see 394.
2974 **MISTER RAIDER 10** [9] 8-7-10 (38)(bl) (60h) D Kinsella (7) 20/1: -00008: Front rank, wknd 3f out.   1½   20
2535 **ORIEL STAR 28** [2] 4-8-1 (42)(vis)(1ow) R Mullen 11/1: 006009: With ldrs 3f, wknd into 9th: op 6/1.   shd   25
2250 **LANDICAN LAD 40** [4] 3-8-13 (58) S Carson (3) 12/1: 00500: Prsd ldrs 3f, wknd into last: 6 wk abs.   6   22
10 ran   Time 1m 0.7   (David W Chapman)   D W Chapman Stillington, N Yorks

CARLISLE MONDAY AUGUST 7TH Righthand, Stiff Track, Uphill Finish

Official Going FIRM. Stalls: Inside, except 12f - Outside.

3192 **6.15 CUMBRIAN APPR HCAP 3YO+ 0-70 (E)** **1m rnd Firm 11 +03 Fast** [55]
£2912 £832 £416 3 yo rec 7 lb

2063 **HYDE PARK 48** [1] D Nicholls 6-9-7 (48) Clare Roche (5) 11/1: -00001: 6 b g Alzao - Park Elect 53
(Ahonoora) Made all, clr over 1f out, rdn & held on well ins last: 7 wk abs: failed to win in '99, plcd numerous
times (rtd 72a & 63, h'caps): '98 wnr at Brighton, Pontefract & Chester (h'caps, rtd 72): suited by 7f/1m on firm,
gd/soft, soft & any trk: likes to force the pace & can carry big weights: runs well fresh: well h'capped.
1680 **CHINABERRY 65** [5] M Brittain 6-9-3 (44) D Mernagh 14/1: -04002: 6 b m Soviet Star - Crimson Conquest 1 44
(Diesis) Towards rear, rdn & styd on fnl 2f, not reach wnr: 2 month abs: 1 win in 35 starts: see 299 (AW).
2958 **RAINSTORM 10** [3] P D Evans 5-9-0 (41) Joanna Badger (3) 5/1: 000-03: 5 b g Rainbow Quest - Katsina nk 40
(Cox's Ridge) Dwelt/rear, styd on fnl 2f, not reach wnr: clr rem: handles firm & equitrack, sharp/stiff trk.
2883 **STITCH IN TIME 14** [2] G C Bravery 4-8-9 (36) G Baker (3) 4/1 FAV: 302054: Chsd ldrs, held 1f out. 4 27
2533 **BRANDON MAGIC 28** [4] 7-9-1 (42) T Hamilton (5) 9/2: 305505: In tch 6f: stablemate of wnr: see 497. ¾ 32
3011 **YOUNG ROSEIN 8** [9] 4-9-10 (51) Angela Hartley (5) 6/1: 003006: Chsd ldrs, btn 2f out: btr 2542. 1¼ 38
3045 **BITTER SWEET 7** [6] 4-8-13 (40)(vis) R Cody Boutcher (3) 9/2: 540057: Prom 7f: see 1272, 1100. ½ 26
2970 **BY THE GLASS 10** [7] 4-8-3 (30) Giorgia Lamberti (5) 33/1: 600068: Dwelt & al bhd: see 1132 (sell). 2½ 11
3138 **FASTWAN 3** [8] 4-7-12 (25) P Hanagan (3) 14/1: 000059: Al towards rear: qck reapp: see 2523. 4 0
9 ran Time 1m 39.4 (0.6) (Ian Hewitson) D Nicholls Sessay, N.Yorks.

3193 **6.45 HORSLYX MDN AUCT 2YO (E)** **5f rnd Firm 11 -17 Slow**
£2828 £808 £404

3009 **GIBNEYS FLYER 8** [3] A Berry 2-7-12 P Fessey 9/2: -61: 2 br f Magical Wonder - Wisdom To Know 70
(Bay Express) Trkd ldr, led 2f out & rdn/in command 1f out, styd on well: progressed from debut: apprec drop
to a stiff 5f, 6f will suit: acts on firm grnd: open to further improvement.
2652 **MIDNIGHT VENTURE 24** [4] Mrs L Stubbs 2-8-9 W Supple 5/2: 03022: 2 b c Night Shift - Front Line 1¾ 75
Romance (Caerleon) Led, rdn/hdd 2f out, kept on, al held after: handles firm & soft grnd: see 2652, 812.
2778 **FLYING ROMANCE 18** [5] D W Barker 2-7-11 J Bramhill 14/1: -0553: 2 b f Flying Spur - State Romance ¾ 61
(Free State) Rear, rdn & styd on fnl 2f, no threat: op 12/1: see 2360, 2100.
2933 **TYPE ONE 11** [2] T G Mills 2-8-10 L Carter 1/1 FAV: 034: Held up, keen, no room over 1f out, nk 73
switched & kept on onepace ins last: hvly bckd, op 6/4: more expected here: see 2933.
2200 **ANGELAS HUSBAND 42** [1] 2-8-9 (bl) J Fanning 16/1: 60035: Chsd ldrs, btn/no room 1f out: abs. 3 65$
2990 **TANCRED WALK 9** [6] 2-7-11 Kimberley Hart 20/1: 06: Chsd ldrs 3f: mod form. 5 44
6 ran Time 1m 0.9 (1.4) (Mrs U O'Reilly) A Berry Cockerham, Lancs.

3194 **7.15 BARCLAYS HCAP 3YO 0-60 (F)** **6f rnd Firm 11 -06 Slow** [67]
£2865 £818 £409

*3161 **PIPS STAR 2** [16] J S Goldie 3-8-13 (52)(6ex) A Culhane 4/1: 400011: 3 b f Pips Pride - Kentucky 58
Starlet (Cox's Ridge) Prom, rdn/led over 1f out, styd on well, rdn out: op 7/2, qck reapp after: recent
Doncaster wnr (h'cap): '99 W'hampton wnr (seller, rtd 68a, plcd on turf earlier, rtd 77): eff at 5/6f on
firm, fast & fibresand, sharp or stiff/gall trk: looks nicely h'capped & is now in fine form, hat-trick beckons.
3033 **NATSMAGIRL 7** [5] Martyn Wane 3-8-5 (44) P Fessey 16/1: -50562: 3 b f Blues Traveller - Top The ¾ 47
Rest (Top Ville) Dwelt/bhd, rdn & styd on fnl 2f, nrst fin: gd run, could find similar, poss at 7f: see 74.
3161 **BEST BOND 2** [9] N P Littmoden 3-9-3 (56)(vis) R Winston 11/1: 056063: 3 ch c Cadeaux Genereux - ¾ 57
My Darlingdaughter (Night Shift) Mid-div, short of room over 2f out, rdn & kept on onepace fnl 2f: qck reapp:
handles firm & gd/soft grnd: also bhd this wnr in 3161.
2885 **FEAST OF ROMANCE 14** [14] Miss Gay Kelleway 3-9-5 (58) D Holland 15/2: 603004: Held up, rdn/no nk 58
room 2f out, styd on ins last, no threat to wnr: acts on firm, fast & fibresand: see 2216, 275.
*3035 **SOBA JONES 7** [10] 3-9-5 (58)(bl) (6ex) K Darley 2/1 FAV: 234315: Led, rdn/hdd over 1f out, no nk 57
extra ins last: hvly bckd, op 3/1: acts on firm & gd grnd: see 3035 (mdn, 5f).
3010 **CHRISTOPHERSSISTER 8** [15] 3-8-11 (50) J Fanning 25/1: 400006: Rear, rdn/late gains, no threat. 2½ 42
1365 **CROESO ADREF 80** [8] 3-8-3 (42) G Baker (5) 33/1: 434007: Mid-div, nvr on terms: abs, new stable. 2 29
3103 **JEPAJE 5** [4] 3-8-11 (50)(bl) G Duffield 12/1: 064458: Mid-div at best: qck reapp: see 105. 3 30
2733 **COMEX FLYER 20** [12] 3-9-1 (54) T Hamilton (7) 11/1: 001009: Dwelt, rcd mid-div, held 2f out. shd 34
3010 **HOWARDS LAD 8** [7] 3-9-7 (60)(bl) V Halliday 16/1: 510200: Rdn/towards rear, no impress: 10th. nk 39
2964 **PRIDE OF PERU 10** [1] 3-8-4 (43) D Egan (7) 33/1: -00550: Prom 4f: 11th: btr 2964, 2731 (7f/1m). 2 17
1600 **NEEDWOOD TRIBESMAN 68** [14] 3-8-11 (50) W Supple 25/1: -00000: Al rear: 12th: abs: mod form. ½ 22
2864 Reds Desire 15 [3] 3-7-10 (35)(13oh) D Mernagh (1) 66/1:
2919 Were Not Joken 12 [2] 3-8-10 (49)(VIS) R Fitzpatrick (3) 25/1:
2864 Annakaye 15 [6] 3-7-10 (35)(2oh) Dale Gibson 12/1: 2374 Collision Time 35 [11] 3-8-9 (48)(vis) F Norton 16/1:
16 ran Time 1m 13.1 (1.0) (Colin Barnfather & Frank Steele) J S Goldie Uplawmoor, E.Renfrews.

3195 **7.45 HORSLYX HCAP 3YO 0-80 (D)** **1m4f Firm 11 -72 Slow** [84]
£4624 £1156

2842 **RAPID DEPLOYMENT 16** [2] J G Smyth Osbourne 3-8-4 (60) F Norton 3/1: 0-0021: 3 b g Deploy - City 63
Times (Last Tycoon) Dictated pace, increased tempo over 2f out, styd on well ins last & always holding rival under
hands-and-heels riding: op 9/4: slow time: plcd once in '99 (auct mdn, rtd 75): eff at 11f, stayed slowly run
12f tonight, may get further: acts on firm & gd grnd, sharp or stiff trk: first success tonight.
*2643 **SPECTROMETER 24** [1] Sir Mark Prescott 3-9-7 (77) G Duffield 2/9 FAV: 6-4112: 3 ch c Rainbow Quest -1¼ 77
Selection Board (Welsh Pageant) Trkd wnr, hard rdn over 1f out, looking held when sltly hmpd/switched well
ins last: hvly bckd at long odds on: acts on firm & gd/soft: see 2643.
2 ran Time 2m 40.7 (9.9) (Mrs E T Smyth-Osbourne & Partners) J G Smyth Osbourne Adstone, Northants.

CARLISLE
MONDAY AUGUST 7TH   **Righthand, Stiff Track, Uphill Finish**

3196
8.15 RIVERSIDE CLAIMER 3YO (F)   **7f rnd**   **Firm 11**   **-03 Slow**
£2299   £657   £328

2882 **DIHATJUM** 14 [2]   T D Easterby 3-8-7 K Darley 9/4 FAV: -32401: 3 b g Mujtahid - Rosie Potts (Shareef   66
Dancer) Held up in tch, prog/chsd ldr 1f out, rdn & styd on well ins last to lead cl-home: bckd: first win: plcd on
several '99 starts (clmr, rtd 66): eff btwn 6f/1m on firm & fast grnd, sharp/stiff trk: best without a visor.
3037 **BAJAN BELLE** 7 [3]   M Johnson 3-8-2 J Fanning 100/30: 403002: 3 b f Efisio - With Love (Be My   ½   59
Guest) Bhd ldrs, rdn/led 2f out & lkd in command 1f out, rdn/wknd & hdd nr fin: see 1855, 1138.
*3004 **SPEEDFIT FREE** 9 [6]   M A Buckley 3-8-8 A Culhane 6/1: 504413: 3 b g Night Shift - Dedicated Lady   1½   62$
(Pennine Walk) Trkd ldrs, rdn & onepace fnl 2f: acts on firm & fast grnd: see 3004 (1m, made most).
*617 **DIRECT REACTION** 159 [4]   Miss Gay Kelleway 3-8-13 (vis) D Holland 100/30: 514114: Led 1f, cl-up   3   61
till rdn/held 1f out: bckd: 5 mth abs: handles gd & fibresand, equitrack/Lingfield specialist: see 617.
3033 **ABSINTHER** 7 [5]   W Supple 3-8-7 (VIS) W Supple 5/1: -02005: Led after 1f till 2f out, sn held: visor, no improv.   2½   50
3080 **GREMLIN ONE** 5 [1]   3-8-2 T Williams 50/1: 06: Rear, eff 2f out, no impress: qck reapp, lngr 7f trip.   1   43
6 ran   Time 1m 26.5 (1.0)   (The Gordon Partnership)   T D Easterby Great Habton, N.Yorks.

3197
8.45 NSPCC CLASSIFIED STKS 3YO+ 0-60 (F)   **7f rnd**   **Firm 11**   **+07 Fast**
£2299   £657   £328   3 yo rec 6 lb

2376 **QUIET VENTURE** 35 [6]   I Semple 6-9-2 (tvi) R Winston 11/4: 000041: 6 b g Rainbow Quest - Jameelaty   60
(Nureyev) Made all, clr 2f out, rdn & held on well ins last: bckd: gd time: plcd form in '99 (rtd 81, h'cap): '98
Redcar, Musselburgh (class stks), Newcastle (h'cap) & W'hampton wnr (AW h'cap, rtd 88a & 81): suited by forcing
tactics at 6f/1m on firm, fast & fibresand, any trk: has run well fresh, eff with/without a vis, suited by a t-strap.
2147 **BAHRAIN** 45 [3]   N P Littmoden 4-9-2 K Darley 15/8 FAV: 400062: 4 ch c Lahib - Twin Island   1¾   56
(Standaan) Held up, drvn/styd on from over 2f out, al held by wnr: hvly bckd, 6 wk abs: eff over a stiff 7f,
return to 1m+ shld suit: handles firm grnd: t-strap omitted tonight: prev with J W Hills: see 2147, 961.
3083 **NAISSANT** 5 [1]   J S Goldie 7-9-2 A Culhane 9/2: 312003: 3 b m Shaadi - Nophe (Super Concorde)   5   46
Chsd wnr 3f out, rdn/held over 1f out: qck reapp: busy mare, 17th start since April: see 2641 (6f, h'cap).
3144 **PALACEGATE TOUCH** 2 [4]   A Berry 10-9-2 (bl) P Bradley (5) 14/1: 365004: Held up, keen, eff 3f   2½   41
out, sn held: qck reapp: see 1139.
1905 **ROYAL ARROW FR** 54 [2]   4-9-2 (VIS) W Supple 6/1: 000055: Dwelt & al bhd: visor: abs: see 1070.   3   35
2761 **KEEN HANDS** 19 [5]   4-9-5 (vis) R Fitzpatrick (3) 7/1: 104006: Chsd wnr, btn 3f out: op 5/1: btr 1504.   1¼   35
6 ran   Time 1m 25.8 (0.3)   (Gee Kay Gee Gees)   I Semple Carluke, S.Lanarks.

CATTERICK
TUESDAY AUGUST 8TH   **Lefthand, Undulating, Very Tight Track**

Official Going: GOOD/FIRM. Stalls: Inside

3198
2.15 HORSESMOUTH MDN 2YO (D)   **7f rnd**   **Good/Firm 27**   **-12 Slow**
£2951   £908   £454   £227

1169 **SPETTRO** 94 [2]   P F I Cole 2-9-0 J Fortune 13/8: 51: 2 b c Spectrum - Overruled (Last Tycoon)   91
Made all, increased tempo over 2f out, al holding rivals fnl 1f, styd on well: hvly bckd from 9/4, 3 month abs:
apprec step up to 7f, will get further: dam a 1m juv wnr: acts on fast grnd & a sharp trk: runs well fresh.
2921 **MARK ONE** 13 [4]   B W Hills 2-8-9 A Culhane 1/1 FAV: -32: 2 b f Mark Of Esteem - One Wild Oat   1¼   82
(Shareef Dancer) Trckd front pair, rdn/chsd wnr over 1f out, kept on tho' al held: nicely bckd though op 4/6,
5L clr 3rd: better expected after promising debut in 2921, shld win a mdn.
2862 **EDDYS LAD** 16 [3]   R M H Cowell 2-9-0 K Darley 4/1: -23: 2 b c Lahib - Glamour Model (Last Tycoon)   5   77
Trkd ldr, rdn/held over 1f out: bckd from 11/2: see 2862.
2316 **SOLO DANCE** 38 [1]   T D Easterby 2-8-9 J Carroll 25/1: 44: Sn outpcd in rear, lost tch over 2f out.   20   42
4 ran   Time 1m 25.7 (2.7)   (Luciano Gaucci)   P F I Cole Whatcombe, Oxon

3199
2.45 DONCASTER SELLER 3-5YO (G)   **1m7f177y**   **Good/Firm 27**   **-34 Slow**
£1806   £516   £258   3 yo rec 15lb

2776 **LUDERE** 19 [4]   B J Llewellyn 5-9-8 R Havlin 9/2: 400-41: 5 ch g Desse Zenny - White Jasmin (Jalmood)   36
Led/dsptd lead, rdn clr 1f out, eased nr fin: no bid, op 7/2: 99/00 hdles wnr at Sedgefield (2m1f nov, firm,
rtd 88h, P Monteith): dual '99 rnr up on the level (rtd 40, h'cap): '98 Musselburgh wnr (clmr, rtd 62): eff
at 12f/sharp 2m on firm & gd/soft: likes a sharp track & apprec this drop to selling grade.
2457 **SYRAH** 32 [7]   W R Muir 4-9-3 D Holland 8/1: 0-6002: 4 b f Minshaanshu Amad - La Domaine (Dominion)   5   25
Held up, prog to chase ldrs 3f out, chsd wnr 1f out, rdn op 10/1: stays a sharp 2m: see 1880 (11f).
2393 **ROOFTOP PROTEST** 35 [3]   Mrs M Reveley 3-8-13 (BL) K Darley 11/10 FAV: 031623: 3 b g Thatching -   3   33
Seattle Siren (Seattle Slew) Reluctant to go to post, trkd ldrs 4f out, no impress fnl 2f: well bckd: tried blnks.
2989 **IRANOO** 10 [5]   R Allan 3-8-7 (t) R Winston 20/1: 2-0004: Led/dsptd lead halfway till 2f out, fdd.   3½   24
3050 **PHARAOHS HOUSE** 7 [1]   3-8-7 (bl) J Carroll 3/1: 000555: Prom, rdn/btn 2f out: see 1681.   5   19
2999 **KISSED BY MOONLITE** 10 [2]   4-9-3 T G McLaughlin 14/1: 200-06: Bhd 3f out: op 7/1: longer 2m   dist   0
trip: rtd 51 at best in '99 (flattered, stks): only mod form prev in '98 (rtd 54 at best, unplcd).
2887 **ARANA** 15 [6]   5-9-3 Sophie Mitchell 20/1: 000607: Bhd 4f out, t.o.: longer 2m trip, no form.   shd   0
7 ran   Time 3m 30.5 (9.7)   (The Trade Import Agency Ltd)   B J Llewellyn Fochriw, Caerphilly

3200
3.15 SHAME NOT TO HCAP 3YO+ 0-60 (F)   **7f rnd**   **Good/firm 27**   **-03 Slow**   **[60]**
£2677   £765   £382   3 yo rec 6 lb

2420 **LUNCH PARTY** 34 [18]   A Berry 8-9-8 (54) J Carroll 16/1: 0-4061: 8 b g Beveled - Crystal Sprite   60
(Crystal Glitters) Mid div/wide, smooth prog to lead dist, in command ins last, rdn out: '99 wnr here at Catterick
(class stks) & Thirsk (h'cap, rtd 67): '98 Musselburgh & Catterick wnr (2, h'caps, rtd 67): 7f sharp trk specialist,
stays 1m: acts on firm & soft, likes to front run, loves Catterick & Musselburgh: now well h'capped, shld follow-up.
3011 **THATCHED** 9 [2]   R E Barr 10-8-11 (43) P Fessey 12/1: 056302: 10 b g Thatching - Shadia (Naskra)   1¼   44

Rear, switched wide & styd on for press fnl 2f, nrst fin: game veteran, best over 1m/9f: see 1254.
3033 **OSCAR PEPPER 8** [1]   T D Barron 3-9-8 (60) J P Spencer 9/1: 220303: 3 b g Brunswick - Princess ½ 60
Baja (Conquistador Cielo) Rear, no room/switched 1f out, rdn & styd on well inside last, nrst fin: improved
eff with blinks omitted: acts on fibresand & fast grnd: fairly h'capped on turf, should win similar: see 534, 365.
3129 **ROYAL REPRIMAND 4** [11]   R E Barr 5-8-6 (38) P Goode (3) 16/1: 000524: Chsd ldrs, not much room 1 36
when rdn & outpcd over 1f out, kept on, no threat: eff btwn 7/9f: handles fast & gd/soft, best without a visor.
3037 **PRIX STAR 8** [7]   5-9-8 (54)(vis) J Fanning 10/1: 040005: Handy, led over 1f out till dist, no extra. hd 51
2882 **ACID TEST 15** [9]   5-10-0 (60)(VIS) R Fitzpatrick (3) 10/1: 000506: Chsd ldrs, held over 1f out: visor. 1¼ 54
2820 **SAND HAWK 18** [16]   5-8-9 (41)(bl) J Bramhall 16/1: 423507: Chsd ldrs, not much room 3f out, sn held. hd 34
2385 **SEVEN SPRINGS 36** [12]   4-8-6 (38) P M Quinn 40/1: 300008: Keen/led till over 1f out, fdd. shd 31
3144 **SYCAMORE LODGE 3** [10]   9-8-13 (45) A Nicholls (3) 9/2 FAV: 060309: Rear, rdn & mod gains fnl 2f. nk 37
3138 **KNAVES ASH 4** [3]   9-8-8 (40) J McAuley 16/1: 360060: Rear, late gains when no room 1f out, position ¾ 31+
accepted: 10th: this run best forgotten, well h'capped & will apprec 1m in similar company: see 1190.
2081} **COOL AFFAIR 416** [5]   5-8-13 (45) J Bramhill 33/1: 0/00-0: Mid div, held/no room inside last: 11th: ¾ 35
reapp: unplcd from just 2 starts in '99 for K Hogg, no form prev: with J G Given.
*3082 **CITY FLYER 6** [15]   3-8-13 (51)(6ex) R Winston 6/1: 006010: Chsd ldrs till over 1f out: 12th: btr 3082. ¾ 40
3138 **BROCTUNE GOLD 4** [4]   9-8-8 (40) A Culhane 10/1: 0-5040: Towards rear, keeping on when no room 1f 0
out & badly hmpd inside last, position accepted after: 15th: quick reapp: best forgotten: see 1658.
3080 Tancred Arms 6 [17] 4-9-0 (46) F Lynch 16/1:   2932 River Blest 13 [13] 4-9-7 (53) G Duffield 12/1:
3144 Napier Star 3 [14] 7-8-1 (33)(t) D Mernagh (3) 25/1:   2188 Moon Dream 43 [6] 4-8-1 (33) T Williams 50/1:
17 ran   Time 1m 25.1 (2.1)   (S Aitken)   A Berry Cockerham, Lancs

---

3201   3.45 REDCAR HCAP 3YO+ 0-70 (E)   1m5f175y Good/Firm 27 -01 Slow   [66]
£3656   £1125   £562   £281   3 yo rec 12lb

3011 **BHUTAN 9** [4]   Mrs M Reveley 5-10-0 (66) A Culhane 4/1: -16001: 5 b g Polish Patriot - Bustinetta 70
(Bustino) Mid div, smooth prog to chase ldrs 2f out, drvn & gamely styd on to lead well ins last: bckd: earlier
won at Hamilton (h'cap): hat-trick scorer over hdles in 99/00 at M Rasen (mdn), Newcastle & Wetherby (h'caps, rtd
118h): '99 Flat scorer at Newcastle (h'cap) & here at Catterick (class stks, rtd 66): eff at 10/14f on firm or
soft, any track, likes Catterick: a tricky ride who is best delivered late & runs well for A Culhane.
3102 **SING AND DANCE 6** [5]   J R Weymes 7-8-13 (51) R Winston 9/1: -25532: 7 b m Rambo Dancer - ½ 54
Musical Princess (Cavo Doro) Chsd ldrs, prog to lead over 2f out, rdn/hdd well inside last & no extra: eff at
10/14f: looks to be coming to hand, likes Musselburgh, see 1147.
-2793 **REDOUBLE 19** [8]   J Akehurst 4-9-8 (60) K Darley 2/1 FAV: 0-0223: 4 b g First Trump - Sunflower 1¼ 61
Seed (Mummy's Pet) Al prom, rdn/every ch 1f out, held nr fin: op 7/2: styd longer 14f trip: see 1878.
2785 **MARMADUKE 19** [11]   Miss Gay Kelleway 4-9-4 (56)(vis) D Holland 16/1: 366034: Held up, prog/ch 2½ 53
2f out, sn onepace: stays a sharp 14f: see 2785 (seller).
2643 **NEEDWOOD MYSTIC 25** [6]   5-8-11 (49) A Nicholls (3) 8/1: 400105: Held up, rdn/kept on onepcd fnl 3f. hd 45
3052 **PENNYS FROM HEAVEN 7** [10]   6-9-3 (55) Clare Roche (7) 7/1: 245046: Held up, keen, badly hmpd nk 50
over 3f out, late gains fnl 2f, no threat: would have finished closer without interference: see 2139.
3025 **SPOSA 9** [7]   4-8-8 (46) T G McLaughlin 8/1: 114437: Prom 12f: btr 2776 (claimer, 12f). 5 34
2951 **HASTA LA VISTA 11** [3]   10-8-10 (48)(vis) T Lucas 10/1: 143508: Led 6f out till over 2f out, wknd: op 8/1. nk 35
2279 **LAWNETT 40** [12]   4-8-2 (40) J McAuley 16/1: 600509: Held up, nvr any impression: abs: see 1363, 437. 4 21
2930 **CONCINO 13** [1]   3-7-11 (47)(1ow)(9oh) P Fessey 66/1: 00-030: Led 1m: 10th: flattered 2930. 17 9
2746 **WILLIAM THE LION 20** [2]   3-7-13 (49) P Bradley(4) 8/1: 552040: Bhd 4f out: btr 2141 (mdn h'cap). shd 11
3050 **COMANCHE QUEEN 7** [9]   3-7-10 (46)(5oh) G Bardwell 66/1: 0-0000: Chsd ldrs, btn 3f out: mod form. 4 2
12 ran   Time 2m 59.3 (3.9)   (P D Savill)   Mrs M Reveley Lingdale, N Yorks

---

3202   4.15 WETHERBY CLAIMER 3YO+ (F)   1m4f   Good/Firm 27 -18 Slow
£2383   £681   £340   3 yo rec 11lb

2538 **WRANGEL 5** [5]   J G FitzGerald 6-9-0 J Carroll 16/1: 001: 6 ch g Tropular - Swedish Princess 48
(Manado) Chsd ldrs, styd on well fnl 2f to lead inside last, rdn out: claimed by J Llewellyn for £5,000: first
success: 99/00 Stratford hdles wnr (nov h'cap, subs rtd 99h), eff arnd 2m/2m1.5f on firm & gd/soft): eff at
12f on the level, could get further: acts on fast grnd: enjoys claiming grade.
2800 **FIELD OF VISION 18** [9]   Mrs A Duffield 10-9-0 G Duffield 9/2: 214522: 10 b g Vision - Bold Meadows 1½ 45
(Persian Bold) Trckd ldrs, rdn & styd on fnl 2f, not pace of wnr: btr 2800.
2866 **SANDABAR 16** [2]   Mrs M Reveley 7-9-5 (t) A Culhane 8/11 FAV: 321563: 7 b g Green Desert - 1 49
Children's Corner (Top Ville) Prom, rdn/every ch 1f out, held inside last: hvly bckd: btr 2203 (h'cap, 2m).
2904 **METEOR STRIKE 14** [11]   D Nicholls 4-8-8 (t) A Nicholls (3) 5/1: 160034: Led till inside last, no extra. 1 42
2865 **LA CINECITTA 16** [1]   4-8-7 K Darley 50/1: -00605: Held up, rdn/late gains, no threat: see 1415. 2 33$
2932 **JATO DANCER 13** [8]   5-9-8 Carrie Jessop (7) 50/1: 406006: Trckd ldrs over 1f out, sn held: see 1353, 359. 1 34$
2776 **CLASSIC DEFENCE 19** [3]   7-9-0 Sophie Mitchell 10/1: 0B0/30: In tch 10f: op 8/1: btr 2776. 6 30
2161} **FORTUNE HOPPER 412** [6]   6-8-12 J McAuley 33/1: 03/0-8: Al rear: Flat reapp: 10 week jumps abs, 1¼ 26
99/00 Hexham wnr (h'cap, rtd 74h): unplcd sole '99 Flat start (rtd 35, mdn h'cap): stays 2m, suited by 12f:
acts on gd & gd/soft grnd: best without a visor.
822 **MISS ARCH 125** [10]   4-8-7 J Fanning 25/1: 200-59: In tch 9f: abs: 4 month abs: see 822. 4 15
-- **GOLDEN GROOVE 4** [4]   4-8-10 (BL) O Pears 9/1: 0: Bhd 5f out: 10th: blinks: Flat debut, 8 wk bmpr 29 0
abs (mod form): tried blinks today for J Norton.
1100 **CIEL DE REVE 98** [7]   6-9-0 (tBL) T G McLaughlin 100/1: 00-000: Cl up till halfway: 11th: blnks. 19 0
11 ran   Time 2m 36.6 (5.4)   (Mrs R A G Haggie)   J G FitzGerald Norton, N Yorks

---

3203   4.45 HORSEMOUTH HCAP 3YO+ 0-65 (F)   5f rnd   Good/Firm 27 +05 Fast   [64]
£2499   £714   £357   3 yo rec 3 lb

*2753 **NOBLE PATRIOT 20** [4]   R Hollinshead 5-8-8 (44) Stephanie Hollinshead (7) 8/1: 534111: 5 b g Polish 49
Patriot - Noble Form (Double Form) Dwelt, held up in tch, no room when prog over 1f out, rdn & styd on well
ins last to lead nr line: earlier scored at Doncaster (2, appr h'caps): plcd in '99 (mdn h'cap, rtd 39a & 33):
eff at 5/6f, stays 7f well, acts on firm, gd/soft & both AWs: handles a sharp or gall track: in fine form.
2929 **TANCRED TIMES 13** [7]   D W Barker 5-9-1 (51) Kimberley Hart 14/1: 411552: 5 ch m Clantime - nk 53
Mischievous Miss (Niniski) Chsd ldrs, rdn/led over 1f out, just hdd line: op 12/1: see 2395.
2753 **TORRENT 20** [8]   D W Chapman 5-9-8 (58)(bl) D Holland 6/1: 444633: 5 ch g Prince Sabo - Maiden shd 60
Pool (Sharpen Up) Trkd ldrs, rdn/chall ins last, just held nr fin: has a high head carriage & a v tricky ride.

CATTERICK TUESDAY AUGUST 8TH Lefthand, Undulating, Very Tight Track

3091 **SIHAFI 6** [5] D Nicholls 7-9-9 (59) Alex Greaves 9/4 FAV: 104324: Mid div, styd on fnl 2f, not pace pace of front trio: hvly bckd op 7/2: quick reapp: still on a fair mark: see 2326. 1¼ 58
2925 **AMERICAN COUSIN 13** [1] 5-8-11 (47) A Nicholls (3) 9/2: 000005: Dwelt/rear, late gains, no threat. nk 45
2925 **OFF HIRE 13** [3] 4-9-5 (55)(vis) R Fitzpatrick (3) 14/1: 044156: Chsd ldrs, held 1f out: see 2732. hd 52
3091 **SOUNDS ACE 6** [9] 4-8-10 (46)(bl) J Fanning 16/1: 030007: In tch, held 1f out: qck reapp: see 1923. 1½ 39
3180 **BOWCLIFFE GRANGE 1** [12] 8-7-11 (33)(bl) Claire Bryan (5) 25/1: 300608: Led till over 1f out, fdd. 1 24
2743 **SWYNFORD DREAM 20** [13] 7-9-6 (56) G Bardwell 20/1: 042609: Dwelt, nvr on terms: see 798. hd 46
+3123 **MILL END QUEST 4** [6] 5-9-4 (54)(bl)(6ex) T Lucas 11/2: 00-010: Dwelt, al towards rear: 10th. ½ 42
3180 **THORNCLIFF FOX 1** [10] 3-9-6 (59)(vis) O Pears 25/1: 360330: Mid div at best: 11th: qck reapp. ½ 45
3091 **NORTHERN SVENGALI 6** [2] 4-9-10 (60) J P Spencer 6/1: 004050: Restless in stalls, sn outpcd & bhd fnl 2f: fin 12th, nicely bckd: eyecatching in 3091 & better expected. 2½ 39
2931 **KERRIDGE CHAPEL 13** [11] 3-7-12 (36)(bl)(1ow) N Carlisle 100/1: 0-0060: Al rear: 13th: mod form. 3 9
13 ran Time 58.4 (1.1) (The Four Dreamers) R Hollinshead Upper Longdon, Staffs

BATH TUESDAY AUGUST 8TH Lefthand, Turning Track with Uphill Finish

Official Going GOOD TO FIRM. Stalls: Straight - Far Side: Round Course - Inside.

3204 2.00 FRANCASAL SELLER 2YO (F) 5f rnd Firm 10 -38 Slow
£2247 £642 £321

2628 **MONTEV LADY 26** [16] W G M Turner 2-8-6 A Daly 25/1: 01: 2 ch f Greensmith - Flair Lady (Chilibang) Nvr far away, rdn to lead below dist, ran on well: bought in for 4,000gns: reportedly finished lame on debut: April first foal, dam 6f wnr: apprec drop back to 5f on firm grnd & ease in grade. 61
3015 **TUSCAN 9** [8] M R Channon 2-8-6 T Quinn 15/8 FAV: -4602: 2 b g f Charnwood Forest - Madam Loving (Vaigly Great) Trckd ldrs, shaken up 2f out, kept on inside last, not pace of wnr: nicely bckd, claimed for £6,000: clearly unsuited by drop back to 5f, cld win one of these over 6f: handles firm grnd. 1¼ 58
2248 **GEMTASTIC 41** [13] P D Evans 2-8-6 R Mullen 8/1: -603: 2 b f Tagula - It's So Easy (Shaadi) Cl up, led ent fnl 2f till below dist, onepace: 6 week abs, prob hndles firm grnd. 1¼ 54
3038 **SOOTY TIME 8** [1] J S Moore 2-8-11 B Marcus 12/1: 066234: Led till entering fnl 2f, same pace. ¾ 56
2772 **QUEENS SONG 19** [18] 2-8-6 F Norton 20/1: -0365: In tch, styd on bef fnl 1f, had to be switched ins last. ½ 49
3038 **PAT THE BUILDER 8** [14] 2-8-11 N Callan 8/1: 54046: Chsd ldrs wide, onepace appr fnl 1f: op 5/1. hd 54
3038 **DESIRE ME 8** [11] 2-8-6 J Quinn 14/1: 57: In tch, eff halfway, styg on but no chance with ldrs when short of room nr fin: tchd 20/1: 6f will suit. nk 48
2773 **ACORN CATCHER 19** [4] 2-8-11 D McGaffin (5) 10/3: 0138: Chsd ldrs, chall under press 2f out, fdd. nk 52
2723 **DISTANT DAWN 21** [5] 2-8-6 (VIS) Cheryl Nosworthy (7) 25/1: 40269: Nvr better than mid div: vis reapp. ½ 45
3028 **UNVEIL 8** [3] 2-8-6 D O'Donohoe 25/1: 446650: Nvr dangerous: 10th, back in trip. hd 44
2772 **Bayrami 19** [7] 2-8-6 K Dalgleish (5) 33/1: -- **So Foxy** [17] 2-8-6 M Tebbutt 33/1:
-- **Eccentricity** [6] 2-8-6 Paul Eddery 16/1: 2933 **Lady Liffey 12** [10] 2-8-6 L Newman (3) 14/1:
2778 **Mulsanne 19** [2] 2-8-11 G Hannon (7) 50/1: -- **Beacons A Light** [9] 2-8-11 A Mackay 20/1:
2939 **Dancing Milly 12** [12] 2-8-6 S Whitworth 20/1: 2949 **Flowline River 11** [15] 2-8-6 P Doe 50/1:
18 ran Time 1m 02.7 (2.4) (Mrs M S Teversham) W G M Turner Corton Denham, Somerset

3205 2.30 COLERNE FILL AUCT MDN 2YO (E) 5f161y rnd Firm 10 -04 Slow
£2762 £850 £425 £212

-- **GOLDIE** [9] D J Coakley 2-8-0 Martin Dwyer 16/1: 1: 2 b f Celtic Swing - Hotel California (Last Tycoon) Waited with, hdwy appr fnl 2f, led bef dist & qcknd clr: equalled crse record: 6,200gns Mar foal, dam 7.5f juv wnr: eff over extended 5f, lks sure to improve over further: acts on firm grnd & runs well fresh: impressive debut. 80
2868 **FIAMMA ROYALE 16** [6] Mrs P N Dutfield 2-8-5 L Newman (3) 9/4 FAV: 225242: 2 b f Fumo Di Londra - Ariadne (Bustino) Handy, rdn appr fnl 1f, kept on for 2nd but no hope with wnr: well bckd, caught a tartar. 7 72
2886 **LITTLE CALLIAN 15** [7] T M Jones 2-8-0 P Doe 7/1: -6043: 2 ch f Charmer - Eucharis (Tickled Pink) Set fair pace till hdd appr fnl 1f, onepace: op 5/1: drop back to 5f/sharper track may suit. hd 66
2821 **MRS PERTEMPS 18** [2] J R Fanshawe 2-8-11 D Harrison 13/2: 034: Chsd ldrs, pushed along thro'out, nvr pace to chall: op 5/1: may do better in 7f nurseries now: see 2821. 1½ 72
2916 **ABBY GOA 13** [1] 2-8-12 W Supple 7/2: 45: Rear, moderate late hdwy: unsuited by the drop in trip. ½ 71
3020 **BLUE LADY 9** [4] 2-8-1 J Quinn 14/1: -06506: Outpcd, late prog: op 10/1, tchd 20/1: win a seller. shd 60
3044 **LEGGIT 8** [13] 2-8-10 (t) T Quinn 16/1: 07: Nvr troubled ldrs & raced wide fnl 2f: Ir£12,000 Night Shift half-sister to a 1m juv wnr, dam 1m/12f wnr: with M Channon. 1¾ 63$
2227 **TURBO BLUE 41** [11] 2-8-5 G Hind 11/1: 08: Dwelt, imprvg but no threat when short of room & eased dist. ½ 56
-- **BRANSTON GEM** [3] 2-8-10 M Hills 11/2: 9: Pressed wnr till 2f out: debut: 16,000gns So Factual March first foal, dam decent sprint juv, sire a sprinter: dropt to a sharp 5f for now?: with M Johnston. nk 60
3101 **MRS TIGGYWINKLE 6** [5] 2-8-2 G Baker (5) 20/1: -64000: Chsd ldrs till appr fnl 2f: 10th, nds sellers. ½ 50
2854 **ARMIDA 17** [8] 2-8-3 F Norton 33/1: -000: Al bhd: 11th. 8 31
11 ran Time 1m 09.9 (0.8) (Chris Van Hoorn) D J Coakley West Ilsley, Berks

3206 3.00 AUGUST HCAP 3YO 0-75 (E) 1m3f144y Firm 10 -18 Slow [76]
£2749 £846 £423 £211

2980 **FLYOVER 11** [8] B R Millman 3-8-6 (54) G Hind 4/1: 0-0051: 3 b f Presidum - Flash By (Ilium) Mid-div, lost grnd bend over 4f out, recovered well 2f out & ran on under press to get up towards fin: tchd 5/2: '99 wnr at Salisbury (fill mdn auction, rtd 74): clearly suited by this step up to 11.5f: acts on firm & gd grnd, suited by a stiff finish: eff in blnks though prob best without. 60
3045 **SPIRIT OF TENBY 8** [1] S Dow 3-9-1 (63) P Doe 5/1: 330402: 3 b g Tenby - Asturiana (Julio Mariner) Held up, prog 3f out, led dist, worn down nr fin: tchd 7/1: improved for longer 11.5f trip, but still a mdn. ¾ 67
*2727 **CYBER BABE 21** [4] A G Newcombe 3-8-8 (56) L Newman (3) 11/4 FAV: 100213: 3 ch f Persian Bold - Ervedya (Doyoun) In tch, prog & every ch appr fnl 1f, onepace inside last: nicely bckd: prob ran to best over longer 11.5f trip tho' shorter trip may suit best: see 2727 (10f). 1¼ 58
2554 **DANDES RAMBO 29** [2] D W P Arbuthnot 3-8-0 (48) M Henry 7/1: 563604: Trckd ldrs, rdn appr fnl 1f, not pace to chall: handles firm & gd grnd, needs mdn h'caps: see 1967. hd 50
2967 **TWIST 11** [3] 3-8-12 (60) Martin Dwyer 4/1: 505025: Sn led, under press entering 3f out, hdd 1f 1¼ 60

out, no extra: different tactics, better held up in 2967.
1455 **MORNINGSIDE** 77 [7] 3-9-7 (69) R Thomas (7) 7/1: 6-646: Nvr dangerous: top-weight on h'cap bow. 3½ 64
2553 **DAJAM VU** 29 [6] 3-7-12 (46) F Norton 16/1: 0007: Struggling after halfway: h'cap bow, nds sellers. 23 21
2332 **GOLDFAW** 38 [5] 3-7-11 (45)(1ow)(8oh) J Quinn 50/1: 0-0008: Early ldr, lost place 5f out, t.o. dist 0
8 ran   Time 2m 28.8 (3.3)   (R J Tory)   B R Millman Kentisbeare, Devon

3207
3.30 TOTE HCAP 3YO+ 0-80 (D)   1m rnd   Firm 10   00 Fast   [80]
£6743   £2075   £1037   £518   3 yo rec 7 lb

2890 **MINETTA** 15 [7] M L W Bell 5-9-3 (69) M Fenton 9/1: -65001: 5 ch m Mujtahid - Minwah (Diesis) 74
Settled last, gd prog 2f out, led dist, rdn out: op 6/1, well rdn: fair time: '99 wnr at Windsor (2) & Thirsk
(fill h'cap, rtd 77): '98 Newmarket (h'cap) & Bath wnr (stks, rtd 77): eff arnd 1m, loves firm/fast grnd, poss
hndles gd/soft & fibresand: likes Windsor & Bath: best without blnks & can carry big weights: nicely h'capped.
2942 **TAPAGE** 12 [1] Andrew Reid 4-8-9 (61) M Henry 11/2: 111162: 4 b g Great Commotion - Irena ¾ 64
(Bold Lad) Sn led, hdd 2f out, still every ch, kept on under press: tough, remains in grand form: see 2726.
3170 **SHAANXI ROMANCE** 2 [2] M J Polglase 5-7-11 (49)(vis)(6ex) F Norton 9/4 FAV: 661123: 5 b g Darshaan ½ 51
- Easy Romance (Northern Jove) Chsd ldrs, chall appr fnl 1f, sn short of room, kept on: well bckd, clr rem,
would not have btn the wnr though wld prob have got 2nd: ran 48hrs ago & is proving tough: see 3078.
2942 **TWIN TIME** 12 [8] J S King 6-9-1 (67) D Harrison 10/3: 231434: Early ldr, again 2f out, hdd dist, fdd. 4 61
3041 **DILKUSHA** 8 [4] 5-9-10 (76) Pat Eddery 7/1: -00435: In tch, eff 2f out, no impress: tchd 10/1, up in trip. 3½ 64
2978 **ADDITION** 11 [3] 4-8-1 (53) J Quinn 11/1: 0-0046: Al towards rear: op 8/1: longer trip, see 1799. shd 41
2855 **CREAM TEASE** 17 [5] 3-9-3 (76) R Studholme 16/1: 0-0007: Chsd ldrs, btn qckly 3f out: btr 2855. ¾ 62
2942 **HARMONY HALL** 12 [6] 6-8-13 (65) T Quinn 13/2: 422208: Al bhd: op 5/1: see 2645, 1973. ½ 50
8 ran   Time 1m 39.1 (0.8)   (Mrs G Rowland-Clark)   M L W Bell Newmarket, Suffolk

3208
4.00 FIGURE IT OUT CLAIMER 3YO+ (E)   5f161y rnd   Firm 10   -23 Slow
£2736   £842   £421   £210   3 yo rec 4 lb

*2747 **LABRETT** 20 [3] B J Meehan 3-9-6 (bl) Pat Eddery 11/8 FAV: 044011: 3 b g Tragic Role - Play The Game 77
(Mummy's Game) In tch, prog ent fnl 2f, led bef dist, rdn out: nicely bckd: recent Kempton wnr (clmr): '99 wnr at
Redcar & Chester (nov stks, rtd 98): eff at 5/6f on firm & gd/soft grnd, any trk, wears blks: better than a clmr.
2944 **ARAB GOLD** 12 [1] M Quinn 5-8-6 (vis) Martin Dwyer 33/1: 400302: 5 b g Presidium - Parklands Belle 2 50$
(Stanford) Chsd ldr, prog to chall appr fnl 1f, rdn & outpcd by wnr: flattered at the weights but likes firm grnd.
2944 **MR STYLISH** 12 [5] I A Balding 4-9-4 (t) M Hills 7/4: 305053: 4 b g Mazilier - Moore Stylish ½ 61
(Moorestyle) Keen, held up in tch, improving when short of room 2f out, styd on but chance had gone:
nicely bckd, would have been 2nd at worst: acts on firm & hvy grnd: mdn after 20: see 1438.
2690 **ONES ENOUGH** 24 [7] G L Moore 4-9-0 I Mongan (5) 12/1: 001004: Held up, wide, prog & edged left 1¾ 51
2f out, chance dist, sn no extra under press: stiff task: see 1994.
1966 **MISTER JOLSON** 53 [4] 11-8-6 F Norton 8/1: 000-45: Held up, late hdwy but not threaten ldrs when nk 42
short of room inside last: op 5/1, 8 week abs: see 1966.
2680 **ORLANDO SUNSHINE** 24 [6] 3-8-2 (b) L Newman (3) 16/1: 0-0006: Led till appr fnl 1f: see 1944. 5 27
2907 **SPLIT THE ACES** 14 [2] 4-8-6 (bl) A Daly 33/1: 550007: Chsd ldrs till halfway: stablemate 5th. 4 15
7 ran   Time 1m 11.0 (1.9)   (Mrs E A Lerpiniere)   B J Meehan Upper Lambourn, Berks

3209
4.30 SUMMER SPRINT HCAP 3YO+ 0-85 (D)   5f rnd   Firm 10   +04 Fast   [82]
£3789   £1166   £583   £291   3 yo rec 3 lb

*3191 **SOAKED** 1 [7] D W Chapman 7-7-10 (50)(bl) J Quinn 9/1: 00R211: 7 b g Dowsing - Water Well 57
(Sadler's Wells) Bmpd start & bhd, gd wide prog 2f out, drvn below dist, kept on gamely to get up fnl strides:
fair time: 2nd win in 20 hrs, yesterday evening won at Windsor (h'cap): '99 Lingfield wnr (AW h'cap, rtd 87a):
'98 wnr at Musselburgh (2), Hamilton, Southwell (3) & Lingfield (2, h'caps, rtd 83a & 65): eff at 5/6f on
firm, gd/soft grnd & both AW: with/without blnks, any track: has really come to the boil, quick hat-trick?
2925 **PALAWAN** 13 [4] I A Balding 4-9-4 (72) R Cochrane 10/1: 301062: 4 br g Polar Falcon - Krameria nk 77
(Kris) Stalked leading duo, hdwy 2f out, led bef dist, rdn inside last & hdd nr fin: clr rem: gd run,
acts on firm, gd grnd & fibresand: cld make amends on a sharper track if reappearing qckly: see 1881.
2869 **BANDANNA** 16 [12] R J Hodges 3-9-13 (84) Paul Eddery 12/1: 065163: 3 gr f Bandmaster - Gratclo 2½ 83
(Belfort) Dwelt, mid div, kept on appr fnl 1f but not pace of frnt pair: back to near best at 5f, see 2787 (C/D).
2845 **NINEACRES** 17 [8] J M Bradley 9-9-2 (70)(bl) W Supple 8/1: 110304: Rear, shaken up from halfway, ½ 67
styd on but nvr dangerous: tchd 10/1, not clearest of passages: worth another chance back at 6f: see 2054.
2929 **RUDE AWAKENING** 13 [10] 6-7-11 (51)(1ow)(4oh) P Doe 16/1: 310105: Held up, keen, not much shd 48
room appr fnl 1f, ran on: see 2743.
3176 **CAUDA EQUINA** 2 [2] 6-9-7 (75) M Tebbutt 7/2 FAV: 040046: Waited with, kept on fnl 1f dispite ¾ 70
not much room: nicely bckd at favourite track but needs plenty of luck in running: see 905.
*2947 **BRANSTON FIZZ** 11 [5] 3-8-11 (68) R Ffrench 10/1: 40017: Off the pace till some late hdwy: 1 60
op 8/1, h'cap bow, bck on turf: return to 6f will suit: see 2947.
3056 **THAT MAN AGAIN** 7 [11] 8-9-2 (70)(bl) M Fenton 11/1: 100438: Led till halfway, no extra bef dist. ½ 61
*2976 **RITAS ROCK APE** 11 [13] 5-9-3 (71) D Harrison 15/2: 060019: Pressed ldr, went on halfway till ¾ 60
bef dist, grad wknd: tchd 9/1: unsuited being taken on for the lead: see 2976.
2428 **MANGUS** 34 [6] 6-7-13 (53) Martin Dwyer 12/1: 500050: In tch, rdn 2f out, no impress/hmpd 1f out: 10th. nk 41
2432 **SPEED ON** 34 [3] 7-9-10 (78) C Rutter 6/1: 063050: In tch, rdn appr fnl 1f, keeping on same pace ½ 65
pace when badly hmpd entering fnl 1f: 11th, nicely h'capped: see 1013.
1887 **TOLERATION** 56 [1] 3-9-10 (81) N Pollard 25/1: 41-000: In tch till halfway: 12th, 8 wk abs, see 1371. 14 48
2247 **JACKIES BABY** 41 [9] 4-10-0 (82) A Daly 10/1: 540040: Sn out the bck: 13th, bckd from 14/1, 6 wk abs. 1 46
13 ran   Time 1m 00.6 (0.3)   (David W Chapman)   D W Chapman Stillington, N Yorks

Official Going   GOOD TO FIRM

3210   **2.45 GR 3 PRIX DE CABOURG 2YO   6f   Good/Firm**
£21134   £7685   £3842

--   **CRYSTAL CASTLE** J E Hammond 2-8-11 C Asmussen 37/10: -21: 2 b c Gllded Time - Wayage   103
(Mr Prospector) Front rank, rdn into lead just ins last, drvn out: earlier rnr-up on debut: eff arnd a gall
6f on fast grnd: smart, well regarded juvenile who holds Gr 1 entries.
--   **EURIBOR** O Pessi 2-8-11 M Demuro 39/10: -1222: 2 b c Indian Ridge - Anna Grassi (Bound For Honour)   ½   101
Led, increased pace 3f out, rdn/hdd ins last, rall cl-home: earlier won on debut & dual rnr-up: eff at 6f on fast.
--   **LUNASALT** A Fabre 2-8-11 O Peslier 3/2 FAV: -13: 2 b c Salse - Lunafairy (Always Fair)   nk   100
Prom, rdn & kept well ins last, nvr nrr: earlier successful on debut: stays 6f on fast ground.
7 ran   Time 1m 12.5   (J Raw)   J E Hammond France

Official Going   GOOD

3211   **2.20 GR 3 PRIX DE PSYCHE 3YO FILL   1m2f   Good**
£21134   £7685   £3842   £2305

1457   **HIDALGUIA 76** J de Roualle 3-8-11 G Mosse 8/1: 1-1231: 3 b f Barathea - Halesia (Chief's Crown)   110
Settled rear, gd hdwy over 2f out, led appr fnl 1f, drvn out: earlier made a wng reapp, subs plcd in Gr 1
company: eff at 9/10f on gd & hvy grnd: smart & consistent filly.
--   **FALL HABIT** L Camici 3-8-11 F Jovine 141/10: -22142: 3 b f Hamas - Hard Bob (Hard Fought)   1½   107
Waited with, gd hdwy over 2f out, ran on well fnl 1f: reportedly lost a shoe: eff at 10f on gd: v useful.
--   **MOSQUERA** P Schiergen 3-8-11 T Hellier 60/1: -15633: 3 ch f Acatenango - Midnight Society   snk   107
(Imp Society) Bhd, rdn/hdwy over 2f out, ev ch till no extra well ins last: German raider: eff at 10f on gd.
-2501   **SOLAIA 28** P F I Cole 3-8-11 T Jarnet 46/10: -41024: Prom, chall ldr over 2f out, drvn & fdd ins   1½   104
last: not disgraced on this drop to 10f, shld relish a return to 12f, as in 2501.
12 ran   Time 2m 05.9   (E Sarasola)   J de Roualle France

Official Going   GOOD

3212   **2.15 GR 1 PRIX MAURICE DE GHEEST 3YO+   6f110y   Good**
£48031   £19212   £9606   £4803   3 yo rec 4 lb

2115   **BOLD EDGE 45** R Hannon 5-9-2 Dane O'Neill 91/10: 1-0341: 5 ch h Beveled - Daring Ditty (Daring   120
March) Jinked right leaving stalls, made all, drvn & ran on strongly when pressed ins last: 6 wk abs: in '99
won at Newmarket (List, reapp) & Ascot (2, Gr 2's, Cork & Orrery & Diadem, rtd 120): '98 wnr at Leicester,
Newbury & Newmarket: stays 7f, best when able to dominate arnd 6f: handles any grnd & likes a stiff or gall
trk, esp Ascot/Newmarket: can go well when fresh: v tough & high-class sprinter.
2615   **LEND A HAND 24** Saeed bin Suroor 5-9-2 L Dettori 1/1 FAV: -61352: 5 b h Great Commotion - Janaat   nk   119
(Kris) Prom, switched over 2f out, drvn & styd on strongly fnl 1f, not btn far: ran close to best, see 2615.
*2574   **GORSE 26** H Candy 5-9-2 G Mosse 6/1: -36213: 5 b h Sharpo - Pervenche (Latest Model)   1½   115
Trkd ldrs, drvn & not pace of front 2 ins last: fine run on grnd faster than ideal: v smart & in fine form.
*2646   **HOT TIN ROOF 23** T D Easterby 4-8-11 K Darley 167/10: 123614: Hmpd leaving stalls, rear, hdwy   shd   110
when short of room appr fnl 1f, ran on well fnl 1f: smart run & would have gone closer with a clear run.
2960   **SIR NICHOLAS 9** 3-8-11 J Weaver 75/10: -12657: Hmpd start, waited with, rdn/no impress fnl 2f: 106
stiff task upped in grade, will apprec a drop to List/Gr 3 company: see 2115.
2615   **WINNING VENTURE 24** 3-8-11 J Reid 55/1: 023009: Nvr a dngr: highly tried, needs a drop in grade.   98
11 ran   Time 1m 16.0   (Lady Whent And Friends)   R Hannon East Everleigh, Wilts

Official Going   GOOD

3213   **2.35 TIVOLI SPRINT CUP 4YO+   6f   Good**
£2538   £1269   £635

2847   **GAELIC STORM 3** M Johnston 6-9-11 K Andersen : 046441: 6 b g Shavian - Shannon Princess (Connaught)   107
Prom, rdn/hdwy over 1f out, drvn out to get up cl-home: qck reapp: 4th in a Listed race in Norway 3 days ago:
'99 wnr at Goodwood (stks), Sweden (2, incl Listed) & Newmarket (Listed, rtd 114): eff at 6/7f: acts on firm,
suited by good or soft grnd: acts on any trk: smart at best.
--   **PRIME MATCH** Denmark 8-9-2 N Cordrey : 2: 8 ch g Primo Dominie - Last Blessing (Final Straw)   1   95
--   **EUGEN** Denmark 5-9-6 M Larsen : 3: 5 b g Diaghlyphard - Eulalia (Level Par)   4   89
8 ran   Time 1m 10.0   (H C Racing Club)   M Johnston Middleham, N Yorks

Official Going GOOD TO FIRM Stalls: Stands Side.

3214 6.00 LADIES AMAT HCAP 3YO+ 0-70 (E) 5f Good/Firm 28 +12 Fast [48]
£2808 £864 £432 £216 3 yo rec 3 lb

3144 **MISS BANANAS** 4 [8] C N Kellett 5-9-5 (39) Miss S Phizacklea (5) 11/1: 000001: 5 b m Risk Me - **46**
Astrid Gilberto (Runnett) Made all, rdn & styd on strongly appr fnl 1f: fast time, quick reapp: earlier
won at Pontefract (sell): '99 wnr at Leicester (amat h'cap, this race, rtd 41 & 57a): prev term scored at
Lingfield (h'cap, rtd 63a): loves to race up with/force the pace at 5/6f, has tried 7f: acts on fast, soft
& both AWs, handles any trk & likes Leicester.
2840 **FRANKLIN LAKES** 18 [7] M R Bosley 5-9-3 (37)(bl)(5oh) Miss G Browne (4) 50/1: 546002: 5 ch g 1¾ **38$**
Sanglamore - Eclipsing (Baillamont) Waited with, rdn to improve over 1f out, ran on ins last but no threat.
3123 **KOSEVO** 5 [6] D Shaw 6-9-5 (39)(bl) Mrs C Williams 12/1: 000003: 6 b g Shareef Dancer - Kallista 1 **38**
(Zeddaan) Rear, rdn & ran on well appr fnl 1f, held well ins last: qck reapp & best run for a while: see 2701, 673.
2796 **SURPRISED** 19 [4] R A Fahey 5-11-7 (69) Miss S Brotherton (5) 9/4 FAV: -00154: Sn outpcd, ran ½ **66**
on late, nvr nrr: both wins over 6f as in 1905.
2931 **ANSELLMAN** 14 [5] 10-11-2 (64)(bl) Miss E J Jones 4/1: 400145: Sn rdn in tch, no extra appr fnl 1f. 1 **59**
3077 **LEGAL VENTURE** 7 [10] 4-9-9 (43)(bl) Ms D Goad (7) 9/1: 402046: Trkd ldrs, drvn/fdd over 1f out. 1½ **34**
3046 **TWO STEP** 9 [1] 4-9-7 (41)(t) Miss C Cooper (5) 12/1: 001057: Mid-div at best: btr 2632 (fibresand). 1½ **28**
2976 **NICKLES** 12 [2] 5-10-1 (49) Miss S Rowe (5) 9/2: 0-0648: Nvr dangerous: see 2976. nk **35**
1487 **RUN MACHINE** 76 [11] 3-9-7 (44) Miss C Stretton (5) 50/1: 000-09: Prom, rdn/wknd appr fnl 1f: abs. 2 **25**
2650 **MINIMUS TIME** 26 [9] 3-9-3 (40)(bl)(3oh) Miss S A Karlsson (1) 16/1: 640000: V slow start, al bhd, 10th. 7 **8**
3180 **CARMARTHEN** 2 [3] 4-9-6 (40)(tvi) Miss K Smith (7) 33/1: 000000: Jinked left start, al bhd, 11th. 1 **6**
11 ran Time 59.1 (0.8) (W Meah) C N Kellett Smisby, Derbys

3215 6.30 TATTERSALLS MDN AUCT 2YO (E) 6f Good/Firm 28 -04 Slow
£3971 £1222 £611 £305

2328 **CLANBROAD** 39 [14] Mrs A J Perrett 2-8-3 T Ashley 7/1: 41: 2 ch c Clantime - Under The Wing **79**
(Aragon) Trkd ldrs, rdn over 2f out, led appr fnl 1f, rdn out: 8,500 gns Apr foal, half brother to a wnr abroad,
dam a mdn: apprec this step up to 6f & further could suit: acts on fast grnd & a stiff/gall trk: on the upgrade.
3064 **KAI ONE** 8 [7] R Hannon 2-8-12 Dane O'Neill 11/10 FAV: 32: 2 b c Puissance - Kind Of Shy (Kind Of ½ **85**
Hush) Handy, drvn & ran on ins last, closing at fin: well bckd, clr rem: consistent, win similar sn: see 3064.
2711 **RAMBLIN MAN** 23 [13] V Soane 2-8-3 Martin Dwyer 33/1: -0503: 2 b c Blues Traveller - Saborinie 5 **64**
(Prince Sabo) Front rank, went on 2f out, hdd appr fnl 1f, not pace of front 2: imprvd at 6f, handles fast: see 1993.
3047 **RESPLENDENT FLYER** 9 [11] P W Harris 2-8-9 T G McLaughlin 14/1: 04: Led after 3f, hdd 2f out, 2½ **63**
btn appr fnl 1f: left debut run bhd: see 3047.
2854 **LONG WEEKEND** 18 [4] 2-8-9 D Harrison 7/2: -05: Outpcd early, ran on well under hands & heels 1½ **59**
appr 1f, nvr nrr: bred to apprec further in time & looks sure to do better: see 2854.
3020 **TALAT** 10 [2] 2-7-12 M Baird 50/1: 06: Mid-div, mod late gains: see 3020. ¾ **46**
2653 **PILGRIM GOOSE** 26 [15] 2-8-5 A Whelan 25/1: 07: Nvr dangerous: needs sells: se 2653. ½ **51**
2488 **MINUSCOLO** 32 [9] 2-8-0 R Ffrench 33/1: 08: Led, hdd 3f out, wknd qckly: see 2488. ¾ **44**
-- **ZOZARHARRY** [3] 2-8-7(2ow) R Cochrane 11/1: 9: Dwelt, al rear: op 8/1 on debut: 11,500gns shd **51**
Apr foal, half-brother to a 2yo scorer abroad, sire a high-class miler: with D Cosgrove.
2972 **BOISDALE** 12 [1] 2-8-12 M Tebbutt 40/1: 00: Al bhd, 10th: see 2972. ¾ **54**
-- **REVOLVER** [2] 2-8-7 T E Durcan 8/1: 0: Al well outpcd, 11th: op 6/1: IR 15,500gns gldg, ½ **47**
half brother to 2 2yo scorers: with W J Haggas.
-- **Florida** [6] 2-8-0 C Adamson 33/1: 2588 **Rock And Skip** 28 [8] 2-8-3 J Tate 50/1:
13 ran Time 1m 11.7 (1.9) (Derek Broad) Mrs A J Perrett Pulborough, W Sussex

---

3216 7.00 MACE NURSERY SELL HCAP 2YO (G) 6f Good/Firm 28 -25 Slow [71]
£1991 £569 £284

+2898 **RIVER OF FIRE** 15 [3] J M P Eustace 2-9-3 (60)(VIS) J Tate 9/2: 011: 2 ch g Dilum - Bracey Brook **67**
(Gay Fandango) Made all, ran on strongly appr fnl 1f, rdn out: bought in for 3,200gns: earlier won at Yarmouth
(sell): half-brother to a 10f juv wnr: eff forcing the pace at 6/7f, 1m could suit in time: acts on firm/fast
& a fair stiff/gall trk: runs well fresh & apprec a visor today: imprvg & is prob better than a plater.
2991 **CIRCUIT LIFE** 11 [11] A Berry 2-8-12 (55) T E Durcan 14/1: 306662: 2 ch c Rainbows For Life - 1¼ **57**
Alicedale (Trempolino) Front rank, rdn/prog appr fnl 2f, onepcd fnl 1f: drop in trip, blnks omitted: see 2862.
3028 **BANNINGHAM BLIZ** 9 [4] D Shaw 2-8-9 (52)(VIS) R Cochrane 7/1: 430223: 2 ch f Inchinor - Mary From ½ **52**
Dunlow (Nicholas Bill) Bhd, rdn & ran on well appr fnl 1f, closing at fin: 1st time visor (prev blnkd): see 3026.
1981 **ASTAIREDOTCOM** 54 [9] K R Burke 2-8-11 (54) D Harrison 7/1: -4504: Cl-up, chall wnr appr fnl 2f, ½ **52**
fdd ins last: 8 wk abs: visor omitted: see 1208.
2052 **MISSING A BIT** 51 [6] 2-8-3 (46) R Ffrench 12/1: 4455: Mid-div, rdn to improve appr fnl 1f, sn held. 1 **42**
2962 **IVANS BRIDE** 12 [10] 2-9-1 (58) M Fenton 9/1: 06406: Dwelt, sn prom, wknd qckly fnl 1f: see 1577. 3 **47**
3168 **ITALIAN AFFAIR** 3 [8] 2-9-3 (60) Jonjo Fowle (5) 7/2 FAV: 050467: Trkd ldrs, chall wnr over 2f 1½ **45**
out, sn lost tch: bckd from 6/1, quick reapp: better expected on this drop to sell grade: see 3168.
3055 **SLIPPER ROSE** 8 [5] 2-8-9 (52) P M Quinn 9/1: 060008: Nvr dangerous: disapp since 730. 2½ **30**
2880 **CATCH THE CHRON** 16 [12] 2-8-12 (55) W Supple 7/1: 2049: Nvr a factor: btr 1492 (clmr, soft). ¾ **31**
2741 **IZZET MUZZY** 21 [1] 2-9-7 (64) T G McLaughlin 20/1: 055460: Sn rdn, al bhd, 10th: btr 2417. 7 **27**
2898 **HARRY JUNIOR** 15 [7] 2-8-10 (53) Paul Eddery 14/1: 052W00: In tch, bhd halfway, fin last: op 10/1. 2½ **9**
11 ran Time 1m 13.00 (3.2) (J C Smith) J M P Eustace Newmarket

---

3217 7.30 LUMBERS HCAP 3YO 0-70 (E) 1m2f Good/Firm 28 -08 Slow [76]
£5044 £1552 £776 £388

3043 **BANDLER CHING** 10 [9] C N Allen 3-9-6 (68) Martin Dwyer 4/1 JT FAV: 33-521: 3 b g Sri Pekan - Stanerra's **76**
Wish (Caerleon) Trkd ldrs, led going well appr fnl 2f, rdn clr, readily: 1st win, plcd twice in '99 (h'caps, rtd 72,
P Mitchell): impvd since tubed/stepped up to 10f: acts on firm & gd grnd, sharp or stiff/gall trks.
2376 **EASTWOOD DRIFTER** 37 [6] W R Muir 3-9-0 (62) R Cochrane 10/1: 036262: 3 ch g Woodman - 3 **64**
Mandarina (El Gran Senor) Held up, imprvd 2f out, styd on und press for 2nd, nvr nr wnr: shapes likes 12f may suit.

2579 **LAHAAY 28** [9] M P Tregoning 3-9-7 (69) W Supple 6/1: -00453: 3 ch g Lahib - Jasarah (Green Desert) hd 70
Waited with, gd wide prog to chall appr fnl 2f, sn rdn & onepace: ran to best off top weight, clr rem, stays 10f.
2958 **RED CANYON 12** [5] M L W Bell 3-9-0 (62) M Fenton 4/1 JT FAV: 123404: Led till appr fnl 2f, no extra. 3 59
3034 **RAINWORTH LADY 9** [12] 3-7-10 (44)(6oh) P M Quinn (3) 50/1: 000635: Bhd, hmpd appr fnl 2f, switched ½ 40
& styd on, nvr nr to chall: clr rem & appears to have imprvd last twice: return to 12f will suit.
2627 **MAGIC SYMBOL 27** [3] D Harrison 20/1: -0056: Chsd ldrs, outpcd 4f out: h'cap bow. 7 46
2506 **COMMONWOOD 32** [2] 3-9-0 (62) Paul Eddery 10/1: 6-4007: Nvr better than mid-div: lngr trip, see 1726. ½ 47
2908 **LOUP CERVIER 15** [14] 3-7-13 (47) R Ffrench 13/2: 003448: Handy till step pl 3f out: tchd 9/1, btr 2908. ¾ 31
2871 **SUPREME SILENCE 17** [16] 3-8-11 (59) D Holland 20/1: -0009: Al around same place: h'cap bow. 2 40
3095 **SKY HOOK 7** [1] 3-8-10 (58) J Tate 20/1: 305-50: Nvr a factor: 10th, quick reapp, see 3095, 153. 2½ 35
3033 **FOREST QUEEN 9** [15] 3-8-6 (54) J Bramhill 25/1: 0-0000: Nvr dangerous: 11th, big step up in trip: 3 27
'99 rnr-up (btn 8L in a 5f nov, rtd 69): with K Hogg.
2789 **SEEKING UTOPIA 20** [11] 3-9-5 (67) R Fitzpatrick (3) 11/1: 5040P0: Chsd ldrs 7f: 12th, see 2023, 727. 2½ 36
2331 **JUMP 39** [4] 3-7-10 (44)(2oh) C Adamson 33/1: 040000: Well plcd till wknd qckly 3f out: 13th, see 328. 8 4
4121} **HORTA 317** [13] 3-9-1 (63) T E Durcan 25/1: 6060-0: In tch till 4f out: 14th, reapp: unplcd 12 10
up to 1m as a juv (nurs, rtd 65, G Bravery): now with B Case.
14 ran   Time 2m 06.1 (3.6)   (Newmarket Connections Ltd)   C N Allen Newmarket, Suffolk

---

3218   8.00 TRAVELSPHERE CLAIMER 3YO (F)   7f str   Good/Firm 28 -02 Slow
£2478   £708   £354

2364 **FOOTPRINTS 37** [3] M Johnston 3-9-5 D Holland 11/8 FAV: 100201: 3 b f College Chapel - Near Miracle 65
(Be My Guest) Led till bef halfway, again appr fnl 2f, drvn bef dist & hard prsd, kept on well: nicely bckd,
clmd for £10,000: earlier won reapp at Warwick (class stks): '99 Redcar wnr (auct mdn, rtd 75): eff at
5/7f: acts on fast & hvy grnd, any trk, likes to force the pace: runs well fresh & is a genuine filly.
2658 **LEEN 26** [9] C G Cox 3-8-1 Jonjo Fowle (5) 14/1: 000602: 3 b f Distant Relative - St James's Antigua 1 44
(Law Society) Held up, rdn 2f out, kept on to chall ent fnl 1f, held 10p: op 10/1, gd effort: stays 7f.
3078 **CHILWORTH 7** [6] T M Jones 3-9-7 (bl) D Harrison 14/1: 420003: 3 ch g Shalford - Close The Till 4 56
(Formidable) Chsd ldrs, no extra bef dist: op 10/1: qk reapp, stiff task at the weights, blnks reapplied.
3033 **NOWT FLASH 9** [7] B S Rothwell 3-9-9 M Fenton 8/1: 500404: Held up, went thro' btn horses fnl 2f. 5 40
2621 **LEEROY 27** [5] 3-9-10 Dane O'Neill 9/2: 4-2005: Sn bmpd, chsd ldrs till appr fnl 2f: see 840. 2 45
3081 **VILLA ROMANA 7** [2] 3-8-10 T G McLaughlin 3/1: 150-06: Al towards rear: quick reapp, see 3081. 2½ 26
3033 **SIRENE 9** [4] 3-8-10 (bl) R Fitzpatrick (3) 14/1: 000357: Bmpd start, led after 2f bef 2f out, wknd. 1¼ 23
2450 **AIR MAIL 34** [1] 3-9-10 (vis) J Tate 20/1: 050008: In tch till 3f out: se 651 (without headgear, e/track). 4 29
-- **SANDOWN CLANTINO** [8] 3-8-4 V Halliday 33/1: 9: Al bhd: debut: Clantime filly with J Given. 2½ 6
9 ran   Time 1m 24.1 (2.1)   (Mrs Joan Keaney)   M Johnston Middleham, N Yorks

---

3219   8.30 EVANS CLASSIFIED STKS 3YO+ 0-65 (E)   1m3f183y   Good/Firm 28 -33 Slow
£2938   £904   £452   £226   3 yo rec 11lb

2872 **THREE WHITE SOX 17** [5] P W Harris 3-8-5 W Supple 9/2: 032551: 3 ch f Most Welcome - Empty Purse 66
(Pennine Walk) Mid-div, prog appr fnl 2f, rdn to lead bef dist, kept on strongly: slow time, tchd 11/2, 1st
win: unplcd sole juv start: eff at 12f, tried further & shld stay: acts on firm & gd/soft grnd, any trk.
3043 **MALARKEY 9** [11] J A Osborne 3-8-8 Dane O'Neill 9/2: 554532: 3 b g Mukaddamah - Malwiya 2½ 64
(Shahrastani) Towards rear, rdn to chase wnr appr fnl 1f, sn no impress: styd longer 12f trip: see 3043.
3049 **KENNET 2** [2] P D Cundell 5-9-5 D Holland 7/2 FAV: 020223: 5 b g Kylian - Marwell Mitzi (Interrex) 1 63
Waited with, keen, kept on under press appr fnl 1f, not pace to chall: tchd 6/1, in tch, rem, best, see 2527, 512.
1091 **I TINA 99** [6] M P Tregoning 4-9-2 A Daly 16/1: 64-604: Led till appr fnl 1f, onepace: op 12/1: 10f? ¾ 59$
3093 **ELMS SCHOOLGIRL 7** [8] 4-9-2 J Tate 9/1: 060645: Rear, wide prog under press 2f out, sn no extra. 1¼ 57
2755 **FLITE OF ARABY 21** [9] 3-8-8 Martin Dwyer 14/1: 00-346: Nvr a factor tho' not clearest of runs 2f out. 6 51
2771 **KINGS VIEW 21** [4] 3-8-8 T E Durcan 4/1: 50-047: Chsd ldrs till 3f out: needs a drop in trip, see 2771. 3 47
2667 **GEMINI GUEST 26** [7] 4-9-5 R Cochrane 8/1: -05038: Handy till 3f out: tchd 10/1, btr 2667. nk 46
2815 **WINDMILL LANE 19** [1] 3-8-7 M Fenton 10/1: 210359: Front rank till lost place appr fnl 3f: op 7/1. ¾ 44
9 ran   Time 2m 34.4 (6.1)   (Les McLaughlin)   P W Harris Aldbury, Herts

---

Official Going   GOOD TO FIRM. Stalls: Inside

3220   2.20 GENTS AMAT HCAP 3YO+ 0-80 (E)   1m2f   Good/Firm 36 -36 Slow   [41]
£2756   £848   £424   £212   3 yo rec 9 lb

3084 **PROTOCOL 7** [9] Mrs S Lamyman 6-9-13 (40)(t) Mr S Dobson (5) 5/1: 042231: 6 b g Taufan - Ukraine's 46
Affair (The Minstrel) Held up, prog to chall over 1f out, drvn & styd on gamely ins last to lead cl-home, all out:
'99 Nottingham scorer (amat stks, rtd 63, unplcd on sand, rtd 51a, h'cap): '98 Doncaster & Leicester wnr (h'caps,
rtd 84 & 61a): eff btwn 10f & 2m1f, tried 2m5.5f: acts on firm & gd, relishes soft & hvy grnd, handles both AWs:
best in a t-strap, has tried a visor: likes a stiff/gall trk & runs well for an amat.
3111 **RARE TALENT 5** [2] S Gollings 6-11-4 (59) Mr T Best (5) 2/1 FAV: 261522: 6 b g Mtoto - Bold As hd 64
Love (Lomond) Held up, prog/led 3f out, hard rdn & duelled with wnr ins last, hdd nr line: bckd, tough.
3111 **IL DESTINO 5** [5] B W Hills 5-11-0 (55) Mr C B Hills (3) 6/1: -65003: 5 b g Casteddu - At First Sight 2 57
(He Loves Me) Held up, chsd front pair over 1f out, kept on tho' al held: bckd: clr of rem: blnks omitted.
2751 **BOULDER 21** [3] L M Cumani 3-11-13 (77) Mr N Bertran de Balanda 3/1: 6454: Dwelt, in tch, held fnl 3f. 8 70
2802 **CLASSIC EAGLE 19** [6] 7-10-1 (42) Mr S Rees 20/1: -00005: Dwelt/bhd, mod gains: see 1272. 4 29
2831 **MARGARETS DANCER 19** [8] 5-10-3 (44)(t) Mr J A Richardsor (6) 10/1: 50-006: In tch, btn 2f out. ½ 30
3081 **GRAND AMBITION 7** [4] 4-12-0 (69) Mr B Wharfe (7) 33/1: 505007: Chsd ldrs 7f: see 3081, 1352 (mdn). 2 52
3007 **AVERHAM STAR 11** [1] 5-9-10 (37)(12oh) Mr Ashlee Price (7) 50/1: -00068: Led 7f, sn btn: see 2188. 1¼ 18
1690 **CASSANDRA 67** [7] 4-11-0 (55) Mr W Fearon (7) 12/1: 250209: Prom, wknd qckly 3f out: op 8/1, abs. 4 30
9 ran   Time 2m 15.3 (7.2)   (P Lamyman)   Mrs S Lamyman Louth, Lincs

PONTEFRACT WEDNESDAY AUGUST 9TH Lefthand, Undulating Track, Stiff Uphill Finish

3221

2.50 MATTY BOWN MDN 3YO+ (D) 1m rnd Good/Firm 36 -15 Slow
£3412 £1050 £525 £262 3 yo rec 7 lb

2679 **SEEKING SUCCESS 25** [1] Sir Michael Stoute 3-8-9 Pat Eddery 13/8: 002261: 3 b f Seeking The Gold - Testy Trestle (Private Account) Made all, styd on strongly fnl 2f to assert under hands & heels riding: hvly bckd: eff at 1m, may get further: acts on firm & gd/soft grnd, stiff/gall trk: eff forcing the pace. **80**

-- **COUTURE** [3] N A Callaghan 3-8-9 K Darley 8/1: 2: 3 ch f Night Shift - Classic Design (Busted) Dwelt, chsd ldrs, rdn/onepace & held over 1f out: op 5/1, debut: eff over a stiff/undul 1m on fast grnd: 130,000 gns yearling purchase, shld find a race on this evidence. *3* **72**

3048 **NASHAAB 9** [4] R W Armstrong 3-9-0 W Supple 5/1: -553: 3 b c Zafonic - Tajannub (Dixieland Band) Held up racing keenly, rdn/outpcd fnl 2f: op 7/2: see 2860. *1* **75**

2832 **FREE WILL 19** [2] L M Cumani 3-9-0 J P Spencer 11/8 FAV: -5634: Cl-up, rdn/btn 1f out, hvly bckd, op 2/1: prob needs further & h'cap company: btr 2832 (10f). *hd* **74**

4 ran Time 1m 45.9 (4.1) (R Barnett) Sir Michael Stoute Newmarket, Suffolk

3222

3.20 CHAPLINS CLUB HCAP 3YO+ 0-70 (E) 5f rnd Good/Firm 36 +04 Fast [70]
£3802 £1170 £585 £292 3 yo rec 3 lb

-3123 **WILLIAMS WELL 5** [16] M W Easterby 6-10-0 (70)(bl) T Lucas 8/1: 552221: 6 ch g Superpower - Catherines Well (Junius) Al prom, led ins last, styd on strongly, rdn out: best time of day: earlier scored at Nottingham (h'cap): '99 wnr at Carlisle & Catterick (h'caps, rtd 70 at best): eff at 6f, all wins at 5f: acts on firm & soft, handles any trk, likes Catterick: well suited by blnks & a gd weight carrier: fine run from a tricky high draw. **77**

3077 **QUITE HAPPY 7** [3] W J Musson 5-8-13 (55) P McCabe 12/1: 364222: 5 b m Statoblest - Four Legged Friend (Aragon) Held up, rdn/prog to press wnr ins last, al just held: prev with M H Tompkins: see 3077, 897. *½* **59**

3203 **NORTHERN SVENGALI 1** [4] T D Barron 4-9-4 (60) T G McLaughlin 12/1: 040503: 4 b g Distinctly North - Trilby's Dream (Mansooj) Al prom, rdn & kept on well ins last: unplcd at Catterick yesterday: see 3091, 631. *¾* **62**

3046 **PREMIUM PRINCESS 9** [17] J J Quinn 5-8-10 (52) Pat Eddery 8/1: 333624: Dwelt/rear, prog when no room over 1f out, styd on well ins last when in clr, not reach ldrs: no luck in running: deserves to find similar. *hd* **53**

3203 **SIHAFI 1** [9] 7-9-3 (59) Alex Greaves 4/1 FAV: 043245: Mid-div, kept on fnl 2f, not able to chall: well bckd, fin 4th at Catterick yesterday: see 2326. *¾* **58**

3113 **MARINO STREET 5** [2] 7-9-2 (58) T E Durcan 10/1: 11W566: Led halfway till ins last: see 2252. *nk* **56**

3136 **STATOYORK 5** [12] 7-9-0 (56) Paul Eddery 16/1: 500007: Dwelt/towards rear, hdwy 2f out, no impress. *1* **52**

3144 **GRAND ESTATE 4** [6] 5-9-0 (56) D Holland 6/1: 350348: Held up, late gains: bckd, needs 6f. *½* **50**

3037 **MALADERIE 9** [14] 6-8-11 (53) F Norton 40/1: 000009: Chsd ldrs, btn 1f out: see 908. *1½* **43**

2444 **UNSHAKEN 34** [8] 6-9-12 (68) W Supple 9/1: 000000: Dwelt, nvr on terms: 10th, likes cut. *¾* **56**

2969 **BOLLIN RITA 12** [18] 4-9-2 (58) K Darley 12/1: 002040: Dwelt, mid-div at best: 11th: see 2505, 2158 *nk* **45**

2701 **SUGAR CUBE TREAT 24** [15] 4-8-8 (50) J Bramhill 20/1: 035000: Al towards rear: 12th: see 910. *¾* **35**

2944 **SQUARE DANCER 13** [10] 4-9-5 (61) A Clark 11/1: 540260: Chsd ldrs, btn/hmpd 1f out: 13th. *hd* **45**

2929 **WESTCOURT MAGIC 14** [5] 7-10-0 (70) G Parkin 16/1: 0-0000: Narrow lead till halfway, sn btn: 14th. *1¼* **51**

2165 **Branston Pickle 46** [11] 3-9-8 (67) R Ffrench 40/1: 2586 **Prime Recreation 28** [7] 3-9-3 (62) Dale Gibson 20/1:

2632 **Snap Cracker 26** [13] 4-8-5 (47) Claire Bryan (5) 40/1:

17 ran Time 1m 02.9 (1.6) (Mr K Hodgson & Mrs J Hodgson) M W Easterby Sheriff Hutton, N Yorks

3223

3.50 CORNMILL MDN 2YO (D) 6f rnd Good/Firm 36 -31 Slow
£3575 £1100 £550 £275

2363 **TIME TO REMEMBER 37** [10] T D Easterby 2-9-0 K Darley 1/1 FAV: 31: 2 b c Pennekamp - Bequeath (Lyphard) Prom, led 1f out, held on well ins last, rdn out: hvly bckd, op 11/8: eff over a stiff/undul 6f, 7f+ will suit (dam a 9f French wnr): acts on fast grnd & a stiff/undul trk: op to further improv, particularly over further. **78**

2106 **SOLDIER POINT 48** [7] P C Haslam 2-9-0 Dale Gibson 50/1: 02: 2 ch c Sabrehill - Reel Foyle (Irish River) Led, rdn/hdd 1f out, styd on well for press: abs, left debut bhd: eff at 6f, 7f+ will suit: acts on fast grnd. *¾* **75**

2500 **TROYS GUEST 32** [3] E J Alston 2-8-9 W Supple 8/1: 53: 2 gr f Be My Guest - Troja (Troy) Chsd front pair over 1f out, kept on well for press ins last: op 5/1: stays a stiff/undul 6f, looks sure to relish 7f+. *½* **68**

2248 **TALBOT AVENUE 42** [1] R F Johnson Houghton 2-9-0 D Holland 3/1: 44: Trkd ldrs, sltly hmpd over 2f out, kept on fnl 1f, no threat to ldrs: 6 wk abs: styd longer 6f trip, will appreciate 7f+: see 2248. *1¾* **69**

-- **ALPHAEUS** [11] 2-9-0 M Worrell (7) 20/1: 5: Dwelt/rear, kept on fnl 2f, nrst fin: Sillery gelding, Mar foal, a 1st foal: dam a mdn: sire a high-class 9f/10f performer: will relish 7f+, sharper/improve next time. *1* **67**

3009 **RATHKENNY 10** [13] 2-9-0 S Finnamore (5) 14/1: -56: Dwelt/mid-div, nvr threat to ldrs: op 10/1. *¾* **65$**

1918 **RAINBOW RIVER 56** [2] 2-9-0 C Lowther 25/1: 07: Drvn/mid-div halfway, held 2f out: 8 wk abs. *2* **60**

2576 **SOME WILL 28** [12] 2-9-0 Pat Eddery 16/1: 048: Al towards rear: longer priced stablemate of wnr. *1¾* **56**

3162 **LEATHERBACK 4** [4] 2-9-0 F Norton 20/1: 009: Al bhd: op 12/1, quick reapp: see 2106. *2* **51**

1774 **ALBURACK 63** [9] 2-9-0 G Faulkner (3) 12/1: 00: Chsd ldrs 4f: 10th: abs, op 16/1: btr 1774. *3* **44**

2730 **FATHERS FOOTSTEPS 22** [8] 2-9-0 J Stack 50/1: 0000: Bhd 2f out: 11th: no form. *dist* **0**

11 ran Time 1m 18.1 (4.0) (Reg Griffin & Jim McGrath) T D Easterby Great Habton, N Yorks

3224

4.20 ROGERTHORPE HCAP 3YO+ 0-90 (C) 1m4f Good/Firm 36 -03 Slow [88]
£6922 £2130 £1065 £532 3 yo rec 11lb

2446 **SENSE OF FREEDOM 34** [3] M Johnston 3-8-9 (80) M Hills 3/1 FAV: 22231: 3 ch f Grand Lodge - Greatest Pleasure (Be My Guest) Trkd front pair, prog to lead just ins last, readily asserted under hands & heels riding despite swishing tail: well bckd: 1st win: eff at 10/12f, may get further: acts on firm & gd, any trk: consistent filly, typical of the stable, can win again on this evidence. **87**

3024 **ARCHIE BABE 10** [4] J J Quinn 4-9-5 (79) D Holland 13/2: 010102: 4 ch g Archway - Frensham Manor (Le Johnstan) Handy, rdn/led over 1f out, hdd ins last & sn held by wnr: gd run, loves Pontefract: see 2562 (10f). *3* **80**

3024 **KOMISTAR 10** [6] P W Harris 5-9-10 (84) K Darley 7/2: 020003: 5 ch g Komaite - Rosie's Gold (Glint Of Gold) Led till over 1f out, sn held: bckd, op 9/2: prob stays a stiff 12f, best form at 1m/10f: see 1031. *2½* **81**

3013 **CASHMERE LADY 10** [2] J L Eyre 8-8-3 (63) J Stack 5/1: 110204: Held up, eff 3f out, no hdwy. *3½* **55**

3001 **CARLYS QUEST 11** [1] 6-9-13 (87)(tvi) F Norton 5/1: 300405: Rear, eff 3f out, no hdwy: op 4/1: see 2852. *4* **73**

3122 **FANTAIL 5** [7] 6-9-1 (75) A Clark 12/1: 0/0006: Held up, drvn/btn over 2f out: quick reapp: see 2530. *¾* **60**

2883 **GREEN BOPPER 16** [5] 7-8-0 (60) W Supple 10/1: 105507: Chsd ldrs, drvn/btn over 2f out: op 8/1. *1* **44**

7 ran Time 2m 38.8 (4.7) (Salem Suhail) M Johnston Middleham, N Yorks

3225　　4.50 AUGUST CLASSIFIED STKS 3YO 0-70 (E)　　6f rnd　Good/Firm 36　-37 Slow
£2860　£880　£440　£220

*3076 **HAND CHIME** 7 [4] W J Haggas 3-9-6 M Hills 4/6 FAV: 112311: 3 ch g Clantime - Warning Bell　81
(Bustino) Held up, rdn & prog fnl 2f to lead ins last, styd on strongly: hvly bckd: earlier scored at Catterick
(auct mdn), Carlisle & Kempton (h'caps): eff over a stiff 6f/1m, may get further: acts on firm & soft grnd, sharp
or stiff trk: has run well fresh: progressive gelding, can win more races.

2395 **GARTH POOL** 36 [6] A Berry 3-9-0 C Lowther 10/1: 511002: 3 b g Sri Pekan - Millionetta (Danehill)　2 68
Led till ins last, no extra: op 7/1: see 1205 (AW, made all).

3010 **POLAR HAZE** 10 [3] Miss S E Hall 3-9-0 G Faulkner (3) 16/1: 6-2303: 3 ch g Polar Falcon - Sky Music　hd 67
(Absalom) Chsd ldr, drvn & kept on for press fnl 2f, not pace of wnr: op 10/1: see 2204, 1688.

*3056 **RYTHM N TIME** 8 [1] E J Alston 3-8-13 W Supple 7/2: 040014: Chsd ldrs, btn over 1f out: btr 3056 (5f).　4 56

1409 **BULAWAYO** 81 [2] 3-9-0 D Holland 20/1: 140465: Towards rear, nvr pace to chall: abs: see 362 (7f).　¾ 55

1665 **BERKELEY HALL** 68 [7] 3-8-11 (bl) K Darley 13/2: -00126: Chsd ldrs 4f: op 9/2, abs: btr 1665, 1273.　3½ 43
6 ran　　Time 1m 15.5 (4.4)　　(Mrs M M Haggas)　　W J Haggas Newmarket, Suffolk

3226　　5.20 TALLY HO HCAP 3YO 0-65 (F)　　1m rnd　Good/Firm 36　-13 Slow　　[72]
£2457　£702　£351

2782 **RUDETSKI** 20 [5] M Dods 3-8-5 (49) A Clark 20/1: 006561: 3 b g Rudimentary - Butosky (Busted)　54
Mid-div, keen, styd on well fnl 2f for press to lead well ins last: 1st win: appreciated drop to 1m, has tried
11f: acts on fast grnd & a stiff/undul trk.

3093 **SHAMSAN** 7 [1] M Johnston 3-9-4 (62) D Holland 2/1 FAV: 320522: 3 ch c Night Shift - Awayil　¾ 65
(Woodman) Al handy, rdn/led over 1f out till well ins last, no extra: hvly bckd, op 5/2: see 3093, 709 & 266.

2918 **HELLO HOLLY** 14 [11] Mrs A L M King 3-8-5 (49) A McGlone 33/1: 00-603: 3 b f Lake Coniston -　3½ 45
Amandine (Darshaan) Prom, ch/rdn over 1f out, held ins last: eff at 1m on fast grnd: see 2180.

2882 **STORMSWELL** 16 [7] R A Fahey 3-8-8 (52) T Lucas 10/1: 315304: Twds rear, kept on fnl 2f, no threat.　¾ 47

2026 **DISTANT GUEST** 52 [3] 3-9-7 (65)(bl) G Faulkner (3) 16/1: 202405: Chsd ldrs over 2f out, sn held: abs.　2 56

2918 **TIMELESS CHICK** 14 [8] 3-8-13 (57)(vis) C Lowther 11/1: 305106: Led till over 1f out, fdd: op 8/1.　½ 47

2829 **KUUIPO** 19 [14] J Bramhill 3-7-12 (42)(t) J Bramhill 8/1: 602657: Mid-div, outpcd over 2f out, btn/eased ins last.　2½ 27

3095 **SECRETARIO** 7 [13] 3-7-10 (40)(bl) (5oh) J McAuley 50/1: 600008: In tch, btn 2f out: see 2484, 328.　nk 24

2914 **SILOGUE** 14 [10] 3-7-10 (40) G Gibbons (3) 25/1: -0069: Chsd ldrs 6f: h'cap bow.　3½ 17

2980 **BAJAN SUNSET** 12 [6] 3-8-7 (51) K Darley 3/1: -06220: Held up, efft 3f out, no impress: 10th: bckd.　nk 27

2542 **JUST BREMNER** 30 [2] 3-9-1 (59) G Parkin 11/1: 004-00: Chsd ldrs 6f: 11th: see 125 (AW).　3 29

2506 **Caldey Island** 32 [12] 3-8-1 (45) Iona Wands 25/1:　1665 **Boomshadow** 68 [9] 3-8-11 (55) J Stack 25/1:

3095 **Chiko** 7 [4] 3-9-7 (65)(BL) V Halliday 20/1:
14 ran　　Time 1m 45.7 (3.9)　　(A F & P Monk)　　M Dods Piercebridge, Co Durham

---

Official Going　GOOD (GOOD/FIRM places). Stalls: Sprint Crse - Far Side; Rnd Crse - Inside except 14f - Outside.

3227　　5.50 CHAMPAGNE APPR HCAP 3YO+ 0-80 (E)　　1m rnd　Good Slow　　[76]
£2785　£857　£428　£214　　3yo rec 7lb

2877 **RIBERAC** 16 [1] M Johnston 4-9-9 (71) K Dalgleish 6/1: 020001: 4 b f Efisio - Ciboure (Norwich):　82
Trkd ldrs, imprvd to lead 3f out, clr over 1f out, won eased down: value for 4L+: highly tried in '99 for W
Haggas (stks, rtd 91): '98 Windsor wnr (mdn, rtd 98), also plcd in List company: eff at sprint trips, apprec
this step up to 1m: acts on gd & firm, handles any trk: took advantage of a decent h'cap mark, cld follow up.

*2790 **SAMMYS SHUFFLE** 20 [5] Jamie Poulton 5-7-11 (45)(bl) D Kinsella (5) 4/1: 223212: 5 b h Touch Of　1¾ 48
Grey - Cabinet Shuffle (Thatching): Rear, imprvd to chase wnr 2f out, plugged on all the way to the line, no ch
with wnr: 4L clr 3rd: not apprec this drop back to 1m all wins at 10f on sharp trks: see 2790 (10f).

2942 **FIONN DE COOL** 13 [3] J Akehurst 9-7-13 (45)(2ow) P Fitzsimons 5/1: 3-0053: 9 b g Mazaad - Pink　4 42
Fondant (Northfields) Rear, kept on to take mod 3rd nr line: again hinted at a return to form: well h'capped.

2922 **HILLTOP WARNING** 14 [6] S P C Woods 3-9-10 (79) L Newman 3/1 JT FAV: 3-0154: Trkd ldr, onepace　shd 74
final 2f: well bckd from 4/1, top weight: btr 1947 (7f).

2726 **MUTABASSIR** 22 [7] 6-9-0 (62) P Dobbs 3/1 JT FAV: 543025: Chsd ldrs, left bhd final 2f: well bckd.　1½ 54

3063 **INSIGHTFUL** 8 [2] 3-9-5 (74) R Smith (3) 8/1: 264406: Prom till wknd qckly 2f out: see 2325 (blnkd).　10 46

2872 **FIELD MASTER** 17 [4] 3-7-13 (54) A Nicholls (3) 20/1: 050007: Set pace 5f, sn wknd: mkt drifter.　1½ 23
7 ran　　Time 1m 45.85 (6.85)　　(Mr & Mrs G Middlebrook)　　M Johnston Middleham, Nth Yorks.

3228　　6.20 HERSHAM NURSERY HCAP 2YO (D)　　5f str　Good Slow　　[88]
£4368　£1344　£672　£336

-3101 **BLAKESHALL BOY** 7 [4] M R Channon 2-9-2 (76) Craig Williams 9/2: 140321: 2 b g Piccolo - Giggleswick　82
Girl (Full Extent): Mid-div, not much room over 1f out, strong run final 1f to lead on line: op 7/2: earlier won
at Brighton (mdn): dam 6f wnr: eff at 5f, has tried 6f & that trip will suit: acts on fast & gd/soft grnd,
handles any trk: well rdn by C Williams today.

*2901 **CLARION** 15 [10] Sir Mark Prescott 2-9-7 (81) S Sanders 2/1 FAV: -212: 2 ch c First Trump - Area Girl　shd 85
(Jareer): In tch, rdn to lead ent final 1f & kicked for home, caught on line: hvly bckd, top weight: win similar.

2933 **AMELIA** 13 [7] J Cullinan 2-8-10 (70) P Dobbs 20/1: 423343: 2 b f General Monash - Rose Tint　2 68
(Salse): Nvr far away, led halfway till ent final 1f, kept on but no pace of first 2: op 14/1: grad improving.

*3075 **THERESA GREEN** 7 [9] Mrs P N Dutfield 2-8-10 (70)(6ex) L Newman (3) 5/1: 003014: Chsd ldrs, ev ch　hd 68
dist, not qckn inside last: gamble from 10/1: 6lb pen for 3075 (6f, gd/firm).

2868 **IF BY CHANCE** 17 [8] 2-8-6 (66) R Hughes 20/1: -04205: Led till halfway, ev ch dist, fdd cl-home.　1½ 60

1838 **TROJAN PRINCE** 60 [5] 2-9-0 (74) R Hills 7/1: -00256: Dwelt, held up, styg on nicely when no room　2½ 61 +
ins fnl 1f, eased: tchd 10/1, 9 wk abs: eye-catching run & one to keep a cl eye on in similar, poss over 6f.

2357 **HARD TO CATCH** 38 [6] 2-8-7 (67) C Catlin (7) 20/1: -53467: Chsd ldrs, btn over 1f out: btr 1612.　½ 53

3149 **ONCE REMOVED** 4 [3] 2-8-10 (70) A Nicholls (3) 8/1: 402348: Rear, prog & ch 2f out, btn final 1f.　1¼ 52

SANDOWN   WEDNESDAY AUGUST 9TH   Righthand, Galloping Track, Stiff Finish

2766 **RENEE** 21 [2] 2-8-5 (65) R Mullen 9/1: -3559: Hdwy from rear over 2f out, btn dist: op 6/1. *1* **44**
2939 **MISTY BELLE** 13 [1] 2-8-10 (70) G Hind 16/1: 3234D0: Front rank, wknd fnl 1½f: fin last: see 2939. *16* **9**
10 ran   Time 1m 03.64 (4.04)   (M Bishop)   M R Channon West Isley, Berks.

3229   6.50 ELMBRIDGE MDN 3YO+ (D)   5f str   Good   Slow
£4134   £1272   £636   £318   3yo rec 3lb

2919 **CHORUS** 14 [5] B R Millman 3-8-9 (VIS) G Hind 7/2: 632321: 3 b f Bandmaster - Name That Tune **73**
(Fayruz): Prom, imprvd to lead over 1½f out, rdn clr fnl 1f: deserved win in 1st time visor, plcd sev times
prev: 2nd twice as a juv (rtd 71): eff at 5/6f on firm, hvy & f/sand: woken up by first time visor today.
2900 **STAR PRINCESS** 15 [2] K T Ivory 3-8-9 C Catlin (7) 6/4 FAV: 642242: 3 b f Up And At 'Em - Princess *2½* **66**
Sharpenup (Lochnager): In tch, hdwy to chase wnr 1f out, kept on: well bckd: often the bridesmaid.
1843 **NEEDWOOD TROOPER** 60 [6] B C Morgan 3-9-0 S Sanders 20/1: 0-443: 3 br c Puissance - Blueit (Bold *2½* **64**
Lad): In tch, chsd front pair fnl 1f, onepcd when slightly hmpd ins last: mkt drifter, 9 wk abs: see 1280.
1605 **GASCON** 70 [1] D J Coakley 4-9-3 J Fortune 13/2: -024: Rdn in rear, some late hdwy, nvr dngrs: 10 *3* **55**
wk abs: btr 1605 (6f, soft grnd).
2977 **SECOND GENERATION** 12 [3] 3-9-0 N Pollard 9/2: -05: In tch, btn over 1f out: see 2977. *1½* **51**
95 **HOPEFUL HENRY** 260 [4] 4-9-3 W Ryan 33/1: 0-6: Front rank, led halfway till dist, wknd: reapp: unplcd *2* **45**
in a Lingfield mdn (AW) on sole '99 start: with G Moore.
2326 **BREW** 39 [7] 4-9-3 R Hughes 11/2: -06007: Led 3f, saddle slipped & wknd qckly, virtually p.u. *18* **5**
7 ran   Time 1m 03.49 (3.89)   (B R Millman)   B R Millman Kentisbeare, Devon.

3230   7.20 BERKELEY GROUP COND STKS 3YO+ (C)   1m1f   Good   Slow
£6515   £2409   £1204   £547

2475 **ALBARAHIN** 33 [5] M P Tregoning 5-8-12 R Hills 2/5 FAV: 612-21: 5 b h Silver Hawk - My Dear Lady **115**
(Mr Prospector): Made all, clr fnl 2f, v easily: hvly bckd: '99 wnr at Leicester (reapp), here at Sandown &
Newbury (h'caps, rtd 105): eff btwn 1m & 10f, acts on fast & hvy grnd: likes a stiff/gall trk, esp Sandown: runs
well fresh & a gd weight carrier: v smart entire who deserves a step up into Listed/Group company.
2675 **SURE DANCER** 25 [3] P F I Cole 5-8-12 J Fortune 9/4: 110-62: 5 b h Affirmed - Danlu (Danzig): *6* **104**
Chsd wnr, easily outpcd by wnr fnl 2f: nicely bckd: met a smart rival here: see 2675 (Listed).
2630 **RIVERTOWN** 27 [2] Mrs A J Perrett 6-8-12 D M Oliver 16/1: 1/43: 6 b g Oak Ridge - Star Habit (Habituate): ½ **103$**
Waited with, styd on under press fnl 1f, not quite get 2nd: useful performer, hndles gd grnd: see 2630.
-- **TRISTACENTURY** [1] M A Buckley 7-8-12 J Quinn 33/1: -5424: Rear, bhd final 2f, t.o: long abs: *16* **78**
prev rcd in Australia: eff at 10f on easy grnd: now with M Buckley.
-- **RASHIK** [4] 6-8-12 R Havlin 50/1: 1/5: Chsd ldrs till wknd qckly 2f out, t.o: comeback, last rcd *2½* **72**
back in '97, won sole start at Newbury (mdn): eff at 1m on fast grnd: sharper for this.
5 ran   Time 1m 56.97 (5.77)   (Hamdan Al Maktoum)   M P Tregoning Lambourn, Berks.

3231   7.50 CREDIT SUISSE HCAP 3YO+ 0-90 (C)   1m6f   Good   V Slow   [88]
£6955   £2140   £1070   £535   3yo rec 13lb

*3025 **KING FLYER** 10 [3] H J Collingridge 4-8-5 (65)(t) J Quinn 7/2: 605211: 4 b g Ezzoud - Al Guswa **69**
(Shernazar): Trkd ldr, imprvd to lead over 2f out, held on well fnl 1f, drvn out: slow time: recent Newmarket
wnr (h'caps): '99 wnr again at Newmarket (clmr, rtd 70 & 59a): eff at 10/14.7f on gd, firm grnd & equitrack:
handles any trk, likes a stiff/gall one, esp Newmarket: eff with/without a t-strap: in gd form.
2923 **COPYFORCE GIRL** 14 [2] Miss B Sanders 4-8-2 (62)(t) S Carson(3) 9/2: -13222: 4 b f Elmaamul - Sabaya *1¼* **63**
(Seattle Dancer): Slowly away, imprvd 3f out, ev ch dist, no pace of wnr cl-home: another consistent run.
2647 **FIRST OFFICER** 26 [4] J R Fanshawe 3-8-13 (86) R Hills 4/1: 021063: 3 b c Lear Fan - Trampoli *½* **86**
(Trempolino): Trkd ldrs, not much room 2f out, onepcd ent final 1f till ran on cl-home: stays 14f: see 1539.
2953 **DANEGOLD** 12 [5] M R Channon 8-7-11 (57)(1ow)(2oh) P Doe 6/1: 540004: Dwelt, sn well bhd, hdwy *2* **54**
2f out, no further impress: best in big fields: see 2953.
*2923 **FLETCHER** 14 [1] 6-8-6 (63)(3ow) R Hughes 2/1 FAV: 232115: Waited with, nvr a factor: well bckd: *½* **62**
not one of his going days today, better with a faster pace: beat todays 2nd over C/D in 2923.
2709 **HELVETIUS** 24 [6] 4-10-0 (88) W Ryan 16/1: 60-546: Set pace 12f, wknd: top weight: btr 2028. *11* **69**
6 ran   Time 3m 11.51 (16.51)   (In The Know (2))   H J Collingridge Exning, Suffolk.

3232   8.20 GENERAL MDN 3YO+ (D)   1m2f   Good   V Slow
£4248   £1338   £669   £334   3yo rec 9lb

-- **SILKEN WHISPER** [4] J H M Gosden 3-8-7 J Fortune 5/1: -1: 3 b f Diesis - Yaguda (Green Dancer): **90+**
Led after 3f & made rest, pushed clr final 1½f, cmftbly: $100,000 purchase: half-sister to a couple of US
mid-dist wnrs: eff at 10f, will stay 12f: acts on gd grnd on a stiff/gall trk, runs well fresh: impressive
debut, sure to rate more highly & win more races.
-- **AZAAN** [1] M P Tregoning 3-8-12 R Hills 7/4 FAV: -2: 3 ch c Lure - Crystal Cross (Roberto): *4* **85**
Early ldr, chsd wnr after, outpcd final 1½f: well bckd, debut: IR 260,000gns purchase: middle dist bred colt
who handles gd grnd: met a potentially decent rival here.
4061} **OCTAVIUS CAESAR** 321 [2] P F I Cole 3-8-12 D Sweeny 11/2: 20-3: 3 ch c Affirmed - Secret Imperatrice *3½* **80**
(Secretariat): In tch, lost place after 4f, onepcd final 2f: op 7/2, reapp: twice rcd juv, Epsom rnr-up on debut
(mdn, rtd 80): half-brother to a couple of wnrs in the USA: dam stayed 9f: handles firm grnd & a sharp/undul trk.
1200 **SEEK THE LIGHT** 93 [5] H R A Cecil 3-8-12 W Ryan 3/1: -64: Rcd keenly in rear, no impress final 2f. *¾* **79**
-- **LUNA FLIGHT** [3] 3-8-7 R Hughes 7/2: -5: Trkd ldrs, lost place 2f out, sn eased on debut: nicely *6* **65**
bckd: bred to apprec middle dist+: M Johnston filly who is sure to learn from this.
5 ran   Time 2m 14.43 (10.33)   (R E Sangster & Mr B V Sangster)   J H M Gosden Manton, Wilts.

Official Going   GOOD. Stalls: 1m6f - Stands Side, Str Crse - Far Side; Rem - Inside.

3233   **5.40 BOTTON BROS LADIES HCAP 3YO+ 0-75 (F)**   **1m6f**   **Good 50**   **-25 Slow**   [37]
£2236   £639   £319   3 yo rec 13lb

2607 **NOSEY NATIVE** 27 [2] J Pearce 7-10-7 (44) Mrs L Pearce 6/1: 226241: 7 b g Cyrano de Bergerac - Native   49
Flair (Be My Native): Settled rear, gd hdwy appr 3f, led over 1f out, styd on strongly, rdn out: plcd in '99
(rtd 34a & 42): '98 wnr at Ripon & Catterick (h'caps, rtd 47 & 50a at best): eff btwn 12f & 2m on fast, hvy &
fibresand, handles equitrack: best without a visor & handles any trk: runs well for an amateur.

*3026 **MONACLE** 9 [6] John Berry 6-10-4 (41)(5ex) Mrs S Bosley 3/1 FAV: F-3412: 6 b g Saddlers' Hall -   1   44
Endless Joy (Law Society): Bhnd, prog appr fnl 3f, ev ch till not pace of wnr well ins last: return to 2m will suit.

1711 **REPTON** 66 [3] B Smart 5-9-7 (30) Mrs V Smart (5) 20/1: 0-0003: 5 ch g Rock City - Hasty Key (Key   2   30
To The Mint): Dwelt, sn chsd ldrs, led 3f out till dist, sn btn: 9 wk abs, clr rem: signs of a return to form.

2958 **SILENT SOUND** 12 [9] Mrs A J Perrett 4-11-4 (55) Miss L J Harwood (7) 15/2: 002534: Rear, drvn/prog   3½   51
over 2f out, hung left & onepcd over 1f out: op 6/1: consistent: see 2958, 2689.

*2008 **DURHAM** 53 [1] Mrs J Moore 9-11-7 (58)(bl) Mrs J Moore 9/2: 00-015: Waited with, late gains, no threat: 5   49
op 7/2, 7 wk abs: do better with stronger handling, see 2008.

*2827 **MISCHIEF** 19 [8] Miss J Ellis (5) 7/1: 050616: Sn led, hdd appr final 4f, sn lost tch.   8   18

*3102 **INDIGO BAY** 7 [7] 4-10-6 (43)(tbl)(5ex) Miss R Bastiman (5) 9/1: 000517: Led early, remnd with   3½   23
ldrs, led again 4f out, sn hdd/wknd: op 7/1: much btr 3102 (12f).

2923 **PRINCESS TOPAZ** 14 [4] 6-10-13 (50) Mrs S Moore (5) 11/2: 5-2608: Cl-up, rdn & wknd qckly final   16   15
3f: op 9/2: 48hrs ago landed a nov sell hdle at N Abbot (2m1f, gd grnd, rtd 80h): see 2411.

2971 **JANE ANN** 12 [5] 4-10-5 (42) Miss S Arnold (7) 33/1: 00-0R9: Trkd ldrs, wknd rapidly final 5f, t.o.   dist   0
9 ran   Time 3m 08.3 (10.5)   (Jeff Pearce)   J Pearce Newmarket.

3234   **6.10 STRUMPSHAW CLAIMER 3YO+ (E)**   **1m2f**   **Good 50**   **+04 Fast**
£2847   £876   £438   £219   3 yo rec 9 lb

*2981 **WILLIE CONQUER** 12 [7] Andrew Reid 8-9-4 J Reid 5/4 FAV: 001011: 8 ch g Master Willie - Maryland   71
Cookie (Bold Hour): Settled rear, short of room 2f out, qcknd well to lead ins last, rdn clr: earlier won at
Brighton (2, sell for D Elsworth & clmr) & Salisbury (clmr): '99 Brighton wnr (reapp, h'cap, rtd 88, t-strap):
best at 10/12f on firm, gd/soft & any trk, loves Brighton: goes well fresh: hard to beat in sells/clmrs.

2775 **HADLEIGH** 20 [9] H J Collingridge 4-9-6 (VIS) Dean McKeown 14/1: -00002: 4 b c Perugino - Risacca   3   66$
(Sir Gaylord): Dwelt, rcd keenly & sn cl-up, chall over 2f out, drvn & not pace of wnr inside last: op 10/1 &
an imprvd effort in this first time visor: eff at 7/10f on fast & gd: see 2170.

2920 **HUGWITY** 14 [1] G C Bravery 8-9-4 Pat Eddery 5/2: 140153: 8 ch g Cadeaux Genereux - Muit d'Ete   2   60
(Super Concorde): Front rank, drvn/no impress appr final 1f: capable of better: see 2411.

3021 **EMALI** 10 [10] C E Brittain 3-8-11 P Robinson 11/2: 6-2204: Prom, went on over 3f out, hdd dist, wknd.   1   60

2671 **SPONTANEITY** 25 [5] 4-8-8 (VIS) Joanna Badger (7) 20/1: 062505: Led, hdd 3f out, gradually wknd: 3½   43$
op 12/1, first time visor: treat rating with caution: see 2245.

215 **MOONSHIFT** 232 [2] 6-8-11 (tvi) L Newton 33/1: 1050-6: Sn rdn, nvr dngrs: 8 mth abs, v stiff task.   3   41$

2587 **CAERDYDD FACH** 28 [4] 4-8-6 J Mackay 50/1: -04007: Nvr a factor: stiff task, see 1772.   10   20

2727 **NAKED OAT** 22 [3] 5-9-0 J Bosley (5) 20/1: 001608: Chsd ldrs, wknd qckly fnl 2f: op 14/1: see 1933.   hd   28

2875 **ESPERTO** 16 [6] 7-8-13 G Bardwell 16/1: 610449: Rear, effort halfway, sn lost tch: see 2875, 1546.   2   24

-- **MISTRESS BANKES** [8] 4-8-9 Darren Williams (5) 33/1: 0: Dwelt, al bhd: Petardia filly.   13   5
10 ran   Time 2m 08.8 (4.6)   (A S Reid)   Andrew Reid Mill Hill, London NW7.

3235   **6.40 BANHAM POULTRY COND STKS 3YO+ (C)**   **6f str**   **Good 50**   **+08 Fast**
£5950   £2200   £1100   £500   3 yo rec 4 lb

4100} **VISION OF NIGHT** 318 [4] J L Dunlop 4-8-10 Pat Eddery 5/2: 10-301: 4 b c Night Shift - Dreamawhile   107
(Known Fact): Rcd keenly in rear, gd hdwy appr final 1f, led dist, drvn out: best time of day: rcd in the US
last 2 starts, plcd once (1m, firm): '99 scorer at Newbury (stks) & Deauville (Gr 3, rtd 115 at best): juv scorer
at Ripon (mdn) & Doncaster (stks, 3rd in a Gr 1, rtd 107): suited by 6f, has tried further: acts on firm, soft &
any trk: runs well fresh: smart sprinter, back to form today.

2151 **DOCTOR SPIN** 47 [1] R F Johnson Houghton 4-8-10 J Reid 2/1 FAV: 0-1502: 4 b h Namaqualand -   ½   105
Madam Loving (Vaigly Great): Waited with, gd hdwy to chall appr final 1f, no extra cl-home: 7 wk abs & a gd
run at these weights: shld win again sn: see 1338, 1182.

2960 **DANCING MAESTRO** 12 [3] N A Callaghan 4-8-10 J Mackay (5) 20/1: 5-0063: 4 gr c Nureyev - Ancient   ½   103
Regime (Olden Times): Led till just ins last, held cl-home: seemingly imprvd for forcing the pace here, well
btn in a similar contest over 5f last time: eff at 6f on gd grnd: see 2496.

3172 **CRETAN GIFT** 3 [2] N P Littmoden 4-9-4 (vis) T Quinn 5/1: 002344: Front rank, effort when short   shd   111$
of room inside last, sn held: qck reapp: stiff task at these weights & prob a shade flattered: see 2847, 952.

2574 **TOMBA** 29 [5] 6-8-10 (BL) P Robinson 3/1: 0-2035: Prom, rdn & slightly outpcd over 1f out, late   ¾   101
hdwy, no threat: nicely bckd tho' op 2/1, first time blnks: see 2574, 1453.
5 ran   Time 1m 12.9 (2.5)   (Hesmonds Stud)   J L Dunlop Arundel, West Sussex.

3236   **7.10 HORSEY SELL HCAP 3-4YO 0-60 (G)**   **1m str**   **Good 50**   **-30 Slow**   [50]
£2044   £584   £292   3 yo rec 7 lb

1819 **ON PORPOISE** 61 [16] P W D'Arcy 4-9-2 (38) P Robinson 12/1: -00001: 4 b g Dolphin Street - Floppie   45
(Law Society): Dwelt/rear, gd hdwy appr final 2f, led dist, rdn & sn wnt clr: no bid, 9 wk abs: unplcd prev
this term: unplcd in '99 (rtd 62, mdn): mod form prev: eff over an easy 1m on gd grnd: clearly apprec this
drop to sell company & has benefited from a recent breathing operation.

3031 **BROWNS DELIGHT** 9 [15] S Dow 3-9-2 (45) J Reid 16/1: 650002: 3 b f Runnett - Fearless Princess   3   46
(Tyrnavos): Front rank, drvn/not pace of wnr ins last: imprvd here, win a sell h'cap: stays 1m on gd: see 287.

3048 **PEPPERCORN** 9 [18] M D I Usher 3-8-11 (40) G Baker (5) 16/1: 0-6003: 3 b f Totem - Sparkling Roberta   2   37
(Kind Of Hush): Mid-div, rdn & ran on appr final 1f, nvr nrr: first time in the frame, stays 1m on gd grnd.

2731 **ALABAMA WURLEY** 22 [14] D Morris 3-9-3 (46)(vis) D McGaffin (5) 8/1: 600104: Chsd ldrs, rdn into   1   41
lead appr final 2f, hdd over 1f out, sn fdd: twice below prev 2413 (non-h'cap sell).

3094 **EDEIFF** 7 [11] 3-9-10 (53)(t) Darren Williams (5) 33/1: 605055: Waited with, rdn/styd on over   ½   47

1001

YARMOUTH
WEDNESDAY AUGUST 9TH Lefthand, Flat, Fair Track

1f out, nrst fin: qck reapp: see 3094, 1439.

2974 **ANGUS THE BOLD** 12 [17] 4-8-9 (31)(vis) S Righton 33/1: 0-0006: Mod late gains from rear: up in trip. 2½ 21
2914 **JENSENS TALE** 14 [10] 3-8-2 (31) G Bardwell 33/1: 000007: Rear, late hdwy: see 830. ¾ 20
3094 **SWEET HAVEN** 9 [4] 3-8-11 (40)(vis) Joanna Badger (7) 6/1: 000028: Front rank, rdn, hung left & wknd final 2f: op 9/2, qck reapp: better expected after 3094 (clmr). 2 25
3021 **SPANISH STAR** 10 [8] 3-10-0 (57) N Callan 14/1: 136069: Chsd ldrs, dropped rear after 4f, brief effort 2f out, sn lost tch: top-weight: drop in trip: see 565. 1¾ 40
3103 **RED WOLF** 7 [13] 4-9-3 (39) Dean McKeown 7/4 FAV: -00320: Dsptd lead, rdn & wknd qckly over 2f out: gamble from 4/1: v disapp here, something amiss?: much btr 3103, 2834. 6 12
2658 **ROSE OF HYMUS** 26 [7] 3-9-3 (46) Pat Eddery 12/1: 0-0000: Nvr dngr, 11th: no form. ¾ 18
2914 **SNATCH** 14 [1] 3-9-1 (44) J Mackay (5) 12/1: 6400: Led, hdd 3f out, wknd qckly, 12th: h'cap bow. nk 16
2506 **OZAWA** 32 [5] 3-9-3 (46)(t) J P Spencer 12/1: 0-0000: Al in rear, 13th: modest form. 3½ 12
2914 **SOBER AS A JUDGE** 14 [6] 3-8-9 (38) T Quinn 6/1: 000300: Rear, rdn/lost tch fnl 4f, 14th: btr 2143. 2½ 0
2017 **Double Fault** 52 [3] 3-9-4 (47) D O'Donohoe 16/1: 2136 **Broughton Belle** 47 [2] 4-7-10 (18)(6oh) J Lowe 50/1:
2533 **Sitting Pretty** 30 [12] 4-8-2 (24)(BL) L Newton 16/1:
17 ran Time 1m 41.5 (6.4) (Paul d'Arcy) P W D'Arcy Newmarket.

3237
7.40 S JOSEPH NOV STKS 2YO (D) 7f str Good 50 -50 Slow
£4134 £1272 £636 £318

*2563 **LONDONER** 29 [3] H R A Cecil 2-9-5 T Quinn 1/2 FAV: 11: 2 ch c Sky Classic - Love And Affection (Exclusive Era): Made all, prsd inside last, rdn out: slow time: earlier won on debut at Newmarket (mdn, impress): Mar foal, half-brother to sev wnrs in the US, dam 5f/1m wnr: sire 9/12f performer: eff arnd 7f, sure to apprec 1m+ in time: acts on gd grnd & a stiff or easy trk: potentially smart & can rate more highly. 98
-- **REFERRAL** [1] K R Burke 2-8-8 N Callan 16/1: 2: 2 ch c Silver Hawk - True Joy (Zilzal): Trkd wnr, slightly short of room over 1f out, ran on strongly twrds fin: 26,000gns Mar 1st foal, sire a high-class miler: eff at 7f on gd grnd: fine debut & should win a mdn. ½ 85
3027 **TISSALY** 9 [5] C E Brittain 2-8-7 P Robinson 6/4: 23: 2 b f Pennekamp - Island Ruler (Ile de Bourbon) Keen/prom, rdn & not pace of front 2 inside last: up in trip, stays 7f: slightly better on debut in 3027. 2 80
3121 **GAY CHALLENGER** 5 [4] N A Callaghan 2-8-12 J Mackay (5) 33/1: -504: Settled last, outpcd over 2f out, late hdwy: qck reapp: mod form in 2 starts prev & probably flattered off this slow pace today: see 2959. hd 85$
4 ran Time 1m 29.6 (7.0) (HRH Prince Fahd Salman) H R A Cecil Newmarket.

3238
8.10 PILSON GREEN HCAP 3YO+ 0-80 (D) 7f str Good 50 -15 Slow [79]
£4062 £1250 £625 £312 3 yo rec 6 lb

2932 **ITALIAN SYMPHONY** 14 [9] P D Evans 6-8-1 (52)(vis) Joanna Badger (7) 25/1: 056351: 6 b g Royal Academy - Terracotta Hut (Habitat): Chsd ldrs, rdn to lead ins last, drvn out & just prevailed: '99 Lingfield (stks), W'hampton (h'cap, rtd 97a at best), Newmarket, Warwick, Catterick, Musselburgh & Southwell wnr (rtd 58): '98 Southwell (2), Lingfield (2) & W'hampton wnr (5, clmrs/h'caps, rtd 89a & 40): suited by 7f/1m, stays 9f: acts on firm & gd/soft, loves both AWs: eff in a visor, has tried blnks: runs well for an apprec jockey & handles any trk, likes a sharp one: v tough gelding (19 wins from 109 career starts). 56
3118 **PROSPECTORS COVE** 5 [11] J Pearce 7-9-3 (68) T Quinn 7/1: 104662: 7 b g Dowsing - Pearl Cove (Town And Country): Rear, shaken up & prog to chall ins last, just btn under hands-&-heels riding: qck reapp: gd run, jockey once again lkd reluctant to use his whip: see 1611. shd 71
*3030 **DARYABAD** 9 [14] N A Graham 8-7-13 (50)(bl) (6ex) Dale Gibson 3/1 FAV: 003013: 8 b g Thatching - Dayanata (Shirley Heights): Front rank, rdn/led dist, hdd well ins last, not btn far: nicely bckd: see 3030 (C/D). ½ 52
1444 **BLUE STREAK** 78 [6] Sir Michael Stoute 3-8-13 (70) J Mackay (5) 6/1: -0044: Waited with, effort when hung left appr final 1f, ran on inside last, no threat: 11 wk abs, h'cap bow: stays 7f on gd: see 1444, 972. 2 68
2870 **THUNDER SKY** 17 [12] 4-9-12 (77)(vis) P Robinson 16/1: 451005: Dsptd lead till went on appr final 2f, hdd inside last, sn btn: not disgrcd under top weight: see 2293 (mdn). hd 75
2804 **GUEST ENVOY** 19 [4] 5-7-10 (47)(3oh) G Baker (5) 16/1: 550546: Prom, rdn to chall appr final 1f, fdd. 3 39
2104 **JAHMHOOR** 49 [2] 3-9-1 (72) J Reid 20/1: -0657: Waited with, rdn/prog over 2f out, no impress: nk 63
7 wk abs, h'cap bow: see 2104, 972.
3030 **INDIAN WARRIOR** 9 [3] 4-7-10 (47)(2oh) J Lowe 9/1: 006028: Nvr a factor: btr 3030. nk 38
2899 **SEA DEER** 15 [5] 11-9-5 (70) Dean McKeown 20/1: 000609: Bhd, effort/hung left over 2f out, sn btn. 1¼ 59
2690 **HYPERACTIVE** 25 [1] 4-9-4 (69) D O'Donohoe 8/1: -02000: Prom, rdn/wknd over 1f out, 10th: op 6/1. 1¼ 56
3030 **QUALITAIR PRIDE** 9 [8] 8-7-10 (47)(8oh) Claire Bryan (5) 33/1: 100060: Led after 2f to over 2f out, 11th. 19
2950 **TROJAN WOLF** 12 [13] 5-8-6 (56)(1ow) N Callan 33/1: 006150: Wide, led early, lost tch after halfway, 12th. 17
3118 **ELLWAY PRINCE** 5 [7] 5-8-0 (51) G Bardwell 8/1: 432400: Chsd ldrs, wknd rapidly final 2f, t.o., 13th. 0
13 ran Time 1m 27.2 (4.6) (J E Abbey) P D Evans Pandy, Gwent.

BRIGHTON
WEDNESDAY AUGUST 9TH Lefthand, V Sharp, Undulating Track

Official Going GOOD (GOOD/FIRM in places). Stalls: Inside, except 10f & 1m4f - Outside.

3239
2.40 AMPLICON MDN AUCT 2YO (E) 7f rnd Good/Firm 38 -25 Slow
£2763 £789 £394

3079 **CARNOT** 7 [4] G C Bravery 2-8-8 L Newman (3) 16/1: 051: 2 b g General Monash - Pamiers (Huntercombe) 76
Trkd ldrs going well, squeezed thro' to lead dist, ran on well, drvn out: op 10/1, qck reapp: dam 7/9f wnr: apprec step up to a sharp/undul 7f on fast grnd.
2916 **SOONA** 14 [5] A P Jarvis 2-8-5 N Callan 11/2: 055522: 2 ch f Royal Abjar - Presently (Cadeaux 1¼ 70
Genereux) Made most till drifted left & hdd appr fnl 1f, styd on: bckd from 8/1: see 2916.
2886 **LOOKING FOR LOVE** 16 [1] J G Portman 2-8-0 N Pollard 15/8 FAV: -0333: 2 b f Tagula - Mousseux nk 64
(Jareer) Led after 1f till halfway, not much room 2f out, kept on: nicely bckd: styd longer 7f trip, flattered 2886?
2494 **HAWKES RUN** 32 [8] B J Meehan 2-8-11 D R McCabe 5/1: 664: Well off the pace till kept on ½ 73+
appr fnl 1f, nvr nrr: eye-catching h'cap qual run, did not seem at home on this undul trk: eff at 7f on fast grnd, step up to 1m will suit: acts on fast grnd: keep in mind in nursery h'caps, see 2494, 1472.
2724 **MOONLIGHT DANCER** 22 [10] 2-8-12 P Dobbs(5) 3/1: 422025: Chsd ldrs, same pace appr fnl 1f. shd 74
2599 **BILLIE H** 28 [9] 2-8-0 A Nicholls (3) 25/1: 0006: Mid-div, und press halfway, styd on without threatening. 1 60

1002

-- **TOMENOSO** [3] 2-8-8 A Daly 12/1: 7: Mid-div, onepce fnl 2f: op 7/1: half-brother to a sprinter. *5* **58**
2357 **CAPTAIN GIBSON 38** [2] 2-8-6 J Quinn 50/1: -508: Slow away, al bhd & not handle track: no form. *3* **50**
1988 **SAAFEND FLYER 53** [7] 2-8-10 P Fitzsimons (5) 20/1: 009: Al bhd: stablemate 5th, 8 wk abs. *½* **53**
-- **OUTRAGEOUSE** [6] 2-8-5 M Henry 16/1: 0: Nvr trbld ldrs, wide: 10th, debut, op 8/1: Be My Chief gldg. *15* **23**
10 ran Time 1m 24.2 (4.4) (Ott Partnership) G C Bravery Newmarket.

3240

3.10 CMP EUROPE SELLER 2YO (F) 7f rnd Good/Firm 38 -43 Slow
£2194 £627 £313

2723 **LOOK FIRST 22** [5] A P Jarvis 2-8-11 N Callan 7/4: 231: 2 b c Namaqualand - Be Prepared (Be My Guest) **65**
Sn led, rdn dist, ran on well, rdn out: bt in for 6,000gns: eff at 7f on fast & gd/soft grnd, sharp/undul trk.
2841 **HARD TO LAY 18** [4] D J S Cosgrove 2-8-6 G Carter 6/4 FAV: 25002: 2 br f Dolphin Street - Yavarro *1* **57**
(Raga Navarro) Early ldr & then chsd wnr, kept on but held: bckd, clr rem: stays 7f, handles fast & soft grnd.
2867 **FATHER SEAMUS 17** [1] P Butler 2-8-11 D Sweeney 7/2: -00003: 2 b c Bin Ajwaad - Merry Rous *7* **48**
(Rousillon) In tch, outpcd appr fnl 2f: down in grade, prob flattered 2867.
-- **MEADOW SONG** [2] J A Osborne 2-8-6 R Havlin 10/1: 4: Slow away, sn struggling: op 3/1 on *23* **13**
debut: Rock City half-sister to a couple of juv wnrs: with J Osborne.
4 ran Time 1m 25.5 (5.7) (Miss Ann Jarvis) A P Jarvis Aston Upthorpe, Oxon.

3241

3.40 ELECTRONICS MDN 3-4YO (D) 1m4f Good/Firm 38 +15 Fast
£3721 £1145 £572 £286 3 yo rec 11lb

1661 **APPLE TOWN 68** [4] H R A Cecil 3-8-5 T Quinn 10/11 FAV: -321: 3 br f Warning - Applecross (Glint **75**
Of Gold) Held up, closed on bit appr str, went on bef 2f out, shkn up, v cmftbly: hvly bckd, easily the quickest
time of the day, 10 wk abs: unrcd juv: eff at 12f on fast & gd grnd, further shld suit: handles a sharp/undul trk.
2659 **RAINBOW SPIRIT 26** [5] A P Jarvis 3-8-10 N Callan 5/1: 034342: 3 b g Rainbows For Life - Merry *8* **66**
Moment (Taufan) Led till 2½f out, sn outpcd by wnr: will apprec a return to h'caps, see 2321.
3023 **BLOSSOM WHISPERS 10** [6] C A Cyzer 3-8-5 S Sanders 5/1: 064323: 3 b f Ezzoud - Springs Welcome *4* **56**
(Blakeney) Rcd in 2nd, chall appr fnl 2f, sn onepace: needs a drop in grade: see 3023, 2659.
2691 **CHIEF WALLAH 25** [3] D R C Elsworth 4-9-7 N Pollard 14/1: 6-04: Nvr troubled ldrs: tchd 25/1. *½* **60$**
2590} **STAND ASIDE 396** [2] 4-9-7 J Quinn 33/1: 0000-5: In tch till halfway: op 14/1 on reapp: well btn *15* **45**
all prev starts, rtd 65 in '99 & rtd 66 in '98: with Lady Herries.
2265 **CALDIZ 41** [1] 3-8-10 (t) R Hughes 5/1: -666: Cl-up for 3f, struggling halfway, virtually p.u.: abs. *dist* **0**
6 ran Time 2m 30.9 (2.7) (Dr Catherine Wills) H R A Cecil Newmarket.

3242

4.10 EPD AND DPA MDN HCAP 3YO 0-60 (F) 7f rnd Good/Firm 38 -21 Slow [64]
£2467 £705 £352

2896 **FLIGHT OF DREAMS 16** [4] M Wigham 3-7-11 (32)(1ow) J Quinn 15/2: 0-0061: 3 b f College Chapel - **43**
Lady Portobello (Porto Bello) Mid-div, imprvd 3f out, ran on strongly ins last to lead fnl 100y, going away: op
6/1: well btn juv, first sign of ability last time in first time blnks (not worn here): eff at 7f, tried 12f: acts
on fast grnd & a sharp/undul trk: late-maturing filly, at right end of h'cap.
2977 **MASTER LUKE 12** [10] G L Moore 3-8-9 (45)(BL) S Whitworth 9/1: 0002: 3 b g Contract Law - Flying *2* **50**
Wind (Forzando) Cl-up, led after 2f till well ins last, no extra: tchd 16/1, clr rem on h'cap bow: woken up
by forcing tactics & first time blnks: stays 7f on fast grnd.
2592 **HAZY HEIGHTS 28** [3] B J Meehan 3-8-11 (47) B Marcus 7/1: 000043: 3 b f Shirley Heights - Dancing *5* **42**
Spirit (Ahonoora) In tch, prog 3f out, chsd ldrs appr fnl 1f, sn onepace: op 5/1: see 915.
2489 **ST IVES 32** [6] V Soane 3-8-7 (43) G Hind 33/1: -06004: Prom, ch 2f out, grad wknd: op 20/1. *1¼* **35**
2896 **CEDAR LIGHT 16** [2] 3-8-9 (45) P Doe 13/2: 000035: Dwelt, bhd, kept on wide & late, nvr nrr: op 4/1. *hd* **37**
2824 **SUPER DOMINION 19** [12] 3-9-7 (57) R Hughes 11/4 FAV: 4336: Dwelt, bhd, late hdwy, nvr dngrs: *2* **45**
well bckd from 10/1 on h'cap bow, top-weight: poss worth another chance in similar on a more galloping track.
2512 **FLYING RUN 32** [1] 3-8-6 (42) N Pollard 33/1: 000007: Chsd ldrs till 2f out: now with J Portman. *½* **29**
2976 **BORN TO RULE 12** [16] 3-9-5 (55) R Havlin 12/1: 500008: Mid-div, not much room dist: tchd 33/1. *1¾* **39**
2896 **UBITOO 16** [18] 3-7-13 (34)(bl)(1ow) C Rutter 12/1: 053009: Prom, lost pl 2f out: poor draw. *hd* **19**
2592 **RING MY MATE 28** [11] 3-9-3 (53) R Brisland (5) 16/1: 34-000: Al same pl: 10th, see 48. *1¼* **35**
2999 **FOX STAR 11** [5] 3-8-6 (42)(bl) A Daly 12/1: 053000: Early ldr, wknd qckly appr fnl 2f: 11th, btr 1930. *2½* **19**
2795 **DOM MIGUEL 20** [17] 3-8-8 (44) G Carter 12/1: -00000: Nvr in it: 16th, tricky high draw, see 804. **0**
4461} **Magical River 293** [8] 3-9-2 (52) S Sanders 14/1: 1349 **Bottelino Joe 83** [7] 3-9-6 (56) J Weaver 25/1:
1955 **Medooza 55** [13] 3-8-7 (43) A Nicholls (3) 25/1: 2658 **Who Da Leader 26** [14] 3-8-13 (49) P Dobbs (5) 14/1:
2980 **Father Ted 12** [9] 3-8-4 (40) M Henry 33/1: 3045 **Cedar Lord 9** [15] 3-9-2 (52)(BL) L Newman (3) 20/1:
18 ran Time 1m 23.9 (4.1) (Cable Media Consultancy Ltd) M Wigham Newmarket.

3243

4.40 NEW ELECTRONICS HCAP 3YO+ 0-65 (F) 6f rnd Good/Firm 38 -15 Slow [65]
£2599 £742 £371 3 yo rec 4 lb

3138 **CHAKRA 5** [3] M S Saunders 6-8-8 (45) R Havlin 11/1: 213021: 6 gr g Mystiko - Maracuja (Riverman) **51**
Bhd ldrs, hdwy appr fnl 1f & kept on well to lead fnl 100y, rdn out: qck reapp: earlier won at Lingfield (AW
h'cap, rtd 37a) & Folkestone (clmr, J Bradley): '99 rnr-up (h'cap, rtd 45): '98 wnr at Warwick (2, h'caps, rtd
54): stays a sharp 7f, suited by 5/6f: acts on firm, gd grnd & equitrack, any trk, likes sharp/turning ones.
3046 **ABSOLUTE FANTASY 9** [14] E A Wheeler 4-8-13 (50)(bl) S Carson (3) 10/1: 420242: 4 b f Beveled - *1¼* **52**
Sharp Venita (Sharp Edge) Cl-up, led 2f out till fnl 100y: back to form at fav trk, poor high draw: see 2428, 1211.
*3209 **SOAKED 1** [11] D W Chapman 7-9-5 (56)(bl)(6ex) J Quinn 11/4 FAV: 0R2113: 7 b g Dowsing - Water *½* **56**
Well (Sadler's Wells) Chsd ldrs, rdn appr fnl 1f, onepce till styd on towards fin: well bckd from 9/2, 3rd run
in 3 days & another sound effort up in trip: tough: see 3209.
2840 **JAMES DEE 18** [10] A P Jarvis 4-9-10 (61) Lisa Jones (7) 14/1: 262004: Well plcd & ev ch till no *nk* **60**
extra fnl 100y: op 11/1: apprec return to 6f & softer grnd: poor high draw: see 462.
2777 **AUNT DORIS 20** [6] 3-9-1 (56) N Pollard 7/1: 600425: Towards rear, gd hdwy appr fnl 1f, ran onto heels *¾* **53**
of ldrs & no room, position accepted fnl 100y, fin lame: unlucky not to have gone close, worth another chance.
2882 **SANTANDRE 16** [7] 4-8-8 (45) B Marcus 25/1: 000506: In tch, late hdwy, nvr a threat: better effort. *½* **41**
2840 **REACHFORYOURPOCKET 18** [1] 5-8-11 (48) R Hughes 14/1: 000107: Led till 2f out, btn when hmpd *shd* **44**
& eased towards fin: better run, see 2728 (7f, here).
2230 **FAIRYTIME 42** [13] 4-7-10 (33)(4oh) R Brisland (5) 33/1: 00-008: Bhd, mod late hdwy: 6 wk abs, *1* **26**

BRIGHTON
WEDNESDAY AUGUST 9TH Lefthand, V Sharp, Undulating Track

stiffish task, new stable: modest for J Arnold in '99, plcd sole juv start (mdn, rtd 65): handles gd/soft grnd.

2899	**RAINBOW RAIN 15** [12] 6-9-10 (61)(t) P Doe 14/1: 002009: Dwelt, wide into str, nvr better than mid-div.		nk	53
2623	**HALF TONE 27** [2] 8-8-0 (37)(bl) C Rutter 16/1: 305000: Outpcd, some late hdwy: fin 10th.		hd	29
*2896	**MARNIE 16** [9] 3-9-4 (59) J Weaver 3/1: 602210: Well plcd till wknd appr fnl 1f: 11th, tchd 4/1:		hd	50

progressive earlier, see 2896 (C/D mdn h'cap, beat wnr of prev race).

*2907	**CELTIC VENTURE 15** [4] 5-9-0 (51) A Daly 14/1: 0-6610: Mid-div till 2f out: 12th: see 2907 (clmr, here).		4	32
*2905	**CITY REACH 15** [16] 4-9-8 (59)(vis) D Sweeney 12/1: 130510: Handy till after halfway: 13th, back up		2	34

in trip: see 2905 (5.3f, here, beat this rnr-up).

109)	**Panther 616** [8] 3-9-0 (33)(2oh) M Henry 33/1:	1638	**Bold Saboteur 69** [5] 3-8-10 (51) L Branch (7) 16/1:
15 ran	Time 1m 11.0 (3.2)	(Brian McFadzean)	M S Saunders Haydon, Somerset.

3244
5.10 EPR ECLIPSE APPR HCAP 3YO + 0-60 (F) 1m2f Good/Firm 38 -34 Slow [53]
£2208 £631 £315 3 yo rec 9 lb

2958 **SHEER FACE 12** [4] W R Muir 6-10-0 (53) Michael Doyle (5) 14/1: 133501: 6 b g Midyan - Rock Face **61**
(Ballad Rock) Rear, imprvd 4f out, not clr run & switched dist, qcknd to lead towards fin, sn clr: val for 5L+:
earlier won here at Brighton (clmr): plcd in '99 (h'cap, rtd 73): '98 Goodwood wnr (h'cap, rtd 77 & 57a): eff
at 7/10f on firm & gd/soft grnd, sharp/undul trks, likes Brighton: nicely h'capped & cld follow up.

2725	**DONT WORRY BOUT ME 22** [10] T G Mills 3-9-6 (54)(vis) K Lavelle (5) 12/1: 016262: 3 b g Brief		2½	55

Truce - Coggle (Kind Of Hush) Handy, led ent fnl 2f till fin 100y, no extra: tchd 16/1: ran well, eff at 10/12f.

3192	**STITCH IN TIME 2** [2] G C Bravery 4-8-11 (36)(VIS) S Clancy (3) 13/2: 020543: 4 ch g Inchinor -		1	35

Late Matinee (Red Sunset) Chsd ldrs, rdn appr fnl 1f, styd on, unable to chall: op 5/1, visored, ran 48hrs ago.

3031	**LEVEL HEADED 9** [11] P W Hiatt 5-9-1 (40) P Shea 7/1: 044134: Led till appr fnl 1f, onepce: btr 2789.		1½	37
*2655	**WHISTLING DIXIE 26** [7] 4-9-8 (47) T Hamilton (3) 5/4 FAV: 601415: Held up, closed 4f out, rdn		1¼	42

2f out, fdd: well bckd: Nicholls stable has not had a Brighton wnr since '96: btr 2655 (gd).

2936	**ABLE SEAMAN 13** [9] 3-9-12 (60) S Hitchcott (7) 7/1: 333436: Chsd ldrs, wknd bef dist: clr rem.		1	53
2887	**PIPS BRAVE 16** [1] 4-9-3 (42) M Cotton (5) 16/1: 000157: Nvr a factor: see 2381 (fibresand clmr).		10	20
2627	**BROMEIGAN 27** [6] 3-8-13 (47) N Esler 25/1: 0068: Mid-div, no extra 4f out: h'cap bow, op 12/1.		5	18
683	**RAED 145** [12] 7-10-0 (53) W Hutchinson 25/1: 60-369: Nvr dngrs: nr 5 month abs, see 369.		2½	20
2908	**ARROGANT 15** [8] 3-8-6 (40) G Sparkes 11/2: 000-30: Al bhd: 10th, tchd 10/1: btr 2908 (C/D).		2½	4
3008	**BOLDER ALEXANDER 10** [5] 3-8-6 (40)(bl) D Glennon 33/1: 0000F0: Bhd from halfway: 11th.		3½	0
11 ran	Time 2m 05.0 (7.2)	(A J de V Patrick)	W R Muir Lambourn, Berks.	

NEWCASTLE
WEDNESDAY AUGUST 9TH Lefthand, Galloping, Stiff Track

Official Going GOOD (GOOD/FIRM in places). Stalls: Str - Stands Side; Rnd - Inside.

3245
2.30 DIGITAL SERVICE MED AUCT MDN 2YO (F) 6f Good 54 -18 Slow
£2709 £774 £387 Field raced in 2 Groups - Stands Side favoured

2692 **PETONGSKI 25** [5] D W Barker 2-9-0 F Lynch 7/2: 21: 2 b g Petong - Madam Petoski (Petoski) **92**
Made all stands side, clr 2f out, easily: val for 6L+, op 2/1: Jan foal, full brother to a 6f wnr: eff at 6f,
shld stay further: acts on gd & a gall trk: v useful from the front here, shld go in again.

2106	**STRETTON 48** [12] J D Bethell 2-9-0 R Winston 5/2 FAV: 032: 2 br c Doyoun - Awayil (Woodman)		4	79

Handy stands side, eff to chase wnr 2f out, onepce: well bckd, abs: shld win a race, prob at 7f: see 2106.

2692	**PASITHEA 25** [11] T D Easterby 2-8-9 M Fenton 7/2: 4533: 2 b f Celtic Swing - Midnight's Reward		2	68

(Night Shift) Handy stands side, outpcd over 3f out, kept on over 1f out: op 2/1: scope: will apprec 7f.

2990	**FRENCH BRAMBLE 11** [16] J Balding 2-8-9 (BL) J Edmunds 6/1: 600064: Chsd wnr stands side, hung		½	67

left & wknd 2f out: bckd from 20/1: better run in 1st time blnks: see 2990, 1304.

3047	**SUN BIRD 9** [10] 2-9-0 G Duffield 16/1: 505: In tch stands side, late gains, nvr dangerous: scope.		2½	65$
2835	**KIRKBYS TREASURE 18** [13] 2-9-0 J Carroll 20/1: -0366: Chsd wnr, wknd halfway: see 2639.		½	63
--	**GONE TOO FAR** [3] 2-9-0 T Williams 33/1: 7: In tch far side, kept on over 1f out, no ch with		½	62

stands side group: ndd race: Feb foal, cost 3,000 gns: dam 10f wnr: will apprec 7f in time: encouraging run
racing on the unfavoured side & looks sure to rate higher.

2692	**MR BOUNTIFUL 25** [4] 2-9-0 R Thomas (7) 25/1: 008: Led far side group till wknd over 1f out.		1¼	59
2649	**CONGENIALITY 26** [8] 2-8-9 P Fessey 14/1: 09: Al bhd, stands side: see 2649.		1¼	50
--	**MISDEMEANOR 25** [5] 2-8-9 O Pears 33/1: 0: In tch far side, wknd 2f out: 10th: dam juv 5/6f wnr.		shd	49
--	**FOLLOW FREDDY** [1] 2-9-0 J Fanning 10/1: 0: Handy far side, wknd over 1f out: 15th: Mar foal:			0

dam hdle wnr: bred to apprec further, with M Johnston.

--	**Sorayas Quest** [6] 2-8-9 A Beech (5) 33/1:	--	**Kundalila** [14] 2-8-9 J McAuley 33/1:
--	**Quazar** [2] 2-9-0 A Culhane 20/1:	1844	**Strictly Pleasure 60** [7] 2-9-0 D Mernagh (3) 14/1:
15 ran	Time 1m 15.3 (4.3)	(P Asquith)	D W Barker Scorton, N Yorks

---

3246
3.00 PUBS&CLUBS NURSERY HCAP 2YO (E) 7f str Good 54 -09 Slow [86]
£2782 £856 £428 £214 Field raced stands side

2927 **CYNARA 14** [14] G M Moore 2-7-10 (54) A Polli (3) 10/1: 0521: 2 b f Imp Society - Reina (Homeboy) **62**
Made all stands side, clr 2f out, kept on, pushed out: rnr-up last time (sell last time): Apr foal, cost 4,200 gns:
half sister to a 5f juv wnr: stays 7f well, 1m will suit: acts on fast, gd & any trk: improved from the front.

2881	**PERFECT PLUM 16** [2] Sir Mark Prescott 2-9-2 (74) G Duffield 8/1: 5232: 2 b f Darshaan - Damascene		2½	76

(Scenic) In tch centre, eff over 1f out, kept on ins last: op 5/1: looks sure to follow up: shld win 1m & shld win a race.

*2991	**DOMINAITE 11** [4] M W Easterby 2-9-2 (74) A Culhane 13/2: 003213: 2 b g Komaite - Fairy Kingdom		shd	76

(Prince Sabo) Waited with, switched right start, eff to chase wnr over 1f out, onepace: ran to wng form of 2991.

*2155	**BULA ROSE 46** [13] E W Tuer 2-8-1 (58)(1ow) O Pears 7/1: -52314: In tch, eff over 1f out, onepace:		1¼	76

7 wk abs & prev with W G M Turner: well clr of rem & a gd gun on step out of sell grade, see 2155.

2441	**BOMBAY BINNY 34** [16] 2-7-10 (54)(3oh) P Fessey 33/1: 020555: Handy stands side, no extra over 1f		7	41

out: no blnks, see 2441, 1764.

2218	**TENERIFE FLYER 43** [3] 2-7-10 (54)(7oh) P Hanagan (3) 33/1: 6046: Switched right start, bhd,		1	39

some late gains: swtg, lengthy: 6 wk abs: see 2218, 974.

*2926	**TIMES SQUARE 14** [10] 2-9-6 (78) O Urbina 6/1: -4317: In tch, eff 2f out, sn wknd: small, lngr trip.		hd	62
2521	**SIR EDWARD BURROW 31** [15] 2-7-12 (56) J McAuley 33/1: -0408: Chsd ldrs, wknd over 2f out.		½	39

*3032 **CUMBRIAN HARMONY** 9 [5] 2-8-11 (69)(6ex) T Williams 13/2: 055219: In tch, wknd 2f out: btr 3032. hd 51
2678 **MON SECRET** 25 [12] 2-9-7 (79) R Cody Boutcher (7) 10/1: 324140: In tch, wknd over 1f out: 10th. 2 57
2575 **ORANGE TREE LAD** 28 [6] 2-8-12 (70) P Goode (3) 5/1 FAV: 232000: In tch, wknd 2f out: 11th, lngr trip. hd 7
2700 **THE FANCY MAN** 24 [8] 2-8-4 (62) J Fanning 10/1: -4060: Al bhd: 12th, lacks scope: see 1823. 2 35
2983 **APORTO** 11 [9] 2-8-0 (58) A Mackay 16/1: 0030: In tch, wknd 2f out: 13th: see 2983 (6f, sell). 1¼ 29
2741 **MAGIC OF YOU** 21 [11] 2-8-12 (70) M Fenton 7/1: 130: In tch, wknd halfway: 14th: see 2741, 2377. 7 27
3057 **Eaglet** 8 [1] 2-8-12 (70) F Lynch 25/1: 1653 **Eyes Dont Lie** 68 [7] 2-8-1 (59) D Mernagh (3) 33/1:
16 ran Time 1m 28.48 (4.38) (R I Graham) G M Moore Middleham, N Yorks

---

3247 3.30 READY APPRENTICE SELLER 3YO+ (G) 1m4f93y Good 54 -30 Slow
£1890 £540 £270 3 yo rec 11lb

2742 **MITHRAIC** 21 [1] W S Cunningham 8-9-6 K Parkin (7) 10/1: 13-561: 8 b g Kefaah - Persian's Glory 37
(Prince Tenderfoot) Prom, hdwy to lead over 1f out, kept on, pushed out: no bid, tubed: '99 wnr of this v
race here at Newcastle (appr sell, rtd 44): missed '98, 97/98 hdle wnr at Newcastle & Southwell (sell h'cap,
stays 2m4f on fast & hvy): eff at 12f, stays 14f on firm, hvy & any trk, likes Newcastle: eff with/without blnks.
2989 **FOSTON SECOND** 11 [10] C B B Booth 3-8-4 A Polli 12/1: 00-42: 3 ch f Lycius - Gentle Guest nk 31
(Be My Guest) Handy, hdwy over 2f out, kept on ins last, just btn: better for race: stays 12.4f on gd/firm & gd.
2951 **MARIANA** 12 [13] T T Clement 5-9-1 P Clarke (5) 16/1: 000303: 5 b h Anshan - Maria Cappuccini ½ 30
(Siberian Express) Led till over 1f out, kept on for press, not btn far: stays 12.4f: mdn after 37, see 2381.
2800 **RED ROSES** 19 [5] Don Enrico Incisa 4-9-1 Giorgia Lamberti (7) 20/1: 004004: In tch, eff over ¾ 29
2f out, sn no impress: flattered: stays 12.4f: see 825.
2964 **THREEFORTYCASH** 12 [11] 3-8-9 R Thomas (5) 20/1: 060005: Prom, onepace well over 1f out. 1½ 32
2826 **THREE CHERRIES** 19 [6] 4-9-1 P Goode 14/1: 000455: In tch, wknd 2f out: see 2742, 1191. ¾ 26
3007 **GUNBOAT DIPLOMACY GB** 11 [2] 5-9-12 T Eaves (7) 4/1: -00157: Al bhd: best 2143 (10f). 1¾ 34
2989 **WEST END DANCER** 11 [4] 3-8-4 Dean Williams (7) 9/1: 050338: Nvr a factor: see 2989, 2715. ½ 22
2834 **SAVOIR FAIRE** 18 [12] 4-9-1 P Hanagan (5) 33/1: 0-0009: In tch, wknd over 3f: mod. 1½ 20
4393 **HOUSE OF DREAMS** 298 [3] 8-9-6 R Studholme (3) 6/5 FAV: 6624-0: Bhd, brief eff over 4f out, sn 2½ 21
wknd: 10th, well bckd, burly: last rcd over hdles back in Feb, scored at Wetherby (h'cap hdle, rtd 128h, stays
2m3f on fast & hvy): rnr-up in '99 on the Flat, at Pontefract (appr h'cap, rtd 54, with G M Moore): back in '98
won at Catterick, Carlisle & Thirsk (h'caps): stays 14f on fast, hvy & on any trk.
3008 **FRENCH MASTER** 10 [9] 3-9-1 (vis) R Cody Boutcher (5) 15/2: 332000: Slow away, al bhd: 11th. 0
-- **Caribbean Summer** [14] 3-8-9 P Bradley (3) 20/1: 2244 **Camair Crusader** 42 [7] 6-9-6 A Beech (3) 14/1:
455 **Shamokin** 187 [8] 8-9-6 D Mernagh 14/1:
14 ran Time 2m 47.14 (9.24) (A R Boocock) W S Cunningham Hutton Rudby, N Yorks

---

3248 4.00 RACING CHANNEL MDN 3YO+ (D) 1m1f Good 54 -44 Slow
£3770 £1160 £580 £290 3 yo rec 8 lb

1449 **TOUCH FOR GOLD** 78 [5] Sir Michael Stoute 3-8-8 F Lynch 1/1 FAV: 01: 3 br f Mr Prospector - Daijin 66
(Deputy Minister) Prom, led over 2f out, kept on, rdn out: hvly bckd after an abs: dam 6f/1m wnr: stays 9f on gd.
1072 **TOUGH TIMES** 100 [3] T D Easterby 3-8-13 R Winston 9/4: -5602: 3 b g Ezzoud - Shahaamh (Reference ½ 70
Point) Handy, eff to chall over 1f out, kept on for press, not btn far: nicely bckd, clr rem, abs: stays 9f on gd.
-- **FREE KEVIN** [1] Miss L C Siddall 4-9-7 A Culhane 20/1: 3: 4 b g Midyan - Island Desert (Green 6 61
Desert): Waited with, effort over 2f out, onepace: bred to apprec mid-dists.
-- **RUBY RAVEN** [4] J R Turner 3-8-8 O Pears 25/1: 4: Slow away, bhd, eff over 3f out, sn no impress. ¾ 54
3034 **WILD RIVER** 9 [2] 3-8-13 J Fanning 3/1: 045: Led till over 2f out, wknd: see 3034. 6 47
5 ran Time 2m 0.94 (8.84) (Teruya Yoshida) Sir Michael Stoute Newmarket.

3249 4.30 7 DAYS A WEEK HCAP 3YO+ 0-65 (F) 1m6f97y Good 54 [57]
£2730 £840 £420 £210 3 yo rec 13lb

1597 **FREE** 70 [3] Mrs M Reveley 5-9-7 (50) T Eaves (7) 9/1: 23-001: 5 ch g Gone West - Bemissed (Nijinsky): 58
Made all, sn well clr, kept on well, pushed out: unplcd chase rnr 2 mths ago, last term scored at Carlisle &
Sedgefield (rtd 125c, stays 2m5f on fast & gd/soft): '99 Flat wnr at Newcastle (this v race, h'cap, rtd 59): 98/99
hdle wnr at Kelso & Catterick (rtd 117h): eff at 14.4f, stays 2m on firm/fast, gd & any trk, loves Newcastle.
*2801 **PAPI SPECIAL** 19 [10] I Semple 3-8-8 (56) R Winston 4/1 FAV: 24012D: 3 b g Tragic Role - Practical 5 57
(Ballimore) Waited with, effort to chase wnr 3f out, sn no impress: fin 2nd, disq & plcd last: well bckd,
jockey received a 14 day riding ban: stays 14.4f & in gd form: see 2801.
2879 **LUCKY JUDGE** 16 [8] W W Haigh 3-9-1 (57) F Lynch 11/1: 504642: 3 b g Saddlers' Hall - Lady Lydia 2 55
(Ela Mana Mou): Handy, effort over 2f out, onepcd: fin 3rd, plcd 2nd: see 2879 (mdn h'cap).
2516 **HIGHFIELD FIZZ** 32 [12] C W Fairhurst 8-8-8 (37) T Williams 8/1: 016063: Waited with, effort over 3f 2 33
out, onepace: fin 4th, plcd 3rd: best at 2m: see 1563.
1597 **BOLD CARDOWAN** 70 [9] 4-8-11 (40)(BL) O Pears 15/2: -00004: Waited with, rdn over 3f out, some ½ 35
late gains: better for race after 10 wk abs in first time blnks: see 876.
3036 **HAYSTACKS** 9 [6] 4-9-10 (53)(vis) G Duffield 5/1: 6-0425: Waited with, effort 3f out, sn no impress. 3 44
2879 **ALBARDEN** 16 [2] 3-8-4 (44)(2ow) J Carroll 10/1: -55006: In tch, wknd over 3f out: see 2879, 1255. hd 37
2945 **RED SEPTEMBER** 12 [11] 3-8-1 (43)(bl) P Hanagan (3) 20/1: 5-0607: Chsd ldrs, wknd over 4f out. 1 33
2382 **ASTON MARA** 37 [4] 3-8-13 (55) A Culhane 8/1: 000008: Al bhd: now with Mrs M Reveley: see 990. ¾ 44
3053 **NOIRIE** 8 [5] 6-8-11 (40) D Mernagh (3) 20/1: 302009: Chsd ldrs, badly hmpd halfway, not recover. 5 23
3026 **NUBILE** 9 [7] 6-8-6 (34)(tbl)(1ow) O Urbina 12/1: 002550: Bhd, effort over 4f out, sn wknd: 10th. 5 12
3036 **DESERT MUSIC** 9 [1] 4-9-3 (46) J Fanning 25/1: -05550: Chsd clr ldr, wknd over 3f out: 11th. 18 3
12 ran Time 3m 12.5 (P D Savill) Mrs M Reveley Lingdale, Nth Yorks.

3250 5.00 ON CABLE HCAP 3YO+ 0-85 (D) 7f str Good 54 +10 Fast [76]
£3835 £1180 £590 £295 3 yo rec 6 lb

2580 **MISTER MAL** 28 [7] J A Glover 4-9-9 (71) G Duffield 11/4: -05001: 4 b g Scenic - Fashion Parade 78
(Mount Hagen): Led after 1f, clr over 1f out, kept on well final 1f: '99 wnr at Catterick (mdn), Leicester &
Redcar (h'caps, rtd 77 & 75a): unsuited by 6f earlier this term, all 4 wins at 7f & likes gd & soft grnd, handles
firm & fast, does stay 1m: likes a gall trk: game, loves to dominate & has slipped to a fair mark.
2719 **WELCOME TO UNOS** 23 [2] M Dods 3-8-10 (64) T Williams 14/1: -06302: 3 ch g Exit To Nowhere - Royal 3 64

NEWCASTLE   WEDNESDAY AUGUST 9TH   Lefthand, Galloping, Stiff Track

Loft (Homing): Led 1f, cl up, not pace of wnr over 1f out: stays 7f on fast & gd: see 2440.

3170 **DONNAS DOUBLE 3** [6] D Eddy 5-9-8 (70) A Beech (5) 4/1: 352103: 5 ch g Weldnaas - Shadha (Shirley ½ 69
Heights): Prom, kept on same pace over 1f out: acts on fast gd: ran to form of 2694.

*2999 **PETERS IMP 11** [3] A Berry 5-9-12 (74) J Carroll 5/2-FAV: 530114: Waited with, effort over 2f out, 2 69
onepace: nicely bckd: rtd higher 2999 (Lady riders h'cap).

3119 **PEPPIATT 5** [5] 6-8-13 (61) J Fanning 7/2: 002535: Waited with, effort over 2f out, no impress: 1¼ 54
qck reapp, best at 6f: see 3119.

2882 **NORTHGATE 16** [1] 4-8-1 (49)(bl) D Mernagh (3) 15/2: 142006: Prom, wknd over 3f out: see 2612. 16 12
6 ran   Time 1m 27.15 (3.05)   (Mrs Andrea M Mallinson)   J A Glover Carburton, Notts.

CHEPSTOW   THURSDAY AUGUST 10TH   Lefthand, Undulating, Galloping Track

Official Going: GOOD/FIRM (GOOD PLACES)   Stalls: Straight Course - Stands Side, Round Course - Inside

3251	**2.10 MADEMOISELLE LADIES HCAP 3YO+ 0-70 (E)**	**1m str Good/Firm 28 -03 Slow**	**[38]**
	£2814 £804 £402 3 yo rec 7 lb		

749 **MANIKATO 135** [14] R Curtis 6-9-3 (27)(1oh) Miss M Gunstone (5) 14/1: 00-461: 6 b g Clever Trick - 36
Pasampsi (Crow) Chsd ldrs, smooth prog to lead over 1f out, pushed clr, readily: op 20/1, jumps fit (mod form):
earlier with R Beckett on the level: unplcd in '99 (rtd 36a & 34, D Cosgrove & T T Clement): rcd in '98 (mdn, rtd
57a): suited by 7f/1m, poss stys 12f: acts on fast & gd/soft grnd, prob handles both AWs: best without a visor.

2840 **DOBERMAN 19** [10] P D Evans 5-10-8 (46)(vis) Miss E Folkes (5) 5/1: 100222: 5 br g Dilum - Switch 6 46
Blade (Robellino) Led till over 1f out, held by wnr after: see 2840, 2378 & 550.

2974 **MUJKARI 13** [11] J M Bradley 4-10-0 (38)(vis) Mrs C Williams 7/1: 040023: 4 ch g Mujtahid - Hot 8 26
Curry (Sharpen Up) Chsd ldrs, onepace/held fnl 2f: see 323 (AW).

3110 **ARBENIG 7** [13] B Palling 5-10-12 (50) Mrs S Bosley 4/1-FAV: 105204: In tch, held fnl 2f: op 7/2. 2 34

2892 **MUSTANG 17** [8] 7-10-4 (42)(vis) Mrs L Pearce 15/2: 610545: In tch, outpcd 2f out: see 2040 (sell). 3 20

2974 **PRIORY GARDENS 13** [4] 6-10-6 (44) Miss Hayley Bryan (5) 11/2: 461036: Rear, mod gains: see 2658. 1¼ 19

2999 **ROBELLION 12** [2] 9-11-7 (59) Miss S Newby Vincent (5) 6/1: -51307: Rear, mod prog: op 5/1. 1 32

3094 **DOVES DOMINION 8** [6] 3-10-8 (53)(vis) Miss E J Jones 14/1: 005508: Prom 4f: see 2776, 2379 & 841. 1 24

3078 **FLASHFEET 8** [7] 10-9-10 (34) Miss A Purdy 25/1: 406009: Al rear: see 398. hd 4

2840 **DEFIANCE 19** [5] 5-9-6 (30) Mrs S Moore (5) 14/1: 000000: In tch 6f: 10th: op 20/1: see 1578. ¾ 0

2971 **Little Tara 13** [1] 3-9-3 (34)(9oh) Miss Sarah Jane Durman (7) 66/1:

3144 **Pips Tango 5** [3] 3-9-9 (40) Miss M Mullineaux (7 50/1:

492 **Just A Stroll 182** [15] 5-9-3 (27)(9oh) Miss S Owen (5) 50/1:

2292 **Earley Session 41** [12] 3-9-9 (40)(VIS) Miss S Higgins (5) 25/1:

-- **Belle Dancer** [9] 6-9-5 (29)(2ow)(9oh) Miss D Lewis Price (0) 50/1:
15 ran   Time 1m 34.4 (2.5)   (The Popsi Partners)   R Curtis Lambourn, Berks

3252	**2.40 TUTSHILL MED AUCT MDN 2YO (E)**	**5f** **Good/Firm 28 -24 Slow**	
	£2800 £800 £400		

-- **KYLLACHY** [5] H Candy 2-9-0 C Rutter 7/4: 1: 2 b c Pivotal - Pretty Poppy (Song) 86
Prom, briefly outpcd halfway, narrow lead ins last, held on well: Feb foal, cost 36,000gns: half brother to 2 juv
5f wnrs & useful 5f h'capper Speed On: dam a 5f juv wnr: eff over 5f, shld get 6f: acts on fast & runs well fresh.

-2082 **ATTORNEY 50** [1] M A Jarvis 2-9-0 P Robinson 6/4-FAV: -0222: 2 ch g Wolfhound - Princess Sadie nk 84
(Shavian) Led/dsptd lead till ins last, styd on well, just held: well bckd, 7 wk abs: can find similar sn.

3044 **ROXANNE MILL 10** [3] M D I Usher 2-8-9 Martin Dwyer 33/1: 503: 2 b f Cyrano de Bergerac - It Must 2 74$
Be Millie (Reprimand) Bhd ldrs, rdn to chall dist, onepace inside last: op 20/1: eff at 5f on fast grnd.

2886 **TWILIGHT MISTRESS 17** [2] D W P Arbuthnot 2-8-9 J D Smith 5/1: -004: Cl up, ch 1f out, no extra ½ 72
inside last: big gamble from 50/1: left prev 2 starts bhd: apprec drop to 5f, acts on fast grnd.

-- **LORD LIAM** [4] 2-9-0 P Doe 16/1: 5: Outpcd early, mod gains halfway, no threat: Foxhound colt, 3½ 68
March foal, a 32,000gns 2yo: dam a 7f juv wnr: sire a high class sprinter: with N Littmoden.

-- **BANDARELLO** [9] 2-8-9 N Pollard 16/1: 6: Chsd ldrs outpcd halfway, rdn & mod late gains fnl 1¾ 59
1f: op 14/1: Distant Relative filly, May foal: dam a 5f juv wnr: with D J Coakley.

2784 **YNYSMON 21** [8] 2-9-0 R Mullen 14/1: 57: Unruly stalls, in tch till halfway: op 12/1: see 2784. ½ 62

1962 **SAAFEND ROCKET 55** [12] 2-9-0 R Hughes 9/1: 558: In tch till halfway, sn outpcd: 8 week abs. shd 62

-- **WINTER DOLPHIN** [11] 2-8-9 L Newman (3) 33/1: 9: Struggling halfway: Dolphin Street filly, Jan 10 38
foal, 13,000gns 2yo: half sister to a 5f juv wnr: dam unrcd: with I Wood.

-- **SUNNY STROKA** [7] 2-9-9 R Havlin 50/1: 0: Dwelt & al rear: 10th: May foal, dam unrcd. ½ 36

-- **SPINETAIL RUFOUS** [6] 2-9-0 A Clark 25/1: 0: Sn bhd: 11th: May foal, dam a mdn. 0
11 ran   Time 59.4 (2.6)   (Thurloe Thoroughbreds V)   H Candy Wantage, Oxon

3253	**3.10 WHITEBROOK SELLER 3YO+ (F)**	**7f str** **Good/Firm 28 -21 Slow**	
	£2303 £658 £329 3 yo rec 6 lb		

2834 **SHARP SHUFFLE 19** [11] Ian Williams 7-9-2 L Newman (3) 7/4-FAV: 002321: 7 ch g Exactly Sharp - Style 60
(Traffic Judge) Chsd ldrs, rdn & prog to lead inside last, styd on well, rdn out: well bckd: no bid: '99 wnr at
W'hampton (2, sells, rtd 63a & 60): '98 Newmarket wnr (2, seller & claimer, rtd 70, with R Hannon): suited by
7f/1m stays a sharp 10f: acts on firm, gd/soft & both AWs, any track: loves sells/clmrs.

2777 **ZEPPO 21** [9] B R Millman 5-9-2 G Hind 5/2: 064452: 5 ch g Fayruz - Chasse Paperchase (Malinowski) 1 56
Chsd ldrs halfway, rdn/led over 1f out, hdd inside last & no extra: bckd tho' op 2/1: stys 7f, best at 5/6f.

1418 **WHITE SETTLER 449** [5] Miss S J Wilton 7-9-2 D Sweeney 12/1: 1/00-3: 7 b g Polish Patriot - Oasis 1¾ 53
(Valiyar) Rear, prog/swtchd over 1f out, kept on, no threat to front pair: op 6/1: reapp: mod form from 2 starts last
term (rtd 49): '98 Leicester wnr (R Hodges) & here at Chepstow (sellers, rtd 56): eff at 7f/1m on firm & hvy grnd,
undulating or stiff track, likes Chepstow: best without blinks.

2974 **MISS MONEY SPIDER 13** [8] J M Bradley 5-8-11 R Hughes 6/1: 000004: Led, hdd over 1f out, fdd. 3½ 41

2460 **TITAN 34** [7] 5-9-2 A Clark 25/1: 005005: Rear, mod late gains: stayed on with M Muggeridge: see 817. 1¾ 43$

2892 **PURNADAS ROAD 17** [2] 5-8-11 N Pollard 33/1: 0-6036: Chsd ldr, btn over 1f out: see 2892, 226. 1 36

-- **MOGUL** [6] 6-9-2 R Havlin 50/1: 0600/7: Sn outpcd: reapp, long abs: mod jumps form in 99/00: 2 37
only mod form on the level prev.

2372 **NUNKIE GIRL 38** [4] 3-8-5 (bl) P Fitzsimons (5) 8/1: 00608: Sn bhd: flattered 1481. 1¼ 29
2785 **QUEENS STROLLER 21** [12] 9-8-11 P Doe 50/1: 0/0009: Chsd ldrs 5f: see 2186. ½ 28
2561 **CHARLTON IMP 30** [10] 7-8-11 Paul Eddery 25/1: 006/00: Chsd till halfway: 10th: mod form in recent seasons: '96 wnr at Bath & Chepstow (sellers): eff at 1m on fast & gd grnd. 2 24
2680 **Castrato 26** [3] 4-9-2 C Rutter 50/1: 2950 **Phoebus 13** [1] 3-8-10 (t) Martin Dwyer 12/1:
12 ran Time 1m 22.2 (3.4) (G A Gilbert) Ian Williams Alvechurch, Worcs

3254

3.40 OFFA'S DYKE HCAP 3YO 0-90 (C) 1m str Good/Firm 28 +07 Fast [94]
£6483 £1995 £997 £498

2661 **KELTECH GOLD 27** [2] B Palling 3-8-5 (71) D Sweeney 9/1: -02151: 3 b c Petorius - Creggan Vale Lass (Simply Great) Made all, rdn over 1f out, styd on strongly inside last, unchall: op 7/1: earlier scored at Bath (h'cap, 1st win): rtd 69 in '99 (auction mdn): suited by forcing tactics at 1m on fast & gd/soft grnd: prog colt. 77
2762 **FLAMENCO RED 22** [4] R Charlton 3-9-7 (87) Paul Eddery 12/1: 235-42: 3 b f Warning - Spanish Wells (Sadler's Wells) Held up, switched & prog to chase wnr over 1f out, kept on, al held: op 10/1: stays 1m. 2½ 87
2792 **KNOCKTOPHER ABBEY 21** [7] B R Millman 3-8-12 (78) G Hind 12/1: 0-5053: 3 ch g Pursuit Of Love - Kukri (Kris) In tch, onepace/held over 1f out: see 1826. ½ 77
3022 **SIR FERBET 11** [8] B W Hills 3-9-5 (85) R Hughes 11/1: 001004: Held up, no room 2f out till 1f out, styd on inside last, nvr a threat: op 8/1: plcd with a clr run here, worth another chance: see 1853. 1¼ 81
2733 **MAMZUG 23** [3] 3-9-0 (80) P Robinson 5/1: 414235: Chsd wnr, held fnl 1f: see 2733, 1435. hd 75
2999 **DANIYSHA 12** [9] 3-8-10 (76) L Newman (3) 11/4: -43106: Chsd ldrs, btn 1f out: bckd: see 2471 (7f). ¾ 70
2922 **FALCONIDAE 15** [1] 3-9-2 (82) A Clark 9/4 FAV: -05127: Held up, eff over 2f out, sn held: bckd. ¾ 75
3095 **BISHOPSTONE MAN 8** [6] 3-8-1 (67) C Rutter 8/1: 351028: Keen/chsd ldrs till over 1f out: btr 3095. ¾ 59
8 ran Time 1m 33.6 (1.7) (D Brennan) B Palling Cowbridge, Vale Of Glamorgan

3255

4.10 PIERCEFIELD HCAP 3YO+ 0-65 (F) 1m4f Good/Firm 28 -08 Slow [64]
£2499 £714 £357 3 yo rec 11lb

2681 **CUPBOARD LOVER 26** [3] D Haydn Jones 4-9-0 (50) A McGlone 6/1: 656631: 4 ch g Risk Me - Galejade (Sharrood) Dwelt, prog to lead over 1f out, styd on strongly, eased down nr fin: val for 4L: '99 wnr at Hamilton & Nottingham (h'cap, rtd 64): eff at 12/14f on fast & gd, stiff/gall trks: well h'capped, could win again. 57
3049 **TULSA 10** [1] L Montague Hall 6-7-13 (35)(bl) N Pollard 8/1: 00-552: 6 b g Priolo - Lagrion (Diesis) Dwelt/rear, rdn & styd on well fnl 3f, not reach wnr: eff at 10/12f: see 2793. ¾ 36
*3053 **LOST SPIRIT 9** [15] P W Hiatt 4-8-2 (38)(6ex) L Newman (2) 13/2: 640113: 4 b g Strolling Along - Shoag (Affirmed) Led & sn clr, rdn/hdd 2f out, no extra inside last: op 5/1: another bold run under a 6lb pen. 4 33
3049 **KIRISNIPPA 10** [9] Derrick Morris 5-9-0 (50) P Doe 12/1: 403504: Chsd ldr, held 1f out: see 1784, 1128. 2 42
2943 **ROYAL SIGNET 14** [5] 5-8-1 (37) C Rutter 20/1: 500-45: Rear, nvr on terms: see 2943. 1 28
3084 **WATER LOUP 8** [16] 4-7-12 (34)(2ow)(4oh) Martin Dwyer 5/1 JT FAV: 062226: Chsd ldrs, btn 2f out. ½ 24
2463 **TOWN GOSSIP 34** [10] 3-8-13 (60) A Clark 12/1: 0-0507: Rear, mod gains for press: op 10/1. ½ 49
3045 **DIM OFAN 10** [7] 4-9-4 (54) R Hughes 10/1: 600048: Chsd ldrs, no impress fnl 4f: see 326 (AW, 1m). 2½ 39
2656 **STAFFORD KING 27** [6] 3-8-4 (51) Jonjo Fowle (5) 10/1: 000649: Rear, nvr on terms: op 8/1. 3 32
2941 **NOTEWORTHY 14** [12] 4-7-13 (35) Claire Bryan (5) 16/1: 000000: Chsd ldrs 9f: 10th: see 1440. 1¼ 14
*2875 **LOKOMOTIV 17** [14] 4-8-4 (40)(bl) P Fitzsimons (5) 15/2: 600010: Sn bhd: 11th: btr 2875. 1¼ 17
2491 **PING ALONG 33** [17] 3-7-13 (46) N Carlisle 5/1 JT FAV: -6050: In tch 7f: 16th: op 10/1, h'cap bow. 0
2565} **Notagainthen 398** [13] 4-8-7 (43) R Havlin 50/1: 2554 **Taxmere 31** [4] 3-7-10 (43)(3oh) Joanna Badger (7) 50/1:
2096} **Mazilla 418** [2] 8-7-10 (32) J McAuley 14/1: -- **Monongahela** [11] 6-9-10 (60) S Carson (3) 20/1:
16 ran Time 2m 35.5 (4.4) (Mrs Judy Mihalop) D Haydn Jones Efail Isaf, Rhondda C Taff

3256

4.40 ROMAN ROAD MDN 3YO+ (D) 7f str Good/Firm 28 -03 Slow
£3770 £1160 £580 £290 3 yo rec 6 lb

1376 **BORDER SUBJECT 83** [9] R Charlton 3-8-13 (t) R Hughes 8/11 FAV: -601: 3 b c Selkirk - Topicality (Topsider) Trkd ldrs going well, smooth prog to lead ins last, sn clr with rider doing little: val for 6L+, hvly bckd, 12 week abs: suited by application of t-strap: eff at 7f, return to 1m shld suit: acts on fast & gd/soft grnd: likes a gall/undul track: runs well fresh: useful colt, win more races. 90
3048 **DIGITAL 10** [6] M R Channon 3-8-13 Craig Williams 7/2: -42: 3 ch g Safawan - Heavenly Goddess (Soviet Star) Mid div, styd on fnl 2f, no ch with wnr: op 4/1: handles fast grnd: return to 1m shld suit. 2 78
3119 **KAREEB 6** [8] W R Muir 3-8-13 (bl) Martin Dwyer 11/2: 500343: 3 b g Green Desert - Braari (Gulch) Rdn early to lead, hdd inside last & sn held: op 3/1, quick reapp: see 3119,2977 & 1183. nk 77
3048 **COOL SPICE 10** [5] B Palling 3-8-8 D Sweeney 25/1: -04: Dwelt, keen/held up, late gains, no threat. 2 68
2709 **MOORLANDS AGAIN 25** [2] 5-9-5 N Pollard 40/1: 65: Rear, drvn/mod prog fnl 2f: see 2709. 2½ 68
2957 **TAW PARK 13** [11] 6-9-5 Paul Eddery 20/1: -566: Rear, rdn/mod gains: see 2709 (10f). 4 60
2531 **HERRING GREEN 32** [7] 3-8-13 S Carson (3) 100/1: -007: Chsd ldrs 5f: mod form at 10f prev. 4 52
2548 **SOLO BID 31** [4] 3-8-8 G Hind 14/1: 48: Chsd ldrs 3f, btn 2f out: op 10/1: see 2548 (soft). 1 45
2977 **ASHLEEN 13** [3] 3-8-8 R Mullen 40/1: 409: Al bhd: trainer reported filly swallowed her tongue. 3 39
2548 **RED WHITE AND BLUE 31** [1] 3-8-8 P Doe 100/1: 00-000: Dwelt & al rear: 10th: mod form. 6 30
10 ran Time 1m 22.00 (2.2) (K Abdulla) R Charlton Beckhampton, Wilts

3257

5.10 LEVY BOARD HCAP 3YO+ 0-75 (E) 6f Good/Firm 28 +01 Fast [75]
£2814 £804 £402 3 yo rec 4 lb

3209 **NINEACRES 2** [2] J M Bradley 9-9-9 (70)(bl) P Fitzsimons (5) 11/2: 103041: 9 b g Sayf El Arab - Mayor (Laxton) Prom, narrow lead 2f out, held on well ins last, gamely: qck reapp: earlier won at Bath (2), W'hampton, Southwell (rtd 58) & Windsor (h'caps): '99 W'hampton wmr (clmr, rtd 59a & 42): suited by 5/6f, stys 7f: likes firm & gd & both AWs, any trk, esp W'hampton: suited by blnks/vis, likes to force the pace: tough. 75
3209 **RUDE AWAKENING 2** [9] C W Fairhurst 6-8-0 (47) P Doe 6/1: 101052: 6 b g Rudimentary - Final Call (Town Crier) Prom halfway, rdn to chall inside last, just held cl home: qck reapp: again bhd todays wnr in 3209. nk 51
3123 **CRUSTY LILY 6** [10] J M Bradley 4-7-10 (43) Claire Bryan (5) 10/1: 200663: 4 gr f Whittingham - Miss Crusty (Belfort) Chsd ldrs, rdn & kept on fnl 2f, not pace to chall: op 14/1: quick reapp: see 2221. ¾ 45
2845 **BEYOND CALCULATION 19** [3] J M Bradley 6-9-7 (68) R Hughes 9/2: 501644: Prom, ch 1f out, onepcd. nk 69
2621 **PARKER 28** [6] 3-9-7 (72) D Sweeney 8/1: -24635: Chsd ldrs, ch 2f out, held fnl 1f: see 1266 (mdn). ½ 71
3097 **BANDBOX 8** [7] 5-9-1 (62) C Rutter 9/2: 306236: In tch, hard rdn halfway, not pace to chall: see 511. ¾ 59

CHEPSTOW   THURSDAY AUGUST 10TH   Lefthand, Undulating, Galloping Track

*2944 **RING DANCER 14** [4] 5-10-0 (75) A Clark 4/1 FAV: -00017: Held up rear, keen, nvr a factor.   1¾   68
3123 **SWINO 6** [1] 6-8-1 (48)(vis) Joanna Badger (7) 14/1: 002008: Sn rdn/twds rear, nvr on terms: op 10/1.   shd   41
1794 **TRUMP STREET 63** [5] 4-8-6 (53) L Newman (3) 20/1: 250109: Led 4f, sn btn: abs: btr 1557 (hvy, C/D).   1½   42
148 **MADAME JONES 248** [8] 5-9-4 (65) A McGlone 50/1: /000-0: Chsd ldrs 4f: 10th: 8 month abs: mod   1   52
form in '99: '98 wnr at Nottingham (ltd stakes), Goodwood (h'cap, M Buckley) & Chester (class stks, current
connections, rtd 76, unplcd on sand, rtd 54a): eff at 6/7f on fast & gd/soft grnd, any track.
2673 **RIFIFI 26** [11] 7-8-13 (60)(tvi) P Shea (5) 20/1: 030000: Sn bhd, eased/no ch halfway: 11th: see 320.   24   2
11 ran   Time 1m 10.4 (1.6)   (J M Bradley)   J M Bradley Sedbury, Gloucs

BRIGHTON   THURSDAY AUGUST 10TH   Lefthand, V Sharp, Undulating Track

Official Going   GOOD TO FIRM. Stalls: Inside except 1m2f & 1m4f - Outside.

3258   2.20 BROADLAND NURSERY HCAP 2YO (D)   6f rnd   Goof/Firm 39   +02 Fast   [89]
£3461   £1065   £532   £266

1995 **SIR FRANCIS 54** [7] J Noseda 2-9-7 (82) J Weaver 4/1: 521061: 2 b g Common Grounds - Red Note   90
(Rusticaro) Led after 1f, readily made rest: tchd 11/2, best time of day, 8 week abs: h'cap bow: earlier won here
at Brighton (mdn): half-brother to 2 juv wnrs: eff at 5/6f: acts on fast & soft, poss nt hvy: suited by
sharp/undul trks, likes Brighton & forcing the pace: goes well fresh & can carry big weights: improving.
2575 **DENSIM BLUE 29** [1] J Pearce 2-9-1 (76) T Quinn 5/2 FAV: 241452: 2 b c Lake Coniston - Surprise   2½   76
Visitor (Be My Guest) Early ldr, chsd wnr after, nvr any impress: op 7/2: ran well, eff at 5/6f, see 1463.
2894 **WATTNO ELJOHN 17** [2] D W P Arbuthnot 2-8-3 (64) D R McCabe 8/1: 000163: 2 b c Namaqualand -   ½   62
Caroline Connors (Fairy King) Rear, shaken up to go 3rd dist, nvr nrr: eff at 5/6f on fast & gd/soft grnd.
2687 **CHAWENG BEACH 26** R Hannon 2-7-11 (57)(1ow) J Quinn 3/1: 0164: Prom, same pace appr fnl 1f.   1   53
2985 **PAY THE SILVER 12** [4] G Duffield 5/1: 04355: Chsd ldrs, no extra appr fnl 1f: h'cap bow.   ¾   65
*2891 **LONDON EYE 17** [3] 2-8-4 (65) C Catlin (7) 12/1: 320016: Sn handy, fdd 2f out: blnks omitted, h'cap bow.   3   49
*3028 **PRESENTOFAROSE 10** [6] 2-7-11 (58)(7ex) D Glennon (7) 20/1: 234317: Bhd from halfway: h'cap bow.   14   12
7 ran   Time 1m 11.0 (2.2)   (L P Calvente)   J Noseda Newmarket, Suffolk

3259   2.50 BROADLAND CLASS STKS 3YO+ 0-70 (E)   7f rnd   Good/Firm 39   -11 Slow
£2804   £801   £400   3 yo rec 6 lb

*3041 **HAIL THE CHIEF 10** [4] R Hannon 3-9-0 R Smith (5) 7/2: 426011: 3 b c Be My Chief - Jade Pet   71
(Petong) In tch, imprvd appr fnl 2f, led bef dist, edged left under press but ran on well: bckd from 9/2: recent
Folkestone wnr (h'cap): unplcd in '99: eff at 7f, tried 1m: acts on fast grnd & sharp/undul trks: on the upgrade.
2999 **BUTRINTO 12** [6] B R Johnson 3-9-0 T Quinn 10/3: 140232: 6 ch g Anshan - Bay Bay (Bay Express)   ¾   65
Held up, styd on well under hands/heels appr fnl 1f, nvr nrr: ran to best at the weights at fav track, see 1462, 1335.
3097 **REDOUBTABLE 8** [1] D W Chapman 9-9-6 J Quinn 5/1: 004143: 9 b h Grey Dawn II - Seattle Rockette   1¼   65
(Seattle Slew) Trckd ldrs, rdn dist, unable to quckn: back up in trip, capable of better, see 2994.
1590 **PAGAN KING 71** [5] J A R Toller 4-9-3 S Whitworth 6/1: 56-004: Not travel well early & rdn in rear,   nk   61
hdwy 2f out, short of room & switched dist, unable to chall: op 4/1, 10 wk abs: sharper next time, likes Brighton.
2978 **AMORAS 13** [3] 3-8-8 B Marcus 9/1 FAV: 400425: Chsd ldrs, onepace appr fnl 1f: nicely bckd, clr rem.   hd   58
2896 **MALAAH 17** [7] 4-9-3 (bl) J Mongan (5) 50/1: 050056: Led/dsptd lead till appr fnl 1f, sn btn: flattered.   6   46$
2747 **BLUNDELL LANE 22** [2] 5-9-3 G Duffield 12/1: 006047: Led - dsptd lead till appr fnl 2f, fdd: up in trip.   4   38
1005 **MISS DANGEROUS 108** [9] 5-9-0 G Hannon (7) 50/1: 355008: In tch till 3f out: 15 wk abs, v stiff task.   2½   30
2943 **AMITGE 14** [8] 6-9-0 Darren Williams (5) 50/1: 303/59: Sn struggling: poss getting fit for jmps campaign.nk   29
9 ran   Time 1m 23.3 (3.5)   (Peter M Crane)   R Hannon East Everleigh, Wilts

3260   3.20 GRAHAM SELL HCAP 3YO+ 0-60 (F)   1m4f   Good/Firm 39   -01 Slow   [60]
£2299   £657   £328   3 yo rec 11lb

2887 **BLOWING AWAY 17** [11] J Pearce 6-7-10 (28)(5oh) G Bardwell 9/2 JT FAV: 005031: 6 b m Last Tycoon -   26
Taken By Force (Persian Bold) Held up, imprvd halfway, hard rdn appr fnl 1f, kept on gamely to lead nr fin:
tchd 7/1, no bid: no form in '99, plcd in '98 (h'caps, rtd 49, M Tompkins), last win in '97, at Leicester (clmr,
rtd 48): 97/98 hdls wnr (2m, gd & soft, rtd 76h): eff at 1m, suited by 12f, tried 2m on firm & soft, without vis.
3040 **REMEMBER STAR 10** [8] R J Baker 7-7-11 (29)(1ow)(4oh) J Quinn 5/1: 0-4322: 7 ch m Don't Forget Me -   ¾   26
Star Girl Gay (Lord Gayle) Cl up, led appr fnl 2f, drvn bef dist & hdd towards fin: op 7/2: eff at 12f/2m on fast.
2902 **BLAYNEY DANCER 16** [5] Jamie Poulton 3-7-10 (39)(3oh) D Kinsella (7) 33/1: 365003: 3 b c Contract   1½   34
Law - Lady Poly (Dunbeath) Held up, styd on entering fnl 2f & went 3rd inside last, not trouble front pair:
stays a sharp/undulating 12f on fast grnd: see 461.
2904 **LUNAR LORD 16** [7] J S Moore 4-8-5 (37) B Marcus 9/2 JT FAV: 202244: Mid div, improved 2f out,   3½   28
sn rdn & no extra: mdn after 16: btr 2904 (also bhd this 2nd), 2254.
2904 **SCENIC LADY 16** [1] 4-7-10 (28)(bl)(7oh) A Polli (3) 10/1: 6-0025: Dwelt, improved halfway, led &   1¼   17
came stands side appr fnl 3f, hdd bef 2f out, hung badly left 2f out: stiff task, see 2904.
2971 **WINSOME GEORGE 13** [12] 5-8-0 (32)(vis) G Sparkes (7) 14/1: 040506: In tch, prog to chase ldrs   3   17
3f out, sn onepace: op 10/1, tchd 20/1: visor reapplied, see 682.
3002 **ACTION JACKSON 12** [4] 8-7-10 (28)(1oh) S Righton 12/1: 4-0507: Al around same place: see 2843.   2½   10
3050 **BEE GEE 9** [2] 3-7-11 (39)(1ow) Dale Gibson 16/1: 430508: Chsd ldrs till halfway, no threat after.   ½   21
3002 **STICKS AND STONES 12** [9] 8-8-2 (34) A Mackay 9/1: 020049: Chsd ldrs fdd wknd 2f out, eased.   3½   11
2958 **FULL EGALITE 13** [3] 4-8-8 (40)(bl) T Quinn 11/2: 001200: Led till 5f out, fdd: 10th, see 2181.   nk   16
2958 **ROMAN REEL 13** [6] 9-8-0 (32)(tbl) R Brisland (5) 12/1: -00000: Handy 1m: 11th, t-strap & blnks reapp.   9   0
2981 **COSMO JACK 13** [10] 4-10-0 (60)(vis) Darren Williams (5) 10/1: 025000: Al bhd: 12th under top-weight.   17   7
12 ran   Time 2m 33.0 (4.8)   (Mr & Mrs S Fernandes)   J Pearce Newmarket, Suffolk

BRIGHTON
THURSDAY AUGUST 10TH   Lefthand, V Sharp, Undulating Track

3261
3.50 TOMMY JUDGE HCAP 3YO 0-75 (E)   1m rnd   Good/Firm 39   -10 Slow   [82]
£3558   £1095   £547   £273

2858 **BOLD EWAR** 19 [2] C E Brittain 3-9-7 (75)(bl) B Marcus 10/3: 505201: 3 ch c Persian Bold - Hot Curry   83
(Sharpen Up) Held up, switched & gd wide prog appr fnl 1f, led below dist, sn clr: '99 wnr at Southwell (nurs,
rtd 76a & 86): eff at 1m/10f: acts on fast, gd grnd & fibresand, any trk: can force the pace, wears blinks.
2908 **DUSKY VIRGIN** 16 [7] S Woodman 3-7-11 (51) R Brisland (5) 14/1: -00402: 3 b f Missed Flight - Rosy   4   51
Sunset (Red Sunset) Prom, led over 2f out till ent fnl 1f, sn outpcd: return to form, eff at 7f/1m on firm/fast.
*3094 **COLLEGE ROCK** 8 [4] R Brotherton 3-8-7 (61)(vis)(6ex) I Mongan (5) 8/1: 414613: 3 ch g Rock   shd   61
Hopper - Sea Aura (Roi Soleil) Rear, prog & slightly hmpd 2f out, rdn bef dist, same pace: clr rem, ran to best.
3227 **INSIGHTFUL** 1 [3] R Hannon 3-9-6 (74) J Weaver 12/1: 644064: Held up, mod late hdwy: ran yesterday. 3½   67
2895 **BOLD STATE** 17 [1] 3-9-2 (70) T Quinn 5/2: 011225: Mid div, progress & not much room 2f out, no extra. 3   57
2906 **PINHEIROS DREAM** 16 [5] D R McCabe 14/1: 031046: Led after 2f till bef 2f out, fdd.   hd   48
2814 **TRAJAN** 20 [6] 3-9-2 (70)(VIS) J Quinn 12/1: 5-4067: Early ldr, lost pl 2f out: visored: longer trip.   4   49
4526J **CORUSCATING** 288 [8] G Duffield 9/4 FAV: 005-8: Well plcd, bmpd appr fnl 2f & btn: 1¾   42
bckd on reappr/h'cap bow: promise fnl '99 start (mdn, rtd 70): thought capable of better: with Sir M Prescott.
8 ran   Time 1m 35.9 (3.9)   (A J Richards)   C E Brittain Newmarket, Suffolk

---

3262
4.20 CLUB 4 KIDS MED AUCT MDN 3YO (E)   1m2f   Good/Firm 39   -33 Slow
£2717   £836   £418   £209

3126 **CABALLE** 6 [3] S P C Woods 3-8-9 T Quinn 4/5 FAV: 233221: 3 ch f Opening Verse - Attirance (Crowned   78
Prince) Easily made all: well bckd, slow time, qk reapp, finally shed mdn tag, nvr out of the first 3 in 6 prev
starts, incl when rnr-up sole '99 start (fill mdn, rtd 87): eff at 1m/10f on fast & soft grnd, any track.
3004 **NO REGRETS** 12 [2] M Quinn 3-9-0 G Hannon (7) 50/1: 050002: 3 b c Bin Ajwaad - Marton Maid   10   53$
(Silly Season) Bhd, went a moderate 2nd: looks flattered, well btn in a seller in 2448.
1281 **BRIG OTURK** 89 [1] Mrs A J Perrett 3-9-0 G Duffield 6/5: 0-43: 3 ch g Inchinor - Sharmood (Sharpen   ¾   51
Up) Chsd wnr till appr fnl 2f: nicely bckd, 3 month abs: poss worth another ch on a flatter track, see 1281 (g/s).
3116 **DAZZLING DAISY** 6 [4] Pat Mitchell 3-8-9 J Tate 14/1: 44: Prom 7f: op 7/1, qk reapp, lngr trip.   2½   42
3006 **STAR ATTRACTION** 12 [5] 3-8-9 B Marcus 50/1: 405: Sn struggling: stablemate 2nd, see 2449.   24   12
5 ran   Time 2m 05.0 (7.2)   (B Allen, R Hine, R Dawson & A Duke)   S P C Woods Newmarket, Suffolk

---

3263
4.50 CHICKEN DANCE FILL HCAP 3YO 0-65 (F)   1m2f   Good/Firm 39   -15 Slow   [72]
£2714   £775   £387

3089 **PERFECT MOMENT** 8 [8] C A Dwyer 3-9-7 (65) A Beech (5) 5/2 FAV: 211161: 3 b f Mujadil - Flashing   70
Raven (Maelstrom Lake) Always up, prog to lead 3f out, rdn to repel rnr up ins last, gamely: bckd: prev ran up a hat-
trick at Nottingham (sell h'cap), Pontefract (sell, G McCourt, cost current connections 13,000gns) & W'hampton
(h'cap, rtd 60a): '99 Leicester wnr (auct mdn, A Jarvis, rtd 74): eff at 1m/10f on fast, soft & fibresand.
2906 **COLNE VALLEY AMY** 16 [10] G L Moore 3-9-7 (65) I Mongan (5) 4/1: 211432: 3 b f Mizoram -   1¼   67
Panchelita (Pancho Villa) Waited with, gd wide prog 4f out to chall appr fnl 1f, held towards fin: lost nothing
in defeat & styd this sharp/undulating 10f well though drop back to 1m will probably suit: see 2467.
2561 **IMARI** 30 [11] N P Littmoden 3-9-5 (63) T Quinn 7/2: 013263: 3 b f Rock City - Misty Goddess   2   62
(Godswalk) Towards rear, prog to chase ldrs 2f out, rdn & onepace: clr rem, ran near to best, see 1955, 1772.
*2908 **ADRIANA** 16 [5] C E Brittain 3-8-2 (46) A Nicholls (3) 7/2: 001014: In tch, outpcd 3f out, onepace.   6   36
2811 **CUMBRIAN PRINCESS** 20 [3] 3-8-1 (45) Dale Gibson 12/1: 000605: Led/dptd lead till 3f out, fdd.   3½   30
3049 **CORAL SHELLS** 10 [9] 3-8-1 (45)(BL) J Quinn 25/1: 000006: Chsd ldrs, not much rm 3f out & lost pl: 4   24
blnkd: drop back to 1m in a sell h'cap will suit: see 1511.
2795 **PICCALILLI** 21 [2] 3-7-10 (40)(30h) R Brisland (5) 50/1: 060607: Al towards rear: longer trip, no form.   nk   16
1955 **PAMELA ANSHAN** 56 [4] 3-7-10 (40)(2oh) G Bardwell 33/1: 00-008: Led after 3f till 5f out, btn: 8 wk abs.   1   16
2548 **FFYNNON GOLD** 31 [6] 3-9-0 (58) G Duffield 25/1: 0009: Cl up, keen, hmpd appr straight & drpd rear.   19   14
9 ran   Time 2m 04.3 (6.5)   (Casino Racing Partership)   C A Dwyer Newmarket, Suffolk

---

HAYDOCK
THURSDAY AUGUST 10TH   Lefthand, Flat, Galloping Track

Official Going   GOOD TO SOFT. Stalls: 10f & 12f - Outside; 5f, 6f & 14f - Centre; 7f & 1m - Inside.

3264
2.00 RAINHILL NURSERY HCAP 2YO (E)   5f str   Good/Soft 61   -25 Slow   [99]
£3108   £888   £444

2500 **EFFERVESCE** 33 [3] M A Buckley 2-7-13 (67)(3ow) A Daly 12/1: 4601: 2 b f Sri Pekan - Arcitc   73
Winter (Briartic) Led, narrowly hdd appr fnl 1f, rallied well ins last, led again nr fin, all out: h'cap bow:
IR 34,000gns half-sister to sev wnrs: eff at 5f on gd/soft & a gall trk: apprec switch to h'caps: lks genuine.
3168 **LOVE TUNE** 4 [6] K R Burke 2-7-10 (67)(3oh) D Mernagh (5) 5/1: 536222: 2 b f Alhijaz - Heights Of   nk   69
Love (Persian Heights) Trkd wnr, rdn into narrow lead appr fnl 1f, kept on well but collared cl-home: qck reapp:
eff on fast, gd/soft & fibresand: deserves to win similar, see 3168, 2665.
3027 **BYO** 10 [4] M C Chapman 2-10-0 (99) R Studholme (5) 10/1: 151243: 2 gr c Paris House - Navan Royal   nk   100
(Dominion Royale) Sn outpcd, drvn & ran on strongly ins last, closing at finish: op 6/1: excellent run under
10-0 burden: acts on fast & gd/soft grnd: see 2664, 2483.
2874 **EMISSARY** 17 [5] M Johnston 2-7-10 (67)(1oh) J Mackay (5) 4/1 JT FAV: 664024: Mid-div, rdn/hdwy   1½   64
over 2f out, hung left appr fnl 1f, not pace of ldrs: handles gd/soft & firm, shld apprec a return to 5f: see 2874.
2664 **PRINCESS OF GARDA** 27 [2] 2-9-4 (89) S Sanders 4/1 JT FAV: 312145: Front rank, drvn/onepcd appr   ¾   84
fnl 1f: capable of better, see 2248 (nov stks, fast grnd).
2915 **SEANS HONOR** 15 [11] 2-7-10 (67)(6oh) G Baker (5) 25/1: 54406: Handy, drvn & no impress from   4   52
halfway: stiffish task: op 16/1: see 1706.
2849 **DIVINE WIND** 19 [7] 2-8-4 (75) K Darley 9/2: 033407: Prom, lost tch appr fnl 1f: btr 2318.   1¾   56
2717 **BALL GAMES** 24 [1] 2-7-10 (67)(2oh) J Bramhill 12/1: 6468: Dwelt, sn chasing ldrs, wknd qckly fnl 2f.   1½   44
2874 **CLANSINGE** 17 [10] 2-7-10 (67) P Fessey 13/2: 531349: V slow to start, al bhd: btr 2665, 1918.   nk   44
9 ran   Time 1m 03.14 (4.34)   (C C Buckley)   M A Buckley Upper Helmsley, N.Yorks.

3265 **2.30 THREEPWOOD MDN 3YO+ (D)** **1m2f120y** **Good/Soft 61** **00 Slow**
£4082 £1256 £628 £314 3 yo rec 10lb

2548 **GOLDEN WAY 31** [6] E A L Dunlop 3-8-9 J Reid 8/1: 0-61: 3 ch f Cadeaux Genereux - Diavolina (Lear 85
Fan) Settled in tch, smooth hdwy to lead appr fnl 1f, rdn clr ins last: unplcd sole '99 start (fill mdn, rtd 68):
half-sister to sev wnrs, dam 10f wnr: clrly relished this step up to a gall 10f & further shld suit: acts on gd/soft
grnd: clearly going the right way & could win again, prob over 12f next time.
2679 **AYMARA 26** [5] J H M Gosden 3-8-9 K Darley 11/2: 42: 3 b f Darshaan - Chipaya (Northern Prospect) 3 80
Trkd wnr, rdn to improve over 3f out, ev ch till outpcd by wnr fnl 1f: op 4/1: imprvd on this step up to a
gall 10.5f on gd/soft, could win similar: see 2679.
2751 **SHATTERED SILENCE 22** [10] R Charlton 3-8-9 Pat Eddery 7/4 FAV: -0333: 3 b f Cozzene - Sunday 3½ 75
Bazaar (Nureyev) Led till over 1f out, sn drvn/wknd: well bckd: a return to 12f & faster grnd shld suit: see 2751.
-- **DANCE DIRECTOR** [2] J H M Gosden 3-9-0 J Fortune 7/1: 4: Dwelt, bhd, rdn/gd hdwy over 3f out, 3½ 75+
sn onepcd & not given a hard time: cl rem: related to high-class 6/7f mnr: gd debut & shld know more next time.
-- **CHIEF WARDANCE** [8] 6-9-10 A Culhane 33/1: 5: Bhd, mod late gains, no threat: Flat debut: 7 65
3 months ago scored over timber at Wetherby (h'cap, rtd 116h at best, eff forcing the pace over 2m on fast &
soft, sharp or gall trk): apprec further on the level for Mrs S Lamyman.
2558 **GREEN WILDERNESS 30** [9] 3-8-9 D Harrison 3/1: -626: Prom, rdn/outpcd over 3f out, no impress 2 56
after: disapp but prob not handle this softer grnd, btr 2558, 2258 (fast/firm).
1668 **SWEMBY 69** [1] 3-8-9 D Holland 33/1: 07: Keen/mid-div, lost tch fnl 3f: 10 wk abs: see 1668. 1¾ 53
-- **CHAIN** [4] 3-9-0 Dane O'Neill 16/1: 8: Missed break, al bhd: Last Tycoon colt, with R Charlton. shd 58
2439 **SANDROS BOY 35** [7] 3-9-0 J Carroll 33/1: 329: Al bhd: new stable: btr 2439 (13.5f). 6 50
2889 **TRAVELLERS REST 17** [3] 3-9-0 S Sanders 25/1: -050: Handy, wknd rapidly half-way, t.o. in 10th. dist 0
10 ran Time 2m 16.36 (6.36) (Ahmed Ali) E A L Dunlop Newmarket.

3266 **3.00 TWO NECKS MDN CLAIMER 3YO (F)** **1m30y rnd** **Good/Soft 61** **-01 Slow**
£2492 £712 £356

2992 **OSTARA 12** [12] K A Ryan 3-8-10 F Lynch 14/1: 030051: 3 b g Petorius - Onde de Choc (L'Enjoleur) 65
Chsd ldrs, gd hdwy to lead appr fnl 1f, pushed clr ins last, val 4/5L: plcd once in '99 (seller, first time
blnks, rtd 61): eff btwn 6f & 1m: acts on fast, gd/soft & a gall track: best without blnks now.
3080 **NIGHT DIAMOND 8** [1] I A Balding 3-8-6 (t) K Darley 9/2: 004042: 3 b g Night Shift - Dashing 2½ 52
Water (Dashing Blade) Mid-div, gd hdwy to lead appr fnl 1f, hdd appr fnl 1f, not pace of wnr: op 3/1: styd
this longer 1m trip well, visor omitted here: see 2549.
2947 **SLAM BID 13** [8] R Charlton 3-8-6 S Sanders 10/1: 00-563: 3 b g First Trump - Nadema (Artaius) nk 52
Waited with, prog over 3f out, sn chall, drvn/no extra fnl 1f: op 7/1: btr 2585 (mdn).
2946 **STANDIFORD GIRL 13** [6] J G Given 3-8-6 G Baker (5) 11/1: 000324: Prom, drvn/no impress appr 2½ 43$
fnl 1f: turf return, treat rating with caution: btr 2946 (AW clmr).
3094 **FOSTON FOX 8** [9] 3-8-0 (bl) J Bramhill 33/1: 006005: Bhd, gd hdwy over 2f out, sn held. 1 40
3082 **DOLFINESSE 8** [14] 3-8-1 (vis) D Mernagh (3) 14/1: 406206: In tch, rdn to improve over 3f out, sn held. 2 37
2411 **WENSUM DANCER 36** [2] 3-8-3 J Mackay (5) 11/1: 040647: In tch, boxed in on rails 4f out, no room till nk 39
switched appr fnl 1f & styd on under hands-&-heels: tchd 14/1 & no luck in running, worth a look in a mdn h'cap.
3082 **NORTHERN ECHO 8** [10] 3-8-10 (bl) A Culhane 14/1: 053208: Mid-div at best: better on firm in 2731. 2½ 42
2662 **LITIGIOUS 27** [3] 3-8-7 N Callan 5/1: -229: Front rank, wknd qckly fnl 2f: op 7/2 & a disapp 4 32
run on this softer grnd: btr 2662 (gd), 2198 (fast).
-- **VICKY SCARLETT** [11] 3-8-3 J Fanning 33/1: 0: Bhd, eff/sltly hmpd 2f out, no threat after, 10th. 4 21
2585 **FLYING BACK 29** [7] 3-8-10 Dane O'Neill 4/1 FAV: -440: Dwelt, nvr dngrs, 11th: up in trip, btr 2585. shd 28
3004 **CENTAUR SPIRIT 12** [5] 3-8-8 P Dobbs (3) 20/1: 0-040: In tch, wknd fnl 2f, 12th: see 3004. hd 26
2914 **SKELTON MONARCH 15** [15] 3-8-3 (t) P M Quinn (3) 14/1: 000030: Al bhd, 13th: btr 2914 (sell, fast). ½ 20
472 **ALL MINE 185** [13] 3-8-8 M Fenton 40/1: 60650: Led early, rcd keenly, wknd rapidly fnl 2f, 14th: abs. 22 0
2297 **BALLY CYRANO 41** [4] 3-8-8 (vis) D Holland 50/1: 00-000: Sn led, hdd 2f out, wknd qckly, 15th. 7 0
15 ran Time 1m 45.53 (5.03) (J Nixon) K A Ryan Hambleton, N.Yorks.

3267 **3.30 TOTE JACKPOT HCAP 3YO 0-95 (C)** **1m2f120y** **Good/Soft 61** **-15 Slow** **[98]**
£7377 £2270 £1135 £567

*2750 **POLAR RED 22** [6] M J Ryan 3-9-7 (91) P McCabe 4/6 FAV: 124311: 3 ch g Polar Falcon - Sharp Top 102
(Sharpo) Mid-div, smooth hdwy to lead over 2f out, pushed clr over 1f out, hvly easily fnl 100y, val 7/8L:
hvly bckd at odds-on: earlier won here at Haydock (rtd h'cap) & Kempton (h'cap): juv wnr at Windsor (nurs,
rtd 73): eff btwn 1m & 12f on fast, soft & any trk, likes Haydock: v prog this term, can extend win run.
2553 **CAPRICCIO 31** [5] C G Cox 3-8-5 (75) J Mackay (5) 9/1: 4352: 3 gr g Robellino - Yamamah (Siberian 1¼ 75
Express) Front rank 4f, sn outpcd, rallied & styd on strongly fnl 2f, closing on hvly eased wnr cl-home:
gd effort on this h'cap bow & caught a useful/progressive rival today: shld apprec 12f next time: see 2211.
1198 **FRONTIER 94** [3] R Hannon 3-9-4 (88) Dane O'Neill 8/1: 21-533: 3 b c Indian Ridge - Adatiya nk 88
(Shardari) Handy, gd hdwy to lead over 2f out, sn hdd, not pace of easy wnr: gd effort, just sharper for this.
2666 **RHODAMINE 27** [4] J L Eyre 3-7-10 (66) G Baker (5) 15/2: 143404: Dwelt, bhd, gd hdwy to chall ¾ 65
ldrs appr fnl 2f, sn hdd/no extra: 8L clr rem: see 1560.
*2832 **ROUSING THUNDER 20** [1] 3-8-9 (79)(VIS) J Reid 9/1: -02015: Led, hdd appr fnl 2f, sn drvn/fdd: 8 68
op 7/1: shade disapp in first time visor & on this softer grnd: btr 2832 (mdn, fast).
*198 **ELEGANT ESCORT 237** [2] 3-9-1 (85) S Sanders 33/1: 31-6: Trkd ldrs, wknd qckly over 2f out: 8 64
turf/h'cap bow, 8 month abs: sharper next time: see 198 (1m fibresand mdn).
2235 **HIGHLAND GOLD 43** [7] 3-7-10 (66)(1oh) P M Quinn (3) 20/1: 65-357: Mid-div, wknd fnl 3f: up in trip. ¾ 44
7 ran Time 2m 18.0 (8.0) (M Byron) M J Ryan Newmarket.

3268 **4.00 BADGEHOLDERS AUCT MDN 2YO (E)** **6f str** **Good/Soft 61** **-28 Slow**
£3038 £868 £434

-- **ST ANTIM** [14] J A Osborne 2-8-4 J Fanning 25/1: 1: 2 b f Petardia - Efficient Funding (Entitled) 73
Chsd ldrs, eff when short of room over 2f out, rdn/prog appr fnl 1f, styd on strongly to lead fnl nr fin, drvn out:
IR 11,500gns Feb foal, full sister to 5f 2yo scorer Petrovna: eff at 6f, 7f will suit: runs well fresh on
gd/soft grnd & a gall trk: can rate more highly & this was a welcome win for trainer J Osborne.

-- **TRACK THE CAT** [9] B A McMahon 2-8-9 D Holland 12/1: 2: 2 b c Catrail - Snowtop (Thatching) *shd* 76
Mid-div, hdwy to lead well ins last, styd on well for press, collared fnl strides: 20,000gns half-brother
to sev wnrs abroad: dam Irish 2yo wnr: eff over a gall 6f on gd/soft grnd: gd debut & can win a mdn.

-- **CARBON COPY** [18] W J Haggas 2-8-8 K Darley 3/1 FAV: 3: 2 ch f Pivotal - Astolat (Rusticaro) ¾ 73
Trkd ldrs, switched appr fnl 2f, went on over 1f out, hdd well ins last, rall, not btn far: nicely bckd: 23,000gns
Mar foal, half-sister to a couple of 7f wnrs: eff over a gall 6f on gd/soft, 7f will suit next time.

2029 **FLYING TURK** 53 [17] J A Osborne 2-8-9 J P Spencer 20/1: -304: Waited with, hdwy when short *nk* 73
of room over 2f out, hmpd again appr fnl 1f, styd on well ins last, closing at fin: 7 wk abs: acts on gd/soft
& soft: unlucky in running here & can find a mdn soon.

2828 **ARMAGNAC** 20 [2] 2-8-9 S Sanders 9/2: 640425: Trkd ldr, led 4f out, hdd appr fnl 1f, no extra ½ 72
nr fin: 6L clr rem: mkt drifter for new stable: prev with D Sasse: handles fast & gd/soft: see 2828.

2810 **TEMPLES TIME** 20 [13] 2-8-0 A Daly 9/2: -436: Mid-div, onepcd fnl 2f: op 7/2: btr 2810 (firm, 7f). 6 48

2608 **WEET A WHILE** 28 [7] 2-8-9 N Callan 25/1: -07: Prom, rdn/wknd appr fnl 1f: see 2608. *nk* 56

-- **HENRY PEARSON** [12] 2-8-13 M Fenton 33/1: 8: Dwelt, sn handy, btn when sltly hmpd appr fnl 1f: 1¾ 56
Mar foal, dam a wnr in the States: with T H Caldwell.

2756 **JUST AS YOU ARE** 22 [11] 2-8-5 (1ow)(BL) Pat Eddery 14/1: -009: Led, hdd over 4f out, became 1 45
unbalanced & drpd rear 2f out, not given hard time after: first time blnks, longer 6f trip: see 2539.

1918 **VODKA** 57 [8] 2-8-5 Dean McKeown 16/1: 560: Mid-div at best: see 1476. *hd* 45

2454 **YOUNG TERN** 34 [15] 2-8-5 T Williams 25/1: 00: In tch, rdn/onepcd fnl 2f, 11th: see 2454. *shd* 45

-- **GRAIN STORM** [10] 2-8-8 J Reid 9/1: 0: Dwelt, al outpcd, 12th: op 7/1: IR 28,000gns Marju filly, ¾ 46
dam scored over 12f: shld improve over further in time for E Dunlop.

-- **GRAIG PARK** [6] 2-8-5 J Carroll 9/1: 0: Al bhd, 15th: op 7/1: Apr foal, dam related to a smart 0
miler: half-brother to sev wnrs: with A Berry, can do better in time.

2841 Limburg 19 [5] 2-8-5 D Harrison 25/1: -- Beau Sauvage [4] 2-8-13 T Lucas 33/1:
-- Basinet [16] 2-8-9 F Lynch 33/1: 2692 Mauld Segoisha 26 [1] 2-8-4 D Mernagh (3) 14/1:
2730 Got Alot On 23 [3] 2-8-5 R Winston 33/1:
18 ran Time 1m 16.66 (5.36) (Mrs H J Clarke) J A Osborne Lambourn, Berks.

3269 4.30 TILSTON HCAP 3YO 0-70 (E) 7f30y rnd Good/Soft 61 -10 Slow [75]
£3122 £892 £446

*3033 **DAKOTA SIOUX** 10 [15] R A Fahey 3-8-10 (57)(bl)(6ex) G Parkin 4/1 JT FAV: -36011: 3 ch f College 61
Chapel - Batilde (Victory Piper) Sn led, hdd appr fnl 1f, rall for press to get up nr fin, drvn out: op 5/2:
earlier won at Newcastle (h'cap, 1st win, first time blnks): plcd sole '99 start (auct mdn, rtd 71): prev eff at
5f, now best dominating at 7f: handles fast, gd/soft, poss not soft: best on a stiff/gall trk: improving in blnks.

2918 **MOONLIGHT SONG** 15 [2] W Jarvis 3-9-0 (61) M Tebbutt 9/1: 000122: 3 b f Mujadil - Model Show ¾ 63
(Dominion) Chsd ldrs, gd hdwy to lead over 2f out, styd on but hdd nr fin: acts on fast, gd/soft & fibresand.

3033 **HEATHYARDS LAD** 10 [8] R Hollinshead 3-8-9 (56) Pat Eddery 14/1: 655003: 3 b c Petardia - *nk* 57
Maiden's Dance (Hotfoot) In tch, short of room & switched over 2f out, ran on strongly ins last, closing at fin.

1665 **THE PROSECUTOR** 69 [4] B A McMahon 3-9-5 (66) D Holland 11/1: 500144: Prom, drvn & hmpd over 2 63
2f out, ran on ins last, no impress: 10 wk abs, eff at 6/7f: would have gone close with a clear run: see 1665.

1889 **SHINING STAR** 58 [7] 3-9-0 (61) J P Spencer 14/1: 65-405: Waited with, prog when short of room ½ 57
over 1f out, switched ins last & styd on: 8 wk abs: handles gd/soft & soft: see 1606.

3163 **DILSAA** 5 [6] 3-9-4 (65) J Fortune 6/1: 000646: Prom, drvn/btn appr fnl 1f: nicely bckd: qck reapp. 1 59

1793 **STRAND OF GOLD** 63 [3] 3-9-1 (62) Dane O'Neill 12/1: 550507: Bhd, rdn to improve over 2f out, *nk* 56
kept on but no dngr: see 1537 (flattered).

3033 **INDY CARR** 10 [14] 3-8-12 (59) A Culhane 14/1: 046608: In tch rdn/imprvg when continually hmpd fnl 1½ 50
1f, no ch after: would have gone much closer with a clear run & this effort can prob be forgotten: see 900.

800 **FOR HEAVENS SAKE** 133 [16] 3-8-11 (58) O Pears 20/1: -43269: Mid-div, rdn & hung badly right 2½ 45
over 1f out, no threat: long abs: btr 636 (firmish).

1266 **CAREW CASTLE** 90 [12] 3-9-2 (63) D Harrison 25/1: -5500: Mid-div, lost tch fnl 2f, 10th: 3 month abs. ¾ 49

*2243 **CRYFIELD** 43 [11] 3-9-2 (63) J Fanning 4/1 JT FAV: 201310: Keen/prom, hung left & wknd qckly ½ 48
appr fnl 1f, 11th: well bckd after 6 wk abs & better expected: btr 2243.

2811 **VERDURA** 20 [10] 3-9-6 (67)(BL) K Darley 14/1: 0-6400: Rear, eff/no room 2f out, no dngr, 12th: blnks. 1 50
846 Canny Hill 124 [1] 3-9-2 (63) J Bramhill 33/1: 2512 Aljazir 33 [9] 3-8-8 (55) T E Durcan 16/1:
1979 Dontbesobold 55 [5] 3-8-13 (60)(vis) M Fenton 16/1:
15 ran Time 1m 32.21 (5.11) (Mrs Una Towell) R A Fahey Butterwick, N.Yorks.

3270 5.00 LEVY BOARD HCAP 3YO 0-85 (D) 1m3f200y Good/Soft 61 +10 Fast [90]
£3984 £1226 £613 £306

3014 **PRINCIPLE** 11 [8] Sir Mark Prescott 3-9-2 (78) S Sanders 5/1: -43141: 3 b c Caerleon - Point Of Honour 85
(Kris) Trkd ldrs, led appr fnl 4f, strongly pressed ins last, all out to hold on: fast time: earlier won here at
Haydock (h'cap, 1st win): '99 rnr-up (auct mdn, rtd 79 at best): eff at 1m/10f, suited by 12f & even further
could suit: acts on fast, gd/soft & a gall trk, likes Haydock: won in a fast time here, could win again.

3122 **SUDDEN FLIGHT** 6 [2] E A L Dunlop 3-9-2 (78) J Reid 8/1: 130252: 3 b c In The Wings - Ma Petite *shd* 84
Cherie (Caro) Hld up, switched/imprvd over 2f out, chall well ins last, drvn out, just failed: clr rem, qk reapp.

3014 **RAGDALE HALL** 11 [10] J H M Gosden 3-9-7 (83) J Fortune 11/2: -5103: 3 b c Bien Bien - Gift Of 5 82
Dance (Trempolino) Mid-div, smooth hdwy over 3f out, not pace of front 2 appr fnl 1f: first try on easy grnd.

*906 **ROYAL MINSTREL** 118 [5] M H Tompkins 3-9-6 (82) D Holland 14/1: 64-314: Prom, rdn/wknd fnl 2f: 3 76
4 month abs & shld be sharper for this: btr 906 (soft).

*2943 **FRANGY** 14 [9] 3-9-2 (78) J P Spencer 4/1 JT FAV: -3115: Chsd ldrs, chall over 2f out, wknd *nk* 72
qckly appr dist: h'cap bow, btr 2943 (firm).

2562 **ASTRONAUT** 30 [1] 3-9-0 (76) K Darley 4/1 JT FAV: 041226: Handy, outpcd appr fnl 3f & not given 4 64
hard time after: longer 12f trip & better expected: see 2562, 2450.

2610 **AZUR** 28 [7] 3-9-1 (77) D Harrison 25/1: 01-007: Mid-div at best: up in trip: see 2610. 14 49

2936 **MAKASSEB** 14 [3] 3-8-12 (74) A Culhane 12/1: 060448: Nvr dngrs: see 2523. *hd* 46

3042 **EL ZITO** 10 [4] 3-9-7 (83) T E Durcan 10/1: 110339: Set fast pace to 4f out, sn btn: btr 1919 (firm). 9 43

2175 **CLEAR PROSPECT** 46 [6] 3-8-10 (72) J Carroll 20/1: 3-0040: Lost tch halfway & virtually p.u. fnl 3f, *dist* 0
t.o. in 10th: 7 wk abs & reportedly became unbalanced: longer 12f trip: see 2175.
10 ran Time 2m 33.85 (6.05) (Sir Edmund Loder) Sir Mark Prescott Newmarket.

WOLVERHAMPTON (Fibresand)   FRIDAY AUGUST 11TH   Lefthand, Sharp Track

Official Going   STANDARD. Stalls: Inside, except 7f/14f - Outside.

3271

2.10 FAMILY FUN HCAP 3YO+ 0-65 (F)   5f aw rnd   Going 26   -02 Slow   **[63]**
£2275   £650   £325   3 yo rec 3 lb

3191 **SOTONIAN** 4 [7] P S Felgate 7-9-5 (54) G Duffield 4/1 FAV: 453651: 7 br g Statoblest - Visage (Vision)   59a
Al prom, rdn/led over 1f out, styd on well, drvn out: op 6/1: '99 scorer at W'hampton, Lingfield (2), Warwick &
Catterick (h'caps, rtd 68 & 64a at best): '98 W'hampton wnr (h'cap, rtd 45a & 50): stays 6f, suited by a sharp/
turning 5f: acts on fast, gd/soft & both Aws: best without blnks: looks on a fair mark, can win again.
2650 **SAMWAR** 28 [10] Mrs N Macauley 8-9-8 (57)(vis) R Fitzpatrick (3) 8/1: 225632: 8 b g Warning - Samaza   1 58a
(Arctic Tern) Outpcd/bhd & wide early, rdn/styd on well fnl 2f, nrst fin: see 1237.
3123 **COOL PROSPECT** 7 [1] K A Ryan 5-8-13 (48)(bl) F Lynch 5/1: 322003: 5 b g Mon Tresor - I Ran Lovely shd   49a
(Persian Bold) Rdn/chsd ldrs halfway, styd on for press fnl 1f, not pace of wnr: see 1143.
3113 **BRANSTON LUCY** 7 [6] T J Etherington 3-9-8 (60) R Ffrench 6/1: 021224: Bhd ldrs, rdn/kept on fnl 2f: shd   60a
acts on fast, gd/sft & fibresand: see 2535.
*3180 **YOUNG IBNR** 4 [2] P Mullen 5-9-4 (53)(7ex) R Mullen 8/1: 430015: Led/dsptd lead 3f: 7lb pen, op 11/2.   1 51a
3077 **MARENGO** 9 [9] 6-9-8 (57) T G McLaughlin 8/1: 000636: Rear/outpcd early, mod gains: see 1073 (6f). shd 55a
3191 **YABINT EL SHAM** 4 [5] 4-9-9 (58) P Mundy (7) 20/1: 000007: Chsd ldrs, btn over 2f out: see 466, 191. 2½ 49a
1923 **PALVIC LADY** 58 [8] 4-9-3 (52) J Stack 20/1: 10-008: Chsd ldrs wide halfway, sn held: 8 wk abs: AW shd 43a
bow: '99 Beverley mdn wnr (rtd 72): eff at 5f on gd & gd/sft grnd.
3056 **JACK TO A KING** 10 [4] 5-9-12 (61)(bl) R Studholme (5) 14/1: 200009: Led/dsptd lead 3f: see 609. 3 45a
2777 **FASTRACK TIME** 22 [11] 3-9-5 (57) Paul Eddery 33/1: 00-000: Rear/wide, nvr factor: 10th: AW bow, 2 36a
unplcd last term (rtd 72, auct mdn, flattered).
3180 **SWEET MAGIC** 4 [3] 9-9-1 (50)(t) J Fanning 12/1: 000000: Bhd/eased fnl 2f: saddle slipped. 4 19a
11 ran   Time 1m 01.60   (Tim Dean)   P S Felgate Newmarket

3272

2.40 BRING THE KIDS MDN 3YO (D)   1m1f79y aw   Going 26   +03 Fast
£2834   £872   £436   £218

2838 **JOONDEY** 20 [1] M A Jarvis 3-9-0 P Robinson 11/8 FAV: 032521: 3 b c Pursuit Of Love - Blueberry   80a
Walk (Green Desert) Made all, rdn clr from over 1f out, readily: nicely bckd, AW bow: effective btwn 9/10f on
fast, gd and fibresand: handles any track: eff forcing the pace: could make his mark in h'cap company.
1269 **PEACHES** 91 [7] C A Cyzer 3-8-9 J Fanning 33/1: -002: 3 b f Selkirk - Off The Blocks (Salse) 8 61a
Trkd ldrs halfway, outpcd by wnr fnl 2f: 3 mth abs: AW bow: now qualified for h'caps.
2945 **AIWIN** 14 [10] G C H Chung 3-9-0 (t) M Henry 8/1: 453053: 3 b c Forzando - Great Aim (Great 1½ 63a
Nephew) Held up, rdn/prog to chase ldrs 2f out, no further hdwy: see 1977, 1388.
2617 **KARAJAN** 29 [3] J W Hills 3-9-0 S Whitworth 9/4: 3-04: Trkd ldrs 7f, AW bow, op 7/4: see 2617. 2 59a
3379} **BUSY BUSY BEE** 363 [6] 3-8-9 C Cogan (5) 8/1: 002-5: In tch 6f: reapp: rnr-up on fnl start last term 1¾ 51a
(rtd 65a, mdn): stays 7f, 1m+ shld suit: handles fibresand.
2770 **FLAVIA** 23 [7] 3-8-9 Dale Gibson 14/1: 66: Trkd ldrs, btn over 2f out: longer 9f trip. 1½ 48a
3095 **COST AUDITING** 9 [2] 3-8-9 R Ffrench 20/1: 0-5007: Cl up, fdd fnl 3f: longer 9f trip, mod form. 11 32a
2592 **LATINO BAY** 30 [5] 3-9-0 T G McLaughlin 33/1: 00-068: Trkd ldrs when stumbled badly and lost place 12 19a
halfway: AW bow: longer 9f trip: see 2026.
2604 **OVERSLEPT** 29 [8] 3-9-0 R Mullen 25/1: 009: Dwelt, al bhd: longer 9f trip, no form. 8 7a
2449 **ABERNANT LADY** 36 [4] 3-8-9 Paul Eddery 50/1: 050: Sn bhd: 10th: AW bow: mod form. 18 0a
10 ran   Time 2m 0.40 (2.2)   (Sheikh Ahmed Al Maktoum)   M A Jarvis Newmarket

3273

3.10 GREENWELL NURSERY HCAP 2YO (E)   7f aw rnd   Going 26   -14 Slow   **[95]**
£2831   £809   £404

2966 **RIVER RAVEN** 14 [9] Sir Mark Prescott 2-9-7 (88) G Duffield 6/4 FAV: 2141: 2 b c Efisio - River   97a
Spey (Mill Reef) Cl-up going well halfway, led 2f out, styd on well ins last, rdn out: nicely bckd: earlier scored
at Hamilton (mdn): eff at 7f, 1m+ shld suit: acts on fast, gd & fibresand: handles a stiff/undul or sharp trk: gd
weight carrier: progressive type, shld win more races.
2718 **CARRABAN** 25 [6] B J Meehan 2-8-1 (68) D R McCabe 12/1: 5W3362: 2 b f Mujadil - Bayazida (Bustino) 1½ 72a
Prom, rdn/ch 2f out, not pace of wnr: AW bow: eff at 7f: acts on fibresand, handles gd/soft & fast grnd.
2916 **EL HAMRA** 16 [1] B A McMahon 2-8-1 (68) R Mullen 8/1: 50333: 2 gr c Royal Abjar - Cherlinoa (Crystal nk 71a
Palace) Chsd ldrs, styd on for press fnl 2f, no threat to wnr: clr of rem: see 2916.
3149 **CHURCH MICE** 6 [2] M L W Bell 2-8-6 (73)(vis) J F Egan 6/1: 215364: Led till 2f out, held 1f out. 5 66a
2894 **REPEAT PERFORMANCE** 18 [7] 2-8-2 (69)(t) P Fitzsimons (5) 8/1: 444055: Bhd, mod late gains, ½ 61a
no threat: AW bow, longer 7f trip: see 1463, 1124 & 891.
2468 **BLUE ORLEANS** 35 [5] 2-7-12 (65) T Williams 14/1: 30006: Al bhd: mod form since eyecatching in 1136. 5 47a
2383 **BORDER EDGE** 39 [11] 2-7-11 (64) Dale Gibson 16/1: 04057: Al outpcd: see 1236. 2½ 41a
3175 **TRUSTED MOLE** 5 [10] 2-8-2 (69) Paul Eddery 7/1: 630448: Bhd halfway: qck reapp: btr 3175, 2468. 1¾ 43a
2948 **ORCHARD RAIDER** 14 [3] 2-8-0 (67) R Ffrench 7/2: 412029: Prom 5f: btr 2948 (6f). nk 40a
2773 **MAYSBOYO** 22 [8] 2-7-10 (63)(18oh) G Baker 33/1: -30000: Sn bhd: 10th: longer 7f trip, AW bow. 5 26a
10 ran   Time 1m 29.8 (3.6)   (Hesmonds Stud)   Sir Mark Prescott Newmarket.

3274

3.40 EXPRESS & STAR HCAP 3YO 0-85 (D)   1m100y aw rnd   Going 26   +03 Fast   **[86]**
£3789   £1166   £583   £291

2666 **INVER GOLD** 28 [1] A G Newcombe 3-9-1 (73) S Whitworth 7/1: 004301: 3 ch c Arazi - Mary Martin (Be My   78a
Guest) Trkd ldrs, rdn over 3f out, drvn to narrowly assert ins last, gamely: earlier won a mdn at Southwell: rnr-up
in '99 (rtd 77a, rtd 79 on turf, M Johnston): suited by 1m/10f on both AWs, fast & gd/soft: likes a sharp track.
2999 **MANXWOOD** 13 [3] D J S Cosgrove 3-8-12 (70) J F Egan 7/2 FAV: 421002: 3 b g Petorius - Eliza   ½ 73a
Wooding (Faustas) Cl up, led after 1f, duelled with wnr final 2f, hdd just ins last, styd on well, just held clr home:
well bckd: appreciated this return to sand, can win again: see 1726.
2499 **FAYRWAY RHYTHM** 34 [5] M A Jarvis 3-9-7 (79) P Robinson 4/1: 445103: 3 b c Fayruz - The Way She 1¼ 79a
Moves (North Stoke) Led early, rem cl-up, kept on fnl 2f: AW bow: acts on firm, soft & fibresand.
2947 **TOYON** 14 [6] Sir Mark Prescott 3-8-7 (65) G Duffield 4/1: 652234: Trkd ldrs, drvn/held fnl 2f: mdn. 2½ 60a
2980 **SOFISIO** 14 [2] 3-9-0 (72) B Marcus 7/1: -03245: Sn rdn/rear, in tch, nvr any impress on ldrs: see 2661. 4 59a

WOLVERHAMPTON (Fibresand) FRIDAY AUGUST 11TH Lefthand, Sharp Track

3182 **GERONIMO** 4 [7] 3-8-12 (70) O Pears 6/1: 0-2166: Chsd ldrs 5f: qck reapp: btr 2604 (mdn, 6f). 8 45a
3163 **ANYHOW** 6 [4] 3-8-12 (70) M Henry 6/1: -04107: Held up in tch, btn 3f out: fin lame: btr 2591 (7f, gd). 3½ 38a
7 ran   Time 1m 48.4 (2.2)   (M Patel)   A G Newcombe Huntshaw, Devon

---

3275 4.10 SUMMER SELLER 3YO+ (G) 6f aw rnd Going 26 -12 Slow
£2023 £578 £289   3 yo rec 4 lb

1920 **ROYAL CASCADE** 58 [8] B A McMahon 6-9-2 (bl) R Mullen 5/1: 020201: 6 b g River Falls - Relative 64a
Stranger (Cragador) Rdn/bhd early, styd on strongly fnl 2f for press to lead nr line: op 4/1, no bid: 2 month
abs: '99 hat-trick scorer at Southwell (2, clmr & h'cap) & Southwell, rtd 38 on turf, h'cap):
'98 wnr again at Southwell (2, clmr & seller, first time blnks) & W'hampton (2, clmrs): suited by 6/7f, tried 1m:
fibresand specialist, handles gd grnd: best in blnks: runs well fresh: enjoys claim/sell grade.
2796 **DISTINCTIVE DREAM** 21 [7] A Bailey 6-9-7 J Bosley (7) 10/1: 050002: 6 b g Distinctly North - Green ¾ 65a
Side (Green Dancer) Rdn/bhd early, rdn & styd on fnl 2f, not pace of wnr: op 7/1: see 1250, 598.
2819 **PURPLE FLING** 21 [8] A J McNae 9-9-2 T G McLaughlin 4/1 JT FAV: 6-0023: 9 ch g Music Boy - Divine nk 59a
Fling (Imperial Fling) Prom, rdn/led over 1f out, hdd well ins last: op 3/1: see 82.
2819 **FEATHERSTONE LANE** 21 [9] Miss L C Siddall 9-9-7 Dean McKeown 8/1: 633634: Rdn/outpcd early, ½ 62$
styd on fnl 2f, not pace to chall: see 1235.
1298 **MAITEAMIA** 88 [1] 7-9-2 (bl) N Mitchell (7) 11/2: 120-55: Led till over 1f out, fdd: op 5/2, 12 wk abs. 2 54a
2785 **COLONEL CUSTER** 22 [5] 5-9-7 (vis) P Fitzsimons (5) 25/1: 650406: Prom, btn 1f out: see 408 (12f). hd 56$
2193 **KOMASEPH** 46 [12] 8-9-2 (t) D R McCabe 25/1: 064007: Held up, nvr on terms: 6 wk abs: t-strap. 3 44$
*2680 **SUPERBIT** 27 [4] 8-9-7 G Faulkner (3) 5/1: 1-0618: Chsd ldrs, held over 1f out: see 2680 (seller). nk 48a
630} **RING THE CHIEF** 517 [6] 8-9-2 G Hannon (7) 25/1: 2306-9: Nvr on terms: reapp: '99 Southwell wnr 2½ 36a
(appr h'cap, rtd 39a): '98 wnr at Southwell (2, h'caps, rtd 39a) & Salisbury (appr h'cap, rtd 39): eff btwn
7/12f on a stiff or sharp trk: acts on fast, gd/soft, fibresand & prob hvy: can have ability with/force the pace.
2329 **CORNISH ECLIPSE** 41 [13] 3-8-12 G Baker 33/1: 000-60: Chsd ldrs 4f: 10th: abs: AW bow. 6 25a
427 **NIGHT AND DAY** 193 [3] 3-8-7 (tVl) J F Egan 4/1 JT FAV: 3-2230: Drvn mid-div, btn 2f out: 11th: 1½ 16a
op 7/2, visor: 6 month abs: btr 427, 362 & 278.
3080 **ROISTERER** 9 [11] 4-9-2 G Parkin 25/1: 000: Sn outpcd/bhd: 12th: AW bow, no form. dist 0a
12 ran   Time 1m 15.1 (2.3)   (R L Bedding)   B A McMahon Hopwas, Staffs.

3276 4.40 APPRENTICE HCAP 3YO+ 0-60 (G) 1m6f166y aw Good/Firm 26 -35 Slow [57]
£1928 £551 £275   3yo rec 14lb

*2904 **BEAUCHAMP MAGIC** 17 [10] M D I Usher 5-8-1 (30) G Baker (3) 9/2 JT FAV: 543011: 5 b g Northern Park - 37a
Beauchamp Buzz (High Top) Held up, prog to lead over 2f out, held on gamely, all out: recent Brighton wnr (sell
h'cap, rtd 30): '99 W'hampton wnr (AW h'cap, rtd 37a & 54, t-strap, tried blnks): also rtd 38 (rtd 69, h'cap):
suited by 12f/2m on f/sand & firm, handles gd grnd: likes a sharp/undul trk: best form without visor/blnks.
2672 **BLACK WEASEL** 27 [3] A Bailey 5-8-6 (35) Claire Bryan (3) 7/1: 4-0562: 5 br h Lahib - Glowlamp nk 41a
(Glow) Chsd ldr, led 4f out till over 2f out, styd on well for press, just held: clr of rem: eff btwn 12f/2m on
fibresand, fast & gd grnd: see 141, 124.
2298 **SIPOWITZ** 42 [6] C A Cyzer 6-9-0 (43) J Bosley (5) 16/1: 03/503: 6 b g Warrshan - Springs Welcome 6 40a
(Blakeney) Chsd ldrs halfway, eff/no room & snatched up over 2f out, held after: 6 wk abs: see 1975.
2941 **MU TADIL** 15 [5] R Dickin 8-7-12 (27) Clare Roche (3) 16/1: 000604: Rear, mod gains fnl 3f, no threat. hd 23a
2689 **HOTELIERS PRIDE** 27 [1] 3-8-12 (55) Jonjo Fowle (3) 33/1: 0-0505: Held up, eff 5f out, held 2f out. 1¼ 49a
*2951 **AQUAVITA** 17 [7] 6-8-4 (33) P Fitzsimons 6/1: 354416: Towards rear, mod gains: op 4/1: recent 6 18a
jumps rnr (rnr-up, h'cap hdle): see 2951 (2m).
3181 **YANKEE DANCER** 4 [8] 5-8-7 (36) A Hawkins (5) 33/1: 000007: Held up, nvr factor: qck reapp: see 1496. 4 15a
2951 **STEAMROLLER STANLY** 14 [12] 7-9-12 (55) R Studholme (5) 6/1: 412208: Trkd ldrs 11f: op 4/1: see 2606. 4 28a
1915 **MALCHIK** 58 [11] 4-10-0 (57) P Hanagan (5) 8/1: 026009: In tch, btn 3f out: 2 month abs: see 922. 1¼ 28a
2951 **MACHALINI** 14 [4] 7-9-11 (54)(t) C Cogan (5) 9/2 JT FAV: 030/50: Nvr a factor: 10th: op 6/1, abs. 2½ 21a
2075 **IRISH CREAM** 51 [2] 4-8-13 (42)(vis) R Cody Boutcher (5) 5/1: 062620: Led 11f, fdd: 11th: 7 wk abs. 1 8a
3112 **UNIMPEACHABLE** 7 [9] 3-8-8 (51) P Dobbs (3) 8/1: 442250: Held up, eff halfway, no impress: 12th. 12 4a
12 ran   Time 3m 18.6 (9.0)   (The Magic & Dance Partnership)   M D I Usher Newmarket.

LINGFIELD FRIDAY AUGUST 11TH Lefthand, Sharp, Undulating Track

Official Going GOOD/FIRM (FIRM places). Stalls: Str - Far Side; 10f - Inside; 11f - Outside.

3277 2.00 EBF PRIME MDN 2YO (D) 5f str Firm 13 +01 Fast
£3750 £1154 £577 £288

3044 **SENIOR MINISTER** 11 [3] J M P Eustace 2-9-0 J Tate 6/5 FAV: 21: 2 b c Lion Cavern - Crime Ofthecentury 95
(Pharly) Dsptd lead, went on over 2f out, styd on well for press: well bckd, gd time: Feb foal, cost 55,000
gns: half brother to useful sprinter Tussle: dam 5f wnr: eff at 5f, 6f will suit: acts on firm/fast: useful.
-- **LEOZIAN** [2] Miss Gay Kelleway 2-9-0 N Callan 16/1: 2: 2 b c Lion Cavern - Alzianah (Alzao) 1¼ 90$
Prom, kept on over 1f out, no pace of wnr: debut: well bckd, 23,000 gns: half brother to a 5f juv wnr: dam
useful sprinter: eff at 5f on firm grnd, 6f will suit: clr of rem, can improve & win a race.
3044 **MADRASEE** 11 [7] M Blanshard 2-8-9 D Sweeney 14/1: 36303: 2 b f Beveled - Pendona (Blue Cashmere) 4 73
Cl up, eff on fnl 2f, no extra: handles firm & gd: see 2711.
3109 **HOT PANTS** 8 [4] K T Ivory 2-8-9 C Catlin (7) 20/1: 053064: Led till over 2f out, outpcd under hand riding. ½ 72
2209 **MAGIC GEM** 48 [8] 2-9-0 R Cochrane 33/1: 05: In tch, outpcd 3f out: well btn on debut: abs: 2 71
Feb foal, cost 16,000 gns: sprint bred.
-- **NERA ZILZAL** [5] 2-8-9 O Urbina 20/: 6: Dwelt, sn in tch, btn over 2f out: Apr foal, cost 24,000 ½ 65
gns: half sister to a 5f juv wnr: dam sprint wnr: bred to apprec 6/7f in time.
3133 **REEL BUDDY** 7 [1] 2-9-0 R Hughes 6/4: 62007: Missed break (jockey failed to remove hood till after nk 69
stalls had opened!), nvr in it: bckd: this run must be ignored: his jockey can look inspirational coming late
in big fields at times, but also v modest on some other occasions: prob flattered 3133, see 2849.
-- **SWANTON ABBOT** [10] 2-9-0 S Sanders 12/1: 8: Al bhd on debut: op 8/1: Feb foal, cost 85,000 gns: hd 68
dam won as a juv: bred to apprec 6/7f: with M Tompkins.
-- **ONE CHARMER** [9] 2-9-0 P McCabe 33/1: 9: Dwelt, sn bhd on debut: Mar foal, cost 1,400 gns: 6 50

half brother to 2 juv wnrs: bred to apprec 6/7f in time: with P S McEntee.
9 ran Time 57.4 (0.6) (R Carstairs) J M P Eustace Newmarket

3278 **2.30 PRIME TIME FILLIES SELLER 2YO (G) 6f str Firm 13 -41 Slow**
£1907 £545 £272

-- **DELTA SONG** [1] W R Muir 2-8-11 Martin Dwyer 9/1: 1: 2 b f Delta Dancer - Song Of Gold (Song) **64**
Chsd ldrs, hdwy to lead over 1f out, pushed out: wng debut: Mar foal, bought for 11,600 gns: half sister to wnrs over 5/7f: dam sprint juv wnr: eff at 6f on firm, further shld suit: win again in this grade.
3028 **TEENAWON 11** [6] K R Burke 2-8-11 D Harrison 9/2: 32: 2 ch f Polar Falcon - Oasis (Valiyar) *2* **56**
Led till over 1f out, not pace of wnr: stays 6f on fm & a sharp/undul trk: better run: see 3028.
*2983 **MISS EQUINOX 13** [8] N Tinkler 2-9-2 T Quinn 5/4 FAV: 022313: 2 b f Presidium - Miss Nelski *nk* **60**
(Most Secret) Keen, prom, eff 2f out, onepace for press: well bckd: not disgraced: see 3044.
-- **MONASH LADY** [4] J S Moore 2-8-11 R Hughes 12/1: 4: Slow away, hld up, eff 2f out, no impress: *1¾* **51**
Feb first foal: dam unraced: bred to apprec 6/7f in time.
-- **MISS SUTTON** [3] 2-8-11 L Carter 8/1: 5: Bhd, hdwy over 2f out, wknd fnl 1f: Feb foal, cost *½* **49**
6,200 gns: dam 5f juv wnr: bred to apprec 6/7f in time.
2949 **RAGING TIMES 14** [7] 2-8-11 A Daly 7/1: -06: Cl up, wknd 2f out: see 2949. *4* **37**
1737 **POWDER 67** [5] 2-8-11 S Sanders 7/1: 07: Prom, keen, wknd 2f out: abs, see 1737. *½* **35**
-- **CARRICK LADY** [2] 2-8-11 A Nicholls (3) 16/1: 8: Hld up, keen, rdn & wknd 2f out: uninspired *3* **26**
gamble from 33/1: debut: cheaply bt Apr foal: half sister to a 6/7f wnr: sprint bred.
8 ran Time 1m 12.05 (3.25) (Mrs A G Loriston-Clarke) W R Muir Lambourn, Berks

3279 **3.00 PRIME TIME FILLIES HCAP 3YO+ 0-65 (F) 7f str Firm 13 -06 Slow** **[64]**
£2660 £760 £380 3 yo rec 6 lb 2 Groups - Stands Side Favoured.

3188 **WHO GOES THERE 4** [15] T M Jones 4-9-2 (52) D Harrison 10/1: 030161: 4 ch f Wolfhound - **56**
Challenging (Mill Reef) Dwelt, stands side, bhd, hdwy to lead ins last, styd on, drvn out: earlier won at Chepstow (h'cap): rnr-up in '99 (rtd 53 & 29a): suited by 7f, stays 9f on any trk: likes firm, handles soft.
2920 **CAPPELLINA 16** [17] P G Murphy 3-8-11 (53) F Norton 12/1: 0-0042: 3 b f College Chapel - Santa Ana *½* **56**
Wind (Busted) Prom stands side, led over 1f out till ins last, no extra: gd run back at 7f on fm: see 1796.
3030 **ANNIJAZ 11** [16] J G Portman 3-9-0 (56) G Carter 10/1: 330103: 3 b f Alhijaz - Figment (Posse) *1¼* **57**
Bhd stands side, hdwy 2f out, ev ch just ins last, onepace: ran to best: see 2794.
2999 **CALCAVELLA 13** [3] M Kettle 4-9-11 (61) N Callan 14/1: -40504: Hld up far side, hdwy to lead that *1¼* **59**
gr 1f out, no ch with favoured stands side group: fine run from wrong side under top-weight: shld win a race.
3030 **EMANS JOY 11** [14] 3-9-9 (65) R Cochrane 6/1 FAV: -35145: In tch stands side, outpcd 2f out, late gains. *hd* **62**
2786 **ENTROPY 22** [11] 4-8-12 (48) I Mongan (5) 10/1: 051036: Chsd ldrs stands side, no impress fnl 1f: bckd. *½* **44**
3076 **LADYWELL BLAISE 9** [8] 3-9-4 (60) Martin Dwyer 16/1: 012007: Led far side group till 1f out, wknd. *1¼* **53**
3041 **L A TOUCH 11** [18] 7-9-1 (51) J Quinn 10/1: 0-0368: Prom stands side, wknd 2f out: see 2840. *½* **43**
3045 **GRANDMA ULLA 11** [10] 3-8-10 (52) J Tate 25/1: 000009: Chsd ldr far side, wknd over 1f out: wrong side *1¼* **42**
2759 **GAELIC FORAY 23** [2] 4-8-9 (45) A Nicholls (3) 25/1: 003530: Chsd ldrs far side, wknd over 1f out: 10th. *½* **34**
2899 **MILADY LILLIE 17** [1] 4-9-0 (50) R Hughes 10/1: 040660: No danger far side: 11th, wrong side. *½* **38**
2918 **TAFFETA 16** [5] 3-9-9 (65) T Quinn 7/1: 50640: Keen, in tch far side till 2f out: 12th, bckd, wrong side. *shd* **52**
2795 **SANGRA 22** [7] 3-9-6 (62) R Hills 15/2: 6-4250: Al bhd far side: 13th, btr 1855. *hd* **48**
2794 **BETTINA BLUE 22** [13] 3-9-0 (56) W Ryan 9/1: -66000: Led stands side till over 1f out: 14th. *nk* **41**
1801 **NOCCIOLA 63** [12] 4-9-2 (52) S Sanders 9/1: 0-0600: In tch stands side, wknd 2f out: fin last. **0**
3412} **Swing Job 360** [9] 4-8-13 (49) P McCabe 33/1: 3110 **Night Shifter 8** [6] 3-9-2 (58) O Urbina 20/1:
17 ran Time 1m 21.72 (1.32) (The Rest Hill Partnership) T M Jones Albury, Surrey

3280 **3.30 TOTE HCAP 3YO 0-80 (D) 6f str Firm 13 +04 Fast** **[84]**
£7202 £2216 £1108 £554

2855 **BANAFSAJYH 20** [4] A C Stewart 3-9-5 (75) R Hills 9/2: -10401: 3 b f Lion Cavern - Arylh (Lyphard) **82**
Made all, kept on for press ins last, drvn out: gd time: earlier won at Nottingham (med auct mdn): plcd fnl 2 '99 starts (fill mdn, rtd 78): v eff at 6f on firm/fast & any trk: runs well fresh: genuine.
1569 **CHIQUITA 74** [5] J A R Toller 3-9-4 (74) W Ryan 7/1: -50002: 3 ch f College Chapel - Council Rock *½* **79**
(General Assembly) Hld up, hdwy 2f out, kept on ins last, too much to do: encouraging after 10 wk abs, see 982.
2934 **BALFOUR 15** [2] C E Brittain 3-8-4 (60) A Nicholls (3) 8/1: 560343: 3 b c Green Desert - Bandawi *nk* **64**
(Diesis) Bhd, hdwy 2f out, kept on ins last, not btn far: handles fm & hvy: sole win has come at 7f: see 1787.
2885 **DOCTOR DENNIS 18** [8] B J Meehan 3-8-13 (69) S Clancy (7) 13/2: 201224: Cl up, ev ch 1f out, wknd. *½* **71**
3010 **JAMES STARK 12** [7] 3-9-3 (73)(vis) J Quinn 13/2: 342445: In tch, eff 2f out, onepace fnl 1f: see 3010. *½* **74**
2294 **SUSSEX LAD 42** [1] 3-9-2 (72) R Hughes 8/1: 040646: Handy, onepace over 1f out: see 2294. *1¼* **69**
2919 **NEEDWOOD TRICKSTER 16** [6] 3-8-11 (67) S Sanders 20/1: -03367: Bhd, eff 2f out, sn no impress. *1* **61**
2804 **CUPIDS CHARM 21** [9] 3-9-7 (77) D Harrison 12/1: 010168: In tch, rdn over 1f out, wknd & eased. *½* **69**
3130 **CASTLE SEMPILL 7** [12] 3-9-5 (75)(vis) R Cochrane 16/1: 510609: In tch, short of room over 1f out, *nk* **66**
no extra ins last: btr 852.
2885 **KISSING TIME 18** [10] 3-9-5 (75) I Mongan (5) 3/1 FAV: 06-050: Prom, wknd 2f out: 10th, bckd, see 2885. *1* **63**
1795 **Stoney Garnett 64** [3] 3-8-13 (69) G Carter 16/1: 1138 **Hoxton Square 99** [11] 3-8-12 (68) O Urbina 33/1:
12 ran Time 1m 09.33 (0.53) (Hamdan Al Maktoum) A C Stewart Newmarket

3281 **4.00 CLASSIFIED STKS 3YO+ 0-70 (E) 1m2f Firm 13 -18 Slow**
£2856 £816 £408 3 yo rec 9 lb

4414} **FASHION 298** [7] Sir Mark Prescott 3-8-6 S Sanders 9/4 JT FAV: 4331-1: 3 b f Bin Ajwaad - New **74**
Generation (Young Generation) Missed break, sn in tch, hdwy to lead over 1f out pushed out, cmftbly: reapp, well bckd: juv wnr at Pontefract (nursery h'cap, rtd 69): eff at 1m, stays 10f & further will suit (half sister to wnrs up to 2m): acts on firm, gd/soft & any trk: runs well fresh: type to win again & improve over further.
*3043 **KELTIC BARD 11** [9] S P C Woods 3-8-12 G Carter 9/4 JT FAV: 000512: 3 b g Emperor Jones *2* **74**
- Broughton Singer (Common Grounds) Led after 1f till over 1f out, not pace of wnr: bckd: another gd run.
2967 **EVE 14** [2] M L W Bell 3-8-7(1ow) R Hughes 6/1: 42343: 3 b f Rainbow Quest - Fade (Persepolis) *1¼* **66**
Cl up, onepace for press over 1f out: prob stays 10f on firm & soft, tho' rated higher in 2426 & 2211.
2895 **BARBASON 18** [1] G L Moore 8-9-7 I Mongan (5) 15/2: 515534: In tch, onepace 2f out: ran to form. *nk* **70**

LINGFIELD   FRIDAY AUGUST 11TH   Lefthand, Sharp, Undulating Track

1364 **LORD EUROLINK** 84 [10] 6-9-4 R Cochrane 8/1: 044645: Led 1f, btn 2f out: abs, better off in h'caps.   2   **64**
2920 **GULF SHAADI** 16 [5] 8-9-4 N Callan 10/1: 540536: Keen bhd, eff over 3f out, sn no impress: frustrating.   nk   **63**
1690 **ROGER ROSS** 69 [6] 5-9-4 R Smith (5) 25/1: -50007: Chsd ldrs, btn over 4f out: stiff task.   14   **43**
2527 **SASEEDO** 33 [8] 10-9-4 G Bardwell 33/1: 000608: Slow away, al bhd: poorly placed (offic rated 30).   2   **40$**
2814 **MINT LEAF** 21 [4] 3-8-6 (t) O Urbina 25/1: -00009: In tch, btn over 4f out: stiff task.   1   **36**
2871 **BATWINK** 19 [4] 3-8-6 Martin Dwyer 33/1: -0000: In tch, btn over 5f out: last, modest.   6   **27**
10 ran   Time 2m 07.33 (3.13)   (H R H Prince Fahd Salman)   Sir Mark Prescott Newmarket

3282   4.30 PRIME TIME HCAP 3YO+ 0-75 (E)   1m3f106y   Firm 13   -25 Slow   [71]
£2898   £828   £414   3 yo rec 10lb

3031 **LADY JO** 11 [3] S Dow 4-8-11 (54) R Smith (5) 6/1: 606051: 4 ch f Phountzi - Lady Kalliste (Another   **59**
Realm) Hld up, gd hdwy to lead 2f out, pushed clr, cmftbly: '99 scorer at Yarmouth & Lingfield (fill h'caps,
rtd 67): eff 10f, suited by 12f now: acts on firm, gd & equitrack: handles any trk: on a handy mark.
2370 **FOREST DREAM** 39 [9] L A Dace 4-8-8 (45) A Nicholls (3) 16/1: 023002: 5 b m Warrshan - Sirenivo (Sir   3½   **44**
Ivor) Bhd, eff over 2f out, kept on to chase wnr ins last, no impress: gd run: has worn a t-strap: see 43.
3110 **SUCH BOLDNESS** 8 [2] Miss Gay Kelleway 6-8-7 (50)(2ow) R Hughes 5/1: -00003: 6 b g Persian Bold -   1½   **47**
Bone China (Sadler's Wells) In tch, hdwy over 2f out, sn onepace: encouraging run, has run well from the front.
2793 **TOMMY CARSON** 22 [4] Jamie Poulton 5-8-7 (50)(bl) I Mongan (5) 13/2: -62504: Chsd ldrs, led over   hd   **47**
2f out, sn hdd & onepace: clr rem: see 2081.
3111 **SURE FUTURE** 7 [7] 4-8-6 (49)(bl) A Polli (3) 14/1: 02-005: Led over 3f out till over 2f out, wknd.   4   **40**
1364 **TOMASZEWSKI** 84 [1] 5-9-3 (60) G Bardwell 13/2: 650/06: Handy, wknd 3f out: 3 month abs, see 1364.   ½   **50**
3043 **MURJAN** 11 [6] 3-9-3 (70) G Carter 100/30 FAV: 4-5047: Prom, wknd 2f out: see 3043.   shd   **60**
3206 **TWIST** 3 [5] 3-8-7 (60) Martin Dwyer 6/1: 050258: Hld up, rdn over 4f out, wknd over 2f out: qk reappr.   1½   **47**
3007 **ROGUE SPIRIT** 13 [8] 4-9-10 (67) T Quinn 7/1: 002009: Led till over 3f out, wknd: lngr trip.   5   **47**
9 ran   Time 2m 27.81 (4.41)   (Ken Butler)   S Dow Epsom, Surrey

HAYDOCK   FRIDAY AUGUST 11TH   Lefthand, Flat, Galloping Track

Official Going   GOOD (GOOD TO SOFT in places). Stalls: 10/12f - Outside; 7f/1m - Inside; Rem - Centre.

3283   6.05 ROSSETT CLAIMER 3YO+ (F)   6f str   Good/Firm 53   -06 Slow
£2425   £693   £346   3 yo rec 4 lb

3144 **CZAR WARS** 6 [4] P T Dalton 5-8-7 (bl) D Mernagh (3) 66/1: 003461: 5 b g Warrshan - Dutch Czarina   **53**
(Prince Sabo) Rear, rdn/hdwy appr fnl 2f, led dist, styd on well, drvn out for a shock 66/1 success: qck reappr:
plcd once in '99 (clmr, rtd 43 & 45a): rcd 58 in '98: won twice back in '97, at Warwick (auct mdn, rtd 70):
eff at 6/7f, stays 11f: acts on fast, soft & fibresand: a remarkable effort at these weights.
2833 **CAPE COAST** 21 [9] R M Beckett 3-8-10 R Winston 16/1: 163042: 3 b g Common Grounds - Strike It Rich   1   **57**
(Rheingold) Towards rear, rdn to impr over 2f out, styd on well for press ins last, nvr nrr: btr 1423 (gd/soft).
2820 **RUSSIAN ROMEO** 21 [3] B A McMahon 5-9-1 (bl) K Dalgleish (5) 7/1: 220023: 5 b g Soviet Lad -   ¾   **56**
Aoteraroa (Flash Of Steel) Front rank, went on 2f out, drvn/hdd dist, not pace of wnr: shade btr 2820 (AW).
*3077 **KING OF PERU** 9 [10] D Nicholls 7-9-13 Alex Greaves 7/2: 220114: Prom, rdn/prog over 2f out,   3   **60**
sn chall ldrs, wknd ins last: op 11/4 on hat-trick bid: btr 3077 (5f).
2701 **HIGH ESTEEM** 26 [7] 4-9-5 Dale Gibson 33/1: -10005: Led, hdd appr fnl 2f, edged right over 1f out, fdd.   ½   **51$**
3180 **PRESS AHEAD** 4 [5] 5-8-9 (vis) A Culhane 20/1: 000006: Handy, drvn/lost tch fnl 2f: qck reappr.   nk   **41**
*1663 **BLUSHING GRENADIER** 70 [1] 3-8-8 (8) S Finnamore (5) 12/1: 660217: Chsd ldrs, wknd fnl 2f: abs.   1   **38**
2505 **LORD HIGH ADMIRAL** 34 [1] 12-8-5 (vis) P M Quinn 33/1: 400468: Handy, wknd qckly over   ¾   **32**
2f out: veteran, best when dominating over 5f, see 673.
2845 **ACE OF PARKES** 20 [6] 4-9-13 J Carroll 6/1: 506509: With ldr, rdn/lost tch over 2f out: see 1245.   2½   **48**
2663 **WELCHS DREAM** 28 [11] 3-8-9(3ow) T E Durcan 12/1: 560060: Al bhd, 10th: see 2663.   hd   **33**
3123 **ZIGGYS DANCER** 7 [8] 9-9-4 K Darley 10/3 FAV: 400000: In tch, wknd qckly for press fnl 2f, 11th: hd   **44**
nicely bckd tho' op 3/1, qck reappr: out of form at present, but v well h'capped: see 2247.
2555 **JOHNNY STACCATO** 32 [2] 6-8-5 Paul Eddery 66/1: 000000: Al outpcd, fin last.   9   **6**
12 ran   Time 1m 14.88 (3.58)   (Mrs Julie Martin)   P T Dalton Bretby, Derbyshire.

3284   6.35 RADIO CITY HCAP 3YO+ 0-60 (F)   1m4f   Good 53   +01 Fast   [60]
£2740   £783   £391   3 yo rec 11lb

3008 **BOLLIN NELLIE** 12 [18] T D Easterby 3-8-7 (50) K Darley 6/1: 505021: 3 ch f Rock Hopper - Bollin   **54**
Magdalene (Teenoso) Mid-div, prog apppr fnl 4f, led over 1f out, styd on strongly, rdn out: gd time: first win:
plcd fnl start in '99 (rtd 63, h'cap): eff btwn 1m & 12f: acts on firm, gd & gall trk: apprec this return to 12f.
2482 **SKYERS A KITE** 35 [19] Ronald Thompson 5-8-11 (43) T Williams 14/1: 653152: 5 b m Deploy - Milady   1½   **46**
Jade (Drumalis) In tch, led briefly over 2f out, not pace of wnr ins last: in gd heart, see 2219 (clmr, fm, made all).
2893 **SECRET DROP** 18 [1] K McAuliffe 4-9-4 (50)(e) R Winston 25/1: 000043: 4 b f Bustino - Safe House   shd   **53**
(Lyphard) Hdwy from rear over 4f out, ran on well for press ins last, nvr nrr: wore an eye-shield, 4L clr of rem:
imprvd form today & shld appreci a return to further: see 1091.
3026 **RAYWARE BOY** 11 [3] D Shaw 4-8-7 (39)(bl) Paul Eddery 33/1: 452004: Rear, rdn/prog over 2f out,   4   **36**
late hdwy, no threat to ldrs: see 1660 (seller).
3036 **MELODY LADY** 11 [4] 4-9-2 (48) K Dalgleish (5) 10/1: 022035: Set strong pace, hdd over 2f out,   nk   **45**
wknd appr fnl 1f: op 8/1: see 2309, 1496.
2763 **WESTERN COMMAND** 23 [7] 4-9-0 (46) R Fitzpatrick (3) 25/1: 106206: Mid-div, prog 3f out, held fnl 2f.   hd   **43**
2139 **CAMARADERIE** 49 [10] 4-9-2 (48) A Culhane 6/1: 34-337: Rear, rdn/prog fnl 2f, nrst fin: 7 wk abs.   1¼   **43**
752 **MI ODDS** 136 [13] 4-9-2 (46)(2ow) Alex Greaves 33/1: 3058: Waited with, switched/prog over 2f out,   1¼   **41**
onepcd nr fnl out: long abs, turf/h'cap bow: see 603.
2463 **BROUGHTONS MILL** 35 [11] 5-8-8 (40) S Finnamore (4) 10/1: 042369: Settled rear, smooth hdwy   1½   **31**
over 3f out, wknd qckly appr dist: op 8/1: btr 2141 (mdn h'cap).
3053 **MANZONI** 10 [15] 4-9-2 (48)(VIS) T Lucas 14/1: -00600: Prom, rdn/fdd over 2f out, 10th: visor, see 2279.   ¾   **38**
3084 **OPPORTUNE 9** [8] 5-8-8 (40) J Fanning 12/1: 314/50: Nvr dngrs: see 3084.   5   **23**
3125 **OPTION 7** [6] 3-8-11 (54) G Duffield 20/1: -50050: Mid-div at best, 12th: qck reappr: see 3125.   4   **31**
3053 **ALS ALIBI** 10 [20] 7-9-12 (58) O Pears 11/2 FAV: 021420: Front rank, chall 4f out, wknd rapidly   2½   **31**

1015

HAYDOCK   FRIDAY AUGUST 11TH   Lefthand, Flat, Galloping Track

fnl 2f, 13th: nicely bckd & capable of much better, see 3053 (h'cap).
2461 **MURCHAN TYNE** 35 [12] 7-9-1 (47) T E Durcan 16/1: 043060: Al towards rear, 14th: see 2461.   6   12
1949 **Ptah** 57 [9] 3-8-13 (56) D Mernagh (3) 20/1:   2971 **Tajar** 14 [14] 8-8-5 (36)(1ow) S Whitworth 14/1:
3013 **Aldwych Arrow** 12 [17] 5-9-7 (53) J Carroll 14/1:   3706) **Zsarabak** 345 [2] 3-8-13 (56) F Lynch 25/1:
3122 **Fiery Waters** 7 [5] 4-9-3 (49) J Stack 25/1:   2244 **Berty Boy** 44 [16] 4-8-7 (39)(BL) P M Quinn (3) 40/1:
20 ran   Time 2m 34.02 (6.22)   (Lady Westbrook)   T D Easterby Great Habton, N.Yorks.

3285   7.05 MOSCHINO HCAP 3YO+ 0-75 (E)   1m2f120y   Good 53 -12 Slow   [75]
£3250   £1000   £500   £250   3 yo rec 10lb

2817 **NOMINATOR LAD** 21 [2] B A McMahon 6-9-11 (72)(BL) K Dalgleish (5) 14/1: 000441: 6 b g   78
Nomination - Ankara's Princess (Ankara) Settled mid-div, gd hdwy over 2f out, led dist, drvn out & just held on:
top-weight, first time blnks: '99 Pontefract wnr (h'cap, rtd 83): '98 W'hampton & Ayr wnr (h'caps, rtd 74a & 81):
eff btwn 7/10.5f on firm, hvy & f/sand & any trk: took advantage of a handy mark & woken up by 1st time blnks.
*2836 **MINI LODGE** 20 [4] J G FitzGerald 4-9-3 (64) K Darley 7/4 FAV: 00-012: 4 ch g Grand Lodge - Mirea   hd   69
(The Minstrel) Dwelt/rear, rdn over 2f out, ran on strongly for press ins last, closing at fin, just failed:
would have won in few more strides, regain winning ways soon: see 2836.
3226 **SHAMSAN** 2 [10] M Johnston 3-8-5 (62) J Fanning 4/1: 205223: 3 ch c Night Shift - Awayil (Woodman)   1   65
Prom, went on appr fnl 3f, hdd dist, no extra cl-home: ran 48hrs ago & remains in fine form: see 3226.
*3093 **PAARL ROCK** 9 [7] G Barnett 9-8-9 (56)(vis)(6ex) G Gibbons (7) 7/1: 003214: Led, hdd over 3f out,   1½   56
no extra appr fnl 1f: in gd heart: see 3093.
3141 **THORNTOUN GOLD** 7 [8] 4-7-13 (46) J Bramhill 10/1: 002355: Waited with, prog over 3f out,   1   44
sltly outpcd over 1f out, ran on ins last, no dngr: see 2970, 2875.
1927 **PAS DE PROBLEME** 58 [9] 4-9-4 (65) Dale Gibson 13/2: 153146: Front rank, drvn/onepcd appr fnl 1f.   nk   63
2080 **ARMENIA** 31 [3] 3-8-1 (58) T Williams 33/1: 432007: Handy, chal ldrs over 3f out, wknd qckly   1¾   53
fnl 2f: 7 wk abs: see 882 (seller, AW).
2883 **DIAMOND FLAME** 18 [6] 6-8-3 (50)(1ow) R Winston 12/1: -00048: Dwelt, hdwy halfway, btn fnl 2f.   hd   45
2379 **AREISH** 39 [11] 7-8-1 (48) J Edmunds 40/1: 135609: Nvr dngrs: turf return: see 2121, 611.   6   34
3217 **FOREST QUEEN** 2 [5] 3-7-11 (54) P M Quinn (3) 50/1: -00000: Al bhd, 10th: ran 48hrs ago.   5   33
2758 **HARLEQUIN DANCER** 23 [1] 4-9-4 (65) Paul Eddery 25/1: 0-0000: Sn bhd, fin last: see 1445.   hd   44
11 ran   Time 2m 16.85 (6.85)   (J D Graham)   B A McMahon Hopwas, Staffs.

3286   7.35 COUNTRYWIDE COND STKS 2YO (C)   6f str   Good 53 -04 Slow
£6069   £2244   £1122   £510

2849 **WHERES JASPER** 20 [2] K A Ryan 2-9-2 J Carroll 7/4: 21201: 6 ch g Common Grounds - Stifen (Burslem)   94
Sn led, rdn over 2f out, edged right ins last, drvn out: earlier won here at Haydock (mdn): cost 18,000gns,
related to sev wnrs: eff at 5/6f, 7f cold suit: acts gd/soft & a gall trk, likes Haydock: tough & useful.
*2886 **GALAPAGOS GIRL** 18 [5] B W Hills 2-8-11 K Darley 10/11 FAV: -12: 2 b f Turtle Island - Shabby   3   80
Doll (Northfields) Settled mid-div, rdn, switched over 2f out, hung badly left for press over 1f out, styd on
but no ch with wnr: lost ch by hanging today, shade better on debut in 2886.
*3174 **FOLEY MILLENNIUM** 5 [3] M Quinn 2-9-2 Paul Eddery 6/1: 513413: 2 ch c Tagula - Inshirah (Caro)   nk   84
Trkd wnr thr'out, drvn/no extra appr fnl 1f: clr rem: qck reapp & remains in gd form: see 3174 (5f, fast).
-- **IRIDESCENT** [1] W M Brisbourne 2-8-3 J Fanning 33/1: 4: Rear, nvr dngrs: debut: Feb foal,   6   56
half-sister to a 5f 2yo scorer, dam won over 6f: shld improve for this experience.
2966 **ANTHONY ROYLE** 14 [4] 2-8-11 D Allan (7) 25/1: 665: Chsd ldrs, hung badly left over 2f out &   nk   64
sn lost tch: stiff task, needs sellers: see 2664.
5 ran   Time 1m 14.7 (3.4)   (Jimm Racing)   K A Ryan Newmarket.

3287   8.05 EBF MDN 2YO (D)   7f30y rn   Good 53 -09 Slow
£4101   £1262   £631   £315

2468 **ZELOSO** 35 [2] J L Dunlop 2-9-0 J F Egan 2/1 FAV: -03021: 2 b c Alzao - Silk Petal (Petorius)   85
Led, styd on strongly fnl 2f, rdn out: plcd twice prev: 72,000gns Jan foal, half-brother to 4 wnrs, dam useful
7f/1m wnr: eff at 6/7f, 1m shld suit: acts on fast, gd/soft & a gall/gall trk: rate more highly & win again.
-- **SKY QUEST** [1] P W Harris 2-9-0 A Culhane 4/1: 2: 2 b c Spectrum - Rose Vibert (Caerleon)   1¾   81
Handy, rdn & chsd wnr fnl 2f, no impress ins last: Mar first foal, dam unrcd: sire high-class at 1m/10f:
eff at 7f on gd grnd: promising debut, holds some big race entries & lks sure to win a mdn soon.
3003 **DREAMIE BATTLE** 13 [8] R Hollinshead 2-8-9 P M Quinn (3) 50/1: 33: 2 b f Makbul - Highland Rossie   1¾   73
(Pablond) Bhd, drvn & ran on well fnl 2f, no impress on front 2: much imprvd run today on this step up to
7f, shld apprec 1m: handles gd grnd: nursery h'caps shld suit in time: see 3003.
2649 **QUI WARRANTO** 28 [6] J G FitzGerald 2-9-0 J Carroll 20/1: 04: Slow start, rear, hdwy over 2f out,   hd   78
rdn/styd on, nvr nrr: stays a gall 7f on gd but bred to come into his own over mid-dists next term: see 2649.
3020 **FRUIT PUNCH** 12 [5] 2-8-9 R Winston 11/2: 55: Wide/mid-div, drvn/onepcd over 1f out: btr 3020.   3½   67
-- **REVIEWER** [3] 2-9-0 K Darley 10/3: 6: Dwelt, sn in tch, rdn/no extra appr fnl 1f: Feb foal, brother   1½   69
to a high-class juv, dam well related gd/soft wnr: with J Gosden, sure to know more next time & will improve.
2926 **BOLLIN THOMAS** 16 [7] 2-9-0 G Duffield 20/1: 07: Cl-up to halfway, sn rdn/btn: see 2926.   ½   68$
3039 **MY PLACE** 11 [4] 2-8-9 Paul Eddery 10/1: 38: Trkd ldrs, wknd 2f out, eased when btn: btr 3039.   ½   62
8 ran   Time 1m 31.6 (4.5)   (Tom Wilson)   J L Dunlop Arundel, W.Sussex.

3288   8.35 WILMSLOW HCAP 3YO+ 0-70 (E)   1m30y   Good 53 +07 Fast   [66]
£3164   £904   £452   3 yo rec 7 lb

3192 **YOUNG ROSEIN** 4 [12] Mrs G S Rees 4-8-13 (51) J F Egan 16/1: 030061: 4 b f Distant Relative -   59
Red Rosein (Red Sunset) Prom, switched wide & ran on well to lead 2f out, strongly pressed ins last, drvn out:
qck reapp, best time of day: '99 wnr at Musselburgh (h'cap, rtd 57, first win): unplcd in '98 (fill mdn, flattered,
rtd 62): eff around 7f/1m on fast & gd grnd: handles a sharp or gall track.
2863 **YENALED** 19 [1] J S Goldie 3-8-9 (54) A Culhane 8/1: 162462: 3 gr g Rambo Dancer - Fancy Flight   hd   61
(Arctic Tern) Waited with, gd hdwy appr fnl 2f, ran on strongly to chall ins last, just failed: clr rem: gd
effort & back on a winning mark, can win again soon: see 1434.
3083 **SAFFRON** 9 [14] D Shaw 4-8-4 (42) T Williams 33/1: 000543: 4 ch f Alhijaz - Silver Lodge (Homing)   3   43
Rear, rdn/gd hdwy over 2f out, kept on but not pace of front 2 ins last: first time in the frame this term on

this step up to 1m, v well h'capped on old form: see 1842.

2844 **VICTORIET 20** [5]   A T Murphy 3-8-3 (48) R Winston 20/1: 550444: Rcd keenly, chsd ldrs, went on 3f out, hdd 2f out, onepace ins last: flattered 2844.   ¾ 48

2508 **WEETMANS WEIGH 34** [11] 7-10-0 (66) J Stack 12/1: 464065: Mid-div, rdn/styd on appr fnl 1f, nvr nrr: top-weight: on a fair mark but best on the all-weather: see 49.   2½ 61

3200 **KNAVES ASH 3** [8] 9-8-2 (40) K Dalgleish (5) 10/1: 600606: Waited with, gd hdwy when badly hmpd appr fnl 1f, ran on fnl 1f, no dngr: no luck here & would prob have fin 3rd with a clr run: also unlucky in 3200.   hd 35

2882 **PACIFIC ALLIANCE 18** [1] 4-9-9 (65) Dean McKeown 33/1: -34407: Led to 3f out, wknd qckly appr dist.   ¾ 55

2799 **FALLS OMONESS 21** [2] 6-8-9 (47) J Bramhill 14/1: 002008: Dwelt, late hdwy, no threat: btr 2062.   3½ 35

2380 **TIME TO WYN 39** [10] 4-8-8 (46) J Carroll 25/1: 000-09: Rear, late gains, no dgnr: '99 Carlisle wnr (class stks, rtd 63): '98 wnr at Beverley (sell nurs, rtd 61 at best): eff at 7f/1m, stays 10f: acts on firm, gd & a stiff trk, best with waiting tactics.   2 30

3054 **AL MABROOK 10** [17] 5-9-4 (56) F Lynch 33/1: -10000: Al bhd, 10th: best on AW, see 270.   hd 40

3083 **BODFARI ANNA 9** [3] 4-9-7 (59) (vis) K Darley 4/1 FAV: 031430: Mid-div, drvn/lost tch fnl 2f, 11th.   5 34

3200 **CITY FLYER 3** [13] 3-8-6 (51) (6ex) Paul Eddery 8/1: 060100: Prom, wknd qckly fnl 3f, 13th: qck reapp.   0

*2795 **MUST BE MAGIC 22** [4] 3-9-8 (67) (vis) S Whitworth 5/1: 634310: Mid-div, eff when badly hmpd & nrly went through rails 2f out, not recover & eased: 17th: ignore this run: see 2795.   0

1190 **NOBLE CYRANO 96** [18] 5-9-2 (54) J Fanning 11/1: 100040: Al well bhd, t.o.: fin last: 3 month abs.   0

3082 Sea Emperor 9 [15] 3-8-2 (47)(vis) G Duffield 16/1:   3129 Swynford Elegance 7 [7] 3-7-13 (44) D Mernagh(3) 25/1:

2831 Rimatara 21 [16] 4-8-10 (48) T Lucas 20/1:   3124 Colonel Sam 7 [6] 4-8-2 (40)(bl) Dale Gibson 16/1:

18 ran   Time 1m 44.19 (3.69)   (J W Gittins)   Mrs G S Rees Preston, Lancs.

Official Going   GOOD/FIRM (GOOD Places). Stalls: 6f - Far Side; 7f & 1m - Centre; 12f - Stands Side

---

3289   2.20 MORRISTON FILLIES MDN 3YO (D)   1m str   Good/Firm 38   -30 Slow
£3640   £1120   £560   £280

894 **BLOODY MARY 120** [6] R Hannon 3-8-11 Dane O'Neill 6/1: 234-01: 3 ch f Prince Of Birds - Royaltess (Royal And Regal) Made all, qcknd 2f out, ran on strongly, rdn out: long abs: plcd sev times in '99 (h'caps, rtd 70): eff at 7f/1m, v0 may suit: acts on gd & firm, runs well fresh: given a fine tactical ride from the front.   69

1447 **ADRIFT 80** [4] B Hanbury 3-8-11 L Newman 33/1: -002: 3 ch f Irish River - Dream Play (Blushing Groom) Chsd ldrs, rdn 2f out, switched dist, styd on well but not rch wnr: 12 wk abs: eff at 1m on fast grnd.   1¼ 65

-- **DUSTY SHOES** [1] D R C Elsworth 3-8-11 N Pollard 7/1: -3: 3 b f Shareef Dancer - Run Faster (Commanche Run) Rear, styd on fnl 2f under a kind ride, nvr nrr: op 5/1 on debut: eff at 1m on fast grnd, 10f will suit: not given a hard time today & sure to improve, esp over further.   1¼ 62

2232 **HATHEETHAH 44** [5] L M Cumani 3-8-11 J P Spencer 11/10 FAV: 0554: Trkd ldr going well, chall 2f out till no extra cl home: well bckd, 6 wk abs: worth a try in headgear: see 1857 (10f).   ½ 61

-- **PAPARAZZA** [2] 3-8-11 Pat Eddery 7/2: -5: Chsd ldrs, ev ch 2f out, grad fdd on debut: drifted from 9/4: bred to apprec 1m/10f: with P Harris & shld be capable of better.   5 51

2472 **ANGELAS PET 35** [3] 3-8-11 C Rutter 66/1: 066-66: Rear, bhnd fnl 2f, t.o.: flattered 2472 (6f).   23 1

4474) **CATALONIA 294** [7] M Fenton 5/1: 65-W: Withdrawn not under orders: ref to enter stalls, bckd from 6/1: twice rcd juv, 5th in a Doncaster mdn (rtd 78, trained by J Glover): half sister to a useful mid-dist wnr, dam scored over 12f: eff at 7f on soft grnd: with M Bell.   0

7 ran   Time 1m 44.59 (5.49)   (Gamahada Partners)   R Hannon East Everleigh, Wilts

---

3290   2.50 H S LESTER HCAP 3YO 0-70 (E)   1m4f   Good/Firm 38   +09 Fast   [76]
£3006   £925   £462   £231

3014 **AFTER THE BLUE 12** [4] M R Channon 3-9-4 (66) Craig Williams 7/2: 122451: 3 b c Last Tycoon - Sudden Interest (Highest Honor) Dwelt, came centre/stands side home str, prog to lead 2f out, rdn clr: nicely bckd, best time of day: earlier won at Nottingham (class stks), also plcd sev times: eff at 10/12f, 14f bhid suit: acts on firm & gd/soft grnd: handles a stiff/gall trk: likes to come off a strong pace & well ridden today.   79

*3073 **EXILE 9** [1] R T Phillips 3-9-7 (69) G Sparkes (7) 9/2: -25212: 3 b g Emperor Jones - Silver Venture (Silver Hawk) Chsd ldrs, led 3f out till 2f out, kept on but no ch with wnr: 4L clr 3rd, op 7/2: see 3073.   4 74

3125 **MARJEUNE 7** [9] P W Harris 3-9-5 (67) A Beech (5) 5/1: 41-023: 3 b f Marju - Ann Veronica (Sadler's Wells) Prom, rdn & onepcd fnl 2f: lightly rcd this term, shld win a h'cap: see 3125 (fill h'cap).   4 66

3073 **PINCHANINCH 9** [8] J G Portman 3-9-5 (67) S Carson(3) 8/1: 421244: Prom, ev ch 2f out, onepcd.   hd 66

2789 **SEEKING SANCTUARY 22** [10] 3-7-10 (44) J Lowe 11/2: 0-0045: Rear, hdwy 2f out, no impress fnl 1f.   ¾ 42

*3206 **FLYOVER 3** [2] 3-8-11 (59) (5ex) G Hind 3/1 FAV: -00516: Nvr better than mid-div: too sn after 3206?   ¾ 56

2889 **CITRUS MAGIC 18** [6] 3-9-3 (65) C Rutter 33/1: -4007: Nvr a factor on h'cap bow: see 1912.   ½ 61

2554 **MUCHANA YETU 32** [3] 3-8-9 (62) L Newman 14/1: 060658: Early ldr, chsd ldrs till btn 2f out: bckd from 25/1: clearly shown something at home: see 1177 (10f here).   1¾ 51

2727 **BLESS 24** [5] 3-7-10 (44)(vis)(1oh) D Kinsella (7) 25/1: 003309: Made most till 3f out, wknd into last.   1½ 36

9 ran   Time 2m 35.93 (3.53)   (Timberhill Racing Partnership)   M R Channon West Ilsley, Berks.

3291   3.20 LISTED SOVEREIGN STKS 3YO+ (A)   1m str   Good/Firm 38   -13 Slow
£14446   £5126   £2563   £1165   3yo rec 7lb

*2228 **HOPEFUL LIGHT 44** [2] J H M Gosden 3-8-7 Dane O'Neill 11/4: 1-4011: 3 b g Warning - Hope (Dancing Brave) Tried to make all, hdd ins last, forced head in front cl home in a driving fin: op 9/4, 6 wk abs: recent wnr here at Salisbury (stks): '99 Doncaster wnr (mdn, rtd 92): eff at 6/7f, stays 1m: acts on fast & hvy, handles a stiff/gall trk: runs well fresh: gelded since last run: useful, may go for a Gr race abroad.   110

+2670 **LATE NIGHT OUT 27** [1] W Jarvis 3-9-0 M Tebbutt 5/2: 24-012: 5 b g Lahib - Chain Dance (Shareef Dancer) Trkd ldr & rcd keenly, chall fnl 2f, led briefly ins last, just btn in a driving fin: nicely bckd: stays a stiff 1m: useful gelding, see 2670.   shd 109

-- **CRIMSON TIDE** [4] J W Hills 6-9-0 J P Spencer 8/1: 3150/3: 6 b h Sadler's Wells - Sharata (Darshaan) Rear, no room 2f out, switched dist, fin well but too late: op 6/1: missed '99, prev term won at Epsom (Gr 3, rtd 113): '97 wnr at Bath (stks), Dusseldorf & Capannelle (Gr 2, rtd 115): eff at 1m, stays 12f well: acts on firm & hvy grnd: handles any trk, likes a sharp one: smart colt, prob wnr with a clear run, spot on next time.   ¾ 108

3155 **SMART RIDGE 6** [3] K R Burke 3-8-7 Pat Eddery 11/8 FAV: 020234: Trkd ldrs, ev ch dist, no extra ins last: well bckd, qck reapp: useful, up in grade after 3155. ¾ **106$**
4 ran Time 1m 43.21 (4.11) (K Abdulla) J H M Gosden Manton, Wilts.

3292

3.50 DOUGLAS FILLIES MDN 2YO (D) 7f str Good/Firm 38 -03 Slow
£3815 £1174 £587 £293

-- **FANTASY RIDGE** [10] M R Channon 2-8-11 Craig Williams 5/1: -1: 2 ch f Indian Ridge - Footlight Fantasy (Nureyev) Held up, smooth hdwy to lead 2f out, pulled right away fnl 1f, v easily despite flashing tail: nicely bckd, gd juv time: Apr foal, half-sister to a couple of juv wnrs: dam a 7f wnr, sire a high-class sprinter: eff over a stiff 7f on fast grnd, runs well fresh: highly impressive, potentially high-class & one to follow. **91+**
-- **S W THREE** [7] M P Tregoning 2-8-11 J Lowe 33/1: -2: 2 b f Slip Anchor - Anna Karietta (Precocious) Slowly away, imprvd 2f out, styd on well under hands-and-heels riding, no ch with wnr: Apr foal, sister to a wnr abroad: half-sister to a couple of 7f/1m wnrs: dam a winning sprinter, sire a top-class mid-dist performer: eff at 7f, 1m+ will suit: handles fast grnd: plenty to like about this eye-catching debut, caught a tartar today. *8* **76+**
-- **PLANET GIRL** [16] J L Dunlop 2-8-11 D O'Donohoe 12/1: -3: 2 b f Mtoto - Galactic Miss (Damister) Slowly away, pushed in rear, kept on stdly fnl 1f, nrst fin: op 7/1: Feb foal, half-sister to mid-dist wnr Mowelga: dam a 10f wnr, sire a top-class mid-dists performer: eff over a stiff 7f on fast grnd, mid-dist bred & will relish 1m+ now: stable's juv invariably improve for first effort & one to keep a close eye on in mdns over further. *1* **74+**
-- **CAPE COD** [12] J W Hills 2-8-11 M Tebbutt 12/1: -4: Rear, switched 2f out, styd on fnl 1½f, nrst fin on debut: May foal, cost 38,000gns: sister to smart miler Abeyr, half-sister to a 6/7f juv scorer: sire a top-class mid-dist performer: eff at 7f on fast grnd, 1m+ will suit: sure to benefit from this promising debut. *1½* **71+**
-- **PUFFIN** [6] 2-8-11 J P Spencer 8/1: -5: Mid-div, styd on fnl 1f under minimal press, nvr nrr on debut: op 5/1, shorter priced stablemate of 3rd: Apr foal, half-sister to useful miler Inglenook: dam a mid-dist/stayer, sire a top-class miler: looks sure to apprec 1m+ given time: looks certain to benefit from this run. *½* **70**
2748 **IT GIRL 23** [5] 2-8-11 G Hind 9/1: -246: Rear, improving when short of room dist, no ch after. *1¾* **66**
2390 **EXOTIC FAN 38** [3] 2-8-11 N Pollard 8/1: -47: Nvr far away, led 3f out till 2f out, no extra: big gamble from 25/1: imprvd effort, prob found a hot race here: see 2390. *hd* **66**
2259 **TOUCHY FEELINGS 44** [11] 2-8-11 Dane O'Neill 11/4 FAV: -38: Prom, ev ch 2f out, fdd: 6 wk abs: better expected after promising debut in 2259. *1* **64**
-- **FLASH OF LIGHT** [14] 2-8-11 C Rutter 25/1: -9: Slowly away, nvr a factor on debut: May foal, cost IR 13,500gns: half-sister to numerous wnrs abroad: dam a 2yo wnr in Ireland: sire a high-class 1m/10f performer. *nk* **63**
3020 **ST FLORENT 12** [8] 2-8-11 R Havlin 10/1: -200: Slowly away, nvr nr ldrs: see 2316 (debut). *½* **62**
2810 **KWAHERI 21** [13] 2-8-11 L Newman (3) 9/1: -R040: Speed 4f, fdd into 11th: see 2810. *1¾* **58**
2583 **GOLDEN BEACH 30** [15] 2-8-11 P Doe 50/1: -000: Led 4f, wknd into 12th: see 1876. *hd* **58**
-- **SUPER VALUE** [9] 2-8-11 Pat Eddery 4/1: -0: Speed 4f, wknd: fin 13th, debut, nicely bckd: Mar foal, half-sister to a French 1m scorer: dam from a gd family, sire a smart 6f/1m performer: with Mrs A Perrett. *1¾* **54**
-- **TAMILIA** [2] 2-8-11 J D Smith 50/1: -0: Nvr a factor on debut, fin 14th. *1¾* **50**
-- **SUNDOWN** [1] 2-8-11 R Perham 20/1: -0: V slowly away, imprvd to hold ch 2f out, sn btn & fin last, eased considerably: stablemate of rnr-up. *5* **40**
15 ran Time 1m 28.43 (2.93) (Helena Springfield Ltd) M R Channon West Isley, Berks.

3293

4.20 S JOSEPH FILLIES HCAP 3YO+ 0-70 (E) 6f str Good/Firm 38 -09 Slow [65]
£3136 £965 £482 £241 3yo rec 4lb

2978 **DAYS OF GRACE 14** [13] L Montague Hall 5-9-1 (52) C Rutter 5/2 FAV: 200531: 5 gr m Wolfhound - Inshirah (Caro) Nvr far away, went on 2f out, ran on strongly, rdn out: hvly bckd from 4/1: earlier won at Southwell & W'hampton (fill h'caps, rtd 69a): '99 Southwell & W'hampton wnr (h'caps, rtd 62a & 56): eff at 7f, prob just best at 5/6f: acts on firm, hvy grnd & on both AWs: handles any trk, likes Southwell & W'hampton: gd weight carrier: v tough & consistent, well h'capped on turf & could follow up. **62**
3046 **BRAMBLE BEAR 11** [3] M Blanshard 6-8-12 (49) G Hind 11/2: 040332: 6 b m Beveled - Supreme Rose (Frimley Park) Waited with, imprvd 2f out, chall dist, not pace of wnr ins fnl 1f: op 7/1: another consistent run. *2½* **51**
2976 **WAFFS FOLLY 14** [12] D J S ffrench Davis 5-9-0 (51) Craig Williams 7/1: -00353: 5 b m Handsome Sailor - Shirl (Shirley Heights) Nvr far away, ev ch 1f out, no extra cl-home: fair effort: see 2230 (C/D), 1082. *nk* **52**
2978 **FLEETING FANCY 14** [5] S Dow 3-8-12 (53) P Doe 16/1: 300504: Rdn in rear, imprvd 1f out, nvr nrr. *1¼* **50**
2980 **DANCING LILY 14** [11] 3-8-2 (43) R Brisland(5) 20/1: 000205: Mid-div, eff 2f out, not pace to chall. *¾* **37**
2885 **ENDYMION 18** [4] 3-9-7 (62) L Newman (3) 10/1: 003046: Chsd ldrs till onepcd fnl 1½f: see 2885. *nk* **55**
3161 **ZOENA 6** [6] 3-9-0 (55) S Carson(3) 14/1: 045637: Chsd ldrs, no room halfway, effort & btn dist, drifted right: qck reapp since 3161 (5f). *½* **47**
2978 **MAGIQUE ETOILE 14** [2] 4-9-2 (53) M Tebbutt 10/1: 622668: Nvr nr ldrs: best 2230. *1* **42**
3046 **STRIDHANA 11** [10] 4-9-4 (55)(VIS) N Pollard 9/1: -00409: Chsd ldrs, ev ch 2f out, wknd: 1st time visor. *½* **43**
2794 **SKYLARK 22** [14] 3-9-10 (65) Dane O'Neill 10/1: 465300: Nvr a factor in 10th: jt top-weight. *1¼* **49**
2654 **PALO BLANCO 28** [1] 9-9-3 (54) J P Spencer 13/2: 324620: Al bhd, fin 11th: much btr 2654. *6* **20**
2036 **BALIDARE 53** [9] 3-8-0 (41)(4ow)(5oh) Sophie Mitchell 33/1: 0-0000: Led till halfway, wknd & fin 12th: 8 wk abs, stiffish task: modest form. *2½* **1**
3056 **TOPLESS IN TUSCANY 10** [8] 3-9-10 (65) Darren Williams (5) 50/1: -03600: Speed to halfway, fin last: jt top-weight: well below 2472 (gd/soft grnd). *1¾* **20**
13 ran Time 1m 14.95 (2.85) (Stephen & Michelle Bayless) L Montague Hall Tadworth, Surrey.

3294

4.50 HANDS&HEELS APPR HCAP 3YO+ 0-70 (E) 7f str Good/Firm 38 -13 Slow [67]
£2704 £832 £416 £208 3yo rec 6lb

2974 **KNOBBLEENEEZE 14** [4] M R Channon 10-8-2 (41)(vis) M Mathers (6) 8/1: 005241: 10 ch g Aragon - Proud Miss (Semi Pro) Chsd ldrs, eff 2f out, ran on strongly to lead fnl 50yds, won going away: failed to win in '99, rnr-up on reapp (rtd 63, stks): '98 wnr at Newbury (h'cap, rtd 69 at best): '97 Ripon & Ayr wnr (h'caps): eff at 7f/1m: acts on firm, relishes gd/soft & hvy grnd: handles any trk, likes Newbury: best in a visor. **42**
2749 **LAW COMMISSION 23** [2] D R C Elsworth 10-9-12 (65) R Thomas(3) 11/4: -60142: 10 ch g Ela Mana Mou - Adjala (Northfields) Dwelt, prog 3f out, short of room 2f out, fin fast but too late: op 4/1, top-weight. *1* **65**
2690 **ALHUWBILL 27** [3] J J Bridger 5-7-12 (37) D Kinsella (3) 20/1: -60043: 5 b g Full Extent - Hale Lane (Comedy Star) Chsd ldrs, imprvd to lead briefly ins fnl 1f, no extra cl-home: ran to v best, stays a stiff 7f. *nk* **36**
2980 **AEGEAN FLOWER 14** [9] R M Flower 3-8-4 (49)(bl) M Worrell(3) 14/1: 000034: Led till ins last, no extra. *nk* **47**
3144 **ARZILLO 6** [6] 4-8-10 (49)(1ow) P Shea 14/1: 040305: Prom, ev ch dist, no extra cl-home: qck reapp. *¾* **45**
2974 **MY MAN FRIDAY 14** [7] 4-8-0 (39) Michael Doyle (3) 8/1: 00-006: Prom, wknd fnl 1f: bckd from 16/1. *¾* **33**

SALISBURY FRIDAY AUGUST 11TH Righthand, Galloping Track, Stiff Finish

2661 **SHERATON HEIGHTS 28** [10] 3-8-9 (54) Cheryl Nosworthy (9) 14/1: 560-07: Pushed in rear, not pace to chall: op 10/1: will apprec stronger handling: see 2661. *2* **44**
3251 **FLASHFEET 1** [11] 10-7-10 (35)(1oh) R Naylor(3) 50/1: 060008: Nvr a factor: ran yesterday. *¾* **23**
2303 **SCISSOR RIDGE 42** [5] 8-8-7 (46) D Glennon 10/1: 306059: Chsd ldrs 5f, wknd: 6 wk abs, shorter priced stablemate of 3rd: see 2303. *1¼* **31**
3115 **BLUE ACE 7** [1] 7-8-10 (49) A Hall (9) 14/1: 666460: Well bhd, some late prog, nvr dngrs in 10th. *1½* **31**
*3129 **LIONS DOMANE 7** [8] 3-8-2 (47)(6ex) G Sparkes 15/8 FAV: 260610: Chsd ldr 5f, wknd into last: disapp after 3129 & this came too soon? *¾* **27**
11 ran Time 1m 29.09 (3.59) (Anthony Andrews) M R Channon West Isley, Berks.

NEWMARKET (July) FRIDAY AUGUST 11TH Righthand, Stiff, Galloping Track

Official Going GOOD TO FIRM. Stalls: Stands Side.

3295 **5.45 MYKAL HCAP 3YO+ 0-90 (C) 2m24y Firm 15 +05 Fast [85]**
£6760 £2080 £1040 £520

3171 **VIRGIN SOLDIER 5** [3] M Johnston 4-10-0 (85) D Holland 2/1 FAV: 102421: 4 ch g Waajib - Never Been Chaste (Posse) Prom, led appr fnl 3f, hung left und press dist, held on well: hvly bckd, gd time, qk reapp, front 2 clr: earlier won at Newcastle (h'cap): '99 wnr at Lingfield (2, h'caps, rtd 84a), Musselburgh (h'cap, rtd 58), Southwell & W'hampton: plcd in '98 (mdn, rtd 62, T Etherington): eff at 12f, suited by 2m, prob stays 2½m: acts on firm, gd/soft, both AWs, any trk: runs well fresh, without blnks & can carry big weights: progressive. **93**
2953 **GENEROUS WAYS 14** [9] E J Alston 5-8-2 (56)(3ow) D McGaffin (0) 10/1: 540102: 5 ch g Generous - Clara Bow (Coastal) Rear, closed appr fnl 3f, drvn to press wnr dist, held nr fin: 8L clr rem, back to best: 8lbs o/w proved very costly: deserves to win more h'caps: see 2173. *¾* **65**
2953 **LITTLE BRAVE 14** [1] J M P Eustace 5-8-4 (59)(2ow) D Sweeney 13/2: 051433: 5 b g Kahyasi - Littlemisstrouble (My Gallant) Prom, eff 2f out, onepace: consistent, see 2763. *8* **60**
3025 **HILL FARM BLUES 12** [7] Miss S E Baxter 7-8-4 (61) L Newton 6/1: 500024: Rear, wide prog 3f out, sn same pace: grnd faster than ideal, see 809. *2* **58**
*2812 **BID ME WELCOME 21** [6] 4-9-9 (80) J Reid 11/2: 052315: Chsd ldrs, fdd ent fnl 2f: btr 2812. *5* **73**
1170} **CANDLE SMILE 464** [4] 8-9-4 (75) J Fortune 12/1: 6/20-6: Led till appr fnl 3f, lost pl: reapp: rnr-up 1st of just 2 '99 starts (h'cap, rtd 87): last won in '96 at Ayr & Goodwood (rtd h'cap, rtd 94, Sir M Stoute): eff at 14f, stays 2m4f on firm, gd/soft & any trk: gd weight carrier, forces the pace: v well h'capped now. *6* **63**
1222 **MAZZELMO 93** [2] 7-8-5 (62) Pat Eddery 11/1: 1-0507: Al towards rear: 3 month abs, see 876. *8* **44**
3025 **ALHAWA 12** [5] 7-9-10 (81) J Weaver 6/1: 25B048: Al bhd: bckd, won this in '99 (off 5lbs lower). *3½* **60**
2812 **WOODYS BOY 21** [8] 6-8-3 (60) A Daly 12/1: 31/56P: Prom when pulled up after 1m, lame: see 2131. **0**
9 ran Time 3m 24.1 (1.6) (J David Abell) M Johnston Middleham, N Yorks

3296 **6.15 MINERAL STAR SELLER 2YO (E) 7f str Firm 15 -45 Slow**
£3445 £1060 £530 £265

2903 **CHAUNTRY GOLD 17** [2] B J Meehan 2-8-11 Pat Eddery 10/11 FAV: 00321: 2 b g Desert Style - Ervedya (Doyoun) Sn led, easily made rest: hvly bckd, sold for 18,000 gns, slow time: plenty in hand: 6,000 gns Apr gldg: eff at 7f, will stay further: acts on firm grnd, stiff/gall trk & forcing the pace: prob better than a seller. **77**
3128 **TIP THE SCALES 7** [6] R M Whitaker 2-8-11 (vis) A Mackay 12/1: 0502: 2 b g Dancing Spree - Keen Melody (Sharpen Up) Well plcd, rdn appr fnl 1f, outpcd by wnr: quick reapp: gets 7f on firm. *3* **65**
2214 **GAME MAGIC 45** [5] R Hannon 2-8-11 J Fortune 15/8: 443: 2 b c Mind Games - Mia Fillia (Formidable) Early ldr, bhd ldrs, not much room appr fnl 1f & hung left, onepace: hvly bckd, abs: prob stays 7f. *shd* **65**
2599 **STAR BRIEF 30** [7] W J Musson 2-8-11 L Newton 16/1: 04: Held up, short of room ent fnl 2f, nvr dngrs. *2½* **58**
2898 **SUGAR ROLO 17** [3] 2-8-6 D McGaffin (3) 20/1: 65: Dwelt, in tch, hung left 3f out & fdd bef dist. *1¼* **49**
2599 **BROUGHTON STORM 30** [8] 2-8-11 P McCabe 25/1: -006: Keen, well plcd & ch till hung right bef fnl 1f. *5* **39**
2898 **PELLI 17** [4] 2-8-7(1ow) J Quinn 20/1: -0037: Keen, chsd ldrs till 2f out: stiff task, see 2898. *½* **34**
7 ran Time 1m 28.08 (4.18) (J S Dunningham) B J Meehan Upper Lambourn, Berks

3297 **6.45 B LLOYD HCAP 3YO+ 0-85 (D) 6f Firm 15 +04 Fast [82]**
£4182 £1287 £643 £321 3 yo rec 4 lb

2961 **BAHAMIAN PIRATE 14** [10] D Nicholls 5-9-10 (78) L Dettori 5/4 FAV: 112221: 5 ch g Housebuster - Shining Through (Deputy Minister) Chsd ldrs, rdn appr fnl 1f, kept on to lead towards fin: well bckd, fair time: deserved, rnr-up thrice since wins at Carlisle & Southwell (h'caps, rtd 75a): '99 Ripon wnr (mdn, rtd 72): eff at 5/6f, stays 7f: acts on firm, gd grnd & fibresand, any trk: goes well fresh: progressive & tough. **87**
1871 **RUSHCUTTER BAY 60** [4] P L Gilligan 7-9-9 (77) D Harrison 16/1: 0-2602: 7 br g Mon Tresor - Llwy Bren (Lidhame) Nvr far away, led below dist, hdd fnl 100y: 9 wk abs: had the rest covered & is nicely h'capped. *nk* **84**
3243 **SOAKED 2** [2] D W Chapman 7-8-2 (56)(bl)(6ex) J Quinn 13/2: R21133: 7 b g Dowsing - Water Well (Sadler's Wells) Cl-up, led after halfway till ent fnl 1f, onepace: 4th run in 5 days & is holding his form v well. *2* **57**
-- **DANES LADY** [1] E J Alston 4-9-2 (70) W Supple 33/1: 2104-4: Chsd ldrs, unable to qckn appr fnl 1f: promising Brit bow, abs: ex-Irish, '99 wnr at Roscommon (7f mdn on fast grnd): return to 7f will suit. *1¾* **66**
2631 **COLD CLIMATE 29** [6] 5-8-1 (55)(vis) A Daly 12/1: 000405: Bhd, late hdwy, nvr a threat: capable of better, won this in '99 off a 3lbs higher mark: see 2431, 1028. *1* **48**
2704 **DOUBLE SPLENDOUR 26** [7] 10-9-3 (71) J Weaver 20/1: -00006: Al around mid-div: see 1840. *1¾* **59**
*1783 **LAKELAND PADDY 64** [3] 3-9-8 (80) D Sweeney 16/1: 336417: In tch, eff after halfway, no impress. *hd* **68**
2813 **SLUMBERING 21** [13] 4-9-2 (70)(bl) Pat Eddery 9/1: 006348: Led till after halfway, fdd bef dist: tchd 12/1. *¾* **56**
2961 **LAS RAMBLAS 14** [8] 3-9-8 (80)(vis) J Reid 11/2: 004239: Dwelt, al towards rear: 2nd time visor. *¾* **64**
3044} **DOUBLE BOUNCE 377** [11] 10-9-2 (70) J Tate 33/1: /060-0: Chsd ldrs till appr fnl 2f: 10th on reapp: lightly rcd in '99 (rtd 73): last won way back in '96 at Newcastle (h'cap, rtd 90, P Makin): best at 6f, poss stays 7f on firm, gd/soft, handles hvy: with H Morrison. *nk* **53**
2355 **SARSON 40** [14] 4-9-11 (79) J Fortune 25/1: 00-000: Chsd ldrs till hung left under press & wknd 2f out: 11th, 6 wk abs: better at 5f & lks well h'capped nowadays, see 1676. *1* **59**
3238 **GUEST ENVOY 2** [9] 5-7-10 (50)(6oh) J Mackay (5) 33/1: 505460: Dwelt, nvr in it: 12th, ran 48hrs ago. *hd* **30**
2961 **Bintang Timor 14** [15] 6-9-0 (68) L Newton 14/1: 1682 **Woodlands 69** [12] 3-9-13 (85) R Cochrane 20/1:
3123 **Luanshya 7** [5] 4-8-11 (65) D Holland 16/1: P

NEWMARKET (July)   FRIDAY AUGUST 11TH   Righthand, Stiff, Galloping Track

15 ran   Time 1m 11.64 (0.64)   (H E Lhendup Dorji)   D Nicholls Sessay N Yorks

3298

7.15 CITY TRUCK MDN 2YO (D)   7f str   Firm 15 -35 Slow
£4163   £1281   £640   £320

2649 **EMMS 28** [4] P F I Cole 2-9-0 J Fortune 8/15 FAV: 231: 2 gr c Fastness - Carnation (Carwhite)   94
Made most till appr fnl 1f, led again below dist, edged right, rdn out: hvly bckd: last time plcd bhd 2 subs wnrs:
half brother to a miler: eff at 7f, 1m is going to suit: acts on firm/fast, handles soft, stiff/gall trks: improving.

-- **MUQTADI** [3] J H M Gosden 2-9-0 R Hills 7/2: 2: 2 b c Marju - Kadwah (Mr Prospector)   ¾ 91+
Dwelt, clsd trav well halfway, led bef dist & shkn up, hdd ins last & kept on same pace: fine debut, clr of 3rd:
Feb foal, half-brother to a cple of decent juvs at 6f/1m: dam 1m/10f wnr: eff at 7f, stay further in time:
acts on firm grnd, stiff/gall trk: mdn looks a formality & shld go on to better things.

-- **STEEL BAND** [6] H Candy 2-9-0 D Harrison 12/1: 3: 2 b c Kris - Quaver (The Minstrel)   2½ 86
Handy, eff appr fnl 1f, not pace of front pair: sound debut: dam 7f wnr: gets 7f on firm & shld pick up a mdn.

-- **KINGS OF EUROPE** [7] B W Hills 2-9-0 M Hills 11/2: 4: Dwelt, ran green in rear, styd on ins last: 1 84+
300,000gns Rainbow Quest Feb foal, half-brother to sev wnrs, notably Oaks heroine Jet Ski Lady: bred in the
purple & shld come into his own over mid-dists next term: improvement almost certain.

-- **DR STRANGELOVE** [10] 2-9-0 J Reid 14/1: 5: Chsd lrds, outpcd appr fnl 1f: stablemate 4th: 1 82
145,000 gns Dr Devious Feb foal, half-brother to a couple of decent juv sprinters: some promise here.

3003 **BENEVOLENCE 13** [8] 2-8-9 N Callan 33/1: 046: Handy, hmpd appr fnl 2f & no extra: qual for h'caps.   1¾ 73
-- **LAMBAY RULES** [9] 2-9-0 F Norton 25/1: 7: Al bhd: IR 70,000gns Dr Devious Feb foal, bred for 10f+.   2 74
2619 **EXPLOSIVE 29** [1] 2-9-0 S Sanders 66/1: 08: Front rank, ev ch till fdd appr fnl 2f: highly tried.   1¾ 70
-- **MARTINS SUNSET** [2] 2-9-0 Pat Eddery 20/1: 9: Chsd lrds till appr fnl 2f: 44,000 gns Royal   3½ 64
Academy Apr foal, half-brother to 5 sprinters: with W Muir.

-- **ROYAL SATIN** [9] 2-9-0 J Quinn 33/1: 0: Sn struggling: 10th: 28,000 gns Royal Academy colt.   23 34
10 ran   Time 1m 27.37 (3.47)   (Sir George Meyrick)   P F I Cole Whatcombe, Oxon

3299

7.45 DR MARTENS NURSERY HCAP 2YO (D)   7f str   Firm 15 -27 Slow   [89]
£4143   £1275   £637   £318

2683 **PALATIAL 27** [6] J R Fanshawe 2-9-7 (82) D Harrison 2/1: 2221: 2 b f Green Desert - White Palace   90
(Shirley Heights) Bhd lrds, qcknd to lead when gap appeared below dist, ran on well: well bckd, wng h'cap bow:
rnr-up all 3 prev starts over 6f: clrly suited by step up to 7f, acts on firm & gd grnd, stiff/gall or sharp trk.

2894 **PATHAN 18** [5] S P C Woods 2-9-1 (76) B Marcus 8/1: 05142: 2 b c Pyramus - Langton Herring   nk 81
(Nearly A Hand) Well plcd, led appr fnl 1f till ent fnl 1f, kept on: well clr rem & imprvd in defeat against
unexposed wnr: acts on firm & gd grnd: see 2653.

2948 **MONICA GELLER 14** [1] C N Allen 2-8-0 (61) G Bardwell 25/1: -06303: 2 b f Komaite - Rion River   4 59
(Taufan) Sn dsptng lead, ran green but ev ch till hung left appr fnl 1f & no extra: fair turf bow over longer
7f trip: worth another chance back at 6f: see 2635.

1954 **GROVE DANCER 57** [4] M H Tompkins 2-8-9 (70) S Sanders 7/1: 134: Cl-up & ev ch till hung left, rdn   1 66
& fdd appr fnl 1f: 8 wk abs, h'cap bow: unsuited by step up to 7f, easier grnd will suit: see 1612.

2886 **MAINE LOBSTER 18** [2] 2-9-2 (77) Pat Eddery 1/1 FAV: -0325: Narrow lead till appr fnl 1f, sn btn: nk 72
hvly bckd, h'cap bow: lkd ready for this step up to 7f, poss unsuited by forcing tactics: see 2886, 2285 (worked out).

2903 **MAID OF ARC 17** [3] 2-8-2 (63)(t) J Mackay (5) 10/1: 022446: Dwelt, al bhd: btr 2417.   10 38
6 ran   Time 1m 26.81 (2.91)   (Cheveley Park Stud)   J R Fanshawe Newmarket

3300

8.15 R BOLTON COND STKS 3YO+ (C)   1m2f   Firm 15 -08 Slow
£6249   £2370   £1185   £538   3yo rec 9 lb

2476 **REACH THE TOP 35** [7] J H M Gosden 3-8-7 J Fortune 6/1: 161: 3 b c Zafonic - Andaleeb (Lyphard)   106
Bhd lrds, shaken up appr fnl 2f, kept on to lead 1f out, styd on strongly: earlier won debut at Goodwood
(mdn): half-brother to Gr 1 wng juv filly Prophecy: eff at 1m, suited by this step up to 10f: acts on firm
& gd/soft grnd, stiff or sharp/undul trks: useful & progressive colt, worth a try in Listed/Group 3 company.

1752 **MASTERMIND 68** [3] P F I Cole 3-8-4 D Sweeney 4/1: 1-0402: 3 ch c Dolphin Street - Glenarff   1¼ 100
(Irish River) Prom, led appr fnl 2f till dist, hvld towards fin: 10 wk abs, nicely bckd, lkd to best: clrly
suited by the return to quicker grnd: met a v useful rival: see 1340, 1171.

4543 **AUTONOMY 287** [1] M L W Bell 3-8-7 M Fenton 9/2: -151-3: 3 b c Doyoun - Debbie's Next (Arctic   1 101
Tern) Held up in tch, prog to chall ent fnl 2f, same pace under press: reapp: '99 wnr at Sandown (mdn) & here
at Newmarket (stks, rtd 102): eff at 1m, stays 10f on firm & gd/soft, stiff/gall trks: runs well fresh: useful.

1592 **PEGNITZ 72** [6] C E Brittain 5-8-13 P Robinson 11/4 FAV: -04434: Led till ent fnl 3f, onepace: 1½ 96
nicely bckd, 10 wk abs: much btr 1592, 1174.

2578 **DYNAMIC DREAM 30** [2] 3-7-13 J Mackay (5) 9/2: 1-35: Held up, ev ch till appr fnl 2f, btn appr fnl 1f: Ingr trip.   4 85
1841 **GARDEN SOCIETY 62** [5] 3-8-7 Pat Eddery 4/1: 1336: Chsd lrds till appr fnl 2f: abs, btr 1841, see 1157.   ½ 92
6 ran   Time 2m 04.16 (2.26)   (K Abdulla)   J H M Gosden Manton, Wilts

ASCOT   SATURDAY AUGUST 12TH   Righthand, Stiff, Galloping Track

Official Going   GOOD/FIRM (GOOD Places). Stalls: Str Crse - Stands Side; Rnd Crse - Inside; except 1m - Centre

3301

1.30 SHERGAR DISTAFF RTD HCAP 3YO+ 0-105 (B)   6f str   Good/Firm 35 -00 Slow   [112]
£25000   £9000   £5000   £3500   3yo rec 4lb

-1833 **ROMANYLEI 63** [6] J G Burns 3-9-0 (102) M J Kinane 12/1: 1-6201: 3 gr f Blues Traveller -   105
Krayyalei (Krayyan) Rear, switched & prog 2f out, strong run to lead dying strides: op 10/1, fair time: Irish
raider, won both juv starts, at Cork & Naas (h'cap): eff at 5/6f on fast & gd/soft grnd: handles a stiff/gall trk:
v useful, speedy filly who showed a fine turn of foot here: cld win in List/Gr 3 company.

3120 **PRESENTATION 8** [9] R Hannon 3-8-5 (92)(1ow) G Hall 20/1: 266052: 3 b f Mujadil - Beechwood   nk 95
(Blushing Groom) Chsd lrds, prog to lead ent fnl 1f, v hard drvn when rider became unbalanced ins fnl 1f, caught
& eased slightly cl home: gd run & 1lb o/w proved v costly: rider given a lenient 4-day whip ban.

2997 **BOAST 14** [7] R F Johnson Houghton 3-8-9 (97) M Demuro 5/1: 635103: 3 ch f Most Welcome - Bay Bay   nk 98

(Bay Express) Chsd ldrs, chall strongly fnl 1f, just btn in a cl fin: well bckd: apprec return to 6f & ran to best.
2343 **ICICLE 42** [3] J R Fanshawe 3-9-3 (105) Pat Eddery 7/1: 4-0354: Rear, imprvng when short of room dist, fin well but too late: 6 wk abs: not much luck & a return to 7f will suit: one to keep in mind, see 2343. *1¼* **102**
3104 **CLARANET 9** [10] 3-8-7 (95) B Marcus 9/1: 100025: Front rank, led briefly dist, no extra cl home. *½* **91**
2646 **MAGIC OF LOVE 29** [1] 3-8-11 (99) T Quinn 11/2: -33046: Waited with, no room ver 1f out till ins last, no ch after: tchd 13/2: no room at any stage & this shld be forgiven: see 2646, 1830 (7f). *½* **94**
2669 **FLANDERS 28** [4] 4-9-3 (101) D M Oliver 10/1: 6-1007: Chsd ldrs, onepcd fnl 1f: all wins at 5f. *1½* **92**
3016 **SERAPHINA 13** [2] 3-8-12 (100) M Ebina 33/1: 203008: Rear, eff dist, nvr nr ldrs: btr 1833. *¾* **88**
1232 **DESERT MAGIC 96** [5] 4-9-7 (105) J Murtagh 5/1: 00-129: Set pace till dist, fdd: 3 month abs, top-weight: prev trained in Ireland by C Collins, now with N Clement: btr 1232, 1122. *1* **90**
4137} **ELAFLAAK 319** [8] 3-9-1 (103) L Dettori 4/1 FAV: 1110-0: Rear, rdn & btn over 1f out on reapp: well bckd, belated reapp: '99 wnr at Beverley & Newbury (2, inc List, rtd 100), bolted to start when unplcd in Gr 1 Cheveley Park: eff at 5/6f on fast/firm grnd: runs well fresh: smart filly, better than this. *¾* **85**
10 ran Time 1m 15.22 (2.12) (Mrs J A Dene) J G Burns The Curragh, Co Kildare

3302

2.05 SHERGAR STAYERS RTD HCAP 4YO+ 0-105 (B) 2m45y Good/Firm 35 -09 Slow [112]
£25000 £9000 £5000 £3500

*2153 **DOMINANT DUCHESS 50** [3] J W Hills 6-8-8 (92) T Quinn 11/4 FAV: 22-111: 6 b m Old Vic - Andy's Find (Buckfinder) Rear, prog 2f out, strong run to lead on line: well bckd, 7 wk abs: unbtn this term, prev scored at York (h'cap) & R Ascot (Queen Alexandra): '99 Kempton wnr (reapp), also rnr-up in Cesarewitch (rtd 85): eff at 14f, suited by 2m/2m6f: acts on gd & firm, any trk, likes Ascot: best caught fresh: useful stayer. **94**
2705 **SPIRIT OF LOVE 27** [5] M Johnston 5-9-7 (105) M Demuro 10/1: -03032: 5 ch g Trempolino - Dream Mary (Marfa) Chsd ldrs till lost pl 5f out, rallied 3f out, led well ins fnl 1f, just btn in a thrilling fin: fine run under top-weight, met a useful & progressive mare: may re-oppose today's wnr in the Doncaster Cup. *shd* **106**
2336 **BIENNALE 42** [4] Sir Michael Stoute 4-9-6 (104) J Murtagh 5/1: 3-4453: 4 b h Caerleon - Malvern Beauty (Shirley Heights) Hld up, prog to chall strongly fnl 1f, just btn in a 3-way photo: bckd, abs, stays 2m. *hd* **105**
*3171 **FANTASY HILL 6** [9] J L Dunlop 4-8-11 (95)(bl) Pat Eddery 7/2: 534014: Rcd keenly in tch, went on 2f out till ins last, not btn far in a v close fin: op 9/4, qck reapp: 2nd time blnks: see 3171. *1* **95**
2153 **EILEAN SHONA 50** [7] 4-8-13 (97) M Ebina 14/1: 1-0545: Prom, keeping on well & ev ch when badly hmpd dist, no ch after: 7 wk abs: wld have gone v close & must be given another chance: see 2153 (2m6f). *½* **96+**
3058 **AFTERJACKO 11** [6] 4-8-7 (91)(2oh) B Marcus 7/1: 120056: Rear, steady prog 2f out, ch dist, no extra cl home: poss not quite stay this longer 2m trip: shade unlucky over 14f in 3058. *1½* **88**
*2705 **KNOCKHOLT 27** [8] 4-8-13 (97) K Darley 8/1: -00017: Early ldr, led again after 6f till 2f out, hmpd dist & wknd: well clr of rem: front rnr, not disgraced: see 2705. *2½* **91**
2705 **ASHGAR 27** [1] 4-8-12 (96) L Dettori 14/1: 564048: Mid-div till btn 2f out, t.o.: see 2705. *19* **70**
2982 **HERBSHAN DANCER 15** [2] 6-8-7 (91)(43oh) J Saimee 200/1: 56025P: Led after 1f till 10f out, wknd qckly, t.o. & p.u. fnl 1f: dismounted: imposs task at today's weights: see 2268 (14f). **0**
9 ran Time 3m 33.08 (7.08) (Mrs Diana Patterson) J W Hills Lambourn, Berks.

3303

2.40 SHERGAR CUP SPRINT 3YO (B) 6f str Good/Firm 35 +05 Fast
£50000 £18000 £10000 £7000

1171 **BERNSTEIN 98** [1] A P O'Brien 3-8-12 M J Kinane 5/1: 115-01: 3 b c Storm Cat - La Affirmed (Affirmed) Nvr far away, forced head in front cl home, drvn out: best time of day, 3 month abs: prob not stay 1m when unplcd in 2000 Guineas earlier: '99 wnr at The Curragh (2, incl Gr 3, rtd 117): v eff at 6f on fast & gd/soft grnd: runs well fresh: smart sprinter, Haydock Stanley Leisure Sprint looks the target. **111**
+2847 **AUENKLANG 21** [4] Saeed bin Suroor 3-9-4 L Dettori 1/1 FAV: 121-12: 3 ch c Big Shuffle - Auenglocke (Surumu) Tried to make all, worn down cl home: hvly bckd, top-weight: fine eff with visor left off: will reoppose this wnr in the Haydock Sprint on 6lb better terms & must go close: see 2847. *hd* **116**
2960 **VITA SPERICOLATA 15** [2] J S Wainwright 3-8-7 J Saimee 33/1: -24033: 3 b f Prince Sabo - Ahonita (Ahonoora) Rear, hdwy when briefly short of room dist, chall strongly fnl 1f, just btn in a thrilling fin: 5L clr of 4th: career best run, shld win a List/Gr 3 with a repeat of this: see 2960 (5f). *nk* **104**
*2706 **AWAKE 27** [7] M Johnston 3-8-12 J Murtagh 25/1: 420314: Prom, ev ch dist, fdd ins last: stiff task. *5* **94**
2670 **BALLY PRIDE 28** [6] 3-8-12 M Ebina 40/1: 2-4035: Chsd ldrs till btn dist: btr 2670 (7f). *1* **91**
3076 **MISTER SUPERB 10** [8] 3-8-12 G Hall 100/1: 210636: Waited with, prog on outside halfway, v hard drvn & jockey again became unbalanced (as in first race) 2f out, btn dist: treat rating with caution: see 3076. *½* **90$**
3152 **TRINCULO 7** [9] 3-8-12 (BL) K Darley 25/1: 404007: Chsd ldrs 4½f, wknd: tried blnks. *nk* **89**
3172 **SELKING 6** [5] 3-8-12 T Quinn 12/1: 324028: In tch till btn dist: qck reapp: btr 3172. *3* **80**
*3120 **LITTLEFEATHER 8** [3] 3-8-7 Pat Eddery 5/2: 35-519: Rcd keenly in rear, wknd fnl 2f & fin last: well bckd: much better expected after 3120, rcd too keenly for own gd here. *½* **74**
9 ran Time 1m 14.94 (1.84) (Mr Tabor, Mrs Magnier & Mrs Maxwell Moran) A P O'Brien Ballydoyle, Co Tipperary

3304

3.15 SHERGAR CUP JUVENILE 2YO (B) 1m rnd Good/Firm 35 -33 Slow
£25000 £9000 £5000 £3500

-- **TURNBERRY ISLE** [1] A P O'Brien 2-8-12 M J Kinane 9/4 FAV: -11: 2 ch c Deputy Minister - Blush With Pride (Blushing Groom) Waited with, prog 2f out, led dist, held on gamely, drvn out: hvly bckd, 7 wk abs, Irish raider: landed a Gowran Park mdn on sole prev start: brother to a 9f juv wnr in the USA: eff at 7f/1m, mid-dists will suit: acts on gd & fast grnd, runs well fresh: smart colt, may be back here for the Royal Lodge. **104**
+2881 **VICIOUS KNIGHT 19** [3] L M Cumani 2-8-12 J Murtagh 6/1: -612: 2 b c Night Shift - Myth (Troy) Rear, imprvng when short of room 2f out till dist, fin strongly but just failed: fine run & prob unlucky: eff over a stiff 1m on gd & fast grnd: connections keen to take on today's wnr in the Royal Lodge & must run well. *nk* **103**
2613 **SHADOWLESS 30** [2] C E Brittain 2-8-12 J Saimee 13/2: -4023: 2 b c Alzao - Warning Shadows (Cadeaux Genereux) Hld up, not much room 2f out till dist, kept on but not pace of front 2: stays 1m: must win sn. *2* **99**
*2677 **FORWOOD 28** [6] M A Jarvis 2-8-12 K Darley 11/4: -114: Trkd ldrs, ev ch dist, no extra ins fnl 1f: well bckd: prob stays a stiff 1m: gd run on this step up in grade: see 2677 (7f here). *½* **98**
2848 **IMPERIAL DANCER 21** [9] 2-8-12 M Demuro 33/1: 130245: In tch, prog to lead briefly dist, no extra. *1¼* **95**
2848 **BLUEBERRY FOREST 21** [4] 2-8-12 Pat Eddery 5/1: -12226: Front rank, losing pl when hmpd dist, fdd. *5* **85**
2514 **SPIRIT HOUSE 35** [8] 2-8-12 B Marcus 20/1: -27: Prom, led 3f out till over 1f out, wknd: highly tried. *1¾* **81**
2921 **NORTHFIELDS DANCER 17** [7] 2-8-12 D M Oliver 25/1: -0228: Led 5f, wkng when hmpd dist: see 2921. *7* **66**
2935 **MUSIC MAID 16** [5] 2-8-7 G Hall 66/1: -61309: Chsd ldrs, wide into str, grad wknd & fin last. *2* **57**
9 ran Time 1m 43.95 (5.45) (Mrs John Magnier & Mr M Tabor) A P O'Brien Ballydoyle, Co Tipperary

ASCOT SATURDAY AUGUST 12TH Righthand, Stiff, Galloping Track

3305
3.50 EBF SHERGAR CUP OAKS 3YO+ (B) 1m4f **Good/Firm 35 -09 Slow**
£30000 £9000 £5000 £3500 3yo rec 11lb

2857 **SAILING** 21 [5] P F I Cole 3-8-9 D M Oliver 9/1: 214101: 3 ch f Arazi - Up Anchor (Slip Anchor) **112**
Trkd ldrs, prog to chall over 1f out, went on cl home, rdn out: earlier won at San Siro (2, incl Gr 3): '99 wnr at
Goodwood (fill mdn) & Sandown (stks, rtd 100): eff at 1m/12f on fast & hvy grnd: handles any trk: runs well
fresh, likes to run up with/force the pace: shld run well in the Park Hill Stakes at Doncaster.

2739 **LITTLEPACEPADDOCKS** 27 [1] M Johnston 3-8-6 K Darley 6/5 FAV: 1-3142: 3 b f Accordion - Lady In hd **107**
Pace (Burslem) Tried to make all, worn down cl home: well bckd, clr of 3rd: smart, gd run: see 2739, 1945.

2889 **SHAMAIEL** 19 [3] C E Brittain 3-8-6 M Ebina 33/1: -44043: 3 b f Lycius - Pearl Kite (Silver Hawk) 3½ **102$**
Trkd ldr till over 1f out, rdn & onepcd: offic rtd this rating with caution: see 2169 (10f).

2739 **MILETRIAN** 27 [2] M R Channon 3-8-11 T Quinn 3/1: 040164: Lost many lengths start, given time to 3 **103**
recover & in tch after 4f, no impress fnl 2f: nicely bckd: lost all ch at the start today: see 2112 (gd).

1459 **DIGNIFY** 83 [4] L Dettori 3/1: 310-45: In tch, rdn & btn 2f out: 12 wk abs: see 1459. 3½ **96**
5 ran Time 2m 34.36 (5.36) (H R H Prince Fahd Salman) P F I Cole Whatcombe, Oxon

3306
4.25 SHERGAR CUP CLASSIC 3YO+ (B) 1m4f **Good/Firm 35 +01 Fast**
£56000 £18000 £10000 £7000 3yo rec 11lb

2114 **ARCTIC OWL** 51 [1] J R Fanshawe 6-9-3 J Murtagh 9/2: 26-301: 6 b g Most Welcome - Short Rations **116**
(Lorenzaccio) Bhnd, imprvd 3f out, went on dist, held on gamely cl home, drvn out: fair time, 7 wk abs: '99 wnr
at Sandown (Gr 3, rtd 123), subs 2nd thrice in Gr company: '98 wnr at York (h'cap), Deauville (Gr 2) & Newmarket
(2, incl Gr 3, rtd 121): eff btwn 12f & 2m on fast & hvy grnd: handles any trk: high-class
gelding who can rate more highly: shld run well in the Irish St Leger.

*3134 **MURGHEM** 8 [2] M Johnston 5-9-3 B Marcus 7/4 FAV: 211112: 5 b h Common Grounds - Fabulous hd **115**
Pet (Somethingfabulous) Led 3f, remained prom till led again 3f out, collared dist, rallied & only just btn: hvly
bckd, clr of rem: remains in top form, hds for the Geoffrey Freer & ultimately the Melbourne Cup.

*2566 **LITTLE ROCK** 32 [6] Sir Michael Stoute 4-9-8 Pat Eddery 3/1: 1-1613: 4 b c Warning - Much Too 5 **112**
Risky (Bustino) Chsd ldrs, smooth prog 2f out, hit by wnrs whip, sn onepcd: bckd, top-weight, btr 2566.

1321 **MUKHALIF** 90 [3] Saeed bin Suroor 4-9-3 L Dettori 5/1: 210-04: In tch, ch dist, wknd: 3 month abs. 4 **101**
1848 **KINGSCLERE** 63 [4] 3-8-6 K Darley 6/1: 3-1505: Led after 3f, hdd 3f out, wknd qckly, t.o.: abs. 24 **71**
2336 **KUMATOUR** 42 [5] 5-9-3 J Saimee 20/1: 63-306: Trkd ldrs till wknd qckly 2f out, t.o.: 6 wk abs. 1 **70**
6 ran Time 2m 33.13 (4.13) (The Owl Society) J R Fanshawe Newmarket

REDCAR SATURDAY AUGUST 12TH Lefthand, Flat, Galloping Track

Official Going FIRM (GOOD TO FIRM PLACES) Stalls: Stands Side, except 1m6f - Centre.

3307
2.30 MARKET CROSS SELLER 2YO (F) 6f **Firm 17 -28 Slow**
£2310 £660 £330

2983 **DANCING PENNEY** 14 [8] K A Ryan 2-8-12 F Lynch 6/1: 001221: 2 b f General Monash - Penultimate Cress **62**
(My Generation) Al prom, rdn/led over 1f out, styd on well for press: no bid: earlier scored at Catterick (seller):
eff at 5/6f, 7f could suit: acts on firm, fast & fibresand, any trk: likes to race with/force the pace in sells.

2983 **LATE AT NIGHT** 14 [7] T D Barron 2-8-11 (bl) G Duffield 15/2: 00042: 2 b g Twilight Agenda - 1½ **56**
Fullocherries (Full Out) Led till over 1f out when wandered badly, rider lost whip but kept on ins last: also behind
this winner today: op 10/1: acts on firm & fast ground, eff in blnks: see 2983.

3145 **NEW WONDER** 7 [2] J G Given 2-8-6 N Pollard 11/10 FAV: 304203: 2 b f Presidium - Miss Tri Colour nk **50**
(Shavian) Keen/chsd ldrs, rdn/carried left over 1f out, held in last: hvly bckd: handles firm, soft & fibresand.

2928 **PETIT TOR** 17 [9] J Norton 2-8-6 O Pears 11/2: 425264: Prom, onepcd/held fnl 1f: op 9/2: btr 2441. ¾ **48**
2949 **MISS PROGRESSIVE** 15 [3] 2-8-6 J Fanning 15/2: 000025: Cl up, hampered over 1f out, fdd: btr 2949. 1¾ **44**
-- **FOREVER FABULOUS** [4] 2-8-11 D McGaffin (5) 12/1: 6: Sn rdn, nvr pace of leaders: op 7/1: Timeless ½ **47**
Times colt, Feb foal, cost 7500gns: brother to a 7f juv wnr: dam a 2yo wnr abroad: with W Jarvis.

2880 **RED OCARINA** 19 [10] J Stack 12/1: 07: Sn rdn/in tch, outpcd fnl 2f: lnger 6f trip, mod form. 12 **19**
1679 **TINY MIND** 70 [1] P Fessey 100/1: 0008: Dwelt, sn well bhd: 10 wk abs: no form. dist **0**
8 ran Time 1m 11.6 (2.7) (Robert Chambers) K A Ryan Hambleton, N Yorks

3308
3.00 EBF SHEPHERD FILLIES MDN 2YO (D) 7f str **Firm 17 -10 Slow**
£2834 £872 £436 £218

2806 **ELREHAAN** 22 [1] J L Dunlop 2-8-11 W Supple 1/3 FAV: 21: 2 b f Sadler's Wells - Moss (Woodman) **85**
Bhd ldrs, led going easily over 2f out, readily asserted with rider just steering fnl 2f: val for 10L+: heavily bckd:
confirmed debut promise: eff at 7f, bred to relish 1m+: acts on firm & fast, stiff/gall trk: can rate more highly.

3020 **PRINCESS TITANIA** 13 [3] N A Callaghan 2-8-11 F Lynch 9/2: 402: 2 b f Fairy King - Chiquelina 7 **70**
(Le Glorieux) Cl up, rdn fnl 3f, no ch with easy wnr: fin clr of rem: see 2683.

3039 **DANCING VENTURE** 12 [6] S P C Woods 2-8-11 G Duffield 11/2: 543: 2 b f Shareef Dancer - Adeptation 6 **60**
(Exceller) Led 4f, sn held: op 4/1: rated higher 3039 (gd/firm), 1957.

2862 **PENTAGON LADY** 20 [2] J L Eyre 2-8-11 R Cody Boutcher (7) 66/1: -00054: Held up in tch, held fnl 3f. 1¾ **57**
-- **TOP QUALITY** [5] 2-8-11 G Parkin 20/1: 5: Chsd ldrs 4f, sn btn: Simply Great filly, Feb foal, full 1¾ **54**
brother to high class chaser Simply Dashing, dam a winning hurdler: will need further in time.

2968 **FERNDOWN** 15 [4] 2-8-11 R Winston 66/1: 46: Prom till halfway: longer 7f trip, mod form. 5 **44**
6 ran Time 1m 23.7 (1.9) (Hamdan Al Maktoum) J L Dunlop Arundel, W Sussex

1022

3309
3.30 A HUMPHREYS HCAP 3YO+ 0-85 (D)   1m str   Firm 17   +09 Fast   [80]
£5170   £1591   £795   £397   3 yo   rec 7 lb

*2861 **THWAAB** 20 [5] F Watson 8-8-2 (54)(bl) G Duffield 5/2 JT FAV: -06111: 8 b g Dominion - Velvet Habit   58
(Habitat) Held up, rdn fnl 3f, drvn to chall dist, styd on gamely to lead nr line, all out: gd time: completed hat-
trick after h'cap wins at Carlisle & here at Redcar (C/D): unplcd last term (rtd 39): '98 Doncaster wnr (h'cap, rtd
62): eff at 7f/1m on gd/gd/soft, relishes firm & fast grnd: handles any trk, loves Redcar: eff with/without vis or blnks.
3011 **PENTAGON LAD** 13 [6] J L Eyre 4-9-8 (74) R Winston 4/1: 625142: 4 ch g Secret Appeal - Gilboa   shd   77
(Shirley Heights) Handy, efft/hmpd over 1f out, led 1f out, drvn/hung left & just hdd nr line: bckd, tough.
3054 **MEHMAAS** 11 [2] R E Barr 4-8-3 (55)(vis) P Fessey 10/1: 000053: 4 b g Distant Relative - Guest List (Be   2½   53
My Guest) Led hung right/hdd 1f out, sn held: op 12/1: vis reapplied: see 1920.
3159 **COURT EXPRESS** 7 [3] W W Haigh 6-9-13 (79) F Lynch 6/1: 205304: Held up, efft 2f out, held fnl 1f.   shd   77
2167 **LOVE YOU TOO** 49 [4] 3-9-9 (82) Paul Eddery 8/1: 0-0405: Cl up till over 1f out: abs: btr 1186 (7f).   5   70
3142 **GOLDEN CHANCE** 8 [1] 3-9-5 (78) J Fanning 5/2 JT FAV: 130426: Cl up 6f: btr 3142, 2955 & 2159.   1½   63
6 ran   Time 1m 35.4 (0.6)   (F Watson)   F Watson Sedgefield, Co Durham

3310
4.05 CASTLEFIELD MDN HCAP 3YO+ 0-75 (E)   1m2f   Firm 17   -14 Slow   [67]
£4111   £1265   £632   £316   3 yo   rec 9 lb

3167 **PETEURESQUE** 7 [4] T D Barron 3-9-7 (69) G Duffield 5/1 FAV: 200203: 3 ch g Petoski - Miss Ultimo   74
(Screen King) Chsd ldrs, rdn/prog to lead over 1f out, styd on well, rdn out: debut rnr-up in '99 (rtd 78, mdn):
eff at 10f, tried 12f, may yet suit: acts on firm & fast ground: likes a galloping track.
3082 **GLEN VALE WALK** 10 [10] Mrs G S Rees 3-7-10 (44)(2oh) J McAuley 13/2: 004022: 3 ch g Balla Cove -   1½   46
Winter Harvest (Grundy) Bhd, prog to chase ldrs over 1f out, styd on for press ins last, no threat to wnr: eff at
1m/10f on firm & gd/soft grnd: headgear could help: see 3082, 887.
2863 **STEPASTRAY** 20 [12] R E Barr 3-8-4 (52) P Fessey 8/1: 003633: 3 gr g Alhijaz - Wandering Stranger   2   51
(Petong) Rear, rdn/styd on fnl 3f, nrst fin: eff at 10/11f on firm and fast grnd: see 2863.
3140 **GARGOYLE GIRL** 8 [11] J S Goldie 3-7-13 (47) G Baker (5) 10/1: 455544: Rear, styd on fnl 3f for press.   nk   45
2958 **MINJARA** 15 [1] 5-7-12 (37) R Brisland (5) 11/2: 550045: Twds rear, kept on fnl 3f, no threat: bckd.   ½   34
3266 **NORTHERN ECHO** 2 [13] 3-8-6 (54) T Williams 25/1: 532006: Chsd ldrs, held 2f out: qck reapp: see 2731.1   50
2824 **MOON GLOW** 22 [2] 4-10-0 (67) Paul Eddery 10/1: 00-427: Led 4f out till over 1f out, fdd: see 2159 (1m).   nk   62
2353 **KELBURNE** 41 [14] 3-8-11 (59) F Lynch 16/1: -5448: Rear, eff at 10/11f out, no impress: abs, h'cap bow.   ½   53
2564 **FINAL LAP** 32 [7] 4-10-0 (67) D McGaffin (5) 16/1: 45-009: Mid-div, btn 2f out: see 56 (AW).   1¾   59
2671 **BUTTERSCOTCH** 28 [5] 4-8-6 (45) R Winston 9/1: 033500: Held up, held over 2f out: 10th: btr 1705.   hd   36
2888 **MONKEY BUSINESS** 19 [6] 3-9-4 (66) W Supple 10/1: 4-0600: Chsd ldrs 4f out, sn held: 11th: btr 1853.   3   53
3014 **EMPIRE DREAM** 13 [3] 3-9-11 (73) J Fanning 13/2: 42200: Led 6f, sn btn: 13th: btr 2560, 2222.   0
2930 **Pies Ar Us** 17 [9] 3-8-7 (55) P Goode (3) 50/1:   2611 **Shalbeblue** 30 [8] 3-9-4 (66) V Halliday 33/1:
14 ran   Time 2m 05.4 (3.1)   (J Baggot)   T D Barron Maunby, N Yorks

3311
4.40 M REVELEY CLAIMER 3YO+ (F)   1m6f   Firm 17   -17 Slow
£2769   £852   £426   £213   3 yo   rec 13lb

2436 **HULLBANK** 37 [8] W W Haigh 10-9-4 F Lynch 1/1 FAV: 5-1451: 10 b g Uncle Pokey - Dubavarna (Dubassoff)   50
Held up, al trav well, led 2f out, shaken up to readily extend, styd on strongly: hvly bckd: earlier won a Catterick
seller: '99 wnr here at Redcar (h'cap, rtd 68): '98 Southwell & Redcar wnr (h'caps, rtd 60a & 70): eff btwn 14f/2m
on firm, gd & fibresand: handles any trk, loves Redcar: gd weight carrier: well suited by clmrs/sells.
2826 **RIGHTY HO** 22 [3] W H Tinning 6-9-8 J McAuley 11/1: -00022: 6 b g Reprimand - Challanging (Mill Reef) 5   46
Led 2f, led again over 3f out till 2f out, sn held by wnr: clr rem: prob stys 14f: see 1272 (10f).
2742 **GO WITH THE WIND** 24 [6] R A Fahey 7-9-4 P Hanagan (7) 9/2: 203-03: 7 b g Unfuwain - Cominna   10   31
(Dominion) Held up, prog & ch 3f out, sn held: op 3/1: see 2742.
3084 **ULSHAW** 10 [1] J D Bethell 3-9-1 (vis) R Winston 20/1: 030004: Prom, held fnl 3f: see 3084, 2144.   3   37
1353 **CHARITY CRUSADER** 85 [5] 9-9-0 (bl) T Eaves (7) 9/1: 00-005: Led after 2f & sn clr, hdd over 3f out/sn   6   14
btn: recent jmps rnr (mod form): rnr-up twice in '99 (rtd 55, h'cap, c/d): '98 wnr at Musselburgh (h'cap, rtd 53):
suited by 14f/2m on firm and soft grnd, sharp/gall trk: suited by blnks.
3099 **SECONDS AWAY** 10 [4] 9-9-0 Dawn Rankin (7) 10/1: 343336: In tch 10f: op 8/1: see 2875, 1191.   1¼   12
3099 **LOYAL TOAST** 10 [2] 5-9-4 G Duffield 10/1: 053367: In tch till 4f out: see 2783, 670.   ½   15
2866 **RUNNING FREE** 20 [7] 6-9-10 O Pears 33/1: 145/08: Well bhd 4f out: see 2866.   28   0
8 ran   Time 3m 02.5 (4.7)   (Mrs V Haigh)   W W Haigh Melsonby, N Yorks

3312
5.15 GO RACING HCAP 3YO+ 0-60 (F)   6f   Firm 17   +02 Fast   [59]
£3250   £1000   £500   £250   3 yo   rec 4 lb

2721 **JOHAYRO** 26 [7] J S Goldie 7-9-8 (53) A McGlone 6/1 CO FAV: 430001: 7 ch g Clantime - Arroganza   58
(Crofthall) Led/chsd lead till went on 2f out, held on gamely for press cl home, drvn out: blnks omitted: '99 wnr
at Musselburgh (2), Ayr & Thirsk (h'caps, rtd 75): '98 Ayr wnr (h'cap, rtd 70): suited by 5/6f, stays a sharp 7f:
eff with/without blnks or vis: likes fm, handles soft, likes Ayr & Musselburgh: inconsistent, but v well h'capped.
3200 **PRIX STAR** 4 [12] C W Fairhurst 5-9-7 (52)(vis) J Fanning 11/1: 400052: 5 ch g Superpower - Celestine   nk   56
(Skyliner) Chsd ldrs halfway, rdn & styd on well fnl 1f, post came too soon: turn not far away: see 82.
3200 **TANCRED ARMS** 4 [16] D W Barker 4-9-2 (47) F Lynch 14/1: 030203: 4 b f Clantime - Mischievous Miss   ½   49
(Niniski) Rdn/chsd ldrs halfway, kept on well ins last, not rch wnr: qck reapp: acts on firm & soft: see 3080, 698.
3123 **CRYSTAL LASS** 8 [10] J Balding 4-8-8 (39) J Stack 25/1: 050504: Chsd ldrs, kept on for press fnl 1f.   hd   40
3037 **VENIKA VITESSE** 12 [1] 4-9-9 (54) G Duffield 10/1: 000005: Prom, rdn/onepace over 1f out: see 1074.   1   53
2820 **PETITE DANSEUSE** 22 [9] 6-8-8 (39) Joanna Badger (7) 16/1: 052546: In tch, kept on fnl 2f, no threat.   nk   37
3222 **MALADERIE** 3 [14] 6-9-5 (50)(vis) C Lowther 14/1: 000007: Drvn early, kept on fnl 1f, no threat: op 10/1.   ¾   46
1976 **JACKERIN** 57 [5] 5-9-0 (45)(t) V Halliday 25/1: 066408: Prom, held fnl 1f: abs, now with Miss J F Craze.   ½   39
2877 **YOUNG BIGWIG** 19 [13] 6-9-10 (55) G Parkin 6/1 CO FAV: 453349: Prom, held over 1f out: btr 2877, 2796.1   47
3056 **TIME TO FLY** 15 [6] 7-8-11 (42)(bl) D McGaffin (5) 11/1: 000500: Dwelt/rear, mod hdwy over 2f out: 10th.   hd   40
2969 **DOMINELLE** 15 [20] 8-9-6 (51) P Fessey 6/1 CO FAV: 040610: Prom 4f: 11th: btr 2969.   ¾   40
2796 **EASTERN PROPHETS** 22 [18] 7-9-6 (51)(bl) T Williams 10/1: 000440: In tch, btn 2f out: 13th: see 1258.   0
3037 **JACOBINA** 12 [3] 5-9-4 (49)(t) W Supple 10/1: 600-00: Bhd, nvr on terms: 15th: see 3037.   0
3037 **WISHBONE ALLEY** 12 [19] 5-9-1 (46)(vis) R Winston 8/1: 003050: In tch 3f: 18th: see 312 (AW).   0

4554) **Key** 288 [8] 4-9-10 (55) L Enstone (7) 66/1: 3161 **Lady Sandrovitch** 7 [4] 3-8-7 (42) P Hanagan (7) 25/1:
3124 **Rudcroft** 8 [15] 4-7-10 (27)(7oh) J McAuley 50/1: 2753 **Baritone** 24 [2] 6-8-5 (36)(vis) Paul Eddery 33/1:
3103 **Qualitait Survivor** 10 [17] 5-8-3 (34) O Pears 25/1:
19 ran Time 1m 09.8 (0.9) (Frank Brady) J S Goldie Uplawmoor, E Renfrewshire

---

NEWMARKET (July) SATURDAY AUGUST 12TH Righthand, Stiff, Galloping Track

Official Going GOOD TO FIRM. Stalls: Stands Side.

3313

2.00 MONTANA MDN 3YO+ (D) 1m4f Good/Firm 20 -06 Slow
£4706 £1448 £724 £362 3 yo rec 11lb

2897 **TROILUS** 18 [2] J H M Gosden 3-8-10 (BL) J Fortune 4/5 FAV: -03221: 3 ch c Bien Bien - Nakterjal 80
(Vitiges) V easily made all: well bckd, tried blnks: unplcd in 2 '99 starts (rtd 81): half-brother to smart mid-
dist wnr Bienanado: eff forcing the pace at 12f: acts on firm/fast grnd: prev visored, blnkd today.
2897 **SEEKER** 18 [3] H R A Cecil 3-8-5 W Ryan 6/4: 32: 3 ch f Rainbow Quest - Sarmatia (Danzig) 9 63
Chsd wnr, left bhd 3f out: hvly bckd: similar dist bhd this wnr in 2897.
-- **CHANCERY** [1] A King 4-9-7 R Hughes 7/1: 430-23: 4 ch g St Jovite - Big E Dream (Persian Bold) 13 55
Held up, nvr dngrs: 12 wk abs, Brit bow: ex-Irish, rnr-up in May (12f mdn on fast grnd, J Bolger).
2897 **DOUBLE ROCK** 18 [4] P Howling 4-9-2 J Quinn 50/1: 54: Chsd ldrs till 4f out: highly tried. 12 38
4 ran Time 2m 31.34 (3.14) (J Toffan & T McCaffery) J H M Gosden Manton, Wilts.

3314

2.35 LADY RIDERS HCAP 3YO+ 0-65 (F) 1m2f Good/Firm 20 -28 Slow [47]
£4862 £1496 £748 £374 3 yo rec 9 lb

*3049 **MYSTERIUM** 12 [6] N P Littmoden 6-10-5 (52) Mrs C Williams 9/1: 002511: 6 gr g Mystiko - Way To Go 56
(Troy) Waited with, gd prog to lead ent fnl 2f, hung badly left dist, pushed out: op 12/1: earlier won at
W'hampton (h'cap, rtd 54a) & Windsor (h'cap): '99 wnr at Yarmouth (rtd 44) & W'hampton (h'caps, rtd 53a): eff
at 9/12f on fast, gd grnd & fibresand, likes W'hampton: goes on any trk, without a visor: best coming late.
3206 **DANDES RAMBO** 4 [8] D W P Arbuthnot 3-9-6 (48) Miss J Reich Rorhwig 14/1: 636042: 3 gr g Rambo 1¾ 49
Dancer - Kajetana (Caro): Led 4f & briefly appr final 1f, kept on: op 8/1, qck reapp: goes on fast & gd.
3227 **SAMMYS SHUFFLE** 3 [11] Jamie Poulton 5-9-12 (45)(bl) Mrs S Bosley 9/2: 232123: 5 b h Touch shd 46
Of Grey - Cabinet Shuffle (Thatching) Held up, prog to chall 2f out, slightly hmpd ent final 1f, styd on:
nicely bckd tho' op 3/1, qck reapp: in form, see 2790.
3220 **RARE TALENT** 3 [1] S Gollings 6-10-13 (60) Miss E J Jones 7/2 FAV: 615224: Mid-div, wide, styd on 1¼ 58
to chase ldrs appr final 1f, unable to chall: nicely bckd, clr rem, qck reapp: not far off best, see 2883.
3186 **SILVER SECRET** 5 [4] 4-6-9-10 (43)(bl) Miss A Deniel 10/1: 060555: Held up, chsd ldrs halfway till 2f out. 5 33
3007 **INDIAN NECTAR** 14 [3] 7-10-8 (55) Miss D Lopez (3) 12/1: 205236: Chsd ldrs, fdd appr final 1f: btr 3007. 2 42
2802 **HIGH SUN** 22 [12] 4-10-0 (47) Mrs I Got 33/1: 000507: Nvr a factor, wide: see 942. hd 33
2884 **ASCARI** 19 [10] 4-11-0 (61) Mrs C Bocskai 10/1: -02038: Led after 4f till ent final 2f, wknd: op 8/1. nk 46
3031 **JOIN THE PARADE** 12 [9] 4-10-0 (60) Miss L Jarven 7/1: -03029: In tch till 4f out: btr 3031. 1 43
2518 **SOPHOMORE** 35 [5] 6-10-13 (60) Miss J Allison 33/1: 016000: Handy fr 1m: 10th: see 1731 (1m clmr). 4 37
2771 **SWINGING THE BLUES** 24 [7] 6-10-9 (56)(vis) Miss E Johnson Houghton 8/1: -00100: Nvr trbld ldrs: 11th. 11 19
3021 **SHARP BELLINE** 13 [2] 3-10-3 (59)(VIS) Mrs N Traber Renk 20/1: 4340: Chsd ldrs 6f: 12th, tchd 33/1. 2 19
12 ran Time 2m 06.72 (4.82) (Alcester Associates) N P Littmoden Newmarket, Suffolk.

3315

3.05 JOE JENNINGS HCAP 3YO+ 0-105 (B) 7f str Good/Firm 20 +14 Fast [105]
£19500 £6000 £3000 £1500 3 yo rec 6 lb

3119 **PREMIER BARON** 8 [17] P S McEntee 5-7-13 (76) L Newman (1) 33/1: 644461: 5 b g Primo Dominie - 85
Anna Karietta (Precocious) Bhd ldrs, led appr final 1f, qcknd clr: fast time: earlier won at Kempton (reapp,
h'cap): '99 wnr at Sandown (h'cap, rtd 88 & 68a, P Mitchell): rtd 83 in '98 for T Clement: all 3 wins at 7f,
prob stays 1m: acts on fast, soft grnd & fibresand, any trk: runs well fresh: on a fair mark, qk follow-up?
3152 **HO LENG** 7 [7] Miss L A Perratt 5-10-0 (105) R Hughes 9/1: -30302: 5 ch g Statoblest - Indigo Blue 2 108
(Bluebird) Waited with, prog & short of room appr final 1f, swtchd & kept on, not trouble wnr: qck reapp, jockey
given 3 day ban for irresp ride: fine weight carrying performance from this v useful gelding: see 1182.
2997 **FREE OPTION** 14 [4] B Hanbury 5-9-5 (96) D Harrison 12/1: 303103: 5 ch g Indian Ridge - Saneena 1¼ 97
(Kris) Rear, prog & carried left appr final 1f, styd on for pressure: back to form, see 2870 (1m).
3152 **SECOND WIND** 7 [13] C A Dwyer 5-8-6 (83)(t) A Beech (5) 8/1: 124054: Trkd ldrs, briefly short of ¾ 82
room 2f out, hard rdn & ch before final 1f, onepace: consistent, see 2287, 2133.
3155 **EASY DOLLAR** 7 [15] 8-8-9 (86)(bl) R Cochrane 25/1: 600055: Set gd pace, rdn ent final 2f, sn hdd shd 85
& no extra: qck reapp, blnks back on, see 2954, 1674.
2954 **PERUVIAN CHIEF** 15 [11] 3-8-5 (88) J Quinn 12/1: 204336: In tch, prog & ch before final 1f, fdd. 2½ 82
3063 **ELMHURST BOY** 11 [8] 4-8-3 (80)(vis) F Norton 25/1: 304527: Wide, rear, prog & ch ent final 2f, wknd. nk 73
2997 **CATCHY WORD** 14 [10] 3-9-3 (100)(VIS) W Ryan 33/1: 205408: Held up, wide, hdwy under press 2f out, 1¼ 91
no further impress when short of room below dist: visored, see 2809, 1830.
3130 **TEODORA** 8 [12] 3-8-2 (85)(t) P Doe 25/1: 062009: Nvr better than mid-div: stablemate 7th, btr 2567. nk 75
2999 **CARLTON** 14 [6] 6-8-0 (77) G Bardwell 33/1: 002400: Not go pace, wide, nvr dngrs: 10th, see 76. nk 66
2986 **KARAMEG** 14 [3] 4-8-8 (85) J Fortune 8/1: -04220: Nvr a factor, wide, eased fnl 1f: 11th, btr 2986, 2694. 3 68
2706 **KAYO** 27 [16] 5-9-9 (100) M Hills 9/2: 231220: Cl-up till lost place ent fnl 2f: 12th, tchd 10/1, not his form. nk 82
2870 **CHOTO MATE** 20 [1] 4-8-12 (89) Dane O'Neill 25/1: 041000: Bhd from halfway: 13th, see 1989. shd 71
+2954 **ROYAL ARTIST** 15 [14] 4-8-13 (90) J P Spencer 6/4 FAV: 262110: Chsd ldrs, wknd qckly 2f out: 14th, 1¼ 70
hvly bckd: surely something amiss: v progressive earlier & must be given another chance: see 2954.
3132 **Debbies Warning** 8 [9] 4-8-13 (90) J Tate 33/1: 2809 **Trouble Mountain** 22 [5] 3-9-6 (103) J Mackay(5) 33/1:
16 ran Time 1m 24.33 (0.43) (Miss T J Fitzgerald) P S McEntee Newmarket, Suffolk.

3316 **3.35 LISTED SWEET SOLERA STKS 2YO (A) 7f str Good/Firm 20 -09 Slow**
£12470 £4730 £2365 £1075

2935 **PEACEFUL PARADISE 16** [5] J W Hills 2-8-8 M Hills 7/1: -3151: 2 b f Turtle Island - Megdale (Waajib) **105**
Prom, led halfway, rdn clr before final 1f, pushed out: earlier won at Kempton (fillies mdn): eff at 7f, 1m looks likely to suit: acts on firm/fast, handles gd/soft, sharp or stiff/gall trk: progressive, useful filly.
2935 **BRING PLENTY 16** [8] J H M Gosden 2-8-8 J Fortune 4/1: 0132: 2 b f Southern Halo - Alcando *1¼* **101**
(Alzao) Chsd ldrs, chsd wnr ins last, kept on but no impress: imprvg tho' was in front of this wnr in 2935, see 1957.
2935 **RIZERIE 16** [4] L M Cumani 2-8-8 J P Spencer 5/1: 1203: 2 gr f Highest Honor - Riziere (Groom Dancer) *¾* **99**
Held up, hdwy to dispute 2nd appr final 1f, same pace under press: nicely bckd: acts on fast & gd grnd.
2565 **LADY LAHAR 32** [2] M R Channon 2-8-8 Craig Williams 9/4 FAV: 134: Chsd ldrs, no extra appr final *1* **97**
1f: well bckd tho' op 6/4: unsuited by step up to 7f?: see 2565 (Gr 2), 1968 (gd).
*2940 **CHAGUARAMAS 16** [6] 2-8-8 R Hughes 6/1: 115: Led, hung badly left after 2f & ended up on far rail, *1½* **94**
hdd halfway, wknd inside last: well bckd: lost unbtn record but not disgrcd & will apprec a return to sprinting.
2565 **GOODIE TWOSUES 32** [7] 2-8-8 Dane O'Neill 8/1: -13456: Prom till ent final 2f: st/mate 5th, up in trip. *nk* **93**
2306 **FASTINA 43** [3] 2-8-8 D Harrison 25/1: -437: Slow to stride, al bhd: 6 wk abs, highly tried, fill mdns suit. *½* **92$**
7 ran Time 1m 25.92 (2.02) (Karen Scott Barrett (Abbott Racing Ptnrs)) J W Hills Upper Lambourn, Berks.

3317 **4.10 NEW ZEALAND FILLIES HCAP 3YO+ 0-80 (D) 1m str Good/Firm 20 -17 Slow [77]**
£4836 £1488 £744 £372 3 yo rec 7 lb

2974 **BEADING 15** [4] J W Hills 3-8-9 (65)(t) M Hills 12/1: -00251: 3 b f Polish Precedent - Silver Braid **70**
(Miswaki) Held up wide, smooth prog to lead ent final 2f, sn edged right, pshd out, cmftbly: first win: unplcd sole '99 start: eff at 7f, apprec step up to 1m: acts on fast grnd, stiff/gall trk: wears a t-strap: progressive.
2767 **JESSINCA 24** [12] A P Jones 4-7-10 (45)(2oh) F Norton 14/1: 001422: 4 b f Minshaanshu Amad - Noble *1½* **47**
Soul (Sayf El Arab) Chsd ldrs, styd on appr fnl 1f & went 2nd towards fin, no ch wnr: return to 10f?: see 1511.
3188 **CAUTION 5** [10] S Gollings 6-8-5 (54) J Quinn 6/1: 422523: 6 b m Warning - Fairy Flax (Dancing *nk* **55**
Brave) Mid-div, prog to dispute 2nd dist, styd on: qck reapp, see 2561, 645.
2855 **TIME VALLY 21** [14] S Dow 3-9-0 (70) P Doe 10/1: 010554: Dwelt, rear, short of room appr final 1f, *½* **70**
swtchd & finished well: back to form, apprec the return to 1m: see 1855.
*2914 **BINT HABIBI 17** [13] 3-8-0 (56) G Bardwell 20/1: 166315: Held up, briefly short of room ent final *½* **55**
2f, styd on but not pace to chall: in gd heart & now with J Pearce: see 2914 (seller).
*2980 **EVERGREEN 15** [9] 3-9-1 (71) R Hughes 5/1 FAV: 400216: Wide, rear, chsd ldrs appr final 1f, onepace. *1¼* **67**
3160 **OMNIHEAT 7** [8] 3-9-8 (78) P McCabe 20/1: 165407: Held up, prog into mid-div trav well bef fnl 1f, *1¾* **70**
sn short of room & ch went, position accepted: blnks omitted, plcd with clr run: apprec a return to 10f: see 1649.
3022 **TRIPLE WOOD 13** [7] 3-9-2 (72) D Harrison 25/1: 543108: Led till 2f out, no extra: btr 2824 (7f). *1* **62**
3011 **SWYNFORD PLEASURE 13** [11] 4-8-2 (51) J Mackay (5) 8/1: 533439: Rear, hmpd after 1f, not much *shd* **41**
room before dist, nvr in it: tchd 10/1: see 2180, 1939.
3160 **LADY HELEN 7** [5] 3-9-4 (74) J Fortune 8/1: 510100: Prom, chall 2f out, wknd: 10th, qk reapp, see 2988. *2½* **59**
2890 **SILVER QUEEN 19** [3] 3-8-7 (63)(vis) R Cochrane 14/1: 002460: Chsd ldrs till 2f out: 11th, btr 2296. *3* **42**
3081 **PICTURE PUZZLE 10** [6] 4-9-12 (75) W Ryan 9/1: -32120: Front rank till appr final 2f: 12th: top-weight. *3½* **48**
2994 **SEA DRIFT 14** [2] 3-9-2 (72) J P Spencer 11/2: -53130: Mid-div till 3f out: 13th, up in trip, see 2860 (mdn). *1* **43**
3110 **BAY VIEW 9** [1] 5-9-2 (65) Dane O'Neill 50/1: 2-3000: Bhd final 3f: 14th, see 833. *4* **28**
14 ran Time 1m 39.79 (2.59) (Wyck Hall Stud) J W Hills Upper Lambourn, Berks.

3318 **4.45 BAY OF PLENTY CLAIMER 3YO+ (E) 7f str Good/Firm 20 -14 Slow**
£3562 £1096 £548 £274 3 yo rec 6 lb

2747 **PLEADING 24** [6] M A Buckley 7-8-13 (VIS) R Hughes 10/1: 050061: 7 b g Never So Bold - Ask Mama **62**
(Mummy's Pet) Waited with, prog 2f out, rdn to lead before dist, ran on strongly: back to form in a visor: '99 Chepstow wnr (h'cap, first time blnks, W Musson, rtd 69): '98 Pontefract wnr (h'cap, rtd 69): eff at 6/7f on fast, hvy & fibresand: can go well fresh, any trk, likes stiff ones: woken up by visor today.
3196 **DIRECT REACTION 5** [9] Miss Gay Kelleway 3-9-0 (vis) R Cochrane 6/1: 141142: 3 b g College Chapel - *3* **66**
Mary's Way (Night Shift): Held up, prog 2f out, ch bef fnl 1f, same pace for press: qk reapp, capable of better.
3030 **REDSWAN 12** [4] S C Williams 5-9-3 (t) W Ryan 11/4: 000203: 5 ch g Risk Me - Bocas Rose (Jalmood) *½* **62**
Held up, styd on appr final 1f, nvr pace to chall: can win similar: nicely bckd: see 2775, 1810.
2920 **LAKOTA BRAVE 17** [2] C N Allen 6-9-3 (t) R Morse 12/1: 0/64: Rear, wide prog 2f out, no extra dist. *nk* **61**
*2582 **CRISS CROSS 31** [10] 3-8-13 R Smith (5) 5/2 FAV: 245415: Cl-up, led briefly appr final 1f, fdd: *nk* **62**
well bckd: unsuited by return to 7f on fast grnd?: see 2582 (6f, gd/soft).
2947 **STOP THE TRAFFIC 15** [12] 3-8-2 (t) L Newman (3) 25/1: 000556: Led till 2f out, sn btn: stiff task. *4* **43**
2981 **PENALTA 15** [1] 4-9-5 J Quinn 33/1: 007: Al towards rear: stiff task. *7* **40$**
115 **YALAIL 260** [3] 4-8-13 Dane O'Neill 33/1: 0000-8: Al bhd: reapp: flattered 6th of 7 in '99 (rtd 65). *2* **30**
3123 **DANDY REGENT 8** [8] 6-8-13 J Fortune 11/2: 100409: Prom till appr final 2f: see 1315 (sell). *½* **29**
3117 **PRIVATE SEAL 8** [5] 5-8-10 (t) G Faulkner (3) 40/1: 660040: Handy 5f: 10th, stiff task. *8* **11**
3045 **WELODY 12** [7] 4-9-1 J Tate 14/1: 000000: In tch till halfway: 11th, see 658. *16* **0**
11 ran Time 1m 26.28 (2.38) (Stamford Bridge Partnership) M A Buckley Upper Helmsley, Nth Yorks.

3319 **5.20 SOUTH ISLAND MDN 3YO (D) 6f Good/Firm 20 -17 Slow**
£4065 £1251 £625 £312

1773 **ETIENNE LADY 66** [5] J H M Gosden 3-8-9 W Ryan 10/1: 61: 3 gr f Imperial Frontier - Petula (Petong) **78**
Made all, rdn out: op 7/1, bigger-priced stablemate of rnr-up, 9 wk abs: unrcd juv, half-sister to a sprinter: eff forcing the pace at 6f on fast grnd, stiff trk: runs well fresh: going the right way.
2807 **DOUBLE PLATINUM 22** [3] J H M Gosden 3-8-9 J Fortune 11/8 FAV: 0-3622: 3 ch f Seeking The Gold - *½* **76**
Band (Northern Dancer) Chsd ldrs, went after wnr appr final 1f, hung left & kept on, not btn far: well bckd stablemate of wnr, clr rem: return to 7f will suit, as will headgear: goes on fast & gd/soft grnd.
1951 **JABUKA 58** [2] J A R Toller 3-8-9 S Whitworth 3/1: 43: 3 b f Shareef Dancer - Neptunalia (Slip Anchor) *3* **67**
Held up, feeling pace 2f out, kept on for 3rd & hung left, no ch ldrs: nicely bckd, 8 wk abs: return to 7f needed.
3985} **DIZZY KNIGHT 329** [1] B Palling 3-8-9 Craig Williams 25/1: 0-4: Keen, held up, chsd ldrs appr final *1¾* **62**
2f till before dist: reapp: unplcd for M F Godley sole '99 start (mdn, rtd 66): half-sister to a mid-dist/stayer.
2294 **ALMASHROUK 43** [4] 3-9-0 J Quinn 14/1: 664065: Chsd ldrs till 2f out: 6 wk abs, needs sellers. *7* **47**

3163 **PORT ST CHARLES** 7 [6] 3-9-0 R Hughes 7/2: -24506: Keen, prsd wnr till appr final 2f: qck reapp.   2½   41
6 ran   Time 1m 13.2 (2.2)   (Owen Promotions Ltd)   J H M Gosden Manton, Wilts.

HAYDOCK   SATURDAY AUGUST 12TH   Lefthand, Flat, Galloping Track

Official Going   GOOD. Stalls: 10f/12f - Outside, 7f/1m - Inside, 5f/6f/14f - Centre.

3320

2.20 EBF FILLIES NOV STKS 2YO (D)   6f str   Good/Firm 25   -45 Slow
£3679   £1132   £566   £283   Raced stands side

*3090 **SHEPPARDS WATCH** 10 [3] M P Tregoning 2-9-2 Martin Dwyer 9/4 FAV: -411: 2 b f Night Shift - Sheppard's 101
Cross (Soviet Star) Al prom, rdn/went on over 1f out, styd on strongly ins last: hvly bckd: recent Goodwood wnr
(mdn): eff at 6f, will get further: dam a 7f wnr: acts on fast & a sharp/undul or gall trk: useful & progressive.
2565 **ALINGA** 32 [6] M L W Bell 2-8-13 J F Egan 5/2: 51302: 2 b f King's Theatre - Cheyenne Spirit (Indian 1¾   92
Ridge) Prom, keen early, rdn/narrow lead 2f out, hdd over 1f out, not pace of wnr: nicely bckd tho' op 6/4.
2344 **ASH MOON** 42 [4] K R Burke 2-9-6 D Holland 16/1: -1103: 2 ch f General Monash - Jarmar Moon   2   94
(Unfuwain) Led, rdn/hdd 2f out, kept on for press: op 12/1, 6 wk abs: see 2014.
*2748 **SWEET PROSPECT** 24 [7] C F Wall 2-8-13 R Mullen 5/1: -014: Chsd ldrs, rdn/outpcd 2f out, kept on   ½   85
ins last, no threat: bckd, op 7/1: 7f may now suit: see 2748.
2683 **SUNSHINE NSHOWERS** 28 [1] 2-8-9 G Carter 11/1: 35: In tch, held 2f out: see 2683.   2½   74
-- **SHADED MEMOIR** [8] 2-8-5 R Havlin 12/1: 6: In tch, rdn/btn 2f out: op 10/1: Jan foal, dam won over   hd   69
1m in the US: looks sure to apprec 7f+ in time: likely to improve & could go close in a maiden next time.
1759 **PROMISED** 66 [2] 2-8-13 D Mernagh (3) 33/1: 1307: Chsd ldrs, btn 2f out: 2 month abs: btr 1558.   hd   76
-- **MINT ROYALE** [5] 2-8-5 J Carroll 12/1: 8: Dwelt, al outpcd rear: Cadeaux Genereux filly, Jan foal,   3   61
38,000gns 2yo: full sister to top-class juv Bahamian Bounty: dam a 5f juv wnr: with T D Easterby.
8 ran   Time 1m 15.52 (4.22)   (Major & Mrs R B Kennard & Partners)   M P Tregoning Lambourn, Berks.

3321

2.50 GR 3 ROSE OF LANCS STKS 3YO+ (A)   1m2f120y Good/Firm 25   -04 Slow
£23200   £8800   £4400   £2000   3 yo rec 10lb

*2709 **EKRAAR** 27 [4] M P Tregoning 3-8-7 R Hills 7/4 FAV: 3-3411: 3 b c Red Ransom - Sacahuista (Raja Baba) 117
Led/dsptd lead till went on over 3f out, rdn & al holding rivals fnl 2f, styd on well: hvly bckd: earlier scored at
Newbury (stks): '99 Goodwood wnr (Gr 3), subs 3rd in Gr 1 Racing Post Trophy (first time blnks, rtd 114): suited
by 10f, 12f will suit: acts on firm, soft & any trk: eff with/without blnks & likes to race with/force the pace:
runs well fresh: smart colt, can win more races in Group company.
2596 **FORBEARING** 31 [1] Sir Mark Prescott 3-8-7 S Sanders 5/1: 011122: 3 b c Bering - For Example   1¾   113
(Northern Baby) Chsd ldrs, rdn to press wnr 2f out, held ins last tho' kept on for press cl-home to snatch 2nd:
tough & genuine, imprvd again here: can find a Listed contest & could apprec 12f: see 2596, 2471.
*2578 **FRENCH FELLOW** 31 [7] T D Easterby 3-8-7 J Carroll 6/1: 1-2013: 3 b c Suave Dancer - Mademoiselle nk   112
Chloe (Night Shift) Chsd ldrs, rdn/chsd wnr ins last, al held: op 5/1: stays 10.5f: win another Listed race.
2066 **INGLENOOK** 53 [9] J L Dunlop 3-8-7 G Carter 5/1: -51104: Rear, rdn & kept on well fnl 3f, no   nk   111
threat to wnr: op 7/2, 8 wk abs: styd longer 10f trip: acts on fast & soft grnd: see 1530 (List, 1m).
2475 **KINGS MILL** 36 [3] 3-8-7 R Hills 20/1: 111055: Held up, eff 3f out, held 2f out: see 1310 (rtd h'cap). 2½ 107$
3061 **ST EXPEDIT** 11 [8] 3-8-7 D Holland 12/1: 120306: Chsd ldrs, rdn/held over 2f out: see 3061, 1103.   1½ 105
2851 **DEHOUSH** 21 [6] 4-9-3 R Mullen 20/1: 4-1037: Led after 1f till 3f out, btn over 2f out: btr 2851, 1592. ¾ 104
1174 **HAPPY CHANGE** 98 [2] 6-9-3 J Weaver 14/1: /21-38: Chsd ldrs, btn over 2f out: abs: see 1174.   nk 103
2997 **SPEEDFIT TOO** 14 [5] 5-9-3 (vis) T E Durcan 20/1: 012309: Al bhd: see 2997, 2229 (h'caps, 7f/1m).   5   96
9 ran   Time 2m 13.07 (3.07)   (Hamdan Al Maktoum)   M P Tregoning Lambourn, Berks.

3322

3.20 CORAL EUROBET HCAP 3YO+ 0-100 (C)   5f str   Good/Firm 25   +03 Fast   [97]
£14885   £4580   £2290   £1145   3 yo rec 3lb Raced across track, no advantage

3016 **IVORYS JOY** 13 [7] K T Ivory 5-9-3 (86) C Carver (3) 16/1: 604501: 5 b m Tina's Pet - Jacqui Joy 94
(Music Boy) Al prom, led 2f out, styd on strongly ins last, rdn out: gd time: earlier won at Brighton (h'cap):
'99 wnr at Thirsk, Haydock & W'hampton (h'caps, rtd 82 & 87a): suited by 5f, stays 6f on firm & fibresand, loves
gd & hvy, best without blnks or a visor: tough & useful mare.
1980 **SAPHIRE** 57 [17] C B B Booth 4-9-1 (84) J Reid 40/1: 056502: 4 ch f College Chapel - Emerald Eagle 1½   86
(Sandy Creek) Chsd ldrs, outpcd halfway, styd on well for press fnl 2f, not rch wnr: 8 wk abs: well h'capped,
a stiffer 5f with give in the grnd should prove ideal: one to keep close tabs on: see 1133.
2987 **SHARP HAT** 14 [8] D W Chapman 6-7-13 (68) Claire Roche(6) 16/1: 261163: 6 b g Shavian - Madam   ½   68
Trilby (Grundy) Prom, ch 2f out, rdn & kept on, not pace of wnr: see 2721.
3152 **FURTHER OUTLOOK** 7 [3] D Nicholls 6-10-0 (97) D Holland 7/1: 325364: Chsd ldrs, rdn/kept on fnl 2f.   ½   95
3016 **SHEER VIKING** 13 [18] 4-9-13 (96) R Hills 16/1: 320005: Rdn/towards rear till styd on fnl 2f, nrst fin. nk   93
2987 **XANADU** 14 [15] 4-8-9 (78) A Nicholls (3) 10/1: 012436: Dwelt, sn prom, onepace fnl 1f: see 2505 (C/D).shd 75
2261 **THREAT** 45 [12] 4-7-12 (67)(t) P M Quinn (3) 6/1: 000607: Reared start, rdn/towards rear, styd on nk   63
well for press from over 1f out, nrst fin: hvly bckd & subject of a morning gamble: 6 wk abs: t-strap fitted: well
h'capped & made eye-catching late progress here, looks one to note for similar events: see 1989.
2003 **RAILROADER** 56 [9] 3-8-11 (83) D Mernagh (3) 12/1: -61028: Cl-up, ch 2f out, sn held: op 8/1: abs.   hd   78
3016 **SUNLEY SENSE** 13 [10] 4-9-1 (84) J Weaver 14/1: 200209: Dwelt, rear, hdwy over 2f out, no prog fnl 1f. 1   77
3176 **BRECONGILL LAD** 6 [19] 8-9-1 (84) Alex Greaves 5/1 FAV: 003120: Nvr on terms: 10th: qck reapp.   1   75
2676 **TADEO** 28 [13] 7-9-13 (96) K Dalgleish (5) 14/1: 4-0300: Held up, nvr pace to chall: 11th: op 16/1.   ¾   85
3176 **POLLY GOLIGHTLY** 6 [5] 7-7-10 (65)(bl) (1oh) Dale Gibson 25/1: 640000: Led 3f, wknd: 12th.   ½   52
3183 **PIPS MAGIC** 5 [14] 4-9-1 (84) A Culhane 14/1: 100100: Rdn/rear, nvr on terms: 13th: op 12/1.   shd   71
2929 **Cartmel Park** 17 [11] 4-8-9 (78)(vis) J Carroll 16/1:   3172 **Demolition Jo** 6 [2] 5-8-3 (72)(vis) Martin Dwyer 20/1:
3135 **Melanzana** 8 [6] 3-8-13 (85) G Carter 14/1:   3222 **Unshaken** 3 [1] 6-7-13 (68) J Bramhill 20/1:
2929 **Taras Girl** 17 [4] 3-8-8 (80) J F Egan 33/1:
18 ran   Time 59.91 (1.11)   (K T Ivory)   K T Ivory Radlett, Herts.

3323 3.55 GROSVENOR HCAP 3YO+ 0-85 (D) 1m6f Good/Firm 25 -04 Slow [83]
£2984 £1226 £613 £306 3 yo rec 13lb

-3270 **SUDDEN FLIGHT** 2 [11] E A L Dunlop 3-8-10 (78) J Reid 7/2 FAV: 302521: 3 b c In The Wings - Ma 86
Petite Cherie (Caro) Mid-div, prog/hung right over 1f out, styd on gamely for press to lead well ins last, drvn out:
earlier scored at Thirsk (class stks, reapp): '99 Yarmouth wnr (nurs h'cap), subs plcd at Nottingham (unlucky,
rtd 70): eff at 12f/14f on fast & soft grnd: runs fresh well fresh: handles a stiff/gall or sharpish track.
2852 **SEREN HILL** 21 [6] G A Butler 4-9-9 (78) D Holland 7/1: 0-0002: 4 ch f Sabrehill - Seren Quest ½ 84
(Rainbow Quest) Cl-up halfway, rdn/led 1f out, hdd well ins last & no extra: back to form, can find similar: see 997.
2600 **WEET FOR ME** 31 [1] R Hollinshead 4-9-8 (77) J F Egan 16/1: 030163: 4 b c Warning - Naswara 2½ 79
(Al Nasr) Led/dsptd lead, drvn/hdd 1f out, no extra: see 2319.
*2993 **MAJESTIC BAY** 14 [8] P W Harris 4-9-11 (80) J Weaver 7/1: 301314: Led/dsptd lead, drvn/held fnl 1f. ½ 81
2584 **BUSY LIZZIE** 31 [9] 3-8-11 (79) G Carter 5/1: -20625: Chsd ldrs, held 1f out: op 7/2: see 2584, 964. nk 79
2936 **TYPHOON TILLY** 16 [4] 3-8-4 (72) R Mullen 7/1: 311126: Chsd ldr 3f out, sn held: btr 2936, 2681. 3½ 67
-- **COLUMBUS** [7] 3-8-10 (78)(bl) S Sanders 25/1: 0-6417: Chsd ldrs, btn 2f out: British debut, 7 63
ex-Irish, July mdn wnr at Roscommon: eff at 12f, suited by 2m: acts on fast grnd: with C Grant.
3135} **ANGUS G** 374 [5] 8-10-0 (83) J Carroll 40/1: 2305-8: Al towards rear: reapp: rnr-up in '99 (h'cap, rtd 5 61
92): mod form sole '98 start: '97 wnr at Newmarket & York (h'caps, rtd 94): eff at 10/12f on firm & gd grnd.
3013 **SHAFFISHAYES** 13 [2] 8-7-13 (54) Dale Gibson 12/1: 546539: Keen/chsd ldrs, btn 3f out: op 10/1. nk 31
2256 **JASEUR** 45 [3] 7-9-6 (75)(vis) T G McLaughlin 33/1: -00060: Chsd ldrs halfway, btn 3f out: 6 wk abs. 3 48
2691 **ROUTE ONE** 28 [12] 7-9-0 (69) R Hills 40/1: 6450: Chsd ldrs halfway, strugg 4f out: 11th: h'cap bow. 4 36
2446 **LINEA G** 37 [10] 6-8-7 (62) A Culhane 8/1: 120-60: Chsd ldrs 5f out, btn/eased fnl 2f: 12th: op 6/1. 23 4
12 ran Time 3m 01.99 (3.99) (Maktoum Al Maktoum) E A L Dunlop Newmarket.

3324 4.30 MTB GROUP MDN 3YO (D) 1m4f Good/Firm 25 -24 Slow
£3926 £1208 £604 £302

-- **SCHEMING** [7] W M Brisbourne 3-9-0 Martin Dwyer 33/1: 1: 3 br g Machiavellian - Alusha (Soviet Star) 82
Keen in tch, prog to chase ldrs 2f out, switched & styd on well to lead cl home: debut: 3,000gns purchase: eff
at 12f, 14f+ could suit: acts on fast & a gall trk: runs well fresh.
2963 **SHAIR** 15 [4] J H M Gosden 3-9-0 R Havlin 4/6 FAV: 422: 3 b g Warning - Sahima (Shareef Dancer) ¾ 81
Trkd ldrs, prog/led 3f out, rdn over 1f out & hdd well ins last, no extra: hvly bckd: see 2963, 2617.
4473} **ZEYAARAH** 295 [9] M P Tregoning 3-8-9 R Hills 15/8: 30-3: 3 ch f Rahy - Princess Haifa (Mr Prospector) 1½ 74
Trkd ldrs, rdn & onepace fnl 2f: nicely bckd tho' op 5/4: clr of rem: reapp: plcd on first of just two '99 starts
(rtd 86): styd this longer 12f trip: acts on fast & gd grnd & a gall track.
2879 **TYCOONS LAST** 19 [3] W M Brisbourne 3-9-0 T G McLaughlin 50/1: 435304: Led, rdn/hdd 3f out, sn held.5 67$
2722 **SPIRIT OF PARK** 26 [1] 3-9-0 K Dalgleish (5) 50/1: 55: Rear, mod gains: longer 12f trip: see 2722. 6 63$
2774 **BLUE HAWK** 23 [2] 3-9-0 J Weaver 50/1: 00-006: Keen in tch, btn 3f out: longer 12f trip: see 1352. 3½ 58
2560 **BETTER MOMENT** 32 [8] 3-9-0 J Carroll 10/1: 47: Keen/trk ldr, btn 3f out: op 14/1: see 2560. 7 48
2691 **ARTHUR K** 28 [5] 3-9-0 J Reid 40/1: 648: Chsd ldrs halfway, btn 4f out: needs low-grade h'caps. hd 47
-- **ATTACKER** [6] 3-9-0 A Culhane 66/1: 9: Sn bhd: debut: with Miss L C Siddall. dist 0
9 ran Time 2m 33.66 (5.86) (Christopher Chell) W M Brisbourne Great Ness, Shropshire.

3325 5.05 HPR RTD HCAP 3YO+ 0-90 (C) 1m30y rnd Good/Firm 25 +04 Fast [101]
£6192 £2348 £1174 £533 3 yo rec 7 lb

*3147 **ADOBE** 7 [6] W M Brisbourne 5-8-4 (77) K Dalgleish (5) 9/2: 341211: 5 b g Green Desert - Shamshir 82
(Kris) Held up, stdy run from over 2f out to lead ins last, edged left, styd on gamely, drvn out: bckd from 6/1,
gd time: earlier scored at W'hampton, Hamilton (2), Bath, Goodwood, Doncaster & Thirsk (h'caps): '99 wnr at Bath
& Nottingham (h'caps, rtd 55 & 49a): suited by 7f/1m on firm, gd & fibresand, handles soft grnd: acts on any trk,
likes Hamilton/Bath: eff with/without a t-strap: most tough, genuine & progressive, credit to connections.
*2986 **TONY TIE** 14 [3] J S Goldie 4-9-0 (87) A Culhane 6/1: 020212: 4 b g Ardkinglass - Queen Of The ¾ 90
Quorn (Governor General) Held up, rdn & prog to lead 1f out, hard rdn/hdd ins last, held by wnr cl-home.
3250 **PETERS IMP** 3 [10] A Berry 5-8-4 (76)(1ow) J Carroll 8/1: 301143: 5 b g Imp Society - Catherine 2½ 75
Clare (Sallust) Held up, rdn/prog to press ldr dist, wknd ins last: op 6/1: qck reapp: stays 1m, suited by 6/7.5f.
2090 **WELSH WIND** 52 [5] D J Murphy 4-9-3 (90) J F Egan 10/1: 0-2204: Rear, rdn & kept on fnl 2f, not 1¾ 87
pace to chall: 8 wk abs, top-weight: prev with R Ingram: see 1262, 851.
*2844 **KATHIR** 21 [2] 3-8-7 (87) R Hills 3/1 FAV: -03215: Led till 4f out, fdd: bckd: see 2844. 2 81
3170 **NOMORE MR NICEGUY** 6 [1] 6-8-3 (79)(3oh) J Bramhill 14/1: 040066: Chsd ldrs, led 4f out, rdn/hdd ½ 69
over 2f out & sn held: see 977.
3018 **NIMELLO** 13 [9] 4-9-0 (87)(bl) D Sweeney 10/1: -01007: Trkd ldrs, led over 2f out, rdn/hdd over nk 79
1f out, fdd: op 12/1: blnks reapplied: see 1042.
*3118 **SMOOTH SAILING** 8 [8] 5-8-9 (82) O Urbina 7/1: 400518: Al towards rear, op 11/2: see 3118. 1¼ 72
2197 **SUDRA** 47 [7] 3-8-8 (88) G Carter 16/1: 10-009: Chsd ldrs, rdn/btn 3f out: op 12/1: 7 wk abs. 3½ 73
2922 **COTE SOLEIL** 17 [4] 3-8-1 (81) R Mullen 16/1: 000500: Al rear: 10th: see 2117, 977. 1½ 64
2999 **THE EXHIBITION FOX** 14 [11] 4-8-3 (78)(2oh) A Nicholls(3) 16/1: -03000: Chsd ldrs 3f out, sn btn. 1½ 57
11 ran Time 1m 42.17 (1.67) (P R Kirk) W M Brisbourne Great Ness, Shropshire.

Official Going FIRM (GOOD/FIRM places). Stalls: Str Crse - Stands Side; 2m - Centre, Rem - Inside.

3326 2.35 FAMILY TICKET MED AUCT MDN 3-4YO (E) 1m1f Firm 04 -28 Slow
£2964 £912 £456 £228

2548 **BERZOUD** 34 [10] J Noseda 3-8-7 Paul Eddery 2/1: 021: 3 b f Ezzoud - Bertie's Girl (Another Realm): 69
Rear, rdn & styd on well final 2f to lead well inside last: op 6/4: eff at 1m/9f on firm & soft grnd, sharp/gall trk.
3012 **WHAT A DANCER** 14 [4] W W Haigh 3-8-12 F Lynch 25/1: -02: 3 b g Dancing Dissident - Cool Gales 1½ 70
(Lord Gayle): Dwelt, held up, smooth prog to lead over 1f out, rdn/hdd well inside last: eff at 9f on firm grnd.

--   **BEAUTY ROSE** [8] J H M Gosden 3-8-7 K Darley 11/10 FAV: 3: 3 ch f Bien Bien - Small World   ½   **64+**
(Transworld): Held up, rdn/outpcd 3f out, styd on well inside last for press, not reach front pair: nicely bckd,
debut, needed this: stays 9f, looks sure to relish 10f+: much sharper in a similar contest next time.
3247   **THREE CHERRIES** 4 [3] R E Barr 4-9-1 P Goode (3) 50/1: 004554: Prom, onepace/held final 2f.   3½   **65$**
3019   **ANASTASIA VENTURE** 14 [2] 3-8-7 J Fanning 9/2: -53245: Led till over 1f out, fdd: op 7/2: see 1388.   nk   **56**
1597   **MILDON** 74 [6] 4-9-6 R Winston 66/1: 00-006: Prom till outpcd final 3f: needed this, abs: mod form.   9   **53$**
2994   **ST PACOKISE** 15 [1] 3-8-7 W Supple 50/1: 504-07: Cl-up, rdn/btn 2f out: unplcd in '99 (rtd 63, debut).   6   **30**
4002}   **JAZZ NIGHT** 329 [5] 3-8-12 J Stack 50/1: 0-8: Prom 6f: reapp, needed this: unplcd sole '99 start   hd   **34**
for G Woodward (rtd 54): tall, scopey gelding, with J Balding.
3012   **MY LINE** 14 [7] 3-8-12 A Culhane 33/1: -09: Sn bhd: no form.   ¾   **33**
--   **HAMISH G** [9] 3-8-12 T Eaves (7) 50/1: 0: Slowly away, sn bhd: 10th: debut.   1¾   **30**
10 ran   Time 1m 51.7 (2.9)   (Mike F Sullivan)   J Noseda Newmarket, Suffolk.

3327   **3.05 NORTHERN ECHO NURSERY HCAP 2YO (C)**   **6f**   **Firm 04**   **-18 Slow**   **[88]**
          £7605   £2340   £1170   £585

*2687   **BECKY SIMMONS** 29 [9] A P Jarvis 2-9-6 (80) N Pollard 11/2: 111: 2 b f Mujadil - Jolies Eaux   **88**
(Shirley Heights): Cl-up, drvn/led inside last, styd on well: padd pick: remains unbtn after wins at Hamilton
(auct mdn) & Salisbury (nov auct stks): eff at 6f, 7f will suit: acts on firm & gd grnd, stiff/undul or gall trk:
goes well fresh: gd weight carrier: fine h'cap bow from this tough & prog filly: scopey, can win again.
*2778   **MILLIKEN PARK** 24 [8] Miss L A Perratt 2-8-7 (67) K Dalgleish (5) 12/1: -612: 2 ch f Fumo Di Londra -   ¾   **72**
Miss Ironwood (Junius): Led, hung left over 2f out, hdd inside last, kept on well for press: op 10/1: acts
on firm & fast grnd: tall, sturdy & scopey filly, fine h'cap bow: see 2778.
3047   **SNOWEY MOUNTAIN** 13 [5] N A Callaghan 2-9-3 (77) W Supple 7/2 FAV: -6443: 2 gr c Inchinor - Mrs   1¾   **78**
Gray (Red Sunset): Mid-div, hdwy final 2f, styd on well for press inside last, nrst fin: well bckd, op 5/1: lengthy,
scopey type who will relish a return to 7f: handles firm & gd grnd: see 2005.
2928   **WINDCHILL** 18 [4] T D Easterby 2-8-0 (60) P Fessey 10/1: 221134: In tch, no extra final 1f: acts on   1   **59**
firm & gd/soft grnd: see 2312 (sell).
2100   **CARK** 53 [1] P Bradley (5) 20/1: -145: Led/dsptd lead, no extra final 1f: abs: see 2100 (5f).   nk   **67**
3184   **XIPE TOTEC** 6 [11] 2-9-7 (81) K Darley 6/1: -0136: Cl-up, held 1f out: bckd: see 3184, 2700.   shd   **77**
3168   **FRANICA** 7 [3] 2-9-4 (78) P Hanagan (7) 12/1: 152247: Rear, styd on final 1f, no threat: see 2557.   hd   **75**
3165   **SYLVAN GIRL** 8 [10] 2-8-8 (68) P M Quinn (3) 13/2: 32538: Al mid-div, no impress final 2f: op 5/1.   2½   **58**
2532   **NOWT BUT TROUBLE** 34 [12] 2-8-8 (68) J Fanning 12/1: 6359: Dwelt, nvr factor: btr 1429 (7f).   ¾   **56**
3098   **LE MERIDIEN** 11 [2] 2-8-7 (67) F Lynch 12/1: -0440: Mid-div, held 2f out: 10th: op 20/1: btr 2700.   ¾   **53**
3101   **FLINT** 11 [15] 2-8-13 (73) T Lucas 20/1: 054150: In tch stands side, outpcd final 3f: 11th: btr 2880 (5f).   3   **52**
2091   **The Names Bond** 53 [16] 2-9-5 (79) A Culhane 33/1:*3143 **Tomthevic** 8 [13] 2-9-6 (80)(t) D Mernagh (3) 12/1:
*2990   **Berezina** 15 [6] 2-8-9 (69) R Winston 14/1:   *2948 **Cedar Tsar** 16 [7] 2-8-5 (65) Claire Bryan (5) 11/1:
15 ran   Time 1m 10.2 (1.3)   (Mrs D B Brazier)   A P Jarvis Aston Upthorpe, Oxon.

3328   **3.40 OWN A HORSE HCAP 3YO+ 0-80 (D)**   **7f str**   **Firm 04**   **+09 Fast**   **[73]**
          £4771   £1468   £734   £367   3 yo   rec 6 lb

3083   **PUPPET PLAY** 11 [7] E J Alston 5-8-11 (56) W Supple 7/1: 041321: 5 ch m Broken Hearted - Fantoccini   **62**
(Taufan): Prom, rdn/led over 2f out, clr dist, styd on well for press: op 6/1, fast time: earlier won at Pontefract
(fills h'cap): rnr-up on turf in native Ireland & on sand in '99 (rtd 52a, AW mdn): likes to race with/force the
pace at 7f/1m, stays 9f: acts on firm, fast & both AWs, any trk: likes a stiff/gall one: best without blnks.
2999   **PERFECT PEACH** 15 [1] C W Fairhurst 5-9-7 (66) P Goode (3) 10/1: 043462: 5 b m Lycius - Perfect   1   **68**
Timing (Comedy Star) Dwelt, hld up, stdy hdwy final 2f under hands & heels riding riding, not rch wnr:
eyecatching, stewards accepted explanation that the mare does not respond to strong pressure: see 1250.
2612   **ARPEGGIO** 31 [8] D Nicholls 5-9-10 (69) Alex Greaves 12/1: 004103: 5 b g Polar Falcon - Hilly (Town   3   **65**
Crier): Chsd ldrs, rdn & styd on final 2f, no threat to wnr: lkd well: acts on firm & soft grnd: see 2437.
1517   **SECRET CONQUEST** 78 [3] D W Barker 3-9-7 (72) F Lynch 25/1: 0-0064: Prom, held final 1f: abs.   ¾   **67**
3147   **SUPREME SALUTATION** 8 [10] 4-10-0 (73) K Darley 100/30 FAV: 060355: Reared & slowly away, rear till nk   **67**
styd on final 2f, nrst fin: op 4/1: plenty of ability but a tricky ride (can pull hard): see 1011.
*3144   **ENCOUNTER** 8 [6] 4-8-8 (53) A Beech (5) 8/1: 211016: Dwelt, bhd till styd on final 2f, nrst fin: hmpd   nk   **46**
chances with a slow start today: see 3114 (sell h'cap, 6f).
*3309   **THWAAB** 1 [13] 8-8-9 (54)(bl)(6ex) K Dalgleish (5) 6/1: 061117: Chsd ldrs, onepace final 2f: qck   2   **43**
reapp under a 6lb pen: won over this C/D yesterday: see 3309.
*3197   **QUIET VENTURE** 6 [4] 6-9-5 (64)(tvi)(6ex) R Winston 8/1: 000418: Led 4f, sn held: see 3197.   hd   **52**
3037   **MOTHER CORRIGAN** 13 [12] 4-8-6 (51)(vis) D Mernagh (3) 33/1: 000009: Led halfway till over 2f out, fdd. 3   **33**
2878   **GLENDAMAH** 20 [9] 3-9-6 (71) N Pollard 20/1: 033-00: Sn rdn, chsd ldrs 5f: 10th: still ndd this.   3½   **46**
3309   **MEHMAAS** 1 [11] 4-8-10 (55) P Fessey 10/1: 000530: Rcd alone stands side, in tch 3f: 11th: qck reapp.   ¾   **29**
3259   **REDOUBTABLE** 5 [5] 9-9-1 (70)(bl) A Culhane 9/2: 041430: Nvr on terms: 12th: qck reapp: btr 2994.   3   **38**
*2299   **Zig Zig** 44 [14] 3-9-7 (72) L Enstone (7) 14/1:   1920 **Cyran Park** 60 [2] 4-7-11 (42)(VIS)(1ow)(2oh) T Williams 25/1:
2833   **Nite Owl Mate** 23 [15] 3-8-4 (55) J Fanning 20/1:
15 ran   Time 1m 21.7 (u0.1)   (Mrs F D McAuley)   E J Alston Longton, Lancs.

3329   **4.15 CLARION HCAP 3YO 0-90 (C)**   **1m3f**   **Firm 04**   **-51 Slow**   **[91]**
          £7150   £2200   £1100   £550

*3178   **SANTIBURI GIRL** 7 [3] J R Best 3-8-3 (66) A Polli (3) 7/2: 230011: 3 b f Casteddu - Lake Mistassiu   **71**
(Tina's Pet): Trkd ldrs, led over 2f out, styd on well, eased cl-home: slow time, op 5/2: earlier won at
Lingfield (class stks) & Newbury (fill h'cap): '99 wnr at Salisbury (nov auct, rtd 87): eff at 7f, relished step
up to 10/11f last twice: acts on firm, gd & a sharp/undul or gall trk: progressive filly.
3159   **ABUZAID** 8 [2] J L Dunlop 3-9-7 (84) W Supple 5/2: 001532: 3 br c Nureyev - Elle Seule (Exclusive   1   **85**
Native): Al prom, briefly led over 2f out, sn hard rdn & onepce/held inside last: bckd, op 3/1: topweight.
*3012   **TIGRE** 14 [6] B W Hills 3-9-5 (82) Paul Eddery 2/1 FAV: 400213: 3 b c Mujtahid - Vice Vixen (Sure   1¼   **81**
Regent): Dictated pace, increased tempo/rdn over 3f out, hdd over 2f out & sn held: lkd well: stays a slow run 11f.
3005   **ADAMAS** 15 [5] Andrew Turnell 3-8-10 (73) A Culhane 20/1: 041004: Held up rear, in tch, effort 2f   hd   **71**
out, not pace to chall: see 2222 (1m,mdn).
2829   **LULLABY** 23 [4] 3-8-3 (66) J Fanning 16/1: 401205: Rear, in tch, efft 3f out, not able to chall: op 14/1.   4   **58**
2889   **CIRCUS PARADE** 20 [1] 3-9-2 (79) K Darley 4/1: -5036: Handy, ch 2f out, fdd: h'cap bow: see 2889.   ¾   **70**
6 ran   Time 2m 21.5 (6.0)   (Alan Turner)   J R Best Hucking, Kent.

3330   4.50 FAMILY DAY CLASS STKS 3YO+ 0-65 (E)   1m str   Firm 04   -09 Slow
£3042   £936   £468   £234   3 yo rec 7 lb

3141 **BOWCLIFFE 9** [4] E J Alston 9-9-7 W Supple 6/1: 9 b g Petoski - Gwiffina (Welsh Saint): **62**
Chsd ldrs, rdn & styd on strongly from over 1f out to lead ins last, drvn out: earlier scored at Carlisle (class
stks): plcd over hdles in 99/00 (nov h'cap, rtd 78h): '99 Musselburgh wnr (class stks, rtd 67), prev term won at
W'hampton & Doncaster (h'caps, rtd 77a & 68): suited by 1m/9f, stays 10f: acts on firm, soft & fibresand: runs
well fresh & best without blnks: gd weight carrier: genuine gelding.
3011 **ROUTE SIXTY SIX 14** [1] Jedd O'Keeffe 4-9-1 J Fanning 11/2 FAV: 0-0002: 4 b f Brief Truce - Lyphards ½ **54**
Goddess (Lyphard's Special): Al prom, led going well 2f out, hdd inside last, no extra: nicely h'capped for similar.
3200 **ROYAL REPRIMAND 5** [3] R E Barr 5-9-4 P Goode (3) 16/1: 005243: 5 b g Reprimand - Lake Ormond 2 **53$**
(King's Lake): Al prom, kept on onepace for press final 2f: swtg: qck reapp: see 1009.
3200 **THATCHED 5** [5] R E Barr 10-9-4 P Fessey 8/1: 563024: Dwelt/twds rear, stdy hdwy final 2f, no threat. ½ **52$**
2994 **MARTON MERE 15** [14] 4-9-7 F Lynch 25/1: 001005: Rdn/rear halfway, styd on final 2f, nrst fin. 1¼ **52**
2895 **EASTERN CHAMP 20** [11] 4-9-4 (t) N Callan (7) 50/1: 206346: Chsd ldrs, onepace final 2f: paddock pick. ½ **48**
3142 **FOUR MEN 9** [6] 3-8-11 Mark Flynn (7) 50/1: 656537: Led halfway till over 2f out, fdd: see 2682. 2 **44$**
3030 **DON BOSCO 13** [15] 4-9-4 A Culhane 6/1: 000308: Nvr better than mid-div: see 2107, 1286. hd **43**
3033 **LADY LOVE 13** [9] 3-8-8 R Winston 7/1: -50209: Chsd ldrs 5f: lengthy, scopey: btr 1579. 7 **28**
2834 **FOURTH TIME LUCKY 22** [7] 4-9-4 K Dalgleish (5) 50/1: 0-0060: Sn rdn mid-div, nvr on terms: 10th. 3 **25**
3312 **RUDCROFT 1** [8] 4-9-4 J McAuley 66/1: 000000: Led, hdd halfway, sn btn: 15th: unplcd yesterday. **0**
2994 **Abstract 15** [12] 4-9-1 (vis) P Hanagan (7) 66/1:   3144 **Time For The Clan 8** [13] 3-8-11 N Pollard 50/1:
827 **Paddy Mul 130** [2] 3-8-11 (t) T Williams 50/1:   2542 **The Castigator 34** [16] 3-8-11 D Mernagh (3) 66/1:
15 ran   Time 1m 35.8 (1.0)   (Philip Davies)   E J Alston Longton, Lancs.

3331   5.20 ENDLESS HCAP 3YO+ 0-75 (E)   2m   Firm 04   -27 Slow   [65]
£2886   £888   £444   £222   3 yo rec 15lb

2516 **MENTAL PRESSURE 36** [3] Mrs M Reveley 7-9-6 (57) A Culhane 11/2: /32521: 7 ch g Polar Falcon - **61**
Hysterical (High Top): Held up, stdy prog final 4f, drvn/led inside last, styd on gamely: lightly raced in recent
seasons: plcd in 6 of 7 starts back in '96 (rtd 84, h'caps): prev suited by 12/14f, now stays 2m well: acts on firm
& gd grnd, prob handles any trk: belated first win for this 7yo.
3295 **GENEROUS WAYS 2** [11] E J Alston 5-9-5 (56) W Supple 7/2: 401022: 5 ch g Generous - Clara Bow ¾ **58**
(Coastal): Chsd ldrs, al travelling well, ev ch 2f out, rdn & not pace of wnr cl-home: bckd, tho' op 3/1, qck reapp.
3026 **XELLANCE 13** [7] M Johnston 3-9-2 (68) K Dalgleish (5) 3/1 FAV: 214123: 3 b g Be My Guest - Excellent hd **69**
Alibi (Exceller): Prom, led over 2f out till inside last, no extra: bckd: jockey given 2-day careless riding ban.
3249 **HIGHFIELD FIZZ 4** [9] C W Fairhurst 8-8-0 (37) T Williams 7/1: 160634: Held up, effort 3f out, al held. 3 **35**
3053 **SPA LANE 12** [5] 7-8-3 (40) R Winston 10/1: 325005: Prom, led 3f out till 2f out, fdd: see 2482, 1276. nk **37**
2659 **BARROW 30** [2] 3-9-5 (71) K Darley 4/1: -00126: Prom, hard rdn/btn 2f out: see 2659. 2 **66**
2681 **ALLOTROPE 29** [8] 5-9-4 (55) T Eaves (7) 20/1: 460-07: Rear, nvr a factor: still needed this. 11 **42**
3008 **PORTRACK JUNCTION 14** [1] 3-7-10 (48)(10oh) D Mernagh (3) 66/1: 000008: Led till over 3f out, fdd. nk **34**
3084 **MINALCO 11** [6] 4-7-10 (33)(14oh) P Fessey 66/1: 0-0009: Prom till 2f out: see 3084. 4 **15**
2993 **SALSKA 15** [10] 9-9-8 (59) N Callan 9/1: 054250: Chsd ldrs, btn 3f out, eased: 10th: something amiss? 3½ **38**
10 ran   Time 3m 29.7 (4.9)   (The Mary Reveley Racing Club)   Mrs M Reveley Lingdale, Nth Yorks.

Official Going   GOOD/FIRM. Stalls: Stands Side.

3332   2.25 PETER EBDON SELLER 3-4YO (F)   7f str   Good/Firm 20   -22 Slow
£2352   £672   £336   3yo rec 6lb

3117 **TERM OF ENDEARMENT 9** [13] J Pearce 3-8-5 R Mullen 5/2 FAV: 520021: 3 b f First Trump - Twilight **50**
Secret (Vaigly Great) In tch, short of room 2f out, kept on gamely to lead cl-home, drvn out: well bckd, bt in for
3,700gns: '99 wnr at Bath (claim auct, rtd 81): eff at 7f/1m, has tried 10f: acts on fast & gd/soft, stiff trks.
2215 **GREEN PURSUIT 47** [5] J A Osborne 4-9-2 F Norton 8/1: 06-002: 4 b g Green Desert - Vayavaig 1¼ **52**
(Damister) Tried to make all, collared ins fnl 1f, just btn: 7 wk abs: apprec drop to sell: stays 7f on fast.
3010 **PRINTSMITH 14** [11] J Norton 3-8-10 O Pears 8/1: 010603: 3 br f Petardia - Black And Blaze (Taufan) 2 **48**
Prom, short of room 2f out, imprvd & ev ch dist, not qckn cl-home: clr rem: ran nr to best over this longer 7f trip.
2964 **WISHEDHADGONEHOME 16** [2] J Balding 3-8-5 (vis) J Edmunds 10/1: 560044: Chsd ldrs, fdd 2f out. 6 **31**
3124 **MEGS PEARL 9** [1] 4-8-11 (bl) T G McLaughlin 11/2: 0-0R25: Front rank 5½f, wknd: btr 3124 (6f). 1¼ **28**
2907 **BONNIE DUNDEE 19** [3] 4-8-11 J D Kinsella (7) 33/1: 000456: Chsd ldrs, bmpd 2f out, wknd. 2 **24**
-- **EVERBOLD** [15] 3-8-5 G Bardwell 50/1: -7: Dwelt, nvr a factor on race crse debut: 1,200gns purchase. 1½ **21**
2538 **BODFARI SIGNET 34** [8] 4-9-2 (tVIS) J Bosley (7) 66/1: 000608: Prom 5f, wknd: tried a visor: 3 **20**
unplcd in a sell h'cap hdle 7 days ago: see 1969.
2914 **LADY CYRANO 18** [6] 3-8-5 R Fitzpatrick(2) 10/1: 602009: Slowly away, eff halfway, btn 2f out. nk **14**
-- **BRIGHT BLUE** [7] 4-9-2 P McCabe 25/1: -0: Slowly away, al bhd & t.o. in 10th on debut: dam sprinter. 12 **0**
3138 **MISS GRAPETTE 9** [9] 4-8-11 J Weaver 7/1: 050200: Slowly away, no ch after: fin 11th, op 11/2: 2½ **0**
reportedly slipped leaving stalls & this is best forgotten: see 2533 (1m).
2555 **Arcadian Chief 34** [10] 3-8-10 G Baker (5) 40/1:   3006 **Fastbeat Racing 15** [12] 3-8-5 L Newman (3) 50/1:
13 ran   Time 1m 25.0 (3.0)   (Saracen Racing)   J Pearce Newmarket.

3333   2.55 EBF J VIRGO MDN 2YO (D)   7f str   Good/Firm 20   -12 Slow
£3851   £1185   £592   £296

2867 **GLEAMING BLADE 21** [10] Mrs A J Perrett 2-9-0 W Ryan 1/1 FAV: -21: 2 ch c Diesis - Gleam Of Light **91**
(Danehill) Rcd keenly & nvr far away, led after 2f, ran on strongly, rdn out: hvly bckd: dam a 7f wnr: eff over
a stiff/gall 7f, 1m will suit: acts on fast & firm, runs well fresh: likes to run-up with the pace: improving.
1667 **SINGLE HONOUR 72** [12] R Hannon 2-8-9 L Newman (3) 9/2: -52: 2 b f Mark Of Esteem - Once Upon 1½ **82**
A Time (Teenoso) Rcd keenly in bhd ldrs, eff when hmpd 2f out, kept on well but not quite pace of wnr: op

7/2, 10 wk abs: eff over a stiff 7f on fast grnd: shld find similar, see 1667 (debut, gd/soft).
-- **AZKABAN** [15] B J Meehan 2-9-0 M Tebbutt 14/1: -3: 2 ch c Ashkalani - Lanasara (Generous) *1½* **84**
Waited with, imprvd 2f out, kept on under press fnl 1f on debut: op 10/1: Mar foal, cost 35,000gns: dam unrcd but from a gd family, sire a smart miler: eff over a stiff 7f on fast grnd, 1m will suit: pleasing debut.
2867 **PERSIAN PRIDE 21** [7] P W Harris 2-9-0 T G McLaughlin 14/1: -04: Chsd ldrs, onepcd fnl 1f: see 2867. *1½* **81**
-- **ESHER COMMON** [4] 2-9-0 R Mullen 25/1: -5: Trkd ldrs, ev ch when went left dist, sn onepcd: *hd* **81**
mkt drifter, debut: Jan foal, cost 27,000gns: first foal, sire a smart miler: likely to apprec 1m+ given time.
-- **HASTY PRINCE** [2] 2-9-0 D Sweeney 14/1: -6: Slow away, imprvd from rear halfway, no impress fnl *1¼* **78**
1f on debut: 62,000gns purchase: Apr foal, half-brother to sev wnrs, incl decent miler Port Lucaya: dam a 10f wnr in the USA, sire a high-class mid-dist performer: likely to apprec 1m+ next term: sure to learn from this.
-- **PENNY FARTHING** [9] 2-8-9 C Rutter 14/1: -7: Mid-div, no impress fnl 2f: racecourse bow: *3* **67**
5,500gns Apr foal: related to sev wnrs, incl a couple of 2yo scorers: sire a high-class 2yo wnr: H Candy filly.
-- **TOKEN** [1] 2-9-0 A Daly 11/1: -8: Prom till halfway, hung right & sn btn: tchd 14/1, debut: May *2½* **67**
foal, dam a 1m 2yo wnr in France: sire a high-class miler: likely to do better at 1m+ next term: with M Tregoning.
-- **ROYAL ENCLOSURE** [14] 2-9-0 D R McCabe 14/1: -9: Nvr a factor on debut: Mar foal, cost IR 100,000 *3½* **60**
gns: brother to a 7f wnr & half-brother to numerous scorers, incl a Gr winning 2yo abroad: dam an Irish 2yo wnr, sire a high-class miler: with B Meehan.
-- **CHESTERS BOY** [5] 2-9-0 J Bramhill 100/1: -0: Slowly away, nvr a factor in 10th on debut: Mar *2½* **55**
foal, half-brother to a couple of wnrs abroad: sire a decent 7f performer: with B Leavy.
2862 **TOBYTOO 21** [8] 2-9-0 R Fitzpatrick (3) 66/1: 000000: Early ldr, sn wknd & fin 13th: see 2862. **0**
-- **Regatta Point** [13] 2-9-0 D Harrison 33/1: 3051 **Uncle Folding 12** [11] 2-9-0 F Norton 50/1:
3029 **Polwhele 13** [3] 2-9-0 M Fenton 50/1: 3092 **Rozary 11** [6] 2-8-9 J Tate 66/1:
15 ran Time 1m 24.3 (2.3) (K Abdulla) Mrs A J Perrett Pulborough, W.Sussex.

3334

3.25 R WOOD HCAP 3YO+ 0-85 (D) 1m str Good/Firm 20 +28 Fast [85]
£7442 £2290 £1145 £572 3yo rec 7lb

3118 **DERRYQUIN 9** [11] P L Gilligan 5-7-13 (56)(bl) F Norton 16/1: 020401: 5 b g Lion Cavern - Top Berry **67**
(High Top) Made all, clr dist, cmftbly: best time of day: earlier won at Redcar (h'cap): failed to score in '99 (rtd 56, 1st time blnks): back in '97 won at Lingfield (mdn) & Doncaster (stks, rtd 100): suited by 1m: acts on gd/soft, loves fast/firm: suited by blnks now: apprec switch to forcing tactics & could make a qk follow up.
2610 **FLITWICK 31** [3] H R A Cecil 3-9-4 (82) W Ryan 7/1: -0162: 3 b c Warning - Flit (Lyphard) *3½* **85**
Nvr far away, kept on fnl 1f but not pace of ready wnr: met a well h'capped rival here: apprec a return to 10f.
2757 **SERGEANT YORK 25** [14] C Smith 4-9-7 (78)(vis) R Fitzpatrick (3) 20/1: 360453: 4 b g Be My Chief - *1¾* **77**
Metaphysique (Law Society) Chsd ldr, rdn & onepcd fnl 1½f: first time visor in 2757 (highly tried), see 2578.
3018 **COOL TEMPER 14** [6] J M P Eustace 4-9-2 (73) J Tate 10/1: 550544: Slowly away, imprvd 2f out, kept *1* **70**
on under press & nrst fin: mkt drifter: needs 10f now: see 3018.
*2890 **MADAM ALISON 20** [1] 4-9-12 (83) R Smith (5) 11/2: -31315: Prom, 6½f, fdd: top-weight: btr 2890. *nk* **79**
3118 **ITS MAGIC 9** [2] 4-9-1 (72)(bl) D Harrison 4/1 FAV: -06206: Rear, late hdwy under press, nvr nrr: *1¾* **64**
well bckd: twice below par after eye-catching effort in 3018.
3089 **DENS JOY 11** [12] 4-8-6 (63) D McGaffin(4) 14/1: 200547: Mid-div, eff 2f out, btn fnl 1f: see 3089. *½* **54**
-- **BABA AU RHUM** [8] 8-8-6 (63) L Newman (3) 25/1: 4500/8: Imprvd from rear halfway, btn dist: last *¾* **52**
rcd over hdles in 98/99, won twice at Ludlow (h'cap, rtd 101h, eff at 2m on fast/firm grnd): last rcd on the Flat in '98, 4th at Leicester (h'cap, rtd 66): '97 Sandown & Haydock Flat wnr (rtd 71): eff over a gall 1m on gd/soft & fast grnd, handles any trk: can force the pace: well h'capped now but 8yo.
2888 **STROMSHOLM 20** [7] 4-8-10 (67) R Mullen 11/2: 324239: Rcd keenly & trkd wnr, wknd over 1f out. *¾* **54**
3317 **SWYNFORD PLEASURE 1** [9] 4-7-10 (53)(2oh) G Bardwell 16/1: 334300: Nvr a factor in 10th: qk reapp. *1¾* **37**
2870 **RESPLENDENT STAR 21** [4] 3-9-3 (81)(bl) T G McLaughlin 10/1: 10-400: Nvr a factor, fin 11th. *½* **64**
3054 **ONE DINAR 12** [13] 5-8-5 (62) J Lowe 20/1: 050360: Slowly away, nvr a factor in 12th: btr 2752. *nk* **44**
3136 **PETRUS 9** [5] 4-8-11 (68)(t) C Rutter 11/1: 050000: Rear, hmpd halfway, nvr a factor in 13th. *½* **49**
776 **CHURCHILLS SHADOW 137** [10] 6-7-10 (53)(1oh) G Baker (5) 66/1: 3-5000: Speed 5f, wknd into *3* **28**
last: rnr-up in a nov sell hdle since 776.
14 ran Time 1m 33.7 (u0.7) (Lady Bland) P L Gilligan Newmarket.

3335

4.00 JIMMY WHITE RATED HCAP 3YO 0-105 (B) 6f str Good/Firm 20 -08 Slow [105]
£9639 £3656 £1828 £831

3130 **MERSEY MIRAGE 9** [8] R Hannon 3-8-8 (85) L Newman (3) 7/2: 302-01: 3 b c King's Signet - Kirriemuir **88**
(Lochnager) Chsd ldr till went on over 1f out, hdd ent fnl 1f, rallied gamely to regain lead cl-home, all out: '99 Brighton wnr (mdn, rtd 87): v eff at 6f on firm & gd/soft grnd: handles a stiff/gall or sharp/undul trk: lightly raced this season, can improve further & win again.
2900 **PEDRO JACK 19** [6] B J Meehan 3-8-5 (82)(bl) D Glennon (7) 5/1: 603522: 3 b g Mujadil - Festival *hd* **83**
Of Light (High Top) Led till dist, rallied gamely fnl 1f & just btn in a close fin: another sound run: see 2900.
3135 **BABY BARRY 9** [3] Mrs G S Rees 3-8-8 (85) F Norton 7/1: 343033: 3 b c Komaite - Malcesine (Auction *½* **85**
Ring) Trkd ldrs, switched dist, ran on strongly & btn under 1L in a close fin: stays 6f well: see 3135 (5f).
2769 **BAILEYS WHIRLWIND 25** [9] M L W Bell 3-9-1 (92) M Fenton 6/1: 503444: Dwelt, prog to lead ent *shd* **92**
fnl 1f, swamped by rivals cl-home: ran nr to best: see 2568, 2197.
3130 **BLUE VELVET 9** [2] 3-8-13 (90) C Carver (3) 10/3 FAV: 001165: In tch, edged right & onepcd fnl 1f. *2* **84**
3130 **GLENROCK 9** [5] 3-8-10 (87) A McGlone 7/1: 502006: Chsd ldrs, wknd fnl 1f: best 2568. *2½* **74**
2568 **KELSO MAGIC 33** [1] 3-8-11 (88)(BL) D R McCabe 25/1: 6-0007: Al outpcd in first time blnks: *7* **55**
well below form this term, grad coming down the weights: see 1078.
3158 **SEVEN NO TRUMPS 8** [4] 3-9-7 (98) R Naylor (7) 12/1: 000038: Al outpcd, nvr a factor: top-weight. *¾* **62**
8 ran Time 1m 11.5 (1.7) (Speedith Group) R Hannon East Everleigh, Wilts.

3336

4.35 CLASSIFIED STKS 3YO+ 0-75 (D) 1m3f183y Good/Firm 20 -57 Slow
£3796 £1168 £584 £292 3yo rec 11lb

*3122 **FAHS 9** [6] N Hamilton 8-9-7 D Harrison 10/11 FAV: 501211: 8 br g Riverman - Tanwi (Vision) **84**
Trkd ldrs, led dist, rdn clr for a decisive victory: well bckd, slow time, top-weight: earlier scored at Yarmouth & Newmarket (h'caps): '99 wnr at Yarmouth & Lingfield (h'cap, rtd 77 & 79a): '98 Lingfield wnr (amat h'cap, rtd 80a & 81): eff at 10/12f, stays 14f: acts on gd, firm grnd & equitrack, handles soft: likes Yarmouth: suited by waiting tactics, a gd weight carrier: continues in fine form.
2917 **ANGELS VENTURE 18** [4] J R Jenkins 4-9-3 (tvi) S Whitworth 5/1: 000432: 4 ch c Unfuwain - City Of *5* **72**

Angels (Woodman) Rear, imprvd to chase wnr dist, sn no impress: well clr of 3rd: met a fast improving rival.
2950 **BURNING** 16 [5] B D Leavy 8-9-3 (bl) J Bramhill 100/1: 000003: 8 b g Bering - Larnica (Alydar)   12 54$
Rear, eff 4f out, wkng when left 3rd ins fnl 1f: offic rtd just 24, treat this rating with extreme caution: see 2950.
*2876 **ALEXANDRINE** 20 [7] Sir Mark Prescott 3-8-11 G Duffield 5/2: 114114: Pulled hard & in tch, rdn &   2 56
btn 2f out: nicely bckd: puzzling run, this is not her form: much btr 2876.
3081 **EL KARIM** 11 [2] J Bosley (7) 100/1: /00-05: Led & sn in clr led, drifted left & wknd 2f   13 31
out, hdd dist, t.o.: see 3081 (1m).
1329 **HIGH POLICY** 88 [1] 4-9-3 A Daly 9/1: 63-106: Chsd ldr 10th, wknd, t.o.: 12 wk abs: btr 519 (AW).   ¾ 30
1674} **TENBY HEIGHTS** 439 [3] 4-9-3 (t) L Newman (3) 100/1: 0000-7: Prom 1m, wknd & t.o. on reapp: dist 0
prev trained by R Hollinshead & little Flat or hdles form: now with H Howe, wears a t-strap.
2032 **RUSSIAN MUSIC** 56 [8] 7-9-3 (t) O Pears 100/1: 00-00P: Rear, 3rd & staying on when broke leg   0
ins fnl 1f, sadly had to be destroyed.
8 ran   Time 2m 37.6 (9.3)   (City Industrial Supplies Ltd)   N Hamilton Epsom, Surrey.

3337   5.10 R. O'SULLIVAN HCAP 3YO+ 0-85 (D)   1m2f   Good/Firm 20 -36 Slow   [84]
£4046   £1245   £622   £311   3yo rec 9lb

2805 **INDUCEMENT** 23 [1] Mrs A J Perrett 4-9-11 (81) W Ryan 13/2: 400-41: 4 ch g Sabrehill - Verchinina   86
(Star Appeal) Held up, imprvd 3f out, went on dist, styd on strongly, pushed out: bckd from 10/1: '99 Sandown
wnr (h'cap, rtd 88, with B Hills): eff at 10f on fast & soft: likes a stiff/gall trc: gd weight carrier.
3102 **TROIS** 11 [5] J G Given 4-7-13 (55) G Baker (5) 12/1: 050452: 4 b g Efisio - Drei (Lyphard)   ½ 59
Rear, imprvd & ev ch 2f out, styd on well & not btn far: apprec this drop back to 10f: see 1279, 271.
3060 **CULZEAN** 12 [4] R Hannon 4-9-13 (83) L Newman (3) 5/1: 041203: 4 b g Machiavellian - Eileen Jenny   1 85
(Kris) Rear, imprvd 3f out, kept on under press & nrst fin: see 2844, 2287.
3285 **PAARL ROCK** 2 [8] G Barnett 5-7-12 (54) (vis) D Glennon (7) 5/1: 032144: Set pace till collared   1 54
dist, no extra: op 7/2, 4L clr rem: qck reapp since 3285, see 3093.
3166 **ANOTHER TIME** 8 [9] 8-9-8 (78) R Mullen 9/4 FAV: 050435: Hdwy from rear 3f out, btn fnl 1f: 4 72
well bckd: better expected after 3166.
3173 **PIPED ABOARD** 7 [6] 5-8-10 (66) M Fenton 16/1: 500606: Rear, imprvd & ev ch 2f out, btn dist: see 2502.   1½ 58
2955 **AMJAD** 16 [10] 3-8-0 (65)(BL) A Daly 25/1: 445507: Trkd ldr, ev ch 2f out, sn btn: first time blnks.   ¾ 56
2750 **LOVERS LEAP** 25 [3] 4-9-2 (72) C Rutter 10/1: 006008: Chsd ldrs till slipped on bend 5f out, sn btn   18 39
& eased considerably, t.o.: forget this: see 1969 (first time visor, 7f).
3186 **CITY GAMBLER** 6 [7] 6-7-11 (53) G Bardwell 7/1: 500109: Prom when slipped on bend 5f out,   12 2
wknd & eased, t.o.: qck reapp: btr 3031.
9 ran   Time 2m 08.1 (5.6)   (J B Dale)   Mrs A J Perrett Pulborough, W.Sussex.

Official Going   GOOD/FIRM (GOOD in places). Stalls: Str Course - Stands Side; Round - Inside, Except 1m - Centre.

3338   2.15 MAIL ON SUNDAY HCAP 3YO+ 0-100 (C)   1m str   Good/Firm 39 +00 Fast   [99]
£8404   £2586   £1293   £646   3yo rec 7lb

*3022 **KIROVSKI** 14 [3] P W Harris 3-8-6 (84) T Quinn 11/4 JT FAV: 0-2111: 3 b c Common Gounds - Nordic   90
Doll (Royal Academy) Led over 1f, led again well over 1f out, kept on well for press: hvly bckd, fair time:
landed hat-trick after wins at Carlisle & Newmarket (h'caps, fast times): rtd 71 on 3 unplcd juv starts: suited
by a stiff 1m on fast & gd: useful & game 3yo, thriving on his racing & open to further improvement.
3107 **MAYARO BAY** 10 [4] R Hannon 4-10-0 (99) R Hughes 14/1: 160302: 4 b f Robellino - Down The Valley   2 100
(Kampala) Cl-up, ev ch over 1f out, not pace of wnr: useful eff under top weight bhd a prog 3yo: see 2707.
*3018 **SALTY JACK** 14 [6] V Soane 6-8-13 (84) R Cochrane 11/2: 054513: 6 b h Salt Dome - Play The Queen   shd 85
(King Of Clubs) Held up, hdwy 2f out, kept on same pace ins last: tough (9 wins from 49 starts): see 3018.
2858 **ARGENTAN** 22 [11] J H M Gosden 3-8-8 (86)(bl) J Fortune 6/1: 220144: Held up, hdwy well over 1f   ¾ 85
out, short of room but kept on ins last, nvr dangerous: things did not go his way today & shld rate higher.
*3261 **BOLD EWAR** 3 [5] 3-8-2 (80)(bl)(5ex) S Carson(3) 8/1: 052015: Waited with, hdwy 2f out, onepace: 1 77
quick reapp under a pen having landed 3261 (minor trk).
2229 **TAMMAM** 46 [8] 4-9-1 (86) C Lowther 20/1: 053446: Dwelt, waited with, onepace over 1f out: abs.   2½ 78
2645 **STYLE DANCER** 30 [13] 6-7-13 (70) (vis) J Mackay(5) 14/1: 401107: Led after 1f till well over 1f   2½ 57
out, no extra: new tactics did not work, better waited with as in 2481.
3107 **SILK ST JOHN** 10 [10] 6-9-6 (91) D Holland 14/1: 316408: Waited with, brief eff 2f out, no extra.   hd 77
3063 **NAVIASKY** 12 [12] 5-8-7 (78) Martin Dwyer 9/1: 466349: Reluctant to post, waited with, rdn & btn   ¾ 62
over 2f out: a 'character' these days: see 2063, 2792.
2330 **STRASBOURG** 43 [7] 3-9-2 (94) Dean McKeown 11/1: -00220: In tch, wknd over 1f out: 10th, 6 wk abs: 2½ 73
prev trained by J Gosden, now with N Tinkler: btr 2330, 2108.
2564 **DOLPHINELLE** 33 [4] 4-7-10 (67)(4oh) M Henry 33/1: 031600: In tch, wknd over 2f out: 11th, btr 1926.   ¾ 44
2768 **TEMERAIRE** 25 [1] 5-8-12 (83) J F Egan 14/1: 042300: Al bhd: fin last, swtg: btr 2261, 1989 (7f).   1¾ HetS
12 ran   Time 1m 41.82 (3.12)   (Batten, Bowstead, Gregory & Manning)   P W Harris Aldbury, Herts.

3339   2.45 ANDREX HCAP 3YO+ 0-100 (C)   1m2f   Good/Firm 39 +06 Fast   [98]
£8170   £2514   £1257   £628   3yo rec 9lb

2805 **MYNAH** 23 [6] A C Stewart 3-8-10 (89) J P Spencer 11/2: 01221: 3 b f Selkirk - Reyah (Young Generation)   94
Waited with, hdwy travelling well over 1f out, sn led, drvn out ins last: gd time: earlier scored at Newmarket
(mdn): unraced juv: suited by a stiff 10f on firm/fast grnd: useful, genuine & lightly raced 3yo.
3110 **THE GREEN GREY** 10 [11] L Montague Hall 6-7-13 (69) Martin Dwyer 12/1: 100152: 6 gr g Environment   ½ 73
Friend - Pea Green (Try My Best) Cl-up, led 2f out till dist, kept on for press, not btn far: tough, likes Windsor.
2995 **ORMELIE** 15 [1] J H M Gosden 5-9-8 (92) J Fortune 4/1: 51-053: 5 b h Jade Hunter - Trolley Song   1½ 93
(Caro) Waited with, hdwy well over 1f out, kept on same pace ins last: bckd: ran close to best: see 2707.
3166 **EASTWAYS** 8 [7] M Johnston 3-8-5 (84) D Holland 3/1 FAV: 004224: Waited with, hdwy & short of   nk 85
room over 2f out, kept on same pace ins last: hvly bckd & running well in defeat: see 3166.
3060 **HUDOOD** 12 [8] 5-9-10 (94) T E Durcan 11/1: 001D05: Waited with, eff well over 1f out, onepace.   1¼ 93
1246 **THARI** 94 [5] 3-9-2 (95) R Hills 33/1: 136-06: Hld up, eff 2f out, sn no impress: abs, stays 10f.   shd 94

3134 **JUST IN TIME 9** [10] 5-9-8 (92) J Reid 10/1: 403057: Led till 2f out, no extra: see 3134, 874.   2½   87
2955 **IMPERIAL ROCKET 16** [2] 3-8-7 (86) R Hughes 11/2: 600228: In tch, wknd 2f out: bckd, btr 2955.   3   77
3060 **CHIEF CASHIER 12** [9] 5-8-10 (80) S Carson (3) 16/1: 001469: With ldr till over 6f out, wknd over   8   59
3f out: prefers softer: see 2750, 25522.
1528 **SPRING PURSUIT 78** [4] 4-9-0 (84) P Fitzsimons (5) 33/1: 130050: Dwelt, bhd, btn over 2f out: nk   63
10th, 11 wk abs & will be looking for softer grnd this autumn: see 1187.
2647 **J R STEVENSON 30** [3] 4-9-7 (91) A Nicholls (3) 11/1: 000650: Cl-up, wknd qckly over 2f out: 11th.   8   58
11 ran   Time 2m 07.31 (3.31)   (Hamish Leslie-Melville & Lord Hartington)   A C Stewart Newmarket

3340   3.15 LISTED VALIANT STKS 3YO+ (A)   1m rnd   Good/Firm 39 -01 Slow
£20670   £6360   £3180   £1590   3yo rec 7lb

*2167 **PAPABILE 50** [1] W Jarvis 3-8-9 R Cochrane 100/30: -24111: 3 b f Chief's Crown - La Papagena   105
(Habitat) Keen early in rear, gd hdwy to lead dist, rdn clr: nicely bckd, 7 wk abs: landed hat-trick after wins
at Yarmouth (mdn) & Ascot (List rtd h'cap): rnr-up as a juv (rtd 92): all 3 wins over a gall 1m, further shld suit:
acts on fast, handles soft & any trk, likes a gall one, esp Ascot: runs well fresh: fast improving & v useful.
*2487 **COURTING 38** [7] W J Haggas 3-8-9 R Hughes 3/1 FAV: 00-312: 3 gr f Pursuit Of Love - Doctor's Glory   1½   102
(Elmaamul) Set pace till dist, not pace of wnr: well bckd, clr of rem & prob career best run in defeat: see 2487.
4559} **ALPENGLOW 288** [5] J H M Gosden 4-8-12 R Havlin 7/2: 1613-3: 4 b f Ezzoud - Aquaglow (Caerleon)   3½   91
Prom, hdwy over 2f out, no extra appr fnl 1f: in '99 scored at Newmarket (fills mdn) & Leicester (stks, rtd 98
at best): stays a stiff 1m on firm & soft: runs well fresh: useful, sharper for this.
2274 **TOTAL LOVE 45** [6] E A L Dunlop 3-8-5 G Carter 7/2: -02534: Prom, eff 2f out, wknd over 1f out: ½   90
nicely bckd after a 6 wk abs: see 2274, 2150.
*1837 **CROWN LODGE 64** [2] 3-8-5 J P Spencer 6/1: -215: Waited with, eff over 2f out, sn no extra: 2 month   hd   89
abs & a stiff task after mdn win in 2837: shld find easier opportunities.
2857 **SHADY POINT 22** [4] 3-8-5 (vis) T E Durcan 25/1: 210606: Waited with, btn over 2f out: needs h'caps.   14   65
6 ran   Time 1m 41.72 (3.22)   (Exors Of The Late Howard de Walden)   W Jarvis Newmarket

3341   3.50 SANATOGEN HCAP 3YO+ 0-80 (D)   5f str   Good/Firm 39 -25 Slow   [80]
£6906   £2125   £1062   £531   3yo rec 3lb

3152 **DANCING MYSTERY 8** [11] E A Wheeler 6-10-0 (80) S Carson (3) 16/1: 510301: 6 b g Beveled - Batchworth   84
Dancer (Ballacashtal) Cl-up, hdwy to lead dist, kept on well for press ins last: earlier scored at Salisbury
(h'cap): '99 wnr at Lingfield, Southwell (rtd 82a), Warwick (h'caps) & Redcar (stks, rtd 78): '98 wnr at Windsor
& Goodwood (h'cap, rtd 57 & 74a): stays 6f, suited by 5f on fast, gd/soft & both AWs: handles any trk & runs well
fresh, with/without blnks: v tough & genuine (10 wins from 59 starts).
3136 **MISS HIT 9** [12] G A Butler 5-9-3 (69) J P Spencer 8/1: 00-102: 5 b m Efisio - Jennies' Gem   hd   72
(Sayf El Arab) Waited with, hdwy over 1f out, bumped 1f out, kept on ins last, just held: lightly rcd this term.
*3136 **FLAK JACKET 9** [3] D Nicholls 5-9-7 (73)(t) D Holland 11/8 FAV: 021113: 5 b g Magic Ring - Vaula   shd   76
(Henbit) Slow away, waited with, barged thro' appr fnl 1f, kept on for press ins last, just held: hvly bckd,
jockey received a 4 day careless riding ban which also triggered another 5 day ban: win again, see 3136 (6f).
3119 **DIAMOND GEEZER 9** [6] R Hannon 4-9-3 (69) R Hughes 13/2: 614224: Handy, eff to chall over 1f out,   ½   71
kept on, not btn far: just beat over a sharp 6f: see 3119.
2877 **MUNGO PARK 20** [15] 6-9-11 (77)(bl) A Clark 10/1: 022225: Held up, hdwy over 1f out, held head v   1   76
high & onepace for press: often plcd & on a long losing sequence: see 2877.
2999 **VIOLET 15** [7] 4-7-13 (51)(bl) J Mackay (5) 20/1: 010506: Dwelt, sn bhd, kept on over 1f out, nrst   1   47
fin: handles fast & soft: see 2631.
3046 **IVORY DAWN 13** [14] 6-9-10 (76) J F Egan 14/1: 301507: Waited with, eff 2f out, sn onepace.   ½   70
3209 **RITAS ROCK APE 5** [4] 5-9-5 (71) I Mongan (5) 20/1: 600108: Led till over 1f out, no extra ins last.   ¾   63
3091 **FORGOTTEN TIMES 11** [8] 6-9-7 (73)(vis) C Catlin (7) 16/1: 212069: Hld up, btn when hampd dist.   shd   64
2732 **POLAR MIST 26** [13] 5-8-6 (58)(tbl) Dean McKeown 25/1: 106020: In tch, btn over 1f out: 10th.   nk   48
2925 **Prince Prospect 18** [5] 4-9-9 (75) C Lowther 33/1:   3176 **Tiger Imp 7** [10] 4-9-1 (67) J Fortune 14/1:
3209 **That Man Again 5** [1] 8-9-3 (69)(bl) G Faulkner (3) 14/1:
13 ran   Time 1m 02.19 (3.19)   (Austin Stroud & Co Ltd)   E A Wheeler Whitchurch On Thames, Oxon

3342   4.25 IDEAL PRINTERS FILLIES MDN 2YO (D)   6f str   Good/Firm 39 -31 Slow
£6760   £2080   £1040   £520

2926 **EARLY MORNING MIST 18** [3] M Johnston 2-8-11 D Holland 4/1: -31: 2 b f Alzao - Welsh Mist   84
(Damister) Held up, hdwy & short of room over 2f out, styd on well for press to lead ins last, going away:
Jan 1st foal: dam useful 5f juv scorer: stays a stiff 6f well, 7f looks sure to suit: handles fast grnd &
any trk: type to progress with racing/over further, win again.
2901 **FARHA 19** [1] B Hanbury 2-8-11 R Hills 11/10 FAV: -32: 2 b f Nureyev - Arutua (Riverman)   1½   77
Led over 2f out, kept on for press till collared ins last, not pace of wnr: hvly bckd & shld win similar
on a minor trk: stays 6f on fast grnd: see 2901.
2714 **CARPET LADY 27** [8] Mrs P N Dutfield 2-8-11 P Doe 11/1: -33: 2 b f Night Shift - Lucky Fountain   1¼   73
(Lafontaine) Held up, hdwy 2f out, kept on same pace despite jumping path halfway: handles gd & fast:
shld apprec 7f on a minor trk: see 2714.
-- **TARA GOLD 9** [9] R Hannon 2-8-11 R Hughes 13/2: -4: Slow away, sn in tch, eff & not clr run   shd   73
over 2f out, kept on ins last: op 4/1, clr of rem on debut: Feb foal, cost 100,000 gns: full sister to a
v smart miler: bred to apprec 7f/1m in time & showed promise here: sure to rate higher.
-- **DANE DANCING** [6] 2-8-11 J Fortune 5/1: -5: Slow away, rdn & btn over 1f out on debut: 4   63
drifted from 9/4: Feb foal: half sister to sev wnrs: dam 10/12f scorer: bred to apprec 7f/1m+ in time.
3162 **THATS ALL JAZZ 8** [2] 2-8-11 A Mackay 50/1: -006: Led 2f out, wknd: see 993.   10   33
2583 **PHARMACYS PET 32** [4] 2-8-11 A Nicholls (3) 40/1: -007: With ldr, wknd 2f out, virtually p.u.: see 2357.   13   0
7 ran   Time 1m 16.68 (3.58)   (Alan Lillingston)   M Johnston Middleham, N Yorks

ASCOT SUNDAY AUGUST 13TH Righthand, Stiff, Galloping Track

3343 **5.00 CARBINE CLUB MDN 3YO (D) 7f str Good/Firm 39 -06 Slow**
£6695 £2060 £1030 £515

1837 **GREY EMINENCE 64** [5] R Hannon 3-9-0 R Hughes 6/4 JT FAV: 5-2221: 3 gr c Indian Ridge - Rahaam (Secreto) Waited with, gd hdwy to lead over 1f out, pushed clr ins last: well bckd after a 2 month abs: rnr-up 3 prev starts: apprec step back to 7f, stays a stiff 1m on fast & soft: runs well fresh: tough & useful. **84**
2999 **HARMONIC 15** [6] D R C Elsworth 3-8-9 T Quinn 4/1: 022202: 3 b f Shadeed - Running Melody (Rheingold) Chsd ldrs, hdwy to chall over 1f out, not pace of wnr ins last: rnr-up again: see 2621, 2232. *2½* **72**
-- **HUGS DANCER** [2] J G Given 3-9-0 Dean McKeown 20/1: -3: 3 b g Cadeaux Genereux - Embracing (Reference Point) Held up, eff 2f out, onepace: cost 14,000 gns: dam 12/14f scorer: bred to need 1m+: improve. *1½* **75**
3048 **ENTAIL 13** [1] J H M Gosden 3-8-9 J Fortune 6/4 JT FAV: 3-534: Led till over 1f out, wknd: hvly bckd & better expected after 3048 (rcd in touch). *3½* **63**
2531 **DAWN TRAVELLER 35** [4] 3-8-9 G Faulkner(3) 50/1: -005: With ldr, wknd over 1f out: see 1708. *9* **45**
-- **CHICANERY** [3] 3-9-0 C Lowther 20/1: -6: Dwelt, al bhd on debut: dam 6f juv scorer: with Mrs L Stubbs. *9* **32**
6 ran Time 1m 29.14 (3.14) (Jeffen Racing) R Hannon East Everleigh, Wilts

THIRSK MONDAY AUGUST 14TH Lefthand, Flat, Oval Track

Official Going GOOD (GOOD TO SOFT places). Stalls: Rnd Crse - Inside; Str Crse - Stands Side.

3344 **5.55 HORSESMOUTH SELL HCAP 3YO+ 0-60 (F) 1m rnd Good/Firm 31 -28 Slow [53]**
£3027 £865 £432 3 yo rec 7 lb

3220 **MARGARETS DANCER 5** [5] J L Eyre 5-9-5 (44)(t) K Darley 13/2: 0-0061: 5 b g Rambo Dancer - Cateryne (Ballymoss) Prom, rdn over 3f out, rdn & styd on gamely ins last to lead nr line, all out: no bid: rnr-up in '99 (class stks, rtd 61): '98 Pontefract, Thirsk (sells) & Beverley wnr (h'cap, rtd 61): suited by 1m on fast & hvy grnd, prob handles any trk: tried blnks, suited by a t-strap: apprec this drop in trip & return to sell grade. **49**
3118 **TRYSOR 10** [7] S C Williams 4-9-8 (47)(VIS) G Faulkner (3) 16/1: 000002: 4 b c Then Again - Zahiah (So Blessed) Led after 1f, hung right on bend from halfway, rdn & styd on well ins last, just hdd cl-home: op 14/1, fine run in first time visor: eff at 1m on fast grnd, only mod form previously. *hd* **51**
3288 **AL MABROOK 3** [2] K A Ryan 5-9-10 (49) F Lynch 8/1: 100003: 5 b g Rainbows For Life - Sky Lover (Ela Mana Mou) Mid-div, drvn & styd on fnl 2f, not pace to chall front pair: qck reapp: op 12/1: see 270 (AW) *1½* **50**
2994 **KIERCHEM 16** [18] C Grant 9-8-10 (35) T Hamilton (7) 16/1: 146004: Wide/rear, rdn & styd on well fnl 2f, nrst fin: op 25/1: a creditable run from a tricky high draw: see 2099. *1¾* **33**
3200 **BROCTUNE GOLD 6** [17] 9-8-13 (38) A Culhane 12/1: -50405: Held up, rdn/hdwy 2f out, held ins last. *½* **35**
2861 **RAASED 22** [8] 8-8-11 (36)(tvi) D Mernagh (3) 10/1: 0-0006: Chsd ldrs halfway, held 1f out: see 2861. *nk* **32**
3251 **MUJKARI 4** [4] 4-8-13 (38)(vis) G Baker (5) 12/1: 400237: Rear, rdn/mod gains fnl 3f: qck reapp. *1½* **31**
3081 **JAMMIE DODGER 12** [3] 4-9-2 (41) V Halliday 16/1: 01U068: Chsd ldrs, btn 2f out: see 2533. *shd* **34**
2950 **HEATHYARDS JAKE 17** [9] 4-9-6 (45) M Tebbutt 20/1: 500549: Dwelt/rear, mod gains, nrst fin. *shd* **37**
2946 **SHONTAINE 17** [10] 7-8-11 (36)(bl) C Lowther 25/1: 300000: Hmpd/drpd towards rear after 2f, mod late gains, no threat: 10th, blnks reapplied: see 383, 297. *nk* **27**
*3138 **CODICIL 10** [15] 4-9-0 (39) T Williams 8/1: 003410: In tch, btn 2f out: 11th: op 6/1: btr 3138 (7f). *1* **28**
2861 **KUSTOM KIT KEVIN 22** [14] 4-9-0 (39)(BL) G Duffield 16/1: 030000: Al twds rear: 12th: blnks. *4* **20**
3080 **CAIRN DHU 12** [1] 6-8-7 (32) F Norton 33/1: 000050: Dwelt, nvr on terms: 13th: see 159 (AW seller). *1½* **10**
3288 **FALLS OMONESS 3** [12] 6-9-8 (47) W Supple 11/4 FAV: 020000: Keen/chsd ldrs halfway, btn 2f out: 14th: well bckd, op 4/1: qck reapp: see 2062, 931. *¾* **24**
3200 **COOL AFFAIR 6** [6] 5-9-6 (45) J Bramhill 16/1: /00-00: Led 1f, prom 6f: 15th: op 14/1: qck reapp. *1½* **19**
1939 **Scarlet Livery 60** [16] 4-9-3 (42) K Hodgson 33/1: 3181 **Buzz The Agent 7** [11] 5-8-11 (36)(bl) T Lucas 12/1:
3251 **Mustang 4** [13] 7-9-3 (42)(vis) G Bardwell 20/1:
18 ran Time 1m 40.1 (4.7) (J Bladen) J L Eyre Sutton Bank, N.Yorks.

3345 **6.25 SAFFIE JOSEPH HCAP 3YO 0-80 (D) 1m rnd Good/Firm 31 -09 Slow [83]**
£4121 £1268 £634 £317

*3266 **OSTARA 4** [6] K A Ryan 3-8-4 (59)(6ex) F Lynch 13/2: 300511: 3 b g Petorius - Onde de Choc (L'Enjoleur) Held up, prog to chall fnl 2f, rdn & narrow lead well ins last, just held on, all out: qck reapp under a 6lb pen: recent wnr at Haydock (mdn clmr): plcd once in '99 (seller, first time blnks, rtd 61): prev eff at 6/7f, now seems suited by 1m on fast & gd/soft grnd, gall or sharp track: eff with/without blnks. **65**
3288 **YENALED 3** [1] J S Goldie 3-7-13 (54) G Baker (5) 2/1 FAV: 624622: 3 gr g Rambo Dancer - Fancy Flight (Arctic Tern) Held up, rdn/prog to lead over 1f out, hdd well ins last, just held: well bckd: see 1434. *nk* **59**
3095 **NOBLE PASAO 12** [5] Andrew Turnell 3-9-0 (69) R Thomas (7) 8/1: 553133: 3 b g Alzao - Belle Passe (Be My Guest) Cl-up, rdn/led over 3f out till over 1f out, onepace after: op 6/1: see 2970 (C/D, made all). *3* **68**
3269 **HEATHYARDS LAD 4** [8] R Hollinshead 3-7-12 (53) P M Quinn (3) 7/1: 550034: Rear/in tch, styd on for press fnl 2f, no threat: qck reapp: eyecatching latest but only one win previously: see 976, 294. *¾* **51**
3033 **DIAMOND OLIVIA 14** [4] 3-8-1 (56)(1ow) O Pears 11/2: 340625: Chsd ldrs, held over 1f out: btr 3033 (7f) *2* **50**
2733 **STORMVILLE 27** [7] 3-8-7 (62) D Mernagh (3) 8/1: 640026: Prom, btn 2f out: op 6/1: btr 2733. *9* **43**
2918 **DESERT SAFARI 19** [3] 3-9-5 (74) W Supple 14/1: 011367: Chsd ldrs 6f: btr 2699, 2438 (7f). *6* **46**
3147 **SHAAN MADARY 9** [2] 3-9-7 (76) A Culhane 6/1: -02148: Led till over 3f out, btn/eased over 1f out. *8* **36**
8 ran Time 1m 38.6 (3.2) (J Nixon) K A Ryan Hambleton, N.Yorks.

3346 **6.55 UNION TRUCKS MED AUCT MDN 2YO (E) 5f Good/Firm 31 -03 Slow**
£3038 £935 £467 £233 Raced across track, no advantage

3143 **FOREVER TIMES 9** [3] T D Easterby 2-8-9 K Darley 9/4 FAV: 36221: 2 b f So Factual - Simply Times (Dodge) Al prom far side, rdn/led halfway, styd on strongly ins last, rdn out: nicely bckd tho' op 7/4: eff at 5f, stays 6f & a return to that trip shld suit: acts on fast grnd: op to further improv when tackling further. **77**
3092 **CRIMSON RIDGE 12** [8] R Hollinshead 2-8-9 N Carter (7) 16/1: -3642: 2 b f King's Signet - Cloudy Reef (Cragador) Al prom in centre, rdn & styd on well fnl 1f, not pace of wnr: rest well covered: eff at 5f on fast. *1¾* **71**
2608 **QUEENS MUSICIAN 32** [13] M Dods 2-9-0 A Culhane 3/1: -3303: 2 b c Piccolo - Queens Welcome *2½* **69**

(Northfields) Al prom stands side, drvn & styd on fnl 2f, no threat to front pair: bckd: eff at 5f, needs return to 6f.
3143 **BOLD MCLAUGHLAN 9** [12] J S Goldie 2-9-0 T E Durcan 33/1: 000654: Went left start, chsd ldrs stands side, kept on onepace fnl 2f: see 700 (debut). ½ **67**
-- **EFIDIUM** [7] 2-9-0 J McAuley 100/1: 5: In tch centre, held over 1f out: Presidium colt, Apr foal, a first foal, cost only 900gns: dam a 1m wnr: creditable intro for N Bycroft. *shd* **67**
2088 **DOUBLE FANTASY 54** [10] 2-8-9 M Tebbutt 5/2: 06: Badly bmpd start, towards rear stands side, drvn & kept on fnl 2f, nvr threat to ldrs: hvly bckd, 8 wk abs: lost winning ch at start, can improve on this: see 2088. *hd* **61**
3009 **BOLLIN TOBY 15** [11] 2-9-0 (BL) R Winston 100/1: -07: Hmpd start, towards rear stands side, mod gains: blnks: well bhd on debut prev: Mar foal, half-brother to 2 wnrs: dam a winning sprint h'capper. *1* **64**
2730 **PAID UP 27** [1] 2-9-0 T Lucas 16/1: 468: In tch far side 4f: btr 2360. *hd* **63**
2821 **WHITE STAR LADY 24** [5] 2-8-9 W Supple 33/1: 5059: Nvr on terms far side: see 1304. ½ **56**
-- **DOUBLE PING** [4] 2-8-9 G Parkin 100/1: 0: Dwelt, nvr on terms far side: 10th: Petong filly, Apr foal: half-sister to mid-dist/staying h'capper Sandbaggedagain: dam unrcd: with M W Easterby. ¾ **54**
1294 **DISPOL CHIEFTAN 91** [2] 2-9-0 G Duffield 25/1: 0550: Cl-up far side 3f: 11th: abs: btr 1294. *1* **57**
2277 **RISING PASSION 46** [9] 2-9-0 A Nicholls (3) 25/1: 000: Badly bmpd start, al rear centre: 12th: abs. 3½ **48**
3092 **HEATHYARDS SIGNET 12** [6] 2-9-0 F Norton 66/1: 560: Led far side till halfway, sn held: 13th. *2* **43**
13 ran Time 58.7 (1.7) (Times Of Wigan) T D Easterby Great Habton, N.Yorks.

3347

7.25 CALVERTS MDN AUCT 2YO (E) 7f rnd Good/Firm 31 -38 Slow
£3103 £955 £477 £238

2862 **KINGS WELCOME 22** [3] C W Fairhurst 2-8-6 P Goode (3) 4/1: -31: 2 b c Most Welcome - Reine de Thebes (Darshaan) Held up, rdn/hdwy 2f out & led ins last, styd on strongly & pushed clr cl-home, readily: op 7/2: confirmed promise of debut: eff at 7f, looks sure to relish 1m+: acts on fast grnd: should win more races. **78+**
3032 **CERALBI 14** [6] R Hollinshead 2-8-9 W Supple 3/1: 622: 2 b c Goldmark - Siwana (Dom Racine) Chsd ldrs, briefly led over 1f out, styd on ins last, no ch with wnr: bckd, tho' op 9/4: stays 7f, handles fast & gd. *4* **70**
3079 **TEFI 12** [8] T D Easterby 2-8-9 K Darley 5/4 FAV: -53223: 2 ch g Efisio - Masuri Kabisa (Ascot Knight) Handy, rdn/narrow lead halfway till over 1f out, held ins last: hvly bckd: handles firm & fast grnd: see 3079, 1558. 2½ **65**
2985 **CHEMICALATTRACTION 16** [9] D W Barker 2-8-9 F Lynch 33/1: 004: Led, rdn/pressed halfway, hdd over 1f out & no extra: imprvd for forcing tactics: stays 7f & handles fast grnd: h'cap company shld suit. ¾ **64**
1864 **CAVERNARA 63** [2] 2-8-1 P Fessey 13/2: 45: Chsd ldrs, no room 1f out, hmpd/no extra ins last: abs. ½ **55**
-- **LANCE FEATHER** [7] 2-8-12 R Winston 20/1: 6: Bhd, mod late gains, nrst fin: Petardia colt, Feb foal, a first foal: dam a mdn: sire a smart juv/high-class miler: will know more next time, shld improve for J L Eyre. *3* **60**
-- **TIME PROOF** [1] 2-8-9 G Duffield 20/1: 7: Towards rear/rdn halfway, no impress: Clantime gelding, Apr foal, a first foal: dam sister to smart h'capper Jo Mell: with R Fahey. 1¼ **54**
3009 **HIGH SOCIETY LADY 15** [10] 2-8-1 J McAuley 100/1: 000008: Prom till halfway: mod form. 3½ **39**
3127 **TOMAMIE 10** [11] 2-8-1 O Pears 100/1: 000009: Cl-up, btn 2f out: mod form. *3* **33**
2828 **POUR NOUS 24** [5] 2-8-6 A Culhane 33/1: 000: Bhd halfway: longer 7f trip. *dist* **0**
10 ran Time 1m 27.7 (4.8) (G H & S Leggott) C W Fairhurst Middleham, N.Yorks.

3348

7.55 BLACK SHEEP HCAP 3YO+ 0-60 (F) 2m Good/Firm 31 -56 Slow [56]
£2957 £845 £422 3 yo rec 15lb

*3276 **BEAUCHAMP MAGIC 3** [4] M D I Usher 5-8-2 (30) G Baker(5) 4/1 JT FAV: 430111: 5 b g Northern Park - Beauchamp Buzz (High Top) Held up in tch, rdn/prog to lead over 2f out, strongly pressed ins last, rdn & styd on gamely to narrowly prevail: slow time: op 7/2, qck reapp: earlier scored at Brighton (sell h'cap) & W'hampton (AW appr h'cap, rtd 37a): '99 W'hampton wnr (AW h'cap, rtd 37a & 54, t-strap, tried blnks): plcd in '98 (rtd 69, h'cap): eff arnd 12f/2m on f/sand, firm & gd grnd: likes a sharp/undul trk, esp W'hampton: best form without vis or blnks. **33**
3112 **NEEDWOOD TRIDENT 10** [6] J Pearce 3-7-10 (39)(5oh) P M Quinn (3) 14/1: 050042: 3 b f Minshaanshu Amad - Needwood Nymph (Bold Owl) Held up, prog to press wnr ins last, just held: stays a slowly run 2m on fast. *shd* **41**
3053 **YES KEEMO SABEE 13** [1] D Shaw 5-9-3 (45) L Newton 4/1 JT FAV: 002533: 5 b g Arazi - Nazeera (Lashkari) Held up in tch, rdn & prog to press wnr fnl 1f, held nr fin: acts on fast, soft & fibresand: see 2461. ¾ **46**
*2902 **KING FOR A DAY 20** [7] Bob Jones 4-9-1 (43)(vis) F Norton 5/1: -00414: In tch, onepace/held 1f out. *2* **42**
3233 **MONACLE 5** [5] 6-9-1 (43) O Pears 11/2: -34125: Led 4f out till over 2f out, sn held: qck reapp. ½ **41**
2436 **RIGADOON 39** [8] 4-9-11 (53)(bl) G Parkin 9/1: -45046: Dictated pace, increase tempo halfway till hdd 4f out, sn held: op 7/1: topweight: see 797. *2* **49**
*3099 **TOP OF THE CHARTS 12** [3] 4-8-12 (40)(bl) A Culhane 9/2: 4-5017: Chsd ldrs, ch 2f out, sn held. 1¾ **34**
3002 **ACQUITTAL 16** [2] 8-8-7 (35)(vis) J Bramhill 8/1: 044538: Held up, outpcd fnl 3f: op 7/1: see 3002. *shd* **29**
8 ran Time 3m 36.7 (13.9) (The Magic & Dance Partnership) M D I Usher Kingston Lisle, Oxon.

3349

8.25 WEATHERBYS BANK HCAP 3YO 0-80 (D) 5f Good/Firm 31 +11 Fast [87]
£4303 £1324 £662 £331 Majority racing stands side always ahead

*2919 **OUR FRED 19** [11] T G Mills 3-9-2 (75)(bl) K Darley 7/1: 440211: 3 ch g Prince Sabo - Sheila's Secret (Bluebird) Made all stands side, drvn & held on well ins last: best time of night: nicely bckd, op 9/1: earlier scored at Leicester (auct mdn): plcd on 3 of 4 juv starts in '99 (rtd 79, nurs): eff at 5f, stays 6f: acts on firm & soft grnd, sharp or stiff/gall trk: well suited by blnks & forcing tactics. **82**
*3194 **PIPS STAR 7** [15] J S Goldie 3-7-13 (58)(6ex) G Baker (5) 5/1: 000112: 3 b f Pips Pride - Kentucky Starlet (Cox's Ridge) Al prom stands side, ev ch ins last, kept on tho' just held nr fin: bckd: see 3194. ¾ **62**
3194 **SOBA JONES 7** [8] T D Easterby 3-7-13 (58)(bl) T Williams 15/2: 343153: 3 b g Emperor Jones - Soba (Most Secret) In tch stands side, styd on fnl 2f, not pace of front pair: see 3035 (mdn). 1¾ **58**
3225 **RYTHM N TIME 5** [17] E J Alston 3-8-11 (70) W Supple 12/1: 400144: Chsd ldrs stands side, held fnl 1f. *nk* **69**
3037 **ZESTRIL 14** [12] 3-8-4 (63)(vis) R Winston 16/1: 066005: Stands side, nvr pace to chall: see 3037. 1¼ **59**
2684 **HONESTY FAIR 30** [3] 3-9-7 (80) D Mernagh (3) 13/2: 000466: Prom far side, led that group over 1f out, styd on, no ch with ldrs stands side: first home on unfav'd far side, worth another chance: see 1384 (C/D). ¾ **74**
-- **SOMESESSION** [14] 3-9-5 (78)(bl) T E Durcan 4/1 FAV: 0-0017: Chsd ldrs stands side, held over 1f out: bckd, op 5/1: Irish raider: recent wnr of a h'cap at The Curragh: eff at 5f on fast grnd: eff in blnks. 1¼ **69**
3010 **PERTEMPS FC 15** [2] 3-7-10 (55)(t)(3oh) P Fessey 8/1: 000008: Chsd ldrs far side, held over 1f out. ½ **44**
2541 **MARON 35** [5] 3-8-2 (61) P Bradley (5) 14/1: 032109: Dwelt/bhd far side, nvr on terms: 10th: op 16/1. ½ **48**
2820 **LYDIAS LOOK 24** [1] 3-7-13 (58) F Norton 50/1: 410000: Chsd far side ldrs, held 2f out: 10th. *1* **43**
3135 **MAROMITO 10** [9] 3-9-2 (75) O Pears 12/1: 10-000: Prom till halfway: 11th: op 10/1: see 2644. *shd* **60**
3135 **SABRE LADY 10** [16] 3-9-5 (78) A Nicholls (3) 16/1: -34000: Al bhd stands side: 12th: op 14/1. *hd* **62**
2929 **DISTINCTLY BLU 19** [7] 3-8-13 (72) F Lynch 10/1: 252100: Led far side till over 1f out, sn held: 13th. ¾ **54**

THIRSK
MONDAY AUGUST 14TH Lefthand, Flat, Oval Track

844 **Shatin Beauty 128** [13] 3-8-5 (64) P Hanagan (7) 50/1:
3113 **Palmstead Belle 10** [6] 3-7-13 (58)(t) Dale Gibson 25/1:
2418 **Alustar 40** [4] 3-8-7 (66) J McAuley 25/1:   3161 **Mount Park 9** [10] 3-7-10 (55)(bl)(6oh) Claire Bryan (4) 25/1:
17 ran   Time 58.00 (1.0)   (Sherwoods Transport Ltd)   T G Mills Headley, Surrey.

WINDSOR
MONDAY AUGUST 14TH Sharp, Figure 8 Track

Official Going   GOOD (GOOD/FIRM in places). Stalls: Inside.

3350
2.00 YORKSHIRE FOG MDN 3YO+ (D)   **1m67y rnd**   **Good   Inapplicable**
£2951   £908   £454   £227   3 yo rec 7 lb

2611 **ALWAYS VIGILANT 32** [10] R Charlton 3-8-9 R Hughes 4/1 CO FAV: -031: 3 b f Lear Fan - Crowning
Ambition (Chief's Crown) Made all, kept on well over 1f out, rdn out: drifted from 9/4: full sister to a 12f wnr:
stays 8.3f well, further will suit: handles fast & gd: improved & useful from the front today.   91

1108 **CAFE OPERA 103** [8] J W Hills 3-8-9 M Hills 4/1 CO FAV: 42-02: 3 b f Sadler's Wells - Takreem
(Mr Prospector) Held up, hdwy over 2f out, chsd wnr over 1f out, no impress: op 9/4: fair run after a 3 month
abs & stays 8.3f on gd & firm grnd: sharper from this over further: see 1108.   3½   83

3048 **COOLING OFF 14** [13] G Wragg 3-8-9 D Holland 11/2: -03: 3 b f Brief Truce - Lover's Parlour (Beldale
Flutter) In tch, hdwy over 2f out, sn onepace: clr of rem: better run & could improve again over further.   2½   78$

-- **FARAWAY LOOK** [6] J R Fanshawe 3-9-0 D Harrison 7/1: 4: In tch, modest late gains: half-brother
to a 7f juv scorer: bred to apprec 1m.   10   67

-- **EUROLINK ZANTE** [7] 4-9-7 J Reid 16/1: 5: Held up, outpcd over 3f out, some late gains, nvr
dngrs: op 8/1: bred to apprec 1m+: shld prove sharper & improve for this.   1½   65

4606} **CENTER STAGE 283** [4] A Daly 10/1: 46-6: In tch, rdn & no impress over 2f out: reapp, op 5/1:
unplcd on 2 juv starts (rtd 81): dam 1m juv wnr: eff at 7f on hvy grnd.   1   63

2924 **SHADOWBLASTER 19** [9] 3-9-0 Dane O'Neill 4/1 CO FAV: -5227: Keen bhd, eff over 2f out, sn wknd.   3   57

478 **KUWAIT FLAVOUR 188** [11] 4-9-7 D McGaffin (5) 16/1: 4/3-68: Nvr a factor: long abs since 478.   4   49

3048 **LIVELY FELIX 14** [5] 3-9-0 C Rutter 50/1: -09: Prom, wknd over 2f out.   3½   42

2325 **GROVE LODGE 44** [12] 3-9-0 S Whitworth 50/1: 000000: Al bhd: 10th, abs: see 1024.   ½   41

1343 **Miss Amber Nectar 88** [1] 3-8-9 S Carson (3) 50/1:   2384} **Red Thatch 409** [3] 3-9-0 T G McLaughlin 50/1:
12 ran   Time 1m 45.1   (K Abdulla)   R Charlton Beckhampton, Wilts.

3351
2.30 TIMOTHY SELLER 3-4YO (G)   **1m3f135y**   **Good   Inapplicable**
£1886   £539   £269   3 yo rec 11lb

3008 **TITUS BRAMBLE 15** [6] B R Millman 3-9-2 R Hughes 11/4 FAV: 060141: 3 b g Puissance - Norska
(Northfields) Held up, hdwy 2f out, kept on to lead ins last, rdn out: bckd, op 9/4: bt in for 4,000gns: earlier
won at Yarmouth (seller): unplcd & tried blnks in '99 (rtd 74, prob flattered): eff at 10f, stays 11.6f on firm & gd.   52

3313 **DOUBLE ROCK 2** [3] P Howling 4-9-4 J Quinn 9/1: 542: 4 b f Rock Hopper - Rockin' Rosie (Song)
Led, rdn & hdd ins last, just held off: clr of rem & stays 11.6f on gd grnd in sell grade.   nk   42

3050 **INDIANA SPRINGS 13** [9] J G Given 3-8-12 J Tate 14/1: 400603: 3 b g Foxhound - Moss Agate (Alias
Smith) Keen, held up, hdwy over 2f out, sn onepace: stays 11.3f on gd grnd in sell grade.   3½   42

2981 **ALBERGO 17** [10] M Blanshard 3-8-12 Dane O'Neill 9/1: 002004: Chsd ldrs, outpcd over 3f out, some
late gains: see 1234, 937.   1¼   40

2887 **ERIN ANAM CARA 21** [8] 3-8-7 C Rutter 100/30: -00005: Bhd, brief eff over 2f out, wknd over
1f out: bckd tho' op 2/1: see 2887.   7   26

3262 **NO REGRETS 4** [1] 3-8-12 G Hannon (7) 8/1: 500026: Bhd, brief effort over 2f out, wknd over 1f out.   1   30

-- **LANTIC BAY** [5] 3-8-7 R Havlin 16/1: 7: Slow away, bhd, btn over 3f out: jump bred.   ¾   23

2914 **SWALDO 19** [1] 3-8-12 T G McLaughlin 5/1: 3-0008: In tch, wknd over 2f out: now with M Muggeridge.   1½   26

3048 **WHITE MAGIC 14** [2] 3-8-7 S Carson 12/1: 0-09: Al bhd: poor form.   2   18

9 ran   Time 2m 36.8   (Henry Rix)   B R Millman Kentisbeare, Devon.

3352
3.00 RBS COND STKS 2YO (C)   **6f**   **Good   Inapplicable**
£5307   £2013   £1006   £457

*3062 **PICCOLO PLAYER 13** [6] R Hannon 2-8-12 Dane O'Neill 6/4 FAV: -21411: 2 b g Piccolo - The Frog Lady
(Al Hareb) Dsptd lead, led over 3f out, clr over 1f out, eased: val 5L+, hvly bckd: Mar foal, cost 12,000gns:
half-brother to a juv 7f wnr: earlier won at Windsor (auct mdn) & Goodwood (nurs h'cap): eff at 6f, shld stay
further: acts on fast, gd & on easy trks, likes Windsor: can force the pace: improved & useful now since gelded.   102

*2132 **WARDEN WARREN 52** [7] M A Jarvis 2-9-0 P Robinson 5/1: -012: 2 b c Petong - Silver Spell (Aragon)
Handy, hdwy to go 2nd over 1f out, no impress on wnr: op 3/1: abs & progressing well: lightly rcd, see 2132.   3½   89

2915 **NEARLY A FOOL 19** [5] B A McMahon 2-9-4 J Fortune 10/1: 331333: 2 b g Komaite - Greenway Lady
(Prince Daniel) In tch, eff 2f out, sn onepace: op 6/1: useful & consistent: see 2915.   1   90

2849 **THREEZEDZZ 23** [3] J G Portman 2-8-12 T Quinn 7/1: 12634: Led till over 3f out, wknd over 1f out.   ½   83

1176 **PALACE AFFAIR 99** [1] 2-8-2 (BL) S Carson (3) 9/1: W5: Went left start, sn handy, wknd over
1f out: abs, blnks, op 6/1: see 1176.   3½   63

3105 **STREGONE 11** [4] 2-9-0 Pat Eddery 5/2: 204206: Prom, wknd well over 1f out: bckd, btr 2850.   2   69

2867 **COURT ONE 22** [2] 2-8-10 P Fitzsimons (5) 50/1: -007: Al well bhd: see 1403.   24   15

7 ran   Time 1m 13.4   (Park Walk Racing)   R Hannon East Everleigh, Wilts.

3353
3.30 BROWNTOP HCAP 3YO+ 0-70 (E)   **1m3f135y**   **Good   Inapplicable**   **[70]**
£2996   £856   £428   3 yo rec 11lb

3219 **KENNET 5** [8] P D Cundell 5-9-6 (62) S Sanders 6/1: 202231: 5 b g Kylian - Marwell Mitzi (Interrex)
Held up, hdwy over 2f out, styd on to lead ins last, drvn out: qck reapp & deserved win after sev plcd runs:
in '99 won at Lingfield (mdn, rtd 72a), Windsor & Bath (class stks, rtd 72): eff over 10/12f on any grnd:
likes sharp trks & has run well fresh: proving tough & consistent.   68

2852 **FIRST IMPRESSION 23** [11] Mrs A J Perrett 5-10-0 (70) Pat Eddery 5/1 FAV: 45-202: 5 b g Saddlers'
Hall - First Sapphire (Simple Great) Led, rdn & hdd ins last, not pace of wnr: clr of rem & a fine run under 10-0.   1¼   72

3049 **THE SHADOW** 14 [7] D W P Arbuthnot 4-7-12 (40) (vis) J Quinn 20/1: 005003: 4 br g Polar Falcon - Shadiliya (Red Alert) Prom, rdn & btn 1f out: prob just best at 10f: see 854. 4 38
3049 **MY PLEDGE** 14 [4] C A Horgan 5-9-2 (58) T Quinn 6/1: -21034: Held up, brief eff over 2f out, sn btn. ½ 55
2793 **HALF TIDE** 25 [9] 6-8-5 (47) J Mackay (5) 9/1: 062105: Held up, hdwy over 2f out, sn onepace: op 6/1. ¾ 43
3045 **COMPATRIOT** 14 [6] 4-9-6 (62) W Ryan 14/1: 602536: Bhd, brief eff over 2f out, no impress: see 3045. ¾ 57
*3045 **QUEENS PAGEANT** 14 [1] 6-10-1 (71) M Roberts 15/2: 446517: Held up, wknd well over 1f out: top-weight & prob not stay 11.5f: btr 3045 (10f). 3 62
3014 **IGNITE** 15 [2] 3-8-13 (66) J Reid 7/1: 40-068: Bhd, wknd 2f out: nicely bckd: see 2750. nk 56
1862 **UNDER THE SAND** 64 [3] 3-9-1 (68) P Robinson 13/2: 000429: Bhd, wknd over 2f out: 2 month abs. 1¼ 56
1425 **CONSTANT** 84 [10] 3-9-0 (67) M Hills 12/1: 5-0500: Al bhd: 10th, 3 month abs: see 1225, 979. 23 25
3049 **DIZZY TILLY** 14 [5] 6-8-4 (46) J Tate 9/1: 010600: Prom, wknd over 3f out: fin last: see 2370. 5 0
11 ran   Time 2m 31.0   (Miss M C Fraser)   P D Cundell Compton, Berks.

3354	4.00 TATTERSALLS FILLIES NURSERY HCAP 2YO (D 6f Good Inapplicable	[90]
	£3575 £1100 £550 £275	

2990 **SHARP SECRET** 16 [3] M Johnston 2-8-0 (62) R Ffrench 8/1: -5251: 2 b f College Chapel - State Treasure (Secretariat) Nvr far away, led dist, rdn clr fnl 1f: op 6/1: earlier rnr-up at Hamilton (mdn auct): 10,000gns purchase, sire a high-class 6/7f wnr: eff over an easy 6f on gd & fast grnd: likes to run-up with the pace: decisive wnr here & can follow up. 75
2940 **QUIZZICAL LADY** 18 [2] M Quinn 2-8-8 (70) C Rutter 16/1: 040642: 2 b f Mind Games - Salacious (Sallust) Rear, eff 2f out, styd on for 2nd fnl 1f, no ch with wnr: eff at 5/6f on fast & hvy grnd: see 1000. 5 70
3029 **JETHAME** 14 [9] B J Meehan 2-8-7 (69) Pat Eddery 7/1: 003533: 2 ch f Definite Article - Victorian Flower (Tate Gallery) Rear, eff halfway, kept on under press & nrst fin: eff at 6f, will apprec a return to 7f. nk 68
2678 **QUANTUM LADY** 30 [4] B R Millman 2-8-11 (73) G Hind 12/1: 122364: Set pace till dist, no extra. 1¼ 68
3258 **CHAWENG BEACH** 4 [6] 2-7-12 (60) (2ow)(3oh) J Quinn 8/1: 01645: In tch, rdn & onepcd fnl 1f. 1¼ 52
2891 **QUEENS COLLEGE** 21 [5] 2-8-3 (65) J Mackay (5) 10/1: -0526: Rear, not pace to chall: see 2891 (5f). 1 54
3174 **MILLYS LASS** 8 [8] 2-8-13 (75) Craig Williams 15/2: 132037: Nvr nr ldrs: op 11/2: btr 3174, 2657. 1¾ 60
2849 **MILLENNIUM MAGIC** 23 [7] 2-9-7 (83) A Beech 9/1: 342008: In tch till halfway: btr 2172. nk 67
2368 **FACE D FACTS** 42 [1] 2-9-2 (78) R Mullen 11/2: -5139: Dwelt, nvr a factor on h'cap debut: 6 wk abs: lost all ch at the start today: much btr 2368, 2214. 2 56
2589 **EBULLIENCE** 33 [10] 2-9-3 (79) T Quinn 7/4 FAV: 0120: Speed 4f, wknd & fin last: hvly bckd from 5/2, h'cap debut: much better clrly expected, something amiss here? btr 2589, 1883. ½ 55
10 ran   Time 1m 13.9   (T T Bloodstocks)   M Johnston Middleham, N.Yorks.

3355	4.30 PERENNIAL RYE HCAP 3YO+ 0-80 (D) 1m67y rnd Good Inapplicable	[76]
	£3945 £1214 £607 £303 3 yo rec 7 lb	

3207 **TAPAGE** 6 [6] Andrew Reid 4-8-12 (60) Pat Eddery 11/4 FAV: 111621: 4 b g Great Commotion - Irena (Bold Lad) Made all, held on well fnl 1f, drvn out: well bckd from 9/2, qck reapp: earlier won at Lingfield (2, AW h'caps, rtd 53a), Bath & Brighton (h'caps): rnr-up twice in '99 (clmr, rtd 69, with W Muir): '98 Lingfield wnr (mdn auct, rtd 78a, with D Gillespie): eff at 7f/1m on fast, firm grnd & equitrack: handles any trk, loves a sharp one, esp Lingfield: has tried blnks, best without: ideally suited by forcing tactics, tough, genuine & v game. 65
3078 **LEGAL SET** 12 [12] K R Burke 4-9-8 (70) T Quinn 7/1: 033602: 4 gr g Second Set - Tiffany's Case (Thatching) Mid-div, imprvd to chall fnl 1f, no extra cl-home under hands-and-heels riding: 4L clr 3rd: often plcd but remains a mdn: tried a visor in 2629. ¾ 73
3115 **OUT OF SIGHT** 10 [8] B A McMahon 6-9-0 (62) J Fortune 11/1: 000143: 6 ch g Salse - Starr Danias (Sensitive Prince) Rear, rdn to impr 3f out, onepcd ins fnl 1f: btr 2682 (class stks). 4 58
3188 **WARRING** 7 [1] M S Saunders 6-7-12 (46) (2ow)(7oh) N Carlisle 12/1: 030034: Mid-div, kept on under press late, nvr dngrs: stiffish task: see 3188. ¾ 40
3078 **PIPE DREAM** 12 [4] 4-7-10 (44) (3oh) R Brisland (5) 14/1: 050435: Hdwy from rear 2f out, nvr nrr. shd 38
*2906 **TAKE MANHATTAN** 20 [5] 3-9-1 (70) Craig Williams 12/1: 000016: Prom till wknd over 1f out: mkt drifter: btr 2906 (firm grnd). shd 63
2499 **GRUINART** 37 [7] 3-9-2 (71) R Hughes 12/1: 431407: Nvr a factor & reportedly fin distressed. 5 54
1077 **FLOATING CHARGE** 105 [9] 6-10-0 (76) M Hills 11/2: 1-2U08: Nvr better than mid-div: top-weight, abs. 3 53
3018 **TEOFILIO** 15 [11] 6-9-6 (68) (bl) T G McLaughlin 10/1: 002309: Dwelt, nvr a factor: btr 2814. 2½ 40
2974 **MAGICAL BAILIWICK** 17 [14] 4-8-7 (55) Paul Eddery 33/1: 0-0000: In tch 5f, fdd into 10th. 1¾ 23
2759 **SUPER MONARCH** 26 [15] 6-8-10 (58) S Whitworth 33/1: 040000: Rear, imprvd 3f out, btn 2f out: 11th. 5 19
3118 **KHALED** 10 [3] 5-9-6 (68) D McGaffin 10/1: 50-030: Nvr a factor in 12th: see 3118. ½ 25
2549 **FOXS IDEA** 35 [2] 3-8-8 (63) S Sanders 10/1: 505430: Al towards rear, fin 13th: btr 2549 (6f, soft). 2½ 15
2230 **SATWA BOULEVARD** 47 [13] 5-7-10 (44) (t)(10oh) J Mackay (3) 40/1: 000200: Prom early, btn over 2f out: fin 14th, 7 wk abs, stiff task: see 2043. hd 0
3163 **STARLIGHT** 9 [10] 3-9-1 (70) G Carter 12/1: -10150: Al struggling, fin last: something clrly amiss. 4 13
15 ran   Time 1m 45.1   (A S Reid)   Andrew Reid Mill Hill, London NW7

3356	5.00 CHEWINGS APPR HCAP 3YO+ 0-80 (E) 1m2f Good Inapplicable	[70]
	£2814 £804 £402 3 yo rec 9 lb	

2958 **CAPTAIN MCCLOY** 17 [3] P Mitchell 5-8-0 (41) (bl)(1ow) A Beech 14/1: 633301: 5 ch g Lively One - Fly Me First (Herbager) Chsd ldr, chall strongly fnl 2f & led 1f out till ins last, regained lead nr line: op 8/1: sole prev win came in '99 at Warwick (sell h'cap, rtd 48): eff at 1m/10f, has tried further: acts on gd, fast grnd & equitrack: eff in blnks/visor, handles any trk: not the most resolute in a battle but gained a deserved win. 44
2763 **NIGHT CITY** 26 [6] K R Burke 9-8-12 (54) Darren Williams (3) 13/2: 152252: 9 b g Kris - Night Secret (Nijinsky) Tried to make all, just btn in a thrilling fin: op 9/2: has a superb wins to runs record (21 wins from 88 starts): see 2544 (C/D), 1814. shd 55
3244 **WHISTLING DIXIE** 5 [4] D Nicholls 4-8-5 (47) J Mackay 7/2: 014153: 4 ch g Forest Wind - Camdens Gift (Camden Town) Rcd keenly rear, switched & hdwy 2f out, fin well & only just btn: qck reapp: see 2655. nk 47
*3111 **KINNINO** 10 [2] G L Moore 6-8-2 (43) (1ow) I Mongan 4/1: 403214: Rear, imprvd 2f out, kept on under press & nrst fin: see 3111. 1¾ 41
3314 **SAMMYS SHUFFLE** 2 [1] 5-8-5 (bl) D Kinsella (5) 5/2 FAV: 321235: Rear, imprvd 3f out, onepace fnl 1f: well bckd, qck reapp: see 3314, 2790. ½ 41
2470 **YOU DA MAN** 38 [7] 3-9-10 (75) P Fitzsimons 11/2: 125106: Waited with, eff 2f out, not pace to chall: tchd 7/1, top-weight: twice below 2131 (12f, fast grnd). 2 68

WINDSOR   MONDAY AUGUST 14TH   Sharp, Figure 8 Track

2527 **OSCIETRA 36** [2] 4-8-8 (50) S Carson 7/1: 055567: Nvr a factor, fin last: tried a vis in 2527.   *13* **23**
7 ran   Time 2m 09.2   (D W Smith)   P Mitchell Epsom, Surrey.

KEMPTON   MONDAY AUGUST 14TH   Righthand, Flat, Fair Track

Official Going   GOOD TO FIRM. Stalls: Str Course - Far Side; Rem - Inside.

3357   5.40 FAST TRACK APP HCAP 3YO 0-70 (E)   1m1f   Good/Firm 22   -37 Slow   [75]
£2749   £846   £423   £211

*2892 **SPARK OF LIFE 21** [8] T D McCarthy 3-8-4 (51)(bl) G Sparkes (3) 9/2: 032311: 3 b f Rainbows For Life   **58**
- Sparkly Girl (Danehill) Held up, smooth prog halfway, switched to lead dist, v cmftbly: nicely bckd, slow
time: 3 wks ago scored at Brighton (sell, P Chamings, bght by current connections for 15,000gns): rtd 64 in 1st
time blnks when an unplcd juv: eff at 1m/9f on firm/fast grnd, sharp/undul trk: progressive, quick hat-trick likely.
3045 **WAVERLEY ROAD 14** [11] A P Jarvis 3-8-12 (59) Lisa Jones (7) 7/1: 506502: 3 ch g Pelder - Lillicara   *4* **60**
(Caracolero) Cl-up, left in lead appr str, hdd 2f out, same pace: ran well against an improver: eff at 9f on fast.
2961 **BILLY BATHWICK 17** [1] E J O'Neill 3-9-3 (64) M Worrell (5) 16/1: 010003: 3 ch c Fayruz - Cut It   *nk* **64**
Fine (Big Spruce) Rear, prog over 3f out to lead 2f out, hard rdn & hdd dist, no extra: big step up in
trip, poss gets 9f tho' looks likely to apprec 1m: see 2278.
3095 **NICOLAI 12** [9] M L W Bell 3-8-0 (47) C Catlin (3) 12/1: -00004: Chsd ldrs, feeling pace ent str, late rally.   *1* **45**
2688 **SPIRIT OF LIGHT 30** [5] 3-9-5 (66) M Mathers (5) 7/1: 230005: Led till bef halfway, fdd ent fnl 2f.   *nk* **63**
3236 **PEPPERCORN 5** [7] 3-7-10 (43)(3oh) Michael Doyle (5) 10/1: -60036: Nvr a factor: qck reapp, op 8/1.   *shd* **40**
3261 **COLLEGE ROCK 4** [2] 3-8-8 (55)(vis) R Cody Boutcher 5/2 FAV: 146137: Held up, hmpd appr str,   *2* **48**
nvr any impress on ldrs: nicely bckd, quick reapp: see 3094.
3309} **PRINCE OF MYSTERY 368** [3] 3-8-7 (54) S Finnamore 12/1: 630-8: Pulled hard, al towards rear: *9* **32**
reapp/h'cap bow: well btn last of 3 for A Jarvis in '99 (mdn, rtd 75% & 52): now with N Littmoden.
3095 **RONNI PANCAKE 12** [6] 3-8-3 (50) N Farmer (7) 12/1: 506009: In tch when hmpd appr str, bhd after.   *nk* **27**
3167 **XIBALBA 9** [10] 3-9-7 (68)(VIS) N Esler (3) 9/1: -1400U: Cl-up, led bef halfway till slipped/u.r. bef str: visor.   **0**
10 ran   Time 1m 55.34 (5.34)   (A D Spence)   T D McCarthy Godstone, Surrey

3358   6.10 FAST TRACK MED AUCT MDN 2YO (E)   6f   Good/Firm 22   +11 Fast
£4446   £1368   £684   £342

2550 **POMFRET LAD 35** [3] P J Makin 2-9-0 S Sanders 10/3: 01: 2 b c Cyrano de Bergerac - Lucky Flinders   **99+**
(Free Bay) Trkd ldrs, shkn up appr fnl 2f, sn sprinted a long way clr, impressive: nicely bckd, v fast time:
reported v green when well bckd/btn fav on soft grnd debut: half-brother to a wng juv sprinter, dam a miler, sire a
sprinter: eff at 6f, shld get 7f: acts on fast grnd: well regarded colt, will hold his own in better company.
-- **SISTER CELESTINE** [10] W Jarvis 2-8-9 Craig Williams 9/1: 2: 2 b f Bishop Of Cashel - Pipistrelle   *9* **74**
(Shareef Dancer) Chsd ldrs, styd on for 2nd below ldrs, no hope with wnr: op 6/1: 3,800 gns half-sister to a 1m
wnr, dam 13f wnr, sire a miler: step up to 7f will suit & will not al meet one this smart in an auct mdn.
-- **LUNEVISION** [12] H J Collingridge 2-8-9 M Roberts 10/1: 3: 2 b f Solid Illusion - Lumiere Celeste   *1* **71+**
(Always Fair) In tch, gd prog to dispute 2nd dist, no extra towards fin: tchd 12/1: on debut: moderately
bred but some promise here & not given a hard time: improvement likely.
3047 **AVERY RING 14** [9] A P Jarvis 2-9-0 D Harrison 5/2 FAV: 6234: Front rank & ev ch till onepace bef fnl 1f.   *2½* **70**
3162 **COSMIC RANGER 9** [7] 2-9-0 J Quinn 8/1: 05: Chsd ldrs, onepace 2f out: tchd 12/1: see 3162.   *½* **68**
-- **INVESTOR RELATIONS** [11] 2-9-0 D R McCabe 20/1: 6: Al mid-div tho' keeping on ins last: debut: *hd* **68**
23,000 gns Goldmark Mar gldg, half-brother to 4 wnrs, dam mid-dist performer: improvement likely at 7f+.
-- **GEORGES WAY** [1] 2-9-0 J Reid 8/1: 7: Went left start, nvr nr ldrs: tchd 12/1: speedily bred first foal.   *3* **59**
2711 **MISHKA 28** [4] 2-9-0 A Daly 20/1: 08: Set gd pace till hdd 2f out, fdd: drop back to 5f will suit.   *hd* **58**
3096 **ANNE SOPHIE 12** [8] 2-8-9 M Fenton 12/1: 09: Handy till after halfway, eased dist: op 8/1, see 3096.   *1½* **49**
3015 **NELSONS FLAGSHIP 15** [13] 2-9-0 P Doe 20/1: -000: Al bhd: 10th, see 3015.   *1¼* **51**
-- **ANKASAMEN** [6] 2-8-9 N Pollard 14/1: 0: Dwelt, al rear: 12th: Muhtarram foal, dam 1m juv wnr.   **0**
1488 Cricketers Club 80 [5] 2-9-0 P Robinson 50/1:   --   Monash Freeway [2] 2-9-0 J Tate 20/1:
13 ran   Time 1m 11.74 (0.64)   (Mrs Pauline Smith & Four Seasons Racing)   P J Makin Ogbourne Maisey, Wilts

3359   6.40 FAST TRACK FILLIES MDN 2YO (D)   7f rnd   Good/Firm 22   -25 Slow
£4368   £1344   £672   £336

-- **SHAHIRAH** [7] M P Tregoning 2-8-11 R Hills 6/5 FAV: 1: 2 b f Diesis - Shemaq (Blushing John)   **99**
Bhd ldrs, pushed into lead 2f out, shkn up to pull clr: hvly bckd on debut: Mar foal, half-sister
to 6f juv wnr Shafaq, dam 7f juv wnr: eff at 7f, 1m likely to suit: acts on fast grnd & goes well fresh:
useful debut, shld develop into a Group performer.
-- **BYLAW** [9] J H M Gosden 2-8-11 J Fortune 14/1: 2: 2 b f Lear Fan - Byre Bird (Diesis)   *3* **91**
Dwelt, held up, prog appr str, onepace after till styd on ins last & went 2nd nr fin: op 7/1: $225,000 first
foal, dam unrcd, sire a miler: eff at 7f, 1m is going to suit: handles fast grnd: shld win similar & improve.
1176 **PASHMEENA 99** [5] R Hannon 2-8-11 R Hughes 11/1: -263: 2 b f Baratheа - Auriga (Belmez)   *shd* **91**
Led till 2f out, same pace: 14 wk abs, op 6/1: prob stays 7f, 6f cld prove ideal: acts on fast & gd/soft grnd.
-- **LADY PAHIA** [4] A P Jarvis 2-8-11 D Harrison 33/1: 4: Mid-div, shkn up 2f out, styd on but no threat: *nk* **90**
op 20/1 on debut: 11,500lr gns Pivotal half-sister to a couple of wnrs, dam & sire sprinters: shld find a fill mdn.
3090 **MILLENNIUM LADY 12** [6] 2-8-11 M Hills 7/1: -05: Chsd ldrs, no extra 2f out: bckd from 10/1.   *3½* **83**
-- **FOLLOW A DREAM** [2] 2-8-11 Pat Eddery 15/2: 6: Chsd ldrs till fdd ent fnl 2f: well bckd on debut: *3½* **76**
Gone West first foal: dam useful mid-dist performer, sire a miler: worth another chance: with Sir M Stoute.
-- **LYNA** [8] 2-8-11 G Carter 20/1: 7: Al towards rear: op 12/1, debut: Slip Anchor half-sister   *hd* **75**
to a decent 7f juv: needs 1m+: with J Dunlop.
3187 **GIRL BAND 7** [3] 2-8-11 Craig Williams 33/1: 008: Nvr a factor: quick reapp, needs a drop in grade.   *shd* **75**
3205 **LEGGIT 6** [1] 2-8-11 (t) T Quinn 33/1: 009: Prom till 3f out: quick reapp.   *1¼* **73$**
9 ran   Time 1m 27.38 (3.28)   (Hamdan Al Maktoum)   M P Tregoning Lambourn, Berks

3360   7.10 YOURFASTTRACK HCAP 3YO+ 0-85 (D)   2m   Good/Firm 22 -12 Slow   [80]
£6825   £2100   £1050   £525   3 yo rec 15lb

3058 **QUEDEX** 13 [5] E L James 4-10-0 (80) I Mongan (5) 4/1: 014001: 4 b c Deploy - Alwal (Pharly) 86
Towards rear, imprvd ent str, rdn to lead bef dist, styd on strongly: nicely bckd: earlier won at Haydock (h'cap):
'99 wnr at Goodwood (h'cap) & Bath (class stks, rtd 71): eff at 14f, suited by step up to 2m: acts on firm,
soft grnd & any trk: can carry big weights: improving, unexposed stayer, win again.

*3023 **ALRISHA** 15 [2] D R C Elsworth 3-8-13 (80) T Quinn 3/1: 0212: 3 b f Persian Bold - Rifaya (Lashkari) 1¼ 84
Trkd ldrs, led 4f out till ent fnl 2f, styd on: nicely bckd on h'cap bow & well clr of rem: imprvd again
up in trip, eff at 14.7f/2m: progressive 3yo, sure to win more races

2953 **RENZO** 17 [6] J L Harris 7-9-12 (78) S Sanders 6/1: 301203: 7 b g Alzao - Watership (Foolish Pleasure) 9 73
Chsd ldrs, carried wide ent str, same pace: op 9/2: see 2498.

3153 **HIGH TOPPER** 9 [3] M Johnston 3-8-13 (80) J Reid 5/2 FAV: 441164: Led 4f, prom, slipped on bend nk 74
appr str tho' lost little momentum, rdn & wknd 2f out: well bckd: back up in trip, see 2973.

2092 **GALAPINO** 54 [7] 7-7-10 (48)(1oh) M Henry 20/1: 005: All towards rear: 8 wk abs: nicely h'capped. 9 35

3231 **DANEGOLD** 5 [4] 8-8-3 (55) Craig Williams 6/1: 400046: Nvr troubled ldrs: quick reapp, see 714. 3½ 40

2923 **READING RHONDA** 19 [1] 4-7-10 (48)(10oh) J Mackay (5) 33/1: 000367: Led after 4f till 4f out, sn btn. 22 18
7 ran   Time 3m 29.68 (5.48)   (L Van Hijkoop)   E L James East Garston, Berks

---

3361   7.40 FAST TRACK COND STKS 2YO (C)   7f rnd   Good/Firm 22 -23 Slow
£5703   £2108   £1054   £479

3164 **CRAZY LARRYS** 9 [4] J Noseda 2-9-2 D Holland 4/6 FAV: -121: 2 ch c Mutakddim - No Fear Of Flying 102
(Super Concorde) Trkd ldrs, shaken up & qknd to lead appr fnl 1f, pushed out, cmftbly: hvly bckd from 6/4:
earlier won debut at Newcastle (mdn): 22,000 gns foal, dam dual wnr in the States: eff at 7f, 1m likely to
suit: acts on fast & gd grnd, stiff/gall or easy trks: useful & progressive, earned a step up in grade.

-- **KHITAAM** [5] B Hanbury 2-8-8 R Hills 3/1: 2: 2 b c Charnwood Forest - Queen's Ransom (Last 1¼ 90
Tycoon) Pulled hard, held up, prog ent str & led briefly 2f out, kept on but not pace of wnr: nicely bckd
tho' op 6/4 on debut: IR£140,000 Mar foal, half-brother to juv sprinter & later 1m wnr Cair Paravel, dam 7f
wnr, sire a miler: eff at 7f, 1m shld suit: handles fast grnd: v well regarded Group entry, sure to win before long.

*970 **ICE MAIDEN** 117 [3] M R Channon 2-8-11 T Quinn 11/1: -13: 2 b f Polar Falcon - Affair Of State 2½ 88
(Tate Gallery) Led till 2f out, no extra: op 6/1, 4 month abs: not disgraced, handles fast & gd/sft: 6f suit for now?

2966 **ADJOURNMENT** 17 [1] P F I Cole 2-9-2 J Fortune 4/1: 01624: Cl-up, fdd 2f out: nicely bckd: see 1988. 2½ 88
4 ran   Time 1m 27.25 (3.15)   (Crazy Radio Ltd)   J Noseda Newmarket, Suffolk

---

3362   8.10 CITY INDEX HCAP 3YO+ 0-70 (E)   7f rnd   Good/Firm 22 -11 Slow   [69]
£3770   £1160   £580   £290   3 yo rec 6 lb

2899 **UNCHAIN MY HEART** 20 [5] B J Meehan 4-8-12 (53)(VIS) Pat Eddery 8/1: 300141: 4 b f Pursuit Of Love - 61
Addicted To Love (Touching Wood) Towards rear, wide into str, gd hdwy und press 2f out to lead dist, kept
held on well: 1st time visor: earlier won at Lingfield (AW clmr, rtd 63a) & Doncaster (fill h'cap): '99 Lingfield
mdn wnr (rtd 62a & 70): eff at 7f/1m, stays a sharp 10f on firm & soft grnd, likes equitrack/Lingfield:
goes on any trk tho' likes easy ones: best in blnks or visor & can go well fresh: improving.

*2978 **APLOY** 17 [6] R F Johnson Houghton 3-9-7 (68) J Reid 7/1: 644512: 3 b f Deploy - Amidst (Midyan) ½ 74
Mid-field, prog 2f out to chase wnr ins ldrs, nt trbld: improving filly, see 2978.

2425 **SUMMER CHERRY** 40 [13] D J Murphy 3-8-13 (60)(t) M Fenton 16/1: 0-4463: 3 b g Summer Squall - 1½ 63
Cherryrob (Roberto) Held up, prog to chase ldrs 2f out, styd on but nt trouble 1st 2: 6 wk abs & sound run
for new connections with t-strap applied: eff at 7f, return to 1m+ will suit: handles fast grnd.

*2749 **WHITE EMIR** 26 [8] L G Cottrell 7-9-7 (62) A Clark 5/1: 0-3214: Prom, chall 2f out, onepace bef dist. nk 64

2612 **GREEN GOD** 32 [3] 4-9-5 (60) S Sanders 33/1: -05005: Rear, late wide hdwy, nvr a threat: op 20/1. 2 58

2749 **MYTTONS MISTAKE** 26 [10] 7-9-0 (55) G Carter 12/2: 421366: Cl-up, led ent fnl 3f till bef fnl 1f, fdd. 1¼ 50

3188 **MOON AT NIGHT** 7 [2] 5-10-0 (69) M Roberts 11/1: -10307: Chsd ldrs, ch 2f out, onepace when hmpd 1 62
bef dist: tchd 14/1, top weight, quick reapp: see 1129.

2922 **PROUD CHIEF** 19 [11] 3-9-8 (69)(vis) D Harrison 16/1: 600008: Bmpd start, rear, mod late wide prog. hd 62

2922 **CEDAR PRINCE** 19 [9] 3-9-3 (64)(bl) P Doe 16/1: 006009: Nvr a factor: see 1744. ½ 50

3833} **PURPLE FLAME** 341 [12] 4-9-0 (55) Paul Eddery 33/1: 6500-0: Nvr in it tho' was staying on fin: nk 46
10th on reapp: unplcd 3yo last year (h'cap, rtd 61): unrcd juv: stays 1m & will be sharper next time at that trip.

*1801 **SOLLYS PAL** 66 [1] 5-8-11 (52)(vis) D Sweeney 14/1: 4-5310: Prom till fdd 2f out: 11th, op 10/1, abs. 1½ 40

2761 **MYSTIC RIDGE** 26 [16] 6-9-8 (63) J P Spencer 9/2 FAV: 040060: Led till appr fnl 2f, lost place: 12th. 3½ 45

3078 **Salory** 12 [7] 4-9-0 (55)(BL) J Bosley (7) 16/1:   2974 **Anstand** 17 [15] 5-8-9 (50) S Whitworth 50/1:

2961 **Midhish Two** 17 [4] 4-9-9 (64)(BL) R Hughes 14/1:   1348 **Storm Cry** 88 [14] 5-9-11 (66)(t) R Havlin 14/1:
16 ran   Time 1m 26.38 (2.28)   (Mascalls Stud)   B J Meehan Upper Lambourn, Berks

---

Official Going   GOOD (GOOD TO SOFT places on back straight). Stalls: Rnd Crse - Outside; Str Crse - Stands Side.

3363   2.15 BELLISLE MED AUCT MDN 2YO (E)   7f rnd   Good 40 -24 Slow
£3087   £950   £475   £237

2873 **BAILEYS CREAM** 22 [4] M Johnston 2-8-9 D Holland 4/1: 021: 2 ch f Mister Baileys - Exclusive Life 84
(Exclusive Native) Prom, led appr final 1f, ran on strongly, pushed out: imprvd with every run: 26,000 gns
half-sister to 2 juv wnrs: dam sprint wnr: eff at 7f, 1m is going to suit: goes on firm & gd, gall trk.

3000 **MAGNUSSON** 17 [7] J H M Gosden 2-9-0 K Darley 1/3 FAV: 32: 2 b c Primo Dominie - Nunsharpa 2 83
(Sharpo) Led till appr final 1f, not pace of wnr: bckd at odds-on: defeat not expected after promising debut
over 6f: possibly unsuited forcing the pace & prob worth another ch: acts on fast & gd grnd: see 3000.

3154 **GILDED DANCER** 10 [5] W R Muir 2-9-0 S Sanders 8/1: 363: 2 b c Bishop Of Cashel - La Piaf 1 81
(Fabulous Dancer) Held up, prog to chase ldrs appr final 1f, edged left & onepace dist: tchd 10/1, clr rem.

3015 **ORIENTAL MIST** 16 [3] Miss L A Perratt 2-9-0 L Newman (3) 20/1: 543304: Held up, moderate late prog. 5 71

2717 **LENNEL** 29 [9] 2-9-0 A Nicholls (3) 33/1: 635: Chsd ldrs, no extra 2f out: up in trip, qual for h'caps.   nk 70
1859 **ARJAY** 65 [8] 2-9-0 P Fessey 66/1: -56: Handy till fdd appr final 2f: 9 wk abs, see 1859.   5 60
700 **HOBO** 145 [1] 2-9-0 A Culhane 100/1: 07: Missed break & detached, some late gains: 5 mth abs since   1½ 57
running in the Brocklesby: 8,000 gns Timeless Times brother to decent 5f juv Foreman: with D Barker.
3246 **EYES DONT LIE** 6 [6] 2-9-0 (VIS) R Winston 100/1: 04008: Al towards rear: visored, needs sells.   1¾ 53
1628 **QUIET TRAVELLER** 75 [10] 2-9-0 C Lowther 100/1: 09: Sn in rear: stablemate 4th, 11 wk abs.   nk 52
3246 **SIR EDWARD BURROW** 6 [11] 2-9-0 Dean McKeown 100/1: -04000: Chsd ldrs till 3f out: 10th, stiff task.   1½ 49
2417 **Dance Queen** 41 [12] 2-8-9 J Bramhill 100/1:   **Mister Doc** [2] 2-9-0 F Lynch 100/1:
12 ran   Time 1m 28.28 (4.48)   (G R Bailey Ltd Baileys Horse Feeds)   M Johnston Middleham, Nth Yorks.

3364   2.45 LADY ISLE SELLER 3YO (F)   7f rnd   Good 40   -30 Slow
£2282   £652   £326

3138 **MYTTONS AGAIN** 11 [4] A Bailey 3-8-12 (bl) J Bramhill 7/2: 500631: 3 b g Rambo Dancer - Sigh   61
(Highland Melody) Held up, imprvd ent str, led before dist, drifted left, dbn out: stays 1m: acts on fast & hvy grnd, any trk: wears blnks.
Chester (nursery), rtd 74 & 68a): eff at 7f, stays 1m: acts on fast & hvy grnd, any trk: wears blnks.
3194 **JEPAJE** 8 [8] A Bailey 3-8-12 S Sanders 16/1: 644502: 3 b g Rambo Dancer - Hi-Hunsley (Swing Easy)   1 57$
Rear, kept on well appr final 1f, nvr nrr: stablemate of wnr, poss flattered: goes on gd, gd/soft & equitrack.
3196 **ABSINTHER** 8 [6] E J Alston 3-8-12 W Supple 9/1: 020053: 3 b g Presidium - Heavenly Queen (Scottish hd 56
Reel) Towards rear, swtchd & hdwy appr fnl 1f, rdn & onepace in last: visor omitted, best 2205 (led, 1m).
3194 **NATSMAGIRL** 8 [3] Martyn Wane P Fessey 10/1: 505624: Mid-div, rdn appr final 1f, styd on   ½ 49
without threatening: tchd 12/1, stiff task, apprec return to 7f: see 74.
2541 **LORDOFENCHANTMENT** 36 [2] 3-8-12 (vis) A Culhane 7/2: 522055: Pulled hard bhd ldrs, shkn up 2f   nk 53
out, rdn dist, no impress: nicely bckd from 5/1: visor reapplied, up in trip, btr 1768 (6f, hvy grnd h'cap).
2136 **WATERGOLD** 53 [9] 3-8-12 (BL) O Pears 20/1: 500006: Bhd, styd on thro' btn horses final 1f: op 14/1: 1½ 49$
stiff task, 8 wk abs: tried blnks & prob flattered: worth a try at 1m: see 1105.
*2798 **THEOS LAD** 25 [1] 3-9-4 R Winston 11/2: 0-5017: Cl-up, led before 2f out till appr final 1f, fdd.   ½ 53
3269 **INDY CARR** 5 [10] 3-8-7 K Darley 3/1 FAV: 466008: Trkd ldrs, shkn up when slightly checked 2f   ½ 40
out, held when hmpd dist: qck reappr, bckd: see 3269, 900.
1923 **SCHATZI** 62 [11] 3-8-7 J Fanning 20/1: -02009: In tch, onepace 2f out: 9 wk abs, lngr trip: see 872. 1½ 37
3082 **BLUE SAPPHIRE** 13 [7] 3-8-7 Kimberley Hart 33/1: 030300: Al towards rear, 10th, stiff task, see 1081. 7 23
3226 **SECRETARIO** 6 [5] 3-8-7 (bl) J McAuley 33/1: 000000: Led till appr final 2f, wknd qckly: 11th, stiff task. 16 3
11 ran   Time 1m 28.67 (4.87)   (Gordon Mytton)   A Bailey Little Budworth, Cheshire.

3365   3.15 TOTE EXACTA HCAP 3YO+ 0-90 (C)   1m rnd   Good 40   -13 Slow   [87]
£6857   £2110   £1055   £527   3 yo rec 7 lb

*3227 **RIBERAC** 6 [1] M Johnston 4-8-12 (71) J Fanning 2/1 FAV: 200011: 4 b f Efisio - Ciboure (Norwich)   81
Nvr far away, led 2f out & qcknd 3L clr dist, shkn up, readily: nicely bckd, qck reappr: recent Sandown wnr (appr
h'cap, easily): highly tried in '99 for W Haggas (stks, rtd 91): '98 Windsor wnr (mdn, rtd 98): former sprinter,
now found a new lease of life at 1m: acts on firm & gd, any trk: has given trble at the start: well h'capped.
3325 **TONY TIE** 3 [5] J S Goldie 4-10-0 (87) A Culhane 11/4: 202122: 4 b g Ardkinglass - Queen Of The   1¾ 92
Quorn (Governor General) Trkd ldrs, rdn & unable to qckn when wnr went on 2f out, styd on for press in last but
no threat: nicely bckd from 4/1, qck reappr, top-weight: not disgrcd against a well h'capped filly, remains in form.
3170 **INTRICATE WEB** 9 [8] E J Alston 4-8-11 (70) W Supple 7/1: 133053: 4 b g Warning - In Anticipation   1 73
(Sadler's Wells) Well plcd, ch 2f out, sn outpcd by wnr: ran to best but both wins over 7f: see 2241.
*2878 **RYEFIELD** 22 [4] Miss L A Perratt 5-8-2 (61) J McAuley 8/1: -0R214: Held up, styd on onepace for   1½ 61
4th, nvr dngrs: won this in '99 (off 4lbs higher mark): btr 2878 (7f here, beat this 2nd).
3078 **SKY DOME** 13 [2] 7-8-13 (72) S Sanders 5/1: 230325: Chsd ldrs, onepace ent final 2f: bckd tho' op 4/1. ¾ 70
*3238 **ITALIAN SYMPHONY** 6 [7] 6-7-13 (58)(vis)(6ex) Joanna Badger (7) 11/1: 563516: Chsd ldrs, fdd 2f out. 1½ 53
2799 **ARIZONA LADY** 25 [3] 3-8-3 (68)(1ow) R Winston 12/1: 032157: Led till 2f out, lost pl: btr 2397 (trkd ldr). 2 60
3267 **HIGHLAND GOLD** 5 [6] 3-7-13 (65) A Nicholls (2) 50/1: 5-3508: Al bhd, hung left in str: qck reappr. 1 54
8 ran   Time 1m 40.85 (4.25)   (Mr & Mrs G Middlebrook)   M Johnston Middleham, Nth Yorks.

3366   3.45 STINCHAR CLASSIFIED STKS 3YO+ 0-80 (D)   6f   Good 40   +02 Fast
£3828   £1178   £589   £294   3 yo rec 4 lb

1192 **ABBAJABBA** 100 [7] C W Fairhurst 4-9-2 J Fanning 7/4 FAV: -31131: 4 b g Barrys Gamble - Bo' Babbity   83
(Strong Gale) Mid-div going well, swtchd & prog appr final 1f, led from 150y, readily: nicely bckd from 11/4,
best time of day, 14 wk abs: earlier won at Hamilton & Epsom (h'cap): unplcd in '99 (rtd 67): juv rnr-up
(nursery, rtd 82): eff at 6f, tried 7f: acts on fast, suited by gd & hvy, any trk: runs whole fresh, on the upgrade.
*2807 **STRONG PRESENCE** 25 [3] T P Tate 3-9-1 T Lucas 7/2: 5-12: 3 b c Anshan - Lazybird Blue   ¾ 82
(Bluebird) Cl-up, rdn appr final 1f, onepce till styd on towards fin: gd run on only 3rd start, win at 7f.
3283 **ACE OF PARKES** 4 [9] A Berry 4-9-2 D Holland 12/1: 065003: 4 b g Teenoso - Summerhill Spruce   hd 78
(Windjammer) Led till final 150y, onepace: clr of next, qck reappr, back to form: see 1245.
2334 **PRINCELY DREAM** 45 [6] R A Fahey 4-9-2 K Darley 11/4: 0-0004: Chsd ldrs, outpcd appr final 1f: 4 68
6 wk abs, bckd: won this in '99 but has been lightly rcd & out of sorts this term: see 1533.
602 **AMBUSHED** 169 [5] 4-9-2 R Winston 100/1: -00105: Held up, swtchd & hdwy 2f out, no extra dist: over   1 65$
5 mth abs & looks flattered (offic rtd 36) for new stable: see 585 (1m appr mdn h'cap, fibresand).
3056 **PALACEGATE JACK** 14 [10] 9-9-2 P Bradley (5) 66/1: 305456: Chsd ldrs till 2f out: stiff task, best at 5f. 4 53$
3152 **GET STUCK IN** 10 [1] 4-9-2 C Lowther 5/1: 544007: Cl up wide till wknd qckly 2f out: not his form. 1½ 49
3312 **BARITONE** 3 [4] 6-9-2 (vis) O Pears 100/1: 536008: Al towards rear: qck reappr, impossible task.   3 40$
2877 **FACILE TIGRE** 22 [2] 5-9-2 P Hanagan (7) 66/1: 503009: Bhd from halfway: stiff task, see 146.   hd 39
3103 **CLEAR MOON** 13 [8] 3-8-12 (bl) J McAuley 100/1: 05000R: Dwelt & sn refused to race: see 929.   0
10 ran   Time 1m 11.55 (2.25)   (Northern Cheshire Trading & Storage Ltd)   C W Fairhurst Middleham, Nth Yorks.

3367   4.15 BRODICK BAY HCAP 3YO+ 0-70 (E)   1m7f   Good 40   -59 Slow   [63]
£2762   £680   £425   £212   3 yo rec 14lb

3331 **HIGHFIELD FIZZ** 2 [7] C W Fairhurst 8-8-2 (37) T Williams 4/1: 606341: 8 b m Efisio - Jendor   38
(Condoret) Held up, imprvd ent str, rdn to lead dist, styd on strongly: slow time, ran 48hrs ago: earlier won
at Redcar (h'cap): '99 wnr at Musselburgh (h'cap, rtd 47): '98 wnr at Pontefract & Musselburgh (rtd 53):

AYR TUESDAY AUGUST 15TH Lefthand, Galloping Track

eff at 14f/2m, stays 2m2f on firm, hvy grnd, any trk, likes Musselburgh: v tough.

2482 **SMUDGER SMITH 39** [3] B S Rothwell 3-8-2 (51)(vis) W Supple 7/1: 346462: 3 ch g Deploy - Parfait 1¾ 49
Armour (Clantime) Set slow pace, hdd 3f out, rall to take 2nd inside last: 6 wk abs: eff at 12f, stays 15f.
2993 **PLEASANT MOUNT 17** [5] Miss J A Camacho 4-10-0 (63) K Darley 13/8 FAV: 503023: 4 b g First Trump - ½ 60
Alo Ez (Alzao) Well plcd, led 3f out till 1f out, onepace: nicely bckd from 11/4: remains in form, see 918.
3084 **HAPPY DAYS 13** [2] D Moffatt 5-8-3 (38) J Bramhill 5/1: 625244: Chsd ldrs, briefly short of room ¾ 34
appr final 2f, unable to qckn: op 7/2: back up in trip, faster pace would have suited: see 552.
2734 **TOTALLY SCOTTISH 28** [4] A Culhane 5/1: 4-0565: Trkd ldrs, shkn up over 2f out, no ¾ 38
impress: op 7/2: needs a faster pace, see 2734.
1222 **EMBRYONIC 97** [1] 8-9-11 (60) Dean McKeown 7/1: -00606: Mid-div, eff 2f out, onepace: abs, new stable. ½ 54
-- **JORDANS RIDGE** [6] 4-9-0 (49) R Winston 25/1: 650-07: Chsd ldrs, ch 2f out, fdd bef dist: rnr-up in 1¾ 41
a sell hdle last wk (stays 2m1f on gd, rtd 75h, blnkd): ex-Irish mdn up to 12f: drop back in trip will prob suit.
7 ran   Time 3m 24.66 (14.86)   (Mrs P J Taylor-Garthwaite)   C W Fairhurst Middleham, Nth Yorks.

3368 4.45 NO SHOW HCAP 3YO+ 0-75 (E) 1m2f Good 40 -02 Slow [69]
£3984 £1226 £613 £306 3 yo rec 9 lb

2884 **ZAGALETA 22** [2] Andrew Turnell 3-8-13 (63) K Darley 16/1: -00021: 3 b f Sri Pekan - Persian Song 68
(Persian Bold) Pulled hard, in tch, prog 2f out, led 1f out, rdn clr: op 12/1, tchd 20/1: first win, plcd all 3
juv starts (6f mdns, rtd 81): has apprec the step up to 10f: acts on firm & gd grnd, any trk: on a handy mark.
3285 **THORNTOUN GOLD 4** [4] J S Goldie 4-8-5 (46)(BL) F Lynch 9/1: 023552: 4 ch f Lycius - Gold Braisim 2 47
(Jareer) Chsd ldrs, rdn ent final 2f, same pace towards fin: qck reapp: ran to best in blnks & stays 10f.
3141 **IMPULSIVE AIR 11** [9] J R Weymes 8-8-3 (44) R Winston 13/2: 020043: 8 b g Try My Best - Tracy's shd 45
Sundown (Red Sunset) Off the pace till styd on wide final 2f, nvr nrr: worth a try over 12f?: see 569.
3013 **OCEAN DRIVE 16** [3] Miss L A Perratt 4-8-5 (46) L Newman (3) 8/1: 422454: In tch, shkn up apr nk 46
final 2f, styd on, unable to chall: op 10/1: return to 12f should suit: see 2309, 846.
3192 **RAINSTORM 8** [5] 5-8-0 (41) Joanna Badger (7) 13/2: 00-035: Prom, led ent final 2f, sn edged nk 40
left & hdd, onepace: stays 10f, shade btr 3192 (1m).
2562 **NIAGARA 35** [10] 3-9-6 (70) S Sanders 8/1: 0-0036: Rear, styd on appr final 1f, nvr dngr: tchd 10/1. 1 67
3159 **FREEDOM QUEST 10** [7] 5-9-5 (60) W Supple 11/2: 521407: Led bef halfway till ent final 2f, onepace. nk 56
*3141 **CYBERTECHNOLOGY 11** [1] 6-9-7 (62) J Fanning 7/2 FAV: 031618: Held up, prog 2f out, no extra ½ 56
before final 1f: nicely bckd from 5/1: btr 3141 (9f here).
2999 **PARKSIDE 17** [6] 4-9-12 (67) D Holland 10/1: 030009: Nvr better than mid-div: top-weight, lngr trip. hd 61
2781 **KIDZ PLAY 26** [8] 4-9-0 (57) Dean McKeown 14/1: 014040: Led till before halfway, wknd 2f out: 10th. ½ 50
864} **KONKER 11** [11] 5-9-2 (57) A Culhane 25/1: 0/06-0: Dwelt, al bhd: 11th on reapp: lightly rcd in 1¾ 48
'99 for G M Moore (rtd 60): '98 wnr at Newbury (clmr, rtd 78, W Haggas): eff at 10/11f on gd & hvy grnd.
11 ran   Time 2m 08.58 (4.18)   (Dr John Hollowood)   Andrew Turnell Sandhutton, Nth Yorks.

DEAUVILLE SATURDAY AUGUST 12TH Righthand, Galloping Track

Official Going GOOD

3369 2.55 LIST PRIX RIDGWAY 3YO C&G 1m2f Good
£13449 £4611 £3458

-- **CHESHIRE** [3] J Hammond 3-9-2 C Soumillon : -1: 3 b g Warning - Dance To The Top (Sadler's Wells) 109
-- **SKIPPING** [2] France 3-9-2 T Thulliez : -2: 3 b c Rainbow Quest - Minskip (The Minstrel) ½ 108
2675 **SPENCERS WOOD 28** [5] P J Makin 3-9-2 G Mosse : 1-143: 3 b c Pips Pride - Ascoli (Skyliner) 1½ 105
Set stdy pace till dist, onepace: not disgraced on step up to 10f: see 2675, 1186.
9 ran   Time 2m 07.5   (P Willmott)   J Hammond France

3370 3.25 GR 3 PRIX GONTAUT-BIRON 4YO+ 1m2f Good
£21134 £7685 £3842 £2305

2072 **AGOL LACK 58** [8] A Fabre 4-8-11 O Peslier 64/10: -51231: 4 ch c Gulch - Garvin's Gal (Seattle Slew) 117
Cl-up, led over 1f out, kept on well: smart French trained colt: stays 10f on gd.
1433} **TIJIYR 450** [7] A de Royer Dupre 4-8-11 G Mosse 49/10: 3-1222: 4 gr c Primo Dominie - Tijara 1½ 113
(Darshaan) Held up, hdwy over 2f out, kept on ins last, nrst fin: stays 10f, 12f shld suit.
1115 **KABOOL 104** [5] Saeed bin Suroor 5-8-9 C Soumillon 38/10: 34-443: 5 b h Groom Dancer - Sheroog 2½ 107
(Shareef Dancer) In tch, eff to lead over 2f out, hdd & no extra appr fnl 1f: 3 month abs: can rate higher.
2975 **CAPE GRACE 15** [3] R Hannon 4-8-6 T Jarnet 125/10: 150524: Handy, rdn & onepace fnl 2f. 1 102
*2410 **ALRASSAAM 41** [4] 4-9-4 P Robinson 17/10 FAV: 2-0418: Set pace till over 2f out, wknd qckly, eased: 74
reportedly 'gurgled' & is much better than this: convincing Gr2 wnr in 2410.
8 ran   Time 2m 10.4   (Sultan Al Kabeer)   A Fabre France

LEOPARDSTOWN SUNDAY AUGUST 13TH Lefthand, Galloping Track

Official Going GOOD

3371 2.50 LIST BALLYROAN STKS 3YO+ 1m4f Good
£16250 £4750 £2250 £750 3yo rec 11lb

*949 **GRAND FINALE 119** [3] D K Weld 3-9-0 P J Smullen 9/4 FAV: 3-111: 3 b c Sadler's Wells - Final Figure 110
(Super Concorde) Held up, hdwy to lead dist, kept on well for press: bckd tho' op 6/4: 4 month abs since
wng here at Leopardstown (List), earlier scored at Gowran (stks): eff at 10f, stays 12f well on gd & soft:
runs well fresh: proving smart, tough & progressive.
-- **PALACE ROYALE** [6] M J Grassick 4-9-3 E Ahern 12/1: 24-202: 4 b f Perugino - Trojan Tale (Critique) ½ 101
Handy, hdwy to chall over 1f out, kept on ins last, not btn far: useful filly who stays 12f on gd grnd.

LEOPARDSTOWN SUNDAY AUGUST 13TH Lefthand, Galloping Track

-- **ROSTROPOVICH** [2] A P O'Brien 3-8-9 M J Kinane 6/1: -313: 3 gr c Sadler's Wells - Infamy (Shirley nk **103**
Heights) Prom, hdwy to lead briefly well over 1f out, btn less than 1L: earlier won at
Galway (mdn): stays 12f well, further shld suit: acts on gd grnd: lightly raced, op to further improvement.
2153 **WINGED HUSSAR** 51 [12] J Oxx 7-9-6 J P Murtagh 8/1: -31504: Held up, rdn over 1f out, onepace. 2½ **100**
12 ran   Time 2m 33.4   (Moyglare Stud Farm)   D K Weld Curragh, Co Kildare

3372   3.25 GR 1 HEINZ 57 STKS 2YO   6f   Good
£98350 £33600 £16100 £5600

3000 **MINARDI** 15 [9] A P O'Brien 2-9-0 M J Kinane 7/2: -21: 2 br c Boundary - Yarn (Mr Prospector) **122**
Prom, hdwy to lead over 1f out, qcknd clr fnl 1f, impress: btn in a mdn at Ascot on debut: Mar foal, cost
$1,650,000: half brother to wnrs in the US: dam 3yo scorer: v eff at 6f, 7f sure to suit: acts on gd:
reportedly only stable's 2nd string here but demolished a useful field & must be kept on the right side.
+ 2849 **SUPERSTAR LEO** 22 [1] W J Haggas 2-8-11 M Hills 7/2: 211112: 2 b f College Chapel - Council Rock 5 **106**
(General Assembly) Prom, eff & edged right over 1f out, kept on ins last but no ch with impress wnr: smart
filly who stays 6f, but could well return to wng ways at 5f in the Flying Childers at Doncaster: see 2849.
+ 2565 **DORA CARRINGTON** 33 [6] P W Harris 2-8-11 Pat Eddery 3/1 FAV: -113: 2 b f Sri Pekan - Dorothea ¾ **103**
Brooke (Dancing Brave) Prom, eff 2f out, kept on same pace: op 9/4: poss just below form of 2565 (Gr2).
-- **LONGUEVILLE LEGEND** [8] C Collins 2-8-11 P Shanahan 20/1: -24: Led till over 1f out, ½ **102**
onepace: eff over 6/7f on gd grnd: v useful, would relish a drop into Listed/Gr3 company.
2399 **LA VIDA LOCA** 46 [7] 2-8-11 J A Heffernan 10/1: -5215: Waited with, eff 2f out, kept on same pace: 1½ **98**
recent Curragh (5f) mdn wnr: see 2399.
2698 **SILCA LEGEND** 29 [4] 2-9-0 J Murtagh 16/1: 422126: Cl-up, rdn & hmpd over 1f out, wknd: big step 2½ **94**
up in class from nurs h'caps & will relish a return to that company as in 2698.
2738 **PIRATE OF PENZANCE** 28 [5] 2-9-0 P J Smullen 10/1: -127: Nvr a factor: see 2738. **0**
2850 **PRINCE OF BLUES** 22 [11] 2-9-0 J A Quinn 25/1: -52658: In tch, btn 2f out: needs mdns, see 2595. **0**
3133 **SPEEDY GEE** 9 [10] 2-9-0 Craig Williams 16/1: 610569: Al bhd: v stiff task: see 3133, 2808. **0**
-- **CASHEL PALACE** [3] 2-9-0 P J Scallan 25/1: -2150: Prom, wknd 2f out. **0**
10 ran   Time 1m 12.2   (Michael Tabor)   A P O'Brien Ballydoyle, Co Tipperary

3373   4.0 GR 3 PHOENIX SPRINT STKS 3YO+   6f   Good
£22750 £6650 £3150 £1050   3yo rec 4lb

3059 **EASTERN PURPLE** 12 [8] K A Ryan 5-9-2 B Marcus 2/1 FAV: 005621: 5 b g Petorius - Broadway (Absalom) **113**
Set pace till over 1f out, headed gamely for press to get up again cl-home: earlier just tchd off in the Gr 3
King George at Goodwood: '99 scorer at The Curragh (Gr3, rtd 113): '98 Haydock scorer (rtd h'cap, rtd 108, with
R Fahey): eff at 5f, suited by 6f & handles firm, likes gd & gd/soft, any trk: eff with/without blnks, has
tried a visor: v tough & smart, right back to best since gelding operation in June.
4241} **CONORMARA** 316 [7] D Hanley 3-8-12 N G McCullagh 12/1: -01152: 3 b c Carr de Naskra - Teeming shd **112**
Shore (L'Emigrant) Prom, hdwy to lead just ins last, kept on till collared cl-home: earlier won at Naas (mdn)
& The Curragh (h'cap): suited by around 6f on gd & gd/soft: proving v progressive & tough, only lightly raced.
*1834 **ONE WON ONE** 64 [6] Mrs J Morgan 6-9-2 J Murtagh 9/2: 301203: 6 b g Naevus - Harvard's Bay ½ **111**
(Halpern Bay) Cl-up, hdwy 2f out, kept on for press ins last, not btn far: tough & smart, poss just best at 7f.
1122 **ARETHA** 104 [3] J S Bolger 3-8-9 K J Manning 8/1: 5-2424: In tch, eff over 1f out, kept on ins last, hd **108$**
not btn far: tried blnks today: tried blnks in 1122, see 948.
3235 **CRETAN GIFT** 4 [5] 9-9-2 (bl) J A Quinn 7/1: 023445: In tch, rdn over 2f out, some late gains: tough. ¾ **108**
8 ran   Time 1m 12.5   (T C Chiang)   K A Ryan Hambleton, N Yorks

DEAUVILLE TUESDAY AUGUST 15TH Righthand, Galloping Track

Official Going   GOOD/FIRM

3374   2.50 GR 2 PRIX GUILLAUME D'ORNANO 3YO   1m2f   Good/Firm
£28818 £11527 £5764 £2882

2225 **BEST OF THE BESTS** 51 [4] Saeed bin Suroor 3-8-11 L Dettori 5/2: 2-3441: 3 ch c Machiavellian - **119**
Sueboog (Darshaan) Made all, qcknd over 1f out, styd on well, cmftbly: 7 wk abs: earlier 10L 4th in the Epsom
Derby: juv scorer at Sandown (with C Brittain, Gr 3, rtd 112): suited by 10f, tried 12f: acts on firm & soft,
stiff trks: v smart colt who is not over-raced this term.
1752 **KUTUB** 72 [5] F Head 3-9-2 D Bonilla 6/4 JT FAV: 1-1242: 3 b c In The Wings - Minnie Habit (Habitat) 4 **117**
Prom, eff to chase wnr ins last, no danger: back to form with blnks discarded at 10f: see 1752, 864.
2736 **HESIODE** 32 [2] J C Rouget 3-8-11 T Jarnet 52/10: 113033: 3 gr c Highest Honor - Elite Guest 1½ **109**
(Be My Guest) Chsd wnr, rdn & no extra over 1f out: see 2736 (blnks).
5 ran   Time 2m 06.7   (Godolphin)   Saeed bin Suroor Newmarket

HAMILTON WEDNESDAY AUGUST 16TH Righthand, Undulating Track, Stiff Uphill Finish

Official Going   SOFT. Stalls: 1m/9f - Inside, Rem - Stands Side.

3375   5.50 CLASS CLAIMER 3YO+ 0-60 (F)   1m1f36y   Good/Soft 60 -05 Slow
£2744 £784 £392   3 yo rec 7 lb

3011 **ALAMEIN** 17 [5] W Storey 7-8-6 (t) T Williams 14/1: 002301: 7 ch g Roi Danzig - Pollination (Pentotal) **41**
Held up, prog to lead ins last, styd on well, rdn out: op 12/1: '99 Lingfield wnr (clmr & h'cap, rtd 77a, with
D Nicholls, rtd 54 on turf): '98 Southwell wnr (clmr, rtd 78a & 74): eff btwn 7f/9f on firm, gd/soft & both AWs:
handles any trk: loves Lingfield: gd weight carrier who is eff with/without blnks: eff in a t-strap nowadays.
3199 **ROOFTOP PROTEST** 8 [12] Mrs M Reveley 3-8-5 P Bradley (5) 13/2: 316232: 3 b g Thatching - Seattle ¾ **45**
Siren (Seattle Slew) Chsd ldrs, eff/hung badly right over 1f out, styd on ins last, not pace of wnr; op 5/1:

eff btwn 9/11f: acts on fast & gd/soft grnd: see 1909.
3141 **CLAIM GEBAL CLAIM 12** [6] P Monteith 4-8-6 V Halliday 14/1: 001603: 4 b g Ardkinglass - Infra Blue ¾ 38
(Bluebird) Led till ins last, held nr fin: well clr of rem: op 12/1: see 2780 (C/D).
3141 **ACE OF TRUMPS 12** [1] J Hetherton 4-8-8 (t) J McAuley 5/1: 002564: Cl-up, btn 1f out: see 1195. 10 26
1239 **GO THUNDER 97** [7] 6-9-0 (t) Iona Wands 100/1: 0-0005: Chsd ldrs till over 1f out: 3 month abs. ¾ 31
3247 **FRENCH MASTER 7** [11] 3-8-7 (vis) D O'Donohoe 20/1: 320006: Held up, rdn 3f out, sn held: see 3008. ½ 30
*2642 **PEGASUS BAY 33** [8] 9-9-12 A Beech (5) 9/2: 62-117: Held up, eff 2f out, no impress: btr 2642. 2½ 39
2831 **LAUND VIEW LADY 26** [13] 3-8-0 P Hanagan (6) 25/1: 060008: Dwelt, nvr on terms: see 1351 (seller). 2½ 17
*2538 **ROCK SCENE 37** [3] 8-9-4 P Dobbs (5) 7/2 FAV: 655419: Dwelt & al rear: op 4/1: btr 2538. nk 27
3192 **FASTWAN 9** [10] 4-8-6 A McGlone 33/1: 000500: Chsd ldrs 6f: 10th: see 3138. ½ 14
1819 **TIME LOSS 68** [9] 5-9-0 (VIS) M Fenton 20/1: 540000: Prom, btn 2f out: 11th: visor: 2 month abs. ½ 21
2861 **POWER GAME 24** [2] 7-8-10 A Mackay 200/1: -04000: Mid-div, btn 4f out: 12th: see 2046, 1685. 5 11
2655 **VANBOROUGH LAD 33** [4] 11-8-6 O Pears 7/1: 21000P: Held up, broke down/p.u. 2f out: 13th: op 5/1. 0
13 ran Time 2m 0.1 (6.0) (R J H Limited) W Storey Muggleswick, Co.Durham.

3376

6.20 ROSEBANK SELLER 2YO (F) 5f Good/Soft 60 -20 Slow
£2646 £756 £378 Raced stands side

3216 **CATCH THE CHRON 7** [4] N Tinkler 2-8-7 A Beech (5) 7/1: 20401: 2 b f Claintime - Emerald Gulf 69
(Wassl) Dwelt, prog to lead ins last, styd on strongly, rdn out: op 4/1: first win: apprec this drop to 5f, tried 6f: acts on gd/soft grnd & a stiff/undul trk: eff in sell grade.
3264 **SEANS HONOR 6** [2] C N Kellett 2-8-7 T Williams 4/1: 544062: 2 b f Mukaddamah - Great Land (Friend's 3 61
Choice) Led till ins last, sn held by wnr: op 7/2, qck reapp: prob handles fast & gd/soft grnd: see 1706.
3204 **GEMTASTIC 8** [10] P D Evans 2-8-7 A Mackay 11/4 FAV: -6033: 2 b f Tagula - It's So Easy (Shaadi) 2½ 55
Cl-up, rdn/ch over 1f out, held ins last: well bckd: handles firm & gd/soft grnd: see 3204.
2948 **EASTERN RED 19** [6] K A Ryan 2-8-7 Iona Wands 14/1: 562054: Dwelt, prog 2f out, no hdwy fnl 1f. 2 51
2983 **FAYZ SLIPPER 18** [7] 2-8-7 M Fenton 11/2: 424555: Prom, rdn/btn 1f out: see 2435, 1918. 1 49
2880 **LADY AMBITION 23** [8] 2-8-7 A McGlone 16/1: -0506: Rcd towards centre, hung right/btn 2f out. ½ 48
2507 **CAPTAINS FOLLY 39** [9] 2-8-7 J McAuley 12/1: -0057: Al outpcd: mod form prev for Miss J F Craze. 1½ 45
2507 **GOLGOTHA 39** [5] 2-8-7 O Pears 33/1: 0508: Chsd ldrs till over 1f out: mod form. nk 44
-- **MEIKLE PRINCE** [11] 2-8-12 C Lowther 20/1: 9: Dwelt, sn well bhd, mod gains 2f out: op 10/1: nk 48
Contract Law colt, May foal, cost 2,400gns: a first foal: dam unrcd: sire 6f juv Gr 2 wnr: with Miss L A Perratt.
2277 **BLOOM 48** [1] 2-8-7 Dean McKeown 20/1: 500: In tch 3f: 10th: 7 wk abs: prev with D Moffatt. 1½ 40
3128 **PAT PINKNEY 12** [3] 2-8-7 D O'Donohoe 9/1: 545460: Cl-up 3f: 11th: btr 2268 (fast). ¾ 39
11 ran Time 1m 02.1 (4.0) (The Oldham Chronicle Racing Club) N Tinkler Langton, N.Yorks.

3377

6.50 ARTHUR BALDING HCAP 3YO+ 0-70 (E) 6f Good/Soft 60 +03 Fast [70]
£3916 £1205 £602 £301 3 yo rec 3 lb Field raced centre - far side

*3097 **TOM TUN 14** [8] Miss J F Craze 5-10-0 (70)(t) T Lucas 10/1: 050011: 5 b g Bold Arrangement - B Grade 75
(Lucky Wednesday) Al prom, rdn/led 1f out, held on well for press nr fin: op 8/1: recent Leicester wnr (class stks): '99 wnr at Southwell (2, h'caps, rtd 75a), Newcastle (h'cap) & Doncaster (2, h'cap & stks, rtd 82): '98 wnr at Newcastle & Southwell (h'caps, rtd 62a & 65): eff at 5/6f on firm, soft & both AWs: handles any trk, likes Southwell & Doncaster: gd weight carrier, eff with/without t-strap: in great heart at present.
*3080 **TREASURE TOUCH 14** [5] P D Evans 6-10-0 (70) Joanna Badger (7) 16/1: 313012: 6 b g Treasure Kay - hd 74
Bally Pourri (Law Society) In tch, prog to chall ins last, styd on well, just held: in great form: see 3080 (clmr).
*1780 **CHARMING LOTTE 70** [3] N Tinkler 3-9-7 (66)(vis) A Beech (5) 25/1: 000513: 3 b f Nicolotte - 1 67
Courtisane (Persepolis) Chsd ldrs, styd on for press fnl 1f: 10 wk abs: acts on gd, loves gd/soft & soft grnd: can win again granted similar conditions: see 1780 (clmr).
3200 **SAND HAWK 8** [18] D Shaw 5-7-13 (41)(bl) J McAuley 8/1: 235004: Held up, styd on fnl 2f, not ¾ 40
able to chall: bckd, op 10/1: return to 7f & similar company shld suit: see 323 (AW, 7f).
3103 **FOUND AT LAST 14** [13] 4-8-9 (51)(BL) Dean McKeown 14/1: 222435: Dwelt, towards rear, rdn/prog 2 45
2f out, no hdwy ins last: tried blnks: see 3103 (mdn h'cap).
3097 **INDIAN MUSIC 14** [14] 3-9-9 (68) R Winston 6/1: 555326: Cl-up, rdn/ch 1f out, held ins last: bckd. ½ 60
3083 **LADY OF WINDSOR 14** [12] 3-9-6 (65)(bl) J Fanning 25/1: 230067: Led till 1f out, fdd: blnks reapp. hd 56
3170 **LADY BOXER 10** [16] 4-9-0 (56) A Mackay 14/1: -00008: Dwelt/rear, mod gains fnl 2f: op 10/1: '99 ½ 45
Chester wnr (class stks, rtd 79): '98 Leicester debut wnr (auct mdn, rtd 84): eff at 6f on firm & hvy grnd, any trk.
3197 **NAISSANT 9** [17] 7-8-11 (53) A Culhane 3/1 FAV: 120039: Chsd ldrs, btn over 1f out: hvly bckd, op 5/1. 1¾ 38
2240 **SHARP EDGE BOY 49** [2] 4-8-9 (50)(1ow) T Eaves (0) 20/1: 000020: Rear, nvr on terms: 10th: abs. 1 34
2559 **BOWLERS BOY 36** [9] 7-9-1 (57) C Lowther 7/1: 121540: Prom, btn 2f out: 11th: btr 1941. nk 39
2697 **DOUBLE ACTION 32** [10] 6-9-7 (63)(bl) M Fenton 8/1: 266060: Rdn/rear, mod prog: 12th: op 6/1. hd 44
3123 **BENZOE 12** [11] 10-9-1 (57) Iona Wands 12/1: 061530: Cl-up 4f: 16th: op 10/1: btr 2701 (fast). 0
2969 **Mujagem 19** [7] 4-8-1 (43)(bl) P Hanagan (7) 20/1: 1910 **Red Symphony 63** [6] 4-8-8 (50)(vis) O Pears 25/1:
2612 **Jaypeecee 34** [15] 4-8-4 (46)(vis) T Williams 16/1: 3080 **San Michel 14** [1] 8-8-4 (46)(vis) D O'Donohoe 33/1:
3161 **Shalarise 11** [4] 3-8-11 (56)(vis) A McGlone 50/1:
18 ran Time 1m 13.2 (3.4) (Mrs O Tunstall) Miss J F Craze Elvington, N.Yorks.

3378

7.20 CARLTON HCAP 3YO+ 0-70 (E) 1m5f Good/Soft 60 +04 Fast [70]
£2973 £915 £457 £228 3 yo rec 11lb

3284 **SKYERS A KITE 5** [9] Ronald Thompson 5-8-1 (43) T Williams 4/1: 531521: 5 b m Deploy - Milady Jade 51
(Drumalis) Held up, prog ent str, led bef dist, sn clr: best time of night: earlier won at Beverley (clmr): '99 wnr again at Beverley (h'cap, rtd 45): '98 wnr at Beverley & Catterick (sell h'cap, rtd 50): eff at 10f, suited by 12/13f: acts on firm & gd, soft grnd suits: goes on any trk, likes a stiff fin, esp Beverley.
3249 **PAPI SPECIAL 7** [8] I Semple 3-8-3 (56) R Winston 3/1 FAV: 4012D2: 3 b g Tragic Role - Practical 6 57
(Ballymore) Prom in chsg pack, prog to chall 2f out, onepace: nicely bckd, qck reapp: remains in form.
2801 **ONCE MORE FOR LUCK 26** [1] Mrs M Reveley 9-9-10 (66) T Eaves (7) 4/1: 312523: 9 b g Petorius - 1½ 66
Mrs Lucky (Royal Match) Rear, prog & ch ent fnl 2f, sn no extra: tchd 5/1: nk bhd this 2nd in 22801, see 2098.
1894 **TURGENEV 64** [7] R Bastiman 11-7-10 (38)(10oh) J McAuley 16/1: 050664: Handy, outpcd appr fnl 1f. 1 37$
3255 **LOST SPIRIT 6** [4] 4-7-11 (39) Joanna Badger (7) 8/1: 401135: Sn in a clr lead, hdd ent fnl 2f, fdd: 1½ 37
qck reapp: poss went off too fast on this rain softened grnd over longer 13f trip: see 3053.
2461 **TOTEM DANCER 40** [6] 7-9-2 (58) D O'Donohoe 6/1: 024206: Held up, eff 3f out, no impress: 6 wk abs. 1½ 55
3201 **SING AND DANCE 8** [5] 7-8-7 (49) A Beech (5) 11/2: 255327: In tch, wknd appr fnl 2f: reportedly 12 36

unsuited by this rain-softened grnd: see 3201, 1147.
2801 **LORD ADVOCATE 26** [3] 12-7-12 (40)(vis)(2ow)(17oh) A Mackay 66/1: 060668: Led chsg pack, lost pl 3f out.*1* **23**
2742 **TEN PAST SIX 28** [10] 8-7-10 (38)(vis)(12oh) Iona Wands 100/1: 560009: Chsd ldrs till after halfway.   *19* **6**
9 ran   Time 2m 52.8 (7.3)   (G A W Racing Partnership)   Ronald Thompson Stainforth, S.Yorks.

3379

7.50 HAZELBANK HCAP 3YO+ 0-80 (D) **1m3f**   **Good/Soft 60 -19 Slow**   **[75]**
£4192   £1290   £645   £322   3 yo rec 9 lb

4410} **CAPTAIN BRADY 303** [8] J S Goldie 5-8-4 (51) A McGlone 20/1: 0030-1: 5 ch g Soviet Lad - Eight Mile   **55**
Rock (Dominion) Led, increased pace 2f out, hard rdn dist, just held on: drifter from 12/1 on debut, fine ride:
'99 wnr here at Hamilton & Ripon (h'caps, rtd 54): missed '98, mdn plcd in '97 (rtd 58a, W Turner): eff at
9f/11f on firm, soft grnd & fibresand: goes well fresh, without blnks & likes to force the pace.
3368 **OCEAN DRIVE 1** [7] Miss L A Perratt 4-7-13 (46) A Beech (5) 11/2: 224542: 4 b g Dolphin Street -   *shd* **49**
Blonde Goddess (Godswalk) Towards rear, prog 2f out, gaining on wnr thr' fnl 1f, just failed: ran yesterday,
wnr in another stride: acts on fast & gd/soft grnd, see 846.
3049 **WADI 16** [9] Dr J R J Naylor 5-9-4 (65) Dean McKeown 3/1 FAV: 410143: 5 b g Green Desert - Eternal   *2* **65**
(Kris) Prom, hdwy to chase wnr appr fnl 1f, onepace: nicely bckd from 4/1: sound run, grnd softer than ideal.
3368 **FREEDOM QUEST 1** [6] B S Rothwell 5-8-13 (60) M Fenton 9/2: 214004: Held up, switched & hdwy   ½ **59**
to chase ldrs fnl 1f, no extra ins last: bckd, ran yesterday: stamina just stretched back up in trip on easy grnd?
3267 **CAPRICCIO 6** [1] 3-9-5 (75) J Fanning 5/1: 43525: Cl-up & ev ch till fdd & edged left appr fnl 1f.   2½ **71**
3181 **HUNTERS TWEED 9** [2] 4-9-9 (70) A Culhane 8/1: 202066: Chsd ldrs till 2f out: tchd 10/1: see 1194   5 **61**
3368 **IMPULSIVE AIR 1** [4] 8-7-11 (44) P Hanagan (7) 5/1: 200437: Handy till wknd appr fnl 2f: up in trip   3 **32**
& prob came too soon after yesterday: see 3368, 569
-- **SLANEYSIDE** [5] 3-8-11 (67) R Winston 9/1: 5-3608: Prom till 3f out: 12 wk abs, Brit bow, tchd 20/1:   *1* **54**
ex-Irish, earlier plcd over 10f on soft grnd for J Bolger: cost 20,000gns, with I Semple.
3173 **HERACLES 10** [3] 4-10-0 (75) P Bradley (5) 20/1: 634109: Al bhd: top-weight, see 2930 (13f mdn, fast).   ½ **61**
9 ran   Time 2m 27.5 (8.7)   (Frank Brady)   J S Goldie Uplawmoor, E.Remfrews.

3380

8.20 S JOSEPH MDN HCAP 3YO+ 0-65 (F) **1m65y rnd** **Good/Soft 60 -15 Slow**   **[63]**
£3055   £940   £470   £235   3 yo rec 6 lb

3129 **ENTITY 12** [2] T D Barron 3-8-13 (54) D O'Donohoe 10/1: 005001: 3 ch g Rudimentary - Desert Ditty   **60**
(Green Desert) Waited with, closed 3f out, shkn up to lead bef dist, readily: op 8/1: promise more than once
last term (nursery, rtd 71): eff at 1m on firm & gd/soft grnd, any trk, without blnks.
2970 **KUWAIT THUNDER 19** [9] J L Eyre 4-7-12 (31)(vis)(2ow) T Williams 10/1: 050502: 4 ch c Mac's   *3* **33**
Imp - Romangoddess (Rhoman Rule) In tch, drvn & hdwy 2f out, chall bef dist, sn outpcd by wnr: tchd 12/1:
back to form on this rain-softened grnd: see 368.
3310 **GARGOYLE GIRL 4** [5] J S Goldie 3-8-6 (47) A McGlone 8/1: 555443: 3 b f Be My Chief - May Hills   *1½* **44**
Legacy (Be My Guest) Held up, under press 2f out, kept on ins last, nvr nrr: qck reapp, unsuited by drop
back to 1m, prob handles firm & gd/soft grnd.
1263 **MOVING EXPERIENCE 96** [4] D W P Arbuthnot 3-9-7 (62) A Culhane 3/1 FAV: 04-04: Towards rear,   *1¾* **55**
hard rdn 2f out, styd on without threatening: well bckd, over 3 month abs, h'cap bow: try 10f?
3103 **CLOHAMON 14** [13] 5-7-10 (31)(vis) J McAuley 20/1: 00-605: Prom, shkn up to lead 3f out, hdd   ½ **23**
2f out, hung left & btn: interesting back at 7f in a sell h'cap.
1435 **THE LONELY WIGEON 86** [7] 3-7-13 (40)(t) A Beech(1) 25/1: 0506: Nvr better than mid-div: abs, h'cap bow.*2* **28**
2799 **CUTE CAROLINE 26** [3] 4-8-9 (44)(vis) P Bradley (5) 16/1: 623007: Mid-div, prog & ch 3f out, no extra.   *hd* **32**
3365 **HIGHLAND GOLD 1** [10] 3-9-10 (65) C Lowther 16/1: -35008: Prom till appr fnl 2f: ran yesterday.   *2* **49**
3226 **DISTANT GUEST 7** [6] 3-9-10 (65)(bl) M Fenton 9/2: 024059: In tch till 3f out: bckd, qk reapp, see 1367.   *1* **54**
2603 **PUPS PRIDE 34** [8] 3-8-6 (47) P Hanagan (7) 13/2: 000340: Bhd ldrs, lost pl appr fnl 2f: 10th, bckd.   *1¼* **27**
3141 **SPIRIT OF KHAMBANI 12** [12] 3-8-4 (45)(BL) J Fanning 5/1: 042500: Led till 3f out, wknd: 11th.   *8* **11**
4590} **Rattle 287** [1] 7-7-12 (33)(t)(2ow)(10oh) A Mackay 100/1: 3139 **Little Les 12** [11] 4-8-5 (40) R Winston 25/1:
3236 **Sitting Pretty 7** [14] 4-7-10 (31)(bl) (7oh) Joanna Badger (7) 33/1:
14 ran   Time 1m 50.0 (6.2)   (Mrs J Hazell)   T D Barron Maunby, N.Yorks.

Official Going   GOOD TO FIRM Stalls: Str Course - Stands Side, Rem - Inside

3381

2.20 GREAT DAYS OUT MDN 3YO+ (D) **1m2f21y** **Good/Firm 34 +04 Fast**
£4062   £1250   £625   £312   3 yo rec 8 lb

3012 **SCACHMATT 17** [3] L M Cumani 3-8-12 J P Spencer 7/2: 502421: 3 b c Zafonic - Svanzega (Sharpen Up)   **84**
Chsd ldr, led over 1f out, al just holding rival ins last, rdn out: eff at 10/12f on fast & gd: consistent.
3042 **TOLSTOY 16** [8] Sir Michael Stoute 3-8-12 T Quinn 11/10 FAV: 2-5222: 3 b c Nashwan - Millazure   *nk* **83**
(Dayjur) Led, rdn/hdd over 1f out, rallied for press cl home, just held: hvly bckd, clr of rem: stays 10f.
2554 **AMRITSAR 37** [5] P Howling 3-8-12 Paul Eddery 8/1: 543233: 3 ch c Indian Ridge - Trying For Gold   *8* **74**
(Northern Baby) Held up, rdn/outpcd by front pair fnl 2f: op 6/1: prev with Sir M Stoute: see 2554, 2175.
2774 **BREEZE HOME 27** [9] C M Kinane 4-9-6 J Stack 25/1: 7: Prom, rdn/btn 2f out: see 2774.   *1½* **72**
2957 **POLAR STAR 19** [4] 3-8-12 R Mullen 11/2: 02-045: Dwelt, held up, keen, mod hdwy 3f out: op 7/2.   ½ **71**
2963 **VARIETY 19** [6] 3-8-7 O Urbina 12/1: 036: Held up, hdwy 3f out, sn held: op 8/1: see 2963 (12f).   ½ **65**
-- **MISTER MCGOLDRICK 1** [1] 3-8-12 T G McLaughlin 50/1: 7: Held up, keen, rdn/no impress fnl 3f: *nk* **69**
debut: brother to a plcd hdler, dam a 10f wnr: with J G Given.
-- **PAS FARIBOLE 7** [7] 3-8-7 J Lowe 25/1: 8: Held up, bhd 3f out: debut, with Dr J D Scargill.   *16* **46**
8 ran   Time 2m 07.2 (3.0)   (Scuderia Rencati Sri)   L M Cumani Newmarket, Suffolk

3382

2.50 GREATER YARMOUTH CLAIMER 3YO (F)   1m2f21y   Good/Firm 34   -04 Slow
£2184   £624   £312

3263 **IMARI** 6 [4] N P Littmoden 3-8-4(2ow) T Quinn 5/6 FAV: 132631: 3 b f Rock City - Misty Goddess   65
(Godswalk) Trkd ldrs, prog to lead over 1f out, rdly asserted ins last, pushed out: hvly bckd: quick reapp:
earlier opened here at Yarmouth (sell h'cap): unplcd in '99 for J Given (rtd 70, nov stks): suited by 1m/10f on
fast, soft & prob fibresand: likes a sharp/fair trk, loves Yarmouth: enjoys sell/clmg grade.
3236 **EDEIFF** 7 [5] W G M Turner 3-7-10 (t) A Polli (3) 12/1: 050552: 3 b f Tragic Role - Flying Amy   6   47
(Norwick) Held up, prog/chsd ldr 4f out, led over 2f out till over 1f out, sn held: see 3094.
3234 **EMALI** 7 [7] C E Brittain 3-8-13 P Robinson 11/2: -22043: 3 b g Emarati - Princess Poquito (Hard   5   57
Fought) Held up, hdwy 2f out, sn held: see 2685, 2345.
3266 **WENSUM DANCER** 6 [6] R Guest 3-8-4 R Mullen 20/1: 406404: Held up, rdn/mod gains, no threat.   3   44$
3103 **WOODBASTWICK CHARM** 14 [1] 3-8-7 J Quinn 40/1: 000005: Led 7f, sn held: see 2506, 850.   1   46$
3116 **NEGRONI** 12 [2] 3-8-12 M Henry 5/2: 6-336: Keen/trkd ldrs 6f, sn held: longer trip, too keen.   ¾   50
2767 **HANOI** 28 [3] 3-7-12 (bl) J Lowe 40/1: -05007: Prom 7f: debut, with Dr J D Scargill.   7   26
7 ran   Time 2m 08.00 (3.8)   (J R Good)   N P Littmoden Newmarket, Suffolk

3383

3.20 WINTERTON CLASS STKS 3YO+ 0-60 (F)   1m2f21y   Good/Firm 34   +05 Fast
£2912   £896   £448   £224   3 yo rec 8 lb

2893 **IMPREVUE** 23 [7] R J O'Sullivan 6-9-1 (bl) T Quinn 4/1 FAV: 14-631: 6 ch m Priolo - Las Bela (Welsh   57
Pageant) Held up, prog over 1f out, styd on to lead nr fin, hands & heels: op 3/1: best time of day: '99 wnr
twice at Lingfield (h'cap & class stks, rtd 62a), Brighton (amat rider's h'cap) & Nottingham (class stks, rtd 64):
suited by 10f, stays 12f on firm, hvy & equitrack: handles any trk, likes Lingfield: eff with/without blnks.
3188 **MAWINGO** 9 [1] G Wragg 7-9-4 Paul Eddery 13/2: 54-002: 7 b g Taufan - Tappen Zee (Sandhurst Prince)hd   60
Held up, prog over 2f out & rdn/led ins last, sn hdd, kept on well, just held: eff at 7f/1m, stays 10f now.
2958 **EIGHT** 19 [12] C G Cox 4-9-4 M Roberts 9/1: 055403: 4 ch g Thatching - Up To You (Sallust)   3½   55
Chsd ldrs, rdn & onepace fnl 1f: eff around 1m/10f in a visor: see 1807.
3244 **ABLE SEAMAN** 7 [9] C E Brittain 3-8-10 P Robinson 15/2: 334364: Held up, styd on fnl 2f, nrst fin.   ½   54
3011 **HORMUZ** 17 [10] J P Spencer 4-9-6 5/1: 000105: Led, hdd/fdd ins last: top-weight, see 2834 (sell, 1m).   ½   55
-- **ALVARO** [2] 3-8-10 R Mullen 20/1: -06206: Chsd ldrs, no extra when not much room ins last: nk   52
Brit debut, ex-Irish mdn: stays 12f & handles gd/soft grnd.
3159 **YOUNG UN** 11 [3] 5-9-4 P McCabe 11/2: 255007: Held up, eff 3f out, no hdwy fnl 1f: see 786.   shd   52
1388 **SHERZABAD** 88 [6] 3-8-10 G Carter 14/1: 00-08: Held up, rdn 3f out, no threat: op 12/1, 12 wk abs: 2   49
mod form at up to 9.4f prev for Sir M Stoute, now with H J Collingridge.
2593 **ESTABELLA** 35 [11] 3-8-7 (vis) N Callan 10/1: 055549: Hld up, eff 3f out, fdd fnl 1f: vis reapp.   2½   42
1388 **ABLE MILLENIUM** 88 [4] 4-9-4 Dale Gibson 25/1: 30-000: Strugg 3f out: 10th: 12 wk abs: see 133.   1   44
2012 **LATE ARRIVAL** 60 [5] 3-8-10 D McGaffin (5) 16/1: -42000: Prom 1m: 11th: op 12/1, 2 month abs.   1½   42
3030 **LION GUEST** 16 [8] 3-8-10 (t) J Quinn 20/1: -40500: Chsd ldrs/keen, btn 2f out: 12th: no blnks.   dist   0
12 ran   Time 2m 07.1 (2.9)   (Mrs Barbara Marchant)   R J O'Sullivan Epsom, Surrey

3384

3.50 ALDERBY HCAP 3YO+ 0-80 (D)   7f str   Good/Firm 34   -06 Slow   [77]
£5265   £1620   £810   £405   3 yo rec 5 lb

3238 **DARYABAD** 7 [7] N A Graham 8-8-3 (50)(bl)(2ow) Dale Gibson 4/1: 030131: 3 b g Thatching - Dayanata   55
(Shirley Heights) Trkd ldrs, rdn/led 1f out, edged left ins last, styd on well, rdn out: op 3/1: earlier won
at Yarmouth (C/D h'cap): '99 scorer for R McGin, at Lingfield (2, class stks & h'caps, rtd 69a): '98 Catterick
wnr: eff at 1m, suited by 7f on firm, gd/soft & both AWs: loves Yarmouth & Lingfield & suited by blnks: tough.
2999 **ALMASI** 18 [8] C F Wall 8-9-10 (73) R Mullen 4/1: -53402: 8 b m Petorius - Best Niece (Vaigly   1   73
Great) Held up, prog to chase wnr ins last, kept on, al just held: op 6/1: stays 7f, all wins at 6f: see 2999.
3238 **PROSPECTORS COVE** 7 [6] J Pearce 7-9-5 (68) T Quinn 11/4 FAV: 046623: 7 b g Dowsing - Pearl Cove   ½   67
(Town And Country) Held up, prog/switched left over 1f out, styd on onepace: well bckd, op 3/1: see 2768, 1611.
3030 **MEZZORAMIO** 16 [10] K A Morgan 8-7-12 (47)(vis) D Glennon (7) 6/1: 350204: Led 6f, no extra.   ½   45
2878 **AMBER FORT** 23 [3] 7-9-7 (70)(bl) J P Spencer 8/1: 555345: Hld up, late gains, flashed tail.   ½   67
3279 **L A TOUCH** 5 [5] 7-8-2 (51) Paul Eddery 16/1: -03606: Held up, eff 2f out, held 1f out: quick reapp.   2½   43
3297 **GUEST ENVOY** 5 [9] 5-7-10 (45) M Henry 20/1: 054607: Held up, outpcd fnl 2f: quick reapp.   1½   43
*2899 **TOPTON** 22 [1] 6-9-12 (75)(bl) J Quinn 11/2: 023518: Prom, rdn/btn over 1f out: op 4/1, topweight.   ¾   63
*3116 **ELLWAY QUEEN** 12 [2] 3-9-8 (76) W Supple 7/1: -0619: Chsd ldrs 6f: h'cap bow: see 3116 (1m, mdn).   3½   57
3942] **VICTORS CROWN** 335 [4] 3-9-0 (68) A Whelan 33/1: 6200-0: Keen/prom till over 1f out: 10th: reapp.   3   43
rnr-up in '99 (auct mdn, rtd 75): eff at 6f on fast grnd.
10 ran   Time 1m 25.4 (2.8)   (The Three Amigos)   N A Graham Newmarket, Suffolk

3385

4.20 EBF WAXHAM MDN 2YO (D)   6f   Good/Firm 34   -29 Slow
£3461   £1065   £532   £266

-- **CAFETERIA BAY** [6] K R Burke 2-9-0 N Callan 5/1: 2: 2 ch c Sky Classic - Go On Zen (Zen)   87
Prom, led 4f out, styd on well & al holding rivals fnl 1f, pushed out: op 8/1: Jan foal, 60,000 gns 2yo purchase:
dam a US wnr: eff at 6f, 7f+ will suit: acts on fast grnd & runs well fresh: v pleasing debut.
3162 **STATUE GALLERY** 11 [3] J A R Toller 2-9-0 S Whitworth 8/11 FAV: 52: 2 ch c Cadeaux Genereux -   1¼   82
Kinlochewe (Old Vic) Prom, rdn/ev ch 1f out, no pace of wnr ins last: hvly bckd, tchd 5/4: shld win a race.
-- **LA NOTTE** [4] W Jarvis 2-8-9 M Tebbutt 12/1: 3: 2 b f Factual - Miss Mirror (Magic Mirror)   hd   76
Dwelt/outpcd early, switched & styd on well fnl 2f, nor pace of wnr: clr rem: op 7/1: May foal, half-sister to a
wnr abroad: dam a 1m wnr: eff at 6f, 7f sure to suit: acts on fast grnd: learn plenty from this & rate higher.
2828 **PEACE BAND** 29 [5] M H Tompkins 2-9-0 T Quinn 8/1: 54: Prom till over 1f out: see 2828.   4   71
3187 **MANUKA TOO** 9 [2] 2-8-9 R Mullen 20/1: 05: Led 2f, rdn/btn 2f out: op 10/1: see 3187.   ¾   64
-- **HALLAND** [1] 2-9-0 M Roberts 7/2: 6: Unruly stalls, slowly away & al bhd: op 9/4: Halling colt,   2½   62
Feb foal, cost 140,000 gns: half brother to sev wnrs abroad, incl a Gr2 Italian wnr: dam a 7f juv wnr.
-- **CALIBAN** [7] 2-9-0 J Quinn 20/1: 7: Dwelt & al outpcd rear: Rainbows For Life colt, May foal,   8   47
2,000 gns 2yo: brother to a 7f juv wnr abroad: dam a mdn: with N P Littmoden.
7 ran   Time 1m 14.20 (3.8)   (Kenneth Lau)   K R Burke Newmarket, Suffolk

YARMOUTH WEDNESDAY AUGUST 16TH Lefthand, Flat, Fair Track

3386 4.50 SCRATBY FILL HCAP 3YO 0-70 (E) 6f Good/Firm 34 -04 Slow [73]
£3607 £1110 £555 £277

2885 **WATER BABE** 23 [3] J W Payne 3-9-5 (64) J P Spencer 4/1: 0-4101: 3 b f Lake Coniston - Isabella 68
Sharp (Sharpo) Bhd ldrs, hdwy over 1f out, styd on to lead nr line, drvn out: op 7/2: earlier scored at Leicester
(fills h'cap): rtd 64 when unplcd in '99 (mdns): eff over a stiff/gall 6f on fast grnd.
1405 **FIRST DRAW** 88 [4] J R Fanshawe 3-9-7 (66) O Urbina 5/2 JT FAV: 350-02: 3 b f Night Shift - Brook's nk 68
Quest (Ahonoora) Sn cl-up travelling well, went on over 1f out, rdn in last & hdd nr fin, just btn: hvly bckd:
12 wk abs: travelled well on this drop to 6f, acts on fast grnd: see 1405.
*2313 **BIRDSONG** 47 [8] C F Wall 3-9-5 (64) R Mullen 5/2 JT FAV: -0013: 3 b f Dolphin Street - Gay France nk 65
(Sir Gaylord) Cl-up, led over 3f out, rdn/hdd over 1f out, kept on well for press: abs, h'cap bow: new stable.
3076 **DANZIGEUSE** 14 [7] C B B Booth 3-8-11 (56) S Whitworth 20/1: 00-004: Prom, btn 1f out: see 3076. 4 47
3275 **NIGHT AND DAY** 5 [2] 3-9-2 (61) T G McLaughlin 14/1: -22305: Al outpcd: see 118. 2 47
2918 **KIRSCH** 21 [1] 3-8-10 (55)(vis) Paul Eddery 7/1: 005306: Outpcd, nvr on terms: see 361 (AW). 2½ 34
3318 **STOP THE TRAFFIC** 4 [6] 3-8-1 (46)(t) J Quinn 14/1: 005567: Led 2f, btn 2f out: quick reapp. 1¼ 22
3030 **BALLETS RUSSES** 16 [5] 3-8-4 (49) G Carter 9/1: -43008: Slowly away & sn well bhd: see 2036, 1609. 25 0
8 ran Time 1m 12.7 (3.8) (Raymond Tooth) J W Payne Newmarket, suffolk

SALISBURY WEDNESDAY AUGUST 16TH Righthand, Galloping Track, Stiff Finish

Official Going GOOD (GOOD/FIRM places). Stalls: 6f - Far Side; 7f - Centre; 10f - Inside; 12f - Stands Side.

3387 2.10 EBF SANDOWN MDN 2YO (D) 6f str Good/Firm 34 -07 Slow
£3601 £1108 £554 £277

3000 **JENTZEN** 18 [11] R Hannon 2-9-0 R Hughes 8/13 FAV: -41: 2 b c Miswaki - Bold Jessie (Never So Bold): 92+
Trkd ldr, went on dist, readily came clr: hvly bckd, fair dky time: 19,000gns purchase: brother to smart 6f wnr
Abou Zous, dam a useful 6f 2yo scorer: eff over a gall 6f, will stay 7f: acts on fast grnd: held in some regard,
holds Gr 1 entries: sure to rate more highly & win more races.
3064 **AINTNECESSARILYSO** 15 [3] D R C Elsworth 2-9-0 N Pollard 33/1: -00602: 2 ch g So Factual - Ovideo 4 79
(Domynsky): Set pace till dist, sn outpcd by ready wnr: gd front running eff, met a potentially smart rival.
3047 **NOSY BE** 16 [9] P J Makin 2-9-0 S Sanders 12/1: -53: 2 b c Cyrano de Bergerac - Blossomville (Petong): 1¼ 75+
Rear, swtchd 2f out, kept on ins last no ch with ldrs: again shwd promise: sure to rate higher over 7f+ next time.
3009 **ANNATTO** 17 [1] I A Balding 2-8-9 R Cochrane 6/1: -24: Chsd ldrs, rdn & onepcd fnl 1f: not disgraced. hd 70
2550 **CEARNACH** 37 [8] 2-9-0 D R McCabe 100/1: -005: Mid-div, nvr dangrs: 34,000gns May foal: 2 69
half-brother to numerous wnrs both here & abroad: dam scored over 1m: promise here, sure to benefit from 7f/1m.
3215 **BOISDALE** 7 [2] 2-9-0 A Nicholls (3) 25/1: -006: Chsd ldrs, grad fdd final 1½f: poor low draw. hd 69
3047 **LUCKY BREAK** 10 [10] 2-9-0 I Mongan (5) 66/1: -07: Mid-div, some late hdwy, nvr dngrs under a kind shd 69
ride: again shwd some promise, needs 1 more run to qual for nurseries: see 3047.
2091 **GRAND FIVE** 56 [5] 2-9-0 A Clark 20/1: -208: In tch, no impress final 2f: 8 wk abs: best 1573 (g/s). 1¼ 65
2808 **CHARENTE** 26 [13] 2-9-0 Martin Dwyer 66/1: -509: Nvr a factor: see 2189. ½ 64
3000 **DANE FLYER** 18 [7] 2-9-0 (t) Pat Eddery 10/3: -00: Rdn in rear, nvr a factor: 10th, reportedly gurgled. 5 49
3162 **Saorsie** 11 [6] 2-9-0 L Newman(3) 100/1: -- **Level Best** [4] 2-9-0 D Sweeney 66/1:
3162 **Dominion Prince** 11 [12] 2-9-0 Dane O'Neill 25/1:
13 ran Time 1m 14.57 (2.47) (Jeffen Racing) R Hannon East Everleigh, Wilts.

3388 2.40 BEMBRIDGE CLAIMER 2YO (F) 7f str Good/Firm 34 -25 Slow
£2247 £642 £321

3187 **ZANDOS CHARM** 9 [3] R Hannon 2-8-6 Dane O'Neill 16/1: -501: 2 b f Forzando - Silver Charm (Dashing 67
Blade): Front rank till lost place halfway, rallied to lead 2f out, held on well, drvn out: op 12/1: first foal:
sire a smart 9f performer: apprec this step up to 7f, shld stay 1m: acts on fast: apprec drop into claimer.
*3128 **FAZZANI** 12 [2] P C Haslam 2-8-9 K Darley 4/1: 443012: 2 b f Shareef Dancer - Taj Victory (Final Straw): nk 68
Chsd ldrs, imprvd to lead briefly 2f out, ev ch fnl 1f & just btn in a cl fin: prev trained by M Channon, see 3128.
2760 **JOLLANDS** 28 [4] D Marks 2-9-5 D Sweeney 50/1: -03: 2 b c Ezzoud - Rainbow Fleet (Nomination): 1¾ 74
Dwelt, swtchd & prog 2f out, no impress cl home: imprvd form reported into clmg company: eff at 7f on fast grnd.
2784 **TINY TIM** 27 [1] I A Balding 2-8-11 R Cochrane 16/1: -64: Hdwy from rear halfway, ev ch 2f out, 1¾ 62
fdd cl-home: possibly not quite see out this lngr 7f trip: see 2784.
2886 **MARGARITA** 23 [8] 2-8-10 J Reid 33/1: -0005: In tch, outpcd 2f out: little form: see 2628. 4 53
2328 **MONTE MAYOR GOLF** 46 [5] 2-8-2 A Nicholls (3) 9/1: -0506: Set pace 5f, fdd: mkt drifter, 7 wk abs. 3½ 38
3273 **REPEAT PERFORMANCE** 5 [9] 2-9-5 (t) P Fitzsimons (5) 8/1: 440557: Front rank, ev ch 2f out, ¾ 53
grad fdd: qck reapp: see 3273 (AW).
3240 **MEADOW SONG** 7 [12] 2-7-10 D Kinsella (7) 50/1: -48: Dwelt, modest late prog, nvr dngrs: see 3240. 3 24
2990 **FORMAL PARTY** 18 [11] 2-8-4 Pat Eddery 10/11 FAV: -6639: Rdn in rear, nvr a factor: hvly bckd: 2 28
below par effort, reportedly in season: much better expected after 2990 (6f).
3204 **DISTANT DAWN** 8 [7] 2-8-0 (vis) Cheryl Nosworthy(6) 20/1: 402600: Front rank 5f, wknd into 10th. ½ 23
3204 **Mulsanne** 8 [13] 2-8-5 G Hannon (7) 66/1: -- **Debrief** [6] 2-8-7 L Newman (3) 20/1:
12 ran Time 1m 29.68 (4.18) (J C Smith) R Hannon East Everleigh, Wilts.

3389 3.10 LISTED UPAVON FILL STKS 3YO+ (A) 1m2f Good/Firm 34 -04 Slow
£15152 £5747 £2873 £1306 3yo rec 8lb

2696 **FIRST FANTASY** 32 [3] J R Fanshawe 4-9-0 R Cochrane 13/2: 510501: 4 b f Be My Chief - Dreams (Rainbow 96
Quest): Stdd start, imprvd from rear 2f out, led ent fnl 1f, held on well, drvn out: op 8/1: earlier won at Warwick
(stks): '99 Warwick, Yarmouth (2) & Folkestone wnr (h'caps, rtd 82): eff arnd 10f on firm & gd/soft, any trk:
tough & genuine filly who often swishes her tail under press (6 wins from 17 starts): useful.
3001 **DASHIBA** 18 [5] D R C Elsworth 4-9-0 J Reid 7/1: -30662: 4 ch f Dashing Blade - Alsiba (Northfields): shd 95
Rear, imprvd over 2f out, chall strongly final 1f & just btn in a thrilling fin: op 11/2: ran to best here.
1282 **DREAM QUEST** 95 [6] J L Dunlop 3-8-6 (t) Pat Eddery 7/2 FAV: -133: 3 ch f Rainbow Quest - Dreamawhile nk 94

1045

(Known Fact): Waited with, swtchd & imprvd 2f out, kept on well & just btn in a cl-fin: well bckd, 3 mth abs: imprvd eff in first time t-strap, will prob apprec a return to 12f: acts on fast & hvy grnd: see 1282, 1045.
*3189 **PURPLE HEATHER 9** [1] R Hannon 3-8-6 (bl) Dane O'Neill 7/1: 530214: Led till 3f out, remnd prom ½ **93$**
till no extra cl-home: fine run, btn arnd 1L: offic rtd 83, so treat this rating with caution: see 3189.
3134 **BALLADONIA 12** [9] 4-9-0 D Harrison 10/1: 024-65: Chsd ldrs till slightly outpcd 3f out, rallied *nk* **92**
final 1f & btn just over 1L: only 2nd run this year, open to improvement & will enjoy a return to 12f.
2975 **SECRET DESTINY 19** [7] 3-8-6 K Darley 8/1: 3-5156: Mid-div, keeping on when hmpd 2f out, onepcd. 1½ **90**
*2627 **TWIN LOGIC 34** [4] 3-8-6 W Ryan 10/1: 543217: In tch, imprvd to lead 2f out will ent final 1f, *1* **88**
no extra: stiff task: see 2627 (mdn, gd/soft grnd).
2889 **MISS RIVIERA GOLF 23** [2] 3-8-6 D Holland 7/1: -028: Chsd ldrs, imprvd to lead 3f out till 2f out, 2½ **85**
gradually fdd: bckd from 11/1: has shwn enough to find a mdn, see 2889.
3285 **ARMENIA 5** [8] 3-8-6 L Newman 66/1: 320009: Chsd ldr, led briefly 3f out, wknd: qck reapp & *2* **82$**
highly tried, offic rtd just 55: see 882 (AW).
2274 **BLUSIENKA 48** [10] 3-8-6 N Pollard 11/2: -43540: Al towards rear, nvr a factor in last: 7 wk abs: *4* **76**
reportedly unsuited by today's fast grnd: see 2274, 995.
10 ran Time 2m 08.30 (3.80) (Nigel & Carolyn Elwes) J R Fanshawe Newmarket.

3390

3.40 VIOLET APPLIN HCAP 3YO+ 0-70 (E) 1m2f Good/Firm 34 +08 Fast [68]
£3058 £941 £470 £235 3yo rec 8lb

2322 **GUARDED SECRET 46** [2] P J Makin 3-9-7 (69) S Sanders 7/2 FAV: 3-0221: 3 ro c Mystiko - Fen Dance **77**
(Trojan Fen): In tch, kept on under press to lead cl-home, drvn out: bckd from 6/1, best time of day, 7 wk abs, rider reportedly given a 1-day whip ban: apprec this step up to 10f, will stay further: acts on fast, firm grnd & fibresand & on a sharp or stiff/gall trk: continues to improve as he steps up in trip, should win more races.
2445} **BROWNING 410** [3] M P Tregoning 5-9-3 (57) Martin Dwyer 8/1: 2200-2: 5 b g Warrshan - Mossy Rose 1½ **62**
(King Of Spain): Chsd ldrs, went on 3f out, not pace to repel wnr cl-home: belated reapp: trained by D Coakley in '99, rnr-up in 2 h'caps (rtd 61): '98 Windsor wnr (h'cap, rtd 59 & 68a): eff at 10/12f on fast, firm grnd & equitrack: handles a sharp or stiff/gall trk: fine reapp, deserves to go one better.
3031 **SUPERSONIC 16** [5] R F Johnson Houghton 4-9-11 (65) (t) J Reid 16/1: 460403: 4 b f Shirley Heights - 3½ **65**
Bright Landing (Sun Prince): Mid-div, kept on under press fnl 1f, not rch front 2: sound effort, see 679 (AW).
2980 **ALQAWAASER 19** [12] Major D N Chappell 3-9-6 (68) R Havlin 16/1: 30-564: Rear, rdn to impr 3f 2½ **64**
out, kept on & nrst fin: lngr 10f trip: see 2980, 2679.
3166 **NO MERCY 11** [8] 4-9-13 (67)(BL) Pat Eddery 11/2: -50205: Front rank, led after 4f til 3f out, 1¾ **61**
gradually fdd: tchd 9/1, first time blnks, top weight: best 2888.
2688 **DICKIE DEADEYE 32** [15] 3-9-7 (69) S Carson (3) 12/1: 05656: Imprvd from rear 3f out, onepcd fnl 2f. 2½ **59**
4597} **MOMENTOUS JONES 286** [7] 3-8-10 (58) L Newman(3) 25/1: 0552-7: Chsd ldrs racing keenly, no ½ **47**
impress fnl 2f: reapp: trained by M Channon & rnr-up at Windsor (sell, rtd 63$) in '99: eff arnd 7f/1m: now with M Madgwick & rcd too keenly for own gd here.
2846 **ATALYA 25** [14] 3-9-5 (67) P Fitzsimons (5) 14/1: -24528: Chsd ldrs 1m, sn btn: btr 2846 (1m). ¾ **54**
3110 **THATCHMASTER 13** [16] 9-9-10 (64)(t) I Mongan (5) 11/1: 144-09: Nvr a factor: tchd 14/1: see 3110. *1* **49**
2789 **SHARP SPICE 27** [1] 4-9-0 (54) D Holland 15/2: 525530: Dwelt, rcd keenly rear, short of room *nk* **38**
over 3f out till over 1f out: fin 10th: forget this, btr 2789 (firm grnd).
1509 **ZIDAC 82** [13] 8-9-11 (65) A Clark 11/1: 013-00: In tch 7f, sn btn: fin 11th, 12 wk abs: see 1509. *nk* **48**
2467 **COUGHLANS GIFT 40** [6] 4-8-11 (51) R Smith(5) 16/1: 00U050: Rear, effort 3f out, sn btn: 12th, abs. ¾ **32**
2836 **EDIFICE 25** [11] 4-9-13 (67) R Hughes 9/1: 00-560: Al bhd, fin 14th: see 2199. **0**
3012 **MUSALLIAH 17** [10] 3-9-3 (65)(VIS) R Hills 12/1: -0400: Al rear, fin 15th: first time visor on h'cap bow. **0**
2749 **Magic Flute 28** [4] 4-9-9 (63) K Darley 16/1: -- **Hisar** [9] 7-9-11 (65) Dane O'Neill 25/1:
16 ran Time 2m 07.18 (2.68) (D M Ahier) P J Makin Ogbourne Maisey, Wilts.

3391

4.10 ISLE OF WIGHT NOV STKS 2YO (D) 7f str Good/Firm 34 -32 Slow
£3484 £1072 £536 £268

*2979 **TRILLIE 19** [7] D R C Elsworth 2-9-0 N Pollard 16/1: -11: 2 b f Never So Bold - Trull (Lomond): **87**
Front rank, slightly outpcd 2f out, rallied well to force hd in front on line: op 8/1, time slower than the 2yo clmr: prev won here at Salisbury (mdn, debut): 14,000gns half-sister to 2 juv wnrs: eff at 6/7f, 1m shld suit: acts on fast grnd & on a stiff/gall trk, runs well fresh: improving filly.
3154 **REPULSE BAY 11** [4] M R Channon 2-8-12 Pat Eddery 4/5 FAV: -42: 2 b c Barathea - Bourbon Topsy *shd* **84**
(Ile de Bourbon): Chsd lds, drvn into lead inside final 1f, caught on line: hvly bckd from 7/4: ran green today & this probably cost him the race: must sn gain compensation, see 3154.
-- **OVERSPECT** [2] P F I Cole 2-9-5 F Jovine 9/1: -13: 2 b c Spectrum - Portelet (Night Shift): *nk* **90**
Rear, imprvd to lead dist, collared inside last, kept on & not btn far: won at San Siro on debut 12 wks ago: Jan foal, cost IR 30,000gns: dam a multiple sprint wnr, sire a top class 1m/10f performer: eff at 6/7f on gd & fast grnd: runs well fresh, can force the pace: gd run under top-weight.
3121 **NATIVE TITLE 12** [6] M Blanshard 2-8-12 R Cochrane 10/1: -54: Led till dist, no extra cl-home *1* **81**
under hands & heels: op 6/1: may benefit from a drop back to 6f & mdn company: see 3121.
3062 **SMITH AND WESTERN 15** [1] 2-9-2 Dane O'Neill 4/1: 501235: In tch, not qckn final 1f: just btr 3062. 3½ **78**
2494 **PERSUADE 39** [3] 2-8-12 (t) K Darley 12/1: -446: Chsd ldrs 5f, wknd: see 2494. 1½ **71**
-- **LAZZAZ** [5] 2-8-8 R Hills 15/2: -7: Chsd ldrs 5f, wknd: big drifter from 3/1, debut: Mar foal, dam a *10* **47**
wng miler: sire a smart 10f performer: bred to apprec mid-dists in time: with M Tregoning.
7 ran Time 1m 30.12 (4.62) (Sir Stanley & Lady Grinstead) D R C Elsworth Whitsbury, Hants.

3392

4.40 NEWPORT FILL HCAP 3YO+ 0-80 (D) 1m4f Good/Firm 34 +03 Fast [73]
£3861 £1188 £594 £297 3yo rec 10lb

3206 **CYBER BABE 8** [10] A G Newcombe 3-8-1 (56) L Newman (3) 7/1: 002131: 3 ch f Persian Bold - Ervedya **62**
(Doyoun): Rcd keenly in bhd ldrs, rdn & styd on well to lead ins fnl 1f, asserted cl-home: fair time: earlier won at W'hampton (AW sell, with A Reid, rtd 51a) & Brighton (h'cap): dual '99 rnr-up for M Tompkins (rtd 58): eff btwn 1m & 12f on firm, gd/soft grnd & fibresand: likes to run up with/force the pace, handles a sharp/undul or stiff/gall trk: has tried a visor, best without: in gd form.
*3125 **SWEET ANGELINE 12** [7] G G Margarson 3-8-10 (65) K Darley 9/4 FAV: 054312: 3 b f Deploy - Fiveofive 1¾ **68**
(Fairy King): Rear, imprvd to lead 2f out, collared ins fnl 1f & not pace of wnr: bckd from 7/2: see 3125.
2446 **MONO LADY 41** [5] D Haydn Jones 7-9-9 (68)(bl) R Cochrane 9/2: 451443: 7 b m Polish Patriot - Phylella ½ **70**
(Persian Bold): In tch, ch 2f out, no extra cl-home: op 7/2, clr of rem, 6 wk abs: see 2075 (sand).

SALISBURY   WEDNESDAY AUGUST 16TH   Righthand, Galloping Track, Stiff Finish

3045 **DION DEE 16** [6] Dr J R J Naylor 4-8-4 (49) A Daly 14/1: 102564: Led after 2f till 2f out, grad fdd. 3 46
3049 **CRYSTAL FLITE 16** [8] 3-8-5 (60) Martin Dwyer 14/1: 002605: Chsd ldrs 10f, wknd: btr 2246. 2 54
2751 **SALZGITTER 28** [3] 3-9-7 (76) C Rutter 8/1: 5-3306: Rdn in rear, modest late hdwy: not disgrcd, ½ 69
reportedly needs softer grnd: see 1343, 961 (7f, soft grnd).
2924 **QUEEN OF FASHION 21** [11] 4-9-9 (68) P Fitzsimons (5) 20/1: -0437: Chsd ldrs 10f, wknd: op 12/1. ¾ 60
3178 **SWEET CICELY 10** [9] 3-8-8 (63) N Pollard 15/2: 0-3508: Slowly away, nvr a factor: best 1287 (sft). 1¾ 53
2689 **WATER FLOWER 32** [4] 6-9-10 (69)(vis) G Hind 8/1: -01009: Rcd keenly & led 2f, remnd prom till nk 58
wknd 2f out: mkt drifter, top weight: usually runs well here at Salisbury: much btr 2023 (C/D).
2509 **BONNIE FLORA 39** [1] 4-9-3 (62) R Perham 10/1: -003U0: Al bhd, fin last: op 7/1: see 2270 (10f). 7 41
10 ran   Time 2m 36.20 (3.80)   (Advanced Marketing Services Ltd)   A G Newcombe Huntshaw, Devon.

BEVERLEY   WEDNESDAY AUGUST 16TH   Righthand, Oval Track with Stiff, Uphill Finish

Official Going   GOOD/FIRM (GOOD in places). Stalls: Inside.

3393   2.00 ALLDERS CLAIMER 3YO+ (E)   1m100y rnd   Good 45 -07 Slow
£3062   £875   £437   3 yo   rec 6 lb

3330 **MARTON MERE 3** [5] A J Lockwood 4-9-9 R Winston 25/1: 010051: 4 ch g Cadeaux Genereux - Hyatti 64
(Habitat) Hld up, hdwy 2f out, styd on well ins last to get up cl-home, rdn out: op 14/1: qck reapp under
top-weight: earlier won here at Beverley (sell h'cap): rtd 58 & 43a for T Easterby in '99: stays a 8.5f
on gd & gd/firm: loves Beverley & claiming/selling grade.
*3196 **DIHATJUM 9** [1] T D Easterby 3-9-3 J Carroll 7/1: 324012: 3 b g Mujtahid - Rosie Potts (Shareef ½ 63
Dancer) Hld up, hdwy 3f out, led over 1f out, rdn & collared cl-home, not btn far: stays 8.5f.
2816 **FUTURE COUP 26** [14] J Norton 4-9-3 (BL) J Weaver 10/1: 004053: 4 b g Lord At War - Holymoly 1 55
(Halo) Slow away & lost at least 8L, bhd, hdwy over 2f out, styd on strongly ins last, nrst fin: improved run in
first time blnks & wld surely have won but for sloppy start: interesting in this grade if headgear works again.
3266 **NIGHT DIAMOND 6** [8] I A Balding 3-8-11 (t) M Hills 100/30 FAV: 040424: Held up, effort over 2f ½ 54
out, kept on same pace: qck reapp, see 3266.
*3117 **TOUJOURS RIVIERA 12** [2] 10-9-5 A Culhane 5/1: 2/0015: In tch, eff to chall 2f out, sn no extra. ½ 55
3196 **SPEEDFIT FREE 9** [15] 3-9-1 Dean McKeown 6/1: 044136: Led till 3f out, wknd over 1f out: see 3196. 1¾ 55
3082 **CITY BANK DUDLEY 14** [4] 3-8-7 R Lappin 20/1: 364647: In tch, hdwy to lead over 2f out till over 1f out. ½ 46$
3082 **AFRICA 14** [6] 3-8-8 G Duffield 7/1: 604168: In tch, wknd over 2f out: op 5/1, twice below 2731. 4 39
2994 **TOEJAM 18** [7] 7-9-1 (vis) P Fessey 14/1: 150469: In tch, wknd well over 1f out: flattered 2994. 1 38
2826 **FIRST LEGACY 26** [11] 4-9-0 D Mernagh 2 50/1: 000060: Chsd ldrs, wknd over 3f out: 10th, flattered. 1 35$
2882 **Detroit City 23** [13] 5-8-11 J Bramhill 14/1:   1300 **Bunty 93** [10] 4-8-8 J Mackay (5) 25/1:
3503} **Night Of Glory 361** [12] 5-9-4 Suzanne France (7) 50/11073 **Trapper Norman 107** [9] 8-8-13 R Fitzpatrick 16/1:
2732 **Seahorse Boy 29** [3] 3-8-7 K Hodgson 50/1:
15 ran   Time 1m 48.2 (4.4)   (A J Lockwood)   A J Lockwood Brawby, Nth Yorks.

3394   2.30 KINGSTON FILL NURSERY HCAP 2YO (D)   5f   Good 45 -53 Slow   [82]
£3591   £1105   £552   £276

3101 **COZZIE 14** [7] J G Given 2-8-2 (56) P Fessey 10/1: 511661: 2 ch f Cosmonaut - Royal Deed (Shadeed): 59
Held up, hdwy to chall over 1f out, kept on for press to lead ins last, drvn out: earlier won at Musselburgh &
Lingfield (sells, rtd 65a): dam 5f juv wnr: v eff at 5f on any trk: acts on firm, gd & both A/Ws: tough juv.
3109 **CELOTTI 13** [1] R Hollinshead 2-9-7 (75) A Culhane 20/1: 35102: 2 b f Celtic Swing - Zalotti nk 77
(Polish Patriot): Waited with, effort well over 1f out, kept on for press inside last, not btn far: gd run
under top weight: handles fast & gd: wld worth another try at 6f now: see 2818.
2901 **RED RYDING HOOD 22** [2] C A Dwyer 2-9-6 (74) J Weaver 8/1: -63423: 2 ch f Wolfhound - Downeaster ¾ 74
Alexa (Red Ryder) Prom, hdwy & ev ch over 1f out, onepace, not btn far: acts on firm & gd: pinch a race.
3055 **PEYTO PRINCESS 15** [3] C W Fairhurst 2-9-3 (71) J Fanning 9/1: 3224: Cl-up, gd hdwy to lead over ½ 70
1f out, hdd & wknd under press ins last: lkd wnr at dist & worth a try in headgear now (plcd 3 prev starts).
2539 **CHARTLEYS PRINCESS 37** [5] 2-9-0 (68) J Mackay (5) 10/1: -5335: Held up, hdwy & swtchd left 2f ¾ 65
out, slightly short of room inside last, onepace: should rate higher: see 2539.
*3307 **DANCING PENNEY 4** [4] 2-8-12 (66)(7ex) D Mernagh (3) 10/1: 012216: Chsd ldrs, rdn & onepcd well 1 60
over 1f out: qck reapp & not disgrcd after 3307 (6f, sell).
3055 **REGAL AIR 15** [10] 2-9-1 (69) T E Durcan 6/1: 353037: Cl-up, effort to chall when badly hmpd ½ 61
over 1f out, not recover: must have gone closer with a clear run & can rate higher: see 3055, 1249.
3327 **BEREZINA 3** [8] 2-9-1 (69) R Winston 8/1: 640108: Cl-up, wknd well over 1f out: twice below 2990. ¾ 59
*3038 **SCREAMIN GEORGINA 16** [9] 2-9-2 (70)(t) G Faulkner (3) 4/1 FAV: 02119: Led till over 1f out, wknd: 1 57
much btr 3038 (clmr, fast grnd).
3264 **CLANSINGE 6** [11] 2-8-13 (67) J Carroll 7/1: 313400: In tch, wknd & hmpd over 1f out: 10th, see 2665. 3½ 45
3055 **TUPGILL TIPPLE 15** [6] 2-7-13 (53)(VIS) P M Quinn 33/1: 23400: Cl-up, wknd over 2f out: last, visor. 1 28
11 ran   Time 1m 06.2 (4.9)   (D Bass)   J G Given Willoughton, Lincs.

3395   3.00 CHARLES ELSEY HCAP 3YO+ 0-80 (D)   2m   Good 45 -07 Slow   [79]
£4342   £1336   £668   £334   3 yo   rec 14lb

3085 **BUSTLING RIO 14** [7] P C Haslam 4-9-0 (65) P Goode (3) 11/4 FAV: 011151: 4 b g Up And At 'Em - Une 70
Venitienne (Green Dancer) Hld up, plenty to do over 3f out, styd on well fnl 2f to get up cl-home, rdn out, going
away: earlier won at Southwell (rtd 68a), Pontefract & Beverley (h'caps): '99 scorer at Southwell (2) &
Pontefract (h'caps): suited by 2m/2m2f on firm, gd & fibresand: handles any trk & runs well fresh: tough & genuine.
2993 **STAR RAGE 18** [2] M Johnston 10-10-0 (79) J Weaver 4/1: 225542: 10 b g Horage - Star Bound (Crowned 1 83
Prince): Trkd ldr, led after 4f, clr well over 2f out, hard rdn & collared cl-home: clr of rem & back to form
under a big weight: most tough (19 wins from 90 starts): see 2993.
*2455 **FOUNDRY LANE 40** [4] Mrs A J Reveley 9-9-11 (76) A Culhane 7/2: 0-4213: 9 b g Mtoto - Eider 6 74
(Niniski) Trkd ldr, ev ch well over 3f out, outpcd over 2f out: 3 wks ago landed a h'cap chase at M Rasen: see 2455.
2953 **SANDBAGGEDAGAIN 19** [1] M W Easterby 6-9-5 (70)(bl) G Parkin 11/2: 055204: Held up, hdwy over 8 61
3f out, wknd over 2f out: twice below 2455 back in blnks.
*760 **SWIFTWAY 141** [3] 6-7-11 (48) J Bramhill 9/1: /34-15: Led 4f, sn bhd: prob ndd this. ¾ 38

1047

3323 **COLUMBUS 4** [6] 3-8-13 (78)(bl) G Duffield 20/1: -64106: Prom, wknd over 3f out: see 3323.   6   63
3125 **WINDMILL 12** [5] 3-8-2 (67) D Mernagh (3) 6/1: -41447: Hmpd start, sn in tch, wknd 3f out: lngr trip.   12   42
7 ran   Time 3m 38.7 (8.4)   (Rio Stainless Engineering Ltd)   P C Haslam Middleham, Nth Yorks.

3396   **3.30 HULL DAILY MAIL HCAP 3YO 0-70 (E)**   **1m2f**   **Good 45   +04 Fast**   [73]
£3864   £1189   £594   £297

*3281 **FASHION 5** [4] Sir Mark Prescott 3-9-12 (71)(5ex) G Duffield 8/11 FAV: 331-11: 3 b f Bin Ajwaad - New   75
Generation (Young Generation) Cl-up trav well, hdwy to lead over 1f out, styd on gamely ins last, drvn out: hvly
bckd, qck reapp, fast time: earlier scored at Lingfield (class stks): juv scorer at Pontefract (nursery h'cap, rtd
69): eff at 1m, stays 10f & further will suit (half-sister to wnrs up to 2m): acts on firm, gd/soft & any trk: runs
well fresh: progressive & game, no surprise to see her go in again, especially over further.
2902 **NOBLE CALLING 22** [9] N A Graham 3-9-1 (60)(bl) J Weaver 10/1: 302062: 3 b c Caller ID - Specificity   nk   63
(Alleged) Keen, held up, hdwy over 2f out, edged right over 1f out, kept on for press ins last, just btn: gd run.
2746 **SORRENTO KING 28** [8] M W Easterby 3-7-12 (43)(bl) J Mackay (5) 9/1: -00023: 3 ch g First Trump -   nk   45
Star Face (African Sky) Cl-up, short of room & outpcd over 1f out, swtchd outside & styd on ins last, not btn far.
3167 **INVISIBLE FORCE 11** [5] M Johnston 3-8-0 (45)(VIS) R Ffrench 7/2: 613444: Cl-up, led over 2f out   nk   47
till over 1f out, no extra well ins last, not btn far: fair run in first time visor back at 10f: see 2883 (blnks).
3033 **TANGERINE 16** [10] 3-8-2 (47)(bl) D Mernagh (3) 40/1: 000005: Handy, eff for press 2f out, onpcd: 3   45
jockey given 4-day whip ban & trained reportedly fined £260 for giving unacceptable riding instructions.
3124 **SILVER SOCKS 12** [3] 3-7-13 (44) J Bramhill 50/1: 00-006: Keen, in tch, rdn & btn 2f out: modest.   1   40
1444 **GRANTLEY 85** [1] 3-8-8 (53) J Tate 40/1: 00-07: Chsd ldrs, wknd over 2f out: 3 mth abs, modest form.   ½   48
*2685 **FISHER ISLAND 32** [2] 3-8-8 (53) P M Quinn (3) 14/1: 404018: Led till over 2f out, wknd: btr 2685.   3½   43
3201 **COMANCHE QUEEN 8** [7] 3-7-12 (43)(BL)(2ow)(9oh) Kimberley Hart 100/1: -00009: Hmpd start, al bhd.   13   15
3217 **RAINWORTH LADY 7** [8] 3-7-12 (43)(2ow)(5oh) S Righton 14/1: 00635P: Al bhd, hmpd start, t.o/p.u.   0
final 1f: reportedly lost action: see 3217.
10 ran   Time 2m 06.4 (4.1)   (HRH Prince Fahd Salman)   Sir Mark Prescott Newmarket.

3397   **4.00 EBF JOURNAL MDN 2YO (D)**   **7f100y rnd**   **Good 45   -32 Slow**
£4121   £1268   £634   £317

3108 **PAGE NOUVELLE 13** [1] B W Hills 2-8-9 M Hills 30/100 FAV: 31: 2 b f Spectrum - Page Bleue (Sadler's   88
Wells) Prom, hdwy to lead on bit over 1f out, rdn out to hold on ins last: well bckd: half-sister to a German
Gr 3 wnr: stays 7.5f well, further will suit: handles gd & any trk: type to rate higher & progress with racing.
--   **ESYOUEFFCEE** [7] M W Easterby 2-8-9 T Lucas 33/1: 2: 2 b f Alzao - Familiar (Diesis):   hd   86
Keen, hld up, hdwy over 2f out, edged right but styd on for press ins last, just btn on debut: Apr foal, cost IR60,000
gns: bred to relish 1m+ in time & showed plenty of promise here, should win races.
3057 **SIMPATICH 15** [5] L M Cumani 2-9-0 T E Durcan 8/1: -4363: 2 ch c First Trump - Arc Empress Jane   ¾   89
(Rainbow Quest) Led till over 1f out, no extra: clr of rem & an improved run over this stiff/undul 7.5f: see 2620.
3057 **PRINCESS CLAUDIA 15** [2] T D Easterby 2-8-9 J Carroll 9/1: 034: Prom, rdn & btn well over 1f out.   2½   72$
2862 **BARNINGHAM 24** [6] 2-9-0 J Tate 20/1: -645: In tch, wknd over 2f out: see 2862.   7   72
2966 **FORMULA VENETTA 19** [3] 2-9-0 J Weaver 50/1: 0506: Cl-up, wknd well over 2f out: see 2333.   1   70
--   **LOUGH BOW** [8] 2-9-0 G Parkin 50/1: 7: Al bhd: Mar foal, half-brother to a sprint wnr.   2   66
3198 **SOLO DANCE 8** [4] 2-8-9 R Winston 50/1: 448: Held up, effort over 2f out, sn wknd: see 2316.   1   59
8 ran   Time 1m 36.6 (5.8)   (E D Kessly)   B W Hills Lambourn, Berks.

3398   **4.30 TOTE HCAP 3YO+ 0-80 (D)**   **5f**   **Good 45   +09 Fast**   [80]
£7904   £2432   £1216   £608   3 yo rec 2 lb High No's Favoured

3341 **MUNGO PARK 3** [18] M Dods 6-9-11 (77) A Culhane 4/1 FAV: 222251: 6 b g Selkirk - River Dove   84
(Riverman) In tch, gd hdwy over 1f out to lead ins last, rdn out: nicely bckd, gd time, qck reapp: rnr-up num
times earlier this term: '99 wnr at Thirsk (class stks, rtd 84 at best): '98 wnr at Newcastle (2), Beverley &
Nottingham (h'caps, with Mrs J Ramsden): stays 6f, all 8 wins at 5f: likes to come late on any grnd or trk,
loves Newcastle: eff in blnks, sharper today without: consistent, consented to put his head in front today.
2925 **MIZHAR 21** [19] D Nicholls 4-9-6 (72)(BL) Alex Greaves 9/1: 000002: 4 b g Dayjur - Futuh (Diesis):   ½   78
Prom, hdwy to lead dist, rdn & collared ins last, not btn far: back to form from a gd draw in first time blnks:
eff at 5/7f: h'capped to win if headgear works for 2nd time: see 1173.
3203 **TORRENT 8** [2] D W Chapman 5-8-6 (58)(bl) Lynsey Hanna (7) 20/1: 446333: 5 ch g Prince Sabo -   1   61
Maiden Pool (Sharpen Up) Hld up, kept on nicely over 1f out, nrst fin: has ability but frustrating this term.
3214 **SURPRISED 7** [8] R A Fahey 5-9-3 (69)(VIS) G Parkin 20/1: 001544: Steadied start, swtchd to far   nk   71+
rail, bhd, gd hdwy 2f out, short of room & swtchd over 1f out, styd on strongly: eye-catching from modest draw
in first time visor & should go close over 6f next time: see 3214, 1905.
3271 **MARENGO 5** [16] 6-8-4 (56) R Ffrench 20/1: 006365: In tch, hdwy & short of room over 1f out, kept   1¼   54
on for press inside last: qck reapp: see 3077, 1073.
3203 **TANCRED TIMES 8** [20] 5-7-13 (50) Kimberley Hart 7/1: 115526: Led halfway till over 1f out, no extra.   1   46
2987 **MISS FIT 18** [14] 4-8-8 (60) G Duffield 11/1: 000557: In tch, effort 2f out, sn no impress: see 926.   ¾   53
3056 **BOLLIN ANN 15** [10] 5-8-13 (65) J Carroll 14/1: 023068: Held up, effort & short of room over   ¾   56
1f out, onepace: see 2340, 2107.
3257 **RUDE AWAKENING 6** [15] 6-7-10 (48)(1oh) J Mackay (5) 8/1: 010529: Cl-up, wknd 2f out: btr 3257.   nk   38
3214 **KOSEVO 7** [11] 6-7-10 (48)(bl)(9oh) P M Quinn (3) 25/1: 000030: Nvr a factor: 10th: btr 3214.   ¾   36
3091 **GAY BREEZE 14** [17] 7-9-3 (69) J Weaver 11/1: 500600: Led till halfway, wknd over 1f out: 11th.   nk   56
3119 **POLES APART 12** [13] 4-9-8 (74)(BL) M Hills 16/1: 005400: In tch, btn over 2f out: 12th, blnks.   1   58
3136 Smart Predator 12 [1] 4-9-11 (77) T E Durcan 16/1:   3222 Northern Svengali 7 [4] 4-8-8 (60) J Tate 25/1:
2961 Bundy 19 [3] J Fanning 25/1:   3037 Trinity 16 [12] 4-9-0 (66) D Mernagh (3) 16/1:
3341 Violet 3 [6] 4-7-13 (51)(bl) P Fessey 20/1:   2830 Shirley Not 26 [9] 4-9-4 (70) G Faulkner (3) 20/1:
2987 Blessingindisguise 18 [7] 7-9-12 (78)(bl) T Lucas 20/1:
19 ran   Time 1m 03.1 (1.8)   (Exors Of The Late Mrs H M Carr)   M Dods Piercebridge, Co Durham.

BEVERLEY WEDNESDAY AUGUST 16TH Righthand, Oval Track with Stiff, Uphill Finish

3399 5.00 DOWNEY'S DIARY CLASS STKS 3YO+ 0-60 (F)   1m4f   Good 45 -21 Slow
£2310   £660   £330   3 yo rec 10lb

3122 **BLUE STREET** 12 [1] S C Williams 4-9-4 G Faulkner (3) 5/6 FAV: 060231: 4 b c Deploy - Kumzar   57
(Hotfoot) Chsd ldr, led over 2f out, kept on for press ins last: well bckd, first win: stays 12f on a stiff/undul
trk: handles gd & gd/firm: in gd form.
3031 **LADY DONATELLA** 16 [4] M L W Bell 3-8-5 J Mackay (5) 11/4: 600-62: 3 b f Last Tycoon - Nekhbet   ½   53
(Artaius) Hld up, hdwy to chase wnr over 1f out, ev ch ins last, not btn far: clr of rem & stays 12f on gd.
2879 **HORTON DANCER** 23 [7] M Brittain 3-8-8 D Mernagh (3) 20/1: 400303: 3 b g Rambo Dancer - Horton .   4   50$
Lady (Midyan): Led till over 2f out, wknd over 1f out: flattered by rating: see 2439, 752.
3011 **LEGACY OF LOVE** 17 [3] Miss S E Hall 4-9-1 (VIS) J Weaver 5/1: 4-0204: Held up, effort over 2f   1¾   44
out, no impress: big step up in trip in first time visor: btr 2781.
1073 **KINGS CHAMBERS** 107 [2] 4-9-4 P Fessey 50/1: 0-0005: Prom, wknd over 2f out: now with J Parkes &   13   29$
virtually refused to race over hdles 3 mths ago: poor form.
2776 **REPUBLICAN LADY** 27 [6] 8-9-1 P Shea (5) 33/1: -0466: In tch, wknd over 3f out: see 2776.   18   2
3081 **FAS 14** [9] 4-9-4 J Tate 33/1: 000007: Al bhd: flattered 3081.   3   1
3285 **FOREST QUEEN** 5 [8] 3-8-5 P M Quinn (3) 25/1: 000008: In tch, wknd over 3f out: see 3217.   1½   0
8 ran   Time 2m 39.2 (7.9)   (Tymest Ltd)   S C Williams Newmarket.

EPSOM WEDNESDAY AUGUST 16TH Lefthand, V Sharp, Undulating Track

Official Going   GOOD (GOOD/FIRM Places). Stalls: 6f - Outside; 1m4f - Centre; Rem - Inside.

3400 5.35 J CROWDEN MDN AUCT 2YO (E)   6f rnd   Good/Firm 25 -36 Slow
£3542   £1090   £545   £272

-2972 **SCOTISH LAW** 19 [3] P R Chamings 2-8-8 A Nicholls (3) 11/8 FAV: 21: 2 ch g Case Law - Scotia Rose   74
(Tap On Wood) Held up, hdwy under press 2f out, led below dist, ran on strongly: well bckd, 10,000 gns
Mar foal, dam 12f wnr: eff at 6f, needs 7f: acts on fast grnd, sharp/undul trk.
2983 **VISLINK** 18 [1] A P Jarvis 2-8-11 Lisa Jones (7) 33/1: 00002: 2 br c Shalford - Wide Outside   1½   72$
(Don't Forget Me) Sn in clr lead, hdd ent fnl 1f, onepace: much imprvd from the front, stays 6f on fast grnd.
3032 **BAJAN BLUE** 16 [5] M Johnston 2-8-0 F Norton 5/1: 63: 2 b f Lycius - Serotina (Mtoto)   hd   60
Rear, eff 2f out, switched & kept on ins last: imprvd, shld progress further at 7f: handles fast grnd.
3165 **TOP NOLANS** 11 [4] M H Tompkins 2-8-11 G Sparkes (7) 5/1: 033304: Handy in chasing pack, prog,   ½   69
switched & ch appr fnl 1f, onepace: visor omitted: btr 2724.
3228 **ONCE REMOVED** 7 [2] 2-8-3 P Doe 11/4: 023405: Held up, gd prog to chall appr fnl 1f, fdd fnl 100y.   1   58
2748 **EAGALITY** 28 [7] 2-8-3 (BL) D R McCabe 20/1: 0006: Led chsg pack, ev ch ent fnl 2f, sn btn, eased.   2½   50
-- **MYSTERI DANCER** [6] 2-8-11 G Bardwell 12/1: 7: Dwelt, al bhd: op 7/1 on debut: Rudimentary   hd   57
half-brother to several wnrs, incl a dual 6f juv: with R O'Sullivan.
7 ran   Time 1m 11.44 (3.64)   (P R Channings)   P R Chamings Baughurst, Hants

3401 6.05 JOHN HARTNETT HCAP 3YO 0-75 (E)   1m114y rnd   Good/Firm 25 -04 Slow   [77]
£4270   £1314   £657   £328

3261 **DUSKY VIRGIN** 6 [3] S Woodman 3-8-2 (51) F Norton 7/1: 004021: 3 b f Missed Flight - Rosy Sunset   60
(Red Sunset) In tch, hands & heels hdwy 2f out, led dist, cmftbly: qk reapp: '99 Brighton wnr (sell, rtd 63, M
Quinn): eff at 7f/8.5f, tried further: goes on firm/fast grnd, sharp/undul trks: qk follow up at Brighton next week?
2265 **RASMALAI** 48 [4] R Hannon 3-9-4 (67) R Hughes 12/1: 0302: 3 b f Sadler's Wells - Raymouna (High   3½   68
Top) Early ldr, chsd ldrs, not clr run & switched bef dist, styd on under press to grab 2nd nr line: 7 wk
abs, h'cap bow: better run back at 8.5f, handles fast & hvy grnd: rtd higher 1032.
*3357 **SPARK OF LIFE** 2 [2] T D McCarthy 3-8-2 (51)(bl) J Sparkes (7) 13/8 FAV: 323113: 3 b f Rainbows   nk   51
for Life - Sparkly Girl (Danehill) Unruly bef start, dwelt, sn off the pace & pushed along, styd on strongly
ins last, nvr dangerous: well bckd, ran 48hrs ago: poss came to sn & will apprec a return to 9f+: see 3357.
3163 **OCEAN RAIN** 11 [5] C G Cox 3-9-7 (70) S Sanders 8/1: 004034: Well plcd, led ent fnl 3f, till   shd   70
1f out, fdd: more positively rdn here, suited by shorter: see 954.
2012 **RATIFIED** 60 [1] 3-8-8 (57) G Bardwell 10/1: -21405: Al towards rear: 9 wk abs, back in trip, see 1022..   ¾   55
3238 **BLUE STREAK** 7 [6] 3-9-7 (70) J Reid 5/2: -00446: Sn led, hdd 2½f out, grad wknd: bckd tho' op   3   62
13/8, quick reapp, joint top-weight, btr 3238 (7f).
6 ran   Time 1m 44.25 (2.45)   (Mrs W Edgar)   S Woodman East Lavant, W sussex

3402 6.35 TOTE BOOKMAKERS HCAP 3YO+ 0-85 (D)   1m4f   Good/Firm 25 +14 Fast   [79]
£7052   £2170   £1085   £542   3 yo rec 10lb

3001 **GENTLEMAN VENTURE** 18 [6] J Akehurst 4-9-10 (75) P Doe 6/1: 642551: 4 b g Polar Falcon - Our Shirley   82
(Shirley Heights) Nvr far away, led 3f out, hard prsd & rdn 2f out, held on bravely: fast time, front 2 well clr:
'99 Redcar wnr (mdn, h'cap plcd, rtd 84, S Woods): eff at 10f/12f on firm, soft grnd & any trk.
3073 **MANA DARGENT** 14 [3] M Johnston 3-9-6 (81) D Holland 5/2 FAV: 303132: 3 b c Ela Mana Mou -   nk   87
Petite D'Argent (Noalto) Trkd ldrs, shaken up to chall ent fnl 2f, kept on but held fnl 100y: well bckd, 11L
back to 3rd: improved stage in defeat & is a progressive 3yo: shld score again: see 3014.
845 **LADY COLDUNELL** 130 [9] N A Callaghan 4-8-7 (58) R Hughes 16/1: 505-03: 4 b f Deploy - Beau's   11   53
Delight (Lypheor) Held up, hdwy ent str, styd on at the onepace to take 3rd nr fin: op 12/1, 4 month abs,
blnks omitted: '99 wnr at Lingfield (fill h'cap, rtd 61a & 63); rtd 70 in '98: eff at 12f, return to 14f
shld suit, tried 2m: acts on firm, gd grnd & equitrack.
2852 **TOTOM** 25 [4] J R Fanshawe 5-9-6 (71) Martin Dwyer 5/1: 434454: Rear, prog to dspte a remote   hd   66
3rd 2f out, no impression on ldrs: nicely bckd, see 2268, 1288.
+2793 **LEGAL LUNCH** 27 [7] F 5-9-6 (71)(bl) Pat Eddery 6/1: 135615: In tch, prog 3f out, sn rdn & onepace: nk   65
3122 **ORDAINED** 12 [1] 7-7-10 (47) G Baker 6/1: 041226: Al towards rear: btr 2829 (fill h'cap).   3½   37
*3186 **RAYIK** 9 [8] 5-8-2 (53)(6ex) A Nicholls (3) 9/1: 120017: Early ldr, again halfway till 3f out, wknd: 15   31
op 6/1: much better 3186 (amat h'cap).

3110 **HIBERNATE** 13 [5] 6-9-4 (69) S Sanders 12/1: 20S008: Led after 2f till halfway, lost place ent str.   ¾   46
2626 **GOODBYE GOLDSTONE** 34 [2] 4-9-2 (67) F Norton 16/1: -05069: Al bhd: tchd 20/1, see 1288.   21   29
9 ran   Time 2m 36.09 (1.29)   (Canisbay Bloodstock Ltd)   J Akehurst Epsom, Surrey

---

3403   7.05 RON SMYTH CLASS STKS 3YO+ 0-75 (D)   1m2f   Good/Firm 25 -11 Slow
£4173   £1284   £642   £321   3 yo rec 8 lb

2581 **FLIGHT SEQUENCE** 35 [5] Lady Herries 4-9-1 (VIS) R Hughes 9/2 JT FAV: -60201: 4 b f Polar Falcon   75
- Doubles (Damister) Early ldr, again appr fnl 2f, rdn out: op 7/2: 1st win, earlier banned for 'schooling in
public': juv rnr-up (rtd 82): eff at 1m, apprec step-up to 10f on firm, gd & any trk: improved for visor.
2958 **PHEISTY** 19 [9] R F Johnson Houghton 3-8-9 (BL) J Reid 6/1: 541652: 3 b f Faustus - Phlirty   ¾   75
(Pharly) Mid-div, prog appr fnl 2f, rdn bef dist, kept on, nearest fin: gd run in first time blnks: see 2387.
3356 **YOU DA MAN** 2 [3] R Hannon 3-8-12 P Fitzsimons (5) 12/1: 251063: 3 b c Alzao - Fabled Lifestyle   ½   77
(King's Lake) Bhd ldrs, rdn to press wnr appr fnl 1f, held fnl 100y: ran 48hrs ago, ran to best: see 2131 (h'cap).
3110 **FORZA FIGLIO** 13 [7] M Kettle 7-9-4 K Darley 6/1: /03344: Rear, prog & not much room 2f out,   nk   74
rdn dist, not pace to chall: ran well enough & clr rem: not an easy task at the weights: see 1729.
1677 **ADMIRALS PLACE** 74 [6] 4-9-4 D Holland 16/1: 314205: Chsd ldrs, fdd appr fnl 1f: 11 wk abs.   5   66
3024 **BACCHUS** 17 [1] 6-9-6 F Norton 9/2 JT FAV: 322156: Al towards rear: tchd 11/2, see 2671.   ¾   67
2626 **ACHILLES SKY** 34 [8] 4-9-4 N Callan 6/1: 002307: In tch till 2f out: see 805.   shd   65
1466 **BREMRIDGE** 84 [2] 3-8-10 Pat Eddery 8/1: 002-58: Al bhd: op 6/1, 12 wk abs, see 1466.   19   45
2842 **LATOUR** 25 [4] 3-8-7 (BL) R Hills 7/1: -23209: Sn led, hdd ent fnl 3f, wknd qckly: nicely bckd,   shd   42
unsuited by blnks & forcing tactics & is better at 7f/1m, see 1428.
9 ran   Time 2m 07.36 (3.56)   (Tony Perkins)   Lady Herries Angmering, W Sussex

---

3404   7.35 STAFF INGHAM CLAIMER 3YO+ (E)   1m114y rnd   Good/Firm 25 -10 Slow
£2834   £872   £436   £218   3 yo rec 7 lb

3110 **CHINA RED** 13 [2] J W Hills 6-9-10 R Hills 3/1: -00001: 6 br g Red Ransom - Akamare (Akarad)   77
Made all, rdn 2f out, ran on strongly, rdn out: nicely bckd, top-weight: '99 wnr at Lingfield (2, AW h'cap,
rtd 98a): '98 Goodwood wnr (2, h'caps, rtd 88): eff forcing the pace around 8.5f: acts on firm, gd grnd &
equitrack, any trk, likes a sharp one: can carry big weights & run well fresh: relished drop to claiming grade.
2981 **LAKE SUNBEAM** 19 [11] W R Muir 4-9-7 Martin Dwyer 4/1: 561132: 4 b g Nashwan - Moon Drop   1¼   72
(Dominion) Chsd ldrs, went after wnr ent str, kept on but nvr any impress: bckd from 6/1: ran to best back in trip.
3063 **STOPPES BROW** 15 [10] G L Moore 8-9-7 J Mongan (5) 11/4 FAV: 652563: 8 b g Primo Dominie -   1¼   69
So Bold (Never So Bold) Rear, imprvd halfway, chsd ldrs appr fnl 1f, onepace: nicely bckd: btr 2433, see 662.
3236 **BROWNS DELIGHT** 7 [3] S Dow 3-8-1 P Doe 25/1: 500024: Well off the pace till styd on strongly   2   52$
appr fnl 1f, nvr nrr: prob flattered tho' imprvd last twice: see 3236.
2229 **VIRTUAL REALITY** 49 [6] 9-9-5 S Sanders 9/2: 30-055: Mid-div, chsd ldrs briefly 3f out, same pace.   1½   60
3234 **HUGWITY** 7 [4] 8-9-5 R Hughes 7/1: 401536: Held up, not much room appr str, nvr troubled ldrs.   2   56
2907 **JUST FOR YOU JANE** 22 [7] 4-8-9 R Brisland (5) 33/1: 000437: Al towards rear: stiff task, btr 2907.   8   32
2790 **MAX** 27 [9] 5-8-12 D Holland 33/1: 003006: Pld hard mid-div, lost pl 3f out: see 2433.   1   31
2728 **ANNIE APPLE** 29 [8] 4-9-0 Pat Eddery 20/1: 504509: Prom till ent str: stiff task, best in sellers, see 594.   hd   34
2759 **HENRY HEALD** 28 [5] 5-9-0 (BL) J Reid 33/1: 21/000: Pulled hard bhd, v wide into str & btn: 10th.   6   24
2715 **FULHAM** 30 [1] 4-8-13 F Norton 50/1: 200400: Chsd ldrs, hmpd bef halfway & bhd after: 11th, see 2433.   ¾   22
11 ran   Time 1m 44.76 (2.96)   (N N Browne & Partners)   J W Hills Upper Lambourn, Berks

---

3405   8.05 EPSOM DOWNS HCAP 3YO 0-70 (E)   6f rnd   Good/Firm 25 -12 Slow   [77]
£4270   £1314   £657   £328

2794 **KINSMAN** 27 [13] I A Balding 3-9-3 (66) (vis) K Darley 7/1: 231601: 3 b g Distant Relative - Besito (Wassl)   68
Cl-up, led dist, drvn out: bckd: earlier won at Brighton (h'cap): '99 wnr again at Brighton (nurs, rtd 70 & 62a):
eff at 6/7f on firm, soft grnd, prob both AWs: eff up with/forcing the pace on sharp/undul trks: wears blnks or visor.
3261 **TRAJAN** 6 [9] A P Jarvis 3-9-7 (70) N Callan 10/1: -40602: 3 b g Dolphin Street - Lavezzola   1   69
(Salmon Leap) Held up, carried wide & feeling pace ent str, hard rdn dist, ran on strongly, nvr nrr: op 8/1, qk
reapp, top-weight: much better run with visor omitted & apprec drop back to 6f, 7f shld be ideal: see 651.
2896 **LADY STALKER** 23 [1] Andrew Reid 3-7-12 (47) M Henry 25/1: 0-0003: 3 b f Primo Dominie - Tarvie   shd   46
(Swing Easy) Led till 1f out, kept on: took advantage of stall 1, eff at 6f on fast grnd.
2896 **WILLOW MAGIC** 23 [7] S Dow 3-8-9 (58) P Doe 5/1: 034344: Bhd, kept on appr fnl 1f, nrst fin: shd   57
op 7/2, bckd: consistent but is becoming a frustrating maiden: see 1512, 234.
2976 **PARDY PET** 19 [2] 3-7-10 (45) (bl) (5oh) G Bardwell 10/1: -00005: Prom, shaken up appr fnl 1f, onepace.   ¾   41
*3124 **LUCKYS SON** 12 [11] 3-7-13 (48) N Pollard 4/1 FAV: 000216: Pulled hard mid-div, prog to chase ldrs   ¾   41
appr fnl 1f, sn no impression: bckd, new stable, gone from J Dunlop to P Howling: see 3124.
2591 **MUFFIN MAN** 35 [5] 3-8-0 (49) G Baker (5) 13/2: 000467: Swire away, towards rear, feeling pace 3f   nk   41
out, styd on without threatening: back in trip, see 2489.
3191 **AROGANT PRINCE** 9 [3] 3-8-6 (55) R Brisland 12/1: 004038: Towards rear, late hdwy: op 8/1.   shd   47
2603 **BANGLED** 34 [12] 3-7-10 (45) (2oh) F Norton 7/1: 000039: Rear, prog to chase ldrs 2f out, fdd: btr 2603.   3   28
3095 **TIME BOMB** 14 [6] 3-7-12 (47) Martin Dwyer 20/1: 006000: Held up, wide into str, no threat: 10th.   1¾   25
3046 **BELIEVING** 16 [10] 3-9-3 (66) R Hughes 13/2: -46000: Held up, carr wide appr str, sn btn: 11th, see 751.   2   38
11 ran   Time 1m 10.02 (2.22)   (Miss A V Hill)   I A Balding Kingsclere, Hants

---

BEVERLEY   THURSDAY AUGUST 17TH   Righthand, Oval Track with Stiff, Uphill Finish

Official Going   GOOD TO FIRM. Stalls: Inside.

3406   2.10 ST JOHN SELL HCAP 3YO+ 0-60 (D)   2m35y   Good/Firm 39 -26 Slow   [40]
£2296   £656   £328   3 yo rec 14lb

3002 **BEST PORT** 19 [8] J Parkes 4-9-5 (31) A Culhane 3/1 FAV: 430021: 4 b g Be My Guest - Portree (Slip   35
Anchor) Hld up, smooth prog over 2f out, shkn up to lead over 1f out, styd on well, rdn out: no bid: op 4/1:
first win: unplcd in '99 (rtd 42 & 5a): suited by 14f/2m on fast & gd/soft: likes a stiff trk & selling grade.

3036 **SWANDALE FLYER 17** [7] N Bycroft 8-8-3 (15) J McAuley 33/1: -00502: 8 ch g Weldnaas - Misfire (Gunner B): Led, sn clr, rdn/hdd over 1f out, kept on for press: eff at 2m on fast: see 1657. ¾ **17**
3050 **UNICORN STAR 16** [11] J S Wainwright 3-9-6 (46) R Winston 8/1: 362523: 3 b g Persian Bold - Highland Warning (Warning) Chsd ldrs, prog to chall 2f out, onepace/held ins last: op 7/1: stays 2m on firm & gd. 2½ **45**
2763 **CASHIKI 29** [5] B Palling 4-9-9 (35) K Darley 7/2: 026104: Chsd ldrs, rdn/chall 3f out, no extra fnl 1f. 3 **31**
2734 **NOTATION 30** [4] 6-8-6 (18) G Duffield 7/1: 004005: Chsd ldrs halfway, btn 3f out: see 561, 494. 8 **6**
2537 **PHASE EIGHT GIRL 38** [3] 4-8-13 (25) O Pears 10/1: 3-0006: Bhd, nvr a factor: op 8/1: see 2219. 9 **4**
3247 **THREEFORTYCASH 8** [10] 3-8-13 (39) P Fessey 16/1: 600057: Chsd ldr, btn 2f out: lngr 2m trip. 1¼ **17**
2007 **MACHE 61** [6] 3-9-0 (40) G Parkin 25/1: 000-08: Chsd ldrs, struggling 4f out: 2 mth abs, lngr 2m trip. 6 **12**
*3002 **ITALIAN ROSE 19** [9] 5-9-6 (32) M Fenton 7/1: 6-0619: Chsd ldrs 5f out, sn btn: btr 3002 (14f). 8 **0**
3201 **WILLIAM THE LION 9** [2] 3-9-10 (50) P Bradley (5) 9/1: 520400: Held up, struggling 5f out: 10th. 11 **6**
3050 **LAMMOSKI 16** [1] 3-8-9 (35) D Mernagh (3) 20/1: 500040: Chsd ldrs 1m, bhd/eased 2f out: 11th. dist **0**
11 ran Time 3m 40.9 (10.6) (W A Sellers) J Parkes Upper Helmsley, Nth Yorks.

3407

2.45 BOLLINGER AMAT HCAP 3YO+ 0-75 (E) 1m100y rnd Good/Firm 39 -43 Slow [41]
£2873 £884 £442 £221 3 yo rec 6 lb

3115 **OPEN ARMS 13** [11] Mrs A L M King 4-11-10 (65) Mr T Scudamore 7/1: 3-0001: 4 ch g Most Welcome - Amber Fizz (Effervescing) Led, rdn fnl 3f, hdd over 1f out, styd on well for press to lead again ins last, gamely: op 10/1: slow time: first win: plcd sole '99 start (h'cap, rtd 74): plcd in '98 (rtd 76, nursery, C Brittain): suited by 8.5f on firm & gd grnd: gd weight carrier. **67**
2861 **FLASHTALKIN FLOOD 25** [8] J L Eyre 6-9-11 (38) Mr R L Moore (5) 8/1: /00402: 6 ch g Then Again - Linguistic (Porto Bello): Al handy, rdn/narrow lead over 1f out, drvn/hdd inside last, kept on well, just held. nk **39**
3045 **OLLIES CHUCKLE 17** [1] J J Quinn 5-9-10 (37)(4oh) Mr Nicky Tinkler (5) 20/1: 660603: 5 b g Mac's Imp - Chenya (Beldale Flutter): Rear, prog final 3f & styd on well for press inside last, not pace to chall front pair. ¾ **37**
3220 **CLASSIC EAGLE 8** [6] Pat Mitchell 7-10-1 (42)(VIS) Mr S Rees (5) 20/1: 000054: Dwelt/rear, rdn & styd on final 2f, no threat: tried a visor: eff at 1m, prob stays 12f: handles fast & soft grnd: see 1272. ½ **41**
*2802 **PADHAMS GREEN 27** [10] 4-12-0 (69) Mr C B Hills (3) 11/8 FAV: -36215: Rear, prog/chsd ldrs over 2f out, drvn/held final 1f: hvly bckd: reportedly unruly & unseated jockey in paddock: see 2802. 1 **66**
*582 **SEA YA MAITE 175** [5] 6-9-10 (37)(5oh) Mr J J Best (1) 10/1: 565216: Keen/held up, prog/ch 2f out, sn no extra: 6 mth abs: see 582 (AW, 7f). 4 **26**
1614 **SEPTEMBER HARVEST 78** [9] 4-9-12 (39) Mr W Worthington (2) 20/1: 400007: Rear, mod hdwy: 6 wk jumps abs (rtd 67h, mdn): see 261. ½ **27**
4604} **TRAIKEY 287** [2] 8-10-10 (51) Mr S Dobson (5) 33/1: 0000-8: Chsd ldrs, btn 2f out: Flat reapp, 5 mth jumps abs (no form): unplcd in '99 (rtd 50, h'cap): back in '94 scored at Yarmouth (mdn): eff at 1m/10f on gd. 3½ **32**
3052 **HEVER GOLF GLORY 16** [3] 6-9-10 (37)(vis)(4oh) Mr P Collington (7) 20/1: 005609: Chsd ldrs 6f. 2 **14**
2347 **MARCHING ORDERS 47** [12] 4-11-5 (60)(bl) Mr B Wharfe (7) 40/1: 000000: Dwelt/rear, brief effort over 2f out, no impress: 10th: 7 wk abs: blnks reapplied: see 1217. hd **36**
479 **CHAMPAGNE N DREAMS 41** [4] 8-10-5 (46) Mr R Walford 8/1: U60000: Keen/cl up 6f: 11th: abs. ¾ **21**
11 ran Time 1m 50.8 (7.0) (Aiden Murphy) Mrs A L M King Wilmcote, Warwick.

3408

3.15 WESTWOOD FILLIES MDN 2YO (D) 5f Good/Firm 39 -13 Slow
£3727 £1147 £573 £236

2766 **RACINA 29** [7] W J Haggas 2-8-11 M Hills 4/11 FAV: 21: 2 ch f Bluebird - Swellegant (Midyan): Made all, clr final 2f, styd on well under hands-&-heels riding, readily: value for 5L+: hvly bckd at odds-on: confirmed promise of debut: eff at 5f, 6f shld suit: acts on firm & gd, stiff/fair trk: op to further improvement. **83**
3003 **NIGHT HAVEN 19** [4] M L W Bell 2-8-11 M Fenton 10/1: 22: 2 gr f Night Shift - Noble Haven (Indian King): Chsd ldrs, rdn/chsd wnr final 2f, al held: op 8/1: handles fast grnd: see 3003. 4 **68**
2652 **TAR FIH 34** [6] J L Dunlop 2-8-11 W Supple 10/1: 43: 2 b f Gone West - Najiya (Nashwan): Chsd ldrs, onepace/held over 1f out: op 7/1: bred to need further: see 2652 (6f). ¾ **66**
-- **ROSALIA** [8] T D Easterby 2-8-11 K Darley 6/1: 4: Slowly away & bhd, prog to chase ldrs over 1f out, kept on inside last, no threat: op 7/2: Red Ransom filly, Jan foal, cost 95,000 gns: dam a US wnr: shld improve. ½ **64**
-- **ENCYCLOPEDIA** [2] 2-8-11 J Weaver 33/1: 5: Dwelt/bmpd start, rear till kept on final 2f, no threat: lngr prcd stablemate of 4th: So Factual filly, Apr foal: half-sister to a 5f juv wnr: dam a 5f juv wnr: will improve. 3½ **55**
3098 **OLYS DREAM 15** [5] 2-8-11 Dean McKeown 33/1: 506: Keen/chsd ldrs 3f: btr 898 (debut). 3 **48**
2926 **PEGGYS SONG 22** [3] 2-8-11 J Carroll 33/1: 07: In tch till outpcd from halfway: mod form. 13 **24**
3009 **CATALAN BAY 18** [1] 2-8-11 O Pears 100/1: -008: Keen/chsd wnr, rdn/wknd qckly halfway: no form. 1¼ **21**
8 ran Time 1m 03.90 (2.6) (I A Southcott) W J Haggas Newmarket, Suffolk.

3409

3.50 HOLDERNESS NOV AUCT STKS 2YO (E) 7f100y rnd Good/Firm 39 -05 Slow
£2912 £896 £448 £224

*3127 **HARRIER 13** [9] T D Easterby 2-8-12 J Weaver 6/1: 33011: 2 b g Prince Of Birds - Casaveha (Persian Bold): Made all, rdn final 2f, styd on strongly & al holding rivals inside last: earlier scored at Thirsk (clmr): well suited by step up to 7f/7.5f recently, 1m will suit: acts on fast, handles soft: loves to force the pace: progressive last twice with forcing tactics, can win again. **87**
*3100 **CASHNEEM 15** [6] P W Harris 2-8-13 A Culhane 5/2 JT FAV: 412: 2 b c Case Law - Haanem (Mtoto): Trkd ldrs, rdn/chsd wnr over 1f out, flashed tail, kept on, al held: nicely bckd: rest well covered: acts on fast & gd. 2 **82**
2985 **PRINCESS EMILY 19** [2] B S Rothwell 2-8-1 D Mernagh (3) 50/1: 03: 2 b f Dolphin Street - Partita (Polish Precedent): Rear, rdn & styd on final 2f, no threat to front pair: left debut bhd: see 2985. 4 **62**
3175 **TRUMPINGTON 11** [4] I A Balding 2-8-7 G Duffield 12/1: -03104: Bmpd start, chsd ldrs, btn 1f out. 2½ **63**
-- **KENNYTHORPE BOPPY** [8] 2-8-6 R Winston 40/1: 5: Rear, mod gains final 2f: Aragon gelding, Apr foal, cost 5,000 gns: half-brother to a 6f wnr & a 10f sell wnr: dam a 6f juv wnr, subs styd 10f: 1m+ will suit. 2 **58**
*2741 **MONTANA MISS 29** [5] 2-8-11 K Darley 5/2 JT FAV: 4116: Cl-up, hard rdn/btn over 1f out: hvly bckd: mucj better expected after 2741. 4 **55**
2613 **MUJALINA 35** [3] 2-9-0 M Fenton 15/2: 02107: Slightly hmpd/rear early, effort halfway, btn over 1f out: op 6/1: prob flattered latest when highly tried: see 2613, 2383. 1¼ **55**
2539 **ALPHACALL 38** [7] 2-8-1 W Supple 20/1: 458: Al rear: lngr 7.5f trip: see 2539, 1294. 2½ **37**
*2985 **BRILLIANTRIO 19** [1] 2-8-13 K Hodgson 5/1: 19: Unruly before start, chsd ldrs 5f, sn btn: op 3/1. 1½ **46**
9 ran Time 1m 34.1 (3.3) (The Rumpole Partnership) T D Easterby Great Habton, Nth Yorks.

BEVERLEY THURSDAY AUGUST 17TH Righthand, Oval Track with Stiff, Uphill Finish

3410 **4.25 RAPID LAD HCAP 3YO+ 0-90 (C) 1m2f Good/Firm 39 +03 Fast [84]**
£6922 £2130 £1065 £532 3 yo rec 8 lb

3130 **KIND REGARDS 13** [1] M Johnston 3-9-4 (82) K Darley 15/8 FAV: 525451: 3 b f Unfuwain - Barari (Blushing Groom): Trkd ldrs, prog to lead 2f out, rdn clr over 1f out, styd on strongly under hands-&-heels riding: best time of day: well bckd: '99 wnr here at Beverley (fillies mdn, rtd 88): eff at 7f/1m, well suited by this step up to 10f: acts on firm & gd/soft grnd, prob handles any trk, likes Beverley: tough, should win again. **88**
2304 **LITTLE AMIN 48** [8] W R Muir 4-9-7 (77) J Weaver 4/1: 001632: 4 b g Unfuwain - Ghassanah (Pas de Seul): Trkd ldrs, rdn/chsd wnr over 1f out, al held: 7 wk abs: in gd form: see 2304, 1762 (1m). *3* **78**
*2556 **WERE NOT STOPPIN 37** [2] R Bastiman 5-8-4 (60) O Pears 9/2: 111413: 5 b g Mystiko - Power Take Off (Aragon): Handy, led 3f out, rdn/hdd 2f out & held after: nicely bckd, op 6/1: in fine form this term. *1½* **59**
3147 **COLWAY RITZ 12** [6] W Storey 6-10-0 (84) T Williams 9/2: 112024: Held up, effort over 2f out, onepace: op 7/2: topweight: see 3147, 2157 & 2102. *½* **82**
3122 **NORCROFT JOY 13** [5] 5-9-4 (74) J Carroll 10/1: 331045: Held up, effort 2f out, sn held: op 6/1. *3½* **67**
3368 **CYBERTECHNOLOGY 2** [3] 6-8-6 (62) A Culhane 7/1: 316106: Held up, efft final 3f, no hdwy: qck reapp. *2* **52**
4479} **TO THE LAST MAN 300** [7] 4-8-2 (58) G Bardwell 25/1: 0506-7: Led 7f, sn btn: Flat reapp, 6 mth jumps abs (rnr-up, nov hdle, rtd 94h, stays 2m1f on soft): '99 wnr at Salisbury (appr h'cap) & Brighton (class stks, rtd 63, M D I Usher): rnr-up twice in '98 (rtd 74 & 57a at best): suited by 1m, stays 10.8f well: handles firm & fibresand, loves gd & hvy grnd: handles a stiff/undul or sharp trk: best without a visor: with G M Moore. *8* **39**
7 ran Time 2m 05.9 (3.6) (Maktoum Al Maktoum) M Johnston Middleham, Nth Yorks.

3411 **5.00 TOLL GAVEL NURSERY HCAP 2YO (D) 7f100y rnd Good/Firm 39 -10 Slow [88]**
£3818 £1175 £587 £293

3245 **PASITHEA 8** [3] T D Easterby 2-8-9 (69) K Darley 9/2: 45331: 2 b f Celtic Swing - Midnight's Reward (Night Shift): Chsd ldrs, rdn/led 2f out, styd on well inside last, rdn out: bckd: first win on h'cap bow: apprec step up to 7.5f, 1m shld suit: acts on fast & gd grnd, stiff/gall trk: op to further improvement in similar. **75**
2928 **SIENA STAR 22** [1] J L Eyre 2-8-13 (73) A Culhane 12/1: 044322: 2 b g Brief Truce - Gooseberry Pie (Green Desert): Held up rear, prog when hmpd/forced to switch over 1f out, rdn & styd on strongly inside last, nrst fin: eff arnd 7f/7.5f on fast, 1m will suit: lookes v unlucky & one to keep in mind. *¾* **78+**
3299 **PATHAN 6** [9] S P C Woods 2-9-2 (76) G Duffield 5/2 FAV: 051423: 2 b c Pyramus - Langton Herring (Nearly A Hand): Al prom, rdn/ch 2f out, kept on onepace for press: bckd, op 3/1: qck reapp: see 3299, 2653. *1¼* **78**
3062 **SANDLES 16** [10] S C Williams 2-8-13 (73) G Faulkner (3) 9/1: 1544: Trkd ldrs, ev ch when not much room over 1f out, held dist: op 6/1: prob styd longer 7.5f trip: handles fibresand & fast grnd: see 1236 (5f, AW). *1¼* **72**
*3246 **CYNARA 8** [2] 2-8-0 (60)(6ex) G Bardwell 13/2: 05215: Led, edged right/hdd 2f out, no extra. *hd* **58**
3128 **SOMERS HEATH 13** [6] 2-8-2 (62) D Mernagh (3) 14/1: 001056: Chsd ldrs 2f out, no extra when hmpd over 1f out: op 12/1: lngr prcd stablemate of wnr: see 1981 (6f). *shd* **60**
*3079 **GALAXY RETURNS 15** [7] 2-8-12 (72) J Carroll 12/1: -02617: In tch 5f: op 7/1: btr 3079 (6f, mdn auct). *10* **55**
*3057 **PORT MORESBY 16** [4] 2-9-7 (81) W Supple 4/1: -0018: Dwelt, chsd ldrs 5f: nicely bckd: topweight. *1½* **61**
3246 **BULA ROSE 8** [5] 2-8-1 (58)(3ow) O Pears 16/1: 523149: Al bhd: op 12/1: btr 3246, 2155. *1½* **38**
9 ran Time 1m 34.5 (3.7) (Lady Legard) T D Easterby Great Habton, Nth Yorks.

EPSOM THURSDAY AUGUST 17TH Lefthand, V Sharp, Undulating Track

Official Going GOOD TO FIRM (GOOD places). Stalls: Inside, except 1m4f - Centre.

3412 **2.00 CONSTRUSTION NEWS MDN 2YO (D) 7f rnd Good/Firm 40 -26 Slow**
£4212 £1296 £648 £324

3074 **JOHNSONS POINT 15** [7] B W Hills 2-8-9 R Cochrane 11/4 FAV: 21: 2 ch f Sabrehill - Watership (Foolish Pleasure) Chsd ldrs, shkn up 2f out, slightly hmpd dist, hard rdn ins last & ran on to lead fnl strides: nicely bckd: Apr foal, half-sister to a 10f wnr: eff at 7f, 1m+ is sure to suit: acts on fast grnd, sharp/undul trks tho' did not appear totally at ease here: improving filly. **81**
2598 **SPY MASTER 36** [3] Sir Michael Stoute 2-9-0 Pat Eddery 9/2: 02: 2 b c Green Desert - Obsessive (Seeking The Gold) Prom, led appr fnl 1f, rdn ins last & hdd cl home: apprec step up to 7f on fast grnd. *nk* **85**
3051 **WAINAK 16** [9] J L Dunlop 2-9-0 R Hills 7/2: 0223: 2 b c Silver Hawk - Cask (Be My Chief) In tch, not handle trk well, feeling pace ent str, styd on dist & fin strgly, nvr nrr: not btn far, op 5/2: acts on fast & gd/soft grnd & can find similar over further/more gall trk. *nk* **84**
3154 **MURRENDI 12** [2] M R Channon 2-9-0 T Quinn 6/1: -5054: Led till appr final 1f, one pace: tchd 10/1. *1¾* **80**
2894 **BARAKANA 24** [8] 2-9-0 (bl) D R McCabe 6/1: 332635: Prom, shkn up & no extra/hung left bef fnl 1f. *2½* **75**
2810 **PERSIAN SPIRIT 27** [6] 2-8-9 M Roberts 10/1: -06: Dwelt, nvr a factor: nursery type. *6* **60**
-- **THUNDERED** [5] 2-9-0 W Ryan 20/1: 7: Al bhd: 34,000gns Apr foal: half-brother to 3 wnrs. *4* **57**
3268 **GRAIN STORM 7** [1] 2-8-9 J Reid 16/1: 08: Sn struggling & hmpd halfway: qck reapp. *3½* **46**
2979 **HELLOFABUNDLE 20** [10] 2-9-0 R Smith (5) 50/1: 039: Nvr a factor: Phountzi gelding, moderately bred. *1¼* **49**
1472 **MENAS ERN 85** [4] 2-9-0 P Doe 25/1: 00: Dwelt, sn btn: 10th, 12 wk abs. *nk* **48**
10 ran Time 1m 24.75 (4.65) (W J Gredley) B W Hills Lambourn, Berks.

3413 **2.35 HILL MCGLYNN MDN 3YO+ (D) 1m114y rnd Good/Firm 40 -03 Slow**
£4095 £1260 £630 £315

3190 **FINISHED ARTICLE 10** [2] D R C Elsworth 3-8-13 D Holland 15/8 FAV: 463521: 3 b c Indian Ridge - Summer Fashion (Moorestyle) Waited with, imprvd appr fnl 2f, shkn up 1f out, kept on to lead nr fin, cleverly: hvly bckd: rtd 74 last term: brother to high class Definite Article: eff at 1m/10f: acts on fast & gd, any trk. **78**
3116 **MUSICAL HEATH 13** [6] P W Harris 3-8-13 (t) T Quinn 4/1: -422: 3 b c Common Grounds - Song Of The Glens (Horage) Led, pushed along appr final 1f, worn down nr fin (not tchd with whip): bckd from 6/1: similar level of form all 3 starts & appeared suited being out in front today: eff at 1m on firm/fast grnd. *nk* **77**
3019 **ARDUINE 18** [3] J H M Gosden 3-8-8 R Cochrane 10/3: -33033: 3 ch f Diesis - Ardisia (Affirmed) Held up, prog & ch appr fnl 1f, unable to qckn ins last: bckd tho' op 7/4, clr rem: nds headgear: see 1901, 1200. *1* **70**
3288 **VICTORIET 6** [1] A T Murphy 3-8-8 A McGlone 33/1: 504444: Trkd ldrs, losing tch when slightly short *7* **56$**

of room before final 1f: stiff task, looks flattered, qck reapp.

3221 **COUTURE 8** [4] 3-8-8 Pat Eddery 9/4: 25: Pulled hard, chsd ldr till effort & btn ent final 2f: nicely ½ 55
bckd from 3/1: jockey felt unwell & gave up remaining rides: poss best forgiven: see 3221.

3179 **ELLWAY HEIGHTS 11** [5] 3-8-13 R Mullen 25/1: -06: Chsd ldrs till appr final 2f: see 3179. 2 56
6 ran   Time 1m 45.45 (3.65)   (Dr D B Davis)   D R C Elsworth Whitsbury, Hants.

3414
3.05 CATERPILLAR HCAP 3YO+ 0-90 (C)   7f rnd   Good/Firm 40   -07 Slow   [88]
£6955   £2140   £1070   £535   3 yo rec 5 lb

3152 **AL MUALLIM 12** [4] D Nicholls 6-9-13 (87)(t) Alex Greaves 5/1 JT FAV: 000401: 6 b g Theatrical - 91
Gerri N Jo Go (Top Command) In tch, clsd 2f out, swtchd, rdn & ran on 1f out, led towards fin: op 7/2: '99
rnr-up (stks, rtd 100): plcd sev times in '98 (val h'caps, rtd 99): last won in '97 at Lingfield & Newmarket:
eff at 6/7f: acts on firm & gd/soft grnd, any trk: wears a t-strap now: useful & well h'capped.

2922 **WILLOUGHBYS BOY 22** [6] B Hanbury 3-9-5 (84) W Ryan 7/1: 316162: 3 b c Night Shift - Andbell 1¾ 85
(Trojan Fen) Chsd ldrs, strong chall final 1f, outpcd by wnr towards fin: ran well, progressive, see 2768.

*2813 **ALPEN WOLF 27** [9] W R Muir 5-10-0 (88) T Quinn 5/1 JT FAV: 021013: 5 ch g Wolfhound - Oatfield shd 89
(Great Nephew) Bhd ldrs, shkn up to lead below dist, kept on, hdd towards fin: fine effort under top-
weight back up in trip: poss just better at 6f: see 2813.

2814 **SUSANS PRIDE 27** [11] B J Meehan 4-9-1 (75) R Cochrane 12/1: 034054: Waited with, hdwy 2f out, shd 76
kept on well inside last, nvr nrr: gd run, return to 1m?: see 780.

2999 **MISTER RAMBO 19** [3] D R McCabe 11/1: 520605: Towards rear, shkn up appr final 2f, styd 1½ 77
on without threatening: tchd 14/1: signs of a return to form & easier grnd would suit: see 817.

3041 **ARETINO 17** [10] A Beech 10/1: 050026: Led till 1f out, no extra: tchd 12/1. shd 74

3315 **ELMHURST BOY 5** [8] 4-9-6 (80)(vis) B Marcus 11/2: 045207: In rear, effort appr final 2f, mod hdwy. 1 76

3163 **NAJEYBA 12** [1] 3-8-12 (77) M Roberts 10/1: 13408: Al towards rear, hung left 2f out: btr 2577 (led). ½ 72

2858 **CAIR PARAVEL 26** [7] 3-9-8 (87)(bl) A Daly 12/1: 000109: Well plcd & ev ch till btn bef dist, eased. 2½ 77

2918 **SARENA PRIDE 22** [5] 3-8-11 (76) S Sanders 16/1: 243000: Lost lengths start, nvr in it: 10th. 3½ 63

3076 **SHOUF AL BADOU 15** [2] 3-9-1 (80) J Reid 8/1: 000650: Al bhd, btn bef fnl 2f, eased: 11th, see 765. 1 62
11 ran   Time 1m 23.39 (3.29)   (Neil Smith)   D Nicholls Sessay, Nth Yorks.

3415
3.40 DRAKE HCAP 3YO 0-85 (D)   1m2f   Good/Firm 40   -11 Slow   [92]
£5005   £1540   £770   £385

3089 **MUSCHANA 15** [4] J L Dunlop 3-9-4 (82) M Roberts 7/2: -31031: 3 ch f Deploy - Youthful (Green Dancer) 90
Made ev yd, qcknd into a commanding lead appr final 1f, eased inside last: val 5L+, well bckd: earlier won
at Windsor (h'cap, easily): plcd final 2 '99 starts (rtd 83): eff at 1m/10f: acts on gd/soft, suited by fast:
goes on any trk & loves to force the pace: v progressive filly, worth following.

*3329 **SANTIBURI GIRL 4** [7] J R Best 3-8-8 (72)(6ex) A Polli (3) 7/2: 300112: 3 b f Casteddu - Lake Mistassiu 3½ 74
(Tina's Pet) Held up, prog ent str, styd on appr final 1f, nvr nr wnr: well bckd, qck reapp: lost little in
defeat on hat-trick attempt: improving: see 3329.

*3217 **BANDLER CHING 8** [1] C N Allen 3-8-11 (75)(6ex) Martin Dwyer 3/1 FAV: 3-5213: 3 b g Sri Pekan - 2 74
Stanerra's Wish (Caerleon) Rcd in 2nd, feeling pace bef fnl 2f & held: well bckd, clr rem: fnd this tougher than 3217.

2842 **SHRIVAR 26** [5] M R Channon 3-8-7 (71) T Quinn 10/1: 641404: Rear, prog & in tch ent str, sn no 7 60
extra: tchd 14/1: ran into 3 progressive sorts but is better than this: see 2463 (mdn h'cap).

3088 **TORRID KENTAVR 15** [6] 3-9-7 (85) S Sanders 7/1: 331005: Al towards rear: best forcing pace. 4 68

3076 **DESERT FURY 15** [3] 3-9-4 (82) J Reid 13/2: 006046: Held up, not come down hill well & bhd after. 8 55

2337 **FLYING TREATY 47** [2] 3-8-11 (75) R Cochrane 10/1: 5237: Chsd ldrs till appr final 3f, virtually dist 0
p.u: op 7/1, 9 wk abs, h'cap bow: reportedly lost action, worth another ch on a more gall trk: see 2129.
7 ran   Time 2m 08.91 (5.11)   (Nigel & Carolyn Elwes)   J L Dunlop Arundel, West Sussex.

3416
4.15 ATKINS MDN 3YO+ (D)   1m4f   Good/Firm 40   00 Fast
£4153   £1278   £639   £319   3 yo rec 10lb

2493 **CLEPSYDRA 40** [3] H R A Cecil 3-8-6 T Quinn 2/1: 22351: 3 b f Sadler's Wells - Quandary (Blushing Groom) 80
Waited with, clsd 4f out, sn hung left, swtchd to lead below dist, pushed out: nicely bckd, fair time, 6 wk abs:
unrcd juv, apprec return to 12f & shld stay further: acts on firm & soft grnd, has forced the pace: goes on any trk.

3185 **SOUTH SEA PEARL 10** [4] M Johnston 3-8-6 D Holland 5/4 FAV: -66022: 3 b f Southern Halo - 1¼ 78
Naturalracer (Copelan) Led till 1f out, onepace: hvly bckd, clr of 3rd: stays 12f, return to 10f will suit.

2943 **HAVANA 21** [2] Mrs A J Perrett 4-9-2 M Roberts 3/1: 3-4233: 4 b f Dolphin Street - Royaltess 11 65
(Royal And Regal) Chsd ldrs till 4f out: nicely bckd, btr 2627 (10f, gd/soft).

3157 **VILLIAN 12** [1] J G Smyth Osbourne 5-9-2 J Reid 12/1: 34: Rcd in 2nd till halfway, btn over 3f out. 2 65
4 ran   Time 2m 39.58 (4.78)   (K Abdulla)   H R A Cecil Newmarket, Suffolk.

3417
4.50 SWIFT HCAP 3YO 0-75 (E)   1m4f   Good/Firm 40   +02 Fast   [73]
£4270   £1314   £657   £328

3206 **SPIRIT OF TENBY 9** [3] S Dow 3-9-3 (62) P Doe 11/2: 304021: 3 b g Tenby - Asturiana (Julio Mariner) 68
Trkd ldrs, prog to lead ent str, went 3L clr 2f out, kept on strongly: best time of day, tchd 7/1: first win:
plcd on '99 debut (auct mdn, rtd 80): prob imprvd since stepped up to 12f: acts on firm & gd grnd, any trk.

*3290 **AFTER THE BLUE 6** [2] M R Channon 3-9-13 (72)(6ex) T Quinn 11/8 FAV: 224512: 3 b c Last Tycoon - 3 73
Sudden Interest (Higher Honor) Waited with, prog 3f out, hung left final 2f, styd on for 2nd but no ch with wnr:
well bckd, top-weight, qck reapp under a penalty: not disgrcd tho' btr 3290 (gall trk).

3167 **NINNOLO 12** [5] C N Allen 3-9-6 (65)(t) Martin Dwyer 11/4: 300523: 3 b c Perugino - Primo Stampari shd 66
(Primo Dominie) Rear, chsd wnr appr fnl 2f, same pace/short of room ent fnl 1f: bckd: clr rem & imprvd at 12f.

3167 **SAMARARDO 12** [6] C N Allen 3-8-4 (49) J Tate 12/1: 3-5464: Chsd ldrs, no extra appr final 2f. 2½ 47

3219 **MALARKEY 8** [4] 3-9-6 (65) D Holland 11/2: 545325: Led till ent str, lost pl: op 9/2, btr 3219, see 3043. 5 58

2651 **ESTABLISHMENT 34** [1] 3-9-6 (65) S Sanders 10/1: 021566: Handy till 3f out: btr 1935. 4 54
6 ran   Time 2m 39.37 (4.57)   (John Lever)   S Dow Epsom, Surrey.

SALISBURY THURSDAY AUGUST 17TH Righthand, Galloping Track, Stiff Finish

Official Going GOOD/FIRM. Stalls: Stands Side.

3418 **1.50 TATTERSALLS MDN AUCT 2YO DIV I (E) 7f str Good/Firm 37 -17 Slow**
£2938 £904 £452 £226

-- **RIDGEWAY DAWN** [3] M R Channon 2-8-0 Craig Williams 11/2: 1: 2 ch f Mujtahid - Soviet Maid (Soviet Star) Held up, gd hdwy 2f out, led ins last, shade cosily: debut: Feb foal, IR£10,500: stays a stiff 7f well, 1m looks sure to suit: runs well fresh on gd/firm: nice introduction, shld improve for this. **73**
3175 **PASO DOBLE 11** [2] B R Millman 2-8-7 G Hind 5/4 FAV: -03422: 2 b c Dancing Spree - Delta Tempo (Bluebird) In tch, hdwy to lead 2f out, edged right over 1f out & hdd ins last, not pace of wnr: well bckd. *¾* **76**
2972 **SHIRAZI 20** [4] J W Hills 2-8-7 M Henry 6/1: 563: 2 b c Mtoto - Al Shadeedah (Nureyev) Held up, hdwy to chall over 1f out, no extra ins last: better run over this stiff 7f on fast, bred to stay further. *¾* **74**
2841 **DILLY 26** [7] P R Chamings 2-7-12 S Righton 6/1: 24: Led till 2f out, wknd fnl 1f: btr 2841. *2½* **60**
-- **TEEHEE** [8] 2-8-5 D Sweeney 14/1: 5: Bhd, modest late gains on debut: Apr foal, cost IR 9,800gns: full brother to a 7f juv scorer: dam 12f wnr: bred to apprec 1m+ in time. *4* **59**
2454 **CAREFULLY 41** [6] 2-8-7 P Robinson 25/1: 006: Held up, brief eff 2f out, sn btn: 6 wk abs: Apr first foal, cost 12,000gns: dam 5f scorer: bred to apprec 7f/1m. *3* **55**
2628 **SPIRIT OF TEXAS 35** [5] 2-8-9 (BL) T E Durcan 33/1: 0007: In tch, wknd over 2f out: tried blnks. *1½* **54**
-- **PHILIPPI** [1] 2-8-12 F Norton 12/1: 8: In tch, wknd over 2f out on debut: op 6/1: Apr foal, cost IR 26,000gns: half-brother to sev wnrs: bred to apprec 1m+ in time: with J Osborne. *3½* **50**
-- **BARBERELLO** [9] 2-8-4 R Havlin 14/1: 9: Slow away, sn in tch, wknd well over 2f out: op 10/1: Apr foal, cost 16,000gns: half-sister to smart sprinter Andreyev: bred for 6/7f. *15* **12**
9 ran Time 1m 29.3 (3.8) (Ridgeway Downs Racing) M R Channon West Isley, Berks.

3419 **2.20 AXMINSTER APPR HCAP 3YO+ 0-80 (E) 6f Good/Firm 37 +14 Fast** **[78]**
£2782 £856 £428 £214 3 yo rec 3 lb

3280 **SUSSEX LAD 6** [6] R Hannon 3-9-5 (72) P Dobbs (3) 12/1: 406461: 3 b g Prince Sabo - Pea Green (Try My Best) Chsd ldrs, hdwy over 1f out to lead ins last, going away: best time of day, qck reapp: rtd 80 when unplcd as a juv: stays 6f well on gd/firm grnd: handles a stiff trk: apprec patient tactics today. **77**
3136 **REFERENDUM 13** [5] D Nicholls 6-9-9 (73) Clare Roche (8) 9/4 FAV: 266022: 6 b g Common Grounds - Final Decision (Tap On Wood) Chsd ldr, led over 2f out till ins last, kept on: bckd, deserves a win: see 3136. *1* **74**
3091 **KILCULLEN LAD 15** [7] Lady Herries 6-9-0 (64)(vis) P Fitzsimons 5/1: 300603: 6 b g Fayruz - Royal Home (Royal Palace) Handy, eff well over 1f out, kept on same pace: returning to form & h'capped to win. *½* **63**
2777 **GOLDEN POUND 28** [4] Miss Gay Kelleway 8-7-10 (46)(1oh) G Baker 9/1: -45404: Bhd, eff 2f out, sn onepace: op 7/1, see 2631. *3½* **36**
3209 **CAUDA EQUINA 9** [8] 6-9-10 (74) M Mathers (8) 6/1: 400465: Slow away & bhd, some late gains. *shd* **63**
3063 **LOCH LAIRD 16** [1] 5-9-6 (70) A Eddery 12/1: 000006: Bhd, modest late gains: see 3063. *nk* **58**
3091 **BORDER GLEN 15** [11] 4-8-0 (50)(bl) R Brisland 12/1: 600507: Led till over 2f out, wknd: see 292. *1¾* **33**
3097 **KEBABS 15** [2] 3-8-9 (62) C Catlin (5) 16/1: 003058: In tch, wknd well over 1f out: see 736. *nk* **44**
3257 **CRUSTY LILY 7** [9] 4-7-10 (46)(3oh) Claire Bryan (3) 8/1: 006639: In tch, wknd 2f out: see 3257. *1½* **24**
3124 **BRITTAS BLUES 13** [3] 3-7-11 (50) K Dalgleish (3) 7/1: -03450: In tch, wknd over 2f out: 10th. *½* **26**
3289 **ANGELAS PET 6** [10] 3-7-10 (49) D Kinsella (5) 33/1: 66-660: Al bhd: last, see 2472. *9* **1**
11 ran Time 1m 13.49 (1.39) (Peter M Crane) R Hannon East Everleigh, Wilts.

3420 **2.55 TATTERSALLS MDN AUCT DIV II 2YO (E) 7f str Good/Firm 37 -23 Slow**
£2925 £900 £450 £225

-- **BOURGAINVILLE** [7] I A Balding 2-8-9 R Hughes 2/1 FAV: 1: 2 b c Pivotal - Pentocia (Petoski) Slow away, sn in tch, hdwy to lead dist, kept on, rdn out: well bckd from 7/2 on debut: Mar foal, cost 16,000 gns: half-brother to a 6/7f wnr: eff over a stiff 7f, 1m suit: runs well fresh on gd/firm: gd debut. **96**
-- **UP ON POINTS** [9] R Hannon 2-8-2 L Newman (3) 13/2: 2: 2 ch f Royal Academy - Champagne N Roses (Chief Singer) Handy, hdwy to lead well over 1f out, sn hdd & not pace of wnr on debut: Apr foal, cost 15,000gns: dam 7f wnr: eff over a stiff 7f on gd/firm: shld come on for this & win a race. *1¼* **86**
-- **POLE STAR** [1] J R Fanshawe 2-8-7 D Harrison 9/1: 3: 2 b c Polar Falcon - Ellie Ardensky (Slip Anchor) Waited with, hdwy 2f out, onepace fnl 1f: op 6/1 on debut: Apr first foal, cost 12,000gns: dam useful 9/10f wnr: some promise here & looks sure to relish 1m+ & time. *1¼* **89**
2921 **BALLADEER 22** [5] J W Hills 2-8-7 S Whitworth 9/1: -04: In tch, outpcd over 2f out, late gains: will need 1m+: see 2921. *½* **88**
3108 **SPREE LOVE 14** [8] 2-8-0 J Quinn 7/2: 245: Led 2f, wknd over 1f out: btr expected after 3108. *3½* **74**
2583 **MISS PITZ 36** [2] 2-8-4 G Carter 5/1: 66: Led after 2f, clr over 3f out, hdd & wknd qckly over 1f out. *4* **70**
2773 **EVERMOORE 28** [3] 2-7-12 F Norton 66/1: -04647: In tch, btn over 2f out: see 2773 (6f). *6* **52**
-- **FLIPSIDE** [4] 2-8-5 M Henry 25/1: 8: Slow away, al bhd: op 14/1 on debut: Apr foal, cost 10,000gns: bred to apprec 7f/1m: with J Hills. *6* **47**
-- **PEKANOORA** [6] 2-8-7 P Robinson 16/1: 9: Al bhd on debut: Apr first foal, cost IR£15,000: dam 5f wnr. *¾* **47**
9 ran Time 1m 29.68 (4.18) (Robert Hichins) I A Balding Kingsclere, Hants.

3421 **3.25 CHEVIOT CLASSIFIED STKS 3YO 0-90 (C) 1m str Good/Firm 37 -24 Slow**
£7029 £2666 £1333 £606

*2871 **SUMMER VIEW 25** [2] R Charlton 3-9-1 R Hughes 4/7 FAV: -11: 3 ch c Distant View - Miss Summer (Luthier) Made virtually all, kept on well over 1f out, hands-and-heels: hvly bckd: earlier won at Kempton (mdn, easily), had reportedly earlier had a wind op & suffered sore shins: stays 1m well on any trk, further will suit: acts on firm/fast & has run well fresh: likes to front run & proving v useful, can improve again. **100**
2858 **BLUE SUGAR 26** [6] J R Fanshawe 3-8-13 D Harrison 5/2: 1-4222: 3 ch c Shuailaan - Chelsea My Love (Opening Verse) Trkd ldrs, eff to chase wnr over 1f out, onepace: another gd rnr-up placing: see 2858. *1¼* **93**
2917 **MINKASH 22** [4] B Hanbury 3-8-13 (BL) P Robinson 10/1: -06443: 3 b c Caerleon - Ingabelle (Taufan) In tch, eff well over 1f out, kept on to take 3rd ins last: not disgraced in first time blnks stepped back to 1m. *1¾* **89**
2805 **KINGSDON 27** [3] R Hannon 3-8-13 (t) Dane O'Neill 11/2: 300654: Trkd wnr, wknd well over 1f out. *¾* **87**
2591 **CAPPUCINO LADY 36** [1] 3-8-10 L Newman (3) 100/1: 050005: Keen bhd, btn over 2f out: see 357. *25* **44**
5 ran Time 1m 43.95 (4.85) (K Abdulla) R Charlton Beckhampton, Wilts.

3422   4.00 STELLA ARTOIS FILL HCAP 3YO+ 0-85 (D)   1m str   Good/Firm 37   -06 Slow   [85]
£3783   £1164   £582   £291   3yo rec 6lb

3110 **NATALIE JAY** 14 [4] M R Channon 4-8-5 (62) Craig Williams 7/1: 304301: 4 b f Ballacashtal - Falls   70
Of Lora (Scottish Rifle) Rear, imprvd 2f out, led dist, pushed clr, cmftbly: '99 wnr here at Salisbury (this race,
rtd 6/9), also rnr-up on sand (h'cap, rtd 68a): eff at 1m/10f on fast, hvy grnd & equitrack: handles any trk,
likes Salisbury: could make a quick follow up.
2789 **DANIELLA RIDGE** 28 [3] R Hannon 4-7-13 (56) J Quinn 33/1: 0-0002: 4 b f Indian Ridge - Daniella   3½ 58
Drive (Shelter Half) In tch, led briefly dist, kept on but not pace of wnr: back to form with blnks omitted.
2629 **RED LETTER** 35 [7] R Hannon 3-9-6 (83) R Hughes 6/1: -32603: 3 b f Sri Pekan - Never Explain   1¾ 81
(Fairy King) Rdn in rear, styd on under press to take 3rd cl-home, no ch with front 2: s/mate of rnr-up: see 1853.
3089 **FREDORA** 15 [9] M Blanshard 5-10-0 (85) D Sweeney 12/1: 101404: Chsd ldrs, led halfway till   ½   82
2f out, no extra cl-home: tchd 16/1, top-weight: see 2629.
3263 **COLNE VALLEY AMY** 7 [8] 3-8-2 (65) L Newman (3) 5/1: 114325: Led 4f, again 2f out till dist, fdd.   1¼ 59
2889 **CELTIC BAY** 24 [1] 3-8-3 (66) M Henry 20/1: -6666: Nvr a factor on h'cap debut: drifted from   3½ 53
12/1: back in trip, see 2354 (12f mdn).
*3365 **RIBERAC** 2 [6] 4-9-6 (77)(6ex) J Fanning 5/4 FAV: 000117: Chsd ldrs, ev ch 2f out, grad fdd: 3   58
hvly bckd & poss just too soon after 3365 (gd grnd).
3188 **SILENT NIGHT** 10 [5] 3-8-7 (70)(bl) P Robinson 40/1: 0-0508: Front rank 6f, fdd: see 1177 (10f here).   1½ 48
3089 **COMMON CONSENT** 15 [2] 4-7-13 (56) F Norton 11/2: 610429: Rear, eff 2f out, sn btn & fin last: 3   28
tchd 8/1, reportedly fin lame: btr 3089.
9 ran   Time 1m 42.57 (3.47)   (Peter Jolliffe)   M R Channon West Isley, Berks.

3423   4.35 NICHOLSON MDN 3YO (D)   7f str   Good/Firm 37   -06 Slow
£3497   £1076   £538   £269

-- **BURGUNDY** [7] R Charlton 3-9-0 R Hughes 7/4 FAV: -1: 3 b g Lycius - Decant (Rousillon)   80
Dwelt, imprvd from rear halfway, strong run to lead ent fnl 1f, pulled clr, cmftbly: well bckd tho' drifted from
8/11 on debut: half-brother to a 1m wnr: eff over a stiff 7f, 1m sure to suit: acts on fast grnd & on a
stiff/gall trk: reportedly held in some regard, can rate more highly & win more races.
-- **BADAAWAH** [8] B Hanbury 3-8-9 Dane O'Neill 6/1: -2: 3 ch f Lion Cavern - Wanisa (Topsider)   2½ 67
Chsd ldrs, styd on into 2nd ins fnl 1f, not reach wnr: debut, op 4/1: eff at 7f, 1m+ sure to suit: improve.
2462 **TEE CEE** 41 [9] R Guest 3-8-9 D Harrison 6/1: -53343: 3 b f Lion Cavern - Hawayah (Shareef Dancer)   nk 66
Chsd ldr, imprvd to lead over 2f out till dist, no extra cl-home: 6 wk abs: see 1886 (C/D).
2919 **RUSSIAN RHAPSODY** 22 [11] M A Jarvis 3-8-9 P Robinson 7/1: -54: Chsd ldrs, onepcd fnl 2f: nk 65
tchd 10/1, 6L clr rem: up in trip, shapes as tho' further will suit: see 2919.
3238 **JAHMHOOR** 8 [5] 3-9-0 (t) G Carter 6/1: -06505: Rdn in rear, late hdwy, nvr a factor: tchd 9/1.   6   58
2846 **TALENT STAR** 26 [13] 3-9-0 S Righton 50/1: -046: Dwelt, recovered to chase ldrs 5f, wknd: see 2846.   2   54
3293 **DANCING LILY** 6 [14] 3-8-9 R Brisland (5) 33/1: 002057: Front rank, led over 3f out till 2f out, fdd.   nk 48
3179 **WOODYATES** 11 [10] 3-8-9 L Branch (7) 33/1: -068: Chsd ldrs till halfway, wknd: see 3179 (9f).   4   40
3190 **DANGEROUS DEPLOY** 10 [4] 3-9-0 D Cosgrave (7) 33/1: -559: Nvr a factor: see 3190.   ¾   43
1708 **HAREEBA** 74 [3] 3-8-9 A Clark 6/1: -400: Rear, eff over 2f out, sn btn & fin 10th: 10 wk abs.   2   34
-- **BATHWICK DREAM** [12] 3-8-9 A Nicholls (3) 33/1: -0: Led till halfway, wknd & fin last on debut.   0
2889 **Denarius Secundus** 24 [1] 3-9-0 R Perham 33/1:   --   **Finlays Folly** [6] 3-9-0 R Havlin 50/1:
13 ran   Time 1m 28.51 (3.01)   (Highclere Thoroughbred Racing Ltd)   R Charlton Beckhampton, Wilts.

3424   5.10 FRESHWATER HCAP 3YO+ 0-70 (E)   1m6f   Good/Firm 37   -03 Slow   [69]
£2892   £890   £445   £222   3yo rec 12lb

3231 **FLETCHER** 8 [7] H Morrison 6-9-8 (63) R Hughes 3/1 FAV: 321151: 6 b g Salse - Ballet Classique   68
(Sadler's Wells) Rear, plenty to do 2f out, switched left dist, strong run to lead ins fnl 1f, won going away:
bckd from 5/1: earlier won at Salisbury & Sandown (h'caps): '98 wnr at Ascot (amat
h'cap, rtd 79): stays 2m, winning form over 12/14f: acts on firm & soft grnd, best held up for a late run &
likes a stiff finish: can be a tricky ride but revitalised this summer.
2689 **MISCONDUCT** 33 [13] J G Portman 6-8-11 (52) G Baker(5) 5/1: 20-232: 6 gr m Risk Me - Grey Cree   2½ 53
(Creetown) Mid-div, imprvd to lead over 2f out, not pace to repel wnr ins fnl 1f: tchd 7/1: stays 14f: see 2689.
2937 **ALCAYDE** 21 [15] J Akehurst 5-9-0 (55) F Norton 33/1: 5/0053: 5 ch g Alhijaz - Lucky Flinders   nk 55
(Free State) Rear, styd on strongly fnl 2f, nrst fin: bckd to form over this longer 14f trip: v well h'capped.
3049 **OUT ON A PROMISE** 17 [10] B J Meehan 8-8-3 (44) C Rutter 7/1: /00104: In tch, kept on under press   1   42
fnl 1f: op 5/1: stays 14f: best 2971 (12f).
2971 **DESERT VALENTINE** 20 [9] 5-8-2 (43) P Fitzsimons(4) 7/1: 50-025: Rcd keenly rear, imprvd to chall   hd 41
2f out, no extra ins last: prob stays 14f: see 2971.
2982 **NIGHT MUSIC** 20 [12] 3-8-4 (57) R Havlin 10/1: 053036: Mid-div, onepcd fnl 2f: see 2982 (C/D).   nk 54
3073 **RISING SPRAY** 15 [1] 9-9-4 (59) N Pollard 20/1: 06-007: Mid-div, btn fnl 1f: see 2552.   1½ 54
2923 **URGENT SWIFT** 22 [4] 7-9-10 (65) D Harrison 12/1: 124058: Slowly away, late prog, nvr dngrs: 3   56
top-weight: gave away plenty of grnd at the start: see 2164, 1959.
2982 **HIGHLY PRIZED** 20 [8] 6-9-9 (64) S Carson (3) 25/1: -16009: Led till 3f out, grad fdd: see 277 (AW).   ½   54
*2982 **SEA DANZIG** 20 [3] 7-8-12 (53) L Newman(3) 10/1: 004010: Chsd ldrs 12f, wknd into 10th: btr 2982.   2   40
3282 **TOMMY CARSON** 6 [14] 3-8-9 (50)(bl) M Henry 14/1: 625040: Rcd keenly in bhd ldrs, led 3f out   1   35
till 2f out, sn btn: fin 11th: qck reapp: see 1350 (12f here).
2902 **AEGEAN WIND** 23 [6] 3-9-0 (67) G Carter 14/1: 0-5000: Chsd ldrs 10f, wknd: fin 12th: see 1929.   4   46
3219 **I TINA** 8 [16] 4-9-7 (62) A Daly 10/1: 4-6040: Chsd ldrs, ev ch 3f out, sn wknd & fin 14th: btr 3219.   0
2879 **Golden Rod** 24 [5] 3-8-4 (57) A Clark 20/1:   2681 **Alnajashee** 33 [2] 4-9-5 (60)(t) D Sweeney 33/1:
2942 **Starboard Tack** 21 [11] 4-9-5 (60) I Mongan (5) 33/1:
16 ran   Time 3m 03.63 (5.63)   (Lady Margadale)   H Morrison East Ilsley, Berks.

Official Going　GOOD. Stalls: Inside, except 10f - Stands Side.

3425　2.30 EBF COMBERMERE FILLIES COND STKS 2YO (B)　6f rnd　Good/Firm 36　-11 Slow
£9371　£3465　£1732　£787

*2683 **MAURI MOON** 34 [3] G Wragg 2-8-11 F Norton 9/2: 511: 2 b f Green Desert - Dazzling Heights　97
(Shirley Heights) Unruly bef start, handy, kept on over 1f out to lead ins last, rdn out, shade cmftbly: op 11/4:
earlier won at Nottingham (fill mdn): half sister to wnrs over 7f/mid-dists: dam useful over mid-dists: eff at
6f, 7f+ sure to suit: acts on fast grnd: useful & improving, win more races if keeping temperament in check.
2529 **MILLENIUM PRINCESS** 40 [2] R Hannon 2-8-11 J Weaver 4/1: -1262: 2 b f Eagle Eyed - Sopran Marida nk　95
(Darshaan) Dsptd lead till went on 2f out, flashed tail & collared ins last, just btn: abs, clr rem back at 6f.
*2756 **COLUMBINE** 30 [1] A Berry 2-8-11 J Carroll 7/4 FAV: -13: 2 b f Pivotal - Heart Of India (Try My　5　82
Best) Dwelt, bhd, eff over 1f out, onepace: well bckd: stays 6f: will apprec a return to a more gall trk.
*3003 **TEREED ELHAWA** 20 [4] E A L Dunlop 2-8-11 G Carter 9/1: 6314: Dsptd lead till 2f out, no extra　¾　80
over 1f out: drifted from 11/2: up in class after 3003 (fill mdn).
*3327 **BECKY SIMMONS** 5 [5] 2-8-8 G Duffield 3/1: 1115: In tch, btn over 1f out: op 9/4: prob not　shd　77
enjoy this v sharp trk & a qk reapp: unbtn earlier, see 3327 (h'cap, stiff).
5 ran　Time 1m 15.94 (2.84)　(Peter R Pritchard)　G Wragg Newmarket

3426　3.00 KEMIRA AGRO HCAP 3YO 0-90 (C)　1m2f75y　Good/Firm 36　-01 Slow　[89]
£7085　£2180　£1090　£545

2955 **SPORTING GESTURE** 21 [4] M W Easterby 3-8-9 (70) J Fanning 15/2: 000161: 3 ch g Safawan - Polly　73
Packer (Reform) Prom, led over 3f out, clr over 1f out, rdn out: earlier won at York (h'cap, this jockey) & a
strange run under a different jockey last time: '99 winner at Catterick (nurs h'cap, rtd 77): eff at 7f, stays
10.3f on gd/firm, gd & any trk: best forcing the pace & is on the upgrade.
2666 **KAIAPOI** 35 [2] R Hollinshead 3-9-4 (79) R Mullen 7/1: 1U3502: 3 ch c Elmaamul - Salanka (Persian　½　81
Heights) Hld up, hdwy & short of room over 2f out, fin well fnl 1f: can be considered unlucky & loves this crse.
2988 **SALIM** 20 [3] Sir Michael Stoute 3-9-5 (80) W Supple 15/2: -14043: 3 b c Salse - Moviegoer (Pharly)　1¾　79
Cl up, eff to chase wnr over 1f out, kept on samepace: stays a sharp 10.3f on gd & fast: see 1159.
3159 **FAIR LADY** 13 [5] B W Hills 3-9-2 (77) G Duffield 5/1: -16304: Hld up, eff over 2f out, sn wknd: btr 2863.　5　68
3131 **PEDRO PETE** 14 [6] 3-9-2 (77) J Weaver 7/4 FAV: 331105: Keen, handy, wknd 2f out: well bckd　1½　66
but twice well below 2955 & again raced too keenly.
3042 **CARENS HERO** 18 [1] 3-9-7 (82) G Carter 13/2: -31046: Led till over 3f out, wknd 2f out: top-weight.　5　64
3317 **LADY HELEN** 6 [7] 3-8-13 (74) J Carroll 13/2: 100107: Dwelt, hld up, rdn & btn 3f out: thrice below 2988.　4　50
7 ran　Time 2m 12.31 (3.81)　(Steve Hull)　M W Easterby Sheriff Hutton, N Yorks

3427　3.30 MOLLINGTON RATED HCAP 3YO+ 0-100 (B)　7f rnd　Good/Firm 36　+03 Fast　[107]
£9387　£3560　£1780　£809　3 yo rec 5 lb

+3170 **CANTINA** 12 [1] A Bailey 6-8-9 (88) J Mackay (5) 7/4 FAV: 143111: 6 b m Tina's Pet - Real　96
Claire (Dreams To Reality) Made all, clr 2f out, 5L clr when eased cl home: well bckd, gd time: landed hat-trick,
earlier won at Beverley (ladies h'cap) & Carlisle (fill h'cap): '99 scorer at Redcar (amat stks, rtd 73 & 72a):
loves to force the pace at 7/7.5f & likes firm, handles gd/soft & any trk, loves Chester: genuine, in top form.
1470 **RAYYAAN** 86 [5] N A Graham 3-8-6 (90) W Supple 7/1: -11162: 3 ch c Cadeaux Genereux - Anam　2　90
(Persian Bold) Hld up, hdwy & short of room over 2f out, kept on ins last but wnr had flown: gd run after abs.
3315 **KAYO** 6 [3] M Johnston 5-9-7 (100) J Fanning 8/1: 312203: 5 b g Superpower - Shiny Kay (Star Appeal) 2½　95
In tch, eff over 2f out, sn onepace: not disgraced under top-weight: tough, see 2706.
2151 **NIGRASINE** 56 [7] J L Eyre 4-9-0 (99) (bl) J Carroll 12/1: 045104: Cl up, rdn & btn 1f out: 8 wk abs　½　93
& just best at 6f as in 1952.
3016 **SHATIN VENTURE** 19 [6] 3-8-8 (92) G Duffield 20/1: -30005: Bhd, rdn over 2f out, no impress.　2½　81
3155 **KUMAIT** 13 [2] 6-8-11 (90) G Carter 7/1: -40606: Prom, wknd 2f out: best left alone, see 1946.　4　71
-2670 **SILCA BLANKA** 34 [4] 8-9-2 (95) J Weaver 11/4: 110327: Prom, wknd 2f out: something amiss?　4　68
7 ran　Time 1m 27.35 (2.35)　(R Kinsey, Mrs M Kinsey & Miss B Roberts)　A Bailey Little Budworth, Cheshire

3428　4.00 THWAITES NURSERY HCAP 2YO (C)　7f rnd　Good/Firm 36　-17 Slow　[87]
£6240　£1920　£960　£480

2935 **LILS JESSY** 22 [3] J Noseda 2-9-5 (78) J Weaver 5/4 FAV: 5101: 2 b f Kris - Lobmille (Mill Reef)　91
Led fnl 1f, led over 1f out, rdn clr: well bckd: earlier won at Yarmouth (fill mdn): half sister to sev wnrs: eff
at 7f, 1m+ will suit: acts on firm/fast & on a sharp or fair trk: runs well fresh: type to progress with racing.
3044 **LONER** 18 [5] N A Callaghan 2-8-11 (70) F Norton 11/5: 0462: 2 ch g Pivotal - Euridice (Woodman)　2½　77
In tch, eff over 1f out, kept on in last, kept on pace of wnr: well bckd: improved stepped up to 7f on fast.
2962 **DUSTY CARPET** 21 [1] C A Dwyer 2-9-7 (80) G Duffield 5/1: 64643: 2 ch g Pivotal - Euridice　½　86$
(Woodman) Led after 1f till over 1f out, no extra ins last: top-weight: clr rem & prob stays a sharp 7f.
3029 **POLISH PADDY** 18 [4] R Hannon 2-8-9 (68) J Mackay (5) 10/1: 06644: Al bhd: see 3029.　9　58
2619 **MOMENTS IN TIME** 36 [2] 2-8-6 (65) P Fessey 11/1: 6465: Al bhd: op 7/1: btr 2619.　1½　52
3137 **LITTLE TASK** 14 [6] 2-8-13 (72) J Carroll 10/1: 302426: Sn bhd, t.o.: something amiss? btr 3137.　dist　0
6 ran　Time 1m 28.69 (3.69)　(Razza Pallorsi)　J Noseda Newmarket

3429　4.30 DAVID MCLEAN FILLIES MDN 3YO+ (D)　1m4f66y　Good/Firm 36　-01 Slow
£4212　£1296　£648　£324　3 yo rec 10lb

2930 **BAYSWATER** 23 [5] B W Hills 3-8-11 G Duffield 5/1: 0221: 3 b f Caerleon - Shining Water (Kalaglow)　75
Made all, tried to run out over 7f out, kept on ins last despite flashing tail: sister to high-class 10f
wnr Tenby: eff at 12/13f on fm/fast, any trk: improved today but also signs of temperament.
3265 **AYMARA** 8 [2] J H M Gosden 3-8-11 W Supple 9/4: 422: 3 b f Darshaan - Chipaya (Northern Prospect)　1¾　73
In tch, hdwy 3f out, onepace fnl 1f & held when snatched up cl home: op 6/4: stays 12.3f & shld find similar.
-- **JUNO BEACH** [3] D Morris 4-9-7 J Mackay (5) 20/1: 3: 4 ch f Jupiter Island - Kovalevskaia (Ardross)　2½　69
Sn rdn bhd, eff 2f out, onepace over 1f out: last raced in bumpers 4 months ago, earlier won at M Rasen (1m5.5f):

CHESTER   FRIDAY AUGUST 18TH   Lefthand, Very Tight Track

handles fast grnd: eff at 12.3f, 14f+ will suit: some promise here.
3157 **SECOND AFFAIR** 13 [4] C F Wall 3-8-11 R Mullen 4/5 FAV: 324: Chsd ldrs, wandered & wknd appr   ½   68
fnl 1f: well bckd & better expected after 3157.
3232 **LUNA FLIGHT** 9 [1] 3-8-11 J Fanning 10/1: -55: In tch, wknd over 4f out, t.o.: see 3232.   21   38
5 ran   Time 1m 40.94 (4.54)   (K Abdulla)   B W Hills Lambourn, Berks

3430	5.00 AMAT RDRS HCAP 3YO+ 0-80 (E) 1m4f66y Good/Firm 36 -23 Slow	[47]

£3055   £940   £470   £235   3 yo rec 10lb

2309 **BACHELORS PAD** 49 [2] Miss S J Wilton 6-10-9 (56) Mr J J Best (7) 10/1: 423461: 6 b g Pursuit Of Love   61
- Note Book (Mummy's Pet) In tch, hdwy over 2f out, led fnl 1f, rdn out: 7 wk abs, op 6/1: earlier won at
Southwell (appr h'cap) & last winter at W'hampton (3, 2 clmrs, 1 for D Nicholls, sell, rtd 65a): rnr-up in '99
(rtd 63): eff at 7f/12.3f on firm, gd/soft & fibresand: likes a sharp trk, handles any: runs well fresh: tough.
2953 **JAMAICAN FLIGHT** 21 [8] Mrs S Lamyman 7-10-12 (59) Mr S Dobson (5) 9/2: 655442: 7 b h Sunshine   1¼   61
Forever - Kalamona (Hawaii) Led till over 5f out, led again over 2f out till ins last: needs 14f+.
3173 **CAPRIOLO** 12 [6] R Hannon 4-11-10 (71)(bl) Mr S Callaghan (7) 9/4 FAV: 600163: 4 ch g Priolo -   4   67
Carroll's Canyon (Hatim) Led over 5f out till over 2f out, wknd fnl 1f: well bckd: best 2667 (made all).
3186 **CLASSIC CONKERS** 11 [5] Pat Mitchell 6-9-10 (43)(5oh) Mr S Rees (5) 7/2: 015024: Slow away, bhd,   ¾   38
eff over 2f out, nrst fin: btr 3186.
2309 **RUTLAND CHANTRY** 49 [7] 6-11-3 (64) Mr R L Moore (5) 8/1: 256605: In tch, eff 2f out, onepace: abs.   nk   59
3111 **HOH GEM** 14 [3] 4-10-0 (47) Mr G Richards (5) 11/2: 102046: Slow away, al bhd: lngr trip, see 3111.   6   33
668 **BREAK THE RULES** 157 [4] 8-10-9 (56) Mr T Scudamore (5) 4/0-07: Prom, wknd over 5f out: long abs.   9   28
4307} **FLYING EAGLE** 312 [1] 9-12-0 (75) Mr C Bonner 10/1: 4153-8: Bhd, hmpd & stumbled 1m out, btn   9   33
over 4f out, t.o.: fit from hdlg, earlier won at Fontwell (clmr, rtd 117h, eff at 2m/2m2f on fast & hvy, tried blnks):
99/00 Plumpton wnr (hdle, G L Moore): in '99 won on the Flat at Epsom (amat h'cap, rtd 77): stays 12f on fast & hvy.
8 ran   Time 2m 43.65 (7.25)   (John Pointon And Sons)   Miss S J Wilton Wetley Rocks, Staffs

SANDOWN   FRIDAY AUGUST 18TH   Righthand, Stiff, Galloping Track

Official Going   GOOD TO FIRM (GOOD places). Stalls: 5f - Far Side; Rem - Inside.

3431	5.25 PLATINUM NURSERY HCAP 2YO (D) 5f Good 44 -16 Slow	[90]

£4212   £1296   £648   £324

3228 **CLARION** 9 [2] Sir Mark Prescott 2-9-5 (81) S Sanders 2/1 FAV: -2121: 2 ch c First Trump - Area Girl   86
(Jareer) Chsd ldrs, rdn/led over 1f out, checked at path inside last, styd on well for press close home: well bckd
tho' op 6/4: earlier scored at Yarmouth (mdn): eff at 5f, 6f shld suit: acts on fm, gd & fbrsand: tough.
2545 **FAIR PRINCESS** 39 [6] B W Hills 2-9-6 (82) W Ryan 7/1: 22062: 2 b f Efisio - Fair Attempt   ¾   83
(Try My Best) Chsd ldrs, rdn & styd on inside last, not reach wnr: handles gd & gd/soft grnd: see 1538.
*3109 **SOLDIER ON** 15 [4] M R Channon 2-9-2 (78) Craig Williams 9/2: 155013: 2 b c General Monash -   shd   79
Golden Form (Formidable) Held up, rdn & styd on well final 1f, not reach wnr: bckd, op 11/2: see 3109.
3062 **RISQUE SERMON** 17 [1] Miss B Sanders 2-9-2 (78) B Marcus 16/1: 0104: Chsd ldr, led halfway till over   1   77
1f out, held inside last: op 12/1: handles firm & gd grnd: see 2760 (mdn, 6f).
+3101 **CANDOTHAT** 16 [5] 2-9-7 (83) T Quinn 3/1: 061515: Rdn/bhd, styd on well final 1f, nrst fin: return   ¾   80
to 6f in similar company should suit: see 3101.
2067 **RARE OLD TIMES** 59 [3] 2-9-6 (82) L Newman (3) 7/1: 5106: In tch, btn over 1f out: abs: btr 1426 (stks).   5   70
2818 **COUNT CALYPSO** 28 [8] 2-8-5 (67) Martin Dwyer 16/1: 00037: Led 3f, sn held: btr 2818 (AW).   8   40
7 ran   Time 1m 02.6 (3.0)   (Neil Greig)   Sir Mark Prescott Newmarket, Suffolk.

3432	5.55 DORKING FILLIES MDN 3YO (D) 1m2f Good 44 -28 Slow	

£4309   £1326   £663   £331

-- **GWENEIRA** [6] J H M Gosden 3-8-11 K Darley 7/2: 1: 3 gr f Machiavellian - English Spring (Grey Dawn   84
II) Held up, prog over 2f out & rdn/styd on well to lead inside last: op 3/1, debut: half-sister to 6 wnrs: eff
over a stiff/gall 10f, 12f shld suit: acts on gd grnd & runs well fresh: op to further improvement.
-- **SUMMER DREAMS** [1] Major D N Chappell 3-8-11 A McGlone 16/1: 2: 3 b f Sadler's Wells -   1¼   81
Marie de Beaujeu (Kenmare) Dwelt/near, styd on well final 2f, not pace of wnr: debut: half-sister to
stable's wng mid-dist h'capper Livius: eff at 10f, 12f+ likely to suit: acts on gd grnd: shld win soon.
3006 **LAND AHEAD** 20 [3] H R A Cecil 3-8-11 T Quinn 5/4 FAV: 5-3123: 3 ch f Distant View - Nimble Folly   ½   80
(Cyane) Keen/led, rdn/hdd inside last & no extra: hvly bckd: possibly needed a lead here: shwn enough to
win similar prev: acts on fast & gd grnd: see 3006, 2449.
2558 **KALEMAAT** 38 [5] R W Armstrong 3-8-11 L Newman (3) 14/1: 54: Chsd ldrs, outpcd final 2f: see 2558.   1   79
3179 **FUNNY GIRL** 12 [2] 3-8-11 Martin Dwyer 11/4: 5-5625: Cl-up, drvn/wknd final 1f: well bckd: btr 3179.   3   75
2963 **ARDANZA** 21 [4] 3-8-11 Dane O'Neill 7/1: 246: Keen/held up, outpcd final 2f: op 11/2: see 2693, 1343.   8   66
6 ran   Time 2m 11.29 (7.19)   (Sheikh Mohammed)   J H M Gosden Manton, Wilts.

3433	6.25 ESHER FILLIES COND STKS 2YO (C) 1m rnd Good 44 -27 Slow	

£5649   £2088   £1044   £474

*2806 **CRYSTAL MUSIC** 28 [4] J H M Gosden 2-8-12 K Darley 1/3 FAV: 11: 2 b f Nureyev - Crystal Spray   100
(Beldale Flutter) Trkd ldrs, led over 3f out & readily asserted over 1f out under hands & heels riding, styd on
strongly: confirmed promise of wng debut at Newmarket (mdn): well suited by this step up to 1m (dam a 14f wnr) &
mid-dists will suit in '01: acts on fast & gd grnd, stiff trk: v useful, will hold her own in Listed/Gr company.
2996 **ZAHEEMAH** 20 [1] C E Brittain 2-8-9 B Marcus 7/2: 6452: 2 b f El Prado - Port Of Silver (Silver Hawk):   1¼   92
Cl-up, chf 2f out, sn outpcd by easy wnr: stayed this lngr 1m trip & has shown more than enough to win a mdn.
-- **CONSPIRE** [3] G A Butler 2-8-6 T Quinn 8/1: 3: 2 b f Turtle Island - Mild Intrigue (Sir Ivor):   1½   86
Dwelt, chsd front pair 3f out, sn held: Feb foal, cost £115,000 Irish gns: half-sister to 4 wnrs, incl a 1m/9f juv
wnr: dam a 10f wnr: 1m+ looks sure to suit: highly tried on intro, drop to mdn company should suit.
2550 **IMMACULATE CHARLIE** 39 [5] A T Murphy 2-8-9 A McGlone 50/1: 3204: Keen, led till over 3f out, sn   20   49
held: lngr 1m trip: needs a return to sell grade: see 2052, 1553.

4 ran   Time 1m 44.70 (5.7)   (Lord Lloyd-Webber)   J H M Gosden Newmarket, Suffolk.

3434   6.55 EQUANET HCAP 3YO+ 0-70 (E)   **2m78y**   Good 44 -03 Slow   **[67]**
                £3623   £1115   £557   £278   3 yo rec 14lb

2866 **OUR MONOGRAM** 26 [9] A C Stewart 4-8-4 (43) M Roberts 5/1: -00031: 4 b g Deploy - Darling Splodge   **48**
(Elegant Air) In tch, prog ent final 3f, led before dist, sn clr, readily: first win, nicely bckd: rtd 74 on
debut last term (mdn): eff at 2m on fast & gd grnd, galloping trks: gd confidence booster.
3360 **GALAPINO** 4 [8] Jamie Poulton 7-8-8 (47)(bl) O Urbina 12/1: 405052: 7 b g Charmer - Carousella   4 **45**
(Rousillon) Not travel well early & rdn, held up, imprvd appr final 2f, styd on for 2nd, no ch wnr: qk reapp, blnks.
3360 **DANEGOLD** 4 [5] M R Channon 8-9-2 (55) T Quinn 8/1: 000463: 8 b g Danehill - Cistus (Sun Prince)   ¾ **52**
Waited with, effort appr final 2f, no impress till styd on towards fin: qck reapp: better run, well h'capped.
3348 **KING FOR A DAY** 4 [1] Bob Jones 4-8-4 (43)(vis) Paul Eddery 14/1: 004144: In tch, prog 5f out, ch   nk **40**
appr final 2f, kept on same pace: qck reapp, ran well, stays 2m, drop back to 14f may suit: see 2902 (mdn h'cap).
3040 **FAST FORWARD FRED** 18 [4] 9-8-3 (52) A Clark 8/1: 0-0035: Cl-up, outpcd appr final 2f, not much   1¾ **47**
room final 2f, onepace: won this in '98 off a 2lb higher mark: see 1800.
3231 **COPYFORCE GIRL** 9 [2] 4-9-9 (62)(t) S Carson (3) 8/1: 132226: In tch, prog to lead appr final   ½ **56**
2f till before dist, fdd: unsuited by step up to 2m?: btr 2923 (14f here), see 2429.
2763 **MARTHA REILLY** 30 [3] 4-7-12 (37)(2ow)(6oh) Martin Dwyer 20/1: 346-27: Led till bef fnl 2f, no extra.   ½ **30**
*3085 **LAFFAH** 16 [10] 5-10-0 (67)(t) R Hughes 3/1 FAV: 134118: Chsd ldrs, lost place 2f out, eased fnl 1f: ¾ **59**
well bckd, top-weight, had a hardish race over a marathon trip in 3085.
2856 **ZINCALO** 27 [7] 4-9-4 (57)(t) B Marcus 10/1: 013369: Al towards rear: up in trip, see 1874.   2 **47**
*3249 **FREE** 9 [1] 5-9-3 (56)(6ex) T Eaves (7) 4/1: 3-0010: Handy till 5f out: 10th: reportedly never   1 **45**
trav & may have been feeling the effects of recent win in 3249 (14f, made all).
10 ran   Time 3m 37.57 (7.77)   (The Foxons Fillies Partnership)   A C Stewart Newmarket.

3435   7.25 ORLEANS HCAP 3YO 0-95 (C)   **1m rnd**   Good 42 +02 Fast   **[100]**
                £7150   £2200   £1100   £550

3022 **OGILIA** 19 [6] I A Balding 3-8-3 (75) Martin Dwyer 10/1: -00461: 3 b f Bin Ajwaad - Littlemisstrouble   **81**
(My Gallant) Trkd ldrs, rdn dist, kept on strgly to get up fnl stride: best time of evening: '99 Bath wnr (fill mdn
auct, rtd 91 at best): eff at 1m nowadays: acts on firm & soft, any trk: runs well fresh, slipped to a v handy mark.
2870 **MOSSY MOOR** 26 [7] Mrs A J Perrett 3-9-3 (89) R Hughes 11/2: 531042: 3 ch f Sanglamore - Moss   hd **94**
(Alzao) Tried to make all, 2L clr & rdn dist, pushed out thro' final 150y & caught line: nicely bckd: held
on with a more forceful ride?: clr of rem & is a progressive filly: see 2084.
2858 **TUMBLEWEED TOR** 27 [4] B J Meehan 3-9-5 (91) M Tebbutt 10/1: 106363: 3 b g Rudimentary - Hilly   3 **90**
(Town Crier) Prom, rdn 2f out, kept on till no extra final 100y: gd run tho' is prob best forcing it: see 1366.
3018 **TRAVELLING LITE** 19 [1] B R Millman 3-8-10 (82) G Hind 7/1: 342034: Towards rear, outpcd 2f out,   1¾ **77**
styd on towards fin: btr 3018, see 727.
*3005 **TRICCOLO** 20 [8] 3-8-11 (83) M Roberts 4/1: 151315: Mid-div thro'out: nicely bckd, btr 3005.   nk **77**
1283 **PEKANSKI** 97 [3] 3-9-7 (93) Dane O'Neill 10/1: 16-06: Rear, effort & no impress 2f out: over 3 mth   ½ **86**
abs, h'cap bow: should get 1m tho' has clearly had training problems: see 1283.
3130 **SHADOW PRINCE** 14 [2] 3-8-7 (79) S Sanders 7/1 FAV: 501337: Held up, not clr run appr final 2f &   nk **71**
swtchd, rdn & clsg when hmpd again & snatched up dist, position accepted: well bckd, forgive this: see 3130.
3022 **ATAVUS** 19 [5] 3-8-13 (85) K Darley 10/1: 410358: Cl-up & ch till fdd ent final 2f: see 1183 (with W Muir).   1¾ **74**
8 ran   Time 1m 42.34 (3.34)   (Exors of the late G M Smart)   I A Balding Kingsclere, Hants.

3436   7.55 SUMMER HCAP 3YO 0-75 (E)   **5f**   Good 44 +01 Fast   **[75]**
                £4309   £1326   £663   £331   3 yo rec 2 lb

3222 **PREMIUM PRINCESS** 9 [3] J J Quinn 5-8-8 (55) K Darley 8/1: 336241: 5 b m Distant Relative - Solemn   **60**
Occasion (Secreto) Rear, imprvd appr final 1f, ran on well under press to get up nr fin: fair time: '99 Newcastle
wnr (h'cap, rtd 62): '98 rnr-up (mdn, rtd 64): eff at 5/6f: acts on gd/soft, suited by firm: tough.
2934 **WORSTED** 22 [4] Major D N Chappell 3-8-10 (59) R Hughes 16/1: 00-352: 3 ch f Whittingham -   hd **63**
Calamanco (Clantime) Held up, prog appr fnl 1f, drvn to lead towards fin, sn hdd: lightly rcd 3yo, shld win similar.
-3419 **REFERENDUM** 1 [7] D Nicholls 6-9-12 (73) Clare Roche (7) 5/1: 660223: 6 b g Common Grounds - Final   1 **74**
Decision (Tap On Wood): Handy, rdn appr final 1f, kept on but unable to chall: bckd under top-weight, qk reapp.
2716 **SHADY DEAL** 32 [10] M D I Usher 4-8-5 (52) G Baker (5) 13/2: 022134: Cl-up, led 2½f out till below dist.   ½ **51**
3191 **PRICE OF PASSION** 11 [8] 4-9-6 (67)(vis) R Cochrane 3/1 FAV: -00045: Chsd ldrs, prog & ev ch dist,   hd **66**
no extra towards fin: nicely bckd: gradually returning to form, see 1441.
*3113 **PLEASURE TIME** 14 [9] 7-9-6 (67)(vis) R Fitzpatrick 8/1: 060016: Led 2f, drvn appr final 1f, fdd: btr 3113.   ¾ **63**
3113 **ECUDAMAH** 14 [1] 4-8-12 (59)(bl) J Bosley (7) 16/1: 640337: Nvr troubled ldrs: see 40.   ½ **54**
*2925 **MOUSEHOLE** 23 [2] 8-9-9 (70) S Sanders 9/2: 020218: Nvr going pace: needs firm/fast grnd.   1¾ **60**
3091 **KNOCKEMBACK NELLIE** 16 [5] 4-8-13 (60)(bl) B Marcus 16/1: 100509: Prom till ent fnl 2f.   1¼ **46**
-- **AKEBONO** [6] 4-9-2 (63) P McCabe 10/1: 0-1410: Sn struggling: last on Brit bow, 6 wk abs: 5 **39**
ex-Irish, won 2 of last 3 starts at Tipperary & Leopardstown (h'caps): eff at 5/6f on fast & gd/soft grnd.
10 ran   Time 1m 01.73 (2.13)   (Derek Bloy)   J J Quinn Settrington, Nth Yorks.

Official Going   GOOD TO SOFT (GOOD places). Stalls: Inside.

3437   5.45 AMAT RDRS HCAP 3YO+ 0-75 (F)   **1m4f**   Good 50 -24 Slow   **[47]**
                £2268   £648   £324   3 yo rec 10lb

*3233 **NOSEY NATIVE** 9 [6] J Pearce 7-10-2 (49)(5ex) Mrs L Pearce 4/1: 262411: 7 b g Cyrano de Bergerac   **50**
- Native Flair (Be My Native) Cl-up 5f out, rdn & styd on well to lead ins last: recent Yarmouth wnr (ladies
h'cap): plcd in '99 (rtd 34a & 42): '98 wnr at Ripon & Catterick (h'caps, rtd 47 & 50a): suited by 12f/2m on
fast, hvy & fibresand, handles equitrack: best without a vis & handles any trk.
3378 **LOST SPIRIT** 2 [1] P W Hiatt 4-9-10 (43)(4oh) Miss A Bruton (7) 11/1: 011352: 4 b g Strolling Along -   ½ **42**

Shoag (Affirmed) Led & sn clr, hdd ins last, no extra: qck reapp: another bold front running effort: see 3053.
3344 **KIERCHEM** 4 [8] C Grant 9-9-10 (43)(8oh) Mr L Bates (0) 25/1: 460043: 9 b g Mazaad - Smashing Gale 2½ 38
(Lord Gayle) Chsd ldrs, styd on fnl 2f, not pace of wnr: qck reapp: see 3344, 2099 (sell h'cap, 1m).
3201 **PENNYS FROM HEAVEN** 10 [4] D Nicholls 6-10-7 (54) Mrs S Bosley 7/2 FAV: 450464: Held up, kept shd 49
on onepace fnl 2f: see 2139.
2827 **WAFIR** 28 [3] 8-10-1 (48) Miss H Cuthbert (5) 9/2: 642135: Mid-div, outpcd fnl 3f: btr 2827, 2638. 5 36
3344 **BUZZ THE AGENT** 4 [11] 5-9-10 (43)(tbl)(7oh) Miss S Brotherton (5 12/1: 3-2006: Chsd clr ldr 1 30
halfway, btn 2f out: op 10/1, qck reapp: btr 3052 (10f, gd/soft).
3368 **RAINSTORM** 3 [2] 5-9-10 (43)(2oh) Mrs S Owen (5) 10/1: 0-0357: Chsd ldrs, btn 3f out: qck reapp. 5 23
1170} **THE BUTTERWICK KID** 471 [9] 7-12-0 (75) Mr S Edgar (7) 9/1: /120-8: Al bhd: reapp, op 6/1: '99 1½ 53
reapp wnr at Hamilton (h'cap, rtd 76): Dec '98 Wetherby wnr over timber (h'cap, rtd 117h, stays 2m7f, gd/soft &
hvy, has ref to race): '98 Flat wnr at Southwell & Redcar (h'caps, rtd 69 & 60a): eff btwn 11f/2m on fast, f/sand
& loves soft/hvy: best without blnks & handles any trk: sharper fr this.
-- **TROOPER** [10] 6-10-13 (60) Mr A Hopkins (7) 25/1: 2002/9: Al rear: long Flat abs, jumps fit (mod 1½ 36
form): last rcd on the level in '97 (rnr-up, AW h'cap): stays 14f, prob handles fibresand.
3284 **RAYWARE BOY** 7 [5] 4-9-10 (43)(bl)(8oh) Mrs C Williams 7/1: 520040: Bhd 4f out: 10th: see 1660. 3 15
3251 **PIPS TANGO** 8 [7] 3-9-10 (53)(19oh) Miss M Mullineaux (7 100/1: 00-000: Chsd clr ldr 6f, sn bhd. 19 4
11 ran   Time 2m 40.10 (8.9)   (Jeff Pearce)   J Pearce Newmarket.

3438   6.15 TATTERSALLS SELLER 2YO (G)   7f rnd   Good 50   -33 Slow
£1918   £548   £274

3307 **PETIT TOR** 6 [7] J Norton 2-8-6 P Hanagan (7) 9/2: 252641: 2 b f Rock City - Kinoora (Kind Of Hush) 60
Chsd ldrs, styd on well fnl 2f & led ins last, drvn out: first win, no bid: qck reapp: eff at 7f on fast & gd/soft
grnd: handles a stiff/gall or sharp/turning track: well suited by selling grade.
2435 **NETTLES** 43 [11] Denys Smith 2-8-11 K Dalgleish (5) 33/1: 000062: 2 br g Cyrano de Bergerac - ½ 63
Sylvandra (Mazilier) Chsd ldrs, styd on well fnl 1f, not reach wnr: abs: stays sharp 7f, acts on gd: mod form prev.
3128 **GAZETTE IT TONIGHT** 14 [9] A Berry 2-8-6 O Pears 4/1: 633133: 2 b f Merdon Melody - ½ 57
Balidilemma (Balidar) Led, rdn/hdd ins last & no extra: acts on fast & gd grnd: see 2927 (C/D).
2983 **ECKSCLUSIVE STORY** 20 [10] J J Quinn 2-8-6 F Lynch 6/1: 044064: Al prom, onepace/held ins last. ½ 56$
3223 **RAINBOW RIVER** 9 [13] Dean McKeown 5/1: 005: Chsd ldrs, styd on fnl 1f, not pace to chall. ½ 60
-- **GORDONS FRIEND** [14] 2-8-11 J Bramhill 20/1: 6: Prom, held over 1f out: Clantime colt, May foal, 3½ 53
cheaply bght first foal: dam a mdn: with B Rothwell.
3009 **CHILLI BOY** 19 [4] J McAuley 16/1: -007: Mid-div, not pace to chall: longer 7f trip. ½ 52
3128 **CHORUS GIRL** 14 [6] 2-8-6 A Culhane 10/1: 046508: Dwelt, nvr on terms: see 2513. ½ 46$
1492 **DOUBLE DIGIT** 84 [12] 2-8-11 D Mernagh (3) 50/1: 09: Prom 5f: 12 wk abs: see 1492 (5f). 3½ 39
3057 **THE BARNSLEY CHOP** 17 [2] 2-8-11 G Parkin 10/1: 00: Nvr on terms: 10th: op 8/1: see 3057. ½ 43
2239 **UTMOST** 51 [3] 2-8-6 Joanna Badger 12/1: 000: Al rear: 11th: op 25/1, 7 wk abs: longer 7f trip. 0
2454 **JEANNIES GIRL** 42 [1] 2-8-6 P Goode (3) 10/1: 00000: Al bhd: 13th: op 8/1, abs: longer 7f trip. 0
2949 Conspiracy Theory 21 [5] 2-8-6 P Bradley (5) 33/1: 2927 Aries Firecracker 23 [8] 2-8-11 (BL) Iona Wands 50/1:
14 ran   Time 1m 28.8 (5.8)   (J Wightman)   J Norton High Hoyland, S.Yorks.

3439   6.45 RMC AGGREGATES NURSERY HCAP 2YO (D)   6f rnd   Good 50   -07 Slow   [89]
£4251   £1308   £654   £327

3168 **UHOOMAGOO** 12 [2] D Nicholls 2-8-13 (74) O Pears 11/2: -21131: 2 b c Namaqualand - Point of Law 86
(Law Society) Dwelt, prog & rdn to lead ins last, drvn out: improving: earlier won at Thirsk (clmr, R
Fahey) & Southwell (clmr, rtd 76a): eff at 5f/sharp 6f on firm, soft & fbrsnd, any trk.
*3354 **SHARP SECRET** 4 [3] M Johnston 2-8-7 (68)(6ex) R Ffrench 6/4 FAV: -52512: 2 b f College Chapel - 2½ 73
State Treasure (Secretariat) Rdn/bhd halfway, kept on fnl 2f, no threat to wnr: qck reapp under a pen, bckd.
+3258 **SIR FRANCIS** 8 [5] J Noseda 2-9-13 (88)(6ex) J Weaver 11/4: 210613: 2 b g Common Grounds - Red shd 93
Note (Rusticaro) Led, increased tempo 2f out, hdd & held ins last: 6lb pen for latest: see 3258.
2797 **WILSON BLYTH** 28 [6] A Berry 2-9-4 (79) J Carroll 16/1: 221434: Prom, rdn/held 1f out: btr 2237. 4 74
3307 **LATE AT NIGHT** 6 [1] 2-7-10 (57)(bl)(2oh) D Mernagh (0) 14/1: 000425: Prom 4f: btr 3307 (sell, firm). 4 42
+3055 **ERRACHT** 17 [4] 2-9-7 (82) Dean McKeown 4/1: 216: Prom 4f: h'cap bow: btr 3055 (5f, mdn). 15 39
6 ran   Time 1m 13.7 (3.4)   (The David Nicholls Racing Club)   D Nicholls Sessay, N.Yorks.

3440   7.15 D & P HAULAGE HCAP 3YO+ 0-70 (E)   7f rnd   Good 50   + 03 Fast   [70]
£3932   £1210   £605   £302   3 yo rec 5 lb

3377 **SAND HAWK** 2 [14] D Shaw 5-7-13 (41)(bl) J McAuley 10/1: 350041: 5 ch g Polar Falcon - Ghassanah 46
(Pas de Seul) Held up, prog halfway, drvn & styd on well to lead well ins last: qck reapp: earlier this year scored
at Southwell & W'hampton (AW h'caps, rtd 67a): '99 W'hampton mdn wnr (rtd 54a & 40): plcd in '98 (h'caps, rtd
51 & 50a): suited by 6/7f, stays 1m: acts on fast, gd/sft & fibresand: handles any trk, loves W'hampton: suited
by blnks/vis: has run well fresh: welcome wnr for this prev out of form stable, several inmates look well h'capped.
3312 **PRIX STAR** 6 [13] C W Fairhurst 5-8-10 (52)(vis) Dean McKeown 8/1: 000522: 5 ch g Superpower - hd 56
Celestine (Skyliner) Chsd ldrs wide halfway, drvn to chall fnl 1f, styd on well, just held: qck reapp: see 3312.
3243 **SANTANDRE** 9 [5] R Hollinshead 4-8-3 (45) P M Quinn (3) 12/1: 005063: 4 ch g Democratic - Smartie hd 48
Lee (Dominion) Trkd ldrs, rdn/prog to lead over 1f out till ins last, just btn in a 3-way photo: see 687.
3377 **TREASURE TOUCH** 2 [17] P D Evans 6-10-0 (70) Joanna Badger (7) 10/1: 130124: Mid-div, rdn/styd on 1¼ 70
fnl 2f, not pace to chall: qck reapp: 3377, 3080.
3054 **KASS ALHAWA** 17 [16] A Culhane 8/1: 244225: Rear, rdn/kept on fnl 2f, nrst fin: see 3054. 1½ 65
2932 **MAMMAS BOY** 23 [11] 5-8-9 (51) D Allan (7) 11/1: 110046: Twds rear, rdn/kept on fnl 2f, no threat. 1¾ 45
3250 **WELCOME TO UNOS** 9 [10] 3-9-3 (64) T Williams 14/1: 063027: Cl up, fdd over 1f out: see 3250, 2440. ¾ 57
*3192 **HYDE PARK** 11 [15] 6-8-6 (48) F Norton 5/1 FAV: 000018: Cl up wide, rdn/led over 2f out, hdd nk 40
over 1f out & no extra: tricky high draw, much btr 3192 (1m).
2340 **BIFF EM** 48 [18] 6-7-12 (40) K Dalgleish 25/1: 304269: Mid-div, not pace to chall: 7 wk abs. ½ 31
1631 **RAFTERS MUSIC** 78 [9] 5-9-0 (56) T Hamilton 9/1: 033130: Twds rear, nvr able to chall: 10th: abs. ¾ 46
1606 **PRINCESS RIA** 79 [6] 3-9-3 (64) J Bramhill 20/1: 500-00: Mid-div, held over 1f out: 11th: abs. 3 48
3094 **HAZIRAAN** 16 [18] 3-9-1 (62) P Hangan (7) 33/1: 0300: Wide, nvr a factor: 12th: h'cap bow. nk 45
2994 **PRECISION** 20 [2] 5-8-0 (42)(2ow) R Ffrench 10/1: 060000: Narow lead till over 2f out: 13th: see 1714. 4 15
176 **ROYAL WAVE** 249 [7] 4-8-13 (55) J Carroll 10/1: 0000-0: Al twds rear: 14th: reapp: '99 reapp nk 29
Pontefract wnr (rtd 76, Mrs A Swinbank, subs disapp): rtd 73 on sole '98 start for Sir M Stoute: eff over a stiff/

1059

CATTERICK
FRIDAY AUGUST 18TH   Lefthand, Undulating, V Tight Track

undul 6f, tried 1m: acts on gd grnd & has run well fresh: with J L Eyre.
409   **Poliziano 204** [1] 4-9-12 (68) F Lynch 25/1:   3141 **Mr Perry 14** [12] 4-8-3 (45)(vis) Dale Gibson 50/1:
2804 **Swynford Welcome 28** [4] 4-8-4 (46) O Pears 20/1:
17 ran   Time 1m 26.3   (J C Fretwell)   D Shaw Averham, Notts

3441
7.45 TENNANTS CLAIMER 3YO+ (F)   **5f**   **Good 50**   **+04 Fast**
£2268   £648   £324   3 yo rec 2 lb

2987 **BEDEVILLED 20** [4] T D Barron 5-8-11 D Mernagh (3) 5/2: W02001: 5 ch g Beveled - Putout (Dowsing)   **66**
Trkd ldr, slty hmpd early on, rdn/switched over 1f out & styd on well ins last to lead nr line: claimed for
£8,000 by J Pearce: earlier scored at Newcastle (h'cap): '99 Beverley wnr (mdn, rtd 71): suited by 5/6f
on fast & soft, handles fibresand & any trk: well suited by this drop to claim grade today.
3283 **KING OF PERU 7** [2] D Nicholls 7-9-3 Alex Greaves 9/4: 201142: 7 b g Inca Chief - Julie's Star   nk   **72**
(Thatching) Chsd ldrs, rdn/led 1f out, hard rdn ins last, hdd nr line: remains in gd heart: see 3077.
3271 **BRANSTON LUCY 7** [7] M Johnston 3-8-3 R Ffrench 7/4 FAV: 212243: 3 b f Prince Sabo - Softly Spoken ½   **58**
(Mummy's Pet) Prom, hard rdn 2f out, led over 1f out, sn hdd & no extra nr fin: bckd: reportedly claimed by
J Pearce for £7,000: prev with T J Etherington: see 3271.
2505 **TICK TOCK 41** [5] M Mullineaux 3-8-11 (VIS) F Norton 16/1: 220004: Led, hdd over 1f out & no   2   **61$**
extra: 6 wk abs, first time visor: see 1512, 1256.
3180 **UPPER CHAMBER 11** [8] 4-8-6 K Dalgleish (5) 33/1: -00005: Prom, outpcd fnl 2f: see 3144.   1¾   **50$**
3161 **BENNOCHY 13** [6] 3-8-7 O Pears 8/1: 504546: Reared start, chsd ldrs 4f: see 777.   ½   **51**
3275 **ROISTERER 7** [1] 4-8-8 A Culhane 6/1: 0007: Al outpcd rear: mod form.   2½   **43**
3271 **SWEET MAGIC 7** [3] 9-8-7 (t) G Duffield 33/1: 000008: Chsd ldr, drvn/btn over 1f out: see 1392 (AW).   1   **40**
8 ran   Time 59.60 (2.3)   (Mrs J Hazell)   T D Barron Maunby, N.Yorks.

3442
8.15 DURHAM MDN HCAP 3YO+ 0-70 (E)   **1m7f177y Good 50**   **-14 Slow**   **[65]**
£2884   £824   £412   3 yo rec 14lb

2879 **OLD FEATHERS 25** [4] J G FitzGerald 3-7-10 (47)(1oh) K Dalgleish (5) 3/1: 006001: 3 b g Hernando -   **54**
Undiscovered (Tap On Wood) Chsd ldrs 5f out, sn drvn, prog to lead 2f out, held on gamely ins last, drvn out:
well bckd: only mod form/unplcd prev: eff around a sharp 2m on gd grnd: handles a tight trk.
3167 **COCO LOCO 13** [5] J Pearce 3-7-11 (48) Dale Gibson 12/1: 006502: 3 b f Bin Ajwaad - Mainly Me   ¾   **53**
(Huntingdale) Keen/trkd ldrs, chsd wnr over 1f out, kept on well: clr rem: styd longer 2m trip: handles fast & gd.
3112 **SEND ME AN ANGEL 14** [1] S P C Woods 3-8-13 (64) G Duffield 5/1: 442263: 3 ch f Lycius - Niamh   7   **62**
Cinn Oir (King Of Clubs) Trkd ldrs, led over 6f out till over 2f out, btn 3f out: see 2902, 1997 & 1157.
3034 **ROVERETTO 18** [7] Mrs M Reveley 5-10-0 (65) A Culhane 15/8 FAV: 0/624: Held up, prog 7f out,   nk   **62**
drvn/outpcd fnl 2f: op 5/4: longer 2m trip on h'cap bow: see 3034 (12f).
3367 **SMUDGER SMITH 3** [3] 3-8-0 (51)(vis) J Bramhill 6/1: 464625: Led till 6f out, btn dist: qck reapp.   ¾   **47**
2490 **HERSELF 41** [6] 3-7-10 (47)(2oh) P M Quinn (3) 10/1: 060356: Strugg 5f out: abs: new stable.   8   **35**
3888) **MISS LACROIX 340** [8] 5-7-10 (33)(13oh) N Carter (7) 50/1: 0000-7: Chsd ldrs, drvn/btn 4f out: 5   **16**
8 wk jump abs, earlier won at M Rasen (h'cap, rtd 76h), eff at 2m1f on firm & gd/soft): only mod form on turf prev.
2681 **STREET WALKER 34** [2] 4-8-5 (42) F Norton 12/1: 400648: Trkd ldrs, btn 2f out: see 2370, 853 (11f).   ¾   **24**
2879 **STREAK OF DAWN 25** [9] 3-7-10 (47)(17oh) J McAuley 66/1: -00009: Held up, bhd 5f out: see 2624.   3   **26**
9 ran   Time 3m 30.90 (10.1)   (Marquesa de Moratalla)   J G FitzGerald Malton, N.Yorks.

FOLKESTONE
FRIDAY AUGUST 18TH   Righthand, Sharpish, Undulating Track

Official Going   GOOD TO FIRM. Stalls: Str Crse - Stands Side, Rnd Crse - Inside.

3443
2.20 EBF AUCT MDN 2YO (F)   **6f**   **Good/Firm 34**   **-01 Slow**
£2499   £714   £357

--   **SONATINA** [4] J W Payne 2-8-9 R Cochrane 11/2: 1: 2 b f Distant Relative - Son Et Lumiere   **88**
(Rainbow Quest) Trkd ldrs, qcknd to lead dist, ran on strgly: op 4/1: wng debut: 30,000gns Apr foal, half-sister
to 4 wnrs, incl a juv: eff at 6f, 7f is going to suit: acts on fast & a sharp/undul trk: runs well fresh, shld improve.
--   **PLEASURE DOME** [6] J M P Eustace 2-8-9 J Tate 6/1: 2: 2 b f Most Welcome - Hickleton Lady   1¾   **82**
(Kala Shikari) Cl-up, led 2f out till 1f out, not pace of wnr: tchd 8/1, bckd: 7,000gns Jan foal, half-sister
to a 6f winning juv, dam 7f/1m wnr: eff at 6f, bred to apprec 1m+: handles fast grnd & an undul track.
3098 **EXTRA GUEST 16** [1] M R Channon 2-8-9 Craig Williams 2/1 FAV: 242223: 2 b f Fraam - Gibaltarik   3   **73**
(Jareer) Trkd ldrs, boxed in & seemingly going well appr fnl 1f, styd on for 3rd one clr, ldrs had flown:
well bckd from 4/1: luckless filly, worth one more chance in this grade: see 2029.
2029 **ANNIE RUAN 61** [2] D Haydn Jones 2-8-9 A McGlone 6/1: -034: Sn led, hdd 2f out & onepace: op 7/2.   nk   **72**
3223 **ALPHAECA 9** [5] S Sanders 9/4: 55: Front rank, outpcd bef fnl 1f: bckd frm op 6/4, needs further.   ½   **76**
--   **DEAR PICKLES** [11] 2-8-9 G Baker (5) 33/1: 6: Wide, prom, no extra bef fnl 1f: Apr foal, with J Portman.   1   **68**
2227 **RED FANFARE 51** [8] 2-8-9 R Havlin 33/1: 007: Nvr a factor: 7 wk abs, see 2009.   nk   **67**
--   **EAST OF JAVA** [9] 2-9-0 N Callan 7/1: 8: Chsd ldrs 3f: tchd 14/1: 2,200gns May foal: half-brother   8   **56**
to a wnr abroad: sire a miler: with K Burke & unfancied.
3205 **TURBO BLUE 10** [7] 2-8-9 M Fenton 12/1: 009: Al bhd: needs a drop in grade, see 2227.   2½   **46**
--   **TARRANAKI KNIGHT** [3] 2-9-0 Paul Eddery 25/1: 0: Dwelt, nvr in it: 10th: 7,500gns Brief Truce colt.   1   **48**
2214 **BOSRA BADGER 52** [10] 2-9-0 N Pollard 11/1: 000: Speed till halfway: 7 wk abs.   2½   **41**
1667 **COPY CAT 77** [12] 2-8-9 D Harrison 50/1: 400: Speed 2f: 10th, 11 wk abs, routine test ordered, see 1197. 3   **27**
12 ran   Time 1m 13.1 (2.1)   (Mrs R A C Vigors)   J W Payne Newmarket.

3444
2.50 HEADLINE NURSERY HCAP 2YO (E)   **7f str**   **Good/Firm 34**   **-22 Slow**   **[79]**
£2856   £816   £408

2972 **SHINING OASIS 21** [3] P F I Cole 2-9-5 (70) P Dobbs (5) 5/1: -4351: 2 b f Mujtahid - Desert Maiden   **75**
(Green Desert) Trkd ldr, rdn appr fnl 1f, kept on gamely to lead line: winning h'cap bow: shwd lots of pace in 3
prev runs tho' apprec step up to 7f, get further on this evidence: acts on fast grnd: can force the pace, sharp trks.
2962 **EL MAXIMO 21** [1] M G Quinlan 2-9-7 (72)(tBL) T E Durcan 7/1: 326152: 2 b c First Trump - Kentucky shd   **76**

Starlet (Cox's Ridge) Rear but in tch, gd prog to lead 1f out, hard rdn & collared post: tchd 10/1: back to form
with t-strap & blnks & clr rem: carried top-weight & is a tough colt: see 2620 (C/D auct mdn).

3149 **FLUTED 13** [2] M R Channon 2-9-4 (69) Craig Williams 3/1 FAV: 40303: 2 ch c Piccolo - Champagne Grandy (Vaigly Great) Bhd, imprvd appr fnl 2f, led briefly bef fnl 1f, onepace: clr rem, stays 7f on fast grnd.	2	69
3128 **EMMA CLARE 14** [6] J A Osborne 2-8-11 (62) S Sanders 4/1: 00024: Prom, led halfway till ent fnl 2f, fdd.	6	52
*3216 **RIVER OF FIRE 9** [7] 2-9-1 (66)(vis)(6ex) J Tate 5/1: 0115: Led till halfway, sn btn: up in grade in second time visor but surely something amiss: see 3216 (sell nursery, made all).	6	46
2784 **ITS SMEE AGAIN 29** [5] 2-9-0 (65) R Cochrane 5/1: 4446: Trkd ldrs, wknd qckly 2f out: went out like a light on h'cap bow, unsuited by step up to 7f?: see 1870 (5f mdn).	shd	45
3029 **ALLTHEDOTCOMS 18** [4] 2-9-1 (66) J Quinn 16/1: 0467: Dwelt, in tch till 2f out: op 8/1, h'cap bow.	11	26

7 ran   Time 1m 28.1 (3.9)   (Elite Racing Club)   P F I Cole Whatcombe, Oxon.

3445	**3.20 GOMEZ HCAP 3YO+ 0-75 (E) 7f str Good/Firm 34 +03 Fast**			[69]
	£3024 £864 £432 3 yo rec 5 lb 2 horses went far side, rest stands side.			

2026 **TRIBAL PRINCE 61** [2] P W Harris 3-9-10 (70) M Fenton 12/1: 25-001: 3 b g Prince Sabo - Tshusick   76
(Dancing Brave) Mid-div stands side, eff 2f out, strong run under press ins last to get up line: 9 wk abs, jt
top-weight, first win, best time of day: dual '99 rnr-up (h'cap, rtd 74): eff at 7f, get 1m on this evidence:
acts on firm & hvy grnd, any trk, without visor: can carry big weights: runs well fresh, back to form.

3041 **RULE OF THUMB 18** [10] G L Moore 3-9-10 (70) I Mongan (5) 11/2: -00052: 3 ch g Inchinor - Rockin'   shd   75
Rosie (Song) Nvr far away stands side, chall dist, led 100y out, hdd post: tchd 10/1: game run, clrly gets 7f,
acts on fast & gd grnd & looks nicely h'capped: see 954.

2974 **FLYING PENNANT 21** [4] J M Bradley 7-8-1 (42rq)(bl))(2ow) J Tate 12/1: 610363: 7 gr g Waajib - Flying   ½   46
Beckee (Godswalk) Pushed along in tch stands side, prog to lead that group ent fnl 2f, hdd dist, held nr fin:
ran to best, likes sharp/undul trks: see 2427.

3253 **MISS MONEY SPIDER 8** [14] J M Bradley 5-7-13 (40) C Rutter 10/1: 000044: Overall ldr far   3   38
side, joined by stands side 2f out, no extra ent fnl 1f: stablemate 3rd & probably a sound effort: see 2840.

3030 **CLONOE 18** [12] 6-8-0 (41)(t) J Quinn 6/1: 000535: Chsd ldr far side thr'out, onepace bef fnl 1f.   2   35
*3294 **KNOBBLEENEEZE 7** [6] 10-8-0 (41)(vis) M Mathers (7) 8/1: 052416: Al around same pl stands side.   2   31
*3279 **WHO GOES THERE 7** [11] 4-9-3 (58)(6ex) D Harrison 7/1: 301617: Never better than mid-div stands   3   42
side: qck reapp with penalty, capable of better: see 3279.

3243 **REACHFORYOURPOCKET 9** [8] 5-8-7 (48) G Baker (5) 20/1: 001008: Chsd ldrs stands side till 2f out.   ¾   31
1834) **MOROCCO 437** [1] 11-8-9 (50) A Eddery (5) 33/1: 0006-9: Handy stands side 5f: reapp: unplcd for   2½   28
M Channon last term (claim h'cap, rtd 55): '98 Leicester wnr (h'cap, rtd 63): eff at 7f/1m on firm & gd/soft grnd.

3115 **ITS OUR SECRET 14** [7] 4-9-8 (63) S Sanders 12/1: 240050: Prom stands side, chsd ldr ent fnl 2f: 10th, op   4   33
8/1: poss unsuited by drop in trip but stable has been struggling all season: see 1279.

2978 **MAGIC BABE 21** [5] 3-8-13 (59) M Henry 10/1: 412450: Nvr dngrs stands side: 12th: much btr 1787.   0
*3046 **ROUGE 18** [9] 5-8-11 (52) N Callan 11/4 FAV: 13161P: Led stands side 4f, sn wknd, p.u.: hvly bckd   0
from 5/1: reportedly broke a blood vessel: see 3046.

2976 **Uzy 21** [3] 4-7-13 (38)(bl)(1ow) P Fitzimons (0) 40/1:   1038 **Polar Ice 112** [13] 4-9-10 (65) R Cochrane 14/1:
14 ran   Time 1m 26.4 (2.2)   (The Tribe)   P W Harris Ringshall, Bucks.

3446	**3.50 MOTORLINE NOV STKS 2YO (D) 5f Good/Firm 34 -12 Slow**	
	£2847 £876 £438 £219	

*3114 **THE TRADER 14** [2] M Blanshard 2-9-5 D Sweeney 1/1 FAV: 332211: 2 ch c Selkirk - Snowing (Tate   92
Gallery) Trkd ldrs, led bef fnl 1f, pushed out: well bckd: recent Nottingham wnr (mdn): eff at 5f, gets 6f: acts
on firm & soft grnd, any trk, up with the pace: improving.

*3278 **DELTA SONG 7** [1] G L Moore 2-8-8 (1ow) R Cochrane 5/1: 12: 2 b f Delta Dancer - Song Of Gold (Song)   ½   80
Led halfway, rallied under press & ch below dist, held towards fin: clr rem, qck reapp, tchd 9/1: fine run
in this better grade, prev with W Muir: eff at 5f, return to 6f will suit: acts on firm/fast: see 3278 (fill sell).

3358 **MISHKA 4** [4] Julian Poulton 2-8-12 M Roberts 12/1: 003: 2 b g Mistertopogigo - Walsham Witch (Music   3   74
Maestro) Shkn up in tch, switched appr fnl 1f, no impress: tchd 20/1: qck reapp: cld win a seller, see 3358, 2711.

3361 **ICE MAIDEN 4** [3] M R Channon 2-9-0 M Mathers (7) 6/4: -134: Pressed ldr, led halfway till ent   shd   76
fnl 2f, wknd: nicely bred: much btr in trip, too soon after 3361 (stks)?, see 970 (gd/soft).

3277 **MAGIC GEM 7** [5] 2-8-12 Paul Eddery 25/1: 055: Al last: qck reapp, see 3277.   7   54
5 ran   Time 1m 00.7 (2.3)   (Mrs C J Ward)   M Blanshard Upper Lambourn, Berks.

3447	**4.20 COCO THE CLOWN SELLER 3YO+ (G) 1m4f Good/Firm 34 -71 Slow**		
	£1897 £542 £271 3 yo rec 10lb		

*2785 **DUELLO 29** [7] M C Pipe 9-9-11 (vis) M Roberts 13/8 FAV: -33311: 9 b g Sure Blade - Royal Loft   51
(Homing) Waited with, hdwy appr fnl 1f, strong run under hands-&-heels ins last, got up line: well bckd, bght by
trainer for 3,000gns: hdles rnr-up since won at Bath (sell): '99 Leicester wnr (clmr, rtd 58, M Blanshard): '98
Nottingham wnr (h'cap, rtd 59): eff at 12/14f on any grnd, fibresand, any trk: best in sellers now & wears a visor.

3260 **FULL EGALITE 8** [5] B R Johnson 4-9-11 (bl) C Rutter 14/1: 012002: 4 gr g Ezzoud - Milva   shd   50$
(Jellaby) Chsd ldrs, prog to lead appr fnl 1f & went 3L clr, pshd out, jockey peeked over shoulder & got cght line:
clr rem, prob have held on with a more forceful ride: back to form nevertheless, acts on fast, soft grnd & equitrack.

3002 **OCEAN LINE 20** [1] G M McCourt 5-9-11 R Studholme (5) 4/1: 001203: 5 b g Kefaah - Tropic Sea   3   46
(Sure Blade) Led till bef fnl 1f, held on for 3rd: recent hdles rnr: just best at 10f: see 2587.

*2887 **ARTIC COURIER 25** [3] D J S Cosgrove 9-9-11 R Cochrane 5/2: 114414: Towards rear, prog to dspt   nk   45
3rd ins last, onepace: btr 2887 (sell h'cap).

1666 **OLD SCHOOL HOUSE 77** [2] 7-9-6 P Fitzsimons (5) 33/1: 000-05: Prom, no extra appr fnl 1f: 11 wk abs.   1¾   38
3244 **PIPS BRAVE 9** [8] 4-9-6 G Baker 6/1: 001506: In tch, outpcd fnl 2f: stiff task, longer trip.   ½   37
3263 **PICCALILLI 8** [4] 3-8-5 J Quinn 33/1: 606007: Trkd ldr, wknd under press 2f out: stiff task, see 682.   1½   29
3260 **WINSOME GEORGE 8** [6] 5-9-6 (vis) Paul Eddery 20/1: 405068: Trkd ldr, wknd under press 2f out.   shd   34$
8 ran   Time 2m 44.1 (12.6)   (T M Hely-Hutchinson)   M C Pipe Nicholashayne, Devon.

FOLKESTONE   FRIDAY AUGUST 18TH   Righthand, Sharpish, Undulating Track

3448
4.50 PIEROT HCAP 3YO+ 0-65 (F)   2m93y   Good/Firm 34   -04 Slow   [61]
£2373   £678   £339   3 yo rec 14lb

3186 **GOLD MILLENIUM** 11 [3] C A Horgan 6-8-11 (44) I Mongan(5) 8/1: 413631: 6 gr g Kenmare - Gold 45
Necklace (Golden Fleece) In tch, hdwy 6f out, chsd 2f out, led well ins last, pshd out: prev won at Warwick (mdn
h'cap): plcd last term (h'cap, rtd 43): eff at 12f, suited by step up to 2m: acts on fast & gd, sharp/undul trks.
3112 **HARD DAYS NIGHT** 14 [6] M Blanshard 3-7-12 (45)(9oh)(2ow) J Quinn 20/1: 646202: 3 b g Mujtahid - 1 44$
Oiche Mhaith (Night Shift) Prom, led 2f out, hard rdn & hdd cl home: back to form: acts on gd & fast.
3295 **LITTLE BRAVE** 7 [9] J M P Eustace 5-9-12 (59) J Tate 3/1 FAV: 514333: 5 b g Kahyasi - ½ 57
Littlemisstrouble (My Gallant) In tch, prog bef fnl 2f, kept on, nvr nrr: qck reapp, op 4/1: prob ran to best
tho' let ldrs get away somewhat & return to a more gall trk may suit: see 2763.
3241 **STAND ASIDE** 9 [13] Lady Herries 4-9-3 (50)(BL) R Cochrane 25/1: 000-54: Keen, chsd ldrs, left ½ 47
in lead first bend, hdd 2f out & no extra: tchd 10/1: handles fast.
2971 **FANDANGO DREAM** 21 [2] 4-8-5 (38) G Baker (5) 7/1: 441355: Held up, prog 5f out, styd on, no threat. nk 35
2763 **SIRINNDI** 30 [7] 6-8-13 (46) S W Kelly(3) 7/1: /05006: Bhd, late hdwy, nvr nrr: tchd 10/1: handles fast. nk 42
3255 **TULSA** 8 [10] 6-8-4 (37)(bl) N Pollard 5/1: 0-5527: Mid-div thr'out: op 7/2: back up in trip, btr 3255. 1¾ 31
3260 **BLAYNEY DANCER** 8 [8] 3-7-10 (43)(7oh) M Henry 20/1: 650038: Nvr a factor: tchd 33/1, stiffish task. 2½ 35
2953 **TREASURE CHEST** 21 [5] 5-9-5 (52)(vis) P Dobbs (5) 7/1: 405069: V slow away, al towards rear. hd 44
3201 **MARMADUKE** 10 [4] 4-9-9 (56)(vis) M Fenton 12/1: 660340: Held up, nvr dngrs: 10th, lngr trip, btr 3201. 3½ 45
3276 **SIPOWITZ** 7 [11] 6-9-3 (50) N Callan 14/1: 3/5030: Mid-div, fdd appr fnl 2f: 11th, qk reapp, up in trip. 14 29
2982 **NORTHERN FLEET** 21 [1] 7-10-0 (61) D Sweeney 14/1: 0-4500: Pulled hard prom, lost pl 6f out: 12th. 19 25
3125 **WHAT A CRACKER** 14 [12] 3-8-0 (47)(4ow) C Rutter 11/1: 000-60: Led & v keen, went v wide first _dist_ 0
bend & dropped to last after: tchd 14/1: 13th, see 3125.
13 ran   Time 3m 37.5 (6.2)   (Mrs L M Horgan)   C A Horgan Pulborough, W.Sussex.

NEWBURY   FRIDAY AUGUST 18TH   Lefthand, Flat, Galloping Track

Official Going   GOOD/FIRM. Stalls: Centre, except 7f Rnd - Outside.

3449
2.10 OXFORD FILLIES MDN 2YO (D)   6f str   Firm 07   -13 Slow
£5102   £1570   £785   £392

3090 **TEMPTING FATE** 16 [10] J W Hills 2-8-11 M Hills 11/10 FAV: -21: 2 b f Persian Bold - West Of Eden 95+
(Crofter): Waited with, prog to lead ent fnl 1f, sprinted clr, hands & heels: hvly bckd from 7/4: 27,000gns half-
sister to juv wnrs over 5f/1m: eff over a gall 6f on fast & firm grnd, 7f will suit: runs well fresh: useful &
progressive filly who deserves a step up in grade & can win more races.
-- **JACANA** [1] J H M Gosden 2-8-11 K Darley 11/4: -2: 2 ch f Woodman - Storm Teal (Storm Bird): 2½ 85+
Prom, ev ch 2f out, kept on ins fnl 1f, hands & heels: drifted from 6/4 on debut: first foal, dam unrcd but
from a gd family: sire a decent 2yo wnr: eff over a stiff 6f on firm, 7f will suit: improve & win soon.
-- **THERES TWO** [3] M R Channon 2-8-11 T Quinn 11/1: -3: 2 b f Ashkalani - Sudden Interest (Highest 1¾ 80
Honor): Chsd ldrs, kept on fnl 1f, not pace to chall on debut: mkt drifter: IR 35,000gns Feb foal: half-sister
to mid-dist wnr After The Blue: dam a dual wnr in France, sire a top class miler: sure to improve over further.
-- **ANOTHER SECRET** [5] M R Channon 2-8-11 L Newman 25/1: -0: 4 Rear, some late hdwy, not pace to ¾ 77
chall: racecourse bow: Apr foal, cost 18,000gns: dam unrcd but from a speedy family: sire a decent 6f/1m
performer: likely to apprec 7f/1m given time: will learn from this.
-- **PEARLY BROOKS** [4] 2-8-11 R Hughes 20/1: -5: Led till ent final 1f, wknd: debut, Apr foal: related 1 74
to sev wnrs, notably smart Pip's Pride: shwd gd speed here & not helped by bndgs coming loose over 1f out.
3090 **RICHENDA** [11] 2-8-11 Dane O'Neill 11/1: -0066: Prom till wknd 2f out: btr 3090. 1 71
2285 **TAKESMYBREATHAWAY** 49 [7] 2-8-11 M J Kinane 7/1: -67: Dwelt, rear, some late prog under a kind 2 65
ride, nvr nrr: tchd 10/1, 7 wk abs: better clearly expected, prob lost any ch at the start: see 2285.
-- **SALTWOOD** [9] 2-8-11 J Reid 11/1: -0: V slowly away, al bhd on debut: mkt drifter, unsettled at the 1¾ 60
start: Mar foal, half-sister to 10f scorer Shamrock City: dam a mid-dist wnr in France: mid-dist bred filly
who lost any ch at the start here: with B Hills & must be given another chance.
3187 **GONE WITH THE WIND** 11 [8] 2-8-11 R Hills 40/1: -009: Rear, no impress final 2f, eased: see 1782. 3 51
-- **ANN SUMMERS** [6] 2-8-11 Pat Eddery 16/1: -0: Rear, bhd final 1½f: fin 10th, debut: Jan foal, 4 39
dam only modest: sire a decent juv performer in the USA: with P Meehan.
-- **CELERITY** [2] 2-8-11 R Fitzpatrick 33/1: -0: Dwelt, recovered to chase ldrs 3f, wknd into last: debut: 7 19
cost 28,000gns: Apr foal, half-sister to a 10f wnr in France: dam won in France: with M Polglase.
11 ran   Time 1m 12.84 (1.24)   (Michael Kerr - Dineen & Partners)   J W Hills Lambourn, Berks.

3450
2.40 LISTED W'INGTON SINGER STKS 2YO (A)   7f str   Firm 07   -02 Slow
£12343   £3798   £1899   £949

*2692 **PRIZEMAN** 34 [2] R Hannon 2-8-11 R Hughes 8/13 FAV: -11: 2 b c Prized - Shuttle (Conquistador Cielo): 101
In tch, imprvd to lead 1½f out, ran on strongly, drvn out: well bckd from 4/5, fair juv time: debut wnr at York
(mdn auct): 30,000gns purchase: eff on gd & firm grnd, shld stay 1m: runs well fresh: smart, improving juv who holds Group race entries.
3156 **PERFECT SUNDAY** 13 [1] B W Hills 2-8-11 M Hills 8/1: -32: 2 br c Quest For Fame - Sunday Bazaar ½ 99
(Nureyef): Nvr far away, chall strongly final 2f, not pace of wnr cl-home: op 6/1: acts on fast & firm grnd:
v useful & bred to apprec further: muts win soon, see 3156.
*3051 **LUCAYAN CHIEF** 17 [5] S P C Woods 2-8-11 M J Kinane 6/1: -513: 2 b c With Approval - Little Lady Leah 1½ 96
(Shareef Dancer): Led till 1½f out, kept on fnl 1f: sound effort, acts on firm & gd/soft: see 3051.
3015 **SWING BAND** 19 [4] G B Balding 2-8-11 A Daly 9/2: -124: Trkd ldrs, ev ch 2f out, no extra inside last: 1½ 93
op 7/2: gd run in this better grade: see 3015, 2708.
3164 **FREEFOURINTERNET** 13 [3] 2-8-11 Pat Eddery 6/1: -35: Chsd ldrs, ev ch 2f out till dist, fdd: op 7/1: 1¼ 90
not disgrcd in this decent event, has shwn enough to win a mdn: see 3164.
5 ran   Time 1m 24.94 (0.64)   (Highclere Thor'bred Racing Ltd)   R Hannon East Everleigh, Wilts.

3451
3.10 VINEYARD RATED HCAP 3YO+ 0-100 (B)   1m3f   Firm 07 -31 Slow   [100]
£9309   £3531   £1765   £802   3yo rec 9lb

2995 **WESTENDER** 20 [3] W J Haggas 4-9-7 (93) R Hughes 11/4 FAV: 225021: 4 b g In The Wings - Trude   98
(Windwurf): Made all, held on well cl-home, all-out: well bckd: deserved win, rnr-up twice this term: '99 wnr
at Yarmouth (reapp, mdn) & Ripon (h'cap, rtd 89): eff at 10/12f, shld stay further: acts on firm & gd/soft grnd,
handles a sharpish or stiff/gall trk: can come from bhd or force the pace & has run well fresh: tough/consistent.
3088 **CRACOW** 16 [2] J W Hills 3-8-5 (86) M Hills 4/1: 431052: 3 b c Polish Precedent - Height Of Secrecy   nk   90
(Shirley Heights): Nvr far away, chall strongly final 3f, just btn in a cl fin: acts on firm & gd/soft grnd.
3339 **ORMELIE** 5 [6] J H M Gosden 5-9-6 (92) K Darley 4/1: 1-0533: 5 b h Jade Hunter - Trolley Song   1¾   94
(Caro): Chsd ldrs, onepcd inside final 1f: qck reapp: sound effort: see 3339, 2707 (1m here).
3131 **FATHER JUNINHO** 14 [1] A P Jarvis 3-8-11 (92) M J Kinane 4/1: 523354: Waited with, effort 3f out,   1½   92
kept on but not pace to chall: clr of rem: consistent, but rcd a shade too freely here: see 2596.
3166 **CHEMS TRUCE** 13 [4] 3-8-1 (82) Martin Dwyer 8/1: 000345: Nvr nr to chall: btr 3166 (1m).   4   76
*2917 **MANTUSIS** 23 [5] 5-9-6 (92) Pat Eddery 9/2: 214016: In tch, ev ch till wknd 3f out: puzzling after 2917.   7   76
6 ran   Time 2m 20.07 (4.27)   (Khalifa Dasmal)   W J Haggas Newmarket.

3452
3.40 GR 3 HUNGERFORD STKS 3YO+ (A)   7f64y rnd   Firm 07 +26 Fast
£21000   £8050   £4025   £1925   3yo rec 5lb

3087 **ARKADIAN HERO** 16 [5] L M Cumani 5-9-2 J P Spencer 5/2: 404161: 5 ch h Trempolino - Careless Kitten   120
(Caro): Held up travelling well, swtchd & qcknd to lead dist, sprinted right away for an impress victory: hvly
bckd from 10/3, v fast time: earlier won at Newmarket (Gr 3): '99 wnr here at Newbury & Newmarket (List), also
fine 2L 3rd in Gr 1 Sprint Cup (rtd 119): eff at 6/7.3f on gd & firm grnd, handles soft, has tried 1m: acts on
any trk, likes a stiff one, esp Newbury & Newmarket: runs v well fresh: high class entire with a good turn of
foot: looks sure to win more Gr races around 7f, hds for the Challenge Stks at Nemarket next.
2066 **CAPE TOWN** 59 [1] R Hannon 3-8-8 R Hughes 13/2: -10302: 3 gr c Desert Style - Rossaldene   3½   109
(Mummy's Pet) Chsd ldrs, bmpd 2f out, kept on well fnl 1f but no ch with impress wnr: nicely bckd, 8 wk abs:
gd eff on today's faster grnd, acts on firm & soft: eff at 7f/1m: see 1623, 969.
764 **SIEGE** 146 [7] Saeed bin Suroor 4-8-13 J Reid 6/1: -15103: 4 br g Indian Ridge - Above Water   nk   108
(Reference Point): Early ldr, remnd prom & regained lead 3f out till dist, no extra: long abs: fine run back
after a break over a trip short of his best: sharper next time over 1m in similar company, see 764.
2997 **SHOWBOAT** 20 [8] B W Hills 6-8-13 (BL) M Hills 16/1: 030304: Trkd ldrs, prog & ev ch over 1f out,   shd   108$
no extra: better run in first time blnks & best around 1m: see 657
3107 **OMAHA CITY** 15 [3] 6-8-13 K Darley 33/1: 005035: Chsd ldrs, onepace final 1½f: highly tried, rating   ¾   106$
is best treated with caution: better off in h'caps & loves Goodwood, see 3107.
*2997 **TILLERMAN** 20 [4] 4-8-13 M J Kinane 2/1 FAV: -35016: Held up, effort 2f out, nvr nr ldrs: hvly bckd: 1   104
up in grade after showing an impressive turn of foot in 2997 (val h'cap).
2087 **UMISTIM** 58 [6] 3-8-11 Dane O'Neill 9/2: -16527: Led after 3f till 3f out, wknd: nicely bckd, 8 wk abs.   5   97
3132 **TUMBLEWEED RIDGE** 14 [2] 7-9-2 (t) M Tebbutt 7/1: 31304P: In tch till wknd over 3f out, p.u. &   17   63
dismounted fnl 1f: op 12/1: reportedly lost action, but subs fine: see 2226, 2070.
8 ran   Time 1m 26.36 (u1.44)   (Lindy Regis & Mrs Sean Kelly)   L M Cumani Newmarket.

3453
4.10 FURLONG CLUB HCAP 3YO 0-100 (C)   1m2f   Firm 07 -23 Slow   [107]
£7202   £2216   £1108   £554

2596 **KOOKABURRA** 37 [2] B J Meehan 3-9-4 (97) Pat Eddery 5/2 JT FAV: 046341: 3 b c Zafonic - Annoconnor   106
(Nureyev): Trkd ldrs racing keenly, went on 5f out, clr dist, pushed out: well bckd, decisive win: earlier won
at Doncaster (mdn), subs 3rd at R Ascot (val h'cap): plcd sev times in '99 (rtd 92, nurs h'cap): eff forcing the
pace at 1m/10f, acts on firm & gd/soft, handles soft: handles any trk, runs well fresh: imprvg, a useful colt.
3417 **AFTER THE BLUE** 1 [3] M R Channon 3-7-10 (75)(5ex)(4oh) D Kinsella(7) 13/2: 245122: 3 b c Last Tycoon 4   76
- Sudden Interest (Highest Honor): Bhd, imprvd 2f out, fin well but no ch with wnr: nicely bckd, the op 5/1:
rnr-up at Epsom 24hrs prev over 12f: see 3417, 3290.
*2499 **THUNDERING SURF** 41 [4] J R Jenkins 3-8-4 (83) S Whitworth 5/2 JT FAV: 5-0013: 3 b c Lugana Beach 3½   79
- Thunder Bug (Secreto) Mid-div, imprvd & ch 2f out, sn onepcd: hvly bckd, 6 wk abs: slightly disapp after 2499.
*2703 **STAGE DIRECTION** 33 [7] J H M Gosden 3-8-8 (87)(t) K Darley 7/2: -4414: Prom till fdd final 3f.   7   73
3061 **OPTIMAITE** 17 [5] 3-9-7 (100) G Hind 11/1: 310505: Chsd ldrs, ch 3f out, sn wknd: top weight.   2   83
3267 **FRONTIER** 8 [1] 3-8-9 (88) R Hughes 6/1: 1-5336: Led till halfway, hmpd ent str, wknd qckly final   2   68
2f: did not get the run of the race today: see 3267.
6 ran   Time 2m 05.87 (3.07)   (Mrs Susan Roy)   B J Meehan Lambourn, Berks.

3454
4.40 LEVY BOARD HCAP 3YO+ 0-90 (C)   1m5f61y   Firm 07 -55 Slow   [88]
£6760   £2080   £1040   £520   3yo rec 11lb

2852 **MASAMADAS** 27 [5] N J Henderson 5-9-10 (84) J Reid 4/1: 330/21: 5 ch g Elmaamul - Beau's Delight   90
(Lypheor): Waited with, prog to lead ent fnl 1f, ran on strongly, rdn out: fit from hdles, 99/00 wnr at Stratford
(h'cap, stays 3m2f on firm & hvy, rtd 131h): 98/99 hdle wnr at Newbury & Worcester: back on the Flat in '98 won
at Windsor (h'cap, rtd 84): eff arnd 13.3f on firm, soft grnd & fibresand: handles any trk: in gd form.
3058 **ST HELENSFIELD** 17 [3] M Johnston 5-9-12 (86) M Hills 3/1: 201102: 5 ch g Kris - On Credit (No   1½   89
Pass No Sale): Tried to make all, collared ent fnl 1f, not pace of wnr: sound front running eff under top weight.
991 **WILCUMA** 118 [1] P J Makin 9-9-9 (83) A Clark 11/1: 155303: 9 b g Most Welcome - Miss Topville   1¾   84
(Top Ville): Waited with, imprvd 3f out, no impress ins fnl 1f: long abs, 5L clr rem: 9yo, enjoys easy grnd.
*3013 **NAJJM** 19 [2] J L Dunlop 3-8-10 (81) R Hills 6/4 FAV: 3-6514: Chsd ldr till wknd 2f out: hvly bckd   5   74
from 5/2: better expected, not stay this lngr 13.3f trip?: much btr 3013 (12f).
3173 **HANNIBAL LAD** 12 [4] 4-9-9 (83) T G McLaughlin 7/2: 441355: Chsd ldrs 10f, gradually wknd: nicely   2   73
bckd, swtg: earlier in grand form: see 3173, 2674.
5 ran   Time 2m 53.43 (8.33)   (Thurloe Thor'breds IV)   N J Henderson Lambourn, Berks.

NEWBURY   FRIDAY AUGUST 18TH   Lefthand, Flat, Galloping Track

3455	5.10 JACK COLLING APPR HCAP 3YO+ 0-75 (E) 6f str Firm 07 -13 Slow	[73]
	£3152 £970 £485 £242 3yo rec 3lb	

3243 **ABSOLUTE FANTASY 9** [9] E A Wheeler 4-8-5 (50)(bl) D Kinsella (5) 11/2: 202421: 4 b f Beveled -
Sharp Venita (Sharp Edge): Nvr far away, went on over 1f out, sn clr, styd on strongly, rdn out: earlier won
at Brighton (mdn h'cap), also plcd sev times: eff at 6/7f, acts on firm, soft & equitrack: **54**
handles any trk, likes Brighton: suited by blnks: well rdn by D Kinsella today.

2777 **MUJAS MAGIC 29** [7] Mrs N Macauley 5-8-6 (51)(vis) C Catlin (5) 10/1: 501002: 5 b m Mujadil -   2 **51**
Grave Error (Northern Treat): Mid-div, styd on well final 2f, not reach wnr: sound run, see 2415.

2861 **TOBLERSONG 26** [4] Mrs L Stubbs 5-7-11 (42)(vis) Kristin Stubbs (5) 10/1: 420403: 5 b g Tirol -   hd **42**
Winsong Melody (Music Maestro): Dwelt, imprvd halfway, fin well but too late: see 2411, 958.

3113 **FAIRY PRINCE 14** [5] Mrs A L M King 7-9-1 (60) Jonjo Fowle (3) 6/1: 510044: Front rank, led halfway   hd **60**
till over 1f out, no extra: tried blnks in 3113, see 2192.

3294 **SCISSOR RIDGE 7** [10] 8-8-1 (46) R Brisland 12/1: 060505: Chsd wnr till onepcd final 2f: see 2303.   ¾ **43**

2944 **RED DELIRIUM 22** [6] 4-8-10 (55) Michael Doyle(5) 8/1: 000506: Nvr better than mid-div: out of form,   1½ **48**
subs coming down the weights: see 746 (reapp).

3294 **LAW COMMISSION 7** [8] 10-9-6 (65) R Thomas (5) 9/4 FAV: 601427: Dwelt, nvr nr ldrs: well bckd   nk **55**
from 9/2: lost all chance at the turn today: 10yo, see 3294 (7f).

2976 **CALANDRELLA 21** [3] 7-7-10 (41)(4oh) Claire Bryan 14/1: 063308: Led till halfway, fdd fnl 1f.   1¾ **26**

2761 **CLAN CHIEF 30** [2] 7-9-1 (60) A Beech 6/1: 0/0209: Speed 4f, wknd: now with M Blanshard.   3 **36**

3005 **SOVEREIGN STATE 20** [1] 3-9-13 (75) Lindsey Rutty (7) 12/1: 105460: Prom 4f, wknd into last.   nk **50**
10 ran   Time 1m 12.80 (1.20)   (The Red Square Partnership)   E A Wheeler Whitchurch On Thames, Oxon.

NEWMARKET   FRIDAY AUGUST 18TH   Righthand, Stiff, Galloping Track

Official Going   GOOD/FIRM. Stalls: Far Side, except 12f - Stands Side.

3456	5.35 GREENWOOD ELLIS CLAIMER 3YO (E) 1m str Good/Firm 28 +02 Fast	
	£3523 £1084 £542 £271	

3081 **SEA SQUIRT 16** [14] M Johnston 3-8-13 D Holland 11/10 FAV: 416231: 3 b g Fourstars Allstar -   **71**
Polynesian Goddess (Salmon Leap) Held up, plenty to do over 2f out, styd on well appr fnl 1f to lead ins last,
all out in a driving finish: hvly bckd, fair time: earlier scored at Carlisle (class stks): suited by a stiff
1m, stays 12f: can front run or come from bhd on firm & soft grnd: relished drop into claim grade.

3261 **PINHEIROS DREAM 8** [11] B J Meehan 3-8-4(1ow) Pat Eddery 4/1: 310462: 3 ch f Grand Lodge -   hd **61**
Nikki's Groom (Shy Groom) Dwelt, held up bhd, hdwy over 1f out to lead ins last, sn hdd, just held in
a driving fin: well clr of rem but 1ow prob cost her the race: C/D wnr in this company in 2345.

3021 **FINERY 19** [2] C A Dwyer 3-8-6 T E Durcan 14/1: 023003: 3 ch g Barathea - Micky's Pleasure (Foolish   6 **53**
Pleasure) Set pace, rdn & hdd ins last, no extra: gd run with visor discarded back at 1m: see 2284, 1502.

2489 **LIVELY MILLIE 41** [13] R M Beckett 3-7-11 J Lowe 25/1: 0-0004: Dwelt, held up, eff & switched left   shd **43**
over 2f out, nrst fin: 6 wk abs: fair run at these weights with visor discarded: see 2489, modest form.

3226 **CALDEY ISLAND 9** [12] 3-8-1 G Sparkes (7) 40/1: 000005: Held up, rdn & btn 2f out: see 2331, 1545.   2½ **42**

3117 **DISTANT FLAME 14** [8] 3-7-10 M Baird 25/1: 000056: In tch, eff to chall over 1f out, sn wknd: mod.   2½ **32**

3266 **FOSTON FOX 8** [5] 3-7-10 (bl) A Polli (3) 25/1: 060057: In tch, wknd over 2f out: needs sell h'caps.   5 **22**

3236 **SOBER AS A JUDGE 9** [10] 3-8-2 G Bardwell 40/1: 003008: Cl-up, wknd 2f out: see 2413 (seller).   ¾ **26**

3236 **ALABAMA WURLEY 9** [6] 3-8-7 (vis) D McGaffin (5) 16/1: 001049: Prom, wknd over 2f out: best 2413.   3 **25**

3049 **NORTHERN TRIO 18** [4] 3-8-6 R Havlin 40/1: -00000: In tch, wknd over 2f out: 10th, modest.   5 **14**

2842 **WINDFALL 27** [9] 3-9-0 (VIS) S Finnamore (5) 33/1: 030000: Slow away & al bhd: 11th, visored.   4 **14**

-- **FEEL THE STEEL** [3] 3-8-1 N Carlisle 40/1: 0: Slow away, al bhd: 12th, with Mrs A Johnson.   7 **0**

3146 **DIANEME 13** [1] 3-8-7 D O'Donohoe 6/1: 450020: Iron broke soon after start, t.o. in last.   dist **0**
13 ran   Time 1m 39.28 (2.08)   (M J Pilkington)   M Johnston Middleham, N.Yorks.

3457	6.05 H&K COMMISSIONS HCAP 3YO+ 0-80 (D) 6f Good/Firm 28 -02 Slow	[80]
	£4953 £1524 £762 £381 3 yo rec 3 lb	

3297 **RUSHCUTTER BAY 7** [8] P L Gilligan 7-9-11 (77) D Harrison 7/4 FAV: -26021: 7 br g Mon Tresor -   **83**
Liwy Bren (Lidhame) Made all, kept on well for press ins last, just held on, drvn out: hvly bckd under top-
weight: '99 wnr at Windsor (class stks, rtd 90): '98 Newmarket scorer (h'cap, rtd 84): suited by 6f now on
any trk: acts on firm & gd, without a visor: best up with/forcing the pace & can carry big weights:
took advantage of a handy mark & only lightly rcd this term.

3037 **TECHNICIAN 18** [3] E J Alston 5-8-13 (65)(bl) T E Durcan 13/2: 123222: 5 ch g Archway - How It   shd **70**
Works (Commanche Run) Prom, eff to chall ins last, kept on for press, just held: tough & progressive.

3341 **IVORY DAWN 5** [4] K T Ivory 6-9-10 (76) C Carver (3) 8/1: 015003: 6 b m Batshoof - Cradle Of Love   1¾ **76**
(Roberto) In tch, eff & switched left over 1f out, kept on ins last, no dngr: qk reapp: tough: see 2761 (sharp).

3123 **FULL SPATE 14** [1] J M Bradley 5-9-5 (71) Pat Eddery 6/1: 410304: In tch, eff over 1f out, sn onepace.   ¾ **69**

2813 **PETARGA 28** [10] 5-9-5 (71) P Robinson 11/1: 00-005: Prom, no impress over 1f out: on a fair mark.   1 **66**

3200 **OSCAR PEPPER 10** [6] 3-8-1 (56) D O'Donohoe 9/2: 203036: Held up, short of room when hdwy 2f   ½ **49**
out, nvr dngrs: see 3200.

3115 **MAJOR REBUKE 14** [2] 3-8-6 (60)(vis)(1ow) D Holland 20/1: 000207: Nvr a factor: see 2786, 1786.   shd **54**

2747 **KUWAIT ROSE 30** [7] 4-8-13 (65) D McGaffin (5) 16/1: 540258: Slow away, sn handy, wknd 2f out.   ½ **57**

2925 **BRIMSTONE 23** [5] 5-8-1 (53) P Doe 25/1: 06-009: Keen, trkd wnr till wknd over 1f out: see 268.   ½ **43**

3119 **DETECTIVE 14** [9] 4-8-3 (55) J Lowe 16/1: 00-500: Slow away, al bhd: fin last, see 2833.   3 **36**
10 ran   Time 1m 12.78 (1.78)   (Treasure Seekers Partnership)   P L Gilligan Newmarket.

3458 **6.35 HOPKINS HOMES MDN 2YO (D) 1m str Good/Firm 28 -61 Slow**
£4065 £1251 £625 £312

2563 **ROSIS BOY 38** [3] J L Dunlop 2-9-0 Pat Eddery 11/8 JT FAV: 21: 2 b c Caerleon - Come On Rosi (Valiyar) Cl-up, eff well over 1f out, styd on to lead cl-home, rdn out: bckd tho' op 8/11: Apr foal, brother to a 7f/1m scorer: dam 6f wnr: stays a stiff 1m, shld get further: acts on gd & gd/firm grnd & a stiff trk. **85**
2956 **TAABEER 21** [4] E A L Dunlop 2-9-0 R Hills 11/8 JT FAV: 02: 2 b c Caerleon - Himmah (Habitat) With ldr, led over 2f out, edged right over 1f out & collared cl-home, just btn: bckd: stays 1m on gd/firm. *nk* **83**
2708 **DENNIS OUR MENACE 33** [5] S Dow 2-9-0 P Doe 6/1: 033: 2 b c Piccolo - Free On Board (Free State) Prom, eff for press over 1f out, kept on same pace: ran to form of 2708 & stays 1m: shld be plcd to win. *1½* **80**
3121 **TEDSTALE 14** [6] L M Cumani 2-9-0 J P Spencer 12/1: 04: Led over 5f, wknd fnl 1f: shld stay 1m. *½* **79**
3268 **ARMAGNAC 8** [1] 2-9-0 P D'Arcy 14/1: 404255: Waited with, keen, brief effort over 2f out, onepace. *¾* **77**
-- **WHEN IN ROME** [2] 2-9-0 M Hills 33/1: 6: Sn bhd, modest late gains on debut: Mar first foal: dam mid-dist/hdle scorer: will need 10f+ next term. *1¾* **73**
6 ran Time 1m 43.52 (6.32) (Wafic Said) J L Dunlop Arundel, W.Sussex.

3459 **7.05 R&W PUBLICATIONS FILLIES MDN 2YO (D) 7f str Good/Firm 28 -39 Slow**
£4065 £1251 £625 £312

2285 **ASHLINN 49** [6] S Dow 2-8-11 P Doe 7/4 FAV: -21: 2 ch f Ashkalani - Always Fair (Alydar) Made all, clr dist, styd on well, pushed out: well bckd, 7 wk abs: bckd tho op 1/1: Apr foal, sire top-class miler: eff at 6f on fast, apprec this step up to 7f: handles a stiff trk, runs well fresh: useful, rate higher. **90**
-- **NAFISAH** [2] B Hanbury 2-8-11 R Hills 13/2: -2: 2 ch f Lahib - Alyakkh (Sadler's Wells) Prom, chsd wnr under a kind ride fnl 1f, nvr nrr: Apr foal, half sister to 1m wnr Hawas & 12f scorer Bashashah: dam scored over 1m, sire a top-class miler: eff at 7f on fast grnd, 1m will suit: sure to improve & win soon. *¾* **87+**
2172 **MIN MIRRI 55** [4] M R Channon 2-8-11 R Havlin 16/1: -453: 2 b f Selkirk - Sulitelma (The Minstrel) Rcd keenly in rear, styd on well fnl 1f, nvr plcd to chall: 7 wk abs: eyecatching h'cap qual run: stays 7f & acts on fast grnd: spot on next time & one to keep in mind in a nursery h'cap: see 1957 (debut). *1½* **84+**
2748 **PRIYA 30** [8] C E Brittain 2-8-11 P Robinson 7/2: -46224: Chsd ldrs, fdd ins fnl 1f: see 2748 (7f). *1½* **81**
-- **SCARPE ROSSE** [7] 2-8-11 Pat Eddery 7/2: -5: Rear, short of room 2f out, ran on, nvr nrr: debut: Jan foal, cost 180,000gns: half sister to sev wnrs, incl useful Irish 10f performer Red Affair: sire a top-class mid-dist performer: not much luck today: plenty of promise & will improve as she steps up in trip. *nk* **80+**
-- **MISSOURI** [9] 2-8-11 T E Durcan 25/1: -6: Waited with, late hdwy, nvr nrr on debut: IR 16,000gns purchase: Feb foal, dam a 12f wnr: likely to apprec further given time: with M Tompkins. *1½* **77**
-- **GOLDEN FORTUNA** [1] 2-8-11 D Holland 25/1: -7: Not pace to chall on debut: May foal, dam styd mid-dists: sire a top-class miler: J Hills filly. *¾* **75**
3108 **ENGLISH HARBOUR 15** [5] 2-8-11 M Hills 14/1: -08: Chsd wnr 4f, grad wknd: see 3108. *3* **69**
-- **ANTIPODES** [3] 2-8-11 D Harrison 25/1: -9: Speed till halfway, wknd into last: Apr foal, half sister to sev wnrs, incl 6/7f performer Matelot: dam a French sprinter: with J Dunlop & shld improve given time. *½* **68**
9 ran Time 1m 28.57 (4.67) (R E Anderson, J M Connolly & W Thornton) S Dow Epsom, Surrey

3460 **7.35 DAVID SMITH FILLIES HCAP 3YO+ 0-85 (D) 7f str Good/Firm 28 -22 Slow [84]**
£4810 £1480 £740 £370 3yo rec 5lb

*2885 **RAVINE 25** [2] R Hannon 3-8-10 (71) R Hills 13/2: 6-0411: 3 ch f Indian Ridge - Cubby Hole (Town And Country) Chsd ldr till went on dist, styd on well, drvn out: nicely bckd: recent Windsor scorer (h'cap): eff at 6/7f, has tried 1m: acts on fast: likes to run up with/force the pace: lightly raced & improving. **76**
3269 **MOONLIGHT SONG 8** [8] W Jarvis 3-8-0 (61) J Quinn 11/4: 001222: 3 b f Mujadil - Model Show (Dominion) Early ldr, rem prom, styd on well ins last but not pace of wnr: bckd: tough & consistent, see 3269. *1½* **63**
3063 **COMPRADORE 17** [7] M Blanshard 5-8-9 (65) P Robinson 7/1: 103003: 5 b m Mujtahid - Keswa (King's Lake) Rear, styd on well fnl 1f, nvr nrr: promising run, see 1467. *1* **65**
3076 **WILDFLOWER 16** [1] R Charlton 3-8-8 (69) Pat Eddery 9/1: 10004: Led after 1f till dist, no extra. *shd* **69**
2999 **ROUGE ETOILE 20** [5] 4-7-10 (52)(3oh) G Bardwell 16/1: 006005: Rcd keenly & prom, outpcd 2f out, rallied fnl 1f: rcd too keenly for own good: better effort & shld be plcd to win: see 2999. *¾* **50**
1174 **NOUF 104** [6] 4-9-6 (76) D McGaffin (5) 16/1: 002066: Stumbled start, imprvd 2f out, btn fnl 1f: long abs: prob lost chance at the start: see 831. *2½* **69**
3118 **GWENDOLINE 14** [3] 3-9-9 (84) D Harrison 7/4 FAV: -2127: Trkd ldrs, rdn & btn fnl 1f: hvly bckd, wandered under pressure: well bckd: lightly raced & better expected after 3118 (1m here). *1¾* **73**
2918 **CIBENZE 23** [9] 3-8-4 (65) R Havlin 10/1: 602608: Nvr a factor in last: btr 2699. *½* **53**
8 ran Time 1m 27.42 (3.52) (Lord Carnarvon) R Hannon East Everleigh, Wilts

3461 **8.05 EBF TESCO HCAP 3YO+ 0-90 (C) 1m4f Good/Firm 28 Inapplicable [89]**
£6760 £2089 £1040 £620 3yo rec 10lb

3159 **WARNING REEF 13** [4] E J Alston 7-7-12 (59) P Doe 7/2 JT FAV: 333121: 7 b g Warning - Horseshoe Reef (Mill Reef) Trkd ldrs, imprvd to lead dist, rdn clr fnl 1f: well bckd: earlier won at Kempton (h'cap): plcd sev times in '99 (h'caps, rtd 65): '98 wnr at Carlisle, Sandown & Ascot (h'caps, rtd 65): suited by 10/12f, stays 14f on firm, gd/soft & f/sand, any trk: consistent & well h'capped, stable have a fine record with southern raiders. **67**
3058 **MARDANI 17** [7] M Johnston 5-9-12 (87) D Holland 7/2 JT FAV: -00002: 5 b g Fairy King - Marmana (Blushing Groom) Set pace till 2f out, readily outpcd by wnr: nicely bckd: apprec return to 12f: see 3058. *5* **87**
3173 **MORGANS ORCHARD 12** [6] A G Newcombe 4-8-0 (61) J Quinn 5/1: 552023: 4 ch g Forest Wind - Regina St Cyr (Doulab) Chsd ldr, led 2f out till dist, no extra: see 3173 (sharp trk). *nk* **60**
3014 **SPEED VENTURE 19** [2] S P C Woods 3-7-13 (70) N Pollard 12/1: 225504: Rear, imprvd 2f out, onepcd fnl 1f: clr of rem: unproven over 12f: see 3014. *shd* **69**
3173 **GREYFIELD 12** [5] 4-8-10 (71) Pat Eddery 4/1: -45045: Hdwy from rear 1f out, sn no impress: see 3173. *6* **61**
*3282 **LADY JO 7** [1] 4-7-10 (57)(5ex) J Lowe 4/1: 060516: Prom 10f, fdd: much btr 3282. *3* **42**
1850 **NAUTICAL STAR 69** [3] 5-10-0 (89) M Hills 6/1: 2-0007: Prom till 2f out, wknd: 10 wk abs: see 1850. *16* **54**
7 ran Time Not Taken (Valley Paddocks Racing Ltd) E J Alston Longton, Lancs.

RIPON SATURDAY AUGUST 19TH Righthand, Sharpish Track

Official Going GOOD/FIRM Stalls: Straight course - stands side, Rnd course - inside

3462 2.20 CATHEDRAL MDN 3YO+ (D) 5f Good/Firm 22 -24 Slow
£3471 £1068 £534 £267 3 yo rec 2 lb

| -- | SANTIBURI LAD [9] A Berry 3-9-0 C Lowther 16/1: 1: 3 b g Namaqualand - Suggia (Alzao) | | 70 |

Dwelt/outpcd early, hung right/prog fnl 2f, rdn & styd on well to lead well ins last: debut, op 12/1: eff at 5f,
6f shld suit: acts on fast ground & a sharpish track: runs well fresh: open to further improvement.
2919 **AMAZED 24** [1] I A Balding 3-8-9 K Darley 4/6 FAV: 6-42: 3 ch f Clantime - Indigo (Primo Dominie) hd 64
Dwelt, sn rdn, prog to chall fnl 1f, styd on well, just held: h'caps & 6f+ shld now suit: handles fast.
2919 **DAVEYS PANACEA 24** [4] R D Wylie 3-8-9 P Bradley (5) 5/1: 2533: 3 ch f Paris House - Pampoushka 1¾ 60
(Pampabird) Prom, led over 2f out till well ins last, no extra: eff at 5/6f on firm & fast: h'cap company shld suit.
3170 **FIRST VENTURE 13** [5] C N Allen 3-9-0 (bl) J Weaver 9/2: 223004: Bhd, late gains/nrst fin: needs 6f+. 2 60
3035 **ZILUTTE 19** [6] R D Wylie 3-9-0 G Parkin 25/1: 45: Prom till over 1f out: progressed from debut: see 3035. ¾ 58
1710 **T GS GIRL 76** [3] 3-8-9 O Pears 14/1: 040-06: Led halfway, sn held: 11 wk abs, op 10/1: unplcd 3½ 44
in '99 (rtd 60, fillies mdn, R Hannon): has tried 7f prev: low grade h'cap company will suit better.
1771 **EXECUTIVE GHOST 73** [7] 3-9-0 K W Marks 25/1: 07: Chsd ldrs, hung right/btn 1f out: abs, new stable. ¾ 47
3203 **KERRIDGE CHAPEL 11** [8] 3-8-9 (bl) G Duffield 50/1: -00608: Sn behind: mod form. 4 32
1678 **PETERS PRINCESS 77** [2] 3-8-9 J Carroll 25/1: 650-69: Chsd ldrs 3f: mod form. 1¼ 29
-- **TRINITY BAY** [10] 3-8-9 J Edmunds 25/1: 0: Went right start, sn bhd: 10th: debut. 12 6
10 ran Time 1m 00.1 (2.3) (E A Brook) A Berry Cockerham, Lancs

3463 2.50 HORN BLOWER COND STKS 2YO (C) 6f Good/Firm 22 - 40 Slow
£5783 £2138 £1069 £486 Raced centre - stands side

*3184 **HEALEY 12** [3] J D Bethell 2-9-2 J Weaver 6/1: 11: 2 ch c Dr Devious - Bean Siamsa 94
(Solinus) Dwelt, in tch/keen, outpcd halfway, rdn/strong run from over 1f out to lead well ins last, won going away:
op 5/1: slow time: earlier made a winning debut here at Ripon (C/D, stks): eff at 6f, 7f+ sure to suit (sire a
Derby wnr): acts on fast & a sharpish trk, likes Ripon: has run well fresh: progressive, win again over further.
*3245 **PETONGSKI 10** [4] D W Barker 2-8-11 F Lynch 4/5 FAV: 212: 2 b g Petong - Madam Petoski (Petoski) 1¼ 85
Led/dsptd lead, hung right throughout, hdd ins last & no extra: hvly bckd: acts on fast & gd: see 3245 (auct mdn).
*3168 **FAIRGAME MAN 13** [5] A Berry 2-9-0 J Carroll 9/2: -3113: 2 ch c Clantime - Thalya (Crofthall) ½ 86
Led/dsptd lead, bmpd with rnr-up sev times, rdn/hdd & no extra ins last: op 7/2: ran to form of 3168 (nursery).
2344 **MIDNIGHT ARROW 49** [2] I A Balding 2-8-11 K Darley 100/30: -15004: Sn rdn/outpcd, btn 2f out: abs. 6 72
3286 **ANTHONY ROYLE 8** [1] P Bradley (5) 33/1: 6655: Sn drvn/bhd: mdn, highly tried: see 2664. 14 45
5 ran Time 1m 13.70 (3.7) (www.Clarendon Racing.Com) J D Bethell Middleham, N Yorks

3464 3.25 GT ST WILFRID HCAP 3YO+ 0-105 (B) 6f Good/Firm 22 -00 Slow [104]
£24375 £7500 £3750 £1875 3 yo rec 3 lb Raced both sides, first three home stands side

*3222 **WILLIAMS WELL 10** [4] M W Easterby 6-7-13 (75)(bl) Dale Gibson 14/1: 522211: 6 ch g Superpower - 82
Catherines Well (Junius) Al prom stands side, rdn/led over 1f out, styd on well for press: earlier won h'caps at
Nottingham & Pontefract: '99 wnr at Carlisle & Catterick (h'caps, rtd 70 at best): eff at 5/6f: acts on firm &
soft, handles any trk, likes Catterick: well suited by blnks & a gd weight carrier: tough & in the form of his life.
.3152 **BLUE MOUNTAIN 14** [1] R F Johnson Houghton 3-8-13 (92) K Darley 5/1 JT FAV: 221102: 3 ch c ½ 96
Elmaamul - Glenfinlass (Lomond) In tch stands side, drvn/styd on well fnl 2f, not pace of wnr: useful/progressive.
*3297 **BAHAMIAN PIRATE 8** [9] D Nicholls 5-8-8 (84) F Norton 10/1: 122213: 5 ch g Housebuster - Shining nk 87
Through (Deputy Minister) Trkd ldrs stands side trav well, ch 2f out, onepace/held ins last: in great heart.
-3152 **BON AMI 14** [21] A Berry 4-8-13 (89) P Bradley (5) 5/1 JT FAV: 346024: Rdn chasing leaders far ¾ 90
side, drvn/hung left ins last, styd on: first home on far side: jockey given a 2-day ban for careless riding: bckd.
3152 **CADEAUX CHER 14** [6] 6-8-7 (83) N Pollard 12/1: 001005: Prom stands, onepace in last: gd run. hd 83
3176 **ANTHONY MON AMOUR 13** [20] 5-7-11 (73) Clare Roche (7) 20/1: 101356: Dsptd overall lead far side 4f. 1 71
3183 **BOLDLY GOES 12** [19] 4-8-5 (81)(bl) T Williams 16/1: 310067: Chsd ldrs far side, rdn/held/hmpd near fin. shd 79
3183 **AMARANTH 12** [22] 4-8-7 (83) R Cody Boutcher 6/1: 012658: Chsd ldrs far side 5f: bckd: see 1654. nk 80
3136 **ZUHAIR 15** [16] 7-8-3 (79) O Pears 16/1: 033159: Chsd ldrs far side, rdn/staying on to chall when shd 76+
badly hmpd 1f out, not recover: much closer with a clr run & remains one to keep in mind: see 3091.
3152 **CRYHAVOC 14** [7] 6-9-3 (93) Alex Greaves 14/1: 102000: Chsd ldrs far side 4f: 10th: see 2432. ¾ 88
3322 **PIPS MAGIC 7** [14] 4-8-7 (83) A Culhane 20/1: 001000: In tch twds centre, keeping on without 1 76
threatening when hmpd fnl 1f: 11th: can rate higher: see 3037.3322
    FURTHER OUTLOOK 7 [5] 6-9-7 (97) G Carter 10/1: 253640: Led stands side till over 1f out, fdd: 12th. ½ 88
*3176 **AMBITIOUS 13** [13] 5-9-0 (90) C Catlin (7) 16/1: 141010: Chsd ldrs far side 4f: 13th: see 3176 (5f). 3½ 72
3322 **XANADU 7** [12] 4-8-2 (78) J Mackay 20/1: 124360: Dwelt, sn led/dsptd lead far side, btn 2f out: 14th.shd 60
3136 **DOUBLE OSCAR 15** [2] 7-7-10 (72) T Hamilton (7) 33/1: 321000: Chsd ldrs stands side 4f: 15th. 1 52
3183 **FRIAR TUCK 12** [15] 5-8-5 (81) K Dalgleish (5) 14/1: 301130: Chsd ldrs twds centre 4f: 16th: btr 3183. shd 61
+2859 **GUINEA HUNTER 28** [18] 4-9-10 (100) J Carroll 14/1: 010010: Al rear far side: 17th: btr 2859 (6f). 1 78
3183 **ATLANTIC VIKING 12** [10] 5-8-6 (82)(bl) G Duffield 16/1: 004040: Prom stands 4f: 18th: see 1861. ½ 58
*1763 **SUTTON COMMON 73** [3] 3-7-10 (75) Iona Wands 33/1: -20210: Sn outpcd stands side: 19th: abs. ¾ 49
3152 **ALASTAIR SMELLIE 14** [8] 4-8-0 (76) J Bramhill 14/1: 050400: Dwelt, al twds rear: 20th: see 1173. 1¼ 47
3322 **TARAS GIRL 7** [11] 3-7-10 (75) P Fessey 40/1: 000000: Sn outpcd: 21st: needs softer grnd: see 2568. nk 45
3322 **TADEO 7** [17] 7-9-3 (93) J Weaver 16/1: -03000: Led far side 1f, btn 2f out: 22nd: see 2310. nk 62
22 ran Time 1m 11.3 (1.3) (Mr K Hodgson & Mrs J Hodgson) M W Easterby Sheriff Hutton, N Yorks

3465 4.00 EBF FILLIES HCAP 3YO+ 0-80 (D) 1m2f Good/Firm 22 -03 Slow [68]
£6864 £2112 £1056 £528 3 yo rec 8 lb

3024 **SUMMER SONG 20** [1] E A L Dunlop 3-10-0 (76) G Carter 1/1 FAV: 311131: 3 b f Green Desert - High 84
Standard (Kris) Held up, prog to lead over 2f out, sn rdn/duelled with rnr-up, drvn ins last & prevailed on line, all
out: well bckd: earlier won at Windsor, Folkestone (h'caps) & Redcar (class stks): landed a private stakes event at
Newmarket in '99 (rtd 79): eff btwn 1m/10f on fast & gd/soft, prob handles any trk: v tough/genuine & progressive.
*3054 **BOLLIN ROBERTA 18** [3] T D Easterby 4-9-8 (62) J Carroll 9/2: 205312: 4 b f Bob's Return - Bollin shd 69
Emily (Lochnager) Led till over 2f out, drvn & styd on gamely fnl 2f, just held: clr rem: eff at 1m/10f: battled

1066

RIPON SATURDAY AUGUST 19TH Righthand, Sharpish Track

on most bravely here & can find another race on this evidence: see 3054 (8.5f).

3217 **SEEKING UTOPIA** [2] S P C Woods 3-9-2 (64) N Callan 14/1: 040P03: 3 b f Wolfhound - Sakura **10 60**
Queen (Woodman) Prom, rdn/btn 2f out: little encouragement of late: see 2023, 727.

*2774 **EUROLINK ARTEMIS 30** [4] J L Dunlop 3-9-13 (75) K Darley 11/4: 43514: Trkd ldrs, btn 2f out: **6 62**
better expected after 2774 (auct mdn).

3082 **COSMIC SONG 17** [5] 3-8-1 (49) K Dalgleish (5) 15/2: 144605: Cl up halfway, btn 2f out: btr 1722 (g/s). **5 29**
5 ran   Time 2m 05.8 (2.5)   (Maktoum Al Maktoum)   E A L Dunlop Newmarket

---

3466   4.35 TATTERSALLS AUCT MDN 2YO (E)   6f   Good/Firm 22 -30 Slow
£4371   £1345   £672   £336

3055 **LOVE THING 18** [4] R A Fahey 2-7-12 (VIS) R Ffrench 10/1: -601: 2 b g Phountzi - Devils Dirge (Song) **70**
Made virtually all, styd on strongly ins last, rdn out: op 8/1: half sister to smart sprinter Superior Premium:
appr this step up to 6f, 7f could suit: acts on fast: improved by forcing tactics today in first time visor.

2828 **EAGLES CACHE 29** [3] A Berry 2-8-5 J Carroll 10/1: 436262: 2 b c Eagle Eyed - Cache (Bustino) **2 70**
Al prom, rdn/styd on well ins last, al held by wnr: op 7/1: return to 7f shld suit on this evidence: see 1838, 1550.

3184 **PURE SHORES 12** [10] M Johnston 2-8-5 J P Spencer 3/1 FAV: 43: 2 b c Mt Livermore - Symphony Lady **½ 75**
(Theatrical) Al prom, drvn/kept on onepace fnl 1f: hvly bckd: acts on fast grnd: see 3184.

3009 **PRINCE PYRAMUS 20** [11] C Grant 2-8-3 T Hamilton (7) 8/1: -44: Prom, held 1f out: see 3009. **1¼ 63**

-- **LUMIERE DU SOLEIL** [9] 2-8-2 G Carter 11/2: 5: Mid-div, outpcd halfway, kept on fnl 1f, no threat: **nk 61**
op 8/1: Tragic Role filly, Apr foal, cost 10,500gns: half-sister to smart 7f performer Lots Of Magic: dam a 7f juv
wnr: looks sure to relish 7f+, will improve for this intro & shld rate more highly.

3187 **LADY WARD 12** [8] 2-8-2 Dale Gibson 11/2: 036: Prom, onepace fnl 2f: op 4/1: see 3187, 2653. **nk 60**

1294 **ARRAN MIST 96** [7] 2-7-12 Kimberley Hart 16/1: 037: Mid-div, not pace to chall: op 14/1, abs: see 1294. **¾ 54**

3268 **GOT ALOT ON 9** [1] 2-8-3 O Pears 33/1: 008: Chsd ldrs 4f: mod form prev. **shd 59**

3055 **GILLS DIAMOND 18** [14] 2-8-2 Iona Wands 20/1: 359: Chsd ldrs 4f: prev with J J O'Neill. **¾ 56**

2730 **WONDERGREEN 32** [5] 2-8-3 G Parkin 20/1: 600: Mid-div at best: 10th: see 2360 (5f). **1¼ 54**

-- **MIDSHIPMAN** [15] 2-8-3 K Dalgleish (5) 25/1: 0: Sn rdn mid-div, nvr a threat: 11th: cheaply bought **2 49**
March foal, brother to two winners abroad: dam a winner abroad as a 3/4yo.

-- **OUR INDULGENCE** [12] 2-8-3 D O'Donohoe 20/1: 0: Al twds rear: 12th: Prince Of Birds gelding, **2½ 42**
a first foal: dam a maiden, sire an Irish 2000 Guineas wnr: with T D Easterby.

3127 **Just Missed 15** [2] 2-8-0 J McAuley 25/1:   3308 **Ferndown 7** [16] 2-8-2 P Fessey 50/1:

2692 **Darwin Tower 35** [6] 2-8-3 J Fanning 33/1:   -- **Live In Lover** [13] 2-8-5 Dean McKeown 16/1:
16 ran   Time 1m 13.1 (3.1)   (Giles W Pritchard Gordon)   R A Fahey Butterwick, N Yorks

---

3467   5.05 SAFFIE JOSEPH HCAP 3YO 0-90 (C)   1m4f60y   Good/Firm 22 +03 Fast   [93]
£7020   £2160   £1080   £540

*2967 **MICKLEY 22** [1] J D Bethell 3-8-11 (76)(vis) J Weaver 4/1: 536311: 3 b g Ezzoud - Dawsha (Slip **82**
Anchor) Made all, rdn over 2f out, styd on strongly & in command ins last under hands & heels riding: earlier made
all to land a Thirsk h'cap: '99 Musselburgh (auct mdn) & Chester wnr (nurs, rtd 86): suited by 12f nowadays, may
get further: acts on firm, soft & any trk: has run well fresh: suited by blnks/vis: well suited by forcing tactics.

2837 **ORIGINAL SPIN 28** [5] J L Dunlop 3-9-6 (85)(BL) K Darley 15/8 FAV: -21122: 3 b f Machiavellian - Not **4 85**
Before Time (Polish Precedent) Handy, drvn 2f out, held ins last: tried blnks, ran creditably: consistent.

*2897 **GOLD QUEST 25** [3] Sir Michael Stoute 3-9-7 (86) F Lynch 7/2: 523313: 3 ch c Rainbow Quest - My **¾ 85**
Potters (Irish River) Prom, drvn/held by wnr 1f out: op 3/1: see 2897.

3415 **SANTIBURI GIRL 2** [4] J R Best 3-8-7 (72) A Polli (3) 7/2: 001124: Chsd ldrs, held 2f out: qck reapp. **hd 70**

3270 **ROYAL MINSTREL 9** [2] 3-9-2 (81) Dale Gibson 15/2: 4-3145: Prom, outpcd fnl 2f: btr 906 (sft). **nk 78**
5 ran   Time 2m 35.8 (2.3)   (Www.Clarendon Racing.Co.Uk)   J D Bethell Middleham, N Yorks

---

SANDOWN SATURDAY AUGUST 19TH Righthand, Galloping Track, Stiff Finish

Official Going   GOOD (GOOD/SOFT places). Stalls: Sprint - Far Side; 14f - Outside; Rem - Inside.

3468   2.05 TONI & GUY SELL NURSERY HCAP 2YO (E)   7f rnd   Good 43 -75 Slow   [79]
£3250   £1000   £500   £250

3307 **MISS PROGRESSIVE 7** [1] N Tinkler 2-7-13 (49)(1ow) C Rutter 6/1: 000251: 2 b f Common Grounds - **54**
Kaweah Maid (General Assembly) Keen, cl up, led over 1f out, drvn out: no bid: Feb foal: suited by 7f on
any trk: acts on gd & fibresand: looked genuine here, suited by selling grade.

3216 **IVANS BRIDE 10** [4] G G Margarson 2-8-4 (54)(1ow) S Sanders 12/1: 064062: 2 b f Inzar - Sweet **1½ 55**
Nature (Classic Secret) Hld up, eff over 3f out, ev ch 2f out, wandered under press dist, onepace: stays 7f.

3100 **KALUKI 17** [2] W R Muir 2-9-7 (72) T Quinn 7/2: 342033: 2 ch c First Trump - Wild Humour (Fayruz) **1¼ 70**
Led till over 2f out, onepace over 1f out: ran to form of 3100 under top-weight: plcd again.

3216 **MISSING A BIT 10** [7] J A Osborne 2-7-11 (48)(1ow)(4oh) J Quinn 14/1: 44554: Keen, hld up, eff & not **1½ 43**
clr run 2f out, onepace: prob stays 7f: see 3216.

2723 **SEL 32** [5] 2-8-10 (61)(bl) R Hughes 15/8 FAV: 35125: Handy, hdwy to chall over 3f out, switched **½ 55**
left 2f out, wknd: well bckd: jockey received a 5-day irresponsible riding ban: btr 2723.

2949 **BOBANVI 22** [6] 2-7-10 (47)(1oh) G Bardwell 6/1: 540036: Nvr a factor: btr 2949 (a/w). **¾ 39**

3216 **ASTAIREDOTCOM 10** [3] 2-8-2 (53) P Doe 8/1: -45047: Hld up, hdwy to lead over 2f out till over 1f **1 43**
out, wknd qckly: not stay 7f? btr 3216.
7 ran   Time 1m 34.64 (8.24)   (J P Hardiman)   N Tinkler Langton, N Yorks

---

3469   2.40 LISTED ATALANTA STKS 3YO+ (A)   1m rnd   Good 43 -02 Slow
£14820   £4560   £2280   £1140   3 yo rec 6 lb

3104 **OUT OF REACH 16** [3] B W Hills 3-8-8 T Quinn 6/1: -52141: 3 b f Warning - Well Beyond (Don't Forget **111**
Me) Handy al trav best, led over 2f out, rdn clr appr fnl 1f, unchall: nicely bckd: earlier won at Newmarket
(rtd h'cap): won sole '99 start, at Newbury (mdn, rtd 86): stays a stiff 1m well, further shld suit: acts on
fast, hvy & likes stiff trks: has run well fresh: smart, shld win a Gr race if reproducing this.

SANDOWN   SATURDAY AUGUST 19TH   Righthand, Galloping Track, Stiff Finish

3104 **MOSELLE 16** [9] W J Haggas 3-8-8 B Marcus 10/1: 201362: 3 b f Mtoto - Miquette (Fabulous Dancer)   5   102
In tch, eff & edged right over 2f out, kept on same pace: useful, caught a smart sort: see 3104.

*2769 **ROSSE 31** [8] G Wragg 3-8-8 M Roberts 9/2: -41513: 3 ch f Kris - Nuryana (Nureyev)   shd   102
Hld up, eff over 2f out, kept on well up the hill: stays a stiff 1m & well worth a try over further on this form.

3301 **CLARANET 7** [10] K Mahdi 3-8-8 Paul Eddery 16/1: 000254: Led till 2f out, onepace: see 3104 (sharp).   1½   99

2167 **PLEASURE CENTER 56** [5] 3-8-8 J Quinn 14/1: 4-1405: In tch, eff 3f out, no impress: abs, see 2167.   nk   98

*2585 **CAYMAN SUNSET 38** [4] 3-8-8 S Sanders 13/2: 16: Hld up, eff over 2f out, no impress: stiff task.   1½   95

*3089 **AEGEAN DREAM 17** [7] 4-9-0 R Hughes 9/1: 433117: Nvr a factor: needs h'caps as in 3089.   5   86

2597 **BEDAZZLING 38** [6] 3-8-8 P Robinson 7/2 FAV: 0-0148: Hld up, eff over 2f out, wknd: best 2597.   ¾   84

3104 **MY HANSEL 16** [11] 3-8-8 D Harrison 9/1: 3-0109: Prom, wkng when hmpd over 2f out: best 2274.   6   74

4289} **PENANG PEARL 315** [2] 4-9-0 J P Spencer 5/1: 3241-0: Hld up, btn over 3f out: reapp: '99 wnr at   7   62
Windsor (reapp, h'cap), Kempton (h'cap) & Ascot (Listed, rtd 104): '98 rnr-up for M Quinn (rtd 70): eff at
1m/10f on any trk: acts on firm & soft grnd: tough, consistent & progressive last term.

10 ran   Time 1m 42.6 (3.6)   (K Abdulla)   B W Hills Lambourn, Berks

---

3470 3.10 GR 3 SOLARIO STKS 2YO (A)   7f rnd   Good 43   -29 Slow
£18000   £6900   £3450   £1650

2613 **KINGS IRONBRIDGE 37** [7] R Hannon 2-8-11 R Hughes 10/1: -2151: 2 b c King's Theatre - Dream Chaser   105
(Record Token) Chsd ldr, led 1f out, drvn out: Mar foal: half brother to wnrs over sprint trips/1m: dam 6f wnr:
earlier won at Newmarket (mdn): stays a stiff 7f well on fast, stiff trk: runs well fresh: useful & improving.

*3121 **STORMING HOME 15** [4] B W Hills 2-8-11 M Roberts 9/1: -012: 2 b c Machiavellian - Try To   ½   104
Catch (Shareef Dancer) Hld up, eff over 2f out, short of room over 1f out, switched right ins last, kept on, just
btn: acts on gd & fast: gd run stepped up in class & 1m is sure to suit: lightly raced & can win again.

*2966 **BARKING MAD 22** [6] M L W Bell 2-8-11 M Fenton 12/1: 316213: 2 b c Dayjur - Avian Assembly   1¼   101
(General Assembly) Led, sn clr, hdd dist, no extra: useful front running effort: see 2966.

2363 **DAYGLOW DANCER 47** [2] M R Channon 2-8-11 S Whitworth 33/1: -1324: Hld up, eff 2f out, sn no   3   95
impress: useful run after 7 wk abs stepped up to 7f: see 2363.

*2613 **VACAMONTE 37** [3] 2-9-0 T Quinn 1/4 FAV: 15: Hld up, eff 2f out, sn btn: hvly bckd: looked   1¾   94
a colt of great potential on debut in 2613 (bt this wnr, fast grnd) & must have another chance.

*2916 **LOYAL TYCOON 24** [5] 2-8-11 P Doe 33/1: 316: Hld up, eff 2f out, sn wknd: stiff task, see 2916.   1¾   87

-- **EASTWELL MANOR** [1] 2-8-11 R Brisland 100/1: 7: Dwelt, bhd, eff 3f out, wknd 2f out on debut: 17   53
Mar foal: half brother to a 10/12f wnr: bred to apprec 1m+ in time & shld be more sensibly placed next time.

7 ran   Time 1m 31.45 (5.05)   (T A Johnsey)   R Hannon East Everleigh, Wilts

---

3471 3.45 WILLIAM HILL HCAP 3YO+ 0-90 (C)   1m2f   Good 43   -03 Slow   [90]
£9750   £3000   £1500   £750   3 yo rec 8 lb

3060 **POLISH SPIRIT 18** [1] B R Millman 5-9-4 (80) J P Spencer 6/1: 030601: 5 b g Emarati - Gentle Star   87
(Comedy Star) In tch, hdwy to lead over 2f out, kept on gamely for driving ins last: earlier won at Windsor
(h'cap, crse rec), Pontefract (class stks), Sandown & Ascot (h'caps): '99 wnr at Windsor (h'cap, rtd 63): '98
Warwick wnr: eff at 1m, stays 10f on any trk, likes Windsor & Sandown: handles fast, likes gd & hvy: has run
well fresh: most tough & progressive, being aimed at the 9f Cambridgeshire.

3060 **ULUNDI 18** [5] Lady Herries 5-10-0 (90) R Hughes 5/1: 300252: 5 b g Rainbow Quest - Flirt (Lyphard)   ½   96
Hld up, hdwy trav well 2f out, rdn & kept on fnl 1f but wnr had more: clr rem & a v useful run under a big weight.

3166 **SWEET REWARD 14** [3] J G Smyth Osbourne 5-8-5 (66)(1ow) M Fenton 5/1: 440353: 5 ch g Beveled -   4   66
Sweet Revival (Claude Monet) Hld up, eff 2f out, kept on some pace over 1f out: ran to his mark: see 2527.

*3110 **JUNIKAY 16** [7] R Ingram 6-8-10 (72) M Roberts 9/2 JT FAV: 320414: Hld up, eff over 2f out,   2½   68
no extra: shade btr 3110 (sharp trk).

*3336 **FAHS 6** [10] 8-9-9 (85) T Quinn 9/2 JT FAV: 012115: Hld up, eff over 2f out, sn wknd: well bckd   2½   77
but prob best at around 12f now: in fine form earlier, see 3336.

3224 **FANTAIL 10** [4] 6-8-8 (70)(vis) D Harrison 20/1: /00066: In tch, rdn & wknd 2f out: see 3122.   4   56

2696 **TONIGHTS PRIZE 35** [9] 6-9-1 (77) S Sanders 5/1: 5-1467: Handy, wknd over 2f out: btr 2696, 2190.   ½   62

3060 **LOCOMBE HILL 18** [2] 4-9-6 (82) J Quinn 25/1: -30308: Led 3f out, sn hdd & wknd: see 1474.   2½   63

1635 **PRINCE DU SOLEIL 79** [6] 4-8-13 (75) Paul Eddery 20/1: -00009: Al bhd: 11 wk abs, bckd.   1   54

3147 **AL GHABRAA 14** [8] 3-8-8 (78) S Whitworth 14/1: -65000: Keen, led till 3f out, wknd: fin last.   11   39

10 ran   Time 2m 08.7 (4.6)   (Mrs Izabel Palmer)   B R Millman Kentisbeare, Devon

---

3472 4.20 SUNLEY HCAP 3YO+ 0-80 (D)   1m6f   Good 43   -25 Slow   [80]
£5200   £1600   £800   £400   3 yo rec 12lb

2856 **MAGIC COMBINATION 28** [3] B J Curley 7-8-13 (65) J P Spencer 9/4 FAV: /1-451: 7 b g Scenic - Etage   72
(Ile de Bourbon) In tch, hdwy to lead on bit 2f out, sn clr, easily: val 5L+, well bckd: recent unplcd hdle
rnr: last term won here at Sandown (val Imperial Cup, rtd 123h, stays 2m4f on gd & hvy): won sole '99 Flat
start, at Galway (h'cap, rtd 55): eff over 12f/2m on fast & soft grnd: likes a gall trk, esp Sandown.

*3231 **KING FLYER 10** [7] H J Collingridge 4-9-3 (69)(t) J Quinn 7/2: 052112: 4 b g Ezzoud - Al Guswa   1¾   70
(Shernazar) Hld up, eff over 2f out, kept on ins last but flattered by losing margin: in fine form.

3201 **REDOUBLE 11** [6] J Akehurst 4-8-8 (60) S Sanders 6/1: -02233: 4 b g First Trump - Sunflower Seed   ¾   60
(Mummy's Pet) Cl up, led briefly over 3f out, onepace: mdn after 26 but picking up place money: clr rem, see 3201.

3014 **ABLE NATIVE 20** [1] R W Armstrong 3-7-13 (63)(bl) P Doe 20/1: 021004: Hld up, hdwy to lead over   12   49
3f out, onepace: longer trip, best 2217.

2984 **MARAHA 21** [5] 3-8-13 (77) T Quinn 9/2: 0-4325: Prom, wknd over 2f out: see 2984.   3½   58

1203 **CHALCEDONY 103** [2] 4-8-3 (55) R Mullen 14/1: 404036: Bhd, eff 4f out, sn no impress: with G L Moore.   ½   35

3186 **ELAANDO 12** [4] 5-8-12 (64) M Roberts 25/1: 3/0-07: Led till over 3f out, wknd: see 3186.   10   32

3122 **IL PRINCIPE 15** [8] 6-8-2 (54) Paul Eddery 20/1: 000008: Al bhd: likes soft, see 3122, 89.   ¾   21

3001 **TOTAL DELIGHT 21** [9] 4-10-0 (80)(vis) R Hughes 15/2: 412009: Al bhd: losing his way, see 2305.   9   35

9 ran   Time 3m 04.51 (9.51)   (Mrs B J Curley)   B J Curley Newmarket

3473   4.50 GRAND VAC RTD HCAP 3YO+ 0-100 (B)   5f   Good 43   +04 Fast   [107]
£8700   £3300   £1650   £750   3 yo rec 2 lb

3059 **SEE YOU LATER** 18 [10] Major D N Chappell 3-8-12 (93) D Harrison 12/1: 633001: 3 b f Emarati -   **97**
Rivers Rhapsody (Dominion) Cl up, led over 1f out, drvn out: won debut last term, at Sandown (fill mdn, rtd
92 at best): suited by 5f, just stays 6f: acts on gd/fm & gd: handles a stiff trk.
+3183 **LAGO DI VARANO** 12 [2] R M Whitaker 8-8-7 (86)(bl) J P Spencer 10/1: 530012: 8 b g Clantime   1   **87**
- On The Record (Record Token) Prom, outpcd 2f out, rallied well ins last, just held: in fine form.
3016 **DORCHESTER** 20 [11] Sir Mark Prescott 3-8-5 (86)(2oh) S Sanders 5/1: 000053: 3 b g Primo Dominie   shd   **87**
- Penthouse Lady (Last Tycoon) Cl up, eff to chase wnr 1f out, onepace: on a fair mark & has won at Doncaster.
3322 **SAPHIRE** 7 [6] C B B Booth 4-8-7 (86) S Whitworth 5/1: 565024: In tch, eff over 1f out, kept   hd   **86**
on same page: one to keep close tabs on when the grnd comes up soft: see 3322.
*3016 **MAGIC RAINBOW** 20 [9] 5-8-7 (86) M Fenton 11/2: 006515: In tch, eff over 1f out, onepace.   1   **83**
3322 **SUNLEY SENSE** 7 [3] 4-8-7 (86)(3oh) R Mullen 16/1: 002006: Led till over 1f out, no extra: see 2676.   1   **80**
3152 **SARTORIAL** 14 [1] 4-9-7 (100) T Quinn 9/2: -14107: Dwelt, nvr a factor: best 1173 (6f, gd/firm).   1   **91**
3335 **SEVEN NO TRUMPS** 6 [12] 3-8-13 (94) R Naylor (7) 25/1: 000308: Dwelt, nvr a factor: qk reappb.   1½   **81**
3303 **AWAKE** 7 [4] 3-9-4 (99) Paul Eddery 9/1: 203149: Al bhd: all 3 wins at 6f, see 3303.   ½   **85**
1531 **PASSION FOR LIFE** 84 [5] 7-8-9 (88) P Doe 12/1: 1-1000: In tch, wknd over 1f out: 10th, abs.   2   **68**
3016 **DASHING BLUE** 20 [7] 7-9-4 (97) R Hughes 8/1: -06000: Slow away, al bhd: last, see 2496.   5   **65**
11 ran   Time 1m 01.54 (1.94)   (Rex L Mead)   Major D N Chappell Pulborough, W Sussex

3474   5.25 DOWNTOWN FILLIES MDN 3YO (D)   1m rnd   Good 43   -21 Slow
£3900   £1200   £600   £300

3179 **MARRAKECH** 13 [4] P W Harris 3-8-11 T Quinn 5/2: -41: 3 ch f Barathea - Nashkara (Shirley Heights)   **91**
In tch, hdwy to lead over 1f out, drvn clr & flashed tail: half sister to sev wnrs: stays 1m well, further
will suit: acts on gd grnd & on stiff trk: useful type.
3190 **WOOLFE** 12 [5] J H M Gosden 3-8-11 J Quinn 5/4 FAV: 332: 3 ch f Wolfhound - Brosna (Irish River)   13   **70**
Led over 3f out till over 1f out, outpcd by wnr: well bckd: ran to form of 3190.
1537 **IPANEMA BEACH** 84 [3] J W Hills 3-8-11 S Whitworth 10/1: 6-03: 3 ch f Lion Cavern - Girl From   1½   **67**
Ipanema (Salse) Hld up, onepace under hands & heels fnl 2f: 3 month abs & shld prove sharper in h'caps now.
3048 **SPRING GIFT** 19 [1] K Mahdi 3-8-11 Paul Eddery 12/1: -64: Hld up, rdn 3f out, onepace: needs 10f+.   ½   **66**
3289 **CATALONIA** 8 [6] R Mullen 5/1: 65-W5: Unruly stalls, prom, wknd 3f out: see 3289.   1½   **63**
2262 **BLINDING MISSION** 52 [7] 3-8-11 J P Spencer 11/2: 0-0306: Led till over 3f out, wknd: abs, best 2086.   5   **53**
3272 **FLAVIA** 8 [2] 3-8-11 S Sanders 33/1: 667: Al bhd: see 3272.   6   **39**
7 ran   Time 1m 44.13 (5.13)   (Millennium Crossing)   P W Harris Aldbury, Herts

Official Going   GOOD/SOFT (GOOD Places). Stalls 5f/6f - Centre, 1m/2m - Inside, 1m2f/1m4f - Outside.

3475   5.50 FULLERS MOOR NURSERY HCAP 2YO (D)   5f   Good/Soft 69   -25 Slow   [90]
£4023   £1238   £619   £309   Those in centre (low numbers) appeared favoured

2698 **TIME MAITE** 35 [1] M W Easterby 2-8-1 (63) P Hanagan (7) 10/1: 313531: 2 b g Komaite - Martini   **70**
Time (Ardoon) Prom, wide, rdn bef fnl 2f, narrow lead dist, held on well: op 8/1: earlier won at Newcastle (clmr):
eff at 5/6f: acts on good & gd/sft grnd, prob handles hvy & fibresand, gall trks: best up with/forcing the pace.
*3264 **EFFERVESCE** 9 [2] M A Buckley 2-8-9 (71) A Culhane 15/2: 46012: 2 b f Sri Pekan - Arctic   nk   **77**
Winter (Briartic) Led, und press appr fnl 1f, hdd dist, ev ch held nr fin: op 6/1: improving, see 3264.
3143 **VENDOME** 14 [3] J A Osborne 2-8-11 (73) F Norton 11/1: 00033: 2 b c General Monash - Kealbra Lady   ¾   **77**
(Petong) Trkd ldrs, rdn appr fnl 1f, kept on, unable to chall: op 8/1, h'cap bow: jockey rec a 1-day whip ban:
handles fast & gd/sft grnd: see 3143.
3252 **ROXANNE MILL** 9 [4] M D I Usher 2-8-8 (70) R Fitzpatrick 14/1: 5034: With ldrs & ev ch till onepace   nk   **73**
ins last: sound h'cap bow & clr of rem: handles fast & gd/sft grnd: sharper trk may suit.
2152 **BANJO BAY** 57 [6] 2-8-11 (73) P M Quinn 33/1: 5305: Slow away, chsd ldrs halfway till bef dist.   3½   **69**
3145 **FENWICKS PRIDE** 14 [9] 2-9-1 (77) J Mackay (5) 14/1: 533266: Rear, switched 1f out & kept on: try 6f?   hd   **73**
3165 **HUMES LAW** 14 [8] 2-8-13 (75) T E Durcan 12/1: 046107: Bhd on stands rail, kept on fnl 1f, nvr dngrs.   nk   **70**
*2668 **KARITSA** 35 [7] 2-8-12 (74) N Pollard 5/1: 2518: Handy, rdn 2f out, edged right, fdd: h'cap bow: 1¼   **66**
much better 2668 (5 runner mdn on fast, made all).
*2055 **MUJA FAREWELL** 61 [5] 2-9-7 (83) W Ryan 7/2 FAV: 12219: Chsd ldrs, no extra ent fnl 3f: well bckd   nk   **74**
from 7/1, 9 wk abs: unsuited carrying top-weight on easy ground on h'cap bow?: see 2055 (made all on fast).
3098 **SENSIMELIA** 17 [12] 2-8-11 (63) A Mackay 20/1: -53650: Al towards rear: 10th: btr 3098, 1835.   1½   **50**
3327 **CARK** 6 [11] 2-8-5 (67) P Bradley (5) 8/1: -1450: Sn outpcd: 11th, qk reappb, op 5/1, see 2100.   1¾   **50**
3264 **LOVE TUNE** 9 [10] 2-8-7 (69) D Mernagh 3) 15/2: 362220: Mid-div, wknd 2f out: 12th, op 6/1: btr 3264.   1½   **49**
12 ran   Time 1m 03.52 (4.72)   (Tom Beston & Bernard Baugh)   M W Easterby Sherriff Hutton, N Yorks

3476   6.20 RADIO CITY HCAP 3YO 0-75 (E)   2m45y   Good/Soft 69   -23 Slow   [78]
£2800   £800   £400

2446 **INTRUM MORSHAAN** 44 [5] J L Dunlop 3-9-7 (71) P Robinson 2/1 FAV: 63-021: 3 b f Darshaan - Auntie   **83**
Maureen (Roi Danzig) In tch, prog appr str, led bef 2f out, rdly drew clr, easing down: well bckd, first win,
top-weight, abs: plcd juv (mdn, rtd 72): eff at 12f, relished step up to a gall 2m on fast & gd/sft grnd:
runs well fresh: open to further improvement over long trips.
3167 **FURNESS** 14 [2] J G Smyth Osbourne 3-8-4 (54) F Norton 9/1: 00-252: 3 b g Emarati - Thelma (Blakeney) 9   **54**
Prom, chall 3f out, sn swept aside by wnr: tchd 12/1: cght a tartar over longer 2m trip, see 2815.
3112 **JACK DAWSON** 15 [1] John Berry 3-9-1 (65) T E Durcan 9/1: 501223: 3 b g Persian Bold - Dream Of   1½   **64**
Jenny (Caerleon) Rear, prog & ev ch ent str, rdn & onepace fnl 3f: handles fast & gd/soft: see 2659.
TURNED OUT WELL 15 [8] P C Haslam 3-7-10 (46)(2oh) J Mackay (5) 5/1: -55134: Led, rdn/hdd   shd   **45**
appr fnl 2f, no extra: nicely bckd, well clr of remainder: prob ran to best, see 2879 (mdn h'cap).

3219 **WINDMILL LANE 10** [3] 3-8-10 (60) P Hanagan (7) 8/1: 103505: Held up, eff 5f out, nv nr ldrs: see 2244. 23 **44**
3284 **PTAH 8** [7] 3-8-0 (50) D Mernagh (3) 16/1: 323006: Prom till appr str: op 12/1, longer trip, see 1270. 1¼ **33**
3112 **NICIARA 15** [6] 3-7-10 (46)(bl) (2oh) P M Quinn (3) 16/1: 322407: Nvr a factor: needs mdn/sell h'caps. 3½ **27**
1446 **WADENHOE 88** [4] 3-8-3 (53) N Pollard 12/1: 0-6008: Handy, wknd qckly 4f out: 3 mth abs, up in trip. dst **0**
3140 **FIRST BACK 15** [10] 3-8-0 (50) T Williams 12/1: -40039: Struggling halfway: lngr trip, btr 3140 (fast). 10 **0**
1581 **DEBS SON 81** [9] 3-8-3 (53) J Bramhill 33/1: 4-6660: In tch 1m, t.o.: 10th, up in trip, 12 wk abs. dist **0**
10 ran   Time 3m 41.67 (14.67)   (Mrs Maria Mai Goransson)   J L Dunlop Arundel, W Sussex

3477   6.50 OUMO? BY MOSCHINO MDN 3YO (D)   1m30y rnd   Good/Soft 69   +01 Fast
£3867   £1190   £595   £297

2957 **BADR RAINBOW 22** [2] M A Jarvis 3-9-0 P Robinson 6/5 FAV: 042-31: 3 b c Rainbow Quest - Baaderah **76**
(Cadeaux Genereux) Prom, led 3f out, drvn bef fnl 1f, just lasted: well bckd, front 2 clr, fair time: rnr-up fnl
'99 start (nursery, rtd 89 at best): eff at 7f/1m, poss 10f: acts on gd/sft & soft grnd, handles fast, any trk.
2610 **MAC BE LUCKY 37** [5] J Noseda 3-9-0 J Carroll 4/1: 20-002: 3 b c Magic Ring - Take Heart (Electric) shd **75**
In tch, prog 4f out to chall bef dist, just failed: bckd, clr rem: eff at 7f/1m, acts on gd/sft & hvy grnd.
-- **KING OF SPAIN** [4] M Johnston 3-9-0 J Fanning 6/1: 3: 3 ch c Rahy - Royal Fandango (Slew O'Gold) 8 **63**
Rear, chsd ldrs 4f out, sn edged left, same pace: first foal of a 10f wnr: sharper for this.
-- **SIMPLY SENSATIONAL** [1] P F I Cole 3-9-0 D Griffiths 7/1: 4: Hld up, prog to go 3rd 3f out, sn 2 **60**
rdn & no extra: debut, op 11/2: 150,000gns Cadeaux Genereux yearling, related to 4 winners.
-- **GLENQUOICH** [3] 3-9-0 K Darley 5/1: 5: Prom, eff & fdd 3f out: op 3/1: Ir62,000gns Indian Ridge colt. 11 **45**
4493} **PLAZZOTTA 301** [6] 3-9-0 L Gueller (7) 50/1: 0-6: Sn in clr lead, rdn/hdd/btn 3f out: reapp, new stable. 7 **33**
6 ran   Time 1m 45.94 (5.44)   (Sheikh Ahmed Al Maktoum)   M A Jarvis Newmarket, Suffolk

3478   7.20 PONY CLUB MDN 2YO (D)   6f   Good/Soft 69   -30 Slow
£4043   £1244   £622   £311

-- **COUNT DUBOIS** [4] W J Haggas 2-9-0 K Darley 9/4 FAV: 1: 2 b c Zafonic - Madame Dubois (Legend Of **90+**
France) Cl up, led going well 2f out, hard prsd dist, held on well und press & edged left: nicely bckd newcomer,
green/carried head high: 42,000gns half-brother to 3 wnrs up to 12f, dam useful stayer: eff at 6f, further will suit:
acts on gd/sft & a gall track: runs fine well fresh: front two clear, looks the type to improve/rate higher next time.
3268 **MAULD SEGOISHA 9** [6] J G FitzGerald 2-8-9 F Norton 33/1: 002: 2 br f Dolphin Street - September hd **83+**
Tide (Thatching) Mid-div, gd prog ent fnl 2f to chall ins last, carr left fnl 100y, held nr fin under hands &
heels: improved & clr rem: eff at 6f on gd/sft grnd: 7f will suit & shld find a race this autumn: see 2692.
-- **BAILLIESTON** [3] J S Goldie 2-9-0 A Culhane 12/1: 3: 2 ch g Indian Ridge - Bathilde (Generous) 3 **81**
Veered left start, bhd, shaken up & hdwy to go 3rd ins last, nvr nrr: 47,000gns first foal, dam mid-dist performer:
will apprec 7f+ next time: handles gd/sft grnd & looks sure to improve next time.
-- **LION IN THE COURSE** [10] M Johnston 2-9-0 J Fanning 5/1: 4: Mid-div, shkn up 2f out, edged left & 1 **78**
styd on but no threat: op 7/2, debut: 22,000gns Chimes Band half-brother to 5 US wnrs, sire a sprinter.
3268 **HENRY PEARSON 9** [11] 2-9-0 P Robinson 11/1: 05: Mid-div, prog & edged left 2f out, onepace: clr rem.1¼ **75**
3168 **KATIES DOLPHIN 13** [1] 2-8-9 D Mernagh (3) 10/1: 623056: Led after 2f till bef fnl 2f, fdd: needs sells. 8 **54**
3287 **QUI WARRANTO 8** [7] 2-9-0 J Carroll 7/2: 047: Well plcd & ev ch till wknd qckly appr fnl 1f: tchd 5/1, ¾ **57**
much shorter priced stablemate of rnr-up: unsuited by drop in class: rain-softened grnd?: see 3287.
3268 **BEAU SAUVAGE 9** [5] 2-9-0 T Lucas 40/1: 08: V Slow away, nvr in it: 30,000gns Wolfhound gldg, 3½ **50**
half-brother to wnrs at 7f/1m2f, sire 5/7f performer: with M W Easterby.
3277 **SWANTON ABBOT 8** [9] 2-9-0 W Ryan 20/1: 09: Chsd ldrs 3f: see 3277. nk **49**
2454 **TONY 43** [12] 2-9-0 G Parkin 33/1: 00: V slow away, al bhd: 10th, 6 wk abs, see 2454. 5 **39**
2700 **Longchamp Du Lac 34** [8] 2-9-0 O Pears 25/1:   2692 **Kimoe Warrior 35** [2] 2-9-0 A Mackay 33/1:
12 ran   Time 1m 17.21 (5.91)   (Wentworth Racing)   W J Haggas Newmarket, Suffolk

3479   7.50 BROXTON COND STKS 3YO+ (C)   1m4f   Good/Soft 69   -01 Slow
£6727   £2387   £1193   £542

1482 **MONSAJEM 86** [2] E A L Dunlop 5-9-1 K Darley 10/3: 604351: 5 ch h Woodman - Fairy Dancer **108**
(Nijinsky) Nvr far away, switched & rdn to lead ent fnl 1f, ran on strgly: freshened up by 12 wk abs, well rdn, blnks
omitted: '99 wnr at Epsom (1st time visor), Newbury & Ascot (val h'caps, rtd 111): '98 Yarmouth wnr (2, stks
& h'cap) eff at 10/12f on firm, likes gd or softer: eff with/without blnks/visor: runs well fresh: v useful.
1247 **CAPRI 100** [4] H R A Cecil 5-9-1 W Ryan 8/11 FAV: 10-202: 5 ch h Generous - Island Jamboree ¾ **107**
(Exploded) Cl-up, led ent str, rdn & hdd ent fnl 1f, onepace: nicely bckd, 14 wk abs: can rate higher, see 987.
2341 **MAYLANE 49** [1] A C Stewart 6-9-4 P Robinson 3/1: -04633: 6 b g Mtoto - Possessive Dancer ¾ **109**
(Shareef Dancer) Dwelt/nrly u.r., grad imprvd, trkd ldrs ent str, cocked jaw dist, not run on: abs, avoid.
3230 **TRISTACENTURY 10** [3] M A Buckley 7-9-1 A Culhane 25/1: -54244: Led till ent str, sn btn, eased. dist **76$**
4 ran   Time 2m 36.19 (8.39)   (Khalifa Sultan)   E A L Dunlop Newmarket, Suffolk

3480   8.20 ASHCHURCH HCAP 3YO+ 0-70 (E)   1m2f120y Good/Soft 69   -26 Slow   [63]
£3248   £928   £464   3 yo rec 9 lb

3353 **UNDER THE SAND 5** [8] M A Jarvis 3-9-10 (68) P Robinson 7/1: 004201: 3 b g Turtle Island - **77**
Occupation (Homing) Prom going well, led ent fnl 2f, pshd clr, not extended: qk reapp, 1st win, top-weight: unrcd
juvenile: eff at 10f, prob stays 12f: acts on sharp or gall trks: imprvg.
3181 **KATIE KOMAITE 12** [5] Mrs G S Rees 7-8-0 (35) A Mackay 11/2: 002352: 7 b m Komaite - City To City 4 **36**
(Windjammer) Rear, imprvd 4f out to chse ldrs 3f out, sn sltly short of room, kept on for press: likes soft grnd.
3159 **ANNADAWI 14** [2] C N Kellett 5-9-1 (50) T Williams 8/1: 022363: 5 b g Sadler's Wells - Prayer's n ½ **50**
Promises (Foolish Pleasure) Mid-div, shkn up 4f out, rdn 2f out, kept on, no ch with wnr: back to best on fav'd grnd.
3226 **KUUIPO 10** [14] B S Rothwell 3-7-10 (40)(t) D Mernagh (3) 20/1: 026504: Prom, ch 3f out, sn onepace. ¾ **39**
3288 **TIME TO WYN 8** [10] 4-8-7 (42) J Carroll 11/2: 00-005: In tch, rdn 3f out, not pace to chall: see 3288. 1 **40**
3323 **SHAFFISHAYES 7** [12] 8-9-3 (52) A Culhane 7/2 FAV: 465306: Rear, eff 3f out, nvr nr to chall: 1¼ **48**
nicely bckd: prob unsuited by drop in trip, esp with only a moderate pace on: see 943.
3285 **DIAMOND FLAME 8** [11] 6-8-12 (47) K Darley 12/1: 000407: Sn in clr lead, und press/hdd bef dist & btn. nk **43**
3226 **STORMSWELL 10** [9] 3-8-7 (51) P Hanagan (7) 8/1: 153048: Mid-div, rdn 2f out, hung left & fdd 2f out. 3½ **43**
3310 **GLEN VALE WALK 7** [3] 3-8-3 (43) J McAuley 8/1: 040229: In tch till appr str: qk reapp, btr 3310 (fast). 3 **35**
-- **SAHHAR** [1] 7-8-0 (35) J Bramhill 33/1: 4400/0: Nvr trbld ldrs: 10th, abs: '98 Worcester hdles 5 **17**

HAYDOCK   SATURDAY AUGUST 19TH   Lefthand, Flat, Galloping Track

wnr (2m sell h'cap, fast & gd/sft, rtd 77h, P Bevan): 2 year Flat abs, moderate form up to 14f.
3375 ROCK SCENE 3 [13] 8-8-13 (48) P M Quinn (3) 8/1: 554100: Rear, brief wide eff 4f out: 12th, qk reapp.   0
2467 Susans Dowry 43 [6] 4-9-5 (54) F Norton 40/1:   1296 Wonderful Man 96 [7] 4-9-4 (53) G Parkin 16/1:
48   Charlotte Russe 278 [4] 3-7-10 (40)(5oh) P Bradley (5) 33/1:
14 ran   Time 2m 19.99 (9.99)   (David Barker)   M A Jarvis Newmarket, Suffolk

NEWBURY   SATURDAY AUGUST 19TH   Lefthand, Flat, Galloping Track

Official Going GOOD/FIRM. Stalls: Str Crse - Stands Side; Rnd Crse - Inside.

3481   2.0 LADBROKE RTD HCAP 3YO+ 0-95 (C)   7f str Good/Firm 20 +17 Fast   [102]
£6760   £2564   £1282   £582   3yo rec 5lb

2997 WAHJ 21 [9] C A Dwyer 5-9-7 (95) D Holland 13/2: 011201: 4 ch g Indian Ridge - Sabaah (Nureyev):   98
Made all, held on well fnl 1f, pushed out: bckd from 10/1, top weight, best time of day: earlier won at
Haydock (2, incl rtd h'cap): plcd in '99 for Sir M Stoute (List, rtd 100): '98 wnr at Windsor (mdn) & Chepstow
(stks, rtd 109): eff at 7f/1m on firm & soft, handles any trk, likes Haydock: likes to run-up with/force the
pace & runs well fresh: gd weight carrier: useful & progressive gelding.
2900 ALJAWF 25 [1] E A L Dunlop 3-8-12 (91) R Hills 14/1: 061002: 3 gr c Dehere - Careless Kitten (Caro):   ½ 92
Waited with, swtchd outside & imprvd 2f out, fin well but just too late: op 10/1: stays a stiff 7f well, suited
by fast grnd: given plenty to do here & shld win again with a more positive ride: unsuited by visor in 2900.
2495 BIG FUTURE 42 [4] Mrs A J Perrett 3-8-10 (89) Dane O'Neill 9/2: -14153: 3 b c Bigstone - Star Of The   ½ 89
Future (El Gran Senor) Held up, imprvd 2f out, ran on fnl 1f & nrst fin: 6 wk abs: useful, cld win again at 1m.
3179 FREDDY FLINTSTONE 13 [8] R Hannon 3-8-1 (81)(1oh) L Newman(3) 12/1: 400234: Chsd wnr, no extra ¾ 78
inside fnl 1f: not disgraced, consistent: see 3179, 2938 (1m).
*2464 MORNINGS MINION 43 [5] R Perham 9/1: -4415: Dwelt, recovered to chase ldrs, kept on   1½ 80
under press but not pace to chall: op 13/2, 6 wk abs: not disgraced on h'cap bow, a return to 1m will suit.
2997 DUKE OF MODENA 21 [6] 3-9-2 (95) S Carson (3) 5/2 FAV: 151446: Chsd ldrs, wknd fnl 1f: well bckd.   nk 89
3297 SARSON 8 [10] 4-8-1 (81)(6oh) Martin Dwyer 33/1: 0-0007: Pushed in rear, imprvg when not much   hd 69
room dist, no impress inside last: some promise here, v fav h'capped nowadays: see 1676.
-3183 EMERGING MARKET 12 [3] Pat Eddery 7/1: 000528: Rdn in rear, all struggling: btr 3183.   1½ 75
3152 ROYAL RESULT 14 [2] 7-9-0 (88) A Nicholls (3) 5/1: 036449: In tch 5f, wknd into last, eased   10 59
considerably: saw too much daylight today & this is not his form: btr 3152 (6f), 728.
9 ran   Time 1m 24.54 (0.24)   (S B Components (International) Ltd)   C A Dwyer Newmarket.

3482   2.30 LISTED ST HUGH'S STKS 2YO (A)   5f34y str Good/Firm 20 -02 Slow
£12025   £3700   £1850   £925

2565 STRANGE DESTINY 39 [5] A Berry 2-8-8 J Reid 6/1: -31461: 2 b f Mujadil - Blue Birds Fly   100
(Rainbow Quest): Chsd ldrs, imprvd to lead 1½f out, held on well, drvn out: fair juv time: earlier won at
Warwick (fill mdn auct), subs 4th at R Ascot (Gr 3 Queen Mary): apprec return to a stiff 5f, shld stay 6f:
acts on firm & gd/soft grnd, handles a sharp or stiff/gall trk: likes to run up with/force the pace: useful.
*2868 SILLA 27 [2] I A Balding 2-8-8 R Cochrane 7/1: -03112: 2 b f Gone West - Silver Fling (The Minstrel):   nk 99+
Stdd start, short of room when imprvg 1f out, fin fast but just too late: gamble from 12/1: lkd most unlucky
& is a fast improving filly: prob worth a try at 6f next time: lightly raced & shld win similar: see 2868.
2996 KACHINA DOLL 21 [10] M R Channon 2-8-8 Craig Williams 7/1: 052403: 2 br f Mujadil - Betelgeuse   1¼ 95
(Kalaglow): Rear, imprvg when swtchd fnl 1f, fin well but not rch front 2: no luck in running, will apprec
is a return to 6f: useful filly, must be given another chance: see 2996 (Gr 3).
2469 SECRET INDEX 43 [7] Mrs P N Dutfield 2-8-11 L Newman 12/1: -11544: Prom, led 2f out till dist,   nk 97$
no extra: 6 wk abs, jnt top weight: not disgraced, see 2469 (6f, gd/soft).
+3145 PROUD BOAST 14 [1] 2-8-8 W Supple 12/1: 102315: Dwelt, sn prom till slightly outpcd halfway, stopped   ½ 93+
in run toward end fnl 1f, fin well but ch had gone: would have gone v cl with a clr run & one to keep in mind.
3027 QUIESCENT 19 [4] 2-8-8 R Hills 20/1: -0136: Chsd ldrs, ev ch 2f out, no extra ins fnl 1f: op 14/1.   nk 92
*3092 BOIS DE CITRON 17 [9] 2-8-8 Dane O'Neill 7/1: -3417: Chsd ldr, ev ch 2f out, fdd ins last: stiff task.   nk 91
*3027 DANCE ON 19 [3] 2-8-11 Pat Eddery 5/1: -10618: Chsd ldrs, ev ch till wknd final 1f: jnt top weight.   shd 94
*3320 SHEPPARDS WATCH 7 [6] 2-8-8 Martin Dwyer 10/3 FAV: -4119: Front rank till wknd fnl 1f: well   nk 90
bckd: disapp effort & prob not apprec this drop back to 5f: see 3320.
*2968 SEVEN SING 22 [8] 2-8-8 M Hills 13/2: -310: Led till 2f out, wknd into last: up in grade after 2968.   1¾ 85
10 ran   Time 1m 01.42 (1.12)   (Team Valor)   A Berry Cockerham, Lancs.

3483   3.00 GR 2 GEOFFREY FREER STKS 3YO+ (A)   1m5f61y Good/Firm 20 -18 Slow
£36000   £13800   £6900   £3300   3yo rec 11lb

3306 MURGHEM 7 [6] M Johnston 5-9-3 D Holland 7/4 FAV: 111121: 5 b h Common Grounds - Fabulous Pet   113
(Somethingfabulous): Made all, styd on v gamely fnl 1f, drvn out: hvly bckd: earlier won at Epsom (rtd h'cap),
Leicester, Newmarket (List) & Goodwood (List rtd h'cap): '99 Sandown wnr (h'cap, rtd 100, with B Hanbury): '98
Kempton wnr (mdn, rtd 105 at best): stays 2m, suited by 12/13f: acts on firm, soft grnd & fibresand, loves to
run up with or force the pace: has triple blnks, better without, runs well fresh: gd weight carrier: smart,
progressive & most genuine entire who looks sure to give a gd account in the Irish St Leger.
*2957 SAVOIRE VIVRE 22 [7] J H M Gosden 3-8-6 Pat Eddery 2/1: -12: 3 b c Sadler's Wells - Oh So Sharp   1¼ 109
(Kris): Rcd keenly in tch, chsd wnr 2f out, kept on well but no ch with this ultra-game wnr: hvly bckd: fine
run on only 2nd start, stays 13.3f well: smart colt who will win Gr races judged on this: see 2957 (debut).
3171 YORKSHIRE 13 [3] P F I Cole 6-9-3 D Sweeney 20/1: 655/53: 6 ch g Generous - Ausherra (Diesis):   3 104
Rcd keenly rear, imprvd 2f out, styd on into 3rd but no ch with ldrs: sharper next time & a more suitable 2m+ trip.
3106 RAINBOW WAYS 16 [5] B W Hills 3-8-6 M Hills 9/1: 223404: Held up, drvn 2f out, btn final 1f.   4 98
3618↓ NOWHERE TO EXIT 357 [4] 4-9-3 J Reid 10/3: 1125-5: Trkd ldrs till wknd over 1f out: belated reapp: 1¾ 96
trained by J Dunlop in '99, won at Haydock (reapp, rtd h'cap), Chantilly (List) & Longchamp (Gr 3), subs 4L 2nd
to Montjeu in the Gr 1 French Derby (rtd 118): eff at 12f, shld stay further: handles fast, much prefers soft
& hvy: can run well fresh: high class, now with Saeed Bin Suroor: shld leave this bhd on softer grnd next time.
3302 ASHGAR 1 [1] 4-9-3 R Cochrane 50/1: 640406: Chsd wnr till 2f out, fdd: highly tried.   4 90
6 ran   Time 2m 50.24 (5.14)   (A Al-Rostamani)   M Johnston Middleham, Nth Yorks.

1071

3484   **3.35 EBF THEHORSESMOUTH MDN 2YO (D)**   7f str   Good/Firm 20   -08 Slow
£4446   £1368   £684   £342

3121 **TEMPEST** 15 [7] Sir Michael Stoute 2-9-0 Pat Eddery 6/4 FAV: -41: 2 b c Zafonic - Pidona (Baillamont): **100+**
Front rank, led after 2f & made rest, clr fnl 1f, easily: Mar foal, dam a 1m wnr abroad: sire a top class miler:
eff over a stiff 7f, 1m will suit: acts on fast grnd & on a stiff/gall trk: held in some regard, holds sev big
race entries: useful colt who looks one to follow.

-- **MOSAAHIM** [10] J L Dunlop 2-9-0 R Hills 7/1: -2: 2 b c Nashwan - Azdihaar (Mr Prospector): 4 **89+**
Held up, swtchd & imprvd 2f out, squeezed thro' to chase wnr fnl 1f, no ch: op 5/1, debut: Jan foal, half-brother
to a 7f French 2yo scorer: dam scored over 7f, sire a top class mid-dist performer: eff at 7f, likely to apprec
1m+ given time: handles fast grnd: met an above average rival here, will improve & win a mdn.

-- **TAKE ANOTHER BOW** [2] J H M Gosden 2-9-0 R Havlin 8/1: -3: 2 ch c Theatrical - Shy Princess 2 **85**
(Irish River): Rcd keenly rear, ran green when asked for eff 2f out, onepace fnl 1f on debut: Jan foal, related
to sev wnrs, incl smart 6/7f scorer Diffident: dam a French 6/7f wnr, sire a high class mid-dist performer: likely
to apprec 1m+ given time: promising debut, rcd much too keenly here: looks sure to win in mdn company.

-- **LYSANDERS QUEST** [3] L Montague Hall 2-9-0 Dane O'Neill 33/1: -4: Mid-div, styd on nicely final 1¼ **82**
1f, nrst fin: 24,000gns purchase: Apr foal, dam a juv rnr in France: sire a top class mid-dist performer.

2956 **CHANGING SCENE** 22 [8] 2-9-0 R Cochrane 9/1: -05: Trkd ldrs, eased once held final 1f: see 2956. nk **81**
2708 **ARC EN CIEL** 34 [4] 2-9-0 J Reid 20/1: -06: Pushed in rear, some late hdwy, nvr dngrs: stablemate ½ **80$**
of wnr: middle dist bred & sure to impr once qual for h'caps next season: see 2708 (C/D).

-- **CLEAR AMBITION** [9] 2-9-0 S Clancy (7) 33/1: -7: Nvr nr to chall on debut: Feb foal, cost 13,000gns: nk **79**
first foal, sire a decent 10/12f performer: B Meehan gelding.

-- **CAPITAL LAD** [12] 2-9-0 P McCabe 50/1: -8: Rcd keenly & chsd ldrs 5f, sn btn: debut: Mar foal, 5 **69**
cost 7,500gns: half-brother to a 1m wnr: dam scored over 1m in Ireland: with G Brown.

3137 **SMOOTHIE** 15 [11] 2-9-0 D Sweeney 3/1: -39: Early ldr, remnd prom till wknd & eased final 1f: nk **68**
gamble from 6/1: better expected after 3137 (6f, debut).

3333 **ROYAL ENCLOSURE** 6 [5] 2-9-0 M Tebbutt 33/1: -00: Al bhd, fin 10th: qck reapp. 1¼ **64**
-- **RAPTOR** [1] 2-9-0 M Hills 16/1: -0: Al bhd, fin last on debut: 8,000gns Mar foal. 7 **50**
11 ran   Time 1m 26.29 (1.99)   (Cheveley Park Stud)   Sir Michael Stoute Newmarket.

3485   **4.10 R BLACKMAN HCAP 3YO+ 0-95 (C)**   5f34y   Good/Firm 20   +04 Fast   [84]
£6604   £2032   £1016   £508   3yo rec 2lb

*3135 **SMOKIN BEAU** 15 [2] J Cullinan 3-9-7 (79) P Dobbs (5) 5/1: 003611: 3 b g Cigar - Beau Dada **84**
(Pine Circle): Chsd ldrs, went on over 1f out, held on well despite drifting right ins last, drvn out: gd time:
recent Goodwood wnr (h'cap): '99 Southwell scorer (mdn, rtd 81a & 76): eff at 5/6f on fast & soft/hvy grnd, acts
on both AWs: handles a sharp or stiff/gall trk: has tried a visor, better without: gd weight carrier: in gd form.

3322 **BRECONGILL LAD** 7 [3] D Nicholls 8-10-0 (84) A Nicholls (3) 3/1 JT FAV: 031202: 8 b g Clantime - ½ **87**
Chikala (Pitskelly): Waited with, smooth hdwy when short of room dist, hmpd & swtchd inside last, fin well but
just too late: well bckd, top weight: no luck today & almost certainly unlucky: see 3176, 2987.

3091 **ANTONIAS DOUBLE** 17 [4] A Berry 5-9-3 (73) Dane O'Neill 8/1: 300203: 5 ch m Primo Dominie - Mainly ¾ **73**
Sunset (Red Sunset): Led till dist, no extra: op 13/2: sound front running effort, see 2987.

3209 **SPEED ON** 11 [1] H Candy 7-9-6 (76) C Rutter 11/2: 630504: In tch, not qckn ins fnl 1f: see 3209. hd **76**
3209 **PALAWAN** 11 [5] 4-9-6 (76) R Cochrane 3/1 JT FAV: 010625: Trkd ldrs, outpcd final 1f: nicely bckd. ½ **75**
+2569 **RECORD TIME** 39 [6] 4-8-4 (60) Pat Eddery 4/1: 004016: Chsd ldrs, wknd over 1f out: btr 2569 (gd). 6 **44**
6 ran   Time 1m 01.12 (0.82)   (Turf 2000 Ltd)   J Cullinan Quainton, Bucks.

3486   **4.40 LEVY BOARD NURSERY HCAP 2YO (C)**   7f64y rnd   Good/Firm 20   -07 Slow   [89]
£6420   £1920   £960   £480

3246 **TIMES SQUARE** 10 [4] G C H Chung 2-9-3 (78) M Henry 14/1: -43101: 2 b c Timeless Times - Alaskan **87**
Princess (Prince Rupert): Chsd ldrs, went on 2f out, held on gamely cl-home, all-out: op 10/1: earlier won at
Catterick (mdn): eff at 6/7.3f, suited by fast, handles gd/soft: can run well fresh: battled on gamely today.

2962 **ANALYZE** 22 [2] M R Channon 2-8-5 (66) Craig Williams 20/1: 03502: 2 b c Anabaa - Bramosia nk **74**
(Forzando) Hdwy from rear 2f out, kept on well & only just btn: op 14/1, 6L clr 3rd: stays 7.3f on fast & gd/soft.

2430 **NOBLE DOBLE** 45 [1] B W Hills 2-9-4 (79) M Hills 9/1: -4523: 2 b c Shareef Dancer - Kshessinskaya 6 **75**
(Hadeer): Chsd ldrs, left bhd by front 2 final 1f: btr 12/1, 6 wk abs: see 2430.

3268 **FLYING TURK** 9 [8] J A Osborne 2-9-3 (78) R Cochrane 7/2: -3044: Stdd start & rcd keenly rear, ½ **73**
imprvd 2f out, no impress ins fnl 1f: well bckd on h'cap bow: rcd too keenly over this lngr 7.3f trip: see 3268.

2959 **AMEN CORNER** 28 [3] 2-9-7 (82) D Holland 5/1: -4135: Led till 2f out, eased fnl 1f: top-weight. nk **76**
3149 **NIGHT FALL** 14 [6] 2-9-3 (78) P Fitzsimons (5) 16/1: 561406: In tch 5f, wknd: btr 2125. 4 **64**
3239 **MOONLIGHT DANCER** 10 [9] 2-9-1 (76) P Dobbs (5) 14/1: 220257: Nvr a factor: consistent in mdns. ½ **61**
3149 **MERIDEN MIST** 14 [5] 2-8-13 (74) A Beech (5) 11/2: 254148: In tch, stumbled ent home str & went 5 **49**
v wide, no ch after: forget this: much btr 2894.

*3039 **SAUCE TARTAR** 19 [7] 2-9-1 (76) Pat Eddery 9/4 FAV: -619: In tch when hmpd & pushed v wide ½ **50**
ent str, no ch after: hvly bckd on h'cap debut: forget this, see 3039.
9 ran   Time 1m 29.81 (2.01)   (Ian Pattle)   G C H Chung Newmarket.

3487   **5.15 EBF TRIUMVIRATE CLASS STKS 3YO+ 0-90 (C**   1m4f   Good/Firm 20   -20 Slow
£6217   £2358   £1179   £536   3yo rec 10lb

3134 **FAIR WARNING** 15 [5] J W Hills 4-9-3 M Hills 7/1: 2-5001: 4 b g Warning - Fairy Bluebird (Be My Guest): **91**
In tch, imprvd to chall dist, went on ins last, just prevailed in a driving fin: '99 wnr at Yarmouth (mdn) &
York (class stks, rtd 93): plcd form in '98 (rtd 87): eff at 1m/12f on firm & gd/soft grnd: handles any trk: has
reportedly suffered illness problems this year, back to form here.

*2531 **KIFTSGATE** 41 [2] Sir Michael Stoute 3-8-11 Pat Eddery 6/5 FAV: -612: 3 ch c Kris - Blush Rambler nk **94**
(Blushing Groom): Chsd ldr, chall strongly 2f out, led dist till ins last, just btn in a driving fin: well bckd,
6 wk abs: stays a stiff 12f well, acts on gd & fast grnd: continues to improve, see 2531 (mdn).

3088 **UNAWARE** 17 [3] R Charlton 3-8-7 J Reid 5/2: -53403: 3 b c Unfuwain - Rainbow Lake (Rainbow Quest): 1 **88**
Waited wth, stdy hdwy to chall dist, no extra cl-home: sound effort, btn just over 1L: see 1225.

2857 **TRUE CRYSTAL** 28 [6] H R A Cecil 3-8-8 A McGlone 10/3: -104: Led till dist, no extra: nicely bckd. ½ **88**

NEWBURY SATURDAY AUGUST 19TH Lefthand, Flat, Galloping Track

3281 **BATWINK** 8 [4] 3-8-4 A Beech (5) 66/1: -00005: In tch till lost place 3f out, t.o: v highly tried. *dist* 0
5 ran Time 2m 34.15 (4.85) (M Wauchope, Sir Simon Dunning, R Cottam) J W Hills Upper Lambourn, Berks.

LINGFIELD SATURDAY AUGUST 19TH Lefthand, Sharp, Undulating Track

Official Going GOOD TO FIRM (FIRM in places). Stalls: Str Crse - Stands Side; 9f - Inside; 14f - Outside.

3488 5.15 CLAIRE FRANCIS HCAP 3YO+ 0-85 (D) 1m1f Firm 10 -40 Slow [82]
£4043 £1244 £622 £311

2630 **PHILATELIC LADY** 37 [2] M J Haynes 4-9-10 (78) S Carson (3) 4/1: 533031: 3 ch f Pips Pride - Gold 82
Stamp (Golden Act): Held up rear, rdn & styd on well inside last to lead nr line: op 7/2: '99 wnr here at Lingfield
& Windsor (h'caps, rtd 80): '98 wnr again at Lingfield (AW mdn, rtd 75a), earlier rtd 75 on turf: suited by 1m/10f,
stays 11.8f: acts on fast, hvy & equitrack: has run well fresh: handles any trk, loves a sharp/undul one.
2726 **COPPLESTONE** 32 [3] P W Harris 4-9-3 (71) B Marcus 3/1: 440432: 4 b g Second Set - Queen Of The *shd* 74
Brush (Averof): Led, rdn & styd on well for press final 1f, just hdd nr line: plcd again: mdn after 15, see 1744.
3207 **HARMONY HALL** 11 [1] J M Bradley 6-8-8 (62) L Newman (3) 4/1: 222003: 6 ch g Music Boy - Fleeting 2 61
Affair (Hotfoot): Trkd ldrs, effort final 2f, onepace/held inside last: op 3/1: 1 win in 41 starts: see 2645.
3118 **BYZANTIUM GB** 15 [5] W Jarvis 6-9-0 (68) Martin Dwyer 15/8 FAV: 350-54: Chsd ldr, held 1f out: op 5/2. 1 65
835 **FUSUL** 134 [4] 4-8-9 (63) I Mongan (5) 15/2: 113025: Keen, saddle slipped, btn 3f out, eased: op 11/2: 17 35
4 mth abs: this is best forgotten: btr 835, 441 (AW, 12f).
5 ran Time 1m 55.00 (4.5) (G B Farmer) M J Haynes Epsom, Surrey.

3489 5.40 BETTY BARCLAY MDN 3YO+ (D) 1m6f Firm 10 -71 Slow
£2834 £872 £436 £218 3 yo rec 12lb

964 **AWTAAN** 123 [4] M P Tregoning 3-8-7 W Supple 7/4: 43-41: 3 b f Arazi - Bashayer (Mr Prospector): 72
Cl-up, led halfway, hdd over 2f out, duelled with rnr-up after & styd on gamely for press to lead on line: op 1/1:
4 mth abs: rtd 91 in '99 (fill mdn): eff at 14f, 2m could suit: handles firm & gd/soft, any trk: runs well fresh.
2981 **IORANA** 22 [5] M C Pipe 4-9-10 Martin Dwyer 22: 4 ch g Marignan - Fareham (Fast Topaze): *shd* 76
Chsd ldr halfway, led over 2f out, duelled with wnr after, hdd line: well clr rem: op 2/1, stays 14f on firm/fast.
3023 **TUFTY HOPPER** 20 [2] P Howling 3-8-12 A Clark 5/2: 220453: 3 b g Rock Hopper - Melancolia 8 65
(Legend Of France): Chsd ldrs, outpcd final 4f: op 7/2: see 3023, 2710.
3189 **LEILA** 12 [6] J S King 5-9-5 R Havlin 25/1: 04: Chsd ldrs, btn 4f out: lngr 14f trip, see 3189. 23 34
571 **KENTISH ROCK** 178 [1] 5-9-10 I Mongan (5) 25/1: 045: Rear, strugg 3f out: 6 mth abs: lngr 14f trip. 10 25
731} **SALSIFY** 506 [3] 4-9-10 R Studholme (5) 16/1: 0/0-6: Led till halfway, sn bhd: long abs: unplcd on *dist* 0
2 starts at 1m prev for R Charlton (rtd 70, debut): now with G A Ham.
6 ran Time 3m 07.89 (11.39) (Hamdan Al Maktoum) M P Tregoning Lambourn, Berks.

3490 6.10 CHILDREN FREE SELLER 3YO+ (G) 1m2f Firm 10 -42 Slow
£2002 £572 £286 3 yo rec 8 lb

3330 **DON BOSCO** 6 [1] N A Callaghan 4-9-3 R Hughes 15/8 FAV: 003001: 4 ch g Grand Lodge - Suyayeb 53
(The Minstrel): Made all, rdn/asserted over 1f out, in command when eased down inside last: value for 6L+:
op 11/10: bght in for 7,800 gns: qck reapp: '99 Ripon scorer (h'cap, J Banks, rtd 75): prev eff at 6f, styd this
longer 10f trip well: acts on firm & soft, likes a sharp/undul trk: best without blnks: apprec drop to sell grade.
2764 **WAIKIKI BEACH** 31 [10] G L Moore 9-9-3 (bl) I Mongan (5) 12/1: 040062: 9 ch g Fighting Fit - Running 3 44
Melody (Rheingold): Keen/chsd ldrs, chsd wnr lst as held: acts on firm, gd/soft & both AWs: see 136.
3031 **BAY OF BENGAL** 19 [4] J S Wainwright 4-8-12 G Sparkes (7) 8/1: 320603: 4 ch f Persian Bold - Adjamiya ½ 38
(Shahrastani) Chsd ldrs, onepace/held final 2f: op 6/1: acts on firm & gd grnd: interesting in sell h'caps.
4280} **MINNESOTA** 316 [9] M C Pipe 4-9-3 (vis) Martin Dwyer 6/1: 0040-4: Prom, chsd wnr 4f out, held 2f out: 3½ 38
op 8/1: Flat reapp, 11 wk jumps abs (mod form, visor): unplcd for N Callaghan in '99 (rtd 58 & 50a): '98 wnr at
Southwell (mdn, rtd 76a) & Newmarket (nurs, rtd 83): eff at 7f on firm & fibresand, handles soft: best without blnks.
4078} **PETARA** 330 [7] 5-9-3 (vis) C Rutter 8/1: 0100-5: Slowly away/bhd, some hdwy 3f out, no impress on ½ 37
ldrs: op 12/1, reapp: '99 Lingfield wnr (sell h'cap, rtd 42): rnr-up in '98 (h'cap, rtd 53): eff at 7f/1m, stays 10f:
acts on firm & soft grnd, suited by blnks/visor: enjoys sell grade.
2914 **SHAW VENTURE** 24 [5] 3-8-9 R Havlin 8/1: 606056: Chsd ldrs, btn 3f out: see 638 (AW, 6f). 5 30
3318 **PRIVATE SEAL** 7 [6] 5-9-3 B Marcus 25/1: 600407: Rear, mod gains late on: see 262 (AW, 6f). 2 27
4387} **JEWEL FIGHTER** 308 [8] 6-8-12 Claire Bryan (5) 8/1: /340-8: Mid-div, btn 3f out: reapp, op 5/1: 2 19
plcd on first of just 3 '99 starts for P D Evans (rtd 60, mdn): rtd 61 in '98 (C Smith, mdn): only mod form
over hdles: eff arnd 1m, handles soft & hvy grnd: now with J M Bradley.
455 **MIGWAR** 197 [11] 7-9-3 L Newman (3) 11/2: -06039: Rear, nvr a factor: 4 mth jumps abs (no form): nk 23
prev win N Littmoden, now with J M Bradley: now with J M Bradley: see 224 (AW).
2212 **BON GUEST** 53 [2] 6-9-3 W Supple 20/1: 501/00: Cl-up, btn 2f out: 10th: 8 wk abs: new stable. 8 14
3183} Hail Sheeva 379 [12] 3-8-4 C Carver (3) 25/1: 2999 **Fourdaned** 21 [3] 7-9-3 A Clark 25/1:
12 ran Time 2m 09.39 (5.19) (Mrs Patricia E Cunningham) N A Callaghan Newmarket, Suffolk.

3491 6.40 BOB & KATH NURSERY HCAP 2YO (E) 5f Firm 10 +02 Fast [85]
£2954 £844 £422

3109 **JACK SPRATT** 16 [7] R Hannon 2-9-7 (78) L Newman (3) 7/2: 033101: 2 b c So Factual - Raindancing 85
(Tirol): Chsd ldr, rdn/led over 1f out, styd on well: op 5/1: best time of night: earlier scored at Chepstow (nov
stks): eff at 5f, 6f shld suit (dam a useful 6f juv wnr): acts on firm, gd/soft & a sharp/undul or gall trk.
3277 **MADRASEE** 8 [11] M Blanshard 2-9-0 (71) J Quinn 11/2: 363032: 2 b f Beveled - Pendona (Blue 1¼ 73
Cashmere): Al prom, onepace inside last: gd h'cap bow from this mdn: see 3277, 2711.
2730 **YETTI** 32 [9] H Candy 2-8-12 (69) C Rutter 3/1 FAV: 2253: 2 ch f Aragon - Willyet (Nicholas Bill): ½ 69
Chsd ldrs, drvn/onepace inside last: btn 2328 (auct mdn).
3258 **LONDON EYE** 7 [12] K T Ivory 2-8-6 (63)(bl) C Carver (3) 12/1: 200164: Chsd ldrs, not able to chall. 1 61
3228 **IF BY CHANCE** 10 [9] 2-8-5 (62) M Roberts 9/1: 042055: Rdn/chsd ldrs, held 1f out: op 7/1: see 1236. 3 53
3204 **QUEENS SONG** 11 [10] 2-7-10 (53)(2oh) G Sparkes (4) 16/1: -03656: Rear/rdn, styd on final 1f, no 2 39

threat: looks ready for step up to 6f: see 2551.
3204 **ACORN CATCHER 11** [6] 2-8-2 (59) P Doe 12/1: 01307: Unruly before start, mid-div at best: op 8/1. *shd* **45**
2488 **BALI ROYAL 42** [2] 2-8-9 (66) P Fitzsimons (5) 12/1: 2008: Rear, nvr on terms: op 10/1, 6 wk abs. *1½* **49**
3168 **MISS BRIEF 13** [8] 2-9-2 (73) J P Spencer 6/1: 244209: Led till over 1f out, held when no room 1f out. *nk* **55**
1396 **MOLLY IRWIN 91** [5] 2-7-12 (55) Martin Dwyer 20/1: 312000: Dwelt, rdn/al bhd: 10th: op 14/1, abs. *¾* **35**
3204 **SOOTY TIME 11** [1] 2-8-0 (57) G Bardwell 9/1: 662340: Sn bhd: 11th: op 7/1: btr 3038, 2772 (sell). *7* **25**
11 ran Time 57.22 (0.42) (Lady Davis) R Hannon East Everleigh, Wilts.

3492

7.10 HARRISON JONES MDN 2YO (D) 6f Firm 10 -59 Slow
£2925 £900 £450 £225

-- **ALSHADIYAH** [3] J L Dunlop 2-8-9 R Hills 2/7 FAV: 1: 2 gr f Danzig - Shadayid (Shadeed): **95+**
Handy, led over 2f out, readily asserted under hands-&-heels riding from over 1f out: value for 5L: hvly bckd at long odds-on: slow time: Feb foal, half-sister to smart 1m performer Bint Shadayid, a 6/7f juv wnr: dam a 1,000 gns wnr, subs 3rd in Oaks: eff at 6f, step up to 7f+ sure to suit: acts on firm grnd & a sharp/undul trk: runs well fresh: well regarded, made an impressive intro here, looks one to follow in a higher grade.
-- **KIRTHAR** [4] M A Jarvis 2-9-0 G Hind 6/1: 2: 2 b c Mt Livermore - Kazadancoa (Green Dancer): *2* **85**
Keen, chall 2f out, sn outpcd by easy wnr: op 3/1: May foal, cost $70,000: half-brother to a Gr 2 2yo US wnr: dam a 3yo wnr abroad: eff at 6f & handles firm grnd: caught a tartar on intro, will not al meet one so smart.
3252 **LORD LIAM 9** [9] N P Littmoden 2-9-0 P Doe 8/1: 53: 2 b c Foxhound - Crackling Sike (Salse): *3½* **76**
Keen/led till over 2f out, sn outpcd by front pair: op 6/1: see 3252 (5f).
2714 **SUMMER SHADES 33** [7] C A Cyzer 2-8-9 I Mongan (5) 12/1: -364: Chsd ldrs, held 2f out: op 7/1. *½* **69**
-- **WILD SPIRIT** [2] 2-9-0 J D Smith 20/1: 5: Cl-up, btn 2f out: op 8/1: Salse gelding, Apr foal, cost *7* **59**
23,000gns: dam a 5f 2yo wnr: with D W P Arbuthnot.
3047 **AMBASSADOR LADY 19** [1] 2-8-9 S Whitworth 33/1: 06: Keen/chsd ldrs, strugg over 2f out: well bhd *nk* **53**
on debut prev: Apr foal, a first foal: dam a mdn: with A G Newcombe.
-- **FAREHAM** [5] 2-8-9 M Baird 25/1: 7: Sn cl-up, hard rdn/btn 2f out: op 10/1: Mar foal, dam a 7f wnr. *5* **42**
-- **MER LOCK** [8] 2-8-9 A Clark 25/1: 8: Slowly away & sn bhd: op 12/1: Piccolo filly, May foal, cost *7* **27**
8,000gns: half-sister to wnrs between 7f/2m: dam a 7f 2yo wnr: with T J Naughton.
8 ran Time 1m 12.96 (4.16) (Hamdan Al Maktoum) J L Dunlop Arundel, West Sussex.

3493

7.45 SUE PAMMEN HCAP 3YO+ 0-65 (F) 6f Firm 10 -01 Slow [65]
£2656 £759 £379 3 yo rec 3 lb Raced centre - stands side, no advantage

*3293 **DAYS OF GRACE 8** [20] L Montague Hall 5-9-8 (59) C Rutter 11/4 FAV: 005311: 5 gr m Wolfhound - **64**
Inshirah (Caro): Chsd ldrs, drvn & styd on well inside last to lead nr line: nicely bckd, op 4/1: earlier scored at Southwell & W'hampton (AW fillies h'caps, rtd 69a) & Salisbury (fillies h'cap): '99 Southwell & W'hampton wnr (h'caps, rtd 62a & 56): eff at 7f, suited by 5/6f on firm, hvy & both AWs: handles any trk, loves a sharp/turning one: gd wght carrier: v tough & consistent mare, could win again in this grade.
2999 **MY EMILY 21** [18] G L Moore 4-10-0 (65) I Mongan (5) 8/1: 216002: 4 b f King's Signet - Flying Wind *shd* **69**
(Forzando): Chsd ldrs, rdn/led & edged left over 1f out, hdd nr line: back to form: both wins at 7f: see 1884.
3293 **BRAMBLE BEAR 8** [12] M Blanshard 6-8-13 (50) G Hind 3/1: 403323: 6 b m Beveled - Supreme Rose *1½* **51**
(Frimley Park): Chsd ldrs, drvn/chall dist, onepace inside last: op 5/1: see 1464.
2976 **MUTASAWWAR 22** [6] M S Saunders 6-8-2 (39) L Newman (3) 14/1: -50004: Trkd ldrs, rdn/onepace *1½* **36**
final 1f: op 16/1: acts on firm, gd/soft & both AWs: looks nicely h'capped: see 1508 (sell).
3419 **BORDER GLEN 2** [9] 4-8-13 (50)(bl) M Roberts 14/1: 005005: Led after 1f, hdd over 1f out, fdd. *1¾* **43**
*3243 **CHAKRA 10** [16] 6-8-13 (50) R Havlin 11/2: 130216: Trkd ldrs, onepace over 1f out: see 3243. *nk* **42**
3362 **ANSTAND 5** [15] 5-8-13 (50)(bl) S Carson (3) 25/1: 060007: Towards rear, kept on final 2f, nrst fin. *½* **40**
3046 **SEREN TEG 19** [14] 4-8-7 (44)(bl) A Clark 16/1: 006468: Dwelt/outpcd rear, kept on final 2f: see 440. *½* **32**
2438 **RIOS DIAMOND 44** [11] 3-8-11 (51) K Parkin (7) 11/1: 051349: Cl-up, btn 2f out: abs: btr 2036. *nk* **38**
-3214 **FRANKLIN LAKES 10** [19] 5-8-3 (40)(bl) S Righton 20/1: 460020: Dwelt, sn rdn/rear, mod gains: 10th. *½* **25**
2944 **RIVER TERN 23** [8] 7-9-7 (58) P Fitzsimons (5) 12/1: 036000: Chsd ldrs, btn 2f out: 11th: op 10/1. *nk* **42**
3257 **SWINO 9** [13] 6-8-9 (46)(vis) W Supple 14/1: 020000: Rdn/mid-div, btn 2f out: 12th: op 12/1: see 177. *1½* **27**
3279 **LADYWELL BLAISE 8** [4] 3-9-4 (58) Martin Dwyer 16/1: 120000: Mid-div, drvn/btn 2f out: 13th: op *1* **37**
12/1: acts on firm, gd & both AWs: btr 2320 (7f, fillies h'cap).
3384 **L A TOUCH 3** [3] 7-8-12 (49) R Hughes 7/1: 036060: Mid-div, btn 2f out: 14th: qck reapp: see 2840. *2* **23**
1712 **PIETA 76** [5] 3-8-10 (50) B Marcus 20/1: 00050: Led 1f, btn 2f out: 16th: 11 wk abs: mod form. **0**
2919 **White Summit 24** [17] 3-8-10 (50) P Doe 20/1: 3243 **Bold Saboteur 10** [10] 3-8-6 (46) G Sparkes (7) 20/1:
3118 **Chase The Blues 15** [1] 3-9-11 (65) J Stack 16/1:
18 ran Time 1m 09.47 (0.67) (Stephen & Michelle Bayless) L Montague Hall Tadworth, Surrey.

WOLVERHAMPTON (Fibresand) SATURDAY AUGUST 19TH Lefthand, Sharp, Track

Official Going STANDARD. Stalls: 7f - Outside; Rem - Inside.

3494

7.00 CHEMIQUE APPR MDN HCAP 3YO+ 0-65 (G) 1m4f aw Going 26 -33 Slow [54]
£1809 £517 £258 3 yo rec 10lb

1671 **STRICTLY SPEAKING 78** [3] P F I Cole 3-9-4 (54) Darren Williams 6/1: -06601: 3 b c Sri Pekan - Gaijin **64a**
(Caerleon) Handy, imprvd to lead appr fnl 3f, sn well clr, eased considerably: val 10L: op 9/2 on AW bow, 11 wk abs, blnks omitted: plcd juv (mdn, rtd 79): half-brother to smart miler Hawksley Hill: eff at 1m, suited by this step up to 12f: goes on hvy grnd, clrly suited by fibresand, sharp trk: type to rate higher & win again.
2606 **TOPAZ 37** [5] H J Collingridge 5-8-0 (26) Jonjo Fowle 8/1: -04002: 5 b g Alhijaz - Daisy Topper *5* **26a**
(Top Ville) Rear, styd on fnl 2f to go 2nd, no hope with wnr: clr rem: stays 12f on fibresand, handles soft.
3112 **ODYN DANCER 15** [10] M D I Usher 3-8-3 (39) G Hannon 5/1: 604003: 3 b f Minshaanshu Amad - *9* **30a**
Themeda (Sure Blade) Off the pace, went past btn horses fnl 2f: btr 537 (Southwell).
3318 **YALAIL 7** [2] K Mahdi 4-9-6 (46) D McGaffin 20/1: 000-04: Chsd ldrs till fdd appr fnl 2f: op 14/1. *1½* **36a**
2712 **QUIET READING 33** [11] 3-10-0 (64) J Bosley 16/1: 036405: Handy till 4f out: top-weight, btr 2213 (10f). *3* **51a**
3284 **BROUGHTONS MILL 8** [6] 5-8-4 (30) R Smith 5/2 FAV: 423606: Nvr better than mid-div: see 1707. *2½* **15a**
2765 **SAINT GEORGE 31** [7] 4-8-12 (38) D Watson 6/1: 042407: Pulled v hard & led after 4f till ent fnl *9* **14a**
4f, lost place: ran way too free over a trip that stretches his stamina, see 1715.

3111 **TIYE** 15 [9] 5-9-5 (45) D Meah (5) 20/1: 306/08: Al towards rear: op 14/1.   7   14a
3007 **WITH RESPECT** 21 [4] 3-8-10 (46) S Finnamore 7/1: -00549: Nvr in it: btr 2382.   6   10a
3914} **COMBINED VENTURE** 339 [1] 4-8-7 (33)(t) D Glennon (3) 16/1: 0366-0: Led 4f, bhd after: 10th,   16   0a
op 12/1 on reapp, AW bow: plcd in '99 (clmr, rtd 41S): '98 rnr-up (mdn, rtd 66): stays 10f on gd, without t-strap.
3236 **ANGUS THE BOLD** 10 [8] 4-8-2 (28) Joanna Badger 14/1: -00060: In tch till halfway: 11th, longer trip.   1¾   0a
11 ran   Time 2m 40.7 (7.1)   (P F I Cole Ltd)   P F I Cole Whatcombe, Oxon

---

3495   7.30 BRINDLEY HCAP 3YO+ 0-85 (D)   1m1f79y aw   Going 26   -06 Slow   [85]
£3799   £1169   £584   £292   3 yo rec 7 lb

3337 **TROIS** 6 [5] J G Given 4-8-13 (70) G Baker (5) 5/1: 504521: 4 b g Efisio - Drei (Lyphard)   75a
Held up, prog after halfway, led going well appr fnl 2f, kept on well: tchd 8/1, quick reapp: back in Jan
won at W'hampton (h'cap): '99 wnr again here at W'hampton (mdn, rtd 67a & earlier modest on turf for L
Cumani, op 9/10f: goes on firm/fast, loves fibresand & W'hampton.
*3272 **JOONDEEY** 8 [12] M A Jarvis 3-9-2 (80) M Tebbutt 5/1: 325212: 3 b c Pursuit Of Love - Blueberry Walk   2   81a
(Green Desert) In tch, prog to chase wnr appr str, styd on for press but no impress: tchd 7/1 & a sound run
on h'cap bow: will win again on fibresand.
3334 **ONE DINAR** 6 [1] K Mahdi 5-9-7 (78) D McGaffin (5) 11/1: 503603: 5 b h Generous - Lypharitissima   ½   78a
(Lightning) Rear, prog halfway, chsd ldrs ent str, kept on onepace: qck reapp: back to form on fav surface.
2950 **RAMBO WALTZER** 22 [11] Miss S J Wilton 3-9-1 (72) R Lake (7) 10/1: 320024: Chsd ldrs, feeling pace   ½   71a
appr fnl 2f, styd on ins last: op 8/1: not far off best, see 517 (C/D clmr).
868 **FAILED TO HIT** 130 [8] 7-8-5 (62)(vis) J Tate 20/1: 634365: Sn in rear & rdn halfway, last 3f out,   1½   59a
kept on well up the str: clr rem, finds this trip inadequate nowadays: spot on next time at 12f: see 530.
*3285 **NOMINATOR LAD** 8 [3] 6-9-1 (72)(bl) R Mullen 10/1: 004416: Led after 2f till bef 3f out, onepace.   6   59a
*3314 **MYSTERIUM** 7 [2] 6-8-1 (58) R Brisland (5) 3/1 FAV: 025117: Nvr going pace to chall: op 5/1,   1   43a
stablemate of 5th, quick reapp: reportedly not face kickback on return to fibresand: see 3314.
3274 **MANXWOOD** 8 [9] 3-8-9 (73) Dean McKeown 8/1: 210028: Early ldr, again appr fnl 3f, hdd & btn   2½   54a
appr 2f out: much btr 3274, see 1726 (8.5f, see 1726).
3281 **LORD EUROLINK** 8 [13] 6-8-10 (67)(vis) T G McLaughlin 12/1: 446459: In tch till 3f out: op 8/1, vis.   2½   44a
*2950 **BARON DE PICHON** 22 [6] 4-9-12 (83) N Callan 20/1: 6-0510: Prom till halfway: 10th, tchd 16/1.   3   55a
3042 **DANCE IN TUNE** 19 [7] 3-9-5 (83) Q Duffield 13/2: 430-50: Bhd after halfway: 12th: see 3042.   0a
2524 Sign Of The Tiger 41 [10] 3-8-9 (73) P Goode (3) 16/12298 **Danzino** 5 [4] 5-10-0 (85)(BL) P McCabe 25/1:
13 ran   Time 2m 01.2 (3)   (Mrs Jo Hardy)   J G Given Willoughton, Lincs

---

3496   8.00 WEATHERBYS DASH COND STKS 2YO (B)   6f aw rnd   Going 26   +04 Fast
£19140   £7260   £3630   £1650

3228 **AMELIA** 10 [12] J Cullinan 2-8-6 R Mullen 9/1: 233431: 2 b f General Monash - Rose Tint (Salse)   79a
With ldrs, went on halfway, hard rdn fnl 1f, edged right, ran on: op 6/1, best time of evening, 1st win, first foal,
front 2 clr: eff at 5f, suited by step up to 6f: handles firm, soft grnd & fibresand, any trk: imprv'g & genuine filly.
2152 **FALCON GOA** 57 [3] N Tinkler 2-8-6 G Duffield 2/1 JT FAV: -04162: 2 b f Sri Pekan - Minden (Bluebird)   ¾   76a
Chsd ldrs, rdn to chase wnr appr fnl 1f, kept on: well clr rem, 8 wk abs, AW bow, nicely bckd: fine run,
goes on gd, soft grnd & fibresand: shld win soon on sand: see 1698.
3205 **BLUE LADY** 11 [9] N P Littmoden 2-8-6 J Tate 20/1: 065063: 2 b f College Chapel - Dancing Bluebird   5   61a
(Bluebird) Struggled to go pace, wide, kept on appr fnl 1f, nvr nr: op 14/1: handles fibresand, fast grnd.
*2766 **WARLINGHAM** 31 [4] Miss Gay Kelleway 2-9-1 M Fenton 6/1: 636214: Chsd ldrs, under press 3f out,   ½   69a
onepace till keepr on nr fin: AW bow, prob handles fibresand, btr 2766 (6f).
2588 **LAW BREAKER** 38 [2] 2-8-11 D O'Donohoe 16/1: 0405: Led 3f, onepace appr fnl 1f: AW bow.   shd   65$
*2635 **SEBULBA** 36 [1] 2-8-11 Dean McKeown 2/1 JT FAV: 216: Prom, no extra 2f out: btr 2635 (Southwell).   shd   65a
-- **FAZENDA** [8] 2-8-6 N Callan 20/1: 7: Nvr on terms: debut: Piccolo filly, cost 1,600gns.   5   48a
2653 **STARRY MARY** 36 [13] 2-8-6 Dale Gibson 16/1: 0408: Al towards rear: AW bow, op 8/1, see 2010.   10   28a
-- **NICOL** [5] 2-8-6 P McCabe 20/1: 9: Outpaced: debut, op 12/1: Nicolotte half-sister to 2 wnrs.   8   8a
3239 **TOMENOSO** 10 [6] 2-8-11 M Tebbutt 25/1: 00: Nvr a factor: 10th, op 10/1 on AW bow.   2   8a
2784 **AUCTIONEERS CO UK** 30 [7] 2-8-11 D Sweeney 7/1: 3P: Chsd ldrs, p.u. after 2f, lame on AW bow.   0a
-- **Mr Tod** [11] 2-8-11 T G McLaughlin 25/1:   -- **Aunt Susan** [10] 2-8-6 G Faulkner 25/1:
13 ran   Time 1m 14.1 (1.3)   (Turf 2000 Ltd)   J Cullinan Quainton, Bucks

---

3497   8.30 EBF FASHION MDN 2YO (D)   7f aw rnd   Going 26   -04 Slow
£3445   £1060   £530   £265

2760 **ACT OF REFORM** 31 [3] R Charlton 2-9-0 M Tebbutt 8/1: 51: 2 b c Lit de Justice - Bionic Soul   84a
(Bionic Light) Towards rear, gd prog over 3f out, rdn to chall 2f out, sn led, kept on well: op 6/1 on AW bow:
Apr foal, dam 1m wnr: apprec step up to a sharp 7f on fibresand: progressive colt, win more AWs.
2565 **JAMILA** 39 [6] E J O'Neill 2-8-9 G Duffield 5/4 FAV: -02202: 2 b f Green Desert - Virelai (Kris)   1½   75a
Led till ent fnl 2f, styd on: nicely bckd: back to best on fibresand: deserves a race, see 2251, 1974.
1774 **CARNIVAL LAD** 73 [1] Sir Michael Stoute 2-9-0 F Lynch 5/1: 253: 2 ch c Caerleon - Fun Crowd (Easy   4   72a
Goer) Trkd ldrs, rdn ent str, onepace: 10 wk abs, AW bow: return to 6f may suit, see 1774, 1612.
3347 **CAVERNARA** 5 [5] T D Barron 2-8-9 P Fessey 11/1: 454: Bhd ldrs, sltly hmpd/stumbled halfway,   1½   64a
unable to qckn ent fnl 2f: quick reapp & again lkd capable of better: keep in mind for a nursery.
3074 **FLIT ABOUT** 17 [8] 2-8-9 M Fenton 3/1: 235: Prom till 2f out: AW bow, btr 3074, 2488.   3½   58a
1924 **MY VERY OWN** 66 [2] 2-9-0 J Tate 20/1: 06: Nvr trbled ldrs: 9 wk abs, AW bow: Persian Bold filly.   3   57a
3003 **CHOCOLATE FOG** 21 [7] 2-8-9 (tVl) R Mullen 33/1: 05057: Front rank 3f, sn btn: t-strap/visor for AW bow.15   22a
-- **JUST MIDAS** [4] 2-9-0 N Callan 16/1: 8: Slow away, al rear: tchd 12/1 on debut: 4,800gns Merdon   5   17a
Melody foal: brother to 2 7f juv wnrs: with K Burke.
3029 **ST NICHOLAS** 19 [9] 2-9-0 Dean McKeown 25/1: 09: Slow away, al bhd: AW bow.   3½   11a
9 ran   Time 1m 28.3 (2.1)   (Highclere Thoroughbred Racing)   R Charlton Beckhampton, Wilts

WOLVERHAMPTON (Fibresand)   SATURDAY AUGUST 19TH   Lefthand, Sharp, Track

3498
9.00 SUPERMODEL SELLER 3-5YO (G)   1m1f79y aw   Going 26   -10 Slow
£1862   £532   £266   3 yo rec 7 lb

2713 **CANADIAN APPROVAL** 33 [2] I A Wood 4-9-5 M Tebbutt 6/1: 211401: 4 ch f With Approval - Atasteforlace   63a
(Laomedonte) Led, pushed clr appr str, unchall, v cmftbly: op 4/1, sold for 9,200gns: earlier won at Lingfield
(AW h'cap) & Southwell (2, sell & clmr): plcd in '99 (val h'cap, rtd 78, P W Harris): eff btwn 1m & 11f: acts
on firm & gd, likes both AWs, run well fresh, forcing the pace: better than a seller.
3272 **AIWIN** 8 [9] G C H Chung 3-8-11 (tBL) M Henry 5/2 FAV: 530532: 3 b c Forzando - Great Aim (Great   7   52a
Nephew) Mid-div, went 2nd bef halfway, styd on till no extra dist: t-strap & blnkd in this lesser grade: claimed
by F Jordan for £5,000 but this was disappointing after 3272 (mdn over C/D).
2765 **INDIAN SWINGER** 31 [10] P Howling 4-9-4 N Callan 12/1: 330003: 4 ch c Up And At 'Em - Seanee   4   46a
Squaw (Indian Ridge) Rear, prog to chase ldrs 4f out till 2f out: tchd 20/1, stiff task, suited by shorter.
2367 **HARD LINES** 47 [5] I A Balding 4-9-4 M Fenton 7/2: -00004: Chsd ldrs till 2f out: bckd on AW bow, abs.   1   45a
2587 **BILLICHANG** 38 [4] 4-9-10 R Mullen 14/1: 100445: Prom 5f: stiff task back in trip, see 775.   7   42a
2946 **PIPPAS PRIDE** 22 [7] 5-9-10 T G McLaughlin 11/4: 030236: Nvr nr ldrs: new stable, likes Southwell.   2   39a
3220 **AVERHAM STAR** 10 [6] 5-9-4 A Hawkins (7) 33/1: 000607: Bhd from halfway: v stiff task, flattered.   1¾ 31$
3094 **AQUADAM** 17 [8] 3-8-11 D McGaffin (5) 25/1: 08: Nvr going pace: AW bow, looks modest.   5   24a
4460} **VALENTINES VISION** 303 [3] 3-8-11 J Tate 16/1: 650-9: Handy 4f: best on debut last term (5f   3   19a
auct mdn on fast grnd, rtd 63): with N Littmoden.
2510 **THIRTY SIX CEE** 42 [1] 3-8-6 Dean McKeown 16/1: 050500: Speed 3f: 10th, stiff task, 6 wk abs.   4   8a
-- **JAY DEES GIRL** [11] 3-8-6 G Faulkner (1) 25/1: 0: Al bhd: 11th on debut.   dist   0a
11 ran   Time 2m 01.6 (3.4)   (Nigel Marris)   I A Wood Upper Lambourn, Berks

3499
9.30 D HARRISON HCAP 3YO+ 0-70 (E)   1m100y aw rnd   Going 26   -23 Slow   [67]
£2779   £794   £397   3 yo rec 6 lb

2634 **ROBBIES DREAM** 36 [2] R M H Cowell 4-8-9 (48)(t) R Mullen 9/2: 500121: 4 ch g Balla Cove - Royal   55a
Golden (Digamist) Well off the pace, still plenty to do 2f out, kept on strgly for hands & heels in the str to get
up final 50y, shade rdly: earlier won at Southwell (h'cap): lightly rcd/unplcd for D Morris in '99 (stks, rtd 51):
unplcd in '98 (mdn, rtd 75): eff around 1m, 10f looks sure to suit on this evidence: acts on fibresand, sharp
trks: goes well fresh, wears a t-strap, without visor: imprvg/unexposed on fibresand.
2946 **AIR OF ESTEEM** 22 [10] P C Haslam 4-9-10 (63) P Goode (3) 14/1: 350452: 4 b g Forzando - Shadow   ¾   67a
Bird (Martinmas) Slow away, imprvd halfway & gd prog to lead well ins last, sn hdd/outpcd by wnr: visor omitted.
3244 **STITCH IN TIME** 10 [12] G C Bravery 4-8-10 (49)(vis) G Baker (5) 10/1: 205433: 4 ch g Inchinor - Late   1¾ 49a
Matinee (Red Sunset) Cl-up, led appr fnl 2f till ins last: op 7/1, clr rem, AW bow: mdn: handles fm, sft & f/sand .
3355 **TEOFILIO** 5 [7] A J McNae 6-10-0 (67)(bl) T G McLaughlin 10/1: 023004: Rear, imprvd halfway, prsd   3   61a
ldr 2f out, no extra dist: top-weight, gd reapp: handles fibresand, will apprec a drop back to 7f/1m, see 594.
*3355 **TAPAGE** 5 [13] 4-9-11 (64)(6ex) M Henry 7/4 FAV: 116215: Chsd ldrs, outpcd appr str & not   4   51a
persevered with: bckd from 7/2, quick reapp: nvr 6 out of 4 here at W'hampton: see 3355.
2634 **APPROACHABLE** 36 [6] 5-8-8 (47) D Glennon (7) 9/1: 202336: In tch, chsd ldrs halfway till 2f out.   ½   33a
2633 **GYPSY SONG** 36 [9] 3-8-6 (51) F Lynch 10/1: -0057: Nvr better than mid-div: h'cap bow, see 2633.   nk 37a
2802 **CRUAGH EXPRESS** 29 [5] 3-8-7 (47) J Tate 20/1: 5-5608: Nvr troubled ldrs: AW bow, mdn, see 1775.   shd 33a
3274 **TOYON** 8 [1] 3-9-5 (64) G Duffield 6/1: 522349: Chsd ldrs till 3f out: mdn, much btr 3274, see 2187.   1¼ 48a
3251 **DOBERMAN** 9 [3] 5-8-3 (42)(vis) Joanna Badger (7) 11/2: 002220: Nvr a factor: 10th, see 2378, 550.   2   22a
3318 **WELODY** 7 [11] 4-9-12 (65)(bl) D McGaffin (5) 25/1: 000000: Led after 3f till appr fnl 2f, sn lost pl: 11th.   5   37a
2890} **PRIMEVAL** 393 [4] 6-8-11 (50) P McCabe 33/1: 0010-0: Al bhd: 12th on reapp: '99 wnr at W'hampton   7   12a
(sell, rtd 57a, 1st time visor): rnr-up sole '98 start (AW bow, mdn, P Harris, rtd 69a): eff at 10/12f on
both AWs: can go well fresh with/without visor, prob best in a t-strap: with K Comerford.
3217 **SKY HOOK** 10 [11] 3-8-7 (52)(BL) M Fenton 11/1: 05-500: Early ldr, btn halfway: 13th, blnkd.   shd 14a
13 ran   Time 1m 50.4 (4.2)   (James Brown)   R M H Cowell Six Mile Bottom, Cambs

PONTEFRACT   SUNDAY AUGUST 20TH   Lefthand, Undulating Track, Stiff Uphill Finish

Official Going   GOOD/FIRM. Stalls: 2m1f - Centre, Remainder - Inside

3500
2.15 SUNDAY PLATE MDN 2YO (D)   5f   Firm 00   -42 Slow
£6032   £1856   £928   £464

1642 **AMIS ANGEL** 79 [12] D Carroll 2-8-9 T Quinn 13/2: 21: 2 b f Fayruz - Khunasira (Nishapour)   80
Al prom, rdn/led inside last, all out to hold on: 11 week abs: slow time: confirmed promise of debut: eff over a
stiff/undul or gall 5f, 6f should suit: acts on firm & gd/soft grnd: runs well fresh.
2113 **FLINT RIVER** 59 [11] R F Johnson Houghton 2-9-0 K Darley 5/4 FAV: 2202: 2 b c Red Ransom - She's   ½   82+
All Class (Rahy) Trckd ldrs, rdn/poised to chall when hmpd & snatched up dist, styd on well inside last, post
came too sn: unlucky, must surely have won this with a clr run: hvly bckd, 2 month abs: acts on firm & gd grnd.
3098 **LADY ROCK** 18 [10] R Bastiman 2-8-9 O Pears 16/1: -00463: 2 b f Mistertopogigo - Bollin Victoria   shd 77$
(Jalmood) Led, rdn/edged left & hdd ins last, kept on: bckd at long odds, op 33/1: jockey given 2-day careless
riding ban: imprvd effort: eff at 5f on firm: interesting for a nursery h'cap: see 1659.
3252 **YNYSMON** 10 [13] A Berry 2-9-0 C Lowther 33/1: 504: Chsd ldrs, rdn/onepace inside last: eff at 5f on   ¾   80
firm grnd: progressed from prev 2 efforts, h'cap company should suit: see 2784.
2668 **SMIRFYS PARTY** 36 [7] 2-9-0 J Weaver 13/2: 625: Keen/prom, held inside last: op 5/1: see 2668.   1½ 76
-- **GOOD TIMING** [3] 2-9-0 F Lynch 33/1: 6: Dwelt, handy halfway, no extra when not much room ins   ¾   74
last: Timeless Times gelding, Jan foal, cost 4,500gns: brother to 7f h'cap wnr Time Vally, dam a 1m/9f wnr.
3174 **DEIDAMIA** 14 [14] 2-8-9 A Culhane 14/1: -47: Held up, mod gains fnl 2f, no threat: op 12/1: see 3174.   ¾   67$
3092 **EAGER ANGEL** 18 [9] 2-8-9 F Lappin 50/1: 58: Prom, held over 1f out: see 3092.   ½   65
2926 **MR PIANO MAN** 25 [1] 2-9-0 J Quinn 15/2: -3059: In tch, held when no room over 1f out: btr 2360.   1   68
-- **YORKER** [8] 2-9-0 J Tate 10/1: 0: Dwelt & al rear: 10th: op 6/1: Boundary colt, Feb foal, cost   nk 67
$15,000: a first foal: dam a mdn: with J Eustace.
1727 **Global Explorer** 76 [15] 2-9-0 M Fenton 50/1:   -- **Northern Castle** [6] 2-9-0 Dale Gibson 25/1:
-- **Distinctive Manna** [4] 2-9-0 P Goode (3) 50/1:

1076

13 ran   Time 1m 03.4 (2.1)   (R McDiarmid)   D Carroll Southwell, Notts

3501
2.45 GO RACING HCAP 3YO+ 0-65 (F)   2m1f22y Firm 00 -37 Slow   [65]
£3802   £1170   £585   £292   3 yo rec 16lb

2734 **KEEP IKIS** 33 [9] Mrs M Reveley 6-9-5 (56) A Culhane 3/1: 143151: 6 ch m Anshan - Santee Sioux   62
(Dancing Brave) Held up, prog halfway, rdn/styd on well to lead ins last, styd on strongly & in command when
eased cl home: bckd, tho' op 5/2: earlier scored at Ripon & Catterick (h'caps): plcd fnl 2 '99 starts (rtd 41,
h'cap), formerly a bmpr rnr up for S Gollings: eff btwn 15f/2m2f, looks a thorough stayer & shld get further:
acts on firm, gd & any track: has run well fresh: tough mare, having a fine season.
3241 **CHIEF WALLAH** 11 [13] D R C Elsworth 4-9-6 (57) N Pollard 9/1: 6-042: 4 b c Be My Chief - Arusha   1½ 59
(Dance Of Life) Prom, rdn/chsd wnr fnl 1f, kept on tho' al held: op 6/1: fine h'cap bow over this longer 2m1f
trip: acts on firm grnd: lightly rcd & open to improvement in similar: see 2691 (mdn).
*3395 **BUSTLING RIO** 4 [7] P C Haslam 4-10-6 (71)(6ex) P Goode (3) 11/4 FAV: 111513: 4 b g Up And At 'Em -hd 72
Une Venitienne (Green Dancer) Held up, prog to lead 3f out till 1f out, onepace/held inside last: bckd, op 7/2.
2951 **VINCENT** 23 [1] J L Harris 5-8-4 (41) Paul Eddery 10/1: -10134: Held up, hdwy 3f out, onepace/held ins 2½ 40
last: op 8/1: creditable turf effort, acts on firm & fast, fibresand specialist: see 2606 (AW).
3026 **RUM BABA** 20 [6] 6-7-12 (35)(bl) P Fessey 16/1: 02-565: Chsd ldrs, outpcd fnl 3f: op 12/1: see 2866.   nk 34
2516 **IRELANDS EYE** 43 [14] 5-9-1 (52) J Weaver 7/1: -33206: Prom 5f out, held over 1f out: abs: see 1276.   3   48
2037 **CAPTIVATING** 62 [10] 5-7-11 (34)(1ow)(14oh) G Bardwell 66/1: 0/0007: Led 14f, fdd: 2 month abs.   ½   29
*3220 **PROTOCOL** 11 [15] 6-8-7 (44)(t) J Quinn 11/2: 422318: Mid div, hdwy 4f out, held 2f out: btr 3220.   1   38
3406 **NOTATION** 3 [5] 6-7-10 (33)(15oh) Joanna Badger (7) 100/1: 040059: Prom halfway, btn 3f out.   1½ 26
2951 **BLACK ICE BOY** 23 [8] 9-7-11 (34)(vis) J McAuley 12/1: Chsd ldrs halfway, btn 3f out: 10th.   4   23
3331 **Allotrope** 7 [4] 5-8-11 (48) G Parkin 25/1:   3331 **Portrack Junction** 7 [16] 3-7-10 (49)(11oh) D Mernagh (0) 100/1:
--   **Peep O Day** [12] 9-7-10 (33)(4oh) P Hanagan (3) 100/1:
2297 **Eastwell Minstrel** 51 [3] 9-8-3 (40)(BL) P Bradley (5) 100/1:
14 ran   Time 3m 46.6 (6.3)   (T McGoran)   Mrs M Reveley Lingdale, N Yorks

3502
3.15 STANLEY HCAP 3YO+ 0-65 (F)   5f rnd Firm 00 -02 Slow   [65]
£4641   £1428   £714   £357   3 yo rec 2 lb

*3436 **PREMIUM PRINCESS** 2 [11] J J Quinn 5-9-4 (55)(6ex) K Darley 13/2: 362411: 5 b m Distant Relative   63
- Solemn Occasion (Secreto) Mid div, rdn/styd on well from over 1f out to lead well inside last: qck reapp under
a pen: recent Sandown wnr (h'cap): '99 Newcastle wnr (h'cap, rtd 62): '98 rnr up (mdn, rtd 64, also rtd 48a):
suited by 5f, stays 7f well: acts on gd/soft, suited by fast/firm: handles any track, loves a stiff/gall one.
3222 **QUITE HAPPY** 11 [14] W J Musson 5-9-7 (58) P Hanagan (7) 7/1: 642222: 5 b m Statoblest - Four   ¾ 62
Legged Friend (Aragon) Handy, rdn/briefly led inside last, kept on well: op 9/1: see 3222, 897.
3113 **PIERPOINT** 16 [8] D Nicholls 5-9-12 (63)(bl) Alex Greaves 8/1: 010053: 5 ch g Archway - Lavinia   2 62
(Habitat) Handy, rdn & kept on onepace in last: op 7/1: fine run under topweight: blinks reapp: see 1868 (C/D).
3297 **SOAKED** 9 [3] D W Chapman 7-9-10 (61)(bl) A Culhane 10/1: 211334: Led & clr over 1f out, rdn/hdd nk 59
& no extra inside last: op 8/1: fine effort under a big weight: remains in gd heart: see 3209.
3222 **SQUARE DANCER** 11 [16] 4-9-9 (60) T Quinn 12/1: 402605: Held up, rdn/kept on fnl 2f, no threat.   1½ 55
3341 **POLAR MIST** 7 [5] 5-9-7 (58) Paul Eddery 14/1: 060206: Chsd ldrs 4f out: op 10/1: see 1487.   ¾ 51
-3349 **PIPS STAR** 6 [2] 3-9-4 (57) F Lynch 11/4 FAV: 001127: Handy, outpcd 1f out: hvly bckd, op 4/1.   hd 49
2650 **FRILLY FRONT** 37 [6] 4-9-3 (54) Lynsey Hanna (7) 20/1: 500428: Mid div, rdn/hung left & btn 1f out.   1 44
3180 **PISCES LAD** 13 [4] 4-9-2 (53) D Mernagh (3) 14/1: 000029: Held up, nvr pace to chall: op 12/1.   ½ 41
3203 **SWYNFORD DREAM** 12 [15] 7-9-3 (54) G Bardwell 25/1: 426000: Mid div at best: 10th: see 798.   ¾ 40
2701 **MOOCHA CHA MAN** 35 [1] 4-9-11 (62)(bl) J Weaver 14/1: 005000: Mid div, rdn/no room over 2f out, hd 47
sn held: fin 11th: see 844, 622.
3455 **MUJAS MAGIC** 2 [18] 5-9-0 (51)(vis) R Fitzpatrick 14/1: 010020: Rear/wide, nvr factor: 12th: op 10/1. nk 35
3283 **Welchs Dream** 9 [3] 3-9-6 (59)(BL) L Swift (7) 50/1:   2833 **Albert The Bear** 30 [3] 7-9-7 (58)(vis) C Lowther 12/1:
3271 **Cool Prospect** 9 [10] 5-9-8 (59) Clare Roche (7) 14/1:
2732 **Lizzie Simmonds** 33 [12] 3-9-5 (58) Joanna Badger (7) 14/1:
3056 **Coco De Mer** 19 [17] 3-9-11 (64) G Parkin 50/1:   3222 **Prime Recreation** 11 [7] 3-9-7 (60) J Quinn 25/1:
18 ran   Time 1m 01.4 (0.1)   (Derrick Bloy)   J J Quinn Settrington, N Yorks

3503
3.45 LISTED FLYING FILLIES STKS 3YO+ (A)   6f rnd Firm 00 +07 Fast
£17793   £5475   £2737   £1368   3 yo rec 3 lb

2167 **ARABESQUE** 57 [9] H R A Cecil 3-8-11 T Quinn 8/1: 314041: 3 b f Zafonic - Prophecy (Warning)   101
Al prom, led inside last, styd on gamely for press, just held on: fast time: 8 week abs: earlier scored at
Salisbury (mdn): rtd 93 in '99: eff at 6f, stys 1m well: acts on firm & soft, loves a stiff/undul or gall
track: likes to race with/force the pace: useful filly, could win again in similar grade.
3120 **JEZEBEL** 16 [8] C F Wall 3-8-11 R Mullen 10/1: -25322: 3 b f Owington - Just Ice (Polar Falcon) hd 100
Chsd ldrs, rdn & styd on well from over 1f out, pcd came too sn, just held: op 7/1: most tough & consistent,
fine run on step up to Listed grade: deserves a race: see 1078.
3120 **JEMIMA** 16 [11] T D Easterby 3-8-11 (BL) J Weaver 14/1: 000603: 3 b f Owington - Poyle Fizz   nk 99
(Damister) Mid div, rdn, switched & strong run fnl 1f, pcd came too sn: woken up by blnks: worth another ch at 7f.
3301 **BOAST** 8 [4] R F Johnson Houghton 3-8-11 C Lowther 9/1: 351034: Chsd ldrs, rdn/onepace ins last.   1 97
3172 **DAMALIS** 14 [12] 4-9-0 F Lynch 20/1: 010035: Led till inside last, no extra: fine eff, stays 6f, all nk 96
wins at 5f: loves Chester: see 2247 (h'cap).
2646 **DANDY NIGHT** 37 [10] 3-8-11 D Harrison 14/1: -01306: Handy, onepace inside last: op 10/1: see 2289. hd 95
3328 **PERFECT PEACH** 7 [1] 5-9-0 P Goode 66/1: 434627: Held up, prog/chsd ldrs over 1f out, sn held.   1 93$
3212 **HOT TIN ROOF** 14 [3] 4-9-4 K Darley 11/8 FAV: 236148: Rear, eff 2f out, no hdwy/held inside last: 2 92
hvly bckd, tchd 6/4: connections reportedly blamed firm grnd for this below-par effort: topweight here: see 2646.
3301 **MAGIC OF LOVE** 8 [13] 3-8-11 M Fenton 12/1: 330469: Held up, nvr pace to chall: see 3301, 1830.   shd 88
3155 **KASHRA** 15 [14] 3-8-11 M Roberts 12/1: 400020: Dwelt, keen/al towards rear: 10th: btr 3155 (7f).   ½ 86
3152 **ALEGRIA** 15 [2] 4-9-0 J Tate 33/1: 010600: Held up, eff/no room over 2f out, sn held: 11th: see 2151. 2½ 79
3120 **FLOWINGTON** 16 [6] 3-8-11 J Quinn 33/1: 042030: Chsd ldrs 4f: 12th: btn 3120, 1371.   2½ 72
3059 **MAY CONTESSA** 19 [5] 3-8-11 N Pollard 5/1: -11300: In tch, btn over 1f out: 13th, wants easier grnd. ½ 70
13 ran   Time 1m 13.7 (u0.4)   (K Abdulla)   H R A Cecil Newmarket, Suffolk

3504
4.15 SILENTNIGHT BEDS HCAP 3YO+ 0-100 (C) 1m4f **Firm 00 -36 Slow** [88]
£6792 £2090 £1045 £522 3 yo rec 10lb

2127 **LIDAKIYA 58** [1] Sir Michael Stoute 3-9-8 (92) T Quinn 6/4 FAV: 41121: 3 b f Kahyasi - Lilissa (Doyoun) 96+
Prom, rdn/led over 1f out, styd on strongly to pull clr under hands & heels riding fnl 1f, eased nr fin: hvly bckd,
tchd 2/1: earlier won at Thirsk (mdn) & Newbury (fillies h'cap): eff at 10/12f, 14f+ should suit: acts on firm &
gd/soft, stiff or sharpish track: prog filly, decisive success here, one to keep on your side.
3058 **THREE GREEN LEAVES 19** [4] M Johnston 4-9-12 (86) J Weaver 5/2: 313662: 4 ch f Environment 3½ 84
Friend - Kick The Habit (Habitat) Prom, outpcd 2f out, chsd wnr inside last, no threat: nicely bckd tho' op 2/1.
3173 **JUST GIFTED 14** [2] R M Whitaker 4-9-4 (67) F Lynch 10/1: 622203: 4 b g Rudimentary - Parfait nk 64
Armour (Clantime) Led till over 1f out, no extra: op 8/1: acts on firm & gd/soft grnd: see 1499 (C/D).
2600 **MONTECRISTO 39** [5] R Guest 7-10-0 (88) N Pollard 8/1: 0-3554: Held up, rdn/outpcd fnl 2f: op 6/1. 2½ 81
3224 **ARCHIE BABE 11** [3] K Darley 4/1: 101025: Chsd ldrs, drvn/held 1f out: bckd: btr 3224. 2½ 69
5 ran Time 2m 38.4 (4.3) (H H Aga Khan) Sir Michael Stoute Newmarket, Suffolk

3505
4.45 WAKEFIELD MDC HCAP 3YO 0-90 (C) 1m rnd **Firm 00 -05 Slow** [96]
£6955 £2140 £1070 £535

*1352 **EVEREST 93** [4] P F I Cole 3-9-2 (84) K Darley 6/4 FAV: -23211: 3 ch c Indian Ridge - Reine d'Beaute 88
(Caerleon) Chsd ldrs, chsd ldr fnl 2f, drvn & styd on gamely ins last to lead nr line: nicely bckd, 3 mth abs:
earlier won at Thirsk (mdn), plcd all 4 starts prev: suited by 1m, stays a sharp 9f, cld get further: acts on
firm & hvy grnd, sharp/stiff trk: runs well fresh: tough & consistent colt, open to further improvement.
3254 **SIR FERBET 10** [3] B W Hills 3-9-3 (85) A Culhane 5/2: 010042: 3 b c Mujadil - Mirabiliary (Crow) hd 88
Cl up, led over 2f out, strongly pressed/hard rdn ins last, just hdd nr fin: op 2/1: loves fast/firm: see 3254, 1853.
*3221 **SEEKING SUCCESS 11** [2] Sir Michael Stoute 3-9-3 (85) T Quinn 7/4: 022613: 3 b f Seeking The Gold - 7 77
Testy Trestle (Private Account) Led till over 2f out, sn held by front pair: bckd: btr 3221 (C/D mdn).
3158 **JAMADYAN 15** [1] H Akbary 3-9-7 (89) J Stack 12/1: 1-6464: Chsd ldrs 5f: btr 3158, 2228 (6/7f). 9 68
4 ran Time 1m 42.2 (0.4) (H R H Prince Fahd Salman) P F I Cole Whatcombe, Oxon

3506
5.15 KIDS COME FREE MDN 3YO+ (D) 1m rnd **Firm 00 -21 Slow**
£4543 £1398 £699 £349 3 yo rec 6 lb

3189 **BEDEY 13** [8] A C Stewart 3-8-12 M Roberts 8/13 FAV: -4221: 3 b c Red Ransom - Mount Helena 83
(Danzig) Chsd ldrs, went on over 2f out, styd on strongly & in command inside last when eased down twds fin: val
for 3L+: well bckd at odds on: eff at 1m, prob stays a sharp 10f: acts on firm & gd, sharp or stiff/undul track.
3746} **MUSH 352** [13] N P Littmoden 3-8-12 C Carver (3) 16/1: 03-2: 3 b c Thatching - Petite Jameel 1 77
(Ahonoora) Held up, prog/rdn to press wnr 2f out, kept on tho' al held ins last: clr rem, reapp: plcd on 2nd
of just 2 '99 starts (rtd 70, auct mdn): stys a stiff/undul 1m on firm grnd: encouraging reapp, qual for h'caps.
3343 **HUGS DANCER 7** [5] J G Given 3-8-12 M Fenton 5/1: -33: 3 b g Cadeaux Genereux - Embracing 6 66
(Reference Point) Chsd ldrs, rdn/held fnl 2f: bred to apprec 1m+: rtd higher on debut in 3343.
-- **GLENHURICH** [2] M Johnston 3-8-7 K Darley 7/1: 4: Prom, no room over 3f out, rdn/held fnl 2f: ¾ 60
op 9/2: debut: Sir Pekan filly, likely to apprec 7f/1m.
3116 **CARRIE CAN CAN 16** [20] 3-8-7 J Tate 25/1: 65: Held up, hdwy 3f out, sn held: see 3116. 6 49
3477} **CARRADIUM 723** [19] 4-9-4 P Goode (3) 66/1: 6556/6: Held up, hdwy 3f out, no prog fnl 2f: reapp, 1¼ 51
long abs: missed '99: tried up to 7f in '98 (rtd 65).
3126 **MAYBEE 16** [16] 4-8-13 N Pollard 40/1: 37: Held up, hdwy 4f out, btn 2f out: btr 3126. 2½ 41
-- **VITUS BERING** [18] 3-8-12 (t) J Quinn 16/1: 8: Held up, rdn/btn 2f out: debut: t strap: brother 1 44
to high class 1m performer Matiara: gelding, with D J Murphy.
3201 **CONCINO 12** [1] 3-8-12 C Lowther 100/1: 0-0309: In tch, btn 3f out: flattered 2930 (13f). ½ 43$
2187} **LADY FLORA 423** [9] 4-8-13 G Bardwell 66/1: 6-0: Strugg halfway: 10th: reapp: no form sole '99 start. hd 37
-- **HICKLETON DREAM** [10] 3-8-7 F Lynch 66/1: 0: Dwelt al bhd: 11th: debut with G Woodward. nk 36
3326 **HAMISH G 7** [11] 3-8-12 T Eaves (7) 66/1: 00: Slowly away & al bhd: 12th: no form. ½ 40
3326 **MY LINE 7** [12] 3-8-12 A Culhane 66/1: -000: Al bhd: 13th: improve in low-grade h'caps over further. nk 39
3012 **LA SYLPHIDE Gb 21** [6] 3-8-7 T Williams 33/1: 360: Chsd ldrs, btn 3f out: 14th: btr 3012. hd 33
3343 Dawn Traveller 7 [7] 3-8-7 J Stack 50/1: 3330 Time For The Clan 7 [3] 4-8-12 J McAuley 66/1:
2865 Stamford Hill 28 [3] 5-9-4 D Allan (7) 100/1: 2543 Butterwick Chief 41 [15] 3-8-12 P Hanagan (7) 50/1:
-- Ashville Lad [14] 3-8-12 J Weaver 16/1:
19 ran Time 1m 43.5 (1.7) (Sheikh Ahmed Al Maktoum) A C Stewart Newmarket, Suffolk

Official Going GOOD. Stalls: 10f - Stands Side; Rem - Inside.

3507
2.25 BARNARDOS COND STKS 2YO (C) 6f rnd **Good/Firm 36 -30 Slow**
£5890 £2090 £1045 £475

3372 **SILCA LEGEND 7** [2] M R Channon 2-8-13 J Reid 5/4: 221261: 2 ch c Efisio - Silca Cisa (Hallgate): 97
Unruly before start, sn led, rdn & styd on well appr final 1f, rdn out: well bckd, qck reapp: recent Newcastle
wnr (mdn), plcd sev times: half-brother to Irish Guineas 2nd Golden Silca: suited by 6f, 7f should suit: acts on
firm & gd/soft, handles soft & likes to force the pace: acts on a gall or sharp trk: v tough & still improving.
*3273 **RIVER RAVEN 9** [3] Sir Mark Prescott 2-8-13 G Duffield 6/5 FAV: 21412: 2 b c Efisio - River Spey 1¼ 93
(Mill Reef): Trkd ldrs, rdn to chall appr final 1f, carried hd high & onepcd final 1f: apprec a return to 7f.
-- **JUST WOODY** [1] A Berry 2-8-7 T E Durcan 12/1: 3: 2 br c Charmwood Forest - Zalamera (Rambo 1 84
Dancer) Cl-up, drvn & not pace of front 2 final 1f: 16,000 gns Mar foal, dam modest: sire high class
at 7f/1m: eff at 6f on fast grnd: gd debut.
3062 **WALLY MCARTHUR 19** [4] A Berry 2-9-4 J Carroll 8/1: 321104: Dwelt, rear, lost tch final 2f: op 6/1, 13 61
stablemate of 3rd: again disapp & twice below 2754.
4 ran Time 1m 17.09 (3.99) (Aldridge Racing Ltd) M R Channon West Isley, Berks.

3508   2.55 EBF MBNA MDN 2YO (D)   7f rnd   Good/Firm 36   -07 Slow
£3503   £1078   £539   £269

3064 **PUTRA PEKAN** 19 [1] M A Jarvis 2-9-0 (BL) P Robinson 11/2: 061: 2 b c Grand Lodge - Mazarine Blue **88**
(Bellypha): Prom, chall ldr appr final 1f, styd on strongly & drvn out to lead final strides: first time blnks:
up in trip: 42,000gns half-brother to 3 juv wnrs, one smart: dam a sprinter: eff at 7f on fast grnd & a sharp
trk: apprec this step up in trip & sharpened up by blnks.
-- **ATTACHE** [6] M Johnston 2-9-0 R Hills 7/1: 2: 2 ch c Wolfhound - Royal Passion (Ahonoora): hd 87
Mid-div, gd hdwy to lead appr final 1f, kept on well but hdd nr fin: op 5/1, 8L clr rem: Mar foal, half-brother
to smart sprinter Tadeo, dam won over 10f: eff at 7f on fast: good debut & will go one better sn.
3223 **TROYS GUEST** 11 [9] E J Alston 2-8-9 W Supple 15/2: 533: 2 gr f Be My Guest - Troja (Troy): 8 68
Dsptd lead, led briefly appr final 1f, wknd qckly dist: lngr 7f trip: see 3223.
3156 **REGENT COURT** 15 [5] T D Easterby 2-8-9 J Carroll 9/2: 54: Hmpd after 1f, rear, rdn/hdwy over 1½ 65
2f out, no extra final 1f: op 3/1: shade btr 3156.
2873 **SEDUCTIVE** 27 [4] 2-9-0 G Duffield 3/1 FAV: 0235: Led, drvn/hdd over 1f out, wknd qckly: btr 2873. 2 66
-- **A C AZURE** [2] 2-9-0 T E Durcan 25/1: 6: Dwelt/rear, nvr dngr: 46,000 Dolphin Street colt, half- 2 62
brother to sev wnrs abroad & a wng hdler: will learn from this, with P D Evans.
3121 **FOLLOW YOUR STAR** 16 [7] 2-9-0 Pat Eddery 4/1: 667: Chsd ldrs, hmpd 2f out & sn wknd: btr 3121. nk 61
3169 **ACADEMIC RECORD** 14 [3] 2-9-0 N Callan 20/1: -08: Missed break, al last: op 12/1: see 3169. 12 37
8 ran   Time 1m 27.99 (2.99)   (HRH Sultan Ahmad Shah)   M A Jarvis Newmarket.

3509   3.25 CHESTER LISTED RTD HCAP 3YO+ 0-110 (A)   1m5f89y   Good/Firm 36   +06 Fast   [116]
£19399   £6883   £3421   £1564   3 yo rec 11lb

1401 **ZAAJER** 92 [1] E A L Dunlop 4-9-7 (109) R Hills 9/2: 04-331: 4 ch h Silver Hawk - Crown Quest **111**
(Chief's Crown): Made all, edged left for press when strongly prsd inside last, all-out & just prevailed:
3 mth abs: in '99 won on reapp at York (Listed, rtd 111), prev term won at Ascot (stks, rtd 105+): eff at
10.4/13.4f: acts on fast & soft grnd: runs well fresh on any trk: tough & smart.
3134 **LIGHTNING ARROW** 16 [2] H J Dunlop 4-9-6 (108) Pat Eddery 1/3 FAV: 024122: 4 br g Silver Hawk - shd 109
Strait Lane (Chieftain II): Slow to start, sn prom, rdn to chall dist, ev ch inside last, just held:
well bckd at long odds-on: v tough, useful & consistent: see 2803.
1474 **TAUFANS MELODY** 88 [3] Lady Herries 9-9-0 (102) J Reid 9/1: 4/0023: 9 b g Taufan - Glorious Fate ½ 102
(Northfields): Trkd ldrs, short of room over 2f out, gd hdwy when squeezed for room & hmpd dist, swtchd, drvn &
ran on strongly well ins last, not btn far: 3 mth abs: v unlucky: tough 9yo, see 1247.
1225 **FIRST TRUTH** 102 [4] A Bailey 3-7-10 (95)(3oh) J Mackay 14/1: -64204: Al last, lost tch final 28 65
3f, t.o: op 10/1: longer 13.4f trip: would probably apprec a drop in trip: see 990.
4 ran   Time 2m 53.79 (3.99)   (Hamdan Al Maktoum)   E A L Dunlop Newmarket.

3510   3.55 LINDEN HOMES HCAP 3YO+ 0-100 (C)   7f122y rnd   Good/Firm 36   +07 Fast   [99]
£14820   £4560   £2280   £1140   3 yo rec 6 lb

3377 **LADY BOXER** 4 [5] M Mullineaux 4-7-11 (68)(1ow)(12oh) A Mackay 50/1: 000001: 4 b f Komaite - Lady **74**
Broker (Petorius): In tch, rdn & ran on well to lead inside last, rider dropped whip & pushed out: best time
of day, qck reapp: well btn prev this term: '99 wnr here at Chester (class stks, rtd 79), also a fine 4th in
the Ayr Silver Cup: '98 Leicester debut wnr (auct mdn, rtd 84 at best): eff at 6/7.5f on firm, likes gd & hvy:
handles any trk but clearly goes well here at Chester: runs well when fresh: back to form from 12lbs o/h.
3322 **DEMOLITION JO** 8 [7] W M Brisbourne 5-7-13 (70)(vis) K Dalgleish (5) 20/1: 000602: 5 gr m Petong - 2½ 71
Fire Sprite (Mummy's Game): Rcd keenly cl-up, chall ldr over 3f out, went on appr final 1f, hdd inside last
& not pace of wnr: stays 7.5f: gd run, likes Chester: see 1074.
3325 **PETERS IMP** 3 [3] A Berry 5-8-4 (75) J Carroll 10/1: 011433: 5 b g Imp Society - Catherine Clare nk 75
(Sallust): Bhd, rdn/prog over 2f out, styd on well, nvr nrr: continues in gd form: see 3325, 2999.
3325 **NOMORE MR NICEGUY** 8 [10] E J Alston 6-8-2 (73) W Supple 14/1: 400664: Bhd, ran on strongly nk 72
for press inside last, nrst fin: well h'capped but on a long losing run: see 977.
2616 **GIFT OF GOLD** 38 [11] 5-8-12 (83) Pat Eddery 9/1: 013005: In tch, drvn over 1f out, ran on inside ¾ 80
last: gd effort on grnd faster than ideal: see 2616, 1483.
3427 **SILCA BLANKA** 2 [2] 8-9-10 (95) J Reid 7/1: 100608: Mid-div, late hdwy, no threat: ran 48hrs ago. 1 90
*3427 **CANTINA 2** [12] 6-9-3 (88)(6ex) J Mackay (5) 7/2 FAV: 431117: Led after 1f, hdd appr final 1f, ¾ 81
wknd inside last: ran 2 days ago: nicely bckd tho' op 3/1 & better expected but this poss came too sn after 3427.
2528 **ESPADA** 42 [8] 4-9-5 (90) S Sanders 11/1: 621008: Bhd, eff/no room over 1f out, no dngr: 6 wk abs. nk 82
3297 **LAKELAND PADDY** 9 [13] 3-8-1 (78) A Nicholls (3) 25/1: 364109: Nvr a factor: poor draw: see 1783. nk 69
2696 **PENSION FUND** 36 [4] 6-8-7 (78) T Lucas 7/1: 6-3000: Bhd, prog/short of room over 2f out, sn 1¼ 67
btn, eased, fin 10th: drop in trip: see 1217.
-- **CONTACT** [1] 3-9-2 (93) P Robinson 20/1: 3616-0: Slow to start, al bhd, 11th: reapp/British bow: 3 76
'99 scorer at Leopardstown (6f mdn, gd/soft): now with M Wigham.
+3250 **MISTER MAL** 11 [6] 4-8-6 (77) G Duffield 11/2: 050010: Led early, no room appr final 3f, swtchd 1½ 57
& wknd for press final 2f, fin 12th: op 9/2: likes to dominate, made most in 3250.
*3130 **ZIETZIG** 16 [14] 3-8-3 (80) N Callan 12/1: 064010: Dwelt, sn rdn & prom, wknd for press final 1 58
2f, 13th: likes to front run & unable to dominate here: much btr 3130.
2997 **BOLD KING** 22 [9] M Hills 7/1: -10300: Front rank, wknd qckly final 2f, fin last. 6 58
14 ran   Time 1m 34.57 (2.17)   (Esprit de Corps Racing)   M Mullineaux Alpraham, Cheshire.

3511   4.25 WHITE FRIARS HCAP 3YO+ 0-85 (D)   2m   Good/Firm 36   -11 Slow   [72]
£4394   £1352   £676   £338   3 yo rec 14lb

3323 **BUSY LIZZIE** 8 [6] J L Dunlop 3-9-7 (79) Pat Eddery 9/4 FAV: 206251: 3 b f Sadler's Wells - Impatiente **90**
(Vaguely Noble): Settled rear, smooth hdwy appr final 2f, led over 1f out, pushed well clr ins last: nicely bckd,
1st win: unplcd in both '99 starts: full sister to useful, late maturing styr Eminence Grise: suited by recent
step up to 14f/2m: acts on fast, soft & a sharp trk: runs well fresh: imprvg stayer, can win more staying races.
3323 **JASEUR** 8 [3] G Barnett 7-9-12 (70)(bl) L Vickers (7) 25/1: 000602: 7 b g Lear Fan - Spur Wing 7 72
(Storm Bird): Sn led & clr, drvn/hdd appr final 1f, not pace of wnr: well h'capped but has not won for nrly 3 yrs.
2672 **NORTHERN MOTTO** 36 [2] J S Goldie 7-8-3 (47) W Supple 9/2: 333443: 7 b g Mtoto - Soulful (Zino): 1½ 47

CHESTER SUNDAY AUGUST 20TH Lefthand, Very Tight Track

Front rank, drvn/dropped rear over 2f out, kept on final 1f but no ch with wnr: consistent form: see 2672.
3181 **ASHLEIGH BAKER 13** [4] M Johnston 5-8-7 (51) K Dalgleish (5) 4/1: 161244: Prom, drvn/outpcd *hd* **51**
over 2f out, late hdwy, no dngr: unproven at 2m: see 2783 (12f).
3276 **BLACK WEASEL 9** [3] 5-7-10 (40) Claire Bryan (5) 9/1: -05625: Lead early, remnd cl-up, rdn/btn fnl 2f. *1* **39**
3331 **SALSKA 7** [1] 9-8-12 (56) N Callan 12/1: 542506: Mid-div, rdn/held final 2f: see 3331. *2* **53$**
1180 **DISTANT STORM 105** [5] 7-8-7 (51)(bl)(1ow) S Sanders 11/1: 22-407: Mid-div, rdn/lost tch appr *3½* **57**
final 2f: op 8/1: plcd twice over timber (2m h'caps, rtd 109h, acts on any grnd) since 1180.
1711 **MY LEGAL EAGLE 77** [7] 6-9-2 (60) G Hannon (7) 12/1: 360608: Nvr a factor: 11 wk abs: see 1023. *½* **52**
3348 **YES KEEMO SABEE 6** [8] 5-8-1 (45) O Pears 6/1: 025339: In tch, wknd qckly final 3f: qck reapp. *15* **22**
3095 **IT CAN BE DONE 18** [10] 3-8-2 (60) P M Quinn (3) 25/1: 600600: Dwelt, rear, t.o. final 5f, *dist* **0**
fin 10th: reportedly fin distressed: big step up in trip: see 1645 (1m, soft).
10 ran Time 3m 30.18 (7.48) (Nigel Clark (Susan Abbott Racing)) J L Dunlop Arundel, West Sussex.

3512 4.55 ROWTON MOOR HCAP 3YO+ 0-85 (D) 5f rnd Good/Firm 36 -09 Slow [82]
£5947 £1830 £915 £457 3 yo rec 2 lb

3123 **CLASSY CLEO 16** [6] P D Evans 5-9-1 (69) T E Durcan 14/1: 464001: 5 b m Mujadil - Sybaris (Crowned **74**
Prince): Chsd ldrs, gd hdwy to lead fnl 1f, drvn out, just held on: unplcd on turf prev this term & tumbled
down weights: '99 Redcar wnr (h'cap, rtd 99a & 100 at best): '98 Chester (2) & Redcar wnr (h'caps, rtd 96):
6-time wnr in '97 (rtd 100a & 86): eff at 5/6f on any grnd/trk, likes Chester: v tough & on a handy mark.
3222 **STATOYORK 11** [7] D Shaw 7-7-12 (52) T Williams 14/1: 000002: 7 b g Statoblest - Ultimate Dream *nk* **56**
(Kafu) Unruly in stalls, bhd, short of room over 2f out, drvn & ran on well final 1f, just failed: back to form.
*1662 **BODFARI KOMAITE 79** [4] M W Easterby 4-9-4 (72) T Lucas 4/1: -W2113: 4 b g Komaite - Gypsy's *1* **73**
Barn Rat (Balliol): Led, hdd after 1f, remnd cl-up, led again appr final 1f, hdd inside last, held cl-home:
11 wk abs: should be just sharper for this & shld go in again: see 1662.
3322 **POLLY GOLIGHTLY 8** [3] M Blanshard 7-8-8 (62)(bl) Dale Gibson 5/1: 400004: Prom, drvn/onepcd *¾* **61**
inside last: op 4/1: won this last year off a 1lb higher mark: see 1980, 1005.
3135 **NIFTY MAJOR 16** [1] 3-9-4 (74) J Reid 14/1: 000005: Led after 1f, hdd over 1f out, sn btn. *½* **71**
3283 **ZIGGYS DANCER 9** [2] 9-9-4 (72) W Supple 14/1: 000006: Waited with, prog over 2f out, no danger. *nk* **68**
3398 **MARENGO 4** [14] 6-8-2 (56) R Ffrench 20/1: 063657: Bhd, rdn to impr over 1f out, styd on well *hd* **51**
final 1f, nrst fin: qck reapp & not disgrcd from a poor draw today: see 1073.
3222 **SIHAFI 11** [5] 7-8-7 (61)(BL) Pat Eddery 3/1 FAV: 432458: Waited with, eff/short of room over *¾* **54**
1f out, styg on when hmpd ins last, no ch after, eased: nicely bckd in 1st time blnks, unlucky not to have fin clsr.
*3271 **SOTONIAN 9** [9] 7-8-4 (58) A Nicholls (3) 12/1: 536519: Prom, rdn/fdd appr final 1f: btr 3271. *¾* **49**
3398 **MISS FIT 4** [8] 4-8-6 (60) G Duffield 12/1: 005500: Nvr dngr, fin 10th: qck reapp. *½* **49**
3257 **MADAME JONES 10** [10] 5-8-5 (59) K Dalgleish (5) 33/1: 000-00: Rear, nvr a factor, 11th: see 3257. *3½* **38**
3322 **THREAT 8** [12] 4-8-13 (67)(t) G Faulkner (3) 12/1: 006000: Dwelt, sn in tch, eff 3f out, sn btn, 12th. *3½* **36**
3222 **WESTCOURT MAGIC 11** [11] 7-8-13 (67) S Sanders 16/1: -00000: Sn rdn, wknd qckly over 2f out, 13th. *1½* **32**
3322 **CARTMEL PARK 8** [13] 4-9-10 (78) O Pears 25/1: 010300: Early speed, wknd fnl 2f, 14th: poor draw. *5* **29**
14 ran Time 1m 02.06 (2.26) (J E Abbey) P D Evans Pandy, gwent.

BATH SUNDAY AUGUST 20TH Lefthand, Turning Track with Uphill Finish

Official Going GOOD. Stalls: Straight Course - Far side: Round Course - Inside.

3513 2.35 SUNDAY AUCT MDN 2YO (D) 5f rnd Good/Firm 20 -02 Slow
£4104 £1263 £631 £315

3277 **REEL BUDDY 9** [6] R Hannon 2-8-12 P Dobbs (5) 6/4 FAV: 620001: 2 ch c Mr Greeley - Rosebud **95**
(Indian Ridge) With ldrs going well, led 2f out, pushed out, readily: hvly bckd: not btn far into 7th in a Gr 3
earlier: 23,000gns foal: eff at 5f should stay 6f: acts on fast & gd/soft grnd, prob any track: useful colt.
3187 **TICKLE 13** [7] P J Makin 2-7-12 A Beech (3) 7/2: 022: 2 b f Primo Dominie - Funny Choice *3* **70+**
(Commanche Run) Rear & pushed along, gd wide progress appr fnl 1f, styd on to go 2nd nr fin, nvr nr wnr:
found this drop back to 5f against her: handles fast grnd: interesting at 6f next time: see 3187.
3252 **TWILIGHT MISTRESS 10** [4] D W P Arbuthnot 2-8-0 F Norton 10/1: -0043: 2 b f Bin Ajwaad - By *nk* **71**
Candlelight (Roi Danzig) Led till 2f out, onepace: op 6/1: ran to best from the front.
3055 **ELLENDUNE GIRL 19** [2] D J S ffrench Davis 2-7-12 P Doe 25/1: 0504: Mid div, eff over 2f out, no *1¾* **64**
impress on ldrs: improved run, could win a seller & will apprec 6f.
3109 **LAI SEE 17** [10] 2-8-3 B Marcus 11/2: 022255: Prom till no extra appr fnl 1f: tchd 7/1, btr 2868, 2360. *1* **66**
3252 **WINTER DOLPHIN 10** [1] 2-8-0 L Newman (1) 50/1: 06: Prom, fdd appr fnl 1f. *1½* **59**
3143 **BARON CROCODILE 15** [9] 2-8-5 (BL) D O'Donohoe 12/1: 450247: Chsd ldrs, rdn 2f out & btn: *5* **51**
blnkd, drifter from 7/1: softer grnd suits, see 2532.
-- **FESTIVE AFFAIR** [3] 2-8-9 M Tebbutt 8/1: 8: Dwelt, nvr in it: op 5/1 on debut: 18,000gns *2* **50**
Mujadil colt, dam & sire sprinters: with B Smart.
3169 **JUNIOR BRIEF 14** [8] 2-8-5 Craig Williams 33/1: -00009: Nvr dangerous, swished tail: needs sells. *nk* **45**
2933 **MY FRIEND JACK 24** [5] 2-8-3 A Daly 14/1: -5060: Bhd bef halfway: 10th, btr 2933, 993. *2* **38**
10 ran Time 1m 01.4 (1.1) (Speedlith Group) R Hannon East Everleigh, Wilts

3514 3.05 DICK REYNOLDS HCAP 3YO+ 0-80 (D) 1m rnd Good/Firm 20 -05 Slow [74]
£4095 £1260 £630 £315 3 yo rec 6 lb

3355 **WARRING 6** [6] M S Saunders 6-7-10 (42)(4oh) R Brisland (5) 10/1: 300341: 6 b g Warrshan - Emerald **45**
Ring (Auction Ring) In tch, chsd ldr 2f out, hard rdn bef dist, kept on gamely to lead fnl 50y: qck reapp: dual
'99 rnr up (h'cap, rtd 54): '98 Windsor wnr (2, h'caps, rtd 61): poor jmps form: eff arnd 1m on firm & gd/soft
grnd, has tried a t strap: likes Windsor: well h'capped despite 4lbs o/h.
*3139 **BARABASCHI 16** [2] J H M Gosden 4-10-0 (74) G Baker (5) 7/2 JT FAV: -22612: 4 b g Elmaamul - Hills' *¾* **75**
Presidum (Presidum) Keen & led after 2f, rdn ent fnl 1f, worn down towards fin: gd run but uphill finish &
top-weight just found out this hard-puller: eff at 1m, worth another try back at 7f: see 3139.
3259 **PAGAN KING 10** [3] J A R Toller 4-9-6 (66) J P Spencer 9/1: 6-0043: 4 b g Unblest - Starinka *hd* **66**
(Risen Star) Bhd, under press appr fnl 2f, styd on bef dist, nvr nrr: eff at 7f, apprec return to 1m: see 895.
3207 **SHAANXI ROMANCE 12** [10] M J Polglase 5-8-6 (52)(vis) F Norton 4/1: 611234: Mid div, shaken up 3f *nk* **51**

out, improving & short of room bef 2f out, styd on for hands & heels, not btn far: nicely bckd, clr rem: hmpd at a crucial stage & prob unlucky not to have made the frame: remains in form & is worth another ch, see 3078
3365 **ITALIAN SYMPHONY 5** [8] 6-8-10 (56)(vis) D Sweeney 14/1: 635165: Outpcd, rdn halfway, styd on late. 4 **48**
3254 **KNOCKTOPHER ABBEY 10** [1] 3-9-12 (78) G Hind 9/2: -50536: In tch, lost pl halfway, kept on inside last: bckd from 11/2: appeared unsuited by this turning track: see 3254, 1826. ¾ **68**
*3207 **MINETTA 12** [9] 5-10-0 (74) P Doe 7/2 JT FAV: 650017: Nvr a factor: btr 3207 (C/D, beat this 4th). *shd* **64**
3355 **MAGICAL BAILIWICK 6** [4] 4-8-9 (55)(BL) S Carson (3) 33/1: -00008: Early ldr, prom till lost place 2f out & hung left: quick reapp, blinkd, see 2270. *nk* **44**
3230 **RASHIK 11** [7] 6-9-12 (72) R Havlin 33/1: 1/59: Chsd ldrs 5f: see 3230. 2½ **57**
9 ran Time 1m 40.3 (2) (Chris Scott) M S Saunders Haydon, Somerset

3515

3.35 DICK HERN COND STKS 3YO+ (B) 1m rnd Good/Firm 20 +10 Fast
£9187 £3484 £1742 £792 3 yo rec 6 lb

3107 **FULL FLOW 17** [6] B W Hills 3-8-7 J P Spencer 6/1: 0-4401: 3 b c Eagle Eyed - Fast Flow (Riverman) **104**
Confidently held up, prog halfway, rdn below dist & ran on to lead fnl strides: fast time, well rdn: '99 debut wnr at Newcastle (mdn, Listed rnr up, rtd 102): eff at 7f/1m on firm & gd/soft, any trk: useful colt, nds to come late.
2995 **BRILLIANT RED 22** [4] Mrs L Richards 7-9-2 (t) I Mongan 6/1: 000362: 7 b g Royal Academy - Red Comes Up (Blushing Groom) Well plcd, rdn to lead ent fnl 1f, hdd cl home: ran to best conceding weight. *hd* **106**
3107 **PULAU TIOMAN 17** [5] M A Jarvis 4-8-13 Craig Williams 6/4 FAV: 242203: 4 b c Robellino - Ella Mon Amour (Ela Mana Mou) Held up, shaken up 2f out, rdn bef dist, kept on strongly fnl 100y, too late: well bckd from 5/2: given a lot to do & still below early season form, see 115. *shd* **103**
3177 **CIRCLE OF LIGHT 14** [3] P W D'Arcy 3-8-2 B Marcus 9/1: 323304: Set gd clip, under press & hdd ent fnl 1f, held fnl 50y: op 5/1: not disgraced & clr rem, back in trip: acts on fast & gd/soft grnd, see 1374, 1108. ¾ **96**
3230 **RIVERTOWN 11** [1] 6-8-13 T Ashley 12/1: 1/435: Outpcd, nvr a factor: op 7/1: will apprec return to 9f+. 4 **93$**
*3179 **GRAMPAS 14** [7] 3-8-11 R Cochrane 3/1: -216: Held up, wide, progress 3f out, wknd bef dist: bckd: not disgraced up in grade tho shade btr 3179 (9f mdn). ¾ **95**
3256 **MOORLANDS AGAIN 10** [2] 5-8-13 A Daly 100/1: 657: Prom 4f: impossible task. 6 **79$**
7 ran Time 1m 39.1 (0.8) (K Abdulla) B W Hills Lambourn, Berks

3516

4.05 STAN JAMES HCAP 3YO+ 0-90 (C) 5f161y rnd Good/Firm 20 -08 Slow [84]
£6857 £2110 £1055 £527 3 yo rec 3 lb

3152 **BOLD EFFORT 15** [3] K O Cunningham Brown 8-9-8 (78)(bl) D O'Donohoe 10/1: 210501: 8 b g Bold Arrangement - Malham Tarn (Riverman) Waited with, gd wide prog appr fnl 1f, rdn dist, hung left, led fnl 50y: op 8/1: earlier won at Lingfield (rtd 81a) & Salisbury (h'caps): '99 wnr at Lingfield (h'cap, rtd 97a & 83): '98 wnr at Sandown & Kempton (h'caps, rtd 96 & 87a): eff at 5/6f, stays 1m: acts on firm, gd/soft & both AWs, any track: wears blinks & can go well fresh: nicely h'capped, tough 8yo. **81**
3419 **CAUDA EQUINA 3** [1] M R Channon 6-9-4 (74) Craig Williams 9/2 FAV: 004652: 6 gr g Statoblest - Sea Fret (Habat) Held up, prog & nowhere to go ent fnl 2f till below dist, strong burst, too late: nicely bckd from 3/1, qk reapp: shld have won this but but always needs plenty of luck in running & loves Bath: see 905. ½ **77**
3208 **MR STYLISH 12** [11] I A Balding 4-8-13 (69)(tvi) J P Spencer 9/2: 050533: 4 b g Mazilier - Moore Stylish (Moorestyle) Mid div, wide prog to lead ent fnl 2f, drvn dist, hdd fnl 50y: better run with visor reapplied. *nk* **71**
2999 **EASTER OGIL 22** [4] I A Balding 5-9-8 (78)(vis) Leanne Masterton (7) 10/1: 250004: Mid-div, imprvg when gap clsd 2f out, switched & kept on, no threat: op 6/1: needs plenty of luck in running: see 1517 (class stks). 1½ **76**
3209 **BANDANNA 12** [5] 3-9-11 (84) F Norton 4/1: 651635: Rear, prog to chase ldrs 2f out, onepace when bmpd dist: nicely bckd from 6/1, top-weight: see 2787 (5f, here). *shd* **82**
2931 **LA PIAZZA 25** [10] 4-9-7 (77) R Cochrane 11/2: 002336: Prom, eff & hmpd bef fnl 1, onepce: new stable. 1¾ **70**
3218 **SIRENE 11** [8] 3-7-10 (55)(bl)(10oh) D Kinsella (7) 25/1: 003507: Front rank, led briefly 2f out, fdd. *2* **42**
3259 **BLUNDELL LANE 10** [2] 5-8-8 (64) B Marcus 10/1: 060408: Prom, bmpd appr fnl 1f, no extra, eased fnl 1f. 3 **43**
3257 **TRUMP STREET 10** [6] 4-7-10 (52) G Baker (5) 25/1: 501009: Led, hdd 2f out & sn badly hmpd. *1* **28**
9 ran Time 1m 10.7 (1.6) (A J Richards) K O Cunningham Brown Stockbridge, Hants

3517

4.35 MYSTERY MDN 3YO (D) 1m3f144y Good/Firm 20 -04 Slow
£5499 £1692 £846 £423

3232 **OCTAVIUS CAESAR 11** [9] P F I Cole 3-9-0 D Sweeney 6/1: 20-31: 3 ch c Affirmed - Secret Imperatrice (Secretariat) Led, went clr after halfway, shkn up, cmftbly: tchd 10/1: juv rnr up (mdn, rtd 80): clrly suited by step up to 11.5f & forcing tactics: goes on firm/fast grnd, sharp/undulating or turning track. **86**
1985 **SALUEM 65** [12] R Guest 3-8-9 Craig Williams 13/8 FAV: -32: 3 b f Salse - Pat Or Else (Alzao) Rear, prog 5f out, went 2nd bef 2f out, chsd wnr in vain after: well bckd from 3/1, clr rem, 9 wk abs: not disgraced over lngr 11.5f trip tho' gave wnr plenty of rope: worth another chance. *5* **76**
-- **FLAME OF TRUTH** [6] J H M Gosden 3-8-9 R Cochrane 5/1: 3: 3 b f Rainbow Quest - River Lullaby (Riverman) Rear, went thro' btn horses fnl 3f, nvr dangerous: debut: related useful performers up to 12f. *8* **66**
2553 **HIGH TOWER 41** [4] Mrs A J Perrett 3-9-0 A McGlone 7/2: 44: Chsd ldrs, no extra 4f out: 6 wk abs. *3* **67**
2611 **CHOCSTAW 38** [2] 3-9-0 L Newman (3) 12/1: -005: Prom 7f: now qual for h'caps. *5* **60**
2445 **KISTY 45** [11] 3-8-9 C Rutter 8/1: -03336: Handy, wide 5f out, fdd 3f out: op 6/1, 6 wk abs, back in trip. 1½ **53**
3189 **LORD GIZZMO 13** [1] 3-9-0 G Hind 50/1: -067: Rcd in 2nd till 4f out: v stiff task. *12* **42**
1692 **ROCCIOSO 78** [5] 3-9-0 R Smith (5) 66/1: 00-08: Pulled hard, mid div till 6f: imposs task: 11 wk abs. *20* **16**
3179 **BISHOPS BLADE 14** [13] 3-9-0 R Havlin 50/1: -09: Bhd from halfway: see 3179. *9* **4**
895} **TOPMAN 492** [8] 3-9-0 G Baker (5) 50/1: 0-0: Nvr in it: 10th, reapp, new stable, no form. *3* **0**
2907 **PETRIE 26** [7] 3-9-0 A Daly 50/1: 503000: Sn struggling, 11th, stiff task, new stable. *10* **0**
11 ran Time 2m 27.8 (2.8) (Sir George Meyrick) P F I Cole Whatcombe, Oxon

3518

5.05 FAMILY DAY OUT HCAP 3YO+ 0-75 (E) 1m5f22y Good/Firm 20 -09 Slow [72]
£3493 £1075 £537 £268 3 yo rec 11lb

*3353 **KENNET 6** [7] P D Cundell 5-9-10 (68)(6ex) A Beech (5) 9/2: 022311: 5 b g Kylian - Marwell Mitzi (Interrex) Waited with, prog appr fnl 3f, styd on strgly to lead below dist, pshd out: defied a pen for wng 6 days ago at Windsor (h'cap): '99 wnr at Lingfield (mdn, rtd 72a) Windsor & Bath (class stakes, rtd 72): eff at 11.5f/13f: acts on any grnd, likes sharp/turning tracks, especially Windsor & Bath: can go well fresh: tough. **73**
3255 **KIRISNIPPA 10** [3] Derrick Morris 5-8-1 (45) P Doe 10/1: 035042: 5 b g Beveled - Kiri Te (Liboi) ¾ **48**

Prom, led appr fnl 3f, hard rdn & hdd below dist, kept on: op 8/1, ran to best, see 1784, 1128, 474.
3157 **DOODLE BUG 15** [6] T R Watson 3-9-1 (70) Craig Williams 16/1: 30-353: 3 b f Missed Flight - Kaiserlinde (Frontal) Rear, rdn ent fnl 3f, kept on well appr fnl 1f, too much to do: sound h'cap bow & stays 13f. ½ 72+
*3255 **CUPBOARD LOVER 10** [9] D Haydn Jones 4-9-2 (60) A McGlone 3/1 FAV: 566314: Pulled hard, dwelt, improved to lead halfway till appr fnl 3f, no extra: well bckd: prob ran to form of 3255. 3½ 57
3233 **REPTON 11** [10] 5-7-10 (40)(10oh) D Kinsella (7) 16/1: -00035: Bhd, some late hdwy, nvr a threat: op 12/1: stiff task but clear signs of a return to form: well h'capped: see 1499. 1¾ 35$
2866 **ROYAL PATRON 28** [4] 4-9-11 (69) J P Spencer 6/1: -23546: Towards rear, prog to go 3rd 3f out, sn hard rdn & outpcd: return to 14f+ may suit: see 1440, 853. 3 60
3018 **PUNISHMENT 21** [1] 9-10-0 (72)(t) D O'Donohoe 12/1: 062467: Nvr better than mid div: top-weight. 3½ 58
1996 **PARADISE NAVY 64** [12] 11-8-6 (50)(bl) G Sparkes(7) 20/1: 60-008: Ran in snatches, btn 4f out: abs. 2 33
2982 **REAL ESTATE 23** [13] 6-9-12 (70) R Cochrane 4/1: 3/3209: Handy 1m: will apprec a drop in trip. 9 41
1613 **TORMENTOSO 81** [8] 3-8-4 (59) A Daly 33/1: -46050: Led till bef halfway, no threat after: 10th, new stable. 1½ 28
3255 **Notagainthen 10** [11] 4-7-10(40)(2oh) G Baker(5) 40/1:
3255 **Royal Signet 10** [5] 5-7-13 (43)(3ow)(13oh) C Rutter 16/1:
2327 **Premiere Valentino 50** [2] 3-7-11 (52)(BL)(1ow)(2oh) F Norton 16/1:
13 ran Time 2m 49.3 (3.8) (Miss M C Fraser) P D Cundell Compton, Berks

NOTTINGHAM MONDAY AUGUST 21ST Lefthand, Galloping Track

Official Going GOOD. Stalls: 5/6f - Stands Side; Rem - Inside.

3519 2.15 COME RACING NURSERY HCAP 2YO (E) 6f str Good 47 -05 Slow [89]
£2912 £896 £448 £224

3075 **IMPERIAL MEASURE 19** [4] B R Millman 2-9-7 (82) G Hind 8/1: 15021: 2 b c Inchinor - Fair Eleanor (Saritamer): Cl-up, rdn/led over 1f out, styd on well for press inside last: earlier made a wng debut at Windsor (mdn): eff at 5/6f, 7f shld suit: acts on fast & gd/soft, sharp/gall trk: gd wght carrier: progressive type. 91
*3096 **INJAAZ 19** [3] J L Dunlop 2-9-5 (80) A Beech (5) 3/1 FAV: 012: 2 ch f Sheikh Albadou - Ferber's Follies (Saratoga Six) Trkd ldrs, rdn/chsd wnr fnl 1f, kept on but al held: bckd: lightly rcd, acts on fast & gd. 1½ 84
*3228 **BLAKESHALL BOY 12** [2] M R Channon 2-9-5 (80) Craig Williams 7/2: 403213: 2 b g Piccolo - Giggleswick Girl (Full Extent): Held up in tch, kept on final 2f, not pace to chall: op 4/1: prob stays 6f. 2 79
3149 **VALDESCO 16** [5] M A Jarvis 2-9-1 (76) P Robinson 9/2: 34104: Bhd ldrs, held 1f out: see 2724 (mdn). ½ 73
3165 **ONLY ONE LEGEND 16** [7] 2-9-4 (79) J Weaver 7/1: 033105: Led, rdn/btn over 1f out: btr 2575 (5f). 1¾ 72
3109 **HAMATARA 18** [1] 2-9-0 (75)(t) K Darley 4/1: 404126: Bhd ldrs, rdn/btn 1f out: op 7/2: btr 3109 (5f). 2½ 61
2915 **TICCATOO 26** [6] 2-8-1 (62) P M Quinn (3) 20/1: 100027: Dwelt, held up, btn 2f out: btr 2915, 865 (5f). 5 39
7 ran Time 1m 13.9 (3.1) (Southern Cross Racing) B R Millman Kentisbeare, Devon.

3520 2.45 TATTERSALLS MDN AUCT 2YO (E) 6f str Good 47 -16 Slow
£3770 £1160 £580 £290

3090 **ZIETUNZEEN 19** [8] A Berry 2-8-3(1ow) G Carter 5/4 FAV: 233551: 2 b f Zieten - Hawksbill Special (Taufan) Cl-up trav well, shkn up to assert under hands-&-heels riding fnl 1f: well bckd: has run well in gd company (rtd 91): eff at 5/6f on firm & gd/soft, stiff/gall or sharp trk: shld rate higher in stronger company. 81
3075 **HALCYON MAGIC 19** [13] Pat Mitchell 2-8-3 R Brisland (5) 50/1: 004552: 2 b g Magic Ring - Consistent Queen (Queens Hussar): Led, rdn/hdd 1f out, kept on for press: eff at 6f, prob handles fast, gd & fibresand. ¾ 75
2550 **SALSA 42** [11] W R Muir 2-8-9 Martin Dwyer 16/1: 53: 2 b c Salse - Lana Turrel (Trempolino): Trkd ldrs, rdn & kept on for press final 2f, no threat: op 14/1, 6 wk abs: sure to apprec 7f+: see 2550. 2 76
2985 **GARDOR 23** [2] J G FitzGerald 2-8-3 L Newman (3) 11/1: 444: Towards rear, rdn & styd on final 2f, nrst fin: type to do better with a more positive ride at 7f+ now he has qualified for nursery h'caps. 1½ 66
3268 **WEET A WHILE 11** [6] 2-8-7 D Sweeney 33/1: -005: In tch, onepcd/held dist: see 2608. ¾ 68
3100 **DAWN ROMANCE 19** [14] 2-8-0(2ow) Craig Williams 25/1: 005066: Prom, outpcd final 2f: btr 2810. 1 59
-- **ITS ECCO BOY** [9] 2-8-7 N Callan 20/1: 7: Chsd ldrs till over 1f out: Clantime colt, Apr foal, 13,000 gns 2yo: brother to a 6f juv wnr: dam a juv mdn: with K Burke. nk 65
3215 **RAMBLIN MAN 12** [1] 2-8-3 G Hind 50/1: -05038: Rcd alone far side, rdn & kept on onepace final 2f tho' held by ldrs stands side dist: prob not helped by racing alone: see 3215, 1993. nk 60
3358 **INVESTOR RELATIONS 7** [7] 2-8-12 D R McCabe 25/1: 69: Trkd ldrs, fdd over 1f out: see 3358. nk 68$
3162 **SHEER PASSION 16** [10] 2-8-7 M Hills 3/1: 00: Chsd ldrs, rdn/held over 1f out: 10th: btr 3162. ¾ 61
-- **PREMIER AMBITIONS** [5] 2-8-7 F Norton 16/1: 0: Dwelt/towards rear, al bhd: 11th: op 12/1: Bin Ajwaad colt, Feb foal, cost 11,500 gns: half-brother to 3 wnrs: dam a 7f juv wnr: with W J Haggas. ½ 59
-- **Yanus** [3] 2-8-9 M Fenton 20/1: 3292 **Tamilia 10** [15] 2-8-0 J Quinn 50/1:
-- **Cincinnati** [4] 2-8-5 K Darley 50/1:
14 ran Time 1m 14.6 (3.8) (Chris & Antonia Deuters) A Berry Cockerham, Lancs.

3521 3.15 TALK LISTEN COND STKS 3YO+ (C) 5f str Good 47 +21 Fast
£6351 £2409 £1204 £547 3 yo rec 2 lb

+2960 **LORD KINTYRE 24** [7] B R Millman 5-9-6 M Roberts 6/1: 440211: 5 b g Makbul - Highland Rowena (Royben): Trkd ldrs, prog/rdn to lead 1f out, styd on well inside last, drvn out: fast time, top-weight: op 7/1: earlier won at Newmarket (cond stks): unplcd both '99 starts, reportedly broke blood vessels & subs gelded: plcd sev times in '98 (rtd 109, Gr 3): smart juv (rtd 112): suited by 5f, stays 6f: acts on firm & hvy, any trk: runs well fresh: likes to race with/force the pace: v smart sprinter & shld win a Listed/Gr 3 events in this form. 114
3158 **PROUD NATIVE 16** [10] D Nicholls 6-9-0 Alex Greaves 11/4: 220622: 6 b g Imp Society - Karamana (Habitat): Held up, swtchd right over 1f out, prog when briefly no room dist, styd on well inside last, not reach wnr: well bckd tho' op 2/1: shade unlucky, run stopped at a crucial stage & can rate higher: tough & smart. ½ 106
3152 **HALMAHERA 16** [1] I A Balding 5-8-11 K Darley 5/1: 560403: 5 b g Petardia - Champagne Girl (Robellino): Dwelt, sn chsd ldrs, onepace over 1f out without jockey resorting to the whip: consistent: see 734. ¾ 101
3152 **COASTAL BLUFF 16** [9] N P Littmoden 8-8-11 J Quinn 16/1: 210204: Chsd ldrs, drvn/styd on onepace: offic rtd 87, treat rating with caution: see 1871 (h'cap). ½ 99$
3059 **ELLENS LAD 20** [11] 6-8-11 Pat Eddery 2/1 FAV: 501105: Held up, rdn/kept on final 2f, no threat. shd 99
1078 **KALINDI 112** [8] 3-8-4 Craig Williams 33/1: 00-006: Rear, late gains: 4 mth abs: better run, see 1078. 1¼ 91

3152 **REPERTORY** 16 [5] 7-8-11 R Price 6/1: 323507: Led & clr after 2f, rdn/hdd 1f out, wknd: see 914.   shd   96
3493 **MUTASAWWAR** 2 [2] 6-8-11 L Newman (3) 100/1: 500048: Twds rear, outpcd: qck reapp: highly tried.   1¾   92$
3183 **OCKER** 14 [12] 6-9-0 J Weaver 33/1: 045509: Dwelt, al rear: surprise wnr of this race last year: see 47.   2   90$
3056 **DISTANT KING** 20 [4] 7-8-11 Clare Roche (7) 100/1: 060000: Al rear: 10th: see 1256.   2   82$
3366 **PALACEGATE JACK** 6 [3] 9-8-11 D Allan (7) 100/1: 054560: In tch 3f: 11th: qck reapp: see 191 (AW).   hd   81$
3209 **JACKIES BABY** 13 [6] 4-8-11 Darren Williams (5) 66/1: 400400: Cl-up 3f: 12th: stiff task, see 394 (AW).   8   61
12 ran   Time 59.8 (1.3)   (M Calvert)   B R Millman Kentisbeare, Devon.

3522   3.45 TOTE CREDIT HCAP 3YO 0-80 (D)   1m6f   Good 47   -22 Slow   [85]
         £5720   £1760   £880   £440

2863 **FANTASTIC FANTASY** 29 [7] J L Dunlop 3-9-5 (76) Pat Eddery 4/1: -11621: 3 b f Lahib - Gay Fantasy   80
(Troy) Keen/held up, kept on well for hard driving fnl 2f to lead nr line: well bckd: earlier won at Southwell
& Yarmouth (h'caps): rtd 80 in '99 (fillies mdn): eff at 10f, stayed this 14f trip well & 2m will suit: acts
on fast & gd, sharp/gall trk: progressive & game filly, continues to improve as she steps up in trip.
*2554 **BRISBANE ROAD** 42 [6] I A Balding 3-8-11 (68)(t) K Darley 5/1: 0-4512: 3 b g Blues Traveller - Eva   ¾   70
Fay (Fayruz) Led, drvn/strongly prsd over 2f out, kept on till hdd well near line: bckd: 6 wk abs: styd lngr
14f trip well: eff in a t-strap: acts on gd & gd/soft: progressive 3yo, 8lbs higher than 2554 (mdn h'cap).
2173 **BARCELONA** 58 [2] J Noseda 3-9-7 (78) J Weaver 7/2: -31163: 3 b c Barathea - Piptina (Bustino):   shd   80
Held up, drvn/prog to chall & briefly led inside last, just held cl-home: op 4/1, 2 mth abs: apprec drop to 14f.
3166 **THREE LIONS** 16 [3] R F Johnson Houghton 3-8-10 (67) T Quinn 6/1: 0-0164: Bhd ldrs over 3f out,   1½   67
eff over 1f out, no extra ins last: op 5/1: prob styd lngr 14f trip, drop to 12f could prove ideal: see 2884 (10f).
3167 **SKYE BLUE** 16 [1] 3-8-11 (68) Craig Williams 16/1: 023205: Hld up, eff over 2f out, sn held: lngr trip.   2½   64
*3284 **BOLLIN NELLIE** 10 [5] 3-7-10 (53) J Quinn 5/2 FAV: 050216: Chsd ldrs, rdn to chall over 2f out,   shd   49
held over 1f out: nicely bckd: lngr 14f trip: btr 3284 (12f).
2774 **MILLENNIUM SUMMIT** 32 [4] 3-9-1 (72) R Cochrane 16/1: 4647: Chsd ldr, rdn/btn 3f out: longer trip.   22   43
7 ran   Time 3m 07.9 (9.6)   (Windflower Overseas Holdings Inc)   J L Dunlop Arundel, West Sussex.

3523   4.15 NETHERFIELD NOV STKS 2YO (E)   1m54y rnd   Good 47   -35 Slow
         £3493   £1075   £537   £268

*3198 **SPETTRO** 13 [4] P F I Cole 2-9-5 K Darley 7/4: 511: 2 b c Spectrum - Overruled (Last Tycoon):   98
Made all, hard rdn/strongly prsd from over 2f out, drvn/styd on gamely inside last: well bckd: earlier scored at
Catterick (mdn): apprec step up to 1m, should go further: acts on fast & gd grnd, sharp/gall trk: likes to force
the pace & has run well fresh: useful/prog colt with a willing attitude, should hold his own in higher company.
*2873 **SNOWSTORM** 28 [2] M L W Bell 2-9-5 M Fenton 9/4 FAV: 2612: 2 gr c Environment Friend - Choral   nk   97
Sundown (Night Shift): Keen/trkd ldrs, prog/hard rdn to press wnr over 1f out, just held cl-home: pulled
clr of the other pair: stays a gall 1m well: useful colt: see 2873.
--   **ACADEMIC GOLD** [1] K R Burke 2-8-8 N Callan 16/1: 3: 2 ch c Royal Academy - Penultimate   6   75
(Roberto): Keen/trkd ldrs, sn outpcd by front ppair: op 10/1: Feb foal, cost 16,500 gns: half-brother to a 10f
wnr: dam unrcd: this 1m trip will suit: highly tried but not disgrcd on intro, mdn company shd suit.
*2862 **GULCHIE** 29 [3] H R A Cecil 2-9-5 T Quinn 5/2: -14: Trkd ldr, ch 2f out, sn held: longer 1m trip.   shd   86
4 ran   Time 1m 46.00 (6.6)   (Luciano Gaucci)   P F I Cole Whatcombe, Oxon.

3524   4.45 RACING'S FREE HCAP 3YO+ 0-75 (D)   1m2f   Good 47   -25 Slow   [70]
         £3107   £956   £478   £239   3 yo rec 8 lb

3337 **PAARL ROCK** 8 [13] G Barnett 5-8-13 (55)(vis) G Gibbons (7) 5/1: 321441: 5 ch h Common Grounds -   58
Markievicz (Doyoun): Made all, rdn final 3f & strongly prsd 2f out, held on well for press inside last, gamely:
op 4/1: earlier scored at Leicester, first win): plcd in '99 (h'cap, blnkd, rtd 52): loves to force the
pace at 10f on fast & gd grnd: eff in visor/blnks: handles any trk: 5yo entire, in fine form.
*3244 **SHEER FACE** 12 [8] W R Muir 6-9-4 (60) Martin Dwyer 5/1: 335012: 6 b g Midyan - Rock Face (Ballad   ½   61
Rock) Towards rear, rdn & styd on well from over 1f out, not nearest wnr: op 6/1: in gd form: see 3244 (Brighton).
1917 **SIFAT** 68 [10] J R Jenkins 5-9-10 (66)(vis) Pat Eddery 9/4 FAV: -51123: 5 b m Marju - Reine Maid   1¼   65
(Mr Prospector): Held up, rdn & styd on onepace final 2f: 10 wk abs: bckd, op 7/2: see 1917, 1775.
3011 **AGIOTAGE** 22 [4] S C Williams 4-9-1 (57) T G McLaughlin 7/1: 161554: Chsd ldrs, ch 2f out, no   1¾   54
extra 1f out: stays 10f, wng form at 1m/9f & likes Mussekburgh: see 2378 (Musselburgh).
2685 **BAJAN BROKER** 37 [12] 3-9-0 (64) M Tebbutt 16/1: 3-0405: Mid-div, prog/chsd ldrs 2f out, onepace: ½   60
prev with N Callaghan, now with E Stanners: see 2111.
3234 **MOONSHIFT** 12 [2] 6-7-10 (38)(tvi)(10oh) K Dalgleish (5) 20/1: 050-66: Towards rear, rdn & styd on   hd   34
final 2f, nrst fin: lightly rcd in '99, scored at Yarmouth (appr h'cap, rtd 30, subs unplcd on sand): unplcd in '98
(rtd 44 & 37a): eff at 10f on fast grnd: wears a t-strap & visor.
1101 **STERLING HIGH** 110 [11] 5-7-10 (38)(t)(2oh) S Righton 25/1: 000007: Rear, hdwy 3f out, sn held: abs.   nk   33
3234 **HADLEIGH** 12 [9] 4-9-7 (63)(vis) J Quinn 7/1: 000028: Chsd ldrs, btn 2f out: btr 3234 (clmr).   hd   57
3407 **HEVER GOLF GLORY** 4 [5] 6-7-10 (38)(bl) P M Quinn (3) 33/1: 056009: Mid-div, prog/ch 3f out, fdd.   2½   28
3498 **AVERHAM STAR** 2 [14] 5-7-10 (38)(bl) (13oh) N Carter (7) 50/1: 006000: Chsd wnr, btn 3f out: 10th.   1   27
2037] **THUNDERING PAPOOSE** 791 [7] 5-7-10 (38)(8oh) K Pierrepont (1) 40/1: 0/00/0: Al rear: 11th: long   6   18
abs, missed '99: only mod form prev at up to 14f for N Graham, now with J Jenkins.
4600} **THE PROOF** 291 [1] 3-8-0 (50) D Mernagh (3) 25/1: 000-0: Chsd ldrs, btn 4f out: 12th: reapp/h'cap   nk   29
bow: unplcd at up to 1m in '99 (tsd 55, mdn): bred to apprec mid-dists.
3181 **THE BARGATE FOX** 14 [3] 4-8-6 (48) L Newman (3) 11/2: 300030: Chsd ldrs, rdn/btn 4f out: 13th.   1¼   25
13 ran   Time 2m 09.5 (7.2)   (J C Bradbury)   G Barnett Stoke-On-Trent, Staffs.

BRIGHTON MONDAY AUGUST 21ST Lefthand, V Sharp, Undulating Track

Official Going FIRM. Stalls: 1m2f & 1m4f - Outside; Rem - Inside.

3525 2.30 EBF FILLIES AUCT MDN 2YO (F) 6f rnd Firm Slow
£2341 £669 £334

3096 **KOMENA 19** [1] J W Payne 2-8-11 J P Spencer 6/4 FAV: 421: 2 b f Komaite - Mena (Blakeney) **86**
Trkd ldrs, went on appr final 1f, pshd clr, v cmftbly: nicely bckd from 9/4: Mar 1st foal: imprvd at 6f, 7f shld suit: acts on firm/fast grnd, sharp/undul trk: going the right way.

3394 **REGAL AIR 5** [2] B I Case 2-8-11 T E Durcan 5/1: 530302: 2 b f Distinctly North - Dignified Air (Wolver Hollow) Led till ent fnl 2f, onepace: qck reapp: should stay 6f: handles fm, gd/soft & fibresand. *7* **70**

3443 **EXTRA GUEST 3** [7] M R Channon 2-8-11 J Reid 5/2: 422233: 2 b f Fraam - Gibaltarik (Jareer) *½* **69**
Hmpd early, prom, led briefly ent final 2f, sn rdn & btn & hung right: bckd from 7/2, qck reapp: btr 3443, 2029.

3239 **SOONA 12** [8] A P Jarvis 2-8-11 D Harrison 4/1: 555224: Chsd ldrs, no extra 2f out: jockey given 2-day *2½* **63**
ban for careless riding at the start: much btr 3239, 2916 (7f).

2526 **SONG N DANCE 43** [9] 2-8-11 G Baker (5) 16/1: -05: Handy till fdd 2f out: 6 wk abs. *1¼* **60$**

2939 **PINK CHAMPAGNE 25** [5] 2-8-11 R Havlin 50/1: 06: Chsd ldrs till wknd ent final 2f: see 2939. *12* **40**

-- **BEL TEMPO** [3] 2-8-11 I Mongan(5) 16/1: 7: Sn detached: op 10/1: 3,000 gns Petong 1st foal, dam 6f wnr *20* **0**

7 ran Time 1m 10.8 (3) (The Frankland Lodgers) J W Payne Newmarket, Suffolk.

3526 3.00 PETER & DENISE CLAIMER 4YO+ (F) 1m2f Firm Slow
£2310 £660 £330

*3234 **WILLIE CONQUER 12** [2] Andrew Reid 8-9-4 J Reid 1/2 FAV: 010111: 8 ch g Master Willie - Maryland Cookie **72**
(Bold Hour) Well plcd, led 3f out, sn hard prsd, held on narrowly und press: well bckd to land the odds: earlier won here at Brighton (2, sell for D Elsworth & clmr), Salisbury & Yarmouth (clmrs): '99 wnr at Brighton (h'cap, rtd 88, t-strap): eff at 10/12f on firm, gd/soft grnd & any trk, loves Brighton: hard to beat in sells/clmrs.

2304 **NO EXTRAS 52** [3] G L Moore 10-9-4 S Whitworth 9/4: -11602: 10 b g Efisio - Parkland Rose *hd* **71**
(Sweet Candy) In tch, prog to chall appr final 2f, styd on but being held: bckd tho' op 6/4, 7 wk abs, 10L to next: probably gets a sharp 10f in clmg grade tho' likely to apprec a drop back to 1m: see 1690.

3253 **PURNADAS ROAD 11** [4] Dr J R J Naylor 5-7-13(2ow) N Pollard 50/1: -60363: 5 ch m Petardia - Choral *10* **32**
Park (Music Boy) In tch, outpcd by front pair 2f out: v stiff task, offic rtd 33: see 226.

3260 **SCENIC LADY 11** [7] L A Dace 4-8-1 G Bardwell 33/1: -00254: Held up, nvr a factor: flattered, see 2904. *hd* **34$**

3255 **LOKOMOTIV 11** [1] 4-8-10 (bl) P Fitzsimons (5) 16/1: 000105: Al bhd: see 2875 (sell). *1½* **41**

3186 **PADDYS RICE 14** [5] 9-8-12 C Rutter 66/1: 00/006: Led till 3f out, lost place: stiff task. *13* **23**

3234 **MISTRESS BANKES 12** [6] 4-7-13 A Daly 100/1: 07: Cl-up till after halfway: no form. *7* **0**

7 ran Time 2m 03.5 (5.7) (A S Reid) Andrew Reid Mill Hill, London NW7

3527 3.30 S J & M YALLOP HCAP 3YO+ 0-70 (E) 1m rnd Firm Slow [68]
£3094 £884 £442 3 yo rec 6 lb

3227 **MUTABASSIR 12** [13] G L Moore 6-9-6 (60) I Mongan (5) 11/4 FAV: 430251: 6 ch g Soviet Star - Anghaam **64**
(Diesis) Prom, led appr final 2f, rdn out: nicely bckd: '99 wnr here at Brighton (h'cap, rtd 72): '98 wnr again at Brighton (mdn h'cap), Epsom, Folkestone (h'caps), Lingfield & Southwell (AW h'caps, rtd 56a): eff at 7f, 1m suits, stays 10f: acts on gd/soft, both AWs, likes firm grnd: loves sharp trks, esp Brighton & can run well fresh.

3243 **RAINBOW RAIN 12** [11] S Dow 6-9-5 (59)(t) P Doe 12/1: 020002: 6 b g Capote - Grana (Miswaki) *1* **60**
Held up, wide prog 3f out to chase wnr 2f out, styd on for press but unable to chall: tchd 16/1, likes Brighton.

3288 **PACIFIC ALLIANCE 10** [2] M Wigham 4-9-5 (59) Dean McKeown 10/3: 344003: 4 b g Fayruz - La *hd* **60**
Gravotte (Habitat) Led till appr final 2f, styd on: op 8/1, ran to best: acts on firm, gd grnd & equitrack: see 463.

2764 **COLONEL NORTH 33** [10] Andrew Reid 4-9-3 (57) J Reid 10/1: 066554: Mid-div, rdn & outpcd 2f out, *1½* **55**
kept on ins last: recent 20L 4th on hdles bow (rtd 81h): v well h'capped & interesting on a stiffer trk next time.

3078 **ARDENT 19** [5] 6-8-2 (42) S Carson (3) 12/1: 640005: Trkd ldrs, slightly hmpd appr final 2f, unable to *nk* **40**
qckn, eased cl-home: tchd 20/1, jockey given 2-day ban for easing down prematurely: on a fair mark, see 23.

3093 **CABARET QUEST 19** [9] 4-8-2 (42) C Carver (3) 11/1: 060336: Chsd ldrs, onepace appr final 1f: op 7/1. *1¼* **38**

1892 **LARAZA 69** [1] 3-9-2 (62) J P Spencer 14/1: 3-5507: Bhd, swtchd & late wide prog: op 10/1, blnks off. *nk* **57**

3314 **ASCARI 9** [15] 4-9-6 (60) D McGaffin (5) 12/1: 020308: Same place thro'out: op 8/1, see 2130, 1973 *½* **54**

2546 **DR MARTENS 42** [8] 6-8-1 (41) N Pollard 25/1: 6-0009: Rear, not much room ent final 3f, nvr a factor. *1½* **32**

3118 **SYLVA LEGEND 17** [7] 4-9-12 (66)(tvi) T E Durcan 14/1: 033000: Chsd ldrs till 2f out: 10th, top-weight. *1* **55**

3129 **HEATHER VALLEY 17** [6] 4-8-2 (42) G Bardwell 11/1: -05540: Keen, handy till wknd qckly fnl 2f: 14th. **0**

2942 **Democracy 25** [4] 4-8-5 (45) D Harrison 16/1: 3117 **Philistar 17** [14] 7-8-0 (40)(bl) J Bramhill 25/1:
1930 **Robber Red 67** [12] 4-8-10 (50) C Rutter 33/1: 3124 **Countess Parker 17** [3] 4-8-4 (44) P Fitzsimons (5) 25/1:

15 ran Time 1m 35.3 (3.3) (Stanley W Clarke) G L Moore Woodingdean, East Sussex.

3528 4.00 DOUG WOOD HCAP 3YO+ 0-80 (D) 5f59y rnd Firm Fair [80]
£6909 £2126 £1063 £531 3 yo rec 2 lb

2961 **SYLVA PARADISE 24** [9] C E Brittain 7-9-2 (68)(vis) T E Durcan 11/1: 450301: 7 b g Dancing Dissident - **72**
Brentsville (Arctic Tern) Held up, imprvd appr fnl 1f, ran on strgly ins last & pshd into lead nr fin: op 8/1: plcd sev times in '99 (h'caps, rtd 84): last won in '96 at Yarmouth (h'cap, rtd 92): stays 7f, suited by 5/6f: acts on firm, soft grnd: goes on any trk, likes sharp ones, with/without blnks/visor: v well h'capped.

3341 **RITAS ROCK APE 8** [3] R Brotherton 5-9-4 (70) I Mongan (5) 9/2: 001002: 5 b m Mon Tresor - Failand *¾* **71**
(Kala Shikari) With ldrs, rdn, slightly outpcd & swtchd appr final 1f, rallied & ev ch final 100y, outpaced by wnr nr fin: back to form, likes Brighton: see 2976.

3091 **TUSCAN DREAM 19** [1] A Berry 5-9-9 (75) P Bradley (5) 7/2 FAV: 512403: 5 b g Clantime - Excavator *hd* **75**
Lady (Most Secret) Led, under press appr final 1f, hdd well inside last, nicely bckd from 5/1: bt this wnr in 2326.

*3341 **DANCING MYSTERY 8** [10] E A Wheeler 6-10-3 (83) S Carson (3) 4/1: 103014: Slow away, wide, in tch, *1¼* **80**
eff ent fnl 2f, kept on towards fin: top-weight: handles firm, acts on fast, gd/soft & both AWs: see 3341 (Ascot).

3341 **THAT MAN AGAIN 8** [7] 8-9-1 (67)(bl) G Faulkner (3) 9/1: 043005: Cl-up & ev ch till no extra 1f out. *1¾* **59**

3203 **SOUNDS ACE 13** [2] 4-7-11 (49)(bl)(1ow)(6oh) J Mackay (5) 20/1: 300006: Chsd ldrs, nvr any impress. *1¼* **37**

3516 **TRUMP STREET 1** [8] 4-8-0 (52)(BL) G Baker (5) 25/1: 010007: Chsd ldrs, no extra ent final 2f: blnkd. *¾* **37**

3280 **CUPIDS CHARM 10** [6] 3-9-8 (76) D Harrison 4/1: 101608: Al bhd: nicely bckd from 6/1: see 2280. *2* **55**

3176 **WHIZZ KID 15** [5] 6-9-5 (71) Claire Bryan (5) 8/1: 010009: Nvr going pace: op 6/1, see 2451. *¾* **48**

BRIGHTON   MONDAY AUGUST 21ST   Lefthand, V Sharp, Undulating Track

9 ran   Time 1m 01.8 (1.8)   (Eddy Grimstead Honda)   C E Brittain Newmarket, Suffolk.

3529   4.30 KATHY AND PHIL FILLIES MDN 3YO+ (D)   7f rnd   Firm   V Slow
£3835   £1180   £590   £295   3 yo rec 5 lb

3279 **TAFFETA** 10 [1] J L Dunlop 3-8-13 J Reid 6/5: 506401: 3 ch f Barathea - Almela (Akarad)   69
Set slow pace, incrsd tempo 2f out, drvn out, unchall: nicely bckd, canny ride, v slow time: unrcd juv: eff
forcing the pace 7f on firm/fast grnd, sharp/undul or gall trk.
3319 **JABUKA** 9 [3] J A R Toller 3-8-11 S Whitworth 8/11 FAV: 432: 3 b f Shareef Dancer - Neptunalia   1½ 65
(Slip Anchor) Pulled hard, trkd wnr halfway, effort & hung left dist, nvr able to chall: nicely bckd: back up in
trip, looks in need of headgear & a faster pace: in front of this wnr in 1951.
3279 **SWING JOB** 10 [4] P S McEntee 4-9-4 G Faulkner (3) 40/1: 060-03: 4 b f Ezzoud - Leave Her Be   2½ 57$
(Known Fact) Chsd ldrs, outpcd appr fnl 1f: no form last term, promise in '98 starts (fill mdn, rtd 71, T Mills).
3293 **TOPLESS IN TUSCANY** 10 [5] P W Hiatt 3-8-13 G Baker (5) 25/1: 036004: Rcd in 2nd till halfway, hung   3 48
left & btn after: stiffish task, up in trip, see 2472 (gd/soft, set pace).
4 ran   Time 1m 24.2 (4.4)   (Capt J Macdonald-Buchanan)   J L Dunlop Arundel, W Sussex.

3530   5.00 TEDDY AND CAROL HCAP 3YO 0-65 (F)   1m2f   Firm   Slow   [71]
£2436   £696   £348

*3008 **HIGHCAL** 22 [6] Ronald Thompson 3-7-11 (40) J Bramhill 5/1: 000011: 3 gr g King's Signet - Guarded   47
Expression (Siberian Express) Mid-div, prog appr fnl 2f, led bef dist, pshd out, rdly: earlier won at Ripon (sell
h'cap): unplcd last term (rtd 64): eff at 10f, tried 12f: acts on firm/fast grnd, sharp/undul trks: progressing.
2908 **SHAMAN** 27 [7] G L Moore 3-9-6 (63) I Mongan (5) 5/2 FAV: 101322: 3 b g Fraam - Magic Maggie   3½ 64
(Beveled) Bhd ldrs, led 3f out till ent final 2f, no ch with wnr: tchd 7/2, clr rem: consistent: see 2041 (C/D).
3242 **FLYING RUN** 12 [12] J G Portman 3-7-10 (39)(2oh) G Baker (5) 25/1: 000003: 3 b f Lake Coniston -   3½ 35
Kaskazi (Dancing Brave) Handy, rdn appr final 2f, plugged on for 3rd: lngr 10f trip will prob suit in a mdn h'cap.
3357 **COLLEGE ROCK** 7 [2] R Brotherton 3-9-2 (59) J P Spencer 8/1: 461304: In tch, prog to go 3rd appr   2½ 52
final 1f, sn onepace: op 10/1, qck reapp: unsuited by this return to 10f in a h'cap?: see 3094 (1m clmr).
2908 **CHEZ BONITO** 27 [10] 3-7-13 (41)(1ow) N Pollard 10/1: 054005: Dwelt, held up, styd on late, nvr a threat. ½ 34
3030 **ASSURED PHYSIQUE** 21 [13] 3-9-5 (62)(tvi) D Harrison 8/1: 366556: Chsd ldrs, shkn up 3f out, no extra. ½ 53
2884 **AFRICAN PETE** 28 [8] 3-9-4 (61) G Faulkner (3) 10/1: 602657: Nvr nr ldrs: op 8/1: btr 2332.   1¼ 50
3362 **CEDAR PRINCE** 7 [3] 3-9-7 (64)(VIS) A Nicholls (3) 20/1: 060008: Keen, led after 5f till 3f out, fdd.   shd 53
2908 **LOMOND DANCER** 27 [4] 3-8-6 (49) P Doe 11/2: 050009: Chsd ldrs, not much room 3f out, sn btn: see 1495. 8 28
tchd 20/1: has styd a v slow run 11.5f but shapes like a drop back to 7f would suit.
1725 **NEW FORTUNE** 77 [5] 3-9-6 (63) J Reid 10/1: 0-040: Nvr in it: 10th, 11 wk abs, h'cap bow.   1 41
2774 **BOSSCAT** 32 [1] 3-9-2 (59)(BL) T E Durcan 12/1: 0-0500: Led 5f, sn lost place: 13th, blnkd, see 2621.   0
2264 **Count Tirol** 53 [11] 3-8-10 (53) A Daly 33/1:   2908 **Bond Diamond** 27 [15] 3-8-11 (54) M Tebbutt 12/1:
80 **Actually** 275 [14] 3-7-11 (40) M Henry 25/1:
14 ran   Time 2m 02.1 (4.3)   (J Bradwell)   Ronald Thompson Stainforth, Sth Yorks.

HAMILTON   TUESDAY AUGUST 22ND   Righthand, Undulating Track, Stiff Uphill Finish

Official Going: SOFT. Stalls: 1m/9f - Inside, Rem - Stand Side

3531   2.20 CHANNEL APPR HCAP 3YO+ 0-60 (F)   1m4f   Good/Soft 63 -43 Slow   [56]
£2408   £688   £344   3 yo rec 10lb

3501 **NOTATION** 2 [9] D W Chapman 6-7-10 (24)(6oh) Claire Bryan 50/1: 400501: 6 b g Arazi - Grace Note   28
(Top Ville) Dictated pace, styd on well fnl 2f, al holding rivals: slow time: unplcd in '99 (rtd 23a, h'cap):
plcd in '98 (rtd 55a & 31): '97 Southwell wnr (2, h'caps, rtd 52a): eff at 12f/2m on f/sand & gd/soft grnd.
3480 **KATIE KOMAITE** 3 [3] Mrs S Rees 7-8-7 (35) Angela Hartley (5) 5/1: 023522: 7 b m Komaite - City   1¼ 36
To City (Windjammer) Keen/chsd wnr, ev ch 3f out, not pace of wnr fnl 2f: op 7/2, qck reapp: see 3181, 2453.
2298 **NEEDWOOD MAESTRO** 53 [1] B C Morgan 4-8-4 (32)(vis) P M Quinn 12/1: 0-5003: 4 b g Sizzling Melody 1 32
- Needwood Poppy (Rolfe) Chsd ldrs, rdn/kept on fnl 2f, not pace to chall: 8 week abs: eff over a slowly run 12f,
handles gd/soft & hvy grnd: eff in a visor: see 1523 (claimer).
3379 **OCEAN DRIVE** 6 [4] Miss L A Perratt 4-9-4 A Beech 3/1: 245424: Prom 10f: bckd, quick reapp.   3½ 43
*3378 **SKYERS A KITE** 6 [8] 5-9-7 (49)(6ex) T Hamilton (5) 15/8 FAV: 315215: Held up, btn 3f out: bckd.   4 42
2202 **AN SMEARDUBH** 57 [7] 4-8-3 (31)(BL) A Polli 14/1: -00606: Prom, btn 3f out: op 12/1, blnks, abs.   4 20
3052 **SMARTER CHARTER** 21 [6] 7-10-0 (66) Kristin Stubbs 7/1: 325637: Al bhd: op 7/2: see 2081, 871.   1½ 44
2453 **MANSTAR** 46 [2] 3-8-13 (51)(vis) P Goode 16/1: 050008: Held up, rdn/btn 3f out: abs: see 1446, 1193.   2 37
8 ran   Time 2m 44.5 (12.7)   (David W Chapman)   D W Chapman Stillington, N Yorks.

3532   2.50 RACING CHANNEL MDN 2YO (D)   1m65y rnd   Good/Soft 63 -37 Slow   [3]
£3867   £1190   £595   £297

3169 **SMYSLOV** 16 [1] J L Dunlop 2-9-0 G Carter 1/3 FAV: -0441: 2 b c Rainbow Quest - Vlaanderen (In The   77
Wings) Chsd ldr, shaken up & led dist, styd on well under hands & heels riding: hvly bckd, slow time: eff over
1m, mid dists will suit in time: handles firm & gd/soft grnd: loves a gall or stiff/undul trk: easy task here.
-- **SIMPLY ERIC** [4] J L Eyre 2-9-0 R Cody Boucher (7) 33/1: 2: 2 b c Simply Great - Sanjana   1½ 71
(Priamos) Dwelt/rear, rdn & styd on fnl 2f, no threat to wnr: op 20/1: April foal, cost IR 5,200gns: brother to
a juv wnr abroad: dam a juv wnr abroad: stays a stiff 1m, mid dists shld suit: handles gd/soft: encouraging intro.
2873 **THORNTON DANCER** 29 [3] J S Goldie 2-8-9 W Supple 20/1: -00563: 2 b f Unfuwain - Westry   2 62
(Gone West) Chsd ldrs, rdn & styd on onpace fnl 2f: bred to apprec this longer 1m trip, will get further: low
grade h'cap will suit: handles gd/soft: see 843.
3363 **ORIENTAL MIST** 7 [8] Miss L A Perratt 2-9-0 A Beech (5) 7/1: 433044: Keen/chsd ldrs, rdn/hung   nk 66
right & held over 1f out: op 4/1: longer 1m trip: see 1146.
1513 **SANTISIMA TRINIDAD** 87 [5] 2-8-9 J Weaver 7/1: 05: Led/clr halfway, hdd over 1f out, fdd: op 5/1, abs. 6 51
2828 **WESTERNMOST** 32 [6] 2-9-0 D O'Donohoe 20/1: 006: Prom, rdn/held 2f out: longer 1m trip: see 2360 (5f). 2 52
3246 **TENERIFE FLYER** 13 [7] 2-8-9 O Pears 33/1: 60467: Rear, btrn 4f out: longer 1m trip: see 974.   1¼ 44

3363 **QUIET TRAVELLER 7** [2] 2-9-0 C Lowther 50/1: 008: Struggling halfway: longer 1m trip: see 1628.   ½ 48
8 ran   Time 1m 52.1 (8.3)   (Benny Andersson)   J L Dunlop Arundel, West Sussex

---

3533   **3.25 RACING CHANNEL NOV STKS 2YO (D)   6f   Good/Soft 63 -40 Slow**
£3620 £1114 £557   £278   Raced stands side

3320 **ALINGA 10** [3] M L W Bell 2-8-11 M Fenton 1/1 FAV: 513021: 2 b f King's Theatre - Cheyenne Spirit   86
(Indian Ridge). Prom, led over 1f out & styd on strongly to go clr under hands & heels riding inside last: nicely
bckd: earlier scored at Ayr (auct mdn): eff at 5/6f on firm & gd/soft grnd, stiff/gall or undulating track.
*755 **BLUE FOREST 147** [2] J Noseda 2-9-5 Paul Eddery 11/10: 12: 2 b c Charnwood Forest - Vian   3 84
(Far Out East) Cl up, ch over 1f out, sn outpcd: hvly bckd: abs: topweight: handles gd/soft & soft: see 755 (5f).
3327 **MILLIKEN PARK 9** [4] Miss L A Perratt 2-8-11 A Beech (5) 8/1: -6123: 2 ch f Fumo Di Londra   ¾ 74
- Miss Ironwood (Junius) Reluctant to go to post, led till over 1f out, sn held: handles firm & gd/soft: see 3327.
2717 **SHATIN PLAYBOY 36** [5] Miss L A Perratt 2-8-12 M Scott (7) 33/1: 44: In tch 3f: highly tried.   6 63
4 ran   Time 1m 16.00 (6.2)   (Peter G Ward)   M L W Bell Newmarket, Suffolk

---

3534   **4.00 R CHANNEL SELL HCAP 3YO+ 0-60 (F)   1m65y rnd   Good/Soft 63 -04 Slow**   [59]
£2618 £748 £374   3 yo rec 6 lb

3344 **TRYSOR 8** [11] S C Williams 4-9-2 (47)(vis) G Carter 6/1 JT FAV: 000021: 4 b c Then Again - Zahiah   57
(So Blessed) Chsd ldrs, rdn/outpcd 3f out, switched & strong run fnl 1f to lead nr fin: no bid, 1st sucess: eff
at 1m on fast & gd/soft: handles a stiff/undul or sharpish track: galvenised by visor last twice: can win again.
3375 **CLAIM GEBAL CLAIM 6** [3] P Monteith 4-8-7 (38) V Halliday 10/1: 016032: 4 b g Ardkinglass - Infra   2 42
Blue (Bluebird) Cl up, rdn/led over 3f out, hdd well inside last: op 8/1: clr rem: see 2780 (claimer).
3375 **ACE OF TRUMPS 6** [16] J Hetherton 4-8-7 (38)(t) M Fenton 12/1: 025643: 4 ch g First Trump -   4 35
Elle Reef (Shareef Dancer) Led till over 3f out, onepace/held after: op 7/1: quick reapp: see 1195 (claimer).
3344 **HEATHYARDS JAKE 8** [12] R Hollinshead 4-9-0 (45) P M Quinn (3) 16/1: 005404: Held up, eff/briefly   hd 41
no room over 3f out, rdn & styd on inside last, no threat to ldrs: see 229 (AW mdn).
3170 **LYNTON LAD 16** [2] 8-10-0 (59) W Supple 8/1: 001005: Prom halfway, rdn/held 1f out: top-weight.   hd 54
3380 **KUWAIT THUNDER 6** [5] 4-8-0 (31)(vis) Claire Bryan (5) 7/1: 505026: Handy, hung right/btn 1f out.   1¾ 23
3380 **CLOHAMON 6** [10] 5-7-13 (30) P Hanagan (6) 10/1: 0-6057: Mid div, rdn/btn over 1f out: see 3103.   hd 21
3440 **MR PERRY 4** [9] 4-9-0 (45) G Duffield (3) 33/1: 006008: Mid div, eff 3f out, no impression: see 1149.   1½ 33
3332 **MISS GRAPETTE 9** [15] 4-8-6 (37) O Pears 14/1: 502009: Mid div, rdn/btn 2f out: see 3332, 2533.   ½ 24
*3375 **ALAMEIN 6** [7] 7-8-12 (43)(t)(6ex) T Williams 7/1: 023010: Held up, eff 3f out, no hdwy: 10th.   nk 29
3344 **SHONTAINE 8** [8] 7-8-6 (36)(bl) (1ow) C Lowther 16/1: 000000: Held up, eff 3f out, sn held: 11th.   3½ 17
3393 **FUTURE COUP 6** [1] 4-9-3 (48)(bl) J Weaver 6/1 JT FAV: 040530: Keen in tch, btn 3f out: 12th.   nk 23
2950 **PRIDEWAY 25** [14] 4-9-7 (52) D O'Donohoe 9/1: 600060: Al bhd: 13th: see 1419 (AW).   shd 28
3138 Mister Westsound 18 [6] 8-8-10 (41)(bl) A Beech (5) 25/1:   3328 Cyran Park 9 [4] 4-8-7 (38) Iona Wands 25/1:   5 23
2965 Breakin Glass 25 [13] 3-8-3 (40)(BL) P Fessey 16/1:
16 ran   Time 1m 49.4 (5.6)   (Tymest Ltd)   S C Williams Newmarket, Suffolk

---

3535   **4.30 J C STEWART RTD HCAP 3YO+ 0-90 (C)   1m1f36y   Good/Soft 63 +04 Fast**   [90]
£6240 £2367 £1183   £538   3 yo rec 7 lb

*3410 **KIND REGARDS 5** [1] M Johnston 3-9-2 (85)(3ex) J Fanning 11/8 FAV: 254511: 3 b f Unfuwain - Barari   95+
(Blushing Groom) Trckd ldrs, led over 2f out, readily asserted under hands & heels riding fnl 1f: hvly bckd, best
time of day, qck reapp: 3lb pen for recent Beverley win (h'cap): '99 wnr again at Beverley (fill mdn, rtd 88): eff
at 7f/1m, suited by 9/10f: acts on firm & gd/soft, handles any trk, likes Beverley: progressive & useful filly.
2988 **GRANTED 24** [3] M L W Bell 3-8-12 (81) M Fenton 8/1: 211432: 3 b f Cadeaux Genereux - Germane   3½ 82
(Distant Relative) Held up, prog/chsd wnr over 1f out, no match: eff at 1m/9f: see 2579.
3182 **CLEVER GIRL 15** [7] T D Easterby 3-8-11 (80) J Weaver (7): D00043: 3 b f College Chapel - Damezao   1 79
(Alzao) Cl up, outpcd over 1f out: see 1645, 823.
3250 **DONNAS DOUBLE 13** [4] D Eddy 5-8-8 (70) A Beech (5) 10/1: 521034: Chsd ldrs, rdn/held over 1f out.   ¾ 68
3054 **INDIAN PLUME 21** [2] 4-9-4 (80) W Supple 6/1: 010035: Led, hdd over 2f out, sn held: btr 3054, 1598.   5 69
*3182 **ARANYI 15** [5] 3-9-7 (90) G Carter 7/2: 133316: Chsd ldrs, btn 2f out: op 3/1: btr 3182 (led).   nk 78
2108 **FOREST FRIENDLY 61** [6] 3-8-4 (73) P Hanagan (7) 16/1: 4-0057: Rear, struggling halfway: 2 month   6 51
abs: prev with B Hills, now with R Fahey: see 2108.
7 ran   Time 1m 59.5 (5.4)   (Maktoum Al Maktoum)   M Johnston Middleham, N Yorks

---

3536   **5.00 RACING CHANNEL HCAP 3YO+ 0-60 (F)   5f   Good/Soft 63 -01 Slow**   [58]
£2996 £856 £428   3 yo rec 2 lb   Raced centre - far side

2779 **ROBIN HOOD 33** [14] Miss L A Perratt 3-9-0 (46) A Beech (5) 11/1: 444061: 3 b g Komaite - Plough   52
Hill (North Briton) Held up, prog to lead over 1f out, rdn/hung left inside last, styd on well: first win: eff at
5/6f, likes gd/soft & soft grnd, stiff/undulating or gall track.
3366 **FACILE TIGRE 7** [1] P Monteith 5-9-5 (49) W Supple 40/1: 030002: 5 gr g Efisio - Dancing Diana   1 51
(Raga Navarro) Held up, rdn & styd on well from over 1f out, not reach wnr: well h'capped & back to form here.
*2819 **GARNOCK VALLEY 32** [4] A Berry 10-9-12 (56) G Carter 12/1: 252013: 10 b g Dowsing - Sunley   ½ 56
Sinner (Try My Best) Rear, rdn & styd on strongly inside last, nrst fin: op 8/1: remains in gd form: see 2819 (AW).
3200 **SEVEN SPRINGS 14** [10] R Hollinshead 4-8-5 (35)(VIS) P M Quinn (3) 20/1: 000004: Prom, rdn/no   hd 34
extra inside last: imprvd eff in first time vis: acts on fibresand, enjoys gd/soft & hvy grnd: see 1005, 647.
3144 **SUPERFRILLS 17** [18] 7-8-4 (34) Iona Wands 12/1: 004005: Held up, styd on onepace fnl 1f: op 10/1.   nk 32
2015 **PANDJOJOE 65** [13] 4-9-13 (57) P Hanagan (7) 5/1 FAV: 055606: Prom, onepace inside last: bckd: nk 54
9 wk abs: jockey given a 2-day whip ban.
3203 **OFF HIRE 14** [3] 4-9-11 (55)(vis) M Fenton 12/1: 441567: Prom, hung right/btn 1f out: see 2732.   1 50
3197 **PALACEGATE TOUCH 15** [16] 6 10-9-2 (46)(bl) Mark Flynn (7) 25/1: 650048: Rear, rdn/mod late gains.   ½ 39
3440 **BIFF ME 4** [12] 6-8-10 (40) C Lowther 25/1: 042609: Chsd ldrs 4f: stablemate of wnr: qck reapp.   nk 32
2732 **DAZZLING QUINTET 35** [5] 4-9-3 (47) R Fitzpatrick 14/1: 302000: Prom, hung right/btn 2f out: 10th.   1½ 35
3502 **POLAR MIST 2** [17] 5-10-0 (58)(tbl) Paul Eddery 33/1 FAV: 602060: Led till over 1f out, fdd: 11th: op 5/1.   ½ 44
3349 **PERTEMPS FC 8** [3] 9-10-0 (58)(vis) M Fenton 40/1: 000000: Dwelt, al towards rear: 12th: see 1412.   2 33
3377 **RED SYMPHONY 6** [16] 4-9-6 (50)(vis) O Pears 16/1: 001000: Al bhd: 13th: 1st time vis, hvy).   nk 30
3377 **NAISSANT 6** [12] 7-9-8 (52) P Goode (3) 7/1: 200300: Chsd ldrs 3f: 14th: quick reapp: btr 2641.   ½ 30

HAMILTON TUESDAY AUGUST 22ND Righthand, Undulating Track, Stiff Uphill Finish

3144 **Tong Road** 17 [9] 4-8-4 (34) (BL) T Williams 25/1: 3312 **Jackerin** 10 [15] 5-8-13 (43) V Halliday 12/1:
3144 **Kalar** 17 [7] 11-8-13 (43) (bl) Claire Bryan (5) 33/1:
17 ran Time 1m 01.3 (3.2) (Cree Lodge Racing Club) Miss L A Perratt Ayr, Strathclyde

YORK TUESDAY AUGUST 22ND Lefthand, Flat, Galloping Track

Official Going: GOOD. Stalls 5f & 6f - Stands Side: Round Course - Inside.

3537	2.05 LISTED ACOMB STKS 2YO (A) 7f rnd Good 40 -16 Slow
	£19992 £7392 £3696 £1680

*3072 **HEMINGWAY** 22 [1] A P O'Brien 2-9-1 M J Kinane 8/13 FAV: 11: 2 b c Spectrum - Welsh Love (Ela Mana 113
Mou) Made all, given a smack with whip & flashed tail dist, pshd out & ran on strongly: hvly bckd Irish raider,
gave 2nd 5lbs, front 2 clr: earlier won debut at Galway (mdn, easily): 500,000Ir gns half-brother to high-class
juv miler Second Empire, dam 12f wnr: eff at 7f, 1m will suit & shd stay at least 10f next term: runs well fresh
on gd & any trk: likes to force the pace: smart, progressive colt with plenty of scope, win in Group company.
3162 **EMINENCE** 17 [3] Sir Michael Stoute 2-8-10 Pat Eddery 5/2: 32: 2 b c Machiavellian - Divine Danse 1¼ 105
(Kris) Trck ldrs, shaken up & qcknd to chase wnr 2f out, ch bef dist, sn rdn, held fnl 100y: well bckd, 7L clr of
3rd: apprec step up to 7f, acts on fast & gd grnd: useful, scopey & well regarded colt, win a nice prize soon.
*3015 **SARATOV** 23 [5] M Johnston 2-9-1 K Darley 6/1: -3113: 2 b c Rudimentary - Sarabah (Ela Mana Mou) 7 96
Keen, trckd wnr, eff 2f out, sn outpcd: strong colt, not disgraced tho'shade btr 3015 (fast grnd, auct stks).
2921 **REDUIT** 27 [2] G A Butler 2-8-10 L Dettori 33/1: -44: In tch, shkn up 3f out, sn no ch with ldrs & not 1 89
persevered with: op 20/1, edgy/warm in padd: highly tried & still bckwd, will apprec a mdn confidence booster.
3237 **REFERRAL** 13 [4] 2-8-10 N Callan 40/1: 25: Chsd ldrs, no extra appr fnl 2f: looked fit & well but 1¾ 85
was out of his depth here: neat sort: has shown enough to win a mdn in 3237.
5 ran Time 1m 25.12 (3.92) (Michael Tabor) A P O'Brien Ballydoyle, Co Tipperary

3538	2.35 GR 3 LONSDALE STKS 3YO+ (A) 2m Good 40 -13 Slow
	£44625 £16500 £8250 £3750 3 yo rec 14lb

*3106 **ROYAL REBEL** 19 [3] M Johnston 4-9-6 (vis) M J Kinane 2/1 JT FAV: 012211: 4 b g Robellino - 118
Greenvera (Riverman) Rcd in 2nd, shaken up appr straight, styd on to chall appr fnl 1f, hard rdn to lead nr fin,
v gamely: well bckd, gave weight all round: earlier won at Leopardstown (Listed) & Goodwood (Gr 2, 1st time visor):
'99 wnr at Newcastle (mdn) & Leopardstown (stks, rtd 108): 5th in a Gr 1 in '98 (rtd 102): eff at 14f, improved
since stepped up to 2m with a visor: acts on firm & gd/soft grnd, any trk, likes gall ones: eff with/without blnks,
best visored: responds very well to pressure & is a high class, tough & very geniune stayer.
3106 **RAINBOW HIGH** 19 [2] B W Hills 5-9-4 M Hills 2/1 JT FAV: 21-542: 5 b h Rainbow Quest - Imaginary shd 115
(Dancing Brave) Trckd ldrs, prog to lead 2f out, sn hard prsd & rdn, hdd towards fin, just btn: well bckd, clr rem:
lost nothing in defeat, also bhd this wnr last time: gives the impression he needs holding up as late as possible.
*2953 **SKI RUN** 25 [1] G A Butler 4-8-12 L Dettori 14/1: 01-013: 4 b f Petoski - Cut And Run (Slip Anchor) 3 110
Waited with, gd prog to chall appr fnl 2f, saddle began slipping & was unrideable by dist, held on uncomfortably for
3rd: poss unlucky, may have gone very cl: vastly improved since stepped up to 2m: useful, deserves a val prize.
3302 **SPIRIT OF LOVE** 10 [5] M Johnston 5-9-1 R Hills 4/1: 030324: Led, incrsd pace appr str, hdd 2f out, ¾ 108
onepce: bandaged in front, nicely bckd, stablemate wnr: gd run tho' will apprec a return to Listed, see 1565.
3371 **ROSTROPOVICH** 9 [4] 3-8-1 G Duffield 6/1: -3135: In tch, eff appr fnl 2f, no impress: Irish raider, 1½ 107
far from disgraced on only 4th ever run & against elders tho' poss not see out this longer 2m trip: see 3317.
5 ran Time 3m 28.21 (8.41) (P D Savill) M Johnston Middleham, N Yorks

3539	3.10 GR 1 INTERNATIONAL STKS 3YO+ (A) 1m2f85y Good 40 +21 Fast
	£261000 £99000 £49500 £22500 3 yo rec 8 lb

+3087 **GIANTS CAUSEWAY** 20 [5] A P O'Brien 3-8-11 M J Kinane 10/11 FAV: 221111: 3 ch c Storm Cat - 126
Mariah's Storm (Rahy) Trckd pacemaker, went on appr fnl 2f, rdn bef dist & went a hd down, rall most bravely for
press to regain lead nr fin, all-out: hvly bckd, fast time, good pick: a remarkable 4th Gr 1 in 2 mths, earlier
won at Ascot (St James Palace), Sandown (Eclipse) & Goodwood (Sussex), prev won at The Curragh (Gr 3) & rnr up
in both English & Irish 2000 Guineas: juv wnr at Naas, The Curragh (Gr 3) & Longchamp (Gr 1, rtd 118): eff at
1m/10.5f on fast, any trk: runs well fresh, up with the pace: high-class, as game & tough as they come.
-2497 **KALANISI** 45 [6] Sir Michael Stoute 4-9-5 Pat Eddery 5/4: 1-2122: 4 b h Doyoun - Kalamba (Green hd 125
Dancer) Rcd in 3rd, trkd eventual wnr, pulled out to chall 2f out, hard rdn to lead narrowly dist, edged left &
hdd cl home, just btn by the gamest wnr: bckd, well clr rem, jockey given 2 day whip ban, 6 week abs: lost
nothing in defeat & a hd bhd this wnr in the Eclipse last time in another pulsating fin: deserves a Group 1 win.
769 **LEAR SPEAR** 150 [4] D R C Elsworth 5-9-5 T Quinn 14/1: 0-203: 5 b h Lear Fan - Golden Gorse 7 115
(His Majesty) Towards rear, shaken up 3f out, styd on same pace for 3rd but no ch with high-class front
pair: sound effort after 5 month abs & better for race: will apprec a return to Gr 2/3 company, see 655.
2409 **SHOAL CREEK** 51 [3] A P O'Brien 3-8-11 (VIS) P J Scallan 150/1: -53104: Set furious gall, edged ½ 114
right to let stablemate thro' & hdd 2f out, no extra: qk reapp: pacemaker for wnr in first time visor.
3071 **BARATHEA GUEST** 23 [1] B W Hills 3-8-11 L Dettori 16/1: 134055: Held up, brief eff 3f out: strong colt, 1st run 3½ 109
for M Channon: drop to Gr 3 will suit: see 1171, 950.
3087 **ALMUSHTARAK** 20 [2] 7-9-5 R Cochrane 40/1: 0-3606: Al last: better at 1m: see 1043. 5 102
6 ran Time 2m 09.3 (2) (Mrs John Magnier & Mr M Tabor) A P O'Brien Ballydoyle, Co Tipperary

3540	3.45 GR 2 GREAT VOLTIGEUR STKS 3YO (A) 1m4f Good 40 -12 Slow
	£89250 £3300 £16500 £7500

3061 **AIR MARSHALL** 21 [2] Sir Michael Stoute 3-8-9 J Murtagh 7/2: 14-221: 3 ch c In The Wings - Troyanna 117
(Troy) Trckd ldrs, going well/short of room appr fnl 2f, squeezed thro' & qcknd to lead ent fnl 1f, shade readily:
hvly bckd: earlier unlucky shd 2nd in a Gr 3: '99 Goodwood wnr (mdn, Gr 1 4th, rtd 104): eff at 12f, should get
the extended 14f of the St Leger: acts on firm & gd grnd, any track: can force the pace but has a smart of foot
that is best delivered from bhd: angular, v smart, improving colt, should go close at Doncaster next month.
*2503 **MARIENBARD** 45 [4] M A Jarvis 3-8-9 P Robinson 6/1: 1112: 3 b c Caerleon - Marienbad (Darshaan) 2½ 112

1087

Last but in tch, pshd along appr fnl 2f, carried head akwdly & slightly bmpd bef dist, styd on well for press ins last, no ch wnr: 6 wk abs, op 4/1: lost unbtn record tho' improved again in defeat: strong colt, sharper for this & lks sure to apprec the 14f+ of the St Leger trip where he again crosses swords with Air Marshall: beat him in 2503.
*2068 **DALAMPOUR 63** [5] Sir Michael Stoute 3-8-9 Pat Eddery 15/8 FAV: -0113: 3 b c Shernazar - Dalara (Doyoun) Led, hdd briefly 3f out, rdn & hdd dist, onepace: hvly bckd from 5/1, stablemate wnr, lkd well after 9 wk abs: gd run from this smart colt & shld be seen to even better effect with a return to 14f+: see 2068. *shd* **112**
3321 **FRENCH FELLOW 10** [3] T D Easterby 3-8-9 K Darley 8/1: -20134: Prom, led briefly 3f out, rdn, onepce & hung left below dist: looked superb: stays 12f, will apprec return to Gr 3 company: see 2578. *2* **109**
*2148 **SUBTLE POWER 60** [1] 3-8-12 T Quinn 11/4: 1215: Cl up, chall 3f out till appr fnl 1f, fdd: well bckd, 9 wk abs, padd pick: shade below par (as have a few of his stablemates recently): see 2148. *1½* **110**
5 ran Time 2m 33.01 (6.21) (Lord Weinstock) Sir Michael Stoute Newmarket, Suffolk

3541

4.15 LADBROKE HCAP 3YO+ 0-95 (C) 1m4f Good 40 -08 Slow [91]
£19977 £6147 £3073 £1536 3 yo rec 10lb

2695 **SEEK 38** [10] L M Cumani 4-9-9 (86) J P Spencer 4/1 FAV: 21-251: 4 br c Rainbow Quest - Souk (Ahonoora) Mid div, trckd ldrs going well 3f out, rdn appr fnl 1f, ran on strongly to get up fnl 100y: hvly bckd: won fnl of just 2 '99 starts at Pontefract (mdn, rtd 82): eff at 12f, stays 14f & return to that trip will suit: acts on gd & soft, handles firm, stiff/gall trcks: stocky colt, progressing well, rate higher & win more races. **92**
3461 **MORGANS ORCHARD 4** [7] A G Newcombe 4-7-12 (61) G Baker (5) 20/1: 520232: 4 ch g Forest Wind - Regina St Cyr (Doulab) Nvr far away, pshd into lead ent fnl 2f, rdn dist, hdd towards fin: nicely bckd: fine run from the bottom of the h'cap from this attractive gelding: acts on firm, gd grnd & fibresand: see 607. *¾* **64**
2178 **RIYAFA 58** [3] Sir Michael Stoute 3-9-0 (87) J Murtagh 11/1: 2153: 3 b f Kahyasi - Riyama (Doyoun) Held & last ent str, prog when sltly short of room 3f out, weaved thro' fnl 2f & kept on strgly, nvr nrr: op 9/1, 8 wk abs: fine h'cap bow from this lightly rcd, scopey filly: give too much to do here, sure to win more races. *½* **89+**
*3461 **WARNING REEF 4** [15] E J Alston 7-8-0 (63)(4ex) P Doe 10/1: 331214: Wide, mid-div, styd on well for press fnl 2f, grabbed 4th cl home: qk reapp: gd run from difficult high draw: also 4th in this last year: v tough. *2* **63**
2594 **CANFORD 41** [12] 3-8-12 (85) R Cochrane 12/1: 4-1355: Led after 2f till ent fnl 2f, rdn bef dist, no extra & eased cl home/lost 4th: 6 wk abs: back in trip on h'cap bow: stays 12f: see 1588 (10f mdn on soft). *hd* **85**
3461 **MARDANI 4** [18] 5-9-10 (87) R Hills 20/1: 000026: Prom, rdn 3f out, hung left 2f out, unable to qckn. *¾* **86**
3131 **RICH VEIN 18** [2] 3-8-12 (85)(vis) G Duffield 7/1: 112147: Bhd, shaken up 3f out, styd on nicely but nvr nr to chall: bckd: hold up tactics overdone over lngr 12f trip: not given a hard time & is worth another ch. *¾* **83**
3353 **QUEENS PAGEANT 8** [14] 6-8-8 (71) M Roberts 33/1: 465108: Keen, early ldr, no extra appr fnl 1f. *nk* **68**
*3140 **WESTGATE RUN 18** [11] 3-7-12 (71) J Quinn 10/1: 311219: Cl up, ch 3f out, sn hmpd & lost grnd, no threat after: hard fit: not disgraced, this was a lot more competitive than what she is used to: see 3140 *¾* **67**
2279 **FATEHALKHAIR 54** [6] 8-8-3 (66) D Mernagh (3) 20/1: 023150: Chsd ldrs, lost pl & drpd towards rear halfway, hdwy und press appr fnl 2f, onepace bef dist: 10th, bckd from 33/1, swtg, edgy in paddock: won a nov chase at Sedgefield (2m gd/fm, rtd 116c) 19 days ago: see 2061. *hd* **62**
3451 **FATHER JUNINHO 4** [8] 3-9-5 (92)(VIS) N Callan 16/1: 233540: Towards rr, eff 3f out, no impress: 11th. *1¾* **86**
2518 **RINGSIDE JACK 45** [1] 4-8-2 (65)(vis) A Nicholls (3) 25/1: 106040: Held up, rdn 3f out, onepace: 12th. *½* **58**
*3159 **GRALMANO 17** [5] 5-9-8 (85) F Lynch 12/1: 164110: Cshd ldrs, lost place 3f out: 13th, unsuited by step up to 12f, see 3159 (beat this 4th over 10f). *1¼* **76**
3058 **WAIT FOR THE WILL 21** [16] 4-9-8 (85)(bl) M J Kinane 7/1: 223130: Keen, mid-div, wknd qckly fnl 3f: 14th. *5* **71**
2596 **AIR DEFENCE 41** [9]. 3-9-7 (94) M Hills 10/1: 2-2100: Hmpd after 4f & al bhd: 15th, 6 week abs. *shd* **80**
3173 **Night Venture 16** [4] 4-9-8 (85) J Reid 16/1: 3058 **Batswing 21** [13] 5-8-13 (76) F Norton 16/1:
3323 **Angus G 10** [17] 8-9-3 (80) A Culhane 50/1:
18 ran Time 2m 32.54 (5.74) (Fittocks Stud) L M Cumani Newmarket, Suffolk

3542

4.45 LINKS NURSERY HCAP 2YO (C) 7f rnd Good 40 -26 Slow [102]
£11609 £3572 £1786 £893

3304 **IMPERIAL DANCER 10** [1] M R Channon 2-9-7 (95) Craig Williams 10/1: 302451: 2 b c Primo Dominie - Gorgeous Dancer (Nordico) Held up on ins rail, prog & got a dream run thro' appr fnl 1f, led dist, shkn up, readily: top-weight, h'cap bow: earlier won at Warwick (4 rnr mdn): eff at 7f, tried 1m last time: acts on firm, suited by gd or hvy grnd, any track: can carry big weights: useful & progressive colt. **103**
3246 **DOMINAITE 13** [8] M W Easterby 2-8-2 (76) A Nicholls (3) 10/1: 032132: 2 b g Komaite - Fairy Kingdom (Price Sabo) Towards rear, switched appr fnl 2f, styd on for press & went 2nd nr fin, no ch wnr: tall gelding, tough & improving, will appreciate 1m next time: see 2991. *1¼* **80**
3086 **PEREGIAN 20** [6] M Johnston 2-8-13 (87) R Hills 9/1: 011103: 2 b c Eagle Eyed - Mo Pheata (Petorius) Led, rdn & edged right ent fnl 2f, hdd ent fnl 1f, onepace: op 7/1: strong & consistent, see 2928. *nk* **90**
*3223 **TIME TO REMEMBER 13** [11] T D Easterby 2-8-4 (78) K Darley 5/2 FAV: 314: Trkd ldrs, shkn up to press ldr & hung left appr fnl 1f, unable to qckn: bckd, h'cap bow, tricky draw: well regarded, worth another ch. *nk* **80**
3108 **AKER WOOD 19** [2] 2-8-8 (82) N Callan 20/1: 0205: Mid div, trckd ldrs 3f out, shkn up 2f out & not clr run, switched & bmpd dist, no extra: would have been considerably closer on h'cap bow: worth another look. *3½* **78**
2962 **LUNAR LEO 25** [3] 2-8-11 (85) G Faulkner (3) 11/2: -4136: Keen in mid-div, rdn appr fnl 1f, no impress on ldrs: well bckd, clr rem: will apprec a stronger pace: see 2459 (made all in a mdn auction). *shd* **81**
3127 **VISITATION 18** [4] 2-7-10 (70)(8oh) J Mackay (5) 25/1: -0127: Chsd ldrs, onepace 2f out: stiff task. *3* **60**
3164 **SABANA 17** [10] 2-8-9 (83) M J Kinane 8/1: 0258: Dwelt, nvr in it: attractive colt, h'cap bow, see 2881. *1¼* **71**
3245 **STRETTON 13** [13] 2-8-4 (78) L Newman (3) 9/1: 0329: Wide, nvr nr ldrs: gd looking colt, forget this h'cap bow from stall 13: well worth another chance at 7f/1m. *shd* **66**
2991 **AFFARATI 24** [12] 2-8-0 (74) J Quinn 20/1: 216050: Al wide & towards rear: 10th, forgive from stall 12. *3* **56**
3228 **TROJAN PRINCE 13** [9] 2-7-10 (70)(1oh) F Norton 8/1: 002560: Not settle & prsd ldr till halfway, no extra/hmpd & eased 2f out: leggy, scopey but headstrong: 6f may prove ideal for now: see 3228, 1513. *1¾* **49**
3428 **LITTLE TASK 4** [7] 2-7-13 (73) P Bradley (4) 25/1: 024260: Chsd ldrs till ent straight: 12th, qk reapp. *1* **50**
*2316 **CASPIAN 52** [5] 2-8-1 (75) G Duffield 11/1: 210: Bhd ldrs, drpd away quickly appr fnl 2f: 13th, abs. *2* **48**
13 ran Time 1m 25.92 (4.62) (Imperial Racing) M R Channon, West Isley, Berks

3543

5.15 HAREWOOD HCAP 3YO+ 0-100 (C) 6f Good 40 +02 Fast [100]
£17290 £5320 £2660 £1330 3yo rec 3lb 3 rcd stands side for 3f - centre favoured

2348 **NIGHT FLIGHT 51** [15] R A Fahey 6-9-0 (86) J Reid 25/1: 060001: 6 gr g Night Shift - Ancestry (Persepolis) Bhd ldrs in centre going well, led bef dist, rdn out, readily: freshened up by 7 week abs, fair time: '99 wnr here at York, Haydock & Ascot (val h'cap, rtd 105): '98 Newcastle wnr (h'cap, rtd 80): eff at 5/6f on firm **94**

& soft, prob fibresand: can carry big weights & runs well fresh: nicely h'capped for the Ayr Gold Cup.

*2961 **ANTONIO CANOVA 25** [11] Bob Jones 4-8-3 (75) Dale Gibson 9/1: -30012: 4 ch g Komaite - Joan's   ½ 78
Venture (Beldale Flutter) Chsd ldrs, eff appr fnl 1f styd on well inside last, nvr btn far: nicely bckd,
sweating: in grand form, see 2961 (first win).

3485 **BRECONGILL LAD 3** [8] D Nicholls 8-8-12 (84) A Nicholls (3) 16/1: 312023: 8 b g Clantime - Chikala   ½ 85
(Pitskelly) Waited with, smooth prog when ran into back of ldrs appr fnl 1f, kept on, nvr nrr: op 12/1, qck
reapp, v fit: remains in cracking form, lkd unlucky here & deserves another win: see 2987.

*2900 **LORD PACAL 28** [17] N A Callaghan 3-8-8 (83) L Newman (3) 20/1: 002214: Led centre group till   nk 83
veered left & hdd bef dist, kept on onepace: gd run, in form, acts on firm & gd grnd: see 2900.

3427 **KAYO 4** [9] 5-10-0 (100) K Darley 20/1: 122035: Front rank, edged left & outpcd 2f out, rallied fnl 1f.   nk 99

3152 **DANIELLES LAD 17** [23] 4-9-9 (95) D McGaffin (5) 33/1: 110406: Rcd stand side & sn clr overall ldr,   shd 94
shkn up & drifted to centre halfway, sn hdd, kept on: edgy in paddock & went down early: back to form, see 1531.

3464 **PIPS MAGIC 3** [12] 4-9-3 (89) A Culhane 25/1: 010007: Towards rear, shaken up halfway, not much   nk 81
room bef dist, kept on for press inside last: quick reapp, not far off best, see 3037.

3315 **PERUVIAN CHIEF 10** [13] 3-8-13 (88) J P Murtagh 20/1: 043368: Held up, rdn 2f out, no impress   ½ 84
till kept on nicely ins last, nvr dngrs: bckd tho' op 16/1: stiffer 6f or return to 7f should suit.

3130 **CAPRICHO 18** [20] 3-8-11 (86) M J Kinane 5/1: -21129: In tch, not clr run appr fnl 1f, eff & no   hd 82
impress inside last: nicely bckd: unsuited by drop to 6f, see 2855.

3473 **LAGO DI VARANO 3** [21] 8-9-0 (86)(bl) Dean McKeown 16/1: 300120: In tch stands side, pushed   1 79
along halfway, badly bmpd appr fnl 1f, nvr nr ldrs: 10th: quick reapp: see 3183 (first win at 6f).

3464 **GUINEA HUNTER 3** [22] 4-10-0 (100) J Carroll 20/1: 100100: Held up stands side for 2f, switched   ½ 91
to centre & chased ldrs, edged left under press appr fnl 1f, onepace: 11th, jt top-weight, qk reapp: btr 2859 (5f).

3341 **FLAK JACKET 9** [16] 5-8-3 (75)(t) F Norton 7/2 FAV: 211130: Cl up, pushed along & onepace when   shd 66
carried left bef dist: 12th, well bckd: been busy & is better coming from off the pace: see 3136.

3440 **TREASURE TOUCH 4** [4] 6-7-12 (70) Joanna Badger (7) 16/1: 301240: Al around same place: 13th.   ¾ 59

2504 **CARD GAMES 45** [10] 3-8-7 (82) T Lucas 25/1: 001200: Mid div, briefly short of room appr fnl 1f,   shd 71
no ch with ldrs & eased: 14th, 6 week abs: see 1133.

3341 **MISS HIT 3** [14] 5-7-13 (71) J Quinn 9/1: 0-1020: Bhd, hmpd appr fnl 1f, late hdwy: 15th, bckd, lkd well.   1 57

*3398 **MUNGO PARK 6** [19] 6-8-11 (83)(bl)(6ex) T Quinn 20/1: 222510: Waited with, bmpd appr fnl 1f, nvr   hd 69
dangerous: 16th, quick reapp: better at 5f, see 3398.

3464 **BON AMI 3** [7] 4-9-3 (89) P Bradley (5) 7/1: 460240: Nvr going pace: 17th, bandaged, quick reapp: 1 72
has had some hard races recently, see 3130 & 3341.

3136 **Teyaar 18** [2] 4-8-6 (75)(3ow) N Callan 25/1:   3170 **The Gay Fox 16** [1] 6-8-2 (74)(tbl) G Duffield 20/1:
3464 **Cryhavoc 3** [6] 6-9-7 (93) Alex Greaves 20/1:   1307 **Adelphi Boy 98** [3] 4-7-12 (70) K Dalgleish (5) 50/1:
2569 **Fearby Cross 42** [5] 4-8-8 (80) Pat Eddery 16/1:   1250 **Blue Star 103** [18] 4-8-0 (72)(vis) J Tate 33/1:
23 ran   Time 1m 11.65 (2.25)   (C H Stevens)   R A Fahey Butterwick, N Yorks

---

Official Going   GOOD TO FIRM

3544   2.55 GR 1 PRIX DU HARAS 3YO+ 1m Good/Firm
£115274   £46110   £23055   £11527   3 yo rec 7 lb

2064 **MUHTATHIR 54** Saeed bin Suroor 5-9-4 L Dettori 215/10: 4-3161: 5 ch h Elmaamul - Majmu (Al Nasr)   125
Keen, chsd ldrs, went on appr fnl 2f, styd on well & drvn clr: 8 wk abs: earlier won at San Siro (Gr 2):
'99 wnr again at San Siro (Gr 1, rtd 118 at best), prev term scored at Doncaster, Newbury, Goodwood (Gr 2)
& rnr-up at Longchamp (French 2,000 Guineas, rtd 120): loves to race up with/force the pace at 7f/1m on
firm, gd & dirt: runs well fresh on a stiff/gall trk: top-class miler, career best effort today.

2089 **SENDAWAR 53** A de Royer Dupre 4-9-4 G Mosse 7/10 FAV: 11-142: 4 b c Priolo - Sendana (Darshaan)   3 120
Settled mid-div, gd prog appr fnl 1f, styd on but no impress on wnr: 8 wk abs: apprec this drop back to 1m
but still below v best form: top-class miler: see 2089, 1458.

2571 **KINGSALSA 36** A Fabre 4-9-4 O Peslier 76/10: 132133: 4 b c Kingmambo - Caretta (Caro)   1½ 117
Bhd, rdn/hdwy over 2f out, drvn & onepaced appr fnl 1f: v tough, smart & consistent: relish a return to Gr 3.

*3151 **CRIMPLENE 8** C E Brittain 3-8-8 P Robinson 28/10: 311114: Led, hdd appr fnl 2f, drvn &   ½ 113
no extra over 1f out: qck reapp: reportedly became upset in the stalls & this poss came too sn after 3151.

*1321 **TIMBOROA 91** 4-9-4 T Jarnet 25/10: -13115: Waited with, hmpd nr halfway, styd on late   2 112
for press, nvr nrr: new stable, prev trained in Italy, now with A de Royer Dupre: apprec a return to 10f.

1901 **NEW STORY 63** 3-8-8 S Pasquier 57/1: -16006: Mid-div, unable to qckn fnl 2f: see 1901.   hd 109

2997 **SUGARFOOT 15** 6-9-4 C Asmussen 446/10: 155100: Nvr dangerous: needs a drop in grade: see 2997.   110
11 ran   Time 1m 34.6   (Godolphin)   Saeed bin Suroor Newmarket

---

Official Going   GOOD TO FIRM

3545   1.55 LISTED PRIX MICHEL HOUYVET 3YO 1m7f Good/Firm
£13449   £4611   £3458

2594 **SHUWAIB 35** M R Channon 3-8-11 Craig Williams : 131: 3 b c Polish Precedent - Ajab Alzamaan   104
(Rainbow Quest) Made all, pressed appr fnl 1f, pushed out to assert cl-home, shade cosy: earlier won on debut
at Goodwood (mdn): eff at 12f, apprec this step up to 15f, even further could suit: acts on fast grnd & a
sharp or gall trk: lightly raced & progressive colt who can win more valuable races.

3065 **BOURGEOIS 19** Mme C Head 3-8-11 O Doleuze : 412342: 3 ch c Sanglamore - Bourbon Girl (Ile De   ¾ 102
Bourbon) -:

--   **STROMNESS** France 3-8-11 O Peslier : 3: 3 ch c Trempolino - Caithness (Roberto)   ¾ 101
4 ran   Time 3m 22.1   (Ahmed Al Maktoum)   M R Channon West Isley, Berks

DEAUVILLE

SATURDAY AUGUST 19TH   Righthand, Galloping Track

Official Going   GOOD TO FIRM

3546   **3.15 GR 3 PRIX DE LA NONETTE 3YO FILL**   1m2f   **Good/Firm**
£21134   £7685   £3842

*2401 **DI MOI OUI 50** P Bary 3-9-0 T Thulliez 24/10: 341011: 3 b f Warning - Biosphere (Pharly)   111
Settled last, gd hdwy to lead appr fnl 1f, drvn out: returned with a badly cut leg: 7 wk abs: dual wnr prev
this term, incl a Gr 3 at Chantilly: eff at 9/10f on fast & gd grnd: runs well fresh: tough/useful filly.
--   **TRES RAVI** A Wohler 3-9-0 A Suborics 87/10: 4-1242: 3 br f Monsun - Tres Magnifique (Gay Fandango) 1½ 108
Chsd ldrs, rdn to chall over 1f out, sn not pace of wnr: useful run, eff over a gall 10f on fast grnd.
1901 **REVE DOSCAR 69** Mme M Bollack Badel 3-9-0 A Badel 22/10 FAV: -22143: 3 gr f Highest Honor -   shd 108
Numide (Baillamont) Waited with, rdn/prog appr fnl 1f, kept on, no impress on wnr: plcd since 1901, see 1457.
6 ran   Time 2m 13.1   (Grundy Bloodstock Ltd)   P Bary France

3547   **3.45 LISTED COUP DU FONDS 4YO+ FILLIES**   1m2f   **Good/Firm**
£38425   £15370   £11527

3177 **LIMELIGHTING 13** J H M Gosden 4-8-11 O Peslier : 2-4541: 4 b f Alleged - Stealthethunder (Lyphard)   107
Made most, comfortably: '99 wnr at York (mdn) & Doncaster (fillies stks, rtd 98): stays 12f, suited by 10f:
acts on firm, hvy & any trk: likes racing up with/forcing the pace: useful, well plcd to land this val prize.
3538} **STAR OF AKKAR 364** J C Rouget 4-8-11 T Jarnet : 1211-2: 4 b f Distant Relative - Donna Star   2½ 103
(Stately Don) -:
3177 **FARFALA 13** P F I Cole 4-8-11 G Mosse : 10-523: 4 gr f Linamix - Fragrant Hill (Shirley Heights)   ½ 102
In tch, prog appr fnl 1f, sn not pace of wnr: may apprec a return to 12f: shade btr 3177.
10 ran   Time 2m 12.8   (George Strawbridge)   J H M Gosden Manton, Wilts

FAIRYHOUSE

SATURDAY AUGUST 19TH   Righthand, Galloping Track

Official Going   FIRM

3548   **3.30 LISTED BELGRAVE STKS 3YO+**   6f   **Firm**
£16250   £4750   £2250   3 yo rec 3 lb

2151 **SOCIAL HARMONY 57** D K Weld 6-9-0 P J Smullen 11/4: -02041: 6 b g Polish Precedent - Latest Chapter   113
(Ahonoora) With ldr, went on 3f out, rall strongly for press over 1f out, comfortably: won h'caps in '99 at The Curragh & Galway
(rtd 108): suited by 6f, stays 7f: acts on fast & hvy grnd: smart run here, win a Gr 3 on this form.
3373 **ONE WON ONE 6** Ms J Morgan 6-9-5 J Murtagh 11/4: 012032: 6 b g Naevus - Harvard's Bay (Halpern   3½ 106
Bay) Settled rear, styd on well for press fnl 2f, no ch with wnr: qck reapp: not disgraced conceding weight.
988 **GALLOWAY BOY 119** D K Weld 3-8-11 (t) F M Berry 16/1: 040-03: 3 ch c Mujtahid - Supportive   1 98
(Nashamaa) Bhd, rdn & styd on appr fnl 1f, nvr nrr: stablemate of wnr: gd run for new connections after
4 month abs: dual wnr in '99, incl on debut (with S J Mahon): eff arnd 5/6f on gd/soft grnd: with D K Weld.
7 ran   Time 1m 11.7   (S Creaven)   D K Weld Curragh, Co Kildare

ARLINGTON (USA)

SATURDAY AUGUST 19TH   --

Official Going   YIELDING

3549   **11.27 GR 1 SECRETARIAT STKS 3YO**   1m2f   **Yielding**
£146341   £48780   £26829

2409 **CIRO 48** A P O'Brien 3-8-8 M J Kinane 48/10: -31631: 3 ch c Woodman - Gioconda (Nijinsky)   119
Trkd ldrs, dropped rear 3f out, rall strongly for press over 1f out, drvn out to lead well in last: 7 wk abs:
earlier won at Longchamp (Gr 1 Prix Lupin): '99 wnr at Galway (mdn), subs awarded a Gr 1 at Longchamp (rtd 112):
eff at 1m/12f on gd/soft grnd: high-class colt who will reportedly continue his career in the USA.
--   **KING CUGAT** W Mott 3-8-11 J D Bailey 3/5 FAV: 1-1112: 3 b c Kingmambo - Tricky Game (Majestic   1 120
Light) -:
2225 **GUILLAMOU CITY 55** J C Rouget 3-8-5(3ow) C Nakatani 34/1: -11163: 3 b c Lesotho - Star Emily (Tasso) 4½ 107
2736 **COMPTON BOLTER 36** G A Butler 3-8-2 (BL) A Solis 47/1: 405045: Settled last, mod late gains,   99
no impress on ldrs, fin 5th: below-par in 1st time blnks: needs a drop in grade: see 2736.
8 ran   Time 2m 01.64   (Jayeff B Stables)   A P O'Brien Ballydoyle, Co Tipperary

DEAUVILLE

SUNDAY AUGUST 20TH   Righthand, Galloping Track

Official Going   GOOD TO SOFT

3550   **1.40 GR 1 PRIX MORNAY 2YO**   6f   **Good/Soft**
£76849   £30740   £15370   £7685

*3044 **BAD AS I WANNA BE 20** B J Meehan 2-9-0 G Mosse 144/10: 011: 2 ch c Common Grounds -   119
Song Of The Glens (Horage) Made all, qckd & impress went clr fnl 2f, rdn out: earlier won a mdn at Windsor
(comfortably): 62,000gns Mar foal, brother to a 7f juv wnr: v eff at 6f, 7f sure to suit: acts on fast, clearly
well suited by gd/soft grnd: runs well fresh on a sharp or gall trk: making rapid improvement & this was a top-class
performance (2nd & 3rd won Gr races last time out): potential Champion 2yo, keep on your side.
*3105 **ENDLESS SUMMER 17** J H M Gosden 2-9-0 O Peslier 11/10 FAV: -112: 2 b c Zafonic - Well Away   6 110

DEAUVILLE
SUNDAY AUGUST 20TH   Righthand, Galloping Track

(Sadler's Wells) Chsd ldrs, rdn/prog appr fnl 1f, kept on but no threat to impress wnr: caught a top-class
rival here: acts on fm & gd/soft, will reportedly prefer a sounder surface: win more Gr races & 7f will suit.

*2595 **NOVERRE 39** D R Loder 2-9-0 L Dettori 3/1: -1113: 2 b c Rahy - Danseur Fabuleux	1	107

(Northern Dancer) Cl-up, drvn/not pace of wnr appr fnl 1f: lost unbeaten record in top company, 7f shld now suit.

*3066 **ROLLY POLLY 22** B Grizzetti 2-8-10 M Demuro 37/10: -11114: Front rank, ev ch till not	3	96

qckn from 2f out: Italian raider, unbeaten prev: reportedly lost a shoe & returned a cut leg: see 3066.

3105 **PYRUS 17** 2-9-0 M J Kinane 9/2: 125: With ldr, drvn/fdd appr fnl 1f: reportedly unsuited by this	1½	97

rain-softened grnd: much better on good in 3105 (Gr 2, again bhd today's rnr-up).

*2956 **RED MAGIC 23** 2-9-0 R Hughes 78/10: 216: Waited with, lost tch fnl 2f, fin last:	5	87

v disapp & somthing surely amiss, but this was his first run on grnd softer than fast: impress mdn wnr in 2956.
6 ran   Time 1m 10.3   (Joe L Allbritton)   B J Meehan Upper Lambourn, Berks

---

3551   2.50 LISTED PRIX NORMANDY 3YO FILLIES   1m   Good/Soft
£13449   £4611   £3458

*2679 **MAY BALL 36** J H M Gosden 3-8-12 L Dettori : -12411: 3 b f Cadeaux Genereux - Minute		101

Waltz (Sadler's Wells) Trkd ldr, went on appr fnl 1f, strongly pressed ins last, drvn out: earlier won at
Newmarket (meaningless 2-rnr chall race) & Ascot (mdn): half-sister to a 1m/9f wnr: loves to race up with/
force the pace over 1m/9f: acts on fast, good/soft & a gall trk: improved today, useful.

3069 **PEONY 21** D Sepulchre 3-9-2 C Asmussen : -11252: 3 ch f Lion Cavern - Persiandale (Persian Bold)	snk	104
-- **EVER IN LOVE** France 3-9-2 J B Eyguem : 3: 3 b f Neverneyev - French Love (Zino)	1	102

9 ran   Time 1m 44.1   (Lord Hartington)   J H M Gosden Manton, Wilts

---

3552   3.20 GR 2 PRIX KERGORLAY 3YO+   1m7f   Good/Soft
£28818   £11527   £5764   £2882

3106 **PERSIAN PUNCH 17** D R C Elsworth 7-9-4 R Hughes 32/10: 201651: 7 ch g Persian Heights - Rum Cay		115

(Our Native) Made all, clr appr fnl 1f, eased well ins last: val 4/5L: earlier won at Sandown (Gr 3): below
best in '99, tho' did win fnl start at Doncaster (stks, rtd 110 at best): '98 wnr at Newmarket, Sandown & York
(Gr 3's), also plcd in the Melbourne Cup (Gr 1, rtd 118): '97 wnr at Newbury & Sandown (Gr 3, rtd 120): eff
at 12f, suited by 14f/2m & does stay 2m4f: runs well fresh on firm & hvy grnd: best up with/forcing the pace:
v tough, game & high-class stayer: may now head to Australia for another crack at the Melbourne Cup.

2402 **WAJINA 51** A Fabre 4-9-1 O Peslier 23/10: 5-2232: 4 b f Rainbow Quest - Wajd (Northern Dancer)	2	107

Chsd ldrs, rdn appr fnl 2f, styd on but no impress on wnr: plcd on all 4 starts this term, debut wnr in '99:
eff arnd a gall 15f on gd & gd/soft grnd: useful & consistent filly.

3106 **THREE CHEERS 17** J H M Gosden 6-9-4 (bl) L Dettori 23/10: 2-1203: 6 br g Slip Anchor - Three	¾	109

Tails (Blakeney) Handy, rdn after halfway, drvn & ran on ins last, no threat to wnr: see 2153, 1857.

*2909 **PAIRUMANI STAR 29** J L Dunlop 5-9-4 G Mosse 18/10 FAV: -01214: Front rank, drvn over 4f out,	2½	107

no extra for press fnl 2f: reportedly unsuited by the rain-softened grnd: see 2909 (Listed).

1456 **LE TINTORET 91** 7-9-4 O Doleuze 32/10: 4-1025: Settled rear, late hdwy, no dngr: long abs, see 1456.	¾	106

7 ran   Time 3m 14.4   (J C Smith)   D R C Elsworth Whitsbury, Hants

---

DIELSDORF (SWITZERLAND)
SUNDAY AUGUST 20TH   --

Official Going   GOOD

3553   2.45 SILBERBLAUES BAND VON ZURICH 3YO+   2m   Good
£5647   £2259   £1694

3060 **AKBAR 19** M Johnston 4-9-13 J Fanning : 110641: 4 b c Doyoun - Akishka (Nishapour)		99

Trkd ldr, went on 4f out, easily went clr: earlier won twice here in Switzerland (stks, incl reapp): mainly
with J Oxx in '99, plcd sev times, incl List (rtd 101): eff at 10f/2m on fast & hvy: tough & useful colt.

4349] **EAGLES CROSS 667** Switzerland 5-9-8 Brigitte Renk : 0056/2: 5 b h Trempolino - Shining Bright	5	86

(Rainbow Quest) -:

1903 **HARISHON 69** Switzerland 4-10-1 J M Breux : 23: 4 b c Waajib - Cheyna (Beldale Flutter)	3	90

6 ran   Time 3m 14.7   (Markus Graff)   M Johnston Middleham, N Yorks

---

CURRAGH
SUNDAY AUGUST 20TH   Righthand, Stiff, Galloping Track

Official Going   GOOD

3554   3.00 GR 3 DESMOND STKS 3YO+   1m   Good
£27950   £8170   £3870   3 yo rec 6 lb

3087 **GOLDEN SILCA 18** M R Channon 4-9-0 J Murtagh 7/4: 410541: 4 ch f Inchinor - Silca Cisa (Hallgate)		114

Trkd ldr, swtchd appr fnl 1f & sn led, drvn clr: jockey received a 2-day careless riding ban: earlier won at
Epsom (List): rnr-up in 3 of 4 '99 starts, incl Gr 1 Irish 1,000 Guineas & Coronation Stks (rtd 115): v tough
juv, wnr at Newbury (4, incl Gr 2) & also in Germany: eff at sprint trips, now seems best arnd 1m: acts on firm,
hvy & any trk, likes Newbury: runs well fresh: v tough/smart filly, win more races in this grade.

2675 **DUCK ROW 36** A R Toller 5-9-3 S Whitworth 2/1: -12232: 5 ch g Diesis - Sunny Moment (Roberto)	3½	109

Settled last, hdwy when bumped 2f out, styd on but not pace of wnr: admirably tough & consistent this term
& sorely deserves to win another race: see 1847.

1752 **MUAKAAD 77** D K Weld 3-8-11 (t) P J Smullen 6/4 FAV: -13013: 3 b c Muhtarram - Forest Lair	shd	109

(Habitat) Led, drvn/hdd over 1f out, not qckn: recent wnr at Leopardstown (10f stks, fast): see 1314.
3 ran   Time 1m 41.7   (Aldridge Racing Limited)   M R Channon West Isley, Berks

CURRAGH

SUNDAY AUGUST 20TH   Righthand, Stiff, Galloping Track

3555   3.30 LISTED DEBUTANTE FILL STKS 2YO   7f   Good
£16250   £4750   £2250

--   **AFFIANCED** J S Bolger 2-8-10 (BL) K J Manning 7/1: -211: 2 b f Erin's Isle - La Meilleure   **101**
(Lord Gayle) Rear, rdn/hdwy over 1f out, ran on strongly to get up nr fin, drvn out: 1st time blnks: recent
Leopardstown wnr (mdn): eff at 7f on fast & gd grnd: progressive filly, apprec fitting of blnks today.

2408   **SEQUOYAH** 49 A P O'Brien 2-8-10 C O'Donoghue 4/1 FAV: -312: 2 b f Sadler's Wells - Brigid (Irish   shd   **100**
River) Mid-div, gd hdwy to lead dist, collared cl-home: clr rem: Tipperary wnr (7f mdn, fast) since 2408.

--   **IMAGINE** A P O'Brien 2-8-10 P J Scallan 10/1: 3: 2 b f Sadler's Wells - Doff The Derby (Master   3   **94**
Derby) Sn led, drvn/hdd dist, not pace of front 2: gd debut, stablemate of rnr-up: stays 7f on good.

13 ran   Time 1m 28.5   (A G Moylan)   J S Bolger Coolcullen, Co Carlow

---

3556   4.30 GR 2 ROYAL WHIP STKS 3YO+   1m2f   Good
£39000 £11400 £5400 £1800   3 yo rec 8 lb

*3068   **TAKALI** 22 J Oxx 3-8-8 J Murtagh 13/8 FAV: 144511: 3 ch c Kris - Takarouna (Green Dancer)   **113**
Cl-up, went on 2f out, styd on well when pressed fnl 1f, all out: earlier won at Cork (mdn) & The Curragh (Gr 3),
also 5th at 200/1 in the Irish Derby: eff at 10/12f on fast & soft: tough, smart & consistent.

--   **MOLOMO** N Meade 3-8-5 P Shanahan 5/1: -322: 3 b f Barathea - Nishan (Unknown)   hd   **109**
Waited with, swtchd/imprvd 2f out, chall ldrs last, styd on well, just failed: 10 wk abs: recently plcd twice
in mdns: eff at 10/12f on fast & soft: improving & sure to win a race sn.

3068   **JAMMAAL** 22 D K Weld 3-8-8 (bl) P J Smullen 9/4: 121243: 3 b c Robellino - Navajo Love Song   1   **110**
(Dancing Brave) Prom, chall wnr 2f out, not qckn well ins last: clr rem: also bhd this wnr in 3068.

*2071   **ANNIEIRWIN** 67 F Ennis 4-8-13 F M Berry 12/1: 4-6104: 3 b f Distinctly North - Golden Diamond   4   **101**
top-weight: 6 wk abs: unplcd in List company (1m) since 2071.

1627   **APOLLO VICTORIA** 84 3-8-8 J A Heffernan 11/2: 1-2405: Led, hdd 2f out, fdd: 12 wk abs: see 818.   3   **99**

5 ran   Time 2m 13.7   (H H Aga Khan)   J Oxx Currabeg, Co Kildare

---

BRIGHTON

WEDNESDAY AUGUST 23RD   Lefthand, V Sharp, Undulating Track

Official Going   FIRM. Stalls: 10f - Outside; Rem - Inside.

3557   5.25 ARGUS APPR HCAP 3YO+ 0-70 (E)   1m2f   Firm 08   -25 Slow   **[68]**
£2834   £872   £436   £218   3 yo rec 8 lb

3527   **ARDENT** 2 [9] Miss B Sanders 6-8-2 (42) D Kinsella (5) 9/1: 400051: 6 b g Aragon - Forest Of Arden   46
(Tap On Wood): Chsd ldrs, rdn/led over 1f out, styd on well inside last, pushed out cl-home: qck reapp: '99 Kempton
wnr (h'cap, rtd 49, rnr-up on sand, rtd 49a): '98 won 3 here at Brighton (h'cap, rtd 52, also rtd 43a, C Benstead): eff
at 1m/sharp 10f on firm, gd/soft & equitrack: best without blnks: enjoys a sharp/undul or easy trk, likes Brighton.

3188   **LITTLE TUMBLER** 16 [12] S Woodman 5-8-5 (45) R Brisland 8/1: -56502: 5 b m Cyrano de Bergerac -   1   47
Glass Minnow (Alzao): Rear, slightly hmpd after 2f, rdn & styd on well final 3f, not reach wnr: see 1807.

2622   **GEE BEE BOY** 41 [4] G M McCourt 6-8-1 (41) Jonjo Fowle (3) 12/1: 06-063: 6 ch g Beveled - Blue And   ½   42
White (Busted): Prom, ch over 1f out, onepce inside last: recent Worcester wnr over hdles (sell, rtd 92h, eff
arnd 2m on firm & soft): eff at 10/12f on the level, acts on firm & gd: see 2622.

2887   **REGAL ACADEMY** 30 [6] C A Horgan 6-7-11 (37)(tbl)(1ow)(3oh) A Beech 25/1: 004-04: Dwelt/twds rear,   ¾   37
styd on fnl 2f, nrst fin: plcd in '99 (rtd 48, h'cap): rtd 47 in '98: eff at 10/12f on firm & fast: eff in t-strap/blnks.

3244   **RAED** 14 [8] 7-8-5 (45) M Mathers (5) 20/1: 0-3605: Led halfway till over 1f out, fdd: see 369 (AW).   4   39

3357   **WAVERLEY ROAD** 9 [2] 3-8-11 (59) Lisa Jones (7) 15/2: 065026: Led till halfway, btn 3f out: op 5/1.   3   38

2767   **SWING BAR** 35 [3] 7-7-13 (39) Claire Bryan 8/1: -00007: Mid-div, btn 2f out: see 965.   3   25

3018   **CALLDAT SEVENTEEN** 24 [11] 4-10-0 (68) D McGaffin (3) 5/1 FAV: 460608: Chsd ldrs 1m: topweight.   3   50

3314   **JOIN THE PARADE** 11 [13] 4-9-6 (60) I Mongan 15/2: 030209: Prom, btn 3f out: see 2033.   1   41

3382   **EMALI** 7 [7] 3-9-0 (62)(VIS) S Hitchcott (7) 16/1: 220430: In tch, btn 2f out: 10th: visor: btr 3382, 3234.   6   34

3053   **SACREMENTUM** 22 [5] 5-8-7 (47) C Catlin (5) 11/2: 24424F: Chsd ldrs, crashed into rails & fell.   0

2893   **PARISIAN LADY** 30 [10] 5-8-7 (47) G Sparkes (3) 7/1: 44202U: Rear, badly hmpd/u.r. after 2f: see 2893.   0

12 ran   Time 2m 01.1 (3.3)   (R Lamb)   Miss B Sanders Epsom, Surrey.

3558   5.55 EVENING ARGUS AUCT MDN 2YO (E)   7f rnd   Firm 08   -21 Slow
£2775   £854   £427   £213

3239   **BILLIE H** 14 [2] C E Brittain 2-7-11 J Lowe 5/1: 00061: 2 ch f Cool Jazz - Rachels Eden (Ring Bidder)   67
Cl-up, rdn/led 3f out, just held on for press cl-home: only mod form prev: eff over a sharp/undul 7f on firm grnd.

2488   **NUN LEFT** 46 [3] R M Beckett 2-8-3 G Hind 1/3 FAV: 3242: 2 b f Bishop Of Cashel - Salsita (Salse):   hd   72
Chsd ldrs, drvn/strong chall dist, kept on, just held: well bckd at odds-on: abs: eff at 6/7f on firm & fast grnd.

2653   **MERRY DANCE** 40 [4] A P Jarvis 2-8-2 A Beech (5) 14/1: 03: 2 ch f Suave Dancer - Sarah Byrne (Star   1½   68$
Way): Led 4f, held over 1f out: 6 wk abs: mod form prev.

2841   **DATIN STAR** 32 [1] D J Coakley 2-8-0 P Doe 14/1: 6064: In tch, btn over 1f out: op 8/1: see 2251.   2½   61$

2214   **AGILE DANCER** 57 [5] 2-8-6 D O'Donohoe 20/1: 005: In tch, hung left/btn 2f out: abs: Ingr 7f trip.   4   59

5 ran   Time 1m 21.8 (2.0)   (C E Brittain)   C E Brittain Newmarket, Suffolk.

3559   6.25 EVENING ARGUS SELLER 3YO+ (F)   7f rnd   Firm 08   -03 Slow
£2352   £672   £336   3 yo rec 5 lb

3404   **ANNIE APPLE** 7 [1] N Hamilton 4-8-12 D Harrison 13/2: 045001: 4 ch f Petardia - Art Duo (Artaius):   45
Held up, prog final 3f, drvn inside last to lead nr line: bght in for 4,800 gns: '99 scorer at Lingfield (sell, rtd 59a,
R Hannon), subs plcd sev times for G Lewis & current connections (rtd 54 at best, h'cap): '98 Folkestone wnr (sell,
rtd 59): eff btwn 6f/1m on firm, soft & equitrack, any trk: best without a visor: all 3 wins in sell grade.

3445   **REACHFORYOURPOCKET** 5 [4] M D I Usher 5-9-9 I Mongan (5) 8/1: 010002: 5 b g Royal Academy -   hd   55$
Gemaasheh (Habitat) Chsd ldrs, led over 1f out, drvn/strongly prsd ins last, hdd nr fin: clr rem, qck reapp.

1092

BRIGHTON WEDNESDAY AUGUST 23RD Lefthand, V Sharp, Undulating Track

*3332 **TERM OF ENDEARMENT** 10 [2] J Pearce 3-8-13 D O'Donohoe 4/1 FAV: 200213: 3 b f First Trump -   4 **42**
Twilight Secret (Vaigly Great): Mid-div, kept on final 2f for press, no threat: op 3/1: prefer a stiffer trk: see 3332.

2794 **TEA FOR TEXAS** 34 [13] J Akehurst 3-8-13 P Doe 8/1: 160004: Held up, effort halfway, onepace fnl 2f.   ½ **41**

2765 **ERTLON** 35 [5] 10-9-3 A Nicholls (3) 14/1: 060355: Mid-div, rdn/hung left 2f out, sn held: op 12/1.   nk **39**

2970 **DANZAS** 26 [6] 6-9-9 (bl) Claire Bryan (5) 12/1: 625046: Slowly away/rear, late gains: see 2043, 326.   1¾ **30**

3355 **SATWA BOULEVARD** 9 [8] 5-8-12 (t) A Beech (5) 16/1: 002007: Prom 5f: btr 2907 (C/D clmr).   nk **40**

3243 **CELTIC VENTURE** 14 [11] 5-9-9 A Daly 12/1: -66108: Prom 5f: btr 2040 (1m).   4 **32**

3344 **MUSTANG** 9 [3] 7-9-9 (vis) T G McLaughlin 25/1: 054509: Chsd ldrs 5f: btr 2040 (1m).   ½ **25**

602 **LORD BERGERAC** 177 [7] 4-9-3 G Hind 20/1: 600-00: Led till over 1f out, fdd: 10th: abs: see 602.   ¾ **24**

3144 **MR CUBE** 18 [14] 10-9-3 (bl) D Watson (7) 14/1: 524000: Towards rear, nvr on terms: 11th: op 10/1.   ¾ **0**

3208 **ONES ENOUGH** 15 [12] 4-9-9 A Clark 11/2: 010040: Dwelt, sn prom, btn 2f out: 14th: t-strap.

2032 **Hunan Scholar** 66 [10] 5-9-3 D R McCabe 50/1:   2907 **Night Adventure** 29 [15] 4-9-3 L Newman (3) 20/1:

3094 **Burcot Girl** 21 [9] 3-8-7 A Mackay 33/1:

15 ran   Time 1m 20.60 (0.8)   (City Industrial Supplies Ltd)   N Hamilton Epsom, Surrey.

3560   6.55 EVENING ARGUS HCAP 3YO 0-70 (E)   1m3f196y Firm 08 -02 Slow   [72]
£2740   £843   £421   £210

*3167 **WELSH DREAM** 18 [4] A C Stewart 3-9-3 (61) S Whitworth 11/10 FAV: 000-11: 3 b c Mtoto - Morgannwg   **67**
(Simply Great): Dwelt/waited with rear, prog final 3f & rdn/styd on well inside last to lead nr line: hvly bckd:
earlier made a wng h'cap bow at Newmarket: unplcd in 3 '99 mdns (rtd 69): well suited by step up to 12f last twice,
shld get further: acts on firm & fast grnd, stiff/gall or sharp trk: has run well fresh: op to further improvement.

3102 **ALPHA ROSE** 21 [5] M L W Bell 3-9-7 (65) A Beech (5) 6/1: 531142: 3 b f Inchinor - Philgwyn   hd **70**
(Milford): Mid-div, rdn/prog to lead 2f out, hdd nr fin: clr rem: still improving: see 2893 (C/D, fill h'cap).

3241 **RAINBOW SPIRIT** 14 [8] A P Jarvis 3-9-7 (65) D Harrison 13/2: 343423: 3 b g Rainbows For Life - Merrie   6 **61**
Moment (Taufan): Led till 2f out, sn held by front pair: see 2321, 1362 & 916.

*3417 **SPIRIT OF TENBY** 6 [6] S Dow 3-9-13 (71)(6ex) P Doe 7/1: 040214: Prom, ch 2f out, sn held: op 5/1.   4 **61**

2332 **THE FROG QUEEN** 53 [3] 3-8-6 (50) L Newman (3) 16/1: 040305: Prom, btn 2f out: onepace: blnkrs.   5 **33**

3417 **ESTABLISHMENT** 6 [7] 3-9-7 (65)(BL) I Mongan (5) 20/1: 215666: Rear, efft 4f out, no menace: see 74.   2½ **44**

3530 **SHAMAN** 2 [1] 3-9-5 (63) W Ryan 13/2: 013227: Held up, keen, btn 2f out: too soon after 3530 (10f)?   ½ **41**

3317 **SILVER QUEEN** 11 [2] 3-9-3 (61) B Marcus 16/1: 024608: Prom, btn 3f out: btr 2296 (10f).   8 **30**

8 ran   Time 2m 29.4 (1.2)   (Mr K J Mercer & Mrs S Mercer)   A C Stewart Newmarket, Suffolk.

3561   7.25 ARGUS FILLIES HCAP 3YO 0-60 (F)   1m rnd Firm 08 -02 Slow   [65]
£2830   £808   £404

3242 **HAZY HEIGHTS** 14 [13] B J Meehan 3-8-8 (45) B Marcus 14/1: 000431: 3 b f Shirley Heights - Dancing   **51**
Spirit (Ahonoora): Held up, prog wide/hung left over 1f out, rdn/led well in last, styd on strongly: op 12/1:
1st win: eff at 7f, apprec this step up to 1m, has tried 10f: acts on firm & gd: fine win from a tricky high draw.

*3401 **DUSKY VIRGIN** 9 [9] S Woodman 3-9-4 (55)(6ex) I Mongan (5) 4/1 FAV: 040212: 3 b f Missed Flight   1¾ **57**
- Rosy Sunset (Red Sunset): Held up, prog to lead/rdn over 1f out, hdd inside last & no extra: rest well covered.

3317 **BINT HABIBI** 11 [5] J Pearce 3-9-5 (56) G Bardwell (5): 663153: 3 b f Bin Ajwaad - High Stepping   3½ **51**
(Taufan): Chsd ldrs, ch 2f out, onepace/held over 1f out: op 7/1: see 3317, 2914.

3386 **NIGHT AND DAY** 7 [3] P S McEntee 3-9-7 (58)(vis) G Faulkner (3) 25/1: 223054: Held up, prog/briefly   1½ **50**
led 2f out, no hdwy: prob stays a sharp 1m & handles firm grnd: see 118.

3279 **ANNIJAZ** 12 [7] 3-9-5 (56) A Beech (5) 8/1: 301035: In tch halfway, held 2f out: btr 2794 (7f).   hd **47**

3364 **NATSMAGIRL** 8 [6] 3-8-9 (46) A Clark 12/1: 056246: Twds rear, mod gains fnl 2f: see 74 (sell).   1½ **34**

3242 **MAGICAL RIVER** 14 [12] 3-8-10 (47) D Harrison 10/1: 600-07: Prom, ch 2f out, sn held: op 7/1:   shd **35**
unplcd in '99 (rtd 64, 4 nvr stks).

3493 **RIOS DIAMOND** 4 [1] 3-9-0 (51) K Parkin (7) 20/1: 513408: Trkd ldrs, wknd qckly 1f out: qck reapp.   ½ **38**

3345 **DIAMOND OLIVIA** 9 [2] 3-9-4 (55) R Fitzpatrick 10/1: 406259: Mid-div, held 2f out: see 3033, 1024.   1½ **39**

3226 **TIMELESS CHICK** 14 [14] 3-9-4 (55)(vis) L Newman (3) 20/1: 051060: Prom 6f: 10th: btr 2460.   2½ **34**

3293 **FLEETING FANCY** 12 [4] 3-9-0 (51) P Doe 12/1: 005040: Al rear: 11th: op 10/1: btr 1877 (6f).   1½ **27**

3183 **BETTY BATHWICK** 383 [8] 3-9-5 (56) W Ryan 20/1: 0002-0: Led 6f: 15th: reapp, h'cap bow: rnr-up in   **0**
'99 (rtd 55, sell, B Smart): eff over a sharp/undul 6f on firm grnd, bred to apprec further: now with E J O'Neill.

3046 **Sunleys Picc** 23 [11] 3-9-3 (54) T G McLaughlin 33/1: 3266 **Litigious** 13 [10] 3-9-1 (52) D Sweeney 16/1:

3386 **Ballets Russes** 7 [15] 3-8-12 (49) S Whitworth 33/1:

15 ran   Time 1m 32.8 (0.8)   (Wyck Hall Stud)   B J Meehan Upper Lambourn, Berks.

3562   7.55 ARGUS CLASSIFIED STKS 3YO+ 0-60 (F)   5f59y rnd Firm 08 +08 Fast
£2431   £694   £347   3 yo rec 2 lb

3398 **TORRENT** 7 [4] D W Chapman 5-9-4 (bl) Lynsey Hanna (7) 9/4: 463331: 5 ch g Prince Sabo - Maiden Pool   **62**
(Sharpen Up): Trkd ldr travelling well, dsptd lead from over 1f out, styd on under hands-&-heels riding to prevail
on line: best time of night: plcd num times prev this term: '99 wnr at Lingfield (2, h'caps,
rtd 73a) & Beverley (class stks, rtd 75): '98 Catterick (mdn) & Thirsk wnr (h'cap, rtd 83, T D Barron): suited
by 5/6f on firm, gd/soft & both AWs, prob soft: suited by blnkrs: runs well from the kind urgings of Lynsey Hanna.

*3455 **ABSOLUTE FANTASY** 5 [5] E A Wheeler 4-9-1 (bl) S Carson (3) 15/8 FAV: 024212: 4 b f Beveled - Sharp hd **58**
Venita (Sharp Edge): Hld up, prog to dispute lead over 1f out, rdn inside last, just hdd line: nicely bckd: clr rem.

3243 **CITY REACH** 14 [9] P J Makin 4-9-7 (vis) D Sweeney 13/2: 305103: 4 b g Petong - Azola (Alzao):   5 **52**
Rear, kept on final 2f, no threat to front pair: topweight: see 2905 (C/D).

3161 **WILLRACK TIMES** 18 [7] B A McMahon 3-8-13 A Nicholls (3) 50/1: 000004: Prom, ch 2f out, sn held.   1 **44**

3293 **ZOENA** 12 [8] 3-8-13 L Newman (3) 10/1: 456305: Mid-div, nvr pace to chall: see 2252.   2 **39**

3180 **WINDRUSH BOY** 16 [6] 10-9-4 Joanna Badger (7) 25/1: 004446: Rear, mod hdwy/no room over 1f out.   hd **41$**

3214 **LEGAL VENTURE** 14 [1] 4-9-4 A Daly 25/1: 020467: Led till over 1f out, fdd: see 639, 440 & 291.   1¼ **38**

3293 **BALIDARE** 12 [10] 3-8-13 C Rutter 50/1: -00008: Mid-div, rdn/btn over 1f out: see 3293.   1¾ **31**

3209 **MANGUS** 15 [3] 6-9-4 D O'Donohoe 12/1: 00509: Prom till halfway: 10th: see 2586.   2½ **27**

2905 **AZIRA** 29 [2] 3-8-13 S Righton 25/1: 6-0060: Towards rear, drvn 2f out, no hdwy & eased final 1f.   11 **3**

10 ran   Time 1m 00.0 (0.0)   (Mrs J Hazell)   D W Chapman Stillington, Nth Yorks.

Official Going GOOD. Stalls: Sprint - Stands Side; Rnd - Inside.

3563 **2.05 MOTABILITY RTD HCAP 3YO+ 0-105 (B)** **1m2f85y Good/Firm 22 +16 Fast** **[108]**
£16882 £6403 £3201 £1455 3 yo rec 8 lb

*3024 **PRINCE ALEX 24** [1] Mrs A J Perrett 6-8-13 (93)(t) M J Kinane 100/30 FAV: 102-11: 6 b g Night Shift - Finalist (Star Appeal) Hld up, keen, hdwy over 3f out to lead over 1f out, hit by rival's whip, gamely pushed clr: hvly bckd, lkd superb, best time of day: earlier scored at Newmarket (val h'cap, reapp): landed a hat-trick in '99, at Kempton (2) & Ascot (h'caps, rtd 88): missed '98, '97 Newmarket wnr (h'cap, with A Stewart): eff over 10/12f on fast, gd/soft & a stiff or easy trk: best in a t-strap & has run well fresh: most progressive, tough & genuine 6yo, only twice raced this term & looks worth following again. **102**

2696 **NOOSHMAN 39** [16] Sir Michael Stoute 3-8-11 (99) Pat Eddery 8/1: 150132: 3 ch g Woodman - Knoosh (Storm Bird) Hld up, plenty to do over 3f out, hdwy & not clr run over 2f out, swtchd right & styd on strongly ins last, nrst fin: lkd unlucky & sure to apprec further: v progressive & can land a val prize: see 2696, 2358. *¾* **104+**

3300 **MASTERMIND 12** [10] P F I Cole 3-8-12 (100) J Fortune 14/1: -04023: 3 ch c Dolphin Street - Glenarff (Irish River) Prom, hdwy to lead over 3f out till over 1f out, onepace: ran to v best but 1m/9f may prove ideal. *2½* **101**

2995 **HIMSELF 25** [12] H R A Cecil 5-8-11 (91) T Quinn 8/1: 14-434: In tch, effort over 2f out, kept on same pace over 1f out: nicely bckd: running well in defeat: see 2995, 1845. *½* **91**

3389 **DASHIBA 7** [7] 4-8-10 (90) J Reid 12/1: 306625: Held up, hmpd sev times from over 3f out, styd on strongly inside last: clr of rem & no luck in running: clearly coming to hand & should win again on this form. *hd* **90+**

3060 **PANTAR 22** [2] 5-9-0 (94) K Darley 14/1: 300236: Waited with, effort over 2f out, onepace: see 3060. *4* **88**

3155 **ADJUTANT 18** [4] 5-9-3 (97) O Peslier 33/1: 120607: Waited with, brief effort over 2f out, no dngr: rcd freely to post: big step up in trip: all wins at 7f: see 1514, 1286. *1¾* **88**

2995 **NOBELIST 25** [9] 5-9-5 (99)(VIS) T E Durcan 25/1: 610008: Held up, modest late gains tried in a visor. *¾* **89**

2596 **VINTAGE PREMIUM 42** [5] 3-8-12 (100) R Cochrane 8/1: 022169: Prom, wknd well over 1f out: 6 wk abs, better than this earlier: see 2596, 2351. *1* **88**

3024 **JULIUS 24** [13] 3-7-13 (87) R Ffrench 20/1: 111040: Led 2f, hung left & wknd over 2f out: 10th. *½* **74**

3107 **SHARP PLAY 20** [8] 5-9-7 (101) R Hills 14/1: 204100: Nvr a factor: top weight, twice below 3060. *3* **84**

3060 **PRAIRIE WOLF 22** [3] 4-8-12 (92) J Mackay (5) 12/1: -34020: Prom, wkng when hmpd over 2f out: 12th. *7* **65**

757 **AL AZHAR 148** [11] 6-8-12 (92) J Carroll 33/1: 430-50: Slowly away, al bhd: 13th: long abs since 757. *1¾* **61**

4580} **DABUS 296** [15] 5-8-12 (92) G Duffield 100/1: 3/36-0: Nvr a factor: 14th: fit from hdling, earlier scored at Stratford & M Rasen (h'cap hdles, rtd 104h, 2m1.5f, firm & gd/soft): rtd 99 on first of 2 '99 Flat starts for H Cecil: '98 Sandown wnr (mdn, rtd 92): eff at 10f on fast grnd & a stiff trk. *3½* **56**

3017 **TACTFUL REMARK 24** [17] 4-9-0 (94) J P Spencer 25/1: 054030: Led 1m out till over 3f out, wknd: 15th. *1½* **56**

*3451 **WESTENDER 5** [14] 4-9-2 (96)(3ex) J Murtagh 11/1: 250210: Cl-up, wknd over 2f out: 16th, nicely bckd: tough & progressive earlier, this possibly came too sn after wng 3451. *hd* **58**

2475 **TRAHERN 47** [6] 3-9-3 (105) F Norton 14/1: 421400: Prom, wknd over 2f out: 6 wk abs, btr 2148. *2½* **63**

17 ran Time 2m 07.98 (0.68) (M Dawson, K Mercer & A Jones) Mrs A J Perrett Pulborough, West Sussex.

3564 **2.35 GR 1 YORKSHIRE OAKS 3YO+ (A)** **1m3f195y Good/Firm 22 +00 Fast**
£127600 £48400 £24200 £11000 3 yo rec 10lb

*2739 **PETRUSHKA 38** [1] Sir Michael Stoute 3-8-8 J Murtagh 5/4 FAV: -13411: 3 ch f Unfuwain - Ballet Shoes (Ela Mana Mou) Hld up, hdwy over 2f out, drvn to lead dist, styd on well: hvly bckd: earlier won at Newmarket (Gr 3) & The Curragh (Gr 1 Irish Oaks, by 5½L), also 3rd in the 1,000 Guineas: won sole juv start, at Leicester (mdn): eff at 1m, well suited by 12f now & shld stay further: acts on firm, gd/soft & likes a gall trk: top-class filly who can quicken, lightly raced & can win more top grade contests. **122**

*1828 **LOVE DIVINE 75** [2] H R A Cecil 3-8-8 T Quinn 2/1: 2-112: 3 b f Diesis - La Sky (Law Society) Cl-up, kept on to lead over 2f out, hdd dist, not pace of wnr: bckd: 11 wk abs & ran to wng Oaks form (had this wnr 4L bhd, gd/soft): acts on fast, gd/soft, handles hvy: lightly rcd & high class, lost little in defeat here. *1¼* **119**

1152 **RAMRUMA 110** [5] H R A Cecil 4-9-4 M J Kinane 15/2: 112-03: 4 ch f Diesis - Princess Of Man (Green God) Set pace till over 2f out, onepace: prob ran to same level of form as when landing this race last term. *2* **116**

3305 **MILETRIAN 11** [6] M R Channon 3-8-8 C Williams 33/1: 401644: Waited with, rdn & outpcd 3f out. *3½* **111**

3151 **ELA ATHENA 18** [3] 4-9-4 M Roberts 6/1: -04125: Chsd ldr, rdn & wknd over 2f out: rnr-up in this race last term & better expected after 3151. *1¾* **108**

*3070 **INTERLUDE 24** [4]. 3-8-8 Pat Eddery 16/1: 1-3416: Prom, btn 2f out: not up to this class, see 3070. *nk* **107**

6 ran Time 2m 29.41 (2.61) (Highclere Thor'bred Racing Ltd) Sir Michael Stoute Newmarket.

3565 **3.10 TOTE EBOR HCAP 3YO+ (B)** **1m5f194y Good/Firm 22 +06 Fast** **[109]**
£113750 £35000 £17500 £8750 3 yo rec 12lb

3061 **GIVE THE SLIP 22** [16] Mrs A J Perrett 3-8-8 (101) Pat Eddery 8/1: 312141: 3 b c Slip Anchor - Falafil (Fabulous Dancer) Made all from tricky high draw, styd on well for press over 1f out, drvn out: hvly bckd, gd time: earlier scored at Royal Ascot (val King George V H'cap) & Windsor (auct mdn), 1L 4th in a Gr 3 last time: eff at 12f, relished this step up to 14f: acts on firm, gd/soft & any trk: best up with/forcing the pace: given a top-class ride by Pat Eddery: tough, v useful & smart, type to win in Listed/Gr class. **110**

*2647 **BOREAS 40** [7] L M Cumani 5-9-0 (95) J P Spencer 11/4 FAV: 143/12: 5 b g In The Wings - Reamur (Top Ville) Hld up, gd hdwy over 2f out, styd on over 1f out, wnr wld not be denied: not btn far, big ante post gamble: 6 wk abs & stays 14f well: reportedly suffered an over-reach: useful, deserves a val prize: see 2647. *¾* **102**

*3295 **VIRGIN SOLDIER 12** [8] M Johnston 4-8-8 (89)(4ex) K Dalgleish (5) 14/1: 024213: 4 ch g Waajib - Never Been Chaste (Posse) Al cl-up, rdn & kept on for press over 1f out: tough & genuine, will enjoy a return to 2m. *nk* **96**

3302 **AFTERJACKO 11** [1] D R C Elsworth 4-8-8 (89) N Pollard 20/1: 200564: Handy, effort & slightly short of room over 2f out, kept on same pace of press over 1f out: running well in defeat & suited by 14f: see 3302. *2½* **92**

3302 **BIENNALE 11** [4] 4-9-9 (104) J Murtagh 16/1: -44535: In tch, rdn & slightly outpcd over 3f out, kept on over 1f out: will apprec a return to 2m as in 3302. *shd* **107**

3088 **ALVA GLEN 21** [11] 3-8-10 (103) F Norton 12/1: 601236: Held up bhd, plenty to do over 3f out, styd on, nrst fin: set too much to do: stays 14f & deserves another nice prize with a more positive ride: see 3088. *½* **105+**

3058 **EMINENCE GRISE 22** [20] 5-9-0 (95) T Quinn 20/1: -02107: Held up, hdwy over 2f out, kept on inside last, nrst fin: stays well & would have apprec a more positive ride, but had a poor high draw: see 2695. *½* **96**

3177 **RADAS DAUGHTER 17** [19] 4-9-2 (97) R Cochrane 20/1: 000108: Held up, effort over 2f out, onepace: probably stays 14f: has a poor high draw here: see 2502. *nk* **97**

3134 **LIGNE GAGNANTE 19** [12] 4-8-13 (94) J Mackay (5) 12/1: 602239: In tch, effort to chall 2f out, wknd *nk* **94**

final 1f: appeared not to see out this lngr 14f trip: btr 3134 (12f).
3171 **PRAIRIE FALCON 17** [2] 6-8-3 (84) M Roberts 33/1: F06040: Handy, onepcd 2f out: 10th: see 3171, 917. ¾ **83**
*3173 **FLOSSY 17** [15] 4-8-10 (91)(7ex) P Robinson 20/1: -04410: Held up, hmpd sev times in str, nvr 3 **86**
dngrs: 11th, will do better: see 3173.
2696 **INCH PERFECT 39** [3] 5-8-6 (87) G Duffield 9/1: 313100: Keen, waited with, effort over 3f out, wknd *shd* **82**
over 2f out: 12th: twice below 1982.
3058 **MOWBRAY 22** [9] 5-9-2 (97) J Fortune 10/1: 560440: Hld up, eff & hmpd over 1f out, no dngr: 13th. 1¾ **89**
3058 **LOOP THE LOUP 22** [17] 4-8-11 (92) M Hills 50/1: -50000: Al bhd: 14th: see 732. 2½ **81**
*3058 **TEMPLE WAY 22** [21] 4-9-0 (95)(vis)(7ex) M J Kinane 12/1: 022210: Prom, wknd 2f out: fin 15th: 1 **83**
had a poor high draw: much btr 3058 (first time visor).
2695 **BAY OF ISLANDS 39** [18] 8-9-2 (97)(vis) K Darley 16/1: 003130: Bhd, brief effort over 3f out, *hd* **84**
sn btn: rare below par run, poor high draw: see 2695 (C/D), 2336.
2336 **INIGO JONES 53** [13] 4-8-12 (93) O Peslier 16/1: -14560: In tch, wkng when short of room over 2f 1¼ **78**
out: 17th, 8 wk abs: see 2336.
1982 **RUM POINTER 68** [5] 4-8-13 (94) J Carroll 33/1: 002100: In tch, wknd over 2f out: 18th, 10 wk abs. 7 **71**
3339 **SPRING PURSUIT 10** [22] 4-8-3 (84) P Fitzsimons (5) 66/1: 300500: Slow away, al bhd: 19th, likes soft. *hd* **61**
3483 **YORKSHIRE 4** [14] 6-9-10 (105) P Dobbs (5) 25/1: 55/530: Bhd, btn over 3f out: 20th, qck reapp. 1¼ **80**
-- **PIRANESI** [6] 4-9-0 (95)(t) J Reid 33/1: 150050: Al bhd: 21st: Irish raider, earlier scored *nk* **70**
at Leopardstown (h'cap): stays 12f on fast grnd: wears a t-strap.
3504 **THREE GREEN LEAVES 3** [10] 4-8-7 (88) R Hills 25/1: 036620: Prom, btn over 4f out: last, qck reapp. ½ **62**
22 ran Time 2m 55.62 (2.22) (John E Bodie) Mrs A J Perrett Pulborough, West Sussex.

3566

3.45 GR 2 GIMCRACK STKS 2YO (A) 6f str Good/Firm 22 -30 Slow
£72500 £27500 £13750 £6250

3162 **BANNISTER 18** [2] R Hannon 2-8-11 J Murtagh 11/1: 221: 2 ch c Inchinor - Shall We Run (Hotfoot) **107**
Led over 4f out till over 1f out, rallied most gamely for press to get up again inside last, styd on: nicely bckd,
rangy: Apr foal, cost 66,000gns: half-brother to useful 5/6f wnr Roo: dam sprinter: v eff over a stiff 6f,
should stay further: acts on fast, handles gd/soft: genuine & v smart colt.
3064 **ZILCH 22** [5] R Hannon 2-8-11 J Fortune 20/1: 242: 2 ch c Zilzal - Bunty Boo (Noalto) *nk* **106**
Bhd, gd hdwy to lead over 1f out, edged right & hdd ins last, just held by stablemate: much imprvd over this stiff
6f on fast: showed a gd turn of foot to reach the front here, prob best covered up till late & must win a val prize.
-- **JUNIPER** [3] A P O'Brien 2-8-11 M J Kinane 9/2: 3: 2 b c Danzig - Montage (Alydar) *hd* **106+**
Handy, eff to chall dist, bmpd slightly ins last but styd on, just held in a 3-way photo: scopey, debut: Feb
foal: half-brother to wnrs over 1m/12f: eff at 6f, sure to apprec 7f/1m in time: handles fast: v smart first
run, open to plenty of further improvement & looks sure to win valuable prizes.
*3162 **HURRICANE FLOYD 18** [9] J Noseda 2-8-11 R Cochrane 5/4 FAV: 214: Waited with, hdwy & short of 1¾ **104**
room over 1f out, hmpd again ins last, kept on, not recover: hvly bckd, padd pick: must have gone cl with a clr
run & worth another try in similar company: smart, see 3162.
*2009 **GAME N GIFTED 67** [4] 2-8-11 T Quinn 25/1: 215: Led over 1f, ev ch over 1f out, onepace: stocky: 1½ **98**
useful run after a 10 wk abs on step into Gr class & stays 6f on fast, handles gd/soft: see 2009.
2595 **MEDIA MOGUL 42** [10] 2-8-11 K Darley 7/2: 13126: Waited with, effort well over 1f out, onepace: ½ **96**
nicely bckd: 6 wk abs & better expected after rnr-up in a Gr 3 in 2595.
*3029 **LOST AT SEA 23** [8] 2-8-11 (t) N Callan 33/1: -02017: In tch, wknd over 1f out: stocky, see 3029 (7f). 2 **90**
3133 **TARAS EMPEROR 19** [7] 2-8-11 Pat Eddery 20/1: 141058: With ldr, bmpd over 1f out, wknd: see 3133. 1¾ **85**
3105 **MAMMAS TONIGHT 20** [1] 2-8-11 G Carter 20/1: 315409: Prom, wknd over 1f out: see 2113. 4 **73**
-- **FRENCH EMPIRE** [6] 2-8-11 O Peslier 20/1: 0: Al bhd: fin last on debut: Feb foal, cost 23,000 gns: *dist* **0**
US raider: bred to apprec 7f.
10 ran Time 1m 12.5 (3.1) (The Royal Ascot Racing Club) R Hannon East Everleigh, Wilts.

3567

4.15 LISTED ROSES STKS 2YO (A) 5f str Good/Firm 22 -24 Slow
£18053 £5555 £2777 £1388

3133 **BOUNCING BOWDLER 19** [5] M Johnston 2-8-11 K Darley 6/4 FAV: 212221: 2 b c Mujadil - Prima Volta **106**
(Primo Dominie) Broke well & made all, kept on fnl 1f despite drifting right, drvn out: hvly bckd: dam 6f juv
wnr: earlier won at Ripon (mdn), subs rnr-up twice in Gr 3: eff over a stiff 5f, will stay 6f: acts on fast &
soft, any trk: can force the pace: tough, v genuine & smart colt.
*3277 **SENIOR MINISTER 12** [2] J M P Eustace 2-8-11 J Tate 9/2: 212: 2 b c Lion Cavern - Crime Ofthecentury ½ **103**
(Pharly) Chsd ldrs, rdn & ev ch ins fnl 1f, just btn in a cl fin: well bckd from 6/1: scopey, useful colt: see 3277.
3352 **NEARLY A FOOL 9** [3] B A McMahon 2-8-11 J Fortune 20/1: 313333: 2 b g Komaite - Greenway Lady 2 **97**
(Prince Daniel) Waited with, imprvd over 1f out, kept on final 1f & nrst fin: improved run: see 1995.
3372 **SPEEDY GEE 10** [7] M R Channon 2-8-11 Craig Williams 14/1: 105604: Dwelt, hld up trav well, only ½ **95+**
asked for eff appr fnl 1f, styd on well but far too late: poor ride, much closer with a more positive ride.
3264 **BYO 13** [4] 2-8-11 G Duffield 10/1: 512435: Speed till halfway, grad left bhd by ldrs: just btr 3264. ¾ **93**
-- **JOPLIN** [1] 2-8-11 M J Kinane 11/4: -16: Trkd ldrs, rdn & btn 2f out: well bckd, 10 wk abs: Irish ¾ **91**
raider, cost $600,000: debut wnr at Navan (stks): eff at 6f on gd grnd, runs well fresh: dam a juv wnr in the
States, sire a top class miler: much better clearly expected, worth another ch on softer grnd.
3149 **SHUSH 18** [6] 2-8-11 P Robinson 25/1: 560107: Al outpcd: unsuited by this drop back to 5f. 2½ **84**
7 ran Time 59.1 (2.3) (Paul Dean) M Johnston Middleham, Nth Yorks.

3568

4.45 MOORESTYLE MDN 2YO (D) 6f str Good/Firm 22 -25 Slow
£14755 £4540 £2270 £1135

3000 **GHAYTH 25** [8] Sir Michael Stoute 2-9-0 R Hills 9/2: 61: 2 b c Sadler's Wells - Myself (Nashwan) **106+**
Prom, went on after 2f, styd on strongly fnl 1f, rdn out: well bckd: 300,000gns purchase: dam smart 6f 2yo wnr:
sire a top class mid-dist wnr: eff at 6f on fast, 7f+ sure to suit: potentially high-class, keep on your side.
-- **KING CHARLEMAGNE** [6] A P O'Brien 2-9-0 M J Kinane 4/5 FAV: 2: 2 b c Nureyev - Race The Wild 1¾ **100+**
Wind (Sunny's Halo) Trkd ldrs, swtchd dist, ran on well but not pace of wnr: v hvly bckd Irish raider:
$1,500,000 Mar foal: half-brother to a wnr in the USA, dam a smart 1m performer in the US: sire a top class
miler: eff at 6f on fast grnd, 7f will suit: bred in the purple, sure to improve & go one better.
3090 **NASMATT 21** [9] M R Channon 2-8-9 C Williams 5/1: -33: 2 b f Danehill - Society Lady (Mr Prospector) *shd* **94**
Trkd ldrs, eff over 1f out, styd on well & not btn far: nicely bckd: 7f suit: met 2 smart sorts, must win sn.
3009 **LOVE EVERLASTING 24** [11] M Johnston 2-8-9 Paul Eddery 20/1: -34: Front rank till left bhd fnl 1f: 2 **88**

scopey filly who will improve over 7f+: type to progress with racing, over further: shld be wng sn: see 3009.
-- **POLISH OFF** [2] 2-9-0 M Hills 20/1: 4: Dwelt, imprvg when short of room dist, styd on nicely & nrst *dht* **93$**
fin on debut: ddhtd for 4th: Mar foal, cost 70,000gns: dam a mid-dist wnr, sire a top class miler: plenty to like about this eye-catching debut, one to keep in mind over 7f+.
3009 **VICIOUS DANCER 24** [1] 2-9-0 J Quinn 66/1: -06: Hdwy from rear 2f out, no impress final 1f: still *¾* **91**
needed this: will find much easier races, see 3009.
3064 **LILLEMAN 22** [5] 2-9-0 J P Spencer 14/1: 57: Chsd ldrs, onepcd final 1½f: op 10/1: scopey colt. *3½* **81**
3287 **FRUIT PUNCH 12** [4] 2-8-9 J Carroll 33/1: 558: Chsd ldrd 5f, gradually fdd: see 3020. *3½* **66**
3051 **MATADI 22** [7] 2-9-0 P Robinson 66/1: -459: Led 2f, remnd prom till btn dist: see 2754 (debut). *hd* **70**
-- **REBEL STORM** [10] 2-9-0 J Fortune 10/1: 0: Unruly in stalls & slow away, recovered & sn prom 4f, *¾* **68**
wknd into 10th: drifted from 7/1 on debut: 110,000gns Mar foal: dam unrcd but from a smart family: likely to apprec 7f/1m given time: scopey, lost all ch in the stalls today: sure to learn from this, with J Gosden.
-- **MANICANI** [3] 2-9-0 R Cochrane 25/1: 0: Slowly away, no ch after on debut: fin last, ndd race: *1* **65**
IR 19,000gns purchase: Mar foal, half-brother to sev wnrs both here & abroad: sire a smart 7f performer.
11 ran Time 1m 12.25 (2.85) (Hamdan Al Maktoum) Sir Michael Stoute Newmarket.

3569

5.15 FALMOUTH HCAP 3YO 0-100 (C) 5f str Good/Firm 22 -32 Slow **[99]**
£15827 £4870 £2435 £1217 Those racing in the centre seemed favoured

3349 **HONESTY FAIR 9** [12] J A Glover 3-8-9 (80) D Mernagh (3) 12/1: 004661: 3 b f Reprimand - Truthful **87**
Image (Reesh) Waited with, imprvd 2f out, strong run to lead cl-home, rdn out: earlier won at Beverley (mdn) & Thirsk (h'cap), unlucky in running sev times subs: eff at 5/6f on firm & gd/soft: shrewd stable returning to form.
3016 **KATHOLOGY 24** [10] D R C Elsworth 3-9-6 (91) N Pollard 14/1: 114002: 3 b c College Chapel - Wicken *nk* **97**
Wonder (Distant Relative) Trkd ldrs, ev ch fnl 1f, just btn in a tight fin: fine eff conceding this wnr 11lbs.
3016 **ROZEL 24** [16] R Guest 3-9-1 (86) G Baker (5) 12/1: 01343: 3 ch f Wolfhound - Noirmant (Dominion) *hd* **92**
Rear, prog halfway, led ins fnl 1f, caught cl-home: fine effort, may well have held on with a more forceful jockey: only lightly rcd, still imprvg & should regain wng ways: see 3016, 1609.
3136 **COMPTON BANKER 19** [6] G A Butler 3-9-3 (88) J P Spencer 3/1 FAV: 510244: Slowly away & bhd, fin *1* **92**
v fast but not rch ldrs: hvly bckd from 9/2: did not have the best of draws today: see 3136.
3135 **TRAVESTY OF LAW 19** [2] 3-8-13 (84)(bl) Pat Eddery 13/2: 000325: Chsd ldr, went on dist till ins *1* **84**
last, no extra: well bckd from 8/1: had to use up plenty of speed overcoming poor low draw: well h'capped & due a change of luck: see 3135, also poorly drawn.
3280 **JAMES STARK 12** [1] 3-8-1 (72)(bl) K Dalgleish (5) 20/1: 424456: Led till over 1f out, no extra: *½* **70**
unfav low draw: reportedly boiled over in the preliminaries: see 3010.
*2934 **LA CAPRICE 27** [8] 3-8-10 (81) G Carter 14/1: 202017: Prom, onepcd final 1f: just btr 2934. *½* **78**
+3010 **DESRAYA 24** [13] 3-8-6 (77)(bl) J Quinn 10/1: 231118: Imprvg from rear when hmpd dist, no ch *hd* **73**
after: not much luck here: completed a hat-trick in 3010 (6f).
3130 **CD FLYER 19** [5] 3-8-5 (76) Craig Williams 14/1: 463309: Rear, styd on final 1f, nrst fin: btr 2885. *1¾* **67**
2663 **ROYAL ROMEO 40** [17] 3-8-5 (76) P Fessey 20/1: 016300: Rear, rdn to impr over 1f out, nvr a *nk* **66**
factor in 10th: 6 wk abs: see 2663.
3427 **SHATIN VENTURE 5** [15] 3-9-7 (92) G Duffield 33/1: 300050: Nvr a factor in 11th: swtg, qck reapp. *1* **79**
3183 **PIPADASH 16** [9] 3-9-1 (86) K Darley 16/1: 000300: Chsd ldrs 3f, sn bhd & fin 12th: btr 2859. *hd* **72**
3349 **SOMESESSION 9** [11] 3-8-7 (78)(bl) T E Durcan 14/1: -00100: Al outpcd, fin 13th: see 3349. *½* **62**
2197 **SHINBONE ALLEY 58** [4] 3-9-5 (90) M J Kinane 12/1: 5-5100: Nvr better than mid-div, btn fnl 1f: abs. *¾* **72**
3161 **ELVINGTON BOY 18** [14] 3-8-7 (78) J Mackay (5) 9/2: 325220: Speed to halfway, sn btn: fin 15th, *½* **58**
hvly bckd: much better clearly expected, see 3161, 3010.
2859 **HALF MOON BAY 32** [18] 3-9-5 (90) J Fortune 20/1: 511-60: Chsd ldrs till btn over 1f out: fin *1½* **66**
16th: only 2nd start this term & capable of much better: see 2859.
2663 **SINGSONG 40** [3] 3-9-6 (91) J Carroll 14/1: 430330: Speed 3f, fin last: 6 wk abs. *½* **65**
17 ran Time 59.48 (2.68) (P & S Partnership) J A Glover Carburton, Notts.

CARLISLE WEDNESDAY AUGUST 23RD Righthand, Stiff Track, Uphill Finish

Official Going GOOD (GOOD/FIRM places) Stalls: All Races Inside, Except 12f - Outside

3570

2.25 CFM RADIO CLAIMER 3YO+ (F) 1m4f Firm 13 -05 Slow
£2278 £651 £325 3yo rec 10lb

3311 **RIGHTY HO 11** [7] W H Tinning 6-9-4 K Hodgson 5/1: 000221: 6 b g Reprimand - Challanging (Mill Reef) **43**
Chsd ldr, led 2f out, rdn/hdd ins last, rallied gamely for press to lead on line: plcd in '99 (clmr, rtd 66$, rtd 56 in a h'cap for C Booth): missed '98, '97 Salisbury & Epsom wnr for P Walwyn (amat h'caps, rtd 70): prev eff at 1m, now seems best at 10/14f on firm & soft grnd, any trk: eff with/without visor.
3202 **FIELD OF VISION 15** [8] Mrs A Duffield 10-9-2 L Enstone (7) 3/1 FAV: 145222: 10 b g Vision - Bold *shd* **41**
Meadows (Persian Bold) Held up, prog to chall over 1f out, rdn/narrow lead ins last, hdd line: nicely bckd.
3202 **MISS ARCH 15** [6] M A Buckley 4-8-6 Dean McKeown 33/1: 00-503: 4 gr f Archway - Zanskar (Godswalk) *1½* **29$**
Rear, rdn & styd on fnl 2f, not pace of front pair: eff at 10/12f: handles firm & fast, poss soft: see 822 (h'cap).
3202 **SANDABAR 15** [10] Mrs M Reveley 7-9-12 A Culhane 7/2: 215634: Held up, rdn/kept on onepace fnl 2f: *½* **48**
op 9/4: top weight: see 2203 (h'cap, 2m).
3199 **IRANOO 15** [5] 3-8-6 (t) R Winston 11/1: -00045: Handy, btn over 1f: see 1940. *5* **30$**
3399 **LEGACY OF LOVE 7** [9] 4-9-7 (vis) F Lynch 5/1: -02046: Mid-div, btn 3f out: see 1940 (1m). *2* **32**
3247 **MARIANA 14** [4] 5-8-11 P M Quinn (3) 14/1: 003037: Led till 2f out, sn btn: op 12/1: see 3247, 2381. *4* **16**
3125 **BITTY MARY 19** [11] 3-7-11 (vis)(1ow) T Williams 25/1: 005608: Keen/prom, strugg 4f out: see 807. *1¾* **10**
3247 **CARIBBEAN SUMMER 14** [2] 3-8-6 O Pears 33/1: -09: Mid-div, rdn/bhd 5f out: no form. *7* **9**
3284 **OPTION 12** [3] 3-8-3 (VIS) J Fanning 6/1: 500500: Keen/chsd ldrs 9f: 10th: vis, op 9/2: mod form. *17* **0**
10 ran Time 2m 33.0 (2.2) (W H Tinning) W H Tinning Thornton le Clay, W Yorks

3571 **2.55 EBF MED AUCT MDN 2YO (F)** **5f rnd** **Firm 13 -23 Slow**
£2879 £822 £411

-- **YELLOW TRUMPET** [2] M L W Bell 2-8-9 M Fenton 5/1: -1: 2 b f Petong - Daffodil Fields (Try My Best) **75**
Dwelt, switched right from start, trkd ldrs halfway, switched & rdn/prog to lead ins last, styd on well: op 4/1: Feb foal, cost 37,000 gns: sister to useful juv sprinter Petula: dam a mdn: eff at 5f, 6f will suit: acts on firm grnd & a stiff trk: runs well fresh: open to further improvement.
2784 **SILKEN WINGS 34** [11] I A Balding 2-8-9 J Fanning 8/13 FAV: -322: 2 b f Brief Truce - Winged Victory *1¼* **70**
(Dancing Brave) Led, rdn/hdd ins last not extra: hvly bckd & better expected after 2784, see 2357.
-- **CHAIRMAN BOBBY** [1] T D Barron 2-9-0 A Culhane 10/1: -3: 2 ch g Clantime - Formidable Liz *1¼* **72+**
(Formidable) Dwelt, rdn rear, styd on well from over 1f out, nrst fin: op 8/1: Clantime gldg, Mar foal, first foal: dam a 6f wnr: eff over a stiff 5f, will apprec 6f on this evidence: acts on firm: sure to improve plenty.
-- **VIEWFORTH** [6] Miss L A Perratt 2-9-0 Dale Gibson 11/1: -4: Dwelt/towards rear, rdn & styd on fnl *hd* **72**
2f, not pace to chall: op 9/1: Emarati colt, Jan foal, cost 22,000 gns: dam a 5f juv wnr: will appr 6f: handles firm.
3245 **KIRKBYS TREASURE 14** [8] 2-9-0 C Lowther 12/1: -03665: Prom, onepace over 1f out: see 2639, 1835. *nk* **71$**
3215 **MINUSCOLO 14** [9] 2-8-9 T Williams 14/1: -006: Trkd ldrs, onepace fnl 1f: op 12/1: dropped in trip. *½* **65**
3346 **EFIDIUM 9** [10] 2-9-0 J McAuley 12/1: -57: In tch, outpcd fnl 2f: op 10/1: see 3346. *hd* **70$**
3137 **JOHNSTONS DIAMOND 19** [7] 2-9-0 J Bramhill 12/1: -48: Prom, rdn/wandered over 1f out, fdd. *1¾* **65**
1252 **JUST MURPHY 103** [4] 2-9-0 F Lynch 16/1: -69: Al towards rear: 3 month abs: see 1252. *nk* **64**
3466 **FERNDOWN 4** [5] 2-8-9 G Parkin 33/1: -4600: Mid-div, btn 2f out: 10th: quick reapp: see 2968. *3½* **49**
3346 **BOLLIN TOBY 9** [12] 2-9-0 (bl) R Winston 16/1: -000: Sn rdn/al outpcd rear: 11th: rtd higher 3346. *¾* **51**
-- **LADY LENOR** [3] 2-8-9 P Goode (3) 25/1: -0: Reared start & almost u.r., al bhd: 12th: Presidium *9* **21**
filly, Apr foal, cheaply bought: dam a 1m wnr: with J Weymes.
12 ran Time 1m 01.3 (1.8) (Cheveley Park Stud) M L W Bell Newmarket, Suffolk

3572 **3.30 CARLSBERG HCAP 3YO+ 0-80 (D)** **5f rnd** **Firm 13 +05 Fast** **[78]**
£4738 £1458 £729 £364 3yo rec 2lb

3512 **STATOYORK 3** [10] D Shaw 7-8-2 (52) T Williams 4/1 FAV: 000021: 7 b g Statoblest - Ultimate Dream **62**
(Kafu) Slow to start, settled rear, smooth hdwy halfway, edged right & led ins last, shade cmftbly: jockey rec a 3 day irresponsible riding ban: gd time: '99 wnr at Carlisle (class stks) & Ripon (2, h'caps, rtd 73): '98 Pontefract wnr (h'cap, rtd 49 & 53a): stays 7f, suited by 5f: acts on firm, soft & fibresand: needs to be held up for a late challenge: has prev broken blood vessels: well h'capped, could follow up.
3398 **NORTHERN SVENGALI 7** [6] T D Barron 4-8-11 (61) J Fanning 9/1: 050302: 4 b g Distinctly North - *1½* **66**
Trilby's Dream (Mansooj) Waited with, gd hdwy when short of room appr fnl 1f, styd on strongly ins last, nvr nrr: gd run & is h'capped to win sn: see 631.
3222 **BOLLIN RITA 14** [12] T D Easterby 4-8-6 (56)(bl) R Winston 7/1: 020403: 4 b f Rambo Dancer - Bollin *1½* **57**
Harriet (Lochnager) Mid-div, rdn/prog over 2f out, chall dist, no extra well ins last: see 2505.
3312 **MALADERIE 11** [2] M Dods 6-7-12 (48) Dale Gibson 20/1: 000004: In tch, drvn/prog over 1f out, styd *nk* **48**
on well ins last, nvr nrr: vis omitted: gd run from an unfavourable wide draw & has slipped right donw the weights.
3283 **RUSSIAN ROMEO 12** [9] 5-8-10 (60)(bl) M Fenton 10/1: 200235: Cl-up, rdn/chall appr fnl 1f, sn held. *shd* **60**
3349 **RYTHM N TIME 9** [3] 3-9-1 (67) C Lowther 12/1: 001446: Chsd ldrs, went on appr fnl 1f, hdd well *½* **66**
ins last & sn btn: both wins at Beverley: shade btr 3056 (gd/soft).
2701 **PURE COINCIDENCE 38** [8] 5-9-11 (75) Dean McKeown 11/2: 000037: Dwelt/bhd, rdn/prog over 1f out, *nk* **73**
staying on but no impress when hmpd cl-home: op 9/2: won this race off a 2lb higher mark last term: see 2701.
1842 **BOW PEEP 74** [1] 5-8-5 (55)(bl) G Parkin 20/1: -12408: Bhd, late hdwy, nvr dangerous: 11 wk abs: *½* **52**
just sharper for this & shld apprec an easy surface: see 1244.
2559 **ABLE AYR 43** [4] 3-8-11 (63) Dawn Rankin(6) 25/1: 500009: Slow to start, late gains, no threat: abs. *nk* **59**
3136 **SHAROURA 19** [11] 4-9-11 (75) Alex Greaves 7/1: 000200: Prom, fdd appr fnl 1f, 10th: btr 2684. *½* **70**
3377 **INDIAN MUSIC 7** [5] 3-9-2 (68) F Lynch 14/1: 553260: Mid-div at best, 11th: qck reapp: btr 3097 (6f). *nk* **62**
3010 **COLLEGE MAID 24** [15] 3-9-1 (67) A Culhane 12/1: 100500: Handy, rdn & imprvg when short of *1¼* **57**
room over 1f out, staying on when hmpd & snatched up ins last, not recover & eased, 12th: ignore this run.
870 **MARITUN LAD 134** [14] 3-8-6 (58)(bl) J McAuley 25/1: 431640: Al rear: 13th: 4 month abs: see 624. *shd* **48**
3349 **SHATIN BEAUTY 9** [7] 3-8-12 (64) P Hanagan(7) 33/1: 40-000: Chsd ldrs, fdd fnl 2f, 14th: '99 debut *3* **45**
wnr at Hamilton (nov auct stks, rtd 77): half-sister to a 6f juv wnr: eff arnd 5f on firm/fast: runs well fresh.
3366 **ACE OF PARKES 8** [13] 4-9-11 (75) O Pears 12/1: 650030: Led, rdn/hdd over 1f out, sn badly squeezed *1½* **52**
for room, not recover & eased into 15th: see 3366.
15 ran Time 59.9 (0.4) (M D H Racing) D Shaw Averham, Notts

3573 **4.05 KEITH/PAT CLASSIFIED STKS 3YO+ 0-65 (E)** **7f rnd** **Firm 13 -08 Slow**
£2873 £884 £442 £221 3yo rec 5lb

3322 **UNSHAKEN 11** [2] E J Alston 6-9-0 F Lynch 6/1: 000001: 6 b h Environment Friendly - Reel Foyle **69**
(Irish River) Slow to start, bhd, no room appr fnl 1f, ran on strongly ins last, got up cl-home, drvn out: unplcd this term prev: '99 wnr at Hamilton (2) & Newcastle (h'caps, rtd 81 at best): '98 wnr at Carlisle & Hamilton (stks, rtd 68): eff at 6/7f on firm, hvy & likes a stiff/uphill fin, esp Hamilton: back to form & v well h'capped.
2878 **PERSIAN FAYRE 30** [1] A Berry 8-9-3 P Bradley (5) 8/1: 010002: 8 b g Persian Heights - Dominion *¾* **68**
Fayre (Dominion) Led, clr halfway, rdn & tired ins last, hdd nr fin: bold front running eff: 7f specialist.
2694 **CAUTIOUS JOE 39** [7] R A Fahey 3-8-6 G Parkin 8/1: 035503: 3 b f First Trump - Jomel Amou (Ela *½* **61**
Mana Mou) Trkd ldrs, drvn/outpcd over 2f out, rallied & styd on fnl 1f: gd eff, could win a 3yo h'cap: see 2047.
3377 **LADY OF WINDSOR 7** [6] I Semple 3-8-6 (vis) R Winston 9/1: 300604: Prom, stly outpcd over 2f out, *¾* **59**
rallied for press ins last, staying on but held when hmpd nr fin: visor reapplied: see 2017.
2986 **CUSIN 25** [10] 4-9-0 O Pears 5/1: 050005: Settled rear, rdn/prog over 2f out, styd on, no dngr: see 926. *¾* **60**
3440 **WELCOME TO UNOS 5** [5] 3-8-9 T Williams 10/1: 630206: Front rank, drvn/btn appr fnl 1f: qck reapp. *½* **59**
3275 **DISTINCTIVE DREAM 12** [8] 6-9-0 M Fenton 15/2: 500027: Slow start, nvr dngrs: btr 3275 (6f, AW). *¾* **57**
3170 **RYMERS RASCAL 17** [3] 8-9-0 A Culhane 5/2 FAV: 342538: Mid-div at best: stablemate of wnr. *nk* **56**
2787 **KILBRANNAN SOUND 34** [4] 3-8-6 Dean McKeown 12/1: 500009: Handy, lost tch fnl 2f: see 1219. *9* **35**
3386 **DANZIGEUSE 7** [9] 3-8-6 K Hodgson 20/1: 0-0040: Chsd ldrs to halfway, sn btn, 10th: quick reapp. *2½* **30**
10 ran Time 1m 27.0 (1.5) (G G Sanderson & M Twentyman & A J Picton) E J Alston Longton, Lancs

CARLISLE
WEDNESDAY AUGUST 23RD   Righthand, Stiff Track, Uphill Finish

3574   **4.35 CARLISLE UTD FILLIES HCAP 3YO+ 0-70 (E)**   1m rnd   Firm 13   +08 Fast   [64]
£2925   £900   £450   £225   3yo rec 6lb

*3288   **YOUNG ROSEIN** 12 [8]   Mrs G S Rees 4-9-7 (57) A Culhane 9/2: 300611: 4 b f Distant Relative - Red   61
Rosein (Red Sunset) Mid-div, prog 2f out, rdn to lead dist, just held on: op 3/1: gd time: recent Haydock wnr
(h'cap): '99 wnr at Musselburgh (h'cap, rtd 57, 1st wnr): rtd 62 in '98 (fill mdn): eff at 7f/1m on firm & gd grnd.
2946   **MAI TAI** 26 [14]   D W Barker 5-8-3 (39)(vis) Kimberley Hart 10/1: 256662: 5 b m Scenic - Oystons   shd   42
Propweekly (Swing Easy) Trkd ldrs, not clr run appr fnl 2f & switched, chsd wnr ins last, just failed: new stable.
3548}   **HUTCHIES LADY** 365 [1]   J S Goldie 8-7-10 (32)(9oh) J McAuley 25/1: 5400-3: 8 b m Efisio - Keep Mum   ½   34$
(Mummy's Pet) Rear, prog ent fnl 2f, kept on well, not btn far: abs: '99 rnr-up (appr h'cap, rtd 36): last won in
'96 at Hamilton (h'cap, rtd 39): has tried hdles: eff at 1m/10f, stays 12f on firm & hvy: best fresh, likes Hamilton.
2831   **WINTZIG** 33 [9]   M L W Bell 3-9-2 (58) M Fenton 8/1: 503304: Held up, prog to chase ldrs appr fnl   ¾   58
1f, same pace towards fin: btr 2345, see 924.
2823   **GYMCRAK FLYER** 33 [13]   R Winston 5/1: 000005: Trkd ldrs, boxed in appr fnl 2f   1½   37
till fnl 150y, ch had gone: poss unlucky, won this in '99 off a 4lbs higher mark, see 2561.
3288   **SAFFRON** 12 [2]   4-8-6 (42) T Williams 11/2: 005436: Held up, imprvg when not clr run appr fnl   1   37
2f, switched & rdn, unable to qckn: see 3288, 1842.
1649   **DILETIA** 82 [5]   3-9-3 (59) Dean McKeown 8/1: -04567: Nvr troubled ldrs: 12 wk abs, op 6/1, blnks off.   ½   53
*3269   **DAKOTA SIOUX** 13 [10]   3-9-5 (61)(VIS) G Parkin 11/4 FAV: 360118: Prom, rdn to lead 2f out till dist,   2½   50
wknd & hmpd ins last: op 6/4, visored on hat-trick attempt & up in trip: better without over 7f in 3269.
3226   **HELLO HOLLY** 14 [11]   3-8-7 (49) F Lynch 8/1: 0-6039: Cl-up, led briefly appr fnl 2f, btn & eased dist.   1½   35
3006   **NILOUPHAR** 25 [6]   3-7-10 (38)(3oh) P M Quinn (3) 33/1: 0-0000: Al bhd: 10th, no form.   2   20
1891   **TOP OF THE CLASS** 71 [12]   3-9-6 (62) C Teague 14/1: 000300: Led till appr fnl 2f, sn lost place: 1th.   9   26
1430]   **DANCE MELODY** 821 [7]   6-7-10 (32)(12oh) P Hanagan(3) 33/1: 00000/0: Mid-div 4f: 12th, no form.   14   0
12 ran   Time 1m 39.2 (0.4)   (J W Gittins)   Mrs G S Rees Sollom, Lancs

3575   **5.05 J NOBLE MDN HCAP 3YO+ 0-60 (F)**   2m1f52y   Firm 13   -22 Slow   [52]
£2247   £642   £321   3yo rec 14lb

3406   **SWANDALE FLYER** 6 [7]   N Bycroft 8-7-10 (20)(5oh) J McAuley 11/1: 005021: 8 ch g Weldnaas - Misfire   23
(Gunner B) Made all kept on gamely when prsd appr fnl 1f, pushed out: op 8/1, quick reapp: 1st Flat win:
unplcd last term (h'cap, rtd 30): back in 97/98 won over hdles at Sedgefield: eff at 2m/2m1f on firm/fast grnd.
3367   **JORDANS RIDGE** 8 [3]   P Monteith 4-9-11 (49) R Winston 20/1: 50-002: 4 b g Indian Ridge - Sadie   ¾   50
Jordan (Hail The Pirates) Held up, prog to chall appr fnl 1f, held towards fin: stays 2m1f on firm grnd.
3324   **ARTHUR K** 11 [8]   H Morrison 3-8-7 (45) J Fanning 9/1: -6403: 3 ch g Greensmith - Classy Miss   ½   45
(Homeboy) Prom, prog & ev ch ent fnl 2f, no extra fnl 50y: op 7/1, clr rem on h'cap bow: stays 2m1f on firm.
3311   **ULSHAW** 11 [10]   J D Bethell 3-7-11 (39)(vis)(1ow)(4oh) T Williams 20/1: 300044: Rcd in 2nd, prsd wnr 3f   6   29
out, sn no extra: stiffish task, see 1386.
3442   **SMUDGER SMITH** 5 [4]   3-8-13 (51)(vis) M Fenton 13/2: 646255: In tch, rdn 3f out, no impress: 1½   43
quick reapp, suited forcing the pace over shorter, see 3367.
3501   **IRELANDS EYE** 3 [6]   5-10-0 (52) P Hanagan (7) 4/1: 332066: In tch, chsd ldrs 6f out till appr fnl 2f.   5   39
3367   **TOTALLY SCOTTISH** 8 [1]   4-9-5 (43) A Culhane 9/1: -05657: Al towards rear: see 3367, 2734.   ½   29
3406   **UNICORN STAR** 6 [2]   3-8-8 (46) F Lynch 10/1: 625238: In tch till 3f out: op 7/1, quick reapp.   4   28
3348   **NEEDWOOD TRIDENT** 9 [9]   3-7-10 (34) P M Quinn (3) 2/1 FAV: 500429: Mid-div, fdd 4f out: bckd: 3½   12
better last time, but that was in a very slow-run race: see 3348.
348   **FIFTEEN REDS** 218 [5]   5-9-6 (44) P Goode (3) 14/1: 00-260: Al bhd: 10th, abs, new stable.   3   19
10 ran   Time 3m 48.0 (6.1)   (Barrie Abbott)   N Bycroft Norton, N Yorks

LINGFIELD
WEDNESDAY AUGUST 23RD   Lefthand, Sharp, Undulating Track

Official Going   GOOD TO FIRM (FIRM In Places). Stalls: Str Course - Far side; Round Course - Inside.

3576   **2.15 EBF MDN 2YO (D)**   5f   Firm 17   -31 Slow
£3640   £1120   £560   £280

3228   **HARD TO CATCH** 14 [9]   K T Ivory 2-9-0 (BL) C Catlin (7) 16/1: 534601: 2 b c Namaqualand - Brook's   74
Dilemma (Known Fact) Cl-up, dsptd lead from halfway, rdn to lead bef dist, narrowly: woken up by blnks: IR 28,000
gns half-brother to wnrs up to 1m: eff at 5f, stays 6f: acts on firm & gd/soft, handles hvy, sharp trks.
3047   **UNPARALLELED** 23 [7]   I A Balding 2-9-0 B W Ryan 8/15 FAV: 452: 2 b f Primo Dominie - Sharp Chief   nk   68
(Chief Singer) Sn led, prsd from halfway, hdd appr fnl 1f, rallied for press, just btn: nicely bckd: more expected
after v promising debut & prob unsuited by drop back to 5f: make amends at 6f, acts on firm/fast grnd.
3385   **PEACE BAND** 7 [8]   M H Tompkins 2-9-0 S Sanders 12/1: 543: 2 b c Desert Style - Anita's Love   1½   69
(Anita's Prince) Chsd ldrs, under press 2f out, styd on but no impress on ldrs: qk reapp, back in trip, handles firm.
--   **STRAWBERRY DAWN** [1]   N Hamilton 2-9-0 D Harrison 12/1: 4: Early ldr, front rank till no extra   1¼   60
appr fnl 1f: debut: 15,000 gns Fayruz Feb foal, dam & sire sprinters.
3009   **ZIETING** 24 [5]   2-9-0 D Sweeney 20/1: -05: Green & shaken up in rear, no impress till kept on   ½   63
nicely ins last: back in trip, looks capable of better, possibly in 6f+ nurseries.
2711   **RUSHBY** 37 [4]   2-9-0 W Supple 40/1: 636206: Handy, fdd appr fnl 1f: has been gelded.   2½   57
3114   **ATEMME** 19 [3]   2-8-9 T G McLaughlin 12/1: 037: Dwelt, nvr in it: see 3114.   5   37
7 ran   Time 59.18 (2.38)   (E H Maloney)   K T Ivory Radlett, Herts

3577   **2.45 BODDINGTONS MED AUCT MDN 2YO (F)**   7f140y str   Firm 17   -15 Slow
£2530   £723   £361

3020   **ZULFAA** 24 [11]   J L Dunlop 2-8-9 W Supple 13/8: 41: 2 b f Bahri - Haniya (Caerleon)   90
Trkd ldrs, led 3f out, pushed out, v rdly: front 2 clr: Feb foal, half sister to a 7f juv wnr, dam 12f wnr: eff
at 7.5f, 10f+ will suit next term: goes on firm & gd, sharp or stiff/gall trk: progressive & potentially useful.
2091   **DUBAI SEVEN STARS** 63 [8]   M C Pipe 2-8-9 Martin Dwyer 6/4 FAV: 452: 2 ch f Suave Dancer - Her   1½   85
Honour (Teenoso) Well plcd, chall appr fnl 2f, sn drvn & kept on but easily outpcd by wnr: nicely bckd from

5/2, clr rem, 9 wk abs: caught a decent sort, handles firm & gd grnd: shld go one better soon.
-- SHII TAKES GIRL [10] Mrs A J Perrett 2-8-9 T Ashley 20/1: 3: 2 ch f Deploy - Super Sally 5 70+
(Superlative) In tch, ran in snatches, shaken up & styd on for 3rd, no ch front pair: pleasing debut: 8,000 gns
Mar foal, sister to decent 7f wnr Shii Take, dam 1m/10f AW wnr: bred to apprec mid-dists: improvement likely.
-- COMPANION [14] W J Haggas 2-8-9 M Tebbutt 9/1: 4: Dwelt & rear, late hdwy, nvr a threat: op 5/1, hd 70+
shld come on plenty for this green debut: sister to a 1m juv wnr, dam 7f/1m wnr: apprec 10f+ next term.
3478 SWANTON ABBOT 4 [2] 2-9-0 A Beech (5) 40/1: 005: Wide, prom, kept on same pace appr fnl 1f. 1¾ 70
2708 TRILLIONAIRE 38 [9] 2-9-0 L Newman (3) 12/1: 62347: Chsd ldrs, wide, no extra ent fnl 2f. 1¼ 66
3358 AVERY RING 9 [18] 2-9-0 D Sweeney 10/1: 62347: Bhd ldrs, fdd 2f out: tchd 14/1, lngr trip: see 3047. ½ 64
-- ABRACADABJAR [5] 2-9-0 S Sanders 25/1: 8: Slow away, wide, prog/in tch 2f out, hung left/no extra ½ 62
1f out: 27,000gns purchase: half-brother to v smart miler Princess Ellen, sire a miler: some promise here.
3074 DODONA 21 [6] 2-8-9 I Mongan (5) 16/1: 409: Chsd ldrs, wknd 2f out: see 2583. 2½ 51
2488 FLOOT 46 [13] 2-8-9 J Weaver 16/1: 000: Wide, rear, went thro' btn horses ins last: 10th, 7 wk abs: hd 55
stablemate wnr, not given a hard time on h'cap qualifying run: see 1472.
2619 Impero 41 [17] 2-9-0 Paul Eddery 40/1: -- Waikiki Dancer [15] 2-8-9 D McGaffin (5) 33/1:
2748 Classic Millennium 35 [3] 2-8-9 R Brisland (5) 25/1: 3358 Monash Freeway 9 [12] 2-9-0 T G McLaughlin 50/1:
3358 Cricketers Club 9 [16] 2-9-0 S Whitworth 40/1: -- Magic Air [7] 2-8-9 A McGlone 33/1:
2791 Pickett Point 34 [4] 2-9-0 C Rutter 50/1:
17 ran   Time 1m 30.22 (2.42)   (Hamdan Al Maktoum)   J L Dunlop Arundel, W Sussex

3578	3.20 HEINEKEN SELL HCAP 3YO+ 0-60 (G) 6f Firm 17 -01 Slow	[60]
	£2233 £638 £319 3 yo rec 3 lb 2 Groups, stands side (high numbers) had the edge	

3253 ZEPPO 13 [12] B R Millman 5-9-10 (56) G Hind 7/1: 644521: 5 ch g Fayruz - Chase Paperchase 61
(Malinowski) Prom stands side, rdn appr fnl 1f, ran on to lead towards fin: bt in for 4,800gns: '99 Chepstow
wnr (h'cap, rtd 61): '98 Lingfield wnr (h'cap, rtd 63): eff at 5/6f, stays 7f: acts on firm, gd grnd, any trk,
likes Lingfield: best without blnks & appreciated this drop back to 6f
3445 MISS MONEY SPIDER 5 [20] J M Bradley 5-8-8 (40) L Newman (3) 4/1: 000442: 5 b m Statoblest - 1¼ 41
Dream Of Jenny (Caerleon) Led stands side & went clr 3f out, stride shortened ent fnl 1f, hdd towards fin: tchd
6/1, quick reapp: eff at 6f, suited by 7f, stays 1m: a bold effort: see 2840.
*3283 CZAR WARS 12 [9] J Balding 5-8-9 (41)(bl) S Sanders 8/1: 034613: 5 b g Warrshan - Dutch Czarina nk 41
(Prince Sabo) Prom stands side, drvn appr fnl 1f, styd on but not pace to chall: tchd 12/1: fair first run
for new connections & handles firm grnd: rtd higher in 3283 (clmr).
3293 PALO BLANCO 12 [11] Andrew Reid 9-9-8 (54) M Henry 12/1: 246204: Handy stands side, onepace fnl 1f. 1¼ 50
1734 ITHADTOBEYOU 79 [8] 5-8-13 (45) M Tebbutt 7/2 FAV: 223005: Prom stands side, rdn appr fnl 2f, fdd. nk 40
3208 ARAB GOLD 15 [19] 5-8-12 (44)(vis) Martin Dwyer 16/1: 003026: Rcd in 2nd stands side till 2f out, 1 36
same pace: op 12/1: flattered last time.
3312 PETITE DANSEUSE 11 [14] 6-8-6 (38) Lynsey Hanna (7) 12/1: 525467: Held up, stands side, short of hd 30
room 2f out, switched & late hdwy, nvr dangerous: see 1422.
3493 FRANKLIN LAKES 4 [16] 5-8-8 (40)(bl) D Sweeney 16/1: 600208: Nvr dngrs stands side: qck reapp. hd 31
2331 VILLAGE NATIVE 17 [17] 7-9-5 (51)(bl) D O'Donohoe 14/1: 000629: Prom stands side, hung left/btn 2f out.¾ 40
3208 MISTER JOLSON 15 [15] 11-9-7 (53) Paul Eddery 12/1: 00-450: In tch stands side, wknd appr fnl 1f: 10th. 2 38
3251 ROBELLION 13 [13] 9-9-11 (57) R Havlin 14/1: 513000: Al towards rear stands side: 11th, op 10/1: ¾ 38
3436 ECUDAMAH 5 [4] 4-9-13 (59)(bl) J Bosley (7) 16/1: 403300: Cl-up centre & led that group after 3f, 1 37
ev ch till no extra bef fnl 1f, eased: 12th, qck reapp, top-weight: best forgiven over longer trip: see 40.
3238 Qualitair Pride 14 [1] 8-8-6 (38) Claire Bryan (5) 16/1:3180 Sunset Harbour 16 [7] 7-8-11 (43) S Carson(3) 16/1:
2367 Betchworth Sand 51 [10] 4-8-12 (44) C Rutter 33/1: 2428 Sounds Lucky 49 [5] 4-9-3 (49)(vis) A Beech(5) 16/1:
3194 Needwood Tribesman 16 [3] 3-8-9 (44) S Whitworth 16/1:
2777 Sonbelle 34 [2] 3-9-10 (59) D McGaffin (5) 16/1: 3124 Bold Emma 19 [18] 3-9-5 (54) J Weaver 25/1:
2788 Sandpoint 34 [6] 4-8-7 (39)(VIS) A Daly (5) 16/1:
20 ran   Time 1m 09.9 (1.1)   (The Plyform Syndicate)   B R Millman Kentisbeare, Devon

3579	3.55 LEISURE CLUB MDN 3YO+ (D) 6f Firm 17 +01 Fast	
	£3016 £928 £464 £232 3 yo rec 3 lb	

2977 TRUE NIGHT 26 [10] H Candy 3-9-0 C Rutter 6/5 FAV: 41: 3 b c Night Shift - Dead Certain (Absalom) 79
With ldrs, led appr fnl 1f, rdn out: well bckd, best time of day: just sharper for debut: dam a smart juv:
eff at 6f on firm/fast grnd, sharp or stiff trk: eff up with/forcing the pace: going the right way.
3337 AMJAD 10 [6] C E Brittain 3-9-0 (bl) W Supple 20/1: 455002: 3 ch g Cadeaux Genereux - Babita ¾ 76$
(Habitat) Bmpd start, keen, rear, prog appr fnl 1f & chsd wnr ins last, al held: tchd 33/1: clrly suited by drop
back to 6f on firm grnd, 7f/1m could be ideal.
3319 DOUBLE PLATINUM 11 [8] J H M Gosden 3-8-9 R Havlin 5/2: -36223: 3 ch f Seeking The Gold - shd 71
Band (Northern Dancing) Bhd ldrs, rdn & ch appr fnl 1f, onepace ins last: bckd from 4/1 & clr rem but btr 3319.
2965 HONEST WARNING 26 [14] B Smart 3-9-0 S Sanders 8/1: 424: Trkd ldrs, shaken up 2f out, rdn bef 2½ 70
dist, onepace: op 6/1: can do better.
3229 STAR PRINCESS 14 [12] 3-8-9 (BL) C Catlin (7) 5/1: 422425: Led/dstpd lead, no extra under press nk 64
appr fnl 1f: op 7/1, blnkd: see 2900, 1021.
3384 VICTORS CROWN 7 [3] 3-9-0 A Beech (5) 25/1: 200-06: Chsd ldrs, fdd appr fnl 1f: quick reapp. 1 66
3263 PAMELA ANSHAN 13 [9] 3-8-9 D O'Donohoe 50/1: 0-0007: Nvr a factor: v stiff task. 4 51$
3297 WOODLANDS 12 [11] 3-9-0 J Weaver 9/1: 30-308: Trkd ldrs till 2f out: lclry. nk 55
2604 EXECUTIVE WISH 41 [7] 3-8-9 Martin Dwyer 50/1: 009: Pulled hard, al bhd: 6 wk abs, new stable. 5 35
3146 REPLACEMENT PET 18 [4] 3-8-9 T G McLaughlin 14/1: 40: In tch till 2f out: 10th: tchd 33/1. ½ 34
2293 Dizzie Lizzie 54 [13] 3-8-9 Paul Eddery 33/1: -- Artyfactual [2] 3-9-0 I Mongan (5) 33/1:
3229 Hopeful Henry 14 [1] 4-9-3 W Ryan 33/1: 595 Chartwell 179 [5] 3-9-0 A Nicholls (3) 50/1:
14 ran   Time 1m 09.77 (0.97)   (The Hon Mrs M A Marten)   H Candy Wantage, Oxon

3580	4.25 STRONGBOW HCAP 3YO 0-80 (D) 7f140y str Firm 17 00 Fast	[85]
	£4225 £1300 £650 £325	

3280 BALFOUR 12 [2] C E Brittain 3-8-4 (61)(vis) A Nicholls (3) 9/1: 603431: 3 b c Green Desert - Badawi 67
(Diesis) Waited with, prog after halfway, drvn ot lead below dist, going away: tchd 14/1: fair time:
earlier won at Warwick (reapp, h'cap): unplcd 3 juv starts (rtd 70$): eff at 6f, suited by 7/7.5f: acts on
firm & hvy grnd, likes sharp trks, with/without visor: improving.

LINGFIELD WEDNESDAY AUGUST 23RD Lefthand, Sharp, Undulating Track

2844 **CEDAR MASTER 32** [7] R J O'Sullivan 3-9-7 (78)(VIS) L Newman (3) 14/1: 556032: 3 b c Soviet Lad - Samriah (Wassl) Led, rdn appr fnl 1f, hdd below dist & outpcd by wnr: gd run in 1st time visor under top-weight & clr rem: eff at 7.5f forcing the pace, tried 1m: see 1029. **2** **79**

3257 **PARKER 13** [14] B Palling 3-9-1 (72) D Harrison 12/1: 246353: 3 b c Magic Ring - Miss Loving (Northfields) Keen, towards rear, kept on stdly appr fnl 1f, nvr nr to chall: worth a try at 1m/stiffer trk: see 1266. **3** **67**

3405 **TRAJAN 7** [5] A P Jarvis 3-8-9 (66) D Sweeney 7/1: 406024: Well plcd, ch appr fnl 1f, sn no extra. **nk** **60**

2216 **WAFFLES OF AMIN 57** [13] 3-9-0 (71) S Sanders 14/1: 004005: Bhd, bmpd 2f out, some late hdwy. **¾** **63**

*3095 **JUDICIOUS 21** [15] Paul Eddery 6/4 FAV: -03016: Dwelt & bhd, imprvg when short of room 2f out, styd on but no threat: well bckd, unsuited by drop back to a sharp 7.5f, worth another chance: see 3095. **nk** **67**

3445 **RULE OF THUMB 5** [11] 3-8-13 (70) I Mongan (5) 7/2: 000527: Chsd ldrs, edged left & no extra bef dist. **½** **60**

3076 **ANDYS ELECTIVE 21** [18] 3-8-8 (65)(vis) S Whitworth 16/1: 051008: In tch, onepace when hung left appr fnl 1f: much btr 2044 (made all in 1st time visor, mdn h'cap). **1½** **52**

3254 **BISHOPSTONE MAN 13** [8] 3-8-12 (69) C Rutter 14/1: 510209: Pld v hard, trkd ldrs till btn appr fnl 1f. **1½** **53**

3095 **MIND THE SILVER 21** [1] 3-8-0 (56)(1ow) A Daly 14/1: 060040: Wide, nvr a factor: 10th, btr 3095. **1** **39**

3033 **SHOWING 23** [6] 3-8-0 (57)(t) Martin Dwyer 12/1: -00600: Chsd ldrs wide 4f, eased: 16th, see 2655, 839. **0**

636 **Ridgecrest 172** [4] 3-7-12 (55) Joanna Badger (7) 33/1: 2885 **Carnage 30** [3] 3-7-10 (53)(1oh) G Bardwell 14/1:

3445 **Magic Babe 5** [9] 3-8-2 (59) M Henry 14/1: 4491} **Sparkling Isle 305** [10] 3-8-8 (65) G Hind 25/1:

3423 **Dancing Lily 6** [16] 3-7-10 (53)(12oh) R Brisland (5) 50/1:

3188 **So Dainty 16** [12] 3-7-12 (55)(2ow)(5oh) A Mackay 50/1:

17 ran   Time 1m 29.11 (1.31)   (Sheikh Marwan Al Maktoum)   C E Brittain Newmarket, Suffolk

---

3581 4.55 STELLA FILLIES HCAP 3YO+ 0-65 (F) 1m2f Firm 17 -18 Slow [61]
£2604 £744 £372 3 yo rec 8 lb

3244 **LEVEL HEADED 14** [3] P W Hiatt 5-8-7 (40) A Mackay 9/1: 441341: 5 b m Beveled - Snowline (Bay Express) Led, went 4L clr ent str, pushed out, rdly: earlier won at Bath (fill h'cap, 1st win): unplcd for E Wheeler in '99 (mdn, rtd 40): eff forcing the pace at 10f on firm, hvy grnd, sharp/turning trks. **49**

*3368 **ZAGALETA 8** [7] Andrew Turnell 3-10-0 (69)(6ex) J Weaver 4/1 FAV: 000212: 3 b f Sri Pekan - Persian Song (Persian Bold) Confidently held up, well off the pace ent str, gd hdwy 2f out, went 2nd dist, nvr nr wnr: gd run under top-weight tho' set a lot to do: progressive, win again, see 3368. **1¾** **74**

3390 **SHARP SPICE 7** [12] D J Coakley 4-9-7 (54) S Sanders 8/1: 255303: 4 b f Lugana Beach - Ewar Empress (Persian Bold) Held up, hdwy 2f out, dsptd 2nd dist, same pace for press: qk reapp, back to form: see 2041. **1** **57**

3314 **INDIAN NECTAR 11** [10] R Brotherton 7-9-7 (54) L Newman (3) 9/1: 052364: Wide, mid-div, prog to chase wnr briefly appr fnl 2f onepace bef dist: better run tho' won this in '99 (off 8lbs lower mark): see 1332. **¾** **56**

2774 **SAIL WITH THE WIND 34** [4] 3-8-8 (49) S Whitworth 12/1: 00-05: In tch, prog appr fnl 2f, sn rdn, btn: op 33/1 on h'cap bow: well btn all 3 prev starts, rtd 59$ as a juv: with T McCarthy. **nk** **50$**

3188 **BECKON 16** [16] 4-8-3 (36) C Rutter 6/1: 501506: Bhd, wide prog appr fnl 2f, rdn & no impress. **1** **35**

3282 **FOREST DREAM 12** [2] 5-8-12 (45) A Nicholls (3) 9/1: 230027: Mid-div, hmpd appr fnl 2f, nvr dngrs: see 43. **½** **43**

3031 **SILK STOCKINGS 23** [6] 3-9-10 (65) W Supple 12/1: 030008: Nvr better than mid-div: moderate. **4** **57**

2887 **IN THE STOCKS 30** [1] 6-9-0 (47) S Carson (3) 9/2: -00629: Al towards rear, hmpd 2f out: unsuited by drop back to 10f?: worth another look: see 1100. **½** **38**

2211 **MAIDEN AUNT 58** [9] 3-9-2 (57) D Harrison 16/1: 5000: Chsd ldrs till ent str: 10th on h'cap bow, abs. **¾** **47**

2533 **RED CAFE 44** [15] 4-8-7 (40)(VIS) Paul Eddery 10/1: 004240: Rear, prog to go 2nd 3f out, sn rdn & lost place: 1th, 6 wk abs, visored, unsuited by step up to 10f: see 854. **1¾** **28**

2484 **POLISHED UP 47** [8] 3-8-6 (47) Martin Dwyer 12/1: 0-6030: Handy 5f: 12th, 7 wk abs: see 2484. **½** **34**

3526 **Purnadas Road 2** [13] 5-8-0 (33) G Bardwell 25/1: 3360 **Reading Rhonda 9** [5] 4-8-5 (38) W Ryan 16/1:

1909 **Dulzie 70** [11] 3-9-0 (55) D Sweeney 14/1:

15 ran   Time 2m 07.74 (3.54)   (Anthony Harrison)   P W Hiatt Hook Norton, Oxon

---

FOLKESTONE THURSDAY AUGUST 24TH Righthand, Sharpish, Undulating Track

Official Going: GOOD/FIRM. Stalls: Round Course- Outside, Straight Course - Stands Side.

3582 2.15 RADIO KENT SELLER 2YO (F) 7f str Good/Firm 34 -17 Slow
£2331 £666 £333 Field raced far side

2182 **SAWBO LAD 60** [10] J Akehurst 2-8-11 F Norton 16/1: 60001: 2 b c Namaqualand - Maafi Esm (Polish Precedent) Chsd ldr halfway, drvn & styd on well to lead well inside last: bought in for 4,000gns: op 12/1, 2 mth abs: first win: unplcd previously for R J O'Sullivan: eff at 7f, 1m should suit: acts on fast grnd & a sharp/ undul track: runs well fresh: woken up by change of stable & appreciated this drop to sell grade. **72**

3468 **KALUKI 5** [11] W R Muir 2-8-11 Martin Dwyer 5/2 FAV: 420332: 2 ch c First Trump - Wild Humour (Fayruz) Led, rdn fnl 2f, hdd well inside last & no extra: hvly bckd, op 3/1: quick reapp: acts on fast & gd/soft. **¾** **69**

3240 **HARD TO LAY 15** [14] D J S Cosgrove 2-8-6 G Carter 7/1: 250023: 2 b f Dolphin Street - Yavarro (Raga Navarro) Chsd ldrs, rdn & kept on fnl 2f, not able to chall: see 3240. **2** **60**

3296 **SUGAR ROLO 13** [2] D Morris 2-8-6 D McGaffin (3) 25/1: 654: Rear/rdn early, hdwy 3f out, held fnl 1f. **3½** **53**

3292 **GOLDEN BEACH 13** [12] 2-8-6 P Doe 12/1: -0005: Chsd ldrs, briefly no room 3f out, sn held: op 6/1. **1¼** **50**

3047 **STYLISH FELLA 24** [8] 2-8-11 D Sweeney 9/1: 006: Chsd ldrs, held 2f out: op 5/1: see 2598 (6f). **2½** **50**

3428 **MOMENTS IN TIME 6** [3] 2-8-6 Craig Williams 8/1: 64657: Dwelt/rear, mod gains: quick reapp. **3** **39**

3388 **REPEAT PERFORMANCE 8** [7] 2-8-11 (t) A Daly 12/1: 405508: Held up, eff 3f out, sn held: op 7/1. **shd** **44**

878 **SIZE DOESNT MATTER 134** [5] 2-8-11 M Roberts 33/1: 039: Slowly away, rear, mod late gains: abs. **¾** **43**

3296 **STAR BRIEF 13** [9] 2-8-11 L Newton 10/1: 040: Sn bhd, mod late prog: 10th: op 6/1: see 2599. **4** **35**

3204 **ECCENTRICITY 16** [6] 2-8-6 Paul Eddery 10/1: 00: Chsd wnr 4f, sn btn: 11th: longer 7f trip. **6** **19**

-- **Yura Madam** [1] 2-8-6 G Faulkner (0) 25/1: 3278 **Teenawon 13** [13] 2-8-6 J Quinn 12/1:

3204 **Beacons A Light 16** [4] 2-8-11 A Mackay 33/1:

14 ran   Time 1m 27.8 (3.6)   (Normandy Developments (London))   J Akehurst Epsom, Surrey

---

1100

FOLKESTONE THURSDAY AUGUST 24TH Righthand, Sharpish, Undulating Track

3583 2.45 KENT HEADLINE FILL MDN 2YO (D) 7f str Good/Firm 34 -13 Slow
£4407 £1356 £678 £339 Field raced far side

2686 **BREAKFAST BAY 40** [8] R Charlton 2-8-11 R Perham 6/4 FAV: 31: 2 b f Charnwood Forest - Diavolina (Lear Fan) Sn cl up, styd on well to prevail thrilling fin: nicely bckd tho' op 5/4, 6 week abs: eff over a stiff or sharp/undul 7f, will apprec 1m+: acts on fast & gd grnd: showed a fine attitude here, op to further improvement. **82**
1856 **BOGUS PENNY 74** [6] S P C Woods 2-8-11 J Quinn 3/1: 42: 2 b f Pennekamp - Dreams Are Free (Caerleon) Led after 1f, jnd fnl 2f, styd on well, just hdd line: nicely bckd & clr of rem: styd longer 7f trip well after 11 week abs: handles firm & fast grnd: lost little in defeat, can find a race: see 1856. *shd* **81**
-- **MISS MOSELLE** [2] P W Harris 2-8-11 R Mullen 10/1: 3: 2 b f Zieten - Topseys Tipple (Hatim) Slowly away & rear, rdn & styd on well from over 1f out, no threat to front pair: op 8/1: May foal, cost IR24,000 gns: half sister to a 6/7f Irish juv wnr: dam a 3yo 9f Irish wnr: looks sure to relish 1m in time: handles fast. *5* **71**
3079 **ROSELYN 22** [9] I A Balding 2-8-11 Martin Dwyer 14/1: 644: Went left start, led 1f, outpcd fnl 2f. *nk* **70**
3039 **RAMBAGH 24** [4] 2-8-11 G Carter 5/1: 425: Trckd ldrs, outpcd over 2f out: btr 3039, 2306. *3* **64**
-- **SODFAHH** [3] 2-8-11 A Daly 12/1: 6: Dwelt, sn keen/trckd ldrs, rdn/btn over 1f out: mkt drifter, op 6/1: Lion Cavern filly, April foal: half-sister to a 12f wnr: dam a juv 5f wnr: with M P Tregoning. *1½* **61**
3187 **ARABIAN WATERS 17** [5] 2-8-11 S Carson (3) 33/1: 07: Prom, outpcd fnl 2f: longer 7f trip: see 3187. *1¾* **58**
3039 **GRECIAN HALO 24** [1] 2-8-11 M Fenton 20/1: 68: Al bhd: op 12/1: see 3039. *1½* **55**
3215 **TALAT 15** [7] 2-8-11 P McCabe 25/1: 069: Hmpd start & al bhd: see 3020. *1½* **52**
9 ran Time 1m 27.5 (3.3) (F M Alger) R Charlton Beckhampton, Wilts

3584 3.20 O FISHER MED AUCT MDN 3-4YO 5f Good/Firm 34 -08 Slow
£2772 £792 £396 3 yo rec 2 lb Field raced stands side

3341 **TIGER IMP 11** [7] I A Balding 4-9-2 (t) Martin Dwyer 9/4 FAV: 3-0601: 4 b g Imp Society - Mrs Merry Man (Bellypha) Prom, led halfway, drvn over 1f out, styd on well ins last: well bckd: improved eff in a t-strap: plcd all 3 '99 starts (rtd 77, mdn): eff over a sharp/undulating 5/7f on fast & gd grnd: h'caps shld suit. **70**
2947 **TOP OF THE PARKES 27** [8] N P Littmoden 3-8-9 J Tate 8/1: 50-302: 3 b f Mistertopogigo - Bella Parkes (Tina's Pet) Chsd ldrs, rdn/prog to chase wnr ins last, kept on: op 6/1: handles firm, fast & fibresand. *1¼* **61**
2716 **CORBLETS 38** [5] S Dow 3-8-9 P Doe 5/2: 000363: 3 b f Timeless Times - Dear Glenda (Gold Song) Badly hmpd start & slowly away, chased ldrs halfway, rdn/kept on onepace inside last: bckd, op 4/1: lost winning ch at start, gd eff in circumstances: return to h'caps should suit: see 1427, 1098. *1½* **57**
2820 **DANCEMMA 34** [10] M Blanshard 3-8-9 J Quinn 11/2: 250004: Prom, onepace over 1f out: op 4/1. *nk* **56**
3180 **LUNALUX 17** [1] 3-8-9 (vis) J Stack 12/1: 024005: Led till halfway, outpcd fnl 1f: op 10/1: see 2095. *nk* **55$**
-- **MELLEDGAN** [2] 3-8-9 M Roberts 8/1: 6: Handy, outpcd from halfway: op 3/1: Catrail filly, will enjoy step up to 6f+ on this evidence: with R Guest. *1¼* **52**
3279 **BETTINA BLUE 13** [4] 3-8-9 N Pollard 14/1: 660007: Hmpd start & slowly away, al rear: see 745. *½* **50**
2779 **PACIFIC PLACE 35** [3] 3-9-0 F Norton 14/1: 322008: Prom till over 1f out: op 9/1: btr 2243 (6f). *hd* **54**
3186 **ROYAL CZARINA 17** [6] 3-8-9 G Baker (5) 33/1: 0-0009: Went left start & slowly away, sn outpcd. *7* **34**
9 ran Time 1m 0.5 (2.1) (Mrs Angela Brodie) I A Balding Kingsclere, Hants.

3585 3.55 HBLB NEWS HCAP 3YO 0-80 (D) 1m1f149y Good/Firm 34 +02 Fast **[85]**
£4030 £1240 £620 £310

3281 **KELTIC BARD 13** [7] S P C Woods 3-9-4 (75) G Carter 9/4 JT FAV: 005121: 3 b g Emperor Jones - Broughton Singer (Common Grounds) Made all, rdn clr over 2f out, in command ins last & eased nr fin: nicely bckd tho' op 6/4, gd time: earlier won here at Folkestone (h'cap): '99 W'hampton wnr (nov auct, rtd 88a & 80): eff at 1m/10f on firm, fast & f/sand: loves to force the pace on a sharp/undul trk, esp Folkestone: progressive. **82**
3178 **YOUR THE LADY 18** [9] M R Channon 3-9-3 (74) Craig Williams 6/1: 851102: 3 b f Indian Ridge - Edwina (Caerleon) Chsd wnr 2f, chsd wnr again fnl 2f, rdn & kept on, al held: clr rem: stays 9.7f: see 2895. *½* **76**
3334 **RESPLENDENT STAR 11** [6] P W Harris 3-9-7 (78)(vis) M Fenton 13/2: 0-4003: 3 b g Northern Baby - Whitethroat (Artaius) Rear, hdwy over 2f out, rdn/no prog inside last: visor reapp: topweight: see 1341 (1m) *5* **72**
1912 **HEFIN 71** [4] S C Williams 3-7-12 (55)(2ow)(5oh) J Quinn 33/1: -0004: Trckd ldrs, rdn/held over 1f out: op 14/1 on h'cap bow: 10 week abs: only mod form prev. *¾* **48**
3351 **NO REGRETS 10** [8] 3-7-12 (55) F Norton 33/1: 000265: Chsd ldrs, outpcd fnl 3f: see 2250, 629. *1¾* **45**
3456 **WINDFALL 6** [1] 3-8-5 (62) Martin Dwyer 33/1: 300006: Chsd ldrs 7f: see 3456, 1912. *7* **40**
3530 **ASSURED PHYSIQUE 3** [5] 3-8-5 (62)(tvi) D O'Donohoe 8/1: 665567: Dwelt/rear, no impress: op 11/2. *1¼* **37**
3046 **SHAFAQ 24** [3] 3-9-4 (75) R Price 20/1: -06008: Rear, hdwy 4f out, btn 2f out: op 10/1: see 1676 (6f). *½* **49**
*3185 **PHANTOM RAIN 17** [2] 3-9-4 (75) M Roberts 9/4 JT FAV: 02519: Prom 7f: bckd, op 9/2: jockey reported filly lost her action: btr 3185 (mdn). *14* **28**
9 ran Time 2m 01.1 (3.1) (G A Roberts) S P C Woods Newmarket, Suffolk

3586 4.25 KENT MESSENGER HCAP 3YO+ 0-70 (E) 1m4f Good/Firm 34 -05 Slow **[70]**
£3108 £888 £444 3 yo rec 10lb

3437 **LOST SPIRIT 6** [15] P W Hiatt 4-7-10 (38) G Baker (5) 9/2: 113521: 4 b g Strolling Along - Shoag (Affirmed) Made all, rdn clr over 2f out, held on gamely for press nr fin: bckd, qck reapp: earlier won h'caps at Lingfield (AW, rtd 49a), Warwick & Beverley: '99 wnr at Southwell (clmr) & W'hampton (h'cap, rtd 66a & 49): loves to dominate at 12f on firm, gd/soft & both AWs, sharp or stiff/undul trk: eff with/without blnks: tough & genuine. **40**
3448 **SIRINNDI 6** [4] B J Curley 6-8-4 (46) S W Kelly (1) 5/1: 050062: 6 b g Shahrastani - Sinntara (Lashkari) Dwelt, prog 3f out, drvn when hmpd dist, styd on well for strong press ins last, just held: tchd 7/1: can be rtd an unlucky loser, can find compensation: acts on fast & hvy grnd: see 1416. *½* **48**
3402 **RAYIK 8** [1] G L Moore 5-8-11 (53) I Mongan (5) 14/1: 200103: 5 br g Marju - Matila (Persian Bold) Trckd ldrs, rdn/chsd wnr 2f out, just held inside last: op 8/1: back to form here, acts on fast, gd & both AW's. *nk* **54**
3353 **MY PLEDGE 10** [10] C A Horgan 5-9-2 (58) N Pollard 15/2: 210344: Dwelt/rear, hdwy 3f out, sn onepace. *1* **58**
3282 **SURE FUTURE 13** [14] 4-8-4 (46)(bl) A Polli (3) 25/1: 2-0055: Sn chsd wnr, held fnl 2f: see 3111. *1* **44**
3424 **TOMMY CARSON 7** [12] 5-8-8 (50)(bl) O Urbina 20/1: 250406: Held up, eff 3f out, kept on onepace. *½* **48**
3217 **SUPREME SILENCE 15** [16] 3-8-2 (54) R Mullen 12/1: -00007: Chsd wnr 2f, btn 2f out: op 10/1. *shd* **52**
3402 **ORDAINED 8** [13] 7-8-5 (47) Martin Dwyer 12/1: 412268: Twds rear, eff 3f out, no impress: op 9/1. *hd* **44**
3461 **LADY JO 6** [6] 4-9-4 (60) R Smith (5) 10/1: 605169: Dwelt/rear, eff 3f out, no impression: see 3282. *¾* **56**
3201 **NEEDWOOD MYSTIC 16** [9] 5-8-4 (46) J Tate 16/1: 001050: Prom, btn 2f out: 10th: see 2422. *1½* **40**

FOLKESTONE
THURSDAY AUGUST 24TH   Righthand, Sharpish, Undulating Track

3447 **ARTIC COURIER 6** [5] 9-8-5 (47) G Carter 12/1: 144140: Rear, eff 2f out, sn held, eased ins last: 11th. 8 32
3353 **FIRST IMPRESSION 10** [3] 5-10-0 (70) M Roberts 11/4 FAV: 5-2020: Chsd ldrs 10f: 12th: nicely bckd. 5 48
3424 **RISING SPRAY 7** [8] 9-9-3 (59) Paul Eddery 8/1: 6-0000: Reared start & lost many lengths, al rear: 15th.   0
3263 Adriana 14 [7] 3-7-11 (49) (1ow) (3oh) F Norton 12/1:   1942 **Sibertigo 70** [11] 4-8-3 (45) C Rutter 33/1:
2691 Bamboozle 40 [2] 4-9-9 (65) J Quinn 33/1:
16 ran   Time 2m 36.2 (4.7)   (Red Lion Chipping Norton Partnership)   P W Hiatt Hook Norton, Oxon

3587
4.55 ARENA CLASSIFIED STKS 3YO+ 0-65 (E)   6f   Good/Firm 34   +04 Fast
£3033   £868   £434   3 yo rec 3 lb Two groups - majority stands side

3257 **BANDBOX 14** [11] M Salaman 5-9-0 J Quinn 7/1: 062361: 5 ch g Imperial Frontier - Dublah (Private   67
Account) Prom far side, led overall 2f out & rdn clr 1f out, held on well, drvn out: best time of day: earlier
scored at Southwell (AW claimer, rtd 70a): '99 Leicester wnr (class stakes, rtd 67): dual '98 rnr up (h'cap, rtd
74): eff at 5/7f on firm, gd/soft & fibresand: eff with/without vis or blinks, tried a t-strap: has run well fresh.
3297 **DOUBLE BOUNCE 13** [2] H Morrison 10-9-0 M Roberts 12/1: 060-02: 10 b g Interrex - Double Gift   ¾ 64
(Cragador) Chsd ldrs stands side, rdn/styd on ins last, not rch wnr far side: see 3297.
*3562 **TORRENT 1** [1] D W Chapman 5-9-0 (bl) Lynsey Hanna (7) 11/2: 633313: 5 ch g Prince Sabo - Maiden   ½ 62
Pool (Sharpen Up) Led stands side, shaken up over 1f out, no extra inside last: stays 6f, prob just best at 5f.
*3493 **DAYS OF GRACE 5** [6] L Montague Hall 5-9-0 R Cutter 6/1: 053114: Prom stands side, onepace fnl 1f.   hd 64
3419 **KILCULLEN LAD 7** [5] 6-9-0 (vis) P Fitzsimons (5) 4/1 JT FAV: 006035: Prom stands side, held dist.   1½ 57
3362 **MIDHISH TWO 10** [12] 4-9-0 (bl) I Mongan (5) 16/1: 000006: Led overall far side 4f, fdd: op 20/1.   2½ 50
3562 **ABSOLUTE FANTASY 1** [8] 4-8-11 (bl) S Carson (3) 7/1: 242127: Prom stands side, btn/eased   nk 46
inside last: rnr up at Brighton yesterday: see 3455.
2839 **MUFFLED 33** [4] 3-8-8 G Carter 9/1: -00208: Twds rear stands side, nvr pace to chall: op 5/1.   ½ 44
3243 **FAIRYTIME 15** [10] 4-8-11 R Brisland (5) 50/1: 0-0009: Rear far side, struggling 2f out: see 3243.   ½ 42
3280 **NEEDWOOD TRICKSTER 13** [3] 3-8-11 J Tate 14/1: 033600: Dwelt, chsd ldrs stands side 5f: 10th.   hd 44
*3386 **WATER BABE 8** [9] 3-9-0 N Pollard 4/1 JT FAV: -41010: Chsd ldrs stands side 4f: 11th: btr 3386.   1½ 44
3269 **SHINING STAR 14** [7] 3-8-8 F Norton 14/1: 5-4050: Al bhd stands side: 12th: see 3269, 1606.   1½ 34
12 ran   Time 1m 12.8 (1.8)   (R Brooks, G Else, M Salaman)   M Salaman Baydon, Wilts

3588
5.25 HEADLINE APPR HCAP 3YO 0-70 (F)   2m93y   Good/Firm 34   -21 Slow   [72]
£2268   £648   £324

2554 **LORD ALASKA 45** [8] J A R Toller 3-8-11 (55) C Carver 25/1: 00501: 3 b g Sir Harry Lewis - Anchorage   63
(Slip Anchor) Held up, hdwy 3f out, no room/switched over 1f out, rdn & styd on well inside last to lead nr fin, won
going away: jockey given 2-day careless riding ban: first win: apprec step up to 2m, could get further: acts on
fast grnd & a sharp/undulating track: runs well fresh: op to further improvement in similar contests.
3417 **SAMARARDO 7** [7] N P Littmoden 3-8-5 (49) G Baker (3) 11/1: -54642: 3 b g Son Pardo - Kinlet   1¼ 54
Vision (Vision) Dwelt, keen & sn led/dsptd lead, rdn & every ch inside last, hdd/held nr fin: stays 2m: handles
fast & fibresand: could find a similar modest h'cap: see 80 (AW)..
*3112 **ESTABLISHED 20** [2] J R Best 3-7-13 (43) A Polli 2/1 FAV: 355013: 3 b g Not In Doubt - Copper   shd 48
Trader (Faustus) Prom, forced wide on bend 3f out, drvn & ev ch 2f out, just held whn hmpd nr line: well
bckd, op 5/2: confirmed improvement of latest: see 3112.
3448 **HARD DAYS NIGHT 6** [1] M Blanshard 3-7-10 (40) (4oh) A Beech 7/2: 462024: Trckd ldrs, rdn/led over   hd 44
2f out, sn strongly pressed & hdd well inside last, no extra: op 5/2: eff around 2m on fast & gd: see 1911.
3290 **MUCHANA YETU 13** [4] 3-8-8 (52) S W Kelly 10/1: 606505: Chsd ldrs, btn 2f out: see 1177.   9 49
3290 **PINCHANINCH 13** [6] 3-9-7 (65) S Carson 9/1: 212446: Keen/held up, outpcd fnl 3f: op 6/1.   shd 62
3383 **ABLE SEAMAN 8** [5] 3-9-0 (58) (VIS) S Hitchcott (7) 5/1: 343647: Trkd ldr, led 5f out till 4f out, ran   5 50
wide over 3f out, sn hung left & btn: suffered steering problems in first time visor, prob needs stronger handling.
3241 **BLOSSOM WHISPERS 15** [3] 3-9-7 (65) I Mongan 9/2: 643238: Held up, rdn/btn 3f out: op 6/1.   3 54
8 ran   Time 3m 40.3 (9.0)   (Mrs Claire Smith)   J A R Toller Newmarket, Suffolk

MUSSELBURGH
THURSDAY AUGUST 24TH   Righthand, Sharp Track

Official Going   GOOD TO FIRM (FIRM In Places). Stalls: 5f - Stands Side; Rem - Inside.

3589
2.25 WHITELAW SELLER 2YO (F)   5f str   Good/Firm 31   -41 Slow
£2716   £776   £388

3346 **WHITE STAR LADY 10** [8] J R Weymes 2-8-6 R Winston 8/1: 50501: 2 ch f So Factual - Cottonwood   59
(Teenoso) Prom, eff/hung left over 1f out, led ins last, rdn out: no bid, 1st win: cheaply bt Apr foal, half-sister
to a wnr abroad: dam 10f wnr: eff arnd a sharp 5f, further shld suit: apprec drop to sells.
3145 **AMAMACKEMMUSH 19** [1] K A Ryan 2-8-11 Iona Wands 6/4 FAV: 022352: 2 b g General Monash -   ¾ 61
Paganina (Galetto) Led, hdd well ins last, held cl-home: nicely bckd: apprec this drop to sell company.
-- **HEAD SCRATCHER** [6] W W Haigh 2-8-11 T E Durcan 7/1: 3: 2 ch g Alhijaz - Sabrata (Zino)   ½ 60
Sn well detached, rdn, swtchd & ran on strongly ins last, nrst fin: claimed for £6,000: Mar foal, dam a 5f 2yo
wnr abroad: eff at 5f, 6f will suit: acts on fast & a sharp trk: sure to learn from this & can land a seller.
1659 **ALICIAN SUNHILL 83** [2] Mrs A Duffield 2-8-6 L Enstone (7) 9/1: -0304: Mid-div, rdn/ran on ins   nk 54
last, nvr nrr: 12 wk abs & just sharper for this, handles fast grnd: see 1359, 1146.
3376 **GOLGOTHA 8** [4] 2-8-6 P Bradley 25/1: 05005: Fly-jumped start, prom, switched appr dist, sn held.   ¾ 52
2968 **LAS LLANADAS 27** [9] 2-8-6 J Fanning 16/1: 56: Sn outpcd, late gains for press, no dngr: see 2968.   1¾ 48
3028 **MRS MITCHELL 24** [10] 2-8-6 O Pears 16/1: 67: Prom, short of room over 1f out, sn btn: bckd from 50/1.   ½ 47
3408 **OLYS DREAM 7** [3] 2-8-6 Kim Tinkler 10/1: 5068: Sn rdn in mid-div, nvr dangerous: quick reapp.   hd 47
3193 **ANGELAS HUSBAND 17** [5] 2-8-11 (VIS) P Hanagan (7) 10/1: 600359: Front wknd, wknd fnl 2f: visor.   1 49
3216 **ITALIAN AFFAIR 15** [7] 2-8-11 P Fessey 11/2: 504600: Prom, eff/hmpd over 1f out, sn btn/eased, 10th.   ¾ 47
10 ran   Time 1m 01.1 (3.6)   (White Star Racing)   J R Weymes Coverham, N Yorks

3590 **2.55 ROYAL SCOTS CUP HCAP 3YO+ 0-75 (E)**   1m6f   Good/Firm 31 -15 Slow   **[70]**
£3445   £1060   £530   £265

3284 **MANZONI** 13 [3] M W Easterby 4-8-1 (43) P Hanagan (7) 7/2: 006001: 4 b g Warrshan - Arc Empress Jane   48
(Rainbow Quest) Led, qcknd pace halfway, strongly prsd fnl 2f, held on gamely, drvn out: nicely bckd: up in trip:
visor omitted: '99 wnr at Southwell (AW h'cap, rtd 54a), rnr-up on turf (rtd 56): loves to force the pace around
12/14f: acts on fast, gd, fibresand & a sharp trk: eff with/without blnks, has tried a visor: battled well today.
*3201 **BHUTAN** 16 [4] Mrs M Reveley 5-10-0 (70) A Culhane 11/4: 160012: 5 b g Polish Patriot - Bustinetta   ½ 74
(Bustino) Rcd keenly, chsd ldr, chall on bit with jockey looking round 2f out, drvn & found little well ins last: clr rem,
top-weight: nicely bckd: looked reluctant to go past wnr here, worth a try in headgear now: see 3201.
*3367 **HIGHFIELD FIZZ** 9 [1] C W Fairhurst 8-8-0 (42)(6ex) T Williams 8/1: 063413: 8 b m Efisio - Jendor   6 38
(Condorcet) Settled rear, eff after halfway, not pace of front 2 fnl 3f, late rally: 6lb pen for scoring in 3367.
2643 **COSMIC CASE** 41 [2] J S Goldie 5-8-4 (46) K Dalgleish (5) 8/1: 421134: Prom, drvn, hung right & wknd   6 34
fnl 3f: mkt drifter, 9 wk abs: see 2643, 2392.
3378 **SING AND DANCE** 8 [6] R Winston 8/1: 553205: Handy, drvn/grad wknd fnl 3f: btr 3201.   hd 40
3331 **GENEROUS WAYS** 11 [5] 5-9-2 (58) T E Durcan 9/4 FAV: 010226: Dwelt, rear, prog after halfway, wknd   8 33
qckly fnl 3f: nicely bckd & surely something amiss: see 3295, 2173.
6 ran   Time 3m 03.0 (6.5)   (Bodfari Stud Ltd)   M W Easterby Sheriff Hutton, N Yorks

3591 **3.30 NISH & THOMSON CLAIMER 3YO 0-65 (E)**   1m1f   Good/Firm 31 +09 Fast
£3445   £1060   £530   £265

3364 **ABSINTHER** 9 [5] E J Alston 3-8-12 T E Durcan 13/8 FAV: 200531: 3 b g Presidium - Heavenly Queen   57
(Scottish Reel) Trkd ldr, hdwy to lead dist, rdn & qcknd up well ins last: well bckd, best time of day: 1st win:
plcd once as a juv (rtd 67, 7f, hvy): apprec this step up to 9f & further could suit: acts on fast grnd & a
sharp or easy trk: best without a visor: imprvd for this step up in trip.
*2989 **WISHFUL THINKER** 26 [4] N Tinkler 3-8-12 O Pears 2/1: 003012: 3 b g Prince Sabo - Estonia (King's   3½ 49
Lake) Led, hdd dist, drvn & not pace of wnr: in good form but will prob apprec a return to further: see 2989.
3330 **PADDY MUL** 11 [2] W Storey 3-8-2 (t) T Williams 16/1: 00-003: 3 ch c Democratic - My Pretty Niece   2½ 34
(Great Nephew) Handy, dropped rear over 2f out, rall fnl 1f, no dngr: 1st sign of form this term, stays 9f on fast.
3125 **PIX ME UP** 20 [1] K A Ryan 3-7-13 Iona Wands 2/1: 005404: Prom, rdn/fdd over 1f out: btr 2946 (AW).   nk 31
3364 **SECRETARIO** 9 [3] 3-7-13 (bl) K Dalgleish (5) 25/1: 000005: Dsptd lead despite hanging thr'out,   3 25
wknd qckly over 1f out: mod form.
5 ran   Time 1m 52.6 (1.9)   (J E Abbey)   E J Alston Longton, Lancs

3592 **4.05 ROYAL SCOTS NURSERY HCAP 2YO (D)**   7f130y rnd   Good/Firm 31 -26 Slow   **[81]**
£4127   £1270   £635   £317

2991 **LADY BEAR** 26 [1] R A Fahey 2-8-11 (64)(vis) R Winston 4/1: 633441: 2 b f Grand Lodge - Boristova   74
(Royal Academy) Led, hdwy to lead over 1f out, qcknd well & rdn out: 1st win: cost IR10,500gns, dam 9f Irish
juv wnr: eff at 7f, 1m shld suit: acts on fast, gd & fibresand: best visored: improving.
3439 **SHARP SECRET** 6 [5] M Johnston 2-9-1 (68)(6ex) J Fanning 5/2: 525122: 2 b f College Chapel - State   2 73
Treasure (Secretariat) Trkd ldrs, led 2f out, hdd appr fnl 1f, held well ins last: nicely bckd, clr rem, stays 7f.
*3439 **UHOOMAGOO** 6 [2] D Nicholls 2-9-13 (80)(6ex) Darren Williams 5/2: 211313: 2 b c   3½ 79
Namaqualand - Point Of Law (Law Society) Prom, rdn/no extra over 1f out: top weight, quick reapp, well bckd:
longer 7f trip, may apprec a drop back to 6f: ahead of today's rnr-up in 3439 (6f).
1429 **PHARAOH HATSHEPSUT** 94 [6] J S Goldie 2-8-6 (59) P Fessey 9/1: -40004: Led, hdd 2f out, sn   ½ 57
onepace: 3 month abs & this longer 7f trip prob not suit: btr 796.
3127 **ORIGINAL SINNER** 20 [3] 2-9-0 (67) A Culhane 4/1: 6465: Dwelt, rear, eff 3f out, sn held: btr 2841.   1 63
2990 **NOT JUST A DREAM** 26 [7] 2-8-9 (62) C Lowther 10/1: 43046: Rear, nvr dangerous: see 1700.   nk 58
2301 **OLYS GILL** 55 [4] 2-7-10 (49)(10oh) K Dalgleish (5) 33/1: 4007: Prom to halfway, sn lost tch: 5 37
8 wk abs, stiff task: prev with J J O'Neill, now with A Berry.
7 ran   Time 1m 29.0 (4.1)   (A & K Lingerie)   R A Fahey Butterwick, N Yorks

3593 **4.35 MANSON HCAP 3YO 0-70 (E)**   7f130y rnd   Good/Firm 31 -10 Slow   **[77]**
£3094   £952   £476   £238

*3364 **MYTTONS AGAIN** 9 [12] A Bailey 3-9-2 (65)(bl) (6ex) J Bramhill 10/1: 006311: 3 b g Rambo Dancer -   71
Sigh (Highland Melody) Hld up, eff & switched over 2f out, ran on well to lead nr fin: rdn out: earlier won at
Ayr (sell): '99 wnr at Chester (nurs, rtd 74 & 68a): suited by 7f, stays 1m on fast, hvy, any trk & in blnks.
3269 **FOR HEAVENS SAKE** 14 [2] C W Thornton 3-8-7 (56) Dean McKeown 8/1: 432602: 3 b g Rambo   nk 60
Dancer - Angel Fire (Nashwan) Led, drvn appr fnl 1f, styd on but hdd cl-home: clr rem: acts on fast & fibresand.
3364 **THEOS LAD** 9 [8] R Allan 3-8-5 (54) T Williams 8/1: -50103: 3 b g Shareef Dancer - Inshirah (Caro)   2 54
Front rank, rdn to improve appr fnl 2f, not pace of front 2: tchd 12/1: consistent, likes sell grade.
2719 **CALLING THE SHOTS** 3 [3] W Storey 3-8-3 (52)(vis) Iona Wands 9/2: 000424: Handy, drvn/not   nk 52
qckn appr fnl 1f: see 2719.
3328 **SECRET CONQUEST** 11 [9] 3-9-7 (70) J Fanning 9/4 FAV: -00645: Cl-up, rdn/onepcd over 1f out: 2 66
nicely bckd, top weight: see 1517, 1308.
*3103 **GRANITE CITY** 22 [11] 3-8-5 (54) A Culhane 4/1: 030216: Mid-div, prog halfway, btn appr fnl 1f: 1½ 47
nicely bckd, shade btr 3103 (mdn h'cap, C/D, gd).
3124 **RED MITTENS** 20 [5] 3-7-10 (45)(4oh) J McAuley 14/1: -00667: Rear, late hdwy, no threat: see 1723.   4 31
3194 **HOWARDS LAD** 17 [6] 3-8-10 (59)(vis) V Halliday 14/1: 100208: Handy, wknd qckly over 2f out.   2½ 41
3124 **FANTASY ADVENTURER** 20 [1] 3-8-1 (50) O Pears 10/1: 404009: Nvr a factor: see 2541.   shd 32
2964 **LADY TILLY** 27 [10] 3-7-10 (45)(7oh) K Dalgleish (5) 16/1: 544000: Dwelt, rear, eff halfway, nvr dngrs: 5 19
3366 **CLEAR MOON** 9 [7] 3-7-10 (45)(bl) (7oh) P Fessey 50/1: 5000RR: Refused to race: one to avoid.   0
11 ran   Time 1m 27.9 (3.0)   (Gordon Mytton)   A Bailey Little Budworth, Cheshire

MUSSELBURGH
THURSDAY AUGUST 24TH   Righthand, Sharp Track

3594
5.10 BRYDIE APPR HCAP 3YO+ 0-65 (F)   5f str   Good/Firm 31   -03 Slow   [62]
£2828   £808   £404   3 yo rec 2 lb

3512 **SIHAFI** 4 [11] D Nicholls 7-9-13 (61) Clare Roche (5) 9/2: 324501: 7 ch g Elmaamul - Kit's Double (Spring Double) Settled in tch, gd hdwy over 2f out, styd on to lead ins last, rdn clr: op 3/1, qck reapp: top weight: blnks omitted: earlier won at Lingfield (h'cap): plcd twice in '99 (h'caps, rtd 71): won 9 times in '98, at Lingfield (2), Windsor, Bath, Folkestone, Salisbury, Sandown, Haydock & W'hampton (h'caps, rtd 71 & 81a): stays 6f, best at 5f: acts on both AWs & gd/soft, likes gd & firm: eff weight carrier & prob best without blnks: v tough. **71**

*3312 **JOHAYRO** 12 [3] J S Goldie 7-9-8 (56) Dawn Rankin (5) 4/1 JT FAV: 300012: 7 ch g Clantime - Arroganza (Crofthall) Chsd ldrs, rdn & styd on well ins last, no impress on wnr: well h'capped & likes Musselburgh, see 3312. 2   **58**

3536 **FACILE TIGRE** 2 [6] P Monteith 5-9-1 (49) R Lake (7) 7/1: 300023: 5 gr g Efisio - Dancing Diana (Raga Navarro) Towards rear, ran on well ins last, nvr nrr: ran 48hrs ago: see 3536 (gd/soft). nk   **50**

*3203 **NOBLE PATRIOT** 16 [4] R Hollinshead 5-9-0 (48) Stephanie Hollinshead (5) 4/1 JT FAV: 341114: Mid-div, eff when hung right over 2f out, no extra well ins last: not disgraced on this 4 timer bid, see 3203. nk   **49**

3203 **BOWCLIFFE GRANGE** 16 [8] 8-7-10 (30) Joanna Badger (3) 7/1: 006005: Sn clr ldr, hdd well ins last. ½   **30**

3144 **E B PEARL** 19 [7] 4-8-1 (35) P Hanagan (3) 8/1: 500426: Prom, drvn/not pace of ldrs 1f out: see 3144. nk   **34**

3502 **PISCES LAD** 4 [9] 4-9-5 (53) R Cody Boutcher (3) 10/1: 000207: Rear, late hdwy, no threat, bckd from 16/1, quick reapp: see 3180. ½   **51**

3222 **BRANSTON PICKLE** 15 [10] 3-9-12 (62) (bl) K Dalgleish 12/1: 000008: Speed 3f: prev with T Etherington, now with M Johnston & new connections have rejuvenated horses from this stable prev, keep an eye on. ¾   **58**

3377 **SHALARISE** 8 [5] 3-9-6 (56) (vis) P Goode 14/1: 502009: Dwelt, al rear: see 2864. 1   **49**

3441 **BENNOCHY** 6 [2] 3-9-3 (53) P Bradley 10/1: 045460: Trkd ldrs, wknd qckly fnl 2f, 10th: see 777. 1¼   **43**

3222 **SNAP CRACKER** 15 [1] 4-8-8 (42) Claire Bryan 20/1: 000000: Al well in rear, 11th. 5   **22**

11 ran   Time 59.2 (1.7)   (John Gilbertson)   D Nicholls Sessay, N Yorks

---

YORK
THURSDAY AUGUST 24TH   Lefthand, Flat, Galloping Track

Official Going: GOOD (GOOD/FIRM places). Stalls: Inside, except 5f/6f - Stands side.

3595
2.05 LISTED GALTRES STKS 3YO+ (A)   1m3f195y   Firm 08   -07 Slow
£28486   £8765   £4382   £2191   3 yo rec 10lb

2857 **FIRECREST** 33 [6] J L Dunlop 3-8-9 T Quinn 7/1: 111141: 3 b f Darshaan - Trefoil (Blakeney) Towards rear, imprvd ent str, led bef fnl 2f, rdn clr, styd on strongly: lkd well, tchd 11/2: earlier landed a 4 timer at Leicester (2), Newbury & Salisbury (h'caps): uncrd juv: eff at 12f, shld stay further: acts on firm & gd/soft, stiff trk: can go well fresh: v progressive & tough, has a turn of foot & shld be kept on the right side. **107**

-- **FANTASIA GIRL** [3] J Oxx 3-8-8 J Murtagh 10/3 FAV: 2112: 3 b f Caerleon - Dreamboat (Mr Prospector) Patiently rdn, improved appr fnl 3f, styd on under press inside last to take 2nd, no ch with wnr: warm, well bckd Irish raider, earlier won at Tipperary (mdn) & Curragh: uncrd juv: eff at 10f, stays a gall 12f: acts on firm/fast grnd: wiry, lightly raced, useful & improving. 3½   **101**

3017 **HIDDNAH** 25 [1] M Johnston 3-8-8 J Reid 9/1: 315-23: 3 ch f Affirmed - L'Extra Honor (Hero's Honor) Chsd ldrs, prog to chall appr fnl 2f, kept on same pace: bckd: stays a gall 12f & shapes like further will suit: tough & useful, shld be placed to win more races over 12f+: see 3017. nk   **100**

3151 **NEW ASSEMBLY** 19 [10] Sir Michael Stoute 3-8-8 M J Kinane 10/1: -21164: Held up, prog 4f out, dsptd 3rd 2f out, onepace for press: bckd tho' op 8/1, swtg: stays 12f, return to 10f may suit: see 2190. 1½   **98**

*2509 **METRONOME** 47 [4] J P Spencer 6/1: 02215: Cl up, led appr fnl 3f till bef 2f out, rdn & no extra: well bckd: 7 week abs: stable has a cracking record in this race & not disgraced up in class: see 2509. ½   **97**

-- **REVE RUSSE** [9] 3-8-8 (VIS) R Cochrane 33/1: 032136: Held up, prog going well & hmpd appr fnl 2f, switched & hmpd again bef dist, nvr dngrs: Irish raider, much closer with a clr run: earlier won at D Royal (0-90 h'cap): eff at 9/10f, well worth another try at 12f: acts on firm & gd grnd: tried a visor, eff without. ¾   **96**

3547 **FARFALA** 3 [5] 4-9-4 J Fortune 6/1: 0-5237: Rear, wide prog 3f out, fdd fnl 2f: too sn after 3547? ½   **95**

2112 **CLIPPER** 63 [8] 3-8-8 R Hills 33/1: 1-3008: Chsd ldrs, lost pl halfway: op 20/1, dull coat, 9 wk abs. ½   **94**

3305 **SHAMAIEL** 12 [2] 3-8-8 P Robinson 20/1: 440439: Handy, eff appr fnl 2f, weakening when checked bef dist: sturdy filly could do with a confidence boosting maiden win. 4   **90**

*3177 **MISS LORILAW** 18 [7] 3-9-0 M Hills 12/1: 336010: Chsd ldrs till wknd quickly entering straight: 10th, small, looked well: improvement considerably to win in 3117. 9   **88**

*3034 **HELENS DAY** 24 [11] 4-9-4 K Darley 16/1: -2210: With ldrs till wknd quickly 4f out: 11th, up in grade. ¾   **81**

3370 **CAPE GRACE** 13 [13] 4-9-10 (VIS) R Hughes 20/1: 505240: Led 1m, sn btn: 12th & visored, btr 2975. 5   **82**

2112 **UNSEEDED** 63 [12] 3-8-8 Pat Eddery 14/1: 4-1060: Chsd till after halfway: 13th, stablemate wnr, abs. 15   **64**

13 ran   Time 2m 28.55 (1.75)   (Sir Thomas Pilkington)   J L Dunlop Arundel, W Sussex.

3596
2.35 GR 2 LOWTHER STKS 2YO (A)   6f   Firm 08   -47 Slow
£46400   £17600   £8800   £4000

*2996 **ENTHUSED** 26 [6] Sir Michael Stoute 2-9-0 J Murtagh 9/4: -1211: 2 b f Seeking The Gold - Magic Of Life (Seattle Slew) Stdd start, trkd ldrs appr fnl 2f, short of rm bef dist so switched, rdn & qcknd smartly to lead ins last despite hanging left, readily drew clr: val 3L+, well bckd, slow time: earlier won at Newmarket (mdn) & Ascot (Gr 3): half-sister to 3 mid-dist wnrs: dam high class 1m wnr: v eff at 6f, shld stay at least 1m next term: acts on firm & gd, stiff trks: high-class, has a terrific turn on foot & shld be kept on the right side. **114+**

*2618 **KHULAN** 42 [3] J L Dunlop 2-8-11 R Hills 5/6 FAV: 12: 2 b f Bahri - Jawlaat (Dayjur) Keen, led, rdn & edged left bef dist, kept on but had no answer as wnr swept by fnl 100y: hvly bckd, abs, padd pick: not disgraced having to set pace: acts on firm/fast: considered high-class by connections, cld rate higher. 1½   **105**

2996 **AUTUMNAL** 26 [1] B J Meehan 2-8-11 Pat Eddery 14/1: -31123: 2 b f Indian Ridge - Please Believe Me (Try My Best) Trckd ldrs, hdwy under press & ch appr fnl 1f, kept on: looked well: improved in defeat in this higher grade: useful, would relish a drop to Listed class: see 2996. hd   **104**

2849 **ROMANTIC MYTH** 33 [1] T D Easterby 2-9-0 K Darley 5/1: 11164: Chsd ldrs, hdwy under press 2f out, rdn & edged right bef dist, onepace/short of room towards fin: back to form: stays 6f on firm & soft: see 2849. 1   **104**

3164 **PARTY CHARMER** 19 [7] 2-8-11 P Robinson 66/1: 14065: Held up in tch, not much room when pace qcknd 2f out, switched & no impress on ldrs: stiff task, prob flattered, see 1059. 2½   **94$**

1104

*3500 **AMIS ANGEL** 4 [4] 2-8-11 J P Spencer 66/1: 216: Pulled hard bhd ldrs, outpcd ent fnl 2f: shd **94$**
quick reapp, highly tried: unfurnished filly, up in trip & grade here: see 3500.
3320 **ASH MOON** 12 [5] 2-8-11 N Callan 66/1: -11037: Chsd ldrs till 2f out: looked well but had a stiff task.   ¾ 92
7 ran   Time 1m 12.72 (3.32)   (Niarchos Family)   Sir Michael Stoute Newmarket, Suffolk

---

3597   3.10 B & B RTD HCAP 3YO+ 0-105 (B)   1m rnd   Firm 08 +09 Fast   [112]
£27898 £10582 £5291 £2405   3 yo rec 6 lb

3107 **PEARTREE HOUSE** 21 [3] D Nicholls 6-8-3 (91)(4oh) J Mackay (5) 12/1: 440661: 6 b g Simply Majestic -   94
Fashion Front (Habitat) Led after 1f, made rest at a gd clip, rdn out: gd time, op 10/1: earlier won at Ayr
(class stks): '99 rnr up for W Muir (rtd 94): '98 Lingfield wnr (ltd stks, rtd 94): eff at 7.5f/1m: acts on firm,
gd/soft, any trk: best without visor & back to form under a gd positive ride from the front, usually comes from bhd.
3365 **TONY TIE** 9 [4] J S Goldie 4-8-6 (91)(1oh) A McGlone 14/1: 021222: 4 b g Ardkinglass - Queen Of   2 92
The Quorn (Governor General) Chsd wnr throughout, drvn appr fnl 1f, kept on but al held: v tough, see 2986.
3338 **MAYARO BAY** 11 [5] R Hannon 4-9-2 (100) R Hughes 10/1: 603023: 4 b f Robellino - Down The Valley   1 100
(Kampala) Trkd ldrs, pld hard, rdn appr fnl 1f, unable to qckn: paddock pick, nicely bckd: useful, see 1327.
3107 **JOHN FERNELEY** 21 [2] P F I Cole 5-9-4 (102)(bl) J Fortune 4/1 FAV: -31244: Fought for hd for 4f,   nk 101
well plcd, shkn up 2f out, kept on at the onepace: hvly bckd: another useful run: tough, see 3107.
3147 **DURAID** 19 [9] 8-8-3 (91)(4oh) D Mernagh (3) 25/1: 214165: Mid-div, prog 2f out, styd on for press   nk 85
inside last, nvr nr to chall: ran to best in this v competitive h'cap: see 2648 (C/D).
3315 **FREE OPTION** 12 [6] 5-8-12 (96) J Reid 8/1: 031036: In tch when badly buffeted after 1f, eff 3f out,   1¾ 91
styd on without threatening: nicely bckd, tchd 10/1: gd run in the circumstances: see 2870.
*3325 **ADOBE** 12 [8] 5-8-1 (91)(9oh) K Darley 16/1: 412117: Keen, towards rear, shkn up appr fnl 2f, late   1¾ 76
hdwy, no threat: stocky, lked well, unable to get competitive here: better than this: see 3325 (beat this rnr up).
3107 **CALCUTTA** 21 [7] 4-8-10 (94)(BL) M Hills 12/1: 006308: Mid div, switched & eff 3f out, no impression.   1¼ 83
1382 **PARADISE GARDEN** 96 [12] 3-8-2 (92) R Ffrench 33/1: -03049: Early ldr, fdd 2f out: ndd it after absence. 2 77
3107 **RED N SOCKS** 21 [11] 3-8-4 (94) Pat Eddery 6/1: 200100: Rear, wide, rdn & prog into mid-div over   shd 79
2f out, sn btn: 10th, bckd: better expected after catching the eye in 3107.
+3315 **PREMIER BARON** 12 [16] 5-8-1 (91)(6oh) L Newman (3) 25/1: 444610: Chsd ldrs till wknd 2f out: 11th.   ¾ 69
3018 **RICH IN LOVE** 25 [1] 6-8-1 (91)(7oh) S Sanders 25/1: 310050: Bdly hmpd 1f, al bhd: 12th, ignore.   shd 69
*3414 **AL MUALLIM** 7 [13] 6-8-6 (91)(t)(3ex)(1oh) A Nicholls (3) 12/1: 004010: V slow away, switched,   3½ 68
keen, al bhd: 13th, stablemate wnr, quick reapp, btr 3414 (7f).
+3107 **PERSIANO** 21 [10] 5-9-3 (101) D Harrison 9/2: 132510: Al rear: 14th, bckd, beat sev of these in 3107.   6 69
3338 **STRASBOURG** 11 [15] 3-8-4 (94) J Carroll 33/1: 002200: Dwelt, nvr on terms: 15th btr 2330, 2108.   3½ 56
3107 **PYTHIOS** 21 [14] 4-9-7 (105)(tVl) T Quinn 12/1: -04200: Nvr a factor: 16th, swtg, top-weight, visored.   9 52
16 ran   Time 1m 35.72 (u0.08)   (G Vettraino & Fayzad Throughbreds)   D Nicholls Sessay, N Yorks

---

3598   3.45 GR 1 NUNTHORPE STKS 2YO+ (A)   5f   Firm 08 -15 Slow
£101500 £38500 £19250 £8750   3 yo rec 2 lb

*2065 **NUCLEAR DEBATE** 65 [1] J E Hammond 5-9-9 G Mosse 5/2 FAV: 0-6111: 5 b g Geiger Counter -   123
I'm An Example (Cox's Ridge) Mid-div going well, trckd ldrs 2f out, qcknd to lead dist, readily: hvly bckd French
raider, 9 wk abs: earlier won at Chantilly & R Ascot (Gr 2): '99 wnr at M-Laffitte, Deauville (List) & San Siro
(Gr 3, rtd 113): '98 wnr at Thirsk & Newcastle: eff at 5f, stays 6f: acts on firm & hvy grnd: runs well fresh:
high-class, flying gelding, looks the Champion Sprinter.
2615 **BERTOLINI** 42 [14] Saeed bin Suroor 4-9-9 (vis) L Dettori 13/2: 0-2362: 4 b h Danzig - Aquilegia   1¼ 118
(Alydar) Cl up going well, led 2f out till dist, not pace of wnr (not tchd with whip): lked superb, 6 wk abs:
v smart entire, deserves another Group race: see 766.
2615 **PIPALONG** 42 [10] T D Easterby 4-9-6 K Darley 7/1: 121033: 4 b f Pips Pride - Limpopo (Green   1½ 111
Desert) Bhd ldrs, niggled halfway, styd on for press inside last but no ch with front pair: 6 wk abs & not
disgraced on grnd faster than ideal: apprec a return to 6f & can win a nice prize on easy grnd this autumn.
3059 **WATCHING** 23 [6] R Hannon 3-9-7 R Hughes 20/1: 220144: Mid-div, rdn entering fnl 2f, styd on, nvr   hd 114
dangerous: op 16/1: smart, back to form, shld find a Group race, esp on easier grnd: see 2496.
2065 **PERRYSTON VIEW** 65 [3] 8-9-9 J Reid 33/1: 100105: Led till bef halfway, no extra appr fnl 1f: 1¾ 109
better run tho' appears slightly flattered by 1566 (very weak Gr 2).
3059 **RAMBLING BEAR** 23 [15] 7-9-9 R Cochrane 25/1: 330056: Rear, stands rail, improved appr fnl 1f,   1¼ 105
sn rdn, fdd: not quite up to this company: see 1172.
3059 **RUDIS PET** 23 [12] 6-9-9 (bl) S Sanders 40/2: 6-1037: Front rank, led bef halfway till appr fnl 1f, wknd: nk 104
nicely bckd, lked well, bandaged: better than this, beat this 4th in 3059 (missed break), see 1757.
*3373 **EASTERN PURPLE** 11 [11] 5-9-9 B Marcus 10/1: 056218: Nvr going pace: bckd, looked superb.   hd 104
2847 **HARMONIC WAY** 33 [4] 5-9-9 J Fortune 16/1: 421629: V slow away & detached, went through beaten   1¼ 100
horses inside last: stiffish task tho' unsuited by drop bck to 5f (stays 7f): see 2151 (6f Wokingham h'cap).
3172 **MANORBIER** 18 [13] 4-9-9 F Lynch 33/1: 414050: Bmpd start, al bhd: 10th, lked well, highly tried.   1½ 95
*3303 **BERNSTEIN** 12 [2] 3-9-7 (VIS) M J Kinane 6/1: 15-010: Sn struggling: fin 11th, well bckd: 1¾ 90
more expected tho' was back in trip here & fitted with a visor: btr 3303 (6f).
3059 **ROSSELLI** 23 [8] 4-9-9 J Carroll 50/1: 600260: Chsd ldrs 2f: stiff task: 12th, see 927.   3 81
3059 **EMERALD PEACE** 23 [5] 3-9-4 P Robinson 33/1: 112-00: Bhd from halfway: 13th, stiff task.   1¾ 73
13 ran   Time 57.83 (1.13)   (J R Chester)   J E Hammond France

---

3599   4.15 C HEIDSIECK RTD HCAP STKS 3YO 0-100 (B)   1m5f194y Firm 08 +02 Fast   [105]
£20558 £7797 £3898 £1772

3058 **RIDDLESDOWN** 23 [17] S P C Woods 3-9-7 (98) R Hughes 40/1: 221001: 3 ch c Common Grounds -   107
Neat Dish (Stalwart) Waited with, gd wide prog 3f out to lead 2f out, sn rdn & edged left, hdd fnl 100y: fin 2nd,
plcd 1st, defied top-weight & difficult high draw, lked well: earlier won at Haydock (ltd h'cap): '99 wnr at Bath
(mdn auct, rtd 94): eff at 12f/14f, tried 2m: acts on firm, soft grnd, gall or turning track: can go well fresh &
force the pace, improved from bhd here: gd weight carrier & has developed into a useful stayer.
3088 **ROMANTIC AFFAIR** 22 [11] J L Dunlop 3-9-0 (91) Pat Eddery 5/1: 021142: 3 ch g Persian Bold -   ½ 99
Broken Romance (Ela Mana Mou) Patiently rdn, squeezed thro' to chse ldrs 3f out, rdn & briefly not clr run bef
fnl 1f, kept on but was held by front 2: fin 3rd, plcd 2nd, hvly bckd, swtg: gets a gall 14f, acts on firm & soft.
-3402 **MANA DARGENT** 8 [7] M Johnston 3-8-4 (81) M Hills 4/1 FAV: 031323: 3 b c Ela Mana Mou - Petite   1¼ 88
D'Argent (Noalto) In tch, going well but not much room appr fnl 3f, clr & hdwy 2f out, rdn dist, kept on till
no extra nr fin: fin 4th, plcd 3rd, hvly bckd: lked well: stays 14f, likely to apprec return to 12f.

YORK THURSDAY AUGUST 24TH Lefthand, Flat, Galloping Track

3360 **ALRISHA 10** [3] D R C Elsworth 3-8-4 (81)(1oh) J Mackay (5) 12/1: 02124: Off the pace, last ent str, hdwy 3f out, hmpd & switched 2f out, kept on for press, nvr nr to chall: fin 5th, plcd 4th, bckd: gd run, clr of rem: acts on firm & gd grnd, win again when rdn closer to the pace: see 3023 (mdn). 2 86$

*2852 **DUCHAMP 33** [16] 3-8-11 (88) K Darley 8/1: 540215: Waited with, pushed along 3f out, mid-div 2f out, no further impress on ldrs: fin 6th, plcd 5th, bckd, looked superb: see 2852, 6 88

*3153 **FANFARE 19** [10] 3-8-8 (85) J P Spencer 12/1: 102416: Slow away, bhd, eff & not much room appr fnl 3f, moderate late hdwy: lkd well: btr 3153. ¾ 84

3088 **IL CAPITANO 22** [13] 3-8-12 (89)(BL) R Cochrane 40/1: 2-0507: Keen, chsd ldrs, eff & btn 2f out, eased inside last: tried blnks: trying sev trips: see 2068 (2m), 1216. nk 88

3426 **KAIAPOI 6** [4] 3-8-4 (81)(2oh) P M Quinn (3) 25/1: U35028: Held up, not much room entering fnl 3f, no ch with ldrs & not given a hard time: quick reapp: bck up in trip, worth another ch, see 1225. 1¾ 79

*3142 **WHITE HOUSE 20** [1] 3-8-4 (81)(2oh) S Sanders 20/1: -44319: In tch, prog to chse ldrs 3f out, sn no extra: not quite get home?: see 3142 (10f, class stakes). 1¾ 78

*3467 **MICKLEY 5** [15] 3-8-4 (81)(3ex)(2oh) D Harrison 20/1: 363110: Early ldr, feeling the pinch when hmpd appr fnl 3f: 10th, qck reapp: up in trip: best dominating in lesser class: see 3467 (5 days ago). 8 72

3153 **COVER UP 19** [5] 3-9-1 (92)(VIS) J Murtagh 7/1: 2-1030: Chsd ldrs, wknd appr fnl 2f: 11th, hvly bckd, visor. ¾ 82

+3270 **PRINCIPLE 14** [12] 3-8-7 (84) G Duffield 10/1: 431410: Led/dsptd lead till ent straight, lost pl: 12th: longer trip: btr 3270. 2½ 72

3058 **GIVE NOTICE 23** [6] 3-8-9 (86) T Quinn 14/1: 611100: Nvr troubled ldrs: 13th, off the boil since 2584. 19 60

3270 **FRANGY 14** [14] 3-8-4 (81)(4oh) B Marcus 16/1: -31150: Keen, dsptd lead till appr fnl 4f, btn/hmpd: 14th. 1¾ 54

1400 **POMPEII 96** [8] 3-8-6 (83) J Fortune 33/1: -21160: Mid div till 4f out: 15th, 14 week abs, see 1064. 1 55

*2936 **TAKWIN 28** [9] 3-9-4 (95)(t) R Hills 12/1: 322110: Chsd ldrs till appr fnl 3f, eased: 16th, btr 2936. 1½ 67

3058 **JARDINES LOOKOUT 23** [2] 3-9-1 (92) M J Kinane 10/1: 62121D: Mid-div, prog & switched appr fnl 3f, drvn to chall bef dist, edged right, got on top towards fin: fin 1st, harshly disq & plcd last: jockey dealt a 6 day ban for irresp riding, nicely bckd: clearly the wnr on merit: acts on firm & gd/soft grnd: scopey & useful. 102

17 ran Time 2m 54.21 (0.81) (The Storm Again Syndicate) S P C Woods Newmarket, Suffolk

3600

4.45 LISTED CITY OF YORK STKS 3YO+ (A) 7f rnd Firm 08 -05 Slow
£22717 £6990 £3495 £1747 3 yo rec 5 lb

3291 **LATE NIGHT OUT 13** [7] W Jarvis 5-9-0 M Tebbutt 14/1: 4-0121: 5 b g Lahib - Chain Dance (Shareef Dancer) In tch, rdn appr fnl 1f, kept on gamely to lead well inside last: earlier won at Chester (stks): '99 wnr at Haydock (List h'cap, rtd 106): '98 Redcar wnr (stks rtd 100): eff at 6f, stays 1m, best at 7f: acts on firm & soft grnd, any track: runs well fresh: smart, progressive & career best effort today. 110

*2443 **MAHFOOTH 49** [8] Saeed bin Suroor 3-8-9 R Hills 4/1: 3-0212: 3 ch c Diesis - I Certainly Am (Affirmed) Well plcd, prog to lead 1f out, sn rdn, hdd fnl 30y: well bckd, lkd well after 7 wk abs: improving v useful & lightly raced: acts on firm & soft grnd: see 2443 (mdn). ¾ 108

-3315 **HO LENG 12** [9] Miss L A Perratt 5-9-0 M J Kinane 3/1 FAV: 303023: 5 ch g Statoblest - Indigo Blue (Bluebird) Held up, prog appr fnl 1f, rdn dist, ch inside last, hung left, held: looked well, nicely bckd: not disgraced in this higher grade: v useful: see 1182. nk 107

3104 **LAST RESORT 21** [1] B W Hills 3-8-4 M Hills 12/1: 413634: Towards rear, prog ent fnl 2f, ch ins last, no extra towards fin: another sound run: acts on firm & gd/soft grnd: see 1224. ¾ 100

2578 **MEADAAAR 43** [4] 3-8-9 W Supple 16/1: 13-025: Cl up, led after 3f till 1f out, one pace: looked well & scopey, 6 week abs: useful: see 2578, 1693. ¾ 103

3503 **JEMIMA 4** [2] 3-8-4 (bl) G Duffield 13/2: 006036: Rear, rdn & switched appr fnl 1f, kept on but nvr threatened: hvly bckd from 12/1, qk reapp: less than inspired ride: see 3503, 953. 1¾ 94

+3152 **TAYSEER 19** [5] 6-9-0 R Hughes 4/1: 031317: Waited with, mod late hdwy, nvr on terms: well bckd: up in grade & trip: btr 3152 (Stewards Cup). hd 99

3303 **VITA SPERICOLATA 12** [6] 3-8-4 Pat Eddery 8/1: 240338: Keen, rear, pushed along appr fnl 2f, nvr a factor: bckd: rcd too keenly over longer 7f trip: btr 3303 (6f). ½ 93

3235 **TOMBA 15** [11] 6-9-0 (bl) P Robinson 14/1: -20359: Chsd ldrs till 2f out: grnd totally against him. 2½ 93

3543 **KAYO 2** [10] 5-9-0 K Darley 16/1: 220350: Handy till 2f out: 10th, op 12/1, sweating, been busy. 4 85

*3172 **YORKIES BOY 18** [12] 5-9-5 J Carroll 20/1: 416010: Led for 3f: 11th, best at 6f. 2½ 85

11 ran Time 1m 22.24 (0.94) (J M Greetham) W Jarvis Newmarket, Suffolk

NEWCASTLE FRIDAY AUGUST 25TH Lefthand, Galloping, Stiff Track

Official Going GOOD/FIRM. Stalls: Str Course - Stands Side, Round Course - Inside

3601

5.35 TYNE BRIDGE NOV AUCT STKS 2YO (F) 1m str Firm 15 -03 Slow
£2212 £632 £316

*2841 **SPECIFIC SORCEROR 34** [2] A P Jarvis 2-9-4 K Darley 1/1: 511: 2 ch c Definite Article - Mystic Dispute (Magical Strike) Handy, drvn to lead ins last, styd on well: nicely bckd: earlier scored at Warwick (auct mdn): eff at 7f/1m, will get further: acts on firm & fast grnd, sharp or stiff/gall trk: progressive. 93

3411 **PATHAN 8** [3] S P C Woods 2-8-9 J Carroll 10/11 FAV: 514232: 2 b c Pyramus - Langton Herring (Nearly A Hand) Led, increased tempo halfway, hdd ins last & no extra: clr of rem, stays 1m: see 3299. 1¼ 81

-- **TIYOUN** [1] D W Barker 2-8-9 F Lynch 16/1: 3: 2 b g Kahyasi - Taysala (Akarad) 6 70
Held up, outpcd fnl 3f: Mar foal, cost IR£9,000: dam unrcd: sire top-class performer at 12f: will apprec mid-dists.

-- **FFIFFIFFER** [4] A Dickman 2-8-9 T Lucas 20/1: 4: Keen/held up rear, outpcd fnl 3f: Definite Article colt, Mar foal, cost 7,000 gns: half brother to a juv 1m Irish wnr: dam a mdn. ¾ 69

4 ran Time 1m 38.40 (1.4) (The Aston Partnership) A P Jarvis Aston Upthorpe, Oxon

3602

6.05 WEATHERBYS NOV STKS 2YO (D) 5f Firm 15 -12 Slow
£3386 £1042 £521 £260

3408 **NIGHT HAVEN 8** [4] M L W Bell 2-8-7 M Fenton 15/8: 221: 2 gr f Night Shift - Noble Haven (Indian King) Chsd ldrs, rdn/led over 1f out, styd on strongly, rdn out: nicely bckd: eff at 5f, tried 6f, will suit: acts on firm & fast grnd: likes a stiff/gall trk: clearly going the right way. 76

3439 **WILSON BLYTH 7** [3] A Berry 2-9-0 J Carroll 8/1: 214342: 2 b c Puissance - Pearls (Mon Tresor) Trkd ldrs, led/hung left over 1f out, sn hdd & held ins last: acts on firm & gd/soft grnd: eff at 5/6f: see 2237 (6f). 2 76

3165 **OUR DESTINY 20** [1] A P Jarvis 2-9-2 K Darley 13/8 FAV: -01363: 2 b c Mujadil - Superspring (Superlative) Chsd ldrs, rdn/ch 2f out, held ins last & eased nr fin: btr 2808, 2454 (6f). *4* **68**
*3098 **NORDIC SABRE 23** [2] Mrs L Stubbs 2-8-11 C Lowther 3/1: 614: Led, hung left, hdd over 2f out & sn btn: twice disapp on firm grnd: btr 3098 (gd). *7* **48**
4 ran Time 59.56 (1.36) (B H Farr) M L W Bell Newmarket

3603 **6.35 S EASTEN HCAP 3YO+ 0-70 (E) 1m1f rnd Firm 15 +04 Fast [70]**
£2989 £854 £427 3 yo rec 7 lb

3141 **KESTRAL 21** [5] T J Etherington 4-8-0 (42) R Ffrench 6/1 JT FAV: 062321: 4 ch g Ardkinglass - Shiny Kay (Star Appeal) Held up, prog to lead dist, rdn clr ins last: best time of night, 1st win: unplcd in '99 (rtd 55, h'cap): rtd 62 in '98 (unplcd): suited by 1m/9f: acts on firm & gd grnd: best without a t-strap. **49**
3366 **AMBUSHED 10** [14] P Monteith 4-7-10 (38)(2oh) J McAuley 15/2: 001052: 4 b g Indian Ridge - Surprise Move (Simply Great) Led, rdn/hdd over 1f out, kept on tho' sn held by wnr: acts on fibresand & firm grnd: eff at 1m/9f: see 3366, 585 (AW mdn h'cap). *4* **36**
3330 **ROUTE SIXTY SIX 12** [4] Jedd O'Keeffe 4-9-0 (56) O Pears 8/1: -00023: 4 b f Brief Truce - Lyphards Goddess (Lyphards Special) Chsd ldrs, rdn & kept on onepace from over 1f out: see 3330, 3011. *¾* **53**
3141 **LINCOLN DEAN 21** [7] J S Goldie 4-8-1 (43) Kimberley Hart 12/1: 003204: Chsd ldrs, held over 1f out. *¾* **39**
4574} **GREENAWAY BAY 298** [6] 6-9-2 (58) D Harrison 6/1 JT FAV: 6463-5: Trkd ldrs, onepace fnl 2f: reapp: '99 Brighton scorer (h'cap, rtd 59): plcd sev times in '98 for W J Musson (rtd 62 & 59a): suited by 1m/10f on firm & soft, any trk: has run well fresh: could prove sharper for this & can find similar. *2½* **49**
2994 **LOVE KISS 27** [3] 5-8-5 (47) T Williams 33/1: 002006: Prom 6f: see 2542, 2063 & 1583. *¾* **37**
3379 **IMPULSIVE AIR 9** [16] 8-8-3 (45)(1ow) R Winston 12/1: 004307: Mid-div, held 2f out: see 3368, 569. *¾* **34**
3407 **OLLIES CHUCKLE 8** [1] 5-7-11 (39)(6oh)(1ow) Dale Gibson 12/1: 606038: In tch, held 2f out: see 908. *½* **27**
2758 **WOORE LASS 37** [2] 4-8-5 (47) Kim Tinkler 12/1: 002459: Mid-div, btn 2f out: see 1658. *½* **34**
3368 **KONKER 10** [15] 5-9-1 (57) A Culhane 20/1: /06-00: Rear, mod prog: 10th: see 3368 (10f). *½* **43**
2453 **A DAY ON THE DUB 49** [9] 7-8-5 (47) M Fenton 16/1: 140050: Dwelt, al towards rear: 11th: 7 wk abs. *1½* **30**
2242 **EL SALIDA 58** [12] 4-9-9 (65) T Lucas 8/1: 4-0000: In tch, btn 2f out: 12th: 8 wk abs: see 73. *hd* **47**
3330 **THATCHED 12** [13] 10-8-2 (44) P Fessey 7/1: 630240: Rear, nvr factor: 13th: see 3200, 1254. *¾* **25**
3362 **PROUD CHIEF 11** [8] 3-9-6 (69)(vis) K Darley 10/1: 000000: Chsd ldrs, btn 2f out: 16th: see 1826, 792. **0**
4590} **Turtle 296** [17] 4-8-4 (46)(1ow) J Fanning 50/1: 3314 **Swinging The Blues 13** [18] 6-8-13 (55)(BL) J Carroll 14/1:
3534 **Cyran Park 3** [11] 4-7-10 (38) Iona Wands 33/1: 3440 **Poliziano 7** [10] 4-9-12 (68) F Lynch 33/1:
18 ran Time 1m 53.05 (0.95) (The R And R Partnership) T J Etherington Norton, N Yorks.

3604 **7.05 S. JOSEPH MDN 3YO+ (D) 7f str Firm 15 -02 Slow**
£3662 £1127 £563 £281 3 yo rec 5 lb

784 **SLOANE 149** [7] M L W Bell 4-9-5 M Fenton 6/4 FAV: 620-21: 4 ch c Machiavellian - Gussy Marlowe (Final Straw) Made all, rdn/styd on well fnl 2f: 5 month abs: '99 rnr-up for G Wragg (rtd 80, mdn): eff at 7f/1m, shld stay 10f: acts on firm & gd grnd, stiff/gall trks: runs well fresh & can force the pace. **70**
3330 **ROYAL REPRIMAND 12** [6] R E Barr 5-9-5 P Goode (3) 40/1: 052432: 5 b g Reprimand - Lake Ormond (King's Lake) Held up, prog/chsd wnr over 1f out, kept on tho' al held: offic rtd 45, treat rating with caution. *2* **65$**
3456 **DIANEME 7** [4] T D Easterby 3-8-9 J Carroll 7/1: 500203: 3 b f Primo Dominie - Aunt Jemima (Busted) Prom, ev ch over 2f out, sn outpcd: see 3146, 826. *5* **50**
4171} **BENOUI SPRINGS 330** [3] J H M Gosden 3-9-0 K Darley 5/2: 0-4: Chsd ldrs, held fnl 2f: reapp: unplcd on sole start for P W Chapple-Hyam in '99 (mdn, rtd 76): bred to apprec mid-dists this term. *1¼* **52**
3506 **GLENHURICH 5** [1] 3-8-9 J Fanning 5/1: 45: Prom, ch 3f out, sn held: qck reapp: btr 3506 (1m). *½* **46**
3326 **WHAT A DANCER 12** [2] 3-9-0 F Lynch 14/1: -026: Keen/held up, btn 2f out: btr 3326 (9f). *9* **35**
6 ran Time 1m 25.0 (0.9) (Mrs John Van Geest) M L W Bell Newmarket

3605 **7.35 GREAT NORTH ROAD HCAP 3YO+ 0-65 (F) 6f Firm 15 -07 Slow [63]**
£2548 £728 £364 3 yo rec 3 lb Raced both sides of track, no advantage

3312 **EASTERN PROPHETS 13** [20] M Dods 7-9-0 (49)(vis) M Fenton 11/1: 004401: 7 b g Emarati - Four Love (Pas de Seul) Al prom, styd on well for press to lead well ins last: visor reapplied: '99 Nottingham wnr (appr h'cap, rtd 66, 1st time visor), plcd numerous times subs: '98 Doncaster wnr (clmr, rtd 69 & 71a, G Lewis): likes to race with/force the pace over 5/6f on firm, gd/soft & on both AWs: best in blnks/visor: well h'capped. **54**
3330 **LADY LOVE 12** [3] Denys Smith 3-9-6 (58) R Winston 33/1: 502002: 3 b f Pursuit Of Love - Lady Day (Lightning) Prom far side, led over 1f out, hdd ins last, kept on well: acts on firm & gd/soft: see 1579. *¾* **60**
3440 **PRIX STAR 7** [9] C W Fairhurst 5-9-5 (54)(vis) J Fanning 7/1: 005223: 5 ch g Superpower - Celestine (Skyliner) Chsd ldrs, styd on for press ins last: consistent: see 82 (AW). *½* **54**
3440 **RAFTERS MUSIC 7** [19] D Nicholls 5-9-7 (56) Alex Greaves 9/2 FAV: 331304: Chsd ldrs, rdn/led over 1f out, hdd ins last & no extra: well bckd: see 1519. *nk* **55**
3502 **SQUARE DANCER 5** [16] 4-9-11 (60) K Darley 5/1: 026055: Chsd ldrs, kept on, not pace to chall. *nk* **58**
3144 **BALLINA LAD 20** [7] 4-8-8 (43) P Goode (3) 25/1: -00506: Led/dsptd lead till over 1f out: see 2118. *½* **39**
3312 **TANCRED ARMS 13** [11] 4-8-13 (48) F Lynch 12/1: 302037: Chsd ldrs, onepace fnl 2f: see 3312, 698. *1* **42**
3312 **WISHBONE ALLEY 13** [18] 5-8-10 (45) Dale Gibson 12/1: 030508: Chsd ldrs, held 1f out: see 312 (AW). *shd* **39**
3203 **AMERICAN COUSIN 17** [6] 5-8-12 (47) T Hamilton (7) 10/1: 000059: Chsd ldrs 4f: see 1278. *hd* **40**
3536 **BIFF EM 3** [8] 6-8-5 (40) R Ffrench 33/1: 426000: Led/dsptd lead till over 1f out, sn held: qck reapp. *¾* **31**
3377 **DOUBLE ACTION 9** [12] 6-10-0 (63)(bl) J Carroll 16/1: 660600: Mid-div, nvr threat: 11th: topweight. *nk* **53**
3572 **MALADERIE 2** [15] 6-8-13 (48) T Williams 8/1: 000040: Prom, 4f: 12th: quick reapp: btr 3572 (5f). *¾* **36**
3222 **GRAND ESTATE 16** [10] 5-9-8 (57) A Culhane 11/1: 503400: Dwelt, nvr on terms: 13th: see 2396. *¾* **43**
3269 **Cryfield 15** [5] 3-9-11 (63) D Harrison 16/1: 3144 **Souperficial 20** [13] 9-8-11 (46) Kim Tinkler 20/1:
2559 **Green Ginger 45** [1] 4-9-11 (60)(vis) Jonjo Fowle (5) 33/1: 3312 **Crystal Lass 13** [17] 4-8-5 (40) O Pears 12/1:
3455 **Toblersong 7** [4] 5-8-7 (42)(vis) C Lowther 14/1: 892} **Knotty Hill 497** [2] 8-9-1 (50) C Teague 50/1:
3493 **L A Touch 6** [14] 7-9-0 (49) P Hanagan (7) 20/1:
20 ran Time 1m 12.35 (1.05) (Graham & Barbara Spencer) M Dods Piercebridge, Co Durham

NEWCASTLE FRIDAY AUGUST 25TH Lefthand, Galloping, Stiff Track

3606

8.05 ANGEL HCAP 3YO 0-75 (E)   1m4f93y   Firm 11 -20 Slow   [79]
£2870   £820   £410

3167 **CHAKA ZULU** 20 [4] W J Haggas 3-9-0 (65) K Darley 2/5 FAV: 131131: 3 b g Muhtarram - African Dance   69
(El Gran Senor) Trkd ldrs, went on over 2f out, styd on well for press ins last: hvly bckd at odds-on: prog this
term, earlier won h'caps at Bath (reapp), Catterick & Newcastle (C/D): mod in '99 (rtd 38): eff at 10f, suited by
12f, shld get further: acts on firm, gd & a sharp/turning or stiff/gall trk, likes Newcastle: progressive gelding.
3310 **NORTHERN ECHO** 13 [2] M Dods 3-8-1 (52) T Williams 11/1: 320062: 3 b g Pursuit Of Love - Stop Press 1 53
(Sharpen Up) Chsd ldrs, rdn fnl 3f, styd on ins last, not pace to chall: styd this longer 12f trip: see 2731 (clmr).
3329 **ADAMAS** 12 [5] Andrew Turnell 3-9-7 (72) A Culhane 5/1: 410043: 3 b f Fairy King - Corynida ¾ 72
(Alleged) Trkd ldr, rdn/ch 2f out, onepace/held ins last: topweight: stays 12f: see 2222 (1m, mdn).
3270 **CLEAR PROSPECT** 15 [3] M A Buckley 3-9-1 (66) F Lynch 16/1: -00404: Held up, rdn/outpcd fnl 2f. 2 63
3043 **FAHAN** 25 [1] 3-8-8 (59)(BL) J Carroll 7/1: 0-0555: Led, rdn/hdd over 2f out, sn held & eased ins 24 31
last: 1st time blnks: longer 12f trip, not certain to stay on breeding: see 1812.
5 ran   Time 2m 41.7 (3.8)   (J D Ashenheim)   W J Haggas Newmarket

NEWMARKET (JULY) FRIDAY AUGUST 25TH Righthand, Stiff, Galloping Track

Official Going   GOOD/FIRM. Stalls: Stands Side.

3607

2.00 BLUE PETER FILLIES MDN 2YO (D)   7f str   Good 43 -23 Slow
£4875   £1500   £750   £375

-- **KARASTA** [6] Sir Michael Stoute 2-8-11 T Quinn 10/11 FAV: 1: 2 b f Lake Coniston - Karliyka   100+
(Last Tycoon) Slow away, waited with in touch, hdwy over 2f out to lead over 1f out, qcknd clr, v cmftbly: slow
run race, hvly bckd, debut: Jan foal: half sister to a 9f wnr, dam also scored at that trip: stys 7f well,
1m will suit: runs well fresh on gd: looks v useful & sure to win races in better company, keep on your side.
-- **TIME AWAY** [1] J L Dunlop 2-8-11 M Roberts 16/1: 2: 2 b f Darshaan - Not Before Time 3 91+
(Polish Precedent) In tch, rdn 2f out, styd on nicely appr fnl 1f, hands & heels: debut: Feb foal, half
sister to a couple of mid dist wnrs: eff at 7f, mid dist will suit next term: looks potentially useful,
will rate more highly, especially over further & looks to have a promising long term future.
2618 **ECSTATIC** 43 [9] R Hannon 2-8-11 R Hughes 5/2: -243: 2 ch f Nashwan - Divine Quest (Kris) 2 87
Led 5f out till over 1f out, not pace of front 2: bckd, abs: stys 7f & shown enough to win an ordinary mdn.
-- **LADY ANGOLA** [12] J L Dunlop 2-8-11 M Hills 33/1: 4: V slow away, sn in tch, eff over 1f out, 1¼ 85
onepace: debut: Feb foal, half sister to a 1m scorer: apprec 1m in time: stablemate of rnr up: shld improve.
-- **BARANOVA** [7] 2-8-11 J Fortune 16/1: 5: Bhd, kept on late, no danger: debut: Feb first foal: nk 84+
bred to come into her own over mid dists next term & this was a pleasing start.
-- **SILLY GOOSE** [2] 2-8-11 Pat Eddery 13/2: 6: Led 2f, bhd over 1f out, debut: Feb foal, cost 2 82
340,000IR gns: half sister to a 7f scorer: bred to apprec 1m+ in time: stablemate of rnr up & 4th.
2952 **CLOUDY** 28 [10] 2-8-11 J Reid 33/1: 567: In tch, wknd 2f out: see 2598. 2 78
-- **HALCYON DAZE** [3] 2-8-11 J P Spencer 14/1: 8: Slow away, al bhd on debut: May foal: half hd 77
sister to useful stayer Ashgar: dam 10f scorer: bred to relish 10f+ next term & will do better in time.
3121 **MAY PRINCESS** 21 [4] 2-8-11 R Cochrane 50/1: 09: Keen, bhd, eff 2f out, wknd well over 1f out. 1 75
-- **WHALAH** [8] 2-8-11 P Robinson 25/1: 0: Prom, wknd 2f out: debut: fin 10th: Feb foal, 2 71
cost $200,000: bred to apprec 1m in time: with C Brittain.
1059 **DEGREE OF POWER** 116 [5] 2-8-11 D McGaffin (5) 50/1: 40: Al bhd: 11th, now with Miss D McHale. 5 61§
-- **PLAYONETOONEDOTCOM** [11] 2-8-11 M Mullen 50/1: 0: With ldrs, wknd over 2f out on debut: 12th. 15 31
12 ran   Time 1m 28.5 (4.6)   (H H Aga Khan)   Sir Michael Stoute Newmarket, Suffolk

3608

2.30 GIRTON MDN 2YO (D)   7f str   Good 43 -40 Slow
£4862   £1496   £748   £374 Slow run race

-- **FAIR QUESTION** [1] J L Dunlop 2-8-11 J Reid 14/1: 1: 2 b c Rainbow Quest - Fair Of The Furze 88+
(Ela Mana Mou) Waited wth, hdwy & short of room dist, switched right & styd on well ins last to lead cl home,
going away: debut, slow run race: April foal, cost 45,000gns: half brother to top class mid dist scorer White
Muzzle: dam high class 10f scorer: stys a stiff 7f, will do better over mid dists next term: acts on gd grnd
& runs well fresh: potentially smart, will come on plenty for this & win in better company.
-- **NATION** [8] Sir Michael Stoute 2-8-11 R Hills 20/1: 2: 2 b c Miesque's Son - Erica's Fault hd 85
(Muttering) Cl up, eff & rdn 2f out, switched left & styd on to lead ins last, collared cl home, just btn
on debut: Apr foal, cost 50,000gns: eff over a stiff 7f, 1m will suit in time: useful debut, should win races.
-- **IRISH STREAM** [3] R Charlton 2-8-11 R Hughes 3/1: 3: 2 ch c Irish River - Euphonic (The Minstrel) ½ 84+
Hld up, eff to chall dist, kept on ins last, not btn far on debut: well bckd: Feb foal: dam smart over 7f/1m:
bred to apprec 7f/1m: should learn plenty from this & win a mdn sn.
-- **PRINCES THEATRE** [4] I A Balding 2-8-11 R Cochrane 20/1: 4: Slow away, waited with, hdwy 2f out, ½ 83
styd on to chall inside last, not btn far on debut: op 12/1: Apr foal, cost 16,000gns: dam unrcd: stays 7f on
gd grnd: should come on from this & would certainly win a mdn on a minor track.
-- **ADIOS** [2] 2-8-11 T Quinn 1/1 FAV: 5: Handy, hdwy to lead 2f out till inside last, no extra: hvly ½ 82
bckd on debut, clr rem: April foal: full brother to a useful 1m juv wnr: dam mid dist/staying wnr: bred to
need 1m+ in time & can win one of these.
-- **TOMMY LORNE** [2] 2-8-11 M Roberts 20/1: 6: Prom, outpcd over 2f out, late gains: debut: Apr 4 74
foal, cost 8,500gns: dam 7f scorer: bred to apprec 7f: stablemate of wnr & a step up to 1m shld suit.
2956 **WOODFIELD** 28 [9] 2-8-11 B Marcus 8/1: 037: Led 5f, wknd over 1f out: btr 2956. 1½ 71
3047 **PARTY PLOY** 25 [6] 2-8-11 N Callan 33/1: 08: Keen, prom till wknd 2f out: see 3047. ½ 70
-- **DRESS REHEARSAL** [5] 2-8-11 Pat Eddery 15/2: 9: Keen, cl up, wknd over 1f out on debut: op 4/1: ½ 69
Feb foal: full brother to a 10f wnr: dam useful 7f juv scorer: bred to apprec 1m in time: with Sir M Stoute.
-- **CONQUERING LOVE** [11] 2-8-11 M Mullen 33/1: 0: Slow away, hld up, brief eff over 2f out, sn btn: 2 65
10th: Apr foal, cost 80,000gns: half brother to sprint wnrs: dam 1m scorer: bred to apprec 1m in time.
10 ran   Time 1m 29.74 (5.84)   (Tessona Racing Limited)   J L Dunlop Arundel, W Sussex

3609 **3.00 SAXHAM NURSERY HCAP 2YO (C) 1m str Good 43 -25 Slow [92]**
£6240 £1920 £960 £480

3411 **SIENA STAR 8** [2] J L Eyre 2-8-9 (73) J P Spencer 7/2: 443221: 2 b g Brief Truce - Gooseberry Pie (Green Desert) Hung right start, held up, hdwy over 1f out to lead & hung right ins last, styd on, drvn out: deserved win: Mar first foal: suited by step up to 1m & acts on fast, gd & any track: in fine heart. **78**
3304 **NORTHFIELDS DANCER 13** [7] R Hannon 2-9-7 (85) R Hughes 9/2: -02202: 2 ch c Dr Devious - Heartland (Northfields) Held up, hdwy & short of room appr fnl 1f, swithched left & kept on ins last: shade unlucky under top-weight: stays 1m on firm & gd: should win a race with a more positive ride, poss over further: see 2921. *½* **89**
3149 **DENNIS EL MENACE 20** [6] W R Muir 2-8-13 (77)(BL) Pat Eddery 6/1: 643203: 2 b c College Chapel - Spanish Craft (Jareer) Prom, styd on to lead over 1f out till inside last, no extra: back to form in first time blinks over this stiff 1m: shown enough to win a race: see 2962, 2468. *¾* **79**
3175 **COUNTRYWIDE PRIDE 19** [1] K R Burke 2-8-5 (69) N Callan 25/1: -04304: Keen, handy, eff to chall over 1f out, sn onepace: clr rem: better run over this stiff 1m & handles fast & gd: see 2841. *½* **70**
3187 **ESPANA 18** [3] 2-8-5 (69) M Hills 9/1: 0305: Hmpd start, bhd, brief eff 2f out, sn wknd: longer trip. *5* **61**
3327 **SNOWEY MOUNTAIN 12** [5] 2-8-13 (77) J Fortune 100/30 FAV: -64436: Cl up, led over 2f out till over 1f out, wknd: poss not stay this longer trip: btr 3327 (6f). *1¾* **65**
3409 **TRUMPINGTON 8** [10] 2-8-11 (75) A Nicholls (3) 20/1: 031047: Led over 5f, wknd & hmpd over 1f out. *1* **61**
3057 **INVESTMENT FORCE 24** [8] 2-9-0 (78) R Hills 10/1: 00528: In tch, eff to chall over 2f out, sn wknd. *1½* **61**
3292 **ST FLORENT 14** [4] 2-8-6 (70)(VIS) R Havlin 12/1: -2009: Hmpd start, nvr a factor: tried a visor. *¾* **51**
2698 **FIENNES 41** [9] 2-8-5 (69) R Mullen 20/1: 506360: In tch, wknd 2f out: see 1480. *1½* **47**
10 ran Time 1m 42.67 (5.47) (R Peel, J H A Hopkinson, J M H Binney) J L Eyre Sutton Bank, N Yorks

3610 **3.30 LISTED HOPEFUL STKS 3YO+ (A) 6f str Good 43 +10 Fast**
£13398 £5082 £2541 £1155 3 yo rec 3 lb

*3235 **VISION OF NIGHT 16** [4] J L Dunlop 4-9-0 Pat Eddery 11/4: 0-3011: 4 b c Night Shift - Dreamawhile (Known Fact) Cl up, led over 1f out, drvn out: fast time, bckd: earlier won at Yarmouth (stks): plcd in the US earlier: '99 wnr at Newbury (stakes) & Deauville (Gr 3, rd 115): juv scorer at Ripon & Doncaster (stks): all wins at 6f on firm, soft & any track: runs well fresh: smart & tough, shld continue to give a gd account. **115**
3303 **LITTLEFEATHER 13** [1] Sir Mark Prescott 3-8-6 Dean McKeown 10/1: 5-5102: 3 b f Indian Ridge - Marwell (Habitat) Slow away, held up, hdwy & short of room over 1f out, styd on well ins last: smart sprinter who would have gone closer with a clr run: won for stable jockey G Duffield in 3210. *1½* **105**
3600 **HO LENG 1** [6] Miss L A Perratt 5-9-0 R Cochrane 6/1: 030233: 5 ch g Statoblest - Indigo Blue (Bluebird) Hld up, short of room over 1f out, styd on well ins last, nrst fin: nicely bckd: v tough & useful, plcd at York yesterday: best held up, but set too much to do here: see 3600. *½* **109**
*3158 **FATH 20** [9] Saeed bin Suroor 3-8-11 (t) R Hills 7/4 FAV: 2-0614: Set pace till over 1f out, no extra: hvly bckd: better expected after dominating a less classy field in 3158. *hd* **108**
3373 **CRETAN GIFT 12** [3] 9-9-4 (vis) J Tate 14/1: 234455: Handy, onepace over 1f out: clr of rem. *1* **109**
2425} **ROSEUM 419** [5] 4-8-9 M Roberts 33/1: 1101-6: Waited with, rdn & btn over 1f out: reapp: won 3 of 4 '99 starts, at Pontefract (fill mdn, reapp), Newbury & Haydock (h'caps, rtd 94): suited by 6f on gd/soft & hvy: likes a gall track & has run well fresh: useful, sharper in h'caps on easier grnd this autumn. *5* **86**
3132 **MITCHAM 21** [7] 4-9-0 J Fortune 16/1: -04007: Prom, btn over 1f out: has failed to fire this term. *1½* **87**
3152 **CUBISM 20** [2] 4-9-0 (t) M Hills 11/2: -03538: In tch, btn 2f out: much btr 3152, see 1952. *2½* **80**
8 ran Time 1m 12.96 (1.96) (Hesmonds Stud) J L Dunlop Arundel, W Sussex

3611 **4.05 BREHENY HCAP 3YO+ 0-95 (C) 1m6f175y Good 43 -50 Slow [87]**
£6873 £2115 £1057 £528 3 yo rec 12lb

3153 **FAIT LE JOJO 20** [6] S P C Woods 3-8-10 (81) R Hughes 4/1: 411351: 3 b g Pistolet - Pretty Davis (Trempolino) Made all, kept on well over 1f out, drvn out: earlier scored at Salisbury & Goodwood (h'caps): '99 wnr at W'hampton (mdn, rtd 83a): suited by 14f, stays 2m on firm, gd, fibresand & any track: v tough. **83**
3295 **BID ME WELCOME 14** [7] Miss D A McHale 4-9-6 (79) J Reid 5/1: 523152: 4 b g Alzao - Blushing Barada (Blushing Groom) Prom, rdn & onepace over 1f out: ran to form of 2812. *¾* **80**
3171 **TENSILE 19** [3] M C Pipe 5-9-13 (86) Pat Eddery 3/1: 600433: 5 b g Tenby - Bonnie Isle (Pitcairn) Hld up, eff over 2f out, kept on same pace for press over 1f out: clr rem, top-weight: 1 win in 22 starts. *nk* **87**
*2856 **FINAL SETTLEMENT 34** [1] J R Jenkins 5-8-9 (68) S Whitworth 4/1: 653414: In tch, rdn & btn 2f out. *6* **62**
3001 **COOL INVESTMENT 27** [4] 3-9-6 (91) R Hills 5/2 FAV: 644135: Cl up, wknd well over 1f out: well bckd: not see out this longer trip? btr 3001, 2547. *13* **69**
5 ran Time 3m 19.21 (13.71) (G A Roberts) S P C Woods Newmarket, Suffolk

3612 **4.35 LONSDALE CLAIMER 3YO (E) 7f str Good 43 -11 Slow**
£3532 £1087 £543 £271

3456 **PINHEIROS DREAM 7** [1] B J Meehan 3-8-8 Pat Eddery 4/1: 104621: 3 ch f Grand Lodge - Nikki's Groom (Shy Groom) Slow away, held up, hdwy & carried right but led ins last, rdn clr: nicely bckd, claimed for £12,000: earlier scored here at Newmarket (claimer): plcd once in '99 (rtd 81): eff over 7f/1m, stys 10f on firm, gd & likes Newmarket: eff with/without blinks & enjoys claiming grade. **58**
3383 **LATE ARRIVAL 9** [3] D Morris 3-8-11 (VIS) R Cochrane 25/1: 420002: 3 b g Emperor Jones - Try Vickers (Fuzzbuster) Waited with, hdwy over 1f out, kept on inside last, nrst fin: back to form in first time visor back at 1m, stays 10f: mdn but has ability: see 1770. *1¼* **58**
3130 **NORFOLK REED 21** [14] R Hannon 3-9-5 (VIS) R Hughes 7/2: 500003: 3 b g Thatching - Sawaki (Song) Hld up rear, hdwy & short of room sev times fnl 2f, styd on well ins last, not btn far: prob unlucky in first time visor dropped into claiming grade: his jockey often sets his mounts plenty to do & subs finds trouble. *¾* **66**
3456 **FINERY 7** [8] C A Dwyer 3-8-11 T E Durcan 16/1: 230034: Led far side racing alone, hung right over 2f out, collared & no extra inside last: gd run: see 2456. *1¾* **53**
3005 **PAGEANT 27** [5] 3-9-2 M Tebbutt 9/4 FAV: 126255: Prom, wknd inside last: bckd: rtd higher 3005, 2855. *2* **54**
3225 **POLAR HAZE 16** [15] 3-9-1 T Quinn 8/1: -23036: In tch, rdn over 2f out, sn no impression: see 3325. *3* **47**
3218 **LEEN 16** [7] 3-8-0 A Nicholls (3) 16/1: 006027: In tch, wknd well over 1f out: claimed for £4,000. *1½* **29**
3266 **SLAM BID 15** [11] 3-8-7 (BL) J Reid 10/1: 0-5638: Held up, rdn & btn over 1f out: claimed for £6,000. *¾* **34**
3194 **FEAST OF ROMANCE 18** [12] 3-9-3 N Callan 16/1: 030049: In tch, wknd well over 1f out: btr 3194 (6f). *hd* **43**

NEWMARKET (JULY)   FRIDAY AUGUST 25TH   Righthand, Stiff, Galloping Track

2946 **LOUS WISH 28** [9] 3-8-8 (bl) R Fitzpatrick 50/1: 000000: In tch, wknd over 2f out: 10th: see 346. 1½ 31
3456 **Alabama Wurley 7** [2] 3-8-4 D McGaffin (1) 20/1:   -- **Serpent Systems** [6] 3-8-2 S Carson 25/1:
3129 **Mr Stickywicket 21** [4] 3-8-5 J Tate 66/1:   3272 **Latino Bay 14** [10] 3-8-11 T G McLaughlin 33/1:
3382 **Hanoi 9** [13] 3-8-0 (bl) J Lowe 66/1:   3332 **Everbold 12** [16] 3-8-2 G Bardwell 50/1:
16 ran   Time 1m 27.66 (3.76)   (The Chantilly Partnership)   B J Meehan Upper Lamborn, Berks

3613   5.10 NGK APPR HCAP STKS 3YO+ 0-80 (E)   6f str   Good 43   +00 Fast   [75]
£3540 £1120 £560 £280   3 yo rec 3 lb

2391 **BE MY WISH 52** [6] W A O'Gorman 5-8-12 (59)(bl) J Mackay (3) 13/2: -32251: 5 b m Be My Chief - 66
Spinner (Blue Cashmere) Slow away, held up, gd hdwy over 1f out to lead inside last, going away: 7 week abs:
rtd 55 at best for S Woods in '99 (first time blinks): '98 wnr at Ascot (mdn, rtd 77 & 76a with Miss G Kelleway):
eff at 6/7f on firm/fast, equitrack & handles gd/soft: runs well fresh with/without blinks: well rdn.
3297 **DOUBLE SPLENDOUR 14** [5] P S Felgate 10-9-7 (68) G Faulkner 25/1: 000062: 10 b g Double Schwartz 2 68
- Princess Pamela (Dragonara Palace) Held up, hdwy over 1f out, styd on well inside last, nrst fin: 10yo,
but has slipped down the weights & could pinch another race on this evidence: see 1840.
3214 **TWO STEP 16** [12] R M H Cowell 4-7-10 (43)(t)(4oh) A Polli 25/1: 010503: 4 b g Mujahid - Polka ½ 41
Dancer (Dancing Brave) Handy, hdwy to lead over 1f out, hdd & no extra ins last: stays 6f on fibresand & gd.
3543 **TREASURE TOUCH 3** [10] P D Evans 6-9-9 (70) Joanna Badger (5) 6/1 JT FAV: 012404: Prom, rdn & ½ 67
onepace over 1f out: quick reapp: see 3440.
3238 **SEA DEER 16** [11] 11-9-5 (66) D Watson (7) 16/1: 006005: Prom, lost place over 3f out, rallied & ¾ 61
not clr run over 1f out, nrst fin: see 2580, 1952.
1273 **BLUE KITE 105** [7] 5-9-0 (61) P M Quinn 12/1: 100246: Held up, eff & switched right over 1f out, ¾ 54
kept on same pace: 3 month abs & sharper next time: see 1196, 645.
2999 **EVENTUALITY 27** [14] 4-9-9 (70) S Carson 6/1 JT FAV: 001207: Prom, wknd over 1f out: btr 2845. 2 58
3460 **MOONLIGHT SONG 7** [15] 3-8-13 (63) D McGaffin (3) 13/2: 012228: Al bhd: consistent over 7f prev. hd 50
3516 **MR STYLISH 5** [3] 4-9-8 (69)(tvi) A Nicholls 10/1: 505339: Held up, btn over 1f out: quick reapp. ½ 54
3457 **PETARRA 7** [2] 5-9-10 (71) C Carver 6/1 JT FAV: 0-0050: Held up, btn well over 1f out: 10th, see 3457. ¾ 54
3341 **PRINCE PROSPECT 12** [1] 4-9-12 (73) Kristin Stubbs(7) 16/1: 040000: Led alone on far side, hdd 0
& wknd over 1f out: fin 13th: see 2266, 3104.
3398 **Kosevo 9** [13] 6-7-10 (43)(bl)(5oh) M Mathers(0) 14/1: 3502 **Mujas Magic 5** [9] 5-8-4 (51)(vis) C Catlin (5) 12/1:
3229 **Gascon 16** [8] 4-9-11 (72) A Beech 14/1:
2241 **Three Angels 58** [4] 5-9-6 (67) S Finnamore (3) 20/1:
15 ran   Time 1m 13.59 (2.59)   (W A O'Gorman)   W A O'Gorman Newmarket, Suffolk

THIRSK   FRIDAY AUGUST 25TH   Lefthand, Flat, Oval Track

Official Going   GOOD/FIRM. Stalls: Round Course - Inside: Straight Course - Stands Side.

3614   2.20 EBF MDN 2YO (D)   6f str   Good/Firm 29   -06 Slow
£4257 £1310 £665 £327

3154 **TAKAROA 20** [8] I A Balding 2-9-0 K Darley 3/1: -331: 2 b c Tagula - Mountain Harvest (Shirley 89
Heights) Chsd ldrs, pushed halfway, styd on well to lead ent fnl 1f, drvn out: well bckd from 4/1: half brother
to a wnr abroad, cost 36,000gns: stys 7f, apprec this drop bck to 6f: acts on gd & firm: improving colt.
3162 **PROLETARIAT 20** [10] H Candy 2-9-0 C Rutter 9/4 FAV: -242: 2 gr c Petong - Primulette (Mummy's Pet) ½ 88
Never far away, led over 2f out till ent fnl 1f, styd on well & just btn in a driving fin: op 7/4, clr of 3rd:
another sound eff, must sn go one better: see 3162, 2979.
3156 **MAWHOOB 20** [1] J L Dunlop 2-9-0 W Supple 5/2: -643: 2 gr c Dayjur - Asl (Caro) 3½ 78
Chsd ldrs, pushed along halfway, kept on fnl 1f, no ch with front 2: well bckd: unsuited by this drop bckd to 6f.
-- **STARBECK** [4] J D Bethell 2-8-9 D Harrison 20/1: -4: Dwelt, improved halfway, nrst fin on debut: 1¾ 68
March foal, cost 15,000gns: sire a top class mid dist performer: will apprec 7f judged on this: sure to
benefit from todays experience.
3508 **A C AZURE 5** [6] 2-9-0 P McCabe 25/1: -65: Outpcd, improving when hmpd dist, kept on & nrst fin: 1¼ 69+
quick reapp: encouraging eff, in need of 7f/1m+: one to keep in mind, see 3508.
3408 **ROSALIA 8** [7] 2-8-9 J Weaver 10/1: -46: Slowly away, imprvd 2f out, nvr nr ldrs & eased ins last: hd 64
lost ch at the start & not given a hard time here: coming along nicely, needs one more run to qualify for nurseries.
1503 **MARKUSHA 91** [11] 2-9-0 Alex Greaves 20/1: -437: Nvr a factor: 3 month abs, not given a hard ride: nk 68
h'cap qualifying run, can do better: see 1503. (AW).
-- **FLYING PETREL** [5] 2-8-9 J Fanning 12/1: -8: Front rank till drftd left 2f out, grad wknd: debut: ½ 62
Jan foal, related to sev wnrs, incl smart 7f juv scorer Putra: dam a dual wnr in the States: with M Johnston.
3137 **FINMAR 21** [12] 2-9-0 C Lowther 50/1: -59: Set pace 4f, grad fdd: see 3137. hd 67
-- **BRILLYANT DANCER** [3] 2-8-9 R Ffrench 33/1: -0: In tch till halfway, no ch after on debut: May nk 61
foal, cost 2,500gns: sire a top class 10f performer: with Mrs A Duffield.
1698 **EL UNO 82** [9] 2-9-0 R Cody Boutcher (7) 50/1: -00: Slowly away, al struggling & fin 11th: 12 ½ 65
week abs: prev with Miss Craze, now J L Eyre: shown little todate, see 1698.
2683 **MAID TO DANCE 41** [2] 2-8-9 G Parkin 16/1: -50: Speed 2f, sn well bhd & vertually p.u. t.o. in 20 20
last: 6 week abs: something clearly amiss: see 2683.
12 ran   Time 1m 11.6 (2.1)   (Robert Hitchins)   I A Balding Kingsclere, Berks

3615   2.50 HELMSLEY SELLER 2YO (F)   7f rnd   Good/Firm 29   -39 Slow
£2975 £850 £425

3438 **GAZETTE IT TONIGHT 7** [10] A Berry 2-8-12 G Carter 10/3 FAV: 331331: 2 b f Merdon Melody - 63
Balidilemma (Balidar) Nvr far away, imprvd to lead 2f out, pushed clr fnl 1f, comftbly: nicely bckd from 4/1,
no bid: earlier won at Catterick (sell), also plcd numerous times: eff at 7f, shld stay 1m: acts on gd & fast
grnd, handles a sharp track: enjoys selling grade, decicive wnr here.
*3438 **PETIT TOR 7** [8] J Norton 2-8-12 P Hanagan (7) 9/2: 526412: 2 b f Rock City - Kinoora (Kind Of 2½ 60
Hush) Trckd ldrs, kept on for 2nd fnl 1f, not rch wnr: sound run: see 3438.
3299 **MAID OF ARC 14** [13] M L W Bell 2-8-6 M Fenton 5/1: 224463: 2 b f Patton - Holy Speed (Afleet) 1 52
Rcd wide mid div, imprvd halfway, ev ch 2f out, not qckn ins last: apprec this drop into sell comp: stays 7f.

3246 **APORTO 16** [11] D W Barker 2-8-11 T Williams 10/1: 00304: Trckd ldrs, ev ch 2f out, sn onepcd. 2½ 52
3397 **SOLO DANCE 9** [4] 2-8-6 (BL) K Darley 10/1: -4405: Led till 2 out, grad fdd: tchd 14/1, first time 1¼ 44
blnks: better expected on drop into sell grade & with application of blnks: bred to apprec further: see 2316.
-- **FINN MCCOOL** [9] 2-8-11 G Parkin 6/1: -6: Dwelt, improved halfway, btn dist: tchd 8/1, debut: 1¼ 46
March foal, sire a high class mid dist performer: R Fahey gelding, better expected.
3127 **LIGHT OF ARAGON 21** [6] 2-8-6 R Cody Boutcher(7) 20/1: -0007: Rear, mod late gains, nvr dngrs. 4 33
3363 **DANCE QUEEN 10** [12] 2-8-6 J Bramhill 14/1: 600608: Switched start, imprvd 2f out, btn dist. 1½ 30
2949 **LASTOFTHEWHALLEYS 28** [1] 2-8-12 F Lynch 8/1: 001609: Rcd keenly in bhd ldrs, ev ch 2f out, fdd. ½ 35
-- **THANKS MAX** [3] 2-8-11 C Lowther 12/1: -0: Dwelt, nvr a factor in 10th on debut: 1,500gns ¾ 32
purchase: March foal, sire a 1m 2yo wnr in France: with Miss L Perratt.
3376 **Bloom 9** [14] 2-8-6 A Culhane 20/1: 1890 **Itsakindofmagic 73** [2] 2-8-6 K Hodgson 50/1:
3376 **Captains Folly 9** [5] 2-8-6 R Winston 20/1: 3500 **Distinctive Manna 5** [7] 2-8-11 P Goode (3) 25/1:
14 ran   Time 1m 27.7 (4.8)   (The Gazetters)   A Berry Cockerham, Lancs

---

3616   **3.20 EBF CLASSIFIED STKS 3YO+ 0-90 (C)   1m rnd   Good/Firm 29 -22 Slow**
£5904   £2239   £1119   £509   3yo rec 6lb

3254 **FLAMENCO RED 15** [6] R Charlton 3-8-6 K Darley 1/25 FAV: 35-421: 3 b f Warning - Spanish Wells 45
(Sadler's Wells) Waited with, smooth hdwy to lead 2f out, won hard held: '99 Nottingham wnr (mdn, rtd 90+): eff
at 1m, acts on gd & fast: handles a stiff/gall trk: has tried a visor: had sev stone in hand on official ratings.
3330 **FOUR MEN 12** [1] A Berry 3-8-9 Mark Flynn 7/1 16/1: 565302: 3 b g Nicolotte - Sound Pet (Runnett) 1½ 37
Led till 2f out, kept on but no ch with facile wnr: pulled 9L clr 3rd: rtd 53lbs inferior to this wnr on official
ratings but conceded 3lbs today: prob stys 1m & acts on fast grnd: see 2682.
2522 **INITIATIVE 47** [4] B W Murray 4-9-1 P McCabe 50/1: 5-0003: 4 ch g Arazi - Dance Quest (Green 9 19
Dancer) Chsd ldrs, rdn & btn 2f out: 7 wk abs: won for H Cecil last term, but has completely lost his form.
3399 **FAS 9** [2] J D Bethell 4-9-1 (vis) L Gueller(7) 100/1: 000004: Trckd ldr till left bhd 3f out: officially hd 19
rtd just 19 & had an impossible task today: see 2147.
3506 **STAMFORD HILL 5** [3] 5-9-1 D Allan (7) 100/1: 056005: Waited with, outpcd 3f out, fin last: 3 13
quick reapp, impossible task at todays weights: no form.
5 ran   Time 1m 39.5 (4.1)   (K Abdulla)   R Charlton Beckhampton, Wilts.

3617   **3.55 TATTERSALLS AUCT MDN 2YO (E)   7f rnd   Good/Firm 29 -36 Slow**
£3851   £1185   £592   £296

3032 **SMART DANCER 25** [4] T D Easterby 2-8-9 J Weaver 14/1: -50441: 2 b c Spectrum - Plessaya 79
(Nureyev) Broke well & made all, rdn clr dist, styd on well, pushed out: op 10/1: improved form under an
enterprising ride: 16,000gns half brother to a couple of wnrs abroad: eff at 7f on fast grnd.
3245 **GONE TOO FAR 16** [9] M Dods 2-8-3 T Williams 10/1: -02: 2 b g Reprimand - Blue Nile (Bluebird) 1¼ 71
Chsd ldrs, chsd wnr 1½f out, kept on but nvr going to get there: eff at 7f on fast grnd, 1m will suit: has
shown enough to win a minor event, see 3245.
3478 **LION IN THE COURSE 6** [5] M Johnston 2-8-12 J Fanning 11/8 FAV: -43: 2 b c Chimes Band - Late 3 74
Flight (Caracolero) Chsd ldrs, kept on under press fnl 1f, not pace of front 2: well bckd tho' op 11/10, qck
reapp: prob stys 7f, handles fast & gd/soft grnd: more expected after 3478 (debut).
3215 **LONG WEEKEND 16** [6] J L Dunlop 2-8-9 D Harrison 9/2: -054: Chsd ldrs, onepaced fnl 1½f: 3 65
tchd 6/1: now qualified for nursery h'caps & 1m+ will suit: see 3215.
2927 **SPORTS EXPRESS 30** [10] 2-7-12 F Fessey 14/1: -445: Unruly start, rear till late hdwy, nvr dngrs: 1½ 51
drifted from 10/1: encouraging h'cap qual run, unlucky in 2927 (sell): one to keep an eye on in a nursery h'cap.
3079 **COMEUPPANCE 23** [8] 2-8-4(1ow) G Carter 50/1: -606: In tch, no impress fnl 2f: see 2377 (debut). shd 57
3347 **CHEMICALATTRACTION 11** [3] 2-8-7 F Lynch 20/1: -0047: In tch racing keenly, hmpd & lost pl early 1¼ 57
on, imprvd 2f out, btn dist: drifted from 12/1: did not get the run of today's race: see 3347 (C/D).
3347 **LANCE FEATHER 11** [12] 2-8-7 R Cody Boutcher 7/1 16/1: -68: Dwelt, recovered to ch ldrs 5f, wknd. 1¾ 53
-- **GREY IMPERIAL** [2] 2-8-7 A Culhane 12/1: -9: Slowly away, al bhd on debut: drifted from 10/1: 1½ 50
1,500gns March foal, sire a decent juv wnr: with P Harris & should improve given time.
1538 **EASY FREE 90** [1] 2-7-12 R Ffrench 16/1: -00: Slowly away, al bhd & fin 10th: 3 month abs. 1¼ 38
3347 **TIME PROOF 11** [11] 2-8-5 G Parkin 25/1: -00: Al towards rear, fin 11th: see 3347. nk 44
-- **LUCEFER** [7] 2-8-7 O Urbina 13/2: -0: Rcd keenly & hmpd early on, saddle slipped & virtually 24 6
p.u. fnl 2f: tchd 8/1, debut: Feb foal, cost 1,400gns: sire a decent 6f/1m juv performer: forgive this.
12 ran   Time 1m 27.5 (4.6)   (Bernard Hathaway)   T D Easterby Great Habton, Yorks

---

3618   **4.25 JOE BAGGOTT HCAP 3YO+ 0-85 (D)   2m   Good/Firm 29 +01 Fast**   **[83]**
£4101   £1262   £473   £473   3yo rec 14lb

3395 **STAR RAGE 9** [2] M Johnston 10-9-10 (79) J Weaver 10/11 FAV: 255421: 10 b g Horage - Star Bound 82
(Crowned Prince) Trkd ldrs, imprvd to lead over 2f out, held on well fnl 1f, drvn out: hvly bckd, fair time, top
weight: plcd over timber in 99/00 (val h'cap hdle, rtd 137h, eff at 2m/3m on gd & firm): incredibly tough &
progressive on the Flat in '99, won at Lingfield (AW h'cap, rtd 84a), Beverely (2), Redcar & Goodwood (h'caps, rtd
86): rcd over fences in 98/99 (rtd 109c, with D Elsworth), also tried blnks & rtd 149h prev: '98 W'hampton wnr
(h'cap, rtd 81a): best arnd 2m on firm, gd/soft grnd & on both AW's: can carry big weights, acts on any trk:
amazingly tough 10yo, this was his 20th Flat win from 91 starts, a real credit to all concerned.
3367 **EMBRYONIC 10** [1] R F Fisher 8-8-5 (60) G Carter 5/1: 006062: 8 b g Prince Rupert - Belle Viking 2 60
(Riverman) Waited with, imprvd into 2nd over 1f out, no impress on wnr cl home: sound run, well h'capped.
3430 **JAMAICAN FLIGHT 7** [4] Mrs S Lamyman 7-8-4 (59) J Fanning 2/1: 554423: 7 b h Sunshine Forever - 1¼ 57
Kalamona (Hawaii) Led till 2f out, no extra: ddhtd for 3rd: front rnr who acts in very well h'capped: see 2953, 253.
3249 **LUCKY JUDGE 16** [3] W W Haigh 3-7-10 (65)(8oh) P Fessey 8/1: 046423: Trckd ldr, eff 2f out, dht 63$
onepace fnl 1f: ddhtd for 3rd: fair run from out of the h'cap, treat this rating with caution: see 3249 (14f).
4 ran   Time 3m 27.3 (4.5)   (J David Abell)   M Johnston Middleham, Yorks

THIRSK
FRIDAY AUGUST 25TH   Lefthand, Flat, Oval Track

3619   **4.55 HORSESMOUTH APP HCAP 3YO+ 0-70 (E)**   **5f str**   **Good/Firm 29**   **+03 Fast**   **[66]**
£3685   £1134   £567   £283   3yo rec 2lb   Stalls 1-2-4 rcd far side - no chance

3572 **NORTHERN SVENGALI 2** [15] T D Barron 4-9-9 (61) Lynsey Hanna (5) 3/1 FAV: 503021: 4 b g Distinctly **69**
North - Trilby's Dream (Mansooj) Chsd ldrs, imprvd to lead 1f out, ran on strongly, rdn out: best time of day, qck
reapp, bckd from 5/1: plcd form in '99 (rtd 79, h'cap): '98 wnr at Catterick (2, mdn & nursery, rtd 84), also plcd
on sand (rtd 80): eff at AW5, handles any trk: acts on firm, hvy & on both AW's: has slipped to a v attractive
h'cap mark & could follow up now he has got his head bck in front.
3594 **JOHAYRO 1** [9] J S Goldie 4-9-9 (56) Dawn Rankin (5) 8/1: 000122: 7 ch g Clantime - Arroganza   1¼ **58**
(Crofthall) Chsd ldrs, led briefly dist, kept on well & not btn far: saddle reportedly slipped, fine run in the
circumstances: rnr up at Musselburgh yesterday, op 7/1: see 3594, 3312.
3349 **SOBA JONES 11** [13] T D Easterby 3-9-4 (58)(bl) P Dobbs 7/2: 431533: 3 b g Emperor Jones -   hd **60**
Soba (Most Secret) Chsd ldrs, kept on under press fnl 1f, not btn far: well bckd: running well: see 3349 (C/D).
3377 **BENZOE 9** [3] D Nicholls 10-9-5 (57) Clare Roche (5) 9/1: 615304: Dwelt, swithched right start, styd   1 **56**
on well fnl 1m, nrst fin: fine run from poor low draw, op 7/1: loves to come with a late run, likes Thirsk.
3502 **SWYNFORD DREAM 5** [11] 7-9-2 (54) A Robertson (5) 16/1: 260005: Set pace till dist, no extra: nk **52**
quick reapp: better eff & v well h'capd now: see 798 (reapp).
3502 **COOL PROSPECT 5** [7] 5-9-7 (59) R Cody Boutcher (3) 20/1: 200306: Chsd ldrs & sn rdn along,   1½ **53**
onepaced fnl 1f: quick reapp, not disgraced from low draw: see 3271 (AW).
3191 **ORIEL STAR 18** [12] 4-8-2 (40)(vis) D Meah(5) 25/1: 060007: Chsd ldrs, no impression fnl 1f.   nk **33**
3124 **EMMA AMOUR 21** [17] 3-8-1 (41) P Bradley 16/1: 000008: Front rank 4f, grad fdd: front rnr, showed   nk **33**
up well for a long way from a fav draw: has tried blnks: see 62 (AW).
3271 **FASTRACK TIME 14** [16] 3-8-10 (50) K Parkin (5) 20/1: 0-0009: Rear, some late hdwy, nvr dngrs.   ¾ **39**
2976 **INDIAN BAZAAR 28** [6] 4-8-8 (46) Jonjo Fowle(3) 16/1: 100560: Chsd ldrs 4f, wknd & eased: ½ **34**
poor low draw: op 12/1: much btr 2223.
2743 **MUKARRAB 37** [4] 6-8-13 (51) D Allan (5) 16/1: 044450: Led on far side, no ch with stands side   hd **39**
from halfway: foget this: see 2340, 1714 (well h'capd nowadays).
3493 **RIVER TERN 6** [14] 7-9-6 (58) Claire Bryan 10/1: 360000: Slowly away, nvr a factor: see 2644.   shd **46**
2697 **RED CHARGER 41** [8] 4-9-9 (61) N Chalmers(5) 25/1: -00000: Nvr a factor: 6 week abs, stablemate   ½ **48**
of 4th: mod draw: see 1781.
3502 **COCO DE MER 5** [5] 3-9-10 (64) P Hanagan (5) 25/1: 000000: Slowly away, al bhd: top weight,   hd **51**
quick reapp, poor low draw: see 2663.
*3536 **ROBIN HOOD 3** [1] 3-8-12 (52)(6ex) G Sparkes(3) 12/1: 440610: Rcd far side & al bhd, fin last: **0**
foget this, quick reapp since 3536 (gd/soft).
3312 **Time To Fly 13** [10] 7-8-2 (40)(bl) D Kinsella(5) 16/1:   2947 **Danakim 28** [2] 3-9-5 (59) (bl) J Bosley (3) 20/1:
17 ran   Time 58.3 (1.3)   Timothy Cox)   T D Barron Maunby, N Yorks

---

BATH
FRIDAY AUGUST 25TH   Lefthand, Turning Track With Uphill Finish

Official Going   FIRM. Stalls: Str Course - Far Side; Round Course - Inside.

3620   **5.25 NUNNEY NOV AUCT STKS 2YO (E)**   **5f161y rnd**   **Firm -05**   **-06 Slow**
£2775   £854   £427   £213

3062 **SIBLA 24** [7] Mrs P N Dutfield 2-8-10 L Newman (3) 15/2: 521251: 2 b f Piccolo - Malibasta (Auction   **89**
Ring) Nvr far away, led appr fnl 1f, ran on strongly, readily: dam 6f juv wnr: earlier won here at Bath (auct
mdn): eff around 6f, shld get 7f: acts on firm & gd, likes this stiff/turning trk: improving.
*3205 **GOLDIE 17** [4] D J Coakley 2-8-7 Martin Dwyer 8/11 FAV: 12: 2 b f Celtic Swing - Hotel California   2½ **79**
(Last Tycoon) Well plcd & ev ch till outpcd below dist: well bckd to land the odds: shade better expected aftr
impressive debut win over C/D in 3205 & probably needs further now.
3354 **EBULLIENCE 11** [5] R Charlton 2-8-11 Paul Eddery 7/1: 01203: 2 b f Makbul - Steadfast Elite   1¾ **78**
(Glenstal) Led till appr fnl 1f, onepace: ran to best, acts on firm & gd grnd: see 1883.
*3215 **CLANBRAZAN 16** [6] Mrs A J Perrett 2-8-12 T Ashley 6/1: 414: Bhd ldrs, feeling pace 2f out, late rally.   nk **78**
3286 **FOLEY MILLENNIUM 14** [8] 2-9-4 F Norton 12/1: 134135: Stumbled start, in tch, prog & ch 2f out,   ½ **82**
fdd dist: stiff task giving weight away: see 3286, 3174.
2328 **SHEER FOCUS 55** [1] 2-8-12 (t) N Pollard 33/1: 0506: Dwelt, keen, nvr a factor: 8 wk abs.   2 **70**
3400 **EAGALITY 9** [3] 2-8-4 (bi) D R McCabe 40/1: 00067: Nvr dangerous: needs sells.   2½ **56**
-- **LIGHT OF FASHION** [2] 2-8-4 D Sweeney 14/1: 8: Sn bhd: debut: Common Grounds filly with B Smart. nk **55**
8 ran   Time 1m 09.2 (0.1)   (D Bevan)   Mrs P N Dutfield Axmouth, Devon

3621   **5.55 MENDIP FILLIES MDN 2YO (D)**   **5f rnd**   **Firm -05**   **-05 Slow**
£3503   £1078   £539   £269

3346 **DOUBLE FANTASY 11** [4] B Smart 2-8-11 Paul Eddery 3/1: 061: 2 b f Mind Games - Song's Best   **85**
(Never So Bold) Bhd ldrs, switched & ran on strongly to lead ins last, cmftbly: bckd, much improved: 36,000
gns half-sister to a juv sprinter: eff over a stiff/turning 5f on firm grnd: going the right way.
3431 **FAIR PRINCESS 7** [3] B W Hills 2-8-11 F Norton 6/5 FAV: 220622: 2 b f Efisio - Fair Attempt   1½ **80**
(Try My Best) Cl-up, rdn & ev ch appr fnl 1f, led briefly ins last, no ch with wnr fnl 100y: quick reapp:
fair run & handles firm grnd tho' poss suited to dam higher 3431 (gd grnd nursery).
-- **HIRAETH** [2] B Palling 2-8-11 D Sweeney 14/1: 3: 2 b f Petong - Floppie (Law Society)   ½ **78**
Front rank, chall appr fnl 1f, onepace towards fin: 5,600 gns half sister to a decent Irish juv mdn, dam
3yo wnr: eff at 5f but needs ground: handles firm grnd: pleasing start.
3443 **ANNIE RUAN 7** [7] D Haydn Jones 2-8-11 A McGlone 11/1: -0344: Led till appr fnl 1f, same pace.   ¾ **75**
-- **PICCOLO ROSE** [1] 2-8-11 Craig Williams 13/2: 5: Nvr going pace: debut: Piccolo half sister to   3 **66**
a 5f juv wnr, dam 6f juv wnr: bred for speed: with M Channon.
-- **CALANDA** [6] 2-8-11 L Newman (3) 6/1: 6: Nvr a factor: 7,000 gns Aragon half-sister to several wnrs.   1½ **62**
2939 **YUKA SAN 29** [5] 2-8-11 G Hannon (7) 40/1: 6047: Chsd ldrs till after halfway: needs sells.   2½ **56**
-- **ANNE MCCOL** [8] 2-8-11 G Baker (5) 50/1: 8: Nvr in it: debut: Faustus first foal, dam unrcd.   7 **41**
8 ran   Time 1m 00.3 (0)   (Willie McKay)   B Smart Upper Lambourn, Berks

---

3622   **6.25 BATHWICK CLASSIFIED STKS 3YO+ 0-80 (D)   5f rnd   Firm -05   +05 Fast**
£3711   £1142   £571   £285   3 yo rec 2 lb

3516 **CAUDA EQUINA** 5 [4] M R Channon 6-9-2 Craig Williams 1/1 FAV: 046521: 6 gr g Statoblest - Sea Fret   80
(Habat) Held up in tch, imprvd appr fnl 1f, rdn & ran on to lead towards fin: quick reapp, hvly bckd: '99
wnr here at Bath (2) & Lingfield (class stks, rtd 84): '98 Bath (2, clmr & h'cap) & Salisbury (h'cap, rtd 80):
eff at 5/6f on firm & soft grnd, any trk, Bath specialist (7th career win here): tough.
*2977 **WHISTLER** 28 [3] R Hannon 3-9-3 L Newman (3) 11/4: 3-2412: 3 ch g Selkirk - French Gift (Cadeaux   ½ 80
Genereux) Prom, led ent fnl 2f drvn dist, hdd nr fin: ran to best back in trip against the ultimate Bath
specialist: acts on firm/fast grnd, handles gd/soft: progressive type, a return to 6f shld suit: see 2977.
3493 **BORDER GLEN** 6 [7] J J Bridger 4-9-2 (vis) Martin Dwyer 33/1: 050053: 4 b g Selkirk - Sulitelma   1¾ 71$
(The Minstrel) Rear & pushed along, rdn 2f out, styd on fnl 1f, nvr nr to chall: quick reapp: lks flattered
at the weights tho' acts on firm, gd/soft grnd & both AWs: visor reapplied (usually blnkd): see 96.
3512 **CARTMEL PARK** 5 [6] A Berry 4-9-5 (vis) D Sweeney 7/2: 03004: Sn in clr lead, hdd/no extra ent fnl 2f.   ½ 73
3512 **MADAME JONES** 5 [2] 5-8-13 A McGlone 25/1: 00-005: Prom till 2f out: quick reapp, stiff task.   1½ 63$
2022 **DOUBLE M** 68 [5] 3-9-0 A Mackay 14/1: 404-06: Nvr on terms: 10 wk abs: see 2022.   nk 65
313 **DANCING JACK** 226 [1] 7-9-2 R Brisland (5) 50/1: 06-507: Bhd from halfway, v stiff task, long abs.   5 50$
7 ran   Time 59.8 (u0.8)   (Michael A Foy)   M R Channon West Isley, Berks

---

3623   **6.55 C SAUNDERS HCAP 3YO+ 0-65 (F)   1m rnd   Firm -05   -15 Slow**   [64]
£2977   £916   £458   £229   3 yo rec 6 lb

3188 **MULLAGHMORE** 18 [4] M Kettle 4-8-10 (46) L Newman (3) 9/1: 500051: 4 b g Petardia - Comfrey Glen   51
(Glenstal) Slow away, prog halfway, switched appr fnl 1f & ran on to lead fnl 100y, going away: earlier won
at Lingfield (2, AW, mdn & h'cap, rtd 71a): plcd in '99 (h'cap, rtd 67): eff at 1m/10f: goes on firm, gd grnd,
likes equitrack: handles any trk, with/without blnks, tried a t-strap: can go well fresh & carry big weights.
3527 **CABARET QUEST** 4 [9] J M Bradley 4-8-6 (42) R Havlin 20/1: 603362: 4 ch g Pursuit Of Love - Cabaret   1½ 43
Artiste (Shareef Dancer) Nvr far away, led 2f out till well in last: quick reapp, gd run: acts on firm/fast grnd.
*3514 **WARRING** 5 [12] M S Saunders 6-8-8 (44)(6ex) R Brisland (5) 9/2 FAV: 003413: 6 b g Warrshan -   1¼ 43
Emerald Ring (Auction Ring) Chsd ldrs, briefly outpcd 3f out, wide rally & ch dist, onepace for press: in form.
2775 **SAMARA SONG** 36 [13] Ian Williams 7-9-5 (55) Darren Williams (5) 7/1: 600404: Rear, prog to chase   1 52
ldrs 2f out, kept on same pace: back up in trip, see 1003.
3383 **HORMUZ** 9 [16] 4-9-10 (60) P Fitzsimons (5) 20/1: 001055: Cl-up, led 3f out till 2f out, no extra.   nk 56
3186 **TARSKI** 18 [15] 6-8-10 (46)(VIS) Craig Williams 8/1: 033546: Rear, late hdwy, nvr a threat: unsuited   2 38
by big drop in trip & visor?: see 2552, 1395.
*3236 **ON PORPOISE** 16 [14] 4-8-8 (44) P D'Arcy 10/1: 000017: Hld up, mod gains: btr 3236 (sell).   shd 36
3251 **ARBENIG** 15 [1] 5-8-13 (49) D Sweeney 10/1: 052048: Chsd ldrs till 2f out: see 1732.   hd 40
*2729 **THE THIRD CURATE** 38 [3] 5-8-12 (48) S W Kelly (3) 5/1: -00119: Nvr better than mid-div: bckd: 1 37
needs strong handling, much btr 2729 (sharp trk).
2379 **SOUHAITE** 53 [6] 4-8-7 (43) Martin Dwyer 20/1: 001000: Led after 3f till 3f out, lost place: 10th, 8 wk abs.   3 26
3317 **JESSINCA** 13 [10] 4-8-11 (47) F Norton 5/1: 014220: Rear, eff & not clr run ent fnl 2f, nvr dngrs: 12th.   0
3279 **ENTROPY** 11 [11] 4-8-11 (47) G Baker (5) 12/1: 510360: Mid-div till 3f out: 13th, see 2331 (clm h'cap).   0
3170 Hadeqa 19 [2] 4-8-12 (48)(bl) Paul Eddery 33/1:   2899 My Bold Boyo 31 [5] 5-8-11 (47)(bl) M Henry 25/1:
3294 Aegean Flower 14 [7] 3-8-7 (49)(bl) P Doe 20/1:   4392] Cymmeriad O Gymru 668 [8] 5-9-0 (50) A Clark 25/1:
16 ran   Time 1m 38.8 (0.5)   (Greenacres)   M Kettle Blewbury, Oxon

---

3624   **7.25 SUMMER SELLER 3-4YO   1m3f144y Firm -05   -58 Slow**
£2289   £654   £327   3 yo rec 10lb

3404 **BROWNS DELIGHT** 9 [3] S Dow 3-8-6 P Doe 3/1: 000241: 3 b f Runnett - Fearless Princess (Tyrnavos)   47
Mid-div, gd prog to lead 2f out, easily went clr: val 10L: no bid: rnr-up in '99 (h'cap, AW bow, rtd 62a & 62):
eff at 1m, suited by step up to 11.5f: handles firm grnd & equitrack: appears to be on the up-grade.
3526 **LOKOMOTIV** 4 [12] J M Bradley 4-9-12 (bl) P Fitzsimons (5) 10/1: 001052: 4 b g Salse - Rainbow's   6 46
End (My Swallow) Rear, late hdwy & went 2nd nr fin, no dr win: quick reapp, back to form: see 2875.
3490 **SHAW VENTURE** 6 [5] B Palling 3-8-11 D Sweeney 16/1: 060563: 3 ch g Whittingham - Al Shany   ½ 40
(Burslem) Well plcd, led briefly appr fnl 2f, same pace: quick reapp, longer trip: sole win at 5f: see 638.
3351 **LANTIC BAY** 11 [9] J C Tuck 3-8-6 R Havlin 20/1: 04: Chsd ldrs, no extra appr fnl 2f.   ¾ 34
*3351 **TITUS BRAMBLE** 11 [6] 3-9-2 Craig Williams 5/2 FAV: 601415: In tch, hdwy & not clr run appr fnl   ¾ 43
1f, nvr dangerous: may have made the frame but had no ch with: btr 3351.
3234 **SPONTANEITY** 16 [1] 4-9-2 (vis) S W Kelly (3) 6/1: 625056: Led till appr fnl 2f, fdd: stiff task, lngr trip.   3½ 29
3447 **PICCALILLI** 7 [11] 3-8-6 R Brisland (5) 25/1: 060007: Handy till wknd ent fnl 2f: stiff task.   shd 29
1731 **THE FLYER** 81 [7] 3-8-11 N Pollard 4/1: -60208: Mid-div till wknd 3f out: 12 wk abs, btr 1572 (1m, g/s).   2 32
3336 **TENBY HEIGHTS** 12 [10] 4-9-7 (tBL) L Newman (3) 40/1: 000-09: Bhd ldrs till lost place 3f out.   16 17
3262 **STAR ATTRACTION** 15 [4] 3-8-6 G Hannon (7) 33/1: 4050: Al towards rear: stiff task, no form.   6 7
3351 Albergo 11 [2] 3-8-11 (VIS) F Norton 12/1:   2715 Titan Lad 39 [8] 3-8-11 Paul Eddery 33/1:
12 ran   Time 2m 31.2 (6.2)   (Cecil Brown)   S Dow Epsom, Surrey

---

3625   **7.55 PULTENEY STAYERS HCAP 3YO+ 0-75 (E)   2m1f34y Firm -05   -47 Slow**   [62]
£3088   £950   £475   £237

*3434 **OUR MONOGRAM** 7 [7] A C Stewart 4-9-1 (49)(6ex) M Roberts 6/4 FAV: 000311: 4 b g Deploy - Darling   55
Splodge (Elegant Air) Handy, went on appr fnl 1f, cmftbly: nicely bckd, defied a penalty for last week's win at
Sandown (h'cap): rtd 74 last term (mdn): eff at 2m/2m1f on firm & gd grnd, stiff/gall trks: progressive stayer.
3434 **FAST FORWARD FRED** 7 [5] L Montague Hall 4-9-4 (52) A Clark 9/2: -00352: 9 gr g Sharrood - Sun   2 52
Street (Ile de Bourbon) Led halfway till 1½f out, styd on but no ch dist: qk reapp, also bhd this wnr in 3434.
3085 **RENAISSANCE LADY** 23 [6] T R Watson 4-9-10 (58) Craig Williams 11/4: 112533: 4 ch f Imp Society -   ½ 57
Easter Morning (Nice Havrais) Led till halfway, prom, outpcd 2f out, staying on nr fin: tho' styr, see 3085, 2461.
2941 **SHERIFF** 29 [3] J W Hills 9-9-0 (48) M Henry 9/1: 021034: Led briefly halfway, chsd ldrs till 2f out.   4 44
3424 **SEA DANZIG** 8 [1] 7-9-5 (53) L Newman (3) 12/1: 404105: Chsd ldrs, no extra appr fnl 3f: longer trip.   ½ 48
3447 **WINSOME GEORGE** 7 [2] 5-7-10 (30)(vis)(2oh) F Norton 33/1: 050606: Held up, lost tch 4f out.   17 12
2622 **LAJADHAL** 43 [4] 11-7-10 (30)(16oh) G Baker (5) 100/1: /00-07: Detached by halfway: 6 wk abs.   dist 0

1113

BATH   FRIDAY AUGUST 25TH   Lefthand, Turning Track With Uphill Finish

7 ran   Time 3m 48.0 (7.1)   (The Foxons Fillies Partnership)   A C Stewart Newmarket, Suffolk

NEWMARKET   SATURDAY AUGUST 26TH   Righthand, Stiff, Galloping Track

Official Going: GOOD/FIRM. Stalls: Far side

3626

2.00 FCI VERA VERRALL MDN 3YO+ (D)   1m str   Good/Firm 22 -00 Slow
£4992 £1536 £768 £384 3 yo rec 6 lb Majority raced far side

-- **YOU ARE THE ONE** [3] L M Cumani 3-8-6 J P Spencer 13/8 FAV: 1: 3 b f Unfuwain - Someone Special (Habitat) Held up, prog fnl 3f, led ins last, held on well for press: bckd from 2/1: bred in the purple, related to smart mid-dist performers One So Wonderful & Alnasr Alwasheek: eff at 1m, 10f+ will suit: acts on fast grnd & on a stiff/gall trk: runs well fresh: open to improvement, ran green today: potentially useful. **81**
3232 **AZAAN 17** [14] M P Tregoning 3-8-11 R Perham 9/2: -22: 3 ch c Lure - Crystal Cross (Roberto) Led till ins last, rallied well, just held: drifted from 3/1, 5L clr of rem: acts on fast & gd grnd: eff at 1m, a return to 10f & similar company shld suit: shld win a mdn, see 3232. *hd* **85**
3256 **DIGITAL 16** [4] M R Channon 3-8-11 J Fortune 4/1: -423: 3 ch g Safawan - Heavenly Goddess (Soviet Star) Chsd ldrs, ch over 1f out, no extra inside last: op 5/1: h'caps shld now suit: see 3256, 3048. *5* **75**
3350 **KUWAIT FLAVOUR 12** [18] K Mahdi 4-9-3 D McGaffin (5) 66/1: /3-604: Led stands side group over 3f out, hung left/held 1f out: offic rtd just 58, treat this rating with caution: see 478. *½* **74$**
2211 **PAGAN PRINCE 61** [7] 3-8-11 W Ryan 33/1: 05: Chsd ldrs 6f: 2 month abs: see 2211. *½* **73**
-- **WODHILL FOLLY** [9] 3-8-6 J Quinn 50/1: 6: Dwelt, held up far side, drvn & kept on fnl 2f, nrst fin: debut: mid-dists could suit on this evidence: with N Callaghan. *1¾* **65**
3189 **SOPHALA 19** [8] 3-8-6 G Hind 20/1: 0-37: Mid div, btn 2f out: see 3189 (10f):. *½* **64**
3293 **SKYLARK 15** [13] 3-8-6 M Roberts 20/1: 653008: Led stand side group 4f, sn held: btr 2585 (7f). *shd* **64**
-- **LEMARATE** [2] 3-8-11 P Robinson 16/1: 9: Dwelt, nvr on terms on debut: dam a top-class miler Sayyedati: bred to apprec 1m: lost all chance at the start today: with C Brittain & shld be capable of better. *1¾* **66**
109 **MABROOKAH 274** [5] 4-8-12 L Newman (3) 66/1: 6245-0: Prom 6f: 10th: 9 month abs: see 109. *hd* **60**
3179 **CULMINATE 20** [1] 3-8-11 J Tate 100/1: -000: Nvr on terms: 11th: mod form prev. *1¾* **62**
-- **KADINSKY** [10] 3-8-11 M Fenton 12/1: 0: Dwelt, al rear: cost 30,000gns: half bro to 7f wnr. *1¾* **59$**
-- **Salem** [15] 3-8-11 R Price 25/1:   3262 **Dazzling Daisy 16** [11] 3-8-6 R Brisland (5) 66/1:
3289 **Paparazza 15** [16] 3-8-6 T E Durcan 20/1:   1758 **Moose Malloy 80** [12] 3-8-11 P McCabe 66/1:
3189 **Pembroke Star 19** [6] 4-8-12 T G McLaughlin 100/1:
17 ran   Time 1m 38.97 (1.77)   (Helena Springfield (Ltd))   L M Cumani Newmarket, Suffolk

3627

2.35 EBF COURAGE MDN 2YO (D)   6f   Good/Firm 22 -24 Slow
£4810 £1480 £740 £370 Raced far side

-- **HAMADEENAH** [7] K Mahdi 2-8-9 D McGaffin (5) 20/1: 1: 2 ch f Alhijaz - Mahbob Dancer (Groom Dancer) Al prom, led & hung left 2f out, held on well, drvn out: op 14/1: Mar foal, cost 3,700gns: sire a smart juv: eff over a stiff/gall 6f on fast grnd: runs well fresh: ran green today, shld improve. **82**
3358 **LUNEVISION 12** [4] H J Collingridge 2-8-9 M Hills 11/4: 32: 2 b f Solid Illusion - Lumiere Celeste (Always Fair) Led, hdd 2f out, kept on for press tho' held when hmpd nr line: nicely bckd: acts on fast grnd. *1¾* **76**
-- **MINE** [6] L M Cumani 2-9-0 J P Spencer 11/10 FAV: 3: 2 b c Primo Dominie - Ellebanna (Tina's Pet) Trkd ldrs, not much room 2f out, onepcd fnl 1f: hvly bckd: April foal, cost 64,000gns: half brother to a 7f 2yo wnr, dam a sprint wnr: eff at 6f on fast grnd, 7f shld suit: sharper next time & shld win similar. *½* **79**
3162 **HARD TO KNOW 21** [3] D J S Cosgrove 2-9-0 G Carter 14/1: 404: Prom, rdn & outpcd over 2f out, kept on ins last: bred to apprec 7f+ & nursery h'caps will now suit: see 2760. *1¾* **75**
3162 **PENTLAND 21** [1] 2-9-0 M Roberts 11/2: 05: Chsd ldrs, outpcd fnl 2f: op 9/2: Apr foal, cost 110,000gns: dam a wnr in the States: sire top class 12f performer: sure to apprec 7f+. *nk* **74**
1924 **RAW SILK 73** [8] 2-9-0 P McCabe 33/1: 006: Held up, rdn/btn over 2f out: 10 week abs: mod form. *3½* **65**
-- **DUNKIRK SPIRIT** [2] 2-9-0 T G McLaughlin 25/1: 7: Dwelt & al rear: Whittingham colt, April foal, 7,000gns 2yo: dam a wnr abroad: with J Pearce. *1* **63**
-- **SIR DESMOND** [9] 2-9-0 R Cochrane 10/1: 8: Slowly away & al bhd: Petong colt, March foal, cost 8,000gns: a first foal, dam a 6/7f wnr: with R Guest. *5* **51**
8 ran   Time 1m 13.73 (2.73)   (Mrs Debbie Mountain)   K Mahdi Newmarket, Suffolk

3628

3.05 DANEPAK RTD HCAP 3YO+ 0-95 (C)   1m2f   Good/Firm 22 -10 Slow   [101]
£10770 £4085 £2042 £928 3 yo rec 8 lb Raced centre - stands side in straight.

3421 **BLUE SUGAR 9** [6] J R Fanshawe 3-8-8 (89) R Cochrane 5/2 FAV: -42221: 3 ch c Shuailaan - Chelsea My Love (Opening Verse) Held up, prog fnl 3f, led over 1f out, styd on well for press: well bckd: '99 Lingfield wnr (med auct mdn, rtd 89, sole start): eff at 1m, apprec this step up to 10f: acts on fast & soft grnd: handles a sharp/undul or stiff/gall track: useful & progressive colt. **93**
3337 **ANOTHER TIME 13** [1] S P C Woods 8-8-7 (83)(3oh) M Tebbutt 20/1: 504352: 8 ch g Clantime - Another Move (Farm Walk) Held up, rdn/prog to chall 1f out, every ch inside last, just held nr fin: see 1170. *½* **82**
3339 **HUDOOD 13** [2] C E Brittain 5-9-5 (92) T E Durcan 13/2: 01D053: 5 ch h Gone West - Fife (Lomond) Held up, rdn & styd on fnl 2f, not pace of front pair: back to form, likes Newmarket: see 2805 (C/D). *2½* **90**
3024 **CAPTAINS LOG 27** [7] M L W Bell 5-8-8 (81) M Fenton 12/1: 141504: Led, hdd 6f out, kept on onepace. *½* **78**
*3337 **INDUCEMENT 13** [8] 4-8-13 (86) W Ryan 5/1: 00-415: Held up, eff 2f out, held ins last: see 3337. *½* **82**
3337 **CULZEAN 13** [4] 4-8-11 (84) J Fortune 9/1: 412036: Held up, eff 2f out, no impress: see 2844, 2287. *1* **79**
3013 **BAILEYS PRIZE 27** [9] 3-8-1 (82) L Newman (3) 7/1: 223147: In tch, eff fnl 2f, sn held: btr 3013, 2805. *2½* **73**
2475 **IPLEDGEALLEGIANCE 50** [5] 4-9-6 (93) G Carter 10/1: -30008: Trkd ldr racing keenly, led over 6f out & sn clr, rdn/hung right & hdd over 1f out, fdd: 7 wk abs: ran much too free for own gd today: see 757. *5* **77**
3155 **SWAN KNIGHT 21** [3] 4-9-7 (94) T Quinn 13/2: 400269: Chsd ldrs, btn fnl 2f: top-weight: see 2648 (1m). *5* **71**
9 ran   Time 2m 05.05 (3.15)   (G Algranti)   J R Fanshawe Newmarket, Suffolk

---

3629

3.35 CHRIS BLACKWELL HCAP 3YO 0-90 (C)   7f str Good/Firm 22 +05 Fast   **[94]**
£7221   £2222   £1111   £555 Raced far side

3543 **LORD PACAL** 4 [14] N A Callaghan 3-9-3 (83) J Fortune 7/1: 022141: 3 b g Indian Ridge - Please **90**
Believe Me (Try My Best) Chsd ldrs, prog to lead ins last, held on well, drvn out: gd time, qck reapp: earlier won
at Yarmouth (h'cap): '99 debut wnr at Newbury (mdn, subs Gr 3 4th, rtd 100): eff at 5f, suited by 6/7f: acts on
firm & gd grnd, handles any trk: tough, progressive & genuine gelding, reportedly heads for Ayr Gold Cup.
3163 **SHATHER** 21 [13] J W Hills 3-8-6 (72) M Hills 9/2 JT FAV: 034322: 3 b c Goofalik - Western Pride ½ 77
(Priamos) Dwelt, rdn & prog over 1f out, styd on well ins last, bckd from 6/1: again shaped
as if a return to 1m will suit: tough & consistent: see 3163, 2855 & 1204 (mdn).
*3445 **TRIBAL PRINCE** 8 [12] P W Harris 3-8-8 (74) M Fenton 10/1: 5-0013: 3 b g Prince Sabo - Tshusick hd 78
(Dancing Brave) Held up, rdn/prog & ch 1f out, not pace of wnr ins last: fine run, imprvd in defeat: see 3445.
*3335 **MERSEY MIRAGE** 13 [8] R Hannon 3-9-7 (87) L Newman (3) 10/1: 02-014: Prom halfway, led 2f out, 1¾ 88
hdd ins last & no extra: gd run under top-weight: stays 7f: see 3335 (rtd h'cap, 6f).
3335 **BABY BARRY** 13 [10] 3-9-5 (85) M Tebbutt 14/1: 430335: Chsd ldrs, onepace fnl 2f: see 3335, 954. ¾ 85
2947 **GINGKO** 29 [3] 3-8-2 (68) A Beech (5) 33/1: -4446: Chsd ldrs, hmpd over 1f out, styd on inside last, hd 67
no threat to ldrs: creditable eff on h'cap bow: step up to 1m should suit: see 2947, 1072.
1406 **FOLLOW SUIT** 98 [1] 3-8-13 (79) G Carter 25/1: 15-07: Held up, late gains, no threat: h'cap bow, abs. ½ 77
*2770 **DANCE WEST** 38 [5] 3-9-5 (85) T Quinn 9/2 JT FAV: 004218: Held up, briefly no room over 1f out, ¾ 82
sn rdn & held: hvly bckd: found little once press applied today: see 2770 (mdn).
3303 **MISTER SUPERB** 14 [2] 3-9-3 (83) G Hind 20/1: 106369: Held up, efft fnl 2f, no hdwy: see 3076, 2183. nk 75
3163 **SUMTHINELSE** 21 [15] 3-8-10 (76) J Quinn 20/1: 021460: Held up, efft 2f out, no impress: 10th. hd 71
3130 **WIND CHIME** 22 [11] 3-8-10 (76) P Robinson 20/1: 24-200: Mid div, btn 2f out: 11th: see 3130. nk 70
3076 **COWBOYS AND ANGELS** 24 [16] 3-8-10 (76) Darren Williams (5) 12/1: 042120: Prom 5f: 12th. 1 68
3414 **WILLOUGHBYS BOY** 9 [9] 3-9-4 (84) J P Spencer 6/1: 161620: Led 5f, sn held: 13th: btr 3414, 2768. 3½ 69
3147 **Hadath** 21 [6] 3-9-3 (83) M Roberts 14/1:   3353) **Random Task** 378 [4] 3-8-12 (78) T G McLaughlin 33/1:
15 ran   Time 1m 25.08 (1.18)   (Paul & Jenny Green)   N A Callaghan Newmarket, Suffolk

---

3630

4.10 TOTE TRIFECTA NURSERY HCAP 2YO (B)   6f Good/Firm 22 -05 Slow   **[96]**
£17745   £5460   £2730   £1365 Raced far side

+2972 **RED CARPET** 29 [7] M L W Bell 2-9-2 (84) J P Spencer 7/4 FAV: 2511: 2 ch c Pivotal - Fleur Rouge **97+**
(Pharly) Made most, drvn ins last, styd on strongly to forge clr: hvly bckd, h'cap bow: earlier won at Chepstow
(auct mdn): eff over a stiff/gall or undul 6f, stays 7f & a return to that trip could suit: acts on fast grnd:
useful, progressive type: held in high regard, holds Gr entries & well worth a step up in grade.
3394 **RED RYDING HOOD** 10 [11] C A Dwyer 2-8-6 (74) A Beech (5) 12/1: 634232: 2 ch f Wolfhound - 3 76
Downeaster Alexa (Red Ryder) Cl up 4f, left bhnd by wnr fnl 1f: met a fast improving, useful rival here: eff
at 5/6f: still a mdn, but can find similar: see 3394.
3062 **STRUMPET** 25 [9] R F Johnson Houghton 2-8-9 (77) J Quinn 14/1: -20163: 2 b f Tragic Role - Fee nk 78
(Mandamus) Prom, rdn & styd on onepace from over 1f out: eff at 5/6f: see 2227 (fillies mdn, 5f).
3327 **SYLVAN GIRL** 13 [2] C N Allen 2-7-13 (67) P M Quinn (3) 20/1: 325304: Held up, no room over 1f ½ 66
out, styd on ins last, no threat: eff at 6f, again shaped as if 7f will suit: can find a race: see 3165, 1954.
3431 **SOLDIER ON** 8 [8] 2-8-11 (79) T E Durcan 9/1: 550135: Held up, eff fnl 2f, onepace: see 3109 (5f). nk 77
3352 **WARDEN WARREN** 12 [5] 2-9-7 (89) P Robinson 4/1: -0126: Chsd ldrs, onepace/held over 1f out: bckd. ½ 85
2972 **PRINCE MILLENNIUM** 29 [6] 2-8-10 (78) J Fortune 9/1: -5637: Rdn/chsd ldrs, nvr on terms: op 7/1. 1 72
*3486 **TIMES SQUARE** 7 [1] 2-9-4 (86)(BL) M Henry 8/1: 431018: Dwelt, chsd ldrs 4f, no hdwy: btr 3486. shd 80
3428 **DUSTY CARPET** 8 [4] 2-8-12 (80) G Carter 14/1: 646439: Dwelt, sn prom, btn 2f out: op 10/1: mdn. 5 64
3463 **MIDNIGHT ARROW** 7 [3] 2-9-7 (89) R Cochrane 25/1: 150040: Al rear: 10th: see 1169 (5f). ½ 71
*3466 **LOVE THING** 7 [10] 2-8-6 (74)(vis) T Quinn 9/1: -60010: Prom 4f: 11th: h'cap bow: see 3466 (auct mdn). 1 54
11 ran   Time 1m 12.6 (1.6)   (Cheveley Park Stud)   M L W Bell Newmarket, Suffolk

---

3631

4.40 LADY AMAT RIDERS HCAP 3YO+ 0-85 (E)   5f Good/Firm 22 +08 Fast   **[68]**
£3474   £1069   £534   £267   3 yo rec 2 lb Raced far side

3464 **AMARANTH** 7 [12] J L Eyre 4-11-0 (82) Miss Diana Jones 7/2 FAV: 126501: 4 b g Mujadil - Zoes **87**
Delight (Hatim) Rear, prog fnl 2f, led ins last, styd on strongly, rdn out: nicely bckd: earlier scored at Ayr
(h'cap): '99 wnr at Newcastle & Newmarket (h'caps, incl this race, rtd 83): '98 juv wnr at Redcar (auct mdn, rtd
76): eff at 5/6f on firm or soft, loves a stiff/gall track: eff with/without a t-strap: gd weight carrier.
+3349 **OUR FRED** 12 [10] T G Mills 3-10-12 (82)(bl) Miss Karen Jones (5) 10/1: 402112: 3 ch g Prince Sabo 1 84
- Sheila's Secret (Bluebird) Prom, led bef halfway, rdn/hung left over 1f out & hdd ins last, kept on: in gd form.
3214 **ANSELLMAN** 17 [9] A Berry 10-9-9 (63)(bl) Miss E J Jones 16/1: 001453: 10 gr g Absalom - Grace 1¼ 62
Poole (Sallust) Chsd ldrs, rdn/kept on fnl 1f, not pace of wnr: 10yo, suited by clmrs nowadays: see 2788 (clmr).
*3208 **LABRETT** 18 [5] B J Meehan 3-10-7 (77)(bl) Miss J Allison 8/1: 440114: Dwelt/outpcd rear early, 2 71
not much room over 1f out, styd on ins last, nrst fin: return to h'caps, looks on a fair mark: see 3208 (5.7f).
3297 **LAS RAMBLAS** 15 [4] 3-10-9 (79)(vis) Miss E Johnson Houghton 10/1: 042305: Prom 3f, sn onepace. hd 72
*3441 **BEDEVILLED** 8 [11] 5-9-11 (65) Mrs L Pearce 7/1: 020016: Prom, held fnl 1f: now with J Pearce. nk 54
3502 **PIERPOINT** 6 [8] 5-9-9 (63)(bl) Mrs S Bosley 9/2: 100537: Led 2f, held fnl 1f: op 7/1, quick reapp. nk 54
3613 **MUJAS MAGIC** 1 [6] 5-8-11 (51)(vis) Mrs M Morris (3) 20/1: 002008: Al outpcd: unplcd here yesterday. ½ 40
2934 **JUDIAM** 30 [11] 3-9-11 (67) Miss Michelle Saunders (7) 20/1: 005109: Dwelt, al outpcd: see 2586. 1 54
3203 **MILL END QUEST** 18 [7] 5-9-2 (56)(bl) Miss J Foster 10/1: 0-0100: Prom 3f: 10th: btr 3123 (6f). 3 36
+3214 **MISS BANANAS** 17 [2] 5-8-10 (50)(5oh) Miss S Phizacklea (5) 20/1: 000010: Prom 3f: 11th: btr 3214. nk 29
3341 **DIAMOND GEEZER** 13 [3] 4-10-2 (70) Mrs S Moore (5) 11/2: 142240: Prom, rdn/hmpd 1f out, sn btn 1 47
& eased inside last: 12th: see 2716, 2371 (6f).
12 ran   Time 59.22 (0.72)   (M Gleason)   J L Eyre Sutton Bank, N Yorks

Official Going FIRM (GOOD/FIRM Places). Stalls: Str Crse - Stands' Side; 14f - Centre; Rem - Inside.

3632 5.30 LADIES EVENING NOV AUCT STKS 2YO (E) 5f str Good/Firm 24 -16 Slow
£2828 £808 £404

3327 **TOMTHEVIC** 13 [1] J J Quinn 2-9-0 (t) O Pears 4/1 FAV: 032101: 2 ch g Emarati - Madame Bovary 83
(Ile de Bourbon) Trkd ldrs, prog to lead ins fnl 1f, styd on well, drvn out: earlier won at Thirsk (mdn): half
brother to a 7f 2yo wnr: dam a 1m/10f wnr: eff at 6f, better over 5f: acts on fast grnd, will reportedly prefer
some give: handles a gall or easy trk: wears a t-strap: tough & consistent, shld do well in 5f nursery h'caps.
3519 **ONLY ONE LEGEND** 5 [3] T D Easterby 2-9-2 R Winston 9/2: 331052: 2 b g Eagle Eyed - Afifah nk 84
(Nashwan) Tried to make all, hdd ins last, rallied & only just btn: qck reapp: jockey given a 3-day whip ban:
apprec this return to 5f & best run to-date: loves to force the pace, see 2575 (h'cap).
3101 **SHATIN DOLLYBIRD** 24 [7] Miss L A Perratt 2-8-3 G Bardwell (5) 5/1: 233103: 2 ch f Up And At 'Em - 1¼ 67
Pumpona (Sharpen Up) Chsd ldrs, eff & ev ch 1f out, no extra cl home: op 7/2: fav by today's weights.
3245 **FRENCH BRAMBLE** 17 [6] J Balding 2-7-13 (bl) N Carlisle 9/1: 000644: Hmpd start, styd on fnl 2f, ½ 62
nvr nrr: return to 6f will suit: see 3245 (first time blnks).
3376 **SEANS HONOR** 10 [9] 2-8-1 T Williams 14/1: 440625: Prom, outpcd halfway, rallied fnl 1f: op 10/1. 1 61
3500 **GLOBAL EXPLORER** 6 [10] 2-8-12 R Fitzpatrick 25/1: -006: Dwelt, late prog, nvr dngrs on h'cap qual 3 63
run: qck reapp: bred to need further & 6/7f+ nursery h'caps will now suit: see 1727.
*3193 **GIBNEYS FLYER** 19 [5] 2-8-5 C Lowther 9/2: -617: Speed 4f, wknd: btr 3193. hd 56
3205 **BRANSTON GEM** 18 [2] 2-8-5 J Fanning 8/1: -08: Cl-up 3½f, wknd: op 6/1: see 3205. ½ 55
3478 **TONY** 7 [4] 2-8-6 Dale Gibson 50/1: -009: Slowly away, al bhnd: see 2454. 6 38
-- **FILLE DE DAUPHIN** [8] 2-7-13 J McAuley 50/1: -0: Slowly away, al bhnd on debut: fin last: cost ½ 30
1,800gns: May foal, half sister to sev wnrs both here & abroad, incl 12f scorer Spirit Of Tenby.
10 ran Time 58.5 (2.0) (Derrick Bloy) J J Quinn Settrington, N Yorks.

3633 6.00 BETTER HALF SELLER 3YO+ (F) 1m6f Good/Firm 24 -50 Slow
£2278 £651 £325

3247 **HOUSE OF DREAMS** 17 [2] Mrs M Reveley 8-9-5 A Culhane 4/1: 624-01: 8 b g Darshaan - Helens 48
Dreamgirl (Caerleon) Rear, imprvd 3f out, forged ahd cl home, drvn out: no bid, slow time: Feb '00 hdles wnr at
Wetherby (h'cap, rtd 128h, eff at 2m3f on fast & hvy): rnr-up in '99 (appr h'cap, rtd 54, with G M Moore): '98 wnr
at Catterick, Carlisle & Thirsk (h'caps): eff at 14f on fast & hvy grnd: handles any trk: could rate higher.
3311 **GO WITH THE WIND** 14 [7] R A Fahey 7-9-5 P Hanagan(7) 7/2: 03-032: 7 b g Unfuwain - Cominna ¾ 46
(Dominion) Chsd ldrs, went on 2f out, worn down cl home: 4L clr 3rd, rider given a 4 day whip ban: see 3311.
3255 **WATER LOUP** 16 [6] W R Muir 4-9-0 C Lowther 4/1: 622263: 4 b f Wolfhound - Heavenly Waters 4 35
(Celestial Storm) Rear, imprvd to chase ldrs 2f out, kept on but no ch with front 2: nicely bckd: see 3084.
3472 **IL PRINCIPE** 7 [3] John Berry 6-9-5 F Norton 3/1 FAV: 000004: Chsd ldrs, onepcd fnl 2f: been 1¼ 38
tubed: well h'capped now & interesting in h'caps on softer grnd: see 3122, 89.
3399 **KINGS CHAMBERS** 10 [8] 4-9-5 (t) P Fessey 50/1: -00055: Led till 2f out, wknd: off rtd just 20. 2½ 35$
2734 **ICE PACK** 39 [10] 4-9-0 Kim Tinkler 6/1: 003436: Chsd ldr, wkng when hmpd dist: see 2734 (2m). nk 29
-- **GO FOR IT SWEETIE** [9] 7-9-0 (t) J Bramhill 50/1: -7: Eff from rear 3f out, sn btn on Flat debut: 5 21
mod hdle & chase form prev: wears a t-strap: with B Leavy.
3331 **MINALCO** 13 [4] 4-9-0 P Goode (3) 33/1: -00008: Chsd ldrs 11f, wknd: no form. 5 13
3002 **SMARTS MEGAN** 28 [1] 4-9-0 G Baker (5) 10/1: -00009: Nvr a factor: bckd from 33/1: see 3002. 2½ 10
3202 **LA CINECITTA** 18 [5] 4-9-0 K Hodgson 50/1: 006050: Mid-div till btn 3f out, fin last: see 1415 (AW). 11 0
10 ran Time 3m 08.2 (10.4) (J & M Leisure/Unos Restaurant) Mrs M Reveley Lingdale, N Yorks.

3634 6.30 RYCROFT HCAP 3YO+ 0-80 (D) 1m str Good/Firm 24 +16 Fast [79]
£5369 £1652 £826 £413 3yo rec 6lb

+3334 **DERRYQUIN** 13 [3] P L Gilligan 5-8-13 (64)(bl) F Norton 6/1: 204011: 5 b g Lion Cavern - 75
Top Berry (High Top) Made all, clr fnl 1f, easily: best time of day: recent Leicester wnr, earlier won here at
Redcar (h'caps): failed to win in '99 (tried blnks): '97 wnr at Lingfield (mdn) & Doncaster (stks, rtd 100):
suited by 1m: acts on gd/soft, loves fast/firm: eff in blnks & likes to force the pace: land qk-fire hat-trick.
3365 **RYEFIELD** 11 [4] Miss L A Perratt 5-8-10 (61) Dean McKeown 4/1 JT FAV: 0R2142: 5 b g Petong - Octavia 3 63
(Sallust) In tch, chsd wnr in vain fnl 1f: nicely bckd: change of tactics, usually held up: likes Ayr.
3338 **STYLE DANCER** 13 [6] R M Whitaker 6-9-4 (69)(vis) C Lowther 8/1: 011003: 6 b g Dancing Dissident - 1 69
Showing Style (Pas de Seul) Mid-div, styd on under press fnl 1f, nvr nrr: back to form, see 2481.
3328 **MEHMAAS** 13 [1] R E Barr 4-8-2 (53)(vis) P Fessey 16/1: 005304: Prom on far side, onepcd fnl 1f: hd 53
fair run racing away from rivals & has slipped down the weights: see 3309 (C/D).
3345 **YENALED** 12 [12] 3-8-4 (59)(2ow) A McGlone 5/1 JT FAV: 246225: Rear, styd on fnl 2f, nvr nrr: op 7/2. 1½ 58
3309 **PENTAGON LAD** 14 [2] 4-9-11 (76) K Darley 11/2: 251426: Prom till wknd fnl 2f: tchd 7/1, top-weight. 1 71
*3440 **SAND HAWK** 8 [8] 5-7-10 (47)(bl)(3oh) J McAuley 8/1: 500417: Nvr better than mid-div: needs 7f. 1¾ 38
2994 **ORIOLE** 28 [5] 7-7-10 (47)(4oh) Kim Tinkler 14/1: 000048: Chsd ldrs till btn over 2f out: flattered 2994. 3 32
3365 **INTRICATE WEB** 11 [9] 4-9-5 (70) J Carroll 7/1: 330539: Mid-div till btn 2f out: see 3365. 1 53
3328 **ENCOUNTER** 13 [7] 4-8-2 (53) O Pears 12/1: 110160: Chsd ldrs 6f, wknd: fin 10th: btr 3144 (6f). 2 32
3410 **TO THE LAST MAN** 9 [10] 4-8-6 (57) F Lynch 33/1: 506-00: Nvr a factor in 11th: see 3410. nk 35
2349 **TOM DOUGAL** 55 [11] 5-9-6 (71) R Fitzpatrick 9/1: -00500: Al rear, fin last: tchd 16/1, 8 wk abs: 1¼ 46
well h'capped now & better clearly expected: see 1490.
12 ran Time 1m 35.5 (0.7) (Lady Bland) P L Gilligan Newmarket

---

3635 7.00 GREEN NOV MED AUCT STKS 2YO (E) 7f str Good/Firm 24 -26 Slow
£3656 £1125 £562 £281

3508 **ATTACHE** 6 [9] M Johnston 2-8-12 K Darley 1/2 FAV: -21: 2 ch c Wolfhound - Royal Passion (Ahonoora) 85
Trkd ldrs going well, went on dist, styd on well, rdn out: well bckd, qck reapp: half brother to useful sprinter
Tadeo: dam a 10f wnr: eff at 7f on fast, 1m will suit: runs well fresh, handles a gall or sharp trk: improving,
potentially useful colt: shld rate more highly & win more races.
-- **BOUCHRA** [5] M L W Bell 2-8-7 A Culhane 5/1: -2: 2 ch f Inchinor - My Darlingdaughter (Night 2½ 74
Shift) Chsd ldrs, chsd wnr fnl 1f, no impress on debut: Jan foal, sire a high-class 7f performer: eff at 7f

on fast grnd, 1m will suit: sure to learn from this & shld win a mdn.

3316 **FASTINA** 14 [2] R Guest 2-8-7 C Lowther 4/1: -4303: 2 b f Dunphy - Farandole (Gay Baron)   hd   74$
Dwelt, recovered to chase ldrs, kept on fnl 1f, nvr nrr: drifted from 9/4: flattered 3316, see 2306.

-- **ALS ME TRAINER** [4] A Dickman 2-8-12 J Fanning 33/1: -4: Led till dist, no extra on debut: 4   71
Mar foal, cost 5,000gns: showed up well for a long way & sharper next time.

3478 **BEAU SAUVAGE** 7 [6] G Parkin 66/1: -005: Prom, ev ch 2f out, wknd: clr of rem.   3½   64$
3333 **CHESTERS BOY** 13 [1] J Bramhill 66/1: -06: Speed 5f, sn wknd: see 3333.   10   44
3051 **SAVE THE POUND** 25 [3] 2-8-12 J Carroll 33/1: -507: Chsd ldrs 5½f, wknd: see 2271 (debut).   nk   43
3492 **FAREHAM** 7 [7] 2-8-7 M Baird 20/1: -08: Dwelt, al bhnd: see 3492.   3½   31
-- **ARISTAEUS** [8] 2-8-12 R Lappin 66/1: -9: Slowly away, al bhnd, t.o.: Mar foal, sire a decent sprinter.   25   6
9 ran   Time 1m 25.0 (3.5)   (J R Goad)   M Johnston Middleham, N Yorks.

3636   7.30 DAILY STAR HCAP 3YO+ 0-70 (E)   1m3f   Good/Firm 24 -44 Slow   [68]
      £4030   £1240   £620   £310   3yo rec 9lb

*2755 **DOUBLE BLADE** 38 [7] Mrs M Reveley 5-9-10 (64) A Culhane 9/2: 0-2011: 5 b g Kris - Sesame   69
(Derrylin) Waited with, imprvd 2f out, led ins fnl 1f, readily: slow time, top-weight: recent Doncaster wnr (h'cap):
won 4 times over hdles in 99/00 (novs, rtd 123h, eff at 2m on gd & firm): dif 4/1 on fast & gd/soft: tried
blnks, better without: runs well fresh & gd weight carrier: still fairly h'capped & cld complete hat-trick.

3379 **FREEDOM QUEST** 10 [9] B S Rothwell 5-9-5 (59) R Lappin 7/1: 140042: 5 b g Polish Patriot -   ½   61
Recherchee (Rainbow Quest) Rcd keenly mid-div, imprvd to lead dist, not pace of wnr cl home: see 3379.

3392 **SWEET ANGELINE** 10 [2] G G Margarson 3-9-5 (68) K Darley 5/2 FAV: 543123: 3 b f Deploy - Fiveofive   1¾   68
(Fairy King) Hdwy from rear 3f out, ev ch 2f out, no extra cl home: consistent: see 3392, 3125.

3181 **FALCON SPIRIT** 19 [10] G M Moore 4-8-11 (51)(bl) J Carroll 25/1: 20-004: Rear, hdwy & ev ch 2f out,   nk   50
no extra ins fnl 1f: blnks back on: lightly rcd this term: mdn, see 2836.

3344 **AL MABROOK** 12 [6] 5-8-10 (50) F Lynch 8/1: 000035: Led till dist, no extra: see 3344 (sell h'cap).   2½   45
2482 **BOLT FROM THE BLUE** 50 [3] 4-7-10 (36)(1oh) Kim Tinkler 12/1: 005606: Rear, hdwy, nvr dngrs: abs.   hd   31
3249 **DESERT MUSIC** 17 [11] 4-7-10 (36)(2oh) G Baker (5) 33/1: 055507: Chsd ldrs till wknd over 1f out.   ½   30
3310 **STEPASTRAY** 14 [1] 3-8-3 (52) P Fessey 15/2: 036338: Rcd keenly & chsd ldrs 9f, wknd: btr 3310.   1   44
3368 **THORNTON GOLD** 11 [4] 4-8-6 (46)(bl) A McGlone 7/1: 235529: Prom 9f, wknd: btr 3368 (gd).   shd   38
3247 **GUNBOAT DIPLOMACY GB** 17 [12] 5-7-11 (37) Dale Gibson 10/1: 001500: Rear, hdwy & ev ch 2f out,   hd   29
sn btn: fin 10th, longer priced stablemate of wnr: won a poor race in 2143 (10f here, clmr).

3140 **WINGED ANGEL** 22 [5] 3-8-8 (57) F Norton 9/1: 000150: Chsd lds 1m, wknd into 11th: btr 2863.   5   41
3336 **BURNING** 13 [8] 8-7-10 (36)(bl)(2oh) J Bramhill 12/1: 000030: Rear, eff & chsd ldrs 4f out, sn btn.   2½   16
12 ran   Time 2m 23.0 (7.5)   (The Mary Reveley Racing Club)   Mrs M Reveley Lingdale, N Yorks.

3637   8.00 BEST DRESSED HCAP 3YO 0-70 (E)   1m6f   Good/Firm 24 -36 Slow   [72]
      £3591   £1105   £552   £276

3476 **JACK DAWSON** 7 [1] John Berry 3-9-5 (63) F Norton 9/4 FAV: 012231: 3 b g Persian Bold - Dream Of   70
Jenny (Caerleon) In tch, prog to lead 2½f out, held on well, drvn out: nicely bckd: in gd form, earlier won
at Chepstow (h'cap), also plcd sev times: unplcd for J Noseda in '99 (mdns, rtd 75): much imprvd since upped
to 14f/2m: acts on fast & gd/soft grnd: tough, consistet & in-form gelding.

*2651 **VANISHING DANCER** 43 [8] A Dickman 3-9-7 (65) J Fanning 9/1: W03312: 3 ch g Llandaff -   ½   71
Vanishing Prairie (Alysheba) Led till lost place halfway, rallied & ev ch 3f out, just btn in a tight fin: 6 wk abs,
9L clr 3rd, top-weight: prev trained by K Burke: stays 14f, acts on fast, gd/soft & equitrack: improving, see 2651.

3050 **WELCOME BACK** 25 [6] K A Ryan 3-7-10 (40)(3oh) G Baker (5) 12/1: 055363: 3 ch g Most Welcome -   9   32
Villavina (Top Ville) Rdn in rear, styd on into 3rd, no ch with front 2: prob stays 14f: see 2964 (1m).

3247 **FOSTON SECOND** 17 [9] C B B Booth 3-7-10 (40)(11oh) A Polli (3) 10/1: 00-424: Mid-div, rdn & ch   shd   32
3f out, wknd fnl 2f: stiff task: prob not stay this longer 14f trip: see 3247 (12f).

3399 **HORTON DANCER** 10 [7] 3-7-13 (43) T Williams 9/1: 003035: Chsd ldrs, imprvd to lead 4f out till 2f   4   29
out, sn wknd: flattered 3399 (12f), see 2439 (mdn).

3396 **SORRENTO KING** 10 [10] 3-8-0 (44)(bl) Dale Gibson 10/3: 000236: Chsd ldrs till btn 3f out: tchd 5/1.   ½   29
3181 **WETHAAB** 19 [2] 3-8-11 (55)(bl) K Darley 9/1: 401607: Led/dsptd lead, led halfway till 4f out, fdd.   ½   39
2825 **WORTH THE RISK** 36 [3] 3-7-10 (40)(2oh) Kim Tinkler 9/1: 0-3508: Al towards rear: see 2222 (1m).   8   12
3396 **GRANTLEY** 10 [4] 3-8-4 (48) J Carroll 9/2: 00-009: Nvr a factor: mkt drifter: longer trip.   3½   15
3448 **WHAT A CRACKER** 8 [5] 3-7-12 (42) J Lowe 9/1: 00-600: In tch 10f, sn btn: fin last: see 3125.   10   0
10 ran   Time 3m 06.3 (8.5)   (The Premier Cru)   John Berry Newmarket

---

Official Going   GOOD Stalls: Inside.

3638   5.20 EBF NOV MED AUCT STKS 2YO (E)   6f   Good   Inapplicable
      £3705   £1140   £570   £285

3162 **WHALE BEACH** 21 [9] B W Hills 2-8-12 W Ryan 10/3: 01: 2 b c Known Fact - Zulu Dance (Danzatore)   81
Dwelt, sn mid-div, hdwy when short of room/switched dist, ran on strongly to lead post, drvn out: op 9/4:
IR60,000gns Feb 1st foal, dam multiple wnr in the States: eff at 6f, further will suit: acts on gd grnd &
a sharp/turning trk: improving & will apprec further.

3443 **DEAR PICKLES** 8 [8] J G Portman 2-8-7 R Brisland (5) 14/1: 62: 2 b f Piccolo - Freddie's Recall   hd   75
(Warrshan) Dsptd lead, led ins last, drifted left & hdd nr fin: stays 6f: win with a more experienced jockey.

3223 **TALBOT AVENUE** 17 [2] M R F Johnson Houghton 2-8-12 S Carson (3) 4/1: 443: 2 b c Puissance -   1¼   77
Dancing Daughter (Dance In Time) Led, rdn/hdd well ins last, held nr fin: handles fast & gd: gd run.

1166 **BABY BUNTING** 112 [5] M L W Bell 2-8-7 J Mackay (5) 6/1: -444: Front rank, ev ch till no extra   hd   72
for press well ins last: not disgraced after a nr 4 month abs & just sharper for this: stays 6f on gd: see 970.

2868 **MY LUCY LOCKET** 34 [6] 2-9-1 P Dobbs (5) 13/8 FAV: 332105: Cl-up, drvn/not pace of ldrs fnl 1f: nk   79
nicely bckd on this step up to 6f: twice below a useful run in 2665 (h'cap).

3239 **CAPTAIN GIBSON** 17 [7] 2-8-12 D Sweeney 50/1: -5006: Dwelt, raced keenly & sn chsg ldrs, ev ch   1   73$
till not qckn for press fnl 1f: treat this rating with caution, only mod form prev: see 3239.

2854 **SAVING LIVES ATSEA** 35 [3] 2-8-12 C Rutter 33/1: -607: Handy, lost tch appr fnl 1f: see 1426.   5   61

1117

3252 **SPINETAIL RUFOUS** 16 [1] 2-8-12 J D Smith 33/1: 08: In tch to halfway, fdd: see 3252.   8   45
--   **BELTANE** [4] 2-8-8 Sophie Mitchell 40/1: 9: Dwelt, al bhd: speedily bred colt.   ½   40
9 ran   Time 1m 14.7   (Mr C Wright & The Hon Mrs J M Corbett)   B W Hills Lambourn, Berks

3639   5.50 DAILY STAR SELLER 2YO (F)   5f   Good   Inapplicable
£2380   £680   £340

--   **MY LOVELY** [1] D J S Cosgrove 2-8-6 C Rutter 10/1: 1: 2 b f Dolphin Street - My Bonus (Cyrano de   62
Bergerac) Bhd, rdn/prog halfway, led appr fnl 1f, styd on well, rdn out: debut, bought in for 10,000gns:
Feb 1st foal, dam a 5f wnr: eff over a sharp 5f, gd grnd: goes well fresh: encouraging debut.
3376 **GEMTASTIC** 10 [6] P D Evans 2-8-6 W Ryan 9/2: -60332: 2 b f Tagula - It's So Easy (Shaadi)   1   58
Led, prsd sn after halfway, hdd over 1f out, rall ins last, held cl-home: tch 7/2: consistent: see 3376.
3204 **UNVEIL** 18 [4] G M McCourt 2-8-6 D Kinsella (7) 33/1: 466503: 2 b f Rudimentary - Magical Veil   3½ 50
(Majestic Light) Waited with, short of room after 2f, gd hdwy over 1f out, no extra ins last: see 3204, 1136.
3278 **MISS SUTTON** 15 [9] T G Mills 2-8-6 J Mackay (5) 10/1: 54: In tch, rdn & late hdwy but no threat   1   47
to ldrs: tchd 14/1: fin clr rem: 6f shld suit: see 3278.
3359 **LEGGIT** 12 [2] T Quinn 2-8-6 C Rutter 9/2: 0005: Prom, drvn/btn over 1f out: prob flattered in 3359. 4 37
2772 **SAVANNA MISS** 37 [8] 2-8-6 D Sweeney 16/1: 5006: Dwelt, sn detached, late gains, no dngr.   3½ 29
3491 **MOLLY IRWIN** 7 [7] B Marcus 20/1: 120007: Sn well bhd, mod late gains: qck reapp.   3   26
3388 **MULSANNE** 10 [3] G Hannon (7) 50/1: -0008: Handy, wknd qckly fnl 2f: of little account.   nk 25
3015 **THE WALL** 27 [14] 2-8-6 A Nicholls (3) 50/1: -05009: Chsd ldrs to halfway, fdd: mod form.   1   17
3466 **GILLS DIAMOND** 7 [13] Pat Eddery 15/8 FAV: 3500: Prom, rdn & wknd rapidly after halfway,   1   14
fin 10th: nicely bckd, qck reapp: reportedly unsuited by this rain-softened grnd: see 3055, 1823.
2550 **Truth Be Known** 47 [5] 2-8-11 (BL) S Carson (3) 33/1:3278 **Carrick Lady** 15 [12] 2-8-6 A Mackay 50/1:
3277 **One Charmer** 15 [10] 2-8-11 P McCabe 20/1:   3296 **Broughton Storm** 15 [11] 2-8-11 D R McCabe 33/1:
14 ran   Time 1m 01.1   (Mrs J I McGinn)   D J S Cosgrove Newmarket

3640   6.20 3 DAY FESTIVAL COND STKS 3YO+ (C)   1m3f135y Good   Inapplicable
£5962   £2261   £1130   £514   3 yo rec 10lb

3321 **HAPPY CHANGE** 14 [1] M Johnston 6-9-1 M Hills 4/1: 21-301: 6 ch g Surumu - Happy Gini (Ginistrelli) 108
Led early, remnd cl-up, went on again 3f out, strongly prsd appr fnl 1f, styd on gamely, drvn out: tchd 6/1:
rnr-up over hdles in '99/00 (2m, rtd 112m, Miss V Williams): '99 Epsom wnr (stks, rtd 110): ex-German, '98 wnr
at Baden-Baden (Gr 3, rtd 115): eff at 10/12f on fast, soft & a sharp or undul trk: tough & useful gelding.
*3088 **BLUE GOLD** 24 [5] R Hannon 3-8-2 L Newman (3) 10/3: 012012: 3 b c Rainbow Quest -   ¾ 103
Relatively Special (Alzao) Front rank, chall wnr 2f out, styd on ins last, no extra cl-home: nicely bckd:
useful & remains in fine form, capable of landing similar: see 3088.
1174 **AZOUZ PASHA** 112 [6] H R A Cecil 4-9-1 T Quinn 9/2: 21-553: 4 b c Lyphard - Empress Club (Famesio) ½ 105
Settled rear, rdn/hdwy 2f out, ev ch fnl 1f, no extra well in last: 9L clr rem: fine effort after a near 4
month abs: acts on gd, likes firm/fast grnd: just sharper for this: see 1014.
2995 **SHABLAM** 28 [2] Sir Michael Stoute 3-8-5 (VIS) Pat Eddery 9/1: -54404: Sn led, keen, raced alone   9 93
stands side 3f out, sn hdd & lost tch: 1st time visor: longer 11.6f trip: see 1246, 955.
2720 **PORT VILA** 40 [3] R Hills 11/4 FAV: 4-3135: Cl-up, wknd qckly fnl 2f: drifted from 2/1:   ¾ 99
6 wk abs: disapp here & poss not suited by this step up to 11.6f: see 2720, 2169.
1578▶ **MARCUS MAXIMUS** 457 [4] 5-8-12 W Ryan 15/2: 4/01-6: Al towards rear on belated reapp: raced just   5 82
twice in '99, wng 2nd start, at Newcastle (cond stks, rtd 115): '98 wnr at Yarmouth (mdn) & Doncaster (stks,
rtd 106+): eff at 10/12.5f on fast/firm, sharp or gall trks: smart at best, just sharper for this run.
6 ran   Time 2m 30.3   (The Winning Line)   M Johnston Middleham, N Yorks

3641   6.50 GR 3 WINTER HILL STKS 3YO+ (A)   1m2f   Good   Inapplicable
£23400   £8970   £4485   £2145   3 yo rec 8 lb

*3150 **ADILABAD** 21 [5] Sir Michael Stoute 3-8-9 Pat Eddery 6/4 FAV: 11-511: 3 b c Gulch -   117
Adaiyka (Doyoun) Cl-up, went on appr fnl 1f, held on gamely, drvn out: hvly bckd: recent Goodwood wnr (List):
wnr of both juv starts, at Sandown & Newmarket (stks, rtd 96): eff at 7f, stays 10f well on firm, gd/soft &
any trk: runs well fresh: lightly raced & smart colt, still improving & likely to win more Group races.
*3230 **ALBARAHIN** 17 [3] M P Tregoning 5-9-0 R Hills 2/1: 12-212: 5 b h Silver Hawk - My Dear   ½ 116
Lady (Mr Prospector) In tch, gd hdwy to lead 3f out, prsd 2f out, hdd appr fnl 1f, not pace of wnr well in last:
nicely bckd: smart & progressive entire, looks sure to win in Listed/Gr 3 soon: see 3230.
3321 **FORBEARING** 14 [4] Sir Mark Prescott 3-8-6 S Sanders 11/2: 111223: 3 b c Bering - For Example   1¼ 114
(Northern Baby) Dwelt, settled rear, gd hdwy to chall over 2f out, ev ch fnl nt qckn ins last: op 4/1:
8L clr rem: another smart run, not out of the frame in last 6 starts: see 3321, 2596, 2471.
2720 **ISLAND HOUSE** 40 [9] G Wragg 4-9-0 M Roberts 8/1: -11154: Waited with, rdn/outpcd over 2f out,   8 102
sn btn: 6 wk abs: shld apprec a drop back to List class, see 2260.
3291 **CRIMSON TIDE** 15 [8] 6-9-0 M Hills 14/1: 150/35: Raced keenly in rear, gd hdwy over 2f out,   1 101
ev ch fnl wknd qckly appr fnl 1f: see 3291.
3150 **MERRY MERLIN** 21 [1] 3-8-6 J P Spencer 20/1: 105636: Front rank, led after halfway, hdd 3f out, fdd. hd 101
2089 **RHYTHM BAND** 66 [6] 4-9-4 L Dettori 8/1: -32167: Mid-div, lost tch fnl 3f: op 12/1, abs: see 2089.   2 102
3132 **YAKAREEM** 27 [7] 4-9-0 D McGaffin 66/1: 0-0508: Prom, wknd qckly fnl 3f: v stiff task: see 1847.   11 84
3306 **KINGSCLERE** 14 [2] 3-8-6 Martin Dwyer 16/1: -15059: V keen, sn led, hdd 5f out, wknd rapidly, t.o. dist 0
9 ran   Time 2m 07.4   (H H Aga Khan)   Sir Michael Stoute Newmarket

3642   7.20 GREENOAKS RTD HCAP 3YO+ 0-90 (C)   1m67y   Good   Inapplicable   [95]
£6301   £2390   £1195   £543   3 yo rec 6 lb

*3256 **BORDER SUBJECT** 16 [6] R Charlton 3-9-0 (87) Pat Eddery 11/10 FAV: -6011: 3 b c Selkirk - Topicality 92
(Topsider) Led at steady pace, increased tempo 2f out, drvn to maintain adv ins last, shade cosy: hvly bckd
on h'cap bow: recent impress h'cap mdn wnr (wore t-strap): likes to race up with/force the pace over
7f/8.3f: acts on fast, good/soft & any trk: eff with/without a t-strap: runs well fresh: useful & progressive.
3325 **WELSH WIND** 14 [8] D J Murphy 4-9-7 (88) M Fenton 10/1: -22042: 4 b g Tenby - Bavaria (Top Ville)   ½ 90
Raced keenly cl-up, drvn/styd on ins last but al held by wnr: tchd 20/1: gd run under top-weight: see 3325.
3355 **LEGAL SET** 12 [10] K R Burke 4-8-7 (74)(1oh) J P Spencer 10/1: 336023: 4 gr g Second Set -   1 74

WINDSOR SATURDAY AUGUST 26TH Sharp, Figure 8 Track

Tiffany's Case (Thatching) Mid-div, rdn/imprvd 3f out, not pace of wnr fnl 1f: mdn, ran to form of 3355.
-3107 **PARISIEN STAR 23** [5] N Hamilton 4-9-6 (87) T Quinn 5/2: 045124: Settled rear, rdn & outpcd over 2f out, ran on late, no threat: well bckd: shade btr 3107 (Goodwood). ¾ **86**
3597 **ADOBE 2** [2] 5-9-1 (82) T G McLaughlin 8/1: 121105: In tch, dropped rear 3 out, ran on late: op 6/1: ran 48hrs ago: v tough: ran to form of win in 3325. *hd* **81**
3410 **LITTLE AMIN 9** [7] 4-8-10 (77) Martin Dwyer 11/1: 016326: Chsd ldrs, rdn/btn fnl 2f: see 3410 (10f). ¾ **74**
2858 **CHAPEL ROYALE 35** [3] 3-8-9 (82) D McGaffin (5) 12/1: 203107: Bhd, nvr dngrs: btr 2614. ¾ **78**
4615} **ABAJANY 294** [9] 6-8-10 (77) Craig Williams 20/1: 3524-8: Nvr a factor: reapp: failed to win from 20 '99 starts (plcd sev times, h'caps, rtd 87 at best), subs plcd over timber (2m h'cap, rtd 101h): '98 wnr at Bath (class stks) & Ayr (h'cap, rtd 90): '97 Leicester & Sandown wnr (h'caps, rtd 77): eff at 1m/10f, poss stays 12f: acts on firm, soft & any trk: just sharper for this. *3* **68**
3325 **SUDRA 14** [1] 3-8-10 (83) M Hills 14/1: 0-0009: Prom, wkng qckly when hmpd 2f out: see 1534. *3* **69**
9 ran Time 1m 47.4 (K Abdulla) R Charlton Beckhampton, Wilts

3643 **7.50 S JOSEPH FILLIES HCAP 3YO+ 0-85 (D) 1m67y Good Inapplicable [84]**
£4062 £1250 £625 £312 3 yo rec 6 lb

3259 **AMORAS 16** [4] J W Hills 3-8-8 (70) M Hills 15/2: 004251: 3 b f Hamas - Red Lory (Bay Express) Handy, gd hdwy over 2f out, ran on strongly to lead post, drvn out: op 6/1: '99 Bath wnr (nursery, rtd 76): suited by 7f/1m on firm & gd grnd, handles gd/soft & any trk: genuine. **72**
3334 **DENS JOY 13** [7] Miss D A McHale 4-8-6 (62) D McGaffin (4) 14/1: 005402: 4 b f Archway - Bonvin (Taufan) Dwelt, hdwy from rear 2f out, styd on strongly fnl 1f, just failed: gd run, likes Windsor: see 1917. *hd* **63**
3317 **CAUTION 14** [11] S Gollings 6-7-13 (55) J Quinn 5/1: 225233: 6 b m Warning - Fairy Flax (Dancing Brave) Front rank, hdwy to lead ins last, styd on, collared nr line: nicely bckd: consistent: see 3317, 2561. *shd* **56**
3160 **MIDNIGHT ALLURE 21** [10] C F Wall 3-9-1 (77)(t) S Sanders 9/1: 116234: Cl-up, went on appr fnl 1f, hdd well ins last, sn held: remains in good form: see 3160, 2713. 1½ **75**
3422 **FREDORA 9** [3] 5-10-0 (84) D Sweeney 12/1: 014045: Chsd ldrs, hdwy to lead halfway, hdd appr fnl 1f, sn rdn/not qckn: top-weight: see 2629 (gd/soft). 1¼ **80**
3178 **SAFARI BLUES 20** [1] 3-9-3 (79) P Dobbs (5) 12/1: 505266: In tch, late gains: see 2811 (10f). ¾ **73**
*3422 **NATALIE JAY 9** [2] 4-8-13 (69) Craig Williams 11/2: 043017: Nvr dngrs: op 7/2: btr 3422 (Salisbury). ½ **62**
3309 **LOVE YOU TOO 14** [5] 3-9-3 (79) N Callan 16/1: -04058: Led to halfway, grad wknd: see 1186. 1½ **69**
2871 **SASH 34** [6] 3-8-0 (62) P Doe 20/1: -5059: Dwelt, nvr a factor: h'cap bow: see 2322. ¾ **51**
3460 **NOUF 8** [8] 4-9-2 (72) M Roberts 16/1: 020660: Al twrds rear, 10th: see 3460. ½ **60**
*3289 **BLOODY MARY 15** [9] 3-8-5 (67) L Newman (3) 15/2: 34-010: Held up, eff 2f out, sn btn/eased, 11th: op 6/1: better expected after a front-running mdn win in 3289. *nk* **55**
*3160 **JAWLA 21** [12] 3-9-8 (84) R Hills 7/2 FAV: -32110: Front rank, wknd qckly 2f out, fin last: v disapp on this hat-trick bid, connections baffled by this poor run: much btr 3160. ½ **71**
12 ran Time 1m 46.5 (Espresso Racing) J W Hills Upper Lambourn, Berks

GOODWOOD SATURDAY AUGUST 26TH Righthand, Sharpish, Undulating Track

Official Going GOOD. Stalls: Str - Stands Side; Rnd - Inside. No pace Figs due to Rain throughout afternoon.

3644 **1.45 BRISSAC GENTS AMAT HCAP 3YO+ 0-85 (E) 1m1f Good Slow [51]**
£3575 £1100 £550 £275 3 yo rec 7 lb

3110 **BOUND FOR PLEASURE 23** [6] J H M Gosden 4-11-10 (75)(t) Mr T Scudamore 11/8 FAV: 00-231: 4 gr c Barathea - Dazzlingly Radiant (Try My Best) Hld up, gd hdwy to lead over 2f out, pushed clr, easily under top weight: lightly rcd in '99 (rtd 80, with G L Moore): '98 Lingfield scorer (mdn, rtd 81): eff at 7f, stays 9f well on firm, hvy & likes a sharp/undul trk: best without blnks but with a t-strap: in fine form, qk follow up? **86**
3390 **THATCHMASTER 10** [5] C A Horgan 9-10-12 (63)(t) Mr A Evans 13/2: 44-002: 9 b g Thatching - Key Maneuver (Key To Content) Led 1f, in tch, eff again over 1f out, took 2nd ins last: tough 9yo, 3 wins at Goodwood. *8* **63**
*3407 **OPEN ARMS 9** [9] Mrs A L M King 4-11-1 (66) Mr D N Russell 11/1: -00013: 4 ch g Most Welcome - Amber Fiz (Effervescing) Handy, chsd ldrs over 5f out, kept on same pace: ran to form of 3407. *nk* **66**
3404 **STOPPES BROW 10** [12] G L Moore 8-11-5 (70)(bl) Mr R L Moore (5) 9/2: 525634: Bhd, late gains, nvr dngrs: likes a sharp trk: see 3404, 2433. *shd* **70**
2802 **IRON MOUNTAIN 22** [8] 5-11-7 (72) Mr S Callaghan (7) 6/1: 014305: Chsd ldrs, hung badly right 2f out, no extra: btr 2802, 2564. 2½ **68**
3403 **PHEISTY 10** [2] 3-11-2 (74)(bl) Mr E Hennau 9/1: 416526: Bhd, some late gains: btr 3403, 2387. 1¼ **68**
3404 **MAX 10** [7] 5-9-10 (47)(14oh) Mr T Steeger 66/1: 030007: In tch, btn over 2f out: stiff task, see 2433. *nk* **40**
3078 **KAFIL 24** [11] 6-9-10 (47)(8oh) Mr G Arizkorreta 66/1: 003068: In tch, short of room & wknd 2f out. 2½ **36**
3186 **TWOFORTEN 19** [10] 5-9-10 (47)(vis)(15oh) Mr R Lucey Butler (7) 66/1: 500069: In tch, onepace when hmpd 2f out, sn btn: stiff task: see 2347 (7f). *nk* **35**
3407 **CLASSIC EAGLE 9** [4] 7-9-10 (47)(vis)(7oh) Mr S Rees (5) 25/1: 000540: Al bhd, 10th: btr 2407. *1* **33**
3334 **BABA AU RHUM 13** [1] 8-10-12 (63) Mr Edgar Byrne 20/1: 500/00: Slow away & al bhd: 11th: see 3334. 1¾ **45**
3011 **MODUS OPERANDI 27** [14] 4-11-4 (69) Mr J J Best (5) 25/1: 640000: Led after 1f, clr 6f out till hdd & wknd 2f out: 12th: see 3011, 593. 2½ **47**
2527 **SABOT 48** [13] 7-9-10 (47)(1oh) Mr M Sheridan (7) 33/1: -04000: Chsd ldr after 1f till over 5f out, no extra: 13th, 7 wk abs: see 1335. *17* **0**
2347 **LANDICAN LANE 56** [3] 4-9-10 (47)(21oh) Mr T Radford (7) 66/1: 00000U: V keen bhd, slightly hmpd & u.r. over 5f out: 8 wk abs, v stiff task: his 64 year-old jockey is sadly in a critical condition. **0**
14 ran Time 1m 58.53 (8.03) (Action Bloodstock) J H M Gosden Manton, Wilts.

3645 **2.15 LISTED MARCH STKS 3YO+ (A) 1m6f Good Fair**
£15515 £5885 £2942 £1337 3 yo rec 12lb

3565 **ALVA GLEN 3** [5] Sir Michael Stoute 3-8-7 Pat Eddery 5/2: 012361: 3 b g Gulch - Domludge (Lyphard) Held up, gd hdwy to lead over 2f out, sn clr, cmftbly: qck reapp having been set plenty to do in Ebor, earlier scored at York (rtd h'cap): '99 Nottingham wnr (mdn, rtd 96): eff at 12f, apprec step up to 14f & further could suit: acts on firm, soft & on any trk: v useful & open to further improvement over long dists. **111**
3061 **KUWAIT TROOPER 25** [2] G A Butler 3-8-7 K Darley 5/1: 031052: 3 b c Cozzene - Super Fan (Lear Fan) *3* **105**

Waited with, hdwy to lead over 6f out till over 2f out, not pace of wnr: useful & apprec return to 14f: see 1311.

*3065 **SAMSAAM** 29 [1] J L Dunlop 3-8-12 R Hills 7/4 FAV: 113213: 3 b c Sadler's Wells - Azyaa (Kris) 2 107
Cl-up travv well, rdn & no extra final 2f: not disgraced conceding weight all-round & will apprec softer grnd.

3061 **GOING GLOBAL** 25 [6] S P C Woods 3-8-7 R Hughes 6/1: 320604: Led till over 6f out, wknd over 2f out. 3½ 97

3509 **TAUFANS MELODY** 6 [4] 9-9-7 J Reid 11/2: /00235: Sn handy, btn over 3f out: qck reapp: btr 3509. 11 85
5 ran   Time 3m 05.13 (6.33)   (Sheikh Mohammed)   Sir Michael Stoute Newmarket.

3646   2.45 LADBROKES HCAP 3YO+ 0-95 (C)   6f   Good Fair   [92]
£22717 £6990 £3495 £1747   3 yo rec 3 lb

3398 **SURPRISED** 10 [21] R A Fahey 5-8-6 (70)(vis) S Sanders 8/1: 015441: 5 b g Superpower - Indigo 78
(Primo Dominie) In tch, hdwy halfway to lead over 1f out, styd on well, rdn out: caught the eye over 5f last
time, earlier scored at Hamilton (amat class stks): '99 wnr at Pontefract (h'cap, rtd 72): all 3 wins over 6f,
does stay 7.4f: acts on firm, gd/soft & on any trk: best without blnks, suited by a visor now: qck follow-up?

1471 **MARSAD** 94 [18] J Akehurst 6-9-8 (86) P Doe 11/1: -50002: 6 ch g Fayruz - Broad Haven (Be My Guest) 1 90
Slow away, sn in tch, hdwy over 2f out, kept on inside last, but not pace of wnr: 3 mth abs & looks to have
been saved for a soft grnd autumn campaign: see 728.

*3257 **NINEACRES** 16 [12] J M Bradley 9-8-10 (74)(bl) P Fitzsimons (5) 25/1: 030413: 9 b g Sayf El Arab - 1 75
Mayor (Laxton) Handy, hdwy to lead over 2f out till over 1f out, kept on same pace: most tough: see 3257.

*3502 **PREMIUM PRINCESS** 6 [19] J J Quinn 5-8-4 (68) K Darley 9/1: 624114: Handy, effort 2f out, kept on ½ 68
same pace: continues in fine form: all 3 wins over a stiff 5f as in 3502.

3464 **ZUHAIR** 7 [5] 7-9-1 (79) Alex Greaves 10/1: 331505: Outpcd & rdn along, kept on over 1f out, shd 79
nrst fin: could well go in again: see 3464, 3091.

*3464 **WILLIAMS WELL** 7 [20] 6-9-2 (80)(bl) T Lucas 10/1: 222116: Cl-up, ev ch over 1f out, no extra ½ 78
inside last: gd run having been raised 5lb for 3464.

3510 **ZIETZIG** 6 [8] 3-8-13 (80) N Callan 25/1: 640107: Handy, effort over 1f out, sn btn: best 3130 (7f). shd 77

3464 **BLUE MOUNTAIN** 7 [4] 3-10-0 (95) J Reid 9/2 FAV: 211028: Sn rdn & bhd, hdwy halfway, late gains, nk 91
no threat: nicely bckd under a big weight: suited: see 3464, 2355.

3315 **EASY DOLLAR** 14 [11] 8-9-6 (84)(bl) D Sweeney 20/1: 000559: Cl-up, led 3f out till over 2f out, wknd. 1 77

3457 **FULL SPATE** 8 [9] 5-8-6 (70) Martin Dwyer 25/1: 103040: Handy, rdn & btn final 1f: see 2877, 2444. nk 62

*3457 **RUSHCUTTER BAY** 8 [10] 7-9-4 (82) R Hughes 14/1: 260210: Bhd, plenty to do over 2f out, late hd 73
gains: 11th: much better when forcing the pace under a more positive jockey in 3457.

3464 **CADEAUX CHER** 7 [16] 6-9-5 (83) R Hills 12/1: 010050: Bhd, modest late gains: 12th: see 3152, 2845. ¾ 72

*3485 **SMOKIN BEAU** 7 [17] 3-9-2 (83) P Dobbs (5) 14/1: 036110: In tch, btn over 1f out: 13th, btr 3458 (5f). ¾ 70

3457 **IVORY DAWN** 8 [1] 6-8-12 (76) C Carver (3) 20/1: 150030: Sn rdn & nvr a factor: 14th: see 3457. 1 60

3473 **SEVEN NO TRUMPS** 7 [7] 3-9-9 (90) R Naylor (7) 40/1: 003000: Nvr a factor: 15th: btr 3158. ½ 72

3335 **PEDRO JACK** 13 [2] 3-9-2 (83)(bl) Pat Eddery 14/1: 035220: In tch, wknd over 3f out: 16th: btr 3335. shd 65

3322 **SHARP HAT** 14 [6] 6-8-6 (70) G Bardwell 25/1: 611630: Led till halfway, wknd 2f out: last, see 3322. 0

3176 Midnight Escape 20 [3] 7-9-4 (82) A Daly 20/1:   3436 Referendum 8 [13] 6-8-10 (74) Clare Roche (7) 16/1:
2444 Hill Magic 51 [15] 8-8-12 (76) A Clark 16/1:   1047 Barringer 20 [14] 3-9-6 (87) Craig Williams 25/1:
21 ran   Time 1m 11.69 (1.69)   (D R Brotherton)   R A Fahey Butterwick, Nth Yorks.

3647   3.20 GR 2 CELEBRATION MILE 3YO+ (A)   1m rnd   Good Fast
£46400 £17600 £8800 £4000   3 yo rec 6 lb

3087 **MEDICEAN** 24 [4] Sir Michael Stoute 3-8-9 Pat Eddery 5/2: 113031: 3 ch c Machiavellian - Mystic 123
Goddess (Storm Bird) Chsd ldr, hdwy to lead 3f out, styd on well for press despite edging right just ins fnl 1f:
earlier scored at Sandown (stks) & Ayr (class stks), subs arnd 1L 3rd to Giants Causeway in Gr 1 St James Palace
& 2 1/4L 3rd bhd that same horse here in the Gr 1 Sussex: suited by 1m, shld stay 10f: acts on fast, handles
hvy & any trk: has progressed into a tough & high-class colt, shld continue to give a good account.

*3132 **OBSERVATORY** 22 [7] J H M Gosden 3-8-9 K Darley 9/4 FAV: 1-2112: 3 ch c Distant View - Stellaria 1 120
(Roberto) Keen, handy, effort 2f out, pressing wnr when slightly hmpd just ins last, swtchd left & kept on for
press, al just held: bckd: high class run stepped up to 1m & should certainly win more Gr races: see 3132 (7f).

3452 **CAPE TOWN** 8 [3] R Hannon 3-8-9 R Hughes 7/1: 103023: 3 g r c Desert Style - Rossaldene (Mummy's 1¼ 117
Pet) In tch, eff to chall 2f out, no extra ins last: smart run & should certainly win a Listed/Gr 3 this autumn.

2150 **SEAZUN** 64 [5] M R Channon 3-8-6 Craig Williams 16/1: -24404: Held up, brief effort over 2f out, 4 107
no extra: 2 mth abs: see 2150, 1626.

2066 **BACHIR** 67 [2] 3-9-1 L Dettori 5/2: 121165: Led till over 3f out, wknd 2f out: op 4/1, 10 wk abs under 3½ 109
top weight & twice below 1623 (Gr1, made all, gd/soft).

2410 **SARAFAN** 55 [6] 3-8-9 S Sanders 10/1: 21-536: In tch, brief effort 3f out, wknd over 2f out: 8 20 67
wk abs, op 6/1: needs Listed/Gr 3: see 2410, 2066.
6 ran   Time 1m 38.65 (1.25)   (Cheveley Park Stud)   Sir Michael Stoute Newmarket.

3648   3.50 CHICHESTER RTD HCAP 3YO+ 0-105 (B)   7f rnd   Good Slow   [103]
£9616 £3647 £1823 £829   3 yo rec 5 lb

3155 **MUCHEA** 21 [6] M R Channon 6-9-7 (96) Craig Williams 8/1: 540041: 6 ch h Shalford - Bargouzine 101
(Hotfoot) In tch, hdwy over 2f out, styd on nicely on rails when bmpd ins last, led cl home, rdn out: rnr-up
twice prev term: unplcd in Hong Kong in '99: '98 wnr at the Curragh & Newmarket (Gr 3, rtd 113): best at
7f, does stay 1m: acts on firm & hvy, on any trk: can run well fresh: tough, useful & has slipped down the weights.

3452 **OMAHA CITY** 8 [5] B Gubby 6-9-6 (95) J Reid 11/4 JT FAV: 050053: 6 b g Night Shift - Be Discreet hd 99
(Junius) With ldr, hdwy to lead over 1f out, hung right for press but kept on till collared cl-home, just btn:
likes Goodwood & appreciated this return to 7f: see 3107, 1450.

2090 **BLACK SILK** 66 [3] C F Wall 4-9-5 (94) S Sanders 100/30: 03-163: 4 b g Zafonic - Mademoiselle Chloe ¾ 96
(Night Shift) Chsd ldrs, eff to chall appr fnl 1f, kept on same pace, not btn far: edgs for autumn campaign.

2616 **STRAHAN** 44 [9] J H M Gosden 3-9-7 (101) K Darley 11/4 JT FAV: 122304: Led till well over 1f out, 2 99
wkng when hmpd 1f out: 6 wk abs: see 2151, 1470.

3414 **MISTER RAMBO** 9 [4] 5-8-3 (78) D R McCabe 16/1: 206055: Handy, rdn & btn over 1f out: see 3414. ¾ 74

3503 **KASHRA** 6 [8] 3-8-13 (93) R Hills 9/1: 000206: Nvr a factor: qck reapp & twice below 3155 (fm). 1¼ 87

3315 **TEODORA** 14 [1] 3-8-3 (83)(t) P Doe 16/1: 620007: Went badly left start & well bhd, some late gains. 3 71

3120 **FAIRY GEM** 22 [2] 3-8-12 (92)(VIS) P Fitzsimons (5) 20/1: 04660R: Refused to race: tried a visor, see 995. 0
8 ran   Time 1m 28.23 (3.73)   (Andy J Smith)   M R Channon West Isley, Berks.

GOODWOOD   SATURDAY AUGUST 26TH   Righthand, Sharpish, Undulating Track

3649   4.20 DAILY STAR MDN AUCT 2YO (E)   6f   Good Slow
£4290   £1320   £660   £330

3193 **MIDNIGHT VENTURE 19** [8] Mrs L Stubbs 2-8-11 S W Kelly (3) 13/2: 030221: 2 b c Night Shift - Front   78
Line Romance (Caerleon) Made all, kept on well for press ins last, drvn out: deserved win: Feb foal, cost 9,000
gns: half-brother to a 6f juv wnr, dam 7f juv scorer: loves to front run over 6f & handles firm, soft & any trk.
2748 **AUNT RUBY 38** [7] M L W Bell 2-8-9 R Hills 20/1: 02: 2 ch f Rubiano - Redress (Storm Cat)   hd   75
In tch, chsd wnr 2f out, strong chall ins last, just held: imprvd for debut over this sharp/undul 6f on gd.
3215 **KAI ONE 17** [5] R Hannon 2-9-0 P Fitzsimons (5) 11/10 FAV: 323: 2 b c Puissance - Kind Of Shy   1   77
(Kind Of Hush) Prom, slightly outpcd 2f out, kept on again same pace fnl 1f: well bckd: shwn enough to win a race.
2854 **SENOR MIRO 35** [3] R F Johnson Houghton 2-9-0 J Reid 5/1: -054: Bmpd start, held up, kept on nicely   2½   70
at same pace final 2f, hands-&-heels: encouraging here & may do better now he qualifies for nursery h'caps.
3446 **MISHKA 8** [1] A Daly 16/1: 0035: In tch, rdn over 2f out, no impress over 1f out: see 3446   1½   63
-- **SHARED HARMONY** [6] 2-9-0 P Doe 25/1: 6: Sn bhd, brief effort 2f out, sn wknd: debut: Jan foal,   3   58
cost 21,000 gns: half-brother to a useful sprinter: bred to apprec 6f.
3215 **RESPLENDENT FLYER 17** [4] 2-9-0 Pat Eddery 8/1: 047: Slow away & bhd, some gains: bred for further.   ¾   56
3044 **PACKIN EM IN 26** [2] 2-9-0 Martin Dwyer 50/1: 08: Went right start, chsd wnr 3f, sn btn: Apr foal,   3   47
cost 16,000 gns: half-brother to a 6f juv wnr: dam 5f juv scorer: with N Hamilton.
2972 **WINFIELD 29** [10] 2-9-0 S Sanders 7/1: 040: In tch, effort over 2f out, sn wknd: op 5/1, btr 2972.   shd   47
9 ran   Time 1m 13.04 (3.04)   (The Midnight Venture Partnership)   Mrs L Stubbs Newmarket.

3650   4.55 EBF SOLENT MDN 2YO (D)   7f rnd   Good V Slow
£4251   £1308   £654   £327

3298 **MUQTADI 15** [3] J H M Gosden 2-9-0 R Hills 8/13 FAV: 21: 2 b c Marju - Kadwah (Mr Prospector)   87
Held up, rdn & slightly outpcd 2f out, rallied for press over 1f out & despite edging right got up cl-home,
drvn out: hvly bckd: Feb foal, half-brother to juv wnrs over 6f/1m: dam 1m/10f scorer: stays 7f, sure to
relish 1m: acts on firm, gd & any trk: open to improvement over further.
2921 **ELMONJED 31** [2] J L Dunlop 2-9-0 P Doe 10/1: -002: 2 b c Gulch - Aqaarid (Nashwan)   nk   86
Led, edged right dist, kept on, collared last strides: better from the front over this sharp/undul 7f on gd.
3342 **TARA GOLD 13** [4] R Hannon 2-8-9 R Hughes 9/4: -43: 2 b f Royal Academy - Soha (Dancing Brave)   1¼   78
Handy, effort to chall 2f out, hung right dist, held when slightly hmpd inside last: stays 7f: see 3342.
-- **JAMIE MY BOY** [1] K R Burke 2-9-0 N Callan 9/1: 4: Chsd ldr, wknd over 2f out on debut: op   14   57
12/1: Apr foal, cost 25,000 gns: full brother to a smart 10f wnr: with K Burke.
4 ran   Time 1m 30.62 (6.12)   (Hamdan Al Maktoum)   J H M Gosden Manton, Wilts.

BEVERLEY   SATURDAY AUGUST 26TH   Righthand, Oval Track with Stiff, Uphill Finish

Official Going   FIRM (GOOD TO FIRM Straight). Stalls: Inside.

3651   2.20 WATTS MDN 3YO+ (D)   5f   Good/Firm 30 -18 Slow
£3893   £1198   £599   £299   3 yo rec 2 lb

1609 **VILLA VIA 87** [8] J A R Toller 3-8-9 S Whitworth 5/4 FAV: -53221: 3 b f Night Shift - Joma Kaanem   70
(Double Form) Prom, led appr final 1f, ran on strongly: nicely bckd after 3 mth abs: consistent in defeat
previously, unrcd juv: eff at 5/6f on firm & gd/soft grnd, any trk: well fresh.
3377 **FOUND AT LAST 10** [5] J Balding 4-9-2 G Baker (5) 15/2: 224352: 4 b g Aragon - Girton (Balidar)   2½   67$
In tch, not clr run bef fnl 1f, kept on inside last, nvr nrr: tchd 11/1, stiff task, looks flattered, blnks
omitted: appears to apprec this drop back to a stiff 5f: handles fast grnd & fibresand.
3462 **DAVEYS PANACEA 7** [7] R D Wylie 3-8-9 P Bradley (5) 7/1: 25333: 3 ch f Paris House - Pampoushka   nk   61
(Pampabird) Well plcd, rdn ent final 2f, onepace: op 5/1, qck reapp, shwn enough to win a seller: see 3462.
3462 **FIRST VENTURE 7** [3] C N Allen 3-9-0 (VIS) J Weaver 7/1: 230044: Led till appr fnl 1f, onepace: vis.   2½   59
2519 **DAYLILY 49** [9] 3-8-9 G Parkin 5/2: 033235: Prom, eff 2f out, outpcd: op 7/2, 7 wk abs: see 2313.   2½   47
2965 **BOLLIN ROCK 29** [10] 3-9-0 R Winston 20/1: 56: Nvr going pace: stablemate 5th, back in trip.   1½   47
3229 **BREW 17** [6] 4-9-2 J Carroll 33/1: 060007: Dwelt, prom till after halfway: stiff task, new stable.   1½   42
4360] **COTTAM LILLY 317** [11] 3-8-9 J Fanning 66/1: 0-8: Al towards rear: reapp, unplcd sole '99 start.   2   31
87 **MISS PIPPIN 2** [4] 4-8-11 P Mundy (7) 33/1: 4050-9: Speed 2f: 4th in a C/D mdn in '99 (g/s, rtd 66).   1½   26
2839 **LUCKY COVE 35** [1] 4-9-2 Kim Tinkler 100/1: 000000: Bhd from halfway: 10th, stiff task.   2½   25
3266 **BALLY CYRANO 16** [2] 3-9-0 (tbl) F Norton 100/1: 0-0000: Dwelt, nvr in it: 11th: has shwn nothing   ½   24
since plcd on debut last term (auct mdn, rtd 72): eff at 5f on fast grnd: with B McMahon.
11 ran   Time 1m 03.7 (2.4)   (Harry R D McCalmont)   J A R Toller Newmarket, Suffolk.

3652   2.50 STANLEY RACING HCAP 3YO+ 0-70 (E)   7f100y rnd   Good/Firm 30 +02 Fast   [70]
£4992   £1536   £768   £384   3 yo rec 5 lb

3054 **TIPPERARY SUNSET 25** [8] D Shaw 6-9-3 (59)(BL) T Williams 7/1: 664D41: 6 gr g Red Sunset - Chapter   64
And Verse (Dancer's Image) In tch, smooth prog appr fnl 2f, kept on to lead before dist, rdn out: best time of
day: '99 wnr again here at Beverley (h'cap, rtd 66, J Quinn): '98 Hamilton wnr (h'cap, rtd 60): eff at 7.5f/10f:
acts on firm & soft grnd, any trk, blnks favoured: sharpened by blnks: stable back in form.
3279 **CALCAVELLA 15** [3] M Kettle 4-9-5 (61) F Norton 10/1: 405042: 4 b f Pursuit Of Love - Brightside   1¼   63
(Last Tycoon) Towards rear, wide prog und press appr fnl 1f: op gd run, poor draw, eff at 7/7.5f: see 2320.
3334 **SWYNFORD PLEASURE 13** [10] J Hetherton 4-8-8 (50) O Pears 14/1: 343003: 4 b f Reprimand -   nk   51
Pleasuring (Good Times) Bhd ldrs, kept on fnl 1f, unable to chall: ran to best, see 2180, 1939.
2777 **ANGEL HILL 37** [1] K A Ryan 5-8-12 (54) F Lynch 25/1: 061004: Off the pace, rng/hmpd 2f out, kept on   1   53
strgly ins last, nvr nrr: wld have gone close for new connections: poor draw, no visor: stays 7.5f, likes Newcastle.
2673 **ONLY FOR GOLD 42** [12] 5-8-12 (54) J Carroll 6/1: 302005: Led till appr final 1f, no extra: 6 wk abs.   nk   52
3503 **PERFECT PEACH 6** [2] 5-9-13 (69) J Fanning 5/1: 346206: Towrds rear, prog & not clr run dist, unable   1   65
to chall: qck reapp, not much luck in running but hard to win with: flattered last time, see 1250.
3514 **ITALIAN SYMPHONY 6** [7] 6-9-0 (56)(vis) Joanna Badger (7) 16/1: 351657: Mid-div, no room/switched   nk   51

1121

1f out, kept on: forget this, see 3238.
3440 **KASS ALHAWA 8** [14] 7-9-12 (68)(bl) A Culhane 7/2 FAV: 442258: Prom, rdn & ch bef fnl 1f, onepace.   hd   63
*3318 **PLEADING 14** [4] 7-9-4 (60)(vis) Dean McKeown 12/1: 500619: Lost any ch with v slow start: tchd 16/1.   2½   50
3317 **TRIPLE WOOD 14** [5] 3-9-8 (69) J Weaver 20/1: 431000: Well plcd til 2f out: 10th, see 2824.   hd   58
3170 **DOVEBRACE 20** [9] 7-8-13 (55) J Bramhill 10/1: 662300: Slow away, al bhnd: 11th, see 3141, 2420.   ¾   42
3194 **Best Bond 19** [13] 3-8-9 (56)(vis) R Winston 14/1:   2193 **Mybotye 61** [11] 7-9-2 (58)(t) G Faulkner (3) 20/1:
3480 **Wonderful Man 7** [6] 4-8-7 (49) G Parkin 25/1:
14 ran   Time 1m 32.9 (2.1)   (Harold Bray)   D Shaw Averham, Notts.

3653	3.25 NETBETSPORTS.COM HCAP 3YO+ 0-75 (E) 5f Good/Firm 30 -10 Slow [75]
	£6344 £1952 £976 £488 3 yo rec 2 lb

3191 **BEYOND THE CLOUDS 19** [17] J S Wainwright 4-9-4 (65) R Winston 4/1 FAV: 141421: 4 b g Midhish -   70
Tongabezi (Shernazar) Bhd ldrs, burst thro' to lead before final 1f, rdn out: earlier won at Hamilton &
Windsor (h'caps): plcd last term (h'cap, rtd 54): all 3 wins at 5f, stays 6f: acts on fast & gd grnd, any
trk, likes stiff finishes: best without a visor now: tough, improving.
3257 **BEYOND CALCULATION 16** [18] J M Bradley 6-9-7 (68) F Norton 9/2: 016442: 6 ch g Geiger Counter -   ½   71
Placer Queen (Habitat) Trkd ldrs tho' hemmed in, switched & ran on ins last, not btn far: win again at 6f.
3455 **FAIRY PRINCE 8** [8] Mrs A L M King 7-8-13 (60)(bl) A McGlone 16/1: 100443: 7 b g Fairy King - Danger   ½   61
Ahead (Mill Reef) In tch, not much room 2f out till dist, kept on well: gd run with blnks reapplied, see 2192.
*3572 **STATOYORK 3** [12] D Shaw 7-9-1 (62)(6ex) T Williams 5/1: 000214: Mid-div, trav well eff & swithced   2   57
bef fnl 1f, 2f out, kept on without threatening: qck reapp & penalty, shade btr 3572.
3398 **BOLLIN ANN 10** [15] 5-9-2 (63) J Weaver 11/2: 230605: Front rank, led ent fnl 2f till dist, no extra.   nk   57
3619 **TIME TO FLY 1** [13] 7-7-10 (43)(bl) (3oh) T Hamilton (7) 25/1: 504006: Rider lost irons start & bhd,   ¾   34
imprvd when short of room 2f out, clr dist & ran on well, nvr dngrs: unplcd at Thirsk yesterday: see 2525.
2777 **AMARO 37** [11] 4-7-10 (43)(5oh) C Catlin (4) 25/1: 563607: Handy, effort & no impress appr final 1f.   hd   34
*3512 **CLASSY CLEO 6** [5] 5-9-13 (74) Joanna Badger (7) 16/1: 640018: Nvr a factor: poor draw.   1¼   61
3349 **MARON 12** [14] 3-8-11 (60) J Carroll 20/1: 321009: Chsd ldrs, fdd fnl 1f: see 2440 (6f, soft).   1   44
3613 **KOSEVO 1** [9] 6-7-10 (43)(bl) (5oh) G Baker (5) 25/1: 000300: With ldrs wide till ent final 2f: 10th.   1   24
3605 **SQUARE DANCER 1** [10] 4-8-11 (58) G Parkin 14/1: 260550: Prom 3f: 11th, op 10/1, qck reapp.   1   36
3349 **MAROMITO 12** [16] 3-9-7 (70) O Pears 12/1: 0-0000: Led till ent fnl 2f, wknd: 13th, op 8/1, see 2644.   0
3502 **SOAKED 4** [4] 7-9-0 (61)(bl) A Culhane 12/1: 113340: Chsd ldrs till lost pl 2f out: 15th, poor draw, see 3209.   0
3271 Yabint El Sham 15 [7] 4-8-8 (55)(t) P Mundy (7) 33/1:1778 **Bergen 80** [1] 5-9-9 (70) F Janning 16/1:
3312 **Jacobina 14** [3] 5-7-12 (45) J Bramhill 33/1:   3312 **Dominelle 14** [6] 8-8-4 (51) P Fessey 16/1:
3528 **Whizz Kid 5** [2] 6-9-10 (71) Claire Bryan (5) 40/1:
18 ran   Time 1m 03.3 (2)   (P Charalambous)   J S Wainwright Kennythorpe, Nth Yorks.

3654	3.55 CLASSIFIED STKS 3YO+ 0-80 (D) 1m4f Good/Firm 30 -03 Slow
	£4355 £1340 £670 £335 3 yo rec 10lb

2936 **DARARIYNA 30** [6] Sir Michael Stoute 3-8-8 F Lynch 10/3: 22151: 3 b f Shirley Heights - Dararita   82
(Halo) Trkd ldrs, led appr final 1f, ran on well: earlier won at Chester (mdn), unrcd juv: eff at 12/13.5f:
acts on fast & gd/soft grnd, prob any trk: progressive filly.
*3517 **OCTAVIUS CAESAR 6** [3] P F I Cole 3-8-11 A Culhane 8/11 FAV: 20-312: 3 ch c Affirmed - Secret   1¼   83
Imperatrice (Secretariat) Keen, bhd ldrs, rdn appr final 1f, kept on but not pace of wnr: nicely bckd,
qck reapp: shade better expected after 3517 (made all).
*3262 **CABALLE 16** [2] S P C Woods 3-8-8 Dean McKeown 9/2: 332213: 3 ch f Opening Verse - Attirance   hd   79
(Crowned Prince) Led till appr final 1f, same pace: clr rem & tho' imprvd over lngr 12f trip, return to 10f cld suit.
3472 **TOTAL DELIGHT 7** [1] Lady Herries 4-9-7 (t) J Carroll 10/1: 120004: Chsd ldrs, effort & outpcd   5   75
2f out: qck reapp, vis omitted, t-strap reapplied: btr 1991 (14f h'cap).
3501 **PORTRACK JUNCTION 6** [8] 3-8-9 R Lappin 100/1: 000005: Prom till 3f out: v stiff task, flattered.   12   53$
891} **PENMAR 498** [10] 8-9-5 G Faulkner (3) 100/1: 01/0-6: Al bhd: ran once in '99, '98 Musselburgh wnr   1¼   51
(h'cap, rtd 55, M Peill): '96 W'hampton wnr (h'cap, rtd 57a): eff at 1m/9f, stays 12f on fast, soft & fibresand.
3053 **GENUINE JOHN 25** [11] 7-9-5 J Weaver 33/1: 053007: Chsd ldrs, in tch till 4f out: v stiff task.   2   47$
3053 **TIGER TALK 25** [4] 4-9-5 P Bradley (5) 50/1: 000058: Mid-div till lost place 4f out: see 1743.   hd   46
3616 **STAMFORD HILL 1** [9] 5-9-5 D Allan (7) 100/1: 560059: Nvr dngrs: impossible task, ran yesterday.   1½   42
3099 **PARISIENNE HILL 24** [5] 4-9-2 K Hodgson 100/1: 0-0000: Prom 7f: 10th, stiff task.   16   19
10 ran   Time 2m 35.2 (3.9)   (H H Aga Khan)   Sir Michael Stoute Newmarket, Suffolk.

3655	4.25 NETBETSPORTS EBF FILLIES MDN 2YO (D) 7f100y rnd Good/Firm 30 -26 Slow
	£3705 £1140 £570 £285

3397 **ESYOUEFFCEE 10** [5] M W Easterby 2-8-11 J Carroll 1/1 FAV: 21: 2 b f Alzao - Familiar (Diesis)   94
Led, qcknd over 10L clr appr final 1f, eased considerably inside last: well bckd: IR60,000 gns Apr foal: eff at
7.5f, should stay at least 10f next term: acts on fast & gd grnd, stiff trk: impressive from the front here & this
well regarded filly should hold her own in better company.
3108 **IFFAH 23** [1] J L Dunlop 2-8-11 F Lynch 2/1: 62: 2 ch f Halling - Taroob (Roberto)   5   77
Trkd ldrs, unbalanced/nrly slipped 3f out, kept on for 2nd but no hope with wnr: cght a tartar, shld find a fill mdn.
3400 **BAJAN BLUE 10** [3] M Johnston 2-8-11 J Weaver 3/1: 633: 2 b f Lycius - Serotina (Mtoto)   10   57
Prom, no extra 2f out: lngr trip, should stay: now qualified for nurseries, see 3400.
3245 **CONGENIALITY 17** [2] T D Easterby 2-8-11 G Parkin 25/1: 004: Keen, chsd wnr till fdd appr final 2f.   2½   52
-- **LEANADIS ROSE** [4] 2-8-11 P Bradley (5) 50/1: 5: Sn struggling: cheaply bght Namaqualand filly.   11   32
5 ran   Time 1m 35.0 (4.2)   (M P Burke)   M W Easterby Sheriff Hutton, Nth Yorks.

3656	5.00 HANDS/HEELS APPR MDN HCAP 3YO+ 0-60 (F) 1m2f Good/Firm 30 -17 Slow [51]
	£2236 £639 £319 3 yo rec 8 lb

3357 **NICOLAI 12** [12] M L W Bell 3-9-0 (45) C Catlin 7/2: 000041: 3 b g Piccolo - Fair Eleanor (Saritamer)   51
In tch, prog to lead ent final 2f, pushed out, cmftbly: unrcd juv, apprec step up to 10f on fast grnd.
3396 **SILVER SOCKS 10** [15] M W Easterby 3-8-8 (39) D Allan (3) 3/1 FAV: 0-0062: 3 gr g Petong - Tasmin   4   39
(Be My Guest) Led chsg pack, imprvd & ch fnl 1f, kept on but not as well as wnr: bckd from 5/1: stays 10f on fast.
3318 **PENALTA 14** [7] M Wigham 4-9-0 (37) A Hawkins (3) 25/1: 0003: 4 ch g Cosmonaut - Targuette   ½   36

(Targowice) In tch, kept on appr final 1f, nvr pace to chall: h'cap bow: stays 10f on fast grnd.
3314 **SHARP BELLINE 14** [3] J L Harris 3-9-7 (52) N Esler 8/1: 43404: Towards rear, prog 2f out, hmpd *1¼* **39**
before dist, onepace: tchd 10/1, visor omitted: see 3021, 2765.
3326 **THREE CHERRIES 13** [11] 4-8-11 (34) L Enstone (6) 10/1: 045545: Held up, kept on 2f out till fnl 150y. *1* **29**
3382 **WOODBASTWICK CHARM 10** [13] 3-8-8 (39) L Paddock (3) 14/1: 000056: In tch, onepace final 2f. *3* **30**
3506 **CONCINO 6** [4] 3-8-7 (38) Lynsey Hanna 40/1: -03007: Nvr better than mid-div: qck reapp. *2* **26**
3294 **ARZILLO 15** [8] 4-9-10 (47)(BL) R Thomas 12/1: 403058: Sn in a clr lead, saddle slipped, no extra *nk* **34**
3f out, hdd ent fnl 2f, wknd: blnkd, jnt top-weight: big step up in trip, btr 3129.
684 **FORTHECHOP 162** [14] 3-8-9 (40) D Meah (3) 25/1: 454309: In tch till 3f out: abs, btr 555. *5* **20**
3357 **PEPPERCORN 12** [6] 3-8-8 (39) S Clancy (3) 8/1: 600360: Al towards rear: 10th, btr 3236. *11* **8**
3124 **SILVER TONGUED 22** [10] 4-8-5 (28) M Mathers (3) 7/1: 006040: Nvr dngrs: 11th: much longer trip. *1¼* **0**
3236 **Jensens Tale 17** [1] 3-7-11 (28) N Carter (6) 25/1: 4037} **Loch Sound 340** [5] 4-8-9 (32) M Salvidge (6) 40/1:
3310 **Kelburne 14** [9] 3-9-10 (55) D Glennon 11/1:
14 ran Time 2m 07.0 (4.7) (Mrs Anne Yearley) M L W Bell Newmarket, Suffolk.

GOODWOOD SUNDAY AUGUST 27TH Righthand, Sharpish, Undulating Track

Official Going GOOD Stalls: Str Course - Stands Side, Round Course - Inside, 12f - Outside

3657 **2.15 GOING PLACES HCAP 3YO+ 0-85 (D) 1m4f Good 57 -09 Slow [83]**
£15275 £4700 £2350 £1175 3yo rec 10lb

1982 **LIVIUS 72** [2] Major D N Chappell 6-10-0 (83) R Hills 8/1: 21-341: 6 b g Alzao - Marie de Beaujeu **88**
(Kenmare) Rear, prog to trk ldrs over 2f out, switched & rdn to lead dist, styd on strongly ins last: 10 wk abs:
'99 wnr at Ascot (h'cap, rtd 83): rtd 79 at best in '98: suited by 12f, has tried 14f: acts on firm & gd/sft grnd,
any trk: best without blnks: runs well fresh & a gd weight carrier: progressive, could win again.
3001 **VERIDIAN 29** [8] N J Henderson 7-9-13 (82) T Quinn 5/1: 2/1342: 7 b g Green Desert - Alik (Targowice) *1¼* **83**
Rear, smooth prog fnl 3f, ch ins last, not pace of wnr nr fin: sound run, see 2069, 1251.
+3402 **GENTLEMAN VENTURE 11** [7] J Akehurst 4-9-12 (81) P Doe 7/2 FAV: 425513: 4 b g Polar Falcon - Our *1½* **80**
Shirley (Shirley Heights) Prom, rdn/led over 1f out till dist, kept on for press: op 3/1: remains in gd heart.
3461 **GREYFIELD 9** [10] M R Channon 4-9-1 (70) Craig Williams 8/1: 450454: Dwelt/held up rear, hdwy *nk* **68**
3f out, styd on onepace fnl 1f: need to come with a late run: see 1984.
3339 **THE GREEN GREY 14** [5] 6-9-2 (71) A Clark 10/1: 001525: Led/dsptd lead 10f, fdd: jockey given a *1¼* **67**
2-day careless riding ban: see 2888 (10f, Windsor).
*3399 **BLUE STREET 11** [6] 4-8-4 (59) D Harrison 12/1: 602316: Handy, led over 2f out till over 1f out, fdd. *3* **50**
1709 **REVIVAL 84** [4] 3-9-4 (83) J P Spencer 4/1: 0-127: Trkd ldrs travelling well, shaken up over 1f out, *hd* **74**
sn btn: nicely bckd on h'cap bow after 12 wk abs: longer 12f trip, shaped as is a return to 10f will suit: see 1709.
3353 **HALF TIDE 13** [9] 6-7-10 (51)(6oh) A Beech(0) 16/1: 621058: Mid-div, eff & hmpd over 2f out, lost pl, *2* **39**
kept on ins last, no threat to ldrs: cl-up with a clr run, unlikely to have troubled principals: see 2626.
3392 **WATER FLOWER 11** [13] 6-8-11 (66) S Sanders 20/1: 010009: Trkd ldrs, btn over 1f out: see 2023. *shd* **54**
3586 **ORDAINED 3** [11] 7-8-0 (55)(4ow)(10oh) N Pollard 33/1: 122600: Rear, eff 3f out, sn held: 10th. *4* **37**
2785 **MUTADARRA 38** [3] 7-8-4 (59) P Robinson 20/1: 251020: Twds rear, eff 3f out/sn held: 11th: btr 2785. *9* **26**
3514 **SHAANXI ROMANCE 7** [1] 5-7-12 (52)(vis)(1ow) F Norton 14/1: 112340: Keen/led after 3f till over 3f *7* **10**
out, wkng when hmpd 2f out, sn btn: 12th: btr 3514, 3170 (1m).
3073 **SUPLIZI 25** [12] 9-7-11 (52) A Nicholls(0) 16/1: 060600: Bhd halfway: 13th: vis omitted: see 1788. *4* **3**
13 ran Time 2m 39.72 (7.92) (Mrs G McClintock & Miss E Kilfeather) Major D N Chappell Pulborough, W Sussex

3658 **2.45 BRITANNIA RESCUE HCAP 3YO 0-95 (C) 1m1f Good 57 +01 Fast [97]**
£15210 £4680 £2340 £1170

*3505 **EVEREST 7** [4] P F I Cole 3-9-2 (85) R Hughes 7/2: 232111: 3 ch c Indian Ridge - Reine d'Beaute **90**
(Caerleon) Trkd ldrs, chsd wnr 3f out, sustained chall for press ins last, prevailed cl-home: bckd from 5/1, gd
time: completed hat-trick after wins at Thirsk (mdn) & Pontefract (h'cap), plcd all 4 starts prev: suited by 1m/
sharp 9f, cld get further: acts on firm & hvy grnd, sharp or stiff trks: runs well fresh: tough & progressive.
3325 **KATHIR 15** [1] A C Stewart 3-9-2 (85) R Hills 8/1: 032152: 3 ch c Woodman - Alcando (Alzao) *shd* **89**
Led, rdn/strongly prsd from over 1f out, styd on well, just hdd nr line: bold front running effort, can find similar.
2358 **SCOTTISH SPICE 56** [7] I A Balding 3-8-13 (82) J P Spencer 14/1: -60053: 3 b f Selkirk - Dilwara *2* **82**
(Lashkari) Trkd ldrs, chsd front pair over 1f out, kept on tho' al held: 8 wk abs: jockey given a 2-day whip ban.
3300 **DYNAMIC DREAM 16** [12] P W Harris 3-9-4 (87) M Fenton 14/1: 1-354: Twds rear, hdwy 2f out, sn held. *3½* **81**
3435 **SHADOW PRINCE 9** [11] 3-8-10 (79) S Sanders 5/2 FAV: 013305: Rear, hdwy over 2f out, sn btn: *2* **69**
well bckd, op 3/1: longer trip, prev fast finishing over 7f: btr 3130, 2261 (7f/1m).
3355 **TAKE MANHATTAN 13** [3] 3-8-1 (70) Craig Williams 16/1: 000166: Chsd ldr, hung left/btn 2f out. *hd* **60**
3317 **OMNIHEAT 15** [6] 3-8-9 (78) P Robinson 9/1: 654007: Mid-div, held 2f out: see 3317, 1649 (10f). *2½* **64**
*3435 **OGILIA 9** [9] 3-8-11 (80) A Nicholls (3) 7/1: 004618: Rear, eff 3f out, sn held: op 6/1: btr 3435. *1* **64**
3317 **TIME VALLY 15** [10] 3-8-1 (70) P Doe 16/1: 105549: Slowly away, rear, nvr factor: btr 1855 (7f). *1¼* **51**
3338 **BOLD EWAR 14** [8] 3-8-11 (80)(bl) B Marcus 12/1: 520150: Twds rear, btn 2f out: 10th: btr 3261. *1½* **58**
2757 **DIVULGE 39** [2] 3-9-7 (90) F Norton 9/1: -5140: Trkd ldrs 7f: 11th: op 7/1, h'cap bow: see 1960 (mdn). *3½* **62**
11 ran Time 1m 55.55 (5.05) (H R H Prince Fahd Salman) P F I Cole Whatcombe, Oxon

3659 **3.15 GR 3 ATS PRESTIGE STKS 2YO (A) 7f rnd Good 57 +01 Fast**
£24000 £9200 £4600 £2200

2565 **FREEFOURRACING 47** [3] B J Meehan 2-8-9 T Quinn 8/1: -1101: 2 b f French Deputy - Gerri N Jo Go **105**
(Top Command) Trkd ldrs, pushed along/briefly no room 2f out, styd on strongly to lead nr fin, rdn out: 7 wk abs,
gd time: reportedly scoped badly after disapp eff latest: earlier scored at Beverley (val stks, fast time) &
Windsor (stks): apprec step up to 7f, 1m will suit: acts on gd & gd/soft, untried on faster: handles a sharp or
stiff trk: runs v well fresh: smart juv filly, should continue to give a good account.
*3020 **SUMMER SYMPHONY 28** [4] L M Cumani 2-8-9 J P Spencer 3/1: -12: 2 gr f Caerleon - Summer Sonnet *nk* **103**
(Baillamont) Held up, smooth prog to lead over 1f out, drvn & hdd nr fin: bckd from 5/1: only 2nd start & fast
improving: smart filly, poss hit the front too sn: hds for the Gr 1 Fillies Mile, see 3020.
*3074 **WAKI MUSIC 25** [6] R Charlton 2-8-9 R Hughes 15/8 FAV: -13: 2 b f Miswaki - Light Music (Nijinsky) *2½* **98**

Led, eff & hung left 2f out, hdd over 1f out & sn held: hvly bckd: acts on fast & gd grnd: see 3074.

3316 **CHAGUARAMAS 15** [5] R Hannon 2-8-9 S Sanders 20/1: -1154: Rear/in tch, eff fnl 2f, held over 1f out: return to 5/6f would suit: see 3316, 2940. — **1 96**

*3292 **FANTASY RIDGE 16** [2] 2-8-9 Craig Williams 2/1: -15: Trkd ldr, shaken up/btn 1f out: hvly bckd tho' op 7/4: more expected after easy debut success in 3292 (fill mdn). — **¾ 94**

*3391 **TRILLIE 11** [1] 2-8-9 N Pollard 14/1: -116: Chsd ldrs, btn 2f out: op 10/1: btr 3391 (nov stks). — **7 80**

6 ran   Time 1m 28.48 (3.98)   (Roldvale Ltd)   B J Meehan Upper Lambourn, Berks

---

3660   3.50 CSMA NURSERY HCAP 2YO (C)   7f rnd   Good 57 -01 Slow   [95]
£7020   £2160   £1080   £540

3428 **LONER 9** [2] N A Callaghan 2-8-5 (72) F Norton 5/1: -04621: 2 b g Magic Ring - Jolis Absent (Primo Dominie) Trkd ldr, rdn/led over 1f out, al holding rivals ins last, pushed out: op 6/1, 1st win: eff at 7f, shld apprec 1m+: acts on fast & gd grnd, likes a sharp/undul trk: v well h'capped on 5th to Bad As I Wanna Be at Windsor in 3044: showed a decent turn of foot & can win more races. — **80**

3165 **FOODBROKER FANCY 22** [1] D R C Elsworth 2-8-12 (79) T Quinn 2/1 FAV: -24102: 2 ch f Halling - Red Rita (Kefaah) Rear/in tch, prog to chase wnr 1f out, styd on tho' al held: op 5/2: eff at 6/7f on fast & gd. — **½ 85**

3165 **KNOCK 22** [7] R Hannon 2-8-13 (80) R Hughes 7/2: 415243: 2 b c Mujadil - Beechwood (Blushing Groom) Trkd ldrs, no room over 2f out till over 1f out, onepace ins last: op 3/1: prob stay longer 7f trip. — **3 79**

3444 **FLUTED 9** [4] M R Channon 2-8-1 (66) Craig Williams 5/1: 403034: Rear/in tch, eff/no room over 2f out till over 1f out, no ch with ldrs after: no luck in running, closer with a clr run, this best forgotten: see 3444. — **3½ 61**

3292 **IT GIRL 16** [3] 2-8-7 (74) A Nicholls (3) 9/2: -2465: Led till halfway, close up 6f: h'cap bow. — **hd 67**

3047 **ZHITOMIR 27** [5] P Doe 10/1: -6406: Keen/cl-up, led halfway till over 1f out, fdd: op 8/1, h'cap bow: longer 7f trip: btr 2854 (6f). — **¾ 61**

6 ran   Time 1m 28.58 (4.08)   (N A Callaghan)   N A Callaghan Newmarket, Suffolk

---

3661   4.20 PROTON CARS FILLIES MDN 2YO (D)   6f str   Good 57 -11 Slow
£4192   £1290   £645   £322

3449 **THERES TWO 9** [3] M R Channon 2-8-11 Craig Williams 2/1: -31: 2 b f Ashkalani - Sudden Interest (Highest Honor) Held up, prog/cl-up 2f out, shaken up to lead 1f out, asserted under hands & heels riding: nicely bckd: eff at 6f, half sister to mid-dist wnr After The Blue: eff at 6f, 7f+ will suit: acts on firm & gd grnd, clrly going the right way & op to further improvement when tackling 7f+. — **89**

-- **ATAMANA** [2] M P Tregoning 2-8-11 R Hills 2/1: -2: 2 b f Lahib - Dance Ahead (Shareef Dancer) Cl-up, led over 2f out/hdd 1f out, kept on, al just held: bckd: Mar foal, cost IR 60,000gns: half sister to smart Irish juv wnr Dance Clear: dam a 7f juv wnr: eff at 6f, 7f will suit: acts on gd grnd: encouraging. — **1 85**

-- **HIDDEN MEANING** [1] R Hannon 2-8-11 R Hughes 15/8 FAV: -3: 2 ch f Cadeaux Genereux - Cubby Hole (Town And Country) Trkd ldrs, shaken up fnl 2f, sn outpcd by front pair: nicely bckd: Feb foal, half sister to v smart 1m performer Niche: dam plcd at 12f: eff at 6f, likely to apprec 7f+: acts on gd grnd. — **2½ 78**

-- **MISS BEETEE** [5] J J Bridger 2-8-11 A Nicholls (3) 12/1: -4: Went right start, pushed along/rear, nvr on terms: bckd from 50/1: Brief Truce filly, May foal, cost 1,700gns: half sister to an Irish 1m/9f wnr. — **6 63**

2488 **FIRE BELLE 50** [4] 2-8-11 S Sanders 25/1: -005: Led till over 2f out, sn btn: 7 wk abs, mod form. — **10 38**

5 ran   Time 1m 14.13 (4.13)   (Timberhill Racing Partnership)   M R Channon West Isley, Berks

---

3662   4.50 TOUCHDOWN CLASSIFIED STKS 3YO+ 0-75 (D)   7f rnd   Good 57 -08 Slow
£4192   £1290   £645   £322   3yo rec 5lb

*3622 **CAUDA EQUINA 2** [9] M R Channon 6-9-3 Craig Williams 9/2: 465211: 6 gr g Statoblest - Sea Fret (Habat) Held up racing keenly, smooth prog to lead over 1f out, al holding rivals under hands & heels riding: qck reapp: scored at Bath 2 days ago (class stks): '99 wnr at Bath 2 (i) & Lingfield (class stks), plcd sev times (rtd 84): '98 Bath (2, clmr & h'cap) & Salisbury wnr (h'cap, rtd 80): eff at 5/6f, now stays a sharp 7f: acts on fast & soft grnd: handles any trk, relishes Bath: tough & genuine gldg who has hit form in fine style. — **81**

3384 **ALMASI 11** [10] C F Wall 8-9-0 S Sanders 10/3: 534022: 8 b m Petorius - Best Niece (Vaigly Great) Rear, in tch, rdn/prog to chase wnr ins last, kept on tho' al held, see 3384, 1531. — **1 75**

3644 **KAFIL 1** [7] J J Bridger 6-9-3 A Nicholls(3) 66/1: 030603: 6 b g Housebuster - Alchaasibiyeh (Seattle Slew) Chsd ldr 2f, styd onepace over 1f out: unplcd here at Goodwood yesterday (amat h'cap): offic rtd 39. — **¾ 76$**

*3460 **RAVINE 9** [6] R Hannon 3-8-13 R Hughes 10/3: -04114: Sn trkd ldr, ch over 1f out, no extra: op 5/2. — **1 75**

3414 **SUSANS PRIDE 10** [1] 4-9-3 D R McCabe 3/1 FAV: 340545: Chsd ldrs, outpcd from over 1f out: bckd. — **1¼ 71**

3613 **PRINCE PROSPECT 2** [5] 4-9-3 J P Spencer 10/1: 400006: Led, hdd over 1f out, fdd: op 8/1, qck reapp. — **¾ 69**

*2472 **STEPPIN OUT 51** [2] 3-8-11 P Doe 7/1: -17: Rear, eff/no room 2f out, sn held: op 11/2: 7 wk abs. — **¾ 66**

3644 **MAX 1** [3] 5-9-3 D Harrison 50/1: 300008: Rear, rdn/btn 2f out: ran yesterday: see 256. — **3½ 60$**

838 **END OF STORY 142** [4] 4-9-3 R Brisland(5) 66/1: 000-09: Chsd ldrs, wknd qckly 2f out: 5 month abs: unplcd in '99 (rtd 72, mdn, R Hannon): rtd 68 in '98 (unplcd): with P Butler. — **25 20**

9 ran   Time 1m 29/08 (4.58)   (Michael A Foy)   M R Channon West Isley, Berks

---

3663   5.25 MOTORING MDN HCAP 3YO+ 0-70 (E)   1m1f192y   Good 57 -03 Slow   [68]
£4875   £1500   £750   £375   3yo rec 8lb

3393 **NIGHT DIAMOND 11** [16] I A Balding 3-8-6 (54)(t) A Nicholls (3) 13/2: 404241: 3 b g Night Shift - Dashing Water (Dashing Blade) Mid-div, prog to chall 1f out, narrowly asserted well ins last, drvn out: plcd once in '99 (mdn, rtd 78 at best): eff at 1m, suited by this step up to 10f: acts on fast & gd/soft grnd, prob handles soft: best without a visor, eff in a t-strap: handles a gall or sharp trk. — **57**

3031 **MA VIE 27** [18] J R Fanshawe 3-8-13 (61)(VIS) D Harrison 7/1: 0-0202: 3 b f Salse - One Life (L'Emigrant) Al prom, led over 2f out till well ins last, kept on: return to form in visor: see 2463 (mdn h'cap). — **½ 63**

3644 **TWOFORTEN 1** [1] P Butler 5-7-10 (36)(4oh) R Brisland(5) 33/1: 000603: 5 b g Robellino - Grown At Rowan (Gabitat) Rear, rdn & styd on stdly fnl 3f, not pace to chall front pair: unplcd here yesterday: see 524 (AW). — **½ 37**

3293 **MAGIQUE ETOILE 16** [19] M P Muggeridge 4-8-11 (51) M Fenton 20/1: 226604: Led 1f, remained handy, ch ins last, no extra: stays a sharp 10f: see 114, 25 (6f, AW). — **1½ 50**

3423 **WOODYATES 10** [4] 3-8-7 (55) L Branch(7) 16/1: -0605: Rear, stdy gains fnl 3f under hands & heels riding, no threat: styd longer 10f trip on h'cap bow, bred up to 12f shld suit: eye-catching late hdwy here. — **½ 53**

3192 **BITTER SWEET 20** [10] 4-7-13 (39) A Mackay 14/1: 400506: Towards rear, rdn/late gains, no threat. — **½ 36**

3380 **MOVING EXPERIENCE 11** [9] 3-8-11 (59) T Quinn 5/1: 04-047: Trkd ldr, ch 2f out, sn no extra. — **1¾ 53**

GOODWOOD SUNDAY AUGUST 27TH Righthand, Sharpish, Undulating Track

3390	**MOMENTOUS JONES** 11 [14] 3-8-6 (54) F Norton 14/1: 552-08: Mid-div, eff over 2f out, sn onepace/held.	*1*	46
2888	**THIHN** 34 [11] 5-8-10 (50) J P Spencer 9/1: 203609: Trkd ldrs, wknd over 1f out: see 2888, 1395.	1	40
3392	**QUEEN OF FASHION** 11 [6] 4-9-11 (65) D McGaffin(5) 20/1: -04300: Dwelt/rear, mod gains: 10th.	½	54
3383	**EIGHT** 11 [17] 4-9-5 (59)(vis) S Sanders 9/1: 354030: Trkd ldrs, wknd over 1f out: 11th.	hd	48
3281	**EVE** 16 [12] 3-9-6 (68) R Hughes 4/1 FAV: 423430: Led after 1f till over 2f out, sn held: 12th.	shd	57
2554	**JOHN STEED** 48 [3] 3-7-13 (47) A Beech(3) 12/1: 00-040: Rear, eff 3f out, no hdwy: 13th: 7 wk abs.	nk	35
3323	**ROUTE ONE** 15 [5] 7-9-6 (60) B Marcus 20/1: 64500: Mid-div, btn 3f out: 14th: big drop in trip.	hd	54
3383	**SHERZABAD** 11 [8] 3-8-7 (55) A Clark 10/1: 00-000: Rear, no prog: 15th: op 12/1: see 1388.	5	35
2211	Tarcoola 62 [15] 3-8-8 (56) G Hind 20/1:	1556	Valdero 90 [13] 3-9-8 (70) P Doe 20/1:
2770	April Star 39 [7] 3-8-1 (49) S Carson(1) 14/1:	627}	My Little Man 533 [2] 5-8-8 (48) N Pollard 25/1:

19 ran Time 2m 10.20 (6.00) (J C Smith) I A Balding Kingsclere, Hants

---

YARMOUTH SUNDAY AUGUST 27TH Lefthand, Flat, Fair Track

Official Going GOOD TO FIRM. Stalls: Str Crse - Far Side; 14f - Stands Side; Rem - Inside.

3664 2.05 INTENSIVE CARE HCAP 3YO+ 0-75 (E) 1m6f Good/Firm 26 -39 Slow [68]
£3542 £1090 £545 £272 3 yo rec 12lb

3442	**SEND ME AN ANGEL** 9 [6] S P C Woods 3-8-10 (62) N Callan 5/1: 422631: 3 ch f Lycius - Niamh Cinn Oir		70
	(King Of Clubs): Led early, remnd with ldrs, went on again 2f out, rdn clr appr dist: 1st win: plcd thrice prev		
	this term: unplcd since '99 start (rtd 63, mdn): eff at 11.5/14f, tried 2m: acts on firm, gd & an easy of sharp trk.		
3219	**ELMS SCHOOLGIRL** 18 [4] J M P Eustace 4-9-6 (60) J Tate 20/1: 606452: 4 ch f Emarati - Ascend	5	60
	(Glint Of Gold) In tch, rdn & chsd wnr appr final 2f, styd on no threat: stays 14f: all 3 wins at Brighton.		
3437	**PENNYS FROM HEAVEN** 9 [3] D Nicholls 6-8-12 (52) Clare Roche (7) 13/2: 504643: 6 gr g Generous -	nk	52
	Heavenly Cause (Grey Dawn II): Keen/rear, plenty to do 3f out, ran on for press appr fnl 1f, nvr nrr: see 2139.		
3348	**MONACLE** 13 [3] John Berry 6-8-2 (42) J Mackay (5) 3/1 FAV: 341254: Waited with, rdn to impr over	shd	42
	3f out, kept on late, no dngr: a return to 2m should suit, as in 3026.		
3282	**TOMASZEWSKI** 16 [1] J Reid 16/1: 50/065: Front rank, rdn/outpcd appr fnl 2f: longer 14f trip.	1	54
3284	**MI ODDS** 16 [11] 4-8-5 (45) J Quinn 16/1: 30506: Keen, led after 3f, hdd 2f out, sn btn: up in trip.	¾	43
3233	**DURHAM** 18 [7] 9-9-2 (56)(bl) I Mongan 6/1: 0-0157: In tch, drvn/eff over 2f out, sn btn: op 5/1.	nk	54
3434	**DANEGOLD** 9 [9] 8-9-1 (55) R Havlin 6/1: 004638: Nvr better than mid-div: shade btr 3434 (2m).	1½	51
3247	**WEST END DANCER** 18 [10] 3-7-10 (48)(14ch) D Kinsella (7) 33/1: 503309: At rear: new stable.	3	40$
3424	**URGENT SWIFT** 10 [5] 7-9-10 (64) D Sweeney 8/1: 240500: Effort from rear over 3f out, wknd fnl 2f, 10th.	5	50
3531	**AN SMEARDUBH** 5 [2] 4-7-10 (36)(bl) (5oh) M Baird 40/1: 006060: Struggling 4f out, t.o., 11th.	6	16

11 ran Time 3m 06.9 (9.1) (Kaniz Bloodstock Investments Ltd) S P C Woods Newmarket.

3665 2.35 LOWESTOFT MDN AUCT 2YO (E) 1m str Good/Firm 26 -57 Slow
£3510 £1080 £540 £270

3075	**MAGIC BOX** 25 [7] A P Jarvis 2-8-7 N Callan 5/2: 644341: 2 b c Magic Ring - Princess Poquito		81
	(Hard Fought): Chsd ldrs, smooth hdwy to lead appr 1f, rdn clr inside last: fav foal, cost 50,000 gns,		
	dam related to sev wnrs: stays 1m on fast grnd: handles a flat/easy trk: consistent, deserved this win.		
3333	**REGATTA POINT** 14 [5] A P Jarvis 2-8-7 D Sweeney 16/1: -02: In tch, hdwy 2f out, styd on nicely under hands-&-heels riding: 12,000gns Feb foal, half	2½	75+
	(Maelstrom Lake): Held up, hdwy 2f out, styd on nicely under hands-&-heels riding: 12,000gns Feb foal, half		
	sister to a 7f 2yo wnr: eff at 1m on fast: stablemate of wnr & looks sure to improve with a more positive ride.		
3100	**OCEAN LAKE** 25 [1] M L W Bell 2-8-0 J Mackay (5) 5/4 FAV: 523: 2 b f Dolphin Street - Scuba Diver	1¼	66
	(King's Lake): Outpcd 4f out, styd on for press fnl 1f, no dngr: nicely bckd: cld improve in nurseries.		
3239	**OUTRAGEOUSE** 18 [4] Andrew Reid 2-8-3 M Henry 33/1: 04: Led, hdd appr fnl 1f, sn held: needs sells.	¾	68
3385	**CALIBAN** 11 [3] 2-8-7 J Quinn 14/1: 05: Dwelt, sn prom, ran green/no extra appr fnl 1f: lngr 1m trip.	1¾	69
--	**KURANDA** [2] 2-7-12 R Ffrench 4/1: 6: Bhd, eff/ran green over 2f out, sn held: 3,200gns Apr foal,	2	56
	half-sister to a 7f 2yo wnr: eff at 1m on fast: stablemate of wnr with M Johnston, should be capable of better.		
3205	**ARMIDA** 19 [6] 2-8-0 J Tate 33/1: -0007: Rcd v keenly, cl-up, wknd qckly final 2f: big step up in trip.	½	57
--	**GRANDMA GRIFFITHS** [8] 2-7-12 A Polli (3) 14/1: 8: Veered left start, sn front rank, wknd qckly	6	46
	final 2f: cheaply bought Apr foal, half-sister to a wng hdler: dam 2yo wnr abroad: with Mrs L Stubbs.		

8 ran Time 1m 41.8 (6.7) (Quadrillian Partnership) A P Jarvis Aston Upthorpe, Oxon.

3666 3.05 BROADLAND 102 FILL HCAP 3YO+ 0-80 (D) 7f str Good/Firm 26 -22 Slow [74]
£4062 £1250 £625 £312 3 yo rec 5 lb

3209	**BRANSTON FIZZ** 19 [1] M Johnston 3-9-0 (65) R Ffrench 5/1: 400101: 3 b f Efisio - Tuxford Hideaway		75
	(Cawston's Clown): Rdn in rear, gd hdwy appr final 1f, qcknd well for press & readily under clr: op 7/2: earlier		
	won at Southwell (AW med auct mdn, rtd 68a): rnr-up twice in '99 (mdn, rtd 85): half-sister to sev wnrs, incl		
	v tough sprinter Branston Abbey: eff at 6/7f on fast, soft & fibresand, not equitrack: handles a sharp or		
	stiff/undul trk & runs well fresh: clearly relished this step up to 7f & can win more races at this trip.		
3317	**SEA DRIFT** 15 [6] L M Cumani 3-9-5 (70) W Supple 4/1: 531302: 3 gr f Warning - Night At Sea (Night	5	70
	Shift): In tch, rear 2f out, rall & styd on well fnl 1f, no threat: tchd 6/1: worth another try at 1m: see 2860.		
3254	**DANIYSHA** 17 [8] Sir Michael Stoute 3-9-9 (74) L Newman (3) 4/1: 431063: 3 b f Doyoun - Danishara	shd	74
	(Slew O'Gold): Cl-up, chall 2f out, kept on inside last but no dngr to wnr: see 2491.		
3160	**STEALTHY TIMES** 22 [7] J G Given 3-9-5 (70) T G McLaughlin 11/1: 000554: Rear, rdn/prog over 2f	1	68
	out, no extra inside last: see 2564, 1138.		
3384	**GUEST ENVOY** 11 [12] 5-7-10 (42) M Henry 12/1: 546005: Bhd, prog over 2f out, nvr dangerous: see 811.	½	39
3043	**CLEAR CRYSTAL** 27 [4] 3-7-10 (47) A Polli (2) 20/1: 006606: Dsptd lead till 2f out, sn btn: see 930.	¾	42
3046	**OARE KITE** 27 [5] 5-8-4 (50)(bl) Dale Gibson 16/1: 010007: Rcd keenly & sn led, hdd appr fnl 1f, wknd.	1¾	42
3280	**HOXTON SQUARE** 16 [10] 3-8-12 (63) J Quinn 25/1: -02008: Chsd ldrs, lost tch after halfway, eased.	11	40
3160	**DIAMOND RACHAEL** 22 [9] 3-9-1 (66)(vis) R Fitzpatrick 3/1 FAV: 660129: Al bhd, eased fnl 2f:	½	42
	nicely bckd tho' op 5/2 & better expected here: much btr 3160, 2918.		

9 ran Time 1m 26.0 (3.4) (J David Abell) M Johnston Middleham, N Yorks

---

3667   **3.35 GREAT YARMOUTH COND STKS 3YO+ (C)**   6f   Good/Firm 26   00 Slow
£5945   £2255   £1127   £512   3 yo rec 3 lb

3152 **DEEP SPACE** 22 [1] E A L Dunlop 5-8-8 J Reid 5/4 FAV: 354301: 5 br g Green Desert - Dream Season   105
(Mr Prospector) Cl up, eff/short of room over 2f out, found gap dist & ran on strongly for press to lead cl-home,
drvn out: nicely bckd: in fine '99 form, Lingfield (h'cap), Royal Ascot (val Wokingham h'cap) & Nottingham wnr
(stks, rtd 108 at best): '98 Sandown & Newmarket wnr (h'caps, rtd 85): suited by 6/7f on any trk: handles
gd/soft, likes firm/fast: tough/v useful gelding with a turn of foot, would have won by further with a clear run.
3235 **DANCING MAESTRO** 18 [5] N A Callaghan 4-8-8 L Newman (3) 13/2: -00632: 4 gr c Nureyev - Ancient   ½   101
Regime (Olden Times) Rcd keenly & sn led, drvn & collared by wnr fnl fin: acts on fast & gd grnd: improved
recently for forcing the pace: useful: see 3235, 2496.
1338 **TEAPOT ROW** 101 [6] J A R Toller 5-8-8 S Whitworth 4/1: 12-503: 5 b h Generous - Secrage   1¾   97
(Secreto) Front rank, drvn & no extra well inside last: 3 month abs, will apprec a return to 7f: see 952.
1283 **ALHUFOOF** 106 [4] M P Tregoning 3-8-0 W Supple 11/4: 31-404: Prom, drvn & not pace of ldrs   hd   92
appr fnl 1f: op 9/4, long abs: just sharper of this when returning to 7f: see 953.
3158 **ALFIE LEE** 22 [3] 3-8-5 (tBL) J Quinn 33/1: 005005: Rear, well bhd fnl 2f: blnkd, v stiff task.   14   72
3152 **ALFAILAK** 22 [7] 3-8-5 D O'Donohoe 16/1: 0-0506: Al well in rear, fin last: see 2458.   1¾   70
6 ran   Time 1m 12.0 (1.6)   (Maktoum Al Maktoum)   E A L Dunlop Newmarket, Suffolk

---

3668   **4.10 DFDS SEAWAYS HCAP 3YO+ 0-90 (C)**   5f43y   Good/Firm 26   -07 Slow   [87]
£5887   £2233   £1116   £507   3 yo rec 2 lb

3398 **SMART PREDATOR** 11 [8] J J Quinn 4-9-4 (77) J Quinn 9/2: 520301: 4 gr g Polar Falcon -   87
She's Smart (Absalom) Chsd ldrs, rdn into lead appr fnl 1f, drvn clr inside last: op 7/2: earlier scored at
Redcar (class stks), also produced creditable efforts in competitive h'caps: '99 York wnr (mdn, rtd 84):
eff between 5f & 1m: acts on firm, soft & any track: likes racing up with/forcing the pace: tough/versitile.
3398 **MIZHAR** 11 [2] D Nicholls 4-9-3 (76)(bl) Alex Greaves 9/4 FAV: 000022: 4 b f Dayjur - Futuh   2½   78
(Diesis) Trckd ldr, rdn & not pace of wnr ins last: nicely bckd: improved with recent fitting of blnks: see 3398.
3528 **THAT MAN AGAIN** 6 [6] S C Williams 4-8-8 (67)(bl) G Faulkner (3) 12/1: 430053: 8 ch g Prince Sabo -   1¾   65
Milne's Way (The Noble Player) Led, hdd appr fnl 1f, onepace inside last: qck reapp: see 2022.
3280 **CASTLE SEMPILL** 16 [3] R M H Cowell 3-8-12 (73)(vis) J Mackay (5) 16/1: 106004: In tch, rdn/no   1   68
extra appr fnl 1f: prob unsuited by this drop in trip: see 852 (6f).
3077 **ARGENT FACILE** 25 [4] 3-10-0 (89) J Reid 16/1: 223055: Cl up, drvn over 2f out, not qckn appr   nk   83
fnl 1f: op 12/1, top weight & a tough task conceding weight to elders: see 3077.
3516 **LA PIAZZA** 7 [1] 4-9-2 (75) T E Durcan 12/1: 023366: Nvr dangerous: qck reapp: see 2931 (clmr).   nk   69
3398 **GAY BREEZE** 11 [5] 7-8-7 (66) Dale Gibson 7/1: 006007: Sn rdn in rear, wknd fnl 2f: op 10/1: see 905.   1¼   57
3436 **MOUSEHOLE** 9 [7] 8-8-11 (70) R Cochrane 11/4: 202108: Handy, rdn/fdd fnl 2f: nicely bckd.   1¾   57
8 ran   Time 1m 01.8 (1.7)   (B Shaw)   J J Quinn Settrington, N Yorks

---

3669   **4.40 CLASSIFIED STKS 3YO+ 0-90 (C)**   1m2f121y   Good/Firm 26   +10 Fast
£7041   £2670   £1335   £507   3 yo rec 8 lb

*2889 **WELSH MAIN** 34 [4] H R A Cecil 3-8-12 W Ryan 11/4: -11: 3 br c Zafonic - Welsh Daylight   97
(Welsh Pageant) Waited with, slightly outpcd over 2f out, ran on strongly for press to lead well ins last,
drvn out: nicely bckd, fast time: earlier won on debut at Windsor (mdn): half brother to a useful miler:
eff at 10f 12f will suit in time: runs well fresh on fast grnd & a sharp or easy track: progressive & unbtn.
2567 **VIA CAMP** 47 [1] E A L Dunlop 3-8-5 W Supple 7/1: 10-462: 3 b f Kris - Honeyspike (Chief's   1   87
Crown) Rcd keenly in rear, rdn/improved over 2f out, ran on strongly inside last, not btn far: op 6/1,
7 wk abs: eff at 1m/10f: fine run on this step up in trip & caught a useful rival, should win again: see 2171.
3159 **WEET A MINUTE** 22 [5] N P Littmoden 7-9-2 D Sweeney 10/1: 600543: 7 ro h Nabeel Dancer - Ludovica   ½   89$
(Bustino) Led early, remnd prom, led again appr fnl 1f, hdd well ins last, held cl-home: gd run: see 3159, 230.
3339 **JUST IN TIME** 14 [6] T G Mills 5-9-4 J Reid 9/4 FAV: 030504: Keen cl up, outpcd over 2f out,   ¾   90
styd on well inside last: nicely bckd: see 3134, 874.
2955 **TARABAYA** 30 [2] 3-8-9 L Newman (3) 5/2: -6135: 12f: 7-6135: Led 7f out, rdn/hdd appr fnl 1f, onepace ins last.   ½   88
3338 **TAMMAM** 14 [3] 4-9-2 C Lowther 16/1: 534466: Dwelt, bhd, lost tch fnl 2f: up in trip: see 1744.   8   75
6 ran   Time 2m 05.8 (1.6)   (K Abdulla)   H R A Cecil Newmarket, Suffolk

---

Official Going   GOOD/FIRM. Stalls: Inside.

3670   **2.00 BRITANNIA CLAIMER DIV 1 3YO (E)**   7f100y rnd   Good/Firm 38   -08 Slow
£2394   £684   £342

2515 **NODS NEPHEW** 50 [2] Miss J A Camacho 3-9-2 J Weaver 9/1: 104001: 3 b g Efisio - Nordan Raider   69
(Domynsky) Led, went 3L clr appr fnl 1f, unchall: freshened up by 7 wk abs: earlier won here at Beverley (h'cap):
unplcd both '99 starts (rtd 61): suited by this stiff 7.5f: acts on fast & hvy grnd, forcing the pace: goes well fresh.
3364 **LORDOFENCHANTMENT** 12 [7] N Tinkler 3-8-7 Kim Tinkler 8/1: 220552: 3 ch g Soviet Lad - Sauvignon 2½   55
(Alzao) Chsd wnr thr'out, rdn appr fnl 1f, no impress: visor omitted, suited by sltly shorter?: see 1600.
2733 **CELEBRE BLU** 40 [5] K A Ryan 3-8-9 F Lynch 10/3: 330003: 3 b g Suave Dancer - Taufan Blu (Taufan)   ¾   55
Towards rear & pshd along, rdn ent fnl 2f, kept on to go 3rd ins last: 6 wk abs: stays 7.5f: btr 1562 (gd/soft).
3393 **SPEEDFIT FREE** 11 [1] M A Buckley 3-8-10 Dean McKeown 8/1: 441364: Mid-div, prog 2f out, sn onepace.   2   52
3456 **LIVELY MILLIE** 9 [11] 3-8-2 G Duffield 3/1 FAV: -00045: Chsd ldrs, no extra appr fnl 1f: op 7/1, stiff task.   1   42
3506 **TIME FOR THE CLAN** 7 [9] 3-8-4 O Pears 66/1: 000006: Well plcd till 2f out: flattered, qck reapp.   shd   44$
3456 **CALDEY ISLAND** 9 [4] 3-8-6 G Sparkes (7) 25/1: 000057: Nvr a factor: stiff task, flattered   ½   45$
3324 **BLUE HAWK** 15 [8] 3-8-6 Paul Eddery 8/1: 0-0068: In tch till 2f out: back in trip, see 1352.   1¾   41
3332 **WISHEDHADGONEHOME** 14 [12] 3-8-0 (vis) A Daly 20/1: 600449: Al towards rear: stiff task.   hd   35
3194 **CROESO ADREF** 20 [13] 3-7-13 G Baker (5) 16/1: 300000: Dwelt, nvr nr ldrs: 10th, stiff task, see 589.   shd   34
3616 **FOUR MEN** 2 [3] 3-8-5 P Bradley(5) 10/1: 653020: Prom 4f: 11th: flattered, likewise 3330, 3142.   shd   40$

--   **MUJAALED** [10] 3-8-11 A Culhane 25/1: -0: Sn out the back: 12th, debut: Elmaamul gelding.   23   6
12 ran   Time 1m 34.3 (3.5)   (Brian Nordan)   Miss J A Camacho Norton, N.Yorks.

3671   2.25 BRITANNIA CLAIMER DIV 2 3YO (E)   7f100y rnd   Good/Firm 38 -11 Slow
£2380   £680   £340

2704 **JAMESTOWN** 42 [5] C Smith 3-9-2 Dean McKeown 5/1: 6-0461: 3 b g Merdon Melody - Thabeh (Shareef   70
Dancer) Led, rdn appr fnl 1f, held on well: 6 wk abs, op 7/2: '99 Warwick wnr (auct mdn, rtd 78): eff at
7/7.5f: acts on firm & gd/firm grnd, any trk: runs well fresh: effective forcing the pace & apprec drop in grade.
3196 **BAJAN BELLE** 20 [1] M Johnston 3-8-6 M Roberts 10/3: 030022: 3 b f Efisio - With Love (Be My Guest)   ½   59
Cl-up, prog to press wnr fnl 1f, al being held: clr rem, stays a stiff 7.5f on firm/fast grnd, sole win at 5f.
3393 **DIHATJUM** 11 [10] T D Easterby 3-8-11 K Darley 1/1 FAV: 240123: 3 b g Mujtahid - Rosie Potts (Shareef 2½   59
Dancer) Chsd ldrs, short of room & switched 1f out, no impress: bckd, clr rem: btr 3393, see 3196.
3393 **AFRICA** 11 [4] T D Barron 3-8-2 G Duffield 6/1: 041604: Chsd wnr, no extra appr fnl 1f: stiff task.   4   42
3326 **ST PACOKISE** 14 [11] 3-8-10 R Winston 33/1: 04-005: Al around same place: stiff task, flattered.   hd   50$
3462 **KERRIDGE CHAPEL** 8 [8] 3-8-2 (bl) P Hanagan (7) 50/1: 006006: Keen, prom, fdd bef dist: flattered.   1   40$
3393 **CITY BANK DUDLEY** 11 [2] 3-8-7 R Lappin 25/1: 646407: Al towards rear: stiff task.   ¾   43
3218 **SANDOWN CLANTINO** 18 [12] 3-8-1 G Baker (5) 50/1: -08: Dwelt, nvr in it: no form.   3   31
3364 **WATERGOLD** 12 [6] 3-8-6 (bl) O Pears (5) 25/1: 000069: Mid-div, wide 3f out & bhd: stiff task.   ¾   34
3330 **THE CASTIGATOR** 14 [3] 3-8-4 J McAuley 50/1: -60000: Dwelt, at rear: 10th, stiff task.   5   22
3266 **VICKY SCARLETT** 17 [7] 3-7-13 K Dalgleish (5) 40/1: -00: Keen, al bhd: 11th, no form.   1½   14
11 ran   Time 1m 34.5 (3.7)   (A E Needham)   C Smith Temple Bruer, Lincs.

3672   2.55 DAILY STAR MDN DIV 1 3YO+ (D)   1m2f   Good/Firm 38 +01 Fast
£4117   £1267   £633   £316   3yo rec 8lb

--   **OUR SOUSY** [5] E A L Dunlop 3-8-8 G Carter 5/4: 46-3441: 3 b f Silver Hawk - Sous Entendu (Shadeed)   83
Chsd ldrs, rdn to lead 1f out, drew clr towards fin: bckd on Brit bow: ex-French, 19 days ago btn just over 2L into
4th in a Listed (12f): eff at 10f, return to 12f will suit: acts on fast grnd, stiff track: useful.
2006 **GLEDSWOOD** 71 [4] Lady Herries 3-8-8 K Darley 1/1 FAV: -322: 3 ch f Selkirk - Horseshoe Reef (Mill   3   77
Reef) Well plcd, led 3f out till 1f out, no extra: bckd, clr of rem, 10 wk abs: stays 10f, return to 1m will suit.
3265 **CHIEF WARDANCE** 17 [6] Mrs S Lamyman 3-9-7 A Culhane 14/1: -303: 6 ch g Profilic - Dolly   11   72
Wardance (Warpath) Rear, went past btn horses fnl 2f: staying h'caps will suit soon.
3324 **BETTER MOMENT** 15 [1] J FitzGerald 3-8-13 J Carroll 20/1: -404: Handy till 2f out: back in trip.   shd   64
3344 **SCARLET LIVERY** 13 [7] 4-9-2 F Lynch 100/1: -00005: Led till 3f out, sn wknd: stiff task, flattered.   6   50$
3034 **ANGEL DUST** 27 [3] 4-9-2 G Duffield 20/1: -56: Chsd ldrs till 3f out: new stable.   ⅓   45
3012 **LETS REFLECT** 28 [2] 3-8-8 M Roberts 33/1: -047: Al towards rear: see 2832.   23   15
--   **JULIES GIFT** [9] 3-8-8 J McAuley 40/1: -8: Dwelt, al bhd: debut: Presidium filly with N Bycroft.   16   0
--   **TIGONTIME** [10] 3-8-8 R Lappin 100/1: -9: Sn struggling: debut: Tigani filly with N Wilson.   16   0
3645] **DAUNTING ASSEMBLY** 722 [8] 5-9-2 K Hodgson 100/1: -00/0: Dwelt, sn t.o.: 10th, 2 yr abs, no form.   26   0
10 ran   Time 2m 06.0 (3.7)   (Maktoum Al Maktoum)   E A L Dunlop Newmarket.

3673   3.25 JOHN SMITH'S NURSERY HCAP 2YO (C)   5f str   Good/Firm 38 -32 Slow   [92]
£7289   £2243   £1121   £560

3475 **VENDOME** 8 [7] J A Osborne 2-8-10 (74) J Weaver 14/1: 000331: 2 b c General Monash - Kealbra Lady   81
(Petong) Made all, rdn out, unchall: first win, first foal: bred from 20/1: eff at 5f on fast
& gd/soft grnd, stiff/gall trk tho' has plenty of toe & shld go well on sharp ones.
3101 **ROUGH SHOOT** 25 [4] T D Barron 2-8-10 (74)(hd) M Roberts 12/1: -1532: 2 ch g King's Signet - Tawny   ½   78
(Grey Ghost) Chsd wnr, outpcd ent fnl 2f, rallied well towards fin: not btn far, tchd 16/1: yet to run a
bad race, step up to 6f will suit now: see 2100, 1418.
*3431 **CLARION** 9 [5] Sir Mark Prescott 2-9-7 (85) G Duffield 7/2 FAV: -21213: 2 ch c First Trump - Area   1½   85
Girl (Jareer) Chsd ldrs, rdn appr fnl 1f, kept on for 3rd but not ch front pair: op 5/2, top-weight: tough, see 3431.
*3394 **COZZIE** 11 [11] J G Given 2-7-10 (60)(10h) G Baker (5) 5/1: 116614: Towards rear, not much room   nk   59
2f out, wide prog ins last, nvr nr to chall: tchd 8/1: not much luck in running, see 3394 (C/D fill nursery).
3519 **BLAKESHALL BOY** 6 [3] 2-9-2 (80) A Culhane 10/1: 032135: Last, prog & not clr run thr'out fnl   nk   78
2f, kept on: qck reappr, forget this from poor draw: see 3228.
3394 **CLANSINGE** 11 [2] 2-7-12 (62) K Dalgleish (5) 20/1: 134006: Rear, short of room appr fnl 2f till   ½   59
dist, kept on, nvr dngrs: see 1918 (made all in a clmr).
3394 **CHARTLEYS PRINCESS** 11 [10] 2-8-2 (66) P Fessey 9/2: -53357: Mid-div, rdn appr fnl 1f, no impress.   shd   63
*3346 **FOREVER TIMES** 13 [1] 2-8-9 (73) K Darley 8/1: 362218: Wide, in tch till appr fnl 1f: forget from stall 1.   hd   70
2868 **FANTASY BELIEVER** 35 [6] 2-9-3 (81) F Lynch 14/1: 422169: Dwelt, prom till hung right under   nk   77
press appr fnl 1f: op 10/1: btr 2532 (gd/soft).
3475 **HUMES LAW** 8 [9] 2-8-8 (72) J Carroll 9/1: 461000: Nvr a factor: see 2730.   3½   58
3533 **MILLIKEN PARK** 5 [8] 2-8-7 (71) G Carter 7/1: -61230: Well plcd till appr fnl 2f, btn/hmpd dist: 11th.   6   42
2754 **TOMMY SMITH** 39 [2] 2-7-13 (63) J McAuley 50/1: 411650: Wide, in tch till 2f out: 12th, poor draw.   ¾   31
12 ran   Time 1m 04.8 (3.5)   (John Livock)   J A Osborne Lambourn, Berks.

3674   4.00 OWN A HORSE HCAP 3YO+ 0-75 (E)   1m4f   Good/Firm 38 -17 Slow   [57]
£3835   £1180   £590   £295   3yo rec 10lb

*3531 **NOTATION** 5 [2] D W Chapman 6-7-10 (25)(7oh) Claire Bryan 12/1: 005011: 6 b g Arazi - Grace Note   28
(Top Ville) Mid-div, pshd along appr fnl 2f, styd on well to lead cl-home: qck reapp: 5 days won at Hamilton (50/1,
appr h'cap): mod since '97 wnr at Southwell (2, h'caps, rtd 52a): eff at 12f/2m on fast, gd/soft grnd & fibresand.
3511 **YES KEEMO SABEE** 7 [6] D Shaw 5-9-4 (45)(BL) T Williams 8/1: 253302: 5 b g Arazi - Nazeera   shd   47
(Lashkari) In tch, prog appr fnl 2f, led below dist, hdd nr fin: qck reapp, back to form in blnks: eff at 12f/2m2f.
3233 **INDIGO BAY** 18 [11] R Bastiman 4-8-12 (41)(bl) O Pears 9/1: 005103: 4 b g Royal Academy - Cape   nk   42
Heights (Shirley Heights) Sn in a clr lead, hung left appr fnl 2f, hdd ent fnl 1f, styd on: not btn far, likely
wnr if he'd maintained a straight crse & appreciated the return to 12f: see 3102.
2755 **SIMPLE IDEALS** 39 [14] Don Enrico Incisa 6-8-11 (40) Kim Tinkler 10/1: 055654: Towards rear,   2½   37
late hdwy, nvr a factor: see 1563.
3217 **EASTWOOD DRIFTER** 18 [10] 3-9-10 (63) K Darley 5/2 FAV: 362625: Mid-div, prog 2f out, no extra   nk   59

towards fin: op 7/2: longer trip, prob stays a stiff 12f, sharper track or return to 10f will suit: see 2053
1478 **HOME COUNTIES 94** [3] 11-8-12 (41)(t) G Duffield 25/1: -00006: Held up, went past btn horses appr fnl 1f: 3 month abs, t-strap reapplied: see 845. 1½ **35**
3348 **ACQUITTAL 13** [7] 8-8-2 (31)(vis) J Bramhill 20/1: 445307: Nvr better than mid-div: see 3002, 1852. ½ **24**
3331 **SPA LANE 14** [9] 7-8-10 (39) K Dalgleish (5) 6/1: 250058: Al around same pl: see 2482, 1276. *shd* **32**
3654 **PORTRACK JUNCTION 1** [12] 3-7-11 (36) P Hanagan (7) 66/1: 000059: Pld hard, chsd ldr till 2f out. *1* **27**
2540 **DALYAN 48** [4] 3-9-0 (53) J Weaver 14/1: 004050: In tch till 3f out: 10th, jumps rnr 5 wks ago. *3* **39**
3284 **ALDWYCH ARROW 16** [5] 5-9-4 (47) Dean McKeown 20/1: 0-0000: Nvr troubled ldrs: 11th: see 2836. ½ **32**
3378 **PAPI SPECIAL 11** [8] 3-9-5 (58)(vis) R Winston 11/2: 012D20: Prom 1m: 12th: better than this, unsuited by reapplication of visor? see 3249, 2801. 2½ **39**
3654 **Genuine John 1** [1] 7-8-1 (30) P Fessey 25/1: 3084 **Flintstone 25** [13] 3-8-13 (52) G Baker (5) 16/1:
14 ran Time 2m 38.0 (6.7) (David W Chapman) D W Chapman Stillington, N.Yorks.

3675

4.30 BEVERLEY LIONS MED AUCT MDN 2YO (E) 1m100y rnd Good/Firm 38 -30 Slow
£3737 £1150 £575 £287

3443 **ALPHAEUS 9** [9] Sir Mark Prescott 2-9-0 G Duffield 9/4: -551: 2 b g Sillery - Aethra (Trempolino) Keen, trkd ldrs, shkn up to lead appr fnl 1f, v cmftbly: nicely bckd: first foal: clrly appr step up to 8.5f, 10f+ shld suit next term: acts on fast grnd, stiff trk: progressive. **80**
2985 **BOLSHOI BALLET 29** [2] J L Dunlop 2-9-0 K Darley 6/4 FAV: -0332: 2 b c Dancing Spree - Broom Isle (Damister) Led after 2f till appr fnl 1f, outpcd by wnr: nicely bckd: prob stays 8.5f: poor low draw: see 2290. 3½ **72**
3245 **QUAZAR 18** [6] J J O'Neill 2-9-0 F Lynch 33/1: -03: 2 b c Inzar - Evictress (Sharp Victor) Towards rear, gd wide prog appr fnl 1f, nvr nrr: 6,200gns half-brother to a 3yo wnr: dam a mdn: sire 6/7f performer: promise here & suited by step up in trip. 2½ **67**
3245 **KUNDALILA 18** [13] J Hetherton 2-8-9 Dean McKeown 50/1: -04: Pulled hard, early ldr, no extra appr fnl 1f: River Falls first foal, dam mid-dist wnr, sire a sprinter: better run. 1½ **59**
3287 **DREAMIE BATTLE 16** [7] 2-8-9 P M Quinn (3) 3/1: -335: Towards rear, not much room 2f out, again bef dist, nvr dngrs: rough passage, worth another chance in a nursery, see 3287. *nk* **58**
-- **LAST OF THE MICE** [11] 2-9-0 J Weaver 16/1: -6: Green & well off the pace, moderate late wide hdwy: debut: Deploy half-brother to sev wnrs, inc a juv: dam stoutly bred: bred for mid-dists & further. 1¾ **59**
3347 **HIGH SOCIETY LADY 13** [8] 2-8-9 J McAuley 66/1: 000007: Prom onepace appr fnl 1f: stiff task. *2* **50**
3287 **BOLLIN THOMAS 16** [1] 2-9-0 J Carroll 14/1: -008: Prom, wide, fdd appr fnl 1f: difficult low draw. ½ **54**
3409 **KENNYTHORPE BOPPY 10** [4] 2-9-0 R Winston 25/1: -58: Chsd ldrs, wknd qckly appr fnl 1f: see 3409. *dht* **54**
3397 **LOUGH BOW 11** [12] 2-9-0 G Parkin 50/1: -00: Prom 5f: 10th, see 3397. 3½ **47**
3438 **CONSPIRACY THEORY 9** [5] 2-8-9 O Pears 66/1: 464000: Nvr troubled ldrs: 11th, stiff task. *10* **22**
3333 **Tobytoo 14** [3] 2-9-0 K Dalgleish (5) 100/1: -- **Kingfisher Eve** [14] 2-8-9 M Roberts 14/1:
13 ran Time 1m 49.6 (5.8) (Hesmonds Stud) Sir Mark Prescott Newmarket.

3676

5.05 CLOWN FILLIES HCAP 3YO+ 0-80 (D) 1m2f Good/Firm 38 +05 Fast [78]
£4468 £1375 £687 £343 3yo rec 8lb

*3465 **SUMMER SONG 8** [4] E A L Dunlop 3-9-10 (82) G Carter 4/1: 111311: 3 b f Green Desert - High Standard (Kris) Held up, switched & gd prog 2f out, led below dist, pshd out: op 3/1: earlier won at Windsor, Folkestone (h'caps), Redcar (class stks) & Ripon (fill h'cap): landed a private stks race at Newmarket in '99 (rtd 79): eff at 1m, suited by 10f, may get further: acts on fast & gd/soft grnd, any trk: genuine & v progressive. **87**
3465 **BOLLIN ROBERTA 8** [8] T D Easterby 4-9-3 (67) R Winston 3/1 FAV: 053122: 4 b f Bob's Return - Bollin Emily (Lochnager) Cl-up, led appr fnl 2f till ent fnl 1f, styd on: bckd: imprvd again in defeat, progressive: see 3465 (also bhd this wnr), 3054. 1½ **69**
3541 **QUEENS PAGEANT 5** [6] J L Spearing 6-9-6 (70) A Culhane 7/1: 651003: 6 ch m Risk Me - Mistral's Dancer (Shareef Dancer) In tch, eff 3f out, kept on well towards fin, nvr nrr: qck reapp, apprec return to 10f. ½ **71**
3220 **CASSANDRA 18** [7] M Brittain 4-8-3 (53) T Williams 25/1: 502004: Led till appr fnl 2f, onepace. 2½ **50**
2696 **MCGILLYCUDDY REEKS 43** [9] 9-9-9 (73) Kim Tinkler 7/1: 523105: Prom, no extra ent fnl 2f: abs. *shd* **70**
3178 **RESOUNDING 21** [5] 3-9-8 (80) M Roberts 10/3: 1-3246: Nvr dngrs: tchd 5/1: see 3178, 2614. *6* **68**
3178 **CHELONIA 21** [2] 3-8-8 (66) G Duffield 12/1: -05637: Held up, rdn appr fnl 2f, sn short of rm, onepce. *2* **51**
3490 **BAY OF BENGAL 8** [1] 4-7-10 (46)(8oh) G Sparkes(3) 40/1: 206038: Nvr in it: stiff task, see 3490. *5* **23**
*3248 **TOUCH FOR GOLD 18** [3] 3-9-1 (73) K Darley 9/2: -019: Prom till 3f out: h'cap bow, much btr 3248 (9f). *1* **48**
9 ran Time 2m 05.6 (3.3) (Maktoum Al Maktoum) E A L Dunlop Newmarket.

3677

5.35 DAILY STAR MDN DIV 2 3YO+ (D) 1m2f Good/Firm 38 -27 Slow
£4095 £1260 £630 £315 3yo rec 8lb

3476 **FIRST BACK 8** [6] C W Fairhurst 3-8-13 T Williams 2/1 FAV: 400301: 3 b g Fourstars Allstar - Par Un Nez (Cyrano de Bergerac) Cl-up, led halfway, kept on strongly, rdn out: nicely bckd from 7/2: unplcd last term (mdn, rtd 70): eff forcing the pace at 10f, stays 11f: acts on fast grnd, stiff track. **57**
2897 **STARDREAMER 33** [10] B Hanbury 3-8-13 J Carroll 9/2: -062: 3 ch g Arazi - Hafwah (Gorytus) Early ldr, prom, rdn appr fnl 1f, kept on for 2nd but not bother wnr: op 7/2: stays 10f on fast. 2½ **52**
4263} **BRAVE KNIGHT 326** [7] N Bycroft 3-8-13 J McAuley 10/1: 0-3: 3 b c Presidium - Agnes Jane (Sweet Monday) Bolted bef start, held up, imprvd 3f out to dispute 2nd bef fnl 1f, onepace: op 8/1, reapp, unplcd sole '99 start (auct mdn, rtd 58): stays 10f, return to 1m may suit: handles fast grnd. *1* **50**
2989 **MISS CASH 29** [9] M E Sowersby 3-8-8 O Pears 7/2: -424: Trkd ldrs, unable to qckn 2f out: new stable. 3½ **40**
3506 **HICKLETON DREAM 7** [1] 3-8-8 A Culhane 7/1: -05: Dwelt, nvr nr ldrs: no form. *5* **32**
2223 **LUCKY UNO 61** [8] 4-9-7 K Dalgleish (5) 16/1: 06-006: Slow away, nvr a factor: 9 wk abs, big step up in trip: yet to make the frame, rtd 42 iast term over 5f. *hd* **37**
3654 **PARISIENNE HILL 1** [5] 4-9-2 K Hodgson 50/1: -00007: Al towards rear: ran yesterday, v stiff task. *1* **30$**
3248 **RUBY RAVEN 18** [4] 3-8-8 F Lynch 13/2: -48: Held up, prog to chase ldrs 5f out, wknd 3f out: see 3248. ½ **29**
-- **KAILAN SCAMP** [2] 7-9-2 P Fessey 33/1: -9: Led till 5f out, btn 3f out: Flat bow, nr 3 yr bmpr absence. *22* **0**
2012] **EMMAS SUNSET 799** [3] 4-9-2 R Winston 40/1: -00/0: Bhd fnl 4f: 10th, 2 yr abs, new stable, no form. *dist* **0**
10 ran Time 2m 08.0 (6.5) (Twinacre Nurseries Ltd) C W Fairhurst Middleham, N.Yorks.

CHEPSTOW   MONDAY AUGUST 28TH   Lefthand, Undulating, Galloping Track

Official Going   GOOD TO FIRM (Good Places) Stalls: Str Course - Stands Side, Round Course - Inside

3678   **2.25 EBF MDN 2YO (D)   1m str   Good/Firm 26 -08 Slow**
£3484 £1072 £536 £268

3020 **CANDICE 29** [8] E A L Dunlop 2-8-11 G Carter 4/5 FAV: 331: 2 br f Caerleon - Criquette (Shirley Heights) Al handy, duelled with rnr-up fnl 2f, rdn & narrowly prevailed in a bobbing head finish: hvly bckd: apprec this step up to 1m, sure to relish further in time: acts on firm & gd, any trk: on the upgrade. **94**
3333 **SINGLE HONOUR 15** [10] R Hannon 2-8-11 L Newman (3) 9/2: -522: 2 b f Mark Of Esteem - Once Upon A Time (Teenoso) Keen/led, rdn & duelled with wnr fnl 2f, just hdd on line: op 6/1: styd longer 1m trip well: rest well covered, can find a race: see 3333, 1667. *shd* **93**
-- **BRANICKI** [7] J H M Gosden 2-8-11 W Ryan 33/1: 3: 2 b f Spectrum - Karinski (Palace Music) Towards rear, hdwy over 2f out, sn outpcd by front pair: Mar foal, half sister to a 6f juv wnr: dam unrcd: sire top-class performer at 1m/10f: eff at 1m on fast grnd, will apprec further in time: shld improve & win a race. *3½* **86**
-- **SEYOOLL** [11] M R Channon 2-8-11 Craig Williams 8/1: 4: Held up, kept on under hands & heels riding fnl 2f, no threat to front pair: op 6/1: Feb foal, cost 100,000 gns: dam a smart 1m performer: improve. *1* **84+**
3198 **MARK ONE 20** [2] 2-8-11 M Hills 6/1: -325: Keen/trkd ldrs, held fnl 2f: clr rem: btr 3198, 2921 (7f). *nk* **83**
-- **STARDARA** [5] 2-8-11 W Supple 14/1: 6: Held up, outpcd/btn over 2f out: op 7/1: Theatrical filly, Apr foal: half sister to 7f wnr Sporting Lad: dam sprint wnr: with P Cole. *8* **69**
-- **GAMITAS** [9] 2-8-11 N Pollard 50/1: 7: Trkd ldrs 6f: Dolphin Street filly, Feb foal, cost 3000gns: a 1st foal: dam a mdn: sire top-class 6/7f performer: with A P Jarvis. *1½* **66**
-- **HWISPRIAN** [4] 2-8-11 G Hind 66/1: 8: Held up, rdn/btn 3f out: Definite Article filly, Mar foal: half sister to a 1m juv wnr & subs wng stayer: dam a mdn: likely to appreciate mid-dists for V Soane. *hd* **65**
2259 **AWAY WIN 61** [6] 2-8-11 D Sweeney 50/1: -59: Prom 6f: 2 month abs: see 2259 (7f). *hd* **64**
3292 **CAPE COD 17** [3] 2-8-11 Jonjo Fowle (5) 16/1: -40: Prom 6f: 10th: op 12/1: btr 3292 (7f). *½* **63**
-- **COPPELIUS** [1] 2-8-11 R Havlin 33/1: 0: Held up, rdn/btn over 2f out, eased fnl 1f: 11th: stewards enquired into run, noted explanations that filly was slowly away, started to hang & ran green: Apr foal, half sister to a 6f/1m juv wnr: dam a 7f juv wnr, subs scored at 9f: may do better in time for J H M Gosden. *1½* **60**
11 ran   Time 1m 34.6 (2.7)   (Maktoum Al Maktoum)   E A L Dunlop Newmarket, Suffolk

3679   **2.55 SUZUKI NURSERY HCAP 2YO (D)   5f   Good/Firm 26 -22 Slow   [91]**
£3425 £1054 £527 £263

+3491 **JACK SPRATT 9** [4] R Hannon 2-9-7 (84) L Newman (3) 9/4 FAV: 331011: 2 b c So Factual - Raindancing (Tirol) Made all, styd on well ins last, rdn out: nicely bckd: slow time: earlier scored here at Chepstow (nov stks) & Lingfield (nurs h'cap): dam useful 6f wnr: eff at 5f, 6f shld suit: acts on firm, gd/soft & any trk, likes Chepstow: likes to force the pace: proving tough & progressive. **90**
3354 **MILLYS LASS 14** [2] M R Channon 2-8-12 (75) Craig Williams 11/4: 320302: 2 b f Mind Games - Millie's Lady (Common Grounds) Held up, rdn & prog to chase wnr ins last, kept on, wnr had flown: bckd, op 7/2: another C Williams mount asked plenty to do from the rear: worth another try at 6f: see 3174. *1½* **76**
3496 **WARLINGHAM 9** [5] Miss Gay Kelleway 2-9-1 (78) G Carter 5/1: 362143: 2 b c Catrail - Tadjnama (Exceller) Trkd ldrs, rdn/onepace from over 1f out: see 3496, 2766 (mdn). *1½* **76**
*3204 **MONTEV LADY 20** [1] W G M Turner 2-7-11 (60) A Polli (3) 7/1: 014: Went left start, rcd alone towards centre, drifted left/btn ins last: h'cap bow: closer here if keeping a straight course: see 3204 (sell). *¾* **56**
3513 **LAI SEE 8** [3] 2-8-10 (73)(VIS) D Sweeney 7/2: 222555: Prom till over 1f out: visor: btr 2360. *1¾* **65**
1916 **NINE TO FIVE 75** [6] 2-8-2 (65) W Supple 33/1: 334456: Struggling halfway: 11 wk abs: h'cap bow. *16* **27**
6 ran   Time 59.2 (2.4)   (Lady Davis)   R Hannon East Everleigh, Wilts

3680   **3.25 EBF MDN 2YO (D)   1m str   Good/Firm 26 -03 Slow**
£3493 £1075 £537 £268

3298 **STEEL BAND 17** [2] H Candy 2-8-11 D Sweeney 100/30: 31: 2 b c Kris - Quaver (The Minstrel) Held up, rdn/prog to lead over 1f out, styd on well ins last, hands & heels: op 4/1: confirmed promise of debut: apprec step up to 1m, mid-dists will suit next term: acts on firm & fast, stiff trk: rate higher. **84**
3298 **KINGS OF EUROPE 17** [4] B W Hills 2-8-11 M Hills 3/1 FAV: 42: 2 b c Rainbow Quest - Bemissed (Nijinsky) Chsd ldrs, rdn/briefly outpcd 2f out, styd on well ins last, not reach wnr under hands & heels: stays 1m, sure to relish further: acts on fast & firm grnd: type to progress with racing, esp over further: see 3298. *1* **80+**
2708 **ALBASHOOSH 43** [3] E A L Dunlop 2-8-11 G Carter 7/1: 03: 2 b c Cadeaux Genereux - Annona (Diesis) Keen/cl-up, led after 3f till over 1f out, no extra: op 4/1, 6 wk abs: left debut bhd over 1m on fast grnd. *1½* **77**
3391 **LAZZAZ 12** [8] M P Tregoning 2-8-11 W Supple 20/1: -04: Mid-div, kept on onepace fnl 2f: op 14/1: styd longer 1m trip, will relish 10f+ in time: see 3391. *1¾* **74**
3000 **SEATTLE PRINCE 30** [5] 2-8-11 L Newman (3) 6/1: 05: Towards rear, rdn & mod gains fnl 2f, no threat: op 4/1: this longer 1m trip shld suit: see 3000 (6f). *nk* **73**
3015 **MONSIEUR LE BLANC 29** [6] 2-8-11 N Pollard 4/1: -6356: Trkd ldrs, btn 2f out: op 5/1: btr 2494 (7f). *½* **72**
-- **MORSHID** [9] 2-8-11 Craig Williams 10/1: 7: Held up, rdn/outpcd fnl 3f: Gulch colt, May foal: half brother to enigmatic but v useful mid-dist performer Maylane: dam an Irish Oaks wnr: will need mid-dists. *1½* **69**
-- **LAGO** [7] 2-8-11 G Hind 40/1: 8: Dwelt/rear, btn 2f out: Mar foal, cheaply bought: dam a wnr abroad. *11* **52**
3287 **REVIEWER 17** [1] 2-8-11 (BL) R Havlin 14/1: 69: Led 3f, sn btn: op 7/1, poor effort in 1st time blnks. *1½* **49**
9 ran   Time 1m 34.2 (2.3)   (Girsonfield Ltd)   H Candy Wantage, Oxon

3681   **3.55 JOHN & IRIS CLAIMER 3YO+ (F)   1m4f23y   Good/Firm 26 -57 Slow**
£2422 £692 £346   3 yo rec 10lb

3424 **HIGHLY PRIZED 11** [2] J S King 6-9-11 L Newman (3) 3/1: 160001: 6 b g Shirley Heights - On The Tiles (Thatch) Led/dsptd lead thr'out, rdn fnl 2f & narrowly asserted over 1f out, held on well for press: op 5/2: earlier scored at W'hampton (AW h'cap, rtd 63a): rnr-up in '99 (h'cap, rtd 70): '98 Salisbury wnr (rtd 73, h'cap): eff at 12/15f, tried 2m+: acts on firm, hvy & both AWs, any trk: gd weight carrier: apprec drop to clmg grade. **60**
-- **QUALITY** [1] P J Hobbs 7-9-3 N Pollard 7/2: 1403/2: 7 b g Rock City - Queens Welcome (Northfields) Chsd ldrs, not much room over 2f out, switched & rdn/styd on well ins last, al just held: long Flat abs, 10 mth jumps abs, 99/00 Taunton wnr (sell, rtd 100h, eff at 2m): last rcd on the level in '96, scored at Lingfield (stks) & Yarmouth (h'cap, W A O'Gorman): eff at 12f on fast, gd & equitrack, with/without visor: runs well fresh. *½* **50**

CHEPSTOW MONDAY AUGUST 28TH Lefthand, Undulating, Galloping Track

3202 **CLASSIC DEFENCE 20** [7] B J Llewellyn 7-8-13 R Havlin 10/1: B0/303: 7 b g Cyrano de Bergerac - My Alanna (Dalsaan) Chsd wnr, rdn/led over 2f out, hdd over 1f out & no extra: op 8/1: eff at 10/12f: see 2776.   `2`   `43`
3530 **CHEZ BONITO 7** [3] J M Bradley 3-8-1(1ow) Craig Williams 9/2: 540054: Held up, eff fnl 2f, al held.   `1½`   `39`
2448 **CASTLEBRIDGE 53** [4] 3-8-2 (vis) W Supple 9/4 FAV: 153045: Chsd ldrs, rdn/eff 2f out, sn held: `1¼`   `38`
op 5/4, recent jumps rnr (plcd, rtd 74, nov clmr): suited by an easier surface: see 1002 (10f, h'cap, hvy).
-- **MONTICELLO** [5] 8-8-13 D Kinsella (7) 25/1: 6: Held up, rdn/btn 3f out: Flat debut, long hdles   `14`   `24`
abs, rnr-up in 98/99 (c.j. nov, rtd 63h): stays 2m4f, handles gd grnd.
3941J **BOCA CHICA 347** [6] 3-7-12 A Mackay 50/1: 0000-7: Held up, rdn/btn 3f out: reapp: no form at up   `7`   `9`
to 1m in '99 for N Tinkler, now with M Mullineaux.
7 ran   Time 2m 41.1 (10.0)   (Mrs Marygold O'Kelly)   J S King Broad Hinton, Wilts

---

3682 4.25 MERLIN COND STKS 3YO+ (C)   7f str Good/Firm 26 +23 Fast
£6032 £2288 £1144 £520   3 yo rec 5 lb

3060 **SIR EFFENDI 27** [1] M P Tregoning 4-8-11 W Supple 7/2: 12-201: 4 ch c Nashwan - Jeema (Thatch)   `92`
Led/dsptd lead till went on halfway, rdn & styd on strongly ins last: op 3/1: fast time: plcd 3 times in '99,
also scored at Lingfield (nov, rtd 93): eff btwn 7f/9f, poss stays sharp 10f: acts on firm & fast grnd, any trk:
has run well fresh: lightly raced & useful colt.
*1181 **WELCOME FRIEND 113** [2] R Charlton 3-8-10 W Ryan 1/1 FAV: 12: 3 b c Kingmambo - Kingscote   `1¾`   `92`
(King's Lake) Trkd ldrs, rdn/ch over 1f out, kept on, not pace of wnr: 4 month abs: op 5/4: effat 7f, poss longer 7f trip suited
well, 1m could suit: acts on firm & fast grnd: useful run on only start, open to improvement: see 1181 (mdn).
3452 **SHOWBOAT 10** [3] B W Hills 6-9-0 (bl) M Hills 6/4: 303043: 6 b h Warning - Boathouse (Habitat)   `¾`   `90`
Cl-up, ch 2f out, sn rdn/outpcd by wnr: clr rem: hvly bckd tho' op 5/4: eff at 7f, poss best at 1m/9f: see 3452, 657.
3515 **MOORLANDS AGAIN 8** [6] D Burchell 5-8-11 R Price 66/1: 6504: Prom 4f: highly tried, needs h'caps.   `6`   `78$`
3518 **TORMENTOSO 8** [5] 3-8-6 L Newman (3) 100/1: 460505: Led after 1f till over 3f out, sn btn: see 3518.   `5`   `68$`
3517 **PETRIE 8** [4] 3-8-6 R Havlin 150/1: 030006: Al bhd: highly tried: see 3517, 2291 & 42.   `13`   `48$`
6 ran   Time 1m 20.00 (0.2)   (Hadi Al Tajir)   M P Tregoning Lambourn, Berks

---

3683 4.55 DAILY STAR HCAP 3YO+ 0-70 (E)   1m2f36y Good/Firm 26 -11 Slow   [64]
£2947 £842 £421   3 yo rec 8 lb

3581 **INDIAN NECTAR 5** [7] R Brotherton 7-9-4 (54) L Newman (3) 7/1: 523641: 7 b m Indian Ridge - Sheer   `59`
Nectar (Piaffer) Chsd ldrs, rdn/chsd ldr over 2f out, led 1f out, styd on strongly, rdn out: quick reapp: '99 wnr
at Nottingham, Lingfield (fill h'caps) & Chepstow (h'cap, this race, rtd 58): 98/99 hdles wnr at Worcester (nov) &
Hereford (nov h'cap, rtd 84h): suited by 10/12f on firm, gd/soft & any trk, likes Chepstow: on a fair mark.
3524 **SHEER FACE 7** [6] W R Muir 6-9-10 (60) Michael Doyle (7) 11/2: 350122: 6 b g Midyan - Rock Face   `2½`   `61`
(Ballad Rock) Towards rear, rdn & styd on fnl 2f, al held by wnr: loves Brighton: see 3524, 3244.
3499 **STITCH IN TIME 9** [1] G C Bravery 4-8-0 (36)(vis) A Polli 7/2: 054333: 4 ch c Inchinor - Late   `shd`   `37`
Matinee (Red Sunset) Handy, led over 3f out, rdn/hdd 1f out & no extra: stays 10f: eff in a visor: mdn: see 3499.
3182 **WILFRAM 21** [8] J M Bradley 3-9-3 (61) Craig Williams 7/2 FAV: 316324: Chsd ldrs, held 2f out: bckd.   `3½`   `57`
3422 **CELTIC BAY 11** [12] 3-9-4 (62) M Hills 12/1: -66665: Chsd ldrs 1m: see 3422, 2354.   `2½`   `54`
3314 **DANDES RAMBO 16** [2] 3-8-7 (51) W Supple 13/2: 360426: Led over 4f out till over 3f out, sn held.   `1¼`   `41`
3294 **SHERATON HEIGHTS 17** [15] 3-8-5 (49) Cheryl Nosworthy (7) 16/1: 60-007: Twds rear, mod gains fnl 3f.   `1`   `38`
3557 **SWING BAR 5** [13] 7-8-3 (39) R Havlin 16/1: 000008: Mid-div at best: op 12/1, qck reapp: see 965.   `1½`   `26`
3095 **PRINISHA 26** [10] 3-9-5 (63) G Carter 9/1: 202209: Rear, mod late prog: op 7/1: flattered 2745 (7f).   `3`   `46`
1395 **LALA SALAMA 100** [4] 4-8-11 (47) N Pollard 14/1: 00-000: Chsd ldrs, btn 2f out: 10th: 3 month abs: `½`   `29`
unplcd in '99 (rtd 61, debut).
1179 **MISTER WEBB 113** [9] 3-9-6 (64) D Sweeney 14/1: 64-500: Mid-div, btn 2f out: 11th: op 16/1, abs.   `1½`   `44`
3392 **BONNIE FLORA 12** [5] 4-9-6 (56) A Mackay 12/1: 003U00: Al twds rear: 12th: op 8/1: see 2270, 1343.   `3½`   `31`
3014 **KATHAKALI 29** [14] 3-9-0 (58) G Hind 7/1: 005000: Al bhd: 13th: bckd, op 8/1: btr 2450 (C/D).   `¾`   `32`
-- **COLD ENCOUNTER** [11] 5-9-10 (60) W Hutchinson (7) 33/1: 0/32-0: Al towards rear: 14th: reapp: `12`   `21`
7 month jumps abs (rnr-up thrice, rtd 97h, 1st time visor, mdn hdle, handles firm & gd grnd, P Eccles): ex-French,
10f Flat wnr in the provinces in '98 (hvy grnd): with S Mellor.
3404 **HENRY HEALD 12** [3] 5-8-7 (43) (bl) W Ryan 25/1: 1/0000: Led/sn clr, ran wide on bend over 4f out   `24`   `0`
& sn hdd, sn bhd: longer 10f trip: see 3404, 2759.
15 ran   Time 2m 07.90 (3.8)   (Mrs Carol Newman)   R Brotherton Elmley Castle, Worcs

---

EPSOM MONDAY AUGUST 28TH Lefthand, Very Sharp, Undulating Track

Official Going GOOD. Stalls: Str - Stands Side; 6f - Outside; 12f - Centre; Rem - Inside.

3684 2.05 TOKYO TROPHY COND STKS 3YO+ (C)   1m2f Good 40 -01 Slow
£6307 £2332 £1166 £530   3 yo rec 8 lb

2341 **NATIONAL ANTHEM 58** [3] Sir Michael Stoute 4-8-13 Pat Eddery 1/1 FAV: 4-1441: 4 b h Royal Academy -   `106`
Heart's Harmony (Blushing Groom) Cl up, styd on well for press to lead 1f out, rdn clr ins last: hvly bckd
after an 8 week abs: earlier scored on reapp at Newmarket (h'cap): '99 Sandown scorer (mdn, rtd 97): well
suited by 10f, stays 12f on firm, gd/soft & any trk: runs well fresh: v useful & fairly lightly raced 4yo.
2497 **GOLD ACADEMY 51** [4] R Hannon 4-9-2 B Marcus 9/4: 4-6662: 4 b h Royal Academy - Soha (Dancing   `2`   `105`
Brave) Trckd ldr, chall well over 2f out & ev ch till not qckn ins last: abs & not disgraced under top-weight.
3315 **CATCHY WORD 16** [1] E A L Dunlop 3-8-5 J Fanning 20/1: 054003: 3 ch c Cadeaux Genereux -   `½`   `101`
Lora's Guest (Be My Guest) Set pace, rdn & hdd dist, no extra: improved run, with no visor, stepped up to 10f.
*3488 **PHILATELIC LADY 9** [2] M J Haynes 4-8-8 S Carson (3) 33/1: 330314: Dwelt, bhd, eff over 2f out,   `3½`   `91$`
sn onepace: ran well up in class but will apprec a return to h'cap company as in 3488.
1848 **ZYZ 79** [5] 3-8-5 J Carroll 4/1: -23305: Held up, brief eff 3f out, sn btn: 11 week abs & dropped in   `5`   `89`
class: a candidate for headgear now: see 1246, 996.
5 ran   Time 2m 07.69 (4.11)   (Mrs Denis Haynes)   Sir Michael Stoute Newmarket, Suffolk

3685   2.35 AVENUES HCAP 3YO+ 0-90 (C)   1m114y rnd   Good 40   -06 Slow   [85]
£8463   £2604   £1302   £651   3 yo rec 7 lb

3422 **RIBERAC** 11 [7] M Johnston 4-9-8 (79) J Fanning 8/1: 001101: 4 b f Efisio - Ciboure   91
(Norwick) Handy, gd hdwy to lead over 2f out, sn pushed clr, v readily: val 6L+, op 6/1: earlier won at Sandown
& Ayr (h'caps): highly tried in '99 for W Haggas (stakes, rtd 91): former sprinter, revelation since stepped up to
1m/8.5f & even further cld suit: acts on firm, gd & any track: most progressive & useful now, cld well go in again.
3488 **COPPLESTONE** 9 [1] P W Harris 4-9-1 (72) I Mongan (5) 10/1: 404322: 4 b g Second Set - Queen Of   4 74
The Brush (Averof) Led after 1f till over 2f out, kept on but with no ch with impress wnr: deserves to go one better.
3471 **JUNIKAY** 9 [11] R Ingram 6-9-1 (72) J Carroll 12/1: 204143: 6 b g Treasure Kay - Junijo (Junius)   1¾ 70
Hld up, eff over 2f out, kept on same pace: likes a sharp/undulating track & ran close to form of 3110.
3365 **SKY DOME** 13 [3] M H Tompkins 7-9-1 (72) Dale Gibson 9/1: 303254: In tch, eff over 2f out, no impress.   3 65
3063 **MUYASSIR** 27 [2] P Doe 5/1: 011355: Held up rear, mod late gains, nvr dangerous: ½ 75
return to 9f & more positive tactics will suit: see 3063, 2304.
3422 **COMMON CONSENT** 11 [6] A Nicholls (3) 20/1: 104206: Hld up, eff 2f out, no impress.   nk 47
3499 **TAPAGE** 9 [9] J Mackay (5) 8/1: 162157: Cl up, wknd over 2f out: see 3499, 3355.   2½ 69
3421 **MINKASH** 11 [12] 3-9-10 (88)(bl) G Faulkner (3) 1/1: 064438: Waited with, brief eff 2f out, wknd.   2½ 69
3338 **SALTY JACK** 15 [5] 6-10-0 (85) T G McLaughlin 13/2: 545139: Held up, brief eff over 2f out, sn btn.   3 60
3110 **EASTERN SPICE** 25 [4] 3-9-3 (81) B Marcus 10/1: 130100: Sn rdn in tch, btn well over 3f out: 10th.   2½ 51
*3190 **POLAR CHALLENGE** 21 [8] 3-9-4 (82)(t) Pat Eddery 4/1 FAV: 352310: Handy, rdn & btn over 2f out: shd 52
eased: 11th, well bckd: much better expected after making all in 3190 (mdn).
2666 **LAGO DI COMO** 45 [10] 3-8-3 (67) S Carson (3) 50/1: 304100: Led 1f, wknd well over 3f out: last,   15 9
twice below 2322 (made all, med auction mdn).
12 ran   Time 1m 45.74 (3.94)   (Mr & Mrs G Middlebrook)   M Johnston Middleham, N Yorks

3686   3.10 MOET GENTS AMAT HCAP 3YO+ 0-90 (C)   1m4f   Good 40   -29 Slow   [58]
£10432   £3210   £1605   £802   3 yo rec 10lb   Horses strung across track like washing

3314 **RARE TALENT** 16 [4] S Gollings 6-10-4 (67) Mr B Hitchcott 8/1: 152241: 6 b g Mtoto - Bold   67
As Love (Lomond) Held up, hdwy over 2f out, styd on to lead ins last, drvn out: earlier won at Beverley (h'cap)
& plcd num times: '99 scorer at Beverley (ladies h'cap) & Windsor (amat h'cap, rtd 61): '98 wnr at Doncaster &
Chester (h'caps, rtd 65): suited by 10/12f & handles gd/soft, gd & firm & any track: best without a visor
& runs v well for an amat pilot: well rdn in a race in which these unprofessional jockeys drifted all over the str.
2943 **WASP RANGER** 32 [1] G L Moore 6-11-7 (79) Mr E Hennau 4/1 JT FAV: 231622: 6 b g Red Ransom -   2½ 80
Lady Climber (Mount Hagen) Dwelt, sn handy, styd on to lead alone on far side 3f out, hdd ins last, not pace of
wnr: nicely bckd & continues to run well: see 2943, 2530.
*3518 **KENNET** 8 [7] P D Cundell 5-11-0 (72) Mr T Steeger 4/1 JT FAV: 223113: 5 b g Kylian - Marwell   hd 73
Mitzi (Interrex) Hld up, hdwy in centre of course to ch ldr over 2f out, ev ch 1f out, sn wknd: clr of rem, bckd.
2812 **NAVARRE SAMSON** 38 [8] P J Hobbs 5-10-7 (65)(t) Mr L Jefford 8/1: 002/04: Handy, lost place after   4 60
5f, some late gains towards stands side: op 11/2: recently won a claiming hdle at Stratford (rtd 120h): see 2812.
3560 **SPIRIT OF TENBY** 5 [3] 3-10-0 (68) Mr Edgar Byrne 11/2: 402145: Held up, came stands side in   2 60
straight, rdn & btn over 1f out: quick reapp: see 3417.
3336 **ANGELS VENTURE** 15 [5] 4-10-12 (70)(tvi) Mr O Sauer 11/2: 004326: Held up, came stands side in   1 61
straight, btn well over 1f out: see 3336, 2917.
3110 **TARAWAN** 25 [9] 4-11-1 (73)(bl) Mr C Bonner 16/1: 005007: Slow away, keen & led after 1f,   8 54
came stands side & hdd 3f out, no extra: see 580.
3402 **HIBERNATE** 12 [10] 6-10-7 (65)(vis) Mr A Evans 14/1: 0S0008: Keen, led 1f, came stands side   5 39
straight & sn wknd: can do better: see 1829, 422.
3461 **NAUTICAL STAR** 10 [2] 5-12-0 (86) Mr C B Hills 10/1: -00009: Handy, wknd ent straight: see 1850.   14 40
9 ran   Time 2m 43.11 (8.31)   (John King, Bill Hobson, Graham King)   S Gollings Scambleby, Lincs

3687   3.40 TOTE EXACTA HCAP 3YO+ 0-105 (B)   5f   Good 40   +21 Fast   [102]
£19093   £5875   £2937   £1468   3 yo rec 2 lb

3521 **REPERTORY** 7 [7] M S Saunders 7-10-0 (102) Darren Williams (5) 16/1: 235001: 7 b g Anshan -   107
Susie's Baby (Balidar) With ldrs, styd on to lead dist, edged left but kept on gamely for press ins last: fast
time, top weight: plcd in List company earlier (rtd 104): won 3 times in '99, rtd 106: last win came in this
race in '98, here at Epsom (h'cap, rtd 106), also won at The Curragh (List h'cap): all wins at 5f: acts on firm,
hvy & any trk, likes Epsom: has run well fresh: can carry big weights: v speedy, useful & tough/genuine.
*3322 **IVORYS JOY** 16 [18] K T Ivory 5-9-5 (93) C Carver (3) 5/1 FAV: 045012: 5 b m Tina's Pet -   shd 97
Jacqui Joy (Music Boy) In tch, hdwy over 1f out, kept on for press ins last, just held: at the top of her form.
3646 **SHARP HAT** 2 [13] D W Chapman 6-7-10 (70) Claire Bryan (5) 20/1: 116303: 6 b g Shavian - Madam   ¾ 72
Trilby (Grundy) Dwelt, bhd, hdwy over 2f out, kept on nicely inside left, not btn far nrst fin: quick
reapp & back to form: could go in again this term: see 3322, 2721.
3512 **BODFARI KOMAITE** 8 [1] M W Easterby 4-7-13 (73) Dale Gibson 12/1: W21134: With ldr, ev ch till   shd 74
no extra cl home, not btn far: in fine form: see 3512, 1662.
3528 **TUSCAN DREAM** 7 [11] 5-8-1 (75) Iona Wands 12/1: 124035: With ldrs, tchd left over 1f out, onepace.   1½ 72
3473 **SUNLEY SENSE** 9 [2] 4-8-8 (82) Pat Eddery 14/1: 020066: Made most till dist, no extra: tough.   hd 78
3464 **ANTHONY MON AMOUR** 9 [3] 5-7-12 (72) A Nicholls (3) 12/1: 013567: With ldrs, wknd fnl 1f: see 2944.   1 65
2676 **CORRIDOR CREEPER** 44 [6] 3-8-10 (86) I Mongan (5) 20/1: 300638: With ldrs, btn dist: abs, see 2676.   shd 78
3528 **DANCING MYSTERY** 7 [5] 6-8-9 (83) S Carson (3) 16/1: 030149: Bhd, some late gains: see 3528.   hd 75
3543 **PERUVIAN CHIEF** 6 [15] 3-8-12 (88) J Mackay (5) 14/1: 433600: Sn rdn & outpcd, styd on nicely   nk 79
late, nrst fin: 10th: quick reapp & looks sure to go closer next time over 6/7f: see 2954, 2568.
3016 **HENRY HALL** 29 [9] 4-9-6 (94) Kim Tinkler 20/1: 311000: With ldrs, held when short of room dist: ½ 83
11th, risen in the weights after landing 2310.
3569 **SINGSONG** 5 [17] 3-9-1 (91) D Allan (7) 16/1: 303300: Sn outpcd, switched left 1f out, mod   shd 79
gains, 12th: quick reapp: see 2663, 2348.
3341 **FORGOTTEN TIMES** 15 [16] 6-7-12 (72)(vis) C Catlin (7) 8/1: 120600: Sn rdn in tch, wknd 1f out: 13th.   ½ 58
3521 **COASTAL BLUFF** 7 [19] 8-8-13 (87) S W Kelly (3) 10/1: 102040: Nvr a factor: 14th, flatted 3521.   ¾ 73
3135 **ANSELLAD** 24 [8] 3-8-7 (83) J Carroll 20/1: -00250: Al bhd: 15th: btr 2787, 1285.   nk 66
3091 **PURE ELEGANCIA** 26 [10] 4-7-11 (71)(1ow)(2oh) P Doe 10/1: -02430: Cl up, held when hmpd over 1f out.   ½ 53

EPSOM MONDAY AUGUST 28TH Lefthand, Very Sharp, Undulating Track

*3528 **SYLVA PARADISE 7** [8] 7-8-4 (74)(vis)(4ow)(6ex) B Marcus 16/1: 503010: Al bhd: 17th: btr 3528. *3* **51**
3473 **DASHING BLUE 9** [14] 7-9-5 (93)(BL) J Fanning 14/1: 060000: Sn rdn & al bhd: 18th, tried blinks. *nk* **65**
3059 **AFAAN 27** [12] 7-9-5 (93)(bl) T G McLaughlin 20/1: 020400: In tch, wknd over 1f out: 19th. *2* **59**
19 ran Time 55.26 (0.96) (M S Saunders) M S Saunders Haydon, Somerset

3688 4.10 EBF NOV STKS 2YO (D) 7f rnd Good 40 -87 Slow
£4800 £1477 £738 £369

3304 **MUSIC MAID 16** [4] H S Howe 2-8-11 A Nicholls (3) 10/1: 613001: 2 b f Inzar - Richardstown Lass (Muscatite) Made all, kept on for press fnl 2f, rdn to assert cl home: earlier scored at Lingfield (mdn auct): 2,800gns Apr foal: half sister to 2 wnrs: stys 7f on fast, gd/soft & any trck: improved for forcing tactics. **85**
*3478 **COUNT DUBOIS 9** [3] W J Haggas 2-9-5 B Marcus 11/8: 12: 2 b c Zafonic - Madame Dubois (Legend Of France) Keen, held up, eff to chall over 1f out, not pace of wnr: hvly bckd & came out best of these at the weights: stays 7f on gd & gd/soft: see 3478. *½* **93**
3412 **SPY MASTER 11** [2] Sir Michael Stoute 2-8-12 Pat Eddery 10/11 FAV: 023: 2 b c Green Desert - Obsessive (Seeking The Gold) Trckd ldr, eff 2f out, onepace over 1f out: similar form to 3412. *1½* **83**
3492 **LORD LIAM 9** [1] N P Littmoden 2-8-12 P Doe 11/1: 534: Keen bhd, rdn & btn 2f out: see 3492. *2½* **78**
4 ran Time 1m 29.01 (8.91) (R J Parish) H S Howe Oakford, Devon

3689 4.40 DAILY STAR CLAIMER 3YO+ (E) 6f rnd Good 40 -03 Slow
£3640 £1120 £560 £280 3 yo rec 3 lb

3283 **CAPE COAST 17** [3] R M Beckett 3-8-5 S Carson (3) 13/2: 630421: 3 b g Common Grounds - Strike It Rich (Rheingold) Held up, hdwy over 1f out, styd on well ins last to get up cl home: claimed by N Littmoden for £7,000: earlier scored at Nottingham (seller with J Osborne): rtd 77 when rnr up for D Marks in '99: suited by 6f on any track: acts on fast & gd/soft: best without blinks: should be plcd to win similar. **68**
3493 **MY EMILY 9** [4] G L Moore 4-8-5 I Mongan (2) 7/2: 160022: 4 b f Kings's Signet - Flying Wind (Forzando) Held up, styd alone far side straight, overall ldr 2f out, hard rdn & collared cl home: just btn, clr of rem, bckd tho' op 5/2: both prev wins over 7f: win in this grade: see 3493, 1884. *½* **63**
3631 **ANSELLMAN 2** [8] A Berry 10-8-12 (bl) J Carroll 12/1: 014533: 10 gr g Absalom - Grace Poole (Sallust) Handy, onepace fnl 2f: 10yo, quick reapp, see 3631. *3* **62**
3441 **KING OF PERU 10** [1] D Nicholls 7-9-8 Alex Greaves 6/1: 011424: Held up, eff 2f out, hung left & no extra fnl 1f: ran to form of 3441, 3077. *nk* **71**
3436 **KNOCKEMBACK NELLIE 10** [2] 4-8-9 (bl) Dale Gibson 20/1: 005005: Led till 2f out, no extra: stiff task: better off in mod h'caps, see 2788. *¾* **56**
3493 **CHAKRA 9** [6] 6-8-10 P Doe 25/1: 302166: Bhd, no impress over 1f out: stiff task, best 3243. *1* **54$**
*3405 **KINSMAN 12** [7] 3-8-11 (vis) A Nicholls (3) 100/30: 316017: Prom, btn 2f out: better expected on drop in class after 3405 (C/D). *1¾* **53**
3297 **SLUMBERING 17** [5] 4-8-12 (bl) Pat Eddery 5/2 FAV: 063408: Chsd ldr, btn over 2f out, eased: hvly bckd & clearly much better expected: see 2813, 2631. *1½* **47**
8 ran Time 1m 10.4 (2.6) (Willie McKay) R M Beckett Lambourn, Berks

3690 5.15 TATTENHAM CORNER NURSERY HCAP 2YO (C) 7f rnd Good 40 -19 Slow [89]
£7085 £2180 £1090 £545

3354 **CHAWENG BEACH 14** [2] R Hannon 2-7-11 (58)(1ow)(2oh) A Nicholls (0) 16/1: 016451: 2 ro f Chaddleworth - Swallow Bay (Penmarric) Cl up, led 2f out, rdn clr fnl 1f, readily: earlier scored at Lingfield (seller): March foal, dam 6f juv scorer: eff at 6f, apprec step up to 7f on gd: likes a sharp/undul track. **66**
*3444 **SHINING OASIS 10** [1] P F I Cole 2-8-12 (73) Darren Williams (5) 6/1: -43512: 2 b f Mujtahid - Desert Maiden (Green Desert) Set pace, leather broke 2f out, kept on but no ch with wnr fnl 1f: gd run in the circumstances: handles gd/firm & gd: should go in again, see 3444. *4* **72**
*3388 **ZANDOS CHARM 12** [7] J Akehurst 2-8-5 (66) P Doe 10/1: -5013: 2 b f Forzando - Silver Charm (Dashing Blade) Cl up, rdn & onepace over 1f out: prev with R Hannon & ran cl to form of 3388 (claimer). *¾* **63**
3258 **PAY THE SILVER 18** [5] A P Jarvis 2-8-9 (70) S W Kelly (3) 14/1: 043554: Held up, eff 2f out, kept on same pace: see 2161, 2005. *nk* **66**
*3660 **LONER 1** [6] 2-8-11 (72)(6ex) J Mackay (5) 11/4 FAV: 046215: Slow away, sn in tch, no impress over 1f out: bckd tho' op 9/4, this prob came too soon after winning at Goodwood yesterday in 3660. *2* **64**
3609 **COUNTRYWIDE PRIDE 3** [3] 2-8-8 (69) Pat Eddery 4/1: 043046: Held up, eff over 2f out, eased when btn inside last: nicely bckd, quick reapp, btr 3609. *1½* **58**
3149 **MEDIA BUYER 23** [9] 2-9-1 (76)(bl) D R McCabe 14/1: 003207: Pressed ldr till 3f out, no extra. *2* **61**
*3412 **JOHNSONS POINT 11** [8] 2-9-7 (82) J Carroll 9/2: 218: In tch, btn over 2f out: bckd: btr 3412 (mdn). *4* **60**
3400 **TOP NOLANS 12** [4] 2-8-10 (71) Dale Gibson 12/1: 333049: Keen in tch, btn over 2f out: longer trip. *2* **45**
9 ran Time 1m 24.22 (4.12) (F Coen) R Hannon East Everleigh, Wilts

WARWICK MONDAY AUGUST 28TH Lefthand, Sharp, Turning Track

Official Going GOOD. Stalls: Inside.

3691 2.00 SYMBIO SELLER 3YO+ (G) 1m2f188y Good Inapplicable
£2060 £588 £294 3 yo rec 9 lb

2981 **DIVORCE ACTION 31** [16] R M Stronge 4-9-6 K Dalgleish (5) 9/2: 250051: 4 b g Common Grounds - Overdue Reaction (Be My Guest) Dwelt, hdwy halfway, went on 2f out, styd on well, drvn out: new stable, bght in for 5,400gns: 99/00 hdles wnr at Newbury (2m juv nov h'cap, fast, rtd 95h): '99 Kempton Flat wnr (clmr, rtd 68, P Cole): eff at 9/11f on firm & gd/soft: runs well fresh on a sharp or easy trk: apprec drop to sell grade. **61**
3390 **ZIDAC 12** [5] P J Makin 8-9-6 A Clark 7/2 FAV: 13-002: 8 b g Statoblest - Sule Skerry (Scottish Rifle) Front rank, went on over 2f out, sn hdd, styd on, not pace of wnr ins last: can win similar: see 1509. *1½* **58**
3447 **FULL EGALITE 10** [8] B R Johnson 4-9-11 (bl) C Rutter 6/1: 120023: 4 gr g Ezzoud - Milva (Jellaby) Bhd, hdwy over 4f out, ev ch till onepcd appr fnl 1f: treat rating with caution, needs a return to 12f: see 3447. *2* **59$**
2680 **ERUPT 44** [14] Miss S J Wilton 7-9-11 R Lake (7) 20/1: 300004: In tch, eff 3f out, held fnl 2f: *5* **52**

6 wk abs: big step up in trip: see 1799, 1601.
3351 **INDIANA SPRINGS 14** [4] 3-8-11 J Tate 16/1: 006035: Prom, rdn/btn over 2f out: see 3351. 2 **43$**
3117 **GAME TUFTY 24** [10] 4-9-6 N Callan 9/2: 0-0006: Handy, eff 3f out, sn fdd: nicely bckd from 14/1. 1½ **41**
3534 **HEATHYARDS JAKE 6** [1] 4-9-6 P M Quinn (3) 14/1: 054047: Dwelt, late gains: qck reapp, up in trip. ¾ **40**
869 **MURRON WALLACE 139** [12] 6-9-1 S Finnamore(5) 20/1: 0/0008: Hdwy from rear 3f out, sn held: abs. *shd* **35**
1911 **KINGS TO OPEN 75** [13] 3-8-11 Paul Eddery 15/2: 0-0609: Prom, wknd fnl 2f: abs: see 1911, 1035. ½ **39**
3456 **DISTANT FLAME 10** [6] 3-8-6 O Urbina 25/1: 000560: Mid-div at best, fin 10th: mod form. 1½ **32**
3524 **AVERHAM STAR 7** [15] 5-9-6 (vis) A Hawkins (7) 50/1: 060000: Led early, led again halfway, hdd 2f out, qckly lost tch, 11th: quick reapp, stiff task. 2 **34$**
3498 **THIRTY SIX CEE 9** [3] 3-8-6 M Tebbutt 50/1: 505000: Trkd ldrs, wknd rapdily fnl 3f, 12th: see 171. 2 **26**
594 **REGENT 184** [11] 5-9-6 G Baker (5) 33/1: 400-00: V keen, led after 1f, hdd halfway, wknd rapidly, 17th: 6 month abs: prev with C Morlock, now with P W Hiatt. **0**
4078} **Protaras Bay 339** [18] 6-9-6 (vis) G Bardwell 33/1:
4048} **Toby Grimes 341** [2] 3-8-11 A Daly 40/1:
3332 **Bright Blue 15** [7] 4-9-6 D McGaffin (5) 66/1:
3094 **Time To Skip 26** [9] 3-8-6 S Righton 50/1:
569 **Untold Story 188** [17] 5-9-6 R Brisland (5) 50/1:
18 ran Time 2m 22.8 (Kevin Elliott) R M Stronge Beedon, Berks

3692

2.35 FELLOWES AUCT MDN 2YO (F) 7f26y rnd Good Inapplicable
£2446 £699 £349

3558 **NUN LEFT 5** [6] R M Beckett 2-8-4 N Callan 11/4 FAV: 32421: 2 b f Bishop of Cashel - Salsita (Salse) **81**
Led, styd on well & al in command, drvn out: plcd 3 of 4 prev starts: 7,000gns Mar foal, dam a juv wnr abroad, sire high-class at 7f/1m: eff at 6/7f on firm & gd: handles a sharp or stiff/undul trk: genuine, deserved this.
3239 **LOOKING FOR LOVE 19** [9] J G Portman 2-7-13 G Baker (5) 7/2: -03362: 2 b f Tagula - Mousseux (Jareer) Front rank, chsd ldrs fnl 1f, al held: op 3/1: acts on fast & gd grnd, needs nurs h'caps: see 3239. 1¼ **73**
3418 **DILLY 11** [11] P R Chamings 2-7-13 S Righton 8/1: 243: 2 br f Dilum - Princess Rosananti (Shareef Dancer) Waited with, prog over 3f out, styd on ins last, held cl-home: 4L clr rem: now qual for h'caps & that sphere shld suit in time: stays 7f on fast & gd: see 2841. 1¾ **70**
3358 **SISTER CELESTINE 14** [2] W Jarvis 2-8-5 M Tebbutt 3/1: 24: Prom, rdn/held appr fnl 1f: up in trip, shade better on debut in 3358 (6f). 4 **69**
3273 **EL HAMRA 17** [4] 2-8-8 C Rutter 8/1: 503335: Speed 5f, wknd appr dist: see 3273 (h'cap). ¾ **71**
-- **MARSHAL BOND** [8] 2-8-4 Paul Eddery 12/1: 6: Mid-div at best on debut: 15,000gns Mar foal, half brother to numerous wnr incl a couple of 7f 2yo scorers: dam well related: with B Smart. 3½ **61**
2091 **SILVER INFERNO 68** [1] 2-8-4 R Brisland (5) 66/1: 07: Nvr dangerous: 9 wk abs: see 2091. 1¾ **58**
3057 **CHICKASAW TRAIL 27** [12] 2-7-13 P M Quinn (3) 50/1: 08: Al in rear: see 3057. 2 **49**
2214 **BEE J GEE 62** [7] 2-8-10 G Bardwell 40/1: 609: Mid-div, lost tch fnl 2f: 9 wk abs: up in trip: see 1962. 1¼ **58**
-- **BELLINO EMPRESARIO** [3] 2-8-8 A Clark 25/1: 0: Dwelt, al rear, 10th: Apr foal, dam a wng stayer. 6 **47**
-- **Cosmic Pearl** [5] 2-7-13 K Dalgleish (5) 20/1:
3268 **Graig Park 18** [10] 2-8-8 O Pears 33/1:
12 ran Time 1m 28.7 (The Millennium Madness Partnership) R M Beckett Lambourn, Berks

3693

3.05 PLEDGE NURSERY HCAP 2YO (E) 6f21y Good Inapplicable [96]
£2821 £806 £403

2599 **JOINT INSTRUCTION 47** [6] M R Channon 2-7-11 (65) M Mathers (3) 13/2: 520201: 2 b g Forzando - Edge Of Darkness (Vaigly Great) Chsd ldrs, led appr fnl 1f, styd on well, drvn out: 7 wk abs: earlier won at Brighton (nov med auct): eff at 5/6f on firm & hvy grnd, 7f shld suit: poss acts on any trk, likes a sharp/turning one. **70**
3439 **SIR FRANCIS 10** [8] J Noseda 2-9-7 (89) Paul Eddery 10/3 FAV: 106132: 2 b g Common Grounds - Red Note (Rusticaro) Rcd wide in lead, hdd appr fnl 1f, rallied well ins last, not btn far: fine eff conceding upwards of 13lbs all round, remains in gd heart: see 3439, 3258. ¾ **91**
3466 **EAGLES CACHE 9** [1] A Berry 2-8-7 (75) O Pears 11/2: 362623: 2 b c Eagle Eyed - Cache (Bustino) Mid-div, till ran on strongly for press well ins last, closing at fin: worth another try at 7f: see 3466. *nk* **77**
-3258 **DENSIM BLUE 18** [5] J Pearce 2-8-8 (76) G Bardwell 11/2: 414524: Rcd keenly/prom, rdn/held appr dist: op 9/2: shade btr 3258. 1½ **74**
3466 **LADY WARD 9** [7] 2-8-2 (70) A Clark 10/1: 0365: Sn outpcd, prog over 2f out, held appr fnl 1f: op 7/1, h'cap bow: see 3187, 2683. 1½ **64**
3175 **TROUBLESHOOTER 22** [3] 2-8-0 (68)(BL) R Brisland (5) 9/2: 020206: Keen in tch, btn fnl 2f: blnkd. *shd* **62**
3264 **DIVINE WIND 18** [4] 2-8-4 (72) K Dalgleish (5) 10/1: 334007: Chsd ldrs, fdd over 2f out: op 7/1, see 2318. 4 **57**
3354 **QUIZZICAL LADY 14** [2] 2-8-2 (70) C Rutter 7/1: 406428: Al last: op 6/1: btr 3354. 2 **50**
8 ran Time 1m 16.7 (Ridgeway Downs Racing) M R Channon West Isley, Berks

3694

3.35 FIVE STAR CLAIMER 3YO+ (F) 5f Good Inapplicable
£2446 £699 £349 3 yo rec 2 lb

3214 **NICKLES 19** [16] L G Cottrell 5-8-4 A Daly 14/1: -06401: 5 b g Lugana Beach - Instinction (Never So Bold) Front rank, led appr fnl 1f, rdn clr well ins last: claimed for £2,000: '99 Lingfield wnr (clmr, rtd 63): plcd twice in '98 (mdn, rtd 73): best racing up with the pace arnd 5f on gd, soft & a sharp trk: likes clmrs. **55**
3136 **GDANSK 24** [13] A Berry 3-9-2 O Pears 6/1: 004002: 3 b g Pips Pride - Merry Twinkle (Martinmas) Led, hdd appr fnl 1f, kept on but not pace of wnr well ins last: see 2663, 1712. 2 **62**
3464 **TADEO 9** [10] M Johnston 7-9-10 K Dalgleish (5) 10/11 FAV: 030003: 7 ch g Primo Dominie - Royal Passion (Ahonoora) Trkd ldrs, dropped rear over 2f out, ran on well ins last: nicely bckd under top weight: much better expected at these weights (officially 22lbs+ ahd of all these rivals): see 2310. *hd* **68**
2240 **APPLES AND PEARS 61** [15] M H Tompkins 4-8-5 C Rutter 50/1: 000004: Prom, drvn/btn over 1f out: 9 wk abs, treat rating with caution (offic only 38): see 312. 2½ **43$**
3562 **WILLRACK TIMES 5** [4] 3-8-1 G Baker (5) 25/1: 000045: Chsd ldrs, rdn/no extra appr dist: qck reapp. *shd* **41**
3493 **WHITE SUMMIT 9** [14] 3-8-10 P Fitzsimons (5) 66/1: 0-0006: Handy, wknd qckly ins last: see 2919. ½ **48**
3562 **WINDRUSH BOY 5** [6] 10-8-4 Joanna Badger (7) 33/1: 044467: Outpcd halfway, late hdwy: qck reapp. *nk* **39**
3283 **BLUSHING GRENADIER 17** [1] 8-8-8 (bl) S Finnamore (5) 6/1: 602108: Al bhd: op 10/1: btr 1663 (6f). 1¾ **38**
3521 **MUTASAWWAR 7** [3] 6-8-8 R Brisland (5) 14/1: 000409: Bhd, no room over 2f out, sn btn: qck reapp. *shd* **38**
3405 **PARDY PET 12** [9] 3-8-5 (bl) A Clark 25/1: 000050: Dwelt, al bhd, 10th: see 2432. 1 **34**
2701 **Gad Yakoun 43** [11] 7-8-12 Angela Hartley (7) 66/1:
3283 **Press Ahead 17** [2] 5-8-6 M Tebbutt 33/1:
3243 **Panther 19** [5] 10-8-8 G Bardwell 50/1:
2976 **Ladycake 31** [8] 4-8-2(3ow) Paul Eddery 50/1:
3161 **Clansman 23** [7] 3-8-4 (BL) N Callan 25/1:
15 ran Time 1m 00.1 (Inforfivecents) L G Cottrell Dulford, Devon

3695   **4.05 EUROTEK HCAP 3YO+ 0-80 (D)**   **2m39y**   **Good**   Inapplicable   [74]
£3818   £1175   £587   £293   3 yo   rec 14lb

3331 **XELLANCE** 15 [6] M Johnston 3-8-10 (70) K Dalgleish (5) 2/1 FAV: 141231: 3 b g Be My Guest - Excellent   74
Alibi (Exceller) Prom, hdwy to chall 3f out, led 2f out, styd on well, rdn out: v consistent this term, wng at
Southwell (2), W'hampton (AW h'caps, rtd 53a), Musselburgh, Redcar (2) & Chepstow (h'caps): suited by 14f/2m2f
on firm, gd & fibresand: handles any trk & runs well fresh: typically tough, genuine & prog M Johnston stayer.

3148 **PALUA** 23 [3] Mrs A J Bowlby 3-9-2 (76) Paul Eddery 13/2: 320332: 3 b c Sri Pekan - Reticent Bride   1¼   78
(Shy Groom) Waited with, gd hdwy appr fnl 1f, ev ch until drvn & lkd reluctant to go past wnr ins last: op
5/1: up in trip, stays 2m: looks a tricky ride & worth a try in headgear: see 2872.

3518 **PARADISE NAVY** 8 [5] C R Egerton 11-7-11 (43)(bl) G Sparkes (4) 10/1: 0-0003: 11 b g Slip Anchor -   5   40
Ivory Waltz (Sir Ivor) Led early, led again over 6f out, hdd 2f out & not pace of front 2: op 6/1: well h'capped.

3511 **MY LEGAL EAGLE** 8 [1] R J Price 6-8-11 (57) P Fitzsimons (5) 9/1: 606004: Settled rear, prog   3½   50
over 3f out, btn fnl 2f: btr 1023 (hvy).

3295 **CANDLE SMILE** 17 [2] 8-9-10 (70) G Gibbons (7) 9/2: /20-65: Sn led, hdd over 6f out, lost tch fnl 2f.   7   57
3448 **LITTLE BRAVE** 10 [4] 5-8-12 (58) J Tate 5/2: 143336: Bhd, brief eff over 3f out, sn wknd: btr 3448.   4   41
6 ran   Time 3m 37.3   (T T Bloodstocks)   M Johnston Middleham, N Yorks

---

3696   **4.35 ESSELTE MDN 3YO+ (D)**   **7f26y rnd**   **Good**   Inapplicable
£4225   £1300   £650   £325   3 yo   rec 5 lb

3457 **KUWAIT ROSE** 10 [10] K Mahdi 4-9-4 J Tate 8/1: 402501: 4 b c Inchinor - Black Ivor (Sir Ivor)   67
Front rank, went on 2f out, switched stands side & pushed clr ins last: up in trip: plcd on turf in '99 (mdn,
rtd 61): eff at 6f, suited by 7f: acts on gd, soft, f/sand & a sharp/turning trk: could follow up.

3350 **FARAWAY LOOK** 14 [8] J R Fanshawe 3-8-13 O Urbina 5/2 JT FAV: 42: 3 b c Distant View - Summer   5   59
Trip (L'Emigrant) Handy, dropped rear over 3f out, rallied & ran on well appr fnl 1f, wnr had flown:
prob unsuited by this drop back to 7f (bred to apprec 1m+): see 3350.

-- **THREE OWLS** [4] L M Cumani 3-8-8 G Sparkes (7) 4/1: 3: 3 b f Warning - Three Terms (Arctic Tern)   1   52
Settled rear, gd hdwy 3f out, no extra appr dist: op 3/1: related to sev wnrs: prob stays 7f on gd: shld imprv.

3350 **LIVELY FELIX** 14 [12] S Mellor 3-8-13 C Rutter 66/1: -004: Chsd ldrs, rdn/held appr fnl 1f: only   nk   57$
mod form prev: poss get 7f on gd.

3626 **KUWAIT FLAVOUR** 2 [14] 4-9-4 D McGaffin (5) 14/1: 3-6045: Bhd, prog 3f out, no extra over 1f out: shd   57
op 10/1, ran 48hrs ago: stablemate of wnr: flattered 3626.

3256 **COOL SPICE** 18 [9] 3-8-8 P Fitzsimons (5) 11/1: -046: Mid-div at best: btr 3256.   1¼   50
3189 **MACS DREAM** 21 [6] 5-9-4 (t) M Tebbutt 33/1: -00057: Bhd, late hdwy, no dngr: flattered 3189 (10f).   3   49
3190 **REGAL VISION** 11 [3] 3-8-13 G Hannon (7) 66/1: 08: Nvr a factor: see 3190.   4   42
3529 **TOPLESS IN TUSCANY** 7 [2] 3-8-8 G Baker (5) 33/1: 360049: Prom, lost tch appr fnl 1f: qck reapp.   ½   36
2978 **ROYAL TARRAGON** 31 [1] 4-8-13 R Brisland (5) 66/1: 000000: Led over 3f out, hdd 2f out, wknd, 10th.   hd   36
3390 **ATALYA** 12 [11] 3-8-13 K Dalgleish (5) 16/1: 245000: Chsd ldrs, fdd over 2f out, 11th: drop in trip.   ½   40
2579 **IN THE ARENA** 47 [13] 3-8-13 Paul Eddery 5/2 JT FAV: -43400: Led till 3f out, wknd/eased: 12th, abs.   5   32
2232 **No Tomorrow** 61 [7] 3-8-8 (t) N Callan 40/1:   2232 **Kerrich** 61 [5] 3-8-8 A Daly 50/1:
14 ran   Time 1m 28.7   (Greenfield Stud)   K Mahdi Newmarket

---

Official Going   GOOD (GOOD TO FIRM in places). Stalls: Str Crse - Stands Side; Rnd Crse - Inside.

3697   **2.30 GRASSINGTON SELLER 2YO (F)**   **6f**   **Good 40**   -35 Slow
£2282   £652   £326   2 Groups, no discernible advantage

3444 **ITS SMEE AGAIN** 10 [15] B W Hills 2-8-6 R Hills 7/2 FAV: 44461: 2 ch f Mizoram - Mountain Dew   59
(Pharly) Cmftbly made all far side: tchd 9/2, sold for 9,000 gns: eff forcing the pace at 6f on gd grnd in a seller.

3278 **MISS EQUINOX** 17 [7] N Tinkler 2-8-11 D O'Donohoe 11/2: 223132: 2 b f Presidium - Miss Nelski   3½   56
(Most Secret) Cl-up stands side, led that pack ent final 2f, no impress on wnr: op 7/2: consistent in sellers.

3216 **CIRCUIT LIFE** 19 [2] A Berry 2-8-11 C Lowther 10/1: 066623: 2 ch g Rainbows For Life - Alicedale   ¾   54
(Trempolino) Prom stands side, styd on appr final 1f: worth another try at 7f, see 3216.

3223 **RATHKENNY** 19 [6] J G Given 2-8-11 Dean McKeown 4/1: -564: Front rank stands side, onepace final 1f.   ½   52
3346 **DOUBLE PING** 14 [17] 2-8-6 T Lucas 16/1: 05: Towards rear far side, late hdwy, nvr a threat: nds 7f+.   2½   41
3376 **EASTERN RED** 12 [16] 2-8-6 S Sanders 16/1: 620546: Prom far side till onepace 2f out: stiff task.   2½   35
3127 **MARE OF WETWANG** 24 [13] 2-8-6 P Robinson 16/1: 6007: Nvr dngrs far side: op 12/1, moderate.   ½   34
3055 **EMMA THOMAS** 27 [3] 2-8-6 R Ffrench 12/1: 008: Bhd ldrs stands side, fdd ent final 2f: see 2539.   1¼   31
2985 **PREMIER BOY** 30 [12] 2-8-11 J Bramhill 33/1: 09: Nvr a factor stands side: Blues Traveller half   1¼   33
brother to sev wnrs: needs further: with B Rothwell.

2862 **KUMAKAWA** 36 [1] 2-8-11 V Halliday 33/1: -0000: Dwelt, al towards rear stands side: 10th, no form.   nk   32
3438 **ECKSCLUSIVE STORY** 10 [5] 2-8-6 (VIS) K Darley 7/1: 440640: Bhd final 3f stands side: 11th: visored.   2   21
3438 **DOUBLE DIGIT** 10 [10] 2-8-6 T Williams 33/1: 000: Led stands side till ent final 2f, sn btn: 14th.   0
3143 **BLUE FALCON** 23 [4] 2-8-11 G Parkin 8/1: 060: Nvr a factor stands side, hmpd halfway: 15th: tchd 10/1.   0
3438 **Gordons Friend** 10 [9] 2-8-11 M Fenton 20/1:   -- **Dispol Foxtrot** [8] 2-8-6 A McGlone 33/1:
1713 **Dusty Princess** 84 [11] 2-8-6 (BL) S Whitworth 33/1:
16 ran   Time 1m 14.5 (4.5)   (The Anglo Irish Choral Society)   B W Hills Lambourn, Berks.

3698   **3.00 B NEVETT HCAP 3YO 0-80 (D)**   **6f**   **Good 40**   -20 Slow   [87]
£5154   £1586   £793   £396   2 Groups, probably no avantage.

3280 **CHIQUITA** 17 [9] J A R Toller 3-9-3 (76) P Robinson 9/1: 500021: 3 ch f College Chapel - Council Rock   81
(General Assembly) In tch stands side, prog appr final 1f, qcknd to lead inside last, rdn on strongly, rdn out:
'99 wnr at W'hampton (rtd 80a) & Sandown (nurseries, rtd 80, W Haggas): eff at 6f, tried 7f: acts on firm, hvy
grnd & fibresand, any trk: back to form, no surprise to see her go in again soon.

3130 **BUDELLI** 24 [11] M R Channon 3-9-5 (78) P McCabe 8/1: 312502: 3 b c Elbio - Eves Temptation   ¾   80

(Glenstal) Nvr far away stands side, kept on final 1f, not btn far: back to form, apprec return to 6f: see 1399.

3161 **LAYAN 23** [20] J Balding 3-7-10 (55)(3oh) J Bramhill 20/1: 034203: 3 b f Puissance - Most Uppitty nk 56
(Absalom) Prsd ldrs far side, led that side appr fnl 2f & ev ch, kept on: fine run 3lbs o/h: eff at 5/6f.

3414 **ARETINO 11** [1] P W Harris 3-9-3 (76) M Fenton 8/1: 500264: Handy stands side, rdn ent fnl 2f, ½ 75
held towards fin: clr rem, back in trip: see 1262.

3619 **SOBA JONES 3** [4] 3-7-13 (58)(bl) R Ffrench 9/2: 315335: Led stands side group till ent final 2 51
1f, fdd: qck reapp, btr 3619 (5f), see 3035.

3605 **CRYFIELD 3** [19] 3-8-4 (63) D O'Donohoe 20/1: 131006: Towards rear far side, kept on appr final shd 56
1f, nvr nr to chall: signs of a return to form, see 2243.

3010 **POP SHOP 29** [2] 3-8-5 (63)(1ow) Dean McKeown 8/1: 000007: Cl-up stands side, onepace ent fnl 2f. ½ 55

3569 **ROYAL ROMEO 5** [5] 3-9-3 (76) T Lucas 11/1: 163008: Bhd ldrs stands side, outpcd 2f out: qck reapp. ¾ 64

3572 **ABLE AYR 5** [17] 3-8-4 (63) G Parkin 20/1: 000009: Prom far side till 2f out: qck reapp, see 1768, 1074. nk 50

3135 **TIME FOR MUSIC 24** [8] 3-9-7 (80) T Williams 20/1: 261-00: Front rank stands side, fdd/eased fnl 1f: 10th. nk 66

3136 **BOANERGES 24** [12] 3-9-7 (80) S Sanders 12/1: 113060: Al armd same place stands side: 11th, op 8/1. 3½ 57

3593 **SECRET CONQUEST 4** [16] 3-8-11 (70) Kimberley Hart 20/1: 006450: Led far side till appr final 2f, hd 46
sn wknd: 12th, qck reapp, back in trip: see 1308.

3377 **CHARMING LOTTE 12** [15] 3-8-8 (67)(vis) R Fitzpatrick 12/1: 005130: Nvr dngrs far side: 15th, see 3377. 0

*2640 **MI AMIGO 45** [14] 3-9-1 (74) K Darley 4/1 FAV: -24310: Chsd stands side ldrs 3f: 17th, abs, h'cap bow. 0

3136 **Corunna 24** [10] 3-9-4 (77) C Lowther 25/1:   3579 **Victors Crown 5** [7] 3-8-4 (63) R Hills 33/1:

3135 **Needwood Truffle 24** [18] 3-8-13 (72) S Whitworth 20/1:

3225 **Bulawayo 19** [13] 3-8-5 (64) L Newton 25/1:   3328 **Nite Owl Mate 15** [3] 3-7-10 (55)(t)(5oh) D Glennon(5) 25/1:

19 ran   Time 1m 13.4 (3.4)   (Buckingham Thor'breds)   J A R Toller Newmarket, Suffolk.

3699   3.30 RIPON ROWELS HCAP 3YO+ 0-100 (C)   1m rnd   Good 40   +01 Fast   [95]
     £6994   £2152   £1076   £538   3 yo rec 6 lb

3366 **STRONG PRESENCE 13** [9] T P Tate 3-8-7 (80) T Lucas 8/1: 5-121: 3 b c Anshan - Lazybird Blue 87+
(Bluebird) V keen, trkd ldr, rdn to lead below dist, shkn up, readily: fair time: earlier won reapp at Newmarket
(mdn): 5th sole '99 start (mdn, rtd 80): eff at 6f, relished being sharp to 1m: acts on fast & hvy grnd, sharp or
stiff trk: runs well fresh: big, progressive colt, likely to rate higher & win more races.

3535 **INDIAN PLUME 6** [5] C W Thornton 4-8-13 (80) M Fenton 14/1: 100352: 4 b c Efisio - Boo Hoo 1¼ 82
(Mummy's Pet) Led, under press appr final 1f, hdd below dist, kept on: qck reapp, back to form at 1m, see 1598.

2768 **HONEST BORDERER 40** [3] J L Dunlop 5-8-13 (80) S Sanders 5/1: 6-6143: 5 b g Selkirk - Tell No Lies nk 81
(High Line) Keen, in tch, shkn up 2f out, styd on but nvr able to chall: 6 wk abs: suited by return to 1m.

3309 **COURT EXPRESS 16** [6] W W Haigh 4-8-11 (77) P McCabe 14/1: 053044: Rear, effort, not much hd 78
room & swtchd ent final 2f, styd on for press, nvr nrr: gd run, see 1279.

*3456 **SEA SQUIRT 10** [10] 3-8-2 (75) R Ffrench 8/1: 162315: Chsd ldrs, onepace appr final 1f: ran to best. ½ 75

3597 **DURAID 4** [4] 8-9-6 (87) A McGlone 6/1: 141656: Trkd ldrs, rdn appr final 1f, unable to qckn: won 1¾ 83
this in '99 off a 20lbs lower mark: see 2648.

3078 **ZULU DAWN 24** [8] 3-9-5 (92) P Robinson 8/1: -04008: In tch, hemmed in on inside rail 3f out till nk 67
dist, onepace: nicely bckd: may pay to forget this: see 1879.

3130 **LAGOON 24** [11] 4-8-5 (84) R Hills 5/1: 330057: Towards rear, effort 2f out: up in trip, see 1470, 1153. 1¼ 84

1854 **CHAMPION LODGE 78** [1] 3-9-10 (97) S Whitworth 11/1: -21109: Rear, eff/btn appr fnl 2f: abs, h'cap bow. 4 82

991 **DEE PEE TEE CEE 128** [11] 6-9-3 (84) G Parkin 20/1: 100-00: Al bhd & wide up the str: 10th, op 1¾ 66
14/1, 4 mth abs: '99 wnr at Chester, Pontefract, Hamilton & York (2, h'caps, rtd 86): won twice over hdles last
winter (2m/2m1f, gd & soft, rtd 114h): '97 wnr at Beverley (2), Redcar, Carlisle & Musselburgh (h'caps, rtd 73):
eff at 10f, stays 12f: acts on fast & hvy grnd, any trk, likes York: sharper next time at 10f+.

3510 **PENSION FUND 8** [7] 6-8-9 (76) K Darley 9/2 FAV: -30000: Al towards rear, wide in the str: 11th, bckd. 1½ 55

3267 **ELEGANT ESCORT 18** [2] 3-8-9 (82) Dean McKeown 33/1: 31-60: Chsd ldrs, fdd 2f out & hmpd: 12th. 2 57

12 ran   Time 1m 40.6 (3.1)   (T P Tate)   T P Tate Tadcaster, Nth Yorks.

3700   4.00 LISTED CHAMPION 2YO TROPHY 2YO (A)   6f   Good 40   -13 Slow
     £13888   £4928   £2464   £1120

3086 **BAARIDD 26** [2] M A Jarvis 2-8-11 P Robinson 3/1: -1251: 2 b c Halling - Millstream (Dayjur) 105
Bmpd start, chsd ldrs, shkn up to chall appr fnl 1f, got on top ins last, rdn clr nr fin: earlier won debut at
Goodwood (mdn), subs rnr-up at R Ascot (List): first foal, dam a sprinter, sire 10f performer: eff at 6/7f:
acts on gd & gd/soft grnd, sharp or stiff/gall trk: useful colt.

*3352 **PICCOLO PLAYER 14** [4] R Hannon 2-9-0 K Darley 6/4 FAV: 214112: 2 b g Piccolo - The Frog Lady 1½ 103
(Al Hareb) Tried to make all, rdn 2f out, hdd dist, outpcd by wnr: well bckd: ran to best giving weight away.

*3542 **IMPERIAL DANCER 6** [1] M R Channon 2-8-11 S Sanders 7/1: 024513: 2 b c Primo Dominie - Gorgeous nk 99
Dancer (Nordico) Bhd ldrs, pshd along & imprvg when bmpd & short of room appr final 1f, kept on once clr but
unable to chall: op 5/1, qck reapp: 2nd with a clr run but was unsuited by drop back to 6f.

3086 **SHAARD 26** [3] B W Hills 2-8-11 (bl) R Hills 2/1: -134: Went left start, trkd ldr, shkn up & outpcd/bmpd ¾ 97
appr final 1f: unsuited by drop back to 6f?: see 3086 (7f Gr 3, in front of this wnr, fast grnd).

4 ran   Time 1m 13.2 (3.2)   (Sheikh Ahmed Al Maktoum)   M A Jarvis Newmarket, Suffolk.

3701   4.30 DAILY STAR MDN 3YO+ (D)   1m4f60y   Good 40   -03 Slow
     £4173   £1284   £642   £321

1157 **SOLITARY 114** [1] B W Hills 3-8-13 (BL) S Sanders 11/10 FAV: 4-221: 3 b c Sanglamore - Set Fair 88
(Alleged) Rcd in 2nd, pushed into lead appr final 2f, rdn clr, readily: nicely bckd, 4 mth abs, sharpened by blnks:
4th sole '99 start (rtd 80): made all at 12f, lks a thoro' styr: goes well fresh on gd & poss hvy: can force the pace.

3432 **KALEMAAT 10** [3] R W Armstrong 3-8-8 R Hills 4/1: 542: 3 ch f Unfuwain - Ardassine (Ahonoora) 7 79
Last but in tch, feeling pace appr final 2f, kept on at onepace & flashed tail, nvr nrr, went 2nd nr fin: lngr trip:
prob stays 12f but needs a drop in grade: see 2558.

3416 **SOUTH SEA PEARL 11** [4] M Johnston 3-8-8 P Robinson 13/8: 660223: 3 b f Southern Halo - nk 78
Naturalracer (Copelan) Led till appr final 2f, fdd: crying out for a drop back to 10f: see 3416, 3185.

3185 **ALI OOP 21** [2] J D Bethell 3-8-13 T Williams 25/1: 64: Prom till ent str, t.o: plating class so far. dist 53

4 ran   Time 2m 28.8 (5.3)   (K Abdulla)   B W Hills Lambourn, Berks.

RIPON

MONDAY AUGUST 28TH   Righthand, Sharpish Track

3702   **5.05 PATELEY BRIDGE HCAP 3YO 0-70 (E)**   **1m2f**   **Good 40**   **+07 Fast**   [77]
  £3796   £1168   £584   £292

2783 **ALTAY** 39 [14] R A Fahey 3-8-2 (51) R Ffrench 9/2: 036351: 3 b g Erin's Isle - Aliuska (Fijar Tango) 61
Set fair pace, pshd clr ent fnl 2f, readily: op 6/1, gd time, 6 wk abs: first win, unplcd juv (mdn, rtd 63):
poss stays 14f, suited by drop back to 10f & forcing tactics: acts on firm & gd/soft, sharp or stiff/gall trk.
*3380 **ENTITY** 12 [5] T D Barron 3-8-11 (60) D O'Donohoe 7/1: 050012: 3 ch g Rudimentary - Desert Ditty 2 66
(Green Desert) Dropped out last, prog on bit ent str, briefly hmpd 2f out, sn clr & kept on to go 2nd below dist,
wnr had flown: clr rem: waiting tactics overdone over lngr 10f trip but clrly stays & is on the upgrade: win again.
3140 **SHOTACROSS THE BOW** 24 [13] B W Hills 3-9-4 (67) R Hills 4/1 FAV: 000323: 3 b c Warning - Nordica 4 67
(Northfields) Chsd wnr, outpcd appr final 1f: clr rem but shade btr 2552 (gd/soft).
3267 **RHODAMINE** 18 [11] J L Eyre 3-9-2 (65) K Darley 11/2: 434044: Well plcd, same pace ent final 2f. 3 61
3248 **TOUGH TIMES** 19 [8] S Whitworth 14/1: -56025: Chsd ldrs, rdn appr final 2f & hung 5 59
left, sn btn: op 10/1: unsuited by step up in trip on h'cap bow?: clr rem.
3531 **MANSTAR** 6 [10] R Fitzpatrick 33/1: 500006: Al arnd mid-div: qck reappr, visor omitted. 3 37
2829 **IRISH DANCER** 38 [12] 3-8-11 (60) J Bramhill 14/1: 031107: Mid-div thro'out: op 10/1: sharper 1¼ 44
for this & return to 12f will suit, see 2540 (here).
3244 **DONT WORRY BOUT ME** 19 [15] (vis) T Williams 7/1: 162628: Chsd ldrs, rdn & wknd 2f out. 1 40
3530 **LOMOND DANCER** 7 [3] 3-8-2 (49) (2ow) G Parkin 33/1: 500009: Nvr trbld ldrs, wide in the str. qk reapp. 3 30
3368 **NIAGARA** 13 [2] 3-9-5 (68) S Sanders 10/1: -00360: Nvr better than mid-div: 10th, tchd 8/1, see 1153. nk 46
3480 **GLEN VALE WALK** 9 [9] 3-7-11 (46) D Glennon (6) 12/1: 402200: Prom, going well ent str, sn btn: 11th. 2½ 21
*495 **SPECIAL PROMISE** 200 [7] 3-9-7 (70) Dean McKeown 8/1: -11110: Al bhd, drvn & btn before final 3f: 14th. 0
3310 **Shalbeblue** 16 [6] 3-8-11 (60) V Halliday 33/1:
3095 **Bebe De Cham** 26 [4] 3-7-13 (48) (3ow) (5oh) Kimberley Hart 25/1:
1863 **Flow Beau** 78 [1] 3-8-4 (50) (3ow) A McGlone 25/1:
15 ran   Time 2m 06.6 (3.3)   (John T Robson)   R A Fahey Butterwick, Nth Yorks.

NEWCASTLE

MONDAY AUGUST 28TH   Lefthand, Galloping, Stiff Track

Official Going   GOOD/FIRM (GOOD places); GOOD/SOFT after 1st race; SOFT after 3rd race. Stalls: Str Crse - Stands
Side; Rnd Crse - Inside; 3.20 & 4.50 stalls moved to far side due to false grnd: Heavy Rain throughout afternoon.

3703   **2.20 LISTED RTD HCAP 3YO+ 0-105 (A)**   **1m2f32y**   **Good**   **Inapplicable**   [100]
  £12928   £4903   £2451   £1114   3yo rec 8lb

*3535 **KIND REGARDS** 6 [11] M Johnston 3-8-8 (88) J Reid 5/1: 545111: 3 b f Unfuwain - Barari (Blushing 100
Groom) Waited with, smooth hdwy to lead 1½f out, ran on strongly, cmftbly: nicely bckd, qck reapp: completed
hat-trick after wins at Beverley & Hamilton (h'caps): '99 Beverley wnr (fill mdn, rtd 88): eff at 1m, suited by
9/10f: acts on firm & gd/soft, handles any trk: progressive, useful filly, keep on your side this autumn.
3565 **FLOSSY** 5 [4] C W Thornton 4-9-0 (86) A Culhane 15/2: 044102: 4 b f Efisio - Sirene Bleu Marine 3 90
(Secreto) Trkd ldrs, went in pursuit of wnr fnl 1f, no impress: op 10/1: fine effort over this
inadequate 10f trip: interesting at 12/14f next time: met a fast imprvg rival here: see 3173.
3389 **SECRET DESTINY** 12 [6] J H M Gosden 3-8-10 (90) J Fortune 20/1: -51563: 3 b f Cozzene - Dramatrix 2½ 90
(Forty Niner) Trkd ldrs till outpcd 2f out, rallied fnl 1f but ch had gone: looks a smart filly of note now: consistent.
3389 **BALLADONIA** 12 [2] Lady Herries 4-9-6 (92) R Winston 14/1: 24-654: Led till 1½f out, no extra: 5L hd 92
clr rem: spot-on next time & a return to 12f will suit: in front of today's 3rd in 3389.
*3339 **MYNAH** 15 [12] 3-8-13 (93) T E Durcan 11/2: 012215: Slowly away, imprvd from rear 2f out, nvr 5 85
nr ldrs: prev progressive on fast & firm grnd: see 3339.
*3042 **GOLCONDA** 28 [3] 4-9-1 (87) J Weaver 12/1: 000016: Held up, late hdwy: better on fast. ¾ 78
3340 **CROWN LODGE** 15 [7] 3-8-10 (90) J P Spencer 9/1: -2157: Nvr nr to chall on h'cap debut: lightly rcd. nk 80
*3616 **FLAMENCO RED** 3 [1] 3-8-8 (88) F Lynch 14/1: 5-4218: Rear, effort 2f out, btn final 1f: op 10/1, 1 76
qck reapp: facile wnr of a non-event in 3616.
*2475 **LADY ANGHARAD** 52 [9] 4-9-3 (89) R Cochrane 4/1 FAV: 0-1119: In tch till btn over 1f out: nicely 1¼ 75
bckd, 7 wk abs: uncharacteristic below par performance this time on this rain-softened grnd: much btr 2475.
2610 **BROADWAY LEGEND** 46 [8] 3-8-5 (85) P Fessey 11/1: -10020: Rcd keenly mid-div, btn over 1f out: ¾ 70
fin 10th, 7 wk abs: much btr 2610 (gd/fm).
3340 **TOTAL LOVE** 15 [10] 3-9-3 (97) G Duffield 16/1: 025340: Nvr a factor in 11th: see 2274 (1m, fast). 1½ 80
*3504 **LIDAKIYA** 8 [5] 3-9-7 (101) T Quinn 11/2: 411210: Chsd ldrs 1m, saddle slipped & eased considerably, 6 75
fin last: top weight: most progressive earlier, this run must be forgotten: see 3504 (12f, firm grnd).
12 ran   Time 2m 12.51 (6.01)   (Maktoum Al Maktoum)   M Johnston Middleham, Nth Yorks.

3704   **2.50 TRAVIS PERKINS NURSERY HCAP 2YO (B)**   **1m str**   **Good/Soft**   **Inapplicable**   [97]
  £26000   £8000   £4000   £2000   Two groups, far side favoured

3246 **PERFECT PLUM** 19 [4] Sir Mark Prescott 2-8-7 (76) G Duffield 10/1: 52321: 2 b f Darshaan - Damascene 87
(Scenic) Trkd ldrs far side, qcknd into lead 2f out, ran on strongly, rdn out: first success, well plcd to land this
val h'cap: half-sister to an Irish 7f 2yo wnr, sire a high class mid-dist performer: eff at 7f, relished this
step up to 1m: acts on firm & gd/soft, handles a stiff/gall trk: sure to progress further & win more decent races.
*3298 **EMMS** 17 [15] P F I Cole 2-9-7 (90) J Fortune 4/1: -2312: 2 gr c Fastness - Carnation (Carwhite) 2 95+
Trkd ldrs on stands side, led that group 2f out, styd on strongly but no ch with wnr on far side: well bckd from
11/2, top weight: fine effort from an unfav high draw, fin well clr of rem on his side: stays a stiff 1m well,
acts on firm & gd/soft, handles soft grnd: will sn regain wng ways, see 3298 (mdn).
3542 **DOMINAITE** 6 [3] M W Easterby 2-8-7 (76) T Quinn 7/1: 321323: 2 b g Komaite - Fairy Kingdom ½ 80
(Prince Sabo) Chsd ldrs far side, ev ch 1f out, sn left bhd by wnr: op 11/2, gd/soft grnd, 6L clr rem: fine run,
stays a stiff 1m: reportedly not apprec today's rain-softened grnd but this was a fine run: see 3542, 2991.
3486 **NOBLE DOBLE** 9 [16] B W Hills 2-8-8 (77) R Cochrane 14/1: -45234: Held up stands side, prog 2f out, 6 71
ran on well but no ch with ldrs: fair run from a poor high draw, interesting in similar next time: see 3486, 2430.
2935 **CARIBBEANDRIFTWOOD** 32 [12] 2-9-4 (87) P Dobbs (5) 25/1: -2105: Waited with stands side, kept on 3 76
final 1f but no ch with ldrs: change of tactics, set the pace when successful in 2583 (fillies mdn).

3149 **ACHILLES SPIRIT 23** [17] 2-8-12 (81) J Weaver 10/1: -0136: Prom on stands side, btn over 1f out. *nk* **69**
*3149 **FOREVER MY LORD 23** [2] 2-8-12 (81) J Quinn 13/2: 601117: Chsd ldrs on far side, wknd final 1f: *½* **68**
probably not stay this lngr 1m trip on today's rain-softened grnd: see 3149 (7f, firm).
3486 **SAUCE TARTAR 9** [8] 2-8-7 (76) R Winston 20/1: -6108: Led till 2f out far side, wknd: saddle *3* **58**
reportedly slipped: may apprec a drop back to 7f for now: see 3039 (fillies mdn, fast grnd).
3169 **BORDERS BELLE 22** [5] 2-8-10 (79) J P Spencer 20/1: -4329: Chsd ldrs 6f far side: see 3169 (7f, fm). *1* **59**
3411 **GALAXY RETURNS 11** [18] 2-8-0 (69) P Fessey 33/1: 026100: Prom 6f stands side, fin 10th: btr 3079. *shd* **49**
3051 **GOLD STATUETTE 27** [6] 2-8-9 (78) M Henry 14/1: -0640: Chsd ldrs far side, btn over 1f out: 11th. *shd* **58**
3327 **THE NAMES BOND 15** [19] 2-8-6 (75) R Thomas (7) 33/1: 314000: Led stands side 6f, fdd into 12th: *½* **54**
poor high draw: see 1252 (5f mdn).
2991 **THEWHIRLINGDERVISH 30** [10] 2-8-2 (71) R Mullen 10/1: -00320: Al bhd stands side: 13th: btr 2991. *shd* **50**
3411 **SANDLES 11** [9] 2-8-3 (72) A Beech (5) 16/1: 15440: Al bhd stands side, fin 14th: btr 3411, 3062. *7* **39**
3149 **DANCE ON THE TOP 23** [14] 2-9-5 (88) J Reid 5/2 FAV: -6120: Trkd ldrs stands side, btn 2f out: *shd* **55**
15th, well bckd from 4/1: poorly drawn & not apprec today's rain-softened grnd: btr 3149, 2867.
3169 **CEZZARO 22** [11] 2-8-13 (82) M Roberts 14/1: -5030: Speed to halfway on far side: fin 16th. *1¾* **46**
2514 **CO DOT UK 51** [13] 2-8-4 (73) F Lynch 25/1: 013450: Chsd ldrs 4f stands side, wknd & fin last: abs. *7* **24**
17 ran Time 1m 40.69 (stalls moved 40y forward) (Sir Edmund Loder) Sir Mark Prescott Newmarket.

3705

3.20 EBF UKBETTING.COM MDN 2YO (D) 7f str Good/Soft Inapplicable
£2814 £804 £402

-- **LOTS OF LOVE** [2] M Johnston 2-9-0 M Roberts 5/1: -1: 2 b c Woodman - Accountable Lady **88+**
(The Minstrel) Chsd ldrs, prog to lead dist, kept on strongly, rdn out on debut: Apr first foal, cost $80,000:
sire a high-class juv performer, dam smart in the US: eff over a stiff 7f, bred to apprec 1m+ next term: acts on
gd/soft grnd, runs well fresh: open to plenty of improvement & potentially useful colt.
3617 **LUCEFER 3** [4] G C H Chung 2-9-0 M Henry 25/1: -02: 2 b g Lycius - Maharani (Red Ransom) *2* **83**
In tch, imprvd to chase wnr fnl 1f, no impress cl-home: qck reapp after saddle slipped on debut in 3617:
eff at 7f on gd/soft grnd: should find a mdn judged on this.
-- **STAGING POST** [9] H R A Cecil 2-9-0 T Quinn 3/1 FAV: -3: 2 b c Pleasant Colony - Interim *1½* **80**
(Sadler's Wells) Chsd ldrs, eff & ev ch dist, no extra ins last: not given a hard time, 4L clr rem: Mar foal,
dam a decent 10f wnr: sire smart in the USA: bred to apprec 1m+ next term: handles gd/soft grnd: reportedly
lost a shoe here & must be given another chance.
3458 **TEDSTALE 10** [1] L M Cumani 2-9-0 J P Spencer 4/1: -044: Set pace till dist, no extra: acts on *4* **72**
fast & soft grnd, well clr of rem here: see 3121.
-- **RICH GIFT** [8] 2-8-9 D Harrison 25/1: -5: Rear, prog when swtchd 2f out, nvr nr ldrs on debut: Feb foal, *6* **57**
cost 25,000gns: sire a top class sprinter, dam plcd over 1m as a 2yo: shld apprec 7f/2m: know more next time.
-- **CATEEL BAY** [6] 2-8-9 K Hodgson 33/1: -6: Rear, short of room halfway, nvr nr ldrs on debut: Mar *2½* **53**
foal, half-sister to a 12f/2m wnr: dam won over 12f, sire a high class mid-dist performer: mid-dist bred.
3466 **LUMIERE DU SOLEIL 9** [10] 2-8-9 J Fortune 8/1: -57: Front rank 5f, fdd: see 3466. *½* **52**
3154 **ACHILLES SUN 23** [12] 2-9-0 J Weaver 33/1: -U408: Prom till 2f out, wknd: see 2677. *¾* **55**
-- **BLIND SPOT** [7] 2-9-0 J Reid 7/2: -9: Nvr a factor on debut: bckd from 5/1: 180,000 gns purchase: *½* **54**
Feb foal, half-brother to sev wnrs, incl top class middle dist performer High Rise: dam a 14f/2m wnr, sire a
high-class 7f performer: E Dunlop colt, much better clearly expected.
3051 **BUY A VOWEL 27** [5] 2-9-0 F Lynch 6/1: -060: Rear, nvr a factor in 10th: see 2708. *1¾* **51**
1835 **VAIL PEAK 79** [11] 2-9-0 G Duffield 14/1: -50: Al bhd, fin 11th: 11 wk abs. *8* **36**
-- **CELTIC SPRING** [3] 2-9-0 A Culhane 33/1: -0: Slowly away, al detached, t.o. in last: 26,000gns Mar *10* **21**
foal: dam a sprint wnr, sire a top class mid-dist performer: with W Cunningham.
12 ran Time 1m 30.27 (6.17) (M Doyle) M Johnston Middleham, Nth Yorks.

3706

3.50 UKBETTING.COM CLAIMER 2YO (E) 1m rnd Soft Inapplicable
£2744 £784 £392

3388 **FAZZANI 12** [4] P C Haslam 2-8-8 A Beech (5) 15/8 FAV: 430121: 2 b f Shareef Dancer - Taj Victory **69**
(Final Straw) Trkd ldrs, prog to lead over 1f out, ran on strongly, cmftbly: earlier trained by M Channon to win
at Thirsk (clmr): dam 10/13f wnr: eff at 7f/1m, further shld suit: acts on fast & soft: suited by clmg grade.
3127 **BORDER TERRIER 24** [6] R A Fahey 2-8-13 G Duffield 9/1: -042: 2 b c Balnibarbi - Ring Side (Alzao) *3* **64**
Nvr far away, led 2f out till dist, kept on but not pace of wnr: eff at 1m on soft grnd: shld win a clmr/seller.
3128 **JEZADIL 24** [1] M Dods 2-8-8 F Lynch 7/1: -06443: 2 b f Mujadil - Tender Time (Tender King) *¾* **57**
Trkd ldrs, ev ch 2f out, onepace fnl 1f: lngr 1m trip: handles fast & soft: see 3128.
3532 **TENERIFE FLYER 6** [8] J Norton 2-8-6 P Hanagan (7) 25/1: 604604: Rear, styd on under press fnl 2f, *1¼* **52$**
nvr nr ldrs: qck reapp: best effort to date, offic rtd just 47: apprec this drop into clmg company, see 974.
3466 **JUST MISSED 9** [10] 2-8-12 J Reid 6/1: -00505: Led/dsptd lead till went on 3f out, hdd 2f out, no *½* **57**
extra: bckd from 12/1 on this return to clmg grade: see 1698 (debut, 5f).
3542 **LITTLE TASK 6** [5] 2-9-3 R Winston 13/2: 242606: Rdn in rear, imprvd 2f out, onepcd when hmpd *1½* **59**
dist: qck reapp: thrice below 3137 (6f, fast grnd).
2983 **PICTURE MEE 30** [9] 2-8-0 J McAuley 33/1: 0007: Rear, imprvg when badly hmpd 2f out, no ch after: *nk* **41**
can rate higher: prob benefited from today's softer grnd: see 1864 (debut).
3438 **NETTLES 10** [3] 2-8-7 M Roberts 4/1: 000628: Rdn mid-div, nvr nr ldrs: btr 3438 (7f, gd grnd). *1¼* **45**
3100 **FIRST MEETING 26** [7] 2-8-12 A Culhane 8/1: -259: In tch 6f, wknd: much btr 2218 (debut, firm grnd). *½* **49**
1418 **PERCY VERANCE 98** [2] 2-9-3 J P Spencer 33/1: -000: Led/dsptd lead 5f, wknd & fin 10th: 3 mth *12* **39**
abs: much lngr 1m trip today: no form.
3307 **TINY MIND 16** [11] 2-8-1 (VIS) L Enstone(3) 50/1: 00000: Slowly away, al well bhd, t.o. in last: *28* **0**
much lngr 1m trip & first time visor to little effect here: no form.
11 ran Time 1m 51.08 (12.08) (S A B Dismore) P C Haslam Middleham, Nth Yorks.

3707

4.20 UKBETTING.COM MDN 3YO (D) 1m rnd Soft Inapplicable
£3760 £1157 £578 £289

3350 **CAFE OPERA 14** [5] J W Hills 3-8-9 R Cochrane 9/4: 42-021: 3 b f Sadler's Wells - Takreem (Mr **81**
Prospector) Made all, held on well fnl 1f, drvn out: well bckd: rnr-up in '99 (rtd 89): eff over a stiff 1m,
bred to apprec mid-dists: acts on firm & soft, seems eff when held up or forcing the pace: deserved victory.
3432 **LAND AHEAD 10** [3] H R A Cecil 3-8-9 T Quinn 2/1 JT FAV: -31D232: 3 ch f Distant View - Nimble Folly *1¾* **77**
(Cyane) Trkd wnr thro'out, styd on final 1f but not pace of wnr: eff over a stiff 1m, return to 10f will suit:

NEWCASTLE   MONDAY AUGUST 28TH   Lefthand, Galloping, Stiff Track

acts on fast & soft grnd: see 3432, 2449 (first past the post, subs disq).

4542} **GALLANT 304** [8] Sir Michael Stoute 3-9-0 J Reid 2/1 JT FAV: 0-3: 3 b c Rainbow Quest - Gay Gallanta ¾ 80
(Woodman) Trkd ldrs, ev ch ent fnl 1f, sn no extra: well bckd from 3/1, clr of rem: unplcd in a Newmarket mdn
on sole '99 start : dam a smart juv performer, sire top class over mid-dists: eff over a stiff 1m on soft grnd.
3477 **SIMPLY SENSATIONAL 9** [2] P F l Cole 3-9-0 D Griffiths 10/1: -44: Rear, some late hdwy, no ch 6 70
with front 3: see 3477 (debut).
2831 **NOBLE SPLENDOUR 38** [1] 3-9-0 J P Spencer 14/1: 023345: Effort from rear 3f out, sn btn: see 2524. 11 54
3324 **ATTACKER 16** [7] 3-9-0 M Roberts 66/1: -06: Slowly away, nvr a factor: highly tried: see 3324 (12f). 2½ 50
3006 **SUN SILK 30** [4] 3-8-9 J Fortune 14/1: -057: Rear, bhd final 2f: see 2232. ½ 44
7 ran   Time 1m 47.61 (8.61)   (Christopher Wright)   J W Hills Upper Lambourn, Berks.

3708   4.50 UKBETTING.COM HCAP 3YO+ 0-90 (C)   7f str   Soft   Inapplicable   [85]
£6581   £2025   £1012   £506   3yo rec 5lb

3464 **BOLDLY GOES 9** [12] C W Fairhurst 4-9-9 (80)(bl) R Cochrane 15/2: 100601: 4 b c Bold Arrangement - 89
Reine de Thebes (Darshaan) Held up, prog 2f out, went on ins fnl 1f, sprinted clr: bckd from 10/1: earlier won
at York (h'cap, first time blnks): unplcd in '99 (stks, rtd 91), prev term won at Pontefract, W'hampton (rtd 86a),
Thirsk (stks) & Ripon (List, rtd 104): eff at 6/7f on firm, hvy grnd & fibresand: can run well fresh, handles a
sharp or stiff/gall trk: suited by blnks: well h'capped & a clear cut success here.
3170 **JEFFREY ANOTHERRED 22** [9] M Dods 4-9-9 (66) T Quinn 2/1 FAV: 006042: 6 b g Emarati - First 3½ 67
Pleasure (Dominion) Held up, imprvd 2f out, styd on final 1f but wnr had flown: hvly bckd from 7/2: back to
form on fav soft grnd: likes Doncaster: h'capped to win on this grnd soon: see 2163.
3328 **SUPREME SALUTATION 15** [13] T D Barron 4-9-1 (72) J Fortune 7/1: 603553: 4 ch g Most Welcome - shd 73
Cardinal Press (Sharrood) Slowly away, recovered to chase ldrs, kept on under press fnl 1f: acts on firm & soft.
3355 **OUT OF SIGHT 14** [8] B A McMahon 6-8-4 (61) R Mullen 12/1: 001434: Hdwy from rear 2f out, kept on ½ 61
under press & nrst fin: acts on firm, soft grnd & fibresand: see 2682.
3328 **REDOUBTABLE 15** [14] 9-8-11 (68) M Roberts 12/1: 414305: Rear, styd on under press fnl 2f, nvr nrr. 2 64
3605 **DOUBLE ACTION 3** [6] 6-8-5 (62) R Winston 12/1: 606006: Led till inside final 1f, no extra: qck hd 58
reapp: likes 7f trip: loves soft grnd: see 1869, 1011.
3440 **MAMMAS BOY 10** [1] 5-7-10 (53)(4oh) P Fessey 20/1: 100467: Prom 6f, fdd: see 2046 (firm grnd). 3½ 42
*3328 **PUPPET PLAY 15** [11] 5-8-5 (62) T E Durcan 5/1: 413218: Chsd ldrs, ev ch 1f out, wknd: btr 3328. 2½ 46
3170 **MANTLES PRIDE 22** [3] 5-9-9 (80)(bl) G Duffield 10/1: 600509: Chsd ldrs, rdn & ev ch 1f out, sn btn. 1½ 61
1645 **AUTUMN RAIN 87** [4] 3-9-4 (80) J Reid 8/1: -20130: Mid-div till btn 2f out: fin 10th, 3 mth abs. 5 51
3535 **DONNAS DOUBLE 6** [7] 5-8-12 (69) J Weaver 10/1: 210340: Slowly away, al bhd & fin 11th: qck reapp. 5 30
3464 **SUTTON COMMON 9** [2] 3-8-11 (73) F Lynch 10/1: 202100: Chsd ldrs till halfway, sn btn & fin 2 30
last: tchd 16/1 & better clearly expected: twice below 1763.
12 ran   Time 1m 29/99 (5.89)   (G H & S Leggott)   C W Fairhurst Middleham, Nth Yorks.

3709   5.20 DAILY STAR HCAP 3YO+ 0-80 (D)   1m6f97y   Soft   No Standard Time   [78]
£3602   £1127   £563   £281   3yo rec 12lb

3522 **BARCELONA 7** [6] J Noseda 3-9-2 (78) J Weaver 2/1 FAV: 311631: 3 b c Barathea - Pipitina (Bustino) 84
Held up, gd prog 2f out, went on dist, styd on well, drvn out: well bckd: earlier won at Nottingham (h'cap) &
Kempton (class stks): plcd in '99 (mdn, rtd 80): eff at 14f, has tried 2m: acts on fast & soft grnd, handles a
sharp or gall trk: in form young stayer.
3402 **LADY COLDUNELL 12** [3] N A Callaghan 4-8-4 (54) G Duffield 11/2: 05-032: 4 b f Deploy - Beau's 1¼ 57
Delight (Lypheor) Trkd ldr till went on 2f out, collared dist, kept on but no pace of wnr: apprec this return
to 14f, acts on firm, soft grnd & equitrack: see 3402.
3442 **ROVERETTO 10** [1] Mrs M Reveley 5-9-1 (65) A Culhane 9/2: 0/6243: 5 b g Robellino - Spring Flyer 3½ 63
(Waajib) Trkd ldrs, onepcd final 1½f: tchd 11/2, 8L clr rem: just btr 3034.
2674 **VRIN 44** [7] L M Cumani 5-10-0 (78) J P Spencer 9/4: 01:04: Rear, effort 3f out, sn btn: 6 wk abs, 8 64
top weight: longer 14f trip: see 2674.
3360 **HIGH TOPPER 14** [2] 3-9-3 (79)(BL) J Reid 7/2: 411645: Led till 2½f out, sn btn: keen in 1st time blnks. nk 64
5 ran   Time 3m 19.46   (K Y Lim)   J Noseda Newmarket.

RIPON   TUESDAY AUGUST 29TH   Righthand, Sharpish Track

Official Going: GOOD.   Stalls: Straight Course - Stands Side: Round Course - Inside.

3710   2.30 NAGSHEADPICKHILL AUCT MDN 2YO (F)   5f str   Good/Firm 26   -30 Slow
£3081   £948   £474   £237

3475 **FENWICKS PRIDE 10** [8] B S Rothwell 2-8-10 M Fenton 5/2 FAV: 332661: 2 b g Imperial Frontier - 76
Stunt Girl (Thatching) Rear, improved ent fnl 2f, kept on well under press to get up towards fin: op 6/4:
eff at 5f, shld improve at 6f: acts on fast & soft grnd, sharp or gall track.
3513 **BARON CROCODILE 9** [9] A Berry 2-8-10 T E Durcan 10/1: 502402: 2 b g Puissance - Glow Again ½ 74
(The Brianstan) Rear, rdn appr fnl 1f, hdd well ins last: drifter from 11/2: ran to best: acts on fast & hvy grnd.
3346 **DISPOL CHIEFTAN 15** [2] S E Kettlewell 2-8-10 (t) J Fortune 16/1: 05503: 2 b c Clantime - Ski ¾ 72
Baby (Petoski) Held up, prog appr fnl 1f, rdn inside last, no extra towards fin: drifter from 8/1:
improved for fitting of a t-strap, eff at 5f on fast grnd.
2588 **HIGHLAND FLIGHT 48** [3] Bob Jones 2-7-12 F Norton 14/1: 04: Well plcd & ev ch till no extra below nk 59
dist: tchd 25/1: clr rem, 7 wk abs: 1,900gns Missed Flight first foal: eff at 5f on fast, further will suit.
2983 **FAIR STEP 31** [1] P Fessey 40/1: 2305: Chsd ldrs, outpcd appr fnl 1f: back in trip, see 2772. 3½ 50
3520 **HALCYON MAGIC 8** [11] 2-8-3 R Brisland (5) 11/2: 045526: Wide, nvr a factor: op 7/2, tricky draw. 2½ 49
2933 **TIMELESS FARRIER 33** [6] 2-8-6 (t) Pat Eddery 13/2: 6607: Wide & in tch till appr fnl 1f, eased dist. 1¼ 48
-- **MARTHA P PERKINS** [10] 2-8-1 R Mullen 9/2: 8: Wide, prom 3f: bckd: 2,800gns Fayruz first foal. 1 40
3342 **THATS ALL JAZZ 16** [5] 2-7-12 G Baker (5) 16/1: -0069: Chsd ldrs till halfway: op 12/1. nk 36
2821 **MADIES PRIDE 39** [4] 2-8-1 J Quinn 10/1: 400: In tch till halfway: 10th, op 8/1, 6 week abs, see 2539. 2½ 33
3408 **CATALAN BAY 12** [7] 2-8-1 J McAuley 50/1: -0000: Went right start, sn struggling, 11th, no form. 11 13
11 ran   Time 1m 00.6 (2.8)   (J H Tattersall)   B S Rothwell Musley Bank, N Yorks

1138

RIPON TUESDAY AUGUST 29TH Righthand, Sharpish Track

3711 3.00 DEVERELL CLAIMER 3YO+ (F) 1m rnd Good/Firm 26 00 Fast
£2632 £752 £376 3 yo rec 6 lb

3117 **ARTFUL DANE 25** [14] C G Cox 8-8-8 (bl) G Duffield 20/1: 503001: 8 b g Danehill - Art Age (Artaius) **54**
Made all, rdn clr appr fnl 1f, unchall: plcd in '99 (h'cap, rtd 51): last won in '97 at Doncaster (val h'cap, rtd 78): eff at 1m, tried further: acts on firm & gd/soft grnd: best in blinks or visor, forcing the pace.
3314 **SOPHOMORE 17** [13] J L Harris 6-8-10 K Dalgleish (5) 7/1: 160002: 6 b g Sanglamore - Livry *3½* **50**
(Lyphard) Chsd ldrs, went after wnr appr fnl 2f, no threat: op 5/1: down in trip & grade, softer grnd suits, see 1731.
3671 **DIHATJUM 2** [6] T D Easterby 3-8-8 J Fortune 4/1: 401233: 3 b g Mujtahid - Rosie Potts (Shareef *½* **53**
Danacer) Mid-div, improved appr fnl 2f, styd on but unable to chall: nicely bckd: see 3393, 3196.
3534 **ALAMEIN 7** [8] W Storey 7-8-8 (t) T Williams 12/1: 230104: Bhd, gd prog appr fnl 2f, onepace fnl 1f. *½* **46$**
3314 **HIGH SUN 17** [12] 4-9-5 A Nicholls (3) 20/1: 005005: Towards rear, rdn & not much room 3f out, *½* **56$**
styd on towards fin: op 33/1, stiff task: interesting in lowly h'cap grade on softer grnd: see 942.
3404 **HUGWITY 13** [9] 8-9-0 K Darley 5/1: 015366: Mid div, shaken up 3f out, short of room 2f out, *½* **50**
nvr nr to chall: op 7/2: capable of better with more luck in running: see 2411.
2882 **SKYERS FLYER 36** [15] 6-8-9 J Bramhill 33/1: 000067: Chsd ldrs, no extra ent fnl 2f: stiff task. *1½* **42$**
3334 **SERGEANT YORK 16** [7] 4-9-10 (vis) G Faulkner (3) 11/8 FAV: 604538: Towards rear, wide eff *1½* **55**
3f out, no impress: well bckd, looked favoured by these weights: 1 win in 29 starts: see 1291.
936 **BORDERLINE 134** [11] 3-9-0 L Gueller (7) 66/1: -09: Off the pace, gd prog on ins rail to go 2nd briefly *2* **47**
2f out, fdd: over 4 mnth abs & has been bght out of H Cecil's stable for 2,200gns.
2799 **NOBBY BARNES 39** [10] 11-8-9 Kim Tinkler 33/1: 302600: Nvr a factor: 10th, 6 week abs, stiff task. *nk* **35**
3234 **Naked Oat 20** [5] 5-8-10 J Bosley (7) 33/1:
3141 **Rooftop 25** [1] 4-8-8 A Culhane 33/1:
3549} **Ribble Assembly 371** [3] 5-8-12 F Lynch 33/1:
3603 **Cyran Park 4** [2] 4-8-8 (vis) G Parkin 50/1:
-- **Fabi** [4] 5-8-12 J Fanning 50/1:
15 ran Time 1m 39.6 (2.1) (S P Lansdown Racing) C G Cox Lambourn, Berks

3712 3.30 STEVE NESBITT NURSERY HCAP 2YO (D) 6f str Good/Firm 26 -26 Slow **[92]**
£4212 £1296 £648 £324

3145 **SAMADILLA 24** [2] T D Easterby 2-9-0 (78) K Darley 10/3: -1441: 2 b f Mujadil - Samnaun (Stop The **80**
Music) In tch, prog under press appr fnl 1f, ran on to lead well inside last: bckd, swtg: saddle reportedly slipped last time: earlier won debut at Pontefract (auct mdn): apprec step up to 6f, stay further (half-sister to a 10f wnr): acts on fast & gd grnd, sharp or stiff/undulating track: progressive filly.
3354 **FACE D FACTS 15** [1] C F Wall 2-8-10 (74) R Mullen 10/1: -51302: 2 b f So Factual - Water Well *nk* **75**
(Sadler's Wells) Held up in tch, improved & qcknd to lead 1f out, rdn & hdd fnl 50y: op 12/1: stays sharp 6f.
3475 **KARITSA 10** [3] M R Channon 2-8-7 (71) Craig Williams 12/1: 25103: 2 b f Rudimentary - Desert *1¾* **67**
Ditty (Green Desert) Led/dsptd lead & travelled well on stands rail, rdn & hdd dist, no extra: stays a sharp 6f, drop back to 5f is kely to suit: see 2668.
3264 **PRINCESS OF GARDA 19** [7] Mrs G S Rees 2-9-7 (85) G Duffield 14/1: 121454: Pld v hard & led/dsptd *nk* **80**
till rdn & edged left dist, onepace: not disgraced over lngr trip but this fierce puller will apprec a return to 5f.
*3009 **RIDGE RUNNER 30** [4] 2-9-7 (85) Pat Eddery 1/1 FAV: -215: Rear, wide, rdn halfway, unable to *¾* **78**
chall: nicely bckd on h'cap bow: not disgraced considering ran away from the pace: see 3009.
3394 **DANCING PENNEY 13** [5] 2-7-10 (60) Iona Wands 16/1: 122166: Chsd ldrs, onepace appr fnl 1f. *½* **51**
3327 **CEDAR TSAR 16** [6] 2-7-12 (62) Claire Bryan (5) 25/1: 333107: Bhd from halfway: best on fibresand. *11* **33**
3246 **EAGLET 20** [9] 2-8-2 (66) J Bramhill 50/1: 545508: Unruly & went right start, in tch till halfway: maiden. *hd* **36**
3431 **CANDOTHAT 11** [8] 2-9-5 (83) A Culhane 6/1: 615159: Wide, al bhd: btr 3171 (gd). *1* **50**
9 ran Time 1m 13.1 (3.1) (W T Whittle) T D Easterby Great Habton, N Yorks

3713 4.00 TOTE EXACTA HCAP 3YO+ 0-90 (C) 1m2f Good/Firm 26 +06 Fast **[85]**
£7176 £2208 £1104 £552 3 yo rec 8 lb

3024 **ANDROMEDES 30** [9] H R A Cecil 3-9-1 (80) T Quinn 9/2: 431061: 3 b c Sadler's Wells - Utr (Mr **84**
Prospector) Bhd ldr, shkn up to lead ent fnl 2f, pshd out: tchd 11/2, best time of day: earlier won at Warwick (mdn): plcd sole juv start (rtd 86): eff at 10f/12f, tried further: acts on fast & hvy, any trk: progressive colt.
3285 **MINI LODGE 18** [3] J G FitzGerald 4-8-10 (67) A Culhane 7/2 FAV: 0-0122: 2 ch g Grand Lodge - *¾* **69**
Mirea (The Ministrel) Held up, prog 3f out, rdn bef dist, kept on to chase wnr fnl 100y, not btn far: nicely bckd: gd run, in form, worth a try at 12f now: see 2836.
*3379 **CAPTAIN BRADY 13** [8] J S Goldie 5-7-10 (53)(1oh) J Quinn 15/2: 030-13: 5 ch g Soviet Lad - Eight *1¼* **53**
Mile Rock (Dominion) Led, incrsd pace 3f out, hdd ent fnl 2f, same pace inside last: op 6/1: in gd heart.
3329 **ABUZAID 16** [6] J L Dunlop 3-9-6 (85) R Hills 13/2: 015324: Handy, shaken up appr fnl 2f, rdn bef *½* **84**
dist, keeping on nr fin but nvr able to chall: ran well tho' appeared unsuited by drop back to 10f: see 2270.
3410 **COLWAY RITZ 12** [1] 6-9-13 (84) T Williams 11/2: 120245: Bhd, last turning in, shkn up & imprvd *½* **82**
into mid-div 3f out, onepace bef fnl 1f: bckd, clr rem & prob ran nr to best: likes Ripon: see 2102 (C/D).
3541 **GRALMANO 7** [4] 5-10-0 (85) F Lynch 8/1: 641106: Al towards rear & carr head awkwardly in the straight. *5* **76**
1053 **YOURE SPECIAL 122** [10] 3-8-7 (72) Dean McKeown 33/1: 2-1007: Al bhd: 4 month abs, see 319. *5* **56**
3510 **CONTACT 9** [7] 3-9-9 (88) P Robinson 33/1: 616-08: Well plcd till wknd qckly 3f out: lngr trip, see 3510. *1* **71**
2464 **EJTITHAAB 53** [2] 3-9-1 (80) W Supple 14/1: 440039: In tch till 3f out: 8 wk abs, up in trip, btr 2464. *3* **59**
*3148 **WASEEM 24** [5] 3-8-12 (77) K Dalgleish (5) 6/1: 210310: Pld hard, nvr in it: 10th, too sn after 3148 (12f)? *1* **55**
10 ran Time 2m 05.3 (2) (Mr M Tabor & Mrs John Magnier) H R A Cecil Newmarket, Suffolk

3714 4.30 CLARO CONDITIONS STKS 2YO (C) 5f str Good/Firm 26 -12 Slow
£5591 £2120 £1060 £482

*3513 **REEL BUDDY 9** [5] R Hannon 2-9-0 J Fortune 9/4: 200011: 2 ch c Mr Greeley - Rosebud (Indian Ridge) **101**
Chsd ldrs, qcknd to lead appr fnl 1f, rdn out: nicely bckd tho' tchd 6/4: last wk won at Bath (auct mnd), earlier not btn far in a Gr 3: eff at 5f, shld get 6f: acts on fast & gd/soft grnd, any track: useful, improving colt.
3482 **PROUD BOAST 10** [3] Mrs G S Rees 2-8-9 A Culhane 11/8 FAV: 023152: 2 b f Komaite - Red Rosein *¾* **93**
(Red Sunset) Stdd start, in tch, shaken up 2f out, ran on to chase wnr inside last, being held: well bckd: ran to best, consistent filly: see 3482, 3145.
*3446 **THE TRADER 11** [2] M Blanshard 2-9-4 D Sweeney 8/1: 322113: 2 ch c Selkirk - Snowing (Tate Gallery) *¾* **100**
Held up in tch, short of room ent fnl 2f & switched wide, ran on strgly ins last, nvr nrr: well clr rem &

RIPON
TUESDAY AUGUST 29TH   **Righthand, Sharpish Track**

much improved: useful colt, gave weight away all round & lkd unlucky: shld win again sn, poss over 6f.

3145 **LAUREL DAWN 24** [7] A Berry 2-8-10 K Darley 10/1: 012134: Led till appr fnl 1f, no extra: ran to best.   3½   83
2901 **TALISKER BAY 35** [1] 2-8-10 R Fitzpatrick 66/1: 055: Chsd ldr, onepace und press fnl 1f: poss flattered   ½   81
3567 **BYO 6** [6] 2-9-2 L Gueller (7) 7/1: 124356: Outpcd, wide, improved appr fnl 1f, saddle slipped, no   ½   85
no extra & u.r. passing the line: quick reapp: see 3264.
*3576 **HARD TO CATCH 6** [4] 2-9-0 (bl) C Catlin (7) 33/1: 346017: Chsd ldrs till appr fnl 2f: stiff task after 3576. 2   77
3463 **ANTHONY ROYLE 10** [9] 2-8-10 Mark Flynn (7) 100/1: 66558: Keen, cl up 3f, btn & hmpd bef dist.   shd   73$
--   **HELALI MANOR** [8] 2-8-2 J McAuley 200/1: 9: Veered right, al bhd: debut: stoutly bred Muhtarram filly.   22   15
9 ran   Time 59.7 (1.9)   (Speedlith Group)   R Hannon East Everleigh, Wilts

---

3715   **5.00 WEATHERBYS HCAP 3YO+ 0-75 (E)**   **2m**   **Good/Form 26**   **-09 Slow**   **[70]**
£3458   £1064   £532   £266   3 yo rec 14lb

3270 **MAKASSEB 19** [6] M R Channon 3-9-2 (72) Craig Williams 8/1: 604401: 3 ch g Kris - Shefoog   75
(Kefaah) Trckd ldrs, went on appr fnl 2f, rdn out: first win, dual '99 rnr up (mdn, rtd 89): eff at 12f, relished
step up to 2m: acts on fast & gd/soft grnd, sharp or gall tracks: unexposed at this trip.
*3406 **BEST PORT 12** [7] J Parkes 4-7-10 (38)(3oh) J Quinn 13/2: 300212: 4 b g Be My Guest - Portree   1   38
(Slip Anchor) Held up, keen, prog to chase ldrs 3f out, styd on but not trouble wnr: tchd 8/1:
gd run from 3lbs o/h: at right end of h'cap & could have done with a stronger gallop: see 3406.
*3331 **MENTAL PRESSURE 16** [8] Mrs M Reveley 7-9-4 (60) A Culhane 9/4 FAV: 325213: 7 ch g Polar   shd   60
Falcon - Hysterical (High Top) Mid-div, prog to chase wnr appr fnl 1f, styd on for press: bckd, clr rem.
3501 **VINCENT 9** [3] J L Harris 5-7-13 (41) G Baker (5) 5/1: 101344: Held up, wide into str/outpcd, late rally.   5   37
+3429 **BAYSWATER 11** [1] 3-9-2 (72)(BL) Pat Eddery 3/1: 02215: Led till 3f out, no extra: blnkd   1¾   67
for h'cap bow & step up in trip: better without headgear in 3429 (12f fillies mdn).
3511 **SALSKA 9** [2] 9-8-10 (52)(vis) K Darley 7/1: 425066: Prom till 3f out: visor reapplied, see 2273.   4   44
3570 **MISS ARCH 6** [5] 4-7-10 (38)(15oh) K Dalgleish (5) 33/1: 0-5037: Held up, eff ent str, sn btn: stiff task.   14   20
7 ran   Time 3m 30.6 (5.8)   (Ahmed Al Shafar)   M R Channon West Isley, Berks

---

DEAUVILLE
FRIDAY AUGUST 25TH   **Righthand, Galloping Track**

Official Going   GOOD TO FIRM

3716   **1.55 LISTED PRIX DU HARAS 2YO**   **7f**   **Good/Firm**
£13449   £4611   £3458

3210 **LUNASALT 22** A Fabre 2-9-2 O Peslier : -131: 2 b c Salse - Lunafairy (Always Fair)   100
3470 **DAYGLOW DANCER 6** M R Channon 2-9-2 L Dettori : -13242: 2 b c Fraam - Fading (Pharly)   1½   97
Set pace, drvn/hdd ins last, not pace of wnr: qck reapp: eff at 6/7f: again imprvd in defeat, useful: see 3470.
--   **STORM BOY** France 2-9-2 G Mosse : 3: 2 ch c Bering - Princess Bilbao (Highest Honour)   1½   94
5 ran   Time 1m 21.2   (J-L Lagardere)   A Fabre France

3717   **2.55 GR 3 PRIX QUINCEY 3YO+**   **1m**   **Good/Firm**
£21134   £7685   £3842   3 yo rec 6 lb

1754 **PENNYS GOLD 82** P Bary 3-8-7 T Thulliez 36/10: -15211: 3 b f Kingmambo - Penny's Valentine (Storm Cat)   115
Chsd ldrs, gd hdwy to lead over 1f out, styd on well, rdn out: dual wnr prev this term, incl a Gr 3: eff at
1m on fast & soft grnd: tough, smart & improving filly.
1536} **ISLAND SANDS 461** Saeed bin Suroor 4-9-2 L Dettori 9/10 FAV: 1/15-2: 4 b h Turtle Island - Tiavanita   1½   114
(J O Tobin) Set fast pace, rdn/hdd dist, not pace of wnr: belated reapp after being sidelined with a foot injury:
high-class 3yo in '99, wng the 2000 Guineas on reapp (by a hd, rtd 118), subs 5th in Irish 2000 Guineas: wnr of
both '98 juv starts for D Elsworth, both at Salisbury (rtd 108 at best): half-brother to a 1m/10f wnr: suited by
1m on firm & gd/soft grnd: handles a stiff/gall trk: runs well fresh, forcing the pace: top-class colt at best,
entitled to just need this run & shld rate higher.
1433} **LEAVE US LEAP 463** A Fabre 4-9-0 O Peslier 76/10: 12-243: 4 b c Summer Squall - Sporades (Vaguely *snk* 111
Noble) Cl-up going well, ev ch till drvn/no extra well ins last: eff at 1m on fast: smart.
6 ran   Time 1m 32.8   (Overbrook Farm)   P Bary France

CLAIREFONTAINE
SATURDAY AUGUST 26TH   --

Official Going   GOOD

3718   **3.10 LISTED GRAND PRIX DE CLAIREFONTAINE 3YO**   **1m4f**   **Good**
£12488   £4227   £3170

3061 **TALAASH 25** M R Channon 3-8-12 D Boeuf : 1361: 3 b c Darshaan - Royal Ballet (Sadler's Wells)   107
Trkd ldr going well, drvn appr fnl 1f, led ins last, rdn out, shade cosy: earlier won on debut at Goodwood (mdn,
v easily), subs not disgraced when tried in Gr company: 380,000gns purchase: eff at 10/12f, will stay further:
acts on fast & gd/soft ground: progressing with every run & now v useful:
2225 **CRIMSON QUEST 62** A Fabre 3-9-2 O Peslier : 1-1202: 3 ch c Rainbow Quest - Bex (Explodent)   ¾   108
--   **KATHMANDU** France 3-9-2 C Asmussen : 3: 3 br c Kaldounevees - Midnight Lady (Mill Reef)   nse   108
--   **ANTICLES** Ian Williams 3-8-12 T Jarnet : -156: Front rank, wknd appr fnl 1f, eased, fin 6th: 10½   92
highly tried: recent debut wnr at Chantilly (stks), subs down the field in List company: apprec a drop in grade.
6 ran   Time   (Sheikh Ahmed Al Maktoum)   M R Channon West Isley, Berks

Official Going   Straight Course - YIELDING; Round Course - GOOD

3719   2.50 GR 3 KING OF KINGS EBF STKS 2YO   7f   Good
£32500   £9500   £4500   £1500

3316 **LADY LAHAR** 14 M R Channon 2-8-9 J Murtagh 5/1: 1341: 2 b f Fraam - Brigadiers Bird (Mujadil)   109
Settled rear, rdn & plenty to do over 1f out, ran on strongly to lead nr fin, drvn out: earlier won on debut at
Chepstow (nov stks), subs 3rd in the Gr 2 Cherry Hinton at Newmarket: Feb foal, sire a smart miler: dam unraced:
eff at 6/7f, 1m should suit: acts on good & a stiff/gall or undul trk: smart & progressive.
3086 **BONNARD** 24 A P O'Brien 2-8-12 M J Kinane 6/4 FAV: -1322: 2 b c Nureyev - Utr (Mr Prospector)   ½   110
Prom, eff & ran green appr fnl 1f, styd on well to claim 2nd cl-home: gd run: smart, see 3086 & 2613.
-- **BECKETT** A P O'Brien 2-8-12 J A Heffernan 6/1: -13: 2 b c Fairy King - Groom Order (Groom Dancer)   shd   110
Cl-up, rdn into lead dist, hdd cl-home: stablemate of rnr-up: 10 wks ago landed a Leopardstown mdn (6f, gd):
styd this longer 7f trip well: shld win in List company.
-- **DERIVATIVE** J S Bolger 2-8-12 K J Manning 8/1: -14: Nvr dngrs: recent Curragh mdn wnr (7f, fast).   5   102
*1844 **DOWN TO THE WOODS** 77 2-8-12 R Ffrench 5/2: 15: Led, 3L clr 2f out, wknd qckly & hdd dist,   ½   101
sn lost tch: 11 wk abs: shld stay 7f & this was a big step up in class after 1844 (easy mdn auct win, gd/fm).
7 ran   Time 1m 35.7   (Barry Walters Catering)   M R Channon West Ilsley, Berks

3720   3.55 TATTERSALLS BREEDERS STKS 2YO   6f   Yielding
£98000   £38000   £23000   £13000   Those drawn high held a big advantage.

*2714 **BLUE GODDESS** 40 R Hannon 2-8-7 D Harrison 5/1 FAV: 111: 2 b f Blues Traveller - Classic   107
Goddess (Classic Secret) Front rank, went on after halfway, shaken up & went clr over 1f out, comfortably:
6 wks abs: unbeaten filly, earlier won at Chepstow (auct mdn, debut) & Windsor (stks): half-sister to 2 wnrs
abroad: suited by 6f, 7f shld suit in time: acts on gd, gd/soft & prob any trk: runs well fresh: v useful &
fast improving filly, win in List class: trainer R Hannon landed a remarkable 5th successive win in this race.
-- **SWEET DILEMMA** K Prendergast 2-8-7 D P McDonogh 16/1: 352112: 2 b f Dolphin Street - Night Roofer   2   98
(Thatching) Cl-up, chall wnr over 1f out, rdn/no extra ins last: dual recent wnr, at Down Royal (mdn) &
Leopardstown (stks): eff at 6/7f on firm & gd/soft grnd: tough/consistent.
3174 **MISS DOMUCH** 20 R Hannon 2-8-7 E Ahern 12/1: 23123: 2 ch f Definite Article - Eliza Orzeszkowa   nk   97
(Polish Patriot) Chsd wnr thro'out, drvn/held fnl 1f: stablemate of wnr, improved on this gd/soft, handles fm.
-- **GALANTA** J S Bolger 2-8-12 K J Manning 10/1: -124: Dwelt, settled rear, rdn & styd on well   1½   98
fnl 2f, nrst fin: earlier won on debut at Galway (7f mdn, gd grnd).
3090 **BEE ONE** 24 2-8-7 N Pollard 14/1: -54045: Speed 4f, wknd ins last: gd run form poor draw.   hd   92
-- **TENDER COVE** 2-8-12 F M Berry 14/1: 426146: In tch, late hdwy, nvr nrr: D Royal mdn wnr (5f, fast).   shd   97
3320 **PROMISED** 14 2-8-7 C O'Donoghue 25/1: 13007: Waited with, drvn/btn over 1f out: see 1558.   0
2849 **INNIT** 35 2-8-7 M J Kinane 10/1: 543408: Mid-div at best: poor draw: see 2849 (5f, gd/fm).   0
3482 **KACHINA DOLL** 7 2-8-7 R Havlin 10/1: 520339: Cl-up, ev ch till wknd qckly fnl 1f: btr 3482 (List).   0
2514 **WITNEY ROYALE** 49 2-8-12 W J O'Connor 16/1: 140: Waited with, mod gains, 11th: 7 wk abs: see 2514.   0
3145 **OPEN WARFARE** 21 2-8-7 D M Grant 25/1: 353300: Nvr a factor, 13th: stiff task.   0
*2277 **FIAMMA ROYALE** 18 2-8-7 R Ffrench 16/1: 252420: Prom, fdd fnl 2f, 14th: btr 3205 (auct mdn).   0
3162 **BIJAN** 58 2-8-7 Paul Eddery 14/1: 5310: Al bhd, 17th: 8 wk abs: btr 2277 (auct mdn, fm).   0
3162 **BRANDON WIZZARD** 21 2-8-12 (t) D O'Donohoe 8/1: 60: Led, hdd over 2f out, wknd/eased, 22nd.   0
3513 **JUNIOR BRIEF** 6 2-8-12 (bl) W Supple 66/1: 000000: Al rear, 24th: v highly tried.   0
24 ran   Time 1m 14.9   (David Mort)   R Hannon East Everleigh, Wilts

3721   4.30 LISTED BALLYCULLEN STKS 3YO+   1m6f   Yielding
£16250   £4750   £2250   £750   3 yo rec 12lb

*2069 **KATIYKHA** 67 J Oxx 4-9-8 J Murtagh 13/8 FAV: -24111: 4 b f Darshaan - Katiyfa (Auction Ring)   109
Cl-up, went on over 1f out, ran on well, rdn out: 9 wk abs: hat-trick landed after wins at Gowran Park
(List) & notably the val Duke Of Edinburgh H'cap at R Ascot: '99 wnr for L Cumani at Newmarket (2, mdn &
rtd h'cap) & Leicester (stks, rtd 105): eff at 12/14f, even further could suit: acts on gd and soft ground,
likes a stiff/gall trk: v smart & progressive filly, win a Gr race in this form.
3068 **CHIMES AT MIDNIGHT** 28 L Comer 3-8-8 (BL) D A Stamp 40/1: 131002: 3 b c Danzig - Surely Georgies   ½   106
(Alleged) Held up, hdwy to chall dist, styd on, held cl-home: clr rem: imprvd in blnks, eff at 14f on gd: see 3028.
2409 **MEDIA PUZZLE** 55 D K Weld 3-8-8 (bl) P J Smullen 3/1: 113013: 3 ch c Theatrical - Market Slide   4½   100
(Gulch) In tch, drvn & styd on fnl 1f, no dngr: Down Royal wnr (12f List h'cap, firm) since 2409, see 1899.
2153 **KAHTAN** 64 J L Dunlop 5-9-11 W Supple 7/2: 1-4464: With ldr, went on 3f out, rdn/hdd over 1f out,   1   104
sn btn: 9 wk abs: top-weight: see 2153.
8 ran   Time 3m 05.0   (H H Aga Khan)   J Oxx Currabeg, Co Kildare

Official Going   GOOD TO SOFT

3722   2.20 GR 3 PRIX DU CALVADOS 2YO FILLIES   7f   Good/Soft
£21134   £7685   £3842   £2305

*2850 **ASCENSION** 36 M R Channon 2-8-9 C Asmussen 19/10 FAV: -111: 2 ch f Night Shift - Outeniqua   108
(Bold Lad) Chsd ldrs, led going well appr fnl 1f, easily gd/soft clr: unbeaten, recently won at Leopardstown
(mdn, with D Wachmann) & Newbury (Listed): Mar foal, cost IRE22,000: eff at 6/7f, 1m will suit: acts on
firm, good/soft & a gall trk: smart & prog filly with a fine turn of foot, win more Gr races.
-- **WOODEN DOLL** Mme C Head 2-8-9 O Doleuze 23/10: -12: 2 ch f Woodman - Kingscote (King's Lake)   2½   103
Waited with, ran on well for press fnl 1f, no ch with wnr: recent debut wnr: eff at 7f on gd/soft, 1m suit.
*3316 **PEACEFUL PARADISE** 15 J W Hills 2-8-9 M Hills 59/10: -31513: 2 b f Turtle Island -   snk   103
Megdale (Waajib) Front rank, drvn/not pace of wnr fnl 1f: acts on firm & gd/soft: prob ran to form of 3316 (List).
*2935 **SILVER JORDEN** 31 J L Dunlop 2-8-9 Pat Eddery 4/1: -11014: Led, hdd appr fnl 1f, sn held: 1½   100

1141

DEAUVILLE   SUNDAY AUGUST 27TH   Righthand, Galloping Track

eff on fast grnd, handles gd/soft & soft: apprec a drop back to List class as in 2935.
7 ran   Time 1m 25.3   (Norman Cheng)   M R Channon West Isley, Berks

3723   3.30 GR 2 GRAND PRIX DE DEAUVILLE 3YO+   1m4f110y   Good/Soft
£48031   £19212   £9606   £4803

1461 RUSSIAN HOPE 97 H A Pantall 5-9-4 C Soumillon 91/10: 2-1141: 5 ch h Rock Hopper - Dievotchka   116
(Dancing Brave) Made all, held on all out fnl 1f: 3 month abs: dual wnr earlier this term, incl a Gr 3 at
Saint Cloud: eff at 10/12.5f, clearly relishes gd/soft & hvy grnd: v smart & tough entire.
2406 DARING MISS 56 A Fabre 4-9-4 O Peslier 7/10 FAV: -41122: 4 b f Sadler's Wells - Bourbon Girl   hd 115
(Ile De Bourbon) Waited with, rdn to chall ins last, kept on, just held: 8 wk abs: see 2406, 1902.
--   MONT ROCHER J E Hammond 5-9-4 C Asmussen 47/10: 11-123: 5 b g Caerleon - Cuixmala (Highest   hd 115
Honor) Settled rear, smooth hdwy to chall dist, ran on, not btn far: eff at 12.5f on gd/soft: gd run, v consistent.
3306 LITTLE ROCK 15 Sir Michael Stoute 4-9-7 Pat Eddery 11/2: -16134: Trkd wnr, drvn over 1f out,   2   115
onepcd well ins last: not disgraced conceding weight all round: see 3306, 2566.
6 ran   Time 2m 40.5   (Baron Edouard de Rothschild)   H A Pantall France

3724   4.05 GR 3 PRIX DE MEAUTRY 3YO+   6f   Good/Soft
£21134   £7685   £3842   £2305

3132 THREE POINTS 23 J L Dunlop 3-8-11 Pat Eddery 7/2: 244121: 3 b c Bering - Trazi (Zalazi)   114
Made all, rdn & went clr appr fnl 1f, pshd out, cosily: earlier won at Newbury (stks, smashed trk record),
subs 2nd in a Gr 3 at Goodwood: '99 Kempton (mdn) & Nottingham (nov, rtd 103) wnr: suited by 6/7f, stays 10f:
acts on firm, gd/soft & a stiff or easy trk: v smart, tough & versatile.
2574 DANGER OVER 47 P Bary 3-8-11 T Thulliez 14/10 JT FAV: 5-1122: 3 b c Warning - Danilova (Lyphard)   1   109
Chsd wnr, rdn/prog over 1f out, styd on but no ch with comfortable wnr: 7 wk abs: see 2574, 945.
2226 MOUNT ABU 63 J H M Gosden 3-8-11 J Fortune 86/10: -41163: 3 b c Foxhound - Twany Angel (Double   1½ 105
Farm) Settled rear, imprvd 2f out, kept on, no threat to wnr: 9 wk abs: btr 2226, 1674.
10 ran   Time 1m 10.1   (Hesmonds Stud)   J L Dunlop Arundel, W Sussex

YORK   WEDNESDAY AUGUST 30TH   Lefthand, Flat, Galloping Track

Official Going   GOOD Stalls: 5/6f - Stands Side, 7f/Round Course - Inside

3725   2.10 BATLEYS HCAP STKS 3YO+ 0-85 (D)   1m3f195y   Good/Firm 29   -21 Slow   [82]
£8079   £2486   £1243   £621   3 yo rec 10lb

3430 CAPRIOLO 12 [4] R Hannon 4-9-2 (70)(bl) J Fortune 11/2: 001631: 4 ch g Priolo - Carroll's Canyon   77
(Hatim) Led, increased tempo 5f out, rdn & styd on well from 2f out, al holding rivals: nicely bckd, tchd 13/2:
earlier made all in a Chester class stks event: '99 wnr at Salisbury (mdn h'cap) & Leicester (h'cap, rtd 73):
suited by 10/12f on gd/soft grnd: tried a visor, earlier blnkered by blnks: handles any trk: loves to force the pace.
3674 SIMPLE IDEALS 3 [7] Don Enrico Incisa 6-7-10 (50)(10oh) Kim Tinkler 16/1: 556542: 6 b g Woodman -   1½ 53$
Comfort And Style (Be My Guest) Chsd wnr thr'out, rdn & kept on fnl 2f, al held: bckd, best at 14/15f now.
3159 CLARENDON 25 [2] V Soane 4-9-9 (77) M Tebbutt 7/1: 622303: 4 ch c Forest Wind - Sparkish (Persian   ½   79
Bold) Towards rear, rdn & styd on fnl 2f, no threat to wnr: paddock pick: cld rate higher: see 968.
4618\N NICHOL FIFTY 298 [6] M H Tompkins 6-9-7 (75) M Birch 16/1: 2500-4: Mid-div, rdn & styd on   2½ 73
onepace fnl 3f, no threat to front pair: ndd this on reapp: rtd 95h over timber in 99/00 (h'cap, unplcd): '99
wnr at Nottingham (h'cap) & Kempton (class stks, rtd 80): suited by 12/14f, stays 2m: acts on firm & soft grnd,
sharp/gall trk: runs well fresh: encouraging reapp, fin clr of rem here, interesting at 14f.
2811 DIVINE PROSPECT 40 [8] 3-8-6 (70) N Callan 9/1: 640235: Bolted riderless bef start, in tch, rdn/btn   10 57
over 2f out: op 6/1, 6 wk abs: surprising decision to run after pre-race antics, shld be forgotten: see 2811, 701 (10f).
3657 SHAANXI ROMANCE 3 [11] 5-7-12 (52) R Ffrench 25/1: 123406: Trkd ldrs, btn fnl 3f: quick reapp.   1½ 37
*3392 CYBER BABE 14 [10] 3-7-13 (63) J Quinn 9/2: 021317: Chsd ldrs, btn 2f out: bckd: btr 3392.   2   45
3541 RINGSIDE JACK 8 [9] 4-8-11 (65)(vis) J Fanning 7/1: 060408: Prom, btn 3f out: bckd, still ndd this.   2   44
3504 ARCHIE BABE 10 [12] 4-9-12 (80) K Darley 10/1: 010259: In tch, btn 3f out: see 3224, 2562.   2   56
2674 RAPIER 46 [3] 6-9-13 (81) Pat Eddery 100/30 FAV: -40130: Trkd ldrs, wknd qckly 4f out: 10th: nk 56
nicely bckd: 6 wk abs: btr 2674, 1788 (clmr).
3220 GRAND AMBITION 21 [5] 4-8-8 (62)(t) F Lynch 33/1: 050000: Al bhd: 11th: see 3081, 1352 (mdn).   8   28
11 ran   Time 2m 32.74 (5.94)   (Taylor Homer Racing)   R Hannon East Everleigh, Wilts

3726   2.40 LISTED STRENSALL STKS 3YO+ (A)   1m1f   Good/Firm 29   +11 Fast
£21645   £6660   £3330   £1665   3 yo rec 7 lb

1899 RIGHT WING 81 [4] J L Dunlop 6-9-8 (vis) J Reid 8/1: -31221: 6 b h In The Wings - Nekhbet (Artaius)   115
Slowly away, held up rear, smooth/stdy prog fnl 3f to trk ldrs over 1f out, rdn/qcknd to lead ins last, styd on
strongly: fast time: op 6/1, lkd superb after 12 wk abs: earlier scored at Kempton (Listed): '99 wnr at Doncaster
(reapp, Lincoln h'cap, rtd 107) & Nottingham (stks): '98 scorer again at Doncaster (rtd h'cap, rtd 102): suited by
1m/10f: handles any grnd but relishes an easy surface: handles any trk, likes Doncaster: runs v well fresh: suited
by a visor, has run well in blnks: loves to come late against horses: v tough & smart entire.
3300 AUTONOMY 19 [1] M L W Bell 3-8-10 M Fenton 10/1: 151-32: 3 b c Doyoun - Debbie's Next (Arctic Tern)   ½   108
Waited with rear, rdn/prog to lead over 1f out, hdd ins last, kept on well: clr rem: op 8/1, still just sharper for
this: v useful & progressive colt, had the rest well covered & a likely type for similar this autumn: see 3300.
*2476 FANAAR 54 [6] J Noseda 3-8-10 Pat Eddery 5/4 FAV: -1013: 3 ch c Unfuwain - Catalonda (African Sky)   4   100
Held up, eff over 2f out, drvn/onepace appr fnl 1f out: hvly bckd, tchd 11/8: abs: longer trip, return to 1m shld suit.
*3291 HOPEFUL LIGHT 19 [9] J H M Gosden 3-9-1 J Fortune 8/1: -40114: Led/dsptd lead, rdn/hdd over 1f   nk 104
out & no extra: op 6/1: see 3291 (1m, Salisbury).
3469 MOSELLE 11 [7] B Marcus 10/1: 013625: Trkd ldrs, rdn & eff when not much room 2f out, onepace nk 93
when not much room ins last: op 7/1: poss 3rd here with a clr run & shld rate higher.
3563 NOBELIST 7 [2] 5-9-3 (vis) T E Durcan 25/1: 100006: Waited with rear, eff fnl 3f, no impress on ldrs.   ½   97
1185 ISSEY ROSE 115 [5] 3-8-5 T Williams 66/1: 140-07: Trkd ldrs, ch 3f out, sn fdd: ndd this after 4   nk 91

mth abs: '99 Folkestone wnr (fillies mdn, rtd 87, subs rtd 102 when 4th in Gr1 fillies mile): acts on firm & soft grnd, sharp/undul or stiff/gall trk: suited by 7f/1m.

*3017 **ASLY 31** [3] 3-8-10 R Hills 7/2: -2118: Trkd ldrs, ch 2f out, sn rdn/btn: nicely bckd, btr 3017.	¾	95
3641 **YAKAREEM 4** [8] 4-9-3 D McGaffin 66/1: -45009: Led/dsptd lead after 1f till 3f out, sn btn: quick reapp.	8	83

9 ran   Time 1m 50.43 (1.63)   (The Earl Cadogan)   J L Dunlop Arundel, W Sussex

---

3727   **3.10 LAWRENCE BATLEY RTD HCAP 3YO+ 0-105 (B)**   **6f**   **Good/Firm 29**   **-05 Slow**   **[112]**
£15848   £6011   £3005   £1366   3 yo rec 3 lb   Raced towards centre

2706 **ANDREYEV 45** [2] R Hannon 6-9-7 (105) J Fortune 16/1: 005041: 6 ch g Presidium - Missish (Mummy's Pet) Held up, prog/rdn to lead over 1f out, styd on strongly ins last under hands & heels riding: op 14/1, 6 wk abs: earlier made a wng reapp at Doncaster (listed): rnr-up twice in '99 (rtd 109, Gr3), subs gelded & had a wind op: '98 Kempton (reapp, stks), Newcastle (Listed) & Deauville (Gr3) wnr, also 3rd in Gr2 at R Ascot (rtd 117): eff at 7f, best at 6f on fast or hvy, any trk: eff with/without blnks: best caught fresh nowadays: smart.   111

*3543 **NIGHT FLIGHT 8** [1] R A Fahey 6-8-7 (91)(3ex)(2oh) G Duffield 9/4 FAV: 600012: 6 gr g Night Shift - Ancestry (Persepolis) Trkd ldr halfway going well, ev ch over 1f out, sn outpcd by wnr: hvly bckd, gd run.   2   92

3464 **FURTHER OUTLOOK 11** [6] D Nicholls 6-8-13 (97) R Winston 10/1: 536403: 6 g g Zilzal - Future Bright (Lyphard's Wish) Early, hdd over 1f out, kept on for press: op 8/1: consistent in defeat.   shd   98

3335 **BAILEYS WHIRLWIND 17** [4] M L W Bell 3-8-5 (92) J Mackay 12/1: 034444: Held up, rdn & short of room over 1f out, kept on fnl 1f: poss worth another try at 7f: see 1186.   ¾   91

3543 **GUINEA HUNTER 8** [12] 4-9-1 (99)(BL) J Carroll 12/1: 001005: Held up towards rear, styd on for press fnl 2f, nvr pace to chall: sound eff in first time blnks: op 10/1: likes Haydock: see 2859 (5f).   nk   97

3543 **CRYHAVOC 8** [3] 6-8-8 (92) A Culhane 16/1: 200006: Chsd ldrs, no impress fnl 1f: see 2432.   nk   89

3335 **BLUE VELVET 17** [7] 3-8-4 (91)(2oh) C Carver (3) 16/1: 011657: Mid-div, held over 1f out: see 3130.   nk   87

3543 **DANIELLES LAD 8** [10] 4-8-11 (95) K Darley 8/1: 104068: Cl-up, btn 2f out: btr 3543, 1531 (soft).   ½   89

3521 **KALINDI 9** [8] 3-8-7 (94) Craig Williams 20/1: 0-0069: Bmpd start & slowly away/bhd, some late gains despite little room: kind ride, shld improve on this h'cap bow: see 1078.   ¾   86

3427 **NIGRASINE 12** [1] 6-8-11 (95)(BL) D O'Donohoe 12/1: 451040: Cl-up, wknd over 1f out: 10th: op 10/1.   ½   85

3315 **ROYAL ARTIST 18** [13] 4-8-7 (91)(1oh) P Robinson 8/1: 621100: Chsd ldrs 4f: 11th: op 5/1.   1   79

3158 **NOW LOOK HERE 25** [11] 4-8-12 (96) W Supple 20/1: 020050: Mid-div, btn 2f out: 12th: see 1337.   1¾   80

2568 **DONT SURRENDER 12** [5] 3-8-7 (94) Pat Eddery 8/1: -02300: Cl-up 4f: 13th: 7 wk abs: see 1178.   ½   76

13 ran   Time 1m 11.43 (2.03)   (J Palmer-Brown)   R Hannon East Everleigh, Wilts

---

3728   **3.40 EMIRATES RTD HCAP 3YO 0-105 (B)**   **1m3f195y**   **Good/Firm 29**   **-27 Slow**   **[111]**
£13705   £5067   £2533   £1151

3451 **CRACOW 12** [1] J W Hills 3-8-5 (88) R Hills 7/2: 310521: 3 b c Polish Precedent - Height Of Secrecy (Shirley Heights) Dictated pace, increased tempo 5f out, held on well from over 1f out, drvn out: well bckd: lkd well: earlier scored at Brighton (mdn): rtd 84 when rnr-up in '99: eff at 10/12f, may get further: acts on firm & gd/soft grnd, stiff/gall or sharp/undul trk: eff forcing the pace: useful colt.   91

3487 **KIFTSGATE 11** [2] Sir Michael Stoute 3-8-10 (93) Pat Eddery 5/2: -6122: 3 ch g Kris - Blush Rambler (Blushing Groom) Trkd ldrs, prog & drvn/chall from over 1f out, styd on well tho' held nr fin: pulled well clr of other pair: useful colt, encouraging h'cap bow & open to further improvement: see 3487, 2531.   ½   94

3014 **ZIBELINE 31** [3] C E Brittain 3-8-4 (87)(2oh) P Robinson 9/2: 441523: 3 b c Cadeaux Genereux - Zia (Shareef Dancer) Held up, rdn over 2f out, sn outpcd by front pair: bckd: scopey type: see 3014.   6   79

3599 **MANA DARGENT 6** [4] M Johnston 3-8-4 (87)(2oh) K Dalgleish (5) 6/4 FAV: 313234: Trkd wnr, eff fnl 3f, rdn/btn over 1f out: hvly bckd: quick reapp: btr 3599, 3014.   2½   75

4 ran   Time 2m 33.54 (6.74)   (N N Browne)   J W Hills Upper Lambourn, Berks

---

3729   **4.10 TRAVEL TRADE MDN AUCT 2YO (E)**   **1m rnd**   **Good/Firm 29**   **-20 Slow**
£6698   £2061   £1030   £515

3409 **PRINCESS EMILY 13** [5] B S Rothwell 2-7-13 D Mernagh (3) 4/1: 031: 2 b f Dolphin Street - Partita (Polish Precedent) Al prom, led 2f out, held on gamely ins last, all out: well bckd, op 5/1: apprec step up to 1m, may stay further in time: acts on fast grnd & a stiff/gall trk: improving with racing.   72

3497 **MY VERY OWN 11** [4] N P Littmoden 2-8-7 C Carver (3) 14/1: 062: 2 ch c Persian Bold - Cossack Princess (Lomond) Mid-div, prog/rdn & chall fnl 1f, styd on well, just held: bckd at long odds, op 20/1: left prev form bhd him over longer 1m trip & further will suit: acts on fast & a gall trk: scopey.   shd   80

3466 **WONDERGREEN 11** [7] T D Easterby 2-8-4 W Supple 16/1: 6003: 2 ch c Wolfhound - Tenderetta (Tender King) Handy, led over 2f out, sn rdn/hdd, kept on for press ins last: clr of rem: styd longer 1m trip well: acts on fast grnd: only mod form prev: tall, scopey type: shld win a race.   1   75

3532 **SIMPLY ERIC 8** [17] J L Eyre 2-8-7 Pat Eddery 7/2 FAV: 24: Chsd ldrs, rdn & onepace/held fnl 2f: lkd well: op 5/2: not disgraced from a awkward high draw though rtd higher 3532.   9   62

— **CAPTAIN KOZANDO** [3] 2-8-4 G Duffield 10/1: 5: Dwelt, towards rear, hdwy 4f out, styd on onepace fnl 2f: ndd this: Komaite gldg, Jan foal, cost 1,400 gns: dam a 7f/1m juv wnr: strong, scopey type.   1   57

3520 **DAWN ROMANCE 9** [10] 2-8-2 Craig Williams 9/1: 050066: Unruly paddock, mid-div, mod gains fnl 2f.   nk   54

— **THE OLD SOLDIER** [11] 2-8-7 A Culhane 16/1: 7: Towards rear, kept on fnl 3f under hands & heels riding, no threat: op 14/1, ndd this: Magic Ring colt, Apr foal, cost 5,400 gns: dam a mdn: strong, backward type.   nk   58

1095 **WESTON HILLS 120** [8] 2-8-10 N Callan 14/1: 08: In tch 6f: op 10/1: lkd well tho' ndd this after 4 month abs: longer 1m trip: see 1095.   3   55

3363 **HOBO 15** [16] 2-8-10 F Lynch 40/1: 009: Rear, mod gains when no room over 1f out, sn no hdwy: lkd well tho' still burly: longer 1m trip today: see 3363, 700.   1¼   52

3558 **MERRY DANCE 7** [18] 2-8-2 J Quinn 8/1: 030: Prom 6f: 10th: op 5/1: poor high draw: btr 3558 (7f).   1¼   41

3412 **PERSIAN SPIRIT 13** [19] 2-8-6(1ow) J Fortune 8/1: -060: Chsd ldrs 5f: 11th: high draw: see 3412.   nk   44

— **SALVIANO** [6] 2-8-7 Kim Tinkler 20/1: 0: Al towards rear: 12th: op 12/1: burly & bkwd on intro: River Falls gldg, May foal, cost 5,500 gns: half brother to a smart 5f juv wnr: dam a 12f wnr: 1m+ will suit in time.   2½   35

3215 **PILGRIM GOOSE 21** [15] 2-8-10 S Finnamore (5) 20/1: 000: Slowly away, keen, al rear: 13th.   2½   33

3216 **IZZET MUZZY 21** [14] 2-8-10 T Williams 40/1: 554600: Prom, led 4f out till over 2f out, wknd: 14th.   2   29

3497 **ST NICHOLAS 11** [1] 2-8-4 J Fanning 33/1: 000: Narrow lead 4f, sn struggling: 15th: longer 1m trip.   5   13

— **Royal Gent** [9] 2-8-4 K Hodgson 33/1:	3466 **Live In Lover 11** [2] 2-8-10 Dean McKeown 40/1:
3500 **Northern Castle 10** [12] 2-8-7 Dale Gibson 33/1:	1558 **Itis Itis 93** [13] 2-8-10 J Carroll 33/1:

19 ran   Time 1m 39.7 (3.9)   (Mrs Julie Mitchell)   B S Rothwell Musley Bank, N Yorks

YORK
WEDNESDAY AUGUST 30TH   Lefthand, Flat, Galloping Track

3730   **4.40 PRINCE OF WALES MDN 2YO (D)   7f rnd   Good/Firm 29   -40 Slow**
£6493   £1998   £999   £499

-- **TOBOUGG** [3] M R Channon 2-9-0 Craig Williams 2/1 FAV: 1: 2 b c Barathea - Locavia (Majestic Light)   105+
Dwelt, settled rear, not much room 3f out till 2f out, prog under hands & heels riding to lead 1f out, sn asserted:
bckd: Feb foal, cost 230,000 gns: half brother to sev wnrs abroad: dam French Oaks wnr: eff at 7f, 1m+ sure to
suit: acts on fast & runs well fresh: defied burly looking appearance, looks sure to win in better company.

3568 **LOVE EVERLASTING** 7 [9] M Johnston 2-8-9 K Darley 100/30: -342: 2 b f Pursuit Of Love - In Perpetuity 1¾   93
(Great Nephew) Handy, dsptd lead over 2f out, sn hdd, kept on: hvly bckd tho' op 2/1: scopey filly: stays 7f well:
caught a gd sort here: can find similar on a minor trk: see 3568, 3009.

-- **LIPICA** [2] K R Burke 2-8-9 N Callan 12/1: 3: 2 b f Night Shift - Top Knot (High Top)   nk   92
Held up, prog/rdn to dspt lead 2f out till 1f out, kept on: lkd fit: Apr foal, half sister to a wnr abroad: dam
a 12f/2m Irish wnr: eff at 7f, 1m+ is sure to suit: shld improve over further.

3361 **KHITAAM** 16 [1] B Hanbury 2-9-0 R Hills 9/4: 24: Trkd ldrs racing keenly, not much room over 1f   ¾   96
out, styd on onepace for press: well bckd: tall, lengthy & scopey colt, looks sure to relish 1m+ in similar company.

2414 **WHERE THE HEART IS** 56 [4] 2-9-0 G Duffield 50/1: 35: Chsd ldrs, rdn & kept on fnl 2f, not pace   ¾   95$
to chall: 8 wk abs: longer 7f trip: see 2414.

3298 **DR STRANGELOVE** 19 [5] 2-9-0 J Reid 10/1: 56: Led 5f, fdd: clr rem: op 12/1: still ndd this.   2½   90
2708 **FREECOM NET** 45 [7] 2-9-0 J Quinn 66/1: U7: Prom, ch 2f out, held when no room over 1f out: abs.   10   72
-- **BEST GUEST** [8] 2-9-0 G Hind 40/1: 8: Al bhd: Barathea colt, Apr foal, cost 40,000 IR gns: half   1¾   69
brother to a wnr: dam a 6f Irish juv wnr: with G G Margarson.

2239 **BEE KING** 63 [6] 2-9-0 (VIS) R Havlin 100/1: -0009: Cl-up 4f: 2 month abs, visor, new stable.   3   63
9 ran   Time 1m 25.93 (4.83)   (Sheikh Ahmed Al Maktoum)   M R Channon West Isley, Berks

---

3731   **5.10 TRAVEL TRADE APPR HCAP 3YO+ 0-70 (E)   1m2f85y   Good/Firm 29   -06 Slow   [63]**
£6344   £1952   £976   £488   3 yo rec 8 lb

2815 **MIDDLETHORPE** 40 [2] M W Easterby 3-8-12 (55)(BL) P Hanagan (3) 20/1: 510301: 3 b g Noble Patriarch   61
- Prime Property (Tirol) Trkd ldrs, led going well over 2f out, styd on strongly fnl 1f, rdn out: 6 wk abs:
earlier scored at Beverley (h'cap, 1st win): plcd in '99 (rtd 59, h'cap): suited by 10.5f/12f on fast & soft
grnd: handles a sharp or stiff/gall trk: runs well fresh: galvanised by first time blnks.

*3603 **KESTRAL** 5 [6] T J Etherington 4-8-13 (48)(6ex) Darren Williams (3) 4/1 FAV: 623212: 4 ch g Ardkinglass 1¾   50
- Shiny Ray (Star Appeal) Mid-div, smooth prog over 3f out, rdn/chsd wnr fnl 2f, kept on, al held: pulled well
clr of rem: fine run under 6lb pen: eff at 1m/10.5f: keep on the right side in similar company: see 3603.

3480 **ANNADAWI** 11 [9] C N Kellett 5-9-0 (49) P Fitzsimons 14/1: 223633: 5 b g Sadler's Wells - Prayers'n   8   40
Promises (Foolish Pleasure) Rear/hmpd after 1f, prog/chsd ldrs over 2f out, sn held: see 1575 (gd/soft).

3557 **PARISIAN LADY** 7 [3] A G Newcombe 5-8-12 (47) C Catlin (3) 20/1: 4202U4: Towards rear, late gains   1½   36
for press, no threat to front pair: see 2893, 528 & 152.

2554 **PILLAGER** 51 [11] 3-9-1 (58) G Hannon (3) 33/1: 264505: Mid-div, mod late gains, no threat: abs.   1   46
3531 **SMARTER CHARTER** 8 [8] 7-9-7 (56) Kristin Stubbs (5) 25/1: 256306: Rear/hmpd after 1f, mod gains.   ¾   43
3410 **WERE NOT STOPPIN** 13 [7] 5-9-10 (59) R Studholme (5) 11/1: 114137: Hmpd after 1f, nvr a factor.   nk   45
3495 **MYSTERIUM** 11 [16] 6-9-9 (58) R Brisland 20/1: 251108: In tch, btn 2f out: btr 3314.   2½   40
*3344 **MARGARETS DANCER** 16 [5] 5-8-13 (48)(t) R Cody Boutcher (3) 16/1: -00619: Chsd ldrs 1m.   1   29
3652 **SWYNFORD PLEASURE** 4 [14] 4-9-1 (50) Claire Bryan 20/1: 430030: Mid-div, eff 3f out, sn held: 10th.   ¾   30
3676 **CASSANDRA** 3 [1] 4-9-4 (53) T Eaves 20/1: 020040: Prom 7f: 11th: quick reapp: see 1496.   1½   31
3511 **ASHLEIGH BAKER** 10 [20] 5-9-1 (50) K Dalgleish 12/1: 612440: Mid-div, btn 3f out: 12th: op 14/1.   1½   26
3356 **WHISTLING DIXIE** 16 [19] 4-9-0 (49)(bl) J Mackay 7/1: 141530: Cl-up, led 5f out till over 2f out, btn/   ¾   24
eased in last: 13th: bckd, op 12/1: btr 2655.

3368 **KIDZ PLAY** 15 [13] 4-9-5 (54) Dawn Rankin (5) 33/1: 140400: Led 5f, sn btn: 14th: see 1689.   nk   28
3111 **MISSILE TOE** 26 [4] 7-9-1 (50) D McGaffin (3) 15/2: 116530: Al bhd: 19th: see 2309.   0
*3495 **TROIS** 11 [12] 4-9-9 (58) S Finnamore (3) 11/1: 045210: Held up, keen, btn 3f out: 20th: btr 3495.   0
1940 Typhoon Ginger 76 [22] 5-9-9 (58) R Smith (3) 20/1: 3073 Acebo Lyons 28 [18] 5-9-8 (57) Lisa Jones (7) 20/1:
3389 Armenia 14 [17] 3-9-3 (60) D Glennon (5) 25/1:   2725 Noble Reef 43 [10] 3-9-3 (60) Angela Hartley (5) 25/1:
20 ran   Time 2m 10.94 (3.64)   (J H Quickfall & A G Black)   M W Easterby Sheriff Hutton, N Yorks

---

BRIGHTON
WEDNESDAY AUGUST 30TH   Lefthand, V Sharp, Undulating Track

Official Going   FIRM. Stalls: 1m2f & 1m4f - Outside; Rem - Inside.

3732   **2.20 EBF/BBC MDN 2YO (D)   6f rnd   Firm 10   -33 Slow**
£3432   £1056   £528   £264

3385 **STATUE GALLERY** 14 [4] J A R Toller 2-9-0 S Whitworth 2/5 FAV: 521: 2 ch c Cadeaux Genereux -   71
Kinlochewe (Old Vic) Early ldr, again appr fnl 1f, rdn ent fnl 1f, pshd out cl-home: hvly bckd: first foal: eff
at 6f, bred for further: acts on firm/fast grnd: possibly not at home on this undul trk & is better the bare from.

3582 **KALUKI** 6 [3] Mrs L Stubbs 2-9-0 S W Kelly (3) 9/1: 303322: 2 ch c First Trump - Wild Humour   ½   68
(Fayruz) Prom, feeling pace ent fnl 2f, rallied to press wnr ins last but al being held: op 6/1, qck reapp, clr
rem: ran well for new connections back at 6f tho' is eff at 7f: acts on firm & gd/soft grnd.

3418 **PHILIPPI** 13 [6] J A Osborne 2-9-0 (BL) J P Spencer 33/1: 03: 2 b c Alzao - Lighted Glitter   2½   61
(Crystal Glitters) Sn led, hdd appr fnl 1f, & no extra: better run in blnks but needs further: see 3418.

3044 **MISS DAMINA** 30 [1] J Pearce 2-8-9 M Roberts 33/1: 0004: Nvr a factor: up in trip, needs sells.   4   46
3576 **STRAWBERRY DAWN** 7 [5] T Quinn 4/1: 45: In tch till halfway, sn btn/eased: something amiss?   23   6
3492 **WILD SPIRIT** 11 [2] 2-9-0 S Sanders 33/1: 56: Sn struggling: op 10/1, see 3492.   4   1
6 ran   Time 1m 10.4 (2.6)   (The Duke Of Devonshire)   J A R Toller Newmarket, Suffolk

---

3733
2.50 ASHFORTH SELLER 2YO (F)   7f rnd   Firm 10 -24 Slow
£2205   £630   £315

3468 **SEL 11** [3] G L Moore 2-8-11 (bl) I Mongan (5) 1/1 FAV: 351251: 2 b f Salse - Frog (Akarad) **61**
Trkd ldr, rdn to lead bef fnl 1f, won going away: bt in for 6,500gns: earlier won here at Brighton (sell, Sir M
Prescott, 1st time blnks): eff at 7f, sure to get further: acts on firm & gd/soft: likes Brighton, best blnkd.
3582 **GOLDEN BEACH 6** [4] Mrs P N Dutfield 2-8-6 P Doe 5/1: -00052: 2 b f Turtle Island - Good As Gold 3½ **48**
(Glint Of Gold) Led, hdd appr fnl 1f & onepace for press: clr rem, qk reapp: stiff task with wnr at the weights.
2079 **PERTEMPS JACK 70** [1] A D Smith 2-8-11 S Whitworth 50/1: 663: 2 br g Silca Blanka - Stella 18 **23**
Royale (Astronef) Al bhd: 10 wk abs, no worthwhile form.
3468 **IVANS BRIDE 11** [5] G G Margarson 2-8-6 S Sanders 6/4: 640624: In tch till halfway: unsuited by 2 **14**
firm grnd/undul trk?: in front of this winner in 3468 (gd grnd, stiffer trk, sell h'cap).
3582 **YURA MADAM 6** [2] 2-8-6 J Tate 33/1: 05: Sn btn: quick reapp: Cosmonaut filly with P McEntee. 4 **8**
5 ran   Time 1m 22.2 (2.4)   (C F Sparrowhawk)   G L Moore Woodingdean, E Sussex

3734
3.20 ARMY HCAP 3YO+ 0-80 (D)   5f59y rnd   Firm 10 -03 Slow   **[80]**
£3916   £1205   £602   £301

3528 **RITAS ROCK APE 9** [2] R Brotherton 5-9-4 (70) I Mongan (5) 7/2: 010021: 5 b m Mon Tresor - Failand **77**
(Kala Shikari) Led, rdn clr & drifted right appr fnl 1f, shade rdly: earlier won at Chepstow (h'cap): '99 wnr
here at Brighton (2, incl stks), Bath, Lingfield & Salisbury (h'cap/appr h'caps, rtd 80): plcd in '98 (rtd 62 &
56a): eff forcing the pace around 5f: acts on gd grnd, handles gd/soft, firbresand & any trk, likes Brighton.
3653 **SOAKED 4** [7] D W Chapman 7-8-9 (61)(bl) G Parkin 12/1: 133402: 7 b g Dowsing - Water Well 2 **62**
(Sadler's Wells) Prom, rdn appr fnl 1f, kept on for 2nd but no chr wnr: op 8/1, qk reapp & back to form: tough.
3687 **FORGOTTEN TIMES 2** [9] K T Ivory 6-9-6 (72)(vis) A Beech (5) 8/1: 206003: 6 ch m Nabeel Dancer - shd **73**
Etoile d'Amore (The Minstrel) Rear, kept on fnl 1f, nvr nr to chall: op 6/1, ran 48 hrs ago & this was a
return to form on grnd faster than ideal: see 2184.
3516 **BLUNDELL LANE 10** [1] A P Jarvis 5-8-9 (61) D Sweeney 10/1: 604004: Cl-up & ev ch till no extra fnl ¾ **60**
1f: op 7/1: better run from fav'ble draw: see 1126 (6f here, reapp).
3689 **CHAKRA 2** [4] 6-7-12 (50) P Doe 12/1: 021665: Rear till kept on well fnl 1f, nvr dangerous: op 8/1, hd **48**
ran 48hrs ago & will apprec a return to 6f: see 3243 (here).
3176 **SAILING SHOES 24** [3] 4-9-10 (76) L Newman (3) 12/1: 000606: Bhd ldrs, no extra appr fnl 1f: op 8/1. ¾ **72**
3687 **SYLVA PARADISE 2** [8] 7-9-8 (74)(vis)(6ex) T Quinn 8/1: 030107: Al bhd, late hdwy: ran 48hrs nk **69**
ago, see 3528 (C/D, beat this wnr).
-2266 **CROWDED AVENUE 62** [6] 8-10-0 (80) (vis) S Sanders 7/1: 0-0328: Chsd ldrs, unable to qckn appr fnl ½ **73**
1f & short of room below dist: op 5/1, top-weight, see 1687.
3687 **PURE ELEGANCIA 2** [5] 4-9-3 (66) A Nicholls (3) 3/1 FAV: 024309: Dwelt, prom, wknd qckly ent fnl 7 **47**
2f, eased: nicely bckd, came to sn after 3687?: see 2525.
9 ran   Time 1m 00.7 (0.7)   (Mrs Janet Pearce)   R Brotherton Elmley Castle, Worcs

3735
3.50 SUN FILLIES HCAP 3YO+ 0-70 (E)   1m3f196y Firm 10 -30 Slow   **[67]**
£2834   £872   £436   £218   3 yo rec 10lb

3560 **ALPHA ROSE 7** [2] M L W Bell 3-9-2 (65) A Beech (5) 8/13 FAV: 311421: 3 ch f Inchinor - Philgwyn **71**
(Milford) Nvr far away, led appr fnl 2f, rdn out: well bckd, quick reapp: earlier won at Musselburgh, Ayr (stks),
Lingfield & here at Brighton (fill h'caps): unplcd for R Williams in '99 (rtd 68): eff btwn 10f & 14f, tried 2m:
suited by firm/fast grnd & equitrack, progressive filly.
3434 **COPYFORCE GIRL 12** [3] Miss B Sanders 4-9-10 (63)(t) S Sanders 10/3: 322262: 4 b f Elmaamul - 2 **65**
Sabaya (Seattle Dancer) Led till bef fnl 2f, styd on: clr rem, bckd & ran to best giving weight to this imprvg
winner: suited by drop back in trip, eff at 12f/14f: see 2429, 1934.
3557 **REGAL ACADEMY 7** [5] C A Horgan 6-7-10 (35)(tbl)(1oh) G Baker (5) 8/1: 04-043: 6 b m Royal Academy 9 **28**
- Polistatic (Free State) Dwelt, keen, chsd ldrs appr str, sn outpcd tho' plodded on for 3rd: qck reapp, tricky ride.
3581 **FOREST DREAM 7** [4] L A Dace 5-8-4 (43) A Nicholls (3) 8/1: 300204: Prom, pld hard, no extra fnl 3f. ¾ **35**
3442 **STREAK OF DAWN 12** [6] 3-7-11 (46)(1ow)(16oh) P Doe 66/1: 000005: Well plcd till 3f out: stiff task. 5 **33**
3581 **READING RHONDA 7** [1] 4-7-12 (37)(t) (2ow)(3oh) A Mackay 20/1: 036006: In tch till appr str: op 14/1. 8 **16**
6 ran   Time 2m 33.0 (4.8)   (Richard J Morris Jr)   M L W Bell Newmarket, Suffolk

3736
4.20 CAT CLUB CLAIMER DIV I 3YO+ (E)   1m rnd   Firm 10 -18 Slow
£2301   £708   £354   £177   3 yo rec 6 lb

3559 **ERTLON 7** [4] C E Brittain 10-8-9 A Nicholls (3) 9/1: 603551: 10 b g Shareef Dancer - Sharpina **52**
(Sharpen Up) Led, rdn clr appr fnl 1f, unchall: op 6/1, quick reapp: bckd thrice in '99 (h'cap, rtd 79a & 71):
last won in '97, at Lingfield (rtd 79a & 71): eff at 7f/1m, tried 10f: acts on firm/fast & equitrack, handles
soft & fibresand: best forcing the pace without blnks: well ridden.
3259 **BUTRINTO 20** [3] B R Johnson 6-9-9 C Rutter 13/8 FAV: 402322: 6 ch g Anshan - Bay Bay (Bay 1¼ **63**
Express) V keen, in tch, belatedly shkn up 2f out, styd on well, too much to do: clr rem but puzzling ride.
3253 **NUNKIE GIRL 20** [5] R Hannon 3-7-11 (bl)(1ow) P Doe 20/1: 006003: 3 ch f Thatching - Ecco Mi 3 **37**
(Priolo) Held up, wide prog to chase wnr 3f out, sn no impress: op 10/1: mod form so far tho' prob handles firm.
*3559 **ANNIE APPLE 7** [8] N Hamilton 4-8-12 T Quinn 3/1: 450014: Chsd ldrs, onepcd ent fnl 3f: quick 2½ **41**
reapp, stiffish task at the weights: see 3559 (7f trk).
3527 **COLONEL NORTH 9** [7] 4-9-9 S Sanders 4/1: 665545: Hmpd & dropped rear after 2f, drvn ent str, ¾ **51**
nvr nr ldrs: bckd tho' op 3/1: see 3527, 90.
3559 **CELTIC VENTURE 7** [9] 5-8-13 D Sweeney 12/1: 661006: Chsd ldrs till 3f out: stiff task, quick reapp. 3½ **34**
3404 **JUST FOR YOU JANE 14** [6] 4-8-8 I Mongan (5) 20/1: 004367: Al bhd: op 12/1, see 2907, 1971. 1 **27**
3242 **UBITOO 21** [1] 3-8-13 (bl) A Clark 33/1: 530008: Handy till halfway: v stiff task: see 2592. 9 **18**
8 ran   Time 1m 34.2 (2.2)   (C E Brittain)   C E Brittain Newmarket, Suffolk

BRIGHTON

WEDNESDAY AUGUST 30TH   Lefthand, V Sharp, Undulating Track

3737

4.50 ANDY AMAT HCAP 3YO+ 0-65 (F)   1m2f   Firm 10 -25 Slow   [39]
£2705   £773   £386   3 yo rec 8 lb

3581 **BECKON** 7 [6] B R Johnson 4-9-11 (36) Miss L Sheen(5) 12/1: 015061: 4 ch f Beveled - Carolynchristensen   42
(Sweet Revenge) Dwelt & held up, stdy wide prog appr fnl 2f, pshd into lead with ins last: tchd 20/1: earlier
won at Lingfield (AW appr h'cap, rtd 52a): '99 wnr again at Lingfield (sell, rtd 53a, flattered on turf, rtd 62):
eff at 10f, tried 12f: acts on firm grnd, loves equitrack/Lingfield & sharp/undul trks & goes well for inexp jockeys.
3557 **LITTLE TUMBLER** 7 [10] S Woodman 5-10-6 (45) Miss R Woodman 7/1: 565022: 5 b m Cyrano de   ¾   48
Bergerac - Glass Minnow (Alzao) Well off the pace, gd prog fnl 2f & ev ch ins last, held nr fin: op 7/1,
quick reapp: acts on firm & gd/soft grnd: in form, see 1807.
*3557 **ARDENT** 7 [3] Miss B Sanders 6-10-3 (42) Miss Diana Jones 7/1: 000513: 6 b g Aragon - Forest Of   1   43
Arden (Tap On Wood) Chsd ldrs, prog to lead dist, hdd towards fin: op 5/1, qk reapp: gd run tho' shade btr 3557.
3356 **KINNINO** 16 [15] G L Moore 6-10-4 (43) Mr R L Moore (5) 5/1 FAV: 032144: In tch, prog appr fnl 1f,   nk   43
ch ins last, no extra fnl 50y: sound run, acts on firm, gd & both AWs, see 3111.
*3251 **MANIKATO** 20 [11] B R Millman 5-10-9 (38) Miss M Gunstone (5) 12/2: 0-4615: Patiently rdn, gd prog appr fnl 1f,   shd   38
kept on, too much to do: back up in trip, remains in form & clrly gets 10f, poss stays 12f: see 3251.
3330 **EASTERN CHAMP** 17 [8] 4-11-7 (60)(t) Mr T Scudamore 8/1: 063466: Bhd till ran on late & wide,   ½   59
nvr dangerous: not disgraced under a massive weight, up in trip, stays 10f: see 1259.
3499 **DOBERMAN** 11 [5] 5-10-7 (46)(vis) Miss E Folkes (5) 25/1: 022207: Chsd ldr & clr, ev ch 2f out, fdd.   2   42
3356 **SAMMYS SHUFFLE** 16 [19] 5-10-9 (48)(bl) Mr H Poulton(7) 13/2: 212358: In tch, no impress appr fnl 2f.   4   38
3561 **NIGHT AND DAY** 7 [20] 3-10-9 (56)(tvi) Mr Paul J Morris (5) 20/1: 230549: Nvr better than mid-div: lngr trip.   ½   45
3663 **TWOFORTEN** 3 [13] 5-9-7 (32) Mr R Lucey Butler (7) 12/1: 006030: Nvr nr ldrs: 10th, btr 3663 (gd).   2½   18
*3581 **LEVEL HEADED** 7 [4] 5-10-6 (45)(5ex) Mrs S Bosley 9/1: 413410: Led & clr with one other, hdd ent fnl   shd   31
2f & wknd qckly: 11th, tchd 11/1, qck reapp: set off way too fast: see 3581.
*3052 **GOLD BLADE** 29 [9] 11-10-8 (47) Mrs L Pearce 11/1: 054610: Al bhd: 15th, much btr 3052 (gd/soft).   0
3437 Rainstorm 12 [16] 5-9-13 (38) Mrs S Owen(5) 20/1:   3644 Classic Eagle 4 [2] 7-10-1 (40)(vis) Mr S Rees(5) 25/1:
3526 Paddys Rice 9 [14] 9-9-13 (35)(t)(3ow) Mr S J Edwards (0) 100/1:
3490 Waikiki Beach 11 [18] 9-10-4 (43)(bl) Mr A Quinn (5) 16/1:
3644 Sabot 4 [17] 7-10-7 (46) Mr M Sheridan(7) 50/1:   2887 Napper Blossom 37 [7] 3-9-7 (40) Miss C Stretton(5) 100/1:
2707] Rockette 772 [1] 5-9-10 (35) Mr K Burke(5) 100/1:   3202 Meteor Strike 32 [12] 6-10-5 (44)(t) Mr J Diment(5) 25/1: U
20 ran   Time 2m 01.3 (3.5)   (B A Whittaker)   B R Johnson Epsom, Surrey

---

3738

5.20 CAT CLUB CLAIMER DIV II 3YO+ (E)   1m rnd   Firm 10 +04 Fast
£2301   £708   £354   £177   3 yo rec 6 lb

3404 **VIRTUAL REALITY** 14 [8] J A R Toller 9-9-7 M Roberts 6/5: 0-0551: 9 b g Diamond Shoal - Warning   76
Bell (Bustino) Led, came stands side in str, in complete control when eased comfortably fnl 100y: nicely bckd,
best time of day: '99 Warwick wnr (class stks, rtd 91): '98 Bath & Salisbury wnr (h'caps, rtd 89): eff at 1m/
10f: acts on firm & gd, best without visor & runs well fresh: gd weight carrier, back to form from the front.
3355 **SUPER MONARCH** 16 [4] L A Dace 4-8-13 (bl) T G McLaughlin 20/1: 400002: 6 ch g Cadeaux   9   48
Genereux - Miss Fancy That (The Minstrel) Mid-div, went after wnr appr fnl 2f, easily outpcd: op 10/1, stiff
task at the weights, blnks reapplied: see 1542.
3559 **SATWA BOULEVARD** 7 [6] P Mitchell 5-8-8 (t) A Beech (5) 33/1: 020003: 5 ch m Sabrehill - Winnie   3½   35
Reckless (Local Suitor) Mid-div, eff 3f out, sn same pace: quick reapp, v stiff task, see 2043, 326.
3534 **SHONTAINE** 8 [2] Mrs L Stubbs 7-8-8 (t) S W Kelly (3) 40/1: 000004: Rcd in 2nd till fdd 2f out.   4   30
3490 **PRIVATE SEAL** 11 [7] 5-8-13 (t) G Baker (5) 50/1: 004005: Al towards rear: stiff task, t-strap.   1½   27
3332 **BONNIE DUNDEE** 17 [1] 4-8-4 (bl) D Kinsella (7) 33/1: 004566: Chsd ldrs till halfway: see 776.   1   16
3526 **NO EXTRAS** 9 [5] 10-9-9 S Whitworth 10/1 FAV: 116027: Rear, pushed along from halfway, sn btn: nk   34
well bckd: clrly not his form, see 3526 (10f here), 1690.
3559 **HUNAN SCHOLAR** 7 [3] 5-8-11 D R McCabe 50/1: 000008: Pulled hard, bhd from halfway: qck reapp.   15   0
8 ran   Time 1m 32.5 (0.5)   (G B Partnership)   J A R Toller Newmarket, Suffolk

---

3739

5.50 J HEAL CLASS STKS 3YO 0-60 (F)   7f rnd   Firm 10 -24 Slow
£2476   £707   £353

2974 **CRUISE** 33 [1] R Hannon 3-8-12 P Dobbs (5) 16/1: -05001: 3 ch c Prince Sabo - Mistral's Dancer   64
(Shareef Dancer) Led, rdn clr appr fnl 1f & ran on strongly: op 12/1, tchd 20/1: late '99 wnr at Lingfield
(auct mdn, rtd 70a): eff forcing the pace at 6/7f on firm, soft grnd & equitrack, sharp/undul trks.
3279 **SANGRA** 19 [4] N A Callaghan 3-8-9 (BL) J P Spencer 9/2: -42502: 3 b f El Gran Senor - Water Song   2   59
(Clever Trick) In tch, drvn appr fnl 1f, chsd wnr ins last but no impress: tchd 6/1: back to form in blnks,
eff without: goes on firm/fast grnd, return to 1m+ will suit: see 1632.
3561 **DUSKY VIRGIN** 7 [10] S Woodman 3-8-12 A Nicholls (3) 11/4 FAV: 402123: 3 b f Missed Flight - Rosy   4   54
Sunset (Red Sunset) Rear, styd on appr fnl 1f, nvr nr to chall: nicely bckd, qck reapp: see 3401 (8.5f, here).
3405 **MUFFIN MAN** 14 [2] M D I Usher 3-8-12 G Baker (5) 20/1: 004604: Handy, rdn & onepace appr fnl 1f.   2   50
3405 **WILLOW MAGIC** 14 [8] 3-8-9 P Doe 11/2: 343445: Pulled hard, chsd ldrs, fdd 2f out: see 1512, 234.   3   41
*3593 **MYTTONS AGAIN** 6 [5] J Bosley (7) 4/1: 063116: Trkd ldrs, keen, prsd wnr 2f out, blnks   nk   49
began slipping, lost action, eased: op 5/2, blnks reapplied: nvr to have been 2nd at worst & deserves compensation.
3269 **STRAND OF GOLD** 20 [7] 3-8-12 (bl) L Newman (3) 9/1: 505007: Chsd ldrs till 2f out: op 5/1 tho'   ½   42
shorter-priced stablemate of wnr: blnks reapplied, unproven beyond 5f: see 1220, 1181.
3263 **CORAL SHELLS** 20 [9] 3-8-9 (bl) C Rutter 50/1: 000068: Handy, wide, lost place appr fnl 2f: stiff task.   2½   34
3457 **MAJOR REBUKE** 12 [3] 3-8-12 (BL) I Mongan (5) 8/1: 002009: Mid-div, not travel well & btn 3f out: 3   31
op 5/1: blnkd, much better without 2786.
2919 **IN SEQUENCE** 35 [6] 3-8-9 G Parkin 20/1: 40-00: Dwelt, nvr in it: 10th, op 12/1, up in trip.   ¾   27
10 ran   Time 1m 22.2 (2.4)   (Heathavon Stables Ltd)   R Hannon East Everleigh, Wilts

Official Going: GOOD/FIRM (GOOD PLACES). Stalls: Inside, except 5f/2m - Stands Side.

3740 2.10 TATTERSALLS AUCT MDN 2YO (E) 1m rnd Good/Firm 32 -31 Slow
£3428 £1055 £527 £263

3444 **EMMA CLARE** 13 [1] J A Osborne 2-7-12 T Williams 7/4 FAV: 000241: 2 b f Namaqualand - Medicosma 59
(The Minstrel) Trckd ldrs, rdn/prog to chall fnl 2f, led dist, styd on well, rdn out: well bckd tho' op 5/4:
apprec this step up to 1m, mid dists may suit in time: acts on fast grnd & a sharp track.
2873 **HO PANG YAU** 38 [2] Miss L A Perratt 2-8-12 J Mackay (5) 3/1: 052: 2 b c Pivotal - La Cabrilla 2 67
(Carwhite) Led, rdn over 2f out, hdd dist, held by wnr & position accepted nr fin: op 4/1: styd longer 1m trip:
acts on fast grnd: nursery h'cap company may now suit best: see 2717.
3363 **SIR EDWARD BURROW** 16 [4] R F Fisher 2-8-3 J McAuley 20/1: 040003: 2 b c Distinctly North - hd 57$
Alalja (Entitled) Cl up, rdn/outpcd 2f out, kept on for press inside last: well clr rem: styd longer 1m trip
well, further should suit on this evidence: handles fast grnd: only mod form previously.
-- **TUPGILL CENTURION** [5] S E Kettlewell 2-8-9 D O'Donohoe 6/1: 4: Slowly away & well bhd, mod 9 47
gains fnl 2f: Emperor Jones gelding, Jan foal, cost 15,000gns, a first foal: dam a mdn: sire high class 1m/10f
performer: should apprec further in time: lost chance at start today.
3615 **THANKS MAX** 6 [3] 2-8-7 G Duffield 25/1: -05: Bhd, mod late prog: quick reapp, longer 1m trip. 1 43
3363 **EYES DONT LIE** 16 [6] 2-8-3 (BL) R Winston 16/1: 040006: Chsd ldrs, drvn/btn 3f out: first time ½ 38
blinks, no improvement: longer 1m trip: see 1359.
-- **DENISE BEST** [8] 2-8-0 P Bradley (5) 10/1: 7: Al bhd: op 3/1: March foal, cost IR 9,000gns. 6 24
722 **DUSTY DEMOCRAT** 159 [7] 2-8-3 S W Kelly (1) 5/1: 28: In tch, btn 3f out: 5 mth abs: btr 722 (5f, AW). 2 23
8 ran Time 1m 42.5 (5.0) (Mrs K Sherry) J A Osborne Lambourn, Berks

3741 2.40 STEWARTS CLASSIFIED STKS 3YO+ 0-65 (E) 1m4f Good/Firm 32 -12 Slow
£2954 £844 £422 3 yo rec 10lb

3379 **SLANEYSIDE** 15 [1] I Semple 3-8-7 G Duffield 4/1: -36001: 3 ch g Project Manager - Erneside (Lomond) 62
Led, rdn over 3f out & hdd over 2f out, switched & rallied gamely for press fnl 1f, led line, all out: op 6/1:
first win, jockey given a 2-day whip ban: ex Irish, plcd over 10f on soft grnd for J Bolger: cost current
connections 20,000gns: eff at 12f on fast & soft grnd: likes a sharp track: battled gamely today.
*3606 **CHAKA ZULU** 6 [2] W J Haggas 3-9-1 A Culhane 1/2 FAV: 311312: 3 b g Muhtarram - African Dance hd 69
(El Gran Senor) Cl up, rdn/led 3f out, drvn inside last & hdd on line: bckd tho' op 1/3: quick reapp.
3139 **LITTLE JOHN** 27 [3] Miss L A Perratt 4-9-3 (vis) J Mackay (5) 3/1: 252423: 4 b g Warrshan - dist 0
Silver Venture (Silver Hawk) Handy, rdn over 5f out, bhd/eased fnl 2f: mdn: see 1656.
3 ran Time 2m 35.9 (5.3) (Gordon McDowall) I Semple Carluke, S Lanarks

3742 3.10 FORTH AM HCAP 3YO+ 0-65 (F) 2m Good/Firm 32 -07 Slow [58]
£2873 £884 £442 £221 3 yo rec 14lb

*3588 **LORD ALASKA** 7 [5] J A R Toller 3-8-11 (55) S Whitworth 5/1: 005011: 3 b g Sir Harry Lewis - 64
Anchorage (Slip Anchor) Mid div, rdn/hdwy 4f out, led over 1f out & pulled clr under hands & heels riding inside
last, eased nr line: earlier scored at Folkestone (appr h'cap, first win): eff at 2m, could get further: acts on
fast grnd & a sharp/undul track: runs well fresh: won with something in hand here, hat-trick on the cards.
3348 **RIGADOON** 17 [1] M W Easterby 4-9-7 (51)(6ex) D O'Donohoe 9/1: 450462: 4 b g Be My Chief - Loucoum 5 53
(Iron Duke) Prom, led halfway & clr 5f out, hdd over 1f out, sn held: met an in-form rival: see 797 (C/D).
*3442 **OLD FEATHERS** 13 [9] J G FitzGerald 3-8-9 (53) G Duffield 9/1: 060013: 3 b g Hernando - 3 52
Undiscovered (Tap On Wood) Chsd ldrs, rdn/chall over 2f out, held by wnr fnl 1f: confirmed
improvement of latest: acts on fast & gd: see 3442 (mdn h'cap).
*3674 **NOTATION** 4 [7] D W Chapman 6-7-10 (26)(6ex)(2oh) Claire Bryan (5) 8/1: 050114: Chsd ldrs, styd 2 23
on onepace fnl 3f: op 6/1: qck reapp: stays 2m, see 3674 (12f).
3586 **SIRINNDI** 7 [12] 6-9-0 (44) S W Kelly (3) 7/4 FAV: 500625: Twds rear, hdwy 4f out, held fnl 2f: well bckd. 3 38
3511 **NORTHERN MOTTO** 11 [8] 7-9-2 (46) T E Durcan 8/1: 130436: Chsd ldrs halfway, btn over 2f out. 3½ 37
*3575 **SWANDALE FLYER** 8 [2] 8-7-10 (26)(6ex)(2oh) J McAuley 10/1: 050217: Handy, led after 4f till 2½ 15
halfway, btn 3f out: op 7/1: btr 3575 (mdn h'cap).
37 **LE SAUVAGE** 293 [11] 5-7-11 (26)(1ow) J Bramhill 25/1: 0560-8: Rear, hdwy 4f out, sn held: reapp, 7 10 9
mth jmps abs (plcd, rtd 87h, nov h'cap): rnr up in '99 (rtd 38a, auct mdn, unplcd on turf, rtd 27, h'cap).
3618 **EMBRYONIC** 6 [6] 8-10-0 (58) J Weaver 8/1: 060629: Mid div, eff 3f out, sn held: btr 3618. 11 32
3406 **PHASE EIGHT GIRL** 14 [10] 4-7-10 (26)(7oh) J Mackay (5) 50/1: -00060: Al bhd: 10th: see 2219. 10 0
3311 **SECONDS AWAY** 19 [3] 9-7-10 (26)(1oh) D Mernagh (1) 20/1: 433360: Led 4f, prom till halfway: 11th. 13 0
3501 **ALLOTROPE** 11 [4] 5-8-11 (41)(bl) A Culhane 14/1: 0-0000: Al bhd: 12th: see 2681. dist 0
12 ran Time 3m 28.8 (6.3) (Mrs Claire Smith) J A R Toller Newmarket, Suffolk

3743 3.40 CAPEL CURE NURSERY HCAP 2YO (C) 5f Good/Firm 32 +04 Fast [86]
£6288 £1935 £967 £483 Raced stands side

3101 **NIFTY ALICE** 29 [8] A Berry 2-9-7 (79) T E Durcan 8/1: 441001: 2 ch f First Trump - Nifty Fifty 83
(Runnett) Al handy, rdn/led inside last, held on well: best time of day, op 6/1: earlier scored here at
Musselburgh (auct mdn) & Ayr (nov auct stks): eff at 5f, 6f shld suit: acts on fast, gd/soft, sharp or gall
trk, likes Musselburgh: gd weight carrier: tough & geniune filly.
*3673 **VENDOME** 4 [3] J A Osborne 2-9-8 (80)(6ex) J Weaver 2/1 FAV: 003312: 2 b c General Monash - nk 83
Kealbra Lady (Petong) Led, rdn over 1f out & hdd inside last, kept on well for press, just held: hvly bckd.
3394 **PEYTO PRINCESS** 15 [2] C W Fairhurst 2-8-12 (70) J Fanning 4/1: 32243: 2 b f Bold Arrangement - hd 72
Bo' Babbity (Strong Gale) Trckd ldrs, rdn/switched to chall dist, just held nr line: nicely bckd: see 3394, 2045.
3632 **SHATIN DOLLYBIRD** 5 [5] Miss L A Perratt 2-9-1 (73) G Duffield 16/1: 331034: Rear, in tch, swtchd/ ¾ 73
drvn & styd on well inside last, not able to chall: op 12/1: see 2797 (nov auct stks).
3394 **SCREAMIN GEORGINA** 15 [1] 2-8-10 (68)(t) G Faulkner (3) 8/1: 021105: Chsd ldrs, drvn/held 1f out. ¾ 66
3228 **RENEE** 22 [9] 2-8-4 (62) J Mackay (5) 11/2: -35506: In tch, btn 1f out: see 2034. 4 50
3491 **MISS BRIEF** 12 [10] 2-8-12 (70) Joanna Badger (7) 10/1: 442007: In tch, btn over 1f out: op 8/1. ¾ 56
3346 **BOLD MCLAUGHLAN** 17 [6] 2-8-7 (65) D Mernagh (3) 10/1: 006548: Sn outpcd rear: see 700. 1½ 47
3589 **AMAMACKEMMUSH** 7 [7] 2-8-7 (65) F Lynch 12/1: 223529: Cl up, fdd fnl 2f: op 10/1: btr 3589. 1¾ 43

9 ran   Time 58.9 (1.4)   (Mrs Norma Peebles)   A Berry Cockerham, Lancs

3744	4.10 COMERACING MED AUCT MDN 3-4YO (F)	7f30y rnd Good/Firm 32 -30 Slow
	£2576 £736 £368 3 yo rec 5 lb	

3529 **JABUKA** 10 [6] J A R Toller 3-8-9 S Whitworth 6/4 FAV: 4321: 3 b f Shareef Dancer - Neptunalia (Slip Anchor) Trkd ldr, led 2f out, styd on well under hands & heels riding fnl 1f: nicely bckd tho' op evens: eff at 7f, 1m could suit: acts on firm & fast grnd, likes a sharp trk: straight forward task, can rate higher. **59**

3651 **FOUND AT LAST** 5 [5] J Balding 4-9-5 J Fanning 7/2: 243522: 4 b g Aragon - Girton (Balidar) Trkd ldrs, prog/ch over 1f out, rdn/no extra inside last: bckd, op 5/1: quick reapp: eff btwn 5/7f: see 3651 (5f). **2 58**

3593 **FOR HEAVENS SAKE** 7 [2] C W Thornton 3-9-0 (BL) Dean McKeown 11/4: 326023: 3 b g Rambo Dancer - Angel Fire (Nashwan) Led, rdn/hdd 2f out, held after: bckd, tho' op 9/4: blinks: see 3593 (C/D h'cap). **1½ 55**

3380 **CUTE CAROLINE** 15 [3] A Berry 4-9-0 (vis) T E Durcan 20/1: 230004: Chsd ldrs, ch over 1f out, sn no extra: drifted from 10/1: btr 2378, 2147 (blinks, 1m). **nk 49$**

1768 **HOUT BAY** 85 [1] 3-9-0 D O'Donohoe 9/2: 453005: In tch, rdn/btn 3f out: 12 week abs, ran as if something amiss here: btr 1354 (g/s, 6f). **21 22**

5 ran   Time 1m 29.3 (4.4)   (Mrs J Toller)   J A R Toller Newmarket, Suffolk

3745	4.40 MINERS HCAP DIV 1 3YO+ 0-60 (F)	1m rnd Good/Firm 32 -01 Slow	[60]
	£2002 £572 £286 3 yo rec 6 lb		

3708 **MAMMAS BOY** 3 [10] A Berry 5-9-3 (49) T E Durcan 8/1: 004601: 5 b g Rock City - Henpot (Alzao) Rear, switched & hdwy to chall dist, led ins last, rdn out: qck reapp: earlier landed hat-trick at Redcar (sell) & here at Musselburgh (2, clmrs): '99 wnr at Thirsk (sell) & again here at Musselburgh (clmr, rtd 62): '98 wnr at Doncaster (mdn h'cap) & Sandown (clmr, rtd 72): eff at 5/6f, now seems best suited by a sharp 7f/1m: acts on firm, hvy & any trk: loves Musselburgh: tried blnks, goes best without: suited by sell/clmrs, did well in a h'cap here. **54**

2412 **SHARP GOSSIP** 57 [4] J A R Toller 4-9-8 (54) S Whitworth 12/1: 000002: 2 b g College Chapel - Idle Gossip (Runnett) Mid div, hdwy to chall fnl 2f, op/briefly led 1f out, not pace of wnr nr fin: op 10/1, 8 wk abs: mdn: eff at 6f/1m on fast & soft grnd: see 1676. **½ 57**

3375 **GO THUNDER** 15 [8] D A Nolan 6-7-12 (30)(t) Iona Wands 20/1: -00053: 6 b g Nordico - Moving Off (Henbit) Handy, led over 5f out, rdn/hdd 1f out, kept on for press: bckd at long odds, op 33/1: ex-Irish, plcd once back in '98 (14f h'cap): mod British form subs: eff around sharp 1m on fast grnd. **½ 32**

3524 **AGIOTAGE** 10 [11] S C Williams 4-9-11 (57) G Faulkner (3) 4/1: 615544: Held up, prog/rdn & ch over 1f out, no extra inside last: see 3524, 2378. **1½ 56**

3574 **MAI TAI** 8 [7] 5-8-7 (39)(vis) Kimberley Hart 7/1: 566625: Rear, rdn/styd on fnl 2f, nrst fin: see 867. **1¾ 35**

3380 **LITTLE LES** 15 [6] 4-7-12 (30) J McAuley 33/1: 606406: Chsd ldrs 3f out, sn held: see 3139, 1655. **4 18**

3236 **RED WOLF** 22 [5] 4-8-9 (41) Dean McKeown 14/1: 003207: Led 3f, cl up till over 2f out: op 12/1. **3½ 22**

3623 **WARRING** 6 [1] 6-8-12 (44) R Brisland (5) 7/1: 034138: Chsd ldrs 6f: quick reapp: btr 3623, 3514. **1 23**

3344 **BROCTUNE GOLD** 17 [14] 9-8-6 (36)(2ow) A Culhane 10/1: 504059: Chsd ldrs 6f: see 1658. **½ 16**

3138 **BANDIDA** 7 [9] 6-7-10 (28)(1oh) P Bradley (0) 50/1: 060000: In tch, btn 2f out: 10th: see 3138, 1244. **1 4**

3188 **MASSEY** 24 [3] 4-9-1 (47)(VIS) G Duffield 20/1: 000000: Prom 6f: 11th: visor: see 752 (mdn, AW). **½ 22**

3362 **MYSTIC RIDGE** 17 [12] 6-10-0 (60) S W Kelly (3) 5/2 FAV: 400600: Towards rear, eff 3f out, no hdwy: 12th: bckd: likes to dominate, unable to do so here: see 476 (AW). **8 23**

3033 **PHILAGAIN** 31 [13] 3-8-5 (43) J Mackay (5) 10/1: 163040: Dwelt & al rear: 13th: see 3033, 2205. **nk 5**

4360} **LUBOHENRIK** 322 [1] 3-8-5 (43) F Lynch 66/1: 0000-0: Al bhd: 14th: reapp: h'cap bow: rtd 55 at best from 4 starts in '99 (mdn): bred to apprec 1m+. **5 0**

14 ran   Time 1m 40.1 (2.6)   (Mrs J M Berry)   A Berry Cockerham, Lancs

3746	5.10 MINERS HCAP DIV 2 3YO+ 0-60 (F)	1m rnd Good/Firm 32 +03 Fast	[60]
	£1988 £568 £284 3 yo rec 6 lb		

3527 **PACIFIC ALLIANCE** 10 [2] M Wigham 4-9-13 (59)(bl) Dean McKeown 5/1: 440031: 4 b g Fayruz - La Gravotte (Habitat) Made all, rdn & styd on well fnl 2f: op 4/1, gd time: '99 Lingfield (auct mdn) & Sandown wnr (h'cap, rtd 68a & 65, R Armstrong): rtd 73 in '98: suited by 1m, tried 10f: acts on firm, gd & eqtrk: well suited by reapp of blinks today, eff without: handles any track, likes to force the pace on a sharp one. **67**

3380 **SPIRIT OF KHAMBANI** 15 [11] M Johnston 3-8-4 (42) J Fanning 12/1: 425002: 3 ch f Indian Ridge - Khambani (Royal Academy) Mid div, rdn/styd on fnl 2f, no threat to wnr: op 14/1: see 2735. **2½ 44**

3534 **CLAIM GEBAL CLAIM** 9 [3] P Monteith 4-8-6 (38) V Halliday 8/1: 160323: 4 b g Ardkinglass - Infra Blue (Bluebird) Prom, rdn/onepace & held fnl 2f: likes to dominate: see 2780 (clmr, made all). **½ 39**

3574 **SAFFRON** 8 [12] D Shaw 4-8-10 (42) T Williams 6/1: 054364: Dwelt, rear, styd on fnl 2f, nrst fin. **1¼ 40**

3192 **CHINABERRY** 24 [6] 6-8-13 (45) D Mernagh (3) 8/1: 040025: Chsd wnr, fdd fnl 2f: see 3192, 299. **1¼ 40**

3593 **GRANITE CITY** 7 [8] 3-9-2 (54) A Culhane 8/1: 302166: Rear, mod late hdwy: btr 3103 (7f, mdn h'cap). **2 45**

3393 **DETROIT CITY** 15 [9] 5-8-3 (35) J Bramhill 5/1: 040007: Chsd ldrs 6f: see 1148. **¾ 25**

3652 **ITALIAN SYMPHONY** 5 [5] 6-9-10 (56)(vis) Joanna Badger (7) 3/1 FAV: 516508: Rear, hdwy 3f out, no prog fnl 2f: well bckd, tchd 4/1: quick reapp: see 3238 (7f). **hd 45**

3266 **STANDIFORD GIRL** 21 [4] 3-8-5 (43) P Fessey 16/1: 003249: Bhd fnl 3f: op 14/1: btr 2816 (clmr, AW). **3 26**

3574 **GYMCRAK FLYER** 8 [1] 9-8-8 (40)(vis) R Winston 13/2: 000050: Trkd ldrs 6f: 10th: op 11/2: see 2561. **2½ 18**

3083 **On Till Morning** 29 [10] 4-9-6 (52) F Lynch 16/1: —   **Megabyte** [14] 6-8-4 (36) O Pears 50/1:

249 **Time And Again** 241 [13] 4-7-10 (28)(1oh) Clare Bryan (5) 50/1:

13 ran   Time 1m 39.8 (2.3)   (Michael Wigham)   M Wigham Newmarket, Suffolk

Official Going GOOD/FIRM (GOOD in places). Stalls: Far Side.

3747

2.20 AXMINSTER APPR HCAP 3YO+ 0-80 (E)   5f str   Firm 17 +02 Fast   **[77]**
£2827   £870   £435   £217   3 yo rec 2 lb

3605 **AMERICAN COUSIN 6** [4] D Nicholls 5-7-12 (47) T Hamilton (5) 7/1: 000501: 5 b g Distand Relative - **51**
Zelda (Sharpen Up) Mid-div, switched/hdwy over 2f out, led dist, hung right ins last, drvn out, just held on:
tchd 11/1, gd time: qck reapp: below best prev this term & dropped down the weights: '99 wnr at Doncaster
(2, appr h'caps, tchd 63 at best): rnr-up in '98 for R Johnson Houghton (rtd 60): eff at 5/6f on firm, gd/soft
& fibresand: best without blnks, likes Doncaster: took advantage of a handy mark today.

3293 **WAFFS FOLLY 20** [17] D J S ffrench Davis 5-8-2 (51) A Beech 4/1 FAV: 003532: 5 b m Handsome   hd **54**
Sailor - Shirl (Shirley Heights) Prom, drvn appr fnl 1f, rdn & ran on strongly towards fin, not btn far: nicely
bckd & another sound run, can go one better soon: see 3293, 1082.

3587 **TORRENT 7** [14] D W Chapman 5-9-3 (66)(bl) (6ex) Lynsey Hanna (5) 5/1: 333133: 5 ch g Prince Sabo - 1 **66**
Maiden Pool (Sharpen Up) Front rank, chall ldr over 1f out, rdn/held well ins last: consistent, see 3587, 3562.

2230 **OARE PINTAIL 64** [16] R M Beckett 3-8-7 (58) G Gibbons (5) 25/1: 60-004: Cl-up, went on appr fnl   ¾ **57**
2f, hdd over 1f out, no extra well ins last: 9 wk abs, new stable: back to 5f, handles firm grnd: see 1345.

3587 **ABSOLUTE FANTASY 7** [2] 4-8-6 (55)(bl) D Kinsella (5) 14/1: 421205: Rear, rdn to impr appr fnl   ½ **53**
1f, ran on strongly ins last, nvr nrr: qck reapp: unsuited by this drop back to 5f, best at 6f+: see 3455.

*3229 **CHORUS 22** [9] 3-9-10 (75)(vis) Cheryl Nosworthy (7) 12/1: 323216: Handy, rdn to chall 2f out, 1¾ **69**
fdd fnl 1f: shade btr 3229 (gd, first time visor).

3631 **DIAMOND GEEZER 5** [6] 4-9-7 (70) R Smith (3) 8/1: 422407: In tch, rdn/btn appr fnl 1f: qck reapp.   ½ **63**
3436 **SHADY DEAL 13** [15] 4-8-3 (52) K Dalgleish 9/2: 221348: Prom, rdn/lost tch ins last: btr 2555 (gd/soft). 1 **42**
3562 **BALIDARE 8** [13] 3-7-10 (47)(13oh) Michael Doyle (5) 66/1: 000009: Dwelt, sn in tch, drvn/fdd fnl 2f.   ½ **36**
3455 **CALANDRELLA 13** [1] 7-7-10 (45)(8oh) G Sparkes (3) 50/1: 633000: Prom to halfway, 10th: see 2428. shd **34**
3493 **ANSTAND 12** [3] 5-7-10 (45) M Mathers (2) 20/1: 600000: Handy, wknd qckly fnl 2f, 11th: drop in trip. hd **34**
2977 **FARRIERS GAMBLE 34** [11] 4-8-6 (55) P Dobbs 33/1: 0-500: Dwelt, nvr dngrs, 12th: h'cap bow.   ¾ **42**
3405 **AROGANT PRINCE 15** [5] 3-8-3 (54) Jonjo Fowle (3) 33/1: 040300: Led till after halfway, wknd, 13th. hd **41**
3619 **River Tern 6** [8] 7-8-6 (55) P Fitzsimons (2) 20/1:   2716 **Perigeux 45** [7] 4-8-13 (62) C Catlin (5) 14/1:
3562 **Mangus 8** [10] 6-8-2 (51) D Glennon (5) 20/1:   3293 **Endymion 20** [12] 3-8-10 (61) D McGaffin (3) 16/1:
17 ran   Time 1m 00.54 (0.74)   (Middleham Park Racing)   D Nicholls Sessay, N.Yorks.

3748

2.50 EBF FILLIES MDN DIV 1 2YO (D)   7f str   Firm 17 -08 Slow
£5044   £1552   £776   £358

3020 **FLIGHT OF FANCY 32** [8] Sir Michael Stoute 2-8-11 W Ryan 1/4 FAV: 21: 2 b f Sadler's Wells - **102+**
Phantom Gold (Machiavellian) Led after 2f, shkn up 2f out, easily qcknd clr, impress: hvly bckd at odds on:
earlier rnr-up on debut: Mar foal, dam a high-class mid-dist 3yo performer: eff over a stiff/gall 7f, 1m will
suit: acts on firm & gd: smart performance, will imprv further & lks capable of winning in List/Gr company.

2174 **ROOFER 67** [11] M R Channon 2-8-11 Craig Williams 12/1: 542: 2 b f Barathea - Castlerahn (Thatching) 6 **84**
Led early, remained chasing ldr till no extra over fnl 1f: 9 wk abs: gd run, stays 7f on firm: caught a tartar.

-- **RANIN** [3] E A L Dunlop 2-8-11 R Hills 14/1: 3: 2 b f Unfuwain - Nafhaat (Roberto) 1 **82**
Waited with, switched/prog appr fnl 1f, styd on nicely ins last: Feb foal, half-sister to a decent miler, dam
scored over 12f: stays 7f on firm grnd: encouraging debut, will improve, prob over 1m.

3449 **SALTWOOD 13** [5] B W Hills 2-8-11 M Hills 20/1: -04: Mid-div, kept on for press ins last, no threat. 3½ **76**
-- **CLIMBING ROSE** [4] C Rutter 33/1: 5: Rcd keenly, chsd ldrs till no extra well over 1f out: ½ **75**
op 16/1: half-sister to numerous wnrs, incl a useful miler & a sprinter, dam a smart/speedy juv: with R Charlton.

3292 **PUFFIN 20** [9] 2-8-11 K Darley 12/1: -56: Front rank, rdn/fdd fnl 2f: shade btr 3292.   ¾ **74**
-- **TRUST IN PAULA** [2] 2-8-11 R Cochrane 20/1: 7: Rear, gd hdwy halfway, wknd qckly appr fnl 1f,   ¾ **73**
eased when btn: 21,000gns Apr foal, half-sister to a wnr abroad, dam scored in the USA: with D Haydn Jones.

3292 **FLASH OF LIGHT 20** [7] 2-8-11 J Reid 33/1: -08: Handy, wknd qckly fnl 2f: op 20/1: see 3292. 4 **66**
-- **GOODGOLLYMISSMOLLY** [1] 2-8-11 G Bardwell 100/1: 9: Keen in mid-div, lost tch & hung left 6 **56**
over 2f out: highly tried on debut: Mar first foal, dam modest: with M Allen.

-- **SOLAR FLARE** [10] 2-8-11 J Fortune 14/1: 0: Prom to halfway, sn bhd, 10th: op 10/1: May foal, 7 **45**
half-sister to a couple of 1m 2yo scorers: dam related to sev wnrs in the States: with J Gosden, shld do better.
10 ran   Time 1m 27.24 (1.74)   (The Queen)   Sir Michael Stoute Newmarket.

3749

3.20 DICK POOLE FILLIES COND STKS 2YO (B)   6f str   Firm 17 -19 Slow
£9252   £3421   £1710   £777

*3449 **TEMPTING FATE 13** [3] J W Hills 2-8-12 M Hills 7/4: -211: 2 b f Persian Bold - West Of Eden **103**
(Crofter) Dwelt, sn in tch, smooth hdwy to lead over 1f out, drvn out: well bckd: earlier scored at Newbury
(fill mdn): 27,000gns half-sister to juv wnrs over 5f/1m: eff over a stiff/gall 6f on firm & fast grnd, 7f shld
suit in time: mostly fresh: tough, useful & consistent, can win more races.

3720 **INNIT 5** [4] M R Channon 2-8-12 Craig Williams 14/1: 434002: 2 b f Distinctly North - Tidal Reach   ¾ **99**
(Kris S) Chsd ldrs, rdn 3f out, switched & ran on well fnl 1f, not reach wnr: qck reapp: see 3720, 2687.

*3492 **ALSHADIYAH 12** [1] J Dunlop 2-8-12 R Hills 11/10 FAV: 13: 2 gr f Danzig - Shadarra (Shadeed) nk **98**
Rcd keenly, trkd ldrs, led after halfway, hdd 2f out, drvn/held well ins last: nicely bckd tho' op 10/11:
shld apprec a step up to 7f now: see 3492.

3425 **MILLENIUM PRINCESS 13** [2] R Hannon 2-8-12 J Fortune 11/2: -12624: Led early, remained 2 **92**
with ldrs till fdd appr fnl 1f: btr 3425.

3175 **MYHAT 25** [5] 2-8-9 M Roberts 66/1: 223265: Rear, nvr dngrs: stiff task: see 2714. 1¾ **82**
5 ran   Time 1m 14.26 (2.16)   (Michael Kerr-Dineen & Partners)   J W Hills Upper Lambourn, Berks.

3750

3.50 EBF FILLIES LOCHSONG HCAP 3YO+ 0-95 (C)   7f str   Firm 17 +15 Fast   **[88]**
£12057   £3710   £1855   £927   3 yo rec 5 lb

3207 **CREAM TEASE 23** [8] D J S ffrench Davis 3-8-8 (73) L Newman (3) 25/1: -00001: 3 b f Pursuit Of Love - **78**
Contralto (Busted) Prom, went on after halfway, kept on strongly for press ins last, drvn out: v fast time:
unplcd prev this term: '99 wnr here at Salisbury (fill mdn, tchd 85): eff around 7f on firm & gd grnd: has tried
blnks, best without: handles a stiff/gall trk & clrly goes best here at Salisbury.

3362 **APLOY 17** [12] R F Johnson Houghton 3-9-7 (72)(10w)(VIS) R Cochrane 6/1: 445122: 3 b f Deploy - Amidst ½ **76**
(Midyan) Front rank, chall wnr appr fnl 1f, held cl-home: op 8/1, sound run in 1st time visor: win sn: see 2978.

3130 **RENDITION** 27 [10] W J Haggas 3-9-10 (89) F Norton 9/2 FAV: -11303: 3 b f Polish Precedent - Rensaler1¾ 90
(Stop The Music) Bhd, switched & ran on over 2f out, no extra well ins last: see 2003, 1308.

*3317 **BEADING** 19 [9] J W Hills 3-8-6 (71)(t) M Hills 9/1: 002514: In tch, eff/switched appr fnl 1f, styd ½ 71
on ins last, no dngr: op 7/1: remains in gd form, see 3317 (1m).

3315 **KARAMEG** 19 [13] 4-9-11 (85) A Beech (5) 13/2: 042205: Rcd keenly cl-up, fdd ins last: top-weight. 1¼ 83

3643 **NATALIE JAY** 5 [14] 4-8-9 (69) Craig Williams 10/1: 430106: Prom, eff when short of room over hd 67
2f out, no extra well ins last: op 8/1: qck reapp: needs a return to 1m+: see 3422.

3160 **QUEENS BENCH** 26 [11] 3-8-11 (73) J Reid 10/1: 400567: Led to halfway, remnd prom, rdn/btn fnl 1f. nk 73

*3613 **BE MY WISH** 6 [5] 5-7-13 (59)(bl) R Ffrench 5/1: 322518: Rear, nvr a factor: qck reapp: btr 3613 (6f). nk 56

3622 **MADAME JONES** 6 [6] 5-7-10 (56)(3oh) K Dalgleish (5) 50/1: 0-0059: Handy, then fnl 2f: qck reapp. 2½ 49

3597 **RICH IN LOVE** 7 [4] 6-9-10 (84) R Hills 20/1: 100500: Al twrds rear, fin 10th: qck reapp: see 3597. 5 69

3405 **BELIEVING** 15 [2] 3-7-11 (62) G Bardwell 33/1: 460000: Nvr dngrs, 11th: see 751. nk 47

3010 **EFFERVESCENT** 32 [3] 3-8-7 (72) K Darley 11/1: 234130: Rcd keenly cl-up, wknd qckly after 2½ 53
halfway: tchd 14/1: see 3010, 2421.

3334 **MADAM ALISON** 18 [1] 4-9-9 (83) J Fortune 12/1: 313150: Al well bhd, 13th: twice below 2890 (1m). 2 60

3163 **ALPHILDA** 26 [7] 3-8-9 (74) W Ryan 20/1: 340300: Lost tch halfway, t.o. in 14th: see 3163. 23 21

14 ran Time 1m 25.67 (0.17) (Badgers Holt) D J S ffrench Davis Letcombe Regis, Oxon.

3751	4.20 FESTIVAL COND STKS 3YO+ (C)		1m6f Firm 17 -06 Slow
	£6322 £2398 £1199 £545	3 yo rec 12lb	Flag start

3106 **CHURLISH CHARM** 28 [8] R Hannon 5-9-7 J Reid 13/8 FAV: 032361: 5 b h Niniski - Blushing Storm 111
(Blushing Groom) Settled off pace, drvn 3f out, strong run fnl 2f to lead nr fin, drvn out: well bckd: plcd thrice in
Group company prev this term: '99 York wnr (Gr 2 Yorkshire Cup, rtd 115), unplcd in Ascot Gold Cup: '99 wnr at
Newmarket (mdn), Goodwood (stks) & Newbury (h'cap, rtd 104 at best): eff at 12/14f, prob may need best suited by 2m:
acts on firm & gd, likes gd/soft & soft: runs well fresh: smart entire,
can rate more highly & holds solid claims in next week's Doncaster Cup, esp with any cut in the ground.

3509 **LIGHTNING ARROW** 11 [1] J L Dunlop 4-9-8 K Darley 9/4: 241222: 4 b g Silver Hawk - Strait Lane nk 111
(Chieftain II) Front rank, went on over 3f out, drvn & strongly pressed appr fnl 1f, collared cl-home: another
fine run, v tough & useful gelding: eff at 10/14f: see 2803.

3565 **MOWBRAY** 8 [5] P F l Cole 5-9-1 (t) R Cochrane 3/1: 604403: 5 b g Opening Verse - Peppy Raja (Raja 3 100
Baba) Led & sn clr, hdd over 3f out, no extra appr dist: clr rem, op 5/2: fine eff up in grade: see 3058 (h'cap).

*2963 **SHEER SPIRIT** 34 [4] D R C Elsworth 3-8-0 (t) N Pollard 8/1: 314: Chsd ldrs, eff 5f out, rdn/fdd 9 87$
fnl 2f: up in trip/grade: see 2963 (12f mdn).

3479 **TRISTACENTURY** 12 [6] 7-9-1 R Cochrane 100/1: 542445: Handy, lost tch halfway: stiff task: see 3230. 15 75$

-- **SILENT COVE** 3 [3] 3-8-5 W Ryan 20/1: -106: Al towards rear: British bow, earlier won on hd 77
debut at San Siro (12f stks, gd): with J L Dunlop.

2691 **WILDERNESS** 47 [2] 3-7-12 K Dalgleish (5) 150/1: -0-07: Al well bhd, t.o.: 7 wk abs, modest form. dist 40

3961} **FLOTSAM** 349 [7] 4-9-1 L Newman (3) 150/1: -0-8: Keen, lost tch halfway t.o.: new stable, no form. dist 0

8 ran Time 3m 01.3 (3.3) (Mohamed Suhail) R Hannon East Everleigh, Wilts.

3752	4.50 EBF FILLIES MDN DIV 2 2YO (D)	7f str	Firm 17 -05 Slow
	£5024 £1546 £773 £386		

3420 **UP ON POINTS** 14 [5] R Hannon 2-8-11 P Dobbs (5) 11/2: 21: 2 ch f Royal Academy - Champagne 91
N Roses (Chief Singer) Front rank, rdn to chall dist, sn led, drvn out: 15,000gns Apr foal, dam a 7f wnr:
eff over a stiff 7f on fast/firm, 1m shld suit: progressive, can win again.

3459 **NAFISAH** 13 [8] B Hanbury 2-8-11 R Hills 2/1 FAV: -22: 2 ch f Lahib - Alyakkh (Sadler's Wells) 1 87
Led, hdd dist, drvn & sn not pace of wnr: nicely bckd: acts on firm/fast grnd, deserves to win similar: see 3459.

-- **DEAR DAUGHTER** 7 [7] Sir Michael Stoute 2-8-11 J Reid 7/1: 3: 2 ch f Polish Precedent - Darayna ½ 86
(Shernazar) Handy, rdn & styd on stdly ins last: 38,000gns Mar foal, half-sister to a juv wnr abroad, dam related
to serv smart wnrs: eff at 7f, 1m will suit: acts on firm & a stiff/gall trk: encouraging debut, improve & win sn.

-- **PELAGIA** 4 [4] R Hannon 2-8-11 L Newman (3) 8/1: 4: Rear, gd hdwy appr fnl 1f, hung right/no extra ¾ 84
appr fnl 1f: half-sister to high-class French juv Lady Of Chad, dam well related: with R Hannon, promising.

-- **HEAD IN THE CLOUDS** [10] 2-8-11 K Darley 4/1: 5: V slow to start, gd hdwy after halfway, held 1¼ 81+
well ins last: May foal, full-sister to high-class mid-dist performer Millenary, dam scored over 7f: lost
all chance at start here, will learn from this & improve for J L Dunlop.

-- **KAZEEM** [3] 2-8-11 M Hills 11/2: 6: Prom, drvn/onepcd appr fnl 1f: bckd 9/1: Feb foal, half- 4 73
sister to a 7f juv scorer, dam won over 1m: with B W Hills, shld improve at 1m.

3333 **PENNY FARTHING** 18 [9] 2-8-11 C Rutter 33/1: -07: Rear, nvr a factor: see 3333. 3½ 66

2182 **ELA DARLIN MOU** 67 [6] 2-8-11 M Roberts 66/1: 08: Prom to halfway, wknd: 9 wk abs: see 2182. 1 64

3359 **GIRL BAND** 17 [1] 2-8-11 (VIS) Craig Williams 16/1: 0609: Prom 4f, sn lost tch: visored. 4 56

-- **BALMAINE** [2] 2-8-11 J Fortune 14/1: 0: Al well bhd, 10th: Apr foal, half-sister to a 6f juv scorer: ½ 55
dam 7f/1m Gr 2 wnr: with J Gosden, shld be capable of better in time.

3096 **LIFFORD LADY** 29 [11] 2-8-11 A McGlone 66/1: 00: Handy, wknd rapidly fnl 3f, 11th: highly tried. ½ 54

11 ran Time 1m 27.09 (1.59) (Vernon Carl Matalon) R Hannon East Everleigh, Wilts.

3753	5.20 WINTERBOURNE HCAP 3YO+ 0-70 (E)	1m str	Firm 17 -06 Slow	[70]
	£3224 £992 £496 £248	3 yo rec 6 lb		

*3188 **WITH A WILL** 24 [8] H Candy 6-9-10 (66) C Rutter 6/1: 331411: 6 b g Rambo Dancer - Henceforth (Full 70
Of Hope) Rear, switched/prog over 2f out, ran on strongly to lead cl-home, drvn out: earlier won twice at
Windsor (class stks & h'cap): back in '98 won at Kempton (appr h'cap) & Lingfield, (rtd 62): eff at 1m, stays
10f well: acts on firm/fast, likes gd, gd/soft & an easy trk, esp Windsor: proving v tough & consistent.

3663 **THIHN** 4 [14] J L Spearing 5-8-8 (50) A Beech (5) 12/1: 036002: 5 ch g Machiavellian - Hasana hd 53
(Private Account) Bhd, prog after halfway, led well over 1f out, styd on well, collared nr fin: qck reapp:
gd run on this drop back to 1m: mdn: eff at 1m/10f on firm & soft: see 1395.

*3623 **MULLAGHMORE** 6 [15] M Kettle 4-8-10 (52)(6ex) L Newman (3) 7/1: 000513: 4 b g Petardia - Comfrey 1½ 52
Glen (Glenstal) Rear, rdn & gd hdwy appr fnl 2f, kept on ins last, nvr nrr: qck reapp: in fine form, see 3623.

3362 **GREEN GOD** 17 [18] C G Cox 4-9-2 (58) J Reid 10/1: 050054: Front rank, rdn & keeping on when 1¾ 55
short of room fnl 1f, sn held: tchd 16/1: eff at 1m, handles firm & soft: see 1542.

3422 **DANIELLA RIDGE** 14 [12] 4-9-0 (56) J Fortune 9/1: -00025: Cl-up, onepcd appr fnl 1f: btr 3422 (C/D). 1¾ 50

3334 **ITS MAGIC** 18 [12] 4-10-0 (70)(bl) R Cochrane 7/1: 062066: Dwelt, gd late hdwy, nvr nrr: top-weight. ½ 63

3445 **KNOBBLEENEEZE** 13 [4] 10-8-2 (44)(vis) M Mathers (7) 14/1: 524167: Handy, rdn/fdd fnl 2f: 2½   33
won here over 7f in 3294 (h/h appr h'cap).
3623 **JESSINCA** 6 [17] 4-8-5 (47) F Norton 12/1: 142208: Prom, swtchd/eff over 2f out, sn held: qck reapp.   1   34
3455 **SCISSOR RIDGE** 13 [5] 8-8-2 (44) G Bardwell 33/1: 605059: With ldr, rdn/lost tch 2f out: best at 6/7f.   2½   27
3578 **VILLAGE NATIVE** 8 [16] 7-8-9 (51)(bl) P Dobbs (5) 20/1: 006200: Rear, late gains, no dngr, 10th.   nk   34
283 **BARRYS DOUBLE** 237 [11] 3-8-7 (55) P Fitzsimons (5) 25/1: 040-40: Nvr a threat, 11th: 8 month   hd   38
abs: new stable, prev with C W Fairhurst, now with P Burgoyne, see 181.
3390 **BROWNING** 6 [2] 5-9-4 (60) K Darley 7/2 FAV: 200-20: Led, hdd well over 1f out, wknd qckly, fin   ½   42
12th: op 9/2: prob unsuited by this drop in trip but better expected after a promising reapp in 3390 (10f).
3708 **REDOUBTABLE** 3 [7] 9-9-12 (68) M Roberts 12/1: 143050: Al towards rear, 13th: qck reapp.   1½   47
3227 **FIONN DE COOL** 22 [13] 9-8-3 (45) A McGlone 11/1: -00530: Al rear, 14th: btr 3227 (gd).   2   20
3580 **Mind The Silver** 8 [9] 3-8-8 (56) Jonjo Fowle (5) 20/1: 3586 **Sibertigo** 7 [10] 4-8-3 (45)(BL) R Ffrench 33/1:
3188 **Fuegian** 24 [3] 5-9-1 (57) K Dalgleish (5) 20/1:   3663 **My Little Man** 4 [6] 5-8-6 (48) N Pollard 33/1:
18 ran   Time 1m 40.95 (1.85)   (Henry Candy)   H Candy Wantage, Oxon.

Official Going TURF: GOOD/FIRM (FIRM Back Str). AW: Standard. Stalls: AW - Outside; Turf: Str Crse - Far Side; Rnd - Out.

3754   2.00 GATWICK MDN 3YO+ (D)   1m3f106y   Firm -04   -39 Slow
£2892   £890   £445   £222   3 yo rec 10lb

3324 **ZEYAARAH** 19 [3] M P Tregoning 3-8-6 R Perham 15/8 JT FAV: 30-31: 3 ch f Rahy - Princess Haifa   82
(Mr Prospector) Led, rdn clr appr fnl 1f, eased considerably: well bckd, slow time, val 6L+: plcd on debut last
term (rtd 86): eff at 12f on firm & gd grnd, sharp/undul or gall tracks: improved from the front: progressive filly.
-- **DISTANT COUSIN** [6] H R A Cecil 3-8-11 T Quinn 3/1: 2: 3 b c Distant Relative - Tinaca (Manila)   3½   80
Held up, shkn up ent str, styd on to go 2nd bef fnl 1f, nvr any ch with wnr: drifter from 5/4 on debut: half-brother
to a modest NH performer: eff at 12f, likely to apprec further: handles firm grnd & should win a mdn on this evidence.
3381 **BREEZE HOME** 15 [4] C M Kinane 4-9-7 M Fenton 9/1: 543D: 4 b g Homo Sapien - Poppy's Pride   7   62
(Uncle Pokey) Rcd in 2nd till 4f out, onepace after: fin 3rd, disqualified for reportedly carrying 8lbs less than
allocated: longer trip today, will appreciate a more galloping track.
3125 **MOUJEEDA** 27 [5] W Jarvis 3-8-6 S Sanders 15/8 JT FAV: -50433: Prom went 2nd ent straight, sn rdn,   1¼   63
fdd appr fnl 1f: fin 4th, plcd 3rd, bckd: needs a return to h'caps.
-- **TOMS DEAL** [1] 6-9-2 A Nicholls (3) 66/1: 4: Al bhd, t.o.: fin 5th, plcd 4th, Flat bow, hdles abs, no form. *dist*   0
3517 **TOPMAN** 11 [2] 3-8-11 T G McLaughlin 66/1: 0-05: Slow away, pulled hard, nvr in it, t.o.: fin 6th, plcd 5th.   0
6 ran   Time 2m 27.48 (4.08)   (Sheikh Ahmed Al Maktoum)   M P Tregoning Lambourn, Berks

3755   2.30 ARENA LEISURE HCAP 3YO+ 0-70 (E)   2m   Firm -04   -37 Slow   [58]
£3052   £872   £436   3 yo rec 14lb

3588 **ESTABLISHED** 7 [6] J R Best 3-7-13 (43) A Polli (3) 7/1: 550131: 3 b g Not In Doubt - Copper Trader   48
(Faustus) Waited with, imprvd 3f out, hard rdn appr fnl 1f, kept on gamely to lead well ins last: op 10/1: slow
time, qk reapp: earlier won at Nottingham (h'cap): unplcd in '99 (h'cap, rtd 49, prev with H Candy): improved
since stepped up to 2m: acts on firm/fast grnd, sharp/undul or gall tracks, without blinks: win more staying h'caps.
*3448 **GOLD MILLENIUM** 13 [12] C A Horgan 6-9-2 (46) T Quinn 9/1: 136312: 6 gr g Kenmare - Gold   ½   49
Necklace (Golden Fleece) Early ldr, went on again appr fnl 2f, rdn below dist, hdd towards fin: op 7/1,
clr rem: clearly improved since stepped up to 2m: acts on firm & gd grnd: see 3448.
1996 **LEGGY LADY** 75 [2] J A R Toller 4-9-5 (43) A Nicholls (3) 7/1: 04-053: 4 b f Sir Harry Lewis - Lady   3   44
Minstrel (Tudor Music) Held up, kept on well fnl 2f, nvr nr to chall: 11 week abs: thoro' styr, should win a race.
3625 **FAST FORWARD FRED** 6 [14] L Montague Hall 9-9-6 (50) A Clark 8/1: 003524: Prom, rdn to chase   3   49
ldr appr fnl 2f, sn onepace: quick reapp, shade btr 3625, see 3560.
3260 **REMEMBER STAR** 21 [11] 7-7-13 (29) J Quinn 14/1: -43225: Handy, prog under press when slightly   1½   27
hmpd 2f out, same pace: back up in trip: consistent this term for one so lowly rated, see 3260.
*3348 **BEAUCHAMP MAGIC** 17 [4] 5-8-1 (31) G Baker (7) 6/1 FAV: 301116: Bhd, prog when not clr run 2f   ½   29
out, kept on, nvr dangerous: set a lot to do, see 3348.
3447 **PIPS BRAVE** 13 [18] 4-8-7 (37) D Holland 25/1: 015067: Chsd ldrs, no extra ent fnl 2f: longer trip.   ½   34
3448 **FANDANGO DREAM** 13 [10] 4-8-7 (37) S Sanders 14/1: 413558: Midfield, gd prog under press 3f out,   1   33
fdd fnl 1f: drop back to 2m may suit: see 2656.
3424 **OUT ON A PROMISE** 14 [15] 8-9-0 (44) D R McCabe 10/1: 001049: Sn led, hdd appr fnl 2f, btn & eased.   nk   40
3217 **RED CANYON** 22 [7] 3-9-4 (62) M Fenton 14/1: 234040: Pld hard, nvr in it: 10th, longer trip.   5   54
3434 **ZINCALO** 13 [9] 4-9-10 (54) P Robinson 12/1: 133600: Nvr dngrs: 16th, tow 25/1, top-weight, see 1874 (14f).   0
3434 **GALAPINO** 13 [3] 7-9-4 (48)(bl) R Mullen 8/1: 050520: Dwelt, al well bhd: last, reportedly disliked firm grnd.   0
1465 **Red Bordeaux** 99 [13] 5-8-10 (40) P Doe 14/1:   3434 **Martha Reilly** 13 [19] 4-8-1 (31) A Mackay 20/1:
3447 **Old School House** 13 [1] 7-8-3 (33) Paul Eddery 20/1:3448 **Stand Aside** 13 [20] 4-9-4 (48)(bl) J P Spencer 14/1:
2452 **Wild Colonial Boy** 56 [5] 5-8-3 (33) M Henry 25/1:   3838 **Laguna Bay** 358 [8] 6-8-10 (40) G Carter 33/1:
18 ran   Time 3m 30.52 (5.32)   (Teapot Lane Partnership)   J R Best Hucking, Kent

3756   3.00 PETTICOAT CLASSIFIED STKS 3YO+ 0-65 (E)   1m aw rnd   Standard   Inapplicable
£2786   £796   £398   3 yo rec 6 lb

3318 **LAKOTA BRAVE** 19 [4] C N Allen 6-9-3 (t) G Hind 16/1: 0/641: 6 ch g Anshan - Pushinia (Pharly)   75a
Trckd ldrs going well, qcknd to lead appr fnl 1f, easily went clr: op 12/1 on AW bow: lightly rcd on turf & has
had several training probs (incl broken jaw): eff at 1m on fibresand in a t-strap: likely to win again on AW.
3269 **VERDURA** 21 [1] G A Butler 3-8-8 (t) D Holland 12/1: -64002: 3 b f Green Desert - Spirit Of The   6   62a
Wind (Little Current) Cl up, led after halfway till bef fnl 1f, easily outpcd by wnr: AW bow, blnks omitted,
t-strap applied: has apprec a drop back in trip: prob handles equitrack.
3465 **SEEKING UTOPIA** 12 [8] S P C Woods 3-8-8 T Quinn 5/1: 40P033: 3 b f Wolfhound - Sakura Queen   1¼   60a
(Woodman) Dwelt, struggling till improved 3f out, ch appr fnl 1f, sn onepace: back in trip on AW bow.
3585 **ASSURED PHYSIQUE** 7 [5] C E Brittain 3-8-11 P Robinson 12/1: 655604: In tch till 2f out: quick   2½   58a
reapp, AW bow: further likely to suit, see 1770.
3499 **TEOFILIO** 12 [7] 6-9-3 (bl) T G McLaughlin 13/8 FAV: 230045: Chsd ldrs, ch ent str, fdd bef dist: see 594.   ½   57a

*3498 **CANADIAN APPROVAL 12** [6] 4-9-9 (BL) M Tebbutt 5/1: 114016: V reluctant to enter stalls, wide, al bhd: new stable: tried blinks, appeared to run to form! will have to pass a stalls test before racing again. ¾ **61a**
3622 **BORDER GLEN 6** [3] 4-9-3 (vis) A Nicholls (3) 8/1: 500537: Led till after halfway, sn btn: tchd 12/1. *12* **35a**
2942 **SUPERCHIEF 35** [2] 5-9-3 (tvi) S Sanders 7/1: 150008: Cl up till 4f out: visor reapplied, see 596. *nk* **34a**
8 ran Time 1m 37.93 (1.73) (Newmarket Connections Ltd) C N Allen Newmarket, Suffolk

3757

3.30 OAKS PUB SELLER 2YO (G) 6f Firm -04 -34 Slow
£1960 £560 £260

3615 **MAID OF ARC 6** [12] M L W Bell 2-8-6 M Fenton 4/1 JT FAV: 244631: 2 b f Patton - Holy Speed (Afleet) Held up, prog going well but short of room appr fnl 2f, switched & hdwy bef dist, switched again to lead ent fnl 1f, drvn out: slow time, bght for 6,600gns, qk reapp: eff at 6/7f: acts on firm/fast grnd, sharp tracks. **61**
3639 **LEGGIT 5** [7] M R Channon 2-8-6 T Quinn 4/1 JT FAV: 00052: 2 b f Night Shift - Scales Of Justice (Final Straw) Mid-div, rdn ent fnl 2f, kept on to chall dist, held fnl 100y: clr rem, qk reapp: claimed for £5,000 & reportedly joins A McNae: ran well, eff at 6f on firm grnd: shown enough to win a seller. ¾ **58**
2818 **TROUBADOUR GIRL 41** [6] M A Jarvis 2-8-6 P Robinson 16/1: 0003: 2 b f Clantime - Nilu (Ballad Rock) Cl up, led after 3f till 1f out, onepace: 6 week abs: stays 6f on firm grnd. *2½* **50**
3388 **DISTANT DAWN 15** [9] B R Millman 2-8-6 (vis) G Hind 12/1: 026004: In tch, prog under press 2f out, same pace inside last: clr rem: stiff task back in trip, poss handles firm & hvy grnd. *1* **47**
3204 **DESIRE ME 23** [11] 2-8-6 J Quinn 11/2: 505: Wide, rear, improved 2f out, wknd fnl 1f: up in trip. *3* **38**
3525 **SONG N DANCE 10** [2] 2-8-6 R Perham 7/1: -056: With ldrs till wknd quickly inside last: op 5/1. *shd* **38**
3387 **SAORSIE 15** [4] 2-8-11 R Mullen 16/1: -007: Detached, mod late hdwy: op 12/1. *nk* **42**
3388 **MARGARITA 15** [5] 2-8-6 (BL) J Tate 7/1: -00058: Sn chsd ldrs, wknd 2f out: op 10/1: blnks. *1¾* **31**
2772 **BONNYELLA 42** [1] 2-8-6 D Sweeney 13/2: 59: Mid-div, lost place 2f out: 6 week abs. *2½* **25**
3307 **FOREVER FABULOUS 19** [3] 2-8-11 M Tebbutt 14/1: 60: Handy till appr fnl 2f: 10th, op 10/1. ¾ **27**
3582 **SIZE DOESNT MATTER 7** [8] 2-8-11 A Polli (3) 20/1: 0300: Chsd ldrs, drvn/btn/short of room 2f out: 11th. ¾ **25**
3443 **BOSRA BADGER 13** [10] 2-8-11 A Nicholls (3) 33/1: 0000: Led 3f, wknd: 12th, no form. *nk* **24**
12 ran Time 1m 10.5 (1.8) (The Hon Mrs J M Corbett) M L W Bell Newmarket, Suffolk

3758

4.00 GOLF CLUB HCAP 3YO+ 0-85 (D) 7f str Firm -04 +10 Fast [85]
£4062 £1250 £625 £312 3 yo rec 5 lb

2814 **SURPRISE ENCOUNTER 41** [7] E A L Dunlop 4-9-8 (79) G Carter 7/2 FAV: 005421: 4 ch g Cadeaux Genereux - Scandalette (Niniski) Chsd ldrs, led bef fnl 1f, ran on strongly to draw clr, readily: nicely bckd, fast time, 6 week abs: '99 wnr at Kempton (mdn, rtd 87): lightly rcd in '98 (stks, rtd 90): eff at 7f, stays 1m: acts on firm/fast grnd, handles gd/soft, likes sharp tracks, handles any: runs well fresh: impressive here. **90**
3107 **VOLONTIERS 28** [8] P W Harris 5-9-13 (84) J P Spencer 13/2: 022002: 5 b g Common Grounds - Senlis (Senstive Prince) Confidently rdn in tch, improved to trck ldrs on bit appr fnl 1f, sn rdn, kept on but no ch with wnr: op 5/1: not disgraced giving 5lbs to wnr: acts on firm, gd/soft & equitrack: see 2758, 1160. *2* **87**
*3119 **POINT OF DISPUTE 27** [6] P J Makin 5-9-13 (84)(vis) S Sanders 4/1: 1-4413: 5 b g Cyrano de Bergerac - Opuntia (Rousillon) Slow away, held up, prog 2f out, rdn bef dist, same pace: tchd 5/1: poss unsuited by return to 7f: see 3119 (stiff 6f). *4* **79**
3207 **DILKUSHA 23** [10] B J Meehan 5-9-5 (76) D R McCabe 14/1: 004354: Rear, feeling pace after halfway, kept on fnl 1f without threatening: see 1989. *½* **70**
2954 **ZUCCHERO 34** [5] 4-9-9 (80)(bl) D Holland 4/1: 6-6165: Set gd pace, hdd appr fnl 1f & no extra: capable of better, beat this wnr in 2814. *shd* **74**
3414 **SHOUF AL BADOU 14** [3] 3-9-0 (76) A Eddery (5) 25/1: 006506: Chsd ldrs, fdd appr fnl 1f: see 765. *1½* **67**
3580 **CEDAR MASTER 8** [1] 3-9-2 (78)(vis) I Mongan (5) 8/1: 560327: With ldr till wknd 2f out: btr 3580. *shd* **69**
3227 **HILLTOP WARNING 22** [2] 3-9-1 (77)(BL) T Quinn 12/1: -01548: Al towards rear: blnkd, btr 1947. *2½* **63**
*3580 **BALFOUR 8** [4] 3-8-5 (67)(vis)(6ex) P Robinson 13/2: 034319: Handy 5f, eased fnl 1f: too sn after 3580? ¾ **52**
331 **STAND BY 230** [9] 3-7-10 (58) G Baker (5) 40/1: 05-330: Al bhd, btn halfway: 10th, abs, new stable. *9* **28**
10 ran Time 1m 19.4 (u1.0) (Ahmed Ali) E A L Dunlop Newmarket, Suffolk

3759

4.30 CARVERY HCAP 3YO 0-70 (E) 6f Firm -04 -10 Slow [76]
£3276 £936 £468 2 Groups, first 5 home raced stands side (high numbers)

3386 **BIRDSONG 15** [19] C F Wall 3-9-3 (65) R Mullen 11/2: -00131: 3 b f Dolphin Street - Gay France (Sir Gaylord) Led stands side group till 2f out, rallied well for press ins last to collar wandering ldr fnl stride: earlier won at Newcastle (fill mdn, R Guest): unrcd juv: eff at 6f, tried 10f: acts on firm/fast grnd & likes forcing the pace on sharp or gall tracks: improving. **70**
563 **TOLDYA 191** [16] M Kettle 3-8-12 (60) M Tebbut 20/1: 432132: 3 b f Beveled - Run Amber Run (Run The Gantlet) Well plcd stands side, led that grp ent fnl 2f & sn overall ldr/began edging left, ended up nr far rail & hdd line: 6 mth abs, new stable: must have won if keeping a straight path: acts on firm grnd & equitrack. *shd* **64**
3580 **BISHOPSTONE MAN 8** [20] S Mellor 3-9-7 (69) W Hutchinson (7) 20/1: 102003: 3 b g Piccolo - Auntie Gladys (Great Nephew) Held up stands side, hdwy under press appr fnl 1f, ran on, just btn: op 14/1, joint top-weight: good run back in trip, acts on firm & soft grnd, see 2512. *nk* **72**
3280 **DOCTOR DENNIS 20** [18] B J Meehan 3-9-7 (69) D R McCabe 7/1: 012244: Cl up stands side, ch 1f out, held nr fin: joint top-weight, ran to best, tough, see 2603, 2549. *nk* **71**
3698 **POP SHOP 3** [10] 3-9-1 (63)(BL) J P Spencer 7/1: 000005: Held up stands side, rdn 2f out, mod hdwy. *2* **59**
3584 **BETTINA BLUE 7** [4] 3-8-4 (52) D Sweeney 16/1: 600006: Led overall far side, till 2f out, no extra. *nk* **47**
3279 **CAPPELLINA 20** [1] 3-8-8 (56) R Havlin 11/1: -00427: Cl up far side, led briefly 2f out, onepace: btr 3579. *nk* **50**
3318 **DIRECT REACTION 19** [2] 3-9-5 (67)(vis) D Holland 9/1: 411428: Chsd ldrs far side, no impress 2f out. *1½* **57**
3579 **AMJAD 8** [7] 3-9-1 (63)(bl) P Robinson 5/1: 550029: Outpcd far side, styd on fnl 1f: op 7/1, nds 7f/1m. *shd* **53**
3405 **TIME BOMB 15** [17] 3-7-12 (46)(2ow)(3oh) A Mackay 25/1: 060000: Nvr a factor stands side: 10th. *1½* **34**
3561 **FLEETING FANCY 8** [9] 3-8-3 (51) P Doe 20/1: 050400: In tch far side till appr fnl 1f: 11th, back in trip. *shd* **33**
3405 **LADY STALKER 15** [15] 3-7-13 (47) M Henry 11/1: -00030: Bhd stands side ldrs, fdd 2f out: 12th, op 8/1. ¾ **29**
3462 **AMAZED 12** [14] 3-9-3 (65) S Sanders 9/2 FAV: 6-420: Slow away & al bhd stands side: 15th, bckd from 7/1 on h'cap bow, see 3462 (5f). *2* **0**
3405 **LUCKYS SON 15** [5] 3-8-2 (47)(3ow) Paul Eddery 12/1: 002160: In tch far side 3f: 16th, op 8/1. *shd* **0**
3493 **Ladywell Blaise 12** [12] 3-8-8 (56) A Nicholls (3) 25/1: 3386 **Kirsch 15** [8] 3-8-5 (53)(vis) J Quinn 20/1:
2591 **Blue Dove 50** [13] 3-8-3 (50)(1ow) A Clark 33/1: 3332 **Arcadian Chief 18** [11] 3-7-10 (44)(9oh) G Baker(5) 40/1:
2729 **Parkside Prospect 44** [3] 3-8-1 (49)(BL) J Tate 33/1:
19 ran Time 1m 09.2 (0.4) (Mrs A G Kavanagh) C F Wall Newmarket, Suffolk

Official Going   GOOD. Stalls: 6f - Outside; Rem - Inside. Heavy showers thr'out afternoon.

3760   2.10 FUJITSU MED AUCT MDN 2YO (E)   7f rnd   Good 44   -29 Slow
£4290   £1320   £660   £330

-- **BLUSHING BRIDE** [7] J Noseda 2-8-9 J Weaver 3/1: -1: 2 b f Distant Relative - Dime Bag (High Line)   82+
Trkd ldrs trav strongly, prog to lead ent fnl 1f, pushed out cl-home: well bckd, debut: 15,000gns Mar foal:
half-sister to a couple of wnrs, notably useful 9f scorer Pawn Broker: dam a winning stayer, sire a top-class
miler: eff over a sharp 7f, will stay 1m: acts on gd grnd, runs well fresh: ran well today & can follow up.

-- **ALAKANANDA** [2] Sir Mark Prescott 2-8-9 G Duffield 9/2: -2: 2 b f Hernando - Alouette (Darshaan)   1¾ 76+
Dwelt & bhd, ran green, imprvd over 1f out, fin fast but too late on debut: big drifter from 3/1: Feb foal, sister
to high-class 1m/10f performer Alborada: dam a mid-dist wnr, sire top-class at 12f: eff over a sharp 7f on gd grnd,
crying out for 1m+: took a while for the penny to drop today, spot on next time & shld not be missed.

1974 **WOLF VENTURE** 77 [4] S P C Woods 2-9-0 B Marcus 14/1: -43: 2 ch c Wolfhound - Relatively Sharp   ½ 80
(Sharpen Up) Tried to make all, collared ent fnl 1f, no extra: 11 wk abs: eff at 7f on gd grnd: see 1974 (AW).

3577 **TRILLIONAIRE** 9 [5] R Hannon 2-9-0 L Newman (3) 14/1: 064: Prom, rdn & onepcd fnl 1f: now qual   1¾ 76
for nurs h'caps: see 3577, 2708.

3688 **LORD LIAM** 4 [10] P Howling 2-9-0 N Callan 16/1: -5345: Nvr btr than mid-div: see 3688, 3492.   ½ 75

2628 **FLY BOY FLY** 50 [1] 2-9-0 D Holland 2/1 FAV: -46: Front rank till wknd over 1f out: nicely bckd,   nk 74
7 wk abs: longer 7f trip: see 2628 (6f here).

2209 **MAROMA** 67 [8] 2-8-9 J Reid 8/1: -547: Slowly away, nvr a factor: 10 wk abs: see 2209, 1486.   5 59

3388 **TINY TIM** 16 [6] 2-9-0 M Hills 16/1: -648: Nvr nr ldrs: see 3388.   ½ 63

3358 **ANKASAMEN** 18 [9] M Fenton 25/1: -09: Al towards rear, t.o. in 9th: see 3358.   13 33

3443 **TARRANAKI KNIGHT** 14 [3] Paul Eddery 33/1: -00: Well bhd from halfway, fin last: see 3443.   1 36
10 ran   Time 1m 25.27 (5.17)   (Mrs D M Solomon)   J Noseda Newmarket.

3761   2.40 GRILLE DIFFUSER NURSERY HCAP 2YO 0-85   6f   Good 44   -03 Slow   [91]
£5096   £1568   £784   £392

3446 **DELTA SONG** 14 [6] G L Moore 2-8-11 (74) D Holland 4/1 CO FAV: -121: 2 b f Delta Dancer - Song Of   85
Gold (Song) Nvr far away, imprvd to lead 1½f out, clr ins fnl 1f, rdn to hold on cl-home: well bckd: debut
Lingfield wnr (fill sell, with W Muir): half-sister to sev wnrs over 5/7f, dam a sprint winning 2yo: eff at 6f on
gd & firm grnd: likes to run up with the pace, handles a sharp trk: lightly rcd, improving filly.

3630 **SOLDIER ON** 6 [4] M R Channon 2-9-2 (79) Craig Williams 4/1 CO FAV: 501352: 2 b g General Monash -   ¾ 87+
Golden Form (Formidable) Held up & last rounding Tattenham Corner, imprvd 2f out, fin v fast but too late:
qck reapp, well bckd, clr of 3rd: given plenty to do here, may well have won with more enterprising tactics.

3109 **EUROLINK SUNDANCE** 29 [3] J L Dunlop 2-9-3 (80) J Reid 4/1 CO FAV: -01343: 2 ch f Night Shift -   3½ 78
Eurolink Mischief (Be My Chief) Nvr far away, ev ch over 1f out, not pace of front 2 ins fnl 1f: stays an easy 6f.

3491 **LONDON EYE** 13 [7] K T Ivory 2-7-12 (61)(bl) C Catlin(5) 12/1: 001644: Chsd ldrs, onepcd fnl   1½ 55
1f: has been busy: see 2891 (firm grnd).

2152 **JOHNNY REB** 70 [8] 2-9-6 (83)(t) L Newman (3) 6/1: -2605: Not pace to chall: clr of rem, nicely   hd 77
bckd, 10 wk abs: change of tactics in first time t-strap, forced the pace prev: see 1691, 1426.

3205 **LITTLE CALLIAN** 24 [2] 2-8-6 (69) R Price 14/1: -60436: Led till dist, fdd: much btr 3205 (firm).   7 48

2419 **LOVE LADY** 58 [1] 2-8-4 (67) R Ffrench 6/1: -4337: Mid-div, btn 2f out: 8 wk abs: btr 2419 (firm).   ½ 45

3620 **FOLEY MILLENNIUM** 7 [5] 2-9-7 (84) Paul Eddery 12/1: 341358: Speed till 2f out, wknd: btr 3286.   3½ 52

3446 **MAGIC GEM** 14 [9] 2-8-4 (67) G Duffield 25/1: -0559: Rear, short of room early on, no ch from   1 32
halfway & fin last: h'cap bow: see 3277.
9 ran   Time 1m 10.63 (2.83)   (Richard Green (Fine Paintings))   G L Moore Brighton, E.Sussex.

3762   3.15 VAILLANT HCAP 3YO 0-70 (E)   1m2f   Good 44   -21 Slow   [73]
£5928   £1824   £912   £456

3290 **FLYOVER** 21 [1] B R Millman 3-8-12 (57) B Marcus 7/1: 005161: 3 b f Presidium - Flash By (Ilium)   63
Broke well & made all, held on well ins fnl 1f, all out: tchd 8/1: earlier won at Bath (h'cap): '99 Salisbury wnr
(fill mdn auct, rtd 74): eff at 10/12f on gd & firm grnd: handles a sharp/undul or stiff trk: eff in blnks, seems
best without: well rdn by B Marcus to take advantage of a fav'able low draw.

3357 **BILLY BATHWICK** 18 [11] E J O'Neill 3-9-4 (63) D Holland 10/1: 100032: 3 ch c Fayruz - Cut It Fine   2 65
(Big Spruce) Rear, gd hdway 2f out, fin strongly but not reach wnr: styd on well over this longer 10f trip,
but wnr had already flown: see 3357.

3396 **NOBLE CALLING** 16 [14] N A Graham 3-9-3 (62)(VIS) J Weaver 5/1 FAV: 020623: 3 b c Caller ID -   nk 63
Specificity (Alleged) Dsptd lead till ent fnl 1f, fdd & caught for 2nd cl-home: sound run in first time visor.

3261 **CORUSCATING** 22 [5] Sir Mark Prescott 3-9-7 (66) G Duffield 10/1: 005-04: Rear, rdn to impr over   ¾ 66
2f out, kept on & nrst fin: top-weight, clr of rem: some promise here & worth keeping in mind over 10f+: see 3261.

2591 **KOINCIDENTAL** 51 [10] N Callan 20/1: -00055: Hdwy from rear 2f out, nrst fin: 7 wk   3 48
abs: longer 10f trip & hinted at ability: see 1268.

3656 **PEPPERCORN** 6 [12] 3-7-10 (41)(20h) G Baker (5) 20/1: 003606: Rear, prog 2f out, nvr nr to chall.   3½ 31

3530 **FLYING RUN** 11 [9] 3-7-10 (41)(4oh) R Brisland(5) 14/1: 000037: Nvr better than mid-div: btr 3530.   hd 31

3110 **BOX CAR** 29 [4] 3-9-1 (60) I Mongan (5) 12/1: 200608: Al around mid-div, no ch with ldrs: see 1199.   shd 50

1446 **DOUBLE RED** 101 [7] 3-9-1 (60) M Fenton 12/1: 2-2309: Rear, some late hdwy, nvr dngrs: long abs.   1¼ 48

2206 **SALIENT POINT** 67 [8] 3-9-4 (63) J Reid 16/1: 500400: Nvr nr to chall after 10 wk abs: see 1803 (AW).   ½ 50

2945 **BELINDA** 35 [15] 3-8-10 (55) D Sweeney (3) 25/1: 010030: Prom to 1m, wknd: see 2945 (AW).   10 27

3530 **CEDAR PRINCE** 11 [16] 3-9-1 (60)(vis) J Quinn 33/1: 600000: Mid-div till btn over 2f out: see 1744.   ¾ 31

3217 **LOUP CERVIER** 23 [13] 3-8-0 (45) P Doe 12/1: 034400: Prom 1m: fin 13th: btr 2908, 2735.   3 11

3585 **NO REGRETS** 8 [3] 3-7-12 (43) F Norton 11/1: 002650: Mid-div till btn over 2f out: flattered 3262.   nk 8

3226 **BAJAN SUNSET** 23 [4] 3-8-6 (51) R Hills 11/1: 062200: Prom 6f, sn wknd & fin last: btr 2980, 2512.   8 4
15 ran   Time 2m 10.36 (6.56)   (R J Tory)   B R Millman Kentisbeare, Devon.

3763

3.45 LISTED FORTUNE STKS 3YO+ (A)   7f rnd   Good 44   +15 Fast
£15340   £4720   £2380   £1180   3yo rec 4lb   All runners came wide to stands side

2997 **NICOBAR 34** [1] I A Balding 3-9-0 M Hills 7/2 CO FAV: 610501: 3 b c Indian Ridge - Duchess Of Alba   112
(Belmez) Nvr far away, went on 2f out, held on gamely, drvn out: well bckd, best time of day: earlier won at
Chester (h'cap) & here at Epsom (List), subs tried in Gr company: '99 Haydock wnr (mdn, rtd 100): eff at 7f/1m,
has tried further: acts on fast & gd/soft grnd, handles firm: loves to run up with or force the pace, handles any
trk, developing into a Epsom specialist: smart colt.

*3155 **VEIL OF AVALON 12** [2] R Charlton 3-8-7(1ow) J Reid 8/1: -62162: 3 b f Thunder Gulch - Wind In   ¾ 102
Her Hair (Alzao) Chsd ldrs, ev ch dist, kept on & not btn far: 6th in a List race at Deauville 12 days ago:
useful filly who continues to progress: see 3155.

1834 **WARNINGFORD 83** [5] J R Fanshawe 6-9-1 O Urbina 7/2 CO FAV: -24263: 6 b h Warning - Barford Lady 1¼ 103
(Stanford) Held up, gd hdwy 2f out, drifted left fnl 1f & no extra ins last: well bckd, 12 wk abs: 7f specialist
who is best off in the grnd: see 1834, 952.

3600 **YORKIES BOY 8** [3] A Berry 5-9-4 J Weaver 16/1: 160104: Set pace 5f, no extra: top-weight: ran   ½ 105
nr to best here over a trip which is sltly further than his optimum: see 3172 (6f).

*3213 **GAELIC STORM 26** [8] 6-9-1 D Holland 7/2 CO FAV: 464415: Rear, eff halfway, kept on, not pace to chall.   ½ 101
2389 **JARN 59** [9] 3-8-11 (t) R Hills 12/1: 0-1026: Prom till wknd fnl 1f: 8 wk abs: reportedly   2 97
needs faster grnd: see 2389, 1371.

3515 **CIRCLE OF LIGHT 12** [4] 3-8-6 G Duffield 12/1: 233047: Mid-div, imprvd halfway, btn & eased fnl 1f.   1½ 89
3104 **INCREDULOUS 29** [6] 3-8-6 M Dwyer 13/2: 241048: Mid-div, imprvd 2f out, btn fnl 1f: see 3104.   1 87
2389 **PRINCE CASPIAN 59** [7] 3-8-11 B Marcus 25/1: -149: Speed till halfway, wknd into last: 8 wk abs.   9 77
9 ran   Time 1m 22.13 (2.03)   (Robert Hitchins)   I A Balding Kingsclere, Hants.

3764

4.20 M J LONSDALE MDN 3YO (D)   1m114y rnd   Good 44   -16 Slow
£4192   £1290   £645   £322   All runners came wide to stands side

3413 **MUSICAL HEATH 15** [6] P W Harris 3-9-0 (t) M Fenton 13/8 FAV: -4221: 3 b c Common Grounds - Song   79
Of The Glens (Horage) Made all, rdn clr fnl 1f, cmftbly: hvly bckd: deserved win, rnr-up twice prev: eff over an
extended 1m, acts on gd & firm grnd: seems suited by forcing the pace & wearing a t-strap: decisive win today.

3423 **RUSSIAN RHAPSODY 15** [3] M A Jarvis 3-8-9 N Callan 6/1: -542: 3 b f Cosmonaut - Hannah's   6 62
Music (Music Boy) Chsd wnr, left bhd fnl 1f: rider reportedly given a 5 day ban for careless riding: stays an
easy 1m, handles gd & fast grnd: see 3423, 2919.

2679 **MADURESE 48** [1] C E Brittain 3-9-0 B Marcus 11/1: -403: 3 b c Machiavellian - Luana (Shaadi)   ½ 66
Rear, rdn to impr 2f out, kept on but no ch with ldrs: 7 wk abs: now quals for h'caps, 10f+ may suit: see 1333.

3413 **ELLWAY HEIGHTS 15** [7] I A Balding 3-9-0 M Hills 25/1: -064: Slowly away, some late hdwy, nvr   3 60
dngrs on h'cap qual run: mid-dist bred & will benefit from a step up in trip & h'cap company: see 3179.

3423 **BADAAWAH 15** [4] 3-8-9 R Hills 2/1: -25: Prom, wknd fnl 2f: well bckd: better expected after 3423.   2 51
3524 **BAJAN BROKER 11** [5] 3-8-9 J Reid 7/1: -04056: Mid-div, prog to chase ldrs when hmpd 2f out, no   6 39
ch after: better off in h'caps: see 3524.

3048 **DUEMILA 32** [2] 3-9-0 C Rutter 50/1: -007: Slowly away, al bhd & fin last: no form.   5 34
7 ran   Time 1m 46.91 (5.11)   (The Highlanders)   P W Harris Tring, Herts.

3765

4.50 H & V NEWS HCAP 3YO+ 0-70 (E)   7f rnd   Good 44   -24 Slow   **[66]**
£4543   £1398   £699   £322   3yo rec 4lb   All runners came wide to stands side

2690 **CONTRARY MARY 48** [5] J Akehurst 5-9-10 (62) R Farmer(7) 6/1 JT FAV: 512201: 5 b m Mujadil - Love   67
Street (Mummy's Pet) Waited with, prog 2f out, forged ahd ins fnl 1f, won all out: 7 wk abs: earlier won at
Salisbury (fill h'cap): '99 Folkestone wnr (class stks, rtd 67): '98 wnr at Lingfield (h'cap) & Pontefract (clmr,
subs disq, rtd 74 & 59a): suited by 6/7f on firm & soft, handles any trk: gd weight carrier who runs well fresh.

3561 **ANNIJAZ 9** [9] J G Portman 3-9-0 (56) G Baker (5) 12/1: 010352: 3 b f Alhijaz - Figment (Posse)   shd 60
Slowly away, imprvd 2f out, chall strongly fnl 1f & just btn in a thrilling fin: fine eff, deserves to go one better.

*3578 **ZEPPO 9** [2] B R Millman 5-9-10 (62)(6ex) N Pollard 12/1: 445213: 5 ch g Fayruz - Chase Paperchase   2 62
(Malinowski) Led till ent fnl 1f, no extra cl-home: sound front running effort: see 3578 (6f, firm grnd).

3580 **TRAJAN 9** [1] A P Jarvis 3-10-0 (70) N Callan 12/1: 060244: Nvr far away, chall fnl 1f, no extra   shd 70
cl-home: not disgraced under top-weight: see 3580, 3405 (6f, fast grnd).

3559 **REACHFORYOURPOCKET 9** [4] 5-8-8 (46) Martin Dwyer 11/1: 100025: Chsd ldrs, no extra fnl 1f.   1 44
3634 **SAND HAWK 6** [11] 5-8-6 (44)(bl) Paul Eddery 6/1 JT FAV: 004106: Slowly away & bhd, fin v   hd 42+
strongly, nrst fin: qck reapp: stable in fine form: eye-catching effort here, see 3634.

3536 **SEVEN SPRINGS 10** [17] 4-7-11 (35) P M Quinn 20/1: 000047: Mid-div when hmpd 2f out, kept on   nk 32
but ch had gone: visor left off today: enjoys gd/soft & hvy grnd, v well h'capped & primed for a return to form.

3445 **CLONOE 14** [13] 6-8-3 (41)(t) J Quinn 14/1: 005358: Prom 5f, fdd: just btr 3030.   ¾ 36
3279 **MILADY LILLIE 21** [12] 4-8-10 (48) A Daly 16/1: 406609: Mid-div, prog 2f out, btn fnl 1f: see 2899.   1½ 40
3445 **FLYING PENNANT 14** [10] 7-8-6 (44)(bl) F Norton 8/1: 103630: Rear, eff 3f out, nvr nr nr ldrs: see 3445.   1 34
3344 **MUJKARI 18** [7] 4-7-10 (36)(vis) M Henry 20/1: 002300: Nvr a factor in 11th: btr 3251, 2974.   3½ 19
3739 **MUFFIN MAN 2** [15] 3-8-5 (47) C Rutter 14/1: 046040: Prog from rear halfway, wkng when hmpd   hd 30
2f out: fin 12th, qck reapp.

2355 **MISTER TRICKY 61** [14] 5-9-12 (64) I Mongan (5) 14/1: 010000: Mid-div till btn dist: fin 13th, abs.   2½ 42
3440 **SANTANDRE 14** [6] 4-8-9 (47) D Holland 10/1: 050630: Speed 5f, wknd: broke a blood vessel.   4 17
2033 **STEP ON DEGAS 74** [16] 7-8-11 (49) D Sweeney 14/1: 00-000: Chsd ldrs, in tch when badly hmpd   20 0
3f out, eased & virtually p.u.: 10 wk abs: v lucky not to be brght down & this must be forgiven: see 1058.

3527 **RAINBOW RAIN 11** [3] 6-9-7 (59)(t) P Doe 10/1: 20002R: Reared badly in stalls & u.r.: see 3527.   0
16 ran   Time 1m 24.90 (4.80)   (Fisher Foods)   J Akehurst Epsom, Surrey.

HAYDOCK FRIDAY SEPTEMBER 1ST Lefthand, Flat, Galloping Track

Official Going SOFT. Stalls: 5f & 6f - Centre; 7f & 1m - Ins; 1m2f & 1m4f - Outside. After 3.00 race the meeting was abandoned due to heavy rain.

3766 **2.00 VALE OF LUNE MED AUCT MDN 2YO (E) 1m30y rnd Soft Inapplicable**
£3066 £876 £438

2956 **MORSHDI 35** [15] M A Jarvis 2-9-0 P Robinson 7/2: 51: 2 b c Slip Anchor - Reem Albaraari (Sadler's Wells) Prom, led 2f out, well in control when eased nr fin: bckd tho' op 5/2: Mar foal: imprvd for debut & apprec step up to 1m, mid-dists shld suit next term: acts on soft grnd & a gall trk: progressive, Gr 2 entered colt. **91**
2583 **LA VITA E BELLA 51** [7] C F Wall 2-8-9 R Mullen 16/1: 02: 2 b f Definite Article - Coolrain Lady (Common Grounds) Towards rear, hdwy 2f out, styd on to go 2nd ins last, no ch wnr: 7 wk abs, op 12/1: suited by step up to 1m, get mid-dists next term: goes on soft grnd. *1¾* **81**
-- **DEUCE OF TRUMPS** [5] J Noseda 2-9-0 J Carroll 12/1: 3: 2 b c Desert Style - Mauras Pride (Cadeaux Genereux) Trkd ldrs, rdn 3f out, kept on, not pace to chall: sound debut, op 8/1: IR 20,000gns Apr foal, brother to a modest mdn: dam unrcd: eff at 1m on soft grnd & shld improve. *1* **84**
3433 **CONSPIRE 14** [13] G A Butler 2-8-9 K Darley 7/4 FAV: 34: Well plcd, feeling pace 3f out, rallied 2f out, onepace fnl 1f: well bckd: stays 1m on gd & soft grnd but more expexted & rated higher on debut (gd). *¾* **78**
-- **LADY SHARP SHOT** [1] 2-8-9 T Quinn 14/1: 5: Held up, prog 3f out, not much room fnl 2f tho' styd on: debut: Son Of Sharp Shot, Feb foal: dam 7f juv wnr: handles soft & will relish mid-dists next term. *1½* **76**
3577 **COMPANION 9** [12] 2-8-9 M Tebbutt 5/1: 46: Wide, held up, gd prog to chase ldrs 2f out, fdd und press. *¾* **75**
-- **THE BYSTANDER** [6] 2-8-9 R Winston 33/1: 7: Bhd ldrs, outpcd 2f out & not much room ins last: debut: 4,000gns Mar foal: half-sister to a 7f juv wnr, dam 11f wnr: with N Littmoden. *2* **71**
2962 **TOTALLY COMMITTED 35** [10] 2-9-0 J Fortune 8/1: 032368: Made most till 2f out, fdd: lngr trip. *½* **75**
-- **SOUTHERN DANCER** [14] 2-9-0 Dean McKeown 40/1: 9: Pld hard & dsptd lead halfway till 2f out, no extra: debut: 4,000gns Makbul first foal: with R Hollinshead. *¾* **74**
-- **GREENHOPE** [2] 2-9-0 J P Spencer 20/1: 0: Nvr a factor: 10th, debut, op 14/1: 30,000gns Definite Article Apr foal: half-brother to several wnrs: with J Osborne. *nk* **73**
3156 **Mount Royale 27** [9] 2-9-0 Kim Tinkler 66/1: 2952 **Four Legs Good 35** [8] 2-8-9 S Sanders 25/1:
-- **Ice Prince** [3] 2-9-0 S W Kelly (3) 33/1: -- **Needwood Brave** [11] 2-9-0 M Roberts 33/1:
-- **Marrel** [4] 2-9-0 G Faulkner (3) 25/1:
15 ran Time 1m 50.16 (9.66) (Sheikh Ahmed Al Maktoum) M A Jarvis Newmarket.

3767 **2.30 EBF NORWEST HOLST MDN 2YO (D) 5f Soft Inapplicable**
£4634 £1426 £713 £356

1782 **KINGS BALLET 85** [5] P J Makin 2-9-0 S Sanders 2/1 FAV: 01: 2 b c Imperial Ballet - Multimara (Arctic Tern) Trkd ldrs, qcknd to lead bef fnl 1f, edged left under press, ran on well: 3 mth abs, bckd from 3/1: brother to smart sprinting stablemate Imperial Ballet: eff fresh over a gall 5f on soft grnd: progressive & potentially useful. **84**
-- **BENEDICTINE** [14] R Hannon 2-9-0 K Darley 7/2: 2: 2 b c Primo Dominie - Benedicite (Lomond) Cl-up, ev ch appr fnl 1f, rdn & held by wnr when dropped whip ins last: op 5/1, debut: 28,000gns Feb foal, dam unrcd: eff at 5f on soft grnd: bred for speed, shld find similar. *1½* **79**
3571 **VIEWFORTH 9** [10] Miss L A Perratt 2-9-0 Dale Gibson 12/1: -43: 2 b c Emarati - Miriam (Forzando) Led till appr fnl 1f, onepace ins last: clr rem, op 8/1: suited by forcing tactics: eff at 5f on soft grnd. *1½* **76**
-- **DARK FINISH** [15] B A McMahon 2-8-9 W Supple 12/1: 4: Prom, outpcd by ldrs appr fnl 1f: debut: IR 19,000gns Night Shift half-sister to 5f juv wnr Cherry Blossom: dam 7f juv wnr: promising. *5* **59**
3484 **SMOOTHIE 13** [13] 2-9-0 J Fortune 13/2: -305: Towards rear, rdn/some hdwy bef fnl 1f, nvr dngrs. *½* **59**
2766 **SO SOBER 44** [8] 2-9-0 R Mullen 11/2: -54206: Saddle soon slipped, front rank, coasted thr' fnl 2f: 6 wk abs, op 9/2: forget this: see 2545. *2½* **57**
-- **NEEDWOOD BLADE** [7] 2-9-0 M Roberts 25/1: 7: Slow to stride, nvr better than mid-div: debut: 33,000gns Mar foal: half-brother to multiple juv wnr Islay Mist: dam scored up to 2m, sire a sprinter: improve. *¾* **54**
2880 **MISS BEADY 39** [3] 2-8-9 Kim Tinkler 50/1: 005508: Al rear: 6 wk abs, new stable, blnks omitted. *1½* **46**
3621 **PICCOLO ROSE 7** [12] 2-8-9 T Quinn 8/1: 59: Chsd ldrs till 2f out, eased: see 3621. *1¾* **38**
3408 **ENCYCLOPEDIA 15** [11] 2-8-9 J Carroll 25/1: 50: Bhd ldrs, wknd qckly 2f out: 10th, see 3408. *4* **0**
2454 **Baby Maybe 56** [4] 2-8-9 P Robinson 25/1: -- **Mahlstick** [6] 2-9-0 J D Smith 33/1:
-- **Mindahra** [9] 2-8-9 J Bramhill 40/1: -- **Lucks Luvly** [1] 2-8-9 O Pears 33/1:
14 ran Time 1m 02.82 (4.02) (Dr Carlos E Stelling) P J Makin Ogbourne Maisey, Wilts.

3768 **3.00 RBF CLASSIFIED STKS 3YO+ 0-90 (C) 6f Heavy Inapplicable**
£7058 £2677 £1338 £608 3 yo rec 2 lb

3569 **SHATIN VENTURE 9** [3] Miss L A Perratt 3-8-8 R Winston 16/1: 000501: 3 b c Lake Coniston - Justitia (Dunbeath) Prom, rdn appr fnl 1f, kept on grimly & got up fnl 50y: '99 debut wnr at Ayr (nov stks, rtd 92): eff at 5f/6f, stays 7f: acts on fast, right back to form on this hvy grnd: suited by gall trks. **85**
*2577 **MOLLY BROWN 51** [5] R Hannon 3-8-11 J Carroll 10/1: 040012: 3 b f Rudimentary - Sinking (Midyan) Cl-up, led halfway, rdn bef fnl 1f, edged left ins last & hdd towards fin: 7 wk abs, op 8/1: an improving filly, acts on fast & hvy grnd: see 2577 (h'cap). *½* **86**
3521 **OCKER 11** [2] Mrs N Macauley 6-8-10 R Fitzpatrick 14/1: 455003: 6 br g Astronef - Violet Somers (Will Somers) In tch, closed ent fnl 2f, rdn & ch bef dist, held/jinked left nr fin: won this race last year & is proving himself a late summer/autumn gelding: see 47. *nk* **82**
2660 **PUNCTUATE 49** [6] W J Haggas 3-8-8 K Darley 7/1: 000034: Chsd ldrs, drvn ent fnl 2f, onepace: 7 wk abs & signs of return to form on grnd much softer than ideal: handles hvy, suited by fast/firm: see 988. *2* **78**
2456 **BOOMERANG BLADE 29** [4] 4-8-7 J Stack 14/1: 226605: Bhd ldrs, rdn appr fnl 1f, no impression. *½* **74**
3727 **BLUE VELVET 2** [12] 3-9-0 C Carver (3) 13/2: 116506: In tch towards stands side, prog & ev ch 2f out, rdn & fdd bef dist: ran 48hrs ago, tough: see 2568. *2½* **78**
3536 **PALACEGATE TOUCH 10** [1] 10-8-13 P Bradley (5) 66/1: 500407: Led till halfway, wknd/edged left fnl 1f. *1* **73$**
3315 **CHOTO MATE 20** [11] 4-9-2 P Dobbs (5) 16/1: 410008: Held up, nvr a factor: stablemate rnr-up: faster grnd suits, see 1989 (h'cap). *½* **75**
3687 **PERUVIAN CHIEF 4** [10] 3-8-8 J Mackay (5) 5/1: 336009: Well plcd, wknd qckly appr fnl 1f: qck reapp, needs faster grnd: promising in 3687, see 2568 & 112. *2½* **64**
3503 **ALEGRIA 12** [9] 4-8-13 (bl) M Tebbutt 12/1: 106000: V keen, cl-up, lost pl 2f out: 10th, blnks reapplied, op 10/1: drop back to 5f will suit as will faster grnd: see 1728. *shd* **67**
3130 **ROO 28** [8] 3-8-5 T Quinn 7/4 FAV: 322500: Sn struggling nr stands side: 11th, well bckd: better *2* **57**

expected, went well in soft grnd as a juvenile: see 1887, 912.

3569 **SHINBONE ALLEY 9** [7] 3-9-0 G Carter 20/1: -51000: Al bhd: 12th: needs faster grnd: see 1843.   2 62

12 ran   Time 1m 18.14 (6.74)   (Shatin Racing Group)   Miss L A Perratt Ayr, Strathclyde.

WOLVERHAMPTON (Fibresand)   SATURDAY SEPTEMBER 2ND   Lefthand, Sharp Track

Official Going   STANDARD. Stalls: Inside, except 7f - Outside.

3769	**7.00 COMEDY MDN HCAP 3YO+ 0-65 (F)** 1m100y aw rnd Going 30 -23 Slow **[64]**
	£2534 £724 £362 3 yo rec 5 lb

3353 **COMPATRIOT 19** [2] P S Felgate 4-9-7 (57) G Duffield 7/1: 025361: 4 b g Bigstone - Campestral   62a
(Alleged) In tch, prog appr str, rdn & kept on to lead towards fin: '99 rnr-up (mdn, rtd 87, N Callaghan): '98
rnr-up (rtd 96): eff at 1m, stays 10f: acts on firm, soft & fibresand, any trk: eff with/without blnks.

3744 **FOR HEAVENS SAKE 2** [9] C W Thornton 3-9-5 (60) Dean McKeown 11/2: 260232: 3 b g Rambo   1½ 62a
Dancer - Angel Fire (Nashwan) Early ldr, again 2f out, drifted left & worn down ins last: qk reapp, stays 8.5f.

3197 **BAHRAIN 26** [8] N P Littmoden 4-9-7 (57) T G McLaughlin 10/3 FAV: 000623: 4 ch c Lahib - Twin   1½ 56a
Island (Standaan) Prom, led halfway till 2f out, onepace: fair AW bow, clr rem: eff at 7f, stays 1m on fm & f/sand.

2601 **LILLAN 51** [5] G A Butler 3-9-7 (62)(t) D Holland 14/1: 644W4: Struggled till went past btn horses   6 51a
fnl 2f: 7 wk abs, AW/h'cap bow: jockey reported the filly lost her action on the bend: see 1640

3573 **WELCOME TO UNOS 10** [1] 3-9-7 (62) A Clark 10/1: 302065: Same pl thro'out: lngr trip, AW bow, btr 3250. ½ 50a

3670 **CELEBRE BLU 6** [3] 3-9-5 (60) F Lynch 10/1: 300036: Nvr better than mid-div: op 8/1, qk reapp.   3 42a

2906 **SPOT 39** [10] 3-9-8 (63) M Henry 25/1: 03407: Nvr going pace: btr 2604 (6f mdn here).   ¾ 44a

4511} **SEA ISLE 312** [4] 4-10-0 (64) A Nicholls (3) 14/1: 6350-8: Led after 1f till halfway, btn 2f out: 2½ 40a
reapp, AW bow: 6th in a Newbury mdn in '99 (rtd 71): stays 1m on firm grnd: with I Balding.

3272 **PEACHES 22** [7] 3-9-7 (62) S Sanders 5/1: -0029: Prom 5f: h'cap bow, much btr 3272 (mdn, here).   2½ 33a

3217 **COMMONWOOD 24** [6] 3-9-3 (58) J Weaver 10/1: -40000: Al bhd: 10th, AW bow: see 1726.   nk 28a

2489 **Slieve Bloom 56** [12] 3-9-5 (60) L Carter 25/1:   3606 **Fahan 8** [13] 3-9-0 (55) W Supple 12/1:

3242 **Ring My Mate 24** [11] 3-9-5 (60) Sophie Mitchell 25/1:

13 ran   Time 1m 50.7 (4.5)   (Foreneish Racing)   P S Felgate Grimston, Leics

3770	**7.30 BET DIRECT CLAIMER 3YO+ (F)** 7f aw rnd Going 30 -11 Slow
	£2436 £696 £348 3 yo rec 4 lb

3218 **AIR MAIL 24** [3] J M P Eustace 3-8-11 J Tate 6/1: 500001: 3 b g Night Shift - Wizardry (Shirley Heights)   57a
Made all, rdn clr bef dist, unchal: op 4/1, clmd by Mrs Macauley for £2,000: earlier won at Lingfield (mdn,
rtd 75a): unrcd juv: suited by 7f, stays 1m: likes both AW's & forcing the pace on sharp trks, without blnks.

3694 **BLUSHING GRENADIER 5** [11] S R Bowring 8-8-11 (bl) S Finnamore (5) 16/1: 021002: 8 ch g - Salt   4 53a
Dome - La Duse (Junius) Chs wnr thro'out, nvr any impress: qk reapp: ran to best at the weights, see 1663.

3275 **FEATHERSTONE LANE 22** [12] Miss L C Siddall 3-8-11 K Darley 7/1: 336343: 9 b g Siberian Express -   1¾ 50a
Try Gloria (My Best) Not go pace till styd on fnl 2f: tchd 14/1: can do better, see 1235 (C/D h'cap).

*2637 **GENERAL KLAIRE 50** [10] D Morris 5-9-1 D McGaffin (5) 7/4 FAV: 640014: Well outpcd, kept on   ¾ 53a
bef dist: bckd, f wk abs: just needed this?: btr 2637 (h'cap).

*3275 **ROYAL CASCADE 22** [8] 6-9-6 (bl) W Supple 9/2: 202015: Outpcd till fnl 2f prog: btr 3275.   1 56a

3274 **GERONIMO 22** [5] 3-8-13 Dean McKeown 9/1: -21666: Chsd ldrs, no extra appr fnl 1f: clmd by   shd 53a
M Wigham for £6,000: see 2604 (6f).

2816 **ABTAAL 43** [7] 10-8-5 (vis) R Fitzpatrick 33/1: 006067: Nvr a factor: stiff task, 6 wk abs, see 1305.   1¼ 39a

677 **COMEOUTOFTHEFOG 170** [6] 5-8-11 R Lake (7) 20/1: 500508: Nvr trbld ldrs: 6 mth abs, see 567 (sell). shd 45a

3253 **PHOEBUS 23** [2] 3-9-2 (t) J Weaver 10/1: 003309: Sn bhd: tchd 14/1, btr 2950, 2633.   7 44a

3275 **COLONEL CUSTER 22** [4] 5-9-9 (vis) T G McLaughlin 50/1: 504060: Prom 4f: 10th, stiff task, see 408. shd 47$

3694 **PRESS AHEAD 5** [1] 5-8-8 (vis) D Holland 20/1: 000600: In tch, wknd 3f out: 1th, qk reapp, lngr trip.   nk 31a

3332 **GREEN PURSUIT 20** [9] 4-9-6 J P Spencer 5/1: 6-0020: In tch 3f: 12th, see 3332, 538.   13 25a

12 ran   Time 1m 29.1 (2.9)   (Gary Coull)   J M P Eustace Newmarket, Suffolk

3771	**8.00 BERNARD HCAP 3YO 0-85 (D)** 7f aw rnd Going 30 -04 Slow **[89]**
	£4101 £1262 £631 £315

*3225 **HAND CHIME 24** [8] W J Haggas 3-9-5 (80) K Darley 11/8 FAV: 123111: 3 ch g Clantime - Warning   86a
Bell (Bustino) Chsd ldrs, rdn to lead appr fnl 1f, kept on well: nicely bckd, AW bow: earlier won at Catterick
(auct mdn), Carlisle, Kempton (h'caps) & Pontefract (class stks): eff at 6f/1m: acts on firm, soft grnd &
fibresand: goes on any trk: can run well fresh: tough & fast improving/versatile gelding.

3457 **OSCAR PEPPER 15** [9] T D Barron 3-8-13 (74) J P Spencer 5/1: 030362: 3 b g Brunswick - Princess   ¾ 77a
Baja (Conquistador Cielo) Rear, imprvd 2f out, styd on for press/drifted left fnl 1f: not btn far, see 2833, 365.

3629 **SUMTHINELSE 7** [10] N P Littmoden 3-8-13 (74) J Quinn 12/1: 214603: 3 ch g Magic Ring - Minnie Love 2 73a
(Homeric) Prom, led briefly ent fnl 2f, onepace: solid AW bow, acts on firm, gd & fibresand, handles gd/sft.

3495 **MANXWOOD 14** [3] D J S Cosgrove 3-8-12 (73) G Duffield 6/1: 100204: Early ldr, prom, no extra 2f out. 3½ 66a

2495 **TAP 56** [6] 3-9-7 (82) S Whitworth 12/1: 2-1605: Cl-up, led bef fnl 2f, sn hdd, fdd: 8 wk abs, AW bow. ¾ 74a

3629 **RANDOM TASK 7** [1] 3-9-5 (80) T G McLaughlin 33/1: 14-06: Chsd ldrs, lost pl appr fnl 2f: '99 wnr   3 66a
here at W'hampton (debut, mdn, rtd 87a), well btn last of 4 on turf, rtd 63): eff at 6f on fibresand.

3242 **BOTTELINO JOE 24** [4] 3-7-10 (57)(7oh) R Brisland (5) 50/1: 5-0007: Sn niggled, handy, wknd 2f out. ½ 42a

3269 **THE PROSECUTOR 23** [7] 3-9-4 (79) J Weaver 6/1: 001447: Rear, brief eff 3f out, sn btn: see 1494.   2 60a

3708 **SUTTON COMMON 5** [2] 3-8-12 (73) F Lynch 12/1: 021009: Sn led, hdd appr fnl 2f, sn wknd: AW bow.   2 50a

3759 **DIRECT REACTION 2** [5] 3-9-4 (79)(vis) D Holland 10/1: 114200: Al bhd: 10th, ran 48 hrs ago, see 3196. 2½ 52a

10 ran   Time 1m 28.6 (2.4)   (Mrs M M Haggas)   W J Haggas Newmarket, Suffolk

---

3772	8.30 SMILING NOV AUCT STKS 2YO (E) 1m100y aw rnd Going 30 -14 Slow
	£2695 £770 £385

3601 **PATHAN 8** [4] S P C Woods 2-8-9 G Duffield 10/11 FAV: 142321: 2 b c Pyramus - Langton Herring   **82a**
(Nearly A Hand) Prsd ldr, went on after halfway, rdly: well bckd, AW bow: earlier won at Lingfield (turf auct mdn):
eff forcing the pace at 7f/8.5f: acts on firm, gd grnd & fibresand: suited by sharp trks, handles any: tough/imprvg.
3692 **EL HAMRA 5** [2] B A McMahon 2-8-5 W Supple 7/1: 033352: 2 gr c Royal Abjar - Cherlinoa (Crystal   3 **70a**
Palace) Prom, went after wnr 3f out, sn held/hung left: op 9/2, well clr of next, qk reapp: stays 1m, see 2916.
3496 **BLUE LADY 14** [5] N P Littmoden 2-8-0 J Tate 6/4: 650633: 2 b f College Chapel - Dancing Bluebell   9 **49a**
(Bluebird) Dwelt, chsd ldrs till ent fnl 3f: bckd: unsuited by step up to 8.5f?: much btr 3496 (6f here).
3015 **VIOLENT 34** [3] Andrew Reid 2-8-4 (vis) M Henry 9/1: 021204: Led till after halfway, fdd: AW bow, lngr trip.3 **47a**
4 ran   Time 1m 50.0 (3.8)   (S P C Woods)   S P C Woods Newmarket, Suffolk

---

3773	9.00 CHUCKLE SELL HCAP 3-5YO 0-60 (G) 1m4f aw Going 30 -37 Slow	[50]
	£1897 £542 £271 3 yo rec 9 lb	

3494 **ODYN DANCER 14** [4] M D I Usher 3-8-4 (35) G Baker (5) 7/1: 040031: 3 b f Minshaanshu Amad -   **41a**
Themeda (Sure Blade), Rear, imprvd ent fnl 3f, led below dist, rdn clr: bght in for 5,300gns: 1st win, '99 rnr up
(auct mdn rtd 59a, unplcd on turf, rtd 55): eff at 12f, tried 2m: acts on both AW's, sharp trks: nicely h'capped.
3276 **IRISH CREAM 22** [11] Andrew Reid 4-9-5 (41)(vis) M Henry 11/4 FAV: 626202: 4 b f Petong - Another   3 **42a**
Baileys (Deploy) Waited with, prog halfway, led appr fnl 1f, rdn & hdd ins last: tchd 9/2: ran to best, see 668.
3437 **RAYWARE BOY 15** [3] D Shaw 4-9-4 (34) A Clark 7/1: 200403: 4 b c Scenic - Amata (Nodouble)   nk **40a**
Towards rear, prog & edged left, not clr run 2f out, kept on: tchd 9/1: eff at 1m, stays 12f, see 1660
3498 **BILLICHANG 14** [2] P Howling 4-9-7 (43)(bl) J Quinn 12/1: 004454: Led till ent fnl 2f, onepace.   2½ **40a**
3002 **FLY LIKE A BIRD 35** [6] 4-8-12 (34) G Duffield 8/1: 040055: Bhd ldrs, eff 3f out, fdd ent fnl 2f: see 2075. 2½ **28a**
3624 **LOKOMOTIV 8** [10] 4-9-1 (37)(bl) P Fitzsimons (5) 8/1: 010526: Nvr better than mid-div: AW bow, op 6/1. 2 **29a**
3260 **COSMO JACK 23** [12] 4-10-0 (50)(vis) K Darley 7/1: 250007: Rear, prog halfway, wknd ent str: AW bow. 4 **38a**
3612 **LATINO BAY 8** [9] 3-9-3 (48) T G McLaughlin 33/1: -06008: Al towards rear: longer trip, see 2026.   4 **32a**
3499 **GYPSY SONG 14** [5] 3-9-3 (48) O Pears 10/1: -00509: Chsd ldrs, wknd qckly 3f out: longer trip.   1¼ **31a**
3637 **WELCOME BACK 7** [7] 3-8-5 (35)(vow) F Lynch 7/1: 553630: Well plcd till ent fnl 3f, rdn/btn/eased 3f out: 10th. 2½ **17a**
2331 **Cool Vibes 63** [1] 5-9-11 (47)(vis) R Fitzpatrick 33/1:   3681 **Boca Chica 5** [8] 3-8-4 (35) A Mackay 50/1:
12 ran   Time 2m 41.6 (8)   (M D I Usher)   M D I Usher Kingston Lisle, Oxon

---

3774	9.30 CHEEKY GRIN HCAP 3YO+ 0-70 (E) 6f aw rnd Going 30 +03 Fast	[70]
	£3080 £880 £440 3 yo rec 2 lb	

3572 **RUSSIAN ROMEO 10** [4] B A McMahon 5-9-10 (66)(bl) W Supple 6/1: 002351: 5 b g Soviet Lad - Aotearoa   **73a**
(Flash Of Steel) Cl-up, led halfway, clr bef dist, ran on strgly: '99 wnr here at W'hampton (h'cap) & Southwell
(class stks, rtd 69a & 64): '98 Chester wnr (clmr, rtd 72 & 73a): eff at 6f, tried 7f: acts on firm, soft grnd &
fibresand: suited by sharp trks, wears blnks or visor: can force the pace
3587 **DAYS OF GRACE 9** [11] L Montague Hall 5-9-12 (68) C Rutter 7/1: 531142: 5 gr m Wolfhound - Inshirah 1¾ **70a**
(Caro) In tch, prog ent fnl 3f, went 2nd bef dist, not trble wnr: fine run back on sand, v tough: see 3493.
3312 **YOUNG BIGWIG 21** [10] D W Chapman 6-9-0 (56) G Duffield 4/1 FAV: 533403: 6 b g Anita's Prince -   1¼ **54a**
Humble Mission (Shack) Chsd ldrs, niggled thro'out, unable to qcken appr fnl 1f: clr rem but can do better, see 425.
3578 **PALO BLANCO 10** [13] Andrew Reid 9-8-6 (48) M Henry 10/1: 462044: Rear till kept on appr fnl 1f.   3 **37a**
3502 **MOOCHA CHA MAN 13** [7] 4-9-3 (59)(VIS) J Weaver 16/1: 050005: Handy, onepce dist: vis, st/mate wnr. ½ **47a**
3653 **KOSEVO 7** [2] 6-8-7 (49)(bl) Dean McKeown 25/1: 030006: Led till halfway, no extra appr fnl 1f: qk reapp. ¾ **35a**
3493 **SEREN TEG 14** [5] 4-9-8 (64)(bl) A Clark 7/1: 064607: Nvr going pace: see 440.   2½ **44a**
3502 **QUITE HAPPY 13** [8] 5-9-6 (62) L Newton 6/1: 422228: Nvr a factor: AW bow, longer trip, btr 3502, see 897. ¾ **40a**
3578 **ITHADTOBEYOU 10** [12] 5-8-8 (50)(t) J Quinn 9/2: 230059: Dwelt, nvr in it: t-strap, see 1139, 879.   shd **28a**
3578 **SOUNDS LUCKY 10** [9] 4-8-13 (55)(BL) C Carver (3) 20/1: 050000: Nvr trbld ldrs: 10th, blnkd, see 563.   nk **32a**
3512 **MARENGO 13** [6] 6-8-12 (54) R Fitzpatrick 8/1: 636500: Rear, brief eff 3f out: 11th, see 1073.   ½ **30a**
3364 **INDY CARR 18** [3] 3-8-9 (53) N Callan 20/1: 660000: Al bhd: 12th, AW bow, see 900.   3 **22a**
3698 **NITE OWL MATE 5** [1] 3-9-12 (70)(t) T G McLaughlin 8/1: 010000: Speed 3f: 13th, qk reapp, top-weight. 9 **19a**
13 ran   Time 1m 14.4 (1.6)   (R L Bedding)   B A McMahon Hopwas, Staffs

---

Official Going   GOOD Stalls: Round Course - Inside; Str Course - Stands Side.

3775	2.20 GOING FORTH SELLER 3YO+ (F) 1m rnd Good/Soft 73 -17 Slow
	£2992 £855 £427 3 yo rec 5 lb

3393 **TOUJOURS RIVIERA 17** [15] J Pearce 10-9-6 T G McLaughlin 9/1: /00151: 10 ch g Rainbow Quest -   **60**
Miss Roulaway (Northfields) Chsd ldr thr'out, styd on to lead 2f out, kept on strongly for press, drvn out: no
bid: earlier won at Newmarket (sell): well btn sole '99 start, prev term won at Lingfield (h'cap, rtd 80a): eff
over 1m/12f: acts on firm, soft, both AWs, any trk: now best in sell grade.
3623 **HORMUZ 8** [4] J M Bradley 4-9-6 F Lynch 11/8 FAV: 010552: 4 b g Hamas - Balqis (Advocator)   ½ **59**
Led, hdd 2f out, kept on for press, no extra well ins last: nicely bckd: consistent, win another sell: see 2834.
1603 **SEVEN 94** [13] Miss S J Wilton 5-9-6 (vis) M Fenton 25/1: 000403: 5 ch g Weldnaas - Polly's   2 **55**
Teahouse (Shack) In tch, rdn/prog over 2f out, chsd front 2 appr fnl 1f but al held: op 16/1, gd eff after
a 3 month abs: eff at 6/7f, stays 1m: see 414.
3534 **FUTURE COUP 11** [3] J Norton 4-9-0 (bl) R Winston 6/1: 405304: Slow to start, gd late hdwy   1¾ **46**
from rear but nvr nrr: tchd 8/1: once again lost ch at start: see 3393.
3407 **CHAMPAGNE N DREAMS 16** [7] 8-8-9 Kim Tinkler 16/1: 660005: Towards rear, prog after halfway,   1¾ **38**
rdn/held appr fnl 1f: see 1275.
3711 **NAKED OAT 4** [9] 5-9-6 J Bosley (7) 33/1: 160006: Mid-div, prog 4f, rdn/fdd over 1f out: qck reapp.   shd **49$**
3691 **HEATHYARDS JAKE 5** [2] 4-9-0 P M Quinn (3) 14/1: 540407: Rear, late gains, no threat: qck reapp.   3 **38**
3672 **SCARLET LIVERY 6** [12] 4-8-9 K Hodgson 20/1: 000058: Sn rdn, mod late gains, no dngr: qck reapp.   5 **25**

1157

3326 **MILDON** 20 [11] 4-9-0 (BL) J Fanning 50/1: 0-0069: Mid-div at best: blnkd: drop in trip.   ½ 29
2331 **SWEET TEDDY** 63 [1] 3-8-4 G Carter 13/2: 4-0000: Nvr a factor, fin 10th: 9 wk abs: see 1234.   ½ 23
3670 **SPEEDFIT FREE** 6 [10] 3-9-1 Dean McKeown 10/1: 413040: Chsd ldrs, wkng when short of room   2½ 30
2f out, sn bhd, 11th: quick reapp: see 3670.
3129 **PETRA NOVA** 29 [14] 4-8-9 V Halliday 33/1: 0-0060: Rcd v keenly, prom, lost tch fnl 2f, 12th.   shd 19
4444} **Minty** 318 [8] 4-9-0 G Parkin 33/1:   3671 **Sandown Clantino** 6 [17] 3-8-4 P Fessey 33/1:
3380 **Sitting Pretty** 17 [6] 4-8-9 D Mernagh (3) 50/1:   --   **Johnstons Fanfan** [18] 4-9-0 C Lowther 20/1:
3226 **Boomshadow** 24 [5] 3-8-9 (t) D O'Donohoe 20/1:
17 ran   Time 1m 42.6 (7.2)   (The Fantasy Fellowship)   J Pearce Newmarket

---

3776   2.55 SINCLAIR MASON AUCT MDN 2YO (F)   7f rnd   Good/Soft 73 -39 Slow
£2925   £900   £450   £225

3617 **GONE TOO FAR** 8 [6] M Dods 2-8-6 J Fanning 11/8 FAV: -021: 2 b g Reprimand - Blue Nile (Bluebird)   71
Front rank, went on over 3f out, hdd appr fnl 1f, rall to lead fnl 50yds, drvn out: nicely bckd: 3,000gns Feb foal,
dam 10f wnr: acts on fast, gd/soft & a flat/easy trk: looks genuine, could win again.
3520 **GARDOR** 12 [12] J G FitzGerald 2-8-6 A Nicholls (3) 2/1: 4442: 2 b c Kendor - Garboesque (Priolo)   ¾ 70
Settled rear, gd hdwy when hmpd over 2f out, ran on well to lead over 1f out, hdd well ins last, held cl-home:
nicely bckd, clr rem: eff at 7f on gd/soft: shown enough to land a mod contest: see 3520.
2873 **SECOND VENTURE** 40 [8] J R Weymes 2-8-6 M Fenton 33/1: 03: 2 b c Petardia - Hilton Gateway (Hello   4 62
Gorgeous) Keen, chsd ldrs, imprvd halfway, no extra over 1f out: 6 wk abs: poss stays 7f on gd/soft: see 2873.
3245 **SORAYAS QUEST** 24 [7] A B Mulholland 2-8-1 A Beech (5) 25/1: 04: Rear, gd late hdwy, nvr nrr: hd 57
cheaply bought Feb 1st foal, dam scored over 13f: 1m+ shld suit in time.
--   **MOON ROYALE** [1] 2-8-5 P Fessey 33/1: 5: Dwelt, hdwy from rear 2f out, nvr dngrs: 6,200gns foal,   hd 61
half sister to a number of wnrs, incl a decent 6f juv scorer: dam a 1m wnr: encouraging debut.
3614 **EL UNO** 8 [9] 2-8-6 R Cody Boutcher (5) 25/1: -006: Ins, rn/hung right over 2f out, wknd: up in trip.   ½ 61
2588 **SUSIE THE FLOOSIE** 52 [2] 2-8-5 Paul Eddery 14/1: 07: Slow to start, sn chasing ldrs, snatched up   4 53
over 2f out, not recover: 7 wk abs: 7,500 gns May foal: forgive this, with B Smart.
2985 **NISAN BIR** 35 [10] 2-8-1 G Parkin 14/1: 040508: Handy, prog/hmpd over 2f out, sn btn: see 1838.   nk 57
3601 **FFIFFIFFER** 8 [3] 2-8-10 T Lucas 8/1: 49: Keen/prom, wknd qckly fnl 2f: btr 3601 (1m, firm).   3½ 51
3617 **EASY FREE** 8 [11] 2-8-1 D Mernagh (3) 50/1: -000: Al towards rear, fin 10th: see 1538.   hd 42
898   **SEA STORM** 142 [13] 2-8-10 R Winston 33/1: 00: Led, hdd over 3f out, sn lost tch, 13th: long abs: 0
prev with M Todhunter, now with R F Fisher: see 898.
1577 **Tupgill Flight** 95 [4] 2-8-1 J Quinn 33/1:   --   **Taras Tipple** [5] 2-8-6 O Pears 25/1:
13 ran   Time 1m 30.8 (7.9)   (Exors Of The Late Mrs H M Carr)   M Dods Piercebridge, Co Durham

---

3777   3.25 BLACK CAT FILLIES HCAP 3YO+ 0-90 (C)   1m rnd   Good/Soft 73 -10 Slow   [79]
£6760   £2080   £1040   £520   3 yo rec 5 lb

2688 **DIVERS PEARL** 49 [1] J R Fanshawe 3-9-5 (75) J Fanning 7/1: -21301: 3 b f Prince Sabo - Seek The   82
Pearl (Rainbow Quest) Made all, rdn & went clr appr fnl 1f, eased fnl 50yds, val 4/5L: 7 wk abs: earlier won on
the AW at W'hampton (med auct mdn, rtd 80a): plcd in '99 (auct mdn, rtd 87): eff at 7f/1m on firm, gd/soft &
fibresand: acts on an easy or sharp/undul trk: goes v well when fresh: cmftble wnr here, could follow up.
3344 **FALLS OMONESS** 19 [4] E J Alston 6-7-10 (47)(4oh) P M Quinn (3) 14/1: 200002: 6 b m River Falls -   2½ 48
Sevens Are Wild (Petorius) Pulled v hard, imprvd over 2f out, styd on ins last, no threat: needs to learn to settle.
3643 **CAUTION** 7 [3] S Gollings 6-8-5 (56) J Quinn 11/4: 252333: 6 b m Warning - Fairy Flax (Dancing Brave)   1¾ 54
Cl-up, rdn to improve 2f out, sn not pace of wnr: quick reapp: consistent form, see 3643, 3188.
2188 **ANGIES QUEST** 68 [2] H R A Cecil 3-9-8 (78) W Ryan 3/1: 630-24: Prom, drvn over 2f out, sn btn: 4 69
10 wk abs, h'cap bow: shade better on reapp in 2188 (mdn, fast).
3432 **ARDANZA** 15 [7] 3-9-4 (74) G Carter 16/1: 2465: Dwelt, nvr nr to chall: drop in trip, apprec 10f+.   nk 65
3432 **FUNNY GIRL** 15 [5] 3-9-10 (80) D O'Donohoe 9/1: -56256: Waited with, brief eff 3f out, sn held: op 7/1.   nk 70
3022 **FLYING CARPET** 34 [6] 3-8-12 (68) Paul Eddery 5/2 FAV: 003137: Handy, drvn & dropped rear appr   1¼ 56
fnl 1f: nicely bckd & better expected, reportedly not apprec this slow pace: prog prev, btr 3022, 2515.
7 ran   Time 1m 42.1 (6.7)   (Cheveley Park Stud)   J R Fanshawe Newmarket

---

3778   4.00 TOTE HAMBLETON CUP HCAP 3YO+ 0-90 (C)   1m4f   Good/Soft 73 -37 Slow   [87]
£4597   £2250   £1125   £562   3 yo rec 9 lb

*3676 **SUMMER SONG** 6 [7] E A L Dunlop 3-9-4 (86) G Carter 11/4 FAV: 113111: 3 b f Green Desert - High   90
Standard (Kris) Front rank, went on appr fnl 1f, styd strongly, drvn out: slow time: nicely bckd: prolific this
term, earlier won at Windsor, Folkestone, Redcar, Ripon & Beverley (h'caps): landed a private stks at Newmarket in
'99 (rtd 79): eff at 1m, suited by 10/12f: acts on fast & gd/soft & any trk: admirably tough & progressive filly.
3541 **WARNING REEF** 11 [6] E J Alston 7-8-6 (65) F Lynch 9/2: 312142: 7 b g Warning - Horseshoe Reef   ¾ 67
(Mill Reef) Mid-div, rdn/prog over 2f out, ran on well ins last, closing at fin: op 7/2: not out of 1st 4 in
last 8 starts: v tough, deserves another win: see 3541, 3461.
3336 **ALEXANDRINE** 20 [2] Sir Mark Prescott 3-8-4 (72) Dean McKeown 10/1: 141143: 3 b f Nashwan -   1 72
Alruccaba (Crystal Palace) Rcd keenly in tch, drvn 2f out, kept on ins last, no threat to wnr: acts on firm &
gd/soft grnd, ran to near best here: see 2876.
3541 **FATEHALKHAIR** 11 [1] B Ellison 8-8-5 (64) R Winston 9/1: 231504: Cl-up, rdn/prog 2f out, held fnl 1f.   nk 64
3504 **MONTECRISTO** 13 [4] A Beech (5) 6/1: -35545: Chasing ldrs when short of room over   ½ 85
2f out, drvn & held when checked well ins last: see 1030.
3541 **MARDANI** 11 [8] 5-9-13 (86) J Fanning 7/2: 000266: Set slow pace, hdd appr fnl 1f, sn btn: see 3461.   nk 85
3453 **AFTER THE BLUE** 15 [5] 3-8-7 (75) R Havlin 9/1: 451227: Waited with, prog over 2f out, sn drvn/wknd.   4 68
3224 **CASHMERE LADY** 24 [3] 8-8-3 (62) D O'Donohoe 14/1: 102048: Nvr a factor, fin last: out of form.   1¾ 53
8 ran   Time 2m 43.1 (13.3)   (Maktoum Al Maktoum)   E A L Dunlop Newmarket

---

3779   4.35 EBF CUCUMBER MDN 2YO (D)   1m rnd   Good/Soft 73 -25 Slow
£3939   £1212   £606   £303

3459 **MIN MIRRI** 15 [2] M R Channon 2-8-9 R Havlin 2/1: -4531: 2 b f Selkirk - Sulitelma (The Minstrel)   83
Prom, hdwy to lead 2f out, rdn & went clr ins last, eased nr fin, val arnd 4L: nicely bckd: 18,500gns Apr foal,
sister to a 1m wnr, dam scored over 5f: apprec this step up to 1m: acts on fast, gd/soft & a stiff/gall or easy trk.

3412 **WAINAK 16** [5] J L Dunlop 2-9-0 G Carter 6/4 FAV: 02232: 2 b c Silver Hawk - Cask (Be My Chief)   2½   79
Sn rdn in last place, drvn/hdwy over 2f out, ran on ins last, no threat to wnr: nicely bckd: poss styd this
longer 1m trip: looks a tricky ride & worth a try in headgear: see 3412.

3156 **DON ALFRED 28** [7] P F I Cole 2-9-0 D Griffiths 10/1: 503: 2 b c Mark Of Esteem - Jezyah (Chief's   1¼   77
Crown) Prom, rdn/prog over 2f out, onepcd appr dist: clr rem, op 7/1: stays 1m on gd/soft, h'caps will suit.

3121 **RED DEER 29** [3] E A L Dunlop 2-9-0 W Ryan 20/1: 004: Led, hdd 2f out, wknd dist: longer 1m trip.   5   68

3508 **REGENT COURT 13** [1] 2-8-9 Paul Eddery 7/2: 545: Dsptd lead, fdd appr fnl 2f: up in trip: see 3156.   7   51

2635 **MR SQUIGGLE 50** [6] 2-9-0 G Parkin 50/1: 066: Trkd ldrs, wknd qckly halfway: 7 wk abs, no form yet.   11   40

-- **MUSADIF** [4] 2-9-0 C Lowther 7/1: R: Reared up as stalls opened & refused to race: Feb foal,   0
full brother to a high-class juv, dam scored over 5f as a 2yo: with B Hanbury.

7 ran   Time 1m 43.3 (7.9)   (Dominion Partners)   M R Channon West Isley, Berks

---

3780	5.10 CHARTERHOUSE MDN 3YO+ (D) 6f Good/Soft 73 +07 Fast

     £4394   £1352   £676   £338   3 yo rec 2 lb

3587 **MUFFLED 9** [12] J L Dunlop 3-8-7 G Carter 4/1 JT FAV: 002001: 3 ch f Mizaaya - Sound It (Believe It)   64
Trkd ldrs, rdn to lead 1f out, drvn clr ins last: nicely bckd, best time of day: flattered 4th in a Leicester mdn
on '99 debut (rtd 70): eff around 6f: acts on fast, clrly apprec gd/soft grnd today: handles a flat/easy trk.

3651 **FIRST VENTURE 7** [2] C N Allen 3-8-12 (vis) D O'Donohoe 14/1: 300442: 3 b g Formidable - Diamond   3   59
Wedding (Diamond Shoal) Led & rcd alone centre trk, hdd dist, kept on but not pace of wnr: op 10/1, quick
reapp: consistent recent form, handles gd, gd/soft & both AWs: see 804.

3180 **IMPALDI 26** [9] B Ellison 5-8-9 R Winston 16/1: 023303: 5 b m Imp Society - Jaldi (Nordico)   ½   53$
Slow to start, hdwy from rear when switched over 2f out, ran on, nvr nrr: mdn after 32 starts: treat rating
with caution, well btn in a sell h'cap off 40 in 3180.

3584 **MELLEDGAN 9** [8] R Guest 3-8-7 W Ryan 8/1: 64: Mid-div, imprvd over 2f out, kept on but not   1½   49
pace of ldrs: up in trip: see 3584.

222 **BOADICEA THE RED 255** [4] 3-8-7 M Fenton 6/1: 6203-5: Prom, rdn/no impress appr fnl 1f: 1½   45
9 month abs: just sharper for this: see 222 (nurs h'cap).

3462 **ZILUTTE 14** [7] 3-8-12 Paul Eddery 14/1: 456: Chsd ldrs, rdn/btn fnl 2f: sell h'caps suit: see 3462.   hd   50

3651 **DAVEYS PANACEA 7** [6] 3-8-7 P Bradley (5) 9/2: 253337: Front rank, drvn/onepcd fnl 2f: qck reapp.   hd   45

3584 **TOP OF THE PARKES 9** [11] 3-8-7 J Quinn 4/1 JT FAV: 0-3028: With ldr, wknd qckly appr fnl 1f: 3½   36
softer grnd here, much better on gd/firm in 3584 (5f).

3651 **DAYLILY 7** [3] 3-8-7 G Parkin 8/1: 332359: Trkd ldrs, wknd appr fnl 1f: btr 2313 (fast).   ½   36

4014} **ZAMAT 348** [14] 4-9-0 V Halliday 66/1: 0-0: Dwelt, al in rear, 10th: reapp: massive drop in trip: 2   34
t.o. in a 12f mdn (hvy grnd) sole '99 start for W Jarvis: now with P Monteith.

3698 **VICTORS CROWN 5** [5] 3-8-12 A Beech 5/1: 0-0600: Al twrds rear, 11th: qck reapp: see 3384.   ½   33

1298 **Trumpet Blues 110** [1] 4-9-0 O Pears 50/1:   3651 **Cottam Lilly 7** [10] 3-8-7 T Lucas 50/1:

3477 **Plazzotta 14** [13] 3-8-12 L Gueller (7) 33/1: P

14 ran   Time 1m 13.5 (4.0)   (P D Player)   J L Dunlop Arundel, W Sussex

---

3781	5.40 IRWIN MITCHELL MDN HCAP 3YO+ 0-60 (F) 5f Good/Soft 73 +01 Fast	[60]

     £3201   £985   £492   £246   3 yo rec 1 lb

3441 **UPPER CHAMBER 15** [5] J G FitzGerald 4-8-3 (35) D O'Donohoe 14/1: 000051: 4 b g Presidium -   37
Vanishing Trick (Silly Season) Front rank, went on appr fnl 1f, strongly prsd well ins last, drvn out & just
prevailed: rnr-up on '99 reapp (rtd 70): eff arnd 5f on firm & gd/soft grnd: handles a flat/easy trk:
firm & gd/soft grnd: has tried blnks/visor, best without.

3536 **TONG ROAD 11** [16] D W Chapman 4-8-3 (34)(1ow) G Parkin 20/1: -00002: 4 gr g Petong - Wayzgoose nk   36
(Diesis) Slow to start, hdwy from rear when switched over, styd on strongly cl-home, just held: mod prev:
jockey put up costly 1lb overweight: looks capable of wng similar: eff at 5f on gd/soft.

3200 **RIVER BLEST 25** [21] Mrs A Duffield 4-9-6 (52) L Enstone (7) 7/1: 500203: 4 b g Unblest - Vaal   hd   53
Salmon (Salmon Leap) Rear, prog over 1f out, strong fnl 1f, not btn far: eff at 5/7.5f, apprec a return to 6f+.

3161 **SASHA 28** [8] J Balding 3-9-0 (47) J Fanning 33/1: 0-4004: Front rank, rdn & kept on ins last,   shd   48
held nr fin: quick reapp: stays 5f on gd/soft: see 2519.

3694 **APPLES AND PEARS 5** [11] 4-8-6 (38) A Beech (5) 8/1: 000045: Led, hdd appr fnl 1f, kept on &   nk   38
not btn far: quick reapp: flattered 3694.

3652 **BEST BOND 7** [6] 3-9-8 (55)(vis) C Lowther 12/1: 606306: Sn outpcd, ran on late, no threat to   ½   53
ldrs: quick reapp & shld apprec a return to 6f: see 3194.

3502 **PRIME RECREATION 13** [20] 3-9-8 (55) W Ryan 14/1: 030007: Trkd ldrs, rdn/held ins last: see 1817.   shd   53

3266 **ALL MINE 23** [10] 3-8-2 (35) D Mernagh (3) 33/1: 606508: Prom, onepcd fnl 1f: drop in trip.   ¾   31

3653 **AMARO 7** [18] 4-8-9 (41) R Winston 5/1 FAV: 636009: Mid-div, dropped rear over 2f out, staying   ¾   35
on but no impress when short of room ins last: see 226.

3670 **TIME FOR THE CLAN 6** [23] 3-7-11 (30)(vis) Michael Doyle (7) 14/1: 000060: Cl-up 4f, sn btn, 10th.   ¾   22

3441 **ROISTERER 15** [13] 4-8-3 (35) Claire Bryan (7) 25/1: 00000: Mid-div at best, 11th: mod form.   ½   26

3441 **TICK TOCK 15** [3] 3-9-2 (49)(vis) L Newton 13/2: 200040: V slow to start, gd hdwy appr fnl 1f, no   1¾   35
extra ins last, fin 12th: lost all ch at start here & poss worth another try in similar: see 3441.

3619 **FASTRACK TIME 8** [17] 3-8-12 (45)(VIS) Paul Eddery 12/1: -00000: Nvr a factor, 13th: visored.   ½   30

2905 **SIMBATU 39** [22] 3-9-10 (57) P Bradley (5) 12/1: 00-650: Al bhd: top weight: see 2511 (6f).   0

2184 **PRINCESS AURORA 69** [19] 3-8-10 (43) M Fenton 12/1: -06000: Hmpd start, al bhd, 19th: 10 wk abs.   0

3462 **PETERS PRINCESS 14** [4] 3-8-3 (34)(2ow) G Carter 12/1: 50-600: Prom 4f, sn bhd, 20th: bckd from 25/1.   0

2535 **Two Jacks 54** [12] 3-9-0 (47)(t) O Pears 25/1:   3593 **Red Mittens 9** [14] 3-8-7 (40) P Fessey 33/1:

3194 **Reds Desire 26** [15] 3-7-10 (29)(7oh) Iona Wands 33/1:

942 **Rathlea 138** [2] 6-8-6 (38) P M Quinn (3) 50/1:

20 ran   Time 1m 00.6 (3.6)   (J G FitzGerald)   J G FitzGerald Norton, N Yorks

HAYDOCK SATURDAY SEPTEMBER 2ND Lefthand, Flat, Galloping Track

Official Going HEAVY (Times suggest straight crse rode appreciably qckr than round crse).
Stalls: 5f/6f - Stands Side; 7f/1m - Ins; 1m6f - Centre; 1m2f - Outside.

3782

2.00 STANLEY RTD HCAP 3YO 0-100 (B) 1m2f120y Soft 116 -03 Slow [107]
£9460 £3588 £1794 £816

*3267 **POLAR RED 23** [1] M J Ryan 3-9-7 (100) P Robinson 11/2: 243111: 3 ch g Polar Falcon - Sharp Top (Sharpo) In tch, smooth prog to lead appr fnl 2f, rdn & ran on strongly: op 9/2, jt top-weight: v progressive, earlier won at Kempton & here at Haydock (2, rtd h'cap & h'cap): juv wnr at Windsor (nurs, rtd 73): eff btwn 1m & 12f on fast, soft grnd: goes on any trk, becoming a Haydock specialist: v useful, win a Listed. **104**

3563 **VINTAGE PREMIUM 10** [4] R A Fahey 3-9-7 (100) G Duffield 9/1: 221602: 3 b c Forzando - Julia Domna (Dominion) Cl-up, led ent str till bef 2f out, kept on well for press: gd run from this useful colt. *1¾* **101**

*2596 **MOON SOLITAIRE 52** [3] E A L Dunlop 3-9-4 (97) J Reid 9/2 CO FAV: 313013: 3 b c Night Shift - Gay Fantastic (Ela Mana Mou) In tch, prog to chase ldrs 2f out, hung left & no extra ent fnl 1f: fine run after 7 wk abs: improving, see 2596 (made all under a canny ride). *½* **97**

3421 **KINGSDON 16** [2] R Hannon 3-8-8 (87)(t) R Hughes 6/1: 006544: Waited with, prog to dispute 2nd ent fnl 2f, onepace for press ins last: well clr of rem, loves soft grnd: stays 10.5f, 1m shld be ideal: see 1382. *¾* **86**

*3658 **EVEREST 6** [6] 3-8-10 (89) L Dettori 9/2 CO FAV: 321115: Held up, under press 3f out, same pace: qck reapp & stamina prob stretched over this longer 10.5f trip on testing grnd: see 3658. *6* **82**

3509 **FIRST TRUTH 13** [7] 3-8-13 (92) Pat Eddery 9/1: 642046: Chsd ldrs, fdd appr fnl 2f: see 990. *5* **80**

3453 **OPTIMAITE 15** [8] 3-9-4 (97) J P Spencer 33/1: 105057: Dwelt but sn led, hdd ent str & no extra. *¾* **84**

-2702 **BONAGUIL 48** [9] 3-8-8 (87) R Mullen 9/2 CO FAV: 113428: In tch till wknd 3f out: bckd tho' tchd 7/2, 7 wk abs: reportedly unsuited by this soft grnd & worth forgiving: see 2702, 1075. *3½* **71**

2475 **CAROUSING 57** [5] 3-8-13 (92) K Darley 14/1: 1-1509: Mid-div, left bhd 3f out: 8 wk abs, see 1703. *4* **72**

9 ran Time 2m 22.53 (12.53) (M Byron) M J Ryan Newmarket.

3783

2.30 STANLEYBET.CO.UK HCAP 3YO+ 0-85 (D) 1m6f Soft 116 -09 Slow [82]
£21108 £6495 £3247 £1623 3 yo rec 11lb

3323 **MAJESTIC BAY 21** [8] P W Harris 4-9-12 (80) J Weaver 25/1: 013141: 4 b g Unfuwain - That'll Be The Day (Thatching) Led, pushed over 2L clr 2f out, wandered & flashed tail under press dist, held on well: earlier won at Yarmouth (mdn) & Redcar (h'cap): dual '99 rnr-up (rtd 90): eff at 10f, suited by 14f/2m: acts on firm & soft, poss hvy, any trk: likes forcing the pace, without blnks: progressive stayer. **86**

*3323 **SUDDEN FLIGHT 21** [16] E A L Dunlop 3-9-5 (84) J Reid 7/1: 025212: 3 b c In The Wings - Ma Petite Cherie (Caro) Patiently rdn, imprvd 2f out, rdn bef dist, ran on to go 2nd nr fin: fine run & is on the upgrade tho' beat this wnr in 3323 (set less to do on fast grnd). *2* **85**

3378 **TOTEM DANCER 17** [14] J L Eyre 7-8-2 (56) R Mullen 33/1: 242063: 7 b m Mtoto - Ballad Opera (Sadler's Wells) Dwelt, towards rear, imprvd appr fnl 1f & drvn to chase wnr ins last, kept on onepace: ran to best. *nk* **56**

3590 **BHUTAN 9** [15] Mrs M Reveley 5-9-4 (72) A Culhane 20/1: 600124: Mid-div, eff 2f out, kept on for press but not pace to chall: tricky ride, ran well: see 3201. *2* **71**

*3472 **MAGIC COMBINATION 14** [1] 7-9-5 (73) J P Spencer 7/1: 1-4515: Held up, prog to chase ldrs 3f out, no impress bef dist: op 5/1: fair run from this Sandown specialist: see 3472. *1* **71**

3541 **MORGANS ORCHARD 11** [9] 4-8-11 (65) G Baker (5) 12/1: 202326: Well pl & ch till no extra appr fnl 1f. *nk* **63**

*3476 **INTRUM MORSHAAN 14** [6] 3-9-5 (84) Pat Eddery 5/2 FAV: 3-0217: Front rank, onepace ent fnl 2f: well bckd: 13lbs higher than in a much less competitive affair in 3476 (2m, gd/soft). *¾* **81**

3323 **SEREN HILL 21** [5] 4-10-0 (82) K Dalgleish (5) 9/2: -00028: Held up, prog 2f out, fdd und press bef dist. *½* **78**

3674 **YES KEEMO SABEE 6** [10] 5-7-10 (50)(bl)(1oh) J McAuley 25/1: 533029: Prom, wknd appr fnl 1f. *2* **45**

3472 **MARAHA 14** [2] 3-8-10 (75)(BL) W Supple 40/1: -43250: Chsd ldrs, rdn appr fnl 2f, sn btn: 10th, blnkd. *½* **69**

3522 **BRISBANE ROAD 12** [4] 3-8-5 (70)(t) G Duffield 12/1: -45120: Chsd ldrs, lost pl appr fnl 2f: 11th. *4* **61**

*3424 **FLETCHER 16** [12] 6-9-0 (68) R Hughes 14/1: 211510: In tch till 3f out: 12th, recent wins on faster grnd. *1¾* **58**

2502 **CELESTIAL WELCOME 56** [11] 5-9-8 (76) K Darley 12/1: 100000: Al towards rear: 13th, 8 wk abs. *3* **64**

2691 **ARMEN 49** [7] 3-9-1 (80) M Roberts 25/1: 0-220: Handy till ent str: last on h'cap bow, 7 wk abs, see 1929. *10* **61**

14 ran Time 3m 15.44 (17.44) (The Quiet Ones) P W Harris Aldbury, Herts.

3784

3.00 GR 1 STANLEY SPRINT CUP 3YO+ (A) 6f Inapplicable Fast
£87000 £33000 £16500 £7500 3 yo rec 2 lb 2 Groups, centre-far side was the place to be.

3598 **PIPALONG 9** [7] T D Easterby 4-8-11 K Darley 3/1: 210331: 4 b f Pips Pride - Limpopo (Green Desert) Prom far side, led bef dist, edged left under press but ran on gamely: well bckd, tchd 4/1, gd time: earlier won at Thirsk (stks), Newmarket (Gr 3) & here at Haydock (List): '99 Ripon (val h'cap) & Doncaster wnr (List, rtd 107): '98 wnr at Ripon, York & Redcar (val 2yo Trophy, rtd 105): eff at 5f, suited by 6f, prob stays 7f: acts on firm & hvy grnd, any trk: runs well fresh: v smart & genuine filly, deserved this. **116**

2115 **SAMPOWER STAR 72** [12] Saeed bin Suroor 4-9-0 L Dettori 6/1: -01522: 4 b h Cyrano de Bergerac - Green Supreme (Primo Dominie) In tch stands side, smooth prog 2f out, rdn to chase wnr & edged right over to far side dist, kept on & not btn far: 10 wk abs & a v smart run conceding weight: loves soft grnd: see 1320. *¾* **117**

3600 **TOMBA 9** [3] M A Jarvis 6-9-0 P Robinson 11/1: 203503: 6 ch h Efisio - Indian Love Song (Be My Guest) Held up in tch far side, gd prog to lead appr fnl 1f, sn hdd, no extra towards fin: well clr rem & suited by omission of blnks: v smart on soft grnd here at Haydock, plcd twice in this race before: see 1453. *1* **115**

3598 **HARMONIC WAY 9** [6] R Charlton 5-9-0 J P Spencer 33/1: 216204: Held up far side, hdwy to chase ldrs appr fnl 1f, onepace for press: v useful h'capper, far from disgraced in Gr 1 company: see 2151. *4* **107**

3598 **PERRYSTON VIEW 9** [11] 8-9-0 S Sanders 20/1: 001055: Chsd ldrs stands side, carr left 2f out, no extra bef dist: ideally suited forcing it over 5f nowadays: see 1566 (Gr 2). *1¼* **105**

3598 **EASTERN PURPLE 9** [2] 5-9-0 B Marcus 25/1: 562106: Cl-up far side, fdd bef fnl 1f: capable of better, will apprec return to Gr 3 & faster grnd: see 3373. *nk* **104**

2615 **LINCOLN DANCER 51** [5] 3-8-12 M Roberts 5/2 FAV: -40127: Bhd ldrs far side, hung left appr fnl 1f, btn below dist & eased: well bckd, 7 wk abs: shorter priced stablemate of 3rd & something amiss: considered a mudlark tho' has yet to win on grnd worse than gd/soft: see 2615 (in front of this wnr), 1534 (C/D). *¾* **102**

3610 **CRETAN GIFT 8** [8] 9-9-0 (vis) J Tate 50/1: 344558: Chsd ldrs stands side, no extra appr fnl 1f. *2* **98**

3212 **WINNING VENTURE 27** [10] 3-8-12 (BL) G Duffield 66/1: 230009: Prom stands side till 2f out: blnkd. *1¼* **95**

*3610 **VISION OF NIGHT 8** [15] 4-9-0 Pat Eddery 11/1: 10-110: Prom stands side, hung badly left ent fnl 2f & btn: 10th: up in grade tho' capable of better: see 3610 (fast). *1¼* **92**

3303 **AUENKLANG 21** [9] 3-8-12 (vis) J Reid 12/1: 21-120: Led stands side till 2f out, sn carr left & wknd: *1¾* **88**

11th, visor reapplied, first try on soft grnd & poss best forgotten: see 2847 (Listed, impressive).
*3212 **BOLD EDGE 27** [4] 5-9-0 R Hughes 7/1: -03410: Led far side till 2f out, wknd qckly: 12th: clrly not his form, suited by faster grnd: see 3212 (beat this 2nd on gd grnd). 1¾ **84**
*2669 **INDIAN SPARK 49** [14] 6-9-0 A Culhane 25/1: 102010: Sn struggling: 13th, 7 wk abs, highly tried. 20 **54**
13 ran Time 1m 15.49 (4.19) (T H Bennett) T D Easterby Geeat Habton, N.Yorks.

3785 **3.35 STANLEY RACING HCAP 3YO+ 0-90 (C) 7f30y rnd Soft 116 +04 Fast [90]**
£7540 £2320 £1160 £580 3 yo rec 4 lb

1836 **PRINCE BABAR 84** [2] R A Fahey 9-9-3 (79) P Hanagan (7) 20/1: 244501: 9 b g Fairy King - Bell Toll (High Line) Held up, gd prog appr fnl 2f, ran on strongly ins last to lead fnl 50y: gd time, 12 wk abs: unplcd in '99 for J Banks (h'caps, rtd 83): former jumps rnr-up (nov, 2m, gd & gd/soft, rtd 99h): '98 Newmarket wnr (h'cap, rtd 97): eff at 7f/1m: acts on firm, soft grnd, any trk, without visor: runs well fresh & is v well h'capped. **82**
3510 **MISTER MAL 13** [11] J A Glover 4-9-1 (77) G Duffield 12/1: 500102: 4 b g Scenic - Fashion Parade (Mount Hagen) Well plcd, led bef 2f out & qcknd clr appr dist, rdn & worn down ins last: tchd 16/1: back to form on fav'd surface, win again whilst conditions suit: see 3250. ¾ **77**
2954 **KINAN 36** [12] G C Bravery 4-9-9 (85) J Weaver 16/1: -01003: 4 b c Dixieland Band - Alsharta (Mr Prospector) Cl-up, rdn appr fnl 1f, kept on but unable to chall: suited by gd/soft & soft, acts on fast: see 2431. ½ **84**
*3708 **BOLDLY GOES 5** [15] C W Fairhurst 4-9-10 (86)(bl)(6ex) B Marcus 5/1 FAV: 006014: In tch, eff 2f out, styd on well fnl 100y: nicely bckd, clr rem: gd run from difficult high draw: tough: see 3708. shd **85**
2961 **CHAMELEON 36** [5] 4-8-12 (74) R Mullen 20/1: 0/105: Off the pace till styd on strongly ins last, nvr nrr: only 4th ever start, acts on soft grnd & fibresand & is well worth a try at 1m: see 478. 2½ **70**
3510 **PETERS IMP 13** [7] 5-8-13 (75) J Carroll 12/1: 114336: Rear, shkn up ent str, kept on ins last, nvr dngrs. ½ **70**
3510 **GIFT OF GOLD 13** [13] 5-9-6 (82) J Reid 8/1: 130057: Same place thr'out: see 1483. 2 **74**
3597 **TONY TIE 9** [10] 4-10-3 (93) A Culhane 7/1: 212228: Mid-div, shkn up appr fnl 2f, onepace & short of room bef dist: unsuited by drop back on trip on easier grnd?: see 2986. 1½ **83**
3535 **CLEVER GIRL 11** [9] 3-8-13 (79)(BL) K Darley 6/1: 000439: Well plcd & ev ch till wknd 2f out: blnkd. 1 **68**
*3510 **LADY BOXER 13** [6] 4-8-12 (74) A Mackay 11/2: 000010: Prom, chsd ldrs, badly hmpd, snatched up & drpd rear after 3f, no threat: 10th, forgive?: see 3510. ½ **62**
3118 **FALLACHAN 29** [1] 4-8-13 (75) P Robinson 12/1: 440300: Chsd ldrs, wknd appr fnl 1f, eased ins last: 11th. 8 **55**
2300 **GIRLS BEST FRIEND 64** [16] 3-9-0 (80) S Sanders 25/1: 0-0560: In tch till 3f out: 12th, 9 wk abs. 5 **55**
3481 **SARSON 14** [8] 4-8-13 (75) R Hughes 14/1: -00000: Led till ent fnl 3f, sn btn: 13th, unprvn at 7f/sft grnd. 6 **44**
13 ran Time 1m 35.12 (8.02) (Giles W Pritchard-Gordon) R A Fahey Butterwick, N.Yorks.

3786 **4.10 STANLEY CASINOS MDN 2YO (D) 7f30y rnd Soft 116 -39 Slow**
£3991 £1228 £614 £307

3333 **ESHER COMMON 20** [10] T G Mills 2-9-0 R Mullen 10/1: -51: 2 b c Common Grounds - Alsahah (Unfuwain) Held up, smooth prog to lead appr fnl 1f, ran on strongly, pushed out: op 7/1: 27,000gns Jan first foal: eff at 7f, 1m+ is going to suit: acts on soft grnd, handles fast, stiff/gall trks: progressive & well regarded colt. **90+**
-- **COME ON PEKAN** [15] M A Jarvis 2-9-0 R Hughes 7/1: 2: 2 b c Sri Pekan - Landrail (Storm Bird) Led till halfway, ev ch, outpcd by wnr dist: op 10/1: IR 25,000gns Feb foal: eff at 7f on soft, shld find a mdn. 2½ **85**
3478 **BAILLIESTON 14** [16] J S Goldie 2-9-0 A Culhane 10/1: 33: 2 ch g Indian Ridge - Bathilde (Generous) Handy, ch appr fnl 1f, rdn dist & hmpd, switched & kept on: eff at 7f on gd/soft & soft: see 3478. 1¾ **83**
-- **FORTUNE POINT** [8] J Noseda 2-9-0 L Dettori 5/1: 4: Cl-up, led appr fnl 2f till bef dist, no extra: bckd tho' op 3/1: IR 100,000gns Cadeaux Genereux Jan foal, dam 10f wnr: handles soft grnd, shld improve. 1¼ **81**
2521 **WORTHILY 55** [5] 2-9-0 J Reid 50/1: -05: Held up, hdwy 2f out, onepace fnl 1f: 8 wk abs: see 2521. 2 **78**
2259 **MISS TRESS 66** [13] 2-8-9 J P Spencer 20/1: -46: Rear, prog appr fnl 2f, same pace bef dist: abs. 1¾ **71**
-- **ROSE PEEL** [9] 2-8-9 B Marcus 25/1: 7: Dwelt/off the pace, prog past btn horses appr fnl 1f: drifter from 10/1, stablemate 6th, debut: Danehill May foal, sister to 3 decent juvs up to 1m, dam unrcd: with P Harris. 1¾ **69**
-- **STOLI** [4] 2-9-0 S Sanders 20/1: 8: Held up, hmpd appr fnl 2f, nvr dngrs: op 12/1 on debut: 33,000gns Feb foal, half-brother to decent 6f juv Acicula: dam 10f wnr: with P Makin. 1¼ **72**
-- **DREAM MAGIC** [12] 2-9-0 P Robinson 50/1: 9: Chsd ldrs, fdd 2f out: Magic Ring Apr first foal. shd **72**
-- **THE JUDGE** [1] 2-9-0 K Darley 6/5 FAV: 0: Dwelt, bhd, prog to chase ldrs ent fnl 3f, sn btn, eased fnl 1f: 10th, well bckd, debut: 24,000gns Feb foal, half-brother to a juv wnr, dam 6f juv wnr: with P Cole. 1½ **70**
-- **SUNNY GLENN** [14] 2-9-0 J Tate 50/1: 0: Prom 4f: 11th, debut: v stoutly bred Rock Hopper colt. hd **70**
2810 **GOLDEN WINGS 43** [7] 2-8-9 Pat Eddery 33/1: -00: Cl-up till wknd 3f out: 12th, 6 wk abs. 1½ **63**
2142 **THE LOOSE SCREW 71** [2] 2-9-0 A Clark 50/1: -600: Front rank, led ent str till 2f out, sn lost pl: abs. ½ **67**
13 ran Time 1m 37.96 (10.86) (David J Archer) T G Mills Headley, Surrey.

3787 **4.40 ACROPOLIS.COM COND STKS 2YO (B) 1m30y rnd Soft 116 -03 Slow**
£8122 £2882 £1441 £655

*3523 **SPETTRO 12** [3] P F I Cole 2-9-0 K Darley 11/4: 5111: 2 b c Spectrum - Overruled (Last Tycoon) Led, rdn 2f out, kept on strongly, readily: nicely bckd tho' op 9/4: hat-trick landed after wins at Catterick (mdn) & Nottingham (nov stks): eff at 1m, shld stay at least 10f next term: acts on fast & soft grnd, sharp or gall trks: likes to force the pace & can run well fresh: useful, progressive colt with a fine attitude. **103**
3450 **LUCAYAN CHIEF 15** [1] S P C Woods 2-8-12 L Dettori 6/4 FAV: -5132: 2 b c With Approval - Littleladyleah (Shareef Dancer) Trkd ldrs, rdn appr fnl 2f, chsd wnr bef dist, nvr any impress: well bckd: probably ran to best: eff at 7f/1m: acts on firm & soft grnd: see 3051 (made all). 2 **96**
*3347 **KINGS WELCOME 19** [4] C W Fairhurst 2-8-10 J Reid 6/1: -313: 2 b c Most Welcome - Reine de Thebes (Darshaan) Last but in tch, outpcd appr fnl 2f, rall fnl 1f: progressive, apprec step up to 1m: acts on fast & soft. ¾ **93**
*3287 **ZELOSO 22** [2] J L Dunlop 2-8-12 Pat Eddery 11/4: 030214: Dwelt but sn chsd wnr, wknd under press 2f out: bckd, stiffish task: not disgraced, first try at 1m/on soft grnd: see 3287. 5 **89**
4 ran Time 1m 50.05 (9.55) (Luciano Gaucci) P F I Cole Whatcome, Oxon.

3788 **5.15 STANLEYBET.CO.UK HCAP 3YO+ 0-95 (C) 5f Inapplicable Fair [90]**
£7507 £2310 £1155 £577 3 yo rec 1 lb Raced down the centre

3653 **STATOYORK 7** [8] D Shaw 7-7-11 (59) J McAuley 12/1: 002141: 7 b g Statoblest - Ultimate Dream (Kafu) Trkd ldrs, gd turn of foot to lead towards fin, clvrly: qck reapp, bckd from 16/1: earlier won at Carlisle (h'cap): '99 wnr at Carlisle (class stks) & Ripon (2, h'caps, rtd 73): '98 Pontefract wnr (h'cap, rtd 49 & 53a): **67**

HAYDOCK SATURDAY SEPTEMBER 2ND Lefthand, Flat, Galloping Track

stays 7f, suited by 5f on firm, soft grnd & fibresand: needs to come late, has brkn blood vessels: well h'capped.
3687 **SHARP HAT 5** [9] D W Chapman 6-8-8 (70) A Culhane 14/1: 163032: 6 b g Shavian - Madam Trilby ¾ 74
(Grundy) Cl-up, led briefly well ins last, kept on: qck reapp: in gd form, see 2721.
3512 **POLLY GOLIGHTLY 13** [5] M Blanshard 7-7-13 (61)(bl) Dale Gibson 12/1: 000043: 7 ch m Weldnaas - 1 63
Polly's Teahouse (Shack) Front rank, narrow lead appr fnl 1f till fnl 100y, onepace: likes soft grnd: see 1005.
3687 **SUNLEY SENSE 5** [7] M R Channon 4-9-6 (82) Pat Eddery 10/1: 200664: Narrow lead till till appr 1¼ 80
fnl 1f, same pace: qck reapp, consistent, see 1245, 926.
3512 **THREAT 13** [4] 4-8-2 (64)(t) R Mullen 14/1: 060005: Rear, prog appr fnl 1f, sn rdn, nvr dngrs: shd 62
clr rem: eff at 5f, suited by 6f: handles soft, best on fast: see 1989.
3572 **RYTHM N TIME 10** [16] 3-8-5 (68) W Supple 33/1: 014466: Mid-div thr'out: likes a stiff fin: see 3056. 2 62
3176 **EASTERN TRUMPETER 27** [19] 4-9-5 (81) K Darley 6/1: 021037: Chsd ldrs, wknd ins last: bckd 1 73
from 10/1: suited by faster grnd?: see 1861.
3473 **SAPHIRE 14** [18] 4-9-10 (86) J Reid 9/1: 650248: Towards rear, nvr dngrs: not given a hard time. 2½ 73
2168 **BLUE HOLLY 70** [6] 3-9-6 (83) A Clark 20/1: 520109: In tch till appr fnl 1f: 10 wk abs, see 1795. nk 69
3464 **TARAS GIRL 14** [17] 3-8-7 (70) T E Durcan 20/1: 000000: Nvr a factor: 10th: see 988. 3 50
3543 **FLAK JACKET 11** [10] 5-8-13 (75) S Sanders 9/2 FAV: 111300: Handy 3f: 11th, bckd from 6/1: see 3136. 1¾ 51
3646 **BARRINGER 7** [3] 3-9-8 (85) M Roberts 10/1: -45300: Prom far side, no ch appr fnl 1f: 12th, op 7/1. ¾ 59
1384 **POWER PACKED 105** [1] 3-10-0 (91) P Robinson 12/1: 12-560: Led far side, saddle sn slipped, btn nk 64
2f out: 13th, 15 wk abs: forget this, see 1047.
4538J **AZIZZI 310** [11] 8-10-0 (90) R Hughes 5/1: 3131-0: Speed till halfway: 15th, bckd from 7/1 on reapp: 0
'99 wnr at Newmarket (reapp, clmr), Pontefract & Windsor (h'caps, rtd 93): prev lightly rcd since dual '97 rnr-up
(List/Gr 3, rtd 99): eff forcing the pace at 5f/7f: acts on fast & soft/hvy grnd, any trk: shld leave this bhd.
*2519 **Bond Boy 56** [12] 3-9-6 (83) A McGlone 25/1: 3512 **Nifty Major 13** [3] 3-8-9 (72) J P Spencer 25/1: R
16 ran   Time 1m 02.94 (4.14)   (M D H Racing)   D Shaw Averham, Notts.

KEMPTON SATURDAY SEPTEMBER 2ND Righthand, Flat, Fair Track

Official Going: GOOD (GOOD/FIRM Places). Stalls: Str Course - Stands Side, 10f - Outside, Rem - Inside.

3789 2.05 MILCARS FILLIES COND STKS 2YO (C) 7f rnd Good/Firm 28 -15 Slow
£6293   £2387   £1193   £542

*3418 **RIDGEWAY DAWN 16** [7] M R Channon 2-8-8 Craig Williams 12/1: 11: 2 ch f Mujtahid - Soviet Maid 92
(Soviet Star) Made all, shaken up over 2f out, styd on strongly & al holding rivals under hands & heels riding
ins last: earlier scored at Salisbury (auct mdn,): eff at 7f, 1m will suit: acts on fast grnd & a stiff/undul
or fair trk: has run well fresh: can force the pace: progressive filly, can rate more highly.
-- **MATOAKA** [5] Sir Michael Stoute 2-8-8 D Harrison 100/30 FAV: 2: 2 b f A P Indy - Appointed One ¾ 89+
(Danzig) Trkd ldrs, styd on well under hands & heels riding fnl 2f, al held by wnr: hvly bckd, tho' op 5/2: Jan foal,
dam a US 1m wnr: sire a top class dirt performer: eff at 7f, 1m will suit: acts on fast grnd: encouraging intro.
*3156 **TARFSHI 28** [8] M A Jarvis 2-8-13 M Tebbutt 9/2: 13: 2 b f Mtoto - Pass The Peace (Alzao) ¾ 92
Keen/chsd wnr, rdn fnl 2f, kept on tho' held in last: bckd: mid-dist bred, step up to 1m shld now suit: see 3156.
-- **KAFEZAH** [6] B Hanbury 2-8-8 R Hills 7/1: 4: Rear/in tch, switched & styd on fnl 2f under minimal 1 85+
press, no threat: bckd: Pennekamp filly, March foal: dam a 5f juv wnr: sire top class juv/miler: encouraging intro.
-- **BARATHEASTAR** [3] 2-8-8 J Fortune 5/1: 5: Dwelt, sn trkd ldrs, outpcd fnl 2f: bckd, 6L clr of rem: ½ 84
Baratheastar filly, March foal: half sister to 10f wnr Sena Desert, also v smart mid dist wnr Best Of The Bests: dam a
high class 7f 2/3yo wnr: looks sure to relish 1m+ in time: superbly bred filly, can improve for C Brittain.
3459 **SCARPE ROSSE 15** [1] 2-8-8 T Quinn 7/2: -56: Chsd ldrs, rdn/btn over 2f out: op 5/2: btn 3f 3459. 6 72
3449 **ANOTHER SECRET 15** [4] 2-8-8 L Newman (3) 8/1: -47: Rear, btn 3f out: highly tried after 3449 (6f). 3 66
-- **WHITE AMIT** [9] A Daly 66/1: 8: Slowly away, keen/rear, btn 3f out: Shaamit filly, April foal, 7 52
cost 4,800gns: half sister to a multiple 5f juv wnr & sprint h'capper White Emir: dam unrcd: sire a Derby wnr.
-- **ZAFILLY** [2] 2-8-8 D Holland 50/1: 9: Al bhd: Zafonic filly, May foal, cost 9,500gns: half-sister to 5 42
a 1m/12f wnr: dam a 12f wnr: will need further in time for G L Moore.
9 ran   Time 1m 27.11 (3.01)   (Ridgeway Downs Racing)   M R Channon West Isley, Berks

3790 2.40 MILCARS COND STKS 2YO (C) 7f rnd Good/Firm 28 -22 Slow
£6351   £2409   £1204   £547

*3420 **BOURGAINVILLE 16** [7] I A Balding 2-8-10 M Hills 13/8 FAV: 11: 2 b c Pivotal - Petonica (Petoski) 97+
Made all, styd on strongly to go clr under hands & heels riding, readily: hvly bckd: earlier made a winning
debut at Salisbury (auct mdn,): eff at 7f, 1m shld suit: acts on fast grnd & a stiff/undul or fair trk: runs
well fresh: eff forcing the pace: prog & clearly useful, well regarded & deserves to tackle Gr/List company.
3333 **AZKABAN 20** [5] B J Meehan 2-8-10 D R McCabe 7/2: -32: 2 ch c Ashkalani - Lanasara (Generous) 2½ 90
Rdn chasing front pair halfway, styd on well fnl 2f, no threat to wnr: hvly bckd, op 5/1: clr of rem: confirmed
promise of debut, step up to 1m should suit: useful colt who looks sure to find a mdn: see 3333.
-- **DANCING MASTER** [4] Sir Michael Stoute 2-8-10 N Pollard 11/2: 3: 2 b c Nashwan - Dance Time 5 80
(Sadler's Wells) With wnr, rdn/no extra from over 2f out: op 7/2: Feb foal, a first foal: dam unrcd tho' related
to smart mid dist performers: sire top class 1m/12f performer: 1m+ will suit in time: acts on fast grnd: had
plenty of use made of him today & showed up well for a long way: will find a mdn on this evidence.
-- **CAPAL GARMON** [8] J H M Gosden 2-8-10 J Fortune 10/1: 4: Rdn chasing front pair halfway, kept on ¾ 79
onepace fnl 2f, no threat: op 6/1: Caerleon colt, Feb foal: brother to a 12f Irish wnr: dam 3yo dual 12f wnr:
looks sure to relish mid dists in time: encouraging intro, should improve over 1m+ next time.
-- **NZAME** [3] 2-8-10 D Harrison 16/1: 5: Held up in tch, eff 3f out, no impress on ldrs: op 12/1: nk 78
Darshaan colt, May foal: half brother to two 7f Irish juv wnrs: dam a 5/6f Irish wnr: sire a French Derby wnr.
-- **ALSYATI** [2] 2-8-10 G Hind 20/1: 6: Rear, rdn halfway, sn btn: Salse colt, Feb foal, cost 36000gns: 2 74
a first foal: dam a 1m wnr: needs a drop in grade on this evidence: with C Brittain.
3387 **DOMINION PRINCE 17** [1] 2-8-10 L Newman (3) 50/1: -007: Chased ldrs, btn 2f out: longer 7f trip. 2 70
-- **OCEAN ROAD** [9] 2-8-10 T Quinn 6/1: 8: Slowly away, al bhd: op 9/1: Inchinor colt, March foal, 6 58
cost 45,000gns: half brother to useful sprinter Midnight Escape & winning miler Midnight Allure: dam modest.
8 ran   Time 1m 27.62 (3.52)   (Robert Hitchins)   I A Balding Kingsclere, Hants

3791 3.15 MILCARS RUISLIP HCAP 3YO+ 0-95 (C) 6f Good/Firm 28 -03 Slow [93]
£15730 £4840 £2420 £1210 3 yo rec 2 lb Stands side group always in command

2609} **CANDLERIGGS 419** [3] E A L Dunlop 4-9-5 (84) R Hills 25/1: 6205-1: 4 ch g Indian Ridge - Ridge Pool (Bluebird) Trkd ldrs stands side, al trav well, led over 1f out, held on well ins last, drvn out: op 20/1: reapp: '99 wnr here at Kempton (reapp, h'cap, rtd 87 at best): rnr up in '98 (mdn, rtd 79): eff at 6f on fast & gd/soft grnd, fair or gall track, likes Kempton: runs v well fresh: useful gelding, cld win again. 91
3646 **IVORY DAWN 7** [1] K T Ivory 6-8-11 (76) C Carver (3) 33/1: 500302: 6 b m Batshoof - Cradle Of Love (Roberto) Twds rear stds side, rdn/prog to chse wnr ins last, styd on well, just held: see 2761. *nk* 81
3152 **LONE PIPER 28** [6] C E Brittain 5-8-9 (74) G Hind 40/1: 000003: 5 b h Warning - Shamisen (Diesis) Held up stands side, prog when briefly no room over 1f out, styd on well inside last, nrst fin: back to form here with t-strap & visor omitted: looks v well h'capped & could find similar soon: see 660 (AW). *1* 76
1728 **LITERARY SOCIETY 89** [7] J A R Toller 7-9-7 (86) S Whitworth 33/1: 0-0004: Held up stands side, hdwy over 1f out, styd on onepace inside last: 3 month abs: see 1173. *shd* 88
3646 **CADEAUX CHER 7** [10] 6-9-3 (82) N Pollard 20/1: 100505: Held up stands side, prog when no room over 1f out & again ins last, nrst fin: no luck in running: heads now for valuable Portland h'cap next week, won the race in '98 (off rtd 89) & loves Doncaster (3 course wins): well h'capped & one to keep in mind: see 2845. *1* 82+
3646 **PEDRO JACK 7** [2] 3-9-2 (83) T Quinn 25/1: 352206: Led overall stands side till over 1f out, fdd. *shd* 83
3646 **ZUHAIR 7** [15] 7-9-0 (79) Clare Roche (7) 12/1: 315057: Held up towards rear far side, switched & styd on well ins last to lead far side group, no ch with ldrs stands side: unlucky, first home on unfavoured side, still fairly h'capped & remains one to keep in mind: see 3464, 3091. *nk* 78+
3646 **RUSHCUTTER BAY 7** [24] 7-9-3 (82) D Harrison 9/1: 602108: Prom far side, led that group halfway & rdn/clr 2f out, wknd inside last: poor high draw: see 3457. *nk* 80
3118 **SOCIAL CONTRACT 29** [5] 3-8-12 (79) J Fortune 25/1: 001349: Chsd ldrs stands side 5f: see 3118. *½* 75
3653 **BEYOND CALCULATION 7** [23] 6-8-6 (71) L Newman (3) 12/1: 164420: Led far side 3f, fdd: 10th. *nk* 66
3646 **NINEACRES 7** [4] 9-8-10 (75)(bl) P Fitzsimons (5) 16/1: 304130: Prom stands side 4f: 11th: op 14/1. *hd* 69
3631 **LAS RAMBLAS 7** [17] 3-8-11 (78) D Holland 16/1: 423050: Cl up far side 5f: 12th: op 20/1. *1¼* 69
3464 **BAHAMIAN PIRATE 14** [20] 5-9-7 (86) Alex Greaves 5/1: 222130: Prom far side 5f: 13th: well bckd. *1¼* 74
2003 **CHARLOTTEVALENTINA 77** [22] 3-8-13 (80) P Dobbs (5) 33/1: -02000: Nvr on terms far side: 14th: abs. *½* 66
3646 **MARSAD 7** [13] 6-9-10 (89) P Doe 8/1: 500020: Prom far side till over 1f out: 16th: op 6/1: appeared poorly drawn & this is poss best forgotton: see 3646, 728. 0
3543 **CAPRICHO 11** [18] 3-9-5 (86) M Hills 4/1 FAV: 211200: Prom far side 4f, btn/eased inside last: 22nd: hvly bckd: dissap effort, but on wrong side: connections unable to offer explaination: see 3543, 2855 (7f). 0
3646 **Easy Dollar 7** [16] 8-9-4 (83)(bl) Craig Williams 25/1: *3651 **Villa Via 7** [9] 3-8-5 (72) J Mackay (5) 25/1:
1110 **Indian Blaze 122** [11] 6-9-4 (83) R Thomas (7) 33/1: 3646 **Zietzig 7** [8] 3-8-12 (79) N Callan 25/1:
3646 **Seven No Trumps 7** [12] 3-9-4 (85) R Naylor (7) 40/1: 2954 **Undeterred 36** [19] 4-9-10 (89) M Tebbutt 20/1:
3135 **Illusive 29** [14] 3-8-7 (74)(bl) F Norton 33/1:
23 ran Time 1m 12.97 (1.87) (The Right Angle Club) E A L Dunlop Newmarket, Suffolk

3792 3.45 GR 3 SEPTEMBER STKS 3YO+ (A) 1m4f Good/Firm 28 +13 Fast
£21000 £8050 £4025 £1925 3 yo rec 9 lb

2149 **MUTAMAM 71** [3] A C Stewart 5-9-0 R Hills 5/2 FAV: 0-2141: 5 b h Darshaan - Petal Girl (Caerleon) Led after 1f, drew clr under hands & heels riding from over 2f out, eased down nr line, comfortably: val for 10L+: well bckd, fast time, 10 wk abs: earlier scored at Goodwood (stks): '99 wnr at Sandown (stks), Haydock & Goodwood (Gr 3's, Gr 1 4th, rtd 120): eff at 10/12f on firm, gd/soft & any trk, likes Goodwood & likes to force the pace: tough & high class entire, in great form: prove hard to beat if tackling Cumberland Lodge Stakes at Ascot. 117
3645 **KUWAIT TROOPER 7** [1] G A Butler 3-8-5 (BL) D Holland 25/1: 310522: 3 b c Cozzene - Super Fan (Lear Fan) Rear, drvn & styd on fnl 2f, took 2nd nr line, no threat to easy wnr: gd run in first time blinks: will relish a return to 14f & reportedly heads for St Leger next week: see 1311. *7* 106
1752 **PAWN BROKER 90** [5] D R C Elsworth 3-8-5 T Quinn 4/1: -12203: 3 ch c Selkirk - Dime Bag (High Line) Held up, smooth prog to chase wnr 3f out, soon rdn/no impress & lost 2nd nr line: bckd, 3 month abs: appeared to not quite see out this 12f trip, return to 10f & similar company should suit: see 1326 (Gr 2). *nk* 105
*3300 **REACH THE TOP 22** [7] J H M Gosden 3-8-5 J Fortune 15/2: 1614: Rear/in tch, eff 3f out, sn held: op 5/1: this longer 12f trip could suit but prob needs a drop in grade: see 3300 (stks). *1¾* 103
*3640 **HAPPY CHANGE 7** [2] 6-9-0 M Hills 8/1: 1-3015: Trkd ldrs, rdn/outpcd 4f out, btn 2f out: op 6/1. *shd* 103
*3645 **ALVA GLEN 7** [4] 3-8-5 D Harrison 3/1: 123616: Led 1f, rdn/chased wnr briefly over 3f out, sn held: nicely bckd tho' op 5/2: has been busy of late: btr 3645 (14f, Listed). *2½* 99
2503 **ZAFONIUM 56** [6] 3-8-5 D Sweeney 11/1: 31-247: Keen/trckd wnr after 2f, ran wide on bend over 3f out & sn hung badly left, t.o.: op 8/1, 8 wk abs: something amiss? see 2503, 2148. *dist* 0
7 ran Time 2m 31.77 (1.77) (Hamdan Al Maktoum) A C Stewart Newmarket, Suffolk

3793 4.20 MILCARS WATFORD HCAP 3YO 0-85 (D) 1m rnd Good/Firm 28 -28 Slow [90]
£7605 £2340 £1170 £585

3535 **GRANTED 11** [9] M L W Bell 3-9-5 (81) J Mackay (5) 13/2 FAV: 114321: 3 b f Cadeaux Genereux - Germane (Distant Relative) Trkd ldrs, rdn to lead ins last, styd on well under hands & heels riding nr fin: hvly bckd from 8/1: earlier scored at Hamilton (first win) & Doncaster (h'caps): rtd 82 in '99: suited by 1m/9f, tried 10f: acts on fast & gd/soft, stiff/gall or fair track: best without a visor: progressive filly. 87
1638 **GLORY QUEST 93** [11] Miss Gay Kelleway 3-9-4 (80) D Holland 20/1: -22342: 3 b c Quest For Fame - Sonseri (Prince Tenderfoot) Mid div, drvn & styd on from over 1f out, not reach wnr: abs: mdn: see 1032, 962. *1½* 82
2688 **PRETRAIL 49** [3] A C Stewart 3-9-0 (76) S Whitworth 14/1: 210023: 3 b c Catrail - Pretty Lady (High Top) Rear, rdn/prog over 2f out, styd on strongly ins last, nrst fin: 7 wk abs: set too much to do here tho' had an awkward low draw: appears progressive & can win again: see 2688, 1675 (mdn). *½* 77+
3658 **TAKE MANHATTAN 6** [15] M R Channon 3-8-8 (70) Craig Williams 16/1: 001664: Led, clr over 2f out, rdn/hdd 1f out, no extra: op 12/1, qck reapp: back to form with front running tactics: see 2906. *nk* 70
3415 **DESERT FURY 16** [10] 3-9-4 (80) D Harrison 10/1: 060465: Chsd ldrs, chsd wnr over 2f out, sn held. *2* 76
3474 **IPANEMA BEACH 14** [6] 3-8-7 (69) M Hills 20/1: 6-036: Rear, styd on steadily under hands & heels riding from over 2f out, nrst fin: can improve in similar granted more positive tactics: h'cap bow today: see 3474. *¾* 64+
2117 **FRENCH HORN 72** [5] 3-9-7 (83) N Esler (7) 10/1: 031107: Wide/towards rear, rdn/mod hdwy fnl 3f. *½* 77
3270 **AZUR 23** [13] 3-8-8 (70)(VIS) O Urbina 25/1: 1-0008: Rdn/mid div halfway, no impress on ldrs: visor. *1* 62

3435 **TRAVELLING LITE 15** [7] 3-9-5 (81) G Hind 7/1: 420349: Chsd ldr halfway till 2f out, fdd: see 1177.   nk 72
3274 **SOFISIO 22** [14] 3-8-2 (64) P Doe 25/1: 032450: Twds rear, eff 3f out, little hdwy: 10th: see 2961.   nk 54
3642 **CHAPEL ROYALE 7** [16] 3 9 5 (81) D McGaffin (5) 11/1: 031000. Rear/hmpd over 3f out, sn held: 11th.   ¾   70
1183 **ROYAL INSULT 118** [2] 3-9-7 (83) N Callan 20/1: 21-000: Chsd ldrs 6f: 12th: 4 month abs: btr 1183.   3½ 65
*3413 **FINISHED ARTICLE 16** [12] 3-9-3 (79) T Quinn 7/1: 635210: Mid div, btn 3f out, 13th: btr 3413 (mdn).   5   51
3426 **SALIM 15** [17] 3-9-3 (79)(VIS) R Hills 9/1: 140430: Chsd ldrs, wknd 3f out: 16th: visor: btr 3426.   0
*3254 **KELTECH GOLD 23** [1] 3-9-1 (77) D Sweeney 10/1: 021510: Keen/prom wide till halfway, sn bhd: 17th: 0
op 8/1: awkward low draw for a confirmed front rnr: progressive earlier, see 3254 (made all).
3261 **Insightful 23** [4] 3-8-8 (70) J Fortune 20/1:   1375 **Hint Of Magic 106** [8] 3-8-8 (75) L Newman (3) 25/1:
17 ran   Time 1m 41.28 (4.48)   (E D Kessly)   M L W Bell Newmarket, Suffolk

---

3794 **4.55 MILCARS STANMORE HCAP 3YO+ 0-85 (D)   1m2f   Good/Firm 28 -10 Slow   [85]**
£5596   £1722   £861   £430   3 yo rec 7 lb

3414 **ELMHURST BOY 4** [4] S Dow 4-9-8 (79) P Doe 33/1: 452001: 4 b c Merdon Melody - Young Whip   86
(Bold Owl) Held up, prog 4f out & led over 2f out, styd on strongly despite carrying head high, rdn out: vis omitted:
earlier scored at Brighton (h'cap): '99 scorer at Epsom (mdn, rtd 80) & Lingfield (h'cap, rtd 84a): all wins prev at
7f, a revelation stepped up to 10f today: acts on firm, hvy & equitrack: likes a sharp/undulating or fair track,
handles any: eff with/without blinks or a visor: on a fair mark & could win again in similar.
2696 **MILLIGAN 49** [3] Miss Venetia Williams 5-10-0 (85) J Mackay (5) 11/1: 00-102: 5 b g Exit To Nowhere   1½ 88
- Madigan Mill (Mill Reef) Slowly away, rear, hdwy fnl 3f & rdn/pressed wnr over 1f out, held inside last: bckd, 7
week abs, top-weight: acts on fast & soft grnd: see 757.
3403 **ADMIRALS PLACE 17** [1] H J Collingridge 4-8-10 (67) F Norton 14/1: 142053: 4 ch c Perugino - Royal   2   67
Daughter (High Top) Al handy, chsd 2f out, held inside last: op 12/1: acts on fast, soft & both AWs: see 965 (soft).
2515 **BELLA BELLISIMO 56** [14] J W Hills 3-8-8 (72) M Hills 25/1: -00604: Rear, rdn & steady prog fnl 2f,   1¼ 70+
nrst fin: abs: eff at 10f on fast & gd grnd: eyecatching late hdwy, could find similar this autumn: see 874.
3453 **THUNDERING SURF 15** [5] 3-9-5 (83) S Whitworth 5/1 FAV: -00135: Rear, eff/no room over 2f out   ¾   80
& again over 1f out, styd on ins last, no threat: bckd, op 7/1: closer with a clr run: in gd heart: see 2499.
3644 **PHEISTY 7** [12] 3-8-10 (74)(bl) S Carson (3) 16/1: 165266: Mid div, rdn/onepace fnl 2f: see 3403.   1¾ 69
3402 **TOTOM 17** [18] 5-8-12 (69) O Urbina 10/1: 344547: Twds rear, mod hdwy fnl 2f: see 2268, 1288.   nk 63
3467 **SANTIBURI GIRL 14** [11] 3-8-8 (72) A Polli 33/1: 011248: Rear, eff/no room over 2f out, sn btn.   1½ 64
3310 **FINAL LAP 21** [6] 4-8-6 (63) D Sweeney 33/1: 5-0009: Rear, eff 3f out, mod hdwy: see 56.   1¾ 53
3426 **PEDRO PETE 15** [8] 3-8-12 (76) Craig Williams 16/1: 311050: Trkd ldrs, btn/eased ins last: 10th.   nk 65
3337 **LOVERS LEAP 20** [13] 4-8-13 (70) C Rutter (5) 33/1: 060000: Prom till over 1f out: 11th: see 3337, 1015.   2½ 55
3403 **FORZA FIGLIO 17** [7] 7-9-3 (74)(bl) T Quinn 10/1: 033440: Led/dsptd lead till over 2f out, btn   nk 58
over 1f out & eased inside last: 12th, nicely bckd: btr 3403, 1729.
632 **SECRET SPRING 182** [17] 8-9-9 (80) I Mongan (5) 33/1: 400550: Rear, eff over 2f out, no hdwy: 2   61
13th, 6 month abs: see 208 (1m, AW, stakes).
3422 **RED LETTER 16** [2] 3-9-4 (82)(VIS) J Fortune 12/1: 326030: Led/dsptd lead 3f, wknd quickly over   1¾ 61
2f out: 14th, tried a visor, op 10/1: btr 3422, 1853 (1m).
2358 **MUSALLY 62** [19] 3-9-5 (83) R Hills 7/1: 4100: Mid div, btn 2f out: 15th: abs: btr 1480 (g/s).   3½ 57
1866 **RUM PUNCH 82** [10] 3-8-13 (77) D Harrison 13/2: 0-0020: Trkd ldrs, lost place 3f out, sn btn: 18th: 0
nicely bckd tho' op 5/1: 12 week abs: btr 1866.
3471 **Tonights Prize 14** [20] 6-9-4 (75) M Tebbutt 12/1:   3390 **Supersonic 17** [9] 4-8-7 (64) N Pollard 20/1:
3334 **Cool Temper 20** [15] 4-9-1 (72) L Newman (3) 12/1:
19 ran   Time 2m 06.08 (3.78)   (R E Anderson)   S Dow Epsom, Surrey

---

Official Going   GOOD. Stalls: Str Crse - Stands Side, Rem - Inside.

3795 **2.20 CITY INDEX EBF FILLIES MDN 2YO (D)   6f str   Good/Firm 23 +06 Fast**
£4602   £1416   £708   £354

3352 **PALACE AFFAIR 5** [5] G B Balding 2-8-11 (bl) S Carson (3) 20/1: W51: 2 ch f Pursuit Of Love - Palace   104+
Street (Secreto) Made all, rdn clr from 2f out, in command when eased down ins last, cmftbly: val for 7L+: op
14/1, gd time: half-sister to tough 1m h'capper Cad Oro: eff at 6f, 7f+ lks sure to suit: acts on fast grnd &
a fair trk: eff forcing the pace: has temperament prob & is suited by blnks: posted a v useful performance here.
--   **GHAZAL** [6] Sir Michael Stoute 2-8-11 W Ryan 9/2: 2: 2 b f Gone West - Tough Of Greatness   3½ 92+
(Hero's Honor) Held up, hdwy over 2f out, styd on strongly under minimal pressure cl home, no threat to easy wnr:
nicely bckd tho' op 3/1: Jan foal, cost $575,000: half-sister to a 7f/1m US wnr, also smart juv Rossini: dam
unrcd: eff at 6f, 7f+ will suit: handles fast grnd: caught a tartar but shld repay this kind intro.
3607 **ECSTATIC 9** [9] R Hannon 2-8-11 R Hughes 4/1: -2433: 2 ch f Nashwan - Divine Quest (Kris)   nk 91
Cl-up, rdn/outpcd by wnr over 2f out: op 11/4: return to 7f & h'cap company shld suit: see 3607, 1568.
--   **OOMPH** [4] W Jarvis 2-8-11 M Tebbutt 10/1: 4: Settled rear, rdn halfway, styd on fnl 2f, no threat to   3   84
ldrs: op 6/1: Shareef Dancer filly, Apr foal: half-sister to a 7f wnr: dam a 5/6f juv wnr: sire an Irish Derby
wnr: looks sure to relish 7f+ & shld rate more highly.
--   **EYE OF GOLD** [3] O Urbina 12/1: 5: Trkd ldrs, outpcd from over 2f out: Wolfhound filly, Jan   hd 83
foal, half-sister to a 5/6f juv wnr: dam a 7f 3yo wnr: with J Fanshawe.
--   **JINAAN** [7] 2-8-11 W Supple 5/1 FAV: 6: Prom, eff over 2f out, sn btn: hvly bckd from 11/4: March   2   78
foal: dam a daughter of high-class performer Salsabil: more expected on intro for J L Dunlop.
3342 **DANE DANCING 21** [10] 2-8-11 J Fortune 14/1: -57: Chsd ldrs, btn 2f out: op 8/1: Danehill filly,   1¼ 73
Feb foal: half-sister to 2 juv wnrs: dam a 10/12f wnr: will relish 1m+ in time for J H M Gosden.
--   **PRINCESS CHLOE** [12] 2-8-11 G Hind 20/1: 8: Prom till halfway, sn struggling: Primo Dominie filly,   2   70
Mar foal, cost 25,000gns: half-sister to a 5f wnr: dam a 5f juv wnr: with M Jarvis.
3342 **CARPET LADY 21** [13] 2-8-11 L Newman (3) 12/1: -339: Chsd ldrs, btn 2f out: op 10/1: btr 3342.   shd 70
3459 **PRIYA 16** [14] 2-8-11 B Marcus 10/1: 462240: Chsd ldrs till halfway: 10th: op 7/1: btr 2748 (C/D).   shd 69
--   **PICCOLITIA** [8] 2-8-11 A Clark 33/1: 0: Keen in rear, btn 2f out: 11th: Mar foal: dam modest.   1¼ 66
--   **BELLA PAVLINA** [11] 2-8-11 S Sanders 33/1: 0: Dwelt, keen & rear, btn: 12th: Sure Blade filly, April   6   51
foal, a first foal: dam 6/7f wnr: with P Mitchell.
12 ran   Time 1m 12.1 (1.0)   (Miss B Swire)   G B Balding Fyfield, Hants.

3796 2.55 CITY INDEX HCAP 3YO+ 0-80 (D) 7f jub rnd Good/Firm 23 -06 Slow [78]
£7767 £2390 £1195 £597 3 yo rec 4 lb

3355 **FLOATING CHARGE 20** [16] J R Fanshawe 6-9-10 (74) O Urbina 8/1: -2U001: 6 b g Sharpo - Poyle Fizz (Damister) Chsd ldrs, prog to lead over 1f out, held on well ins last under hand-and-heels riding: op 6/1: '99 wnr at Windsor & here at Kempton (h'caps, rtd 77): '98 Redcar wnr (class stks, rtd 67): eff btwn 7/9f on firm, hvy & fibresand: handles any trk, likes Kempton: has run well fresh: gd weight carrier, best without blnks/visor. **79**
3646 **HILL MAGIC 8** [11] L G Cottrell 5-9-9 (73) S Sanders 14/1: 000002: 5 br g Magic Ring - Stock Hill Lass (Air Trooper) Hmpd & drpd towards rear after 2f, prog fnl 2f, drvn/chsd wnr ins last, styd on well & only just btn: tchd 16/1: eff at 6/7f: well h'capped, a shade unlucky here, can find similar: see 935. ½ **76**
*3384 **DARYABAD 18** [8] N A Graham 8-8-3 (53)(bl) Dale Gibson 5/1 FAV: 301313: 8 b g Thatching - Dayanata (Shirley Heights) Mid-div, drvn/prog to chall over 1f out, kept on ins last, not pace of wnr: well bckd. *hd* **55**
3756 **TEOFILIO 3** [13] A J McNae 6-9-2 (66) T G McLaughlin 12/1: 300454: Held up rear, no room over 1f out, rdn/styd on well fnl 1f, not pace to chall: op 10/1: poss plcd with a clr run: looks nicely h'capped: see 594. ¾ **67**
3315 **CARLTON 22** [14] 6-9-11 (75) N Pollard 12/1: 024005: Mid-div, eff/briefly no room over 1f out, kept on. *nk* **75**
3256 **KAREEB 24** [15] 3-9-9 (77)(bl) J Reid 10/1: 003436: Towards rear, no room 2f out till ins last, late hdwy, chance had gone: op 6/1: mdn but no luck in running today, much closer with a clr run: can find a race. 1¼ **74+**
2355 **ASTRAC 63** [3] 9-8-10 (60) T Ashley 20/1: 000007: Twds rear/wide, late hdwy, no threat: 9 wk abs. *1* **55**
3460 **COMPRADORE 16** [17] 5-9-1 (65) J Fortune 11/2: 030038: Reared start, towards rear, hdwy 2f out, held over 1f out & eased ins last: bckd: see 1467. 1¼ **57**
3362 **WHITE EMIR 20** [1] 7-8-12 (62) A Clark 15/2: -32149: Chsd ldrs wide, held over 1f out: op 5/1. ¾ **53**
3063 **DANGEROUS FORTUNE 33** [6] 4-9-12 (76) B Marcus 12/1: 5-6000: Slowly away, rear, switched/eff over 2f out, little hdwy: 10th: topweight: op 10/1: see 1015. *hd* **66**
3436 **AKEBONO 16** [2] 4-8-12 (62) D R McCabe 16/1: -14100: Chsd ldrs 5f: 11th: op 10/1: see 3436. ½ **51**
3362 **MOON AT NIGHT 20** [7] 5-9-3 (67) A Daly 14/1: 103000: Led, hdd over 1f out, fdd: 12th: op 10/1. ¾ **55**
3759 **Ladywell Blaise 3** [9] 3-8-2 (56) S Carson (3) 33/1: 1494 **Misty Boy 100** [5] 3-7-11 (51) P Doe 33/1:
1471 **Uplifting 102** [10] 5-9-1 (65) J Lowe 20/1: 3445 **Who Goes There 16** [4] 4-8-6 (56) R Price 14/1:
16 ran Time 1m 26.16 (2.06) (The Leonard Curtis Partnership) J R Fanshawe Newmarket.

3797 3.25 LISTED SIRENIA STKS 2YO (A) 6f str Good/Firm 23 +12 Fast
£12369 £3806 £1903 £951

2996 **SANTOLINA 36** [10] J H M Gosden 2-8-6 J Fortune 9/2: -1241: 2 b f Boundary - Alamosa (Alydar) Rear/in tch, switched over 2f out & prog to lead ins last, styd on strongly, rdn out: fast time: earlier made a winning debut at Leicester (auct mdn): eff at 6f, 7f shld suit: acts on firm & fast grnd, stiff/gall or fair trk: runs well fresh: tough & v useful filly, could still make her mark in Group company this term. **101**
*2106 **PROCEED WITH CARE 73** [4] M Johnston 2-8-11 J Reid 6/1: 512: 2 b c Danehill - Ultra Finesse (Rahy) Led, rdn/hdd ins last, held after: 10 wk abs: fine run on step up to Listed company: useful colt. 1¼ **100**
3105 **TRIPLE BLUE 31** [1] R Hannon 2-8-11 W Ryan 16/1: 352453: 2 ch c Bluebird - Persian Tapestry (Tap On Wood) Rear, briefly no room over 2f out, switched & rdn/styd on ins last, no threat: op 10/1: see 2850. ¾ **98**
3720 **KACHINA DOLL 8** [6] M R Channon 2-8-6 W Supple 8/1: 203304: Prom, held dist: ahd of wnr in 2996. *2* **88**
3105 **DOMINUS 31** [7] 2-8-11 R Hughes 10/1: 22165: Rcd towards centre, rear, rdn/mod late hdwy: op 7/1. *nk* **92**
3482 **SECRET INDEX 15** [8] 2-8-6 L Newman 16/1: 115446: Prom, wknd fnl 1f: op 12/1: see 2469, 1176 (5f). ½ **85**
3482 **SILLA 15** [2] 2-8-6 N Pollard 2/1 FAV: 031127: Chsd ldrs, hard rdn/btn over 1f out: hvly bckd tho' op 13/8: return to 5f looks in order: see 3482, 2868 (5f). 1½ **81**
3566 **GAME N GIFTED 11** [3] 2-8-11 D R McCabe 8/1: 2158: Prom, rdn/btn over 1f out: op 5/1: btr 3566 (Gr 2). ½ **84**
2848 **PREFERRED 43** [9] 2-8-11 B Marcus 9/1: 01139: Prom 4f: 6 wk abs, stablemate of 3rd: btr 2848, 2678. 1¾ **81**
9 ran Time 1m 11.74 (0.64) (H Lascelles, Indian Creek & A Stroud) J H M Gosden Manton, Wilts.

3798 4.00 CITY INDEX HCAP 3YO+ 0-100 (C) 1m4f Good/Firm 23 -10 Slow [96]
£10773 £3315 £1657 £828 3 yo rec 9 lb

3471 **ULUNDI 15** [6] Lady Herries 5-9-10 (92) R Hughes 4/1: 002521: 5 b g Rainbow Quest - Flit (Lyhard) Settled rear, smooth hdwy 3f out, jnd ldr going easily over 1f out, rdn to assert ins last: op 3/1: earlier won at W'hampton (AW mdn, rtd 65a) & Windsor (class stks): 99/00 wnr at N Abbot (2 bmprs), Fontwell (nov) & Cheltenham (nov h'cap hdle, rtd 110h, 2m2f, firm & gd/soft): eff at 10/12f, may get further: acts on firm, soft & fibresand, prob handles any trk: has run well fresh: gd weight carrier: tough & useful gelding. **97**
3541 **RIYAFA 12** [2] Sir Michael Stoute 3-8-13 (90) J Reid 8/11 FAV: 21532: 3 b f Kahyasi - Riyama (Doyoun) Led, rdn/joined over 1f out, held by wnr ins last: hvly bckd: change to forcing tactics: see 3541, 2178 & 1493. ¾ **93**
2336 **FIRST BALLOT 64** [5] D R C Elsworth 4-9-3 (85) N Pollard 14/1: 0-0003: 4 b g Perugino - Election Special (Chief Singer) Cl-up, onepace fnl 3f: op 10/1, 2 mth abs: eff at 12f, return to 14f+ shld suit: see 1222. 1¾ **86**
3178 **DELAMERE 28** [7] J H M Gosden 3-8-6 (83) J Fortune 11/2: 643124: Held up in tch, rdn over 3f out, styd on onepace fnl 2f: bckd tho' op 4/1: prob styd longer 12f trip, 14f+ could suit: see 2722 (10f, mdn). 1½ **82**
815 **LEMON BRIDGE 153** [4] 5-8-7 (75) L Newman (3) 25/1: 220-55: Rear/in tch, eff 3f out, no hdwy: abs. ¾ **73**
3515 **RIVERTOWN 14** [1] 6-9-8 (90) T Ashley 20/1: 1/4356: Chsd ldrs, btn 2f out: see 3230, 2630 (10f). 1¾ **86**
3597 **PARADISE GARDEN 10** [3] 3-8-12 (89) B Marcus 16/1: 030407: Chsd ldrs, rdn/btn 2f out: op 8/1. *5* **78**
7 ran Time 2m 33.97 (3.97) (D Heath) Lady Herries Angmering, W.Sussex.

3799 4.35 CITY INDEX EBF MDN STKS 2YO (D) 1m jub rnd Good/Firm 23 -12 Slow
£4348 £1338 £669 £334

2956 **HILL COUNTRY 37** [10] J H M Gosden 2-9-0 J Fortune 6/1: 01: 2 b c Danehill - Rose Of Jericho (Alleged) Trkd ldr, rdn/led 2f out, styd on well ins last, rdn out: bckd: half-brother to Derby wnr Dr Devious: apprec step up to 1m, mid-dists will suit: acts on fast grnd & a fair trk: useful colt, clrly going the right way. **97**
2956 **BORDER COMET 37** [12] Sir Michael Stoute 2-9-0 R Hughes 11/10 FAV: 42: 2 b c Selkirk - Starlet (Teenoso) Trkd ldrs, switched & rdn/styd on fnl 2f, not pace to chall: hvly bckd tho' op 4/6: styd longer 1m trip well, mid-dists shld suit in time: see 2956. 1½ **92**
-- **STAY BEHIND** [15] Mrs A J Perrett 2-8-9 W Ryan 7/1: 3: 2 ch f Elmaamul - I Will Lead (Seattle Slew) Dwelt, rear/bhd 4f out, styd on strongly under hands-&-heels riding fnl 3f, nrst fin: Mar foal, dam an unrcd half-sister to high-class mid-dist performer Rainbow Quest: sire top-class at 10/12f: stays 1m, will relish mid-dists: acts on fast grnd: most eyecatching, will leave this bhd & merits close consideration next time. *nk* **86+**

KEMPTON SUNDAY SEPTEMBER 3RD Righthand, Flat, Fair Track

3121 **MODRIK 30** [2] R W Armstrong 2-9-0 W Supple 9/2: -034: Trkd ldr, rdn/led 3f out till 2f out, no extra ins last: styd longer 1m trip: h'cap company may now suit best: see 3121. *1½* **88**
2921 **TAMIAMI TRAIL 39** [4] 2-9-0 D R McCabe 16/1: -005: Chsd ldrs, rdn over 2f out, al held: op 25/1: sure to relish 1m+ & h'caps in time: see 2921. *2* **84**
-- **GALLA PLACIDIA** [7] 2-8-9 S Sanders 50/1: 6: Slowly away, towards rear & bhd 4f out, rdn/styd on fnl 2f, no threat: Royal Abjar filly, Mar foal, 2,600gns 2yo: half-sister to a 6f/11f wnr: dam unrcd: will stay 1m+. *¾* **78**
-- **UNSIGNED** [6] 2-9-0 O Urbina 14/1: 7: Mid-div, rdn 3f out: sn held: op 12/1: Cozzene colt, Jan foal, cost 20,000gns: dam a mdn: sire high-class 1m performer: with J Fanshawe. *¾* **82**
3484 **CLEAR AMBITION 15** [5] 2-9-0 M Tebbutt 33/1: -08: Mid-div, held over 2f out: see 3484. *2* **78$**
3154 **WELL MAKE IT 29** [9] 2-9-0 R Mullen 50/1: 609: Mid-div, btn 2f out: longer 1m trip: see 2760. *1½* **75**
3470 **EASTWELL MANOR 15** [1] 2-9-0 L Newman (3) 40/1: 00: Led 5f, fdd: 10th: longer 1m trip: see 3470. *1* **73**
-- **KUT O ISLAND** [13] 2-9-0 J Reid 14/1: 0: Rear, eff 3f out, sn held: 11th: Woodman colt, Feb foal, cost $300,000: half-brother to a 12f wnr: with G Butler. *4* **65**
2867 **Ash Hab 42** [8] 2-9-0 P Doe 20/1: -- **Dr Gordon** [3] 2-9-0 B Marcus 14/1:
2867 **Mad Habit 42** [11] 2-9-0 N Pollard 40/1: 2708 **Brendas Delight 49** [14] 2-8-9 G Hind 50/1:
15 ran Time 1m 39.56 (2.76) (R E Sangster & Mrs J Magnier) J H M Gosden Manton, Wilts.

3800 5.10 JIM BROWN HCAP 3YO+ 0-75 (E) 1m6f92y Good/Firm 23 -36 Slow [72]
£4524 £1392 £696 £348 3 yo rec 11lb

3522 **THREE LIONS 13** [4] R F Johnson Houghton 3-8-12 (67) J Reid 4/1: -01641: 3 ch f Jupiter Island - Super Sol (Rolfe) Trkd ldrs halfway, rdn/led over 2f out, styd on well fnl 1f, rdn out: nicely bckd, tchd 11/2: earlier scored at Beverley (class stks): unplcd in '99 (rtd 67): prev eff at 10f, now suited by 14f, 2m could suit: acts on fast & gd grnd, stiff/fair trk: can force the pace: lightly rcd & op to further improv, esp when tackling 2m. **75**
3588 **ABLE SEAMAN 10** [14] C E Brittain 3-7-13 (54)(vis) Dale Gibson 14/1: 436402: 3 b g Northern Flagship - Love At Dawn (Grey Dawn II) Prom, hard rdn/chsd wnr 2f out, kept on tho' al held: op 10/1: stays 14f well. *2* **58**
3664 **DURHAM 7** [12] G L Moore 9-8-10 (54)(bl) I Mongan (5) 8/1: -01503: 9 ch g Caerleon - Sanctuary (Welsh Pageant) Dwelt/rear, rdn & styd on fnl 2f, nvr pace to chall: see 2008 (sell h'cap). *1½* **56**
3424 **MISCONDUCT 17** [11] J G Portman 6-8-9 (53)(1ow) R Hughes 4/1: 0-2324: Trkd ldrs, hard rdn 2f out, sn held: nicely bckd, op 5/1: see 3424, 2689. *1½* **53**
3424 **ALCAYDE 17** [3] 5-8-11 (55) J Fortune 7/2 FAV: /00535: Chsd ldrs, drvn/held 2f out: hvly bckd, op 4/1. *1½* **53**
3586 **RISING SPRAY 10** [5] 9-8-11 (55) S Sanders 20/1: -00006: Dwelt/rear, hdwy 3f out, no prog over 1f out. *1½* **51**
3518 **ROYAL PATRON 14** [13] 4-9-10 (68) B Marcus 14/1: 235467: Led till over 2f out, btn/eased fnl 1f: op 7/1. *3* **60**
2872 **CHATER FLAIR 42** [7] 3-8-4 (59) Sophie Mitchell 12/1: -04108: Prom 11f: op 6/1, abs: new stable. *2* **48**
3586 **MY PLEDGE 10** [8] 5-9-0 (58)(E) N Pollard 10/1: 103449: Dwelt/rear, eff when no room over 2f out, sn held & eased ins last: op 7/1, wore an eye-shield: see 2263 (12f). *shd* **47**
3625 **SEA DANZIG 9** [6] 7-8-6 (50) L Newman (3) 25/1: 401050: Mid-div, btn 3f out, eased fnl 1f: 10th. *1¾* **37**
3662 **END OF STORY 7** [10] 4-8-0 (44) A Daly 33/1: 00-000: Well bhd halfway: 11th: see 3662 (7f). *dist* **0**
3518 **KIRISNIPPA 14** [2] 5-8-1 (45) P Doe 11/1: 350420: In tch 10f, eased right down fnl 2f: reportedly broke a blood vessel: 12th: op 7/1: see 1784, 1128 & 474. *19* **0**
12 ran Time 3m 11.16 (8.36) (Jim Short) R F Johnson Houghton Blewbury, Oxon.

HAMILTON SUNDAY SEPTEMBER 3RD Lefthand, Undulating Track With Stiff Uphill Finish

Official Going SOFT (HEAVY in places). Stalls: Stands Side, except 1m & 1m1f - Inside.

3801 2.10 SCOTTISH NOV AUCT STKS 2YO (E) 5f str Soft 95 -15 Slow
£3094 £952 £476 £238

3740 **THANKS MAX 3** [6] Miss L A Perratt 2-8-12 C Lowther 33/1: -051: 2 b c Goldmark - Almost A Lady (Entitled) Prom, eff appr fnl 1f, rdn to lead towards fin: qck reapp, much imprvd, drifted from 16/1: 1,500gns Mar foal: clrly suited by drop back to a stiff 5f on soft grnd tho' shld appreciate 6f. **76**
3673 **FANTASY BELIEVER 7** [2] J J Quinn 2-9-2 O Pears 1/1 FAV: 221602: 2 b g Sure Blade - Delicious (Dominion) Well plcd, led bef dist, under press & hdd cl-home: well bckd, qck reapp: ran to best, see 2532. *¾* **78**
3720 **OPEN WARFARE 8** [5] M Quinn 2-8-11 Paul Eddery 3/1: 335003: 2 b f General Monash - Pipe Opener (Prince Sabo) Led till bef fnl 1f, onepace: bckd from 4/1: btr 1166. *2½* **68**
3079 **GARRISON 32** [3] Miss L A Perratt 2-8-1 K Dalgleish (5) 16/1: 04: Chsd ldrs till appr fnl 1f: tchd 33/1. *½* **57**
3508 **ACADEMIC RECORD 14** [4] 2-8-12 Dean McKeown 20/1: -005: Dwelt, nvr in it: back in trip. *9* **48**
3632 **GIBNEYS FLYER 8** [1] 2-8-7 J Carroll 4/1: -610P: Chsd ldrs, p.u. ent fnl 2f, sadly died. **0**
6 ran Time 1m 03.6 (5.5) (T P Finch) Miss L A Perratt Ayr, Strathclyde.

3802 2.45 DOUBLEPRINT NURSERY HCAP 2YO 0-75 (E) 5f str Soft 95 -07 Slow [77]
£3757 £1156 £578 £289

3145 **DA VINCI 29** [12] J A Osborne 2-9-7 (70) R Ffrench 6/1: 1001: 2 b c Inzar - Tuft Hill (Grundy) Well plcd, led appr fnl 1f, rdn & drifted left, pshd out cl-home: earlier won debut at Pontefract (auct mdn): half-brother to 2 juv wnrs: eff at 5f & is clrly suited by soft grnd: can go well fresh: likes stiff/undul trks. **79**
2521 **MR PERTEMPS 56** [10] S C Williams 2-7-10 (45) M Baird 3/1 FAV: -0602: 2 b c Primo Dominie - Amber Mill (Doulab) Led till appr fnl 1f, kept on under pressure: gamble from 10/1 after 8 wk abs on h'cap bow, jockey given 4 day whip ban: clrly suited by return to 5f on soft grnd, forcing the pace. *1½* **50**
*3475 **TIME MAITE 15** [8] M W Easterby 2-9-4 (67) P Hanagan (7) 7/2: 135313: 2 b g Komaite - Martini Time (Ardoon) Trkd ldrs, eff 2f out, onepace till rallied fnl 100y: bckd from 9/2: not far off best, return to 6f will suit. *1¾* **68**
3589 **ALICIAN SUNHILL 10** [11] Mrs A Duffield 2-8-6 (55) A McGlone 12/1: -03044: Mid-div, drvn 2f out, hdwy dist, no extra towards fin: h'cap bow, handles fast & soft. *¾* **54**
2142 **ASTER FIELDS 72** [4] 2-8-5 (54) O Pears 14/1: -0605: Held up, moderate late hdwy: tchd 25/1 on h'cap bow after 10 wk abs: step up to 6f will sut now. *2* **49**
*3376 **CATCH THE CHRON 18** [3] 2-9-2 (65) K Dalgleish (5) 7/1: 204016: Dwelt & bhd, wide prog appr fnl 1f, onepace ins last: op 5/1: much btr 3376 (seller on gd/soft). *¾* **58**
3673 **CLANSINGE 7** [7] 2-8-10 (59) J Carroll 8/1: 340067: Chsd ldrs till 2f out: drifter from 11/2, qk reapp. *¾* **50**
3693 **QUIZZICAL LADY 6** [5] 2-9-7 (70) G Sparkes (7) 14/1: 064208: Al bhd: op 10/1, qck reapp. *¾* **59**
3592 **OLYS GILL 10** [1] 2-7-10 (45)(6oh) Joanna Badger (7) 33/1: 40009: Speed 3f: stiff task, back in trip. *1* **32**

3268 **JUST AS YOU ARE** 24 [13] 2-8-8 (57)(tbl) Paul Eddery 11/1: -0000: Hung badly thr'out, nvr dngrs: 10th. 3 38
3673 **TOMMY SMITH** 7 [6] 2-8-11 (60)(VIS) D Mernagh (3) 33/1: 116500: In tch till halfway: 11th, visored. ¾ 39
2605 **ROYLE FAMILY** 52 [2] 2-8-2 (51) P Bradley (5) 25/1: 454540: Sn struggling: 12th: 7 wk abs, btr 2200. 16 5
12 ran   Time 1m 03.2 (5.1)   (Andy Miller)   J A Osborne Lambourn, Berks.

3803

3.15 EBF FILLIES HCAP 3YO+ 0-85 (D)   6f str   Soft 95 +03 Fast [80]
£7507 £2310 £1155 £577   3 yo rec 2 lb Majority rcd centre, 1st 2 home rcd far side

*2969 **CARRIE POOTER** 37 [11] T D Barron 4-9-4 (70)(bl) D Mernagh (3) 4/1: 000111: 4 b f Tragic Role - Ginny 77
Binny (Ahonoora) Dsptd lead far side, drvn to lead dist, ran on strongly: best time of day, tchd 5/1: hat-trick
landed, earlier won at Southwell (rtd 75a), Pontefract & Thirsk (ddht, fill h'caps): '99 wnr at Southwell & here
at Hamilton (h'caps, rtd 72a & 72): '98 Redcar wnr: eff at 6/7f, stays 1m: acts on fast & hvy & fibresand, any
trk: eff with/without blnks & can run well fresh/carry big weights: improving filly.
3460 **ROUGE ETOILE** 16 [12] E J Alston 4-7-11 (49) N Carlisle 11/2: 060052: 4 b f Most Welcome - Choral 2 51
Sundown (Night Shift) Led/dsptd lead far side, outpcd by wnr fnl 1f: reportedly broke a blood vessel & a fair
run in the circumstance: well h'capped now, suited by return to 6f on soft.
3445 **ROUGE** 16 [1] K R Burke 5-8-0 (52) P Hanagan (7) 10/1: 3161P3: 5 gr m Rudimentary - Couleur de Rose 1 52
(Kalaglow) Chsd ldrs in centre, prog appr fnl 1f, kept on for 3rd but no nr front pair: tchd 12/1: back to
form after breaking a blood vessel: acts on fast, soft grnd & both AWs, see 3046.
3572 **COLLEGE MAID** 11 [9] J S Goldie 3-8-13 (67) A McGlone 9/1: 000004: Prom far side, no extra fnl 1f. 1 65
3671 **BAJAN BELLE** 7 [3] R Ffrench 10/1: 300225: Nvr dngrs centre: qk reapp, faster grnd suits. 3½ 54
3666 **CLEAR CRYSTAL** 7 [5] 3-7-10 (50)(6oh) G Baker (5) 25/1: 066066: Dwelt, nvr got in it centre: qk reapp. hd 42
3510 **DEMOLITION JO** 14 [8] 5-9-5 (71)(vis) K Dalgleish (5) 7/2 FAV: 006027: Slow away, imprvd to lead 1 61
centre bef halfway, fdd ent fnl 2f: bckd from 5/1: btr 3510, see 1074.
3010 **CAUTIONARY** 35 [2] 3-9-6 (74) P Bradley (5) 8/1: 20-068: Nvr on terms centre: see 2364. 2½ 59
3191 **FRAMPANT** 27 [4] 3-8-4 (56)(2ow) Paul Eddery 10/1: 443069: Early ldr centre, hung right & btn 2f out. ¾ 42
3259 **MISS DANGEROUS** 24 [7] 5-7-10 (48)(10oh) G Sparkes (3) 66/1: 550000: Prom centre 3f: 10th, stiff task. 3½ 26
2289 **SHANNON DORE** 65 [10] 3-9-10 (78) J Carroll 11/1: 0-4000: Chsd ldrs far side until after halfway: abs. ½ 55
3349 **SABRE LADY** 20 [6] 3-9-7 (75) C Lowther 20/1: 340000: In tch centre 3f: 12th, see 1219. 6 42
12 ran   Time 1m 15.3 (5.5)   (Stephen Woodall)   T D Barron Maunby, N.Yorks.

3804

3.50 VARIETY CLUB SELLER 3YO+ (E)   1m4f   Soft 95 -25 Slow
£2834 £872 £436 £216   3 yo rec 9 lb

3531 **NEEDWOOD MAESTRO** 12 [1] B C Morgan 4-9-7 (vis) J Carroll 6/1: -50031: 4 b f Sizzling Melody - 41
Needwood Poppy (Rolfe) Set moderate pace, drvn & styd on well fnl 2f, unchal: no bid, 1st win, slow time:
plcd last term (sell, rtd 54): eff forcing the pace over 12f on gd/soft & hvy grnd, stiff/gall trk & wears a visor.
2876 **LANCER** 41 [2] J Pearce 8-9-12 (vis) Dean McKeown 1/1 FAV: 065032: 8 ch g Diesis - Last Bird (Sea 1½ 44
Bird II) Prom, chsd wnr 4f out, styd on but nvr any impression: well bckd, 6 wk abs: capable of much better.
3637 **FOSTON SECOND** 8 [6] C B B Booth 3-8-7 K Dalgleish (5) 7/1: 0-4243: 3 ch f Lycius - Gentle Guest 1¾ 32
(Be My Guest) Prom, no extra appr fnl 1f: ran to best, handles fast & soft grnd.
3570 **FIELD OF VISION** 11 [5] Mrs A Duffield 10-9-12 L Enstone (7) 9/2: 452224: Held up, chsd ldrs 3f 1 41
out till 2f out: op 7/2: btr 3570, 1720.
3233 **MISCHIEF** 25 [7] 4-9-12 (vis) G Sparkes (7) 10/1: 506165: Rcd in 2nd till ent str: see 2827 (14f, firm). 15 29
3742 **SECONDS AWAY** 3 [4] 9-9-7 Dawn Rankin (7) 20/1: 333606: Al bhd: op 10/1, v stiff task, qck reapp. 1 23
2875 **MONACO** 41 [3] 6-9-7 (VIS) P Hanagan (7) 50/1: 000007: In tch 3f out: visored, jumps rnr 48 hrs ago. 11 15
7 ran   Time 2m 46.3 (14.5)   (Needwood Racing Ltd)   B C Morgan Barton-under-Needwood, Staffs.

3805

4.25 HAMILTON APPR HCAP 3YO+ 0-70 (F)   1m3f   Soft 95 -16 Slow [60]
£2926 £836 £418   3 yo rec 8 lb

3574 **HUTCHIES LADY** 11 [4] J S Goldie 8-8-0 (32) Joanna Badger (3) 7/2: 400-31: 8 b m Efisio - Keep Mum 38
(Mummy's Pet) Rear, prog appr fnl 2f, kept on strongly under pressure: '99 rnr-up (appr h'cap, rtd 36): last
won in '97 here at Hamilton (h'cap, rtd 39): has tried hdles: eff at 1m/11f, stays 12f: acts on fast & hvy
grnd: goes well fresh & likes Hamilton.
2774 **PERPETUO** 45 [7] R A Fahey 3-9-8 (62) P Hanagan (3) 5/2 FAV: 3362: 3 b f Mtoto - Persian Fountain 4 63
(Persian Heights) Rear, imprvd appr fnl 2f, drifted left, no ch wnr: bckd from 7/2, 6 wk abs, h'cap bow:
eff at 10/11f on firm & soft grnd.
3396 **INVISIBLE FORCE** 18 [3] M Johnston 3-8-5 (45)(vis) K Dalgleish 3/1: 134443: 3 b c Imperial Frontier - 1¾ 45
Virginia Cottage (Lomond) Cl-up, led ent str till 2f out, no extra: 2nd time vis, needs drop back to 10f?
3625 **WINSOME GEORGE** 9 [6] M Quinn 5-7-10 (28)(vis)(7oh) G Sparkes (3) 20/1: 506064: Led till ent str. hd 28$
3534 **ACE OF TRUMPS** 12 [1] 4-8-5 (37)(t) P Bradley 10/1: 256435: Prom, ch 4f out, fdd appr fnl 2f: 10 30
unsuited by longer 11f trip?: see 1195 (9f, here).
1908 **PRINCE NICHOLAS** 81 [5] 5-9-10 (56) G Gibbons (5) 11/2: 440406: Well plcd till 3f out: op 3/1, abs. 6 44
1191 **COLLEGE DEAN** 119 [2] 4-8-4 (36) R Lake (4) 33/1: 0-6007: Keen, bhd ldrs, lost pl 4f out: abs, longer trip.14 14
7 ran   Time 2m 31.0 (12.2)   (Magteam)   J S Goldie Uplawmoor, E Renfrews.

3806

5.00 WULLIE GOFAR HCAP 3YO 0-75 (E)   1m1f36y   Soft 95 -03 Slow [67]
£4628 £1424 £712 £356

3702 **ENTITY** 6 [2] T D Barron 3-9-7 (60) D Mernagh (3) 1/1 FAV: 500121: 3 ch g Rudimentary - Desert Ditty 64
(Green Desert) Confidently held up, prog on bit 2f out, led below dist, sn idled & had to be drvn out: well bckd
from 11/8, qk reapp: given a lot to do at Ripon last week, prev won here at Hamilton (mdn h'cap): promise more
than once last term (nurs, rtd 71): eff at 1m/10f on firm & soft grnd, any trk, likes Hamilton: best without blnks.
*3591 **ABSINTHER** 10 [1] E J Alston 3-9-1 (54) J Carroll 9/2: 005312: 3 b g Presidium - Heavenly Queen nk 56
(Scottish Reel) Chsd ldrs, prog to press wnr fnl 1f, ran on, just held: op 2/1: gd run, acts on fast & soft grnd.
3419 **BRITTAS BLUES** 17 [6] M Johnston 3-8-8 (47) R Ffrench 4/1: 034503: 3 b f Blues Traveller - Missish 1½ 47
(Mummy's Pet) Led till ent fnl 1f, onepace: tchd 11/2, clr rem, big step up in trip: stays 9f on soft grnd.
3380 **HIGHLAND GOLD** 18 [3] Miss L A Perratt 3-9-7 (60) C Lowther 16/1: 350004: Prom, hung right/btn 2f out. 6 54
3380 **THE LONELY WIGEON** 18 [5] 3-8-1 (40)(t) K Dalgleish (5) 10/1: 05065: Held up in tch, prog to 23 14
chall 3f out, sn edged left & wknd: op 6/1, see 1204.
2534 **BLUE LEGEND** 55 [4] 3-8-6 (42)(3ow) A McGlone 16/1: 0-0456: Cl-up till 3f out: op 10/1, 8 wk abs. 13 9

HAMILTON

SUNDAY SEPTEMBER 3RD   Lefthand, Undulating Track With Stiff Uphill Finish

6 ran   Time 2m 02.9 (8.8)   (Mrs J Hazell)   T D Barron Maunby, N.Yorks.

YORK

SUNDAY SEPTEMBER 3RD   Lefthand, Flat, Galloping Track

Official Going: GOOD Stalls: 5/6f - Stands Side: Remainder - Inside.

3807
2.00 SWALLOW NURSERY HCAP 2YO (C)   6f str   Good 40   -40 Slow   **[97]**
£8079   £2486   £1243   £621

2835 **MY AMERICAN BEAUTY** 2 [1] T D Easterby 2-7-10 (65) J Quinn 6/1: -6031: 2 ch f Wolfhound - Hooray Lady (Ahonoora) Settled mid-div, gd hdwy to lead 2f out, styd on strongly, rdn out: 6 wk abs, h'cap bow: 22,000gns Apr foal, half-sister to a 5f wng juv: goes well fresh at 5/6f on fast, gd & a gall or sharpish track.   72

3507 **WALLY McARTHUR** 14 [5] A Berry 2-8-12 (81) G Carter 16/1: 211042: 2 b c Puissance - Giddy (Polar Falcon) Rear, rdn & ran on strongly inside last, nrst fin: ran to beat, worth a try at 7f now: see 2754.   1¼   83

3673 **BLAKESHALL BOY** 7 [7] M R Channon 2-8-10 (79) T E Durcan 9/1: 321353: 2 b g Piccolo - Giggleswick Girl (Full Extent) Handy, rdn to improve 2f out, ev ch till no extra well inside last: quick reapp: eff at 5/6f, proving tough & consistent: see 3228.   nk   79

3592 **UHOOMAGOO** 10 [11] D Nicholls 2-8-13 (82) A Nicholls (3) 10/1: 113134: Trckd ldrs, rdn & no extra well inside last: tough, yet to finish out of the first 4: see 3592, 3439.   ¾   80

3583 **ROSELYN** 10 [2] 2-8-2 (71) A Beech(5) 20/1: -6445: Bhd, rdn/prog over 1f out, held ins last: clr rem.   1½   65

3542 **TIME TO REMEMBER** 12 [9] K Darley 9/4 FAV: -3146: Led 4f out, hdd appr fnl 2f, wknd: nicely bckd again, stablemate of winner: much better over 7f in 3542.   4   62

3673 **ROUGH SHOOT** 7 [3] 2-8-9 (78)(h) N Callan 9/1: -15327: Slow to start, sn prom, went on over 2f out, sn hdd, fdd appr fnl 1f: quick reapp: btr 3673 (5f, fast).   ½   59

3463 **PETONGSHALL** 15 [10] 2-9-7 (90) F Lynch 11/2: -2128: Led early, remained with ldr, flashed tail for press 2f out & sn place: top-weight: btr 3463, 3245.   ½   70

3431 **RARE OLD TIMES** 16 [4] 2-8-9 (78) S W Kelly(3) 16/1: 51069: Prom, rdn/btn over 2f out: btr 1426.   2½   51

3542 **STRETTON** 12 [8] 2-8-7 (76) D Harrison 50/1: 03200: Chsd ldrs, lost tch halfway: 10th: btr 3245.   8   25

*2835 **MAJESTIC QUEST** 43 [6] 2-8-8 (77) A Culhane 10/1: -4210: Handy, wknd qckly fnl 2f: 11th: btr 2835.   nk   25

11 ran   Time 1m 14.23 (4.83)   (Peter G Gorvin)   T D Easterby Great Habton, N Yorks

3808
2.35 SANDERSON CLAIMER 3YO+ (E)   1m1f   Good 40   +01 Fast
£6214   £1912   £956   £478   3yo rec 6lb

3495 **LORD EUROLINK** 5 [6] C A Dwyer 6-8-12 (vis) A Beech (5) 12/1: 464501: 6 b g Danehill - Lady Eurolink (Kala Shikari) Made all, clr 3f out, styd on strongly, rdn out: op 8/1: gd time: earlier won at W'hampton (2, sell & h'cap) & Southwell (clmr): plcd on turf in '99 (rtd 79, appr h'cap): plcd sole '98 start (h'cap, rtd 92, J Dunlop): eff forcing the pace at 1m/10f on fast, gd/soft & fibresand, handles equitrack: wears a t-strap/visor & handles any trk, likes W'hampton: benefited from an enterprising ride by A Beech.   66

*3526 **WILLIE CONQUER** 13 [13] Andrew Reid 8-9-0 S Whitworth 5/1: 101112: 8 ch g Master Willie - Maryland Cookie (Bold Hour) Mid div, rdn/prog over 3f out, styd on to chase wnr fnl 2f, no impress: rtd higher in 3526.   3   62

3383 **YOUNG UN** 18 [4] M J Ryan 3-8-10 J Weaver 11/2: 550003: 5 b h Efisio - Stardyn (Star Appeal) Front rank, drvn over 2f out, no extra appr fnl 1f: clr rem: shld apprec a return to h'cap company: see 786.   2   54

3676 **BAY OF BENGAL** 7 [17] J S Wainwright 4-8-3 G Baker (5) 50/1: 060304: Towards rear, drvn/prog 3f out, styd on, nvr nrr: qck reapp: gd eff from unfav'ble wide draw: should apprec a return to 10f+: see 3490.   4   40

3781 **TIME FOR THE CLAN** 1 [8] 3-8-1 R Brisland(5) 50/1: 000605: Prom, rdn/onepaced fnl 2f: ran yesterday.   nk   43$

3188 **LILANITA** 27 [5] 5-8-4 J Bramhill 50/1: 000006: Front rank, rdn/held fnl 2f: up in trip, stiffish task.   nk   39

3636 **AL MABROOK** 8 [18] 5-8-12 F Lynch 25/1: 000357: Mid div, rdn/late gains, no dngr: see 3344.   ½   46

2799 **FUTURE PROSPECT** 44 [24] 6-9-0 D Harrison 20/1: -25508: Dwelt, rear, late hdwy for press, no threat.   ½   47

3404 **LAKE SUNBEAM** 18 [9] 4-9-1 S W Kelly(3) 9/2 FAV: 611329: Rear, late gains, no dngr: btr 3404 (8.5f).   1   46

3581 **RED CAFE** 11 [14] 4-8-3 S Righton 50/1: 042400: Slow to start, late hdwy from rear: 10th: see 2040.   shd   34

3591 **PADDY MUL** 10 [2] 3-8-1 (t) A Nicholls(3) 50/1: 0-0030: Mid div at best: 11th: dubious rating.   1   36$

3403 **BACCHUS** 18 [20] 6-9-4 (vis) K Darley 50/1: 221560: Prom, rdn/lost tch over 2f out: 12th: btr 2671.   1¼   45

3603 **IMPULSIVE AIR** 9 [26] 8-8-9 J Quinn 33/1: 043000: Nvr dangerous: 13th: see 3368.   1¾   34

3656 **THREE CHERRIES** 8 [1] 4-8-2 P Fitzsimons(3) 50/1: 455450: Nvr a factor: fin 14th, stiff task.   3   22

3344 **JAMMIE DODGER** 20 [19] 4-8-10 V Halliday 40/1: 1U0600: Nvr dangerous; 15th: stiff task, see 2533.   shd   30

*3330 **BOWCLIFFE** 21 [21] 9-9-0 T E Durcan 10/1: 210010: Chsd ldrs, wknd rapidly fnl 2f: fin 21st: capable of much better, see 3330 (classified stakes, 1m, firm).   0

3677 **Parisienne Hill** 7 [12] 4-8-5 K Hodgson 100/1:   3671 **The Castigator** 7 [7] 3-8-1 J McAuley 100/1:

3711 **Alamein** 5 [10] 7-8-7 (t) J Stack 25/1:   *3393 **Marton Mere** 18 [23] 4-9-2 G Carter 16/1:

3282 **Rogue Spirit** 23 [25] 4-9-2 M Fenton 16/1:   963 **Golden Ace** 138 [11] 7-8-7 (tbl) A Mackay 50/1:

3636 **Thorntoun Gold** 8 [22] 4-8-6 A Culhane 33/1:   3310 **Moon Glow** 22 [16] 4-8-13 R Havlin 16/1:

3248 **Free Kevin** 25 [15] 4-9-2 N Callan 66/1:   3082 **Claudius Tertius** 32 [27] 3-8-6 Iona Wands 50/1:

3393 **Night Of Glory** 18 [7] 5-8-7 Kim Tinkler 66/1:

27 ran   Time 1m 52.31 (3.51)   (Roalco Limited)   C A Dwyer Newmarket, Suffolk

3809
3.05 MONKS CROSS HCAP 3YO+ 0-75 (E)   7f rnd   Good 40   -31 Slow   **[75]**
£8901   £2739   £1369   £684   3yo rec 4lb

3634 **STYLE DANCER** 8 [5] R M Whitaker 6-9-8 (69)(vis) K Darley 8/1: 110031: 6 b g Dancing Dissident - Showing Style (Pas de Seul) Chsd ldrs, hdwy & switched over 1f out, sn led, kept on strongly, drvn out: tchd 12/1: earlier scored at Doncaster & Beverley (h'caps): '99 Haydock wnr (h'cap, rtd 68 at best): prev term won here at York (rtd 74): eff at 7/8.5f: acts on firm, gd/soft & fibresand: handles any track, likes a stiff/gall one, especially York: now best in a visor: tough & consistent.   72

3573 **CUSIN** 11 [3] D Nicholls 4-9-2 (63) T Hamilton(3) 10/1: 500052: 4 ch g Arazi - Fairy Tern (Mill Reef) Towards rear, eff when switched over 2f out, ran strongly inside last, closing at fin: not btn far: back to form here, well h'capped & could go in soon: see 926.   ½   64

3398 **BUNDY** 18 [4] M Dods 4-9-5 (66) A Nicholls (3) 25/1: 311003: 3 b g Ezzoud - Sanctuary Cove (Habitat) In tch, rdn/prog over 3f out, every ch dist, held nr fin: gd run up in trip, eff at 6/7f: see 2559.   hd   67

3629 **TRIBAL PRINCE** 8 [20] P W Harris 3-9-12 (77) M Fenton 10/1: -00134: Rear, gd hdwy appr fnl 2f,   ½   77

ran on well inside last, nrst fin: tchd 14/1 & an excellent run from a poor draw: consistent: see 3629, 3445.
3652 **CALCAVELLA 8** [2] 4-9-1 (62) N Callan 7/1 JT FAV: 050425: Handy, rdn/prog over 2f out, ev ch *shd* **62**
dist, no extra well inside last: remains in gd heart: see 3652.
3510 **NOMORE MR NICEGUY 14** [18] 6-9-12 (73) T E Durcan 16/1: 006646: Settled rear, hdwy when short *¾* **71**
of room over 2f out, ran on inside last, nrst fin: gd run from a bad draw, well h'capped: see 977.
2986 **JORROCKS 36** [14] 6-9-2 (63) G Parkin 8/1: 10-267: Late hdwy from rear, nvr nrr: see 2882. *2½* **56**
3573 **PERSIAN FAYRE 11** [21] 8-9-4 (65) G Carter 20/1: 100028: Led, hdd 2f out, fdd appr fnl 1f: btr 3573. *¾* **56**
3325 **THE EXHIBITION FOX 22** [6] 4-9-12 (73) G Baker(5) 33/1: 030009: Dwelt, rear, hdwy when short of *1* **62**
room 2f out, styd on, no impress: see 1836.
2986 **ITS ALLOWED 36** [8] 3-9-6 (71) D Harrison 16/1: 005000: Front rank, rdn/wknd qckly over 1f out: 10th. *½* **59**
3708 **JEFFREY ANOTHERRED 6** [10] 6-9-5 (66) A Culhane 7/1 JT FAV: 060420: Mid div, nvr dangerous: *nk* **53**
11th: quick reapp: loves soft grnd: see 3708.
3384 **AMBER FORT 18** [23] 7-9-8 (69)(bl) P Fitzsimons (5) 20/1: 553450: Prom, went on 2f out, hdd dist, *nk* **55**
wknd quickly: 12th: best form on a sharp tracks, especially Goodwood: see 2878, 1011.
3514 **RASHIK 14** [1] 6-9-4 (65) R Havlin 33/1: 1/500: In tch, prog when short of room 2f out, sn btn: 13th. *2½* **46**
3119 **AT LARGE 30** [22] 6-9-13 (74) P Shea (7) 20/1: 100000: Gd hdwy from rear 2f out, drvn/no extra *2* **51**
appr fnl 1f: 14th: likes soft grnd, as in 1545.
*3696 **KUWAIT ROSE 6** [19] 4-9-8 (69)(6ex) D McGaffin (5) 16/1: 025010: Dwelt, nvr dngrs: 15th: qck reapp. *¾* **44**
3613 **DOUBLE SPLENDOUR 9** [7] 10-9-8 (69) J Weaver 14/1: 000620: Handy, eff 2f out, sn lost tch: 16th. *3½* **37**
*3377 **TOM TUN 18** [16] 5-9-12 (73)(t) T Lucas 10/1: 500110: Dwelt, al towards rear: 19th: best at 6f, see 3377. **0**
1654 **Morgan Le Fay 93** [15] 5-9-0 (61) Kim Tinkler 33/1: 3328 **Quiet Venture 21** [17] 6-9-0 (61)(tvi) D Sweeney 33/1:
*3670 **Nods Nephew 7** [13] 3-9-2 (67) J Quinn 16/1: 3698 **Secret Conquest 6** [24] 3-9-2 (67) F Lynch 25/1:
1840 **Aberkeen 85** [9] 5-9-5 (66) J Stack 20/1: 2999 **Stylish Ways 36** [12] 8-9-7 (68) G Bardwell 20/1:
23 ran Time 1m 26.29 (4.99) (Mrs C A Hodgetts) R M Whitaker Scarcroft, W Yorks

3810

3.40 POLO SUPERMINT HCAP 3YO+ 0-80 (D) 1m rnd Good 40 -04 Slow [79]
£12577 £3870 £1935 £967 3yo rec 5lb

*3746 **PACIFIC ALLIANCE 3** [1] M Wigham 4-9-2 (67)(6ex) A Mackay 7/1 FAV: 400311: 4 b g Fayruz - La **79**
Gravotte (Habitat) Broke well & sn led, rdn & hung right inside last, ran on strongly, drvn out: nicely bckd,
qck reapp: 3 days ago scored at Musselburgh (h'cap): '99 Lingfield (auct mdn) & Sandown wnr (h'cap, rtd 68a
& 65, R Armstrong): rtd 73 in '98: suited by 1m, has tried 10f: acts on firm, gd & equitrack: eff with/without
blinks & handles any trk: loves to force the pace: fast improving & should complete a hat-trick.
3708 **DONNAS DOUBLE 6** [6] D Eddy 5-9-4 (69) J Weaver 14/1: 103402: 5 ch g Weldnaas - Shadha *3½* **73**
(Shirley Heights) Bhd, drvn/ran on well appr fnl 1f, wnr had flown: qck reapp: ran to best: see 2694 (7f).
3573 **RYMERS RASCAL 11** [24] E J Alston 8-8-9 (60) T E Durcan 16/1: 425303: 8 b g Rymer - City Sound *nk* **63**
(On Your Mark) Waited with, switched wide & ran on strongly inside last, nvr nrr: fine run from the worst
of the draw today: on a long losing run but is back on a winning mark: see 3170, 942.
3078 **ARTERXERXES 32** [4] C G Cox 7-9-7 (72) G Hannon (7) 9/1: -30044: Front rank, chall 2f out, no *nk* **74**
extra for press over 1f out: loves to dominate: see 1250.
3527 **LARAZA 13** [3] 3-8-4 (60) J Quinn 33/1: -55005: Dwelt, sn prom, rdn/no impress appr fnl 1f: *½* **61**
acts on firm & gd grnd: see 3527, 1165.
3634 **RYEFIELD 8** [11] 5-8-11 (62) G Carter 9/1: R21426: Waited with, hdwy over 2f out, edged left for *nk* **62**
press over 1f out, kept on, no danger: jockey recieved a 5 day irresponsible riding ban: see 3634.
2133 **IONIAN SPRING 72** [5] 5-9-9 (74) D Sweeney 16/1: 21/007: In tch, no room over 2f out, styd on late. *nk* **73**
3642 **ABAJANY 8** [18] 6-9-10 (75) R Havlin 16/1: 524-08: Slow to start, rear, late hdwy, no danger: *½* **73**
not disgraced from a poor draw, on a fair mark: see 3642.
3285 **SHAMSAN 23** [12] 3-8-9 (65) K Darley 8/1: 052239: Chsd ldrs, rdn/wknd appr fnl 1f: consistent prev. *1* **61**
3643 **NOUF 8** [14] 4-9-3 (68) S Whitworth 25/1: 206600: Waited with, hdwy/short of room over 1f out: 10th. *nk* **63**
1829 **SCENE 86** [2] 5-9-7 (72) A Culhane 14/1: 000000: Prom, eff when badly hmpd over 1f out, not recover: *¾* **65**
fin 11th: 3 month abs, new stable: fin closer with a clr run, just sharper for this, keep in mind: see 831.
3495 **NOMINATOR LAD 15** [21] 6-9-11 (76)(bl) A Beech(5) 25/1: 044160: Dwelt, late hdwy from rear: 12th. *shd* **69**
3658 **OGILIA 7** [13] 3-9-10 (80) A Nicholls(3) 16/1: 046100: Mid div at best 13th: qck reapp: btr 3435. *nk* **72**
3170 **TAFFS WELL 28** [17] 7-9-6 (71) M Fenton 9/1: 260000: Nvr dangerous, fin 14th: see 3018. *hd* **63**
3636 **FREEDOM QUEST 8** [19] 5-8-10 (61) R Lappin 16/1: 400420: Sn well bhd, late hdwy, no danger: 15th. *1¾* **49**
3634 **PENTAGON LAD 8** [9] 4-9-10 (75) R Cody Boutcher (7) 14/1: 514260: Nvr better than mid div: 18th. **0**
3488 **HARMONY HALL 15** [10] 6-8-11 (62) P Fitzsimons (5) 14/1: 220030: Cl up, rdn/lost tch fnl 2f: 19th. **0**
*3426 **SPORTING GESTURE 16** [22] 3-9-4 (74) T Lucas 12/1: 001610: In tch, wknd qckly fnl 3f: 20th: poor draw. **0**
3573 **Cautious Joe 11** [25] 3-8-6 (62) G Parkin 20/1: 3666 **Stealthy Times 7** [20] 3-8-12 (68) G Baker (5) 33/1:
2870 **Indium 42** [16] 6-9-12 (77) P Shea (7) 25/1: 3317 **Bay View 22** [8] 5-8-7 (58) D McGaffin (5) 40/1:
3005 **Royal Cavalier 36** [26] 3-9-3 (73) P M Quinn (3) 33/1: 3707 **Noble Splendour 6** [15] 3-8-9 (65) D Harrison 25/1:
24 ran Time 1m 39.32 (3.52) (Michael Wigham) M Wigham Newmarket, Suffolk

3811

4.15 MINSTER HCAP 3YO+ 0-95 (C) 1m5f194y Good 40 +07 Fast [95]
£18525 £5700 £2850 £1425 3yo rec 11lb

2319 **SHARP STEPPER 64** [1] J H M Gosden 4-8-11 (78) R Havlin 5/1: 1-3621: 4 b f Selkirk - Awtaar (Lyphard) **86**
Front rank, went on over 2f out, sn clr, styd on strgly, drvn out: 9 wk abs: best time of day: '99 rnr-up
(Newmarket h'cap, rtd 78), subs scored at Southwell (mdn, rtd 78a): eff btwn 10f & 14.6f: acts on fast,
gd/soft & fibresand: runs esp well fresh & acts on a sharp or gall track: progressive staying filly, win again.
1715 **MONTALCINO 90** [5] P J Makin 4-9-9 (90) D Sweeney 16/1: 20-542: 4 b g Robellino - Only Gossip *½* **97**
(Trempolino) Prom, slightly outpcd 4f out, rallied & ran on strongly inside last, closing at fin: clr rem
after 3 month abs: eff at 12/14f: gd eff & should win similar soon: see 1484.
3565 **VIRGIN SOLDIER 11** [4] M Johnston 4-10-0 (95) K Darley 3/1 FAV: 242133: 4 ch g Waajib - Never Been *4* **96**
Chaste (Posse) Handy, went on over 4f out, hdd over 2f out, fdd inside last: top weight: v tough: see 3295.
3657 **GREYFIELD 7** [10] M R Channon 4-8-3 (70) A Mackay 9/1: 504544: Dwelt, hdwy from rear 3f out, *3½* **66**
kept on, no impress: quick reapp: likes to come late off a strong pace, poss stays 14f: see 1984.
3565 **RUM POINTER 11** [6] 4-9-12 (93) T E Durcan 16/1: 021005: Led early, remained with ldrs, drpd rear *2½* **85**
4f out, rallied/late gains: will apprec a return to 2m on soft grnd, see 1791.
3504 **JUST GIFTED 14** [7] 4-7-13 (66) J Quinn 20/1: 222036: Led briefly after 2f, cl-up, fdd fnl 3f: lngr trip. *½* **57**
2722 **IL CAVALIERE 48** [8] 5-8-8 (75) A Culhane 13/2: -3047: Waited with, drvn/late hdwy, no threat: *1* **65**
7 week abs, h'cap bow: big step up in trip for this former bmpr wnr: see 2722, 2155.
3565 **INCH PERFECT 11** [2] 5-9-5 (86) G Carter 5/1: 131008: Keen/mid div, fdd fnl 3f: btr 1982 (C/D, fast). *shd* **76**

1909} **LEONATO 450** [9] 8-9-6 (87)(t) M Fenton 20/1: 0/25-9: Waited with, eff 4f out, sn btn: reapp: rnr-up on 1st of 2 '99 starts (cond stks, P D Evans, rtd 98): plcd in '98 (rtd 101 at best when 3rd in the Chester Cup): last won in native France in '95: eff between 13.4f & 2m2.5f: best on fast: with I Balding. *6* **68**
3541 **ANGUS G 12** [11] 8-8-8 (75) D Harrison 40/1: 05-000: Nvr dangerous: fin 10th: see 3323. *½* **55**
1791 **WAVE OF OPTIMISM 87** [12] 5-9-1 (82) G Bardwell 14/1: -01100: Al twrds rear: 11th: 3 month abs. *5* **54**
3599 **DUCHAMP 10** [3] 3-8-8 (86)(VIS) S Whitworth 13/2: 402150: Rcd keenly, led after 3f, hdd 4f out, wknd rapidly, t.o.: 12th: change of tactics, usually held up: see 2852. *16* **38**
12 ran Time 2m 58.02 (4.62) (Mrs Diane Snowden) J H M Gosden Manton, Wilts

3812 4.50 YORK-ENGLAND MDN AUCT DIV 1 2YO (E) 6f str Good 40 -42 Slow
£5239 £1612 £806 £403

3513 **TICKLE 14** [6] P J Makin 2-7-13 A Beech(3) 13/8 FAV: -0221: 2 b f Primo Dominie - Funny Choice (Commanche Run) Prom, drvn to lead dist, pshd out cl-home: nicely bckd, rnr up twice prev: cheaply bght filly, dam scored at up to 15f: eff at 6f, shld stay further: acts on fast, gd & a gall track: tough & consistent. **72**
3710 **HALCYON MAGIC 5** [7] Pat Mitchell 2-8-4 R Brisland (5) 14/1: 455262: 2 b g Magic Ring - Consistent Queen (Queens Hussar) Led, drvn & hung right 2f out, hdd dist, held cl home: quick reapp: ran to best & should apprec nurseries now: see 3520. *¾* **74**
2209 **PENNY LASS 69** [2] J R Fanshawe 2-8-2 J Quinn 4/1: -63: 2 b f Alhijaz - Strapped (Reprimand) Mid div, rdn/hdwy 2f out, kept on ins last, not btn far: gd run after 10 wk abs, stays 6f on gd: win a mod race. *½* **71**
-- **PLEINMONT POINT** [10] P D Evans 2-8-7 T E Durcan 25/1: -4: Bhd, rdn/prog 2f out, styd on, nvr nrr 5,500gns half-brother to a useful 6f wnr, dam scored over 5f as a 2yo: encouraging debut, stys 6f on gd grnd. *¾* **73**
-- **SECOND STRIKE** [1] 2-8-10 D Sweeney 13/2: -5: Mid div, prog when short of room 2f out, styd on inside last, no danger: 10,000gns Mar foal, brother to juv wnrs at 6/7.4f: with B Smart, gd debut & can improve. *¾* **73**
3032 **ROYAL GLEN 34** [3] 2-8-2 G Baker (5) 14/1: -36: Dwelt, sn mid div, drvn/no extra appr fnl 1f. *¾* **62**
3193 **FLYING ROMANCE 27** [15] 2-7-13 J Bramhill 20/1: -05537: Bhd, drvn/prog 2f out, held inside last. *½* **58**
3710 **THATS ALL JAZZ 5** [4] 2-7-13 (VIS) G Bardwell 20/1: -00608: Cl up, wknd quickly appr fnl 1f: quick reapp, first time visor: prev with T Clement, now C A Dwyer, see 993. *3* **49**
3466 **DARWIN TOWER 15** [9] 2-8-7 K Hodgson 25/1: -00009: Nvr dangerous: mod form, see 2692. *3½* **47**
2480 **FLYING TACKLE 58** [11] 2-8-10 F Lynch 33/1: -00: Hmpd start, al bhd: 10th: 8 week abs. *1½* **46**
3697 **GORDONS FRIEND 6** [14] 2-8-5(1ow) M Fenton 50/1: -600: Al in rear: 11th: quick reapp: see 3438. *1* **38**
2480 **SIAMO DISPERATI 58** [12] 2-8-7 S Whitworth 25/1: -300: Nvr a factor: 12th: 8 wk abs: btr 1764 (hvy). *½* **39**
3347 **TEFI 20** [13] 2-8-10 K Darley 6/1: 532230: Handy, wknd quickly over 1f out: 13th: much btr 3347. *½* **41**
-- **Amy G** [5] 2-8-5 Kim Tinkler 33/1: 3204 **So Foxy 26** [8] 2-7-13 A Nicholls(1) 50/1:
15 ran Time 1m 14.33 (4.93) (Mrs Derek Strauss) P J Makin Ogbourne Maisey, Wilts

3813 5.20 FLAT ROOF MDN 3YO (D) 1m2f85y Good 40 -05 Slow
£6698 £2061 £1030 £515

2617 **ROYAL TRYST 52** [11] Sir Michael Stoute 3-9-0 F Lynch 4/7 FAV: -21: 3 ch c Kingmambo - In On The Secret (Secretariat) Front rank, chall 2f out, sn led, pshd out, rdly: nicely bckd after 7 wk abs, front 2 clr: earlier rnr-up on debut: cost $400,000, related to sev useful wnrs: eff around 10f, 12f should suit: acts on fast, gd & a gall/stiff track: runs well fresh: open to further improvement & could win again. **89**
3265 **DANCE DIRECTOR 24** [1] J H M Gosden 3-9-0 K Darley 4/1: -42: 3 b c Sadler's Wells - Memories (Hail The Pirates) Prom, went on 2f out, hdd appr fnl 1f, not pace of wnr inside last: 7L clr rem: eff at 10f on gd & gd/soft: had rest well covered here, shown enough to win similar: see 3265. *2* **83**
3506 **CARRIE CAN CAN 14** [6] J G Given 3-8-9 G Baker (5) 33/1: -653: 3 b f Green Tune - Maidenhair (Darshaan) Settled rear, rdn & styd on late, no threat to front 2: low grade h'caps should now suit: see 3116. *7* **62**
3506 **HUGS DANCER 14** [3] J G Given 3-9-0 D Sweeney 12/1: -334: Led, hdd 2f out, sn drvn/fdd: stablemate of 3rd, now qualified for h'caps: up in trip: see 3506, 3343. *¾* **67**
3626 **KADINSKY 8** [8] 3-9-0 M Fenton 20/1: -05: Mid div, rdn & no impress fnl 2f: up in trip: see 3626. *2½* **64**
3474 **SPRING GIFT 15** [7] 3-8-9 D McGaffin (5) 20/1: -646: Front rank, rdn/lost tch fnl 2f: up in trip. *3* **54**
3324 **SPIRIT OF PARK 22** [9] 3-9-0 J Quinn 66/1: -557: Dwelt, late gains, no threat: flattered 3324 (12f). *shd* **59**
2135 **TRIPPITAKA 72** [14] 3-8-9 S Whitworth 33/1: -08: Bhd, mod late gains: 10 week abs: see 2135. *1¼* **52**
3636 **STEPASTRAY 8** [2] 3-9-0 P Goode (3) 25/1: 363309: Mid div at best: needs h'caps: see 3310. *½* **56$**
-- **BRANDY COVE** [4] 3-9-0 S W Kelly(3) 20/1: -0: Prom, lost tch fnl 2f, fin 10th: brother to a 10f wnr. *1¼* **54**
3707 **Attacker 6** [10] 3-9-0 N Callan 100/1: 3702 **Tough Times 6** [5] 3-9-0 J Weaver 14/1:
3656 **Concino 8** [13] 3-9-0 A Culhane 100/1: 3672 **Julies Gift 7** [12] 3-8-9 J McAuley 100/1:
14 ran Time 2m 12.07 (4.77) (Sheikh Mohammed) Sir Michael Stoute Newmarket, Suffolk

3814 5.50 YORK-ENGLAND MDN AUCT DIV 2 2YO (E) 6f str Good 40 -36 Slow
£5239 £1612 £806 £403

3568 **VICIOUS DANCER 11** [12] R M Whitaker 2-8-7 J Quinn 6/4 FAV: -061: 2 b g Timeless Times - Yankeedoodledancer (Mashoor Dancer) Front rank al going best, qcknd to lead over 1f out, easily pshd clr: nicely bckd: 3,800gns April foal, dam a mdn: eff arnd 6f, has the pace for 5f: acts on gd grnd & a gall trk. **92+**
3693 **TROUBLESHOOTER 6** [14] W R Muir 2-8-10 (bl) N Callan 12/1: 202062: 2 b c Ezzoud - Oublier L'Ennui (Bellman) Led, drvn/hdd over 1f out, sn well outpcd by impressive wnr: quick reapp: caught a tartar. *8* **72**
3571 **JUST MURPHY 11** [11] W W Haigh 2-8-7 F Lynch 12/1: -603: 2 b g Namaqualand - Bui Doi (Dance Of Life) Waited with, rdn/prog 2f out, styd on, no impress on wnr: tchd 20/1, apprec h'caps now. *nk* **68**
3096 **TOPOS GUEST 32** [10] J G Given 2-7-13 G Baker (5) 12/1: -54: Rear, gd late hdwy, no threat: worth a try over further now: rtd higher on debut in 3096. *1* **57**
3592 **PHARAOH HATSHEPSUT 10** [9] 2-8-2 A Beech (5) 16/1: 400045: Front rank, rdn/btn appr fnl 1f. *1* **57**
3466 **ARRAN MIST 15** [15] 2-7-13 Kimberley Hart 12/1: -0306: Cl-up, rdn/fdd over 1f out: btr 1294 (5f, firm). *1½* **50**
3466 **OUR INDULGENCE 15** [13] 2-8-7 K Darley 14/1: -07: Mid div at best: see 3466. *4* **46**
3571 **CHAIRMAN BOBBY 11** [7] 2-8-7 A Culhane 7/2: -38: Nvr a factor: btr 3571 (debut, 5f, firm). *½* **45**
-- **I T CONSULTANT** [1] 2-8-4 S Whitworth 7/1: -9: Dwelt, sn in tch, every ch until no extra over 1f out, eased: gamble from 50/1 on debut: cheaply bght Rock City half-brother to a 6/7f wnr: shld do better. *nk* **41**
2010 **POLYPHONIC 78** [3] 2-7-13 J Bramhill 20/1: -0650: Handy, lost tch over 2f out: fin 10th: 11 wk abs. *3½* **26**
1981 **Magnanimous 79** [8] 2-8-10 Kim Tinkler 50/1: 3675 **Conspiracy Theory 7** [5] 2-7-13 Iona Wands 100/1:
3193 **Tancred Walk 27** [2] 2-7-13 J McAuley 33/1: 2730 **Charmed 47** [4] 2-8-4 D Sweeney 20/1:
3500 **Eager Angel 14** [6] 2-8-2 G Bardwell 16/1:
15 ran Time 1m 14.01 (4.61) (Mrs C Samuel) R M Whitaker Scarcroft, W Yorks

BATH **MONDAY SEPTEMBER 4TH** **Lefthand, Turning Track With Uphill Finish**

Official Going GOOD (GOOD/FIRM places). Stalls: Str Crse - Far Side; Rnd Crse - Inside.

3815 — 2.00 MATINEE FILLIES AUCT MDN 2YO (E) 5f rnd Good/Firm 30 -12 Slow
£3357 £1033 £516 £258

3090 **NEARCTIC LADY 33** [4] R Hannon 2-8-7 R Hughes 4/1: -401: 2 gr f Night Shift - Snowing (Icecapade) **97**
Made all, rdn/clr 1f out, in command when eased down nr fin, readily: eff at 5f, tried 6f, shld suit: handles firm & fast grnd, stiff/undul trk: eff forcing the pace: useful filly, can win again.
3720 **BEE ONE 9** [3] D R C Elsworth 2-8-7 T Quinn 4/6 FAV: 540452: 2 b f Catrail - Ruwy (Soviet Star) 3½ **86**
Chsd ldrs, rdn & kept on from over 1f out, no threat to wnr: hvly bckd at odds on: ahd of this wnr in 3090 (6f).
1954 **ALEXANDER STAR 81** [6] J A R Toller 2-8-3 S Whitworth 8/1: 43: 2 b f Inzar - Business Centre 2 **77**
(Digamist) Dwelt, sn rdn chasing ldrs, kept on for press fnl 1f, no threat: abs: handles fast, return to 6f shld suit.
2657 **LADY EBERSPACHER 52** [5] Mrs P N Dutfield 2-8-3 L Newman(2) 6/1: 04244: Chsd wnr, btn fnl 1f: abs. ½ **75**
3710 **MARTHA P PERKINS 6** [8] 2-8-3 R Mullen 14/1: 05: Rear, rdn/mod gains fnl 2f: op 16/1, qck reapp. *nk* **74**
-- **THATCHED COTTAGE** [9] 2-8-1 P Doe 20/1: 6: Rear/bhd, mod hdwy: Thatching filly, Feb foal, cost 1¼ **69**
1,000gns: a first foal: dam unrcd: with B Palling.
1197 **DELPHYLLIA 119** [7] 2-8-1 N Pollard 25/1: -007: Dwelt/bhd & sn rdn, nvr on terms: 4 months abs. ½ **67$**
3639 **THE WALL 9** [1] 2-8-1 A Daly 50/1: 050008: Al bhd: offic rtd 36, treat rating with caution. 2 **62$**
3228 **MISTY BELLE 26** [2] 2-8-3 G Hind 16/1: 234D09: Struggling halfway, op 10/1: btr 2214. 4 **54**
9 ran Time 1m 02.4 (2.1) (D Boocock) R Hannon East Everleigh, Wilts.

3816 — 2.30 AUTUMN SELL HCAP 3-4YO 0-60 (F) 1m rnd Good/Firm 30 -10 Slow [55]
£2345 £670 £335 3 yo rec 5 lb

3498 **HARD LINES 16** [1] I A Balding 4-10-0 (55) M Hills 13/2: 000041: 4 b g Silver Hawk - Arctic Eclipse **61**
(Northern Dancer) Chsd ldrs, prog to led 2f out, styd on well ins last, drvn out: bght in for 5,200gns: unplcd sole '99 start (rtd 50a, clmr): '98 sole start wnr at Newbury (debut, mdn, rtd 89): prev eff at 6f, now suited by 1m: acts on firm & fast grnd, stiff/gall trk: has run well fresh: gd weight carrier, eff in sell grade.
3736 **ANNIE APPLE 5** [16] N Hamilton 4-9-2 (43) D Harrison 12/1: 500142: 4 ch f Petardia - Art Duo 1¾ **45**
(Artaius) Rear, rdn/styd on fnl 3f to chase wnr ins last, al held: op 10/1, qck reapp: see 3559 (7f).
3557 **EMALI 12** [4] C E Brittain 3-9-10 (56) P Robinson 12/1: 204303: 3 b g Emarati - Princess Poquito ¾ **57**
(Hard Fought) Chsd ldrs, bmpd over 1f out, no extra ins last: visor omitted: eff at 1m/10f: see 2685.
3574 **DILETIA 12** [7] N A Graham 3-9-10 (56)(bl) M Roberts 9/1: 045604: Slowly away/rear, rdn & kept on 1¾ **54**
fnl 3f, no threat to front trio: blnks reapplied: eff around 1m, tried 10f: prob handles fast & gd/soft grnd.
3580 **RIDGECREST 12** [12] 3-9-5 (51)(t) T E Durcan 20/1: -54505: Rear, prog/chsd ldrs when sltly hmpd 2 **45**
3f out, no impress after: see 236, 150.
3094 **MOUNTRATH ROCK 33** [3] 3-9-3 (49)(vis) T Quinn 13/2: 401566: Dwelt/rear, mod gains fnl 2f: see 2187. ¾ **42**
2413 **OUTSTANDING TALENT 61** [14] 3-8-13 (45) F Norton 16/1: 600247: Chsd ldrs till over 1f out: abs. 1 **36**
3499 **SKY HOOK 16** [2] 3-9-6 (52)(VIS) M Fenton 25/1: 5-5008: Chsd ldrs, bmpd 1f out, btn/eased fnl 1f: vis. 1¾ **40**
3656 **ARZILLO 9** [11] 4-9-6 (47)(bl) Pat Eddery 7/1: 030509: Led 6f, fdd: see 3656, 1211. 2½ **30**
3663 **JOHN STEED 8** [15] 3-9-1 (47) N Pollard 16/1: 0-0400: Rear, eff 4f out, btn 2f out: 10th: see 2264. ½ **29**
2964 **WHITEGATE WAY 38** [6] 3-9-3 (49) J Fortune 16/1: 004000: Al towards rear: 11th: see 2443. 1¾ **28**
2448 **BEDOUIN QUEEN 60** [5] 3-9-4 (50) J Bosley (7) 8/1: 060020: Rear, eff 3f out, sn held: 12th: abs. 1¼ **26**
3559 **TERM OF ENDEARMENT 12** [13] 3-9-3 (49) R Mullen 6/1 FAV: 002130: Rear, rdn/eff when wide on 1¼ **22**
bend over 3f out, sn btn: 13th: btr 3332 (7f).
3008 **CUIGIU 36** [9] 3-9-7 (53) D Nolan (7) 10/1: 400230: Chsd ldrs 6f: 14th: btr 3008 (10f). 1½ **23**
3281 **MINT LEAF 24** [8] 3-9-0 (46)(t) I Mongan (5) 25/1: 000000: Rear, nvr factor: 15th: see 2431. *hd* **15**
15 ran Time 1m 40.7 (3.2) (C H Bothway) I A Balding Kingsclere, Hants.

3817 — 3.00 TALENT NURSERY HCAP 2YO 0-90 (C) 1m rnd Good/Firm 30 -09 Slow [92]
£6938 £2135 £1067 £533

3497 **FLIT ABOUT 16** [7] I A Balding 2-8-13 (77) M Roberts 12/1: 2351: 2 ch f Fly So Free - Oxava (Antheus) **80**
Held up, rdn/prog fnl 2f & led ins last, held on well, rdn out: op 10/1: h'cap bow: apprec step up to 1m, could get further: acts on fast grnd & a stiff/undul trk: op to further improvement.
3412 **MURRENDI 18** [1] M R Channon 2-9-2 (80) Craig Williams 8/1: -50542: 2 b c Ashkalani - Formaestre ¾ **81**
(Formidable) Led, rdn over 2f out, hdd ins last, kept on: fine h'cap bow, styd longer 1m trip well: handles fast/firm.
2921 **BOUND 40** [6] B W Hills 2-8-10 (74) J Reid 16/1: -0003: 2 b c Kris - Tender Moment (Caerleon) *nk* **74**
Rear, drvn & styd on well fnl 2f despite flashing tail, nrst fin: 6 wk abs, h'cap bow: styd longer 1m trip, further shld suit on this evidence: unplcd previously.
3630 **PRINCE MILLENNIUM 9** [2] R Hannon 2-9-0 (78) R Hughes 13/2: -56304: Held up, switched/rdn & *hd* **77**
styd on well from over 1f out, nrst fin: only btn around 1L: op 5/1: styd longer 1m trip well: see 2972.
*3497 **ACT OF REFORM 16** [13] 2-9-5 (83) M Tebbutt 9/2: 514: Mid-div/wide, rdn/prog to chall over 1f *dht* **82**
out, just held nr fin: op 7/2: styd longer 1m trip on h'cap bow: acts on fast grnd & fibresand: see 3497 (7f, AW).
3428 **POLISH PADDY 17** [11] 2-8-1 (65) L Newman (3) 12/1: 066446: Chsd ldrs, rdn over 2f out, kept on *hd* **63**
well for press: stablemate of 4th, op 14/1: btn less than 2L: styd longer 1m trip, handles fast grnd.
3609 **ST FLORENT 10** [12] 2-8-2 (66)(BL) F Norton 14/1: -20007: Held up, rdn over 2f out, mod hdwy: blnks. 2 **60**
3449 **RICHENDA 17** [3] 2-9-2 (80) P Dobbs (5) 12/1: -00668: Chsd ldrs, rdn/fdd over 1f out: op 10/1. *shd* **74**
3418 **SHIRAZI 18** [10] 2-8-9 (73) M Hills 3/1 FAV: 5639: Chsd ldrs wide halfway, prog/ev ch over 1f out, ½ **66**
sn rdn/fdd: bckd, op 5/1: not quite see out this longer 1m trip, drop to 7f in similar could suit: see 3418.
2620 **TRAVELLERS DREAM 53** [5] 2-8-2 (66) N Pollard 20/1: 0360: Mid-div, no room/rdn over 1f out, sn *nk* **58**
held: 10th: h'cap bow, 8 wk abs: bred to apprec this longer 1m trip: see 2125, 1408.
3361 **ADJOURNMENT 21** [4] 2-9-7 (85) J Fortune 9/2: 016240: Trkd ldrs, rdn/fdd fnl 2f: 11th: bckd. 1¼ **74**
3273 **TRUSTED MOLE 24** [9] 2-8-3 (67) R Havlin 12/1: 304400: Prom 6f: 12th: op 10/1: btr 2468 (7f, g/s). 2 **52**
*3582 **SAWBO LAD 11** [8] 2-8-4 (68) P Doe 12/1: 600010: Chsd ldrs 5f: 13th: op 10/1: btr 3582 (7f, sell). 19 **23**
13 ran Time 1m 41.4 (3.1) (Robin F Scully) I A Balding Kingsclere, Hants.

3818

3.30 RENATE MDN 3YO+ (D)   1m3f144y   Good/Firm 30   -05 Slow
£3916   £1205   £602   £301   3 yo rec 9 lb

3595 **SHAMAIEL 11** [4] C E Brittain 3-8-7 P Robinson 6/4 FAV: 404301: 3 b f Lycius - Pearl Kite (Silver Hawk)   90
Led 1f, remained handy till went on 3f out, sn rdn clr, eased down nr fin, cmftbly: value for 10L+:
hvly bckd: apprec this return to mdn company, sev encouraging efforts in List/stks company: eff arnd
11/12f, dam a useful 14f performer, further may suit: acts on fast & gd grnd, stiff/gall trk: a straightforward task.
3517 **FLAME OF TRUTH 15** [8] J H M Gosden 3-8-7 J Fortune 13/2: 32: 3 b f Rainbow Quest - River Lullaby   7   77
(Riverman) Chsd ldrs, rdn/chsd wnr over 2f out, al held: op 9/2: see 3517 (C/D).
3265 **SHATTERED SILENCE 25** [7] R Charlton 3-8-7 R Hughes 4/1: -03333: 3 b f Cozzene - Sunday Bazaar   2   75
(Nureyev) Chsd ldrs, rdn/kept on fnl 3f, no threat: op 7/2: h'cap company shld suit: see 2751, 2531.
3429 **JUNO BEACH 17** [11] D Morris 4-9-2 J Reid 9/1: 34: Held up, rdn/mod hdwy fnl 2f: op 14/1: see 3429.   1   74
-- **ANEEFAH** [14] 3-8-7 R Perham 10/1: 5: Towards rear, mod hdwy under hands-and-heels riding fnl   1¼ 72
3f: op 5/1, debut: dam plcd in Gr company abroad as a 3yo: likely to apprec 12f+ for M P Tregoning.
3416 **VILLIAN 18** [16] 5-9-2 F Norton 33/1: 346: Chsd ldrs 10f: see 3157.   1   71
2751 **SATARRA 47** [1] 3-8-12 T Quinn 4/1: 247: Led aftr 1f till 3f out, sn btn: well bckd: abs: see 2751.   ½   75
3489 **LEILA 16** [15] 5-9-2 L Newman (3) 50/1: 048: Al towards rear: needs low-grade h'caps.   6   61
2981 **ATTO 38** [10] 6-9-7 I Mongan (5) 66/1: -069: Chsd ldrs 1m: longer 12f trip, needs h'caps.   1¼ 64
1510 **EVIYRN 101** [9] 4-9-7 K Pierrepont (7) 50/1: 04-060: Al rear: 10th: 3 month abs: see 920.   7   54
3265 Swemby 25 [6] 3-8-7 Pat Eddery 33/1:   2774 Lady Abai 46 [5] 3-8-7 Craig Williams 50/1:
3189 Caramelle 28 [12] 4-9-2 S Whitworth 50/1:   3048 Joli Eclipse 35 [3] 3-8-7 C Rutter 25/1:
14 ran   Time 2m 29.1 (4.1)   (Saeed Manana)   C E Brittain Newmarket.

3819

4.00 HORSESMOUTH.CO.UK MDN HCAP 3YO+ 0-70 (E)   1m5f   Good/Firm 30   -16 Slow   [70]
£2834   £872   £436   £218   3 yo rec 10lb

2470 **DISTANT PROSPECT 59** [7] I A Balding 3-9-3 (69) M Hills 9/2: -23541: 3 b c Namaqualand - Ukraine's   77
Affair (The Minstrel) Chsd ldrs, rdn/led over 1f out, styd on strongly, rdn out: plcd once as a juv in '99 (rtd 73):
eff at 10/13f, could get further: acts on fast & gd/soft grnd, sharp or stiff/undul track.
3472 **REDOUBLE 16** [12] J Akehurst 4-9-4 (60) T Quinn 5/2 FAV: 022332: 4 b g First Trump - Sunflower   2½ 63
Seed (Mummy's Pet) Led/dsptd lead till over 1f out, rdn & styd on onepace: nicely bckd: see 3201, 1878.
3489 **TUFTY HOPPER 16** [3] P Howling 3-8-13 (65) J Fortune 12/1: 204533: 3 b g Rock Hopper - Melancolia   ¾ 67
(Legend Of France) Chsd ldrs, rdn/ev ch over 2f out, onepace: op 10/1: see 2710.
3683 **MISTER WEBB 7** [5] B Smart 3-8-12 (64) M Tebbutt 33/1: 4-5004: Chsd ldrs, rdn/outpcd over 3f out,   2½ 62
styd on from over 1f out, no threat: longer 13f trip: see 858.
3390 **ALQAWAASER 19** [14] 3-9-0 (66) R Havlin 10/1: 0-5645: Rear, hdwy/rdn 3f out, held over 1f out.   nk 63
3522 **SKYE BLUE 14** [9] 3-8-13 (65) Craig Williams 7/1: 232056: Rear, rdn/mod gains fnl 3f, no threat.   ¾ 61
1888 **ROYAL MEASURE 83** [8] 4-8-7 (49) G Hind 8/1: 00-307: Rear, hdwy 3f out, no prog fnl 2f: abs.   shd 45
3586 **TOMMY CARSON 11** [4] 5-8-4 (46)(bl) D Sweeney 11/1: 504068: Chsd ldrs halfway, btn 2f out.   2½ 38
3353 **CONSTANT 21** [2] 3-8-12 (64) R Hughes 16/1: -05009: al held: see 979 (10f).   1   55
3416 **HAVANA 18** [13] 4-10-0 (70)(BL) M Roberts 8/1: -42330: In tch, btn 3f out: 10th: blnks: btr 3416.   2   58
3663 **QUEEN OF FASHION 8** [11] 4-9-5 (61) A Clark 20/1: 043000: Chsd ldrs, rdn 2f out, eased fnl 1f: 11th.   3   45
2353 **MEMPHIS TEENS 64** [1] 3-9-2 (68) S Whitworth 14/1: 3030: Led 6f out till over 3f out, sn btn: 12th: 1   51
2 month abs, h'cap bow: see 2353, 1293.
1637† **HONEST VILLAIN 464** [6] 3-8-8 (60) T E Durcan 20/1: 300-0: Led 3f, btn 4f out: 14th: reapp/h'cap   0
bow: plcd on first of 3 '99 starts (5f mdn, rtd 69): bred to apprec mid-dists.
1824 Revenge 87 [15] 4-9-9 (65)(BL) S Sanders 33/1:   3664 Tomaszewski 8 [10] 5-8-12 (54) M Fenton 12/1:
15 ran   Time 2m 51.5 (6.0)   (The Rae Smiths & Pauline Gale)   I A Balding Kingsclere, Hants.

3820

4.30 SHERSTON MDN 3YO (D)   5f161y rnd   Good/Firm 30   +04 Fast
£3799   £1169   £584   £292

2472 **ULYSSES DAUGHTER 59** [10] G A Butler 3-8-9 (t) T Quinn 15/8 JT FAV: 421: 3 ch f College Chapel -   72
Trysinger (Try My Best) Chsd ldrs, prog/narrow lead over 1f out, held on well, drvn out: well bckd, abs: eff arnd
6f, 7f+ shld suit: acts on fast & gd/soft, stiff/undul or gall trk: eff in a t-strap: runs well fresh.
1773 **OUR FIRST LADY 89** [5] D W P Arbuthnot 3-8-9 Pat Eddery 7/2: 0-022: 3 b f Alzao - Eclipsing   ½ 69
(Baillamont) Trkd ldrs trav well halfway, rdn/chall fnl 1f, just held nr fin: op 3/1: 12 wk abs: acts on fast & gd.
3562 **ZOENA 12** [9] J G Portman 3-8-9 L Newman (3) 16/1: 563053: 3 ch f Emarati - Exotic Forest   2   64$
(Dominion) Led, rdn/hdd over 1f out & no extra: op 14/1: see 2252 (fill h'cap).
1923 **POLAR LADY 82** [2] D Morris 3-8-9 J Reid 15/8 JT FAV: 6-3504: Chsd ldrs, btn over 1f out: hvly   3   57
bckd: 12 wk abs: see 1923, 877.
623 **RISKY REEF 186** [8] 3-9-0 M Hills 5/1: 52-455: Chsd ldrs 2f out, sn held: 6 month abs: see 549.   shd 62
-- **CURRENCY** [1] 3-9-0 P Fitzsimons (5) 20/1: 6: Dwelt/bhd, mod hdwy: debut: with J Bradley.   1¼ 59
3229 **SECOND GENERATION 26** [4] 3-9-0 N Pollard 16/1: -057: Slowly away & al bhd: mod form.   3   52
3423 **TALENT STAR 18** [3] 3-9-0 S Righton 20/1: -0468: Al outpcd rear: mod form.   2   47
3579 **ARTYFACTUAL 12** [6] 3-9-0 I Mongan (5) 40/1: 09: Chsd ldrs 3f: no form.   hd 46
3696 **KERRICH 7** [7] 3-9-0 C Rutter 50/1: 000: Al outpcd rear: 10th: mod form.   6   26
10 ran   Time 1m 10.6 (1.5)   (The Travellers)   G A Butler Blewbury, Oxon.

3821

5.00 HARD TO FIGURE HCAP 3YO+ 0-80 (D)   5f161y rnd   Good/Firm 30   +02 Fast   [80]
£4231   £1302   £651   £325   3 yo rec 2 lb

3613 **PETARGA 10** [18] J A R Toller 5-9-2 (68) S Whitworth 12/1: -00501: 5 b m Petong - One Half Silver   74
(Plugged Nickle) Towards rear, hdwy wide from halfway & styd on strongly to lead ins last, rdn out: op 9/1: '99
Folkestone wnr (h'cap, rtd 80): plcd twice in '98 (h'cap, rtd 80): eff at 5/6f on firm/gd grnd, sharp or gall trk.
3580 **RULE OF THUMB 12** [16] G L Moore 3-9-5 (73) I Mongan (5) 16/1: 005202: 3 ch g Inchinor - Rockin'   1   75
Rosie (Song) Rear, prog from halfway & rdn/led over 1f out, sn hdd, kept on: eff btwn 5/7f: see 3445, 954.
*3662 **CAUDA EQUINA 8** [14] M R Channon 6-10-1 (81) Craig Williams 15/2: 652113: 6 gr g Statoblast -   hd 82
Sea Fret (Habat) Held up, rdn & styd on from over 1f out, nrst fin: op 6/1: topweight, in fine form: see 3662 (7f).
3578 **MISTER JOLSON 12** [18] R J Hodges 11-7-12 (50) P Doe 25/1: 0-4504: Chsd ldrs halfway, led 2f out   1¼ 48
till over 1f out, onepace: well h'capped 11yo who retains enthusiasm: see 1966.

BATH
MONDAY SEPTEMBER 4TH   Lefthand, Turning Track With Uphill Finish

3543 **MISS HIT** 13 [13] 5-9-5 (71) T Quinn 7/1: -10205: Chsd ldrs, eff/hmpd over 1f out, kept on ins last.   ¾   67

3493 **BRAMBLE BEAR** 16 [11] 6-7-12 (50) Dale Gibson 9/4 FAV: 033236: Rear, rdn & styd on fnl 2f, nvr   ¾   44
pace to chall: hvly bckdm from 12/1: strange gamble on this infrequent wnr: see 1464.

2371 **KILMEENA LAD** 63 [19] 4-8-6 (58) S Carson (3) 25/1: 005007: Led over 2f out, sn hdd & no extra: hd   51
2 month abs: blnks omitted: see 1999, 462.

3613 **GASCON** 10 [12] 4-8-13 (65) D Harrison 33/1: -02408: Rear, no room 2f out, fin fast once in the   nk   57+
clr, chance had gone: lightly rcd & one to keep an eye on, promising here: see 1605 (soft, mdn).

3765 **ZEPPO** 3 [5] 5-8-9 (61) G Hind 14/1: 452139: Chsd ldrs 4f: qck reapp: btr 3765, 3578.   ½   51

3135 **IMPERIALIST** 31 [9] 3-9-12 (80)(bl) R Hughes 20/1: 002000: Rear, switched over 1f out, styd on   nk   69
ins last, nrst fin: 10th: see 2663, 1078.

3653 **CLASSY CLEO** 9 [7] 5-9-8 (74) T E Durcan 12/1: 400100: Chsd ldrs, no room over 1f out, sn held: 11th.   nk   62

*3594 **SIHAFI** 11 [2] 7-9-2 (68) Pat Eddery 4/1: 245010: Chsd ldrs, eff 2f out, sn held: 12th: op 7/2.   1   54

3791 **BEYOND CALCULATION** 2 [17] 6-9-5 (71) P Fitzsimons (5) 16/1: 644200: Led/dsptd lead till over 2f   shd   57
out: 13th: op 10/1, qck reapp: btr 2207 (6f).

2193 **HEAVENLY MISS** 70 [8] 6-8-2 (54)(bl) N Pollard 33/1: 140000: Chsd ldrs, btn/eased ins last: 14th: abs. 1½   36

3516 **EASTER OGIL** 15 [10] 5-9-11 (77)(vis) M Hills 7/1: 500040: Al rear: 15th: see 1517.   1½   55

3587 **KILCULLEN LAD** 11 [6] 6-8-12 (64)(vis) J Reid 8/1: 060350: Prom till halfway: 16th: see 1438.   1¾   38

3791 **ILLUSIVE 2** [4] 3-9-6 (74)(bl) F Norton 16/1: 332000: Chsd ldrs 3f: 17th: qck reapp: see 2934, 2787.   4   38

3528 **TRUMP STREET** 14 [1] 4-7-11 (49)(bl) J Bramhill 40/1: 100000: Led till over 3f out, sn btn: 18th.   9   0

18 ran   Time 1m 10.7 (1.6)   (Mrs R W Gore-Andrews)   J A R Toller Newmarket.

HAMILTON
MONDAY SEPTEMBER 4TH   Righthand, Undulating Track With Stiff Uphill Finish

Official Going   SOFT (HEAVY In Places). Stalls: Stands Side, Except 1m/1m1f - Inside.

3822
2.15 EBF MDN 2YO (D)   **1m65y rnd**   Good/Soft 66   -20 Slow
£3461   £1065   £532   £266

2881 **DOUBLE HONOUR** 42 [4] M Johnston 2-9-0 D Holland 7/4: 241: 2 gr c Highest Honor - Silver Cobra   84
(Silver Hawk) Prom, led 2f out, rdly: 6 wk abs: Ffr 150,000 foal, brother to a juv wnr abroad: eff at 1m,
shld stay mid-dists next term: handles fast grnd, imprvd on gd/soft: handles stiff/undul trks: runs well fresh:
completed fastest ever 1000 Flat wnrs for trainer M Johnston: going the right way.

3292 **EXOTIC FAN** 24 [2] R Guest 2-8-9 K Darley 5/1: -402: 2 b f Lear Fan - Green Moon (Shirley Heights)   4   71
Rcd in 3rd, rdn appr fnl 1f, styd on for 2nd but no ch wnr: stays 1m on gd/soft grnd.

3308 **PRINCESS TITANIA** 23 [5] N A Callaghan 2-8-9 J Quinn 10/11 FAV: 4023: 2 b f Fairy King - Chiquelina   ½   70
(Le Glorieux) Led till 2f out, no extra: well bckd, clr of rem: reportedly failed to handle the rain-softened grnd.

3697 **DISPOL FOXTROT** 7 [1] S E Kettlewell 2-8-9 A Culhane 66/1: 04: In tch till 3f out: sister to a 6/7f juv wnr.17   45

-- **INGLEMOTTE MISS** [3] J S Halliday 66/1: 5: Dwelt, sn struggling: Hatim filly, with Miss Craze.   28   5

5 ran   Time 1m 50.9 (7.1)   (The 4th Middleham Partnership)   M Johnston Middleham, N Yorks

3823
2.45 STONEFIELD SELLER 3YO+ (F)   **1m1f36y**   Good/Soft 66   -22 Slow
£2380   £680   £340   3 yo rec 6 lb

3745 **GO THUNDER** 4 [12] D A Nolan 6-9-4 (t) Iona Wands 8/1: 000531: 6 b g Nordico - Moving Off   36
(Henbit) Led, rdn 2L clr appr fnl 1f, pushed out cl-home: tchd 20/1, no bid, quick reapp: 1st win, ex-Irish,
back in '98 plcd in a 14f h'cap: eff at 1m/9f on fast & gd/soft grnd: wears a t-strap.

3805 **ACE OF TRUMPS** 1 [10] J Hetherton 4-9-9 (t) O Pears 10/1: 564352: 4 ch g First Trump - Elle Reef   2½   37
(Shareef Dancer) Well plcd, chsd wnr ent fnl 2f, onepace ins last: op 11/2, ran yesterday: a fair effort.

3524 **HEVER GOLF GLORY** 14 [8] C N Kellett 6-9-4 T Williams 12/1: 560003: 6 b f Efisio - Zaius (Artaius)   1½   29
In tch, eff appr fnl 2f, kept on but no impress on ldrs: down in grade: see 383.

3746 **CLAIM GEBAL CLAIM** 4 [7] P Monteith 4-9-9 V Halliday 7/2 FAV: 603234: Chsd ldrs, under press appr   nk   33
fnl 2f, kept on same pace: clr rem, quick reapp: see 2780 (C/D, beat this 2nd on fast grnd).

3711 **NOBBY BARNES** 6 [5] 11-9-4 Kim Tinkler 5/1: 026005: Dwelt, late hdwy, nvr a threat: quick reapp.   3   23

1858 **HOT POTATO** 85 [4] 4-9-4 J McAuley 12/1: 050206: Nvr troubled ldrs: 12 wk abs, op 9/1: see 1699.   3   18

3234 **EMISSARY** 26 [3] 7-9-9 G Bardwell 9/2: 104407: Nvr better than mid-div: op 11/2: plcd btr 1546 (sell h'cap). nk   22

3570 **IRANOO** 12 [6] 3-8-12 (t) P Lynch 33/1: 000458: Chsd ldrs till fdd 2f out: back in trip, see 1940.   4   11

3506 **LADY FLORA** 15 [1] 4-8-13 A Culhane 33/1: 6-09: Al towards rear: no worthwhile form.   ½   5

3591 **SECRETARIO** 11 [2] 3-8-7 N Kennedy 25/1: 000050: Nvr a factor: 10th, modest.   hd   5

3375 **FASTWAN** 19 [11] 4-9-4 Dawn Rankin (7) 66/1: 005000: Al bhd: 11th, stiff task, no form.   9   0

2799 **FLOORSOTHEFOREST** 45 [9] 4-9-4 A Beech 6/1: 000500: Handy, btn appr fnl 3f: 6 wk abs, op 5/2.   ½   0

12 ran   Time 2m 02.2 (8.1)   (Miss G Joughin)   D A Nolan Newmains, N Lanarks

3824
3.15 PLUMB CENTER NURSERY HCAP 2YO 0-85 (D)   **6f**   Good/Soft 66   -36 Slow   [81]
£2422   £2422   £570   £285

*3693 **JOINT INSTRUCTION** 7 [6] M R Channon 2-9-4 (71)(6ex) A Culhane 5/2 FAV: 202011: 2 b g Forzando -   77
Edge Of Darkness (Vaigly Great) Well plcd, led appr fnl 2f, 2L clr dist, sn hard rdn, joined on line: nicely bckd,
slow time, quick reapp: earlier won at Brighton (nov med auct) & Warwick (nursery): eff at 5/6f: acts on firm
& hvy grnd, any trk tho' sharper ones probably suit: improving.

2692 **CLASSY ACT** 51 [5] A Berry 2-9-2 (69) K Darley 7/2: 2301: 2 ch f Lycius - Stripanoora (Ahonoora)   dht   75
Led till appr fnl 2f, onepace till strong rally for press ins last to share the spoils: tchd 5/1, wnr in another stride
after 7 wk on h'cap bow: eff at 6f, apprec 7f next time: suited by gd/soft, sharp or stiff/undul trk: goes well fresh.

3387 **GRAND FIVE** 19 [8] J S Moore 2-9-5 (72) Dean McKeown 10/3: -2003: 2 b c Spectrum - Iberian Dancer   2   72
(El Gran Senor) Prom, eff appr fnl 2f, kept on but not pace of front 2: bckd tho' op 5/2 on h'cap bow: ran
near to beat on rain-softened grnd: see 1533.

3327 **LE MERIDIEN** 22 [7] J S Wainwright 2-8-10 (63) Paul Eddery 10/1: -04404: In tch, drvn ent fnl 2f,   1½   59
kept on till no extra fnl 100y: op 8/1: see 3098.

3264 **EMISSARY** 25 [3] 2-8-12 (65) K Dalgleish (5) 8/1: 640245: Handy till onepace appr fnl 1f: op 6/1:   1¼   58
crying out for a drop back to 5f: see 3264.

3508 **TROYS GUEST** 15 [4] 2-9-7 (74) F Lynch 14/1: 5336: Bhd ldrs, fdd appr fnl 1f: h'cap bow, btr 3508.   nk   66

3632 **GLOBAL EXPLORER** 9 [1] 2-8-9 (62) J Quinn 11/2: -0067: Al bhd: bckd from 8/1 on h'cap bow.   1¼   51

1173

7 ran   Time 1m 15.9 (6.1)   (C Shine, I Cunningham, J Lambert)   M R Channon Cockerham, Lancs

---

3825   3.45 HAMILTON APPR HCAP 3YO+ 0-70 (F)   5f   Good/Soft 66   +04 Fast   [67]
£2954   £844   £422   3 yo rec 1 lb   Spread across the track

3594 **BRANSTON PICKLE** 11 [9] M Johnston 3-9-5 (59) K Dalgleish (3) 11/2 FAV: 000001: 3 ch g Piccolo - Indefinite (Indian Ridge) Well plcd, rdn to lead appr fnl 1f, ran on well: op 4/1, best time of day: '99 wnr at W'hampton (2, sell & clmr, rtd 80a) & Catterick (nurs, rtd 80, T J Etherington): eff at 5/6f on gd/soft, soft grnd & fibresand: goes on any trk, likes W'hampton: best up with/forcing the pace: v well h'capped, shld follow up.   63

3619 **ROBIN HOOD** 10 [6] Miss L A Perratt 3-8-11 (51) A Beech (3) 8/1: 406102: 3 b g Komaite - Plough Hill (North Briton) Rear, switched & gd prog 2f out, drvn to chase wnr ins last, no extra cl-home: op 6/1, back to form on favoured easy grnd: see 3536 (C/D).   ¾ 52

3377 **MUJAGEM** 19 [12] M W Easterby 4-8-1 (40)(bl) P M Quinn 33/1: 602003: 4 br f Mujadil - Lili Bengam (Welsh Saint) Slow away, rcd up far rail, hdwy appr fnl 1f, nvr nrr: op 16/1: signs of return to form, goes on fibresand & gd/soft grnd: see 1303.   1¼ 38

3572 **INDIAN MUSIC** 12 [10] A Berry 3-9-11 (65)(bl) P Bradley (3) 6/1: 532604: Bhd ldrs, eff appr fnl 1f, kept on but not pace to chall: tchd 8/1: grnd now turning in his favour, see 3097, 1654.   ½ 62

3502 **LIZZIE SIMMONDS** 15 [17] 3-9-3 (57) S Finnamore (5) 6/1: 165305: Prom, led over 2f out till bef dist, no extra: tchd 10/1: see 2732, 1817.   1¼ 51

3594 **FACILE TIGRE** 11 [1] 5-8-12 (51) R Lake (7) 12/1: 000236: Outpcd, rdn appr fnl 1f, styd on, nvr a threat: op 8/1 crying out for return to 6f: see 146.   shd 45

3803 **MISS DANGEROUS** 1 [16] 5-7-13 (38) Claire Bryan (3) 33/1: 500007: Led till 2½f out, kept on same pace. nk 31

3536 **RED SYMPHONY** 13 [8] 4-8-7 (46)(BL) Joanna Badger (5) 14/1: 010008: Chsd ldrs, lost pl appr fnl 2f. nk 38

3631 **BEDEVILLED** 9 [5] 5-9-12 (65) D Watson (7) 12/1: 200169: Chsd ldrs till appr fnl 1f: op 8/1, top-weight. ½ 56

3123 **RIOJA** 31 [11] 5-9-6 (59) T Hamilton 7/1: 0/0000: Chsd ldrs, outpcd appr fnl 1f: 10th: tchd 20/1: lightly rcd, well h'capped back at 6/7f: see 1580. ¾ 48

3747 **CALANDRELLA** 4 [15] 7-7-12 (37) G Sparkes 9/1: 330000: Speed 3f: 11th, qk reapp: see 2428, 371. shd 26

3605 **BIFF EM** 10 [7] 6-7-12 (37) D Mernagh 20/1: 260000: Towards rear, switched halfway, btn bef dist: 12th. 1½ 23

3037 **JACMAR** 35 [13] 5-8-11 (50) M Scott (7) 12/1: 103000: Slow away, al bhd: 13th, stablemate 2nd. hd 36

3161 **PARADISE YANGSHUO** 30 [14] 3-8-6 (46) P Goode 12/1: 415300: Handy 3f: 14th, see 2204 (fast grnd). ¾ 30

4610} Leaping Charlie 304 [2] 4-9-6 (59) A Robertson (7) 40/1: 3631 **Miss Bananas** 9 [4] 5-8-6 (45) D Meah (7) 20/1:
3594 Shalarise 11 [3] 3-8-13 (53)(bl) G Baker (3) 33/1:
17 ran   Time 1m 01.2 (3.1)   (J David Abell)   M Johnston Middleham, N Yorks

---

3826   4.15 WILLIAM HILL HCAP 3YO+ 0-90 (C)   1m65y   Good/Soft 66   -03 Slow   [80]
£6955   £2140   £1070   £535   3 yo rec 5 lb

3603 **AMBUSHED** 10 [4] P Monteith 4-7-10 (48)(2oh) J McAuley 10/1: 010521: 4 b g Indian Ridge - Surprise Move (Simply Great) Led, pushed clr appr fnl 1f, cmftbly: tchd 14/1: earlier wn at Southwell (appr mdn h'cap, 1st time blnks, rtd 36a, M Johnston): eff at 1m/9f: acts on firm, gd/soft grnd & fibresand, prob any trk: eff with/without blnks & likes to force the pace: improving.   56

3699 **SEA SQUIRT** 7 [3] M Johnston 4-9-4 (75) D Holland 9/2: 623152: 3 b g Fourstars Allstar - Polynesian Goddess (Salmon Leap) Handy, lost place turning in, wide rally appr fnl 2f, went 2nd ins last, no ch wnr: op 11/4, quick reapp: in gd heart: see 3456.   4 75

3810 **RYEFIELD** 1 [7] Miss L A Perratt 5-8-10 (62) Dean McKeown 14/1: 214263: 5 b g Petong - Octavia (Sallust) Slow away, trkd ldrs, shaken up 3f out, chsd wnr 2f out, no extra below dist: drifted from 6/1, ran yesterday: not far off best, likes Ayr (Western meeting next week): see 2878.   ¾ 61

2666 **PIPS WAY** 52 [1] K R Burke 3-9-10 (81) N Callan 6/1: 143154: Chsd ldrs, onepace appr fnl 2f: tchd 7/1, top-weight, 7 wk abs: sharper next time, see 2581.   2½ 76

3785 **CLEVER GIRL** 2 [6] 3-9-8 (79)(bl) K Darley 13/2: 004305: Cl-up, fdd appr fnl 2f: ran 48 hrs ago. nk 73

3713 **CAPTAIN BRADY** 6 [5] 5-8-0 (52) J Quinn 7/4 FAV: 30-136: Sn prom, lost place 3f out: bckd from 5/2, quick reapp: unsuited by grnd or trip?: see 3379 (11f home).   2½ 42

3810 **ABAJANY** 1 [2] 6-9-9 (75) A Culhane 5/1: 24-007: Al bhd: tchd 11/2, ran yesterday: see 3642.   12 50

7 ran   Time 1m 49.5 (5.7)   (Allan W Melville)   P Monteith Rosewell, Midlothian

---

3827   4.45 SOUTERS HCAP 3YO+ 0-60 (F)   1m4f   Good/Soft 66   -29 Slow   [50]
£3220   £920   £460   3 yo rec 9 lb

3805 **WINSOME GEORGE** 1 [9] M Quinn 5-7-13 (21) G Sparkes (6) 20/1: 060641: 5 b g Marju - June Moon (Sadler's Wells) Waited on, stdy wide prog appr fnl 2f to lead ent fnl 1f, held on well, pshd out: op 33/1, ran yesterday (forced the pace), front 2 clr: unplcd in '99 (h'cap, rtd 66): '98 Beverley & Redcar wnr (h'caps, rtd 82): eff at 11/14f, tried 2m1f: acts on fast, gd/soft & fibresand, any trk, with/without visor: v well h'capped.   27

3522 **BOLLIN NELLIE** 14 [5] T D Easterby 3-9-7 (52) K Darley 3/1 FAV: 502162: 3 ch f Rock Hopper - Bollin Magdalene (Teenoso) Nvr far away, went on 3f out till below dist, kept on under press but being held: bckd, clr rem: back to form, suited by return to 12f: acts on firm & gd/soft grnd: improving, see 3284.   nk 57

3247 **RED ROSES** 26 [4] Don Enrico Incisa 4-8-1 (23)(t) Kim Tinkler 16/1: 040043: 4 b f Mukaddamah - Roses Red (Exhibitioner) Held up, styd on wide appr fnl 1f, nvr nr to chall: op 20/1, t-strap: see 3247, 825.   6 21

3480 **SUSANS DOWRY** 16 [8] Andrew Turnell 4-9-10 (46) P Fessey 50/1: 0-0004: In tch, rdn to chase ldrs 2f out, onepace fnl 1f: jt top-weight: lightly rcd/no worthwhile form since '98 Pontefract wn (6f fill auct mdn, rtd 75, T Easterby): tried various plces since then: acts on soft grnd & a sharp/undul trk.   2 42

3378 **LORD ADVOCATE** 19 [18] 12-7-12 (20)(vis) K Dalgleish (5) 16/1: 606605: Mid-div, prog to chall 3f out, no extra appr fnl 1f: op 12/1: see 1689.   1¾ 15

3674 **ALDWYCH ARROW** 8 [1] 5-9-5 (41) D Holland 12/1: -00006: Early ldr, ev ch till fdd appr fnl 1f: see 2836. hd 36

3201 **HASTA LA VISTA** 27 [17] 10-9-9 (45)(vis) T Lucas 10/1: 435007: Led after 3f till ent str, onepace fnl 2f. nk 39

3260 **LUNAR LORD** 25 [10] 4-8-13 (35) Dean McKeown 12/1: 022448: Rear, prog into mid-div appr fnl 1f. ¾ 28

3531 **KATIE KOMAITE** 13 [7] 7-8-13 (35) A Mackay 6/1: 235229: Pld hard mid-div, held 2f out: btr 3181, 890. 1¾ 26

3674 **PAPISPECIAL** 8 [12] 3-9-10 (55)(vis) O Pears 14/1: 12D200: Bhd, nvr threatened ldrs: 10th, joint top-weight: capable of better & appears better without a visor: see 3378, 2801.   ½ 45

3112 **DEE DIAMOND** 31 [2] 3-8-7 (38) J Quinn 25/1: 000500: Well plcd, led briefly 4f out, wknd 2f out: 11th. ¾ 24

3742 **NOTATION** 4 [13] 6-8-8 (30) Claire Bryan (5) 11/2: 501140: Handy till wknd qckly appr fnl 2f: 12th. ¾ 18

3036 **SANTA LUCIA** 35 [15] 4-9-8 (44) A Culhane 12/1: 601140: Front rank & ev ch till wknd appr fnl 2f: 13th. nk 31

3167 **RUNAWAY STAR** 30 [14] 3-8-12 (43) L Newton 7/1: -66500: Al towards rear: 15th, op 11/2, see 3167.   0

3637 Grantley 9 [6] 3-9-0 (45) T Williams 20/1:   3506 **Butterwick Chief** 15 [3] 3-9-4 (49)(BL) G Parkin 33/1:

3804 **Mischief 1** [16] 4-8-11 (33) (vis) G Hannon (7) 33/1:   2425 **Count On Thunder 61** [11] 3-9-6 (51) F Lynch 20/1:
18 ran   Time 2m 43.2 (11.4)   (M B Clemence)   M Quinn Sparsholt, Oxon

---

LINGFIELD (MIXED)   TUESDAY SEPTEMBER 5TH   Lefthand, Sharp, Undulating Track

Official Going TURF - GOOD/FIRM (FIRM Places), AW - STANDARD. Stalls: Turf - Stands Side, AW - Inside

3828   2.00 RACELINE SELL HCAP 3YO+ 0-60 (G)   1m2f aw Standard Inapplicable   [60]
£2012 £575 £287   3 yo rec 7 lb

3499 **CRUAGH EXPRESS 17** [3] P L Gilligan 4-8-11 (43) (bl) D Harrison 16/1: -56001: 4 b g Unblest - Cry   **50a**
In The Dark (Godswalk) Made all, rdn/increased tempo 3f out, styd on well to assert inside last, rdn out: sold
to C Sparrowhawk for 5,600gns: first win: plcd in native Ireland twice in '99 (7f): eff around a sharp 10f:
acts on equitrack & gd/soft grnd: likes a sharp track: wears blinkers.
3773 **BILLICHANG 3** [5] P Howling 4-8-11 (43) (bl) R Mullen 12/1: 044542: 4 b c Chilibang - Swing O' The 2½ **45a**
Kilt (Hotfoot) Cl up, rdn/came clr with wnr from 3f out, no impress inside last: quick reapp: see 775 (C/D).
3052 **THOMAS HENRY 35** [4] J S Moore 4-8-4 (36) N Farmer (7) 5/1: 036463: 4 br g Petardia - Hitopah 3 **34a**
(Bustino) Chsd ldrs, rdn/outpcd over 3f out, kept on fnl 2f, no threat: op 3/1: see 3052, 110 (C/D).
2914 **CUPIDS DART 41** [6] P Howling 3-9-4 (57) D Holland 16/1: 000504: Chsd front pair 3f out, rdn/held 4 **49a**
over 1f out: 6 week abs: apprec return to sand, but prob best around 7f/1m: see 615 (mdn).
3738 **SHONTAINE 6** [9] 7-8-6 (38) (bl) S W Kelly (3) 20/1: 000045: Held up, rdn/mod late hdwy: qck reapp. ½ **29a**
3691 **ZIDAC 8** [11] 8-10-0 (60) S Sanders 4/1 FAV: 3-0026: Held up wide, btn 2f out: bckd: topweight. 1½ **49a**
880 **SERGEANT IMP 146** [8] 5-8-8 (40) I Mongan (5) 9/1: 335437: Held up, eff/btn over 2f out: 5 mth abs. ½ **28a**
2735 **WHITE SANDS 49** [7] 3-7-13 (38) A Nicholls (2) 33/1: 006008: Dwelt/rear, mod hdwy: abs: mod form. 1¼ **24a**
3242 **CEDAR LIGHT 27** [1] 3-8-4 (43) P Doe 7/1: 000359: In tch 7f: op 12/1: longer 10f trip. hd **28a**
2887 **ABLE PETE 43** [12] 4-8-3 (35) L Newman (3) 9/1: 460000: Wide/bhd halfway: 10th: abs. 7 **10a**
3578 **BETCHWORTH SAND 13** [2] 4-8-7 (39) (BL) G Bird 33/1: -00000: Held up, btn 3f out: 11th: blinks. 2 **11a**
3490 **MIGWAR 17** [14] 7-9-5 (51) F Norton 11/1: 060300: Rear, rdn/btn 3f out: 12th: op 8/1: see 3490. 5 **16a**
3737 **METEOR STRIKE 6** [10] 6-8-13 (45) (t) T G McLaughlin 15/2: 0354U0: Mid div/wide, btn 4f out: 14th: fin lame. 1½ **8a**
3094 **LE LOUP 34** [13] 3-8-9 (48) N Callan 10/1: 043040: Mid div/wide, btn 4f out: 14th: AW bow. 9 **0a**
14 ran   Time 2m 06.76 (3.96)   (Mrs Anastasia Keane)   P L Gilligan Newmarket, Suffolk

3829   2.30 EBF FILL MDN DIV 1 2YO (D)   7f str Firm 05 -04 Slow
£3055 £940 £470 £235 Raced centre - stands side

-- **LYONETTE** [10] J Noseda 2-8-11 D Holland 4/1: 1: 2 b f Royal Academy - Inanna (Persian Bold) **88**
Al prom, narrow lead over 1f out, styd on well inside last, pshd out: op 5/2: April foal, cost 80.000gns: half-
sister to a useful 6f juv wnr: dam a 6f/1m winning 2yo, including at Group 3 level: eff over a sharp/undulating 7f,
1m will suit: acts on firm grnd & runs well fresh: open to further improvement.
3387 **ANNATTO 20** [5] I A Balding 2-8-11 K Darley 8/1: -242: 2 b f Mister Baileys - Miss Rossi (Artaius) ¾ **85**
Led, rdn/hdd over 1f out, kept on: op 6/1: stays a sharp 7f, handles firm & fast: h'cap comp should suit.
-- **INDEPENDENCE** [12] E A L Dunlop 2-8-11 G Carter 15/2: 3: 2 b f Selkirk - Yukon Hope (Forty 1¼ **82**
Niner) Rear, switched/rdn & prog to chase ldrs over 1f out, onepace/held nr fin: op 4/1: Feb first foal, dam
modest: sire a top class miler: eff at 7f, 1m will suit: handles firm: encouraging intro.
3650 **TARA GOLD 10** [7] R Hannon 2-8-11 R Hughes 3/1 FAV: -434: Dwelt, sn chsd ldrs, rdn & onepace fnl 1 **80**
1f: op 6/1: handles firm & gd grnd: see 3650, 3342.
-- **GUARANDA** [1] 2-8-11 M Tebbutt 33/2: 5: Held up in tch, rdn/prog to press ldrs over 1f out, sn no nk **79**
extra: op 5/2: Acatenango filly, Feb first foal: dam a 7f/1m 2yo wnr: sire top class at 12f abroad: eff
at 7f, 1m+ will suit: handles firm grnd: finished clr of rem, can improve & find a race.
-- **ESTIHAN** [11] 2-8-11 P Robinson 14/1: 6: Held up, eff & bmpd 2f out, sn outpcd by ldrs: 4 **71**
op 10/1: Silver Hawk filly, March foal, cost $35,000: half sister to a US 2yo wnr: dam unrcd: with C Brittain.
3074 **CAPE ROSE 34** [9] 2-8-11 T Quinn 7/2: 57: Chsd ldrs, outpcd fnl 2f: btn 3074. ½ **70**
3292 **SUPER VALUE 25** [8] 2-8-11 D Harrison 20/1: -08: Keen/chsd ldrs, btn over 1f out: see 3292. 6 **58**
3215 **FLORIDA 27** [3] 2-8-11 Lisa Somers (7) 50/1: 09: Prom till over 1f out: bhd debut prev (6f). 4 **50**
1290 **PAULAS PRIDE 113** [4] 2-8-11 A Polli (3) 33/1: 00: Prom, fdd fnl 2f: 10th: abs: new stable. nk **49**
-- **TENNESSEE WALTZ** [8] 2-8-11 W Supple 25/1: 0: Dwelt, al towards rear: 11th: op 12/1: 1¾ **46**
Caerleon filly, May foal, dam unrcd: sire top class at 10/12f: with E Dunlop.
3525 **BEL TEMPO 15** [8] 2-8-11 P Doe 50/1: 00: Al bhd: 12th: no form. 3 **40**
12 ran   Time 1m 21.00 (0.6)   (Dr T A Ryan)   J Noseda Newmarket, Suffolk

3830   3.00 BET DIRECT NURSERY HCAP 2YO 0-75 (E)   7f str Firm 05 -09 Slow   [82]
£3010 £860 £430 Raced centre - stands side

*3690 **CHAWENG BEACH 8** [12] R Hannon 2-8-8 (62) (6ex) P Fitzsimons (5) 5/2 FAV: 164511: 2 ro f Chaddleworth 68
- Swallow Bay (Penmarric) Chsd ldrs, rdn/prog over 1f out, led inside last, styd on well, rdn out: hvly bckd
under a 6lb pen: earlier scored at Lingfield (seller) & Epsom (h'cap): eff at 6f, now suited by a sharp/undul
7f, may get further: acts on firm & gd grnd: progressive filly.
3418 **PASO DOBLE 19** [3] B R Millman 2-9-7 (75) G Hind 6/1: 034222: 2 b c Dancing Spree - Delta Tempo ¾ **78**
(Bluebird) Led/dstpd lead, rdn/hdd inside last, kept on: op 8/1: acts on fast & firm: can win similar: see 3175.
2368 **TUMBLEWEED TENOR 64** [4] B J Meehan 2-9-2 (70) D R McCabe 16/1: -5203: 2 b g Mujadil - Princess shd **73**
Carmen (Arokar) Keen, in tch towards centre, drvn & styd on fnl 2f, not pace of wnr: 2 month abs: encouraging
h'cap bow, stays a sharp 7f, handles firm grnd: see 1208.
3387 **BOISDALE 20** [8] G C Bravery 2-8-12 (66) J Weaver 4/1: -0064: Led/dsptd lead till ins last, onepace: 1 **67**
op 6/1: stays a sharp 7f: handles firm grnd: encouraging h'cap bow.
3486 **MERIDEN MIST 17** [3] 2-8-9 (63) A Beech (5) 11/2: 341405: Bmpd start, rear, rdn & styd on well fnl ½ **74+**
2f, nrst fin: would have gone close if racing closer to the pace here, one to keep in mind: see 2894.
3299 **MONICA GELLER 25** [2] 2-8-5 (59) G Bardwell 20/1: 063036: Rdn/towards rear halfway, rdn & styd on ¾ **58**
onepace fnl 2f, no threat: prob stys a sharp 7f: handles firm & fibresand: see 2635, 2120.
3620 **SHEER FOCUS 11** [10] 2-8-13 (67) (t) N Pollard 16/1: 05067: Went left start, keen/held up, hdwy shd **66**
over 2f out, no prog inside last: longer 7f trip on h'cap bow: see 1823.
3558 **DATIN STAR 13** [8] 2-8-4 (58) P Doe 20/1: 60648: Chsd ldrs 6f: h'cap bow: see 2251. 2½ **52**

LINGFIELD (MIXED) TUESDAY SEPTEMBER 5TH Lefthand, Sharp, Undulating Track

3443 **RED FANFARE 18** [17] 2-8-12 (66) R Havlin 16/1: 0009: Chsd ldrs 5f: h'cap bow, longer 7f trip. *1* **58**
*3558 **BILLIE H 13** [16] 2-8-10 (64) P Robinson 16/1: 000610: Chsd ldrs 5f: 10th: btr 3558 (auct mdn). *1½* **53**
3444 **ALLTHEDOTCOMS 18** [5] 2-8-5 (59) F Norton 20/1: 04600: Rdn/chsd ldrs 2f out, sn btn: 11th. *nk* **47**
2886 **ANDROMEDAS WAY 43** [15] 2-8-13 (67) S Sanders 12/1: -6400: Trckd front pair, btn 2f out: 12th: abs. *1½* **52**
2748 **MAYTIME 48** [18] 2-8-13 (67) R Mullen 10/1: -0050: Dwelt, al bhd: 16th: op 8/1: abs, longer 7f trip. **0**
3273 **Blue Orleans 25** [13] 2-8-5 (59) S Whitworth 33/1: 3665 **Armida 9** [7] 2-8-0 (53)(1ow) J Tate 33/1:
2290 **Kiriwina 67** [14] 2-7-11 (51) A Nicholls (0) 33/1:
16 ran Time 1m 21.4 (1.0) (F Coen) R Hannon East Everleigh, Wilts

3831

3.30 TOTE QUICK PICK HCAP 3YO+ 0-80 (D) 7f140y str Firm 05 +06 Fast [80]
£7605 £2340 £1170 £585 3 yo rec 5 lb Raced centre - stands side

3328 **ARPEGGIO 23** [14] D Nicholls 5-9-3 (69) J Weaver 7/1: 041031: 5 b g Polar Falcon - Hilly (Town Crier) **77**
Trkd ldrs, no room 2f out till inside last, switched & rdn/qckd to lead nr line: bckd, op 8/1: best time of day: earlier scored at Catterick (class stakes): lightly rcd in '99, scored at Thirsk (reapp, mdn, rtd 84): eff at 6f, well suited by a sharp 7f/7.5f: acts on firm, soft, gall or sharp track, has run well fresh.
3685 **COPPLESTONE 8** [10] P W Harris 4-9-6 (72) T Quinn 7/2 FAV: 043222: 4 b g Second Set - Queen Of *1½* **74**
The Brush (Averof) Led, rdn/hdd well ins last & no extra: nicely bckd, op 5/1: remains a mdn but deserves similar.
3488 **BYZANTIUM GB 17** [3] W Jarvis 6-9-1 (67) R Hughes 9/1: 50-543: 6 b g Shirley Heights - Dulceata *hd* **68**
(Rousillon) Sn prom, rdn/every ch over 1f out, just held well inside last: op 7/1: fine effort from a tricky low draw: effective between 7.5f/10f: can find a race on this evidence: see 3118.
3334 **PETRUS 23** [12] C E Brittain 4-8-13 (65) A Nicholls (3) 8/1: 500004: Chsd ldrs, rdn/ch over 1f out, *shd* **66**
no extra ins last: morning gamble: well h'capd & indicated a return to form here, keep in mind: see 1286.
3514 **KNOCKTOPHER ABBEY 16** [18] 3-9-6 (77) G Hind 12/1: 505365: Mid div, rdn/styd on onepace fnl 1f. *1½* **75**
2562 **LUCKY GITANO 56** [17] 4-9-7 (73) G Carter 9/1: -00246: Trckd ldrs, rdn/switched over 1f out, styd *nk* **70**
on onepace: op 6/1: 8 week abs: big drop in trip, return to 1m+ should suit in similar: see 1729.
3455 **LAW COMMISSION 18** [16] 10-9-0 (66) D Holland 12/1: 014207: Held up, rdn/mod hdwy fnl 2f. *¾* **62**
3648 **MISTER RAMBO 10** [11] 5-9-12 (78)(bl) D R McCabe 12/1: 060558: Mid div, nvr able to chall: see 817. *½* **73**
3809 **AMBER FORT 2** [6] 7-9-3 (69)(bl) P Fitzsimons (5) 14/1: 534509: Held up, eff 2f out, little hdwy: see 1011. *½* **63**
3643 **DENS JOY 10** [4] 4-8-12 (64) K Darley 8/1: 054020: Slowly away/rear, late hdwy, nrst fin: 10th. *1½* **55**
3736 **BUTRINTO 6** [9] 6-8-11 (63) C Rutter 10/1: 023220: Held up, eff over 2f out, no impression: 11th. *¾* **53**
3629 **GINGKO 10** [1] 3-8-11 (68) A Beech (5) 10/1: -44460: Held up towards centre, hdwy 2f out, no prog *nk* **57**
inside last: 12th: op 7/1: tricky low draw, poss worth another ch after 3629 (h'cap bow).
1672 **Final Dividend 94** [8] 4-9-7 (73) J Tate 16/1: 3414 **Sarena Pride 19** [5] 3-9-1 (72) P Doe 25/1:
3355 **Khaled 22** [13] 5-9-1 (67) S Whitworth 33/1: 1384} **Autumn Cover 476** [2] 8-9-2 (68) P Robinson 14/1:
3110 **Glendale Ridge 33** [15] 5-8-8 (60) R Mullen 16/1:
17 ran Time 1m 27.7 (u0.1) (H E Lhendup Dorji) D Nicholls Sessay, N Yorks

3832

4.00 0800 211222 MED AUCT MDN 2YO (F) 6f Firm 05 -02 Slow
£2593 £741 £370 Raced centre - stands side

3385 **LA NOTTE 20** [17] W Jarvis 2-8-9 M Tebbutt 7/2 CO FAV: 31: 2 b f Factual - Miss Mirror (Magic **78**
Mirror) Chsd ldrs, shkn up 2f out, strong burst ins last to lead post, cheekily: May foal, half sister to a wnr abroad, dam a 1m wnr: eff at 6f, 7f+ will suit: acts on fast & firm, sharp/fair track: improving filly.
3400 **MYSTERI DANCER 20** [10] R J O'Sullivan 2-9-0 P Doe 20/1: 02: 2 b g Rudimentary - Mystery Ship *shd* **82**
(Decoy Boy) Al prom, rdn/led over 2f out, drvn/hdd on line: left debut bhd: eff over a sharp 6f on firm grnd.
-- **BREAKING NEWS** [3] M A Jarvis 2-9-0 P Robinson 14/1: 3: 2 b c Emperor Jones - Music Khan *1¼* **79**
(Music Boy) Al prom, every ch fnl 2f, just held well inside last: op 10/1: March foal, cost 17,000gns: full brother to 5/6f wnr Dancing Empress: dam a 6f/1m wnr abroad: eff at 6f, 7f should suit: acts on firm: encouraging intro.
2608 **RINGWOOD 54** [11] C F Wall 2-9-0 R Mullen 7/2 CO FAV: -64: Chsd ldrs, held 1f out: bckd: abs. *2* **74**
3466 **MIDSHIPMAN 17** [5] 2-9-0 K W Marks 33/1: 05: Chsd ldrs towards centre 5f: see 3466. *2½* **67**
-- **MINETTE** [4] 2-8-9 G Carter 8/1: 6: Mid div, mod late hdwy under tender handling: op 6/1: Bishop *½* **60+**
Of Cashel first foal, cost 17,000gns: dam a mdn, sire 7f/1m performer: should repay this kind intro over 7f+ in time.
-- **TRESS** [7] 2-8-9 D Harrison 13/2: 7: Dwelt, sn rcd mid div, onepace/held under hands & heels fnl 2f: *¾* **58**
op 4/1: Wolfhound half sister to 5f 2yo wnr Entwine: dam a multiple 2yo wnr: not given a hard time , can improve.
-- **LOCHSPRITE** [15] 2-8-9 K Darley 7/2 CO FAV: 8: Held up, rdn/btn 2f out: bckd, op 9/2: So Factual *1* **56**
Feb foal, half-sister to 3yo 6f wnr Locharati: dam unrcd half sister to high class sprinter Lochsong.
-- **DIXIES DARTS** [6] 2-9-0 S Sanders 33/1: 9: Chsd ldrs 4f: Mistertopogigo gelding, dam 1m wnr. *½* **59**
3577 **WAIKIKI DANCER 13** [20] 2-8-9 N Callan 20/1: 00: Led till over 2f out, fdd: 10th: no form. *hd* **53**
-- **ASWHATILLDOIS** [1] 2-8-9 C Rutter 25/1: 0: Mid div, btn 2f out: 11th: Blues Traveller filly, March *2½* **46**
foal, cost Ir5,000gns, dam a 7f juv Irish wnr: with D Cosgrove.
3092 **EMPRESS OF AUSTRIA 34** [9] 2-8-9 T Quinn 10/1: 30: Chsd ldrs 4f, btn/eased 1f out: 12th: op 8/1: *2* **41**
jockey reported filly rcd too freely to post & did not appreciate the firm grnd: btr 3092 (5f).
-- **IM LULU** [13] 2-8-9 T Ashley 9/1: 0: Mid div, btn 3f out: 13th: Piccolo filly, Jan foal: half-sister *1* **39**
to a 5f 2yo wnr: dam a 10f wnr abroad: with Mrs A J Perrett.
-- **GILTTRIP** [14] 2-9-0 R Havlin 14/1: 0: Al bhd: 14th: Goldmark colt, Feb foal, cost 15,000gns: *hd* **43**
half brother to a 7f wnr: dam a 1m Irish wnr: with J Osborne.
1408 **Simply Remy 108** [19] 2-9-0 F Norton 33/1: -- **Fox Cottage** [18] 2-8-9 S Whitworth 33/1:
-- **Muted Gift** [12] 2-8-9 A Daly 20/1: -- **Les Girls** [2] 2-8-9 A Nicholls (3) 33/1:
18 ran Time 1m 09.2 (0.4) (A L Harrison) W Jarvis Newmarket, Suffolk

3833

4.30 EBF FILL MDN DIV 2 2YO (D) 7f str Firm 05 -19 Slow
£3038 £935 £467 £233 Raced centre - stands side

2952 **VELVET GLADE 39** [1] I A Balding 2-8-11 K Darley 4/5 FAV: 31: 2 b f Kris S - Vailmont (Diesis) **90+**
Keen, al prom, led halfway, joined 2f out & rdn/narrowly asserted well inside last: hvly bckd, op 6/4, fron 2 well clr: confirmed promise of debut: eff at 6f, apprec this step up to 7f, 1m should suit: acts on firm & fast grnd, stiff/gall or sharp track: potentially useful filly, can rate more highly in better company.
-- **FILLE DE BUCHERON** [4] H R A Cecil 2-8-11 T Quinn 11/8: 2: 2 b f Woodman - Special Secreto *½* **88+**
(Secreto) Dwelt, sn trckd ldrs, prog to chall fnl 2f, styd on well under minimal press, just held inside last: hvly bckd tho' op 10/11: well clr of rem: Feb foal, cost 120,000gns: half sister to a wnr abroad, dam a French wnr: eff at 7f, 1m+ will suit: acts on firm grnd & a sharp track: highly encouraging, should prove hard to beat next time.
-- **SABO ROSE** [7] W J Haggas 2-8-11 P Robinson 25/1: 3: 2 b f Prince Sabo - Crimson Rosella *6* **76+**

(Polar Falcon) Dwelt/held up, eff/no room over 3f out, styd on from over 1f out, no threat to front pair: Feb foal, a first foal: dam a mdn: 7f+ will suit in time: shld improve for this kind intro in similar company.

-- **WATCHKEEPER** [2] J L Dunlop 2-8-11 D Harrison 14/1: 4: Went right start, towards rear, rdn & mod 1 74
hdwy fnl 2f: op 10/1: Rudimentary filly, March foal, cost 50,000gns: half sister to smart mid dist performer Rainwatch: dam a 7f juv wnr & subs a smart 12f wnr: bred to relish mid dists, will leave this bhd over further.

3412 **GRAIN STORM** 19 [3] 2-8-11 M Tebbutt 25/1: 005: Chsd ldrs, rdn/btn over 1f out: see 3412, 3268. ½ 73

-- **ALL GRAIN** [11] 2-8-11 D Holland 10/1: 6: Dwelt/held up, rdn/mod late hdwy: op 8/1: Polish 1½ 70
Precedent filly, May foal: dam a 14f 3yo wnr: likely to relish 1m+ in time for Sir Michael Stoute.

3205 **ABBY GOA** 28 [8] 2-8-11 W Supple 20/1: 457: Chsd ldrs 5f: see 3205, 2916. 1¼ 67

-- **THE FAIRY FLAG** [9] 2-8-11 G Hind 25/1: 8: Chsd ldrs, btn 2f out: Inchinor filly, Feb foal, cost 4 59
8,000gns: half sister to a 7f juv wnr: dam a 7f juv wnr: with R Beckett.

3420 **MISS PITZ** 19 [5] 2-8-11 G Carter 20/1: 669: Keen/held up, nvr any impress: see 2583. ¾ 58

1706 **CEDAR JENEVA** 93 [1] 2-8-11 S Whitworth 50/1: 0U00: Prom 5f: 10th: 3 month abs, longer 7f trip. 9 42

3492 **AMBASSADOR LADY** 17 [6] 2-8-11 S Whitworth 66/1: 060: Led till halfway: 11th: longer 7f trip. 1¼ 39
11 ran Time 1m 22.1 (1.7) (George Strawbridge) I A Balding Kingsclere, Hants

---

3834 5.0 ARENA LEISURE MDN 3YO+ (D) 7f str Firm 05 +01 Fast
£4179 £1286 £643 £321 3 yo rec 4 lb Raced centre - stands side

2365 **BURNING SUNSET** 64 [16] H R A Cecil 3-8-9 (t) T Quinn 2/1: 302231: 3 ch f Caerleon - Lingerie 73
(Shirley Heights) Al prom, led 2f out, styd on well: well bckd from 3/1, 2 mth abs, fair time: plcd in '99
(rtd 89, fill mdn): eff at 7f/10f on firm & hvy grnd, stiff/gall or sharp track: runs well fresh: sharpened by t-strap.

3629 **WIND CHIME** 10 [15] C E Brittain 3-9-0 P Robinson 12/1: 4-2002: 3 ch c Arazi - Shamisen 1¾ 74
(Diesis) Led 5f, hard rdn & held by wnr inside last: bck to form on return to Lingfield: see 839 (C/D).

3626 **SALEM** 10 [2] R W Armstrong 3-9-0 R Price 50/1: 03: 3 b c Sabrehill - Fataana (El Gran Senor) nk 73
Rcd towards centre/rear, rdn & styd on fnl 2f, no threat to wnr: eff at 7f, return to 1m+ shld suit: handles firm.

-- **EYECATCHER** [13] J R Fanshawe 3-9-0 R Hughes 7/1: 4: Slowly away, keen, hdwy over 2f out, 2 69
no impress inside last: eff at 7f, 1m+ should suit: handles firm grnd: encouraging intro.

3579 **HONEST WARNING** 13 [1] 3-9-0 S Sanders 20/1: 4245: Towards rear, rdn & styd on fnl 2f, nrst fin. 1¾ 66

3626 **PAGAN PRINCE** 10 [10] 3-9-0 S Whitworth 50/1: 056: Mid div, onepace/held fnl 2f: see 3626, 2211. nk 65

-- **MOUNT McKINLEY** [17] 3-9-0 D Holland 5/4 FAV: 7: Chsd ldrs, btn 2f out, eased inside last: 1 63
dam well related: more clearly expected on intro for J Noseda who felt the grnd may have been too quick.

1376 **ALMIDDINA** 109 [6] 3-8-9 R Perham 8/1: 48: Mid div, no room 2f out & again inside last, styd on nr shd 58+
fin, nvr nrr: op 5/1, abs: no luck in running, much closer with a clr run: worth another look after 1376 (1m).

1692 **DANDILUM** 94 [8] 3-9-0 G Hind 16/1: 22-4W9: Chs ldrs, rdn/btn 2f out: 3 month abs: btr 983. ½ 62

2464 **YAZAIN** 60 [9] 4-9-4 J Tate 33/1: -300: Prom 5f: 10th: jockey reported colt disliked firm grnd: abs. 3 56

-- **MATASHAWAQ** [5] 3-9-0 (BL) W Supple 7/1: 0: Dwelt, sn rdn, nvr on terms: 13th: blnks, op 5/1. 0

2938 Altara 40 [14] 3-8-9 D Harrison 50/1: -- Pursuit Of Dreams [7] 3-9-0 R Mullen 50/1:

-- Rhiann [11] 4-8-13 P Fitzsimons (5) 40/1: -- Millennium Minx [18] 3-8-9 T G McLaughlin 50/1:

3256 Ashleen 26 [4] 3-8-9 (t) M Tebbutt 50/1:

16 ran Time 1m 20.7 (0.3) (Niarchos Family) H R A Cecil Newmarket, Suffolk

---

3835 5.30 BEST BETS MED AUCT MDN 3-4YO (F) 1m4f aw Standard Inapplicable
£2257 £645 £322 3 yo rec 9 lb

-- **EXCLUSION ZONE** [6] M Johnston 3-8-12 D Holland 4/1: 1: 3 ch g Exit To Nowhere - Exculsive 69a
Virtue (Shadeed) Led halfway, rdn/clr over 2f out, styd on well, rdn out: op 3/1, debut: Ir42,000gns yearling
purchase: dam a half sister to 2,000gns wnr Entrepreneur: eff over a sharp 12f, 14f+ could suit: acts on equitrack
& a sharp track: runs well fresh: decisive wnr here, likely to rate higher & win more races.

3494 **QUIET READING** 17 [3] C A Cyzer 3-8-12 I Mongan (5) 25/1: 364052: 3 b g Northern Flagship - Forlis 6 60a
Key (Forli) Prom, hld up, prog/chsd wnr over 3f out, no impress: prob handles equitrack & soft: well clr rem here.

3326 **ANASTASIA VENTURE** 23 [4] S P C Woods 3-8-7 N Callan 3/1: 532453: 3 b f Lion Cavern - Our Shirley 8 44a
(Shirley Heights) Prom, rdn/outpcd fnl 3f: bckd: btr 1388 (9f, fibresand).

3262 **BRIG OTURK** 26 [5] Mrs A J Perrett 3-8-12 R Hughes 11/4 FAV: 0-434: Led 4f, handy 10f: well bckd 2 46a
tho' op 7/4: AW bow, longer 12f trip: btr 1281 (10f).

3474 **FLAVIA** 17 [10] 3-8-7 (BL) R Price 25/1: 6605: Towards rear, hdwy 4f out, sn no prog: blnks. 3 37a

3501 **CHIEF WALLAH** 16 [7] 4-9-7 N Pollard 5/1: 6-0426: Chsd ldrs, btn 3f out: AW bow: btr 3501 (2m1f). 1¾ 40a

3735 **STREAK OF DAWN** 6 [8] 3-8-7 P Doe 40/1: 000057: Held up, btn 4f out: quick reapp: mod form. 15 16a

2037 **AUDACITY** 78 [1] 3-8-7 D Harrison 33/1: 0-5008: Nvr a factor: 11 week abs: see 1588. 5 16a

3637 **WHAT A CRACKER** 10 [13] 3-8-7 R Perham 20/1: 6-0009: Led after 4f till 6f out, sn fdd: AW bow. 3 7a

3494 **YALAIL** 17 [9] 4-9-7 L Newman (3) 25/1: 00-040: Held up, struggling halfway: 10th: see 3318 (7f). nk 11a

3272 **BUSY BUSY BEE** 25 [12] 3-8-7 K Darley 13/2: 002-50: Chsd ldrs till halfway, 11th: longer 12f trip. 8 0a
11 ran Time 2m 32.16 (2.96) (Sir John Robb) M Johnston Middleham, N Yorks

---

Official Going GOOD/FIRM (GOOD In Places). Stalls: Stands Side.

3836 2.15 CALL RACECHAT FILLIES MDN 2YO (D) 1m str Firm 06 -24 Slow
£3887 £1196 £598 £299

3607 **BARANOVA** 11 [4] J H M Gosden 2-8-11 J Fortune 2/9 FAV: 51: 2 b f Caerleon - Lacandona (Septieme 85
Ciel) Cl-up, led bef halfway, prsd & rdn appr fnl 1f, ran on strongly & pushed out jns last: well bckd from
1/2: Feb first foal: apprec step up to 1m, mid-dists are likely to suit: acts on firm & gd grnd, stiff/gall trk:
lks sure to prove better than the bare form as she was reportedly struck intl.

1856 **GUARDIA** 86 [1] J L Dunlop 2-8-11 Pat Eddery 13/2: 02: 2 ch f Grand Lodge - Gisarne (Diesis) 1¾ 80
Led till appr halfway, rdn & ch appr fnl 1f, held & eased fnl 50y: op 5/1, 12 wk abs: imprvng, clrly apprec
step up to 1m in firm grnd: shld find a fillies mdn.

-- **SIMLA BIBI** [2] B J Meehan 2-8-11 M Roberts 7/1: 3: 2 b f Indian Ridge - Scandalette (Niniski) 2½ 75
Chsd ldrs, shaken up appr fnl 2f, kept on same pace: op 5/1 on debut: Apr foal, half-sister to 3 wnrs, incl
2 juvs, dam unrcd: sire a sprinter: handles firm grnd & will find easier fillies mdns.

-- **KAZANA** [3] S P C Woods 2-8-11 G Duffield 12/1: 4: Keen, prom, outpcd appr fnl 2f: op 7/1, 14 50
debut: 11,000 gns Salse May foal, bred to apprec 10f+.

3692 **COSMIC PEARL** 8 [5] 2-8-11 T Williams 66/1: 05: Handy till 3f out: highly tried: 1,000 gns 3 44
Cosmonaut half sister to sev wnrs: with A Newcombe.

3655 **LEANADIS ROSE** 10 [7] 2-8-11 P Bradley (5) 66/1: 56: Dwelt, prog after 4f, btn 3f out: stiff task. 2½ 39
6 ran   Time 1m 36.8 (2.4)   (R E Sangster)   J H M Gosden Manton, Wilts

3837   2.45 RACECHAT SELL NURSERY HCAP 2YO 0-65 (G)   1m str   Firm 06   -27 Slow   [65]
£1939   £554   £277

3697 **KUMAKAWA** 8 [10] J G Given 2-8-10 (47) J Reid 25/1: -00001: 2 ch g Dancing Spree - Maria 53
Cappuccini (Siberian Express) Cl-up, led fnl 3f, kept on well, pushed out: bt for 4,500gns, goes to M Polglase:
first form, half-brother to a 7f wnr: apprec step up to 1m on firm grnd & drop into a seller: has tried a visor.

3697 **EASTERN RED** 8 [7] K A Ryan 2-8-9 (46) F Lynch 14/1: 205462: 2 b f Contract Law - Gagajulu (Al 1½ 48
Hareb) Well plcd, styd on to chase wnr fnl 2f, nvr any impress: gd run, stays 1m: goes on firm/fast grnd.

3438 **RAINBOW RIVER** 18 [9] P C Haslam 2-9-7 (58) Dean McKeown 10/3 FAV: 0053: 2 ch g Rainbows For ½ 59
Life - Shrewd Girl (Sagace) In tch, prog 3f out, drvn bef dist, styd on: op 5/1, top-weight on h'cap bow: clr rem:
gd run, stays 1m on firm & will apprec mid-dists next term.

3639 **UNVEIL** 10 [2] G M McCourt 2-8-12 (49) D Kinsella (7) 16/1: 665034: Keen & led till ent fnl 3f, 3 44
onepace: not quite see out this longer trip? drop back to 6/7f in similar company will suit.

3468 **BOBANVI** 17 [16] J Carroll 2-8-4 (41) J Carroll 14/1: 400365: Chsd ldrs, onepace ent fnl 2f: longer trip, see 2949. nk 35

3582 **STYLISH FELLA** 12 [11] P Dobbs (5) 12/1: 0066: Bhd ldrs, no extra ent fnl 2f: claimed ¾ 44
by I Williams for £3,000, h'cap bow: see 3582, 2598.

3418 **SPIRIT OF TEXAS** 19 [18] 2-9-5 (56)(tbl) J Fortune 25/1: 00007: Same place thr'out: op 16/1, t-strap. hd 47

3296 **PELLI** 25 [6] 2-8-9 (46) J Quinn 10/1: -00308: Chsd ldrs till 2f out: longer trip, h'cap bow. 1¼ 41

1864 **I GOT RHYTHM** 85 [13] 2-8-13 (50) A Culhane 9/1: 00409: Rear, mod late prog: op 6/1, 12 wk abs. ½ 37

3706 **PICTURE MEE** 8 [15] 2-8-4 (41) J McAuley 6/1: 00000: Keen, in tch till 2f out: 10th on h'cap bow. 1½ 25

3582 **SUGAR ROLO** 12 [1] 2-9-4 (55) D McGaffin 5/1: 6540: Nvr better than mid-div: 11th, op 6/1, lngr trip. 5 29

3216 **Slipper Rose** 27 [4] 2-8-11 (48) Stephanie Hollinshead (7) 25/1:
3438 **Jeannies Girl** 18 [5] 2-8-3 (40)(bl) J Bramhill 25/1:
3127 **Aberfolly** 32 [12] 2-9-0 (51) T E Durcan 16/1:   3620 **Eagality** 11 [14] 2-9-3 (54) Pat Eddery 12/1:
2513 **Beacon Of Light** 59 [3] 2-8-5 (42) P Goode (3) 20/1:   3615 **Bloom** 11 [8] 2-8-8 (45) M Fenton 33/1:
2949 **Essence** 39 [17] 2-8-8 (45) R Fitzpatrick (5) 25/1:   3582 **Moments In Time** 12 [19] 2-9-3 (54) Craig Williams 14/1:
19 ran   Time 1m 37.0 (2.6)   (D Bass)   J G Given Willoughton, Lincs

3838   3.15 PHONE RACECHAT MDN 3YO+ (D)   1m2f   Firm 06   -16 Slow
£4173   £1284   £642   £321   3 yo rec 7 lb

-- **JALISCO** [10] J H M Gosden 3-8-9 J Fortune 9/1: 1: 3 b f Machiavellian - Las Flores (Sadler's Wells) 85+
Mid-div, imprvd appr fnl 2f, shkn up & picked up well in last to get up nr fin: debut, op 6/1: v well-bred, dam
plcd in Italian Oaks: eff at 10f, 12f is going to suit: acts on firm grnd, stiff trk & runs well fresh: rate higher.

3381 **TOLSTOY** 20 [16] Sir Michael Stoute 3-9-0 Pat Eddery 11/4 FAV: -52222: 3 b c Nashwan - Millazure ½ 86
(Dayjur) Prom, led 3f out, hard rdn & 2L up bef dist, hdd well into last: bckd, the bridesmaid again:
consistent filly, will shed mdn tag at some point: see 3381, 2337.

-- **DEAR GIRL** [1] H R A Cecil 3-8-9 W Ryan 10/1: 3: 3 b f Fairy King - Alidiva (Chief Singer) 2 78
Mid-div, prog 3f out, styd on but unable to chall: op 6/1 on debut: bred in the purple, half-sister to 3
Gr 1 wnrs, including miler Sleepytime: eff at 10f on firm grnd: shld improve & win a fillies mdn.

-- **MILLENNIUM DASH** [9] L M Cumani 3-8-9 J Reid 7/2: 4: Mid-div, prog to chase ldr ent fnl 2f, ¾ 77
no extra in last: debut: Nashwan filly out of a top-class miler: stays 10f on firm grnd.

2938 **CONWY CASTLE** 40 [17] 3-9-0 J Carroll 6/1: 55: In tch, prog 3f out, same pace bef dist: tchd 10/1, 1¾ 80
shorter-priced stablemate of wnr, clr rem: sharper for race after 6 wk abs tho' may find h'caps more to his liking.

3672 **GLEDSWOOD** 9 [14] 3-8-9 F Lynch 7/1: -3226: Chsd ldrs, no extra 2f out, eased fnl 1f: better than 6 66
this, will apprec a return to 1m: see 3672, 2006.

3272 **KARAJAN** 25 [11] 3-9-0 M Hills 20/1: 3-047: Prom, wknd appr fnl 2f: drop into h'caps will suit. 3 66

3696 **KUWAIT FLAVOUR** 8 [12] 4-9-7 D McGaffin (5) 100/1: -60458: Nvr troubled ldrs: stiff task. 2½ 63

3179 **SELVORINE** 30 [7] 3-8-9 Craig Williams 16/1: -59: Off the pace, went past btn horses fnl 2f: op 10/1. ½ 57

3672 **CHIEF WARDANCE** 9 [6] 3-9-7 J Quinn 100/1: -530: Nvr a factor: 10th, now qual for h'caps, see 3672. 3½ 65

3012 **DE TRAMUNTANA** 28 [2] 3-8-9 R Hills 10/1: -24250: Made most till appr fnl 3f, sn btn: 11th, op 6/1. ½ 52

2842 **KNIGHTS EMPEROR** 45 [13] 3-9-0 (BL) M Roberts 66/1: -40060: Keen, led after 4f till ent fnl 4f, lost pl: 13th. 0

3626 **Paparazza** 10 [3] 3-8-9 A Culhane 50/1:   3506 **Maybee** 16 [4] 4-9-2 Dean McKeown 100/1:
3423 **Finlays Folly** 19 [8] 3-9-0 A McGlone 66/1:   2317 **Karins Lad** 66 [15] 3-9-0 P M Quinn (3) 100/1:
3677 **Lucky Uno** 9 [5] 4-9-7 (BL) K Dalgleish (5) 66/1:
17 ran   Time 2m 04.5 (2)   (George Strawbridge)   J H M Gosden Manton, Wilts

3839   3.45 RACECOURSE VIDEO HCAP 3YO+ 0-70 (E)   7f str   Firm 06   -18 Slow   [67]
£2912   £896   £448   £224   3 yo rec 4 lb

*3362 **UNCHAIN MY HEART** 22 [2] B J Meehan 4-9-4 (57)(vis) Pat Eddery 5/1 FAV: 001411: 4 b f Pursuit Of 63
Love - Addicted To Love (Touching Wood) Front rank, led ent fnl 2f, drvn out: bckd from 13/2: earlier won
at Lingfield (clmr, rtd 63a), Doncaster (fillh'cap) & Kempton (h'cap, 1st time visor): '99 Lingfield mdn wnr (rtd
62a & 70): eff at 7f/1m, stays a sharp 10f: acts on firm, soft grnd & equitrack, any trk: wears blnks or visor
& can run well fresh: tough & improving filly.

3543 **ADELPHI BOY** 14 [19] M C Chapman 4-10-0 (67) R Studholme (3) 33/1: 146002: 4 ch g Ballad Rock - nk 71
Toda (Absalom) Chsd ldr rdn appr fnl 1f, kept on & not btn far: back to form under a big weight: acts on
firm, soft grnd & both AWs: nicely h'capped, see 488.

3318 **REDSWAN** 24 [16] S C Williams 5-9-9 (62)(t) W Ryan 6/1: 002033: 5 ch g Risk Me - Bocas Rose ½ 65
(Jalmood) Towards rear, wide prog 2f out, kept on for press, held nr fin: op 10/1: often bckd, likes Leicester.

*3652 **TIPPERARY SUNSET** 10 [18] D Shaw 6-9-10 (63)(bl) T Williams 8/1: 64D414: Bhd, gd wide prog appr nk 65
fnl 1f, kept on, nrst fin: made up a lot of late grnd, remains in gd form: see 3652.

3006 **PRIME OFFER** 404 [8] 4-9-12 (65) D McGaffin 33/1: 3410-5: Made most till edged left & hdd shd 67
appr fnl 1f, kept on: reapp: '99 Hamilton wnr (mdn, rtd 71, K Morgan): eff at 6f, stays a stiff 7f: acts on
firm/fast grnd & loves to force the pace: v promising comeback, keep in mind.

3653 **SQUARE DANCER** 10 [20] A Culhane 4-9-7 (60) A Culhane 14/1: 605506: Cl-up, eff & onepace fnl 1f: op 10/1. nk 61

1178

3746 **ITALIAN SYMPHONY 5** [12] 6-9-2 (55)(vis) J Carroll 20/1: 165007: Rear, shaken up & not much room 2f out, switched & kept on fnl 1f, nvr nr to chall: quick reapp: see 3238. *shd* **56**
2934 **SCAFELL 40** [13] 3-9-4 (61) R Fitzpatrick 40/1: 053108: Chsd ldrs, onepace fnl 1f: 6 wk abs: longer trip, probably stays a stiff 7f: see 2096 (5f). *1* **60**
*3573 **UNSHAKEN 13** [17] 6-10-0 (67) T E Durcan 14/1: 000019: Towards rear, styd on appr fnl 1f, nvr dngrs. *nk* **65**
3623 **SAMARA SONG 11** [7] 7-9-1 (54) Darren Williams (5) 7/1: 004040: Hmpd start & bhd, stdly imprvd & was staying on fin but nvr got in it: 10th: well h'capped, one to keep a cl eye on: see 1003. *½* **51+**
3536 **PANDJOJOE 14** [3] 4-9-3 (56) G Duffield 14/1: 556060: In tch, rdn 2f out, kept on onepace when not much room ins last: 11th, op 10/l: unsuited by longer 7f trip?: see 1008. *¾* **51**
3652 **ANGEL HILL 10** [6] 5-9-1 (54) F Lynch 12/1: 610040: Keen, mid-div, prog appr fnl 2f, sn rdn & onepace, eased towards fin: 12th: eye-catching from off the pace in 3652. *hd* **49**
3652 **PLEADING 10** [14] 7-9-7 (60)(vis) J Fortune 12/1: 006100: V slow away, mod late hdwy: 13th. *1¼* **53**
3238 **HYPERACTIVE 27** [5] 4-10-0 (67) M Roberts 15/2: 020000: Chsd ldrs, hung right appr fnl 2f, no extra & eased: 14th, op 6/1: something amiss?: see 1483. *¾* **58**
3123 **BLAKESET 32** [11] 5-9-5 (58)(bl) D Mernagh (3) 6/1: 000600: Prom 5f: 15th, up in trip, blnks reapp. *shd* **49**
3587 **DOUBLE BOUNCE 12** [1] 10-9-9 (62) R Hills 10/1: 60-020: Al bhd: 19th: see 3297. **0**
3605 **Green Ginger 11** [15] 4-9-2 (55)(vis) Jonjo Fowle (5) 33/1: 3580 **Waffles Of Amin 13** [10] 3-9-12 (69) J Reid 16/1:
3676 **Chelonia 9** [9] 3-9-8 (65) M Hills 16/1: 620 **Mr Speaker 188** [4] 7-9-8 (61) S Shaw (7) 33/1:
20 ran Time 1m 23.7 (1.7) (Mascalls Stud) B J Meehan Upper Lambourn, Berks

3840

4.15 EBF RING RACECHAT MDN 2YO (D) 7f str Firm 06 -10 Slow
£4069 £1252 £626 £313

2346 **SIXTY SECONDS 66** [13] J H M Gosden 2-9-0 L Dettori 4/5 FAV: 21: 2 b c Definite Article - Damemill (Danehill) Sn led, rdn appr fnl 1f, ran on strongly & pushed out towards fin: hvly bckd: confirmed debut promise: IR 50,000gns Feb foal, dam 7f wnr: eff at 7f, 1m+ is going to suit next term: acts on firm grnd, stiff/gall trks: suited forcing the pace: useful, progressive colt, shld hold his own in better grade. **96**
3458 **TAABEER 18** [7] E A L Dunlop 2-9-0 R Hills 6/1: 022: 2 b c Caerleon - Himmah (Habitat) Trkd ldrs, rdn to chase wnr fnl 1f, kept on but held: op 5/1: eff at 7f/1m on firm/fast grnd: must go one better sn. *1¼* **91**
-- **KINGS SECRET** [10] Sir Michael Stoute 2-9-0 Pat Eddery 7/1: 3: 2 ch c Kingmambo - Mystery Rays (Nijinsky) Chsd ldrs, switched & kept on well fnl 1f, nvr plcd to chall: op 7/2, better for race: $300,000 Apr foal, half-brother to a French juv wnr & a smart American miler: dam a v useful miler: eff at 1m, shld stay 10f: acts on firm grnd: seldom see such a promising intro, looks nailed on for a mdn bef going on to better things. *¾* **89+**
3568 **POLISH OFF 13** [11] B W Hills 2-9-0 M Hills 3/1: 54: Pulled hard, cl-up, rdn appr fnl 1f, no extra ins last: gd run, stays 7f on firm grnd: shld find a mdn. *1¼* **87**
-- **BEEKEEPER** [8] 2-9-0 F Lynch 20/1: 5: Mid-div, shkn up appr fnl 1f, styd on, educational intro: stablemate 3rd, op 14/1: 135,000gns Rainbow Quest Mar foal, dam 14f wnr: handles firm grnd: sure to improve considerably, esp over mid-dists given time: one to keep a close eye on. *¾* **85+**
3385 **HALLAND 20** [15] 2-9-0 M Roberts 25/1: 66: Chsd ldrs, unable to qckn ent fnl 2f: not disgraced. *2½* **80**
-- **CELTIC MISSION** [14] 2-9-0 J Fanning 20/1: 7: Trkd ldrs, fdd appr fnl 1f: op 14/1, debut: 20,000gns Cozzene Jan foal, dam & sire milers: with M Johnston. *2* **76**
-- **MUTARASED** [3] 2-9-0 T E Durcan 20/1: 8: Bhd, hdwy into mid-div 1f out: debut: Storm Cat Apr foal, half-brother to a 6f juv & a 10f wnr: dam 7f/1m wnr: expect improvement: with J Dunlop. *2½* **71+**
3298 **MARTINS SUNSET 25** [16] 2-9-0 G Duffield 50/1: 09: Well plcd till wknd appr fnl 1f: not disgraced. *¾* **69**
-- **PETROV** [17] 2-9-0 J Fortune 16/1: 0: Mid-div thr'out: 10th, op 12/1, stablemate rnr-up: Cadeaux Genereux half-brother to smart mid-dist performer Annus Mirabilis, dam 10f wnr. *½* **68**
3617 **GREY IMPERIAL 11** [5] 2-9-0 A Culhane 40/1: -00: Prom 4f: 11th, one more run for h'cap mark. *3* **62**
-- **FALSE PROMISE** [4] 2-9-0 J Reid 25/1: 0: Nvr a factor: 12th, st/mate 2nd: Bluebird foal, dam 12f wnr. *1½* **59**
-- **Dance In The Day** [18] 2-9-0 W Ryan 25/1: -- **Credenza Moment** [9] 2-9-0 R Smith (5) 33/1:
3520 **Yanus 15** [2] 2-9-0 Dean McKeown 50/1: -- **Bunkum** [1] 2-9-0 M Fenton 33/1:
3388 **Jollands 20** [12] 2-9-0 D O'Donohoe 33/1: 3635 **Chesters Boy 10** [6] 2-9-0 J Bramhill 66/1:
18 ran Time 1m 23.1 (1.1) (The Smoking/Brady Partnership) J H M Gosden Manton, Wilts

3841

4.45 ALEX HAMMOND COND STKS 3YO+ (C) 5f str Firm 06 +10 Fast
£5805 £2202 £1101 £500 3 yo rec 1 lb

3598 **EMERALD PEACE 12** [7] M A Jarvis 3-7-13 M Henry 9/2: 12-001: 3 b f Green Desert - Puck's Castle (Shirley Heights) Sn led, pshd clr dist, ran on strgly: fast time, ease in grade/back to form: '99 wnr at Lingfield (2, mdn & stks, Gr 2 hd rnr-up, rtd 101): eff at 5f: acts on firm & gd/soft, prob any trk: speedy. **101**
3301 **PRESENTATION 24** [8] R Hannon 3-7-13 J Quinn 2/1: 660522: 3 b f Mujadil - Beechwood (Blushing Groom) Chsd ldrs, chsd wnr fnl 1f, nvr any impression: tchd 5/2: eff at 5f, suited by 6f: see 1016. *2* **95**
3598 **ROSSELLI 12** [6] A Berry 4-8-5 J Carroll 15/8 FAV: 002603: 4 b h Puissance - Miss Rossi (Artaius) Trkd ldrs, rdn & unable to qckn with wnr appr fnl 1f: well bckd: in front of this wnr last 2 starts: see 927. *½* **98**
3687 **COASTAL BLUFF 8** [1] N P Littmoden 8-8-5 Pat Eddery 10/1: 020404: Rcd alone stands rail & prom till appr fnl 1f: op 8/1, stiff task, prob flattered, see 1871. *2½* **91**
3521 **PALACEGATE JACK 15** [9] 9-8-5 P Bradley (5) 100/1: 545605: Prom till outpcd appr fnl 1f: flattered. *1½* **86$**
3756 **BORDER GLEN 5** [4] 4-8-5 (vis) M Roberts 66/1: 005306: Nvr a factor: qck reapp, flattered (offic rtd 51). *1¾* **80$**
3183 **FIRST MAITE 29** [3] 7-8-5 (bl) G Duffield 7/1: 034007: Nvr in it: needs easier grnd: see 35. *shd* **80**
3667 **ALFAILAK 9** [5] 3-8-4 (VIS) Craig Williams 14/1: -05068: Prom till 2f out: visored, see 2458. *5* **65**
3421 **CAPPUCINO LADY 19** [2] 3-7-13 R Brisland (5) 100/1: 500059: Sn struggling: impossible task, flattered. *4* **48$**
9 ran Time 58.1 (u0.2) (M P Burke) M A Jarvis Newmarket, Suffolk

3842

5.15 NEVER ALONE APPR HCAP 3YO+ 0-75 (E) 1m2f Firm 06 -35 Slow **[73]**
£2977 £916 £458 £229 3 yo rec 7 lb

3118 **LYCIAN 32** [6] J A R Toller 5-8-11 (56) C Carver 7/2 FAV: 603401: 5 b g Lycius - Perfect Time (Dance Of Life) In tch, prog to lead on bit bef dist, canter: any amount in hand: '99 wnr at Lingfield (rtd 70a) & Goodwood (h'caps, rtd 63): '98 wnr at Brighton, Bath & Lingfield (h'caps, rtd 57 & 63a): eff at 1m/10f: acts on firm, gd grnd & both AWs, any trk: quick follow up likely **62+**
3166 **AMRAK AJEEB 31** [8] R J Baker 8-10-0 (73) G Sparkes (3) 8/1: 314302: 8 b h Danehill - Noble Dust (Dust Commander) Rear, stdy wide prog fnl 2f, nvr nr to chall: gd run under a big weight, grnd faster than ideal. *2½* **73**
3560 **THE FROG QUEEN 13** [10] D W P Arbuthnot 3-7-10 (48)(2oh) R Brisland 20/1: 403053: 3 b f Bin Ajwaad - The Frog Lady (Al Hareb) Cl-up, keen, led ent str, rdn & hdd bef dist, onepace: ran well back in trip: *shd* **48**

LEICESTER   TUESDAY SEPTEMBER 5TH   Righthand, Stiff, Galloping Track

acts on firm/fast grnd & fibresand.

3702 SHALBEBLUE 8 [17] J G Given 3-8-8 (60) G Baker 25/1: 350004: Held up, rdn ent str, late hdwy,   hd   59
nvr a threat: stays 10f on firm grnd.

3711 HIGH SUN 7 [14] 4-7-13 (44) Michael Doyle (5) 16/1: 050055: Off the pace till kept on well fnl 2f.   ½   42

*3524 PAARL ROCK 15 [4] 5-8-13 (58)(vis) G Gibbons (5) 11/2: 214416: Sn led, hdd ent str, no extra bef fnl 1f.   1¼   54
fnl 1f: shade btr 3524 (gd).

3514 MAGICAL BAILIWICK 16 [3] 4-8-4 (49)(bl) D Mernagh 33/1: 000007: Early ldr, again briefly ent str,   2½   42
fdd 2f out: longer trip, see 2270.

3656 KELBURNE 10 [12] 3-8-0 (52) P Bradley 25/1: 544008: Mid-div, sltly hmpd ent str, nvr any impress.   shd   45

3188 LOVE DIAMONDS 29 [5] 4-7-10 (41)(1oh) P M Quinn 33/1: 206009: In tch, hmpd ent str, nvr a threat.   shd   34

*3663 NIGHT DIAMOND 9 [15] 3-8-5 (57)(t) N Chalmers (5) 9/2: 042410: Al mid-div: 10th, op 3/1, btr 3663.   1¾   48

3691 ERUPT 8 [1] 7-8-9 (54) R Lake (7) 25/1: 000040: In tch when badly hmpd ent str, brief eff 3f out: 11th.   shd   45

*3356 CAPTAIN MCCLOY 22 [16] 5-8-0 (45)(bl) D Glennon (5) 7/1: 333010: Chsd ldrs 7f: 12th, btr 3356 (gd).   2½   33

*1050 DARK VICTOR 129 [9] 4-8-9 (54) S Finnamore (3) 11/2!: 405010: Nvr in it: 13th, over 4 month abs.   5   35

3606 ADAMAS 11 [13] 3-9-5 (71) K Dalgleish 8/1: 10043U: Prom when stmbld/u.r. enter str: tchd 101, see 3606, 2222. 0

3535 Forest Friendly 14 [2] 3-9-2 (68) B McHugh (7) 25/1: 470   Clarinch Claymore 211 [7] 4-8-7 (52) P Bradley 20/1:

3403 Bremridge 20 [18] 3-9-4 (70) A Eddery 25/1: 319   Upper Bullens 236 [11] 3-8-13 (65) R Studholme 25/1:

18 ran   Time 2m 06.6 (4.1)   (A Ilsley)   J A R Toller Newmarket, Suffolk

CHANTILLY   WEDNESDAY AUGUST 30TH   Righthand, Galloping Track

Official Going   GOOD

3843   2.25 GR 3 PRIX D'ARENBERG 2YO   5f110y   Good
£21134   £7685   £3842   £2305

3066 IRON MASK 32 Mme C Head 2-8-11 O Doleuze 1/1 FAV: 122211: 2 b c Danzig - Raise A Beauty (Alydar)   111
Chsd ldrs, hdwy to lead dist, qcknd well for press, cmftbly: crse rec time: dual wnr prev this term, also rnr-up
in a Gr 2: eff arnd 5.5f on gd & hvy grnd: smart & progressive juv with a turn of foot, win more Gr races.

-- SEASONS GREETINGS C Laffon Parias 2-8-8 D Boeuf 112/10: 412142: 2 b f Ezzoud - Dream Season   2½   100
(Mr Prospector) Settled rear, rdn to imprv appr fnl 1f, kept on but no ch with wnr: eff at 5.5f on gd: useful.

*3408 RACINA 13 W J Haggas 2-8-8 M Hills 66/10: 213: 2 ch f Bluebird - Swellegant (Midyan)   2½   94
Front rank, went on halfway, drvn/hdd dist, sn btn: gd run & imprvd in defeat: 6f shld now suit: see 3408.

3133 RED MILLENNIUM 26 A Berry 2-8-8 F Norton 53/10: 121134: Cl-up, rdn & wknd qckly well ins last: 2   89
will reportedly drop back to the minimum trip next time & will apprec a drop in grade: see 3133, 2664.

6 ran   Time 1m 02.9 Track Record   (Wertheimer Et Frere)   Mme C Head France

CURRAGH   SUNDAY SEPTEMBER 3RD   Righthand, Stiff, Galloping Track

Official Going   Round Course - GOOD/FIRM; Straight Course - GOOD

3844   2.30 LISTED ROUND TOWER STKS 2YO   6f   Good
£19500   £5700   £2700

2935 LADY OF KILDARE 38 T J Taaffe 2-8-9 P J Smullen 12/1: 022011: 2 b f Mujadil - Dancing Sunset   100
(Red Sunset) In tch, hdwy to lead dist, strongly pressed cl-home, all out: recent Tipperary wnr (fill mdn):
IR£120,000 purchase: eff at 6f, 7f shld suit: acts on gd grnd: useful & prog filly.

3067 MODIGLIANI 36 A P O'Brien 2-8-12 (BL) J A Heffernan 7/2: 1342: 2 b c Danzig - Hot Princess   shd   102
(Hot Spark) Cl-up, went on over 1f out, sn hdd, rall well ins last, just failed: gd eff in blnks: see 2067.

-- ROSE GYPSY A P O'Brien 2-8-9 J P Spencer 8/1: 3: 2 b f Green Desert - Krisalya (Kris)   1   96
Bhd, drvn & ran on strongly over 1f out, nvr nr front 2: stablemate of 2nd: stays 6f on gd: shld improve.

3567 SPEEDY GEE 11 M R Channon 2-8-12 Craig Williams 7/1: 056046: In tch, gd hdwy appr fnl 1f, drvn   95
& no extra well ins last, fin 6th: op 5/1: prob ran to form of 3567 (List), eyecatching).

9 ran   Time 1m 13.7   (Gerard P Callanan)   T J Taaffe Naas, Co Kildare

3845   4.05 GR 1 MOYGLARE STUD STKS 2YO   7f   Good/Firm
£98250   £33500   £16000   £5500

3555 SEQUOYAH 14 A P O'Brien 2-8-11 J P Spencer 9/4 FAV: -3121: 2 b f Sadler's Wells - Brigid (Irish   110
River) Settled twrds rear, smooth hdwy to lead dist, ran on strongly, pshd out: earlier won at Tipperary
(mdn): eff at 7f, 1m shld suit in time: acts on fast grnd: smart juv, can imprv further & win more val races.

2935 HOTELGENIE DOT COM 38 M R Channon 2-8-11 Craig Williams 7/2: 122: 2 gr f Selkirk - Birch Creek   2½   103
(Carwhite) Bhd, eff over 1f out, strong run fnl 1f, no ch with wnr: excellent run by this v useful & prog
filly: shld relish a step up to 1m & can win in Gr 2/3 company sn: see 2935, 2474.

-- MALA MALA T Stack 2-8-11 W J O'Connor 9/1: -53: 2 b f Brief Truce - Breyani (Commanche Run)   hd   103
Prom, ev ch till drvn/not pace of wnr fnl 1f: recent 5th on debut (List), bhd today's wnr): eff at 7f on fast.

3372 LA VIDA LOCA 21 A P O'Brien 2-8-11 C O'Donoghue 14/1: -52154: Front rank, no extra for press   2½   99
appr fnl 1f: stablemate of wnr, needs a drop in grade: see 3372, 2399.

2088 LITTLE FIREFLY 74 2-8-11 J A Heffernan 7/1: -135: Bhd, rdn/late gains, no dngr: not disgraced   hd   99
after a 10 wk abs upped in trip: stablemate of wnr: this longer 7f trip shld suit in time: see 2088 (5f, Gr 2).

3555 IMAGINE 14 2-8-11 G Duffield 10/1: 36: Prom, drvn/btn fnl 2f: stablemate of wnr: see 3555.   2½   95

*3555 AFFIANCED 14 2-8-11 (t) K J Manning 6/1: -2117: Mid-div at best: btr 3555 (List, beat this wnr).   0

-- ALLEZ LA CLASSE 2-8-11 J Murtagh 12/1: -148: Al twrds rear: Roscommon mdn wnr (7f, fast).   0

-- STAGE PRESENCE 2-8-11 M Hills 10/1: 9: Prom, rdn & went on 2f out, hdd dist, wknd rapidly: 0
debut: Selkirk filly, half-sister to a dual juv wnr: v stiff task on debut, will find easier opposition.

-- JUNGLE MOON 2-8-11 P J Scallan 50/1: -00: Led to over 2f out, sn lost tch, 10th: stiff task.   0

10 ran   Time 1m 26.7   (Mrs John Magnier)   A P O'Brien Ballydoyle, Co Tipperary

3846   **5.10 GR 3 MATRON STKS 3YO+   1m   Good/Firm**
£27950   £8170   £3870   £1290   3 yo   rec 5 lb

3069 **IFTIRAAS** 35 J L Dunlop 3-9-0 G Duffield 11/2: 156031: 3 b f Distant Relative - Ideal Home (Home
Guard) Handy, hdwy to chall over 1f out, styd on well to lead nr fin, drvn out: earlier won on reapp at Newbury
(Gr 3): juv wnr at Lingfield (med auct mdn) & just tchd off in Listed (rtd 104): eff arnd 7f/1m: acts on fast,
likes soft/hvy grnd, handles firm: runs well fresh on any trk: tough & smart: deserved win.   **113**

*3104 **DANCEABOUT** 31 G Wragg 3-8-10 D Holland 4/1: 15312: 3 b f Shareef Dancer - Putupon   *shd*   **108**
(Mummy's Pet) Bhd, rdn/prog over 1f out, ran on well likes last, just held: fine run up in class, stays 1m.

*3469 **OUT OF REACH** 15 B W Hills 3-8-10 M Hills 3/1 FAV: 521413: 3 b f Warning - Well Beyond (Don't   *1*   **106**
Forget Me) Led, drvn & pressed over 1f out, hdd/no extra cl-home: op 9/4: shade btr 3469 (List).

*3340 **PAPABILE** 21 W Jarvis 3-8-10 J P Spencer 11/2: 241114: ln tch, rdn & styd on well fnl 1f, no   *1½*   **103**
threat to ldrs: not disgraced on 4-timer bid: win another List race: see 3340.

--   **LIVADIYA** 4-9-1 W J O'Connor 25/1: 310455: Prom, drvn/no extra fnl 2f: stiffish task (offic only 92).   *2½*   **98**
11 ran   Time 1m 39.6   (Kuwait Racing Syndicate II)   J L Dunlop Arundel, W Sussex

Official Going   SOFT

3847   **2.25 GR 1 PRIX DU MOULIN 3YO+   1m   Soft**
£86465   £34582   £17291   £8646   3 yo rec 5 lb

2064 **INDIAN LODGE** 75 Mrs A J Perrett 4-9-2 C Asmussen 113/10: -11301: 4 b h Grand Lodge - Repetitious   **121**
(Northfields) Trkd ldr, hdwy to chall 2f out, led dist, drvn clr ins last: 11 wk abs: earlier won at Newmarket (Gr
3, reapp) & Sandown (Gr 2), also plcd in Gr 1 Lockinge at Newbury: '99 wnr at Newbury, Yarmouth & Newmarket (2,
List, rtd 121): suited by 1m/9f: goes on fast, relishes soft & hvy grnd: likes a stiff trk, esp Newmarket: runs
well fresh: tough & high class, will take all the beating in the QEII at Ascot if there is give in the ground.

3544 **KINGSALSA** 21 A Fabre 4-9-2 O Peslier 19/10: 321332: 4 b c Kingmambo - Caretta (Caro)   *2*   **117**
Twrds rear, gd hdwy when short of room over 1f out, ran on well for press ins last, no ch with wnr: tough,
smart & v consistent (not out of 1st 3 in 7 starts this term): win another Gr race sn: see 3544.

1755 **DIKTAT** 91 Saeed bin Suroor 5-9-2 L Dettori 19/10cp: 15-623: 5 br h Warning - Arvola (Sadler's Wells)   *nk*   **116**
Front rank, drvn & slightly short of room 2f out, styd on appr fnl 1f, not pace of wnr: not disgraced after
3 mth abs, likely to reoppose this wnr at Ascot in a fortnight: high-class: see 1755.

1847 **FLY TO THE STARS** 85 Saeed bin Suroor 6-9-2 D O'Donohoe 19/10cp: 00-054: Sn clr ldr, pressed 2f   *nse*   **116**
out, hdd dist, held well ins last: 12 wk abs: stablemate of 3rd, best run by far this term: likes soft: see 1847.

3544 **SUGARFOOT** 21 6-9-2 C Rutter 43/10: 551005: Trkd ldrs, ev ch till onepcd for press over 1f out: *hd*   **116**
highly tried & not disgraced in this top-class contest: see 2997 (h'cap), 2675 (List).

-3087 **DANSILI** 32 4-9-2 C Soumillon 6/4 FAV: -11226: ln tch, drvn/fdd fnl 2f: shorter priced   *2½*   **112**
stablemate of 2nd: rare below par effort, much btr 3087 (fast grnd).

*3554 **GOLDEN SILCA** 14 4-8-13 D Boeuf 132/10: 105417: Al bhd: shade btr 3554 (3-rnr Gr 3).   *snk*   **109**

--   **IGMAN** 3-8-12 T Jarnet 56/10: 4-1118: Al in rear: unbeaten prev this term (incl List).   **0**
8 ran   Time 1m 40.8   (S Cohn And Sir Eric Parker)   Mrs A J Perrett Pulborough, W Sussex

3848   **3.45 GR 3 PRIX DE LUTECE 3YO   1m7f   Soft**
£21134   £7685   £3842   £2305

2398 **EPITRE** 67 A Fabre 3-8-11 O Peslier 11/10 FAV: 124211: 3 b c Common Grounds - Epistolienne (Law   **115**
Society) Settled in tch, gd hdwy to lead over 1f out, rdn & easily went clr: dual wnr prev this term, also
4th in a Gr 1: imprvg with every step up in trip, eff at 10/15f on gd & soft: progressive, win more Gr races.

3065 **MISTER KICK** 37 A Fabre 3-8-11 C Soumillon 41/10: 431422: 3 gr c Linamix - Mrs Arkada (Arakad)   *4*   **107**
Led early, remnd with ldr, led again dist, sn hdd, not pace of stablemate: capable of wng similar: see 3065.

--   **SOPRAN MONTANELLI** L Camici 3-8-9 G Mosse 114/10: 110453: 3 b c Tenby - Macchiabelle   *1½*   **103**
(Dominion) Chsd ldrs, drvn/eff over 2f out, held appr fnl 1f: useful Italian raider, stays 15f on soft.

*3545 **SHUWAIB** 18 M R Channon 3-8-9 L Dettori 14/10: 1314: Sn led, hdd appr fnl 1f, sn btn: up in   *¾*   **102**
grade: 1st try on soft grnd, will apprec a return to List class, as in 3545.

3545 **BOURGEOIS** 18 3-8-11 (BL) O Doleuze 71/10: 123425: Al last: blnkd: see 2398.   *½*   **103**
5 ran   Time 3m 24.8   (Baron E de Rothschild)   A Fabre France

Official Going   VERY SOFT

3849   **3.30 GR 1 GROSSER PREIS VON BADEN 3YO+   1m4f   V Soft**
£322581   £96774   £48387   £32258   3 yo   rec 9 lb

--   **SAMUM** A Schutz 3-8-9 A Starke 16/10 FAV: 1-1111: 3 ch c Monsun - Sacarina (Old Vic)   **122**
Waited with, gd hdwy to lead 2f out, drvn & impress qcknd clr: 9 wk abs: unbeaten in 3 prev starts this term
(incl German Derby, easily by 5L): unbeaten juv: suited by 12f: acts on soft & hvy grnd (unraced on faster):
runs well fresh: top-class & still improving colt, has an impressive turn of foot: expect a big run in the Arc.

2911 **CATELLA** 42 P Schiergen 4-9-2 T Hellier 132/10: 122312: 4 ch f Generous - Crystal Ring (Kris)   *2½*   **117**
Settled rear, hdwy 4f out, kept on for press fnl 2f but no ch with wnr: recent scorer at Gelsenkirchen (Gr 1):
eff at 12f on fast & soft grnd: high-class German trained colt, capable of wng more Gr races: see 2911.

*2149 **FRUITS OF LOVE** 72 M Johnston 5-9-6 (vis) M Roberts 72/10: 304-3: 5 b h Hansel - Vallee   *hd*   **121**
Secrete (Secretariat) Chsd ldrs, ev ch till no extra for press well ins last: clr rem: excellent run after a 10 wk
abs, top-class entire who shld continue to give a good account in high-class global mid-dist races: see 2149.

2998 **DALIAPOUR** 36 Sir Michael Stoute 4-9-6 Pat Eddery 26/10: 0-1134: Front rank, drvn & no extra appr   *5*   **115**

BADEN-BADEN SUNDAY SEPTEMBER 3RD Lefthand, Sharpish, Turning Track

fnl 1f, eased when btn ins last: reportedly unsuited by the 'sticky' grnd: see 2998, 1827.
2409 **HOLDING COURT 63** 3-8-9 P Robinson 43/10: -11165: Hmpd leaving stalls, sn led, hung right home *1¾* **111**
turn, hdd 2f out, wknd qckly: 9 wk abs: may be seen to best effect on a RHd trk: twice below 1752 (made all).
-- **ACAMANI** 3-8-9 T Mundry 30/1: 212346: Nvr a factor. *½* **110**
1618 **PAOLINI 98** 3-8-9 A Suborics 263/10: 113027: Bhd, nvr dngrs: see 1618. *½* **109**
*2911 **MUTAFAWEQ 42** 4-9-6 R Hills 113/10: 1-3018: Hmpd start, sn in tch, drvn over 3f out, wknd rapidly *13* **95**
fnl 2f: 6 wk abs: reportedly unsuited by this v soft grnd: produced a top-class run on good in 2911.
11 ran Time 2m 38.95 (Stall Blankenese) A Schutz Germany

LUCERNE (SWITZERLAND) SUNDAY SEPTEMBER 3RD -

Official Going HEAVY

3850 **3.45 SWISS ST LEGER 3YO 1m7f Heavy**
£9412 £3765 £2824

3611 **COOL INVESTMENT 9** M Johnston 3-9-2 J Fanning : 441351: 3 b c Prince Of Birds - Superb Investment **92**
(Hatim) Sn trkg ldr, went on after halfway, rdn clr fnl 2f, comfortably: qckish reapp: earlier won at Windsor
(class stks): won sole juv start at Musselburgh (auct, mdn, rtd 78): eff at 10/12f, suited by this step up
to 15f: acts on fast, likes soft/hvy grnd: handles a sharp trk & runs well fresh: tough & useful.
-- **ETBASH** Switzerland 3-9-2 J-M Breux : 2: 3 b c Triple Buck - Emira (Ivory Tower) *4* **86**
-- **HANOVER HOUSE** Switzerland 3-9-2 E Wehrel : 3: 3 br c Goofalik - Helen Elizabeth (Temperence Hill) *dist* **0**
8 ran Time 3m 58.4 (Markus Graff) M Johnston Middleham, N Yorks

LONGCHAMP TUESDAY SEPTEMBER 5TH Righthand, Stiff, Galloping Track

Official Going GOOD TO SOFT

3851 **3.15 GR 3 PRIX GLADIATEUR 4YO+ 1m7f110y Good/Soft**
£21134 £7685 £3842 £2305

*1109 **ORCHESTRA STALL 125** J L Dunlop 8-9-2 T Thulliez 18/10: 21/611: 8 b g Old Vic - Blue Brocade (Reform) **116**
With ldr early, restrained halfway, chall ldr over 1f out, sn led, styd on strongly, drvn out: 4 mth abs: earlier
won at Ascot (Gr 3): missed '99 & '98, back in '97 won at Ascot, The Curragh & this v race here at Longchamp (all
Gr 3's, rtd 121): suited by 15f/2m: eff on hvy, likes gd/soft grnd & handles firm: runs v well fresh & best on
a stiff/gall trk, esp Ascot: v smart, tough & genuine gelding who retains all his ability.
3552 **WAJINA 16** A Fabre 4-8-10 O Peslier 31/10: -22322: 4 b f Rainbow Quest - Wajd (Northern Dancer) *1* **108**
Dstpd lead, rdn/outpcd over 2f out, rall when short of room dist, styd on well: v consistent: see 3552.
4532} **TAJOUN 317** A de Royer Dupre 6-9-6 G Mosse 11/10 FAV: 12-143: 6 b g General Holme - Taeesha *shd* **118**
(Mill Reef) Chsd ldr, hdwy to lead over 2f out, pressed over 1f out, sn hdd, no extra well ins last: long abs:
dual wnr here at Longchamp in '99 (incl Gr 1, rtd 120): best at 2m on gd & hvy, stays 2½m: high-class at best.
3552 **LE TINTORET 16** Y de Nicolay 7-9-0 D Bonilla 94/10: -10254: Settled last, gd hdwy over 1f out, *nse* **112**
oncepcd for press well ins last: see 3552, 1456.
5 ran Time 3m 23.8 (Sir David Sieff) J L Dunlop Arundel, W Sussex

EPSOM WEDNESDAY SEPTEMBER 6TH Lefthand, Very Sharp, Undulating Track

Official Going GOOD. Stalls: 5f - Stands Side, 6f - Outside, 12f - Centre, Rem - Inside

3852 **1.50 EBF MED AUCT MDN 2YO (E) 6f rnd Good 54 -28 Slow**
£4290 £1320 £660 £330

3660 **ZHITOMIR 10** [4] S Dow 2-9-0 P Doe 9/1: -64061: 2 ch c Lion Cavern - Treasure Trove (The Minstrel) **86**
Handy, rdn fnl 3f, led 1f out, asserted well ins last, rdn out: eff at 6f, tried 7f, shld suit: acts on gd grnd.
3635 **BOUCHRA 11** [3] M L W Bell 2-8-9 M Fenton 11/8 FAV: -22: 2 ch f Inchinor - My Darlingdaughter *1½* **76**
(Night Shift) Cl-up, rdn/led over 1f out till dist, held nr fin: hvly bckd tho' op 4/5: just btr 3635 (7f).
3387 **AINTNECESSARILYSO 21** [1] D R C Elsworth 2-9-0 N Pollard 7/4: 006023: 2 ch g So Factual - Ovideo *2½* **73**
(Domynsky) Led, rdn over 2f out, hdd over 1f out & no extra: bckd, op 2/1: prob handles fast & gd grnd.
3484 **CAPITAL LAD 18** [6] G Brown 2-9-0 P McCabe 25/1: -04: Held up, rdn bef halfway, styd on ins last, *nk* **73**
no threat to ldrs: return to 7f+ shld suit, going the right way after 3484 (debut).
2545 **SHARP ACT 58** [2] 2-9-0 B Marcus 6/1: -0055: Trkd ldr bef halfway, wknd over 1f out: abs: see 1924. *1½* **69**
3000 **REAP 39** [5] 2-9-0 G Bardwell 20/1: 06: Dwelt, sn rdn/al bhd: see 3000. *21* **29**
6 ran Time 1m 12.73 (4.93) (G Steinberg) S Dow Epsom, Surrey

3853 **2.25 JARVIS EBF MDN 2YO (D) 1m114y rnd Good 54 -29 Slow**
£4075 £1254 £627 £313

3484 **CHANGING SCENE 18** [3] I A Balding 2-9-0 S Whitworth 3/1: -051: 2 b c Theatrical - Routilante **86**
(Rousillon) Trkd ldr, led over 3f out, soon pulled clr under hands & heels riding, always holding rivals ins last:
hvly bckd, op 7/2: apprec this step up to 8.5f, 10f will suit in time: acts on gd grnd: progressive colt.
3108 **ZANZIBAR 34** [5] M L W Bell 2-8-9 M Fenton 9/4 FAV: 52: 2 b f In The Wings - Isle Of Spice (Diesis) *1¾* **74**
Dwelt/rear, drvn & styd on fnl 2f, al held: bckd: eff over 8.5f, stay further: handles gd grnd: see 3108.
3680 **SEATTLE PRINCE 9** [2] R Hannon 2-9-0 J Weaver 3/1: 053: 2 gr c Cozzene - Chicken Slew (Seattle *1½* **76**
Slew) Trkd ldrs, chsd wnr 3f out, rdn/held over 1f out: nicely bckd tho' op 9/4: clr of rem: see 3000.
3484 **ARC EN CIEL 18** [4] J L Dunlop 2-9-0 W Supple 9/2: -064: Chsd ldrs, drvn/btn over 2f out: op 7/2. *6* **64**
3577 **ABRACADABJAR 14** [1] 2-9-0 S Sanders 10/1: 05: Held up, bhd 3f out: longer 8.5f trip: see 3577. *15* **39**

3038 **HURLINGHAM STAR** 37 [7] 2-9-0 B Marcus 66/1: 0066: Led, hdd over 3f out, sn btn: longer 8.5f trip. 15 14
3433 **IMMACULATE CHARLIE** 19 [6] 2-8-9 A McGlone 50/1: 32047: Bhd halfway, t.o.: see 3433, 1553. dist 0
7 ran   Time 1m 48.82 (7.02)   (George Strawbridge)   I A Balding Kingsclere, Hants

3854	2.55 TIGER WATKINS HCAP 3YO 0-80 (D) 7f rnd Good 54 -36 Slow	[87]
	£7410 £2280 £1140 £570	

*3689 **CAPE COAST** 9 [12] N P Littmoden 3-8-7 (66)(6ex) S Carson (3) 15/2: 304211: 3 b g Common Grounds - 71
Strike It Rich (Rheingold) Held up, prog 3f out, rdn/led over 1f out, styd on well, rdn out: op 6/1, 6lb pen for
recent win here at Epsom (clmr, R Beckett), earlier scored at Nottingham (sell, J Osborne): rnr-up in '99 (rtd 77,
D Marks): suited by 6/7f on any trk, likes Epsom: acts on fast & gd/soft, best without blnks: in great heart.
*3259 **HAIL THE CHIEF** 27 [3] R Hannon 3-8-12 (71) R Smith (5) 13/2: 260112: 3 b c Be My Chief - Jade Pet 1¼ 72
(Petong) Trkd ldrs, lost pl halfway, styd on fnl 2f, not pace of wnr: acts on gd & fast: loves a sharp/undul trk.
2900 **KING SILCA** 43 [10] M R Channon 3-9-3 (76) W Supple 10/1: 213003: 3 b g Emarati - Silca Cisa nk 76
(Hallgate) Chsd ldrs, switched & rdn/prog to lead over 2f out till over 1f out, onepace ins last: op 12/1, 6 wk abs:
eff around 7f, handles fast, loves cut in the grnd, could win again this autumn: see 1708 (gd/soft, mdn).
3739 **MYTTONS AGAIN** 7 [7] A Bailey 3-8-11 (70)(bl) J Bosley (7) 5/1 FAV: 631164: Rear, rdn/late hdwy, ¾ 69
no threat: bckd: better expected after 3739, see 3593.
3759 **BISHOPSTONE MAN** 6 [4] R Perham 15/2: 020035: Cl-up, led over 3f out till over 2f out, fdd. 2 62
2922 **ROYAL IVY** 42 [11] 3-8-7 (66) S Sanders 15/2: 542006: Handy, hard rdn/btn 2f out: op 6/1, fd wk abs. ¾ 60
*3739 **CRUISE** 7 [9] 3-8-3 (62)(6ex) P Fitzsimons (5) 6/1: 050017: Rdn/towards rear, mod hdwy: jockey 1 54
given a 2-day ban for careless riding: see 3739 (firm).
*2177 **NISR** 73 [8] 3-9-7 (80) A McGlone 20/1: 2-6018: Held up, hmpd early, nvr a factor: op 12/1: abs. 4 64
3739 **WILLOW MAGIC** 7 [5] 3-7-13 (58) P Doe 11/1: 434459: Dwelt/rear, eff wide 3f out, sn held: see 1512. nk 41
3474 **CATALONIA** 18 [6] 3-8-10 (69) M Fenton 11/1: 65-W50: Hmpd/dropped rear halfway, al held: 10th. 1 50
1855 **CULTURED PEARL** 87 [1] 3-8-7 (66) Darren Williams (5) 20/1: -36000: Led 4f, fdd: 11th: abs. nk 46
3561 **BINT HABIBI** 14 [2] 3-7-10 (55) G Bardwell 14/1: 631530: Keen/chsd ldrs, not handle bend over 3f ½ 34
out, sn struggling: 12th: forget this, better on a gall trk in 2914 (sell, M Channon).
12 ran   Time 1m 26.37 (6.27)   (Miss Vanessa Church)   N P Littmoden Newmarket, Suffolk

3855	3.30 LAING HCAP 3YO+ 0-80 (D) 5f Good 54 +06 Fast	[79]
	£5005 £1540 £770 £385 3 yo rec 1 lb Raced stands side	

3734 **FORGOTTEN TIMES** 7 [11] K T Ivory 6-9-7 (72)(vis) A Beech (5) 9/2: 060031: 6 ch m Nabeel Dancer - 76
Etoile d'Amore (The Minstrel) Held up, prog & squeezed thro' on stands rail to lead nr line under hands & heels
riding: gd time: earlier won at Lingfield (h'cap): '99 wnr at Goodwood (2), Folkestone, Brighton, Salisbury &
Windsor (h'caps, rtd 66): '98 Lingfield wnr (AW h'cap, rtd 71a & 51): stays 7f, 5f specialist: acts on firm, suited
by soft/hvy & equitrack: goes on any trk but loves a sharp/undul one: best in blnks/visor: tough & genuine mare.
*3734 **RITAS ROCK APE** 7 [13] R Brotherton 5-9-13 (78)(6ex) I Mongan (5) 3/1 FAV: 100212: 5 b m Mon hd 80
Tresor - Failand (Kala Shikari) Cl-up, led ins last till nr fin, just held: bckd, op 5/1: in fine form.
3687 **TUSCAN DREAM** 9 [10] A Berry 5-9-11 (76) P Bradley (5) 6/1: 240353: 5 b g Clantime - Excavator shd 78
Lady (Most Secret) Sn prom, led after 2f till ins last, styd on well, just held: loves a sharp 5f: see 2107.
3668 **MIZHAR** 10 [8] D Nicholls 4-9-12 (77)(bl) Alex Greaves 5/1: 000224: Chsd ldrs, hard rdn & styd on nk 78
well fnl 1f, just held: bckd tho' op 7/2: see 3668, 3398 & 1173.
*3619 **NORTHERN SVENGALI** 12 [3] 4-9-2 (67) Lynsey Hanna (7) 10/1: 030215: Chsd ldrs, prog/switched & nk 67
chance ins last, just held nr fin: op 8/1: remains in gd heart: see 3619.
2684 **ZARAGOSSA** 53 [12] 4-8-5 (56) Iona Wands 14/1: 005006: Dwelt, styd on fnl 2f, not pace to chall: hd 55
longer priced stablemate of 3rd: 8 wk abs: see 1687.
3398 **TANCRED TIMES** 21 [2] 5-8-2 (53) Kimberley Hart 14/1: 155267: Cl-up, wknd ins last: see 2395. ½ 50
2586 **RED TYPHOON** 56 [14] 3-9-6 (72)(t) S Sanders 14/1: 000028: Held up, keeping on for press when nk 68+
no room over 1f out & again ins last: 8 wk abs, t-strap: closer with a clr run, worth another chance: see 2586.
3312 **KEY** 25 [4] 4-8-1 (52) W Supple 40/1: 500-09: Held up, nvr pace to chall: rnr-up in '99 (rtd 68, h'cap): 2½ 41
'98 Brighton wnr (nurs, rtd 78, R Hannon): eff btwn 5/7f on firm & gd/soft grnd, stiff/gall or sharp/undul trk.
3619 **SWYNFORD DREAM** 12 [1] 7-8-1 (52) G Bardwell 16/1: 600050: Led 2f, btn over 1f out: 10th: see 3619. ½ 39
3587 **MIDHISH TWO** 13 [5] 4-8-6 (57)(VIS) M Henry 25/1: 000060: Al outpcd: 11th: visor, blnks 1110. 1¼ 40
3584 **CORBLETS** 13 [6] 3-8-7 (59) P Doe 25/1: 003630: Slowly away, al bhd: 12th: see 3584, 883. nk 41
1219 **AIRA FORCE** 120 [7] 3-10-0 (80) J Weaver 14/1: 10-200: Towards rear, nvr on terms: 13th: op 8/1, ¾ 60
4 month abs: topweight: btr 774 (AW).
13 ran   Time 56.68 (2.38)   (John Crook)   K T Ivory Radlett, Herts

3856	4.00 BARCLAYS HCAP 3YO 0-75 (E) 1m114y rnd Good 54 -20 Slow	[81]
	£4485 £1380 £690 £345	

*3702 **ALTAY** 9 [13] R A Fahey 3-8-4 (57)(6ex) R Ffrench 100/30 FAV: 363511: 3 b g Erin's Isle - Aliuska 60
(Fijar Tango) Held up, rdn & styd on from over 2f out to lead nr line: bckd: 6lb pen for recent Ripon success
(h'cap, 1st win): unplcd in '99 (rtd 63, mdn): poss stays 14f, suited by 1m/10f: can force the pace: acts on
fast & gd/soft grnd, sharp or stiff/gall trk: in fine form, could complete hat-trick.
3739 **DUSKY VIRGIN** 7 [3] S Woodman 3-8-5 (58) S Whitworth 6/1: 021232: 3 b f Missed Flight - Rosy nk 59
Sunset (Red Sunset) Held up, hmpd 4f out, prog to lead dist, hard rdn/hdd nr line: acts on gd & firm: likes Epsom.
2512 **MISTY MAGIC** 60 [5] P W Harris 3-8-2 (55) W Supple 10/1: 043263: 3 b f Distinctly North - Meadmore ¾ 55
Magic (Mansingh) Led till dist, drvn & kept on, not much room where held nr fin: 2 mth abs: see 2013.
3343 **HARMONIC** 24 [10] D R C Elsworth 3-9-2 (69) D Holland 9/1: 222024: Held up, drvn/prog to chall ¾ 68
over 1f out, onepace when hampered ins last, held after: stays a sharp 8.5f: see 1333 (mdn).
3045 **LADY JONES** 37 [6] 3-8-1 (54) G Bardwell 14/1: 013005: Rear, well bhd till kept on strongly fnl 1f for 1½ 50
press, nrst fin: op 12/1: handles gd & firm, suited by testing conditions: promising, see 2043, 1822 (soft).
3362 **SUMMER CHERRY** 23 [11] 3-8-7 (60)(t) M Fenton 7/2: -44636: Chsd ldrs 6f: bckd: btr 3362 (7f). 1¾ 53
3413 **VICTORIET** 20 [12] 3-7-10 (49)(2oh) M Henry 14/1: 044447: Trkd ldrs 6f: see 1435. hd 41
2688 **MENTIGA** 51 [9] 3-9-4 (71) N Pollard 14/1: 506068: Chsd ldrs 6f: 8 wk abs: btr 810 (easy grnd). 2 59
3357 **PRINCE OF MYSTERY** 23 [9] 3-7-10 (49)(2oh) G Baker (5) 33/1: 630-09: Cl-up 6f: see 3357. hd 36
3455 **SOVEREIGN STATE** 19 [7] 3-9-7 (74) P Robinson 6/1: 054600: Trkd ldrs, struggling halfway: 10th. nk 60
3242 **Dom Miguel** 28 [2] 3-7-10 (49) D Kinsella (5) 50/1:   **Jiemce** [4] 3-8-2 (55) J Quinn 20/1:
3242 **Fox Star** 28 [8] 3-7-13 (52)(bl)(3ow)(13oh) A Daly 50/1:
13 ran   Time 1m 48.06 (6.26)   (John T Robson)   R A Fahey Butterwick, N Yorks

3857   4.30 WATES GROUP CLASS STKS 3YO+ 0-80 (D)   1m2f   Good 54 -14 Slow
£4446   £1368   £684   £342   3 yo rec 7 lb

*3685 RIBERAC 9 [6] M Johnston 4-9-5 J Fanning 5/4 FAV: 011011: 4 b f Efisio - Ciboure (Norwick)   93
Trkd ldr bef halfway, led 3f out & readily pulled clr under hands & hard riding, eased down ins last: val for
8L+, hvly bckd: earlier won at Sandown, Ayr & here at Epsom (h'caps): highly tried in '99 for W Haggas (stks,
rtd 91): former sprinter, revelation since stepped up to 1m/10f: acts on firm, gd & any trk, likes Epsom:
progressive filly, in great heart, can win more races this autumn.
3628 CAPTAINS LOG 11 [2] M L W Bell 5-9-8 M Fenton 7/1: 415042: 5 b g Slip Anchor - Cradle Of Love   4   83
(Roberto) In tch, outpcd over 3f out, kept on ins last, no threat to wnr: prob better at 12f: see 2523 (12f).
3643 SAFARI BLUES 11 [7] R Hannon 3-8-8 S Sanders 12/1: 052663: 3 b f Blues Traveller - North Hut   1¼   74
(Northfields) Led 7f, sn held & lost 2nd nr fin: see 2811, 54.
3451 CHEMS TRUCE 19 [1] W R Muir 3-8-11 B Marcus 7/1: 003454: Held up, eff 3f out, little hdwy: see 3166.   1   76
*3794 ELMHURST BOY 4 [4] 4-9-6 P Doe 100/30: 520015: Handy halfway, rdn/carried head high & btn over   5   71
2f out: op 5/2, quick reapp: btr 3794.
1104 SMOOTH SAND 126 [3] 3-8-11 P Robinson 11/2: 0-1136: Trkd ldr 3f out, btn 3f out: abs: btr 1104, 892.   15   52
3393 BUNTY 21 [5] 4-9-1 W Supple 100/1: 040007: Bhd 4f out, sn rem: see 297 (AW h'cap).   13   35
7 ran   Time 2m 10.64 (6.84)   (Mr & Mrs G Middlebrook)   M Johnston Middleham, N Yorks

3858   5.05 MEZZANINE HCAP 3YO+ 0-75 (E)   1m4f   Good 54   +09 Fast   [75]
£4524   £1392   £696   £348   3 yo rec 9 lb

3581 SHARP SPICE 14 [16] D J Coakley 4-8-6 (53) W Supple 16/1: 553031: 4 b f Lugana Beach - Ewar   62
Empress (Persian Bold) Rear, rdn/stdy hdwy fnl 4f, led 1f out, styd on well, rdn out: tchd 25/1, best time of day:
'99 Goodwood wnr (mdn h'cap, rtd 64 at best): rtd 62 in '98 for Lord Huntingdon: suited by 10/12f on firm & hvy
grnd, any trk: best without a visor: well h'capped, could win again.
3541 BATSWING 15 [1] B Ellison 5-10-0 (75) D Holland 12/1: 012002: 5 b g Batshoof - Magic Milly (Simply   1¼   81
Great) Chsd ldrs, rdn/ev ch ins last, just held nr fin: op 14/1, topweight: see 2002, 1777 (10f).
*3731 MIDDLETHORPE 7 [7] M W Easterby 3-7-13 (55)(bl) J Quinn 5/2 FAV: 103013: 3 b g Noble Patriarch -   3   57
Prime Property (Tirol) Rdn/chsd ldr 3f out, briefly led 1f out, held ins last: bckd: just btr 3731 (10f).
3657 THE GREEN GREY 10 [17] L Montague Hall 6-9-10 (71) W Ryan 20/1: 015254: Rear, rdn/styd on fnl 3f,   1   72
nrst fin: stays a sharp 12f: see 2888 (10f, Windsor).
3657 HALF TIDE 10 [2] 6-7-12 (45) M Henry 10/1: 210505: Held up, hdwy 4f out, onepace fnl 2f: see 2626.   ½   45
*3403 FLIGHT SEQUENCE 21 [4] 4-10-0 (75)(vis) P Fitzsimons (5) 10/1: 602016: Trkd ldrs, rdn/onepace   ¾   74
fnl 2f: top-weight: travelled well, but not stay this longer 12f trip: see 3403 (10f).
*2945 BAHAMAS 40 [18] 3-9-0 (70)(bl) S Sanders 8/1: 233117: Chsd ldrs, led 5f out till 1f out, wknd: abs.   nk   68
3586 SURE FUTURE 13 [22] 4-7-11 (44)(bl) A Polli (3) 20/1: -00558: Trkd ldr, btn 2f out: see 3111.   ½   41
*3263 PERFECT MOMENT 27 [5] 3-9-0 (70) A Beech (5) 10/1: 111619: Rear, mod hdwy fnl 3f under a   3   63
v kind ride: reportedly not travel smoothly on the grnd & checked rnd Tattenham Corner: btr 3263 (10f).
3731 MYSTERIUM 7 [3] 6-8-11 (58) R Brisland (5) 16/1: 511000: Rear, mod late gains: 10th: btr 3314 (10f).   6   42
3448 TULSA 19 [14] 6-7-11 (44)(bl) (1ow)(5oh) P Bradley (0) 16/1: -55200: Rear, eff 4f out, btn 2f out: 11th.   1¾   26
3488 FUSUL 18 [9] 4-9-2 (63) J Weaver 33/1: 130250: Twds rear, eff 4f out, sn btn/eased: 12th: see 835.   1   44
*3683 INDIAN NECTAR 9 [6] 7-8-12 (59)(6ex) I Mongan (5) 14/1: 236410: Chsd ldrs, btn/eased 2f out: 13th.   6   31
3686 SPIRIT OF TENBY 9 [13] 3-8-11 (67) P Doe 14/1: 021450: Al towards rear: 14th: btr 3417.   ½   38
3392 DION DEE 21 [10] 4-8-0 (47) N Pollard 25/1: 025640: Al bhd: 15th: see 2011 (10f).   nk   17
*3586 LOST SPIRIT 13 [21] 4-7-10 (43) G Baker (5) 16/1: 135210: Led 7f, sn btn: 16th: op 12/1: btr 3586.   2½   9
3762 Loup Cervier 5 [11] 3-7-10 (52)(7oh) G Bardwell 50/1: 3007 Flag Fen 39 [8] 9-8-10 (57) B Marcus 33/1:
*1927 Two Socks 84 [20] 7-9-1 (62) S Carson (3) 16/1:
3255 Noteworthy 27 [12] 4-7-10 (43)(VIS)(15oh) D Kinsella (7) 50/1:
2691 Five Of Wands 53 [15] 3-9-0 (70) M Tebbutt 20/1:
3501 Captivating 17 [19] 5-7-10 (43)(18oh) Joanna Badger (7) 50/1:
22 ran   Time 2m 39.85 (5.45)   (The Nags Head Racing Syndicate)   D J Coakley West Ilsley, Berks

Official Going   Str Crse - GOOD (GOOD/FIRM Places); Rnd Crse - GOOD/FIRM (GOOD Places). Stalls: Str Crse -
Stands Side, Rnd Crse - Inside; Rnd Mile - Outside.   A v strong headwind in the straight may have affected times.

3859   1.30 SPORT4CAST.COM COND STKS 2YO (C)   7f str   Good/Firm 29 -34 Slow
£7020   £2160   £1080   £540

3391 OVERSPECT 21 [3] P F I Cole 2-9-1 J Fortune 7/1: -131: 2 b c Spectrum - Portelet (Night Shift)   102
Bhd ldrs, rdn to lead below dist, ran on strongly: op 5/1, lkd well: earlier won debut at San Siro: IR 30,000 gns
Jan foal, dam multiple sprint wnr: eff at 7f, will get further: acts on fast & gd grnd, gall trks: can force
the pace & run well fresh: stocky, useful & progressive colt, from a Group race abroad.
*3484 TEMPEST 18 [5] Sir Michael Stoute 2-9-1 Pat Eddery 2/5 FAV: -412: 2 b c Zafonic - Pidona   ¾   100
(Baillamont) Led, shkn up/hdd dist, kept on but held: well bckd, padd pick, clr rem: rangy colt, needs 1m now?
*3385 CAFETERIA BAY 21 [4] K R Burke 2-9-1 N Callan 11/1: 13: 2 ch c Sky Classic - Go On Zen (Zen)   6   88
Trkd ldr, eff 2f out, sn no extra: drifter from 7/1: scopey colt, not disgraced up in trip & grade: see 3385.
*3463 HEALEY 18 [6] J D Bethell 2-9-7 J Reid 6/1: 114: In tch, feeling pace halfway & left bhd by front   7   81
3: op 9/2, lkd well, on toes: gave weight away: lkd sure to be suited by this step up to 7f: see 3463.
-- JALONS STAR 1 [2] 2-8-8 A Culhane 150/1: 5: Struggling after 3f: tall, highly tried Eagle Eyed gldg,   18   28
bred to apprec 10f+ next term: with M Chapman.
3714 HELALI MANOR 8 [2] 2-8-8 J McAuley 200/1: 06: Sn bhd: burly & outclassed.   dist   0
6 ran   Time 1m 27.62 (4.42)   (Luciano Gaucci)   P F I Cole Whatcombe, Oxon

3860 **2.05 CARRIE FILL NURS HCAP 2YO (B)** **6f110y str Good/Firm 29 -31 Slow** **[93]**
£22620 £6960 £3480 £1740 2 Groups, merged by halfway, high nos prob fav

3749 **INNIT 6** [2] M R Channon 2-9-6 (85) Craig Williams 7/1 JT FAV: 340021: 2 b f Distinctly North - Tidal Reach (Kris S) Nvr far away wide, led ent fnl 2f, drifted right, rdn out: stocky, lkd well, h'cap bow: earlier won at Hamilton (mdn): eff at 6/6.5f on firm & gd/soft grnd, stiff/gall trks: fine run racing away from rivals in centre of crse & overcame poor low draw: tough & improving & potentially useful. **93**
3478 **MAULD SEGOISHA 18** [9] J G FitzGerald 2-8-12 (77) M Roberts 11/1: 0022: 2 br f Dolphin Street - September Tide (Thatching) Slow away, towards rear, prog & briefly short of room appr fnl 2f, kept on well for press & not btn far: op 8/1, h'cap bow: scopey filly, acts on fast & gd/soft grnd: 7f+ will suit now. *nk* **83**
3673 **FOREVER TIMES 10** [10] T D Easterby 2-8-8 (73) J Fortune 16/1: 622103: 2 b f So Factual - Simply Times (Dodge) Rear, wide, rdn ent fnl 2f, kept on well, nrst fin: suited by step up to 6.5f: badly drawn in 3673. *½* **77**
*3525 **KOMENA 16** [5] J W Payne 2-9-6 (85) T Quinn 11/1: 4214: Held up, shkn up/not clr run 2f out, clr below dist, ran on, nrst fin: padd pick: strong filly, much closer with a clr run on h'cap bow: worth another look. *¾* **87+**
3359 **PASHMEENA 23** [21] 2-9-1 (80) R Hughes 16/1: -2635: Led on stands rail till 2f out, kept on till no extra fnl 100y: h'cap bow: rtd higher in 3359 (7f). *nk* **81**
3075 **CHURCH BELLE 35** [22] 2-7-10 (61)(3oh) P Fessey 20/1: 02006: Towards rear, hdwy appr fnl 2f, rdn bef dist, styd on without threatening: v fit, stablemate 5th: eff at 5/6.5f on fast & gd/soft grnd. *hd* **62**
3519 **INJAAZ 16** [16] 2-9-5 (84) Pat Eddery 9/1: 0127: Waited with, going well, imprvg & not clr run 2f out, hdwy dist, eased cl-home when no ch: op 7/1: eyecatching run, one to keep in mind next time: see 3519. *1¼* **82+**
3630 **STRUMPET 11** [15] 2-8-13 (78) J Reid 10/1: 201638: Well plcd & ev ch till no extra appr fnl 1f: op 16/1. *½* **75**
*3712 **SAMADILLA 8** [8] 2-9-4 (83)(5ex) K Darley 7/1 JT FAV: -14419: In tch, wide, feeling pace appr fnl 2f, some late hdwy: quickish reapp & penalty: btr 3712. *2* **74**
3228 **THERESA GREEN 28** [4] 2-8-4 (69) L Newman (3) 14/1: 030140: Prom, wide, drifted right after halfway, onepace: 10th: see 3075. *shd* **60**
3425 **BECKY SIMMONS 19** [12] 2-9-7 (86) N Callan 12/1: 11150: Chsd ldrs, outpcd appr fnl 1f: 11th, v fit. *hd* **76**
3571 **SILKEN WINGS 14** [1] 2-8-6 (71) R Mullen 16/1: -3220: Wide, nvr trbld ldrs: 12th, lkd well, h'cap bow. *2* **55**
3246 **CUMBRIAN HARMONY 28** [17] 2-8-4 (69) T Williams 25/1: 552100: Bhd ldrs, fdd fnl 1f: 13th: see 3032. *hd* **53**
3630 **SYLVAN GIRL 11** [11] 2-8-2 (67) P M Quinn (3) 16/1: 253040: Cl-up & ev ch till wknd appr fnl 1f: 14th. *¾* **49**
3630 **RED RYDING HOOD 11** [3] 2-8-11 (76) J Mackay (5) 14/1: 342320: Early ldr in centre, lost pl 2f out: 15th. *½* **56**
3693 **Divine Wind 9** [20] 2-8-7 (72) K Dalgleish (5) 50/1: 3693 **Lady Ward 9** [19] 2-8-5 (70) G Duffield 40/1:
3127 **Flowing Rio 33** [14] 2-8-7 (72) Dean McKeown 16/1: 3015 **Silk Law 38** [13] 2-9-6 (85) G Carter 14/1:
3697 **Miss Equinox 9** [18] 2-7-10 (61)(4oh) Kim Tinkler 50/1: 3446 **Ice Maiden 19** [6] 2-9-2 (81) M Hills 25/1:
21 ran Time 1m 21.71 (3.91) (Tim Corby) M R Channon West Isley, Berks

3861 **2.35 TOTE PORTLAND HCAP 3YO+ 0-110 (B)** **5f140y Good/Firm 29 -02 Slow** **[107]**
£22327 £6870 £3435 £1717 3 yo rec 2 lb Raced centre

3569 **COMPTON BANKER 14** [8] G A Butler 3-8-8 (89) L Dettori 7/2 FAV: 102441: 3 br c Distinctly North - Mary Hinge (Dowsing) Towards rear, shaken up ent fnl 2f, ran on strongly & qcknd under press to lead fnl 100y, going away: well bckd, big gamble from 8/1: v consistent & sometimes unlucky in defeat in val h'caps since won at Ascot (h'cap): unplcd in '99 (rtd 84): eff at 5/5.5f, stays a sharp 6f: acts on fast & gd grnd, any trk, likes stiff/gall ones: imprvg, tough, useful colt who likes to come with a late run: thoroughly deserved this. **96**
2151 **DELEGATE 75** [11] N A Callaghan 7-8-9 (88) L Newman (3) 33/1: 064202: 7 ch g Polish Precedent - Dangora (Sovereign Dancer) Chsd ldrs, prog when carried left dist, sn led & drifted right, hdd & outpcd by wnr towards fin: v fit & back to form after 11 wk abs: well h'capped, return to 6f will suit: see 1182. *1* **91**
*3668 **SMART PREDATOR 10** [9] J J Quinn 4-8-5 (84) K Darley 11/1: 203013: 4 gr g Polar Falcon - She's Smart (Absalom) Trkd ldrs, drvn appr fnl 1f, chall ins last, no extra towards fin: lkd well: bang in form. *½* **85**
3610 **HO LENG 12** [16] Miss L A Perratt 5-10-0 (107) G Carter 16/1: 302334: Patiently rdn, prog & briefly short of room ent fnl 2f, kept on well, nvr nr to chall: lkd superb & fine run under top-weight: tough, see 1182. *¾* **106**
3791 **CADEAUX CHER 4** [7] 6-8-3 (82) F Norton 12/1: 005055: Waited with far side, going well but not clr run 2f out, ran on ins last, nvr dngrs: rcd away from the pace: won this in '98 (7lbs higher): see 2845. *½* **80**
3648 **KASHRA 11** [10] 3-8-10 (91) M Hills 25/1: 002066: Held up, briefly short of room 2f out, kept on ins last without threatening: tchd 40/1: gd run back in trip from this 3yo filly, return to 6f+ shld suit: see 1090. *nk* **88**
3473 **MAGIC RAINBOW 18** [15] 5-8-7 (86) J Mackay (5) 16/1: 065157: Well plcd & ev ch till no extra dist. *1¼* **80**
3322 **SHEER VIKING 25** [18] 4-9-3 (96) R Hills 11/1: 200058: Waited with, rdn & ran on well appr fnl 1f, nvr nrr: op 8/1, stablemate of 5th: likes to come late but waiting tactics overdone here: see 1182, 702. *nk* **89**
*3516 **BOLD EFFORT 17** [5] 8-8-3 (81)(bl)(1ow) M Roberts 25/1: 105019: Chsd ldrs, far side, rdn appr fnl 1f, not pace to chall: lkd superb, see 3516. *shd* **75**
3521 **ELLENS LAD 16** [2] 6-9-11 (104) L Newton 20/1: 011050: Made most in centre, rdn & edged left appr fnl 1f, hdd below dist & fdd: 10th: see 2676. *shd* **97**
3543 **BRECONGILL LAD 15** [17] 8-8-8 (87) Pat Eddery 13/2: 120230: Held up, hdwy appr fnl 1f, nvr nr ldrs: 11th, op 5/1: needs plenty of luck in running: see 2987. *1¼* **76**
3543 **LAGO DI VARANO 15** [19] 8-8-7 (86)(bl) F Lynch 16/1: 001200: Al around mid-div: 12th: see 3183. *shd* **75**
3727 **CRYHAVOC 7** [13] 6-8-12 (91) A Nicholls (3) 25/1: 000060: In tch, outpcd appr fnl 1f: 13th, qk reapp. *nk* **79**
3473 **DORCHESTER 18** [22] 3-8-5 (86) G Duffield 12/1: 000530: Mid-div, no extra appr fnl 1f: 14th, see 2168. *1¼* **71**
2151 **PEPPERDINE 75** [3] 4-9-2 (95) R Hughes 11/1: 2-3500: Held up far side, nvr a factor: 15th, op 9/1 after 11 wk abs: rcd away from the pace & this lkd a satisfactory tune-up for next week's Ayr Gold Cup where he shld go v well: acts on fast, prob best on easy grnd: see 1173. *hd* **79**
3727 **FURTHER OUTLOOK 7** [1] 6-9-4 (97) J P Murtagh 16/1: 364030: Led far side till after 3f, lost place: 21st. **0**
3727 **Guinea Hunter 7** [6] 4-9-5 (98)(bl) J Fortune 25/1: 3543 **Mungo Park 15** [20] 6-8-5 (83)(1ow) A Culhane 16/1:
3687 **Singsong 9** [12] 3-8-8 (89) D Allan (7) 50/1: 3788 **Azizzi 4** [14] 8-8-11 (90) T Quinn 20/1:
3629 **Baby Barry 11** [4] 3-8-4 (85)(vis) J Carroll 33/1: 3687 **Henry Hall 9** [21] 4-9-1 (94) Kim Tinkler 50/1:
22 ran Time 1m 08.51 (1.71) (E Penser) G A Butler Blewbury, Oxon

3862 **3.10 ST LEGER Y'LING STKS 2YO (B)** **6f Good/Firm 29 -20 Slow**
£155950 £62380 £31190 £15595 5 horses raced stands side & were struggling 2f out

*3064 **GOGGLES 36** [4] H Candy 2-8-11 C Rutter 14/1: -411: 2 b c Eagle Eyed - Rock On (Ballad Rock) Prom, rdn & edged right appr fnl 1f, led dist, kept on strongly: bckd, padd pick: earlier won at Goodwood (mdn): 20,000gns half brother to a 6f juv wnr: eff at 6f, shld get 7f: acts on fast grnd & a sharp/undul or gall trk: **100**

progressive, scopey & useful colt, well plcd to win this v val prize: step up to List/Gr 3 will suit.
*3714 **REEL BUDDY 8** [10] R Hannon 2-9-0 R Hughes 9/1: 000112: 2 ch c Mr Greeley - Rosebud (Indian Ridge) Waited with, travelled well, pulled out & ran on strongly fnl 1f, too much to do: lkd well, not the best-judged ride but remains on the upgrade: eff at 5/6f: useful: see 3714. ½ **101**
*3519 **IMPERIAL MEASURE 16** [3] B R Millman 2-8-11 G Hind 25/1: 150213: 2 b c Inchinor - Fair Eleanor (Saritamer) Mid-div, gd hdwy to press ldrs appr fnl 1f, held towards fin: lkd well: much imprvd: see 3519 (nurs). ½ **96**
3133 **ELSIE PLUNKETT 33** [5] R Hannon 2-8-9 J Fortune 8/1: 113244: Trkd ldrs, went on appr fnl 2f, hdd below dist & onepace for press: stablemate 2nd: eff at 5/6f, see 1586, 1372. *hd* **94**
3320 **SWEET PROSPECT 25** [1] 2-8-6 R Mullen 33/1: -0145: Rear towards far side, styd on appr fnl 1f, onepace cl-home: big, strong, scopey filly: imprvd here & will apprec 7f: see 2748. *1* **88**
2808 **FACTUAL LAD 47** [12] 2-8-11 M Roberts 50/1: 323106: Rear, kept on fnl 1½f, nvr nr to chall: abs. ½ **92$**
3352 **STREGONE 23** [22] 2-8-11 L Dettori 16/1: 042067: Led stands side quintet, under press 2f out, onepace & hung left: always seemed to be playing catch-up with main body of field: see 2850, 743. ¾ **90**
*3620 **SIBLA 12** [21] 2-8-6 R Havlin 33/1: 212518: Chsd ldrs stands side, eff/no impress 2f out: lkd well, btr 3620. *1* **82**
2754 **RUMORE CASTAGNA 49** [20] 2-8-11 A Culhane 50/1: -1539: Pulled hard, chsd ldrs stands side, unable to qckn appr fnl 1f: lengthy gldg, lkd well after 7 wk abs: shade btr 2664, see 1764. *1½* **83**
3286 **GALAPAGOS GIRL 26** [2] 2-8-6 M Hills 20/1: -120: V slow away, hdwy into mid-div appr fnl 1f: 10th. *hd* **78**
*3187 **MUJADO 30** [17] 2-8-6 Pat Eddery 7/4 FAV: 2210: Prom stands side, rdn 2f out, sn btn: 11th, hvly bckd: better than this, prob unfavourably drawn: see 3187 (made all). *1* **75**
3712 **PRINCESS OF GARDA 8** [14] 2-8-6 G Duffield 33/1: 214540: Al mid-div: 12th, see 3712, 2248. ½ **73**
3391 **SMITH AND WESTERN 21** [8] 2-8-11 L Newman 50/1: 012350: In tch, drvn 2f out, onepace: 13th. ½ **77**
*3614 **TAKAROA 12** [11] 2-8-11 K Darley 20/1: -3310: Mid-div, outpcd when short of room 2f out: 14th, bckd. *1* **74**
*3286 **WHERES JASPER 26** [9] 2-9-0 J Carroll 20/1: 212010: Led in centre till 2f out, lost pl: 15th, btr 3286 (gd). ½ **76**
3105 **PAN JAMMER 34** [19] 2-9-4 T Quinn 8/1: 123140: Sn switched to centre, prom 4f: 19th, needs easier grnd? **0**
1312 **Reeds Rains 113** [18] 2-8-6 T E Durcan 33/1:
3354 **Millennium Magic 23** [7] 2-8-6 Dale Gibson 50/1:
3352 **Threezedzz 23** [16] 2-8-11 J Reid 16/1:
*3621 **Double Fantasy 12** [6] 2-8-6 Paul Eddery 16/1:
2088 **Final Pursuit 77** [13] 2-8-6 D Harrison 16/1:
-- **Gianni** [15] 2-8-11 A Helfenbein 50/1:
22 ran Time 1m 13.74 (2.94) (Mrs J K Powell) H Candy Wantage, Oxon

3863

3.40 GR 3 PARK HILL STKS 3YO+ (A) 1m6f132y Good/Firm 29 +16 Fast
£24000 £9200 £4600 £2200 3 yo rec 12lb

3564 **MILETRIAN 14** [3] M R Channon 3-8-10 Craig Williams 10/1: 016441: 3 b f Marju - Warg (Dancing Brave) Waited with, prog ent fnl 3f, rdn & edged left dist, sn led, held on well: bckd, fast time, padd pick: earlier won at R Ascot (Gr 2 Riddlesdale): '99 Redcar wnr (mdn, Gr 1 4th, rtd 108): eff at 12f, suited by step up to 14.5f: acts on firm & gd, handles hvy: best on stiff/gall trks with a strong pace: smart filly. **112**
3565 **RADAS DAUGHTER 14** [1] I A Balding 4-9-3 M Hills 16/1: 001002: 4 br f Robellino - Drama School (Young Generation) Mid-div, hdwy appr fnl 2f, ev ch 1f out, kept on for press but held: lkd v well, tchd 20/1: much imprvd in this higher grade: eff at 12/14.5f: useful: see 2502 (val h'cap). ½ **105**
3538 **SKI RUN 15** [6] G A Butler 4-9-3 L Dettori 9/4 FAV: 1-0133: 4 b f Petoski - Cut And Run (Slip Anchor) Held up, prog 3f out, short of room ent fnl 2f & switched, kept on for press but too late: well bckd: must have gone close with a clr run: luckless tho' clrly v useful filly, will apprec a return to 2m: see 3538, 2953. ½ **104**
3211 **SOLAIA 32** [8] P F I Cole 3-8-5 J Fortune 13/2: 410244: Trkd ldrs, going well 3f out, pshd into lead 2f out, sn rdn, hdd dist & no extra: on toes: unfurnished filly, stays 14.5f, win again back at 12f: see 1223. *1* **102**
3177 **FILM SCRIPT 31** [4] 3-8-6(1ow) R Hughes 11/2: 136135: Set gd clip till bef halfway, led again appr fnl 3f till 2f out, styd on: consistent, ran to best, eff at 10f/14.5f: see 2975. ½ **102**
3595 **HIDDNAH 13** [10] 3-8-6(1ow) J Reid 10/1: 15-236: Mid-div, drvn 2f out, kept on same pace: op 8/1, stiffish task, clr rem: stays 14.5f & looks likely to get further: see 3595, 3017. *shd* **102**
*2594 **CEPHALONIA 56** [7] 3-8-5 Pat Eddery 9/1: -11617: Got loose bef start, in tch till appr fnl 1f: rangy filly, lkd well after 8 wk abs tho' faced a stiffish task at the weights: see 2594. *4* **97**
3595 **CLIPPER 13** [2] 3-8-5 G Duffield 33/1: -30008: Al bhd: dull in coat & stable not quite firing: see 1184. *2½* **94**
3564 **INTERLUDE 14** [11] 3-8-10 J Murtagh 7/1: -34169: Prom, led bef halfway till appr fnl 3f, sn btn, eased: jockey reported the filly hung badly right thr'out & this is best forgotten: see 3070 (gd/soft, Gr 2). *9* **90**
3070 **INFORAPENNY 38** [9] 3-8-5 K Darley 12/1: 235300: Chsd ldrs till 3f out: 10th, unproven beyond 12f. *7* **78**
3487 **TRUE CRYSTAL 18** [5] 3-8-5 T Quinn 33/1: -1040: Trkd ldrs, eff 3f out, sn no impress, eased bef fnl 1f: 11th, lkd well: highly tried on only 4th start, reportedly fin lame: see 2258. ¾ **77**
11 ran Time 3m 04.87 (1.87) (Miletrian Plc) M R Channon West Isley, Berks

3864

4.10 TBA MDN 2YO (D) 1m str Good/Firm 29 -57 Slow
£4251 £1308 £654 £327

-- **THEATRE SCRIPT** [2] J H M Gosden 2-9-0 J Fortune 10/1: 1: 2 ch c Theatrical - Gossiping (Chati) Patiently rdn, clsd ent fnl 2f, pshd into lead 1f out, ran on strgly, shade rdly: slow time, debut, edgy in padd & drifted from 6/1: Feb foal, half-brother to v useful 6/7f wnr Musicale, dam 6f wnr: eff at 1m, get at least 10f next term: acts on fast grnd, gall trk & runs well fresh: useful debut from this green colt, looks sure to rate higher. **98+**
3333 **PERSIAN PRIDE 24** [1] P W Harris 2-9-0 T Quinn 16/1: -042: 2 ch c Barathea - Glenarff (Irish River) Chsd ldrs, prog & ev ch 1f out, not pace of wnr: tchd 20/1: v fit: imprvd again & suited by step up to 1m: acts on firm/fast grnd & shld find a maiden. *1½* **93**
3450 **PERFECT SUNDAY 19** [9] B W Hills 2-9-0 M Hills 10/11 FAV: -323: 2 b c Quest For Fame - Sunday Bazaar (Nureyev) Front rank, shaken up to lead appr fnl 2f, rdn bef dist & sn hdd, kept on: hvly bckd, clr of next: eff at 7f/1m: defeat not expected & a shade disappointing after latest, unsuited by funereal pace? ½ **92**
-- **SNIZORT** [6] J D Bethell 2-9-0 J Reid 50/1: 4: Held up, styd on for hands & heels fnl 1½f, nvr nr to chall: better for race: Bahri Feb foal, dam juv wnr in the States: prob handles fast, apprec 10f next term. *3½* **85+**
3484 **MOSAAHIM 18** [5] 2-9-0 R Hills 7/2: -25: Trkd ldrs, ev ch appr fnl 1f, sn outpcd, eased: lkd well, bckd: failed to improve for debut run but this rangy colt is worth another chance: see 3484. ½ **84**
2867 **THUNDERMILL 45** [4] 2-9-0 K Darley 10/1: -536: Set v slow pace till appr fnl 2f, no extra: leggy & burly after 6 wk abs: needs a drop in grade now. *nk* **82**
-- **DAWARI** [10] 2-9-0 J Murtagh 12/1: 7: Bhd, v green, nvr a factor: big drifter from 6/1 on debut: In The Wings half-brother to 10/14f wnr Darapour: burly colt, apprec mid-dists next term: with Sir M Stoute. *1½* **81**
-- **NORTH POINT** [3] 2-9-0 N Callan 50/1: 8: Al towards rear: better for race: 20,000 gns Definite Article Mar foal, half-brother to sev wnrs, incl sprinter Pip's Song: will find easier mdns: with A Jarvis. *nk* **80$**
3608 **CONQUERING LOVE 12** [7] 2-9-0 T E Durcan 66/1: 09: Slow away, al rear: one more run for h'cap mark. *9* **60**
-- **DINOFELIS** [8] 2-9-0 A Culhane 33/1: 0: Bhd from halfway: 10th, bckwd colt, stablemate rnr-up: *2½* **55**

DONCASTER WEDNESDAY SEPTEMBER 6TH Lefthand, Flat, Galloping Track

150,000 gns Rainbow Quest first foal, needs further/more time.
10 ran Time 1m 43.39 (6.89) (Mr R E Sangster & Mr A K Collins) J H M Gosden Manton, Wilts

3865 **4.40 YORKS DRAGOONS CLASS STKS 3YO+ 0-85 (C) 1m2f60y Good/Firm 29 -14 Slow**
£7377 £2270 £1135 £567 3 yo rec 7 lb

2547 **GREEN CARD 58** [13] S P C Woods 6-9-2 J Reid 7/1: 463041: 6 br h Green Dancer - Dunkellin (Irish River) Waited with, cruised up to ldrs on bit 3f out, led 2f out, pushed out, cmftbly: op 11/2, lkd superb: fit from a couple of facile wins over timber (2m/2m3.5f, firm/fast grnd, rtd 127h): plcd sev times in '99 (Gr 3, rtd 110): '98 Nottingham & Doncaster wnr (stks, rtd 112): eff at 1m/10.3f, tried further: acts on firm & gd grnd, handles soft, any trk, likes Doncaster: best without blnks or visor: once smart entire, in a rich vein of form. **87**
3628 **CULZEAN 11** [12] R Hannon 4-9-6 R Hughes 10/1: 120362: 4 b g Machiavellian - Eileen Jenny (Kris) Off the pace, prog going well ent fnl 3f, chsd wnr bef dist, kept on but no impress: op 8/1, v fit: fine effort at the weights, poss flattered tho was well clr of rem: see 2287. *1¾* **87$**
*1963 **RADIO STAR 82** [11] J R Fanshawe 3-8-13 D Harrison 4/1: 13: 3 b c Storm Cat - Andover Way (His Majesty) Waited with, pushed along ent str, prog bef 2f out, sn drvn, kept on onepace: tchd 6/1, clr rem, 12 wk abs, padd pick: not disgraced, big step up in trip: 1m could prove ideal, see 1963. *3½* **82**
3025 **REFLEX BLUE 38** [5] J W Hills 3-8-9 M Hills 10/1: 442364: Bhd, not much room ent str, switched & styd on bef dist, nvr nr ldrs: op 8/1: needs a return to 12f, see 1400, 1198. *5* **71**
3453 **STAGE DIRECTION 19** [7] 3-8-13 (t) J Fortune 10/1: -44145: Nvr a factor tho' staying on fin: try 12 now? *1¾* **73**
*3324 **SCHEMING 25** [9] 3-8-13 R Mullen 16/1: 16: Held up, eff 3f out, nvr pace to chall: v green in paddock tho' lkd well: return to 12f will suit: see 3324. *2* **70**
*2938 **INVADER 41** [3] 4-9-6 (vis) Pat Eddery 10/1: 500217: Well plcd, led appr str till 2f out, fdd: lkd well, 6 wk abs: unsuited by step up to 10f?: see 2938. *3½* **66**
3669 **WEET A MINUTE 10** [2] 7-9-2 D Sweeney 8/1: 005438: Chsd ldrs, chall appr fnl 2f, sn wknd: op 10/1. *¾* **61**
-3669 **VIA CAMP 10** [1] 3-8-6 T Quinn 3/1 FAV: 0-4629: Trkd ldrs, wknd qckly appr fnl 2f: well bckd, lkd well: much better than this, first 6 home came from off the pace: see 3669, 2171. *2* **55**
2955 **MYTHICAL KING 40** [8] 3-8-13 K Darley 14/1: 314200: Led till 5f out, wknd: 10th, tchd 20/1, abs, lkd well. *3* **58**
3654 **Stamford Hill 11** [6] 5-9-2 D Allan (7) 150/1: 395 **Dennis Bergkamp 225** [4] 3-8-9 P M Quinn (3) 100/1:
3563 **Dabus 14** [10] 5-9-2 L Gueller (7) 40/1:
13 ran Time 2m 10.85 (4.45) (P K L Chu) S P C Woods Newmarket, Suffolk

CHEPSTOW THURSDAY SEPTEMBER 7TH Lefthand, Undualting, Galloping Track

Official Going GOOD TO SOFT. Stalls: Str Crse - Stands Side; Rnd Crse - Inside.

3866 **1.45 MONMOUTHSHIRE MDN 2YO (D) 7f str Good 56 00 Slow**
£3877 £1193 £596 £298

-- **GOLAN** [9] Sir Michael Stoute 2-9-0 F Lynch 5/4 FAV: 1: 2 b c Spectrum - Highland Gift (Generous) Chsd ldrs, led dist, styd on well, pshd out: well bckd on debut: Feb 1st foal, dam 10f wnr: sire high-class at 1m/10f: eff at 7f, 1m will suit: runs well fresh on gd & a gall trk/undul trk: well regarded, rate more highly. **98+**
2269 **CLEARING 70** [5] J H M Gosden 2-9-0 W Ryan 5/2: 22: 2 b c Zafonic - Bright Spells (Alleged) With ldr, went on halfway, hdd dist, kept on nicely but not pace of wnr: nicely bckd after 10 wk abs, pulled 9L clr rem: acts on fast & gd grnd: mdn a formality: see 2269. *1½* **93**
3614 **A C AZURE 13** [2] P D Evans 2-9-0 P McCabe 10/1: -653: 2 br g Dolphin Street - Kelvedon (General Assembly) Keen/prom, not pace of front 2 fnl 1f: bckd from 33/1: another promising run & h'caps shld now suit. *9* **72**
-- **ELSAAMRI** [3] M P Tregoning 2-9-0 R Perham 20/1: 4: Dwelt, ran v green, late gains under hands & heels: Feb foal, half-brother to sev wnrs incl a useful juv: sure to improve plenty on this encouraging debut. *1½* **70+**
-- **ISTIHSAAN** [7] 2-9-0 W Supple 12/1: 5: Mid-div, rdn/late hdwy, no dngr: stablemate of 4th: Feb first foal, dam unrcd, but well related: sire high-class miler: with M Tregoning, will improve. *½* **69**
-- **DAKHIRA** [10] 2-8-9 N Pollard 20/1: 6: Dsptd lead, hdd halfway, sn lost tch: 20,000gns Feb foal, dam scored over 5f as a 2yo: with D Elsworth, improve for this run. *2* **60**
-- **AMBERSONG** [12] 2-9-0 M Fenton 33/1: 7: Waited with, nvr dngrs: 19,000gns Jan first foal, dam scored over 5/6f as a juv: with J W Hills. *¾* **63**
2985 **GHADIR 40** [8] 2-8-9 G Hind 33/1: 08: Nvr a factor after 6 wk abs: see 2985. *nk* **58**
3705 **LUCEFER 10** [11] 2-9-0 M Henry 6/1: -029: Front rank, wknd qckly fnl 2f: much btr 3705 (gd/soft). *nk* **62**
-- **THE DOCTOR** [6] 2-9-0 D Sweeney 20/1: 0: Dwelt, al rear, 10th: op 12/1: 30,000gns May foal, dam a 1m scorer as a 2yo: sure to apprec mid-dists next term: with P Cole. *½* **61**
-- **Nugget** [1] 2-9-0 B Marcus 33/1: -- **Mr Kipling** [13] 2-9-0 S Whitworth 33/1:
3577 **Monash Freeway 15** [4] 2-9-0 T G McLaughlin 50/1:
13 ran Time 1m 23.7 (3.9) (Lord Weinstock) Sir Michael Stoute Newmarket.

3867 **2.15 ORCHARD MED AUCT MDN 2YO (E) 1m str Good 56 +05 Fast**
£2775 £854 £427 £213

3537 **REDUIT 16** [13] G A Butler 2-9-0 J P Spencer 15/8 FAV: -441: 2 ch c Lion Cavern - Soolaimon (Shareef Dancer) Rcd keenly in mid-div, imprvd 3f out, ran on strongly ins last to lead nr fin, rdn out: nicely bckd, best time of day: 19,500gns Feb foal, sire smart 6/7f performer: dam well related: eff at 7f/1m on fast & gd grnd: handles a stiff or gall/undul trk: useful & improving colt, can win more races. **99**
3577 **DUBAI SEVEN STARS 15** [2] M C Pipe 2-8-9 W Supple 11/4: 4522: 2 ch f Suave Dancer - Her Honour (Teenoso) Cl-up, went on after halfway, clr appr fnl 1f, collared nr fin: op 7/4: eff at 7f/1m: win sn, see 3577. *½* **92**
3458 **WHEN IN ROME 20** [14] C A Cyzer 2-9-0 S Sanders 16/1: 63: 2 b c Saddlers' Hall - Seasonal Splendour (Prince Rupert) Mid-div, ran on strongly for press ins last, closing at fin: 7L clr rem: left debut run bhd: eff at 1m on gd grnd, sure to apprec further in time: see 3458. *1½* **94**
3635 **FASTINA 12** [1] R Guest 2-8-9 D Harrison 8/1: -43034: Chsd ldrs, rdn/fdd fnl 2f: tchd 14/1: up in trip. *7* **72**
3418 **TEEHEE 21** [11] 2-9-0 M Fenton 33/1: 55: Front rank, drvn/no extra fnl 2f: up in trip: see 3418. *¾* **76**
-- **TWILIGHT DANCER** [3] 2-8-9 P Doe 20/1: 6: Rear, prog over 2f out, styd on, no threat: 13,000gns Mar foal, dam won over 7f as a juv: shld be suited by 1m: with P W Harris, shld improve. *3* **65**
-- **AMIGO** [8] 2-9-0 B Marcus 33/1: 7: Dwelt, rear, modest late gains: 52,000gns Spectrum colt, half-brother to a useful 6/7f 2yo wnr: with P Mitchell, 1m shld suit: open to improvement. *1* **68**

3757 **SAORSIE** 7 [15] 2-9-0 S Whitworth 100/1: -0008: Rcd keenly, mid-div at best: qck reapp, modest. 1½ 65$
-- **FLYING FAISAL** [12] 2-9-0 S W Kelly (3) 33/1: 9: Cl-up, wknd qckly fnl 2f: 16,000gns first foal, shd 65
dam wnr in the USA: 1m/10f shld suit next term: with J A Osborne.
3729 **THE OLD SOLDIER** 8 [6] 2-9-0 J Stack 33/1: 00: In tch, wknd qckly fnl 2f, 10th: see 3729. 1 63
3292 **PLANET GIRL** 27 [4] 2-8-9 G Carter 13/2: -30: Green, nvr a threat, 11th: op 5/1: btr 3292 (7f, fast). 1 56
2306 **SPAIN** 69 [7] 2-8-9 D Sweeney 14/1: 50: Led, hdd 3f out, sn lost tch, 12th: 10 wk abs: has a ½ 55
v high action & looks in need of softer grnd: see 2306.
-- **The Broker** [5] 2-9-0 Dale Gibson 33/1:   3057 **Dardanus** 37 [16] 2-9-0 W Ryan 16/1:
2901 **Challenor** 44 [17] 2-9-0 G Bardwell 50/1:   -- **Greenlees** [9] 2-8-9 A Daly 50/1:
16 ran   Time 1m 36.0 (4.1)   (Five Horses Ltd)   G A Butler Blewbury, Oxon.

3868   **2.45 CHEPSTOW CASTLE SELLER 3YO+ (F)   1m str   Good 56   +02 Fast**
£2359   £674   £337   3 yo rec 5 lb

*3711 **ARTFUL DANE** 9 [2] C G Cox 8-9-8 (bl) S Sanders 10/1: 030011: 8 b g Danehill - Art Age (Artaius) 60
Rcd alone far side & sn led, ran on well for press, rdn out: op 7/1, gd time: no bid: recent Ripon wnr (clmr):
plcd in '99 (h'cap, rtd 51): '97 Doncaster wnr (val h'cap, rtd 78): suited by 1m on firm & gd/soft: handles any
trk & best in blnks/visor: loves dominating: in fine form & benefited from an enterprising S Sanders ride.
*3736 **ERTLON** 8 [1] C E Brittain 10-9-8 A Nicholls (3) 10/1: 035512: 10 b g Shareef Dancer - Sharpina 3½ 52
(Sharpen Up) Led stands side, drvn over 2f out, styd on but no ch with wnr: op 8/1: remains in fine form &
shld win in this grade again soon: see 3736.
4527} **DARWELLS FOLLY** 316 [16] M Johnston 5-9-3 (vis) J Fanning 11/2: 0010-3: 5 ch g Blushing John - 1½ 44
Hispanolia (Kris) Front rank, eff over 2f out, no extra appr dist: op 4/1 on reapp: '99 Leicester (h'cap, 1st
time blnks, rtd 67) & W'hampton wnr (AW clmr, rtd 60a): '98 wnr again at W'hampton (2 h'caps, rtd 91a): eff at
7f on firm, gd & fibresand: acts on any trk, loves W'hampton: runs well fresh in blnks/visor: gd eff after abs.
3241 **CALDIZ** 29 [18] Mrs M Bridgwater 3-8-12 (t) G Baker (5) 12/1: -6664: Handy, rdn & styd on 3 39
fnl 2f, nvr nrr: op 8/1: new stable, prev with Mrs A Perrett: see 2265 (10f).
3117 **MODEL GROOM** 34 [8] 4-9-3 S Whitworth 14/1: 65: Mid-div, late hdwy for press, no threat: op 10/1. ¾ 38
3775 **HORMUZ** 5 [19] 4-9-8 F Lynch 7/2: 105526: Led stands side early, remained with ldrs, wknd fnl 1f: ¾ 42
qck reapp: capable of better, see 3775 (gd/soft).
3770 **COLONEL CUSTER** 5 [3] 5-9-8 I Mongan (5) 50/1: 040607: Mid-div at best: qck reapp: stiff task. 3½ 36$
2970 **HI MUJTAHID** 41 [9] 6-9-3 M Savage (7) 50/1: 000208: Prom, rdn/fdd fnl 2f: 6 wk abs: see 2907. nk 31
2655 **RENDITA** 55 [13] 4-8-12 A Clark 25/1: 0-0009: Bhd, prog over 2f out, bhd fnl 1f: 6 wk abs: see 2655. 3 21
3559 **MR CUBE** 15 [12] 10-9-3 (bl) Claire Bryan (5) 25/1: 240000: Slow to start, nvr dngrs, 10th, see 3907. hd 26
3694 **PANTHER** 10 [10] 10-9-3 G Bardwell 50/1: 00/000: Al in rear, 11th: modest recent form, way back ¾ 25
in '96 won 4 times (h'cap & clmrs, rtd 72 at best): eff btwn 5/7f on firm, hvy & fibresand: best in blnks/visor.
-- **TEXANNIE** [17] 3-8-7 G Carter 16/1: -0000: Stumbled start, al bhd, 12th: op 10/1: ex-French. 8 7
*3253 **SHARP SHUFFLE** 28 [20] 7-9-8 J P Spencer 3/1 FAV: 023210: Nvr a threat, 13th: v disapp but shd 17
reportedly unsuited by grnd, much better on fast in 3253.
-- **Bandido** [5] 3-8-12 C Carver (3) 50/1:   2785 **Victor Power** 49 [7] 5-9-3 M Fenton 50/1:
3738 **Hunan Scholar** 8 [14] 5-9-3 (bl) P McCabe 66/1:   3117 **Alfahaal** 34 [4] 7-9-3 (VIS) T G McLaughlin 20/1:
3275 **Cornish Eclipse** 27 [6] 3-8-12 D Sweeney 50/1:
18 ran   Time 1m 36.2 (4.3)   (S P Lansdown Racing)   C G Cox Lambourn, Berks.

3869   **3.20 TINTERN ABBEY MDN 3YO (D)   1m4f23y   Good 56   00 Slow**
£4182   £1287   £643   £321

-- **ISADORA** [5] L M Cumani 3-8-9 J P Spencer 4/6 FAV: 1: 3 b f Sadler's Wells - Ahead (Shirley 87+
Heights) Waited with going well, smooth hdwy to chall 2f out, sn led, qcknd well & pushed out, cmftbly: well bckd
on debut: bred in the purple: eff arnd a gall/undul 12f on gd grnd, will stay further: runs v well fresh: fine
debut, op to plenty of improvement: potentially useful & will win more races.
3324 **SHAIR** 26 [3] J H M Gosden 3-9-0 R Havlin 5/1: 4222: 3 b g Warning - Shaima (Shareef Dancer) 3 84
Cl-up, went on over 3f out, hdd appr fnl 1f, not pace of easy wnr: op 5/2, 9L clr rem: acts on fast & gd grnd:
caught a potentially useful rival & shld win in mdn company sn: see 3324.
3313 **SEEKER** 26 [2] H R A Cecil 3-8-9 W Ryan 14/1: 323: 3 ch f Rainbow Quest - Sarmatia (Danzig) 9 67
Led, hdd appr fnl 3f, sn fdd: op 10/1: see 3313.
2710 **AMNERIS** 53 [4] R Charlton 3-8-9 (BL) S Sanders 6/1: -234: Prom, rdn/lost tch fnl 3f: 8 wk abs ½ 66
& a below par run in first time blnks: btr 2710, 2258 (firm grnd).
1009 **MACHRIE BAY** 136 [6] 3-9-0 G Carter 9/2: 03-325: Rcd keenly in rear, eff 3f out, no impress: 2 68
5 month abs, just sharper for this: btr 1009 (hvy grnd).
3167 **ICE CRYSTAL** 33 [7] 3-9-0 D Sweeney 20/1: 004006: Handy, wknd qckly fnl 3f: stiff task: see 3167. 4 63
3350 **MISS AMBER NECTAR** 24 [1] 3-8-9 S Carson (3) 100/1: 0007: In tch, wknd qckly fnl 4f, t.o.: poor. dist 0
7 ran   Time 2m 37.8 (6.7)   (Gerald Leigh)   L M Cumani Newmarket

---

3870   **3.50 MASKREYS HCAP 3YO 0-80 (D)   1m2f36y   Good 56   -30 Slow**   [85]
£4329   £1332   £666   £333

3858 **MIDDLETHORPE** 1 [11] M W Easterby 3-7-12 (55)(bl) P Hanagan (5) 3/1 FAV: 030131: 3 b g Noble 60
Patriarch - Prime Property (Tirol) Chsd ldrs, smooth hdwy to lead 2f out, styd on strongly & rdn out: 3rd at
Epsom 24hrs ago (12f): prev won at Beverley (first win) & York (h'caps): plcd in '99 (rtd 59, h'cap): suited
by 10/12f on fast, soft & any trk: runs well fresh & now best in blnks: tough & improving.
3415 **SHRIVAR** 21 [9] M R Channon 3-8-12 (69)(VIS) W Supple 10/1: 414042: 3 b g Sri Pekan - Kriva 1½ 70
(Reference Point) Waited with, eff when short of room 2f out, switched/prog over 1f out, styd on, no ch with wnr:
ran to best in first time visor, could win similar: see 3415, 2463.
3581 **ZAGALETA** 15 [15] Andrew Turnell 3-8-12 (69) F Lynch 7/1: 002123: 3 b f Sri Pekan - Persian Song hd 70
(Persian Bold) Waited with, gd hdwy over 3f out, chall wnr appr fnl 1f, held ins last: tchd 9/1: v consistent.
3220 **BOULDER** 29 [12] L M Cumani 3-8-3 (74) J P Spencer 10/1: 64544: Mid-div, prog appr fnl 2f, drvn/ ¾ 74
onepcd ins last: op 7/1: eff at 10f on gd grnd: see 2751, 2265.
3683 **WILFRAM** 10 [16] 3-8-4 (61) P Fitzsimons (5) 12/1: 163245: Led early, remained with ldrs, rdn/held nk 60
appr fnl 1f: remains in gd heart: see 3182.
2977 **CALLAS** 41 [13] 3-8-9 (66) N Pollard 12/1: 4-0056: Towards rear, drvn/prog over 2f out, no extra nk 65
over 1f out: 6 wk abs: big step up in trip, poss gets a gall 10f: see 1787.
*3390 **GUARDED SECRET** 22 [8] 3-9-4 (75) S Sanders 9/2: -0217: Keen cl-up, drvn/fdd over 1f out: btr 3390. 2 71
1188

3413 **ARDUINE 21** [7] 3-9-7 (78) R Havlin 8/1: 330338: Held up, rdn/prog 3f out, drvn/btn fnl 1f: tchd 12/1. *5* **67**
3340 **SHADY POINT 25** [6] 3-9-6 (77)(vis) A Nicholls (3) 14/1: 106069: Trkd ldrs, wkng/short of room 2f out. *½* **65**
3392 **SALZGITTER 22** [10] 3-9-4 (75) D Sweeney 9/1: -33060: Al towards rear, 10th: see 3392. *2* **60**
3626 **SOPHALA 12** [3] 3-8-6 (63) G Hind 20/1: 0-300: Settled in tch, nvr dngrs, 11th: h'cap bow: see 3189. *1½* **45**
3095 **STORM PRINCE 36** [4] 3-8-6 (63)(VIS) A Mackay 33/1: -60000: Rcd v keenly, lost tch after halfway: fin 12th: tried a visor: up in trip: see 392. *3* **41**
2299 **SPORTING LADDER 69** [1] 3-9-4 (75) Darren Williams (5) 20/1: 4040: Sn led, hdd 2f out, wknd rapidly, 13th: 10 wk abs, h'cap bow: btr 2299 (A/W). *2½* **49**
*3310 **PETEURESQUE 26** [14] 3-9-4 (75) D Mernagh (3) 9/1: 002010: Al bhd, fin last: much btr 3310 (firm). *15* **34**
14 ran Time 2m 12.9 (8.8) (J H Quickfall & A G Black) M W Easterby Sheriff Hutton, N.Yorks.

3871

4.20 HORSESMOUTH HCAP DIV 1 3YO+ 0-65 (F) 7f str Good 56 -09 Slow [63]
£2240 £640 £320 3 yo rec 4 lb

3623 **SOUHAITE 13** [17] W R Muir 4-8-6 (41) D Harrison 14/1: 010001: 4 b g Salse - Parannda (Bold Lad) Grabbed stands rail & sn led, styd on strongly for press ins last, drvn out to hold on: earlier won at Leicester (h'cap): '99 wnr at Southwell (h'cap, first win, rtd 45a): eff at 7/12f, has tried 2m: acts on firm, gd & f/sand: poss handles any trk & runs well fresh, without t-strap: imprvd here for forcing the pace. **49**
3765 **SAND HAWK 6** [7] D Shaw 5-8-9 (44)(bl) Paul Eddery 3/1 FAV: 041062: 5 ch g Polar Falcon - Ghassanah (Pas de Seul) Chsd ldrs far side, led that group & hung left 1f out, ev ch when hung badly right well ins last, just held: qck reapp: threw away winning chance by hanging across trk, can find compensation. *½* **51**
3445 **MOROCCO 20** [6] J A Osborne 11-8-10 (45) A Eddery (5) 20/1: 006-03: 11 b g Cyrano de Bergerac - Lightning Laser (Monseigneur) Rear, drvn/styd on appr fnl 1f, no threat: gd effort, well h'capped veteran. *3* **47**
*2882 **WILEMMGEO 45** [1] P D Evans 3-8-12 (51) Joanna Badger (7) 7/1: 000114: Ran loose bef start, led after 3f, hdd appr fnl 1f, onepace: 6 wk abs: not disgraced on hat-trick bid, prev with M Chapman: see 2882. *hd* **53**
3775 **SEVEN 5** [10] 5-9-1 (50)(vis) M Fenton 12/1: 040035: Dwelt/stumbled start, hdwy from rear over 2f out, kept on, no threat: qck reapp: not disgraced after a v tardy start: see 3775 (seller). *1½* **49**
3559 **DANZAS 15** [13] 6-8-9 (44)(bl) Claire Bryan (5) 16/1: 250466: Dwelt, rear, late hdwy for press, no threat to ldrs: often ruins chance with a slow start: see 2099. *hd* **43**
3200 **ACID TEST 30** [18] 5-9-9 (58) F Lynch 7/1: 005067: In tch, modest gains: tchd 12/1: visor omitted. *shd* **57**
2820 **GRASSLANDIK 48** [9] 4-9-4 (53) S Whitworth 12/1: 004568: Hdwy from rear after halfway, no dngr: 7 wk abs: turf return: see 175 (A/W). *1* **50**
3745 **MASSEY 7** [5] 4-8-12 (47)(vis) S Sanders 25/1: 000009: Prom, lost tch fnl 2f: qck reapp. *shd* **44**
3643 **SASH 12** [16] 3-9-5 (58) P Doe 20/1: -50500: Cl-up, chall over 2f out, wknd qckly ins last, 10th. *1¾* **52**
3738 **SUPER MONARCH 8** [2] 6-9-4 (53)(bl) T G McLaughlin 20/1: 000020: Handy, wknd qckly fnl 2f, 11th. *1* **45**
3207 **ADDITION 30** [15] 4-9-3 (52) R Havlin 10/1: -00460: Al towards rear, 12th: see 1799. *3½* **39**
3225 **BERKELEY HALL 29** [20] 3-9-12 (65) D Sweeney 12/1: 001260: Al bhd stands side, 13th: btr 1665, 1273. *3* **47**
3574 **HELLO HOLLY 15** [12] 3-8-8 (47) A McGlone 12/1: -60300: Nvr a factor, 14th: twice below 3226. *shd* **29**
3362 **STORM CRY 24** [11] 5-10-0 (63)(BL) Darren Williams (5) 25/1: -00000: Led, hdd appr fnl 3f, wknd qckly, t.o. in last: top-weight, blnkd, see 323. **0**
3691 **Regent 10** [4] 5-8-12 (47) A Mackay 33/1: 3004 **Blackpool Mammas 40** [19] 3-9-6 (59) P Fitzsimons(5) 16/1:
3561 **Magical River 15** [14] 3-8-5 (44) A Nicholls(3) 20/1: 3263 **Cumbrian Princess 28** [3] 3-8-3 (42) Dale Gibson 20/1:
19 ran Time 1m 24.4 (4.6) (J Bernstein) W R Muir Lambourn, Berks.

3872

4.50 SPINNEY HCAP 3YO+ 0-70 (E) 5f str Good 56 -05 Slow [70]
£2990 £920 £460 £230 3 yo rec 1 lb

*3747 **AMERICAN COUSIN 7** [7] D Nicholls 5-8-4 (46) T Hamilton (7) 11/2: 005011: 5 b g Distant Relative - Zelda (Sharpen Up) Waited with, hdwy to chall over 1f out, ran on strongly to lead fnl 50y, rdn out: op 7/2, qck reapp: recent Salisbury scorer (appr h'cap): '99 wnr at Doncaster (2, appr h'caps, rtd 63 at best): rnr-up in '98 for R Johnson Houghton (rtd 60): eff at 5/6f on firm, gd/soft & fibresand: best without blnks & handles any trk, likes Doncaster: well h'capped, in fine heart & has forged a gd partnership with young T Hamilton. **53**
*3587 **BANDBOX 14** [5] M Salaman 5-9-7 (63) S Sanders 9/1: 623612: 5 ch g Imperial Frontier - Dublah (Private Account) Waited with, gd hdwy over 2f out, styd on fnl 1f, not btn far: op 7/1: in gd form: see 3587. *½* **68**
3788 **SHARP HAT 5** [17] D W Chapman 6-10-0 (70) D Mernagh (3) 7/2 FAV: 630323: 6 b g Shavian - Madam Trilby (Grundy) Front rank, went on halfway, hdd well ins last, held cl-home: tchd 5/1, qck reapp: in gd heart. *¾* **73**
3398 **RUDE AWAKENING 22** [4] C W Fairhurst 6-8-7 (49) J Fanning 8/1: 105204: Mid-div, gd hdwy over 2f out, no extra ins last: tchd 16/1: see 3257, 2743. *1* **49**
3419 **CRUSTY LILY 21** [18] 4-8-2 (44) N Pollard 16/1: 066305: Handy, rdn/imprvd over 1f out, held fnl 1f. *1¾* **41**
3619 **BENZOE 13** [16] 10-9-0 (56) Clare Roche (7) 12/1: 153046: Slow to start, hdwy from rear 2f out, no threat to front 2: stablemate of wnr: see 3619. *hd* **53**
3619 **INDIAN BAZAAR 13** [11] 4-8-2 (44) P Fitzsimons (4) 16/1: 005607: Led, hdd 3f out, ev ch till wknd well ins last: op 12/1: see 3619, 2223. *1½* **37**
3781 **TICK TOCK 5** [9] 3-8-6 (49) A Mackay 33/1: 000408: Cl-up, rdn/fdd appr fnl 1f: qck reapp: see 3781. *hd* **41**
3747 **RIVER TERN 7** [6] 7-8-12 (54) R Ffrench 25/1: 000009: Dwelt, rear, modest late gains: qck reapp. *hd* **46**
3653 **WHIZZ KID 12** [20] 6-9-12 (68) Claire Bryan (5) 14/1: 000000: Prom, lost tch appr fnl 1f, fin 10th. *1* **57**
*3584 **TIGER IMP 14** [12] 4-9-12 (68)(t) Martin Dwyer 11/1: -06010: Cl-up, wknd dist, 11th: btr 3584. *nk* **56**
3619 **RED CHARGER 13** [2] 4-9-2 (58) A Nicholls (3) 20/1: 000000: Nvr dngrs, 12th: stablemate of wnr. *½* **45**
3821 **MISTER JOLSON 3** [8] 11-8-8 (50) P Doe 12/1: -45040: Al bhd, 17th: qck reapp: see 3821. **0**
3747 **SHADY DEAL 7** [10] 4-8-10 (52) G Baker (5) 14/1: 213400: Al rear, 19th: qck reapp: much btr 2555. **0**
3623 **Cymmeriad O Gymru 13** [1] 5-8-1 (43) R Brisland (5) 50/1:
3694 **Windrush Boy 10** [14] 10-7-10 (38) Joanna Badger (7) 33/1:
3349 **Lydias Look 24** [3] 3-8-9 (52) S Carson (3) 33/1: 3578 **Ecudamah 15** [19] 4-9-2 (58)(bl) T G McLaughlin 33/1:
3578 **Sunset Harbour 15** [13] 7-8-0 (42) G Bardwell 33/1:
19 ran Time 59.9 (3.1) (Middleham Park Racing) D Nicholls Sessay, N.Yorks.

3873

5.20 HORSESMOUTH HCAP DIV 2 3YO+ 0-65 (F) 7f str Good 56 -09 Slow [63]
£2240 £640 £320 3 yo rec 4 lb

3423 **TEE CEE 21** [4] R Guest 3-9-12 (65) S Sanders 10/1: 533431: 3 b f Lion Cavern - Hawayah (Shareef Dancer) Cl-up, led over 2f out, styd on well & rdn out: top-weight, 1st win: consistent mdn form prev: 18,000gns purchase, dam 7f wnr: eff arnd a gall/undul 7f, 1m shld suit in time: fine run conceding weight to elders. **70**
687 **DAVIS ROCK 174** [2] W R Muir 6-8-12 (47) Martin Dwyer 16/1: 101662: 6 ch m Rock City - Sunny Davis *1¾* **48**

CHEPSTOW THURSDAY SEPTEMBER 7TH Lefthand, Undualting, Galloping Track

(Alydar) Mid-div, gd hdwy appr fnl 1f, styd on but not threat to wnr: excellent effort after nr 6 month abs:
entitled to come on for this run & can win again soon: see 601 (AW).

*3242 **FLIGHT OF DREAMS** 29 [13] M Wigham 3-8-2 (41) Paul Eddery 7/2 FAV: -00613: 3 b f College Chapel -   ¾   41
Lady Portobello (Porto Bello) Prom, drvn & not pace of wnr ins last: nicely bckd & remains in gd heart:
acts on fast & gd grnd: see 3242 (mdn h'cap).

3288 **SEA EMPEROR** 27 [12] Mrs G S Rees 3-8-5 (44)(vis) W Supple 14/1: 044304: Front rank, went on   1¾   41
over 2f out, sn hdd, edged left & no extra fnl 1f: stays 7f/1m on gd grnd: see 3082 (1m), 1085.

3765 **FLYING PENNANT** 6 [9] 7-8-9 (44)(bl) J Fanning 14/1: 036305: Rear, styd on well appr fnl 1f,   ¾   39
nrst fin: qck reapp: see 3445, 2427.

3362 **MYTTONS MISTAKE** 24 [8] 7-9-5 (54) G Carter 6/1: 213666: Hdwy from mid-div fnl 2f, not reach ldrs.   ½   48
3218 **CHILWORTH** 29 [17] 3-8-13 (52) R Price 12/1: 200037: Cl-up, wknd over 1f out: btr 3218 (blnkd).   1¼   44
2355 **HALMANERROR** 67 [19] 10-9-8 (57) D Harrison 9/2: 332468: Bhd, prog halfway, drvn/fdd fnl 1f: nk   49
10 wk abs & just sharper for this, likes Chepstow: see 1636, 790.

3750 **MADAME JONES** 7 [7] 5-9-4 (53) A McGlone 25/1: -00509: Prom, rdn/lost tch appr fnl 1f: qck reapp.   nk   44
1979 **TOP BANANA** 83 [6] 9-9-10 (59) Katie Matthews (7) 16/1: 20-000: Handy, fdd fnl 2f, 10th: 12 wk abs.   ¾   48
3753 **KNOBBLEENEEZE** 7 [10] 10-8-9 (44)(vis) M Mathers (7) 11/1: 241600: Nvr a factor: fin 11th, qck   hd   33
reapp: see 3294 (h/h appr h'cap).

3561 **BETTY BATHWICK** 15 [14] 3-8-12 (51) J Stack 33/1: 002-00: Led, hdd over 2f out, wknd qckly, 14th.   0
3771 Bottelino Joe 5 [3] 3-8-11 (50) R Brisland (5) 40/1:   3116 Flamebird 34 [20] 3-9-2 (55) D Sweeney 25/1:
3043 Lago Di Levico 38 [11] 3-8-0 (49) N Pollard 16/1:   3493 Swino 19 [5] 6-8-9 (44)(vis) Joanna Badger (7) 16/1:
1611 An Jolien 99 [18] 3-9-4 (57)(bl) T G McLaughlin 20/1: 2947 Lady Fearless 41 [16] 3-8-6 (45) A Mackay 25/1:
18 ran   Time 1m 24.4 (4.6)   (Matthews Breeding & Racing)   R Guest Newmarket.

DONCASTER THURSDAY SEPTEMBER 7TH Lefthand, Flat, Galloping Track

Official Going: GOOD/FIRM (GOOD Places). Stalls: Str Crse - Stands Side: Rnd Crse - Inside: Rnd Mile - Outside

3874	1.30 LISTED SCARBROUGH STKS 2YO+ (A) 5f Good/Firm 20 -11 Slow

£14508 £4464 £2232 £1116   3 yo rec 1 lb 2 Groups, centre appeared the place to be

+3521 **LORD KINTYRE** 17 [3] B R Millman 5-9-7 M Roberts 4/1: 402111: 5 b g Makbul - Highland Rowena   112
(Royben) Well plcd centre, ran on strongly appr fnl 1f & rdn to lead ins last: lkd superb: hat-trick landed after
wins at Newmarket & Nottingham (cond stks): unplcd both '99 starts, reportedly brk bld vessels & subs gelded:
plcd in '98 (Gr 3, rtd 109): smart juv (rtd 112): acts on firm & hvy grnd, any trk: runs
well fresh, up with/forcing the pace: smart & is in the best form of his life.

*3473 **SEE YOU LATER** 19 [4] Major D N Chappell 3-9-1 K Darley 16/1: 330012: 3 b f Emarati - Rivers   1   103$
Rhapsody (Dominion) Chsd ldr in centre, went on halfway, under press appr fnl 1f & hdd inside last:
op 12/1, looked well: gd run, progressive & useful: see 3473 (rtd h'cap).

3598 **RAMBLING BEAR** 14 [6] M Blanshard 7-9-7 T Quinn 7/1: 300563: 7 ch h Sharood - Supreme Rose   nk   107
(Frimley Park) Prom stands side, kept on for press appr fnl 1f, nvr nrr: looked superb & a gd run
considering raced on what appeared to be a slower strip of grnd: see 1172.

3652 **PERFECT PEACH** 12 [1] C W Fairhurst 5-9-2 P Goode 100/1: 462064: Held up in tch centre,   1¼   98$
chsd ldrs appr fnl 1f, sn onepace: v stiff task, flattered: capable, tho' only 69 rtd h'capper: see 1250.

3569 **TRAVESTY OF LAW** 15 [8] 3-9-6 D R McCabe 66/1: 003255: Chsd ldrs stands side, eff 2f out, not   shd   103$
pace to chall: stocky gelding, flattered & will apprec a return to h'caps: see 1849.

3784 **PERRYSTON VIEW** 5 [7] 8-10-0 J Reid 11/2: 010-506: Led stands side group, hard rdn after halfway,   hd   109
no extra last dist: quick reapp & not disgraced on what may have been a slower strip of grnd: see 1566.

2496 **ASTONISHED** 61 [5] 4-9-10 J Fortune 5/6 FAV: 0-11417: Held up stands side, nvr in it: dull in coat   ½   104
but hvly bckd: worth forgetting, centre was the place to be: wnr of a Deauville Listed race since 2496, see 1849.

3667 **DANCING MAESTRO** 11 [2] 4-9-7 R Hughes 25/1: 006328: Led centre till after halfway, lost place.   4   89
8 ran   Time 59.76 (1.56)   (M Calvert)   B R Millman Kentisbeare, Devon

3875	2.05 GR 3 WHITE ROSE PARK STKS 3YO+ (A) 1m rnd Good/Firm 20 00 Fast

£21000 £8050 £4025 £1925   3 yo rec 5 lb

1171 **DISTANT MUSIC** 124 [2] B W Hills 3-8-9 M Hills 4/1: 11-201: 3 b c Distant View - Musicanti (Nijinsky)   120
(Nijinsky) In tch, prog 3f out, rdn to chall dist, ran on strongly to get on top fnl 100y: tchd 5/1 after 4 mth abs,
lkd v well: has had training probs since disapp 2nd fav in 2,000 Guineas: unbtn juv, won here at Doncaster (2,
mdn & Gr 2) & Newmarket (Gr 1 Dewhurst, rtd 122): eff at 7f/1m: acts on fast & gd grnd, likes gall trks, esp
Doncaster: runs v well fresh & has a fine turn of foot: high-class colt, can hopefully make up for lost time.

3087 **VALENTINO** 36 [5] J H M Gosden 3-8-9 (t) L Dettori 9/4: 4-3202: 3 ch c Nureyev - Divine Danse   nk   119
(Kris) Waited with, gd prog to chall fnl 1f, sn drvn, hung right, held fnl 100y: padd pick: fine run but gives
impression he needs to be produced as late as poss & may be worth trying in h'caps: see 2066 (Gr 1), 1318.

3647 **CAPE TOWN** 17 [1] R Hannon 3-8-9 R Hughes 13/2: 030233: 3 gr c Desert Style - Rossaldene   ¾   117
(Mummy's Pet) Made most till 1f out, kept on: op 9/2, lkd well: ran to best from the front, will find easier Gr 3's.

3132 **SWALLOW FLIGHT** 34 [3] G Wragg 4-9-0 M Roberts 7/4 FAV: 113134: Cl up, ev ch appr fnl 1f, unable   nk   116
to qckn: well bckd: suited by return to 1m but is capable of better, see 2359 (match).

3539 **BARATHEA GUEST** 16 [6] 3-8-13 Craig Williams 10/1: 340555: Chsd ldrs, outpcd appr fnl 1f: lkd well: 5   110
back in trip & grade, could do with some easier grnd: see 950.
5 ran   Time 1m 38.7 (1.6)   (K Abdulla)   B W Hills Lambourn, Berks

3876	2.35 GR 3 MAY HILL STKS 2YO (A) 1m rnd Good/Firm 20 -03 Slow

£24000 £9200 £4600 £2200

*3607 **KARASTA** 13 [11] Sir Michael Stoute 2-8-9 J Murtagh 5/4 FAV: 11: 2 b f Lake Coniston - Karliyka   107+
(Last Tycoon) Towards rear, hdwy appr fnl 2f, led bef dist, idled inside last & drvn, jinked right cl-home: hvly
bckd: recently made an impressive debut at Newmarket (fill mdn): half-sister & dam won over 9f: eff at 7f/1m:
acts on fast & gd: runs well fresh on gall tracks: rangy, potentially high-class filly, shld not be opposed lightly.

*3108 **AMEERAT** 35 [6] M A Jarvis 2-8-9 L Dettori 4/1: 12: 2 b f Mark Of Esteem - Walimu (Top Ville)   1   103+
Bhd ldrs, lost pl 3f out & short of room till bef dist, picked up well for press to chse wnr ins last, held when hmpd
cl-home: well bckd, unlucky? suited by step up to 1m: acts on fast & gd grnd: lengthy, attractive & useful.

1190

DONCASTER

THURSDAY SEPTEMBER 7TH **Lefthand, Flat, Galloping Track**

---

*3678 **CANDICE** 10 [2] E A L Dunlop 2-8-9 J Reid 16/1: 3313: 3 br f Caerleon - Criquette (Shirley Heights) nk 102
Keen, chsd ldrs, rdn to chse wnr appr fnl 1f, onepace towards fin: looked well & a fine run up in grade: useful.

3316 **BRING PLENTY** 26 [3] J H M Gosden 2-8-9 J Fortune 15/2: 01324: Towards rear, eff 3f out, onepace ½ 101
till rdn & kept on well appr fnl 1f, nvr nrr: op 5/1: apprec the step up to 1m: scopey, will get further next term.

3659 **WAKI MUSIC** 11 [4] 2-8-9 T Quinn 10/1: -135: Waited with, rdn & prog to dispute 2nd appr fnl 1f, 1¼ 98
sn onepace: op 8/1: tall, unfurnished filly, prob ran to best up in trip: see 3659, 3074.

3678 **SINGLE HONOUR** 10 [5] 2-8-9 R Hughes 33/1: -5226: Bhd, wide prog to chse ldrs 2f out, held 1¼ 95
bef dist: highly tried mdn but should definitely win back in that grade.

*3308 **ELREHAAN** 26 [1] 2-8-9 R Hills 14/1: 217: Mid-div, eff 2f out, sn hmpd & rdn, no impress: op 10/1: 1 93
not disgraced in this better grade, longer trip: small, attractive filly, apprec mid-dist next term: see 3308.

*3655 **ESYOUEFFCEE** 12 [12] 2-8-9 J Carroll 9/1: 218: Well plcd, chall 2f out, rdn & wknd bef dist: op 7/1: 2 89
edgy in paddock & is capable of better: see 3655.

*3704 **PERFECT PLUM** 10 [9] 2-8-9 G Duffield 14/1: 523219: Prom, led halfway till ent fnl 2f, sn btn: hd 89
op 10/1: stiff task after 3704 (nursery).

*3661 **THERES TWO** 11 [7] 2-8-9 Craig Williams 25/1: -310: Mid div, rdn to chse wnr briefly appr fnl nk 88
2f, wknd: 10th: tall, unfurnished filly, up in trip & grade: see 3661.

3596 **AMIS ANGEL** 14 [8] 2-8-9 T E Durcan 66/1: 2160: Led till halfway, lost pl: 11th, lngr trip, highly tried. 15 63

2344 **JELBA** 68 [10] 2-8-9 Pat Eddery 25/1: 5350: Al bhd: 12th: attractive, scopey filly but outclassed here. 4 55
12 ran   Time 1m 37.95 (1.85)   (H H Aga Khan)   Sir Michael Stoute Newmarket, Suffolk

---

3877

3.10 GR 3 DONCASTER CUP STKS 3YO+ (A)   2m2f   Good/Firm 20   +18 Fast
£24000   £9200   £4600   £2200

2114 **ENZELI** 77 [7] J Oxx 5-9-7 (BL) J Murtagh 15/2: 14-201: 5 b h Kahyasi - Ebaziya (Darshaan) 120
Trckd ldrs, led ent fnl 2f, sn rdn & edged left, hdd below dist, rallied gamely to regain lead fnl strides: fast
time, 11 wk abs, sharpened up by blnks: '99 wnr at Leopardstown (Listed) & R Ascot (Gr 1 Gold Cup, rtd 121):
eff between 14f & 2m4f: acts on hard, hvy grnd, likes stiff/gall tracks: high class & genuine stayer.

*3751 **CHURLISH CHARM** 7 [5] R Hannon 5-9-0 J Reid 7/1: 323612: 5 b h Niniski - Blushing Storm nk 113
(Blushing Groom)Towards rear, hdwy ent fnl 3f, rdn 2f out, sn carried left, led ent fnl 1f, hdd cl home:
drifter from 7/2, clr rem, quick reapp: clearly stys 2m2f & this was a smart run on grnd faster than ideal.

*3552 **PERSIAN PUNCH** 18 [3] D R C Elsworth 7-9-5 T Quinn 8/1: 016513: 7 ch g Persian Heights - Rum Cay 3 115
(Our Native) Made most till appr fnl 1f, same pace: op 6/1: lkd superb: fine run tho' ideally suited by 2m.

3538 **RAINBOW HIGH** 16 [8] B W Hills 5-9-3 M Hills 3/1 FAV: 1-5424: Held up, clsd to trk ldrs ent fnl 3f, shd 113
rdn bef dist, no impress: well bckd, clr rem: rnr-up in this last year (rtd 114): becoming frustrating: see 1222.

3552 **THREE CHEERS** 18 [1] L Dettori 14/1: -12035: Chsd ldrs, drvn & edged left appr fnl 5 105
2f, fdd bef dist: stiffish task for this quirky customer, see 2153, 1897.

3106 **SAN SEBASTIAN** 35 [4] 6-9-0 (bl) Pat Eddery 10/3: -46436: In tch, niggled appr straight, sn btn: 5 101
much better than this & prob suited by easier grnd: had this 2nd 3rd & 4th in arrears in 3106 (gd), see 1109.

3302 **EILEAN SHONA** 26 [9] 4-8-11 R Hughes 12/1: -05457: Held up, eff 4f out, wknd: stiff task, see 1222. 1 97

3538 **SPIRIT OF LOVE** 16 [6] 5-9-0 D Holland 14/1: 303248: Prom, led halfway till 6f out, fdd ent str. 10 92

*3302 **DOMINANT DUCHESS** 26 [2] 6-8-11 R Hills 11/1: 2-1119: Al bhd: boiled over in paddock, stiffish task. 9 82
9 ran   Time 3m 52.9 (0.4)   (H H Aga Khan)   J Oxx Curragbeg, Co Kildare

---

3878

3.40 LISTED SCEPTRE STKS 3YO+ (A)   7f str   Good/Firm 20   -24 Slow
£15151   £4662   £2331   £1165   3yo rec 4 lb

3727 **KALINDI** 8 [13] M R Channon 3-8-6 A Culhane 25/1: -00601: 3 ch f Efisio - Rohita (Waajib) 104
Waited with, qcknd smartly appr fnl 1f & rdn to lead below dist, ran on strongly: '99 wnr at R Ascot (stks, rtd 98):
prev eff at 5f, suited by step up to 7f: acts on fast grnd, stiff/gall tracks: v useful & has a fine turn of foot.

-3763 **VEIL OF AVALON** 6 [7] R Charlton 3-8-6 K Darley 4/1: 621622: 3 b f Thunder Gulch - Wind In Her 1¼ 101
Hair (Alzao) Chsd ldrs, rdn appr fnl 1f, kept on to take 2nd nr fin but no ch wnr: bckd, quick reapp:
progressive, useful, workmanlike filly, should apprec 1m: see 3155.

3600 **LAST RESORT** 14 [3] B W Hills 3-8-6 M Hills 7/1: 136343: 3 ch f Lahib - Breadcrumb (Final hd 100
Straw) In tch, smooth hdwy to lead appr fnl 1f, rdn & hdd inside last, onepace: tchd 9/1: consistent, useful
has plenty of toe & may do even better back at 6f: see 3600, 1224.

3469 **CAYMAN SUNSET** 19 [11] E A L Dunlop 3-8-6 T Quinn 20/1: 164: Towards rear, progress appr fnl 1f, shd 100
chsd ldrs dist, same pace under hands & heels: looked well: useful filly, apprec drop back to 7f: acts on
fast & gd/soft grnd: jockey given 3 day ban for irresponsible riding: see 2585.

3643 **MIDNIGHT ALLURE** 12 [1] 3-8-6 (t) R Mullen 50/1: 162345: Held up, prog appr fnl 1f, styd on for nk 99$
press, nvr nrr: op 33/1: surely flattered tho' looked superb: strong filly, win again back in h'cap: see 1873.

3750 **RENDITION** 7 [12] F Norton 14/1: 113036: Mid div, travelled well, clsd 2f out, rdn & squeezed 1¼ 96$
for room appr fnl 1f, no extra: lkd well, qk reapp, stiff task, flattered: worth another look in h'caps: see 2003, 1308.

3610 **LITTLEFEATHER** 13 [8] 3-8-6 G Duffield 3/1: -51027: Held up, prog when short of room appr fnl 1f, 1¼ 93
no further hdwy: well bckd, tchd 4/1, v fit: see 3610, 3120.

3104 **FLAVIAN** 35 [2] 4-8-10 C Rutter 20/1: -00108: Prom, led 2f out, hdd bef dist, rdn & btn: awash with sweat. 2 89

3301 **ICICLE** 26 [5] 3-8-6 Pat Eddery 9/4 FAV: -03549: Chsd ldrs, rdn bef dist, wknd: hvly bckd, nvr her form. nk 88

3104 **VERBOSE** 35 [6] 3-8-6 J Fortune 16/1: -12500: Al towards rear: 10th: tchd 20/1, return to 1m will suit. 3½ 82

3510 **CANTINA** 18 [10] 6-8-10 J Carroll 20/1: 311100: Led till 2f out, wknd quickly: 11th, stiff task, see 3427. ½ 81
11 ran   Time 1m 26.28 (3.08)   (Barry Taylor)   M R Channon West Isley, Berks

---

3879

4.10 PRINCE OF WALES NURSERY HCAP 2YO (B)   1m str   Good/Firm 20   -38 Slow   [99]
£15015   £4620   £2310   £1155

3523 **SNOWSTORM** 17 [5] M L W Bell 2-9-7 (92) J Mackay (5) 5/1 FAV: 26121: 2 gr c Environment Friend - 97
Choral Sundown (Night Shift) Early ldr, sent on again 2f out, rdn out nr fin: nicely bckd, lkd well, defied
top-weight: earlier won at Ayr (mdn): eff at 7f, suited by 1m now: acts on firm & gd grnd, stiff/gall trks:
best up with/forcing the pace: Gr 1 entry may be aiming too high tho' is certainly worth a try in Listed: useful.

3609 **NORTHFIELDS DANCER** 13 [7] R Hannon 2-9-4 (89) R Hughes 7/1: 022022: 2 ch c Dr Devious - ½ 92
Heartland (Northfields) Off the pace, improved going well 2f out, ran on to chse wnr inside last, not btn far:
sturdy, improving colt, set a lot to do (again): shld shed mdn tag soon: see 3609.

*3601 **SPECIFIC SORCEROR** 13 [13] A P Jarvis 2-9-3 (88) N Callan 9/1: 5113: 2 ch c Definite Article - shd 91
Mystic Dispute (Magical Strike) Trckd ldrs, drvn ent fnl 2f, kept on well towards fin: btn less than 1L, op 7/1:
sound h'cap bow, jockey given 2 day whip ban: scopey filly, type to improve further next term over 10f: see 3601.

DONCASTER
THURSDAY SEPTEMBER 7TH   Lefthand, Flat, Galloping Track

3766 **TOTALLY COMMITTED** 6 [1] R Hannon 2-8-3 (74) L Newman (3) 33/1: 323604: Mid-div, prog on outer 2f out, went 2nd briefly ent fnl 1f, onepace for press: lkd well, stablemate 2nd: gets 1m, return to 7f may suit.   ½   76

3542 **PEREGIAN** 16 [9] D Holland 9/1: 111035: Trkd ldrs, rdn appr fnl 1f, unable to qckn: stays 1m.   1½   88

3015 **BLACK KNIGHT** 39 [4] 2-9-3 (88) L Dettori 6/1: -31166: Led after 2f till 2f out, fdd fnl 1f: well bckd: 6 week abs, h'cap bow, slightly longer trip: strong colt, poss unsuited forcing the pace: see 2514.   ¾   85+

3680 **MONSIEUR LE BLANC** 10 [8] 2-8-11 (82)(BL) M Roberts 14/1: -63567: Keen towards rear, hdwy appr fnl 2f, hmpd bef dist, held when not clr run/eased ins last: lkd v well, blnkd, h'cap bow: looks capable of better.   ½   78

3690 **LONER** 10 [3] 2-8-9 (80) F Norton 14/1: 462158: Al mid-div: longer trip: btr 3660 (gd grnd).   1¾   72

*3592 **LADY BEAR** 14 [2] 2-8-3 (72)(vis)(2ow) G Duffield 12/1: 334419: Pulled hard & well plcd till wknd ent fnl 2f: tchd 16/1: longer trip & found this tougher than 3592 (Musselburgh).   shd   66

3412 **BARAKANA** 21 [12] 2-8-8 (82)(h) Pat Eddery 20/1: 326350: Nvr trbld ldrs: 10th: see 2894 (led)   1   69

*3411 **PASITHEA** 21 [10] 2-8-3 (74) K Darley 10/1: 453310: Al towards rear: 11th: op 8/1, longer trip.   4   56

3568 **FRUIT PUNCH** 15 [6] 2-7-13 (70) P Fessey 6/1: 5500: In tch till appr fnl 1f: 12th, bckd on h'cap bow: unsuited by step up to 1m?: see 3020.   hd   52

3542 **VISITATION** 16 [14] 2-7-10 (67)(2oh) K Dalgleish (5) 25/1: -01200: Mid-div, outpcd 3f out: 13th, see 2949.   3½   43

3704 **NOBLE DOBLE** 10 [16] 2-8-6 (77) M Hills 12/1: 452340: Al bhd: 14th, stocky colt, see 2430.   nk   52

3577 **SWANTON ABBOT** 15 [15] 2-8-3 (74) A Beech (5) 20/1: 0050: Chsd ldrs till halfway: 15th, h'cap bow.   ½   48

15 ran   Time 1m 41.16 (4.66)   (Lord Blyth)   M L W Bell Newmarket, Suffolk

---

3880   4.40 FREE PRESS HCAP 3YO+ 0-90 (C)   7f str   Good/Firm 20   -29 Slow   [90]
£7605   £2340   £1170   £585   3 yo rec 4 lb

3612 **NORFOLK REED** 13 [21] R Hannon 3-8-13 (79)(vis) L Newman (3) 25/1: 000031: 3 b g Thatching - Sawaki (Song) Towards rear, prog after halfway, hdwy to lead 2f out, 2L clr dist, rdn out: unlucky in running last time: '99 debut wnr at Lingfield (nov stakes, nursery rnr up, rtd 90): eff at 6f, suited by 7f: acts on firm & gd grnd, any track: can go well fresh: poss best visored now: gd ride by L Newman & looks nicely h'capped.   83

2495 **PEACOCK ALLEY** 55 [19] W J Haggas 3-9-6 (88) M Hills 10/1: 111362: 3 gr f Salse - Tagiki (Doyoun) Off the pace, gd progress appr fnl 1f, ran on strongly inside last, too late: set a lot to do after 8 week abs: attractive filly, continues to go the right way: will apprec more positive tactics: see 555.   ½   91

*3831 **ARPEGGIO** 2 [3] D Nicholls 5-8-13 (75)(6ex) J Weaver 4/1 FAV: 410313: 5 b g Polar Falcon - Hilly (Town Crier) Mid-div, hdwy appr fnl 1f, kept on, held nr fin: well bckd from 8/1, qck reapp: gd run with a pen.   ½   77

3708 **SUPREME SALUTATION** 10 [22] T D Barron 4-8-10 (72) T E Durcan 16/1: 035534: Last till halfway, prog & not much room ent fnl 2f, styd on stdly under hands & heels: on toes: hard to win with, see 3708, 1011.   hd   74

3758 **ZUCCHERO** 7 [4] 4-9-4 (80) R Hills 20/1: -61655: Early ldr, again appr fnl 2f till bef dist, onepace well inside last: quick reapp & back to form with blinks omitted: see 2814.   ½   81

3384 **TOPTON** 22 [17] 6-8-13 (75)(bl) J Quinn 16/1: 235106: Mid-div, shaken up 2f out, not much room bef dist, ran on for press inside last, nvr nrr: tchd 20/1: back to form at fav track: see 2899.   nk   75

-3758 **VOLONTIERS** 7 [14] 5-9-8 (84) T Quinn 7/1: 220027: Trckd ldrs going well, boxed in throughout fnl 2f, position accepted fnl 100y: tchd 10/1, qk reapp: forget, must have gone cl with a clr run: see 3758, 1160.   ½   83+

3758 **DILKUSHA** 7 [9] 5-9-0 (76) Pat Eddery 16/1: 043548: Bhd, eff & short of room 2f out, switched & kept on well inside last, nvr dangerous: poss best forgotten & could be worth another try at 1m: see 1989.   1½   72

2869 **PAYS DAMOUR** 46 [12] 3-9-5 (85) R Hughes 16/1: 012139: Cl up & ev ch till fdd bef fnl 1f, eased towards fin: tchd 20/1: stablemate wnr: sharper next time after 7 week abs: see 2792.   ½   80

3785 **BOLDLY GOES** 5 [1] 4-9-10 (86)(bl) T Williams 12/1: 060140: Chsd ldrs wide till dist: 10th.   ½   80

3597 **PREMIER BARON** 14 [8] 5-9-9 (85) J Mackay (5) 11/1: 446100: Travelled well in rear, short of room appr fnl 1f, nvr a factor: 11th, bckd from 16/1: well worth another chance, see 3315.   shd   79

*3404 **CHINA RED** 22 [10] 6-9-2 (78) K Darley 16/1: 000010: Chsd ldrs, wknd bef fnl 1f: 12th, new stable.   hd   71

3481 **EMERGING MARKET** 19 [7] 8-9-8 (84) J Reid 16/1: 005200: Nvr better than mid div: 13th: see 728.   shd   77

2614 **LOCHARATI** 56 [2] 3-9-2 (82) J Tate 33/1: 102000: Held up, mod hdwy appr fnl 1f, nvr dngrs: 14th.   1¼   72

*3666 **BRANSTON FIZZ** 11 [13] 3-8-9 (75) D Holland 7/1: 001010: In tch, badly outpcd halfway, late rally: 15th: had a real 'Flat spot' mid-race, capable of much better: see 3666.   nk   64

3514 **BARABASCHI** 18 [11] 4-8-12 (74) J Fortune 14/1: 226120: Led after 2f till appr fnl 2f, sn btn: 16th, sweating, bck in trip: see 3514, 3139.   shd   63

3785 **MISTER MAL** 5 [15] 4-9-1 (77) G Duffield 10/1: 001020: Sn in rear: 21st, bckd tho' op 6/1, qk reapp: reportedly unruly in stalls & will have to pass a test before running again: see 3785, 3250.   0

3708 **Mantles Pride** 10 [18] 5-9-4 (80)(bl) J Carroll 20/1:   3464 **Alastair Smellie** 19 [16] 4-8-11 (73) Iona Wands 16/1: 3597 **Al Muallim** 14 [20] 6-10-0 (90)(t) Alex Greaves 16/1: 3543 **Pips Magic** 16 [5] 4-9-7 (83) A Culhane 14/1:

21 ran   Time 1m 26.64 (3.44)   (The South Western Partnership)   R Hannon East Everleigh, Wilts

---

GOODWOOD
FRIDAY SEPTEMBER 8TH   Righthand, Sharpish, Undulating Track

Official Going: GOOD Stalls: Straight Course - Stands Side, Round Course - Inside, 12f - Outside

3881   2.15 EBF HARVEST MDN 2YO (D)   6f   Good 55   -01 Slow
£4927   £1516   £758   £379

3044 **APPELLATION** 39 [6] R Hannon 2-9-0 L Newman (3) 8/1: -641: 2 b c Clantime - Chablisse (Radetzky) Trkd ldrs, led over 2f out, styd on well inside last, rdn out: bckd from 12/1: apprec step up to 6f, 7f will suit: acts on fast & gd grnd: likes a sharp/undul trk: has reportedly been sick, making up for lost time now: useful, progressive colt who shld win in Listed company this autumn.   95+

-- **AJWAA** [9] M P Tregoning 2-9-0 W Supple 14/1: 2: 2 ch c Mujtahid - Nouvelle Star (Luskin Star) Trkd ldrs, rdn/ch over 1f out, kept on, not pace of wnr: ran green, op 8/1: March foal, brother to tough/useful sprinter Juwwi: dam a high class wnr at 5f-1m: eff at 6f, 7f should suit: handles gd grnd: encouraging intro.   2   87+

1856 **RASHAS REALM** 89 [4] J L Dunlop 2-8-9 T Quinn 4/1: 23: 2 ch f Woodman - Performing Arts (The Minstrel) Trkd ldrs halfway, styd on fnl 1f: 12 wk abs: acts on firm & gd: step up to 7f will suit.   nk   81

3484 **TAKE ANOTHER BOW** 20 [10] J H M Gosden 2-9-0 R Havlin 10/1: -34: Cl up halfway, onepace over 1f out: op 8/1: return to 7f+ should suit: handles fast & gd grnd: see 3484.   ¾   84

-- **NAJ DE** [1] 2-9-0 J P Spencer 7/4 FAV: 5: Trckd ldrs halfway, held over 1f out: hvly bckd, debut: Zafonic colt, April foal: half brother to 5f Gr 3 juv wnr Dance Parade: dam a 9f 2yo wnr: P Cole newcomer, holds big race entries & better clearly expected.   1   82

3492 **KIRTHAR** 20 [7] 2-9-0 G Hind 6/1: 26: Prom, ch 2f out, sn no extra: op 4/1: see 3492.   shd   82

3576 **UNPARALLELED 16** [5] 2-8-9 Martin Dwyer 14/1: 227: Led till over 2f out, sn held: see 3047. *4* **67**
-- **POLICASTRO** [11] 2-9-0 O Peslier 20/1: 8: Rcd alone towards centre from halfway, btn/eased 1f out: jockey reported colt hung right throughout: Anabaa colt, April foal, 25,000gns 2yo: dam a 10f wnr: with J W Hills. *3* **65**
-- **PULSE** [2] 2-9-0 S Sanders 20/1: 9: Slowly away/rear, mod late gains under tender handling: op 14/1, longer priced stablemate of wnr: Salse colt, Feb foal, cost 10,500gns: half brother to 2 6f wnrs: shld improve. *2* **60+**
3649 **SHARED HARMONY 13** [3] 2-9-0 P Doe 40/1: 60: Sn outpcd/bhd: 10th: btr 3649. *7* **43**
3187 **LADY IN THE NIGHT 32** [12] 2-8-9 J Fanning 50/1: 400: Al bhd: 11th: btr 2227 (5f). *shd* **38**
-- **KOORI** [8] 2-8-9 O Urbina 50/1: 0: Sn struggling: 12th: cheaply bought first foal, dam unrcd. *14* **10**
12 ran Time 1m 13.36 (3.36) (Noodles Racing) R Hannon East Everleigh, Wilts

3882

2.45 LISTED BELLWAY STARDOM STKS 2YO (A) 1m rnd Good 55 +04 Fast
£12902 £3970 £1985 £992

*3164 **ATLANTIS PRINCE 34** [7] S P C Woods 2-8-11 O Peslier 6/1: 111: 2 ch c Tagula - Zoom Lens (Caerleon) Trkd ldrs, rdn over 2f out, styd on well to lead well ins last: best time of day, op 9/2: earlier won at Epsom (auct mdn) & Newmarket (stks): eff at 7f, apprec this step up to 1m, mid-dists may suit: acts on fast & gd: handles a stiff/gall or sharp/undul trk: runs well fresh: smart colt, just the type for the Royal Lodge. **105**
3659 **CHAGUARAMAS 12** [1] R Hannon 2-8-6 J Quinn 25/1: -11542: 2 b f Mujadil - Sabaniya (Lashkari) Rear/in tch, keen early, rdn/hdwy fnl 2f, briefly led ins last, hdd nr fin, just held: appreciated this step up to 1m: acts on firm & gd grnd: useful filly: see 2940. *nk* **98**
2848 **MARINE 48** [5] R Charlton 2-8-11 (BL) Paul Eddery 12/1: 511553: 2 b c Marju - Ivorine (Blushing Groom) Dwelt, swtchd & drvn/styd on well fnl 1f, just held: first time blnks, 7 wk abs: stayed longer 1m trip. *hd* **102**
*3237 **LONDONER 30** [3] H R A Cecil 2-8-11 T Quinn 5/1: 114: Led rdn/hdd ins last, kept on, just held nr fin: nicely bckd: styd longer 1m trip well: fine front running effort on this step up in grade. *hd* **101**
*3154 **ARCHDUKE FERDINAND 20** [6] 2-8-11 W Supple 7/1: -0155: Trkd ldrs, rdn/outpcd over 2f out, kept on: stays an easy 1m, will get further: 5th in a Deauville Listed event since 3154. *1¼* **98**
3304 **VICIOUS KNIGHT 27** [2] 2-8-11 J P Spencer 10/11 FAV: -6126: Chsd ldrs, smooth prog to chall 2f out, sn hard rdn & no extra: hvly bckd: travelled much the best in the race for a long way & connections suggested colt may need a faster surface: stayed 1m in 3304. *2½* **93**
3086 **ECOLOGY 37** [4] 2-8-11 G Carter 10/1: 211107: Trkd ldrs, btn 2f out: op 8/1: btr 2576 (7f). *½* **92**
2935 **CELTIC ISLAND 43** [8] 2-8-6 A Daly 16/1: 220148: Held up in tch, btn 2f out: abs: btr 2935 (7f). *1¼* **84**
8 ran Time 1m 41.46 (4.06) (Lucayan Stud) S P C Woods Newmarket

3883

3.15 DARNLEY HCAP 3YO+ 0-100 (C) 1m1f rnd Good 55 -16 Slow **[100]**
£12285 £3780 £1890 £945 3 yo rec 6 lb

3563 **PANTAR 16** [7] I A Balding 5-9-7 (93) O Peslier 11/1: 002361: 5 b g Shirley Heights - Spring Daffodil (Pharly) Mid div, hdwy fnl 2f to lead ins last, styd on well under hands & heels riding: earlier won at W'hampton (AW stks, rtd 92a): plcd form in '99 (rtd 102, h'cap): '98 Goodwood wnr (val h'cap, rtd 102 at best): eff btwn 1m/10f on firm, soft & f/sand: handles any trk, likes Goodwood: eff with/without blnks: gd weight carrier: prev frustrating, but looks fairly h'capped & could go well under a 5lb pen in the Cambridgeshire. **99**
3642 **WELSH WIND 13** [14] D J Murphy 4-9-4 (90) M Tebbutt 8/1: 220422: 4 b g Tenby - Bavaria (Top Ville) Trkd ldrs, drvn & ev ch 1f out, kept on well: tchd 14/1: see 3325, 1262 & 851. *½* **93**
3793 **CHAPEL ROYALE 6** [6] K Mahdi 3-8-3 (81) B Marcus 33/1: 310003: 3 gr c College Chapel - Merci Royale (Fairy King) Towards rear, hdwy over 2f out, rdn/ch over 1f out, no extra: quick reapp: see 2614. *1¼* **81**
3644 **STOPPES BROW 13** [13] G L Moore 8-7-12 (70)(bl) G Baker (5) 9/1: 256344: Mid div, no room over 2f out, styd on ins last, not rch ldrs: prob plcd with a clr run: nicely h'capped, keep in mind for similar: see 662. *shd* **70+**
*3471 **POLISH SPIRIT 20** [10] 5-8-12 (84) J P Spencer 9/2: 306015: Mid div, no room over 2f out, hdwy over 1f out, sn onepace: bckd: see 3471 (10f). *¾* **83**
3642 **LITTLE AMIN 13** [1] 4-8-5 (77) Martin Dwyer 20/1: 163266: Chsd ldr over 2f out, fdd fnl 1f: see 2304. *nk* **75**
3597 **FREE OPTION 15** [8] 5-9-10 (96) W Supple 11/1: 310367: Rear, hdwy/no room over 2f out, late gains when no room inside last: op 8/1, top-weight: not much luck: see 3597, 2870. *½* **93**
3563 **PRAIRIE WOLF 16** [3] 4-9-5 (91) P Doe 16/1: 340208: Rear, hdwy/no room over 2f out, late gains, no threat: closer without traffic problems, prob worth another look: see 3060, 1797. *¾* **87**
3642 **PARISIEN STAR 13** [15] 4-9-1 (87) J Quinn 6/1: 451248: Rear, eff/no room over 2f out, mod late gains from over 1f out: ddhtd for 8th: another to encounter trouble in running: see 3107, 3063. *dht* **83**
*3857 **RIBERAC 2** [4] 4-8-12 (84)(5ex) J Fanning 5/2 FAV: 110110: Keen, led till rdn/hdd ins last, fdd: fin 10th: hvly bckd under a 5lbs pen: qck reapp & has been v busy of late: jockey reported he would have liked a lead & his mount rcd too freely: prev in great heart tho' may need a break now: see 3857. *1¼* **77**
3642 **ADOBE 13** [16] 5-8-10 (82) T G McLaughlin 14/1: 211050: Bhd, mod gains fnl 2f: 11th: op 12/1. *5* **65**
3563 **Tactful Remark 16** [12] 4-9-4 (90) S W Kelly (3) 25/1 3339 **J R Stevenson 26** [2] 4-9-3 (89)(vis) Alex Greaves 14/1:
3178 **Sabreon 33** [5] 3-8-7 (85) T Quinn 16/1: 3325 **Smooth Sailing 27** [9] 5-8-10 (82) J Lowe 25/1:
15 ran Time 1m 56.86 (6.36) (Robert Hitchins) I A Balding Kingsclere, Hants

3884

3.45 SOUTHERNPRINT COND STKS 3YO+ (C) 7f rnd Good 55 +02 Fast
£6322 £2398 £1199 £545 3 yo rec 4 lb

3646 **BLUE MOUNTAIN 13** [4] R F Johnson Houghton 3-8-12 R Mullen 5/1: 110201: 3 ch c Elmaamul - Glenfinlass (Lomond) Mid div, hdwy over 2f out, drvn/led inside last, styd on well: gd time: earlier won h'caps at Kempton & here at Goodwood: plcd on 2 of 3 juv starts last term (rtd 89, mdns): eff at 5f, suited by 6/7f on firm, gd/soft & any track, likes a sharp/easy one: useful/progressive colt with a turn of foot. **99**
-3682 **WELCOME FRIEND 11** [1] R Charlton 3-9-1 J P Spencer 4/1: 122: 3 b c Kingmambo - Kingscote (King's Lake) Mid div, prog to chall inside last, styd on well, al just held: op 5/1: acts on firm & gd grnd: improved run from this useful, but lightly rcd colt, should win more races: see 3682 (stks). *¾* **100**
3600 **MEADAAAR 15** [8] J L Dunlop 3-8-12 Paul Eddery 9/2: 3-0253: 3 ch c Diesis - Katiba (Gulch) Led, rdn/hdd inside last & no extra: op 3/1: form pick at today's weights: see 2578, 1693. *2* **93**
*2543 **VARIETY SHOP 60** [6] H R A Cecil 4-9-0 T Quinn 6/1: 2-14: Trkd ldrs, kept on onepace from over 1f out: clr of rem, 2 month abs: not disgraced on this step up in grade: acts on gd & hvy: return to 1m+ shld suit. *¾* **90**
2809 **GRANNYS PET 49** [2] 6-9-7 G Carter 13/2: -31605: Held up rear, hdwy over 2f out, sn held: 7 wk abs. *6* **85**
2616 **EXEAT 57** [3] 4-9-2 Alex Greaves 10/1: 3-2006: Rear, eff over 2f out, little hdwy: op 8/1, 8 wk abs: prev with J H M Gosden, now with D Nicholls: see 1489. *1¼* **77**
+3682 **SIR EFFENDI 11** [5] 4-9-7 W Supple 3/1 FAV: 2-2017: Trckd ldr, rdn/wknd quickly over 1f out: hvly bckd: disapp here after beating today's rnr-up on fast grnd in 3682. *¾* **81**

3753 **SCISSOR RIDGE 8** [7] 8-9-2 R Brisland (5) 200/1: 050508: Strugg 3f out: stiff task: see 3753. *2½* **71$**
8 ran Time 1m 28.22 (3.72) (Mrs C J Hue Williams) R F Johnson Houghton Blewbury, Oxon

3885 **4.20 TILNEY HCAP 3YO+ 0-70 (E) 1m rnd Good 55 -04 Slow [67]**
£5245 £1614 £807 £403 3 yo rec 5 lb

2367 **SILVERTOWN 67** [4] B J Curley 5-9-5 (58) J P Spencer 3/1 FAV: 110021: 5 b g Danehill - Docklands (Theatrical) Al prom, smooth prog to lead 3f out, asserted under hands & heels riding fnl 1f: gamble from 8/1, 10 wk abs: earlier scored at W'hampton & Lingfield (AW h'caps, rtd 73a): '99 scorer at Epsom & York (h'caps, rtd 56): suited by 1m/10f, stays 11.5f: acts on firm, gd/soft & both AWs: likes to race with/force the pace & runs well fresh: looks nicely h'capped on turf, could win again on this evidence. **68**
3495 **ONE DINAR 20** [13] K Mahdi 5-9-7 (60) B Marcus 10/1: 036032: 5 b h Generous - Lypharitissima (Lightning) Towards rear, rdn & styd on well from over 2f out, al held by wnr: op 8/1: see 580. *2* **64**
3753 **THIHN 8** [9] J L Spearing 5-8-8 (47) A Beech (5) 4/1: 360023: 5 ch g Machiavellian - Hasana (Private Account) Trkd ldrs 3f out, no room over 1f out till ins last, fin well: prob 2nd with a clr run, no luck here: however, still a mdn after 16 starts: see 3753. *½* **50**
1822 **BOLD RAIDER 91** [5] I A Balding 3-9-9 (67) J Fanning 6/1: 0-1234: Trkd ldrs, styd on onepace fnl 1f: 3 month abs: likes to front run: see 1822, 1671 & 1024 (hvy). *shd* **70**
*3527 **MUTABASSIR 18** [10] 6-9-12 (65) I Mongan (5) 15/2: 302515: Chsd wnr over 2f out, sn held: op 6/1. *1¼* **65**
*3756 **LAKOTA BRAVE 8** [22] 6-9-9 (62)(t)(5ex) Martin Dwyer 10/1: 0/6416: Prom, rdn/held fnl 2f: op 7/1: rcd too keenly & reportedly saw too much daylight: see 3756 (AW). *1½* **59**
3736 **COLONEL NORTH 9** [2] 4-9-3 (56) D O'Donohoe 20/1: 655457: Mid div/wide, nvr pace to threaten. *1¼* **50**
3524 **HADLEIGH 18** [18] 4-9-7 (60)(vis) J Quinn 14/1: 000208: Trkd ldrs, fdd fnl 2f: btr 3234 (clmr, 10f). *nk* **53**
3031 **BOBBYDAZZLE 39** [12] 5-8-13 (52) O Urbina 16/1: 440349: Mid div, hdwy over 2f out, sn no prog. *¾* **44**
854 **HIGHLY PLEASED 151** [3] 5-9-5 (58) D R McCabe 40/1: 006-00: Slowly away, towards rear, stdy late gains under minimal press fnl 2f, no threat to ldrs: 10th: 5 month abs: stewards enquired into run, jockey reported gelding lost his action: unplcd last term (rtd 65, appr h'cap): plcd in mdns in '98 (rtd 75, J Dunlop): eff at 7f/1m on firm & gd grnd: caught the eye under a kind ride here, but remains a mdn. *hd* **49+**
3685 **COMMON CONSENT 11** [8] 4-9-3 (56) T Quinn 16/1: 042060: Towards rear, hdwy over 2f out, sn no prog: 11th: see 3422, 3089 &2296 (10f). *nk* **46**
3737 **SAMMYS SHUFFLE 9** [17] 5-8-9 (48)(bl) R Mullen 16/1: 123500: Held up, efft 3f out, sn held: 12th. *½* **37**
3217 **MAGIC SYMBOL 30** [7] 3-8-11 (55)(VIS) N Pollard 25/1: -00560: Mid div, bmpd over 2f out, sn btn: 13th. **0**
3758 **STAND BY 8** [14] 3-9-0 (58) G Baker (5) 40/1: 5-3300: Led 5f, wknd quickly: 20th: btr 331, 257 (AW, 6/7f). **0**
1926 **Catamaran 86** [15] 5-10-0 (67)(BL) F Lynch 20/1:
3753 **Barrys Double 8** [20] 3-8-11 (55) P McCabe 33/1:
3045 **Salva 39** [16] 4-9-7 (60)(BL) S Sanders 16/1:
3362 **Purple Flame 25** [11] 4-8-12 (51) Paul Eddery 16/1:
-- **Kildare Chiller** [19] 6-9-2 (55) G Carter 20/1:
3289 **Adrift 28** [21] 3-9-4 (62) W Supple 14/1:
2811 **Ribbon Lake 49** [6] 3-8-11 (55) L Newman (3) 20/1:
21 ran Time 1m 42.13 (4.73) (Mrs B J Curley) B J Curley Newmarket, Suffolk

3886 **4.50 DRAYTON NURSERY HCAP 2YO 0-85 (D) 6f Good 55 -02 Slow [92]**
£4446 £1368 £684 £171 Raced centre - stands side, low no's appeared favoured.

*3761 **DELTA SONG 7** [2] G L Moore 2-9-3 (81)(7ex) I Mongan (5) 5/1: -1211: 2 b f Delta Dancer - Song Of Gold (Song) Trckd ldrs, rdn/led over 1f out, held on well nr fin, rdn out: 7lb pen: earlier won at Lingfield (debut, fill sell, W Muir) & Epsom (nursery h'cap): eff at 6f, 7f cld suit: acts on firm & gd grnd: likes to run up with the pace on a sharp trk: lightly rcd & progressive filly: battled well here & looks sure to win more races. **89**
3761 **SOLDIER ON 7** [4] M R Channon 2-9-1 (79) T Quinn 5/2 FAV: 013522: 2 b g General Monash - Golden Form (Formidable) Held up in tch, prog halfway & ev ch fnl 1f, styd on well, just held: hvly bckd from 4/1: again just bhd today's wnr in 3761: deserves to go one better in similar. *nk* **86**
3542 **LUNAR LEO 17** [1] S C Williams 2-9-7 (85) G Faulkner (3) 9/1: -41363: 2 b g Muhtarram - Moon Mistress (Storm Cat) Led till over 1f out, rdn/held ins last: fair run under top-weight: see 2459 (auct mdn). *2½* **85**
3542 **TROJAN PRINCE 17** [12] B W Hills 2-7-13 (63) N Pollard 10/1: 025604: Prom travelling well centre, ev ch dist, sn onepcd: ddhtd for 4th: apprec drop back to 6f, rcd much too keenly over 7f prev: tricky high draw. *1¾* **59**
3712 **FACE D FACTS 10** [7] 2-8-10 (74) R Mullen 7/1: 513024: Dwelt, held up in tch, hdwy 2f out, onepace/ held inside last: ddhtd for 4th: see 3712, 2214. *dht* **70**
3673 **COZZIE 12** [9] 2-7-10 (60)(1oh) G Baker (5) 14/1: 166146: Prom 4f, fdd fnl 1f: btr 3394 (5f). *1¾* **52**
3508 **FOLLOW YOUR STAR 19** [15] 2-9-4 (82) A Beech (5) 25/1: 6607: Prom, ch over 1f out, fdd. *hd* **73**
3520 **RAMBLIN MAN 18** [11] 2-7-12 (62) R Brisland (5) 25/1: 050308: Rear/pushed along early, hdwy halfway, held inside last: h'cap bow: unfav high draw: worth another chance in similar: see 3520, 3215. *3½* **44**
*2652 **CEDAR RANGERS 56** [13] 2-9-0 (78) P Doe 12/1: 519: Prom 3f, sn held: op 8/1: h'cap bow: abs. *1¼* **57**
*3649 **MIDNIGHT VENTURE 13** [8] 2-9-2 (80) S W Kelly (3) 11/1: 302210: Cl up 3f: 10th: btr 3649 (C/D). *½* **57**
3749 **MYHAT 8** [16] 2-9-0 (78)(BL) C Carver (3) 14/1: 232650: Held up, eff halfway, btn over 1f out: 11th: bckd from 25/1: first time blnks & poor high draw: clearly thought capable of better: see 2714 (stks). *1¼* **52**
3679 **WARLINGHAM 11** [10] 2-9-0 (78) G Carter 20/1: 621430: Prom till halfway: 12th: btr 3679, 2766 (5f). *5* **40**
2368 **FOCUSED ATTRACTION 67** [3] 2-8-12 (76) S Sanders 6/1: -6540: Chsd ldrs 4f: 13th: h'cap bow, abs. *nk* **35**
1883 **EASTER ISLAND 87** [6] 2-7-11 (61)(1ow)(10oh) J Quinn 20/1: 00000: Dwelt, in tch 4f: 14th: 12 wk abs. *1¼* **19**
14 ran Time 1m 13.41 (3.41) (Richard Green (Fine Paintings)) G L Moore Woodingdean, E Sussex

3887 **5.20 BOLLINGER GENTS AMAT HCAP 3YO+ 0-80 (E) 1m4f Good 55 -42 Slow [52]**
£3705 £1140 £570 £285 3 yo rec 9 lb

3424 **DESERT VALENTINE 22** [13] L G Cottrell 5-9-12 (50)(2ow)(7oh) Mr L Jefford 8/1: 0-0251: 5 b g Midyan - Mo Ceri (Kampala) Chsd ldrs, prog/chsd ldr over 2f out, rdn/led over 1f out, sn in command: unplcd last term (rtd 47, h'cap): '98 Goodwood wnr (h'cap, rtd 59): prev eff at 1m, now suited by a sharp/undul 12f, stays 14f: acts on fast & gd/soft grnd: has run well fresh: likes Goodwood & runs well for an amateur. **55**
3472 **CHALCEDONY 20** [16] G L Moore 4-9-13 (51) Mr H Poulton (7) 12/1: 040362: 4 ch g Highest Honor - Sweet Holland (Alydar) Held up, dropped rear bef halfway, rdn & styd on from over 2f out, no threat to wnr: op 16/1: acts on both AW's, firm & gd grnd: well h'capped now: see 3472, 343 (AW). *3* **51**
3501 **PROTOCOL 19** [3] Mrs S Lamyman 6-9-10 (48)(t)(4oh) Mr S Dobson (5) 12/1: 223103: 6 b g Taufan - Ukaraine's Affair (The Minstrel) Held up, prog/chsd ldrs halfway, not much room over 2f out, kept on onepace. *1* **47**
3073 **MEILLEUR 37** [9] Lady Herries 6-10-5 (57) Mr T Best (5) 12/1: 630264: Held up, hdwy from halfway, drvn/onepace fnl 2f: see 68 (AW). *nk* **55**
2581 **THE WILD WIDOW 58** [5] 6-12-0 (80)(vis) Mr T Scudamore 5/1: 111105: Led/sn clr, drvn/hdd over *2* **75**

1f out, wknd inside last: 8 wk abs: unproven beyond 10f & seemed not to stay 12f here: see 2493 (10f).
3695 **PARADISE NAVY 11** [7] 11-9-10 (48)(bl)(5oh) Mr R Bliss (6) 20/1: -00036: Held up rear, mod gains fnl 3½ **38**
3f: return to 14f+ should suit: well h'capped veteran performer: see 1784.
3644 **THATCHMASTER 13** [11] 9-10-11 (63)(t) Mr R L Moore (5) 6/1: 4-0027: Held up, hdwy halfway, 3 **49**
btn 3f out: op 8/1: see 3644, 3110 (9f).
*3430 **BACHELORS PAD 21** [2] 6-10-8 (60) Mr J J Best (5) 13/2: 234618: Mid div, btn 3f out: btr 3430. *nk* **45**
3430 **CLASSIC CONKERS 21** [12] 6-9-10 (48)(6oh) Mr S Rees (5) 20/1: 150249: Slowly away/bhd, mod gains. *nk* **32**
2982 **NORTH OF KALA 42** [4] 7-9-10 (48)(5oh) Mr A Quinn (5) 8/1: -13300: Held up, hdwy halfway, btn 1½ **30**
3f out: 10th: recent jumps wnr (won a match at Fontwell, rtd 108h, h'cap): btr 1888.
3654 **TOTAL DELIGHT 13** [1] 4-11-9 (75)(t) Mr P Pritchard Gordon 14/1: 200040: Chsd clr ldr till halfway, *nk* **56**
btn 2f out: 11th: see 3654, 1991 (made all).
3195 **SPECTROMETER 32** [8] 3-11-2 (77) Mr B Hitchcott 7/2 FAV: -41120: Chsd clr ldr halfway till over 2f 2 **55**
out, wknd quickly: 12th: hvly bckd: btr 3195, 2643.
3220 **IL DESTINO 30** [14] 5-10-4 (55)(1ow) Mr C B Hills (0) 10/1: 650030: Al bhd: 13th: op 8/1: see 3220. 3 **30**
3819 **Tommy Carson 4** [6] 5-9-10 (48)(bl)(2oh) Mr R Lucey Butler 33/1:
3683 **Cold Encounter 11** [15] 5-10-8 (60)(vis) Mr A Bradley (5) 50/1:
2381 **Slapy Dam 67** [10] 8-9-13 (51)(3ow)(17oh) Mr R Bailey (0) 50/1:
16 ran Time 2m 43.45 (11.65) (Mrs Lucy Halloran) L G Cottrell Dulford, Devon

DONCASTER FRIDAY SEPTEMBER 8TH Lefthand, Flat, Galloping Track

Official Going GOOD/FIRM (GOOD places). Stalls: Str Crse - Stands Side: Rnd Crse - Inside: Rnd 1m - Outside.

3888 1.30 DBS ST LEGER YEARLING STKS 2YO (B) 6f str Firm 08 -31 Slow
£27000 £10800 £5400 £2700 Field raced centre to stands side

*2933 **BLUE REIGNS 43** [5] N P Littmoden 2-8-11 L Dettori 7/2 FAV: -511: 2 b c Whittingham - Gold And Blue **91**
(Bluebird) Trkd ldrs going well, gd hdwy to lead ins fnl 1f, held on well despite drifting right, drvn out: well
bckd, 6 wk abs: prev scored at Sandown (mdn auct): eff over a stiff 5f, apprec this step up to 6f: acts on fast
& firm grnd, runs well fresh: likes a stiff/gall trk: fast improving, scopey & useful colt.
3621 **FAIR PRINCESS 14** [2] B W Hills 2-8-6 M Hills 5/1: 206222: 2 b f Efisio - Fair Attempt (Try My *nk* **84**
Best) Waited with, gd hdwy to lead 1½f out, collered ins fnl 1f, kept on well despite drifiting right & just
btn in a driving fin: hvly bckd: rnr up on 5 of last 7 starts & deserves a change of luck: stays 6f well.
3609 **SNOWEY MOUNTAIN 14** [21] N A Callaghan 2-8-11 J Fortune 16/1: 644363: 2 gr c Inchinor - Mrs Gray 2½ **82**
(Red Sunset) Rear, prog 2f out, styd on strongly fnl 1f, not rch front 2: again fast fin over 6f, 7f cld prove
ideal: attractive colt who shld win sn: see 3327 (nursery h'cap).
2933 **DOUBLE BREW 43** [20] R Hannon 2-8-11 M Roberts 20/1: 342254: Trkd ldrs, qcknd into lead 2f out & ½ **81**
went 2L clr, hdd over 1f out & fdd ins last: 6 wk abs, lkd well: showed plenty of speed, stays 6f but a drop
bck to 5f could prove ideal: acts on firm & gd/soft grnd, may do best in blnks: see 2357, 2083.
3679 **MILLYS LASS 11** [15] 2-8-6 Craig Williams 16/1: 203025: Hmpd start, recovered to chase ldrs, not 1½ **72**
qckn fnl 1f: see 3679 (nursery h'cap).
3486 **FLYING TURK 20** [22] 2-8-11 Pat Eddery 16/1: -30446: Waited with, kept on under press fnl 1½f, *shd* **77**
nvr nrr: bck in trip after 3486 (nursery h'cap, 7f), see 3268.
3617 **LION IN THE COURSE 14** [7] 2-8-11 J Reid 20/1: -437: Front rank 5f, fdd: plenty of speed over *shd* **77**
this shorter trip: see 3617 (7f).
*3710 **FENWICKS PRIDE 10** [12] 2-8-11 M Fenton 16/1: 326618: Rear, no room when improving 2f out, ½ **76**
onepaced fnl 1f: see 3710 (5f).
3614 **FINMAR 14** [13] 2-8-11 R Winston 50/1: -509: Rear, late hdwy, nvr dngrs on h'cap qual run: ¾ **73**
change of tactics, set the pace in 3614: likely to apprec 7f & nursery h'caps: see 3137.
3592 **SHARP SECRET 15** [17] 2-8-6 R Ffrench 14/1: 251220: Chsd ldrs, no impress fnl 2f & fin 10th. ¾ **65**
3520 **SHEER PASSION 18** [14] 2-8-11 R Hills 25/1: -000: Chsd ldrs, no impress when short of room over 1f ½ **69**
out, fin 11th: longer priced stablemate of rnr up: 7f+ & nurs h'caps will now suit: see 3162 (some promise).
*3400 **SCOTISH LAW 23** [11] 2-8-11 S Whitworth 8/1: -210: Nvr better than mid div, fin 12th: btr 3400, 2972. *1* **66**
3411 **PORT MORESBY 22** [3] 2-8-11 (tBL) R Hughes 12/1: -00100: Chsd ldrs till wknd over 1f out: fin ½ **65**
13th, first time blnks, bckd from 16/1: twice below 3057 (7.5f, gd/soft grnd).
3704 **FOREVER MY LORD 11** [1] 2-8-11 G Duffield 12/1: 011100: Chsd ldrs 4½f, wknd: much btr 3149 (7f). *1* **62**
3500 **YNYSMON 19** [9] 2-8-11 C Lowther 50/1: -5040: Led till halfway, wkng when short of room fnl 1f. *shd* **62**
-- **CEDAR DU LIBAN** [10] 2-8-11 (bl) P J Smullen 10/1: 006310: Mid div when hmpd 2f out, no ch **0**
after: fin 18th: Irish chall, 8 days ago won at Gowran Park (nursery h'cap): eff at 7f/1m on gd/soft & soft
grnd: with D Weld & will do much better back over further & on softer grnd.
3693 **Eagles Cache 11** [19] 2-8-11 J Carroll 20/1: 3358 **Cosmic Ranger 25** [4] 2-8-11 D Sweeney 50/1:
3347 **Ceralbi 25** [8] 2-8-11 K Darley 50/1: 1006 **Thorntoun Diva 137** [6] 2-8-6 (VIS) Dean McKeown 33/1:
*3239 **Carnot 30** [16] 2-8-11 J Weaver 20/1:
21 ran Time 1m 13.18 (2.38) (J R Slater) N P Littmoden Newmarket, Suffolk

3889 2.05 JOY UK COND STKS 3-5YO (B) 1m2f60y Firm 08 +08 Fast
£9750 £3000 £1500 £750 3yo rec 7lb

4543} **FRANCESCO GUARDI 315** [1] P F I Cole 3-8-9 K Darley 11/2: 12-1: 3 b c Robellino - Lamees **106**
(Lomond) Trkd ldr going well, rdn to lead 1½f out, styd on strongly, drvn out: gd time, belated reapp: twice
rcd in '99, debut Catterick wnr (mdn auct), subs rnr up at Newmarket (stks, rtd 97): eff over a stiff 10f, will
sty 12f+: acts on firm & gd/soft grnd, runs v well fresh: has clearly had his problems, but potentially v smart.
*3453 **KOOKABURRA 21** [5] B J Meehan 3-8-11 M J Kinane 4/9 FAV: 463412: 3 b c Zafonic - Annoconnor 3½ **102**
(Nureyev) Tried to make all, collered 1½f out, no extra ins fnl 1f: hvly bckd, padd pick: rcd too freely for
own gd today: met a lightly rcd & improving rival: see 3453 (h'cap).
2851 **TISSIFER 38** [4] M Johnston 4-9-2 (bl) J Carroll 10/3: 200403: 4 b g Polish Precedent - Ingozi 1½ **98**
(Warning) Rear, eff 3f out, some late prog but no ch with front 2: op 9/4, top weight: worth a try over 12f now.
3383 **ALVARO 23** [3] M C Chapman 3-8-9 M Roberts 100/1: 062064: Chsd ldrs, eff 4f out, sn wknd & well 18 **73$**
bhd fnl 2f: faced a v stiff task against today's rivals, officially rtd just 58: see 3383.
4 ran Time 2m 06.41 (0.01) (Richard Green (Fine Paintings)) P F I Cole Whatcombe, Oxon

3890   2.35 MALLARD HCAP 3YO+ 0-105 (B)   1m6f132y Firm 08 -00 Slow   [102]
£22035   £6780   £3390   £1695   3yo rec 12lb

3599 **ROMANTIC AFFAIR** 15 [11] J L Dunlop 3-8-12 (98) Pat Eddery 3/1 FAV: 211421: 3 ch g Persian Bold - Broken Romance (Ela Mana Mou) Waited with, improving when short of room 3f out, squeezed thr' ins fnl 1f, strong run to lead fnl 50y, all out: hvly bckd from 11/2: earlier won at Sandown & Salisbury (h'caps): '99 Newcastle wnr (mdn auct, rtd 74): eff at 12/14f, may stay further: acts on firm & soft, likes a stiff/gall trk: v progressive & useful gelding who is worth a try in Listed comp: given a fine ride by Pat Eddery today.   107

3565 **AFTERJACKO** 16 [2] D R C Elsworth 4-9-3 (91) M J Kinane 15/2: 005642: 4 ch g Seattle Dancer - Shilka (Soviet Star) Mid div, hdwy to lead 2f out, not pace to repel wnr cl home: nicely bckd, clr of 3rd, lkd superb: fine run conceding 5lbs to this useful & prog rival: most consistent, deserves a similar race: see 3565.   hd   98

3565 **BAY OF ISLANDS** 16 [3] D Morris 8-9-9 (97)(vis) K Darley 10/1: 031303: 8 b g Jupiter Island - Lawyer's Wave (Advocator) Waited with, prog 3f out, styd on under press but not pace of front 2: bck to form after poorly drawn when again bhd today's rnr-up in 3565: see 2695.   3½   99

3565 **EMINENCE GRISE** 16 [10] H R A Cecil 5-9-7 (95) W Ryan 7/1: 021004: Trckd ldrs, onepcd fnl 1½f: again bhd today's 2nd in 3565 (poorly drawn).   nk   96

3565 **TEMPLE WAY** 16 [6] 4-9-5 (93)(vis) R Hughes 8/1: 222105: Trkd ldrs travelling strongly, eff 2f out, sn no impress: padd pick, found less than expected here: see 3058.   nk   93

3686 **KENNET** 11 [4] 5-7-12 (72) F Norton 16/1: 231136: Rear, improving when short of room 3f out, nrst fin: not disgraced in this much better company: see 3518.   ¾   71

3599 **COVER UP** 15 [9] 3-8-5 (91) G Duffield 14/1: -10307: Chsd ldrs, left bhd fnl 1½f: see 3153.   ½   89

3565 **PRAIRIE FALCON** 16 [1] 6-8-8 (82) J Mackay (5) 16/1: 060408: Prog from rear 3f out, onepcd when short of room over 1f out: will apprec a return to 2m+: see 3171 (2m+).   hd   80

3088 **PROMISING LADY** 37 [12] 3-8-1 (87)(1ow) Craig Williams (5) 50/1: 060269: Nvr a factor: boiled over.   2½   82

3811 **VIRGIN SOLDIER** 5 [13] 4-9-7 (95) D Holland 11/1: 421330: Led till 2f out, wknd into 10th: qck reapp: prev v consistent, see 3811, 3295 (2m).   2   90

3611 **BID ME WELCOME** 14 [7] 4-8-6 (80) J Reid 20/1: 231520: Chsd ldrs till btn fnl 2f: fin 11th.   hd   72

3302 **KNOCKHOLT** 27 [5] 4-9-9 (97) L Dettori 11/1: 000100: In tch till btn over 2f out: 12th: btr 2705.   nk   88

3751 **MOWBRAY** 8 [8] 5-9-10 (98) J Fortune 11/1: 044030: Al rear, nvr a factor & fin last: top-weight.   hd   89

13 ran   Time 3m 04.25 (1.25)   (The Earl Cadogan)   J L Dunlop Arundel, W Sussex

3891   3.05 GR 2 CHAMPAGNE STKS 2YO (A)   7f str   Firm 08 -27 Slow
£60000   £23000   £11500   £5500

3550 **NOVERRE** 19 [4] D R Loder 2-9-0 L Dettori 7/2: -11131: 2 b c Rahy - Danseur Fabuleux (Northern Dancer) Held up, smooth hdwy 2f out, strong run to lead ins fnl 1f, pushed out, cosily: earlier won 1st 3 at Chantilly, M-Laffitte (List) & Newmarket (Gr 3), subs 7L 3rd to Bad As I Wanna Be in Franace (Gr 1): half brother to sev wnrs, notably champion 2yo Arazi: eff at 6/7f on firm & soft grnd, handles any trk: progressive, smart colt who looks sure to develop into a top class 7f/1m performer next term: hds to the Breeders Cup Juvenile.   113

*2067 **CD EUROPE** 80 [8] M R Channon 2-9-0 Craig Williams 9/2: -112: 2 ch c Royal Academy - Woodland Orchid (Woodman) Trkd ldrs, rdn into lead ent fnl 1f, not pace to repel wnr cl home: fit after 12 wk abs: lost unbtn record but met a smart rival here: eff at 6/7f on firm & gd/soft: runs well fresh: smart colt.   1¼   109

3086 **CHIANTI** 37 [2] J L Dunlop 2-8-10 Pat Eddery 6/1: -1163: 2 b c Danehill - Sabaah (Nureyev) Dwelt, rcd keenly in rear, imprvd 2f out, kept on but not pace of wnr, ddhtd for 3rd: drifted from 9/2: best ever run with a change of tactics, prev forced the pace: see 3086, 2693.   hd   105

*3568 **GHAYTH** 16 [7] Sir Michael Stoute 2-8-10 R Hills 5/2 FAV: -613: Nvr far away, led 2f out till ins last, no extra: ddhtd for 3rd: hvly bckd: stays a stiff 7f, acts on fast & firm grnd: see 3568.   dht   105

*2848 **PATSYS DOUBLE** 48 [1] 2-8-10 D Sweeney 5/1: -1115: Chsd ldrs, kept on fnl 1f, nrst fin: 7 wk abs: swtg: prev unbtn colt, see 2848.   ½   104

3470 **BARKING MAD** 20 [9] 2-8-10 M Fenton 20/1: 162136: Led till 2f out, no extra: not disgraced.   1   102

3086 **TORTUGUERO** 20 [3] 2-8-10 M Hills 20/1: 112447: Rdn in rear, some late hdwy but nvr dngrs.   1¼   99

3797 **DOMINUS** 5 [5] 2-8-10 R Hughes 9/1: 221658: Chsd ldrs, onepcd fnl 2f, fin last: quick reapp.   hd   99

8 ran   Time 1m 25.67 (2.47)   (Godolphin S N C)   D R Loder Evry, France

3892   3.40 LISTED AMCO TROY STKS 3YO+ (A)   1m4f   Firm 08 +09 Fast
£14579   £4486   £2243   £1121   3yo rec 9lb

3539 **LEAR SPEAR** 17 [5] D R C Elsworth 5-9-1 M J Kinane 11/10 FAV: 3-2031: 5 b h Lear Fan - Golden Gorse (His Majesty) Trckd ldr, prog to lead ins fnl 1f, drvn out: hvly bckd, crse record time, padd pick: '99 wnr at Epsom (Gr 3), R Ascot (Gr 2) & Goodwood (Gr 3, rtd 119): '98 wnr at Sandown (mdn) & Newmarket (val h'cap, rtd 104): eff at 1m/10f, stayed this longer 12f trip: acts on firm, gd/soft grnd & dirt: runs well fresh, handles any trk: apprec today's drop in grade, can rate more highly & win more races.   110

1284 **KING O THE MANA** 118 [1] R Hannon 3-8-6 R Hughes 10/1: -04132: 3 b c Turtle Island - Olivia Jane (Ela Mana Mou) Trkd ldrs, briefly short of room 2f out, switched & styd on well fnl 1f, not pce of wnr: op 8/1, long abs: stays a stiff 12f, acts on firm & soft grnd: runs well fresh, spot on next time, see 1089.   ½   108

3640 **BLUE GOLD** 13 [4] R Hannon 3-8-6 J Reid 5/1: 120123: 3 b c Rainbow Quest - Relatively Special (Alzao) Set pace till ins fnl 1f, no extra: gd front running eff, posted a career best eff here: see 3640, 3088.   hd   108

3640 **AZOUZ PASHA** 13 [6] H R A Cecil 4-9-1 W Ryan 7/2: 1-5534: Held up, eff 3f out, not pce to chall: well bckd: won this race last season: again bhd today's 3rd in 3640.   1¾   106

3479 **MAYLANE** 20 [3] 6-9-1 M Roberts 7/1: 046335: Dwelt, rcd v keenly in rear, nvr nr ldrs: enigmatic gelding who possess bags of ability when in the mood: see 3479.   1   104

5 ran   Time 2n 29.67 (u0.13)   (Raymond Tooth)   D R C Elsworth Whitsbury, Hants

3893   4.10 FENNER TROPHY COND STKS 3YO (C)   1m rnd   Firm 08 -25 Slow
£6500   £2000   £1000   £500

3107 **EL GRAN PAPA** 36 [1] J H M Gosden 3-9-0 L Dettori 2/1 FAV: 110201: 3 b c El Gran Senor - Banner Hit (Oh Say) Rear, prog 2f out, strong run to lead fnl 50y, won going away: hvly bckd: earlier won at Newbury (class stakes) & R Ascot (val h'cap), not much luck in a couple of sub outings: eff at 7f/1m on firm & gd/soft: likes stiff/gall trks: useful, progressive colt who has a decent turn of foot: sure to win more races.   109

3523} **SOVIET FLASH** 383 [8] E A L Dunlop 3-8-11 J Reid 6/1: -41-2: 3 b c Warning - Mrs Moonlight (Ajdal)   ½   104

DONCASTER   FRIDAY SEPTEMBER 8TH   Lefthand, Flat, Galloping Track

Tried to make all, rallied well fnl 1f but not pace to repel wnr: fine comeback: twice rcd juv, won at Leicester (rtd 91): half brother to a 1m wnr abroad: eff at 7f/1m, 10f shld suit: loves to force the pace & seems suited by firm grnd: just fitter next time: open to plenty of improvement & a potentially smart colt.

*3421 **SUMMER VIEW** 22 [5] R Charlton 3-9-5 R Hughes 9/4: -113: 3 ch c Distant View - Miss Summer (Luthier) Rear, prog to chall ent fnl 1f, just btn in a cl fin: hvly bckd: lightly rcd & prev unbtn colt, lost little in defeat under top weight today: smart performer, see 3421.	shd	112
1535 **JALAD** 104 [3] B Hanbury 3-8-11 (t) R Hills 9/1: 16-204: Trckd ldrs, not qckn ins fnl 1f: op 7/1, long abs & just better for race: spot on next time, see 1069 (C/D).	1	102$
3866} **DRAMATIC QUEST** 364 [4] 3-8-11 D Holland 14/1: 0115-5: Prom, ev ch till short of room & outpcd 2f out, rallied but no ch after: drifted from 8/1, ndd this reapp: '99 wnr at Pontefract & Ascot (stks), 5th in a Gr2 here at Doncaster on fnl outing (rtd 99): eff at 1m, looks in need of further: acts on gd & firm grnd, runs well fresh: useful, scopey colt who will be much sharper next time.	nk	101
3369 **SPENCERS WOOD** 27 [7] 3-9-4 Pat Eddery 9/2: 1-1436: Rcd keenly in bhd ldrs, onepcd fnl 1½f.	2½	103
3711 **BORDERLINE** 10 [6] 3-8-11 R Studholme (3) 100/1: -007: Trckd ldrs till outpcd fnl 1½f: highly tried & this rating is best treated with caution: see 3711.	1½	93$

7 ran   Time 1m 38.78 (2.68)   (Thomas P Tatham)   J H M Gosden Manton, Wilts

---

3894   4.40 CPL HCAP 3YO+ 0-80 (D)   5f str   Firm 08   -20 Slow   [80]
£3900   £1200   £600   £300   3yo rec 1lb   Field raced up the centre of the crse

3788 **THREAT** 6 [18] S C Williams 4-8-12 (64)(t) D Holland 7/1: 600051: 4 br g Zafonic - Prophecy (Warning) In tch, rdn to lead ins fnl 1f, ran on strongly, won a shade cosily: well bckd, qck reapp: 1st win this term, has tumbled down the weights: rnr up for J Gosden in '99 (rtd 98): '98 Goodwood mdn wnr (rtd 102): eff at 5/6f on gd & firm: can run well fresh, wears a t-strap now: incredibly well h'capd & could follow up.		71
3464 **XANADU** 20 [4] Miss L A Perratt 4-9-11 (77) K Dalgleish (5) 16/1: 243602: 4 ch g Casteddu - Bellatrix (Persian Bold) Nvr far away, led 1½f out till ins fnl 1f, not pace to repel wnr: fine run under joint top weight, met a well h'capped rival here: see 2505.	1½	79
3485 **PALAWAN** 20 [10] I A Balding 4-9-9 (75) K Darley 14/1: 106253: 4 br g Polar Falcon - Krameria (Kris) Set pace till 1½f out, rallied & not btn far: another consistent run: see 3209.	nk	76
2478 **DACCORD** 63 [21] M Kettle 4-9-9 (76) N Callan 25/1: 535064: Rear, improved 2f out, fin well into 4th: 9 wk abs: fine eff, fairly lightly rcd & looks to be improving: see 444 (AW, with E Wheeler).	½	76
*3788 **STATOYORK** 6 [11] 7-8-13 (65)(6ex) T Williams 11/2: 021415: Rear, improved over 1f out, nrst fin: hvly bckd, quick reapp: came with customary late run here: see 3788.	1	62
2900 **CONNECT** 45 [15] 3-9-11 (78) G Duffield 25/1: 043056: Slowy away & well bhd, fin fast but too late: 6 wk abs, joint top weight: stable has had a torried time this season, plenty of promise with this run: see 2900.	nk	74+
3687 **BODFARI KOMAITE** 11 [2] 4-9-7 (73) T Lucas 7/2 FAV: 211347: Chsd ldrs, outpcd halfway, rallied fnl 1f: hvly bckd: better expected after 3687, 1662.	hd	69
3788 **POLLY GOLIGHTLY** 6 [9] 7-8-9 (61)(bl) Dale Gibson 14/1: 000438: Chsd ldrs, no impress fnl 1f.	hd	57
691 **GRAND VIEW** 174 [14] 4-9-0 (66) F Norton 33/1: 0-6139: Outpcd, late hdwy but nvr dangerous after long abs: swtg: in gd form on the AW bck in 691 & 653.	½	61
3135 **POPPYS SONG** 35 [19] 3-9-6 (73) C Rutter 16/1: 002140: Rcd alone on stands rail, no ch with ldrs fnl 1½f: this is best ignored: see 2684.	shd	68
3653 **BOLLIN ANN** 13 [12] 5-8-9 (61) J Fortune 14/1: 306050: Rear, some hdwy 2f out, nvr a factor in 11th.	nk	55
3512 **ZIGGYS DANCER** 19 [7] 9-9-4 (70)(VIS) T E Durcan 25/1: 000060: Speed till halfway: tried a visor.	½	63
2107 **WATERFORD SPIRIT** 78 [1] 4-8-6 (58) R Winston 20/1: 000000: Rear, improved 2f out, btn fnl 1f: fin 13th, 11 wk abs & ndd this: prev trained by T Barron, now with D Nicholls: v well h'capped sprinter, sure to improve for this & one to keep in mind: see 2107.	shd	51+
2697 **DAAWE** 55 [3] 9-9-6 (72) Clare Roche (7) 25/1: 005050: Speed till halfway: 8 wk abs & ndd this.	hd	65
3821 **SIHAFI** 4 [5] 7-9-2 (68) A Culhane 16/1: 450100: In tch, improving when short of room dist, no ch after & eased: 11 wk reapp: forget this, btr 3594.	shd	61
3436 **PRICE OF PASSION** 21 [8] 4-9-2 (68)(vis) R Hughes 12/1: 000450: Al bhd, fin 19th: btr 3191.		0
3687 **ANTHONY MON AMOUR** 11 [13] 4-9-2 A Nicholls (3) 12/1: 135600: Speed 3f, wknd into 21st.		0

3631 Labrett 13 [22] 3-9-9 (76)(bl) Pat Eddery 25/1:   3485 Antonias Double 20 [20] 5-9-7 (73) P Fessey 14/1:
3398 Blessingindisguise 23 [17] 7-9-10 (76)(bl) G Parkin 20/1:3653 Maromito 16 [6] 3-8-12 (65) O Pears 20/1:
2165 Pop The Cork 76 [16] 3-8-9 (62) Dean McKeown 40/1:
22 ran   Time 59.62 (1.42)   (Pertemps Flexipeople Owners Syndicate)   S C Williams Newmarket

---

DONCASTER   SATURDAY SEPTEMBER 9TH   Lefthand, Flat, Galloping Track

Official Going: GOOD/FIRM (GOOD Places). Stalls: Straight Course - stands side: Rnd course - Ins: Rnd mile - Outside

3895   2.00 G.N.E.R. COND STKS 2YO (C)   6f   Firm -07   -30 Slow
£7247   £2230   £1115   £557

3719 **DOWN TO THE WOODS** 14 [6] M Johnston 2-8-13 D Holland 11/8: 151: 2 ch c Woodman - Riviera Wonder (Batonnier) Led, prsd appr fnl 1f, shkn up & qcknd clr ins last, readily: hvly bckd, swtg: earlier won here at Doncaster (auct mdn, by 5L): eff at 6f, tried 7f in a Gr3 latest: acts on firm/fast grnd, gall trks: likes to force the pace: speedy, progressive colt, earned a step up in grade.		102
3450 **FREEFOURINTERNET** 22 [3] B J Meehan 2-8-11 Pat Eddery 6/1: -352: 2 b c Tabasco Cat - Dixie Chimes (Dixieland Band) Well plcd, rdn appr fnl 1f, kept on for 2nd but no ch with wnr: op 9/2: ran well back at 6f but could do with a confidence boosting mdn win now: see 3164.	2½	92
3066 **BRAM STOKER** 42 [1] R Hannon 2-9-1 R Hughes 11/10 FAV: 112333: 2 ch c General Monash - Taniokey (Grundy) Prom, prog to press ldr appr fnl 1f, sn rdn & same pace: swtg, edgy in padd, hvly bckd, 6 wk abs: reportedly not fully wound up for this: 3 times a runner-up this term & trainer feels the colt will be better at 5f: handles firm.	hd	96
3720 **BIJAN** 14 [2] R Hollinshead 2-8-8 P M Quinn (3) 33/1: 53104: Chsd ldrs, onepace ent fnl 2f: leggy filly.	4	77
3245 **MISDEMEANOR** 31 [4] 2-8-6 O Pears 100/1: 05: Dwelt, nvr in it: backward filly, highly tried.	11	45
3449 **CELERITY** 22 [5] 2-8-6 G Duffield 100/1: -06: Bhd from halfway: highly tried.	½	43

6 ran   Time 1m 12.16 (1.36)   (Miller/Richards Partnership)   M Johnston Middleham, N Yorks

DONCASTER   SATURDAY SEPTEMBER 9TH   Lefthand, Flat, Galloping Track

3896   **2.30 BEAZER HOMES HCAP 3YO+ 0-105 (B)   1m4f   Firm -07 +10 Fast   [99]**
£17712 £5450 £2725 £1362 3 yo rec 9 lb

3599 **TAKWIN 16** [1] B Hanbury 3-8-12 (92) P J Smullen 14/1: 221101: 3 b c Alzao - Gale Warning (Last Tycoon) Well plcd, led bef fnl 1f, drvn & held on gamely: fast time: earlier won at Kempton (mdn) & Sandown (h'cap): unrcd juv: eff at 12/14f: acts on firm & gd grnd, any track, up with the pace: eff with/without t-strap: powerful, useful & improving colt. **97**
1401 **MOWELGA 112** [6] Lady Herries 6-10-0 (99) Pat Eddery 7/1: 10/102: 6 ch g Most Welcome - Galactic Miss (Damister) Held up, gd prog appr fnl 2f, prsd wnr ins last, edged left/held towards fin: fine run under top-weight, clr rem, nr 4 month abs: apprec return to 12f: acts on firm & gd/soft grnd: useful, see 968. *nk* **103**
3131 **TANTALUS 36** [2] B W Hills 3-9-1 (95)(t) J Reid 14/1: 134063: 3 ch c Unfuwain - Water Quest (Rainbow Quest) Chsd ldrs, eff ent fnl 3f, styd on but nvr pace to chall: gd run, clearly apprec return to 12f & shapes like will stay further: acts on firm & gd/soft grnd: see 713. *3* **95**
3541 **FATHER JUNINHO 18** [15] A P Jarvis 3-8-9 (89) D Holland 10/1: 335404: Waited with, kept on steadily fnl 2f, nvr nr to chall: eff at 10f/12f, will benefit from more positive tactics next time: see 1055. *½* **88**
1151 **ETHMAAR 127** [4] 3-9-3 (97) W Supple 16/1: 13-45: Cl up, shkn up to lead appr fnl 2f, rdn & hdd bef dist, no extra: 4 mth abs, padd pick, h'cap bow: prob stays 12f, return to 10f likely to suit: tall & unexposed colt. *nk* **96**
3454 **HANNIBAL LAD 22** [7] 4-8-12 (83) T G McLaughlin 16/1: 413556: Bhd, kept on appr fnl 2f, onepce fnl 1f. *¾* **81**
2805 **LUXOR 50** [3] 3-8-10 (90) T Quinn 12/1: 42107: Led till appr fnl 2f, fdd bef dist: 7 week abs, poss unsuited by step up to 12f: see 2135. *4* **84**
3541 **RICH VEIN 18** [13] 3-8-4 (84)(vis) J Mackay (5) 13/2 FAV: 121408: Bhd, mod late hdwy: bckd tho' op 5/1, looked well: remains unproven at 12f: see 3541, 2937. *hd* **78**
3686 **WASP RANGER 12** [11] 6-8-8 (79)(bl) R Hughes 7/1: 316229: Dwelt, mid-div, onepace fnl 3f: btr 3686. *2½* **70**
3451 **ORMELIE 22** [9] 5-9-7 (92) J Fortune 8/1: -05330: In tch, outpcd ent fnl 3f: 10th: see 2707. *1½* **81**
3088 **ROYAL EAGLE 38** [10] 3-8-12 (92) D Sweeney 20/1: 003000: Prom till fdd 3f out: 11th, see 1347, 1089. *3* **78**
3565 **SPRING PURSUIT 17** [5] 4-8-9 (80) P Fitzsimons (5) 33/1: 005000: Nvr a factor: 12th, nds easier grnd. *1½* **64**
*3487 **FAIR WARNING 21** [8] 4-9-5 (90) M Hills 15/2: -50010: Mid div, lost place 3f out: 13th, tchd 6/1: much better than this, see 3487 (class stakes). *2½* **71**
*3654 **DARARIYNA 14** [14] 3-8-4 (84) F Lynch 7/1: 221510: Chsd ldrs 1m: 14th, yet to cut the ice in h'caps. *8* **57**
3565 **THREE GREEN LEAVES 17** [12] 4-9-1 (86) K Darley 20/1: 366200: Nvr in it: 15th: see 1695. *4* **55**
15 ran   Time 2m 27.71 (u2.09)   (Hamdan Al Maktoum)   B Hanbury Newmarket, Suffolk

3897   **3.00 PORCELANOSA RATED HCAP 3YO+ 0-105 (B)   1m str   Firm -07 -20 Slow   [110]**
£14378 £4424 £2212 £1106 3 yo rec 5 lb

3597 **MAYARO BAY 16** [1] R Hannon 4-9-3 (99) R Hughes 11/2: 030231: 4 b f Robellino - Down The Valley (Kampala) Waited with, clsd on bit after halfway, led 2f out & edged right, held on gamely und press: lkd superb: useful in defeat since earlier win at York (Listed rtd h'cap): '99 Goodwood wnr (h'cap, rtd 98): '98 Warwick wnr (mdn, rtd 84): v eff at 1m: acts on gd/soft, loves firm: can run well fresh, any trk: tough, improving & v useful. **102**
3130 **ATLANTIC RHAPSODY 14** [6] M Johnston 3-8-8 (95) M Hills 11/2: 605462: 3 b g Machiavellian - First Waltz (Green Dancer) Slow away, rear, prog appr fnl 2f, chall inside last, held fnl strides: op 4/1, lkd well: suited by return to 1m & this was a useful effort: see 1535. *hd* **98**
3435 **TUMBLEWEED TOR 22** [5] B J Meehan 3-8-3 (90) D R McCabe 14/1: 063633: 3 b g Rudimentary - Hilly (Town Crier) Cl up, led ent fnl 3f, sn hdd, kept on under press for 3rd: v consistent, goes on firm & hvy grnd. *1¾* **89**
3648 **BLACK SILK 14** [9] C F Wall 4-8-12 (94) R Mullen 7/2 FAV: 3-1634: Held up, trav well, prog when not clr run 2f out, sn drvn & switched, unable to chall: nicely bckd: wld have been plcd, well worth another look. *hd* **93**
3505 **SIR FERBET 20** [8] 3-8-2 (89)(4oh) G Duffield 12/1: 100425: In tch, prog & ch appr fnl 1f, onepce under press: gd run from this stocky colt, 4lbs o/h, see 3505, 1853. *½* **87**
3435 **MOSSY MOOR 22** [7] 3-8-6 (93) Pat Eddery 5/1: 310426: Chsd ldrs, chall appr fnl 2f, no extra bef dist: bckd, small: drop back to 7f may suit, see 3435, 2084. *1¾* **88**
2171 **MOON EMPEROR 77** [11] 3-8-9 (96) J Stack 25/1: 5-1057: Held up, nvr trbld ldrs: lkd well, absence. *1½* **88**
3597 **STRASBOURG 16** [4] 3-8-3 (90) Kim Tinkler 40/1: 022008: Trckd ldr, outpcd bef fnl 2f: see 2330, 1826. *3* **76**
3230 **SURE DANCER 31** [10] 5-9-7 (103)(BL) T Quinn 7/1: 10-629: Chsd ldrs, fdd ent fnl 3f: blnkd, tchd 10/1, looked well: more expected on h'cap bow: see 2675. *½* **88**
*3597 **PEARTREE HOUSE 16** [2] 6-9-0 (96) A Nicholls (3) 11/2: 406610: Led till bef fnl 2f, wknd: 10th: surely something amiss, beat this wnr last time in 3597. *1½* **78**
10 ran   Time 1m 37.52 (1.02)   (J R Shannon)   R Hannon East Everleigh, Wilts

3898   **3.35 GR 1 ST LEGER STKS 3YO (A)   1m6f132y   Firm -07 -04 Slow**
£222000 £85100 £42550 £20850

*3061 **MILLENARY 39** [5] J L Dunlop 3-9-0 T Quinn 11/4 FAV: -11011: 3 b c Rainbow Quest - Ballerina (Dancing Brave) Held up in tch, prog ent str, led bef fnl 2f, edged left, drvn & asserted fnl 100y: well bckd, lkd superb after 6 wk abs: earlier won at Newbury (mdn), Chester & Goodwood (Gr 3's): highly tried/ran well both '99 starts (stks, rtd 89): eff at 12f, relished this step up to 14.5f: handles soft but is well suited by firm/fast grnd: goes on any trk & runs well fresh: imprvg, high-class colt, win more Group races. **119**
*3540 **AIR MARSHALL 18** [6] Sir Michael Stoute 3-9-0 J Reid 3/1: 4-2212: 3 ch c In The Wings - Troyanna (Troy) Held up, trav well, hdwy appr fnl 2f & strong chall ent fnl 1f, hard drvn & held towards fin: well bckd tho' op 5/2: lost little in defeat, clrly stays 14.5f tho' longer trip poss just blunted his finishing kick: v smart. *¾* **117**
3721 **CHIMES AT MIDNIGHT 14** [1] Luke Comer 3-9-0 (bl) J Carroll 40/1: 310023: 3 b c Danzig - Surely Georgies (Alleged) Waited with, going well, smooth prog 3f out & ev ch 2f out, sn rdn & styd on but not as well as front 2: Irish raider, clr rem: v smart & improving colt, acts on firm & gd grnd & has improved significantly since blnkd: can win a Group race back at 12f: see 3068. *1* **115**
3721 **MEDIA PUZZLE 14** [3] D K Weld 3-9-0 (bl) P J Smullen 33/1: 130134: Patiently rdn, not much room appr fnl 3f, sn squeezed thro', kept on, but nvr nr ldrs: lkd superb: smart run, stays 14f: acts on firm & soft grnd. *2½* **113**
3540 **DALAMPOUR 18** [12] 3-9-0 Pat Eddery 4/1: -01135: Pulled hard & led after 4f, shkn up appr fnl 3f, hdd bef fnl 2f, eased ins last: nicely bckd, st/mate 2nd: v useful run, just below the v best: see 2068 (Gr 3). *1* **111**
3540 **MARIENBARD 18** [8] 3-9-0 P Robinson 11/2: 11126: Held up, not trav well early, eff & onepace 3f out, late hdwy under press: bckd, padd pick: v useful run over lngr 14.5f trip tho' clsr to 2nd in 3540 & bt him in 2503. *2* **109**
3538 **ROSTROPOVICH 18** [9] 3-9-0 (VIS) G Duffield 33/1: -31357: Early ldr, prom till lost pl ent str: visored. *2* **107**
3305 **LITTLEPACEPADDOCKS 28** [11] 3-8-9 M Hills 11/1: -31428: Prom, wide, fdd appr fnl 2f: fit & well *1½* **100**

tho' drifted from 7/1: poss not stay longer 14.5f trip & a return to Listed/Group 3 will suit: see 1945.
*3718 **TALAASH 14** [2] 3-9-0 Craig Williams 33/1: 13619: Handy, wknd appr fnl 2f: stiffish task/longer trip. 1¾ **103**
3645 **GOING GLOBAL 14** [4] 3-9-0 (VIS) R Hughes 66/1: 206040: Chsd ldrs, losing tch/hmpd 2f out: fin 10th. ¾ **102**
3792 **KUWAIT TROOPER 7** [7] 3-9-0 (bl) D Holland 14/1: 105220: Mid-div, wknd appr straight: 11th, v edgy in padd, qck reapp: not his form, but is going to apprec a drop in grade: see 3792, 1311. 5 **97**
11 ran Time 3m 02.58 (u0.42) (L Neil Jones) J L Dunlop Arundel, W Sussex

3899

4.15 LADBROKES.CO.UK HCAP 3YO+ 0-95 (C) 1m2f60y Firm -07 -05 Slow [92]
£19987 £6150 £3075 £1537 3 yo rec 7 lb

*3644 **BOUND FOR PLEASURE 14** [9] J H M Gosden 4-9-8 (86)(t) J Fortune 11/4 FAV: 0-2311: 4 gr c Barathea - Dazzlingly Radiant (Try My Best) Bhd, eff 3f out, no impress till kept on well appr fnl 1f, drifted left dist & got up dying strides, gamely: well bckd, jockey given 2 day ban for careless riding: recent Goodwood wnr (amat h'cap): lighly rcd in '99 (rtd 80, G L Moore): '98 Lingfield wnr (mdn, rtd 81): eff at 9/10f on firm, hvy grnd, any trk: best without blnks, wears a t-strap: progressive, stocky colt, one for the Cambridgeshire short-list. **92**
3541 **AIR DEFENCE 18** [13] B W Hills 3-9-5 (90) M Hills 14/1: -21002: 3 br c Warning - Cruising Height (Shirley Heights) In tch, gd prog 3f out to lead dist, rdn ins last, collared line: lkd superb: right back to form & clearly apprec return to 10f: acts on firm & gd/soft grnd: strong colt: see 1218. hd **94**
3713 **MINI LODGE 11** [7] J G FitzGerald 4-8-5 (69)(vis) Pat Eddery 6/1: -01223: 4 ch g Grand Lodge - Mirea (The Minstrel) Mid-div, shkn up & kept on ent fnl 2f, styd on for press but lkd held when slightly hmpd by wnr fnl 30y: swtg, bckd: gd run from this improving gelding: acts on firm & hvy grnd, 12f will suit. ¾ **72**
3810 **DONNAS DOUBLE 6** [8] D Eddy 5-8-5 (69) A Beech (5) 16/1: 034024: Mid-div, prog 2f out, drvn bef dist, styd on but unable to chall: fine run from this versatile sort, stays up to 12f tho' yet to win beyond 1m. 1¼ **70**
3685 **MINKASH 12** [10] 3-9-1 (86) W Supple 20/1: 644305: Trckd ldrs, hdwy & narrow lead appr fnl 2f till bef fnl 1f, no extra: gd run with blnks omitted, cld win over sltly shorter: see 1310, 1215. 1½ **85**
3676 **MCGILLYCUDDY REEKS 13** [12] 9-8-8 (72) Kim Tinkler 25/1: 231056: Handy, shkn up/onepace fnl 2f. 1¾ **69**
3339 **EASTWAYS 27** [3] 3-8-13 (84) D Holland 9/1: 042247: Rcd in 2nd, led briefly appr fnl 2f, fdd bef dist. hd **81**
3713 **COLWAY RITZ 11** [6] 6-9-5 (83) T Williams 14/1: 202458: Al mid div: looked well: see 2102. ½ **79**
3658 **SCOTTISH SPICE 13** [5] 3-8-11 (82) K Darley 8/1: 600539: Chsd ldrs, rdn, edged left & no extra 2f out. 2 **77**
3451 **MANTUSIS 22** [11] 5-9-13 (91) A Culhane 25/1: 140160: Off the pace, hdwy into mid-div appr fnl 2f, no impress on ldrs: 10th: strong gelding, unsuited by shorter trip?: see 2917 (12f). ½ **83**
*3686 **RARE TALENT 12** [15] 6-8-2 (66) D Mernagh (3) 16/1: 522410: Nvr a factor: 11th, not given hard time. 1 **57**
3676 **QUEENS PAGEANT 13** [20] 6-8-6 (70) L Newman (3) 20/1: 510030: Al towards rr: 12th, btr 3676, 3045. nk **59**
3541 **WESTGATE RUN 18** [14] 3-8-0 (71) P Hanagan (7) 12/1: 112100: Al wide & around same pl: 13th. hd **59**
2750 **PUZZLEMENT 52** [2] 6-8-5 (69) P Robinson 20/1: 100550: Led till appr fnl 2f, btn/hmpd fnl 1f: 14th, abs. 1 **57**
*1204 **TATE VENTURE 124** [19] 3-8-1 (72) R Mullen 25/1: 0310: Nvr in it: 15th, 4 month abs, h'cap bow, lngr trip. **58**
3648} **Compton Aviator 377** [16] 4-9-2 (80) Craig Williams 25/1: 3725 **Archie Babe 10** [17] 4-9-0 (78) G Duffield 33/1:
3644 **Open Arms 14** [4] 4-8-2 (66) A Daly 25/1: 3628 **Ipledgeallegiance 14** [18] 4-10-0 (92) J Reid 20/1:
19 ran Time 2m 06.21 (u0.19) (Action Bloodstock) J H M Gosden Manton, Wilts

3900

4.45 GR 2 FLYING CHILDERS STKS 2YO (A) 5f Firm -07 -29 Slow
£27000 £10350 £5175 £2475

3372 **SUPERSTAR LEO 27** [3] W J Haggas 2-8-12 M Hills 2/1 FAV: 111121: 2 b f College Chapel - Council Rock (General Assembly) Led, ran on strgly to draw 2L clr dist, unchall: hvly bckd, lkd well: earlier rattled off a 4 timer at Catterick (2, stks), R Ascot (Gr 3 Norfolk) & Newbury (val Super Sprint): 5L Gr 1 rnr-up over 6f last time, clrly suited by return to 5f: acts on firm, soft grnd & on any track: loves to force th epace: v smart & speedy: will tackle her elders in the Gr 1 Prix L'Abbaye at Longchamp on Arc weekend. **112**
*3133 **MISTY EYED 36** [6] Mrs P N Dutfield 2-8-12 L Newman 7/2: 101112: 2 gr f Paris House - Bold As Love (Lomond) Slightly hmpd start, rear, prog & not clr run 2f out, ran on strgly for press below dist, nvr nrr: jockey given 3 day ban for irresp riding: bckd: smart run in the circumstances: acts on firm & gd grnd: tough. ¾ **109**
3566 **ZILCH 17** [2] R Hannon 2-8-12 R Hughes 11/2: 2423: 2 ch c Zilzal - Bunty Boo (Noalto) Stdd start, shkn up & hdwy appr fnl 1f, styd on but not pace of front 2: bckd tho' op 4/1, lkd well: v useful run back at 5f tho' will apprec a return to 6f: acts on firm/fast grnd: mdn a formality/boost his confidence: see 3566. 1½ **105**
3714 **THE TRADER 11** [7] M Blanshard 2-8-12 Dale Gibson 20/1: 221134: Pulled hard, chsd ldrs, chsd wnr 1f out, sn onepace: useful run from this stocky, improving colt up in grade: see 3446. nk **104**
3596 **ROMANTIC MYTH 16** [8] 2-8-12 K Darley 4/1: 111645: Slow away & bmpd, pulled hard, chsd ldrs, prog & ch ent fnl 2f, sn outpcd: lifeless in paddock tho' bckd: see 3596 (6f), 2088. 1¾ **99**
3567 **JOPLIN 17** [4] 2-8-12 G Duffield 20/1: -166: Trcd wnr, feeling pace & left bhd ent fnl 2f: highly tried Irish raider, padd pick, op 14/1: see 3567. 2½ **93**
3797 **KACHINA DOLL 6** [10] 2-8-7 Craig Williams 16/1: 033047: Nvr trbled ldrs: bckd, qk reapp, stiff task. ¾ **86**
-3797 **PROCEED WITH CARE 6** [9] 2-8-12 J Reid 9/1: 5128: Front rank till fdd ent fnl 2f, sn hmpd: lkd well. nk **90**
3566 **TARAS EMPEROR 17** [1] 2-8-12 J Fortune 25/1: 410509: Al towards rear: softer grnd suits, see 1586. 1½ **87**
3567 **NEARLY A FOOL 17** [11] 2-8-12 W Supple 25/1: 133330: Nvr in it: 10th, stiff task: see 1995. 1 **84**
3277 **LEOZIAN 29** [5] 2-8-12 N Callan 25/1: 20: Cl up & fought for head, wknd ent fnl 2f: 11th, v highly tried. nk **83**
11 ran Time 59.32 (1.12) (Lael Stable) W J Haggas Newmarket, Suffolk

3901

5.20 PEGLER NURSERY HCAP 2YO 0-85 (D) 7f str Firm -07 -27 Slow [92]
£7995 £2460 £1230 £615

*3428 **LILS JESSY 22** [12] J Noseda 2-9-7 (85) Pat Eddery 9/4 FAV: 51011: 2 b f Kris - Lobmille (Mill Reef) In tch, going well, qcknd to lead appr fnl 1f, ran on strgly, pshd out cl-home: well bckd, jockey given 2 day ban for careless riding, top-weight: earlier won at Yarmouth (fill mdn) & Chester (nursery): eff at 7f, shld get 1m: acts on firm/fast grnd, sharp or gall track: runs well fresh: can carry big weights: imprvg, potentially v useful. **92**
*3638 **WHALE BEACH 14** [22] B W Hills 2-9-5 (83) M Hills 8/1: 012: 2 b c Known Fact - Zulu Dance (Danzatore) Rear, gd prog 2f out, chsd wnr inside last, not btn far: op 10/1: this was a cracking run from stall 22 on h'cap bow: appreciated the step up to 7f: acts on firm & gd grnd: win more races: see 3638. ½ **88**
3649 **KAI ONE 14** [8] R Hannon 2-9-3 (81) J Fortune 14/1: 3233: 2 b c Puissance - Kind Of Shy (Kind Of Hush) Mid div, picked up well ent fnl 2f under hands & heels, styd on for 3rd, not able to chall: apprec this step up to 7f, acts on firm, fast grnd & has a turn of foot: will win a race: see 3649, 3064. 1½ **83**
3387 **CEARNACH 24** [21] B J Meehan 2-8-2 (66) D R McCabe 16/1: -0054: Held up, prog ent fnl 2f, drvn bef dist, styd on: apprec this step up to 7f on firm grnd on h'cap bow & was clr of rem: see 3387. nk **67**
3807 **UHOOMAGOO 6** [14] 2-9-3 (81) A Nicholls (3) 11/1: 131345: Led, rdn & hdd appr fnl 1f, no extra: 3 **76**

bckd from 20/1, quick reapp: unsuited by return to 7f?: see 3592, 3439 (6f).

3704 **BORDERS BELLE** 12 [15] 2-8-12 (76) P Robinson 25/1: -43206: Chsd ldrs, ch 2f out, same pace.   hd 71
3675 **DREAMIE BATTLE** 13 [19] 2-8-4 (68) P M Quinn (3) 20/1: -3357: Keen, in tch, chsd ldrs 2f out, sn   1¼ 61
onepace: h'cap bow, return to 1m will suit, see 3675, 3287.
3156 **MYTHICAL JINKS** 35 [18] 2-9-1 (79) J Reid 10/1: -5668: Held up, late hdwy, nvr nr ldrs: bckd tho'   ¾ 70
op 8/1 on h'cap bow: 1m is going to suit now.
2692 **MISTER SANDERS** 56 [9] 2-8-2 (66) G Duffield 33/1: 0609: Held up, improving when hmpd 2f out, nvr   nk 56
dangerous: 8 week abs, h'cap bow, worth another look on a minor track.
3475 **BANJO BAY** 21 [5] 2-8-6 (70) L Newman (3) 20/1: 53050: Mid-div throughout; 10th, longer trip.   1 58
3660 **KNOCK** 13 [16] 2-9-1 (79) R Hughes 8/1: 152430: Trckd ldrs wknd bef dist: 11th, op 12/1, st/mate 3rd.   ¾ 65
3660 **FLUTED** 13 [2] 2-8-4 (68) Craig Williams 12/1: 030340: Rear, carried left bef 2f out, nvr on terms: 12th.   shd 54
3299 **GROVE DANCER** 29 [4] 2-8-4 (68) A Beech (5) 20/1: 1340: Speed mid appr fnl 2f: 13th, see 3299, 1612.   1½ 51
3620 **CLANBROAD** 15 [10] 2-8-12 (76) T Ashley 16/1: 4140: Mid-div, unable to qckn ent fnl 2f: 14th, h'cap bow. ¾ 58
3830 **BOISDALE** 4 [7] 2-8-2 (66) W Supple 16/1: -00640: Keen, prom till appr fnl 1f: 15th, quick reapp.   hd 48
3542 **AKER WOOD** 18 [6] 2-9-4 (82) K Darley 8/1: 02050: Chsd ldrs, losing pl when badly hmpd halfway: 22nd.   0
3496 **Sebulba** 21 [13] 2-8-13 (77) Dean McKeown 25/1:   3409 **Mujalina** 23 [20] 2-9-1 (79) D Holland 25/1:
3237 **Gay Challenger** 31 [11] 2-8-7 (71) G Bardwell 25/1:   3617 **Chemicalattraction** 15 [3] 2-8-0 (64) T Williams 33/1:
3720 **Witney Royale** 14 [1] 2-9-4 (82) N Callan 25/1:   3327 **Nowt But Trouble** 27 [17] 2-8-0 (64) N Kennedy 33/1:
22 ran   Time 1m 25.9 (1.4)   (Razza Pallorsi)   J Noseda Newmarket, Suffolk

Official Going: GOOD. Stalls: Straight Course - Stands Side, Round Course - Inside, 12f - Outside.

3902

2.15 MGM RTD HCAP 3YO+ 0-105 (B)   7f rnd   Good 40   -07 Slow   [109]
£9404   £3567   £1783   £810   3 yo rec 4 lb

3648 **OMAHA CITY** 14 [1] B Gubby 6-9-1 (96) J P Spencer 10/3 JT FAV: 503521: 6 b g Night Shift - Be   100
Discreet (Junius) Held up, hdwy when no room over 2f out & again over 1f out, switched & styd on well to lead
line: well bckd: '99 wnr here at Goodwood & York (h'caps, rtd 97): eff at 7f, stays a sharp/undul 1m: acts on
firm & gd/soft, any trk, loves Goodwood: gd weight carrier: useful at best.
*3648 **MUCHEA** 14 [5] M R Channon 6-9-3 (98) R Havlin 10/3 JT FAV: 400412: 6 ch h Shalford - Bargouzine   shd 101
(Hotfoot) Held up, rdn to chase ldr dist, led well ins last till caught on line: ahead of this wnr in 3648 (C/D).
3481 **BIG FUTURE** 21 [7] Mrs A J Perrett 3-8-0 (85) W Ryan 12/1: 141533: 3 b c Bigstone - Star   ¾ 87
Of The Future (El Gran Senor) Tried to make all, collared ins last, no extra: bckd: see 3481, 2325.
3600 **KAYO** 16 [6] M Johnston 5-9-5 (100) J Weaver 11/2: 203504: Keen/trckd ldr till over 1f out, held fnl 1f.   2 98
3791 **EASY DOLLAR** 7 [3] 8-8-7 (95)(vis)(7oh) C Rutter 16/1: 055005: Chsd ldrs till over 2f out, sn btn: 5 76
stablemate of wnr: visor reapp: needs a drop in grade: see 1674.
3727 **BAILEYS WHIRLWIND** 10 [2] 3-8-6 (91) M Fenton 7/1: 344044: Rear, in tch, rdn/eff over 2f out,   1½ 76
no impress inside last: see 1186 (class stks).
1329} **MEXICAN ROCK** 483 [4] 4-8-9 (90) S Sanders 20/1: -105-7: Chsd ldrs, rdn/btn 3f out: reapp/h'cap   14 54
bow: '99 Folkestone debut wnr for J Toller (rtd 89, auct mdn), subs rtd 99$ in List company: eff over a sharp/
undul 6f, 7f+ cld suit: acts on soft grnd & runs well fresh: now with Dr J Naylor.
7 ran   Time 1m 27.78 (3.28)   (Brian Gubby Ltd)   B Gubby Bagshot, Surrey

3903

2.45 GR 3 SELECT STKS 3YO+ (A)   1m1f192y   Good 40   +11 Fast
£24000   £9200   £4600   £2200   3 yo rec 9 lb   Majority raced towards centre fnl 4f

*3321 **EKRAAR** 28 [3] M P Tregoning 3-8-10 R Hills 10/11 FAV: -34111: 3 b c Red Ransom - Sacahuista   120
(Raja Baba) Trkd ldr, led over 3f out, styd on strongly fnl 2f, forged clr under hands & heels riding: hvly bckd,
fast time: completed hat-trick after wins at Newbury (stks) & Haydock (Gr 3): '99 wnr here at Goodwood (Gr 3),
subs 3rd in Gr 1 Racing Post Trophy (1st time blnks, rtd 114): eff at 10f, 12f will suit: acts on firm, soft &
any trk, likes Goodwood: eff with/without blnks & likes to race with/force the pace: runs well fresh: high
class, progressive colt: connections will head for the Dubai Champion Stakes at Newmarket & at the top of his form.
*3684 **NATIONAL ANTHEM** 12 [5] Sir Michael Stoute 4-9-0 J P Spencer 5/1: -14412: 4 b h Royal Academy -   5 106
Heart's Harmony (Blushing Groom) Trkd ldrs, rdn/chsd wnr 2f out, flashed tail, no impress on wnr: op 4/1,
had the rest well covered: v useful, could win in Listed company: see 3684 (stakes).
+3726 **RIGHT WING** 10 [4] J L Dunlop 6-9-0 (vis) G Carter 4/1: 312213: 6 b h In The Wings - Nekhbet   4 100
(Artaius) Held up rear, eff fnl 3f, kept on tho' al held: btr 3726 (9f, Listed).
3684 **GOLD ACADEMY** 12 [1] R Hannon 4-9-0 D Harrison 9/1: -66624: Led 6f, sn btn: op 8/1: see 1057.   3½ 95
*3703 **KIND REGARDS** 12 [2] 3-8-4 J Fanning 13/2: 451115: Trckd ldrs, eff over 2f out, sn btn: btr 3703.   2 91
5 ran   Time 2m 07.08 (2.88)   (Hamdan Al Maktoum)   M P Tregoning Lambourn, Berks

3904

3.20 PHILLIPS HCAP 3YO+ 0-95 (C)   6f   Good 40   +08 Fast   [90]
£14690   £4520   £2260   £1130   3 yo rec 2 lb   Raced centre/stands side, no advantage

3791 **ZUHAIR** 7 [11] D Nicholls 7-9-3 (79) J Quinn 5/1: 150501: 7 ch g Mujtahid - Ghzaalh (Northern   87
Dancer) Chsd ldrs halfway, prog to lead ins last, styd on well, rdn out: nicely bckd from 7/1, gd time: earlier
won here at Goodwood (h'cap): '99 wnr at Lingfield & York (h'caps), also twice in 3 days here at Goodwood (h'caps,
rtd 88): trained by D McCain in '98, '97 W'hampton wnr (rtd 93 & 80a): suited by waiting tactics over 5/6f, handles
gd/soft & f/sand, loves fast & firm: tried blnks, best without: handles any trk, becoming a Goodwood specialist.
3768 **MOLLY BROWN** 8 [15] R Hannon 3-9-10 (88) M Roberts 14/1: 400122: 3 b f Rudimentary - Sinking   1¼ 91
(Midyan) Chsd ldrs, rdn & styd on well fnl 1f, not pace of wnr: remains in gd form: see 3768, 2577.
*3646 **SURPRISED** 14 [17] R A Fahey 5-9-0 (76)(vis) S Sanders 10/1: 154413: 5 b g Superpower -   hd 78
Indigo (Primo Dominie) Trkd ldrs halfway, ev ch 1f out, not pace of wnr fnl 1f: bckd from 9/2: bt this wnr in 3646.
3646 **PREMIUM PRINCESS** 14 [6] J J Quinn 5-8-6 (68) R Hills 10/1: 241144: Prom, rdn fnl 2f, kept on   ¾ 68
onepace: op 12/1: remains in fine form: see 3646, 3502 (5f).
*2804 **GLOWING** 50 [10] 5-9-5 (81) D Harrison 10/1: 202415: Al prom, narrow lead/drvn over 1f out till   shd 81
inside last, no extra: 7 week abs: run to form of 2804.
3485 **SPEED ON** 21 [16] 7-9-0 (76) C Rutter 20/1: 305046: Held up, rdn & styd on fnl 1f, no threat: shd 75
looks nicely h'capped, could win similar this autumn: all wins at 5f: see 1013.

3543 **FEARBY CROSS** 18 [9] 4-9-3 (79) L Newton 20/1: 341007: Held up, rdn over 1f out, mod late gains.   nk   **77**
3791 **IVORY DAWN** 7 [12] 6-9-3 (79) C Carver (3) 12/1: 003028: Prom, ch over 1f out, fdd: btr 3791, 2761.   1½   **73**
*3855 **FORGOTTEN TIMES** 3 [5] 6-9-0 (76)(vis)(4ex) C Catlin (7) 14/1: 600319: Held up, eff fnl 2f, no hdwy.   1¼   **67**
3821 **CAUDA EQUINA** 5 [13] 6-9-5 (81) J P Spencer 10/1: 521130: Held up, eff 2f out, no impress: 10th.   hd   **71**
3322 **RAILROADER** 28 [3] 3-9-5 (83) S Carson (3) 12/1: 610200: Led till over 1f out, fdd: 11th: op 10/1.   hd   **72**
3481 **ROYAL RESULT** 21 [4] 7-9-12 (88) Alex Greaves 6/1: 364400: Held up, rdn/btn 2f out: 14th: nicely   **0**
bckd, op 8/1, stablemate of wnr: top-weight: see 728.
3457 **TECHNICIAN** 22 [2] 5-8-7 (69)(bl) C Lowther 10/1: 232220: Strugg halfway: 15th: btr 2396, 2015.   **0**
3713 **Contact** 11 [8] 3-9-5 (83) A Mackay 20/1:   2577 **Dancing Empress** 59 [14] 3-8-12 (76) K Dalgleish (5) 25/1:
1851 **Russian Fox** 91 [7] 3-9-9 (87) J Weaver 33/1:
16 ran   Time 1m 11.9 (1.9)   (The Gardening Partnership)   D Nicholls Sessay, N Yorks

---

3905   **3.55 PERSIMMON HOMES HCAP 3YO+ 0-85 (D)**   **2m**   **Good 40**   **-09 Slow**   **[84]**
           £7328   £2255   £1127   £563   3 yo rec 13lb   Raced towards centre fnl 4f

3434 **LAFFAH** 22 [8] G L Moore 5-8-10 (66)(t) I Mongan (5) 7/1: 341101: 5 b g   Silver Hawk - Sakiyah   **70**
(Secretariat) Trkd ldrs, prog to lead 2f out, held on gamely ins last, all out: earlier won at Chepstow, Bath
& here at Goodwood (h'caps): prev a wnr over hdles: suited by 2m/2m4f on firm & gd, any trk: loves Goodwood:
suited by a t-strap: thorough stayer, most tough & game: sure to win more long dist h'caps.
3472 **KING FLYER** 21 [3] H J Collingridge 4-9-0 (70)(t) J Quinn 5/1: 521122: 4 b g   Ezzoud - Al Guswa   nk   **72**
(Shernazar) Trkd ldrs, smooth prog to chall over 1f out, styd on well, just btn in a close fin: lkd all over the
wnr, but met a v tough rival today: stayed longer 2m trip well: see 3472, 3231 (14f).
3102} **RATHBAWN PRINCE** 411 [5] D T Hughes 8-9-6 (76) P Dobbs (5) 3/1: 0623-203: 8 ch g   All Haste - Ellis   1¼   **77**
Town (Camden Town) Slowly away, held up rear, rdn/outpcd 3f out, styd on well inside last, no pace to chall
(h'caps): suited by 2m on gd & gd/soft grnd: Irish raider, earlier rnr up in a h'cap at The Curragh: '98 wnr at Dundalk & Tralee:
3625 **RENAISSANCE LADY** 15 [2] T R Watson 4-8-2 (58) K Dalgleish (5) 8/1: 125334: Led after 1f till over   1¼   **58**
3f out, onepace/held inside last: see 3085, 2461 (Warwick).
3454 **NAJJM** 22 [6] 3-8-12 (81) R Hills 9/1: -65145: Trkd ldrs, held over 1f out: not btn far & prob stays 2m.   nk   **81**
3798 **FIRST BALLOT** 6 [1] 4-10-0 (84) N Pollard 11/4 FAV: -00036: Keen/led 1f, led again over 3f out   nk   **83**
till over 2f out, sn no extra: hvly bckd: quick reapp: see 1222.
*3618 **STAR RAGE** 15 [4] 10-10-0 (84) J Weaver 6/1: 554217: Held up rear, eff over 2f out, no impress.   1½   **81**
3783 **YES KEEMO SABEE** 7 [7] 5-7-10 (52)(bl)(4ch) J McAuley 16/1: 330208: Keen/held up in tch, btn   8   **41**
3f out: see 3674, 3348 & 2627.
8 ran   Time 3m 32.09 (7.79)   (Richard Green (Fine Paintings))   G L Moore Woodingdean, East Sussex

---

3906   **4.30 EBF ROYAL NAVY MDN 2YO (D)**   **1m rnd**   **Good 40**   **-23 Slow**
           £4280   £1317   £658   £329   Raced towards centre fnl 4f.

3650 **ELMONJED** 14 [3] J L Dunlop 2-9-0 R Hills 3/1: -0021: 2 b c   Gulch - Aqaarid (Nashwan)   **84**
Keen/trkd ldr, led over 2f out, rdn & strongly pressed fnl 1f out, held on well: apprec this step up to 1m, mid-
dists will suit next term: acts on gd grnd & a sharp/undul trk: prog type, shld hold his own in nursery company.
-- **SPANISH SPUR** [8] J H M Gosden 2-9-0 R Havlin 3/1: 2: 2 b c   Indian Ridge - Las Flores (Sadler's   ¾   **82**
Wells) Held up in tch, rdn/prog to chall over 1f out, kept on well, al just held: bckd, tho' op 7/4: April foal,
dam a useful mid dist performer: sire a high class sprinter: eff at 1m, mid dists shld suit in time: acts on gd
grnd & a sharp/undul trk: encouraging intro, can find similar.
3680 **MORSHID** 12 [1] M R Channon 2-9-0 J P Spencer 5/1: 03: 2 b c   Gulch - Possessive Dancer (Shareef   nk   **81**
Dancer) Held up, rdn & styd on from 3f out, not pace to chall: stys 1m on gd grnd: going the right way.
2686 **PRIZE DANCER** 56 [5] D R C Elsworth 2-9-0 J Weaver 9/4 FAV: 04: Led, rdn/hdd over 2f out & held   2   **77**
over 1f out: hvly bckd, well clr rem, 8 wk abs: styd longer 1m trip, handles gd grnd: more expected.
-- **MIDNIGHT CREEK** [7] 2-9-0 W Ryan 16/1: 5: Rear, left hdd fnl 3f tho' mod late gains: Tragic Role   9   **59**
colt, March foal, cost 3,700gns: dam a 10f/2m wnr: likely to improve over mid dists in time.
-- **KIVOTOS** [2] 2-9-0 G Carter 40/1: 6: Rear, rdn/btn 3f out: Trempolino colt, March foal, 35,000gns   ¾   **58**
2yo: dam a multiple wnr in US: sire high class mid dist performer: will need further in time for E O'Neill.
3790 **DOMINION PRINCE** 7 [6] 2-9-0 D Harrison 20/1: -0007: Chsd ldrs, btn over 2f out: longer 1m trip.   3½   **51**
-- **BAILAMOS** [4] 2-9-0 S Sanders 20/1: 8: Chsd ldrs, btn 3f out: Feb foal, IR32,000gns purchase: 11   **29**
brother to a smart 5f/1m 2yo wnr & half brother to sev wnrs abroad: dam a mdn: with Miss G Kelleway.
8 ran   Time 1m 42.45 (5.06)   (Hamdan Al Maktoum)   J L Dunlop Arundel, W. Sussex

---

3907   **5.00 CITY OF PORTSMOUTH MDN 3YO (D)**   **1m1f192y**   **Good 40**   **-05 Slow**
           £4121   £1268   £634   £317   Raced towards centre fnl 4f

4556} **SALEE** 315 [8] J H M Gosden 3-8-9 R Havlin 7/1: 6-1: 3 b f   Caerleon - Almaaseh (Dancing Brave)   **85+**
Dwelt/held up, hdwy to lead 2f out, styd on strongly to push clr under hands & heels riding ins last: reapp:
unplcd sole '99 start (rtd 85, A G Foster, mdn): apprec step up to 10f, shld get further: acts on gd grnd &
on a sharp/undul trk: runs well fresh: plenty in hand here, shld win more races.
3793 **GLORY QUEST** 7 [3] Miss Gay Kelleway 3-9-0 J Weaver 2/1 FAV: 223422: 3 b c   Quest For Fame -   4   **82**
Sonseri (Prince Tenderfoot) Keen/trkd ldrs, rdn & ev ch over 2f out, held over 1f out: bckd from 7/2: stays 10f.
3432 **SUMMER DREAMS** 22 [7] Major D N Chappell 3-8-9 R Hills 9/4: 23: 3 b f   Sadler's Wells - Marie de   2   **74**
Beaujeu (Kenmare) Trckd ldr, briefly led over 2f out, sn held: well bckd: btr 3432.
3289 **DUSTY SHOES** 29 [4] D R C Elsworth 3-8-9 N Pollard 14/1: -34: Dwelt, held up rear, styd on from   1¼   **72**
over 2f out, no threat to ldrs: op 12/1: improved over longer 10f trip, 12f could suit: see 3289.
3006 **MARENKA** 42 [6] 3-8-9 C Rutter 12/1: 4235: Keen/trckd ldrs, rdn/btn 2f out: 6 wk abs: see 2774.   ½   **71**
3381 **AMRITSAR** 24 [1] 3-9-0 Paul Eddery 14/1: 432336: Led till over 4f out, fdd: op 12/1: see 3381, 2175.   5   **69**
3014 **DIAMOND ROAD** 41 [5] 3-9-0 I Mongan (5) 25/1: 332607: Rear, eff 3f out, no impress: 6 week abs.   8   **57**
2617 **ROSE ADAGIO** 58 [2] 3-8-9 W Ryan 3/1: 58: Led over 4f out, hdd/hmpd over 2f out, wknd: 8 wk abs.   4   **46**
8 ran   Time 2m 08.66 (4.46)   (M Stewkesbury & Mrs J Magnier)   J H M Gosden Manton, Wilts

GOODWOOD   SATURDAY SEPTEMBER 9TH   Righthand, Sharpish, Undulating Track

3908
5.35 NEWS HCAP 3YO 0-75 (E)   5f   Good 40   -04 Slow   [82]
£4043   £1244   £622   £311   Raced centre - stands side

3569 **JAMES STARK** 17 [5] N P Littmoden 3-9-3 (71)(bl) J Quinn 8/1: 244561: 3 b g Up And At 'Em - June Maid (Junius) Prom, rdn/led over 1f out, styd on strongly ins last, rdn out: '99 scorer at Southwell (auct mdn) & Lingfield (AW h'cap, rtd 85a & 64): eff at 5f/sharp 6f: acts on firm & gd/soft grnd, both AWs: suited by blnks/visor & likes to race with/force the pace.   79

*3825 **BRANSTON PICKLE 5** [2] M Johnston 3-8-5 (59) K Dalgleish (5) 2/1 FAV: 000012: 3 ch g Piccolo - Indefinite Article (Indian Ridge) Al prom, drvn fnl 2f, styd on, not pace of wnr: well bckd, op 11/4: qck reapp.   1¾   62

3579 **STAR PRINCESS 17** [8] K T Ivory 3-9-5 (73)(bl) C Carver (3) 16/1: 224253: 3 b f Up And At 'Em - Princess Sharpenup (Lochnager) Al prom, ev ch over 1f out, held inside last: eff with/without blnks.   nk   75

3759 **TOLDYA 9** [7] M Kettle 3-8-8 (62) M Tebbutt 6/1: 321324: Rdn/towards rear, styd on well for press fnl 1f, nrst fin: acts on firm, gd & both AWs: worth another try over a sharp 6f: see 3759, 526 (blnks).   ½   62

3010 **FLY MORE 41** [1] J Weaver 10/1: 455155: Towards rear, rdn & styd on fnl 1f, no threat: op 8/1, 6 wk abs: eff at 5f, suited by 6f: acts on fast & gd grnd: see 2839 (6f).   1¼   67

3135 **QUEEN OF THE MAY 36** [11] J P Spencer 7/1: 654006: Held up towards rear, rdn over 1f out, late hdwy, no threat: op 10/1: see 1098.   nk   71

3747 **CHORUS 9** [15] 3-9-4 (72)(vis) M Roberts 12/1: 232167: Dwelt, sn outpcd towards rear, styd on from over 1f out, no threat: btr 3229 (mdn, first time visor).   nk   67

3572 **MARITUN LAD 17** [16] 3-8-0 (54)(bl) J McAuley 40/1: 316408: Chsd ldrs, held over 1f out: see 624.   shd   49

3781 **PRIME RECREATION 7** [3] 3-8-1 (55) N Pollard 20/1: 300009: Led till over 1f out, fdd: see 1817.   ¾   48

3796 **LADYWELL BLAISE 6** [12] 3-8-0 (53) C Catlin (6) 40/1: 000000: Chsd ldrs, held fnl 2f: 10th.   nk   45

3747 **AROGANT PRINCE 9** [9] 3-7-13 (53) R Brisland (5) 40/1: 403000: Prom till over 1f out, fdd: 11th.   hd   44

3747 **OARE PINTAIL 9** [10] 3-8-4 (58) S Carson (3) 14/1: 0-0040: Sn rdn chasing ldrs, btn 2f out: 12th.   1   47

3386 **FIRST DRAW 24** [13] 3-9-0 (68)(t) D Harrison 5/1: 50-020: Held up, hdwy halfway, hung right/btn over 1f out: 13th: wore a t-strap: btr 3386.   2   52

3694 **Pardy Pet** 12 [6] 3-7-10 (50)(bl)(8oh) G Baker (5) 33/1:
3759 **Lady Stalker** 9 [17] 3-7-10 (50)(4oh) D Kinsella (7) 25/1:
3747 **Balidare** 9 [4] 3-7-13 (53)(3ow)(17oh) C Rutter 50/1:
16 ran   Time 58.88 (2.18)   (Paul J Dixon)   N P Littmoden Newmarket, Suffolk

---

WARWICK   MONDAY SEPTEMBER 11TH   Lefthand, Sharp, Turning Track

Official Going: GOOD/FIRM. Stalls: Inside.

3909
2.00 EBF OSTLER MDN 2YO (D)   7f26y rnd   Good/Firm   Inapplicable
£3835   £1180   £590   £295

2608 **GRANDERA 60** [2] J R Fanshawe 2-8-11 D Harrison 3/1: -51: 2 ch c Grand Lodge - Bordighera (Alysheba) Trkd ldrs trav well, led dist, asserted under hands & heels riding, easily: val for 7L+, nicely bckd, 2 month abs: April foal, dam a French 13f wnr, sire top class at 1m/10f: apprec this step up to 7f, 1m lks sure to suit: acts on fast grnd & a sharp trk: runs well fresh: useful & impressive, worth following.   100+

2854 **BULLSEFIA 51** [1] B W Hills 2-8-11 R Hills (3) -32: 2 gr c Holy Bull - Yousefia (Danzig) Led, rdn/hdd over 1f out, kept on tho' no ch with impressive wnr: hvly bckd, 7 wk abs: stays 7f on fast grnd: caught a tartar, shown enough to win similar: see 2854.   4   86

3608 **NATION 17** [3] Sir Michael Stoute 2-8-11 Pat Eddery 6/4 FAV: 23: 2 b c Miesque's Son - Erica's Fault (Muttering) Chsd ldrs, trav well over 2f out, drvn over 1f out, onepace: well bckd: acts on fast & gd grnd.   ½   85

3608 **PRINCES THEATRE 17** [15] I A Balding 2-8-11 K Darley 9/1: 44: Dwelt, mid div/wide halfway, rdn & styd on well fnl 2f, no threat to front trio: op 11/2: tricky high draw, worth another look in similar: promising 3608.   1   83

3760 **WOLF VENTURE 10** [5] 2-8-11 B Marcus 9/1: -435: Trckd ldr, rdn/no extra over 1f out: op 9/1: acts on fast & gd grnd: h'cap company should now suit: see 3760, 1974.   1¼   78

3790 **OCEAN ROAD 9** [11] 2-8-11 T Quinn 20/1: 06: Chsd ldrs halfway, sn held: left debut bhd.   3½   73

3790 **ALSYATI 9** [8] 2-8-11 P Robinson 33/1: 67: Chsd ldrs, lost pl over 2f out, sn btn: see 3790.   ¾   72

3766 **NEEDWOOD BRAVE 10** [13] 2-8-11 S Sanders 100/1: 08: Chsd ldrs 5f: well bhd on debut prev.   shd   72

3799 **CLEAR AMBITION 8** [12] 2-8-11 D R McCabe 25/1: -009: Chsd ldrs 5f: see 3484.   nk   71

3729 **WESTON HILLS 12** [16] 2-8-11 Darren Williams (5) 40/1: 000: Towards rear, mod hdwy under hands & heels riding fnl 2f: 10th: a return to 1m & h'cap comp should suit, not knocked about here, improve: see 1095.   shd   71+

3766 **LEE PRINCE 10** [4] 2-8-11 S W Kelly (3) 66/1: 00: Held up, eff under minimal press fnl 2f, little hdwy: not knocked about here: March foal, cost 42,000gns: half brother to a 6f 2yo wnr: dam a 5/6f 2yo wnr.   ½   70

3497 **JUST MIDAS 23** [10] 2-8-11 D Sweeney 100/1: 00: Al towards rear: 12th: turf bow: see 3497.   nk   69

3766 **Marrel** 10 [14] 2-8-11 W Ryan 50/1:   -- **Phurtive** [7] 2-8-11 S Carson (3) 50/1:
3638 **Beltane** 16 [9] 2-8-11 R Havlin 100/1:   -- **Illustrious Duke** [6] 2-8-11 A Mackay 100/1:
16 ran   Time 1m 26.60   (Mrs V Shelton)   J R Fanshawe Newmarket, Suffolk

3910
2.30 PERTEMPS EBF FILLIES MDN 2YO (D)   7f26y rnd   Good/Firm   Inapplicable
£3965   £1220   £610   £305

-- **LILIUM** [16] Sir Michael Stoute 2-8-11 F Lynch 9/1: 1: 2 b f Nashwan - Satin Flower (Shadeed) In tch, smooth prog to trk ldrs over 2f out, led dist, asserted ins last under hands & heels riding, readily: op 6/1: April foal, half sister to top class 2yo Lujain: dam a Gr 3 7f wnr: eff at 7f, 1m shld suit: acts on fast & a sharp trk: runs well fresh: decisive scorer despite tricky high draw, shld win more races.   95+

3583 **BOGUS PENNY 18** [10] S P C Woods 2-8-11 J Reid 6/4 FAV: 422: 2 b f Pennekamp - Dreams Are Free (Caerleon) Trkd ldrs, rdn to chall dist, sn outpcd: hvly bckd: shown enough to find a race: see 3583.   1¼   89

2952 **MAMEHA 45** [7] C E Brittain 2-8-11 P Robinson 9/1: 03: 2 b f Rainbow Quest - Musetta (Cadeaux Genereux) Keen/led over 3f till over 1f out, kept on onepace: op 7/1, 7 wk abs: stays 7f, will apprec 1m+: acts on fast grnd, going the right way after debut: see 2952.   1   87

3408 **TAR FIH 25** [19] J L Dunlop 2-8-11 R Hills 9/1: 434: Mid div/wide rdn & styd on well fnl 2f, nrst fin: op 6/1, 5L clr of rem: stays 7f & improved effort from a tricky high draw: clearly going the right way & h'caps/1m+ will now suit: see 2652.   shd   87+

1202

WARWICK   MONDAY SEPTEMBER 11TH   Lefthand, Sharp, Turning Track

2618 **AILINCALA 60** [20] 2-8-11 R Mullen 33/1: -U05: Switched start & held up, rdn & styd on well fnl 3f, no threat to front quartet: 2 mth abs, poor high draw: eyecatching late hdwy, lks sure to apprec 1m & h'caps: would merit close consideration in such company next time: see 2285.   5   77+

-- **SECRET PASSION** [18] 2-8-11 B Marcus 25/1: 6: Mid div, eff over 2f out, no impress: Petong filly, Apr foal, 5,000gns 2yo: dam a useful 1m/9f wnr: with K Mahdi.   1½   74

3766 **FOUR LEGS GOOD 10** [9] 2-8-11 L Newman (3) 50/1: 007: Dwelt, held up towards rear, switched & rdn/steady late hdwy in kind ride, nvr nrr: improved eff under a kind ride, now looks ready for h'caps: see 2952.   ½   73+

3577 **SHII TAKES GIRL 19** [6] 2-8-11 T Ashley 9/2: 38: Chsd ldrs 4f, sn held: op 7/2: btr 3577.   ½   72

3767 **PICCOLO ROSE 17** [1] 2-8-11 Craig Williams 20/1: 509: Rdn chasing ldrs over 2f out, sn held.   ¾   70

-- **RELATIVE DELIGHT** [13] 2-8-11 J P Spencer 33/1: 0: Dwelt, towards rear, mod late hdwy: 10th: Distant Relative filly, Feb foal, cost 2,000gns: a first foal: dam a hdles wnr: with R Hollinshead.   1¼   68

-- **POLAR ROCK** [8] 2-8-11 M Fenton 10/1: 0: Dwelt, keen/towards rear, mod late hdwy: 11th: Polar Falcon filly, April foal, dam a 7f/1m wnr: with M L W Bell.   ½   67

3748 **TRUST IN PAULA 11** [12] 2-8-11 Pat Eddery 20/1: 00: Mid div, btn 2f out: 12th: see 3748.   nk   66

3607 **PLAYONETOONEDOTCOM 17** [5] 2-8-11 D O'Donohoe 66/1: 00: Led till over 4f out, sn btn: 16th.   0

3752 **Lifford Lady 11** [11] 2-8-11 C Rutter 66/1:   3607 **Degree Of Power 17** [3] 2-8-11 D McGaffin (5) 33/1:
-- **Summer Key** [4] 2-8-11 S Sanders 33/1:   3621 **Anne Mccol 17** [1] 2-8-11 R Studholme (3) 100/1:
17 ran   Time 1m 28.10   (Sheikh Mohammed)   Sir Michael Stoute Newmarket, Suffolk

---

3911   3.00 MCDONNELL AUCT MDN DIV 1 2YO (E)   6f21y rnd   Good/Firm   Inapplicable
£2415   £690   £345

3500 **FLINT RIVER 22** [6] R F Johnson Houghton 2-8-13 J Reid 1/2 FAV: 22021: 2 b c Red Ransom - She's All Class (Rahy) Trkd ldrs, poised to chall when badly hmpd dist, recovered & qcknd to lead nr line: hvly bckd at odds on: deserved this, rnr up on 3 of 4 prev starts: eff at 5/6f, 7f shld suit: acts on firm & gd grnd, stiff/gall or sharp trk: consistent colt, showed a decent turn of foot: could make his mark in h'caps.   85

3812 **HALCYON MAGIC 8** [12] Pat Mitchell 2-8-4 R Brisland (5) 11/2: 552622: 2 b g Magic Ring - Consistent Queen (Queens Hussar) Cl up, led 4f out, rdn & hung badly left over 1f out, hdd nr line: op 9/2: jockey given 5-day irresponsible riding ban: nearly overcame poor high draw: see 3812, 3520.   nk   70

2687 **CAMBIADO 58** [17] J R Fanshawe 2-8-9 O Urbina 20/1: 03: 2 ch g Ashkalani - Changed Around (Doulab) Chsd ldrs, rdn/briefly outpcd over 2f out, rdn to chall dist, no extra cl home: 2 month abs, poor high draw: eff over a sharp/turning 6f on fast grnd, 7f should suit: see 2687.   nk   74

3520 **ITS ECCO BOY 21** [13] K R Burke 2-8-10 D Harrison 16/1: 04: Chsd ldrs, rdn/chall over 2f out, no extra inside last: op 14/1, poor high draw: eff at 6f on fast grnd: see 3520.   ¾   73

3832 **ASWHATILLDOIS 6** [5] 2-8-1 C Rutter 50/1: 05: Chsd ldrs, outpcd fnl 2f: qck reapp: see 3832.   3   57

3829 **PAULAS PRIDE 6** [14] 2-8-3 A Polli (3) 33/1: 006: Chsd ldrs, wide on bend over 2f out, sn held.   1   57

3520 **WEET A WHILE 21** [7] 2-8-9 J P Spencer 14/1: -0057: Chsd ldrs 4f: op 12/1: see 2608.   3   56

3388 **MONTE MAYOR GOLF 26** [16] 2-8-1 F Norton 33/1: -05068: In tch 4f: high draw: see 1798.   1   46

3620 **LIGHT OF FASHION 17** [4] 2-8-3 Paul Eddery 25/1: 09: Led till 4f out, btn 2f out: see 3620.   1¼   45

-- **SANAPTA** [15] 2-8-0 Martin Dwyer 33/1: 0: Slowly away, bhd, late gains, nrst fin: 10th: Elmaamul filly, April foal, cost 4,000gns: half sister to a 2yo wnr abroad: dam a 1m wnr: poor high draw & slow start, got the hang of things late on: sure to relish 7f+ & should improve for W R Muir.   1   40+

3814 **CHARMED 8** [11] 2-8-5 J Quinn 50/1: -000: Chsd ldrs 3f: 11th: mod form.   hd   44

-- **DOLPHIN BEECH** [1] 2-7-13 A Nicholls (2) 25/1: 0: Keen, al towards rear: 12th: Dolphin Street filly, April foal, cost 10,000gns 2yo: a first foal: dam a wnr abroad: with R Dickin.   shd   38

-- **PERTEMPS BOYCOTT** [3] 2-8-11 A Culhane 10/1: 0: Slowly away & al bhd: 16th: Indian Ridge gelding, April foal, 28,000gns 2yo: half brother to 6 wnrs, dam a 1m juv wnr: with W Haggas.   0

-- **Mr Uphill** [2] 2-8-7 R Winston 25/1:   2459 **Hetra Reef 66** [10] 2-8-7 L Newton 50/1:
3760 **Tarranaki Knight 10** [9] 2-8-7 R Havlin 66/1:
16 ran   Time 1m 14.60   (Mrs C J Hue Williams)   R F Johnson Houghton Blewbury, Oxon

---

3912   3.30 MCDONNELL AUCT MDN DIV 2 2YO (E)   6f21y rnd   Good/Firm   Inapplicable
£2415   £690   £345

3175 **POTARO 36** [2] B J Meehan 2-8-13 Pat Eddery 4/11 FAV: -53531: 2 b c Catrail - Bianca Cappello (Glenstal) Made all, styd on strongly ins last, eased down: val for 8L+, hvly bckd & made most of fav low draw: eff at 6/7f: acts on fast grnd & a gall or sharp trk: holds big race entries, well regarded & can rate more highly.   93

3729 **CAPTAIN KOZANDO 12** [7] Mrs G S Rees 2-8-4 W Supple 10/1: 52: 2 b g Komaite - Times Zando (Forzando) Dwelt, sn prom, rdn over 1f out, sn outpcd by easy wnr: eff at 6f, return to 7f+ shld suit: see 3729.   4   64

3496 **LAW BREAKER 23** [3] J Cullinan 2-8-6 D Sweeney 20/1: 04053: 2 ch c Case Law - Revelette (Runnett) Cl up, outpcd by wnr over 1f out over 1f out: op 16/1: eff at 6f on fast grnd: should apprec h'cap company.   1   64

3204 **TUSCAN 34** [1] B G Powell 2-8-7 J Reid 9/1: -46024: Trkd ldrs onepace/held over 1f out: op 14/1: return to selling company could suit: handles firm & fast grnd: prev with M Channon: see 3204 (5f).   1   63

3621 **YUKA SAN 17** [13] 2-8-1 G Baker (5) 16/1: 60405: Chsd ldrs, rdn & kept on onepace fnl 2f: op 12/1.   shd   57

3772 **BLUE LADY 9** [14] 2-8-0 J Tate 10/1: 506336: Cl up 5f: poor high draw: see 3772, 3496 (AW).   ¾   54

3215 **REVOLVER 33** [11] 2-8-10 S W Kelly (3) 25/1: 07: Chsd ldrs, rdn/btn 2f out: see 3215.   1¼   61

3520 **PREMIER AMBITIONS 21** [16] 2-8-9 F Norton 25/1: 08: Towards rear, mod late gains: op 14/1.   3   53

2459 **BANITA 66** [15] 2-7-13 J Quinn 33/1: -09: Chsd ldrs 4f: 2 month abs, high draw: see 2459.   hd   42

-- **LADY LAUREATE** [10] 2-8-3 L Newman (3) 33/1: 0: Al outpcd: 10th: Sir Harry Lewis filly, Jan foal, cost 10,000gns: a first foal: with G Bravery.   3   39

-- **BOND MILLENNIUM** [12] 2-8-9 M Tebbutt 25/1: 0: In tch, btn over 2f out: 11th: March foal, cost 12,000gns: dam a multiple wnr at 14f/2m: will need further in time for B Smart.   ¾   43

-- **CALLMEMRWOO** [6] 2-8-4 Dean McKeown 33/1: 0: Sn outpcd rear: 12th: Rock City gelding, May foal, cost 4,900gns: a first foal: dam a 7f juv selling wnr: with J G Given.   nk   37

-- **BROUGHTONS FLUSH** [8] 2-8-11 L Newton 33/1: 0: Slowly away & sn bhd: 13th: First Trump gelding, March foal, cost 15,000gns: half brother to wnrs between 5f/12f: dam unrcd: with W Musson.   9   26

13 ran   Time 1m 13.60   (Mrs Susan McCarthy)   B J Meehan Upper Lambourn, Berks

3913	**4.00 TOTE NURSERY HCAP 2YO 0-95 (C)**	7f26y rnd Good/Firm Inapplicable	[97]
	£7247 £2230 £1115 £557		

*3137 **LAPWING** 38 [10] B W Hills 2-8-9 (78) M Hills 5/1: 411: 2 b c Tagula - Wasaif (Lomond) **81**
Chsd ldr, led dist, drvn & held on well ins last: h'cap bow: earlier scored at Ayr (mdn, made all): eff at 6f,
apprec this step up to 7f, 1m may suit: acts on fast grnd & a sharp or gall trk: can force the pace: progressive.
*3692 **NUN LEFT** 14 [5] R M Beckett 2-8-8 (77) W Supple 9/2: 324212: 2 b f Bishop Of Cashel - Salsita hd **78**
(Salse) Chsd ldrs, outpcd briefly over 2f out, switchd & rdn/styd on strongly ins last, just held: fine h'cap bow.
3705 **TEDSTALE** 14 [4] L M Cumani 2-8-12 (81) J P Spencer 4/1 FAV: -0443: 2 ch c Irish River - Carefree 1 **80**
Kate (Lyphard) Trkd ldrs halfway, rdn & kept on onepace from over 1f out: h'cap bow: eff at 7f: see 3705, 3121.
3688 **SPY MASTER** 14 [8] Sir Michael Stoute 2-9-0 (83)(VIS) Pat Eddery 5/1: 0234: Led, rdn/hdd over nk **81**
1f out, held after: first time visor on h'cap bow, creditable effort: see 3412 (mdn).
3566 **LOST AT SEA** 19 [1] 2-9-7 (90)(t) D Harrison 10/1: 020105: Held up in tch, rdn/hdwy 2f out, held nk **87**
inside last: op 8/1, top-weight: see 3029 (auction mdn).
3165 **NORCROFT LADY** 37 [2] 2-9-6 (89) J Quinn 12/1: 141606: Rear, in tch, rdn & styd on fnl 2f, not ½ **85**
able to chall: op 10/1: improved on debut up to 7f: acts on fast & gd grnd: see 2589 (6f).
3704 **SANDLES** 14 [6] 2-8-3 (72) L Newman (3) 8/1: 154407: Chsd ldr 3f, btn 1f out: see 3411, 1236. ½ **67**
3630 **TIMES SQUARE** 16 [3] 2-9-3 (86) O Urbina 13/2: 310108: Held up, eff over 2f out, hung left/sn held. ½ **80**
2972 **ALQUID NOVI** 45 [9] 2-7-10 (65) F Norton 12/1: 3409: Chsd ldrs, hmpd halfway, sn struggling: abs. 10 **44**
3901 **MUJALINA** 2 [7] 2-8-10 (79)(BL) D Holland 33/1: 210000: Sn pushed along in tch, btn 2f out: nk **57**
10th, tried blnks, qck reapp: see 2383 (AW).
10 ran   Time 1m 26.60   (The Hon Mrs J M Corbett & Mr C Wright)   B W Hills Lambourn, Berks

3914	**4.30 CROSBEE & ATKINS MED AUCT MDN 3YO (F)**	1m22y rnd Good/Firm Inapplicable	
	£2488 £711 £355		

3506 **MUSH** 22 [8] N P Littmoden 3-9-0 T Quinn 3/1: 03-21: 3 b c Thatching - Petite Jameel (Ahonoora) **76**
Trkd ldrs, led 1f out, styd on well under hands & heels riding: bckd from 9/2: plcd on 2nd of just 2 '99 starts
(rtd 71, auct mdn, P Harris): eff arnd a sharp or stiff/undul 1m on fast & firm: open to further improvement.
3580 **PARKER** 19 [4] B Palling 3-9-0 Pat Eddery 15/2: 463532: 3 b c Magic Ring - Miss Loving (Northfields) 1 **73**
Al handy, briefly led over 1f out, just held by wnr ins last: eff btwn 6f/1m: deserves to find a race: see 3580.
3838 **GLEDSWOOD** 6 [3] Lady Herries 3-8-9 K Darley 5/2 FAV: -32263: 3 ch f Selkirk - Horseshoe Reef 1¼ **65**
(Mill Reef) Led, rdn/hdd over 1f out & held inside last: hvly bckd, op 3/1: quick reapp: twice below 3672, 2006.
3031 **VENTO DEL ORENO** 42 [20] L M Cumani 3-8-9 J P Spencer 20/1: 656004: Dwelt, held up in tch, styd on ¾ **64**
well from over 1f out, nrst fin: 6 wk abs: improved effort despite tricky high draw: stays a sharp 1m, handles
fast grnd, return to 10f+ & h'cap company should suit: see 1344.
3350 **COOLING OFF** 28 [7] 3-8-9 D Holland 3/1: -035: Prom, onepace fnl 2f: op 7/4: rtd higher 3350. ¾ **63**
3217 **LAHAAY** 33 [15] 3-9-0 R Hills 4/1: 004536: Mid div, rdn/hdd gains fnl 2f: clr rem: needs 10f+. ½ **67**
1045 **KOSMIC LADY** 136 [1] 3-8-9 S Dweeny 50/1: 007: Mid div, slightly hmpd over 2f out, sn held: abs. 6 **50**
-- **SCENTED AIR** [13] 3-8-9 Dean McKeown 50/1: 8: Mid div, btn 2f out: debut, with T Watson. 1 **48**
1738 **COLLINE DE FEU** 98 [2] 3-8-9 A Culhane 20/1: 049: Held up, nvr a factor: 3 month abs: dropped in 1¼ **45**
trip, return to 10f+ & h'cap company should now suit for Mrs P Sly.
3813 **SPRING GIFT** 8 [19] 3-8-9 B Marcus 20/1: -6460: Mid div, no impress fnl 3f: 10th: see 3048. nk **44**
3696 **REGAL VISION** 14 [12] 3-9-0 G Hannon (7) 66/1: 000: Held up, nvr a factor: 11th: see 3190. shd **49**
3263 **FFYNNON GOLD** 32 [11] 3-8-9 L Newman (3) 66/1: 00000: Handy, btn over 1f out: 12th: mod form. **43**
3579 **Replacement Pet** 19 [17] 3-8-9 S Sanders 50/1:   3696 **Topless In Tuscany** 14 [14] 3-8-9 A Mackay 66/1:
1084 **Flight Refund** 132 [16] 3-9-0 P M Quinn (3) 100/1:   3671 **Kerridge Chapel** 15 [18] 3-8-9 P Hanagan (7) 100/1:
3256 **Herring Green** 32 [6] 3-9-0 S Carson (3) 66/1:   -- **Cosmic Dancer** [9] 3-9-0 R Studholme (3) 66/1:
18 ran   Time 1m 39.20   (Turf 2000 Limited)   N P Littmoden Newmarket, Suffolk

3915	**5.00 CLAIMING HCAP 3YO+ 0-60 (F)**	1m2f188y Good/Firm Inapplicable	[60]
	£2604 £744 £372 3 yo rec 8 lb		

3581 **IN THE STOCKS** 19 [5] L G Cottrell 6-8-13 (45) S Carson (3) 4/1 FAV: 006201: 6 b m Reprimand - **50**
Stock Hill Lass (Air Trooper) Chsd ldrs, drvn/led ins last, held on well, drvn out: bckd: '99 fnl start wnr at
Lingfield (h'cap, rtd 51): '98 Bath wnr (sell h'cap, rtd 55): eff btwn 1m/11.5f on firm, gd/soft, prob handles
soft & any trk: autumn seems to be her time of year, could win similar again.
3623 **ARBENIG** 17 [4] B Palling 5-9-1 (47) D Sweeney 20/1: 520402: 5 b m Anita's Prince - Out On Her ½ **50**
Own (Superlative) Led after 3f, rdn fnl 2f & hdd inside last, just held cl home: eff between 7f/11f: see 1732.
3842 **LOVE DIAMONDS** 6 [20] N P Littmoden 4-8-8 (40) P M Quinn (3) 20/1: 060003: 4 b g Royal Academy - nk **42**
Baby Diamonds (Habitat) Chsd ldrs, rdn/ch fnl 2f, styd on, held cl home: qck reapp: acts on fast, soft & both AWs.
3683 **LALA SALAMA** 14 [7] Lady Herries 4-8-11 (43) D Harrison 20/1: 0-0004: Cl up, chsd ldr 4f out till 1¼ **43**
over 2f out, held inside last: only mod form prev this term in h'caps: eff at 11f on fast grnd.
3681 **CLASSIC DEFENCE** 14 [6] 7-8-9 (41) R Havlin 11/1: 0/3035: Dwelt/rear, styd on fnl 2f, no threat. nk **40**
3657 **ORDAINED** 15 [11] 7-8-11 (43) T Quinn 7/1: 226006: Chsd ldrs 3f out, sn pace/held: see 2829. 1 **41**
3657 **MUTADARRA** 15 [1] 7-9-8 (54) R Studholme (3) 12/1: 510207: Chsd ldrs 10f: see 2544 (10f, soft). ¾ **51**
*3737 **BECKON** 12 [3] 4-8-8 (40) I Mongan (5) 6/1: 150618: In tch, eff over 2f out, no impress: btr 3737 (10f). ¾ **36**
3775 **FUTURE COUP** 9 [9] 4-9-2 (48)(VIS) O Pears 14/1: 053049: In tch 9f: visor: see 3775, 3393 & 1254. 1 **43**
3570 **SANDABAR** 19 [14] 7-9-5 (51)(t) A Culhane 8/1: 156340: In tch 9f: 10th: t-strap: btr 2203 (2m). shd **46**
3490 **PETARA** 23 [18] 5-8-7 (39)(vis) R Winston 12/1: 100-50: Keen/rear, hdwy 5f out, btn 2f out: 11th. 1¼ **32**
3455 **RED DELIRIUM** 24 [16] 4-9-6 (52) K Darley 7/1: 005060: Rear, rdn/mod gains: 12th: see 746 (6f). 1 **44**
3591 **WISHFUL THINKER** 18 [13] 3-8-7 (47) Kim Tinkler (5) 50/1: 030120: Chsd ldrs 7f: 16th: btr 3591, 2989. **0**
3691 **Kings To Open** 14 [2] 3-8-7 (47)(BL) S W Kelly (3) 20/1: 574 **High Shot** 201 [8] 10-9-10 (56) A Hawkins (7) 25/1:
3490 **Bon Guest** 23 [19] 6-8-8 (40) R Mullen 50/1:
154] **Le Grand Gousier** 1003 [17] 6-8-13 (45)(bl) P Fitzsimons (5) 50/1:
3603 **Poliziano** 17 [10] 4-10-0 (60) W Supple 50/1:   3765} **Trouble** 373 [10] 4-9-9 (55) Darren Williams (5) 40/1:
3624 **The Flyer** 17 [15] 3-9-6 (60)(BL) D Holland 25/1:
20 ran   Time 2m 19.20   (E Gadsden)   L G Cottrell Dulford, Devon

WARWICK   MONDAY SEPTEMBER 11TH   Lefthand, Sharp, Turning Track

3916   5.30 S JOSEPH APPR HCAP 3YO+ 0-70 (F)   2m39y   Good/Firm   Inapplicable   [70]
£2467   £705   £352   3 yo rec 13lb

*3742 **LORD ALASKA 11** [7] J A R Toller 3-8-9 (64) P Dobbs 1/1 FAV: 050111: 3 b g Sir Harry Lewis - 69
Anchorage (Slip Anchor) Held up, hdwy halfway, chsd ldrs over 2f out, styd on well for press to lead well ins
last: hvly bckd: completed hat-trick after wins at Folkestone (first win) & Musselburgh (h'caps): eff at 2m,
may get further: acts on fast & a sharp/turning or undul track: runs well fresh: improving.

*3637 **JACK DAWSON 16** [5] John Berry 3-8-13 (68) G Baker 10/1: 122312: 3 b g Persian Bold - Dream Of   1   70
Jenny (Caerleon) Reared up bef start, trkd ldrs, led over 1f out, hung left & hdd inside last, no extra: op 8/1:
consistent gelding: clr of rem here, can win again: see 3637 (14f).

*3755 **ESTABLISHED 11** [13] J R Best 3-7-10 (51)(3oh) Jonjo Fowle (3) 8/1: 501313: 3 b g Not In Doubt -   5   48
Copper Trader (Faustus) Chsd ldrs halfway, led over 2f out till over 1f out, sn held: see 3755.

3040 **GOLDBRIDGE 42** [2] T P McGovern 5-7-12 (40) P Hanagan (3) 5/1: 004/44: Mid div, styd on fnl 2f,   nk   37
not pace to chall: recent jumps wnr (rnr up match, h'cap hdle): see 3040.

3755 **GOLD MILLENIUM 11** [12] 6-8-7 (49) I Mongan 6/1: 363125: Cl up, wknd over 1f out: btr 3755, 3448.   4   42

3674 **ACQUITTAL 15** [10] 8-7-10 (38)(vis)(11oh) D Kinsella (5) 50/1: 453006: Held up, rdn/mod hdwy fnl 4f.   1¾   29

2853} **MIKE SIMMONS 416** [1] 4-7-10 (38)(1oh) C Catlin (3) 20/1: 0/00-7: Mid div, nvr able to chall: Flat   ½   28
reapp, 6 month jumps abs, 99/00 Taunton wnr (mdn hdle, rtd 96h at best, eff around a sharp 2m/1f on soft grnd):
mod form on the level in '99 (rtd 39, mdn): rtd 54 & 12a in '98.

3424 **NIGHT MUSIC 25** [6] 3-8-1 (56) G Sparkes (3) 14/1: 530368: Rear, mod late hdwy: longer 2m trip.   1¼   45

124 **MOON COLONY 286** [11] 7-9-4 (60) A Hawkins (5) 50/1: 0650-9: Mid div, btn 3f out: Flat   nk   49
reapp, 10 wk jumps abs (mod form): with Lady Herries on the level in '99, plcd (rtd 67, h'cap, subs disapp in blnks):
'98 Doncaster & Newmarket wnr (h'caps, rtd 81): stays 2m, suited by 12f on fast & soft & a gall trk: eff in a t-strap.

3695 **MY LEGAL EAGLE 14** [9] 6-8-9 (51) P Fitzsimons 25/1: 060040: Mid div, btn 2f out: 10th: btr 1023.   hd   39

3581 **SILK STOCKINGS 19** [17] 3-8-5 (60) S Hitchcott (7) 33/1: 300000: Slowly away, rear/nvr factor: 11th.   ½   47

2763 **PRINCE DARKHAN 54** [16] 4-7-12 (40) K Dalgleish (3) 33/1: 000460: Keen/led 14f, sn btn: 12th: abs.   1¼   26

3754 **Breeze Home 11** [4] 4-9-13 (69) A Beech 25/1:   *1613 **Open Ground 103** [15] 3-7-13 (54) P Bradley 14/1:
3199 **Arana 34** [3] 5-7-10 (38)(23oh) C Haddon (7) 100/1:
3624 **Tenby Heights 17** [18] 4-7-13 (41)(tbl)(3ow)(21oh) R Cody Boutcher (0) 100/1:
16 ran   Time 3m 32.70   (Mrs Claire Smith)   J A R Toller Newmarket, Suffolk

YARMOUTH   TUESDAY SEPTEMBER 12TH   Lefthand, Flat, Fair Track

Official Going: GOOD TO FIRM   Stalls: Straight course - far side, Remainder - inside.

3917   2.00 BENNETTS CLAIMER 3YO (F)   1m3f101y   Firm 17   -28 Slow
£2324   £664   £332

3681 **CHEZ BONITO 15** [4] J M Bradley 3-8-2 L Newman (1) 4/1: 400541: 3 br f Persian Bold - Tycoon Aly   47
(Last Tycoon) Trckd ldrs, rdn/led over 1f out, styd on well, rdn out: op 7/2: first win: eff between 9f/11f on
firm & fast grnd: handles a sharp/undulating or fair track: eff in claiming grade.

3816 **EMALI 8** [1] C E Brittain 3-8-13 P Robinson 9/4 FAV: 043032: 3 b g Emarati - Princess Poquito   1¾   57
(Hard Fought) Trckd ldrs, rdn fnl 2f, styd on inside last, not pace to chall wnr: well bckd: see 3816, 2685.

3769 **SLIEVE BLOOM 10** [9] T G Mills 3-8-9 T Williams 16/1: 605003: 3 b g Dancing Dissident - Full Of   1¾   51
Sparkle (Persian Heights) Led, rdn over 2f out & hdd over 1f out, no extra: stays 11.5f, handles fast grnd.

3762 **PEPPERCORN 11** [2] M D I Usher 3-7-12 G Baker (5) 7/2: 036064: Trckd ldrs, rdn/held over 1f out.   3   36

3816 **MOUNTRATH ROCK 8** [6] 3-8-0 (vis) Kim Tinkler 11/2: 015665: Held up, hdway 3f out, no prog fnl 1f.   ½   37

3050 **HIGH BEAUTY 42** [3] 3-8-2 J Tate 14/1: 500006: Held up, eff 3f out, no impress: abs: see 3050.   3   35$

3050 **DINKY 42** [5] 3-8-0 D Kinsella (7) 50/1: 000007: Keen/prom, fdd over 1f out: 6 week abs: see 3021.   1¼   31$

3530 **ACTUALLY 22** [8] 3-7-10 M Henry 33/1: 000-08: Prom, wide on bend over 4f out, sn btn: unplcd   dist   0
in '99 (rtd 45, seller): mod form this term, including in blinks.

3736 **UBITOO 13** [10] 3-8-13 C Rutter 50/1: 300009: Bhd fnl 4f: see 2592 (7f).   1   0

3670 **MUJAALED 16** [7] 3-9-3 Claire Bryan (5) 50/1: -00: Dwelt, al bhd: 10th, longer 11.5f trip: no form.   ½   0
10 ran   Time 2m 28.00 (5.2)   (David S Lewis)   J M Bradley Sedbury, Gloucs

3918   2.30 LISTED J MUSKER FILLIES STKS 3YO+ (A)   1m2f21y   Firm 16   +14 Fast
£15990   £4920   £2460   £1230   3 yo rec 7 lb

3340 **COURTING 30** [6] W J Haggas 3-8-10 S Sanders 14/1: 0-3121: 3 grf Pursuit Of Love - Doctor's Glory   107
(Elmaamul) Set gd pace, qcknd over 2L clr 2f out, drvn out ins last: fast time, well rdn: op 12/1: earlier won
a Listed contest in the French provinces: won first 4 in '99, at Catterick (2, auct mdn & auct stks), Thirsk &
Newmarket (stks, rtd 100, Sir Mark Prescott'): prev suited by 7f/1m styd this longer 10f trip well: runs well fresh:
acts on firm, gd & any track: loves to force the pace: v useful/tough, reportedly to be retired to the paddocks now.

*1872 **SACRED SONG 92** [7] H R A Cecil 3-8-6 T Quinn 9/2 FAV: 1-12: 3 b f Diesis - Ruby Ransom   ½   101
(Red Ransom) Held up, switched & rdn/hdwy over 2f out, styd on well inside last, too late: well bckd:
3 month abs: styd this longer 10f trip well: handled step up in grade & can find similar: see 1872 (stks, 1m).

3726 **MOSELLE 13** [3] W J Haggas 3-8-6 M Hills 7/1: 136253: 3 b f Mtoto - Miquette (Fabulous Dancer)   ¾   100
Hld up, short of rm 3f out, rdn/hdwy over 1f out, styd on, unable to chall: possibly unlucky, stablemate of wnr.

2596 **NAVAL AFFAIR 62** [2] Sir Michael Stoute 3-8-6 F Lynch 25/1: 1-4004: Trckd ldrs, not much room/   nk   99
outpcd over 2f out, drvn & styd on inside last, no threat: back to form after 2 month abs: see 1184.

3703 **BALLADONIA 15** [15] 4-8-13 D Harrison 33/1: 4-6545: Sn cl up, rdn/no extra over 1f out: see 3703.   2½   95

3469 **ROSSE 24** [16] 3-8-6 M Roberts 7/1: 415136: Held up, rdn/mod hdwy fnl 3f & hung left: longer 10f trip.   hd   94

*3389 **FIRST FANTASY 27** [13] 4-9-3 Pat Eddery 8/1: 105017: Held up, nowhere to go from over 2f out   1   97$
till switched bef dist, mod hdwy inside last: op 12/1: stiffish task at the weights, prob ran to best: see 3389.

3389 **PURPLE HEATHER 27** [5] 3-8-6 (bl) R Hughes 20/1: 302148: Led 1f, remainder prom, btn over 1f out.   1   92

3232 **SILKEN WHISPER 34** [4] 3-8-6 J Fortune 7/1: -19: Chsd ldrs, rdn/held over 1f out: see 3232 (mdn).   2   89

*3626 **YOU ARE THE ONE 17** [1] 3-8-6 J P Spencer 13/2: 10: Held up, switched/wide hdwy 3f out, btn over   1¾   87
1f out: 10th: jockey reported bit slipped through fillies mouth: op 5/1: longer 10f trip & up in grade after 3626.

3177 **BE THANKFULL 37** [11] 4-8-13 J Reid 33/1: 1-5360: Mid div, outpcd fnl 2f: 11th: see 3177, 2263 (12f).   shd   87

1205

YARMOUTH TUESDAY SEPTEMBER 12TH Lefthand, Flat, Fair Track

*3818 **SHAMAIEL 8** [12] 3-8-6 P Robinson 10/1: 043010: Chsd ldrs, btn 3f out: 12th: op 12/1: btr 3818. *6* **78**
*3474 **MARRAKECH 24** [9] 3-8-6 W Supple 12/1: -410: Prom, wknd over 3f out: 13th: btr 3474 (1m, mdn, gd). *hd* **77**
3595 **FARFALA 19** [14] 4-8-13 K Darley 12/1: -52300: Mid div/wide, eff 3f out, sn btn: 14th: btr 3547. *1½* **75**
3664 **ELMS SCHOOLGIRL 16** [8] 4-8-13 J Tate 100/1: 064520: Al bhd: 15th: highly tried: see 3664, 1332. *8* **66$**
15 ran Time 2m 04.4 (0.2) (Cheveley Park Stud) W J Haggas Newmarket, Suffolk

3919 **3.00 T PRIOR MDN 3YO+ (D) 6f Firm 16 -16 Slow**
£4368 £1344 £672 £336 3 yo rec 2 lb Raced far side

2977 **MUNEEFA 46** [3] E A L Dunlop 3-8-7 (t) J Reid 5/4: 221: 3 b f Storm Cat - By Land By Sea (Sauce Boat) Trkd ldrs, led going best over 1f out, hung left & drvn clr inside last, v cmftbly: well bckd tho' op 4/6: prev with Saeed bin Suroor: eff at 6/7f: handles firm & fast grnd: runs well fresh & wears a t-strap. **81**
3834 **WIND CHIME 7** [2] C E Brittain 3-8-12 P Robinson 1/1 FAV: -20022: 3 ch c Arazi - Shamisen (Diesis) Trkd ldrs, outpcd halfway, rdn & styd on to take 2nd inside last, no threat to wnr: hvly bckd: see 3834, 839. *5* **74**
2977 **AJYAAL 46** [5] J H M Gosden 3-8-12 (t) R Hills 8/1: 003: 3 b g Dayjur - Arjuzah (Ahonoora) Cl up, led halfway till rdn/hdd over 1f out, lost 2nd inside last: abs, blinks omitted, tried a t-strap: mod prev. *1½* **70**
3462 **EXECUTIVE GHOST 24** [1] Mrs D Haine 3-8-12 K Dalgleish (5) 50/1: 004: Led till halfway, sn btn. *½* **66**
3747 **FARRIERS GAMBLE 12** [4] 4-8-9 C Rutter 50/1: 0-5005: Sn outpcd: mod form. *16* **23**
3113 **NOBLE CHARGER 39** [6] 5-9-0 (bl) D Nolan (7) 66/1: 00-006: Sn outpcd: blinks reapp: see 784. *10* **16**
6 ran Time 1m 12.3 (1.9) (Maktoum Al Maktoum) E A L Dunlop Newmarket, Suffolk

3920 **3.30 TOTE HCAP 3YO+ 0-90 (C) 5f43y Firm 16 +01 Fast [90]**
£7572 £2330 £1165 £582 3 yo rec 1 lb Raced both sides, probably no advantage

3687 **DANCING MYSTERY 15** [18] E A Wheeler 6-9-6 (82) S Carson (3) 12/1: 301401: 6 b g Beveled - Batchworth Dancer (Ballacashtal) Al prom stands side, led overall 2f out, styd on well, pshd out: op 10/1, gd time: earlier scored at Salisbury & Ascot (h'caps): '99 wnr at Lingfield, Southwell (rtd 82a), Warwick (h'caps) & Redcar (stks, rtd 78): '98 wnr at Windsor & Goodwood (h'cap, rtd 57 & 74a): stays 6f, suited by 5f: acts on firm, gd/soft & both AWs: handles any track & runs well fresh: eff with/without blinks: most tough/geniune & useful gelding. **91**
3861 **SMART PREDATOR 6** [2] J J Quinn 4-9-8 (84) K Darley 7/2 FAV: 030132: 4 gr g Polar Falcon - She's Smart (Absalom) Chsd ldrs far side, rdn/hdwy to lead that group inside last, styd on strongly for press: op 3/1: had rivals on far side well covered, remains in fine form & could win similar again: see 3668 (C/D). *1½* **87**
3908 **STAR PRINCESS 3** [19] K T Ivory 3-8-10 (73)(VIS) C Carver (3) 16/1: 242533: 3 b f Up And At 'Em - Princess Sharpenup (Lochnager) Chsd ldrs stands side, rdn & styd on well fnl 1f, not pace of wnr: qk reapp: first time visor, fine effort: remains a mdn but shown enough to find a race: see 3908, 2900 & 1021 (mdn). *½* **74**
3874 **TRAVESTY OF LAW 5** [14] B J Meehan 3-9-7 (84) D R McCabe 12/1: 032554: Held up stands side, drvn/styd on well towards centre fnl 1f, nrst fin: op 10/1: qck reapp: nicely h'capped on best 2yo form, see 1849. *½* **83**
3747 **TORRENT 12** [11] 5-8-5 (67)(bl) Lynsey Hanna (7) 16/1: 331335: Chsd ldrs stands side, held fnl 1f. *hd* **65**
3788 **SUNLEY SENSE 10** [6] 4-9-3 (79) Pat Eddery 7/1: 006646: Led far side group till inside last, no extra. *½* **75**
3687 **AFAAN 15** [17] 7-10-0 (90) T G McLaughlin 33/1: 204007: Cl up stands side 4f: top-weight, blnks omitted. *nk* **85**
3747 **DIAMOND GEEZER 12** [13] 4-8-7 (69) R Hughes 20/1: 224008: Led stands side 3f, held over 1f out. *nk* **63**
*3653 **BEYOND THE CLOUDS 17** [12] 4-8-8 (70) R Winston 10/1: 414219: Al same pl stands side: btr 3653. *hd* **63**
3668 **MOUSEHOLE 16** [15] 8-8-7 (69) S Sanders 16/1: 021000: Held up stands side, mod late hdwy: 10th. *½* **60**
*3694 **NICKLES 15** [9] 5-7-11 (59)(1ow)(5oh) J Quinn 33/1: 064010: Chsd ldrs far side, rdn/ch over 1f out, wknd inside last: 11th: see 3694 (claimer, gd). *½* **48**
3464 **AMBITIOUS 24** [1] 5-10-0 (90) A Beech (5) 20/1: 410100: Chsd ldrs far side 4f: 12th: btr 3176. *1½* **76**
3791 **LONE PIPER 10** [4] 5-8-13 (75) P Robinson 16/1: 000030: Nvr on terms far side: 13th: btr 3791 (6f). *½* **59**
3631 **OUR FRED 17** [10] 3-9-7 (84)(bl) S Finnamore (5) 12/1: 021120: Prom 3f stands side: 14th: op 10/1. *nk* **67**
3788 **Blue Holly 10** [8] 3-9-4 (81) J Fortune 25/1: 3668 **Castle Sempill 16** [16] 3-8-8 (71)(vis) K Dalgleish (5) 12/1:
3687 **Corridor Creeper 15** [5] 3-9-7 (84)(t) W Supple 16/1: 2697 **Red Revolution 59** [3] 3-8-12 (75) J P Spencer 25/1:
18 ran Time 1m 0.9 (0.8) (Austin Stroud & Co Ltd) E A Wheeler Whitchurch On Thames, Oxon

3921 **4.00 TOSHIBA SELLER 3YO+ (G) 7f str Firm 16 -28 Slow**
£2191 £626 £313 3 yo rec 4 lb Raced both sides, no advantage

3253 **WHITE SETTLER 33** [1] Miss S J Wilton 7-9-2 S Whitworth 10/1: /00-31: 7 b g Polish Patriot - Oasis (Valiyar) Held up in tch far side, hdwy to lead overall over 1f out, styd on well, drvn out: no bid: op 8/1: mod form from 2 starts last term (rtd 49): '98 Leicester wnr (R Hodges) & Chepstow (sells, rtd 56): eff at 7f/1m on firm & hvy grnd, fair/undul or stiff track, likes Chepstow: best without blinks & relishes selling grade. **54**
3117 **SAIFAN 39** [12] D Morris 11-9-2 (vis) J Weaver 9/2: -00232: 11 ch g Beveled - Superfrost (Tickled Pink) Cl up stands side, rdn/led that group over 1f out, styd on well for press, just held: bckd from 7/1: in form. *½* **52**
3498 **VALENTINES VISION 24** [20] N P Littmoden 3-8-12 J Tate 33/1: 650-03: 3 b g Distinctly North - Sharp Anne (Belfort) Held up in tch stands side, rdn & styd on fnl 1f, not pace to chall: stays 7f, handles firm grnd. *¾* **51**
3894 **GRAND VIEW 4** [6] D Nicholls 4-9-7 Alex Greaves 7/2 FAV: -61304: Held up far side, hdwy to press ldrs over 1f out, sn onepace: nicely bckd tho' op 3/1: quick reapp under topweight: stays 7f, return to 6f may suit. *¾* **55**
92 **AIX EN PROVENCE 294** [10] 5-9-2 J P Spencer 10/1: 5000-5: Sn prom stands side, rdn/led over 2f out till over 1f out, sn held: 10 mth abs: '99 wnr here at Yarmouth (sell h'cap, rtd 60): rtd 83 sole '98 start (M Johnston): eff at 6f/1m, tried 10f: acts on firm & gd, gall/sharp trk, without t-strap: has brkn blood vessels. *hd* **49**
3579 **PAMELA ANSHAN 20** [19] 3-8-7 (VIS) R Hughes 50/1: -00006: Held up stands side, mod gains: vis. *1½* **41$**
3456 **SOBER AS A JUDGE 25** [2] 3-8-12 G Bardwell 33/1: 030007: Chsd ldrs far side, rdn/led over 2f out till over 1f out, no extra: see 2413. *hd* **45$**
3386 **STOP THE TRAFFIC 27** [18] 3-8-7 (t) J Quinn 33/1: 055608: Stands side, led 4f, fdd: see 397. *1½* **37**
3868 **ERTLON 5** [7] 10-9-7 A Nicholls (3) 9/1: 355129: Led 4f far side, btn over 1f out: op 12/1: qck reapp. *1¾* **44**
3816 **TERM OF ENDEARMENT 8** [11] 3-8-12 K Darley 8/1: 021300: Prom stands side 4f: 10th: btr 3559. *½* **38**
3236 **DOUBLE FAULT 34** [16] 3-8-7 (bl) A Daly 50/1: 033000: Prom 5f stands side: 11th: see 1818, 1596. *½* **32**
3344 **CODICIL 29** [5] 4-9-2 T Williams 20/1: 034100: Chsd ldrs 5f far side: 12th: btr 3138. *1* **35**
3868 **DARWELLS FOLLY 5** [9] 5-9-2 (vis) D Holland 4/1: 010-30: Held up stands side, eff over 2f out, no hdwy: 13th: quick reapp: reportedly ran without declared t-strap after vet spotted blood in horses mouth at the start. *½* **34**
3393 **Tripper Norman 27** [17] 8-9-2 R Fitzpatrick 33/1: 3739 **Coral Shells 13** [8] 3-8-7 (bl) C Rutter 50/1:
3579 **Executive Wish 20** [4] 3-8-7 K Dalgleish (5) 50/1: 3275 **Komaseph 32** [3] 8-9-2 (t) D Nolan (7) 40/1:
3770 **Press Ahead 10** [13] 5-9-7 (tvi) S Finnamore (5) 40/1:
18 ran Time 1m 25.7 (3.1) (John Pointon And Sons) Miss S J Wilton Wetley Rocks, Staffs

3922   **4.30 LEADER FILLIES NURSERY HCAP 2YO 0-85 (D   7f str   Firm 16   -28 Slow**   **[87]**
£4543   £1398   £699   £349   Stands side group in command final 2f

3692 **DILLY 15** [11] P R Chamings 2-8-7 (66) A Nicholls (3) 12/1: 2431: 2 br f Dilum - Princess Rosananti   76
(Shareef Dancer) Held up in tch stands side, prog to lead over 2f out, styd on strongly inside last, rdn clr:
op 14/1, h'cap bow: eff at 7f, 1m should suit: acts on firm & gd grnd, prob any trk: improving filly.
3830 **MONICA GELLER 7** [10] C N Allen 2-8-0 (59) G Bardwell 16/1: 630362: 2 b f Komaite - Rion River   3   61
(Taufan) Held up stands side, rdn/prog to chase wnr over 1f out, no impress : stays an easy 7f: see 3830, 2635.
3704 **SAUCE TARTAR 15** [8] N A Callaghan 2-8-13 (72) L Newman (3) 6/1: -61003: 2 ch f Salse - Filly   nk   73
Mignonne (Nashwan) Led stands side 4f, rdn/kept on: bckd: acts on firm & fast grnd: see 3039.
3830 **MERIDEN MIST 7** [12] P W Harris 2-8-13 (72) Pat Eddery 5/2 FAV: 414054: Held up stands side,   ½   72
rdn/hdwy 2f out, onepace/held inside last: hvly bckd: ahead of todays rnr-up when eyecatching 3830.
3411 **CYNARA 26** [4] 2-8-3 (62) K Dalgleish (5) 12/1: 052155: Led far side till halfway, rdn/led that group   2½   57
again over 1f out, no ch with ldrs stands side: op 10/1: first home on unfav far side: acts on firm & gd: see 3246.
3860 **CHURCH BELLE 6** [9] P Fessey 2-7-13 (58) P Fessey 4/1: 020066: Held up far side, hdwy to lead that grp over   1   51
2f out, sn rdn/hdd & held by ldrs stands side: quick reapp: this longer 7f trip should suit: see 3860, 1463.
3817 **RICHENDA 8** [13] 2-9-7 (80) P Dobbs 16/1: 000607: In tch stands side, switched to race far side   hd   72
halfway, mod gains, no threat: op 14/1: topweight: jockey made wrong move here, prob worth another look.
3057 **JUSTINIA 42** [1] 2-8-0 (59) J Quinn 33/1: 03508: Held up far side, nvr on terms: abs: see 2316.   2½   46
1974 **BAREFOOTED FLYER 88** [15] 2-8-6 (65) D Mernagh (3) 16/1: 02439: Prom stands side 5f: op 14/1,   ½   51
12 week abs: longer 7f trip, h'cap bow: see 1974, 1408.
3577 **CLASSIC MILLENNIUM 20** [6] 2-8-0 (59) R Brisland (5) 33/1: -0000: Al rear far side: 10th: h'cap bow.   hd   44
2417 **MULLING IT OVER 69** [7] 2-7-12 (57) G Baker (5) 10/1: 3000: Prom far side, led halfway till over 2f   1¼   39
out, fdd: 11th: op 7/1, 10 week abs: see 1737 (5f).
3690 **ZANDOS CHARM 15** [14] 2-8-7 (66) K Darley 13/2: -50130: Prom stands side 4f: 15th: btr 3690, 3388.   0
3772 **Violent 10** [5] 2-8-4 (63)(vis) M Henry 20/1:   3246 **Magic Of You 34** [2] 2-8-9 (68)(VIS) M Fenton 20/1:
3761 **London Eye 11** [16] 2-8-1 (60)(bl) D Kinsella (7) 25/1:
15 ran   Time 1m 25.7 (3.1)   (Mrs J E L Wright)   P R Chamings Baughurst, Hants

Official Going   GOOD

3923   **2.25 GR 3 FLYING FIVE STKS 2YO+   5f   Good**
£32500   £9500   £4500   £1500   3 yo rec 1 lb

*1622 **NAMID 105** J Oxx 4-9-12 J Murtagh 4/1: 3-3111: 4 b h Indian Ridge - Dawnsio (Tate Gallery)   120
Mid-div, gd hdwy to lead dist, styd on strongly, drvn out & just prevailed: 15 wk abs due to a knee injury:
earlier won at Cork (List) & The Curragh (Gr 3): plcd both '99 starts (rtd 107, Gr 3 & List): eff between
5f & 7f on gd & hvy: acts on a stiff/gall trk & clearly runs v well fresh: smart/prog, win another Gr race.
3172 **TEDBURROW 34** E J Alston 8-9-9 T E Durcan 5/1: 001302: 8 b g Dowsing - Gwiffina (Welsh Saint)   hd   116
Chsd ldr, hdwy over 1f out, styd on well for press & just failed: bold bid to land an historic 3rd successive
win in this race: v tough 8yo who retains all his ability: see 3172, 2669, 2335.
3373 **ARETHA 27** J S Bolger 3-9-5 (bl) K J Manning 10/1: 242443: 3 ch f Indian Ridge - Smaoineamh   1½   109
(Tap On Wood) Led/dsptd lead till hdd just in last, sn held: 4th at Fairyhouse (List) since 3373.
*3548 **SOCIAL HARMONY 21** D K Weld 6-9-9 P Shanahan 7/1: 020414: Cl-up, rdn & not qckn fnl 1f: shd   112
capable of better & may apprec a return to further: see 3548 (6f, Listed).
3598 **WATCHING 16** 3-9-8 M J Kinane 7/4 FAV: 201445: Prom, dsptd lead over 2f out, hdd appr fnl 1f,   2½   106
sn btn: shade disapp on this drop to Gr 3 company, may apprec an easier surface: see 3598 (Gr 1).
9 ran   Time 58.6   (Lady Clague)   J Oxx Currabeg, Co Kildare

3924   **3.25 LISTED FOXROCK STKS 3YO+   1m2f   Good**
£22750   £6650   £3150   £1050   3 yo rec 7 lb

3554 **MUAKAAD 20** D K Weld 3-8-9 (tBL) P Shanahan 3/1: 130131: 3 b c Muhtarram - Forset Lair (Habitat)   113
Mid-div going well, smooth hdwy to lead appr fnl 1f, shaken up & sn clr, comfortably: 1st time blnks:
dual wnr here at Leopardstown this term (incl reapp, mdn & stks): suited by 10f on fast & soft, acts on a
stiff/gall trk, loves Leopardstown: much improved in 1st time blnks.
-- **DOLYDILLE** J S Bolger 4-9-6 K J Manning 12/1: 341012: 4 b f Dolphin Street - Gradille (Home Guard)   6   107
Bhd, rdn & styd on well fnl 2f, no threat to wnr: recent Galway wnr (12f, List): excellent run at the weights.
3595 **FANTASIA GIRL 16** J Oxx 3-8-6 (BL) N G McCullagh 9/2: 21123: 3 b f Caerleon - Dreamboat   shd   100
(Mr Prospector) Prom, chall ldr over 2f out, sn led, hdd over 1f out, no extra: blnkd: see 3595 (12f, firm).
4483) **LERMONTOV 322** A P O'Brien 3-8-9 M J Kinane 5/2 FAV: -112-4: Led/dsptd lead till 2f out, drvn   2   100
& held fnl 1f: belated reapp: v useful 2yo in '99, scored at Gowran (mdn) & The Curragh (Gr 3), subs a fine
rnr-up in the Gr 1 Racing Post Trophy at Doncaster (rtd 115): eff at 1m, bred to apprec mid-dists: runs well
fresh on gd & soft grnd: v smart at best but has clearly had training problems: sharper for this over further.
1945 **IDOLIZE 86** 3-8-6 W J Smith 12/1: 1-0107: Prom, wknd qckly fnl 1f, 7th: 12 wk abs: btr 1797 (g/s).   0
8 ran   Time 2m 04.2   (Hamdan Al Maktoum)   D K Weld The Curragh, Co Kildare

3925   **4.05 GR 1 IRISH CHAMPION STKS 3YO+   1m2f   Good**
£486200   £128200   £59200   £20200   3 yo rec 7 lb

+3539 **GIANTS CAUSEWAY 18** A P O'Brien 3-8-11 M J Kinane 8/11 FAV: 211111: 3 ch c Storm Cat - Mariah's   124
Storm (Rahy) Chsd ldr, led briefly over 2f out, rallied well & led again 1½f out, styd on gamely, drvn out:
amazing 5th successive Gr 1 victory after wins at Ascot (St James Palace), Sandown (Eclipse), Goodwood (Sussex)
& York (International): prev won at The Curragh (Gr 3) & rnr-up in both English & Irish 2,000 Guineas: juv wnr
at Naas, The Curragh (Gr 3) & Longchamp (Gr 1, rtd 118): eff at 1m/10.5f on fast, soft & any trk: runs well
fresh, up with the pace: top-class colt, as tough & game as they come: now heads for the QEII stks at Ascot
where he has an outstanding chance of recording a record-equalling 6th successive Group 1 win.

LEOPARDSTOWN
SATURDAY SEPTEMBER 9TH   Lefthand, Galloping Track

*3071 **GREEK DANCE 41** Sir Michael Stoute 5-9-4 J Murtagh 8/1: -22512: 5 b h Sadler's Wells - Hellenic ½ **121**
(Darshaan) Settled rear, rdn 3f out, styd on strongly for press fnl 1f, closing at fin: 6 wk abs: excellent effort
on grnd a shade faster than ideal: was a v tough & top-class rival, capable of landing more Gr races: see 3071.
*3374 **BEST OF THE BESTS 25** Saeed bin Suroor 3-8-11 L Dettori 3/1: -34413: 3 ch c Machiavellian - Sueboog 1 **119**
(Darshaan) Cl-up, chall wnr over 2f out, sn led, hdd over 1f out, no impress on wnr fnl 1f: another smart run:
likely to reoppose this wnr at Ascot: will reportedly be much stronger after a winter break (as a 4yo): see 3374.
1458 **INDIAN DANEHILL 11** A Fabre 4-9-4 O Peslier 15/2: 2-1124: In tch, rdn/prog appr fnl 2f, sn btn: 2 **116**
French raider, near 4 month abs: best form prev this term has come on an easier surface: see 1458.
3071 **SUMITAS 41** 4-9-4 T Hellier 16/1: -3D225: Cl-up, eff 2f out, onepce: 6 wk abs, German raider: see 3071. 2½ **112**
3556 **APOLLO VICTORIA 20** 3-8-11 P J Scallan 200/1: -24056: Led till over 2f out, fdd: pacemaker for wnr. 15 **92**
3087 **MANHATTAN 38** 3-8-11 J A Heffernan 200/1: 1-107: Handy, wknd qckly fnl 2f: v stiff task. **0**
7 ran   Time 2m 03.1   (Mrs John Magnier)   A P O'Brien Ballydoyle, Co Tipperary

LONGCHAMP
SUNDAY SEPTEMBER 10TH   Righthand, Stiff, Galloping Track

Official Going   GOOD

3926
1.55 GR 3 PRIX DES CHENES 2YO   1m   Good
£21134   £7685   £3842   £2305

-- **EQUERRY USA** A Fabre 2-9-2 L Dettori 4/10 FAV: -111: 2 br c St Jovite - Colour Chart (Mr Prospector) **111**
Chsd ldrs, hdwy to lead appr fnl 1f, styd on for press, rdn out: jockey fined for misuse of the whip: hat-trick
landed, unbeaten prev: eff at 1m on gd grnd: smart & imprvg juv, win more Gr races.
-- **MIZZEN MAST** Mme C Head 2-9-2 O Doleuze 39/10: -12: 2 gr c Cozzene - Kinema (Graustark) nse **110**
Front rank, went on 2f out, hdd over 1f out, rall strongly for press, just held: clr rem: jockey fined for whip
misuse: recent debut wnr: eff over 1m on gd grnd: smart, win similar.
-- **PANIS** P Bary 2-9-2 T Thulliez 125/10: -2143: 2 b c Miswaki - Political Parody (Doonebury) 2½ **105**
In tch, rdn over 2f out, sn not pace of front 2: met a couple of smart rivals: stays a gall 1m on gd grnd.
-- **GREENGROOM** C Laffon Parias 2-9-2 D Boeuf 73/10: -2114: Keen/bhd, drvn over 1f out, no impress. 2½ **100**
3716 **DAYGLOW DANCER 16** 2-9-2 C Asmussen 129/10: 132425: Led to 2f out, fdd: longer 1m trip: see 3716. ¾ **99**
6 ran   Time 1m 38.05   (Sheikh Mohammed)   A Fabre France

3927
2.25 GR 2 PRIX FOY 4YO+   1m4f   Good
£38425   £15370   £7685   £3842

+ 2998 **MONTJEU 43** J E Hammond 4-9-2 M J Kinane 1/10 FAVcp: 4-1111: 4 b h Sadler's Wells - Floripedes **123**
(Top Ville) Settled off slow pace, imprvd over 1f out, led on dist, pshd out, v easily, any amt in hand: 6 wk
abs: unbeaten this term, won Gr 1's at The Curragh, St Cloud & Ascot (King George, v easily): '99 Longchamp (3,
notably Gr 1 Arc, rtd 136), Chantilly (Gr 1 French Derby) & The Curragh wnr (Gr 1 Irish Derby, by 5L): suited to
10/12f on fast & hvy grnd, handles firm: loves a stiff/gall trk: top-class & out of the highest drawer, will
apprec a likely stronger pace/softer grnd in his quest for a 2nd Arc & will be very hard to beat.
1461 **CRILLON 111** E Lellouche 4-9-2 D Bonilla 84/10: 122252: 4 br c Saumarez - Shangrila (Riverman) 1½ **111**
Chsd ldr, eff over 1f out, kept on but no ch with wnr: met a rival of the highest class here: see 1461.
2566 **COMMANDER COLLINS 61** J H M Gosden 4-9-2 J Fortune 8/1: 04-433: 4 b c Sadler's Wells - Kanmary shd **111**
(Kenmare) Prom, went on appr fnl 1f, sn hdd & no ch with facile wnr, just 2nd nr fin: prob ran to best after
a 9 wk abs: will apprec a drop in grade & a softer surface: can find a Gr 3 abroad this Autumn: see 2566.
2406 **STOP BY 70** J E Hammond 5-9-2 O Thiron 1/10 FAVcp: 150-44: Set slow pace to over 1f out: pacemaker.15 **91**
4 ran   Time 2m 32.8   (Michael Tabor)   J E Hammond France

3928
3.35 GR 1 PRIX VERMEILLE 3YO FILLIES   1m4f   Good
£76849   £30740   £15370   £7685

1901 **VOLVORETA 91** C Lerner 3-9-0 M J Kinane 11/2: 11-121: 3 ch f Suave Dancer - Robertiya (Don Roberto) **122**
Settled rear, smooth hdwy over 2f out, ran on to lead ins last, pshd out: 3 month abs, time over 6secs faster
than Montjeu in preceding race! earlier won at St Cloud (Gr 3, reapp) & rnr-up in the Gr 1 French Oaks: unbtn in
'99, incl a Deauville Gr 3: eff at 10/12f on gd & soft: runs v well fresh: high-class with a fine turn of foot.
3546 **REVE DOSCAR 22** Mme M Bollack Badel 3-9-0 G Mosse 16/1: 221432: 3 gr f Highest Honor - Numidie 1½ **118**
(Baillamont) Twrds rear, rdn/prog over 2f out, ran on well for press, closing at fin: best run to date on this
step up in trip, eff at 10/12f: smart, win again sn in Gr 2/3 company: see 3546, 1457.
*1901 **EGYPTBAND 91** Mme C Head 3-9-0 O Doleuze 13/10 FAVcp: 1-113: 3 b f Dixieland Band - Egyptown nk **118**
(Top Ville) Waited with, gd hdwy over 2f out, drvn/no extra fnl 1f: 3 month abs: longer 12f trip & lost unbtn
record: stays a gall 12f but beat this wnr over 10.5f in 1901 (Gr 1 French Oaks).
3564 **LOVE DIVINE 18** H R A Cecil 3-9-0 T Quinn 5/2: 2-1124: Cl-up, went on over 2f out, drvn/hdd dist, 2 **115**
kept on same pace: Brit raider, apprec a bit more cut in the grnd: high-class at best: see 3564, 1828 (Oaks).
2739 **MELIKAH 56** 3-9-0 L Dettori 3/1: -1325: Chsd ldrs, hdwy to chall appr fnl 2f, no extra for press nk **115**
over 1f out: Brit raider, 8 wk abs: smart at best: see 2739.
3070 **SADLERS FLAG 42** 3-9-0 C Asmussen 13/10 FAVcp: 211226: Bhd, late gains, no dngr: abs: see 3070. 4 **109**
11 ran   Time 2m 26.3   (Mme M-S Vidal)   C Lerner France

3929
4.10 GR 2 PRIX NIEL 3YO   1m4f   Good
£38425   £15370   £7685   £3842

*2409 **SINNDAR 70** J Oxx 3-9-2 J Murtagh 3/10 FAVcp: -21111: 3 b c Grand Lodge - Sinntara (Lashkari) **132**
Chsd stablemate, easily went into lead 2f out, rdn & drew well clr fnl 1f, easily: 10 wk abs: earlier won at
Leopardstown (Gr 3), Epsom (Gr 1 Derby, by 5L) & The Curragh (Gr 1 Irish Derby, by amazing 9L): dual '99 wnr
at The Curragh (incl Gr 1, rtd 107): eff at 1m, now suited to 12f on any trk: acts on fast & soft grnd: prev eff
in a t-strap, not worn today: runs v well fresh: most tough, genuine & top-class colt who produced yet another
impressive performance today: now heads for the Arc & shld give Montjeu a run for his money.
3718 **CRIMSON QUEST 15** A Fabre 3-9-2 O Peslier 79/10: -12022: 3 ch c Rainbow Quest - Bex (Explodent) 8 **117**
Chsd clr ldrs, drvn/kept on fnl 2f, no ch with easy wnr: ran to best against a top-class rival: see 1231.

LONGCHAMP SUNDAY SEPTEMBER 10TH Righthand, Stiff, Galloping Track

*2736 **SOBIESKI 58** A Fabre 3-9-2 L Dettori 37/10: 116113: 3 b c Polish Precedent - Game Plan ¾ 116
(Darshaan) Settled rear, rdn/late gains, no impress: 8 wk abs: comfortable Gr 2 wnr in 2736 (10f, soft).
3718 **KATHMANDU 15** D Sepulchre 3-9-2 (bl) C Asmussen 141/10: 411434: Twrds rear, late gains, no threat. nk 116
*2398 **LYCITUS 74** 3-9-2 (bl) G Mosse 78/10: -12115: In tch, eff 2f out, wknd: 10 wk abs, see 2398. 1 114
2998 **RAYPOUR 43** 3-9-2 N McCullagh 3/10 FAVcp: 614616: Set fast pace to 2f out, wknd qckly: pacemaker. 4 109
6 ran Time 2m 26.4 (H H Aga Khan) J Oxx Currabeg, Co Kildare

HANNOVER SUNDAY SEPTEMBER 10TH -

Official Going GOOD

3930	**3.50 GR 3 PREIS DER STADTSPARKASSE 3YO+** 1m4f Good
	£23387 £9356 £4677 £2903

-- **MOONLADY** H Remmert 3-8-9 K Woodburn : 1: 3 b f Platini - Midnight Fever (Sure Blade) 111
Led at slow pace, qcknd tempo 3f out, styd on well, drvn out: eff at 12f on gd: smart German-trained filly.
1459 **WELL MINDED 112** H Blume 3-8-9 A Boschert : 20-432: 3 br f Monsun - Well Proved (Prince Ippi) ¾ 110
Cl-up, drvn to chall over 1f out, no impress fnl 1f: eff at 11/12f: see 1459.
-- **SERINGA** P Rau 3-8-9 R Koplik : 3: 3 b f Acatenango - Seldom (Wavering Monarch) 1¾ 108
Bhd, drvn & styd on late but no threat to front pair: eff at 12f on gd.
*3595 **FIRECREST 17** J L Dunlop 3-8-9 K Darley : 111414: Settled mid-div, rdn/eff over 1f out, unable to ¾ 107
qckn: ran to near best but reportedly not suited by waiting tactics off a slow pace: see 3595.
8 ran Time 2m 36.04 (Gary A Tanaka) H Remmert Germany

TABY (SWEDEN) SUNDAY SEPTEMBER 10TH Lefthand, Sharp Track

Official Going GOOD

3931	**3.05 GR 3 STOCKHOLM CUP INTERNATIONAL 3YO+** 1m4f Good
	£43860 £14620 £7310 £4300 3 yo rec 9 lb

-- **VALLEY CHAPEL** Wido Neuroth 4-9-6 E Ahern 6/1: 1: 4 ch c Selkirk - Valley Springs (Saratoga Six) 111
In tch, hdwy to chall ldr dist, drvn to lead nr fin: eff at 12f on gd: smart Norwegian colt.
4416} **BARRIER REEF 330** A P O'Brien 3-8-11 K Andersen 17/10: 4152-2: 3 b c Perugino - Singing Millie nk 110
(Millfontaine) Prom, went on 4f out, styd on well but collared near line: Irish raider, up in trip on belated reapp:
dual '99 wnr, incl a Navan mdn: prev eff at 1m, now suited by 12f: acts on gd & hvy grnd: useful, fine reapp.
-- **DANO MAST** F Poulsen 4-9-6 M Larsen 20/1: 3: 4 b c Unfuwain - Camera Girl (Kalaglow) 1 108
Bhd, rdn & styd on well fnl 2f, nvr nrr: eff over 12f on gd grnd.
*3483 **MURGHEM 22** M Johnston 5-9-6 D Holland 6/5 FAV: 111214: In tch, drvn & not qckn appr fnl 1f: shd 108
Brit raider, capable of better & likes to dominate: see 3483 (Gr 2, 13f).
2886} **DREAM POWER 774** 5-9-6 Madeleine Smith 36/1: 2210/0: Lost tch halfway, 10th: v long abs. 0
10 ran Time 2m 27.7 (Stall Perlen) Wido Neuroth Norway

BELMONT PARK SATURDAY SEPTEMBER 9TH Lefthand, Easy Track

Official Going FAST

3932	**10.12 GR 1 MAN O'WAR STKS 3YO+** 1m3f Fast
	£182927 £60976 £33537

-2998 **FANTASTIC LIGHT 42** Saeed bin Suroor 4-9-0 J D Bailey 13/20 FAV: -12521: 4 b c Rahy - Jood (Nijinsky) 124
Settled twrds rear, smooth hdwy to lead over 1f out, pshd out, cosily: 6 wk abs: earlier won on reapp in Dubai
(Gr 3, with Sir M Stoute) & subs rnr-up to Montjeu in Gr 1 King George: in fine '99 form, won at Sandown (Gr 3,
reapp), York (Gr 2 Great Voltigeur) & Newbury (List, off 125): dual '98 Sandown wnr: eff at 10/12f on fast, soft
& any trk: runs well fresh: tough & high-class colt who shld give a gd account in the Breeders Cup Turf.
3564 **ELA ATHENA 17** M A Jarvis 4-8-11 M E Smith 35/1: 041252: 4 gr f Ezzoud - Crodelle (Formidable) 1 116
Chsd ldrs, hdwy to lead appr fnl 1f, sn hdd, not pace of wnr: completed a 1-2 for the Brit raiders: smart filly
who loves a sound surface: will reportdly be campaigned in the US for the remainder of the season: see 3151.
-- **DRAMA CRITIC** America 4-9-0 J R Velazquez 33/1: 3: 4 b c Theatrical - Guiza (Golden Act) nk 119
8 ran Time 2m 17.44 (Godolphin) Saeed bin Suroor Newmarket

WOODBINE (CANADA) SUNDAY SEPTEMBER 10TH --

Official Going FIRM

3933	**7.40 GR 1 ATTO MILE 3YO+** 1m Firm
	£253165 £84388 £46414

13] **RIVIERA 1037** R J Frankel 6-8-5 J R Velazquez 106/10: 1135/1: 6 ch h Kris - Manureva (Nureyev) 119
+3452 **ARKADIAN HERO 23** L M Cumani 5-8-7 J P Spencer 21/1: 041612: 5 ch h Trempolino - Careless Kitten nse 120
(Caro) V slow to start & lost many lengths, ran on strongly for press fnl 2f, just failed: v unlucky & would
surely have won this with a level break: eff at 6f/1m: v smart & deserves another chance: see 3452.
-- **AFFIRMED SUCCESS** America 6-8-9 J Chavez 44/10: 3: 6 b g Affirmed - Towering Success (Irish Tower) 1½ 119
*3544 **MUHTATHIR 28** Saeed bin Suroor 5-8-12 M E Smith 4/1: -31615: Front rank, chall over 2f out, drvn 119

WOODBINE (CANADA) SUNDAY SEPTEMBER 10TH --

appr fnl 1f & sn held: Brit raider, capable of better: see 3544.
154} **KAHAL** 637 6-8-9 B Blanc 11/1: 22D5/0: Fin 11th: stablemate of Muhtathir.   **0**
13 ran   Time 1m 33.18   (E A Gann)   R J Frankel USA

CHANTILLY MONDAY SEPTEMBER 11TH Righthand, Galloping Track

Official Going GOOD

3934 1.55 GR 3 PRIX D'AUMALE 2YO FILLIES 1m Good
£21134   £7685   £3842   £2305

--   **GREEN MINSTREL** J M Beguigne 2-8-9 O Peslier 6/5 FAV: -11: 2 b f Green Tune - Shy Minstrel   **106**
(The Minstrel) Chsd ldrs, gd hdwy to lead ins last, pshd out, comfortably: recent debut scorer at Deauville:
eff over a gall 1m on gd grnd: won with something to spare here, win more Gr races.
--   **WINTER SOLSTICE** Mme C Head 2-8-9 O Doleuze 5/2: -12: 2 b f Unfuwain - Hunt The Sun (Rainbow   ¾   **102**
Quest) Led, rdn clr 2f out, hdd ins last, not pace of easy wnr: recent Deauville debut wnr: eff at 1m on gd.
--   **POLYANDRY** R Gibson 2-8-9 C Soumillon 8/1: -153D: 2 b f Unknown - Unknown (Unknown)   2   **98**
Prom, eff over 1f out, drvn & hung left ins last, no extra: fin 3rd, disqual & plcd 5th: stays 1m on gd.
--   **CHOC ICE** R Collet 2-8-9 S Pasquier 118/10: 606133: Rear, eff over 1f out, onepcd: fin 4th, plcd 3rd.   2   **94**
7 ran   Time 1m 42.8   (X Beau)   J M Beguigne France

YARMOUTH WEDNESDAY SEPTEMBER 13TH Lefthand, Flat, Fair Track

Official Going: GOOD/FIRM (GOOD places)   Stalls: Straight Course - Far Side, Remainder - Inside.

3935 2.00 NEWTON SELLER 3-4YO (G) 1m2f21y Firm 16 -15 Slow
£2065   £590   £295   3 yo rec 7 lb

3773 **LOKOMOTIV** 11 [4] J M Bradley 4-9-9 (bl) J Fortune 16/1: 105261: 4 b g Salse - Rainbow's End   **49**
(My Swallow) Dwelt, prog fnl 3f & styd on gamely to lead nr line, all out: bt in for 5,500gns, jockey given 2
day whip ban: earlier scored at Ayr (sell): rnr up in '99 (rtd 57, P D Evans, h'cap): '98 wnr here at Yarmouth
(sell, rtd 75, M Channon): eff at 7f/1m, suited by 10/11f on firm & gd/soft: eff with/without blnks, tried a visor.
3691 **GAME TUFTY** 16 [1] P Howling 4-9-4 J Quinn 6/1: -00062: 4 b g Sirgame - Melancolia (Legend Of   shd   **43**
France) Held up, prog to lead over 3f out, rdn fnl 1f, hdd nr line: op 4/1: acts on firm & gd/soft: see 1210.
3351 **ERIN ANAM CARA** 30 [2] D J S Cosgrove 3-8-6 (BL) C Rutter 14/1: 000053: 3 ch f Exit To Nowhere -   3½   **33**
Honey Heather (Kris) Cl up over 3f out, onepace/held fnl 1f: imprvd in 1st time blnks: eff btwn 1m/10f: see 1572.
3737 **NIGHT AND DAY** 14 [7] P S McEntee 3-8-6 (vis) R Mullen 11/2: 305404: Held up, hdwy 4f out, rdn   2½   **29**
fnl 1f: clr of rem: prob stays 10f: see 3561, 118 (mdn).
2887 **SILKEN LADY** 51 [8] J Weaver 12/1: 003605: Held up, rdn/mod hdwy: 7 week abs: see 2537.   11   **17**
3050 **JEUNE PREMIER** 43 [12] D R McCabe 16/1: 500006: Led after 1f till over 3f out, sn btn: 12   **9**
6 wk abs: first time visor, no improvement: see 3050.
3921 **DOUBLE FAULT** 1 [10] J Mackay (5) 33/1: 330007: Prom 7f: unplcd here yesterday (7f).   5   **0**
3868 **CALDIZ** 6 [11] 3-8-11 (t) R Studholme 13/2: -66648: Sn rdn, al bhd: qck reapp: see 3868, 1912.   1¼   **0**
3835 **ANASTASIA VENTURE** 8 [9] 3-8-7 (VIS)(1ow) J Reid 2/1 FAV: 324539: Trkd ldrs 7f, sn btn: well bckd   1½   **0**
tho' op 7/4: dissap eff in first time visor: btr 1388, 1051 & 745 (mdns).
3456 **FEEL THE STEEL** 26 [3] 3-8-6 N Carlisle 50/1: 00: Led 1f, handy 6f: 10th: longer 10f trip.   1   **0**
3917 **UBITOO** 1 [6] 3-8-11 (bl) T G McLaughlin 50/1: 000000: Chsd ldrs 7f: 11th: unplcd here yesterday.   8   **0**
3445 **UZY** 26 [5] 4-9-4 A Daly 33/1: 0-0000: Al bhd: 12th: mod form this term: scored in '99 (rtd 61, first   8   **0**
time visor, h'cap, I Balding): rtd 66 in '98: eff at 6f, handles gd & gd/soft grnd: with M Ryan.
12 ran   Time 2m 07.3 (3.1)   (Mrs Heather Raw)   J M Bradley Sedbury, Gloucs

3936 2.35 DANNY WRIGHT HCAP 3YO+ 0-80 (D) 1m str Firm 16 -10 Slow [80]
£5850   £1800   £900   £450   3 yo rec 5 lb   Field raced stands side

3839 **ADELPHI BOY** 8 [10] M C Chapman 4-9-1 (67) R Studholme (3) 14/1: 460021: 4 ch g Ballad Rock -   **73**
Toda (Absalom) Made all, in command fnl 1f, rdn out: earlier scored at W'hampton (4 rnr AW sts, rtd 102a): plcd
sev times in '99 (h'caps, rtd 73 & 92a): '98 Southwell wnr (2, mdn & nurs) & Lingfield (h'cap, rtd 91a & 80):
suited by 7/9.4f, tried 12f: acts on firm, soft & both AWs: handles any trk, likes a sharp one: well h'capped.
3809 **TRIBAL PRINCE** 10 [18] P W Harris 3-9-6 (77) J Weaver 9/2: 001342: 3 b g Prince Sabo - Tshusick   1½   **78**
(Dancing Brave) Trkd ldrs, rdn & styd on fnl 1f, al held by wnr: op 6/1: styd longer 1m trip: see 3445 (7f).
3796 **DARYABAD** 10 [17] N A Graham 8-8-2 (54)(bl) Dale Gibson 8/1: 013133: 8 b g Thatching - Dayanata   hd   **54**
(Shirley Heights) Mid div, rdn/styd on fnl 2f, not pace to chall: jockey given 3-day careless riding ban: 3384 (7f).
3885 **BOBBYDAZZLE** 5 [14] C A Dwyer 5-8-0 (52) W Supple 20/1: 403404: Prom, styd on onepce fnl 2f for   nk   **51**
press: op 14/1: qck reapp: on a fair mark, could find similar this autumn: acts on firm, soft & fibresand: see 78.
3810 **NOUF** 16 [16] 4-9-0 (66) S Whitworth 10/1: 500008: Rear, hdwy/kept on fnl 2f: handles firm & soft.   nk   **64**
3384 **PROSPECTORS COVE** 28 [8] 7-9-5 (71) M Roberts 8/1: 466236: Rear, hdwy fnl 2f, keeping on when no   nk   **68**
room ins last, no threat: prob plcd with a clr run: won this race last year, likes Yarmouth: see 1611 (7f).
3238 **THUNDER SKY** 35 [15] 4-9-9 (75)(vis) J Fortune 14/1: 510057: Chsd ldrs 6f: see 2293 (7f, made all, mdn).   2½   **67**
3810 **INDIUM** 10 [3] 6-9-10 (76) P Shea (7) 20/1: 500008: Rear, kept on fnl 2f, nvr plcd to chall: top-weight: 1¾   **65**
jockey/horse banned & trainer fined under the schooling in public rule: back on a winning mark, keep in mind.
3880 **TOPTON** 6 [7] 6-9-9 (75)(bl) J Quinn 10/1: 351069: Held up, hdwy when hmpd over 1f out, held after.   ¾   **63**
3642 **LEGAL SET** 18 [13] 4-9-8 (74) J P Spencer 14/1: 360230: Chsd ldrs, btn 1f out: 10th: see 3642, 854.   1   **60**
3698 **TIME FOR MUSIC** 16 [2] 3-9-7 (78) T Williams 25/1: 61-000: Chsd ldrs 6f: 11th: see 3135 (5f).   1½   **61**
3810 **TAFFS WELL** 10 [11] 7-9-3 (69) D Holland 4/1 FAV: 600000: Trckd ldrs, btn over 1f out: 12th: hvly   3½   **45**
bckd: very much a talking horse this term, has failed to deliver as yet but remains well h'capped: see 715.
3514 **Minetta** 24 [12] 5-9-8 (74) M Fenton 16/1:   3725 **Shaanxi Romance** 14 [9] 5-7-12 (50)(vis) G Bardwell 16/1:
3355 **Starlight** 30 [6] 3-8-11 (68) J Mackay (5) 33/1:   3746 **Saffron** 13 [1] 4-7-10 (48)(6oh) D Glennon (5) 40/1:
16 ran   Time 1m 37.2 (2.1)   (Barry Brown)   M C Chapman Market Rasen, Lincs

3937 **3.10 EASTERN COND STKS 3YO+ (C) 6f Firm 16 +03 Fast**
£5945 £2255 £1127 £512 3 yo rec 2 lb Raced centre - stands side

3120 **FEMME FATALE 40** [6] W Jarvis 3-8-1 J Quinn 7/2: 231-41: 3 b f Fairy King - Red Rita (Kefaah) **94**
Trkd ldrs, rdn/led ins last, held on well: op 5/2, 6 wk abs, gd time: won fnl '99 start at Ayr (List, rtd 108): eff at 6f on firm & gd, likes a gall/fair trk: runs well fresh: useful filly.
3768 **BLUE VELVET 12** [9] K T Ivory 3-8-1 C Carver (2) 20/1: 165062: 3 gr f Formidable - Sweet Whisper *shd* **93**
(Petong) Held up, prog halfway to lead over 1f out, rdn/hdd ins last, battled on & just btn in a thrilling fin.
*3667 **DEEP SPACE 17** [5] E A L Dunlop 5-9-4 J Reid 13/8 FAV: 543013: 5 br g Green Desert - Dream *1* **105**
Season (Mr Prospector) Held up, shaken up for eff over 1f out, styd on onepace: nicely bckd: see 3667 (C/D).
3503 **FLOWINGTON 24** [7] N P Littmoden 3-8-1 R Mullen 16/1: 420304: Dwelt, held up racing keenly, *nk* **89**
briefly outpcd 2f out, rdn/styd on well ins last, no threat: op 14/1: eff at 5/6f, worth a try at 7f: see 1371.
3920 **AFAAN 1** [8] 7-8-9(1ow) T G McLaughlin 33/1: 040005: Held up racing keenly, eff 2f out, sn onepace/ *½* **94$**
held: unplcd in a 5f h'cap here yesterday: see 113 (AW).
3667 **ALHUFOOF 17** [1] 3-8-1 W Supple 3/1: 1-4046: Led, rdn/hdd over 1f out, sn held: hvly bckd, op 7/2. *½* **85**
+3481 **WAHJ 25** [2] 5-9-4 D Holland 9/1: 112017: Chsd ldrs, btn 1f out: btr 3481 (7f, made all). *1½* **96**
3503 **DANDY NIGHT 24** [4] 3-8-13 J Fortune 14/1: 013068: Chsd ldrs till over 1f out: op 12/1: see 2289. *¾* **91**
3744 **FOUND AT LAST 13** [3] 4-8-8 Dale Gibson 66/1: 435229: Prom, outpcd from halfway: highly tried. *9* **62$**
9 ran Time 1m 11.2 (0.8) (Anthony Foster) W Jarvis Newmarket, Suffolk

3938 **3.40 HALVERGATE FILLIES MDN 2YO (D) 6f Firm 16 -24 Slow**
£3558 £1095 £547 £273 Raced centre - stands side

3568 **NASMATT 21** [4] M R Channon 2-8-11 L Dettori 10/11 FAV: -331: 2 b f Danehill - Society Lady (Mr **93**
Prospector) Trkd ldrs, went on 2f out, styd on well ins last, rdn out: hvly bckd, op 5/4: half sister to top class juv filly Bint Allayal, sire a top class miler: eff at 6f, 7f will suit: acts on firm & fast grnd, sharp/undul or gall trk: useful juv, should hold her own in a higher grade.
-- **ROCKERLONG** [5] G Wragg 2-8-11 M Roberts 8/1: 2: 2 b f Deploy - Dancing Rocks (Green *½* **90**
Dancer) Chsd ldrs, rdn/outpcd over 2f out, styd on well for press ins last, not rch wnr: op 9/2: March foal, half sister to smart Gr 3 7f juv wnr Glatisant: dam a smart 10f performer: eff at 6f, looks sure to relish 7f+: acts on firm grnd: most promising intro, should find similar soon.
3795 **OOMPH 10** [9] W Jarvis 2-8-11 M Tebbutt 20/1: 43: 2 b f Shareef Dancer - Seductress (Known *1½* **87**
Fact) Prom, rdn/edged left over 1f out, kept on ins last: op 14/1: step up to 7f+ shld suit: acts on firm grnd.
3789 **KAFEZAH 11** [6] B Hanbury 2-8-11 W Supple 9/1: 44: Chsd ldr, led over 3f out till 2f out, held *hd* **86**
ins last: handles firm & fast grnd: see 3789 (stks).
3876 **JELBA 6** [1] 2-8-11 M Fenton 16/1: 53505: Held up, went left soon after start, prog to chall over 1f *¾* **84**
out, held ins last: op 12/1, qck reapp: back to form after trying 1m in Group company in 3876: see 2132.
3237 **TISSALY 35** [2] 2-8-11 D Harrison 15/2: 236: Held up, eff over 2f out, al held: op 6/1: btr 3027 (5f). *1¾* **80**
-- **YAQOOTAH** [7] 2-8-11 R Hills 4/1: 7: Held up, keen, nvr pace to chall: op 3/1: Gone West filly, March *1¾* **76**
foal, half sister to two useful 6f juv wnrs, Rihan & Elshabiba: dam a high class 1m juv performer in USA: looks sure to relish step up to 7f, shld improve on this considerate intro for E Dunlop.
3795 **DANE DANCING 10** [10] 2-8-11 J Fortune 33/1: -508: Chsd ldrs till over 1f out: see 3342. *1½* **72$**
3385 **MANUKA TOO 28** [8] 2-8-11 R Mullen 50/1: 059: Led over 2f, btn 2f out: needs a drop in grade. *3½* **63**
9 ran Time 1m 12.8 (2.4) (Sheikh Ahmed Al Maktoum) M R Channon West Isley, Berks

3939 **4.15 SEA-DEER APPR HCAP 3YO+ 0-75 (G) 7f str Firm 16 -15 Slow** **[74]**
£1935 £553 £276 3 yo rec 4 lb Raced across track, pair racing far side well ahead

3839 **BLAKESET 8** [3] T D Barron 5-8-12 (58)(bl) L Enstone (7) 16/1: 006001: 5 ch g Midyan - Penset (Red **65**
Sunset) Made all far side, held on well ins last, all out: earlier scored at W'hampton (AW clmr, rtd 84a): '99 Lingfield wnr (h'cap, rtd 82a), rnr up for R Hannon earlier (rtd 85, stks): plcd in '98 (rtd 88, h'cap): eff at 6f, suited by 7/7.5f on firm, gd & both AWs, any trk: best in blnks, tried a t-strap: gd weight carrier.
3816 **ARZILLO 9** [5] J M Bradley 4-8-2 (48)(1ow) M Savage (0) 33/1: 305002: 4 b g Forzando - Titania's Dance *nk* **54**
(Fairy King) Chsd wnr far side thro'out, rdn/strong chall ins last, styd on, just held: clr of rem: see 1211.
3561 **RIOS DIAMOND 21** [6] M J Ryan 3-7-12 (48) D Kinsella (3) 16/1: 134003: 3 b f Formidable - Rio *4* **46**
Piedras (Kala Shikari) Prom centre, rdn & styd on fnl 1f, no threat: acts on firm, fast & fibresand: see 2036.
3873 **FLIGHT OF DREAMS 6** [1] M Wigham 3-7-10 (46)(5oh) S Warren (1) 8/1: 006134: Far side, towards rear, *¾* **43**
switched centre bef halfway, styd strongly on inside last, nrs fin: eyecatching late hdwy, keep in mind: see 3873.
3871 **DANZAS 6** [18] 6-8-3 (44)(bl)(5ow) D Watson (0) 14/1: 504665: Held up stands side, mod hdwy fnl *2* **42**
3f: op 16/1, quick reapp: first home on unfavoured stands side: see 1462, 896.
3626 **MABROOKAH 18** [15] 4-9-2 (62) P Shea 16/1: 245-06: Held up stands side, styd on fnl 2f, nrst fin. *1¾* **52**
3854 **BISHOPSTONE MAN 7** [4] 3-9-6 (70) W Hutchinson 14/1: 200357: Prom stands side, held fnl 1f. *nk* **59**
*3605 **EASTERN PROPHETS 19** [9] 7-8-7 (53)(vis) S Clancy (3) 9/1: 044018: Prom 5f stands side: op 7/1. *nk* **41**
3612 **FINERY 19** [12] 3-8-2 (52) D Meah (5) 9/1: 300349: Chsd ldrs stands side 5f: btr 2612, 3456 (clmrs). *1* **38**
3803 **CLEAR CRYSTAL 10** [10] 3-7-10 (46)(2oh) S Hitchcott (7) 25/1: 660660: Prom 5f stands side: 10th. *nk* **31**
3440 **HYDE PARK 26** [7] 6-8-5 (51)(t) Clare Roche 8/1: 000100: Led stands side 5f: 11th: btr 3192 (1m). *½* **35**
3831 **COPPLESTONE 8** [16] 4-9-12 (72) Carol Packer (7) 7/2 FAV: 432220: Chsd ldrs stands side 5f: 12th: *2* **52**
nicely bckd, op 7/1: remains a mdn: see 3831, 1744 & 1070.
3873 **KNOBBLEENEEZE 6** [17] 10-7-11 (43)(vis) M Mathers 10/1: 416000: Al rear stands side: 13th: btr 3294. *1¾* **20**
3605 **Toblersong 19** [2] 5-7-10 (42)(vis) Kriston Stubbs (2) 20/1: 3579 **Woodlands 21** [13] 3-9-6 (70) C Halliwell (7) 20/1:
15 ran Time 1m 24.8 (2.2) (Nigel Shields) T D Barron Maunby, N Yorks

3940 **4.45 EBF FLEGGBOROUGH MDN 2YO (D) 7f str Firm 16 -30 Slow**
£3753 £1155 £577 £288 Majority racing centre seemed favoured

3568 **REBEL STORM 21** [8] J H M Gosden 2-9-0 J Fortune 8/1: 01: 2 b c Storm Bird - Heavenly Rhythm **86+**
(Septieme Ciel) Dwelt, prom far side, led dist, styd on well ins last under hands & heels riding: eff at 7f, 1m shld suit: acts on firm & a fair trk: lost all ch at the start on debut, clearly going the right way.
3680 **ALBASHOOSH 16** [12] E A L Dunlop 2-9-0 J Reid 6/4 FAV: 032: 2 b c Cadeaux Genereux - Annona *1* **83**
(Diesis) Trkd ldrs far side, rdn/ch over 1f out, kept on inside last, not pace of wnr: hvly bckd, tchd 2/1: acts on fast & firm grnd: eff at 7f, return to 1m should suit: see 3680.

2956 **WANNABE AROUND** 47 [17] T G Mills 2-9-0 T Williams 12/1: 63: 2 b c Primo Dominie - Noble Peregrine ½ 82
(Lomond) Chsd ldrs stands side, led that group 2f out, styd on, not rch front pair far side: 7 week abs: well
clr on stands side, creditable effort: handles firm & fast grnd: can find a race: see 2956.
3169 **TUDOR REEF** 38 [5] J Noseda 2-9-0 J Weaver 16/1: -0464: Led far side, rdn/hdd over 1f out, kept on ¾ 81
onepace: op 14/1: eff at 7f, 1m could suit: handles firm grnd: should apprec h'caps: see 1943.
3840 **CELTIC MISSION** 8 [4] D Holland 2-9-0 J Weaver 10/1: 05: Dwelt, sn in tch far side, styd on onepace fnl 2f. ½ 80
3786 **DREAM MAGIC** 11 [9] 2-9-0 T G McLaughlin 40/1: 06: Dwelt, prom far side, outpcd fnl 2f: see 3786. nk 78
-- **PENDULUM** [6] 2-8-9 M Hills 7/1: 7: Chsd ldrs far side, ch over 1f out, sn held: op 5/1: Pursuit nk 73
Of Love filly, Feb foal, half sister to 2 juv wnrs: sire high class 6f/1m performer: with W J Haggas.
3627 **PENTLAND** 18 [14] 2-9-0 M Roberts 12/1: 058: Dwelt, held up far side, rdn & kept on fnl 2f: op 10/1. 1¾ 75
3627 **MINE** 18 [16] 2-9-0 J P Spencer 7/2: 39: Led stands side 5f, sn held: bckd, tho' op 5/2: raced on 2 71
unfav stands side, poss better judged on 3627 (6f).
-- **AMIR ZAMAN** [3] 2-9-0 A McGlone 25/1: 0: Dwelt, held up far side, mod hdwy: 10th: Salse colt, hd 70
May foal, cost 80,000gns: half brother to smart juv Mudeer: dam unrcd: likely to apprec 1m+: shld improve.
-- **SINJAREE** [1] 2-9-0 M Tebbutt 50/1: 0: Dwelt, held up far side, mod late gains under minimal press: shd 70+
11th: Mark Of Esteem colt, March foal, cost 55,000gns: dam a 7f juv wnr, subs scored at 10f: will apprec 1m+.
2414 **DEFINITE GUEST** 70 [11] 2-9-0 G Hind 25/1: 60: Chsd ldrs far side, rdn over 1f out, wknd fnl 2f (6f). ½ 69
3215 Zozarharry 35 [1] 2-9-0 C Rutter 25/1:   3859 Jalons Star 7 [7] 2-9-0 R Studholme (3) 66/1:
-- Olympic Pride [2] 2-8-9 J Mackay (5) 33/1:   -- Bustle [13] 2-8-9 S Whitworth 10/1:
-- Crossways [15] 2-9-0 R Mullen 33/1:
17 ran   Time 1m 25.8 (3.2)   (R Sangster, B Sangster & A Sangster)   J H M Gosden Manton, Wilts

5.15 BRIAN TAYLOR HCAP 3YO+ 0-90 (C)   1m2f21y Firm 16 +07 Fast   [87]
          £7702   £2370   £1185   £592   3 yo rec 7 lb

*3842 **LYCIAN** 8 [5] J A R Toller 5-7-11 (56) T Williams 13/8 FAV: 034011: 5 b g Lycius - Perfect Time 65
(Dance Of Life) Held up, no room over 2f out, prog to lead dist, held on well, rdn out: nvy bckd: earlier won at
Leicester (appr h'cap): '99 wnr at Lingfield (rtd 70a) & Goodwood (h'caps, rtd 63): '98 wnr at Brighton, Bath &
Lingfield (h'caps, rtd 57 & 63a): eff at 1m, suited by 10f: acts on firm, gd & both AWs: still lks fairly h'capped.
3063 **KRISPIN** 43 [3] G Wragg 3-9-1 (81) D Holland 20/1: 033102: 3 ch c Kris - Mariakova (The Minstre |) nk 87
Chsd ldrs, rdn/ch over 1f out, styd on well, just held: op 14/1: abs: acts on firm & gd/soft grnd: can find similar.
3808 **WILLIE CONQUER** 10 [7] Andrew Reid 8-8-11 (70) J Reid 9/1: 011123: 8 ch g Master Willie - 3 72
Maryland Cookie (Bold Hour) Held up, styd on well fnl 2f, no threat: relishes sell/claiming grade: see 3526.
3415 **BANDLER CHING** 27 [10] C N Allen 3-8-9 (75) J Mackay (5) 16/1: -52134: Led 9f, no extra: see 3217. 1 76
3563 **JORDAN** 21 [13] 3-9-6 (86) M Hills 20/1: 110405: Held up, late hdwy, no threat: see 2434 (class stks). ¾ 86
3899 **PUZZLEMENT** 4 [4] 6-8-10 (69) S Hitchcott (7) 20/1: 005506: Dwelt/held up, rdn/mod hdwy fnl 2f. ½ 68
3270 **RAGDALE HALL** 34 [8] 3-9-2 (82) J Fortune 6/1: -51037: Held up, rdn/mod hdwy fnl 2f, no threat. shd 64
2528 **PRINCE SLAYER** 66 [1] 4-9-7 (80) J Quinn 25/1: 201008: Held up, eff over 2f out, sn held: abs. 1½ 77
3858 **PERFECT MOMENT** 7 [14] 3-8-4 (70) M Roberts 20/1: 116109: Prom, fdd fnl 2f: see 3858, 3263. 2½ 63
3628 **ANOTHER TIME** 18 [2] 8-9-10 (83) M Tebbutt 10/1: 043520: Held up, eff 3f out, no impress when nk 75
hmpd inside last: 10th: op 8/1: see 1170.
3471 **FAHS** 25 [11] 8-9-9 (82) D Harrison 12/1: 121150: Held up, nvr a factor: 11th: op 10/1: btr 3336. 1¼ 72
*3381 **SCACHMATT** 28 [9] 3-9-4 (84) J P Spencer 20/1: 024210: Trkd ldrs, btn 2f out: 13th: op 7/1. 0
3403 Achilles Sky 28 [6] 4-9-1 (74)(VIS) J Weaver 20/1:   3731 Trois 14 [15] 4-7-13 (58) Dale Gibson 25/1:
3270 El Zito 34 [12] 3-9-6 (86) T E Durcan 25/1:
15 ran   Time 2m 05.1 (0.9)   (A Isley)   J A R Toller Newmarket, Suffolk

Official Going   GOOD TO FIRM. Stalls: Sprint Crse - Far Side; 14f - Outside; Rem - Inside.

2.10 CHESTNUT MDN AUCT 2YO (E)   5f str   Good/Firm 36 -07 Slow
          £3688   £1135   £567   £283   Raced in 2 groups - no significant advantage.

3720 **FIAMMA ROYALE** 18 [15] Mrs P N Dutfield 2-8-1 L Newman (1) 3/1 FAV: 524201: 2 b f Fumo Di Londra - 70
Ariadne (Bustino) Led/dsptd lead, led overall appr fnl 1f, styd on strongly, drvn out: well bckd: rnr-up sev
times prev: Apr foal, half-sister to a smart 6f wnr, dam 2m wnr: eff at 5/6f on fast & fair grnd: deserved this.
3761 **LITTLE CALLIAN** 12 [10] T M Jones 2-7-12 P Doe 10/1: 604362: 2 ch f Charmer - Eucharis (Tickled Pink) 1 64
Led over 3f out, prsd by wnr sn after, hdd dist, no extra cl-home: eff at 5f on fast grnd: win similar, see 3205.
3571 **MINUSCOLO** 21 [3] J A Osborne 2-8-1 A Nicholls (3) 33/1: -0063: 2 b f Piccolo - Wrangbrook (Shirley ¾ 65
Heights) Dwelt, bhd near side, rdn/hdwy appr fnl 1f, ran on strongly late, nvr nrr: eff at 5f on fast grnd:
gd effort, worth a look when returning to 6f in a nursery: see 2488.
3055 **ADWEB** 43 [6] J Cullinan 2-7-12 P M Quinn (3) 33/1: 004: Prom nr side, led that group appr fnl 1½ 58
1f, no extra well nss last: 6 wk abs: imprvd form: stays 5f on fast: see 3055.
3486 **MOONLIGHT DANCER** 25 [7] 2-8-4 R Hughes 8/1: 202505: Reared start, sn in tch nr side, cl-up nk 68
halfway, rdn/held appr fnl 1f: drop in trip: see 2724 (6f).
3814 **TROUBLESHOOTER** 10 [4] 2-8-6 (bl) T Quinn 14/1: 020626: Led nr side, hdd appr fnl 1f, sn btn: hd 65
poss unsuited by this drop in trip: see 3814 (6f).
3710 **HIGHLAND FLIGHT** 15 [12] 2-7-12 F Norton 8/1: 047: Handy far side, hdwy appr fnl 1f, wknd fnl 1f. shd 57
3832 **BREAKING NEWS** 8 [2] 2-8-13 P Robinson 4/1: 38: Cl-up nr side, drvn/fdd over 1f out: tchd 1 69
7/1: shade better on debut in 3832 (6f, firm).
2828 **MADAME ROUX** 54 [5] 2-8-4 N Pollard 33/1: -409: Handy nr side, wknd fnl 1f: 8 wk abs: see 1659. 1½ 57
-- **INDIAN GIVER** [9] 2-8-4 P Fitzsimons (2) 14/1: 0: Mid-div far side, lost pl halfway, kept on, no dngr: 1½ 54
10th: cost 15,000gns, dam related to a top-class miler: with R Hannon, shld learn from this & improve over further.
-- **JOE TAYLOR** [14] 2-8-13 Pat Eddery 10/1: 0: Dwelt, al bhd far side, 11th: 19,000gns May foal, 5 51
half-brother to sev wnrs in the States: with D Arbuthnot.
-- **ZILKHA** [16] 2-8-8 K Darley 7/1: 0: Dwelt, sn in tch, wknd after halfway, 12th: op 5/1: 16,000gns ¾ 45
Feb foal, dam scored over 5f as a juv: sire high-class sprinter: with I Balding.
-- Minnies Mystery [13] 2-7-12 G Baker (5) 20/1:   -- Brown Holly [11] 2-8-6 D Sweeney 20/1:
-- Laudable Lad [8] 2-8-4(1ow) R Havlin 33/1:   3044 Bravura 44 [1] 2-8-9 W Ryan 33/1:
16 ran   Time 1m 01.75 (2.15)   (Royal Oak Racing Partnership)   Mrs P N Dutfield Axmouth, Devon.

3943   2.45 EBF FILLIES MDN 2YO (D)   1m rnd   Good/Firm 36 -52 Slow
£4231   £1302   £651   £325

3607 **TIME AWAY 19** [2] J L Dunlop 2-8-11 Pat Eddery 10/11 FAV: 21: 2 b f Darshaan - Not Before Time   **92+**
(Polish Precedent) Cl-up, led going well appr fnl 2f, pushed clr ins last, cmftbly: well bckd: Feb foal, half-
sister to a couple of mid-dists wnrs: eff at 7f/1m, will relish mid-dists next term: acts on fast, gd & a stiff/
gall trk: potentially useful filly who can rate more highly, esp over further next year.
--   **GAY HEROINE** [1] Sir Michael Stoute 2-8-11 T Quinn 3/1: 2: 2 b f Caerleon - Gay Gallanta (Woodman)   2½   83
Dwelt, chsd ldrs, rdn over 2f out, kept on nicely under hands-and-heels: nicely bckd: Feb foal, dam Gr wng juv
at 6f: sire high-class at 10/12f: stays a stiff/gall 1m on fast: kind intro, sure to improve & can win similar.
3678 **SEYOOLL 16** [4] M R Channon 2-8-11 Craig Williams 4/1: 43: 2 b f Danehill - Andromaque (Woodman)   ½   82
Set slow pace, rdn/hdd appr fnl 2f, no extra appr fnl 1f: op 3/1: see 3678.
3786 **MISS TRESS 11** [5] H W Harris 2-8-11 P Doe 25/1: -464: Keen/prom, rdn/no impress fnl 2f: up in trip.   4   75
--   **WESTERN EDGE** [3] 2-8-11 K Darley 7/1: 5: Dwelt, ran green thr'out, nvr dngrs: Mar foal, sister   2   71
to mid-dist wnr Marcus Maximus, also a 7f juv wnr: dam wnr at up to 9f: with J Gosden, sure to improve for this.
5 ran   Time 1m 46.07 (7.07)   (R Barnett)   J L Dunlop Arundel, W.Sussex.

3944   3.20 TOTALBET.COM FILL HCAP 3YO 0-85 (D)   1m rnd   Good/Firm 36 -25 Slow   [90]
£7410   £2280   £1140   £570

3422 **COLNE VALLEY AMY 27** [3] G L Moore 3-8-5 (67) P Doe 16/1: 143251: 3 b f Mixoram - Panchellita   71
(Pancho Villa) Cl-up, led appr fnl 2f, qckly increased pace & sn clr, ran on strongly, rdn out: earlier won at
Salisbury (2, appr h'caps): unplcd in '99 (rtd 58, mdn): suited by 7f/1m, stays a sharp/undul 10f: acts on
firm & gd/soft grnd & likes a stiff/undul trk, esp Salisbury: well rdn by P Doe.
3810 **OGILIA 10** [12] I A Balding 3-9-3 (79) K Darley 5/1 FAV: 461002: 3 b f Bin Ajwaad - Littlemisstrouble   1¼   80
(My Gallant) In tch, rdn to improve over 2f out, ran on for press ins last, no ch with wnr: nicely bckd: back
to best here: ran to form of C/D success in 3435.
3279 **EMANS JOY 33** [11] J R Fanshawe 3-8-1 (63) A Nicholls (3) 11/2: 351453: 3 b f Lion Cavern - Carolside   nk   64
(Music Maestro) Keen/prom, chsd wnr appr fnl 1f, held ins last: consistent, eff at 6f/1m: see 2462.
3505 **SEEKING SUCCESS 24** [1] Sir Michael Stoute 3-9-4 (80) Pat Eddery 9/1: 226134: Cl-up, drvn & kept   1¼   79
on onepace appr fnl 1f: made all in 3221.
3658 **OMNIHEAT 17** [9] G Faulkner (3) 8/1: 540005: Keen, waited with, hdwy when short of   ¾   73
room appr fnl 1f, no extra well ins last: see 3317, 1649.
*3218 **FOOTPRINTS 35** [10] 3-8-13 (75) B Marcus 12/1: 002016: Set stdy pace, hdd appr fnl 2f, ev ch   shd   73
till wknd fnl 1f: prev with M Johnston, now with W R Muir, see 3218 (7f clmr).
3663 **EVE 17** [6] 3-8-4 (66) J Stack 16/1: 234307: Rcd wide in tch, dropped rear over 2f out, late hdwy   1   62
ins last, no dngr: not given a hard time here, shld apprec a return to further: see 3281 (10f class stks, firm).
3856 **DUSKY VIRGIN 7** [4] 3-7-11 (58) (1ow) F Norton 11/2: 212328: Dwelt, nvr dngrs: qck reapp: btr 3856.   shd   55
3317 **EVERGREEN 32** [5] 3-8-9 (71)(t) R Hughes 8/1: 002169: Waited with, hdwy when no room 2f out,   ¾   66+
rdn briefly dist, eased considerably fnl 1f: wld have fin much closer with assistance from the saddle, keep in mind.
3643 **BLOODY MARY 18** [7] 3-8-3 (65) L Newman (3) 20/1: 0A-0100: Bhd, rdn/eff 3f out, sn btn, 10th.   shd   60
3756 **SEEKING UTOPIA 13** [8] 3-7-13 (60)(1ow) N Pollard 20/1: 0P0330: Keen, cl-up, wknd over 1f out, 11th.   2½   52
3707 **LAND AHEAD 16** [2] 3-9-7 (83) T Quinn 6/1: 1D2320: Prom, wknd/short of room over 1f out, sn btn,   2   70
fin 12th: well bckd & v disapp here, capable of much better: see 3707 (mdn, soft).
12 ran   Time 1m 43.95 (4.95)   (Colne Valley Golf (Deluxeward Ltd))   G L Moore Woodingdean, E.Sussex.

3945   3.50 NORWEST CLASSIFIED STKS 3YO+ 0-85 (C)   1m rnd   Good/Firm 36 +09 Fast
£6506   £2002   £1001   £500   3 yo rec 5 lb

3629 **WILLOUGHBYS BOY 18** [3] B Hanbury 3-9-0 Pat Eddery 6/1: 616201: 3 b c Night Shift - Andbell   89
(Trojen Fen) Waited with, hdwy & sltly short of room over 2f out, switched left & chall over 1f out, led well ins
last, shade cosily: op 4/1, fast time: earlier won at Beverley (mdn) & Yarmouth (h'cap): eff at 7f/1m on firm,
gd & a stiff/gall or easy trk: useful & progressive, shld follow up.
3643 **FREDORA 24** [4] M Blanshard 5-9-5 T Quinn 13/2: 140452: 5 ch m Inchinor - Ophrys (Nonoalco)   1½   84
Settled last, rdn/hdwy over 2f out, led appr fnl 1f, hdd well ins last, sn held: ran to best: see 2629.
1958 **DANCING MIRAGE 89** [7] R Hannon 3-8-8 L Newman (3) 9/1: 310-63: 3 ch f Machiavellian - Kraemer   1¼   76
(Lyphard) Chsd ldrs, rdn/sltly outpcd 2f out, ran on ins last, no threat to ldrs: gd run after a 3 month
abs: just sharper for this & worth another try at 10f: see 1958.
3325 **NIMELLO 32** [5] P I Cole 4-9-2 D Sweeney 8/1: 010004: Bhd, gd hdwy over 2f out, chall dist,   nk   79
wknd qckly ins last: op 6/1: btr 1042 (rtd h'cap, hvy).
3865 **INVADER 7** [2] 4-9-5 (vis) P Robinson 11/2: 002105: Keen/dsptd lead, wknd over fnl 1f: qck reapp.   5   74
*3865 **GREEN CARD 7** [1] 6-9-5 R Hughes 5/4 FAV: 630416: Chsd clr ldrs, smooth hdwy appr fnl 2f, drvn &   1½   71
no extra appr fnl 1f, sn btn: well bckd: qck reapp: unsuited by this drop back to 1m: see 3865 (10f class stks).
3662 **KAFIL 17** [6] 6-9-2 A Nicholls (3) 50/1: 306037: Bhd, eff/short of room over 1f out, no dngr: flattered.   3   62$
2167 **TWEED MILL 81** [8] 3-8-8 K Darley 25/1: -21008: Set fast pace, hdd appr fnl 1f, wknd: btr 1032 (mdn, hvy).   9   45
8 ran   Time 1m 41.21 (2.21)   (Mrs G E M Brown)   B Hanbury Newmarket.

3946   4.25 EBF NOV STKS 2YO (D)   7f rnd   Good/Firm 36 -22 Slow
£4914   £1512   £756   £378

*3635 **ATTACHE 18** [2] M Johnston 2-9-2 K Darley 2/1 FAV: -211: 2 ch c Wolfhound - Royal Passion   104
(Ahonoora) Cl-up, hdwy when carried left appr fnl 2f, rdn into lead dist, styd on well, rdn out: well bckd:
earlier won at Redcar (nov auct): half-brother to useful sprinter Tadeo, dam a 10f wnr: eff arnd 7f, 1m shld
suit: acts on fast grnd & a stiff or gall trk: useful & progressive, could complete at hat-trick.
--   **DILSHAAN** [4] Sir Michael Stoute 2-8-8 Pat Eddery 7/2: 2: 2 b c Darshaan - Avila (Ajdal)   1½   92
Chsd ldrs, eff/carr left over 2f out, rdn & kept on nicely but no impress on wnr: op 5/2: 190,000gns Feb foal,
half-brother to a wnr abroad: sire high-class at 12f: eff over a stiff/gall 7f on fast: encouraging, win a mdn.
3086 **CAUVERY 42** [5] S P C Woods 2-9-5 B Marcus 4/1: -2103: 2 ch c Exit To Nowhere - Triple Zee (Zilzal)   ½   102
Led early, remained with ldrs, rdn again appr fnl 1f, hdd dist, not pace of wnr: nicely bckd after 6 wk abs:
gd effort, capable of landing similar: see 2271.
*3333 **GLEAMING BLADE 31** [3] Mrs A J Perrett 2-9-5 W Ryan 11/4: -214: Rcd keenly & sn led, rdn &   1¾   99

hung left appr fnl 2f, hdd over 1f out, fdd: nicely bckd: ran to form of mdn success in 3333.

3484 **LYSANDERS QUEST 25** [1] 2-8-12 T Quinn 8/1: -45: Waited with, drvn appr fnl 2f, late hdwy,   *hd* **92**
no threat: prob in need of 1m+: see 3484.

5 ran   Time 1m 30.47 (4.07)   (J R Good)   M Johnston Middleham, N.Yorks.

3947	**4.55 WILLOW CLAIMER 3YO+ (E)**	**5f str**	**Good/Firm 36 -01 Slow**
	£2951 £908 £454 £227	3 yo rec 1 lb	

3668 **THAT MAN AGAIN 17** [14] S C Williams 8-8-9 (bl) G Faulkner (3) 11/4 FAV: 300531: 8 ch g Prince   **64**
Sabo - Milne's Way (The Noble Player) Made all far side, strongly pressed ins last, all out, just prevailed:
nicely bckd, jockey rec a 1 day whip ban: earlier won at Salisbury (h'cap, gamble): '99 Sandown & Newmarket
wnr (h'caps, rtd 82), '98 Folkestone & Lingfield wnr (rtd 76 & 74a): stays 6f, all wins at 5f: handles hvy, acts on
firm/fast: acts on any trk, likes Sandown: has tried visor, best in blnks, likes dominating, on a fair mark.

3689 **ANSELLMAN 16** [1] A Berry 10-8-11 (bl) R Hughes 10/1: 145332: 10 gr g Absalom - Grace Poole   *shd* **65**
(Sallust) Chsd ldrs, rdn over 2f out, ran on strongly for press ins last, just failed: v tough 10yo, likes clmrs.

3747 **PERIGEUX 13** [13] K T Ivory 4-8-6 (VIS) C Catlin (7) 20/1: 510003: 4 b g Perugino - Rock On   *hd* **60**
(Ballad Rock) Sn chsg wnr, drvn & styd on well ins last, not btn far: gd effort in 1st time visor: tough: see 2428.

3774 **QUITE HAPPY 11** [5] W J Musson 5-8-6 Pat Eddery 15/2: 222204: In tch, rdn/prog over 2f out,   *¾* **58**
styd on late, nvr nr ldrs: see 3502, 897.

3694 **TADEO 16** [7] 7-8-13 K Darley 7/2: 300035: Sn rdn in tch, hdwy over 1f out, kept on, no threat: *nk* **64**
former smart sprinter, looked well in at the weights here: see 3694.

3689 **MY EMILY 16** [4] 4-8-6 T Quinn 5/1: 600226: Handy, rdn/hdwy over 2f out, held well ins last: *1* **54**
nicely bckd: drop in trip: shade btr 3689, 3493 (6f).

3694 **WHITE SUMMIT 16** [2] 3-8-6 P Fitzsimons (5) 50/1: -00067: Chsd ldrs, drvn over 2f out, btn fnl 1f.   *¾* **53$**

3579 **HOPEFUL HENRY 21** [6] 4-8-6 W Ryan 33/1: 0-608: Waited with, hdwy appr fnl 1f, sn btn: mod prev.   *nk* **51$**

3259 **MALAAH 34** [8] 4-8-12 (bl) B Marcus 50/1: 500569: Bhd, switched/late hdwy, no threat: flattered.   *nk* **57$**

3734 **CROWDED AVENUE 14** [3] 3-8-8-9 (vis) S Sanders 5/1: -03200: Bhd, nvr dngrs: 10th: op 4/1: btr 2266.   *¾* **52**

3820 **ZOENA 9** [12] 3-8-13 L Newman (3) 16/1: 630530: Dwelt, sn in tch, wknd over 1f out, eased: 11th.   *½* **56**

3622 **Dancing Jack 19** [10] 7-8-5 R Brisland (5) 66/1:   2716 **Clara Blue 58** [11] 4-8-0 N Pollard 66/1:

3214 **Minimus Time 35** [15] 3-7-13 G Baker (7) 66/1:

14 ran   Time 1m 01.45 (1.85)   (J T Duffy & R E Duffy)   S C Williams Newmarket.

3948	**5.30 SURREY HERALD HCAP 3YO+ 0-80 (D)**	**1m6f**	**Good/Firm 36 -09 Slow**	**[75]**
	£4641 £1428 £714 £357	3 yo rec 11lb		

3025 **HAMBLEDEN 45** [2] M A Jarvis 3-9-8 (80) P Robinson 20/1: 103201: 3 b g Vettori - Dalu (Dancing   **83**
Brave) In tch, hdwy to chall appr fnl 2f, led over 1f out, ran on well, drvn out: 6 wk abs: earlier won on the
AW at W'hampton (h'cap, v easily): showed promise fnl '99 start (rtd 70, mdn): eff btwn 10f & 14f on firm, hvy
& fibresand: prob handles any trk & runs well fresh: improving, win again.

3783 **FLETCHER 11** [6] H Morrison 6-9-5 (66) R Hughes 5/1: 115102: 6 b g Salse - Ballet Classique   *½* **68**
(Sadler's Wells) In tch, rdn/hdwy over 2f out, hung right & styd on ins last, al held by wnr: in gd form, see 3424.

3858 **THE GREEN GREY 7** [8] L Montague Hall 6-9-10 (71) A Clark 9/1: 152543: 6 gr g Environment Friend -   *¾* **72**
Pea Green (Try My Best) Settled rear, rdn/hdwy over 2f out, ran on strongly ins last, closing at fin: op 12/1, qck
reapp: gd run under top-weight on this step up to 14f, can win at this trip: see 3858, 2888.

3695 **PALUA 16** [9] Mrs A J Bowlby 3-9-6 (78) T Quinn 10/1: 203324: Waited with, rdn/late hdwy,   *½* **78**
nvr nrr: often plcd but remains a mdn: see 3695.

*3664 **SEND ME AN ANGEL 17** [7] 3-8-12 (70) P Dobbs (5) 8/1: 226315: Prom, hdwy to lead appr fnl 2f,   *1* **68**
hdd over 1f out, held well ins last: in gd heart, see 3664.

3794 **SANTIBURI GIRL 11** [10] 3-9-0 (72) A Polli (3) 16/1: 112406: Sn well bhd, rdn/hdwy 3f out,   *nk* **70**
styd on well, no impress: op 12/1: clr rem: up in trip & poss stays 14f: sede 3415, 3329.

3557 **JOIN THE PARADE 21** [3] 4-8-11 (58) F Norton 25/1: 302007: Mid-div at best: up in trip: see 2033.   *5* **49**

3657 **WATER FLOWER 17** [13] 6-9-1 (62) B Marcus 20/1: 100008: Bhd, late gains: btr 2023 (12f, firm).   *3* **49**

3800 **SEA DANZIG 10** [11] 7-7-12 (45) R Brisland (5) 33/1: 010509: Bhd, nvr a factor: btr 2982.   *1½* **30**

3783 **BRISBANE ROAD 11** [5] 3-8-12 (70)(t) K Darley 5/1: 451200: Prom, hdwy to chall over 2f out,   *1¾* **53**
wknd qckly appr fnl 1f, 10th: see 3522.

*3522 **FANTASTIC FANTASY 23** [12] 3-9-8 (80) Pat Eddery 11/4 FAV: 116210: Mid-div, lost tch fnl 2f,   *2½* **60**
11th: well bckd, reportedly hung thr'out race: much btr 3522.

*3754 **ZEYAARAH 13** [14] 3-9-8 (80) R Perham 7/1: 30-310: Dsptd lead & set fast pace, hdd/wknd qckly   *½* **59**
over 2f out, 12th: went off too fast here: much btr 3754.

*3681 **HIGHLY PRIZED 16** [1] 6-8-10 (57) L Newman (3) 14/1: 600010: Led/dsptd fast pace, led overall   *shd* **36**
3f out, hdd over 2f out, wknd qckly, 13th: btr 3681 (12f clmr).

13 ran   Time 3m 01.34 (6.34)   (Stag & Huntsman)   M A Jarvis Newmarket.

BEVERLEY   WEDNESDAY SEPTEMBER 13TH   Righthand, Oval Track with stiff uphill finish

Official Going: GOOD TO FIRM. Stalls: Inside.

3949	**1.50 TATTERSALLS MDN AUCT DIV 1 2YO (E)**	**7f100y rnd**	**Good 46 -03 Slow**
	£3051 £939 £469 £234		

3729 **WONDERGREEN 14** [10] T D Easterby 2-8-4(1ow) J Carroll 4/7 FAV: 60031: 2 ch c Wolfhound - Tenderetta   **73**
(Tender King) Pld hard, trkd ldr, went on 2f out, sn hung right, pressed dist, rdn & reasserted towards fin:
nicely bckd: imprvd since stepped up to 7.5f/1m: acts on fast & gd grnd, stiff or gall trk: scopey colt.

2916 **HEATHYARDS GUEST 49** [8] R Hollinshead 2-8-12 A Culhane 14/1: 02: 2 ch c Be My Guest - Noble   *½* **78**
Nadia (Thatching) Chsd ldrs, chall 1f out, kept on but held cl home: op 10/1, clr rem, 7 wk abs: much
improved, conceding wnr 8lbs: runs well fresh, stays 7.5f on gd grnd & shld win similar.

3655 **BAJAN BLUE 18** [3] M Johnston 2-7-12 R Ffrench 4/1: 6333: 2 b f Lycius - Serotina (Mtoto)   *7* **50**
Not go pace, late hdwy thro' btn horses: op 11/4: needs a drop in grade, see 3400.

3697 **PREMIER BOY 16** [4] B S Rothwell 2-8-3 Joanna Badger (7) 50/1: 004: Pld hard, prom, no extra fnl 2f.   *hd* **55**

3740 **TUPGILL CENTURION 13** [6] 2-8-7 G Duffield 14/1: 45: Nvr a factor: op 8/1, see 3740.   *1½* **56**

828 **CENTURY STAR 160** [5] J Tate 16/1: -006: Led till 2f out, fdd: 5 month abs: Bigstone Gldg.   *¾* **52$**

2360 **ROYAL MUSICAL 72** [1] 2-8-0 D Mernagh (3) 25/1: 5007: Went left start, nvr nr ldrs: 10 week abs.   *1*   **45**
3632 **FILLE DE DAUPHIN 18** [2] 2-7-12 J McAuley 40/1: -08: Bhd from halfway: longer trip.   *1¾*   **39**
--   **NIGHT ON THE TOWN** [7] 2-8-7 J Bosley (4) 16/1: 9: Wide, al bhd: op 7/1: Dancing Spree gelding.   *2*   **44**
9 ran   Time 1m 34.5 (3.7)   (Health Mail Ltd)   T D Easterby Great Habton, N Yorks

---

3950   **2.20 OLYMPIC SELL NURSERY HCAP 2YO 0-65 (F)**   **7f100y rnd**   **Good 46**   **-19 Slow**   **[71]**
       £2492   £712   £356

3246 **THE FANCY MAN 35** [12] N Tinkler 2-9-0 (57)(VIS) A Culhane 16/1: -40601: 2 ch c Definite Article - Fanciful (Mujtahid) Mid-div, rdn ent fnl 2f, kept on well bef dist, led fnl 50y: no bid, set alight by visor: clearly suited by step up to a stiff 7.5f on gd grnd & drop in grade.   **65**
3615 **PETIT TOR 19** [3] J Norton 2-8-13 (56) P Hanagan (7) 13/2: 264122: 2 b f Rock City - Kinoora (Kind Of Hush) Chsd ldrs, rdn ent fnl 2f, chall ins last, not pace of wnr: gd run, eff at 7/7.5f: see 3438.   *1¼*   **60**
3837 **EASTERN RED 8** [10] K A Ryan 2-8-13 (46) D O'Donohoe 3/1 FAV: 054623: 2 b f Contract Law - Gagajulu (Al Hareb) With ldrs, led 2f out till fnl 50y: tchd 9/2: fair run, clr rem, acts on firm & gd grnd.   *1*   **48**
3697 **CIRCUIT LIFE 16** [4] A Berry 2-8-12 (55) G Duffield 15/2: 666234: Mid div, styd on for press appr fnl 1f, unable to chall: worth another try at this 7.5f trip, acts on fast grnd.   *3*   **51**
3776 **EL UNO 11** [11] 2-9-7 (64) R Cody Boutcher (7) 14/1: -0065: Led/dsptd lead till 2f out, no extra.   *1½*   **57**
3615 **LIGHT OF ARAGON 19** [7] 2-7-10 (39) Joanna Badger (7) 20/1: -00006: Off the pace till kept on fnl 1f.   *½*   **31**
3615 **SOLO DANCE 19** [1] 2-8-2 (45)(bl) P Fessey 16/1: -44057: Chsd ldrs, onepce ent fnl 2f: no form.   *nk*   **36**
2513 **MASTER COOL 67** [14] 2-8-7 (50) R Winston 16/1: 44558: Rear, kept on late into mid-div: 10 wk abs.   *nk*   **40**
3733 **IVANS BRIDE 14** [6] 2-8-13 (56) J Tate 16/1: 406249: Well plcd till wknd appr fnl 1f: btr 3468.   *nk*   **45**
3675 **HIGH SOCIETY LADY 17** [5] 2-8-9 (52) J McAuley 20/1: 000000: Nvr troubled ldrs: 10th on h'cap bow.   *2*   **37**
3697 **EMMA THOMAS 16** [15] 2-8-1 (44) P Bradley (5) 10/1: 0000: Slow away, nvr in it: 11th, h'cap bow.   *1¾*   **26**
3776 **NISAN BIR 11** [16] 2-9-1 (58) J Carroll 9/1: 405000: In tch till wknd 2f out: 12th, op 7/1, see 1838.   *hd*   **40**
3246 **BOMBAY BINNY 35** [9] 2-8-4 (47)(bl) G Parkin 9/1: 205550: Speed 3f: 15th, op 6/1, blnks reapplied.   **0**
3589 **Angelas Husband 20** [13] 2-8-13 (56)(vis) D Mernagh (3) 16/1:
3697 **Mare Of Wetwang 16** [8] 2-8-4 (47) Paul Eddery 14/1:
2730 **Runaway Bride 57** [2] 2-8-11 (54) R Fitzpatrick 16/1:
16 ran   Time 1m 35.7 (4.9)   (P D Savill)   N Tinkler Langton, N Yorks

---

3951   **2.55 PRICEWATERHOUSE HCAP 3YO+ 0-65 (F)**   **1m100y rnd**   **Good 46**   **+05 Fast**   **[64]**
       £3594   £1106   £553   £276   3 yo rec 5 lb

3885 **THIHN 5** [13] J L Spearing 5-9-3 (53) A Beech (5) 9/2: 600203: 5 ch g Machiavellian - Hasana (Private Account) Bhd ldrs, trav well, pld out & ran on strongly to lead below dist, going away: nicely bckd from 6/1, best time of day: deserved 1st win: rnr up in '99 (h'caps, rtd 55): eff at 1m/10f: acts on firm & soft grnd, any trk: likes a strong pace: has a decent turn of foot for this level & can win again.   **62**
3603 **ROUTE SIXTY SIX 19** [15] Jedd O'Keeffe 4-9-6 (56) J Fanning 7/1: 000232: 4 b f Brief Truce - Lyphards Goddess (Lyphard's Special) Well plcd, led appr fnl 1f, hdd inside last & outpcd by wnr: gd run, win again with a less testing finish, see 3011.   *2½*   **59**
3731 **KESTRAL 11** [16] T J Etherington 4-9-6 (56) G Duffield 5/2 FAV: 232123: 4 ch g Ardkinglass - Shiny Kay (Star Appeal) Cl up, eff ent fnl 2f, kept on same pace: bckd from 10/3: tough, see 3731, 3603.   *1*   **57**
3731 **SWYNFORD PLEASURE 14** [14] J Hetherton 4-9-0 (50) O Pears 14/1: 300304: Handy, rdn appr fnl 1f, no impression: op 10/1: back in trip, ran near to best: see 2180, 1939.   *1*   **49**
3731 **TYPHOON GINGER 14** [9] 5-9-7 (57) R Smith (5) 12/1: -66205: Towards rear, shaken up 2f out, kept on but nvr dangerous: promising run, see 1940 & 1070.   *1*   **54**
3756 **ASSURED PHYSIQUE 13** [17] 3-9-3 (58) D O'Donohoe 14/1: 556046: Led till 2f out, no extra: new tactics.   *½*   **54**
3711 **DIHATJUM 15** [12] 3-9-5 (60) J Carroll 12/1: 012337: Mid-div thro'out: btr 3196 (firm grnd clmr).   *1½*   **53**
3753 **MULLAGHMORE 13** [6] 4-9-2 (52) S W Kelly (3) 11/1: 005138: Towards rear, mod late wide hdwy.   *½*   **44**
1442 **DORISSIO 114** [1] 4-9-13 (63) Martin Dwyer 16/1: -33369: Held up, briefly short of room 2f out, onepace.   *½*   **54**
3410 **CYBERTECHNOLOGY 27** [5] 6-9-11 (61) A Culhane 12/1: 161060: Al rear: 10th, not given a hard ride.   *¾*   **50**
3808 **Future Prospect 10** [2] 6-9-5 (55) F Lynch 16/1:   3808 **Marton Mere 10** [11] 4-9-10 (60) R Winston 16/1:
3745 **Agiotage 13** [4] 4-9-5 (55) J Tate 12/1:   3604 **Dianeme 19** [7] 3-9-1 (56) G Parkin 20/1:
2970 **Nip In Sharp 47** [8] 7-9-0 (50) Paul Eddery 20/1:
15 ran   Time 1m 47.3 (3.5)   (Messrs P Cowan, S Daniels & B Beale)   J L Spearing Kinnersley, Worcs

---

3952   **3.30 TATTERSALLS MDN AUCT DIV 2 2YO (E)**   **7f100y rnd**   **Good 46**   **-09 Slow**
       £3051   £939   £469   £234

3692 **SISTER CELESTINE 16** [9] W Jarvis 2-8-0 Martin Dwyer 7/2: 241: 2 b f Bishop Of Cashel - Pipistrelle (Shareef Dancer) Bhd ldrs, pulled out ent fnl 2f, ran on to lead bef fnl 1f, readily: half-sister to a 1m wnr, dam 13f wnr: apprec step up to a stiff 7.5f & will get further: acts on gd grnd, poss handles fast.   **75**
3692 **MARSHAL BOND 16** [8] B Smart 2-8-3 Paul Eddery 12/1: 62: 2 b c Celtic Swing - Arminda (Blakeney) Chsd ldrs, feeling pace appr fnl 2f, rdn bef dist, no impress till kept on nicely towards fin: op 8/1: suited by step up to 7.5f, should come into his own in mid-dist h'caps next term.   *2½*   **71**
3772 **EL HAMRA 11** [4] B A McMahon 2-8-4(1ow) Dean McKeown 10/1: 332523: 2 gr c Royal Abjar - Cherlinoa (Crystal Palace) Prom, chall appr fnl 1f, onepce: consistent, see 2916.   *1*   **70**
3729 **HOBO 14** [7] D W Barker 2-8-5 F Lynch 25/1: 0004: Led till bef fnl 1f, fdd: new tactics: nds sellers.   *2*   **67$**
3729 **CYBER SANTA** [10] 2-8-7 O Pears 20/1: 5: Outpcd, styd on appr fnl 1f: op 12/1 on debut: 15,000gns Celtic Swing first foal, likely to get mid-dists next term: with J Hetherton.   *2*   **65**
3649 **AUNT RUBY 18** [5] 2-8-4 A Beech (5) 33/1 FAV: 026: Handy, outpcd ent fnl 2f: well bckd, up in trip.   *¾*   **61**
3156 **KATHANN 39** [2] 2-7-12 D Mernagh (3) 50/1: 007: Al same pl: 6 wk abs: Presidium filly, dam useful styr.   *¾*   **53**
3128 **THE MERRY WIDOW 40** [6] 2-7-12 R Ffrench 50/1: 008: Al towards rear: 6 week abs.   *¾*   **55**
3814 **OUR INDULGENCE 10** [1] 2-8-3 P Fessey 12/1: -009: Outpcd: no worthwhile form.   *nk*   **51**
--   **TUPGILL TANGO** [3] 2-8-5 G Duffield 25/1: 0: Dwelt, nvr in it: 10th on debut: 8,500gns half brother to a 1m wnr, dam hdles wnr: with S Kettlewell.   *1¼*   **54**
10 ran   Time 1m 34.9 (4.1)   (Sales Race 2000 Syndicate)   W Jarvis Newmarket, Suffolk

BEVERLEY WEDNESDAY SEPTEMBER 13TH Righthand, Oval Track with stiff uphill finish

3953 4.00 GARROWBY FILLIES MDN 2YO (D) 7f100y rnd Good 46 -14 Slow
£3705 £1140 £570 £285

3730 **LOVE EVERLASTING 14** [12] M Johnston 2-8-11 J Fanning 11/10 FAV: -3421: 2 b f Pursuit Of Love - In Perpetuity (Great Nephew) Prom, boxed in going well 2f out, switched dist, qcknd to lead nr fin: well bckd, deserved, jockey given 3 day ban for irresp. riding: ran into the useful looking Tobougg last time: eff at 7.5f, further is going to suit (half-sister & dam won at 10f): acts on fast & gd grnd, stiff/gall trks: improve further. **85**
3661 **ATAMANA 17** [11] M P Tregoning 2-8-11 Martin Dwyer 2/1: -22: 2 b f Lahib - Dance Ahead (Shareef Dancer) With ldr, rdn to lead ent fnl 1f, hdd nr fin: nicely bckd: eff at 7.5f: shld win similar. *nk* **83**
3614 **ROSALIA 19** [8] T D Easterby 2-8-11 J Carroll 20/1: -463: 2 b f Red Ransom - Normandy Belle (Fit To Fight) Led till just inside fnl 1f, held towards fin: op 12/1: much improved form the front over longer 7.5f trip: should win a fillies mdn if repeating this. *1* **81**
-- **MASAKIRA** [9] Sir Michael Stoute 2-8-11 F Lynch 12/1: 4: Mid-div, chsd ldrs appr fnl 1f, onepace ins last: op 7/1, debut: Royal Academy first foal, dam a mdn: likely to come on plenty for this & win similar. *1½* **78**
-- **PRICKLY POPPY** [6] 2-8-11 G Duffield 14/1: 5: Chsd ldrs, keeping on onepce when hmpd ins last: op 10/1 on debut, stablemate 2nd: Feb foal, dam 10f wnr, sire a miler: promising, sure to improve. *1* **76**
-- **SHAANARA** [10] 2-8-11 P Fessey 25/1: 6: In tch, eff 2f out, same pace: clr rem, debut: 130,000gns Darshaan May foal, half-sister to 7f wnr Cool Edge: promise here in what was a 'hot' fillies mdn for this track. *¾* **74**
3692 **CHICKASAW TRAIL 16** [3] 2-8-11 J Tate 50/1: 007: Al towards rear: needs a drop in grade. *6* **59**
3675 **KUNDALILA 17** [7] 2-8-11 Dean McKeown 25/1: -048: Nvr on terms: now qual for h'caps. *1* **57**
3786 **GOLDEN WINGS 11** [2] 2-8-11 (BL) Paul Eddery 50/1: -009: Dwelt, held up, btn fnl 2f: blnks. *10* **37**
3776 **TUPGILL FLIGHT 11** [4] 2-8-11 R Winston 66/1: 0000: Nvr a factor: 10th, no worthwhile form. *2½* **32**
-- **Our Shellby** [5] 2-8-11 A Culhane 50/1: -- **Born Wild** [1] 2-8-11 D O'Donohoe 20/1:
12 ran Time 1m 35.3 (4.5) (Mr & Mrs G Middlebrook) M Johnston Middleham, N Yorks

3954 4.35 JAGUAR CENTRE HCAP 3YO 0-70 (E) 1m4f Good 46 -22 Slow [74]
£3242 £998 £499 £249

3805 **PERPETUO 10** [3] R A Fahey 3-9-2 (62) P Hanagan (7) 7/1: 33621: 3 b f Mtoto - Persian Fountain (Persian Heights) Slightly hmpd start, held up, prog appr fnl 2f, led below dist, hung left, pshd out: 1st win, unrcd juv: eff at 10/12f, stay further on this evidence: acts on firm & soft grnd: likes uphill finishes: unexposed. *1¼* **67**
3819 **TUFTY HOPPER 9** [15] P Howling 3-9-5 (65) R Winston 10/1: 045332: 3 b g Rock Hopper - Melancolia (Legend Of France) Keen, mid-div, clsd 3f out, sn short of room, clr dist, ran on: op 7/1: poss unlucky. *¾* **67**
3769 **FOR HEAVENS SAKE 11** [13] C W Thornton 3-9-0 (60) J Fanning 12/1: 602323: 3 b g Rambo Dancer - Angel Fire (Nashwan) Trckd ldrs going well, shaken up to lead 2f out, hdd 1f out, onepace: styd this longer, stiff 12f: remains a mdn after 13 tho' has the ability to win, possibly at 10f/with a less testing finish. *1¾* **61**
*3195 **RAPID DEPLOYMENT 37** [10] J G Smyth Osbourne 3-9-3 (63) S Carson (3) 6/1: -00214: Well plcd, chall 2f out, no extra inside last: drifter from 7/2: won a match in 3195. *3* **62**
3764 **ELLWAY HEIGHTS 12** [6] 3-9-0 (60) Martin Dwyer 12/1: -0645: Rear, shaken up & styd on fnl 2f, nvr dngrs: hold up tactics poss overdone over longer 12f trip on h'cap bow: worth another try at 12f: see 3764. *2* **55**
3713 **YOURE SPECIAL 15** [8] 3-9-7 (67) Dean McKeown 13/2: -10006: Wide, mid-div throughout: op 10/1. *nk* **59**
3399 **LADY DONATELLA 28** [14] 3-8-7 (53) A Beech (5) 7/2 FAV: 00-627: Mid-div, came wide appr fnl 2f & no extra: btr 3399 (C/D class stakes). *1¼* **44**
3125 **TOP HAND 40** [11] 3-8-12 (58) O Pears 33/1: 400008: Led till ent fnl 2f, fdd: 6 wk abs, unprvn beyond 1m. *2½* **47**
2425 **LENNY THE LION 70** [4] 3-8-8 (54) A Culhane 6/1: 055309: Nvr a factor: 10 week abs, see 2332. *5* **40**
2195 **PERCUSSION 79** [12] 3-8-7 (53) R Ffrench 4/1: 006400: Chsd ldrs till wknd appr fnl 2f: 10th, 11wk abs. **34**
3663 **Valdero 17** [5] 3-9-7 (67) G Duffield 16/1: 3395 **Windmill 28** [9] 3-9-5 (65)(BL) J Carroll 12/1:
3870 **Storm Prince 6** [1] 3-9-3 (63) A Mackay 33/1: 3819} **Rambo Nine 371** [2] 3-8-9 (55) S Finnamore(5) 33/1:
14 ran Time 2m 39.4 (8.1) (A N Barrett) R A Fahey Butterwick, N Yorks

3955 5.05 GORACING.CO.UK MDN 2YO (D) 5f Good 46 -34 Slow
£4091 £1259 £629 £314 High numbers favoured.

3466 **PRINCE PYRAMUS 25** [9] C Grant 2-9-0 F Lynch 14/1: -441: 2 b c Pyramus - Rekindled Flame (King's Lake) Handy, chall appr fnl 1f, drvn to lead fnl 100y: slow time: apprec drop back to 5f on gd grnd. **79**
3720 **BRANDON WIZZARD 18** [12] I A Balding 2-9-0 D O'Donohoe 9/4: 602: 2 b c Tagula - Topmost (Top Ville) Front rank, led ent fnl 2f drvn & pressed dist, edged left & hdd towards fin: well bckd: suited by drop back to 5f on gd grnd: shown enough to win a race: see 3162. *½* **77**
-- **NIGHT GYPSY** [14] T D Easterby 2-8-9 J Carroll 7/1: 3: 2 b f Mind Games - Ocean Grove (Fairy King) In tch, eff 2f out, kept on well, not rch front 2: tchd 11/2 on debut: Jan first foal, dam 6f juv wnr: plenty of promise here at 5f, should improve & find a Northern mdn, possibly at 6f. *¾* **70**
3500 **DEIDAMIA 24** [16] P W Harris 2-8-9 A Beech (5) 14/1: -404: Chsd ldrs, not clr run & outpcd 2f out, stying on fin: clr rem: worth a try in blnks, now qual for h'caps: see 3174 (debut). *1¾* **65**
3767 **ENCYCLOPEDIA 12** [19] 2-8-9 G Parkin 16/1: 505: Led till ent fnl 2f, onepce: stablemate 3rd, op 12/1. *3* **56**
3812 **AMY G 10** [6] 2-8-9 N Kennedy 50/1: -06: Chsd ldrs, unable to qckn appr fnl 1f: 7,500gns Common Grounds half-sister to a wnr abroad: with N Tinkler, unfav low draw. *2* **50**
3814 **MAGNANIMOUS 10** [13] 2-9-0 (VIS) Kim Tinkler 50/1: -00007: Chsd ldrs till 2f out: visored, needs sellers. *1¾* **50**
-- **BINT ROYAL** [5] 2-8-9 O Pears 33/1: 8: Keen, towards rear, ran green appr fnl 2f, late prog: debut: Royal Abjar first foal, dam juv wnr abroad, sire a miler: poor low draw: with J Glover. *nk* **44**
3852 **BOUCHRA 7** [18] 2-8-9 A Culhane 2/1 FAV: -229: Mid-div throughout: op 6/4, quick reapp, unsuited by drop back in trip?: see 3852 (6f), 3635 (7f). *shd* **44**
1595 **MISTER MIND 105** [10] 2-9-0 D Mernagh (3) 50/1: 00: Nvr a factor: 10th. *1½* **45**
3812 **FLYING TACKLE 10** [8] 2-9-0 R Winston 50/1: -000: Al towards rear: 11th. *½* **44**
3732 **PHILIPPI 14** [3] 2-9-0 (bl) S W Kelly (3) 16/1: 030: Veered badly left start, nvr on terms: 12th poor draw. *½* **43**
-- **BEAT IT** [2] 2-8-9 G Duffield 14/1: 0: Badly hmpd start, al bhd: 15th, op 10/1 on debut: Diesis first foal, dam 1m wnr: poor low draw, forget this: with Sir M Prescott. **0**
1418 **Trudie 114** [4] 2-8-9 V Halliday 33/1: -- **Diamond Jayne** [15] 2-8-9 R Fitzpatrick 50/1:
3500 **Yorker 24** [11] 2-9-0 J Tate 20/1: 1628 **Love 104** [1] 2-9-0 J Fanning 16/1:
3143 **Roghan Josh 39** [17] 2-9-0 Dean McKeown 50/1: 3697 **Double Digit 16** [7] 2-8-9 P Fessey 50/1:
19 ran Time 1m 05.3 (4) (Havelock Racing) C Grant Wolviston, Co Durham

3956   5.40 SAFFIE JOSEPH MDN 3YO+ (D)   5f   Good 46 -02 Slow
£4212   £1296   £648   £324   3 yo rec 1 lb

3613 **MR STYLISH** 19 [19] I A Balding 4-9-0 (tvi) Martin Dwyer 6/4 FAV: 053301: 4 b g Mazillier - Moore Stylish   75
(Moorestyle) Trkd ldrs, went on bef fnl 2f, pshd clr, v cmftbly: nicely bckd, well drawn: plcd sev times prev,
incl in '99 (h'caps, rtd 71): acts on firm & hvy grnd, any track: best with t-strap & visor now.
3780 **TOP OF THE PARKES** 11 [20] N P Littmoden 3-8-8 J Tate 9/1: 30202D: 3 b f Mistertopogigo - Bella   4   58
Parkes (Tina's Pet) Bhd ldrs, edged out 2f out, rdn bef dist, styd on but no ch wnr: fin 2nd, plcd 3rd,
jockey banned 3 days for irresponsible riding: op 7/1: better off in sell h'caps: see 3584.
3820 **POLAR LADY** 9 [7] D Morris 3-8-8 R Winston 6/1: -35042: 3 ch f Polar Falcon - Soluce (Junius)   shd   58
Slowly into stride, mid-div by halfway, keeping on when hmpd 2f out, rallied: fin 3rd, plcd 2nd, tchd 10/1:
will apprec a return to 6f, see 877.
3744 **HOUT BAY** 13 [14] S E Kettlewell 3-8-13 D O'Donohoe 20/1: 530054: Last till picked up well ent fnl   2½   56
2f, nvr nrr: big drop in trip, see 1354, 781.
3194 **PRIDE OF PERU** 37 [17] 3-8-8 S W Kelly (0) 20/1: 005505: Reared start, prom, led bef halfway till   1¾   46$
2f out, no extra: stiff task, well drawn, prob flattered.
3180 **NOW IS THE HOUR** 37 [12] 4-9-0 G Gibbons (7) 50/1: 003656: Chsd ldrs, onepace ent fnl 2f: flattered.   1½   46$
3780 **DAVEYS PANACEA** 11 [10] 3-8-8 P Bradley (5) 12/1: 533307: Al mid-div: btr 3651, 3462 (fast).   hd   41
1024/ **B W LEADER** 505 [16] 3-8-13 (t) D McGaffin (5) 25/1: 0-8: Bhd, late hdwy into mid-div: tchd   1   43
50/1 on reapp, t-strap: unplcd sole '99 start for P Cole: since sold cheaply & now with Miss D McHale.
3698 **LAYAN** 16 [6] 3-8-8 J Edmunds 16/1: 342039: Handy 3f: poor low draw: btr 3698, 2947 (6f).   ¾   35
3780 **MELLEDGAN** 11 [18] 3-8-8 A Culhane 7/1: 640: Prom, wknd appr fnl 1f: 10th, see 3780, 3584.   ½   33
1093 **ICON** 134 [11] 3-8-8 J D Smith 16/1: 000: Nvr a factor: 11th, over 4 month abs, new stable.   1¼   29
3203 **THORNCLIFF FOX** 36 [5] 3-8-13 (vis) G Duffield 16/1: 603300: Nvr troubled ldrs: 12th, stiffish task.   nk   33
3393 Seahorse Boy 28 [13] 3-8-13 (VIS) K Hodgson 33/1: -- **Lakeside Lady** [3] 3-8-8 J Carroll 33/1:
3694 **Willrack Times** 16 [4] 3-8-8 A Beech (5) 33/1:   1040 **Mcquillan** 138 [2] 3-8-13 Dean McKeown 50/1:
3619 **Emma Amour** 19 [15] 3-8-8 T Lucas 16/1: -- **Shapiro** [8] 3-8-8 P McCabe 20/1:
3587 **Needwood Trickster** 20 [1] 3-8-13 J Fanning 16/1:
19 ran   Time 1m 03.7 (2.4)   (T J W Burton)   I A Balding Kingsclere, Hants

Official Going: SOFT. Stalls: Round Course - Inside: Straight Course - Centre.

3957   2.05 MOBIL-ONE AYRSHIRE SELLER 2YO (E)   1m rnd   Soft 105 -16 Slow
£3250   £1000   £500   £250

3697 **RATHKENNY** 17 [7] J G Given 2-8-11 Dean McKeown 11/2: -5641: 2 b c Standiford - Shine (Sharrood)   62
Settled rear, drvn & strong run ins last, led cl home, drvn out: tchd 7/1, bt in for 6,000gns: Mar 1st foal,
dam mdn wnr: apprec this step up to 1m on soft: acts on a gall trk: win again in this grade.
3704 **CO DOT UK** 17 [10] K A Ryan 2-9-2 D O'Donohoe 7/1: 134502: 2 b g Distant Relative - Cubist   1¼   63
(Tate Gallery) Prom, went on appr fnl 2f, hdd fnl 50y, no extra: nicely bckd & apprec this drop to selling
grade: eff at 6f/1m: seems to go best when there is cut in the grnd: see 1602.
3706 **JUST MISSED** 17 [3] M W Easterby 2-8-6 D Holland 11/2: 005053: 2 b f Inchinor - Lucky Round   hd   53
(Auction Ring) In tch, drpd rear over 3f out, rallied & ran on strongly appr fnl 1f, closing at fin: stys 1m on
soft grnd, could win a seller: see 1698.
3706 **JEZADIL** 17 [4] M Dods 2-8-6 A Culhane 6/1: 064434: Front rank, chall ldr over 2f out, no extra   1½   50
well inside last: consistent plating class form: see 3706.
3837 **BOBANVI** 9 [1] 2-8-6 F Norton 50/1: 003655: Waited with, rdn & styd on appr fnl 1f, no threat to   2½   44$
ldrs: treat rating with caution (officially only 39): see 2949.
3822 **DISPOL FOXTROT** 10 [12] 2-8-6 M Fenton 50/1: 046: Led, hdd over 2f out, fdd over 1f out: see 3822.   2   39
3706 **BORDER TERRIER** 17 [14] 2-8-11 S Sanders 9/2 FAV: -0427: With ldr till over 2f out, wknd: ¾   43
nicely bckd tho' op 3/1: much better 3706 (claimer).
3706 **LITTLE TASK** 17 [13] 2-8-11 R Winston 8/1: 426068: Mid div at best: btr 3706.   4   35
2057 **NO SURRENDER** 86 [2] 2-8-6 J Carroll 9/1: 69: Chsd ldrs, wknd qckly appr fnl 1f: 12 wk abs: see 2057.   1   27
2620 **BISHOPS SECRET** 63 [9] 2-8-11 R Hughes 33/1: -000: Nvr dangerous, fin 10th: 9 week abs: modest.   3½   25
3127 **Mud N Bert** 41 [8] 2-8-6 N Kennedy 50/1:   2394 **Daveysfire** 72 [6] 2-8-6 T E Durcan 50/1:
3184 **Wharfedale Lady** 38 [5] 2-8-6 K Darley 25/1: -- **Princess Sophie** [11] 2-8-6 J Bramhill 40/1:
14 ran   Time 1m 46.3 (9.7)   (Ray Monaghan)   J G Given Willoughton, Lincs

3958   2.35 TATTERSALLS AUCT MDN 2YO (E)   6f str   Soft 105 +02 Fast
£3893   £1198   £599   £299

3458 **ARMAGNAC** 27 [6] M H Tompkins 2-8-9 S Sanders 11/1: 042551: 2 b c Young Ern - Arianna Aldini   92
(Habitat) In tch, rdn to improve over 2f out, led over 1f out, drvn clr ins last: op 7/1, gd time: plcd once prev
this term (with D Sasse): Apr foal, half brother to sev wnrs, including smart sprint juv Green's Bid: eff around
6f on fast & soft grnd, has tried up to 1m: improving & stable returning to form, can win more races this Autumn.
3776 **SECOND VENTURE** 12 [11] J R Weymes 2-8-3 F Norton 50/1: 032: 2 b c Petardia - Hilton Gateway   5   74$
(Hello Gorgeous) Prom, went on appr 2f out, hdd appr dist, not pace of wnr: eff at 6/7f on gd/soft & soft, see 3776.
-- **ORIENTOR** [7] J S Goldie 2-8-7 A Culhane 25/1: 3: 2 b c Inchinor - Orient (Bay Express)   1¼   75
Dwelt, sn chsg ldrs, chall over 2f out, onepcd ins last: 12,000gns Feb foal, half brother to a decent 7f
scorer, dam a useful sprinter: stys 6f on soft: encouraging debut, scope to improve.
3156 **CARDINAL VENTURE** 40 [18] K A Ryan 2-8-5 F Lynch 15/2: 04: Rear, rdn/late hdwy, nrst fin: hd   73
6 week abs, drpd in trip: see 3156 (7f).
3268 **CARBON COPY** 35 [16] 2-8-7 K Darley 2/1 FAV: 35: Prom, rdn/no extra appr fnl 1f: hvly bckd   2½   69
& much better expected after a promising debut run in 3268.
3812 **PLEINMONT POINT** 11 [14] 2-8-5 W Winston 10/1: -46: In tch, hdwy when hmpd over 1f out, not   ¾   65
recover: nicely bckd tho' 8/1: btr 3812 (debut, gd grnd).
3801 **GARRISON** 11 [13] 2-7-12 N Kennedy 50/1: 047: Chsd ldrs, rdn/wknd over 1f out: jockey received   ¾   57

1217

a 2 day careless riding ban: needs sellers: see 3079.
3675 **QUAZAR 18** [17] 2-8-3 D O'Donohoe 20/1: -038: Late hdwy from rear, no threat: op 12/1: btr 3675. 2½ **57**
3466 **PURE SHORES 26** [15] 2-8-12 D Holland 13/2: 439: Handy, wknd fnl 2f: op 5/1: btr 3466, 3184 (gd/firm). ¾ **65**
3589 **HEAD SCRATCHER 21** [3] 2-8-5 J Bramhill 50/1: 30: Dwelt, al bhd, 10th: new stable: btr 3589 (5f sell). ½ **57**
3767 **VIEWFORTH 13** [5] 2-8-12 R Hughes 9/2: -430: Cl up, wknd quickly fnl 2f, 14th: better expected **0**
on this step up to 6f, prob needs to dominate: see 3767 (5f).
3635 **ALS ME TRAINER 19** [4] 2-8-3 J McAuley 16/1: -40: Led till over 2f out, wknd, 15th: btr 3635. **0**
3532 **Santisima Trinidad 23** [10] 2-8-4 J Carroll 50/1: -- **Piano Power** [12] 2-8-4 (1ow) Dean McKeown 40/1:
3184 **Royal Wanderer 38** [9] 2-8-3 P Doe 50/1: 3507 **Just Woody 25** [8] 2-8-9 T E Durcan 12/1:
-- **Cash** [2] 2-8-5 D Mernagh (3) 50/1:
17 ran Time 1m 15.46 (6.16) (High Havens Stables) M H Tompkins Newmarket, Suffolk

3959

3.05 LISTED H ROSEBERY STKS 2YO (A) 5f str Soft 105 -05 Slow
£11484 £4356 £2178 £900

*3814 **VICIOUS DANCER 11** [6] R M Whitaker 2-8-11 Dean McKeown 6/1: -0611: 2 b g Timeless Times - Yankeedoodledancer (Mashhor Dancer) Nvr far away, drvn appr fnl 1f, no impress till picked up well fnl 100y & got up nr fin: nicely bckd: recent easy wnr at York (mdn auct): 3,800gns April foal, eff at 5/6f: acts on gd & soft grnd, gall tracks: useful & improving gelding. **99**
3843 **RED MILLENNIUM 15** [10] A Berry 2-8-11 F Norton 5/1: 211342: 2 b f Tagula - Lovely Me (Vision) *hd* **98**
Narrow lead, hard rdn 1f out & hung right, edged left fnl 100y, hdd fnl strides: bckd: suited by return to 5f: acts on fast & soft grnd: useful, see 2664.
3862 **ELSIE PLUNKETT 8** [3] R Hannon 2-8-9 R Hughes 3/1 FAV: 132443: 2 b f Mind Games - Snow Eagle *hd* **96**
(Polar Falcon) Pressed ldr, rdn & every ch appr fnl 1f, edged right, held nr fin: nicely bckd: tough.
3566 **MAMMAS TONIGHT 22** [9] A Berry 2-9-2 (BL) R Winston 16/1: 154004: Slightly hmpd start & rear, 1¼ **100$**
imprvd after halfway, drvn to chse ldrs ent fnl 1f, unable to chall: blnkd, fine run conceding weight all round.
2996 **SIPTITZ HEIGHTS 47** [11] 2-8-9 M Fenton 33/1: 50105: In rear till kept on well fnl 1f, nvr nr to chall: *1* **90**
7 week abs: improved, acts on gd & soft grnd, return to 6f will suit: see 2363.
3714 **PROUD BOAST 16** [12] 2-8-6 A Culhane 9/2: 231526: Held up eff appr fnl 1f, no impress on ldrs: *nk* **87**
bckd tho' op 5/2: possibly suited by faster grnd, see 3145.
*3507 **SILCA LEGEND 25** [2] 2-9-0 Craig Williams 12/1: 212617: Keen, front rank, outpcd appr fnl 1f: *1* **92**
raced a shade too freely back in trip: see 3507 (6f, fast)
+3743 **NIFTY ALICE 14** [4] 2-8-7(1ow) S Sanders 20/1: 410018: Chsd ldrs, rdn appr fnl 1f, sn onepce, eased 1½ **81**
towards fin: stiff task, stablemate 2nd: see 3743 (fast grnd nursery).
3475 **EFFERVESCE 26** [7] 2-8-6 D Holland 50/1: 460129: Mid-div, niggled halfway, onepace: stiff task. *1* **76**
2248 **TIME N TIME AGAIN 78** [1] 2-8-11 T E Durcan 40/1: 10000: Cl up & every ch till wknd fnl 1f: 10th, 2½ **77**
11 week abs, stiff task: see 843 (debut).
3463 **FAIRGAME MAN 26** [5] 2-8-11 J Carroll 12/1: -31130: Chsd ldrs till 2f out: 11th, first try on soft gnd. 1½ **74**
2700 **XALOC BAY 60** [8] 2-8-11 K Darley 12/1: -220: Hmpd start, nvr in it: 12th, 9 wk abs, back in trip. 4 **64**
12 ran Time 1m 02.12 (5.52) (Mrs C Samuel) R M Whitaker Scarcroft, W Yorks

3960

3.35 GAEL SUZUKI AYRSHIRE HCAP 3YO+ 0-85 (D) 5f str Soft 105 +09 Fast [84]
£6500 £2000 £1000 £500 3 yo rec 1 lb Stands Side appeared at a disadvantage

4087} **PTARMIGAN RIDGE 355** [16] Miss L A Perratt 4-9-2 (72) M Fenton 40/1: 0000-1: 4 b c Sea Raven - Panayr **80**
(Faraway Times) Led centre group, overall bef fnl 1f, rdn clr: gd time, reapp: rnr-up here at Ayr last term (h'cap, rtd 86): won sole juv start at Catterick (stks, rtd 81): eff at 5f, tried 6f: loves soft grnd & goes esp well fresh, sharp or gall track: suited forcing the pace here: quick follow up likely.
3366 **GET STUCK IN 30** [10] Miss L A Perratt 4-9-2 (72) S Sanders 25/1: 440002: 4 b g Up And At 'Em - *3* **72**
Shoka (Kaldoun) Led far side/overall till appr fnl 1f, onepce under press: st/mate wnr: back in trip & back to form.
3572 **PURE COINCIDENCE 22** [9] K R Burke 5-9-4 (74) Dean McKeown 10/1: 000303: 5 b g Lugana Beach - *hd* **74**
Esilam (Frimley Park) Cl-up far side, rdn appr fnl 1f, ran on: tchd 14/1: running in well in defeat, see 768.
3788 **NIFTY MAJOR 12** [18] A Berry 3-9-1 (72) T E Durcan 25/1: 0005R3: In tch centre, drvn entering *dht* **72**
fnl 2f, kept on but unable to chall: a return to form, acts on fast & soft grnd, see 1219.
3872 **WHIZZ KID 7** [17] 6-8-12 (68) Claire Bryan (5) 25/1: 000005: Bhd centre, ran on strgly fnl 1f, nvr nrr. *hd* **68**
1663 **SUE ME 104** [13] 8-8-3 (56)(3ow) Craig Williams 14/1: -00106: In tch centre, prog under press 1f *nk* **58**
out, no extra nr fin: gd run after 15 week abs: won this in '99 (off 1lbs higher mark): see 1430.
3646 **SMOKIN BEAU 19** [25] 3-9-12 (83) P Dobbs (5) 16/1: 361107: Slow away stands side, imprvd to lead that ½ **80**
grp by halfway, kept on but nvr on terms with rest: tchd 20/1: top-weight & prob a gd run in the circumstances.
3536 **GARNOCK VALLEY 23** [14] 10-8-0 (56) Dale Gibson 12/1: 520138: Rear centre, late hdwy under press, ½ **52**
nvr dangerous: stablemate of Nifty Major: return to 6f will suit, see 2819 (seller).
3572 **SHAROURA 22** [20] 4-9-4 (74) D Holland 14/1: 002009: Towards rear centre, rdn & prog appr fnl 1f, *shd* **70**
nvr on terms: return to 6f will suit, as will faster grnd: see 2128.
3894 **DAAWE 6** [26] 9-9-2 (72)(bl) O Pears 16/1: 050500: Chsd ldrs stands side, onepce appr fnl 1f: 10th. 1½ **64**
3788 **EASTERN TRUMPETER 12** [27] 4-9-11 (81) K Darley 12/1: 210300: Cl-up stands side, eff & no extra *shd* **73**
appr fnl 1f: 11th: see 2644.
3619 **ORIEL STAR 20** [15] 4-7-10 (52)(15oh) J Bramhill 66/1: 600000: Al same pl: 12th, new stable, vis off. *hd* **44**
3894 **ANTHONY MON AMOUR 6** [5] 5-9-1 (71)(t) A Nicholls (3) 14/1: 356000: In tch far side, wknd *nk* **62**
ent fnl 1f: 13th, t-strap reapplied: see 2830.
3398 **TRINITY 29** [23] 4-8-9 (65) D Mernagh (3) 40/1: 006400: Nvr a factor stands side: 14th: see 2701. *nk* **55**
3791 **SEVEN NO TRUMPS 12** [6] 3-9-9 (80) R Hughes 14/1: 300000: Dwelt, nvr in it far side: 15th. *nk* **70**
2697 **BODFARI PRIDE 61** [2] 5-9-8 (78) Alex Greaves 14/1: 116200: Well plcd far side, fdd appr fnl 1f: 16th. *shd* **68**
3572 **SHATIN BEAUTY 22** [24] 3-8-0 (57) Iona Wands 50/1: 0-0000: Led stands side till after halfway, sn btn. **0**
3908 **BRANSTON PICKLE 5** [12] 3-8-2 (59) D O'Donohoe 7/2 FAV: 000120: Chsd ldrs in centre, wknd **0**
under press ent fnl 2f: 23rd, well bckd, quick reapp: see 3825.
3894 **STATOYORK 6** [19] 7-9-1 (65)(6ow) T Williams 10/1: 214150: Al bhd centre: 25th, reportedly lost **0**
action after losing a shoe & this is best ignored: see 3788.
3825 **Red Symphony 10** [11] 4-7-10 (52)(bl)(6oh) N Kennedy 40/1:
3250 **Peppiatt 36** [1] 6-8-5 (61) R Winston 16/1:
3825 **Jacmar 10** [22] 5-7-10 (52)(2oh) Angela Hartley (3) 50/1: 3825 **Facile Tigre 10** [8] 5-7-10 (52)(1oh) J McAuley 20/1:
3646 **Referendum 19** [4] 6-9-4 (74) F Norton 14/1: 3698 **Soba Jones 17** [7] 3-8-3 (60)(bl) J Carroll 25/1:
3803 **College Maid 11** [3] 3-8-9 (66) A Culhane 20/1: 3662 **Steppin Out 18** [21] 3-9-0 (71) P Doe 33/1:
27 ran Time 1m 01.4 (4.8) (Miss Heather Galbraith) Miss L A Perratt Ayr, Strathclyde

3961   4.05 RBS HCAP 3YO 0-95 (C)   1m7f   Soft 105   -06 Slow   [97]
£7182   £2210   £1105   £552

*3511 **BUSY LIZZIE 25** [1] J L Dunlop 3-9-7 (90) K Darley 7/2: 062511: 3 b f Sadler's Wells - Impatiente   **96**
(Vaguely Noble) Mid-div, prog to lead appr str, hdd bef 3f out, rall for press to regain lead dist, styd on well:
bckd, top-weight: earlier won at Chester (h'cap): unplcd both juv starts: sister to useful, late maturing styer
Eminence Grise: eff around 2m: acts on fast, soft grnd, sharp or gall track: runs well fresh: imprvg young stayer.

3467 **ROYAL MINSTREL 26** [3] M H Tompkins 3-8-11 (80) J Carroll 25/1: -31452: 3 ch c Be My Guest -   ¾ 85
Shanntabariya (Shernazar) Prom, led appr fnl 3f, hdd dist, kept on but not go past wnr: 9L clr rem: back to form
& clearly suited by step up to 15f, loves soft grnd: did not look at all keen & blnks will suit: see 906.

3290 **MARJEUNE 34** [6] P W Harris 3-7-13 (68) F Norton 5/1: 1-0233: 3 b f Marju - Ann Veronica   9 64
(Sadler's Wells) Hld up, chsd ldrs bef str, onepce appr fnl 2f: clr rem, up in trip & a questionable stayer.

3153 **BOX BUILDER 40** [8] M R Channon 3-9-2 (85) Craig Williams 7/2: 335144: Held up, eff ent str, no   7 74
impress: blnks on: reportedly backed for the Cesarewitch after this defeat: btr 3153, 2477 (fm & gd).

3599 **IL CAPITANO 21** [7] 3-9-3 (86) R Hughes 10/1: -05005: Chsd ldrs till wknd 3f out: blnks omitted.   3½ 71

3783 **SUDDEN FLIGHT 12** [4] 3-9-2 (85) S Sanders 3/1 FAV: 252126: Mid div, improved appr straight, wknd   8 62
qckly ent fnl 3f: bckd: something amiss? progressive earlier: see 3783, 3323.

*3741 **SLANEYSIDE 14** [2] 3-7-10 (65)(VIS)(2oh) N Kennedy 16/1: 360017: Led till appr straight, sn btn: dist 0
visored, op 12/1: longer trip, see 3741 (12f, class stakes).

3637 **VANISHING DANCER 19** [5] 3-7-13 (68) D Mernagh (3) 9/1: 033128: Ran in snatches, left bhd 4f out.   dist 0
8 ran   Time 3m 26.46 (16.66)   (Nigel Clark (Susan Abbott Racing))   J L Dunlop Arundel, W Sussex

3962   4.35 EBF MDN 2YO (D)   7f rnd   Soft 105   -11 Slow
£4426   £1362   £681   £340

3748 **SALTWOOD 14** [9] B W Hills 2-8-9 R Hughes 8/1: -041: 2 b f Mujtahid - Actualite (Polish Precedent)   **79+**
Held up, hdwy 3f out, rdn bef dist, switched & ran on strongly to get up fnl 50y: half-sister to useful 10f wnr
Shamrock City, dam mid-dist wnr: eff over a gall 7f on soft grnd but is likely to improve further at 1m+.

3608 **IRISH STREAM 20** [8] R Charlton 2-9-0 K Darley 10/11 FAV: 32: 2 ch c Irish River - Euphonic   ½ 82
(The Minstrel) Well plcd & trav strgly, narrow lead dist, sn hard rdn, hdd fnl 50y: well bckd: found less than
expected on this softer grnd tho' cirly handled it: must win a mdn (Gr 1 entry).

3779 **REGENT COURT 12** [4] T D Easterby 2-8-9 J Carroll 25/1: 5453: 2 gr f Marju - Silver Singing   1½ 74
(Topsider) Handy, led appr fnl 2f till ent fnl 1f, onepce: clr rem: improved: handles fast & soft grnd: see 3156.

3730 **WHERE THE HEART IS 15** [5] M H Tompkins 2-9-0 S Sanders 13/2: 354: In tch, prog 3f out, rdn 2f   5 71
out, hung left, fdd: op 5/1: first try on soft, must be given another ch after 3730, 2414 (fast, both worked out well).

1249 **CHANTAIGNE 126** [1] 2-8-9 A Culhane 25/1: 05: Mid-div, eff/btn appr fnl 2f: 4 mnth abs, lngr trip.   2 62

3705 **LUMIERE DU SOLEIL 17** [3] 2-8-9 F Lynch 25/1: -506: Nvr a factor: see 3466.   2½ 58

3533 **SHATIN PLAYBOY 23** [6] 2-9-0 R Winston 33/1: 447: Led till appr fnl 2f, wknd: lngr trip, nds sells.   1 61

-- **ACTIVIST** [7] 2-9-0 M Fenton 4/1: 8: Held up, shkn up 3f out, wknd: drifter from 2/1 on debut: 1¾ 58
115,000gns foal, brother to 4 juv wnrs, 2 of them useful: dam smart juvs: Gr 1 entry, will do better on faster grnd.

-- **OUR EMILY** [10] 2-8-9 Dean McKeown 20/1: 9: Dwelt, nvr in it: first foal, dam 6/11f wnr.   1¼ 51
9 ran   Time 1m 31.96 (8.16)   (Bodfari Stud Ltd)   B W Hills Lambourn, Berks

3963   5.05 KIDZPLAY AMAT HCAP 3YO+ 0-70 (E)   1m3f   Soft 105   -07 Slow   [32]
£2600   £800   £400   £200   3 yo rec 8 lb

3731 **KIDZ PLAY 15** [14] J S Goldie 4-11-5 (51) Mrs C Williams 16/1: 404001: 4 b g Rudimentary - Saka   58
Saka (Camden Town) Well plcd, went on ent fnl 3f, sn clr, rdn out: tchd 20/1: earlier won at Musselburgh
(h'cap): '99 Hamilton wnr (mdn h'cap, rtd 54): rtd 68 in '98 for M Johnston: eff at 1m/11f: acts on firm &
soft grnd, any track: best up with/forcing the pace.

*3494 **STRICTLY SPEAKING 26** [18] P F I Cole 3-11-6 (60) Mr O Cole (7) 7/1 FAV: 066012: 3 b c Sri Pekan -   4 61
Gaijin (Caerleon) Waited with, styd on fnl 2f without much assistance from the saddle, nvr nr wnr: op 5/1,
tchd 10/1: well worth another look when reunited with a stronger jockey: see 3494.

1065 **MASTER BEVELED 136** [6] P D Evans 4-12-0 (60) Mr T Scudamore 15/2: /0-303: 10 b g Beveled -   2½ 57
Miss Anniversary (Tachypous) Held up, shkn up 3f out, plodded on for 3rd: tchd 10/1, jt top-weight, btr 809.

3842 **CLARINCH CLAYMORE 9** [16] J M Jefferson 4-11-6 (52) Mr Nicky Tinkler (5) 14/1: -23004: Chsd ldrs,   ¾ 48
onepce fnl 2f: see 324, 131.

3773 **GYPSY SONG 12** [11] 3-10-2 (42) Mr M Seston (7) 25/1: 005005: Bhd, not much room 2f out,   hd 38
kept on but stdd, nvr on terms: worth another try at this trip in a mdn h'cap.

3842 **DARK VICTOR 9** [8] 4-11-8 (54) Mr J J Best (5) 12/1: 050106: Rear, improved 2f out, onepce fnl 1f.   1¼ 48

3531 **OCEAN DRIVE 23** [5] 4-11-3 (49) Miss S Brotherton (5) 16/1: 454247: Chsd ldrs, fdd appr fnl 1f: 2½ 40
op 10/1: faster grnd suits, see 3379, 846.

3826 **CAPTAIN BRADY 10** [13] 5-11-7 (53) Miss A Deniel 8/1: 0-1368: Led till appr fnl 2f, lost pl: s/mate wnr.   1¾ 41

3664 **PENNYS FROM HEAVEN 18** [3] 6-11-6 (52) Mrs S Bosley 9/1: 046439: Dwelt, al around mid-div.   3 35

3823 **FLOORSOTHEFOREST 10** [12] 4-11-4 (50) Mr T Best (5) 100/1: 005000: Chsd ldrs till 3f out: 10th.   hd 33

705 **THROWER 175** [2] 9-11-5 (51) Mrs S Owen (5) 9/1: -14500: Prom 1m: 11th, abs & new stable.   shd 24

1167 **GRAND CRU 131** [15] 9-10-12 (44) Miss L Vollaro (5) 16/1: 014600: Held up, eff 4f out, sn wknd: abs.   2½ 24

2238 **SPREE VISION 78** [1] 4-11-7 (53) Mr F King (5) 10/1: 451650: Prsd ldr till ent fnl 3f, wknd qckly: 13th, abs. 3 29

1769 **ATLANTIC CHARTER 99** [17] 4-12-0 (60) Mr P Robson (7) 16/1: -06550: Al bhd: 14th, 14 week   ½ 35
abs, longer trip, needs faster grnd: see 875.

3702 **RHODAMINE 17** [9] 3-11-9 (63) Miss Diana Jones 15/2: 340440: Held up, prog 5f out, btn 3f out: 3 34
15th, tchd 10/1: drop in trip may suit, as will faster grnd: see 1560.

3808 **Al Mabrook 11** [10] 5-11-3 (49) Miss E Ramsden 12/1:

3842 **Upper Bullens 9** [7] 3-11-11 (65) Miss Bridget Gatehouse (3) 33/1:

4591} **Tswalu 316** [4] 3-11-4 (58) Miss M Mullineaux (7) 50/1:
18 ran   Time 2m 28.33 (12.33)   (W M Johnstone)   J S Goldie Uplawmoor, E Renfrews

YARMOUTH THURSDAY SEPTEMBER 14TH Lefthand, Flat, Fair Track

Official Going: GOOD/FIRM. Stalls: Str Course - Far Side, Rem - Inside. ALL TIMES SLOW

3964 **1.55 KITCHENS HCAP DIV 1 3YO+ 0-60 (F) 6f Good/Firm Inapplicable [60]**
£2135 £610 £305 3 yo rec 2 lb Raced centre - stands side, high no's favoured.

3774 **KOSEVO 12** [18] D Shaw 6-8-6 (38)(bl) J Quinn 8/1: 300061: 6 b g Shareef Dancer - Kallista (Zeddaan) **43**
Chsd ldrs, briefly no room over 1f out, swtchd & prog to lead ins last, styd on well, drvn out: '99 Haydock wnr (h'cap, rtd 62 & 57a at best): '98 wnr at Southwell (2, sell & h'cap, 1st for A Kelleway, rtd 51a): eff btwn 5/7f on firm, gd/soft & both AWs: likes to race with/force the pace, handles any trk: eff with/without blnks.
3536 **JACKERIN 23** [15] Miss J F Craze 5-8-8 (40)(vis) V Halliday 16/1: 640002: 5 b g Don't Forget Me - *nk* **44**
Meanz Beanz (High Top) Led, rdn/pressed fnl 2f, hdd ins last, kept on well, just held: op 12/1: visor reapplied: on a handy mark for similar: see 3312, 798.
619 **JANICELAND 197** [10] M Wigham 3-9-12 (60) Paul Eddery 7/1: -10553: 3 b f Foxhound - Rebecca's *½* **62**
Girl (Nashamaa) Chsd ldrs, rdn/bmpd inside last, styd on well: abs: prev with S Kettlewell: see 443 (AW, sell).
3405 **BANGLED 29** [17] D J Coakley 3-8-9 (43) D Harrison 16/1: 000304: Held up, rdn/styd on fnl 2f, *½* **43**
not pace to chall: op 11/1: eff at 6f: handles fibresand & fast grnd: see 1494.
3634 **ENCOUNTER 19** [5] 4-9-6 (52) R Ffrench 8/1: 101605: Al prom, styd on fnl 1f: gd run from low draw. *shd* **52**
3872 **CRUSTY LILY 7** [7] 4-8-12 (44) L Newman (3) 5/1 FAV: 663056: Prom, kept on for press fnl 1f: op 7/1. *¾* **42**
3578 **CZAR WARS 22** [12] 5-8-10 (42)(bl) G Duffield 10/1: 346137: Prom, outpcd halfway, styd on well *1* **38**
cl home, no threat: return to 7f could suit on this evidence: see 3578, 3283 (claimer).
3605 **BALLINA LAD 20** [3] 4-8-11 (43) Pat Eddery 11/2: 005068: Trkd ldrs, rdn over 1f out, held ins last. *shd* **39**
3759 **POP SHOP 14** [2] 3-9-12 (60)(bl) J P Spencer 13/2: 000059: Held up, late gains, no threat: see 3759. *¾* **54**
3457 **BRIMSTONE 27** [6] 5-9-2 (48)(VIS) A Polli (3) 16/1: 6-0000: Mid div, nvr pace to chall: 10th: visor. *½* **40**
2749 **Ok Babe 57** [4] 5-8-0 (32) R Brisland (5) 33/1: 2440 **Ski Free 70** [13] 3-8-4 (38) K Dalgleish (5) 50/1:
3747 **Anstand 14** [11] 5-8-11 (43)(bl) R Havlin 20/1: 3781 **Fastrack Time 12** [9] 3-8-8 (42) J Reid 25/1:
3871 **Massey 7** [1] 4-8-10 (42)(vis) A Daly 25/1: 3919 **Farriers Gamble 2** [8] 4-9-4 (50)(BL) C Rutter 33/1:
16 ran Time 1m 13.5 (3.1) (K Nicholls) D Shaw Averham, Notts

3965 **2.25 GREAT YARMOUTH COND STKS 2YO (C) 6f Good/Firm Inapplicable**
£5713 £2167 £1083 £492 Raced stands side

*3443 **SONATINA 27** [4] J W Payne 2-8-6 J P Spencer 2/1 FAV: 11: 2 b f Distant Relative - Son Et Lumiere **88**
(Rainbow Quest) Held up in tch, no room over 1f out, prog under hands & heels riding fnl 1f to lead nr fin: hvly bckd, tchd 7/2: earlier scored at Folkestone (auct mdn, debut): eff at 6f, 7f will suit: acts on fast grnd & a sharp/undul or fair track: runs well fresh: reportedly heads for the Redcar 2yo trophy next month.
*3047 **GREENWOOD 45** [7] J M P Eustace 2-9-1 J Tate 9/1: 12: 2 ch c Emarati - Charnwood Queen *1¼* **93**
(Cadeaux Genereux) Led, rdn over 1f out, hdd inside last, kept on well: abs: fine eff, useful colt, win more races.
*2959 **RASOUM 48** [6] E A L Dunlop 2-9-1 J Reid 5/2: -313: 2 gr c Miswaki - Bel Ray (Restivo) *shd* **93**
Trkd ldrs, keen, rdn/ch 1f out, not pace of wnr inside last: nicely bckd tho' op 7/4: 7 week abs: see 2959.
2344 **DRESS CODE 75** [2] W Jarvis 2-8-10 J Fortune 16/1: 31004: Trkd ldrs, kept on fnl 1f, nvr pace *1½* **84**
to chall: 11 week abs: h'cap company could suit best: eff at 5/6f on firm & fast grnd: see 1249.
3075 **QUINK 43** [1] 2-9-1 G Duffield 100/30: 13135: In tch twds centre, rdn halfway, btn over 1f out: abs. *1¾* **85**
2318 **IDLE POWER 75** [3] 2-9-1 Pat Eddery 12/1: -25166: Held up, keen, held over 1f out: 11 week abs. *¾* **83**
3027 **MISE EN SCENE 45** [5] 2-8-10 P Robinson 20/1: -01057: Cl up, wknd over 1f out: abs: btr 1986 (5f). *2½* **71**
7 ran Time 1m 14.00 (3.6) (Mrs R A C Vigors) J W Payne Newmarket, Suffolk

3966 **2.55 KITCHENS HCAP DIV 2 3YO+ 0-60 (F) 6f Good/Firm Inapplicable [60]**
£2135 £610 £305 3 yo rec 2 lb Raced both sides, no advantage

*3872 **AMERICAN COUSIN 7** [17] D Nicholls 5-9-11 (57)(6ex) Clare Roche (7) 7/2 FAV: 050111: 5 b g Distant **62**
Relative - Zelda (Sharpen Up) Dwelt, sn trkd ldrs stands side, rdn/led over 2f out, styd on well ins last, rdn out: well bckd: earlier scored at Salisbury & Chepstow (h'caps): '99 wnr at Doncaster (2, appr h'caps, rtd 63): rnr up in '98 for R Johnson Houghton (rtd 60): eff at 5/6f on firm, gd/soft & fibresand: best without blnks & handles any trk, likes Doncaster: in great form, runs well for an apprentice rider.
3613 **TWO STEP 20** [2] R M H Cowell 4-8-10 (42)(t) J Fortune 10/1: 105032: 4 b f Mujtahid - Polka *¾* **44**
Dancer (Dancing Brave) Al prom far side, rdn/led that group over 2f out, kept on well inside last: acts on fibresand, fast & gd grnd: creditable effort, could find similar: see 3613.
3872 **RIVER TERN 7** [4] J M Bradley 7-9-4 (50) R Ffrench 20/1: 000003: 7 b g Puissance - Millaine *hd* **51**
(Formidable) Held up far side, rdn/prog to chall over 1f out, no extra well inside last: return to form here, v well h'capped, could yet pinch similar this autumn, particulary when dropped to 5f: see 1357.
3456 **FOSTON FOX 27** [9] C B B Booth 3-8-6 (40)(bl) S Whitworth 33/1: 600504: Towards rear stands side, *shd* **41+**
rdn & strong run from over 1f out, fin v fast: wnr with another 50yds: eff at 6f, has tried up to 12f prev: handles fast grnd: v eye-catching effort, see 3266 (1m).
3734 **CHAKRA 15** [1] 6-9-4 (50) R Havlin 16/1: 216655: Prom far side, ch 1f out, no extra: see 3243. *½* **49**
3765 **MILADY LILLIE 13** [16] 4-8-13 (45) C Carver (3) 13/2: 066006: Prom stands side 5f: see 2899, 746. *½* **42**
3821 **KILMEENA LAD 10** [7] 4-9-12 (58) S Carson (3) 10/1: 050007: Prom stands side 5f: see 1999, 462. *hd* **54**
3781 **AMARO 12** [5] 4-8-8 (40) J Quinn 14/1: 360008: Prom far side, held dist: op 12/1: see 226. *½* **34**
3080 **SAMMAL 43** [13] 4-8-11 (43) G Duffield 16/1: 620069: Trkd ldrs stands side, held 1f out: 6 wk abs. *1¼* **34**
3774 **PALO BLANCO 12** [3] 9-9-7 (53) M Henry 16/1: 620440: Led 3f far side, sn held: 10th: see 680 (AW). *nk* **43**
1804 **TABBETINNA BLUE 97** [14] 3-8-2 (36) K Dalgleish (5) 25/1: 002060: Led stands side 3f: 11th: abs. *2½* **19**
2767 **SILK ST BRIDGET 57** [15] 3-8-6 (40) P Robinson 14/1: 000060: Chsd ldrs stands side 4f: 12th: abs. *1¾* **19**
3238 **INDIAN WARRIOR 36** [11] 4-9-1 (47) Pat Eddery 11/2: 060200: Al rear stands side: 15th: op 9/2. **0**
1787 **Magic Eagle 98** [12] 3-9-10 (58) I Mongan (5) 14/1: 2421 **Indian Dance 71** [10] 4-8-11 (43) D R McCabe 20/1:
2819 **Tinas Royale 55** [8] 4-7-10 (28) G Bardwell 11/2: 3528 **Sounds Ace 24** [6] 4-8-11 (43)(bl) N Pollard 20/1:
17 ran Time 1m 14.1 (3.7) (Middleham Park Racing XIV) D Nicholls Sessay, N Yorks

3967	**3.25 MILLENNIUM HCAP 3YO+ 0-95 (C)** 2m2f51y Good/Firm Inapplicable		[87]
	£6890 £2120 £1060 £530 3 yo rec 14lb		

3905 **KING FLYER** 5 [3] H J Collingridge 4-8-11 (70)(t) J Quinn 2/1: 211221: 4 b g Ezzoud - Al Guswa — **73**
(Shernazar) In tch, prog to lead dist, held on well, rdn out: nicely bckd: earlier scored at Newmarket & Sandown
(h'caps): '99 wnr again at Newmarket (clmr, rtd 70 & 59a): eff btwn 10/14.7f, now stays a slowly run 2m2f: acts
on firm, gd & equitrack: handles any trk, likes a stiff/gall one, esp Newmarket: eff with/without t-strap: tough.

2092 **EASTWELL HALL** 85 [1] T P McGovern 5-9-11 (84) L Newman (3) 11/2: 4-5152: 5 b g Saddlers' Hall — nk **86**
- Kinchenjunga (Darshaan) Trckd ldrs, rdn/not much room over 1f out, styd on well ins last, just held: op 4/1,
12 wk abs: thorough stayer, denied the gap at a crucial stage, poss would have won otherwise: see 2092.

3085 **SELIANA** 43 [2] G Wragg 4-9-5 (78) J Reid 7/4 FAV: 340223: 4 b f Unfuwain - Anafi (Slip Anchor) — 2 **78**
Dictated pace, qcknd tempo 11f out, hdd over 1f out & held ins last: hvly bckd, 6 wk abs: handles fast & soft.

*3695 **XELLANCE** 17 [4] M Johnston 3-8-2 (75) K Dalgleish (5) 7/2: 412314: Chsd ldrs, rdn/held over 1f out. — 1½ **73**
4 ran   Time 4m 07.30 (13.5)   (In The Know (2))   H J Collingridge Exning, Suffolk

3968	**3.55 L & A. BOTTON NURSERY HCAP 2YO 0-75 (E)** 1m str Good/Firm Inapplicable		[82]
	£3029 £932 £466 £233 Raced stands side		

3888 **SNOWEY MOUNTAIN** 6 [1] N A Callaghan 2-9-7 (75) J Fortune 6/4 FAV: 443631: 2 gr c Inchinor - — **83**
Mrs Gray (Red Sunset) Held up, hdwy over 1f out, strong run to lead cl home, drvn & won going away: hvly bckd,
qck reapp: eff btwn 6f/1m on firm & gd grnd: handles a stiff/gall or sharp trk: goes well.

3308 **DANCING VENTURE** 33 [10] S P C Woods 2-8-12 (66) G Duffield 7/1: 5432: 2 b f Shareef Dancer - — ½ **71**
Adeptation (Exceller) Trkd ldrs, rdn/led over 1f out, hdd well ins last, no extra: styd longer 1m trip, handles fast.

2009 **CHEVENING LODGE** 89 [5] K R Burke 2-7-13 (53) M Henry 16/1: -46003: 2 ch g Eagle Eyed - — 3½ **51**
Meadmore Magic (Mansingh) Trkd ldr, led 5f out till over 1f out, onepace held inside last: op 10/1, 12 week abs:
styd longer 1m trip well on h'cap bow: acts on fast grnd: see 1095.

1974 **KINGS CREST** 90 [11] S C Williams 2-7-10 (50)(1oh) G Bardwell 6/1: 0664: Led 3f, ch 2f out, sn held: — ½ **47**
3 month abs: h'cap bow: bred to apprec this longer 1m trip.

2810 **STRATH FILLAN** 55 [7] 2-8-2 (56) A Daly 10/1: -0005: Trkd ldr, lost pl halfway, rdn & kept on fnl 2f, — nk **52**
no threat: op 8/1, 8 week abs/h'cap bow: this longer 1m trip will suit: see 1864.

3830 **BLUE ORLEANS** 9 [8] 2-8-5 (59) S Whitworth 20/1: 000606: Rdn/twds rear, mod hdwy: lngr 1m trip. — 2 **51**
3901 **GROVE DANCER** 5 [6] 2-9-0 (68) Pat Eddery 7/1: 13407: Trkd ldrs, outpcd over 2f out: quick reapp. — ½ **59**
3333 **UNCLE FOLDING** 32 [3] 2-7-12 (52)(tBL) J Quinn 16/1: -6008: Chsd ldrs 3f out, sn held: tried blnks — hd **42**
& a t-strap, op 12/1: h'cap bow & longer 1m trip.

3627 **RAW SILK** 19 [9] 2-8-8 (62) P Robinson 12/1: 0069: Chsd ldrs, btn 3f out: h'cap bow, longer 1m trip. — 7 **41**
3732 **MISS DAMINA** 15 [4] 2-7-13 (53) R Ffrench 20/1: 00040: Prom 6f: 10th: op 12/1: longer 1m trip. — 3½ **25**
10 ran   Time 1m 39.9 (4.8)   (Gallagher Equine Ltd)   N A Callaghan Newmarket, Suffolk

3969	**4.25 EBF HADDISCOE MDN 2YO (D)** 1m str Good/Firm Inapplicable		
	£3620 £1114 £557 £278 Raced stands side		

--   **MOT JUSTE** [9] E A L Dunlop 2-8-9 W Ryan 9/1: 1: 2 b f Mtoto - Bunting (Shaadi) — **89+**
Dwelt, in tch, not much room 2f out, prog over 1f out, styd on strongly fnl 100y under hands & heels riding to
lead nr fin: Feb foal, half sister to a useful 6f juv wnr: dam a 1m juv wnr, subs useful mid-dist performer:
eff at 1m, mid dist will suit: acts on fast grnd: really got the hang of things cl home, can win more races.

3537 **REFERRAL** 23 [4] K R Burke 2-9-0 J P Spencer 7/1: 252: 2 ch c Silver Hawk - True Joy (Zilzal) — ½ **90**
Trckd ldrs, rdn/led over 1f out, hdd nr line: styd longer 1m trip well: acts on fast & gd grnd: can find similar.

3790 **CAPAL GARMON** 12 [6] J H M Gosden 2-9-0 J Fortune 2/1 JT FAV: 43: 3 b c Caerleon - Elevate — shd **90**
(Ela Mana Mou) Cl up, rdn/led over 2f out, hdd over 1f out, styd on well inside last: well bckd, clr of rem:
left debut bhd over longer 1m trip, lks sure to relish mid dists: acts on fast grnd: see 3790.

--   **FLYING LYRIC** [3] S P C Woods 2-9-0 G Duffield 16/1: 4: Held up in tch, eff over 2f out, sn outpcd — 5 **80**
by front trio: op 10/1: Definite Article colt, May foal, cost 30,000gns: dam unrcd: sire smart 10/12f
performer: encouraging intro, sure to relish further in time.

3790 **AZKABAN** 12 [7] 2-9-0 D R McCabe 2/1 JT FAV: -325: Trckd ldrs, rdn/btn over 1f out: nicely bckd — 2½ **75**
tho' op 6/4: dissap over longer 1m trip: ahead of today's 3rd in 3790 (7f).

--   **FLY WITH ME** [1] 2-9-0 J Reid 5/1: 6: Went left start, sn handy, wknd over 1f out: cost 55,000gns: — nk **74**
brother to smart mid dist performer The Fly: dam a 6f juv wnr: sire top class at 7/10f: should relish 1m+.

--   **MASTER GATEMAKER** [2] 2-9-0 Pat Eddery 10/1: 7: Went left start, held up in tch, btn 2f out: — 7 **60**
op 8/1: Tragic Role colt, March foal, dam a 7f juv wnr: sire a 12f wnr: with P Harris.

3665 **CALIBAN** 18 [8] 2-9-0 J Tate 33/1: 058: Led, hdd/slightly hmpd over 2f out, sn strugg: see 3665, 3385. — 17 **26**
8 ran   Time 1m 39.90 (4.8)   (Mohammed Al Nabouda)   E A L Dunlop Newmarket, Suffolk

3970	**4.55 FESTIVAL MDN HCAP DIV 1 3YO 0-60 (F)** 1m str Good/Firm Inapplicable		[67]
	£2226 £636 £318		

3236 **SNATCH** 36 [18] M L W Bell 3-8-1 (40) J Mackay (5) 16/1: 64001: 3 b f Elmaamul - Tarkhana — **45**
(Dancing Brave) Rear, gd hdwy appr fnl 2f, led appr dist, drvn out: mid dist bred filly: eff at 1m/10f
further could suit: acts on fast grnd & a stiff or easy track.

3810 **LARAZA** 11 [2] Miss I Foustok 3-9-6 (59) J Quinn 8/1: 550052: 2 ch f Arazi - Queen Midas (Glint — 1¾ **60**
Of Gold) Cl up, chall over 1f out, no extra fnl 1f: clr rem: stys 1m on firm & gd, win similar: see 3810, 1165.

3612 **LATE ARRIVAL** 20 [1] D Morris 3-9-3 (56) J Weaver 9/2 FAV: 200023: 3 b g Emperor Jones - Try Vickers — 5 **47**
(Fuzzbuster) Bhd, rdn/prog over 2f out, styd on, no ch with front 2: bckd, visor omitted: rtd higher in 3612.

3561 **LITIGIOUS** 22 [17] K R Burke 3-8-6 (45)(VIS) L Newman (3) 16/1: -22004: Led, rdn/hdd over 1f out, — 1¾ **33**
fdd: first time visor: stys 1m on fast: see 2662.

3762 **KOINCIDENTAL** 13 [13] 3-8-11 (50) J Fortune 9/1: 000055: Late hdwy from rear: btr 3762 (10f). — 2½ **33**
3561 **BALLETS RUSSES** 22 [4] 3-8-5 (44) N Carlisle 33/1: 300006: Nvr dangerous: see 2036. — 1¼ **24**
3380 **DISTANT GUEST** 29 [20] 3-9-7 (60)(VIS) D Harrison 10/1: 240507: Cl up, lost tch appr fnl 1f: — ¾ **39**
op 8/1, top weight: first time visor: see 1397.

2198 **ALZITA** 80 [11] 3-9-6 (59) S Whitworth 9/1: 0-038: Sn rdn/rear, late hdwy, no danger: op 7/1, — 2½ **33**
11 wk abs: better expected on this h'cap bow: rtd much higher in 2198, 2024 (mdns).

3780 **VICTORS CROWN** 12 [5] 3-9-5 (58) G Duffield 20/1: -06009: Keen cl up, lost tch fnl 2f: see 3384. — 1¾ **29**

YARMOUTH THURSDAY SEPTEMBER 14TH Lefthand, Flat, Fair Track

3242 **ST IVES** 36 [12] 3-8-1 (40) C Rutter 16/1: 060040: Mid div at best, 10th: modest. — 1 — 9
3242 **MASTER LUKE** 36 [8] 3-8-9 (48)(bl) I Mongan (5) 7/1: 00020: Keen/in tch, wknd qckly 2f out, 11th. — 2½ — 12
3021 **GAYE CHARM** 46 [14] 3-8-13 (52) T G McLaughlin 25/1: -0600: Nvr a factor, 12th: 7 wk abs, h'cap bow. — 1 — 14
3921 **CORAL SHELLS** 2 [3] 3-7-13 (38)(bl) R Ffrench 33/1: 006000: Dwelt, al bhd, 13th: ran 48 hrs ago. — hd — 0
3612 **SLAM BID** 20 [19] 3-9-0 (53) A Beech (5) 20/1: -56300: Prom, wknd qckly fnl 2f, 14th: new stable. — nk — 13
118 **Mercede** 292 [10] 3-8-1 (40) J Tate 16/1: 3494 **With Respect** 26 [16] 3-8-0 (39) N Pollard 11/1:
3048 **Moon Of Alabama** 45 [7] 3-9-2 (55) Pat Eddery 12/1: 3593 **Fantasy Adventurer** 21 [9] 3-8-8 (47) J Stack 20/1:
18 ran   Time 1m 39.1 (4.0)   (Mrs G Rowland-Clark)   M L W Bell Newmarket, Suffolk

3971 5.25 FESTIVAL MDN HCAP DIV 2 2YO 0-60 (F)   1m str   Good/Firm   Inapplicable   [67]
£2198   £628   £314

3753 **MIND THE SILVER** 14 [20] V Soane 3-8-13 (52) J P Spencer 12/1: 004001: 3 gr g Petong - Marjorie's — 57
Memory (Fairy King) Settled rear, gd hdwy 2f out, ran on well for strong press fnl 1f, led fnl stride, all out:
failed to make the frame in 11 starts prev: unplcd in '99 (rtd 69): eff and an easy 1m on fast grnd.
3288 **SWYNFORD ELEGANCE** 34 [14] J Hetherton 3-8-1 (40) R Ffrench 33/1: 200002: 3 ch f Charmer - — shd — 44
Qualitairess (Kampala) Front rank, went on appr fnl 1f, drvn out, hdd fnl stride: clr rem: eff at 7f/1m on
fast & gd/soft: capable of winning similar: see 1793.
3623 **AEGEAN FLOWER** 20 [18] R M Flower 3-8-9 (48)(bl) D Harrison 16/1: 003403: 3 b g Robellino - — 3 — 46
Bercheba (Bellypha) Led, hdd appr fnl 1f, not pace of ldrs: ran to nr best, handles fast grnd.
3746 **SPIRIT OF KHAMBANI** 14 [17] M Johnston 3-8-6 (45) K Dalgleish (5) 9/2: 250024: Waited with, — hd — 42
rdn/prog over 2f out, no extra inside last: see 3746.
3670 **CALDEY ISLAND** 18 [19] 3-8-0 (39) G Sparkes (7) 9/1: 000505: Waited with, rdn/hdwy over 1f out, — ¾ — 35
styd on, nvr nrr: flatted 3670.
3626 **DAZZLING DAISY** 19 [13] 3-8-8 (47) R Brisland (5) 20/1: 4406: Cl up, rdn/held fnl 2f: h'cap bow. — 1¼ — 40
3266 **DOLFINESSE** 35 [4] 3-8-0 (39)(vis) G Bardwell 14/1: 062067: Sn rdn in tch, eff 3f out, fdd fnl 1f. — 1¾ — 29
3856 **SUMMER CHERRY** 8 [16] Pat Eddery 3/1 FAV: 446368: Rear, eff/no room/swtchd over — ½ — 49
3f out, styd on, nvr nrr: nicely bckd, top weight: shade unlucky in running, worth another chance: see 3362.
3856 **MISTY MAGIC** 8 [7] 3-9-2 (55) J Fortune 9/2: 432639: Mid div, eff 2f out, sn lost tch: btr 3856. — 3½ — 37
3506 **DAWN TRAVELLER** 25 [11] 3-8-4 (43) J Quinn 33/1: -00500: Keen, nvr a factor, 10th: see 1708. — 1¼ — 22
3696 **LIVELY FELIX** 17 [1] 3-9-5 (58) C Rutter 25/1: -0040: Chsd ldrs, lost tch fnl 2f, 11th: h'cap bow. — hd — 36
3816 **CUIGIU** 10 [9] 3-9-0 (53) D Nolan (7) 16/1: 002300: Mid div at best, 12th: btr 3008 (10f). — ½ — 30
3702 **FLOW BEAU** 17 [15] 3-8-8 (47)(BL) A McGlone 33/1: -40600: Dwelt, al bhd, 13th: blnkd: modest. — shd — 24
2554 **ARCTIC HIGH** 66 [10] 3-8-5 (44) R Havlin 33/1: 030000: Prom, wknd/hmpd over 1f out, 14th: abs. — ½ — 20
3873 **CHILWORTH** 7 [2] 3-8-13 (52)(vis) R Price 16/1: 000300: Prom, wknd qckly fnl 2f, 15th: qck reapp. — 1½ — 25
3030 **Satzuma** 45 [3] 3-9-4 (57)(t) J Reid 25/1: 3856 **Prince Of Mystery** 8 [12] 3-8-8 (47) T G McLaughlin 25/1:
3530 **African Pete** 24 [8] 3-9-6 (59)(BL) G Hind 16/1: 2192 **Eltars** 80 [5] 3-8-1 (40) L Newman (1) 20/1:
3578 **Needwood Tribesman** 22 [2] 3-7-13 (38) N Carlisle 33/1:
20 ran   Time 1m 39.00 (3.9)   (The Soane Rangers)   V Soane East Garston, Berks

NOTTINGHAM FRIDAY SEPTEMBER 15TH Lefthand, Galloping Track

Official Going   GOOD/SOFT, SOFT after race 3. Stalls: 6f - Stands Side; Rem - Inside.

3972 1.50 EBF TRENT MDN 2YO (D)   1m54y rnd   Soft 97   -46 Slow
£3900   £1200   £600   £300

-- **WELSH BORDER** [1] H R A Cecil 2-9-0 T Quinn 11/8 FAV: 1: 2 ch c Zafonic - Welsh Daylight (Welsh — 88+
Pageant) Cl-up, led dist, asserted ins last under hands-&-heels riding: nicely bckd tho' op 1/1, slow time: Mar
foal, brother to 10f wnr Welsh Main, dam a 10f wnr in Ireland: eff at 1m on soft, further shld suit: acts on a
gall trk, runs well fresh: held in some regard & likely to rate more highly.
3601 **TIYOUN** 21 [4] D W Barker 2-9-0 J Stack 11/1: 32: 2 b g Kahyasi - Taysala (Akarad) — 2½ — 83
Led, rdn over 2f out & styd on well fnl 1f out, held ins last: op 7/1: stays 1m, acts on firm & soft grnd.
3608 **TOMMY LORNE** 21 [3] J L Dunlop 2-9-0 J P Spencer 7/4: 3: 2 b g Inchinor - Actress (Known Fact) — 3 — 77
Trkd ldrs, rdn/outpcd fnl 2f, eased: nicely bckd: prob handles soft grnd & stays 1m: see 3608.
3840 **PETROV** 10 [5] E A L Dunlop 2-9-0 M Tebbutt 7/2: 04: Held up, eff 2f out, no impress: longer 1m trip. — 1¾ — 75
3420 **PEKANOORA** 29 [2] 2-9-0 A Beech (5) 33/1: 05: Chsd ldrs, drvn over 3f out, sn btn: see 3420. — 8 — 63
5 ran   Time 1m 51.1 (11.7)   (K Abdulla)   H R A Cecil Newmarket.

3973 2.20 EBF CRICKETERS MDN DIV 1 2YO (D)   6f   Soft 97   -01 Slow
£3217   £990   £495   £247 Raced centre - stands side

3342 **FARHA** 33 [12] B Hanbury 2-8-9 W Supple 7/4: -321: 2 b f Nureyev - Arutua (Riverman) — 79
Trkd ldrs going well, prog to lead over 1f out, sn asserted under hands-&-heels riding: nicely bckd, fair juv time:
eff at 6f, further shld suit (dam related to mid-dist performers): acts on firm & fast grnd, relished this soft
surface: likes a stiff/gall trk: reportedly unsuited by forcing the pace earlier: open to further improvement.
3621 **HIRAETH** 21 [2] B Palling 2-8-9 D Sweeney 6/1: 32: 2 b f Petong - Floppie (Law Society) — 2½ — 72
Held up, rdn & styd on well fnl 2f, al held by wnr: nicely bckd: stays 6f on firm & soft grnd: can find a race: see 3621.
3443 **EAST OF JAVA** 28 [11] K R Burke 2-9-0 Dean McKeown 25/1: 03: 2 b c Greensmith - Krakatoa (Shirley — nk — 76$
Heights) Led, rdn/hdd over 1f out, kept on onepace for press: left debut bhd with forcing tactics on soft grnd:
eff at 6f, 7f+ shld suit: fin well clr of rem here: see 3443.
3649 **PACKIN EM IN** 20 [4] N Hamilton 2-9-0 J Spencer 66/1: 004: Chsd ldrs over 2f out, sn btn: imprvd — 7 — 62
effort on soft grnd: h'cap company shld now suit: see 3649.
3096 **SAFINAZ** 44 [5] 2-8-9 P McCabe 25/1: 065: Prom, wknd over 1f out: 6 wk abs: see 2692. — 3½ — 50
3910 **LIFFORD LADY** 4 [6] 2-8-9 C Rutter 16/1: 0006: Prom 4f: qck reapp: btr form previously. — 5 — 40
-- **CALLING DOT COM** [9] 2-9-0 T Quinn 11/10 FAV: 7: Reared start & v slowly away, mod gains under — 1½ — 42+
tender handling: hvly bckd: Halling colt, Feb foal, cost 52,000gns: dam 7f juv wnr: sire tough high-class 10f
performer: lost all chance at start & this must be forgiven.
3627 **SIR DESMOND** 20 [1] 2-9-0 O Pears 33/1: 08: Al towards rear: no form. — 4 — 34
3732 **WILD SPIRIT** 16 [8] 2-9-0 J D Smith 66/1: 569: Al bhd: see 3492. — 3 — 28
3767 **NEEDWOOD BLADE** 14 [3] 2-9-0 D Holland 25/1: 0: Al rear: 10th: see 3767. — ½ — 27

-- **MOYNE PLEASURE** [7] 2-9-0 S W Kelly (3) 25/1: 0: Chsd ldrs 3f, sn btn: 11th: Exit To Nowhere *½* **26**
filly, Mar foal, cost IR £23,000: first foal: dam a 5/7f wnr: with J Osborne.
11 ran Time 1m 16.70 (5.9) (Hamdan Al Maktoum) B Hanbury Newmaket.

3974 **2.50 EBF CRICKETERS MDN DIV 2 2YO (D) 6f Soft 97 -10 Slow**
£3217 £990 £495 £247 Raced centre - stands side

3832 **MIDSHIPMAN 10** [6] Mrs D Haine 2-9-0 T Quinn 20/1: 051: 2 b c Executive Man - Midler (Comedy Star) **79**
Al prom, led over 2f out till dist, rallied well to regain lead near line, drvn out: eff at 6f, 7f+ could suit: relished soft grnd today, handles a gall trk: could improve further in h'cap company.
3363 **ARJAY 31** [1] Andrew Turnell 2-9-0 R Thomas (7) 33/1: -562: 2 b g Shaamit - Jenny's Call (Petong) *hd* **78**
Chsd ldrs, rdn/narrow lead over 1f out, collared cl home: 7L clr of rem: eff at 6f, imprvd on soft grnd.
3678 **CAPE COD 18** [3] J W Hills 2-8-9 M Henry 7/1: -403: 2 b f Unfuwain - Haboobti (Habitat) *7* **59+**
Bhd, styd on under hands-&-heels riding fnl 2f, no threat to front pair: unsuited by drop to 6f: prob handles fast & soft grnd: likely to improve in h'cap company when returned to 7f+: see 3292.
-- **LIBERTY BOUND** [11] D Shaw 2-8-9 O Pears 16/1: 4: Chsd ldrs, btn over 1f out: op 12/1: Primo *shd* **59**
Dominie filly, Feb foal, cost 21,000gns: half-sister to a 7f wnr Tribal Prince: dam a 7f winner.
3705 **VAIL PEAK 18** [2] 2-9-0 J Weaver 7/1: -505: Prom, held fnl 2f: op 4/1: btr 1835 (5f). *2½* **59**
-- **CITY OF LONDON** [7] 2-9-0 J P Spencer 5/4 FAV: 6: Towards rear, mod hdwy over 2f out: bckd *1½* **56**
from 7/4: Grand Lodge colt, Mar foal, cost 130,000gns: half-brother to 6/7f juv wnr Ffestiniog: likely to apprec 7f/1m next term: much better clearly expected & worth another chance on faster grnd.
-- **ARONA** [9] 2-8-9 Dean McKeown 10/1: 7: In tch, outpcd fnl 3f: Spectrum filly, Apr foal, cost *hd* **50**
IR 42,000gns: half-sister to a French 3yo wnr: dam also a wnr in France: sire top-class 1m/10f performer.
-- **IN SPIRIT** [10] 2-9-0 C Rutter 8/1: 8: Led 4f, sn btn: op 11/2: Apr foal, cost IR 34,000gns: *2½* **50**
half-brother to sev wnrs, dam a 3yo wnr: with D J S Cosgrove.
3520 **INVESTOR RELATIONS 25** [4] 2-9-0 D R McCabe 9/1: 609: Slowly away & al rear: btr 3358 (g/f). *1½* **47**
2057 **SPRINGWOOD JASMIN 87** [5] 2-8-9 (t) D Nolan (7) 40/1: 05600: Prom 4f: 10th: 12 wk abs. *3½* **35**
3638 **SPINETAIL RUFOUS 20** [8] 2-9-0 J D Smith 33/1: 000: Prom till halfway, t.o.: 11th: mod form. *15* **15**
11 ran Time 1m 17.2 (6.4) (Mrs V Bayley) Mrs D Haine Newmarket.

3975 **3.20 MARSTONS FILLIES HCAP 3YO+ 0-70 (E) 6f Soft 97 +02 Fast [69]**
£3224 £992 £496 £248 3 yo rec 2 lb Raced centre - stands side

3904 **PREMIUM PRINCESS 6** [1] J J Quinn 5-9-13 (68) D Holland 6/1: 411441: 5 b m Distant Relative - Solemn **73**
Occasion (Secreto) Chsd ldrs, styd on to lead well ins last, drvn out: best time of day, qck reapp, op 7/1: earlier scored at Sandown & Pontefract (h'caps): '99 Newcastle wnr (h'cap, rtd 62): '98 rnr-up (mdn, rtd 64): suited by 5/6f, stays 7f well: acts on firm & soft grnd, handles any trk, loves a stiff/gall one: gd weight carrier: tough.
3222 **MARINO STREET 37** [8] B A McMahon 7-9-3 (58) J Weaver 6/1: 1W5662: 7 b m Totem - Demerger *½* **60**
(Dominion) Al prom, rdn/led over 1f out, drvn & hdd well ins last: acts on firm, soft & fibresand: see 2252 (5f).
3956 **LAYAN 2** [5] J Balding 3-8-13 (56) J Edmunds 10/1: 420303: 3 b f Puissance - Most Uppitty *½* **57**
(Absalom) In tch, rdn & styd on well fnl 1f, not rch wnr: qck reapp, only btn 1L: acts on firm, soft & fibresand.
3587 **SHINING STAR 22** [3] J A Osborne 3-9-2 (59) J P Spencer 20/1: -40504: Bhd, rdn & styd on fnl 2f, nrst *1½* **57**
fin: return to 7f in similar company shld suit: see 1606.
3809 **MORGAN LE FAY 12** [2] 5-9-3 (58) Kim Tinkler 20/1: 0-1005: Chsd ldrs, held fnl 1f: new stable. *¾* **55**
2654 **TALARIA 63** [16] 4-9-7 (62)(t) G Faulkner (3) 7/1: 004056: Held up, keen, mod hdwy: 2 month *2* **55**
abs, t-strap reapplied: visor omitted: btr 1082 (C/D, gd/soft).
*3759 **BIRDSONG 15** [20] 3-9-11 (68) N Pollard 6/1: 001317: Prom, rdn/led 3f out till over 1f out, fdd: op 4/1. *4* **53**
3821 **HEAVENLY MISS 11** [9] 6-8-13 (54)(bl) D Nolan (7) 20/1: 400008: Sn prom, btn fnl 2f: btr 1244 (5f). *½* **38**
3613 **EVENTUALITY 21** [11] 4-10-0 (69) S Carson (3) 12/1: 012009: Chsd ldrs, btn over 1f out: btr 2654 (gd). *¾* **52**
3774 **DAYS OF GRACE 13** [17] 5-9-8 (63) C Rutter 8/1: 311420: Chsd ldrs till over 1f out: 10th: btr 3493 (fm). *½* **45**
811 **INCHALONG 167** [19] 5-9-7 (62)(vis) N Carlisle 14/1: 06-000: Led till halfway, sn held: 11th: 6 mth abs. *1½* **41**
3809 **ITS ALLOWED 12** [15] 3-9-12 (69) W Supple 12/1: 050000: Al rear: 12th: see 1308. *nk* **47**
3666 **Hoxton Square 19** [7] 3-9-1 (58) T G McLaughlin 25/1: 3573 **Kilbrannan Sound 23** [6] 3-9-2 (59) T Quinn 20/1:
2759 **Sontime 58** [4] 3-9-1 (58) D Sweeney 25/1: 3584 **Dancemma 22** [12] 3-9-2 (59) Dale Gibson 20/1:
3809 **Secret Conquest 12** [14] 3-9-8 (65) J Stack 25/1: 3739 **In Sequence 16** [18] 3-8-11 (54) O Pears 33/1:
18 ran Time 1m 16.5 (5.7) (Derrick Bloy) J J Quinn Settrington, N.Yorks.

3976 **3.50 EUROBALE NURSERY HCAP 2YO 0-75 (E) 6f Soft 97 -00 Slow [81]**
£3289 £1012 £506 £253 Raced centre - stands side

3354 **QUANTUM LADY 32** [8] B R Millman 2-9-1 (68) G Hind 7/1: 223641: 2 b f Mujadil - Folly Finnesse **80**
(Joligeneration) Keen/chsd ldrs, rdn/led over 1f out, styd on strongly, rdn clr: bckd from 12/1: earlier scored at Bath (auct mdn): eff at 5/6.8f: acts on gd & fast, imprvd on soft grnd here: handles a sharp/undul or gall trk: decisive scorer here & cld follow up under a penalty.
3525 **REGAL AIR 25** [10] B I Case 2-9-2 (69) A Beech (5) 14/1: 303022: 2 b f Distinctly North - Dignified *4* **70**
Air (Wolver Hollow) Led, rdn/hdd over 1f out, drvn & styd on ins last, no ch with wnr: handles firm, soft & fibresand: encouraging return to h'caps, step up to 7f could now suit: see 865.
3730 **BEE KING 16** [5] M R Channon 2-8-6 (59) J Stack 20/1: -00003: 2 ch c First Trump - Fine Honey *shd* **60**
(Drone) Al prom, rdn & styd on fnl 2f, no impress on wnr: visor omitted: eff at 6f, imprvd on soft grnd: see 3730.
3577 **DODONA 23** [13] T D McCarthy 2-9-0 (67) C Rutter 20/1: 4004: Rear, rdn/styd on well under hands-and- *1* **66+**
heels riding fnl 2f, nrst fin: h'cap bow: handles gd/soft & soft: most encouraging, one to note at 7f+ in similar.
3500 **SMIRFYS PARTY 26** [4] 2-9-4 (71) T Quinn 9/2 FAV: 6255: Chsd ldrs 4f: h'cap bow, op 6/1. *1½* **67**
3466 **GOT ALOT ON 27** [1] 2-8-9 (62) O Pears 14/1: 0006: Chsd ldrs, btn 2f out: h'cap bow: unplcd prev. *3* **52**
3732 **KALUKI 16** [15] 2-9-3 (70) S W Kelly (3) 16/1: 033227: Chsd ldrs 3f: see 3732 (mdn). *1* **58**
3824 **GLOBAL EXPLORER 11** [7] 2-8-9 (62) M Tebbutt 16/1: -00608: Rear, went left over 2f out, little hdwy. *hd* **49**
3649 **SENOR MIRO 20** [17] 2-9-7 (74) D Holland 6/1: -0549: Chsd ldrs 4f: h'cap bow: op 4/1: btr 3649. *1½* **58**
3766 **MOUNT ROYALE 14** [19] 2-8-8 (61) Kim Tinkler 25/1: 0000: Prom till halfway: 10th: h'cap bow. *1½* **42**
3679 **MONTEV LADY 18** [18] 2-8-7 (60) A Daly 14/1: 0140: Prom 3f: 11th: see 3679, 3204 (5f, seller, firm). *½* **40**
-3491 **MADRASEE 27** [16] 2-9-6 (73) Dale Gibson 9/1: 630320: Prom 4f: 12th: op 6/1: btr 3491 (5f, fm). *¾* **52**
3592 **NOT JUST A DREAM 22** [20] 2-8-7 (60) W Supple 14/1: 430460: Chsd ldrs 4f: 13th: see 1146. *5* **29**
13 ran Time 1m 16.60 (5.8) (N W Lake) B R Millman Kentisbeare, Devon.

3977 **4.20 NOTTS CCC MDN 3YO (D) 1m54y rnd Soft 97 -09 Slow**
£3883 £1195 £597 £298

3389 **MISS RIVIERA GOLF 30** [1] G Wragg 3-8-9 D Holland 11/8 FAV: -0201: 3 b f Hernando - Miss Beaulieu **85+**
(Northfields) Chsd ldr, led over 3f out, pulled clr under hands-and-heels riding fnl 1f, readily: val for 7L+: well bckd: eff btwn 1m/10f: acts on fast & soft grnd, sharp or gall trk: plenty in hand here, one to note for h'caps.
3834 **DANDILUM 10** [10] V Soane 3-9-0 G Hind 11/1: 2-4W02: 3 b c Dilum - Renira (Relkino) *5* **79**
Held up, prog to chase wnr over 1f out, al held: op 6/1: met a potentiall useful rival: see 983 (7f).
3707 **SIMPLY SENSATIONAL 18** [12] P F I Cole 3-9-0 D Griffiths 16/1: -443: 3 ch c Cadeaux Genereux - *3½* **74**
Monaiya (Shareef Dancer) Held up, mod gains fnl 2f, no threat: h'cap company shld now suit: see 3707, 3477.
3707 **GALLANT 18** [6] Sir Michael Stoute 3-9-0 T Quinn 4/1: 0-34: Prom/keen, chsd wnr over 2f out till *¾* **73**
over 1f out, sn held: op 2/1: see 3707.
-- **HINDAAM** [13] 3-9-0 W Supple 100/30: 5: Slowly away, held up, mod gains under hands-and-heels *nk* **72+**
riding fnl 2f: bckd from 6/1, debut: half-brother to a wnr abroad at 1m/10f: better clearly expected, worth another chance on faster grnd: with E Dunlop.
2558 **CLASSY IRISH 66** [11] 3-9-0 J P Spencer 10/1: -6246: Held up, eff over 2f out, no impress: 2 mth abs. *¾* **71**
3696 **FARAWAY LOOK 18** [3] 3-9-0 O Urbina 8/1: 427: Keen/prom 6f: op 5/1: btr 3350. *4* **65**
2104 **PORAK 86** [7] 3-9-0 J Stack 50/1: -68: Slowly away, nvr on terms: 12 wk abs: see 2104. *½* **64**
-- **SILVER PRAIRIE** [4] 3-8-9 G Sparkes (7) 33/1: 9: Held up, eff over 3f out, no impress: debut. *1½* **57**
3350 **RED THATCH 32** [2] 3-9-0 R Studholme (3) 66/1: 06-00: Led 4f, btn 2f out: 10th: mod form prev. *1½* **60$**
3813 **KADINSKY 12** [14] 3-9-0 M Tebbutt 20/1: -050: Al rear: 11th: see 3626. *3½* **55**
3834 **PURSUIT OF DREAMS 10** [5] 3-9-0 J Weaver 40/1: 00: Keen/prom, btn 2f out: 12th: no form prev. *½* **54**
3319 **DIZZY KNIGHT 34** [9] 3-8-9 D Sweeney 25/1: 0-40: Keen/prom 6f: 13th: btr 3319 (6f, fast). *2* **46**
13 ran Time 1m 48.1 (8.7) (J L C Pearce) G Wragg Newmarket.

3978 **4.55 COAL INDUSTRY HCAP 3YO+ 0-65 (F) 2m Soft 97 -00 Slow [65]**
£2709 £774 £387 3 yo rec 13lb

4370} **PERSIAN WATERS 336** [6] J R Fanshawe 4-9-11 (62) O Urbina 8/1: 0300-1: 4 b g Persian Bold - Emerald **67**
Waters (King's Lake) Al prom, shkn up to lead dist, styd on strongly under hands-&-heels riding: Flat reapp, 7 month jumps abs: 99/00 wnr at Huntingdon (juv nov, rtd 124h at best): unplcd on the level in '99 (rtd 69, h'cap, with M Pipe): '98 fnl start wnr at Pontefract (nurs, rtd 70, Mrs J Ramsden): prev eff at 10f, now stays 2m well: enjoys gd/soft & hvy, poss handles fast: gd weight carrier, runs well fresh: plenty in hand here, qck follow up.
*3570 **RIGHTY HO 23** [2] W H Tinning 6-8-1 (38) K Hodgson 12/1: 002212: 6 b g Reprimand - Challanging (Mill *4* **37**
Reef) Chsd ldr, rdn & ch over 2f out, sn held by wnr: prob stays 2m: rtd higher 3570 (clmr, 12f, firm).
3695 **CANDLE SMILE 18** [11] G Barnett 8-9-12 (63) L Vickers (7) 16/1: 20-653: 8 b g Pleasant Colony - *¾* **61**
Silent Turn (Silent Cal) Led, rdn/hdd well over 1f out, held ins last: op 10/1, top-weight: see 3295.
3715 **MENTAL PRESSURE 17** [16] Mrs M Reveley 7-9-9 (60) T Quinn 5/1:.252134: Held up, rdn/styd on fnl *hd* **58**
2f, no threat: op 3/1: acts on firm & soft grnd: see 3331.
*3625 **OUR MONOGRAM 21** [15] 4-9-3 (54) J P Spencer 11/4 FAV: 003115: In tch, onepace/held fnl 2f: *1½* **51**
well bckd: handles firm & soft grnd, prob prefers the former: see 3625.
3742 **SIRINNDI 15** [14] 6-8-12 (49) S W Kelly (3) 4/1: 006256: Dwelt/held up, hdwy 5f out, held fnl 2f: clr rem. *1½* **43**
3887 **PARADISE NAVY 7** [12] 11-8-6 (43)(bl) G Sparkes (7) 20/1: 000367: Held up, eff 3f out, little hdwy. *5* **35**
3674 **SPA LANE 19** [5] 7-8-0 (37) N Pollard 16/1: 500508: Held up, eff 3f out, no impress: op 12/1. *1½* **28**
3586 **SUPREME SILENCE 22** [4] 3-8-1 (51) W Supple 14/1: 000009: Handy, btn 2f out: longer 2m trip: op 8/1. *¾* **41**
3575 **TOTALLY SCOTTISH 23** [7] 4-8-2 (39)(tBL) O Pears 20/1: 056500: Held up, eff 3f out, no impress: *5* **25**
10th: first time blnks, longer priced stablemate of 4th: see 2730, 1633.
3800 **Alcayde 12** [13] 5-9-4 (55) J Weaver 12/1: 3434 **King For A Day 28** [1] 4-8-5 (42)(vis) Dale Gibson 20/1:
-- **Scottish Song** [3] 7-8-3 (40) C Rutter 20/1: 3664 **Mi Odds 19** [17] 4-8-6 (43) R Fitzpatrick 16/1:
14 ran Time 3m 39.7 (15.5) (Paul & Jenny Green) J R Fanshawe Newmarket.

3979 **5.30 CONF CENTRE CLASS STKS 3YO+ 0-65 (E) 1m2f Soft 97 -02 Slow**
£3315 £1020 £510 £255 3 yo rec 7 lb

3557 **CALLDAT SEVENTEEN 23** [9] P W D'Arcy 4-9-4 (t) P D'Arcy 14/1: 606001: 4 b g Komaite - Westminster **70**
Waltz (Dance In Time) Made all, clr 2f out, unchall, easily: val for 7L+, op 10/1: '99 Lingfield (auct mdn, rtd 75a) & Epsom wnr (2, stks & h'cap, rtd 79): eff at 1m/10f on fast, soft & equitrack: handles any trk, loves Epsom: eff forcing the pace & in a t-strap: plenty in hand here, could score again granted similar conditions.
3663 **MA VIE 19** [7] J R Fanshawe 3-8-8 (vis) O Urbina 13/2: -02022: 3 b f Salse - One Life (L'Emigrant) *5* **59**
Prom, chsd wnr 2f out, sn held: op 5/1: acts on gd & soft grnd: see 3663, 2463.
3471 **SWEET REWARD 27** [16] J G Smyth Osbourne 5-9-4 M Tebbutt 7/2: 403533: 5 ch g Beveled - Sweet *shd* **62**
Revival (Claude Monet) Held up, rdn/onepace fnl 2f: op 9/2: see 1150.
3762 **BILLY BATHWICK 14** [4] E J O'Neill 3-8-13 D Holland 9/1: 000324: Held up, prog over 3f out, sn held. *1½* **63**
3819 **SKYE BLUE 11** [14] 3-8-11 T Quinn 8/1: 320565: Held up, mod late hdwy: see 2712, 1593. *shd* **61$**
1725 **RED LION FR 102** [15] 3-8-11 D R McCabe 40/1: 0006: Held up, eff over 2f out, little hdwy: 3 mth abs. *1¾* **59**
3674 **EASTWOOD DRIFTER 19** [6] 3-8-11 S Kelly (5) 20/1: 626257: Dwelt/held up, mod late hdwy: btr 2053. *½* **58**
3813 **CARRIE CAN CAN 12** [12] 3-8-8 Dean McKeown 20/1: -6538: Chsd wnr, btn 2f out: op 12/1: see 3813. *½* **54**
3378 **ONCE MORE FOR LUCK 30** [10] 9-9-4 T Eaves (7) 14/1: 125239: Held up, nvr factor: btr 2098 (fm). *½* **56**
3011 **BURNING TRUTH 47** [2] 6-9-4 L Enstone (7) 14/1: 4-6020: Held up, rdn/btn 2f out: 10th: 7 wk abs. *9* **47**
3681 **CASTLEBRIDGE 18** [3] 3-8-11 G Baker (5) 12/1: 530450: Prom 7f: 11th: op 20/1: now with M Usher. *hd* **47**
3474 **BLINDING MISSION 27** [1] 3-8-8 G Hind 20/1: -03060: Slowly away, al rear: 12th: see 2086, 1692. *8* **36**
3524 **SIFAT 25** [5] 5-9-1 (vis) A Clark 5/2 FAV: 511230: Dwelt/held up, al rear: 13th: btr 1917, 1775. *2½* **34**
3390 **Edifice 30** [13] 4-9-4 J P Spencer 16/1: 695 **Swift 179** [11] 6-9-4 R Fitzpatrick 14/1:
15 ran Time 2m 12.2 (9.9) (Keith Harrison & Terry Miller) P W D'Arcy Newmarket.

Official Going GOOD/FIRM (FIRM in places). Stalls: Centre.

3980   **1.40 CITY OF GOLD MDN 2YO (D)**   **6f str**   **Firm 13   -00 Slow**
£5486   £1688   £844   £422

2132 **PALANZO 84** [13] P W Harris 2-9-0 Pat Eddery 7/1: -21: 2 b c Green Desert - Karpacka   **99+**
(Rousillon) Prom, led 2f out till ins last, rallied gamely to regain lead cl home, just prevailed in a driving
fin: nicely bckd, 12 wk abs, fair juv time: first foal, dam a useful 2yo performer abroad: eff over a stiff
6f on fast & firm: likes run up with the pace, runs well fresh: tough & useful, shld develop into a decent 3yo.

3064 **MOOTAFAYILL 45** [17] B W Hills 2-9-0 M Hills 9/4 FAV: -22: 2 b c Danzig - Ruznama (Forty   shd   **98**
Niner) Nvr far away, rdn to lead ins fnl 1f, battled on gamely & just lost out in a driving fin: hvly bckd, clr
of 3rd, 6 wk abs: lost little in defeat, met a potentially smart rival: shld have no trouble in finding a mdn.

-- **GLORIOUS QUEST** [20] M A Jarvis 2-9-0 P Robinson 5/1: -3: 2 ch c Lake Coniston - Lassalia   3½   **88+**
(Sallust) Chsd ldrs, kept on fnl 1f but no ch with front 2: Jan foal, cost IR 26,000gns: related to sev wnrs
incl high class 1m/10f performer Free Flyer: sire a high class sprinter: eff over a stiff 6f on firm grnd, will
stay 7f: nice introduction, met a couple of above average rivals here: shld have no trouble in finding a mdn.

-- **AMICABLE** [16] B W Hills 2-9-0 M Hills 10/1: -4: Mid div, kept on nicely fnl 1f, nrst fin on debut: ¾   **85+**
longer priced stablemate of rnr up: May foal, cost IR 62,000gns: half sister to a couple of wnrs abroad, dam
scored in France: sire a decent miler: eff at 6f on firm grnd, 7f will suit: plenty to like about this most
encouraging debut, looks sure to win in mdn company.

2529 **GIVE BACK CALAIS 68** [5] 2-9-0 S Sanders 11/4: -3235: Prom, onepcd fnl 1f: 10 week abs: nicely   shd   **85**
bckd & better expected on this drop in grade: see 2529 (List).

-- **SMIRK** [12] 2-9-0 M J Kinane 9/1: -6: Mid div, some late hdwy, nrst fin on debut: 67,000gns   2   **79**
purchase: Feb foal, dam a 1m winning 2yo: sire a top class miler: D Elsworth colt, will benefit from this.

-- **PROVIDENT** [21] 2-9-0 J Fortune 16/1: -7: Slowly away, rear, steady hdwy fnl 1f, nvr plcd to chall   2½   **72+**
on debut: Jan foal, dam a useful performer in France: sire a top class performer in the USA: likely to apprec
7f/1m+ next term: J Gosden colt, most promising debut & one to keep a cl eye on.

-- **PIQUET** [2] 2-8-9 R Hughes 10/1: -8: Set pace 4f, grad fdd: debut: cheaply bought March foal: ½   **66**
dam a 7f wnr, sire a v smart juv performer: with R Hannon & bred to be speedy.

-- **OREANA** [6] 2-8-9 B Marcus 14/1: -9: Chsd ldrs till left bhd fnl 1½f: debut: Feb foal, dam a   ½   **65**
high class sprinter: sire a top class sprinter: with J Dunlop, bred to be v speedy.

-- **BEIDERBECKE** [4] 2-9-0 R Perham 20/1: -0: Slowly away, nvr a factor in 10th on debut: April   2½   **63**
foal, dam a 1m/11f wnr abroad: sire smart over 7f: R Charlton colt, likely to apprec 7f+.

-- **CELTIC MISS** [11] 2-8-9 D Harrison 20/1: -0: Rdn in rear, nvr nr ldrs: fin 11th, debut: May foal,   nk   **57**
half sister to sev wnrs, incl 7f 2yo scorer Deputy Governor: dam a useful performer in the US, sire a high class
mid dist performer: with J Dunlop & likely to do much better over mid dist next year.

3752 **ELA DARLIN MOU 15** [19] 2-8-9 C Carver(3) 50/1: -000: Nvr better than mid div, fin 12th: highly tried   nk   **56**
3387 **LUCKY BREAK 30** [8] 2-9-0 Paul Eddery 50/1: -000: Nvr better than mid div: fin 13th: highly tried   nk   **60**
& now qualified for nursery h'caps: 7f will suit, see 3387.

2357 **RYANS GOLD 75** [7] 2-9-0 R Ryan 20/1: -00: Mid div till btn dist: fin 14th, 11 wk abs: see 2357.   ½   **59**
-- **FOREST LIGHT** [1] 2-8-9 J Reid 33/1: -0: Speed till halfway on debut: Jan foal cost 40,000gns: 1¼   **50**
half sister to a couple of winning 2yo's: dam unrcd but from a decent family, sire a top class mid dist performer:
with R Johnson Houghton & likely to do better over 1m+ next term.

1079 **Tropical River 137** [10] 2-9-0 J Mackay (5) 50/1:   --   **Dark Dolores** [14] 2-8-9 R Havlin 33/1:
3092 **Run On 44** [23] 2-9-0 S Clancy (7) 33/1:   --   **Golfagent** [9] 2-9-0 M Palmer (7) 50/1:
-- **Worth A Gamble** [3] 2-9-0 M Roberts 50/1:

20 ran   Time 1m 12.41 (0.81)   (Mrs P W Harris)   P W Harris Tring, Herts

---

3981   **2.10 PRICEWATERHOUSE HCAP 3YO+ 0-95 (C)**   **7f64y rnd   Firm 13   +21 Fast**   **[91]**
£7930   £2440   £1220   £610   3yo rec 4lb

*3796 **FLOATING CHARGE 12** [3] J R Fanshawe 6-9-0 (77) D Harrison 9/2 FAV: 2U0011: 6 b g Sharpo - Poyle   **82**
Fizz (Damister) Chsd ldrs, prog to lead ins fnl 1f, rdn out & won a shade cosily: fast time: recent Kempton wnr
(h'cap): '99 wnr at Windsor & Kempton (h'caps, rtd 77): '98 Redcar scorer (class stks, rtd 67): eff at 7/9f on
firm, hvy grnd & f/sand: handles any trk, likes Kempton: gd weight carrier who can run well fresh: has tried
blnks/visor, seems better without: best held up for a late chall & well rdn by D Harrison today.

3041 **GOODENOUGH MOVER 46** [10] J S King 4-9-0 (77) R Havlin 14/1: 111142: 4 ch g Beveled - Rekindled   ½   **79**
Flame (King's Lake) Nvr far away, went on 3f out & kicked for home, not pace to repel wnr ins fnl 1f: 7 wk abs:
fine eff, loves to run up with/force the pace: runs well fresh: prog gelding, see 2690.

3880 **VOLONTIERS 8** [15] P W Harris 5-9-9 (86) J Reid 8/1: 200203: 5 b g Common Grounds - Senlis   ½   **87**
(Sensitive Prince) Mid div, styd on fnl 1f but no pace to rch front 2: not disgraced from an unfavourable high
draw, must surely win a h'cap bef season's end: unlucky in 3880, see 3758.

3880 **ZUCCHERO 8** [17] D W P Arbuthnot 4-9-2 (79) M Roberts 14/1: 616554: Mid div, improved 1f out,   1   **78**
kept on & nrst fin: change of tactics, has been setting the pace: poor high draw: see 3880, 2814.

3629 **SHATHER 20** [14] 3-8-8 (75) M Hills 12/1: 343225: Mid div, short of room 2f out, fin well but too   ½   **73**
late: poor high draw: crying out for 1m, promising run here: see 3629, 3163.

3796 **CARLTON 12** [7] 6-8-12 (75) M J Kinane 13/2: 240056: Chsd ldrs, no impress fnl 1f: see 2761.   1¼   **70**
3796 **HILL MAGIC 12** [6] 5-8-11 (74) J Lowe 13/2: 000027: Waited with, improved over 1f out, not pace   ½   **68**
to chall: bmpd 2f out, prob cost him his chance: much closer to today's wnr when poss unlucky in 3796.

3414 **ALPEN WOLF 29** [16] 5-9-11 (88) Martin Dwyer 16/1: 210138: Early ldr, remained prom until   nk   **81**
btn dist: prev in gd form, see 3414, 2813.

1534 **ASAAL 111** [2] 3-9-11 (92) R Hills 33/1: 0-5609: Mid div, short of room 2f out, no ch   1   **83**
after: long abs & little luck in running here: sharper next time: see 912 (1m here).

3809 **THE EXHIBITION FOX 12** [12] 4-8-9 (72) T E Durcan 20/1: 300000: Nvr better than mid div, fin 10th: 1¾   **59**
out of form & subs slipping down the weights: see 1836.

3904 **RUSSIAN FOX 6** [1] 3-9-6 (87) R Smith (5) 33/1: 000000: Led after 1f till 3f out, wknd fnl 1f: fin   shd   **74**
11th, qck reapp: has had a mid season break: see 1028.

3796 **TEOFILIO 12** [8] 6-8-3 (66) J Mackay (5) 10/1: 004540: Slowly away, nvr a factor in 12th: lost   1½   **50**
all ch at the start here: see 3796.

3662 **SUSANS PRIDE 19** [9] 4-8-12 (75) Pat Eddery 10/1: 405450: Nvr a factor: see 3414.   3½   **52**
2356 **COMPTON ARROW 75** [11] 4-9-2 (79)(t) L Dettori 8/1: -00000: Held up, badly hmpd over 2f out,   ¾   **54**
no ch after: 11 week abs: lost all ch when hmpd, this must be forgotton: see 1450.

1836 **TUMBLEWEED RIVER** 97 [18] 4-9-1 (78) R Hughes 25/1: 05-000: Rear, nvr a factor in 15th: ½   52
3 month abs, poor high draw: tried blinks in 1836.
3763 **PRINCE CASPIAN** 14 [13] 3-9-11 (92) P Robinson 33/1: -1400: Led briefly after 1f, remained prom   5   56
till btn 2f out: fin last, top weight, unfav high draw: much btr 2389.
16 ran   Time 1m 27.20 (u0.60)   (The Leonard Curtis Partnership)   J R Fanshawe Newmarket

---

3982   2.40 LISTED DUBAI WORLD TROPHY 3YO+ (A)   5f34y str   Firm 13   +13 Fast
£23200   £8800   £4400   £2000   3yo rec 1lb

-3687 **IVORYS JOY** 18 [6]   K T Ivory 5-8-8 C Carver 16/1: 450121: 5 b m Tina's Pet - Jacqui Joy (Music   108
Boy) Prom, led dist & kicked clr, styd on strongly, rdn out: fast time: earlier won at Brighton & Haydock (h'caps):
'99 wnr at Thirsk, Haydock & W'hampton (h'caps, rtd 82 & 87a): suited by 5f, stays 6f: acts on firm, hvy & f/sand:
tried blnks/visor, best without: loves to run up with/force the pace: smart, career best effort.
3784 **EASTERN PURPLE** 11 [11] K A Ryan 5-9-2 B Marcus 11/2: 621062: 5 b g Petorius - Broadway Rosie   1¼   112
(Absalom) Rear, prog 2f out, kept on without ever looking likely to trouble wnr: op 9/2: apprec this drop
in grade & faster grnd: see 3373 (Gr 3).
*3727 **ANDREYEV** 16 [5] R Hannon 6-8-13 J Fortune 6/1: 050413: 6 ch g Presidium - Missish (Mummy's   1¼   105
Pet) Rear, hdwy over 1f out, kept on & nrst fin: eff at 5f, better over 6f as in 3727.
3600 **VITA SPERICOLATA** 22 [1] J S Wainwright 3-8-7 G Bardwell 10/1: 403304: Mid div, prog over 1f out,   shd   100
no impress inside last: bckd from 16/1: apprec this drop bck to 5f, 6f may prove ideal: see 3303.
*3874 **LORD KINTYRE** 8 [9] 5-8-13 M Roberts 5/2 FAV: 021115: Held up, rdn to improve 2f out, onepce   ¾   102
fnl 1f: hvly bckd on bid for 4-timer: change of tactics, prev best up with/forcing the pace: btr 3874.
+3841 **EMERALD PEACE** 10 [4] 3-8-7 P Robinson 16/1: 2-0016: Prom, ev ch dist, no extra: btr 3841.   hd   97
3874 **RAMBLING BEAR** 8 [3] 7-8-13 R Hughes 8/1: 005637: Rear, late hdwy, nvr dngrs: btr 3874.   1   99
+3687 **REPERTORY** 18 [7] 7-8-13 Darren Williams 14/1: 350018: Set fast pace 3f, wknd: seems better off in   ½   98
h'caps, likes Epsom: see 3687 (beat today's wnr).
3569 **KATHOLOGY** 23 [10] 3-8-12 M J Kinane 12/1: 140029: Nvr a factor: much btr 3569.   3   89
3598 **RUDIS PET** 22 [2] 6-9-2 (bl) S Sanders 11/2: -10300: Rcd alone far side & gd speed, jnd rem of   1½   88
field 2f out, wknd fnl 1f, eased: fin 10th, op 9/2: v speedy gelding who has lost his way since 3059.
3610 **MITCHAM** 21 [8] 4-8-13 (BL) L Carter 25/1: 040000: Front rank 3f, wknd: v free in first time blnks.   4   73
11 ran   Time 1m 00.33 (u0.03)   (K T Ivory)   K T Ivory Radlett, Herts

---

3983   3.10 HAYNES/HANSON/CLARK COND STKS 2YO (B)   1m str   Firm 13   -33 Slow
£9439   £3580   £1790   £813

--   **NAYEF** [3] M P Tregoning 2-8-10 R Hills 7/4 FAV: -1: 2 b c Gulch - Height Of Fashion (Bustino)   110+
Held up, smooth hdwy 2f out, went on dist, styd on strongly, rdn out: hvly bckd tho' big drifter from 11/10: May
foal, bred in the purple, half brother to numerous wnrs, notably top class mid dist performers Nashwan & Unfuwain:
dam high class mid dist performer, sire a top class performer in the USA: eff over a stiff 1m, will apprec mid
dists next time: acts on firm grnd & on a gall track, runs well fresh: held in some regard by connections (holds
sev Gr race entries), potentially high class colt who bids to follow some prestigious wnrs of this race.
3154 **TAMBURLAINE** 41 [4] R Hannon 2-8-8 R Hughes 11/4: -22: 2b c Royal Academy - Well Bought   nk   108
(Auction Ring) Nvr far away, went on 2f out till collared dist, battled on well & ev ch till no extra cl home:
big gamble from 9/2, 6 wk abs, 3L clr rem: eff over a stiff 1m: fine run against a potentially v smart rival.
--   **MERSEY SOUND** [6] D R C Elsworth 2-8-10 M J Kinane 14/1: -3: 2 b c Ela Mana Mou - Coral Sound   3   102
(Glow) Dwelt, improved from rear 2f out, kept on nicely but no ch with front 2: op 12/1, debut: 110,000gns Feb
foal: half brother to multiple wnr Golden Glisk: dam a mid dist wnr, sire a top class mid dist performer: eff
at 1m on firm grnd: useful colt, will improve & win races.
*3608 **FAIR QUESTION** 21 [1] J L Dunlop 2-9-1 J Reid 11/2: -14: Waited with, eff when carried left 2f   1½   104
out, onepce fnl 1f: seems to stay 1m & acts on firm grnd: see 3608 (debut).
2608 **RUSSIAN WHISPERS** 64 [8] 2-8-10 Pat Eddery 13/2: -35: Set pace 6f, fdd fnl 1f: op 8/1, 9 wk abs: nk   98$
will have little trouble winning a mdn judged on this: see 2608.
*3508 **PUTRA PEKAN** 26 [2] 2-9-1 (bl) P Robinson 10/1: -0616: Chsd rds racing keenly, btn over 1f out: 3   97
rcd much too keenly here: see 3508, (7f).
3304 **SHADOWLESS** 34 [7] 2-8-10 L Dettori 4/1: -40237: Prom 6f, wknd: swtg: much btr 3304, 2613.   6   80
7 ran   Time 1m 40.53 (3.73)   (Hamdan Al Maktoum)   M P Tregoning Lambourn, Berks

---

3984   3.40 LISTED DUBAI ARC TRIAL STKS 3YO+ (A)   1m3f   Firm 13   -13 Slow
£29000   £11000   £5500   £2500   3yo rec 8lb

3792 **PAWN BROKER** 13 [7] D R C Elsworth 3-8-8 M J Kinane 6/4 FAV: 122031: 3 ch c Selkirk - Dime   113
Bag (High Line) Waited with, no room 2f out till over 1f out, styd on strongly to lead cl home, won going away:
hvly bckd from 9/4: earlier won at Newmarket (List, reapp): '99 Newmarket wnr (mdn): eff at 1m/11f, has tried
12f & prob just failed to stay: acts on firm & hvy, runs well fresh: likes gall track: smart colt.
*3889 **FRANCESCO GUARDI** 7 [6] P F I Cole 3-8-8 R Hughes 4/1: 12-12: 3 b c Robellino - Lamees   ½   110
(Lomond) Chsd ldr, went on 4f out, not pce to repel wnr cl home: nicely bckd: fine run, lightly rcd & progressive.
3151 **DIAMOND WHITE** 11 [5] M J Ryan 5-8-11 L Dettori 11/2: 645453: 5 b m Robellino - Diamond Wedding   2   102
(Diamond Shoal) Mid div, imprvng when drftd left 2f out, onepcd fnl 1f: op 4/1: seems to stay 11f: see 1057.
3792 **REACH THE TOP** 13 [3] J H M Gosden 3-8-8 J Fortune 11/1: 16144: Led till 4f out, no extra: op 9/1.   shd   107
3640 **PORT VILA** 20 [4] 3-8-8 (t) R Hills 7/1: -31355: Dwelt, mid div, no impress fnl 2f: tried a t-strap.   1   105
3792 **ZAFONIUM** 13 [9] 3-8-8 (BL) S Sanders 16/1: 1-2406: Nvr nr to chall in first time blnks: best 2148.   shd   105
3088 **ZAFONICS SONG** 44 [2] 3-8-8 Pat Eddery 5/1: -35127: Dwelt, eff when short of room 2f out,   1¼   103
sn btn: 6 week abs: see 3088, 2386.
7 ran   Time 2m 18.69 (2.89)   (Raymond Tooth)   D R C Elsworth Whitsbury, Hants

---

3985   4.10 DUTY FREE EBF COND STKS 2YO (C)   7f str   Firm 13   -21 Slow
£9674   £3669   £1834   £834

*3299 **PALATIAL** 35 [5] J R Fanshawe 2-8-8 D Harrison 5/1: -22211: 2 b f Green Desert - White Palace   96
(Shirley Heights) Waited with, gd hdwy to lead 2f out, rdn clr fnl 1f: nicely bckd: recent Newmarket wnr (nurs
h'cap): eff at 6/7f on gd & firm: handles a stiff/gall or sharp trk: useful, improving filly.
3108 **SAYEDAH** 43 [6] M P Tregoning 2-8-8 R Hills 10/11 FAV: -22: 2 b f Darshaan - Balaabel (Sadler's   1¼   92

Wells) Nvr far away, led briefly 2f out, not pace of wnr fnl 1f: hvly bckd, 6 wk abs: acts on gd & firm grnd, poss prefers the former: better expected after 3108 (debut).

3829   **ANNATTO** 10 [3]   I A Balding 2-8-8 M Hills 12/1: -2423: 2 br f Mister Baileys - Miss Rossi (Artaius)   ½   91
Set pace 5f, kept on but no ch with front 2: consistent, see 3829.

--   **MISS TEAK** [2]   G A Butler 2-8-8 M J Kinane 8/1: -4: Rear, kept on nicely fnl 1f, nvr nrr on debut: ½   90
May foal, cost 110,000gns: sister to a wnr abroad: sire a smart 2yo: will suit.

*3627   **HAMADEENAH** 20 [9]   2-8-8 B Marcus 14/1: -15: Chsd ldrs, fdd fnl 1f: see 3627 (6f, debut).   3½   88

--   **IRISH VERSE** [8]   2-8-8 J Fortune 10/1: -6: Slowly away, rdn to improve 1f out, eased ins fnl 1f: nk   82
better for debut: May foal, dam a sprint winning 2yo: sire a high class sprinter: may benefit from a drop bck to 6f for now: with J Gosden & sure to improve for this.

--   **NEVER PROMISE** [7]   2-8-8 J Reid 10/1: -7: Nvr a factor on debut: drifted from 7/1: Feb foal,   hd   82
half sister to 1m 2yo scorer Fancy My Chance: dam from a gd family, sire a top class sprinter with B Hills.

3661   **HIDDEN MEANING** 19 [1]   2-8-8 R Hughes 6/1: -38: Speed 5½f, fdd into last: see 3661 (6f, gd).   2½   77
8 ran   Time 1m 26.69 (2.39)   (Cheveley Park Stud)   J R Fanshawe Newmarket, Suffolk

---

3986   4.45 DUBAI HCAP STKS 3YO+ 0-100 (C)   2m   Firm 13 -57 Slow   [97]
     £7150   £2200   £1100   £550   3yo rec 13lb

2092   **BANGALORE** 86 [1]   Mrs A J Perrett 4-9-7 (90) M J Kinane 10/3: 6-3101: 4 ch h Sanglamore - Ajuga   94
(The Minstrel) Chsd ldr till went on 4f out, hdd briefly dist, styd on gamely fnl 1f, drvn out: gamble from 11/2, top weight, 3 month abs, slow time: earlier won at Chester (val h'cap): 99/00 hdle wnr at Fontwell & Uttoxeter (nov, eff at 2m/2½m on firm, hvy grnd, rtd 134h): '99 Pontefract wnr (mdn auct, rtd 86, with B Hills): eff at 12f, suited by 2m+: goes on any grnd & on any trk, runs v well fresh: gd weight carrier who is developing into a useful stayer: looks sure to give a gd account in the Cesarewitch.

3231   **FIRST OFFICER** 37 [3]   J R Fanshawe 3-8-4 (86) D Harrison 9/1: 210632: 3 b c Lear Fan - Trampoli   ¾   88
(Trempolino) Prom, rdn to lead briefly dist, kept on but al being held by wnr: op 7/1: stays a stiff 2m.

3599   **ALRISHA** 22 [2]   D R C Elsworth 3-8-1 (83) J Mackay (5) 15/8 FAV: 021243: 3 b f Persian Bold -   1¼   84
Rifaya (Lashkari) Mid div, lost pl 3f out, rallied fnl 1f, nrst fin: bckd from 11/4: stays 2m, further will suit.

1839   **TAMING** 97 [9]   I A Balding 4-8-10 (79) J Fortune 10/1: /1-044: Waited with, steady hdwy to hold   hd   80
ev ch dist, no extra: op 7/1, 3 month abs: seems to sty this longer 2m trip: see 1839.

3890   **KENNET** 7 [4]   5-8-3 (72) A Beech(5) 8/1: 311365: Mid div, rdn to improve 2f out, short of room   nk   72
& swtchd dist, not pace to chall: up in trip: see 3518 (13f).

3890   **BID ME WELCOME** 7 [6]   4-8-1 (80) J Reid 14/1: 315206: Led till 4f out, no extra: see 3611 (14f).   shd   80

3899   **COMPTON AVIATOR** 6 [11]   4-8-11 (80)(t) W Ryan 14/1: 433-07: Held up, rdn to improve 2f out,   ½   79
no impress fnl 1f: qck reapp, big step up in trip: lightly rcd in '99, plcd in a couple of mdn's (rtd 81 at best): eff at 10f on fast/firm grnd, poss stays 2m: wears a t-strap.

*3360   **QUEDEX** [7]   4-9-2 (85) I Mongan (5) 6/1: 140018: Held up, nvr nr ldrs: rtd higher 3360.   ¾   83

3811   **GREYFIELD** 12 [10]   4-7-13 (68) Martin Dwyer 12/1: 045449: Nvr a factor, fin last: see 3657 (12f).   1   65
9 ran   Time 3m 37.22 (11.22)   (Mike Dawson)   Mrs A J Perrett Pulborough, W Sussex

---

AYR   FRIDAY SEPTEMBER 15TH   Lefthand, Galloping Track

Official Going   SOFT (HEAVY in places). Stalls: Rnd Crse - Inside; Str Crse - Stands Side.

3987   2.00 JAMES BARR NURSERY HCAP 2YO 0-95 (C)   6f   Soft 90 -31 Slow   [91]
     £7540   £2320   £1160   £580

3886   **SOLDIER ON** 7 [11]   M R Channon 2-9-7 (84) Craig Williams 6/1: 135221: 2 b g General Monash - Golden   88
Form (Formidable) In tch, prog 2f out, ran on well to lead fnl 100y: bckd, slow time: prev won at Brighton (mdn) & Goodwood (nurs): eff at 5/6f on firm & soft grnd: goes on a sharp/undul or gall trk: progressive & tough.

+3958   **ARMAGNAC** 1 [5]   M H Tompkins 2-9-11 (88)(7ex) G Duffield 7/1: 425512: 2 b c Young Ern - Arianna   nk   90
Aldini (Habitat) In tch, clsd 2f out, rdn to lead briefly ent fnl 1f, kept on: won a mdn over C/D yesterday: clearly relishes soft grnd & stable back to form & prob worth following: see 3958.

3614   **MARKUSHA** 21 [6]   D Nicholls 2-8-8 (71) F Norton 14/1: -4303: 2 b g Alhijaz - Shafir (Shaadi)   1¾   69
Led till ent fnl 1f, onepace: h'cap bow, tchd 20/1: stays 6f on soft grnd: see 1102.

3879   **LONER** 8 [8]   N A Callaghan 2-9-3 (80) P Hanagan (7) 12/1: 621504: Slow to stride, front rank   shd   78
after 2f, going well 2f out, effort & found little bef fnl 1f: down in trip, goes on fast & soft grnd: see 3660 (7f).

3363   **LENNEL** 31 [2]   A Nicholls (3) 20/1: 6355: Hmpd after 1f & rear, rdn appr fnl 1f, late   nk   69
prog, nvr dngers: clr of rem on h'cap bow: prob handles soft grnd, worth another chance over 7f.

3532   **ORIENTAL MIST** 24 [10]   2-8-13 (76) K Dalgleish (5) 20/1: 330446: Cl-up, fdd bef fnl 1f: h'cap bow.   4   65

*3807   **MY AMERICAN BEAUTY** 12 [4]   2-8-7 (70) K Darley 15/8 FAV: -60317: Bmpd after 1f, cl-up, wknd appr   hd   59
fnl 1f: well bckd, prob worth another chance after 3807 (gd).

3888   **THORNTON DIVA** 7 [7]   2-9-2 (79) F Lynch 12/1: -30208: Nvr a factor: op 8/1 h'cap bow, vis omitted.   1¼   65

3673   **MILLIKEN PARK** 19 [9]   2-8-8 (71) M Fenton 16/1: -30208: Prsd ldr 4f: op 12/1: see 3533, 3327.   6   47

3394   **CELOTTI** 30 [3]   2-9-0 (77) R Winston 14/1: 351020: Al bhd: 10th, btr 3394 (5f), see 2818.   5   43

3712   **CANDOTHAT** 17 [1]   2-9-4 (81) A Culhane 20/1: 151500: In tch, rdn & btn 2f out: 11th: first run on soft.   5   37
11 ran   Time 1m 16.58 (7.28)   (T S M Cunningham)   M R Channon West Isley, Berks.

3988   2.30 BYMAX CLAIMER 3YO+ (E)   1m1f20y   Soft 90   +04 Fast
     £3796   £1168   £584   £292   3 yo rec 6 lb

3782   **CAROUSING** 13 [6]   M Johnston 3-9-2 (BL) K Darley 5/2: -15001: 3 b c Selkirk - Moon Carnival   80
(Be My Guest) Held up, hdwy 2f out, drvn & kept on well to get up towards fin: clmd for £20,000, fair time, first time blnks: earlier won reapp at Pontefract (class stks): '99 wnr at Lingfield (mdn) & Goodwood (nurs, rtd 91): eff at 9/10f on firm & soft, prob any trk: goes well fresh: apprec this drop in grade & woken up by blnks.

*3808   **LORD EUROLINK** 12 [2]   C A Dwyer 6-8-11 (vis) J Carroll 2/1 FAV: 645012: 6 b g Danehill - Lady   1   66
Eurolink (Kala Shikari) Trkd ldr, led ent str, 3L clr 2f out, hard rdn ins last & worn down nr fin: well bckd, 4L clr rem: acts on fast, soft & fibresand, handles equitrack: little ch with wnr at today's weights: see 3808.

3644   **IRON MAIDEN** 20 [4]   N A Callaghan 3-9-5 10-P Hanagan (7) 3/1: 143053: 5 b g Scenic - Merlannah   4   73
(Shy Groom) Mid-div, eff 2f out, styd on for 3rd but no ch with front & ran well at the weights.

*3823   **GO THUNDER** 11 [10]   D A Nolan 6-8-12 (t) Iona Wands 25/1: 005314: Chsd ldrs, onepace appr fnl 1f.   1½   59$

3269 **CANNY HILL** 36 [12] 3-8-4 J Bramhill 20/1: 4-3005: Chsd ldrs, fdd ent fnl 2f: op 14/1: best on sand.   2 54
3873 **LADY FEARLESS** 8 [7] 3-7-13 A Mackay 100/1: 06-006: Bhd, went past btn horses fnl 1f: v stiff task.   7 39
3808 **IMPULSIVE AIR** 12 [9] 8-8-8 J Quinn 33/1: 430007: Mid-div, outpcd fnl 2f: stiff task, faster grnd suits. hd 42
--   **SEOMRA HOCHT** [3] 3-8-11 M Fenton 20/1: 8: Nvr a factor: debut, half-brother to a mid-dist wnr.   4 45
3808 **THORNTOUN GOLD** 12 [11] 4-8-5 (bl) (1ow) F Lynch 33/1: 552008: Al towards rear: stiff task, see 2180. 1½ 31
3813 **TOUGH TIMES** 12 [5] 3-8-6 (BL) R Winston 14/1: 602500: Chsd ldrs, wknd 3f out: 10th, see 3248. 1½ 36
3775 **MINTY** 13 [1] 4-8-10 (VIS) D Mernagh (3) 66/1: 050-00: Keen & led till ent str, sn btn/eased: dist 0
11th, visored: well btn over hdles 3 days ago: 7L Southwell rnr-up last term (h'cap, rtd 58a): stays 11f on f/sand.
3823 **FASTWAN** 11 [8] 4-8-7 A Culhane 150/1: 000000: In tch till ent str: 12th, v stiff task. 1½ 0
12 ran   Time 1m 58.05 (7.75)   (P D Savill)   M Johnston Middleham, N.Yorks.

3989   **3.00 FAUCETS FILLIES HCAP 3YO+ 0-90 (C)**   **1m2f**   **Soft 90** -03 Slow   **[80]**
      £7182   £2210   £1105   £552   3 yo rec 7 lb

*3265 **GOLDEN WAY** 36 [7] E A L Dunlop 3-9-7 (80) K Darley 2/1 FAV: 0-611: 3 ch f Cadeaux Genereux -   88
Diavolina (Lear Fan) In tch, progr to lead 2f out, sn clr, readily: well bckd, h'cap bow: earlier won at Haydock
(mdn, readily): unplcd sole '99 start (fill mdn, rtd 68): much imprvd since stepped up to 10f, will get further:
acts on gd/soft & soft grnd: progressive filly, one to keep on the right side.
3785 **CHAMELEON** 13 [6] M L W Bell 4-9-6 (72) M Fenton 11/2: 0/1052: 4 b f Green Desert - Old Domesday   6 73
Book (High Top) Held up, prog ent str, rdn 2f out, styd on for 2nd, no ch wnr: caught a fast improving sort
& was up in trip here, prob stays 10f: acts on fibresand, prob handles soft grnd: see 478.
3750 **NATALIE JAY** 15 [3] M R Channon 4-9-2 (68) Craig Williams 12/1: 301063: 4 b f Ballacashtal - Falls 1½ 67
Of Lora (Scottish Rifle) Rear, prog & sltly short of room over 2f out, switched to dispute 2nd dist, sn
onepace: mkt drifter: back up in trip & 9L clr rem, see 3422 (1m).
3657 **REVIVAL** 19 [1] Sir Michael Stoute 3-9-10 (83) F Lynch 7/2: 0-1204: Trkd ldrs, ch appr fnl 2f, btn dist   9 72
& eased: bckd, top-weight: grnd & trip shld suit, something amiss? see 3657, 1343.
3676 **BOLLIN ROBERTA** 19 [4] 4-9-2 (68) J Carroll 6/1: 531225: Led till over 2f out, sn wknd: unsuited 1¼ 55
forcing the pace on this easier surface? see 3054.
3701 **SOUTH SEA PEARL** 18 [5] 3-9-0 (73) J Fanning 12/1: 602236: Pressed ldr till ent str, sn lost place. 14 44
6 ran   Time 2m 13.72 (9.32)   (Ahmed Ali)   E A L Dunlop Newmarket.

3990   **3.30 SCOTS NURSERY HCAP 2YO 0-95 (C)**   **1m rnd**   **Soft 90** -13 Slow   **[92]**
      £7572   £2330   £1165   £582

3876 **PERFECT PLUM** 8 [9] Sir Mark Prescott 2-9-7 (85) G Duffield 5/2 FAV: 232101: 2 b f Darshaan -   102
Damascene (Scenic) Cl-up, led ent fnl 3f, sn hard pressed, drvn to assert 1f out & drew clr: hvly bckd: tried Gr 3
company since won at Newcastle (nurs): eff at 1m, mid-dists will suit next term: acts on firm, likes gd/soft &
soft grnd: handles stiff/gall trks: gd weight carrier who shld make the step into List comapny.
*3706 **FAZZANI** 18 [5] M W Easterby 2-8-4 (68) P Hanagan (7) 7/1: 301212: 2 b f Shareef Dancer - Taj   5 75
Victory (Final Straw) In tch, gd prog ent str to chall 2f out, onepace dist: nicely bckd: sound run for new
connections, prev with P Haslam: tough & progressive: see 3706 (clmr).
3817 **ACT OF REFORM** 11 [2] R Charlton 2-9-5 (83) K Darley 8/1: 5143: 2 b c Lit de Justice - Bionic Soul 2½ 86
(Bionic Light) Pressed ldr, led ent str till bef 2f out, no extra: fair run tho' shapes like return to 7f may suit.
*3532 **SMYSLOV** 24 [3] J L Dunlop 2-9-2 (80) F Lynch 4/1: -04414: Trkd ldrs, outpcd 2f out: h'cap bow: ¾ 82
well bckd: already looks in need of 10f+: see 3532.
*3729 **PRINCESS EMILY** 16 [6] 2-8-10 (74) D Mernagh (3) 14/1: 0315: Bhd, prog into mid-div 3f out, ¾ 75
onepace after: op 10/1, h'cap bow, first try on soft: see 3729 (gd/firm).
3635 **SAVE THE POUND** 20 [1] 2-7-10 (60)(2oh) P Fessey 50/1: -5006: Led till ent str, sn lost pl: h'cap bow. 10 46
*3609 **SIENA STAR** 21 [4] 2-9-0 (78) A Culhane 10/1: 432217: In tch till 3f out: prog earlier on faster grnd.   5 56
3532 **THORNTOUN DANCER** 24 [7] 2-7-13 (63) J Quinn 25/1: 005638: Chsd ldrs 5f: h'cap bow, btr 3532 (mdn).6 32
*3779 **MIN MIRRI** 13 [10] 2-9-4 (82) Craig Williams 6/1: -45319: Pulled hard, rear, brief eff 3f out: 3½ 46
h'cap bow, comfortable mdn wnr in 3779 (gd/soft).
3704 **THEWHIRLINGDERVISH** 18 [8] 2-8-7 (71) J Carroll 16/1: 003200: Dwelt, nvr in it: 10th, see 2991, 2521.   4 29
10 ran   Time 1m 44.83 (8.23)   (Sir Edmund Loder)   Sir Mark Prescott Newmarket.

3991   **4.00 HBG PROPERTIES COND STKS 2YO (C)**   **7f rnd**   **Soft 90** -35 Slow
      £6820   £2420   £1210   £550

3304 **BLUEBERRY FOREST** 34 [3] J L Dunlop 2-9-5 K Darley 3/10 FAV: 122261: 2 br c Charnwood Forest -   96
Abstraction (Rainbow Quest) Led, pressed 3f out, drvn & found extra to go clr, readily: well bckd to land
the odds, slow time: 3 time rnr-up since winning debut at Doncaster (mdn): IR 75,000gns colt, eff at 6/7f,
tried 1m last time: acts on firm & soft grnd, gall trks: useful front-runner, easy task here.
3740 **DENISE BEST** 15 [4] A Berry 2-8-7 Mark Flynn (7) 100/1: 02: 2 ch f Goldmark - Titchwell Lass (Lead   4 76
On Time) Chsd ldrs, rdn & ch appr fnl 2f, styd on for 2nd but outpcd by wnr: stays 1m, apprec this softer grnd.
3860 **FOREVER TIMES** 9 [1] T D Easterby 2-8-12 J Carroll 4/1: 221033: 2 b f So Factual - Simply Times   3 76
(Dodge) Trkd ldrs, chall 2f out, sn onepace: bckd, first try on soft, see 3860, 3346 (gd/firm).
3888 **FINMAR** 7 [2] Miss L A Perratt 2-8-12 R Winston 9/1: -5004: Keen, prsd ldrs till wknd/flashed tail 2f out.   6 66
4 ran   Time 1m 32.53 (8.73)   (L Cashman)   J L Dunlop Arundel, W.Sussex.

3992   **4.30 BEAT 106 HCAP STKS 3YO+ 0-90 (C)**   **7f rnd**   **Soft 90** +03 Fast   **[89]**
      £7540   £2320   £1160   £580   3 yo rec 4 lb

1777 **GREAT NEWS** 100 [11] W J Haggas 5-8-6 (67) P Hanagan (7) 11/4 FAV: 000001: 5 b g Elmaamul - Amina   75
(Brigadier Gerard) Nvr far away, led going well 2f out, rdn out: hvly bckd, 14 wk abs, right back to form: '99 wnr
at Ascot & Windsor (val h'cap & rtd h'cap, rtd 86): '98 Lingfield wnr (h'cap, rtd 75): eff at 7f/1m, tried 10f:
acts on any grnd/trk: runs v well fresh & has slipped to a v handy mark, qck follow up likely.
3880 **SUPREME SALUTATION** 8 [4] T D Barron 4-8-11 (72) M Fenton 9/1: 355342: 4 ch g Most 1¼ 77
Welcome - Cardinal Press (Sharrood) Bhd, rdn & rapid prog appr fnl 1f, went 2nd towards fin, nvr nrr: in
gd form, return to 1m may suit: hmpd early on & poss a shade unlucky: see 3708, 1011.
3699 **LAGOON** 18 [3] B W Hills 3-9-10 (89) A Culhane 6/1: 040003: 3 ch c Common Grounds - Secret 1¼ 92
Hideaway (Key To The Mint) Prom, rdn to chall ent fnl 2f, no extra ins last: return to form, acts on firm & soft.
3831 **AMBER FORT** 10 [12] J M Bradley 7-8-7 (68)(bl) F Norton 25/1: 345004: Keen in tch, prog to press hd 71

wnr appr fnl 1f, onepace ins last: sound run, goes well on testing grnd, rcd a shade too keenly here: see 1011.

3839 **UNSHAKEN 10** [16] 6-8-6 (67) F Lynch 20/1: 000105: Rear, gd prog to chase ldrs appr fnl 1f, ¾ 69
same pace ins last: loves soft grnd, prob ran to best: see 3573.

3785 **KINAN 13** [5] 4-9-10 (85) K Dalgleish (5) 10/1: 010036: Rear, short of room over 2f out, switched ¾ 86
bef dist, kept on, nvr a factor: bckd tho' gd 8/1, top-weight: not much luck in running, acts on fast & soft grnd.

3880 **ARPEGGIO 8** [10] 5-9-0 (75)(6ex) A Nicholls (3) 10/1: 103137: Trkd ldrs, hmpd/outpcd & drvn ent nk 75
fnl 2f, unable to qckn: qckish reapp with a penalty, worth another chance: see 844.

3288 **WEETMANS WEIGH 35** [13] 7-8-3 (64) R Winston 12/1: 640658: Bhd, late hdwy into mid-div: see 49. nk 63

3809 **AT LARGE 12** [14] 6-8-11 (72) L Newton 33/1: 000009: Al around same place: see 1545. ½ 70

*3809 **STYLE DANCER 12** [7] 6-8-11 (72)(vis) G Duffield 12/1: 100310: In tch, shaken up & hdwy when 1 68
short of room & snatched up 1½f out, onepace after: fin 10th: badly hmpd & worth forgiving, see 3809.

2986 **ZIRCONI 48** [2] 4-9-0 (75)(VIS) K Darley 10/1: 403300: Cl-up, led appr fnl 2f, sn hdd & fdd: 11th, visor. 3½ 66

3839 **TIPPERARY SUNSET 10** [1] 6-8-2 (63)(bl) T Williams 12/1: 4D4140: Chsd ldrs, lost pl 2f out: 12th. hd 54

1192 **MAGIC MILL 131** [18] 7-8-2 (63) J Quinn 25/1: 0-4000: Led till 2f out, btn: 16th, long abs: see 844. 0

3750 Karameg 15 [8] 4-9-9 (84) M Fenton 16/1:   *3345 Ostara 32 [15] 3-8-1 (65)(1ow) D O'Donohoe 14/1:
3960 Peppiatt 1 [6] 6-8-0 (61) P Doe 20/1:
16 ran   Time 1m 29.86 (6.06)   (Executive Network (Pertemps Group))   W J Haggas Newmarket.

| 3993 | 5.05 SPORRAN HCAP 3YO+ 0-80 (D)   2m1f105y Soft 90 -12 Slow | [78] |
| | £4940 £1520 £760 £380   3yo rec 13lb | |

1701 **GIVE AN INCH 103** [4] W Storey 5-8-10 (60) T Williams 7/4 FAV: 000011: 5 b m Inchinor - Top Heights 68
(High Top) Patiently rdn, imprvd appr straight, led bef 3f out, sn clr, cmftbly: well bckd, 15 wk abs: earlier
won at Pontefract (ddht, h'cap): '99 wnr again at Pontefract & here at Ayr: '98 Redcar
(mdn sell) & Ayr wnr (2, incl this h'cap, rtd 64): eff at 2m/2m2f: acts on fast, suited by gd/soft & hvy grnd,
gall trks: completed a hat-trick in this race & remains unbeaten here at Ayr: tough mare.

3783 **BHUTAN 13** [9] Mrs M Reveley 5-9-7 (71) A Culhane 10/1: 001242: 5 b g Polish Patriot - Bustinetta 11 71
(Bustino) Mid-div, prog to go 2nd 3f out, no ch wnr: fair run tho' stamina poss stretched over lngr 2m1.5f trip.

2951 **CHARMING ADMIRAL 49** [7] Mrs A Duffield 7-8-6 (56)(bl) G Duffield 7/1: 200303: 7 b g Shareef ¾ 55
Dancer - Lilac Charm (Bustino) Bhd, went past toiling rivals up the straight, nvr dngrs: 18 days ago scored
at Cartmel (2m5f h'cap chase, soft grnd, rtd 97c): see 876.

3674 **HOME COUNTIES 19** [2] J Hetherton 11-7-10 (46)(t)(7oh) K Dalgleish (5) 8/1: 000064: Chsd ldrs 14f. 5 42

3511 **BLACK WEASEL 26** [3] 5-7-10 (46)(8oh) P Hanagan 33/1: 056255: Prom, edged left & btn ent 5 39
fnl 3f: 3 wks ago scored over timber at Cartmel (2m6f nov, gd/soft, rtd 88h): stiff task today & is best at 14f.

3709 **HIGH TOPPER 18** [10] 3-9-0 (77) K Darley 11/1: 10456: Nvr a factor: blnks omitted, wins on firm/fast. 2 69

3742 **NORTHERN MOTTO 15** [1] 7-7-10 (46)(2oh) J Quinn 16/1: 344367: Handy till ent str: see 797. 2 37

2406] **SUBTLE INFLUENCE 800** [8] 6-10-0 (78) F Lynch (3) 0534/8: Led till ent str, sn btn: abs, 29 33
98/99 hdles wnr at Huntingdon (nov, debut, 2m, gd grnd, rtd 90a, N Callaghan): ex-French Flat wnr (rtd 91):
eff at 2m on gd & soft, handles firm: tried blnks: now with J Goldie.

3167 **DR COOL 41** [5] 3-7-13 (62)(bl) P Doe 20/1: 054009: Dwelt, imprvd halfway till wknd 4f out. 19 22

*3715 **MAKASSEB 17** [12] 3-8-12 (75) Craig Williams 9/1: 044010: Cl-up & ch till rdn & btn ent str: 29 24
10th, tchd 9/1: much btr 3715 (fast grnd).

3395 **SWIFTWAY 30** [11] 6-7-11 (47) J Bramhill 10/1: 34-150: Mid-div but hung right, lost tch halfway: 11th. *dist* 0

11 ran   Time 4m 00.11 (17.81)   (Black Type Racing)   W Storey Muggleswick, Co.Durham.

Official Going   GOOD/FIRM. Stalls: Rnd - Outside; Str - Centre.

| 3994 | 2.00 TOTE AUTUMN CUP HCAP 3YO+ 0-100 (C)   1m5f61y Firm 10 -01 Slow | [96] |
| | £18443 £5675 £2837 £1418   3yo rec 9lb | |

3890 **AFTERJACKO 8** [14] D R C Elsworth 4-9-13 (95) Pat Eddery 11/4 FAV: 056421: 4 ch g Seattle Dancer - 101
Shilka (Soviet Star) Bhd, plenty to do 3f out, styd on well for strong press fnl 2f to get up cl-home: bckd from
5/1, topweight: earlier scored at Salisbury (h'cap), plcd sev times: '98 Bath wnr (mdn, rtd 83): well suited by
around 14f on fm, gd/soft & likes gall trks: can carry big weights: tough & v useful, still improving.

*3454 **MASAMADAS 29** [4] N J Henderson 5-9-6 (88) J Reid 8/1: 30/212: 5 ch g Elmaamul - Beau's Delight ½ 92
(Lypheor) Chsd ldrs, eff 2f out, kept on ins last to take 2nd, not btn far: useful, improving & still fresh.

3339 **THARI 34** [13] B Hanbury 3-9-2 (93) R Hills 25/1: 36-063: 3 b c Silver Hawk - Magic Slipper (Habitat) nk 96
Handy, hdwy to lead 2f out, kept on for press till collared ins last, not btn far: stays 13.3f, improve at this trip.

2116 **MASTER GEORGE 86** [12] I A Balding 3-8-3 (80) L Newman (3) 16/1: 162504: In tch, eff for press 1½ 81
2f out, kept on same pace: gd run after 3 month abs with visor discarded & stays 13.3f: see 2116, 1400.

3896 **FATHER JUNINHO 7** [9] 3-8-12 (89) R Mullen 14/1: 354045: Slow away, bhd, eff over 1f out, kept on 3 85
ins last, nvr dngrs: prob stays 13.3f: see 3896 (nvr a chance over dist 3541).

3654 **OCTAVIUS CAESAR 21** [10] 3-8-6 (83) P Robinson 13/2: 0-3126: Sn clr ldr till 2f out, wknd: lngr trip. 1½ 77

629 **DONATUS 196** [3] 4-8-2 (70) A Beech (3) 40/1: 260-27: Bhd, some late gains, no dngr: lngr trip. 1¾ 62

3783 **MORGANS ORCHARD 14** [8] 4-7-11 (65) G Baker (5) 16/1: 023268: In tch, wknd well over 1f out: shd 57
best at 12f as in 3541.

*3728 **CRACOW 17** [6] 3-8-13 (90) M Hills 6/1: 105219: In tch, eff over 2f out, sn btn: btr 3728 (12f). 1¾ 80

3811 **DUCHAMP 32** [15] 3-8-8 (85) R Hughes 16/1: 021500: Slow away, al bhd: 10th: btr 3599. 3½ 70

*3783 **MAJESTIC BAY 14** [5] 4-9-3 (85) J Weaver 15/2: 131410: Chsd ldr till 4f out: 11th: btr 3783. 1½ 68

3782 **OPTIMAITE 14** [11] 3-9-1 (92) J P Spencer 25/1: 050500: Al bhd: 12th: best 1347 (12f). 2 72

2584 **ENFILADE 66** [2] 4-8-7 (75)(t) J Mackay 25/1: 501650: Al bhd: 13th: 10 wk abs: see 2584. 2 52

3725 **CLARENDON 17** [7] 4-8-9 (77) M Tebbutt 10/1: 223030: Al bhd: 14th: btr 3725 (12f), 968. ½ 53

3285 **PAS DE PROBLEME 36** [1] 4-7-10 (64) Dale Gibson 25/1: 531460: In tch, wknd 9f out: see 1927, 1570. 7 30

15 ran   Time 2m 46.60 (1.50)   (McDowell Racing)   D R C Elsworth Whitsbury, Hants.

NEWBURY SATURDAY SEPTEMBER 16TH Lefthand, Flat, Galloping Track

3995
2.30 LISTED DUBAI DUTY FREE CUP 3YO+ (A) 7f64y rnd Firm 10 +05 Fast
£23200 £8800 £4400 £2000 3yo rec 3lb

3763 **WARNINGFORD** 15 [1] J R Fanshawe 6-9-0 O Urbina 6/1: 242631: 6 b h Warning - Barford Lady (Stanford) **114**
Cl-up, hdwy to lead dist, styd on well, rdn out: gd time: plcd earlier: '99 scorer at Warwick (stks), Leicester
(Gr 3) & Haydock (List, rtd 114): '98 scorer at Yarmouth & Goodwood (h'caps): eff at 6f, all 7 wins over 7f/7.3f,
stays 1m on fm, likes gd/soft & hvy: eff with/without a vis & runs like fresh: genuine & tough 7f specalist.

3452 **UMISTIM** 29 [5] R Hannon 3-9-0 R Hughes 9/1: 165202: 3 ch c Inchinor - Simply Sooty (Absalom) 1½ **112**
Handy, hdwy to lead 2f out, rdn & hdd 1f out, hmpd ins last when appeared held: back to form & could go in
again on reportedly fav'd easy grnd this autumn: see 1171, 981.

*3884 **BLUE MOUNTAIN** 8 [6] R F Johnson Houghton 3-8-11 J Reid 8/1: 102013: 3 ch c Elmaamul - Glenfinlass ¾ **107$**
(Lomond) Chsd ldrs, eff well over 1f out, kept on same pace: impvd again stepped up in class & stays 7.3f.

4169) **INVINCIBLE SPIRIT** 352 [11] J L Dunlop 3-8-11 Pat Eddery 7/1: 3116-4: Held up, short of room 2f ¾ **105+**
out till dist, kept on: reapp: in '99 won at Goodwood & Ripon (List, rtd 110): eff at 6f, stay 7.3f on firm/fast
& any trk: smart at best, caught the eye here & will surely improve for this & shld be plcd to land a nice contest.

3861 **HO LENG** 10 [2] 5-9-0 R Hills 11/4 FAV: 023345: Keen bhd, eff 2f out, short of room over 1f out, wknd. ½ **104**
3667 **TEAPOT ROW** 20 [8] 5-9-0 J Weaver 11/1: 2-5036: Stdd start, hld up, eff 2f out, no impress. 2½ **99**
*3600 **LATE NIGHT OUT** 23 [10] 5-9-0 M Tebbutt 9/2: -01217: In tch, rdn & wknd over 1f out: btr 3600. ½ **98**
*3878 **KALINDI** 9 [7] 3-8-6 J P Spencer 14/1: 006018: Held up, rdn & no impress fnl 2f: btr 3878. nk **92**
+3763 **NICOBAR** 15 [4] 3-8-11 M Hills 5/1: 105019: Led till 2f out, wknd: much btr 3763 (Epsom). shd **97**
9 ran Time 1m 28.18 (0.38) (Barford Bloodstock) J R Fanshawe Newmarket.

3996
3.05 GR 2 MILL REEF STKS 2YO (A) 6f str Firm 10 -22 Slow
£30000 £11500 £5750 £2750

*3567 **BOUNCING BOWDLER** 24 [4] M Johnston 2-8-12 R Hills 10/1: 122211: 2 b c Mujadil - Prima Volta **109**
(Primo Dominie) Set pace, rdn & collared just ins last, rallied most gamely to get up again cl-home for press:
op 7/1: Feb first foal, dam 6f juv wnr: earlier scored at Ripon (mdn) & York (List), plcd all other 6 starts: eff
over a stiff 5f, stay 6f: acts on fast & soft: acts on any trk: can force the pace: v tough, genuine & smart.

+3358 **POMFRET LAD** 33 [6] P J Makin 2-8-12 Pat Eddery 13/8 FAV: -012: 2 b c Cyranno de Bergerac - shd **108**
Lucky Flinders (Free State) Prom, eff to lead ins fnl 1f, rdn & collared cl-home, just btn: hvly bckd: fine
run from this lightly rcd colt who handles firm/fast grnd & shld win plenty more gd races: see 3358.

3895 **BRAM STOKER** 7 [7] R Hannon 2-8-12 J P Spencer 12/1: 123333: 2 ch c General Monash - Taniokey nk **107**
(Grundy) Hld up, eff over 1f out, kept on for press ins last, not btn far: yet to be out of the frame: most tough.

3797 **TRIPLE BLUE** 13 [1] R Hannon 2-8-12 R Hughes 16/1: 524534: In tch, short of room & dropped rear 1½ **103**
after 2f out, some late gains, nvr dngrs: shapes like 7f will suit in List/Gr 3: see 3900, 3133.

3900 **MISTY EYED** 7 [2] 2-8-10 L Newman 15/8: 011125: Prom, lost pl after 2f, eff 2f out, short of shd **101**
room & wknd dist: hvly bckd: below prev smart best stepped up in trip: prob best at 5f: see 3900, 3133.

3862 **PAN JAMMER** 10 [5] 2-9-1 J Reid 25/1: 231406: Slow away, keen & no impress fnl 2f: btr 3105. 2½ **99**
3566 **HURRICANE FLOYD** 24 [3] 2-8-10 J Weaver 7/2: -2147: In tch, wknd qckly over 1f out, reportedly lame. ½ **95**
7 ran Time 1m 13.56 (1.96) (Paul Dean) M Johnston Middleham, N.Yorks.

3997
3.40 COURAGE BEST HCAP 3YO+ 0-105 (B) 1m2f Firm 10 -08 Slow [105]
£43500 £16500 £8250 £3750 3yo rec 6lb

3224 **KOMISTAR** 38 [9] P W Harris 5-8-6 (83) P Robinson 16/1: 200031: 5 ch g Komaite - Rosie's Gold **87**
(Glint Of Gold) Made all, held on gamely fnl 1f, all out: '99 Doncaster & Newbury wnr (h'caps, rtd 89): has tried
12f, seems best at 1m/10f: acts on firm & gd/soft, handles hvy: likes Newbury & forcing the pace: game.

3782 **BONAGUIL** 14 [2] C F Wall 3-8-4 (87) R Mullen 25/1: 134202: 3 b g Septieme Ciel - Chateaubrook ½ **90**
(Alleged) In tch, styd on well under press fnl 1f, not btn far: apprec this return to firm grnd & ran to best.

3782 **MOON SOLITAIRE** 14 [4] E A L Dunlop 3-9-0 (97) J Reid 10/1: 100133: 3 b ny Night Shift - Gay Fantastic nk **99**
(Ela Mana Mou) Chsd ldrs, went after wnr 2f out, caught for 2nd cl-home: sound run, btn under 1L: tough.

3469 **AEGEAN DREAM** 28 [11] R Hannon 4-8-10 (87) R Hughes 20/1: 331104: Dwelt, imprvd from rear 3f out, ½ **88+**
short of room sev times fnl 2f: best held up for a late run & poss unlucky: in gd form for a Cambridgeshire assault.

*3166 **PINCHINCHA** 42 [5] 6-8-3 (80) Dale Gibson 16/1: 434215: Mid-div, eff halfway, edged left & styd hd **81**
on under press fnl 1f, nrst fin: 6 wk abs, rider reportedly given a 1 day careless riding ban: see 3166.

3563 **SHARP PLAY** 24 [17] 5-9-10 (101) R Hills 20/1: 041006: Rear, hdwy on outside 2f out, nrst fin: fine ½ **101**
run under top-weight: see 3060.

3563 **DASHIBA** 24 [14] 4-9-1 (92) J Weaver 12/1: 066257: Dwelt, rcd keenly rear, switched & styd on nk **91+**
well fnl 1f, nrst fin: once again little luck in running & primed for a return to form: see 3563.

+3563 **PRINCE ALEX** 15 [15] 6-9-8 (99)(t)(5ex) J P Spencer 3/1: 02-118: In tch, onepcd when hmpd ent nk **97**
fnl 1f, wknd & eased: hvly bckd from 9/2: see 3563.

-3563 **NOOSHMAN** 24 [1] 3-9-2 (99) Pat Eddery 7/4 FAV: 501329: In tch, repeatedly denied a run fnl 2f, shd **97+**
nrst fin: hvly bckd: no run at any stage & must be given another chance: ideal type for the Cambridgeshire.

3685 **JUNIKAY** 19 [6] 6-7-10 (73)(1oh) A Beech(0) 25/1: 041430: Hdwy from rear over 2f out, nvr nr ldrs. shd **71**
3941 **FAHS** 3 [3] 8-8-5 (82) J Mackay 33/1: 211500: Held up, imprvd 3f out, btn over 1f out: 11th. 1¼ **78**
-3515 **BRILLIANT RED** 27 [16] 7-9-11 (102)(t) J Mongan 5/1: 003620: Chsd ldrs, no impress when hmpd nk **97**
over 1f out, eased: fin 12th: btr 3515.

3865 **CULZEAN** 10 [12] 4-8-7 (84) L Newman 25/1: 203620: Rear, eff 3f out, nvra factor in 13th. shd **79**
3657 **GENTLEMAN VENTURE** 20 [13] 4-8-5 (81)(1ow) M Hills 14/1: 255130: Mid-div, eff 3f out, btn 2f out: hd **77**
fin 14th: rtd higher over 12f in 3657 & 3402.

2475 **BLUE** 71 [10] 4-9-4 (95) A McGlone 20/1: /15100: Chsd ldr, ev ch 3f out, wknd into 15th: 10 wk 1¼ **88**
abs, longer priced stablemate of Prince Alex (8th): twice below 2170 (gd grnd).

3563 **TRAHERN** 24 [7] 3-9-8 (105)(BL) R Havlin 33/1: 214000: Chsd ldrs 1m, wknd: fin 16th, tried blnks. 3½ **93**
3842 **AMRAK AJEEB** 11 [8] 8-7-10 (73) G Sparkes(5) 33/1: 143020: Dwelt & rcd wide, nvra factor & fin last. ½ **60**
17 ran Time 2m 04.66 (1.86) (Class Act) P W Harris Aldbury, Herts.

3998   **4.10 PORTCHESTER HCAP 3YO 0-100 (C)**   **1m rnd**   **Firm 10**   **+04 Fast**   **[107]**
£9165   £2820   £1410   £705

3796 **KAREEB 13** [5] W R Muir 3-7-11 (76) G Baker (5) 25/1: 034361: 3 b g Green Desert - Braari (Gulch)   **80**
Rear, switched outside & imprvd 2f out, went on at dist, styd on well despite edging left, rdn out: gd time, first
win: rnr-up 3 times in '99 (rtd 84, mdn): eff at 7f, stays 1m well: acts on gd & firm grnd, has disapp on soft:
has tried blnks, better without today: handles a sharp or stiff/gall trk: well rdn by G Baker today.

3658 **SHADOW PRINCE 20** [1] R Charlton 3-7-13 (78) J Mackay (5) 6/1: 133052: 3 ch g Machiavellian -   nk   **81**
Shadywell (Habitat) Rcd keenly & chsd ldrs, lost pl halfway, imprvd 2f out, fin well & not btn far: best
held up for a late run & stays a stiff 1m: see 3130, 2922.

3481 **FREDDY FLINTSTONE 28** [7] R Hannon 3-8-1 (80) L Newman (3) 12/1: 002343: 3 b c Bigstone - Daring   ½   **82**
Ditty (Daring March) Chsd ldrs, rdn to lead 2f out till hdd dist, no extra cl-home: tchd 16/1, btn under 1L.

3453 **FRONTIER 29** [13] R Hannon 3-8-7 (86) R Hughes 16/1: -53364: Early ldr, remained prom till no   ¾   **86**
extra cl-home: see 3267, 1198.

3658 **KATHIR 20** [17] 3-8-9 (88) R Hills 7/2: 321525: Led after 1f till 2f out, no extra: bckd from 6/1:   2½   **83**
better expected after 3658 (beat today's 2nd): see 2844.

3597 **RED N SOCKS 23** [11] Pat Eddery 11/4 FAV: 001006: Prom till lost pl halfway, short of   nk   **87**
room 2f out, styd on but ch had gone: hvly bckd from 9/2: had little luck in running today & shld be given one
more ch: eye-catching in 3170, see 2762.

3793 **FRENCH HORN 14** [15] P Robinson 11/1: 311007: Chsd ldrs, fdd fnl 1f: likes soft.   nk   **75**

3315 **TROUBLE MOUNTAIN 35** [8] 3-9-4 (97) J Reid 25/1: -65008: Rear, prog when no room 3f out, kept on   shd   **90**
but ch had gone: slipping down the h'cap & hinted at return to form here: see 969.

3658 **BOLD EWAR 20** [6] 3-8-0 (79) (bl) A Beech (3) 20/1: 201509: Nvr nr ldrs: best 3261.   2½   **67**

3897 **TUMBLEWEED TOR 7** [10] 3-8-11 (90) S Clancy (7) 14/1: 636330: Chsd ldrs 6f, wknd into 10th: btr 3897.   4   **70**

3626 **DIGITAL 21** [9] 3-7-12 (77) R Brisland(5) 16/1: -4230: Rcd keenly in rear, nvr a factor in 11th.   1   **55**

3897 **STRASBOURG 7** [14] 3-8-7 (86) J P Spencer 33/1: 220000: Chsd ldrs 6f, wknd: fin 12th: see 3338.   6   **52**

3291 **SMART RIDGE 36** [4] 3-9-7 (100) Darren Williams (5) 20/1: 202340: In tch 6f, sn btn: fin 13th.   4   **58**

3435 **Atavus 29** [16] 3-8-4 (83) M Hills 25/1:   3699 **Champion Lodge 19** [18] 3-9-2 (95) J Weaver 16/1:

3254 **Falconidae 37** [12] 3-8-3 (82) R Mullen 16/1: U

16 ran   Time 1m 36.30 (0.50)   (J Bernstein)   W R Muir Lambourn, Berks.

3999   **4.45 PIG & WHISTLE MDN 2YO (D)**   **7f str**   **Firm 10**   **-19 Slow**
£5414   £1666   £833   £416

-- **WEST ORDER** [8] R Hannon 2-9-0 R Hughes 3/1 FAV: -1: 2 ch g Gone West - Irish Order (Irish River)   **90**
Set pace till dist, rallied gamely to regain lead cl-home, rdn out: well bckd, debut, rider reportedly fined £110
for not riding to draw: May foal, cost IR 200,000gns: half-brother to sev wnrs, incl a smart performer in the USA:
dam a useful 2yo wnr in France, sire a top-class 1m/9f performer: eff over a stiff 7f, will stay 1m: acts on firm
grnd, runs well fresh: can force the pace: game & protentially useful colt who shld rate more highly & win again.

-- **HALAWAN** [25] Sir Michael Stoute 2-9-0 J Reid 4/1: -2: 2 b c Muhtarram - Haladiya (Darshaan)   ½   **88**
Trkd ldrs, prog to chall 2f out, led dist till worn down cl-home: nicely bckd, debut: Feb foal, dam lightly rcd
but from a useful French family: sire a top-class 10f performer: eff over a stiff 7f, bred to apprec 1m+ next
term: acts on firm grnd & on a gall trk: shld sn go one better.

-- **MAYVILLE THUNDER** [19] G A Butler 2-9-0 J P Spencer 10/1: -3: 2 ch c Zilzal - Mountain Lodge   1¾   **84+**
(Blakeney) In tch, kept on fnl 1f but not pace of front 2: 75,000gns purchase: Apr foal, half-brother to
numerous wnrs, notably useful stayer Compton Ace: dam a smart stayer, sire a top-class miler: eff at 7f on
firm grnd, 1m looks sure to suit: sure to benefit from this promising introduction & win races.

-- **LORD PROTECTOR** [7] D W P Arbuthnot 2-9-0 J D Smith 40/1: -4: Mth div, kept on nicely fnl 1f,   nk   **83**
nrst fin: debut: IR 38,000gns Mar foal: sire a smart miler: eff at 7f on firm grnd, 1m looks sure to suit:
plenty of promise here & looks sure to improve.

-- **MUTHAABER** [22] 2-9-0 R Hills 5/1: -5: Dwelt, improving from rear when short of room 2f out,   1¾   **79+**
fin well but ch had gone: debut: Feb foal, dam a 10f wnr: sire a high-class miler: J Gosden colt who caught
the eye in some style here: shld not be missed next time.

3786 **STOLI 14** [13] 2-9-0 L Newman(3) 50/1: -06: Chsd ldrs, left bhd fnl 1f: see 3786.   ½   **78**

-- **LEARNED LAD** [20] 2-9-0 J Mackay(5) 25/1: -7: Rear, short of room 3f out, fin well but chance had   1¼   **75**
gone: debut, Apr foal, cost IR 35,000gns: half-brother to a couple of 2yo wnrs, also smart stayer Churlish Charm: dam
a mid-dist performer, sire a top-class miler: with D Elsworth, promising here & shld improve considerably.

-- **HERNANDITA** [10] 2-8-9 A Beech 25/1: -8: Chsd ldrs till wknd over 1f out: debut: May foal,   nk   **69**
half-sister to a 10f wnr: dam won over 7f/1m, sire top-class over mid-dists: J Dunlop filly, improve in time.

-- **CHANCELLOR** [4] 2-9-0 M Hills 12/1: -9: Hmpd start, stdy late hdwy, nvr plcd to chall on debut: hd   **74+**
190,000gns purchase: Feb foal, half-sister to sev wnrs both here & abroad: dam a sprint winning 2yo, sire a
high-class mid-dist performer: B Hills filly who looks sure to leave this effort behind.

3678 **HWISPIRIAN 19** [12] 2-8-9 R Brisland(5) 66/1: -00: Chsd ldrs 5f, wknd into 10th: see 3678.   1   **67**

-- **MAGZAA** [15] 2-9-0 O Urbina 33/1: -0: Rear, some late hdwy, nvr nr ldrs: 11th: Mar foal, dam a   1½   **69**
useful mid-dist wnr: sire a top-class mid-dist performer: with J Dunlop, mid-dist bred & sure to leave this behind.

-- **VALLEY OF DREAMS** [9] 2-8-9 R Perham 25/1: -0: Dwelt, imprvd to chase ldrs 3f out, wknd over   nk   **63**
1f out: fin 12th, bckd at long odds: Feb foal, cost 41,000gns: dam a wnr in the States: with P Howling.

-- **MASQUE TONNERRE** [14] 2-9-0 P Robinson 12/1: -0: Mid-div, no prog fnl 2f, eased: 13th, op 6/1.   2   **64**

-- **COSMOCRAT** [5] 2-9-0 S Clancy (7) 40/1: -0: Hmpd start, eff halfway, no impress fnl 2f: fin 14th.   3½   **57**

-- **SPA GULCH** [16] 2-9-0 N Chalmers(7) 33/1: -0: Chsd ldrs till halfway: fin 15th, debut.   nk   **56**

-- **CHALOM** [6] 2-9-0 Pat Eddery 8/1: -0: Chsd ldrs 4f, wknd into 16th.   1¾   **53**

-- **INDIAN FILE** [2] 2-9-0 J Lowe 12/1: -0: Hmpd start, no ch from halfway: fin 19th, with B Hills.   **0**

-- **Star Glade** [24] 2-8-9 A McGlone 66/1:   -- **Caqui Dor** [18] 2-9-0 J Weaver 16/1:

-- **Doc Davis** [21] 2-9-0 A Eddery(5) 25/1:   -- **Equal Balance** [3] 2-9-0 D Kinsella(7) 50/1:

21 ran   Time 1m 26.36 (2.06)   (Monsun Investments Ltd)   R Hannon East Everleigh, Wilts.

4000   **5.15 DUBAI AIRPORT COND STKS 3YO+ (B)**   **1m1f**   **Firm 10**   **-39 Slow**
£9471   £3592   £1796   £816   3yo rec 5lb

3549 **COMPTON BOLTER 28** [7] G A Butler 3-8-6 (t) J P Spencer 7/2: 050451: 3 b c Red Sunset - Milk And Honey **108**
(So Blessed) Rear, stdly imprvd 2f out, forged ahd cl-home, drvn out: nicely bckd, slow time: earlier 6th in

NEWBURY

SATURDAY SEPTEMBER 16TH Lefthand, Flat, Galloping Track

2,000 Guineas: '99 Chepstow wnr (mdn auct), plcd in Gr 2 company (rtd 107): eff at 7/9f, seems to stay 10f: acts on firm & hvy, handles any trk: can run well fresh: has tried blnks, better without: wears a t-strap, smart colt.

+3515 **FULL FLOW** 27 [5] B W Hills 3-9-1 M Hills 9/2: -44012: 3 b c Eagle Eyed - Fast Flow (Riverman)   nk   114
Chsd ldrs, rdn to lead 2f out, not pace to repel wnr cl-home: op 3/1: stays 9f: best held up, much improved.

3515 **PULAU TIOMAN** 27 [1] M A Jarvis 4-8-11 P Robinson 2/1 FAV: 422033: 4 b c Robellino - Ella Mon Amour 2   102
(Ela Mana Mou) Chsd ldr till lost pl halfway, rallied fnl 1f: well bckd from 7/2: again bhd today's 2nd in 3515.

1627 **ISLAND SOUND** 111 [3] D R C Elsworth 3-8-6 J Reid 5/1: 1-2534: Dwelt, recovered & sn in lead,   hd   102
hdd 2f out, no extra: long abs: see 1627, 980.

3893 **SPENCERS WOOD** 8 [2] 3-9-1 Pat Eddery 13/2: -14365: Rcd keenly rear, eff 3f out, some late hdwy   ½   110
but nvr dngrs: see 3369.

3107 **BOMB ALASKA** 44 [6] 5-8-11 L Newman 11/2: 340006: Rcd keenly rear, effort 2f out, btn when hung   nk   100
left fnl 1f: 6 wk abs: acts on firm, relishes soft grnd: see 1057, 703.

6 ran   Time 1m 53.45 (4.45)   (E Penser)   G A Butler Blewbury, Oxon.

CATTERICK

SATURDAY SEPTEMBER 16TH Lefthand, Undulating, Very Tight Track

Official Going: SOFT (HEAVY PLACES) Stalls: Inside.

4001

2.10 EBF MDN 2YO (D)   6f   Soft 117   -05 Slow
£3068   £944   £472   £236   Raced stands side fnl 2f

3913 **SPY MASTER** 5 [3] Sir Michael Stoute 2-9-0 (vis) F Lynch 6/5 FAV: 02341: 2 b c Green Desert -   80
Obsessive (Seeking The Gold) Sn prom, led halfway, rdn/strongly pressed over 1f out, always holding rival ins last, rdn out: hvly bckd: quick reapp: dam useful 6f wnr: eff at 6f, stys 7f & a return to that trip should suit: acts on fast & soft, likes a sharp/undulating track: consistent.

2357 **WESTERN FLAME** 76 [13] R Guest 2-8-9 Martin Dwyer 7/2: 52: 2 b f Zafonic - Samya's Flame   ¾   72
(Artaius) Went right start, in tch, prog to ch ldr over 1f out, held ins last: abs: eff at 6f, improved on soft grnd.

-- **ATLANTIC MYSTERY** [4] M Johnston 2-8-9 N Pollard 5/1: 3: 2 ch f Cadeaux Genereux - Nottash   2½   67
(Royal Academy) Prom, rdn/forced wide on bend over 2f out, held over 1f out: op 4/1: March foal, cost 16,000gns: dam a 3yo 7f wnr: eff at 6f, 7f should suit: acts on soft grnd: clr of rem here.

3706 **FIRST MEETING** 19 [7] M Dods 2-8-9 P Fessey 20/1: -2504: Chsd wnr halfway, rdn/held fnl 2f.   4   59$

3009 **COLLEGE STAR** 48 [11] V Halliday 40/1: -05: Rear, styd on fnl 2f, nrst fin: 7 week abs: well   3½   57
bhd debut prev: March first foal: dam a mdn: with R Whitaker.

3571 **BOLLIN TOBY** 24 [8] 2-9-0 P Fessey 25/1: -0006: Rear, late hdwy fnl 2f, no threat: see 3346 (5f).   1   55

3571 **EFIDIUM** 24 [9] 2-9-0 J McAuley 14/1: -507: Rear, mod late gains: op 12/1: see 3346 (5f).   1½   52

3143 **CRYSTAL CHANDELIER** 42 [6] 2-8-9 P McCabe 33/1: 08: Cl up, forced wide bend over 2f out, btn: abs.   5   37

3710 **CATALAN BAY** 18 [2] O Pears 25/1: -00009: Led, hung badly wide halfway & sn hdd, sn bhd.   ½   36$

3776 **MOON ROYALE** 14 [1] 2-8-10(1ow) C Teague 12/1: 50: Trkd ldrs, strugg bef halfway: 10th: op 7/1.   1   34

-- **GIRL FRIDAY** [10] 2-8-9 P Goode (3) 33/1: 0: Slowly away & al bhd: 11th: Ajraas filly, April foal,   3   28
a first foal: dam NH mdn: with Ronald Thompson.

-- **COLIN COOK** [5] 2-9-0 G Parkin 40/1: 0: Chsd ldrs 3f: 12th: Presidium colt, May foal, cost 2,800gns.   8   21

12 ran   Time 1m 17.6 (7.3)   (Cheveley Park Stud)   Sir Michael Stoute Newmarket, Suffolk

4002

2.40 SANDHURST SELLER 3YO (G)   1m5f175y   Soft 117   -17 Slow
£1841   £526   £263   Raced stands side fnl 2f

3774 **INDY CARR** 14 [10] M Dods 3-8-5 Iona Wands 3/1 FAV: 600001: 3 b f Pyramus - Miss Adventure   37
(Adonijah) Keen/prom, led over 4f out & rdn clr fnl 2f, eased down nr fin, readily: bought in for 5,500gns: op 2/1: sole juv start wnr at Newmarket (sell, H Collingridge, rtd 78): eff at 1m, well suited by this step up to 14f, relished return to soft grnd: handles a sharp or stiff track: has run well fresh: loves sell grade.

3637 **WORTH THE RISK** 21 [7] Don Enrico Incisa 3-8-5 Kim Tinkler 10/1: -35002: 3 b f Chaddleworth -   6   30
Bay Risk (Risk Me) Al prom, rdn/chsd wnr fnl 2f, no impress: op 7/1: handles soft: only mod form prev: see 2222.

3406 **LAMMOSKI** 30 [4] M C Chapman 3-8-10 R Studholme (3) 33/1: 000403: 3 ch g Hamas - Penny In My   4   31
Shoe (Sir Ivor) Chsd ldrs, held fnl 2f: see 426, 217.

3808 **PADDY MUL** 13 [5] W Storey 3-8-10 (t) T Williams 100/30: -00304: Rear, drvn halfway, mod gains for   2   29
press: op 6/1: longer 14f trip: see 3591 (claimer, 9f).

3674 **PORTRACK JUNCTION** 20 [8] 3-8-10 R Lappin 20/1: 000505: Led/dsptd lead till over 4f out, sn btn.   nk   29$

3265 **SANDROS BOY** 37 [2] 3-8-10 N Pollard 4/1: 3206: Chsd ldrs 10f: op 5/2: btr 2439, 2105 (fast).   7   22

3570 **BITTY MARY** 24 [1] 3-8-5 (BL) Martin Dwyer 33/1: 056007: Sn rdn rear, little hdwy: see 807 (10f).   nk   17$

3823 **IRANOO** 12 [3] 3-8-10 (t) F Lynch 9/1: 004508: Bhd, no ch 3f out: op 9/1: see 1940 (1m).   9   13

3804 **FOSTON SECOND** 13 [6] 3-8-5 J McAuley 4/1: -42439: Chsd ldrs, rdn/struggling 4f out: well bckd.   13   0

2601 **ROYAL PASTIMES** 65 [9] 3-8-5 P Fessey 50/1: -60500: Led/dsptd lead 10f, sn struggling: 10th: dist   0
recent jumps rnr (mod form): see 783.

10 ran   Time 3m 14.2 (18.8)   (N A Riddell)   M Dods Piercebridge, Co Durham

4003

3.15 CONSTANT HCAP 3YO+ 0-80 (D)   1m4f   Soft 117   +05 Fast   [76]
£4621   £1422   £711   £355   3 yo rec 8 lb   Raced stands side fnl 2f

1583 **NOWELL HOUSE** 109 [14] M W Easterby 4-8-12 (60) G Parkin 3/1 FAV: 000001: 4 ch g Polar Falcon -   69
Langtry Lady (Pas de Seul) Keen, chasing group, prog to lead over 3f out & rdn/clr 2f out, comfortably: val for 9L+: best time of day: 4 mth abs: well bckd: '99 wnr of h'caps at Beverley, Pontefract & Redcar (rtd 66): plcd in '98 (rtd 72, mdn): eff at 10/12f, on fast, relishes soft grnd & handles any track: runs well fresh: plenty in hand, qk follow-up?

3905 **YES KEEMO SABEE** 7 [11] D Shaw 5-7-12 (46)(bl) T Williams 12/1: 302002: 5 b g Arazi - Nazeera   5   47
(Lashkari) In tch, rdn & kept on fnl 2f to chase wnr, al held: op 10/1: see 3674, 3348 & 627.

3899 **ARCHIE BABE** 7 [8] J J Quinn 4-10-0 (76) O Pears 50/1: 025003: 4 ch g Archway - Frensham Manor   2½   75
(Le Johnstan) Rear, styd on for press fnl 3f, no threat: top-weight: loves Pontefract: see 2562.

3437 **THE BUTTERWICK KID** 29 [10] R A Fahey 7-9-10 (72) P Goode (3) 16/1: 120-04: Rear, rdn/kept on fnl 2f. 1   70

3725 **SIMPLE IDEALS** 17 [7] 6-8-0 (48) Kim Tinkler 8/1: 565425: Bhd, kept on for press fnl 3f, nrst fin.   hd   46

*3480 **UNDER THE SAND** 28 [15] 3-9-8 (78) P McCabe 4/1: 042016: Handy 3f out, held fnl 2f: op 5/1.   ¾   75

3480 **SHAFFISHAYES** 28 [6] 8-8-5 (52)(1ow) T E Durcan 8/1: 653067: Dwelt/rear, mod hdwy fnl 3f: see 943.   hd   49

3657 **BLUE STREET** 20 [9] 4-8-7 (55) G Faulkner (1) 12/1: 023168: Chsd clr ldr, btn 2f out: btr 3399 (gd).   9   43

3794 **FINAL LAP 14** [12] 4-8-11 (59) N Kennedy 50/1: -00009: Mid div, btn 3f out: see 56 (10f). *shd* **47**
3778 **AFTER THE BLUE 14** [17] 3-9-4 (74) T A O'Sullivan (5) 16/1: 512200: Al rear: 10th: op 10/1: btr 3290. *nk* **61**
3826 **SEA SQUIRT 12** [19] 3-9-4 (74) N Pollard 12/1: 231520: Prom, btn 2f out: 11th: btr 3826, 3456 (1m). *3* **58**
3778 **CASHMERE LADY 14** [5] 8-8-12 (60) R Cody Boutcher (7) 16/1: 020400: Mid div, strugg 3f out: 12th. *¾* **43**
3674 **INDIGO BAY 20** [16] 4-7-12 (46)(bl) J McAuley 16/1: 051030: Sn clr ldr, hdd over 3f out/sn btn: 13th. *1* **28**
2992 **RIPARIAN 49** [3] 3-9-1 (71) F Lynch 9/1: 5-3140: Prom 9f: 15th: 7 week abs: btr 2520 (1m, mdn). **0**
1473 **Wilton 115** [4] 5-9-8 (70) R Lake (7) 20/1: 3048 **Julia Titus 47** [2] 3-8-4 (60) Martin Dwyer 50/1:
1597 **Segaview 108** [13] 4-8-10 (58) J Stack 20/1:
17 ran Time 2m 44.6 (13.4) (Bernard Bargh & John Walsh) M W Easterby Sheriff Hutton, N Yorks

4004

3.50 OPULATOR FILLIES HCAP 3YO+ 0-60 (F) 7f rnd Soft 117 +03 Fast **[57]**
£2880 £823 £411 3 yo rec 3 lb Raced stands side fnl 2f

3839 **ANGEL HILL 11** [16] K A Ryan 5-9-10 (53) F Lynch 10/1: 100401: 5 ch m King's Signet - Tawny (Grey Ghost) Mid div, rdn/prog fnl 2f & led inside last, styd on strongly, going away: earlier scored at Newcastle (h'cap): '99 wnr again at Newcastle (h'cap, first time blinks, rtd 76): eff at 5/6f, suited by 7f now: acts on firm & soft grnd: handles any track, likes Newcastle: eff with/without blinks, has tried a visor: well h'capped at present. **60**
3803 **ROUGE 13** [7] K R Burke 5-9-9 (52) L Enstone (7) 8/1: 161P32: 5 gr m Rudimentary - Couleur de Rose (Kalaglow) Led, drvn over 1f out & hdd inside last, sn held: typical bold front running effort: see 3803, 3046. *4* **53**
3854 **BINT HABIBI 10** [15] J Pearce 3-9-8 (54) N Pollard 20/1: 315303: 3 b g Bin Ajwaad - High Stepping (Taufan) Chsd ldrs, styd on for press fnl 2f, nrst fin: return to 1m shld suit: acts on firm & soft: see 2914 (sell, 1m). *1* **54**
3480 **STORMSWELL 28** [4] J Hetherton 3-9-4 (50) T Williams 12/1: 530404: Rear, kept on for press fnl 2f, nrst fin: op 10/1: clr rem: return to 1m should suit: prev with R Fahey: see 1907 (mdn h'cap). *½* **49**
3666 **OARE KITE 20** [8] 5-9-5 (48)(bl) G Parkin 20/1: 100005: Handy, rdn/held fnl 2f: btr 2031 (Leicester). *4* **41**
3873 **DAVIS ROCK 9** [12] 6-9-6 (49) Martin Dwyer 3/1 FAV: 016626: Dwelt, mod gains fnl 2f: well bckd. *¾* **41**
3288 **BODFARI ANNA 36** [2] 4-10-0 (57)(vis) R Cody Boutcher (7) 8/1: 314307: Mid div, mod hdwy for press. *1½* **47**
3332 **PRINTSMITH 34** [9] 3-9-8 (54) J Bosley (7) 9/1: 106038: Prom 5f: op 7/1: see 3332, 1710. *¾* **43**
1646 **PICCOLO CATIVO 106** [3] 5-9-5 (48) Angela Hartley (7) 9/1: 0-1049: Chsd ldrs 4f: abs: btr 1066. *2* **34**
3572 **BOLLIN RITA 24** [6] 4-9-13 (56)(bl) J Stack 8/1: 204030: Prom 5f: 10th: see 2505, 2158 (6f). *1¾* **40**
4065} **HIGHLY SOCIABLE 358** [17] 3-9-11 (57) P McCabe 25/1: 5300-0: Sn struggling: 11th: reapp: plcd in '99 for S A Brookshaw (auction mdn, rtd 59): eff at 6f on gd/soft grnd & a gall track: with A Bailey. *5* **34**
3605 **TANCRED ARMS 22** [5] 4-9-5 (48) O Pears 16/1: 020300: Sn bhd: 12th: see 3312, 698. *1¾* **23**
3349 **MOUNT PARK 33** [10] 3-9-3 (49)(bl) R Studholme (3) 25/1: 010500: Mid div, btn 2f out: 13th. *nk* **23**
3803 **ROUGE ETOILE 13** [1] 4-9-8 (51) T E Durcan 7/1: 600520: Al bhd: 15th: btr 3803 (6f): **0**
2223 **Swing City 81** [18] 3-9-7 (53) S Finnamore (5) 20/1: 3873 **An Jolien 9** [11] 3-9-8 (54) G Faulkner (3) 25/1:
4589} **Millsec 318** [14] 3-9-13 (59) H Bastiman 25/1:
17 ran Time 1m 31.00 (8.0) (Keith Taylor) K A Ryan Hambleton, N Yorks

4005

4.25 CRANWELL MDN 3YO (D) 7f rnd Soft 117 -03 Slow
£2860 £880 £440 £220 Raced stands side fnl 2f

3048 **MATERIAL WITNESS 47** [1] W R Muir 3-9-0 Martin Dwyer 4/7 FAV: 223021: 3 b c Barathea - Dial Dream (Gay Mecene) Rear, drvn halfway, prog to lead inside last, just held on, all out: well bckd at odds on: abs: plcd both juv starts (mdns, rtd 85): eff at 7f/1m on fast & soft, sharp or gall trk: runs well fresh. **74**
2337 **CHAMPFIS 77** [5] M Johnston 3-9-0 N Pollard 4/1: 03-42: 3 b g Efisio - Champ d'Avril (Northfields) Prom, rdn/led over 1f out till inside last, kept on well, just held: 11 week abs: eff at 7f, return to 1m shld suit: prob handles firm & soft grnd: see 2337. *hd* **73**
2233} **MOTHER MOLLY 449** [8] R Guest 3-8-9 J Stack 9/2: 2-3: 3 b f Irish River - Charming Molly (Diesis) Trkd ldrs, no room 2f out & switched inside last, styd on well: op 7/2: clr rem: reapp: rnr up sole '99 start (rtd 80, fillies mdn): eff at 6/7f, 1m should suit: handles fast & soft grnd: see 2233. *¾* **67**
3951 **DIANEME 3** [2] T D Easterby 3-8-9 G Parkin 20/1: 020304: Chsd ldrs, held fnl 2f: quick reapp. *5* **60$**
3672 **LETS REFLECT 20** [6] 3-8-9 O Pears 25/1: -5405: Led till over 1f out, sn held: see 2832. *3½* **55**
-- **HICKLETON DANCER** [3] 3-9-0 P Fessey 33/1: 6: Dwelt, sn rdn/strugg: debut, with G Woodward. *17* **38**
570 **WHITLEYGRANGE GIRL 206** [4] 3-8-9 R Cody Boutcher (7) 100/1: 6057: Trckd ldr 4f: abs, turf bow. *1¾* **31**
3672 **TIGONTIME 20** [7] 3-8-9 R Lappin 66/1: -08: Struggling halfway: no form. *1½* **29**
8 ran Time 1m 31.4 (8.4) (M J Caddy) W R Muir Lambourn, Berks

4006

4.55 SKYRAM HCAP 3YO+ 0-65 (F) 1m7f177y Soft 117 -28 Slow **[64]**
£2572 £735 £367 3 yo rec 12lb Raced stands side fnl 2f

3442 **COCO LOCO 29** [7] J Pearce 3-8-4 (52) N Kennedy 10/1: 065021: 3 b f Bin Ajwaad - Mainly Me (Huntingdale) Held up in tch wide, smooth prog 4f out & led 2f out, rdn clr over 1f out, readily: op 12/1: first win: unplcd in a mdn sole '99 start (rtd 63): suited by a step up to a sharp 2m last twice: acts on gd & soft grnd, likes a sharp track: decisive scorer here: could win again. **60**
*3633 **HOUSE OF DREAMS 21** [12] Mrs M Reveley 8-8-10 (46) T E Durcan 7/1: 24-012: 8 b g Darshaan - Helens Dreamgirl (Caerleon) Rear, rdn/prog to chase wnr over 1f out, kept on tho' al held: eff at 14f/sharp 2m: see 3633. *5* **48**
3827 **HASTA LA VISTA 12** [10] M W Easterby 10-8-7 (43)(vis) G Parkin 7/1: 350003: 10 b g Superlative - Falcon Berry (Bustino) Led 5f, remained handy, kept on onepace for press fnl 2f: op 5/1: see 1816 (12f). *3½* **42**
2048 **EVENING SCENT 89** [14] J Hetherton 4-9-0 (50) Martin Dwyer 10/1: 320164: Rear, hdwy 4f out, onepce fnl 2f: 12 week abs, op 12/1: see 2048, 1936. *1* **48**
4259} **SNUGFIT ROSIE 347** [4] 4-9-10 (60) S Finnamore (5) 7/1: 3030-5: Cl up, held fnl 2f: op 5/1, Flat reapp, 5 mth jumps abs: won 4 times in 99/00 (including thrice at Newcastle, 2m/2m4f nov hdles, gd & hvy grnd, rtd 117h): plcd twice on the level in '99 for M R Channon (rtd 79, mdn): stays 2m on gd & a stiff/undul trk. *nk* **57**
3531 **SKYERS A KITE 25** [18] 5-9-0 (50) P McCabe 10/1: 152155: Chsd ldrs, led after 5f, rdn/hdd over 2f out, remained far side fnl 2f, sn held: btr 3378, (13f). *5* **42**
3715 **BEST PORT 18** [5] 4-8-2 (38) J McAuley 8/1: 002127: Rear, rdn/mod hdwy fnl 3f: btr 3406 (fast). *¾* **29**
3575 **IRELANDS EYE 24** [6] 5-8-10 (46) J Bosley (7) 9/2 FAV: 320668: Mid div, rdn/held fnl 2f: bckd, op 6/1. *8* **29**
3633 **IL PRINCIPE 21** [20] 6-8-4 (40) J Stack 9/1: 000049: Prom wide, rdn/held 2f out, eased: not given a hard time, once held: loves this grnd & may do better if stable returns to form: see 3122, 89. *1* **22**
3590 **HIGHFIELD FIZZ 23** [3] 8-8-4 (40) T Williams 10/1: 634130: Bhd, hdwy 6f out, btn 3f out: 10th. *nk* **21**
3476 **WINDMILL LANE 28** [9] 3-8-8 (56) R Lappin 14/1: 035050: Chsd ldrs, btn 4f out: 11th: op 10/1. *8* **29**
3437 **Kierchem 29** [8] 9-8-8 (44) Iona Wands 16/1: 2292} **Uncle Doug 446** [2] 9-8-10 (46) R Cody Boutcher (7) 25/1:
1908 **Divine Appeal 94** [11] 5-9-5 (55) C Teague 50/1: 3742 **Embryonic 16** [19] 8-9-10 (60) N Pollard 20/1:

CATTERICK SATURDAY SEPTEMBER 16TH Lefthand, Undulating, Very Tight Track

15 ran Time 3m 43.8 (23.0) (Mr & Mrs J Matthews) J Pearce Newmarket, Suffolk

4007 **5.25 DARTMOUTH NURSERY HCAP 2YO 0-75 (E) 7f rnd Soft 117 -22 Slow [82]**
£3094 £884 £442 Raced stands side fnl 2f

3615 **APORTO 22** [16] D W Barker 2-7-11 (51) J McAuley 9/1: 003041: 2 ch c Clantime - Portvally (Import) **57**
Chsd ldrs wide, styd on well for press to lead nr line: bckd, op 14/1: first win: eff at 7f, 1m could suit: acts on fast & soft grnd: likes a sharp track.
2678 **BLUSHING SPUR 63** [10] D Shaw 2-8-6 (60) T Williams 10/1: 50252: 2 b g Flying Spur - Bogus John (Blushing John) Chsd ldrs, prog to lead over 1f out, rdn/hdd nr line: op 8/1, abs: acts on fibresand & soft grnd. *¾* **64**
*3468 **MISS PROGRESSIVE 28** [12] N Tinkler 2-8-1 (55) Kim Tinkler 10/1: 002513: 2 b f Common Grounds - Kaweah Maid (General Assembly) Mid div, prog to chall over 1f out, drvn/no extra fnl 1f: acts on gd, soft & fbrsand. *1¼* **57**
3812 **FLYING ROMANCE 13** [15] D W Barker 2-8-6 (60) Kimberley Hart 25/1: 055304: Rear/wide, styd on fnl 2f, nrst fin: longer priced stablemate of wnr: styd longer 7f trip: prob handles firm & soft grnd, sharp or stiff track. *1* **61**
3860 **MISS EQUINOX 10** [18] 2-8-3 (57) N Kennedy 14/1: 313205: Chsd ldrs, rdn/held fnl 2f: op 10/1: this longer 7f trip should suit: acts on firm & fast, prob handles soft: see 2983 (6f, seller). *1¾* **56**
*3824 **CLASSY ACT 12** [14] 2-9-5 (73) T E Durcan 4/1 FAV: 23016: Led after 2f, hdd over 1f out, fdd: op 6/1. *½* **71**
*3824 **JOINT INSTRUCTION 12** [11] 2-9-7 (75) M Mathers (7) 7/1: 020117: Held up, eff 2f out, onepace. *2½* **69**
3704 **THE NAMES BOND 19** [5] 2-9-4 (72) R Thomas (7) 16/1: 140008: Rear, hdwy over 1f out, sn held. *¾* **65**
2730 **CHRISTMAS MORNING 60** [3] 2-8-2 (56) G Parkin 10/1: -0009: Rear, mod gains fnl 2f: h'cap bow, abs. *1* **48**
3901 **CHEMICALATTRACTION 7** [13] 2-8-6 (60) Martin Dwyer 25/1: 004000: Dwelt, nvr factor: 10th. *1¾* **50**
3347 **POUR NOUS 33** [17] 2-7-12 (52) P M Quinn (3) 33/1: 0000: Dwelt, al rear: 11th: h'cap bow. *1½* **40**
3712 **DANCING PENNEY 18** [2] 2-8-5 (59) Iona Wands 12/1: 221660: Chsd ldrs 5f: 12th: btr 3307 (6f, fm). *1* **46**
3812 **DARWIN TOWER 13** [1] 2-7-12 (52) C Adamson 12/1: 000000: Chsd ldrs till halfway: 13th, lost action. *1¼* **37**
3901 **MISTER SANDERS 7** [4] 2-8-9 (63) N Pollard 6/1: 06000: Al rear: 14th: see 3901, 1294. *1* **47**
3394 **BEREZINA 31** [9] 2-8-13 (67) P Fessey 20/1: 401000: Cl up 5f: 15th: op 12/1: btr 2990 (6f, fast). *1* **50**
*3697 **ITS SMEE AGAIN 19** [8] 2-8-7 (61) J Stack 10/1: 444610: Led 2f, sn btn: 16th: prev with B Hills. *10* **33**
3411 **BULA ROSE 30** [6] 2-8-4 (58) O Pears 10/1: 231400: Bhd halfway: 17th: op 8/1: btr 2155 (sell, fast). *½* **29**
17 ran Time 1m 32.7 (9.7) (D W Barker) D W Barker Scorton, N Yorks

AYR SATURDAY SEPTEMBER 16TH Lefthand, Galloping Track

Official Going SOFT. Stalls: Round Course - Inside; Str Course - Stands Side.

4008 **1.50 LAND ENGINEERING NOV STKS 2YO (D) 1m rnd Good/Soft 75 -33 Slow**
£4192 £1290 £645 £322

*3409 **HARRIER 30** [5] T D Easterby 2-9-6 M Roberts 8/1: 330111: 2 b g Prince Of Birds - Casaveha (Persian Bold) Led, injected pace ent str, ran on strgly despite drifting right, rdn out: tchd 10/1, slow time: hat-trick landed, earlier won at Thirsk (clmr) & Beverley (nov auct): imprvd since stepped up to 7f/1m: acts on fast & gd/sft, any trk: likes to force the pace: useful, progressive & tough. **97**
*3577 **ZULFAA 24** [6] J L Dunlop 2-8-9 W Supple 1/1 FAV: 412: 2 b f Bahri - Haniya (Caerleon) Nvr far away, shaken up to chall dist, sn rdn, kept on but held nr fin: hvly bckd: handles firm & gd/sft. *½* **84**
3391 **REPULSE BAY 31** [3] M R Channon 2-8-12 J Carroll 3/1: -423: 2 b c Barathea - Bourbon Topsy (Ile de Bourbon) Chsd wnr, rdn appr fnl 1f, hung left, onepace: bckd: subs found to have a breathing prob: handles firm & gd/soft grnd, stays 1m: see 3391. *1½* **84**
-- **TOMASINO** [2] M Johnston 2-8-8 K Darley 7/1: 4: Rear, styd on appr fnl 1f, nvr threatened ldrs: tchd 9/1 on debut: Celtic Swing half-brother to a 1m/14f wnr, dam 11f wnr: bred for mid-dists & further. *¾* **79**
3786 **BAILLIESTON 14** [1] 2-8-12 A Culhane 11/1: 335: Chsd ldrs, onepace appr fnl 1f: longer trip, mdn. *nk* **82**
3740 **HO PANG YAU 16** [4] 2-8-12 R Winston 50/1: 0526: Al bhd, lost tch 2f out, stiff task. *14* **62**
6 ran Time 1m 45.22 (8.62) (The Rumpole Partnership) T D Easterby Great Habton, N Yorks

4009 **2.20 LISTED FIRTH OF CLYDE STKS 2YO (A) 6f Good/Soft 75 -19 Slow**
£12992 £4928 £2464 £1120

3749 **ALSHADIYAH 16** [9] J L Dunlop 2-8-8 W Supple 4/1 CO FAV: 131: 2 gr f Danzig - Shadayid (Shadeed) Mid-div, prog to lead on bit ent fnl 2f, kept on well, rdn out: op 3/1: earlier made a wng debut at Lingfield (mdn): regally bred, half-sister to smart miler Bint Shadayid: eff at 6f, shld stay further: acts on firm & gd/soft grnd, sharp/undul or gall trk, goes well fresh: useful, improving filly. **97**
3596 **ASH MOON 23** [8] K R Burke 2-8-8 D Holland 14/1: 110302: 2 ch f General Monash - Jarmar Moon (Unfuwain) Well plcd, eff appr fnl 1f, kept on but not pace of wnr: apprec the drop in grade: useful: see 2014. *¾* **94**
3482 **DANCE ON 28** [7] Sir Michael Stoute 2-8-11 K Darley 4/1 CO FAV: 106103: 2 ch f Caerleon - Dance Sequence (Mr Prospector) Bhd ldrs, shaken up 2f out, drvn bef dist, onepace till styd on fnl 100y: well bckd from 7/1: useful run giving 3lbs to first 2: step up to 7f will suit: can rate higher: see 3027. *½* **96**
3720 **PROMISED 21** [4] J A Glover 2-8-8 D Mernagh 25/1: 130004: Held up, prog appr fnl 1f, dsptd 2nd ins last, onepace towards fin: clr rem & much imprvd if not flattered: eff at 5/6f, clrly goes well on gd/soft grnd. *hd* **92$**
*3520 **ZIETUNZEEN 26** [5] 2-8-8 J Carroll 12/1: 335515: Rear, rdn 2f out, nvr any impress on ldrs: see 3520. *3* **85**
3482 **BOIS DE CITRON 28** [2] 2-8-8 M Roberts 7/1: -34106: Led, hung left & hdd 1½f out, fdd: will apprec a drop back to 5f & faster grnd: see 3092. *nk* **84**
3959 **SIPTITZ HEIGHTS 2** [1] 2-8-11 A Culhane 12/1: 501057: Handy till 2f out: ran 48hrs ago over 5f here. *hd* **87**
*3533 **ALINGA 25** [10] 2-8-8 M Fenton 4/1 CO FAV: 130218: Al bhd, btn 2f out: bckd: something amiss? *6* **72**
3596 **PARTY CHARMER 23** [3] 2-8-8 G Duffield 8/1: 140659: Cl-up till lost place after halfway: can do better. *5* **60**
9 ran Time 1m14.91 (5.61) (Hamdan Al Maktoum) J L Dunlop Arundel, W Sussex

4010 **2.50 AYR SILVER CUP HCAP 3YO+ (B) 6f Good/Soft 75 -19 Slow [86]**
£11635 £3580 £1790 £895 3 yo rec 2 lb

3785 **LADY BOXER 14** [26] M Mullineaux 4-9-2 (74) A Mackay 33/1: 000101: 4 b f Komaite - Lady Broker (Petorius) Bhd, gd prog ent fnl 2f, ran on strongly for press ins last to get up fnl strides: earlier won at Chester (h'cap): '99 wnr again at Chester (class stks, rtd 79, also 4th in this race): '98 Leicester debut wnr (auct **82**

mdn, rtd 84): eff at 6/7.5f: acts on firm, likes gd & hvy: goes on any trk: in-form filly with a turn of foot.
3791 **NINEACRES 14** [20] J M Bradley 9-9-2 (74)(bl) D Holland 33/1: 041302: 9 b g Sayf El Arab - Mayor (Laxton) Nvr far away, led appr fnl 1f, drvn fnl 1f, hdd cl-home: back to form, acts on firm, gd/soft & both AWs. *hd* **81**
3960 **GET STUCK IN 2** [27] Miss L A Perratt 4-9-0 (72) R Winston 12/1: 400023: 4 b g Up And At 'Em - Shoka (Kaldoun) Rcd all alone on stands rail & led till bef dist, held fnl 100y: bckd: another cracking run: rnr-up over 5f here 48hrs ago: nicely h'capped: see 844. *1* **76**
3904 **SURPRISED 7** [9] R A Fahey 5-9-5 (77)(vis)(7ex) S Sanders 12/1: 544134: Mid-div, travelled well, shkn up & gd prog 2f out, rdn to chall 1f out, onepace towards fin: fine run, tough & v consistent: see 3646. *nk* **80**
3543 **CARD GAMES 25** [23] 3-9-8 (82) K Darley 10/1 JT FAV: 012005: Mid-div, hdwy under press appr fnl 1f, kept on but unable to chall: bckd: ran well: see 1133. *nk* **84**
3880 **MISTER MAL 9** [22] 4-9-5 (77) G Duffield 14/1: 010206: Chsd ldrs, rdn appr fnl 1f, kept on same pace. *¾* **77**
3170 **I CRIED FOR YOU 41** [7] 5-9-10 (82) Dean McKeown 12/1: 321207: Rear, gd prog to chase ldrs 2f out, no extra ins last: bckd from 16/1, 6 wk abs: see 1840 (7f). *nk* **81**
3904 **FEARBY CROSS 7** [28] 4-9-8 (80) L Newton 16/1: 410008: Waited with, styd on for press appr fnl 1f. *¾* **77**
3960 **SMOKIN BEAU 2** [5] 3-9-9 (83) P Dobbs (5) 25/1: 611009: Front rank, fdd below dist: ran 48hrs ago & is better at 5f: see 3485 (gd/firm). *½* **79**
3809 **BUNDY 13** [14] 4-8-8 (66) A Nicholls (3) 20/1: 110030: Mid-div, feeling pace halfway, late rally: 10th. *1¾* **57**
3809 **TOM TUN 13** [16] 5-9-2 (74)(t) W Supple 20/1: 001100: Rear, some hdwy under press appr fnl 1f: 11th. *nk* **64**
3960 **COLLEGE MAID 2** [12] 3-8-7 (67) D Sweeney 40/1: 500400: Early speed, lost place halfway, staying on again fin: 12th: ran 48hrs ago, see 22165. *1¼* **54**
3136 **FRANCPORT 43** [17] 4-9-1 (73) Mark Flynn (7) 20/1: 030600: Nvr better than mid-div: 13th, 6 wk abs. *½* **59**
3880 **BRANSTON FIZZ 9** [29] 3-8-8 (68)(3ex) K Dalgleish (5) 16/1: 010100: Outpcd, late gains: 14th. *shd* **54**
3646 **WILLIAMS WELL 21** [15] 6-9-8 (80)(bl) T Lucas 14/1: 221160: Well plcd, no extra appr fnl 1f: 15th. *1* **63**
3464 **FRIAR TUCK 28** [2] 5-9-9 (81) G Bardwell 16/1: 011300: Slow away, in tch halfway, wknd ins last: 16th. *¾* **62**
3855 **RED TYPHOON 10** [21] 3-8-13 (73)(t) J Quinn 16/1: 000200: In tch, held when bmpd 2f out: 17th, bckd. *1¾* **50**
3880 **ALASTAIR SMELLIE 9** [4] 4-9-1 (73) F Norton 25/1: 040000: Dwelt, nvr on terms: 18th, see 1173. *nk* **49**
3825 **INDIAN MUSIC 12** [25] 3-8-6 (66) M Roberts 25/1: 326040: Al towards rear: 19th, see 3097, 1654. *½* **41**
3960 **DAAWE 2** [8] 9-9-0 (72)(bl) Clare Roche (7) 28/1: 505000: Chsd ldrs till halfway: 20th, ran 48hrs ago. *nk* **46**
*3960 **PTARMIGAN RIDGE 2** [24] 4-9-5 (77)(5ex) M Fenton 10/1 JT FAV: 000-10: Speed 4f: 21st, well bckd, stablemate 3rd: won here over 5f 48hrs ago & a return to that trip will suit: see 3960. *hd* **51**
3569 **DESRAYA 24** [6] 3-9-3 (77)(bl) D O'Donohoe 16/1: 311100: Nvr a factor: 26th, see 3010 (fast). **0**
3894 **XANADU 8** [1] 4-9-5 (77) P Doe 25/1: 436020: Cl-up till 2f out: 29th, stablemate 3rd: faster grnd suits. **0**
3803 **Sabre Lady 13** [19] 3-9-1 (75) J Bramhill 66/1: 3629 **Hadath 21** [13] 3-9-9 (83) P Hanagan (5) 50/1:
3785 **Gift Of Gold 14** [3] 5-9-10 (82) A Culhane 25/1: 3960 **Trinity 2** [10] 4-8-7 (65) D Mernagh (3) 50/1:
3572 **Ace Of Parkes 24** [18] 4-9-4 (76) P Bradley (5) 50/1: 3809 **Persian Fayre 13** [11] 8-8-5 (63) J Carroll 40/1:
29 ran Time 1m 14.91 (5.61) (Esprit de Corps Racing) M Mullineaux Alpraham, Cheshire

4011

3.25 LISTED DOONSIDE CUP STKS 3YO+ (A) 1m2f192y Good/Soft 75 +10 Fast
£13641 £5174 £2587 £1176 3 yo rec 7 lb

3641 **ISLAND HOUSE 21** [4] G Wragg 4-9-1 M Roberts 4/1: 111541: 4 ch c Grand Lodge - Fortitude (Last Tycoon) Rear, smooth prog appr fnl 2f, led bef dist, drvn out: fast time: earlier landed a hat-trick after wins at Newmarket (stks), Goodwood & Kempton (Listed): '99 Pontefract (class stks) & Ayr wnr (stks, rtd 102): eff at 1m, suited by 10/11f: acts on firm & hvy grnd, any trk, likes Ayr: goes well fresh: smart & tough. **116**
3641 **FORBEARING 21** [3] Sir Mark Prescott 3-8-5(1ow) S Sanders 6/5 FAV: 112232: 3 b c Bering - For Example (Northern Baby) Trkd ldrs, led appr fnl 2f, rdn & hdd bef dist, rallied but held: well bckd, clr rem: tough & v useful colt: stays 11f, return to 10f may suit: see 2471. *½* **111**
3782 **VINTAGE PREMIUM 14** [7] R A Fahey 3-8-4 G Duffield 5/1: 216023: 3 b c Forzando - Julia Domna (Dominion) Cl-up, led briefly 2½f out, gdd: bckd: not disgraced but poss unsuited by step up to 11f. *8* **100**
1286} **CHIST 492** [5] M H Tompkins 5-8-11 K Darley 12/1: 3/56-4: Chsd ldrs, fdd ent fnl 3f: reapp: ran just twice last term (Gr 2 5th, rtd 110): '98 reapp wnr at Leicester (mdn, rtd 105 at best): eff at 12f, tried 14f: goes on firm, suited by hvy, stiff/gall trks. *11* **89**
*3509 **ZAAJER 27** [6] 4-9-1 W Supple 5/1: 4-3315: Led after 3f till ent fnl 3f, sn btn: back in trip, much btr 3509. *4* **89**
3827 **LORD ADVOCATE 12** [2] 12-8-11 (vis) A Nicholls 150/1: 066056: Early ldr, wknd ent str: imposs task. *6* **75$**
6 ran Time 2m 23.08 (7.08) (Mollers Racing) G Wragg Newmarket, Suffolk

4012

4.05 AYR GOLD CUP HCAP 3YO+ (B) 6f Good/Soft 75 +05 Fast [111]
£65000 £20000 £10000 £5000 3 yo rec 2 lb

3791 **BAHAMIAN PIRATE 14** [7] D Nicholls 5-8-3 (86) A Nicholls (3) 33/1: 221301: 5 ch g Housebuster - Shining Through (Deputy Minister) Mid-div, qcknd ent fnl 2f, led bef dist, ran on well: gd time: earlier won at Carlisle, Southwell (rtd 75a) & Newmarket (h'caps): '99 Ripon wnr (mdn, rtd 722): eff at 5/6f, stays 7f: acts on firm, gd/soft grnd & fibresand, any trk: goes well fresh: progressive, tough & v useful. **94**
3861 **LAGO DI VARANO 10** [2] R M Whitaker 8-8-3 (86)(bl) A Mackay 50/1: 012002: 8 b g Clantime - On The Record (Record Token) Well plcd, drvn appr fnl 1f, kept on but no ch wnr: fine run, plcd in this in '98. *1¼* **90**
3861 **GUINEA HUNTER 10** [23] T D Easterby 4-9-2 (99)(bl) J Carroll 25/1: 100503: 4 b g Pips Pride - Preponderance (Cyrano de Bergerac) Chsd ldrs, prog to dspt 2nd appr fnl 1f, hung left under press & onepace nr fin: useful run, eff with/without blnks: see 2859. *½* **101**
3763 **GAELIC STORM 15** [10] M Johnston 6-9-10 (107) D Holland 8/1 FAV: 644154: Rear, short of room appr fnl 2f, switched & picked up well, nrst fin: nicely bckd from 16/1: v useful: likes soft grnd: see 3763. *hd* **108**
3904 **ROYAL RESULT 7** [24] 7-8-5 (88) F Norton 25/1: 644005: Held up, hdwy after halfway, styd on ins last without threatening: stablemate wnr, quick reapp: 3rd in this last year, see 728. *½* **87**
3727 **DANIELLES LAD 17** [28] 4-8-12 (95) D Sweeney 20/1: 040606: Prom stands rail, rdn dist, kept on same pace: bckd from 33/1: gd run, grnd now in his favour, see 1531. *¾* **92**
3600 **TAYSEER 23** [5] 6-9-5 (102) J Quinn 10/1: 313107: Rear, prog halfway, rdn bef dist, kept on onepace. *nk* **98**
*3904 **ZUHAIR 7** [14] 7-8-3 (86)(7ex) Clare Roche (7) 33/1: 505018: Rear, kept on well appr fnl 1f, nvr nrr. *hd* **82**
3861 **FURTHER OUTLOOK 10** [1] 6-9-0 (97) R Winston 33/1: 640309: Led & rcd alone nr far side rail, hdd appr fnl 1f & no extra: stablemate of wnr: see 1182. *½* **91**
3880 **AL MUALLIM 9** [8] 6-8-7 (90)(t) J Bramhill 50/1: 401000: Al around same place: 10th, likes fast. *¾* **82**
3791 **MARSAD 14** [15] 6-8-3 (86) P Doe 10/1: 000200: Towards rr, styd on for press fnl 1f, nvr on terms: 11th. *nk* **77**
*3629 **LORD PACAL 21** [27] 3-8-3 (88)(5ex) W Supple 22/1: 221410: Prom, unable to qckn appr fnl 1f: 12th. *½* **77**
3183 **JUWWI 40** [19] 6-8-7 (90) M Fenton 40/1: 000000: Dwelt, styd on late into mid-div: 13th, 6 wk abs. *¾* **77**
3861 **DELEGATE 10** [18] 7-8-5 (88) T Lucas 20/1: 642020: Bhd, not clr run 2f out, styd on: 14th, forgive. *shd* **75**

3861 **CRYHAVOC** 10 [20] 6-8-9 (92) G Bardwell 33/1: 000600: Nvr troubled ldrs: 15th, stablemate wnr.   2½ 73
3727 **NIGRASINE** 17 [11] 6-8-12 (95)(bl) D O'Donohoe 50/1: 510400: Chsd ldrs till fnl 1f: 16th, see 1952.   nk 75
3569 **PIPADASH** 24 [12] 3-8-1 (86) P Hanagan (5) 50/1: 003000: Mid-div thro'out: 17th: see 988.   nk 65
3902 **KAYO** 7 [16] 5-9-2 (99) K Dalgleish (5) 25/1: 035040: Chsd ldrs 4f: 18th, stablemate 4th, qk reapp.   ½ 77
3610 **ROSEUM** 22 [29] 4-8-9 (92) M Roberts 10/1: 101-60: Nvr better than mid-div: 19th, bckd, lightly rcd.   nk 69
2115 **MONKSTON POINT** 86 [4] 4-9-10 (107)(vis) S Sanders 66/1: 101300: Prom 4f: 20th, top-weight, abs.   ½ 83
3543 **BON AMI** 25 [22] 4-8-7 (90) P Bradley (5) 12/1: 602400: Nvr in it: 21st: well bckd from 18/1, see 1004.   nk 65
1567 **ALWAYS ALIGHT** 110 [13] 6-8-7 (90) Dean McKeown 16/1: -01500: Mid-div 3f: 22nd: won this in '98   nk 64
& reportedly returned with a suspensory problem.
3727 **NIGHT FLIGHT** 17 [17] 6-8-10 (93)(7ex) G Duffield 16/1: 000120: Al bhd: 25th, not his form: see 3543.   0
3861 **PEPPERDINE** 10 [3] 4-8-12 (95)(VIS) K Darley 12/1: -35000: Slow away, chsd ldrs till wknd qckly   0
after halfway: last, bckd, visored, reportedly has a breathing prob: see 1173.
1337 **First Musical** 121 [25] 4-8-3 (86) D Mernagh (3) 25/1: 3785 **Tony Tie** 14 [9] 4-8-7 (90)(VIS) A Culhane 22/1:
3880 **Pips Magic** 9 [6] 4-9-0 (83) Jonjo Fowle (5) 40/1:   3473 **Passion For Life** 28 [26] 7-8-3 (86) L Newton 33/1:
28 ran   Time 1m 13.47 (4.17)   (H E Lhendup Dorji)   D Nicholls Sessay, N Yorks

4013	4.40 LADBROKES AYR HCAP 3YO+ 0-100 (C) 1m rnd Good/Soft 75 -05 Slow	[98]
	£19526 £6008 £3004 £1502 3 yo rec 4 lb	

3992 **GREAT NEWS** 1 [3] W J Haggas 5-7-11 (67)(6ex) J Quinn 2/1 FAV: 000011: 5 b g Elmaamul - Amina   79
(Brigadier Gerard) Cl-up, led going well ent fnl 2f, rdly: hvly bckd: won in similar fashion here at Ayr
yestreday (h'cap): '99 wnr at Ascot & Windsor (val h'cap & rtd h'cap, rtd 86): '98 Lingfield wnr (h'cap,
rtd 75): eff at 7f/1m, tried 10f: acts on any grnd/trk: runs v well fresh: fav'bly h'capped & can make it 3.
3992 **STYLE DANCER** 1 [2] R M Whitaker 6-8-2 (72)(vis) G Duffield 14/1: 003102: 6 b g Dancing Dissident -   3½ 74
Showing Style (Pas de Seul) Pulled hard mid-div, prog to go after wnr appr fnl 1f, kept on for press but
no impress: hmpd in running bhd this wnr yesterday, right back to form here: see 3809.
3889 **TISSIFER** 8 [4] M Johnston 4-10-0 (98) J Carroll 16/1: 004033: 4 b c Polish Precedent - Ingozi   3 94
(Warning) Towards rear, rdn appr fnl 2f, styd for 3rd, no ch front 2: not disgraced under a big weight
back in trip, return to 10f will suit: see 1574.
3699 **DURAID** 19 [5] Denys Smith 8-9-5 (89) A Nicholls (3) 16/1: 416564: Held up, mod late hdwy: see 2648.   1 83
3782 **FIRST TRUTH** 14 [12] 3-9-0 (88) K Darley 14/1: 420465: Prom, outpcd ent fnl 2f: back in trip, see 990.   ¾ 81
*3785 **PRINCE BABAR** 14 [6] 9-8-12 (82) P Hanagan (5) 5/1: 445016: Rear, shkn up appr fnl 2f, no impress.   1½ 72
3854 **MYTTONS AGAIN** 10 [8] 3-7-10 (70)(bl) J Bramhill 20/1: 311647: Bhd, imprvd appr fnl 2f, sn no extra.   ½ 59
*3764 **MUSICAL HEATH** 15 [9] 3-8-4 (78)(t) W Supple 12/1: -42218: Led till appr fnl 1f, fdd: first try on   shd 67
an easy surface on h'cap bow: only lightly raced, worth another chance: see 3764.
3510 **ESPADA** 27 [1] 4-9-5 (89) S Sanders 9/2: 210009: Al towards rear: not his form, see 1077.   4 71
2648 **ICE 64** [7] 4-9-9 (93)(vis) D Holland 12/1: 144000: In tch, eff 3f out, sn btn: 10th, stablemate 3rd, 9 wk abs.   5 67
3653 **BERGEN** 21 [13] 5-7-11 (67) F Norton 16/1: 0-0500: Al bhd: 11th, faster grnd suits: see 1514.   5 33
11 ran   Time 1m 42.96 (6.36)   (Executive Network (Pertemps Group))   W J Haggas Newmarket, Suffolk

4014	5.10 ON AIR RTD HCAP 3YO+ 0-95 (C) 1m5f Good/Soft 75 -09 Slow	[99]
	£6660 £2526 £1263 £574 3 yo rec 9 lb	

3595 **HELENS DAY** 23 [3] W Jarvis 4-8-7 (78) F Norton 12/1: -22101: 4 ch f Grand Lodge - Swordlestown   84
Miss (Apalachee) Prom, rdn to lead 2f out, in command below dist & eased nr fin: earlier won at Newcastle
(mdn): unrcd juv: eff at 10f but suited by 12f/13f: acts on fast, gd/soft grnd, stiff/gall trks: clrly suited
by this drop in grade/h'cap bow: improving, potentially useful h'capper.
2695 **RAISE A PRINCE** 63 [5] S P C Woods 7-9-2 (87)(t) P Dobbs (5) 7/1: 566002: 7 b g Machiavellian -   2½ 88
Enfant d'Amour (Lyphard) Waited with, prog to trk ldrs on bit 3f out, sn shaken up, kept on for 2nd but no
ch wnr: bckd, 9 wk abs: back to form on favoured surface, see 987.
3703 **FLOSSY** 19 [4] C W Thornton 4-9-4 (89) D Holland 6/4 FAV: 441023: 4 b f Efisio - Sirene Bleu Marine   hd 89
(Secreto) Trkd ldrs, feeling pace 3f out, drvn bef dist, styd on towards fin: hvly bckd: ran to best, see 3173.
3541 **NIGHT VENTURE** 25 [2] B W Hills 4-9-0 (85) G Duffield 12/1: 000304: Waited with, hung left &   ½ 84
rdn 3f out, no impress till kept on strongly ins last: stays 13f: looks a difficult ride, see 1031.
3811 **RUM POINTER** 13 [6] 4-9-7 (92) J Carroll 13/2: 210055: Cl-up, led 3f out, sn hdd, onepace: top-weight.   ¾ 90
3728 **MANA DARGENT** 17 [1] 3-8-5 (85) K Dalgleish (5) 13/2: 132346: Rear, prog appr str & ev ch till   5 78
no extra bef fnl 1f, eased: drifted from 4/1, see 3599, 3014.
3961 **ROYAL MINSTREL** 2 [8] 3-8-0 (80)(BL) J Quinn 12/1: 314527: Led till 3f out, sn btn: blnkd,   19 58
ran much better now without headgear 48hrs ago (15f): see 906.
3725 **RAPIER** 17 [7] 6-8-9 (80) A Culhane 20/1: 401308: Al bhd: see 2674, 1788.   2 56
3467 **ORIGINAL SPIN** 28 [9] 3-8-6 (86)(VIS) K Darley 7/1: 211229: Prom till lost place 4f out: reportedly   dist 0
choked, visored: see 3467, 2272.
9 ran   Time 2m 55.52 (10.92)   (Mrs M Dearman)   W Jarvis Newmarket, Suffolk

Official Going: SOFT Stalls: Far side

4015	2.35 UAE SPRINT HCAP 3YO+ 0-95 (C) 5f Good 40 +01 Fast	[92]
	£15236 £4688 £2344 £1172 3 yo rec 1 lb Raced centre - far side	

*3920 **DANCING MYSTERY** 4 [3] E A Wheeler 6-9-10 (88)(6ex) S Carson (3) 12/1: 014011: 6 b g Beveled -   96
Batchworth Dancer (Ballacashtal) Made all centre, styd on strongly fnl 1f, rdn out: gd time, qck reapp under 6lb
pen: earlier won at Salisbury, Ascot & Yarmouth (h'caps): '99 wnr at Lingfield, Southwell (r+td 82a), Warwick
(h'caps) & Redcar (stks, rtd 78): '98 wnr at Windsor & Goodwood (h'cap, rtd 57 & 74a): stays 6f, suited by 5f on
fast, gd/soft & both AWs: handles any track & runs well fresh, with/without blnks: v tough, useful & prog gelding.
3791 **RUSHCUTTER BAY** 14 [12] P L Gilligan 7-9-4 (82)(vis) A Polli (3) 14/1: 021002: 7 br g Mon Tresor -   ½ 88
Llwy Bren (Lidhame) Al prom far side, rdn & styd on well fnl 1f: likes Newmarket: see 3457.
*3894 **THREAT** 8 [11] S C Williams 4-8-7 (71)(t) Paul Eddery 11/2 FAV: 000513: 4 br g Zafonic - Prophecy   ¾ 75
(Warning) Trkd ldrs far side, rdn/led that group over 1f out, styd on well: jockey given a 2 day careless riding ban.
3841 **COASTAL BLUFF** 11 [22] N P Littmoden 8-9-11 (89) J Tate 14/1: 204044: Led far side 3f, held fnl 1f.   ¾ 91

3872 **BANDBOX 9** [7] 5-8-3 (67) M Henry 20/1: 236125: Rdn chasing ldrs, styd on well for press fnl 1f, *nk* **68**
not pace to chall: return to 6f in similar company should suit: see 3587 (class stks, 6f).
3788 **SAPHIRE 14** [2] 4-9-8 (86) K Hodgson 14/1: 502406: Chsd ldrs centre, kept on fnl 1f: see 3322, 1133. *½* **86**
3904 **IVORY DAWN 7** [5] 6-9-1 (79) C Carver (3) 16/1: 030207: Held up centre: kept on fnl 2f: see 2761. *½* **77**
1694 **BOLEYN CASTLE 105** [21] 3-10-0 (93) L Carter 25/1: 5-0508: Chsd ldrs far side 4f: 3 month abs. *hd* **90**
3861 **AZIZZI 10** [10] 8-9-10 (88) A Daly 10/1: 31-009: Trckd ldrs centre 4f: op 12/1: see 3788. *hd* **84**
3872 **SHARP HAT 9** [20] 6-8-8 (72) Claire Bryan (5) 8/1: 303230: Sn handy far side, held fnl 1f: 10th. *½* **66**
3904 **SPEED ON 7** [19] 7-8-12 (76) C Rutter 13/2: 050460: Prom far side early, lost pl/hmpd after 1f, rdn/ *½* **68**
mod hdwy late on: 11th: see 1013.
3861 **MUNGO PARK 10** [17] 6-9-5 (83) A Clark 16/1: 251000: Held up far side, nvr on terms: 12th: btr 3398. *½* **74**
3788 **FLAK JACKET 14** [1] 5-8-10 (74) G Hind 14/1: 113000: Chsd wnr centre till over 1f out: 13th: see 3136. *¾* **63**
3791 **Villa Via 14** [23] 3-8-5 (70) R Ffrench 20/1: 3631 **Pierpoint 21** [15] 5-7-11 (61)(bl) T Hamilton (7) 20/1:
3569 **Half Moon Bay 24** [18] 3-9-6 (85) Lynsey Hanna (7) 20/1: 3613 **Blue Kite 22** [9] 5-7-11 (61) N Carlisle 25/1:
2961 **Red Lion Gb 50** [8] 4-9-4 (82) S W Kelly (3) 14/1:
18 ran Time 1m 0.14 (1.94) (Austin Stroud & Co Ltd) E A Wheeler Whitchurch On Thames, Oxon

4016

3.10 ABU DHABI RTD HCAP 3YO+ 0-100 (B) 1m6f Good 40 +16 Fast [103]
£15381 £5834 £2917 £1326 3 yo rec 10lb

*3599 **JARDINES LOOKOUT 23** [4] A P Jarvis 3-9-1 (100) W Ryan 9/4 FAV: 2121D1: 3 b g Fourstars Allstar - **105**
Foolish Flight (Fool's Holme) In tch, prog 5f out, led ins last, drvn out to assert: well bckd, fast time:
deserved this after controversial disqual at York in 3599, earlier scored at Salisbury (mdn): eff at 14f, 2m
shld suit: acts on fast & gd/soft grnd, any track, loves a stiff/gall one: prog gelding, can win more races.
3778 **MARDANI 14** [6] M Johnston 5-8-10 (85) R Ffrench 4/1: 002662: 5 b g Fairy King - Marmana (Blushing *1½* **87**
Groom) Chsd ldrs, rdn & styd on fnl 2f, not pace of wnr: op 3/1: on a fair mark, loves to dominate: see 633.
*3157 **BANCO SUIVI 42** [2] B W Hills 3-7-13 (84) A Daly 9/2: 202313: 3 b f Nashwan - Pay The Bank (High *nk* **86**
Top) Led after 1f, hdd ins last & no extra cl home: 6 wk abs, clr of rem: stays 14f, suited by front running tactics.
3487 **UNAWARE 28** [1] R Charlton 3-8-3 (87)(1ow) Paul Eddery 7/2: 534034: Held up, eff to press ldrs over *6* **83**
2f out, held over 1f out: bckd: eff at 12f on fast & gd grnd, this longer 14f trip looked just beyond him: see 1225.
3811 **LEONATO 13** [7] 8-8-7 (82)(t) J Fortune 7/1: /25-05: Led 1f, btn 2f out: op 10/1: see 3011. *17* **57**
3483 **ASHGAR 28** [3] 4-9-1 (90) C Rutter 20/1: 404066: Prom 10f: see 2114, 1109. *5* **58**
6 ran Time 2m 58.87 (3.37) (Ambrose Turnbull) A P Jarvis Aston Upthorpe, Oxon

4017

4.20 EBF GULF CLASS STKS 3YO+ 0-95 (B) 1m2f str Good 40 -06 Slow
£8850 £3357 £1678 £763 3 yo rec 6 lb

3684 **CATCHY WORD 19** [6] E A L Dunlop 3-8-11 M Tebbutt 4/1 JT FAV: 540031: 3 ch c Cadeaux Genereux - **103**
Lora's Guest (Be My Guest) Cl up, went on appr fnl 1f, styd on well, rdn out: nicely bckd: won 1st & last of 4
juv starts, at Haydock (mdn) & Yarmouth (stks, rtd 106): eff at 7/10f: acts on firm, gd/soft & runs well fresh on
a stiff/gall or easy trk: has tried visor, best without: useful colt, capable of landing a Listed race abroad.
3595 **CAPE GRACE 23** [1] R Hannon 4-9-5 A Clark 7/1: 052402: 4 b f Priolo - Saffron (Fabulous Dancer) *1½* **102**
Mid div, rdn/prog over 2f out, styd on but no ch with wnr: gd run drpd in grade, visor omitted: win similar.
3883 **WELSH WIND 8** [8] D J Murphy 4-9-0 D R McCabe 5/1: 204223: 4 b g Tenby - Bavaria (Top Ville) *1¾* **93**
Led till over 1f out, edged left & no extra inside last: not disgraced at the weights: consistent: see 3883, 1262.
3515 **GRAMPAS 27** [3] J H M Gosden 3-8-13 J Fortune 6/1: -2164: Waited with, improved 3f out, fdd inside *3* **93**
last: drftd from 7/2: up in trip: useful & lightly rcd, shade btr 3179 (9f).
3017 **KRANTOR 48** [10] 3-8-13 W Ryan 9/1: -62155: Prom, drpd rear over 3f out, late hdwy, no threat: *3* **87**
7 week abs, worth a try over 12f now: see 2434.
1347 **AL TOWD 121** [5] 3-8-8 R Ffrench 9/1: 3-0546: Cl up, lost tch fnl 2f: 4 month abs: btr 1347, 1089. *2* **78**
3868 **TEXANNIE 9** [4] 3-8-5 Esther Remmerswaal 100/1: -00007: Nvr a factor: stiff task: see 3868. *9* **59**
4097} **BARAKULA 356** [7] 3-8-5 G Hind 8/1: 15-8: Al towards rear: better expected on reappearance: *1½* **55**
'99 debut scorer at Windsor (stakes), sub not disgraced when 5th in a Gr 1 at Ascot (rtd 95): dam 6/12f wnr:
eff at 6f, bred to apprec 1m+ in time: can run well fresh on fast grnd: capable of much better.
3131 **FOREIGN SECRETARY 43** [11] 3-8-11 Paul Eddery 4/1 JT FAV: -12609: Prom, wknd quickly fnl 2f: *¾* **59**
nicely bckd after 6 week abs: much better expected, something amiss? see 2116.
3117 **HAMERKOP 43** [9] 5-8-11 D Williamson 100/1: 5-0400: Lost tch fnl 3f, 10th: 6 wk abs: hopeless task. *nk* **52$**
10 ran Time 2m 06.67 (4.57) (Abdullah Ali) E A L Dunlop Newmarket, Suffolk

4018

4.50 CORNICHE CLAIMER 3YO+ (F) 7f str Good 40 -00 Slow
£5541 £1705 £852 £426 3 yo rec 3 lb

3839 **REDSWAN 11** [20] S C Williams 5-8-10 (t) W Ryan 10/1: 020331: 5 ch g Risk Me - Bocas Rose **66**
(Jalmood) Waited with, gd hdwy to lead ins last, styd on well, pushed out: '99 Leicester & Doncaster wnr (h'caps,
rtd 74): '98 wnr here at Newmarket (clmr, rtd 74 & 71a): eff at 7f/1m on firm, gd, handles fibresand & best
on a stiff/gall track: eff in a t-strap, with/without blnks.
3880 **MANTLES PRIDE 9** [12] J A Glover 5-9-0 (bl) G Hind 14/1: 050002: 5 br g Petong - State Romance *1¾* **66**
(Free State) Prom, went on appr fnl 1f, hdd inside last, not pce of wnr: see 1514 (h'cap).
3318 **DANDY REGENT 35** [9] J L Harris 6-8-8 N Carlisle 20/1: 004003: 6 b g Green Desert - Tahilla *1½* **58**
(Moorestyle) Front rank, eff/short of room ins last, sn held: op 12/1: ran to best: likes sells/clmrs.
*3671 **JAMESTOWN 20** [10] C Smith 3-8-13 T Hamilton (7) 12/1: -04614: Prom, held fnl 1f: btr 3671 (made all). *½* **65**
3612 **PAGEANT 22** [23] 3-8-9 A Clark 8/1: 262555: Handy, eff over 1f out, onepcd: op 6/1: see 2855. *nk* **60**
3831 **MISTER RAMBO 11** [13] 5-9-3 (bl) D R McCabe 15/2: 605506: Dsptd lead, went on after 3f, hdd *½* **64**
appr dist, no extra: op 10/1: see 817.
3711 **SERGEANT YORK 18** [16] 4-9-0 (vis) R Fitzpatrick 12/1: 045307: Cl up, rdn halfway, no extra for *1½* **58**
press over 1f out: claimed by T Barron for £12,000: see 3711, 1291 (1m).
3750 **BE MY WISH 16** [14] 5-8-9 (bl) R Ffrench 14/1: 225108: Mid div, late hdwy, no threat: btr 3613 (6f). *1¾* **49**
3810 **STEALTHY TIMES 13** [11] 3-8-2 J Tate 20/1: 055409: Led early, lost tch appr fnl 1f: see 2564, 1138. *nk* **44**
2769 **NIGHT EMPRESS 59** [24] 3-8-12 J Fortune 5/2 FAV: 245150: Mid div at best, eased when btn, 10th: *1½* **51**
hvly bckd after 8 week abs & much better expected: rtd much higher on firm in 2769 (stks), 2391 (h'cap).
3765 **TRAJAN 15** [5] 3-8-9 Lisa Jones (7) 14/1: 602440: Nvr a factor, 11th: btr 3765 (h'cap). *2* **44**
3218 **LEEROY 38** [8] 3-8-11 R Smith (5) 20/1: -20050: Al towards rear, 12th: see 840 (mdn). *5* **38**
3856 **SOVEREIGN STATE 10** [21] 3-8-9 M Tebbutt 10/1: 546000: Sn rdn, lost tch halfway, 20th: btr 1387. **0**
3495 **Baron De Pichon 28** [2] 4-8-12 S Carson (3) 25/1: 3580 **Showing 24** [3] 3-8-7 (t) Paul Eddery 33/1:

3578 **Qualitair Pride** 24 [1] 8-8-1 Claire Bryan (5) 33/1: *3871 **Souhaite** 9 [6] 4-9-8 Sophie Mitchell 33/1:
3793 **Sofisio** 14 [17] 3-8-11 S Righton 25/1: 2031 **Haunt The Zoo** 90 [19] 5-8-5 M Henry 33/1:
-- **Defiant** [22] 3-9-0 P D'Arcy 25/1: 3939 **Finery** 3 [15] 3-8-9 (vis) C Rutter 33/1:
2729 **Neronian** 60 [18] 6-8-9 D McGaffin (5) 66/1:
22 ran   Time 1m 25.98 (2.78)   (P Geoghan)   S C Williams Newmarket, Suffolk

4019
5.20 EBF FILLIES MDN 2YO (D)   1m str   Good 40 -12 Slow
£5525   £1700   £850   £425

3678 **BRANICKI** 19 [2] J H M Gosden 2-8-11 J Fortune 6/4: 31: 2 b f Spectrum - Karinski (Palace Music)   87
Easily made all: bckd: March head, half-sister to a 6f juv wnr, dam unrcd: eff forcing the pace over a stiff
1m, will get further next term: acts on fast & gd grnd, handles a gall trk: going the right way.
3829 **GUARANDA** 11 [5] W Jarvis 2-8-11 M Tebbutt 11/8 FAV: 52: 2 b f Acatenango - Gryada (Shirley Heights 2½ 79
Chsd wnr thro'out, nvr any impress: well bckd, cght a tartar: handles firm & gd grnd & stays 1m.
-- **SILVER GREY LADY** [1] J L Dunlop 2-8-11 Paul Eddery 13/2: 3: 2 gr f Saddlers' Hall - Early Rising   3½ 73
(Grey Dawn II) Held up, chsd ldrs 2f out, outpcd bef dist: debut, tchd 25/1: sister to high class mid-dist/stayer Silver
Patriach: likely to come into her own over mid-dists next term.
-- **SEVEN OF NINE** [3] W R Muir 2-8-11 S Carson (3) 10/1: 4: Chsd ldrs till 2f out, tchd 25/1:   8 59
IR 50,000gns Alzao, sister to useful 7f juv & 1m wnr Rabi: dam unrcd: should do better in time.
3678 **STARDARA** 19 [4] 2-8-11 A Clark 20/1: 65: Chsd along, prom, lost tch after halfway: see 3678.   12 39
5 ran   Time 1m 40.7 (4.2)   (R E Sangster)   J H M Gosden Manton, Wilts

4020
5.50 RUSHBROOKE MDN 2YO (D)   7f str   Good 40 -44 Slow
£5590   £1720   £860   £430

-- **LAGUDIN** [10] L M Cumani 2-9-0 G Hind 100/30: 1: 2 b c Eagle Eyed - Liaison (Blushing   90
Groom) Rcd alone centre, led after 2f, ran on strongly, pshd out: op 5/2, v slow time: half-brother to wnrs
btwn 1m & 12f, dam a 10f wnr: eff over a stiff 7f, 1m will suit: acts on gd grnd & runs well fresh: promising.
-- **ALBUHERA** [5] M Johnston 2-9-0 R Ffrench 11/8 FAV: 2: 2 b c Desert Style - Morning Welcome   1¼ 87
(Be My Guest) Early ldr, every ch, rdn fnl 1f, kept on but held: well bckd from 3/1: IR 12,000gns sister
to French/Irish 2,000 Guineas wnr Bachir: eff at 7f on gd grnd: likely to improve & find similar.
-- **VILLA CARLOTTA** [4] J L Dunlop 2-8-9 M Henry 12/1: 3: 2 ch f Rainbow Quest - Subya (Night   1¼ 78
Shift) In tch, kept on to chase front 2 fnl 1f, nvr any impress: op 7/1: 32,000gns Feb foal, dam a useful
5/7f juv wnr: shld be seen to better effect over 10f+ next term.
-- **ANALYSER** [6] J H M Gosden 2-9-0 J Fortune 3/1: 4: Cl up, fdd appr fnl 1f: drifter from 7/4:   3 78
Royal Academy brother to 7f wnr Musical Treat, dam 7f/1m wnr: should leave this behind.
-- **ROSIE** [2] 2-8-9 Paul Eddery 6/1: 5: Held up in tch, outpcd appr fnl 1f: stablemate 3rd,   ¾ 71
op 4/1: Bering first foal, dam 1m juv wnr: bred to appreciate 10f+.
5 ran   Time 1m 29.1 (5.9)   (Miss G Gatto Roissard)   L M Cumani Newmarket, Suffolk

Official Going   STANDARD. Stalls 7f & 14f - Outside; Rem - Inside.

4021
7.00 BET DIRECT MDN HCAP 3YO+ 0-70 (E)   1m100y aw rnd Going 39 +01 Fast   [64]
£3080   £880   £440   3 yo rec 4 lb

3769 **BAHRAIN** 14 [11] N P Littmoden 4-9-7 (57) T G McLaughlin 2/1 FAV: 006231: 4 ch c Lahib - Twin Island   60a
(Standaan) Trkd ldrs, went on over 2f out, styd on strongly, drvn out: nicely bckd, gd time: promise first of
2 '99 starts for A Jarvis (mdn, rtd 77), well btn sole '98 start for Sir M Prescott: eff at 7/8.5f on firm grnd &
fibresand: acts on a sharp trk: has prev tried a t-strap, prob best without.
3656 **SHARP BELLINE** 21 [9] J L Harris 3-8-11 (51) G Baker (5) 10/1: 434042: 3 b g Robellino - Moon Watch   ¾ 52a
(Night Shift) Cl-up, rdn to chall over 1f out, held fnl 50yds: eff at 8.5f on fibresand: gd AW bow, can win similar.
3095 **GROESFAEN LAD** 45 [2] P S McEntee 3-9-5 (59) G Faulkner (3) 16/1: 040063: 3 b g Casteddu - Curious   1 58a
Feeling (Nishapour) Led, hdd over 2f out, wknd well in last: 6 wk abs: new stable, prev wth B Palling: see 857.
1269 **SUCH FLAIR** 127 [4] J Noseda 3-9-13 (67) A Daly 6/1: 0-304: In tch, rdn/prog over 1f out, held ins   shd 66a
fnl 1f: op 4/1: 4 month abs, AW/h'cap bow: see 1010.
555 **TING** 208 [2] 3-8-11 (51) P Goode (3) 25/1: 5-4605: Chsd ldrs, drvn/btn over 1f out: long abs, clr rem. 1¼ 48a
4154 **FORT SUMTER** 353 [13] 4-9-8 (58) S W Kelly (3) 16/1: 6300-6: Mid-div at best: plcd once in '99   6 45a
(h'cap, rtd 66), well btn over hdles: dual '98 rnr-up (mdn, rtd 81, I Balding): see 3238 (7f).
3440 **HAZIRAAN** 29 [12] 3-9-3 (57) B McHugh (7) 12/1: 03007: Chsd ldrs, drvn/btn over 1f out: see 1643.   hd 44a
3401 **BLUE STREAK** 31 [3] 3-10-0 (68)(VIS) F Lynch 5/1: 004468: Mid-div, hmpd after 2f, lost tch   6 46a
fnl 2f: top-weight, AW bow: first time visor: see 3238 (7f).
3185 **ARANUI** 40 [10] 3-9-1 (55) G Gibbons (7) 33/1: 0-0359: Al in rear: 6 wk abs: AW bow.   5 25a
3769 **SEA ISLE** 14 [3] 4-9-10 (60) R Havlin 16/1: 350-00: Prom, wknd rapidly fnl 3f, 10th: see 3769.   5 22a
1414 **JAVELIN** 119 [6] 4-9-1 (51) Darren Williams (5) 6/1: 540600: Dwelt, al well bhd, t.o. & fin last: long abs.   0a
3696 **Atalya** 19 [5] 3-9-11 (65) I Mongan (5) 16/1:   3854 **Cultured Pearl** 10 [7] 3-9-6 (60)(BL) D Griffiths 14/1:
13 ran   Time 1m 49.4 (3.2)   (Mrs Julie Mitchell)   N P Littmoden Newmarket.

4022
7.30 EBF MDN 2YO (D)   1m100y aw rnd Going 39 -01 Slow
£3562   £1096   £548   £274

3508 **SEDUCTIVE** 27 [6] Sir Mark Prescott 2-9-0 S Sanders 3/1: 02351: 2 b c Pursuit Of Love - Full Orchestra   80a
(Shirley Heights) Prom, went on over 3f out, hung right & strongly pressed ins last, hdd fnl 50yds, rallied & led
again fnl stride, all out: up in trip, AW bow: 36,000gns Apr foal, half-brother to sev wnrs, incl a 6/9f wnr,
dam a 10f wnr: apprec this stiff trip & acts on 8.5f: acts on firm, gd/soft & fibresand: acts on a sharp or gall track.
3497 **CARNIVAL LAD** 28 [2] Sir Michael Stoute 2-9-0 F Lynch 7/4 FAV: 2532: 2 ch c Caerleon - Fun Crowd shd 79a
(Easy Goer) Cl-up, hung right over 1f out, led fnl 50y, hdd on line: up in trip, eff at 8.5f on f/sand: win sn.
3273 **CARRABAN** 36 [5] B J Meehan 2-8-9 D R McCabe 13/2: W33623: 2 b f Mujadil - Bayazida (Bustino)   2½ 70a
Led early, dropped rear after halfway, rdn/late hdwy, no threat to front 2: styd longer 8.5f trip: see 3273 (h'cap).

3766 **COMPANION** 15 [10] W J Haggas 2-8-9 S W Kelly (3) 6/1: 464: Dwelt, eff from halfway, rdn/onepcd *nk* **70a**
over 1f out: AW bow: now quals for h'caps & 10f shld suit in that sphere: see 3577.
3799 **GALLA PLACIDIA** 13 [1] R Havlin 5/1: 65: Sn led, hdd 3f out, lost tch ins last: AW bow, *2* **66a**
one more run for h'cap mark: see 3799.
3909 **ICE PRINCE** 5 [8] 2-9-0 Dean McKeown 33/1: 006: Bhd, modest late gains: qck reapp: see 3909. *3* **66a**
3705 **ACHILLES SUN** 19 [7] 2-9-0 D Sweeney 20/1: -U4007: Cl-up, wknd over 2f out: up in trip: see 2677. *2½* **62a**
3608 **PARTY PLOY** 22 [3] 2-9-0 Darren Williams (5) 16/1: 008: Mid-div, fdd over 3f out: op 12/1, AW bow. *1¼* **60a**
3895 **CELERITY** 7 [9] 2-8-9 I Mongan (4) 25/1: -069: Rcd wide, all well bhd, t.o.: qck reapp, up in trip. *23* **30a**
3789 **WHITE AMIT** 14 [4] 2-8-9 (T) A Daly 33/1: 00: Handy, wknd halfway, t.o., 10th: up in trip, t-strap. *8* **20a**
10 ran   Time 1m 49.6 (3.4)   (Mr Charles Walker & Mr Johnathon Carroll)   Sir Mark Prescott Newmarket.

4023	**8.00 BET DIRECT HCAP 3YO+ 0-70 (E)** 6f aw rnd Going 39 +06 Fast		**[68]**
	£3132 £895 £447 3 yo rec 2 lb		

3774 **MOOCHA CHA MAN** 14 [6] B A McMahon 4-9-3 (57)(bl) F Lynch 10/1: 500051: 4 b f Sizzling Melody - **62a**
Nilu (Ballad Rock) Mid-div, rdn to improve over 1f out, styd on strongly to lead ins last, drvn out: best time
of day: '99 Pontefract wnr (clmr, 1st time blnks, rtd 73 at best): '98 wnr here at W'hampton (auct mdn, rtd 69a):
eff at 5/6f on fast, hvy & fibresand: handles any trk, likes W'hampton: best in blnks, has prev tried visor.
2586 **CAROLS CHOICE** 66 [12] D Haydn Jones 3-9-8 (64) A McGlone 10/1: 323562: 3 ch f Emarati - Lucky Song *1* **66a**
(Lucky Wednesday) Trkd ldrs, led 2f out, hdd ins last, held cl-home: not disgraced after 9 wk abs: see 1795, 549.
3562 **CITY REACH** 24 [8] P J Makin 4-9-2 (56)(vis) D Sweeney 6/1: 051033: 4 b g Petong - Azola (Alzao) *2* **53a**
Sn outpcd, rdn & ran on well ins last, nvr nrr: see 2905.
3839 **HYPERACTIVE** 11 [5] A C Stewart 4-9-11 (65)(BL) S Sanders 6/1: 200004: Outpcd early, ran on *nk* **62a**
strongly for press fnl 2f, nrst fin: first time blnks, AW bow: see 1483 (7f).
3218 **VILLA ROMANA** 38 [11] A Clark 3-9-4 (60) 16/1: 50-065: Bhd, rdn/late hdwy: unsuited by drop in trip? *nk* **57a**
3536 **POLAR MIST** 25 [7] 5-9-7 (61)(tbl) Dean McKeown 11/2: 020606: Led early, remained with ldrs, *2* **53a**
lost tch ins last: see 1487.
1519 **DAHLIDYA** 112 [9] 5-9-10 (64) G Baker (5) 20/1: 300007: V slow to start, hdwy from rear over *hd* **56a**
2f out, nvr nr ldrs: 4 month abs & just sharper for this but often loses chance at start: see 1504, 697.
3770 **ROYAL CASCADE** 14 [13] 6-9-8 (62)(bl) Dale Gibson 7/1: 020158: Nvr a factor: btr 3275 (seller). *1½* **51a**
3872 **RUDE AWAKENING** 9 [3] 6-9-6 (60) P Goode (3) 4/1 FAV: 052049: Prom, sltly hmpd 3f out, sn *1¼* **46a**
lost tch: op 11/4: see 3257, 2743.
1734 **XSYNNA** 103 [2] 4-9-2 (56)(bl) A Daly 14/1: 260000: Al bhd: long abs, new stable: see 351. *2* **37a**
3622 **DOUBLE M** 22 [10] 3-10-0 (70)(bl) I Mongan (5) 12/1: 04-060: Led 4f out, hdd 2f out, wknd, 11th. *2* **46a**
3010 **PADDYWACK** 48 [1] 3-9-8 (64)(bl) Claire Bryan (5) 10/1: 020U00: Al well bhd, t.o. in 12th: 7 wk abs. *12* **16a**
3774 **NITE OWL MATE** 14 [4] 3-10-0 (70)(tBL) T G McLaughlin 20/1: 100000: Al well bhd, t.o. in 13th: blnkd. *6* **10a**
13 ran   Time 1m 14.8 (2.0)   (Michael Sturgess)   B A McMahon Hopwas, Staffs.

4024	**8.30 CLASSIFIED STKS 3YO+ 0-60 (F)** 1m6f166y aw Going 39 -30 Slow		
	£2324 £664 £332 3 yo rec 11lb		

3715 **VINCENT** 18 [3] J L Harris 5-9-6 G Baker (5) 8/1: 013441: 5 b g Anshan - Top Anna (Ela Mana Mou) **61a**
Twrds rear, hdwy halfway, went on 2f out, rdn clr fnl 1f: earlier won at Southwell & here at W'hampton (h'caps):
'99 wnr again at Southwell & W'hampton (h'caps, rtd 52a, unplcd on turf, rtd 48a): plcd in '98 (rtd 55a, visor):
eff at 14f/2m on fast, loves fibresand/sharp trks, handles equitrack: runs well fresh: tough fibresand specialist.
3495 **FAILED TO HIT** 28 [11] N P Littmoden 7-9-4 (vis) D Sweeney 10/3 JT FAV: 343652: 7 b g Warrshan - *2½* **55a**
Missed Again (High Top) Trkd ldrs, went on halfway, hdd 2f out, not pace of wnr: nicely bckd tho' op 5/2:
clr rem: eff at 1m/14.7f: consistent AW form: see 3495, 530.
3255 **TOWN GOSSIP** 37 [12] P J Makin 3-8-5(1ow) A Clark 12/1: -05003: 3 ch f Indian Ridge - Only Gossip *4* **48a**
(Trempolino) In tch, rdn/prog 3f out, no impress on front 2: up in trip, AW bow: stays 14.7f on fibresand.
4407} **MAKATI** 334 [5] J G M O'Shea 6-9-4 I Mongan (5) 8/1: 3261-4: Handy, eff 4f out, btn fnl 2f: recent *5* **44a**
well btn 4th on hdles bow (mdn, rtd 57h): '99 Southwell wnr (h'cap, rtd 53a at best, Miss J Camacho), '98 wnr again
at Southwell & W'hampton (h'caps, rtd 50a): eff at 14f/2m & likes fibresand/sharp trks: can go well fresh.
3476 **FURNESS** 28 [6] J Balding 3-8-7 S Carson (3) 10/3 JT FAV: 0-2525: In tch, drvn/fdd fnl 2f: btr 3/1: btr 3476. *2½* **41a**
3494 **TOPAZ** 28 [10] 5-9-4 Jonjo Fowle (5) 20/1: 040026: Waited with, eff halfway, wknd fnl 2f: stiff task. *6* **35$**
3201 **SPOSA** 39 [2] 4-9-5 T G McLaughlin 6/1: 144307: Cl-up, grad wknd from halfway: see 2776. *9* **26a**
3284 **WESTERN COMMAND** 36 [1] 4-9-4 R Fitzpatrick 5/1: 062068: Led 7f, wknd, t.o.: op 5/2: btr 2156. *1¼* **23a**
3586 **BAMBOOZLE** 23 [6] F Lynch 14/1: 05009: Lost tch halfway, t.o.: op 10/1, AW bow. *ist* **0a**
3255 **MONONGAHELA** 37 [4] 6-9-4 S W Kelly (3) 25/1: 506/00: Al well bhd, t.o. in 10th: recently p.u. *19* **0a**
over timber: Flat scorer back in native Ireland back in '97 (eff at 1m/10f on fast & gd).
3448 **SIPOWITZ** 29 [9] 6-9-4 S Sanders 20/1: /50300: Sn rdn in rear, t.o. from halfway, 11th: btr 3276. *3½* **0a**
11 ran   Time 3m 19.8 (10.2)   (P Caplan)   J L Harris Eastwell, Leics.

4025	**9.00 BET DIRECT SELLER 2YO (G)** 7f aw rnd Going 39 -39 Slow		
	£1970 £563 £281		

3615 **FINN MCCOOL** 22 [9] R A Fahey 2-8-11 S Sanders 5/1: -61: 2 b g Blues Traveller - Schonbein (Persian **59a**
Heights) In tch, hdwy to chall 3f out, went on appr dist, styd on well, drvn out: op 7/2, bght in for 5,400gns:
Mar foal, sire high-class mid-dist performer: eff at 7f, 1m shld suit in time: acts on fibresand & a sharp trk.
3830 **RED FANFARE** 11 [1] J A Osborne 2-8-6 R Havlin 7/4 FAV: 00002: 2 ch f First Trump - Corman Style *2* **52a**
(Ahonoora) Front rank, chsd wnr ins last, kept on but no dngr to wnr: nicely bckd but op 6/4: AW bow & apprec
this drop in grade, stays 7f on fibresand: looks capable of winning similar: see 2009.
3950 **EMMA THOMAS** 3 [2] A Berry 2-8-6 F Lynch 14/1: 00003: 2 b f Puissance - Clan Scotia (Clantime) *2* **48$**
Led, hdd over 1f out, no pace of wnr: ran 3 days ago: AW bow: see 2539.
3639 **MISS SUTTON** 21 [5] T G Mills 2-8-6 L Carter 7/1: 544: Cl-up, dropped rear halfway, late hdwy, *hd* **48a**
no threat: up in trip, AW bow: see 3278.
2898 **BILLYJO** 53 [8] 2-8-11 (bl) D R McCabe 10/1: 66445: Handy, rdn/prog over 2f out, no extra *1* **51$**
appr fnl 1f: 8 wk abs: see 1740.
3496 **MR TOD** 28 [3] 2-8-11 G Baker (5) 12/1: 06: Dwelt, sn in mid-div, no extra fnl 2f: 3,200gns. *¾* **50a**
Mar first foal, dam scored over 1m: sire smart sprinter: with J Given.
3812 **SO FOXY** 13 [4] 2-8-6 A Daly 25/1: -007: In tch, dropped rear halfway, no dngr: AW bow, lks modest. *½* **44a**
1381 **DIAMOND MURPHY** 119 [10] 2-8-6 R Fitzpatrick 20/1: 08: Nvr dngrs: 4 month abs: up in trip. *¾* **42a**
Jan foal, half-sister to a 7f 2yo wnr, dam scored over 5f: with P G Murphy.

3757 **BONNYELLA** 16 [12] 2-8-6 D McGaffin (2) 20/1: 509: Al outpcd: see 2772. ½ 41a
3950 **IVANS BRIDE** 3 [11] 2-8-7(1ow) G Faulkner (0) 13/1: 062400: Al well bhd, 10th: ran 3 days ago. ¾ 41a
3837 **UNVEIL** 11 [7] 2-8-6 D Kinsella (7) 11/2: 650340: Lost tch halfway, 11th: see 3837. 2 36a
3740 **DUSTY DEMOCRAT** 16 [6] 2-8-11 (VIS) Darren Williams (5) 10/1: 200: Outpcd, 12th: visor: btr 722. ¾ 40a
12 ran   Time 1m 31.7 (5.5)   (R A Fahey)   R A Fahey Butterwick, N.Yorks.

4026 9.30 BET247.CO.UK HCAP 3YO+ 0-60 (F)   1m4f aw   Going 39 -10 Slow   [60]
£2548 £728 £364   3 yo rec 8 lb

3518 **CUPBOARD LOVER** 27 [9] D Haydn Jones 4-9-2 (48) A McGlone 9/4 FAV: 663141: 4 ch g Risk Me - 58a
Galejade (Sharrood) Waited with, smooth hdwy to lead over 2f out, easily went clr: nicely bckd: earlier won
at Chepstow (h'cap): '99 wnr at Hamilton & Nottingham (h'caps, rtd 64): by 12/14f on fast, gd & fibresand:
acts on a stiff/gall or sharp trk: looks well h'capped on the AW, can follow-up.
2544 **DESERT SPA** 68 [7] P J Makin 5-10-0 (60) A Clark 4/1: 110102: 5 b g Sheikh Albadou - Healing 6 60a
Waters (Temeprence Hill) Mid-div, imprvd halfway & sn led, hdd 2f out, not pace of wnr: 8 wk abs & not disgraced
against a well h'capped rival, loves W'hampton: see 1389.
3858 **MYSTERIUM** 10 [5] N P Littmoden 6-9-6 (52) T G McLaughlin 7/2: 110003: 6 gr g Mystiko - Way To Go 2½ 48a
(Troy) Bhd, rdn/prog over 4f out, kept on but no threat to front 2: well clr rem: see 3314.
3915 **BON GUEST** 5 [4] M P Muggeridge 6-9-8 (54) G Baker (5) 16/1: 1/0004: Trkd ldrs, rdn/lost tch 19 30a
fnl 3f: op 10/1, qck reapp: see 2212.
3637} **GOLDEN HAWK** 384 [10] F Lynch 14/1: 0650-5: Handy, wknd fnl 4f, op 10/1: recently ½ 25a
well btn hdles rnr (h'caps, rtd 82h): unplcd for S Dow in '99 (h'caps, rtd 58), subs won over hdles at Huntingdon
(nov, rtd 100h, stays 2m on firm): eff btwn 1m & 2m, latter prob suits: acts on firm & hvy: now with C A Dwyer.
3769 **COMMONWOOD** 14 [11] 3-8-13 (53) S Carson (3) 16/1: 400006: Waited with, brief hdwy after halfway, 2½ 25a
wknd qckly fnl 3f: up in trip: see 1726.
2284 **BORDER RUN** 78 [1] 3-9-5 (59)(bl) D R McCabe 9/1: 036037: Led 7f, wknd fnl 3f: 11 wk abs. nk 31a
3276 **MALCHIK** 36 [6] 4-9-8 (54) D Sweeney 16/1: 260008: Trkd ldrs, fdd fnl 4f: btr 922 (9.4f seller). ¾ 25a
2581 **PSALMIST** 66 [3] 3-9-6 (60) R Havlin 12/1: 30009: Lost tch halfway, t.o.: op 8/1, 9 wk abs: AW bow. 25 0a
3828 **MIGWAR** 11 [8] 7-8-13 (45)(BL) Claire Bryan 5/1: 603000: Well bhd halfway, t.o., 10th: blnkd. 6 0a
3683 **BONNIE FLORA** 19 [2] 4-9-7 (53) A Daly 16/1: 03U000: Trkd ldrs, dropped rear after 5f, t.o. in 11th. 13 0a
3524 **THE BARGATE FOX** 26 [12] 4-9-8 (54) S Sanders 9/1: 000300: Al last, t.o., 12th: op 13/2: btr 3181. 3½ 0a
12 ran   Time 2m 39.5 (5.9)   (Mrs Judy Mihalop)   D Haydn Jones Efail Isaf, Rhondda.

Official Going   GOOD TO SOFT. Stalls: Stands Side, except 10f - Inside.

4027 2.15 LIGHTNING HCAP 3YO+ 0-80 (D)   5f   Good/Soft 60 +12 Fast   [79]
£4147 £1276 £638 £319   3 yo rec 1 lb   Raced towards centre, no advantage

*3821 **PETARGA** 14 [5] J A R Toller 5-9-8 (73) S Whitworth 12/1: 005011: 5 b m Petong - One Half Silver 78
(Plugged Nickle) Held up, rdn/hdwy from halfway, styd on strongly for press to lead nr fin: op 10/1: best time
of day: recent Bath wnr (h'cap): '99 Folkestone wnr (h'cap, rtd 80): plcd twice in '98 (h'cap, rtd 80): eff at
5/6f on firm & gd/soft grnd, sharp or stiff/gall track: remains fairly h'capped & in top form.
3694 **MUTASAWWAR** 21 [19] J M Bradley 6-7-11 (48)(1ow)(5oh) F Norton 33/1: 004002: 6 ch g Clantime - ½ 50
Keen Melody (Sharpen Up) Held up in tch, rdn & styd on well ins last, not pace of wnr: likes out & firm near mark.
3960 **PURE COINCIDENCE** 4 [21] K R Burke 5-9-9 (74)(VIS) Dean McKeown 9/1: 003033: 5 b g Lugana shd 76
Beach - Esilam (Frimley Park) Sn pushed along, al prom, led halfway till cl-home: fine run in 1st time visor.
3698 **BOANERGES** 21 [15] R Guest 3-9-13 (79) G Duffield 25/1: 130604: Towards rear, styd on well fnl 1f 1¼ 78+
under tender handling, nrst fin: shown enough win again with a more forceful ride: see 3698.
3966 **RIVER TERN** 4 [8] 7-7-13 (50) R Ffrench 11/1: 000035: Mid-div, rdn & styd on onepace fnl 1f, struck shd 49
by rivals whip nr fin: qck reapp: better on faster grnd: see 1357.
1842 **MARY JANE** 100 [9] 5-7-11 (48) Kim Tinkler 11/2: 000006: Dwelt, sn chsd ldrs, rdn to chall over 1f hd 46
out, onepace/held well ins last: op 4/1, subject of a morning gamble from 40/1: 3 month abs: won this last
term off a 9lb higher mark: acts on firm, gd/soft & both AWs: has reportedly broken blood vessels: see 844.
3855 **NORTHERN SVENGALI** 12 [22] 4-9-2 (67) Lynsey Hanna (7) 16/1: 302157: Held up in tch, held fnl 1f. ½ 63
3894 **PALAWAN** 10 [16] 4-9-11 (76) M Hills 10/1: 062538: Trkd ldrs, onepace/held when hamp ins last. nk 71
*3966 **AMERICAN COUSIN** 4 [14] Clare Roche (7) 7/2 FAV: 501119: Rear, drifted left hd 53
thr'out, nvr on terms: hvly bckd, op 9/2: qck reapp under a 7lb pen: btr 3966 (6f, fast).
3872 **SUNSET HARBOUR** 11 [18] 7-7-10 (47)(7oh) Claire Bryan 5/3: 606000: Held up, mod hdwy: 10th. hd 40
3975 **MARINO STREET** 3 [4] 7-8-7 (58) D Holland 13/2: W56620: In tch, nvr pace to chall: 11th: op 8/1. ¾ 50
3975 **HEAVENLY MISS** 3 [12] 6-8-1 (52)(bl) K Dalgleish (5) 25/1: 000000: Prom, fdd over 1f out: 12th. 1 0
3091 **PARADISE LANE** 47 [6] 4-9-9 (74) G Hind 33/1: 200000: Led till halfway: sn btn: 13th: 7 wk abs. nk 0
3653 **FAIRY PRINCE** 23 [20] 7-8-11 (62)(bl) M Roberts 20/1: 004430: V slowly away, lost all chance: 19th: 0
op 14/1: jockey reported he was unable to remove the blinds when stalls opened, best forgotten: see 3653, 2192.
3123 **Euro Venture** 45 [2] 5-9-11 (76) A Culhane 20/1:   3788 **Rythm N Time** 16 [10] 3-9-0 (66) W Supple 20/1:
3436 **Pleasure Time** 31 [7] 7-9-1 (66)(vis) R Fitzpatrick 20/1:
3825 **Miss Bananas** 14 [1] 5-7-10 (47)(3oh) G Baker (5) 25/1:
2415 **Harveys Future** 75 [13] 6-7-10 (47)(BL) A Polli (3) 16/1:
2165 **Lost In Hook** 86 [11] 3-9-7 (73) D Harrison 25/1:
20 ran   Time 1m 0.7 (2.4)   (Mrs R W Gore-Andrews)   J A R Toller Newmarket.

4028 2.50 KEGWORTH NOV STKS 2YO (D)   7f str   Good/Soft 60 -17 Slow
£4199 £1292 £646 £323   Raced towards far side

3859 **CAFETERIA BAY** 12 [4] K R Burke 2-9-5 D Holland 8/1: 131: 2 ch c Sky Classic - Go On Zen (Zen) 88
Made all, held on well fnl 1f, rdn out: op 6/1: earlier scored on debut at Yarmouth (mdn): eff up with/forcing
the pace at 6/7f, 1m shld suit: acts on fast & gd/soft grnd, gall trks: lightly raced & progressing well.
*3680 **STEEL BAND** 21 [6] H Candy 2-9-5 D Harrison 3/1: 312: 2 b c Kris - Quaver (The Minstrel) ¾ 86
Held up in tch, rcd keenly, rdn & styd on well fnl 1f, al just held by wnr: bckd: eff at 7f, return to 1m shld suit:
acts on firm & gd/soft: consistent type: see 3680.

3867 **TEEHEE** 11 [5] B Palling 2-8-12 D McGaffin (5) 33/1: 553: 2 b c Anita's Prince - Regal Charmer (Royal nk 78
And Regal) Chsd wnr, rdn/chall over 1f out, onepace/held in last: eff at 7f, return to 1m will suit: handles
gd/soft grnd: shown enough to find a mdn: see 3867, 3418.

*3705 **LOTS OF LOVE** 21 [3] M Johnston 2-9-5 M Roberts 4/9 FAV: -14: Dwelt, sn trkd ldrs, shkn up from 3 79
halfway & held over 1f out: hvly bckd at odds on: jockey reported colt had gurgled: more expected after 3705.

3675 **KENNYTHORPE BOPPY** 22 [2] 2-8-12 R Winston 66/1: -505: Chsd ldrs, btn 3f out: needs drop in grade. 7 58
5 ran   Time 1m 27.4 (5.4)   (Kenneth Lau)   K R Burke Newmarket.

4029	3.20 GOLDEN HAND SELLER 3YO (G) 1m2f Good/Soft 60 -15 Slow
	£2051 £586 £293

3816 **DILETIA** 14 [3] N A Graham 3-8-6 (bl) M Roberts 100/30 FAV: 456041: 3 b f Dilum - Miss Laetitia 56
(Entitled) Mid-div, smooth prog to lead over 2f out & readily pulled clr under hand-and-heels riding ins last: val for
6L+: bght in for 8,500gns: bckd, op 9/2: first win: eff at 1m/10f on fast & gd/soft grnd: likes a stiff/gall trk:
eff in blnks: enjoys selling grade.

3842 **THE FROG QUEEN** 13 [6] D W P Arbuthnot 3-8-6 K Dalgleish (5) 4/1: 030532: 3 b f Bin Ajwaad - 4 48
The Frog Lady (Al Hareb) Chsd ldrs, rdn/ch over 2f out, sn outpcd by wnr & position accepted cl-home: clmd
by J O'Shea for £6,000: acts on firm, gd/soft & fibresand: better off in sell h'caps: see 3842.

3691 **INDIANA SPRINGS** 21 [11] J G Given 3-8-11 J Tate 25/1: 060353: 3 b g Foxhound - Moss Agate (Alias 3½ 49$
Smith) Held up, rdn/kept on for press fnl 2f, no threat to front pair: prob handles gd & gd/soft: see 3351 (11.5f).

3260 **BEE GEE** 39 [8] M Blanshard 3-8-6 Dale Gibson 25/1: 305004: Chsd ldrs 3f out, sn held: see 1914. 2 41$

3917 **EMALI** 6 [18] A Nicholls (3) 4/1: 430325: Led over 6f out till over 2f out, fdd: needs fast? hd 45

3827 **GRANTLEY** 14 [4] D Harrison 20/1: -00006: Prom, btn 2f out: 1st time vis, mod form prev. 4 40

3266 **CENTAUR SPIRIT** 39 [15] 3-8-11 F Norton 20/1: 0-0407: Keen/mid-div, btn 3f out (1m, fast) 9 30

3816 **BEDOUIN QUEEN** 14 [13] M Hills 10/1: 600208: Rear, rdn 4f out, mod hdwy: op 7/1: btr 2248 (1m). 5 19

3624 **LANTIC BAY** 24 [7] G Duffield 20/1: 049: Chsd ldrs 6f: mod form. 2 16

3581 **DULZIE** 26 [9] A Nicholls (3) 4/1: 465500: Keen/prom 1m: 10th: op 14/1: see 589 (7f, AW). 1 15

3498 **AQUADAM** 30 [5] D McGaffin (5) 50/1: 000: Keen/led till over 6f out, btn 3f out: 11th: no form. shd 20

3624 Albergo 24 [17] 3-8-11 C Rutter 33/1:   3518 Premiere Valentino 29 [16] 3-8-11 (bl) J D Smith 33/1:
--   Boasted (t) 2-3-8-6 (t) W Supple 12/1:   2981 Sigy Point 52 [14] 3-8-6 Jonjo Fowle (5) 50/1:
3008 Minstrel Gem 50 [19] 3-8-11 J Bramhill 33/1:   41   Cromaboo Countess 310 [12] 3-8-7(1ow) A Culhane 50/1:
17 ran   Time 2m 10.3 (7.5)   (T H Chadney)   N A Graham Newmarket.

4030	3.55 EMBASSY FILL NURSERY HCAP 2YO 0-75 (E) 6f Good/Soft 60 -18 Slow	[77]
	£2990 £920 £460 £230 Raced towards centre	

2619 **LADY KINVARRAH** 67 [7] P J Makin 2-9-6 (69) Martin Dwyer 16/1: 06031: 2 b f Brief Truce - Al Corniche 73
(Bluebird) Held up, drvn & strong run fnl 1f to lead nr line: op 12/1: 2 month abs, h'cap bow, prev with J R Arnold:
eff at 6f, tried 7f, return to that trip shld suit: acts on gd/soft grnd & a stiff trk: runs well fresh: rejuvenated.

3860 **DIVINE WIND** 12 [12] B A McMahon 2-9-2 (65) J Weaver 20/1: 400002: 2 ch f Clantime - Breezy Day nk 68+
(Day Is Done) Bhd, drvn & strong run fnl 1f, post came too soon: op 25/1: left recent mod form bhd him: acts
on fast & gd/soft grnd: h'capped on early season form & caught the eye here: see 2318, 2100 & 730.

*3589 **WHITE STAR LADY** 25 [6] J R Weymes 2-8-10 (59) A Beech (3) 14/1: 505013: 2 ch f So Factual - 1 60
Cottonwood (Teenoso) Held up, prog/ch fnl 1f, onepace/held nr fin: op 10/1: eff at 5/6f on fast & gd/soft.

3807 **ROSELYN** 15 [16] I A Balding 2-9-6 (69) J Fanning 9/1: -64454: Trkd ldrs, rdn/ch fnl 1f, held nr fin: ¾ 68
h'cap bow: eff at 6f & prob handles gd/soft grnd: see 3079.

3942 **MINUSCOLO** 5 [2] A Nicholls (3) 8/1: -00635: In tch, rdn & kept on fnl 2f, not pace to 1¾ 57
chall: qck reapp: handles fast & gd/soft grnd: see 3942, 2488.

3491 **YETTI** 30 [5] C Rutter 10/1: 22536: In tch, eff over 2f out, mod hdwy: see 3491 (fm). ¾ 63

1838 **SPICE ISLAND** 100 [13] 2-8-5 (54) D Mernagh (3) 16/1: 5307: In tch, nvr pace to chall: 3 month abs. nk 46

3589 **OLYS DREAM** 25 [9] Kim Tinkler 33/1: 50608: Trkd ldrs halfway, held fnl 1f: h'cap bow. shd 46

3519 **TICCATOO** 28 [11] 2-8-11 (60) M Roberts 20/1: 000209: Led, rdn/hdd well ins last, fdd: see 2915 (fast). shd 51

3729 **MERRY DANCE** 19 [10] 2-8-12 (61) D Holland 20/1: 000: In tch, held fnl 2f: 10th: bckd, op 20/1. shd 52

3639 **GEMTASTIC** 23 [4] 2-8-9 (58) T E Durcan 14/1: 603320: Held up, no impress fnl 2f: 11th: see 3376. 1 47

*3976 **QUANTUM LADY** 3 [3] 2-9-12 (7ex) G Hind 3/1 FAV: 23641B: Held up, brght down over 2f out: 0
12th: qck reapp, 7lb pen under topweight aft 3976.

*2052 Forest Moon 91 [14] 2-8-7 (56) S Whitworth 16/1:   3491 Bali Royal 30 [22] 2-9-0 (63) P Fitzsimons (5) 25/1:
3824 Le Meridien 14 [1] 2-8-11 (60) R Winston 14/1:   3513 Ellendune Girl 29 [17] 2-9-0 (63) P Doe 14/1:
3679 Nine To Five 21 [8] 2-8-10 (59) P M Quinn (3) 33/1:   3830 Maytime 13 [21] 2-9-1 (64) D Harrison 16/1:
3576 Atemme 26 [13] 2-9-2 (65) F Norton 25/1: R
19 ran   Time 1m 14.5 (4.7)   (John Gale & George Darling)   P J Makin Ogbourne Maisey, Wilts.

4031	4.25 CHARNWOOD CLAIMER 3-4YO (F) 6f Good/Soft 60 -02 Slow
	£2429 £694 £347 3 yo rec 2 lb Raced towards centre

3975 **TALARIA** 3 [9] S C Williams 4-8-3 (t)(1ow) G Hind 7/4 FAV: 040561: 4 ch f Petardia - Million At Dawn 62
(Fayruz) Dwelt/towards rear, rdn/hdwy to lead over 1f out, in command/pushed out cl-home: well bckd, op 2/1, qck
reapp: clmd by J Pearce for £5,000: earlier scored at Nottingham (h'cap): '99 Newmarket wnr for G Wragg (mdn, rtd
86): rtd 87 in '98 (stks): eff at 6f on firm & gd/soft grnd: likes a stiff/gall trk: eff with/without a t-strap:
best without a visor: well suited by drop to claim grade today.

3584 **LUNALUX** 25 [11] C Smith 3-8-4 (BL) J Stack 20/1: 240052: 3 b f Emarati - Ragged Moon (Raga 4 52
Navarro) Bhd, rdn/hdd over 1f out, kept on late: op 12/1: sn gd run in first time blnks: eff at 6/7f on gd/soft.

3559 **TEA FOR TEXAS** 26 [12] J Akehurst 3-7-12(2ow) P Doe 14/1: 600043: 3 ch f Weldnaas - Polly's Teahouse 1 44
(Shack) Chsd ldrs, onepace fnl 1f: op 12/1: clmd by P Clinton for £4,000: acts on firm, gd/soft & equitrack.

3670 **LORDOFENCHANTMENT** 22 [5] N Tinkler 3-8-9 Kim Tinkler 9/1: 205524: Mid-div, not pace to chall. 1¼ 52

3960 **ORIEL STAR** 4 [8] 4-7-12 J Bramhill 7/1: 000005: Trkd ldrs, held fnl 1f: op 5/1, qck reapp: see 1092. ½ 37

3871 **BLACKPOOL MAMMAS** 11 [15] 3-8-0 Claire Bryan (5) 16/1: 606606: Mid-div, not pace to chall: see 1061. 1½ 37

3653 **YABINT EL SHAM** 23 [14] 4-9-0 J Weaver 16/1: 000007: Prom till over 1f out: btr 191 (AW, 5f). 1¾ 45

3578 **BOLD EMMA** 26 [7] 3-7-10 J Lowe 33/1: -06008: Handy 4f: see 2621. ¾ 27

3921 **PAMELA ANSHAN** 6 [4] 3-8-12 (vis) D O'Donohoe 33/1: 000069: Dwelt, sn rdn/outpcd, mod hdwy. hd 42$

3825 **PARADISE YANGSHUO** 14 [18] 3-8-4 W Supple 25/1: 153000: Prom till over 1f out: 10th: see 2779. shd 34

3612 **EVERBOLD** 24 [10] 3-7-10 P M Quinn (3) 33/1: -000: Dwelt, nvr on terms: 11th: mod form previously. nk 25

3332 **LADY CYRANO** 36 [19] 3-7-10 (vis) A Mackay 33/1: 020000: Chsd ldrs 6f: 12th: visor reapplied. ¾ 23

1241

LEICESTER

MONDAY SEPTEMBER 18TH   Righthand, Stiff, Galloping Track

3594 **Bennochy** 25 [1] 3-8-1 O Pears 14/1:
3559 **Ones Enough** 26 [22] 4-8-7 (tbl) F Norton 14/1:
3534 **Miss Grapette** 27 [3] 4-7-12 P Bradley (3) 33/1:
3578 **Sonbelle** 26 [21] 3-8-0 D Mernagh (3) 20/1:
20 ran   Time 1m 13.5 (3.7)   (J W Lovitt)

3573 **Danzigeuse** 26 [17] 3-8-4 K Hodgson 20/1:
2861 **Ivors Investment** 57 [20] 4-9-8 J Bosley (7) 25/1:
3770 **Phoebus** 16 [2] 3-8-9 Martin Dwyer 20/1:
3096} **Brother Tom** 412 [6] 3-8-5 P Fitzsimons (5) 33/1:
S C Williams Newmarket.

4032   **5.0 CLASS STKS DIV 1 3YO+ 0-60 (F)**   **1m str**   **Good/Soft 60**   **-05 Slow**
£2466   £759   £379   £189   3 yo rec 4 lb   Raced towards centre

3810 **CAUTIOUS JOE** 15 [1] R A Fahey 3-8-7 P Hanagan (5) 12/1: 550301: 3 b f First Trump - Jomel Amou **59**
(Ela Mana Mou) Al prom, styd on well ins last to lead fnl fin, rdn out: op 10/1: '99 Newcastle wnr (debut, auct mdn,
rtd 76): stays a stiff/gall 1m well: acts on firm & gd/soft grnd: runs well fresh.
3530 **COLLEGE ROCK** 28 [14] R Brotherton 3-9-2 (vis) P M Quinn (3) 12/1: 613042: 3 ch g Rock Hopper - Sea ½ **66$**
Aura (Roi Soleil) Held up, prog/ev ch 1f out, kept on for press: op 10/1: fine run with visor reapp: see 3094.
*3816 **HARD LINES** 14 [7] I A Balding 4-9-3 M Hills 8/1: 000413: 4 b g Silver Hawk - Arcitc Eclipse   shd **63**
(Northern Dancer) Mid-div, drvn & styd on well ins last, nrst fin: op 5/1: acts on firm & gd/soft: see 3816 (sell).
3574 **WINTZIG** 26 [19] M L W Bell 3-8-7 A Beech (3) 5/1 FAV: 033044: Prom, led 2f out till well ins last.   ½ **56**
3345 **HEATHYARDS LAD** 35 [17] M Roberts 3-8-10 M Roberts 14/1: 500345: Trkd ldrs, ch 1f out, held nr fin: op 12/1.   1 **57**
3663 **MOVING EXPERIENCE** 22 [8] 3-8-7 K Dalgleish (5) 9/1: 4-0406: Chsd ldrs, rdn held fnl 1f: see 1263 (mdn).   ¾ **53**
3842 **ERUPT** 13 [13] R Lake (7) 7-9-0 R Lake (7) 16/1: 000407: Chsd ldrs 7f: op 14/1: see 1601 (7f).   1 **54**
*3770 **AIR MAIL** 16 [5] 3-8-13 J Tate 20/1: 000018: Led 6f: new stable: btr 3770 (AW, made all, clmr).   3½ **50**
3288 **CITY FLYER** 38 [15] 3-8-13 (vis) D Harrison 20/1: 601009: Prom till over 1f out, visor: btr 3082 (fast).   1½ **47**
2986 **HAKEEM** 51 [6] 5-9-0 D Mernagh (3) 14/1: 033000: Held up, nvr on terms: 10th: op 12/1, 7 wk abs.   4 **36**
*3769 **COMPATRIOT** 16 [2] 4-9-3 G Duffield 9/1: 253610: Trkd ldrs 6f: 11th: btr 3769 (AW).   3½ **32**
3753 **GREEN GOD** 18 [11] 4-9-0 J Carroll 13/2: 500540: Chsd ldrs 6f: 12th: btr 3753 (h'cap, firm).   1¾ **26**
2546 **ADMIRALS FLAME** 70 [16] 9-9-0 A Culhane 13/2: -01330: Slowly away, al rear: 17th: op 5/1, abs.   **0**
3560 **Silver Queen** 26 [3] 3-8-7 A Nicholls (3) 14/1:
3691 **Murron Wallace** 21 [12] 6-8-11 Dean McKeown 50/1:
3871 **Regent** 11 [20] 5-9-0 A Mackay 50/1:
3936 **Shaanxi Romance** 5 [18] 5-9-6 (vis) D Holland 20/1:
2561 **Little Chapel** 69 [4] 4-8-11 R Price 50/1:
18 ran   Time 1m 39.6 (5.2)   (Tommy Staunton)   R A Fahey Butterwick, N.Yorks.

4033   **5.30 CLASS STKS DIV 2 3YO+ 0-60 (F)**   **1m str**   **Good/Soft 60**   **-05 Slow**
£2466   £759   £379   £189   3 yo rec 4 lb   Raced towards centre

3870 **WILFRAM** 11 [4] J M Bradley 3-8-13 F Norton 8/1: 632451: 3 b g Fraam - Ming Blue (Primo Dominie) **62**
Al handy, rdn/led over 1f out, held on gamely nr line, all out: jockey given 2-day whip ban: op 7/1: earlier
scored at Chepstow (mdn h'cap): stays 10f well: acts on firm & gd/soft, likes a stiff/undul track.
3557 **WAVERLEY ROAD** 26 [13] A P Jarvis 3-8-10 D Holland 20/1: 650262: 3 ch g Pelder - Lillicara   shd **58**
(Caracolero) Chsd ldrs, drvn & styd on well ins last, just held: eff arnd 1m/10f on fast & gd/soft: see 704 (mdn).
*3574 **YOUNG ROSEIN** 26 [8] Mrs G S Rees 4-9-3 G Duffield 8/1: 006113: 4 b f Distant Relative - Red Rosein 2½ **56**
(Red Sunset) Mid-div, drvn & styd on onepace fnl 2f: acts on firm & gd/soft grnd: see 3574 (fill h'cap).
3753 **DANIELLA RIDGE** 18 [3] R Hannon 4-8-11 J Carroll 12/1: 000254: Held up, styd on onepace fnl   shd **50**
2f: handles firm & gd/soft grnd: mdn: see 2789.
3696 **COOL SPICE** 21 [7] 3-8-7 D McGaffin (5) 20/1: -0465: Sn prom, onepace fnl 2f: flattered 3256 (mdn).   1 **48**
-- **GOLDEN TOUCH** [12] 8-9-0 R Price 40/1: 5600/6: Held up/keen, mod late hdwy under min press: 1 **49**
reapp, long abs: last rcd in '97: '96 wnr at W'hampton, Kempton & Newmarket (h'caps, rtd 64, D Cosgrove):
eff btwn 1m/10f on fast & gd/soft, both AWs: handles any trk & best held up: some encouragement here.
3941 **TROIS** 5 [10] 4-9-3 G Baker 16/1: 521007: Held up, rdn/mod hdwy: qck reapp: btr 3495 (AW, 9.5f).   hd **51**
3708 **OUT OF SIGHT** 23 [2] 6-9-3 A Nicholls (3) 6/1: 014348: Chsd ldrs 7f: 9th: btr 3708, 2682.   ½ **50**
3711 **SOPHOMORE** 20 [16] 6-9-0 K Dalgleish (5) 4/1 FAV: 600029: Held up, rdn/prog to lead 2f out, sn   ¾ **46**
hdd & fdd: op 6/1: btr 1731 (C/D, clmr).
3839 **SQUARE DANCER** 13 [5] 4-9-0 A Culhane 12/1: 055060: Chsd ldr, btn 2f out: 10th: btr 2830, 941 (5/6f).1½ **43**
3445 **ITS OUR SECRET** 31 [19] 4-9-0 Dale Gibson 16/1: 400500: Prom till over 1f out: 11th: see 1279.   ½ **42**
3527 **ASCARI** 28 [6] 4-9-0 (BL) Martin Dwyer 12/1: 203000: Led 6f, wknd qckly, 12th: blnks: op 10/1.   hd **41**
*3921 **WHITE SETTLER** 6 [1] 7-9-3 S Whitworth 8/1: 00-310: Nvr on terms: 13th: btr 3921 (sell, 7f, firm).   ¾ **43**
3534 **Lynton Lad** 27 [11] 8-9-3 W Supple 20/1:
4521} **Lady Muck** 328 [15] 4-8-11 R Studholme (3) 33/1:
3762 **Bajan Sunset** 17 [18] 3-8-10 M Roberts 50/1:
3344 **Kustom Kit Kevin** 35 [9] 4-9-0 Dean McKeown 50/1:
3839 **Pleading** 13 [20] 7-9-3 (vis) D Harrison 16/1:
3355 **Foxs Idea** 35 [7] 3-8-7 D Mernagh (3) 16/1:
19 ran   Time 1m 39.6 (5.2)   (R D Willis)   J M Bradley Sedbury, Glos.

KEMPTON

MONDAY SEPTEMBER 18TH   Righthand, Flat, Fair Track

Official Going   SOFT (Sprint course rode faster). Stalls: Str Course - Far Side; Rem - Inside.

4034   **2.0 EBF FILL MDN DIV 1 2YO (D)**   **7f rnd**   **Soft 115**   **-12 Slow**
£3038   £935   £467   £233   Runners came stands side in str

3730 **LIPICA** 19 [15] K R Burke 2-8-11 J P Spencer 6/4 FAV: 31: 2 b f Night Shift - Top Knot (High Top) **85+**
In tch, prog to chall appr fnl 2f, led bef dist, rdn out: hvly bckd tho' op 4/5: 3rd bhd the v smart Tobougg on debut:
half-sister to a wnr abroad, dam won up to 2m: eff at 7f, further will suit: acts on fast & soft (reportedly not
enjoy this grnd): highly regarded filly, likely to prove better than the bare form & win more races.
2182 **ISLAND QUEEN** 85 [7] R Hannon 2-8-11 R Hughes 12/1: 432: 2 b f Turtle Island - Holy Devotion 1¾ **79**
(Commanche Run) Chsd ldrs, feeling pace 2f out, rallied in last & styd on well: gd run: eff at 7f, 1m+
will suit: acts on fast, good & soft (as do many of this sire's progeny): win a race: see 2182.
-- **CHAFAYA** [5] R W Armstrong 2-8-11 M Hills 12/1: 3: 2 ch f Mark Of Esteem - Matila (Persian Bold) 1 **77**
Slow away, mid-div, clsd ent str, hmpd/switched 2f out, ev ch till onepace in last: tchd 16/1: half-sister to
3 wnrs, dam 6f juv wnr: eff at 7f on soft grnd: plenty of promise here, shld improve & find a fillies maiden.
2849 **RECIPROCAL** 58 [8] D R C Elsworth 2-8-11 N Pollard 33/1: 004: With ldr, led after halfway till ¾ **76**
bef dist, same pace: 7 wk abs: imprvd on this soft grnd, stays 7f.
-- **SHEREKIYA** [3] 2-8-11 J Murtagh 8/1: 5: In tch, late hdwy for hands & heels, nvr nrr: op 9/2: ½ **75**
clr rem: Lycius Apr foal, dam unrcd tho' bred to stay: eff at 7f, further will suit: handles soft grnd.

2653 **COCCOLONA 66** [4] 2-8-11 J Reid 33/1: 406: Chsd ldrs, no extra when bmpd 1f out: 9 wk abs.   5   68
2209 **CERTAINLY SO 84** [9] 2-8-11 S Carson (3) 50/1: 07: Mid-div thr'out: 12 wk abs: So Factual   1¾   66
half-sister to 2 wnrs, notably decent 10f performer Cugina, dam 10f wnr: with G Balding.
2583 **UNDERCOVER GIRL 68** [12] 2-8-11 B Marcus 40/1: 508: Bhd ldrs, fdd appr fnl 1f: 10 wk abs.   1   64
2687 **LAY DOWN SALLY 65** [14] 2-8-11 A Daly 20/1: 09: Led till after halfway, wknd qckly 2f out: 9 wk abs.   nk   62
3607 **LADY ANGOLA 24** [11] 2-8-11 K Darley 11/4: 40: Slow away, nvr on terms: 10th: much btr 3607 (gd).   1   61
-- **LA TRAVIATA** [6] 2-8-11 S Sanders 14/1: 0: Al towards rear: 12th on debut: Spectrum half-   0
sister to a 10f wnr, dam a fair juvenile miler: with Sir M Prescott.
-- **AMULETTE** [2] 2-8-11 R Havlin 14/1: 0: Dwelt, pulled hard, al bhd: 13th, drifter from 6/1 on   0
debut: Mark Of Esteem half-sister to sev wnrs, dam 7f/1m wnr: shld leave this bhd: with J Gosden.
-- **Like Blazes** [16] 2-8-11 P Robinson 20/1:   3829 **Florida 13** [1] 2-8-11 Lisa Somers (7) 66/1:
-- **Kiss Curl** [10] 2-8-11 A Eddery (5) 100/1:
15 ran   Time 1m 33.0 (8.9)   (Paul Green)   K R Burke Newmarket, Suffolk

---

4035	2.35 EBF FILL MDN DIV 2 2YO (D) 7f rnd Soft 115 -27 Slow
	£3038 £935 £467 £233

3752 **NAFISAH 18** [2] B Hanbury 2-8-11 R Hills 9/4 JT FAV: -221: 2 ch f Lahib - Alyakhh (Sadler's Wells)   92
Made all, came clr appr fnl 1f, rdly: well bckd tho' op 6/4: half-sister to wnrs up to 12f: dam 1m wnr: eff at
7f, apprec 1m+ in time: acts on firm & soft grnd, stiff or easy trks: eff forcing the pace: going the right way.
-- **PEARL BRIGHT** [11] J L Dunlop 2-8-11 K Darley 14/1: 2: 2 grf Kaldoun - Coastal Jewel (Kris)   3½   84
Went right start, cl-up, chall 2f out, not pace of wnr appr fnl 1f: bckd to a decent 5f juv wnr, dam
unrcd, sire a miler: stays 7f on soft grnd, 1m will suit: pleasing, improve & can win a maiden.
3359 **FOLLOW A DREAM 35** [7] Sir Michael Stoute 2-8-11 J Murtagh 9/4 JT FAV: 63: 2 b f Gone West -   3½   78+
Dance A Dream (Salder's Wells) In tch, outpcd ent str, kept on nicely ins last: bckd: must improve at 1m+.
-- **FIDDLERS MOLL** [1] B J Meehan 2-8-11 D R McCabe 16/1: 4: Cl-up till fdd ent fnl 2f: op 12/1,   1   76
debut: 51,000gns Dr Devious half-sister to decent 1m/10f wnr Blue Sky: sharper for this.
-- **ARAVONIAN** [9] 2-8-11 R Hughes 12/1: 5: Dwelt & bhd, went past btn horses fnl 2f: op 8/1 on   2½   72
debut: 16,000gns Night Shift first foal, dam a mdn: looks sure to improve for this.
3832 **IM LULU 13** [4] 2-8-11 T Ashley 33/1: 06: Front rank till wknd 2f out: see 3832.   ¾   71
3320 **SHADED MEMOIR 37** [5] 2-8-11 R Havlin 8/1: 67: Slow away, in tch till 2f out: tchd 12/1, up in trip.   hd   71
3638 **DEAR PICKLES 23** [10] 2-8-11 S W Kelly 14/1: 628: Chsd ldrs, wknd fnl 2f: op 8/1, btr 3638 (6f, gd).   hd   70
-- **MISS POLLY** [14] 2-8-11 I Mongan 50/1: 9: Nvr a factor: debut: 500gns Democratic filly.   2½   66
3752 **PENNY FARTHING 18** [12] 2-8-11 A McGlone 25/1: -000: Slow & bmpd start, nvr in race: 10th.   1¾   64
3583 **MISS MOSELLE 25** [6] 2-8-11 M Fenton 33/1: 30: In tch till ent str, eased bef dist: 13th: btr 3583 (fast).   0
-- **Phoebe Robinson** [8] 2-8-11 J Reid 33/1:   -- **On My Honour** [3] 2-8-11 R Smith (5) 50/1:
1856 **Shirley Fong 99** [15] 2-8-11 S Sanders 14/1:   3156 **Miss Phantine 44** [13] 2-8-11 D Sweeney 50/1:
15 ran   Time 1m 34.03 (9.93)   (Hamdan Al Maktoum)   B Hanbury Newmarket.

4036	3.05 EBF MDN 2YO (D) 1m rnd Soft 115 -04 Slow
	£3656 £1125 £562 £281

3786 **WORTHILY 16** [10] M R Channon 2-9-0 J Reid 14/1: -051: 2 b c Northern Spur - Worth's Girl (Devil's   93
Bag) Nvr far away, narrow lead appr fnl 1f, rdn to repel rnr-up, gamely: 20,000gns colt, dam wnr in States:
apprec 1m up to 1m, shld get mid-dists next term: clrly goes well in soft grnd: genuine & useful run here.
3840 **KINGS SECRET 13** [9] Sir Michael Stoute 2-9-0 J Murtagh 2/5 FAV: 32: 2 ch c Kingmambo - Mystery   ½   92
Rays (Nijinsky) Cl-up, led after 4f, shkn up ent fnl 2f, sn hdd, rdn & kept on but held: bckd to land the odds, clr
of rem: totally different conditions than eye-catching debut: eff at 7f/1m, handles firm & soft: shld win a maiden.
-- **SERGE LIFAR** [7] R Hannon 2-9-0 R Hughes 4/1: 3: 2 b c Shirley Heights - Ballet (Sharrood)   7   82
Chsd ldrs, switched & effort ent fnl 2f, sn outpcd: op 7/1 on debut: 18,000gns half-brother to useful
1m juv Island Sound: clr of rem here but will prob be seen to better effect over mid-dists next term.
3333 **TOKEN 36** [2] M P Tregoning 2-9-0 A Daly 14/1: -04: Keen, near, moderate hdwy ent str, sn no extra.   8   70
3864 **DINOFELIS 12** [11] M Fenton 20/1: 05: Prom till fdd appr fnl 2f: see 3864.   13   54
3910 **PLAYONETOONEDOTCOM 7** [8] 2-8-9 J Quinn 50/1: 006: Nvr a factor: qck reapp, no form.   4   43
3692 **BELLINO EMPRESARIO 21** [3] 2-9-0 K Darley 50/1: 07: Led till halfway, lost pl: breathing problems.   2   45
-- **LE FANTASME** [4] 2-9-0 O Urbina 25/1: 8: Dwelt, nvr troubled ldrs: debut: 42,000FFr Fairy   ¾   44
King Mar foal, half-brother a wnr at 12f: v stoutly bred, with S Dow.
2583 **PRIMO VENTURE 68** [1] 2-8-9 M Tebbutt 25/1: 609: Sn struggling: 10 wk absence, see 2390.   5   32
3412 **THUNDERED 32** [6] 2-9-0 W Ryan 33/1: 00: Bhd from halfway: 10th: see 3412.   9   27
10 ran   Time 1m 46.3 (9.5)   (Salem Suhail)   M R Channon West Ilsley, Berks.

4037	3.40 TOTE QUICK PICK HCAP 3YO 0-90 (C) 6f Good/Soft Inapplicable	[97]
	£7930 £2440 £1220 £610 2 Groups, stands side had a big advantage	

3771 **RANDOM TASK 16** [2] D Shaw 3-8-2 (70)(BL) (1ow) J Quinn 33/1: 14-061: 3 b c Tirol - Minami (Caerleon)   73
Cl-up stands side, rdn appr fnl 1f, led ins last & ran on well: '99 wnr at W'hampton (debut, mdn, rtd 87a),
well btn last of 4 on turf, rtd 63): suited to drop back to 6f: acts on gd/soft grnd & fibresand, easy trks:
lightly raced, set alight by blnks today.
*3343 **GREY EMINENCE 36** [7] R Hannon 3-9-5 (88) R Hughes 7/1: -22212: 3 gr c Indian Ridge - Rahaam   1   87
(Secreto) Cl-up stands side, kept on for press appr fnl 1f, nrst fin: bckd from 10/1: eff at 6/7f, stays 1m.
3937 **BLUE VELVET 5** [4] K T Ivory 3-9-6 (89) C Carver (3) 11/1: 650623: 3 grf Formidable - Sweet   shd   88
Whisper (Petong) Cl-up stands side, led 2f out, edged right dist, sn hdd, kept on: qck reapp: game filly.
3516 **BANDANNA 29** [5] R J Hodges 3-8-13 (82) J P Spencer 25/1: 516354: Held up stands side, prog to   hd   80
chase ldrs 1f out, onepace nr fin: clr rem, op 16/1: ran to best, acts on firm & gd/soft grnd, see 2787.
*3820 **ULYSSES DAUGHTER 14** [9] 3-8-4 (72)(1) (1ow) W Ryan 12/1: 4215: Dwelt stands side, chsd   3½   64
ldrs by halfway, no extra dist: h'cap bow, shade btr 3820 (mdn).
3791 **PEDRO JACK 16** [3] 3-8-13 (82) D Glennon (7) 25/1: 522066: Led stands side till 2f out, no extra: 1   70
op 16/1: faster grnd suits & poss just better in blnks: see 1289.
3322 **MELANZANA 37** [8] 3-9-0 (83) M Tebbutt 25/1: 425607: Nvr troubled ldrs stands side: op 16/1.   3   64
3894 **LABRETT 10** [18] 3-8-4 (73)(bl) D R McCabe 20/1: 011408: In tch far side, not much room ent   shd   54
fnl 2f, ran on well ins last to lead that group nr fin, no ch stands side: wnr without a pen? keep in mind.
3793 **ROYAL INSULT 16** [1] 3-8-11 (80) Darren Williams (5) 33/1: 1-0009: Al bhd stands side: back in trip.   hd   60
3904 **DANCING EMPRESS 9** [17] 3-8-4 (73)(BL) P Robinson 20/1: 240600: Cl-up far side, led that group   nk   52

halfway till cl-home: 10th, blnkd: wrong side, much better than fin position suggests: see 3904.

3414	**NAJEYBA** 32 [16] 3-8-6 (75) B Marcus 20/1: 134000: Led far side grp after 2f till bef fnl 2f, no extra: 11th.	1	52
3920	**STAR PRINCESS** 6 [20] 3-8-5 (74)(vis) C Catlin (7) 16/1: 425330: Al same pl far side: 12th, st/mate 3rd.	3	44
2003	**RAVISHING** 93 [10] 3-8-11 (80) S W Kelly (3) 14/1: -41000: Chsd far side ldrs till 2f out: 13th, abs.	hd	49
*3698	**CHIQUITA** 21 [15] 3-8-11 (80) K Darley 13/2: 000210: Al bhd far side: 17th, ignore, see 3698.		0
3698	**BUDELLI** 21 [24] 3-8-11 (80) Craig Williams 6/1 FAV: 125020: Rear far side, no room 2f out: 19th, bckd.		0
3904	**MOLLY BROWN** 9 [11] 3-9-7 (90) R Hills 14/1: 001220: Speed till halfway stands side: 21st, stablemate 2nd.		0
3510	**Lakeland Paddy** 29 [13] 3-8-6 (75) D Sweeney 16/1:	3569 **La Caprice** 26 [6] 3-8-12 (81) G Carter 16/1:		
3820	**Risky Reef** 14 [14] 3-8-1 (70) M Henry 33/1:	3750 **Queens Bench** 18 [23] 3-8-6 (73)(2ow) M Fenton 20/1:		
3791	**Las Ramblas** 16 [21] 3-8-8 (76)(1ow) J Reid 20/1:	3750 **Effervescent** 18 [22] 3-8-2 (71) N Pollard 20/1:		
3908	**Chorus** 9 [19] 3-8-1 (70)(vis) J Quinn 20/1:			

23 ran   Time 1m 15.66 (4.56)   (J C Fretwell)   D Shaw Averham, Notts.

4038   **4.10 NORMAN HILL HCAP 3YO+ 0-80 (D)   1m rnd   Soft 115   -02 Slow**   **[80]**
£4836   £1488   £744   £372   3 yo rec 4 lb

3979	**SWEET REWARD** 3 [17] J G Smyth Osbourne 5-8-12 (64) M Fenton 10/1: 035331: 5 ch g Beveled - Sweet Revival (Claude Monet) In tch, trkd ldr going well 2f out, shkn up to lead dist, idled, rdn out: tchd 14/1, qck reapp: plcd sev times in '99 (h'caps, rtd 73): last won in '97 at Leicester (mdn auct, rtd 80): has run over hdles (rtd 101h): eff at 10f, suited by 1m: acts on fast, loves hvy: likes Leicester, RH'd trk: tough.		68
3514	**PAGAN KING** 29 [5] J A R Toller 4-9-0 (66) J P Spencer 10/1: -00432: 4 b g Unblest - Starinka (Risen Star) Rear, hdwy ent fnl 2f, rdn/switched 1f out, grad clsd on wnr, not btn far: in-form, likes soft grnd.	½	69
3885	**BOLD RAIDER** 10 [1] I A Balding 3-8-11 (67) W Ryan 7/1 FAV: -12343: 3 b g Rudimentary - Spanish Heart (King Of Spain) Cl-up, led appr fnl 1f, rdn & hdd 1f out, kpt on: clr rem: consistent, see 1822, 1024.	hd	70
3471	**LOCOMBE HILL** 30 [8] M Blanshard 4-9-11 (77) J Quinn 20/1: 303004: Cl-up, led after halfway till bef fnl 1f, no extra: signs of return to form & well h'capped if so: see 1474.	4	74
*3115	**SILK DAISY** 45 [3] 4-9-0 (66) A McGlone 10/1: 451515: Held up, prog to chase ldrs 2f out, sn onepace: op 7/1, 6 wk abs: btr 3115 (fast grnd).	½	62
-3750	**APLOY** 18 [18] 3-9-6 (76) R Hills 10/1: 451226: Chsd ldrs, rdn 2f out, no impress: visor omitted, clr rem: just better at 7f & prefers faster grnd: see 2978.	¾	71
3826	**ABAJANY** 14 [6] 6-9-6 (72) Craig Williams 14/1: 4-0007: Last, prog into mid-div appr fnl 2f: see 3642.	5	60
3669	**TAMMAM** 22 [15] 4-10-0 (80) S W Kelly (3) 20/1: 344668: Bhd, modest late hdwy: jt top-weight.	1½	66
2770	**SINCERITY** 61 [2] 3-9-7 (77) O Urbina 14/1: -0239: Chsd ldrs till appr fnl 1f: 9 wk abs, h'cap bow.	hd	63
3919	**WIND CHIME** 6 [14] 3-9-4 (74) B Marcus 25/1: 200220: Chsd ldrs till wknd 2f out: 10th, qk reapp.	hd	59
3831	**FINAL DIVIDEND** 13 [20] 4-9-4 (70) D R McCabe 16/1: 0-4500: Nvr a factor: 11th: see 705.	shd	55
3831	**KNOCKTOPHER ABBEY** 13 [12] 3-9-5 (75) S Sanders 12/1: 053650: In tch till appr fnl 2f: 12th.	1¼	59
1765	**INDIAN SUN** 103 [19] 3-9-6 (76)(BL) K Darley 8/1: 460020: Led till after halfway, lost place: 15th: op 5/1, 15 wk abs: blnkd, much btr without 1765, see 792.		0
3831	**BYZANTIUM GB** 13 [16] 6-9-1 (67) R Hughes 10/1: 0-5430: Prom 5f: 17th, op 7/1: needs faster grnd.		0
3857	**SMOOTH SAND** 12 [10] 3-9-8 (78) P Robinson 12/1: -11360: Al bhd: last, op 8/1, regressive since 892.		0
3794	**Secret Spring** 16 [11] 8-9-12 (78) I Mongan (5) 33/1:	3791 **Indian Blaze** 16 [4] 6-10-0 (80) N Pollard 14/1:		
3936	**Time For Music** 5 [7] 3-9-8 (78) L Carter 33/1:	3076 **Jazzy Millennium** 47 [18] 3-8-11 (67) A Clark 33/1:		

19 ran   Time 1m 46.12 (9.32)   (Mrs Andria Dorler & Partners)   J G Smyth Osbourne Adstone, Northants.

4039   **4.45 EBF CLASS STKS 3YO+ 0-90 (C)   1m4f   Soft 115   +06 Fast**
£7058   £2677   £1338   £608   3 yo rec 8 lb

1484	**ZILARATOR** 116 [6] W J Haggas 4-9-4 B Marcus 11/2: 5-6161: 4 b g Zilzal - Allegedly (Sir Ivor) Towards rear, smooth prog ent str, led bef 2f out, drvn clr: nicely bckd tho' 9/2, best time of day, 4 month abs: earlier won at Epsom (val h'cap): '99 Leicester wnr (mdn, rtd 89): eff at 12/15f, acts on gd grnd, loves soft & hvy: handles any trk: goes well fresh: useful & progressive on this grnd, win more races.		97
3918	**PURPLE HEATHER** 6 [8] R Hannon 3-8-9 R Hughes 8/1: 021402: 3 b f Rahy - Clear Attraction (Lear Fan) Cl-up, chall appr fnl 2f, kept on for 2nd but no ch wnr: drifter from 4/1, qck reapp: blnks omitted: prob stays an easy 12f on soft grnd but 10f on fast is ideal: see 3189.	6	89
*3813	**ROYAL TRYST** 3 [3] Sir Michael Stoute 3-8-12 J Murtagh 5/2 FAV: -213: 3 ch c Kingmambo - In On The Secret (Secretariat) Trkd ldrs, ev ch 2f out, no extra dist: hvly bckd: not disgraced up in trip/grade: acts on fast & good with another look, prob back at 10f: see 3813.	2½	90
3669	**JUST IN TIME** 22 [2] T G Mills 5-9-4 J Reid 13/2: 305044: Set decent clip, hdd ent str, same pace.	¾	87
1198	**KUSTER** 133 [5] 4-9-4 J P Spencer 10/3: 20-424: Chsd ldrs, rdn ent str, kept on onepace: bckd from 9/2, over 4 month abs: longer trip, see 1198.	dht	87
3563	**AL AZHAR** 26 [9] 6-9-4 A Clark 25/1: 30-506: Al bhd & btn & eased 2f out: back up in trip, see 757.	15	75
1198	**BOW STRADA** 133 [1] 3-8-10 M Fenton 9/1: 11-57: Prom 1m, losing place when bmpd 2f out: op 6/1, over 4 month abs, longer trip, see 1198.	1¼	74
3049	**FAMOUS** 49 [4] 7-9-4 I Mongan (5) 100/1: 000008: Nvr a factor: abs: impossible task, flattered.	5	67$
3751	**SHEER SPIRIT** 18 [7] 3-8-9 N Pollard 16/1: 3149: Keen, al bhd, t.o.: tchd 20/1, reportedly has breathing problems: first run on soft grnd: see 2963.	dist	0

9 ran   Time 2m 43.11 (13.11)   (Wentworth Racing Pty Ltd)   W J Haggas Newmarket.

4040   **5.15 JOYCE MCCRINDLE MDN 3YO (D)   1m4f   Soft 115   -08 Slow**
£4062   £1250   £625   £312

3813	**DANCE DIRECTOR** 15 [2] J H M Gosden 3-9-0 K Darley 6/4 FAV: -421: 3 b c Sadler's Wells - Memories (Hail The Pirates) In tch, prog to lead 2f out, shkn up, eased cl home, val 5L+: well bckd: unrcd juv, related to a high-class 6/7f performer: clrly apprec step up to 12f: acts on gd & soft grnd, flat/gall trks: progressive colt.		89
3517	**SALUEM** 29 [11] R Guest 3-8-9 S Sanders 8/1: -322: 3 b f Salse - Pat Or Else (Alzao) Chsd ldrs, rdn to chase wnr appr fnl 1f, kept on but no ch: consistent, eff at 12f on fast & soft: shkd win a race.	3	76
3754	**DISTANT COUSIN** 18 [18] H R A Cecil 3-8-9 W Ryan 9/1: 23: 3 b c Distant Relative - Tinaca (Manila) Prom, rdn 2f out, kept on but not pace to chall: op 7/1: handles firm & soft grnd: see 3754.	nk	80
3178	**ISLAND PRINCESS** 43 [3] D R C Elsworth 3-8-9 P Robinson 14/1: 20-504: Keen, wide, led till 2f out, onepace: 6 wk abs: longer trip, drop back to 10f will suit: see 1045.	1¾	74
2249	**GUARD DUTY** 82 [13] 3-9-0 A Daly 10/1: 3-6245: Held up, mod late hdwy, nvr dangs: no blnks.	3½	76
3838	**SELVORINE** 13 [6] 3-8-9 R Hughes 20/1: -506: Well plcd till fdd appr fnl 2f: longer trip, see 3179.	6	66
3381	**POLAR STAR** 33 [12] 3-9-0 J Reid 10/1: 2-0457: Pulled hard bhd ldrs, wknd 2f out: op 7/1, lngr trip.	½	70

1244

KEMPTON MONDAY SEPTEMBER 18TH Righthand, Flat, Fair Track

--	**OCEAN TIDE** [19] 3-9-0 J P Spencer 14/1: 48: Nvr better than mid-div: abs: 4th of 5 prev start in Italy.	1½	69
--	**HIGH BARN** [1] 3-8-9 O Urbina 10/1: 9: Nvr a factor: debut: Shirley Heights filly out of a smart stayer.	6	59
4606}	**DENA** 318 [9] 3-8-9 M Tebbutt 8/1: 5-0: Pulled hard, nvr on terms: 10th, tchd 12/1 on reapp:	2	58

5th of 20 sole '99 start (mdn, rtd 78): stoutly bred filly with W Jarvis

4613} **PRIDE OF INDIA** 317 [15] 3-9-0 G Carter 20/1: -0-0: Nvr nr ldrs: 12th on reapp: unplcd sole '99 start: half-brother to a 14f wnr, shld do better in mid-dist h'caps: with J Dunlop. **0**

1831 **STORM WIZARD** 101 [16] 3-9-0 Craig Williams 9/1: 342200: Nvr a threat: 18th, tchd 12/1, 15 wk abs: broke a blood vessel latest: see 1193. **0**

--	**Terimons Dream** [5] 3-9-0 J Quinn 33/1:	3524	**The Proof** 28 [4] 3-9-0 S Carson (3) 33/1:
3189	**Plain Chant** 42 [8] 3-9-0 M Fenton 33/1:	2924	**Cavania** 54 [17] 3-8-9 B Marcus 20/1:
--	**Followeroffashion** [14] 3-9-0 N Pollard 33/1:	3242	**Super Dominion** 40 [7] 3-9-0 D Sweeney 33/1:
3813	**Attacker** 15 [10] 3-9-0 J Murtagh 50/1:		

19 ran   Time 2m 44.79 (14.79)   (Mr R E Sangster)   J H M Gosden Manton, Wilts

---

BEVERLEY TUESDAY SEPTEMBER 19TH Righthand, Oval Track with Stiff Uphill Finish

Official Going: HEAVY. Stalls: Inside. Racing abandoned after 6th race due to unsafe conditions (hvy rain).

4041 2.00 GO RACING SELLER 3YO+ (G) 1m4f Soft/Heavy 123 -78 Slow
£2054 £587 £293 3 yo rec 8 lb

3804 **FIELD OF VISION** 16 [5] Mrs A Duffield 10-9-10 G Duffield 7/2 JT FAV: 522241: 10 b g Vision - Bold Meadows (Persian Bold) In tch, eff 3f out, kept on well under press to held in ldr ins last, going away: bckd, slow time, no bid: earlier won at Carlisle (claimer): lightly rcd, incl over hdles since '98 wnr at Hamilton & here at Beverley (h'caps, rtd 72 & 67a): eff at 12/14f: acts on firm, soft/hvy, both AW's, likes stiff finishes. **42**

3633 **KINGS CHAMBERS** 24 [4] J Parkes 4-9-5 (t) P Fessey 16/1: 000552: 4 ch g Sabrehill - Flower Girl (Pharly) Tried to make all, rdn & 3L clr ent fnl 2f, onepce & worn down inside last: stays 12f on hvy. 2¾ **33$**

3773 **COOL VIBES** 17 [13] Mrs N Macauley 5-9-5 (vis) R Fitzpatrick 25/1: 000003: 5 br g Rock City - Meet Again (Lomond) In tch, rdn ent fnl 3f, styd on but unable to chall: eff at 1m, stays 12f on firm & soft/hvy. 1¾ **31**

3827 **RED ROSES** 3 [2] Don Enrico Incisa 4-9-0 Kim Tinkler 15/2: 400434: Bhd, late hdwy, nvr a threat. 2¾ **24$**

3677 **KAILAN SCAMP** 23 [14] (t) D Mernagh (3) 50/1: -05: Prom, eff 3f out, no impress: t-strap. 3½ **21**

3916 **MOON COLONY** 8 [8] A Hawkins (7) 9/2: 650-06: Nvr troubled ldrs tho' stying on fin: see 3916. 1½ **25**

3633 **GO WITH THE WIND** 24 [3] 7-9-5 K Darley 7/2 JT FAV: 3-0327: Handy, drvn appr fnl 3f, flashed tail 2f out & btn: op 5/2, faster grnd suits, see 2742. 1½ **24**

3935 **SILKEN LADY** 6 [7] 4-9-0 P Robinson 16/1: 036058: Nvr a factor: stiff task, quick reapp. 5 **14**

3715 **MISS ARCH** 21 [6] 4-9-0 Dean McKeown 14/1: -50309: Al bhd: op 10/1, stiff task, see 3570. ¾ **13**

3808 **NIGHT OF GLORY** 16 [11] 5-9-0 (BL) C Rutter 40/1: 50-000: Struggling halfway: 10th, blnkd, lngr trip. 17 **0**

3808 **GOLDEN ACE** 16 [10] 7-9-5 (tbl) A Mackay 6/1: -45000: Prom till 4f out: 12th, op 5/2, see 791. 3 **0**

438}	**Peter Perfect** 592 [15] 6-9-5 C Teague 50/1:	3344	**Cairn Dhu** 36 [9] 6-9-5 Kimberley Hart 33/1:
51	**Danny Deever** 309 [1] 4-9-5 T Lucas 25/1:		

14 ran   Time 2m 55.5 (24.2)   (Mrs L J Tounsend)   Mrs A Duffield Constable Burton, N Yorks

4042 2.30 THISISHULL NOV STKS 2YO (D) 5f Soft/Heavy 123 +01 Fast
£3679 £1132 £566 £283

*3639 **MY LOVELY** 24 [6] D J S Cosgrove 2-8-9 J Quinn 12/1: 11: 2 b f Dolphin Street - My Bonus (Cyrano de Bergerac) Trckd ldrs, switched & ran on strongly appr fnl 1f, led fnl 100y, readily: best time of day: earlier won a Windsor seller on debut: Feb first foal, dam 5f wnr: eff at 5f, will get 6f: acts on gd, improved on this soft/hvy grnd: handles any track: goes well fresh: improving, shld win again. **86**

*3252 **KYLLACHY** 40 [7] H Candy 2-9-2 C Rutter 11/8 FAV: 12: 2 b c Pivotal - Pretty Poppy (Song) Nvr far away, led appr fnl 1f till fnl 100y, no extra: hvly bckd, clr rem, abs: acts on fast & soft/hvy grnd. 2½ **86**

3844 **SPEEDY GEE** 16 [3] M R Channon 2-9-5 Craig Williams 6/4: 560463: 2 b c Petardia - Champagne Girl (Robellino) Chsd ldr, fdd 1f out: bckd, clr rem: not handle sft/hvy? useful from on gd grnd in 3844. 5 **79**

3576 **ZIETING** 27 [5] K R Burke 2-8-12 N Callan 20/1: -054: Nvr going pace: see 3576 (fm). 11 **47**

3767 **BABY MAYBE** 18 [1] 2-8-7 P Robinson 100/1: 005: Set decent pace, hdd appr fnl 1f, sn btn. 1½ **38**

-- **BEANBOY** [2] 2-8-8 Dean McKeown 100/1: 6: Dwelt, al bhd: debut: 1,250gns Clantime colt. hd **38**

-- **BOLHAM LADY** [9] 2-8-3 J Edmunds 100/1: 7: Bhd halfway: Timeless Times half-sister to a 12f wnr. 3½ **25**

2082 **KENTUCKY BOUND** 90 [8] 2-8-12 J P Spencer 4/1: -08: Sn struggling: bckd from 9/1 after 3 mnth abs. 4 **24**

8 ran   Time 1m 07.4 (6.1)   (Mrs Jean McGinn)   D J S Cosgrove Newmarket, Suffolk

4043 3.00 V & E SMITH COND STKS 3YO+ (C) 5f Soft/Heavy 123 -11 Slow
£5916 £2244 £1122 £510 3 yo rec 1 lb

3841 **ROSSELLI** 14 [6] A Berry 4-8-9 (BL) J Carroll 7/2: 026031: 4 b h Puissance - Miss Rossi (Artaius) Led, drvn appr fnl 1f, kept on well: op 11/4: 5th in a Gr 3 last term (rtd 105): smart juv, won at Newcastle, here at Beverley (stks) & R Ascot (Gr 3, rtd 110): stays 6f, suited by 5f: acts on fast, best on soft/hvy: runs well fresh, any trk, likes stiff/gall ones: eff with/without t-strap: v useful, back to form in blnks. **108**

3982 **VITA SPERICOLATA** 4 [1] J S Wainwright 3-8-3 G Bardwell 2/1: 033042: 3 b g Prince Sabo - Ahonita (Ahonoora) Mid-div, prog to chase wnr appr fnl 1f, kept on but held: bckd from 5/2, quick reapp: sound run: acts on firm & soft/hvy grnd: useful & consistent: see 3982, 1529. ¾ **100**

-3521 **PROUD NATIVE** 29 [10] D Nicholls 6-8-9 K Darley 7/4 FAV: 206223: 6 b g Imp Society - Karamana (Habitat) Well plcd, rdn appr fnl 1f, unable to qckn: nicely bckd tho' op 5/4: capable of better, see 1172. 1¾ **101**

3841 **PALACEGATE JACK** 14 [8] A Berry 9-8-9 P Bradley (5) 66/1: 456054: Bhd ldrs, slightly hmpd ent fnl 2f, outpcd: stablemate of wnr: flattered once again but clearly retains enough ability to win another seller/claimer. 3 **92$**

3521 **DISTANT KING** 29 [3] 7-8-9 A Nicholls 100/1: 600005: Rear, eff halfway, kept on same pace: flattered. 3½ **82$**

2897} **PLUM FIRST** 423 [2] 10-8-9 Kimberley Hart 100/1: 4056-6: Prom till 2f out: reapp, flattered: unplcd in '99 (h'cap, rtd 50, J Wainwright): last won in '95 at Pontefract & Warwick (stakes, rtd 60): eff at 5/6f on hvy grnd, fibresand, any trk: eff with/without blnks or visor: with N Wilson. 3 **73$**

3623} **MELON PLACE** 388 [9] 3-8-8 N Callan 9/1: 231-7: Chsd wnr till 2f out: reapp: landed fnl of 3 '99 starts, at Goodwood (mdn auct, Listed 3rd, rtd 96): eff at 5f on firm/fast grnd, sharp/undulating or gall track: can force the pace & run well fresh: should leave this bhd on a faster surface: with K Burke. 7 **57**

-- **LEVENDI** [11] 3-8-8 R Winston 100/1: 8: Dwelt, nvr in it: Mukaddamah gldg, v highly tried on debut. *¾* **55**
3653 **TIME TO FLY 24** [7] 7-8-9 (bl) K Hodgson 66/1: 040069: V slow away, al bhd: v stiff task, see 2525. *3½* **46$**
2847 **DON PUCCINI 59** [5] 3-8-8 M Tebbutt 8/1: 61-500: Prom till after halfway: 10th, tchd 10/1, *hd* **46**
8 week abs: needs faster grnd: see 1987.
10 ran Time 1m 08.0 (6.7) (T G Holdcroft) A Berry Cockerham, Lancs

4044 **3.30 MERRINGTON HCAP DIV 1 3YO+ 0-70 (E) 7f100y rnd Soft/Heavy 123 -29 Slow [70]**
£2769 £852 £426 £213 3 yo rec 3 lb

2694 **MELODIAN 66** [4] M Brittain 5-9-8 (64)(bl) D Mernagh (3) 8/1: 100001: 5 b h Grey Desire - Mere Melody (Dunphy) Prom, led ent fnl 2f, sn rdn, drftd right, held on well: op 6/1, 9 week abs, slow time: earlier won at Newcastle & here at Beverley (h'caps): '99 wnr again here at Beverley, Doncaster & Catterick (h'caps, rtd 56): '98 Newcastle wnr (h'cap, rtd 44): eff at 7/7.5f, stays 1m: acts on firm, suited by gd/soft & hvy: goes on any track, likes Beverley: wears blnks & best up with/forcing the pace: v tough. **72**
*3951 **THIHN 6** [11] J L Spearing 5-9-3 (59)(6ex) A Beech (3) 7/4 FAV: 002312: 5 ch g Machiavellian - Hasana (Private Account) Towards rear, stdy prog & short of room 2f out, rdn to chase wnr ins last, kept on but held: clr rem, well bckd from 3/1, qk reapp & pen: improving: goes on firm & soft/hvy grnd: see 3951. *1* **65**
3765 **ANNIJAZ 18** [7] J G Portman 3-9-0 (59) G Baker (5) 12/1: 103523: 3 b f Alhijaz -Figment (Posse) Rear, improved to go 3rd dist, nvr dangerous: not handle soft/hvy? see 3765, 2794. *7* **55**
3652 **KASS ALHAWA 24** [1] D W Chapman 7-9-11 (67) A Culhane 9/1: 422504: Bhd, went past btn horses appr fnl 1f: big weight to carry in these conditions: see 38. *4* **56**
3631 **MILL END QUEST 24** [13] 5-8-13 (55)(bl) T Lucas 14/1: -01005: Cl up, eff & not clr run appr fnl 1f, lost place & no threat: longer trip, poss worth another chance at 7.5f: see 3123. *3* **39**
3939 **ARZILLO 6** [9] 4-8-2 (44) F Norton 8/1: 050026: In tch till appr fnl 1f: op 11/2, qck reapp, see 1211. *1¾* **26**
1611 **REX IS OKAY 111** [14] 4-9-11 (67) K Darley 9/1: 026007: Pressed ldr till wknd ent fnl 2f: nr 4 mnth abs. *4* **42**
3809 **CUSIN 16** [2] 4-9-8 (64) T Hamilton (7) 7/1: 000528: Keen, nvr a factor: op 4/1: btr 3809 (gd). *nk* **38**
3407 **TRAIKEY 33** [12] 8-8-2 (44) J Quinn 20/1: 000-09: Hmpd start, al bhd: see 3407. *1½* **15**
3809 **NODS NEPHEW 16** [5] 3-9-6 (65) J P Spencer 6/1: 400100: Led till ent fnl 2f, wknd quickly: 10th, tchd 8/1: much btr 3670 (C/D claimer on fast grnd). *5* **28**
2816 **EVER REVIE 60** [16] 3-8-6 (51) S Whitworth 14/1: 014000: Mid-div till 3f out: 11th, tchd 25/1, 9 wk abs. *9* **0**
3839 **SCAFELL 14** [15] 3-9-1 (60)(vis) R Winston 16/1: 531000: Prom 4f: 12th, vis reapp, needs faster grnd? *9* **0**
12 ran Time 1m 42.2 (11.4) (Mel Brittain) M Brittain Warthill, N Yorks

4045 **4.00 INFO@BEVERLEY HCAP 3YO 0-70 (E) 1m100y rnd Soft/Heavy 123 -13 Slow [77]**
£3360 £1034 £517 £258 First 4 home stayed on inside rail after halfway

*3806 **ENTITY 16** [16] T D Barron 3-9-0 (63) D O'Donohoe 5/2 FAV: 001211: 3 ch g Rudimentary - Desert Ditty (Green Desert) Well plcd, trav strgly, went on 2f out, shkn up & sn clr, easing down: nicely bckd from 7/2: earlier won at Hamilton (2, mdn h'cap & h'cap): promise more than once as a juv (nurs, rtd 71): eff at 1m/10f: acts on firm & soft/hvy grnd, any track, likes stiff finishes: best without blnks: progressive, in fine form. **73**
*3226 **RUDETSKI 41** [14] M Dods 3-8-6 (55) A Clark 7/1: 065612: 3 b g Rudimentary - Butosky (Busted) Rear, kept on stdly fnl 2f & went 2nd well ins last, nvr nr wnr: 6 wk abs: acts on fast & soft/hvy: see 3226. *6* **55**
2945 **BOSS TWEED 53** [15] Ronald Thompson 3-9-2 (65) F Lynch 25/1: 310503: 3 b g Persian Bold - Betty Kenwood (Dominion) Led till 2f out, onepce: clr rem, 8 wk abs: eff on soft/hvy grnd & both AW's: see 827. *2* **61**
2515 **BENBYAS 73** [9] J L Eyre 3-8-8 (57)(BL) R Cody Boutcher (7) 25/1: 061004: Handy, rdn & edged left appr fnl 2f, outpcd: 10 week abs: tried blnks: see 1723 (visored, gd/soft). *6* **43**
3769 **WELCOME TO UNOS 17** [2] 3-8-13 (62) A Culhane 25/1: 020655: Nvr a factor & wide into straight. *10* **30**
3810 **ROYAL CAVALIER 16** [1] 3-9-7 (70) P M Quinn (3) 16/1: 062006: Wide, nvr on terms: see 2250, 720. *5* **30**
3793 **HINT OF MAGIC 17** [4] 3-9-7 (70)(t) G Baker (5) 20/1: -44007: Wide, in tch till 3f out: see 873, 713. *7* **18**
3793 **TAKE MANHATTAN 17** [12] 3-9-7 (70) Craig Williams 7/1: 016648: Chsd ldrs, wide 3f out, sn btn. *3½* **12**
3345 **STORMVILLE 36** [13] 3-8-13 (62) D Mernagh (3) 16/1: 400269: Prom till edged left & wknd 3f out. *1¾* **1**
2524 **MARVEL 72** [10] 3-8-8 (57) Kim Tinkler 12/1: 020360: Wide, nvr trbld ldrs: 10th, 10 wk abs, see 2235. *3* **0**
1964 **YERTLE 95** [6] 3-9-2 (65) S Whitworth 6/1: -00360: Wide, al towards rr: 11th, op 7/2, see 1435 (fast). *2* **0**
3163 **ATYLAN BOY 45** [11] 3-9-2 (65) K Darley 8/1: 524600: Mid div, wide, lost place halfway: 13th, tchd 12/1, abs. **0**
3914 **LAHAAY 8** [7] 3-9-7 (70) W Supple 7/1: 045360: Bhd from halfway: 16th, top-weight, see 3217 (10f, fast). **0**
3764 **Madurese 18** [8] 3-9-3 (66) P Robinson 20/1: 3328 **Glendamah 37** [5] 3-9-3 (66) J Quinn 20/1:
1412 **Aisle 122** [3] 3-8-8 (57) G Duffield 25/1:
16 ran Time 1m 55.4 (11.6) (Mrs J Hazell) T D Barron Maunby, N Yorks

4046 **4.30 FORWARD HCAP DIV 1 3YO+ 0-60 (F) 1m2f Soft/Heavy 123 -01 Slow [60]**
£2184 £624 £312 3 yo rec 6 lb

3737 **LEVEL HEADED 20** [5] P W Hiatt 5-8-12 (44) A Mackay 14/1: 134101: 5 b m Beveled - Snowline (Bay Express) Rcd wide 4f, made all, drew well clr fnl 3f, drvn out: earlier won at Bath & Lingfield (fill h'caps): unplcd in '99 (rtd 40, E Wheeler): eff forcing the pace at 10f on firm & hvy: qk follow-up on similar grnd? **58**
3401 **RATIFIED 34** [2] H Candy 3-9-2 (54) C Rutter 4/1 FAV: 214052: 2 b g Not In Doubt - Festival Of Magic (Clever Trick) Rcd wide for 4f & chsd wnr throughout, left bhd appr fnl 2f: bckd from 7/1, clr rem. *20* **52**
4006 **KIERCHEM 3** [1] C Grant 9-8-12 (44) T Hamilton (7) 16/1: 004303: 9 b g Mazaad - Smashing Gale (Lord Gayle) Nvr a factor tho' went through btn horses to take 3rd inside last: quick reapp: see 2099. *10* **32**
3842 **NIGHT DIAMOND 14** [14] I A Balding 3-9-5 (57)(t) K Darley 7/1: 424104: Chsd ldrs till 3f out. *3½* **42**
3396 **FISHER ISLAND 34** [4] 3-9-1 (53) P M Quinn (3) 16/1: 040105: Handy 7f: btr 2685 (fast grnd). *6* **32**
4021 **SHARP BELLINE 3** [8] 3-8-13 (51) G Baker (5) 7/1: 340426: Nvr better than mid div: bckd from 9/1, quick reapp: see 4021 (fibresand mdn h'cap). *7* **23**
3636 **FALCON SPIRIT 24** [9] 4-9-5 (51)(VIS) J Carroll 16/1: 0-0047: Wide early, nvr on terms: visored. *2½* **20**
3915 **HIGH SHOT 8** [13] 10-9-10 (56) A Hawkins (7) 25/1: 331408: Nvr trbled ldrs: see 505 (equitrack sell). *2* **23**
3674 **DALYAN 23** [6] 3-8-9 (47) R Winston 16/1: 040509: Mid-div, btn 3f out: see 1104. *7* **7**
3951 **ASSURED PHYSIQUE 6** [18] 3-9-6 (58) P Robinson 16/1: 560460: Well plcd, wknd qckly appr 3f out: 10th. *5* **13**
*3530 **HIGHCAL 29** [12] 3-8-10 (48) F Lynch 8/1: 000110: Al rear: 11th: progressive on firm/fast prev. *14* **0**
3839 **MR SPEAKER 14** [10] 7-9-12 (58) A Culhane 20/1: -50000: Nvr in it: 12th: see 431. *10* **0**
3636 **WINGED ANGEL 24** [17] 3-9-3 (55)(VIS) F Norton 11/1: 001500: Chsd ldrs 7f: 13th, visored, op 8/1. *3* **0**
3284 **FIERY WATERS 39** [11] 4-8-10 (42) J P Spencer 10/1: -00600: In tch till 4f out: 14th, op 16/1, 6 wk abs. *5* **0**
*3656 **NICOLAI 24** [19] 3-9-0 (52) M Fenton 11/2: 000410: Bhd from halfway: 15th, op 9/2: see 3656 (fast). *1½* **0**
3951 **Marton Mere 6** [7] 4-10-0 (60) P Hanagan (5) 25/1: 2282 **Peng 82** [15] 3-8-13 (51) O Pears 20/1:

BEVERLEY   TUESDAY SEPTEMBER 19TH   Righthand, Oval Track with Stiff Uphill Finish

17 ran   Time 2m 14.6 (12.3)   (Anthony Harrison)   P W Hiatt Hook Norton, Oxon

4047   5.00 MERRINGTON HCAP DIV 2 3YO+ 0-70 (E)   7f100y rnd
            RACE ABANDONED DUE TO UNSAFE CONDITIONS (HEAVY RAIN)

4048   5.30 FORWARD HCAP DIV 2 3YO+ 0-60 (F)   1m2f
            RACE ABANDONED DUE TO UNSAFE CONDITIONS (HEAVY RAIN)

MAISONS-LAFFITTE   WEDNESDAY SEPTEMBER 13TH   Left & Righthand, Sharpish Track

Official Going   GOOD

4049   2.25 LISTED PRIX HEROD 2YO   7f   Good
            £13449   £5379   £4035

*3860 **INNIT 7** M R Channon 2-8-13 T Thulliez : 400211: 2 b f Distinctly North - Tidal Reach   98
(Kris S) Held up, smooth hdwy to lead over 1f out, easily went clr: earlier won at Doncaster (val nursery):
Jan foal, dam multiple sprint wnr: eff arnd 7f, 1m shld suit in time: acts on fast, gd & a sharpish or gall
trk: can force the pace or come from bhd: tough, useful & progressive colt.
3716 **STORM BOY 19** France 2-9-2 G Mosse : 32: 2 ch c Bering - Princess Bilbao (Highest Honor)   3   92
--   **ASPIRING DIVA** France 2-8-13 O Doleuze : 3: 2 b f Distant View - Queen Of Song (His Majesty)   hd   89
6 ran   Time 1m 23.6   (Tim Corby)   M R Channon West Isley, Berks

4050   2.55 GR 3 LA COUPE DE M-LAFFITTE 3YO+   1m2f   Good
            £21134   £7685   £3842   £2305   3 yo rec 7 lb

*3370 **AGOL LACK 32** A Fabre 4-9-0 O Peslier 33/10: 512311: 4 ch c Gulch - Garvin's Gal (Seattle Slew)   117
Grabbed stands rail & sn led, made rest, drvn out to hold on: earlier scored in a Gr 3 at Deauville: eff over
a sharpish or gall 10f: acts on gd grnd: likes to race up with/force the pace: smart & consistent colt.
3723 **MONT ROCHER 17** J E Hammond 5-8-11 (bl) T Gillet 43/10: 1-1232: 5 b g Caerleon - Cuixmala   hd 113
(Highest Honor) Hld up, hdwy over 1f out, ran on strongly fnl 1f, just failed: stays 12.5f on gd & gd/soft: smart.
3374 **KUTUB 29** F Head 3-8-10 D Bonilla 19/10 JT FAV: -12423: 3 b c In The Wings - Minnie Habit (Habitat)   1 117
Chsd ldrs, drvn 2f out, kept on well but not pace of front pair: gd run at these weights: see 3374 (Gr 2).
2571 **CHELSEA MANOR 67** P Bary 4-8-11 T Thulliez 52/10: 233204: In tch, rdn/styd on fnl 1f, no impress.   hd 111
1625 **GOLDEN SNAKE 108** 4-8-11 T Jarnet 36/10: 160-45: Prom, rdn appr fnl 2f, kept on onepcd for press   ½ 110
fnl 1f: fair run after nr 4 month abs, now with J L Dunlop: may prefer softer grnd: see 1625.
8 ran   Time 1m 59.9   (Sultan Al Kabeer)   A Fabre France

CHANTILLY   FRIDAY SEPTEMBER 15TH   Righthand, Galloping Track

Official Going   GOOD

4051   2.25 LISTED CRITERIUM DE VITESSE 2YO   5f   Good
            £13449   £4611   £3458

3843 **SEASONS GREETINGS 16** C Laffon Parias 2-8-8 D Boeuf : 121421: 2 b f Ezzoud - Dream Season   100
(Mr Prospector) -:
*3679 **JACK SPRATT 18** R Hannon 2-8-11 T Jarnet : 310112: 2 b c So Factual - Raindancing (Tirol)   1½   98
Led, hdd just in last, not pace of wnr: imprvd again on hat-trick bid: useful/prog front-runner: see 3679.
3900 **KACHINA DOLL 6** M R Channon 2-8-8 T Thulliez : 330403: 2 b f Mujadil - Betelgeuse (Kalaglow)   shd 95
In tch, swtchd/prog appr fnl 1f, styd on, no impress on ldrs: qck reapp: gd run, see 3900, 2996.
3797 **SECRET INDEX 12** Mrs P N Dutfield 2-8-8 O Peslier : 154468: Prom, rdn/btn over 1f out, 8th: btr 3482. 86
9 ran   Time 58.3   (Maktoum Al Maktoum)   C Laffon Parias France

4052   3.25 GR 3 PRIX DE SEINE-ET-OISE 3YO+   6f   Good
            £21134   £7685   £3842

3724 **DANGER OVER 19** P Bary 3-8-11 T Thulliez 4/5 FAV: -11221: 3 b c Warning - Danilova (Lyphard)   111
Front rank, went on appr fnl 1f, drvn out: won 1st 2 starts this term, incl a List race at Maisons-Laffitte:
eff at 6/7f on gd & soft grnd: handles a sharp or gall trk: v useful & consistent, deserved Group success.
4197 **KHASAYL 349** J E Hammond 3-8-8 C Asmussen 67/10: 11-102: 3 b f Lycius - Maraatib (Green Desert)   nk 107
Waited with, strong run for press fnl 1f, just held: wnr on reapp prev this term: prog for P Walwyn in '99,
won at Bath (fill mdn), Doncaster (nov), Ayr (List) & Redcar (val stks race, rtd 107): sister to a 6/10f wnr:
eff at 5/6f, stays 7f: acts on fast, soft & a stiff/gall trk: tough & v useful filly, win similar.
3503 **JEZEBEL 26** C F Wall 3-8-8 R Mullen 103/10: 253223: 3 b f Owington - Just Ice (Polar Falcon)   ½ 105
Waited with, drvn/hdwy over 1f out, kept on but no impress: gd run up in grade: see 3503 (List).
7 ran   Time 1m 12.2   (K Abdulla)   P Bary France

Official Going   GOOD TO SOFT

4053   1.35 GR 3 PRIX DU PRINCE D'ORANGE 3YO   1m2f   Good/Soft
£21134   £7685   £3842

-- **HIGHTORI** P Demercastel 3-8-11 G Mosse 79/10: 1511-1: 3 b c Vettori - High Mecene (Highest Honor)   113
Trkd ldr, hdwy to lead over 1f out, rdn out: belated reapp due to injury: won 3 times as a juv, incl a Gr 3:
eff at 10f, 12f shld suit: runs well fresh on gd/soft & a gall trk: open to further imprvment, win more Gr races.
2736 **BLEU DALTAIR** 64 D Smaga 3-8-11 D Boeuf 165/10: 141502: 3 b c Green Tune - Parannda (Bold Lad)   1   110
Led at slow pace, drvn/hdd appr fnl 1f, sn held by wnr: eff over a gall 10f on gd/soft.
2225 **RHENIUM** 83 J C Rouget 3-9-2 T Jarnet 22/10: 113363: 3 ch c Rainbows For Life - Miss Mulaz (Luthier)   1   113
Handy, drvn/no extra appr fnl 1f: acts on gd/soft & hvy grnd: see 2225, 1026.
-2696 **MAN OMYSTERY** 63 J Noseda 3-8-11 O Peslier 33/10: -12426: Dwely, bhd, late gains, no dngr, 6th: 105
9 wk abs & not disgraced on this step up to Gr company: see 2696 (val h'cap).
7 ran   Time 2m 11.0   (Ecurie Bader)   P Demercastel France

4054   2.50 GR 1 PRIX DE LA SALAMANDRE 2YO   7f   Good/Soft
£38425   £15370   £7685   £3842

*3730 **TOBOUGG** 17 M R Channon 2-9-0 Craig Williams 38/10: 11: 2 b c Barathea - Lacovia (Majestic Light)   119+
Chsd ldrs, styd on well to lead over 1f out, readily: recent debut scorer at York (mdn): Feb foal,
cost 230,000gns: half-brother to sev wnrs abroad, dam French Oaks wnr: eff at 7f, 1m+ is sure to suit in time:
acts on fast, gd/soft & runs well fresh on a stiff/gall trk: high-class & lightly raced juv, has a big future.
*2408 **HONOURS LIST** 76 A P O'Brien 2-9-0 M J Kinane 6/4: 112: 2 b c Danehill - Gold Script (Script Ohio)   2   113
Set fast pace, rdn/hdd appr fnl 1f, kept on but no ch with impress wnr: clr rem: 11 wk abs: continues to
improve & not disgraced against a top-class opponent: in again in Gr 2/3 class: see 2408 (Gr 3).
3722 **WOODEN DOLL** 20 Mme C Head 2-8-11 O Doleuze 54/10: -123: 2 ch f Woodman - Kingscote (King's   4   103
Lake) Settled last, rdn/kept on one pace appr fnl 1f: needs a drop in grade: see 3722 (Gr 3).
*3550 **BAD A3 I WANNA BE** 27 B J Meehan 2-9-0 G Mosse 9/10 FAV: 0114: Pulled v hard, sn trkd ldr, ev ch   ½   105
till wknd for press fnl 1f: did himself no favours by racing far too freely today: capable of much better &
prob best when allowed to dominate: looked high-class in 3550 (Gr 1, made all, sole runner on stands rail strip).
4 ran   Time 1m 22.2   (Sheikh Ahmed Al Maktoum)   M R Channon West Isley, Berks

Official Going   Round Course - GOOD; Straight Course - YIELDING

4055   3.45 GR 1 IRISH ST LEGER 3YO+   1m6f   Good
£101800   £33550   £16050   £5550   3 yo rec 10lb

*3306 **ARCTIC OWL** 35 J R Fanshawe 6-9-8 D Harrison 7/2: 6-3011: 6 b g Most Welcome - Short Rations   119
(Lorenzaccio) Mid-div, imprvd to chall ldr over 1f out, led dist, ran on well, drvn out: earlier won at Goodwood
(val stks): '99 wnr at Sandown (Gr 3, rtd 123), subs 2nd thrice in Gr company: '98 wnr at York (h'cap),
Deauville (Gr 2) & Newmarket (2, incl Gr 3, rtd 121): eff between 12f & 2m on fast & hvy grnd: runs well fresh
on any trk: tough & high class stayer, type to make his presence felt in the Melbourne Cup.
2911 **YAVANAS PACE** 34 M Johnston 8-9-8 J Fanning 8/1: 322652: 8 ch g Accordion - Lady In Pace (Burslem)1½   116
Front rank, led 7f out, hard pressed 2f out, hdd dist, styd on, held cl-home: 6L clr rem: most tough & smart
gelding, but is still searching for that elusive first Group 1 victory: see 2586, 987.
3849 **MUTAFAWEQ** 13 Saeed bin Suroor 4-9-8 L Dettori 11/4 FAV: -30103: 4 b h Silver Hawk - The Caretaker   6   108
(Caerleon) In tch, drvn/eff 2f out, sn onepcd: prob best on faster grnd: see 2911.
3898 **ROSTROPOVICH** 7 A P O'Brien 3-8-12 K J Manning 20/1: 313504: Waited with, rdn & styd on fnl 2f,   ½   107
no impress: not disgraced with visor omitted, see 3538, 3317.
3723 **LITTLE ROCK** 20 4-9-8 B Marcus 8/1: 161345: Cl-up, drvn/btn fnl 2f: up in trip: btr 3723, 2566 (12f).   hd   107
3898 **CHIMES AT MIDNIGHT** 7 3-8-12 (bl) J A Heffernan 9/1: 100236: Nvr dngrs: qck reapp: much btr 3898.   ½   106
*3721 **KATIYKHA** 21 4-9-5 J Murtagh 3/1: 241117: Waited with, eff 2f out, sn lost tch: big step up in trip: 0
disapp on 4-timer bid but reportedly returned distressed: much btr 3721 (List).
3924 **LERMONTOV** 7 3-8-12 P J Scallan 16/1: 112-48: Led to halfway, bhd fnl 3f: qck reapp: see 3924.   0
8 ran   Time 3m 02.2   (The Owl Society)   J R Fanshawe Newmarket

4056   4.20 GR 3 BOLAND STKS 3YO+   7f   Good
£26000   £7600   £3600   £1200

3923 **SOCIAL HARMONY** 7 D K Weld 6-9-1 P J Smullen 11/4: 204141: 6 b g Polish Precedent - Latest Chapter   113
(Ahonoora) In tch, hdwy to chall dist, ran on well to lead nr fin, drvn out: earlier won at Fairyhouse (List):
'99 h'cap wnr at The Curragh & Galway (rtd 108): suited by 6/7f on fast & hvy: smart & consistent gelding.
862 **TARRY FLYNN** 160 D K Weld 6-9-1 (bl) P Shanahan 14/1: 246002: 3 br g Kenmare - Danzig Lass   ½   112
(Danzig) Led, clr appr fnl 1f, pressed by wnr ins last, hdd/held cl-home: back to best here after a string
of below-par efforts: see 862 (Gr 3, only narrowly btn by Giants Causeway).
4559) **MAIDAAN** 322 Saeed bin Suroor 4-9-1 L Dettori 5/1: 20-163: 4 b c Midyan - Panache Arabelle (Nashwan)   1   110
Mid-div, hdwy over 2f out, styd on but held by front 2 when no room well ins last: 6 month abs: earlier won
in Dubai (3-rnr List): rnr-up on 1st of 2 juv starts (List, rtd 107): won fnl of 2 juv starts, at Newmarket
(stks, rtd 107, M Channon): eff at 7f/1m: acts on fast & gd, poss not soft grnd: acts on a stiff/gall trk:
runs well fresh but entitled to need this run: useful & lightly raced colt, just sharper for this.
3548 **ONE WON ONE** 28 Ms J Morgan 6-9-1 E Ahern 5/2 FAV: 100324: Prom, chall ldrs 2f out, held fnl 1f.   ¾   108
8 ran   Time 1m 28.9   (S Creaven)   D K Weld Curragh, Co Kildare

Official Going   YIELDING

4057
2.45 GR 3 BLANDFORD STKS 3YO+   1m3f   Good/Soft
£45500   £13300   £6300   £2100   3 yo rec 7 lb

1626 **CHIANG MAI** 112 A P O'Brien 3-8-7 M J Kinane 13/8 FAV: 11-101: 3 b f Sadler's Wells - Eljazzi   108
(Artaius) Waited with, gd hdwy over 1f out, ran on strongly to lead cl-home, drvn out: 4 month abs: earlier won
on reapp here at The Curragh (stks): '99 wnr at Navan (mdn) & Leopardstown (List, rtd 106): eff at 1m/1f,
loves gd/soft & soft: runs well fresh: useful, needs to be produced as late as possible.
4055 **CHIMES AT MIDNIGHT** 1 L Comer 3-8-10 (bl) J A Heffernan 5/1: 002362: 3 b c Danzig - Surely   shd 110
Georgies (Alleged) Prom, chall over 1f out, ran on strongly, just held: gd eff after a below-par run yesterday.
3792 **HAPPY CHANGE** 15 M Johnston 6-9-3 J Murtagh 9/4: -30153: 6 ch g Surumu - Happy Gini (Ginistrelli)   nk 109
Prom, led 3f our, strongly pressed 2f out, styd on well, hdd nr fin: excellent eff on this return to Gr class.
6 ran   Time 2m 27.2   (Mrs Chryss O'Reilly)   A P O'Brien Ballydoyle, Co Tipperary

4058
3.45 GR 1 NATIONAL STKS 2YO   7f   Good/Soft
£114600   £38600   £18600   £6600

3719 **BECKETT** 22 A P O'Brien 2-9-0 J A Heffernan 10/1: -131: 2 b c Fairy King - Groom Order (Groom Dancer)   118
Cl-up, hdwy to lead appr fnl 1f, pushed clr, readily: earlier won on debut at Leopardstown (mdn): eff at 6/7f,
1m will suit: acts on gd & gd/soft grnd: smart & v progressive, win more Gr races.
-- **KINGS COUNTY** A P O'Brien 2-9-0 P J Scallan 12/1: -12: 2 b c Fairy King - Kardelle (Kalaglow)   3   110
Prom, went on 2f out, hdd over 1f out, ran green & no impress fnl 1f: stablemate of wnr: 10 wk abs: earlier
won on debut at Leopardstown (mdn): eff at 6/7f on fast & gd/soft: smart run, win a Gr race on this form.
-- **MARCH KING** T Stack 2-9-0 W J O'Connor 20/1: -423: 2 b c Caerleon - Porphyrine (Habitat)   1   108
Mid-div, styd on well fnl 2f but no ch with wnr: excellent run by this mdn, stys 7f/1m on gd/soft: v useful.
*3895 **DOWN TO THE WOODS** 8 M Johnston 2-9-0 D Holland 13/2: 1514: Keen & sn led, hdd 2f out, drvn &   2½   104
sn btn: 5L clr rem & not disgraced on this step up to Gr 1 company: handles fm & gd/soft: see 3895 (stks, 6f).
2738 **BERLIN** 63 2-9-0 E Ahern 12/1: 135: Nvr a threat: 9 wk abs: see 2738, 2400.   5   96
*1624 **DARWIN** 112 2-9-0 M J Kinane 4/9 FAV: 16: Prom, drvn & fdd appr fnl 2f: reportedly fin lame: 4   89
odds-on after a near 4 month abs: stablemate of wnr & looked a decent prospect when wng on debut in 1624.
-- **AMERICAN GOTHIC** 2-9-0 F M Berry 20/1: 7: Al rear: tough task on debut.   0
3719 **BONNARD** 22 2-9-0 (BL) J P Spencer 7/1: -13228: Al twrds rear: blnkd: see 3719.   0
2400 **ELBADER** 79 2-9-0 (bl) P J Smullen 14/1: 333219: Dwelt, al well bhd: v stiff task.   0
9 ran   Time 1m 29.8   (Mrs John Magnier)   A P O'Brien Ballydoyle, Co Tipperary

4059
4.20 LISTED SOLONAWAY STKS 3YO+   1m1f   Good/Soft
£26000   £7600   £3600   3 yo rec 5 lb

3539 **SHOAL CREEK** 26 A P O'Brien 3-8-10 (bl) M J Kinane 5/2 FAV: 310241: 3 b c Fairy King - Catalonia   109
Express (Diesis) Led, rdn & styd on well fnl 1f, drvn out: earlier won at Cork (maiden): eff at 1m/9f on
gd/soft grnd: has tried a visor, now eff in blnks: apprec this drop in grade.
2320} **MUDAA** EB 427 K Prendergast 4-9-1 S Craine 10/1: 320402: 4 br c Machiavellian - Alkaffeyeh (Sadler's   ¾   107
Wells) Prom, rdn & styd on appr fnl 1f, not pace of wnr: gd run (offic rtd only 95): eff at 9f on gd/soft.
4030} **SCOTTISH MEMORIES** 364 J E Mulhern 4-9-1 D P McDonogh 9/2: 1-0363: 4 ch g Houmayoun - Interj   1   105
(Salmon Leap) In tch, drvn & styd on fnl 2f, al held by front 2: clr rem: eff at 9/10f on gd/soft & soft.
13 ran   Time 1m 54.9   (Michael Tabor)   A P O'Brien Ballydoyle, Co Tipperary

4060
5.20 LISTED BLENHEIM STKS 2YO   6f   Good/Soft
£26050   £7650   £3650

-- **BLACK MINNALOUSHE** A P O'Brien 2-8-11 M J Kinane 1/1 FAV: -11: 2 b c Storm Cat - Coral Dance   103
(Green Dancer) Prom, hdwy to lead appr fnl 1f, styd on well, rdn out: 6 wk abs: earlier won on debut at Cork
(mdn): eff arnd 6f, further could suit: acts on fast & good/soft grnd: useful, type to rate higher.
3700 **IMPERIAL DANCER** 20 M R Channon 2-9-0 Craig Williams 5/1: 245132: 2 b c Primo Dominie - Gorgeous   ¾   103
Dancer (Nordico) Waited with, gd hdwy to chall wnr dist, no impress well ins last: consistent, see 3700.
-- **SAYING GRACE** Miss F M Crowley 2-8-8 P J Smullen 14/1: -41103: 2 b f Brief Truce - Adamparis   nk   96
(Robellino) Mid-div, ran on well fnl 1f: Sligo (mdn) & Cork (stks) wnr prev this term: eff at 6f on fast & gd/soft.
8 ran   Time 1m 16.5   (Mrs John Magnier)   A P O'Brien Ballydoyle, Co Tipperary

Official Going   HEAVY (Soft In Places) Stalls: Str Course - Stands side; Round Course - Inside; 12f - Outside.

4061
2.30 MACPHIE CLASS STKS 3YO+ 0-75 (D)   1m4f   Soft 97   -25 Slow
£3575   £1100   £550   £275   3 yo rec 8 lb   Field stayed far side in str

3794 **PHEISTY** 18 [5] R F Johnson Houghton 3-8-9 S Carson (3) 7/1: 652661: 3 b f Faustus - Phlirty (Pharly)   74
Settled rear, rdn/imprvd over 2f out, led appr dist, kept on strongly, drvn out: earlier won at Yarmouth
(ladies amat h'cap): '99 Leicester debut wnr (auct mdn, rtd 75): eff at 10f, apprec this step up to 12f:
acts on firm, soft & poss any trk: eff with/without blnks: genuine.
3111 **SOVEREIGNS COURT** 47 [10] L G Cottrell 7-9-4 A Clark 13/2: /30162: 7 ch g Statoblest - Clare   ½   74
Celeste (Coquelin) Bhd, rdn/prog over 3f out, hdwy when sltly short of room over 1f out, kept on well ins last,
not btn far: op 5/1, abs: eff at 1m/12f: shade unlucky in running: likes gd/soft & hvy: deserves another ch.
*3725 **CAPRIOLO** 21 [2] R Hannon 4-9-8 (bl) R Hughes 4/1 FAV: 016313: 4 ch g Priolo - Carroll's Canyon   ½   77
(Hatim) Led, strongly prsd appr fnl 1f, hdd just ins last, held cl-home: nicely bckd tho' op 7/2, clr rem:
sound eff conceding weight all round, acts on firm & soft grnd: see 3725.
3270 **ASTRONAUT** 41 [12] W J Haggas 3-8-10 (VIS) J P Spencer 13/2: 412264: Keen/mid-div, bhd 3f out   3   69

rall appr fnl 1f, btn well ins last: op 9/2, 6 wk abs: 1st time visor: poss stays 12f & handles soft: see 2450.

2210	**BLESS THE BRIDE** 86 [13] 3-8-7 Pat Eddery 11/2: 6-1005: Handy, rdn/prog over 2f out, no extra fnl 1f: unproven at 12f, btr 1094 (10f, gd).				3	62
3948	**SANTIBURI GIRL** 7 [9] 3-8-11 A Polli (3) 8/1: 124066: Waited with, hdwy over 2f out, lost tch appr fnl 1f: unproven on soft grnd, see 3948, 3329.				1	64
4039	**FAMOUS** 2 [1] 7-9-4 (bl) I Mongan (5) 100/1: 000007: Mid-div at best: ran 48hrs ago, v stiff task.				1¼	61$
1743	**BLUE STYLE** 106 [3] 4-9-4 (t) J Mackay (5) 7/1: 121008: Al towards rear: v long abs: sharper next time & likes gd/soft & hvy grnd: see 1076.				10	49
3793	**AZUR** 18 [11] 3-8-7 (vis) D Harrison 12/1: -00009: Prom, fdd fnl 2f: see 2610.				4	41
3662	**MAX** 24 [8] 5-9-4 Martin Dwyer 100/1: 000000: Mid-div, eff halfway, lost tch fnl 3f, 10th: stiff task.				½	43$
3737	Twoforten 21 [6] 5-9-4 G Baker (5) 50/1:		2268	Happy Go Lucky 83 [7] 6-9-1 N Callan 16/1:		
413	Park Royal 236 [4] 5-9-4 R Winston 100/1:					

13 ran   Time 2m 46.42 (14.62)   (Mrs R J Johnson Houghton)   R F Johnson Houghton Blewbury, Oxon

---

4062   3.00 UNIGATE MDN 2YO (D)   1m rnd   Soft 97   -31 Slow
£3250   £1000   £500   £250   Field came stands side in str

3879 **NORTHFIELDS DANCER** 13 [7] R Hannon 2-9-0 R Hughes 2/5 FAV: 220221: 2 ch c Dr Devious - Heartland (Northfields) Made all, styd on strongly for press fnl 2f, rdn out, in command when eased nr fin: nicely bckd tho' op 1/4: rnr-up sev times prev under some less than positive rides: eff around 1m on firm & soft grnd, further shld suit next term: prev held up, apprec more positive tactics today.   88

-- **PRECISO** [4] Mrs A J Perrett 2-9-0 S Sanders 7/1: 2: 2 b c Definite Article - Symphony (Cyrano de Bergerac) Prom, rdn/outpcd 3f out, rallied for press appr fnl 1f, closing at fin: 35,000 gns Feb 1st foal, dam related to a smart Irish sprinter: eff arnd 1m on soft: encouraging debut, learn from this & win a mdn.   ½   86

3840 **MARTINS SUNSET** 15 [5] W R Muir 2-9-0 D Harrison 20/1: 003: 2 ch c Royal Academy - Mainly Sunset (Red Sunset) Cl-up, chall 2f out, held well ins last: 6L clr rem: much imprvd on this step up to 1m on soft.   nk   85

3832 **RINGWOOD** 15 [6] C F Wall 2-9-0 A McGlone 9/2: -644: Handy, eff over 2f out, fdd appr fnl 1f: bckd from 8/1: big step up in trip: see 3832, 2608 (6f).   6   76

-- **ALFANO** [2] 2 0 0 M Henry 33/1: 5: Veered left start, rear, nvr dangerous: 9,800 gns Mar 1st foal, dam a successful sprinter: with P Mitchell, could improve.   1½   73

-- **SECRETE CONTRACT** [1] 2-9-0 I Mongan (5) 33/1: 6: Hmpd start, al last: 4,700 gns Mar 1st foal, dam related to sev wnrs: sire high-class sprinting juv: with G L Moore.   1   71

6 ran   Time 1m 47.65 (10.25)   (John Michael)   R Hannon East Everleigh, Wilts

---

4063   3.30 ROA AUCT STKS 2YO (C)   7f rnd   Soft 97   -24 Slow
£6235   £2365   £1182   £537   Field came stands side in str

*3760 **BLUSHING BRIDE** 19 [4] J Noseda 2-8-4 Pat Eddery 1/1 FAV: -11: 2 b f Distant Relative - Dime Bag (High Line) Mid-div, rdn 3f out, ran on well to lead appr fnl 1f, pushed out & rdly went clr, eased cl-home, val 5/6L: well bckd: earlier won on debut at Epsom (med auct mdn): half sister to a couple of wnrs, notably useful 9f wnr Pawn Broker, dam a wng stayer: eff over a sharp/undul 7f, 1m will suit: runs well fresh on gd & soft grnd: useful & prog, can rate more highly & win more races.   93+

3470 **LOYAL TYCOON** 32 [1] S Dow 2-8-9 P Doe 15/2: 3162: 2 br c Royal Abjar - Rosy Lydgate (Last Tycoon) Handy, led appr fnl 2f, hdd over 1f out, not pace of wnr: op 5/1, clr rem: v consistent, acts on fast & soft grnd.   3½   87

3812 **SECOND STRIKE** 17 [11] B Smart 2-8-4 Paul Eddery 8/1: -53: 2 b c Kris - Honeyspike (Chief's Crown) Keen, led over 5f out, hdd appr fnl 2f, sn no extra: poss stys 7f on soft, win a mdn on a minor trk: see 3812.   3½   77

3799 **UNSIGNED** 17 [8] J R Fanshawe 2-8-10 D Harrison 6/1: 04: Bhd, rdn/late hdwy, no threat: op 7/2: drop in trip: will apprec a return to 1m: see 3799.   shd   83

*3268 **ST ANTIM** 41 [7] 2-8-4 J Quinn 13/2: 15: Keen/prom, chall ldr over 2f out, wknd qckly appr dist: 6 wks abs: up in trip & poss not quite get home over 7f on soft: see 3268.   ¾   76

-- **GIN PALACE** [9] 2-8-13 R Hughes 25/1: 6: Dwelt, eff halfway, wknd qckly fnl 2f: IR 26,000 gns Feb foal, half brother to a couple of juv sprint wnrs: with G L Moore, sharper next time.   hd   85

3789 **ZAFILLY** 18 [6] 2-7-13 Martin Dwyer 50/1: 07: Al towards rear: see 3789.   1¼   69$

3240 **FATHER SEAMUS** 42 [5] 2-8-1 G Baker (5) 66/1: 000038: Led early, wknd from halfway: 6 wks abs.   5   64$

3412 **MENAS ERN** 34 [2] 2-8-10 R Smith (5) 66/1: 009: Keen/rear, nvr dangerous: mod prev form.   2   70$

9 ran   Time 1m 32.94 (8.44)   (Mrs D M Solomon)   J Noseda Newmarket

---

4064   4.00 LISTED FOUNDATION STKS 3YO+ (A)   1m1f192y   Soft 97   -04 Slow
£17810   £5480   £2740   £1370   3 yo rec 6 lb   Field came stands side in str

3641 **ALBARAHIN** 25 [2] M P Tregoning 5-9-0 R Hills 4/5 FAV: 2-2121: 5 b h Silver Hawk - My Dear Lady (Mr Prospector) Made all, styd on well fnl 2f, pshd out: well bckd at odds-on: earlier won at Sandown (stks), rnr-up twice: '99 Leicester (reapp), Sandown & Newbury wnr (h'caps, rtd 105): eff btwn 1m & 10f on fast, hvy & prob any trk, likes Sandown: runs well fresh, eff weight carrier: progressive & smart, shld win a Gr race.   118

3903 **RIGHT WING** 11 [5] J L Dunlop 6-9-0 (vis) Pat Eddery 9/2: 122132: 6 b h In The Wings - Nekbet (Artaius) Bhd, swtchd/hdwy appr fnl 1f, ran on strongly fnl 1f: nicely bckd: prob needs more cover: see 3726.   1½   114

3984 **DIAMOND WHITE** 5 [7] M J Ryan 5-8-9 A Daly 9/2: 454533: 5 b m Robelino - Diamond Wedding (Diamond Shoal) Cl-up, eff over 3f out, held fnl 1f: qck reapp: won this last year (rtd 111, hvy grnd): see 3984.   ¾   108

18 **ZOMARADAH** 319 [4] L M Cumani 5-8-9 J P Spencer 7/1: 1213-4: Handy, hdwy over 3f out, rdn/wknd appr fnl 1f: nicely bckd tho' op 4/1 on reapp: '99 star at Doncaster (stks), The Curragh (Gr2, rtd 118) & Capannelle (Gr2): '98 scorer at Brighton (reapp, mdn auct), San Siro (Gr1 Italian Oaks) & Woodbine (Gr2, rtd 110): eff at 10/11f on firm or hvy grnd: acts on any trk & likes to force the pace: can run well fresh but entitled to need this: v smart at best, sharper next time.   2½   104

3857 **ELMHURST BOY** 14 [6] 4-9-0 P Doe 50/1: 200155: Rear, rdn/prog over 3f out, lost tch appr dist: v stiff task at these weights, apprec return to h'cap company: see 3794.   ½   108$

1380 **GARGALHADA** Primal 125 [3] 3-8-8 R Hughes 16/1: 1256: Prom, dropped rear 3f out, btn when short of room appr fnl 1f, eased: 4 month abs & may apprec a drop in grade: see 1380, 1168.   2½   105$

6 ran   Time 2m 14.0 (9.9)   (Hamdan Al Maktoum)   M P Tregoning Lambourn, Berks

4065   4.35 KERRY HCAP 3YO+ 0-70 (E)   5f   Soft 97   +07 Fast   [69]
£3250   £1000   £500   £250   3 yo rec 1 lb   Field raced through centre

3747 **ABSOLUTE FANTASY 20** [13] E A Wheeler 4-9-1 (56)(bl) S Carson (3) 11/1: 212051: 4 b f Beveled -   **61**
Sharp Venita (Sharp Edge) Hmpd start, bhd, hdwy 2f out, ran on strongly to lead cl-home, drvn out: op 9/1, best
time of day: earlier won at Brighton (mdn h'cap) & Newbury (appr h'cap), plcd sev times: eff btwn 5f & 7f, stays
a sharp 1m: acts on firm, soft & equitrack: handles any trk, likes Brighton & best in blnks: tough & versatile.

-4027 **MUTASAWWAR 2** [7] J M Bradley 6-8-2 (43) R Ffrench 11/2 FAV: 040022: 6 ch g Clantime - Keen   nk   **47**
Melody (Sharpen Up) Cl-up, rdn into lead appr fnl 1f, styd on well, hdd cl-home: ran 48hrs ago: remains
in fine form & deserves similar: acts on fast & soft grnd, both AWs: h'capped to win soon: see 1508.

3825 **BEDEVILLED 16** [19] J Pearce 5-9-8 (63) T Quinn 11/1: 001603: 5 ch g Beveled - Putout (Dowsing)   1   **64**
Mid-div, hdwy to chall appr fnl 1f, held well ins last: tchd 14/1: ran to best: see 3441.

3841 **BORDER GLEN 15** [17] J J Bridger 4-8-13 (54)(bl) Martin Dwyer 20/1: 053064: Set fast pace, hdd   ¾   **53**
appr fnl 1f, fdd well ins last: acts on firm & soft grnd: see 3622.

3821 **KILCULLEN LAD 16** [24] 6-9-8 (63)(vis) J Mackay (5) 14/1: 603505: Mid-div, eff 2f out, styd on ins   ¾   **61**
last, nvr nrr: on a fair mark now: see 1438.

3855 **CORBLETS 14** [22] 3-9-1 (57) P Doe 20/1: 036306: Dwelt, rear, hdwy fnl 2f, no dngr: mdn: see 3584.   hd   **55**

2078 **PRIDE OF BRIXTON 91** [2] 7-8-8 (49) M Henry 8/1: 111207: In tch, rdn/onepcd appr fnl 1f: 3 month   1   **45**
abs & poss just sharper for this: see 1140.

3956 **POLAR LADY 7** [18] 3-9-7 (63) R Winston 10/1: 350428: Hdwy from rear over 2f out, styd on ins   nk   **58**
last, no danger: tchd 16/1, quick reapp: needs a return to 6f: see 3956.

3046 **NIGHTINGALE SONG 51** [21] 6-8-3 (43)(1ow) A Clark 25/1: -04009: Cl-up, eff/hmpd over 1f out, not   1   **37**
recover: 7 wk abs: unlucky in running & worth another ch at 6f/stiff 5f: on a gd mark: see 1487.

3796 **ASTRAC 17** [5] 9-9-3 (58) T Ashley 10/1: 000000: Handy, outpcd over 2f out, ran on strongly ins   hd   **51**
last, no threat, 10th: best at 6f: see 4066.

72   **PERTEMPS STAR 306** [4] 3-7-12 (40) G Baker (5) 50/1: 0000-0: Prom, fdd fnl 1f, 11th: abs, modest.   1¼   **30**

3046 **KAYO GEE 51** [8] 4-9-1 (56)(vis) C Rutter 20/1: 030000: In tch, wknd over 1f out, 12th: 9 wk abs.   nk   **45**

3820 **SECOND GENERATION 16** [11] 3-8-13 (55)(BL) N Pollard 33/1: -0500: Prom to halfway, 13th: blnkd.   nk   **43**

3947 **PERIGEUX 7** [12] 4-9-5 (60)(vis) C Catlin (7) 8/1: 100030: Stumbled badly start, sn in tch, styd on   nk   **48**
lost tch with ldrs over 1f out, 14th: quick reapp: see 3947.

3631 **JUDIAM 25** [25] 3-9-10 (66) R Hughes 10/1: 051000: Sn outpcd, 15th: btr 2586.   shd   **54**

3947 **QUITE HAPPY 7** [1] 5-9-7 (62) P McCabe 12/1: 222040: Handy, lost tch fnl 2f, 17th: qck reapp: see 3502.   0

3966 Chakra 6 [6] 6-8-9 (50) R Havlin 20/1:   3841 Cappucino Lady 15 [9] 3-7-10 (38)(3oh) D Kinsella (7) 66/1:
2885 Sea Haze 58 [15] 3-9-7 (63)(BL) Paul Eddery 25/1:   3780 First Venture 18 [3] 3-9-4 (60)(vis) G Hind 16/1:
3825 Calandrella 16 [16] 7-7-10 (37)(2oh) G Sparkes (3) 25/1:

21 ran   Time 1m 01.17 (4.47)   (The Red Square Partnership) E A Wheeler Whitchurch On Thames, Oxon

4066   5.05 PREMIER CLAIM HCAP 3YO+ 0-65 (E)   1m rnd   Soft 97 -10 Slow   [65]
£3250   £1000   £500   £250   3 yo rec 4 lb

*3828 **CRUAGH EXPRESS 15** [11] G L Moore 4-8-13 (50)(bl) I Mongan (5) 10/1: 560011: 4 b g Unblest - Cry   **53**
In The Dark (Godswalk) Cl-up, went on appr fnl 2f, styd on strongly, drvn out: op 8/1, new stable: earlier won
for P Gilligan at Lingfield (AW sell h'cap, 1st win): plcd in native Ireland twice in '99: eff arnd 1m/sharp 10f:
acts on gd/soft, soft & equitrack: likes a sharp trk & eff in blnks: timely first start for new connections.

3842 **MAGICAL BAILIWICK 15** [10] R J Baker 4-8-9 (46)(bl) J P Spencer 16/1: 000002: 4 ch g Magical   ¾   **47**
Wonder - Alpine Dance (Apalachee) Mid-div, edged right for press appr fnl 2f, ran on well ins last, no ch
with wnr: gd run dropped in grade, eff over a sharp 1m on soft: see 2270.

3951 **DORISSIO 7** [15] I A Balding 4-9-12 (63) R Hughes 5/1 FAV: 333603: 4 b f Efisio - Floralia   hd   **64**
(Auction Ring) Hdwy from rear after halfway, short of room 2f out, ran on strongly ins last, not btn far:
nicely bckd & clrly goes best with cut in the grnd these days: see 811.

3831 **GLENDALE RIDGE 15** [13] Jamie Poulton 5-9-2 (53) P Dobbs (5) 25/1: 400004: Chsd ldrs, sltly   2   **50**
hmpd 2f out, btn appr fnl 1f: see 2129.

3831 **BUTRINTO 15** [14] 6-9-11 (62) P Shea (7) 16/1: 232205: Rear, hdwy halfway, ev ch until fdd ins last.   1¼   **57**

3737 **KINNINO 21** [7] 6-8-6 (43) C Rutter 14/1: 321446: Waited with, eff when no room appr fnl 1f,   ½   **37**
styd on fnl 1f, no danger: unlucky in running, worth another look when returning to 10f: see 3737, 3111.

3885 **SALVA 12** [17] 4-9-3 (54) S Sanders 20/1: -46007: Handy, eff 3f out, lost tch appr dist: tchd 33/1.   ½   **47**

3356 **OSCIETRA 37** [8] 4-8-9 (46)(vis) S Carson (3) 6/1: 555608: Hdwy from rear over 2f out, styd on   ¾   **38**
late, no threat: tchd 12/1, visor reapplied: see 2262, 1096.

3887 **THATCHMASTER 12** [18] 9-9-11 (62)(t) Paul Eddery 9/1: -00209: Trkd ldrs, drvn/lost tch fnl 2f: 1¾   **51**
likes Goodwood but prefers faster grnd: see 3644, 3110.

3423 **DENARIUS SECUNDUS 34** [9] 3-9-0 (55)(BL) Martin Dwyer 16/1: -0000: Rear, mod late gains, fin   nk   **44**
10th: blnkd: big drop in grade on h'cap bow: see 2465.

3939 **KNOBBLEENEEZE 7** [1] 10-8-5 (42)(vis) T A O'Sullivan (5) 10/1: 160000: Prom, rdn/fdd fnl 2f, 11th.   nk   **31**

3078 **ORIENT EXPRESS 49** [20] 3-9-7 (62) Pat Eddery 9/1: 030300: Led 6f out-2f out, wknd, 12th: 7 wk abs.   6   **43**

3753 **FUEGIAN 20** [5] 5-9-5 (56)(vis) D Harrison 25/1: 10P000: Led early, ch until wknd qckly fnl 2f, 13th.   5   **30**

--   **GREEN MAGICAL** [4] 4-8-11 (48) S W Kelly (3) 6/1: 0304-0: In tch, wknd fnl 3f, 14th: op 3/1,   4   **16**
reapp/Brit bow: mdn in native Ireland prev (tried btwn 1m & 11f): now with B Curley.

3623 Hadeqa 26 [19] 4-8-6 (43)(bl) N Callan 20/1:   1031 Ilissus 147 [12] 4-10-0 (65) J Mackay (5) 20/1:
3745 Warring 20 [3] 6-8-7 (44) P Doe 16/1:

17 ran   Time 1m 45.97 (8.57)   (C F Sparrowhawk)   G L Moore Woodingdean, E Sussex

4067   5.35 MERBURY HCAP 3YO 0-80 (D)   1m1f192y   Soft 97   +05 Fast   [86]
£3575   £1100   £550   £275

3762 **DOUBLE RED 19** [8] M L W Bell 3-7-12 (56) J Mackay (5) 20/1: -23001: 3 b f Thatching - Local   **65**
Custom (Be My Native) Hdwy from rear after halfway, went on 3f out, rdn clr appr dist, eased cl-home, val
4/5L: gd time, 1st win: rnr-up fnl 2 starts in '99 (incl 1m/10f, h'cap): eff at 1m/10f, poss stays 12f: acts on
gd, soft & poss any trk: cmftble wnr here, shld follow up while conditions remain in his favour.

3379 **CAPRICCIO 35** [3] C G Cox 3-9-2 (74) M Fenton 14/1: 435252: 3 gr g Robellino - Yamamah (Siberian   2   **75**
Express) Rear, prog over 2f out, styd on to wnr: eff arnd 10/10.5f, appr easy grnd: see 3267.

2506 **PRINCE OMID 74** [19] J R Fanshawe 3-8-9 (67) D Harrison 16/1: 340043: 3 b g Shuailaan - Matilda   1¼   **66**

The Hun (Young Bob) In tch, eff over 3f out, styd on fnl 2f but no threat: 10 wk abs & just sharper for this.

3857 **CHEMS TRUCE** 14 [9] W R Muir 3-9-7 (79) B Marcus 11/1: 034544: Rear, rdn/late hdwy, nvr nrr: hd 78
again set too much to do: see 3166.

3585 **RESPLENDENT STAR** 27 [17] 3-9-3 (75)(vis) J P Spencer 12/1: -40035: Rear, eff/switched appr fnl 1 72
1f, kept on, no threat: longer 10f trip: see 3585, 1341.

3167 **EYELETS ECHO** 46 [6] 3-8-9 (67) R Winston 25/1: 001506: Chsd ldrs, rdn/btn fnl 2f: 7 wk abs: nk 64
unproven on soft grnd: see 2276 (fast, 9f).

3731 **ARMENIA** 21 [7] 3-7-11 (55) G Baker (5) 25/1: 000007: Led early, rem cl-up, went on again after 4 46
halfway, hdd 3f out & sn wknd: see 3389, 882.

3423 **DANGEROUS DEPLOY** 34 [16] 3-8-2 (60) N Pollard 14/1: -5508: Rear, late gains, no dngr: h'cap bow. ¾ 50

3390 **DICKIE DEADEYE** 35 [11] 3-8-7 (65) S Carson (3) 13/2: 056569: Prom, fdd fnl 2f: tchd 9/1, btr 2688. 2 52

3856 **MENTIGA** 14 [14] 3-8-10 (68) G Hind 20/1: 060600: Prom, wknd fnl 2f, eased when btn, 10th: likes soft. 2 52

*3416 **CLEPSYDRA** 34 [10] 3-9-6 (78)(BL) T Quinn 10/1: 223510: V slow to start & well bhd, mod late hdwy 4 56
but nvr dangerous, 11th: 1st time blnks & lost all ch at the start here: much btr 3416 (12f mdn).

3477 **MAC BE LUCKY** 32 [15] 3-9-3 (75) Pat Eddery 5/2 FAV: 0-0215: Cl-up, rdn & wknd qckly fnl 2f, 0
14th: well bckd & better expected on grnd which had come in his favour: much btr 3477 (1m mdn).

3465 **EUROLINK ARTEMIS** 32 [20] 3-9-1 (73) S Sanders 9/1: 435140: Handy, wknd fnl 3f, 16th: btr 2774 (fast). 0

213 **WELSH PLOY** 274 [18] 3-9-6 (78) T G McLaughlin 33/1: 0512-0: Sn led, hdd over 4f out, sn lost tch, 0
fin last: v long abs, turf return: see 213, 158.

3793 **Insightful** 18 [13] 3-8-8 (66) R Hughes 20/1:   3580 **Sparkling Isle** 28 [1] 3-8-2 (60) J Quinn 40/1:

2579 **Monduru** 70 [21] 3-8-9 (67) Martin Dwyer 25/1:   3819 **Alqawaaser** 16 [12] 3-8-4 (62) R Havlin 20/1:

18 ran   Time 2m 13.17 (8.97)   (Terry Neill)   M L W Bell, Newmarket

---

Official Going   SOFT (HEAVY in places). Stalls: Inside. No speed figures, inside running rail re-aligned after 1st race.

4068   2.20 LEGAT OWEN MDN 2YO (D)   7f rnd   Soft   Inapplicable
£3672   £1130   £565   £282

3866 **CLEARING** 13 [1] J H M Gosden 2-9-0 J Fortune 4/9 FAV: 221: 2 b c Zafonic - Bright Spells (Alleged) 89
Trkd ldr, went on dist, pushed clr, easily: well bckd: Feb first foal, dam 12f wnr: eff at 7f, shld get 10f
next term: acts on fast & soft grnd, any trk: progressive & useful, type to rate higher.

3888 **EAGLES CACHE** 12 [2] A Berry 2-9-0 J Carroll 12/1: 262302: 2 b c Eagle Eyed - Cache (Bustino) 5 77
Tried to make all, hdd 1f out, easily outpcd by wnr: clr of next, ran to best back up in trip, handles fast & soft.

3359 **MILLENNIUM LADY** 37 [13] B W Hills 2-8-9 M Hills 12/1: -053: 2 ch f Woodman - Salina Cookie (Seattle 9 57
Dancer) Towards rear, prog halfway, btn 2f out: op 7/1, difficult draw: not enjoy softer grnd? btr 3359.

3940 **DEFINITE GUEST** 7 [14] G Margarson 2-9-0 D Holland 25/1: 604: Prom, fdd appr fnl 1f: qck reapp. hd 62

3478 **KIMOE WARRIOR** 32 [10] A Mackay 66/1: 5005: Mid-div thr'out: up in trip, see 1823. 5 54$

3571 **JOHNSTONS DIAMOND** 28 [8] 2-9-0 W Supple 66/1: -406: Chsd ldrs 5f: up in trip, see 3571, 3137. 2½ 50

-- **DOWNPOUR** [6] 2-9-0 G Duffield 8/1: 7: Dwelt, nvr a factor: $85,000 Torrential half-brother to 5 42
sev wnrs in the States: gelding with Sir M Prescott.

3358 **GEORGES WAY** 37 [7] 2-9-0 J Reid 20/1: 08: In tch till halfway: see 3358. 1 40

3156 **REIMS** 46 [9] 2-9-0 T E Durcan 16/1: 09: Dwelt, al bhd: 7 wk abs, tricky high draw. 1¾ 38

-- **RACINGFORYOU LASS** [5] 2-8-9 A Nicholls 66/1: 0: Al bhd: 10th on debut: Moujeeb first foal. 2 30

2686 **LAGGAN MINSTREL** 67 [11] 2-9-0 P Fessey 33/1: 00: Handy, wkng when stmbld badly 2f out/lost pl: 11th. 3 31

-- **SPARTAN SAILOR** [3] 2-9-0 N Kennedy 66/1: 0: Dwelt, sn struggling: 12th on debut: Handsome dist 0
Sailor May foal. half-brother to a couple of winning pt-to-ptrs: with A Senior.

12 ran   Time 1m 31.85 (6.85)   (K Abdulla)   J H M Gosden Manton, Wilts.

4069   2.50 PASTARAZZI CLASS STKS 3YO+ 0-80 (D)   6f rnd   Soft   Inapplicable
£4465   £1374   £687   £343   3 yo rec 2 lb

*4010 **LADY BOXER** 4 [2] M Mullineaux 4-9-3 A Mackay 13/8 FAV: 001011: 4 b f Komaite - Lady Broker 88
(Petorius) In tch, shkn up to lead appr fnl 1f, rdn out: well bckd, qck reapp: prev won here at Chester & 4 days
ago at Ayr (Silver Cup h'cap): '99 wnr again at Chester (this stks, rtd 79): '98 Leicester wnr (auct mdn, rtd 84):
eff at 6/7.5f on firm, loves hvy: goes on any trk, likes Chester: most progressive & has a turn of foot.

2697 **DOWNLAND** 70 [10] G Wragg 4-9-0 (BL) J P Spencer 6/1: 0-0002: 4 b c Common Grounds - Boldabsa 1½ 81
(Persian Bold) In tch, wide, switched ins to chase wnr ent fnl 2f, kept on but nvr able to chall: op 5/1, 10 wk
abs: clr of rem & a sound run from a high draw in first time blnks: acts on firm & soft grnd: see 1173.

3809 **NOMORE MR NICEGUY** 11 [12] E J Alston 6-9-0 W Supple 11/1: 664603: 6 b h Rambo Dancer - Lariston 5 71
Gale (Pas de Seul) Slow into stride, towards rear, imprvg when hmpd/lost grnd over 2f out, late rally for 3rd:
tchd 14/1: no easy task at the weights/from high draw: slipping down the weights: see 977.

3821 **IMPERIALIST** 16 [11] R Hannon 3-8-9 (bl) J Reid 10/1: 020004: Prom, eff appr fnl 1f, unable to qckn. 1 66

3791 **CHARLOTTEVALENTINA** 18 [3] 3-8-9 T E Durcan 8/1: 050025: Trkd ldrs, short of room ent fnl 2f shd 66
& onepace after: tchd 10/1: not much luck in running, faster grnd will suit: see 1220.

3629 **COWBOYS AND ANGELS** 25 [6] 3-9-1 Darren Williams (5) 12/1: 241206: Chsd ldrs till fdd appr fnl 1f. 3½ 65

3785 **SARSON** 18 [15] 4-9-0 J Fortune 20/1: 000007: Al around same place: not given a hard time: see 1676 ¾ 60

4010 **ACE OF PARKES** 4 [1] 4-9-0 J Carroll 12/1: 003008: Led till 1½f out, sn btn: qck reapp: see 1245. nk 59

3612 **FEAST OF ROMANCE** 26 [8] 3-8-12 S Whitworth 33/1: 300409: Stumbled after 1f, al towards rear. 2½ 54

3771 **SUMTHINELSE** 18 [9] 3-9-1 D Holland 14/1: 146030: Prom till halfway: 10th, see 3771, 2250. ½ 56

4043 **Time To Fly** 1 [7] 7-9-0 (bl) K Hodgson 66/1:   3768 **Palacegate Touch** 19 [14] 10-9-0 P Bradley (5) 50/1:

3138 **Taker Chance** 47 [4] 4-9-0 A Robertson (7) 100/1:   3183 **Look Here Now** 44 [16] 3-8-12 K Darley 25/1:

3694 **Gad Yakoun** 23 [13] 7-9-0 (t) P Fessey 100/1:

15 ran   Time 1mm 19.76 (6.66)   (Esprit de Corps Racing)   M Mullineaux Alpraham, Cheshire.

4070 3.20 WEATHERBYS NURSERY HCAP 2YO 0-95 (C) 7f rnd Soft 105 Inapplicable [88]
£6695 £2060 £1030 £515

3901 **BOISDALE 11** [1] G C Bravery 2-8-5 (65) A Nicholls 8/1: 006401: 2 b c Common Grounds - Alstomeria 78
(Petoski) Led, qcknd 3L clr appr fnl 1f, unchall: took full advantage of plum draw: eff forcing the pace over
a sharp 7f: handles firm, imprvd in this soft going (as do many of this sire's progeny).

3879 **PASITHEA 13** [8] T D Easterby 2-9-0 (74) K Darley 9/1: 533102: 2 b f Celtic Swing - Midnight's 3½ 80
Reward (Night Shift) Chsd wnr, outpcd appr fnl 1f: ran well considering drawn 8: acts on fast & soft grnd.

*3832 **LA NOTTE 15** [3] W Jarvis 2-9-5 (79) M Tebbutt 7/2 FAV: 313: 2 b f Factual - Miss Mirror (Magic 1 83
Mirror) Trkd ldrs, lost grnd halfway & had to be snatched up bef 2f out, rallied fnl 1f to go 3rd: bckd on h'cap
bow: ignore this, acts on firm/fast & prob soft & will apprec a return to a more conventional trk: see 3832.

*3615 **GAZETTE IT TONIGHT 26** [6] A Berry 2-8-1 (61) F Norton 5/1: 313314: Chsd ldrs onepace under 1½ 63
press fnl 1f: btr 3615 (fast grnd seller).

3901 **DREAMIE BATTLE 11** [2] 2-8-5 (65) P M Quinn (3) 8/1: -33505: Towards rear, forced wide over 2f 1¼ 65
out, nvr a factor: needs a return to 1m, see 3287.

*3913 **LAPWING 9** [7] 2-9-10 (84)(6ex) M Hills 5/1: 4116: Well plcd, fdd appr fnl 1f: top-weight with a penalty: shd 84
first try on soft grnd & poss came too soon after 3913.

3860 **PASHMEENA 14** [10] 2-9-7 (81) J Fortune 6/1: -26357: Bhd ldrs, shkn up when hmpd over 2f out. 2 78

2916 **SHIMLA 56** [5] 2-7-12 (58) P Fessey 25/1: 0058: Nvr in it: 8 wk abs, h'cap bow. 8 41
8 ran Time 1m 34.08 (9.08) (OTT Partnership) G C Bravery Newmarket.

4071 3.50 TOTE QUICK PICK HCAP 3YO+ 0-80 (D) 1m7f195y Soft Inapplicable [78]
£7670 £2360 £1180 £590 3 yo rec 12lb

3890 **PRAIRIE FALCON 12** [10] B W Hills 6-10-0 (78) M Hills 12/1: 604001: 6 b g Alzao - Sea Harrier (Grundy) 83
Towards rear, trav well/hugged ins rail, clsd halfway, qcknd to lead ent fnl 1f, clvrly: lightly
rcd in '99, 4th in the Chester Cup (rtd 91): '98 wnr at Haydock & Goodwood (amat h'caps, rtd 85): eff at
2m/2m2.7f: acts on firm & soft grnd, any trk, likes Chester: gd weight carrier, can run well fresh: well ridden.

2516 **LASTMAN 74** [5] J J O'Neill 5-8-5 (55) D O'Donohoe 16/1: -52202: 5 b g Fabulous Dancer - Rivala 1½ 59
(Riverman) Ran in snatches early, rear, prog 5f out, led going well bef fnl 1f, hdd just ins last, kept on:
tchd 20/1, clr of rem: first run, eff at 12f/2m1f: suited by soft/hvy, handles fast, see 1767.

3963 **THROWER 6** [6] P D Evans 9-8-1 (51) W Supple 16/1: 145003: 9 b g Thowra - Atlantic Line (Capricorn) 7 50
Cl-up, led 2f out, sn hdd, same pace: qck reapp, back to form at 2m & likes soft: see 470.

3511 **JASEUR 31** [6] G Barnett 7-9-6 (70)(bl) L Vickers (4) 12/1: 006024: Well plcd, led ent fnl 5f hd 69
till 2f out, no extra: gd run, see 1791.

3993 **BLACK WEASEL 5** [7] 5-7-11 (47)(1ow)(9oh) J Bramhill 12/1: 562555: Chsd ldrs, fdd 2f out: op 16/1. 6 41

3916 **MY LEGAL EAGLE 9** [2] 6-8-1 (51) K Dalgleish (5) 10/1: 600406: Al mid-div: op 12/1, see 1023. 7 40

3395 **SANDBAGGEDAGAIN 35** [1] 6-9-5 (69) K Darley 8/1: 552047: Nvr troubled ldrs: blnks omitted. ¾ 57

3611 **FINAL SETTLEMENT 26** [3] 5-9-3 (67) S Whitworth 7/1: 534148: In tch till 4f out: see 2856 (fast grnd). 21 40

*3590 **MANZONI 27** [11] 4-7-11 (47) P Hanagan (4) 12/1: 060019: Chsd ldrs till 5f out: lngr trip, btr 3590 (fast). ¾ 19

2672 **NICELY 67** [8] 4-9-6 (70) G Duffield 7/1: -05000: Chsd ldrs, wknd appr fnl 3f: 10th, bckd, 10 wk abs. 3 40

1548 **BENTYHEATH LANE 114** [1] 3-7-12 (60)(2ow)(10oh) A Mackay 50/1: 00-00: Led till appr fnl 4f, sn dist 0
btn, eased: 11th, stiff task, 4 month abs, h'cap bow.

3916 **JACK DAWSON 9** [12] 3-8-6 (68) F Norton 4/1 FAV: 223120: Reared start, mid-div, eff 6f out, btn 3 0
3f out: 12th, bckd: probably pay to forgive, needs faster grnd: see 3637.

3783 **TOTEM DANCER 18** [4] 7-8-7 (57) D Holland 7/1: 420630: Al bhd: 13th, unproven beyond 14f, see 1087. 5 0

3865 **Scheming 14** [15] 3-9-3 (79) J Carroll 16/1:

1369 **Quigleys Point 124** [9] 4-7-10 (46)(16oh) N Kennedy 100/1: P
15 ran Time 3m 45.77 (23.07) (Mrs B W Hills) B W Hills Lambourn, Berks.

4072 4.20 LEAHURST COND STKS 2YO (C) 7f122y rnd Soft Inapplicable
£5539 £2101 £1050 £477

*2686 **ELNAHAAR 67** [1] E A L Dunlop 2-9-0 W Supple 10/3: 11: 2 b c Silver Hawk - Futuh (Diesis) 98
Chsd ldrs, briefly short of room appr fnl 1f, rdn to lead ins last, ran on strongly: op 5/2, 10 wk abs: unbtn,
earlier won debut at Salisbury (mdn): half-brother to useful sprint/10f wnrs: dam 6f wnr: eff at 7.5f, 1m + is
going to suit: acts on gd & soft grnd, sharp or stiff/gall trks: progressive, useful colt, win more races.

3926 **DAYGLOW DANCER 10** [5] M R Channon 2-9-0 Craig Williams 3/1: 324252: 2 b c Fraam - Fading 2 94
(Pharly) Led till appr fnl 1f, no extra under press: bckd: acts on fast & hvy: consistent in defeat.

3787 **ZELOSO 18** [2] J L Dunlop 2-9-0 (VIS) K Darley 6/1: 302143: 2 b c Alzao - Silk Petal (Petorius) 1¼ 92
Prsd ldr, onepace appr fnl 1f: improvmed for visor, speed on soft grnd: see 3787, 3283.

3991 **DENISE BEST 5** [4] A Berry 2-8-6 Mark Flynn (6) 25/1: 024: Sn badly outpcd, styd on strongly fnl nk 83
2f, nvr nrr: quick reapp: made up a lot of late grnd, could win a soft grnd mdn on a galloping trk.

3786 **SUNNY GLENN 18** [3] 2-8-11 D Holland 66/1: 05: Sn struggling: stiff task. 16 66

*3859 **OVERSPECT 14** [6] 2-9-5 J Fortune 11/8 FAV: -1316: Went right start, prom till halfway, sn btn & 1¾ 72
eased: well bckd: reportedly unable to handle this soft surface: worth another ch after 3859 (fast).
6 ran Time 1m 43.89 (11.59) (Hamdan Al Maktoum) E A L Dunlop Newmarket, Suffolk

---

4073 4.55 TELME.COM HCAP 3YO+ 0-85 (D) 5f rnd Soft Inapplicable [83]
£4043 £1244 £622 £311 3 yo rec 1 lb Low numbers favoured

3894 **POLLY GOLIGHTLY 12** [4] M Blanshard 7-8-6 (61)(bl) Dale Gibson 6/1: 004301: 7 ch m Weldnaas - Polly's 67
Teahouse (Shack) Led, rdn clr ins last: '99 wnr here at Chester (h'cap, rtd 71): '98 wnr again here at
Chester & York (h'caps, rtd 73): stays 7f, all wins at 5f: acts on firm, suited by gd/soft & hvy: wears
blnks or a visor & likes to force the pace on any trk, loves Chester: took advantage of gd draw & h'cap mark.

3960 **BODFARI PRIDE 6** [3] D Nicholls 5-9-9 (78) A Nicholls 3/1 FAV: 162002: 5 b g Pips Pride - Renata's 2½ 78
Ring (Auction Ring) Bhd ldrs, eff & ch appr fnl 1f, kept on onepace: nicely bckd, quick reapp: likes soft.

3821 **CLASSY CLEO 16** [1] P D Evans 5-9-5 (74) T E Durcan 6/1: 001003: 5 b m Mujadil - Sybaris shd 74
(Crowned Prince) Mid-div, prog 2f out, styd on, unable to chall: ran to fair trk: see 3512.

3543 **THE GAY FOX 29** [9] B A McMahon 6-9-4 (73)(tbl) K Darley 10/1: 241004: Hmpd & lost sev lengths hd 72
start, grad imprvd & drvn to dspt 3rd ins last, no extra nr fin: bckd, clr of rem: wld have been plcd: see 2697.

CHESTER   WEDNESDAY SEPTEMBER 20TH   Lefthand, V Tight Track

4015 **THREAT 4** [6] 4-9-2 (71)(t) D Holland 10/3: 005135: Bustled along towards rear, imprvd 2f out, 3½ 63
onepace after: bckd, quick reapp: faster grnd suits: see 3894.
3512 **WESTCOURT MAGIC 31** [5] 7-8-8 (63) J Carroll 8/1: 000006: Prom till appr fnl 1f: won this in '99. 4 47
3894 **BODFARI KOMAITE 12** [12] 4-9-5 (74) T Lucas 12/1: 113407: Chsd ldrs wide till halfway: difficult shd 58
task from stall 12 & is prob worth another ch, see 1662.
3622 **CARTMEL PARK 26** [2] 4-9-5 (74) O Pears 14/1: 030048: Prsd wnr till ent fnl 2f: see 2078. ½ 57
3734 **SAILING SHOES 21** [11] 4-9-5 (74) J Fortune 20/1: 006069: Al bhd: poor draw, see 1810. shd 57
3687 **ANSELLAD 23** [13] 3-9-12 (82) G Carter 33/1: 002500: Nvr a factor: 10th, poor draw, see 1285. ¾ 63
3861 **BOLD EFFORT 14** [7] 8-9-12 (81)(bl) D O'Donohoe 12/1: 050100: Dwelt, nvr in it, 11th, top-weight: 12 42
reportedly lost action, prefers a faster surface: see 3516.
11 ran   Time 1m 06.47 (6.67)   (David Sykes)   M Blanshard Upper Lambourn, Berks

---

4074   5.25 CHESTER FM HCAP 3YO+ 0-70 (E)   1m2f75y   Soft   Inapplicable   [70]
£4459   £1372   £686   £343   3 yo rec 6 lb

3725 **RINGSIDE JACK 21** [5] C W Fairhurst 4-9-7 (63)(vis) J Fanning 12/1: 604001: 4 b g Batshoof - Celestine 71
(Skyliner) In tch, closed going well 3f out, led bef dist, shaken up, rdly: earlier won reapp at Beverley (h'cap):
'99 rnr-up (h'cap, rtd 81): juv wnr at Redcar (mdn, nurs plcd, rtd 82): eff at 1m/10.5f, tried 12f: acts on
fast, suited by soft/hvy: goes on any trk & runs well fresh: eff with/without visor: qk follow up on this grnd?
3794 **ADMIRALS PLACE 18** [13] H J Collingridge 4-9-11 (67) G Carter 8/1: 420532: 4 ch c Perugino - Royal 3 70
Daughter (High Top) Mid-div, prog to lead bef 2f out till appr fnl 1f, same pace: clr rem, op 6/1: sound
weight-carrying performance in these conditions: loves soft: see 3794, 965.
3430 **RUTLAND CHANTRY 33** [2] S Gollings 6-9-5 (61) J Fortune 11/2: 566053: 6 b g Dixieland Band - 3½ 60
Christchurcน (So Blessed) Mid-div, not clr run over 3f out & lost place, rallied bef dist for 3rd, no threat:
bckd from 13/2: gd run, suited by soft grnd: see 601.
3963 **MASTER BEVELED 6** [14] P D Evans 10-9-4 (60)(vis) T E Durcan 7/1: 0-3034: Rear, wide, mod late 1½ 57
hdwy, nvr a threat: quick reapp, difficult task from stall 14 over an inadequate trip: see 809.
3810 **FREEDOM QUEST 17** [8] 5-9-4 (60) R Lappin 20/1: 004205: Dwelt, imprvg when hmpd/forced wide ent ¾ 56
fnl 4f, hmpd again bef 2f out & switched, nvr on terms: vis reapp: forget this, got no kind of run, see 2522.
3858 **BAHAMAS 14** [9] 3-9-6 (68)(bl) G Duffield 4/1 FAV: 331106: Well plcd, led after halfway till bef 4 59
2f out & btn: well bckd: unsuited forcing it?: see 2945.
3887 **BACHELORS PAD 12** [1] 6-9-3 (59) S Whitworth 9/1: 346107: Mid-div, feeling pace halfway, nvr on hd 50
terms: unsuited by drop back to a sharp 10f: see 3430 (12f here).
3994 **PAS DE PROBLEME 4** [3] 4-9-8 (64) Dale Gibson 8/1: 314608: In tch, chsd ldrs briefly 3f out, fdd. 1½ 53
3963 **ATLANTIC CHARTER 6** [6] 4-9-4 (60) D O'Donohoe 25/1: 065509: Al bhd: see 875. 16 34
3871 **ACID TEST 13** [7] 5-9-0 (56) Dean McKeown 20/1: 050600: Led till appr fnl 4f, sn btn: 10th, lngr trip. 2½ 27
3808 **YOUNG UN 17** [10] 5-9-3 (59) D Holland 10/1: 500030: Chsd ldrs till 4f out: 11th, see 786. 3 27
3702 **SHOTACROSS THE BOW 23** [11] 3-9-4 (66) M Hills 12/1: 003230: Chsd ldrs, wknd qckly appr fnl 2f: 1½ 33
12th, op 8/1: much better on faster grnd last thrice, see 3140.
3842 **PAARL ROCK 15** [4] 5-9-2 (58)(vis) J Carroll 12/1: 144160: Trkd ldrs, shaken up 4f out, sn short 5 20
of room & dropped rear: 13th, best ignored: see 3524.
3285 **HARLEQUIN DANCER 40** [12] 4-9-2 (58)(vis) K Darley 25/1: -00000: In tch, wide, prog halfway, wknd dist 0
qckly 3f out: 14th, 6 wk abs, difficult draw, see 1445.
14 ran   Time 2m 22.26 (13.76)   (M J G Partnership)   C W Fairhurst Middleham, N Yorks

---

GOODWOOD   THURSDAY SEPTEMBER 21ST   Righthand, Sharpish, Undulating Track

Official Going: SOFT   Stalls: Straight Course - Stands Side, Round Course - Inside, except 12f - Outside.

4075   2.00 UCELLO&UBU NH JOCKEYS HCAP 3YO+ 0-70 (E)   2m   Soft 114   -26 Slow   [41]
£3835   £1180   £590   £295   3 yo rec 12lb   Raced stands side fnl 3f.

3588 **SAMARARDO 28** [5] N P Littmoden 3-10-0 (53)(4oh) R Hughes 8/1: 546421: 3 b g Son Pardo - Kinlet 58
Vision (Vision) Made all, drvn & styd well till fnl 2f: op 6/1: '99 W'hampton wnr (h'cap, rtd 54a, rtd 60 at best on turf):
suited by 2m on fast, soft & fibresand: likes a sharp/undul track: has run well fresh: best without a visor.
*3978 **PERSIAN WATERS 6** [7] J R Fanshawe 4-11-11 (66)(4ex) M A Fitzgerald 7/4 FAV: 300-12: 4 b g Persian 2 68
Bold - Emerald Waters (King's Lake) Chsd wnr 4f out, hard rdn & kept on fnl 1f, al held by wnr: hvly bckd.
3755 **MARTHA REILLY 21** [6] Mrs Barbara Waring 4-10-0 (41)(12oh) R Wakley 50/1: 6-2003: 4 ch f shd 43
Rainbows For Life - Debach Delight (Great Nephew) Rear, styd on fnl 2f: clr rem: stays 2m on both AWs & soft.
3755 **STAND ASIDE 21** [1] Lady Herries 4-10-5 (46)(bl) L Aspell 25/1: 0-5404: Mid div, prog/rdn & chall 4 45
2f out, no extra fnl 1f: softer grnd: see 3448, 3241.
2475 **ESTACADO 444** [11] 4-10-7 (48) A Bates 9/1: 6/00-5: Chsd ldrs, lost pl after 5f, drvn/mod late 2½ 45
gains: op 6/1: Flat reapp, 4 month jmps abs: 99/00 scorer at Wincanton (juv claimer & juv nov) & Fontwell (juv
nov, rtd 127h at best, stays 2m3f, fast & hvy): unplcd on the Flat prev for B Gubby (rtd 62, tried visor).
3804 **LANCER 18** [9] 8-10-12 (53)(vis) T J Murphy 16/1: 650326: Rear, prog/chsd ldrs 3f out, sn held: lngr trip. 1¾ 48
2951 **SHARAF 55** [10] 7-10-7 (48) Sophie Mitchell 25/1: 230447: Chsd wnr 12f, btn fnl 2f: 8 week abs. 1¼ 42
3755 **GALAPINO 21** [12] 7-10-7 (48)(bl) S Curran 25/1: 505208: Chsd ldrs over 2f out, sn wknd: see 1044. 2½ 40
2750 **GRANNY RICH 432** [4] 6-10-0 (41)(3oh) R Thornton 6/1: 4564-9: Chsd ldrs over 2f out, wknd qckly 2 31
fnl 2f: Flat reapp, 7 month jumps abs, 99/00 wnr of 4 h'caps over timber between 2m/2m3.5f (rtd 108h, gd & soft
grnd): unplcd on the level last term: stays a gall 14f, handles firm & gd grnd.
1411 **CINDESTI 124** [14] 4-10-2 (43) E Husband 33/1: -00000: In tch, btn 2f out: 10th: 3 month jumps abs. 13 23
3800 **MISCONDUCT 18** [2] 6-10-11 (52) C Maude 9/1: -23240: Chsd ldrs 11th: btr 3800, 3424 (14f). nk 32
3835 Chief Wallah 16 [8] 4-11-4 (59) J Culloty 20/1:   4017} Tumbleweed Glen 367 [13] 4-11-10 (65)(bl) V Slattery 25/1:
13 ran   Time 3m 46.75 (22.45)   (Trojan Racing)   N P Littmoden Newmarket, Suffolk

---

4076   2.30 AMISTAR NURSERY HCAP 2YO 0-85 (D)   1m rnd   Soft 114   -26 Slow   [90]
£4416   £1359   £679   £339   Raced stands side fnl 3f

3922 **MONICA GELLER 9** [16] C N Allen 2-7-12 (60)(2ow)(3oh) Martin Dwyer 10/1: 303621: 2 b f Komaite - Rion 64
River (Taufan) Rear, prog halfway & drvn/led over 1f out, held on gamely inside last, drvn out: 1st win: dam
10f wnr: suited by step up to 1m: acts on firm, soft & fibresand: likes a sharp/undulating or fair track.

1254

3824 **GRAND FIVE** 17 [2] J S Moore 2-8-9 (71) R Hughes 10/1: -20032: 2 b c Spectrum - Iberian Dancer   nk 74
(El Gran Senor) Trckd ldrs travelling well over 2f out, rdn/switched & styd on well inside last, just held:
op 8/1: styd longer 1m trip well, further shld suit: enjoys gd/soft & soft grnd: see 3824, 1573.
3901 **CEARNACH** 12 [9] B J Meehan 2-8-5 (67) D R McCabe 10/1: -00543: 2 b c Night Shift - High Matinee   ¾ 69
(Shirley Heights) Chsd ldrs, rdn/outpcd over 3f out, styd on for press inside last, not pace to chall: styd
longer 1m trip on only 2nd h'cap start: acts on firm & soft grnd: see 3901, 3387.
3583 **RAMBAGH** 28 [17] J L Dunlop 2-8-6 (68) T Quinn 12/1: 4254: Chsd ldrs, rdn/ch 2f out, just held   nk 69
ins last: h'cap bow, op 10/1: eff at 1m, handles fast & soft grnd: likes a sharp/undul track: see 3039, 2306.
3239 **HAWKES RUN** 43 [13] M Tebbutt 6/1: 6645: Rear, prog/chsd ldrs 3f out, held fnl 1f: hd 73
h'cap bow, 6 week abs: styd longer 1m trip: handles fast & soft grnd: see 3239, 1472.
3817 **BOUND** 17 [7] J Reid 15/2: -00036: Chsd ldrs, drvn/chall 2f out, fdd: handles fast & soft.   ¾ 74
3409 **CASHNEEM** 35 [10] 2-9-7 (83) Pat Eddery 5/1 FAV: 4127: Led, hdd over 1f out, fdd: btr 3409 (gd/fm).   hd 81
3864 **THUNDERMILL** 15 [1] R Mullen 16/1: -5368: Rear, prog/chsd ldrs over 2f out, sn held.   4 73
3901 **GAY CHALLENGER** 12 [11] 2-8-1 (63) F Norton 25/1: -50409: Rear, eff 3f out, little hdwy: see 2959.   3½ 50
3888 **SCOTISH LAW** 13 [4] 2-9-0 (76) S Whitworth 14/1: -2100: Mid div, btn 3f out: 10th: btr 3400 (6f, fast).   3 59
3817 **POLISH PADDY** 17 [3] 2-8-5 (67) L Newman (3) 12/1: 664460: Chsd ldrs 6f: 11th: op 14/1: btr 3817.   1¼ 48
3799 **WELL MAKE IT** 18 [14] 2-8-10 (72) I Mongan (5) 16/1: 6000: Mid div at best: 12th: op 14/1, h'cap bow.   hd 52
*3733 **Sel** 22 [12] 2-8-0 (62)(bl) J Quinn 14/1:   3830 **Andromedas Way** 16 [5] 2-7-12 (60) J Mackay (5) 20/1:
3154 **Mujalia** 47 [8] P Doe 33/1:   3239 **Saafend Flyer** 43 [15] 2-7-11 (59)(1ow)(2oh) A Nicholls 14/1:
16 ran   Time 1m 48.61 (11.21)   (Newmarket Connections Ltd)   C N Allen Newmarket, Suffolk

---

4077	**3.00 EBF NFU CLASSIFIED STKS 3YO+ 0-95 (B)** 1m rnd Soft 114 -03 Slow
	£8775 £3328 £1664 £756 3 yo rec 4 lb Raced centre - stands side fnl 3f

3510 **BOLD KING** 12 [3] J W Hills 5-9-2 R Hills 7/2: 030001: 5 br g Anshan - Spanish Heart (King Of Spain)   92
Rear, in tch, rdn/prog to lead over 1f out, styd on well inside last, rdn out: op 3/1: earlier made a winning reapp
at Ascot (val h'cap): '99 scorer at Newbury (rtd h'cap, rtd 90) & plcd sev times: '98 Southwell wnr (auction mdn,
rtd 80a): suited by a stiff 7f/sharp 1m, stays 10f: acts on fast, relishes gd/soft & soft grnd: handles any track:
runs well fresh & a gd weight carrier: v useful performer on this testing grnd.
3469 **PENANG PEARL** 33 [4] G A Butler 4-9-1 J P Spencer 9/4 FAV: 241-02: 4 b f Bering - Guapa   3 89
(Shareef Dancer) Rear, in tch, trck ldrs halfway, rdn/every ch 2f out, sn held by wnr: hvly bckd: can rate higher.
3883 **CHAPEL ROYALE** 13 [6] K Mahdi 3-9-1 B Marcus 4/1: 100033: 3 gr c College Chapel - Merci   shd 93$
Royale (Fairy King) Led/dsptd lead till over 1f out, styd on for press inside last: loves soft grnd: see 2614.
2578 **ON TIME** 71 [5] J R Fanshawe 3-8-9 D Harrison 5/2: 13-354: Chsd ldrs, eff over 2f out, al held   2½ 83
by front trio: hvly bckd tho' op 7/4: 10 week abs: see 1574 (7f).
6] **AQUIRE NOT DESIRE** 684 [2] 4-8-13 I Mongan 20/1: 14/5-5: Keen, led/dsptd lead 2f, btn 3f out: 14 68
Flat reapp, 6 month jumps abs (unplcd, rtd 99h, h'cap, C Mann): ex-French, Flat wnr in the provinces in '98
(9f, soft grnd, Mme C Head): now with G L Moore.
3945 **KAFIL** 8 [1] 6-8-13 A Nicholls 66/1: 060306: Led/dsptd lead 6f out till 4f out, sn btn: see 1.   nk 67$
6 ran   Time 1m 46.77 (9.37)   (The Farleigh Court Racing Partnership)   J W Hills Upper Lambourn, Berks

---

4078	**3.30 GR 3 SUPREME STKS 3YO+ (A)** 7f rnd Soft 114 -01 Slow
	£22800 £8740 £4370 £2090 3 yo rec 3 lb Raced centre - stands side fnl 3f

3724 **MOUNT ABU** 25 [5] J H M Gosden 3-8-9 J Fortune 2/1 FAV: 411631: 3 b c Foxhound - Twany Angel   111
(Double Form) Trkd ldr, drvn/strong chall fnl 2f, led over 1f out & held on gamely inside last, all out: hvly bckd,
op 5/2: earlier scored in Listed contests at Ascot & Lingfield: '99 wnr at Newbury (mdn, rtd 105 at best, P C Hyam):
eff at 6/7f on fast, likes soft & any track: smart & geniune, relishes easy grnd, could win again this Autumn.
4056 **ONE WON ONE** 5 [4] Ms J Morgan 6-8-12 Pat Eddery 11/4: 203242: 6 b g Naevus - Harvard's   hd 110
Bay (Halpern Bay) Chsd ldrs, drvn to chall fnl 1f, styd on well, just held: well bckd: quick reapp: relishes
easy grnd & shld certainly win another Listed race: see 1834 (Listed).
3878 **LAST RESORT** 14 [7] B W Hills 3-8-6 R Hills 9/1: 363433: 3 ch f Lahib - Breadcrumb (Final Straw)   ½ 106
Chsd ldrs, rdn/briefly led over 1f out, just held nr fin: op 7/2: smart run up in class & acts on fast & soft.
3469 **BEDAZZLING** 33 [3] J R Fanshawe 3-8-6 D Harrison 9/1: -01404: Rear, in tch, rdn & styd on well   ½ 105
fnl 1f, not reach front trio: op 6/1: likes soft & a gallop/may run stepped up to Gr class: Listed will suit.
3784 **WINNING VENTURE** 19 [8] 3-8-9 J Reid 10/1: 300005: Dwelt/rear, eff 2f out, sn held: blinks omitted.   4 102
3469 **CLARANET** 23 [2] 3-8-6 J Tate 12/1: 002546: Led & soon clr, hdd/wknd over 1f out: see 3104, 934.   3 95
*3902 **OMAHA CITY** 12 [6] 6-8-12 J P Spencer 9/1: 035217: Al rear: stiff task, btr 3902 (rtd h'cap).   1¼ 94
3878 **LITTLEFEATHER** 14 [1] 3-8-6 S Sanders 9/1: 510208: Rear, eff 3f out, sn held: op 5/1: btr 3120 (6f).   ½ 89
8 ran   Time 1m 32.53 (8.03)   (Gary Seidler & Andy J Smith)   J H M Gosden Manton, Wilts

---

4079	**4.00 EBF FARMERS DAY NOV STKS 2YO (D)** 6f Soft 114 +02 Fast
	£4189 £1289 £644 £322

*3881 **APPELLATION** 13 [4] R Hannon 2-9-5 L Newman (3) 4/6 FAV: -6411: 2 b c Clantime - Chablisse   95
(Radetzky) Made all, shaken up/briefly rdn over 1f out to assert, styd on well under hands & heels riding fnl 1f:
hvly bckd at odds on: confirmed improvement of earlier mdn win here at Goodwood (C/D): eff at 6f, 7f will suit:
acts on fast & soft grnd: likes Goodwood: useful colt, found this a straightforward task, can rate more highly.
*3852 **ZHITOMIR** 15 [2] S Dow 2-9-2 P Doe 7/1: 640612: 2 ch c Lion Cavern - Treasure Trove (The Minstrel)   1½ 86
Led/dsptd lead, ev ch over 1f out, sn held by wnr: clr of rem, op 5/1: acts on gd & soft grnd: see 3852 (mdn).
-- **TREMEZZO** [7] B J Meehan 2-8-8 Pat Eddery 11/2: 3: 2 b c Mind Games - Rosa Van Fleet   7 64
(Sallust) Chsd ldrs, btn 2f out: op 9/2: April foal, 22,000gns 2yo: half brother to a 9f wnr.
3661 **MISS BEETEE** 25 [3] J J Bridger 2-8-7 J Quinn 14/1: -44: Dwelt/rear, bhd halfway, mod late gains.   shd 63
*3757 **MAID OF ARC** 21 [1] 2-8-7 D Harrison 12/1: 446315: Bhd 2f out: op 20/1, new stable: btr 3757 (sell).   5 53
-- **DA WOLF** 25 [5] 2-8-8 Martin Dwyer 14/1: 6: Chsd ldrs 4f: op 12/1: Wolfhound colt, April foal, cost   1 52
Ffr180,000: dam unrcd though well related: sire high class 5/7f performer: with W Muir.
6 ran   Time 1m 16.7 (6.7)   (Noodles Racing)   R Hannon East Everleigh, Wilts

GOODWOOD

THURSDAY SEPTEMBER 21ST   Righthand, Sharpish, Undulating Track

---

4080   4.35 PLANTATION HCAP 3YO 0-85 (D)   7f rnd   Soft 114   -09 Slow   **[90]**
£4689   £1443   £721   £360   Raced stands side fnl 3f.

3460 **WILDFLOWER** 34 [10] R Charlton 3-8-6 (68) J Mackay (5) 9/2: 100041: 3 b f Namaqualand - Fajjoura   **77+**
(Fairy King) Made all, asserted under hands & heels riding fnl 2f, comfortably: val for 7L+: earlier scored on
debut at Kempton (mdn): eff at 7f, 1m will suit: handles fast, relishes soft grnd: handles a stiff/gall or
sharp track: can run well fresh: a revelation backs on soft grnd, one to follow in the mud this autumn.
*3854 **CAPE COAST** 15 [7] N P Littmoden 3-8-8 (70) S Carson (3) 100/30: 042112: 3 b g Common Grounds -   5   69
Strike It Rich (Rheingold) Mid div, prog to chase wnr over 2f out, al held: bckd, op 4/1: acts on fast & soft grnd.
-2364 **CLOTTED CREAM** 80 [5] P J Makin 3-9-1 (77) S Sanders 5/2 FAV: 3-3123: 3 gr f Eagle Eyed - Seattle   ½   75
Victory (Seattle Song) Chsd ldrs, rdn/onepce & held fnl 2f: bckd tho' op 2/1: 12 week abs: see 1500 (mdn, 6f).
2579 **ALAWAR** 71 [1] C G Cox 3-7-11 (58)(t)(1ow) A Nicholls 12/1: 000444: Rear, rdn/mod gains: 10 wk abs.   ½   56
3643 **JAWLA** 26 [2] 3-9-7 (83) R Hills 13/2: 321105: Mid div, eff 3f out, no impress: 12 week abs?   1   79
3456 **NORTHERN TRIO** 34 [11] 3-8-2 (64)(6ow)(29oh) J Tate 100/1: 000006: Rear, eff over 2f out, little hdwy.   5   53
3771 **THE PROSECUTOR** 19 [9] 3-8-3 (65) L Newman (2) 16/1: 014407: Chsd ldrs 5f: op 14/1: btr 1494 (6f).   2   51
3971 **ARCTIC HIGH** 7 [6] 3-7-12 (60)(2ow)(16oh) P Doe 50/1: 300008: Fly jmpd start, prom 4f: btr 1040.   1   45
3908 **LADYWELL BLAISE** 12 [12] 3-7-11 (59)(1ow)(9oh) Martin Dwyer 33/1: 000009: Al rear: btr 2320.   6   35
3319 **ALMASHROUK** 40 [4] 3-8-4 (66) B Marcus 12/1: 640650: Chsd wnr, btn 2f out: 10th: abs: see 731 (mdn).4   36
3580 **Magic Babe** 29 [8] 3-7-12 (60)(2ow)(30h) F Norton 33/1:
3970 **Moon Of Alabama** 7 [3] 3-7-10 (58)(3oh) J Quinn 33/1:
12 ran   Time 1m 33.11 (8.61)   (Anglia Bloodstock Syndicate 1998)   R Charlton Beckhampton, Wilts

---

4081   5.05 HORSERACING MDN 3YO (D)   1m1f192y   Soft 114   +02 Fast
£4416   £1359   £679   £339   Raced stands side fnl 3f

3869 **SHAIR** 14 [1] J H M Gosden 3-9-0 J Fortune 5/4 FAV: 42221: 3 br g Warning - Shaima (Shareef Dancer)   86
Trkd ldrs, chsd ldr over 2f out, hard drvn & led narrowly inside last, sn hdd, kept on gamely to lead again nr line,
all out: hvly bckd: eff at 10f, return to 12f should suit: acts on fast & soft grnd: handles a stiff/gall or sharp
track: open to further improvement in h'cap company.
3429 **SECOND AFFAIR** 34 [4] C F Wall 3-8-9 R Mullen 9/2: 3242: 3 b f Pursuit Of Love - Startino (Bustino)   nk   80
Led, rdn/hdd ins last, sn led again till hdd & no extra nr line, just held: eff at 10/12f on fast & soft.
1697 **TIKRAM** 110 [3] H R A Cecil 3-9-0 T Quinn 7/2: -03: 3 ch c Lycius - Black Fighter (Secretariat)   2   83
Chsd ldrs, rdn & kept on fnl 2f, not pce of front pair: clr rem: bckd: eff at 10f, 12f could suit: handles soft.
4474} **ALL GOOD THINGS** 335 [9] R Ingram 3-9-0 L Newman (3) 50/1: 00-4: Rear, rdn/mod hdwy 3f out: 8   75
sn held: unplcd on 2 starts for J Dunlop in '99 (rtd 71, tried up to 7f): mid dists should suit, now qualified for h'caps.
3413 **COUTURE** 35 [10] 3-8-9 R Hughes 10/1: 255: Chsd ldrs, btn 2f out: op 12/1: btr 3221 (1m, fast).   8   62
3350 **GROVE LODGE** 38 [7] 3-9-0 F Norton 100/1: 000006: Chsd ldrs 7f: see 1024 (h'cap).   23   47
2531 **GENERAL JACKSON** 74 [2] 3-9-0 N Pollard 7/1: -04307: Chsd ldr, btn over 2f out: op 5/1, 10 wk abs.   ¾   46
-- **GAY LOVER** [5] 3-8-9 S Sanders 66/1: 8: Al bhd: debut: with Dr Naylor.   3   38
3804} **SUPER STORY** 380 [11] 3-8-9 A Eddery (5) 66/1: 0-9: Al bhd: reapp, no form.   1¾   36
-- **SEASONAL BLOSSOM** [8] 3-8-9 Paul Eddery 33/1: 060: Al bhd: 10th: 12 week abs, British debut, mod.1½   35
-- **FAY KING** [6] 3-9-0 J Quinn 50/1: 0: Bhd halfway: 11th: debut: with J Mullins.   dist   0
11 ran   Time 2m 15.4 (11.2)   (Sheikh Mohammed)   J H M Gosden Manton, Wilts

---

PONTEFRACT

THURSDAY SEPTEMBER 21ST   Lefthand, Undulating Track With Stiff Uphill Finish

---

Official Going   GOOD TO SOFT (SOFT PLACES). Stalls: Inside.

4082   2.15 EBF DIGITAL MDN DIV 1 2YO (D)   6f rnd   Soft 97   -20 Slow
£3363   £1035   £517   £258

3833 **SABO ROSE** 16 [13] W J Haggas 2-8-9 P Robinson 3/1: 31: 2 b f Prince Sabo - Crimson Rosella (Polar   **80+**
Falcon) Dwelt, mid div, switched ent str, ran on strongly to get up towards fin, going away: bckd: Feb first
foal: eff at 6f, 7f+ sure to suit: acts on soft grnd & a stiff/undulating track: impressed today, win more races.
3568 **LILLEMAN** 29 [14] G A Butler 2-9-0 D Holland 11/8 FAV: 502: 2 b c Distant Relative - Lillemor   ¾   82
(Connaught) Front rank, led ent str, hdd & no extra fnl 1f, sn drvn, hdd cl home, not btn far: well bckd: handles fast & soft.
-- **EXCEPTIONAL PADDY** [4] J A Osborne 2-9-0 S W Kelly (3) 25/1: 3: 2 b c Common Grounds - Itkan   1¾   77
(Marju) Dwelt, mid div, gd prog to lead ent fnl 2f, hdd inside last, onepce: clr rem, op 14/1, debut: 28,000 Ir
gns first foal, related to decent juv Painted Madam: eff at 6f on soft grnd: gd debut, should win a mdn.
2939 **HILL WELCOME** 56 [1] B W Hills 2-8-9 M Hills 11/1: 34: Rear, improved ent straight, went 4th   5   60
1f out, nvr nr ldrs: op 7/1, 8 week abs: needs 7f+: see 2939.
-- **GEM BIEN** [7] 2-9-0 P Fessey 33/1: 5: Well plcd, led after 3f till bef fnl 1f, fdd: Bien Bien 1st foal.   1¾   60
-- **MASTER FELLOW** [12] 2-9-0 Dean McKeown 25/1: 6: Sn chsd ldrs, eff 2f out, no impress: debut: hd   60
25,000gns First Trump half brother to 2 juv wnrs in Italy: dam unrcd: with J Given.
-- **DIABOLO** [9] 2-9-0 T Lucas 50/1: 7: Rear, wide, mod late prog: op 25/1, debut: 8,200gns   ¾   58
Magic Ring half brother to a modest mdn: dam 6f wnr: with M Easterby.
3748 **GOODGOLLYMISSMOLLY** 21 [15] 2-8-9 R Ffrench 100/1: 08: Prom 4f: see 3748.   1½   49
-- **DIWAN** [6] 2-9-0 W Supple 20/1: 9: Dwelt, nvr going pace: drifter from 8/1: 75,000 Ir gns   1½   50
Be My Guest half brother to a wnr abroad, dam a juv wnr: with R Armstrong.
-- **CANOVAS KINGDOM** [8] 2-9-0 O Urbina 50/1: 0: In tch 3f: 10th: half brother to sprinter Antonio Canova. nk   49
1486 **AMBER TIDE** 119 [5] 2-8-9 M Fenton 6/1: 340: Dsptd lead till halfway, sn btn: 13th, 4 month abs.   6   0
-- **SEARCH AND DESTROY** [2] 2-9-0 G Duffield 12/1: 0: Dwelt, nvr in it: 14th, debut, op 8/1:   0
$55,000 Sky Classic half brother to sev wnrs, dam a miler: with Sir M Prescott.
3697 **Double Ping** 24 [11] 2-8-9 G Parkin 33/1:   3617 **Time Proof** 27 [10] 2-9-0 P Hanagan (5) 50/1:
-- **Miss Rebecca** [3] 2-8-9 Kim Tinkler 25/1:
15 ran   Time 1m 21.1 (7)   (Don Magnifico Partnership)   W J Haggas Newmarket, Suffolk

PONTEFRACT THURSDAY SEPTEMBER 21ST Lefthand, Undulating Track With Stiff Uphill Finish

4083

2.45 EBF DIGITAL MDN DIV 2 2YO (D) 6f rnd Soft 97 -38 Slow
£3347 £1030 £515 £257

3705 **RICH GIFT 24** [10] J D Bethell 2-8-9 P Robinson 25/1: -51: 2 b f Cadeaux Genereux - Deep Divide (Nashwan) Keen, bhd ldrs, rdn appr fnl 1f, ran on to lead fnl 100y, won on the nod: slow time, left debut bhd: 25,000gns foal, dam stayed 1m: eff over a stiff/undulating 6f on soft grnd: improving. **74**
3955 **NIGHT GYPSY 8** [7] T D Easterby 2-8-9 K Darley 11/8 FAV: 32: 2 b f Mind Games - Ocean Grove (Fairy King) Nvr far away, drvn to chall well inside last, just btn: well bckd: eff at 5/6f on gd & soft: win a race. *shd* **73**
3268 **BASINET 42** [2] D W Barker 2-9-0 F Lynch 40/1: 03: 2 b c Alzao - Valiancy (Grundy) Led till well inside last, onepce: 6 week abs, left debut bhd: 12,000gns half brother to 6 wnrs, dam 10f wnr: eff forcing the pace over a stiff 6f on soft grnd, sure to relish 1m+ next term: pleasing. *1* **75**
-- **DARK SOCIETY** [6] P W Harris 2-9-0 A Culhane 25/1: 4: Towards rear, shkn up ent fnl 2f, kept on, unable to chall: 2,500gns Imp Society first foal, dam 11f wnr: handles soft: green today, relish 7f+. *nk* **74+**
-- **SHAKAKHAN** [3] 2-8-9 M Hills 13/2: 5: Waited with, went for ambitious run up ins rail fnl 2f, hdwy till ran into back of ldrs ins last & position accepted: luckless debut, op 5/1: 9,000gns Night Shift first foal, dam a stoutly bred mdn, sire gets speedy types: acts on soft: sure to rate more highly. *½* **68+**
3832 **MINETTE 16** [1] 2-8-9 G Carter 6/1: 66: Towards rear, prog to chase ldrs fnl 1f, sn onepce & hmpd. *2* **62**
3245 **FOLLOW FREDDY 43** [5] 2-9-0 D Holland 25/1: 07: Prom, no extra appr fnl 1f: 6 wk abs, see 3245. *nk* **66**
-- **MA JOLIE** [14] 2-8-9 J Stack 40/1: 8: Dwelt & bhd, late hdwy into mid div: 2,800gns Shalford filly. *1¼* **58**
-- **NO SAM NO** [8] 2-8-9 S W Kelly (3) 50/1: 9: Nvr better than mid div: 5,800gns Reprimand first foal. *1¼* **55**
3478 **HENRY PEARSON 33** [11] 2-9-0 W Supple 7/1: 050: Prom till halfway: 10th, btr 3478. *½* **59**
-- **EGYPT** [13] 2-9-0 G Duffield 7/1: 0: Veered right start, al towards rear: drifter from 7/2: Green Desert brother to useful miler Distant Oasis & half brother to v smart miler Reprimand: should leave this bhd. *7* **41**
-- **Mamcazma** [4] 2-9-0 K Hodgson 50/1: 3912 **Callmemrwoo 10** [9] 2-9-0 V Halliday 100/1:
-- **Grand Houdini** [12] 2-9-0 T Lucas 33/1:
14 ran Time 1m 22.2 (8.1) (Mrs J E Vickers) J D Bethell Middleham, N Yorks

4084

3.20 FILLIES NURSERY HCAP 2YO 0-85 (E) 1m rnd Soft 97 -12 Slow [87]
£3068 £944 £472 £236

3922 **CYNARA 9** [1] G M Moore 2-8-3 (62) K Dalgleish (5) 8/1: 521551: 2 b f Imp Society - Reina (Homeboy) Chsd ldrs, prog to lead ent fnl 1f, rdn out: badly drawn latest, earlier won at Newcastle (nursery): eff at 7f/1m: acts on firm & soft grnd, any track: improving filly. **69**
3609 **ESPANA 27** [6] B W Hills 2-8-6 (65) M Hills 8/1: 03052: 2 gr f Hernando - Pamela Peach (Habitat) Mid div, prog under press appr fnl 1f, grad clsd on wnr but nvr going to get there: gd run, stys 1m on soft & fast. *½* **71**
3692 **LOOKING FOR LOVE 24** [9] J G Portman 2-8-10 (69) G Baker (5) 6/1: 033623: 2 b f Tagula - Mousseux (Jareer) Well plcd, led ent fnl 3f till below dist, onepce: op 4/1 on h'cap bow: ran to best eff at 7f, stays 1m: acts on fast & soft grnd. *2* **71**
3706 **TENERIFE FLYER 24** [11] J Norton 2-7-10 (55)(1oh) P Hanagan (2) 14/1: 046044: Towards rear, wide, drvn appr fnl 1f, styd on till no extra nr fin: clr rem & a gd effort: stays 1m on soft grnd. *nk* **56**
3867 **FASTINA 14** [13] 2-9-0 (73) D Holland 11/1: 430345: Slow away, hdwy under press over 2f out, nvr nrr. *5* **66**
3409 **BRILLIANTRIO 35** [4] 2-9-6 (79) A Culhane 16/1: 106: Last, improving when short of room 2f out, not given a hard time: h'cap bow, prob worth another look, see 2985. *1¼* **70**
*3817 **FLIT ABOUT 17** [8] 2-9-7 (80) K Darley 10/3 FAV: 23517: Chsd ldrs till fdd ent fnl 2f: bckd, top-weight: first run on soft grnd, much btr 3817 (fast). *2½* **67**
3660 **IT GIRL 25** [5] 2-8-8 (67) M Roberts 10/1: -24658: Al towards rear: tchd 14/1, stablemate of favourite. *1¼* **52**
2948 **SHINNER 55** [3] 2-8-10 (69) J Weaver 16/1: 421409: Led till appr fnl 2f, lost pl: 8 wk abs, lngr trip. *¾* **53**
3397 **PRINCESS CLAUDIA 36** [10] 2-8-4 (63) J Carroll 9/1: 0340: Nvr troubled ldrs: 10th, h'cap bow. *¾* **46**
*3740 **EMMA CLARE 21** [12] 2-8-3 (62) T Williams 14/1: 002410: In tch, chase ldrs appr fnl 2f, sn wknd: 11th. *5* **37**
3990 **PRINCESS EMILY 6** [2] 2-9-1 (74) D Mernagh (3) 12/1: 03150: Prom 5f: 12th, qk reapp, nds faster grnd? *4* **43**
3308 **PENTAGON LADY 40** [7] 2-7-10 (55) Joanna Badger (7) 25/1: 000540: Dwelt, nvr in it wide: abs, 13th. *2½* **20**
13 ran Time 1m 50.5 (8.7) (R I Graham) G M Moore Middleham, N Yorks

4085

3.50 DALBY RATED HCAP 3YO+ 0-95 (C) 1m2f Soft 97 +08 Fast [99]
£6478 £2457 £1228 £558 3 yo rec 6 lb

3731 **ANNADAWI 22** [9] C N Kellett 5-8-1 (72)(29oh) G Baker (5) 50/1: 236331: 5 b g Sadler's Wells - Prayers n' Promises (Foolish Pleasure) Waited with, imprvd ent str, drvn & kept on gamely to lead fnl stride: gd time, overcame a massive 29lbs o/h: earlier won at Leicester (h'cap): mod in '99, incl over jumps: eff at 1m, better arnd 10f: handles fast but well suited by gd/soft or hvy grnd: best without blinks/visor & t-strap. **73**
*3989 **GOLDEN WAY 6** [10] E A L Dunlop 3-8-6 (83)(3ex) K Darley 4/6 FAV: 0-6112: 3 ch f Cadeaux Genereux - Diavolina (Lear Fan) Prom, went on appr fnl 1f, sn rdn, edged left, hdd line: well bckd: progressive. *shd* **83**
3628 **INDUCEMENT 26** [7] Mrs A J Perrett 4-9-0 (85) W Ryan 12/1: 0-4153: 4 ch g Sabrehill - Verchinina (Star Appeal) Mid div, prog 2f out, drvn bef dist, kept on for 3rd: back to form: see 3337. *1¼* **83**
1310 **DANCING BAY 128** [6] Miss J A Camacho 3-8-11 (88) A Culhane 12/1: 0-1104: Held up in tch, eff 2f out, late hdwy but nvr a threat: over 4 mth abs: grnd now in his favour, sharper next time & is worth a try at 12f. *1¾* **84**
3883 **LITTLE AMIN 13** [8] 4-8-7 (77)(1ow)(1oh) D Holland 10/1: 632665: Led after 2f till ent fnl 2f, no extra. *¾* **73**
3899 **SCOTTISH SPICE 12** [3] 3-8-4 (81) G Duffield 11/1: 05306D: Bhd ldrs, prog ent fnl 3f & every ch till fdd appr fnl 1f: fin 6th, disqualified & plcd last, jockey given 5 day ban for irresp riding: wins at 7f. *10* **71**
3810 **NOMINATOR LAD 18** [1] 6-8-5 (76)(2oh) F Lynch 25/1: 441606: Nvr a factor: plcd 6th: blnks omitted. *1¾* **57**
3794 **MUSALLY 19** [2] 3-8-3 (80) W Supple 16/1: 41007: Early ldr, lost place ent str: fin 8th, plcd 7th, op 10/1. *4* **55**
4017 **WELSH WIND 5** [5] 4-9-7 (92)(t) M Fenton 11/1: 042238: Chsd ldrs, under press when hmpd 3f out, eased: fin 9th, plcd 8th, op 7/1, top weight, quick reapp: prob best to ignore this: btr 4017, 3883. *dist* **0**
3505 **JAMADYAN 32** [4] 3-8-5 (82) J Stack 33/1: -64649: Prom till halfway: fin 10th, plcd 9th, longer trip. *28* **0**
10 ran Time 2m 17.0 (8.9) (Sean A Taylor) C N Kellett Smisby, Derby

PONTEFRACT

THURSDAY SEPTEMBER 21ST — Lefthand, Undulating Track With Stiff Uphill Finish

---

4086 4.20 IN PUBS & CLUBS MDN 2YO (D) 1m rnd Soft 97 -28 Slow
£3965 £1220 £610 £305

3972 **TIYOUN** 6 [2] D W Barker 2-9-0 F Lynch 10/1: 321: 2 b g Kahyasi -Taysala (Akarad) **84**
Pld hard, early ldr, regained lead appr fnl 2f, hard rdn, just held on: op 8/1, quick reapp: Ir£9,000 foal,
dam unrcd: eff at 1m on soft grnd & a stiff/undulating or gall track: consistent.

2563 **MR COMBUSTIBLE** 72 [6] B W Hills 2-9-0 M Hills 8/1: 02: 2 b c Hernando - Warg (Dancing Brave) shd **83**
Slow away, mid div, chsd ldrs when short of room appr fnl 1f, styd on strongly & edged left for press ins last,
just failed: 10 wk abs: suited by step up to 1m on soft grnd & will get mid-dists next term: should win a mdn.

3817 **MURRENDI** 17 [13] M R Channon 2-9-0 A Culhane 5/1: 505423: 2 b c Ashkalani - Formaestre 1¾ **80**
(Formidable) Prom & ev ch till onepcd below dist: bckd tho' op 4/1: handles soft but rtd higher on firm/fast prev.

3459 **ENGLISH HARBOUR** 34 [4] B W Hills 2-9-0 M Roberts 10/1: -004: Rear, plenty to do ent straight, shd **75**
gd hdwy when not clr run & switched 1f out, unable to chall: stablemate 2nd: improved on this easier surface:
interesting in 10f+ h'caps next term: see 3108.

3766 **DEUCE OF TRUMPS** 20 [1] 2-9-0 J Weaver 13/8 FAV: 35: Sn led, hdd appr fnl 2f, onepce fnl 1f: nk **79**
well bckd: more expected after promising debut in 3766.

-- **ELLA TINO** [8] 2-8-9 D Mernagh (3) 33/1: 6: Chsd ldrs till 1f out: half-sister to sev wnrs, dam 10f wnr. 5 **64**

3478 **QUI WARRANTO** 33 [11] 2-9-0 J Carroll 10/1: 0407: Nvr trbld ldrs: lngr trip, rtd higher on faster grnd. 3 **64**

2005 **FORUM FINALE** 96 [7] 2-8-9 D Holland 6/1: 258: Stumbled start, al towards rear: over 3 month abs. 1 **54**

3730 **BEST GUEST** 22 [5] 2-9-0 G Hind 20/1: 09: Prom till after halfway: see 3730. 10 **47**

-- **UMBOPA** [3] 2-9-0 M Fenton 14/1: 0: Slow away, al bhd: 10th, debut, op 10/1: $57,000 Gilded 1¾ **45**
Time Apr foal, related to useful miler Tik Fa & half brother to sev wnrs, dam unrcd: should do better in time.

-- **Jawrjik** [10] 2-9-0 W Supple 40/1:   3617 **Lance Feather** 27 [9] 2-9-0 R Cody Boutcher (7) 50/1:
12 ran   Time 1m 51.8 (10)   (Miss Sharon Long)   D W Barker Scorton, N Yorks

---

4087 4.55 SUBSCRIBE HCAP 3YO+ 0-70 (E) 5f rnd Soft 97 -03 Slow **[70]**
£3185 £980 £490 £245 3 yo rec 1 lb

3920 **TORRENT** 9 [16] D W Chapman 5-9-11 (67)(bl) Lynsey Hanna (7) 10/1: 313351: 5 ch g Prince Sabo **72**
- Maiden Pool (Sharpen Up) Towards rear, wide, gd prog appr fnl 1f, kept on well under hands & heels to lead
towards fin: earlier won at Brighton (class stks) & plcd sev times: '99 wnr at Lingfield (2, h'caps, rtd
73a) & Beverley (class stakes, rtd 75): '98 Catterick (mdn) & Thirsk wnr (h'cap, rtd 83, T Barron): eff at
6f, best at 5f: acts on firm, soft grnd, both AW's: wears blinks: admirably consistent this term.

3894 **MAROMITO** 13 [6] R Bastiman 3-9-3 (60) O Pears 14/1: 000002: 3 b c Up And At 'Em - Amtico ¾ **63**
(Bairn) Led, pshd over 2L clr appr fnl 1f, sn rdn, worn down well ins last: back to form, acts on fast & soft.

3377 **BOWLERS BOY** 36 [14] J J Quinn 7-9-1 (57) D Holland 10/3 FAV: 215403: 7 ch g Risk Me - Snow 1½ **56**
Wonder (Music Boy) Mid div, outpcd & short of room ent fnl 2f, switched & ran on inside last, nvr nrr: bckd:
back to form tho' shld apprec a return to 6f: see 1941.

3419 **KEBABS** 35 [17] J A Osborne 3-9-1 (58) S W Kelly (3) 20/1: 030504: Dwelt & well off the pace till 1¾ **52**
ran on strongly appr fnl 1f, nrst fin: return to 6f+ will suit: acts on gd & soft.

2603 **ABSENT FRIENDS** 70 [2] P Dobbs (5) 25/1: -04005: Chsd ldrs, eff appr fnl 1f, onepce. ½ **54**

3956 **NEEDWOOD TRICKSTER** 8 [11] 3-9-3 (60) G Hind 25/1: 360006: Towards rear, short of room appr fnl 1 **50**
1f, late hdwy: return to 6f will suit, see 1266.

3653 **MARON** 26 [9] 3-9-1 (58) J Carroll 20/1: 210007: Rear, nvr dangerous: prefers fast grnd, see 2440. hd **45**

3920 **NICKLES** 9 [8] 3-9-12 (54) A Daly 14/1: 640108: Well plcd till appr fnl 1f: btr 3694 (gd grnd clmr). ¾ **42**

3271 **YOUNG IBNR** 41 [13] 5-8-11 (53) L Newton 16/1: 300159: Prom till appr fnl 1f: 6 week abs: btr 3180. ¾ **39**

3275 **SUPERBIT** 41 [5] 8-9-1 (57) J Weaver 12/1: -06100: Handy 3f: 10th, 6 week abs: see 2680 (fast grnd). 1 **40**

3839 **PANDJOJOE** 16 [15] 4-8-13 (55)(BL) P Hanagan (5) 9/2: 560600: In tch, wknd fnl 1f: 11th, bckd, blnkd. hd **38**

3759 **AMAZED** 21 [12] 3-9-6 (63) A Culhane 10/1: 6-4200: Nvr a factor & not much room appr fnl 1f: 12th. nk **45**

*1162 **SULU** 138 [1] 4-10-0 (70) T Lucas 10/1: -00010: Hmpd early, al bhd: 13th, top-weight, long abs. nk **51**

3056 **LEGS BE FRENDLY** 51 [10] 5-9-8 (64) Alex Greaves 10/1: -W3500: Prom 3f: 14th, 7 week abs. hd **45**

3572 **BOW PEEP** 29 [1] 5-8-11 (53)(bl) G Parkin 11/1: 124000: Nvr in it: 15th: see 1244, 798. shd **34**

1257 **FOREIGN EDITOR** 132 [4] 4-9-8 (60) F Lynch 14/1: 332000: Al bhd: 16th, nr 5 mnth abs, now with K Ryan 5 **33**
16 ran   Time 1m 06.3 (5)   (Mrs J Hazell)   D W Chapman Stillington, N Yorks

---

4088 5.25 7 DAYS CLASSIFIED STKS 3YO+ 0-70 (E) 1m2f Soft 97 -05 Slow
£3068 £944 £472 £236 3 yo rec 6 lb

3870 **SHRIVAR** 14 [7] M R Channon 3-8-12 (vis) W Supple 5/1: 140421: 3 b g Sri Pekan - Kriva (Reference **80**
Point) Mid div, trav well, hdwy & qcknd to lead appr fnl 1f, pshd clr, readily: bckd tho' op 4/1: earlier won
at Warwick (mdn h'cap): eff at 10f, stays 14f: acts on fast, improved on soft today: handles any track: wears
a visor now: progressive type, quick follow up in a h'cap?

3870 **ZAGALETA** 14 [2] Andrew Turnell 3-8-9 K Darley 7/2 FAV: 021232: 3 b f Sri Pekan - Persian Song 3½ **71**
(Persian Bold) Pulled hard bhd ldrs, led briefly ent fnl 2f, sn outpcd by wnr: bckd: handles firm & soft grnd.

3899 **QUEENS PAGEANT** 12 [15] J L Spearing 6-9-1 M Roberts 11/2: 100303: 6 ch m Risk Me - Mistral's 1¾ **69**
Dancer (Shareef Dancer) Rear, closed appr straight & ev ch, onepce bef fnl 1f: tchd 13/2, clr rem: gd run.

3899 **MCGILLYCUDDY REEKS** 12 [1] Don Enrico Incisa 9-9-1 Kim Tinkler 5/1: 310564: Chsd ldrs, onepce 6 **60**
appr fnl 1f: bckd tho' op 7/2: see 2350 (h'cap).

3682 **MOORLANDS AGAIN** 24 [5] 5-9-2 R Price 16/1: 65045: Led till appr fnl 2f, same pace: longer trip. 1¾ **59**

3663 **BITTER SWEET** 25 [19] 4-8-13 A Culhane 33/1: 005066: Rear, late hdwy, nvr a threat: flattered. ¾ **54$**

4069 **TAKER CHANCE** 1 [18] 4-9-2 A Robertson (7) 50/1: 620007: Hld up, eff/no impress 3f out: ran yesterday. nk **56$**

3396 **RAINWORTH LADY** 36 [14] 3-8-7 R Ffrench 33/1: 0635P8: Chsd ldrs till fdd appr fnl 2f: stiff task. nk **52$**

3461 **SPEED VENTURE** 34 [17] 3-8-10 G Duffield 8/1: 255049: Mid div, prog to lead appr fnl 2f till bef ¾ **53**
dist, sn wknd: see 3461, 1640.

4045 **BOSS TWEED** 2 [11] 3-8-10 (t) A Daly 12/1: 105030: Mid div till 3f out: 10th, t-strap, ran 48hrs ago. ¾ **51**

3893 **BORDERLINE** 13 [9] 3-8-10 R Studholme (3) 12/1: -0000: Dwelt, prog 5f out till ent fnl 3f: 13th, op 8/1. **0**

3813 **HUGS DANCER** 18 [14] 3-8-10 Dean McKeown 10/1: -3340: In tch till 4f out: 15th, first run on soft grnd. **0**

2785} **In Good Faith** 432 [16] 8-9-2 P Goode (3) 33/1:   3808 **Bay Of Bengal** 18 [3] 4-8-13 G Baker (5) 33/1:
1300 **Tarradale** 129 [10] 6-9-2 K Hodgson (7) 50/1:   126 **Welcome Heights** 296 [12] 6-9-2 A Mackay 50/1:
2609 **Victory Roll** 70 [8] 4-9-2 M Fenton 25/1:   3808 **Time For The Clan** 18 [4] 3-8-10 O Pears 40/1:
-- **End Of The Day** [6] 4-9-2 D Nolan (7) 40/1:

PONTEFRACT THURSDAY SEPTEMBER 21ST Lefthand, Undulating Track With Stiff Uphill Finish

19 ran Time 2m 18.3 (10.2) (P D Savill) M R Channon West Isley, Berks

HAYDOCK FRIDAY SEPTEMBER 22ND Lefthand, Galloping Track

Official Going HEAVY. Stalls: 6f - Centre; 7f, 1m, 14f - Inside; 10/12f - Outside.

4089 2.20 GLOVER MDN 3YO (D) 1m2f120y Soft 118 -33 Slow
£4374 £1346 £673 £336

3381 **MISTER MCGOLDRICK** 37 [3] J G Given 3-9-0 Dean McKeown 8/1: 01: 3 b g Sabrehill - Anchor Inn **78**
(Be My Guest) Cl up, led over 3f out, pushed out, val 8L (runner-up eased): op 5/1: dam 10f wnr: brother to
a plcd hdler: stays 10.5f & clearly enjoys soft grnd: acts on a gall trk.
3012 **PRECIOUS POPPY** 54 [5] Sir Michael Stoute 3-8-9 Pat Eddery 4/9 FAV: -4332: 3 b f Polish Precedent 14 **69**
- Benazir (High Top) Led till over 2f out, no extra, 8L down when eased down: well bckd: 8 wk abs, softer grnd.
3813 **TRIPPITAKA** 19 [4] N A Graham 3-8-9 W Supple 8/1: -003: 3 b f Ezzoud - Bluish (Alleged) 10 **59**
Chsd ldr, wknd 3f out: see 2135.
-- **ROYAL TEMPTATION** [1] Jedd O'Keeffe 3-9-0 D Harrison 9/1: 504: Nvr a factor, btn over 3f out: 1¼ **63**
soundly btn in 2 Irish mdns 3 months ago.
-- **SAINT CRYSTALGLASS** [2] 3-8-9 M Tebbutt 33/1: 5: Slow away, al bhd: dam 5f wnr. dist **0**
5 ran Time 2m 25.92 (15.92) (Richard Longley) J G Given Willoughton, Lincs

4090 2.50 KENDAL NURSERY HCAP 2YO 0-85 (D) 6f Soft 118 -24 Slow [87]
£3835 £1180 £590 £295

3273 **CHURCH MICE** 42 [3] M L W Bell 2-8-11 (70)(vis) M Fenton 5/1: 153641: 2 br f Petardia - Negria **75**
(Al Hareb) Held up, gd hdwy to lead on bit over 1f out, hard rdn to hold on ins last: 6 wk abs, well bckd:
earlier scored at Leicester (med auct mdn, also soft grnd): suited by 6f now & relishes soft grnd, handles
firm & fibresand: handles any trk, likes a gall one & best in a visor: runs well fresh.
3802 **CATCH THE CHRON** 19 [5] N Tinkler 2-8-6 (65) T Quinn 5/1: 040162: 2 b f Clantime - Emerald Gulf ¾ **68**
(Wassl) Held up, hdwy to lead over 1f out, styd on well ins last, too late: stays 6f on soft grnd & shld win again.
3976 **BEE KING** 7 [4] M R Channon 2-8-1 (59)(1ow) R Mullen 7/1: 000033: 2 ch c First Trump - Fine Honey 1¼ **60**
(Drone) Chsd ldrs, hdwy to lead well over 1f out, sn hdd & onepace: op 5/1: ran to form of 3976.
3860 **SAMADILLA** 16 [10] T D Easterby 2-9-7 (80) K Darley 5/1: 144104: Keen in tch, rdn & onepace over 1¾ **76**
1f out: top-weight, bckd tho' op 3/1: prob handles fast & soft: see 3712.
3888 **FENWICKS PRIDE** 14 [7] 2-9-1 (74) Dean McKeown 11/1: 266105: Chsd ldrs, hung right & no impress 3 **64**
fnl 2f: op 7/1: see 3710 (auct mdn, 5f, gd/firm).
3888 **FLYING TURK** 14 [6] 2-9-3 (76)(t) J P Spencer 7/2 FAV: 304466: Dwelt, held up, eff & hung left 1¾ **62**
over 1f out, no impress: well bckd: softer grnd: see 3888.
3866 **A C AZURE** 15 [9] 2-9-0 (73) P McCabe 10/1: -6537: Cl-up, wknd over 1f out: btr 3866 (gd). 11 **39**
3824 **TROYS GUEST** 18 [2] 2-8-13 (72) W Supple 20/1: 53368: Handy, wknd 2f out, eased ins last: not 3½ **31**
handle grnd?: btr 3508 (fast).
3075 **GOLD AIR** 51 [8] 2-9-2 (75)(BL) Pat Eddery 10/1: 102009: Led till over 1f out, wknd: abs, blnks. hd **33**
3649 **WINFIELD** 27 [1] 2-8-12 (71) J Carroll 20/1: 0400: Sn rdn & al bhd, eased: see 2972. 3½ **22**
10 ran Time 1m 19.81 (8.51) (R P B Michaelson) M L W Bell Newmarket.

4091 3.20 WEATHERBYS COND STKS 3YO+ (C) 1m6f Soft 118 +09 Fast
£6438 £2442 £1221 £555 3 yo rec 10lb

*3599 **RIDDLESDOWN** 29 [4] S P C Woods 3-8-2 R Mullen 7/4 FAV: 210011: 3 ch c Common Grounds - Neat Dish 112
(Stalwart) Held up, gd hdwy to lead on bit over 2f out, sn pushed clr, 7L in command when eased ins last:
hvly bckd, gd time: recently won at York (big field rtd h'cap), earlier scored here at Haydock (rtd h'cap):
'99 wnr at Bath (mdn auct): suited by 14f, 2m shld suit: acts on firm, soft & likes a gall trk, esp Haydock:
has run well fresh & can carry big weights: fast improving stayer, this level of form cld see a listed/Gr 3 win.
3565 **BIENNALE** 30 [8] Sir Michael Stoute 4-8-12 Pat Eddery 9/4: 445352: 4 b h Caerleon - Malvern Beauty 3½ 105
(Shirley Heights) Held up, hdwy to chall 2f out, not pace of wnr: bckd: useful & consistent: see 3565.
3877 **SPIRIT OF LOVE** 15 [7] M Johnston 5-8-12 D Holland 7/2: 032403: 5 ch g Trempolino - Dream Mary 1 104
(Marfa) In tch, rdn over 5f out, onepace fnl 3f: useful, last 2 wins over 2m2f: see 3538, 1565.
4014 **RUM POINTER** 6 [5] T D Easterby 4-8-12 J Carroll 8/1: 100554: In tch, hard rdn over 3f out, kept ½ 104$
on same pace: treat this rating with caution (offic rtd 92), likes soft.
3890 **MOWBRAY** 34 [3] 5-8-12 (VIS) K Darley 8/1: 440305: Set pace till over 2f out, hard rdn & no extra: ½ 103$
not disgraced at these weights in first time visor: see 2795, 1401.
3379 **HERACLES** 37 [6] 4-9-0 C Lowther 100/1: 341006: Chsd ldr, ev ch over 2f out, sn wknd, swished tail. 16 104$
3501 **BLACK ICE BOY** 33 [1] 9-8-12 (vis) Dean McKeown 150/1: 040607: Dwelt, al bhd, t.o.: outclassed. 13 88
3865 **DENNIS BERGKAMP** 16 [2] 3-8-2 N Kennedey 150/1: 0-0008: In tch wknd then o.t., t.o.: dist 76
unplcd jumps rnr & poorly plcd here.
8 ran Time 2m 13.29 (15.29) (The Storm Again Syndicate) S P C Woods Newmarket.

4092 3.50 TOTE EXACTA HCAP 3YO+ 0-90 (C) 1m3f200y Soft 118 -08 Slow [83]
£7735 £2380 £1190 £595 3 yo rec 8 lb

+3241 **APPLE TOWN** 44 [9] H R A Cecil 3-8-13 (76) T Quinn 11/4: -3211: 3 br f Warning - Applecross (Glint 83
Of Gold) Held up, hdwy to lead over 1f out, drvn out: hvly bckd: 6 wk abs since winning at Brighton (mdn):
stays 12f well, further shld suit: relishes winning form on fast, soft grnd & on any trk: lightly rcd & improving.
3899 **MINI LODGE** 13 [4] J G FitzGerald 4-9-2 (71) Pat Eddery 5/1: 012232: 4 ch g Grand Lodge - Mirea 2½ 74
(The Minstrel) Chsd ldr, led over 3f out till over 1f out, outpcd: not disgraced & stays 12f on firm & soft:
in fine heart with visor discarded & well clr of rem: see 3899.
3896 **SPRING PURSUIT** 13 [1] R J Price 4-9-9 (78) M Fenton 11/2: 050003: 4 b g Rudimentary - Pursuit Of 8 73
Truth (Irish River) Slow away, sn in tch, rdn & btn 2f out: likes this grnd & slipping down the weights: see 1187.
3778 **WARNING REEF** 20 [6] E J Alston 7-8-12 (67) W Supple 9/1: 121424: In tch, brief eff over 3f out, 5 57
no impress: prefers a sounder surface?: see 3778, 3461.

1259

3541	**CANFORD** 31 [7] 3-9-8 (85) M Tebbutt 7/2: -13555: In tch, wknd 2f out: bckd, does handle soft.		1¾	73
3599	**KAIAPOI** 29 [5] 3-9-4 (81) J P Spencer 12/1: 350206: Nvr a factor: see 3599, 3426 & 1225.		11	59
3842	**SHALBEBLUE** 17 [2] 3-7-11 (60) N Kennedy 25/1: 500047: In tch, wknd well over 2f out: mdn, see 3842.		8	50
3599	**MICKLEY** 29 [3] 3-9-5 (82)(vis) K Darley 14/1: 631108: Led, sn clr, hdd over 3f out, sn btn: btr 3467.		8	45
8 ran	Time 2m 42.94 (15.14) (Dr Cathering Wills) H R A Cecil Newmarket.			

4093   4.20 WHEATLAND MDN 3YO (D)   7f30y rnd   Soft 118   -09 Slow
£4199   £1292   £646   £323

3834	**ALMIDDINA** 17 [6] R Charlton 3-8-9 T Quinn 2/1: 401: 3 b f Selkirk - Arbela (Persian Bold)			74
	Hld up, hdwy to lead over 2f out, kept on, rdn out: well bckd: stays 7f well on soft & fm: can rate higher.			
3764	**RUSSIAN RHAPSODY** 21 [3] M A Jarvis 3-8-9 P Robinson 7/1: -5422: 3 b f Cosmonaut - Hannah's Music	½		73
	(Music Boy) Prom, ev ch over 2f out, clr rem: improved on this soft grnd, handles fast.			
--	**CONISTON MILL** [7] W R Muir 3-8-9 K Darley 16/1: 3: 3 b f Lake Coniston - Haiti Mill (Free State)	9		60
	Led till over 2f out, no extra: half sister to wnrs up to 7f.			
3499)	**SOPRAN ZANCHI** 398 [4] L M Cumani 3-9-0 G Sparkes (7) 9/2: 23-4: Nvr a factor: reapp: plcd on both	1½		63
	'99 starts (rtd 86): eff at 6f: shld stay further: acts on fast grnd: shld rate higher.			
3364	**JEPAJE** 38 [1] 3-9-0 J Carroll 20/1: 445025: Hld up, eff 4f out, wknd 2f out: flattered, see 3364.	3		59$
3834	**MOUNT MCKINLEY** 17 [2] 3-9-0 Pat Eddery 15/8 FAV: 06: Chsd ldr, wknd 3f out: well bckd, see 3834.	3½		54
3977	**SILVER PRAIRIE** 7 [5] 3-8-9 D Sweeney 33/1: 07: Hld up, wknd over 2f out: see 3977.	6		40
7 ran	Time 1m 36.02 (8.92) (James D Wolfensohn) R Charlton Beckhampton, Wilts			

4094   4.50 LITTLEBOROUGH HCAP 3YO+ 0-85 (D)   1m30y rnd   Soft 118   +08 Fast   [85]
£5031   £1548   £774   £387   3 yo rec 4 lb

3936	**NOUF** 9 [8] K Mahdi 4-8-9 (66) D McGaffin (5) 11/1: 660051: 4 b f Efisio - Miss Witch (High Line)			71
	Held up, gd hdwy over 2f out, styd on well for press to get up ins last, going away: gd time: rtd 79 earlier			
	this term: '99 scorer at Doncaster (debut, mdn, rtd 94): stays 1m well & likes soft grnd & a gall trk: runs			
	well fresh: well h'capped on best form & given a gd polished/strong ride for an apprentice.			
3951	**ROUTE SIXTY SIX** 9 [12] Jedd O'Keeffe 4-7-13 (56) G Sparkes (7) 10/1: 002322: 4 b f Brief Truce -	1		59
	Lyphards Goddess (Lyphard's Special) Held up, eff to lead over 1f out, kept on till collared ins last, not btn far.			
2349	**ROLLER** 82 [1] J G Given 4-9-3 (74) T G McLaughlin 8/1: 220403: 4 b g Bluebird - Tight Spin (High	2		74
	Top) Handy, hdwy to lead over 2f out till over 1f out, onepace: 3 month abs & looks to have been freshened			
	up for an autumn assault on soft grnd h'caps: see 1113, 1007.			
3152	**CHAMPAGNE RIDER** 48 [3] K McAuliffe 4-9-2 (73) P Robinson 33/1: 060004: Prom, edged left over	1		71
	1f out, onepace: on a losing run but slipped down the weights: see 2431, 1173.			
4038	**BOLD RAIDER** 4 [13] 3-8-6 (67) K Darley 9/4 FAV: 123435: Handy, rdn & onepace over 1f out: qk reapp.	¾		64
3945	**FREDORA** 9 [4] 5-9-12 (83) T Quinn 14/1: 404526: In tch, eff 2f out, sn no impress: best form	6		71
	on a sounder surface: see 3945, 2629.			
3810	**SPORTING GESTURE** 19 [10] 3-8-12 (73) T Lucas 20/1: 016107: Led till 4f out, wknd over 2f out:	3		57
	twice below 3426 (10f, gd/firm).			
2287	**COURT OF APPEAL** 84 [18] 3-9-10 (85) D Harrison 12/1: 0-0108: Al bhd: abs, btr 1532.	1¾		66
3981	**THE EXHIBITION FOX** 7 [6] 4-9-1 (72) W Supple 10/1: 000009: In tch, btn 2f out: see 3981, 1836.	2		50
3471	**PRINCE DU SOLEIL** 34 [11] 4-8-13 (70) Paul Eddery 20/1: 000000: Waited with, eff to chall	½		47
	over 2f out, sn wknd: 10th.			
3936	**TRIBAL PRINCE** 9 [7] 3-9-2 (77) M Fenton 10/1: 013420: In tch, btn 4f out: 11th, btr 3936 (firm).	3		50
4038	**ABAJANY** 4 [5] 6-9-1 (72) Pat Eddery 9/1: -00000: Slow away, nvr a factor: qck reapp.			0
3826	**CLEVER GIRL** 18 [14] 3-9-1 (76) J Carroll 16/1: 043050: Led 4f out till over 2f out, wknd, last: see 3785.			0
3944	**Footprints** 9 [2] 3-9-0 (75) D Holland 20/1:	3699	**Dee Pee Tee Cee** 25 [16] 6-9-11 (82) G Parkin 14/1:	
815	**Riverblue** 172 [15] 4-9-7 (78) V Slattery 33/1:			
16 ran	Time 1m 49.31 (8.81) (Solaiman Alsaiary) K Mahdi Newmarket.			

Official Going   AW - STANDARD. Turf - GOOD (GOOD TO SOFT places). Stalls: Str - Stands; 1m6f - Centre; Rem - Ins.

4095   1.30 EBF MED AUCT MDN DIV 1 2YO (F)   5f   Good 46   -04 Slow
£1974   £564   £282

3372	**PRINCE OF BLUES** 21 [9] N P Littmoden 2-9-0 M Roberts 5/4 FAV: 265001: 2 b c Prince Of Birds - Reshift			89
	(Night Shift) Sn led, held on well ins last, pushed out: well bckd: not disgraced in Group company prev (rtd			
	95): eff at 5/6f: acts on firm & gd grnd, sharp or gall trk: useful confidence booster.			
3090	**HOW DO I KNOW** 51 [10] G A Butler 2-8-9 P Doe 4/1: -02: 2 gr f Petong - Glenfield Portion (Mummy's	nk		82
	Pet) Trkd ldrs, prsd wnr fnl 1f, kept on but held: clr rem: apprec drop back to 5f: win a race on this form.			
3942	**TROUBLESHOOTER** 9 [1] W R Muir 2-9-0 (bl) Martin Dwyer 5/1: 206263: 2 b c Ezzoud - Oublier	5		72
	L'Ennui (Bellman) Wide, led early, ev ch till outpcd bef fnl 1f: gd run from: eff at 6f, will stay further.			
3980	**PIQUET** 7 [12] R Hannon 2-8-9 R Hughes 3/1: -04: Cl-up, no extra appr fnl 1f: qck reapp, back in trip.	1¾		62
3757	**BOSRA BADGER** 22 [11] 2-9-0 I Mongan (5) 50/1: 00005: Same place thr'out: poss flattered.	nk		66$
3832	**EMPRESS OF AUSTRIA** 17 [13] 2-8-9 (t) N Callan 20/1: 306: Al around mid-div: t-strap, see 3092.	hd		61
3795	**BELLA PAVLINA** 19 [5] 2-8-9 M Henry 33/1: 07: Nvr a factor tho' late hdwy: needs further, see 3795.	nk		60
3911	**ASWHATILLDOIS** 11 [6] 2-8-9 C Rutter 20/1: 058: Mid-div thr'out under a kind ride: 7f/1m nursery type.	nk		59
--	**BEENABOUTABIT** [14] 2-8-9 F Norton 16/1: 9: Nvr dngrs on debut: Komaite Apr foal, dam a mdn.	¾		57
3757	**SONG N DANCE** 22 [8] 2-8-9 G Baker (5) 50/1: -0560: In tch wide till 2f out: 10th, back in trip.	1¾		52
3942	**Zilkha** 9 [4] 2-8-9 W Ryan 25/1:	3047	**Bevel Blue** 53 [2] 2-9-0 S Carson (3) 25/1:	
3639	**One Charmer** 27 [7] 2-9-0 L Newman (3) 50/1:	--	**Dim Dot** [3] 2-9-0 J Quinn 25/1:	
--	**Case The Joint** [15] 2-9-0 G Hind 25/1:	3832	**Les Girls** 17 [16] 2-8-9 S Sanders 50/1:	
16 ran	Time 59.3 (2.5) (T Clarke) N P Littmoden Newmarket.			

4096

2.00 EBF MED AUCT MDN DIV 2 2YO (F) 5f Good 46 -10 Slow
£1974 £564 £282

3710 **BARON CROCODILE 24** [3] A Berry 2-9-0 T E Durcan 8/1: 024021: 2 b g Puissance - Glow Again (The Brianstan) Trkd ldr, led bef fnl 1f, rdn out: tchd 12/1, first win: dam 5/6f wnr: eff up with/forcing the pace at 5f: acts on fast & hvy grnd, likes sharp trks: best without blnks. **80**
3387 **NOSY BE 37** [5] P J Makin 2-9-0 S Sanders 7/2: -532: 2 b c Cyrano de Bergerac - Blossomville (Petong) Chsd along wide, in tch, styd on for press fnl 1f, nvr nrr: gd run back at 5f on gd, return to 6f or even 7f may suit. 1½ **76**
3627 **LUNEVISION 27** [9] H J Collingridge 2-8-9 M Roberts 5/2 JT FAV: 323: 2 b f Solid Illusion - Lumiere Celeste (Always Fair) Chsd ldrs, rdn 2f out, kept on towards fin: tchd 7/2 unsuited by drop back to 5f, see 3627. ½ **69**
3900 **LEOZIAN 13** [2] Miss Gay Kelleway 2-9-0 S Whitworth 5/2 JT FAV: 204: Switched to stands rail & led till appr fnl 1f, no extra: well bckd: tricky draw, capable of better, see 3900 (Gr 2), 3277 (C/D). ½ **73**
3632 **BRANSTON GEM 27** [13] 2-8-9 R Ffrench 14/1: -005: In tch, not pace of ldrs fnl 2f: further will suit. 1¾ **63**
3513 **WINTER DOLPHIN 33** [14] 2-8-9 Lisa Somers (7) 33/1: 066: Al mid-div, switched bef fnl 1f: nds sellers. 1 **60**
2588 **UNLIKELY 72** [6] 2-9-0 J Weaver 20/1: -307: Chsd ldrs, fdd fnl 1f: ee 1981 (seller). 1½ **61**
3942 **BRAVURA 9** [4] 2-9-0 I Mongan (5) 33/1: 008: Slow away, switched appr fnl 1f & late hdwy: 7,200gns Never So Bold half-brother to decent sprinter/miler Chewit: with G L Moore. ½ **59**
3973 **SAFINAZ 7** [7] 2-8-9 D R McCabe 40/1: 0659: Nvr a factor: qck reapp, needs sellers. 1 **51**
3832 **FOX COTTAGE 17** [12] 2-8-9 K Dalgleish (5) 33/1: 00: Mid-div, wknd bef fnl 1f: 10th, op 20/1: So Factual half-sister to a juv sprint wnr: with D Arbuthnot. ½ **50**
3096 **QUATREDIL 51** [8] 2-8-9 R Hughes 10/1: 040: Nvr in it: 11th, 7 wk abs: btr 3096 (6f). 1½ **46**
3075 **Miss Inform 51** [10] 2-8-9 N Pollard 16/1:
3358 **Anne Sophie 39** [1] 2-8-9 Gemma Sliz (7) 50/1:
3815 **Martha P Perkins 18** [15] 2-8-9 L Carter 14/1:
-- **Raise A Glass** [16] 2-9-0 G Hannon (7) 25/1:
3635 **Fareham 27** [11] 2-8-9 (BL) M Baird 50/1:
16 ran Time 59.6 (2.8) (Chris & Antonis Deuters) A Berry Cockerham, Lancs.

4097

2.30 BET DIRECT CLAIMER 2YO (F) 6f Good 46 -34 Slow
£2548 £728 £364

3910 **PICCOLO ROSE 11** [16] M R Channon 2-8-9 Craig Williams 11/2 FAV: 5001: 2 b f Piccolo - Saunders Lass (Hillandale) Mid-div, prog appr fnl 1f, ran on well & rdn to lead well towards fin: first win: speedily bred filly, apprec drop back to 6f: acts on gd grnd, sharp trk: well ridden. **66**
3802 **CLANSINGE 19** [15] A Berry 2-8-5 T E Durcan 7/1: 400602: 2 ch f Clantime - North Pine (Import) Chsd ldrs, eff 2f out, onepcd till kept on ins last: ran to best up in trip: eff at 5/6f on firm & gd grnd. 1½ **59**
3802 **QUIZZICAL LADY 19** [6] M Quinn 2-8-11 F Norton 13/2: 642003: 2 b f Mind Games - Salacious (Sallust) Led, rdn & hdd 2f out, kept on: op 11/2: up in trip, shade btr 3354. nk **64**
3968 **MISS DAMINA 8** [7] J Pearce 2-8-5 R Ffrench 25/1: 000404: Mid-div, hdwy for press 2f out, kept on but unable to chall: best effort yet, apprec drop back to 6f on gd grnd in a clmr. hd **58$**
1727 **LIGHT EVIDENCE 109** [12] 2-8-1 P Hanagan (5) 12/1: 05: Bhd ldrs, led ent fnl 2f, rdn & hung left & hdd ins last: op 20/1, clr of rem: 15 wk abs & a fair effort, drop back to 5f cld suit: see 1727. nk **53**
3278 **MONASH LADY 42** [19] 2-8-7 R Hughes 6/1: 46: Mid-div, drvn 2f out, same pace: 6 wk abs, tchd 9/1. 5 **44**
-- **DEFINITE RETURN** [9] 2-8-3 J Quinn 20/1: 7: Al around same place: debut: IR 3,200gns Definite Article half-sister to 2 wnrs; bred to need 1m+: with B Palling. 1½ **36**
3912 **REVOLVER 11** [11] 2-9-0 B Marcus 10/1: 008: Slow away, wide, nvr in it: no worthwhile form. hd **46**
3815 **THE WALL 18** [10] 2-8-1 A Daly 33/1: 500009: Dwelt, nvr nr ldrs: stiff task, flattered last time. 1½ **30**
2052 **OSO NEET 95** [8] 2-8-8 L Newman (3) 6/1: 0600: Nvr a factor: over 3 month abs, flattered 1589. ¾ **36**
-- **GHOST OF A CHANCE** [20] 2-8-12 S Sanders 7/1: 0: Nvr dngrs on debut: 16th: Indian Ridge colt. **0**
3278 **Raging Times 42** [1] 2-7-11 K Dalgleish (5) 33/1:
3733 **Golden Beach 23** [5] 2-8-5 P Doe 16/1:
-- **Zetagalopon** [4] 2-8-11 S W Kelly (3) 20/1:
3830 **Kiriwina 17** [13] 2-7-13 A Nicholls 33/1:
3639 **Molly Irwin 27** [17] 2-7-13 N Farmer (7) 25/1:
3258 **Presentofarose 43** [3] 2-8-1 J Mackay (5) 14/1:
3388 **Meadow Song 37** [2] 2-7-11 M Henry 33/1:
-- **Faraway John** [18] 2-9-2 I Mongan (5) 33/1:
19 ran Time 1m 13.6 (4.8) (Mrs Pat Scott) M R Channon West Isley, Berks.

4098

3.00 C & H NURSERY HCAP 2YO 0-85 (D) 5f Good 46 +04 Fast [92]
£4374 £1346 £673 £336 2 raced far side & were never in it

+3496 **AMELIA 34** [11] J Cullinan 2-8-7 (71) D O'Donohoe 10/1: 334311: 2 b f General Monash - Rose Tint (Salse) Chsd ldrs, led 1f out, rdn out: op 8/1: recent W'hampton wnr (stks, rtd 79a): first foal: eff at 5/6f: handles firm, soft grnd & fibresand, any trk: improving & genuine. **79**
-3743 **VENDOME 22** [16] J A Osborne 2-9-3 (81) J Weaver 13/2: 033122: 2 b c General Monash - Kealbra Lady (Petong) Led till 1f out, kept on: op 5/1: gd run conceding 10lbs to wnr: remains on the upgrade: see 3673. 1½ **85**
3431 **RISQUE SERMON 35** [13] Miss B Sanders 2-8-12 (76)(t) B Marcus 8/1: 01043: 2 b g Risk Me - Sunday Sport Star (Star Appeal) Prom, eff 2f out, not pace of front 2: ran well in a t-strap, will apprec a return to 6f. 1½ **76**
3976 **MADRASEE 7** [10] M Blanshard 2-8-9 (73) J Quinn 14/1: 303204: In tch, eff 2f out, nvr pace to chall. ¾ **71**
3942 **LITTLE CALLIAN 9** [20] 2-8-1 (65) P Doe 9/2: 043625: Pressed ldr, no extra appr fnl 1f: op 7/2: rated higher 3942 (fast grnd mdn auct). nk **62**
3475 **ROXANNE MILL 34** [19] 2-8-6 (70) G Baker (5) 11/2: 50346: In tch, onepace fnl 2f: tchd 10/1, btr 3475. nk **66**
3693 **DENSIM BLUE 25** [8] 2-8-11 (75) R Ffrench 14/1: 145247: Al mid-div: btr 3258 (6f), see 1463. hd **71**
3807 **RARE OLD TIMES 19** [6] 2-8-8 (72) L Newman (3) 10/1: 510608: Nvr a threat, wide: tchd 16/1, back in trip. ¾ **66**
3807 **BLAKESHALL BOY 19** [9] 2-9-2 (80) Craig Williams 4/1 FAV: 213539: Nvr dngrs: something amiss? ½ **72**
3743 **SCREAMIN GEORGINA 22** [5] 2-8-1 (65)(t) P Hanagan (5) 10/1: 211050: Rcd far side, sn struggling with stands side: 10th, best forgotten, see 3038 (fast grnd clmr). nk **56**
3801 **OPEN WARFARE 19** [15] 2-8-6 (70) F Norton 12/1: 350030: Dwelt, sn struggling: 13th: see 1166. **0**
3714 **Hard To Catch 24** [3] 2-8-12 (76)(bl) C Catlin (7) 14/1:
3047 **Securon Dancer 53** [12] 2-8-4 (68)(1ow) S Whitworth 16/1:
3621 **Annie Ruan 28** [7] 2-8-9 (73) A McGlone 16/1:
3815 **Delphyllia 18** [17] 2-7-13 (63)(1ow) N Pollard 25/1:
15 ran Time 58.9 (2.1) (Turf 2000 Limited) J Cullinan Quainton, Bucks.

4099　　3.30 BET DIRECT HCAP 3YO 0-70 (E)　　2m aw　　Standard　Inapplicable　　[72]
　　　　　£2852　£815　£407

3383 **ESTABELLA** 37 [10] S P C Woods 3-8-7 (51) R Hughes 8/1: 555401: 3 ch f Mujtahid - Lady In Green **59a**
(Shareef Dancer) Confidently held up, closed going well 5f out, rdn to lead below dist, styd on well: visor
omitted: earlier won at Beverley (fill h'cap): 5th last term (nurs, rtd 55): eff at 12f, relished this step
up to 2m: acts on gd/soft, hvy grnd & both AWs: prob best without blnks or a visor, handles any track.
3476 **PTAH** 34 [1] J L Eyre 3-7-11 (41)(1oh)(1ow) F Norton 7/1: 230062: 3 b g Petardia - Davenport Goddess　nk **48a**
(Classic Secret) Led 4f out till 1f out, kept on: clr rem on AW bow: stays 2m on fast, gd/soft & equitrack: mdn.
3979 **EASTWOOD DRIFTER** 7 [3] W R Muir 3-9-5 (63) Martin Dwyer 6/1: 262503: 3 ch g Woodman -　12 **60a**
Mandarina (El Gran Senor) Chsd ldrs, no extra ent str: op 8/1: qck reapp, AW bow: longer trip: see 2053.
3575 **NEEDWOOD TRIDENT** 30 [11] J Pearce 3-7-10 (40)(2oh) G Baker (5) 7/1: 004204: Al bhd, styd on　7 **30a**
late: AW bow: thorough stayer, see 3348.
3979 **BLINDING MISSION** 7 [4] J Weaver 12/1: 030605: Led till 4f out, sn btn: qck reapp, AW bow.　2 **53a**
3835 **QUIET READING** 17 [7] 3-9-2 (60) I Mongan (5) 9/2 FAV: 640526: Chsd ldrs, fdd 3f out: op 7/1:　7 **41a**
longer trip, back in a h'cap, btr 3835 (12f auct mdn).
3448 **BLAYNEY DANCER** 35 [14] 3-7-10 (40)(1oh) M Henry 25/1: 500307: In tch, outpcd 4f out: hdles rnr.　13 **11a**
3702 **LOMOND DANCER** 25 [5] 3-8-0 (44) A Nicholls 25/1: 000008: Chsd ldrs, wknd 3f out: AW bow, modest.　13 **5a**
3588 **HARD DAYS NIGHT** 29 [12] 3-7-11 (41) J Quinn 5/1: 620249: Al bhd: AW bow: see 3588.　7 **0a**
3769 **FAHAN** 20 [9] 3-8-4 (48) W Ryan 14/1: 055500: Nvr on terms: 10th: longer trip, modest.　13 **0a**
3916 **SILK STOCKINGS** 11 [8] 3-9-2 (60) B Marcus 10/1: 00000P: Nvr dngrs, btn halfway, p.u.: AW bow.　**0a**
2602 **Streccia** 71 [13] 3-8-1 (45) A Daly 25/1:　　　3858 **Loup Cervier** 16 [6] 3-7-12 (42)(2ow) P Doe 20/1:
3754 **Topman** 22 [2] 3-7-10 (40)(15oh) K Dalgleish (5) 33/1:
14 ran　　　Time 3m 21.4 (1.4)　　　　(Ben Allen & Mrs Catherine Hine)　　　S P C Woods Newmarket.

4100　　4.00 BET DIRECT MDN 3YO+ (D)　　1m2f aw　　Standard　Inapplicable
　　　　　£2860　£880　£440　　3 yo rec 6 lb

3762 **CORUSCATING** 21 [8] Sir Mark Prescott 3-9-0 S Sanders 4/1: 05-041: 3 gr h Highest Honor - Mytilene **68a**
(Soviet Star) Trkd ldrs, keen, led appr fnl 2f, rdn ent fnl 1f & flashed tail, all out: winning AW bow: unplcd
juv (mdn, rtd 70): eff at 10f on gd grnd & sharp tracks, improved on equitrack here.
3762 **NOBLE CALLING** 21 [9] N A Graham 3-9-0 (vis) J Weaver 5/1: 206232: 3 b c Caller ID - Specificity　shd **67a**
(Alleged) Slow away, prog to chase ldrs 3f out, onepace till styd on well towards fin, just failed: AW bow:
plcd yet again but appears improved on equitrack, handles fast & gd: deserves a win.
3794 **SUPERSONIC** 20 [1] R F Johnson Houghton 4-9-1 (t) S Carson (3) 7/1: 040303: 4 b f Shirley Heights -　1¼ **60a**
Bright Landing (Sun Prince) Chsd ldrs, shkn up after halfway & sn rdn, styd on in the str but too late: tchd 14/1,
AW bow, gd run, acts on fast, gd/soft grnd & equitrack & is worth a try over at 12f now.
3834 **SALEM** 17 [5] R W Armstrong 3-9-0 R Price 5/2 FAV: 034: Keen, cl-up, led briefly appr fnl 3f,　1¾ **62a**
fdd fnl 1f: tchd 4/1: lngr trip on AW bow & poss best at 1m: see 3834.
3329 **CIRCUS PARADE** 40 [11] 3-9-0 (t) R Havlin 11/2: -50365: Bhd, styd on fnl 1½f, nvr dngrs:　2 **59a**
op 3/1, 6 wk abs, AW bow, t-strap: worth another look on this surface at 12f, see 2889.
3429 **LUNA FLIGHT** 35 [3] 3-8-9 R Ffrench 16/1: -556: Chsd ldrs, outpcd 3f out: AW bow, see 3232.　8 **42a**
3762 **SALIENT POINT** 21 [3] 3-8-9 R Hughes 12/1: 004007: Bhd ldr, wknd ent fnl 3f: op 8/1, drop back to 1m?　6 **33a**
3828 **CUPIDS DART** 17 [7] 3-9-0 J Quinn 20/1: 005048: Led till appr fnl 3f, sn btn: stiff task, see 3828, 80.　6 **29a**
3　　**SWAN LAKE FR** 319 [2] 4-9-1 N Pollard 25/1: 5600-9: Al bhd: reapp: unplcd in '99 (fill mdn, rtd　3 **19a**
66): ex-French, plcd over 1m: with K Cunningham Brown.
3691 **TOBY GRIMES** 25 [12] 3-9-0 Martin Dwyer 33/1: 000-00: Nvr a factor: 10th, v stiff task on AW bow.　3½ **19a**
3818 **Caramelle** 18 [6] 4-9-1 I Mongan (5) 33/1:　　　2699} **Millennium Bug** 435 [10] 4-9-1 A Eddery (5) 33/1:
12 ran　　　Time 2m 05.98 (3.18)　　　　(Mrs F R Watts)　　　Sir Mark Prescott Newmarket.

4101　　4.30 ARENA CLASS STKS 3YO+ 0-70 (E)　　1m4f aw　　Standard　Inapplicable
　　　　　£3060　£880　£440　　3 yo rec 8 lb

3948 **THE GREEN GREY** 9 [17] L Montague Hall 6-9-5 A Clark 9/4 FAV: 525431: 6 gr g Environment Friend - **71a**
Pea Green (Try My Best) Prom, shkn up 3f out, kept on grimly to lead towards fin: bckd, tchd 3/1: earlier won at
Windsor (2, h'caps): lightly rcd in '99 (rtd 66a & 54): '98 wnr at Yarmouth (h'cap), Bath, Brighton (clmr,
W Muir), Kempton & Lingfield (h'caps, rtd 76a, D Morris): eff at 10/12f, stays 14f: acts on firm, gd, equitrack
& handles gd/soft: goes on any trk, likes sharp ones: best without a visor & can carry big weights: v tough.
332 **DAUNTED** 251 [3] G L Moore 4-9-3 (bl) I Mongan (5) 14/1: 00-002: 4 b g Priolo - Dauntess (Formidable)　½ **68a**
In tch, closed 4f out, sn pushed into lead, kept on but worn down nr fin: fine reapp: clrly stays 12f:
loves Lingfield/equitrack & can win again when held up for a later challenge: see 157.
3769 **LILLAN** 20 [5] G A Butler 3-8-6 (t) P Doe 16/1: 644W43: 3 b f Hernando - Lillemor (Connaught)　½ **64a**
Nvr far away, ch appr fnl 1f, kept on, held nr fin: clr rem: styd this longer 12f trip: handles equitrack.
3686 **ANGELS VENTURE** 25 [10] J R Jenkins 4-9-3 (t) S Whitworth 12/1: 043264: Towards rear, prog　6 **60$**
to chase ldrs appr fnl 2f, sn no impress: visor omitted on AW bow: btr 3336, see 1180.
3691 **FULL EGALITE** 25 [4] 4-9-5 (bl) C Rutter 25/1: 200235: Mid-div, eff 3f out, same pace: improving?　1¼ **60a**
4024 **FAILED TO HIT** 6 [13] 7-9-3 (vis) F Norton 8/1: 436526: Trkd ldrs, lost pl 3f out: qck reapp, op 12/1:　1½ **56a**
unsuited by drop back to 12f?: see 4024 (fibresand).
3948 **SEA DANZIG** 9 [8] 7-9-5 J Quinn 12/1: 105007: Nvr a factor: op 8/1: flattered, back in trip.　2 **55a**
3899 **TATE VENTURE** 13 [12] 3-8-9 R Hughes 3/1: 03108: Wide, in tch 1m: op 4/1: unsuited by longer trip?　nk **52a**
*3490 **DON BOSCO** 34 [18] 4-9-5 J Stack 16/1: 030019: Led till appr fnl 3f, sn btn: new stable, AW bow.　¾ **53a**
2945 **KARA SEA** 56 [7] 3-8-6 (VIS) J Mackay (5) 7/1: 10420: Al bhd: 10th, tchd 10/1, 8 wk abs & vis, btr 2945.　6 **42a**
3472 **ABLE NATIVE** 34 [1] 3-8-8 (bl) R Price 12/1: 210040: In tch tdd 4f out: 11th: best without blnks in 2217.　**0a**
3336 **High Policy** 40 [2] 4-9-3 J Weaver 14/1:　　　2941 **Zola** 57 [9] 4-9-3 (VIS) G Hannon (7) 50/1:
1454 **Tuigamala** 850 [16] 9-9-3 L Newman (3) 50/1:　　　3281 **Saseedo** 42 [14] 10-9-3 (bl) A Nicholls 33/1:
2191 **Star Manager** 88 [15] 10-9-3 G Baker (5) 33/1:　　　3753 **Village Native** 22 [11] 7-9-3 (bl) S Sanders 33/1:
2967 **Shareef Khan** 56 [6] 3-8-9 O Urbina 12/1:
18 ran　　　Time 2m 30.86 (1.66)　　　(J Daniels)　　　L Montague Hall Tadworth, Surrey.

LINGFIELD (Mixed) FRIDAY SEPTEMBER 22ND Lefthand, Undulating, Sharp Track

4102
5.00 LEVY BOARD APPR HCAP 3YO+ 0-70 (E) 7f str Good 46 1m 23.7 (3.3) [70]
£3255 £930 £465 3 yo rec 3 lb

*4013 **GREAT NEWS 6** [17] W J Haggas 5-10-3 (73)(6ex) P Hanagan (3) 8/11 FAV: 000111: 5 b g Elmaamul - 85
Amina (Brigadier Gerard) Nvr far away, going well, led ent fnl 2f, pshd clr, v cmftbly: qck hat-trick landed
after 2 facile wins at Ayr last week (h'caps): '99 wnr at Ascot & Windsor (val h'cap & rtd h'cap, rtd 86): '98
wnr here at Lingfield (h'cap, rtd 75): eff at 7f/1m on any grnd/trk: runs well fresh: well h'capped & back to best.
3966 **KILMEENA LAD 8** [11] E A Wheeler 4-8-13 (55) S Carson 12/1: 500002: 4 b g Minshaanshu Amad - 5 55
Kilmeena Glen (Beveled) Chsd ldrs, hdwy appr fnl 1f, drifted left, no ch wnr: tchd 16/1, ran to best back at 7f.
2804 **CARINTHIA 63** [4] C F Wall 5-9-7 (63) A Beech 10/1: 002023: 5 br m Tirol - Hot Lavender (Shadeed) ¾ 61
Wide, towards rear, hdwy under press appr fnl 1f, nvr dngrs: tchd 14/1: fair run, see 2804, 1511.
*3621 **CONTRARY MARY 21** [18] J Akehurst 5-9-10 (66) R Farmer (7) 8/1: 122014: In tch, unable to qckn 2 60
appr fnl 1f: much btr 3765.
3689 **SLUMBERING 25** [14] 4-9-11 (67) G Baker (3) 16/1: 634005: Chsd ldrs, onepace appr fnl 1f: ¾ 59
new stable, gone to B Pearce from B Meehan & will apprec a return to 1m: see 1042.
2371 **AMBER BROWN 81** [12] 4-9-4 (60) C Carver 20/1: 014006: Dsptd lead till ent fnl 2f, fdd: 12 wk 1¾ 48
abs: unsuited by return to 7f without blnks?: see 1542.
3499 **TOYON 34** [7] 3-9-9 (68) M Worrell (7) 12/1: 223407: Nvr a factor: back in trip, see 2817. shd 56
3502 **ALBERT THE BEAR 33** [13] 7-9-1 (57)(vis) P Bradley (3) 16/1: 002008: dsptd lead till appr fnl 2f, wknd. 2 41
3613 **TREASURE TOUCH 28** [9] 6-10-0 (70) Joanna Badger (5) 14/1: 124049: Al towards rear: see 3080 (clmr) 1½ 51
-- **SELLINGERS ROUND** [10] 4-8-13 (55) L Newman 33/1: 363300: Chsd lds till appr fnl 1f: 10th, 2 32
British bow: earlier plcd over 1m on firm/fast grnd in native Ireland (h'caps): with Mrs Jewell.
3947 **MY EMILY 9** [3] 4-9-12 (68) I Mongan 10/1: 002260: In tch till 2f out: 11th, btr 3689, see 1884. ½ 44
2380 **Landing Craft 81** [1] 6-8-12 (54) D Nolan (7) 33/1: 3796 Akebono 19 [2] 4-9-4 (60)(bl) J Mackay 14/1:
3190 **Innkeeper 46** [6] 3-9-7 (66) S W Kelly 20/1: 3257 Rififi 43 [8] 7-8-13 (55)(t) J Bosley (5) 50/1:
3921 **Darwells Folly 10** [16] 5-9-0 (56)(tvi) K Dalgleish (3) 25/1:
1969 **Hoh Hoh Seven 98** [15] 4-8-12 (54) A Nicholls 33/1:
17 ran Time 1m 23.7 (3.3) (Executive Network, Pertemps Group) W J Haggas Newmarket.

HAYDOCK SATURDAY SEPTEMBER 23RD Lefthand, Flat, Galloping Track

Official Going HEAVY (SOFT PLACES) Stalls: Inside, except 5f - centre, 10f -outside

4103
2.10 EBF STANLEY MDN 2YO (D) 7f30y rnd Good/Soft 83 -12 Slow
£4013 £1235 £617 £308 Raced centre - stands side fnl 3f

-- **TURKU** [1] M Johnston 2-9-0 R Ffrench 9/1: 1: 2 b c Polar Falcon - Princess Zepoli (Persepolis) 89
Chsd ldr, led over 2f out, clr over 1f out, styd on strongly, rdn out: op 7/1: Feb foal, full brother to 7f juv wnr Polar
Eclipse: dam a 9f wnr: eff over a gall 7f on gd/sft, 1m will suit: runs well fresh: open to further improvement.
3786 **FORTUNE POINT 21** [6] J Noseda 2-9-0 J Weaver 10/11 FAV: 42: 2 ch c Cadeaux Genereux - Mountains 3 83
Of Mist (Shirley Heights) Held up, prog over 2f out, drvn/held over 1f out: hvly bckd: shld win a race.
1497 **GALY BAY 120** [4] A Bailey 2-8-9 J Bramhill 10/1: 333: 2 b f Bin Ajwaad - Sylhall (Sharpo) 4 71
Sn rdn to lead, hdd over 2f out & sn held: prev with D Morris: abs: now qual for h'caps: see 1497, 828 (5/6f).
1328 **KHAYYAM 129** [5] P F l Cole 2-9-0 J Carroll 2/1: 04: Held up, effrt over 2f out, sn btn: op 5/4. 3½ 70
4001 **BOLLIN TOBY 3** [3] 2-9-0 G Parkin 33/1: -00065: Held up, strugg 3f out: lngr 7f trip: see 3346. 12 50
5 ran Time 1m 33.88 (6.78) (J R Good) M Johnston Middleham, N Yorks

4104
2.40 EBF SALE FILLIES MDN 2YO (D) 1m30y rnd Good/Soft 83 -30 Slow
£4452 £1370 £685 £342 Raced centre - stands side fnl 3f

3766 **LA VITA E BELLA 22** [2] C F Wall 2-8-11 S Sanders 7/2: 021: 2 b f Definite Article - Coolrain 87
Lady (Common Grounds) Held up, hdwy to lead over 1f out, sn in command under hands & heels riding: nicely
bckd: eff at 1m, mid-dists may suit next term: improved last twice on gd/sft & soft & a gall trk: progressive.
3607 **SILLY GOOSE 29** [7] J L Dunlop 2-8-11 D Harrison 6/4 FAV: 62: 2 b f Sadler's Wells - Ducking 2½ 82
(Reprimand) Hld up, prog/chance over 1f out, sn held by wnr: hvly bckd: clr of rem: handles gd/sft: stay further.
3962 **CHANTAIGNE 9** [6] A Bailey 2-8-11 J Carroll 12/1: 053: 2 ch f General Monash - Blue Vista (Pennine 6 72$
Walk) Chsd ldrs, rdn/hdd over 1f out, sn held: stydd longer 1m trip, handles gd/sft: see 1249 (5f).
-- **WATTREY** [5] M A Jarvis 2-8-11 M Tebbutt 6/1: 4: Dwelt, in tch, held fnl 2f: op 9/2: Royal 2½ 67
Academy filly, Jan foal, half-sister to a 1m juv wnr: dam a well related 12f wnr: apprec 1m+ in time: can improve.
2029 **BRUNNHILDE 97** [4] 2-8-11 M Fenton 33/1: -005: Chsd ldr, btn 2f out: 3 mth abs: lngr 1m trip. ½ 66
-- **TREBLE RED** [8] 2-8-11 A Culhane 11/2: 6: Dwelt, always bhd: Shareef Dancer filly, Apr foal, dam 5 56
unrcd, sire a Irish derby wnr: shld appreciate mid-dists & improve in time for M Channon.
-- **GRACIOUS AIR** [1] 2-8-11 W Supple 25/1: 7: Chsd ldrs 4f, sn btn: Bahri filly, March foal, cost 3 50
IR14,000gns: a first foal: dam a US Juvenile wnr: sire a top class miler: with J R Weymes.
-- **MAJESTIC PREMIUM** [3] 2-8-11 P Hanagan (3) 33/1: 8: Chsd ldrs till halfway, sn bhd: Distinctly North 11 30
filly, Apr foal, cost IR13,500gns: dam a maiden: sire a high-class 2yo: with R A Fahey.
8 ran Time 1m 49.69 (9.19) (Ettore Landi) C F Wall Newmarket

4105
3.10 AKZO PREMIER HCAP 3YO+ 0-85 (D) 1m6f Good/Soft 83 -09 Slow [80]
£7605 £2340 £1170 £585 3 yo rec 10lb Raced centre - stands side fnl 3f

4006 **EVENING SCENT 7** [5] J Hetherton 4-7-10 (48) P M Quinn (3) 12/1: 201641: 4 b f Ardkinglass - Fresh Line 55
(High Line) Rear, prog 4f out & led over 2f out, sn rdn clr, eased nr line, readily: op 10/1: earlier scored at
Hamilton (h'cap): '99 Catterick wnr (sell, rtd 60): eff at 12/14f, tried 2m, may yet suit: acts on fast & soft
grnd: handles any trk: can run well fresh: well ridden, qk follow up under a pen?
4003 **SIMPLE IDEALS 7** [11] Don Enrico Incisa 6-7-10 (48)(2oh) Kim Tinkler 10/1: 654252: 6 b g Woodman - 6 47
Comfort And Style (Be My Guest) Held up, styd on for share till 3f, no threat to wnr: op 8/1: clr rem, gd run.
3395 **FOUNDRY LANE 38** [8] Mrs M Reveley 9-9-9 (75) A Culhane 7/1: -42133: 9 b g Mtoto - Eider (Niniski) 3 71
Mid-div, rdn over 3f out, kept on, no threat: see 3395, 2455.

1263

4006 **SNUGFIT ROSIE 7** [12] M W Easterby 4-8-6 (58) T Lucas 9/2 FAV: 030-54: Trkd ldrs 5f out, onepace/   nk   53
held over 2f out: nicely bckd: ahead of this wnr in 4006 (reapp).
3731 **ASHLEIGH BAKER 24** [3] 5-7-11 (49) K Dalgleish (5) 11/1: 124405: Led/dsptd lead 12f: see 2783 (12f).   2½   41
3783 **INTRUM MORSHAAN 21** [10] 3-9-6 (82) J Carroll 5/1: -02106: Held up, efft 3f out, sn held: btr 3476 (2m).1¾   72
3827 **ALDWYCH ARROW 19** [7] 5-7-10 (48)(11oh) P Hanagan (2) 25/1: 000067: Led 1f, cl up 12f: see 2836.   2½   35
3783 **MAGIC COMBINATION 21** [1] 7-9-5 (71) S W Kelly (3) 11/2: -45158: Chsd ldrs, drvn/btn 2f out: op 4/1. 1½   56
4024 **SPOSA 7** [6] 4-7-10 (48)(5oh) Joanna Badger (7) 33/1: 443009: Al rear: btr 2776 (clmr).   ¾   32
2609 **JOHNNY OSCAR 72** [9] 3-9-1 (77) D Harrison 6/1: -4330: Mid-div, btn 4f out: 10th: h'cap bow, 10 wk abs.¾   60
3378 **TURGENEV 38** [4] 11-7-10 (48)(16oh) J McAuley 33/1: 506640: In tch, btn over 3f out: 11th: see 576.   ½   30
2826 **GRAND SLAM GB 64** [5] 5-8-8 (60) W Supple 25/1: 042-40: Chsd ldrs 11f: 12th: abs: see 2826 (12f).   3   39
12 ran   Time 3m 10.87 (12.87)   (H Hetherton)   J Hetherton Malton, N Yorks

---

| **4106** | **3.45 BET DIRECT HCAP 3YO 0-95 (C)** | **7f30y rnd** | **Good/Soft 83** | **+02 Fast** | **[99]** |

£14300   £4400   £2100   £1100   Raced centre - stands side fnl 3f

3574 **DAKOTA SIOUX 31** [2] R A Fahey 3-7-10 (67)(bl)(6oh) P Hanagan (2) 12/1: 601101: 3 ch f College Chapel   72
- Batilde (Victory Piper) Made all & sn well clr, rdn fnl 2f, held on gamely: fair time: earlier scored at Newcastle
& here at Haddock (C/D, h'caps): plcd in '99 (sole start, rtd 71): well suited by dominating at 7f, tried 1m: likes
a gall trk, esp Haydock: acts on fast & gd/soft: well suited by reapp of blnks, disapp in a visor latest.
*3163 **CELEBRATION TOWN 49** [4] D Morris 3-8-12 (83) J Weaver 5/2 FAV: 101612: 3 b g Case Law - Battle   nk   87
Queen (Kind Of Hush) Held up, rdn/hdwy fnl 3f, drvn to press wnr fnl 1f, just held: well bckd: abs, likes soft.
3481 **MORNINGS MINION 35** [10] R Charlton 3-8-12 (83) S Sanders 10/1: -44153: 3 b g Polar Falcon - Fair   1   85
Dominion (Dominion) Hld up, rdn/styd on well fnl 2f, not reach wnr: acts on gd & gd/sft: eff at 7f/1m: see 2464.
4045 **ROYAL CAVALIER 4** [9] R Hollinshead 3-7-13 (70) P M Quinn (3) 20/1: 620064: Rear, eff 3f out, held dist.   2½   68
3698 **ROYAL ROMEO 26** [7] 3-8-3 (1ow) (74) J Carroll 12/1: 630005: Held up, prog 3f out, sn rdn/held.   1   70
3771 **TAP 21** [3] 3-8-9 (80) S Whitworth 9/1: -16056: Chsd wnr, hard rdn/btn 2f out: btr 967 (mdn, reapp).   2½   72
3727 **DONT SURRENDER 24** [1] 3-9-7 (92) D Harrison 11/1: 023007: Chsd ldrs 5f, btn/eased fnl 1f: see 1178. 3½   78
3861 **BABY BARRY 17** [5] 3-8-13 (84) G Duffield 16/1: 033508: Dwelt, al wds rear: unproven at 7f: see 3335.   4   63
4010 **CARD GAMES 7** [8] 3-8-11 (82) T Lucas 7/2: 120059: Chsd ldrs 4f: bckd: btr 1133 (6f).   1¾   59
3345 **DESERT SAFARI 40** [11] 3-8-1 (72) W Supple 25/1: 113600: Al rear: 10th: abs: see 2699, 2438 (fast).   4   42
3945 **TWEED MILL 10** [6] 3-8-9 (80) M Fenton 10/1: 000200: Bhd 3f out: 11th: btr 1032 (mdn, 8.5f).   14   26
11 ran   Time 1m 32.84 (5.74)   (Mrs Una Towell)   R A Fahey Butterwick, N Yorks

---

| **4107** | **4.15 AKZO HOLDINGS HCAP 3YO+ 0-90 (C)** | **5f** | **Good/Soft 83** | **+16 Fast** | **[88]** |

£9782   £3010   £1505   £752   3 yo rec 1 lb   Majority raced centre, winner raced alone far rail

*4073 **POLLY GOLIGHTLY 3** [1] M Blanshard 7-8-7 (67)(bl)(6ex) C Rutter 11/1: 043011: 7 ch m Weldnaas - Polly's   74
Teahouse (Shack) Raced alone far side, al prom/dsptng lead, styd on well, rdn out: gd time, qk reapp, pen:
recent wnr at Chester (h'cap): '99 Chester wnr (h'cap): '98 wnr again at Chester & York (h'caps, rtd 73): stays 7f,
all wins at 5f: acts on firm, suited by gd/sft or hvy: likes Chester: wears blnks/vis & likes to dominate: tough:
*3366 **ABBAJABBA 39** [3] C W Fairhurst 4-9-5 (79) W Supple 5/2 FAV: 311312: 4 b g Barrys Gamble - Bo   1   83+
Babbity (Strong Gale) Hld up, styd on strongly fnl 1f, not reach wnr far side: hvly bckd: win again at 6f.
4015 **SHARP HAT 2** [7] D W Chapman 6-8-12 (72) A Culhane 14/1: 032303: 6 b g Shavian - Madam Trilby   hd   75
(Grundy) Led/dsptd lead till 1f out, styd on well for press: op 10/1: back to form here: see 2721.
3960 **EASTERN TRUMPETER 9** [16] J M Bradley 4-9-6 (80) J Weaver 20/1: 103004: Led/dsptd lead till   nk   82
over 1f out, kept on for press: loves easy ground, tough & suited wn again this autumn: see 2644.
3920 **SMART PREDATOR 11** [2] 4-9-12 (86) M Tebbutt 8/1: 301325: Chsd ldrs, held fnl 1f: topweight, op 6/1.   1   86
4073 **THE GAY FOX 3** [5] 6-8-13 (73)(tbl) T E Durcan 9/1: 410046: Dwelt, late gains from rear, nrst fin.   nk   72
3960 **WHIZZ KID 9** [6] 6-8-8 (68) Claire Bryan (5) 11/1: 000057: Mod late gains, nvr pace to chall ldrs.   2   62
*4087 **TORRENT 2** [14] 5-8-13 (73)(bl)(6ex) Lynsey Hanna (7) 14/1: 133518: In tch, held fnl 1f: op 12/1.   hd   66
4010 **WILLIAMS WELL 7** [12] 6-9-6 (80)(bl) T Lucas 20/1: 211609: Chsd ldrs, held over 1f out: see 3464.   1¼   70
3904 **FORGOTTEN TIMES 14** [10] 6-9-0 (74)(vis) G Duffield 12/1: 003100: Chsd ldrs till over 1f out: 10th.   nk   63
3774 **MARENGO 21** [9] 6-7-10 (56)(2oh) K Dalgleish (5) 33/1: 365000: Sn rdn, al twds rear: 11th: see 1073.   1   43
4010 **PTARMIGAN RIDGE 7** [17] 4-9-6 (80) M Fenton 14/1: 00-100: Led/dsptd lead till over 1f out: 12th.   ½   66
3788 **Barringer 21** [8] 3-9-7 (82) S Whitworth 16/1:   3947 **Ansellman 10** [13] 10-8-5 (65)(bl) C Lowther 25/1:
4012 **Pipadash 7** [15] 3-9-7 (82) J Carroll 20/1:   2820 **Nifty Norman 64** [11] 6-8-5 (65) O Pears 25/1:
4015 **Flak Jacket 7** [4] 5-8-13 (73) S Sanders 20/1:
17 ran   Time 1m 02.13 (3.33)   (David Sykes)   M Blanshard Upper Lambourn, Berks

---

| **4108** | **4.45 EBF FILLIES HCAP 3YO+ 0-90 (C)** | **1m2f120y** | **Good/Soft 83** | **-47 Slow** | **[83]** |

£11017   £3390   £1695   £847   3 yo rec 1 lb   Majority raced centre fnl 3f, wnr remained far side

3324 **TYCOONS LAST 42** [2] W M Brisbourne 3-7-10 (58)(22oh) K Dalgleish (5) 14/1: 353041: 3 b f Nalchik - Royal   61
Tycoon (Tycoon ll) Made all, raced alone far side fnl 3f, rdn & always beating rivals fnl 2f: abs, op 25/1, 22oh:
1st win: unplcd in '99 (rtd 73$): eff at 10f, stays a sharp 12f on fast, likes gd/soft: runs well fresh:
big improvement today for the fourth consecutive race at this meeting jockey tactics proved decisive.
4088 **QUEENS PAGEANT 2** [5] J L Spearing 6-9-0 (69) A Culhane 3/1: 003032: 6 ch m Risk Me - Mistral's   3   67
Dancer (Shareef Dancer) Held up near, rdn/styd on fnl 2f, no impress on wnr: bckd: qck reapp: see 3045.
3381 **VARIETY 38** [1] J R Fanshawe 3-8-3 (65) D Harrison 9/1: 0363: 3 ch f Theatrical - Kamsi (Afleet)   1   62
Chsd wnr, rdn/held fnl 2f: h'cap bow: handles fast & gd/sft grnd.
*3858 **SHARP SPICE 17** [6] D J Coakley 4-8-7 (62) W Supple 7/2: 530314: Hld up, btn 2f: softer grnd.   ½   58
3024 **BEZZAAF 55** [3] 3-9-13 (89) M Tebbutt 9/1: 15P005: Chsd ldrs 1m: abs: btr 1200 (mdn, fast).   1¾   83
3989 **CHAMELEON 8** [4] 4-9-3 (72) M Fenton 9/4 FAV: /10526: Held up, rdn/btn 3f out: bckd: btr 3989.   4   61
6 ran   Time 2m 23.75 (13.75)   (L R Owen)   W M Brisbourne Great Ness, Shropshire

Official Going   GOOD TO SOFT (GOOD in places). Stalls: Str Crse - Stands Side; Rnd Crse - Inside.

4109   2.00 GR 3 CUMBERLAND LODGE STKS 3YO+ (A)   1m4f   Good 40 -14 Slow
£32400   £12420   £6210   £2970   3 yo rec 8 lb

+3792 **MUTAMAM** 21 [6]   A C Stewart 5-9-3 R Hills 4/6 FAV: -21411: 5 b h Darshaan - Petal Girl (Caerleon)   **118**
Led, rdn 3L clr 2f out, pushed out towards fin: hvly bckd: earlier won at Goodwood (stks) & Kempton (Gr 3):
'99 wnr at Sandown (stks), Haydock & Goodwood (Gr 3s, Gr 1 4th, rtd 120): eff at 10f, suited by 12f: acts on
firm & gd/soft grnd, any trk, likes Goodwood & forcing the pace: tough & smart, win more Gr races.
4057 **HAPPY CHANGE** 6 [4]   M Johnston 6-9-0 L Dettori 11/1: 301532: 6 ch g Surumu - Happy Girl (Ginistrelli)   3   **109**
Rcd in 2nd, eff ent str, onepace till rallied to regain 2nd towards fin: op 8/1: qck reapp: useful gelding.
3892 **KING O THE MANA** 15 [2]   R Hannon 3-8-6 R Hughes 12/1: 041323: 3 b c Turtle Island - Olivia Jane   nk   **108**
(Ela Mana Mou) Held up, eff & short of room 2f out, switched & styd on for 3rd ins last, nvr dngrs: useful.
3927 **COMMANDER COLLINS** 13 [7]   J H M Gosden 4-9-0 J Fortune 7/1: 4-4334: Prom, went 2nd appr fnl 1f, nk   **108**
rdn & no extra towards fin: confidence booster in lesser company needed: see 2566, 1057.
2998 **BEAT ALL** 56 [1]   4-9-0 Pat Eddery 4/1: W43245: Rear, prog appr str, sn rdn, no further impression: 1½   **106**
bckd, 8 wk abs: well below par, ideally suited by faster grnd?: see 1248.
3674 **NADOUR AL BAHR** 748 [3]   5-9-0 T Williams 50/1: 2235/6: Al rear, outpcd ent str: 2 yr abs, Brit bow: 7   **97**
ex-German entire, '98 Frankfurt wnr (Gr 3, 2nd in both the Italian & German Derbys, rtd 114): eff at 12f on fast & hvy.
6 ran   Time 2m 35.48 (6.48)   (Hamdan Al Maktoum)   A C Stewart Newmarket.

4110   2.35 GR 1 MEON VALLEY FILLIES MILE 2YO (A)   1m rnd   Good 40 -34 Slow
£116000   £44000   £22000   £10000

*3433 **CRYSTAL MUSIC** 36 [8]   J H M Gosden 2-8-10 L Dettori 4/1: 111: 2 b f Nureyev - Crystal Spray (Beldale   **111**
Flutter) Pulled hard early, in tch, rdn & hdwy ent str, led 1f out, styd on well, rdn out: bckd: hat-trick
landed/unbtn after wins at Newmarket (mdn) & Sandown (fill cond stks): eff at 1m, mid-dists shld suit next term
(dam 14f wnr): acts on fast & gd grnd, stiff trks: smart filly, plenty of scope, looks a Classic prospect.
-3659 **SUMMER SYMPHONY** 27 [10]   L M Cumani 2-8-10 J P Spencer 2/1 FAV: -122: 2 gr f Caerleon -   1¼   **108**
Summer Sonnet (Baillamont) Waited wth, switched wide going well 2f out, rdn bef dist, kept on ins last, held
by wnr: hvly bckd from 3/1: v useful effort & stays 1m: looks sure to win Gr races next term: see 3659.
3845 **HOTELGENIE DOT COM** 20 [6]   M R Channon 2-8-10 Craig Williams 7/2: 1223: 2 gr f Selkirk - Birch   2   **104**
Creek (Carwhite) Rear, smooth prog appr fnl 2f, sn short of room, shkn up bef dist, styd on without threatening:
well bckd: eff at 7f/1m: useful filly, looks capable of rating higher with a more positive ride: see 2935.
3845 **IMAGINE** 20 [1]   A P O'Brien 2-8-10 M J Kinane 14/1: 364: Led till 1f out, no extra: clr rem: 1¼   **101**
fair run from this useful Irish mdn: see 3555.
3910 **MAMEHA** 12 [7]   2-8-10 P Robinson 40/1: 035: Chsd ldr, fdd appr fnl 1f: highly tried mdn, flattered?   3½   **94**
*3833 **VELVET GLADE** 18 [2]   2-8-10 K Darley 9/1: 316: Pulled hard, in tch, lost grnd ent str & no   3   **88**
threat after: nicely bckd: still rather green: find easier races: shade btr 3833 (firm grnd).
*3397 **PAGE NOUVELLE** 38 [3]   2-8-10 M Hills 25/1: 317: Chsd ldrs, wknd ent fnl 2f: op 16/1: not disgraced   1½   **85**
up in grade after winning a Beverley mdn in 3397.
*3363 **BAILEYS CREAM** 39 [5]   2-8-10 D Holland 20/1: 0218: Cl-up, eff appr straight, lost pl 2f out: 1   **83**
free-running sort: will enjoy a drop in grade: see 3363 (7f auct mdn).
*3359 **SHAHIRAH** 40 [4]   2-8-10 R Hills 7/1: 19: Al rear, no ch when hmpd 2f out: abs, see 3359 (mdn).   1   **81**
9 ran   Time 1m 44.44 (5.94)   (Lord Lloyd-Webber)   J H M Gosden Manton, Wilts.

4111   3.20 GR 1 QUEEN ELIZABETH II STKS 3YO+ (A)   1m rnd   Good 40 +04 Fast
£200100   £75900   £37950   £17250   3 yo rec 4 lb

3647 **OBSERVATORY** 28 [6]   J H M Gosden 3-8-11 K Darley 14/1: -21121: 3 ch c Distant View - Stellaria   **126**
(Roberto) Mid-div, imprvd ent str & brght wide, rdn bef fnl 1f, styd on strongly to lead fnl 100y, drvn out: bckd,
gd time: earlier won at R Ascot & Goodwood (Gr 3s): '99 Yarmouth wnr (2, mdn & stks, rtd 100): eff at 7f/1m on
fast & gd, any trk: runs v well fresh: has a smart turn of foot: high-class & still improving, well ridden.
*3925 **GIANTS CAUSEWAY** 14 [9]   A P O'Brien 3-8-11 M J Kinane 11/10 FAV: 111112: 3 ch c Storm Cat -   ½   **125**
Mariah's Storm (Rahy) Prom, led ent fnl 3f, 2L clr appr fnl 1f, sn rdn, hdd fnl 100y, kept on: hvly bckd, clr
rem: 'Iron Horse' finally toppled but lost nothing in defeat: shld remain v hard to beat: see 3925.
3925 **BEST OF THE BESTS** 14 [4]   Saeed bin Suroor 3-8-11 L Dettori 7/1: 344133: 3 ch c Machiavellian -   3½   **119**
Sueboog (Darshaan) Waited wth, imprvd 3f out, short of room & had to be switched 2f out, kept on to
take 3rd ins last, no ch with front 2: bckd: high-class colt, ran to best despite less than clr passage: eff
at 1m, return to 10f will suit: only 1½L bhd this 2nd in 3925, see 3374 (Gr 2).
*3647 **MEDICEAN** 28 [10]   Sir Michael Stoute 3-8-11 Pat Eddery 10/1: 130314: Prom, rdn to chase ldr 2f out,   ¾   **117**
sn onepace: op 8/1: btr 3647 (beat this wnr by 1L).
3847 **GOLDEN SILCA** 20 [2]   4-8-12 Craig Williams 66/1: 054105: Bhd, hdwy on ins rail fnl 2f, nvr dngrs: ¾   **112**
ran nr to best: smart filly, win another Group 3, see 3554.
3847 **DIKTAT** 20 [3]   5-9-1 J Reid 20/1: 5-6236: Wide, towards rear, eff 2f out, nvr any impress on ldrs: ½   **114**
stablemate 3rd, yet to strike top-form this term at 1m, wins at 6/7f: see 1775.
*3847 **INDIAN LODGE** 20 [7]   4-9-1 C Asmussen 3/2: 113017: Chsd ldrs, feeling pace ent str & bhd   ½   **113**
after: bckd tho' op 5/1: ideally suited by easier grnd, see 3847 (soft).
3544 **CRIMPLENE** 41 [1]   3-8-8 P Robinson 6/1: 111148: Pld hard, well plcd, ev ch ent str, sn edged left   ¾   **108**
& wknd: 6 wk abs: again gave trouble at the start & may have had enough for the season: see 3151 (made most).
3539 **ALMUSHTARAK** 32 [5]   7-9-1 M Roberts 66/1: -36069: Nvr a factor: not up to Gr 1 class, see 3539.   5   **101**
3875 **VALENTINO** 16 [8]   3-8-11 (t) G Mosse 12/1: -32020: Rear, shkn up ent str & short of room, no   4   **93**
impress: 10th, tchd 16/1: prob something amiss, only a hd bhd this 2nd in 2066, see 1318.
4055 **LERMONTOV** 7 [11]   3-8-11 Paul Scallan 100/1: 12-400: Led till appr fnl 2f: 11th, pacemaker.   9   **77**
3925 **MANHATTAN** 14 [12]   3-8-11 J A Heffernan 200/1: 1-1000: In tch till 3f out: 12th, stablemate 2nd.   5   **67**
12 ran   Time 1m 41.4 (2.9)   (K Abdulla)   J H M Gosden Manton, Wilts.

ASCOT

SATURDAY SEPTEMBER 23RD   Righthand, Stiff, Galloping Track

4112   3.55 TOTE TRIFECTA HCAP 3YO+ (B)   7f str   Good 40   +06 Fast   [111]
£43500   £16500   £8250   £3750   3 yo rec 3 lb   Low draw lkd an advantage

3481 **DUKE OF MODENA** 35 [1] G B Balding 3-8-9 (95) S Carson (3) 9/1: 514461: 3 ch g Salse - Palace Street **101**
(Secreto) In tch, prog after halfway, rdn to lead 1f out, just held on: has run well in defeat since scoring
at Kempton, Salisbury & Newbury (h'caps): plcd fnl '99 start (mdn, rtd 75): suited by 7f on firm & hvy grnd,
any trk: best up with the pace: v useful & progressive this term.

2997 **NICE ONE CLARE** 3 [3] J W Payne 4-8-7 (90) J P Spencer 8/1: -53202: 4 b f Mukaddamah - Sarah   hd   **95**
Clare (Reach) Towards rear, going well but nowhere to go appr fnl 2f, ran on bef fnl 1f & hmpd again, clr & drvn ins
last, ran on, just failed: bckd from 10/1, lkd v unlucky, 8 wk abs: out of luck all season: deserves a nice prize.

3981 **ZUCCHERO** 8 [10] D W P Arbuthnot 4-7-12 (80)(1ow) A Daly 40/1: 165543: 4 br g Dilum - Legal Sound   1   **84**
(Legal Eagle) Made most till 1f out, kept on: a bold front running effort & is effective with/without blnks
nowadays: acts on firm & gd grnd: see 2814.

4010 **I CRIED FOR YOU** 7 [20] J G Given 5-7-13 (82) F Norton 16/1: 212004: Keen, chsd ldrs, qcknd to   1   **83**
chall appr fnl 1f, edged left, onepace ins last: back to form at 7f: did best of those drawn high: see 1840.

3998 **SMART RIDGE** 2 [2] N Callan 25/1: 023405: Mid-div, shkn up after halfway, not clrst of   nk   **100**
runs 2f out, styd on for press, nvr nrr: tchd 50/1, qck reapp: useful, apprec return to 7f: see 1830, 1055.

3130 **CAMBERLEY** 50 [4] K Darley 10/1: 322106: Held up, rdn appr fnl 1f, kept on, nvr on terms: hd   **93**
bckd, 7 wk abs: prob ran to best: see 1470.

4012 **GAELIC STORM** 7 [19] 6-9-10 (107) D Holland 9/1: 441547: Bhd, wide, hdwy in centre appr fnl 1f,   1½   **104**
nvr a threat: bckd, qck reapp, top-weight: prob ran from outside draw & likes soft: see 3213.

3727 **ROYAL ARTIST** 24 [12] 4-8-7 (90) T Quinn 25/1: 211008: Dwelt, chsd ldrs, no room 2f out till   ¾   **85**
ent fnl 1f, nvr dngrs: prob worth forgetting: see 2954 (6f, here).

3785 **GIRLS BEST FRIEND** 21 [18] 3-7-10 (82)(t) (2oh) J Mackay (5) 66/1: -05609: Wide, rear, prog   hd   **76**
appr fnl 1f, nvr better than mid-div: t-strap reapplied, unfav'ble draw: see 1374.

3510 **SILCA BLANKA** 34 [17] 8-8-10 (93) J Reid 33/1: 032060: Midfield, eff ent fnl 2f, no impress: 10th.   shd   **87**
3992 **KINAN** 8 [11] 4-8-2 (85) A Nicholls 25/1: 100360: Bhd ldrs, outpcd appr fnl 1f: 11th, see 3992, 2431.   nk   **78**
3902 **BIG FUTURE** 14 [22] 3-8-4 (90) W Ryan 20/1: 415330: Chsd ldrs, not much room 2f out, onepce: 12th.   1¼   **80**
4012 **AL MUALLIM** 7 [9] 6-8-7 (90)(t) R Hughes 25/1: 010000: Bhd, kept on appr fnl 1f, nvr a factor: 13th.   shd   **80**
3648 **STRAHAN** 28 [24] 3-9-0 (100) L Dettori 14/1: 223040: Cl-up, fdd appr fnl 1f: 14th, nicely bckd.   shd   **89**
3897 **BLACK SILK** 14 [14] 4-8-11 (94) R Mullen 14/1: -16340: Rear, wide prog 3f out, no extra bef dist: 15th.   shd   **83**
3880 **BARABASCHI** 16 [13] 4-7-10 (79)(5oh) G Baker (5) 50/1: 261200: In tch, wknd appr fnl 1f: 16th, stiff task.   1   **66**
4012 **PIPS MAGIC** 7 [26] 4-8-0 (83) A Beech (3) 50/1: 000000: Front rank, wknd ent fnl 2f: 17th, qk reapp.   nk   **69**
3902 **MUCHEA** 7 [8] 6-9-1 (98) Craig Williams 14/1: 041250: Nvr a factor, not much room appr fnl 1f: 18th.   shd   **84**
3427 **RAYYAAN** 36 [7] 3-8-4 (90) R Hills 15/2 FAV: 111620: Held up, short of room bef fnl 2f, rdn dist,   1½   **73**
nvr in it: 19th, would fancy from 9/1: ideally suited by fast grnd?: see 1153.

*3642 **BORDER SUBJECT** 28 [5] 3-8-6 (92) Pat Eddery 9/1: -60110: Rear, shkn up 3f out, nvr dngrs: 21st,   **0**
bckd: only lightly rcd & is worth another chance: see 3642 (made all over 1m).

3648 **TEODORA** 28 [16] 3-7-12 (84)(2ow)(4oh) P Doe 66/'1: 200000: Led after 2f till halfway, lost place: 25th.   **0**

4012 Tony Tie 7 [25] 4-8-10 (93) A McGlone 33/1:   3880 **Premier Baron** 16 [6] 5-8-2 (85) L Newman (3) 20/1:
3682 Showboat 26 [15] 6-9-9 (106) M Hills 33/1:   3981 **Alpen Wolf** 8 [23] 5-8-5 (88) Martin Dwyer 50/1:
3897 Peartree House 14 [21] 6-9-0 (97) M J Kinane 25/1:

26 ran   Time 1m 28.37 (2.37)   (Miss B Swire)   G B Balding Fyfield, Hants.

4113   4.30 LISTED ROSEMARY RTD HCAP 3YO+ 0-105 (A)   1m str   Good 40   +04 Fast   [107]
£18560   £7040   £3520   £1600   3 yo rec 4 lb

3883 **RIBERAC** 15 [10] M Johnston 4-8-10 (89) K Darley 9/1: 101101: 4 b f Efisio - Ciboure (Norwick)   **97**
Prom, went on appr fnl 1f, rdn clr: tchd 14/1, gd time: earlier won at Sandown, Ayr & Epsom (2, h'caps):
highly tried in '99 for W Haggas (stks, rtd 91): former sprinter, revelation since stepped up to 1m/10f:
acts on firm, gd grnd & any trk, likes Epsom: useful, progressive filly, can go in again.

2167 **MYSTIFY** 17 [13] J H M Gosden 3-8-12 (95) L Dettori 9/2: -15262: 3 b f Batshoof - Santa Linda   2   **98**
(Sir Ivor) Pulled hard mid-div, sltly hmpd 2f out, sn chsd wnr, kept on but no impress: well bckd from 6/1:
not disgraced giving weight to this progressive wnr: useful effort, lightly raced: see 2167, 1134.

3880 **PEACOCK ALLEY** 16 [4] W J Haggas 3-8-7 (90) M Hills 11/4 FAV: 113623: 3 gr f Salse - Tagiki (Doyoun)   ½   **92**
Waited with, prog hmpd 2f, badly hmpd 1½f out & again 1f out, kept on, nvr nr to chall: well bckd, would
have been a least 2nd with a clr run, wnr wld have taken a lot of catching: deserves comp, see 3880, 2163.

1825 **ANNAPURNA** 85 [7] B J Meehan 4-9-5 (98) Pat Eddery 25/1: 234004: Rear, switched & hdwy ent   ½   **98**
fnl 2f, kept on till no extra towards fin: 3 month abs: useful run, see 1482, 1014 (10f).

3703 **CROWN LODGE** 26 [11] B J-8-4 (87) Craig Williams 16/1: -21505: Bhd, rdn 2f out, styd on but nvr on   hd   **86**
terms: prob ran to best tho' return to 10f will suit, as will easier grnd: see 1837.

3878 **RENDITION** 16 [5] 3-8-6 (89) F Norton 16/1: 130366: Held up, kept on appr fnl 1f, nvr dngrs: nk   **87**
stablemate 3rd, op 12/1, tchd 20/1: clrly gets 1m, faster grnd would suit: see 1308.

3897 **MOSSY MOOR** 14 [2] 3-8-9 (92) M J Kinane 12/1: 104267: Prom, unable to qckn appr fnl 1f.   ½   **88**

*3707 **CAFE OPERA** 26 [9] 3-8-3 (86)(2oh) R Hills 16/1: 2-0218: Chsd ldrs, eff & hung right ent fnl 2f,   nk   **81**
same pace: not disgraced in h'cap bow: shade btr 3707 (soft, mdn).

3726 **ISSEY ROSE** 24 [3] 3-8-11 (94) T Williams 33/1: 40-009: Led till appr fnl 2f, fdd: see 3726.   nk   **88**

*3793 **GRANTED** 21 [12] 3-8-3 (86) J Mackay 10/1: 143210: Bhd ldrs, eff & carr right ent fnl 2f, wknd: 10th.   1½   **77**

3340 **ALPENGLOW** 41 [14] 4-9-7 (100) R Havlin 20/1: 613-30: Prom, led appr fnl 2f till bef dist,   2   **97**
lost pl: 11th, 6 wk abs: stablemate 2nd, lightly rcd, see 3340.

1901 **TANZILLA** 104 [1] 3-9-3 (100) P Robinson 20/1: 123000: Prom till 2f out: 12th, abs, back in trip.   hd   **86**

3878 **MIDNIGHT ALLURE** 16 [6] 3-8-7 (90)(t) R Mullen 14/1: 623450: Dwelt, al bhd: 13th, see 1873.   1¼   **73**

3997 **DASHIBA** 7 [8] 4-8-13 (92) J Reid 9/1: 662500: Keen, al bhd: 14th, bckd from 9/1, qck reapp: hd   **74**
unlucky in running last time tho' has proved hard to win with this term: see 1965.

14 ran   Time 1m 41.61 (2.91)   (Mr & Mrs G Middlebrook)   M Johnston Middleham, N.Yorks.

4114   5.00 TSL BLUE SEAL COND STKS 2YO (B)   7f str   Good 40   -04 Slow
£12180   £4620   £2310   £1050

-- **SMALL CHANGE** [1] D R Loder 2-8-8 L Dettori 2/1 FAV: 1: 2 b f Danzig - Blue Note (Habitat)   **97**
Chsd ldrs, rdn 1f out, led fnl 100y: hvly bckd, debut: full sister to high-class sprint juv Blue Duster &

1266

half-sister to Zieten (6/7f): dam got 7f: eff at 7f, 1m will suit: acts on gd grnd, stiff/gall trk
& runs well fresh: useful, potentially v smart filly, shld go well in the Rockfel next month.

3938 **ROCKERLONG** 10 [5] G Wragg 2-8-8 M Roberts 10/3: 22: 2 b f Deploy - Dancing Rocks (Green Dancer)   ¾   94
Well plcd, led 2½f out till well ins last, onepace: bckd: apprec step up to 7f, 1m+ will suit: acts on firm
& gd grnd: sure to win races: see 3938.

3752 **HEAD IN THE CLOUDS** 23 [2] J L Dunlop 2-8-8 Pat Eddery 10/1: 53: 2 b f Rainbow Quest - Ballerina   shd   94+
(Dancing Brave) Keen, mid-div, switched & hdwy appr fnl 1f, kept on for hands-and-heels, nvr nrr: tchd 14/1:
left debut effort bhd, looks sure to win a race over further: see 3752.

3789 **MATOAKA** 21 [6] Sir Michael Stoute 2-8-8 J Murtagh 10/3: 24: Led till appr fnl 2f, onepace fnl   1¼   91
1f: bckd: gd run, will not be long in winning: see 3789.

-- **INCHIRI** [4] 2-8-8 J P Spencer 16/1: 5: Dwelt, bhd, styd on ins last, nvr nr ldrs: op 12/1, tchd 20/1   2   87
on debut: v plaesing debut, sure to improve & apprec 1m+.

-- **SAMARA MIDDLE EAST** [3] 2-8-8 Craig Williams 14/1: 6: In tch, chsd ldrs 2f out till outpcd 1f   ½   86
out: debut: Marju first foal, dam a miler, sire a miler (styd 12f): with M Channon.

3829 **INDEPENDENCE** 18 [10] G Carter 10/1: 37: Prom till edged right & lost pl appr fnl 1f: op 8/1:   5   76
bit reportedly slipped & this can be ignored: see 3829.

3845 **STAGE PRESENCE** 20 [7] M Hills 12/1: 08: Mid-div, prog appr fnl 2f, sn wknd: drop in trip?   6   66

-- **LUMIERE DESPOIR** [9] 2-8-8 P Doe 50/1: 9: Nvr a factor: debut: Saumarez half-sister to sev   6   56
wnrs, up to 12f, dam 10f wnr: bred to need mid-dists next term: with S Dow.

-- **ENCHANTING** [8] 2-8-8 D R McCabe 33/1: 0: Dwelt, nvr in it: 10th, debut: 21,000gns Bigstone   3   50
half-sister to 2 wnrs, incl a useful stayer: with B Meehan.

3985 **HAMADEENAH** 8 [11] 2-8-11 D McGaffin 40/1: -150: Prom till 3f out: 11th, see 3985, 3627.   6   43
11 ran   Time 1m 29.07 (3.07)   (Godolphin)   D R Loder France.

4115   5.35 SPORT4CAST.COM HCAP 3YO+ 0-95 (C)   2m45y   Good 40   -21 Slow   [95]
£14137   £4350   £2175   £1087   3 yo rec 12lb

2068 **MBELE** 95 [5] W R Muir 3-8-13 (92) Martin Dwyer 20/1: -32161: 3 b c Mtoto - Majestic Image   98
(Niniski) Keen, well plcd, went on appr str, styd on strongly, rdn out: 3 month abs, h'cap bow: tried Gr 3
since won at Nottingham (mdn): rnr-up sole '99 start (mdn, rtd 89): eff at 12/14f, relished this stiff 2m:
acts on firm & soft grnd, any trk: goes well fresh: useful, unexposed young stayer.

3811 **MONTALCINO** [9] P J Makin 4-10-0 (95) D Sweeney 10/2: -5422: 4 b g Robellino - Only Gossip   2½   97
(Trempolino) Mid-div, prog ent str, styd on to go 2nd ins last but wnr had flown: useful weight carrying
performance over longer trip: eff at 14f/2m: keep in mind: see 1484.

3986 **BID ME WELCOME** 8 [11] Miss D A McHale 4-8-12 (79) J Reid 25/1: 152063: 4 b g Alzao - Blushing   ½   80
Barada (Blushing Groom) Mid-div, prog over 3f out, went after wnr appr fnl 1f, same pace: gd effort: see 2812.

*2600 **TURNPOLE** 73 [2] Mrs M Reveley 9-8-10 (77) T Quinn 10/1: /06414: Towards rear, rdn ent str,   2   76
late hdwy but nvr a threat: tchd 12/1, 10 wk abs: gd run, see 2600.

3611 **TENSILE** 29 [1] 5-9-6 (87) K Darley 12/1: 004335: Waited with, wide prog 3f out, kept on but nvr   nk   85
*3961 **BUSY LIZZIE** 9 [3] 3-9-4 (97) Pat Eddery 9/1 FAV: 625116: Patiently rdn, imprvd into mid-div ent str,   3½   92
short of room & drvn, no impress: bckd: faster pace would have suited, worth another chance: see 3961.

2498 **BRAVE TORNADO** 77 [14] 9-8-11 (78) S Carson (3) 12/1: 224537: Led till appr fnl 3f, wknd: no extra: 11 wk abs.   ½   72
3890 **PROMISING LADY** 15 [15] 3-8-6 (85) Craig Williams 33/1: 602608: Nvr a factor: up in trip again.   1   78
3783 **SEREN HILL** 21 [7] 4-9-1 (82) D Holland 8/1: 000209: Rear, prog & plenty to do when hmpd twice   ½   74
appr fnl 2f, no dngr: up in trip, best to forget this: see 997.

3986 **FIRST OFFICER** 8 [12] 3-8-7 (86) J Murtagh 13/2: 106320: Prom till fdd ent str: 10th, see 3986, 1539.   6   72
3811 **WAVE OF OPTIMISM** 20 [6] 5-8-13 (80) G Bardwell 14/1: 011000: Keen, nvr in it: 11th, softer suits.   nk   65
3798 **RIVERTOWN** 20 [4] 6-9-6 (87) M J Kinane 25/1: /43560: Handy till wknd over 3f out: 12th, longer trip.   14   62
3905 **RATHBANE PRINCE** 14 [10] 9-8-9 (76) (BL) R Hughes 9/1: 3-2030: Sn prom, rdn 4f out, lost pl: 9   44
13th, nicely bckd Irish raider: blnkd, much btr without 3905.

3986 **COMPTON AVIATOR** 8 [8] 4-8-11 (78) (t) L Dettori 10/1: 33-000: Al towards rear, 14th, see 3986.   10   38
3986 **ALRISHA** 8 [13] 3-8-4 (83) J Mackay (5) 7/1: 212430: Nvr dngrs, btn 4f out: 15th, bckd, btr 3986.   7   38
15 ran   Time 3m 35.68 (9.68)   (Dr & Mrs John Wilson)   W R Muir Lambourn, Berks.

BRIGHTON   SUNDAY SEPTEMBER 24TH   Lefthand, V Sharp, Undulating Track

Official Going   GOOD TO SOFT, becoming SOFT after race 3.

4116   1.50 CYPRUS MDN AUCT DIV 1 2YO (F)   1m rnd   Good/Soft 81   -05 Slow
£1767   £505   £252   Raced stands side fnl 3f

3268 **TEMPLES TIME** 45 [10] R Hannon 2-8-5(1ow) S Sanders 7/2: -4361: 2 b f Distinctly North - Midnight   78
Patrol (Ashmore) Al prom, rdn/led over 2f out, asserted sn over 1f out, rdn out: op 4/1: 6 wk abs: well
suited by step up to 1m, could get further: acts on firm & gd grnd: runs well fresh: can improve.

3906 **MIDNIGHT CREEK** 15 [4] Mrs A J Perrett 2-8-6 W Ryan 12/1: 52: 2 b c Tragic Role - Greek Night Out   5   71
(Ela Mana Mou) Dwelt, mid-div, styd on to take 2nd ins last, no threat to wnr: op 10/1: eff at 1m on gd/soft.

3175 **APRIL LEE** 49 [7] K McAuliffe 2-8-2 (e) W Supple 7/2: 525203: 2 b f Superpower - Petitesse (Petong)   ½   66
Led, rdn/hdd over 2f out, held ins last: 7 wk abs: this longer 1m trip shld suit: prob handles gd & gd/soft grnd.

3906 **KIVOTOS** 15 [3] E J O'Neill 2-8-12 M Tebbutt 16/1: 64: Prom, held fnl 1f: handles gd/soft: see 3906.   1¾   73
3912 **LADY LAUREATE** 13 [1] 2-8-7 A Nicholls 33/1: 05: Cl-up, fdd over 1f out: longer 1m trip: see 3912.   1¾   65
3910 **SECRET PASSION** 13 [6] 2-8-3(3ow) B Marcus 11/2: 66: Rear, eff 3f out, little hdwy: longer 1m trip.   2   57
3952 **MARSHAL BOND** 11 [2] 2-8-4 Paul Eddery 3/1 FAV: 627: Prom, ch over 2f out, fdd: bckd: btr 3952 (gd).   ¾   57
-- **EMPERORS FOLLY** [9] 2-8-11 D Harrison 12/1: 8: Prom 4f: op 10/1: Emperor Jones colt, Jan   15   41
foal, cost 9,000gns: a first foal: dam a multiple wnr abroad as a 2yo: with C A Dwyer.

2459 **SUPREME TRAVEL** 79 [5] 2-8-5 N Pollard 33/1: -009: Bhd 3f out: longer 1m trip.   3   30
-- **HIGH TEMPO** [8] 2-8-13 (t) Darren Williams (5) 14/1: 0: Slowly away/bhd, no ch 3f out & eased   11   22
over 1f out: 10th: op 12/1: Piccolo colt, Mar foal, cost 11,000gns: a first foal: dam a mdn: wore a t-strap here.
10 ran   Time 1m 38.9 (6.9)   (J B Kavangah)   R Hannon East Everleigh, Wilts.

4117   **2.25 CYPRUS MDN AUCT DIV 2 2YO (F)   1m rnd   Good/Soft 81   -29 Slow**
£1767   £505   £252   Raced stands side fnl 3f

3911   **PAULAS PRIDE** 13 [6] J R Best 2-8-6 A Polli (3) 14/1: 0061: 2 ch f Pivotal - Sharp Top (Sharpo)   72
Keen/chsd ldrs, led 3f out, drvn & held on well ins last: improved over this longer 1m trip: acts on gd/soft grnd.

3675   **BOLSHOI BALLET** 28 [7] J L Dunlop 2-8-9 D Harrison 10/11 FAV: -03322: 2 b c Dancing Spree - Broom   ½   73
Isle (Damister), Prom, ch 3f out, sn outpcd, styd on ins last, al held: nicely bckd: acts on fast & gd/soft grnd.

3496   **STARRY MARY** 36 [10] E L James 2-8-0 C Rutter 9/2: 04003: 2 b f Deploy - Darling Splodge (Elegant   1½   61
Air) Dwelt/rear, rdn & styd on well fnl 2f, nrst fin: stays 1m well, further will suit: acts on gd/soft.

3692   **BEE J GEE** 27 [1] J Pearce 2-8-12 T G McLaughlin 33/1: 6004: Led till 3f out, held fnl 1f: clr rem: 2   69$
styd longer 1m trip: acts on gd/soft grnd: see 1962.

3833   **THE FAIRY FLAG** 19 [3] G Hind 8/1: 05: Keen/cl-up, held fnl 3f: longer 1m trip: see 3833.   7   51

3888   **COSMIC RANGER** 16 [2] 2-8-13 D Sweeney 8/1: -0506: Chsd ldrs till halfway: op 10/1: lngr 1m trip.   hd   58

4030   **MERRY DANCE** 6 [5] 2-8-3 N Pollard 12/1: 03007: Prom 6f, op 14/1, qck reapp: see 3558.   1   46

3776   **SUSIE THE FLOOSIE** 22 [8] 2-8-5 Paul Eddery 16/1: 008: Al rear: longer 1m trip, mod form.   4   41

3942   **LAUDABLE LAD** 11 [9] 2-8-4 I Mongan (5) 20/1: 09: Dwelt, al rear: longer 1m trip.   10   25

3836   **COSMIC PEARL** 19 [4] 2-7-12 A Mackay 33/1: 050: Sn bhd: 10th: mod form.   6   10

10 ran   Time 1m 40.8 (8.8)   (Thomas Tanton & Frederick French)   J R Best Hucking, Kent.

4118   **3.00 EBF FILLIES HCAP 3YO+ 0-75 (E)   1m2f   Good/Soft 81   -13 Slow**   **[70]**
£3822   £1176   £588   £294   3 yo rec 6 lb   Raced stands side fnl 3f.

*4046   **LEVEL HEADED** 5 [16] P W Hiatt 5-8-8 (50)(6ex) A Mackay 11/4 FAV: 341011: 5 b Beveled - Snowline   59
(Bay Express) Made all, rdn & styd on strongly fnl 2f, al holding rivals: op 5/2, qck reapp under a 6lb pen: earlier
won h'caps at Bath & Lingfield (fill h'caps) & most recently at Beverley (h'cap, by 20L): unplcd for E Wheeler in
'99 (rtd 40, mdn): eff forcing the pace at 10f on firm & hvy: handles a stiff or sharp/turning trk: tough/prog.

*4094   **NOUF** 2 [13] K Mahdi 4-9-10 (66)(6ex) Paul Eddery 9/1: 600512: 4 b f Efisio - Miss Witch (High Line)   3   70
Held up, prog to chase wnr fnl 1f, kept on, al held: qck reapp under a 6lb pen: styd longer 10f trip: see 4094 (1m).

3989   **NATALIE JAY** 9 [10] M R Channon 4-9-11 (67) T A O'Sullivan 14/1: 010633: 4 b f Ballacashtal -   2   68
Falls Of Lora (Scottish Rifle) Held up, styd on fnl 2f, no threat to wnr: op 12/1: see 3989, 3422 (Salisbury).

*3762   **FLYOVER** 23 [12] B R Millman 3-9-0 (62) B Marcus 11/1: 051614: Chsd wnr, held over 1f out: op 8/1:   ½   62
handles firm & gd/soft grnd: see 3762.

3424   **I TINA** 38 [17] 4-9-2 (58) R Perham 16/1: -60405: Prom, held fnl 2f: see 3563.   2   55

4061   **SANTIBURI GIRL** 4 [11] 3-9-9 (71) I Mongan (5) 12/1: 240666: Rear, hdwy 3f out, held 1f out: op 14/1.   5   61

3819   **HAVANA** 20 [5] 4-9-7 (63) W Ryan 20/1: 423307: Rear, styd on strongly fnl 2f, nrst fin: op 14/1: 4th   nk   52
blnks omitted after latest: see 3819, 2827 & 1343.

4026   **PSALMIST** 8 [19] 3-8-6 (54) W Supple 20/1: 300008: Held up, eff 4f out, held fnl 2f: see 1525.   6   35

3794   **TOTOM** 22 [7] 5-9-12 (68) D Harrison 20/1: 445409: Trkd ldrs, btn 2f out: see 2268, 1288.   5   35

3146   **REEMATNA** 50 [14] 3-9-0 (62) M Tebbutt 16/1: 424630: Chsd ldrs 7f: 10th: op 12/1, abs: see 1675.   1¼   35

3857   **SAFARI BLUES** 18 [4] 3-9-11 (73) P Dobbs (5) 20/1: 526630: Nvr on terms: 11th: see 2811, 54.   1¼   44

*3383   **IMPREVUE** 39 [3] 4-9-4 (60)(bl) S Sanders 6/1: 4-6310: Al rear: 15th: btr 3383 (fast grnd).   0

3474   **WOOLFE** 36 [9] 3-9-10 (72) R Havlin 6/1: 3320: Mid-div, btn 4f out: 17th: op 8/1, h'cap bow, lngr trip.   0

3725   **Divine Prospect** 25 [6] 3-9-8 (70) N Pollard 20/1:   3885   **Common Consent** 16 [2] 4-8-12 (54) A Nicholls 33/1:

3842   **Adamas** 19 [15] 3-9-9 (71) R Thomas (7) 20/1:   3939   **Mabrookah** 11 [18] 4-9-3 (59) S Sanders 33/1:

2270   **In A Twinkling** 87 [20] 3-8-13 (61) A McGlone 33/1:

18 ran   Time 2m 07.2 (9.4)   (Anthony Harrison)   P W Hiatt Hook Norton, Oxon.

4119   **3.35 PUNCH.CO.UK MDN 3YO (D)   1m3f196y   Good/Soft 81   +11 Fast**
£2857   £879   £439   £219   Raced stands side fnl 3f

3838   **CONWY CASTLE** 19 [4] J H M Gosden 3-9-0 R Havlin 8/11 FAV: 551: 3 b c Sri Pekan - Dumayla (Shernazar)   86
Made all, rdn fnl 2f, styd on strongly & al holding rivals: hvly bckd, op 3/1: apprec this step up to 12f with
forcing tactics, shld stay further: acts on sharp/undul trk: significant improvement today on easy grnd.

3869   **MACHRIE BAY** 17 [5] J L Dunlop 3-9-0 S Sanders 11/4: 3-3252: 3 b c Emarati - Fleeting Rainbow   5   79
(Rainbow Quest) Held up, prog to chall over 2f out, sn held: handles gd/soft & hvy grnd: see 1009.

1017   **MANIATIS** 153 [6] P F I Cole 3-9-0 D Sweeney 11/1: 03: 3 b c Slip Anchor - Tamassos (Dance In Time)   nk   78
Cl-up, held over 2f out, op 7/1, 5 month abs: clr of rem: 12f+ shld suit: see 1017.

1785   **NABADHAAT** 108 [8] E A L Dunlop 3-8-9 W Supple 12/1: 40-404: Prom, btn 2f out: op 4/1, 4 mth abs.   12   59

1539   **STRAWMAN** 120 [1] 3-9-0 Paul Eddery 12/1: 0065: Al bhd: op 10/1, 4 month abs: longer 12f trip.   7   56

3856   **DOM MIGUEL** 18 [7] 3-9-0 A Nicholls 33/1: 000006: Dwelt, al bhd: longer 12f trip.   23   31

3232   **SEEK THE LIGHT** 46 [3] 3-9-0 W Ryan 9/2: -647: Prom till halfway: op 5/2, abs: btr 1200 (mdn, fst).   25   4

7 ran   Time 2m 36.6 (8.4)   (John H M Gosden)   J H M Gosden Manton, Wilts.

4120   **4.10 ST MODWEN HCAP 3YO+ 0-75 (E)   6f   Good/Soft 81   -11 Slow**   **[74]**
£3032   £933   £466   £233   3 yo rec 2 lb   Raced stands side fnl 3f

3821   **BRAMBLE BEAR** 20 [18] M Blanshard 6-8-4 (50) D Sweeney 13/2: 332361: 6 b m Beveled - Supreme Rose   60
(Frimley Park) Chsd ldrs, rdn/led 1f out, styd on strongly, rdn out: earlier scored here at Brighton (C/D h'cap):
plcd form in '99 (rtd 62, h'cap): '98 Lingfield wnr (h'cap, rtd 73): eff at 5/6f on firm, well suited by soft grnd
nowadays, handles equitrack: likes a sharp/undul trk, especially Brighton: qk follow-up on similar grnd?

3759   **DOCTOR DENNIS** 24 [16] B J Meehan 3-9-7 (69) D R McCabe 8/1: 122442: 3 b g Last Tycoon - Noble   4   70
Lustre (Lyphard's Wish) Prom, ch 1f out, sn outpcd by wnr: op 8/1: likes soft: see 2603, 2549.

3698   **MI AMIGO** 27 [17] L M Cumani 3-9-7 (69) G Sparkes (7) 8/1: 243103: 3 b c Primo Dominie - Third   nk   69
Movement (Music Boy) Led 5f, held ins last: op 6/1: see 2640 (mdn).

3964   **ENCOUNTER** 10 [10] J Hetherton 4-8-6 (52) A Nicholls 20/1: 016054: Held up, styd on fnl 2f, not pace   hd   51
to chall: reapp gd/soft, loves fast grnd: see 3144.

4015   **BANDBOX** 8 [2] 5-9-7 (67) S Sanders 10/1: 361255: Prom, held over 1f out: see 3587.   1¼   64

4080   **CAPE COAST** 3 [9] 3-9-8 (70) I Mongan (5) 11/4 FAV: 421126: Chsd ldrs, hmpd 2f out, held after: op   hd   66
4/1: closer here without inteference: see 4080, 3854 (7f).

3908   **QUEEN OF THE MAY** 15 [7] 3-9-11 (73) W Supple 10/1: 540067: Chsd ldrs, hmpd halfway, held fnl 1f.   1¼   67

4080   **ALMASHROUK** 3 [12] 3-9-4 (66) T G McLaughlin 20/1: 406508: Mid-div at best: qck reapp: see 731.   1   58

4018 **TRAJAN 8** [5] 3-9-6 (68) D Harrison 16/1: 024409: Mid-div at best: op 12/1: see 3405, 651. *1½* **58**
3854 **WILLOW MAGIC 18** [14] 3-8-8 (56) B Marcus 25/1: 344500: Chsd ldrs, btn 1f out: 10th: see 1512. *3* **40**
2549 **PERLE DE SAGESSE 76** [8] 3-8-10 (58) A Daly 25/1: 021000: Mid-div at best: 11th: abs: btr 1877 (fast). *nk* **41**
3872 **ECUDAMAH 17** [13] 4-8-9 (55)(VIS) C Rutter 25/1: 330000: Chsd ldrs 4f: 12th: visor: btr 40 (AW). *2* **34**
4010 **RED TYPHOON 8** [6] 3-9-10 (72)(t) M Tebbutt 16/1: 002000: Hmpd after 1f & al rear: 13th: op 10/1. *nk* **50**
3919 **Executive Ghost 12** [11] 3-9-7 (69) K W Marks 25/1: 3796 **Uplifting 21** [15] 5-9-2 (62) A Clark 14/1:
3834 **Yazain 19** [4] 4-9-5 (65) S Whitworth 33/1:
16 ran Time 1m 13.2 (5.5) (Vino Veritas) M Blanshard Upper Lambourn, Berks.

4121

4.45 TOTE HCAP 3YO+ 0-85 (D) 7f rnd Good/Soft 81 -05 Slow **[81]**
£4543 £1398 £699 £349 3 yo rec 3 lb Raced stands side fnl 3f.

3796 **WHITE EMIR 21** [18] L G Cottrell 7-8-8 (61) A Clark 12/1: 321401: 7 b g Emarati - White African (Carwhite) Mid-div, not much room over 2f out till ins last, prog to lead ins last, styd on well, rdn out: earlier scored at Kempton (h'cap): plcd in '99 for B Millman (rtd 72, h'cap): eff at 5/6f, now suited by a sharp/easy 7f: acts on firm & hvy, with/without blnks: handles any trk: still on a fair mark, could win again. **66**
3407 **PADHAMS GREEN 38** [15] B W Hills 4-9-2 (69) Paul Eddery 8/1: 362152: 4 b g Aragon - Double Dutch (Nicholas Bill) Held up, prog/ch 1f out, styd on well, not pace of wnr: op 5/1: eff at 7f/1m on firm & gd/sft. *¾* **71**
3796 **COMPRADORE 21** [7] M Blanshard 5-8-12 (65) D Harrison 12/1: 300303: 5 b m Mujtahid - Keswa (King's Lake) Handy, led over 1f out till ins last, held cl-home: op 10/1: just ahead of this wnr in 3796. *1½* **65**
3992 **AMBER FORT 9** [17] J M Bradley 7-9-1 (68)(bl) N Pollard 6/1: 450044: Mid-div, rdn & styd on fnl 2f, not pace to chall: op 8/1: nicely h'capped & loves easy ground: could yet find a race this autumn: see 1011. *¾* **67**
3662 **ALMASI 28** [16] 8-9-7 (74) S Sanders 4/1 FAV: 340225: Rear, styd on fnl 2f, nrst at fin: op 8/1. *1½* **70**
3854 **HAIL THE CHIEF 18** [5] 3-9-2 (72) R Smith (5) 6/1: 601126: Prom 6f: op 8/1: see 3854, 3259 (fast). *1½* **65**
3765 **RAINBOW RAIN 23** [10] 6-8-8 (61) A Nicholls 16/1: 0002R7: Mid-div at best: op 14/1: see 28. *shd* **54**
4018 **MISTER RAMBO 8** [13] 5-9-7 (74)(bl) D R McCabe 12/1: 055068: Chsd ldrs 5f: btr 817. *½* **66**
3885 **MUTABASSIR 16** [6] 6-8-11 (64) I Mongan (5) 8/1: 025159: Led 3f out till over 1f out, fdd: op 6/1. *1¾* **53**
3281 **GULF SHAADI 44** [14] 8-8-12 (65) S W Kelly (3) 16/1: 405360: Towards rear, rdn/some hdwy when hmpd over 1f out, no ch after: 10th: 6 wk abs: closer with a clr run here: see 169. *½* **53**
3758 **CEDAR MASTER 24** [2] 3-9-10 (80)(vis) R Havlin 20/1: 603200: Led 4f: 11th: topweight: see 3580. *nk* **67**
1215 **SPORTY MO 138** [12] 3-9-6 (76)(vis) D Sweeney 9/1: 113100: Prom 5f: 12th: op 14/1, 5 month abs. *4* **56**
3809 **Kuwait Rose 21** [1] 4-9-3 (70) T G McLaughlin 20/1: 1969 **Akalim 100** [3] 7-8-10 (63) A Daly 20/1:
2629 **Shanghai Lady 73** [9] 4-8-12 (65)(t) P D'Arcy 33/1: 4036] **Grand Musica 725** [8] 7-8-2 (55)(bl) G Baker (5) 33/1:
16 ran Time 1m 25.8 (6.0) (Mrs D M Stafford) L G Cottrell Dulford, Devon.

4122

5.20 BE KIND SELLER 3YO+ (G) 1m rnd Good/Soft 81 -45 Slow
£2077 £593 £296 3 yo rec 4 lb Raced stands side fnl 3f

3775 **HEATHYARDS JAKE 22** [10] R Hollinshead 4-9-1 Paul Eddery 14/1: 404001: 4 b c Nomination - Safe Bid (Sure Blade) Chsd ldrs, rdn to chall over 1f out, kept on gamely for press ins last to lead line, all out: no bid: '99 W'hampton wnr (AW mdn, rtd 67a & 60 at best): eff btwn 7f/9f, poss stay 12f: acts on firm, soft & fibresand: handles any trk: eff in sell grade. **52**
*3775 **TOUJOURS RIVIERA 22** [9] J Pearce 10-9-7 T G McLaughlin 6/4 FAV: 001512: 10 ch g Rainbow Quest - Miss Beaulieu (Northfields) Prom, led over 2f out & sn strongly pressed, hdd line: bckd: see 3775. *shd* **57**
2680 **BALANITA 71** [2] B Palling 5-9-1 D Sweeney 6/1: 002543: 5 b g Anita's Prince - Ballybannon (Ballymore) Hld up, hdwy over 2f out, held by front pair ins last: clr rem, abs: stays 1m on fast & gd/soft. *1½* **48**
3868 **MODEL GROOM 17** [1] A G Newcombe 4-9-1 S Whitworth 10/1: 654: Mid-div, nvr able to chall. *7* **37**
2839 **WOOLLY WINSOME 64** [5] 4-9-1 S Sanders 16/1: 000605: Nvr on terms: op 12/1, abs: see 2690. *2* **33**
3775 **NAKED OAT 22** [13] 5-9-7 J Bosley (7) 9/1: 600066: Led 3f out till over 2f out, fdd: see 1933 (10f, fst). *1½* **36**
3939 **DANZAS 11** [4] 6-9-7 (bl) Claire Bryan (5) 10/1: 046657: Dwelt, al towards rear: btr 896. *1* **34**
3868 **HI MUJTAHID 17** [6] 6-9-1 M Savage (7) 25/1: 002008: Al towards rear: flattered 2907 (firm). *¾* **27**
3868 **MR CUBE 17** [8] 10-9-1 (bl) D Watson (7) 14/1: 400009: Chsd ldrs 6f: see 2291, 1336. *1½* **24**
3251 **PRIORY GARDENS 45** [7] 6-9-7 N Pollard 10/1: 610360: Slow away, al bhd: 10th: jmps fit (mod form). *1* **28**
3682 **PETRIE 27** [15] 3-8-11 C Rutter 12/1: 300060: Led 5f: 11th: see 3517, 2291 & 42. *nk* **21**
11 ran Time 1m 42.1 (10.1) (L A Morgan) R Hollinshead Upper Longdon, Staffs.

4123

5.50 LEVY BOARD HCAP 3YO 0-75 (E) 1m3f196y Good/Soft 81 +01 Fast **[82]**
£3009 £926 £463 £231 Raced stands side fnl 3f.

3941 **PERFECT MOMENT 11** [10] C A Dwyer 3-9-0 (68) A Beech (3) 6/1: 161001: 3 b f Mujadil - Flashing Raven (Maelstrom Lake) Handy, led 3f out, styd on strongly under hands & heels riding: gd time: op 10/1: earlier scored at Nottingham (sell h'cap), Pontefract (seller, G McCourt, cost current connections 13,000gns), W'hampton (h'cap, rtd 60a) & here at Brighton (fill h'cap): '99 Leicester wnr (auct mdn, A Jarvis, rtd 74): eff at 1m/10f, now stays sharp 12f well: acts on fast, soft & fibresand: handles any trk, likes Brighton: tough filly. **75**
*3560 **WELSH DREAM 32** [13] A C Stewart 3-9-1 (69) S Whitworth 11/4: 00-112: 3 b c Mtoto - Morgannwg (Simply Great) Held up, prog/chsd wnr 2f out, al held: clr rem: op 2/1: acts on firm & gd/soft: see 3560. *5* **69**
3963 **STRICTLY SPEAKING 10** [7] P F I Cole 3-8-6 (60) S W Kelly (3) 11/8 FAV: 660123: 3 b c Sri Pekan - Gaijin (Caerleon) Chsd ldrs, held over 2f out: op 2/1: btr 3494 (AW mdn h'cap). *9* **50**
4003 **AFTER THE BLUE 8** [9] M R Channon 3-9-5 (73) R Havlin 10/1: 122004: Chsd ldrs, held fnl 3f. *2* **60**
3819 **CONSTANT 20** [6] 3-8-5 (59) Paul Eddery 16/1: 050005: Al towards rear: op 14/1: see 979. *nk* **45**
3517 **KISTY 35** [11] 3-9-0 (68) C Rutter 10/1: 033366: Led after 3f till 3f out, sn btn: see 2445, 1919 & 1094. *5* **48**
3762 **BOX CAR 23** [2] 3-8-2 (56) I Mongan (0) 16/1: 006007: Held up, eff 4f out, sn btn: op 12/1: see 1199. *hd* **35**
3869 **AMNERIS 17** [4] 3-9-0 (68)(bl) W Ryan 10/1: -2348: Led 3f, sn btn: h'cap bow: btr 2710, 2258 (fm). *21* **23**
8 ran Time 2m 37.8 (9.6) (Casino Racing Partnership) C A Dwyer Newmarket.

Official Going: SOFT Stalls: Straight Course - Stands side: Round Course - Inside.

4124

2.00 EUROPEAN TRAINERS COND STKS 2YO (B)   **7f str**   **Good/Soft 80** **-26 Slow**
£12035 £4565 £2282 £1037

-- **LUNAR CRYSTAL** [6] D R C Elsworth 2-8-11 M J Kinane 14/1: 1: 2 b c Shirley Heights - Solar Crystal   **93**
(Alzao) Rear, rdn/hdwy over 2f out, ran on strongly to lead well inside last, rdn out: op 8/1: 80,000gns Jan
first foal, dam Gr wnr at 1m, sire won the Derby: eff at 7f, 1m will suit: runs well fresh on soft grnd & a
stiff/gall track: impress debut, can rate more highly & win again, esp when stepped up to a mile.
-- **KING CAREW** [3] M R Channon 2-8-11 Craig Williams 4/1: 2: 2 b c Fairy King - Kareena   nk **92**
(Riverman) Cl up, led over 1f out, hdd well ins last, just held cl home: IR165,000gns Feb foal, half-brother
to a smart 10f wnr, dam scored over 1m: eff over a stiff/gall 7f on soft: fine debut & can go one better late.
-- **ASKHAM** [4] L M Cumani 2-8-11 J P Spencer 4/1: 3: 2 b c El Gran Senor - Konvincha (Comorant)   1½ **89+**
Prom, rdn/feeling pace over 2f out, styd on for press ins last, no threat to first 2: Jan foal, dam 1m wnr in
the States, sire top class juv: stys 7f on soft, 1m will suit on this evidence: sure to improve & win races.
3786 **COME ON PEKAN** 22 [2] M A Jarvis 2-8-11 R Hughes 11/4 FAV: 24: Led, rdn/hdd over 1f out,   nk **89**
no extra inside last: imprvd on debut run, handles gd/soft & soft: must win a mdn, see 3786.
-- **LANESBOROUGH** [9] 2-8-11 L Dettori 7/1: 5: Veered right start, rear, hdwy halfway, ev ch till   1¼ **87**
fdd fnl 1f: March foal, half-brother to a Gr wnr in the States, dam 1m wnr: stiff/gall track, pleasing debut.
3999 **CHALOM** 8 [7] 2-8-11 K Darley 33/1: -06: In tch, rdn/held appr fnl 1f: 29,000gns April foal,   4 **81**
half brother to a dual 7f 2yo scorer: dam 10/12f Irish wnr: with B J Meehan.
-- **STATEROOM** [5] 2-8-11 S Whitworth 9/2: 7: Handy, wknd fnl 2f: op 3/1: Mar 1st foal, dam US juv wnr.   2 **78**
-- **SAKAMOTO** [1] 2-8-11 T Quinn 25/1: 8: Dwelt, al last: dam 1m wnr: with C Dwyer.   15 **58**
8 ran   Time 1m 33.44 (7.44)   (Michael Poland)   D R C Elsworth Whitsbury, Hants

---

4125

2.35 GR 2 DIADEM STKS 3YO+ (A)   **6f**   **Good/Soft 80** **+10 Fast**
£60000 £23000 £11500 £5500 3 yo rec 2 lb

3784 **SAMPOWER STAR** 22 [4] Saeed bin Suroor 4-9-0 L Dettori 7/4 FAV: 015221: 4 b h Cyrano de Bergerac -   **116**
Green Supreme (Primo Dominie) Held up, rdn/no room 2f out, swtchd appr dist, squeezed thro' to lead well ins last,
pushed out, readily: fast time: earlier won at Longchamp (Gr 3): with R Hannon & very prog in '99, winning at
Windsor (stks), Ascot (List) & York (Gr 3, also Gr1 plcd, rtd 116): '98 wnr at Folkestone (mdn auction) & Salisbury
(novs, rtd 94, R Simpson): suited by 5/6f now, stys 7f/1m: handles firm, suited by gd & loves gd/soft & hvy grnd:
handles any trk, likes Ascot: v smart mud loving sprinter, expect a bold show in the Prix de L'Abbaye next week.
4012 **TAYSEER** 8 [2] D Nicholls 6-9-0 G Mosse 11/1: 131002: 6 ch g Sheikh Albadou - Millfit (Blushing   ½ **113**
Groom) Rear, switched/hdwy appr fnl 1f, ev ch inside last, held by wnr cl home: excellent run on this big step
up in grade, looks certain to win a Listed race at least on this form: see 3152.
3303 **TRINCULO** 43 [8] N P Littmoden 3-8-12 K Darley 50/1: 040003: 3 b c Anita's Prince - Fandangerina   hd **113**
(Grey Dawn II) Led, rdn/hdd ins last, held nr fin: 6 wk abs: excellent run up in grade, blinks omitted: see 2335.
3923 **TEDBURROW** 15 [12] E J Alston 9-9-0 T E Durcan 12/1: 013024: Prom, chal ldrs over 1f out,   shd **113**
led briefly inside last, held fnl 50y: op 10/1: another sound run: v tough, see 3923.
*3995 **WARNINGFORD** 8 [11] 6-9-0 O Urbina 8/1: 426315: In tch, chall ldrs dist, rdn/no extra well   ½ **112**
inside last: op 6/1: excellent run on grnd which has come in his favour: all wins at 7f, win another List race.
3784 **HARMONIC WAY** 22 [1] 5-9-0 R Hughes 12/1: 162046: Patiently rdn in last, drvn & swtchd round whole   shd **112**
field 1f out, ran on, closing at fin: not disgraced but waiting tactics over-done again: see 3784, 2151.
3784 **MONKSTON POINT** 8 [3] 4-9-0 (vis) T Quinn 20/1: 013007: Prom, drvn/fdd fnl 1f: prob ran to best,   2 **107**
needs a drop bck to listed/Gr3 company: see 1529.
3784 **TOMBA** 22 [5] 6-9-0 P Robinson 13/2: 035038: Rear, nvr dngrs: disapp on fvd easy grnd: btr 3784.   2 **102**
3784 **LINCOLN DANCER** 22 [6] 3-8-12 M Roberts 9/2: 401209: Handy, drvn & wknd quickly inside last: 2 **97**
reportedly likes easy grnd but has yet to win on grnd slower than gd/soft: see 3784, 2615.
3995 **KALINDI** 8 [9] 3-8-9 Craig Williams 40/1: 060100: Outpcd, 10th: stiff task: see 3878 (List, 7f, fast).   1¼ **91**
3784 **CRETAN GIFT** 22 [10] 9-9-0 (vis) J Murtagh 25/1: 445500: Prom to halfway, sn btn, 11th.   nk **94**
11 ran   Time 1m 17.29 (4.19)   (Godolphin)   Saeed bin Suroor Newmarket, Suffolk

---

4126

3.10 MAIL ON SUNDAY FINAL HCAP 3YO+ (B)   **1m str**   **Good/Soft 80** **-13 Slow**   **[102]**
£29000 £11000 £5500 £2500 3 yo rec 4 lb

3170 **TORNADO PRINCE** 49 [6] E J Alston 5-7-10 (70) P M Quinn (3) 16/1: 144201: 5 ch g Caerleon - Welsh   **84**
Flame (Welsh Pageant) Mid div, smooth hdwy to lead over 2f out, rdn & pulled well clr fnl 1f: earlier won at
Thirsk (h'cap): '99 won at Ripon, Thirsk & Pontefract (sells & sell h'cap, rtd 67): suited by 7f/1m, stys 9.5f:
prev best on firm & gd grnd, relished gd/soft today: handles any trk & runs well fresh: remarkable performance
on grnd prev thought to be unsuitable, quick follow up likely.
3685 **SALTY JACK** 27 [7] V Soane 6-8-10 (84) J P Spencer 14/1: 451302: 6 b h Salt Dome - Play The Queen   9 **85**
(King Of Clubs) Hdwy from rear after halfway, drvn & chsd wnr in vain fnl 1f: tough, ran to best: see 3018.
*3338 **KIROVSKI** 42 [15] P W Harris 3-8-12 (90) T Quinn 7/1: -21113: 3 b g Common Grounds - Nordic   1¾ **88**
Doll (Royal Academy) Handy, eff & checked over 2f out, hung left & styd on well inside last, wnr had flown:
nicely bckd & not disgraced after a 6 week abs: acts on fast & gd/soft: v tough & consistent: see 3338.
3699 **HONEST BORDERER** 27 [23] J L Dunlop 5-8-6 (80) G Carter 16/1: -61434: Prom, drvn/no extra   hd **78**
fnl 2f: 6L clr rem & not disgraced: see 2768.
4069 **NOMORE MR NICEGUY** 4 [11] 6-7-13 (73) J Lowe 33/1: 646035: Rear, mod late gains: qck reapp.   6 **62**
3998 **BOLD EWAR** 8 [22] 3-8-0 (78)(bl) A Beech (3) 33/1: 015006: Mid div, late hdwy: likes firm/fast.   1¼ **65**
3941 **PRINCE SLAYER** 11 [13] 4-8-4 (78) K Darley 20/1: 010007: Late hdwy, nvr dngrs: btr 1829.   hd **65**
3883 **ADOBE** 16 [16] 5-8-7 (81) G Baker (5) 25/1: 110508: Handy, eff over 2f out, fdd fnl 1f: op 20/1:   ½ **67**
progressive prev this term but seems to have gone off the boil: prefers fast grnd: see 3325.
3338 **SILK ST JOHN** 42 [12] 6-9-2 (90) P Robinson 12/1: 164009: Rear, late gains: 6 wk abs: likes Haydock.   1½ **74**
3981 **COMPTON ARROW** 9 [8] 4-8-1 (75)(t) Craig Williams 11/1: 000000: Led, hdd over 2f out, fdd, 10th.   ½ **58**
3338 **DOLPHINELLE** 42 [2] 4-7-10 (70) D J Bramhill 50/1: 316000: Nvr a factor, 11th: 6 wk abs.   nk **52**
3634 **INTRICATE WEB** 29 [21] 4-7-10 (70)(VIS) N Carlisle 33/1: 305300: Prom, wknd fnl 2f, 12th: visored.   ¾ **51**
4013 **STYLE DANCER** 8 [10] 6-7-13 (73)(vis) Martin Dwyer 14/1: 031020: Late gains from rear, fin 13th.   ½ **53**
3699 **ZULU DAWN** 27 [19] 4-7-11 (71) M Henry 20/1: 300500: Mid div at best, 14th: btr 3699.   shd **51**
*3897 **MAYARO BAY** 15 [17] 4-10-0 (102) R Hughes 16/1: 302310: Al towards rear, 15th: top weight: shd **82**
capable of better & prob just prefers a sounder surface: much btr 3897 (firm).

ASCOT   SUNDAY SEPTEMBER 24TH   Righthand, Stiff, Galloping Track

3998 **FREDDY FLINTSTONE 8** [1] 3-8-5 (83) L Newman (3) 9/1: 023430: Al bhd, 17th: btr 3998 (firm). **0**
*2707 **JUST NICK 70** [3] 6-7-13 (73) P Doe 11/2 FAV: 652110: Cl up, rdn & wknd qckly fnl 2f, 20th: **0**
poss just sharper for this after 10 week abs, may apprec faster grnd: much btr 2707.
4112 Peartree House 1 [14] 6-9-8 (96) M J Kinane 20/1: +3634 Derryquin 29 [24] 5-7-13 (73)(bl) G Bardwell 16/1:
3998 Kathir 8 [9] 3-8-9 (87) R Hills 14/1: 3398 Violet 39 [5] 4-7-10 (70)(22oh) C Adamson 66/1:
4033 Out Of Sight 6 [4] 6-7-10 (70)(10oh) D Glennon (7) 50/1:
4064 Elmhurst Boy 4 [18] 4-8-10 (84) Pat Eddery 20/1:
3944 Omniheat 11 [20] 3-7-10 (74)(bl) (1oh) J Mackay (5) 33/1:
24 ran   Time 1m 46.11 (7.41)   (Mrs J R Ramsden)   E J Alston Longton, Lancs

4127   3.50 GR 2 ROYAL LODGE STKS 2YO (A)   1m rnd   Good/Soft 80 -43 Slow
£72000 £22600 £13800 £6600

*3882 **ATLANTIS PRINCE 16** [1] S P C Woods 2-8-11 L Dettori 11/2: 1111: 2 ch c Tagula - Zoom Lens **112**
(Caerleon) Made all, styd on well for press fnl 1f, drvn out, gamely: unbtn, 4 timer completed after scoring at
Epsom (auction mdn) Newmarket (stks), Goodwood (List): eff at 7f/1m, mid-dists suit next term: acts on fast,
gd/soft & a stiff/gall or sharp/undul trk: runs well fresh: smart & progressive colt, can win more Gr races.
*3304 **TURNBERRY ISLE 43** [8] A P O'Brien 2-8-11 M J Kinane 11/4 FAV: -112: 2 ch c Deputy Minister - ½ **110**
Blush With Pride (Blushing Groom) Chsd ldrs, eff/no room over 2f out, ran on for press ins last, held nr fin:
nicely bckd after 6 week abs: acts on fast & gd/soft grnd: smart Irish raider, win a Gr race sn, see 3304.
*3799 **HILL COUNTRY 21** [4] J H M Gosden 2-8-11 J P Spencer 9/1: 013: 2 b c Danehill - Rose Of Jericho 1¼ **107**
(Alleged) Prom, drpd rear after halfway, rdn/ran on fnl 1f, no threat to 2: op 6/1: acts on fast
& gd/soft: excellent run upped in grade, mid dists will suit next term: win in Gr/Listed company: see 4127.
*3450 **PRIZEMAN 37** [7] R Hannon 2-8-11 R Hughes 6/1: -114: Waited with, eff when no room over 2 out, 1¼ **103**
short of room again when hdwy fnl 1f, no threat: stays 1m on firm & gd/soft: shade unlucky, worth another ch.
*3086 **NO EXCUSE NEEDED 53** [2] J Murtagh 2-9-0 J Murtagh 4/1: -115: Prom, drvn/fdd over 1f out: 8 week abs ½ **105**
& better expected on this step up to 1m, but poss needs faster grnd as in 3086.
3867 **WHEN IN ROME 17** [6] A G Mosse 2-8-11 A G Mosse 33/1: 636: Bhd, outpcd 4f out, late hdwy: stiff task: see 3867. ¾ **101**
3983 **RUSSIAN WHISPERS 9** [5] 2-8-11 Pat Eddery 20/1: -357: Al bhd: stiff task: see 3983. 7 **91§**
3704 **EMMS 27** [3] 2-8-11 K Darley 5/1: -23128: Cl up, rdn & wknd quickly fnl 2f: disappointing run, 9 **79**
something amiss?: much better on similar grnd in 3704 (h'cap).
8 ran   Time 1m 48.32 (9.82)   (Lucayan Stud)   S P C Woods Newmarket, Suffolk

4128   4.25 CORAL EUROBET HCAP 3YO+ (B)   1m4f   Good/Soft 80 -15 Slow   [112]
£45500 £14000 £7000 £3500   3 yo rec 8 lb

3903 **KIND REGARDS 15** [9] M Johnston 3-8-5 (96)(4ex) Craig Williams 15/2: 511151: 3 b f Unfuwain - **107**
Barari (Blushing Groom) Made all, increased pace & pulled well clr fnl 2f, rdn out, comfortably: v prog
this term, earlier won at Beverley, Hamilton (h'caps) & Newcastle (listed rtd h'caps): '99 Beverley wnr
(fillies mdn, rtd 88): eff at 1m, now suited by 10/12f: acts on firm, gd/soft & any trk: apprec forcing
tactics here, wng form prev with waiting tactics: v useful & progressive, win in Listed/Gr 3 on this form.
*3890 **ROMANTIC AFFAIR 16** [3] J L Dunlop 3-8-10 (102)(4ex) Pat Eddery 9/2: 114212: 3 ch g Persian Bold - 8 **104**
Broken Romance (Ela Mana Mou) Prom, hdwy over 3f out, kept on but no ch with easy wnr: op 7/2: ran to nr
best against a v progressive rival, may apprec a return to 14f: see 3890.
4014 **FLOSSY 8** [2] C W Thornton 4-8-4 (88) T Quinn 8/1: 410233: 4 b f Efisio - Sirene Bleu Marine 2 **87**
(Secreto) Rcd keenly in rear, eff when short of room over 2f out, swtchd/ran on well fnl 1f, no danger:
v tough filly, a repeat bid at the November h'cap is on the cards: see 4014, 3173.
3896 **RICH VEIN 15** [6] S P C Woods 3-7-10 (88)(vis)(4oh) J Mackay (5) 25/1: 214004: Bhd, switched/ hd **87**
hdwy over 3f out, styd on, no danger: unproven at 12f: see 3541.
4014 **RAISE A PRINCE 8** [8] 7-8-3 (87)(t) N Callan (5) ⁻: 660025: Late hdwy from rear, no threat to ldr. 1¼ **84**
3657 **LIVIUS 28** [14] 6-8-5 (88)(1ow) M Hills 14/1: 1-3416: Mid div, eff 3f out, wknd fnl 2f: btr 3657. nk **86**
*3778 **SUMMER SONG 22** [11] 3-7-13 (90)(10w)(4ex) G Carter 12/1: 131117: Handy, rdn/fdd fnl 2f: 6 **79**
dissapointing eff on this 4 timer gdly: progressive prev: btr 3778.
*3479 **MONSAJEM 36** [7] 5-9-10 (108) J Reid 20/1: 043518: Mid div, eff over 3f out, sn lost tch: top-weight. 1¼ **94**
-3896 **MOWELGA 15** [12] 6-9-1 (99) K Darley 8/1: 0/1029: Bhd, nvr dangerous: nicely bckd: btr 3896, 968. 6 **77**
*3798 **ULUNDI 21** [1] 5-8-12 (96)(4ex) R Hughes 12/1: 025210: Prom, wknd qckly fnl 3f, 10th: btr 3798 (fast). 5 **66**
*3541 **SEEK 33** [10] 4-8-8 (92) J P Spencer 11/4 FAV: 1-2510: Rear, wknd rapidly fnl 2f, t.o. in 11th: dist **0**
hvly bckd & something surely amiss here: much btr 3541 (gd grnd).
11 ran   Time 2m 40.46 (11.46)   (Maktoum Al Maktoum)   M Johnston Middleham, N Yorks

4129   5.00 SINGAPORE RATED HCAP 3YO+ 0-105 (B)   5f   Good/Soft 80 -01 Slow   [112]
£15648 £5935 £2967 £1349   3 yo rec 1 lb

3861 **ELLENS LAD 18** [17] W J Musson 6-9-5 (103) Pat Eddery 12/1: 110501: 6 b g Polish Patriot - Lady **110**
Ellen (Horage) Rear, prog 2f out, rdn into lead inside last, drvn out: earlier won at York (h'caps),
Doncaster (rtd h'cap) & here at Ascot (h'cap): '99 Newbury, Haydock & Newmarket wnr (h'caps, rtd 95),
prev term won again at Newmarket (h'cap, rtd 86 E J Alston): stys 6f, suited by stiff/gall 5f: acts on firm,
soft & any track, likes Newmarket/Ascot: best without blnks, v eff weight carrier: v tough & useful sprinter.
*4015 **DANCING MYSTERY 7** [7] E A Wheeler 6-8-10 (94) S Carson (3) 12/1: 140112: 6 b g Beveled - 1 **98**
Batchworth Dancer (Ballacashtal) Cl-up, led briefly inside last, sn hdd, held cl home: not disgraced in this
hat-trick bid: v tough & prog this term, shld win again: see 4015.
4012 **FURTHER OUTLOOK 8** [14] D Nicholls 6-8-12 (96) G Carter 14/1: 403003: 6 gr g Zilzal - Future nk **100**
Bright (Lyphard's Wish) Cl up, went on appr fnl 1f, hdd inside last, no extra fnl 50yds: ran to best: see 1182.
3861 **SHEER VIKING 18** [12] B W Hills 4-8-11 (95) M Hills 10/1: 000504: Hdwy from rear 2f out, ½ **98**
chall over 1f out, no extra well inside last: gd eff, see 1182, 702.
4012 **GUINEA HUNTER 8** [13] 4-9-2 (100)(bl) M Roberts 10/1: 005035: Chsd ldrs, hdwy to chall over 1f nk **102**
out, sn no extra: op 8/1, cl under best: may apprec a return to 6f: see 4012, 2859.
4012 **LAGO DI VARANO 8** [18] 8-8-6 (90)(bl) (2oh) J Murtagh 14/1: 120026: Cl up, slightly outpcd over 2 **87**
2f out, late hdwy, no threat: poss best at 6f now: stil prog: see 4012.
4012 **BON AMI 8** [10] 4-8-6 (90)(1oh) P Bradley (5) 20/1: 024007: Sn rdn, late hdwy, no threat: see 1004. hd **87**
3841 **FIRST MAITE 19** [19] 7-8-6 (90)(bl) T Quinn 12/1: 340008: Sn outpcd, rdn/late hdwy no danger: nk **86**
likes soft/hvy grnd & is on a winning mark, could win a race this autumn: see 35.
+ 202 **CAXTON LAD 282** [1] 3-8-6 (90)(5oh) J Mackay (5) 20/1: 0161-9: Led, drvn & hung badly right over ½ **86**
1271

1f out, sn hdd & fdd: not disgraced after a 9 month abs, sharper for this & likes easy grnd: see 202.

4037	**BLUE VELVET** 6 [4] 3-8-7 (92) C Carver (3) 8/1: 506230: Mid div at best, 10th: nicely bckd, qck reapp.		hd	87
3874	**SEE YOU LATER** 17 [11] 3-8-11 (96) K Darley 9/1: 300120: Prom, rdn/fdd fnl 2f, 11th: btr 3874 (fast).		2½	85
3982	**REPERTORY** 9 [2] 7-9-7 (105) Darren Williams (5) 20/1: 500100: Prom, fdd fnl 2f, 12th:		shd	94

op 14/1: speedy, best dominating over a sharp 5f: see 3687.

4012	**JUWWI** 8 [1] 6-8-6 (90)(2oh) L Newman (3) 20/1: 000000: Al bhd, fin 13th: drop in trip.			79
3982	**KATHOLOGY** 9 [16] 3-8-9 (94) M J Kinane 12/1: 400200: Rear, hdwy halfway, wknd fnl 1f, 14th: see 3569.		¾	82
4015	**SAPHIRE** 8 [3] 4-8-6 (90)(3oh) J Reid 12/1: 024060: In tch, wknd over 2f out, 16th: btr 3322.			0
3473	**SARTORIAL** 36 [5] 4-9-2 (100)(VIS) R Hughes 6/1 FAV: 141000: Prom, wknd quickly fnl 2f,			0

17th: nicely bckd & a disappointing run in first time visor: much btr 1173 (6f, fast).

2042} **Hammer And Sickle** 465 [15] 3-8-10 (95) R Hills 25/1: 3503 **Damalis** 14 [8] 4-9-0 (98) T E Durcan 25/1:
-3841 **Presentation** 19 [9] 3-8-9 (94) P Fitzsimons (5) 14/1:
19 ran   Time 1m 03.05 (4.05)   (Mrs Rita Brown)   W J Musson Newmarket, Suffolk

---

4130   **5.35 LISTED HARVEST STKS 3YO+ (A)   1m4f   Good/Soft 80   +01 Fast**
£23400   £7200   £3600   £1800   3 yo rec 8 lb

3798	**RIYAFA** 21 [4] Sir Michael Stoute 3-8-6 J Murtagh 12/1: 215321: 3 b f Kahyasi - Riyama (Doyoun)		104

Bhd, gd hdwy to lead over 1f out, styd on well, pshd out: gd time: recently btn in a h'cap off 90: earlier won at Haydock (fill mdn): eff at 12f, could suit: acts on gd, soft & a stiff or gall track: fast improving filly, won with something in hand here, can follow up.

*3838	**JALISCO** 19 [11] J H M Gosden 3-8-6 Craig Williams 14/1: 12: 3 b f Machiavellian - Las Flores	3	98

(Sadler's Wells) Bhd, rdn/prog over 3f out, sn chasing wnr, no extra inside last: up in trip: eff at 10/12f on firm & gd/soft: lightly rcd & improving filly, win again nr: see 3838.

3564	**RAMRUMA** 32 [7] H R A Cecil 4-9-0 T Quinn 4/5 FAV: 12-033: 4 ch f Diesis - Princess Of Man	1½	96

(Green God) Cl-up, onepcd appr fnl 1f: hvly bckd: again below best & will now reportedly be retired.

3863	**FILM SCRIPT** 18 [6] R Charlton 3-8-9 (VIS) R Hughes 14/1: 361354: Led, drvn/hdd over 1f out,	1	97

wknd: shade better expected in first time visor: see 3863, 2975.

2975	**DRAMA** 58 [5] 3-8-6 M J Kinane 9/1: 2135: Rear, hdwy when hit in face with rivals whip	shd	94

2f out, no extra appr fnl 1f: clr rem: not disgraced up to 12f after an 8 week abs: see 2975.

1282	**BEDARA** 109 [12] 3-8-6 R Hills 33/1: 2-1456: Rear, late gains, no dngr: 4 mth abs: btr 814 (10f mdn).	10	82
3595	**METRONOME** 31 [9] 3-8-6 J P Spencer 16/1: 022157: Bhd, eff halfway, sn btn: btr 3595 (firm).	6	74
3863	**CLIPPER** 18 [3] 3-8-6 M Hills 33/1: 300008: Prom, wknd quickly fnl 3f: out of form: see 1184.	10	62
3918	**SILKEN WHISPER** 12 [8] 3-8-6 M Roberts 33/1: -109: Rcd keenly in tch, drpd rear 4f out, brief	3	58

eff 3f out, sn lost tch: first try at 12f & softer grnd: much btr 3918, 3232.

3863	**SKI RUN** 18 [1] 4-9-0 L Dettori 7/2: -01330: Al well bhd, 10th: nicely bckd & reportedly felt 'flat':	3	54

capable of much better & will apprec a return to further, as in 3863 (Gr3, 14f).

3863	**CEPHALONIA** 18 [10] 3-8-9 Pat Eddery 16/1: 116100: Prom, wknd 4f out, btn/hmpd 3f out, 11th: btr 2594.	6	51

11 ran   Time 2m 38.42 (9.42)   (H H Aga Khan)   Sir Michael Stoute Newmarket, Suffolk

---

Official Going   GOOD TO SOFT (SOFT PLACES) Stalls: 5f/2m - Stands Side; Rem - Inside.

4131   **2.10 CRAIGLEITH MDN 2YO (D)   5f   Good/Soft 66   -08 Slow**
£3672   £1130   £565   £282

3888	**YNYSMON** 16 [4] A Berry 2-9-0 C Lowther 13/2: -50401: 2 b c Mind Games - Florentynna Bay (Aragon)		79

Hmpd start, hmpd again over 3f out, gd hdwy from rear to lead well ins last, drvn out: Jan foal, cost 10,000 gns: half brother to multiple sprint h'cap wnr Albert The Bear: eff around 5f, has tried 6f: acts on firm, gd/soft & a stiff/undul or sharp trk: imprvg, speedy colt, overcame trouble in running today.

2990	**MICKLOW MAGIC** 57 [10] C Grant 2-8-9 L Newton 10/1: 22: 2 b f Farfelu - Scotto's Regret (Celtic	½	73

Cone) Cl-up, chall over 1f out, onepcd fnl 50y: clr rem, abs: acts on fast & gd/soft: going the right way.

3714	**TALISKER BAY** 26 [9] C Smith 2-9-0 R Fitzpatrick 9/1: 0553: 2 b c Clantime - Fabulous Rina	2	73

(Fabulous Dancer) Led, hung right/hdd fnl 1f: sn btn: 1st try on easier grnd: stays 5f on gd/soft: see 2318.

3958	**SECOND VENTURE** 10 [11] J R Weymes 2-9-0 M Fenton 7/1: 0324: Sn outpcd, rdn & styd on well	1¼	70

fnl 1f, no danger: will apprec a return to 6f+: see 3958.

3955	**LOVE** 11 [15] 2-9-0 K Dalgleish (5) 7/2 JT FAV: 505: Trkd ldrs, drvn/onepcd over 1f out: see 1628.	shd	70
3500	**LADY ROCK** 35 [14] 2-8-9 O Pears 7/1: 004636: Handy, drvn/btn fnl 1f: softer grnd: btr 3500 (firm).	½	64
3710	**DISPOL CHIEFTAN** 26 [1] 2-9-0 (t) A Culhane 7/1: 055037: Sn rdn in mid-div, late hdwy: btr 3710 (fast).	½	68
3974	**LIBERTY BOUND** 9 [13] 2-8-9 R Winston 14/1: 48: Veered left start, sn chasing ldrs, btn appr fnl 1f.	¾	61
--	**NIGHT OF NIGHTS** [2] 2-8-9 T Williams 33/1: 9: Sn outpcd, mod late gains: late foal, sister	½	60

to a useful sprinter, dam scored over 12f: with M Dods.

3714	**ANTHONY ROYLE** 26 [8] 2-9-0 Mark Flynn (7) 25/1: 665500: Al bhd, fin 10th: see 2664.	¾	63
--	**TATANTE** [5] 2-8-9 G Duffield 7/2 JT FAV: 0: Hmpd start, chsd ldrs, fdd fnl 2f, 11th: 60,000gns	1¼	55

Mar foal, dam smart 6/7f 2yo: with Sir M Prescott, surely capable of better in time, poss on faster grnd.

4001 **Catalan Bay** 8 [7] 2-8-9 J McAuley 100/1:   -- **Orangino** [12] 2-9-0 F Lynch 66/1:
-- **Minus Four** [3] 2-9-0 V Halliday 50/1:
14 ran   Time 1m 01.2 (3.7)   (Chris & Antonia Deuters)   A Berry Cockerham, Lancs

---

4132   **2.45 FIDRA NURSERY HCAP 2YO 0-80 (D)   1m rnd   Good/Soft 66   +12 Fast**   [86]
£5232   £1610   £805   £402

3968	**KINGS CREST** 10 [11] S C Williams 2-7-10 (54)(5oh) Joanna Badger (7) 10/1: 06641: 2 b g Deploy -		63

Classic Beauty (Fairy King) Cl-up, went on appr fnl 2f, ran on strongly, rdn out: tchd 8/1, fast time, 1st win: 17,000gns Feb 1st foal, dam an 11f wnr, sire won over 12f: apprec recent step up to 1m, further will suit next term: acts on gd/soft grnd & a sharp trk: won in a fast time here, can make a quick follow up.

3879	**LADY BEAR** 17 [9] R A Fahey 2-9-0 (72) P Hanagan (5) 6/1: 344102: 2 b f Grand Lodge - Boristova	2	78

(Royal Academy) In tch, hdwy to chall 2f out, styd on, no threat to wnr: pulled 8L clr rem: eff at 7f/1m on fast & gd/soft: front 2 well and of the rest, can win similar: see 3592.

3950	**CIRCUIT LIFE** 11 [12] A Berry 2-7-10 (54)(1oh) P Fessey 14/1: 662343: 2 ch g Rainbows For Life -	8	48

MUSSELBURGH SUNDAY SEPTEMBER 24TH Righthand, Sharp Track

Alicedale (Trempolino) Front rank, drvn/no extra over 1f out: up in trip: softer grnd: see 3950.

3990 **SIENA STAR** 9 [3] J L Eyre 2-9-6 (78) R Cody Boutcher (7) 10/1: 322104: In tch, late gains, no threat to ldrs: twice below 3609 (faster grnd). — 1¼ 70

3901 **SEBULBA** 15 [2] 2-9-0 (72) M Fenton 16/1: 21605: Led early, remained with ldrs, led again briefly 2f out, sn btn: disapp on turf, much btr 2635 (AW, 6f). — hd 64

*4022 **SEDUCTIVE** 8 [6] 2-9-7 (79) G Duffield 5/1 FAV: 023516: Pulled hard, prom, rdn/btn fnl 2f: nicely bckd under top weight: better expected, see 4022 (fibresand). — 1¼ 69

*4007 **APORTO** 8 [1] 2-7-12 (56) J McAuley 9/1: 030417: Handy, wknd appr fnl 1f: up in trip, btr 4007 (7f). — 4 40

3814 **PHARAOH HATSHEPSUT** 21 [13] 2-7-13 (57) K Dalgleish (5) 12/1: 000458: Nvr a factor: up in trip. — 2½ 37

3910 **FOUR LEGS GOOD** 13 [5] 2-8-6 (64) A Culhane 11/2: 0009: AI towards rear: h'cap bow: see 3910. — 3½ 39

4070 **GAZETTE IT TONIGHT** 4 [7] 2-8-3 (61) J Carroll 7/1: 133140: Mid-div, fdd fnl 3f, 10th: quick reapp. — 1 34

3987 **ORIENTAL MIST** 9 [14] 2-9-1 (73) C Lowther 20/1: 304460: AI bhd, fin 11th. — 1¼ 44

3609 **INVESTMENT FORCE** 30 [10] 2-9-0 (72) R Winston 9/1: 005200: Sn led, hdd 2f out, wknd qckly, 12th. — 9 30

3532 **QUIET TRAVELLER** 33 [8] 2-7-10 (54) (3oh) D Mernagh (1) 25/1: 0000: Sn struggling, 13th: h'cap bow. — 3 8

13 ran   Time 1m 41.8 (4.3)   (Ivyclose)   S C Williams Newmarket, Suffolk

---

4133 3.15 EYEBROUGHY MDN 3YO+ (D)   1m4f   Good/Soft 66   -16 Slow
£3068   £944   £472   £236   3 yo rec 8 lb

-3429 **AYMARA** 37 [2] J H M Gosden 3-8-6 J Carroll 7/4: 4221: 3 b f Darshaan - Chipaya (Northern Prospect) Front rank, led briefly after 2f, led again over 3f out, ran on strongly, rdn out: nicely bckd: rnr-up twice prev: eff at 10/12.3f on fast & gd/soft grnd: handles a sharp or gall trk: deserved this. — 83

3838 **TOLSTOY** 19 [8] Sir Michael Stoute 3-8-11 F Lynch 6/4 FAV: 522222: 3 b c Nashwan - Millazure (Dayjur) Prom, hdwy over 2f out, ev ch when hung in bhd rival appr fnl 1f, sn btn: 10L clr rem: styd longer 12f trip: rnr-up for 5th consecutive time & does not look the easiest of rides, worth a try in headgear: see 3838. — 3½ 83

3811 **IL CAVALIERE** 21 [14] Mrs M Reveley 5-9-5 A Culhane 10/3: -30403: 5 b g Mtoto - Kalmia (Miller's Mate) Waited with, eff 3f out, kept on but no ch with front 2: op 3/1: needs h'caps & further: see 3811. — 10 69

3988 **SEOMRA HOCHT** 9 [1] J G Given 3-8-11 M Fenton 100/1: 04: Bhd, rdn/late gains, no dngr: up in trip. — 1 67

1449} **BARNEY KNOWS** 492 [3] 5-9-5 K Hodgson 25/1: 0-5: Mid-div, no extra fnl 3f: useful over timber in 99/00 for M Peill, won at Doncaster (Gr 2 nov, rtd 130h, earlier rnr-up in a Gr 1 & Gr 2, 2m/2½m, fast & soft, poss any trk): well btn sole '99 Flat start (14f mdn): with R Fahey, sharpener for a jumps campaign. — 6 59

3827 **COUNT ON THUNDER** 20 [7] 3-8-11 K Dalgleish (5) -56506: Led 9f out-3f out, wknd: stiff task. — 2½ 55$

3506 **CARRADIUM** 35 [10] 4-9-5 P Goode (3) 20/1: 556/67: Mid-div at best: see 3506. — 5 48

3701 **ALI OOP** 27 [12] 3-8-11 T Williams 100/1: 648: Nvr a factor: needs sell h'caps. — 6 41

3808 **FREE KEVIN** 21 [15] 4-9-5 O Pears 100/1: -309: Prom, wknd rapidly 3f: up in trip, twice below 3248. — 1¾ 38

3808 **THE CASTIGATOR** 21 [5] 3-8-11 J McAuley 100/1: 000000: AI rear, 10th: mod form. — 2½ 34$

3988 **FASTWAN** 9 [6] 4-9-5 (VIS) Dawn Rankin (7) 200/1: 500000: Rcd v keenly, led till ran v wide & hdd after 2f, wknd rapidly fnl 4f, 15th: visored: poor performer. — 0

1141} **Dancing King** 510 [9] 4-9-5 G Duffield 33/1:   3745 **Lubohenrik** 24 [11] 3-8-6 R Winston 100/1:
-- **Royal Plum** 4 [4] 4-9-5 T Eaves (7) 50/1:   1193 **Spectre Brown** 140 [13] 10-9-8(3ow) A Scholes 200/1:
15 ran   Time 2m 40.4 (9.8)   (Lord Hartington)   J H M Gosden Manton, wilts

---

4134 3.45 BASS ROCK HCAP 3YO+ 0-90 (C)   2m   Good/Soft 66   -43 Slow   [81]
£8502   £2616   £1308   £654   3 yo rec 12lb

3890 **COVER UP** 16 [5] Sir Michael Stoute 3-9-10 (89) F Lynch 3/1 FAV: 103001: 3 b g Machiavellian - Sought Out (Rainbow Quest) Mid-div, gd hdwy to lead over 2f out, styd on well despite flashing tail, pushed clr ins last, eased cl-home: nicely bckd: earlier won on reapp at Windsor (mdn): plcd both '99 starts (mdn stks, rtd 88): eff at 12/14f, relished this step up to 2m: acts on firm, gd/soft, poss hvy: eff weight carrier: useful & right back to best here, win again. — 95

4091 **HERACLES** 2 [1] A Berry 4-9-3 (70) C Lowther 20/1: 410062: 4 b g Unfuwain - La Masse (High Top) Led at slow pace, qcknd over 2f out, sn hdd, not pace of winr: ran 48 hrs ago, stays 2m: flattered 4091. — 3½ 71

3978 **MENTAL PRESSURE** 9 [9] Mrs M Reveley 7-8-7 (60) P Fessey 13/2: 521343: 7 ch g Polar Falcon - Hysterical (High Top) In tch, rdn 2f out, styd on late, no threat to wnr: see 3978, 3331. — ¾ 60

3709 **ROVERETTO** 2 [2] Mrs M Reveley 5-8-11 (64) A Culhane 11/2: /62434: Prom, drvn/btn appr fnl 2f: recent jumps rnr, in the frame when falling 4 out at Worcester 15 days ago (2½m h'cap): see 3034. — 3 61

*3224 **SENSE OF FREEDOM** 46 [4] 3-9-8 (87) J Carroll 10/3: 222315: Bhd, chsd ldrs after halfway, drvn/held fnl 3f: tchd 9/2, 6 wk abs: big step up in trip, shade btr 3224 (12f, fast). — 4 80

4003 **THE BUTTERWICK KID** 8 [7] 7-9-3 (70) P Hanagan (5) 7/2: 20-046: Bhd, eff 6f out, rdn/btn fnl 3f. — 3½ 60

4006 **HIGHFIELD FIZZ** 8 [8] 8-7-12 (51)(2ow)(15oh) T Williams 50/1: 341307: Nvr a factor: stiff task. — 5 37

3993 **NORTHERN MOTTO** 9 [6] 7-7-10 (49)(7oh) D Mernagh (1) 20/1: 443608: AI towards rear: stiffish task. — 4 31

3751 **TRISTACENTURY** 24 [3] 7-8-12 (65) G Duffield 12/1: 424459: Keen/prom, wknd fnl 3f: up in trip. — 10 39

9 ran   Time 2m 40.0 (17.5)   (Lord Weinstock)   Sir Michael Stoute Newmarket,

---

4135 4.20 DUNBAR CLASSIFIED STKS 3YO+ 0-75 (D)   1m rnd   Good/Soft 66   -07 Slow
£4446   £1368   £684   £342   3 yo rec 4 lb

*3810 **PACIFIC ALLIANCE** 21 [5] M Wigham 4-9-8 M Fenton 5/1: 003111: 4 b g Fayruz - La Gravotte (Habitat) Led, hdd over 2f out, rallied gamely for press to lead again well ins last, all out: hat-trick landed after scoring here at Musselburgh & York (h'caps): '99 Lingfield (auct mdn) & Sandown (h'cap, rtd 58a & 65, R Armstrong): suited by 1m, has tried 10f: acts on firm, gd/soft & equitrack: eff with/without blnks & handles any trk, likes Musselburgh: likes to force the pace: v tough, genuine & prog. — 81

3426 **FAIR LADY** 37 [2] B W Hills 3-8-9 K Dalgleish (5) 5/1: 163042: 3 b f Machiavellian - Just Cause (Law Society) Handy, gd hdwy to lead over 2f out, hdd ins last, rallied, not btn far: nicely bckd & ran to near best here: eff at 1m/11f: see 2863, 467. — nk 71

3810 **PENTAGON LAD** 21 [11] J L Eyre 4-9-5 R Cody Boutcher (7) 9/1: 142603: 4 ch g Secret Appeal - Gilboa (Shirley Heights) Dwelt, hdwy from near over 3f out, drvn/kept on, no ch with front 2: see 3309, 2799. — 2 73

4003 **SEA SQUIRT** 8 [12] M Johnston 3-9-1 R Winston 10/1: 315204: Waited with, rdn/prog over 3f out, styd on, no threat to ldrs: op 8/1: see 3826. — nk 73

-- **MASTER COOPER** 1 [6] 6-9-2 (bl) J M O'Dwyer (7) 7/1: 202225: Dwelt, sn prom, drvn/btn fnl 2f: op 5/1: Irish raider, rnr-up thrice this term (h'caps): in '98 won 3 h'caps: eff btwn 1m & 14f on fast & soft grnd. — 1 68

4094 **ROLLER** 2 [10] 4-9-2 A Culhane 15/8 FAV: 204036: Late gains from rear, nvr dngrs: nicely bckd, ran 48hrs ago & poss just too soon after 4094. — ½ 67

MUSSELBURGH SUNDAY SEPTEMBER 24TH Righthand, Sharp Track

3634 **TOM DOUGAL 29** [6] 5-9-2 R Fitzpatrick 14/1: 005007: Mid-div at best: see 3634, 1490. ½ **66**
3081 **HI NICKY 53** [4] 4-8-13 T Williams 100/1: 000048: Chsd ldrs, drvn/btn fnl 2f: 8 wk abs, stiff task. 6 **54$**
3612 **POLAR HAZE 30** [14] 3-8-12 P Hanagan (5) 15/1: 230369: Prom, wknd fnl 2f: up in trip: btr 3225 (6f). 2½ **53**
3603 **THATCHED 30** [13] 10-9-2 P Fessey 33/1: 302400: Nvr dgnrs, 10th: stiff task. 8 **43**
3365 **ARIZONA LADY 40** [7] 3-8-12 G Duffield 16/1: 321500: Front rank, wknd qckly fnl 2f, 11th: 6 wk abs. 1½ **41**
4088 **Taker Chance 3** [9] 4-9-2 A Robertson (7) 100/1: 4088 **Time For The Clan 3** [8] 3-8-12 O Pears 100/1:
4088 **Bay Of Bengal 3** [3] 4-8-13 J McAuley 66/1:
14 ran Time 1m 43.4 (5.9) (Michael Wigham) M Wigham Newmarket.

4136 **4.50 S JOSEPH HCAP 3YO+ 0-85 (D) 7f rnd Good/Soft 66 -21 Slow [80]**
£4407 £1356 £678 £339 3 yo rec 3 lb

3634 **YENALED 29** [8] J S Goldie 3-8-4 (59) K Dalgleish (5) 10/1: 462251: 3 gr g Rambo Dancer - Fancy Flight (Arctic Tern) Waited with, smooth hdwy appr fnl 1f, styd on strongly rdn out: earlier won here at Musselburgh (h'cap, first win): plcd sev times in '99 (h'caps, rtd 64 at best): eff at 7f/10f: acts on firm, gd/soft, poss soft: clrly runs esp well here at Musselburgh. **64**
4004 **BODFARI ANNA 8** [3] J L Eyre 4-8-3 (55)(vis) Joanna Badger (7) 14/1: 143002: 4 br f Casteddu - Lowrianna (Cyrano de Bergerac) Rear, ran on strongly for press fnl 2f, no threat to wnr: ran to nr best: see 2673. 1¾ **56**
3826 **RYEFIELD 20** [7] Miss L A Perratt 5-8-9 (61) A Culhane 8/1: 142633: 5 b g Petong - Octavia (Sallust) Keen in rear, gd hdwy to chall over 1f out, held well ins last: tough, likes Ayr: see 3826, 2878. hd **62**
3809 **JEFFREY ANOTHERRED 21** [12] M Dods 6-9-0 (66) F Lynch 6/1: 604204: Front rank, drvn/no extra appr fnl 1f: on a fair mark & likes soft grnd, keep in mind: see 3708. 2½ **63**
3366 **PRINCELY DREAM 40** [2] 4-9-9 (75) P Hanagan (5) 10/1: -00045: Rear, late hdwy, nvr nrr: 6 wk abs: best run to date this term: see 1533. hd **72**
*3745 **MAMMAS BOY 24** [1] 5-8-0 (52) Iona Wands 10/1: 046016: Rear, gd hdwy to chall ldrs fnl 2f, drvn/onepcd over 1f out: shade btr 3745 (1m, fast). 1 **47**
3699 **INDIAN PLUME 27** [11] 4-10-0 (80) M Fenton 11/2 JT FAV: 003527: Dsptd lead, wknd qckly over 1f out: drop in trip: see 3699 (1m). 1½ **72**
4010 **BUNDY 8** [14] 4-9-1 (67) D Mernagh (3) 9/1: 100308: Mid-div, hdwy 2f out, ev ch till wknd qckly fnl 1f. 4 **52**
*3200 **LUNCH PARTY 47** [13] 8-8-7 (59) J Carroll 11/2 JT FAV: -40619: Bhd, gd hdwy to dspt lead over 2f out, fdd over 1f out: 7 wk abs, btr 3200. 2 **40**
3880 **CHINA RED 17** [10] 6-9-10 (76) O Pears 20/1: 000100: Front rank, dropped rear after halfway, 10th: twice below best for new connections, btr 3404 (8.5f clmr, fast). ½ **56**
3803 **BAJAN BELLE 21** [5] 3-8-5 (60) R Winston 16/1: 002250: Mid-div, hdwy to chall over 2f out, fdd sn after, 11th: likes faster grnd: see 3671. ½ **39**
3605 **PRIX STAR 30** [9] 5-8-3 (55)(vis) T Williams 8/1: 052230: Cl-up, lost tch fnl 2f, 12th: btr 3605, 82. 2½ **30**
3809 **QUIET VENTURE 21** [4] 6-8-7 (59)(tvi) G Duffield 20/1: 041000: Mid-div, wknd 2f out, 13th: likes fast. 4 **28**
3573 **LADY OF WINDSOR 32** [6] 3-8-7 (62)(bl) R Lappin 16/1: 006040: Led, hdd 2f out, wknd rapidly, 14th. 2 **28**
14 ran Time 1m 31.0 (6.1) (Martin Delaney) J S Goldie Uplawmoor, E.Renfrewshire.

BATH MONDAY SEPTEMBER 25TH Lefthand, Turning Track With Uphill Finish

Official Going SOFT (Heavy Rain Throughout The Afternoon). Stalls: Str Course - Far Side; Round Course - Inside. Runner came stands side in str all races

4137 **2.00 TORMARTON MDN DIV I 2YO (D) 5f161y rnd Soft Inapplicable**
£2918 £898 £449 £224

-- **CANTERLOUPE** [5] P J Makin 2-8-9 S Sanders 20/1: 1: 2 b f Wolfhound - Missed Again (High Top) Led till 1f out, rall gamely for press to regain lead fnl strides: 3,500 gns half-sister to 6f/10f wnr Failed To Hit, dam 10f wnr: eff fresh at 5.7f, sure to apprec further: acts on gd/soft grnd, stiff/undul trk: can only improve. **75**
3832 **LOCHSPRITE 20** [8] I A Balding 2-8-9 R Hughes 12/1: 02: 2 ch f So Factual - Lochspring (Precocious) Prsd ldr, led 1f out, rdn, hdd nr fin, just btn: op 8/1: eff at 5.7f on gd/soft, up with the pace: win a mdn. shd **74**
-- **MUNIR** [3] B W Hills 2-9-0 R Hills 9/4 FAV: 3: 2 ch c Indian Ridge - Al Bahathri (Blushing Groom) Prom, rdn & strong chall fnl 1f, held nr fin: nicely bckd, clr rem, debut: half-brother to sev wnrs btwn 6f & 1m: dam high-class sprinter/miler: eff at 6f on gd/soft, 7f suit: pick up a mdn with a stronger ride. ½ **77**
-- **NOON GUN** [13] W R Muir 2-9-0 Martin Dwyer 33/1: 4: Towards rear, feeling pace halfway, kept on ins last: op 20/1: 12,000 gns Ashkalani half-brother to decent 6f juv Lima, dam 10f wnr: improve over 7f+. 4 **66**
-- **MANOR LAKE** [15] 2-8-9 J Reid 20/1: 5: Mid-div, chsd ldrs ent fnl 2f, outpcd ins last: op 14/1 on debut: Puissance half-sister to a 5f juv wnr, dam unrcd, sire a sprinter: with R Johnson Houghton. hd **60**
-- **HIGH PASTURE** [1] 2-8-9 T Quinn 8/1: 6: Towards rear, prog 2f out, sn onepace: op 6/1, tchd 10/1 on debut: El Gran Senor 1st foal, dam 7f wnr: bred to need at least 1m: with R Charlton. shd **60**
3980 **PROVIDENT 10** [12] 2-9-0 J Fortune 5/2: -07: Slow away & bhd, went past btn horses fnl 1f: bckd: more expected after promising debut, but sure to rate higher over 7f+. ½ **64+**
3268 **YOUNG TERN 46** [10] 2-9-0 N Pollard 33/1: 008: Nvr a factor: 7 wk abs, see 2454. 2 **58**
3973 **EAST OF JAVA 10** [6] 2-9-0 J P Spencer 6/1: 039: Chsd ldrs till ent fnl 2f: much btr 3973. 1¾ **53**
3815 **ALEXANDER STAR 21** [9] 2-8-9 S Whitworth 10/1: 430: Handy till 2f out: 10th: btr 3815, 1954 (fast) 4 **38**
4079 **TREMEZZO 4** [7] 2-9-0 Pat Eddery 10/1: 30: Front rank till after halfway: 11th, qck reapp, see 4079. 1½ **40**
3767 **Mahlstick 24** [14] 2-9-0 J D Smith 50/1: 3484 **Raptor 37** [4] 2-9-0 M Hills 25/1:
2711 **Flapdoodle 70** [11] 2-8-9 C Rutter 66/1: 4030 **Atemme 7** [2] 2-8-9 (BL) J Tate 50/1:
15 ran Time 1m 13.4 (4.3) (R A Ballin & The Billinomas) P J Makin Ogbourne Massey, Wilts

4138 **2.30 TORMARTON MDN DIV II 2YO (D) 5f161y rnd Soft Inapplicable**
£2908 £895 £447 £223

1346 **FROMSONG 130** [8] B R Millman 2-9-0 B Marcus 16/1: 51: 2 b c Fayruz - Lindas Delight (Batshoof) Led, went clr ins last, cmftbly: over 4 mth abs: reportedly jarred up on debut: 9,000Ir gns speedily-bred colt: eff forcing the pace at 5.7f on gd/soft: handles a stiff/undul trk: runs well fresh & looks useful, win more races. **103**
3980 **MOOTAFAYILL 10** [12] B W Hills 2-9-0 R Hills 1/2 FAV: -222: 2 b c Danzig - Ruznama (Forty Niner) Well plcd, tried to go after wnr & edged right appr fnl 1f sn outpcd: hvly bckd: acts on firm & gd/soft. 5 **92**
2916 **MARABAR 61** [11] P J Makin 2-8-9 S Sanders 16/1: 63: 2 b f Sri Pekan - Erbaya (El Gran Senor) 2½ **81**

In tch, prog 2f out, styd on but nvr dngrs: clr rem, 9 wk abs: left fast grnd debut bhd for new stable: see 2916.

--	**POLONAISE** [6] I A Balding 2-8-9 J Fortune 16/1: 4: Out the back till styd on thro' btn horses fnl 2f: green, op 10/1: 9,000 gns Pivotal half-sister to a cple of wnrs: dam 10f wnr: shld know more next time.		5	69
2652	**FOREST DANCER** 73 [10] 2-9-0 R Hughes 10/1: 35: Chsd ldrs, no extra 2f out: op 8/1, 10 wk abs.		4	64
--	**DANCING TSAR** [5] 2-9-0 J P Spencer 9/1: 6: Rear, mod late hdwy: op 6/1 on debut: 30,000 gns Salse 1st foal, dam a mdn: bred to apprec at least 1m: with G Butler.		1½	60
3852	**AINTNECESSARILYSO** 19 [2] 2-9-0 (BL) Pat Eddery 12/1: 060237: Handy till after halfway: blnkd.		nk	59
3387	**DANE FLYER** 40 [1] 2-9-0 Craig Williams 8/1: -008: Nvr better than mid-div: abs, see 3000.		nk	58
--	**POYLE PICKLE** [7] 2-8-9 M Tebbutt 16/1: 9: Al towards rear: Piccolo half-sister to wnrs btwn 5f & 9f.		1½	49
3909	**PHURTIVE** 14 [9] 2-9-0 J Reid 50/1: 00: Nvr a factor: 10th: Factual gldg, half-brother to a 5f juv wnr.		5	49
--	**CURTSEY** [4] 2-8-9 C Rutter 10/1: 0: In tch for 2½f: 15th, op 8/1 on debut: Mark Of Esteem half-sister to useful 1m/10f performer Cap Juluca, dam 6f wnr, sire a miler: with R Charlton.			32
--	**Dusky Swallow** [14] 2-8-9 W Supple 50/1:	3832 **Gilt Trip** 20 [3] 2-9-0 S W Kelly (3) 33/1:		
--	**Sashay** [13] 2-8-9 N Pollard 50/1:	3252 **Sunny Stroka** 46 [15] 2-8-9 R Havlin 50/1:		
15 ran	Time 1m 12.4 (3.3)	(Mrs E Nelson, Mr Gary Dormer)	B R Millman Kentisbeare, Devon	

4139 3.00 WEATHERBYS HCAP 3YO+ 0-80 (D) 2m1f34y Soft Inapplicable [69]
£4124 £1269 £634 £317 3 yo rec 12lb

3625	**SHERIFF** 31 [9] J W Hills 9-8-6 (47) M Henry 7/1: 210341: 9 b g Midyan - Daisy Warwick (Ribot) Nvr far away, went on appr fnl 3f, rdn out: tchd 9/1: earlier won here at Bath (C/D h'cap): '99 rnr-up (h'cap, rtd 77a), hdles wnr at N Abbot (3m, firm & gd/soft, rtd 118h at his peak): '98 hat-trick scorer at Lingfield (h'caps, rtd 76a & 55): eff at 2m/2m1f: acts on firm, soft grnd, equitrack/Lingfield specialist, handles any trk: best up with/forcing the pace & can carry big weights.		51
4075	**SHARAF** 4 [6] W R Muir 7-8-7 (48) Martin Dwyer 10/1: 304402: 7 b g Sadler's Wells - Marie de Flandre (Crystal Palace) Chsd ldrs, eff 2f out, onepace till kept on to grab 2nd nr fin: qk reapp, gd run, see 1087.	3	49
3948	**PALUA** 12 [11] Mrs A J Bowlby 3-9-10 (77) J Bramhill 25/1: 033243: 3 b c Sri Pekan - Reticent Bride (Shy Groom) Rear, prog 4f out, rdn to chase wnr appr fnl 1f, sn onepace: pulled away from next & this was a fair run up in trip under top weight in desperate conditions: eff at 12f/2m1f on fast & soft grnd: mdn.	nk	77
3916	**MIKE SIMMONS** 14 [12] L P Grassick 4-7-10 (37)(6oh) C Catlin 4/1: /00-04: Rear, kept on same pace from 2f out to go 4th in last: op 16/1, stiff task: see 3916.	11	29
3232}	**HILLSWICK** 413 [10] 9-7-10 (37)(2oh) A Polli (3) 16/1: 0223-5: Held up, imprvd after halfway, prsd ldrs 4f out till wknd 2f out: op 12/1, reapp, plcd 3 of 4 '99 starts (h'caps, rtd 36), landed sole hdles start at Fontwell (2m4f c.j. h'cap, stays 3m, firm & gd, forcing the pace, rtd 94h): rnr-up sole '98 start over this C/D (h'cap, rtd 36): '97 wnr here at Bath (h'cap, rtd 40): eff at 2m1f, acts on firm & gd grnd & likes Bath.	nk	29
3978	**CANDLE SMILE** 10 [2] 8-9-8 (63)(VIS) J Fortune 4/1: 0-6536: Led till appr fnl 3f, no extra: visored.	½	54
3715	**SALSKA** 14 [4] 9-8-7 (48) S Carson (3) 16/1: 250667: Chsd ldrs till 5f out: op 12/1, visor omitted.	dist	0
3978	**OUR MONOGRAM** 10 [7] 4-8-13 (54) Pat Eddery 4/1: 031158: Mid-div, lost tch 6f out: op 3/1: conditions had gone against him, see 3978, 3625.	2½	0
3664	**DANEGOLD** 29 [3] 8-8-10 (51) Craig Williams 11/4 FAV: 046309: Nvr on terms: tchd 5/1, see 714.	26	0
9 ran	Time 4m 03.0 (22.1)	(The Sheriff Partnership)	J W Hills Lambourn, Berks.

4140 3.30 DODINGTON MDN 2YO (D) 1m2f46y Soft Inapplicable
£3415 £1051 £525 £262

3969	**CAPAL GARMON** 11 [2] J H M Gosden 2-9-0 J Fortune 5/6 FAV: 431: 2 b c Caerleon - Elevate (Ela Mana Mou) Trkd ldrs, went on going easily appr fnl 2f, sn clr: bckd: stoutly bred colt, clrly relished this step up to 10f, 12f+ suit: acts on fast & soft grnd, sharp or stiff/undul trk: promising staying prospect for next term.		88
3799	**TAMIAMI TRAIL** 22 [8] B J Meehan 2-9-0 Pat Eddery 5/1: -0052: 2 ch c Indian Ridge - Eurobird (Ela Mana Mou) Handy, rdn appr fnl 2f, chsd wnr bef fnl 1f, no impress: got this longer 10f trip: acts on fast & soft.	4	80
2956	**COMPTON COMMANDER** 59 [7] G A Butler 2-9-0 J P Spencer 5/1: 03: 2 ch c Baratheea - Triode (Sharpen Up) Held up, hdwy under press over 3f out, onepace appr fnl 1f: 8 wk abs: suited by step up to 10f on soft.	¾	79
3680	**REVIEWER** 28 [5] J H M Gosden 2-9-0 R Havlin 20/1: 604: Led till ent fnl 2f, no extra: stablemate wnr.	1½	77
--	**LA MONDOTTE** [4] 2-8-9 S W Kelly (3) 20/1: 5: Nvr a factor: debut: IR 76,000gns Alzao filly.	4	68
3853	**SEATTLE PRINCE** 19 [6] 2-9-0 R Hughes 11/2: 0536: Prom, wknd ent fnl 3f: longer trip on softer grnd.	2½	70
3866	**THE DOCTOR** 18 [10] 2-9-0 D Sweeney 12/1: 07: Mid-div, btn 3f out: longer trip, see 3866.	12	55
3799	**MAD HABIT** 22 [1] 2-9-0 J Reid 50/1: -008: Nvr a factor: Minshaanshu Amad first foal.	8	54
2810	**POCKET VENUS** 66 [3] 2-8-9 S Whitworth 33/1: -09: Chsd ldrs till halfway: 9 wk absence.	24	20
9 ran	Time 2m 19.1 (13.1)	(Mrs R E Sangster & Mr A K Collins)	J H M Gosden Manton, Wilts.

4141 4.00 HORSEMOUTH FILLIES MDN 3YO+ (D) 1m2f46y Soft Innapplicable
£3955 £1217 £608 £304 3 yo rec 6 lb

3838	**MILLENNIUM DASH** 20 [2] L M Cumani 3-8-10 J P Spencer 5/4 FAV: 41: 3 b f Nashwan - Milligram (Mill Reef) Sn trkd ldrs, led bef halfway, shkn up 2f out, cmftbly: nicely bckd: unrcd juv: dam a top-class miler: eff at 10f: handles firm, clrly goes well on soft, forcing the pace: handles a stiff/undul trk & is improving.		88
3818	**FLAME OF TRUTH** 21 [10] J H M Gosden 3-8-10 J Fortune 7/2: 322: 3 b f Rainbow Quest - River Lullaby (Riverman) Chsd ldrs, chsd wnr appr fnl 2f, nvr any impression & eased towards fin: op 5/2: was back in trip: prob handles fast & soft: see 3818.	10	78
--	**HOLY ISLAND** [4] L M Cumani 3-8-10 G Sparkes (7) 20/1: 3: 3 b f Deploy - Bells (Sadler's Wells) Patiently rdn, went thr' btn horses appr fnl 1f, nvr dngrs: stablemate wnr, debut: stoutly bred first foal: stewards inquired into running/riding: reportedly a nervy filly who needed the experience: will improve.	6	72
3178	**VETORITY** 50 [8] B Smart 3-8-10 M Tebbutt 16/1: -35304: Held up, eff appr fnl 3f, nvr a factor: abs	6	66
--	**ALBARSHA** [13] 3-8-10 W Supple 8/1: 5: Chsd ldrs, fdd 2f out: op 5/1: Mtoto half-sister to 2yo wnr.	3½	62
1796	**MUTASADER** 109 [15] 3-8-10 R Hills 14/1: 0-506: Nvr nr ldrs: 15 wk abs, best 1447 (gd grnd).	3½	58
--	**BROKEN SPECTRE** [8] 3-8-10 R Hughes 50/1: 7: Trkd ldrs, wknd appr fnl 2f, eased: op 5/1, stablemate 2nd, debut: Rainbow Quest sister to high-class 12/14f performer Armiger.	hd	58
3663	**WOODYATES** 29 [12] 3-8-10 Pat Eddery 12/1: -06058: Chsd ldrs till wknd 4f out: stiff task.	11	47
84	**BEAUCHAMP NYX** 308 [14] 4-9-2 S Righton 100/1: /006-9: In tch till 4f out: reapp, new stable, no form.	4	43$
3834	**RHIANN** 20 [6] A J Edwards 4-9-2 F Pitzsimons (5) 50/1: 00: Nvr a factor: 10th, longer trip: Anshan filly.	7	36
3403	**LATOUR** 40 [11] 3-8-10 M Hills 12/1: 232000: Led till bef halfway, lost pl: 11th, 6 wk abs, btr 2543 (1m).	4	32
3683	**Sheraton Heights** 28 [5] 3-8-10 G Hind 33/1:	-- **Colliers Treasure** [7] 3-8-10 D R McCabe 50/1:		
13 ran	Time 2m 18.3 (12.3)	(Helena Springfield Ltd)	L M Cumani Newmarket.

1275

MONDAY SEPTEMBER 25TH Lefthand, Turning Track With Uphill Finish

4142 4.30 MORRIS DANCER COND STKS 3YO+ (C) 1m rnd Soft Inapplicable
£6104 £2315 £1157 £526 3 yo rec 4 lb

3628 **SWAN KNIGHT** 30 [9] J L Dunlop 4-8-11 Pat Eddery 7/1: 002601: 4 b c Sadler's Wells - Shannkara **96**
(Akarad) Confidently held up, gd prog 3f out, led appr fnl 1f, pshd out, cmftbly: Newmarket debut wnr last term
(stks, rtd 89): unrcd juv: eff at 1m, tried 10f: acts on fast, goes well in soft, any trk & runs well fresh.
3563 **ADJUTANT** 33 [8] N P Littmoden 5-8-11 R Hughes 7/1: 206002: 5 b g Batshoof - Indian Love Song 4 **91**
(Be My Guest) Cl-up, led 3f out till bef fnl 1f, no extra: tchd 10/1: stays 1m, all wins at 7f: see 1286.
4000 **PULAU TIOMAN** 9 [5] M A Jarvis 4-8-11 P Robinson 8/11 FAV: 220333: 4 b c Robellino - Ella Mon 1½ **89**
Amour (Ela Mana Mou) Mid-div, prog & ch appr fnl 1f, sn rdn, no impress: well bckd: not his form, see 1015.
4088 **MOORLANDS AGAIN** 4 [1] D Burchell 5-8-11 R Price 50/1: 650454: Led till 3f out, same pace: stiff task. 1 **86$**
1151 **AKEED** 143 [10] J Fortune 7/1: 144-55: Rear chsd ldrs 3f out, fdd 2f out: abs, faster grnd suits 6 **76**
2975 **GLEN ROSIE** 59 [7] D Nicholls 3-8-2 N Pollard 8/1: -24006: Chsd ldrs till after halfway: 8 wk abs, see 913 (7f). 2 **68**
3726 **ASLY** 26 [11] R Hills 7/1: -21107: Al towards rear: first try on soft grnd: see 3017. 3½ **78**
4080 **LADYWELL BLAISE** 4 [2] R Hannon 3-8-4 C Catlin (7) 66/1: 000008: Pulled hard, in tch till 3f out: v stiff task. 4 **57**
690 **ROYMILLON** 191 [6] 6-9-8 M Tebbutt 33/1: -14109: Al bhd: 6 month abs, Brit bow: ex-multiple 3½ **66**
wnr in Germany (9f/10.5f, one Listed, soft grnd & AW): now with D J Wintle.
4122 **PETRIE** 1 [4] 3-8-7 Jonjo Fowle (5) 66/1: 000600: Held up, gd prog 4f out, wknd qckly 3f out: 10th. 5 **44$**
10 ran Time 1m 48.5 (7.2) (Mr & Mrs Gary Pinchen) J L Dunlop Arundel, W.Sussex.

4143 5.00 LETHEBY APPR MDN HCAP 3YO+ 0-60 (F) 1m rnd Soft Inapplicable [60]
£2695 £770 £385 3 yo rec 4 lb

4066 **MAGICAL BAILIWICK** 5 [8] R J Baker 4-9-0 (46)(bl) G Gibbons (5) 5/2 FAV: 000021: 8 ch g Magical **53**
Wonder - Alpine Dance (Apalachee) Sn led, made rest, drvn out: qck reapp: plcd last term (mdn, rtd 75):
eff at 1m, clrly suited by soft grnd, forcing the pace: wears blnks, prob handles any trk.
3745 **SHARP GOSSIP** 25 [15] J A R Toller 4-9-10 (56) C Catlin 3/1: 000022: 4 b g College Chapel - Idle 3 **58**
Gossip (Runnett) In tch, prog appr fnl 2f, chsd wnr & ch briefly dist, sn onepace: bckd tho' op 2/1: gd run.
3816 **RIDGECREST** 21 [11] P D Evans 3-8-13 (49)(t) Joanna Badger 14/1: 545053: 3 ch g Anshan - Lady 1 **49**
Sabo (Prince Sabo) In tch, shkn up 3f out, chsd ldrs appr fnl 1f, no impress: clr rem: goes on equitrack & soft.
4232} **MARTELLO** 357 [12] R Charlton 4-10-0 (60) C Haddon (7) 8/1: 6005-4: Rear, imprvd to go 4th 2f out, 5 **52**
sn no extra: unplcd last term (mdn, rtd 77, h'cap, rtd 61): yet to find a trip, tried 12f: has tried a visor/hdles.
3971 **LIVELY FELIX** 11 [4] 3-9-5 (55) W Hutchinson (3) 20/1: -00405: Held up, moderate late hdwy: btr 3696. 4 **40**
3588 **MUCHANA YETU** 32 [16] 3-9-3 (48)(BL) Darren Williams 8/1: 065056: Held up, prog to chase ldr 3f 1¾ **30**
out, fdd: blnkd, big drop in trip, see 1177.
4032 **MOVING EXPERIENCE** 7 [1] 3-9-6 (56) R Smith 5/1: -04067: Chsd ldrs, wknd appr fnl 2f: tchd 8/1. 1½ **35**
3682 **TORMENTOSO** 28 [6] 3-9-1 (51) D Watson (5) 12/1: 605058: Nvr a factor: usually forces the pace. 3 **25**
3663 **EIGHT** 29 [10] 4-9-10 (56)(vis) G Hannon 8/1: 540309: Trkd ldrs, lost pl appr fnl 2f: see 3383, 1807. 4 **23**
2548 **MISS MANETTE** 77 [5] 3-9-3 (53) Jonjo Fowle (5) 16/1: -6000: Nvr dngrs: 10th, 11 wk abs, h'cap bow. 6 **11**
3885 **Barrys Double** 17 [13] 3-8-12 (48)(vis) S Clancy (5) 25/1:
2839 **Consideration** 65 [14] 3-8-12 (48) D Kinsella (5) 20/1:
421 **Inviramental** 240 [9] 4-9-0 (46) R Thomas (3) 20/1:
13 ran Time 1m 50.0 (11.9) (Island Racing Connection) R J Baker Stoodleigh, Devon.

WEDNESDAY SEPTEMBER 20TH Righthand, Galloping Track

Official Going SOFT

4144 2.25 GR 3 RRIX LA ROCHETTE 2YO 1m Soft
£21134 £7685 £3842

-- **OKAWANGO** Mme C Head 2-8-11 O Doleuze 2/5 JT FAVcp: -11: 2 b c Kingmambo - Krissante (Kris) **103**
Trkd ldr, smooth hdwy to lead dist, easily/not extended: recent debut scorer: eff arnd a gall 1m: acts on
soft grnd: highly rated & unbeaten colt, can win more Gr races.
-- **VAHORIMIX** A Fabre 2-8-11 O Peslier 22/10: -612: 2 gr c Linamix - Vasda Honor (Highest Honor) ¾ **97**
Settled last, rdn to imprv over 1f out, styd on well but no ch with easy wnr: eff over a gall 1m on soft.
3787 **LUCAYAN CHIEF** 18 S P C Woods 2-8-11 M Gosse 72/10: -51323: 2 b c With Approval - Littleladyleah ¾ **96**
(Shareef Dancer) With ldr, led 3f out, rdn/hdd dist, sn no extra: gd run upped in grade: see 3787 (stks).
6 ran Time 1m 41.45 (Wertheimer Et Frere) Mme C Head France

SATURDAY SEPTEMBER 23RD Righthand, Stiff, Galloping Track

Official Going GOOD TO SOFT

4145 2.55 LISTED PREMIO NOVELLA 2YO 7f110y Good/Soft
£22772 £10020 £5465 £2733

*4049 **INNIT** 10 M R Channon 2-8-11 F Jovine : 002111: 2 b f Distinctly North - Tidal Reach **100**
(Kris S) Settled rear, gd hdwy to lead 2f out, qcknd up well, rdn out: hat-trick landed after wins at Doncaster
(val nursery) & M-Laffitte (List): Jan foal, dam a multiple sprint wnr: eff at 7/7.5f, 1m whod suit: acts on
fast, gd/soft & a sharpish or gall trk: can force the pace or come from bhd: tough, useful & in fine form.
-- **FEDINA** Italy 2-8-9 M Tellini : 2: 2 b f Shaamit - Dance Mania (Danzig) 2½ **92**
-- **PURSUIT OF LIFE** Italy 2-8-9 M Demuro : 3: 2 b f Pursuit Of Love - Biosphere (Pharly) shd **92**
6 ran Time 1m 35.2 (Tim Corby) M R Channon West Isley, Berks

COLOGNE   SUNDAY SEPTEMBER 24TH   Righthand, Fair Track

Official Going   SOFT

4146   1.35 LISTED HOLDING-SPRINT-PREIS 3YO+   5f   Soft
£6452   £2581   £1290   £645   3 yo rec 1 lb

--	**TRINIDAD** U Ostmann 3-8-11 J Palik : 1 : 3 ch f Big Shuffle - Tirajana (Riboprince)		**101**
3569	**ROZEL** 32 R Guest 3-8-7 D Holland : 013432: 3 ch f Wolfhound - Noirmant (Dominion)	1¼	93

Trkd ldr, rdn & styd on well fnl 1f, no impress on wnr: acts on fast & soft: gd run upped to Listed class.

--	**SOUND DOMINO** Germany 4-8-10 A Starke : 3 : 4 b g Dashing Blade - Swift Connection	shd	95

(Conquistador Cielo) :
7 ran   Time 57.7   (H Schroer-Dreessmann)   U Ostmann Germany

4147   3.50 GR 1 PREIS VON EUROPA 3YO+   1m4f   Soft
£96774   £38710   £19355

4050   **GOLDEN SNAKE** 11 J L Dunlop 4-9-6 D Bonilla : 60-451: 4 b h Danzig - Dubian (High Line)   **117**
Chsd ldrs, rdn/imprvd over 1f out, strong run fnl 1f to get up on line, all out: '99 wnr at Newmarket (List)
& Chantilly (Gr 1, rtd 119, B W Hills): '98 Doncaster wnr (mdn, rtd 93+): eff at 9/12f on fast & soft grnd,
prob best on the latter: likes a stiff/gall trk & runs well fresh: tough & high-class entire.

4055   **YAVANAS PACE** 8 M Johnston 8-9-6 D Holland : 226522: 8 ch g Accordion - Lady In Pace (Burslem)   nse   116
Cl-up, went on after halfway, clr appr fnl 1f, caught on line by wnr's late rattle: 6L clr rem: yet another
fine run by this most tough, smart & genuine gelding: sorely deserves a change of luck: see 4055.

3849   **CATELLA** 21 P Schiergen 4-9-2 T Hellier : 223123: 4 ch f Generous - Crystal Ring (Kris)   6   104
Bhd, rdn/hdwy over 3f out, drvn/not pace of front 2 appr fnl 1f: btr 3849.
11 ran   Time 2m 32.49   (The National Stud)   J L Dunlop Arundel, W Sussex

DIELSDORF (SWITZERLAND)   SUNDAY SEPTEMBER 24TH   Sharp Track

Official Going   GOOD

4148   3.15 GRAND PRIX JOCKEY CLUB 3YO+   1m4f82y   Good
£18824   £7529   £5647   3 yo rec 8 lb

*3553   **AKBAR** 35 M Johnston 4-9-9 D O'Donohoe : 106411: 4 b c Doyoun - Akishka (Nishapour)   **102**
Led early, remnd with ldrs, led again 3f out, qcknd & styd on well, readily: earlier won thrice here in
Switzerland, incl 2 races at this trk (stks): mainly with J Oxx in '99, plcd sev times (incl List, rtd 101):
eff between 10f & 2m on fast & hvy grnd: loves this sharp trk at Dielsdorf: tough, genuine & useful.

--	**NATIONAL ACADEMY** Switzerland 5-9-11 A Schikora : 2 : 5 b h Royal Academy - Narola (Nebos)	1¾	99
3553	**HARISHON** 35 Switzerland 4-9-11 J-M Breux : 233: 4 b c Waajib - Chenya (Beldale Flutter)	2¾	95
-4016	**MARDANI** 8 M Johnston 5-9-11 R Ffrench : 026626: 5 b h In tch, rdn/onepcd fnl 2f, fin 6th:	9	83

stiff task at the weights against his stablemate, apprec a return to h'caps: see 4016.
*3850   **COOL INVESTMENT** 21 3-9-3 J Stack : 413518: Nvr a factor, 8th: stablemate of wnr: btr 3850 (1m7f).   0
8 ran   Time 2m 37.5   (Markus Graff)   M Johnston Middleham, N Yorks

SOUTHWELL (Fibresand)   TUESDAY SEPTEMBER 26TH   Lefthand, Sharp, Oval Track

Official Going: STANDARD   Stalls: Inside.

4149   1.25 DIRECT AMAT HCAP 3YO+ 0-65 (G)   2m aw   Going 39 -85 Slow   [39]
£2117   £605   £302   3 yo rec 12lb

*4024   **VINCENT** 10 [3] J L Harris 5-11-2 (55) Mr S Walker (5) 11/4 FAV: 134411: 5 b g Anshan - Top Anna   **59a**
(Ela Mana Mou) Held up, hdwy to lead 2f out, styd on well inside last, rdn out: op 5/2: slow time: earlier scored
at Southwell (h'cap) & twice at W'hampton (h'caps & class stakes): '99 wnr again at Southwell & W'hampton (h'caps,
rtd 52a, unplcd on turf, rtd 48): plcd in '98 (rtd 55a, visor): eff at 14f/2m on fast, fibresand/sharp track
specialist, handles equitrack: has run well fresh & a gd weight carrier: all wins on fibresand & in fine form.

3664   **MONACLE** 30 [9] John Berry 6-10-0 (39)(e) Mr M Murphy (5) 6/1: 412542: 6 b g Saddlers' Hall   1   40a
- Endless Joy (Law Society) Held up, styd on for press fnl 3f, not pace of wnr: recent jumps rnr (unplcd, rtd 84h).

3887   **MEILLEUR** 18 [4] Lady Herries 6-11-1 (54) Miss R Woodman (7) 7/1: 302643: 6 b g Nordico - Lucy   ¾   54a
Limelight (Hot Spark) Bhd, rdn & styd on fni 3f, nrst fin: op 11/2: gd run: see 68.

3963   **PENNYS FROM HEAVEN** 12 [11] D Nicholls 6-10-13 (52) Mrs S Bosley 10/1: 464304: Chsd ldrs, onepace 1¼   51a
fnl 2f: stays a sharp 2m: acts on fm, gd/soft & fibresand: see 2139 (11f).

3737   **CLASSIC EAGLE** 27 [5] Mr S Rees (5) 33/1: 054005: Led 14f: see 3407, 1272 (10f).   5   33a
*3202   **WRANGEL** 15 [15] 6-10-9 (48) Miss E J Jones 16/1: 0016: Chsd ldrs 5f out, btn 3f out: recent jumps   4   38a
wnr (unplcd, rtd 83h, h'cap): prev with J FitzGerald: AW bow today: btr 3202 (12f, fast).

3978   **SPA LANE** 11 [10] 7-9-8 (33) Mr S Dobson (5) 10/1: 005007: Handy 14f, btn/eased fnl 1f: see 2482.   1¾   21a
3889   **ALVARO** 18 [8] 3-10-7 (58) Mr W Worthington (7) 20/1: 620648: Prom 14f: see 3383 (10f).   6   40a
3978   **PARADISE NAVY** 11 [7] 11-11-7 (60)(bl) Mr R Bliss (7) 25/1: 003609: Rear, hdwy halfway, sn held.   5   37a
3827   **MISCHIEF** 22 [14] 4-9-3 (28)(vis)(2oh) Miss J Ellis (5) 20/1: 616500: Trckd ldrs 12f: 10th: see 2827.   3   2a
*3260   **BLOWING AWAY** 47 [2] 6-9-4 (29) Mrs L Pearce 7/1: 050310: Trckd ldrs 12f: 11th: lngr trip.   5   0a
*3773   **Odyn Dancer** 24 [12] 3-9-6 (43) Mr K Burke (1) 4/1: 3827 **Notation** 22 [6] 6-9-3 (28) Miss A Deniel 12/1:
--   **The Boy King** [13] 8-10-10 (36)(bl)(13ow) Mr O Cole (0) 66/1:
3311   **Loyal Toast** 45 [16] 5-9-8 (33) Mr Nicky Tinkler (5) 25/1:
3399   **Republican Lady** 41 [1] 8-9-8 (33) Miss P Drew (7) 50/1:
16 ran   Time 3m 45.80 (19.8)   (P Caplan)   J L Harris Eastwell, Leics

---

4150 **1.55 CLAIMER DIV I 3YO+ 0-60 (F)** **1m3f aw** **Going 39 -23 Slow**
£1841 £526 £263 3 yo rec 7 lb

1207 **BE WARNED** 141 [6] R Brotherton 9-9-6 (vis) L Newman (3) 13/2: 012001: 9 b g Warning - Sagar 60a
(Habitat) Chsd ldrs halfway, rdn/led over 1f out, styd on well, pushed out nr fin: 5 mth abs: earlier scored here
at Southwell (claimer): '99 W'hampton scorer (claimer, rtd 85a & 60a): '98 wnr at Southwell (2) & W'hampton
(h'caps, rtd 81a & 66): eff between 7/12f on fast, hvy & both AWs: handles any track, loves W'hampton/Southwell:
suited by a visor, tried blinks: enjoys claiming grade & runs well fresh: v tough.
4003 **INDIGO BAY** 10 [1] R Bastiman 4-9-10 (bl) O Pears 4/1 FAV: 510302: 4 b g Royal Academy - Cape 2 60a
Heights (Shirley Heights) Chsd ldrs halfway, led over 3f out till over 1f out, held inside last: topweight: acts on
firm, gd & both AWs: see 3102.
4029 **BEE GEE** 8 [8] M Blanshard 3-8-4 Dale Gibson 8/1: 050043: 3 b f Beveled - Bunny Gee (Last nk 46$
Tycoon) Rdn twds rear halfway, styd on for press fnl 3f, nrst fin: acts on both AWs: see 1540 (12f, sell).
2008 **SOCIALIST** 101 [10] J A Osborne 4-8-10 S W Kelly (3) 33/1: 630004: Trckd ldrs, kept on onepce fnl nk 44$
3f: 3 month abs, clr rem: handles fibresand & gd/soft grnd: eff around 11/12f: see 893.
3935 **NIGHT AND DAY** 13 [7] J A Osborne 4-8-12 R Ffrench 6/1: 054045: Chsd ldrs, held fnl 2f: clr rem: see 3935, 3561. 3 41a
2119 **PICKENS** 96 [3] 8-8-12 Kim Tinkler 11/2: 060146: Rear, mod late hdwy: 3 mth abs: btr 1415 (c/d). 8 33a
3052 **PURSUIVANT** 56 [15] 6-8-10 (vis) R Fitzpatrick 20/1: 040007: Rdn/twds rear halfway, nvr factor: abs. 1¼ 29a
2782 **ILE DISTINCT** 68 [5] 6-9-6 (bl) G Duffield 13/2: 3-2048: Cl up, led 5f out till over 3f out, fdd: 8 wk 2 36a
jumps abs (unplcd, rtd 72h, nov): tried blinks on AW bow: see 2061.
3125 **GYMCRAK FIREBIRD** 53 [14] 3-8-6 (BL) W Supple 14/1: -00009: Mid div, btn/eased fnl 1f: blnks, abs. 1½ 27a
*3935 **LOKOMOTIV** 13 [4] 4-9-2 (bl) P Fitzsimons (5) 7/1: 052610: Al bhd: 10th, needs turf? 9 20a
3919 **NOBLE CHARGER** 14 [13] 5-9-6 P McCabe 40/1: 0-0060: Al rear: 11th: blinks omitted: see 784. 6 15a
3199 **KISSED BY MOONLITE** 49 [9] 4-8-11 C Carver (3) 33/1: 00-060: Led 6f, sn btn: 12th: abs, AW bow. ½ 5a
3915 **Trouble** 15 [16] 4-9-0 A Mackay 25/1: 3094 **Concierge** 55 [11] 3-8-9 A Culhane 16/1:
1022 **Cacophony** 155 [12] 3-8-11 Dean McKeown 16/1:
15 ran Time 2m 28.10 (6.8) (Paul Stringer) R Brotherton Elmley Castle, Worcs

---

4151 **2.25 CLAIMER DIV II 3YO+ 0-60 (F)** **1m3f aw** **Going 39 +07 Fast**
£1830 £523 £261 3 yo rec 7 lb

3236 **SPANISH STAR** 48 [15] W Jarvis 3-8-13 K Darley 6/1: 360601: 3 b g Hernando - Desert Girl (Green 68+
Desert) Mid div, prog halfway & led over 3f out, rdn clr fnl 1f, easily: fast time: claimed by T D Barron for
£8,000: 7 week abs: earlier scored at W'hampton (mdn): promise both turf starts in '99 (rtd 77, mdn): eff at
11/12f on gd/soft & soft grnd, loves fibresand: handles any trk & runs well fresh: plenty in hand here.
2121 **SHARP STEEL** 96 [8] Miss S J Wilton 5-9-6 M Tebbutt 5/1: 212532: 5 ch g Beveled - Sharp Over 13 60a
(Night Shift) Keen, mid div, hdwy to press wnr 2f out, sn well held: op 9/1, 3 month abs: poss stays 11f.
3915 **LOVE DIAMONDS** 15 [11] N P Littmoden 4-9-8 P M Quinn (3) 5/2 FAV: 600033: 4 b g Royal Academy - 2½ 58a
Baby Diamonds (Habitat) Rear/wide, mod late hdwy: see 3915.
3050 **COLOMBE DOR** 56 [5] P C Haslam 3-8-9 P Goode (3) 12/1: 600034: Trckd ldrs 1m: op 7/1, jmps fit. 5 45a
3963 **AL MABROOK** 12 [6] 5-8-12 (bl) F Lynch 10/1: 035005: Led/dsptd lead 1m: fdd: blinks: see 270. nk 40a
2843 **RONQUISTA DOR** 66 [7] 6-9-0 (bl) R Havlin 20/1: 604006: Trckd ldrs 9f: 2 month abs: see 277. 6 33a
3868 **COLONEL CUSTER** 19 [14] 5-9-4 L Newman (3) 25/1: 406007: Rear, mod late hdwy: see 408. ¾ 36a
2816 **JIBEREEN** 67 [2] 8-9-6 R Winston 5/1: 100048: Trckd ldrs, btn 4f out: 2 month abs: see 866. 10 27a
3490 **JEWEL FIGHTER** 38 [9] 6-8-9 G Duffield 20/1: 340-09: Chsd ldrs, struggling halfway: see 3490. 8 7a
3915 **LALA SALAMA** 15 [3] 4-8-9 A Clark 6/1: -00040: Led after 1f till over 6f out, sn btn: 10th: op 4/1. 2½ 3a
3570 **MARIANA** 34 [12] 5-8-11 T G McLaughlin 33/1: 030300: Bhd 4f out: 11th: see 3247, 2381. ¾ 4a
1772 **Mikes Double** 11 [4] 6-8-10 (vis) R Fitzpatrick 33/1: 3775 **Scarlet Livery** 24 [13] 4-8-11 J McAuley 40/1:
3838 **Maybee** 21 [1] 4-8-11 Dean McKeown 20/1: 4041 **Miss Arch** 7 [10] 4-8-7 (VIS) A Culhane 33/1:
15 ran Time 2m 24.8 (3.5) (Miss V R Jarvis) W Jarvis Newmarket, Suffolk

---

4152 **3.00 EBF NOV MED AUCT STKS 2YO (E)** **1m aw rnd** **Going 39 -09 Slow**
£2886 £888 £444 £222

3990 **ACT OF REFORM** 11 [3] R Charlton 2-9-6 K Darley 6/5 JT FAV: 51431: 2 b c Lit de Justice - Bionic 85a
Soul (Bionic Light) Led, drvn/strongly pressed fnl 2f, just holding rival when jinked right cl home, gamely: bckd:
earlier scored at W'hampton (mdn): eff at 7f/1m on fibresand & fast grnd, likes a sharp track: eff forcing the pace.
*3675 **ALPHAEUS** 30 [7] Sir Mark Prescott 2-9-4 G Duffield 6/5 JT FAV: -5512: 2 b g Sillery - Aethra nk 81a
(Trempolino) Keen/cl up, drvn to chall fnl 2f, just held when slightly hmpd cl home: bckd: AW bow: well clr of
rem here: acts on fast grnd & fibresand: see 3675.
3969 **MASTER GATEMAKER** 12 [8] P W Harris 2-8-12 A Culhane 9/1: 03: 2 b c Tragic Role - Girl At The Gate 10 55a
(Formidable) Handy, outpcd over 2f out: op 25/1: AW bow: see 3969.
-- **GOLDEN NEEDLE** [6] Noel T Chance 2-8-7 R Havlin 25/1: 4: Prom 5f: Prince Of Birds filly, March 1 48a
foal, a first foal: dam a 1m/10f wnr, also a winning hdler: 1m+ will suit in time.
3953 **TUPGILL FLIGHT** 13 [5] R Winston 66/1: 00005: Towards rear, held 3f out: AW bow, mod form. 12 26a
-- **COPCOURT ROYALE** [2] 2-8-7 P Doe 66/1: 6: In tch 5f: Rock City filly, Feb foal: half sister to hd 25a
sev wnrs: dam a 1m wnr: with D J G Murray Smith.
4001 **COLLEGE STAR** 10 [4] 2-8-12 V Halliday 33/1: -057: Cl up till halfway: AW bow: longer 1m trip. 7 19a
3949 **TUPGILL CENTURION** 13 [1] 2-8-12 D O'Donohoe 66/1: 458: Sn bhd: AW bow: btr 3949, 3740. 11 0a
8 ran Time 1m 43.2 (3.8) (Highclere Throughbred Racing Ltd) R Charlton Beckhampton, Wilts

---

4153 **3.35 BOOT FILLIES HCAP 3YO+ 0-70 (E)** **7f aw rnd** **Going 39 +03 Fast** **[68]**
£2954 £844 £422 3 yo rec 3 lb

3613 **MOONLIGHT SONG** 32 [8] W Jarvis 3-9-6 (63) M Tebbutt 8/1: 122201: 3 b f Mujadil - Model Show 67a
(Dominion) Chsd ldrs, drvn & styd on well to lead well inside last: earlier won here at Southwell (C/D claimer): ex-
German mdn wnr: eff over a stiff/undulating or sharp 7f: acts on fibresand, fast & gd/soft grnd: tough & consistent.
3708 **PUPPET PLAY** 29 [7] E J Alston 5-8-9 (49) W Supple 5/1: 132102: 5 ch m Broken Hearted - Fantoccini ½ 51a
(Taufan) Handy, led 3f out till well ins last, not btn far: op 4/1: nicely h'capped on sand: see 3328.
4018 **HAUNT THE ZOO** 10 [15] J L Harris 5-9-6 (60) J Bramhill 11/1: 010303: 5 b m Komaite - Merryhill ¾ 61a
Maid (M Double M) Chsd ldrs wide halfway, rdn & styd on fnl 1f: op 8/1: tricky high draw, gd effort: see 1506 (C/D).

1278

*4004 **ANGEL HILL 10** [12] K A Ryan 5-9-7 (61) F Lynch 8/1: 004014: Chsd ldrs wide, drvn/onepace fnl   hd   **61a**
2f: AW bow: acts on firm, soft & fibresand: remains in gd form: see 4004.
3825 **MUJAGEM 22** [13] 4-8-11 (51)(bl) A Culhane 14/1: 020035: Held up wide, mod late hdwy under min   2½   **46a**
press: reportedly broke a blood vessel: op 12/1: see 3825, 1303 (1m).
3770 **GENERAL KLAIRE 24** [3] 5-10-0 (68) R Winston 5/1: 400146: Sn rdn rear, late hdwy for press.   ½   **62a**
3605 **CRYSTAL LASS 32** [14] 4-9-6 (60) Dale Gibson 16/1: 050407: Chsd ldrs wide 4f: see 513.   5   **44a**
3745 **MAI TAI 26** [9] 5-9-2 (56)(vis) Kimberley Hart 14/1: 666258: Bhd, mod hdwy: see 867 (C/D).   1   **38a**
2582 **TERRA NOVA 76** [2] 3-9-8 (65) R Price 25/1: 6-3039: Mid div, btn 3f out: 11 week abs: AW bow.   4   **39a**
*3975 **PREMIUM PRINCESS 11** [4] 5-9-9 (63) K Darley 3/1 FAV: 114410: Chsd ldrs 4f: 10th: op 4/1:   ¾   **36a**
not handle fibresand? much btr 3975 (turf).
3762 **BELINDA 25** [1] 3-9-6 (63) J Bosley (7) 20/1: 100300: Dwelt, al rear: 11th: btr 2945, 1977.   1   **34a**
3328 **Mother Corrigan 44** [6] 4-8-8 (48)(vis) D Mernagh (3) 40/1:
3780 **Boadicea The Red 24** [10] 3-9-8 (65) Dean McKeown 14/1:
4023 **Dahlidya 10** [16] 5-9-9 (63) P Doe 16/1:   3975 **Hoxton Square 11** [5] 3-8-10 (53) T G McLaughlin 25/1:
15 ran   Time 1m 29.10 (2.5)   (Rams Racing Club)   W Jarvis Newmarket, Suffolk

---

4154   **4.10 BET DIRECT SELLER 2YO (G)**   7f aw rnd   Going 39   -21 Slow
        £1932   £552   £276

3830 **SHEER FOCUS 21** [2] B W Hills 2-8-11 (t) G Duffield 3/1: 050601: 2 b c Eagle Eyed - Persian Danser   **71a**
(Persian Bold) Trkd ldrs, led over 2f out, pulled clr under hands & heels riding fnl 1f, eased down nr fin, comfortably:
val for 10L+: bought by E Alston for 8,500gns: op 9/4: first win on AW bow: eff at 7f on fibresand: eff in a t-strap:
apprec this drop to sell grade: should win again on sand on this evidence.
3969 **CALIBAN 12** [16] N P Littmoden 2-8-11 K Darley 11/2: 0502: 2 ch g Rainbows For Life - Amour   7   **55+**
Toujours (Law Society) Slowly away, bhd/wide, rdn & styd on well fnl 2f, no dnfr with wnr: AW bow: closer without
tricky high draw: prob handles fibresand: caught a tartar in this grade, could find similar: see 3385.
3837 **SUGAR ROLO 21** [14] D Morris 2-8-6 R Winston 16/1: 65403: 2 b f Bin Ajwaad - Spriolo (Priolo)   ¾   **49a**
Outpcd, hdwy 3f out, nvr threat: op 12/1: not disgraced from high draw: prob handles fast & fibresand.
4063 **MENAS ERN 6** [12] S Dow 2-8-11 P Doe 33/1: 0004: Prom, onepce/held fnl 2f: quick reapp: AW bow.   ¾   **53a**
1304 **WORTH A RING 134** [15] 2-8-6 D O'Donohoe 14/1: 05: Rear/rdn, mod hdwy: op 12/1, 5 month abs.   2½   **43a**
3911 **MR UPHILL 15** [9] 2-8-11 (VIS) M Tebbutt 33/1: 06: Led till over 2f out, sn btn: visor: longer 7f trip.   1¾   **45a**
3837 **PELLI 21** [13] 2-8-6 N Callan 20/1: 003007: Bhd, mod hdwy: AW bow: see 2898.   1¼   **37a**
3952 **THE MERRY WIDOW 13** [11] 2-8-6 W Supple 25/1: 0008: Prom, btn 2f out.   1   **35a**
3812 **GORDONS FRIEND 23** [4] 2-8-11 J Bramhill 33/1: -6009: Mid div, btn 3f out: see 3438.   1   **38a**
3957 **CO DOT UK 12** [1] 2-9-2 F Lynch 3/8 FAV: 345020: Dwelt, mod hdwy: 10th: bckd: btr 3957.   1½   **40a**
1602 **Divebomb 118** [8] 2-8-6 S Carson (3) 20/1:   2841 **Only When Provoked 66** [7] 2-8-11 R Havlin 50/1:
2949 **Sweet Veleta 60** [10] 2-8-6 D Mernagh (3) 14/1:   3867 **Greenlees 19** [5] 2-8-6 P Fitzsimons (5) 33/1:
4025 **Mr Tod 10** [6] 2-8-11 Dean McKeown 25/1:
15 ran   Time 1m 30.8 (4.2)   (R J Arculli)   B W Hills Lambourn, Berks

---

4155   **4.40 BET HCAP DIV I 3YO+ 0-60 (F)**   6f aw rnd   Going 39   -26 Slow   [59]
        £2016   £576   £288   3 yo rec 2 lb

4107 **MARENGO 3** [14] M J Polglase 6-9-7 (52) P Doe 9/1: 650001: 6 b g Never So Bold - Born To Dance   **57a**
(Dancing Brave) Held up, prog halfway & led inside last, styd on well, rdn out: op 12/1: qck reapp: earlier
scored at Doncaster (claimer, rtd 60): '99 wnr at Southwell, W'hampton, Epsom (h,caps, rtd 69a & 68) & Southwell
again (J Akehurst, h'cap): all wins at 6f, tried 7f: acts on firm, soft & fibresand: likes Southwell.
4065 **MUTASAWWAR 6** [1] J M Bradley 6-9-10 (55) K Darley 100/30 FAV: 400222: 6 ch g Clantime - Keen   1   **56a**
Melody (Sharpen Up) Chsd ldrs, rdn/ev ch fnl 1f, just held nr fin: nicely bckd: quick reapp: see 4065, 1508.
4023 **RUDE AWAKENING 10** [10] C W Fairhurst 6-10-0 (59) P Goode 8/1: 520403: 6 b g Rudimentary -   nk   **59a**
Final Call (Town Crier) Chsd ldrs, drvn & styd on fnl 1f, not pce of wnr: op 7/1: see 2743.
3975 **MORGAN LE FAY 11** [16] Don Enrico Incisa 5-9-12 (57) Kim Tinkler 20/1: -10054: Mid div/wide,   hd   **56a**
rdn & styd on strongly fnl 1f, nrst fin: fine AW bow: acts on firm, soft & fibresand: gd run from high draw.
3770 **FEATHERSTONE LANE 24** [6] 9-9-8 (53) M Tebbutt 12/1: 363435: Rear, late hdwy, no threat: op 10/1.   ¾   **50a**
3855 **TANCRED TIMES 20** [8] 5-9-2 (47) Kimberley Hart 8/1: 552606: Led till ins last, no extra: see 2395.   nk   **43a**
3605 **GRAND ESTATE 32** [2] 5-9-0 (45) A Culhane 5/1: 034007: In tch, btn fnl 1f: op 4/1: see 614.   2½   **34a**
3271 **JACK TO A KING 46** [13] 6-9-13 (58)(bl) P Fitzsimons (5) 16/1: 000008: Held up, nvr factor: abs.   2   **42a**
1600 **CHILI PEPPER 118** [12] 3-9-11 (58) K Hodgson 20/1: 610309: Al outpcd: abs: btr 1390, 706.   5   **33a**
3578 **PETITE DANSEUSE 34** [13] 6-9-1 (46) Claire Bryan (5) 14/1: 254600: Held up, btn 2f out: 10th: op 12/1.   1   **19a**
*3964 **KOSEVO 12** [7] 6-9-2 (47)(bl) N Callan 7/1: 000610: Held up, eased halfway: 15th: something amiss?   **0a**
3921 **Press Ahead 14** [11] 5-9-3 (48)(vis) Dean McKeown 20/1: 2779 **Pape Diouf 68** [5] 3-9-9 (56) T Williams 16/1:
2183 **Ejder 93** [15] 4-9-2 (47) S Carson (3) 50/1:   2732 **Dance Little Lady 70** [3] 3-9-7 (54) G Parkin 12/1:
15 ran   Time 1m 17.2 (3.9)   (Brian Androlia)   M J Polglase Southwell, Notts

---

4156   **5.10 BET HCAP DIV II 3YO+ 0-60 (F)**   6f aw rnd   Going 39   -14 Slow   [59]
        £2016   £576   £288   3 yo rec 2 lb

3966 **PALO BLANCO 12** [5] Andrew Reid 9-9-2 (47) L Newman (3) 8/1: 204401: 9 b m Precocious - Linpac   **53a**
Mapleleaf (Dominion) Chsd ldrs, rdn/led inside last, styd on well, rdn out: op 12/1: no form sole '99 start: plcd
sev times in '98 (rtd 65a & 61, G Moore & R Ryan): '97 Sandown scorer (claimer, rtd 70): eff at 5/7f on firm, gd/soft
& both AWs: handles a sharp or stiff track: has slipped down the weights.
3964 **BANGLED 12** [14] D J Coakley 3-9-0 (47) P Doe 8/1: 003042: 3 ch g Beveled - Bangles (Chilibang)   1¼   **48a**
Handy, led over 2f out till inside last, held nr fin: op 10/1: see 3964, 1494.
3113 **AJNAD 53** [13] R F Marvin 6-9-13 (58) P McCabe 16/1: 660403: 6 b g Efisio - Lotte Lenta (Gorytus)   2   **54a**
Rear, prog to chase ldrs over 1f out, held inside last: op 12/1, 8 week abs: 1 win in 35 starts: see 282.
2415 **THATCHAM 83** [10] R W Armstrong 4-9-7 (52)(bl) R Price 11/2: 041234: Prom, onepce fnl 2f: abs: 1   **46a**
acts on fast, gd/soft & both AWs: see 1953.
3825 **LEAPING CHARLIE 22** [11] 4-9-12 (57) G Duffield 16/1: 020-05: Chsd ldrs, onepce fnl 2f: AW bow: hd   **50a**
'99 Hamilton scorer (h'cap, rtd 61): plcd in '98 (rtd 69, auction mdn): eff at 5f, 6f should suit: acts on fast &
gd/soft grnd, prob handles fibresand: handles a sharp or stiff/undulating track.
3271 **SAMWAR 46** [6] 8-9-12 (57)(vis) R Fitzpatrick 8/1: 256326: Outpcd early, mod hdwy: 6 week abs.   hd   **49a**
3271 **PALVIC LADY 46** [15] 4-9-2 (47) J Stack 25/1: 0-0007: Cl up 4f: 6 week abs: see 3271.   ¾   **37a**
3816 **SKY HOOK 22** [8] 3-9-0 (47)(vis) S W Kelly (3) 20/1: -50008: Chsd ldrs till over 1f out: see 3816.   ½   **35a**

```
4102  TREASURE TOUCH 4 [7] 6-9-7 (52) K Darley 2/1 FAV: 240409: Sn outpcd: bckd: qck reapp.          1¾   36a
3781  BEST BOND 24 [1] 3-9-8 (55)(vis) S Carson (3) 14/1: 063060: Dwelt, nvr on terms: 10th: op 8/1.   hd   38a
3516  SIRENE 37 [2] 3-9-9 (56)(bl) T G McLaughlin 14/1: 035000: Led till over 2f out, sn btn: 15th: op 10/1.  0a
4004  Printsmith 10 [16] 3-9-4 (51) G Bardwell 25/1:          3269 Aljazir 47 [4] 3-9-5 (52) W Supple 20/1:
3180  Bold Aristocrat 50 [3] 9-9-1 (46) P M Quinn (3) 14/1:   4045 Aisle 7 [12] 3-9-10 (57)(tbl) Dean McKeown 20/1:
1072  Indiana Jones 148 [9] 3-9-3 (50) A Culhane 33/1:
16 ran      Time 1m 16.5 (3.2)        (A S Reid)        Andrew Reid Mill Hill, London NW7
```

Official Going   GOOD TO SOFT. Stalls: Far Side.

4157

1.05 JERSEY NURSERY HCAP 2YO (B)   7f str   Good 40   -12 Slow   [103]
£20800   £6400   £3200   £1600 Raced far side

```
*3985  PALATIAL 11 [16] J R Fanshawe 2-9-0 (89) D Harrison 7/1 JT FAV: 222111: 2 b f Green Desert - White          94
Palace (Shirley Heights) Dwelt but sn trckd ldrs, qcknd to lead appr fnl 1f & sn clr, drvn inside last, kept on
well: bckd: hat-trick landed after wins here at Newmarket (nursery) & Newbury (cond stks): eff at 6f, suited by
7f: acts on firm & gd grnd, stiff/gall tracks, likes Newmarket: progressive, tough & useful, has a turn of foot.
*3953  LOVE EVERLASTING 13 [7] M Johnston 2-8-13 (88) D Holland 7/1 JT FAV: -34212: 2 b f Pursuit Of        ½   91
Love - In Perpetuity (Great Nephew) Midfield, pushed along & hdwy to chall appr fnl 2f, sn outpcd by wnr,
rallied well towards fin: nicely bckd: fine run: improving, win again at 1m: see 3953.
3955  BOUCHRA 13 [12] M L W Bell 2-7-10 (71)(1oh) J Mackay (5) 25/1: -2203: 2 ch f Inchinor - My          hd   74
Darlingdaughter (Night Shift) Chsd ldrs, prog to go after wnr appr fnl 1f, kept on: sound h'cap bow
& clearly suited by return to 7f: acts on fast & gd grnd & should break her duck sn: see 3635.
3748  ROOFER 26 [8] M R Channon 2-8-4 (79) Craig Williams 25/1: 5424: Chsd ldrs, eff 2f out, styd          nk   81
on well inside last, nvr nrr: improved on h'cap bow: acts on firm & gd grnd, 1m will suit now.
-3867  DUBAI SEVEN STARS 19 [17] 2-8-9 (84) M Roberts 8/1: 45225: Bhd, shaken up 2f out, styd on        ½   84
over 1f out despite short of room dist:  gd run: will apprec a return to 1m & a stronger ride: see 3867, 3577.
*4076  MONICA GELLER 5 [10] 2-7-10 (71)(6ex)(5oh) T Hamilton (7) 16/1: 036216: Dwelt & rear, prog        ½   70
on outer appr fnl 1f, nvr nr to chall: op 12/1: quick reapp & pen: in gd form, return to 1m will suit: see 4076.
3991  FOREVER TIMES 11 [4] 2-8-1 (76) K Dalgleish (5) 16/1: 210337: Mid div, prog to chase ldrs          1¾   71
2f out, onepce fnl 1f: not disgraced but is prob just better at 6f, see 3860, 3346.
3910  BOGUS PENNY 15 [6] 2-8-4 (79) B Marcus 14/1: 4228: Cl up, led halfway till appr fnl 1f, no extra.   shd   74
*3962  SALTWOOD 12 [11] 2-8-3 (78) G Carter 7/1: -0419: Rear, rdn 2f out, no impress till ran on well fnl  shd   72
200y: h'cap bow, crying out for further, well worth another chance: see 3962.
3860  BECKY SIMMONS 20 [14] 2-8-10 (85) W Ryan 20/1: 111500: Rear, wide, mod late hdwy: 10th, see 3327.nk   78
3860  INJAAZ 20 [13] 2-8-8 (83) L Dettori 12/1: 01200: Steadied start, prog appr fnl 2f, fdd inside last: 11th.  ½   75
2583  EARLY WISH 76 [1] 2-8-1 (76) A Beech (3) 20/1: -6330: Prom, outpcd halfway, mid div after: 12th.  shd   68
3860  SYLVAN GIRL 20 [9] 2-7-10 (71)(5oh) Joanna Badger (7) 40/1: 530400: Mid div, drvn to chase ldrs    ½   61
appr fnl 1f, sn no impress: 13th, stiffish task, up in trip, see 1954.
3913  NUN LEFT 15 [1] 2-8-5 (80) S Carson (3) 20/1: 242120: Chsd ldrs on outer for 4f: 14th, tricky draw in 1.  hd   69
3630  MIDNIGHT ARROW 31 [21] 2-8-8 (83) Martin Dwyer 33/1: 500400: Trckd ldrs, lost pl 2f out: 15th.   ¾   70
3882  CELTIC ISLAND 18 [2] 2-9-7 (95) A Daly 16/1: 201400: Sn led, hdd over 3f out, fdd: 16th, h'cap bow.   ½   81
3860  KOMENA 20 [18] 2-8-12 (87) T Quinn 10/1: 42140: Early ldr, cl up till wknd appr fnl 2f: last, something amiss?   0
3922  Church Belle 14 [5] 2-7-10 (71)(t)(11oh) D Kinsella (7) 66/13327 Franica 44 [3] 2-8-2 (77) Claire Bryan (5) 33/1:
4030  Divine Wind 8 [15] 2-7-10 (71)(5oh) G Baker (5) 16/1: 3659 Trillie 30 [20] 2-9-2 (91) M J Kinane 20/1:
3901  Aker Wood 17 [22] 2-8-7 (82) J Quinn 33/1:
22 ran      Time 1m 26.89 (3.69)        (Cheveley Park Stud)        J R Fanshawe Newmarket, Suffolk
```

4158

1.35 TATTS HOUGHTON STAKES 2YO (B)   7f str   Good 40   -02 Slow
£229200   £113600   £54800   £22920 Raced in 2 Groups

```
*2407  MOZART 86 [2] A P O'Brien 2-9-0 M J Kinane 11/10 FAV: 11: 2 b c Danehill - Victoria Cross          112
(Spectacular Bid) Led centre group, rdn to lead overall inside last, ran on strongly, rdn out: hvly bckd Irish
raider, 12 wk abs: earlier made a wng debut at The Curragh (mdn, by 8L): 340,000gns half-brother to wnrs in the
US: eff at 7f, will get 1m: acts on gd grnd, stiff/gall trks: smart & improving, looks well up to Gr class.
--     PRETTY GIRL [8] Wido Neuroth Norway 2-8-9 E Ahern 25/1: 11112: 2 ch f Polish Precedent - Petal    1   104
Girl (Caerleon) Trckd far side ldrs qcknd to lead appr fnl 1f, hdd ins last, kept on for press: tchd 33/1:
Norwegian raider, won 4 prev starts: 120,000gns half-sister to v smart mid-dist performer Mutamam, dam a miler:
eff at 6/7f, 1m will suit: acts on gd & soft grnd, prob any track: useful & was clr of rem on the far side.
3688  COUNT DUBOIS 29 [1] W J Haggas 2-9-0 (VIS) B Marcus 20/1: 123: 2 b c Zafonic - Madame Dubois    hd   108
(Legend Of France) Chsd ldrs in centre, chsd wnr appr fnl 1f, kept on under press despite lugging right:
clr of rest & this was a v useful run with visor applied: 1m should suit next term, see 3688, 3478.
3891  TORTUGUERO 18 [11] B W Hills 2-9-0 M Hills 16/1: 124404: Overall ldr far side till appr fnl 1f, onepce.  3½   101
3840  BEEKEEPER 21 [15] 2-9-0 J Murtagh 16/1: 55: Towards rear, shaken up halfway, kept on nicely        1¾   97
inside last, nvr nr to chall: tchd 20/1: highly tried mdn, sure to win a race at 1m+ & shld have a bright future.
2613  EARL GREY 75 [19] 2-9-0 L Dettori 16/1: 1466: Mid div, rdn 2f out, kept on same pace: op 12/1, abs.   2   93
3965  DRESS CODE 12 [4] 2-8-9 J Carroll 50/1: 310047: In tch centre outpcd appr fnl 1f: stiffish task.   shd   88
--     QUEENIE [3] 2-8-9 R Hills 33/1: 8: In tch centre, no extra appr fnl 1f: highly tried on debut:     ½   86
30,000gns Indian Ridge filly, dam 10f wnr: with B Hills.
--     RANDOM QUEST 16 [16] 2-9-0 J Fortune 20/1: 9: Slow away & well off the pace far side till kept   shd   91+
on strongly inside last: debut: 90,000gns Rainbow Quest colt, half brother to a 13f wnr, dam 1m/10f wnr:
bred to relish mid dists & one to keep an eye on next term over further.
3969  AZKABAN 12 [10] 2-9-0 D R McCabe 33/1: -3250: Nvr better than mid div: 10th, stiffish task.        shd   90
--     HEAVENLY WHISPER [21] 2-8-9 M Fenton 33/1: 0: Al around same pl: 11th on debut: 55,000gns        ½   84
Halling half sister to a decent German sprinter: with M Bell.
3985  ANNATTO 11 [5] 2-8-9 W Ryan 50/1: -24230: Nvr a factor in centre: 12th, stiff task, see 3985, 3333.   nk   83
3829  TARA GOLD 21 [20] 2-8-9 R Hughes 33/1: -4340: Chsd ldrs, fdd ent fnl 2f: 13th, stiff task, mdn.   nk   82
*3583  BREAKFAST BAY 33 [27] 2-8-9 S Sanders 25/1: 310: With ldrs till wknd 2f out: 14th, stiff task     1   80
tho' hails from last season's winning stable: see 3583.
```

3704　**CEZZARO** 29 [14] 2-9-0 (VIS) Martin Dwyer 50/1: -50300: Same pl throughout, 15th, visored maiden.　¾　83

--　**JALOUSIE** [9] 2-8-9 N Callan 50/1: 0: Nvr a factor: 16th on debut: 50,000gns Baratinea　2　74
half sister to 3 juv wnrs up to 1m, dam 6f juv wnr: with S Woods.

3864　**PERSIAN PRIDE** 20 [26] 2-9-0 T Quinn 25/1: -0420: Chsd ldrs, wknd appr fnl 1f: 17th: much btr 3864.　1¼　76

3537　**EMINENCE** 35 [17] 2-9-0 Pat Eddery 9/4: 32R: Refused to race, disapp: well bckd: see 3537, 3162.　　0

3953　**Shaanara** 13 [7] 2-8-9 P Fessey 66/1:　　3608　**Woodfield** 32 [25] 2-9-0 P Robinson 50/1:
3704　**Dance On The Top** 29 [6] 2-9-0 J Reid 25/1:　　3940　**Amir Zaman** 13 [23] 2-9-0 A McGlone 66/1:
3980　**Forest Light** 11 [18] 2-8-9 R Mullen 50/1:　　3940　**Pentland** 13 [24] 2-9-0 M Roberts 33/1:
3799　**Kut O Island** 23 [22] 2-9-0 (t) J Quinn 50/1:　　1691　**Carraca** 115 [12] 2-9-0 D Harrison 66/1:
26 ran　　Time 1m 26.15 (8.2)　　(Mr M Tabor & Mrs John Magnier)　　A P O'Brien Ballydoyle, Co Tipperary

---

4159　2.05 GR 1 CHEVELEY PARK STKS 2YO (A)　6f　Good 40 -09 Slow
£75400　£28600　£14300　£6500

*2952　**REGAL ROSE** 60 [2] Sir Michael Stoute 2-8-11 L Dettori 11/2: 11: 2 b f Danehill - Ruthless Rose　114
(Conquistador Cielo) Keen, mid div, closed appr fnl 2f, ran on to lead ent fnl 1f, drvn out: op 9/2, abs: earlier
made a winning debut at Ascot (mdn, in season): half-sister to a couple of juv wnrs: eff at 6f, shld stay 7f/1m:
acts on fast, gd & stiff/gall tracks: runs well fresh: smart, unbeaten & highly regarded filly.

--　**TOROCA** [6] A P O'Brien 2-8-11 Paul Scallan 66/1: 362: 2 ch f Nureyev - Grand Falls (Ogygian)　1　109
Led till 1f out, kept on under press: biggest priced of the 3 O'Brien rnrs: well btn both prev starts, incl
in a Listed: $350,000 sister to a fair 6/7f juv: eff forcing the pace at 6f on gd grnd: must win a Gr race.

3845　**MALA MALA** 23 [7] T Stack 2-8-11 W J O'Connor 25/1: -533: 2 b f Brief Truce - Breyani　nk　108
(Commanche Run) Towards rear, feeling pace 2f out, ran on best of all ins last to grab 3rd nr line: Irish
raider, half-sister to high class miler Tarascon, dam won over 2m: already looks in need of 1m: acts on
fast & gd grnd: type to rate higher & win Gr races over further.

3596　**AUTUMNAL** 33 [1] B J Meehan 2-8-11 Pat Eddery 25/1: 311234: Well plcd, rdn to chall appr fnl　nk　107
1f, same pace towards lip: gd run from this useful filly, who ran back in Listed/Gr 3 comp, see 3596, 2152.

*3845　**SEQUOYAH** 23 [8] 2-8-11 M J Kinane 7/1: -31215: Bhd ldrs, eff & ev ch appr fnl 1f, onepce: op 11/2:　hd　106
better priced of the 3 O'Brien rnrs & was poss unsuited by drop bck in trip: see 3845 (7f, fast, beat this 3rd).

*3596　**ENTHUSED** 33 [4] 2-8-11 J Murtagh 11/8 FAV: -12116: Pld hard towards rear, unable to pick up when　1　103
pace qcknd appr fnl 1f, styg on fin: hvly bckd stablemate of wnr: no sign of the turn of foot she displayed
in 3596 (firm) on this easier grnd: worth another chance tho' trainer feels she is over the top: see 3583.

+3797　**SANTOLINA** 23 [10] 2-8-11 J Fortune 10/1: -12417: Chsd ldrs, outpcd fnl 1f: stiff task, not disgraced.　¾　100

2152　**DIETRICH** 95 [13] 2-8-11 R Hughes 40/1: 248: Waited with, eff & hdwy appr fnl 1f, fdd dist:　½　98
stiff task, stablemate 2nd, 9 week abs: wnr at Tipperary in July: eff at 5f on fast & soft grnd.

--　**SUNSETTER** [5] 2-8-11 D Holland 50/1: 9: Cl up, losing pl when short of room dist: v highly tried on　¾　95
debut: 250,000gns Diesis half-sister to 2 wnrs, dam useful in the States: gd run, mdn looks formality.

*3719　**LADY LAHAR** 31 [3] 2-8-11 Craig Williams 14/1: 13410: Al bhd tho' staying on fin: 10th: unsuited　nk　94
by drop bck to 6f: see 3719, (7f, the 3rd has since won a Gr3).

3843　**RACINA** 27 [11] 2-8-11 M Hills 50/1: 2130: Nvr troubled ldrs: 11th, stiff task up in trip, see 3408.　1¼　90

3862　**FINAL PURSUIT** 20 [12] 2-8-11 D Harrison 50/1: 01000: Nvr dngrs: 12th, highly tried: see 1667.　¾　87

3596　**KHULAN** 33 [9] 2-8-11 R Hills 9/2: 120: Pld hard bhd ldrs, not much room 2f out, sn btn: 13th, bckd from ¾　84
11/2: easier grnd & pulled too hard: highly regarded by stable, see 3596, 2618.
13 ran　　Time 1m 13.75 (2.95)　　(Cheveley Park Stud)　　Sir Michael Stoute Newmarket, Suffolk

---

4160　2.40 CHOKE JADE APPR HCAP 3YO+ 0-85 (E)　1m2f　Good 40 -12 Slow　[82]
£5086　£1565　£782　£391　3 yo rec 6 lb　Raced far side

3941　**JULIUS** 13 [5] M Johnston 3-9-11 (85) K Dalgleish 12/1: 104051: 3 b f Persian Bold - Babushka　90
(Dance Of Life) Handy, qcknd to lead 3f out, held on well under press: earlier won at Nottingham (stakes),
Musselburgh (h'cap), Ripon (stakes), Chester (fill h'cap) & Newcastle (stakes): ex-Irish: eff at 10/12f: acts
on firm, gd grnd, prob any track: can force the pace/come from bhd: v tough & progressive filly.

2755　**FOREST HEATH** 69 [7] H J Collingridge 3-9-4 (78) Jonjo Fowle (3) 16/1: 0-2122: 3 gr g Common　hd　82
Grounds - Caroline Lady (Caro) Towards rear, prog appr fnl 1f, chsd wnr inside last, strong chall
100y, held nr fin: 10 week abs: cracking run from this progressive gelding: see 2755, 2308.

3750　**MADAM ALISON** 26 [13] R Hannon 4-10-0 (82) R Smith (3) 20/1: 131503: 4 b f Puissance - Copper　1　84
Burn (Electric) Held up, prog appr fnl 2f, chsd front 2 inside last, onepce: op 16/1, fnd easier grnd: stays 10f.

*3941　**LYCIAN** 13 [4] J A R Toller 5-8-10 (64) P Dobbs 11/2 JT FAV: 340114: Towards rear, prog 2f out,　2½　62
rdn 1f out, not pace to chall: in gd form, see 3941.

3410　**NORCROFT JOY** 40 [14] 5-9-5 (73) P Hanagan (3) 25/1: 310455: Mid div, shaken up 3f out, outpcd　2　68
till kept on towards fin: 6 wk abs: not disgraced bck at 10f but sure to apprec return to 12f+: see 2482.

1875　**GYPSY 106** [10] 4-8-11 (65) S Finnamore (3) 16/1: 443056: Held up, mod late hdwy: 15 week abs.　nk　59

*4085　**ANNADAWI** 5 [2] 5-8-1 (55)(6ex) C Catlin (3) 11/2 JT FAV: 363317: Held up, wide, prog to chase ldrs　hd　49
2f out, sn no impress: bckd: too soon under a pen after 4085 (soft grnd, 29lbs o/h)?

3811　**ANGUS G** 23 [17] 8-9-0 (68) T Eaves 25/1: 5-0008: Chsd ldrs, fdd appr fnl 1f: tchd 50/1, bck in trip.　1¼　60

4224}　**ASPIRANT DANCER** 358 [8] 5-9-3 (71) J Mackay 16/1: 3016-9: Waited with, short of room appr fnl　shd　63+
2f, styd on into mid div: running a hard time on reapp: 99/00 hdles wnr at M Rasen (2m3f mdn, gd & soft,
forcing the pace, rtd 115h, Mrs Wadham): '99 wnr at Pontefract (3, h'cap & 2 class stks, rtd 72, current
trainer): '98 wnr at Southwell, Folkestone & Haydock (h'caps, rtd 72 & 70a): eff at 12f, suited by 10f:
acts on firm, hvy grnd & fibresand: can go well fresh & force the pace: spot on next time.

4003　**BLUE STREET** 10 [11] 4-7-12 (52) Joanna Badger (3) 12/1: 231600: Nvr a factor: 10th, back in trip.　½　43

3794　**BELLA BELLISIMO** 24 [19] 3-8-11 (71) I Mongan 8/1: 006040: Al towards rear: 11th, op 10/1, bckd 874.　3　57

3530　**NEW FORTUNE** 36 [15] 3-7-12 (58) G Baker 25/1: 0-0400: Al bhd: 12th: mdn see 1725.　½　43

2955　**NEVER DISS MISS** 60 [12] 3-9-1 (75) Darren Williams (3) 12/1: 513250: Prom, fdd 2f out: 13th, abs.　6　52

3643　**LOVE YOU TOO** 31 [6] 3-9-1 (75) N Esler (5) 40/1: 040500: Nvr troubled ldrs: 14th: see 1186.　1¼　50

3339　**CHIEF CASHIER** 44 [16] 5-9-11 (79) F Keniry 16/1: 014600: Chsd ldrs till 3f out: 15th, 6 week abs.　½　53

3989　**SOUTH SEA PEARL** 11 [1] 3-8-9 (69) R Cody Boutcher (3) 20/1: Led till 3f out: 17th: btr 3701, 3416.　　0

*3979　**CALLDAT SEVENTEEN** 11 [3] 4-9-6 (74)(t) A Beech 13/2: 06001R: Went badly left start & refused　　0
to race: bckd: see 3979 (soft class stakes).

3899　**Open Arms** 17 [20] 4-8-11 (65) G Sparkes (3) 25/1:
4003　**Julia Titus** 10 [18] 3-7-10 (56)(2oh) Michael Doyle (5) 50/1:
19 ran　　Time 2m 07.26 (5.16)　　(Mrs K E Daley)　　M Johnston Middleham, N Yorks

4161

3.10 SOLTYKOFF MDN 2YO (D)　　1m str　　Good 40　-09 Slow
£5707　£1756　£878　£439　Raced far side

3983 **TAMBURLAINE** 11 [12] R Hannon 2-8-11 R Hughes 13/8 FAV: -221: 2 b c Royal Academy - Well Bought 　　106
(Auction Ring) Nvr far away, led ent fnl 3f, & easily qcknd clr, impressive: well bckd: 110,000gns colt: eff
at 1m, 10f sure to suit: goes on firm & gd grnd, prob any trk: v useful, improved today & looks Gr class.

-- **PAINTED ROOM** [8] H R A Cecil 2-8-11 T Quinn 9/4: 2: 2 ch c Woodman - All At Sea (Riverman)　　6　93
Keen, trkd ldrs, eff to chase wnr appr fnl 1f, onepce: nicely bckd/cght a tartar on debut: half brother to a couple
of useful 6f/1m performers: dam high-class over 10/12f: eff at 1m, further suit: sure to find a maiden.

3864 **DAWARI** 20 [5] Sir Michael Stoute 2-8-11 J Murtagh 10/1: 03: 2 b c In The Wings - Dawala　　½　92
(Lashkari) In tch, eff appr fnl 1f, onepce till styd on well towards fin: tchd 14/1: already crying for 10f+, improve.

-- **STERLING GUARANTEE** [7] J H M Gosden 2-8-11 J Fortune 12/1: 4: Held up, went past btn horses　　2　88
appr fnl 1f: op 12/1: $120,000 Silver Hawk May foal, half brother to a juv wnr in the States, dam useful: apprec 10f.

-- **MILLENNIUM CADEAUX** [11] 2-8-11 J Reid 20/1: 5: Mid div, feeling pace halfway, kept on towards　　3　82
fin: debut: 32,000gns Cadeaux Genereux March foal, dam & half brother won abroad: gd start.

-- **MUNADIL** [13] 2-8-11 R Hills 12/1: 6: Mid div, not much room ent fnl 2f, sn onepce: debut:　　½　81+
Nashwan Feb foal, dam a miler: looks capable of better, will improve over further in time.

-- **LAZEEM** [9] 2-8-11 G Carter 33/1: 7: Cl up, fdd appr fnl 1f: debut: $45,000 Tabasco Cat　　shd　81
first foal, dam useful miler in the States: sire top class dirt performer at 1m/12f: with E Dunlop.

3906 **PRIZE DANCER** 17 [2] 2-8-11 Pat Eddery 14/1: 048: Led till 3f out, wknd: needs h'caps.　　hd　80$

3298 **LAMBAY RULES** 46 [4] 2-8-11 S Whitworth 40/1: 09: Cl-up till halfway: see 3298.　　5　70

-- **ART EXPERT** [14] 2-8-11 D Holland 25/1: 0: Chsd ldrs, lost pl 2f out: 10th, debut:　　1¼　67
32,000gns Pursuit Of Love March foal, dam unrcd: with P Cole.

-- **BOY BAND** [10] 2-8-11 Craig Williams 25/1: 0: Dwelt, al bhd: 11th: 30,000Ir gns Desert Style,　　4　59
half brother to smart sprinter Mitcham, dam unrcd: sprint bred: with M Channon.

3223 **LEATHERBACK** 48 [6] 2-8-11 Paul Eddery 66/1: 0000: Nvr a factor: 12th: 7 week abs, stiff task.　　nk　58

-- **RANVILLE** [3] 2-8-11 P Robinson 25/1: 0: Slow away, nvr in it: 13th: 15,000gns Deploy　　nk　57
half brother to 7f/12f wnr Colleville: stoutly bred, with M Jarvis.

3909 **NEEDWOOD BRAVE** 15 [1] 2-8-11 S Sanders 66/1: 000: In tch wide till appr fnl 2f: 14th, stiff task.　　½　56

-- **RIPCORD** [15] 2-8-11 L Dettori 10/1: 0: Chsd ldrs 4f: 15th, op 6/1: 1,000,000 Ffr　　¾　54
Diesis half brother to 2 wnrs, dam 6f wnr: with J Gosden.

15 ran　　Time 1m 40.44 (3.94)　　(Jeffen Racing)　　R Hannon East Everleigh, Wilts

4162

3.45 NGK PLUGS RTD HCAP 3YO+ 0-100 (B)　　1m4f　　Good 40　+10 Fast　　[104]
£9625　£3651　£1825　£829　3 yo rec 8 lb

4128 **FLOSSY** 2 [3] C W Thornton 4-8-13 (89) D Holland 8/1: 102331: 4 b f Efisio - Sirene Bleu Marine　　95
(Secreto) Confidently held up, closed on bit appr fnl 3f, led bef dist, ran on strongly: fast time, unlucky 48 hrs
ago: earlier won at Chester (h'cap): '99 wnr at Beverley, Musselburgh, Newbury, Ripon (subs disq), Newcastle,
Haydock & Doncaster (November h'cap, rtd 88): eff at 12f, stys 13f: acts on any grnd/track: needs to come with
a late run: should give a good account in defence of the November h'cap.

3896 **ORMELIE** 17 [5] J H M Gosden 5-9-1 (91)(BL) J Fortune 20/1: 053302: 5 b h Jade Hunter - Trolley　　½　95
Song (Caro) Patiently rdn, prog 3f out, ran on to press wnr inside last, kept on but held: back to form
in blinkers: eff at 10/12f, stys 13f: see 2707.

3918 **BE THANKFULL** 14 [11] Major D N Chappell 4-9-2 (92) S Sanders 50/1: -53603: 4 gr f Linamix - Thank　　2½　93
One's Stars (Alzao) Chsd ldrs, hdwy & ev ch ent fnl 2f, onepce inside last: ran to best bck up in trip, stiff 12f.

*3811 **SHARP STEPPER** 23 [7] J H M Gosden 4-8-10 (86) L Dettori 3/1 FAV: -36214: Mid div, rdn 3f out,　　2½　84
styd on but nvr pce to chall: well bckd stablemate of 2nd, tchd 5/1: return to 14f will suit: see 3811.

*4039 **ZILARATOR** 8 [2] 4-9-3 (93)(3ex) B Marcus 5/1: -61615: Held up, niggled 4f out, late hdwy, nvr dngrs:　　nk　90
nicely bckd, tchd 6/1: poss too soon after last week's win & remains one to keep in mind on soft/hvy this autumn.

3994 **OPTIMAITE** 10 [19] 3-8-3 (87) Cheryl Nosworthy (7) 40/1: 505006: Cl up, led over 2f out till bef fnl 1f.　　¾　83

+3896 **TAKWIN** 17 [18] 3-8-13 (97) R Hills 7/1: 211017: Led/dsptd lead till wknd appr fnl 1f: capable of better.　　2　90

3918 **BALLADONIA** 14 [4] 4-9-3 (93) D Harrison 25/1: -65458: Led/dsptd lead till 4f out, no extra: see 3134.　　½　85

4013 **TISSIFER** 10 [17] 4-9-7 (97) J Carroll 25/1: 040339: Nvr a factor: top-weight, longer trip, see 1574.　　shd　89

3153 **THE WOODSTOCK LADY** 52 [16] 3-8-3 (87) R Mullen 25/1: 002400: Al mid div: 10th, back in trip.　　2　76

*3701 **SOLITARY** 29 [15] 3-8-4 (88)(bl) W Ryan 12/1: 4-2210: Nvr better than mid div: 11th, btr 3701.　　1¾　75

2202‡ **SIR ECHO** 460 [6] 4-8-9 (85) C Rutter 33/1: 4215-0: Al towards rear: 12th, reapp: '99 Newbury　　nk　71
wnr (h'cap, rtd 85): rtd 76 as a juv: eff at 12f, shld get further: acts on fast & hvy grnd, sharp or
gall track: likes to force the pace: with H Candy.

*3988 **CAROUSING** 11 [13] 3-8-6 (90)(bl) G Carter 33/1: 150010: Nvr a factor: 13th, new stable, btr 3988 (sft).　　6　70

3899 **MANTUSIS** 17 [14] 5-9-0 (90) T Quinn 20/1: 401600: Prom, wide till wknd appr fnl 2f: 14th, needs cover.　　½　69

3153 **DOLLAR BIRD** 52 [12] 3-8-12 (96) Pat Eddery 9/1: 320020: In tch till 3f out: btr 3153 (14f, firm)　　1¼　73

-- **EIGHTY TWO** [9] 4-8-11 (87) R Hughes 14/1: 2250-0: Bhd ldrs till wknd quickly 4f out:　　6　58
16th, op 10/1, reapp/Brit bow: ex-French, '99 wnr in Toulouse (10f, v soft): with S Woods.

3865 **Reflex Blue** 20 [8] 3-7-13 (83)(3oh) M Henry 25/1:　　3467 **Gold Quest** 38 [10] 3-8-1 (85) J Quinn 16/1:
18 ran　　Time 2m 32.34 (3.54)　　(Guy Reed)　　C W Thornton Coverham, N Yorks

Official Going　　SOFT Stalls: 6/7f - Stands Side, 1m - Far Side, 10f - Inside

4163

2.20 MARLBOROUGH MDN 2YO (D)　　1m str　　Good/Soft 73　-33 Slow
£4147　£1276　£638　£319　Raced both sides, far side favoured

3665 **REGATTA POINT** 31 [14] A P Jarvis 2-9-0 Pat Eddery 7/1: -021: 2 b c Goldmark - Flashing Raven　　85
(Maelstrom Lake) In tch far side, drvn/prog to lead ins last, styd on well nr fin, rdn out: 12,000 gns Feb foal:
eff at 1m, shld get further: acts on fast, improved on gd/soft: open to plenty of further improvement.

-- **RAMPANT** [15] R M Beckett 2-9-0 G Hind 20/1: 2: 2 b c Pursuit Of Love - Flourishing (Trojan Fen)　　¾　83
Chsd ldrs far side, led over 2f out & sn hard rdn, hdd ins last, held nr line: op 16/1: Mar foal, cost 40,000 gns:

half brother to useful 10f wnr Musally: dam a 7f juv wnr: eff over a stiff/gall 1m on gd/soft: can improve & win.
-- **OVAMBO** [13] P J Makin 2-9-0 D Sweeney 8/1: 3: 2 b c Namaqualand - Razana (Kahyasi) *nk* **82+**
Dwelt/bhd far side, styd on well from over 1f out, not reach front pair: op 10/1, Feb foal, cost 15,000 gns: a 1st foal: dam a 10f wnr: eff over a stiff/gall 1m, looks sure to apprec further: handles gd/soft grnd: good intro.
3867 **DARDANUS 20** [12] E A L Dunlop 2-9-0 S Sanders 50/1: 404: Bhd far side, styd on fnl 2f, no threat: *1½* **79+**
clr rem: stays a stiff/gall 1m & handles gd/soft: sure to relish h'caps & further on this evidence: improving.
3906 **SPANISH SPUR 18** [7] 2-9-0 J Fortune 4/6 FAV: 25: Led stands side, rdn/prsd overall ldr 3f out, *4* **72+**
held ins last: hvly bckd: first home on unfav stands side: handles gd & gd/soft: well worth another chance.
4035 **ARAVONIAN 9** [3] 2-8-9 R Hughes 13/2: 56: Chsd ldrs stands side, held over 1f out: see 4035. *2½* **63**
4036 **DINOFELIS 9** [18] 2-9-0 G Bardwell 66/1: 057: Chsd ldrs far side 3f out, sn held: see 4036, 3864. *2½* **64**
-- **KINGS SIGNAL** [2] 2-9-0 A Clark 50/1: 8: Chsd ldrs stands side till over 1f out: Red Ransom *3* **58**
colt, Feb foal, cost 32,000 gns: dam a 7f juv wnr: with J J Sheehan.
-- **STAR OF WONDER** [4] 2-8-9 P Fitzsimons (5) 33/1: 9: Rcd alone in centre, nvr on terms: Celtic *1½* **50**
Swing filly, Mar first foal: dam a 12f/2m wnr: looks sure to relish mid-dists in time for Lady Herries.
-- **SKI WELLS** [1] 2-9-0 J Reid 10/1: 0: Slowly away & al towards rear far side: 10th: Sadler's Wells *1½* **53**
colt, Apr foal: half brother to 2 12f wnrs, dam an Oaks wnr: sure to relish mid-dists in time for E Dunlop.
3999 **MAGZAA 11** [6] 2-9-0 R Hills 12/1: -00: Chsd ldrs stands side 5f: 11th: op 10/1: see 3999 (7f). *2* **49**
-- **ASHKAAL** [8] 2-9-0 M Henry 14/1: 0: Al outpcd stands side: 12th: Sheikh Albadou colt: Feb *nk* **48**
foal, cost 150,000IR gns: half brother to French 2,000 Guineas wnr Victory Note: dam a mdn: with M Channon.
3864 **North Point 21** [10] 2-9-0 W Ryan 25/1: -- **Indefinite Stay** [11] 2-9-0 Martin Dwyer 33/1:
3840 **Credenza Moment 22** [16] 2-9-0 L Newman (3) 50/1: 3999 **Equal Balance 11** [5] 2-9-0 N Pollard 66/1:
3972 **Pekanoora 12** [17] 2-9-0 P Doe 66/1: 4025 **Dusty Democrat 11** [9] 2-9-0 Darren Williams (5) 66/1:
18 ran Time 1m 47.6 (8.5) (Grant & Bowman Ltd) A P Jarvis Aston Upthorpe, Oxon

4164 2.50 SMITH COND STKS 2YO (C) 6f Good/Soft 73 -20 Slow
£6252 £2371 £1185 £539 Raced far side

*1161 **INSPECTOR GENERAL 144** [6] P F I Cole 2-9-4 J Fortune 3/1: 111: 2 b c Dilum - New Generation (Young **100**
Generation) Rear, in tch, drvn/prog to lead ins last, styd on well, pushed out, shade cosy: nicely bckd tho' op 2/1, abs, top-weight: unbtn after earlier wins at Newbury & Thirsk (stks): dam won at up to 1m: suited by step-up to 6f, 7f+ suit: acts on gd & soft, stiff/gall trk: runs well fresh: v useful colt, keep on the right side.
*3886 **DELTA SONG 19** [4] G L Moore 2-8-7 I Mongan (5) 6/5 FAV: -12112: 2 b f Delta Dancer - Song Of Gold *1* **84**
(Song) Chsd ldrs, rdn/kept on to chase wnr ins last, al held: hvly bckd, op 2/1: acts on firm & gd/soft grnd.
*2545 **SING A SONG 79** [1] R Hannon 2-8-10 R Hughes 4/1: 13: 2 b f Blues Traveller - Raja Moufana (Raja *½* **85**
Baba) Led, rdn/hdd ins last & no extra: op 9/2: 12 wk abs: stays 6f: only twice raced, improving.
3862 **SMITH AND WESTERN 21** [2] R Hannon 2-8-12 L Newman (3) 8/1: 123504: Keen/cl-up, onepace from *½* **85**
over 1f out: op 6/1: return to 7f could suit: see 3062, 2430 (7f).
3876 **THERES TWO 20** [3] 2-8-10 J Reid 7/1: -3105: Cl-up over 3f out, wknd fnl 1f: op 11/2: btr 3661 (gd). *2½* **77**
3342 **PHARMACYS PET 45** [5] 2-8-7 S Sanders 100/1: -0006: Bhd fnl 2f: 6 wk abs, highly tried: see 2357. *7* **57**
6 ran Time 1m 17.65 (5.55) (The Blenheim Partnership) P F I Cole Whatcombe, Oxon

4165 3.20 TOTE TRIFECTA RTD HCAP 3YO+ 0-95 (C) 6f Good/Soft 73 +14 Fast [101]
£9877 £3746 £1873 £851 3 yo rec 2 lb Raced far side

2706 **FIRE DOME 73** [6] Andrew Reid 8-9-0 (87) M Henry 12/1: 111001: 8 ch g Salt Dome - Penny Habit **93**
(Habitat) Rear, switched & strong run for press from over 1f out, led nr line: fast time: 10 wk abs: earlier scored at Redcar, Windsor (clmrs, D Nicholls, cost current connections £10,000), Lingfield & Epsom (h'caps): '99 wnr at Sandown & Redcar (clmrs, rtd 83): '98 Thirsk & Sandown wnr (Listed, rtd 107): stays 7f, suited by 6f on firm, hvy or fibresand, any trk: gd weight carrier: best without blnks & runs well fresh: v tough & useful, in great heart.
4010 **NINEACRES 11** [16] J M Bradley 9-8-5 (78)(bl) P Fitzsimons (5) 8/1: 413022: 9 b g Sayf El Arab - *½* **81**
Mayor (Laxton) Cl-up, went on over 2f out, sn rdn, just hdd & no extra cl-home: deserves to win again: see 4010.
3629 **MERSEY MIRAGE 32** [8] R Hannon 3-8-12 (87) L Newman (3) 14/1: 2-0143: 3 b c King's Signet - *shd* **90**
Kirriemuir (Lochnager) Mid-div, rdn/prog to chall fnl 1f, just held nr fin: op 12/1: useful, see 3629 & 3335.
4129 **JUWWI 3** [9] J M Bradley 6-9-1 (88) M Savage (7) 20/1: 000004: Bhd, strong run fnl 1f, not reach *1½* **88**
front trio: longer priced stable-mate of rnr-up: quick reapp: signalled return to form here: see 1337.
3904 **CAUDA EQUINA 18** [5] 6-8-9 (82) J Reid 16/1: 211305: Rear, kept on fnl 2f, no threat: see 3662 (7f). *½* **80**
3975 **DAYS OF GRACE 12** [12] 5-8-4 (77)(14oh) N Pollard 33/1: 114206: Chsd ldrs, onepace fnl 2f: stiff task. *nk* **74**
3629 **MISTER SUPERB 32** [11] 3-8-6 (81) S Sanders 20/1: 063607: Dwelt/rear, late gains: see 3076, 2183. *¾* **76**
4012 **PASSION FOR LIFE 11** [17] 7-8-11 (84) P Doe 8/1: 100008: Led till over 2f out, fdd: best fresh. *¾* **77**
3947 **TADEO 14** [14] 7-8-5 (78) K Dalgleish (5) 10/1: 000359: Chsd ldrs till over 1f out: op 14/1: see 2310. *nk* **70**
4121 **AMBER FORT 3** [7] 7-8-4 (77)(bl)(9oh) G Baker (5) 20/1: 500440: In tch, outpcd fnl 3f: 10th: needs 7f. *hd* **68**
3981 **RUSSIAN FOX 12** [15] 3-8-8 (83) R Hughes 33/1: 000000: Chsd ldrs 4f: 11th: see 1028. *nk* **73**
4107 **ABBAJABBA 4** [1] 4-8-6 (79) A Clark 9/4 FAV: 113120: In tch, rdn over 2f out, sn btn: 14th: hvly **0**
bckd, quick reapp: disapp eff, connections blamed poor draw & race poss came too soon after 4107.
2676 **LIVELY LADY 74** [4] 4-8-13 (86)(vis) Pat Eddery 8/1: 033000: Al rear: 16th: 10 wk abs, visor reapp. **0**
4012 **DANIELLES LAD 11** [13] 4-9-7 (94) D Sweeney 9/2: 406060: Prom till halfway: 17th, top-weight, see 1531. **0**
2473 **Supreme Angel 82** [10] 5-8-4 (77)(14oh) Martin Dwyer 33/1:
3904 **Railroader 18** [3] 3-8-6 (81) S Carson (3) 11/1:
3646 **Midnight Escape 32** [2] 7-8-8 (81) J Fortune 20/1:
17 ran Time 1m 15.66 (3.56) (A S Reid) Andrew Reid Mill Hill, London NW7

4166 3.50 ELDRIDGE POPE HCAP 3YO+ 0-70 (E) 1m6f Good/Soft 73 -21 Slow [69]
£3107 £956 £478 £239 3 yo rec 10lb

3167 **TE DEUM 53** [11] J C Fox 3-8-4 (55) P Fitzsimons (5) 25/1: 0-0501: 3 ch c Ridgewood Ben - Tabessa **58**
(Shahrastani) Mid-div, prog 4f out, rdn/led over 1f out, styd on well, rdn out: 8 wk abs: 1st win: plcd on 2nd of 3 '99 starts (mdn, rtd 73): apprec step up to 14f, 2m shld suit: acts on gd/soft & a stiff trk: runs well fresh.
3819 **REDOUBLE 23** [19] J Akehurst 4-9-4 (59) S Sanders 7/1: 223322: 4 b g First Trump - Sunflower Seed *¾* **60**
(Mummy's Pet) Chsd ldrs, rdn/chall over 2f out, kept on for press tho' held nr fin: consistent mdn.
3560 **RAINBOW SPIRIT 35** [17] A P Jarvis 3-8-12 (63) J Fortune 9/1: 434233: 3 b g Rainbows For Life - *shd* **64**
Merrie Moment (Taufan) Chsd ldrs, rdn & kept on onepace fnl 2f: stays 14f, tried 2m: handles firm, poss soft.
2305 **AMANCIO 89** [1] Mrs A J Perrett 9-10-0 (69) W Ryan 16/1: 30/234: Prom/keen early, restrained in *¾* **69**
mid-div halfway, styd on well fnl 3f, not reach front trio: op 12/1: 12 wk abs, top-weight: acts on fast & gd/soft.

3392 **CRYSTAL FLITE 42** [8] 3-8-6 (57) Martin Dwyer 20/1: 026055: Led, drvn 3f out, hdd over 1f out, no ½ **56**
extra: 6 wk abs: stays 14f: mdn but on a fair mark: see 2246, 979.
2498 **MANE FRAME 81** [2] 5-9-13 (68) J Reid 6/1: 021066: Trkd ldrs, onepace fnl 2f: op 10/1: see 1711. 1½ **65**
3948 **FLETCHER 14** [3] 6-9-12 (67) R Hughes 6/1: 151027: Mid-div, rdn/held over 2f out: see 3424 (C/D). 2 **61**
3978 **SIRINNDI 12** [13] 6-8-5 (46) G Sparkes (7) 8/1: 062568: Hmpd start, slowly away/bhd, mod hdwy *nk* **39+**
fnl 3f under minimal press, nvr threat: op 5/1: closer without tardy start: always one to watch in market: see 3586.
3219 **GEMINI GUEST 49** [15] 4-9-7 (62) P Doe 20/1: 050309: Chsd ldrs 12f: 7 wk abs: btr 2667 (12f, gd). 2½ **51**
3476} **TOM TAILOR 404** [20] 6-9-2 (57) N Pollard 25/1: 1000-0: Chsd ldrs till over 2f out: 10th: reapp: 1½ **44**
'99 Sandown wnr (h'cap, rtd 62): 97/98 hdles wnr at Sandown & Exeter (juv novs, 2m/2m6f, gd/soft & hvy,
rtd 118h): eff at 12f/14f, suited by a stiff 2m nowadays: acts on fast & gd/soft grnd.
3961 **MARJEUNE 13** [12] 3-9-0 (65) Pat Eddery 4/1 FAV: -02330: Chsd ldrs 12f: 11th: see 3961, 3125 (12f). 3½ **47**
3819 **ROYAL MEASURE 23** [7] 4-8-5 (46) G Hind 10/1: 0-3000: Chsd ldrs over 3f out, sn btn: 12th: op 12/1. 2 **25**
*3887 **DESERT VALENTINE 19** [6] 5-8-13 (54) A Clark 10/1: -02510: Saddle slipped after 5f, t.o./p.u. 2f out. **0**
3800 **Rising Spray 24** [18] 9-8-12 (53) G Bardwell 20/1: 1730 **Legendary Lover 114** [16] 6-8-12 (53) P Dobbs (5) 20/1:
4075 **Galapino 6** [9] 7-8-7 (48)(bl) M Henry 33/1: 4225} **Mighty Magic 359** [4] 5-8-8 (49) L Newman (3) 20/1:
626 **Leading Spirit 209** [5] 8-9-10 (65) R Perham 66/1: 3265 **Travellers Rest 48** [10] 3-9-4 (69) S Carson (3) 25/1:
-- **Bandore** [14] 6-9-10 (65) D Sweeney 50/1:
20 ran Time 3m 11.18 (13.18) (Lord Mutton Racing Partnership) J C Fox Collingbourne Ducis, Wilts

4167 **4.20 AUTUMN NOV STKS 2YO (D) 7f str Good/Soft 73 -28 Slow**
£3718 £1144 £572 £286 Raced far side

3862 **TAKAROA 21** [2] I A Balding 2-9-5 J Reid 1/1 FAV: -33101: 2 b c Tagula - Mountain Harvest (Shirley **88**
Heights) Made all, drvn/strongly prsd over 1f out, rdn out: hvly bckd: earlier scored at Thirsk (mdn): stays
7f, 1m could suit: acts on firm & gd/soft grnd, any trk: useful colt.
2500 **BARATHIKI 81** [3] P F I Cole 2-9-0 J Fortune 11/4: -1462: 2 gr f Barathea - Tagiki (Doyoun) 1¾ **81**
Chsd wnr, drvn to chall over 1f out, held ins last: 12 wk abs: lngr trip: acts on fast & gd/soft.
-- **HAASIL** [4] J L Dunlop 2-8-8 R Hills 15/8: 3: 2 b c Machiavellian - Mahasin (Danzig) 7 **64**
Slowly away, closed on ldrs over 2f out, sn btn: op 6/4: Apr foal, half brother to a 1m wnr: dam 7f/1m wnr.
3 ran Time 1m 32.55 (7.05) (Robert Hitchins) I A Balding Kingsclere, Hants

4168 **4.50 AXMINSTER APPR HCAP DIV I 3YO+ 0-70 (F) 1m2f Good/Soft 73 -18 Slow [67]**
£2103 £601 £300 3 yo rec 6 lb

4067 **DICKIE DEADEYE 7** [9] G B Balding 3-9-6 (65) P Dobbs 9/1: 565601: 3 b g Distant Relative - Accuracy **70**
(Gunner B) Rear, hdwy fnl 3f & rdn/led 1f out, asserted under hands & heels riding fnl 1f: 1st win: eff at 10f,
12f could suit: acts on soft grnd & a stiff/gall trk: lightly raced.
4021 **FORT SUMTER 11** [15] P R Hedger 4-9-3 (56) J Bosley (3) 20/1: 300-62: 4 b g Sea Hero - Gray And Red 2½ **57**
(Wolf Power) Led 2f, remained cl-up, led again over 1f out, sn hdd, onepace/held ins last: see 4021 (AW).
4066 **OSCIETRA 7** [12] G B Balding 4-8-7 (46)(vis) Darren Williams 3/1 FAV: 556003: 4 b f Robellino - Top 3½ **43**
Treat (Topsider) Bhd, rdn & styd on fnl 2f, not pace to chall: nicely bckd stablemate of wnr: see 1096.
3683 **SWING BAR 30** [17] J M Bradley 7-7-10 (35) Joanna Badger (3) 25/1: 000004: Chsd ldrs, led over 2f 1½ **30**
out, hung left/hdd over 1f out & sn held: see 965.
*3915 **IN THE STOCKS 16** [7] 6-8-11 (50) P Fitzsimons 9/1: 062015: Chsd ldrs 4f out, btn 1f out: op 7/1. 3 **41**
4061 **FAMOUS 7** [5] 7-7-11 (36)(bl)(1ow)(9oh) D Cosgrave (0) 12/1: 000006: Chsd ldrs, switched to stands ½ **26**
side over 4f out, btn 2f out: modest ride (far side was clearly the place to be on earlier races): see 90.
3294 **ALHUWBILL 47** [13] 5-7-12 (37) D Kinsella (5) 20/1: 600437: Dwelt/bhd, prog/chsd ldrs over 2f out, 1½ **26**
sn no extra: 7 wk abs: longer 10f trip: btr 3294, 2690 (6/7f, fast & gd).
3819 **QUEEN OF FASHION 23** [1] 4-9-3 (56) S Finnamore 25/1: 430008: Led after 2f till over 4f out, fdd. *nk* **44**
3586 **RAYIK 34** [4] 5-9-0 (53) I Mongan (3) 6/1: 001039: Chsd ldrs, strangely switched to race stands 2½ **38**
side 4f out, sn btn: jockey given a 10-day ban for irresponsible riding & a poor ride from a usually competant appr.
3430 **HOH GEM 40** [16] 4-8-5 (44) Jonjo Fowle (3) 7/1: 020460: Dwelt/bhd, prog to lead over 3f out, *shd* **29**
hdd over 2f out & sn btn: 10th: 6 wk abs: see 1520.
3917 **PEPPERCORN 15** [6] 3-7-10 (41)(5oh) G Baker (3) 20/1: 360640: Chsd ldrs 6f: 11th: btr 3236 (1m). ½ **25**
3971 **SPIRIT OF KHAMBANI 13** [18] 3-8-0 (45) K Dalgleish (3) 9/2: 500240: Chsd ldrs 7f: 14th: btr 3971 (1m). **0**
2774 **Prince Elmar 69** [11] 3-9-3 (62) Michael Doyle (5) 20/1: 2199 **En Grisaille 93** [10] 4-8-2 (41) R Smith 16/1:
3355 **Gruinart 44** [2] 3-9-10 (69) G Sparkes (3) 20/1: 2033 **Hathni Khound 100** [3] 4-8-1 (40) R Naylor (5) 25/1:
1884 **Olly May 106** [8] 5-8-1 (40)(5ow)(16oh) G Hannon (0) 66/1:
17 ran Time 2m 13.63 (9.13) (Miss B Swire) G B Balding Fyfield, Hants

4169 **5.20 AXMINSTER APPR HCAP DIV II 3YO+ 0-70 (F 1m2f Good/Soft 73 -14 Slow [65]**
£2103 £601 £300 3 yo rec 6 lb

3390 **COUGHLANS GIFT 42** [18] J C Fox 4-8-12 (49) R Smith 6/1: 0U0501: 4 ch f Alnasr Alwasheek - Superfrost **55**
(Tickled Pink) Rear, hdwy from over 3f out, led over 1f out, styd on well, rdn out: op 8/1: 6 wk abs: '99 scorer
at Bath (h'cap, rtd 60 & 54a at best): plcd on fnl '98 start (rtd 57): prev suited by 7f/1m, now stays 10f well:
acts on gd & soft, prob handles equitrack: handles a stiff/gall or turning trk: runs well fresh: on a handy mark.
3858 **TWO SOCKS 21** [14] J S King 7-9-10 (61) P Dobbs 12/1: 614102: 7 ch g Phountzi - Mrs Feathers 1¾ **63**
(Pyjama Hunt) Prom, rdn & chsd wnr fnl 1f, al held: op 10/1: best at 12f: see 1927.
3110 **GIKO 55** [1] Jane Southcombe 6-8-9 (46) Jonjo Fowle (3) 40/1: 600003: 6 b g Arazi - Gayane (Nureyev) 3½ **44**
Chsd ldr, led over 2f out till over 1f out, sn held: abs, new stable: prob stays 10f, wng form at 1m/9f: see 1033.
2945 **MOST STYLISH 61** [15] C G Cox 3-9-5 (62) G Hannon (6) 10/1: 234464: Chsd ldrs, wknd fnl 1f: abs. ½ **59**
4061 **MAX 7** [7] 5-8-0 (37) D Kinsella (5) 40/1: 000005: Led till over 2f out, sn held: see 256. ½ **33**
*4067 **DOUBLE RED 7** [12] 3-9-5 (62)(6ex) Gemma Sliz (10) 9/4 FAV: 230016: Mid-div, smooth prog/cl-up 2 **55**
over 2f out, wknd over 1f out: nicely bckd under a 6lb pen: btr 4067.
4088 **BITTER SWEET 6** [8] 4-8-0 (37) T Hamilton (5) 7/1: 050667: Chsd ldrs 1m: qck reapp: see 1272. 1 **29**
4046 **FIERY WATERS 8** [13] 4-8-5 (42)(BL) G Sparkes (3) 20/1: 006008: Dwelt/bhd, nvr factor: blnks. 4 **29**
3581 **MAIDEN AUNT 35** [5] 3-8-9 (52) K Dalgleish 20/1: 50009: Chsd ldrs, drvn/chall 3f out, sn btn. *nk* **38**
4151 **JEWEL FIGHTER 1** [9] 6-8-1 (38) Joanna Badger (3) 33/1: 40-000: Chsd ldrs 1m: 10th: qk reapp. 2½ **21**
3255 **DIM OFAN 48** [11] 4-9-1 (52) S Finnamore 14/1: 000400: Chsd ldrs 1m: 11th: 7 wk abs: see 326. 9 **25**
2025 **MANY HAPPY RETURNS 101** [17] 3-8-2 (45) Darren Williams 16/1: 0-0500: Al bhd: 12th: 3 month abs. 2 **15**
*3382 **IMARI 42** [10] 3-9-6 (63) J Bosley (3) 9/1: 326310: Al bhd: 13th: op 6/1, abs: now with R G Frost. 2½ **30**
*3917 **CHEZ BONITO 15** [16] 3-8-3 (46) P Fitzsimons 8/1: 005410: Chsd ldrs 5f: 18th: btr 3917 (firm, 11.5f, clmr). **0**

SALISBURY WEDNESDAY SEPTEMBER 27TH Righthand, Galloping Track, Stiff Finish

4548} **Kaluana Court 334** [6] 4-7-10 (33)(3oh) Michael Doyle (5) 25/1:
3979 **Castlebridge 12** [2] 3-9-5 (62) G Baker (3) 16/1:
4576} **How High 331** [3] 5-7-12 (35) I Mongan 40/1: 3045 **Ripsnorter 58** [4] 11-7-10 (33)(9oh) R Naylor (4) 66/1:
18 ran Time 2m 13.24 (8.74) (Mrs J A Cleary) J C Fox Collingbourne Ducis, Wilts

BRIGHTON WEDNESDAY SEPTEMBER 27TH Lefthand, V Sharp, Undulating Track

Official Going SOFT. Stalls: 1m2f & 1m4f - Outside; Rem - Inside. Majority of horses came stands side final 3f.

4170 2.10 PREMIER NURSERY HCAP 2YO 0-85 (D) 6f rnd Soft 105 +08 Fast [90]
£3636 £1118 £559 £279

2377 **INZACURE 86** [4] R M Beckett 2-7-10 (58)(3oh) P M Quinn (3) 9/1: 0051: 2 b g Inzar - Whittingham Girl (Primo Dominie) Led, under press appr fnl 1f, held on well: tchd 40/1, best time of day, 12 wk abs, jockey given 3 day ban for irresp riding, h'cap bow: unplcd in 3 auct mdns prev: eff forcing the pace over 6f on soft. **62**
4090 **BEE KING 5** [1] M R Channon 2-7-12 (60) J Quinn 7/2: 000332: 2 ch c First Trump - Fine Honey (Drone) Nvr far away, rdn & ev ch fnl 1f, held nr fin: tchd 9/2, clr rem, qck reapp: clrly suited by soft grnd. ½ **62**
2948 **THOMAS SMYTHE 61** [8] N P Littmoden 2-8-11 (73) Craig Williams 8/1: -02263: 2 ch c College Chapel - Red Barons Lady (Electric) Bhd, rdn appr fnl 1f, kept on, nvr dngrs: tchd 11/1, 9 wk abs: handles gd & prob soft. 3 **68**
3901 **KNOCK 18** [3] R Hannon 2-9-2 (78) M Roberts 3/1 FAV: 524304: Chsd ldrs, no extra appr fnl 1f: bckd tho' tchd 9/4: back in trip, see 1648 (C/D, gd). ½ **72**
3922 **LONDON EYE 15** [2] 2-7-10 (58)(bl)(1oh) C Catlin (4) 14/1: 164405: Styd alone far side, prom till dist. 1¼ **49**
*3732 **STATUE GALLERY 28** [9] 2-9-7 (83) S Whitworth 6/1: 5216: Chsd ldrs, fdd ent fnl 2f: op 4/1, top-weight on h'cap bow: first run on soft grnd, worth another chance on a quicker surface: see 3732. 6 **62**
3886 **FOLLOW YOUR STAR 19** [5] 2-9-1 (77)(VIS) G Duffield 9/1: 66007: Bhd from halfway: op 13/2, visor. 1½ **53**
3909 **WOLF VENTURE 16** [6] 2-9-3 (79) B Marcus 7/1: -4358: Prom 4f: h'cap bow, btr 3909, 3760 (gd & fast). nk **54**
3955 **PHILIPPI 14** [7] 2-8-0 (62) R Ffrench 16/1: 0309: Sn struggling: op 9/1: h'cap bow, see 3732. 1¼ **34**
9 ran Time 1m 13.6 (5.8) (The Inzacure Partnership) R M Beckett Lambourn, Berks

4171 2.40 TENANTRY DOWN SELLER 2YO (G) 5f59y rnd Soft 105 -27 Slow
£1884 £538 £269

3886 **EASTER ISLAND 19** [4] B R Millman 2-8-6 M Roberts 14/1: 000001: 2 b f Turtle Island - Port Queen (Nashamaa) Cl-up, styd far side till switched sharply towards stands side after halfway, led bef fnl 1f, rdn out: no bid, jockey given 3 day ban for irresp riding: eff at 6f on soft grnd: apprec the drop into a seller. **59**
4030 **BALI ROYAL 9** [7] J M Bradley 2-8-6 J Tate 7/1: 200002: 2 b f King's Signet - Baligay (Balidar) Chsd ldrs stands side, shaken up & hmpd by wnr appr fnl 1f, kept on: acts on gd/soft & soft grnd: see 2641. 1¼ **55**
3802 **ALICIAN SUNHILL 24** [6] Mrs A Duffield 2-8-6 (BL) G Duffield 3/1: 030443: 2 br f Piccolo - Midnight Spell (Night Shift) In tch, prog to chase ldrs 2f out, onepace fnl 1f: blnkd: btr without 3802. 2½ **49**
3038 **JUSTALORD 58** [3] W G M Turner 2-9-2 A Daly 3/1: 161524: Chsd ldrs, sltly hmpd appr fnl 1f, same pace: op 2/1, 8 wk abs: better on faster grnd over 5f earlier: see 3038, 1381. 1¼ **56**
2545 **VINE COURT 79** [9] 2-8-6 L Carter 5/2 FAV: 0605: Nvr going pace: bckd, 11 wk abs, down in grade. 4 **36**
3491 **QUEENS SONG 39** [5] 2-8-6 J Quinn 16/1: 036566: Handy till ent fnl 2f: 6 wk abs, op 12/1, see 2551. 1¼ **33**
4030 **NINE TO FIVE 9** [1] 2-8-11 P M Quinn (3) 25/1: 445607: Led, styd far side & hdd appr fnl 1f, wknd/eased. 1¼ **35**
3639 **CARRICK LADY 32** [2] 2-8-6 A Nicholls 33/1: 008: Held up, styd far side, btn appr fnl 1f: no form. 2 **25**
3639 **SAVANNA MISS 32** [8] 2-8-6 M Fenton 20/1: 50069: Nvr in it: op 14/1, stiff task. hd **25**
9 ran Time 1m 07.0 (7) (Normandy Developments (London) B R Millman Kentisbeare, Devon

4172 3.10 SANS FRONTIERE MDN 2YO (D) 7f rnd Soft 105 -05 Slow
£3807 £1171 £585 £292

3840 **MUTARASED 22** [2] J L Dunlop 2-9-0 W Supple 11/4 FAV: 01: 2 b c Storm Cat - Sajjaya (Blushing Groom) Well plcd, led appr fnl 2f, rdn clr: nicely bckd tho' op 7/4: Apr foal, half-brother to a 6f juv & a 10f wnr: dam 7f/1m wnr: eff at 7f, will get 1m: acts on soft grnd & an undul trk: going the right way. **90**
3866 **LUCEFER 20** [18] G C H Chung 2-9-0 O Urbina 9/2: -0202: 2 b c Lycius - Maharani (Red Ransom) Chsd ldrs, chsd wnr appr fnl 1f, kept on but not a threat: op 6/1, clr rem: gd run, acts on gd/soft & soft. 3 **83**
3833 **ABBY GOA 22** [8] B Hanbury 2-8-9 (BL) M Roberts 20/1: 4503: 2 b f Dr Devious - Spring Reel (Mill Reef) Handy, eff 2f out, unable to qckn: blnkd, will appreciate h'caps: see 3205. 4 **70**
2400 **POUNCE 89** [5] J A Osborne 2-8-9 R Ffrench 13/2: 444: Front rank & ev ch till no extra ent fnl 2f. 3 **64**
3913 **TEDSTALE 16** [10] 2-9-0 S W Kelly (3) 9/1: -04435: Al around same place: much btr 3913 (fast). 2½ **64**
3910 **AILINCALA 16** [16] 2-8-9 R Mullen 10/1: -U056: Keen, prom, onepace appr fnl 1f: op 20/1: see 3910. ¾ **58**
3879 **BARAKANA 20** [9] 2-9-0 (bl) D R McCabe 14/1: 263507: Nvr troubled ldrs: see 2894 (firm grnd here) 1½ **61**
3909 **JUST MIDAS 16** [1] 2-9-0 T G McLaughlin 33/1: 008: Nvr better than mid-div: see 3909. ½ **60**
2686 **KELLS 74** [12] 2-9-0 J Quinn 33/1: 09: Dwelt, nvr nr ldrs: 11 wk abs. 1 **58**
3840 **BUNKUM 22** [7] 2-9-0 J Stack 40/1: 00: Nvr a factor: 10th: Robellino first foal with M Bell. 1½ **55**
3980 **DARK DOLORES 12** [3] 2-8-9 Craig Williams 20/1: -00: Led till appr fnl 2f, wknd qckly: 11th, op 14/1: Inchinor half-sister to a 12f wnr: with M Channon. 1 **48$**
4001 **WESTERN FLAME 11** [14] 2-8-9 J Tate 13/2: 520: In tch till 2f out: 12th, op 9/2: much btr 4001 (6f). ½ **47**
3886 **MYHAT 19** [6] 2-8-9 D O'Donohoe 16/1: 326500: Sn bhd, 16th: see 2209. **0**
3864 **Conquering Love 21** [4] 2-9-0 M Fenton 33/1: 3972 **Petrov 12** [11] 2-9-0 M Tebbutt 20/1:
3853 **Abracadabjar 21** [13] 2-9-0 B Marcus 33/1: 1634 **A B My Boy 118** [17] 2-9-0 R Brisland (5) 100/1:
4034 **La Traviata 9** [15] 2-8-9 G Duffield 20/1:
18 ran Time 1m 27.5 (7.7) (Hamdan Al Maktoum) J L Dunlop Arundel, W Sussex

4173 3.40 LIFE CLASS STKS 3YO 0-65 (E) 1m rnd Soft 105 -03 Slow
£2866 £819 £409

3944 **EVE 14** [4] M L W Bell 3-8-11 M Fenton 12/1: 343001: 3 b f Rainbow Quest - Fade (Persepolis) Mid-div, prog & narrow lead appr fnl 1f, drvn out: 1st win, unrcd juv: eff at 1m, prob stays 10f on firm & soft. **65**
3914 **VENTO DEL ORENO 16** [1] L M Cumani 3-8-11 S W Kelly (3) 11/1: 560042: 3 ch f Lando - Very Sweet hd **63**

(Bellypha) Nvr far away, chall appr fnl 1f, just held: tchd 14/1: ran to best at the weights, handles fast & soft.
3810 **SHAMSAN 24** [11] M Johnston 3-9-0 (BL) R Ffrench 13/2: 522303: 3 ch c Night Shift - Awayil (Woodman) Slow away, bhd, switched & kept on for press fnl 2f, nvr nrr: tchd 10/1, clr rem, blnkd: prob ran to best at the weights for new connections: acts on fast, soft grnd & both AWs: see 3093. **¾** **64**
4032 **COLLEGE ROCK 9** [6] R Brotherton 3-9-6 (vis) P M Quinn (3) 14/1: 130424: Towards rear, styd in centre in the str, gd prog & ev ch appr fnl 1f, sn onepace: ran to best giving weight away all round: see 3094. **3½** **63**
4045 **ATYLAN BOY 8** [2] 3-9-0 (bl) D R McCabe 12/1: 246005: Sn led, hdd/held appr fnl 1f: acts on AWs & sft. **1** **55**
4046 **RATIFIED 8** [8] 3-9-0 C Rutter 5/1: 140526: Same place thr'out: op 10/1, stiffish task, see 1022. **nk** **54**
3560 **SHAMAN 35** [14] 3-9-0 A Beech (3) 7/1: 132207: Dwelt, handy halfway, fdd 2f out: back in trip. **1½** **51**
3975 **DANCEMMA 12** [5] 3-8-11 J Quinn 20/1: 000408: In tch till 2f out: stiffish task, longer trip, see 837. **5** **38**
3970 **DISTANT GUEST 13** [9] 3-9-0 (bl) R Mullen 33/1: 405009: Nvr a factor: stiffish task, blnks reapplied. **2½** **36**
3357 **SPIRIT OF LIGHT 44** [10] 3-9-0 T G McLaughlin 7/1: 300050: Struggling after halfway: 10th, 6 wk abs. **1½** **33**
*4100 **CORUSCATING 5** [13] 3-9-3 G Duffield 9/2 FAV: 5-0410: Chsd ldrs 5f: 11th, qk reapp, btr 4100 (AW). **1¾** **33**
2579 **HUTOON 77** [3] 3-9-0 S Whitworth 33/1: 3-6000: Sn in rear: 12th, 11 wk abs, see 1362. **2** **26**
*3146 **SAHAYB 53** [12] 3-9-0 (bl) W Supple 10/1: 2-0010: Dwelt, nvr in it: 13th, 8 wk abs: btr 3146 (fast). **3** **21**
3854 **CRUISE 21** [7] 3-9-3 M Roberts 16/1: 500100: Early ldr, btn halfway: last, reportedly not handle the grnd. **1¾** **22**
14 ran Time 1m 40.6 (8.6) (Lady Carolyn Warren) M L W Bell Newmarket, Suffolk

4174

4.10 SKI & SNOWBOARD HCAP 3YO 0-60 (F) 1m2f Soft 105 -16 Slow [67]
£2695 £770 £385

3870 **SOPHALA 20** [20] C F Wall 3-9-7 (60) R Mullen 20/1: 0-3001: 3 b f Magical Wonder - Fujaiyrah (In Fijar) Towards rear, prog appr fnl 2f, rdn dist, kept on well to lead fnl 100y: first win: unplcd sole '99 start (rtd 62, D Morris): eff over a sharp 10f & clrly goes well in soft grnd. **65**
2825 **TWILIGHT WORLD 68** [8] Sir Mark Prescott 3-9-2 (55) G Duffield 5/2 FAV: 06-132: 3 b g Night Shift - Masskana (Darshaan) Nvr far away, led ent fnl 2f, sn under press, worn down ins last: nicely bckd from 9/2, 10 wk abs: clrly suited by easy grnd, acts on gd/soft & soft: eff at 9/10f: improving. **1¼** **58**
4046 **NIGHT DIAMOND 8** [6] I A Balding 3-9-4 (57)(t) A Nicholls 10/1: 241043: 3 b g Night Shift - Dashing Water (Dashing Blade) Held up, styd towards centre in str & gd hdwy to lead briefly/drifted right appr fnl 1f, no extra for press ins last: op 7/1, tchd 12/1: prob ran to best: acts on fast & soft, see 3663. **2½** **56**
*4029 **DILETIA 9** [3] N A Graham 3-9-7 (60)(bl)(6ex) M Roberts 5/1: 560414: In tch, prog 3f out, no extra bef fnl 1f: quick reapp with a penalty: see 4029 (sell). **2½** **55**
3914 **REGAL VISION 16** [4] 3-9-2 (55) A Daly 25/1: 0005: Mid-div, rdn appr fnl 2f, mod late hdwy: h'cap bow. **2½** **47**
4018 **SOFISIO 11** [5] 3-9-7 (60)(BL) B Marcus 20/1: 245006: Led, styd in centre, hdd 2f out & fdd: blnkd. **nk** **51**
4033 **COOL SPICE 9** [18] 3-9-7 (60) M Fenton 12/1: -04657: Prom, rdn appr fnl 2f, wknd: op 16/1, h'cap bow. **½** **50**
3970 **ALZITA 13** [16] 3-9-1 (54) S Whitworth 16/1: 0-0308: Dwelt, mid-div at best: see 2024. **¾** **43**
3914 **KOSMIC LADY 16** [12] 3-9-2 (55) J Quinn 12/1: 0009: Held up, chsd ldrs halfway till 2f out: h'cap bow. **½** **43**
3971 **MISTY MAGIC 13** [15] 3-9-1 (54) W Supple 10/1: 326300: Nvr nr ldrs: 10th, longer trip, btr 2013. **4** **37**
4026 **COMMONWOOD 11** [13] 3-8-7 (46) R Havlin 10/1: 000060: Chsd ldrs till 3f out: 11th, op 14/1. **1½** **27**
3970 **Koincidental 13** [2] 3-8-8 (47) C Rutter 20/1: 2633 **Presidents Lady 75** [1] 3-8-8 (47) S W Kelly (3) 20/1:
2217 **Buxteds First 92** [19] 3-8-12 (51) R Brisland (5) 16/1: 3517 **Lord Gizzmo 38** [14] 3-8-9 (48) M Tebbutt 33/1:
3885 **Magic Symbol 19** [11] 3-8-11 (50)(vis) A McGlone 20/1: 3357 **Ronni Pancake 44** [10] 3-8-9 (48) D O'Donohoe 16/1:
4004 **An Jolien 11** [9] 3-8-11 (50) T G McLaughlin 33/1: 4080 **Moon Of Alabama 6** [17] 3-8-9 (48) D R McCabe 20/1:
3626 **Culminate 32** [7] 3-8-13 (52) J Tate 40/1:
20 ran Time 2m 09.9 (12.1) (T J Wells) C F Wall Newmarket, Suffolk

4175

4.40 GRAND OCEAN MDN DIV 1 3YO+ (D) 1m rnd Soft 105 -08 Slow
£3282 £1010 £505 £252 3 yo rec 4 lb

4330} **CORK HARBOUR 351** [5] Mrs N Smith 4-9-2 A McGlone 20/1: 63-1: 4 ch g Grand Lodge - Irish Sea (Irish River) Prom, rdn to lead dist, styd on strongly, all out to hold on: reapp/new stable: plcd 2nd of 2 '99 starts (mdn, rtd 82, B Hills): half brother to wnrs abroad, dam mid-dist bred: eff at 1m/10f, 12f could suit: acts on soft & a sharp/undul or gall trk: runs well fresh: fine run for new stable, win again if grnd remains in his fav. **77**
3998 **DIGITAL 11** [1] M R Channon 3-8-12 Craig Williams 7/2: -42302: 3 ch g Safawan - Heavenly Goddess (Soviet Star) Trkd ldr, led briefly over 1f out, rallied ins last, drvn out, just failed: tchd 5/1, 9L clr rem: acts on fast & soft grnd: excellent run & shld win similar, see 3256, 3048. **nk** **77**
3343 **ENTAIL 45** [3] J H M Gosden 3-8-7 R Havlin 11/10 FAV: 3-5343: 3 b f Riverman - Estala (Be My Guest) Handy, led over 3f out, hdd over 1f out, wknd: nicely bckd, 6 wk abs: poss not handle soft grnd: see 3048 (fast). **9** **56**
3914 **GLEDSWOOD 16** [7] Lady Herries 3-8-7 (VIS) J Quinn 2/1: 322634: Cl-up, wknd qckly appr fnl 1f: nicely bckd in first time visor: below best on first try on soft grnd: btr 3672 (10f, fast). **6** **46**
-- **SAVED BY THE BELLE** [8] 3-8-7 J Tate 66/1: 5: Al towards rear on debut: Emarati filly, with L Dace. **11** **26**
3914 **COSMIC DANCER 16** [2] 3-8-12 R Studholme (3) 50/1: 06: Sn well bhd, t.o.: mod form. **13** **6**
3910} **BROOKFURLONG 379** [6] 4-8-11 R Thomas (7) 50/1: 00-7: Al towards rear, t.o.: well btn in 2 '99 mdn starts for J Fanshawe, now with D R C Elsworth. **nk** **0**
3970 **ST IVES 13** [4] 3-8-12 (VIS) C Rutter 66/1: 600408: Led, hdd over 3f out, wknd qckly, t.o.: visored. **5** **0**
1884 **LADY DEALER 106** [9] 5-8-11 P McCabe 50/1: 0/00U9: Sn lost tch, t.o.: long abs, no form. **8** **0**
9 ran Time 1m 41.0 (9) (Martin Ingram) Mrs N Smith Eastbury, Berks

4176

5.10 BOLLINGER AMAT MDN HCAP 3YO+ 0-70 (E) 1m4f Soft 105 -10 Slow [34]
£2873 £884 £442 £221 3 yo rec 8 lb

3656 **PENALTA 32** [5] M Wigham 4-10-3 (37) Mr S Callaghan (5) 6/1: 00031: 4 ch g Cosmonaut - Tarquette (Targowice) Settled mid-div, gd hdwy to lead appr fnl 1f, styd on well, drvn out: tchd 8/1: up in trip: stays 10f, relished this step up to 12f on soft grnd, handles fast: runs well for an inexperienced jockey. **44**
3683 **STITCH IN TIME 30** [3] G C Bravery 4-10-2 (36) Mr D Crosse (5) 7/1: 543332: 4 ch g Inchinor - Late Matinee (Red Sunset) Mid-div, hdwy halfway, went on 3f out, hdd appr fnl 1f, not pace of wnr: op 11/2: visor omitted: stays 10/12f & deserves to win similar: see 3683 (10f, fast, visored). **4** **38**
3827 **LUNAR LORD 23** [13] J S Moore 4-9-11 (31) Mr J J Best (3) 5/1: 224403: 4 b g Elmaamul - Cache (Bustino) Bhd, prog halfway, ev ch until no extra appr fnl 1f: tchd 9/1, well clr rem: btr 2656 (fast grnd). **2½** **30**
3755 **REMEMBER STAR 27** [6] R J Baker 7-9-10 (30)(3oh) Mr B Hitchcott 15/2: 432254: Led bef halfway, hdd 3f out, sn lost tch: poss not handle this rain softened grnd, btr 3260 (C/D, fast). **8** **21**
4061 **TWOFORTEN 7** [11] 5-10-2 (36) Mr R Lucey Butler (7 20/1: 603005: In tch, eff over 4f out, sn btn: quick reapp: btr 3663 (10f, gd). **1¾** **25**

4024 **BAMBOOZLE 11** [8] 4-10-11 (45) Mr T Best (5) 25/1: 050006: Nvr a factor: btr 2265. *8* **27**
4041 **PETER PERFECT 8** [1] 6-9-10 (30)(5oh) Mr S Dobson (5) 50/1: /00-07: Al in rear: mod form. *3¾* **9**
3885 **CATAMARAN 19** [12] 5-12-0 (62)(bl) Mr P Pritchard Gordo 14/1: 450008: Nvr dangerous: up in trip. *2½* **39**
-- **CHIPPEWA** [7] 6-11-0 (48)(t) Mr T Scudamore 3/1 FAV: 000/9: Prom, wknd qckly after halfway: *hd* **25**
op 7/1: jumps fit, recent wnr at N Abbot & Plumpton (clmrs, rtd 106h, 2m/2m3f, fast & hvy, sharp/undul trks): 99/00 hdles wnr at Stratford (h'cap, rtd 104h): mod form on the Flat in native France back in '97.
3526 **SCENIC LADY 37** [15] 4-9-10 (30)(2oh) Mr Ray Barrett (3) 25/1: 002540: Dwelt, al rear, 10th: see 2904. *1½* **6**
3581 **SAIL WITH THE WIND 35** [2] 3-10-5 (47) Mr S Walker (5) 13/2: 00-050: Prom, wknd rapidly fnl 3f, 11th. *5* **18**
3971 **Dazzling Daisy 13** [4] 3-10-2 (44) Mr S Rees (5) 33/1:
2253 **Rock On Robin 91** [14] 3-10-1 (43) Mr T Waters (7) 50/1:
13 ran Time 2m 42.0 (13.8) (John Smallman) M Wigham Newmarket

4177

5.40 GRAND OCEAN MDN DIV 2 3YO+ (D) 1m rnd Soft 105 -43 Slow
£3282 £1010 £505 £252 3 yo rec 4 lb

3696 **THREE OWLS 30** [3] L M Cumani 3-8-7 S W Kelly (3) 7/2: 31: 3 b f Warning - Three Terns (Arctic Tern) **80**
Bhd, gd hdwy over 3f out, led 2f out, rdn & pulled clr appr fnl 1f: up in trip, left debut bhd: related to sev wnrs: stays 7f, relished step up to 1m: acts on soft, handles gd: apprec testing conditions.
3777 **ARDANZA 25** [7] B Hanbury 3-8-7 M Roberts 9/2: 24652: 3 b f Hernando - Arrastra (Bustino) *9* **65**
Prom, rdn & not pace of wnr fnl 2f: clr rem: may apprec a return to 10f: see 3777, 1343.
1491 **BREAK THE GLASS 124** [4] E A L Dunlop 3-8-12 M Tebbutt 8/13 FAV: 4-3233: 3 b g Dynaformer - *4* **62**
Greek Wedding (Blushing Groom) Bhd, prog halfway, drvn/held appr fnl 1f: 4 month abs: btr 1491 (10f h'cap).
3935 **DOUBLE FAULT 14** [5] J A Gilbert 3-8-7 (bl) A Daly 50/1: 300004: Led early, remained with ldrs, *5* **47$**
wknd qckly fnl 2f: stiff task (offic only 36), treat rating with caution.
3820 **ARTYFACTUAL 23** [1] 3-8-12 J Quinn 33/1: 005: Al bhd: big step up in trip. *11* **32**
-- **TAYEED** [6] 3-8-12 W Supple 14/1: 6: In tch, wknd qckly fnl 3f: with R W Armstrong. *3½* **26**
4109] **BOLD BYZANTIUM 722** [2] 4-8-11 D R McCabe 66/1: 0/7: Led 6f out, hdd 2f out, wknd rapidly: *11* **1**
v long abs: missed '99, well btn sole '98 start for E J Alston, now with K Bell.
156 **WINNIPEG 294** [8] 4-8-11 A Nicholls 66/1: 00-8: Cl-up, wknd qckly fnl 3f, t.o.: reapp/new stable. *6* **0**
8 ran Time 1m 43.8 (11.8) (Mrs A Rothschild) L M Cumani Newmarket

NEWMARKET (ROWLEY) THURSDAY SEPTEMBER 28TH Righthand, Stiff, Galloping Track

Official Going GOOD. Stalls: Far Side.

4178

1.30 SPORT4CAST.COM CLAIMER 3YO+ (E) 1m4f Good 40 -13 Slow
£5021 £1545 £772 £386 3 yo rec 8 lb

4003 **FINAL LAP 12** [16] W Jarvis 4-8-13 J Fortune 16/1: 000001: 4 b g Batshoof - Lap Of Honour (Final **57**
Straw) Settled mid div, gd hdwy to chall 2f out, led appr dist, rdn out: first win: rnr-up in '99 (rtd 78): eff at 1m/12f on gd & soft: handles a stiff or gall track: apprec drop to claimers.
3382 **WENSUM DANCER 43** [11] R Guest 3-8-2 J Mackay (5) 50/1: 064042: 3 b f Shareef Dancer - Burning *1* **52$**
Ambition (Troy) Keen/rear, prog 3f out, rdn & styd on inside last, no threat to wnr: fine run at these weights tho' treat rating with caution: eff at 1m/12f on fast & gd: see 3382, 3266.
2659 **FLIQUET BAY 76** [3] Mrs A J Perrett 3-8-9 (bl) M Roberts 16/1: 420303: 3 b g Namaqualand - *1¼* **57**
Thatcherite (Final Straw) Held up, improved over 4f out, sn chasing ldrs, rdn/onepcd fnl 1f: gd run after abs.
3979 **SKYE BLUE 13** [6] M R Channon 3-8-9 Craig Williams 7/1: 205654: Bhd, rdn & styd on fnl 2f, nvr nrr. *1¾* **54**
4067 **DANGEROUS DEPLOY 8** [8] 3-9-5 Pat Eddery 12/1: -55005: Bhd, rdn/prog over 2f out, no impress *hd* **64**
inside last: up in trip/drop in grade: see 3190.
3018 **YAROB 60** [14] 7-9-13 L Dettori 4/1 FAV: 260606: Led, hdd 5f out, rallied to lead again over 2f out, *½* **63**
hdd over 1f out, wknd: nicely bckd tho' op 2/1: below best dropped in class & better around 10f: see 2522.
3869 **ICE CRYSTAL 21** [7] 3-9-0 C Rutter 16/1: 040067: Cl up, led 5f out, hdd appr fnl 2f, wknd: clr rem. *nk* **58**
4077 **AQUIRE NOT DESIRE 7** [10] 4-9-5 D Holland 20/1: 4/5-58: Nvr a factor: quick reapp: see 4077. *11* **42**
3686 **NAUTICAL STAR 31** [1] 5-9-8 M Hills 10/1: 000009: Cl up, wknd appr fnl 2f: out of form, see 1850. *½* **44**
3800 **ABLE SEAMAN 25** [4] 3-9-0 (vis) B Marcus 8/1: 364020: Nvr dangerous, fin 10th: btr 3800 (14f). *5* **37**
1034] **MEDAILLE MILITAIRE 879** [13] 8-9-8 M J Kinane 11/2: -560/0: Al towards rear, t.o. in 16th: **0**
long abs: new stable: 4th over timber for M Pipe in 99/00 (h'cap, rtd 114h), prev term won 4 races (nov, rtd 119h, 2m1f, fast & soft): rtd 109 at best from 4 starts in '97 (listed, with J Dunlop), rtd 111 prev term: eff at 1m/10f, stys 12f: acts on fast, likes gd/soft & has run well fresh: now with Mrs A Perrett.
3522 **Millennium Summit 38** [12] 3-8-11 O Urbina 16/1: 668 **Katies Cracker 198** [9] 5-8-7 F Norton 50/1:
4141 **Woodyates 3** [5] 3-9-0 (t) R Thomas (7) 25/1: *3827 **Winsome George 24** [15] 5-8-13 G Sparkes (7) 25/1:
4029 **Boasted 10** [2] 3-7-13 (t) J Quinn 50/1:
16 ran Time 2m 35.25 (6.45) (T C Blackwell and Partners) W Jarvis Newmarket, Suffolk

4179

2.05 BAILEYS NURSERY HCAP 2YO 0-95 (C) 5f Good 40 -15 Slow [99]
£7254 £2232 £1116 £858

3475 **MUJA FAREWELL 40** [13] T D Barron 2-8-10 (81) M J Kinane 9/1: 122101: 2 ch f Mujtahid - **85**
Highland Rhapsody (Kris) In tch, switched left over 3f out, ran on strongly to lead well ins last: abs: earlier won at Redcar (debut, mdn auctn) & Windsor (stakes): loves to race up with/force the pace around 5f on fast & gd, handles gd/soft: runs well fresh & handles any track: tough, geniune & speedy filly.
*4098 **AMELIA 6** [3] J Cullinan 2-8-7 (78)(7ex) D O'Donohoe 6/1: 343112: 2 b f General Monash - Rose *½* **80**
Tint (Salse) Bhd centre group, gd hdwy over 1f out, styd on well ins last, nvr nrr: in fine form: see 4098.
4098 **VENDOME 6** [1] J A Osborne 2-8-10 (81) J Weaver 13/2: 331223: 2 b c General Monash - Kealbra *hd* **83**
Lady (Petong) Broke well & led centre group, styd on well fnl 1f, not btn far: tough & consistent.
*3602 **NIGHT HAVEN 34** [2] M L W Bell 2-8-7 (78) M Fenton 9/1: 2214: Mid div, eff & edged left appr *hd* **80**
fnl 1f, ran on strongly nr fin: lightly raced & remains on the upgrade: acts on firm & gd: 6f will suit.
3860 **RED RYDING HOOD 22** [15] 2-8-4 (75) A Beech (3) 20/1: 423205: Rcd far side & led overall, *nk* **76**
hdd well inside last, held nr fin: consistent form but remains a mdn, see 3630, 3394.
3888 **DOUBLE BREW 20** [7] 2-8-9 (80) M Roberts 20/1: 422546: Outpcd early, styd on well fnl 1f, *½* **79**

nvr nrr: needs further: see 3888 (val stakes).

3888 **MILLYS LASS** 20 [9] 2-8-6 (77) Craig Williams 16/1: 030257: Towards rear centre group, ran on   *shd* **76**
fnl 1f, nvr nrr: worth another try at 6f: see 3679.

3576 **PEACE BAND** 36 [4] 2-8-0 (71) Dale Gibson 20/1: 5438: Trckd ldrs, slightly outpcd appr fnl 1f,   *nk* **69**
rallied inside last, no threat: h'cap bow: see 3576.

3965 **RASOUM** 14 [8] 2-9-7 (92) J Reid 5/1 FAV: -3139: Towards rear centre, styd on late, no threat   *shd* **90**
to ldrs: top-weight: prob ran to nr best on h'cap bow, but will apprec a return to 6f: see 2959.

3959 **EFFERVESCE** 14 [14] 2-8-4 (75) J Quinn 12/1: 601200: Chsd ldr far side, drvn/no extra appr   *1* **70**
fnl 1f: 10th: btr 3475, 3264 (gd/soft).

3987 **CANDOTHAT** 13 [10] 2-8-9 (80) B Marcus 25/1: 515000: Mid div, late gains: 11th: see 3987, 3101.   *1¾* **70**

3638 **MY LUCY LOCKET** 33 [12] 2-8-10 (81) R Hughes 7/1: 321050: Trckd ldrs, rdn/fdd appr fnl 1f,   *½* **70**
12th: has been a shade disappointing since a useful nursery win in 2665.

3743 **Shatin Dollybird** 28 [5] 2-8-1 (72) K Dalgleish (5) 14/13987 **Celotti** 13 [11] 2-8-6 (77) T Quinn 25/1:
14 ran   Time 1m 00.95 (2.75)   (T Hollins P Huntbach D Rutter W Carson)   T D Barron Maunby, N Yorks

---

4180 **2.35 LISTED JOEL STKS 3YO+ (A)** **1m str** **Good 40** **-09 Slow**
£16182 £6138 £3069 £1395 3 yo rec 4 lb

3726 **HOPEFUL LIGHT** 29 [9] J H M Gosden 3-9-0 J Fortune 20/1: 401141: 3 b g Warning - Hope (Dancing   **112**
Brave) Led, grad wound it up after halfway, found extra & pressed bef fnl 1f, pushed out: earlier won at Salisbury
(2, stakes & List): '99 Doncaster wnr (mdn, rtd 92): eff at 7f/1m, tried 9f last time: acts on fast & hvy, stiff
tks: runs well fresh, from the front: lightly raced, smart & progressive, looks well up to Gr 3 class.

1975 **ON THE RIDGE** 471 [1] H R A Cecil 5-9-0 T Quinn 10/1: 2/20-2: 5 ch h Risk Me - Star Ridge (Storm   *¾* **106**
Bird) Towards rear, gd prog 2f out, pressed wnr 1f out, kept on but held: fine reapp: rnr up first of just 2
'99 starts (Gr 2, rtd 116): '98 York wnr (mdn, rtd 103 at best): eff at 1m/10f: acts on firm & soft grnd:
runs well fresh on a gall trk: smart at best, should come on for this.

*3893 **EL GRAN PAPA** 20 [5] J H M Gosden 3-8-10 L Dettori 13/2: 102013: 3 b c El Gran Senor - Banner   *nk* **106**
Hit (Oh Say) Hld up, prog appr fnl 1f, kept on but unable to chall: bckd, stablemate of wnr & still improving.

3893 **SOVIET FLASH** 20 [8] E A L Dunlop 3-8-10 J Reid 14/1: -41-24: Bhd ldrs, outpcd ent fnl 2f, kept on   *1* **104**
towards fin: only 4th ever start for this progressive, useful colt: step up to 10f may suit now: see 3893.

3875 **SWALLOW FLIGHT** 21 [11] M Roberts 4-9-4 M Hills 2/1 FAV: 131345: Chsd ldrs, pushed along 2f out, kept on   *½* **107**
onepace: hvly bckd: rated higher earlier this term: needs a break?: see 2359 (match).

2851 **TRUMPET SOUND** 68 [7] 3-8-10 (t) B Marcus 16/1: -10426: In tch, outpcd by ldrs & drftd right   *2* **99**
appr fnl 1f: 10 week abs, t-strap: return to 10f will suit, see 2851, 1127.

-2343 **CHAGALL** 89 [4] 3-8-10 M J Kinane 14/1: 2661237: Pulled hard in rear, kept on appr fnl 1f, nvr nr   *hd* **99**
to chall: German raider, up in trip here & looks well worth another ch at 1m tho' btr 2343 (7f, here).

4000 **FULL FLOW** 12 [3] 3-8-10 M Hills 10/1: 440128: Chsd ldrs, no extra appr fnl 1f: op 8/1, btr 4000.   *nk* **99**

3150 **MANA MOU BAY** 54 [2] 3-8-10 R Hughes 33/1: -02459: At towards rear: 8 week abs, stiffish task.   *1* **97**

3995 **HO LENG** 12 [6] 5-9-0 G Carter 20/1: 233450: Dwelt, pulled hard, al bhd: 10th: up in grade &   *1½* **94**
trip, capable of btr: see 1182.

1185 **AUNTY ROSE** 144 [10] 3-8-5 Pat Eddery 10/1: 30-300: Towards rear, wide prog 2f out, sn   *shd* **89**
btn, eased inside last: 11th, op 8/1, 5 month abs: see 953 (7f).

-3726 **AUTONOMY** 29 [12] 3-8-10 M Fenton 7/1: 51-320: Chsd ldrs, wknd 2f out: last, bckd: had   *5* **86**
this wnr bhd in 3726, surely something amiss.
12 ran   Time 1m 40.39 (3.89)   (K Abdulla)   J H M Gosden Manton, Wilts

---

4181 **3.10 GR 1 MIDDLE PARK STKS 2YO (A)** **6f** **Good 40** **+07 Fast**
£89320 £33880 £16940 £7700

*3372 **MINARDI** 46 [3] A P O'Brien 2-8-11 M J Kinane 5/6 FAV: -211: 2 br c Boundary - Yarn   **120**
(Mr Prospector) Dwelt, sn in tch, improved 2f out, led 1f out, ran on strongly for press: hvly bckd, gd time, abs:
Irish raider, earlier won at Leopardstown (Gr 1, by 5L): $1,650,000 half brother to a wnr in the US: eff at 6f,
shld stay at least 7f & prob 1m: acts on fast & gd, stiff trks: high-class & lightly raced, win more Gr 1's.

3550 **ENDLESS SUMMER** 39 [10] J H M Gosden 2-8-11 J Fortune 9/1: -1122: 2 b c Zafonic - Well Away   *1½* **114**
(Sadler's Wells) Sluggish start, rear, hdwy to chase wnr appr fnl 1f, styd on well without being a serious threat:
another fine run, now rnr-up in 2 Gr1's: smart colt, shld win more Gr races with a step up in trip: see 3550.

*3630 **RED CARPET** 33 [4] M L W Bell 2-8-11 J Murtagh 25/1: 25113: 2 ch c Pivotal - Fleur Rouge   *¾* **112**
(Pharly) Front rank, led after halfway, edged right appr fnl 1f & btn, kept on: tchd 40/1:
massive step up in grade & was not found wanting: v useful colt who looks well up to wng in Gr 2/3 class.

4054 **BAD AS I WANNA BE** 12 [2] B J Meehan 2-8-11 Pat Eddery 11/2: 01144: Prom, rdn & ev ch appr   *1½* **108**
fnl 1f, unable to qckn: nicely bckd from 13/2: useful colt but high-class win in 3550 (Gr 1) looks dubious
form (beat this 2nd by 6L but raced alone under the stands rail).

3996 **POMFRET LAD** 12 [9] 2-8-11 S Sanders 20/1: -0125: Held up, gd hdwy to press ldrs 2f out, sn rdn,   *nk* **108**
onepace: op 12/1: another gd run tho' looks below the v best, will apprec a drop to listed/Gr 3 company.

*3700 **BAARIDD** 31 [7] 2-8-11 L Dettori 9/1: -12516: Held up, prog to chase ldrs ent fnl 2f, no   *1* **105**
extra under press inside last: op 7/1: ran well but needs a return to Listed/Gr 3: see 3700.

3996 **BRAM STOKER** 12 [5] 2-8-11 J Reid 25/1: 233337: Mid div, outpcd appr fnl 1f: first time   *1¼* **102**
out of the frame, btr 3996 (firm), 1367.

3900 **JOPLIN** 19 [6] 2-8-11 P J Scallan 33/1: -1668: Led till bef halfway, fdd appr fnl 1f: *3½* **94**
stablemate/pacemaker of wnr & did a gd job.

3891 **GHAYTH** 20 [1] 2-8-11 R Hills 14/1: -6139: Rear, left bhd appr fnl 1f: much btr 3891, 3568 (firm).   *6* **82**

*3566 **BANNISTER** 36 [8] 2-8-11 R Hughes 16/1: 2210: Pulled v hard, chased ldrs, btn ent fnl 3f: *1¾* **78**
10th: pulled too hard: see 3566.
10 ran   Time 1m 12.75 (1.95)   (Mr M Tabor & Mrs John Magnier)   A P O'Brien Ballydoyle, Co Tipperary

---

4182 **3.40 LISTED ROUS STKS 3YO+ (A)** **5f** **Good 40** **+15 Fast**
£16066 £6094 £3047 £1385 3 yo rec 1 lb

4015 **RUSHCUTTER BAY** 12 [12] P L Gilligan 7-8-12 (vis) F Norton 20/1: 210021: 7 br g Mon Tresor -   **106**
Llwy Bren (Lidhame) Nvr far away, led appr fnl 1f, drvn out, just lasted: minor gamble from 40/1: earlier
won here at Newmarket (h'cap): '99 wnr at Windsor (class stakes, rtd 90): '98 wnr here again at Newmarket (h'cap,
rtd 84): eff at 5/6f: acts on firm & gd, with/without visor: best up with/forcing the pace: reserves best
for Newmarket: incredible improvement on step up to Listed company on 47th! career start.

3874 **ASTONISHED 21** [18] J E Hammond 4-9-1 C Asmussen 11/2 FAV: 114102: 4 ch g Weldnaas - Indigo (Primo Dominie) Hld up, hdwy but only asked for eff fnl 1f, too much to do, would have won next stride: would have won if asked for his effort earlier & his jockey rarely endears himself to backers: smart, can rate higher. **shd** **108**
3301 **SERAPHINA 47** [10] B A McMahon 3-8-6 S Sanders 33/1: 030003: 3 ch f Pips Pride - Angelic Sounds (The Noble Player) Towards rear, ran on appr fnl 1f, took 3rd nr fin, nvr nrr: abs: gd run, likes easier grnd. **1½** **96**
3982 **EMERALD PEACE 13** [11] M A Jarvis 3-8-6 M Roberts 20/1: -00164: Chsd ldrs, eff appr fnl 1f, kept on but unable to chall: not far off best, poss ideally suited by firm grnd: see 3841. **nk** **95**
4043 **VITA SPERICOLATA 9** [13] 3-8-6 (VIS) G Bardwell 16/1: 330425: Keen, bhd ldrs, eff & onepce appr fnl 1f, kept on fnl 100y: visored: not far off best: see 4043, 1529. **hd** **95**
3982 **ANDREYEV 13** [1] 6-9-1 J Fortune 7/1: 504136: Off the pace till strong run fnl 1f, nvr nrr: nicely bckd: return to 6f needed, see 3727. **hd** **102**
4015 **COASTAL BLUFF 12** [8] 8-8-12 R Hughes 40/1: 040447: Well plcd, narrow lead appr fnl 2f, hdd bef dist, onepace: stiff task, looks flattered: see 1871. **shd** **99$**
4125 **CRETAN GIFT 4** [3] 9-9-1 J Tate 33/1: 455008: Mid div, eff appr fnl 1f, no impress till styd on nr fin: quick reapp, unsuited by drop bck to 5f without headgear?: see 952 (6f, here). **shd** **102**
+3982 **IVORYS JOY 13** [16] 5-8-10 C Carver 13/2: 501219: Pulled hard, cl up & every ch till no extra fnl 1f: poss rcd too freely, much btr 3982. **½** **96**
3874 **PERFECT PEACH 21** [17] 5-8-7 P Goode 100/1: 620640: Dwelt, bhd, prog when short of room 1f out, nvr nr ldrs: 10th: highly tried again, see 1250. **½** **91$**
4043 **PROUD NATIVE 9** [2] 6-8-12 M J Kinane 9/1: 062230: Held up, eff 2f out, unable to qckn: 11th: can do better, see 1172. **nk** **95**
*3861 **COMPTON BANKER 22** [9] 3-8-11 L Dettori 6/1: 024410: Al bhd tho' staying on fin: 12th, well bckd tho' op 5/1: up in grade & not disgraced: see 3861 (h'cap). **shd** **95**
3982 **RAMBLING BEAR 13** [7] 7-8-12 T Quinn 12/1: 056300: Al towards rear: 13th, not given hard time. **½** **93**
3763 **YORKIES BOY 27** [6] 5-9-1 J Weaver 25/1: 601040: Led till appr fnl 2f, sn btn & hmpd: 15th, btr 3172. **0**
*3937 **FEMME FATALE 15** [14] 3-8-6 Pat Eddery 8/1: 31-410: Well plcd till lost pl appr fnl 1f: 16th, see 3937. **0**
3937 **Afaan 15** [4] 7-8-12 T G McLaughlin 66/1: *4043 **Rosselli 9** [5] 4-8-12 (bl) J Carroll 16/1:
1757 **Mrs P 115** [15] 3-8-6 C Lowther 40/1:
18 ran Time 59.47 (1.27) (Treasure Seekers Partnership) P L Gilligan Newmarket, Suffolk

4183

4.15 EBF WESTLEY MDN DIV 1 2YO (D) 7f str Good 40 -29 Slow
£5102 £1570 £785 £392

-- **DEMOPHILOS** [13] Mrs A J Perrett 2-9-0 Pat Eddery 9/2: 1: 2 b c Dr Devious - Graecia Magna (Private Account) Sn well plcd, shkn up to lead 2f out, ran on strgly, rdn out: nicely bckd from 11/2 on debut: half-brother to a cple of useful wnrs btwn 6f & 12f, dam smart mid dist performer: eff at 7f, should get at least 10f: acts on gd grnd & a stiff/gall track: runs well fresh & looks a useful prospect, shld go on from here. **97**
-- **BIG MOMENT** [7] B W Hills 2-9-0 M Hills 33/1: 2: 2 ch c Be My Guest - Petralona (Alleged) Bhd, going well but nowhere to go 2f out, clr & strong run bef fnl 1f, fin well, too late: unlucky: first foal, dam 12f wnr: eff at 7f but 1m+ looks sure to suit: has a turn of foot & must be kept on the right side. **nk** **96+**
-- **SILKY DAWN** [4] H R A Cecil 2-8-9 (t) T Quinn 7/4 FAV: 3: 2 b f Night Shift - Bluffing (Darshaan) Mid div, prog & ev ch appr fnl 1f, held towards fin: hvly bckd on debut: 320,000gns first foal, dam decent 1m juv wnr, sire gets mainly sprinters: eff at 7f on gd grnd, wore a t-strap: will win a mdn. **nk** **90**
-- **MOSAYTER** [18] M P Tregoning 2-9-0 R Hills 7/1: 4: Cl up & ev ch till onepce ent fnl 1f: Storm Cat half brother to wnrs at 12/14f, dam 1m/12f performer: stays 7f, 1m suit: fine debut, rate more highly. **1½** **92**
3748 **RANIN 28** [9] 2-8-9 W Supple 11/1: 35: Rear, eff & onepce 2f out, styd on nicely ins last: Unfuwain half sister to sev wnrs, some of them useful, dam 12f wnr: bred to be decent over mid dists & will improve. **1** **85+**
-- **DRAGNET** [6] 2-8-9 J Murtagh 10/1: 6: Held up, outpcd & short of room 2f out, picked up well inside last but all too late: tchd 14/1: Rainbow Quest sister to high class 1m/10f performer Spectrum, dam 5f juv wnr & later miler: eye-catching intro, already needs 1m+: keep in mind: with Sir M Stoute. **nk** **84+**
-- **FREEDOM NOW** [15] 2-9-0 J Reid 14/1: 7: Sn chsd ldrs, fdd fnl 1f: op 10/1, tchd 14/1: Sadler's Wells half-brother to 10f wnr Trumpet Sound: dam 7f juv wnr: will need 1m+: with L Cumani. **1¾** **85**
MACDUNE [12] 2-9-0 G Carter 25/1: 8: Front rank & every ch till outpcd appr fnl 1f: stablemate of 5th: 22,000gns Machiavellian first foal, dam 7f wnr: promise here. **½** **84**
2952 **CANOPY 62** [1] 2-8-9 R Hughes 7/1: 59: Chsd ldrs, unable to qckn appr fnl 1f: 9 wk abs, see 2952. **½** **78**
-- **CONTRABAND** [3] 2-9-0 B Marcus 33/1: 0: Well off the pace till fnl 1f hdwy: 10th, green: 59,000gns Red Ransom first foal, dam decent 10f performer: improvement likely: W Haggas. **¾** **81**
-- **REFRACT** [17] 2-9-0 M Fenton 50/1: 0: Led till 3f out, gradually wknd: 11th, debut: 7,000gns Spectrum half brother to sev wnrs: stoutly bred: with Don Cantillon. **hd** **81**
-- **COLLECTIVITY** [10] 2-8-9 J Carroll 33/1: 0: Al around same pl & short of room over 3f out: 12th, stablemate 2nd: 5,800gns Dr Devious first foal: stoutly bred. **½** **75**
2956 **ASTRAL PRINCE 62** [8] 2-9-0 D Holland 33/1: 00: Chsd ldrs till appr fnl 2f: 13th. **nk** **79**
3999 **Caqui Dor 12** [16] 2-9-0 J Weaver 33/1: -- **Mumbling** [14] 2-9-0 S Sanders 33/1:
-- **Winning Pleasure** [5] 2-9-0 J Fortune 33/1: -- **Loose Chippins** [11] 2-8-9 S Whitworth 33/1:
17 ran Time 1m 28.06 (4.86) (Athos Christodoulou) Mrs A J Perrett Pulborough, W Sussex

4184

4.45 EBF WESTLEY MDN DIV 2 2YO (D) 7f str Good 40 -33 Slow
£5086 £1565 £782 £391

-- **MALHUB** [8] J H M Gosden 2-9-0 R Hills 11/2: 1: 2 br c Kingmambo - Arjuzah (Ahonoora) Trkd ldrs, rdn appr fnl 1f, ran on well to lead fnl 30y: tchd 13/2: half-brother to a 6f juv wnr, dam decent 7f performer: eff at 7f, 1m looks likely to suit: acts on gd grnd & a stiff/gall trk: will rate higher. **91**
3980 **AMICABLE 13** [17] B W Hills 2-9-0 M Hills 2/1 FAV: -42: 2 b c Common Grounds - Bahia Laura (Bellypha) Nvr far away, led appr fnl 2f, sn rdn, hdd nr fin: well bckd: eff at 7f on firm & gd: win a mdn. **nk** **90**
-- **HARMONY ROW** [15] E A L Dunlop 2-9-0 G Carter 25/1: 3: 2 ch c Barathea - Little Change (Grundy) Chsd ldrs, prog appr fnl 1f & chance inside last, held fnl 100y: op 14/1: 30,000gns half brother to sev wnrs: eff at 7f on gd grnd, should improve & find similar. **1½** **87**
-- **TOFFEE NOSED** [13] B W Hills 2-8-9 J Carroll 25/1: 4: Keen, held up, gd wide progress appr fnl 1f & ch inside last, no extra towards fin: clr rem: Selkirk half sister to a 6f/1m wnr: dam 10f wnr: eff at 7f, get 1m in time: has a turn of foot, shld improve & can win a fillies mdn. **1½** **80**
-- **CASSIUS** [5] 2-9-0 O Urbina 25/1: 5: Bhd, keeping on when slightly hmpd appr fnl 1f, nvr nrr: op 40/1: Machiavellian half brother to a fair 6f/7f wnr, dam 6f juv wnr: educational intro, imprve for J Fanshawe. **3½** **79**
3980 **RYANS GOLD 13** [10] 2-9-0 M Roberts 33/1: -006: Prom, onepce appr fnl 1f: impvd over longer trip. **hd** **79$**

NEWMARKET (ROWLEY) THURSDAY SEPTEMBER 28TH Righthand, Stiff, Galloping Track

-- **SMASHING TIME** [6] 2-8-9 M J Kinane 7/1: 7: Al mid div: 5,800gns Smart Strike half sister *hd* **74**
to a 3yo wnr in the States, dam useful in France, sire a dirt miler in the States: with Mrs A Perrett.
-- **ALDWYCH** [16] 2-9-0 Pat Eddery 8/1: 8: Chsd ldrs, no extra/eased fnl 1f: In The Wings half brother *½* **78**
to sev wnrs, including useful mid-dist performer Spout, dam 10f wnr: should improve over mid dists next term.
-- **HARLEQUIN** [12] 2-9-0 F Lynch 20/1: 9: Chsd ldrs, onepce fnl 2f: 90,000gns Halling colt, *nk* **77**
dam a wnr abroad: with Sir M Stoute.
-- **EMPORIO** [1] 2-9-0 G Sparkes (7) 25/1: 0: Trckd ldrs, outpcd 2f out: 10th: 16,000gns *1¼* **75**
Emperor Jones half brother to 2 wnrs abroad, dam also won abroad: with L Cumani.
3790 **NZAME 26** [4] 2-9-0 D O'Donohoe 20/1: 50: Handy, lost pl 2f out: 11th, shade btr 3790. *2* **71**
-- **STOCK PROOF** [3] 2-9-0 J Murtagh 10/1: 0: Led till bef fnl 2f, sn btn: 12th, op 6/1: *1¼* **69**
Green Desert first foal, dam modest miler: with Sir M Stoute.
-- **Jennash** [7] 2-8-9 T E Durcan 33/1: -- **Lavanter** [2] 2-9-0 J Reid 20/1:
3298 **Royal Satin 48** [14] 2-9-0 F Norton 33/1:
15 ran Time 1m 28.31 (5.11) (Hamdan Al Maktoum) J H M Gosden Manton, Wilts

4185 **5.15 FITZWILLIAM HCAP 3YO 0-80 (D) 5f Good 40 +01 Fast [87]**
£5248 £1615 £807 £403

3622 **WHISTLER 34** [16] R Hannon 3-9-6 (79) R Hughes 12/1: -24121: 3 ch g Selkirk - French Gift (Cadeaux **85**
Genereux) Chsd ldrs centre, rdn ent fnl 1f, ran on to lead twrds fin, just held on: tchd 14/1: earlier won at
Salisbury (mdn): '99 rnr up (stks, rtd 80): eff at 5/6f on firm & gd: handles gd/soft, any track: progressive.
3894 **DACCORD 20** [1] M Kettle 3-9-3 (76) N Callan 12/1: 350642: 3 ch g Beveled - National Time *shd* **81**
(Lord Avie) Towards rear centre, gd hdwy ent fnl 2f, ran on to press wnr inside last, just failed:
improving: fine run from stall 1: deserves to go one better: acts on firm, soft & equitrack, see 234.
4087 **ABSENT FRIENDS 7** [15] J Cullinan 3-8-2 (61) D O'Donohoe 33/1: 040053: 3 b c Rock City - *1* **63**
Green Supreme (Primo Dominie) Well plcd centre, ev ch till held nr fin: ran to best, mdn: acts on gd & soft.
4037 **ULYSSES DAUGHTER 10** [25] G A Butler 3-8-13 (72)(t) T Quinn 15/2 FAV: 42154: Rear far side, *nk* **73**
switched & ran on strongly fnl 1f, nvr nrr: tchd 9/1: return to 6f will suit, see 3820.
*3908 **JAMES STARK 19** [30] 3-9-5 (78)(bl) J Quinn 9/1: 445615: Cl up, led appr fnl 1f till fnl 100y, no extra. *¾* **77**
3908 **PRIME RECREATION 19** [2] 3-7-10 (55)(1oh) J Lowe 33/1: 000006: Rear, imprvg when ran into back *shd* **54**
of rival ent fnl 2f, kept on, unable to chall: bck to form with waiting tactics: acts on gd & gd/soft, see 1817.
696 **CLOPTON GREEN 192** [24] 3-7-10 (55)(7oh) G Baker (5) 50/1: 333527: Rear far side, weaved thro' *½* **52**
appr fnl 1f, nvr nrr: stiff task, over 6 month abs & this should have put him spot on: acts on gd & both AW's.
4037 **BUDELLI 10** [5] 3-9-7 (80) Craig Williams 12/1: 250208: Held up centre, ran on well fnl 1f, nvr nrr: *shd* **77**
top-weight: should be suited by a return to 6f next time: see 1399.
3908 **FIRST DRAW 19** [7] 3-8-9 (68) O Urbina 25/1: 0-0209: Chsd ldrs centre, onepce ent fnl 1f: *hd* **65**
t-strap omitted & a better eff without it today: see 3386, 1405.
4027 **BOANERGES 10** [8] 3-9-6 (79) D Holland 11/1: 306040: Struggling/outpcd in centre, qcknd thro' *hd* **75**
horses fnl 1f, nvr dangerous: 10th, appears to have plenty of untapped ability: see 2504, 2288.
3960 **BRANSTON PICKLE 14** [14] 3-8-4 (63) K Dalgleish (5) 10/1: 001200: Chsd ldrs, onepce fnl 1f, 11th. *hd* **59**
4015 **VILLA VIA 12** [27] 3-8-7 (66) S Whitworth 33/1: 221000: Bhd far side, prog 2f out, btn fnl 1f, 12th. *shd* **62**
3894 **CONNECT 20** [13] 3-9-4 (77) S Sanders 16/1: 430560: Nvr a factor: 13th, see 3894, 1186. *1¼* **69**
4037 **LABRETT 10** [20] 3-9-0 (73)(bl) Pat Eddery 12/1: 114000: Nvr dangerous tho' stying on fin: *½* **63**
fin 14th: unsuited by this drop back to 5f: see 3208.
3894 **POPPYS SONG 20** [23] 3-8-13 (72) C Rutter 20/1: 021400: Led far side till 2f out, fdd: 15th, btr 2684. *½* **61**
3825 **ROBIN HOOD 24** [6] 3-7-10 (55)(1oh) G Bardwell 20/1: 061020: Nvr dngrs centre, 16th: see 3825, 3536. *¾* **42**
3825 **LIZZIE SIMMONDS 24** [29] 3-7-11 (56) J Mackay (5) 14/1: 653050: Speed far side to halfway, 23rd: op 33/1. **0**
4037 **DANCING EMPRESS 10** [11] 3-9-0 (73)(bl) L Dettori 14/1: 406000: Al bhd: 25th, unsuited by drop to 5f. **0**
3919 **AJYAAL 16** [12] 3-8-11 (70)(tbl) R Hills 14/1: 0030: Bhd after 3f, 28th: back in trip, blnks reapplied. **0**
3584 **Pacific Place 35** [3] 3-7-12 (57) F Norton 33/1:
4065 **Second Generation 8** [18] 3-7-10 (55)(bl) Karen Peippo (7) 40/1:
3920 **Blue Holly 16** [17] 3-9-6 (79) J Fortune 20/1: 3960 **Shatin Beauty 14** [22] 3-7-10 (55)(4oh) R Brisland (5) 50/1:
3135 **Fly Like The Wind 55** [10] 3-9-0 (73) P Robinson 20/1:4027 **Rythm N Time 10** [21] 3-8-7 (66) W Supple 33/1:
4065 **Judiam 8** [26] 3-8-7 (66) A Beech (3) 33/1: 3441 **Branston Lucy 41** [9] 3-8-0 (59) R Ffrench 25/1:
3855 **Aira Force 22** [4] 3-9-1 (74) J Reid 25/1: 982 **Brandon Rock 161** [28] 3-9-0 (73) M Fenton 25/1:
4120 **Almashrouk 4** [19] 3-8-7 (66)(BL) B Marcus 40/1:
30 ran Time 1m 00.16 (1.92) (Raymond Tooth) R Hannon East Everleigh, Wilts

LINGFIELD (MIXED) FRIDAY SEPTEMBER 29TH Lefthand, Sharp, Undulating Track

Official Going: TURF - SOFT, AW - STANDARD Stalls: AW - Inside, Turf - Far Side

4186 **1.55 AMAT CLASS STKS 3YO+ 0-65 (G) 1m4f aw Going Standard Inapplicable**
£2014 £575 £287 3 yo rec 8 lb

3887 **CHALCEDONY 21** [15] G L Moore 4-11-3 Mr R L Moore (5) 5/6 FAV: 403621: 4 ch g Highest Honor - **60a**
Sweet Holland (Alydar) Held up, prog to trck ldrs over 3f out, hard rdn/chsd wnr inside last, kept on tho' al held:
fin 2nd, btn 1 1/4 lengths, awarded race: hvly bckd: earlier scored at Southwell (h'cap, T D Barron): '99
Lingfield & Southwell wnr (h'caps, rtd 66a & 62): plcd in '98 nursery, rtd 56a & 58): eff at 10/12f, stays 14f:
acts on firm, gd & both AWs: best without blinks & likes a sharp track: has run well fresh.
3284 **TAJAR 49** [4] T Keddy 8-11-3 Mrs H Keddy (5) 40/1: 103002: 8 b g Slew O Gold - Mashaarif (Mr *1* **58$**
Prospector) Held up, styd on steadily fnl 3f, nvr dangs, fin 3rd, plcd 2nd: abs: acts on firm, soft & equitrack.
4101 **FAILED TO HIT 7** [11] N P Littmoden 7-11-3 (vis) Miss L Johnston (5) 9/1: 365263: 7 b g Warrshan - *4* **52a**
Missed Again (High Top) Held up, effort wide fnl 3f, kept on onepace fnl 2f: loves claimers & W'hampton.
3737 **ARDENT 30** [5] Miss B Sanders 6-11-3 Miss Diana Jones 9/1: 005134: Chsd ldrs, led over 2f out till *1* **51$**
over 1f out, fdd: not disgraced but prob best at 1m/sharp 10f: see 3557 (10f).
3954 **FOR HEAVENS SAKE 16** [12] 3-10-9 Mr Nicky Tinkler (5) 5/1: 023235: Chsd ldrs 10f: op 3/1: see 3954. *4* **45a**
3375 **PEGASUS BAY 44** [6] 9-11-5 Mr R H Fowler (3) 9/1: 2-1106: Slowly away, eff over 3f out, sn held: abs. *1¼* **45a**
4024 **TOPAZ 13** [14] 5-11-3 Miss A L Hutchinson 66/1: 400267: Mid div at best: see 3494 (h'cap). *½* **42$**
3111 **PROUD CAVALIER 56** [9] 4-11-3 Mr S J Edwards (7) 50/1: 500408: Led 5f out till over 2f out, fdd: *¾* **41$**
8 week abs: mod form: treat rating with caution.

3858 **LOST SPIRIT 23** [1] 4-11-9 Miss A Bruton (7) 16/1: 352109: Led 7f, soon fdd: op 14/1: see 3586 (fast). *11* **35a**
3233 **SILENT SOUND 51** [8] 4-11-3 Miss L J Harwood (7) 9/1: 025340: Chsd ldrs 7f: 10th: op 7/1, 7 wk abs. *3* **25a**
4101 **FULL EGALITE 7** [3] 4-11-3 (bl) Miss L Sheen (5) 14/1: 02351D: Held up, prog to lead over 1f out, **63a**
rdn & styd on well ins last, won by one & a quarter lengths: disqualified & plcd last after weighing in a stone
under correct weight: earlier scored at Lingfield (first time blinks, C/D seller): unplcd last term for W Haggas,
(rtd 63): '98 wnr at Brighton (mdn, rtd 70, R Simpson): suited by 12f on soft grnd & equitrack: eff in blinks.
4119 **Dom Miguel 5** [10] 3-10-9 Miss A Elsey 25/1:   268 **Ihtimaam 268** [16] 8-11-3 Mr D Ross (7) 66/1:
4018 **Qualitair Pride 13** [13] 8-11-2 Miss Michelle Saunders (7) 33/1:
2527 **Tudor Romance 82** [2] 15-11-3 Mr M Sheridan (7) 66/1:
3489 **Kentish Rock 41** [7] 5-11-3 Mrs K Hills (7) 66/1:
16 ran   Time 2m 33.90 (4.7)   (Lancing Racing Syndicate)   G L Moore Woodingdean, East Sussex

---

4187   **2.25 EBF OFFICE PARTY MDN 2YO (D)**   **5f**   **Soft 90**   **+ 10 Fast**
                £3909   £1203   £601   £300   Raced towards centre

4096 **LEOZIAN 7** [15] Miss Gay Kelleway 2-9-0 N Callan 5/1: 2041: 2 b c Lion Cavern - Alzianah (Alzao)   **82**
Made all, held on well fnl 1f, rdn out: best time of day: eff at 5f on firm & soft grnd, likes a sharp/undul track.
3767 **SO SOBER 28** [12] C F Wall 2-9-0 G Duffield 7/2: 542062: 2 b c Common Grounds - Femme Savante   *¾*   **79**
(Glenstal) Chsd ldrs, rdn & styd on strongly fnl 1f, not reach wnr: nicely bckd: step up to 6f shld suit: see 2545.
3449 **PEARLY BROOKS 42** [10] T J Naughton 2-8-9 Paul Eddery 3/1 FAV: -53: 2 b f Efisio - Elkie Brooks   *1½*   **71**
(Relkino) Trkd ldrs, rdn & styd on fnl 2f, not pace of wnr: 6 wk abs, op 7/2: acts on firm & soft: see 3449 (6f).
-- **BRAINWAVE** [4] H Candy 2-8-9 C Rutter 10/1: 4: In tch, kept on under hands & heels riding fnl 2f,   *1½*   **68+**
no threat to front trio: op 7/1: Mind Games filly, Feb foal, cost 11,000gns: half sister to sev wnrs: dam a
sprinter: sire a high class sprinting 2yo: handles soft grnd: sure to improve for this kind intro.
-- **NOSE THE TRADE** [6] 2-9-0 S W Kelly (3) 12/1: 5: Rear, rdn/mod hdwy fnl 2f, no threat: Cyrano   *3*   **67**
de Bergerac gelding, cost a 5/6f juv wnr: spint bred: with J Osborne.
4095 **BELLA PAVLINA 7** [9] 2-8-9 J Fanning 25/1: 006: Chsd ldrs 4f: see 4095, 3795.   *2½*   **57**
-- **FAST FORTUNE 7** [7] 2-8-9 J Tate 13/2: 7: Chsd ldrs 4f: op 8/1: Forzando filly, Feb foal, a first foal: *nk*   **56**
dam plcd as a 2yo over 5f, with J Eustace.
4095 **BOSRA BADGER 7** [8] 2-9-0 I Mongan (5) 16/1: 000058: Towards rear, nvr on terms: mod form prev.   *1*   **59**
2711 **FIRST DEGREE 74** [5] 2-8-9 G Hind (5) 7/1: 009: Held up, mod hdwy under min press fnl 2f: 10 week   *½*   **53+**
abs: not knocked about here, now qual for h'caps & looks sure to do better over 6f+ in that sphere.
-- **KILMEENA STAR 13** [3] 2-9-0 S Carson (3) 20/1: 0: Towards rear, nvr a factor: 10th: So Factual colt,   *1*   **56**
March foal, half brother to 6/7f wnr Kilmeena Lad: dam unrcd: with E Wheeler.
3815 **LADY EBERSPACHER 25** [1] 2-8-9 P Doe 7/1: 042440: Prom early, rdn/btn halfway: btr 3815, 2227 (fast).   **0**
-- **Kingscross** [2] 2-9-0 R Havlin 12/1:   **Pertemps Reverend** [14] 2-9-0 G Faulkner (3) 16/1:
4095 **Bevel Blue 7** [11] 2-9-0 P Dobbs (5) 16/1:   3942 **Brown Holly 16** [3] 2-9-0 G Baker (5) 25/1:
15 ran   Time 1m 0.8 (4.0)   (Mr & Mrs Gary Pinchen)   Miss Gay Kelleway Lingfield, Surrey

---

4188   **2.55 EBF RACE NIGHTS MDN DIV 1 2YO (D)**   **6f**   **Soft 90**   **+ 08 Fast**
                £3484   £1072   £536   £268   Raced stands side

2935 **TRUSTTHUNDER 64** [12] N P Littmoden 2-8-9 P McCabe 11/2: -02201: 2 ch f Selkirk - Royal Cat (Royal   **87**
Academy) Chsd ldrs trav well halfway, rdn/led over 1f out, sn pulled clr & eased nr fin: val for 5L+: op 9/2, abs:
gd time: eff at 6f, stays 7f well: acts on firm & soft, gall or sharp/undul trk: runs well fresh: improved here.
3832 **MYSTERI DANCER 24** [11] R J O'Sullivan 2-9-0 P Doe 5/1: 022: 2 b g Rudimentary - Mystery Ship   *3*   **82**
(Decoy Boy) Led 2f, rdn & kept on fnl 1f, not pace of wnr: op 3/1: acts on firm & soft: confirmed improv of 3832.
-- **EASTERN BREEZE** [2] P W Harris 2-9-0 A Culhane 9/1: 3: 2 b c Sri Pekan - Elegant Bloom (Be   *1¼*   **79+**
My Guest) Bhd early, stdy hdwy from halfway under hands & heels riding, nrst fin: op 6/1: Feb foal, cost 40,000
gns: half brother to Rolo Tomasi, useful 5/7f: eff at 6f, 7f will suit: handles soft: eyecatching late hdwy.
3940 **DREAM MAGIC 16** [7] M J Ryan 2-9-0 A Clark 8/1: 064: Chsd ldrs, rdn & kept on onepace from over 1f   *1½*   **76**
out: handles firm & soft grnd, return to 7f & h'caps could suit: see 3940, 3786.
4001 **ATLANTIC MYSTERY 13** [13] 2-8-9 J Fanning 11/8 FAV: 35: Led/dsptd lead 2f, fdd: hvly bckd.   *3*   **65**
-- **SHARPINCH** [8] 2-9-0 S Righton 25/1: 6: Chsd ldrs halfway, no impress fnl 2f: Beveled colt,   *½*   **69**
May foal, cost 3,000gns, a first foal: dam lightly rcd mdn: with P Chamings.
-- **WHISKY NINE** [1] 2-9-0 M Tebbutt 11/1: 7: Chsd ldrs 4f: op 6/1: Makbul colt, April foal, cost   *6*   **57**
7,500gns: half brother to a 5f juvenile wnr: dam a mdn: with M Jarvis.
4034 **LAY DOWN SALLY 11** [6] 2-8-9 S Carson (3) 14/1: 008: Led towards centre after 2f, hdd 2f out, btn/   *1*   **50**
eased fnl 1f: only mod form prev: see 2687.
4086 **BEST GUEST 8** [14] 2-9-0 G Hind 20/1: 009: Rear, rdn halfway, mod hdwy: see 3730.   *nk*   **54**
3980 **WORTH A GAMBLE 14** [15] 2-9-0 G Baker (5) 33/1: -00: Chsd ldrs 3f: 10th: mod form.   *shd*   **54**
4035 **ON MY HONOUR 11** [10] 2-8-9 R Smith (5) 33/1: 00: Al towards rear, 11th: mod form.   *shd*   **48**
4068 **DOWNPOUR 9** [3] 2-9-0 G Duffield 9/1: 00: Al bhd: 13th: see 4068.   **0**
4137 **Mahlstick 4** [5] 2-9-0 J D Smith 33/1:   4076 **Mujalia 8** [4] 2-9-0 O Urbina 25/1:
-- **Map Boy** [9] 2-9-0 C Rutter 33/1:
15 ran   Time 1m 13.7 (4.9)   (Tallulah Racing)   N P Littmoden Newmarket, Suffolk

---

4189   **3.25 EBF RACE NIGHTS MDN DIV 2 2YO (D)**   **6f**   **Soft 90**   **- 00 Slow**
                £3461   £1065   £532   £266   Raced towards stands side

4072 **SUNNY GLENN 9** [14] N P Littmoden 2-9-0 J Tate 33/1: 051: 2 ch c Rock Hopper - La Ballerina   **81**
(Lafontaine) Chsd ldrs, rdn/pressed wnr fnl 2f, styd on for press to lead cl home: apprec this drop to 6f, 7f shld
suit: acts on soft & a sharp/undulating track: clearly going the right way.
3942 **BREAKING NEWS 16** [3] M A Jarvis 2-9-0 M Tebbutt 9/1: 302: 2 b c Emperor Jones - Music Khan   *nk*   **79**
(Music Boy) Led, strongly pressed fnl 2f & drvn inside last, just hdd nr line: acts on firm & soft: see 3832.
-- **FATHER THAMES** [7] J R Fanshawe 2-9-0 O Urbina 9/1: 3: 2 b c Bishop of Cashel - Mistress Thames   *½*   **78+**
(Sharpo) Chsd ldrs halfway, rdn & kept on well under hands & heels riding fnl 1f, not pace of front pair: April
foal, half brother to a 10f wnr abroad: dam a mdn: eff at 6f, 7f will suit: handles soft grnd: encouraging intro.
789 **ANOTHER SECRET 27** [12] R Hannon 2-8-9 P Fitzsimons (5) 6/1: -404: Prom, rdn/no extra inside   *¾*   **72**
last: clr rem: handles firm & soft grnd: eff at 6f: see 3449.
3047 **SINGLE TRACK MIND 60** [4] 2-9-0 J Bosley (7) 33/1: 05: Chsd ldrs, outpcd halfway, kept on fnl 1f,   *4*   **69**
no threat to ldrs: 2 month abs: not given a hard ride: 7f+ should suit in the future.
3980 **BEIDERBECKE 14** [9] 2-9-0 C Rutter 15/2: -06: Trkd ldr, outpcd over 2f out: see 3980.   *2*   **65**
1291

3881 **RASHAS REALM 21** [2] 2-8-9 G Carter 13/8 FAV: 237: Chsd ldrs 4f: fdd: hvly bckd: btr 3881 (gd). *shd* **60**
-- **AMONG WOMEN** [8] 2-8-9 S Whitworth 25/1: 8: Towards rear, mod hdwy: Common Grounds filly, ¾ **59**
April foal, cost 8,000gns: dam unrcd: sire a high class 2yo miler: with N Callaghan.
-- **SHORE VISION** [10] 2-9-0 A Culhane 16/1: 9: Towards rear, little hdwy: Efisio colt, March foal, *1¾* **61**
cost 10,000gns: half brother to a 7f Listed wnr abroad: dam a 3yo 12f wnr: looks sure to relish further in time.
-- **BRIEF CONTACT** [1] 2-9-0 P Dobbs (5) 33/1: 0: Slowly away & rdn in rear early, no impress: 10th: *3* **55**
Brief Truce gelding, March foal, 9,500gns 2yo: a first foal: dam unrcd: sire top class 1m/10f performer.
4082 **SEARCH AND DESTROY 8** [15] 2-9-0 G Duffield 6/1: 00: Al towards rear: 11th: bhd on debut prev. ½ **0**
-- **Jetstream Flyer** [5] 2-8-9 J Tate 25/1: 3840 **Yanus 24** [6] 2-9-0 W Ryan 33/1:
-- **In Touch** [13] 2-8-9 G Hind 25/1: -- **Far South Trader** [11] 2-9-0 P Doe 33/1:
15 ran Time 1m 14.2 (5.4) (Mrs H F Mahr) N P Littmoden Newmarket, Suffolk

4190

4.00 BET DIRECT CLAIMER 2YO (F) 6f Soft 90 - 17 Slow
£2660 £760 £380 Majority racing stands side favoured

3901 **CLANBROAD 20** [17] Mrs A J Perrett 2-9-7 T Ashley 6/1: 41401: 2 ch c Clantime - Under The Wing **78**
(Aragon) Cl up stands side going well at halfway, rdn/led over 1f out, styd on well inside last, rdn out: earlier won at Leicester (auct mdn): eff at 6f, tried 7f, should suit in time: acts on fast & soft, stiff/gall or sharp trk.
3468 **ASTAIREDOTCOM 41** [18] K R Burke 2-8-4 N Callan 25/1: 450402: 2 b f Lake Coniston - Romantic *1½* **57**
Overture (Stop The Music) Cl up stands side, rdn/led over 2f out, hdd over 1f out, kept on well for press: back to form on return to 6f: 6 week abs: handles firm & soft grnd: best form without visor.
4097 **CLANSINGE 7** [4] A Berry 2-8-6 (BL) T E Durcan 9/2: 006023: 2 ch f Clantime - North Pine (Import) *nk* **58**
Chsd ldrs stands side, rdn/chall over 1f out, no extra cl home: gd run in blinks: op 7/2: acts on firm & soft grnd.
4025 **UNVEIL 13** [13] G M McCourt 2-7-10 B Callaghan (7) 14/1: 503404: Mid div stands side, drifted left *1½* **45**
but styd on strongly under hands & heels fnl 1f, nrst fin: seems best around 5/6f, handles gd, soft & fibresand.
3258 **WATTNO ELJOHN 50** [8] 2-8-13 J Weaver 11/1: 001635: Bhd stands side early, late hdwy, nvr a *2½* **57**
threat: op 9/1, 7 week abs: handles fast & soft grnd: see 3258.
4096 **QUATREDIL 7** [3] 2-8-6 P Fitzsimons (5) 16/1: 0406: Prom towards centre, rdn & kept on fnl 2f tho' ¾ **49**
flashed tail, no chance with ldrs stands side: first home on unfav centre/stands side: see 3096, 2748.
-- **FARAUDE** [12] 2-8-8 B Marcus 25/1: 7: Bhd, rdn/mod late hdwy: Farfelu filly, April foal: cost ½ **50**
1,000gns: dam a 12f wnr: likely to need 7f+ on this evidence: with W Muir.
4097 **LIGHT EVIDENCE 7** [10] 2-8-2 P Hanagan (5) 4/1 FAV: 058: In tch, btn 2f out: op 5/1: btr 4097 (6f, gd). *hd* **43**
4097 **QUIZZICAL LADY 7** [5] 2-8-10 Paul Eddery 9/2: 420039: Chsd ldrs 4f: btr 3354, 1000. *1½* **48**
-- **MEADOWSWEET** [2] 2-8-2 C Rutter 8/1: 0: In tch far side, btn 2f out: 10th: op 5/1: Fumo Di Londra ½ **39**
filly, April foal, cost 6,500gns: half sister to a wnr abroad, dam unrcd tho' well related: sire a smart juv.
4097 **OSO NEET 7** [9] 2-8-7 R Smith (5) 20/1: 06000: Mid div at best: 11th: see 2052, 1589. ½ **43**
3949 **CENTURY STAR 16** [15] 2-8-13 (BL) J Tate 33/1: -0060: Led till over 2f out, wknd: 17th, blinks: btr 3949. **0**
4097 **Ghost Of A Chance 7** [16] 2-8-9 A Clark 20/1: 4098 **Delphyllia 7** [11] 2-8-4 G Baker (5) 11/1:
3832 **Simply Remy 24** [7] 2-8-9 R Fitzpatrick 33/1: 3999 **Spa Gulch 13** [14] 2-9-7 G Duffield 12/1:
-- **Magic Lawyer** [1] 2-8-2 D R McCabe 14/1: 3162 **Amarone 55** [6] 2-8-13 (BL) G Carter 25/1:
18 ran Time 1m 15.2 (6.4) (Derek Broad) Mrs A J Perrett Pulborough, West Sussex

4191

4.35 3663 NURSERY HCAP 2YO 0-75 (E) 7f str Soft 90 - 00 Slow **[82]**
£3342 £955 £477 Raced stands side

*4070 **BOISDALE 9** [10] G C Bravery 2-9-4 (72)(7ex) J Weaver 7/2 FAV: 064011: 2 b c Common Grounds - **80**
Alstomeria (Potsiki) Made all, styd on well fnl 2f, rdn out: nicely bckd: earlier scored at Chester (nursery h'caps): loves to force the pace over a sharp/undul 7f: handles firm, improved last twice on soft grnd: progressive type.
4084 **LOOKING FOR LOVE 8** [1] J G Portman 2-9-4 (72) S W Kelly (3) 12/1: 336232: 2 b f Tagula - Mousseux *3½* **74**
(Jareer) Prom, rdn/chance 2f out, sn outpcd by wnr: op 8/1: consistent in defeat: see 4084.
3577 **FLOOT 37** [3] J L Dunlop 2-8-11 (65) B Marcus 16/1: 0003: 2 b c Piccolo - Midnight Owl (Ardross) *shd* **67**
Al prom, rdn/ev ch 2f out, kept on onepce: fine h'cap bow: eff at 7f on soft grnd.
3767 **SMOOTHIE 28** [14] P F I Cole 2-9-0 (68) G Baker (5) 10/1: -3054: Chsd ldrs, rdn & kept on onepace *3* **66**
fnl 2f: h'cap bow: prob stays 7f, handles fast & soft grnd: see 3137.
3913 **SANDLES 18** [2] 2-9-2 (70) G Hind 16/1: 544005: In tch, lost plce halfway, no threat after: see 3411. *1½* **66**
2599 **HOMELIFE 79** [12] 2-8-12 (66) P D'Arcy 20/1: 64066: Rear, switched halfway, hard rdn & late hdwy, *shd* **62**
no threat: jock given 3-day iresponsible riding ban: abs: h'cap bow: prev with D Sasse, now with P W d'Arcy.
3938 **DANE DANCING 16** [11] 2-9-0 (68) R Havlin 9/1: -5007: Prom 5f: h'cap bow, op 6/1: rtd higher 3938. ½ **63**
3444 **RIVER OF FIRE 42** [16] 2-8-9 (63) J Tate 20/1: 01158: In tch, outpcd fnl 3f: 6 wk abs: btr 3216 (sell). *3½* **53**
*3830 **CHAWENG BEACH 24** [4] 2-9-1 (69) P Fitzsimons (5) 13/2: 645119: In tch 5f: btr 3830 (firm, C/D). ½ **58**
3976 **DODONA 14** [17] 2-8-12 (66) C Rutter 5/1: 40040: Mid div at best: 10th: op 10/1: eyecatching 3976 (6f). *hd* **54**
3860 **SILKEN WINGS 23** [5] 2-9-0 (68) G Duffield 12/1: -32200: Prom 5f: op 8/1: 11th, btr 3571, 2784. *5* **49**
3888 **PORT MORESBY 21** [15] 2-9-7 (75)(t) I Mongan (5) 10/1: 001000: Held up, eff 3f out, sn btn: 12th. *1* **55**
3938 **Manuka Too 16** [8] 2-8-10 (64) M Tebbutt 25/1: 3617 **Long Weekend 35** [7] 2-8-10 (64) G Carter 11/1:
*1577 **Numerate 122** [9] 2-9-7 (75) W Ryan 12/1: 3943 **Miss Tress 16** [6] 2-9-6 (74) A Culhane 25/1:
3760 **Tiny Tim 28** [13] 2-8-10 (64) J Fanning 16/1: 2791 **Hammock 71** [18] 2-8-11 (65)(VIS) R Winston 25/1:
18 ran Time 1m 26.7 (6.3) (Ott Partnership) G C Bravery Newmarket, Suffolk

4192

5.10 HBLB LINGFIELD HCAP 3YO 0-70 (E) 7f str Soft 90 - 09 Slow **[77]**
£3640 £1040 £520 Raced stands side

3561 **DIAMOND OLIVIA 37** [8] John Berry 3-8-4 (53) R Fitzpatrick 7/1: 062501: 3 b f Beveled - Queen Of **61**
The Quorn (Governor General) Held up, prog to lead over 1f out, pulled clr under hands & heels riding fnl 1f despite edging left, readily: val for 6L+: bckd: first win: plcd in '99 for W Turner (rtd 67a): eff at 7f/1m on gd, likes soft & hvy grnd: handles a sharp or stiff/gall track: comfortable wnr here, qk follow-up?
4032 **AIR MAIL 11** [13] Mrs N Macauley 3-8-11 (60) J Tate 25/1: 000102: 3 b g Night Shift - Wizardary *4* **60**
(Shirley Heights) Led, rdn/hdd over 1f out, sn held by wnr: acts on both AW's & soft grnd: see 3770 (AW, clmr).
3970 **LARAZA 15** [5] Miss I Foustok 3-8-11 (60) T E Durcan 8/1: 500523: 3 ch f Arazi - Queen Midas *1* **59**
(Glint Of Gold) Chsd ldrs, rdn & kept on onepce fnl 2f: handles firm & soft grnd: see 3970 (mdn h'cap).
4044 **ANNIJAZ 10** [10] J G Portman 3-8-10 (59) G Baker (5) 5/1 FAV: 035234: Held up, eff 3f out, onepace: ½ **57**
prob handles hvy, prefer a faster surface?: bckd, tchd 7/1: see 2794 (gd).
4102 **TOYON 7** [2] 3-9-5 (68) G Duffield 12/1: 234005: Rear, kept on fnl 2f, no threat: see 2817 (AW, 1m). *hd* **65**
3939 **BISHOPSTONE MAN 16** [3] 3-9-6 (69) C Rutter 16/1: 003506: Rear, hdwy over 1f out, sn no impress. *shd* **66**

LINGFIELD (MIXED)
FRIDAY SEPTEMBER 29TH   Lefthand, Sharp, Undulating Track

3666 **SEA DRIFT** 33 [12] 3-9-7 (70) B Marcus 5/1: 313027: Prom 6f: bckd: btr 2860 (fast, mdn).   2½   63
3739 **STRAND OF GOLD** 30 [18] 3-8-8 (57)(bl) P Fitzsimons (5) 9/1: 050008: Cl up 5f: see 3739, 1220.   1¼   48
2549 **LADY NOOR** 81 [9] 3-8-3 (52) C Carver (3) 20/1: 000059: Chsd ldrs 4f: 12 week abs: see 2549 (6f).   3   39
4040 **SUPER DOMINION** 11 [6] 3-8-5 (54) P M Quinn (3) 16/1: 433600: Mid div at best: 10th: see 3242.   ¾   40
3854 **ROYAL IVY** 23 [1] 3-9-1 (64) P Doe 12/1: 420060: AI towards rear: 11th: se 2325, 421.   ½   49
3274 **ANYHOW** 49 [7] 3-9-6 (69) I Mongan (5) 15/2: 041000: Chsd ldrs 5f: 12th: 7 wk abs: btr 2591 (C/D).   ½   53
3936 **Starlight 16** [14] 3-9-2 (65) G Carter 12/1:   3762 Cedar Prince 28 [17] 3-8-7 (56)(vis) R Havlin 16/1:
3666 **Diamond Rachael 33** [4] 3-9-2 (65)(vis) Joanna Badger (7) 12/1:
3269 **Carew Castle 50** [16] 3-8-11 (60) S Whitworth (7) 12/1:
3750 **Believing 29** [11] 3-8-8 (57) R Smith 25/1:
17 ran   Time 1m 27.3 (6.9)   (Diamond Racing Ltd)   John Berry Newmarket, Suffolk

4193
5.40 BET DIRECT MDN 3YO+ (D)   **1m5f aw**   **Going Standard**   **Inapplicable**
£2973   £457   £228   3 yo rec 9 lb

4040 **DISTANT COUSIN** 11 [3] H R A Cecil 3-8-12 W Ryan 15/8 FAV: 231: 3 b c Distant Relative - Tinaca   80+
(Manila) Trckd ldr, led over 5f out, pulled clr from over 3f out under hands & heels riding, eased down inside
last, comfortably: val for 12L+: hvly bckd: AW bow: eff at 12/13f, further could suit: acts on equitrack & soft
grnd: sharp/easy track: plenty in hand here: looks to be going the right way & h'cap company will now suit.
3290 **CITRUS MAGIC** 49 [2] K Bell 3-8-12 J Bosley (7) 14/1: -40002: 3 b c Cosmonaut - Up All Night   7   62a
(Green Desert) Chsd ldrs halfway, rdn/outpcd by wnr fnl 3f, narrowly prevailed in battle for 2nd: 7 week abs:
caught a tartar here, will apprec a return to h'caps: AW bow today & prob handles equitrack.
1637 **DESTINATION** 120 [8] C A Cyzer 3-8-12 G Carter 5/1: 524453: 3 ch g Deploy - Veuve (Tirol)   hd   61a
Prom, rdn/outpcd by easy wnr fnl 3f: bckd: 4 month abs: longer 13f trip may yet suit: stays a sharp 12f &
handles gd, hvy & prob equitrack: clr of rem: see 1425 (h'cap).
858 **BOLD BAHAMIAN** 172 [7] J Noseda 3-8-12 J Weaver 6/1: 540-64: In tch wide halfway, btn 3f out: 8   49a
op 8/1: 6 month abs, longer 13f trip/AW bow: see 858.
3707 **SUN SILK** 32 [12] R Havlin 12/1: -0505: Chsd wnr over 4f out till over 2f out, sn btn: AW bow.   4   38a
2305 **STORMY SKYE** 91 [1] 4-9-7 (t) I Mongan (5) 15/2: 2-3246: Held up, nvr threat: 3 mth abs, AW bow.   2½   39a
3818 **JUNO BEACH** 25 [9] 4-9-2 R Winston 11/2: 347: Strugg 4f out: op 8/1: AW bow, longer 13f trip.   ¾   33a
-- **MOUNT LOGAN** [13] 5-9-7 A Culhane 14/1: 8: Slowly away & wide on bend 9f out, al bhd: op 8/1.   2½   34a
4099 **EASTWOOD DRIFTER** 7 [6] 3-8-12 B Marcus 7/1: 625039: Bhd 5f out: op 5/1: btr 4099 (h'cap, 2m).   ½   33a
3762 **FLYING RUN** 28 [4] 3-8-7 G Baker (5) 40/1: 000300: Led till over 5f out, sn btn: 10th: longer 13f trip.   3½   23a
3978 **Mi Odds 14** [5] 4-9-7 R Fitzpatrick 33/1:   -- **Somalia** [10] 3-8-12 (BL) O Urbina 66/1:
4100 **Salient Point 7** [11] 3-8-7 N Callan 20/1:
13 ran   Time 2m 43.76 (1.46)   (Wafic Said)   H R A Cecil Newmarket, Suffolk

NEWMARKET
FRIDAY SEPTEMBER 29TH   Righthand, Stiff, Galloping Track

Official Going   GOOD. Stalls: Far side.

4194
2.05 LISTED GODOLPHIN STKS 3YO+ (A)   **1m4f**   **Good 44**   **+10 Fast**
£15834   £6006   £3003   £1305   3 yo rec 8 lb

1848 **WELLBEING** 111 [5] H R A Cecil 3-8-6 T Quinn 7/4 FAV: 3-1151: 3 b c Sadler's Wells - Charming   117
Life (Sir Tristram) Hld up, hdwy to lead over 2f out, styd on well, pushed out, readily: well bckd, abs, fast
time: earlier 13L 5th in Derby, also won twice here at Newmarket (mdn & stks): stays 12f well, further will suit:
acts on fast & gd, loves Newmarket: runs well fresh: lightly raced, improving, Gr 3 St Simon at Newbury looks ideal.
*3984 **PAWN BROKER** 14 [6] D R C Elsworth 3-8-10 M J Kinane 4/1: 220312: 3 ch c Selkirk - Dime Bag   5   114
(High Line) Hld up, trav bed & chased wnr over 2f out, onepace over 1f out: well bckd: clr rem, gd run.
3863 **HIDDNAH** 23 [4] M Johnston 3-8-1 Craig Williams 6/1: 5-2363: 3 ch f Affirmed - L'Extra Honor (Hero's   7   97
Honor) Led over 5f out till over 2f out, no extra: caught 2 smart sorts: see 3595.
3061 **HATAAB** 59 [2] E A L Dunlop 3-8-10 R Hills 8/1: 1-1204: Hld up, eff over 2f out, sn outpcd: abs.   ¾   105
3898 **GOING GLOBAL** 20 [3] 3-8-7 (t) (1ow) J Reid 25/1: 060405: Cl up, outpcd over 2f out: vis discarded.   8   91
3984 **ZAFONIUM** 14 [7] 3-8-6 J Fortune 25/1: -24066: In tch, hdwy to chall over 2f out, sn wknd: no blnks.   4   86
3645 **TAUFANS MELODY** 34 [1] 9-9-0 (VIS) D Harrison 25/1: 002357: Dsptd lead over 6f, wknd 3f out: visored.   8   76
7 ran   Time 2m 32.85 (4.05)   (Exors Of The Late Lord Howard de Walden)   H R A Cecil Newmarket

4195
2.35 H & K RTD HCAP 3YO+ 0-100 (B)   **7f str**   **Good 44**   **-02 Slow**   [107]
£10407   £3947   £1973   £897   3 yo rec 3 lb

3791 **CAPRICHO** 27 [16] W J Haggas 3-8-4 (86) P Robinson 8/1: 112001: 3 gr g Lake Coniston - Star   92
Spectacle (Spectacular Bid) Cl up, strong hdwy to lead over 1f out, styd on well, drvn out: prog earlier, won at
Ayr & Newmarket (h'cap): suited by a stiff 7f on fast & gd/soft: loves Newmarket: useful, has a turn on foot.
4112 **STRAHAN** 6 [3] J H M Gosden 3-9-4 (100) L Dettori 7/1: 230402: 3 b c Catrail - Soreze (Gallic   ½   104
League) Held up, hdwy over 2f out, kept on for press in last, not btn far: back to best: tough & consistent.
3884 **GRANNYS PET** 21 [1] P F I Cole 6-9-7 (100) J Fortune 25/1: 316053: 6 ch g Selkirk - Patsy   1   104+
Western (Precocious) Held up, hdwy & no room over 2f out till just ins fnl 1f, styd on well, too late: eyecatching
under top-weight & prob unlucky: relatively lightly raced this term & can win a back-end 7f contest: see 1574.
3981 **VOLONTIERS** 14 [2] P W Harris 5-8-8 (87) T Quinn 7/1: 002034: Held up, bhd, some late gains.   1½   87
*4012 **BAHAMIAN PIRATE** 13 [4] 5-9-0 (93) A Nicholls 10/1: 213015: Cl up, eff to chall 2f out, ev ch   shd   92
dist, no extra ins last: nicely bckd, could well go in again over favourite 6f trip as in 4012 (Ayr Gold Cup).
4112 **ZUCCHERO** 6 [4] 4-8-4 (83)(3oh) K Dalgleish (5) 11/1: 655436: Held up, eff over 3f out, onepace   ½   81
over 1f out: btr 4112.
3883 **FREE OPTION** 21 [15] 5-9-3 (96) J Reid 10/1: 103607: Handy, rdn & slightly short of room well   shd   93
over 1f out, onepce: see 3883, 3597.
4012 **NIGRASINE** 13 [6] 6-8-12 (91)(bl) R Cody Boutcher (7) 20/1: 104008: Cl up, led over 3f out   hd   87
till 2f out, onepce: best on faster grnd, has slipped down the weights: see 1952 (6f).
4037 **GREY EMINENCE** 11 [10] 3-8-6 (88) R Hughes 6/1 FAV: 222129: Prom, rdn & outpcd over 1f out: nk   83
well bckd: better expected after 4037.
3998 **RED N SOCKS** 13 [17] 3-8-10 (92) Pat Eddery 8/1: 010060: Led 2f out till over 1f out, wknd: 10th.   1   85

3414 **CAIR PARAVEL 43** [1] 3-8-4 (86)(bl) L Newman (3) 33/1: 001000: Prom, wknd over 1f out: ¾ 77
11th, abs: twice below 2858, best 2688 (1m, made all).
3902 **BAILEYS WHIRLWIND 20** [11] 3-8-8 (90) J Mackay (5) 33/1: 444460: In tch, rdn & short of room over ½ 80
1f out, sn wknd: 12th: see 1186.
4078 **OMAHA CITY 8** [7] 6-9-6 (99) K Darley 20/1: 352100: Slow away, al bhd: 13th: best 3902 (Goodwood). ¾ 87
3750 **RICH IN LOVE 29** [5] 6-8-4 (83)(1oh) A Beech (3) 33/1: 005000: Al bhd: 14th: see 3597. nk 70
4013 **ESPADA 13** [9] 4-8-8 (87)(VIS) S Sanders 20/1: 100000: Al bhd: 15th, needs a rest? best 1077 (1m). nk 73
3703 **TOTAL LOVE 32** [8] 3-8-12 (94) M J Kinane 16/1: 253400: Bhd, brief eff over 2f out, sn wknd: 16th. ½ 79
4129 **FIRST MAITE 5** [14] 7-8-11 (90)(bl) Dean McKeown 25/1: 400000: Led till over 3f out, wknd: 17th. 2 71
17 ran Time 1m 26.41 (3.21) (M Tabor) W J Haggas Newmarket, Suffolk

4196

3.05 GR 3 SOMERVILLE TATTS STKS 2YO (A) 7f str Good 44 -02 Slow
£20300 £7700 £3850 £1750

3568 **KING CHARLEMAGNE 37** [6] A P O'Brien 2-8-9 M J Kinane 11/2: 211: 2 b c Nureyev - Race The Wild 104
Wind (Sunny's Halo) Cl up, eff to chall dist, styd on well for hard driving to get up cl home, all out: Irish
raider who earlier scored at Leopardstown (mdn): $1,500,000 Mar foal: dam smart 1m performer: stys a
stiff 7f on gd/firm & gD, 1m will suit: useful, genuine effort here.
*3909 **GRANDERA 18** [4] J R Fanshawe 2-8-9 D Harrison 11/2: -512: 2 ch c Grand Lodge - Bordighera nk 103
(Alysheba) Cl up, led over 2f out till inside last, kept on for press, just held: fine run on only 3rd start.
3891 **PATSYS DOUBLE 21** [8] M Blanshard 2-8-9 T Quinn 10/1: -11153: 2 b c Emarati - Jungle Rose shd 103
(Shirley Heights) Prom, eff for press to lead inside last, hdd cl home under hands & heels riding:
another useful run dropped in class & deserves a Listed success: see 3891, 2848.
3304 **FORWOOD 48** [5] M A Jarvis 2-8-9 P Robinson 20/1: -1144: Keen, chsd wnr, hard rdn over 1f out, 1 101
kept on for press: another useful run after 7 week abs: see 3304, 2677.
4060 **IMPERIAL DANCER 12** [3] 2-8-9 Craig Williams 20/1: 451325: Held up rear, kept on appr fnl 1f, shd 101+
nrst fin, too much to do: another unenterprising ride from his Australian jockey: stays 7f well & can do better.
3859 **TEMPEST 23** [12] 2-8-9 J Murtagh 11/1: -4126: Keen bhd, eff over 1f out, nvr nrr: apprec 1m+. hd 100
3946 **CAUVERY 16** [9] 2-8-10(1ow) O Peslier 25/1: -21037: Held up, brief eff over 1f out, no extra: useful. nk 99
*3980 **PALANZO 14** [2] 2-8-9 R Mullen 14/1: -218: Hld up, rdn over 2f out, no extra over 1f out: stays 7f. hd 98
3470 **STORMING HOME 41** [11] 2-8-9 J Reid 7/1: -0129: Handy, wknd over 1f out: rtd higher 3470. 1 96
*3790 **BOURGAINVILLE 27** [10] 2-8-9 K Darley 14/1: 110: Prom, wknd well over 1f out: 10th, up in class. 3½ 89
3996 **TRIPLE BLUE 13** [1] 2-8-9 R Hughes 25/1: 245340: Al bhd: been busy, see 3996 (6f, Gr2). 1½ 86
*3840 **SIXTY SECONDS 24** [13] 2-8-9 L Dettori 5/2 FAV: 210: Held up, rdn & btn 2f out: well bckd 3 80
& clearly better expected after mdn win in 3840 (firm).
3372 **CASHEL PALACE 47** [7] 2-8-9 Paul Scallen 66/1: -21500: Led till over 2f out, wknd: 12th: 1½ 77
Gowran mdn wnr (7f, soft).
13 ran Time 1m 26.97 (3.77) (Mr M Tabor & Mrs John Magnier) A P O'Brien Ballydoyle, Ireland

4197

3.40 J LEVETT HCAP 3YO 0-100 (C) 1m2f str Good 44 -11 Slow [107]
£8918 £2744 £1372 £686

*4088 **SHRIVAR 8** [1] M R Channon 3-7-10 (75)(vis)(5ex) M Henry 9/1: 404211: 3 b g Sri Pekan - Kriva 81
(Reference Point) Held up, eff & short of room over 2f out, styd on strongly dist to get up cl home, going
away, gd strong ride: well bckd: earlier scored at Warwick (mdn h'cap) & Pontefract (class stakes): suited
by 10f, stays 14f: acts on fast & soft, any track: best in a visor: on the upgrade & has a vital turn of foot.
*1242 **BARTON SANDS 141** [9] L M Cumani 3-8-6 (85) K Darley 12/1: 212: 3 b c Tenby - Hetty Green ½ 90
(Bay Express) Held up, hdwy over 2f out to chall inside last, kept on for press, just held: fine run after a 4
month abs & stays 10f: lightly raced & should land another nice prize: see 1242.
3997 **BONAGUIL 13** [14] C F Wall 3-8-10 (89) R Mullen 8/1: 342023: 3 b g Septieme Ciel - Chateaubrook nk 93
(Alleged) Cl up, eff to dispute lead dist, no extra cl home, not btn far: v prog & tough this term: see 3997.
3794 **THUNDERING SURF 27** [11] J R Jenkins 3-8-3 (82) Craig Williams 10/1: 001354: Held up, hdwy & 1 86+
short of room twice 2f out, kept on ins last, too late: poss unlucky & lacked the strength of the wnr's ride.
*3415 **MUSCHANA 43** [18] 3-8-10 (89) Pat Eddery 12/1: 310315: Led 4f out till inside last, no extra: 1½ 90
op 8/1: 6 week abs & prob ran to winning form of 3415 (fast grnd, made all).
3435 **TRICCOLO 42** [16] 3-8-3 (82) M Roberts 25/1: 513156: Prom, rdn & no extra appr fnl 1f: 6 week ¾ 82
abs: poss stys 10f, return to 1m will suit: see 3005.
.3793 **PRETRAIL 27** [8] 3-7-11 (76) Martin Dwyer 16/1: 100237: Held up, eff 2f out, nvr dangerous. ¾ 75
1990 **ECSTASY 104** [15] 3-7-13 (78) A Nicholls 25/1: 0-0138: Held up, eff over 2f out, sn no extra: abs. nk 76
3896 **ETHMAAR 20** [7] 3-9-4 (97) R Hills 15/2: 13-459: In tch, rdn & btn over 1f out: see 3896. ¾ 94
3718 **ANTICLES 34** [10] 3-9-5 (98) J Mackay (5) 40/1: -1560: Nvr a factor: 10th: see 3718. 1½ 93
3997 **MOON SOLITAIRE 13** [12] 3-9-5 (98) J Reid 8/1: 301330: In tch, wknd over 1f out: 11th, btr 3997. 1½ 91
3150 **CORNELIUS 55** [6] 3-9-7 (100) J Fortune 25/1: 502040: Al bhd: 12th, 8 week abs. 1½ 91
3941 **BANDLER CHING 16** [21] 3-7-10 (75)(1oh) T Hamilton (7) 25/1: 521340: Prom, wknd over 2f out: 13th. 3 62
1366 **KING SPINNER 133** [3] 3-8-3 (82) N Pollard 50/1: 451-00: In tch, wknd 3f out: 14th, long abs. hd 68
*1466 **SOLO FLIGHT 128** [5] 3-8-8 (87) M Hills 12/1: 45-210: Held up, gd hdwy over 2f out, sn btn: ½ 72
15th, needed this after 4 month abs? much btr 1466 (med auction mdn, soft).
*2924 **CLOUD HOPPING 65** [17] 3-8-6 (85) T Quinn 10/1: -610: In tch, btn 2f out: 2 month abs & btr 2924. 3 66
3941 **RAGDALE HALL 16** [4] 3-8-1 (80)(BL) J Quinn 14/1: 510300: Led till 4f out, no extra: 21st, blnks. 0
3654 **Caballe 34** [19] 3-8-1 (80) R Ffrench 25/1: 3893 **Jalad 21** [13] 3-9-6 (99)(t) W Supple 25/1:
3945 **Dancing Mirage 16** [22] 3-8-2 (81)(1ow) L Newman (3) 25/13728 **Zibeline 30** [20] 3-8-6 (85) P Robinson 25/1:
3865 **Radio Star 23** [2] 3-8-3 (82) D Harrison 14/1:
22 ran Time 2m 07.75 (5.55) (P D Savill) M R Channon East Everleigh, Wilts

4198

4.15 BOADICEA FILL RTD HCAP 3YO+ 0-105 (B) 6f Good 44 +00 Fast [104]
£9767 £3704 £1852 £842 3 yo rec 2 lb

*3569 **HONESTY FAIR 37** [11] J A Glover 3-8-6 (84) D Mernagh (3) 5/1: 046611: 3 b f Reprimand - 94
Truthful Image (Reesh) Hdwy to lead over 2f out, sn clr & won pushed out, v comfortably despite drifting
left: earlier scored at Beverley (mdn), Thirsk & York, (h'caps): eff over 5/6f on firm, gd/soft & on a
stiff or easy track: v useful & progressive this term.
1229 **AREYDHA 145** [3] M R Channon 3-9-1 (93) L Dettori 10/1: 00-002: 3 b f Cadeaux Genereux - Elaine's 4 94
Honor (Chief's Crown) Held up, hdwy well over 1f out, kept on inside last, no ch with wnr: encouraging run

after a 4 month abs & stays 6f on gd & soft grnd: useful, sharper for this.

4037	**MOLLY BROWN 11** [7] R Hannon 3-8-12 (90) J Carroll 10/1: 012203: 3 b f Rudimentary - Sinking (Midyan) Dsptd lead, rdn & onepce over 1f out: see 3904, 3768.		1	89
4012	**ROSEUM 13** [1] R Guest 4-9-0 (90) M Roberts 9/2 FAV: 01-604: Held up, brief eff 2f out, onepace.		¾	87
3120	**TABHEEJ 56** [4] 3-9-4 (96) R Hills 10/1: -60065: Handy, rdn & onepce over 1f out: 8 week abs.		nk	92
3937	**DANDY NIGHT 16** [9] 3-9-6 (98) J Reid 20/1: 130606: Led over 3f, btn over 1f out: see 2289.		½	93
3904	**GLOWING 20** [5] 5-8-5 (81) D Harrison 15/2: 024157: Handy, rdn & btn over 1f out: btr 3904, 2804.		1	73
4165	**LIVELY LADY 2** [10] 4-8-10 (86) (vis) Pat Eddery 10/1: 330008: Hld up, rdn & no impress over 1f out.		½	76
2289	**SCARLETT RIBBON 91** [8] 3-9-3 (95) S Sanders 7/1: 10-259: In tch, btn 2f out: 3 month abs.		1½	81
3503	**MAGIC OF LOVE 40** [6] 3-9-7 (99) M Fenton 14/1: 304600: Al bhd: 10th, top weight.		¾	83
1833	**OUT OF AFRICA 111** [2] 3-8-12 (90) K Darley 14/1: 1-0060: In tch, btn halfway: last, now with T Easterby.		11	48
11 ran	Time 1m 13.45 (2.65) (P And S Partnership) J A Glover Notts			

4199   4.45 FURTHER FLIGHT CLASS STKS 3YO+ 0-90 (C)   1m str   Good 44   -12 Slow
£7076   £2684   £1342   £610   3 yo rec 4 lb

3992	**LAGOON 14** [11] B W Hills 3-8-10 D Holland 7/2 FAV: 400031: 3 ch c Common Grounds - Secret Hideaway (Key To The Mint) Held up, hdwy over 1f out to lead inside last, styd on well, drvn out: in '99 scored at Pontefract (mdn, rtd 93 at best): eff at 6f, styd this stiff 1m well: acts on firm, gd/soft & likes a gall track, handles any: has run well fresh: useful at best, on a handy mark.			95
3883	**PRAIRIE WOLF 21** [7] M L W Bell 4-9-0 M Fenton 7/1: 402002: 4 ch g Wolfhound - Bay Queen (Damister) Cl up, eff to lead over 1f out till ins last, kept on, not btn far: ran to best: see 3883, 3060.		1¼	92
3703	**FLAMENCO RED 32** [1] R Charlton 3-8-9 K Darley 12/1: -42103: 3 b f Warning - Spanish Wells (Sadler's Wells) Prom, eff for press 2f out, kept on same pace: gd run back at 1m: see 3616.		¾	89
2858	**FERZAO 69** [10] Mrs A J Perrett 3-8-10 (t) T Quinn 12/1: 315004: Chsd ldr far side, btn appr fnl 1f: gd run after 10 week abs: see 1198.		½	89
3535	**ARANYI 38** [3] 3-8-12 Pat Eddery 9/1: 333165: Bmpd start, soon handy, onepce over 1f out: gd run.		nk	90
*4077	**BOLD KING 8** [6] 5-9-2 M Hills 5/1: 300016: Hld up, eff over 2f out, sn no impress: btr 4077 (soft).		2½	85
2648	**EL CURIOSO 77** [4] 3-8-10 J Reid 10/1: 160307: Reared & went left start, sn in tch, wknd 2f out: abs.		2	79
4094	**FREDORA 7** [9] 5-8-13 J Quinn 16/1: 045268: In tch, btn appr fnl 1f: see 4094.		1	76
3782	**KINGSDON 27** [5] 3-8-10 (t) R Hughes 8/1: 065449: Prom, wknd 2f out: btr 3782.		shd	77
*3945	**WILLOUGHBYS BOY 16** [2] 3-9-0 L Dettori 8/1: 162010: Al bhd: btr expected after 3945 (gd/firm).		4	73
3902	**MEXICAN ROCK 20** [8] 4-9-0 S Sanders 33/1: 105-00: Led till over 2f out: see 3902.		1	67
11 ran	Time 1m 41.01 (4.51) (Guy Reed) B W Hills Lambourn, Berks			

4200   UNUSED NUMBER

4201   UNUSED NUMBER

Official Going: SOFT (HEAVY PLACES). Stalls: Inside, except straight course - Far Side.

4202   2.15 BETONSPORTS NURSERY HCAP 2YO 0-85 (D)   5f   Soft 123   -13 Slow   [92]
£4660   £1434   £717   £358   Raced far side

3942	**ADWEB 17** [11] J Cullinan 2-7-10 (60) (4oh) M Henry 9/1: 0041: 2 b f Muhtarram - What A Present (Pharly) Dwelt, towards rear, prog/no room & snatched up over 2f out, sn hdwy again & led ins last, styd on well, rdn out: first win: eff over a stiff 5f, tried 6f, shld suit: handles fast, improved on soft here.			64
-4042	**KYLLACHY 11** [7] H Candy 2-9-7 (85) C Rutter 9/4 FAV: 122: 2 b c Pivotal - Pretty Poppy (Song) Held up, rdn & styd on well from over 1f out, ev ch fnl 100y, just held: well bckd: fine run under topweight.		nk	88
4098	**ROXANNE MILL 8** [3] M D I Usher 2-8-5 (69) Martin Dwyer 12/1: 503463: 2 b f Cyrano de Bergerac - It Must Be Millie (Reprimand) Led till over 2f out, led again over 1f out till inside last, no extra nr fin: op 8/1: handles fast & soft grnd: gd effort from a tricky low draw: see 3475.		1¼	69
3712	**KARITSA 32** [4] M R Channon 2-8-4 (68) R Havlin 9/1: 251034: Prom, led over 2f out till over 1f out, fdd fnl 1f: op 7/1: handles soft grnd, prob prefer a faster service: btr 2668 (mdn, fast).		2½	63
3795	**CARPET LADY 27** [10] 2-8-8 (72) Darren Williams (5) 12/1: -3305: Chsd ldrs, btn over 1f out: op 10/1: btr 3342, 2714, (6f, gd & fast).		4	59
*3802	**DA VINCI 27** [8] 2-9-1 (79) S W Kelly (3) 11/4: 10016: Trkd ldrs, btn 1f out: bckd, btr 3802.		shd	66
3165	**WESTERN HERO 56** [2] 2-9-1 (79) T Quinn 6/1: 332157: Chsd ldrs 3f: 8 week abs: btr 2711 (gd).		2½	61
3955	**DEIDAMIA 17** [6] 2-8-0 (64) N Pollard 14/1: -4048: Al rear: op 12/1, h'cap bow: btr 3955 (gd).		shd	46
4096	**UNLIKELY 8** [5] 2-8-0 (64) C Adamson 20/1: -3009: Prom till over 1f out: h'cap bow: btr 1981 (sell).		2½	41
3965	**MISE EN SCENE 16** [1] 2-9-0 (78) Paul Eddery 33/1: 010500: Al twds rear: 10th: btr 1986 (C/D, fast).		7	41
10 ran	Time 1m 06.15 (6.75) (Adweb Ltd) J Cullinan Quainton, Bucks			

4203   2.45 BETONSPORTS COND STKS 2YO (C)   1m rnd   Soft 123   -19 Slow
£6351   £2409   £1204   £547   Raced centre in straight

3789	**TARFSHI 28** [7] M A Jarvis 2-8-10 G Hind 4/1: 131: 2 b f Mtoto - Pass The Peace (Alzao) Led 1f, remained cl up, led again over 1f out & held on well under hands & heels riding fnl 1f: earlier scored on debut at Doncaster (mdn): dam high-class over 6f/1m: eff at 7f, well suited to this step up to 1m: acts on fast & soft grnd, stiff/gall track: can rate higher.			93
*4036	**WORTHILY 12** [6] M R Channon 2-9-1 R Havlin 5/2 FAV: -0512: 2 b c Northern Spur - Worth's Girl (Devil's Bag) Chsd ldrs, rdn/ch over 1f out, kept on inside last, just btn: bckd: acts on soft: useful.		½	96
3879	**BLACK KNIGHT 23** [5] S P C Woods 2-9-1 P Dobbs (5) 11/1: 311663: 2 b c Contract Law - Another Move (Farm Walk) Prom, rdn/every ch over 1f out, no extra inside last: op 8/1: clr of rem: acts on fast & soft grnd.		¾	95
*2921	**MATLOCK 66** [2] P F I Cole 2-9-1 T Quinn 11/4: -14: Led after 1f till over 1f out, fdd: 2 month abs:		5	88

up in trip & much softer grnd: see 2921.
3450 **SWING BAND 43** [1] 2-9-1 S Carson (3) 9/2: -1245: Chsd ldr, chance 2f out, fdd: op 10/3, 6 week abs. *5* **81**
3946 **LYSANDERS QUEST 17** [4] 2-8-11 C Rutter 12/1: -456: Held up, btn 2f out: highly tried: see 3946. *5* **70**
4063 **FATHER SEAMUS 10** [8] 2-8-11 Martin Dwyer 66/1: 000307: Held up, rdn/btn 2f out: highly tried mdn. *2* **67**
4124 **SAKAMOTO 6** [3] 2-8-11 O Urbina 66/1: 08: Held up, eff over 2f out, no impress: see 4124 (7f). *20* **37**
8 ran Time 1m 50.36 (11.36) (Sheikh Ahmed Al Maktoum) M A Jarvis Newmarket, Suffolk

4204

3.20 BETONSPORTS HCAP 3YO+ 0-80 (D) 7f rnd Soft 123 -17 Slow [80]
£6344 £1952 £976 £488 3 yo rec 3 lb Raced centre in straight

4102 **SLUMBERING 8** [14] B A Pearce 4-8-13 (65) O Urbina 25/1: 340051: 4 b g Thatching - Bedspread (Seattle Dancer) Prom, rdn fnl 2f, narrow lead inside last, drvn & held on gamely fnl 1f, all out: plcd earlier this term for B Meehan: unplcd 3 '99 starts (h'caps, rtd 83): '98 York wnr (mdn, rtd 89 at best): eff at 6/7f, stys a stiff 1m: acts on gd & hvy grnd: handles any track: likes to race with/force the pace: eff in blinks, best without. **69**
3981 **TUMBLEWEED RIVER 15** [16] B J Meehan 4-9-8 (74) D O'Donohoe 20/1: 5-0002: 4 ch g Thatching - Daphne Indica (Ballad Rock) Towards rear, prog & rdn/strong chall fnl 1f, kept on well, just held: likes soft. *nk* **77**
*4080 **WILDFLOWER 9** [2] R Charlton 3-9-8 (77) P Dobbs (5) 5/2 FAV: 000413: 3 b g Namaqualand - Fajjoura (Fairy King) Trkd ldrs, rdn/styd on well fnl 1f, not pace of wnr: hvly bckd, op 7/2: in gd form. *nk* **79**
4069 **SARSON 10** [13] R Hannon 4-9-4 (70) P Fitzsimons (5) 20/1: 000004: Chsd ldr, led after 2f, rdn/hdd inside last & no extra nr fin: op 12/1: stays a stiff 7f: handles fast & soft grnd: see 1676. *½* **71**
694 **STORMY RAINBOW 194** [11] 3-9-0 (69) G Hind 16/1: 0-225: Mid div, rdn over 2f out, not able to chall: handles equitrack & soft grnd: op 12/1, 6 month abs, h'cap bow: see 591 (AW, 1m). *2* **67**
*2621 **TAKE FLITE 79** [7] 3-9-8 (77) Martin Dwyer 10/1: 200316: Held up, rdn/mod hdwy fnl 2f: op 8/1: abs: acts on firm & soft grnd: see 2621. *nk* **74**
3785 **FALLACHAN 28** [1] 4-9-6 (72) Darren Williams (5) 16/1: 403007: Mid div, btn over 1f out: see 1490. *4* **63**
1969 **CAD ORO 106** [8] 7-9-0 (66) S Carson (3) 7/1: -03028: Held up, eff 2f out, no impress: abs: see 1058. *¾* **56**
4038 **LOCOMBE HILL 12** [4] 4-9-11 (77) D Sweeney 11/1: 030049: Chsd ldrs 6f: see 1474. *2* **64**
3981 **SHATHER 15** [6] 3-9-6 (75) T Quinn 8/1: 432250: Keen/held up, eff 2f out, no impress: 10th: op 6/1. *hd* **61**
3821 **EASTER OGIL 26** [15] 5-9-9 (75)(vis) Leanne Masterton (7) 14/1: 000400: Nvr factor: 11th: op 10/1. *2½* **57**
4037 **QUEENS BENCH 12** [9] 3-9-3 (72) N Pollard 12/1: 506000: Led 2f, btn 2f out: 12th: see 954. *1¾* **52**
4066 **DORISSIO 10** [3] 4-8-12 (64) J Stack 15/2: 336030: slowly away/bhd, in tch wide halfway, sn btn: 15th. **0**
3115 **Most Saucy 57** [5] 4-9-13 (79) J Bosley (7) 16/1: 3297 **Bintang Timor 50** [12] 6-8-13 (65) P McCabe 14/1:
15 ran Time 1m 36.2 (9.8) (Mrs Christine Painting) B A Pearce Newchapel, Surrey

4205

3.55 BETONSPORTS MDN 3YO (D) 1m2f Soft 123 -20 Slow
£4179 £1286 £643 £321 Raced centre in straight

-- **RETURN** [1] H R A Cecil 3-8-9 T Quinn 7/4 FAV: 1: 3 b f Sadler's Wells - Slightly Dangerous (Roberto) Held up, hdwy fnl 3f, no room/swtchd over 1f out, led inside last & styd on well under hands & heels riding: well bckd, op 3/1: eff at 10f, 12f+ looks sure to suit: acts on soft grnd & a stiff/gall track: runs well fresh: open to further improvement. **82**
4119 **MANIATIS 6** [10] P F I Cole 3-9-0 D Sweeney 10/1: 032: 3 b c Slip Anchor - Tamassos (Dance In Time) Led/dsptd lead, rdn/hdd & no extra inside last: op 6/1: eff at 10f on soft: shown enough to win. *½* **85**
-- **MOONJAZ** [4] Saeed bin Suroor 3-9-0 D O'Donohoe 2/1: 3: 3 ch c Nashwan - Harayir (Gulch) Prom, led over 2f out till 1f out, onepace inside last: clr rem: well bckd: eff at 10f on soft, 12f could suit. *1* **84**
4040 **HIGH BARN 12** [3] J R Fanshawe 3-8-9 O Urbina 16/1: 04: Shaken up rear halfway, kept on fnl 2f, no threat to front trio: op 8/1: prob handles soft grnd: 12f+ h'caps will suit later. *6* **73**
3764} **ROBOASTAR 392** [16] 3-9-0 Martin Dwyer 25/1: 033-5: Unruly/u.r. bef start: held up, eff halfway, no impress on ldrs: reapp: plcd twice last term (rtd 79, mdn): stays a sharp 8.5f, mid dists could suit this term: handles firm & gd grnd, sharp or stiff track. *½* **76**
2627 **POLI KNIGHT 79** [9] 3-8-9 C Rutter 16/1: -5536: Held up, eff 3f out, held over 1f out: op 12/1, abs. *5* **67**
-- **GENERAL ALARM** [8] 3-9-0 J Stack 16/1: 7: Towards rear, prog 4f out, btn over 1f out: op 8/1, debut. *1¾* **70**
4536} **COLETTE 338** [5] 3-8-9 A McGlone 20/1: 0-8: Held up, eff 4f out, no impress: op 12/1, reapp: unplcd sole '99 start (rtd 74, mdn). *3* **62**
2053 **BOLD GUEST 103** [14] 3-9-0 G Hind 20/1: -03349: Held up, eff 3f out, no impress: stablemate of 6th: 3 month abs: btr 2053, 1668 (fast & gd). *8* **59**
4040 **ISLAND PRINCESS 12** [17] 3-8-9 N Pollard 10/1: 0-5040: Prom 1m: 10th: btr 4040, 1045. *8* **46**
-- **BRADY BOYS** [13] 3-9-0 (BL) R Havlin 20/1: 0: Chsd ldrs, btn over 2f out, 11th: blinks, op 10/1: debut: Cozzene gelding, mid dists should suit: with J H M Gosden. *7* **44**
3626 **LEMARATE 35** [12] 3-9-0 S Carson (3) 16/1: 00: Chsd ldrs, btn 3f out: 12th: op 10/1: see 3626 (1m). *1* **43**
4040 **Followeroffashion 12** [11] 3-9-0 Jonjo Fowle (5) 50/1: 3110 **Katiypour 58** [6] 3-9-0 Paul Eddery 12/1:
4040 **Ocean Tide 12** [7] 3-9-0 S W Kelly (3) 20/1: 2516} **Barnaby 450** [2] 3-9-0 P Dobbs (5) 66/1:
-- **Amica Bella** [15] 3-8-9 A Clark 100/1:
17 ran Time 2m 18.4 (14.3) (K Abdulla) H R A Cecil Newmarket, Suffolk

4206

4.25 BETONSPORTS HCAP 3YO 0-90 (C) 1m rnd Soft 123 -27 Slow [96]
£12041 £3705 £1852 £926 raced centre in straight.

3998 **FRONTIER 14** [11] R Hannon 3-9-4 (86) R Smith (5) 14/1: 533641: 3 b c Indian Ridge - Adatiya (Shardari) Prom, rdn/chall 3f out, led 2f out, styd on well inside last, drvn out: op 12/1: '99 Lingfield wnr (mdn, rtd 92): eff at 7f/1m, stays 10f: acts on firm & gd/soft grnd, clearly relishes a soft surface: has run well fresh: handles any track: genuine, could win again in these conditions. **92**
4085 **SCOTTISH SPICE 9** [16] I A Balding 3-8-11 (79) Martin Dwyer 14/1: 5306D2: 2 b f Selkirk - Dilwara (Lashkari) Prom, ev ch fnl 2f, rdn & kept on, not pace of wnr: acts on firm & soft: on a fair mark. *1* **83**
3750 **BEADING 30** [9] J W Hills 3-8-3 (71)(t) M Henry 16/1: 025143: 3 b f Polish Precedent - Silver Braid (Miswaki) Held up, rdn/prog to chall over 1f out, no extra inside last: acts on fast & soft grnd: see 3317. *2½* **71**
+1528 **PIPSSALIO 126** [8] Jamie Poulton 3-8-11 (79) P Dobbs (5) 5/1 FAV: 214014: Dwelt/held up, rdn & kept on fnl 2f, no threat: op 6/1, abs: loves this grnd, not helped by tardy start here: win again at 10f. *1* **78**
3676 **RESOUNDING 34** [18] 3-8-11 (79)(VIS) T Quinn 10/1: -32465: Chsd ldrs, btn over 1f out: op 8/1, vis. *1½* **76**
3883 **SABREON 22** [6] 3-9-0 (82) D O'Donohoe 16/1: 0-2506: Held up, hdwy halfway, no prog over 1f out. *3½* **74**
3914 **COOLING OFF 19** [1] 3-8-7 (75) Paul Eddery 20/1: -0357: Chsd ldrs 6f: h'cap bow: see 3350, 3048. *2½* **63**
3998 **FALCONIDAE 14** [7] 3-9-0 (82) A Clark 16/1: 5120U8: Held up, eff 3f out, no impress: btr 2922 (fast). *nk* **69**
*3998 **KAREEB 14** [2] 3-8-12 (80) S Carson (3) 14/1: 343619: Mid div, btn 2f out: btr 3998 (firm). *nk* **66**

*3944 **COLNE VALLEY AMY 17** [14] 3-8-3 (71) I Mongan (1) 12/1: 432510: Led 6f: 10th: btr 3944 (fast). 1¼ 55
3793 **TRAVELLING LITE 28** [10] 3-8-11 (79)(VIS) J Lowe 16/1: 203400: Prom 6f: 11th: visor: btr 1177 (firm). 1¼ 61
3977 **DANDILUM 15** [4] 3-8-12 (80) G Hind 16/1: -4W020: Chsd ldrs 5f: 12th: btr 983 (mdn, 7f). 3 58
*3777 **DIVERS PEARL 28** [3] 3-8-13 (81) O Urbina 7/1: 213010: Hld up, eff 3f out, no impress: 13th, btr 3777. 1¾ 57
*1796 **TRIPLE SHARP 114** [17] 3-9-0 (82) S W Kelly (3) 9/1: 410: In tch 5f: 16th: abs: btr 1796 (10f mdn). 0
3782 **EVEREST 28** [15] 3-9-7 (89) D Sweeney 6/1: 211150: Mid div, btn over 2f out: 17th: bckd: btr 3658 (gd). 0
2938 **Hamlyn 65** [12] 3-8-6 (74) N Pollard 33/1: 2581 **Dixielake 80** [13] 3-8-13 (81) C Rutter 14/1:
3658 **Divulge 34** [5] 3-9-4 (86) R Havlin 16/1:
18 ran Time 1m 51.01 (12.01) (Highclere Thoroughbred Racing Ltd) R Hannon East Everleigh, Wilts

4207

5.00 BETONSPORTS CLAIMER 3YO+ (E) 5f Soft 123 +13 Fast
£3120 £960 £480 £240 3 yo rec 1 lb Majority raced far side, no advantage

3981 **CARLTON 15** [1] D R C Elsworth 6-9-7 N Pollard 10/1: 400561: 6 ch g Thatching - Hooray Lady 75
(Ahonoora) In tch stands side, rdn/hdwy over 1f out & led inside last, styd on well, rdn out: best time of day: op 6/1: '99 wnr at Doncaster (subs disq), Epsom (h'caps, G Lewis), Windsor (2, h'caps, rtd 77), Southwell (h'cap) & W'hampton (class stakes, rtd 70a): '98 wnr again at Windsor & Newbury (h'caps, rtd 69 & 52a): eff at 7f/1m, suited by 5/6f on firm, hvy & fibresand: handles any track: has run well fresh with/without blinks.
1591 **AGENT MULDER 122** [15] P D Cundell 6-8-6 (bl) D Sweeney 5/1: -23302: 6 b g Kylian - Precious 2 55
Caroline (The Noble Player) Prom far side, rdn & ev ch/briefly led inside last, kept on well, held by wnr stands side nr fin: 4 month abs: eff at 5f, suited by 6f on soft: see 816.
4065 **BORDER GLEN 10** [8] J J Bridger 4-8-9 (bl) Martin Dwyer 16/1: 530643: 4 b g Selkirk - Sulitelma ½ 57
(The Minstrel) Prom far side, led over 1f out, hdd inside last & no extra nr fin: op 20/1: see 4065, 3622 & 96 (AW).
4120 **ECUDAMAH 6** [16] Miss Jacqueline S Doyle 4-8-7 (vis) C Rutter 33/1: 300004: Mid div far side, not 3½ 48
pace to chall fnl 2f: see 40 (AW).
4107 **ANSELLMAN 7** [11] 10-8-11 (bl) D O'Donohoe 7/1: 533205: Prom far side, onepce fnl 2f: see 2788. ¾ 51
4027 **HARVEYS FUTURE 12** [10] 6-8-5 J Stack 10/1: -32W06: Held up far side, eff 2f out, sn btn: see 1910. 3 39
3873 **MADAME JONES 23** [3] 5-8-6 (BL) P Fitzsimons (5) 50/1: 005007: Led stands side group 4f: blnks. 1¼ 37
3947 **MALAAH 17** [2] 4-8-12 (bl) O Urbina 33/1: 005608: Chsd ldrs stands side 3f: see 1092. 3 37
3816 **MINT LEAF 26** [13] 3-8-2 Sophie Mitchell 50/1: 000009: Dwelt, nvr on terms far side: see 2431. 2 24
3788 **POWER PACKED 28** [9] 3-9-7 G Hind 11/2: 2-5600: Mid div far side, btn 2f out: 10th: btr 1384, 1047. 3 37
4027 **LOST IN HOOK 12** [14] 3-8-4 (VIS) S W Kelly (1) 16/1: 300000: Held up far side, btn 2f out: 11th: vis. 1½ 17
4073 **CARTMEL PARK 10** [17] 4-8-11 (BL) I Mongan (5) 4/1 FAV: 300400: Overall ldr far side 3f: 14th: blnks. 0
3947 **Crowded Avenue 17** [6] 8-8-9 (vis) A Clark 12/1: 4181} **Run For Glory 365** [12] 3-9-7 N Pollard 33/1:
4065 **Perigeux 10** [7] 4-8-6 C Catlin (7) 12/1: 3821 **Trump Street 26** [5] 4-8-5(1ow) R Havlin 33/1:
4065 **Pertemps Star 10** [4] 3-8-5 J Lowe 66/1:
17 ran Time 1m 05.1 (5.5) (City Slickers) D R C Elsworth Whitsbury, Hants

4208

5.35 HANDS AND HEELS APPR HCAP 3YO+ 0-70 (E) 1m2f Soft 123 -44 Slow [70]
£2925 £900 £450 £225 3 yo rec 6 lb Raced towards centre in straight.

3871 **WILEMMGEO 23** [12] P D Evans 3-8-3 (51) D Meah (5) 12/1: 001141: 3 b f Emarati - Floral Spark 57
(Forzando) Held up, rdn & strong run from over 2f out to lead inside last, styd on well, rdn out: op 10/1: earlier with M C Chapman, scored at W'hampton (2sell, rtd 55a) & twice at Beverley (h'caps): '99 wnr again at W'hampton (seller, rtd 55a & 62): eff between 7.5f/10f on firm, soft & fibresand: handles any track, likes W'hampton & Beverley: eff with/without a visor: tough & consistent filly: runs well for an apprentice rider, in fine form.
3828 **ZIDAC 25** [2] P J Makin 8-9-3 (59) W Hutchinson 14/1: -00262: 8 b g Statoblest - Sule Skerry 1 62
(Scottish Rifle) Chsd ldrs, smooth prog to lead over 1f out, hdd inside last, not pce of wnr: op 10/1, likes sells.
1738 **ARIALA 117** [18] K R Burke 3-8-5 (53) G Gibbons (3) 20/1: 6003: 3 b f Arazi - Kashtala (Lord Gayle) nk 55
Mid div, rdn/prog to chall 1f out, onepce inside last: h'cap bow, 4 month abs: eff over a stiff 10f on soft.
3731 **SMARTER CHARTER 31** [6] Mrs L Stubbs 7-8-12 (54) Kristin Stubbs (8) 10/1: 563064: Held up, rdn & 1¾ 54
styd on fnl 3f, not pace to chall: see 2081 871.
3828 **THOMAS HENRY 25** [1] 4-7-11 (39) N Farmer (8) 12/1: 364635: Held up, mod hdwy fnl 3f: see 3052. 1½ 37
4066 **KINNINO 10** [10] 6-8-1 (43) R Naylor (5) 9/1: 214466: Held up, late hdwy, no threat: acts on firm, ½ 40
soft & both AW's: see 3737, 3111.
3858 **HALF TIDE 24** [8] 6-8-2 (44) D Kinsella (3) 6/1: 105057: Towards rear, mod late hdwy: btr 2626 (12f). shd 41
3731 **PARISIAN LADY 31** [15] 5-8-3 (45) S Hitchcott (7) 12/1: 202U48: Mid div at best: op 10/1: see 2893. 1½ 40
4496} **KYLKENNY 341** [7] 5-8-13 (55) N Esler 20/1: 055-9: Led over 2f out till over 1f out, fdd: reapp/ shd 50
h'cap bow: unplcd at up to 10f in '99 (rtd 61, mdn).
1699 **CHRYSOLITE 118** [16] 5-8-2 (44) M Palmer (6) 20/1: 000-00: Held up, no room/lost pl 4f out, no ½ 38
impress on ldrs after: 10th: 4 month abs: prev with M Sowersby: unplcd last term (rtd 64, h'cap): '98 Lingfield wnr (h'cap, rtd 79, current connections): eff at 9f: acts on firm grnd.
3401 **SPARK OF LIFE 45** [11] 3-8-10 (57)(bl)(1ow) P Shea 13/2: 231130: Chsd ldrs 1m: 11th: 6 wk abs. hd 51
4122 **WOOLLY WINSOME 6** [19] 4-7-10 (38)(2oh) Michael Doyle (5) 25/1: 006050: Nvr a factor: 12th. 1¼ 30
4168 **OSCIETRA 3** [9] 4-8-2 (44)(vis) D Watson (3) 11/2 FAV: 560030: Al towards rear: 13th: qck reapp. ¾ 35
4074 **YOUNG UN 10** [5] 5-9-2 (58) K Parkin (8) 10/1: 000300: Led 1f, btn 3f out: 14th: op 8/1: see 786. 1½ 47
2295 **FIFE AND DRUM 92** [14] 3-8-9 (57) R Thomas 12/1: 000100: Led after 1f till over 2f out, sn fdd: 1¼ 45
15th: op 8/1, 3 month abs: prev with E Dunlop, now with J Akehurst: see 2007 (mdn h'cap, gd, blinks).
4146} **ZURS 367** [17] 7-9-12 (68) S Clancy (3) 10/1: 0000-0: Slowly away & al bhd: 20th: reapp, 10 mth 0
Jump abs (Nov '99 Plumpton wnr, h'cap, rtd 102h at best, eff at 2m on fast & gd grnd): '99 Sandown scorer (C/D h'cap, rtd 74): '98 wnr again at Sandown & Salisbury (appr h'caps, rtd 71): eff at 1m/10f on firm, soft & equitrack: best without blinks: handles any track, likes Sandown.
3842 **Kelburne 25** [13] 3-8-3 (51) N Carter (7) 20/1: 4492} **Charlies Quest 343** [4] 4-8-9 (51) M Worrell (3) 25/1:
4175] **Chai Yo 721** [3] 10-10-0 (70) O Kozak (8) 16/1: 492 **Danka 233** [20] 6-7-10 (38)(6oh) C Halliwell (7) 33/1:
20 ran Time 2m 20.8 (16.7) (R J Hayward) P D Evans Pandy, Gwent

NEWMARKET SATURDAY SEPTEMBER 30TH Righthand, Stiff, Galloping Track

Official Going GOOD. Stalls: Far Side.

4209

1.50 EBF ALINGTON FILLIES MDN 2YO (D) 6f str Good/Firm 30 -15 Slow
£5638 £1735 £867 £433

3795 **GHAZAL 27** [7] Sir Michael Stoute 2-8-11 R Hills 11/8 FAV: 21: 2 b f Gone West - Touch Of Greatness (Hero's Honor) Cl-up, led over 1f out, styd on strongly, pushed out, readily: hvly bckd tho' op 1/1: Jan foal, cost $575,000: half sister to sev wnrs, incl smart sprinter Rossini: dam unrcd: eff at 6f, 7f sure to suit: handles fast grnd: useful filly with a turn of foot, type to win in List/Gr company. **101+**

-- **CIELITO LINDO** [6] R Hannon 2-8-11 R Hughes 20/1: 2: 2 b f Pursuit Of Love - Seal Indigo (Glenstal) With ldr, led over 1f out, sn hdd & not pace of wnr under hands & heels: op 12/1 on debut: Mar foal: half sister to a 6f scorer: dam mid-dist performer: eff at 6f, 7f/1m will suit: handles fast: useful, v encouraging. *3½* **89+**

-- **RED CARNATION** [2] M A Jarvis 2-8-11 P Robinson 20/1: 3: 2 b f Polar Falcon - Red Bouquet (Reference Point) Slow away, bhd, kept on nicely over 1f out, nrst fin: debut: Feb 1st foal, cost 24,000 gns: most encouraging debut at 6f, already needs 7f+: handles fast: improve bundles for this, keep an eye on. *1½* **85+**

3938 **JELBA 17** [10] N P Littmoden 2-8-11 J Reid 20/1: 535054: Held up, hdwy over 1f out, kept on nicely ins last: highly tried & shld find a mdn on a minor trk: see 3938. *nk* **85**

3449 **JACANA 43** [13] 2-8-11 J Fortune 2/1: -25: Prom, rdn & no extra appr fnl 1f: hvly bckd from 7/2 & more expected after promising debut in 3449. *2* **80**

-- **EMERALD PALM** [9] 2-8-11 J Weaver 14/1: 6: Prom, rdn & no extra appr fnl 1f: op 10/1 on debut: Apr foal, dam 14f scorer: bred to need 7f/1m+ in time & showed some promise here. *¾* **78**

2886 **STARFLEET 68** [1] 2-8-11 Pat Eddery 12/1: -57: Led over 4f, no extra over 1f out: see 2886. *1½* **74**

2599 **THE CHOCOLATIER 80** [8] 2-8-11 A Polli (3) 66/1: 658: In tch, wknd 2f out: 11 wk abs, see 2010. *¾* **72**

-- **DRAMA PREMIERE** [14] 2-8-11 J Fanning 33/1: 9: Handy, wknd well over 1f out: Apr foal, cost 30,000 gns: half sister to a useful 6/7f juv wnr: speedily bred, with I Balding. *2½* **65**

3607 **MAY PRINCESS 36** [11] 2-8-11 R Mullen 66/1: 000: Al bhd: 10th: see 3121. *nk* **64**

-- **TIBBIE** [5] 2-8-11 T E Durcan 66/1: 0: In tch, wknd over 2f out: 11th on debut. *2* **58**

-- **LONG DAY** [16] 2-8-11 L Newman (3) 33/1: 0: In tch, wknd over 2f out on debut: 12th. *¾* **56**

-- **ELYSIAN FIELDS** [15] 2-8-11 M Hills 33/1: 0: Nvr a factor: 13th on debut. *¾* **54**

2328 **Modesty 91** [17] 2-8-11 Dale Gibson 66/1:
-- **Miss Devious** [3] 2-8-11 W Ryan 50/1:
3814 **Polyphonic 27** [4] 2-8-11 F Norton 66/1:
3910 **Summer Key 19** [12] 2-8-11 D Holland 66/1:

17 ran Time 1m 13.52 (2.72) (Hamdan Al Maktoum) Sir Michael Stoute Newmarket, Suffolk

4210

2.20 LISTED OH SO SHARP STKS 2YO (A) 7f str Good/Firm 30 -17 Slow
£12365 £4690 £2345 £1066

*3910 **LILIUM 19** [10] Sir Michael Stoute 2-8-9 J Fortune 9/2 JT FAV: 11: 2 b f Nashwan - Satin Flower (Shadeed) Held up, hdwy & flashed tail fnl 1f, but styd on well for press to get up cl-home: nicely bckd: unbtn after debut win at Warwick (fills mdn): half sister to top-class 6f juv wnr Lujain: dam smart at 7f: eff at 7f, 1m sure to suit: acts on fast grnd: runs well fresh: useful & progressive. **100**

*4035 **NAFISAH 12** [5] B Hanbury 2-8-9 R Hills 12/1: -2212: 2 ch f Lahib - Alyakkh (Sadler's Wells) Trkd ldr till went on over 1f out, kept on well for press ins last till collared cl-home, just btn: improved in defeat & will relish a step up to 1m: shld win in similar company, see 4035. *nk* **99**

*3901 **LILS JESSY 21** [4] J Noseda 2-8-9 Pat Eddery 9/2 JT FAV: 510113: 2 b f Kris - Lobmille (Mill Reef) Hld up, eff 2f out, onepace over 1f out: op 3/1: another gd run stepped up in class & crying out for 1m. *1¼* **96**

*3938 **NASMATT 17** [7] M R Channon 2-8-9 Craig Williams 9/1: -3314: Set pace till over 1f out, no extra. *2½* **91**

3862 **SWEET PROSPECT 24** [2] 2-8-9 R Mullen 20/1: -01455: Held up, rdn 2f out, late gains, nvr dangerous: stays 7f & 1m looks sure to suit: see 3862, 2748. *hd* **90**

3789 **BARATHEASTAR 28** [8] 2-8-9 J Reid 25/1: 56: In tch, rdn & sltly outpcd 2f out, some late gains: sure to relish a step up to 1m & a confidence boosting mdn win shld be the plan: see 3789. *½* **89**

*3459 **ASHLINN 43** [9] 2-8-9 P Doe 11/1: -217: Dwelt, sn handy, wknd over 1f out: 6 wk abs, see 3459 (mdn). *1½* **86**

3882 **CHAGUARAMAS 22** [3] 2-8-9 R Hughes 6/1: 115428: Waited with, eff over 2f out, wknd over 1f out. *nk* **85**

3316 **RIZERIE 49** [6] 2-8-9 D Harrison 9/1: 12039: Prom, wknd well over 1f out: 7 wk abs, useful earlier. *3½* **78**

3015 **FIGURA 62** [1] 2-8-9 T E Durcan 25/1: -61640: In tch, wknd over 2f out: 2 month abs, highly tried. *1¼* **76**

3066 **SHAMO 63** [11] 2-8-9 G Carter 7/1: -160: Prom, wknd over 2f out, eased ins last: fin last, 2 month abs. *7* **62**

11 ran Time 1m 26.47 (3.27) (Sheikh Mohammed) Sir Michael Stoute Newmarket

4211

2.55 GR 2 SUN CHARIOT STKS 3YO+ (A) 1m str Good/Firm 30 +01 Fast
£34800 £13200 £6600 £3000 3 yo rec 4 lb

3846 **DANCEABOUT 27** [1] G Wragg 3-8-9 D Holland 9/2: 153121: 3 b f Shareef Dancer - Putupon (Mummy's Pet) Hld up, hdwy over 1f out to lead ins last, edged right but styd on well for press, drvn out: gd time: earlier scored at Goodwood (2, fills mdn & List): unrcd juv: eff over 7f/1m on fast, gd/soft & any trk, likes Goodwood: relatively lightly rcd & smart: genuine & holding her form well. **108**

*2597 **ALSHAKR 80** [4] B Hanbury 3-8-12 R Hills 3/1 FAV: 4-1312: 3 b f Bahri - Give Thanks (Relko) Led over 5f, styd on again to lead dist, sn hdd & carried slightly right ins last, kept on, just held: abs, smart. *nk* **110**

*3551 **MAY BALL 41** [3] J H M Gosden 3-8-9 J Fortune 8/1: 124113: 3 b f Cadeaux Genereux - Minute Waltz (Sadler's Wells) Trkd ldr till went on over 2f out till dist, onepace: 6 wk abs: lightly raced & progressive. *2* **103**

2064 **HASTY WORDS 102** [2] B W Hills 4-8-13 M Hills 33/1: -16404: Held up, rdn 2f out, kept on ins last, nvr nrr: 3 month abs & runs well fresh: interesting with a return to 9/10f: see 967, 703. *hd* **102**

4126 **MAYARO BAY 6** [5] 4-8-13 R Hughes 14/1: 023105: Prom, onepace well over 1f out: back to form. *1½* **99**

*3069 **LADY OF CHAD 62** [9] 3-8-12 J Reid 4/1: -10016: With ldr, wknd well over 1f out: 2 month abs & best form has come with plenty of cut in the grnd as in 3069 (Gr 2, gd/soft). *1* **100**

3647 **SEAZUN 35** [7] 3-8-9 Craig Williams 7/1: 244047: Prom, no impress well over 1f out: btr 2647, 2150. *1¾* **93**

3846 **PAPABILE 27** [8] 3-8-9 Pat Eddery 7/1: 411148: Nvr a factor: ready for a break? btr 3846, 3340 (List). *hd* **92**

3918 **MOSELLE 18** [6] 3-8-9 P Robinson 16/1: 362539: Prom, wknd 2f out: see 3918 (10f), 3726. *1¾* **88**

9 ran Time 1m 38.79 (2.29) (Bloomsbury Stud) G Wragg Newmarket

NEWMARKET SATURDAY SEPTEMBER 30TH Righthand, Stiff, Galloping Track

4212 3.35 TOTE CAMBRIDGESHIRE HCAP 3YO+ (B) 1m1f Good/Firm 30 +09 Fast [112]
£69600 £26400 £13200 £6000 3 yo rec 5 lb Five (incl wnr) raced on far side

*715 **KATY NOWAITEE 190** [34] P W Harris 4-8-8 (92) J Reid 6/1: 512-11: 4 b f Komaite - Cold Blow (Posse) **104**
Held up far side, hdwy to lead overall over 2f out, styd on strongly fnl 1f, rdn out, readily: has reportedly had a throat infection & a 6 month abs since landing reapp at Doncaster (Lincoln consolation h'cap): '99 wnr at Newmarket (mdn) & Redcar (h'cap, rtd 86): eff over 1m/9f on firm & gd/soft: loves a gall trk, esp Newmarket: runs esp well fresh: most progressive, lightly raced & v useful, shld make up into a Listed/Gr class performer.
3997 **NOOSHMAN 14** [15] Sir Michael Stoute 3-8-10 (99) Pat Eddery 11/2 JT FAV: 013202: 3 ch g Woodman - Knoosh (Storm Bird) Handy, led main group over 2f out, rdn clr of those rivals dist but not pace of wnr on far side: hvly bckd: another v useful eff & surely deserves a val prize: type to progress into Listed/Gr class. *1¾* **107+**
3997 **PINCHINCHA 14** [20] D Morris 6-7-10 (80) Dale Gibson 16/1: 342153: 6 b g Priolo - Western Heights (Shirley Heights) Handy, eff for press 2f out, kept on fnl 1f, no impress on front 2: caught two most prog types & is in excellent heart himself: just best at 10f as in 3166. *3½* **82**
4053 **MAN OMYSTERY 14** [33] J Noseda 3-8-13 (102) D Holland 12/1: 124264: Dwelt, switched to race main group & bhd, kept on well fnl 2f, nrst fin: eye-catching run, sure to relish a return to 10f+ & one to keep in mind. *hd* **103+**
3107 **TRIPLE DASH 58** [35] 4-8-4 (88)(BL) M Roberts 14/1: 000405: Keen, handy far side, eff over 1f out, no impress: 2 month abs & a gd run in first time blnks: see 3107, 2696. *2* **86**
3918 **FIRST FANTASY 18** [24] 4-8-9 (93) Craig Williams 33/1: 050106: Bhd, eff over 3f out, onepace over 1f out: gd run, see 3389 (listed). *½* **90**
3554 **DUCK ROW 41** [22] 5-9-10 (108) S Whitworth 40/1: 122327: Dwelt, held up, eff & short of room over 2f out, late gains: 6 wk abs & shld rate higher: rnr-up in a Gr 3 in 3554, see 1847. *¾* **103**
3899 **AIR DEFENCE 21** [18] 3-8-5 (94) M Hills 16/1: 210028: Held up, brief eff over 2f out, no impress. *hd* **88**
3684 **ZYZ 33** [13] 3-9-2 (105) R Hills 66/1: 233059: Handy main group, wknd over 1f out: see 3684. *nk* **99**
3997 **BRILLIANT RED 14** [14] 7-9-4 (102)(t) N Callan 40/1: 036200: Led over 3f out till over 2f out: 10th. *½* **95**
3703 **GOLCONDA 33** [6] 4-8-3 (87) A Beech (3) 50/1: 000160: In tch, onepace fnl 2f: 11th, best 3042. *hd* **79**
3998 **ATAVUS 14** [31] 3-7-10 (85)(2oh) G Baker (5) 50/1: 035000: Bhd far side, no impress over 1f out: 12th. *½* **76**
3997 **AEGEAN DREAM 14** [3] 4-8-3 (87) L Newman (3) 20/1: 311040: Nvr a factor in 13th: see 3997, 3089. *shd* **78**
4085 **LITTLE AMIN 9** [9] 4-7-10 (80)(3oh) P M Quinn (3) 66/1: 326650: Bhd, late gains: 14th, likes soft. *hd* **70**
2304 **MAKE WAY 92** [27] 4-7-11 (81) D Glennon (7) 66/1: 322550: Cl-up, wknd 2f out: 15th, 3 month abs. *¾* **70**
4000 **BOMB ALASKA 14** [29] 5-9-7 (105) R Hughes 20/1: 400060: Led far side till over 2f out, wknd: 16th: nk 2nd in this race off a 10lbs lower mark last term: see 4000. *¾* **93**
3997 **CULZEAN 14** [16] 4-8-0 (84) P Doe 50/1: 036200: Al bhd: 17th: twice below 3865. *hd* **71**
*2858 **JATHAABEH 70** [10] 3-8-4 (93) P Robinson 14/1: 0-1010: Dwelt, bhd, btn over 1f out: 18th, 10 wk abs. *shd* **80**
3897 **ATLANTIC RHAPSODY 21** [26] 3-8-6 (95) J Fanning 14/1: 054620: In tch, brief eff over 2f out, sn btn: 19th, nicely bckd, btr 3897. *1* **80**
3703 **LADY ANGHARAD 33** [32] 4-8-5 (89) D Harrison 25/1: -11100: In tch far side, wknd over 2f out: 20th. *1* **73**
3699 **COURT EXPRESS 33** [8] 6-7-11 (81)(1ow)(4oh) N Carlisle 66/1: 530440: In tch, btn over 2f out: 21st. *½* **64**
*3883 **PANTAR 22** [7] 5-9-1 (99)(5ex) K Dalgleish (5) 28/1: 023610: Bhd, no impress fnl 2f: 22nd, btr 3883. *1½* **80**
2857 **FANTAZIA 70** [11] 4-8-11 (95) R Mullen 33/1: 11-250: Al bhd: 23rd, abs. *½* **75**
*3899 **BOUND FOR PLEASURE 21** [2] 4-7-10 (80)(t)(5ex) F Norton 11/2 JT FAV: -23110: Al bhd, eased over 1f out: 24th, well bckd: much better expected after 3899. *1½* **57**
3865 **WEET A MINUTE 24** [19] 7-7-13 (83) J Tate 66/1: 054300: Led main group till over 3f out, wknd: 25th. *2* **57**
3794 **MILLIGAN 28** [30] 5-8-1 (85) J Mackay (5) 14/1: 0-1020: Dwelt, switched to main group, al bhd in 32rd. **0**
3597 **PYTHIOS 37** [28] 4-9-7 (105)(t) W Ryan 20/1: 042000: Al bhd, eased over 1f out: 34th: see 3597. **0**
4038 **Tammam 12** [4] 4-7-13 (83) Joanna Badger (7) 100/1:
4011 **Vintage Premium 14** [12] 3-8-11 (100) P Hanagan (5) 28/1:
4126 **Prince Slayer 6** [25] 4-7-10 (80) R Brisland (5) 66/1:
1077 **For Your Eyes Only 152** [21] 6-8-11 (95)(bl) T E Durcan 66/1:
3131 **Sir Ninja 57** [5] 3-8-9 (98) J Fortune 100/1: 4077 **Chapel Royale 9** [1] 3-7-10 (85)(3oh) A Polli (3) 66/1:
2528 **The Whistling Teal 83** [23] 4-7-10 (80) J Quinn 50/1: 703 **Dancing Kris 191** [17] 7-8-11 (95)(BL) J Weaver 66/1:
35 ran Time 1m 51.05 (1.85) (The Stable Maites) P W Harris Aldbury, Herts

4213 4.10 C HEIDSIECK HCAP 3YO 0-95 (C) 1m6f Good/Firm 30 +06 Fast [102]
£14046 £4322 £2161 £1080

3994 **THARI 14** [13] B Hanbury 3-9-7 (95) R Hills 7/1: 6-0631: 3 b c Silver Hawk - Magic Slipper (Habitat) **101**
Hld up, hdwy to lead over 1f out, edged right but styd on well for press ins last, drvn out: well bckd, gd time, joint top weight: '99 Chepstow wnr (mdn, rtd 96, with P Walwyn): eff at 10f, suited by 14f now: acts on firm, soft & likes gall trks: has tried blnks: useful & genuine, improved at this trip.
*3916 **LORD ALASKA 19** [15] J A R Toller 3-7-10 (70) F Norton 7/2 FAV: 501112: 3 b g Sir Harry Lewis - Anchorage (Slip Anchor) Held up, hdwy & switched right over 1f out, kept on well for press fnl 1f, just failed: hvly bckd to land 4 timer & narrowly failed: v progressive & would enjoy a return to 2m as in 3916. *nk* **75**
3994 **MASTER GEORGE 14** [2] I A Balding 3-8-6 (80) L Newman (3) 10/1: 625043: 3 b g Mtoto - Topwinder (Topsider) In tch, hdwy to lead over 2f out till over 1f out, onepace: shld find a staying h'cap: see 3994. *3* **81**
3870 **BOULDER 23** [11] L M Cumani 3-7-13 (73)(BL) P Doe 20/1: 645444: Cl-up, led over 4f out till over 2f out, onepace: fair run in first time blnks stepped up to 14f: see 3870 (10f), 2751. *1¾* **72**
4040 **SALUEM 12** [7] 3-8-1 (75) J Mackay (5) 12/1: -3225: Held up, travelling well over 2f out, wknd appr fnl 1f: poss stays 14f & worth a try in headgear: see 4040. *¾* **73**
3896 **TANTALUS 21** [4] 3-9-7 (95) M Hills 12/1: 340636: Held up, eff 2f out, sn onepace: longer trip. *1½* **91**
*3735 **ALPHA ROSE 31** [17] 3-7-13 (73) A Beech (3) 20/1: 114217: Held up, eff to chall 2f out, sn no extra. *nk* **69**
3961 **BOX BUILDER 16** [6] 3-8-10 (84) Craig Williams 16/1: 351448: Bhd, outpcd 2f out, some late gains. *nk* **79**
*3800 **THREE LIONS 27** [1] 3-8-0 (74) J Quinn 9/1: 016419: Keen, cl-up, sltly short of room over 2f out, wknd. *½* **68**
3599 **FANFARE 37** [8] 3-8-9 (83) D Holland 10/1: 024160: Handy, wknd over 2f out: 10th best 3153. *10* **65**
2594 **FULL AHEAD 80** [5] 3-8-10 (84) T E Durcan 20/1: 322160: Nvr a factor: 11th: see 2594. *2½* **62**
4071 **JACK DAWSON 10** [16] 3-7-10 (70) G Baker (5) 16/1: 231200: Al bhd: 12th: been busy, see 4071, 3637. *7* **39**
2068 **KEW GARDENS 102** [12] 3-9-0 (88) Pat Eddery 12/1: 6-2300: Chsd ldr till wknd over 2f out: 13th, abs. *1½* **55**
3948 **SEND ME AN ANGEL 17** [9] 3-7-10 (70)(2oh) K Dagleish (5) 20/1: 263150: Led over 9f, wknd 3f out: 15th. **0**
*3954 **Perpetuo 17** [10] 3-7-10 (70)(2oh) P Hanagan (3) 16/12470 **Colonial Rule 85** [14] 3-8-1 (75) Dale Gibson 25/1:
*3948 **Hambleden 17** [3] 3-8-9 (83) P Robinson 12/1:
17 ran Time 2m 58.91 (3.41) (Hamdan Al Maktoum) B Hanbury Newmarket

4214   4.45 NGK NURSERY HCAP 2YO 0-95 (C)   6f str   Good/Firm 30   -02 Slow   [99]
£8866   £2728   £1364   £682

3165 **CAUSTIC WIT 56** [8] E A L Dunlop 2-9-7 (92) J Reid 5/2 FAV: -50121: 2 b c Cadeaux Genereux -   99
Baldemosa (Lead On Time) Led after 1f, switched to race far rail & clr over 1f out, rdn out: 8 wk abs, joint
top weight: earlier scored at Doncaster (mdn): dam 1m scorer: eff at 6f, 7f shld suit: acts on fast grnd & a
gall trk: likes to dominate & runs well fresh under big weights: useful & on the up-grade.

3862 **THREEZEDZZ 24** [7] J G Portman 2-9-5 (90) D Harrison 25/1: 263402: 2 ch c Emarati - Exotic Forest   1   93
(Dominion) Led centre group thr'out, kept on over 1f out, not reach wnr: back to form & stays 6f: see 2849.

-4079 **ZHITOMIR 9** [11] S Dow 2-9-0 (85) P Doe 12/1: 406123: 2 ch c Lion Cavern - Treasure Trove (The   ½   86
Minstrel) Slow away, sn recovered & chsd wnr after 2f, onepace over 1f out: handles fast & soft: consistent.

3444 **EL MAXIMO 43** [18] M G Quinlan 2-8-3 (74)(tbl) F Norton 25/1: 261524: Dwelt, bhd far side, kept   nk   74
on late, nrst fin: 6 wk abs & needs a return to 7f as in 3444.

3630 **WARDEN WARREN 35** [17] 2-9-4 (89) P Robinson 16/1: -01265: Led 1f far side, bhd over 2f out,   ½   87
late gains: worth a try over 7f now: see 3552, 2132.

4070 **PASHMEENA 10** [12] 2-8-9 (80) L Newman (3) 20/1: 263507: Chsd wnr 5f out till 4f out, wknd 2f out.   nk   75

3987 **ARMAGNAC 15** [6] 2-9-5 (90) T E Durcan 12/1: 255128: Bhd, some late gains: see 3987 (soft grnd).   1   82

*3911 **FLINT RIVER 19** [13] 2-8-13 (84) R Mullen 7/1: 220219: Nvr dangerous: nicely bckd, btr 3911.   shd   63

3952 **AUNT RUBY 17** [4] 2-8-2 (73) A Beech (3) 16/1: 0260: Bhd, nvr dangerous: 10th: see 3649.   hd   69

3959 **XALOC BAY 16** [19] 2-8-9 (80) N Callan 25/1: -2200: In tch, wknd over 1f out: 11th, see 2700.   hd   69

3987 **MY AMERICAN BEAUTY 15** [16] 2-7-12 (69) J Quinn 8/1: 603100: In tch far side, wknd over 1f out: ¾   56
12th, nicely bckd: twice below 3807.

3602 Our Destiny 36 [5] 2-8-9 (80) J Fortune 25/1:   3987 Loner 15 [10] 2-8-7 (78) P Hanagan (5) 16/1:

3246 Mon Secret 52 [2] 2-8-7 (78) Joanna Badger (7) 25/1: 3801 Fantasy Believer 27 [14] 2-8-6 (77) J Mackay (5) 20/1:

1214 Y To Kman 144 [1] 2-9-3 (88) R Hughes 14/1:   3862 Factual Lad 24 [3] 2-9-7 (92) M Roberts 16/1:

18 ran   Time 1m 12.72 (1.92)   (Maktoum Al Maktoum)   E A L Dunlop Newmarket

4215   5.20 LINKS HCAP 3YO+ 0-90 (C)   7f str   Good/Firm 30   -00 Slow   [86]
£7631   £2348   £1174   £587   3 yo rec 3 lb

725 **SEA MARK 189** [13] B W Hills 4-9-8 (80) M Hills 20/1: 2/1-01: 4 ro c Warning - Mettlesome (Lomond)   85
Handy far side, kept on over 1f out to get up close home, drvn out: 6 month abs: won sole '99 start, at
Leicester (appr mdn, rtd 74): eff at 7f, shld stay 1m: runs esp well fresh on fast & gd/soft, gall trks.

3880 **PAYS DAMOUR 23** [17] R Hannon 3-9-9 (84) L Newman (3) 25/1: 121302: 3 b c Pursuit Of Love - Lady   shd   88
Of The Land (Wollow) Led far side, kept on for press over 1f out, collared cl-home: likes to dominate, genuine.

3758 **HILLTOP WARNING 30** [21] S P C Woods 3-8-13 (74) D Glennon (7) 25/1: 015403: 3 b c Reprimand -   ¾   76
Just Irene (Sagaro) Hld up, eff over 1f out, kept on ins last, only btn 1L: better run with blnks discarded.

3528 **CUPIDS CHARM 40** [22] R Guest 3-9-0 (75) D Harrison 16/1: 016004: Bhd, eff over 1f out, kept on   hd   76
ins last: 6 wk abs: stays 7f: see 2280.

*4018 **REDSWAN 14** [20] 5-8-11 (69)(t) W Ryan 12/1: 203315: In tch, eff over 1f out, kept on ins   hd   69
last, not btn far: in gd form, would certainly win another clmr as in 4018 (likes it here).

3904 **CONTACT 21** [2] 3-9-3 (78) P Robinson 15/2: 6-0006: Prom, rdn over 1f out, onepace: nicely bckd: ½   77
much more encouraging: stays 7f on fast & gd/soft: could be more to come.

3992 **SUPREME SALUTATION 15** [18] 4-9-3 (75) T E Durcan 11/2 FAV: 553427: Dwelt, held on, kept on over   ½   73
1f out, nrst fin: nicely bckd: see 3992.

4038 **APLOY 12** [27] 3-9-1 (76) J Reid 20/1: 512268: Held up, kept on late, nrst fin: see 4038.   ½   73

-3981 **GOODENOUGH MOVER 15** [4] 4-9-7 (79) D Holland 7/1: 111429: Led, edged right over 1f out, hdd &   shd   75
onepace: well bckd, tough: see 3981.

3880 **BOLDLY GOES 23** [19] 4-10-0 (86)(bl) Pat Eddery 14/1: 601400: In tch, eff to chall over 1f out, wknd: 10th.½   81

3936 **PROSPECTORS COVE 17** [14] 7-8-13 (71) M Roberts 10/1: 662360: Slow away, some late gains: 11th.   ¾   64

3759 **AMJAD 30** [26] 3-8-9 (70)(bl) P Doe 33/1: 500200: With ldrs, no extra over 1f out: 12th: see 3759.   nk   64

4118 **NOUF 6** [28] 4-9-2 (74) J Quinn 16/1: 005120: Nvr a factor: 13th: btr 4118 (10f, gd/soft).   ½   65

3899 **DONNAS DOUBLE 21** [3] 5-8-11 (69) K Dalgleish (5) 12/1: 340240: In tch, no impress fnl 2f: 14th.   1   58

2869 **ELLENS ACADEMY 69** [11] 5-9-7 (79) J Fortune 10/1: 303040: Al bhd: 15th: 10 wk abs: see 2869.   ½   67

3992 **ARPEGGIO 15** [6] 5-9-4 (76) J Weaver 10/1: 031300: In tch, btn 2f out: 16th: see 3992, 3831.   1¾   60

*3880 **NORFOLK REED 23** [16] 3-9-7 (82)(vis) R Hughes 10/1: 000310: Al bhd: 2nd: much btr 3880.   0

4112 Teodora 7 [5] 3-9-5 (80) A Polli (5) 33/1:   3543 Blue Star 39 [25] 4-8-10 (68)(vis) L Paddock (7) 20/1:

3758 Shouf Al Badou 30 [7] 3-8-11 (72) P Hanagan (5) 20/1: 3163 Kamareyah 56 [30] 3-9-1 (76) R Hills 20/1:

3880 Locharati 23 [29] 3-9-4 (79) J Tate 33/1:   3325 Cote Soleil 49 [15] 3-9-4 (79) A Beech (3) 25/1:

4037 Melanzana 12 [10] 3-9-5 (80) G Carter 33/1:   4094 Champagne Rider 8 [9] 4-9-0 (72)(BL) F Norton 20/1:

3936 Topton 17 [8] 6-9-2 (74)(bl) R Mullen 20/1:   935 Touch Of Fairy 166 [1] 4-9-12 (84)(t) S Whitworth 33/1:

4500} Picot 341 [23] 3-9-8 (83) Craig Williams 20/1:

28 ran   Time 1m 25.32 (2.12)   (K Abdulla)   B W Hills Lambourn, Berks

Official Going   SOFT (HEAVY places in back straight). Stalls: Str - Centre; 1m6f - Centre; Rem - Inside.

4216   2.10 EBF FILLIES HORSESMOUTH MDN 2YO (D)   7f str   Good/Soft 75   -08 Slow
£3146   £968   £484   £242

--   **QUITTE LA FRANCE** [2] J G Given 2-8-11 Dean McKeown 25/1: 1: 2 b f Saddlers' Hall - Tafila   89
(Adonijah) In tch, prog to lead appr fnl 1f, rdn & wandered ins last, kept on well: debut: half-sister to wnrs
at 1m/12f, dam 1m/10f wnr: eff at 7f, bred to apprec mid-dists: acts on gd/soft grnd & a gall trk: runs well fresh.

--   **STARRY LADY** [3] M R Channon 2-8-11 A Culhane 12/1: 2: 2 b f Marju - Caroline Lady (Caro)   ½   87
Rear, imprvd after halfway, ch ent fnl 1f, held towards fin: op 7/1, clr ent, debut: IR 28,000gns half-sister
to 2 10f wnrs, dam 12f wnr: eff at 7f, bred for 10f+: handles gd/soft grnd & shld find similar.

4035 **PHOEBE ROBINSON 12** [13] G C Bravery 2-8-11 M Fenton 33/1: 03: 2 b f Alzao - Savelli (Vision)   6   77

Mid-div, wide, prog to press ldrs 2f out, sn onepace: left debut bhd: IR 17,000gns half-sister to a 5f juv wnr, dam 9f juv wnr: some promise here.

3607 **HALCYON DAZE 36** [12] L M Cumani 2-8-11 G Sparkes (7) 8/1: 04: In tch, eff 2f out, not pace to chall: op 6/1, tchd 10/1: see 3607 (Newmarket). ¾ **75**

4086 **ELLA TINO 9** [6] 2-8-11 D Mernagh (3) 12/1: 65: Chsd ldrs, no extra ent fnl 2f: tchd 16/1. ½ **74**

3953 **ROSALIA 17** [9] 2-8-11 K Darley 5/1: -4636: Hmpd start, led till appr fnl 1f, fdd: flattered last time. *1* **72**

3359 **BYLAW 47** [7] 2-8-11 M Tebbutt 4/6 FAV: 27: Al same place: well bckd, 7 wk abs: much btr 3359 (fast). *nk* **71**

-- **SITARA** [4] 2-8-11 S Sanders 12/1: 8: Nvr troubled ldrs: stablemate 4th: Salse half-sister to fair mid-dist performers Puce & Seek: dam 7f wnr: shld apprec mid-dists next term. *1¾* **68**

3614 **BRILLYANT DANCER 36** [15] 2-8-11 R Ffrench 25/1: -09: Nvr dngrs: see 3614. *3½* **62**

3974 **ARONA 15** [1] 2-8-11 J Carroll 40/1: 00: In tch 4f: 10th, stablemate winner. *1¼* **60**

-- **Eastern Lilac** [11] 2-8-11 F Lynch 50/1: -- **Brief Key** [5] 2-8-11 Kim Tinkler 50/1:

3614 **Maid To Dance 36** [8] 2-8-11 G Parkin 33/1: 3408 **Peggys Song 44** [10] 2-8-11 O Pears 50/1:

1890 **Impreza 109** [14] 2-8-11 (vis) C Lowther 33/1:

15 ran Time 1m 27.6 (5.8) (D Morrison) J G Given Willoughton, Lincs.

4217

2.40 TETLEY'S HCAP 3YO+ 0-85 (D) 1m str Good/Soft 75 +05 Fast [85]
£6578 £2024 £1012 £506 3 yo rec 4 lb

3810 **RYMERS RASCAL 27** [18] E J Alston 8-8-4 (60)(1ow) M Fenton 14/1: 253031: 8 b g Rymer - City Sound (On Your Mark) Mid-div, gd prog appr fnl 2f, led below dist, pshd out: gd time of day: '99 Chester wnr (h'cap, rtd 68): '98 wnr here at Redcar (h'cap, rtd 63): eff at 7f/1m: acts on firm, hvy grnd, any trk, likes Redcar. **67**

3808 **BACCHUS 27** [15] Miss J A Camacho 6-8-13 (70)(vis) K Darley 14/1: 215602: 6 b g Prince Sabo - Bonica (Rousillon) Held up, prog ent fnl 3f, kept on to chase wnr ins last, nvr nrr: gd run back in trip, see 2671. *1¾* **72**

*4044 **MELODIAN 11** [11] M Brittain 5-8-12 (69)(bl) D Mernagh (3) 12/1: 000013: 5 b h Grey Desire - Mere Melody (Dunphy) Front rank, led after halfway till ent fnl 1f, onepace: stays 1m, see 4044 (soft/hvy). ¾ **69**

3777 **CAUTION 28** [14] S Gollings 6-7-12 (55) A Nicholls 14/1: 523334: Held on, kept on appr fnl 1f, nvr nr to chall: tchd 20/1, clr rem: hard to win with this term, see 3561, 645. ½ **54**

4005 **CHAMPFIS 14** [9] 3-8-11 (72) R Ffrench 10/1: 03-425: Cl-up, chall 2f out, onepace bef fnl 1f: tchd 14/1: back up in trip, only lightly rcd, worth another chance at 7f?: see 4005. *2½* **66**

3652 **ONLY FOR GOLD 35** [5] 5-7-11 (54)(2oh) Iona Wands 25/1: 020056: Swerved right start, chased ldrs, onepcd appr fnl 1f: see 780. *1* **46**

3777 **FALLS OMONESS 28** [12] 6-7-10 (53)(6oh) J Bramhill 25/1: 000027: Prom, & ev ch till fdd appr fnl 1f. *1* **43**

4576} **SHARP SCOTCH 334** [10] 7-7-10 (53)(3oh) S Righton 25/1: 0003-8: Al around same place, stiffish task, reapp: landed a Southwell 4-timer in '99 (h'caps, rtd 83a & 52): ex-Irish, '98 wnr at Naas (h'cap), later at W'hampton (h'cap, rt 65a): eff at 1m/9.3f, tried further: acts on fast, soft grnd, fibresand/Southwell specialist. *hd* **42**

3979 **BURNING TRUTH 15** [4] 6-8-5 (62) L Enstone (7) 25/1: -60209: In tch, rdn 3f out, onepce: back in trip. *hd* **51**

3810 **SCENE 27** [1] 5-9-0 (71) S Sanders 9/1: 000000: Prom, no extra appr fnl 2f: 10th, op 7/1: see 831. ¾ **58**

4135 **ROLLER 6** [3] 4-9-3 (74) T G McLaughlin 6/1 JT FAV: 040360: Nvr dngrs: qk reapp, bckd from 9/1. *shd* **61**

1892 **PENNYS PRIDE 109** [19] 5-8-13 (70) A Culhane 14/1: 023030: Dwelt, nvr a factor: 12th, 15 wk abs. *1½* **54**

3753 **ITS MAGIC 30** [13] 4-8-11 (68)(bl) M Tebbutt 12/1: 620660: Nvr on terms tho' staying on fin: 13th. ½ **51**

4038 **PAGAN KING 12** [23] 4-8-12 (69) J Carroll 6/1 JT FAV: 004320: Outpcd, btn fnl 2f: 22nd, btr 4038, 3514. **0**

3634 **Mehmaas 35** [2] 4-7-11 (54)(vis)(1ow)(3oh) P Fessey 25/1: 3899 **Colway Ritz 21** [21] 6-9-10 (81) T Williams 25/1:

3634 **Oriole 35** [7] 7-7-10 (53)(10oh) Kim Tinkler 50/1: 4094 **Clever Girl 8** [8] 3-8-12 (73) G Parkin 33/1:

4033 **Young Rosein 12** [22] 4-8-2 (59) G Bardwell 16/1:

3988 **Impulsive Air 15** [6] 8-7-10 (53)(14oh) G Sparkes (3) 66/1:

4088 **Tarradale 9** [16] 6-7-10 (53)(9oh) A Mackay 66/1: 1495 **Favorisio 127** [17] 3-9-2 (77) R Winston 33/1:

1498 **Windshift 127** [24] 4-8-1 (57)(bl)(1ow) O Pears 33/1: *3826 **Ambushed 26** [20] 4-7-13 (56) J McAuley 14/1:

24 ran Time 1m 40.4 (5.6) (Brian Chambers) E J Alston Longton, Lancs.

4218

3.15 BETABET.COM COND STKS 3YO+ (C) 7f str Good/Soft 75 +01 Fast
£6351 £2409 £1204 £547 3 yo rec 3 lb

4112 **GAELIC STORM 7** [15] M Johnston 6-9-4 J Carroll 2/9 FAV: 415401: 6 b g Shavian - Shannon Princess (Connaught) Held up, prog after 3f, rdn to lead appr fnl 1f, qcknd clr towards fin: bckd to land short odds, qck reapp, fair time: earlier won at Klampenborg: '99 wnr at Goodwood (stks), Sweden (2, incl List) & Newmarket (List, rtd 114): eff at 6/7f: acts on firm, suited by gd or soft grnd, any trk: smart at best. **108**

3884 **EXEAT 22** [3] D Nicholls 4-8-9 K Darley 5/1: -20062: 4 b c Dayjur - By Your Leave (Private Account) Slow away, clsd by halfway & ev ch till outpcd by wnr ins last & eased towards fin: signs of a return to form. *3* **92**

3604 **ROYAL REPRIMAND 36** [6] R E Barr 5-8-9 P Goode (3) 14/1: 524323: 5 b g Reprimand - Lake Ormond (King's Lake) Held up, prog appr fnl 2f & ch bef fnl 1f, sn onepace: surely flattered again, see 1009. *1½* **89$**

3780 **ZAMAT 28** [8] P Monteith 4-8-9 R Winston 100/1: 0-04: Led till appr fnl 1f, no extra: stiff task, flattered. *2* **84$**

3696 **MACS DREAM 33** [1] 5-8-9 (t) M Tebbutt 33/1: 000505: Handy, eff 2f out, outpcd: stiff task, flattered. *5* **72$**

3670 **FOUR MEN 34** [5] 3-8-6 D Allan (7) 66/1: 530206: Prom, rdn appr fnl 2f, fdd: stiff task, flattered. *1* **70$**

2925 **SEALED BY FATE 66** [11] 5-8-9 F Lynch 50/1: 502007: Nvr nr ldrs: stiff task, flattered after 9 wk abs. *1½* **66$**

4032 **REGENT 12** [14] 5-8-9 A Mackay 100/1: -00008: Dwelt, nvr better than mid-div: stiff task, flattered. *1½* **62$**

3823 **HOT POTATO 26** [7] 4-8-9 (vis) J McAuley 200/1: 502069: In tch till halfway: v stiff task, see 1858. ¾ **60$**

4043 **DISTANT KING 11** [9] 7-8-9 A Nicholls 100/1: 000050: Nvr nr ldrs: 10th, flattered again up in trip. *1½* **57$**

4043 **Levendi 11** [4] 3-8-6 G Bardwell 200/1: 4133 **The Castigator 6** [10] 3-8-6 O Pears 200/1:

3775 **Sitting Pretty 28** [2] 4-8-4 P Bradley (5) 200/1: 3865 **Stamford Hill 24** [12] 5-8-9 D Mernagh (3) 200/1:

2223} **Strensall 463** [13] 3-8-6 P Fessey 200/1:

15 ran Time 1m 27.0 (5.2) (H C Racing Club) M Johnston Middleham, N.Yorks.

4219

3.50 BETABET 2-Y-O TROPHY 2YO (B) 6f str Good/Soft 75 +01 Fast
£58000 £22000 £11000 £5000

*3165 **DIM SUMS 56** [6] T D Barron 2-8-4 K Darley 6/4 FAV: 21111: 2 b g Repriced - Regal Baby (Northern Baby) Nvr far away, went on 2f out, sn clr, rdly: 8 wk abs, hvly bckd from 11/4, fair time: 4-timer landed, earlier won at Southwell (mdn, rtd 72a), Pontefract & Newmarket (nurs): eff at 6f, shld get 7f: acts on fast, gd/soft grnd & fibresand, any trk: runs v well fresh: progressive & v useful gelding with a turn of foot. **104**

4009 **ZIETUNZEEN 14** [17] A Berry 2-8-7 C Lowther 25/1: 355152: 2 b f Zieten - Hawksbill Special (Taufan) Rear, sn niggled, ran on appr fnl 2f, went 2nd ent fnl 1f, no ch wnr: jockey given 3 day ban for irresp ride: imprvd here, 7f will now suit: well plcd to land some val prize money here: see 3520. *2½* **98**

3807 **WALLY MCARTHUR 27** [24] A Berry 2-8-1 R Ffrench 33/1: 110423: 2 b c Puissance - Giddy (Polar Falcon) Rear, prog fnl 2f, styd on, nvr nrr: stablemate 2nd, ran to best: acts on fast & gd/sft: must try 7f. *2* **86**
3507 **RIVER RAVEN 41** [22] Sir Mark Prescott 2-8-10 S Sanders 20/1: 214124: Towards rear, prog & hung left appr fnl 2f, kept on till no extra fnl 1f: 6 wk abs: may do better with headgear back at 7f: see 3273. *½* **93**
3862 **WHERES JASPER 24** [16] 2-8-12 J Carroll 33/1: 120105: Well plcd & ch till onepace bef fnl 1f. *1* **92**
3938 **OOMPH 17** [7] 2-8-5 M Tebbutt 16/1: 436: Mid-div, chsd ldrs 2f out till 1f out: stiffish task for this mdn. *½* **83**
3891 **BARKING MAD 22** [20] 2-8-12 M Fenton 7/1: 621367: Towards rear, improving when not clr run 2f out, no threat: stopped at a crucial stage, worth another look: see 3470, 2966. *nk* **89**
3860 **STRUMPET 24** [5] 2-7-10 J Bramhill 33/1: 016308: Nvr better than mid-div: stiff task but btr 2227 (fast). *½* **71**
3862 **PRINCESS OF GARDA 24** [21] 2-7-13 A Mackay 25/1: 145409: Chsd ldrs till 2f out: see 3712, 2248. *hd* **73**
3959 **ELSIE PLUNKETT 16** [8] 2-7-13 A Daly 7/1: 324430: Bhd ldrs, lost pl appr fnl 1f: 10th, return to 5f? *1½* **69**
*3688 **MUSIC MAID 33** [11] 2-7-13 A Nicholls 33/1: 130010: Chsd ldrs, fdd ent fnl 2f: 11th, btr 3688 (7f). *hd* **68**
4051 **SECRET INDEX 15** [15] 2-7-10 G Bardwell 12/1: 544600: Mid-div when short of room 2f out: 12th. *5* **53**
3807 **PETONGSKI 27** [1] 2-8-7 F Lynch 33/1: -21200: Led till 2f out, wknd: 13th, see 3245. *1½* **60**
4009 **PROMISED 14** [4] 2-7-13 D Mernagh 7/1: 300040: Mid-div, rdn & btn appr fnl 2f, eased fnl 1f: 19th. **0**
3497 **Jamila 42** [3] 2-8-9 (BL) T G McLaughlin 100/1: *1993 **Nashira 105** [13] 2-8-2 R Winston 20/1:
3797 **Preferred 27** [19] 2-8-7 Dean McKeown 12/1: 3959 **Silca Legend 16** [2] 2-8-10 A Culhane 20/1:
3807 **Majestic Quest 27** [10] 2-8-7 G Faulkner 66/1: 3513 **Festive Affair 41** [23] 2-8-7 P Fessey 100/1:
4131 **Liberty Bound 6** [18] 2-8-7 O Pears 100/1: 4090 **Winfield 8** [25] 2-8-7 (BL) G Hannon 100/1:
2488 **Upstream 84** [9] 2-8-2 T Williams 25/1:
23 ran Time 1m 13.3 (4.4) (Executive Network (Pertemps Group)) T D Barron Maunby, N.Yorks.

4220

4.20 NSPCC CLASSIFIED STKS 3YO+ 0-70 (E) 5f str Good/Soft 75 -07 Slow
£3029 £932 £466 £233 3 yo rec 1 lb

3694 **GDANSK 33** [15] A Berry 3-8-13 J Carroll 15/2: 040021: 3 b g Pips Pride - Merry Twinkle (Martinmas) Well plcd, rdn to lead appr fnl 1f, pushed out towards fin: earlier won at Warwick (mdn): unplcd juv (mdns, rtd 70): eff at 6f, suited by 5f: acts on gd & gd/soft grnd, prob any trk: likes to be up with/forcing the pace. **68**
4107 **WHIZZ KID 7** [16] J M Bradley 6-9-0 Claire Bryan (5) 9/2 JT FAV: 000502: 6 b m Puissance - Panienka (Dom Racine) In tch, prog appr fnl 1f, kept on ins last, nvr nr to chall: bckd, qk reapp: ran nr to best: see 1391. *¾* **67**
4107 **TORRENT 7** [20] D W Chapman 5-9-6 (bl) Lynsey Hanna (7) 13/2: 335103: 5 ch g Prince Sabo - Maiden Pool (Sharpen Up) Chsd ldrs, ch appr fnl 1f, unable to qckn towards fin: back to nr best, qck reapp: *nk* **72**
3651 **LUCKY COVE 35** [14] N Tinkler 4-9-0 (BL) Kim Tinkler 66/1: 000004: Mid-div, rdn appr fnl 1f, kept on but not pace of ldrs: v stiff task, flattered here in blnks for new connections: see 808. *1* **63$**
4010 **DAAWE 14** [13] 9-9-0 (bl) Clare Roche (7) 8/1: 050005: Well plcd & ev ch till no extra fnl 1f: see 1074. *¾* **61**
3872 **TICK TOCK 23** [19] 3-8-10 (vis) A Mackay 20/1: 004006: Rear, late hdwy, nvr a threat: dubious rating. *½* **56$**
4043 **PALACEGATE JACK 11** [9] 9-9-0 D Allan (7) 33/1: 560547: Bhd ldrs, eff 2f out, outpcd: stablemate wnr. *1½* **55**
3775 **PETRA NOVA 28** [2] 4-8-11 (BL) V Halliday 100/1: -00608: Dwelt, styd on late into mid-div: blnkd. *½* **50$**
2663 **JAILHOUSE ROCKET 78** [7] 3-8-13 S Sanders 9/2 JT FAV: 000009: Slow away, ran on fnl 1f: 11 wk abs, bckd from 6/1: struggling to rediscover useful juvenile form: see 2168. *1½* **50**
3781 **SASHA 28** [12] 3-8-13 M Fenton 16/1: -40040: Led till bef halfway, fdd appr fnl 1f: fin 10th. *shd* **50**
4087 **NICKLES 9** [10] 5-9-3 K Darley 14/1: 401000: Led bef halfway till appr fnl 1f, btn: 11th: see 3694. *nk* **52**
4087 **SULU 9** [6] 4-9-0 T Lucas 7/1: 000100: Nvr a factor: 12th: see 1162. *½* **47**
4069 **Palacegate Touch 10** [3] 10-9-0 P Bradley (5) 33/1: 4069 **Time To Fly 10** [5] 7-9-0 T Hamilton (7) 25/1:
4155 **Jack To A King 4** [4] 5-9-0 A Nicholls 33/1: 4069 **Gad Yakoun 10** [21] 7-9-0 (t) Angela Hartley (7) 50/1:
4004 **Millsec 14** [17] 3-8-10 O Pears 25/1: 4135 **Time For The Clan 6** [18] 3-8-13 J McAuley 50/1:
2243 **General Dominion 94** [22] 3-8-13 D Mernagh (3) 16/1: 4043 **Plum First 11** [11] 10-9-0 Kimberley Hart 33/1:
3536 **Superfrills 39** [8] 7-8-11 M Tebbutt 20/1: 3619 **Danakim 36** [1] 3-8-13 R Winston 16/1:
22 ran Time 1m 00.6 (4.1) (Chris & Antonia Deuters) A Berry Cockerham, Lancs.

4221

4.55 NTL HCAP 3YO+ 0-80 (D) 1m2f Good/Soft 75 -12 Slow [79]
£5573 £1715 £857 £428 3 yo rec 6 lb

*4003 **NOWELL HOUSE 14** [1] M W Easterby 4-9-7 (72) G Parkin 7/2: 000011: 4 ch g Polar Falcon - Langtry Lady (Pas de Seul) Prom, led 3f out, hard rdn & hdd ent fnl 1f, rallied gamely to regain lead fnl strides, all out: nicely bckd: recent Catterick wnr (h'cap): '99 wnr at Beverley, Pontefract & here at Redcar (h'caps, rtd 66): plcd in '98 (mdn, rtd 72): eff at 10/12f: acts on fast, suited by soft, any trk, likes Redcar: runs well fresh. **78**
*1411 **KATHRYNS PET 133** [6] Mrs M Reveley 7-10-0 (79) T Eaves (7) 16/1: 41-612: 7 b m Blakeney - Starky's Pet (Mummy's Pet) Held up, gd hdwy ent str, rdn to lead below dist, hdd nr fin: tchd 20/1, clr rem, long abs: gd run tho' appeared to be out-ridden near finish: see 1411. *shd* **84**
3603 **KONKER 36** [13] Mrs M Reveley 5-8-2 (53) P Fessey 20/1: 06-003: 5 ch g Selkirk - Helens Dreamgirl (Caerleon) Towards rear, styd on thr' btn horses fnl 2f, nvr dngrs: stablemate 2nd: see 3368. *6* **50**
4074 **RUTLAND CHANTRY 10** [8] S Gollings 6-8-9 (60) K Darley 6/1: 660534: Prom, rdn 3f out, same pace. *shd* **57**
3806 **ABSINTHER 27** [10] 3-7-13 (55)(1ow) R Ffrench 8/1: 053125: Well plcd & ev ch till fdd appr fnl 1f. *1¾* **51**
4108 **QUEENS PAGEANT 7** [4] 6-9-4 (69) A Culhane 8/1: 030326: Nvr troubled ldrs: qck reapp, see 3045. *3½* **59**
4370} **BOOGY WOOGY 351** [2] 4-8-11 (62) R Winston 25/1: 0333-7: Nvr on terms: reapp: '99 Thirsk wnr (h'cap, rtd 67): '98 wnr at Redcar (clmr) & Doncaster (nurs h'cap, rtd 71): 99/00 hdles wnr at M Rasen (2m1.5f juv nov, firm & gd/soft, rtd 118h): eff at 12f, stays 14f: goes on firm & gd/soft & prob best blnkd (not worn). *½* **51**
*4118 **LEVEL HEADED 6** [9] 5-8-7 (58) A Mackay 11/4 FAV: 410118: Led till 3f out, lost pl: bckd from 4/1 to land a qck-fire hat-trick & it possibly came too soon after 4118. *1½* **45**
4003 **SHAFFISHAYES 14** [11] 8-8-1 (52) A Nicholls 12/1: 530609: Nvr a factor: stablemate 2nd, see 943. *1* **38**
4003 **UNDER THE SAND 14** [7] 3-9-7 (78) M Tebbutt 10/1: 420160: Al towards rear: 10th: much btr 3480. *1* **62**
3992 **Ostara 15** [5] 3-8-8 (65) J Carroll 20/1: 4582} **Stone Cold 333** [15] 3-7-11 (54) P Fessey 50/1:
3988 **Canny Hill 15** [14] 3-7-10 (53)(3oh) J Bramhill 40/1: 2205 **Haikal 96** [12] 3-8-5 (62) O Pears 50/1:
14 ran Time 2m 11.0 (8.7) (Bernard Bargh & John Walsh) M W Easterby Sheriff Hutton, N.Yorks.

4222

5.25 HORSESMOUTH HCAP 3YO+ 0-70 (E) 1m6f Good/Soft 75 -29 Slow [66]
£3133 £964 £482 £241 3 yo rec 10lb

2319 **MR FORTYWINKS 91** [6] J L Eyre 6-9-7 (59) K Darley 10/1: 041341: 6 ch g Fool's Holme - Dream On (Absalom) Well plcd, eff 2f out, squeezed thro' to lead ent fnl 1f, rdn out: slow time, 3 mth abs: earlier won at Newcastle (class stks): '99 wnr at Hamilton, Ripon (ladies) & Carlisle (h'caps, rtd 70): '98 wnr at W'hampton, Southwell & Nottingham (rtd 63 & 71a): eff up with/forcing the pace at 12/14f on firm, hvy grnd & fibresand: **62**

runs v well fresh & handles any trk: well rdn by K Darley here.
4105 **ALDWYCH ARROW 7** [10] M A Buckley 5-7-13 (37) A Daly 10/1: 000602: 5 ch g Rainbows For Life - Shygate (Shy Groom) Cl-up, led 2f out, hard rdn bef fnl 1f, hdd ins last, kept on: qck reapp, gd run: see 2836. ½ **38**
4006 **HOUSE OF DREAMS 14** [13] Mrs M Reveley 8-8-10 (48) A Culhane 5/1 FAV: 4-0123: 8 b g Darshaan - Helens Dreamgirl (Caerleon) Rear, shkn up & hdwy appr fnl 2f, drvn ins last, kept on, nvr nrr: in form, see 3633. ½ **48**
4105 **SIMPLE IDEALS 7** [12] Don Enrico Incisa 6-8-7 (45) Kim Tinkler 6/1: 542524: Mid-div, prog to chall 2f out, onepace ins last: qck reapp, ran near to best, only btn arnd 1L: see 1563. *shd* **45**
3978 **RIGHTY HO 15** [1] 6-8-3 (41) K Hodgson 10/1: 022125: Led till 2f out, no extra: btr 3570 (12f). 2 **38**
4105 **ASHLEIGH BAKER 7** [5] 5-8-10 (48) R Ffrench 14/1: 244056: Prom, eff appr str, same pace: qck reapp. 4 **40**
4134 **HIGHFIELD FIZZ 6** [9] 8-7-11 (35) L Enstone (1) 16/1: 413007: Nvr better than mid-div: qck reapp. 1½ **25**
1536 **ALPINE PANTHER 126** [14] 7-9-1 (53) T Eaves (7) 20/1: 360/08: Nvr troubled ldrs: stablemate 3rd, jumps rnr-up 7 wks ago, see 1536. ¾ **42**
4006 **BEST PORT 14** [11] 4-7-13 (37) A Nicholls 16/1: 021209: Held up, brief eff 3f out: tchd 25/1. *shd* **26**
1767 **DAME FONTEYN 115** [4] 3-9-1 (63) M Fenton 8/1: 226130: Rear, chsd ldrs 4f out, wknd 2f out: 10th, abs. 7 **45**
*3181 **DARK SHADOWS 54** [7] 5-9-10 (62) T Williams 13/2: 536310: In tch till ent str: 11th, top-weight, 8 wk abs: much btr 3181 (12f, fast). ¾ **43**
3367 **Happy Days 46** [3] 5-8-0 (38) J Bramhill 20/1:
*4002 **Indy Carr 14** [15] 3-8-2 (50) O Pears 14/1:
3963 **Spree Vision 16** [2] 4-8-13 (51) R Winston 20/1:
4259} **Pretty Obvious 361** [16] 4-9-5 (57) P Fessey 16/1:
3249 **Noirie 52** [8] 6-7-10 (34) D Mernagh (0) 20/1:
16 ran Time 3m 12.3 (14.5) (Miss Nuala Cassidy) J L Eyre Sutton Bank, N.Yorks.

WOLVERHAMPTON (Fibresand) SATURDAY SEPTEMBER 30TH LH, Oval, Sharp Track

Official Going STANDARD. Stalls: 7f - Outside; Rem - Inside.

4223

7.00 BET DIRECT HCAP 3YO+ 0-65 (F) 6f aw rnd Going 39 +04 Fast **[65]**
£2590 £740 £370 3 yo rec 2 lb

4023 **CITY REACH 14** [10] P J Makin 4-9-5 (56)(vis) S Sanders 4/1 JT FAV: 510331: 4 b g Petong - Azola (Alzao) Sn rdn in tch, hdwy to lead dist, rdn clr: tchd 6/1, gd time: earlier won at Southwell (AW auct mdn, 1st time visor) & Brighton (class stks): plcd in '99 (rtd 57a & 75), rtd 77 sole '98 start: eff at 5.3/6f, stays a sharp 7f, tried further: acts on firm, hvy, both AWs & a sharp/undul or gall trk & best now in a visor. **68a**
3668 **GAY BREEZE 34** [13] P S Felgate 7-9-12 (63) S Finnamore (5) 14/1: 060002: 7 b g Dominion - Judy's Dowry (Dragonara Palace) Trkd ldr, eff to chall appr fnl 1f, sn not pace of wnr, op 8/1: gd effort under top-weight on this AW debut, acts on fibresand: can win similar this winter: see 905. 4 **65a**
4156 **SAMWAR 4** [3] Mrs N Macauley 8-9-6 (57)(vis) R Fitzpatrick 9/1: 563263: 8 b g Warning - Samaza (Arctic Tern) Sn rdn & outpcd, rdn & styd on well fnl 1f, nvr nrr: op 6/1, qck reapp: shade btr 3271. 1½ **55a**
4087 **LEGS BE FRENDLY 9** [2] D Nicholls 5-9-11 (62) Paul Eddery 11/1: W35004: Outpcd early, late hdwy from rear but no threat to ldrs: see 3056, 2721. 1½ **56a**
4023 **PADDYWACK 14** [1] 3-9-9 (62)(bl) R Studholme (3) 25/1: 20U005: Led/dsptd lead at a decent clip, hdd dist, wknd: paid price for setting too fast a pace here: see 1742. *hd* **56a**
*4023 **MOOCHA CHA MAN 14** [8] 4-9-11 (62)(bl) L Newton 6/1: 000516: Prom, drvn/fdd fnl 2f: btr 4023 (C/D). ¾ **54a**
3759 **CAPPELLINA 30** [5] 3-9-3 (56) P M Quinn (3) 20/1: 004207: Nvr dngrs: btr 3279 (7f, firm). *shd* **48a**
4023 **VILLA ROMANA 14** [7] 3-9-5 (58) J Bosley (7) 9/1: 0-0658: In tch, no impress halfway: see 3081 (1m). 1½ **47a**
4023 **POLAR MIST 14** [9] 5-9-8 (59)(tbl) Dean McKeown 9/1: 206069: Led/dsptd lead till hdd over 1f out, wknd qckly fnl 1f: op 6/1: see 1487 (gd/soft). *shd* **48a**
3774 **YOUNG BIGWIG 28** [4] 6-9-5 (56) J Fanning 4/1 JT FAV: 334030: Al outpcd, 10th: btr 3774 (C/D). *shd* **45a**
4155 **RUDE AWAKENING 4** [12] 6-9-8 (59) P Goode (3) 10/1: 204030: Al rear, 11th: qck reapp: btr 4155. *hd* **48a**
3855 **ZARAGOSSA 24** [11] 4-9-5 (56) Iona Wands 9/1: 050060: Prom, wknd qckly fnl 2f, 12th: up in trip. 1½ **41a**
12 ran Time 1m 14.9 (2.1) (T W Wellard Partnership) P J Makin Ogbourne Maisey, Wilts

4224

7.30 BET DIRECT CLAIMER 3YO+ (F) 7f aw rnd Going 39 -05 Slow
£2534 £724 £362 3 yo rec 3 lb

4018 **BARON DE PICHON 14** [10] K R Burke 4-9-1 N Callan 11/2: 051001: 4 b g Perugino - Ariadne (Bustino) Sn rdn/rear, hdwy to lead fnl 1f, drvn out: op 7/2, clmd for £8,000 by A Reid: prev won at Southwell (clmr): well btn in 2 runs in the US since trained by N Littmoden to win here at W'hampton (3), Southwell & Lingfield (AW h'caps, rtd 84a) in '99: suited by 7f/1m on both AWs: likes a sharp trk, esp W'hampton: likes claim grade. **71a**
4023 **ROYAL CASCADE 14** [5] B A McMahon 6-9-1 (bl) L Newton 12/1: 201502: 6 b g River Falls - Relative Stranger (Cragador) Ouptcd, drvn over 2f out, ran on fnl 1f, closing at fin: likes sell/claim grade, win similar. 1¾ **67a**
3920 **CASTLE SEMPILL 18** [9] R M H Cowell 3-9-2 (vis) Dale Gibson 6/1: 600403: 3 b g Presidium - La Suquet (Puissance) Front rank, went on 2f out, hdd ins last, btn fnl 50y: op 7/2: prob needs a drop back to 6f: see 852. ½ **70a**
3753 **REDOUBTABLE 30** [8] D W Chapman 9-9-9 S Sanders 5/2 FAV: 430504: Prom, sltly outpcd over 2f out, modest late gains, no dngr: see 2994. 2 **70a**
3868 **RENDITA 23** [11] 4-8-5(1ow) Dean McKeown 16/1: -00005: Dwelt, bhd, late hdwy, no dngr: stiff task. 1¼ **50$**
4122 **DANZAS 6** [6] 6-8-7 (bl) Iona Wands 33/1: 466506: Late hdwy from rear, no dngr: qck reapp, stiff task. ½ **51$**
3770 **BLUSHING GRENADIER 28** [7] 8-8-7 (bl) S Finnamore (4) 15/2: 210027: Keen, led halfway till 2f out, sn hung right & wknd: shade btr 3770 (C/D). 3 **46a**
3765 **SANTANDRE 29** [2] 4-9-9 P M Quinn (3) 7/1: 506308: Led to halfway, wknd qckly fnl 2f, reportedly again broke a blood vessel: bckd from 12/1: see 3765, 687. ¾ **60a**
4102 **DARWELLS FOLLY 8** [4] 5-8-5 (vis) J Fanning 4/1: 0-3009: Mid-div at best: qck reapp: see 3921. 1¼ **40a**
3236 **SWEET HAVEN 52** [12] 3-8-5 (vis) G Baker (5) 20/1: 000200: Dwelt, al bhd, 10th: 8 wk abs: see 3094. 1¼ **41a**
3770 **Abtaal 28** [3] 10-8-5 (vis) R Fitzpatrick 33/1:
4031 **Ivors Investment 12** [1] 4-9-0 J Bosley (7) 33/1:
12 ran Time 1m 29.3 (3.1) (DGH Partnership) K R Burke Newmarket.

4225

8.00 BET DIRECT MED AUCT MDN 2YO (F) 6f aw rnd Going 39 +01 Fast
£2404 £687 £343

-- **ELLAS PAL** [13] W Jarvis 2-8-9 M Tebbutt 8/1: 1: 2 ch f Alhijaz - Rattle Along (Tap On Wood) Sn rdn in tch, switched/improved over 2f out, smooth hdwy on bit to lead well ins last, pshd out, v cmftbly: gd juv time: Apr foal, half-sister to a 6f juv scorer, dam won over 9/10f: eff over a sharp 6f, further will suit: acts **75+**

on fibresand & runs well fresh: impressive debut, sure to rate higher & win again.

4082 **LILLEMAN** 9 [3] G A Butler 2-9-0 D Holland 4/6 FAV: 5022: 2 b c Distant Relative - Lillemor | 1 | 72a
(Connaught) Prom, went on appr fnl 1f, hdd well ins last, not pace of cmftble wnr: nicely bckd at odds on
& better expected on this AW bow, handles fibresand: rtd higher on turf on 4082 (soft).

3976 **SMIRFYS PARTY** 15 [6] B A McMahon 2-9-0 S Sanders 10/1: 62553: 2 ch c Clantime - Party Scenes | nk | 72a
(Most Welcome) Set fast pace, hdd over 1f out, no extra fnl 50y: op 8/1: prob ran to nr best & a return to
nurs h'caps shld suit: acts on fast & fibresand: see 2268, 2248.

4035 **DEAR PICKLES** 12 [5] J G Portman 2-8-9 G Baker (5) 16/1: 6204: Cl-up, drvn/no impress fnl 1f: | 1¼ | 64a
op 10/1, well clr rem: AW bow: twice below 3638.

3814 **CHAIRMAN BOBBY** 27 [11] 2-9-0 J Quinn 16/1: -305: Chsd ldrs, drpd rear over 2f out, no threat: op | 7 | 54a
8/1: twice below a promising racecourse bow in 3571 (5f, firm).

3760 **LORD LIAM** 29 [12] 2-9-0 N Callan 7/2: -53456: Handy, drvn & grad wknd from halfway: drop in | ¾ | 52a
trip: disapp AW bow: much btr 3492 (6f mdn, firm).

3911 **MONTE MAYOR GOLF** 19 [1] 2-8-9 Dean McKeown 50/1: 050607: Nvr a factor: modest form so far. | 3½ | 39a
3632 **FRENCH BRAMBLE** 35 [10] 2-8-9 (bl) N Carlisle 20/1: 006448: In tch, wknd qckly fnl 2f: see 3245. | ½ | 38a
-- **MAGGIE FLYNN** [2] 2-8-9 N Pollard 16/1: 9: Dwelt, al bhd: op 12/1 on debut: Apr foal, dam | 1½ | 34a
won over sprint dists: sire high-class in the US: with A P Jarvis.

4042 **BOLHAM LADY** 11 [9] 2-8-9 J Edmunds 50/1: 00: Nvr dngrs, 10th: looks poor. | hd | 34a
4082 **HILL WELCOME** 9 [7] 2-8-9 Paul Eddery 9/1: 340: Al bhd, 11th: AW bow, better on turf in 4082 (soft). | 1½ | 30a
4138 **Gilt Trip** 5 [8] 2-9-0 S W Kelly (3) 50/1:   3840 **Chesters Boy** 25 [4] 2-9-0 (BL) J Bosley (7) 50/1:
13 ran   Time 1m 15.1 (2.3)   (Miss E G Macgregor)   W Jarvis Newmarket.

| **4226** | 8.30 BET247.CO.UK HCAP 3YO+ 0-85 (D)   1m4f aw   Going 39   -12 Slow | | [85] |
| | £4140   £1274   £637   £318   3 yo   rec 8 lb | | |

3415 **TORRID KENTAVR** 44 [8] T G Mills 3-9-4 (83) L Carter 10/1: 310051: 3 b c Trempolino - Torrid Tango | 89a
(Green Dancer) Waited with, smooth hdwy to lead over 3f out, styd on strongly & rdn clr well ins last: op 7/1, 6
wk abs: highly tried since won at Bath (mdn): well btn 4th in Italy sole juv start (8.5f, hvy): eff at 10/12f,
further shld suit: acts on firm, fast & fibresand: clrly apprec drop in grade & switch to AW, win again.

2509 **SURE QUEST** 84 [5] D W P Arbuthnot 5-8-1 (58) J Quinn 8/1: 122342: 5 b m Sure Blade - Eagle's | 3 | 59a
Quest (Legal Eagle) Chsd ldr, rdn to chall over 1f out, drvn & not pace of wnr last: not disgraced after a
12 wk abs: v tough & consistent, shld regain winning ways sn: see 2509, 1555.

4024 **WESTERN COMMAND** 14 [10] Mrs N Macauley 4-8-2 (58)(1ow) R Fitzpatrick 14/1: 620603: 4 b g | 1 | 58a
Saddlers' Hall - Western Friend (Gone West) Waited with, rdn & styd on fnl 2f, no threat to ldrs: op 10/1:
may apprec a return to 14f+ now, see 2156, 1501.

*4026 **CUPBOARD LOVER** 14 [12] D Haydn Jones 4-8-5 (62) D Harrison 13/8 FAV: 631414: Bhd, gd hdwy to | 1 | 59a
chall over 1f out, drvn/btn fnl 1f: nicely bckd & remains in fine form: C/D scorer in 4026.

4046 **FALCON SPIRIT** 11 [3] 4-7-10 (53)(3oh)(vis) K Dalgleish (4) 16/1: -00405: Mid-div, sltly outpcd after | nk | 50$
halfway, modest late gains, no threat: mdn: see 2836.

4122 **TOUJOURS RIVIERA** 6 [4] 10-8-8 (65) T G McLaughlin 10/1: 015126: Cl-up, dropped rear fnl | 2 | 59a
4f, no threat after: op 8/1: qck reapp: best in sellers these days, as in 3775.

3961 **SLANEYSIDE** 16 [2] 3-7-11 (62)(vis) G Bardwell 20/1: 600107: Led 1m out, hdd over 3f out, grad | 4 | 50a
wknd/eased: twice below 3741 (3 rnr class stks, fast grnd).

3599 **POMPEII** 37 [1] 3-9-3 (82) J Fortune 7/2: 211608: Led early, wknd fnl 4f: AW bow: btr 1064 (soft). | 16 | 50a
3702 **SPECIAL PROMISE** 33 [6] 3-9-0 (79) Dean McKeown 8/1: 111109: Prom, wknd qckly after halfway: | ½ | 46a
once again disapp stepped up in trip: much btr 495 (8.5f).

*3585 **KELTIC BARD** 37 [7] 3-9-6 (85) G Carter 9/1: 051210: Dwelt, eff from rear halfway, wknd qckly | 14 | 37a
fnl 3f, t.o. in 10th: op 7/1: well below par on this first try at 12f: much btr 3585 (Folkestone, 9.7f).

690 **WHITE PLAINS** 196 [9] 7-9-12 (83) N Callan 11/1: 333500: Al well bhd, 11th: 6 month abs/new stable. | ¾ | 34a
3495 **DANZINO** 42 [11] 5-10-0 (85)(vis) S Sanders 33/1: 35/00P: V reluctant to race, al well bhd & | | 0a
p.u. after 5f: 6 wk abs, top-weight.
12 ran   Time 2m 39.8 (6.2)   (Kentavr (UK) Ltd)   T G Mills Headley, Surrey.

| **4227** | 9.00 MILLION SELLER 2YO (G)   5f aw rnd   Going 39   -23 Slow | |
| | £1970   £563   £281 | |

3491 **ACORN CATCHER** 42 [13] B Palling 2-8-11 N Callan 10/1: 013001: 2 b f Emarati - Anytime Baby (Bairn) | 63a
Prom, led halfway, edged right & styd on well, rdn out: 6 wk abs, no bid: prev wnr at Leicester (sell):
dam 5f scorer: eff at 5f, does stay 6f: acts on fast & fibresand, poss isn't soft: runs well fresh, enjoys sellers.

4171 **JUSTALORD** 3 [3] W G M Turner 2-9-2 Darren Williams (5) 11/4 FAV: 615242: 2 b g King's Signet - Just | 1 | 65a
Lady (Emarati) Chsd ldr, drvn & styd on fnl 1f, no threat to wnr: op 9/4, qck reapp: clmd for £5,000: acts on
fast, gd & fibresand: looks capable of winning similar: see 3038.

3639 **GILLS DIAMOND** 35 [4] N Tinkler 2-8-6 G Carter 9/1: 35003: 2 ch f College Chapel - Yafford | 1 | 52a
(Warrshan) Sn well outpcd, plenty to do 2f out, rdn & flew home: op 7/1: acts on fibresand & looks sure to
relish step up to 6f+ next time: see 1823.

3974 **SPINETAIL RUFOUS** 15 [2] D W P Arbuthnot 2-8-11 J Quinn 25/1: 0004: Outpcd, rdn/prog over 1f out, | hd | 57$
styd on strongly, nvr nrr: much imprvd form on this AW debut, stays 5f on fibresand, 6f looks sure to suit.

3632 **SEANS HONOR** 35 [10] 2-8-6 (VIS) T Williams 10/1: 406255: Trkd ldr, sltly hmpd 2f out, drvn/btn | shd | 52a
fnl 1f: op 8/1, first time visor: see 3376.

1937 **SUNRIDGE ROSE** 107 [12] 2-8-6 Dean McKeown 14/1: 36: Mid-div at best: long abs: see 1937. | 1¾ | 48a
3743 **AMAMACKEMMUSH** 30 [9] 2-8-11 R Winston 5/1: 235207: Led to halfway, wknd qckly fnl 1f: AW bow. | nk | 53a
3957 **NO SURRENDER** 16 [11] 2-8-7(1ow) S Sanders 16/1: 608: Nvr a factor: big drop in trip for new stable. | 3½ | 41a
4096 **BRANSTON GEM** 8 [1] 2-8-6 J Fanning 7/2: -0059: Mid-div, eff 2f out, nvr dngrs: AW bow: see 4096. | nk | 40a
3589 **MRS MITCHELL** 37 [5] 2-8-6 O Pears 20/1: 600: Al well bhd, 10th: modest efforts so far, see 3028. | nk | 39a
3439 **LATE AT NIGHT** 43 [8] 2-8-11 (bl) D Harrison 12/1: 004250: Dwelt, al rear, 11th: 6 wk abs: AW bow. | 3 | 36a
4095 **ONE CHARMER** 8 [6] 2-8-11 Paul Eddery 50/1: 0000: Sn in rear, fin last: poor form. | nk | 35a
12 ran   Time 1m 03.3 (3.1)   (N C Phillips & T Davies)   B Palling Cowbridge, Vale Of Glamorgan.

WOLVERHAMPTON (Fibresand) SATURDAY SEPTEMBER 30TH LH, Oval, Sharp Track

4228 9.30 POOLS HCAP 3YO+ 0-70 (E) 1m1f79y Going 39 -12 Slow **[69]**
£3094 £854 £442 3 yo rec 5 lb

1933 **JUST WIZ 107** [3] N P Littmoden 4-9-11 (66) T G McLaughlin 7/2 FAV: 002221: 4 b g Efisio - Jade Pet **72a**
(Petong) Mid-div, rdn after 2f, gd hdwy to lead dist, styd on well, rdn out: long abs, new stable: prev briefly
with A Reid: '99 scorer for R Hannon at Southwell (h'cap) & Lingfield (2, h'caps, rtd 86a): rtd 54 & 61a in '98
(h'caps): eff btwn 7f & 10f: acts on firm, gd/soft & both AWs: acts on any trk, likes Lingfield: eff with/without
blnks/visor & runs v well fresh: v tough & a fine debut for new connections.
4135 **ARIZONA LADY 6** [6] I Semple 3-9-5 (65) R Winston 14/1: 215002: 3 ch f Lion Cavern - Unfuwaanah 1½ **67a**
(Unfuwain) Dwelt, sn mid-div, eff over 2f out, styd on ins last, al held by wnr: qck reapp: encouraging AW debut,
acts on firm, gd/soft & fibresand: see 2397.
4074 **SHOTACROSS THE BOW 10** [2] B W Hills 3-9-5 (65) Paul Eddery 5/1: 032303: 3 b c Warning - Nordica 1 **65a**
(Northfields) Front rank, led briefly appr fnl 1f, no extra well ins last: op 4/1, clr rem: acts on fast & fibresand.
3979 **BILLY BATHWICK 15** [9] E J O'Neill 3-9-4 (64) D Holland 6/1: 003244: Waited with, prog 3f out, 6 **54a**
styd on but no threat to front 3: btr 3762 (10f, gd grnd).
3407 **SEA YA MAITE 44** [8] 6-9-11 (66) S Finnamore (5) 12/1: 652165: Cl-up, went on 2f out, hdd appr 1¼ **54a**
fnl 1f, wknd qckly: 6 wk abs: unproven over this longer 9.4f trip, apprec a return to 7f/1m: see 582.
3557 **SACREMENTUM 38** [10] 5-9-1 (56) S W Kelly (3) 9/1: 4424F6: Bhd, late hdwy, nvr dngrs: see 3557. ½ **43a**
3285 **AREISH 50** [11] 7-9-0 (55) J Edmunds 8/1: 356007: Bhd, eff halfway, no threat: op 7/1, 7 wk abs. 1½ **39a**
4153 **MAI TAI 4** [13] 5-9-1 (56) J Quinn 12/1: 662508: Mid-div at best, eased when btn: qck reapp: btr 867. 2½ **36a**
4151 **SHARP STEEL 4** [1] 5-9-3 (58) M Tebbutt 6/1: 125329: Led, hdd 4f out, wkng qckly when hmpd 5 **30a**
2f out: op 8/1: qck reapp: btr 4151 (11f).
3480 **DIAMOND FLAME 42** [7] 6-9-3 (58) G Baker (5) 16/1: 004000: Rear, lost tch fnl 4f, 10th: 6 wk abs. 3 **25a**
3831 **AUTUMN COVER 25** [4] 8-9-5 (60) S Sanders 14/1: /30-00: Cl-up, led halfway till 2f out, wknd 4 **21a**
rapidly, 11th: plcd on first of 2 '99 starts (h'cap, rtd 71): '98 Brighton wnr (ltd stks, rtd 79, reapp), prev term
won at Kempton (h'cap, reapp, rtd 79): won 4 races in '96: best over 1m/9f, stays 10f on firm & gd/soft, also
equitrack: can go well fresh: likes a sharp easy trk, esp Brighton/Goodwood.
3702 **DONT WORRY BOUT ME 33** [5] 3-9-2 (62)(vis) L Carter 12/1: 626200: Nvr a factor, fin last: btr 3244. 6 **15a**
12 ran Time 2m 03.0 (4.8) (Turf 2000 Ltd) N P Littmoden Newmarket.

PONTEFRACT MONDAY OCTOBER 2ND Lefthand, Undulating Track With Stiff Uphill Finish

Official Going HEAVY (SOFT in places). Stalls: 2m1f - Centre; Rem - Inside.

4229 2.15 PONTEFRACT APP HCAP 3YO+ 0-60 (F) 1m4f Soft 117 -15 Slow **[58]**
£2278 £651 £325 3 yo rec 7 lb

4075 **LANCER 11** [15] J Pearce 8-9-5 (49)(vis) G Baker 9/1: 503261: 8 ch g Diesis - Last Bird (Sea Bird II) **54**
Waited with, imprvd after halfway, led 2f out, drvn out: earlier won at Warwick (h'cap): '99 Folkestone wnr
(amat stks, rtd 74): '98 wnr at Leicester, Folkestone & York (h'caps, rtd 75 & 45a): best at 12f, stays 14f,
tried 2m: acts on firm, likes hvy grnd, any trk: wears a visor: can carry big weights: qk York follow-up?
3963 **CLARINCH CLAYMORE 18** [1] J M Jefferson 4-9-5 (49) P Hanagan 12/1: 230042: 4 b g Sabrehill - 1¾ **51**
Salu (Ardross) Well plcd, led appr fnl 3f, hdd 2f out, styd on: eff at 1m/12f: see 324, 131.
3284 **SECRET DROP 52** [11] K McAuliffe 4-9-6 (50) G Sparkes 7/1 CO FAV: 000433: 4 b f Bustino - 1¾ **49**
Safe House (Lyphard) Rear, imprvd appr fnl 4f, chsd ldrs bef dist, styd on: 7 wk abs: eff at 10/12f on soft & hvy.
4208 **SMARTER CHARTER 2** [6] Mrs L Stubbs 7-9-10 (54) Kristin Stubbs (5) 14/1: 630644: Held up, prog 2 **52**
ent str, styd on without threatening: ran 48hrs ago, see 2081, 871.
3887 **PROTOCOL 24** [9] 6-9-1 (45)(t) Sarah Thomas (7) 7/1 CO FAV: 231035: Patiently rdn, prog after hd **43**
halfway, ch appr str, sn onepace: clr rem, btr 3220 (here).
3731 **WHISTLING DIXIE 33** [7] 4-9-4 (48) T Hamilton 9/1: 415306: In tch, rdn & no extra 2f out: op 7/1: 8 **38**
ideally suited by 10f on faster grnd: see 2655.
1446 **MAYBEN 132** [18] 3-8-11 (48) J Bosley 14/1: 60-567: Nvr better than mid-div: over 4 month abs. 1¼ **37**
4074 **MASTER BEVELED 12** [3] 10-10-0 (58)(vis) Joanna Badger 7/1 CO FAV: -30348: In tch, prog 4f out, 2½ **45**
wknd appr fnl 2f: had a big weight to carry around in this group: see 809.
3606 **NORTHERN ECHO 38** [2] 3-9-1 (52) T Eaves 20/1: 200629: Prom till 4f out: see 3606 (firm), 2731. 14 **27**
4149 **PENNYS FROM HEAVEN 6** [8] 6-9-8 (52) Clare Rocke 16/1: 643040: Led till 4f out, wknd qckly: 10th. ½ **26**
3181 **JONLOZ 56** [16] 3-8-13 (50) L Enstone (5) 11/1: 660120: Chsd ldrs till 5f out: last, tchd 14/1, 8 wk abs. **0**
3284 **Zsarabak 52** [12] 3-9-1 (52)(t) N Carter (7) 20/1:
3407 **Flashtalkin Flood 46** [5] 6-8-8 (38) R Cody Boutcher 16/1:
1730 **Coy Debutante 119** [17] 6-9-1 (45) P Shea 14/1: 3838 **Paparazza 27** [10] 3-8-12 (49) Carol Packer (7) 33/1:
2920 **Http Flyer 68** [13] 3-8-8 (45) D Kinsella (3) 25/1:
16 ran Time 2m 51.0 (15.9) (Chris Marsh) J Pearce Newmarket.

4230 2.45 EBF CLAXTON BAY MDN 2YO (D) 1m2f Soft 117 -29 Slow
£3828 £1178 £589 £294

4086 **DEUCE OF TRUMPS 11** [3] J Noseda 2-9-0 Pat Eddery 4/1: 351: 2 b c Desert Style - Mauras Pride **83**
(Cadeaux Genereux) Handy, shkn up after halfway, led 2f out, rdn to hold on nr fin: IR 20,000gns colt: clrly suited
by step up to 10f & will get further: has rcd exclusively on soft grnd: handles a stiff/undul trk: front 2 well clr.
4086 **ENGLISH HARBOUR 11** [1] B W Hills 2-8-9 M Roberts 11/4 FAV: -0042: 2 ch f Sabrehill - Water Woo nk **77**
(Tom Rolfe) Chsd ldrs, eff 3f out, kept on to chase wnr appr fnl 1f, ev ch till held nr fin: nicely bckd,
well clr of next: imprvd last twice on soft grnd: eff at 1m/10f.
3779 **DON ALFRED 30** [2] P F I Cole 2-9-0 K Darley 7/2: 5033: 2 b c Mark Of Esteem - Jezyah (Chief's 12 **70**
Crown) Prom, led appr fnl 3f till 2f out, no extra: nicely bckd from 9/2: longer trip on softer grnd: see 3779.
3949 **HEATHYARDS GUEST 19** [8] R Hollinshead 2-9-0 A Culhane 6/1: 024: In tch, btn 2f out: lngr trip. 4 **65**
4140 **REVIEWER 7** [7] 2-9-0 (bl) J Fortune 9/2: 6045: Led till appr fnl 3f, sn hmpd & lost pl: qck reapp, blnks. 14 **50**
3740 **SIR EDWARD BURROW 32** [4] 2-9-0 J McAuley 50/1: 400036: Al bhd: stiff task, flattered last time. 6 **41**
3953 **OUR SHELLBY 19** [6] J Quinn 100/1: 07: Al in rear: Petardia sister to modest styr Ptah: with J Eyre.23 **9**
-- **NARJIS FLOWER** [5] 2-8-9 D Holland 14/1: 8: Sn struggling: mkt drifter: $50,000 Pleasant Colony 2½ **6**

1305

half-sister to a decent sprinter: dam a useful sprinter: with M Johnston.
4086 **UMBOPA 11** [9] 2-9-0 M Fenton 33/1: 09: Dwelt, nvr in it: big drifter from 14/1.   **3   7**
9 ran   Time 2m 22.7 (14.6)   (Mrs & Mrs John Poynton)   J Noseda Newmarket.

4231	3.15 TRINIDAD HCAP 3YO+ 0-70 (E) 2m1f22y Soft 117 -15 Slow	[70]

£3737   £1150   £575   £287   3 yo rec 11lb

4075 **MARTHA REILLY 11** [5] Mrs Barbara Waring 4-7-13 (40) (1ow) A Mackay 10/1: -20031: 4 ch f Rainbows   **42**
For Life - Deback Delight (Great Nephew) Mid-div, closed 3f out, rdn to lead 1f out, styd on strongly: op 8/1:
'99 wnr at Southwell (fill sell, rtd 58a): rtd 61 & 48a in '98: eff at 12f, suited by 2m1f nowadays: acts on
both AWs, likes soft grnd: goes on any track, without blnks.
4091 **BLACK ICE BOY 10** [6] R Bastiman 9-7-11 (39) (vis) (1ow) (9oh) D Mernagh (0) 5/1: 406002: 9 b g Law   **2   39**
Society - Hogan's Sister (Speak John) Led till 2f out, kept on: op 4/1: back to form 10lbs o/h, won this in '99.
4006 **IRELANDS EYE 16** [16] J Norton 5-8-0 (42) P Hanagan (5) 16/1: 206603: 5 b g Shareef Dancer - So   **1½ 41**
Romantic (Teenoso) Held up, prog to chall till 1f out, onepace: op 12/1, clr rem: eff at 2m/2m1f.
4071 **MY LEGAL EAGLE 12** [9] R J Price 6-7-13 (41) K Dalgleish (5) 15/2: 004064: Held up, prog to   **12 31**
chase ldrs appr fnl 2f, fdd: tchd 9/1: see 1023.
*4149 **VINCENT 6** [15] 5-8-2 (44) (4ex) G Baker (5) 10/1: 344115: Held up, prog to chall appr straight,   **1½ 33**
wknd under press: op 6/1: qck reapp with a penalty: unproven on soft grnd, 6 time winner on fibresand.
4139 **SHARAF 7** [12] 7-8-1 (43) Martin Dwyer 15/2: 044026: Prom, eff & btn 3f out: tchd 9/1: qck reapp.   **4   29**
3511} **SUGGEST 407** [14] 5-7-10 (38) (10oh) Iona Wands 16/1: 0550-7: Nvr a factor: 4 month jumps abs,   **12 15**
ran up a qck hat-trick in May at Hexham (2) & Catterick (h'caps, 2m4f/3m2f, firm, hvy, rtd 104h): unplcd in
'99 (rtd 53\$ & 33): plcd in '98 (h'cap, rtd 49): last won as a juv (clmr & seller): eff at 12f, unproven over
long dists on the Flat: acts on fast & gd/soft grnd & wears a visor: with W Storey.
3276 **MU TADIL 52** [1] 8-7-10 (38) (13oh) G Sparkes (2) 33/1: 006048: Nvr nr ldrs: 7 wk abs, new stable.   **5   11**
3249 **BOLD CARDOWAN 54** [13] 4-7-10 (38) (bl) (2oh) N Kennedy 11/2: 000049: Mid-div till 4f out: 8 wk abs.   **nk 10**
3633 **ICE PACK 37** [3] 4-7-10 (38) (9oh) Kim Tinkler 33/1: 034360: In tch for 12f: 10th, stiff task, see 2734, 1894. **3   8**
*3993 **GIVE AN INCH 17** [10] 5-10-0 (70) T Williams 5/2 FAV: 000110: Held up, brief effort 6f out: 13th: **0**
nicely bckd, stablemate of 7th, top-weight: not her form, came too quckly?: see 3993.
3442 **Herself 45** [4] 3-7-12 (51) (2ow) (8oh) J Quinn 16/1:
4040 **Attacker 14** [7] 3-8-4 (57) (t) (8ow) (19oh) M Roberts 66/1:
3988 **Lady Fearless 17** [11] 3-7-10 (49) (1ow) C Adamson 50/1:
14 ran   Time 4m 02.5 (22.5)   (J McDonnell, A Shapter, P Haggarty)   Mrs B Waring Welford-On-Avon, Warwicks.

4232	3.45 TOTE TRIFECTA HCAP 3YO 0-80 (D) 1m rnd Soft 117 +11 Fast	[83]

£7600   £2400   £1200   £600

*4208 **WILEMMGEO 2** [9] P D Evans 3-7-10 (51) Joanna Badger (7) 4/1: 011411: 3 b f Emarati - Floral   **58**
Spark (Forzando) In tch, imprvd after halfway, rdn to lead appr fnl 1f, ran on well: nicely bckd, fast time,
qck reapp: earlier won at W'hampton (2, sellers, rtd 55a), Beverley (2, appr h'cap & h'cap) & 48hrs ago at
Sandown (appr h'cap): '99 wnr again at W'hampton (seller, rtd 55a & 62): eff btwn 7.5f & 10f: acts on firm,
soft grnd & fibresand, any trk: eff with/without a visor: progressive & tough.
3580 **JUDICIOUS 40** [6] G Wragg 3-9-7 (76) M Roberts 9/2: 030162: 3 b c Fairy King - Kama Tashoof   **1   80**
(Mtoto) Nvr far away, led appr straight till bef fnl 1f, rallied: nicely bckd, clr rem, 6 wk abs, top-weight:
imprvd against the handicapper: acts on fast & soft grnd: see 3095.
4045 **BENBYAS 13** [13] J L Eyre 3-8-0 (55) (bl) K Dalgleish (5) 16/1: 610043: 3 b g Rambo Dancer - Light   **6   49**
The Way (Nicholas Bill) Off the pace, drvn appr str, styd on for 3rd, nvr nr front 2: suited by good grnd.
3971 **SWYNFORD ELEGANCE 18** [18] J Hetherton 3-7-10 (51) (8oh) P M Quinn (3) 33/1: 000024: Rear,   **2½ 41**
late hdwy, nvr a threat: stiff task 8lbs 'wrong': see 3971.
4080 **ALAWAR 11** [16] 3-8-2 (57) (t) A Nicholls 14/1: 004445: In tch, eff ent straight, no impress: see 1793. **2   43**
4045 **MARVEL 13** [3] 3-8-0 (55) Kim Tinkler 25/1: 203606: Rear, imprvd into mid-div 3f out, no further hdwy.   **4   34**
*3856 **ALTAY 26** [12] 3-8-6 (61) R Ffrench 13/2: 635117: Prom, lost pl appr straight: first run on soft   **¾   39**
grnd: progressive earlier on a sounder surface & is probably worth another chance: see 3856.
4018 **JAMESTOWN 16** [2] 3-9-1 (70) Dean McKeown 16/1: 046148: Well plcd, chall appr straight, sn wknd.   **½   47**
3769 **CELEBRE BLU 30** [5] 3-8-5 (60) F Lynch 25/1: 000369: Bhd ldrs, wknd appr fnl 2f: see 3670, 1562.   **1½ 35**
4106 **ROYAL CAVALIER 9** [10] 3-8-13 (68) Pat Eddery 12/1: 200640: Mid-div, eff 3f out, sn btn: 10th.   **1   41**
4045 **GLENDAMAH 13** [8] 3-8-5 (60) (BL) J Quinn 25/1: 3-0000: Led till appr fnl 2f, sn btn: 11th, blinkered.   **3½ 27**
*4045 **ENTITY 13** [14] 3-9-3 (72) D O'Donohoe 4/4 FAV: 012110: Trkd ldrs, rdn & wknd ppr fnl 2f: 13th: **0**
well bckd: been busy on testing grnd lately, may need a rest: see 4045.
2611 **Lady Two K 81** [1] 3-9-3 (72) R Winston 50/1:   4004 **Bint Habibi 16** [17] 3-7-13 (54) G Bardwell 14/1:
4005 **Dianeme 16** [11] 3-7-13 (54) D Mernagh (2) 25/1:   164 **Ash Bold 297** [4] 3-7-10 (51) (2oh) A Polli (2) 20/1:
3462 **T Gs Girl 44** [15] 3-7-11 (52) (1ow) (2oh) J Bramhill 33/1: 3975 **Secret Conquest 17** [7] 3-8-7 (62) A Culhane 33/1:
18 ran   Time 1m 50.3 (8.5)   (R J Hayward)   P D Evans Pandy, Gwent.

4233	4.15 J & B. BIRD CLAIMER 3YO (F) 6f rnd Soft 117 -05 Slow	

£2520   £720   £360

4107 **PIPADASH 9** [8] T D Easterby 3-8-9 K Darley 7/2: 300001: 3 b f Pips Pride - Petite Maxine (Sharpo)   **75**
Cl-up, rdn 2f out, led 1f out, pshd out nr fin: nicely bckd: juv scorer at Haydock (auct mdn), here at Pontefract
& Ascot (stks, rtd 96): eff at 5/6f on fast & hvy, stiff/gall trks: eff with/without blnks: rate higher.
*3462 **SANTIBURI LAD 44** [14] A Berry 3-9-0 C Lowther 8/1: 12: 3 b g Namaqualand - Suggia (Alzao)   **1½ 74\$**
Bhd, imprvd ent str, kept on to go 2nd ins last, not trouble wnr: op 6/1: eff at 5/6f on fast & soft grnd.
3698 **CHARMING LOTTE 35** [13] N Tinkler 3-8-6 (vis) C Rutter 7/2: 051303: 3 b f Nicolotte - Courtisane   **1½ 62**
(Persepolis) Slow away, imprvd after 3f, drvn to chase ldrs 2f out, onepace towards fin: bckd from 5/1:
gd run, had it to do at the weights with the first 2 on official ratings: see 1406.
4156 **SKY HOOK 6** [11] J A Osborne 3-8-3 (bl) S W Kelly (0) 33/1: 500004: Towards rear, clsd und press 2f   **nk 58\$**
out, no extra fnl 100y: qck reapp, blnks reapplied: lks flattered tho' best prev run was also on an easier trk.
2980 **MOBO BACO 66** [1] 3-8-4 S Carson 25/1: 600005: Prom, led 2f out till 1f out, no extra: 9 wk abs.   **2½ 52\$**
4031 **LUNALUX 14** [4] 3-8-0 (bl) A Nicholls 14/1: 400526: Led till 2f out, onepace: stiffish task, see 4031. **1½ 45**
4018 **STEALTHY TIMES 16** [3] 3-8-2 G Bower 5/1: 554007: Chsd ldrs, chall 2f out, fdd: back in trip.   **1½ 43**
3966 **FOSTON FOX 18** [16] 3-7-13 (bl) J Quinn 16/1: 005048: Nvr better than mid-div: op 33/1, stiff task.   **½   38**
4037 **RAVISHING 14** [10] 3-8-9 M Hills 11/4 FAV: 410009: In tch, rdn & wknd ent fnl 2f: nicely bckd: **nk 47**
more expected down in grade, faster grnd prob suits: see 1406.

3694 **CLANSMAN 35** [5] 3-8-4 K Dalgleish (5) 25/1: 000000: Hmpd start, nvr troubled ldrs: 10th, new stable.   **7 26**
3144 Blue Line Lady 58 [6] 3-8-1 Iona Wands 33/1:   3218 Nowt Flash 54 [2] 3-8-6 R Lappin 40/1:
4031 Lordofenchantment 14 [7] 3-8-5 (vis) Kim Tinkler 25/1:   4080 Northern Trio 11 [18] 3-8-8 A Mackay 66/1:
1932 Breezy Louise 109 [15] 3-7-12 (bl) F Norton 16/1:   3593 Theos Lad 39 [12] 3-8-4 T Williams 25/1:
2250 Peggys Rose 96 [9] 3-8-0(2ow) J Tate 20/1:
17 ran   Time 1m 21.4 (7.3)   (T H Bennett)   T D Easterby Great Habton, N.Yorks.

4234   4.45 CARONI MDN 3YO (D)   1m rnd   Soft 117 -23 Slow
£2912 £896 £448 £224

3542} **ATLANTIC ACE 405** [3] B Smart 3-9-0 Paul Eddery 16/1: 0-1: 3 b c First Trump - Risalah (Marju)   **78**
Rear, gd prog 3f out, rdn to lead bef fnl 1f, pshd out fnl 100y: op 12/1, tchd 20/1 on reapp: beat one home sole
'99 start (mdn, rtd 69): suited by this step up to 1m: acts on soft grnd, stiff/undul trk: runs well fresh.
4040 **DENA 14** [9] W Jarvis 3-8-9 Pat Eddery 7/4 FAV: 5-02: 3 b f Deploy - Isabena (Star Appeal)   **5 65**
Chsd ldrs, led 3f out, under press & hdd 1½f out, onepace: nicely bckd, clr rem: back in trip & attracted
some surprisingly large bets considering moderate level of form thus far: prob stays 1m on soft.
1783 **STRATTON 116** [2] C F Wall 3-9-0 R Mullen 3/1: 6-403: 3 b g Fairy King - Golden Bloom (Main Reef)   **5 61**
Keen bhd, prog to chase ldrs appr fnl 2f, sn no extra: bckd from 4/1, 4 month abs: longer 1m trip & softer grnd.
3350 **SHADOWBLASTER 49** [8] B Hanbury 3-9-0 K Darley 2/1: -52204: Chsd ldrs till appr fnl 2f: nicely   **10 45**
bckd, 7 wk abs: much better on faster grnd earlier in the season, see 2924, 2770.
2140 **SIGN OF THE DRAGON 101** [1] 3-9-0 R Winston 16/1: 45: Led till 3f out, wknd: op 12/1, 15 wk abs.   **½ 44**
3677 **HICKLETON DREAM 36** [4] 3-8-9 P Fessey 33/1: -056: Chsd ldrs till halfway: stiff task.   **12 19**
4005 **LETS REFLECT 16** [7] 3-8-9 O Pears 16/1: -54057: Prsd ldr 4f, bhd after: stiff task, see 3012.   **2 15**
3818 **JOLI ECLIPSE 28** [6] 3-8-9 C Rutter 33/1: -008: Sn struggling: no form.   **21 0**
8 ran   Time 1m 53.0 (11.2)   (Richard Page)   B Smart Upper Lambourn, Berks

---

4235   5.15 S JOSEPH NURSERY HCAP 2YO 0-75 (E)   6f rnd   Soft 117 -06 Slow   **[80]**
£3263 £1004 £502 £251

4030 **SPICE ISLAND 14** [17] J A Glover 2-8-1 (53) D Mernagh (3) 16/1: 53001: 2 b f Reprimand - Little   **65**
Emmeline (Emarati) Well plcd, led after halfway, shkn up, rdly drew clr: tchd 20/1: eff 6f, shld get 7f: acts
on gd grnd, much imprvd on this soft surface: handles a stiff/undul trk & is at the right end of the h'cap.
4170 **THOMAS SMYTHE 5** [4] N P Littmoden 2-9-7 (73) K Darley 11/2: 022632: 2 ch c College Chapel - Red   **5 73**
Barons Lady (Electric) Rear, imprvd & ch appr fnl 2f, sn hard rdn, kept on same pace for 2nd: op 8/1,
top-weight, quick reapp: consistent colt, deserves a race: see 4170.
4007 **BLUSHING SPUR 16** [16] D Shaw 2-8-11 (63) T Williams 13/2: 502523: 2 b g Flying Spur - Bogus John   **1½ 59**
(Blushing John) In tch, drvn to chase ldrs 2f out, sn wknd: tchd 12/1, 5wnd (7f).
4132 **APORTO 8** [3] D W Barker 2-8-4 (56) J McAuley 16/1: 304104: Slow away, imprvd 2f out, rdn/onepace.   **1½ 48**
3958 **QUAZAR 18** [18] 2-9-1 (67) D O'Donohoe 16/1: -0305: Towards rear, prog 2f out, nvr nr ldrs: h'cap bow.   **1¾ 54**
*3776 **GONE TOO FAR 30** [14] 2-9-5 (71) J Fanning 12/1: -0216: Led till appr fnl 2f, no extra: h'cap bow.   **shd 58**
3911 **WEET A WHILE 21** [11] 2-8-10 (62) N Callan 12/1: -00507: Al around same place: h'cap bow, see 3520.   **5 37**
3245 **SUN BIRD 54** [9] 2-8-10 (62)(BL) S Sanders 11/2: 5058: Nvr troubled ldrs, tho' staying on fin: **1½ 33**
op 9/2, blnkd, 8 wk abs, h'cap bow.
3478 **KATIES DOLPHIN 44** [6] 2-8-10 (62)(BL) Dale Gibson 20/1: 230569: Mid-div, hdd 2f out: blnkd, abs.   **2 28**
3055 **PATRICIAN FOX 62** [7] 2-8-6 (58) R Ffrench 16/1: 343260: Chsd ldrs till appr fnl 2f: 10th, 9 wk abs.   **8 8**
4090 **CATCH THE CHRON 10** [13] 2-9-2 (68) Pat Eddery 7/2 FAV: 401620: Mid-div, eff & btn after halfway: **4 10**
11th, nicely bckd from 9/2: clearly not her best: see 4090, 3376.
3830 **DATIN STAR 27** [10] 2-8-3 (55) J Quinn 10/1: 606400: Mid-div 4f: 15th, op 12/1: needs sellers.   **0**
3168 Naughty Knight 57 [15] 2-8-3 (55) R Mullen 14/1:   *4097 Piccolo Rose 10 [5] 2-9-3 (69) A Culhane 14/1:
4007 Miss Equinox 16 [1] 2-8-3 (55) Kim Tinkler 25/1:   2880 Braithwell 70 [8] 2-8-10 (62) O Pears 20/1:
3635 Beau Sauvage 37 [12] 2-8-11 (63) T Lucas 20/1:
17 ran   Time 1m 21.5 (7.4)   (Mrs R Morley)   J A Glover Carburton, Notts

---

LONGCHAMP   SATURDAY SEPTEMBER 30TH   Righthand, Stiff, Galloping Track

Official Going GOOD

4236   1.40 GR 2 PRIX ROYALLIEU 3YO+ FILLIES   1m4f110y   Good
£28818 £11527 £5764 £2882 3 yo rec 9 lb

4614} **MOURAMARA 329** [8] J Oxx 3-8-7 G Mosse 33/10: 3-3111: 3 b f Kahyasi - Mamoura (Lomond)   **112**
Settled twrds rear, switched wide & hdwy 2f out, led appr fnl 1f, styd on strongly, rdn out: earlier won at
Roscommon (mdn) & The Curragh (h'cap): plcd in a mdn for L Cumani in '99 (rtd 79+): eff at 1m, suited by this
gall 12.5f: acts on gd & gd/soft, handles hvy: useful & v prog filly who shld win more Group races.
1114 **BEYOND THE WAVES 153** [1] J E Pease 3-8-7 T Jarnet 84/10: 323412: 3 b f Ocean Crest - Excedent   **1½ 108**
(Exceller) Prom, eff appr fnl 1f, styd on, no threat: recent Chantilly List wnr: eff at 9/12f on gd & hvy: v useful.
2572 **PLAYACT 83** [10] N Clement 3-8-7 T Gillet 38/10: 422123: 3 ch f Hernando - Play Or Pay (Play Fellow)   **shd 108**
Bhd, gd hdwy appr fnl 1f, styd on fnl 1f but no ch with wnr: recent Vichy List wnr: acts on gd & hvy: see 2572.
*2617 **INAAQ 79** [3] Saeed bin Suroor 3-8-7 L Dettori 31/10: 14: Trkd ldrs, chall appr fnl 1f, no extra well   **½ 107**
ins last: 11 wk abs: stays 12.5f on fast & gd: only twice raced & open to improvement, win a List/Gr 3.
3928 **SADLERS FLAG 20** [11] 3-8-7 O Doleuze 27/10 FAV: 112265: Bhd, eff over 1f out, no dngr: see 3928.   **2 104**
*4057 **CHIANG MAI 13** [2] 3-8-7 M J Kinane 10/1: 1-1016: Front rank, eff when short of room appr fnl 2f,   **½ 103**
no extra appr fnl 1f: would probably prefer softer grnd: shade btr 4057 (11f, gd/soft).
*3547 **LIMELIGHTING 20** [7] 4-9-2 O Peslier 84/10: 454149: Cl-up, went on over 2f out, hdd appr fnl 1f,   **5 96**
wknd qckly, fin 9th: 4th in a Listed race at Deauville since scoring in 3547 (10f, Listed, fast).
11 ran   Time 2m 37.5   (H H Aga Khan)   J Oxx Currabeg, Co Kildare

LONGCHAMP SATURDAY SEPTEMBER 30TH Righthand, Stiff, Galloping Track

4237 2.40 GR 3 PRIX DE CONDE 2YO 1m1f Good
£21134 £7685 £3842 £2305

3926 **PANIS** 20 [3] P Bary 2-9-2 T Thulliez 74/10: -21431: 2 b c Miswaki - Political Parody (Doonesbury) **105**
Towards rear, plenty to do appr fnl 1f, switched & ran on strongly ins last, led nr fin, rdn out: wnr of
1 of prev 3 starts: eff around a stiff/gall 1m/9f on gd grnd: smart & progressive juv.

4072 **DAYGLOW DANCER** 10 [2] M R Channon 2-9-2 L Detorri 129/10: 242522: 2 b c Fraam - Fading ¾ **103**
(Pharly) Trkd ldrs, went on over 1f out, rdn out, hdd nr fin: best run to date on this step up to Gr 3 company:
eff at 7/9f: acts on fast & hvy grnd, reportedly prefers the latter: see 4072.

-- **SLIGO BAY** [6] A P O'Brien 2-9-2 M J Kinane 23/10: -213: 2 b c Sadler's Wells - Angelic Song 1 **101**
(Halo) Prom, drvn appr fnl 1f, outpcd just ins last, ran on strongly to take 3rd cl-home: recent wnr at
The Curragh (mdn): eff at 1m/9f, mid-dists sure to suit next term: acts on fast & gd: useful prospect.

-- **BERMUDA GRASS** [4] A de Royer Dupre 2-9-2 T Jarnet 17/2: -02114: Hld up, eff over 1f out, onepace. shd **101**
7 ran Time 1m 53.9 (Ecurie Jean-Louis Bouchard) P Bary France

4238 3.10 GR 2 PRIX DOLLAR 3YO+ 1m1f165y Good
£28818 £11527 £5764 £2882 3 yo rec 6 lb

*2072 **SLICKLY** 42 [4] Saeed bin Suroor 4-9-1 L Dettori 7/10 FAVcp: 25-101: 4 gr c Linamix - Slipstream **120**
Queen (Conquistador Cielo) Made all, strongly prsd appr fnl 1f, found extra fnl 100yds, drvn out: well btn in a
Gr 1 in the US (v fast grnd) since scoring on reapp here at Longchamp (Gr 3): '99 wnr again at Longchamp (2, Gr 1
& Gr 2, rtd 119, A Fabre), prev term won at Chantilly (Gr 2, rtd 110): eff at 10/12f on gd & soft: handles
a stiff/gall trk, likes Longchamp: tough & high-class colt, has the Champion Stakes as his next target.

*4064 **ALBARAHIN** 10 [1] M P Tregoning 5-9-1 W Supple 26/10: -21212: 5 b h Silver Hawk - My Dear Lady 1 **118**
(Mr Prospector) Cl-up, chall wnr appr fnl 2f, ev ch till no extra for press ins last: clr rem: fine run, consistent.

*3641 **ADILABAD** 35 [3] Sir Michael Stoute 3-8-9 G Mosse 13/10: 1-5113: 3 b c Gulch - Adaiyka (Doyoun) 6 **109**
Chsd ldrs, not pace of front 2 fnl 2f: below par on this hat-trick bid: something amiss?: btr 3641.

3929 **SOBIESKI** 20 [2] A Fabre 3-9-0 O Peslier 7/10 FAVcp: 161134: Chsd ldrs, rdn/no extra appr fnl 2f: 1½ **111**
may apprec more give in the grnd: btr 3929, 2736.
4 ran Time 1m 59.3 (Godolphin) Saeed bin Suroor Newmarket

4239 3.40 GR 2 PRIX HUBERT 3YO 1m7f Good
£28818 £11527 £5764 £2882

*3848 **EPITRE** 27 [2] A Fabre 3-9-2 O Peslier 3/5 FAV: 242111: 3 b c Common Grounds - Epistolienne (Law **115**
Society) Cl-up, rdn to lead appr fnl 1f, styd on well, drvn out: wnr thrice prev this term, incl a Gr 3 here at
Longchamp last month & also 4th in a Gr 1: eff at 10/15f on gd, soft & a stiff/gall trk: smart & progressive.

*4091 **RIDDLESDOWN** 8 [6] S P C Woods 3-9-2 T Thulliez 10/1: 100112: 3 ch c Common Grounds - Neat 1½ **113**
Dish (Stalwart) Waited with, plenty to do over 2f out, gd hdwy appr fnl 1f, styd on strongly ins last, fin
well: excellent run on this step up to Gr company, 2m will now suit: should win a Listed/Gr 3: see 4091.

4055 **ROSTROPOVICH** 14 [7] A P O'Brien 3-9-2 M J Kinane 8/1: 135043: 3 gr c Sadler's Wells - Infamy nk **113**
(Shirley Heights) Towards rear, eff when short of room 2f out, styd on well ins last, no threat to ldrs:
eff at 12/15f on gd grnd: will apprec a return to Gr 3 company: see 4055, 3538.

4109 **KING O THE MANA** 7 [1] R Hannon 3-9-2 G Mosse 69/10: 413234: Front rank, sltly outpcd 2f out, ½ **112**
rall appr fnl 1f, no extra well ins last: clr rem, qck reapp: ran to best: styd longer 15f trip: see 3892.

1380 **BONNET ROUGE** 135 [4] 3-9-2 D Boeuf 58/10: 11245: Mid-div, drvn/wknd fnl 2f: longer trip. 5 **107**
3898 **TALAASH** 21 [3] 3-9-2 L Dettori 111/10: 136106: Led, hdd appr fnl 1f, sn fdd: needs a drop in grade. 1 **106**
1828 **GOLD ROUND** 113 [5] 3-8-13 O Doleuze 104/10: 1-3107: Al towards rear: 4 month abs, loves hvy grnd. ½ **102**
7 ran Time 3m 12.2 (Baron E de Rothschild) A Fabre France

CURRAGH SATURDAY SEPTEMBER 30TH Righthand, Galloping Track

Official Going Straight course - SOFT; Round Course - GOOD TO SOFT

4240 4.00 GR 3 C L WELD PARK STKS 2YO 7f Good/Soft
£32500 £9500 £4500 £1500

4110 **IMAGINE** 7 A P O'Brien 2-8-11 P J Scallan 5/2 FAV: -36141: 2 b f Sadler's Wells - Doff The Derby **108**
(Master Derby) Made all & sn clr, styd on strongly when prsd ins last, all out: quick reapp: won at Gowran Park
(1m maiden) prior to most recent start: eff around 7f, 1m & further will suit in time: acts on gd, gd/soft grnd
& a gall trk: v useful colt who apprec this drop to Gr 3 company, can win again in this grade.

-- **KATHERINE SEYMOUR** M J Grassick 2-8-11 E Ahern 7/1: -12: 2 b f Green Desert - Sudeley (Dancing ½ **106**
Brave) Cl-up, smooth hdwy over 3f out, styd on strongly ins last, just held: stays 7f, 1m suit: acts on gd/soft.

-- **ENRICH** J Oxx 2-8-11 J Murtagh 5/1: -13: 2 b f Dynaformer - Eternal Reve (Diesis) 1½ **103**
Chsd ldr, drvn 1f out, styd on but no ch with wnr: clr rem, op 7/2: Cork mdn wnr: stays 7f on fast & gd/soft.

1621 **CONEY KITTY** 126 D Hanley 2-8-11 F M Berry 12/1: -224: Late hdwy from rear, no danger: see 1621. 5½ **94**
12 ran Time 1m 32.9 (Mrs John Magnier) A P O'Brien Ballydoyle, Co Tipperary

4241 5.30 LISTED DIAMOND VISION STKS 3YO+ 1m2f Good/Soft
£22750 £6750 £3250 3 yo rec 6 lb

3924 **DOLYDILLE** 21 J S Bolger 4-9-7 K J Manning 9/4 FAV: 410121: 4 b f Dolphin Street - Gradille (Home **111**
Guard) Prom, hdwy to lead 1f out, sn led, rdn clr ins last: earlier won here at The Curragh (h'cap) &
Galway (Listed): eff at 10/12f on fast & gd/soft: v useful & improving, win more of these.

3924 **FANTASIA GIRL** 21 J Oxx 3-8-11 (bl) J Murtagh 7/2: 211232: 3 b f Caerleon - Dreamboat (Mr 4½ **100**
Prospector) Cl-up, chall over 3f out, drvn & not pace of wnr fnl 1f: acts on firm & gd/soft: see 3924.

2909 **TOBARANAMA** 70 D K Weld 3-8-11 P J Smullen 6/1: -14503: 3 b f Sadler's Wells - Ridge The Times hd **100**
(Riva Ridge) Led, rdn/pressed 2f out, hdd appr fnl 1f, onepace: eff at 10f on gd/soft: see 2909.

CURRAGH   SATURDAY SEPTEMBER 30TH   Righthand, Galloping Track

9 ran   Time 2m 18.1   (Mrs K Twomey)   J S Bolger Coolcullen, Co Carlow

SAN SIRO   SUNDAY OCTOBER 1ST   Righthand, Stiff, Galloping Track

Official Going   HEAVY

4242   1.25 PREMIO VERGIATE 2YO   7f110y   Heavy
£8133   £3578   £1952

3397 SIMPATICH 15 L M Cumani 2-8-11 M Demuro : 436311: 2 ch c First Trump - Arc Empress Jane   90
(Rainbow Quest) Cl-up, chall ldr 2f out, led dist, rdn out: recent wnr of a similar event at this trk:
half-brother to a 12f wnr: eff arnd a stiff/gall 7.5f, further will suit: acts on gd grnd: improving colt.
--   BETASITO Italy 2-8-9 M Esposito : 2: 2 b c Petit Loup - Capitelli (Vision)   1   85
--   PLATINUM Italy 2-8-9 M Tellini : 3: 2 b c Dancing Dissident - Mach One (Welnor)   4   79
4 ran   Time 1m 40.9   (Suderia Rencati Srl)   L M Cumani Newmarket

4243   1.55 LISTED PREMIO DEL DADO 2YO   1m   Heavy
£22772   £10020   £5465

--   SOPRAN GLAUMIX B Grizzetti 2-8-11 M Demuro : 1: 2 gr c Linamix - Glauce (Superlative)   103
*4020 LAGUDIN 15 L M Cumani 2-8-9 F Jovine : 12: 2 b c Eagle Eyed - Liaison (Blushing Groom)   4   93
Settled rear, gd hdwy over 1f out, styd on, no ch with wnr: eff at 7f/1m on gd & hvy grnd: see 4020.
*3991 BLUEBERRY FOREST 16 J L Dunlop 2-8-9 G Carter : 222613: 2 b c Charnwood Forest - Abstraction   1½   90
(Rainbow Quest) With ldr, slightly outpcd 2f out, rall ins last, no threat to wnr: will stay 1m+: see 3991.
6 ran   Time 1m 43.5   (Suderia Belforte)   B Grizzetti, Italy

WOLVERHAMPTON (Fibresand)   TUESDAY OCTOBER 3RD   Lefthand, Sharp Track

Official Going   STANDARD   Stalls: Inside

4244   1.40 BOOKER CLAIMER DIV 1 2YO (F)   6f aw rnd   Going 34 -34 Slow
£1736   £496   £248

3912 BLUE LADY 22 [8] N P Littmoden 2-8-6 J Tate 8/1: 063361: 2 b f College Chapel - Dancing Bluebell   70a
(Bluebird) Rdn chasing ldrs halfway, styd on strongly to lead ins last, rdn out: op 6/1: 1st win: eff at 6f,
shld stay further (dam 11f): acts on fibresand & a sharp trk: enjoys claiming grade.
3860 FLOWING RIO 27 [10] P C Haslam 2-8-10 P Goode (3) 7/2: 153302: 2 b f First Trump - Deanta In Eirinn   1¼   69a
(Red Sunset) Al prom wide, rdn/led over 2f out, hdd ins last & no extra: clr rem: acts on fast & fibresand.
3168 HAMBLETON HIGHLITE 58 [9] K A Ryan 2-8-7 (VIS) F Lynch 11/2: 304403: 2 ch g Paris House -   6   54a
Sempreverde (Lear Fan) Briefly led halfway, rdn/no impress fnl 2f: op 4/1: 1st time visor: 2 month abs, AW bow.
--   STORM FROM HEAVEN [3] P C Haslam 2-9-0 Dean McKeown 16/1: 4: Outpcd twds rear, styd on fnl 2f,   ½   59a
no threat: op 12/1: 1st outing 6,000 gns: dam a 7f juv wnr: step up to 7f will suit.
3837 SLIPPER ROSE 28 [1] 2-8-6 P M Quinn (3) 40/1: 000005: Dwelt, mod hdwy fnl 3f: AW bow.   1¾   47a
4190 CLANSINGE 4 [4] 2-8-5 (bl) J Carroll 9/2: 060236: Prom 4f: quick reapp: AW bow: btr 4190, 4097.   ½   44a
4190 MAGIC LAWYER 4 [6] 2-8-1 D Glennon (7) 16/1: 07: Sn rdn, nvr a factor: quick reapp, no form.   3   33a
4154 MR TOD 7 [5] 2-8-6 G Baker (5) 33/1: 0608: Led 1f, btn 2f out: rtd higher 4025 (7f).   ½   36a
801   FIRE PRINCESS 186 [7] 2-8-3 A Beech (3) 11/1: 59: Led after 1f till halfway, sn btn/eased fnl 1f: op   1¼   30a
7/1, 6 month abs: mod form at 5f on sole start prev for J Wharton: now with P Felgate.
3757 FOREVER FABULOUS 33 [11] 2-8-11 M Tebbutt 16/1: 600: Prom 3f: 10th: AW bow, mod form.   1½   34a
2927 LIMBO DANCER 69 [12] 2-8-4 A Mackay 33/1: 60000: Al rear: 11th: 10 wk abs: mod form, new stable.   2   22a
3712 CEDAR TSAR 35 [2] 2-8-11 D Holland 5/2 FAV: 331000: Sn bhd: 12th: fin lame: op 2/1: btr 2948.   dist   0a
12 ran   Time 1m 16.9 (4.1)   (T Clarke)   N P Littmoden Newmarket, Suffolk

4245   2.10 CENTRAL HCAP 3YO+ 0-75 (E)   1m4f aw   Going 34 -19 Slow   [68]
£2758   £788   £394   3 yo rec 7 lb

4186 FAILED TO HIT 4 [5] N P Littmoden 7-9-0 (54)(vis) J Tate 7/2 FAV: 652631: 7 b g Warrshan - Missed   63a
Again (High Top) Made all, rdn/clr over 1f out, styd on strongly ins last, rdn out: nicely bckd, op 5/1: quick reapp:
earlier scored here at W'hampton (C/D clmr): '99 W'hampton (h'cap) & Lingfield (clmr, rtd 74a): '98 wnr at Lingfield
(3, h'caps, & ltd stks) & W'hampton (3, clmr & h'caps, rtd 68a): suited by 12f, further: handles fast grnd,
AW/sharp trk specialist, loves W'hampton: suited by blnks/visor & likes to force the pace: nicely h'capped.
4101 HIGH POLICY 11 [9] D J G Murray Smith 4-9-2 (56)(VIS) J Weaver 16/1: -10602: 4 ch g Machiavellian -   3½   59a
Road To The Top (Shirley Heights) Mid-div halfway, styd on for press fnl 3f, no threat to wnr: first time visor.
3353 THE SHADOW 50 [10] D W P Arbuthnot 4-9-11 (65)(vis) J Quinn 10/1: 050033: 4 br g Polar Falcon -   shd   68a
Shadiliya (Red Alert) Chsd ldrs wide, rdn/chsd wnr 4f out, no impress fnl 2f: abs: stays 12f, best at 9/10f.
3778 ALEXANDRINE 31 [12] Sir Mark Prescott 3-9-11 (72) S Sanders 4/1: 411434: Pushed along chasing ldrs   2   72a
halfway, onepace/no impress over 2f out: well clr rem: op 8/1: btr 1501 (14f, Southwell).
4226 WESTERN COMMAND 3 [8] 4-9-4 (58) R Fitzpatrick 10/1: 206035: Held up in tch, rdn/btn 3f out: 9   48a
quick reapp: op 8/1: see 1501 (14f, Southwell).
4101 ABLE NATIVE 11 [6] 3-9-6 (67)(bl) R Price 20/1: 100406: Chsd wnr 6f out till 4f out, sn btn: btr 2217.   1¾   55a
4026 DESERT SPA 17 [11] 5-9-7 (61) A Clark 4/1: 101027: Rear, eff 4f out, sn btn/eased over 1f out: op 3/1.   2½   45a
3954 YOURE SPECIAL 20 [2] 3-9-13 (74) Dean McKeown 5/1: 100068: Rear, rdn halfway, no impress: bckd,   7   49a
op 10/1: yet to convince beyond 9f: see 319 (mdn, 9f).
3741 CHAKA ZULU 31 [1] 3-9-9 (70) F Norton 9/2: 113129: Mid-div, btn/eased 3f out: op 3/1: AW bow.   9   35a
4075 CINDESTI 12 [7] 4-9-11 (65)(bl) D Holland 20/1: 000000: In tch, btn 3f out: 10th: see 860.   3   26a
2902 WESTERN BAY 70 [3] 4-9-0 (54) R Hughes 33/1: -60000: Chsd wnr 6f, t.o. fnl 2f: 11th, abs.   dist   0a
11 ran   Time 2m 39.9 (6.3)   (M C S D Racing Ltd)   N P Littmoden Newmarket, Suffolk

1309

4246   2.40 BOOKER CLAIMER DIV 2 2YO (F)   6f aw rnd   Going 34   -18 Slow
£1729   £494   £247

3673   **CLARION** 37 [8]   Sir Mark Prescott 2-9-5 S Sanders 4/6 FAV: 212131: 2 ch c First Trump - Area Girl   **88a**
(Jareer) Chsd ldrs, rdn over 1f out, led dist & rdn clr ins last: well bckd: earlier scored at Yarmouth (mdn) &
Sandown (nurs h'cap): eff over a stiff 5f/6f, 7f will may yet suit: acts on firm, gd & fibresand: handles a sharp or
stiff trk: apprec this drop to claiming grade, can win more races.
3439   **ERRACHT** 46 [6]   P C Haslam 2-9-11 Dean McKeown 11/2: 2162: 2 gr f Emarati - Port Na Blath (On Your   3   **71a**
Mark) Chsd ldr, rdn & kept on fnl 1f, not pace of wnr: op 4/1, 6 wk abs: AW bow: stays a sharp 6f: acts on
gd/soft & hvy grnd, handles fibresand: rtd higher 3055 (auct mdn, 5f).
4007   **DANCING PENNEY** 17 [3]   K A Ryan 2-8-2 J Quinn 12/1: 216603: 2 b f General Monash - Penultimate   hd   **61$**
Cress (My Generation) Chsd ldrs, rdn & kept on onepace from over 1f out: op 8/1: see 3307 (sell).
4227   **AMAMACKEMMUSH** 3 [4]   K A Ryan 2-8-7 F Lynch 16/1: 352004: Led, rdn/hdd dist, no extra: qck reapp.1¾   **62$**
3973   **MOYNE PLEASURE** 18 [10]   2-9-4 S W Kelly (3) 25/1: 05: Rdn in tch, nvr pace to chall: AW bow.   nk   **72a**
3205   **MRS TIGGYWINKLE** 56 [7]   2-8-4 J Tate 10/1: 640006: Mid-div, outpcd fnl 3f: 8 wk abs: see 1136.   4   **48a**
3802   **OLYS GILL** 30 [9]   2-8-2 K Dalgleish (5) 50/1: 400007: Al outpcd: mod form.   6   **34a**
4154   **WORTH A RING** 7 [5]   2-8-6 D O'Donohoe 14/1: 058: Al bhd: mod form.   1½   **34a**
4025   **EMMA THOMAS** 17 [2]   2-8-4 J Carroll 16/1: 000039: Sn struggling: flattered 4025 (7f).   11   **11a**
--   **INZARMOOD** [1]   2-8-10 Darren Williams (5) 16/1: 0: Slowly away & al bhd: 10th: op 12/1: Inzar   ½   **15a**
filly, Apr foal, cost 7,500 IR gns: dam an Irish juv wnr: sire a high-class 6/7f performer: with K Burke.
3912   **TUSCAN** 22 [11]   2-8-12 R Hughes 9/1: 460240: Sn outpcd: AW bow: btr 3912, 3204 (firm & fast).   8   **2a**
11 ran   Time 1m 15.9 (3.1)   (Neil Greig)   Sir Mark Prescott Newmarket, Suffolk

---

4247   3.10 MALT HOUSE NOV STKS 2YO (D)   5f aw rnd   Going 34   +10 Fast
£3406   £1048   £524   £262

*2034   **DANEHURST** 106 [2]   Sir Mark Prescott 2-9-0 S Sanders 10/11 FAV: 11: 2 b f Danehill - Miswaki Belle   **103+**
(Miswaki) Made all & rdn clr from over 1f out, eased nr line, cmftbly: fast time: hvly bckd on AW bow after 3
month abs: earlier made a wng debut at Warwick (fills mdn): dam a lightly rcd mdn, sire a top class sprinter/
miler: eff around a sharp/turning 5f, 6f looks sure to suit: acts on fast grnd & fibresand: runs fresh:
produced a juvenile career record time, entered in a Listed contest on Saturday & not to be underestimated.
*4095   **PRINCE OF BLUES** 11 [5]   N P Littmoden 2-9-0 M Roberts 7/4: 650012: 2 b c Prince Of Birds - Reshift   5   **85a**
(Night Shift) Chsd wnr halfway, no impress from over 1f out: op 6/4: AW bow: well clr of rem: acts on firm,
gd & fibresand: caught a tartar here, shld win again: see 4095 (auct mdn).
3425   **COLUMBINE** 46 [1]   A Berry 2-9-0 J Carroll 9/2: -133: 2 b f Pivotal - Heart Of India (Try My Best)   7   **69a**
Chsd ldrs, outpcd from halfway: op 3/1: 6 wk abs: AW bow: see 3425, 2756 (fast).
4030   **TICCATOO** 15 [6]   R Hollinshead 2-8-9 R Hughes 25/1: 002004: Sn outpcd: see 2915, 865.   2½   **57a**
--   **BETTER OFF** [3]   2-8-8 R Fitzpatrick 50/1: 5: Slowly away, al bhd: Bettergeton gldg, Apr foal: ¾   **54a**
dam a mdn: sire a 7f/1m 2/3yo wnr: with Mrs M Macauley.
--   **PIDDINGTON FLYER** [7]   2-8-8 D R McCabe 20/1: 6: Sn struggling: op 12/1: Case Law gldg, Mar   1¾   **50a**
foal: cost 6,000 gns: dam lightly rcd, sire a smart sprinter & a speed influence: with B Meehan.
3786   **THE LOOSE SCREW** 31 [4]   A Clark 50/1: -6007: Sn outpcd: AW bow, mod form prev.   6   **41a**
7 ran   Time 1m 01.4 (1.2)   (Cheveley Park Stud)   Sir Mark Prescott Newmarket, Suffolk

---

4248   3.40 BOOKER HCAP 3YO+ 0-70 (E)   1m100y aw rnd   Going 34   -08 Slow   [67]
£2786   £796   £398   3 yo rec 3 lb

4121   **PADHAMS GREEN** 9 [12]   B W Hills 4-10-0 (67) R Hughes 11/2: 621521: 4 b g Aragon - Double Dutch   **83a**
(Nicholas Bill) Chsd ldrs wide, al travelling well, prog to lead over 2f out & sn clr, eased ins last, cmftbly:
val for 12L+: earlier scored at Newmarket (amat h'cap, rtd 70): trained by M Tompkins in '99 & scored at Salisbury
(appr h'cap, rtd 69): suited by 7f/8.5f on firm, gd/soft & fibresand: handles any trk: gd weight carrier, plenty in
hand here, type to win again if reappearing quickly under a pen.
3981   **TEOFILIO** 18 [6]   A J McNae 6-9-9 (62)(bl) J Weaver 7/1: 045402: 6 ch h Night Shift - Rivoltade   8   **66a**
(Sir Ivor) Towards rear, styd on wide fnl 3f, no ch with wnr: prob handles fibresand, Lingfield/equitrack
specialist, on a fair mark & one to note back on that surface: see 594.
3499   **WELODY** 45 [2]   K Mahdi 4-9-7 (60)(bl-1) J Tate 16/1: 000003: 4 ch g Weldnaas - The Boozy News   2½   **59a**
(L'Emigrant) Led till over 3f out, sn rdn & no impress: op 33/1, 6 wk abs: see 658 (C/D mdn).
3745   **MYSTIC RIDGE** 33 [4]   B J Curley 6-9-11 (64) J Stack 10/1: 006004: Chsd ldr, led over 3f out till   2½   **58a**
over 2f out, sn btn: op 6/1: see 476 (7f).
4033   **SOPHOMORE** 15 [10]   6-9-7 (60) K Dalgleish (5) 14/1: 000205: Held up, rdn/mod hdwy fnl 4f: acts on   ¾   **53a**
fast, gd/soft & fibresand: see 1731 (clmr).
4032   **COMPATRIOT** 15 [5]   4-9-9 (62) Dean McKeown 9/1: 536106: Prom 5f: op 7/1: btr 3769 (C/D).   nk   **54a**
4153   **ANGEL HILL** 7 [3]   5-9-8 (61) F Lynch 9/2: 040147: Chsd ldrs, btn 2f out: btr 4153, 4004 (7f).   1¾   **50a**
4013   **MYTTONS AGAIN** 17 [13]   3-9-9 (65) C McCavish (7) 16/1: 116408: Mid-div, btn 3f out: see 3593 (fast).   3½   **47a**
4173   **CORUSCATING** 6 [11]   3-9-9 (65) S Sanders 7/1: -04109: Dwelt, rdn halfway, no hdwy: quick reapp.   3½   **40a**
*4021   **BAHRAIN** 17 [9]   4-9-8 (61) T G McLaughlin 4/1 FAV: 062310: Mid-div, rdn/btn halfway, 10th: btr 4021.   2   **32a**
1732   **Be The Chief** 120 [7]   4-9-7 (60)(VIS) L Vickers (2) 33/1:   3979   **Edifice** 18 [8]   4-9-7 (60)(BL) M Roberts 25/1:
1022   **Miss World** 162 [1]   3-9-10 (66) J Quinn 33/1:
13 ran   Time 1m 49.8 (3.6)   (Mrs B W Hills)   B W Hills Lambourn, Berks

---

4249   4.10 TUCK SHOP MDN AUCT DIV 1 2YO (F)   1m100y aw rnd   Going 34   -18 Slow
£1694   £484   £242

2653   **BROWSER** 81 [6]   K R Burke 2-8-8 N Callan 9/2: 031: 2 b g Rubiano - Just Looking (Marju)   **83a**
Al prom, led 3f out, rdn/duelled with rnr-up fnl 2f, narrowly asserted for press ins last, all out: 12 wk abs: apprec
step up to 8.5f, dam related to a high-class stayer, mid-dists shld suit: acts on fibresand, handles gd grnd: likes a
sharp/turning trk & runs well fresh: improved for being gelded & open to further improvement.
3729   **MY VERY OWN** 34 [9]   N P Littmoden 2-8-7 C Carver (3) 6/4 FAV: 0622: 2 ch c Persian Bold - Cossack   ½   **80a**
Princess (Lomond) In tch, rdn/prog to press wnr & duel fnl 2f, carried right when just held ins last, kept on
well: well clr rem: nicely bckd: acts on fast grnd & fibresand: win similar on this form: see 3729.
3950   **EASTERN RED** 20 [1]   K A Ryan 2-8-2 F Norton 16/1: 546233: 2 b f Contract Law - Gagajulu (Al Hareb)   13   **49a**

1310

Prom, rdn/btn 2f out: better off in sell h'caps: see 3950 (h'cap, 7.5f).
4097 **DEFINITE RETURN 11** [3] B Palling 2-8-1 J Quinn 25/1: 04: Chsd ldrs, btn 3f out: longer 8.5f trip. 3 **42a**
3867 **TWILIGHT DANCER 26** [8] 2-8-5 P Doe 5/1: 65: Held up, nvr a threat: AW bow: btr 3867. *nk* **45a**
3852 **CAPITAL LAD 27** [4] 2-8-10 P McCabe 8/1: -046: Led after 2f till 3f out, sn btn: AW bow, lngr trip. 2½ **45a**
3950 **EL UNO 20** [2] 2-8-6 A Clark 25/1: -00657: Led 2f, sn btn: longer 8.5f trip, AW bow: see 3614. 2½ **36a**
4072 **DENISE BEST 13** [5] 2-8-4(1ow) J Carroll 3/1: 0248: In tch 4f: op 6/4, AW bow: btr 4072, 3991 (sft). 13 **8a**
4154 **THE MERRY WIDOW 7** [7] 2-8-1 Joanna Badger (7) 50/1: 00009: Ref to race & al t.o.: see 3128 (7f). *dist* **0a**
9 ran Time 1m 50.6 (4.4) (Mrs Julie Mitchell) K R Burke Newmarket, Suffolk

4250

4.40 TUCK SHOP MDN AUCT DIV 2 2YO (F) 1m100y aw rnd Going 34 -22 Slow
£1694 £484 £242

3952 **EL HAMRA 20** [5] B A McMahon 2-8-7 S Sanders 100/30: 335231: 2 gr c Royal Abjar - Cherlinoa (Crystal Palace) Prom, led over 4f out & rdn/clr over 1f out, al holding rivals ins last & eased nr line: op 5/2: eff btwn 7.5f/8.5f on fibresand, fast & gd grnd: handles a sharp/turning or stiff/gall trk. **75a**
4076 **HAWKES RUN 12** [9] B J Meehan 2-8-10 D R McCabe 7/2: 66452: 2 b g Hernando - Wise Speculation (Mr Prospector) Held up, rdn & styd on from over 2f out, no threat to wnr: op 9/4: AW bow: handles fast, soft & fibresand: fin well clr of rem: shown enough to win a modest race: see 4076 (h'cap). 1½ **73a**
2182 **NO NAME CITY 100** [3] J W Hills 2-8-9 S Whitworth 20/1: 003: 2 ch c Royal Abjar - Broadway Gal (Foolish Pleasure) Prom, chsd wnr over 2f out, wknd ins last: abs, AW bow: longer 8.5f trip, mod form prev. 10 **52a**
4116 **SECRET PASSION 9** [7] K Mahdi 2-8-1 J Quinn 5/1: 664: Dwelt, mod late hdwy: AW bow: see 4116. *hd* **43a**
4068 **EAGLES CACHE 13** [4] 2-8-9 J Carroll 15/8 FAV: 623025: Led 4f: bckd, AW bow: btr 4068 (7f). *nk* **50a**
4116 **LADY LAUREATE 9** [1] 2-8-4 M Henry 12/1: 056: Al twds rear: op 10/1: AW bow: btr 4116 (gd/soft). 12 **21a**
3949 **PREMIER BOY 20** [6] 2-8-6 (t) M Roberts 16/1: 0047: Chsd ldrs 5f: op 10/1: AW bow, t-strap. ½ **22a**
3729 **NORTHERN CASTLE 34** [2] 2-8-7 Dean McKeown 33/1: 008: Sn bhd: AW bow, no form. 20 **0a**
8 ran Time 1m 51.00 (4.8) (R Thornhill) B A McMahon Hopwas, Staffs

4251

5.10 HAPPY SHOPPER HCAP 3YO 0-65 (F) 1m1f79y aw Going 34 -10 Slow [71]
£2296 £656 £328

3977 **FARAWAY LOOK 18** [8] J R Fanshawe 3-9-7 (64) D Harrison 13/2: 4201: 3 br c Distant View - Summer Trip (L'Emigrant) Al prom, rdn/led 2f out, held on well ins last, drvn out: nicely bckd, op 8/1: AW/h'cap bow: first win: eff at 7f/9.5f, may get further: acts on fibresand & gd: likes a sharp/turning trk: op to further improv. **71a**
4221 **ABSINTHER 3** [9] E J Alston 3-8-12 (55) J Carroll 5/1: 531252: 3 b g Presidium - Heavenly Queen (Scottish Reel) Rdn/bhd, hdwy wide fnl 3f, styd on for press tho' held nr fin: op 4/1, quick reapp: acts on fast, soft & fibresand: forced a little wide in closing stages by wnr: well clr rem & a gd AW bow: see 3591. ¾ **60a**
3885 **ADRIFT 25** [12] B Hanbury 3-9-2 (59)(t) J Weaver 20/1: -00203: 3 ch f Irish River - Dream Play (Blushing Groom) In tch, briefly led over 2f out, sn rdn/fdd: AW bow: t-strap: btr 3289 (fillies mdn, fast). 9 **50a**
3835 **BUSY BUSY BEE 28** [13] N P Littmoden 3-9-0 (57) T G McLaughlin 20/1: 02-504: Held up, hdwy halfway, btn 2f out: see 3272 (C/D mdn). *hd* **47a**
4021 **GROESFAEN LAD 17** [11] 3-9-2 (59) G Faulkner (3) 7/1: 400635: Prom, btn over 1f out: see 4021, 857. 4 **41a**
4150 **NIGHT AND DAY 7** [2] 3-8-11 (54)(t) P McCabe 25/1: 540456: Led 7f, sn btn: t-strap: see 3935, 3561. *shd* **36a**
4174 **TWILIGHT WORLD 6** [6] 3-8-12 (55) S Sanders 11/8 FAV: 6-1327: In tch halfway, wknd over 2f out: hvly bckd, tchd 5/2: quick reapp: not handle a/w: btr 4174, 2534. 9 **23a**
3956 **ICON 20** [7] 3-8-12 (55)(t) D Holland 20/1: 0008: Al towards rear: op 14/1, h'cap/AW bow: t-strap. 1½ **20a**
3167 **SHAM SHARIF 59** [3] 3-8-12 (55) F Norton 20/1: 105009: Prom 5f: abs, AW bow: blnks omitted. 2 **16a**
4032 **HEATHYARDS LAD 15** [5] 3-9-7 (64) Dean McKeown 10/1: 003450: Bhd after 3f: 10th: op 8/1: see 976. ½ **24a**
3288 **MUST BE MAGIC 53** [10] 3-9-4 (61)(vis) M Roberts 6/1: 343100: Al bhd: 11th: op 4/1, abs: btr 2795. 1 **19a**
3756 **VERDURA 33** [4] 3-9-5 (62) J Quinn 10/1: 640020: Bhd halfway: 12th: op 7/1: btr 3756 (equitrack). ¾ **19a**
12 ran Time 2m 02.3 (4.1) (Cheveley Park Stud) J R Fanshawe Newmarket, Suffolk

CATTERICK TUESDAY OCTOBER 3RD Lefthand, Undulating, V Tight Track

Official Going SOFT (HEAVY In Places). Stalls: Inside. Fields came stands side in the straight
Pace Figs inapplicable due to course realignment

4252

2.0 LANCASHIRE MDN DIV 1 2YO (D) 5f rnd Soft Inapplicable
£2730 £840 £420 £210

3955 **BINT ROYAL 20** [12] J A Glover 2-8-9 O Pears 5/2 FAV: 01: 2 ch f Royal Abjar - Living Legend (Septieme Ciel) Made all going well, rdn out cl home: poorly drawn on debut: 1st foal, dam a juv wnr: eff forcing the pace at 5f on soft grnd: handles a sharp trk: made most of fav high draw here. **68**
3812 **SIAMO DISPERATI 30** [11] C B B Booth 2-9-0 A Culhane 10/1: -3002: 2 ch c Aragon - Jambo (Rambo Dancer) Prsd wnr, drvn appr fnl 1f, kept on but al held: mudlark, acts on soft/hvy: see 1764 (debut). ¾ **70**
3955 **TRUDIE 20** [1] Miss J F Craze 2-8-9 N Carlisle 14/1: 603: 2 b f Komaite - Irish Limerick (Try My Best) Chsd front pair, no extra ent fnl 1f: clr of rem, op 20/1: gd eff from poor low draw: eff at 5f on soft grnd. 2 **59**
-- **DIAMOND ZOE** [3] J L Eyre 2-8-9 D Mernagh (3) 20/1: 4: Chsd ldrs, onepace ent fnl 2f: 1,100 gns 1st foal: dam 6f juv wnr: sprint bred: poor low draw, shld improve. 6 **44**
-- **STATOSILVER** [4] 2-9-0 Paul Eddery 12/1: 5: Al same pl: 7,500 gns Puissance 1st foal, sprint bred. 2½ **43**
4083 **MAMCAZMA 12** [6] 2-9-0 K Hodgson 50/1: 06: Nvr a factor: half brother to a 6/7f wnr. 1¾ **38**
2277 **CLOONDESH 96** [8] 2-9-0 P Hanagan (5) 7/1: 507: Mid-div thr'out: op 5/1, 14 wk abs: see 1595. *hd* **38**
-- **ARCHIRONDEL** [9] 2-9-0 M Fenton 14/1: 8: Nvr troubled ldrs: op 7/1, debut: 5,000 gns Bin Ajwaad colt, dam a wnr abroad: with John Berry. *hd* **37**
-- **LAST TIME** [10] 2-8-9 K Darley 9/2: 9: Dwelt, al towards rear: op 5/2 on debut: half sister to a couple of juv wnrs: lost all ch at the start today, shld be capable of better: with T Easterby. *nk* **31**
4082 **DIABOLO 12** [5] 2-9-0 T Lucas 5/1: 00: Slow away, nvr in it: 10th: see 4082. ½ **35**
3859 **HELALI MANOR 27** [2] 2-8-9 Clare Roche (7) 66/1: 060: Sn struggling: 11th. ½ **29**
-- **WITHIN THE LAW** [7] 2-8-9 T Williams 12/1: 0: Slow away, al bhd: last: Contract Law filly. 1¾ **26**
12 ran Time 1m 02.5 (5.2) (Miss V Haigh) J A Glover Carburton, Notts

CATTERICK TUESDAY OCTOBER 3RD Lefthand, Undulating, V Tight Track

4253 2.30 LANCASHIRE MDN DIV 2 2YO (D) 5f rnd Soft Inapplicable
£2730 £840 £420 £210

-- **HILTON HEAD** [8] T D Easterby 2-8-9 P Fessey 20/1: 1: 2 b f Primo Dominie - Low Hill (Rousillon) **82**
Trkd ldrs, led appr fnl 1f, kept on well, rdn out: op 14/1 on debut: 11,500gns half sister to 2 wnrs, incl decent juv Aix en Provence, dam juv wnr abroad: eff at 5f, shld get 6f: acts on soft, tight trk & runs well fresh.
3571 **LADY LENOR 41** [3] Mrs G S Rees 2-8-9 Angela Hartley (7) 66/1: -02: 2 b f Presidium - Sparkling *1¾* **77**
Roberta (Kind Of Hush) Keen & led till appr fnl 1f, styd on, drifted left: 6 wk abs & much imprvd for new connections, prev with J Weymes: eff at 5f on soft grnd, runs well fresh.
4137 **LOCHSPRITE 8** [10] I A Balding 2-8-9 K Darley 4/9 FAV: 023: 2 ch f So Factual - Lochspring *2* **71**
(Precocious) Prsd ldr till appr fnl 1f, onepace: nicely bckd to land the odds: quickish reapp, btr 4137.
3760 **FLY BOY FLY 32** [11] M Johnston 2-9-0 J Fanning 5/2: -464: Handy, rdn 2f out, kept on onepace: *nk* **75**
back in trip, well clr rem: handles gd & soft grnd.
4083 **GRAND HOUDINI 12** [1] 2-9-0 G Parkin 50/1: 05: Chsd ldrs, no extra 2f out: 800gns Primo Dominie *7* **57**
half brother to a 6f juv wnr, dam unrcd: poor low draw: with M W Easterby.
-- **THE SCAFFOLDER** [2] 2-9-0 R Lappin 33/1: 6: Dwelt, nvr nr ldrs: 2,000gns 1st foal: poor draw. *1½* **54**
4131 **ORANGINO 9** [7] 2-9-0 O Pears 100/1: 07: Nvr a factor: Primo Dominie brother to a 6f juv wnr. *¾* **52**
-- **STORMY CREST** [4] 2-9-0 M Fenton 20/1: 8: Slow away, al towards rear: 5,000gns half brother to *6* **37**
wnrs abroad, dam mid-dist/stayer: with John Berry.
3836 **LEANADIS ROSE 28** [5] 2-8-9 P Hanagan (5) 25/1: 569: Slow away, al bhd: see 3836 (1m). *1½* **28**
4216 **IMPREZA 3** [12] 2-8-9 (vis) C Lowther 100/1: 04000: Nvr dangerous: 10th, quick reapp, no form. *nk* **28**
3955 **Diamond Jayne 20** [9] 2-8-9 D Mernagh (3) 20/1: -- **Ellieberry** [6] 2-8-9 R Winston 25/1:
12 ran Time 1m 02.0 (4.7) (Mr & Mrs John Poynton) T D Easterby Great Habton, N Yorks

4254 3.00 FILL NURSERY HCAP 2YO 0-85 (D) 7f rnd Soft Inapplicable [86]
£5876 £1808 £904 £452

4007 **CLASSY ACT 17** [11] A Berry 2-9-1 (73) G Carter 10/1: 230161: 2 ch f Lycius - Stripanoora (Ahonoora) **78**
Bhd, imprvd 2f out, kept on well und press to lead ins fnl 1f, narrowly: op 7/1: prev won at Hamilton (ddht, nurs): eff at 6/7f: acts on gd/soft & soft grnd, prob any trk: can go well fresh & force the pace: on the upgrade.
4070 **PASITHEA 13** [3] T D Easterby 2-9-3 (75) K Darley 5/1: 331022: 2 b f Celtic Swing - Midnight's *nk* **78**
Reward (Night Shift) Nvr far away, chall appr fnl 1f, kept on under press, just held: tough: see 4070, 3411.
3409 **MONTANA MISS 47** [15] B Palling 2-9-6 (78) D Sweeney 14/1: 41163: 2 b f Earl Of Barking - Cupid *¾* **79**
Miss (Anita's Prince) Cl-up, led appr fnl 2f, rdn & hdd ent fnl 1f, onepace: 7 wk abs: back to form on h'cap bow: acts on firm & soft grnd: gd run from fav high draw, btn under 1L: see 2741.
3950 **PETIT TOR 20** [6] J Norton 2-8-2 (60) P Hanagan (5) 14/1: 641224: Mid-div, eff 2f out, kept on ins *¾* **60**
last, not pace to chall: op 10/1: consistent, acts on fast & soft grnd: see 3438 (C/D sell).
4157 **ROOFER 7** [5] 2-9-7 (79) Craig Williams 7/4 FAV: 54245: Rear & outpcd early, prog when hmpd appr *½* **78**
fnl 1f, kept on well: well bckd, top weight, qck reapp: no run at any stage & prob unlucky: acts on firm & soft grnd: crying out for 1m now: one to keep in mind, see 4157, 3748.
2778 **KANDYMAL 75** [2] 2-7-11 (55)(1ow)(2oh) Dale Gibson 33/1: -06066: Chsd ldrs, onepace appr fnl 1f: *hd* **54**
11 wk abs, h'cap bow: 6,200gns half sister to a decent sprinter: prob stays 7f on soft grnd: with R Fahey.
3901 **BORDERS BELLE 24** [14] 2-9-2 (74) Paul Eddery 16/1: 432067: Towards rear, eff & short of room ent *¾* **71**
fnl 2f, nvr nrr: worth another chance: see 3169.
4086 **FORUM FINALE 12** [7] 2-8-8 (66) J Fanning 11/1: 2508: Chsd ldrs, outpcd when hmpd appr fnl 1f. *¾* **62**
4116 **APRIL LEE 9** [12] 2-8-7 (65)(e) R Ffrench 10/1: 252039: Led till appr fnl 2f, onepace: op 14/1. *hd* **60**
4007 **FLYING ROMANCE 17** [1] 2-8-2 (60) J McAuley 12/1: 553040: In tch till 2f out: 10th: see 4007. *9* **39**
4007 **MISS PROGRESSIVE 17** [10] 2-7-12 (56) Kim Tinkler 10/1: 025130: Prom, wknd qckly appr fnl 2f: 11th, *5* **25**
op 7/1: not her form, in front of this wnr in 4007, see 3468.
3881 **Unparalleled 25** [9] 2-8-13 (71)(BL) R Mullen 20/1: 3655 **Congeniality 38** [4] 2-8-0 (58) P Fessey 20/1:
3953 **Kundalila 20** [13] 2-8-3 (61) T Williams 25/1:
14 ran Time 1m 34.6 (11.6) (C Shine, I Cunningham, J Lambert) A Berry Cockerham, Lancs

4255 3.30 CUMBRIA MDN AUCT 3YO (F) 6f rnd Soft Inapplicable
£2310 £660 £330

3873 **BETTY BATHWICK 26** [7] E J O'Neill 3-8-9 A Culhane 50/1: 02-001: 3 b f Common Grounds - Tynaghmile **64**
(Lyphard's Special) Prom, shaken up appr fnl 2f, rdn to lead bef fnl 1f, ran on well: shock 50/1 wnr, prev btn off 51 in a h'cap: rnr-up fnl '99 start (sell, rtd 55, B Smart): eff at 6f on firm & soft grnd, prob any trk.
4217 **CHAMPFIS 3** [10] M Johnston 3-9-0 K Darley 4/5 FAV: 3-4252: 3 b g Efisio - Champ d'Avril (Northfields) *2½* **63**
Chsd ldrs, rdn 2f out, styd on for 2nd but not bother wnr: nicely bckd, qk reapp: better over 7f/1m: see 4217.
3780 **DAYLILY 31** [1] T D Easterby 3-8-9 M Fenton 11/1: 323503: 3 ch f Pips Pride - Leaping Water (Sure *1* **55**
Blade) Led till appr fnl 1f, no extra: tchd 14/1: win a seller, see 2313.
3975 **LAYAN 18** [5] J Balding 3-8-9 J Edmunds 9/2: 203034: In tch, prog appr fnl 1f, no extra: see 3975. *¾* **53**
3364 **SCHATZI 49** [6] 3-8-9 (VIS) J Bramhill 50/1: 020005: Rear, mod late hdwy: vis, jmps rnr since 3364. *2½* **47**
4005 **WHITLEYGRANGE GIRL 17** [3] 3-8-9 R Cody Boutcher (7) 100/1: 60506: Nvr nr ldrs: v stiff task. *5* **32$**
3956 **LAKESIDE LADY 20** [8] 3-8-9 T Williams 33/1: 07: Nvr on terms: Handsome Sailor filly, no form. *4* **22**
-- **THE PRIEST** [11] 3-9-0 J Fanning 7/1: 8: Chsd ldrs wide till lost place appr fnl 2f: debut: *2½* **21**
College Chapel gldg with J Osborne.
3977 **DIZZY KNIGHT 18** [4] 3-8-9 D Sweeney 9/1: 0-409: Chsd ldrs 4f: tchd 16/1: btr 3319 (fast). *nk* **15**
-- **PRINCE HUSSAR** [2] 3-9-0 R Winston 14/1: 0: Dwelt, al rear: 10th, tchd 20/1 on debut: Emarati *9* **0**
colt, related to decent sprinter Westcourt Magic, dam 11f wnr: with P Howling.
1340} **JEMINAR 507** [9] 3-8-9 T Lucas 20/1: -064-0: Handy till halfway: 11th, op 33/1 on reapp: 4th fnl *16* **0**
of 3 '99 starts (gd/soft grnd clmr, rtd 61): with M Easterby.
11 ran Time 1m 19.1 (8.8) (The Parrot Club) E J O'Neill Newmarket, Suffolk

4256

4.0 NOTTS HCAP 3YO 0-70 (E) 1m4f Soft Inapplicable [77]
£3510 £1080 £540 £270

3827 **BOLLIN NELLIE** 29 [3] T D Easterby 3-8-8 (57) K Darley 5/2 FAV: 021621: 3 ch f Rock Hopper - Bollin 65
Magdalene (Teenoso) Mid-div, clsd 4f out, chall when badly hmpd & lost place ent str, rall gamely to lead ins
last: bckd from 7/2: earlier won at Haydock (h'cap): plcd fnl '99 start (h'cap, rtd 63): suited by 12f now,
tried further: acts on firm & soft, any trk: tough & progressive filly, value for bigger winning margin today.
4074 **BAHAMAS** 13 [16] Sir Mark Prescott 3-9-4 (67)(bl) D Sweeney 5/1: 311062: 3 b g Barathea - Rum Cay ½ 72
(Our Native) Pulled hard mid-div, imprvd appr str & led on bit over 2f out, went 4L clr appr fnl 1f, sn rdn, worn
down ins last: 9L clr rem: back to form with hold up tactics: acts on gd, soft & fibresand: see 2945.
*4174 **SOPHALA** 6 [4] C F Wall 3-9-2 (65)(5ex) R Mullen 6/1: -30013: 3 b f Magical Wonder - Fujaiyrah 9 61
(In Fijar) Rear, prog after 6f, chsd ldrs 2f out, sn onepace: op 4/1, quick reapp with a pen: poss failed
to see out this longer 12f trip in testing grnd: see 4174 (10f).
3517 **CHOCSTAW** 44 [9] Sir Michael Stoute 3-8-11 (60) L Newman (3) 12/1: -0054: Cl-up shaken up appr str, 3 53
sn short of room, onepace after: op 8/1, 6 wk abs: looks v onepaced, worth a try at 2m.
3012 **GRACILIS** 65 [6] 3-8-5 (54) C Lowther 20/1: -4005: Rear, prog into mid-div appr str, no further 2½ 44
hdwy: tchd 33/1 on h'cap bow, 9 wk abs: more galloping trk may suit, see 2520.
3954 **TUFTY HOPPER** 20 [10] 3-9-6 (69) R Winston 8/1: 453326: Chsd ldrs, eff/short of room ent str, onepace. ½ 58
3954 **LENNY THE LION** 20 [2] 3-8-5 (52)(2ow) A Culhane 14/1: 553007: Nvr better than mid-div: see 2332. 1¾ 44
1005 **ROMAN EMPEROR** 162 [7] 3-7-10 (45)(BL)(1oh) J McAuley 14/1: 00-008: In tch till ent str: op 10/1, ½ 31
tchd 25/1, over 5 mth abs, new stable: prev campaigned btwn 5f & 7f, incl when a modest juv for G Kelly.
3375 **FRENCH MASTER** 48 [15] 3-7-10 (45)(vis)(2oh) Iona Wands 33/1: 200069: Cl-up, chall ent str & sltly ¾ 30
hmpd, sn lost place: 7 wk abs: jockey given 1 day ban for careless riding: see 806.
3780 **COTTAM LILLY** 31 [13] 3-7-11 (46)(1ow)(11oh) Dale Gibson 50/1: 0-000: In tch 9f: 10th, h'cap bow. hd 31
4149 **ALVARO** 7 [1] 3-8-9 (58) R Studholme (3) 10/1: 206400: Bhd fnl 4f: 11th, op 25/1, quick reapp. 10 33
2715 **ROOM TO ROOM MAGIC** 78 [11] 3-7-10 (45)(3oh) D Mernagh(0) 20/1: 602520: Led till appr str, sn btn: abs. 0
1071 **CHIEF OF JUSTICE** 155 [12] 3-9-5 (68) T Williams 11/1: -11300: Chsd ldrs, chall appr str, sn badly 0
hmpd/snatched up, eased: 15th, 5 month abs: forget this: see 640 (AW).
2879 **Sadlers Song** 71 [14] 3-7-10 (45)(5oh) J Bramhill 25/1:3506 **My Line** 44 [5] 3-7-10 (45)(2oh) P Fessey 25/1:
3310 **Empire Dream** 52 [8] 3-9-7 (70) J Fanning 20/1:
16 ran Time 2m 49.0 (17.8) (Lady Westbrook) T D Easterby Great Habton, N Yorks

4257

4.30 DERBYS APPR CLASS STKS 3YO+ 0-85 (F) 6f rnd Soft Inapplicable
£2289 £654 £327 3 yo rec 1 lb

3768 **BOOMERANG BLADE** 32 [2] B Smart 4-8-9 R Studholme (3) 9/2: 266051: 4 b f Sure Blade - Opuntia 84
(Rousillon) Well plcd, led appr fnl 2f, rdn clr: op 3/1: '99 rnr-up (stks, rtd 94): '98 Folkestone (mdn) &
Doncaster wnr (val stks, rtd 103): eff at 6/7f, tried 10f: acts on firm & soft grnd, any trk: runs well fresh.
4073 **BODFARI PRIDE** 13 [12] D Nicholls 5-8-12 A Nicholls 9/4 FAV: 620022: 5 b g Pips Pride - Renata's Ring 6 77
(Auction Ring) Early ldr, rechall after halfway, sn edged left & outpcd by wnr: well bckd from 4/1: likes soft.
4220 **PALACEGATE TOUCH** 3 [8] A Berry 10-8-12 D Allan (7) 10/1: 400003: 10 gr g Petong - Dancing ½ 75$
Chimes (London Bells) Mid-div, kept on for press appr fnl 1f: v stiff task, flattered, quick reapp: see 1139.
3603 **LOVE KISS** 39 [5] W Storey 5-8-12 P Hanagan (5) 200/1: 020064: Rear, ran on thro' btn horses fnl 1f: 1¼ 71$
flattered: best prev run also on soft grnd, interesting back in a h'cap granted similar ground: see 2542.
4012 **FIRST MUSICAL** 17 [11] 4-8-9 D Mernagh 6/1: -05005: Chsd ldrs, no extra appr fnl 1f: see 824. hd 68
4112 **KINAN** 10 [4] 4-9-1 L Newman 3/1: 003606: Chsd ldrs, onepace 2f out: bckd tho' op 7/4: unsuited 1 71
by drop back in trip, better prev over 7f: see 3992, 2431.
4165 **CAUDA EQUINA** 6 [10] 6-9-4 T A O'Sullivan (5) 10/1: 113057: Nvr nr ldrs: op 7/1, quick reapp. nk 73
3335 **GLENROCK** 51 [3] 3-8-11 P Bradley (5) 8/1: 020068: Front rank, wknd qckly 2f out: stablemate 3rd. 1¾ 62
4102 **LANDING CRAFT** 11 [9] 6-8-12 D Nolan (7) 33/1: 200009: Dwelt, nvr in it: stiff task, see 1066, 1007. nk 61$
4106 **BABY BARRY** 10 [1] 3-8-11 Angela Hartley (5) 12/1: 335000: Slow away tho' sn led, hdd appr fnl 1¼ 57
2f & wknd: 10th, op 10/1: see 3335 (fast grnd), 954.
4218 **Distant King** 3 [6] 7-8-12 Clare Roche (5) 100/1: 4220 **Danakim** 3 [7] 3-8-11 G Sparkes (5) 100/1:
12 ran Time 1m 17.6 (7.3) (John W Ford) B Smart Upper Lambourn, Berks

4258

5.0 LEICESTERSHIRE HCAP 3YO+ 0-60 (F) 1m7f177y Soft Inapplicable [57]
£3010 £860 £430 3 yo rec 11lb

4166 **SIRINNDI** 6 [11] B J Curley 6-9-3 (46) G Carter 13/2: 625601: 6 b g Shahrastani - Sinntara (Lashkari) 50
Waited with, gd prog appr str, led bef fnl 1f, pshd out: op 4/1, quick reapp: ex-Irish, '97 wnr at Curragh (mdn)
& Cork (stks), tried hdles: eff at 12f, suited by 2m: acts on fast & hvy grnd, any trk: slipped to a v low mark.
3819 **REVENGE** 24 [15] C G Cox 4-9-12 (55)(bl) M Fenton 100/1: 04-002: 4 b g Saddlers' Hall - Classic 1¾ 56
Heights (Shirley Heights) Bhd ldrs, shaken up appr str, badly hmpd 2f out, switched & rallied: op 33/1:
clrly suited by this step up to 2m on soft grnd: eff in blnks: see 1824.
4340} **FAIRTOTO** 356 [5] D J Wintle 4-9-2 (45) D Sweeney 11/1: -003-3: 4 b g Mtoto - Fairy Feet (Sadler's 1 45
Wells) Held up, prog after halfway, led appr fnl 2f till bef fnl 1f, no extra: jumps fit, earlier won at Stratford
(nov hdle, 2m6.5f, firm grnd, rtd 96h): well btn 3rd fnl '99 start (mdn h'cap, rtd 41a): plcd for Mrs Ramsden
in '98 (mdns, rtd 63): stays 2m on soft grnd, firm over hdles.
3348 **TOP OF THE CHARTS** 50 [1] Mrs M Reveley 4-8-9 (38)(bl) A Culhane 14/1: -50104: In tch, eff & hdwy 2 36
when sltly hmpd 2f out, styd on but unable to chall: op 10/1, clr rem: jumps fit: acts on fast & soft grnd.
4222 **ALDWYCH ARROW** 3 [3] 5-8-8 (37) A Daly 9/2: 006025: Trkd ldrs & ev ch till fdd appr fnl 1f: 5 30
bckd from 6/1, jockey given 1 day careless riding ban: too soon after 4222? see 2836.
941} **ROBBO** 532 [8] 6-10-0 (57)(bl) T Eaves (7) 12/1: 30-6-6: Ran in snatches, nvr troubled ldrs: op 8/1, 2½ 48
top-weight: 99/00 chse wnr at Ayr, Kelso, Newcastle & Carlisle (nov h'caps, 2m4f/2m6.5f, gd & hvy, with or
without blnks, rtd 145c): well btn sole '99 Flat start, last won in '97 at Southwell & W'hampton (2, ltd stks
& amat h'caps, rtd 62): eff at 14f/2m: acts on fast, soft grnd & fibresand, with/without blnks.
3819 **MISTER WEBB** 29 [6] 3-9-5 (59) K Darley 4/1 JT FAV: -50047: Led after 4f till appr fnl 2f, sn btn: 15 40
bckd from 8/1: better run expected over this longer 2m trip tho' has yet to make the frame.
4006 **HASTA LA VISTA** 17 [7] 10-8-12 (41)(vis) T Lucas 6/1: 500038: Early ldr, rechall ent str, wknd qckly. hd 22
949} **ONE LIFE TO LIVE** 890 [2] 7-9-0 (43) T Williams 100/1: 0-40/9: Handy 12f: 2 year abs, back in '97 2½ 22
rnr-up in a h'cap (rtd 51): eff at 10f on fast & gd grnd, has tried a visor, prob better blnkd.

CATTERICK
TUESDAY OCTOBER 3RD   Lefthand, Undulating, V Tight Track

2120} **MRS JODI 470** [4] 4-9-9 (52) P Hanagan (5) 12/1: 0300-0: In tch till appr str: 10th: 99/00 hdles   hd   **31**
wnr at Newcastle, M Rasen (juvs) & Haydock (nov h'cap, 2m/2m1f, fast & soft, rtd 111h): flattered (rtd 63$) in '99.
2516 **OLD HUSH WING 87** [10] 7-8-9 (38) P Fessey 4/1 JT FAV: 000000: Held up, imprvd 6 out till wknd   1¾   **16**
4f out: 11th, bckd from 10/1, stablemate 4th, 3 month abs: see 714.
*3805 **HUTCHIES LADY 30** [14] 8-8-9 (38) D Mernagh (3) 6/1: 00-310: Mid-div for 1m, 12th: unsuited   dist   **0**
by big step up in trip?: see 3805 (11f).
779   **Moonlight Monty 188** [13] 4-9-13 (56) R Winston 16/1:   4095} **Sail On Bun 374** [12] 4-8-13 (42) C Lowther 100/1:
14 ran   Time 3m 52.1 (31.3)   (P Byrne)   B J Curley Newmarket, Suffolk

LONGCHAMP
SUNDAY OCTOBER 1ST   Righthand, Stiff, Galloping Track

Official Going   GOOD.

4259   **12.55 GR 2 PRIX DU ROND POINT 3YO+**   **1m**   **Good**
£38425   £15370   £7685   £3842   3 yo rec 4 lb

3370 **KABOOL 50** Saeed bin Suroor 5-9-1 L Dettori 47/10: 4-4431: 5 b h Groom Dancer - Sheroog (Shareef   **118**
Dancer) Led, under press & narrowly hdd ent fnl 1f, rallied gamely to regain lead fnl 100y: 7 wk abs: plcd
in Gr 1 & 2 company in '99 (rtd 122): '98 wnr at Maison Lafitte (Gr 3) & Deauville (Gr 2, rtd 118, N Clement):
eff at 1m/10f on fast & hvy grnd, any trk: runs well fresh: tough & smart entire.
3847 **KINGSALSA 28** A Fabre 4-9-1 O Peslier 4/5 FAV: 213322: 4 b c Kingmambo - Caretta (Caro)   snk   **117**
Waited on, imprvd appr str, narrow lead ent fnl 1f, sn rdn, hdd fnl 100y: ultra consistent tho' prob needs
to arrive as late as possible: see 1619.
3847 **SUGARFOOT 28** N Tinkler 6-9-1 W Ryan 123/10: 510053: 6 ch h Thatching - Norpella (Northfields)   ¾   **115**
Keen, chsd ldrs, eff over 2f out, kept on & not btn far: not far off best tho' ideally suited by soft: see 3847, 2675.
3875 **BARATHEA GUEST 24** M R Channon 3-8-11 Craig Williams 115/10: 405554: Patiently rdn, kept on   hd   **115**
well appr fnl 1f, nvr nr to chall: back to form, fnl only 1L: see 950.
*3717 **PENNYS GOLD 37** 3-8-8 T Thulliez 5/2: 152115: In tch, rdn appr fnl 1f, no impress on ldrs: btr 3717.   1   **110**
3069 **DANZIGAWAY 63** 4-8-11 O Doleuze 182/10: 41-206: Al towards rear: 7 wk abs, see 10 (hvy).   2½   **105**
3641 **CRIMSON TIDE 21** 6-9-1 M Hills 325/10: 0/3507: Chsd wnr till fdd appr fnl 1f: see 3291.   3   **104**
8 ran   Time 1m 36.4   (Godolphin)   Saeed bin Suroor Newmarket

4260   **2.00 GR 1 PRIX MARCEL BOUSSAC 2YO**   **1m**   **Good**
£76849   £30740   £15370   £7685

-- **AMONITA** P Bary 2-8-11 T Jarnet 115/10: -211: 2 b f Anabaa - Spectacular Joke (Spectacular Bid)   **113**
Trkd ldrs, niggled ent fnl 2f, strong run & burst thro' to lead ins last, going away: earlier won here at
Longchamp (C/D, made all): eff at 1m, shld stay at least 10f next term: acts on gd grnd, stiff/gall trk:
v useful, progressive filly with a turn of foot: Classic prospect for next term.
*3876 **KARASTA 24** Sir Michael Stoute 2-8-11 J Murtagh 14/10 FAV: 112: 2 b f Lake Coniston - Karliyka   2   **107**
(Last Tycoon) Towards rear, slipped appr str, gd prog under press 2f out, not pace of wnr towards fin:
gd eff in the circumstances, met a potentially high-class filly: remains a filly to follow next term.
3934 **CHOC ICE 20** R Collet 2-8-11 G Mosse 414/10: 061333: 2 b f Kahyasi - Sherkiya (Goldneyev)   nk   **107**
Chsd ldrs, led appr fnl 1f, rdn & hdd ins last, onepace: prev won in the provinces: eff at 1m on fast & gd/soft.
3845 **LA VIDA LOCA 28** A P O'Brien 2-8-11 M J Kinane 274/10: 521544: Mid-div, prog to chall appr fnl   1½   **104**
1f, kept on onepace: Irish raider, imprvd stepped up to 1m & even further will suit: see 3845.
-- **BORN SOMETHING** 2-8-11 O Doleuze 17/1: -15: Rear, gd prog 2f out, no extra under press dist: hd   **104**
earlier won debut at Chantilly (1m, gd grnd): with Mme C Head.
*3722 **ASCENSION 35** 2-8-11 Craig Williams 31/10: -1116: Well plcd & w ch till fdd appr fnl 1f: ¾   **102**
lost unbtn record over this longer 1m trip, return to 7f will suit for now: btr 3722 (7f, gd/soft).
3934 **WINTER SOLSTICE 20** 2-8-11 Pat Eddery 72/10cp: -127: Al towards rear: stable-mate 5th: see 3934.   nse   **102**
*3934 **GREEN MINSTREL 20** 2-8-11 O Peslier 3/1: -118: Nvr nr ldrs: up in grade after 3934.   nse   **102**
-- **PROVE** 2-8-11 T Thulliez 72/10cp: -19: Led till appr fnl 1f, sn btn: eased: earlier C/D wnr (1m, g/s).   2½   **98**
3876 **BRING PLENTY 24** 2-8-11 (BL) L Dettori 17/1: 013240: Chsd ldrs 6f, 10th: tried blnks: btr 3876.   2   **94**
10 ran   Time 1m 36.3   (Mme P de Moussac)   P Bary France

4261   **2.35 GR 1 PRIX DE L'ABBAYE 2YO**   **5f**   **Good**
£48031   £19212   £9606   £4803   2 yo rec 18lb

*3923 **NAMID 22** J Oxx 4-9-11 J Murtagh 52/10: -31111: 4 b c Indian Ridge - Dawnsio (Tate Gallery)   **125**
Chsd ldrs, led appr fnl 1f, pushed out, rdly: 4-timer landed, earlier won at Cork (List), Then Curragh, then
defied a 15 wk abs due to knee surgery to win at Leopardstown (Gr 3's): plcd both '99 starts (rtd 107): eff
at 5/6f, gets 7f: acts on gd & hvy, any trk: goes well fresh: v progressive & high-class, Champion sprinter.
*3900 **SUPERSTAR LEO 22** W J Haggas 2-8-4 M Hills 41/10: 111212: 2 b f College Chapel - Council Rock   1½   **117**
(General Assembly) Led after 1f till appr fnl 1f, kept on: clr of rem & a cracking run from this smart/u tough 2yo.
*3784 **PIPALONG 29** T D Easterby 4-9-8 K Darley 61/10: 103313: 4 b f Pips Pride - Limpopo (Green Desert)   3   **109**
Chsd ldrs, eff 2f out, unable to qckn: capable of better, suited by 6f as in 3784.
3874 **PERRYSTON VIEW 24** J A Glover 8-9-11 (bl) J Reid 60/1: 105564: Led early, cl-up till fdd fnl 1f: 1½   **108**
not disgraced in the highest grade: see 1566 (Gr 2).
*3843 **IRON MASK 32** 2-8-7 O Doleuze 46/10: 222115: Struggled to go pace till ran on ins last: v useful   nk   **108**
2yo, suited by 5.5f (will get further): see 3843.
2065 **SELTITUDE 103** 4-9-8 G Mosse 36/1: -33006: In tch, eff after halfway, no impress: see 1320.   1½   **102**
3598 **BERTOLINI 38** 4-9-11 (bl) L Dettori 2/1 FAV: -23627: Chsd ldrs, btn appr fnl 1f: not his form, see 1766.   1   **102**
4052 **KHASAYL 16** 3-9-8 C Asmussen 166/10: 1-1028: Al bhd: see 4052.   snk   **99**
2615 **PRIMO VALENTINO 80** 3-9-11 Pat Eddery 111/10: 1-0649: Handy till 2f out: 11 wk abs, btr 2615.   2½   **96**
3923 **WATCHING 22** 3-9-11 R Hughes 431/10: 014450: Early pace, btn halfway: 10th, had a long season.   1   **93**
11 ran   Time 55.1   (Lady Clague)   J Oxx Currabeg, Co Kildare

1314

4262   **3.20 GR 1 PRIX DE L'ARC DE TRIOMPHE 3YO+   1m4f   Good**
£576369   £230548   £115224   £57637   3 yo   rec 8 lb

*3929   **SINNDAR** 21 J Oxx 3-8-11 J Murtagh 8/5cp: 211111: 3 b c Grand Lodge - Sinntara (Lashkari)   **134**
Early ldr, trkd stablemate till went on appr str, sn drvn, styd on v strongly for press: earlier won at
Leopardstown (Gr 3) & both the English & Irish (by 9L) Derbys: dual '99 wnr at The Curragh (incl Gr 1, rtd
107): eff at 12f, will stay 14f: acts on fast & soft grnd, any trk: eff with/without t-strap: runs v well
fresh: tough, genuine, top-class colt: has progressed with every run & is the outstanding 3yo of 2000.

3928   **EGYPTBAND** 21 Mme C Head 3-8-8 O Doleuze 251/10: 1-1132: 3 b f Dixieland Band - Egyptown (Top   1½   **127**
Ville) Waited with, taken wide, gd hdwy on bit, asked for eff appr 1f out, styd on well, nrst fin: pulled clr of
3rd & this was a high-class performance from this imprvg filly, set a fair bit to do: acts on gd & gd/soft grnd:
sure to win Group races & one to keep on your side if kept in training: see 1901.

*3928   **VOLVORETA** 21 C Lerner 3-8-8 O Peslier 86/10: 1-1213: 3 ch f Suave Dancer - Robertiya (Don   3   **122**
Roberto) Trkd ldrs, rdn to press wnr briefly appr fnl 1f, onepace: fine run but had this nk bhd in 3928.

*3927   **MONTJEU** 21 J E Hammond 4-9-5 M J Kinane 4/5 FAV: -11114: 3 b c, Wide, towards rear, slipped 5f out,   2½   **121**
imprvd appr str, drvn appr fnl 1f, unable to qckn: failed to display usual devastating turn of foot: rtd 136
when wng this race last term: grnd prob faster than ideal (returned home stiff): see 3927.

*4053   **HIGHTORI** 15 3-8-11 G Mosse 57/1: 511-15: Chsd ldrs, rdn 2f out, same pace: fine run, big step   nk   **121**
up in grade & longer trip: v smart colt: see 4053 (Gr 3 at 10f).

*3849   **SAMUM** 28 3-8-11 A Starke 15/2: -11116: Bhd, rdn appr fnl 2f, went past btn horses, nvr a threat: 1½   **119**
German colt, lost unbtn record, 1st attempt on grnd faster than soft: high-class on testing grnd, see 3849 (v soft).

3723   **DARING MISS** 35 4-9-2 C Soumillon 49/1: 411227: Mid-div, feeling pace appr str, no danger.   ½   **115**

*3723   **RUSSIAN HOPE** 35 5-9-5 T Jarnet 467/10: -11418: Handy till fdd ent str: stiffish task, not disgraced.   ½   **117**

3374   **HESIODE** 47 3-8-11 (bl) L Dettori 62/1: 130339: Al bhd: 7 wk abs, highly tried.   10   **105**

3929   **RAYPOUR** 21 3-8-11 N G McCullagh 8/5cp: 146160: Sn set gd pace for stablemate, hdd appr str/btn.   8   **96**
10 ran   Time 2m 25.8   (H H Aga Khan)   J Oxx Curragbeg, Co Kildare

4263   **4.05 GR 1 PRIX DE L'OPERA 3YO FILLIES   1m2f   Good**
£67243   £26898   £13449   £6724   3 yo   rec 4 lb

*3564   **PETRUSHKA** 39 Sir Michael Stoute 3-8-12 J Murtagh 9/10 FAV: 134111: 3 ch f Unfuwain - Ballet Shoes   **121**
(Ela Mana Mou) Twrds rear, swtchd & hdwy 2f out, qckd to lead ins last, rdn out: hat-trick landed: earlier won
at Newmarket (reapp, Gr 3), The Curragh (Gr 1 Irish Oaks, by 5½L) & York (Gr 1 Yorkshire Oaks), also 3rd in the
1000 Guineas: sn won juv start, al prmnt (mdn): suited by 10/12f & may stay further: acts on firm, good/
soft & a gall trk: top-class filly with a fine turn of foot: heads for the Breeders Cup.

3928   **REVE DOSCAR** 21 Mme M Bollack Badel 3-8-12 L Dettori 5/2: 214322: 3 gr f Highest Honor - Numidie   ¾   **119**
(Baillamont) Chsd ldrs, hdwy to chall over 1f out, not pace of wnr well ins last: clr rem: still imprvg & this
was a career best eff: may apprec a return to 12f: only 1½L bhd the subs Arc 3rd in 3928: Japan Cup hopeful.

3151   **LADY UPSTAGE** 57 B W Hills 3-8-12 M Hills 45/1: 125103: 3 b f Alzao - She's The Tops (Shernazar)   2½   **115**
Trkd ldr, went on 2f out, hdd just ins last, onepace: gd run after 8 wk abs: apprec return to Gr 2/3: see 3151.

*3211   **HIDALGUIA** 57 J de Roualle 3-8-12 G Mosse 131/10: 123014: Mid-div, gd hdwy to chse ldrs appr   1½   **112**
fnl 1f, no extra well ins last: 8 wk abs & ran to best: win another Gr 3: see 3211.

*3546   **DI MOI OUI** 43 3-8-12 T Thulliez 77/10: 410115: Twrds rear, rdn & ran on well fnl 2f nvr nr to chall: 2   **109**
6 wks abs: tough & consistent, worth a try over further now: see 3546.

--   **AUDACIEUSE** 3-8-12 T Jarnet 25/1: 156516: Bhd, gd late hdwy, nvr nrr: recent C/D wnr (Listed).   1½   **106**

--   **AIRLINE** 3-8-12 O Peslier 138/10: -35117: Rear, eff over 1f out, sn btn: recent Chantilly List wnr (1m).   nse   **106**

*2224   **AMERICA** 98 3-8-12 O Doleuze 158/10: 116108: Nvr a factor: 6 wk abs: unplcd since 2224 (12f).   1½   **103**

4064   **DIAMOND WHITE** 11 5-9-2 K Darley 341/10: 545339: Prom, eff appr fnl 2f, wknd qckly appr fnl 1f: 4   **97**
top-weight: won this race last year on hvy grnd: see 4064.
13 ran   Time 2m 20.0   (Highclere Thoro'bred Racing Ltd)   Sir Michael Stoute Newmarket

4264   **4.40 GR 1 PRIX DU CADRAN 4YO+   2m4f   Good**
£48031   £19212   £9606   £4803

3877   **SAN SEBASTIAN** 24 J L Dunlop 6-9-2 (bl) D Bonilla 122/10: 464361: 6 ch g Niniski - Top Of The League   **120**
(High Top) Trkd ldrs, chall 2f out, rdn into lead ins last, drvn out: creditable efforts in top-class staying races
prev this term: '99 wnr for M J Grassick at R Ascot (2m6f Queen Alexandra stks), also rnr-up in a Gr 1: '98 wnr
at Clonmel, Gowran & R Ascot (h'caps): eff at 2m, relishes extreme distances & suited by 2m4f/2m6f: acts on firm,
likes good & hvy grnd: best in blnks: a deserved Group win for this tough, smart out-&-out stayer.

3877   **PERSIAN PUNCH** 24 D R C Elsworth 7-9-2 R Hughes 138/10: 165132: 7 ch g Persian Heights - Rum Cay   ½   **119**
(Our Native) Led & sn clr, increased pace 6f out, drvn & collared ins last, held cl-home: bold front-running eff,
clearly stays 2m4f v well but has nvr won beyond 2m: tough & game stayer, reportedly fin distressed here.

*3538   **ROYAL REBEL** 40 M Johnston 4-9-2 (bl) M J Kinane 24/10: 122113: 4 b g Robellino - Greenvera (Riverman)¾   **118**
Chsd ldrs, rdn & styd on well appr fnl 1f, despite jockey dropping whip, not btn far: eff at 2m/2m4f: see 3538.

-3877   **CHURLISH CHARM** 24 R Hannon 5-9-2 J Reid 64/10: 236124: In tch, ran on well fnl 2f, no threat: snk   **118**
eff at 2m, stays 2m2f/2m4f: likes a bit of cut in the grnd: see 3877, 3751.

+3877   **ENZELI** 24 5-9-2 (bl) J Murtagh 9/4 FAVcp: 4-2015: Trkd wnr, ev ch till unable to qckn appr fnl   shd   **118**
1f: top-class stayer, a shade below best here: ahead of today's 1st, 2nd & 4th in 3877.

3851   **TAJOUN** 26 6-9-2 G Mosse 4/5 FAVcp: 2-1436: Late hdwy from rear, no dngr: see 3851.   shd   **118**

3851   **LE TINTORET** 26 7-9-2 T Jarnet 196/10: 102547: Al twrds rear: see 3851, 1456.   2½   **115**

3877   **THREE CHEERS** 24 6-9-2 (bl) L Dettori 88/10: 120358: In tch, fdd fnl 2f: highly tried: see 3877.   ¾   **114**
9 ran   Time 4m 14.1   (Mrs Michael Watt)   J L Dunlop Arundel, W Sussex

DORTMUND SUNDAY OCTOBER 1ST --

Official Going HEAVY

4265 3.50 GR 3 GERMAN ST LEGER 3YO 1m6f Heavy
£38710 £15484 £7742

*3930 **MOONLADY** 21 H Remmert 3-8-12 K Woodburn : 11: 3 b f Platini - Midnight Fever (Sure Blade) 108
Cl-up, went on 4f out, clr appr fnl 1f, rdn out: recent Hannover wnr (Gr 3): eff at 12/14f on gd & hvy: smart.
-- **AESKULAP** H Blume 3-9-2 A Boschert : 2: 3 b c Acatenango - Aerope (Celestial Storm) 4 106
Twrds rear, rdn to imprv appr fnl 2f, styd on but no threat to wnr: stays 14f on hvy grnd.
3848 **SHUWAIB** 28 M R Channon 3-9-2 R Havlin : 13143: 3 b c Polish Precedent - Ajab Alzamaan (Rainbow 1 104
Quest) Chsd ldrs, hdwy appr fnl 2f, rdn/no extra over 1f out: Brit raider, ran to best: handles hvy: see 3848.
8 ran Time 3m 19.29 (Gary A Tanaka) H Remmert Germany

CORK SUNDAY OCTOBER 1ST --

Official Going SOFT

4266 3.40 GR 3 CONCORDE STKS 3YO+ 7f Soft
£32500 £9500 £4500 3 yo rec 2 lb

3598 **BERNSTEIN** 38 A P O'Brien 3-8-12 J A Heffernan 5/1: 5-0101: 3 b c Storm Cat - La Affirmed (Affirmed) 115
Prom, eff over 1f out, ran on strongly to lead cl-home, drvn out: visor omitted: prev won at Ascot (val Shergar
Cup Sprint), looked not to stay 1m when well btn in the 2000 Guineas: '99 wnr at The Curragh, (2, incl Gr 3,
rtd 117): v eff at 6/7f, may reportedly try 1m again next time: acts on fast & soft: runs well fresh: v smart.
3397} **COBOURG LODGE** 414 J T Gorman 4-9-0 E Ahern 12/1: 034462: 4 b g Unblest - Rachel Pringle (Doulab)hd 114
Cl-up, hdwy to lead over 1f out, hdd cl-home: career best run, 6th in a List race last time: eff at 7f on soft.
3373 **CONORMARA** 49 D Hanley 3-8-12 F M Berry 8/1: 011523: 3 b c Carr De Naskra - Teeming Shore 2½ 109
(L'Emigrant) Mid-div, imprvd 2f out, chall dist, onepcd ins last: 7 wk abs: eff at 6/7f on gd & soft: see 3373.
3995 **LATE NIGHT OUT** 15 W Jarvis 5-9-0 M Tebbutt 11/2: 012107: Nvr dngrs, fin 7th: twice below 3600 (firm). 0
11 ran Time 1m 30.0 (M Tabor) A P O'Brien Ballydoyle, Co Tipperary

LINGFIELD (Mixed) WEDNESDAY OCTOBER 4TH Lefthand, Sharp, Undulating Track

Official Going TURF - SOFT, AW - Standard Stalls: Turf - Far Side, AW: 1m - Outside, 12f - Inside.

4267 1.30 EBF MDN DIV I 2YO (D) 7f str Soft 100 -04 Slow
£3542 £1090 £545 £272 Raced centre - stands side

-- **FULLY INVESTED** [4] H R A Cecil 2-8-9 T Quinn 5/4 FAV: 1: 2 b f Irish River - Shirley Valentine 88+
(Shirley Heights) Dwelt, sn trckd ldrs, quickened to lead under hands & heels riding to lead ins last, styd on well:
hvly bckd, op 2/1: Apr foal, half sister to smart 10f/14f wnr Memorise: dam a 12f wnr: eff at 7f, looks sure to
apprec mid-dists in time: acts on soft grnd & a sharp/undul trk: runs well fresh: well regarded, rate more highly.
3799 **MODRIK** 31 [1] R W Armstrong 2-9-0 R Hills 7/2: -0342: 2 ch c Dixieland Band - Seattle Summer (Seattle 1¾ 88
Slew) Al prom, rdn & led over 1f out, hdd ins last, not pace of wnr: handles fast & soft grnd: win a race.
4036 **TOKEN** 16 [18] M P Tregoning 2-9-0 W Supple 25/1: -043: 2 b c Mark Of Esteem - Kindergarten 2 85
(Trempolino) Sn led stands rail, hdd over 1f out, kept on onepace: improved on prev effs: eff at 7f, return
to 1m shld suit: handles soft grnd: shown enough to win similar: see 3333.
-- **PARK HALL** [15] C E Brittain 2-9-0 R Hughes 25/1: 4: Prom, onepace fnl 2f: op 12/1: Saddlers ½ 84
Hall colt, Jan foal: half brother to 2 5f juv wnrs: dam a mdn: eff at 7f, 1m+ suit: pleasing debut.
-- **HAYLEYS AFFAIR** [8] J A J Fortune 10/1: 5: Dwelt, sn chsd ldrs, onepace/held fnl 2f: op 16/1: 2½ 75
Night Shift filly, Feb foal: cost 10,000 gns: half sister to a juv 1m wnr: dam unrcd: with P Harris.
3867 **AMIGO** 27 [3] 2-9-0 B Marcus 33/1: 06: Prom till over 1f out: see 3867. 1¾ 78
3187 **ARTIFACT** 58 [6] 2-8-9 L Newman (3) 25/1: 307: Prom 5f: see 3096 (6f, fast). 3 69$
3650 **JAMIE MY BOY** 39 [5] 2-9-0 N Callan (3) 33/1: 48: Chsd ldrs 5f: see 3650. hd 73
-- **DETACHING** [10] 2-8-9 M Hills 16/1: 9: Towards rear, nvr a factor: Thatching filly, Feb foal, 7 58
cheaply bought: half sister to an Irish 1m wnr & 7f/10f wnr Golconda: dam only mod: prob need 1m+ in time.
-- **ANONYMITY** [10] 2-9-0 Pat Eddery 8/1: 0: In tch, outpcd fnl 3f: 10th: op 4/1: Exit To Nowhere 3½ 58
colt, Feb foal, a 1st foal: sire a top-class miler: with Sir M Stoute.
-- **FOLAANN** [12] 2-9-0 P Robinson 5/1: 0: In tch 4f: 11th: op 3/1: Pennekamp colt, Mar first foal, 3 54
cost 82,000 gns: dam unrcd, tho' well related: sire a top class juvenile/miler: with M Jarvis.
-- **PERSEUS WAY** [14] 2-9-0 A Nicholls 33/1: 0: Prom 5f: 12th: Bering colt, May foal, cost nk 53
16,500 gns: dam unrcd: sire top-class 12f performer: with P Chamings.
-- **Alfalfa** [11] 2-9-0 S Carson (3) 25/1: -- **Taffrail** [2] 2-9-0 K Darley 16/1:
-- **Cashdown** [7] 2-9-0 J Lowe 25/1:
15 ran Time 1m 27.7 (7.3) (K Abdulla) H R A Cecil Newmarket, Suffolk

4268 2.00 EBF MDN DIV II 2YO (D) 7f str Soft 100 -13 Slow
£3542 £1090 £545 £272 Raced centre - far side

-- **PAIYDA** [18] E A L Dunlop 2-8-9 J Reid 25/1: 1: 2 b f Danehill - Meadow Pipit (Meadowlake) 88+
Chsd ldrs, smooth prog to lead over 1f out, readily asserted under hands & heels riding fnl 1f: op 20/1: Jan
foal, sister to a 2m hdle wnr: dam a 7f/10f wnr as a 4yo: eff at 7f, looks sure to apprec 1m+: acts on a
sharp/undul trk & runs well fresh: decisive wnr, type to go on & win more races.
-- **YORKSHIRE ROSE** [8] H R A Cecil 2-8-9 T Quinn 9/4 FAV: 2: 2 b f Sadler's Wells - Bush Rose 2½ 82+
(Rainbow Quest) Held up, switched & styd on well under hands & heels riding from over 1f out, no threat to wnr:
nicely bckd tho' op 6/4: Feb first foal, cost 80,000 gns: dam unrcd, sire top-class 1m/12f performer: eff at
7f, looks sure to relish mid-dists next term: acts on soft grnd: sure to win races over further.

LINGFIELD (Mixed) **WEDNESDAY OCTOBER 4TH** **Lefthand, Sharp, Undulating Track**

3866 **ELSAAMRI 27** [7] M P Tregoning 2-9-0 R Hills 9/1: 43: 2 b c Silver Hawk - Muhbubh (Blushing Groom) *1* **86**
Chsd ldrs, ev ch over 1f out, not pace of wnr ins last: op 6/1: acts on soft: going the right way after intro.
-- **COMO** [13] R Charlton 2-8-9 J Fortune 14/1: 4: Chsd ldrs, kept on onepace fnl 2f: op 12/1: *1¼* **79**
Cozzene filly, Mar foal: dam a 1m wnr abroad: sire a high-class 1m wnr: encouraging intro.
-- **PARA GLIDER** [12] 2-9-0 M Hills 33/1: 5: Chsd ldrs, onepace fnl 2f: Jeune Honne colt, Mar foal, *½* **83**
cost 20,000 gns: half brother to a 10/12f wnr: dam unrcd: sire high-class 1m/9f wnr abroad: sure to relish 1m+.
-- **HERETIC** [2] 2-9-0 D Harrison 12/1: 6: Dwelt, mod late hdwy, nvr threat to ldrs: op 10/1: Bishop *2½* **79**
Of Cashel colt: Apr foal, half brother to tough/smart 7f performer Warningford: dam a 7f/1m wnr: improve.
-- **COVENT GARDEN** [14] 2-9-0 Pat Eddery 9/1: 7: Led 1f, handy till rdn/btn when hmpd over 1f out: *1* **78**
mkt drifter, op 4/1: Sadler's Wells colt, Apr foal: half brother to wnrs btwn 1m/12f: dam unrcd: sire top-class 1m/12f performer: likely to relish mid-dists next term & shld improve for Sir M Stoute.
-- **TE QUIERO** [16] 2-9-0 D Holland 33/1: 8: Led after 1f till over 1f out, sn btn: Bering colt, Mar foal, *½* **77**
cost 42,000 gns: dam a wnr abroad, sire a top-class 12f performer: mid-dists will suit: with Miss G Kelleway.
4020 **VILLA CARLOTTA 18** [15] 2-8-9 K Darley 5/1: 39: Trkd ldrs, btn 2f out: op 8/1: btr 4020 (gd). *nk* **71**
3969 **FLY WITH ME 20** [5] 2-9-0 T Williams 5/1: 60: Dwelt, held up, eff halfway, no impress: 10th: *½* **75**
nicely bckd, op 12/1: more expected after debut in 3969.
-- **TRAVEL TARDIA** [6] 2-9-0 P Robinson 33/1: 0: Mid-div, btn 2f out: 11th: Petardia colt, cost *1½* **73**
8,500 gns as a 2yo: first foal: dam unrcd, sire a high-class miler: with I Wood.
3980 **GOLFAGENT 19** [10] 2-9-0 Paul Eddery 33/1: -00: Trkd ldrs 5f: 12th: bhd on debut prev. *4* **67$**
-- **SUNGIO** [9] 2-9-0 G Sparkes (7) 33/1: 60: Al towards rear: well btn on debut in Italy prev. *¾* **66**
-- **SATYR** [3] 2-9-0 R Hughes 9/1: 0: Held up, btn 3f out: 15th: op 6/1: Pursuit Of Love colt, Feb *5* **56**
first foal: dam a 10f wnr: 1m+ shld suit in time, with R Hannon.
4035 **Miss Polly 16** [4] 2-8-9 I Mongan (5) 33/1: -- **Rodoslovnaya** [11] 2-8-9 W Ryan 25/1:
-- **Golden Brief** [17] 2-9-0 N Callan 33/1: -- **Pas De Surprise** [1] 2-9-0 J Quinn 33/1:
18 ran Time 1m 14.2 (5.4) (Mohammed Ali) E A L Dunlop Newmarket, Suffolk

4269 **2.30 BERKELEY NURSERY HCAP 2YO 0-85 (D) 6f Soft 100 -12 Slow [85]**
£4010 £1234 £617 £308 Majority racing towards centre favoured.

*3812 **TICKLE 31** [6] P J Makin 2-9-2 (73) S Sanders 7/1: -02211: 2 b f Primo Dominie - Funny Choice **79**
(Commanche Run) Chsd ldrs, led over 1f out, held on well ins last, drvn out: op 8/1, h'cap bow: earlier scored at York (auct mdn): eff at 6f, shld stay further: acts on fast, soft & a gall or sharp/undul trk: tough & consistent.
3638 **CAPTAIN GIBSON 39** [14] D J S ffrench Davis 2-8-11 (68) T Quinn 12/1: -50062: 2 b g Beveled - Little *1* **71**
Egret (Carwhite) Held up rear, prog fnl 3f despited hanging badly left, chall ins last, onepace nr fin: op 14/1: confirmed improvement of latest: handles gd & soft: wld have gone v close without steering problems: see 3638.
*4090 **CHURCH MICE 12** [2] M L W Bell 2-9-4 (75)(vis) M Fenton 6/1: 536413: 2 br f Petardia - Negria (Al *1½* **75**
Hareb) Dwelt, held up, rdn & kept on fnl 2f, not pace to chall: gd run: see 4090.
2797 **MISS VERITY 75** [12] H Akbary 2-8-12 (69) J Stack 14/1: -62124: Handy, led over 3f out till over 1f *hd* **68**
out, no extra ins last: 11 wk abs: stays a sharp 6f: acts on fast, soft & fibresand: see 2797, 2120 (AW).
4030 **YETTI 16** [9] 2-8-13 (70) C Rutter 16/1: 225365: Chsd ldrs, onepace fnl 2f: acts on firm & soft. *1½* **66**
4098 **MADRASEE 12** [15] 2-9-0 (71) J Quinn 14/1: 032045: Prom, onepace fnl 2f: ddhtd for 5th: op *dht* **67**
12/1: handles firm & soft grnd: remains a mdn: see 2711.
4095 **EMPRESS OF AUSTRIA 12** [13] 2-8-6 (63)(t) D Holland 14/1: 3067: Trkd ldrs, rdn/onepace fnl 2f. *shd* **59**
-4170 **BEE KING 7** [16] 2-8-4 (61) Craig Williams 4/1 FAV: 003328: Prom till over 1f out: bckd: btr 4170. *¾* **56**
4096 **WINTER DOLPHIN 12** [20] 2-8-5 (62) I Mongan (3) 12/1: 0669: Prom, rdn/btn over 1f out: op 10/1. *2½* **52**
3862 **MILLENNIUM MAGIC 28** [18] 2-9-5 (76) S W Kelly (3) 20/1: 200000: Prom, outpcd from halfway: 10th. *1½* **63**
4034 **COCCOLONA 16** [1] 2-8-11 (68) J Reid 16/1: 4060: Held up, nvr factor: 11th: op 20/1, h'cap bow. *nk* **54**
4090 **FLYING TURK 12** [10] 2-9-4 (75) Pat Eddery 12/1: 044660: Mid-div at best: 12th: op 10/1: see 3268. *2½* **56**
4068 **DEFINITE GUEST 14** [17] 2-8-11 (68) K Darley 14/1: 6040: Led till over 3f out, sn btn: 16th: op 10/1. **0**
4063 **ST ANTIM 14** [4] 2-9-7 (78) J Fanning 14/1: 15P: Bhd/p.u. & dismounted 2f out: broke blood vessel. **0**
4095 **Troubleshooter 12** [19] 2-9-1 (72)(bl) Martin Dwyer 20/1: 4096 **Bravura 12** [5] 2-8-3 (60) P Doe 12/1:
4022 **Achilles Sun 18** [11] 2-8-8 (65) N Callan 25/1: 3942 **Moonlight Dancer 21** [7] 2-9-1 (72) L Newman (3) 16/1:
3912 **Law Breaker 23** [8] 2-8-5 (62) D O'Donohoe 12/1:
19 ran Time 1m 15.5 (6.7) (Mrs Derek Strauss) P J Makin Ogbourne Maisey, Wilts

4270 **3.00 COME RACING HCAP 3YO 0-75 (E) 6f Soft 100 +10 Fast [81]**
£3377 £965 £482 Majority racing centre/far side favoured

3908 **TOLDYA 25** [12] M Kettle 3-8-9 (62) N Callan 8/1: 213241: 3 b f Beveled - Run Amber Run (Run The **67**
Gantlet) Chsd ldrs, rdn/led over 1f out, styd on well, rdn out: best time of day: earlier scored at Lingfield (AW h'cap, rtd 62a): unplcd in '99 (rtd 51, rnr-up on sand, rtd 50a, mdn): eff at 5/6f: acts on both AWs, firm & soft grnd: loves a sharp trk: eff with/without blnks: tough & consistent filly.
3698 **CRYFIELD 37** [6] N Tinkler 3-8-8 (61)(VIS) P Robinson 11/1: 310062: 3 b g Efisio - Ciboure (Norwick) *1½* **62**
Held up, styd on for press fnl 2f, not reach wnr: gd run in 1st time visor: acts on fast, soft & fbrsnd: see 2243.
4120 **CAPE COAST 10** [3] N P Littmoden 3-9-3 (70) K Darley 6/1: 211263: 3 b g Common Grounds - Strike It *1* **69**
Rich (Rheingold) Dwelt/bhd, kept on well for press fnl 2f, nrst fin: best at 7f: see 4080, 5854 (7f).
4037 **RISKY REEF 16** [2] I A Balding 3-8-12 (65) M Hills 25/1: -45504: Held up, styd on onepace fnl 2f: *shd* **64**
handles fibresand, gd & soft grnd: see 549 (AW).
4120 **QUEEN OF THE MAY 10** [11] 3-9-4 (71) Craig Williams 10/1: 400605: Prom, onepace/held fnl 1f: *1* **68**
op 8/1: handles firm, soft & equitrack: on a fair mark: see 1098.
3401 **OCEAN RAIN 49** [7] 3-9-2 (69)(BL) J Reid 14/1: 040346: Chsd ldrs, no impress fnl 1f: blnks, 7 wk abs. *½* **65**
4185 **LABRETT 6** [19] 3-9-5 (72)(bl) D R McCabe 12/1: 140007: Started slowly & bhd stands side, stdy hdwy *1* **66+**
from halfway & kept on fnl 2f, no ch with ldrs far side: op 10/1, quick reapp: found himself on the wrong side here, prob worth another look in a similar contest: see 4037, 3208.
4065 **FIRST VENTURE 14** [18] 3-8-5 (58)(vis) L Newman (3) 20/1: 044208: Led stands side till over 2f out, fdd. *1½* **49**
4069 **IMPERIALIST 14** [13] 3-9-7 (74)(bl) R Hughes 12/1: 200049: Dwelt,mid-div, nvr pace to chall: op 10/1. *½* **64**
3243 **MARNIE 56** [1] 3-8-6 (59) P Doe 20/1: 022100: Chsd ldrs 5f: 10th: abs: btr 2896 (mdn h'cap, firm). *2* **45**
4120 **DOCTOR DENNIS 10** [16] 3-9-3 (70) Pat Eddery 4/1 FAV: 224420: Rdn/rear halfway, no impress: 11th: *¾* **55**
well bckd from 6/1 & clearly better expected.
4037 **LAKELAND PADDY 16** [4] 3-9-5 (72) D Sweeney 16/1: 410000: Mid-div at best: 12th: btr 1783 (fast, mdn). *½* **56**
4136 **BAJAN BELLE 10** [5] 3-8-4 (57) J Fanning 16/1: 022500: Prom, hung right & rdn/led over 2f out, hdd **0**
over 1f out & sn btn: 15th: see 3671, 1138.
4185 **ABSENT FRIENDS 6** [20] 3-8-6 (59) D O'Donohoe 11/2: 400530: Prom stands side 4f: 18th: op 8/1. **0**

LINGFIELD (Mixed)   WEDNESDAY OCTOBER 4TH   Lefthand, Sharp, Undulating Track

4120 **Executive Ghost** 10 [8] 3-8-13 (66) T Quinn 33/1:
4185 **Pacific Place** 6 [17] 3-8-4 (57) F Norton 25/1:
3689 **Kinsman** 37 [9] 3-9-1 (68)(vis) M Henry 16/1:
19 ran   Time 1m 14.2 (5.4)   (G Montgomery)

3280 **Stoney Garnett** 54 [14] 3-9-0 (67) A Daly 25/1:
4185 **Almashrouk** 6 [10] 3-8-9 (62) J Quinn 25/1:

M Kettle Blewbury, Oxon

4271   3.30 TOTE TRIFECTA HCAP 3YO+ 0-80 (D)   1m4f aw   Standard   Inapplicable   [80]
£7312   £2250   £1125   £562   3 yo rec 8 lb

*4101 **THE GREEN GREY** 12 [4] L Montague Hall 6-9-5 (71) A Clark 3/1 FAV: 254311: 6 gr g Environment Friend **79a** - Pea Green (Try My Best) Chsd ldrs, led over 2f out, rdn clr over 1f out, styd on strongly fnl 1f & eased nr fin: op 5/2: earlier won at Windsor (2, h'caps, rtd 73 at best) & here at Lingfield (C/D class stks): lightly rcd in '99 (rtd 66a & 54): '98 wnr at Yarmouth (h'cap), Bath, Brighton (clmr, W Muir), Kempton & Lingfield (h'caps, rtd 71 & 59a, D Morris): eff at 10/12f, stays 14f: acts on firm, gd & equitrack, handles gd/soft: goes on any trk, likes a sharp one: best without a visor & a gd weight carrier: tough & genuine gldg, in great form on sand.

4100 **NOBLE CALLING** 12 [12] N A Graham 3-8-5 (65)(vis) M Roberts 8/1: 062322: 3 b c Caller I.D. - **4 66a** Specificity (Alleged) Held up wide, prog to chase wnr fnl 2f, no impress: stays 12f: eff in a vis: see 4100 (mdn).

3997 **FAHS** 18 [9] N Hamilton 8-10-0 (80) D Harrison 8/1: 115003: 8 b g Riverman - Tanwi (Vision) **2 78a** Held up, rdn/outpcd 3f out, late gains, no threat: op 14/1: top weight: see 3336.

3941 **WILLIE CONQUER** 21 [3] Andrew Reid 9-8-5 (71) J Reid 6/1: 111234: Held up, mod hdwy fnl 3f: AW **hd 68a** bow: acts on firm, gd/soft & equitrack: loves sell/clmg grade nowadays: see 3526.

3941 **PUZZLEMENT** 21 [10] 6-9-7 (73) P Robinson 6/1: 055065: In tch 5f out, btn 2f out: op 8/1: btr 791. **5 63a**

4101 **LILLAN** 12 [6] 3-8-4 (64)(t) P Doe 8/1: 44W436: Led over 4f out till over 2f out, wknd: btr 4101. **6 45a**

4101 **DAUNTED** 12 [8] 4-9-1 (67)(bl) I Mongan (5) 8/1: 0-0027: Held up, mod late hdwy: btr 4101, 157. **3 44a**

4108 **SEA DANZIG** 12 [5] 7-8-13 (65)(bl) J Quinn 33/1: 050008: Led after 1f till over 4f out, fdd: blnks reapp. **¾ 41a**

4101 **SHARP SPICE** 11 [7] 4-8-9 (61) W Supple 12/1: 303149: Held up, btn 3f out: btr 3858 (gd). **5 30a**

3444} **BILLADDIE** 413 [11] 7-9-2 (68) C Rutter 33/1: /000-0: Held up, eff wide 4f out, sn btn: 10th: reapp: **2½ 33a** unplcd in '99 (rtd 68, h'cap): '98 wnr at Lingfield, Newmarket, Kempton & Newbury (h'caps, rtd 56a & 71): eff at 10/12f on firm, hvy & equitrack: handles any trk & has run well fresh: best held up.

*4151 **SPANISH STAR** 8 [13] 3-8-7 (67)(6ex) K Darley 9/2: 606010: In tch wide, btn 3f out: 11th: op 5/2: **nk 31a** 6lb pen for latest & now with T Barron: much better on fibresand in 4151 (clmr, 11f).

3114} L S Lowry 427 [2] 4-9-11 (77) J Tate 25/1:   1299 Le Cavalier 142 [1] 3-8-5 (65)(t) L Newman (3) 33/1:
13 ran   Time 2m 29.47 (6.07)   (J Daniels)   L Montague Hall Tadworth, Surrey

---

4272   4.00 ANNUAL MEM'SHIP SELLER 3YO+ (G)   1m aw rnd   Standard   Inapplicable
£1939   £554   £277   3 yo rec 3 lb

3565} **CASTLES BURNING** 406 [5] C A Cyzer 6-8-12 M Hills 9/4 FAV: 4254-1: 6 b g Minshaanshu Amad - Major **54a** Overhaul (Known Fact) Chsd ldrs, rdn/chsd ldr over 1f out, styd on for press to lead nr line: bckd, op 5/2: bought in for 4,200 gns: reapp: '99 scorer at Lingfield (2, class stks, C/D, rtd 71a): '98 Brighton h'cap, rtd 56) & Lingfield wnr (2, rtd 65a): eff btwn 1m/12f on fast, gd/soft & both AWs, loves Lingfield & Brighton.

3756 **SUPERCHIEF** 34 [11] Miss B Sanders 5-9-3 (tbl) S Carson (3) 13/2: 500002: 5 b g Precocious - Rome **nk 58a** Express (Siberian Express) Prom, led 5f out & rdn clr over 2f out, hdd nr line: op 5/1: blnks reapplied, gd run.

4224 **RENDITA** 4 [8] D Haydn Jones 4-8-7 Dean McKeown 8/1: 000053: 4 b f Waajib - Rend Rover **3 42a** (Monseigneur) Held up, rdn & styd on onepace fnl 2f, no threat: op 10/1, quick reapp: see 1259 (C/D).

3921 **VALENTINES VISION** 22 [12] N P Littmoden 3-8-9 J Tate 6/1: 50-034: Prom till over 3f out, fdd: **¾ 46a** op 3/1.

4018 **NERONIAN** 18 [1] 6-9-3 Claire Bryan 25/1: 103005: Held up, mod late hdwy: see 676, 554. **½ 50\$**

3737 **WAIKIKI BEACH** 35 [10] 9-8-12 (bl) I Mongan (5) 10/1: 006206: Slowly away, nvr on terms with ldrs. **3 39a**

841 **COLEY** 180 [2] 3-8-4 G Baker (5) 33/1: -35607: Led 1f, in tch 5f: 6 month abs: now with B A Pearce. **¾ 33a**

3775 **CHAMPAGNE N DREAMS** 32 [9] 8-8-7 K Darley 6/1: 000058: Al towards rear: bckd: see 1275. **10 18a**

3921 **ERTLON** 22 [4] 10-9-3 P Robinson 6/1: 551209: Led after 1f till 5f out, fdd: btr 3736 (clmr). **hd 27a**

1734 **GUNNER SAM** 121 [6] 4-8-12 C Rutter 12/1: 000000: Dwelt, al bhd: 10th: abs: now with B Johnson. **8 10a**

3251 **EARLEY SESSION** 55 [7] 3-8-9 R Havlin 33/1: 0-0000: Al bhd: 11th: 8 wk abs: see 1438. **21 0a**

11 ran   Time 1m 38.52 (2.32)   (R M Cyzer)   C A Cyzer Maplehurst, W Sussex

---

4273   4.30 MILLENNIUM MDN DIV I 3YO+ (D)   7f140y str   Soft 100   -06 Slow
£2561   £788   £394   £197   3 yo rec 3 lb   Raced far side

3907 **GLORY QUEST** 25 [8] Miss Gay Kelleway 3-9-0 D Holland 6/4 FAV: 234221: 3 b c Quest For Fame - **79** Sonseri (Prince Tenderfoot) Chsd ldrs, led over 2f out, held on gamely nr fin, all out: hvly bckd, op 5/2: belated first win, rnr-up sev times prev: (auct mdn, rtd 93): eff btwn 7/10f on fast & hvy, gall/sharp trk.

4093 **RUSSIAN RHAPSODY** 12 [18] M A Jarvis 3-8-9 P Robinson 5/1: -54222: 3 b f Cosmonaut - Hannah's **nk 73** Music (Music Boy) Chsd ldrs, rdn on well, just held: op 9/2: see 4093.

2562 **EL EMPERADOR** 85 [13] J R Fanshawe 3-9-0 D Harrison 11/1: 6-5453: 3 b g Emperor Jones - Car Stop **2 75** (Stop The Music) Chsd ldrs, rdn & styd on onepace from over 1f out: 12 wk abs: op 8/1: handles fast & soft.

3831 **LUCKY GITANO** 29 [14] J L Dunlop 4-9-3 Pat Eddery 6/1: 002464: Led over 3f out till over 2f out, fdd. **3 71**

-- **SUMMER JAZZ** [3] 3-8-9 S Sanders 12/1: 5: Towards rear, late hdwy, no threat: debut, op 8/1: **3½ 61** shld apprec step up to 1m+ on this evidence: with P Makin.

3914 **FFYNNON GOLD** 23 [16] 3-8-9 L Newman 33/1: 000006: Led 5f out till over 2f out, fdd: mod form. **1 60**

4018 **DEFIANT** 18 [2] 3-9-0 P D'Arcy 33/1: 07: Prom till over 1f out: no form prev. **2½ 59**

3350 **EUROLINK ZANTE** 51 [17] 4-9-3 J Reid 16/1: 58: Mid-div, mod late hdwy: op 12/1, 8 wk abs: see 3350. **1¼ 59**

3759 **TIME BOMB** 34 [1] 3-8-9 G Hind 25/1: 600009: Keen/prom, btn 2f out: see 1525. **1¼ 52**

1771 **HARVEY LEADER** 119 [6] 5-9-3 J Quinn 33/1: 300: Mid-div, btn 2f out: 10th, now with Miss D McHale. **½ 56**

-- **MUCH ADO** [11] 3-8-9 J Fortune 7/1: 0: Mid-div at best: 11th: op 4/1, debut: with J Gosden. **3 47**

3834 **HONEST WARNING** 29 [9] 3-9-0 Paul Eddery 11/1: 42450: Mid-div, no impress fnl 3f: 12th: see 2965. **1¾ 50**

2770 **ASSURANCE** 77 [7] 3-9-0 B Marcus 12/1: 50: Led till 5f out, fdd: 16th: 4l, 11 wk abs: see 2770. **0**

4177 Bold Byzantium 7 [4] 4-8-12 D R McCabe 50/1:   4031 Pamela Anshan 16 [5] 3-8-9 (vis) D O'Donohoe 33/1:
4118 Mabrookah 10 [4] 4-8-12 T G McLaughlin 33/1:   -- Boiling Point [12] 4-8-12 S Carson (3) 33/1:
2127} Suhail 471 [15] 4-9-3 G Hannon (7) 33/1:
18 ran   Time 1m 36.00 (8.2)   (Quest To Win Partnership)   Miss Gay Kelleway Lingfield, Surrey

LINGFIELD (Mixed)   WEDNESDAY OCTOBER 4TH   Lefthand, Sharp, Undulating Track

4274   **5.00 MILLENNIUM MDN DIV II 3YO+ (D)**   7f140y str   Soft 100   -10 Slow
£2561   £788   £394   £197   3 yo   rec 3 lb   Raced far side

3977 **HINDAAM** 19 [3] E A L Dunlop 3-9-0 R Hills 11/4: 51: 3 b c Thunder Gulch - Party Cited (Alleged) **77**
Held up, rdn & styd on well fnl 2f to lead well ins last: well bckd, op 4/1: eff around 7.5f, half brother to a wnr
abroad at 1m/10f, 1m+ shld suit: acts on soft grnd & a sharp/undul trk: lightly raced.

4067 **MAC BE LUCKY** 14 [16] J Noseda 3-9-0 J Weaver 8/1: -00202: 3 b c Magic Ring - Take Heart (Electric) *1* **75**
Led 3f out & rdn/clr over 1f out, hdd cl-home: op 4/1: shown enough to win a race, worth a try in headgear.

-- **CELLO SOLO** [6] P J Makin 3-9-0 S Sanders 14/1: 3: 3 b c Piccolo - Whirling Words (Sparkler) *2½* **71**
Dwelt, rdn & styd on fnl 2f, no threat to front pair: op 8/1, debut: eff at 7.5f, shld stay 1m: acts on soft grnd.

2938 **DANZIG WITHWOLVES** 69 [10] H R A Cecil 3-8-9 T Quinn 11/10 FAV: 44: Chsd ldrs, rdn/chsd ldr over *hd* **65**
2f out, no extra ins last: well bckd tho' op 4/5: 10 wk abs: btr 2938 (fast).

3810 **BAY VIEW** 31 [13] 5-8-12 J Reid 33/1: 300005: In tch, eff halfway, btn 2f out: btr 833 (10f). *3* **61$**

-- **COUNTESS COLDUNELL** [1] 3-8-9 G Baker (5) 25/1: 6: Rdn/towards rear, late hdwy, no threat. *hd* **60**

3977 **PORAK** 19 [11] J Stack 33/1: -607: In tch 5f: h'caps will suit: see 2104. *¾* **64**

1947 **FOOL ON THE HILL** 111 [7] 3-9-0 Pat Eddery 11/2: 06-428: Mid-div, no impress fnl 2f: op 7/2: abs. *4* **58**

4081 **GROVE LODGE** 13 [4] 3-9-0 A Nicholls 33/1: 000069: Mid-div, btn 2f out: see 1024. *nk* **57$**

3977 **PURSUIT OF DREAMS** 19 [2] 3-9-0 B Marcus 33/1: 000: Prom 5f: 10th: mod form prev. *1* **56**

3970 **MERCEDE** 20 [15] 3-8-9 P McCabe 50/1: 000-00: Al towards rear, 11th: no form. *8* **41$**

3956 **MELLEDGAN** 21 [5] 3-8-9 M Roberts 20/1: 6400: Led till 3f out: wknd: 13th: longer trip, mod form. **0**

4093 Silver Prairie 12 [18] 3-8-9 D Sweeney 33/1:   3381 Pas Faribole 49 [12] 3-8-9 J Lowe 33/1:
4175 Lady Dealer 7 [9] 5-8-12 Dean McKeown 50/1:   4066 Ilissus 14 [8] 4-9-3 (VIS) J Fanning 33/1:
3781 Rathlea 32 [17] 6-9-3 P M Quinn (3) 33/1:   1708 Profound 122 [14] 4-9-3 R Price 25/1:
18 ran   Time 1m 36.3 (8.5)   (Hamdan Al Maktoum)   E A L Dunlop Newmarket, Suffolk

YORK   THURSDAY OCTOBER 5TH   Lefthand, Flat, Galloping Track

Official Going   SOFT. Stalls 5f/7f - Far side; Round - Inside.

4275   **2.00 CONSTANT CLAIMER 3YO+ (D)**   1m2f85y   Soft 115   -02 Slow
£7020   £2160   £1080   £540   3 yo   rec 5 lb

4006 **SKYERS A KITE** 19 [3] Ronald Thompson 5-8-1 T Williams 7/1: 521551: 5 b m Deploy - Milady Jade **68**
(Drumalis) In tch, hdwy well over 2f out, styd on well for press to lead ins last, going away: earlier won at
Beverley (clmr) & Hamilton (h'cap, rtd 51): '99 wnr again at Beverley (h'cap, rtd 45): '98 wnr at Beverley &
Catterick: winning form over 10/13f & handles firm & gd, loves soft: handles any trk, loves Beverley: tough.

2445 **PRINCE AMONG MEN** 91 [16] M C Pipe 3-8-11 K Darley 6/1: 333322: 3 b g Robellino - Forelino *3* **79**
(Trempolino) Handy, eff to chase ldr 3f out, kept on for press fnl 1f, not pce of wnr: recent hdls wnr at
Worcester (juv nov, rtd 112h, 2m): handles gd/firm & soft: will apprec a return to further: often plcd.

3988 **LORD EUROLINK** 20 [14] C A Dwyer 6-8-6 (vis) J Carroll 7/1: 450123: 6 b g Danehill - Lady Eurolink *½* **68**
(Kala Shikari) Cl up, led 4f out, hung left & hdd inside last, no extra: ran to form of 3988 & 3808.

4291} **ROYAL AMARETTO** 362 [7] B J Meehan 6-9-0 R Hughes 5/1: 0200-4: In tch, eff well over 2f out, sn *3½* **71**
btn: op 3/1 on reapp: rnr up twice in '99, (rtd 105, h'cap): last won in '97 at Newbury (stakes, rtd 114):
likes to force the pace around 10f on firm, gd/soft & any track: v useful at best but has regressed.

3979 **CARRIE CAN CAN** 20 [2] G Baker (5) 16/1: -65305: Slow away, bhd, some late gains, nvr *¾* **57**
dangerous: clr of rem & will be better off in h'cap company over further: see 3116.

.4039 **AL AZHAR** 17 [18] 6-9-7 F Lynch 12/1: 0-5066: Slow away, bhd, mod late gains: top weight *8* **69**

4088 **BOSS TWEED** 14 [1] 3-8-1 (t) O Pears 16/1: 050307: In tch, btn 3f out: btr 4045 (h'cap). *8* **46**

4178 **YAROB** 7 [11] 7-9-2 Alex Greaves 4/1 FAV: 606068: Prom, rdn & btn over 2f out: been busy this *1¼* **55**
term & back on a handy mark now: see 4178, 1070.

3634 **TO THE LAST MAN** 40 [12] 4-8-7 (BL) (1ow) D Holland 25/1: 06-009: Cl up, wknd over 3f out: blnks: *10* **36**
4th in a claiming hdle since 3634.

3686 **HIBERNATE** 38 [6] 6-8-10 N Callan 9/1: S00000: In tch, btn over 3f out: 10th: see 1829, 422. *2* **37**

3672 **ANGEL DUST** 39 [17] 4-8-3 F Norton 20/1: -560: Slow away, al bhd: 11th: see 3672. *3* **27**

3954 **PERCUSSION** 22 [15] 3-8-3 S Whitworth 20/1: 064000: Nvr a factor: 12th: btr 1967 (h'cap). *15* **17**

4228 **DIAMOND FLAME** 5 [5] 6-8-6 (VIS) R Lappin 33/1: 040000: Led till 4f out, wknd: 13th, visored. *3* **10**

4041 Kailan Scamp 16 [8] 7-8-1 (t) D Mernagh (3) 50/1:   3827 Susans Dowry 31 [20] 4-8-1 P Fessey 33/1:
3842 High Sun 30 [4] 4-8-11 J Quinn 25/1:   -- Martial Eagle [13] 4-9-7 Kim Tinkler 33/1:
2744 Nadder 78 [19] 5-8-6 K Dalgleish (5) 50/1:   4085 Jamadyan 14 [9] 3-8-4(1ow) G Hind 20/1:
4222 Righty Ho 5 [10] 6-8-8 K Hodgson 20/1: U
20 ran   Time 2m 19.43 (12.13)   (G A W Racing Partnership)   Ronald Thompson Stainforth, S Yorks

4276   **2.30 EBF CLASSIFIED STKS 3YO+ 0-85 (C)**   1m3f195y   Soft 115   -11 Slow
£7105   £2695   £1347   £612   3 yo   rec 7 lb

4115 **SEREN HILL** 12 [3] G A Butler 4-8-11 Pat Eddery 10/1: 002001: 4 ch f Sabrehill - Seren Quest **86**
(Rainbow Quest) Held up, hdwy over 2f out to lead appr fnl 1f, rdn clr: rnr-up once earlier: '99 wnr at
Haydock (h'cap, rtd 89): '98 Redcar nursery wnr: winning form over 12/14f, stays 2m on fast, prob firm
& loves soft & hvy: likes gall tracks & has run well fresh.

4092 **CANFORD** 13 [7] W Jarvis 3-8-9 J Fortune 14/1: 135552: 3 b c Caerleon - Veronica (Persian *2½* **87**
Bold) Cl up, led 7f out till appr fnl 1f, onepce: lightly rcd & running well: see 3541, 1588.

3778 **MONTECRISTO** 33 [13] R Guest 7-9-0 D Holland 7/1: 355453: 7 br g Warning - Sutosky (Great *3½* **81**
Nephew) Hld up, eff over 2f out, kept on ins last, nvr dngr: slipped back to a winning mark: see 3778.

*4092 **APPLE TOWN** 13 [14] H R A Cecil 3-8-10 T Quinn 7/4 FAV: -32114: In tch, eff over 2f out, *½* **83**
sn onepce: hvly bckd & clr of rem: clearly better expected, but ran to form of 4092 (h'cap).

3896 **DARARIYNA** 26 [8] 3-8-8 F Lynch 16/1: 215105: Cl up, rdn & btn when short of room over 1f out. *8* **73**

4197 **BARTON SANDS** 6 [11] 3-8-9 K Darley 9/2: 2126: Handy, btn over 2f out: nicely bckd: not *5* **69**
handle soft grnd? quick reapp after 4197.

*4160 **JULIUS** 9 [9] 3-8-6 K Dalgleish (5) 5/1: 040517: In tch, eff 3f out, sn btn: not handle soft? *9* **57**

1319

3915 **PETARA 24** [15] 5-9-0 R Winston 100/1: 00-508: Al bhd: no visor, see 3490 (sell, 10f). *7* **51**
4619} **RED RAMONA 334** [10] 5-9-0 P Doe 20/1: 3000-9: In tch, btn over 3f out: reapp: plcd in a val *3½* **47**
h'cap in '99 (rtd 93): '98 scorer at Folkestone (med auct mdn, rtd 92): stays 12/14f & handles firm & soft
grnd: runs well fresh & likes sharp/undul tracks.
4218 **THE CASTIGATOR 5** [4] 3-8-7 O Pears 200/1: 000000: Al bhd: 10th: poorly plcd (offic rtd 28). *nk* **47**
4218 **STAMFORD HILL 5** [6] 5-9-0 T Lucas 500/1: 050000: Led till over 7f out, wknd & fin last: **0**
quick reapp, impossible task (officially rtd only 17).
3674 **Genuine John 39** [1] 7-9-0 D Mernagh (3) 100/1: 1975 **Frontier Flight 111** [12] 10-9-0 Darren Williams(5) 200/1:
4014 **Royal Minstrel 19** [2] 3-8-9 S Sanders 20/1:
14 ran Time 2m 41.92 (15.12) (The Fairy Story Partnership) G A Butler Blewbury, Oxon

4277

3.00 SPORT4CAST.COM COND STKS 2YO (B) 7f rnd Soft 115 -17 Slow
£7766 £2945 £1472 £669

3965 **QUINK 21** [7] Sir Mark Prescott 2-9-0 S Sanders 6/1: 131351: 2 ch g Selkirk - Ink Pot (Green **94**
Dancer) Bhd, hdwy over 3f out to lead over 1f out, held on well under a strong drive: well bckd: earlier won at
Yarmouth & Ayr (nursery h'caps): eff over 6/7f on firm, soft & likes a gall track: has run well fresh: useful.
*4062 **NORTHFIELDS DANCER 15** [2] R Hannon 2-9-0 R Hughes 4/1: 202212: 2 ch c Dr Devious - *nk* **93**
Heartland (Northfields) Handy, hdwy to lead over 1f out, sn.hdd, kept on inside last, but winning jockey
was too strong: clr of rem & a useful run: likes soft grnd: see 4062.
*4103 **TURKU 12** [5] M Johnston 2-9-0 K Darley 7/4 FAV: 13: 2 b c Polar Falcon - Princess Zepoli *12* **76**
(Perspolis) Set pce till over 1f out, no extra: hvly bckd & better expected after wng debut in 4103 (gd/soft).
2985 **SANDORRA 68** [1] M Brittain 2-8-6 D Mernagh 33/1: 064: Bhd, eff 2f out, sn no impress: abs. *1½* **66$**
*4167 **TAKAROA 8** [10] 2-9-3 J Reid 11/2: 331015: Handy, eff over 2f out, sn btn: btr 4167 (gd/soft). *3½* **72**
3940 **JALONS STAR 22** [3] 2-8-11 R Studholme 50/1: 506: Prom, wknd 2f out: see 3859. *shd* **66**
3245 **STRICTLY PLEASURE 57** [8] 2-8-11 T Williams 100/1: 607: In tch, wknd over 2f out: 8 week abs. *15* **44**
-- **ZANGOOEY** [9] 2-8-8 R Winston 66/1: 8: Slow away, al bhd on debut: May foal, cost 2,500gns. *½* **40**
4063 **LOYAL TYCOON 15** [4] 2-8-11 P Doe 5/1: 31629: In tch, wknd qckly 2f out, t.o.: something amiss? *16* **21**
-- **LITTLE PIXIE** [6] 2-8-3 Kim Tinkler 50/1: 0: Handy, wknd qckly over 3f out on debut: fin last: *3½* **8**
April foal, cost 10,000gns: dam 1m/12f scorer.
10 ran Time 1m 30.52 (9.22) (Cheveley Park Stud) Sir Mark Prescott Newmarket, Suffolk

4278

3.30 STERLING RATED HCAP 3YO+ 0-105 (B) 7f rnd Soft 115 +06 Fast **[107]**
£10377 £3936 £1968 £894 3 yo rec 2 lb

4112 **BIG FUTURE 12** [7] Mrs A J Perrett 3-8-9 (90) W Ryan 7/1: 153301: 3 b c Bigstone - Star Of The **95**
Future (El Gran Senor) Early ldr, remained prom, regained lead over 1f out till ins last, rallied gamely to regain
lead on line, all out: bckd from 9/1, fast time: earlier won at Kempton (mdn) & Lingfield (h'cap): does stay 1m,
all winning form at 7f: acts on firm & soft, handles a sharpish or gall trk: likes to run up with the pace: tough.
4195 **GRANNYS PET 6** [6] P F I Cole 6-9-7 (100) J Fortune 3/1: 160532: 6 ch g Selkirk - Patsy *hd* **104**
Western (Precocious) In tch, smooth hdwy 2f out, rdn to lead ins fnl 1f, hdd on line: well bckd, 3L clr rem, top
weight, qck reapp: needs to be held up as late as poss but does win races: eye-catching in 4195, see 1574.
4112 **SILCA BLANKA 12** [8] A G Newcombe 8-8-13 (92) J Reid 20/1: 320603: 8 b h Law Society - Reality *3* **91**
(Known Fact) Prom, not pace of front 2 fnl 1f: rcd a bit too keenly: best dominating on sharp trks: see 2670.
4112 **AL MUALLIM 12** [9] D Nicholls 6-8-10 (89)(t) F Norton 10/1: 100004: Dwelt, hdwy from rear 2f out, *1* **87**
no impress ins fnl 1f: not disgraced on grnd softer than ideal: acts on soft, better on faster grnd: see 3414.
4112 **MUCHEA 12** [3] 6-9-7 (100) Craig Williams 9/1: 412505: Prom, led after 2f till dist, fdd: joint top *3* **94**
weight: beat today's wnr in 3902 (gd grnd), see 3648.
4142 **ADJUTANT 10** [5] 5-9-2 (95) K Darley 7/1: 060026: In tch, btn over 1f out: btr 4142. *3½* **84**
4112 **SMART RIDGE 12** [4] 3-9-4 (99) J Weaver 8/1: 234057: In tch, btn 2f out: beat this 1st & 2nd in 4112. *3* **83**
*4142 **SWAN KNIGHT 10** [1] 4-9-2 (95)(3ex) Pat Eddery 11/4 FAV: 026018: Waited with, switched halfway, *1¼* **77**
rdn & btn over 1f out: well bckd tho' op 2/1: puzz eff, much btr 4142.
4180 **MANA MOU BAY 7** [2] 3-9-5 (100) R Hughes 20/1: 024509: Prom till wknd fnl 2f: btr 3150 (firm). *1¼* **81**
9 ran Time 1m 28.96 (7.66) (K Abdulla) Mrs A J Perrett Pulborough, W Sussex

4279

4.00 GREEN HOWARDS NURSERY HCAP 2YO (C) 7f rnd Soft 115 +08 Fast **[105]**
£7020 £2160 £1080 £540

-4132 **LADY BEAR 11** [8] R A Fahey 2-7-13 (76) P Hanagan (5) 9/2: 441021: 2 b f Grand Lodge - **81**
Boristova (Royal Academy) Held up, prog halfway, led ent fnl 1f, ran on strongly, all out: well bckd from
6/1, fast time: earlier won at Musselburgh (nursery): eff at 7f/1m, will stay 10f+ next term: acts on fast,
soft grnd & fibresand: eff with/without a visor: tough & improving filly.
3990 **FAZZANI 20** [1] M W Easterby 2-7-10 (73)(2oh) J Mackay (5) 8/1: 012122: 2 b f Shareef Dancer - *1¼* **76**
Taj Victory (Final Straw) Trckd ldrs till went on fnl 2f out, hdd ent fnl 1f, kept on but not pace of wnr: nicely
bckd: another sound run from this tough & consistent filly: see 3990.
3630 **DUSTY CARPET 40** [3] C A Dwyer 2-8-2 (79) D O'Donohoe 16/1: 464303: 2 ch g Pivotal - Euridice *1* **80**
(Woodman) Chsd ldrs, kept on under press fnl 1f: 6 wk abs: stays 1m: acts on fast & soft grnd: see 3428.
*4086 **TIYOUN 14** [6] D W Barker 2-8-6 (83) F Lynch 8/1: 3214: Led till 2f out, no extra: well clr of rem *½* **83**
on h'cap debut: not disgraced: see 4086 (mdn).
4034 **ISLAND QUEEN 17** [4] 2-8-3 (80) L Newman (3) 11/2: 4325: Chsd ldrs, rdn & btn 2f out: btr 4034. *8* **69**
4157 **MONICA GELLER 9** [9] 2-7-10 (73)(10oh) T Hamilton (7) 7/1: 362166: Rear, mod late progress, *1¼* **60**
nvr dngrs: op 5/1, stiff task: nvr in the race today: will do better with more positive tactics: see 4076.
*3949 **WONDERGREEN 22** [2] 2-7-11 (74) T Williams 10/1: 600317: Prom 6f, wknd: much btr 3949 (gd). *¾* **60**
3704 **ACHILLES SPIRIT 38** [10] 2-8-4 (80)(1ow) N Callan 10/1: -01368: Mid div till btn fnl 2f: acts on *9* **53**
firm & gd/soft, not handle these testing conditions? btr 3149.
3537 **SARATOV 44** [11] 2-9-7 (98) K Darley 4/1 FAV: -31139: Chsd ldrs 6f, sn btn & fin well bhd: nicely *11* **54**
bckd, 6 wk abs, top weight: this is not his form, grnd much softer today than prev encountered: much btr 3537.
3962 **REGENT COURT 21** [5] 2-7-11 (74) J Quinn 14/1: 54530: Al rear, t.o. in 10th: btr 3962. *7* **20**
*3853 **CHANGING SCENE 29** [7] 2-8-9 (86) M Hills 7/1: -051P: Dwelt, well bhd, p.u. halfway: lame. **0**
11 ran Time 1m 44.35 (8.55) (A & K Lingerie) R A Fahey Butterwick, N Yorks

4280 4.30 RACING GIFTS APPR HCAP 3YO+ 0-75 (E) 1m3f195y Soft 115 -16 Slow [75]
£7283 £2241 £1120 £560 3 yo rec 7 lb

*4105 **EVENING SCENT** 12 [2] J Hetherton 4-8-8 (55) T Hamilton (5) 11/2 CO FAV: 016411: 4 b f Ardinglass - Fresh Line (High Line) Waited with, prog 2f out, led dispite hanging left ins fnl 1f, ran on, pushed out: recent Haydock wnr, earlier scored at Hamilton (h'cap): '99 Catterick wnr (sell, rtd 60): eff at 12/14f, has tried 2m: acts on fast & soft grnd, handles any track: can run well fresh: continues in fine form. **61**

3858 **FIVE OF WANDS** 29 [9] W Jarvis 3-8-6 (60) J Mackay 20/1: 0-2302: 3 b f Caerleon - Overact (Law Society) Tried to make all, not pace to repel wnr cl home: bck to form, acts on fast & soft grnd: stays 12f. ½ **65**

*3870 **MIDDLETHORPE** 28 [20] M W Easterby 3-8-10 (64)(bl) P Hanagan (3) 11/2 CO FAV: 301313: 3 b g Noble Patriarch - Prime Property (Tirol) Dwelt, recovered to race mid div, kept on under press fnl 1f, nvr nrr: well bckd tho' op 9/2: lost little in defeat, see 3870. 2½ **65**

3811 **JUST GIFTED** 32 [14] R M Whitaker 4-9-3 (64) P Shea (5) 16/1: 220364: Prom, every ch 2f out, not qckn fnl 1f: just btr 3504 (firm grnd). 3½ **61**

*4229 **LANCER** 3 [16] 8-8-8 (55)(vis)(6ex) Claire Bryan 11/2 CO FAV: 032615: In tch, onepce fnl 1½f: nicely bckd, quick reapp: see 4229. 1¼ **51**

3963 **DARK VICTOR** 21 [12] 4-8-3 (50) S Finnamore (2) 9/1: 501066: Mid div, late hdwy under press, nvr dngrs: prob stays 12f on soft grnd: see 1050 (10f). 1½ **44**

3994 **MORGANS ORCHARD** 19 [11] 4-9-2 (63) J Bosley (3) 8/1: 232607: Trckd ldrs, rdn & btn over 1f out. hd **57**

4071 **SCHEMING** 15 [15] 3-9-2 (70) K Dalgleish 20/1: 1608: Prom, ev ch 2f out, wknd fnl 1f: lightly rcd: much btr 3324 (debut, fast grnd). 1½ **62**

4105 **TURGENEV** 12 [4] 11-7-10 (43)(15oh) R Brisland 50/1: 066409: Chsd ldrs, no impress fnl 2f: stiff task. 1 **34**

4258 **HUTCHIES LADY** 2 [1] 8-7-10 (43)(5oh) Joanna Badger (3) 20/1: 0-3100: In tch, ev ch 2f out, sn btn & fin 10th: qck reapp, stiffish task: twice below 2805. shd **34**

4178 **WINSOME GEORGE** 7 [5] 5-7-10 (43)(14oh) G Sparkes (3) 33/1: 064100: Rear, eff 2f out, sn btn & fin 11th: v stiff task: see 3827. 4 **30**

4169 **TWO SOCKS** 8 [18] 7-9-0 (61) I Mongan 10/1: 141020: Mid div, no impress fnl 2f: fin 12th. ¾ **47**

1821 **MERRYVALE MAN** 118 [8] 3-9-6 (74) B McHugh (7) 16/1: 102050: Dwelt, recovered to race prom, ev ch 2f out, sn wknd & fin 13th: long abs: prev trained by J Given, now with R Fahey: had soft grnd/AW form earlier this year & will be much fitter next time: see 1071, 782. hd **60**

*4089 **MISTER MCGOLDRICK** 13 [7] 3-9-7 (75) G Baker 8/1: 010: Rear, wide 3f out, btn 1½f out: fin 14th: lightly rcd, much btr 4089 (10f mdn). nk **61**

3663 **Sherzabad** 39 [6] 3-7-10 (50) Jonjo Fowle (0) 40/1:

4067 **Resplendent Star** 15 [10] 3-9-6 (74)(vis) R Cody Boutcher (3) 14/1:

3979 **Once More For Luck** 20 [19] 9-9-3 (64) T Eaves (5) 14/1:

1222 **Royal Expression** 148 [13] 8-9-11 (72) P Fitzsimons 20/1:

4160 **New Fortune** 9 [3] 3-8-4 (58) R Smith 25/1:

19 ran Time 2m 42.53 (15.73) (N Hetherton) J Hetherton Malton, N Yorks

---

Official Going SOFT. Stalls: 5f & 6f - Far Side; Round Course - Inside

4281 2.00 LEVY BOARD MED AUCT MDN 2YO (E) 1m rnd Soft 120 -08 Slow
£7400 £2277 £1138 £569

3766 **THE BYSTANDER** 35 [6] N P Littmoden 2-8-9 R Winston 16/1: 01: 2 b f Bin Ajwaad - Dilwara (Lashkari) Mid-div, prog to lead 2f out, sn hdd, rall und press to regain lead fnl 100y, pshd out: 4,000 gns foal, half sister to a 7f juv wnr, dam 11f wnr: eff at 1m, get at least 10f next term: acts on soft grnd, gall trks: going the right way. **81**

3999 **LORD PROTECTOR** 20 [18] D W P Arbuthnot 2-9-0 T Quinn 9/2: -42: 2 b c Nicolotte - Scared (Royal Academy) Towards rear, gd prog on bit after halfway to lead appr fnl 1f, shkn up & hdd towards fin: op 3/1: eff at 7f/1m: acts on firm & soft grnd & looks sure to win a race. 1 **83**

4083 **MA JOLIE** 15 [14] H Akbary 2-8-9 J Stack 20/1: 03: 2 ch f Shalford - Scalford Brook (Handsome Sailor) Rear, kept on well appr fnl 1f, nrst fin: clrly apprec this step up to 1m on soft grnd: improving. ¾ **76**

3287 **MY PLACE** 56 [8] B W Hills 2-8-9 D Holland 16/1: 304: Mid-div, chsd ldrs appr fnl 1f, unable to chall: 8 wk abs: better run stepped up to 1m on soft grnd & 5L back to next: see 3039. ½ **75**

-- **FOXES LAIR** [12] 2-9-0 J Fanning 33/1: 5: In tch, prog to press ldrs 2f out, fdd fnl 1f: debut: 11,000 gns Muhtarram gldg, brother to decent 10f wnr Muakaad, dam a juv wnr: with M Dods. 5 **70**

4008 **TOMASINO** 20 [3] 2-9-0 K Darley 7/2: 46: Chsd ldrs till wknd appr fnl 1f: op 5/2: btr 4008. 1¼ **68**

3912 **BOND MILLENNIUM** 25 [7] 2-9-0 Paul Eddery 33/1: 07: Nvr out of mid-div: see 3912. 5 **60**

4062 **PRECISO** 16 [15] 2-9-0 S Sanders 3/1 FAV: 28: Dwelt, al around same place: much btr 4062 (debut). 2½ **56**

4163 **ASHKAAL** 9 [21] 2-9-0 Craig Williams 20/1: 09: Mid-div thr'out: not given a hard time. ½ **55**

3705 **CATEEL BAY** 39 [22] 2-8-9 A Culhane 16/1: -60: Nvr troubled ldrs: 10th, 6 wk abs, see 3627. shd **50**

3627 **DUNKIRK SPIRIT** 41 [1] 2-9-0 T G McLaughlin 50/1: 00: Led till 2f out, wknd: 11th, op 25/1, 6 wk abs. ¾ **54**

3950 **HIGH SOCIETY LADY** 23 [4] 2-8-9 (BL) J McAuley 100/1: 000000: Dwelt, nvr on terms: 12th, blnkd. ¾ **48**

3888 **CERALBI** 28 [5] 2-9-0 J Reid 16/1: -62200: Handy 6f: 13th: btr 3347 (fast). ½ **52**

3308 **Top Quality** 55 [2] 2-8-9 G Parkin 33/1: 3909 **Clear Ambition** 25 [17] 2-9-0 Pat Eddery 16/1:

4068 **Kimoe Warrior** 16 [9] 2-9-0 A Mackay 66/1: -- **As Good As It Gets** [11] 2-8-9 A Nicholls 50/1:

3867 **Challenor** 29 [10] 2-9-0 R Ffrench 50/1: 4086 **Jawrjik** 15 [19] 2-9-0 W Supple 50/1:

3952 **Cyber Santa** 23 [20] 2-9-0 O Pears 25/1: 3729 **Salviano** 37 [8] 2-9-0 Kim Tinkler 50/1:

4068 **Reims** 16 [13] 2-9-0 J Carroll 16/1:

22 ran Time 1m 46.01 (10.21) (Mrs D E Sharp) N P Littmoden Newmarket, Suffolk

---

4282 2.30 ALDWARK MANOR HCAP 3YO+ 0-90 (C) 1m2f85y Soft 120 +05 Fast [84]
£7345 £2260 £1130 £565 3 yo rec 5 lb

3794 **PEDRO PETE** 34 [14] M R Channon 3-9-0 (75) Craig Williams 20/1: 110501: 3 ch g Fraam - Stride Home (Absalom) Patiently rdn, imprvd ent str, chall appr fnl 1f, styd on under press to lead ins last: op 14/1, best time of day: earlier won at Lingfield (rtd 69a), Chester & Ascot (h'caps): eff at 10/10.5f: acts on **80**

firm, soft grnd & equitrack, any trk: back to form.
4074 **ADMIRALS PLACE 16** [6] H J Collingridge 4-8-12 (68) J Reid 5/1 FAV: 205322: 4 ch c Perugino - Royal Daughter (High Top) In tch, prog & ev ch appr fnl 1f, briefly outpcd, kept on well towards fin: bckd tho' op 7/2: tough, likes testing grnd: see 965. ½ **71**
4067 **CHEMS TRUCE 16** [15] W R Muir 3-9-3 (78) B Marcus 7/1: 345443: 3 b c Brief Truce - In The Rigging (Topsider) Held up, prog ent str, led appr fnl 1f, hung left & hdd ins last: gd run, eff at 1m/10.5f: see 912. ½ **80**
4094 **COURT OF APPEAL 14** [11] J R Fanshawe 3-9-7 (82) D Harrison 12/1: -01004: In tch, prog to lead appr fnl 2f, hdd bef dist, same pace: stays 10.5f, btr 1532 (1m). 1¼ **82**
4088 **MCGILLYCUDDY REEKS 15** [10] 9-8-13 (69) Kim Tinkler 10/1: 105645: Bhd imprvd appr fnl 2f, styd on but unable to chall: op 8/1, clr rem: not far off best, see 2350. ½ **68**
3997 **GENTLEMAN VENTURE 20** [8] 4-9-10 (80) T Quinn 11/2: 551306: Well plcd & ev ch till wknd ent fnl 2f. 6 **72**
4106 **TAP 13** [7] 3-9-1 (76) S Whitworth 11/1: 160567: Led till 2½f out, sn btn: big step up in trip, see 961. 5 **61**
4003 **ARCHIE BABE 20** [9] 4-9-4 (74) K Darley 10/1: 250038: Dwelt, nvr troubled ldrs: back in trip, see 2562. 6 **52**
4074 **PAS DE PROBLEME 16** [2] 4-8-6 (62) Dale Gibson 16/1: 146009: In tch till 4f out: op 12/1, see 1927, 1570. 1¼ **38**
1076 **SAGAPONACK 158** [4] 4-9-8 (78) D Meah (7) 25/1: 51400: Chsd ldrs till wknd qckly appr fnl 2f: 10th. 5 **49**
4094 **SPORTING GESTURE 14** [13] 3-8-9 (70) T Lucas 16/1: 161000: Bhd ldrs, lost place ent str: 11th. ½ **40**
3941 **KRISPIN 23** [12] 3-9-10 (85) D Holland 11/2: 331020: Chsd ldrs till 3f out: 12th, bckd tho' op 4/1: jt-top-weight: probably needs faster grnd: see 3941, 2558. 1½ **53**
3963 **Captain Brady 22** [3] 5-7-10 (52)(1oh) K Dalgleish (5) 16/1:
3798 **Paradise Garden 33** [1] 3-9-9 (84) J Fanning 16/1:
14 ran Time 2m 19.1 (11.81) (Peter Taplin) M R Channon West Ilsley, Berks

4283

3.00 EBF MDN 2YO (D) 6f Soft 120 -07 Slow
£6581 £2025 £1012 £506

3614 **STARBECK 42** [10] J D Bethell 2-8-9 D Harrison 15/2: -41: 2 b f Spectrum - Tide Of Fortune (Soviet Star) Towards rear, prog to chall when rider dropped whip appr fnl 1f, kept on well under hands & heels to put head in front on line: op 6/1, front 2 well clr, 6 wk abs: come on plenty for debut: 15,000 gns Mar foal: eff at 6f, bred to apprec 1m+: acts on soft grnd, gall trk: progressive filly. **86**
3958 **ORIENTOR 22** [8] J S Goldie 2-9-0 A Culhane 15/2: 32: 2 b c Inchinor - Orient (Bay Express) Bhd ldrs, burst thro' to lead appr fnl 1f, kept on but worn down fnl stride: op 6/1: useful colt, will win a race. *shd* **92**
1328 **FIREWORK 142** [5] W J Haggas 2-9-0 B Marcus 7/2: 223: 2 b c Primo Dominie - Prancing (Prince Sabo) Front rank, dsptd lead halfway till appr fnl 1f, no extra: bckd tho' op 2/1, 5 month abs: first run on soft grnd, worth another ch after 1328, 1169 (firm/fast). 9 **72**
3911 **ITS ECCO BOY 25** [13] K R Burke 2-9-0 N Callan 12/1: 044: Sn cl-up & ev ch till fdd appr fnl 1f. ¾ **69**
-- **KNIGHT CROSSING** [4] 2-9-0 S Sanders 25/1: 5: Chsd ldrs, onepace fnl 2f: 5,000Ir First foal. 2½ **64**
4020 **ALBUHERA 20** [3] 2-9-0 K Darley 11/4 FAV: 26: Trkd ldrs, eff & outpcd fnl 2f: bckd, see 4020 (7f). ½ **63**
-- **TONTO OREILLY** [6] 2-9-0 Paul Eddery 16/1: 7: Nvr a factor: 21,000 gns Mind Games colt, dam 5f wnr. 1¾ **58**
-- **EUROPRIME GAMES** [7] 2-9-0 C Lowther 33/1: 8: Slow away, nvr nr ldrs: debut: 21,000 gns Mind Games half brother to sev wnrs up to 12f: with Miss Perratt. *nk* **57**
4083 **NIGHT GYPSY 15** [9] 2-8-9 J Carroll 11/2: 329: Chsd ldrs till 2f out: much btr 4083. *nk* **51**
2692 **AMY DEE 83** [12] 2-8-9 Kim Tinkler 33/1: 600: Slow away, al rear: 12 wk abs. 7 **35**
3909 **ILLUSTRIOUS DUKE 25** [1] 2-9-0 A Mackay 66/1: 00: Led till halfway, sn btn: 12th: Dancing Spree colt. **0**
3949 **Fille De Dauphin 23** [11] 2-8-9 J McAuley 66/1: -- **Gardrum** [2] 2-9-0 R Winston 33/1: R
13 ran Time 1m 16.89 (7.59) (Www.Clarendon Racing.Com) J D Bethell Middleham, N Yorks

4284

3.30 LADBROKES RTD HCAP 3YO+ 0-100 (B) 1m rnd Soft 120 -02 Slow [102]
£10655 £4041 £2020 £918 3 yo rec 3 lb

4106 **CELEBRATION TOWN 13** [5] D Morris 3-8-9 (86) R Winston 6/1: 016121: 3 b g Case Law - Battle Queen (Kind Of Hush) Waited with, qcknd appr fnl 1f, led ins last, rdn out: op 9/2: earlier won at Southwell, Sandown & Newmarket (h'caps): unplcd for J J O'Neill in '99 (rtd 73): eff at 7f/1m: acts on fast, suited by soft grnd, goes on any trk: runs well fresh: progressive/tough gldg, credit to connections. **91**
*4102 **GREAT NEWS 14** [8] W J Haggas 5-8-9 (83) P Hanagan (5) 6/5 FAV: 001112: 5 b g Elmaamul - Amina (Brigadier Gerard) In tch, prog to lead briefly bef fnl 1f, kept on: well bckd, clr rem: lost nothing in defeat. 1¼ **85**
4112 **TONY TIE 13** [4] J S Goldie 4-9-2 (90) A Culhane 9/1: 220003: 4 b g Ardkinglass - Queen Of The Quorn (Governor General) Led, under press & hdd appr fnl 1f, onepace: tchd 12/1: signs of a return to form. 3 **86**
+3981 **FLOATING CHARGE 21** [3] J R Fanshawe 6-8-7 (81) D Harrison 5/2: U00114: Held up, chsd ldrs 2f out, sn btn: bckd: back up in trip on softer grnd: see 3981. 1¼ **74**
4126 **SILK ST JOHN 12** [1] 6-9-1 (89) G Faulkner (3) 8/1: 640005: Al bhd, wknd 2f out: see 1836 (fav trk). 3½ **76**
3998 **STRASBOURG 20** [7] 3-8-5 (82) Kim Tinkler 33/1: 200006: Chsd ldrs till 2f out: see 2330. 1 **67**
6 ran Time 1m 45.52 (9.72) (Meadowcrest Ltd) D Morris Newmarket, Suffolk

4285

4.00 GOODRAMGATE HCAP 3YO+ 0-80 (D) 5f Soft 120 00 Slow [80]
£7195 £2214 £1107 £553 High numbers probably had a slight edge

-4165 **NINEACRES 9** [11] J M Bradley 9-9-12 (78)(bl) P Fitzsimons (5) 11/2 FAV: 130221: 9 b g Sayf El Arab - Mayor (Laxton) Trkd ldrs, shaken up to lead appr fnl 1f, going away, readily: bckd, fair time, deserved: earlier won at Bath (2), W'hampton, Southwell (rtd 58a), Windsor & Chepstow (h'caps): '99 W'hampton wnr (clmr, rtd 59a & 42): eff at 5/6f, stays 7f: acts on firm, soft grnd, both AWs: goes on any trk: wears blnks or visor: best up with/forcing the pace: ultra-tough & progressive 9yo, credit to trainer. **88**
4153 **PREMIUM PRINCESS 10** [21] J J Quinn 5-9-5 (71) Pat Eddery 14/1: 144102: 5 b m Distant Relative - Solemn Occasion (Secreto) Outpcd till kept on strgly appr fnl 1f, nvr nrr: tchd 20/1: back to best on soft. 3 **72**
4185 **JAMES STARK 8** [12] N P Littmoden 3-9-12 (78)(bl) C Carver (3) 12/1: 456153: 3 b g Up And At'Em - June Maid (Junius) Mid-div, eff/hung left appr fnl 1f, kept on, nvr nrr: acts on firm, soft grnd & both AWs. *shd* **79**
4185 **DACCORD 8** [23] M Kettle 3-9-10 (76) N Callan 10/1: 506424: Bhd, imprvd 2f out, styd on und press. *hd* **76**
4027 **PALAWAN 18** [14] 4-9-10 (76) Martin Dwyer 14/1: 625305: Front rank, led 2f out till bef fnl 1f, onepace: prob ran to best, handles soft grnd, poss suited by faster: see 3209, 1881. *hd* **76**
4220 **WHIZZ KID 6** [6] 6-9-1 (67) Claire Bryan (5) 10/1: 005026: Rear, kept on appr fnl 1f, nvr nr ldrs: see 1391. 1 **64**
4073 **THREAT 16** [9] 4-9-7 (73)(t) K Darley 9/1: 051357: Prom, eff 2f out, unable to qckn: bckd, see 3894. *shd* **70**
4220 **DAAWE 6** [20] 9-9-4 (70)(bl) Clare Roche (7) 20/1: 500058: Chsd ldrs, onepace appr fnl 1f: qk reapp. ¾ **65**
4220 **TORRENT 6** [7] 5-9-7 (73)(bl) Lynsey Hanna (7) 16/1: 351039: Mid-div, not clr run appr fnl 1f, onepce. ½ **67**
4073 **BODFARI KOMAITE 16** [3] 4-9-7 (73) S Sanders 14/1: 134000: Led far side trio, ev ch till fdd appr *nk* **66**

YORK FRIDAY OCTOBER 6TH Lefthand, Flat, Galloping Track

fnl 1f: 10th: prob had a v difficult task on the far side: see 1662.
3894 **ZIGGYS DANCER 28** [22] 9-9-2 (68) W Supple 25/1: 000600: Al around same place: 11th, visor off. *nk* **60**
4107 **BARRINGER 13** [18] 3-9-13 (79) Craig Williams 33/1: 530000: Nvr troubled ldrs: 12th, see 716. *1¾* **66**
4107 **WILLIAMS WELL 13** [13] 6-9-13 (79)(bl) T Lucas 20/1: 116000: Bhd ldrs, fdd appr fnl 1f: 13th, see 3464. *½* **65**
3894 **BLESSINGINDISGUISE 28** [16] 7-9-8 (74)(bl) G Parkin 25/1: 620000: Led till 2f out, sn lost place: 15th. **0**
+4027 **PETARGA 18** [8] 5-9-12 (78) S Whitworth 11/1: 050110: Al towards rear: 17th, nds faster grnd?: see 4027. **0**
*4107 **POLLY GOLIGHTLY 13** [2] 7-9-6 (72)(bl) Dale Gibson 15/2: 430110: Chsd far side ldr till 2f out: 18th, ignore. **0**
4107 **Flak Jacket 13** [4] 5-9-5 (71) Alex Greaves 25/1: 3960 **Nifty Major 22** [19] 3-9-6 (72) J Reid 20/1:
3960 **Anthony Mon Amour 22** [10] 5-9-3 (69)(t) A Nicholls 16/1: 3788 **Bond Boy 34** [17] 3-10-0 (80) J Bosley (7) 33/1:
4107 **Ptarmigan Ridge 13** [1] 4-9-13 (79) K Dalgleish (5) 20/1: 4612} **Harryana 336** [5] 3-9-12 (78) D Holland 20/1:
4015 **Half Moon Bay 20** [15] 3-10-0 (80) D Mernagh (3) 33/1:
23 ran Time 1m 02.79 (5.99) (J M Bradley) J M Bradley Sedbury, Glos

4286

4.30 NORTHERN NURSERY HCAP 2YO (C) 6f Soft 120 -12 Slow [107]
£6581 £2025 £1012 £506

4090 **FENWICKS PRIDE 14** [5] B S Rothwell 2-7-10 (75)(VIS)(8oh) D Mernagh (1) 14/1: 661051: 2 b g Imperial **83**
Frontier - Stunt Girl (Thatching) Held up, imprvd 2f out, rdn bef fnl 1f, got up towards fin despite edging left: defied 8lbs o/h, set alight by visor: earlier won at Ripon (auct mdn): eff at 5f, suited by 6f: acts on fast & soft grnd, sharp or gall trk: improving.
*3955 **PRINCE PYRAMUS 23** [7] C Grant 2-7-10 (75)(5oh) G Bardwell 7/1: -4412: 2 b c Pyramus - Rekindled *½* **81**
Flame (King's Lake) Front rank, led ent fnl 2f, drvn ins last & edged right, hdd towards fin: tchd 9/1, 5lbs o/h on h'cap bow: gd run, eff at 5/6f on gd & soft grnd.
4090 **SAMADILLA 14** [3] T D Easterby 2-7-10 (75)(4oh) P Hanagan (3) 10/3 FAV: 441043: 2 b f Mujadil - *2½* **75**
Samnaun (Stop The Music) Well plcd, chall 2f out, outpcd fnl 1f: bckd, fair run, see 4090, 3712.
3714 **BYO 38** [4] M C Chapman 2-8-10 (89) A Culhane 4/1: 243564: With ldrs, fdd appr fnl 1f: bckd tho' op 11/4.4 **79**
3900 **PROCEED WITH CARE 27** [6] 2-9-7 (100) J Reid 7/2: 51205: Led till ent fnl 2f, no extra: bckd from *3* **82**
9/2, top-weight on h'cap bow: prob needs faster grnd (odds-on debut flop on hvy): see 2106.
3602 **WILSON BLYTH 42** [1] 2-7-10 (75)(3oh) G Baker (5) 8/1: 143426: Chsd ldrs, hung left & btn 2f out. *¾* **55**
3486 **AMEN CORNER 48** [2] 2-7-10 (75) K Dalgleish (5) 9/2: -41357: Prom till wknd qckly 2f out: 7 wk abs. *nk* **54**
7 ran Time 1m 17.34 (7.94) (J H Tattersall) B S Rothwell Musley Bank, N Yorks

4287

5.00 CLASSIFIED STKS 3YO+ 0-75 (D) 6f Soft 120 +02 Fast
£8092 £2490 £1245 £622 3 yo rec 1 lb High numbers probably had the edge

4069 **LOOK HERE NOW 16** [16] B A McMahon 3-8-12 K Dalgleish (5) 33/1: 500001: 3 gr c Ardkinglass - Where's **80**
Carol (Anfield) Rear, switched & strong run appr fnl 1f, led ins last, shade cmftbly: jockey gvn 4 day ban for irresp riding, stable won this in '99: earlier won debut at Doncaster (mdn): eff at 6f on gd & soft grnd, gall trk.
4018 **MANTLES PRIDE 20** [21] J A Glover 5-8-13 (bl) O Pears 14/1: 500022: 5 br g Petong - State Romance *2* **75**
(Free State) In tch, prog when run was blocked appr fnl 1f, switched & rallied to go 2nd nr fin, no ch wnr: fin 3rd, plcd 2nd: ran well in the circumstances, return to 7f will suit: back on a fair mark: see 1514.
3960 **SHAROURA 22** [6] D Nicholls 4-8-10 D Holland 11/1: 020003: 4 ch f Inchinor - Kinkajoo (Precocious) *shd* **72**
Prom, switched appr fnl 1f, ch 1f out, onepace for press: fin 2nd, plcd 3rd, jockey given 1 day ban for careless riding: prob ran to best back at 6f: handles fast & soft: h'capped to win: see 2128.
2241 **DAY BOY 100** [5] Denys Smith 4-8-13 A Nicholls 25/1: -30444: In tch, ran on appr fnl 1f, nvr nr to chall. *1* **72$**
4037 **STAR PRINCESS 18** [7] 3-8-9 (vis) C Carver (3) 12/1: 253305: Chsd ldrs, led appr fnl 1f, sn hard *½* **67**
rdn, hdd ins last & no extra: see 3920, 2900.
3708 **DOUBLE ACTION 39** [4] 6-8-13 T Quinn 16/1: 060066: Rear, wide prog/hmpd appr fnl 1f, nvr nrr. *½* **69**
*3956 **MR STYLISH 23** [1] 4-9-2 (tvi) Martin Dwyer 16/1: 533017: In tch, wide prog 3f out, onepace ins last. *hd* **72$**
4136 **PRINCELY DREAM 12** [8] 4-8-13 (BL) P Hanagan (5) 11/1: 000458: In tch, chsd ldrs ent fnl 2f, *¾* **67**
no extra & short of room ins last: bckd, blnkd: back in trip, see 1533.
3668 **LA PIAZZA 40** [10] 4-8-10 J Carroll 20/1: 233669: Chsd ldrs, onepace appr fnl 1f: back up in trip. *2* **58**
4121 **ALMASI 12** [18] 8-8-10 R Mullen 7/1: 402250: Rear, not clr run halfway, late hdwy, nvr a factor: 10th. *shd* **58$**
3937 **FOUND AT LAST 23** [9] 4-8-13 G Baker (5) 33/1: 352200: Rear, wide prog into mid-div 2f out: 11th. *1* **58**
4107 **SHARP HAT 13** [3] 6-9-5 A Culhane 16/1: 323030: Mid-div, no extra appr fnl 1f: 12th, back up in trip. *1½* **61**
3992 **PEPPIATT 21** [2] 6-8-13 J Fanning 25/1: 535000: Slow away, nvr dangerous: 13th, see 667. *1½* **52**
4233 **SANTIBURI LAD 4** [14] 3-9-1 C Lowther 16/1: 120: Al towards rear: 14th, see 4233, 3462. *shd* **55**
4106 **ROYAL ROMEO 13** [12] 3-8-12 K Darley 10/1: 300050: Chsd ldrs till 2f out: 15th, stablemate 6th. *shd* **52**
4010 **GET STUCK IN 20** [17] 4-8-13 R Winston 4/1 FAV: 000230: Led till ent fnl 2f, sn btn: 16th, bckd from 6/1. *2½* **46**
4073 **CLASSY CLEO 16** [23] 5-8-13 Pat Eddery 8/1: 010030: Al bhd, not much room halfway: 21st, tchd 10/1. **0**
3904 **Technician 27** [11] 5-8-13 S Sanders 16/1: 3920 **Lone Piper 24** [15] 5-8-13 B Marcus 16/1:
2504 **Fine Melody 90** [13] 3-8-9 J Reid 14/1: 2288 **Dawn 98** [22] 3-8-9 N Callan 33/1:
3297 **Danes Lady 56** [20] 4-8-10 W Supple 16/1: 4156 **Ajnad 10** [19] 6-8-13 (bl) T G McLaughlin 33/1:
23 ran Time 1m 16.5 (7.1) (S L Edwards) B A McMahon Hopwas, Staffs

WINDSOR FRIDAY OCTOBER 6TH Sharp, Fig 8 Track

Official Going GOOD/SOFT. Stalls: Inside.

4288

2.05 FILLIES MDN DIV 1 2YO (D) 6f Good/Soft Inapplicable
£2918 £898 £449 £224

-- **GOT TO GO** [5] B W Hills 2-8-11 M Hills 4/6 FAV: 1: 2 b f Shareef Dancer - Ghost Tree (Caerleon) **90+**
Handy, led 2f out, pushed clr ins last: hvly bckd: Mar foal, cost 32,000gns: half sister to a 7f juv wnr: dam 7f scorer: eff over a sharp 6f on gd/soft & runs well fresh: 7f will suit: useful, did well to overcome low draw.
4095 **HOW DO I KNOW 14** [13] G A Butler 2-8-11 P Doe 5/1: -022: 2 gr f Petong - Glenfield Portion *3* **80**
(Mummy's Pet) Handy, rdn & sltly outpcd over 1f out, kept on again to go 2nd ins last: acts on gd & gd/soft.
3292 **SUNDOWN 56** [20] M P Tregoning 2-8-11 R Perham 25/1: -03: 2 b f Polish Precedent - Ruby Setting *1* **78+**
(Gorytus) Held up, kept on nicely over 1f out, kind ride: 8 wk abs: Mar foal: dam 10f scorer: eff at 6f, sure to relish 7f+: handles gd/soft: type to come on plenty for this & one to keep in mind.
3832 **TRESS 31** [3] J R Fanshawe 2-8-11 R Hills 16/1: 04: In tch, eff dist, onepace: stays 6f, poor draw. *hd* **77**

3980 **OREANA 21** [1] 2-8-11 D O'Donohoe 10/1: -05: In tch, onepcd fnl 2f: eff at 6f on gd/soft: poor draw. *shd* **76**
-- **SYRINGA** [17] 2-8-11 D R McCabe 14/1: 6: Led over 3f out till 2f out, no extra on debut: Jan foal, cost IR 45,000gns: bred to apprec 7f in time. *1* **74**
2214 **CHISPA 101** [15] 2-8-11 L Newman (3) 20/1: 007: Handy, wknd fnl 1f: 3 month abs, see 1454. *2* **70$**
3910 **TRUST IN PAULA 25** [19] 2-8-11 A McGlone 14/1: 008: In tch, btn 2f out: see 3748. *½* **69**
4138 **POLONAISE 11** [16] 2-8-11 J Fortune 14/1: 49: In tch, wknd over 2f out: see 4138. *1¼* **66**
4172 **MYHAT 9** [12] 2-8-11 G Duffield 33/1: 265000: In tch, wknd 2f out: 10th: see 2209. *2* **62**
3942 **INDIAN GIVER 23** [21] 2-8-11 R Hughes 20/1: 00: Led over 2f, wknd 2f out: 11th: see 3942. *nk* **61**
4035 **IM LULU 18** [9] 2-8-11 T Ashley 33/1: 060: In tch, btn 2f out: 12th: see 4035. *hd* **60**
-- **MAGIC HARP** [10] 2-8-11 P Robinson 10/1: 0: Nvr a factor: 13th on debut: Apr foal, cost 34,000 gns: half sister to a 5/6f scorer: dam 7f wnr: with M Jarvis. *½* **59**
-- **Saloup** [4] 2-8-11 N Pollard 25/1:
2290 **Fadhah 98** [18] 2-8-11 S W Kelly (3) 11/1:
3583 **Grecian Halo 43** [6] 2-8-11 M Fenton 20/1:
3400 **Once Removed 51** [2] 2-8-11 W Ryan 33/1:
3520 **Tamilia 46** [14] 2-8-11 J D Smith 40/1:
-- **Cape Society** [7] 2-8-11 R Havlin 33/1:
-- **Damages** [11] 2-8-11 Joanna Badger (7) 33/1:
20 ran Time 1m 14.30 (Mrs H Theodorou) B W Hills Lambourn, Berks

4289

2.35 FILLIES MDN DIV 2 2YO (D) 6f Good/Soft Inapplicable
£2908 £895 £447 £223

3795 **PRINCESS CHLOE 33** [19] M A Jarvis 2-8-11 P Robinson 12/1: 01: 2 br f Primo Dominie - Louis Moillon (Mansingh) Handy, hdwy to lead dist, styd on, drvn out: op 8/1: Mar foal, cost 25,000 gns: half sister to a 5f scorer, dam also won at that trip: eff at 6f on gd/soft: much improved from debut. **74**
4095 **BEENABOUTABIT 14** [17] R Ingram 2-8-11 P Doe 25/1: 02: 2 b f Komaite - Tassagh Bridge (Double Schwartz) Set pace till dist, not pace of wnr: imprvd for debut & stays 6f on gd/soft: win a race on this form. *1½* **70**
4131 **TATANTE 12** [6] Sir Mark Prescott 2-8-11 G Duffield 6/1: 03: 2 gr f Highest Honor - Tamnia (Green Desert) Held up, eff 2f out, wandered & no extra ins last: fine run from mod low draw: stays 6f on gd/soft. *1* **68**
4079 **MISS BEETEE 15** [9] J J Bridger 2-8-11 J Quinn 20/1: -444: Prom, rdn & onepace over 1f out: see 3661. *1½* **64$**
4095 **PIQUET 14** [20] 2-8-11 L Newman (3) 10/1: -045: In tch, eff 2f out, onepace: handles firm & gd/soft. *¾* **62$**
4172 **POUNCE 9** [12] 2-8-11 S W Kelly (3) 7/1: 4446: Went left start, in tch, late gains, nvr dangerous: op 5/1: not given a hard time back at 6f: see 2400. *nk* **61**
-- **CAPOSO** [4] 2-8-11 F Norton 14/1: 7: In tch, rdn & btn dist, eased ins last: debut, op 10/1: Apr first foal, cost 16,000 gns: dam wng French juv: with P Harris, had a poor low draw. *½* **60**
-- **SUNLEY SCENT** [2] 2-8-11 R Havlin 5/1: 8: Bhd, kept on late, nrst fin: debut: Mar foal, half sister to wng sprinter Sunley Sense: shaped with promise here from a poor low draw, looks sure to improve. *¾* **58+**
4189 **ANOTHER SECRET 7** [10] 2-8-11 R Hughes 11/2: -4049: Held up, brief eff 3f out, sn btn: btr 4189. *¾* **56**
-- **SPECIAL** [5] 2-8-11 J Weaver 4/1 FAV: 0: Al bhd: 10th on debut: bckd tho' op 5/2: May foal: half sister to high class miler Soviet Line: dam 4th in the Oaks: bred to apprec 1m+ in time, shld do better. *1¾* **52**
4096 **MISS INFORM 14** [13] 2-8-11 J Fortune 20/1: 350000: Prom, wknd well over 1f out: 11th: btr 1639. *hd* **51**
3940 **BUSTLE 23** [14] 2-8-11 T Williams 33/1: 00: Dwelt, sn in tch, btn 2f out: 12th: Mar foal, cost 31,000 gns: half sister to a useful 7f/1m juv wnr: dam sprinter: with J Toller. *nk* **50**
-- **CHORALLI** [1] 2-8-11 N Pollard 10/1: 0: Slow away, al bhd, 13th on debut: poor low draw. *nk* **49**
4083 **MINETTE 15** [15] 2-8-11 G Carter 8/1: 660: In tch, btn over 2f out: 15th: btr 4083. **0**
-- **Scapavia** [11] 2-8-11 G Sparkes (7) 20/1:
4096 **Fox Cottage 14** [18] 2-8-11 J Mackay (5) 33/1:
4034 **Kiss Curl 18** [8] 2-8-11 S Carson (3) 100/1:
4095 **Zilkha 14** [16] 2-8-11 W Ryan 20/1:
-- **Ridgewood Belle** [3] 2-8-11 D R McCabe 12/1:
19 ran Time 1m 14.70 (Mrs Christine Stevenson) M A Jarvis Newmarket, Suffolk

4290

3.05 0800 211222 NURSERY HCAP 2YO 0-75 (E) 1m2f Good/Soft Inapplicable [81]
£2786 £796 £398 4 runners (incl wnr & 3rd) raced far side in str

3609 **TRUMPINGTON 42** [4] I A Balding 2-9-2 (69) W Ryan 8/1: 310401: 2 ch f First Trump - Brockton Flame (Emarati) Prom far side in str, led over 1f out, styd on well, drvn out: op 5/1, 6 wk abs: dam 6f wnr: earlier scored at Newbury (fills auct mdn): eff at 7f, enjoyed step up to 10f on firm & gd/soft, any trk: runs well fresh. **75**
4191 **HOMELIFE 7** [6] P W D'Arcy 2-8-13 (66) P D'Arcy 20/1: 640662: 2 b g Persian Bold - Share The Vision (Vision) In tch, hdwy to lead over 2f out till over 1f out, onepace, only btn 1L: relished this big step up to 10f & acts on gd & gd/soft grnd: shld find a staying race: see 984. *1* **70**
3387 **CHARENTE 51** [15] M C Pipe 2-9-1 (68) P Robinson 14/1: -5003: 2 ch c Hennessy - Zalamalec (Septieme Ciel) Prom, lost place after 2f, trkd over to far side str, ev ch over 1f out, sn no extra: 7 wk abs: improved for big step up to 10f & handles gd/soft grnd: shld win a staying race: see 2189. *1¼* **70**
+4132 **KINGS CREST 12** [22] S C Williams 2-8-9 (62) Joanna Badger (7) 7/2 FAV: 066414: In tch, brief eff 2f out, onepace: prob just stays 10f: risen in the weights since 4132. *1* **63**
3879 **NOBLE DOBLE 29** [12] 2-9-6 (73) M Hills 20/1: 523405: Held up, went far side str, eff well over 1f out, kept on same pace: prob stays 10f: see 2430, 2132. *1¾* **71**
*3957 **RATHKENNY 22** [2] 2-8-12 (65) Dean McKeown 12/1: -56416: Keen, handy, rdn & onepace fnl 2f: up in trip & class after 3957 (sell, 1m). *¾* **62**
4235 **SUN BIRD 4** [14] 2-8-9 (62) G Duffield 5/1: 50507: Handy, rdn & btn well over 1f out: quick reapp & massive step up in trip, but shld stay in time: blnks discarded after 4235, see 2818. *½* **58**
*3240 **LOOK FIRST 58** [18] 2-8-12 (65) J Quinn 16/1: 2318: Nvr a factor: 8 wk abs & a big step up in trip (shld stay in time) & class: see 3240 (sell, 7f, firm). *1* **60**
4076 **GAY CHALLENGER 15** [7] 2-8-3 (56) F Norton 33/1: 504009: Nvr a factor: much longer trip, see 2959. *shd* **51**
4076 **GRAND FIVE 15** [17] 2-9-6 (73) R Hughes 11/2: 200320: Prom, well over 1f out: 10th, up in trip. *¾* **67**
3957 **JEZADIL 22** [16] 2-8-3 (56) T Williams 20/1: 644340: Handy, wknd over 2f out: 11th: see 3957 (1m). *nk* **49**
4022 **CARRABAN 20** [5] 2-9-3 (70) D R McCabe 16/1: 336230: Led till over 2f out, wknd: 12th, longer trip. *½* **62**
3822 **EXOTIC FAN 32** [20] 2-9-7 (74) J Mackay (5) 20/1: -4020: Slow away, al bhd: 13th: btr 3822 (1m). *shd* **66**
4084 **Emma Clare 15** [11] 2-8-7 (60)(BL) S W Kelly (3) 25/1:
3817 **Travellers Dream 32** [21] 2-8-10 (63) G Hind 20/1:
3273 **Border Edge 56** [8] 2-8-7 (60)(VIS) M Tebbutt 33/1:
4076 **Saafend Flyer 15** [1] 2-8-2 (55)(t) L Newman (2) 25/1:
*3950 **The Fancy Man 23** [9] 2-8-11 (64)(vis) J Fortune 16/1:
3853 **Arc En Ciel 30** [19] 2-9-7 (74) G Carter 12/1:
4076 **Polish Paddy 15** [13] 2-8-13 (66) R Smith (5) 33/1:
4137 **Atemme 11** [10] 2-8-12 (65)(bl) J D Smith 33/1:
21 ran Time 2m 13.01 (Park House Partnership) I A Balding Kingsclere, Hants

---

4291	3.35 BET DIRECT HCAP 3YO+ 0-75 (E) 1m2f Good/Soft Inapplicable	[71]
	£2933 £838 £419 3 yo rec 5 lb Runners fanned across the course	

*3885 **SILVERTOWN** 28 [19] B J Curley 5-9-8 (65) S W Kelly (3) 9/2: 100211: 5 b g Danehill - Docklands **72**
(Theatrical) Led after 2f, styd stands side, kept on for press 1f out, flashed tail but won cosily: earlier won at
W'hampton, Lingfield (h'caps, rtd 73a) & Goodwood (h'cap): '99 wnr at Epsom & York (h'caps, rtd 56): suited
by 1m/10f, stays 11.5f on gd/soft & both AWs: best up with/forcing the pace & loves a sharp trk,
handles any: runs well fresh: progressive & the type to go in again.

4044 **THIHN** 17 [8] J L Spearing 5-9-5 (62) A Beech (3) 13/2: 023122: 5 ch g Machiavellian - Hasana hd **66**
(Private Account) Held up, eff over 2f out, kept on for press in last, just held: stays 10f well & in fine heart.

3887 **IL DESTINO** 28 [10] B W Hills 5-8-11 (54) R Hughes 20/1: 500303: 5 b g Casteddu - At First Sight hd **57**
(He Loves Me) Held up, eff in centre over 2f out, kept on well ins last, just failed: likes a sharp/undul
trk & on a handy mark: acts on firm, gd/soft & equitrack: tried blnks in 3111.

3979 **RED LION FR** 21 [3] B J Meehan 3-8-12 (60) D R McCabe 20/1: 00064: Sn bhd, gd hdwy in centre 2f ½ **62**
out, kept on ins last, styd on gd/soft grnd: lightly rcd.

*4168 **DICKIE DEADEYE** 9 [17] P Dobbs 4/1 FAV: 656015: Held up, eff 2f out, nvr dangerous: 3 **59**
not disgraced, tho' rated higher 4168 (stiff trk).

*4066 **CRUAGH EXPRESS** 16 [14] 4-8-10 (53) J Quinn 15/2: 600116: Chsd ldrs, eff 2f out, wknd fnl 1f. hd **50**
4067 **PRINCE OMID** 16 [22] 3-9-5 (67) R Hills 8/1: 400437: In tch, rdn & btn over 1f out: btr 4067. 2 **61**
4135 **FAIR LADY** 12 [5] 3-9-9 (71) M Hills 12/1: 630428: In tch, went far side str, rdn & btn over 1f out. 2 **62**
4045 **YERTLE** 17 [12] 3-8-12 (60) P Robinson 20/1: 003609: Chsd ldrs, went far side str, btn over 1f out. ½ **50**
4208 **YOUNG UN** 6 [4] 5-9-1 (58) J Weaver 20/1: 003000: With ldrs, bhd after 4f, no impress fnl 2f: 1½ **46**
10th: mostly out of form & has subs slipped down the weights: see 786.

3518 **REAL ESTATE** 47 [16] 6-9-11 (68) J Fortune 12/1: /32000: In tch, wknd over 2f out: 11th: 7 wk abs. 1 **54**
*2634 **GUILSBOROUGH** 84 [9] 5-8-12 (55) M Tebbutt 8/1: 0-1110: In tch, went far side str, wknd fnl 1f: 0
14th, 3 month abs & wng run came on an end over a longer trip: v prog on fibresand earlier: see 2634 (1m).
3944 **BLGODY MARY** 23 [6] 3-9-0 (62) L Newman (3) 20/1: -01000: Led 2f, chsd wnr, wknd over 2f out: 0
18th, best 3289 (fills mdn, 1m, gd/firm).

3031	**Fifth Edition** 67 [7] 4-8-8 (51) Dean McKeown 33/1:	3206	**Morningside** 59 [13] 3-9-3 (65) N Pollard 25/1:
4067	**Monduru** 16 [11] 3-8-13 (61) P Doe 33/1:	1018	**Cancun Caribe** 165 [21] 3-9-11 (73) G Hind 20/1:
4166	**Rising Spray** 9 [20] 9-8-10 (53) G Duffield 33/1:	3683	**Prinisha** 39 [2] 3-8-12 (60) A McGlone 20/1:
3362	**Salory** 53 [18] 4-8-9 (52) J D Smith 33/1:	4168	**Prince Elmar** 9 [1] 3-9-0 (62) D O'Donohoe 40/1:

21 ran   Time 2m 11.7   (Mrs B J Curley)   B J Curley Newmarket

---

4292	4.05 BET DIRECT CLASS STKS 3YO+ 0-70 (E) 1m67y rnd Good/Soft Inapplicable	
	£2786 £796 £398 3 yo rec 3 lb Runners fanned across course	

4094 **BOLD RAIDER** 14 [10] I A Balding 3-9-0 W Ryan 9/2 JT FAV: 234351: 3 b g Rudimentary - Spanish Heart **70**
(King Of Spain) In tch, hdwy & went far side str, styd on to lead ins last, rdn out: earlier scored at Nottingham
(reapp, h'cap): suited by 8.3f & likes gd/soft & hvy: handles a sharp trk: has run well fresh.

4045 **TAKE MANHATTAN** 17 [15] M R Channon 3-9-2 R Havlin 14/1: 166402: 3 b g Hamas - Arab Scimetar ½ **71**
(Sure Blade) Hld up, hdwy to lead 2f out till ins last, kept on, just btn: ran to best: see 3793, 2906.

4088 **HUGS DANCER** 15 [8] J G Given 3-9-0 Dean McKeown 16/1: -33403: 3 b g Cadeaux Genereux - 1 **67**
Embracing (Reference Point) In tch, hdwy to chall over 1f out, far side, no extra ins last: apprec drop back
to 8.3f & handles gd/soft, prob firm: lightly rcd.

4094 **PRINCE DU SOLEIL** 14 [11] J R Jenkins 4-9-3 F Norton 25/1: 000004: Held up, short of room over hd **66**
2f out, hdwy over 1f out, kept on ins last, not btn far: in '99 scored at M-Laffitte (stks): suited by 8.3f &
loves gd/soft & hvy grnd: return to form here.

3685 **SKY DOME** 39 [6] 7-9-3 A Beech (3) 8/1: 032545: Held up, eff 2f out, kept on same pace: see 3078. 1¼ **64**
*4143 **MAGICAL BAILIWICK** 11 [17] 4-9-3 (bl) G Gibbons (7) 12/1: 000216: Prom, led over 3f out till ½ **63$**
2f out, wknd fnl 1f: btr 4143.

3883 **STOPPES BROW** 28 [13] 8-9-3 (bl) R Hughes 9/2 JT FAV: 563447: Slow away, bhd, eff 2f out, eased 1¾ **60**
when btn ins last: clr of rem but can rate more highly: see 3883.

4192 **TOYON** 7 [1] 3-9-0 G Duffield 12/1: 340058: Prom, wknd over 2f out: see 2817. 8 **50**
4044 **KASS ALHAWA** 17 [14] 7-9-3 J Weaver 12/1: 225049: Led till over 3f out, no extra: see 4044 (Beverley). 1¾ **48**
4108 **CHAMELEON** 13 [2] 4-9-0 M Fenton 6/1: 105260: In tch, wknd well over 1f out, 10th: btr 3989. hd **44**
4118 **DIVINE PROSPECT** 12 [16] 3-8-11 J Fortune 12/1: 023500: Nvr a factor: 11th: see 3725. 2½ **40**
1003 **POLRUAN** 165 [12] 4-9-3 L Newman 33/1: 4-5640: In tch, btn 2f out: 12th, long abs, see 854. shd **43**
.3831 **DENS JOY** 31 [3] 4-9-0 D Sweeney 15/2: 540200: Nvr a factor: 13th: twice below 3643 (gd grnd) nk **40**

4033	**Lady Muck** 18 [7] 4-9-0 R Studholme (3) 66/1:	2767	**Angel Lane** 79 [12] 3-8-11 S Righton 50/1:
4218	**Regent** 6 [18] 5-9-3 A Mackay 33/1:	3944	**Emans Joy** 23 [9] 3-8-13 R Hills 12/1:
3793	**Ipanema Beach** 34 [4] 3-8-11 M Hills 12/1:		

18 ran   Time 1m 47.3   (The Farleigh Court Racing Partnership)   I A Balding Kingsclere, Hants

---

4293	4.35 SKY TEXT HCAP DIV 1 3YO+ 0-60 (F) 6f Good/Soft Inapplicable	[59]
	£1869 £534 £133 £133 3 yo rec 1 lb Field raced in 2 groups	

*299 **BOUND TO PLEASE** 270 [20] P J Makin 5-9-3 (48) A Clark 8/1: 013-11: 5 b g Warrshan - Hong Kong Girl **52**
(Petong) Chsd ldr, hdwy to lead ins fnl 1f, styd on, drvn out: last rcd back in Jan, won at Southwell (h'cap,
rtd 64a): '99 wnr again at Southwell (h'cap, rtd 55 on turf): eff at 5/6f, stays a sharp 7f: acts on fibresand,
fast & gd/soft: best up with/forcing the pace, likes Southwell: runs esp well fresh: on the upgrade.

3970 **MASTER LUKE** 22 [6] G L Moore 3-9-2 (48)(bl) R Brisland 16/1: 000202: 3 b g Contract Law - nk **51**
Flying Wind (Forzando) Led far side group, kept on for press over 1f out, just held: acts on fast & gd/soft.

3975 **SHINING STAR** 21 [5] J A Osborne 3-9-12 (58) S W Kelly (3) 14/1: 405043: 3 ch f Selkirk - Mystery nk **60**
Ship (Decoy Boy) Chsd ldr far side, ev ch from over 1f out, kept on press ins last, just btn: see 3975.

4207 **BORDER GLEN** 6 [21] J J Bridger 4-9-9 (54)(bl) J Weaver 10/1: 306433: Led stands side group till dht **56**
ins last, no extra, not btn far under hands & heels riding: see 4207.

4120 **ENCOUNTER** 12 [10] 4-9-7 (52) F Lynch 12/1: 160545: Bhd far side, some late gains, nrst fin: 1 **52**
interesting if returned to sell h'cap company: see 4120, 3144.

*4156 **PALO BLANCO** 10 [24] 9-9-12 (57)(7ex) L Newman (3) 11/1: 044016: In tch stands side, onepace over ¾ **55**
1f out: ran to form of 4156 (a/w).

4207	**ECUDAMAH** 6 [7] 4-9-7 (52)(vis) J Quinn 20/1: 000047: Handy far side, btn over 1f out: see 40.	hd	49
4027	**SUNSET HARBOUR** 18 [25] 7-9-0 (45) M Savage (7) 33/1: 060008: In tch stands side, btn over 1f out.	1¼	39
4102	**AKEBONO** 14 [19] 4-9-11 (56)(bl) D R McCabe 7/1 JT FAV: 410009: Bhd stands side, mod late gains.	1	48
4273	**FFYNNON GOLD** 2 [16] 3-9-4 (50) J Mackay (5) 33/1: 000060: In tch far side, btn dist: qck reapp.	hd	41
4102	**AMBER BROWN** 14 [11] 4-10-0 (59)(bl) G Duffield 12/1: 140060: In tch far side, wknd over 1f out: 11th.	nk	49
4066	**GLENDALE RIDGE** 16 [1] 5-9-7 (52) P Dobbs (5) 12/1: 000040: Chsd ldrs far side, btn 2f out: 12th.	hd	41
4065	**ASTRAC** 16 [4] 9-9-10 (55) T Ashley 11/1: 000000: In tch far side, wknd 2f out: 13th, see 4065, 406.	½	42
690	**NAUTICAL WARNING** 202 [22] 5-9-10 (55)(t) C Rutter 7/1 JT FAV: 2-1400: In tch stands side, wknd over 2f out: 16th: long abs, see 337.		0
*4120	**BRAMBLE BEAR** 12 [17] 6-10-0 (59) D Sweeney 10/1: 323610: In tch stands side, btn 2f out: 18th.		0
4015	**BLUE KITE** 20 [23] 5-9-13 (58) J Tate 9/1: 024600: In tch stands side, wknd over 2f out: 20th, see 3613.		0
3947	Hopeful Henry 23 [13] 4-9-3 (48) W Ryan 25/1:		4143 Consideration 11 [9] 3-9-2 (48) R Price 33/1:
4031	Blackpool Mammas 18 [12] 3-9-6 (52) F Norton 25/1:3759		Bettina Blue 36 [18] 3-9-6 (52) P Doe 33/1:
3124	Kind Emperor 63 [14] 3-9-11 (57) Dean McKeown 33/13197		Keen Hands 60 [2] 4-9-11 (56)(vis) R Fitzpatrick 25/1:
2026	Miss Flirtatious 110 [8] 3-9-9 (55) A McGlone 25/1:		4004 Mount Park 20 [3] 3-9-1 (47)(bl) D O'Donohoe 33/1:
24 ran	Time 1m 14.2 (3.9)	(Mrs P J Makin)	P J Makin Ogbourne Maisey, Wilts

---

4294	5.05 SKY TEXT HCAP DIV 2 2YO+ 0-60 (F)	6f	Good/Soft	Inapplicable	[59]
	£1869 £534 £267	3 yo rec 1 lb	Field raced in 2 Groups		

4033	**SQUARE DANCER** 18 [6] J Mods 4-10-0 (59) A Clark 20/1: 550601: 4 b g Then Again - Cubist (Tate Gallery) Led far side group & made most till over 1f out, styd on gamely to regain lead ins last, rdn out under top weight: '99 wnr at Carlisle (auct mdn) & Brighton (stks, rtd 75): stays 7f, all 3 wins at 6f & acts on firm, soft & any trk: gd weight carrier: on a handy mark.		63
4207	**HARVEYS FUTURE** 6 [3] P L Gilligan 6-9-1 (46) A Polli (3) 16/1: 32W062: 6 b g Never So Bold - Orba Gold (Final Crest) Cl-up far side, overall ldr over 1f out till ins last, just held by wnr: gd run: see 1910.	hd	49
3362	**SOLLYS PAL** 53 [5] P J Makin 5-9-3 (48)(vis) D Sweeney 16/1: -53103: 5 gr g Petong - Petriece (Mummy's Pet) Held up far side, eff well over 1f out, kept on onepace: 7 wk abs & acts on both AWs & gd/soft.	1¾	47
4004	**TANCRED ARMS** 20 [8] D W Barker 4-9-2 (47)(vis) F Lynch 25/1: 203004: Held up far side, kept on same pace over 1f out: clr of rem: one win in 41 starts but has slipped down the weights: see 3312, 3080.	1	44
4087	**BOWLERS BOY** 15 [4] 7-9-12 (57) J Fortune 9/1: 154035: Held up far side, brief eff well over 1f out, no impress: btr 4087, see 1941.	4	46
3966	**INDIAN WARRIOR** 22 [19] 4-9-0 (45)(BL) P McCabe 14/1: 602006: Handy stands side, led that group over 2f out, no extra over 1f out: first time blnks: acts on firm & gd/soft: see 3030, 364.	3	28
852	**ON THE TRAIL** 179 [1] 3-9-9 (55) W Ryan 33/1: 06-007: Chsd ldrs far side till no extra over 1f out: abs.	¾	36
4173	**DANCEMMA** 9 [17] 3-9-9 (55) J Quinn 33/1: 004008: Prom stands side, wknd 2f out: see 837.	½	35
4185	**BRANSTON LUCY** 8 [2] 3-9-13 (59) Dean McKeown 20/1: 224309: Slow away far side, nvr a factor.	¾	37
4126	**VIOLET** 12 [13] 4-9-3 (49) T Williams 14/1: 506000: Held up far side, wknd 2f out: 10th: see 3341.	¾	24
4155	**MUTASAWWAR** 10 [21] 6-9-4 (49) F Norton 25/1: 002220: Held up stands side, nvr a factor: 11th.	hd	24
4102	**KILMEENA LAD** 14 [14] 4-9-11 (56) S Carson (3) 4/1 FAV: 000020: Prom, wknd over 2f out: 12th: nicely bckd & better expected after 4102 (7f, gd grnd).	nk	30
2183	**LADY JEANNIE** 103 [23] 3-9-1 (47) J Mackay (5) 20/1: 0600: Led stands side group till 2f out, no extra: 13th: 3 month abs: see 1263.	¾	19
2961	**PRESENT CHANCE** 70 [15] 6-9-12 (57)(bl) L Newton 16/1: 505560: Al bhd stands side: 14th, abs.	½	28
*4155	**MARENGO** 10 [22] 6-10-0 (59)(7ex) R Fitzpatrick 10/1: 500010: In tch stands side, wknd 2f out: 15th.	½	29
4192	**AIR MAIL** 7 [11] 3-9-10 (56) J Tate 10/1: 001020: In tch far side, wknd 2f out: 20th: btr 4129, 3770.		0
3975	Sontime 21 [10] 3-9-7 (53) M Fenton 33/1:		4192 Lady Noor 7 [24] 3-9-6 (52) P Doe 16/1:
4087	Kebabs 15 [18] 3-9-11 (57) S W Kelly (3) 11/1:		4065 Kayo Gee 16 [9] 4-9-7 (52)(vis) G Duffield 33/1:
2264	Brompton Barrage 99 [25] 3-9-8 (54) R Hughes 33/1:		4207 Trump Street 6 [20] 4-9-1 (46) L Newman (3) 33/1:
3966	Magic Eagle 22 [7] 3-9-6 (52) J Weaver 20/1:		3279 Night Shifter 56 [12] 3-9-5 (51) P Dobbs (5) 16/1:
2519}	Regalo 456 [16] 5-9-10 (55) R Havlin 33/1:		
25 ran	Time 1m 13.4	(A Mallen)	M Dods Piercebridge, Co Durham

---

4295	5.35 RACING CHANNEL HCAP 3YO+ 0-70 (E)	5f	Good/Soft	Inapplicable	[70]
	£2940 £840 £420	Runners fanned across the course			

4037	**CHORUS** 18 [1] B R Millman 3-9-11 (67) G Hind 20/1: 216001: 3 b f Bandmaster - Name That Tune (Fayruz) Hdwy to lead far side over 1f out, styd on ins last, rdn out: earlier scored at Sandown (mdn, 1st time visor), also plcd sev times: best at 5f, stays 6f: acts on firm, hvy & fibresand: has won in a visor, not today.		72
4155	**TANCRED TIMES** 10 [10] D W Barker 5-8-11 (53) F Lynch 20/1: 526062: 5 ch m Clantime - Mischievous Miss (Niniski) Handy, eff far side over 1f out, kept on ins last, just held: gd run: likes Hamilton: see 2395.	nk	57
4223	**POLAR MIST** 6 [17] M Wigham 5-9-0 (56)(tbl) Dean McKeown 20/1: 000603: 5 b g Polar Falcon - Post Mistress (Cyrano de Bergerac) Handy, stayed stands side & eff over 1f out, kept on same pace: best 1487.	1½	57
3747	**WAFFS FOLLY** 36 [15] D J S ffrench Davis 4-8-12 (54) R Studholme (3) 10/1: 035324: In tch, outpcd over 2f out, stayed stands side, styd on well ins last: op 7/1: see 3747, 1082.	hd	54
3455	**CLAN CHIEF** 49 [2] 7-9-2 (58) J Quinn 16/1: /02005: In tch, eff over 2f out, no extra ins last.	shd	57
1531	**GORETSKI** 132 [9] 7-9-8 (64) J Fortune 14/1: 000006: Handy, rdn & onepace over 1f out: abs.	nk	62
3689	**KNOCKEMBACK NELLIE** 39 [19] 4-8-13 (55)(bl) R Havlin 20/1: 050056: Led till over 1f out, no extra: see 3689, 2788.	1	51
3619	**MUKARRAB** 42 [21] 6-8-7 (49) J Mackay (5) 14/1: 444508: Nvr a factor: 6 wk abs: see 3619, 2340.	shd	44
3960	**FACILE TIGRE** 22 [5] 5-8-8 (50) G Gibbons (2) 25/1: 023609: In tch, wknd fnl 1f: see 3594.	shd	45
3821	**BEYOND CALCULATION** 32 [4] 6-10-0 (70) F Norton 14/1: 442000: Bhd, mod late gains: 10th.	nk	64
3605	**MALADERIE** 42 [16] 6-8-5 (47) A Clark 11/1: 000040: In tch, eff over 1f out, no impress: 11th, abs.	nk	40
3512	**SOTONIAN** 47 [7] 8-9-0 (56) J Weaver 7/1: 365100: In tch, eff 2f out, no extra ins last: 12th: 7 wk abs, best 3271 (fibresand).	hd	48
3960	**STATOYORK** 22 [25] 7-9-8 (64) T Williams 7/1 JT FAV: 141500: Nvr a factor, 13th: see 3960, 3788.	¾	54
3457	**DETECTIVE** 49 [2] 4-8-9 (51)(BL) J Lowe 25/1: 0-5000: Chsd ldrs, wknd over 1f out: eased ins last: 14th, 7 wk abs, tried blnkrs: see 2833.	hd	40
4065	**KILCULLEN LAD** 16 [13] 6-9-6 (62)(vis) L Newman (3) 8/1: 035050: Sn bhd, kept on late: 15th, see 4065.	½	49
4065	**PRIDE OF BRIXTON** 16 [3] 7-8-7 (49) M Henry 9/1: 112000: In tch, wknd fnl 1f: 16th: see 4065, 1140.	¾	35
*4065	**ABSOLUTE FANTASY** 16 [14] 4-9-6 (62)(bl) S Carson (3) 7/1 JT FAV: 120510: In tch, wknd fnl 1f: 17th.	½	46
4081	**COUTURE** 15 [11] 8-9-6 (65) R Hughes 10/1: 2550: Al bhd: 23rd: btr 3221 (1m, fast grnd).		0
3136	Diamond Decorum 63 [22] 4-9-12 (68) R Fitzpatrick 16/13803		Frampant 33 [6] 3-8-12 (54) M Tebbutt 20/1:

WINDSOR FRIDAY OCTOBER 6TH Sharp, Fig 8 Track

4027 **Fairy Prince 18** [18] 7-9-6 (62)(bl) A McGlone 16/1:   3947 **White Summit 23** [20] 3-8-8 (49)(1ow) M Fenton 25/1:
2555 **Diamond Promise 88** [23] 3-9-0 (56) P Doe 16/1:   3594 **Pisces Lad 43** [24] 4-8-9 (51)(BL) D O'Donohoe 20/1:
24 ran   Time 1m 01.1   (In The Know)   B R Millman Kentisbeare, Devon

---

ASCOT SATURDAY OCTOBER 7TH Righthand, Stiff, Galloping Track

Official Going   HEAVY. Stalls: Rnd Crse - Inside.

4296
1.30 LISTED AUTUMN STKS 2YO (A)   **1m rnd**   **Heavy**   **Inapplicable**
£13487   £4150   £2075   £1037

*3983 **NAYEF 22** [4] M P Tregoning 2-8-11 R Hills 7/4 FAV: -11: 2 b c Gulch - Height Of Fashion   119+
(Bustino) In tch, prog to lead dist, sn clr, impressive: hvly bckd: recent Newbury debut wnr (stks): bred in the
purple, half brother to numerous wnrs, notably top-class Nashwan & Unfuwain: dam a high-class mid-dist performer:
eff over a stiff 1m, will apprec mid-dists next term: acts on firm & hvy, gall trk: runs well fresh: lightly
raced & looks potentially top-class, held in the highest regard & now the winter 2000 Guineas & Derby favourite.
4127 **HILL COUNTRY 13** [2] J H M Gosden 2-8-11 J Fortune 2/1: -0132: 2 b c Danehill - Rose Of Jericho   6   107
(Alleged) Prom, ev ch 2f out, sn left bhnd by impress wnr: well bckd: acts on fast & hvy: met a potentially
top-class rival today: shld win a List/Gr company: see 4127, 3799.
4158 **COUNT DUBOIS 11** [3] W J Haggas 2-8-11 (BL) B Marcus 7/1: -1233: 2 b c Zafonic - Madame Dubois   ¾   105
(Legend Of France) Held up, prog 2f out, no impress ins last: op 5/1: tried blnks & has an awkward head carriage.
*4124 **LUNAR CRYSTAL 13** [6] D R C Elsworth 2-8-11 Pat Eddery 6/1: -14: Chsd ldrs, prog to lead 2f out   ¾   103
till dist, no extra: clr of rem: fine run in this better grade: acts on hvy grnd: see 4124 (7f here).
4124 **KING CAREW 13** [5] 2-8-11 Craig Williams 9/1: -25: Front rank 6f, wknd: again bhnd this 4th in 4124.   6   93
3866 **ISTIHSAAN 30** [1] 2-8-11 W Supple 40/1: -56: Set pace 6f, wknd: stablemate of wnr & highly tried.   10   76
6 ran   Time 1m 49.79 (11.29)   (Hamdan Al Maktoum)   M P Tregoning Lambourn, Berks.

*****Remainder of Meeting Abandoned due to Security Alert*****

YORK SATURDAY OCTOBER 7TH Lefthand, Flat, Galloping Track

Official Going   HEAVY. Stalls: Inside, except 5f/6f/7f - Far Side.

4297
2.10 EBF MDN 2YO (D)   **1m rnd**   **Heavy 169**   **-75 Slow**
£6669   £2052   £1026   £513

3952 **TUPGILL TANGO 24** [3] S E Kettlewell 2-9-0 R Winston 25/1: 01: 2 ch g Presidium - Tangalooma   80
(Hotfoot) Held up, prog 2f out, led 1f out, rdn out: 8,500gns half-brother to a miler, dam hdles wnr: clrly
apprec step up to a gall 1m on hvy grnd & shld get further next term: acts on a gall trk.
4161 **ART EXPERT 11** [4] P F I Cole 2-9-0 D Holland 5/2: 02: 2 b c Pursuit Of Love - Celtic Wing (Midyan)   ¾   77
Well plcd, rdn to lead appr fnl 2f, hdd 1f out, rallied: well bckd: better run, eff at 1m on hvy grnd.
3836 **SIMLA BIBI 32** [7] B J Meehan 2-8-9 G Duffield 2/1 FAV: 33: 2 b f Indian Ridge - Scandalette   nk   71
(Niniski) Bhd ldr, hmpd ent str, led 3f out till appr fnl 2f, kept on: nicely bckd, clr rem: stays 1m on firm & hvy.
--   **FIND THE KING** [5] D W P Arbuthnot 2-9-0 J Weaver 6/1: 4: Held up, imprvd ent fnl 3f, outpcd bef   6   62
fnl 1f: debut: IR26,000gns King's Theatre half-brother to sev wnrs up to 2m: sure to do better next term at 10f+.
4082 **CANOVAS KINGDOM 16** [1] 2-9-0 F Norton 16/1: 05: Chsd ldrs, chall appr fnl 2f, fdd: sprint bred.   3   55
2649 **COTTONTAIL 85** [9] 2-9-0 W Ryan 16/1: 006: Led, edged right ent str, hdd 3f out, sn btn: 3 mth abs.   16   25
3866 **AMBERSONG 30** [4] 2-9-0 S Whitworth 6/1: 07: Mid-div, wknd qckly ent fnl 3f: see 3866.   6   13
7 ran   Time 1m 54.32 (19.52)   (The Tupgill Partnership)   S E Kettlewell Middleham, N.Yorks.

4298
2.40 LISTED ROCKINGHAM STKS 2YO (A)   **6f**   **Heavy 169**   **-04 Slow**
£14352   £5093   £1157   £578

3086 **ATMOSPHERIC 66** [2] P F I Cole 2-9-2 (BL) D Sweeney 7/4 FAV: -12101: 2 ch c Irish River - Magic   106
Feeling (Magical Wonder) Led, rdn & styd on strongly ins last, unchall: well bckd tho' op 11/10, revitalised
by blnks & forcing tactics: earlier won at Pontefract (mdn) & Epsom (List): eff at 5/6f, bred to get at least
1m: acts on gd & hvy grnd, disapp on fast last time: goes well fresh: progressive, v useful colt.
3900 **NEARLY A FOOL 28** [4] B A McMahon 2-8-11 F Lynch 5/2: 333302: 2 b g Komaite - Greenway Lady   2½   95
(Prince Daniel) Chsd wnr thr'out, rdn appr fnl 1f, nvr any impress: ran to best: eff at 5/6f on firm & hvy.
3859 **HEALEY 31** [1] J D Bethell 2-8-11 J Weaver 4/1: 1143: 2 ch c Dr Devious - Bean Siamsa (Solinus)   4   85
Pulled hard, trkd ldrs, eff 2f out, sn onepace: first try on hvy grnd, prob flattered by 3463 (hasn't worked out).
3959 **MAMMAS TONIGHT 23** [5] A Berry 2-9-0 (bl) G Carter 9/4: 540044: Held up in tch, left bhd appr   5   76
fnl 1f: bckd tho' op 7/4, 2nd time blnks up in trip: see 1761.
4 ran   Time 1m 19.76 (10.36)   (Highclere Thoroughbred Racing Ltd)   P F I Cole Whatcombe, Oxon.

4299
3.10 WORSHIPFUL HCAP 3YO+ 0-85 (D)   **1m5f194y**   **Heavy 169**   **-16 Slow**   **[85]**
£8329   £2563   £1281   £640   3 yo rec 9 lb

*3819 **DISTANT PROSPECT 33** [7] I A Balding 3-8-8 (74) Martin Dwyer 10/1: 235411: 3 b c Namaqualand -   80
Ukraine's Affair (The Minstrel) Rear, imprvd ent str, rdn to lead appr fnl 1f, kept on strongly: last time won at Bath
(mdn h'cap): imprvd at 13/14f, shld get 2m: acts on fast & hvy grnd, any trk: progressive styr.
3023 **KADOUN 69** [12] L M Cumani 3-8-10 (76) G Sparkes (7) 12/1: -24432: 3 b c Doyoun - Kumta (Priolo)   1¾   80
Chsd ldrs, prog to lead appr fnl 1f, sn hdd, styd on: 10 wk abs, clr rem, h'cap bow: improving, stays 14f on hvy.
4092 **SPRING PURSUIT 15** [16] R J Price 4-9-7 (78) M Fenton 14/1: 500033: 4 b g Rudimentary - Pursuit Of   4   78
Truth (Irish River) Front rank, led ent str till bef fnl 1f, onepace: clr rem: loves mud, return to 12f suit.
4014 **NIGHT VENTURE 21** [17] B W Hills 4-10-0 (85) D Holland 11/1: 003044: Led till ent str, same pace.   6   80
*4280 **EVENING SCENT 2** [8] 4-7-12 (55) K Dalgleish (5) 9/4 FAV: 164115: Towards rear, imprvd into mid-div   5   46
4f out, no further impression: nicely bckd, won here 48hrs ago in 4280 (12f).

4222 **SIMPLE IDEALS 7** [11] 6-7-10 (53)(8oh) Kim Tinkler 10/1: 425246: Mid-div, onepce ent str: bckd from 20/1. 1¾ 43
4071 **NICELY 17** [13] 4-8-8 (65) M Henry 12/1: 050007: Held up, chsd ldrs 3f out, wknd qckly appr fnl 1f. 3½ 52
4134 **THE BUTTERWICK KID 13** [10] 7-8-12 (69) G Duffield 12/1: 0-0468: Prom till lost pl 3f out: see 3437. 15 44
*4221 **NOWELL HOUSE 7** [2] 4-9-7 (78) P Hanagan (5) 13/2: 000119: In tch till ent str: op 4/1, qck reapp, poss unsuited by step up in trip on this v testing grnd: see 4221 (10f). 18 39
4071 **TOTEM DANCER 17** [9] 7-7-13 (56) T Williams 16/1: 206300: Al bhd, eased when btn appr fnl 2f: 10th. dist 0
3994 **MAJESTIC BAY 21** [5] 4-9-13 (84) J Weaver 12/1: 314100: Handy till 4f out: 11th: see 3783 (made all). shd 0
4105 **MAGIC COMBINATION 14** [3] 7-8-12 (69) S W Kelly (3) 12/1: 451500: Al bhd: 13th, see 3472. 0
3979 **Swift 22** [15] 6-8-1 (58) F Norton 25/1: 3993 **Makasseb 22** [1] 3-8-7 (73) R Mullen 20/1:
14 ran Time 3m 19.24 (25.84) (The Rae Smiths & Pauline Gale) I A Balding Kingsclere, Hants.

4300

3.40 SCHRODERS HCAP 3YO+ 0-80 (D) 1m1f Heavy 169 -09 Slow [79]
£13689 £4212 £2106 £1053 3 yo rec 4 lb

3603 **GREENAWAY BAY 43** [9] K R Burke 6-8-6 (57) D Mernagh (3) 12/1: 463-51: 6 ch g Green Dancer - Raise N Dance (Raise A Native) In tch, prog to trk ldrs on bit appr fnl 2f, rdn ent fnl 1f & ran on to lead fnl 100y: 6 wk abs, cracking ride, 4th in this last year: '99 Brighton wnr (h'cap, rtd 59): plcd sev times in '98 for W Musson (rtd 62 & 59a): eff at 1m/10f: acts on firm & hvy grnd, any trk: goes well fresh. 64
4160 **ANNADAWI 11** [17] C N Kellett 5-10-0 (79) G Baker (5) 25/1: 633102: 5 b g Sadler's Wells - Prayers'n Promises (Foolish Pleasure) Bhd, prog appr fnl 3f, drvn to lead & hung left bef fnl 1f, hdd & edged right towards fin: fine effort under jt top-weight & back to form: clrly suited by soft/hvy grnd: see 4085. 1¾ 83
4094 **ROUTE SIXTY SIX 15** [21] Jedd O'Keeffe 4-8-8 (59) G Sparkes (7) 9/1 CO FAV: 023223: 4 b f Brief Truce - Lyphards Goddess (Lyphard's Special) Patiently rdn, gd prog 3f out to chall 1f out, sn no extra: op 7/1: v consistent filly, stays 9f but will prob apprec a return to 1m: see 3011. 2½ 60
4217 **SCENE 7** [10] N P Littmoden 5-9-4 (69) C Carver (3) 12/1: 000004: Mid-div, feeling pace ent str, imprvd 2f out, not trble ldrs: qck reapp, signs of return to form & on a handy mark: acts on firm, suited by soft. 1 69
4215 **NOUF 7** [22] 4-9-9 (74) S Whitworth 11/1: 051205: Towards rear, prog to chse ldrs ent fnl 2f, sn rdn, edged left & onepace: op 8/1, qck reapp: not far off best back up in trip, likes soft/hvy grnd: see 4094. shd 74
4217 **ROLLER 7** [27] 4-9-7 (72) J Fanning 14/1: 403606: Rear, styd on ent fnl 2f, nvr nr to chall: op 10/1. 1½ 70
4136 **CHINA RED 13** [16] 6-9-9 (74) D Holland 33/1: 001007: Led till bef fnl 1f, fdd: clr rem: a bold attempt on grnd much softer than ideal, see 3404 (fast grnd clmr). ½ 71
4217 **CLEVER GIRL 7** [20] 3-9-1 (70) J Weaver 20/1: 305008: Cl-up & ev ch till wknd appr fnl 1f: see 823. 7 59
4160 **CALLDAT SEVENTEEN 11** [6] 4-9-9 (74)(tVIS) P D'Arcy 16/1: 6001R9: Reluctant to race & nvr got in it: op 12/1, visored: has been uncharacteristically mulish last twice: see 3979. 6 56
1070 **DISPOL ROCK 159** [25] 4-9-4 (69) G Duffield 33/1: 0-000: Nvr better than mid-div: 10th, abs: '99 wnr at Ripon (h'cap, rtd 76, P Calver): '98 wnr at Newcastle (mdn auct, rtd 74): eff at 7f/1m, stays 10f: acts on fast & gd grnd, any trk: can force the pace: clrly had his problems this year: with S Kettlewell. 1½ 49
4085 **NOMINATOR LAD 16** [23] 6-9-9 (74)(bl) F Lynch 20/1: 416060: Chsd ldrs, wknd appr fnl 2f: 11th. 10 44
3731 **WERE NOT STOPPIN 38** [14] 5-8-7 (58) O Pears 10/1: 141300: Handy till lost pl 3f out: 12th, see 2556. ¾ 27
4067 **EYELETS ECHO 17** [11] 3-8-11 (66)(VIS) R Winston 14/1: 015060: Chsd ldrs till 3f out: 13th: visored, back in trip, needs faster grnd: see 2276. ½ 35
4217 **BACCHUS 7** [18] 6-9-7 (72)(vis) J Carroll 9/1 CO FAV: 156020: Rear, prog to chase ldrs appr fnl 2f, sn btn: 14th, op 6/1, qck reapp, faster grnd prob suits: see 2671. 9 32
*3936 **ADELPHI BOY 24** [2] 4-9-6 (71) R Studholme (3) 12/1: 600210: Well plcd till 3f out: 15th, back up in trip after making all on firm grnd in 3936. 3½ 27
4094 **DEE PEE TEE CEE 15** [24] 6-10-0 (79) T Lucas 14/1: 0-0000: In tch till appr str: 16th, jt top-weight. nk 34
3809 **JORROCKS 34** [5] 6-8-11 (62) P Hanagan (5) 9/1 CO FAV: 0-2600: Mid-div, eff & btn 3f out: 17th, op 6/1, unproven beyond 7.5f: see 2882. 5 12
4204 **Dorissio 7** [3] 4-8-13 (64) Martin Dwyer 14/1: 4067 **Welsh Ploy 17** [19] 3-9-5 (74) M Tebbutt 25/1:
4217 **Favorisio 7** [12] 3-9-0 (69) A Culhane 25/1:
20 ran Time 2m 04.84 (16.04) (Asterlane Ltd) K R Burke Newmarket.

4301

4.15 CORAL SPRINT HCAP 3YO+ 0-100 (C) 6f Heavy 169 +13 Fast [100]
£25642 £7890 £3945 £1972 3 yo rec 1 lb 2 Groups, prob no advantage

4129 **FURTHER OUTLOOK 13** [16] D Nicholls 6-9-11 (97) R Winston 14/1: 030031: 6 gr g Zilzal - Future Bright (Lyphard's Wish) Made all stands side, drvn 1f out, ran on strongly: fast time: '99 wnr at Pontefract, Epsom & Doncaster (rtd h'cap, rtd 101): plcd in '98 (h'caps, rtd 84, Mrs Perrett): stays 1m, suited by 5/6f: acts on firm, hvy grnd, any trk: eff up with/forcing the pace: v useful & tough (been busy all turf season). 105
4106 **CARD GAMES 14** [22] M W Easterby 3-8-9 (82) T Lucas 16/1: 200502: 3 b f First Trump - Pericardia (Petong) Chsd wnr stands side, kept on appr fnl 1f but nvr any impression: back to form back in trip: see 1133. 2½ 86
+4165 **FIRE DOME 10** [5] Andrew Reid 8-9-3 (89) M Henry 15/2: 110013: 8 ch g Salt Dome - Penny Habit (Habitat) Chsd ldrs towards far side, prog to lead that group & ev ch appr fnl 1f, no extra fnl 100y: fine run. ½ 92
4165 **ABBAJABBA 10** [12] C W Fairhurst 4-8-9 (81) J Fanning 4/1 FAV: 131204: Prom stands side, eff ent fnl 2f, styd on but nvr pace to chall: well bckd from 8/1: shade btr 3366. 1¾ 80
4129 **LAGO DI VARANO 13** [7] 8-9-2 (88)(bl) Dean McKeown 11/1: 200265: Led group towards far side till appr fnl 1f, edged right & left ins last, onepace: not disgraced up in trip, see 3183. shd 87
4012 **ROYAL RESULT 21** [21] 7-9-2 (88) Alex Greaves 12/1: 440056: In tch stands side, shkn up 2f out, nvr nr to chall: stablemate wnr: not given a hard time but winless this term: see 728. 1 85
4012 **KAYO 21** [6] 5-9-12 (98) D Holland 20/1: 350407: Prom far side, ev ch ent fnl 2f, onepace 1f out. 3 89
4015 **IVORY DAWN 21** [8] 6-8-6 (78) C Carver (3) 20/1: 302008: Chsd ldrs far side till appr fnl 1f: see 2761. 3½ 62
4257 **CAUDA EQUINA 4** [4] 6-8-9 (81) R Mullen 25/1: 130509: Dwelt, nvr got in it far side: qck reapp. 1½ 62
4129 **BON AMI 13** [2] 4-9-2 (88) P Bradley (5) 20/1: 240000: Chsd ldrs far side till 2f out: 10th, see 1004. ½ 68
4012 **ZUHAIR 21** [1] 7-8-12 (84) F Norton 20/1: 050100: Outpcd far side, styd on thr' btn horses fnl 1f: 11th, stablemate wnr, suited by faster grnd: see 3904. ½ 63
4012 **MARSAD 21** [9] 6-9-2 (88) P Doe 10/1: 002000: Reared start, well plcd far side, rdn/btn appr fnl 1f: 12th. hd 67
4165 **JUWWI 10** [13] 6-9-0 (86) M Savage (7) 7/1: 000040: Dwelt, nvr on terms stands side: 13th, bckd from 10/1. 2 61
4010 **FRIAR TUCK 21** [3] 5-8-8 (80) K Dalgleish (5) 25/1: 113000: Front rank far side, lost pl 2f out: 14th. hd 55
4010 **FEARBY CROSS 21** [15] 4-8-6 (78) L Newton 12/1: 100000: Mid-div stands side till wknd after halfway: 21st. 0
3315 **Debbies Warning 56** [19] 4-9-1 (87) S Whitworth 33/1: 3992 **Karameg 22** [10] 4-8-10 (82) A Beech (3) 20/1:
3152 **Return Of Amin 63** [14] 6-8-7 (79)(bl) Martin Dwyer 16/1: 3861 **Brecongill Lad 31** [18] 8-9-1 (87) A Nicholls 16/1:
4195 **First Maite 8** [11] 7-9-0 (86)(tvi) G Duffield 20/1: 2229 **Loch Inch 101** [20] 3-9-0 (87)(bl) M Tebbutt 50/1:
4112 **Pips Magic 14** [23] 4-8-9 (81) A Culhane 33/1:

YORK   SATURDAY OCTOBER 7TH   Lefthand, Flat, Galloping Track

22 ran   Time 1m 18.74 (9.34)   (Mark A Leatham)   D Nicholls Sessay, N.Yorks.

4302   4.45 NEWTON HCAP 3YO+ 0-85 (D)   7f rnd   Heavy 169 -16 Slow   [83]
£10887   £3350   £1675   £837   3 yo rec 2 lb Came stands side in straight

4112 **I CRIED FOR YOU** 14 [19] J G Given 5-9-13 (82) Dean McKeown 9/2 FAV: 120041: 5 b g Statoblest -   88
Fall Of The Hammer (Auction Ring) Trkd ldrs, chall ent fnl 2f, drvn to lead & edged left 1f out, kept on well: bckd
from 7/1: earlier won at Lingfield (class stks) & Doncaster (h'cap): '99 winr at Nottingham (class stks) &
Windsor (h'cap, rtd 76): eff at 6f, stays 1m, best at 7f: acts on firm & hvy, any trk: best without blnks/vis:
has a high cruising speed & this was a good weight carrying performance in testing conditions.

4217 **MELODIAN** 7 [24] M Brittain 5-9-1 (70)(bl) D Mernagh (3) 15/2: 000132: 5 b h Grey Desire - Mere   1½   73
Melody (Dunphy) Trkd ldrs, feeling pace 3f out, rall for press fnl 200y: tchd 10/1, qck reapp: a real mudlark.

4165 **AMBER FORT** 10 [1] J M Bradley 7-9-3 (68)(bl) P Fitzsimons (5) 16/1: 004403: 7 gr g Indian   1¼   69
Ridge - Lammastide (Martinmas) Bhd, kept on well appr fnl 1f, nvr nrr: apprec return to 7f, see 1011.

*4217 **RYMERS RASCAL** 7 [15] E J Alston 8-8-12 (67) M Fenton 12/1: 530314: Mid-div, prog ent fnl 2f,   ¾   67
styd on but nvr nr ldrs: op 10/1, qck reapp: return to 1m will suit: see 4217.

4010 **MISTER MAL** 21 [7] G Duffield 8/1: 102065: Well plcd, led 2f out, drvn & hdd ent fnl   1½   76
1f, fdd: ran nr to best & well clr rem: see 3250.

4010 **GIFT OF GOLD** 21 [12] (BL) D Holland 20/1: 005006: Chsd ldrs, chall 2f out, wknd: blnks.   6   69

3936 **TAFFS WELL** 24 [2] 7-8-11 (66) J Fanning 16/1: 000007: Mid-div thr'out: see 715.   1½   53

1989 **A TOUCH OF FROST** 112 [5] 5-10-0 (83)(bl) G Baker (5) 16/1: 50-148: Towards rear, imprvd ent   5   62
str, rdn & wknd bef fnl 1f: top-weight, 4 month abs, faster grnd suits: see 1716.

4220 **SULU** 7 [3] 4-8-11 (66) T Lucas 20/1: 001009: Nvr troubled ldrs: qck reapp, back up in trip, see 1162.   4   39

*4106 **DAKOTA SIOUX** 14 [18] 3-9-3 (74)(bl) P Hanagan (5) 10/1: 011010: Led till 2f out, sn btn: 10th,   12   32
acts on fast & gd/soft, poss not hvy: see 4106.

3791 **ZIETZIG** 35 [21] 3-9-7 (78) N Callan 25/1: 010000: Mid-div, eff ent str, sn btn: 11th: stole a h'cap 3130 (fast)   ½   35

4204 **TUMBLEWEED RIVER** 7 [4] 4-9-7 (76) D R McCabe 10/1: -00020: Al towards rear: 12th, qk reapp.   ¾   32

2581 **KUWAIT DAWN** 87 [22] 4-9-4 (73) S Whitworth 33/1: 006000: Nvr nr ldrs: 13th, 3 month abs, vis off.   1¼   27

3188 **THE DOWNTOWN FOX** 61 [11] 5-8-12 (67)(bl) L Newton 16/1: 002040: Nvr a factor: 14th, 9 wk abs.   2   18

3785 **PETERS IMP** 35 [17] 5-9-6 (75) J Carroll 20/1: 143360: Al bhd, no ch ldrs when hmpd appr fnl 1f: 15th.   3   21

4126 **NOMORE MR NICEGUY** 13 [16] 9-9-3 (72) A Culhane 16/1: 460350: Nvr dngrs: 16th, stablemate 4th.   nk   17

4112 **GIRLS BEST FRIEND** 14 [10] 3-9-5 (76)(t) K Dalgleish 25/1: 056000: Nvr in it: 17th, see 1374,   nk   20

*4037 **RANDOM TASK** 19 [6] 3-9-4 (77)(bl) R Winston 14/1: 4-0610: Speed 3f: 18th, see 4037 (6f, 1st time blnks).   3   17

3992 **Unshaken** 22 [23] 6-8-11 (66) F Lynch 16/1:   4204 **Most Saucy** 7 [8] 4-9-9 (78) R Mullen 33/1:
4199 **Mexican Rock** 8 [20] 4-9-11 (80) J Weaver 33/1:   4297} **Canovas Heart** 364 [14] 11-9-11 (80) F Norton 20/1: P
22 ran   Time 1m 34.72 (12.97)   (One Stop Partnership)   J G Given Willoughton, Lincs.

AYR   MONDAY OCTOBER 9TH   Lefthand, Galloping Track

Official Going HEAVY. Stalls: Rnd Crse - Inside; Str Crse - Stands Side.

4303   2.10 KIRKOSWALD MDN STKS 2YO   7f rnd   Heavy 182 -52 Slow
£3776   £1162   £581   £290

4008 **BAILLIESTON** 23 [2] J S Goldie 2-9-0 A Culhane 1/5 FAV: 3351: 2 ch g Indian Ridge - Bathilde   81
(Generous) Made all, clr appr fnl 2f, eased ins last: val 10L+: well bckd at long odds on: 47,000gns first
foal, dam mid-dist performer: eff arnd 7f, 1m+ shld suit in time: acts on gd/soft, hvy & a gall trk.

3962 **SHATIN PLAYBOY** 25 [5] Miss L A Perratt 2-9-0 R Winston 8/1: 4402: 2 ch c Goldmark - Skinity (Rarity)   5   66
Keen, chsd wnr, rdn/no impress appr fnl 1f: 18L clr rem: poss stays 7f on hvy, sells shld suit: see 3962, 2717.

3376 **MEIKLE PRINCE** 54 [4] Miss L A Perratt 2-9-0 D Mernagh (3) 33/1: 03: 2 br c Contract Law - Dunston   18   46
Princess (Cyrano de Bergerac) Prom, rdn/no extra fnl 2f: 8 wk abs, up in trip: see 3376 (5f seller, gd/soft).

4252 **WITHIN THE LAW** 6 [3] W Storey 2-8-9 T Williams 40/1: 04: In tch, wknd fnl 2f: qck reapp, up in trip.   nk   41

--   **ROSE OF AMERICA** [1] 2-8-9 K Dalgleish 12/1: 5: V slow to start, sn prom, drvn/wknd rapidly   19   21
ent 2f, t.o.: op 5/1: stablemate of 2nd & 3rd: 20,000gns half-sister to juv wnrs at 6f & 1m: with Miss L Perratt.
5 ran   Time 1m 40.18 (16.38)   (Martin Delaney & Frank Brady)   J S Goldie Uplawmoor, E.Renfrewshire

4304   2.40 FAILFORD CLAIMER 3YO (E)   1m2f192y   Heavy 182 -48 Slow
£2769   £852   £426   £213

2246 **TARA HALL** 103 [5] W M Brisbourne 3-8-1 K Dalgleish (5) 25/1: 50-051: 3 b f Saddlers' Hall - Katie   59
Scarlett (Lochnager) Mid-div, eff 5f out, led appr fnl 1f, drvn clr ins last, eased cl-home: jockey rec a 2 day
whip ban: long abs: clmd for £7,000: unplcd over 1m last term, incl blnkd (with N Littmoden): eff arnd 11f,
further could suit: coped well with v testing conditions today.

4178 **SKYE BLUE** 11 [4] M R Channon 3-8-11 A Culhane 5/1: 056542: 3 b g Blues Traveller - Hitopah (Bustino)   5   57
Mid-div, hdwy 5f out, sn outpcd, rall/styd on appr fnl 1f, no ch with wnr: op 7/1: acts on gd & hvy: see 2712.

3702 **MANSTAR** 42 [11] C W Fairhurst 3-8-5 N Kennedy 20/1: 000063: 3 b g In The Wings - Model Village   1½   48$
(Habitat) Chsd ldrs, hdwy to lead appr fnl 2f, hung left & hdd over 1f out, sn btn: 6 wk abs, treat rating
with caution (offic only 44): handles fast & hvy grnd: see 1193, 827.

4162 **CAROUSING** 13 [2] R M Beckett 3-9-0 (bl) K Darley 11/8 FAV: 500104: Prom, outpcd over 3f out,   3½   53
rallied & styd on late, no threat to ldrs: well bckd: handled soft grnd in 3988 (9f, first time blnks).

4178 **WENSUM DANCER** 11 [9] P Doe 3-8-2 F Norton 8/1: 640425: Trkd ldrs, chall 2f out, wknd qckly appr dist: 9   31
tchd 9/2: much btr 4178 (12f, gd grnd).

4222 **INDY CARR** 9 [3] 3-8-4 Iona Wands 8/1: 000106: Keen, sn led, hdd appr fnl 2f, fdd: twice below 4002.   1½   31

4221 **CANNY HILL** 9 [6] 3-8-11 O Pears 33/1: 300507: Nvr dngrs: up in trip: see 3988.   8   28

4002 **WORTH THE RISK** 23 [1] 3-7-13 Kim Tinkler 20/1: 350028: Chsd ldrs, wknd qckly halfway: stiff task.   4   11

3806 **HIGHLAND GOLD** 36 [7] 3-9-0 J Carroll 25/1: 500049: Led early, remained with ldrs, wknd rapidly   11   16
fnl 4f, t.o.: up in trip: see 2006.

4002 **PADDY MUL** 23 [10] 3-8-2 (VIS) T Williams 33/1: 003040: Al well bhd, t.o. halfway: 10th: visor.   dist   0

3827 **PAPI SPECIAL** 35 [8] 3-8-11 (vis) R Winston 10/1: 2D2000: Trkd ldrs, wknd rapidly fnl 3f, t.o.   23   0
in 11th: seems to have gone off the boil: much btr 3378, 3249.
11 ran   Time 2m 41.32 (25.32)   (John Pugh)   W M Brisbourne Great Ness, Shropshire.

4305 **3.10 JOE CARR NURSERY HCAP 2YO 0-85 (D) 6f str Heavy 182 +05 Fast [87]**
£3656 £1125 £562 £281

4132 **PHARAOH HATSHEPSUT 15** [12] J S Goldie 2-7-10 (55) G Baker (5) 20/1: 004501: 2 b f Definite Article - Maid Of Mourne (Fairy King) Led/dsptd lead, led over 1f out, styd on strongly, rdn out: gd time, first win: May foal, half-sister to a juv wnr, dam 6f 2yo wnr: apprec this drop back to 6f: relishes v testing conditions. **61**
4103 **GALY BAY 16** [8] A Bailey 2-9-2 (75) J Bramhill 5/1 FAV: 3332: 2 b f Bin Ajwaad - Sylhall (Sharpo) Rear, rdn 3f out, gd hdwy appr fnl 1f, no impress well ins fnl 1f: nicely bckd on h'cap bow, clr rem: best run to date over a gall 6f on gd & hvy grnd: see 4103, 1497. *1* **79**
3922 **MULLING IT OVER 27** [7] T D Easterby 2-7-10 (55)(3oh) P Fessey 14/1: 30003: 2 b f Blues Traveller - Wonderment (Mummy's Pet) Chsd ldrs, eff 2f out, onepcd fnl 1f: drop in trip: handles gd/soft & hvy grnd. *5* **48**
4131 **SECOND VENTURE 15** [2] J R Weymes 2-8-11 (70) J Fanning 6/1: 03244: Led, hdd appr fnl 1f, wknd. *2* **59**
3987 **LENNEL 24** [4] 2-8-11 (70) K Darley 6/1: 63555: Prom, drvn 2f out, sn lost tch: btr 3987 (C/D, soft). *2½* **55**
3987 **THORNTOUN DIVA 24** [11] 2-8-12 (71)(t) K Dalgleish (5) 9/1: 302006: Outpcd early, rdn/hdwy over 1f out, no extra ins last: did not wear declared first time t-strap: unproven at 6f: see 1006. *nk* **56**
4030 **OLYS DREAM 21** [9] 2-7-10 (55)(4oh) Kim Tinkler 16/1: 506007: Handy, rdn/grad wknd fnl 2f. *½* **39**
*4096 **BARON CROCODILE 17** [10] 2-9-7 (80) J Carroll 9/1: 240218: Mid-div, lost tch fnl 2f: btr 4096 (5f, gd). *3* **58**
3571 **KIRKBYS TREASURE 47** [1] 2-8-7 (66) P Bradley (5) 16/1: 036659: Chsd ldrs, wknd qckly over 2f out: 9 wk abs, below best on grnd much softer than prev encountered: btr 2369 (5f, fast). *10* **29**
*3801 **THANKS MAX 36** [3] 2-9-2 (75) R Winston 7/1: -0510: Trkd ldrs, wknd halfway, 10th: btr 3801 (5f, soft). *4* **31**
3958 **VIEWFORTH 25** [6] 2-9-2 (75) Dale Gibson 14/1: -4300: Front rank, lost tch fnl 2f, t.o. in 11th. *8* **19**
4007 **JOINT INSTRUCTION 23** [5] 2-9-2 (75) A Culhane 8/1: 201100: In tch, wknd rapidly fnl 2f, fin 12th. *1½* **16**
12 ran Time 1m 19.93 (10.63) (Mike Flynn) J S Goldie Uplawmoor, E Renfrewshire.

4306 **3.40 LOCHRANZA HCAP 3YO+ 0-80 (D) 1m2f Heavy 182 -34 Slow [70]**
£4013 £1235 £617 £308 3 yo rec 5 lb

4257 **LOVE KISS 6** [11] W Storey 5-8-3 (45) T Williams 14/1: 200641: 5 b g Brief Truce - Pendulina (Prince Tenderfoot) Trkd ldrs, led appr fnl 2f, strongly pressed appr fnl 1f, styd on strongly, drvn out: tchd 25/1, qck reapp: first win: promise over an inadequate trip most recent start (6f class stks): lightly rcd & no form prev since plcd as a 2yo in '97 (stks, rtd 86, M Johnston): eff at 1m/10f on gd, loves soft/hvy grnd: has prev broken blood vessels: could follow up while conditions remain in his favour. **51**
4222 **SPREE VISION 9** [13] P Monteith 4-8-7 (49) J Carroll 14/1: 165002: 4 b g Suave Dancer - Regent's Folly (Touching Wood) Patiently rdn, gd hdwy 3f out, chall wnr over 1f out, ev ch till no extra fnl 50y: op 10/1, pulled 16L clr rem: goes v well in v testing conditions & back on a wng mark: see 1908. *1* **53**
4074 **FREEDOM QUEST 19** [5] B S Rothwell 5-9-3 (59) R Lappin 10/1: 042053: 5 b g Polish Patriot - Recherchee (Rainbow Quest) Twrds rear, eff over 2f out, styd on, no ch with front 2: unproven on soft/hvy. *16* **47**
*3963 **KIDZ PLAY 25** [8] J S Goldie 4-9-1 (57) K Darley 7/2 JT FAV: 040014: Led, hdd 4f out, sn no extra: capable of better, see 3963 (11f amat h'cap, soft). *3* **41**
3806 **BRITTAS BLUES 36** [7] 3-7-13 (46) K Dalgleish (5) 9/1: 345035: Prom, outpcd 4f out, no extra fnl 3f: longer 10f trip: btr 3806 (9f, soft). *3½* **26**
4275 **LORD EUROLINK 4** [12] 6-9-13 (69)(vis) M Worrell (7) 10/1: 501236: Dsptd lead, went on 4f out, hdd over 2f out, wknd qckly: op 8/1, qck reapp: best at 1m/9f on faster grnd: see 3808. *6* **43**
2139 **AMRON 108** [4] 13-7-10 (38) J Bramhill 20/1: 006007: Bhd, prog 5f out, drvn/wknd appr fnl 1f: abs. *2½* **9**
4218 **ZAMAT 9** [1] 4-8-5 (47) R Winston 10/1: 0-048: Reared leaving stalls, sn in tch, wknd qckly fnl 3f. *5* **13**
3636 **BOLT FROM THE BLUE 44** [15] 4-7-10 (38)(5oh) Kim Tinkler 14/1: 056069: Al rear: 6 wk abs: see 1683. *1* **3**
*4074 **RINGSIDE JACK 19** [10] 4-10-0 (70)(vis) J Fanning 7/2 JT FAV: 040010: Front rank, wknd rapidly fnl 3f, fin 10th: well bckd & much more expected with conditions in his favour: btr 4074. *½* **34**
4226 **Slaneyside 9** [3] 3-8-13 (60) V Halliday 20/1: 3769} **Oh No Not Him 401** [6] 4-7-10 (38)(3oh) G Baker (5) 25/1:
4133 **Count On Thunder 15** [9] 3-7-12 (45) N Kennedy 16/1: 3963 **Ocean Drive 25** [2] 4-8-5 (47) Dale Gibson 14/1:
4133 **Free Kevin 15** [14] 4-8-1 (42)(1ow) O Pears 20/1:
15 ran Time 2m 26.06 (21.66) (K Knox) W Storey Muggleswick, Co.Durham.

4307 **4.10 SAFFIE JOSEPH HCAP 3YO 0-70 (E) 5f str Heavy 182 +10 Fast [73]**
£3087 £950 £475 £237 Raced across width of track fnl 2f - no advantage.

4185 **PRIME RECREATION 11** [14] P S Felgate 3-8-9 (54) Dale Gibson 8/1: 000061: 3 b g Primo Dominie - Night Transaction (Tina's Pet) Prom stands side, went on appr fnl 1f, rdn & pulled clr ins last: fast time: first win: plcd once prev this term: plcd fnl '99 start (mdn, rtd 74): eff around a sharp or gall 5f on gd & gd/soft, relishes hvy grnd: likely to reappear quickly. **62**
4010 **COLLEGE MAID 23** [5] J S Goldie 3-9-5 (64) A Culhane 14/1: 004002: 3 b f College Chapel - Maid Of Mourne (Fairy King) Prom far side, led that group appr fnl 1f, styd on but no ch with wnr: ran to nr best, acts on firm, goes well on soft/hvy grnd: see 3572, 2165. *3* **66**
4220 **TICK TOCK 9** [19] M Mullineaux 3-8-1 (46)(vis) P Bradley (4) 9/1: 040063: 3 ch f Timesless Times - Aquiletta (Bairn) Prom stands side, led briefly appr fnl 1f, onepcd ins last: tchd 12/1: likes gd/soft & hvy: mdn. *¾* **47**
-4270 **CRYFIELD 5** [1] N Tinkler 3-9-2 (61)(vis) J Fanning 7/1: 100624: Cl-up far side, chall appr fnl 1f, no extra well ins last: op 5/1, qck reapp: will apprec a return to 6f: see 4270. *½* **61**
4185 **RYTHM N TIME 11** [3] 3-9-5 (64) P Doe 16/1: 466005: Led far side, hdd over 1f out, onepcd: poss handles hvy but prev best form has come on a sounder surface: see 3056 (gd/soft). *½* **63**
4255 **DAYLILY 6** [18] 3-8-11 (56) K Darley 10/1: 235036: Handy stands side, rdn/btn appr fnl 1f: qck reapp, h'cap reapp: btr 4255 (6f mdn, soft). *2½* **50**
3194 **CHRISTOPHERSSISTER 63** [4] 3-8-2 (47)(t) J McAuley 33/1: 000067: Sn rdn in mid-div, no extra fnl 2f: 9 wk abs, drop in trip: see 426 (sand, clmr). *1* **39**
4185 **CLOPTON GREEN 11** [10] 3-8-7 (52) G Baker (5) 10/1: 335208: Centre, mid-div at best: btr 4185 (gd). *¾* **42**
4031 **BENNOCHY 21** [17] 3-8-1 (46) P Fessey 20/1: 546009: Rear stands side, eff appr fnl 1f, nvr a threat to ldrs: unproven on hvy grnd: see 777 (fast). *¾* **34**
4185 **ROBIN HOOD 11** [2] 3-8-7 (52) R Winston 12/1: 610200: Prom far side, fdd appr fnl 1f, 10th: btr 3825. *shd* **40**
3698 **ABLE AYR 42** [7] 3-9-1 (60) G Parkin 25/1: 000000: Dwelt, nvr a factor, 11th: 6 wk absence. *1¾* **45**
4185 **SHATIN BEAUTY 11** [15] 3-8-6 (51) D Mernagh (3) 33/1: 000000: Cl-up stands side, wknd fnl 2f, 12th. *shd* **36**
4087 **MAROMITO 18** [12] 3-9-5 (64) O Pears 7/1: 000020: Led stands side 3½f: 13th: op 4/1, btr 4087. *½* **48**
4185 **LIZZIE SIMMONDS 11** [8] 3-8-10 (55) T Williams 20/1: 530500: Nvr a threat, 14th: tchd 50/1. *1¼* **37**

*4220 **GDANSK** 9 [16] 3-9-7 (66) J Carroll 9/2 FAV: 400210: Trkd ldrs, hung left & wknd fnl 2f, fin 15th: 1¾   45
nicely bckd & better expected tho' unproven on grnd softer than gd/soft: much btr 4220 (class stks, gd/soft).
3890} **Maria From Caplaw** 392 [20] 3-7-10 (41)(1oh) K Dalgleish (5) 40/1:
4155 **Pape Diouf** 13 [11] 3-7-10 (41)(3oh) Iona Wands 50/1:
3759 **Kirsch** 39 [9] 3-8-5 (50)(vis) J Bramhill 25/1:   2519 **Mimandi** 93 [6] 3-7-10 (41)(9oh) Clare Roche (7) 50/1:
3593 **Clear Moon** 46 [13] 3-7-10 (41)(3oh) N Kennedy 66/1:
20 ran   Time 1m 05.5 (8.45)   (Moneyleague Ltd)   P S Felgate Grimston, Leics.

4308	4.40 ARRAN COND STKS 3YO (C) 1m rnd Heavy 182 -19 Slow
	£5834 £2213 £1106 £503

4197 **CORNELIUS** 10 [7] P F I Cole 3-8-9 J Carroll 5/1: 020401: 3 b c Baratheo - Rainbow Mountain (Rainbow   101
Quest) Made all, pressed after halfway, styd on strongly, drvn out: tchd 6/1: rnr-up twice prev this term: '99 wnr
at York (debut, mdn), subs 3rd in Gr 3 Coventry at Royal Ascot (rtd 106+): dam a 11.5f wnr: eff at 1m/10f on fast,
both wins on soft/hvy grnd: likes to force the pace: acts on a stiff or gall trk: v useful at best.
4064 **GARGALHADA FINAL** 19 [5] J Noseda 3-9-0 J Weaver 9/4: 12562: 3 b c Sabrehill - Secret Waters (Pharly) 1   104
Mid-div, hdwy to chall wnr over 3f out, drvn/no extra well ins last: nicely bckd & ran to best on this drop back
to 1m: 17L clr rem: acts on fast & hvy grnd: apprec this drop in grade & can win similar: see 4064, 1380.
3389 **BLUSIENKA** 54 [6] G A Butler 3-8-4 P Doe 4/1: 435403: 3 b f Blues Traveller - Pudgy Poppet (Danehill) 17   74
Prom, not pace of front 2 fnl 3f: disapp run on grnd prev thought to be in his favour: abs: see 3389, 995.
4000 **ISLAND SOUND** 23 [8] D R C Elsworth 3-8-9 K Darley 13/8 FAV: -25344: Prom, rdn/wknd over 2f out: 5   73
hvly bckd & much better expected tho' unproven on hvy: see 1627, 1246.
4276 **THE CASTIGATOR** 4 [1] 3-8-9 D Mernagh (3) 100/1: 000005: Lost tch halfway: qck reapp: flattered again. 5   65$
3677 **BRAVE KNIGHT** 43 [4] 3-8-9 A Culhane 100/1: 0-36: Dwelt, al well bhd: 6 wk abs, highly tried.   1¾   62
4218 **LEVENDI** 9 [7] 3-8-9 R Winston 100/1: 007: Al in rear: up in trip, stiff task.   1   60
4220 **TIME FOR THE CLAN** 9 [3] 3-8-9 O Pears 100/1: 050008: Wknd rapidly halfway: impossible task.   4   55$
4218 **FOUR MEN** 9 [2] 3-8-9 Mark Flynn (7) 66/1: 302069: In tch, wknd qckly halfway, t.o.: needs h'caps.   10   43$
9 ran   Time 1m 52.84 (16.24)   (Sir George Meyrick)   P F I Cole Whatcombe, Oxon.

Official Going   HEAVY. Stalls: Stands Side.

4309	1.30 EBF HARE FILLIES MDN DIV 1 2YO (D) 7f str Soft/Heavy Inapplicable
	£3224 £992 £496 £248

--   **GONCHAROVA** [9] Sir Michael Stoute 2-8-11 F Lynch 3/1 FAV: 1: 2 b f Gone West - Pure Grain   86+
(Polish Precedent) In tch, smooth prog to lead 2f out & sn clr, readily: cost £625,000gns first foal, dam
high-class mid-dist performer: eff over a stiff 7f, shld stay at least 10f next term: goes well fresh on soft/
hvy grnd: shld go on to much better things next term, stable saddled Petrushka to win this last year.
3999 **HERNANDITA** 23 [5] J L Dunlop 2-8-11 G Carter 4/1: -02: 2 b f Hernando - Dara Dee (Dara Monarch)   2   78
Cl-up, led 3f out till 2f out, styd on but no clr wnr: op 5/2: met a potentaill decent rival today: eff at 7f,
1m will suit next time: acts on soft/hvy grnd & shld find similar: see 3999.
3748 **CLIMBING ROSE** 39 [7] R Charlton 2-8-11 J Reid 9/1: 53: 2 b f Quest For Fame - Abeer (Dewan)   1   76
Towards rear, imprvd 2f out, nvr able to chall: op 6/1, 6 wk abs: handles soft/hvy grnd.
2806 **VINCENTIA** 80 [11] C Smith 2-8-11 M Fenton 40/1: 044: Cl-up, chall appr fnl 1f, onepace for press: nk   75
imprvd on this soft/hvy grnd after an 11 week break: see 2806 (gd/fm).
--   **FAERIE REALM** [4] 2-8-11 W Ryan 7/1: 5: Rear, shkn up 2f out, styd on nicely ins last, nvr nrr: op 4/1,   nk   74+
stablemate wnr: Fairy King half-sister to smart wnrs btwn 1m & 12f: dam 1m/10f performer: plently to like about
this encouraging debut: mid-dist prospect for 2001 & sure to leave this behind.
3943 **WESTERN EDGE** 26 [6] 2-8-11 J Fortune 6/1: 56: Chsd ldrs, onepace appr fnl 1f: back in trip.   2½   70
--   **GHAY** [1] 2-8-11 W Supple 9/2: 7: Well plcd, chall appr fnl 2f, fdd bef fnl 1f: debut: half-   hd   70
sister to a 7f juv wnr, dam 7f juv wnr: ran well for a long way, shld improve & win a maiden, prob on better grnd.
4216 **SITARA** 9 [3] 2-8-11 G Sparkes (7) 14/1: 08: Nvr trbld ldrs: not given hard time, mid-dist h'caps will suit.   1½   67
--   **BALANOU** [12] 2-8-11 G Duffield 20/1: 9: Al bhd: op 14/1 on debut: half-sister to wnrs at 6f/over   6   57
hdles, dam useful abroad: bred to apprec mid-dists & further next year: with S Williams.
3832 **WAIKIKI DANCER** 34 [2] 2-8-11 D Sweeney 33/1: 000: Led till 3f out, sn btn: 10th: see 3832.   16   32
--   **SPECTINA** [10] 2-8-11 M Hills 10/1: 0: Pulled hard, chsd ldrs till 3f out: 11th, op 6/1, debut: 1½   30
Spectrum half-sister to 3 mid-dist wnrs, dam 6f juv wnr: shld do better: with J Fanshawe.
11 ran   Time 1m 31.6 (9.6)   (Mrs John Magnier & Mr M Tabor)   Sir Michael Stoute Newmarket.

4310	2.00 SHELDUCK FILLIES HCAP 3YO+ 0-70 (E) 1m str Soft/Heavy Inapplicable [67]
	£2003 £2003 £475 £237 3 yo rec 3 lb

*4173 **EVE** 12 [11] M L W Bell 3-9-8 (64) M Fenton 8/1: 430011: 3 b f Rainbow Quest - Fade (Persepolis)   70
Waited with, imprvd appr fnl 2f, kept on gamely under press ins last to lead on line: ddhtd: recent Brighton
wnr (class stks): unrcd juv: eff at 1m, prob stays 10f: acts on firm & soft/hvy grnd, prob any trk: progressive.
4118 **NATALIE JAY** 15 [14] M R Channon 4-10-0 (67) Craig Williams 7/1: 106331: 4 b f Ballacashtal - Falls   dht   73
Of Lora (Scottish Rifle) Prom, led after halfway, under press appr fnl 1f, kept on but jnd nr fin: op 10/1, ddhtd,
clr rem: earlier won at Salisbury (same fill h'cap): '99 wnr again at Salisbury (same fill h'cap, rtd 69 & 68a): eff
at 1m/10f on fast, hvy grnd & equitrack, any trk, likes Salisbury/stiff finishes: game run under 10st.
4217 **YOUNG ROSEIN** 9 [8] Mrs G S Rees 4-9-5 (58) G Duffield 16/1: 611303: 4 b f Distant Relative -   6   55
Red Rosein (Red Sunset) Front rank & ev ch till onepace under press appr fnl 1f: tchd 20/1: better run,
acts on firm & gd/soft, prob handles soft/hvy: see 3574.
4004 **DAVIS ROCK** 23 [1] W R Muir 6-8-10 (49) Martin Dwyer 7/1: 166264: Mid-div, feeling pace appr fnl   1¾   44
2f, rallied ins last: not disgraced back up in trip: see 601 (AW).
4173 **VENTO DEL ORENO** 12 [16] 3-9-6 (62) G Sparkes (7) 5/1 FAV: 600425: Dwelt, imprvd & ev ch 2f out,   nk   56
sn rdn & no extra: clr rem: only a head bhd Eve on 2lbs worse terms in 4173.
3856 **LADY JONES** 33 [3] 3-8-11 (53) Dean McKeown 12/1: 130056: Bhd, went past btn horses fnl 1f: 6   38
worth another try at 10f on similar grnd: see 3856, 2043, 1822.
4224 **SWEET HAVEN** 9 [6] 3-8-2 (43)(vis)(1ow) D R McCabe 50/1: 002007: Cl-up, led briefly after 4f, wknd dist.   nk   28

4004	**PICCOLO CATIVO** 23 [2] 5-8-7 (46) Angela Hartley (7) 25/1: -10408: Chsd ldrs, eff & btn appr fnl 2f.	2½	26
2945	**CAPACOOSTIC** 73 [10] 3-8-3 (45) P Hanagan (5) 33/1: 002009: Bhd ldrs, lost pl appr fnl 2f: 10 wk abs.	1½	23
4217	**FALLS OMONESS** 9 [7] 6-8-8 (47) W Supple 16/1: 000200: Nvr better than mid-div: 10th: see 2062, 931.	2½	22
4136	**BODFARI ANNA** 15 [9] 4-9-3 (56)(vis) R Cody Boutcher (7) 10/1: 430020: Nvr nr ldrs: 11th, op 8/1.	2	28
3401	**RASMALAI** 54 [4] 3-9-11 (67) J Fortune 12/1: 03020: Held up, brief eff after halfway: 12th, 8 wk abs.	8	27
1297	**MY TESS** 147 [20] 4-10-0 (67) R Mullen 11/1: 324250: Held up, imprvd 4f out, wknd qckly bef 2f out: abs.		0
3936	**BOBBYDAZZLE** 26 [19] 5-8-13 (52) J Quinn 8/1: 034040: Nvr in it: 16th, see 3936, 78.		0
3764	**BAJAN BROKER** 38 [12] 3-9-3 (59) J Reid 7/1: 040560: Sn struggling: last, see 2111.		0
4067	Armenia 19 [18] 3-8-10 (52) G Carter 16/1: 4067 Sparkling Isle 19 [13] 3-8-12 (54) F Norton 33/1:		
3921	Term Of Endearment 27 [17] 3-8-5 (46)(1ow) Paul Eddery 33/1:		
3440	Swynford Welcome 52 [15] 4-8-6 (44)(1ow) N Callan 33/1:		
2183	Molly Malone 106 [5] 3-9-7 (63) S Whitworth 33/1:		

20 ran   Time 1m 44.0 (9.6)   (Lady Carolyn Warren)   M L W Bell Newmarket.

4311   2.30 BADGER CLASSIFIED STKS 3YO+ 0-60 (F)   1m str   Soft/Heavy   Inapplicable
£3194   £983   £491   £245   3 yo rec 3 lb

*4032	**CAUTIOUS JOE** 21 [13] R A Fahey 3-8-13 P Hanagan (5) 9/2: 503011: 3 b f First Trump - Jomel Amou (Ela Mana Mou) Mid-div, prog appr fnl 2f, rdn to lead dist, kept on well: recent wnr here at Leicester (class stks): '99 Newcastle wnr (debut, auct mdn, rtd 76): eff over a stiff/gall 1m: acts on firm & soft/hvy grnd, likes Leicester: runs well fresh: on the upgrade.		64
4143	**MARTELLO** 14 [14] R Charlton 4-9-3 C Haddon (7) 12/1: 005-42: 4 b g Polish Precedent - Round Tower (High Top) Chsd ldrs, led after halfway till bef fnl 1f, styd on under press: well clr of 3rd, ran to best: eff over a stiff 1m on soft/hvy grnd: see 4143 (reapp).	2½	60
4032	**HARD LINES** 21 [5] I A Balding 4-9-5 M Hills 4/1: 004133: 4 b g Silver Hawk - Arctic Eclipse (Northern Dancer) Front rank, led halfway, sn hdd, same pace appr fnl 1f: btr 4032, 3816.	6	53
4251	**HEATHYARDS LAD** 6 [18] R Hollinshead 3-9-0 W Ryan 10/1: 034504: Bhd, some hdwy appr fnl 2f, nvr on terms: qck reapp, stiffish task: see 976, 294.	5	44
4248	**SOPHOMORE** 6 [1] 6-9-3 J Quinn 40/1: 002055: Chsd ldrs, eff & no extra 2f out: qck reapp, stiff task.	7	34
2673	**GABLESEA** 86 [9] 6-9-3 (vis) J Bosley (7) 12/1: 500046: In tch, shkn up & not much room appr fnl 2f.	5	27
4168	**HOH GEM** 12 [15] 4-9-3 G Hind 12/1: 204607: Nvr nr ldrs: stiff task back in trip, see 1520.	1	25
4527}	**MARIGLIANO** 348 [2] 7-9-3 W Supple 9/1: 0/06-8: Chsd ldrs till wknd qckly 2f out: abs: 99/00 jmps wnr at Worcester, Huntingdon (h'cap hdles, rtd 122h) & M Rasen (nov chase, 2m/2m2f, any grnd, rtd 102c): ran just twice on the level last term (rtd 60): '98 wnr at Musselburgh & Southwell (clmrs, rtd 74 & 78a): eff at 7f/1m: goes on fast, soft grnd & fibresand, any track: with K Morgan.	nk	24
3383	**MAWINGO** 54 [11] 7-9-3 Paul Eddery 7/2 FAV: 4-0029: Switched left start, nvr troubled ldrs, eased fnl 1f: 8 wk abs, long losing seq: see 3383, 169.	3	20
4033	**WHITE SETTLER** 21 [17] 7-9-3 S Whitworth 12/1: 0-3100: Al towards rear: 10th, stiff task at the weights.	shd	22
4122	**BALANITA** 15 [19] 5-9-3 D Sweeney 16/1: 025430: Pulled hard, mid-div, btn 3f out: 11th, stiffish task.	nk	19
4169	**GIKO** 12 [10] 6-9-3 Jonjo Fowle (5) 7/1: 000030: Chsd ldrs till halfway: 12th, stiff task, see 4169, 1033.	5	12
3954	**RAMBO NINE** 26 [3] 3-9-0 G Duffield 50/1: 560-00: Led till halfway, btn after: 17th, stiff task: modest form.		0
995}	Society King 532 [12] 5-9-3 Darren Williams (5) 25/1: 4032 Green God 21 [20] 4-9-3 (VIS) J Reid 16/1:		
4035}	Rainbow View 384 [8] 4-9-3 Martin Dwyer 20/1: 4099 Silk Stockings 17 [7] 3-8-11 P Robinson 16/1:		
4294	Regalo 3 [6] 5-9-3 (BL) R Havlin 50/1:		

18 ran   Time 1m 44.1 (9.7)   (Tommy Staunton)   R A Fahey Butterwick, N.Yorks.

4312   3.00 EBF HARE FILLIES MDN DIV 2 2YO (D)   7f str   Heavy   Inapplicable
£3211   £988   £494   £247

4035	**PEARL BRIGHT** 21 [2] J L Dunlop 2-8-11 P Robinson 13/8 FAV: 21: 2 gr f Kaldoun - Coastal Jewel (Kris) Led, pushed clr appr fnl 2f, rdn to repel rnr-up towards fin: nicely bckd, front 2 clr: half-sister to a decent 5f juv, dam unrcd: eff forcing the pace at 7f, shld get 1m: acts on soft & hvy grnd, stiff/gall track.		85
4216	**HALCYON DAZE** 9 [11] L M Cumani 2-8-11 G Sparkes (7) 6/1: 042: 2 ch f Halling - Ardisia (Affirmed) Slow away, imprvd halfway & chsd wnr 2f out, switched 1f out, ran on & not btn far: pulled 9L clr of 3rd: imprvd, acts on hvy grnd & will apprec a step up to 1m: see 4216.	½	83
--	**ALLELUIA** [4] Sir Mark Prescott 2-8-11 G Duffield 6/1: 3: 2 b f Caerleon - Alruccaba (Crystal Palace) Dwelt, rear, eff 2f out, styd on same pace for 3rd, nvr nr ldrs: op 5/2 on debut: half-sister to sev wnrs, incl v smart 7f juv/10f scorer Last Second, dam 6f juv wnr: likely to apprec 10f+ next term.	9	68
--	**COYOTE** [1] Sir Michael Stoute 2-8-11 J Fortune 3/1: 4: Chsd ldrs, no extra appr fnl 2f: debut, op 9/4: Indian Ridge first foal: dam v useful 1m/10f performer, sire a sprinter: shld come on for this.	1¾	66
4216	**ARONA** 9 [9] 2-8-11 Dean McKeown 33/1: 005: Chsd ldrs, eff & wknd 2f out: stiff task.	3	61
--	**GARDEN OF EDEN** [8] 2-8-11 F Lynch 9/1: 6: Nvr troubled ldrs, eased when tired ins last: op 5/1 on debut, stablemate 4th: Green Desert first foal, dam a maiden.	8	49
4036	**PLAYONETOONEDOTCOM** 21 [6] 2-8-11 F Norton 50/1: 0067: Keen, cl-up, wknd qckly appr fnl 2f.	7	39
--	**BLUE POOL** [3] 2-8-11 S Whitworth 14/1: 8: Al bhd: op 10/1, debut: Saddlers' Hall half-sister to sev wnrs, notably useful stayer Orchestra Stall: dam 10f wnr: v stoutly bred, with J Toller.	7	29
2430	**PRINCESS EMERALD** 96 [10] 2-8-11 J Quinn 40/1: 09: Sn bhd: over 3 month absence.	2½	25
--	**KRISTINEAU** [5] 2-8-11 R Mullen 20/1: 0: Nvr in it, btn halfway: 10th, debut, op 14/1: 12,000gns Cadeaux Genereux filly: sire a sprinter, but is stoutly bred on dam's side: with C Wall.	3	20

10 ran   Time 1m 33.5 (11.5)   (Pearl Bright Partnership)   J L Dunlop Arundel, W.Sussex.

4313   3.30 STOAT SELLER 3YO (G)   1m2f   Heavy   Inapplicable
£1974   £564   £282

4029	**CENTAUR SPIRIT** 21 [2] A Streeter 3-8-11 F Norton 33/1: -04001: 3 b g Distant Relative - Winnie Reckless (Local Suitor) Restrained, imprvd 3f out, led 2f out, pshd out, eased down: no bid, op 20/1, first win: unplcd sole juv start: cost 50,000gns: eff over a stiff 10f, shld get 12f: revelled in this hvy grnd.		43
3021	**ROYAL EXPOSURE** 71 [3] W J Musson 3-8-11 L Newton 20/1: 02: 3 b g Emperor Jones - Blue Garter (Targowice) Rear, prog appr fnl 3f, ev ch 2f out, styd on but no hope with wnr: 10 wk abs: stays 10f on hvy.	5	36
4029	**BEDOUIN QUEEN** 21 [6] R F Johnson Houghton 3-8-6 G Carter 14/1: 002003: 3 ch f Aragon - Petra's Star (Rock City) Towards rear, prog after halfway, chall bef fnl 2f, sn onepace: best 2448 (fast).	2½	28
4092	**SHALBEBLUE** 17 [13] B Ellison 3-8-11 (VIS) G Duffield 8/1: 000404: In tch, eff 4f out, nvr trbld ldrs.	4	29
3775	**BOOMSHADOW** 37 [9] 3-8-11 (t) R Cody Boutcher (7) 33/1: -60005: Chsd ldrs, wknd qckly 2f out.	8	21

LEICESTER MONDAY OCTOBER 9TH Righthand, Stiff, Galloping Track

-- **OK TWIGGY** [7] 3-8-6 D Kinsella (7) 20/1: 6: Nvr a factor: debut: Kylian filly, dam 10f wnr. *½* **15**
4208 **ARIALA 9** [12] 3-8-6 N Callan 9/4 FAV: 60037: Nvr out of mid-div: better expected after 2408 (appr h'cap). *6* **9**
3816 **OUTSTANDING TALENT 35** [10] 3-8-6 S Righton 20/1: 002408: In tch, chsd ldrs 5f out till 3f out. *1* **8**
4233 **CLANSMAN 7** [1] 3-8-11 R Fitzpatrick 33/1: 000009: Well plcd appr fnl 3f till 2f out, sn btn: qk reapp. *1½* **11**
4141 **SHERATON HEIGHTS 14** [4] 3-8-6 G Hind 20/1: -00000: Led till 3½f out, sn lost pl: 10th, stiffish task. *2½* **3**
3935 **CALDIZ 26** [16] 3-8-11 (t) M Fenton 16/1: 666400: Nvr a factor: 11th, hdles rnr since 3868. *17* **0**
4029 **EMALI 21** [8] 3-8-11 P Robinson 11/2: 303250: Handy 6f: 12th, btr 3917, 3816 (firm & fast). *¾* **0**
4067 **INSIGHTFUL 19** [14] 3-8-11 J Fortune 11/4: 06400P: In tch, brk leg 5f out, sadly had to be destroyed. **0**
3663 **April Star 43** [17] 3-8-6 Dean McKeown 20/1: 3624 **Shaw Venture 45** [5] 3-8-11 D Sweeney 25/1:
3935 **Erin Anam Cara 26** [15] 3-8-6 (bl) J Quinn 16/1: 1955 **Nicks Jule 116** [11] 3-8-6 R Mullen 25/1:
17 ran Time 2m 20.5 (18) (Centaur Racing Ltd) A Streeter Uttoxeter, Staffs.

*****Final Three Races Abandoned due to the Ground*****

SAINT-CLOUD WEDNESDAY OCTOBER 4TH Lefthand, Galloping Track

Official Going GOOD TO SOFT

4314 **2.05 GR 3 PRIX ECLIPSE 2YO 6f110y Good/Soft**
£21134 £7685 £3842

*3912 **POTARO 23** B J Meehan 2-8-11 G Mosse 8/1: 535311: 2 b c Catrail - Bianca Cappello (Glenstal) **104**
Made all, rdn & drew clr appr fnl 1f: 23 days ago easily landed a Warwick auct mdn: eff at 6/7f, 1m will suit: acts on fast, good/soft & a sharp or gall trk: loves dominating: fast improving colt, win more val races.
-- **INZARS BEST** U Suter 2-8-11 T Mundry 57/10: -4112: 2 br c Inzar - Geht Schnell (Fairy King) *3* **97**
Trkd wnr thro'out, drvn/no impress fnl 1f: German raider, recent Listed wnr: eff at 6.5f on gd/soft grnd.
-- **STUNNING** Mme C Head 2-8-8 O Doleuze 2/1 FAV: -2213: 2 b f Nureyev - Gorgeous (Slew O'Gold) *2½* **88**
Chsg ldrs when hmpd after 2f, eff over 1f out, sn btn: recent Chantilly wnr: stays 6.5f on gd/soft.
7 ran Time 1m 20.8 (Mrs Susan McCarthy) B J Meehan Upper Lambourn, Berks

CORK SATURDAY OCTOBER 7TH --

Official Going YIELDING

4315 **3.00 LISTED ENTREPRENEUR STKS 2YO 6f Good/Soft**
£22750 £6650 £3150

4240 **CONEY KITTY 7** D Hanley 2-8-7 N G McCullagh 7/1: -2241: 2 ch f Lycius - Auntie Maureen (Roi Danzig) **100**
Twrds rear, imprvd over 2f out, led dist, styd on well despite edging right, drvn out: qck reapp: dual rnr-up prev: eff at 6f, has tried 7f & shld suit: acts on gd/soft, will reportedly prefer faster grnd: useful.
2113 **KEATS 107** A P O'Brien 2-8-10 M J Kinane 11/10 FAV: 142: 2 b c Hennessy - Alaska Queen (Time For A Change) Sn led, drvn/hdd dist, no extra cl-home: 15 wk abs: eff at 6f on gd/soft grnd: see 2113. *¾* **100**
4060 **SAYING GRACE 20** Miss F M Crowley 2-8-7 P J Smullen 6/1: 411033: 2 b f Brief Truce - Adamparis (Robellino) Sn outpcd, prog 2f out, styd on well, nvr nrr: shld relish 7f next time: see 4060. *hd* **97**
4009 **SIPTITZ HEIGHTS 21** G C Bravery 2-8-7 E Ahern 14/1: 010505: Prom, ev ch appr fnl 1f, sn outpcd: op 10/1, fin 5th: up in grade: see 3959, 2996. *5* **85**
11 ran Time 1m 11.8 (A Doyle) D Hanley Straffan, Co Kildare

BELMONT PARK SATURDAY OCTOBER 7TH Lefthand, Easy Track

Official Going FIRM

4316 **10.12 GR 1 TURF CLASSIC INVITATIONAL 3YO+ 1m4f Firm**
£274390 £91463 £50305 £27439

-- **JOHNS CALL** T Voss 9-9-0 J-L Samyn 104/10: 1: 9 ch h Lord At War - Calling Guest (Be My Guest) **121**
4489} **CRAIGSTEEL 350** United States 5-9-0 J Santos 26/1: /120-2: 5 b h Suave Dancer - Applecross (Glint Of Gold) -: *½* **120**
3932 **ELA ATHENA 28** M A Jarvis 4-8-11 J Bravo 108/10: 412523: 4 gr f Ezzoud - Crodelle (Formidable) *1¾* **114**
Held up, swtchd/hdwy over 1f out, kept on, no dngr: another fine run, loves firm/fast grnd: see 3932.
*3932 **FANTASTIC LIGHT 28** Saeed bin Suroor 4-9-0 L Dettori 7/5 FAV: 125214: Settled rear, hdwy 3f out, swtchd over 1f out, styd on late: reportedly unsuited by slow pace: high-class at best: beat this 3rd in 3932. *1¼* **115**
4109 **COMMANDER COLLINS 14** 4-9-0 E Prado 345/10: -43340: Cl-up, wknd qckly fnl 2f, 11th: see 4109. *13* **100**
12 ran Time 2m 28.58 (Trillum Stable) T Voss North America

MUNICH SUNDAY OCTOBER 8TH Lefthand, Galloping Track

Official Going SOFT

MUNICH   SUNDAY OCTOBER 8TH   Lefthand, Galloping Track

4317   3.25 GR 3 BUCHMACHER SPRINT-PREIS 3YO+   6f110y   Soft
£14516   £5806   £3548   3 yo rec 1 lb

2403 **TERTULLIAN 99** P Schiergen 5-9-0 F Minarik : 32-331: 5 ch h Miswaki - Turbaine (Trempolino)   115
Trkd ldrs, rdn into lead 2f out, sn clr, drvn ins last & held on well: recent C/D Listed wnr: '99 Hoppegarten
wnr (Gr 3, rtd 116): suited by a gall 6.5f on gd & soft grnd: smart & consistent German entire.
*4218 **GAELIC STORM 8** M Johnston 6-8-9 D Holland : 154012: 6 b g Shavian - Shannon Princess   ½ 108
(Connaught) Bhd, hdwy over 1f out, strong run fnl 1f, closing at fin: fine run: smart gelding: see 4218 (stks).
--   **SUNDERLAND** A Wohler 3-8-11 A Suborics : 3: 3 b c Emarati - See Me Well (Common Grounds)   nk 110
Dsptd lead to halfway, ev ch appr fnl 1f, hung left & no extra fnl 50y: eff over a gall 6.5f on soft.
4198 **ROSEUM 9** R Guest 4-8-5 S Sanders : 1-6047: Mid-div, lost tch fnl 2f, 7th: needs a drop in grade.   10 83
7 ran   Time 1m 23.0   (Gestut Schlenderhan)   P Schiergen Germany

SAN SIRO   SUNDAY OCTOBER 8TH   Righthand, Stiff, Galloping Track

Official Going   SOFT

4318   2.55 GR 3 PREMIO DORMELLO 2YO FILLIES   1m   Soft
£44731   £20942   £11793   £5896

*4145 **INNIT 15** M R Channon 2-8-12 Craig Williams 17/10 FAV: 021111: 2 b f Distinctly North - Tidal Reach   103
(Kris S) Trkd ldrs, hdwy to lead over 1f out, rdn out: 4 timer completed after wins at Doncaster (val nursery),
M-Laffitte & here at San Siro (Listed): Jan foal, dam a multiple sprint wnr: eff at 7f/1m on fast, soft & a
sharpish or gall trk: can force the pace or come from bhd: most tough, useful & progressive filly.
--   **ZAZA TOP** A Wohler 2-8-12 M Monteriso 103/10: 2: 2 ch f Lomitas - Zorina (Shirley Heights)   1¼ 100
Mid div, hdwy 2f out, styd on to chase wnr ins last, no dngr: German raider, eff over a stiff/gall 1m on soft grnd.
--   **MACARA** P Schiergen 2-8-12 T Hellier 15/2: 3: 2 b f Acatenango - Midnight Society (Imp Society)   1½ 97
Twrds rear, rdn/imprvd over 2f out, ev ch till no extra fnl 1f: German raider, stays a stiff/gall 1m on soft.
12 ran   Time 1m 42.6   (Tim Corby)   M R Channon West Isley, Berks

4319   3.55 GR 1 PREMIO VITTORIO DU CAPUA+   1m   Soft
£56898   £25594   £15762   3 yo rec 3 lb

*2571 **FABERGER 92** Frau E Mader 4-8-12 L Hammer Hansen 119/10: 341061: 4 b c Dashing Blade - Friedrichslust   118
(Caerleon) Chsd ldrs, hdwy to chall 2f out, led appr fnl 1f, drvn out: earlier landed a surprise win at
Deauville (Gr 3): only 1 win in 15 starts prev (mdn): eff over a stiff/gall 1m on soft: smart, progressive.
3925 **SUMITAS 29** P Schiergen 4-8-12 T Hellier 6/4: 3D2252: 4 b h Lomitas - Subia (Konigsstuhl)   1½ 116
Front rank, hdwy to lead over 3f out, hdd over 1f out, not pace of wnr: apprec a return to 10f: see 3071.
4259 **BARATHEA GUEST 7** M R Channon 3-8-9 Craig Williams 11/10 FAV: 055543: 3 b c Barathea - Western   1½ 113
Heights (Shirley Heights) Settled last, hdwy over 2f out, rdn, hung right & styd on ins last, no threat: qck
reapp: given plenty to do here, signalled a return to something like his best: see 4259.
9 ran   Time 1m 42.0   (Gestut Etzean)   Frau E Mader Germany

LONGCHAMP   SUNDAY OCTOBER 8TH   Righthand, Stiff, Galloping Track

Official Going   SOFT

4320   1.35 GR 1 GRAND CRITERIUM 2YO   1m   Soft
£96061   £38424   £19212   £9606

*4144 **OKAWANGO 18** Mme C Head 2-9-0 O Doleuze 6/5 CO FAVcp: -111: 2 b c Kingmambo - Krissante (Kris)   118+
Held up, smooth hdwy after halfway, led going well over 1f out, rdn out, rdly: unbtn, incl a Gr 3 at Chantilly:
eff arnd a stiff/gall 1m, further cld suit: acts on soft grnd & runs well fresh: high-class, v highly regarded:
a leading fancy for the French 2000 Guineas & looks one to follow as a 3yo.
4058 **KINGS COUNTY 21** A P O'Brien 2-9-0 O Peslier 6/5 CO FAVcp: -122: 2 b c Fairy King - Kardelle   1 115
(Kalaglow) Settled mid-div, hdwy over 1f out, drvn & jockey dropped whip ins last, kept on but no threat to wnr:
clr rem: fine run, eff at 6f/1m on fast & soft: smart colt, sure to win Gr races: see 4058.
4054 **HONOURS LIST 22** A P O'Brien 2-9-0 M J Kinane 6/5 CO FAVcp: 1123: 2 b c Danehill - Gold Script   3 110
(Script Ohio) Front rank, rdn into lead over 2f out, hdd dist, onepcd: s/mate of 2nd: needs faster grnd: see 4054.
3891 **CD EUROPE 30** M R Channon 2-9-0 T Quinn 61/10: -1124: Prom, led after halfway, hdd over 2f out,   1½ 108
fdd ins fnl 1f: ran to best over longer 1m trip & on grnd softer then prev encountered: see 3891 (Gr 2, 7f, firm).
3926 **GREENGROOM 28** 2-9-0 D Boeuf 6/5 CO FAVcp: -21145: Keen/rear, nvr dngrs: see 3926.   6 99
7 ran   Time 1m 41.8   (Wertheimer Et Frere)   Mme C Head France

4321   3.45 LISTED PRIX JOUBERT 3YO FILL   1m4f   Soft
£13449   £4611   £3458

--   **SPACE QUEST** A Fabre 3-8-12 O Peslier : 1: 3 b f Rainbow Quest - Apogee (Shirley Heights)   98
3389 **DREAM QUEST 53** J L Dunlop 3-8-12 Pat Eddery : -1332: 3 ch f Rainbow Quest - Dreamawhile (Known   ½ 97
Fact) Broke out of stalls & ran loose bef race, led, clr appr fnl 2f, wknd ins last & hdd nr fin: 8 wk abs:
fine run considering pre-race exertions: stays 12f: capable of wng in List company sn: see 3389.
--   **TARABELA** France 3-8-12 D Boeuf : 3: 3 b f Johann Quatz - Muirfield (Crystal Glitters)   1 95
4194 **HIDDNAH 9** M Johnston 3-8-12 J Reid : -23636: Sn rdn cl-up, ev ch until fdd appr fnl 1f, fin 6th: 1¾ 92
shade disapp but best form this term has come on faster grnd: see 3595, 3017.
9 ran   Time 2m 36.4   (K Abdulla)   A Fabre France

AYR **TUESDAY OCTOBER 10TH** Lefthand, Galloping Track

Official Going HEAVY. Stalls: Round Course - Inside: Straight Course - Stands Side.

4322 | 2.20 EBF LINFERN FILLIES MDN 2YO (D) 1m rnd Heavy Slow
£3542 £1090 £545 £272

4114 **SAMARA MIDDLE EAST 17** [2] M R Channon 2-8-11 A Culhane 9/4: 61: 2 b f Marju - Modelliste — **89**
(Machiavellian) Trkd ldrs, rdn going well 3f out, rdn appr fnl 2f & sn clr, cmftbly: recently made a promising
debut in a much better race at Ascot: 1st foal, dam & sire milers: eff at 1m, further cld suit in time: handles
gd, goes well on v hvy grnd & on a gall trck: can rate more highly & follow up.
4216 **PHOEBE ROBINSON 10** [5] G C Bravery 2-8-11 M Fenton 10/1: 032: 2 b f Alzao - Savelli (Vision) 7 **77**
Settled rear, rdn ent str, swtchd right & hdwy 3f out, styd on for press fnl 2f, no dngr with wnr: 11L clr rem:
jockey received a 3 day irresponsible riding ban: stays 7f/1m on gd grnd: see 4216.
-- **SWIFTMAR** [1] P F I Cole 2-8-11 K Darley 9/1: 3: 2 b f Marju - Swift Spring (Bluebird) 11 **65**
Led/dsptd lead, led ent str, hdd 3f out, wknd fnl 2f: 9,500gns Apr foal, half-sister to 2 mid-dist wnrs, dam a
7f wnr (styd further): sire made v testing conditions, cld improve on a sounder surface.
-- **THEATRE LADY** [4] M Johnston 2-8-11 J Fanning 10/1: 4: Led/dsptd lead, hdd 4f out, drvn/fdd 1¾ **62**
appr fnl 2f: Mar foal, dam a sprint wnr in Ireland: sire high class at 12f: cld improve in less testing conds.
4034 **SHEREKIYA 22** [3] 2-8-11 F Lynch 11/8 FAV: 55: Chsd ldrs, eff 3f out, sn drvn & btn: well bckd: 4 **56**
much better expected but looked all at sea in this v hvy grnd: btr 4034 (debut, 7f, soft).
3615 **DANCE QUEEN 46** [6] 2-8-11 J Bramhill 100/1: 006006: Bhd, bmpd 3f out, sn btn: abs, v stiff task. 4 **50$**
6 ran Time 1m 53.65 (17.05) (Jaber Abdullah) M R Channon West Isley, Berks

4323 | 2.50 MJ NURSERY HCAP 2YO 0-85 (D) 1m rnd Heavy Slow [88]
£3672 £1130 £565 £282

4132 **ORIENTAL MIST 16** [3] Miss L A Perratt 2-8-8 (68) R Winston 25/1: 044601: 2 gr c Balla Cove - **72**
Donna Katrina (King's Lake) Chsd ldrs, hmpd after 2f, drvn over 3f out, switched & slightly hmpd again appr fnl
1f, styd on strongly to lead ins last, drvn out: first win, rider reportedly given a 2-day whip ban: half
brother to a 7f wnr: eff arnd 1m on hvy grnd & a gall track, further shld suit: proved too fast today.
3990 **THORNTOUN DANCER 25** [6] J S Goldie 2-8-0 (60) D Mernagh (3) 12/1: 056302: 2 b g Unfuwain - 1 **62**
Westry (Gone West) With ldr, rdn to chall over 3f out, led appr fnl 1f, hdd just ins last, drvn & not pace of
wnr: acts on gd/soft & hvy grnd, stays 1m: could win a testing grnd nursery: see 3532, 843.
4132 **CIRCUIT LIFE 16** [5] A Berry 2-7-10 (56)(3oh) J Bramhill 10/1: 623433: 2 ch g Rainbows For Life - 1¾ **55**
Alicedale (Trempolino) Mid div, rdn/outpcd over 3f out, drvn/rallied over 2f out, styd on well for press, nrst fin:
apprec these testing conditions, handles fast & hvy grnd & should appr further in time: see 3950.
3264 **BALL GAMES 61** [2] D Moffatt 2-8-5 (63)(2ow) J Fanning 14/1: 64604: Held up, strong run to chall hd **64**
appr fnl 1f, not qckn fnl 1f: op 10/1, 9 wk abs: up in trip & seems to stay a gall 1m on hvy: see 2717, 821.
4187 **FIRST DEGREE 11** [4] 2-7-11 (57)(1ow)(5oh) Dale Gibson 5/1: 0005: Led, pressed 3f out, rdn/hdd ¾ **55**
appr fnl 1f, sn no extra: op 4/1 on h'cap bow: up in trip & poss not quite get home over 1m on hvy: see 4187.
3957 **BOBANVI 26** [1] 2-7-10 (56)(12oh) G Baker (5) 20/1: 036556: Chsd ldrs, rdn/drpd rear over 3f out, nk **54$**
rall & styd on late, no threat: clr rem: gd run from 12lbs o/h, treat rating with caution: also flattered in 3957.
3968 **DANCING VENTURE 26** [8] 2-8-10 (70) N Callan 4/1: 54327: Settled in tch, eff 3f out, sn drvn, 26 **43**
wknd qckly for press fnl 2f: well bckd & prob not handle these v testing conditions: much btr 3968 (fast).
4167 **BARATHIKI 13** [9] 2-9-7 (81)(BL) P Hanagan (5) 5/2 FAV: -14628: Keen/prom, ev ch till wknd rapidly 2½ **51**
appr fnl 2f, t.o: well bckd, blnkd: up in trip & not sty 1m on hvy grnd: btr 4167 (3 rnr stakes, 7f, gd/soft).
3740 **EYES DONT LIE 40** [7] 2-7-10 (56)(3oh) Joanna Badger (7) 33/1: 400069: Chsd ldrs till halfway, 2 **23**
sn well bhd, t.o.: 6 week abs: first try on hvy, blnks omitted.
3888 **CARNOT 32** [10] 2-9-1 (75) M Fenton 6/1: -05100: Keen, in tch, wknd from halfway, t.o. in 10th: op 2½ **39**
9/2: well below best on this step up to 1m on v hvy grnd: much btr 3239 (sharp/undul 7f, fast).
10 ran Time 1m 55.03 (18.43) (Oriental Mist Partnership) Miss L A Perratt Ayr, Strathclyde

4324 | 3.20 MURRAY JOHNSTONE SELLER 3YO+ (F) 1m1f Heavy Slow
£2478 £708 £354 3 yo rec 4 lb

3808 **RED CAFE 37** [11] P D Evans 4-8-13 J Bramhill 10/1: 424001: 4 ch f Perugino - Test Case **40**
(Busted) Held up, rdn ent str, gd hdwy over 2f out, styd on strongly to lead dist, rdn out: no bid, first win:
plcd twice prev this term: missed '99, plcd on fnl '98 start (seller, rtd 63 at best): eff btwn 6f & 9f: acts
on fast, hvy & a gall trk: likes selling grade.
4280 **HUTCHIES LADY 5** [4] J S Goldie 8-8-13 Joanna Badger (7) 5/1: -31002: 8 b m Efisio - Keep Mum 1¼ **37**
(Mummy's Pet) Rear, rdn & plenty to do over 3f out, ran on well for strong press fnl 2f, nvr nrr: qck reapp:
drop in trip & will appr a return to 10f+ in similar grnd: see 3805.
3823 **ACE OF TRUMPS 36** [5] J Hetherton 4-9-9 (t) M Fenton 7/1: 643523: 4 ch g First Trump - Elle 1¼ **45$**
Reef (Shareef Dancer) Led early on, remained leading ldrs, kept on well for press fnl 1f: tchd 10/1:
excellent run at these weights but treat rating with caution: acts on firm or hvy grnd: see 3805, 1195.
1498 **GINNER MORRIS 137** [12] J Hetherton 5-9-4 (BL) K Dalgleish (5) 10/1: 45-004: Keen, led 7f out, ½ **39**
hdd 3f out, ev ch till onepcd fnl 1f: first time blnks, long abs: plcd over hdles (mdn, rtd 77h) since 1498.
4218 **HOT POTATO 1** [1] 4-9-4 J McAuley 25/1: 002605: Chsd ldrs, slightly outpcd over 2f out, rallied 2 **36**
& styd on fnl 1f, no threat to ldrs: stiffish task at these weights & not disgraced: see 1699.
4217 **AMBUSHED 10** [10] 4-9-9 R Winston 4/1 FAV: 052106: Front rank, rdn to lead 3f out, hdd appr ½ **40**
fnl 1f, no extra: 10L clr rem: btr 3826 (1m, gd/soft).
1936 **PHILMIST 117** [3] 8-8-13 (bl) G Baker (5) 16/1: 4-0007: Sn well bhd, late gains: long abs: see 1361. 10 **18**
3988 **GO THUNDER 25** [7] 6-9-9 (t) Iona Wands 5/1: 053148: Keen/prom, fdd fnl 3f: btr 3823 (gd/soft). 4 **23**
3805 **COLLEGE DEAN 37** [8] 4-9-4 F Lynch 33/1: -60009: Nvr a factor: see 756. 7 **10**
3745 **PHILAGAIN 40** [6] 3-9-0 N Kennedy 16/1: 630400: Prom, lost tch fnl 3f, 10th: abs: best on fast grnd. hd **10**
340 **PRINCIPAL BOY 267** [2] 7-9-4 V Halliday 25/1: 04-600: Al bhd, t.o., 11th: long abs: see 50 (sand). 23 **0**
2202 **MILL AFRIQUE 106** [9] 4-8-13 A Culhane 66/1: 00-000: In tch, wknd rapidly halfway, t.o. in 12th: dist **0**
jumps fit, rnr-up over hdles (sell, rtd 83h, 2m, gd) since 2007.
12 ran Time 2m 10.29 (19.99) (J E Abbey) P D Evans Pandy, Gwent

1335

4325   3.50 TOTE QUICK PICK HCAP 3YO+ 0-95 (C)   1m5f   **Heavy   Slow**   **[87]**
£7247   £2230   £1115   £557   3 yo rec 8 lb

4085 **DANCING BAY** 19 [6] Miss J A Camacho 3-9-6 (87) A Culhane 10/3: -11041: 3 b g Suave Dancer -   **92**
Kabayil (Dancing Brave) Waited with, imprvd ent str, sn hung left, rdn to lead 1f out, styd on well: nicely bckd:
earlier won at Newcastle (mdn) & Pontefract (h'cap): rtd 72 in '99: eff at 10f, relished step up to 13f & may get
further: acts on gd/soft & hvy grnd, stiff/gall trks: can go well fresh: progressive stayer.
3993 **SUBTLE INFLUENCE** 25 [3] J S Goldie 6-8-11 (70) K Darley 20/1: 534/02: 6 b h Sadler's Wells -   ¾ **73**
Campestral (Alleged) Held up, prog 3f out, swtchd & rdn 2f out, ch dist, kept on but held: tchd 33/1: fine
run back in trip, eff at 13f/2m: acts on gd & hvy grnd, handles firm & looks reasonably treated: see 3993.
4128 **RAISE A PRINCE** 16 [1] S P C Woods 7-10-0 (87)(t) N Callan 7/4 FAV: 600253: 7 b g Machiavellian -   1¼ **88**
Enfant d'Amour (Lyphard) Sn prom, rdn to chase ldr 2f out, edged left/ch 1f out, onepce towards fin: well
bckd, clr rem: ran to best under a big weight in these conditions: handles firm, both AW's, likes soft/hvy: see 987.
4134 **HERACLES** 16 [4] A Berry 4-8-11 (70) J Carroll 8/1: 100624: Rcd in 2nd, left in lead after 3f, clr ent   4 **67**
str, onepce/hdd 1f out, btn when hmpd/snatched up ins last: acts on fast, prob handles hvy: see 2930.
3896 **HANNIBAL LAD** 31 [5] 4-9-9 (82) M Fenton 7/1: 135565: Held up, pushed along appr fnl 2f, onepace.   1½ **78**
1167 **EXALTED** 157 [7] 7-8-4 (63) Dale Gibson 13/2: 40-156: Handy till ent straight: tchd 8/1, 5 month abs.   6 **54**
4306 **KIDZ PLAY** 1 [2] 4-7-12 (57) K Dalgleish (5) 12/1: 40014P: V keen & sn in clr lead, hung right/p.u. after 3f.   **0**
7 ran   Time 3m 13.35 (28.75)   (Elite Racing Club)   Miss J A Camacho Norton, N Yorks

---

4326   4.20 MURRAY INCOME MDN 3YO+ (D)   1m2f   **Heavy   Slow**
£3997   £1230   £615   £307   3 yo rec 5 lb

1863 **TAKAMAKA BAY** 121 [1] M Johnston 3-9-0 J Fanning 1/10 FAV: -221: 3 ch c Unfuwain - Stay Sharpe   **80**
(Sharpen Up) Made all, cmftbly drew clr fnl 2f: hvly bckd, 4 mth abs: IR 58,000gns colt, unrcd juv: eff at
9/10f, should get further: acts on fast & hvy grnd, gall trcks: straightforward task today.
4304 **HIGHLAND GOLD** 1 [4] Miss L A Perratt 3-9-0 F Lynch 25/1: 000402: 3 ch c Indian Ridge - Anjuli   11 **55**
(Northfields) Chsd wnr, rdn, hung left & no extra appr fnl 1f: ran yesterday, needs sells: see 2006.
4234 **SIGN OF THE DRAGON** 8 [2] J Semple 3-9-0 R Winston 12/1: 453: 3 b g Sri Pekan - Tartique Twist   9 **45**
(Artic Term) Handy, eff 3f out, sn btn: longer trip, see 2140 (7f).
--   **HEATHERHILL LASS** [5] Miss L A Perratt 5-9-0 J Carroll 50/1: 4: Dwelt, held up, left bhd after 5f: dist **0**
stablemate jumped, debut: jumps bred mare.
4 ran   Time 2m 29.71 (25.31)   (The Chaps Partnership)   M Johnston Middleham, N Yorks

---

4327   4.50 MURRAY JOHNSTONE HCAP 3YO+ 0-70 (E)   6f   **Heavy   Fair**   **[67]**
£3380   £1040   £520   £260   3 yo rec 1 lb 2 Groups, probably no advantage

4136 **RYEFIELD** 16 [5] Miss L A Perratt 5-9-9 (62) J Carroll 20/1: 426331: 5 b g Petong - Octavia (Sallust)   **67**
Dwelt, far siding, imprvd & edged towards stands rail appr fnl 2f, hard rdn ins last, ran on to get up fnl strides:
op 16/1: run well in defeat since earlier win here at Ayr (h'cap): '99 Newcastle & Ayr wnr (h'caps, rtd 68): '98
Carlise wnr (mdn, rtd 80): eff at 6f/7m: acts on firm & hvy grnd, loves Ayr: runs well, without blnks.
4223 **GAY BREEZE** 10 [6] P S Felgate 7-9-10 (63) K Darley 10/1: 600022: 7 b g Dominion - Judy's Dowry   ½ **66**
(Dragonara Palace) Trkd ldrs far side, rdn to lead ent fnl 1f, ran on, hdd nr fin: tchd 14/1, fine run under
top weight: acts on firm, hvy grnd & fibresand & is well h'capped: won race on far side, see 905.
4087 **PANDJOJOE** 19 [2] R A Fahey 4-9-0 (53) P Hanagan (5) 20/1: 606003: 4 b g Archway - Vital   nk **55**
Princess (Prince Sabo) Mid div far side, prog appr fnl 1f, rdn & ch ins last, held nr fin: op 16/1, back to form
with blnks omitted: acts on fast & hvy grnd & is well h'capped: see 1008.
3960 **GARNOCK VALLEY** 26 [24] A Berry 10-9-2 (55) F Lynch 7/1: 201304: Towards rear stands side, hard   1 **54**
rdn after halfway, styd on ins last, unable to chall: tchd 9/1: apprec return to 6f: acts on fast, hvy, both AW's.
3825 **BIFF EM** 36 [10] 6-7-10 (35)(1oh) G Baker (5) 16/1: 600005: Well plcd far side, chall appr fnl 1f, rdn   nk **33**
& onepce towards fin: tchd 20/1, stablemate wnr: not far off best & is nicely h'capped: see 1143.
3534 **MISTER WESTSOUND** 49 [27] 8-7-11 (36)(bl) N Kennedy 14/1: 000006: Slow away & well off the pace   ½ **33**
stands side till styd on appr fnl 1f, nvr on terms: s/mate wnr, clr rem, 7 wk abs: won this in '98: see 1654.
4287 **DOUBLE ACTION** 4 [18] 6-9-7 (60) M Fenton 6/1: 600067: In tch stands side, chsd ldrs ent fnl 2f,   3 **50**
sn onepce: tchd 10/1: quick reapp: flattered last time, see 3708, 623.
4031 **ORIEL STAR** 22 [12] 4-8-5 (44) J McAuley 20/1: 000058: Led far side till ent fnl 1f, no extra: best at 5f.   2 **29**
4287 **PEPPIATT** 4 [14] 6-9-6 (59) J Fanning 16/1: 350009: Slow away stands side, nvr better than mid div.   ¾ **42**
3992 **MAGIC MILL** 25 [19] 7-9-6 (59) K Dalgleish (5) 14/1: -40000: Prom stands side, rdn halfway, onepce: 10th.   ½ **41**
3825 **RIOJA** 36 [21] 5-9-2 (55) N Carlisle 16/1: /00000: Nvr a factor stands side tho' stying on fin: 11th, op 10/1.3 **31**
3960 **RED SYMPHONY** 26 [22] 4-8- (43)(bl) Joanna Badger (7) 25/1: 000000: Nvr dngrs stands side: 12th.   nk **18**
3964 **JACKERIN** 26 [28] 5-8-3 (42)(tvi) V Halliday 16/1: 400020: Led stands side till appr fnl 1f, sn btn: 13th.   hd **17**
3781 **TONG ROAD** 38 [17] 4-7-12 (37) T Hamilton 7/1: 000020: Mid div stands side, prog & ch   1¾ **8**
2f out, sn wknd: 14th, back up in trip: btr 3781 (5f mdn h'cap).
3222 **SUGAR CUBE TREAT** 62 [23] 4-8-8 (47) J Bramhill 9/2 FAV: 350000: Nvr a factor stands side: 15th,   nk **17**
bckd from 6/1 but nvr looked like repeating last season's success in this race (3lbs lower mark today): see 910.
4223 **Young Bigwig** 10 [26] 6-9-0 (53) A Culhane 16/1:   4153 **Boadicea The Red** 14 [3] 3-9-6 (60) D Mernagh(3) 50/1:
3332 **Megs Pearl** 58 [25] 4-8-6 (45)(vis) P Bradley(5) 33/1:
2535 **Pallium** 92 [11] 12-7-10 (35)(tbl)(1ooh) Iona Wands 100/1:
2713 **Smokey From Caplaw** 452 [8] 6-8-12 (51) G Parkin 50/1: 3283 **High Esteem** 60 [7] 4-8-9 (48) Dale Gibson 25/1:
3103 **Doubtless Risk** 69 [1] 3-7-10 (36) P Fessey 50/1:   1941 **Golden Biff** 117 [4] 4-8-7 (46) R Lappin 33/1:
3960 **Jacmar** 26 [13] 5-8-9 (48) N Callan 33/1:   3619 **Johayro** 46 [20] 7-9-5 (58) R Winston 20/1:
25 ran   Time 1m 19.6 (10.3)   (Mrs Elaine Aird)   Miss L A Perratt Ayr, Strathclyde

Official Going STANDARD. Stalls: 5f & 1m - Outside; Rem - Inside.

4328
1.40 WH SMITH CLAIMER DIV 1 3YO+ (F) 7f aw rn Going 18 -03 Slow
£1785 £510 £255 3 yo rec 2 lb

4115 **COMPTON AVIATOR** 18 [11] G A Butler 4-8-3 (t) E Ahern 5/1: 3-0001: 4 ch g First Trump - Rifada **58a**
(Ela Mana Mou) Chsd ldrs, hdwy to lead appr fnl 1f, strongly pressed ins last, all out to hold on: 1st win,
claimed by A Carroll for £2,500: AW bow, big drop in trip: lightly rcd in '99, plcd twice (mdns, rtd 81):
eff at 7/10f, has tried up to 2m: acts on firm/fast & equitrack: eff in a t-strap: apprec drop in trip/grade.
4102 **MY EMILY** 19 [8] G L Moore 4-8-9 J Fortune 2/1 FAV: 022602: 4 b f King's Signet - Flying Wind **shd 63a**
(Forzando) Mid-div, rdn/imprvd 4f out, ran on strongly to chall ins last, just failed: nicely bckd, clr rem:
deserves to go one better: acts on firm, gd & equitrack: see 3689, 1884.
3816 **ANNIE APPLE** 37 [10] N Hamilton 4-8-7 D Harrison 7/1: 001423: 4 ch f Petardia - Art Duo (Artaius) **3½ 54$**
Trkd ldrs, drvn 2f out, no extra for press appr fnl 1f: bckd from 16/1: gd run at the weights, likes sells/clmrs.
4272 **RENDITA 7** [7] D Haydn Jones 4-8-3 (bl) P Doe 12/1: 000534: Prom, went on appr fnl 3f, qcknd **nk 50$**
& sn clr, hdd appr fnl 1f, sn held: qck reapp: better off in h'caps: see 4272, 1259.
3587 **FAIRYTIME** 48 [1] 4-8-9 (t) L Newman (3) 33/1: -00005: Dwelt, sn prom & led over 5f out, hdd **5 48$**
halfway, drvn/no extra appr dist: abs: v stiff task at the weights, treat rating with caution: see 3243 (6f).
3855 **MIDHISH TWO** 35 [6] 4-9-0 M Henry 14/1: 000606: Handy, outpcd halfway, late hdwy: visor omitted. **nk 53a**
4044 **ARZILLO 22** [9] 4-8-8 F Norton 25/1: 500026: Mid-div, hdwy halfway, wknd qcly appr fnl 1f: btr 3939. **½ 46a**
3921 **STOP THE TRAFFIC** 29 [3] 3-8-1 (t) J Quinn 20/1: 556008: Prom to halfway, fdd: see 397. **2 37a**
2729 **CAVERSFIELD** 85 [4] 5-8-6 P Fitzsimons (5) 33/1: 060309: In tch, wknd appr fnl 2f: 12 wk abs. **nk 40$**
2855 **OTIME 81** [5] 3-9-4 (bl) Dean McKeown 4/1: 625000: Nvr dngrs: 10th: tchd 11/2, 11 wk abs: btr 1889. **¾ 53a**
3907] **LUCKY BEA** 750 [15] 7-8-6 Dale Gibson 40/1: 0500/0: Al in rear, 11th: long abs, new stable: **1¼ 37a**
missed '99, prev term unplcd in 2 starts for G Holmes, subs 4th over timber (seller, rtd 67h, 2m, fast & soft):
last won on the Flat in '96, at Newcastle (h'cap, rtd 60): eff arnd 1m on fast, soft & any trk: with K A Ryan.
3581 **PURNADAS ROAD** 49 [2] 5-8-0(2ow) A Daly 33/1: 036300: Led early, rmnd cl-up, wknd fnl 2f, 12th: abs. **1 29a**
3751} **SHADES OF LOVE** 404 [13] 6-9-0 M Tebbutt 8/1: 3005-0: Dwelt, al rear, 13th: op 6/1 on reapp: **1¼ 41a**
early '99 wnr here at Lingfield (h'cap, rtd 75a, unplcd on turf, rtd 34): '98 wnr at Southwell & again here
at Lingfield (h'caps, rtd 70a, 53 on turf): eff at 6/7f, poss stays 1m: acts on firm, soft, fibresand,
Lingfield/equitrack specialist: best on sharp trks & has prev gone well fresh.
3971 **Caldey Island** 27 [14] 3-8-6 S Whitworth 25/1:   3234 **Caerdydd Fach** 63 [16] 4-8-1 G Sparkes (7) 50/1:
15 ran Time 1m 24.3 (1.5) (E Penser) G A Butler Blewbury, Oxon.

4329
2.10 TELEGRAPH MDN HCAP 3YO+ 0-65 (F) 2m aw Going 18 +02 Fast [54]
£2320 £663 £331 3 yo rec 11lb

3978 **SUPREME SILENCE** 26 [6] P W Harris 3-8-10 (47) J Fortune 12/1: 000001: 3 b c Bluebird - Why So **56a**
Silent (Mill Reef) Cl-up, went on briefly after halfway, led again 6f out, clr appr fnl 1f, eased fnl 50y, cmftbly:
op 8/1, gd time: first win, AW bow: unplcd in turf mdns & h'caps prev: eff around 2m & clrly goes v well on
equitrack: acts on a sharp trk: lightly raced & gce to further improvement on equitrack.
4193 **DESTINATION** 12 [9] C A Cyzer 3-10-0 (65) G Carter 6/1: 244532: 3 ch g Deploy - Veuve (Tirol) **6 67a**
Front rank, chsd wnr appr fnl 3f, no extra final 1f: op 4/1: clr rem & a gd run under top-weight: stays 2m.
4193 **CITRUS MAGIC** 12 [4] K Bell 3-9-9 (60) J Bosley (7) 10/1: 400023: 3 b c Cosmonaut - Up All Night **5 58a**
(Green Desert) Bhd, eff halfway, drvn & ran on well fnl 2f, no dngr to ldrs: poss get 2m on equitrack.
4193 **BOLD BAHAMIAN** 12 [11] J Noseda 3-9-9 (60) J Weaver 12/1: 40-644: Prom, drvn 3f out, onepace: **2½ 56a**
longer trip: see 4193, 858.
3683 **DANDES RAMBO** 44 [10] 3-8-13 (50) T Quinn 14/1: 604265: Handy, imprvd into lead after halfway, **4 42a**
hdd 6f out, lost tch fnl 3f: op 10/1, 6 wk abs: big step up in trip: see 3314 (10f).
4256 **TUFTY HOPPER** 8 [3] 3-10-0 (65) R Winston 16/1: 533266: In tch, hdwy 6f out, wknd fnl 2f: top-weight. **3½ 54a**
4099 **PTAH** 19 [12] 3-8-8 (45) F Norton 7/2: 300627: Towards rear, imprvd halfway, wknd qckly fnl 3f: **15 22a**
op 11/2: much better expected after a promising C/D effort in 4099.
3755 **LEGGY LADY** 41 [8] 4-9-3 (43) S Whitworth 2/1 FAV: 4-0538: Prom, grad wknd fnl 6f: nicely **3½ 17a**
bckd after 6 wk abs, much btr 3755 (firm grnd).
3838 **KARAJAN** 36 [13] 3-10-0 (65) B Marcus 12/1: 3-0409: Al towards rear: jt top-weight, in trip. **4 36a**
2024 **ROSE TINA** 115 [1] 3-8-7 (44) S Carson (3) 40/1: 0000: Keen, prom to halfway, sn bhd, t.o. in 10th. **22 0a**
4271 **LE CAVALIER** 7 [2] 3-9-13 (64) L Newman (3) 20/1: 265000: Led, hdd bef halfway, sn lost tch, 11th. **4 16a**
3448 **TREASURE CASTLE** 54 [5] 5-9-8 (48)(vis) R Hughes 12/1: 05060P: Sn struggling & p.u. after halfway: **0a**
AW bow: recently plcd over hdles (nov h'cap, rtd 84h, 2m7f/3m, fast & hvy, t-strap & visor): see 2953.
4102 **Hoh Hoh Seven** 19 [7] 4-9-10 (50) M Henry 25/1:
855] **Winged Greybird** 547 [14] 6-9-0 (40)(t) Sophie Mitchell 33/1:
14 ran Time 3m 22.61 (2.61) (Mrs P W Harris) P W Harris Aldbury, Herts.

4330
2.40 JOHN MENZIES HCAP DIV 1 3YO+ 0-75 (E) 1m aw rn Going 18 +08 Fast [75]
£2299 £657 £328 3 yo rec 3 lb

3685 **TAPAGE** 44 [3] Andrew Reid 4-8-12 (59) M Henry 9/2: 621501: 4 b g Great Commotion - Irena (Bold **64a**
Lad) Trkd ldrs, rdn to chall over 1f out, led just ins last, strongly pressed cl-home, all out & just prevailed:
op 7/2, 6 wk abs: best time of day: earlier won here at Lingfield (2, AW h'caps), Bath, Brighton & Windsor
(h'caps): rnr-up twice in '99 (clmr, rtd 69, W Muir), prev term won here at Lingfield (mdn auct, rtd 78a, D
Gillespie): suited by 7f/1m: acts on firm & fast, loves equitrack/Lingfield, handles any trk: best without
blnks & likes to race up with/force the pace: runs well fresh: most tough & genuine.
4121 **HAIL THE CHIEF** 17 [8] R Hannon 3-9-8 (72) R Smith (5) 9/1: 011262: 3 b c Be My Chief - Jade **shd 76a**
Pet (Petong) Rear, imprvd 4f out, strong run to chall ins last, just failed: acts on fast, gd & equitrack.
4291 **CRUAGH EXPRESS** 5 [9] G L Moore 4-8-6 (53)(bl) D Holland 13/2: 001163: 4 b g Unblest - Cry In The **1½ 54a**
Dark (Godswalk) Led, qcknd appr fnl 1f, wknd/hdd ins last: op 5/1, qck reapp: bold front running bid.
2749 **PENGAMON** 84 [7] M Wigham 4-8-9 (64) J Quinn 7/1 FAV: 302124: Rear, gd hdwy halfway, ev ch till **2 61a**
no extra fnl 2f: well bckd after 12 wk abs, just sharper for this: see 2749.
4126 **COMPTON ARROW** 17 [11] 4-9-11 (72)(t) E Ahern 12/1: 000005: Rear, eff over 2f out, styd on **nk 69a**
fnl 1f but no threat to ldrs: op 8/1: see 3981.
4215 **AMJAD** 11 [5] 3-9-4 (68)(bl) P Robinson 20/1: 002006: Trkd ldrs, rdn/grad wknd appr fnl 2f: see 3759. **½ 64a**
3871 **SASH** 34 [4] 3-8-4 (54) P Doe 33/1: 505007: Dwelt, rear, modest late gains, no threat: AW bow. **2½ 46a**

3884　SCISSOR RIDGE 33 [6] 8-8-8 (55) A Nicholls 20/1: 505008: Prom 4f, no dngr fnl 3f: best at 7f.　nk　47a
4066　ORIENT EXPRESS 21 [1] 3-8-10 (60) D R McCabe 16/1: 303009: Handy, wknd after halfway: see 3078.　1½　50a
3936　LEGAL SET 28 [12] 4-9-12 (73) Darren Williams (5) 12/1: 602300: Cl-up, fdd fnl 3f, 10th: top-weight.　9　49a
4228　SHOTACROSS THE BOW 11 [10] 3-9-1 (65) R Hughes 8/1: 323030: Dsptd lead 4f, qckly lost tch, 11th.　1　39a
3831　KHALED 36 [2] 5-9-4 (65) J Tate 20/1: -03000: Al well in rear, t.o. in 12th: btr 3118, 360.　11　24a
12 ran　Time 1m 37.00 (0.8)　(A S Reid)　Andrew Reid Mill Hill, London NW7.

4331　3.10 WH SMITH CLAIMER DIV 2 3YO+ (F)　7f aw rn　Good 18　-10 Slow
£1778　£508　£254　3 yo rec 2 lb

*4031　TALARIA 23 [2] J Pearce 4-8-9 T Quinn 5/1: 405611: 4 ch f Petardia - Million At Dawn (Fayruz)　64a
Led, pshd clr ent fnl 2f, v cmftbly: drifter from 9/4, AW bow, clmd for £8,000: earlier won at Nottingham (h'cap)
& Leicester (clmr, S Williams): '99 Newmarket wnr for G Wragg (mdn, rtd 86): rtd 87 in '98: eff at 6/7f: acts
on firm, gd/soft grnd & equitrack: goes on any trk, with/without t-strap: best without a visor: hat-trick likely.
4174　SOFISIO 14 [8] W R Muir 3-9-2 (bl) Martin Dwyer 11/2: 450062: 3 ch g Efisio - Legal Embrace　3　66a
(Legal Bid) Mid-div, chsd ldrs 2f out, styd on for 2nd but no ch with wnr: tchd 7/1: eff with/without blnks.
4272　SUPERCHIEF 7 [5] Miss B Sanders 5-9-0 (tbl) S Carson (3) 7/2 JT FAV: 000023: 5 b g Precocious -　2　58a
Rome Express (Siberian Express) Well plcd & ch till onepace ent fnl 2f: tchd 5/1, qck reapp, gd run at weights.
4122　HI MUJTAHID 17 [4] J M Bradley 6-8-8 Claire Bryan (5) 33/1: 020004: Prom, eff 2f out, unable to qckn:　1¾　49$
4208　WOOLLY WINSOME 11 [9] 4-8-3 A Daly 25/1: 060505: Ran in snatches, nvr a threat: stiff task.　1¾　41a
4224　CASTLE SEMPILL 11 [13] 3-8-12 (vis) Dale Gibson 7/2 JT FAV: 004036: Chsd ldrs wide, fdd　shd　52a
appr fnl 1f & rider dropped whip: tchd 9/2, tricky draw: crying out for a drop back to 6f: see 852.
3914　TOPLESS IN TUSCANY 30 [3] 3-7-11 A Mackay 33/1: 004007: Handy till appr fnl 2f: jumps rnr.　1　35a
4018　PAGEANT 25 [14] 3-9-1 A Clark 13/2: 625558: Nvr a factor: op 4/1 on AW bow, see 2026, 1773.　1　51a
4218　MACS DREAM 11 [1] 5-9-10 (t) M Tebbutt 25/1: 005059: Nvr dngrs: stiff task.　nk　58$
3656　SILVER TONGUED 46 [16] 4-8-6 F Norton 40/1: 060400: Al towards rear: 10th, 7 wk absence.　nk　39$
4151　AL MABROOK 15 [11] 5-8-6 (bl) F Lynch 14/1: 350050: Nvr on terms: 11th, op 10/1, back in trip.　½　38$
3970　LITIGIOUS 27 [12] 3-8-3 (vis) L Newman (2) 14/1: 220040: Sn struggling: 14th, op 10/1, AW bow, see 2198.　0a
4207　Mint Leaf 11 [15] 3-8-3(2ow) Sophie Mitchell (5)　4121 Grand Musica 17 [6] 7-8-6 (tbl) L Newman (2) 50/1:
4274　Lady Dealer 7 [10] 5-7-12 G Baker (5) 66/1:
15 ran　Time 1m 24.77 (1.97)　(Saracen Racing)　J Pearce Newmarket.

4332　3.40 G JONES COND STKS 2YO (D)　6f aw rn　Going 18　-04 Slow
£3757　£1156　£578　£289

*3815　NEARCTIC LADY 37 [6] R Hannon 2-8-11 R Hughes 7/4 FAV: -4011: 2 gr f Night Shift - Snowing　95a
(Icecapade) Led, pushed clr ins last, rdly: nicely bckd from 5/2 on AW bow: earlier won at Bath (fill auct mdn):
eff at 5/6f: goes on firm/fast grnd & equitrack, any trk: likes to force the pace: useful, progressive filly.
2966　MAGICAL FLUTE 75 [2] M R Channon 2-8-9 Craig Williams 8/1: -03132: 2 ch f Piccolo - Stride Home　3　83a
(Absalom) Mid-div, rdn appr fnl 2f, sn boxed in, clr ins last & ran on well, too late: tchd 10/1, uninspired ride:
shld have been considerably closer on AW bow after 11 wk abs: acts on firm/fast & equitrack: return to 7f will suit.
-4225　LILLEMAN 11 [13] G A Butler 2-8-11 (t) E Ahern 10/1: 50223: 2 b c Distant Relative - Lillemor　1¼　82a
(Connaught) Mid-div, hdwy under press 2f out, same pace in last: goes on fast, soft grnd & equitrack,
handles firebrand: tried a t-strap today: shown enough to win a maiden.
4247　PRINCE OF BLUES 8 [8] N P Littmoden 2-9-0 J Tate 11/4: 500124: Prom, tried to go after wnr　nk　85a
appr fnl 1f, sn no extra: nicely bckd: goes on firm, gd grnd & both AWs: see 4045.
4157　SYLVAN GIRL 15 [5] 2-8-6 Martin Dwyer 20/1: 304005: Dwelt & bhd till ran on ins last, nvr nrr:　1¼　73$
tchd 50/1 on AW bow: handles fast, gd & equitrack: still a maiden.
4098　HARD TO CATCH 19 [4] 2-9-4 (bl) C Catlin (7) 20/1: 601006: Chsd ldrs, no extra appr fnl 1f:　½　83$
op 16/1 on AW bow: return to 5f will suit: see 3576.
*4187　LEOZIAN 12 [12] 2-9-4 T Quinn 10/1: 20417: Prom till fdd appr fnl 1f: AW bow, op 7/1: return to 5f?　½　82a
3976　MONTEV LADY 26 [1] 2-8-9 A Daly 33/1: 01408: Handy till wknd 2f out: stiff task, AW bow, see 3204.　3　65$
4283　FIREWORK 5 [9] 2-8-11 B Marcus 5/1: 2239: Al towards rear: op 3/1 on AW bow, qck reapp, see 4283.　¾　66a
4030　FOREST MOON 23 [11] 2-8-9 M Henry 33/1: 660100: Sn struggling: 10th, AW bow: see 2052.　5　51a
3913　Alquid Novi 30 [7] 2-8-6 A Clark 50/1:　-- Vals Ring [3] 2-8-9 S Righton 50/1:
4172　Dark Dolores 14 [10] 2-8-8 R Havlin 50/1:
13 ran　Time 1m 11.75 (1.35)　(D Boocock)　R Hannon East Everleigh, Wilts.

4333　4.10 MAIL SELLER 2YO (G)　5f aw rn　Going 18　-18 Slow
£1855　£530　£265

3204　PAT THE BUILDER 64 [2] K R Burke 2-8-11 N Callan 5/1: 540461: 2 b c Common Grounds - Demoiselle　68a
(Midyan) Made all, rdn out: tchd 7/1, bght in for 4,200gns, AW bow, 2 month abs: eff forcing the pace at
5f: acts on equitrack, handles firm grnd, sharp trks: win another AW seller.
4227　BRANSTON GEM 11 [8] M Johnston 2-8-6 D Holland 9/2: -00502: 2 b f So Factual - Branston Jewel　¾　60a
(Prince Sabo) Prom, chsd wnr fnl 2f, held towards fin: better run: eff at 5f on equitrack.
3513　MY FRIEND JACK 52 [5] J Akehurst 2-8-11 S Sanders 4/1 FAV: -50603: 2 b g Petong - Spring Collection1¼　62a
(Tina's Pet) Bhd ldrs, rdn appr fnl 1f, not pace to chall: 7 wk abs, AW bow: gd run, eff at 5f on equitrack.
4095　SONG N DANCE 19 [3] M D I Usher 2-8-6 G Baker (5) 9/1: -05604: Well plcd till no extra appr　2½　51a
fnl 1f, eased ins last: tchd 12/1 on AW bow: prob handles equitrack.
4190　QUIZZICAL LADY 12 [9] 2-8-11 J Fortune 5/1: 200305: Mid-div, feeling pace 2f out: AW bow, see 3354.　½　55a
4190　LIGHT EVIDENCE 12 [10] 2-8-6 G Carter 8/1: 0506: Wide, prom, outpcd appr fnl 1f: tchd 9/2, AW bow.　hd　50a
*4171　EASTER ISLAND 14 [7] 2-8-11 G Hind 5/1: 000017: Dwelt, nvr in it: AW bow: soft grnd wnr in 4171.　2½　49a
4095　DIM DOT 19 [4] 2-8-11 J Quinn 10/1: 08: Bhd from halfway: AW bow: Inzar colt with B Palling.　nk　49a
3278　POWDER 61 [1] 2-8-6 Dale Gibson 25/1: 009: Al bhd: 9 wk abs, AW bow, see 1737.　3½　36a
4171　CARRICK LADY 14 [6] 2-8-6 (BL) D Kinsella (7) 40/1: 0000: Al rear: 10th, blnkd, AW bow, no form.　¾　34a
10 ran　Time 59.64 (1.84)　(James Ryan)　K R Burke Newmarket.

4334
4.40 SURRIDGE DAWSON HCAP 3YO+ 0-60 (F) 1m4f aw Going 18 -12 Slow [60]
£2541 £726 £363 3 yo rec 7 lb

3808 **ROGUE SPIRIT 38** [10] P W Harris 4-10-0 (60) J Fortune 20/1: 200001: 4 b g Petong - Quick Profit 66a
(Formidable) Prom, led appr fnl 3f & drvn, styd on strongly: op 14/1, jt top-weight on AW bow: '99 Folkestone
wnr (mdn, rtd 78): eff at 1m/12f: acts on firm, gd/soft grnd & equitrack, any trk: can carry big weights.

4226 **CUPBOARD LOVER 11** [17] D Haydn Jones 4-10-0 (60) A McGlone 10/1: 314142: 4 ch g Risk Me - 1½ 63a
Galejade (Sharrood) Dwelt, in tch, prog to chall 3f out, styd on but held ins last: op 7/1, tchd 12/1, jt
top-weight who continues to improve: acts on fast, gd grnd & AWs: see 4026.

4186 **FULL EGALITE 12** [9] B R Johnson 4-9-5 (51)(bl) C Rutter 12/1: 2351D3: 4 gr g Ezzoud - Milva 1¾ 51a
(Jellaby) Mid-div, wide prog halfway, rdn 2f out, kept on same pace: gd run, see 4186.

4099 **QUIET READING 19** [6] C A Cyzer 3-9-5 (58) G Carter 16/1: 405264: Rear, styd on fnl 3f, nvr nk 58a
dngrs: back in trip, stays 12f: see 3835.

*4245 **FAILED TO HIT 8** [4] 7-9-9 (55)(vis)(6ex) J Tate 4/1: 526315: Led 4f, outpcd appr fnl 2f: nicely 3 51a
bckd, quckish reapp with a penalty: btr 4245 (fibresand).

3691} **ALPINE HIDEAWAY 407** [2] 7-9-4 (50) F Lynch 33/1: 0163-6: Led after 4f till appr fnl 3f, no extra: 3½ 41a
belated reapp: '99 wnr at Beverley (clmr, rtd 54, M Easterby): '98 rnr-up (amat h'cap, rtd 70): '97 Southwell
(clmr, rtd 81a) & Ripon wnr (clmr, rtd 70, B Hanbury): eff at 7f/8.5f: acts on firm, gd/soft grnd & fibresand,
any trk: best up with/forcing the pace & has tried blnks/hdles: sharper next time back in trip.

3948 **HIGHLY PRIZED 28** [8] 6-9-7 (53) L Newman (3) 10/1: 000107: Prom, eff 4f out, no impress: btr 3681. 3 40a
4100 **SUPERSONIC 19** [15] 4-9-13 (59)(t) S Carson (3) 7/1: 403038: Bhd ldrs, lost pl fnl 2f: see 4100, 679. 8 36a
2537 **NUTMEG 93** [7] 3-8-12 (51) Dale Gibson 33/1: 400669: Nvr better than mid-div: op 20/1, abs, AW bow. 3½ 23a
3586 **LADY JO 48** [16] 4-9-8 (54) R Smith (5) 10/1: 051600: Nvr a factor: 10th, bckd from 14/1, 7 wk abs. ½ 25a
3424 **GOLDEN ROD 55** [18] 3-8-13 (52) P Doe 20/1: 346000: Dwelt 7f to 1m: 11th, 8 wk abs, st/mate wnr 1¾ 21a
4272 **WAIKIKI BEACH 7** [13] 9-8-12 (44) S Whitworth 33/1: 062060: Al rear: 12th, qck reapp, see 3490, 136. 9 1a
3623 **TARSKI 47** [5] 6-8-12 (44) A Clark 14/1: 335460: Nvr troubled ldrs: 13th, 7 wk abs, AW bow & up in trip. 10 0a
*4176 **PENALTA 14** [1] 4-8-13 (45) J Quinn 7/2 FAV: 000310: Dwelt, nvr trav well, brief eff halfway: 6 0a
14th, bckd: reportedly not face the kick-back: much btr 4176 (soft).

3828 Billichang 38 [3] 4-9-0 (46)(bl) R Winston 16/1: 4228 Dont Worry Bout Me 11 [11] 3-9-2 (55)(vis) L Carter 14/1:
3964 Massey 27 [12] 4-9-11 (57) S Sanders 25/1: 4251 Icon 8 [14] 3-9-2 (55)(t) D Holland 40/1:
18 ran Time 2m 32.82 (3.62) (L Grover, P Johns, C Stewart, K Swinden) P W Harris Aldbury, Herts.

4335
5.10 JOHN MENZIES HCAP DIV 2 3YO+ 0-75 (E) 1m aw rn Going 18 -06 Slow [73]
£2299 £657 £328 3 yo rec 3 lb

*4248 **PADHAMS GREEN 8** [5] B W Hills 4-10-0 (73)(6ex) R Hughes 11/10 FAV: 215211: 4 b g Aragon - Double 83a
Dutch (Nicholas Bill) Bhd ldrs, switched & ran on to lead ent fnl 1f, cmftbly: well bckd, defied top-weight/pen:
earlier won at Newmarket (amat h'cap, rtd 70) & W'hampton (h'cap): '99 wnr at Salisbury (appr h'cap, rtd 69,
M Tompkins): eff at 7f/8.5f: acts on firm, gd/soft grnd & both AWs: goes on any trk & can carry big weights.

4101 **DON BOSCO 19** [12] E Stanners 4-8-10 (55) J Stack 25/1: 300102: 4 ch g Grand Lodge - Suyayeb (The 2 57a
Minstrel) Prom, led briefly bef fnl 1f, sn outpcd by wnr: op 16/1: gd run, apprec drop back to 1m:
acts on firm, soft grnd & equitrack, see 3490.

3823 **HEVER GOLF GLORY 37** [7] C N Kellett 6-8-7 (52) G Baker (5) 50/1: 600033: 6 b g Efisio - Zaius 1¼ 52a
(Artaius) Sn outpcd, kept on for press appr fnl 1f, nvr dngrs: op 20/1: better on fibresand: see 383.

4033 **ITS OUR SECRET 23** [8] M H Tompkins 4-8-12 (57) S Sanders 33/1: 005004: Wide, in tch, eff & lost nk 56a
action ent str, no impress on ldrs: AW bow, see 1279.

4100 **SALEM 19** [10] 3-9-3 (65) R Price 12/1: 0345: Handy till no extra appr fnl 1f: h'cap bow, back in trip. nk 63a
3936 **DARYABAD 28** [9] 8-9-10 (69)(bl) Dale Gibson 7/1: 131336: Dwelt, rear, late hdwy: tchd 10/1, see 3384. hd 67a
4077 **KAFIL 20** [4] 6-8-4 (49)(bl) A Nicholls 50/1: 603067: Led till appr fnl 1f, sn btn: blnks reapp: see 1. shd 47a
4204 **STORMY RAINBOW 11** [11] 3-9-5 (67) G Hind 8/1: 0-2258: Nvr nr ldrs: tchd 12/1, see 591. 9 52a
3269 **DILSAA 62** [3] 3-9-0 (62) J Fortune 16/1: 006469: Bhd from halfway: 9 wk abs, AW bow, longer trip. 2½ 43a
*3839 **UNCHAIN MY HEART 36** [2] 4-8-12 (55)(vis) D R McCabe 4/1: 014110: Dwelt, nvr in it: 10th, bckd: ¾ 37a
not her form & it may pay to forget this: see 3839.

3820 **OUR FIRST LADY 37** [6] 3-9-9 (71) T Quinn 16/1: 0-0220: Mid-div, eff 4f out, btn & eased fnl 1f: ¾ 50a
11th, op 8/1, AW/h'cap bow: reportedly ran without declared t-strap & is worth another chance back in trip.

3796 **MOON AT NIGHT 38** [1] 5-9-6 (65) A Clark 10/1: 030000: Chsd ldrs 4f: 12th, AW bow, see 1129 (reapp). 22 19a
12 ran Time 1m 38.14 (1.94) (Mrs B W Hills) B W Hills Lambourn, Berks.

Official Going SOFT. Stalls: Far Side.

4336
1.30 BUCKENHAM SELLER 2YO (E) 7f str Good 40 -41 Slow
£6097 £1876 £938 £469 2 Groups, merged halfway, high no's favoured.

4187 **NOSE THE TRADE 13** [22] J A Osborne 2-8-11 S W Kelly (3) 12/1: 51: 2 b g Cyrano de Bergerac - Lolite 73
(Forzando) In tch, prog 2f out, led 1f out, pushed out: op 8/1, bght in for 16,000gns: dam a sprinter: suited
by step up to 7f: acts on gd grnd, stiff/gall trk: likely to prove better than a plater.

3354 **JETHAME 59** [29] B J Meehan 2-8-6 (BL) Pat Eddery 4/1 FAV: 035332: 2 ch f Definite Article - Victorian 2½ 64
Flower (Tate Gallery) Led till 1f out, no extra under press: 8 wk abs: clr of rem, prob ran to best in blnks.

4190 **WATTNO ELJOHN 13** [24] D W P Arbuthnot 2-9-2 T Quinn 14/1: 016353: 2 b c Namaqualand - Caroline 4 66
Connors (Fairy King) Well plcd & ev ch till onepace fnl 1f: imprvd up in trip: see 4190, 3258 (6f).

4190 **FARAUDE 13** [23] W R Muir 2-8-6 Martin Dwyer 10/1: 04: In tch, prog 2f out, sn edged left & no 3 50
further impression: closer to this 3rd in 4190 (6f).

3957 **BISHOPS SECRET 28** [4] A Beech (3) 50/1: -0005: Held up, styd on appr fnl 1f, nvr 1 53$
dngrs: much imprvd in first time blnks, tho' treat rating with caution: poor low draw: see 2620.

4097 **MONASH LADY 20** [2] 2-8-6 L Newman (3) 20/1: 466: Chsd ldrs till fdd ent fnl 2f: not disgraced, low draw. ¾ 46
3720 **JUNIOR BRIEF 47** [10] R Winston 33/1: 000007: Held up, eff appr fnl 2f, nvr nr ldrs: 7 wk abs. ¾ 49
3950 **SOLO DANCE 29** [27] 2-8-6 (bl) W Supple 25/1: 440508: Handy, rdn appr fnl 2f, wknd: stiff task. ½ 43$

*4025 **FINN McCOOL** 26 [1] 2-9-2 P Hanagan (5) 14/1: -619: Front rank tho' wide, no extra 2f out: no   1¾   49
easy task from stall 1: see 4025 (fibresand).

2683 **BOWFELL** 89 [8] 2-8-6 J Stack 20/1: 060: Chsd ldrs till wknd qckly 2f out: 10th, 3 mth abs, lngr trip.   nk   38

4154 **SUGAR ROLO** 16 [6] 2-8-6 F Norton 25/1: 654030: Al around same place: 11th: btr 4154 (fibresand).   1   36

4097 **MISS DAMINA** 20 [17] 2-8-6 R Ffrench 14/1: 004040: Mid-div thr'out: 12th, flattered 4097.   nk   35

4063 **ZAFILLY** 22 [12] 2-8-6 D Holland 10/1: 000: Nvr trbld ldrs: 13th: tchd 12/1, down in grade, see 3789.   nk   34

2901 **NORTH BY NORTH** 79 [15] 2-8-11 S Sanders 14/1: 00: In tch till 3f out: 14th, 11 wk abs.   1¾   37

3420 **EVERMOORE** 56 [26] 2-8-11 B Marcus 25/1: 046400: Nvr a factor: 15th, 8 wk abs: see 1088.   nk   31

4104 **TREBLE RED** 19 [25] 2-8-6 Craig Williams 10/1: 60: Dwelt, al towards rear: 19th, op 8/1: see 4104.   0

3922 **ZANDOS CHARM** 30 [7] 2-8-11 K Darley 12/1: 501300: Mid-div till halfway: 28th: much btr 3690, 3388.   0

3911 Hetra Reef 31 [19] 2-8-11 P McCabe 33/1:   4246 Inzarmood 9 [11] 2-8-6 B Reilly (7) 33/1:

4097 The Wall 20 [9] 2-8-6 A Polli (3) 50/1:   4246 Worth A Ring 9 [3] 2-8-6 D O'Donohoe 33/1:

4267 Alfalfa 8 [14] 2-8-11 S Carson (3) 50/1:   2880 Rameses 80 [13] 2-8-11 D Harrison 16/1:

3028 Hard To Cash 73 [18] 2-8-11 J Reid 33/1:   4116 High Tempo 18 [28] 2-8-11 N Callan 33/1:

4190 Ghost Of A Chance 13 [16] 2-8-11 A Clark 50/1:   3558 Agile Dancer 50 [5] 2-8-6 R Mullen 20/1:

4117 Laudable Lad 18 [30] 2-8-11 (BL) J Quinn 25/1:   3733 Yura Madam 43 [20] 2-8-8(2ow) G Faulkner (0) 66/1:

29 ran   Time 1m 28.85 (5.65)   (Martyn Booth)   J A Osborne Lambourn, Berks.

4337   2.05 LISTED SEVERALS STKS 3YO+ (A)   1m2f str   Good 40   00 Fast
£14326   £5434   £2717   £1235   3 yo rec 5 lb

*4212 **KATY NOWAITEE** 12 [4] P W Harris 4-9-0 J Reid 11/8 FAV: 12-111: 4 b f Komaite - Cold Blow (Posse)   105
Trkd ldr racing keenly, pshd into lead 2f out, ran on strgly, drvn out: hvly bckd, fair time: hat-trick landed
after wins at Doncaster & here at Newmarket (Cambridgeshire): '99 wnr at Newmarket (mdn, again) & Redcar (h'cap,
rtd 86): eff at 1m/10f on firm & gd/soft, loves gall trks, esp Newmarket: goes well fresh: progressive & useful.

*3907 **SALEE** 12 [2] J H M Gosden 3-8-9 L Dettori 10/1: 6-152: 3 b f Caerleon - Almaaseh (Dancing Brave)   1¾   100
Handy, eff 2f out, rdn 1f out, kept on but no trble wnr: useful run, apprec 12f: 5th in France since 3907 (List).

3177 **ZIBILENE** 67 [1] L M Cumani 3-8-9 S W Kelly 16/1: 3 b f Rainbow Quest - Brocade (Habitat)   ½   99
Led, under press & hdd 2f out, kept on till no extra fnl 100y: tchd 20/1, 10 wk abs: progressive, useful
filly, imprvd with forcing tactics: eff at 10/12f on firm & gd: see 2560.

3595 **NEW ASSEMBLY** 49 [9] Sir Michael Stoute 3-8-9 Pat Eddery 10/1: 211644: Well plcd, rdn 2f out,   1¼   97
onepace fnl 1f: op 8/1, tchd 12/1, 7 wk abs: prob ran to best, acts on firm & gd: see 2190 (h'cap).

4263 **DIAMOND WHITE** 11 [5] 5-9-0 D Holland 6/1: 453305: Waited with, wide effort appr fnl 2f, mod hdwy.   2   94

4212 **FIRST FANTASY** 12 [10] 4-9-3 Craig Williams 10/1: 501066: Held up, imprvd 3f out, sn onepace: ½   96
bckd from 20/1 despite stiffish task at the weights: see 3389.

2501 **FAME AT LAST** 12 [3] 3-8-9 M Hills 16/1: 1-4007: Towards rear, pushed along 3f out, sn no impress.   1¼   91

3918 **YOU ARE THE ONE** 30 [11] 3-8-9 K Darley 9/1: 108: Held up, niggled halfway, nvr on terms: stiff task.   2½   87

4128 **SUMMER SONG** 18 [7] 3-8-9 G Carter 25/1: 311109: Al towards rear: return to h'caps & 12f will suit.   8   75

3924 **IDOLIZE** 33 [8] 3-8-9 D Sweeney 25/1: -01000: Chsd ldrs till appr fnl 2f: 10th, stiff task, see 1797.   ¾   74

4113 **ISSEY ROSE** 19 [6] 3-8-9 L Carter 25/1: 0-0000: Al rear: 11th, stiff task, see 3726.   1   72

4130 **BEDARA** 18 [12] 3-8-9 R Hills 25/1: -14560: Handy till wknd qcky appr fnl 2f: 12th, stiff task, see 814.   7   62

12 ran   Time 2m 06.2 (3.92)   (The Stable Maites)   P W Harris Aldbury, Herts.

4338   2.35 GRANGEWOOD NURSERY HCAP 2YO 0-95 (C)   6f   Good 40   -16 Slow   [98]
£7358   £2264   £849   £849   High numbers favoured

3965 **IDLE POWER** 28 [21] P W Harris 2-9-0 (84) B Marcus 20/1: 251661: 2 b g Common Grounds - Idle   90
Fancy (Mujtahid) Made just about all, found extra when pressed appr fnl 1f, drifted left, rdn out: earlier
won at Kempton (mdn): eff at 5/6f (dam a 1m wnr): acts on fast & gd/soft grnd, prob any trk: imprvd from
the front here: has been gelded, appears on the upgrade, could rate higher.

*3888 **BLUE REIGNS** 34 [22] N P Littmoden 2-9-4 (88) L Dettori 2/1 FAV: -5112: 2 b c Whittingham - Gold   1   90
And Blue (Bluebird) Towards rear, gd prog ent fnl 2f, chsd wnr ins last, nvr nrr: hvly bckd: lost little in
defeat on this easier surface on h'cap bow: acts on firm & gd grnd: see 3888.

3886 **FACE D FACTS** 34 [19] C F Wall 2-8-3 (73) R Mullen 16/1: 130243: 2 b f So Factual - Water Well   nk   74
(Sadler's Wells) Mid-div, eff 2f out, kept on for press ins last: ddht for 3rd: 7f will suit, see 3712, 2214.

*4082 **SABO ROSE** 15 [15] W J Haggas 2-8-11 (81) P Robinson 7/1: 313: Dwelt, bhd, gd prog ent fnl 2f,   dht   82
kept on till no extra fin: ddhtd for 3rd: bckd from 10/1 on h'cap bow: acts on gd & soft grnd: see 4082.

4179 **NIGHT HAVEN** 14 [11] 2-8-10 (80) M Fenton 12/1: 22145: Cl-up/ev ch till no extra fnl 150y: stays 6f.   hd   80

4214 **Y TO KMAN** 12 [17] 2-9-1 (85) R Hughes 14/1: 12406: Chsd ldrs, rdn 1f out, unable to qckn   shd   85
& edged right: gd run, btn just over 1L: stays 6f, see 911, 724.

*4202 **ADWEB** 12 [1] 2-7-12 (68) M Henry 16/1: 00417: In tch, wide, smooth prog on bit appr fnl 1f, sn   ½   66
rdn, no impress: tchd 20/1, gd run from stall 1: stays 6f, one to note back at 5f: see 4202.

4179 **RASOUM** 14 [12] 2-9-7 (91) J Reid 33/1: -31308: Mid-div, eff & not much room appr fnl 1f, styd   shd   89+
on but nvr a threat: top-weight, btn under 2L: not much luck in running, worth another look: see 2959.

3712 **RIDGE RUNNER** 44 [13] 2-9-1 (85) Pat Eddery 14/1: -2159: Dwelt, late wide hdwy, nvr nrr: 6 wk abs.   hd   82

4157 **FOREVER TIMES** 16 [14] 2-8-5 (75) K Darley 12/1: 103300: Towards rear, ran on fnl 1f, nvr dngrs: 10th.   ½   70

4219 **WALLY McARTHUR** 12 [20] 2-9-2 (86) G Carter 12/1: 104230: Prom, eff 2f out, onepace: 11th.   nk   80

4138 **AINTNECESSARILYSO** 17 [4] 2-8-2 (72) N Pollard 33/1: 602300: Well plcd, rdn appr fnl 1f,   nk   65
no impress: 12th, blnks omitted: poor low draw: see 3852.

3802 **TIME MAITE** 39 [9] 2-7-12 (68) P Hanagan (3) 20/1: 353130: Chsd ldrs, shkn up 2f out, unable to   1   58
qckn & sltly hmpd towards fin: op 14/1, 6 wk abs, back up in trip: see 3475 (5f).

4214 **ARMAGNAC** 12 [18] 2-9-5 (89) S Sanders 16/1: 551200: Al around same pl, eased towards fin: 14th.   ¾   76

4170 **WOLF VENTURE** 16 [6] 2-8-7 (77) N Callan 33/1: -43500: Chsd ldrs 4f: 15th, low draw: see 3909.   nk   63

4098 Blakeshall Boy 20 [10] 2-8-8 (78) Craig Williams 25/1:3761 Johnny Reb 41 [3] 2-8-9 (79)(t) L Newman (3) 33/1:

3638 Talbot Avenue 47 [8] 2-8-5 (75) J Reid 20/1:   4214 Loner 12 [16] 2-8-6 (76) F Norton 20/1:

1372 Serviceable 146 [7] 2-8-10 (80) J Tate 25/1:   4214 Mon Secret 12 [5] 2-8-5 (75) J Quinn 33/1:

4172 Western Flame 15 [2] 2-8-2 (72) J Mackay (5) 25/1:

22 ran   Time 1m 14.14 (3.34)   (The Dreamers)   P W Harris Aldbury, Herts.

4339   3.10 UKBETTING.COM RTD HCAP 3YO+ 0-105 (B)   5f   Good 40   +07 Fast   [111]
£9458   £3587   £1793   £815   2 Groups, first 4 home raced in centre

4129 **DANCING MYSTERY** 18 [4]   E A Wheeler 6-8-13 (96) S Carson (3) 8/1: 401121: 6 b g Beveled -   102
Batchworth Dancer (Ballacashtal) Sn led in centre, qcknd clr of that grp appr fnl 1f, edged right & rdn to lead
overall ent fnl 1f, ran on strgly: nicely bckd, fast time: earlier won at Salisbury, Ascot, Yarmouth & here at
Newmarket (h'caps): '99 wins at Lingfield, Southwell (rtd 82a), Warwick (h'caps) & Redcar (stks, rtd 78): '98
wnr at Windsor & Goodwood (h'cap, rtd 57 & 74a): stays 6f, suited by 5f: acts on fast, gd/soft grnd, both AW's:
goes on any trk & runs well fresh, with/without blnks: v tough, useful & still improving.
*3791 **CANDLERIGGS** 40 [1]   E A L Dunlop 4-8-7 (90)(2oh) G Carter 11/1: 205-12: 4 ch g Indian Ridge -   ¾   93
Ridge Pool (Bluebird) In tch centre, prog under press appr fnl 1f, fin strongly, too late: op 8/1, 6 wk abs:
gd run back at 5f, return to 6f will suit: lightly rcd & still improving: see 3791 (reapp).
4012 **NIGHT FLIGHT** 26 [5]   R A Fahey 6-8-8 (91) J Reid 14/1: 001203: 6 gr g Night Shift - Ancestry   1   91
(Persepolis) Handy in centre, eff appr fnl 1f, styd on inside last, nvr nrr: bck to form: see 3543 (6f).
*3631 **AMARANTH** 47 [6]   J L Eyre 4-8-7 (90)(3oh) T Quinn 14/1: 265014: Towards rear, centre, kept on   hd   89
well fnl 1f, nvr dngrs: 7 wk abs: likes Newmarket, see 3631.
*4185 **WHISTLER** 14 [17]   3-8-7 (90)(6oh) L Newman (3) 5/1: 241215: Handy far side, edged left under   shd   89
press appr fnl 1f, no extra towards fin: fine run 6lbs o/h: progressive, see 4185.
4129 **BLUE VELVET** 18 [3]   3-8-9 (92) C Carver (3) 20/1: 062306: Held up centre, late hdwy for press.   ¾   89
4129 **SHEER VIKING** 18 [8]   4-8-12 (95) M Hills 10/1: 005047: Held up centre, going well but short of   ½   90
room appr fnl 1f, kept on, nvr dngrs: bckd tho' op 8/1: see 1182, 702.
4129 **GUINEA HUNTER** 18 [19]   4-9-3 (100)(bl) J Fortune 11/2 FAV: 050358: Prom far side, drvn appr   shd   95
fnl 1f, kept on onepace: bckd from 15/2: btr 4129, see 4012, 2859.
4182 **AFAAN** 14 [14]   7-8-7 (90)(bl) S Finnamore (5) 33/1: 000509: Led & clr far side, hdd ent fnl 1f, onepce.   nk   84
4182 **COASTAL BLUFF** 14 [9]   8-8-9 (92) L Dettori 14/1: 404400: Early ldr centre, same pace fnl 1f: 10th.   nk   85
3473 **AWAKE** 54 [16]   3-9-2 (99) K Darley 16/1: 031400: Towards rr far side mod late hdwy, nvr on terms: abs.   ¾   90
3902 **EASY DOLLAR** 33 [12]   8-8-7 (90)(bl) (9oh) F Norton 40/1: 550050: Al same place far side: 12th.   nk   80
4112 **ALPEN WOLF** 19 [13]   5-8-7 (90)(3oh) Martin Dwyer 33/1: 013000: Handy far side, no fnl 2f: 13th.   1   77
4129 **HAMMER AND SICKLE** 18 [15]   3-8-7 (90) D Holland 33/1: 210-00: Nvr dangerous far side: 14th: hd   77
'99 wnr at Ripon (debut, mdn), Doncaster (subs disq) & Redcar (nov auct, rtd 96): eff forcing the pace at 5f on
firm & gd grnd, any track: with M Johnston.
4012 **DELEGATE** 26 [7]   7-8-7 (90) M J Kinane 10/1: 420200: Nvr dngrs centre: 15th, op 8/1, see 3861, 1182.   ½   75
4301 **FIRE DOME** 5 [11]   8-8-7 (90)(1oh) M Henry 13/2: 100130: Nvr a factor far side: 16th, nicely bckd,   nk   74
qck reapp: back in trip, see 4165 (6f).
4215 **Ellens Academy** 12 [2] 5-8-7 (90)(bl) (13oh) J Mackay (5) 33/1:
3610 **Cubism** 48 [10] 4-9-7 (104) R Hills 20/1:
4015 **Boleyn Castle** 26 [20] 3-8-8 (91) L Carter 14/1:   4043 **Melon Place** 23 [18] 3-8-7 (90)(3oh) N Callan 40/1: U
20 ran   Time 59.86 (1.66)   (Austin Stroud & Co Ltd)   E A Wheeler Whitchurch On Thames, Oxon

---

4340   3.40 GRANGEWOOD HCAP 3YO+ 0-85 (D)   1m str   Good 40   -05 Slow   [83]
£6253   £1924   £962   £481   3 yo rec 3 lb   2 Groups, no obvious advantage

4300 **SCENE** 5 [21]   N P Littmoden 5-9-0 (69) L Dettori 7/1: 000041: 5 b m Scenic - Avebury Ring (Auction   79
Ring) In tch far side, prog 2f out, hdwy to lead ent fnl 1f, going away: tchd 9/1: earlier won at Leicester (fill
h'cap): '99 h'cap wnr at Ascot, Epsom & Nottingham (rtd 80): '98 Thirsk & Haydock wnr (fill h'caps, rtd 77):
eff at 1m/10f: acts on firm, suited by gd & soft & gall trks: best without a visor: can carry big weights.
-4232 **JUDICIOUS** 10 [22]   G Wragg 3-9-4 (76) R Hughes 5/2 FAV: 301622: 3 b c Fairy King - Kama Tashoof   4   79
(Mtoto) Handy far side, qcknd to lead appr fnl 2f, rdn bef dist, sn hdd, onepce: hvly bckd: has a turn of
foot & could do with being held up for a later challenge: see 4232, 3095.
4212 **MAKE WAY** 12 [17]   B J Meehan 4-9-11 (80) Pat Eddery 14/1: 225503: 4 b g Red Ransom - Way Of The   1   81
World (Dance Of Life) Trckd ldrs centre, ran on to lead that group appr fnl 1f, no impress front pair: gd run.
4215 **TOPTON** 12 [10]   P Howling 6-9-4 (73)(bl) R Winston 33/1: 106004: Chsd ldrs centre, under press   1   72
appr fnl 1f, styd on: op 25/1, see 2899.
4199 **KINGSDON** 13 [13]   3-9-13 (85)(tVl) J Fortune 33/1: 654405: In tch centre, prog appr fnl 1f,   ½   83
drifted right, nvr dangerous: tried a visor, see 3782, 1055.
4292 **SKY DOME** 6 [5]   7-9-1 (70) A Beech (3) 33/1: 325456: Waited with centre, ran on fnl 1f, nvr nr to chall.   hd   67
3988 **IRON MOUNTAIN** 27 [23]   5-9-1 (70) L Newman (3) 10/1: 430537: Al arnd same pl far side: op 16/1.   shd   67
4094 **TRIBAL PRINCE** 20 [11]   3-9-5 (77) W Supple 33/1: 134208: Well plcd centre, led that group aftr   ¾   72
halfway till 1f out, fdd: return to 7f may suit, see 3936, 3445.
4135 **PENTAGON LAD** 18 [24]   4-9-3 (72) D Holland 33/1: 426039: Al mid-div far side: btr 2799 (fast).   1   65
4206 **SCOTTISH SPICE** 12 [7]   3-9-10 (82) K Darley 12/1: 306D20: Nvr dngrs centre: 10th, see 4206, 4085.   1   73
4204 **TAKE FLITE** 12 [15]   3-9-3 (75) Martin Dwyer 33/1: 003160: Chsd ldrs centre, wknd appr fnl 1f: 11th.   2½   60
*3753 **WITH A WILL** 42 [4]   6-9-1 (70) C Rutter 14/1: 314110: Nvr on terms centre: 12th, bckd, 6 week abs.   shd   56
2750 **CRYSTAL CREEK** 85 [20]   4-9-6 (75) W Ryan 25/1: -06000: Chsd ldrs far side till 2f out: 13th, 3 mnth abs.   hd   60
4215 **REDSWAN** 12 [2]   5-9-7 (70)(t) J G Hind 14/1: 033150: Switched start, al towards rear centre: 14th, bckd.   1½   52
3883 **SMOOTH SAILING** 34 [30]   5-9-11 (80) F Norton 25/1: 051000: Nvr in it far side: 15th, see 3118.   nk   61
4038 **INDIAN BLAZE** 24 [9]   6-9-6 (75) N Pollard 33/1: 000000: In tch centre, outpcd appr fnl 1f: 16th: 1   54
won this in '99 off 5lbs higher mark, not fired at all this season: see 733.
*4135 **PACIFIC ALLIANCE** 18 [29]   4-9-11 (80) Dean McKeown 14/1: 031110: Led far side till hdd & btn   nk   58
appr fnl 2f: 17th, op 10/1: progressive earlier, see 4135 (class stakes).
1366 **NOBLENOR** 146 [14]   3-9-7 (79) S W Kelly (3) 20/1: -0160: Well plcd centre, led briefly halfway, lost pl: 24th.   0
4126 **BOLD EWAR** 18 [18]   3-9-5 (77)(bl) P Robinson 40/1: 150060: Led centre 4f, sn btn: 26th, see 3261.   0
3794 **Forza Figlio** 40 [19] 7-9-4 (73) N Callan 40/1:   3793 **Finished Article** 40 [6] 3-9-6 (78) M J Kinane 33/1:
4300 **Nouf** 5 [12] 4-9-5 (74) J Quinn 25/1:   4199 **Fredora** 13 [8] 5-10-0 (83) D Sweeney 50/1:
3796 **Dangerous Fortune** 39 [22] 4-9-4 (73) R Hills 40/1:   3794 **Cool Temper** 40 [16] 4-9-1 (70) J Tate 33/1:
*3914 **Mush** 31 [28] 3-9-4 (76) T Quinn 20/1:   3544 **Avanti** 415 [26] 4-9-3 (72) J Reid 66/1:
1840 **Infotec** 12 [1] 3-9-1 (73) J Stack 40/1:   4126 **Honest Borderer** 18 [25] 5-9-11 (80) G Carter 20/1:
1042 **Sharp Rebuff** 167 [3] 9-9-13 (82) S Sanders 50/1:
30 ran   Time 1m 40.09 (3.59)   (Paul J Dixon)   N P Littmoden Newmarket, Suffolk

4341 4.10 EBF SNAILWELL MDN 2YO (D) 6f Good 40 -26 Slow
£7397 £2276 £1138 £569 First 5 home raced down the centre

3881 **AJWAA 34** [7] M P Tregoning 2-9-0 W Supple 12/1: 21: 2 ch c Mujtahid - Nouvelle Star (Luskin Star) **96**
Led centre group till 2f out, outpcd till rallied well in last to regain lead cl home, drvn out: tchd 16/1:
March foal, brother to tough/useful sprinter Juwwi, dam high class up to 1m: eff at 6f, 7f+ is going to suit:
acts on gd grnd, undul or stiff/gall track: game, improving & useful colt.

-- **ISHIGURU** [12] A P O'Brien 2-9-0 M J Kinane 6/5 FAV: 2: 2 b c Danzig - Strategic Maneuver nk **94**
(Cryptoclearance) Nvr far away centre, led appr fnl 1f, sn rdn, hdd nr fin: hvly bckd Irish raider: $1,150,000
April foal, dam high class juv in the States: eff at 6f on gd, shld get further: highly regarded, go one better sn.

-- **MUGHARREB** [5] B Hanbury 2-9-0 R Hills 9/2: 3: 2 b c Gone West - Marling (Lomond) shd **94+**
Chsd ldrs centre, rdn appr fnl 1f, kept on well, just btn in a blanket fin: nicely bckd: $550,000 May foal:
brother to a 7f/1m wnr, dam high class juv sprinter, later miler: eff at 6f, 7f+ will suit: will win a maiden.

-- **KAMA SUTRA** [14] W Jarvis 2-9-0 T Quinn 20/1: 4: Front rank centre, chall ent fnl 1f, held nr fin: hd **93**
op 12/1, clr of rem: Pursuit Of Love half brother to wnrs btwn 6f & 12f: eff at 6f on gd, shld find a mdn.

3000 **STUTTER 75** [3] 2-9-0 B Marcus 16/1: 55: Chsd ldrs centre, eff 2f out, not pace to chall: 11 wk abs: 3 **84**
needs 7f+: looks sure to win with a drop in grade: see 3000.

-- **CLICK ON** [30] 2-9-0 D Harrison 7/1: 6: Overall ldr far side, hdd ent fnl 1f & no extra: tchd 10/1: nk **83**
IR 72,000gns half brother to sev useful juvs: dam a 12f wnr: encouraging start.

4138 **FOREST DANCER 17** [27] 2-9-0 L Newman (3) 50/1: 357: Trck ldr far side, late hdwy: op 20/1: half nk **82**

-- **VICTORIA CROSS** [16] 2-8-9 D Holland 33/1: 8: Towards rear centre, late hdwy: op 20/1: half nk **76+**
sister to useful styer Inchcailloch & high class/enigmatic hdler Pridwell: 1m+ looks sure to suit next term:
plenty to like about this promising debut: with G Wragg & one to keep in mind.

4020 **ANALYSER 26** [17] 2-9-0 J Fortune 33/1: 49: Bhd ldrs centre, fdd appr fnl 1f: bck in trip, see 4020. shd **81**

-- **ALOWMDAH** [11] 2-9-0 M Hills 20/1: 0: Nvr dangerous centre tho' stying on fin: 10th, stablemate 3rd: ¾ **78**
half brother to a couple of useful juvs: sure to benefit from this & improve.

3980 **SMIRK 27** [19] 2-9-0 N Pollard 20/1: -60: Nvr in tch far side, late hdwy, nvr a threat: 11th, needs 1m. 1¼ **73**

-- **AFGHAN** [15] 2-9-0 (t) L Dettori 20/1: 0: Prom centre till 2f out: 12th, op 12/1: $600,000 Hennessy nk **73**
half brother to a wnr in the States: wore a t-strap: shld do better: with J Gosden.

-- **ATLANTIC EAGLE** [10] 2-9-0 K Darley 25/1: 0: In tch centre, outpcd appr fnl 1f: 13th: Mt Livermore ½ **71**
first foal, dam a wnr in the States: shld do better over 7f+ next term: with M Johnston

-- **MAYCOCKS BAY** [9] 2-8-9 R Hills 50/1: 0: Dwelt, nvr a factor centre: 14th: 32,000gns half nk **65**
sister to sev wnrs, incl useful 7f/1m juv Indian Light, dam stoutly bred: with J Glover.

-- **PRIDE IN ME** [21] 2-8-9 J Reid 33/1: 0: Chsd ldrs far side, eff & no extra appr fnl 1f: 15th, op shd **65**
20/1: Indian Ridge first foal, dam useful 5f juv: with E Dunlop & will do better.

4209 **DRAMA PREMIERE 12** [28] 2-8-9 Martin Dwyer 50/1: 00: Handy far side, lost place ent fnl 2f: 16th. 1 **62**

4189 **AMONG WOMEN 13** [4] 2-8-9 S Kelly (3) 50/1: 00: Slow away, nvr in it centre: 17th. hd **61**

-- **CHANTRESS LORELEI** [8] 2-8-9 W Ryan 20/1: 0: Al towards rear centre: 18th, op 14/1: 25,000gns shd **61**
So Factual half sister to sev wnrs, dam a sprinter: with Mrs A Perrett.

-- **Street Life** [22] 2-9-0 P McCabe 50/1: 1367 **Illusionist 146** [20] 2-9-0 G Carter 50/1:
-- **Volte Face** [26] 2-8-9 R Hughes 33/1: -- **Scottys Future** [24] 2-9-0 S Whitworth 50/1:
-- **Pico** [6] 2-8-9 P Robinson 40/1: -- **Bethania** [13] 2-8-9 S Sanders 20/1:
-- **El Giza** [23] 2-9-0 J Stack 40/1: -- **Rateeba** [2] 2-8-9 R Mullen 33/1:
-- **Flying Trapeze** [25] 2-9-0 J Weaver 20/1: -- **Catstreet** [18] 2-9-0 R Price 33/1:
-- **Puzzle** [1] 2-9-0 (t) A Clark 50/1:
29 ran Time 1m 14.74 (3.94) (Hamdan Al Maktoum) M P Tregoning Lambourn, Berks

4342 4.45 GROSVENOR RTD HCAP 3YO+ 0-100 (B) 1m4f Good 40 00 Fast [104]
£9528 £3614 £1807 £821 3 yo rec 7 lb

*4276 **SEREN HILL 7** [17] G A Butler 4-8-7 (83)(3ex) K Darley 7/1: 020011: 4 ch f Sabrehill - Seren Quest **90**
(Rainbow Quest) Slightly hmpd bend & mid div after 2f, clsd 4f out, pshd into lead ent fnl 2f, hard rdn ins last,
edged right, just held on: fair time: recent York wnr (class stks): '99 wnr at Haydock (h'cap, rtd 89): '98
Redcar nursery h'cap wnr: eff at 12/14f, stays 2m: acts on fast, prob firm, loves hvy: suited by gall tracks &
can go well fresh: improving filly, should go well if taking her chance in the Novemeber Handicap.

+4162 **FLOSSY 16** [1] C W Thornton 4-9-4 (94) D Holland 7/2: 023312: 4 b f Efisio - Sirene Bleu Marine shd **100**
(Secreto) Waited with, smooth prog on bit 2f out, went 2nd dist, sn rdn, ran on well, just failed in a thrilling
fin: well bckd, clr rem: fine run, primed for a repeat success in the November H'cap: see 4162.

4148 **MARDANI 18** [6] M Johnston 5-8-11 (87) M J Kinane 12/1: 266263: 5 b g Fairy King - Marmana 4 **87**
(Blushing Groom) Cl up, led after halfway till appr fnl 1f, soon pace: not disgraced against improving fillies.

*4014 **HELENS DAY 26** [18] W Jarvis 4-8-9 (85) F Norton 3/1 FAV: 221014: Chsd ldrs, prog 2f out, rdn bef nk **84**
dist, kept on onepce: nicely bckd from 9/2, clr rem: tough & in-form, see 4014.

3896 **FAIR WARNING 33** [4] 4-9-0 (90) S Whitworth 20/1: 500105: Towards rear, pushed along 4f out, 3 **85**
improved 2f out, no further impression on ldrs: btr 3487 (class stakes).

4197 **ETHMAAR 13** [15] 3-8-13 (96) R Hills 16/1: 3-4506: Rear, improved 3f out, onepce bef fnl 1f: tchd 20/1. 2½ **88**
4039 **KUSTER 24** [8] 4-8-11 (87) S W Kelly (3) 10/1: 0-4247: Held up, hmpd 5f out, nvr pce to chall: stays 12f. ¾ **78**
4016 **BANCO SUIVI 26** [2] 3-8-3 (86) G Carter 20/1: 023138: Chsd ldrs, eff & btn 2f out, eased fnl 1f. ½ **76**
3726 **NOBELIST 43** [19] 5-9-6 (96)(vis) P Robinson 33/1: 000069: Nvr better than mid div: abs, see 1561. nk **86**
4128 **RICH VEIN 18** [9] 3-8-3 (86)(vis) R Mullen 20/1: 140040: Nvr a factor: 10th, see 4128, 2937. 1¾ **74**
4091 **MOWBRAY 20** [10] 5-9-7 (97)(bl) R Hughes 33/1: 403050: Nvr dangerous, eased appr fnl 1f: 11th. ¾ **84**
4197 **SOLO FLIGHT 13** [13] 3-8-2 (85) J Quinn 20/1: 5-2100: Held up, improved 5f out, wknd 2f out: 12th. nk **71**
4162 **SHARP STEPPER 16** [3] 4-8-9 (85) L Dettori 12/1: 362140: Al towards rear: 13th, btr 3811 (14f). 3½ **67**
4213 **KEW GARDENS 12** [11] 3-8-3 (86) W Ryan 25/1: -23000: Led till appr fnl 5f, lost pl: 17th, see 1400, 998.

4304 **Carousing 3** [7] 3-8-3 (86) S Carson (3) 33/1: 3994 **Cracow 26** [16] 3-8-7 (90) M Hills 16/1:
4017 **Al Towd 26** [20] 3-8-6 (89) W Supple 25/1: 4128 **Livius 8** [14] 6-8-12 (88) T Quinn 20/1:
4142 **Akeed 17** [12] 3-8-12 (95) J Fortune 25/1: 3595 **Unseeded 49** [5] 3-8-12 (95) Pat Eddery 25/1:
20 ran Time 2m 33.65 (4.85) (The Fairy Story Partnership) G A Butler Blewbury, Oxon

Official Going   SOFT Stalls: Far Side

4343   1.35 GR 3 PRINCESS ROYAL STKS 3YO+ (A)   1m4f   Good 40   +14 Fast
£16200   £6210   £3105   £1485

-3918   **SACRED SONG** 31 [5]   H R A Cecil 3-8-7 T Quinn 12/1: 1-121: 3 b f Diesis - Ruby Ransom (Red Ransom)   114+
Twrds rear, imprvd over 3f out, went on appr fnl 1f, rdn clr fnl 1f: fast time: earlier won at Nottingham (reapp,
stks): won sole '99 start, again at Nottingham (fills mdn, rtd 94): eff at 1m, stays 12f v well: acts on firm,
gd & a gall/stiff trk, likes Nottingham: goes v well fresh: lightly raced & fast improving, win more Gr races.
3898   **LITTLEPACEPADDOCKS** 34 [11]   M Johnston 3-8-7 D Holland 10/1: 314202: 3 b f Accordion - Lady In   2½   109
Pace (Burslem) Set fast pace, hdd appr fnl 1f, not pace of wnr well ins last: op 8/1: v tough & put up a
career best effort today: reportedly remains in training & can win a val contest as a 4yo: see 3305, 1945.
4236   **INAAQ** 13 [15]   Saeed bin Suroor 3-8-7 L Dettori 4/1: 143: 3 ch f Lammtarra - Elfaslah (Green Desert)   ½   108
Trkd ldrs, chall 3f out, sltly short of room appr fnl 1f, sn held: nicely bckd: imprvd in defeat: see 4236, 2617.
3930   **FIRECREST** 33 [1]   J L Dunlop 3-8-7 G Carter 12/1: 114144: Waited with, rdn to improve 5f out,   2½   104
styd on to chall 3f out, drvn/not qckn appr fnl 1f: op 8/1: ran to best, a return to Listed will suit: see 3930.
*4130   **RIYAFA** 19 [12]   3-8-7 J Murtagh 11/4 FAV: 153215: Mid-div, outpcd 4f out, rdn/late hdwy, nvr   ½   103
dangerous: well bckd & clrly better expected, tho' reportedly never travelling: see 4130 (Listed, gd/soft).
4130   **DRAMA CLASS** 19 [8]   3-8-7 Pat Eddery 16/1: 21356: Bhd, gd hdwy over 2f out, kept on fnl 1f but no   1   101
danger: op 12/1: not disgraced stepped up to Gr company tho' treat rating with caution (offic only 93): see 4130.
-3863   **RADAS DAUGHTER** 37 [6]   4-9-0 K Darley 11/1: 010027: Late hdwy from rear, nvr dangerous: top weight.   3   104
3595   **MISS LORILAW** 50 [3]   3-8-7 M Hills 40/1: 360108: Chsd ldrs, fdd fnl 2f: 7 wk abs: btr 3177 (List).   1¼   95
*4141   **MILLENNIUM DASH** 18 [7]   3-8-7 Craig Williams 14/1: 419: Towards rear, eff halfway, rdn/no extra   nk   95
fnl 2f: op 10/1: lightly rcd & prob imprvd in defeat up in trip: see 4141 (10f, soft).
3863   **SOLAIA** 37 [10]   3-8-7 R Hughes 10/1: 102440: Nvr a factor, 10th: can do better, see 3863 (Gr 3, 14.5f).   1½   93
3918   **SHAMAIEL** 31 [4]   3-8-7 P Robinson 100/1: 430100: Al towards rear, fin 11th: needs a drop in grade.   1¼   91
4085   **GOLDEN WAY** 22 [2]   3-8-7 J Reid 40/1: -61120: In tch, wknd fnl 2f, 12th: see 4085, 3989 (soft).   5   84
*4133   **AYMARA** 19 [13]   3-8-7 R Hills 33/1: 42210: Stumbled leaving stalls, sn chasing ldrs, wknd qckly   9   74
appr fnl 2f, eased, fin 13th: btr 4133 (mdn).
4130   **JALISCO** 19 [9]   3-8-7 J Fortune 11/1: 120: Handy, eff halfway, wknd fnl 3f, eased, 14th: btr 4130.   1½   72
4113   **TANZILLA** 20 [14]   3-8-7 B Marcus 100/1: 230000: Cl-up, rdn/lost tch fnl 4f, eased, t.o. in 15th.   14   57
15 ran   Time 2m 31.86 (3.06)   (Niarchos Family)   H R A Cecil Newmarket

---

4344   2.05 HOUGHTON COND STKS 2YO (B)   7f str   Good 40   -23 Slow
£7569   £2871   £1435   £652

*3999   **WEST ORDER** 27 [5]   R Hannon 2-9-1 R Hughes 8/15 FAV: -11: 2 ch c Gone West - Irish Order (Irish River)   100
Led, rdn & qcknd appr fnl 1f, sn clr, readily: well bckd at odds-on: earlier won on debut at Newbury (mdn):
May foal, cost IR200,000 gns: half brother to sev wnrs, incl a smart performer in the USA: dam useful 2yo
wnr in France: eff around a stiff 7f, will stay 1m: acts on firm, gd & likes to force the pace: runs well
fresh: progressive & potentially v useful colt, one to keep on the right side next term.
--   **CAFE GRANDE** [4]   M A Jarvis 2-8-12 K Darley 7/2: 2: 2 b c Grand Lodge - Olean (Sadler's Wells)   5   85
Cl-up, rdn to chall appr fnl 1f, sn outpcd by wnr: op 6/1: IR 55,000 gns May foal, full brother to 10f
scorer Architect, dam mdn: stays a stiff/gall 7f, 1m will suit: shld have no trouble in finding a mdn.
--   **SCRAMBLE** [6]   J H M Gosden 2-8-12 (t) L Dettori 6/1: 3: 2 ch c Gulch - Syzygy (Big Play)   8   73
V slow to start, sn in tch, hdwy appr fnl 1f: Mar 1st foal, dam smart 1m/12f wnr in South America:
prob capable of better & shld improve when sent over mid-dists next term.
--   **SPEED OF LIGHT** [2]   W R Muir 2-8-12 Martin Dwyer 33/1: 4: Held up, eff 2f out, sn btn: IR 75,000   nk   73
gns Mar foal, half brother to a smart juv wnr, dam wnr abroad: shld apprec 1m in time.
4203   **SAKAMOTO** 13 [1]   2-8-12 J Fortune 100/1: 005: Chsd ldrs, rdn/fdd fnl 3f: highly tried: see 4124.   10   58
--   **SCARROTTOO** [3]   2-8-12 Esther Remmerswaal 66/1: 6: Dwelt, keen/al outpcd: May foal, half brother   2½   54
to a couple of Listed wnrs in France, dam 1m wnr: with S C Williams.
6 ran   Time 1m 27.67 (4.47)   (Monsun Investments Ltd)   R Hannon East Everleigh, Wilts

---

4345   2.35 TATTERSALLS AUTUMN AUCT STKS 2YO (B)   6f   Good 40   -20 Slow
£50825   £20330   £10165   £6099

3316   **GOODIE TWOSUES** 62 [28]   R Hannon 2-8-2(1ow) L Newman 5/1: 134561: 2 b f Fraam - Aliuska (Fijar   92
Tango) In tch, rdn to improve 2f out, hdwy to lead ins last, rdn out: 9 wk abs: earlier won on debut at
Goodwood (fills mdn): Mar foal, dam 5f juv wnr: eff around 6f, has tried 7f: acts on firm, gd/soft & a
sharp/undul or gall trk: runs well fresh: useful & consistent.
4269   **MISS VERITY** 9 [29]   H Akbary 2-7-10 F Norton 50/1: 621242: 2 ch f Factual - Ansellady (Absalom)   1½   81
Trkd ldrs, went on appr fnl 1f, hdd well ins last, not pace of wnr: career best eff: see 4269 (nurs).
3620   **GOLDIE** 49 [17]   D J Coakley 2-7-12(2ow) Martin Dwyer 12/1: 123: 2 b f Celtic Swing - Hotel   nk   82
California (Last Tycoon) In tch, imprvd over 2f out, ran on appr fnl 1f, closing at fin: tchd 16/1: 7 wk
abs: lightly raced & a gd run stepped up to 6f, acts on firm & grnd: see 3205.
3525   **EXTRA GUEST** 53 [1]   M R Channon 2-8-8 Craig Williams 50/1: 222334: Waited with, rdn/prog 2f out,   hd   92$
ran on strongly ins last, nvr nrr: v consistent but prob shade flattered at these weights: see 3443, 2029.
3886   **LUNAR LEO** 35 [16]   2-8-1 (t) G Carter 12/1: 413635: Front rank, drvn over 2f out, edged right   hd   85
& no extra well ins last: consistent, will apprec a return to 7f: see 3886, 2459.
*4117   **PAULAS PRIDE** 19 [14]   2-8-2 A Polli 33/1: 00616: Bhd, drvn/ran on well fnl 1f, nrst at fin: ¾   84$
imprvd in defeat, handles gd & gd/soft: interesting with a return to further: see 4117 (1m mdn auct).
*4188   **TRUSTTHUNDER** 14 [8]   2-7-12 P M Quinn 9/1: 022017: Bhd, eff appr fnl 1f, ran on well ins last,   shd   79
nrst fin: tchd 12/1: caught the eye, keep an eye on over further: see 4188 (soft grnd mdn).
3757   **TROUBADOUR GIRL** 43 [19]   2-7-10 M Henry 100/1: 00038: Late hdwy from mid-div, nvr nrr: 1   75$
6 wk abs: plating class form prev, treat this rating with caution: see 3757 (sell, firm).
3630   **LOVE THING** 48 [30]   2-7-12 (BL) (2ow) R Ffrench 50/1: -60109: Cl-up, led over 2f out, hdd appr   ½   76$
fnl 1f, kept on fnl 1f: 7 wk abs & not disgraced in 1st time blnks: see 3466.
4009   **ASH MOON** 27 [6]   2-8-1 J Quinn 9/2: 103020: Handy, eff over 2f out, no extra appr fnl 1f, 10th: nk   79
op 7/2: capable of better, see 4009 (Listed, gd/soft grnd).
4268   **PARA GLIDER** 9 [13]   2-8-13 M Hills 50/1: 50: Mid-div at best, fin 11th: needs further: see 4268.   1¼   88
*4164   **INSPECTOR GENERAL** 16 [21]   2-9-0 J Fortune 10/3 FAV: 1110: Cl-up, ev ch until short of room twice   ¾   87

1343

& wknd ins last: well bckd on 4 timer bid: unlucky in running fnl 1f, but lkd btn at the time: see 4164.
4083 **DARK SOCIETY 22** [23] 2-8-1 W Supple 25/1: 40: Bhd, prog appr fnl 1f, hung left/btn ins last, 13th. *shd* **74**
3443 **PLEASURE DOME 56** [25] 2-8-0(1ow) J Tate 12/1: 20: Prom, rdn/btn fnl 1f, 14th: 8 wk abs: btr 3443. *nk* **72**
4030 **ELLENDUNE GIRL 25** [20] 2-7-10 A Mackay 50/1: 050400: In tch, mod late hdwy, 15th: prob flattered. *nk* **67$**
3475 **LOVE TUNE 55** [3] 2-7-10 P Fessey 50/1: 622200: Handy, wknd appr fnl 1f, 16th: 8 wk abs: see 3264. *nk* **67**
-- **EL ACTOR** [18] 2-8-12 L Dettori 16/1: 0: Mod late gains from rear, no threat, 17th: recently *1½* **79**
landed a minor event in Italy (6f, gd): 15,000 gns Apr foal, dam mod, sire smart at 9f: with M Quinlan.
3673 **HUMES LAW 47** [15] 2-8-4 J Carroll 50/1: 610000: Nvr a factor, 18th: 7 wk abs: see 2730. *1* **68**
4214 **EL MAXIMO 13** [26] 2-8-7 (tbl) J Murtagh 25/1: 615240: Prom, eff 2f out, sn btn/eased, 19th: see 4214. *1* **68**
4246 **MRS TIGGYWINKLE 10** [4] 2-7-13 (BL) P Doe 100/1: 400060: Led till over 2f out, wknd, 23rd: blnkd. **0**
4250 **Lady Laureate 10** [24] 2-8-2 A Nicholls 100/1:
4098 **Risque Sermon 21** [5] 2-8-12 (t) B Marcus 50/1:
3673 **Chartleys Princess 47** [10] 2-7-10 K Dalgleish 50/1:
3832 **Dixies Darts 38** [12] 2-8-1 G Duffield 66/1:
4277 **Sandorra 8** [7] 2-7-10 D Mernagh 100/1:
1304 **Brief Star 151** [9] 2-7-10 G Bardwell 100/1:
3830 **Armida 38** [22] 2-7-13 G Baker 100/1:
4209 **Modesty 13** [27] 2-7-10 J Mackay 100/1:
3942 **Highland Flight 30** [2] 2-7-10 Dale Gibson 50/1:
3955 **Mister Mind 30** [11] 2-8-10 T Williams 100/1:
30 ran Time 1m 14.38 (3.58) (Mrs Sue Crane & Lady Davis) R Hannon East Everleigh, Wilts

4346

3.10 LISTED BENTINCK STKS 3YO+ (A) 6f Good 40 -07 Slow
£16124 £6116 £3058 £1390 3 yo rec 1 lb

4195 **BAHAMIAN PIRATE 14** [14] D Nicholls 5-8-12 A Nicholls 9/1: 130151: 5 ch g Housebuster - Shining Through **111**
(Deputy Minister) Cl-up far side, went on appr fnl 1f, styd on well & rdn out: tchd 12/1: earlier won at Carlisle, Southwell, Newmarket & notably Ayr (Gold Cup h'cap): '99 Ripon wnr (mdn, rtd 72): suited by 5/6f, just stays 7f: acts on firm, gd/soft, fibresand & any trk: runs well fresh: smart, tough & much improved sprinter.
4182 **ANDREYEV 15** [6] R Hannon 6-8-12 J Fortune 10/3 FAV: 041362: 6 ch g Presidium - Missish (Mummy's *¾* **109**
Pet) Twrds rear centre, imprvd over 1f out, styd on well fnl 1f, nvr nrr: ran to best, likes coming late: see 3727.
+4182 **RUSHCUTTER BAY 15** [11] P L Gilligan 7-8-12 F Norton 14/1: 100213: 7 br g Mon Tresor - Llwy Bren *1¼* **105**
(Lidhame) Prom far side, chall appr fnl 1f, no extra ins last: op 10/1: reportedly broke a blood vessel: another gd run & in the form of his life at the age of 7: confirmed improved form of 4182.
4182 **CRETAN GIFT 15** [8] N P Littmoden 9-8-12 (vis) L Dettori 12/1: 550004: Bhd far side, rdn & ran on *nk* **104**
strongly fnl 1f, nvr nrr: tough: see 4182, 952.
3884 **MEADAAAR 35** [1] 3-8-11 R Hills 12/1: -02535: Rcd alone towards nr side, joined centre group & led *½* **103**
led halfway, drvn, hdd & no extra appr fnl 1f: may apprec a return to further: see 3600, 2578.
4182 **PERFECT PEACH 15** [3] 5-8-7 P Goode 100/1: 206406: Dwelt, sn in tch centre, ev ch till no extra *nk* **97$**
appr fnl 1f: continues to run well in the face of a stiff task tho' prob flattered again (offic rtd 82).
4182 **YORKIES BOY 15** [16] 5-8-12 K Darley 25/1: 010407: Led far side to 4f out, drvn/btn appr fnl 1f. *¾* **100**
4182 **VITA SPERICOLATA 15** [9] 3-8-6 (vis) P Robinson 14/1: 304258: Cl-up far side, rdn/fdd over 1f out. *nk* **95**
4198 **MOLLY BROWN 14** [12] 3-8-6 M Hills 20/1: 122039: Dsptd lead far side till went on over 2f out, *shd* **95**
hdd appr fnl 1f, not qckn: poss a shade flattered: see 4198 (rtd h'cap).
4125 **HARMONIC WAY 19** [10] 5-8-12 R Hughes 4/1: 620460: Bhd centre, mod late gains, nvr dangerous: *hd* **100**
fin 10th: disapp run & capable of much better, see 4125 (Gr 2, gd/soft).
*4069 **LADY BOXER 23** [15] 4-8-7 A Mackay 12/1: 010110: Nvr a factor, fin 11th: needs a drop in grade. *1* **92$**
4125 **MONKSTON POINT 19** [13] 4-8-12 (vis) J Weaver 16/1: 130000: Trkd ldrs far side, wknd qckly appr *nk* **96**
fnl 1f, fin 12th: op 12/1: see 4125, 1529.
*3503 **ARABESQUE 54** [5] 3-8-6 T Quinn 10/1: 140410: Prom, fdd over 1f out, 13th: 8 wk abs: likes fast/firm. *1¾* **87**
4182 **ROSSELLI 15** [4] 4-8-12 (bl) J Carroll 40/1: 603100: Mid-div at best, fdd into 14th: loves soft/hvy. *1½* **88**
3874 **DANCING MAESTRO 36** [7] 4-8-12 J Murtagh 40/1: 063200: Led far side after 2f, hdd over 2f out, *shd* **88**
wknd qckly, eased when btn, fin last: much btr 3667.
15 ran Time 1m 13.63 (2.83) (H E Lhendup Dorji) D Nicholls Sessay, N Yorks

4347

3.40 LISTED DARLEY STKS 3YO+ (A) 1m1f Good 40 -12 Slow
£15892 £6028 £3014 £1370 3 yo rec 4 lb

4238 **ALBARAHIN 13** [5] M P Tregoning 5-9-4 R Hills 6/4 FAV: 212121: 5 b h Silver Hawk - My Dear Lady **119**
(Mr Prospector) Led, strongly prsd 2f out, styd on gamely ins last, drvn out: hvly bckd: not out of the 1st 2 in 6 starts this term, wng at Sandown (reapp, stks) & Goodwood (listed), also rnr-up in Gr 2 company: '98 wnr at Leicester (reapp), Sandown & Newbury (h'caps, rtd 105): suited by 1m/10f on fast, hvy & any trk, likes Sandown: runs v well fresh: eff weight carrier: v smart & game, deserves a win in Group company.
3893 **SUMMER VIEW 35** [10] R Charlton 3-8-10 L Dettori 12/1: -1132: 3 ch c Distant View - Miss Summer *½* **113**
(Luthier) Cl-up, chall 2f out, styd on well ins last, held by wnr fnl 50yds: pulled clr rem: eff at 1m/9f, handles firm & gd grnd: smart & lightly raced, can win similar: see 3421.
4212 **DUCK ROW 13** [1] J A R Toller 5-9-0 S Whitworth 11/1: 223203: 5 ch g Diesis - Sunny Moment (Roberto) *4* **106**
Towards rear, hdwy over 2f out, drvn/no extra well ins last: gd run, v consistent in this grade: see 4212, 1847.
3321 **INGLENOOK 62** [2] J L Dunlop 3-9-0 Pat Eddery 15/2: 511044: Bhd, eff over 3f out, switched & *1½* **107**
imprvd over 1f out, styd on, nvr nrr: 9 wk abs: see 3321.
4180 **ON THE RIDGE 15** [7] 5-9-0 T Quinn 4/1: /20-25: Keen/cl-up, chall over 2f out, wknd appr fnl 1f: *½* **102**
well bckd & better expected after a promising reapp in 4180 (1m).
2410 **KING ADAM 103** [3] 4-9-0 J Murtagh 10/1: 6-1546: Trkd ldrs, outpcd 2f out, no danger after: *¾* **101**
3 month abs & poss just sharper for this run: see 1841.
3995 **UMISTIM 27** [6] 3-9-3 R Hughes 10/1: 652027: Keen, settled rear, tried to go through non-exsistent *1* **106**
gap & hmpd over 1f out, switched wide & mod gains, nvr dangerous: no luck in running: see 3995.
4211 **HASTY WORDS 13** [8] 4-8-13 M Hills 33/1: 164048: Nvr a factor: shade btr 4211 (Gr 2, gd/firm). *½* **97**
4212 **BOMB ALASKA 13** [4] 5-9-0 L Newman 16/1: 000609: Dwelt, sn mid-div, outpcd fnl 2f: see 4000. *½* **97**
4180 **TRUMPET SOUND 15** [9] 3-8-10 (t) S W Kelly 25/1: 104260: Mid-div, drvn/fdd fnl 2f: 10th: see 4180. *2½* **93**
4113 **ANNAPURNA 20** [11] 4-8-9 K Darley 33/1: 340040: Handy, hdwy over 2f out, wknd qckly appr fnl 1f, 11th. *¾* **87**
11 ran Time 1m 53.87 (4.67) (Hamdan Al Maktoum) M P Tregoning Lambourn, Berks

4348

4.15 HEIDSEICK HCAP 3YO+ 0-100 (C) 1m str Good 40 +03 Fast [100]
£7540 £2320 £1160 £580 3 yo rec 3 lb 2 Groups - far side big advantage.

1382 **ELGHANI 146** [11] R W Armstrong 3-9-1 (90) W Supple 25/1: 0121: 3 br c Lahib - Fawaakeh (Lyphard) **96**
Cl-up far side, went on appr fnl 1f, rdn out: 5 month abs (leg injury), jockey rec 3-day whip ban: earlier won at Windsor (mdn): unrcd juv, dam a 6f juv wnr: eff around 1m, further could suit: acts on gd, gd/soft

& any trk: likes racing up with/forcing the pace, goes esp well fresh: lightly rcd & improving, win again.
4302 **MELODIAN 6** [10] M Brittain 5-7-12 (70)(bl) D Mernagh (2) 9/1: 001322: 5 b h Grey Desire - Mere Melody (Dunphy) Led far side, hdd appr fnl 1f, drvn & not pace of wnr well ins last: nicely bckd, quick reapp: in tremendous form, can go one better sn: see 4044. *1* **73**
3597 **JOHN FERNELEY 50** [19] P F I Cole 5-10-0 (100) P Dobbs (5) 6/1: 312443: 5 b g Polar Falcon - I'll Try (Try My Best) Towards rear far side, rdn/imprvd over 1f out, styd on well ins last, nvr nrr: 9 wk abs & an excellent performance under top weight: tough & smart h'capper: see 3107, 733. *nk* **103**
*4199 **LAGOON 14** [15] B W Hills 3-9-4 (93) D Holland 5/1 FAV: 000314: Bhd far side, eff over 1f out, ran on strongly for press fnl 1f, nrst fin: nicely bckd & remains in fine form: see 4199 (C/D, class stks). *½* **95**
3685 **POLAR CHALLENGE 46** [12] 3-8-8 (81)(t)(2ow) J Murtagh 16/1: 523105: In tch far side, drvn 2f out, no extra for press fnl 1f: not disgraced after a 7 wk abs: likes to force the pace, see 3190 (mdn, made all). *1* **83**
4126 **SALTY JACK 19** [20] 6-8-13 (85) Pat Eddery 8/1: 513026: Waited with far side, imprvd over 1f out, hung right/no extra well ins last: shade btr 4126 (gd/soft). *2* **81**
4212 **ATAVUS 13** [18] 3-8-6 (81) G Baker (5) 33/1: 350007: Late hdwy far side, nvr dngrs: see 4212, 1183. *1½* **74**
4197 **JALAD 14** [5] 3-9-8 (97)(tBL) R Hills 20/1: -20408: Led stands side, styd on well for press but no ch with far side group: fine run in first time blnks on the unfavd stands side, keep in mind: see 3893, 1063. *hd* **90**
3897 **SIR FERBET 34** [4] 3-8-12 (87) M Hills 25/1: 004259: Towards rear stands side, late hdwy, nvr nrr: not disgraced on the unfavd stands side: see 3897. *hd* **80**
4160 **MADAM ALISON 17** [16] 4-8-12 (84) R Smith (5) 20/1: 315030: Prom far side, rdn/fdd over 1f out, 10th. *1* **75**
4212 **CHAPEL ROYALE 13** [3] 3-8-6 (81) J Quinn 25/1: 003300: Cl-up stands side, drvn/no extra fnl 1f, fin 11th: twice below 4077 (favd softer grnd). *shd* **72**
3768 **CHOTO MATE 42** [1] 4-9-0 (86) L Newman (3) 33/1: 100000: Front rank stands side, drvn/wknd over 1f out, 12th: 6 wk abs: on a wng mark if returning to form: see 3768, 1989. *¾* **76**
4428} **ILE MICHEL 360** [17] 3-8-13 (88) R Hughes 16/1: 215-0: Dwelt, held up far side, nvr dangerous, 13th: reapp/h'cap bow: '99 wnr at Catterick (mdn, rtd 89): half brother to 2 smart 1m/10f performers: eff at 6f, bred to apprec 1m in time: acts on firm/fast: can go well fresh but entitled to need this, just sharper next time. *1* **76**
4199 **FERZAO 14** [13] 3-8-13 (88)(t) T Quinn 14/1: 150040: In tch far side, rdn/fdd over 1f out, 14th. *nk* **76**
4199 **EL CURIOSO 14** [21] 3-8-13 (88) K Darley 11/1: 603000: Rear, eff 2f out, sn hung left/wknd, 15th. *hd* **76**
*4126 **TORNADO PRINCE 19** [7] 5-8-13 (85) J Fortune 10/1: 442010: Towards rear stand side, eff 3f out, wknd appr fnl 1f, 16th: op 8/1: much better expected after an impress 9L h'cap success in 4126 (gd/soft). *2* **69**
4212 **BRILLIANT RED 13** [8] 7-10-0 (100)(t) K Dalgleish (5) 12/1: 362000: Handy stands side 6f, fin 17th. *8* **72**
3981 **Prince Caspian 28** [2] 3-8-13 (88) P Robinson 33/1: 4284 **Silk St John 7** [6] 6-9-3 (89) L Dettori 14/1:
3883 **Tactful Remark 35** [9] 4-9-1 (87) S W Kelly (3) 40/1:
4302 **Girls Best Friend 6** [14] 3-8-1 (76)(tBL) J Mackay (5) 16/1:
21 ran Time 1m 39.45 (2.95) (Hamdan Al Maktoum) R W Armstrong Newmarket

4349 **4.45 CHESTERTON MDN 2YO (D) 1m str Good 40 -32 Slow**
£7800 £2400 £1200 £600 2 Groups - far side slight advantage.

-- **TERRESTRIAL** [30] J H M Gosden 2-9-0 J Fortune 14/1: 1: 2 ch c Theatrical - Stellaria (Roberto) Trkd ldrs far side, went on 2f out, hung left but styd on strongly ins last, pushed out: Apr foal, half-brother to high-class miler Observatory, dam won at 5f/1m: eff around 1m, further could suit next year: runs well fresh on gd & a stiff/gall trk: fine debut, potentially smart & looks worth following. **96+**
4161 **PAINTED ROOM 17** [6] H R A Cecil 2-9-0 T Quinn 11/10 FAV: 22: 2 ch c Woodman - All At Sea (Riverman) Led centre group, drvn/ran on well fnl 1f but no ch with wnr: hvly bckd: acts on gd: win sn, see 4161. *1¼* **93**
4161 **MUNADIL 17** [13] M P Tregoning 2-9-0 R Hills 16/1: 63: 2 ch c Nashwan - Bintalshaati (Kris) Led overall, hdd 2f out, ev ch till no extra fnl 50yds: must win races & mid-dists will suit in 2001. *½* **92**
4161 **DAWARI 17** [7] Sir Michael Stoute 2-9-0 J Murtagh 15/2: 034: Chsd ldrs in centre, rdn 2f out, styd on fnl 1f, no ch with wnr: consistent, deserves to find a mdn & will apprec further next term: see 4161. *hd* **92**
-- **FOUR EAGLES** [21] 2-9-0 D Holland 33/1: 5: Mid-div far side, rdn & styd on fnl 1f, nvr nrr, hands & heels: IR20,000gns Apr foal, dam smart: sire top-class 1m: sure to improve for this kind intro. *2* **88+**
-- **CAUGHNAWAGA** [17] 2-9-0 W Ryan 16/1: 6: Cl-up far side, onepace under hands & heels: stable-mate of rnr-up: Jan foal: dam Listed wnr in France: with H Cecil, sure to improve & win races. *nk* **87+**
4035 **MISS MOSELLE 25** [18] 2-8-9 B Marcus 50/1: 307: Handy far side, drvn/not pace of ldrs appr fnl 1f: best run to date on this step up to 1m: see 3583 (debut, 7f). *1* **80**
-- **DR GREENFIELD** [12] 2-9-0 J Weaver 40/1: 8: Twrds rear, prog 2f out, hung left appr fnl 1f, sn btn, eased ins last: 20,000 gns Mar foal, dam dual wnr in USA: sire Derby wnr: apprec further in time for G A Butler. *1* **83**
-- **THE GLEN** [11] 2-9-0 M Hills 50/1: 9: Mid-div centre, rdn & styd on nicely appr fnl 1f, nvr dngrs: 60,000gns Mtoto foal, brother to a 10f wnr, dam related to a smart stayer: encouraging debut, relish further in time. *¾* **82**
-- **PLAY TIME** [8] 2-8-9 N Pollard 50/1: 0: Dwelt, sn in tch centre, rd/no extra appr fnl 1f, 10th: Apr lst foal, dam related to a useful 10f wnr, sire top-class at 12f: apprec mid-dists in 2001: with D Elsworth. *½* **76**
-- **AHRAAR** [29] 2-9-0 W Supple 16/1: 0: Bhd far side, late hdwy, nvr dangerous, 11th: Gulch colt, full brother to a top-class 6f/1m scorer: dam well related to a 12f wnr: stable-mate of 3rd, learn from this. *shd* **81**
-- **NICANDER** [20] 2-9-0 L Dettori 14/1: 0: Trkd ldrs far side, rdn/fdd over 1f out, 12th: Feb foal, half brother to a 1m/14f wnr, also a smart hdler: dam 10f wnr: with M Tregoning, apprec mid-dists. *3½* **75**
4035 **FIDDLERS MOLL 25** [19] 2-8-9 D R McCabe 40/1: 40: Mid-div at best, ddhtd for 13th: see 4035. *¾* **68**
-- **RED ROSIE** [14] 2-8-9 Pat Eddery 50/1: 0: Prom centre, btn fnl 2f, ddhtd for 13th: Red Ransom filly. *dht* **68**
-- **MINIHAHA** [3] 2-8-9 A McGlone 50/1: 0: Trkd ldrs centre, rdn/fdd fnl 2f, 15th: First Trump filly. *nk* **67**
-- **ONLYTIME WILL TELL** [25] 2-9-0 P Fessey 66/1: 0: Late hdwy from rear, no dngr, 16th: with C Dwyer. *½* **71**
-- **XTRA** [28] 2-9-0 S W Kelly (3) 15/2: 0: Dwelt, sn outpcd far side, ran on fnl 1f, nvr nrr: 17th: op 7/1: cost 575,000 gns, half brother to a couple of juv wnrs: dam 7f/1m wnr: with L Cumani. *½* **70**
4183 **Mumbling 15** [10] 2-9-0 S Sanders 50/1: -- **Rapt** [2] 2-9-0 M Tebbutt 40/1:
-- **Firewire** [1] 2-9-0 P Doe 66/1: 3864 **Snizort 37** [15] 2-9-0 D Harrison 20/1:
-- **Captain Crusoe** [22] 2-9-0 Paul Eddery 100/1: 3840 **False Promise 38** [26] 2-9-0 J Reid 50/1:
-- **Fouette** [27] 2-8-9 P Robinson 50/1: -- **Silver Chevalier** [23] 2-9-0 Martin Dwyer 100/1:
-- **Is Wonderful** [9] 2-9-0 K Darley 16/1: -- **Athletic Sam** [24] 2-9-0 L Carter 100/1:
-- **Bezza** [16] 2-8-9 G Duffield 50/1: -- **Twilight Haze** [5] 2-9-0 G Carter 50/1:
29 ran Time 1m 42.26 (5.76) (K Abdulla) J H M Gosden Manton, Wilts

4350 5.15 FEN DITTON NURSERY HCAP 2YO 0-95 (D) 1m str Good 40 -22 Slow [95]
£5252 £1616 £808 £404 All bar 2 raced centre field

*4163 REGATTA POINT 16 [1] A P Jarvis 2-8-10 (77) L Dettori 8/1: -0211: 2 b c Goldmark - Flashing Raven 84
(Maelstrom Lake) Towards rear, imprvd over 2f out, rdn & ran on well to lead well ins last, pushed out:
earlier won at Salisbury: 12,000 gns Feb foal: eff at 1m, further will suit next term: acts on
gd & gd/soft, handles fast: lightly raced & improving, shld complete a hat-trick.

3704 DOMINAITE 46 [14] M W Easterby 2-8-13 (80) T Quinn 8/1: 213232: 2 b g Komaite - Fairy Kingdom 1¾ 82
(Prince Sabo) Cl-up, chall appr fnl 1f, rdn & not pace of wnr well ins last: 7 wk abs: v consistent: see 3704.

3901 WHALE BEACH 34 [8] B W Hills 2-9-7 (88) M Hills 13/2 FAV: 0123: 2 b c Known Fact - Zulu Dance hd 90
(Danzatore) Hdwy from rear appr fnl 2f, chall over 1f out, ran on fnl 50y: fine run under top-weight: stays 1m.

*3952 SISTER CELESTINE 30 [11] W Jarvis 2-8-7 (74) Martin Dwyer 20/1: 2414: Mid-div, rdn/prog over ½ 75
2f out, styd on to chall dist, no extra well ins last: eff over a stiff 7.5f/1m: see 3952 (mdn).

4290 KINGS CREST 7 [16] 2-7-10 (63)(1oh) Joanna Badger 2/9/1: 664145: Front rank, went on appr hd 64
fnl 1f, hdd ins last, sn btn: nicely bckd & remains in gd form, handles gd & gd/soft: see 4290, 4132.

4157 BOUCHRA 17 [4] 2-8-6 (73) J Mackay (5) 10/1: -22036: Prom, chall over 1f out, rdn/wknd well 2 70
ins last: longer 1m trip, shade btr 4157 (7f).

3690 COUNTRYWIDE PRIDE 46 [19] 2-8-2 (69) J Quinn 25/1: 430467: Keen/rear, imprvd 3f out, drvn & nk 65
no extra fnl 1f: 7 wk abs: shade btr 3609.

4290 HOMELIFE 7 [21] 2-7-10 (63) M Henry 12/1: 406628: Chsd ldrs, outpcd halfway, rall/no room over nk 58
1f out, swtchd & styd on well fnl 1f: qck reapp & looks sure to relish a return to further, as in 4290 (10f).

*4116 TEMPLES TIME 19 [2] 2-8-10 (77) P Dobbs (5) 20/1: -43619: Handy, rdn 2f out, no extra over hd 72
1f out: shade btr 4116 (mdn auct, gd/soft).

3705 BUY A VOWEL 46 [3] 2-8-3 (70) G Duffield 7/1: -0600: Mid-div, gd hdwy over 1f out, ev ch till 1¼ 62
wknd fnl 1f, 10th: big morning gamble from 16/1: 7 wk abs: up in trip, h'cap bow: see 3705, 2708.

3817 PRINCE MILLENNIUM 39 [13] 2-8-10 (77) R Hughes 20/1: 563040: Late gains from rear, no dngr, 11th. ½ 68

4254 ROOFER 10 [5] 2-8-13 (80) Craig Williams 12/1: 542450: Nvr a factor, 12th: caught the eye in 4254. nk 71

4157 DIVINE WIND 17 [20] 2-8-1 (68) G Baker (5) 33/1: 000200: Led on far side, joined centre group & 1¼ 56
hdd over 1f out, fdd, 13th: up in trip: see 4030 (6f).

4157 SALTWOOD 17 [6] 2-8-11 (78) J Reid 12/1: -04100: Cl-up, rdn/wknd over 2f out, 18th: up in trip. 0

4140 Seattle Prince 18 [12] 2-8-11 (78) L Newman (3) 33/1: 4249 My Very Own 10 [10] 2-8-12 (79) J Tate 16/1:

4184 Ryans Gold 15 [22] M W Ryan 16/1: 4172 Tedstale 16 [17] 2-8-13 (80) S W Kelly (3) 20/1:

3962 Where The Heart Is 29 [9] 2-9-0 (81) S Sanders 33/1: 3458 Dennis Our Menace 56 [7] 2-9-2 (83) P Doe 20/1:

4076 Cearnach 22 [18] 2-8-0 (67) D R McCabe 16/1:

21 ran Time 1m 41.47 (4.97) (Grant & Bowman Ltd) A P Jarvis Aston Upthorpe, Oxon

Official Going GOOD/SOFT. Stalls: 2m2f - Inside; Rem - Stands side.
A class adjustment of +20 was added to each pace figure to compensate for the high-class of runners at this meeting.

4351 1.40 GR 3 JOCKEY CLUB CUP STKS 3YO+ (A) 2m Good 59 +21 Fast
£29000 £11000 £5500 £2500 3yo rec 11lb

4264 PERSIAN PUNCH 13 [3] D R C Elsworth 7-9-5 R Hughes 7/1: 651321: 7 ch g Persian Heights - Rum Cay 122
(Our Native) Shkn up to lead & set a searching gallop, clr thr'out, styd on strongly, unchall: nicely bckd, v fast
time: earlier won at Sandown (Gr 3) & Deauville (Gr 2): '99 Doncaster wnr (stks, rtd 110): '98 Newmarket, Sandown
& York wnr (Gr 3's), plcd in the Melbourne Cup, rtd 118): eff at 14f, best at 2m, stays 2m4f: acts on firm, suited
by gd & hvy grnd & loves to force the pace on stiff/gall trks: high-class, as gd as ever at the age of 7.

4264 ROYAL REBEL 13 [4] M Johnston 4-9-5 (vis) M J Kinane 11/2: 221132: 4 b g Robellino - Greenvera 5 118
(Riverman) Handy in chasing pack, prog to chase wnr 2f out, styd on but nvr any impress: thorough stayer, ran to
best: stays in training next year & shld win more Group races: see 3538.

3877 RAINBOW HIGH 37 [5] B W Hills 5-9-3 M Hills 5/1: -54243: 5 b h Rainbow Quest - Imaginary (Dancing ¾ 115
Brave) Patiently rdn, prog ent fnl 3f, rdn appr fnl 1f, styd on but nvr a threat: clr rem, well bckd: ran to best
tho' hard to win with this term: landed this race in '99 (rtd 116, 3 rnrs): see 1222.

3134 VICIOUS CIRCLE 71 [6] L M Cumani 6-9-0 J P Spencer 4/1 FAV: 211-44: Bhd, prog to go 3rd appr 5 107
fnl 2f, sn rdn, no extra: nicely bckd, clr rem, 10 wk abs: first try at 2m, shade btr 3134 (12f).

+4016 JARDINES LOOKOUT 28 [2] 3-8-3 J Quinn 13/2: 121D15: In tch, prog to dspt 2nd briefly ent fnl 3f, 5 102
fdd 2f out: bckd: big step up in grade & not disgraced over longer trip: only a 3yo, see 4016 (14f rtd h'cap).

4264 CHURLISH CHARM 13 [1] 5-9-0 J Reid 9/2: 361246: Rcd in pack most of way till wknd qckly 3f out: 14 90
bckd: much better than this, less than 1L bhd this wnr on worse terms in 4264, see 3877, 3751.

3645 SAMSAAM 49 [9] 3-8-6 R Hills 25/1: 132137: Prom, dsptd 2nd after 1m till 4f out, sn btn: 7 wk abs. 9 84

3792 ALVA GLEN 42 [7] 3-8-4(1ow) K Darley 14/1: 236168: Al towards rear, btn 4f out: 6 wk abs, op 10/1. 3 79

3552 PAIRUMANI STAR 55 [8] 5-9-0 Pat Eddery 20/1: 012149: In tch till 6f out: op 14/1, 8 wk abs, stiff task. 5 73

9 ran Time 3m 25.72 (2.92) (J C Smith) D R C Elsworth Whitsbury, Hants

4352 2.15 GR 2 CHALLENGE STKS 3YO+ (A) 7f str Good 59 -06 Slow
£58000 £22000 £11000 £5000 3yo rec 2lb Raced stands side

4078 LAST RESORT 23 [7] B W Hills 3-8-9 M Hills 20/1: 634331: 3 ch f Lahib - Breadcrumb (Final Straw) 115
Held up, imprvd 3f out, led appr fnl 1f, rdn & ran on strongly: earlier won at Chester (fill mdn): unrcd juv:
eff at 7f, has the speed for 6f: acts on firm & soft grnd, any trk: v smart & improving filly.

4056 MAIDAAN 28 [8] Saeed bin Suroor 4-9-0 T Quinn 14/1: 0-1632: 4 b h Midyan - Panache Arabelle 2½ 113
(Nashwan) Waited with, prog ent fnl 2f, rdn dist, kept on but no ch wnr: op 10/1: lightly rcd this term & prob
ran a lifetime best: return to 1m may suit: see 4056.

3875 CAPE TOWN 37 [3] R Hannon 3-8-8 R Hughes 7/2: 302333: 3 gr c Desert Style - Rossaldene hd 112
(Mummy's Pet) Cl-up, led appr fnl 2f, rdn & hdd bef fnl 1f, no extra ins last: nicely bckd from 9/2: someway
below his best, softer grnd is ideal: see 3452, 969.

2343 MISRAAH 105 [1] Sir Michael Stoute 3-8-12 R Hills 8/1: 1-1044: Well plcd, shkn up to chall 2f out, 2 108

fdd fnl 1f: tchd 10/1, 15 wk abs: v useful, has had an interrupted campaign & is poss worth a try at 6f: see 955.
3995 **BLUE MOUNTAIN 28** [2] 3-8-12 J Reid 20/1: 020135: In tch, eff 2f out, no impress: imprvg, useful colt. *1* **106**
3995 **INVINCIBLE SPIRIT 28** [5] 3-8-12 Pat Eddery 11/1: 116-46: Chsd ldrs, shkn up 2f out, outpcd: *¾* **104**
op 8/1: capable of better & is prob best covered up (saw plenty of daylight): see 3995.
*4078 **MOUNT ABU 23** [6] 3-8-12 J Fortune 7/1: 116317: Bhd ldrs, wknd appr fnl 1f: bckd: grnd faster *5* **94**
than ideal, best on gd/soft or softer: progressive earlier & beat this wnr in 4078 (soft).
4125 **WARNINGFORD 20** [9] 6-9-0 M J Kinane 5/1: 263158: In tch wide, eff & btn appr fnl 1f: bckd: not *3* **88**
his form, see 3995 (beat this 5th & 6th).
*4259 **KABOOL 13** [4] 5-9-4 L Dettori 11/4 FAV: -44319: Led till appr fnl 2f, btn & eased: hvly bckd s/mate *4* **85**
of 2nd: shorter 7f trip, best over 1m/10f prev: surely something amiss, see 4259 (had a hard race).
9 ran Time 1m 26.34 (3.14) (H R H Prince Fahd Salman) B W Hills Lambourn, Berks

4353

2.55 TOTE CESAREWITCH HCAP 3YO+ (B) 2m2f Good 59 +09 Fast [111]
£78000 £24000 £12000 £6000 3yo rec 12lb

2336 **HEROS FATAL 105** [18] M C Pipe 6-8-1 (83)(1ow) G Carter 11/1: 53-301: 6 ch g Hero's Honor - Femme **92**
Fatale (Garde Royale) In tch, imprvd 6f out, hard rdn to lead appr fnl 2f, held on well, all out: gd time, 15 wk
abs: 99/00 hdles wnr at Cheltenham (2) & M Rasen (2m5f, h'caps, gd & hvy, rtd 146h): 3rd in this race in '99
(rtd 85): ex-French, '98 wnr at Deauville (h'cap) & Toulouse (List): eff at 2m2f, stays 2m4f: acts on fast &
gd/soft grnd, any trk: runs well fresh: genuine, useful stayer, will reportedly go chasing.
4115 **WAVE OF OPTIMISM 21** [6] J Pearce 5-7-13 (82) G Baker (5) 40/1: 110002: 5 ch g Elmaamul - Ballerina *¾* **89**
Bay (Myjinski) Midfield, prog 5f out, chall 3f out, sn rdn, kept on & only just btn: back to form, eff at 2m/2m2f.
*2092 **BARBA PAPA 115** [20] A J Martin 6-8-8 (91)(t) J Murtagh 9/2 FAV: 204-13: 6 b h Mujadil - Baby's *1* **97**
Smile (Shirley Heights) Towards rear, shaken up & hdwy appr fnl 3f, styd on well for press ins last, nrst fin:
well bckd Irish raider, tchd 7/1: 10 wk jumps abs (plcd): useful run, eff at 2m2f/2m4f: see 2092.
-- **TRYPHAENA** [21] W P Mullins 5-7-10 (79)(t) F Norton 10/1: 11-344: In tch, clsd to trk ldrs on bit ent *2* **83**
fnl 4f, shkn up 2f out, hard rdn dist, no extra: op 8/1, tchd 12/1, 10 wk jumps abs: Irish raider, won 4 h'caps
last term, incl at Leopardstown: eff at 2m, just found out by this extra 2f?: acts on fast & soft, wears a t-strap.
3224 **CARLYS QUEST 66** [10] 6-8-3 (86)(tvi) Craig Williams 40/1: 004055: Mid-div, prog to lead & went *3* **87**
clr 5f out, hdd 2f out, onepce: big step up in trip, poss stays 2m2f: 2nd in Nov H'cap prev 2 seasons: see 1373.
*4071 **PRAIRIE FALCON 24** [11] 6-7-13 (82) Dale Gibson 16/1: 040016: In tch, shaken up 5f out, styd on *½* **82**
same pace fnl 2f: tchd 20/1: shade btr 4071.
3986 **QUEDEX 29** [15] 4-8-2 (85) C Rutter 50/1: 400107: Bhd, imprvd 5f out, styd on without threatening. *3* **82**
2336 **ANSAR 105** [5] 4-8-8 (91) P J Smullen 7/1: 020118: Midfield, eff 5f out, nvr able to chall: well *1* **87**
bckd Irish raider, 7 wk abs: won last 2 starts at Galway & Tralee (stks): capable of better: see 1222.
4115 **TENSILE 21** [24] 5-8-4 (87)(VIS) K Darley 20/1: 043359: Rear, gd prog to chase ldrs 5f out, rdn *3* **80**
& wknd 2f out: tried a visor, stablemate of wnr: see 1222.
3360 **RENZO 61** [19] 7-7-10 (79)(3oh) K Dalgleish (5) 66/1: 012030: Bhd, late hdwy thro' btn horses: abs. *nk* **71**
3085 **CHRISTIANSTED 73** [12] 5-8-0 (79)(4ow) W Supple 40/1: 610500: Rear, prog 6f out, wknd 3f out: abs. *6* **70**
4193 **STORMY SKYE 15** [4] 4-7-10 (79)(tbl)(4oh) R Brisland (5) 100/1: -32460: Mid-div, prog to go 2nd 5f *2* **64**
out, wknd ent fnl 4f: 12th, stiffish task, see 1800, 1510.
3085 **SILENT WARNING 73** [1] 5-8-3 (86) G Duffield 12/1: 30-260: Well plcd, eff 5f out, btn 3f out: 13th. *1* **70**
4166 **FLETCHER 17** [26] 6-7-10 (79)(11oh) M Henry 66/1: 510200: Chsd ldrs till 3f out: 14th, stiff task. *2½* **61**
4115 **TURNPOLE 21** [17] 9-7-10 (79)(2oh) J Mackay (5) 10/1: 064140: Nvr dngrs: 15th, bckd, won this in '97. *1½* **60**
3986 **TAMING 29** [2] 4-7-12 (79)(2ow) Martin Dwyer 33/1: 1-0440: Handy till 4f out: 16th: see 3986, 633. *hd* **62**
3967 **EASTWELL HALL 30** [27] 5-8-1 (84) L Newman (1) 8/1: -51520: In tch, brief eff 6f out: 17th, bckd: *½* **64**
plcd in this race last term & is capable of much better: see 1800.
4091 **SPIRIT OF LOVE 22** [16] 5-9-10 (107) D Holland 33/1: 324030: Nvr in it: 22nd, top-weight, won this in '98. **0**
3877 **DOMINANT DUCHESS 37** [3] 6-8-13 (96) M Hills 16/1: -11100: Keen, wide, al rear: fin 23rd, bckd: **0**
2nd in this race in '99 off a 15lbs lower mark: see 3302.
997 **BRIDIES PRIDE 175** [23] 9-7-10 (79)(7oh) Jonjo Fowle (1) 100/1: 00-240: Led till 5f out, sn lost place: 27th. **0**
*3905 **LAFFAH 35** [14] 5-7-10 (79)(t)(13oh) J Quinn 20/1: 411010: Bhd, switched after 4f, btn halfway: **0**
29th, bckd from 28/1 despite 13lbs o/h: see 3905.
4276 **Red Ramona 9** [22] 5-8-2 (85) P Doe 66/1: 4280 **Royal Expression 9** [7] 8-7-10 (79)(7oh) P Hanagan(2) 100/1:
4115 **Bid Me Welcome 21** [13] 4-7-11 (80) G Bardwell 50/1:
3058 **Ravenswood 74** [29] 3-7-11 (91)(t)(1ow) R Ffrench 25/1:
4075 **Granny Rich 23** [33] 6-7-10 (79)(41oh) C Catlin(3) 200/1:
4213 **Full Ahead 14** [32] 3-7-10 (91)(7oh) A Beech(0) 100/1:
4229 **Protocol 12** [9] 6-7-10 (79)(t)(35oh) G Sparkes (4) 200/1: 3295 **Alhawa 64** [31] 7-7-10 (79)(2oh) A Mackay 40/1:
4118 **I Tina 20** [25] 4-7-10 (79)(VIS)(21oh) J Lowe 200/1: 3948 **Water Flower 31** [30] 6-7-10 (79)(17oh) N Carter(5) 200/1:
917 **Kattegat 183** [28] 4-8-7 (90) J Reid 40/1: 3323 **Weet For Me 63** [8] 4-7-10 (79)(1oh) P M Quinn(3) 66/1:
33 ran Time 3m 54.91 (5.41) (Frank A Farrant) M C Pipe Nicholashayne, Devon

4354

3.30 GR 1 DEWHURST STKS 2YO (A) 7f str Good 59 -28 Slow
£124700 £47300 £23650 £10750 Raced stands side

*4054 **TOBOUGG 28** [6] M R Channon 2-9-0 Craig Williams 7/4 FAV: -111: 2 b c Barathea - Lacovia (Majestic **119**
Light) Front rank, led ent fnl 2f, pushed out, rdly: nicely bckd: unbtn, earlier won at York (mdn) & Longchamp
(Gr 1): cost 230,000gns, half brother to sev wnrs, dam won French Oaks: eff at 7f, will stay at least 1m next term:
acts on fast, gd/soft grnd, stiff/gall trks: runs well fresh: high-class, unexposed, on the Guineas short-list.
*3891 **NOVERRE 36** [3] D R Loder 2-9-0 L Dettori 7/1: 111312: 2 b c Rahy - Danseur Fabuleux (Northern *1¼* **115**
Dancer) Held up, prog 2f out, rdn dist, ran on, unable to chall: fine run from this tough, smart French raider.
4196 **TEMPEST 15** [7] Sir Michael Stoute 2-9-0 J Murtagh 40/1: -41263: 2 b c Zafonic - Pidona (Baillamont) *hd* **114**
Held up, imprvd halfway, shaken up to chase ldrs appr fnl 1f, kept on under press: op 25/1: much imprvd:
smart colt with a high cruising speed: see 3484.
*4158 **MOZART 18** [10] A P O'Brien 2-9-0 M J Kinane 11/4: -114: Well plcd but not settle, chall 2f out, rdn *½* **113**
& onepace ent fnl 1f: hvly bckd Irish raider, lost unbtn record tho' prob imprvd in defeat: see 4158.
-- **FREUD** [4] 2-9-0 J P Spencer 11/1: -25: In tch, shaken up 2f out, onepace till hard rdn, switched & *½* **111**
prog fnl 100y: nicely bckd from 16/1: 15 wk abs, stablemate 4th: btn at long odds-on sole prev start: half-
brother to top-class 1m/10f performer Giants Causeway, dam 9f wnr: clrly held in the highest regard by powerful
stable: eff at 7f on gd grnd, 1m is going to suit next term: v useful colt.
3470 **VACAMONTE 56** [8] 2-9-0 T Quinn 6/1: -156: Rear, wide, imprvd appr fnl 2f, sn rdn, no extra: *1* **109**
bckd, 8 wk abs: better run tho' shade below v useful debut performance in 2613 (List, fast grnd).

3891 **CHIANTI** 36 [9] 2-9-0 Pat Eddery 25/1: -11637: Pld hard bhd, nvr a factor: not disgraced, see 3891.   1¾ 105
*3470 **KINGS IRONBRIDGE** 56 [11] 2-9-0 R Hughes 20/1: -21518: Wide, chsd ldrs, lost place ent fnl 2f: 3½ 99
8 wk abs, stiffish task: btr 3470 (Gr 3).
*1691 **VOLATA** 133 [1] 2-9-0 K Darley 33/1: -19: Bhd ldrs, outpcd 2f out: over 4 month abs: see 1691.   3½ 92
4196 **CASHEL PALACE** 15 [2] 2-9-0 P J Scallan 200/1: 215000: Led till 2f out, sn btn: 10th, pacemaker for 4th. 2 88
10 ran   Time 1m 27.93 (4.73)   (Sheikh Ahmed Al Maktoum)   M R Channon West Isley, Berks

4355 **4.10 GR 1 DUBAI CHAMPION STKS 3YO+ (A)   1m2f str   Good 59   +04 Fast**
£232000 £88000 £44000 £20000   3yo rec 5lb   Raced stands side

-3539 **KALANISI** 53 [3] Sir Michael Stoute 4-9-2 J Murtagh 5/1: -21221: 4 b h Doyoun - Kalamba (Green Dancer)   125
Mid-div, clsd going well 3f out, rdn to lead appr fnl 1f, found extra when prsd ins last & ran on v strgly: 8 wk
abs, hvly bckd, gd time: deserved, twice just tchd off by Giants Causeway since won at R Ascot (Gr 2): unbtn in 3
'99 starts for L Cumani, at Folkestone (mdn), Newmarket (stks, rtd 112) & Kempton (List): eff at 1m, suited by 10f,
may get 12f on this evidence: acts on firm, soft grnd, any trk: runs well fresh: high-class & most genuine.
4262 **MONTJEU** 13 [4] J E Hammond 4-9-2 M J Kinane 10/11 FAV: 111142: 4 b c Sadler's Wells - Floripedes   ½ 124
(Top Ville) Waited with, weaved thro' to trk ldrs going well 3f out, switched to chall dist, sn drvn, kept on, only
just btn: v hvly bckd from 13/8: shade better than his Arc performance tho' still 10lbs below 2998.
*3875 **DISTANT MUSIC** 37 [11] B W Hills 3-8-11 M Hills 20/1: 1-2013: 3 b c Distant View - Musicanti   2½ 120
(Nijinsky) Patiently rdn, sltly hmpd 5f out, smooth prog 3f out, chsd ldrs over 1f out, kept on onepce ins last:
tchd 25/1: clrly back to v best: stays 10f, win more Group races next term: see 3875.
3928 **LOVE DIVINE** 34 [12] H R A Cecil 3-8-8 T Quinn 6/1: -11244: Bhd ldrs, chall 2f out, onepce bef   1½ 115
fnl 1f: bckd: smart, but prob needs return to 12f: see 1828 (Oaks).
3925 **INDIAN DANEHILL** 35 [10] 4-9-2 O Peslier 16/1: -11245: Mid-div, drpd rear 4f out, switched bef fnl   1½ 116
1f & some hdwy: op 10/1: French raider, not far off best, ideally suited by soft/hvy grnd: see 1115.
2497 **BORDER ARROW** 98 [8] 5-9-2 (t) J Fortune 33/1: -62306: Rear, prog appr fnl 2f, sn onepce: 14 wk abs.   3 111
*4000 **COMPTON BOLTER** 28 [15] 3-8-11 (t) J P Spencer 150/1: 504517: Switched left start, nvr better than   nk 110
mid-div: stiffish task, ran to best: see 4000.
*4238 **SLICKLY** 14 [7] 4-9-2 L Dettori 20/1: 5-1018: Wide, cl-up, led 3f out till 1½f out, sn btn: made all in 4238. nk 109
2998 **SHIVA** 77 [14] 5-8-13 Pat Eddery 14/1: -01309: Cl-up, led 4f out till 2½f out, lost pace: bckd tho'   5 99
op 8/1, stablemate of 4th, 11 wk abs: needs softer grnd, rnr-up in this last term: high-class on soft grnd in 1587.
3925 **GREEK DANCE** 35 [13] 5-9-2 P J Smullen 10/1: 225120: Mid-div, prog to press ldrs 3f out, sn rdn,   ¾ 101
wknd: 10th, stablemate of wnr, op 13/2: capable of btr, see 3071 (soft).
3903 **GOLD ACADEMY** 35 [2] 4-9-2 R Hughes 150/1: 666240: Chsd ldrs till 3f out: 11th, stiff task, see 1057. shd 101
4111 **LERMONTOV** 21 [6] 3-8-11 Paul Scallan 250/1: 2-4000: Led till 4f out, wknd qckly: 12th, pacemaker.   12 89
4211 **ALSHAKR** 14 [9] 3-8-8 R Hills 66/1: -13120: Pulled hard, trkd ldrs, lost pl appr fnl 3f: 13th, lngr trip.   13 77
4111 **ALMUSHTARAK** 21 [5] 7-9-2 J Quinn 200/1: 360600: Dwelt, chsd ldrs till appr fnl 3f, sn hmpd: 14th.   ½ 75
4319 **BARATHEA GUEST** 6 [1] 3-8-11 Craig Williams 100/1: 555430: Al bhd, switched to centre after 5f: 15th.   2 72
15 ran   Time 2m 05.59 (3.49)   (H H Aga Khan)   Sir Michael Stoute Newmarket, Suffolk

4356 **4.45 GR 2 ROCKFEL STKS 2YO (A)   7f str   Good 59   -29 Slow**
£29000 £11000 £5500 £2500 Raced stands side

3985 **SAYEDAH** 29 [16] M P Tregoning 2-8-9 R Hills 25/1: -221: 2 b f Darshaan - Balaabel (Sadler's Wells)   108
Sn switched to grab stands rail & led, prsd 1f out, rdn to get on top again towards fin: slow time, jockey given
4 day ban for irresp riding: first win: half-sister to a 7f wnr, dam a miler: eff at 7f, bred to apprec 10f+ next
term: acts on firm & gd, sharp/undul or stiff trks: v useful from the front today: strong 1000 Guineas contender.
4240 **KATHERINE SEYMOUR** 14 [14] M J Grassick 2-8-9 E Ahern 7/1: -122D: 2 b f Green Desert - Sudeley   ½ 106
(Dancing Brave) Well plcd, prog to chall dist, sn hung right & rdn, held nr fin: fin 2nd, plcd 3rd, jockey
handed one day ban for careless riding: earlier won a 7f Curragh mdn on debut: useful filly, see 4240.
*4240 **IMAGINE** 14 [15] A P O'Brien 2-8-12 M J Kinane 12/1: 361412: 2 b f Sadler's Wells - Doff The   shd 109
Derby (Master Derby) Chsd ldrs, eff 2f out, rdn bef fnl 1f, kept on & carried right ins last: fin 3rd, plcd
2nd: Irish raider who imprvd again here: 1m+ is going to suit: see 4240.
*3749 **TEMPTING FATE** 44 [5] J W Hills 2-8-9 M Hills 16/1: -2114: Keen, last, shkn up 2f out, strong run   ½ 105
ins last, nvr nrr: 6 wk abs: eff at 7f on firm & gd, 1m will suit: would have gone v close if asked for effort
earlier: held in high regard & will be aimed at the 1000 Guineas next term: v useful, see 3749.
4183 **SILKY SHARM** 16 [1] 2-8-9 (t) T Quinn 10/1: -35: Mid-div, rdn 2f out, staying on fin tho' nvr pace   ¾ 103
to chall: useful run on only 2nd start: nailed on for a mdn, will apprec 10f+ next term: see 4183.
3876 **AMEERAT** 37 [2] 2-8-9 P Robinson 4/1: -126: Sltly hmpd appr 2f, keen, chsd ldrs, rdn & onepce   hd 103
appr fnl 1f: nicely bckd: ran well tho' cld have done with a stronger pace & return to 1m will suit next term.
*4288 **GOT TO GO** 8 [3] 2-8-9 J Reid 14/1: -17: Shuffled back to rear & keen, hdwy 2f out, styd on but   1½ 100
nvr nr ldrs: fair run, quickish reapp: bred to apprec mid-dists next term: see 4288.
4159 **AUTUMNAL** 18 [8] 2-8-9 Pat Eddery 12/1: 112348: Bhd, wide prog appr fnl 1f, rdn/no impress ins last.   nk 99
4009 **ALINGA** 28 [13] 2-8-9 M Fenton 66/1: 302109: Wide, nvr better than mid-div: stiff task, up in trip.   1¾ 95
3659 **FANTASY RIDGE** 48 [12] 2-8-9 Craig Williams 20/1: -150: In tch, outpcd ent fnl 2f: 10th, 7 wk abs.   ¾ 93
*4114 **SMALL CHANGE** 21 [4] 2-8-9 L Dettori 9/4 FAV: -10: Al towards rear: 11th, well bckd French   ½ 92
raider: disappointing after debut win in 4114 (Ascot).
4210 **LILS JESSY** 14 [7] 2-8-9 J Weaver 25/1: 101130: Wide, towards rear, btn fnl 2f: 12th, see 4210, 3901.   1½ 89
4114 **ROCKERLONG** 21 [10] 2-8-9 D Holland 12/1: -220: Chsd ldrs, shaken up when bmpd appr fnl 2f, bhd   nk 86
after: 13th, nicely bckd: poss best forgotten & is bred for 10f+ next term: see 4114, 3938.
4210 **ASHLINN** 14 [11] 2-8-9 P Doe 50/1: -2100: In tch wide, prog & ev ch appr fnl 2f, sn rdn & wknd: 14th.   1 86
*4210 **LILIUM** 14 [9] 2-8-9 J Murtagh 8/1: -110: Rear, eff appr fnl 2f, sn short of room/eased: 15th, ignore.   ½ 65
3876 **AMIS ANGEL** 37 [6] 2-8-9 K Darley 100/1: -21600: Handy, snatched up after 2f, wknd qckly 2f out: 16th. 12 65
16 ran   Time 1m 27.96 (4.76)   (Hamdan Al Maktoum)   M P Tregoning Lambourn, Berks

4357 **5.20 NGK SPARK PLUGS HCAP 3YO+ 0-100 (C)   7f str   Good 59   -35 Slow**   [100]
£7748 £2384 £1192 £596   3yo rec 2lb   2 Groups, prob no advantage

3791 **SOCIAL CONTRACT** 42 [29] R Hannon 3-8-4 (78)(BL) P Fitzsimons (5) 25/1: 013401: 3 b g Emarati - Just   84
Buy Baileys (Formidable) In tch centre, prog appr 2f out, rdn to chall 1f out, got on top well ins last: slow time,
first time blnks, 6 wk abs: earlier won at Leicester (h'cap): '99 Southwell (sell, rtd 80a, T Stack) & Lingfield
wnr (nurs, W Haggas, rtd 79): eff at 6f, best at 7f, stays 1m: acts on firm, hvy & fibresand, any trk.
4012 **LORD PACAL** 28 [28] N A Callaghan 3-8-13 (87) J Fortune 20/1: 214102: 3 b g Indian Ridge - Please   1 90

1348

Believe Me (Try My Best) Well plcd centre, led appr fnl 1f, sn hard prsd, worn down towards fin: clrly suited by return to 7f: improving: see 3629.

4215 **PAYS DAMOUR 14** [3] R Hannon 3-8-13 (87) R Hughes 9/1: 213023: 3 b c Pursuit Of Love - Lady Of   nk   89
The Land (Wollow) Trkd stands side ldr, went on 2f out, ev ch & rdn ins last, held fnl 100y: bckd, stablemate wnr.

4112 **PREMIER BARON 21** [20] P S McEntee 5-8-12 (84) J P Spencer 20/1: 610004: Waited with stands   nk   85
side, switched going well ent fnl 2f, kept on for 4th, nvr nrr: back to form: see 3315.

4013 **PRINCE BABAR 28** [23] P Hanagan (5) 16/1: 450165: Held up stands side, imprvd appr fnl   1¼   79
1f, onepace cl-home: v well h'capped 9yo: see 3785.

4215 **BOLDLY GOES 14** [22] 4-8-13 (85)(bl) P Goode (3) 16/1: 010006: Switched to centre after 2f, led   hd   83
that group halfway till appr fnl 1f, same pace: ran close to best, see 3708.

4112 **ROYAL ARTIST 21** [16] 4-9-2 (88) T Quinn 12/1: 110007: Switched to centre after 2f, chsd ldrs,   nk   85
kept on onepace fnl 1f: op 10/1: see 2954 (6f).

4278 **MUCHEA 9** [1] 6-9-13 (99) Craig Williams 20/1: 125058: In tch stands side, rdn appr fnl 1f,   hd   96
styd on without threatening: fair run giving plenty to weight away: see 3648.

4215 **ARPEGGIO 14** [18] 5-8-3 (75)(BL) A Nicholls 16/1: 313009: Wide, prom stands side group, ev ch   1   70
till hard rdn & no extra appr fnl 1f: tried in blnks, see 3831.

4278 **AL MUALLIM 9** [14] 6-9-2 (88)(t) Alex Greaves 16/1: 000040: Pulled hard, chsd ldrs stands side,   shd   83
onepace appr fnl 1f: 10th, see 4278, 3414.

4215 **NORFOLK REED 14** [8] 3-8-8 (82)(vis) L Newman (3) 20/1: 003100: Handy stands side, rdn 2f out,   hd   76
grad wknd: 11th, stablemate of wnr, btr 3880 (fast grnd).

2599} **CAPTAIN SCOTT 462** [2] 6-9-4 (90)(t) E Ahern 12/1: 2400-0: Bhd stands side, eff & not clr run   ½   83
thr'out fnl 2f, nvr dngrs: 12th, belated reapp: '99 reapp wnr at W'hampton (h'cap, rtd 94a & 93, J Glover): plcd
in '98 (h'caps, rtd 85): '97 wnr at Southwell (mdn) & Ayr (ltd stks, rtd 82): eff at 1m/10f: acts on firm, gd,
fibresand, prob soft, any trk: can go well fresh: likes w'either with/without t-strap: now with G Butler.

4126 **INTRICATE WEB 20** [11] 4-7-11 (69) M Henry 33/1: 053000: Cl-up stands side till onepace appr fnl 1f   shd   62
& sn short of room: 13th, back in trip, visor omitted, see 2241.

4165 **MISTER SUPERB 17** [24] 3-8-6 (80) M Tebbutt 25/1: 636000: Nvr factor centre: 14th, see 3076, 2183.   shd   72

4301 **DEBBIES WARNING 7** [25] 4-8-11 (83)(t) J Quinn 33/1: 005000: Speed in centre 5f: 15th, t-strap reapp.   1   73

4106 **MORNINGS MINION 21** [6] 3-8-9 (83) R Perham 8/1: 441530: In tch stands side till 2f out: 16th.   shd   73

4112 **RAYYAAN 21** [21] 3-9-1 (88) R Hills 9/2 FAV: 116200: Nvr troubled ldrs stands side: 17th, well   shd   79
bckd from 6/1: see 1153.

4287 **DANES LADY 8** [13] 4-7-10 (68)(2oh) P M Quinn (3) 33/1: 04-400: In tch stands side, badly hmpd &   ½   57
snatched up appr fnl 1f, no ch after: forget this: fin 18th, see 3297.

4302 **NOMORE MR NICEGUY 7** [7] 6-7-12 (70) J Lowe 8/1: 603500: Nvr dngrs stands side: 19th, bckd 33/1.   ½   58

4301 **ROYAL RESULT 7** [4] 7-9-1 (87) F Norton 10/1: 400560: Prom stands side till 2f out: 20th, tchd 12/1.   ½   74

3338 **TEMERAIRE 62** [26] 5-8-10 (82) G Duffield 25/1: 423000: Led centre group for 3½f, btn after: 22nd, abs.   0

4301 Cauda Equina 7 [5] 6-8-7 (79) J Reid 25/1:   4233 **Ravishing 12** [17] 3-8-1 (75) Martin Dwyer 33/1:
4302 Gift Of Gold 7 [9] 5-8-6 (78)(bl) K Darley 16/1:   4094 **Footprints 22** [27] 3-7-12 (72) P Doe 33/1:
2167 Miss Kirsty 112 [12] 3-8-12 (86)(t) Pat Eddery 20/1: 4037 **Las Ramblas 26** [15] 3-7-13 (73)(BL) G Sparkes(7) 25/1:
4302 Mexican Rock 7 [19] 4-8-1 (73)(t) G Bardwell 40/1:   4215 **Picot 14** [30] 3-8-4 (73) C Rutter 33/1:
29 ran   Time 1m 28.36 (5.16)   (J G Lambton)   R Hannon East Everleigh, Wilts

Official Going: STANDARD Stalls: 7f - Outside, Remainder - Inside

4358 7.00 BIER KELLER HCAP 3YO+ 0-65 (F)   6f aw rnd Going 35 +12 Fast   [65]
£2534 £724 £362   3yo rec 1lb

*4223 **CITY REACH 14** [8] P J Makin 4-9-13 (64)(vis) S Sanders 13/8 FAV: 103311: 4 b g Petong - Azola   70a
(Alzao) Rdn chsing ldrs, styd on well for press fnl 2f to lead inside last, all out: nicely bckd: earlier scored at
Southwell (auction mdn, first time visor), Brighton (claim stakes, rtd 54) & here at Wolverhampton (C/D h'cap):
plcd in '99 (rtd 57a & 75): eff at 5.3/6f, stays a sharp 7f, tried further: acts on firm, hvy & both AWs: handles
a sharp or gall track, likes Wolverhampton: gd weight carrier & well suited by a visor.

4248 **TEOFILIO 11** [6] A J McNae 6-9-11 (62)(bl) N Pollard 6/1: 454022: 6 ch h Night Shift - Rivoltade   hd   66a
(Sir Ivor) Rdn/outpcd early, styd on strongly fnl 2f, just held: op 9/2: shld win again at 7f/1m: see 4248, 594.

*4294 **SQUARE DANCER 8** [5] M Dods 4-10-0 (65) A Clark 11/2: 506013: 4 b g Then Again - Cubist (Tate   1½   65a
Gallery) Prom, led over 1f out, hdd ins last & no extra nr fin: op 4/1: acts on firm, soft & fibresand.

4136 **LADY OF WINDSOR 20** [12] I Semple 3-9-8 (60)(bl) R Winston 33/1: 060404: Prom, rdn/onepce fnl   1½   56a
2f: AW bow: acts on firm, soft & fibresand: eff in blinks or visor: see 1144 (1m, class stakes).

4223 **SAMWAR 14** [3] 8-9-5 (56)(vis) R Fitzpatrick 9/1: 632635: Outpcd early, late gains, no threat to ldrs.   nk   51a

3908 **MARITUN LAD 35** [1] 3-9-8 (60)(bl) N Callan 25/1: 164006: Chsd ldrs 5f: see 624 (5f, mdn).   nk   54a

4153 **DAHLIDYA 18** [9] 5-9-10 (61) G Baker 20/1: 000007: Slowly away, late gains, no threat: see 697.   1¼   52a

2442 **AUBRIETA 100** [2] 4-9-13 (64)(bl) Dean McKeown 20/1: 011408: Al outpcd: 3 month abs: btr 1913.   2   50a

4294 **BRANSTON LUCY 8** [10] 3-9-5 (57) T G McLaughlin 12/1: 243009: Led till over 1f out, fdd: op 14/1.   hd   42a

3956 **TOP OF THE PARKES 31** [11] 3-9-11 (63) J Tate 9/1: 0202D0: Prom till over 1f out: 10th: see 3584.   1½   44a

4220 **JACK TO A KING 14** [13] 5-9-5 (56) C Teague 25/1: 000040: Chsd ldrs 4f: 11th: see 609 (5f).   hd   36a

4023 **HYPERACTIVE 28** [4] 4-9-13 (64) D Sweeney 13/2: 000040: Al outpcd: 12th: op 11/2: prev with   7   31a
A Stewart, now with B Ellison: see 4023, 1483.

4223 **PADDYWACK 14** [7] 3-9-8 (60)(bl) R Studholme (3) 14/1: 0U0050: Prom 3f: 13th: op 12/1: see 654.   15   0a
13 ran   Time 1m 14.2 (1.4)   (T W Wellard Partnership)   P J Makin Ogbourne Maisey, Wilts

4359 7.30 UMPAH CLAIMER 2YO (F)   6f aw rnd Going 35 -07 Slow
£2275 £650 £325

4190 **ASTAIREDOTCOM 15** [7] K R Burke 2-8-6 N Callan 6/1: 504021: 2 b f Lake Coniston - Romantic Overture   69a
(Stop The Music) Chsd ldrs, drvn/led inside last, styd on well, drvn out: op 4/1: first win on AW bow: eff at
6f, tried 7f: acts on firm, soft & fibresand: likes a sharp/undul trk: best without a vis: enjoys claiming grade.

*4244 **BLUE LADY 11** [6] N P Littmoden 2-8-8 J Tate 3/1: 633612: 2 b f College Chapel - Dancing   1   67a
Bluebell (Bluebird) Prom, rdn/ch over 1f out, kept on onepce fnl 1f: op 2/1: ran to form of 4244 (C/D).

*4227 **ACORN CATCHER 14** [5] B Palling 2-8-4 D Sweeney 7/2: 130013: 2 b f Emarati - Anytime Baby   shd   63a

(Bairn) Led till inside last, no extra nr fin: op 9/4: see 4227 (5f, sell).
4246 **DANCING PENNEY 11** [8] K A Ryan 2-8-4 F Lynch 9/2: 166034: Prom, onepce fnl 1f: see 3307 (sell). 1½ **60a**
3394 **TUPGILL TIPPLE 59** [10] 2-8-2 A Beech (3) 16/1: 234005: Outpcd, late gains, no threat: 2 mth abs: 3½ **49a**
visor omitted: see 2441, 2120 (debut, 5f).
4117 **THE FAIRY FLAG 20** [12] 2-8-12 G Hind 14/1: -056: Outpcd, mod late gains: op 8/1: AW bow. ¾ **57a**
4246 **OLYS GILL 11** [13] 2-8-4 D Allan (7) 33/1: 000007: Al outpcd: mod form. 1 **47$**
4244 **STORM FROM HEAVEN 11** [9] 2-9-4 Dean McKeown 7/2: -48: In tch 4f: op 5/1: see 4244 (debut). 2 **56a**
4190 **MEADOWSWEET 15** [11] 2-8-4 O Pears 12/1: -09: Prom wide 4f: op 8/1: AW bow: see 4190. ¾ **40a**
4227 **SUNRIDGE ROSE 14** [2] 2-8-6 Dale Gibson 16/1: -360: Al outpcd: 10th: op 10/1: see 1937 (5f). nk **41a**
4189 **IN TOUCH 15** [4] 2-8-8 R Winston 10/1: -00: Dwelt, al rear: 11th: op 5/1: AW bow, no form. 2 **38a**
3950 **ANGELAS HUSBAND 31** [1] 2-8-7 J Fanning 16/1: 035000: Strugg halfway: 12th: see 3589, 2200. 10 **12a**
12 ran Time 1m 15.30 (2.5) (Astaire & Partners (Holdings) Ltd) K R Burke Newmarket, Suffolk

4360

8.00 BAVARIAN FILL HCAP 3YO+ 0-75 (E) 1m4f aw Going 35 - 06 Slow [73]
£2723 £838 £419 £209 3yo rec 7lb

4024 **TOWN GOSSIP 28** [5] P J Makin 3-7-11 (49)(1ow)(6oh) A Beech (0) 3/1 JT FAV: 050031: 3 ch f Indian **54a**
Ridge - Only Gossip (Trempolino) Made all, rdn fnl 2f, held on well, rdn out: op 9/4: first win: unplcd/no form sole '99 start: eff at 12f, stys 14.7f: acts on fibresand & a sharp trck: eff with forcing tactics.
4169 **MAIDEN AUNT 17** [9] W R Muir 3-7-11 (49) G Baker (5) 33/1: 500002: 3 b f Distant Relative - Lady ¾ **52a**
Kris (Kris) Rear, styd on fnl 2f to take 2nd ins last, not rch wnr: styd longer 12f trip on AW bow: acts on fbrsnd.
4226 **SURE QUEST 14** [6] D W P Arbuthnot 5-8-13 (58) J Quinn 3/1 JT FAV: 223423: 5 b m Sure Blade - 2 **58a**
Eagle's Quest (Legal Eagle) Chsd wnr 4f out, no impress inside last: clr rem: op 11/4: see 1555.
4228 **ARIZONA LADY 14** [12] I Semple 3-9-1 (67) R Winston 12/1: 150024: Keen/chsd ldrs 10f: op 10/1. 5 **60a**
3392 **MONO LADY 59** [3] 7-10-0 (73)(bl) S W Kelly (3) 9/2: 514435: Rear, prog halfway, no impress fnl 2f: 5 **59a**
op 7/2, 2 month abs: see 2075 (C/D).
4251 **BUSY BUSY BEE 11** [2] 3-8-3 (55) D R McCabe 16/1: 2-5046: Rear, mod late hdwy: see 3272. 7 **31a**
4101 **KARA SEA 22** [7] 3-9-2 (68) C Rutter 14/1: 104207: Trckd ldrs, btn 2f out: op 10/1: visor omitted. 2 **41a**
3284 **MELODY LADY 64** [1] 4-8-1 (46)(t) K Dalgleish (5) 9/1: 220358: Bhd 4f out: abs, recent jumps rnr. 3½ **14a**
2902 **BAILEYS ON LINE 81** [11] 3-8-3 (55) J Fanning 11/2: 000239: Cl up halfway, btn 3f out: op 7/2, abs. 4 **17a**
4176 **SAIL WITH THE WIND 17** [10] 3-7-10 (48)(3oh) G Bardwell 25/1: 0-0500: Prom 1m: 10th: AW bow. 3½ **5a**
3353 **Dizzy Tilly 61** [8] 6-8-0 (45)(4ow)(7oh) J Tate 20/1:3696 **No Tomorrow 47** [4] 3-7-12 (49)(tbl)(1ow) A Nicholls 16/1:
12 ran Time 2m 38.5 (4.9) (Admin Of The Late C Stelling) P J Makin Ogbourne Maisey, Wilts

4361

8.30 STEIN MED AUCT MDN 3YO (F) 7f aw rnd Going 35 -14 Slow
£2233 £638 £319

3773 **LATINO BAY 42** [6] N P Littmoden 3-9-0 T G McLaughlin 7/1: 060001: 3 ch g Perugino - Slightly **44a**
Latin (Ahonoora) Prom, led 2f out, drvn inside last, held on all out: 6 week abs: unplcd last term (rtd 66): eff over a sharp 7f, tried 12f: acts on fibresand & a sharp trck.
3971 **PRINCE OF MYSTERY 30** [4] N P Littmoden 3-9-0 (BL) N Callan 8/1: 0-0002: 3 b g Shalford - Mary ½ **42a**
Kate Danagher (Petoski) Chsd ldr, led over 2f out, sn hdd, styd on well for press inside last: well clr rem: 1st time blinks: stablemate of wnr: eff at 7f on fibresand: AW bow today: see 3357.
3612 **SERPENT SYSTEMS 50** [12] D Shaw 3-8-9 S Carson (3) 12/1: -03: 3 b f Noble Patriarch - Takeall 7 **23a**
(Another Realm) In tch halfway, outpcd by front pair fnl 2f: op 7/1: abs: AW bow: no form sole start prev.
4233 **NORTHERN TRIO 12** [5] Mrs Barbara Waring 3-9-0 A Mackay 14/1: 000604: Outpcd, mod late hdwy. 2½ **23a**
3326 **JAZZ NIGHT 62** [10] 3-9-0 (BL) J Edmunds 12/1: 0-05: Led 5f, wknd: blinks, op 8/1: abs, AW bow. nk **22a**
-- **BLACK SAINT** [2] 3-9-0 L Newton 2/1 FAV: -6: Chsd ldrs 4f: op 3/1, debut: with B McMahon. ¾ **21a**
3914 **KERRIDGE CHAPEL 33** [9] 3-8-9 (bl) R Fitzpatrick 20/1: 600607: Chsd ldrs 5f: mod form. 1¾ **13a**
3671 **WATERGOLD 48** [3] 3-9-0 (bl) O Pears 10/1: 000608: Al outpcd: AW bow: see 3364, 1105. hd **17a**
-- **CRISTOFORO** [1] 3-9-0 S W Kelly (3) 5/2: -9: Al bhd: op evens, half brother to a wng sprinter. hd **10a**
-- **BATTLE GREEN LAD** [11] 3-9-0 C Rutter 16/1: -0: Al bhd: 10th: op 10/1, debut: with J Balding. 9 **0a**
10 ran Time 1m 29.6 (3.4) (The Southgate Seven) N P Littmoden Newmarket, Suffolk

4362

9.00 PUMPERNICKEL FILL SELLER 2YO (G) 1m100y aw rnd Going 35 -11 Slow
£1897 £542 £271

4290 **JEZADIL 8** [2] M Dods 2-8-9 T Williams 9/2: 443401: 2 b f Mujadil - Tender Time (Tender King) **63a**
Led after 1f & clr over 1f out, unchall, easily despite swishing tail: sold to J Harris for 6,000gns: op 5/2: 1st win: AW bow: plcd on turf once prev (rtd 60, claimer): eff around 1m, tried 10f, should suit in time: acts on fast, soft & fibresand: eff forcing the pace: apprec drop to selling grade.
4345 **MRS TIGGYWINKLE 1** [12] N P Littmoden 2-8-9 P McCabe 11/2: 000602: 2 b f Magic Ring - Upper 6 **51a**
Sister (Upper Case) Chsd wnr halfway, no impress fnl 2f: op 4/1: quick reapp, unplcd at Newmarket yesterday.
3957 **DISPOL FOXTROT 30** [11] S E Kettlewell 2-8-9 M Fenton 9/1: 0463: 2 ch f Alhijaz - Foxtrot Pie nk **50$**
(Shernazar) Chsd ldrs, onepcd/no impress fnl 2f: op 7/1: AW bow: mod form prev.
4025 **SO FOXY 28** [3] J A Gilbert 2-8-9 J Quinn 16/1: -0004: Chsd ldrs, btn 2f out: op 10/1: lngr 1m trip. 3 **44a**
4025 **RED FANFARE 28** [4] 2-8-9 R Havlin 7/2 JT FAV: 000025: Led 1f, btn 3f out: btr 4025 (7f). hd **43a**
4290 **EMMA CLARE 8** [8] 2-9-0 (bl) S W Kelly (3) 7/2 JT FAV: 241006: Outpcd, nvr factor: bckd, AW bow: hd **47a**
jockey given a 4-day whip ban: btr 3740.
4244 **SLIPPER ROSE 11** [13] 2-8-9 Stephanie Hollinshead (7) 7/1: 000057: Al outpcd: op 9/1: longer trip. 3 **36a**
4154 **SWEET VELETA 18** [9] 2-8-9 V Halliday 16/1: -34408: Nvr on terms: longer 8.5f trip. hd **35a**
3950 **LIGHT OF ARAGON 31** [1] 2-8-9 Joanna Badger (7) 20/1: 000069: Bhd halfway: AW bow, mod form. nk **34a**
4117 **SUSIE THE FLOOSIE 20** [5] 2-8-9 Paul Eddery 7/1: 0000: Al bhd: 10th: AW bow, mod form. 9 **16a**
4253 **Impreza 11** [10] 2-8-9 N Callan 33/1: 4140 **Pocket Venus 19** [6] 2-8-9 A Nicholls 33/1:
12 ran Time 1m 50.1 (3.9) (Mrs C E Dods) M Dods Piercebridge, Co Durham

4363

9.30 BLUE DANUBE HCAP 3YO+ 0-60 (F) 1m100y aw rnd Going 35 -05 Slow [60]
£2534 £724 £362 3yo rec 3lb

4217 **BURNING TRUTH 14** [4] Mrs A Duffield 6-10-0 (60) L Enstone (7) 12/1: 602001: 6 ch g Known Fact - **65a**
Galega (Sure Blade) Rear, prog over 2f out & led inside last, styd on well, rdn out: op 10/1: first win: plcd twice in '99 (rtd 67 & 57a, h'caps): rnr up twice in '98 (rtd 68, stakes): eff between 1m/9f, prob stys 10f:

acts on firm, gd/soft & fibresand: handles a sharp or stiff/gall trck.
*3499 ROBBIES DREAM 56 [13] R M H Cowell 4-9-7 (53)(t) Dale Gibson 7/4 FAV: 001212: 4 ch g Balla Cove -   ½   56a
Royal Golden (Digamist) Mid div, rdn/prog inside last, kept on, not pace of wnr: nicely bckd: 8 wk abs: see 3499.
4251 GROESFAEN LAD 11 [1] P S McEntee 3-9-9 (58)(VIS) G Faulkner (3) 5/1: 006353: 3 b g Casteddu -   1½   58a
Curious Feeling (Nishapour) Led, rdn/hdd inside last, no extra: op 4/1, vis: stays 8.5f, acts on firm, gd/sft & fbrsnd.
4331 AL MABROOK 3 [10] K A Ryan 5-9-7 (53)(bl) F Lynch 12/1: 500504: Chsd ldrs, ch over 1f out, no   nk   52a
extra inside last: op 10/1, quick reapp, clr rem: on a fair mark: see 270.
4031 YABINT EL SHAM 26 [11] 4-9-8 (54) S Righton 16/1: 000005: Rear, mod hdwy: see 191 (5f).   5   43a
3885 COLONEL NORTH 36 [9] 4-9-8 (54) T Williams 8/1: 554506: Chsd ldrs 6f: op 10/1: see 3527, 90.   ¾   42a
4032 SHAANXI ROMANCE 26 [5] 5-9-7 (53)(vis) R Fitzpatrick 10/1: 406007: In tch halfway, btn 7f out: op 7/1.   3   35a
3593 HOWARDS LAD 51 [8] 3-9-8 (57) V Halliday 25/1: 020008: Slowly away & al bhd: abs: visor omitted.   17   13a
4169 CASTLEBRIDGE 17 [6] 3-9-11 (60)(vis) G Baker (5) 12/1: 045009: Bhd halfway: op 10/1: vis reapp.   ½   15a
3868 SHARP SHUFFLE 37 [2] 7-9-8 (54) A Nicholls 7/2: 232100: Al bhd, eased fnl 1f: 10th: btr 3253 (7f, sell).   ½   8a
4143 Eight 19 [12] 4-9-8 (54)(BL) M Fenton 12/1:   3498 Pippas Pride 56 [3] 5-10-0 (60) T G McLaughlin 12/1:
12 ran   Time 1m 49.6 (3.4)   (Middleham Park Racing IV)   Mrs A Duffield Constable Burton, N Yorks

Official Going STANDARD. Stalls: Inside

4364	1.55 CERUTTI MED AUCT MDN DIV 1 3YO (F) 6f aw rnd Going 39 -03 Slow

£1701   £486   £243

--   SHERINGHAM [8] P J Makin 3-8-9 S Sanders 8/1: 1: 3 b f Robin Des Pins - Kimberley (Paradise Bay)   79a
Dwelt, rear/wide, prog to lead over 1f out, pulled clr under hands & heels riding fnl 1f: debut, drifted from
7/2: 1,500gns 2yo: eff at 6f, 7f shld suit: acts on fibresand & a sharp trk: runs well fresh: improve.
4270 FIRST VENTURE 12 [3] C N Allen 3-9-0 (vis) J Weaver 5/4 FAV: 442002: 3 b g Formidable - Diamond   3½   72a
Wedding (Diamond Shoal), Led, rcd centre fnl 3f, hdd dist & no impress fnl 1f: well bckd, 4L clr rem.
4255 LAYAN 13 [9] J Balding 3-9-0 J Edmunds 9/4: 030343: 3 b f Puissance - Most Uppitty (Absalom)   4   57a
Prom till over 1f out: bckd from 7/2: see 3975 (h'cap).
4293 FFYNNON GOLD 15 [5] J G Portman 3-8-9 L Newman (3) 10/1: 000604: Chsd ldrs 4f: AW bow: see 4273. 1½   53$
4192 SUPER DOMINION 17 [4] 3-9-0 P M Quinn (3) 16/1: 336005: In tch, btn 2f out: op 12/1: AW bow.   2   53$
3769 RING MY MATE 44 [7] 3-9-0 Martin Dwyer 33/1: -00006: Sn rdn/towards rear, nvr on terms: 6 wks abs. 3½   44a
--   SILVER DAWN [2] 3-8-9 A Culhane 10/1: 7: Dwelt, al outpcd, eased fnl 1f: debut, big drifter from   1½   35a
3/1: IR 9,500gns purchase: half sister to a juv 7f wnr: with P W Harris.
4232 ASH BOLD 14 [6] 3-9-0 Dean McKeown 25/1: 000-08: Rdn chasing ldr, btn over 2f out: mod form.   ¾   38a
4175 ST IVES 19 [1] 3-9-0 (vis) M Tebbutt 33/1: 004009: Al outpcd: AW bow: see 4175, 1435.   1¾   34a
9 ran   Time 1m 15.8 (2.5)   (Mrs P J Makin)   P J Makin Ogbourne Maisey, Wilts

4365	2.25 MINOTAUR APPR HCAP 3YO+ 0-75 (G) 1m aw rnd Going 39 -07 Slow	[75]

£1967   £562   £281   3 yo rec 3 lb

4143 SHARP GOSSIP 21 [16] J A R Toller 4-8-9 (56) P Dobbs (3) 8/1: 000221: 4 b g College Chapel - Idle   63a
Gossip (Runnett) Trkd ldrs halfway, led over 1f out & pulled clr under hands & heels riding ins last: op 6/1, 1st
win: ex-Irish mdn, dual '99 rnr-up (off mark of 70): prev eff at 6/7f, now suited to 1m, may get further: acts
on fast, soft & fibresand: best without blnks: fine AW bow from a tricky high draw, should win similar again.
4153 HAUNT THE ZOO 20 [6] J L Harris 5-8-13 (60) Darren Williams (3) 8/1: 103032: 5 b m Komaite -   2½   61a
Merryhill Maid (M Double M) Trkd ldrs halfway, led over 2f out till dist, not pace of wnr fnl 2f: stays 1m well,
poss just best at 6/7f: see 1506 (7f).
3440 ROYAL WAVE 59 [15] J L Eyre 4-8-3 (50) S Carson 12/1: 000-03: 4 b g Polish Precedent - Mashmoon 1¾   48a
(Habitat) Rdn chasing ldrs, onepace fnl 2f: op 20/1, 2 month abs: acts on gd grnd & fibresand: fine effort
from tricky high draw: shld prove sharper for this & could find similar: see 3440.
*4224 BARON DE PICHON 16 [12] Andrew Reid 4-9-12 (73) R Cody Boutcher (5) 8/1: 510014: Towards rear/   1   69a
wide, late hdwy for press, no threat to ldrs: op 7/1: see 4224 (clmr, 7f, W'hampton).
3737 EASTERN CHAMP 47 [5] 4-9-11 (72)(t) N Esler (5) 9/1: 634665: Rear, rdn/late hdwy, nrst fin: abs. 1½   65a
3495 RAMBO WALTZER 58 [2] 8-9-10 (71) R Lake (7) 12/1: 200246: Cl-up, led over 4f out, rdn/hdd over   nk   63a
2f out, fdd: op 10/1, 2 month abs: see 517 (clmr).
*3612 PINHEIROS DREAM 52 [7] 3-8-8 (58) Lindsey Rutty (7) 12/1: 046217: Dwelt, rear/wide, mod gains fnl ½   49a
2f: 7 wk abs: AW bow: see 3612 (7f, clmr).
3007 KING TUT 79 [10] 4-8-1 (48) G Baker (3) 20/1: 220408: Mid-div, nvr any threat: 11 wk abs, AW bow.   1   37a
4311 GABLESEA 7 [11] 6-8-2 (49) G Sparkes (5) 20/1: 000469: Rear, little hdwy: see 890 (hvy, 10f).   hd   37a
4232 BENBYAS 14 [1] 3-8-4 (54)(vis) P M Quinn 12/1: 100430: Al twds rear: 10th: op 9/1: vis reapp.   ½   41a
4155 FEATHERSTONE LANE 20 [14] 9-8-5 (52) S W Kelly 33/1: 634350: Held up, eff wide 3f out, sn btn: 11th. 1¾   36a
4301 KAYO 9 [3] 5-10-0 (75) L Newman 11/4 FAV: 504000: Cl-up halfway, btn 2f out: 12th: topweight.   2½   54a
4228 SEA YA MAITE 16 [13] 6-9-3 (64) M Nicholl (7) 5/1: 521650: Mid-div, btn 3f out: 13th: btr 582 (7f). 1¼   40a
3612 LOUS WISH 52 [4] 3-8-6 (56)(bl) A Nicholls 25/1: 000000: Al bhd: 14th: 8 wk abs: btr 346 (7f).   10   17a
2032 CONSULTANT 120 [9] 4-8-7 (54) D Nolan (5) 33/1: 006000: Led 3f, sn lost place/bhd: 15th: abs.   19   0a
15 ran   Time 1m 43.1 (3.7)   (Buckingham Thoroughbreds)   J A R Toller Newmarket, Suffolk

4366	2.55 CLASSIFIED STKS 3YO+ 0-60 (F) 1m4f aw Going 39 -04 Slow

£2296   £656   £328   3 yo rec 7 lb

4256 CHOCSTAW 13 [1] Sir Michael Stoute 3-8-11 F Lynch 9/1: -00541: 3 b c Mtoto - Cwm Deri (Alzao)   65a
Handy, led over 4f out, rdn & prsd 2f out, pulled clr fnl 1f, readily: op 5/1: 1st win on AW bow: eff at 12f,
14f+ cld suit: acts on fibresand & a sharp trk: can win again.
4151 LOVE DIAMONDS 20 [13] N P Littmoden 4-9-4 P McCabe 10/1: 000332: 4 b g Royal Academy - Baby   5   57a
Diamonds (Habitat) Mid-div, prog to press wnr over 2f out, rdn/no impress fnl 1f: see 3915, 390 (11f).
4245 WESTERN COMMAND 13 [14] Mrs N Macauley 4-9-4 R Fitzpatrick 14/1: 060353: 4 b g Saddlers' Hall   ½   56a
- Western Friend (Gone West) Held up, kept on for press fnl 3f, no threat to wnr: op 12/1: see 1501 (14f).
1933 MAKARIM 123 [9] M R Bosley 4-9-4 D Sweeney 40/1: 5-0504: Trkd ldrs, stumbled/sn rdn & lost place nk   55a
4f out, kept on ins last, no threat: 4 month abs: prob handles firm & fibresand: see 135.

3323 **LINEA G 65** [15] 6-9-1 A Culhane 14/1: 20-605: Rear, late gains fnl 3f, no threat: op 12/1: jmps fit (unplcd, rtd 100h, h'cap): see 2446. 3½ **47a**
4186 **FOR HEAVENS SAKE 17** [16] 3-8-11 Dean McKeown 16/1: 232356: In tch 10f: see 3954, 3769. ½ **49a**
*4150 **BE WARNED 20** [8] 9-9-6 (vis) L Newman (3) 9/1: 120017: Trkd ldrs 10f: op 6/1: btr 4150 (11f). ½ **50a**
2790 **ZAHA 88** [5] 5-9-4 G Bardwell 16/1: 140008: Rdn, rear, mod hdwy: op 12/1: 12 wk abs: btr 1370 (10f). 5 **41a**
4291 **MONDURU 10** [10] 3-8-11 Martin Dwyer 40/1: 350009: Mid-div, btn/eased over 1f out: AW bow. 9 **31a**
3725 **CYBER BABE 47** [7] 3-8-12 J Quinn 7/1: 213100: Handy, btn 3f out, eased fnl 1f: 10th: abs: btr 3392. 2 **29a**
4123 **CONSTANT 22** [12] 3-8-11 F Norton 8/1: 500050: Cl-up 12f: 11th: AW bow: btr 979. hd **27a**
2437 **HAITHEM 102** [3] 3-8-11 T G McLaughlin 40/1: 0-0600: Led, hdd over 4f out, sn btn: 12th: 3 mth abs. ½ **26a**
*4186 **CHALCEDONY 17** [2] 4-9-6 J Weaver 7/4 FAV: 036210: Bhd, rdn halfway, no impress: 13th: nicely bckd from 9/4: not his form, something amiss: see 4186 (equitrack, awarded race). ¾ **27a**
4233 **Nowt Flash 14** [4] 3-8-11 R Lappin 25/1: 3731 **Noble Reef 47** [6] 3-8-11 S Sanders 14/1:
1414 **Thieves Welcome 149** [11] 3-8-8 J Fanning 20/1:
16 ran Time 2m 39.4 (5.1) (Sir Evelyn de Rothschild) Sir Michael Stoute Newmarket, Suffolk

4367

3.25 MARSHALLS NURSERY HCAP 2YO 0-85 (E) 6f aw rnd Going 39 +06 Fast [92]
£2840 £874 £437 £218

*4246 **CLARION 13** [16] Sir Mark Prescott 2-9-7 (85) S Sanders 11/4 FAV: 121311: 2 ch c First Trump - Area Girl (Jareer) Chsd ldrs wide, rdn to lead dist, styd on well, pushed out: best time of day, op 2/1: earlier won at Yarmouth (mdn), Sandown (nurs h'cap, rtd 86) & W'hampton (clmr): eff over 5/6f, 7f cld suit: acts on firm, gd & fibresand: gd weight carrier: tough & prog, fine eff from a tricky high-draw: keep on right side. **92+**
4286 **AMEN CORNER 10** [1] M Johnston 2-9-1 (79) J Fanning 11/1: 413502: 2 ch c Mt Livermore - For All Seasons (Crafty Prospector) Led till dist, kept on fnl 1f, not btn far: AW bow: acts on fast & fibresand. ¾ **83a**
4132 **SEBULBA 22** [12] J G Given 2-8-11 (75) Dean McKeown 9/1: 216053: 2 b g Dolphin Street - Twilight Calm (Hatim) Chsd ldrs wide, rdn & kept on fnl 2f, no threat: encouraging eff from a tricky high draw: see 2635. 3 **72a**
4188 **LAY DOWN SALLY 17** [13] J G Portman 2-7-10 (60) G Baker (5) 20/1: 0004: Dwelt, mod gains fnl 2f: h'cap/AW bow: handles fibresand: see 4188. 1¼ **54a**
2928 **YOUNG ALEX 82** [6] 2-8-6 (70) D Sweeney 9/1: -01145: Slowly away, mod late gains: abs, AW bow. 3½ **55a**
4235 **BLUSHING SPUR 14** [3] 2-8-9 (73) S W Kelly (3) 8/1: 025236: Mid-div, hmpd/stumbled on bend over 3f out, no impress after: travelled well bef interference, poss worth another look in similar: see 4007, 2383 (mdn). ½ **56a**
4022 **CELERITY 30** [4] 2-7-10 (60)(24oh) P M Quinn (3) 33/1: -0607: Dwelt, rear/wide, mod hdwy: h'cap bow. 1 **41a**
4090 **GOLD AIR 24** [11] 2-8-5 (69) D R McCabe 20/1: 020008: Chsd ldrs 4f: blnks omitted: AW bow. 5 **40a**
3420 **SPREE LOVE 60** [2] 2-8-9 (73) S Whitworth 11/1: 2459: Prom 4f: 2 month abs, h'cap bow: btr 3108. nk **43a**
4001 **EFIDIUM 30** [7] 2-7-12 (62) F Norton 14/1: -5000: Chsd ldrs 4f: 10th: op 10/1, h'cap/AW bow. 2½ **25a**
4227 **GILLS DIAMOND 16** [15] 2-7-10 (60)(6oh) Kim Tinkler 16/1: 350030: Mid-div/wide, btn over 2f out: 11th: broke a blood vessel: op 10/1: btr 4227 (5f). 1¾ **19a**
3400 **VISLINK 61** [8] 2-8-6 (70) W Ryan 5/1: 000020: Keen, prom early, sn lost place & btn 3f out: 15th: nicely bckd, op 10/1: AW bow, 2 month abs: flattered 3400 (auct mdn). **0a**
4235 **Aporto 14** [10] 2-7-10 (60)(6oh) J McAuley 14/1:
1782 **The Marshall 130** [9] 2-7-11 (61)(BL)(1ow)(8oh) A Nicholls 25/1:
4244 **Clansinge 13** [5] 2-7-12 (62)(bl)(2ow)(10oh) J Quinn 14/1:
15 ran Time 1m 15.3 (2.0) (Neil Greig) Sir Mark Prescott Newmarket, Suffolk

4368

3.55 CERUTTI MED AUCT MDN DIV 2 3YO (F) 6f aw rnd Going 39 -13 Slow
£1694 £484 £242

3885 **STAND BY 38** [9] B A Pearce 3-8-9 G Baker (5) 8/1: -33001: 3 b f Missed Flight - Ma Rivale (Last Tycoon) Prom, prog to lead 2f out, pushed well clr fnl 1f, easily: bckd from 16/1: unplcd both turf starts in '99 (rtd 40, rtd 62a on sand, T D Easterby): eff at 6f, stays sharp 7f well: acts on fibresand. **61a**
4192 **CAREW CASTLE 17** [2] D W P Arbuthnot 3-9-0 (VIS) J Weaver 10/1: 550002: 3 b g Fayruz - Mirmande (Kris) Dwelt, rear/wide, late hdwy fnl 2f, no threat to wnr: op 6/1, 1st time visor: AW bow: see 837. 9 **53a**
4293 **MISS FLIRTATIOUS 10** [1] D Haydn Jones 3-8-9 A McGlone 25/1: -00003: 3 b f Piccolo - By Candlelight (Roi Danzig) Chsd ldrs, outpcd fnl 2f: AW bow: only mod form prev this term: see 1889, 1289. 3½ **39a**
-- **TOOTORIAL** [8] A C Stewart 3-9-0 S Whitworth 9/4: 4: Dwelt, rdn/towards rear early, eff over 2f out, sn no impress: nicely bckd tho' op 6/4: debut: College Chapel colt, looks one of stables lesser lights. 1¼ **41a**
3161 **SEVEN OF SPADES 72** [5] 3-9-0 A Nicholls 7/2: 5-0005: Keen/led till 2f out, fdd: op 9/4, 10 wk abs: prev with R Fahey, now with D Nicholls: see 1580. 6 **30a**
4120 **TRAJAN 22** [7] 3-9-0 W Ryan 7/4 FAV: 244006: Outpcd from halfway: bckd: see 3261, 651. 1½ **26a**
4361 **SERPENT SYSTEMS 2** [3] 3-8-9 S Carson (3) 16/1: -037: Chsd ldrs 3f: quick reapp, mod form. 6 **10a**
4031 **LADY CYRANO 28** [4] 3-8-9 (vis) R Fitzpatrick 33/1: 200008: Rdn/chsd ldrs halfway, sn btn: see 2036. 2½ **3a**
4005 **HICKLETON DANCER 30** [6] 3-9-0 P Fessey 40/1: 69: Chsd ldrs 2f: AW bow, mod form. 9 **0a**
9 ran Time 1m 16.4 (3.1) (M O'Malley) B A Pearce Newchapel, Surrey

4369

4.25 COCO SELLER 2YO (G) 7f aw rnd Going 39 -37 Slow
£1967 £562 £281

3957 **LITTLE TASK 32** [14] A Berry 2-8-11 (BL) S Sanders 9/1: 260601: 2 b c Environment Friend - Lucky Thing (Green Desert) Prom, chsd ldr over 2f out, led ins last, styd on well, rdn out: no bid, 1st win in 1st time blnks: eff over a sharp 7f, tried 1m: acts on fast & fibresand: handles a gall/sharp trk: eff in sellers. **60a**
4154 **CO DOT UK 20** [6] K A Ryan 2-9-3 (BL) F Lynch 9/2: 450202: 2 b g Distant Relative - Cubist (Tate Gallery) Led, rdn/hdd ins last & no extra: op 7/2: back to form in 1st time blnks: acts on fibresand, gd & soft. 2½ **60a**
4163 **EQUAL BALANCE 19** [13] V Soane 2-8-11 (VIS) M Tebbutt 33/1: -003: 2 ch c Pivotal - Thatcher's Era (Never So Bold) Dwelt/outpcd early, kept on fnl 2f, nrst fin: imprvd eff in 1st time visor on AW bow, poor high draw: handles fibresand, return to 1m shld suit. 3½ **47a**
3817 **SAWBO LAD 42** [4] J Akehurst 2-9-3 F Norton 9/2: 000104: Chsd ldrs, btn 2f out: op 7/2, abs, AW bow. ½ **52a**
4225 **BOLHAM LADY 16** [1] 2-8-6 J Edmunds 25/1: 005: Mid-div, btn 2f out: longer 7f trip. 2½ **36a**
4250 **PREMIER BOY 13** [11] 2-8-11 (t) M Fenton 16/1: 00406: Mid-div, btn 2f out: rtd higher 3949 (gd). 6 **31a**
4131 **MINUS FOUR 22** [5] 2-8-11 Dean McKeown 20/1: 07: Nvr on terms with ldrs: AW bow, longer 7f trip. 4 **23a**
-- **TATTY THE TANK** [2] 2-8-11 Martin Dwyer 6/1: 8: Dwelt, nvr on terms: April first foal: sire a 12f wnr: likely to apprec 1m+ in time for M C Pipe. ½ **22a**
4227 **MRS MITCHELL 16** [9] 2-8-6 Clare Roche (7) 20/1: 6009: Chsd ldr, btn 2f out: longer 7f trip. ¾ **16a**
-- **CHANCE REMARK** [3] 2-8-6 P Fessey 25/1: 0: Dwelt, al towards rear: 10th: IR 3,200gns Mar foal: 1½ **13a**

SOUTHWELL (Fibresand) MONDAY OCTOBER 16TH Lefthand, Sharp, Oval Track

half sister to useful 5f juv performer Gold Futures: dam a 5/7f Irish juv wnr: with M Wane.

4305	**OLYS DREAM** 7 [16] 2-8-6 Kim Tinkler 8/1: 060000: Al towards rear: 11th: op 12/1: AW bow: see 898.		½	12a
4244	**CEDAR TSAR** 13 [12] 2-9-3 A Culhane 4/1 FAV: 310000: Chsd ldrs 4f: 12th: fin lame: see 2948.		2	19a
4227	**One Charmer** 16 [15] 2-8-11 P McCabe 33/1:	4283 **Fille De Dauphin** 10 [10] 2-8-6 J McAuley 33/1:		
--	**Dereks Pride** [8] 2-8-6 S Whitworth 20/1:	1488 **Belando** 143 [7] 2-8-11 T G McLaughlin 33/1:		
16 ran	Time 1m 31.2 (4.6)	(Keith Jackson)	A Berry Cockerham, Lancs	

4370 4.55 OBSESSION HCAP DIV 1 3YO+ 0-70 (E) 1m6f aw Going 39 -15 Slow [70]
£2373 £678 £339 3 yo rec 9 lb

4024	**FURNESS** 30 [15] J G Smyth Osbourne 3-8-2 (53) F Norton 7/1: -25251: 3 b g Emarati - Thelma (Blakeney) Led halfway, clr over 2f out, pushed out fnl 1f, readily: 1st run, unplcd in 3 '99 starts (rtd 59, auct mdn): eff at 12/14f, prob stays 2m: acts on fibresand & gd/soft grnd: plenty in hand here, could score again.		62a
4231	**VINCENT** 14 [16] J L Harris 5-9-2 (58) G Baker (5) 100/30 FAV: 441152: 5 b g Anshan - Top Anna (Ela Mana Mou) Towards rear, prog to chase wnr over 3f out, no impress fnl 1f & position accepted nr fin: op 3/1, 5L clr rem: apprec return to sand, remains in gd heart: see 4149 (2m).	4	59a
4166	**RAINBOW SPIRIT** 19 [3] A P Jarvis 3-8-11 (62) W Ryan 4/1: 342333: 3 b g Rainbows For Life - Merrie Moment (Taufan) Mid-div, rdn/prog to chase ldrs over 3f out, sn onepace/held: op 5/1: AW bow: see 4166.	5	56a
*4222	**MR FORTYWINKS** 16 [9] J L Eyre 6-10-0 (70) R Cody Boutcher (7) 9/2: 413414: Led 7f, fdd fnl 2f.	5	57a
4258	**ONE LIFE TO LIVE** 13 [3] 7-7-10 (38)(1oh) J McAuley 50/1: -40/05: Mid-div/outpcd halfway, no impress.	½	20a
4299	**EVENING SCENT** 9 [4] 4-8-9 (51) P M Quinn (3) 6/1: 641156: Mid-div, btn 3f out: op 5/1: btr 4280 (sft).	8	21a
4258	**MISTER WEBB** 13 [1] 3-8-8 (59) M Tebbutt 12/1: 500407: Towards rear, mod hdwy for press: op 10/1.	8	17a
4141	**BEAUCHAMP NYX** 21 [5] 4-7-10 (38)(5oh) S Righton 50/1: 006-08: In tch 9f: see 4141 (10f).	nk	0a
4149	**NOTATION** 20 [8] 6-7-10 (38)(14oh) Claire Bryan (5) 25/1: 114009: Rear, nvr factor: see 3742, 3674.	½	0a
4231	**ICE PACK** 14 [6] 4-8-3 (45) Kim Tinkler 25/1: 343600: Trkd ldrs 10f: 10th: see 2734, 1894.	1	0a
4149	**Classic Eagle** 20 [13] 7-7-12 (40)(2ow)(5oh) J Quinn 16/12746 **Satire** 89 [2] 3-7-10 (47)(7oh) N Kennedy 50/1:		
2002)	**Royal Alibi** 488 [12] 6-8-3 (45)(t) A Nicholls 33/1:		
3276	**Yankee Dancer** 66 [11] 5-7-10 (38)(10oh) P M Quinn (3) 50/1:		
4101	**Zola** 24 [10] 4-7-10 (38)(6oh) G Sparkes (3) 50/1:		
15 ran	Time 3m 07.4 (7.6) (T D Rootes) J G Smyth Osbourne Adstone, Northants		

4371 5.25 OBSESSION HCAP DIV 2 3YO+ 0-70 (E) 1m6f aw Going 39 -26 Slow [70]
£2362 £675 £337 3 yo rec 9 lb

4208	**HALF TIDE** 16 [8] P Mitchell 6-8-1 (43) A Nicholls 9/2 CO FAV: 050501: 6 ch g Nashwan - Double River (Irish River) In tch, lost pl halfway, rallied fnl 3f, styd on gamely to lead nr line, all out: bckd: earlier won at Epsom (appr h'cap, rtd 48): '99 Lingfield wnr (h'cap, rtd 52a): rtd 43a & 54 when rnr-up in '98: suited by 12/14f on gd/soft & both AWs: likes a sharp/undul trk: battled well today.		48a
*3311	**HULLBANK** 65 [12] W W Haigh 10-8-9 (51) P McCabe 9/2 CO FAV: -14512: 10 b g Uncle Pokey - Dubavarna (Dubassoff) Held up, smooth prog to lead 2f out, rdn/hdd nr line: abs: jock given a 4-day whip ban.	hd	55a
4245	**HIGH POLICY** 13 [14] D J G Murray Smith 4-9-1 (57) J Weaver (5) 106023: 4 ch g Machiavellian - Road To The Top (Shirley Heights) Chsd ldrs, rdn fnl 3f, styd on well ins last, just held: visor omitted: stays 14f.	nk	60a
4229	**PENNYS FROM HEAVEN** 14 [3] D Nicholls 6-8-7 (49) Clare Roche (5) 6/1: 430404: Dwelt/held up, eff 3f out, kept on onepace: see 4149, 2139.	3	48a
4222	**BEST PORT** 16 [9] 4-7-10 (38)(5oh) P Fessey 20/1: 212005: Held up, mod gains fnl 2f: see 3406 (2m).	3	33a
3813	**CONCINO** 43 [16] 3-7-10 (47)(9oh) D Kinsella (7) 25/1: 300006: Prom, lost place 7f out, no impress: abs.	hd	41a
3971	**FLOW BEAU** 32 [2] 3-7-10 (47)(bl) P M Quinn (3) 20/1: 406007: Held up, mod late hdwy: AW bow.	½	40a
3963	**GRAND CRU** 32 [7] 9-8-2 (44)(vis) S Carson (3) 10/1: 146008: Led over 4f out till over 2f out, fdd.	2½	33a
2829	**DANCING MARY** 87 [6] 3-7-10 (47)(1oh) G Baker (5) 9/1: 504369: Chsd ldrs 11f: op 12/1, 12 wk abs.	nk	35a
1874	**KILCREGGAN** 126 [1] 6-8-9 (51) A Culhane 13/2: -03300: Handy over 2f out, sn btn: 10th: abs, AW bow.	2½	35a
4231	**MU TADIL** 14 [11] 8-7-10 (38)(13oh) S Righton 40/1: 060400: Bhd halfway: 11th: see 4231, 1394.	1¼	20a
4245	**THE SHADOW** 13 [4] 4-9-10 (66)(vis) J Quinn 9/1: 500330: Trkd ldrs, btn 3f out: 12th: see 3353, 854.	¾	47a
2537	**AMSARA** 98 [10] 4-7-10 (38)(18oh) Claire Bryan (5) 40/1: 000020: Led 9f, sn btn: 16th: 3 month abs.		0a
4280	**Winsome George** 11 [5] 5-7-10 (38)(10oh) G Sparkes (3) 16/1:		
4222	**Noirie** 16 [15] 6-7-10 (38)(11oh) G Bardwell 50/1:		
606)	**Bamboo Garden** 590 [13] 4-9-1 (57)(bl) O Urbina 25/1:		
16 ran	Time 3m 08.9 (9.1) (The Fruit Cake Partnership) P Mitchell Epsom, Surrey		

PONTEFRACT MONDAY OCTOBER 16TH Lefthand, Undulating Track With Stiff Uphill Finish

Official Going HEAVY (SOFT places). Stalls: Inside, except 2m2f - centre.

4372 2.15 WHITE SWAN MDN AUCT DIV 1 2YO (F) 6f rnd Soft 114 -09 Slow
£1820 £520 £260

4269	**CAPTAIN GIBSON** 12 [6] D J S ffrench Davis 2-8-5 T Quinn 4/1: 500621: 2 b g Beveled - Little Egret (Carwhite) Rear, gd prog ent fnl 2f, hung left ins last, psht out to lead line: imprvd since getting easier grnd: eff at 6f, shld get 7f: acts on gd & soft, any trk, tho' has a tendency to hang & prob best going round a bend.		78
4268	**TRAVEL TARDIA** 12 [3] I A Wood 2-8-11 T Williams 20/1: 02: 2 br c Petardia - Annie's Travels (Mac's Imp) Nvr far away, led appr fnl 2f & sn clr, rdn inside last, hdd fnl stride: clr rem: eff at 6f on soft.	hd	83
4083	**SHAKAHAN** 25 [7] B W Hills 2-8-6 Pat Eddery 11/10 FAV: 53: 2 ch f Night Shift - Sea Wedding (Groom Dancer) Rear, shaken up & no room 2f out till switched 1f out, styd on but ch had gone: nicely bckd, clr of next: another luckless run, worth another chance, prob at 7f: see 4083.	4	68
3729	**SIMPLY ERIC** 47 [10] J L Eyre 2-8-7 K Darley 8/1: 244: Dwelt, bhd, went past beaten horses appr fnl 1f: op 6/1, 7 wk abs: unsuited by drop back to 6f, see 3729 (1m).	7	53
2928	**ALIS IMAGES** 82 [4] 2-8-4(1ow) J Carroll 33/1: 603355: Prom, eff appr fnl 2f, sn btn: 12 wk abs.	hd	48
3812	**TEFI** 13 [1] 2-8-10 J Fortune 12/1: 322306: Last fnl 2f over 2f out, wknd: op 16/1, 6 wk abs, prefers fast?	¾	54
3911	**HALCYON MAGIC** 35 [8] 2-8-4 R Brisland 13/2: 526227: Handy 4f: much btr 3812, 3520 (gd grnd).	1	45
3867	**THE OLD SOLDIER** 39 [2] 2-8-8 J Stack 33/1: 008: In tch till fnl 2f: 6 wk abs, bck in trip, see 3729.	3	40
2818	**RUBY BABE** 87 [5] 2-7-12 Dale Gibson 25/1: 609: Speed till halfway: 3 month abs, see 2480.	5	18
--	**LYCIAT SPARKLE** [9] 2-8-5 D Duffield 33/1: 0: Went right start, nvr in it: 10th: Lycius gldg with Mrs G Rees.	9	5

1353

10 ran   Time 1m 21.6 (7.5)   (M Duthie)   D J S ffrench Davis Letcombe Regis, Oxon

---

4373   2.45 WHITE SWAN MDN AUCT DIV 2 2YO (F)   6f rnd   Soft 114 -34 Slow
£1820   £520   £260

3912 **CAPTAIN KOZANDO** 35 [6] Mrs G S Rees 2-8-4 G Duffield 9/4 FAV: 521: 2 b g Komaite - Times Zando   **67**
(Forzando) Prom, led appr fnl 1f, rdn out: 1,400gns foal: eff at 6f, tried further, shld stay: acts on soft,
handles fast & a stiff/undulating trck: improving.
4007 **DARWIN TOWER** 30 [5] B W Murray 2-8-6 (BL) J Carroll 20/1: 000002: 2 gr c Bin Ajwaad - Floria   *1* **65**
Tosca (Petong) Led after 1f till appr fnl 1f, kept on: big improvement forcing the pace in blnks: eff at 6f on soft.
3500 **GOOD TIMING** 57 [2] J J Quinn 2-8-7 Pat Eddery 10/3: 63: 2 bl g Timeless Times - Fort Vally   ¾ **63**
(Belfort) Bhd ldr, shaken up after halfway, kept on but unable to chall: 8 week abs: handles soft, needs 7f+.
4288 **TAMILIA** 10 [1] D W P Arbuthnot 2-8-4 A Beech (3) 20/1: -0004: In tch, feeling pace ent straight,   1¾ **55**
onepce: first sign of ability on this soft surface.
3729 **ST NICHOLAS** 47 [3] 2-8-3 R Winston 25/1: 0005: Towards rear, improved appr fnl 1f, sn no extra.   nk **53$**
4277 **JALONS STAR** 11 [9] 2-8-10 R Hughes 7/1: 5066: Early ldr, fdd ent fnl 2f: bckd from 16/1: btr 4277.   6 **45**
3729 **LIVE IN LOVER** 47 [4] 2-8-9 P Goode (3) 33/1: 007: Slow away, nvr troubled ldrs: 7 week abs: 11 **14**
6,200 gns speedily bred Up And At 'Em gelding: with P Haslam.
4252 **ARCHIRONDEL** 13 [8] 2-8-7 J Stack 20/1: 08: Struggling after 3f: see 4252.   5 **0**
-- **PERFECT LOVER** [7] 2-8-5 K Darley 11/4: 9: Al bhd: debut: 2,500gns Pursuit Of Love half brother   3 **0**
to wnrs btwn 5f & 12f: sent off 2nd fav, surley capable of better: with D Ffrench Davis.
9 ran   Time 1m 23.0 (8.9)   (Capt James Wilson)   Mrs G S Rees Sollom, Lancs

---

4374   3.15 RACING IN YORKS HCAP 3YO+ 0-70 (E)   1m2f   Soft 114 -20 Slow   [70]
£3133   £964   £482   £241   3 yo rec 5 lb

4021 **SUCH FLAIR** 30 [1] J Noseda 3-9-5 (66) Pat Eddery 11/1: 0-3041: 3 b f Kingmambo - Lady   **71**
Fairfax (Sharrood) Well plcd, pushed into lead 1f out, drvn out: unplcd sole '99 start (fill mdn, rtd 79):
apprec step up to 10f on soft grnd: handles a stiff/undulating track: qck follow-up?
4221 **RUTLAND CHANTRY** 16 [9] S Gollings 6-9-3 (59) J Fortune 9/1: 605342: 6 b g Dixieland Band -   ¾ **62**
Christchurch (So Blessed) Led, under press & hdd 1f out, rallied: a bold attempt, likes soft grnd, see 601.
4325 **KIDZ PLAY 6** [3] J S Goldie 4-9-1 (57) T Quinn 14/1: 0014P3: 4 b g Rudimentary - Saka Saka   1¼ **58**
(Camden Town) Mid div, chsd front 2 appr str, outpcd bef fnl 1f & drvn, keeping on fin: tchd 20/1, clr rem,
quick reapp after p.u. at Ayr: gd run tho' again carried head to one side, see 3963.
4256 **SOPHALA 13** [5] C F Wall 3-9-6 (67) R Hughes 12/1: 300134: Bhd, prog & briefly short of room over   4 **63**
2f out, styd on for press fnl 1f, nvr dngrs: fair run back in trip tho' set a lot to do: see 4256, 4174.
4003 **WILTON 30** [7] 5-9-9 (65) J Reid 16/1: Towards rear, imprvd ent fnl 3f, no extra dist: btr 1203.   6 **54**
4280 **MIDDLETHORPE 11** [10] 3-9-4 (65)(bl) T Lucas 9/2: 013136: Well plcd & travelled well till niggled   3½ **49**
3f out, btn 2f out, eased inside last: nicely bckd, can do much better: see 3870.
4160 **ASPIRANT DANCER 20** [11] 5-10-0 (70) A Beech (3) 10/1: 016-07: Al arnd mid div: op 8/1, top-weight.   5 **47**
38 **RIVERSDALE 338** [4] 4-8-11 (53) D O'Donohoe 33/1: 0020-8: Bhd, went thro' btn horses in str: reapp: hd **30**
'99 rnr up (h'cap, rtd 52, mdn 3rd, rtd 68): rtd 61 as a juv: eff at 1m on gd grnd, shld get 10f: J FitzGerald.
3731 **CASSANDRA 47** [14] 4-8-7 (49) T Williams 33/1: 200409: Chsd ldrs till ent str: 7 wk abs, see 1496.   3½ **22**
4213 **PERPETUO 16** [2] 3-9-5 (66) P Hanagan (5) 12/1: 362100: In tch, outpcd appr str: 10th, back in trip.   ¾ **38**
4280 **JUST GIFTED 11** [15] 4-9-5 (61) K Darley 10/1: 203640: Mid-div, fdd 2f out: 11th, back in trip, btr 3504.   2 **30**
1955 **CAUNTON 123** [6] 3-8-7 (54) G Hind 50/1: 0-0000: Al towards rear: 12th, 4 month abs, see 1184.   1¾ **21**
4226 **SPECIAL PROMISE 16** [12] 3-9-2 (63) P Goode (3) 25/1: 111000: Chsd ldrs till wknd qckly 2f out: 13th.   nk **29**
+4232 **WILEMMGEO 14** [17] 3-8-11 (58) Joanna Badger (7) 7/2 FAV: 114110: Dwelt, nvr on terms: 14th: ½ **23**
nicely bckd from 9/2: progressive earlier, prob best forgotten: see 4232 (1m, here).
4169 **Most Stylish 19** [18] 3-9-1 (62) A Daly 16/1:   4579} **Bronzino 350** [13] 5-8-12 (54)(vis) S Drowne 25/1:
2832 **Joseph Vernet 87** [8] 3-9-2 (63) G Duffield 33/1:   2175 **Mr Cospector 113** [19] 3-9-4 (65) W Supple 16/1:
18 ran   Time 2m 21.5 (13.4)   (Sanford R Robertson)   J Noseda Newmarket, Suffolk

---

4375   3.45 LISTED SILVER TANKARD STKS 2YO (A)   1m rnd   Soft 114 -07 Slow
£12528   £4752   £2376   £1080

4203 **WORTHILY 16** [1] M R Channon 2-8-11 J Reid 11/4 FAV: -05121: 2 b c Northern Spur - Worth's   **103**
Girl (Devil's Bag) Waited with, gd prog to lead appr straight, drvn ent fnl 1f, ran on strongly: nicely bckd:
earlier won at Kempton (mdn), 20,000gns colt, dam a wnr in the States: eff at 1m, 10f+ should suit next
term: clearly at home on soft grnd, prob any trck: useful & progressive colt.
4290 **RATHKENNY 10** [8] J G Given 2-8-11 Pat Eddery 50/1: 564162: 2 b c Standiford - Shine   1¾ **99$**
(Sharrood) Well plcd, pressed wnr ent straight, hard rdn & hung left below dist, held & eased towards fin:
almost certainly flattered tho' clearly suited by 1m in testing grnd: see 3957 (seller).
3882 **MARINE 38** [2] R Charlton 2-9-0 (bl) K Darley 3/1: 115533: 2 b c Marju - Ivorine (Blushing   *1* **100**
Groom) Held up, eff & badly hmpd over 2f out, hdwy appr fnl 1f, rdn inside last, kept on, nvr nrr: bckd, clr
rem: poss unlucky: likely to appr 10f next term: acts on fast & soft grnd: see 3882, 1944.
*4277 **QUINK 11** [5] Sir Mark Prescott 2-9-0 G Duffield 4/1: 313514: Pulled hard towards rear, eff 2f out,   5 **91**
moderate hdwy, nvr threatened: up in trip: see 4277.
4277 **NORTHFIELDS DANCER 11** [3] 2-8-11 R Hughes 7/2: 022125: Chsd ldrs & ch till fdd appr fnl 1f.   2½ **84**
*4297 **TUPGILL TANGO 9** [7] 2-8-11 R Winston 9/1: 016: Slow away, stiffish task, needs hdwy.   5 **74**
4072 **ZELOSO 26** [6] 2-8-11 (vis) T Quinn 12/1: 021437: Slow away, al in rear: see 4072 (1st time vis), 3787.   ½ **73**
*4249 **BROWSER 13** [4] 2-8-11 N Callan 33/1: 0318: Chsd ldrs, wknd qckly 2f out: stiff task, btr 4249 (f/sand).   1½ **70**
*4303 **BAILLIESTON 7** [3] 2-8-11 W Supple 14/1: 33519: Led till appr fnl 2f, lost pl: stiff task, qk reapp.   11 **50**
9 ran   Time 1m 51.5 (9.7)   (Salem Suhail)   M R Channon West Isley, Berks

---

4376   4.15 BLUFF COVE HCAP STKS 3YO+ 0-70 (E)   2m2f   Soft 114 -23 Slow   [60]
£2834   £872   £436   £218   3 yo rec 11lb

*4139 **SHERIFF 21** [1] J W Hills 9-9-5 (51) M Henry 8/1: 103411: 9 b g Midyan - Daisy Warwick (Ribot)   **58**
Mid-div, prog 5f out, led bef 3f out, rdn clr appr fnl 1f, eased down nr fin: earlier won at N Abbot (3m, firm & gd/soft, rtd 77a): hdles wnr at N Abbot (3m, firm & gd/soft, rtd 118h at his peak): '98 Lingfield wnr
(3 h'caps, rtd 76a & 55): eff at 2m/2m2f: acts on firm, soft & equitrack: likes Lingfield & Bath: can force it.

PONTEFRACT MONDAY OCTOBER 16TH   Lefthand, Undulating Track With Stiff Uphill Finish

4105 **SNUGFIT ROSIE 23** [13] M W Easterby 4-9-10 (56) T Quinn 7/1: 30-542: 4 ch f Kris - Sorceress 7 56
(Fabulous Dancer) Well plcd, chall 3f out, sn outstyd by wnr: eff at 2m/2m2f: acts on gd & soft grnd.
4231 **BLACK ICE BOY 14** [2] R Bastiman 9-8-10 (42)(vis) Pat Eddery 11/2: 060023: 9 b g Law Society - 7 37
Hogan's Sister (Speak John) Led till appr fnl 3f, styd on onepce: btr 4231, see 141.
3916 **OPEN GROUND 35** [12] Ian Williams 3-8-8 (51) K Darley 8/1: 016104: Mid-div, prog to go 2nd 1 45
3f out, wknd qckly inside last: return to 2m will suit: see 1613 (claimer).
*4231 **MARTHA REILLY 14** [8] 4-8-11 (43) A Mackay 5/1 FAV: 200315: Al mid-div: btr 4231 (here). 10 29
4231 **IRELANDS EYE 14** [5] 5-8-8 (40)(VIS) P Hanagan (5) 8/1: 066036: In tch, fdd 3f out: visor, btr 4213. 6 22
3476 **NICIARA 58** [11] 3-7-13 (40)(2ow) R Ffrench 14/1: 224007: Nvr a factor: op 20/1: wnr over hdles at 2½ 22
Cartmel & Sedgefield (2m1f juv novs, gd & soft grnd, rtd 109h) since last Flat start: stays 2m on firm, gd & f/sand.
4229 **MAYBEN 14** [6] 3-8-2 (45) Dale Gibson 16/1: 0-5608: Al towards rear: tchd 25/1, big step up in trip. 5 21
3993 **CHARMING ADMIRAL 31** [10] 7-9-8 (54)(VIS) G Duffield 8/1: 003039: Bhd from halfway: visored: 5 26
has won at Sedgefield (2m5f h'cap chse, blnkd) since 3993: see 876 (here).
940 **KIPPANOUR 182** [7] 8-7-10 (28) A Polli (2) 40/1: 45/050: Al bhd: 10th, hdles fit, earlier won over 29 0
fences at Uttoxeter (nov h'cap) & Worcester (h'cap chse, 3m/3m2f, firm & gd, rtd 79c, blnkd or visored): see 940.
4075 **ESTACADO 25** [9] 4-8-12 (44)(vis) J P Spencer 6/1: /00-50: Chsd ldrs, wknd qckly under press 5f out. 28 0
11 ran   Time 4m 16.6 (24.6)   (The Sherrif Partnership)   J W Hills Upper Lambourn, Berks

4377 4.45 TOTE HCAP 3YO+ 0-85 (D)   5f rnd   Soft 114 +16 Fast   [81]
£7605 £2340 £1170 £585

4285 **JAMES STARK 10** [10] N P Littmoden 3-9-12 (79)(bl) K Darley 9/1: 561531: 3 b g Up And At 'Em - 85
June Maid (Junius) Mid-div, improved appr fnl 2f, led 1f out, rdn out: fast time, top-weight: earlier won
at Goodwood (h'cap): '99 winner at Southwell (auct mdn) & Lingfield (AW h'cap, fast 85a & 64): eff at 5f/sharp
6f: acts on firm & soft grnd, both AW's: wears blnks or visor, can force the pace/carry big weights: progressive.
4294 **BOWLERS BOY 10** [12] J J Quinn 7-8-3 (56) P Hanagan (5) 10/1: 540352: 7 ch g Risk Me - Snow 1½ 57
Wonder (Music Boy) Rear, prog 2f out, ran on ins last, not ch wnr: clr rem: gd run, likes soft: see 1941.
4285 **PREMIUM PRINCESS 10** [1] J J Quinn 5-9-5 (72) Pat Eddery 7/2 FAV: 441023: 5 b m Distant Relative - 3 64
Solemn Occasion (Secreto) In tch, chsd ldrs ent straight, ch 1f out, sn onepce: nicely bckd from 6/1:
capable of better, finished in front of this wnr last time: see 3975.
4287 **CLASSY CLEO 10** [18] P D Evans 5-9-7 (74) Joanna Badger (7) 16/1: 100304: Mid-div, wide, 2½ 60
kept on appr fnl 1f, not pace to chall: see 351.
3920 **SUNLEY SENSE 34** [3] 4-9-11 (78)(VIS) T Quinn 12/1: 066465: Led till 1f out, no extra: visor. hd 64
4102 **ALBERT THE BEAR 24** [7] 7-8-2 (55)(vis) R Ffrench 25/1: 026006: Al arnd mid-div tho' stying nk 40
on firm & soft grnd, both AW's: best up with the pace over further, see 1438.
4295 **GORETSKI 10** [9] 7-8-11 (64) J Fortune 7/1: 000067: Chsd ldrs, fdd appr fnl 1f: op 5/1: see 926. hd 49
4156 **LEAPING CHARLIE 20** [16] 4-8-4 (57) G Duffield 14/1: 20-058: Mid-div, wide, nvr a factor: tchd 25/1. 1¼ 39
3894 **WATERFORD SPIRIT 38** [8] 4-8-1 (54) Iona Wands 20/1: 000009: Chsd ldrs, wknd ins last: see 1162. ½ 35
4307 **COLLEGE MAID 7** [13] 3-8-11 (64) W Supple 11/1: 040020: Nvr better than mid div: 10th, quick reapp. ½ 44
4285 **TORRENT 10** [14] 5-9-5 (72)(bl) J Carroll 10/1: 510300: Rear, prog into mid-div halfway, onepce: 11th. 1½ 48
3821 **MISS HIT 42** [4] 5-9-3 (70) J P Spencer 10/1: 102050: Al towards rear: 12th, 6 wk abs, not given hard time. ½ 45
4295 **STATOYORK 10** [17] 7-8-10 (63) T Williams 9/1: 415000: Slow away, nvr in it: 16th, see 3788. 0
-- Fiddlers Rock [6] 5-9-3 (70) J Bramhill 20/1:   4107 Nifty Norman 23 [2] 6-8-10 (63) O Pears 20/1:
4037 Najeyba 28 [5] 3-9-6 (73) B Marcus 25/1:   4185 Blue Holly 18 [15] 3-9-10 (77) R Hughes 12/1:
4285 Daawe 10 [11] 9-9-1 (bl) Alex Greaves 20/1:
18 ran   Time 1m 06.2 (4.9)   (Paul J Dixon)   N P Littmoden Newmarket, Suffolk

4378 5.15 FEATHERS NURSERY HCAP 2YO 0-75 (E)   1m rnd   Soft 114 -27 Slow   [80]
£3198 £984 £492 £246

4161 **LEATHERBACK 20** [16] N A Callaghan 2-8-1 (53) T Williams 10/1: 00001: 2 b g Turtle Island - Phyllode 59
(Pharly) Slow away, imprvd halfway, rdn ent str & styd on well to lead fnl 100y: tchd 14/1: nvr featured in 4
prev races on gd or faster, clrly relished this soft grnd: eff at 1m, get 10f next term: handles a stiff/undul trk.
4070 **SHIMLA 26** [2] R Hannon 2-8-1 (53) A Daly 40/1: 00502: 2 b f Rudimentary - Olivia Jane (Ela ¾ 56
Mana Mou) In tch, hard rdn ent fnl 3f, styd on ins last but held by wnr: suited by step up to 1m on soft grnd.
4323 **THORNTON DANCER 6** [18] J S Goldie 2-8-8 (60) W Supple 14/1: 563023: 2 b f Unfuwain - Westry hd 62
(Gone West) Nvr far away, led appr fnl 1f till fnl 100y, kept on: quick reapp, suited by soft/hvy grnd.
4117 **BOLSHOI BALLET 22** [1] J L Dunlop 2-8-9 (73) D Harrison 8/1: 033224: Prom, ch ent straight, 1 73
no extra final fin: joint top-weight, acts on fast & soft grnd: consistent.
4290 **SUN BIRD 10** [13] 2-8-8 (60)(bl) G Duffield 10/1: 505005: Sn led, hdd appr fnl 1f, onepce ½ 59
inside last: well clr of rem, blinks reapp: eff at 1m on soft grnd.
4290 **BORDER EDGE 10** [5] 2-8-3 (55) R Ffrench 33/1: 405006: Chsd ldrs, outpcd 2f out: nds sellers. 12 34
3675 **BOLLIN THOMAS 50** [9] 2-8-7 (59) B Marcus 20/1: -0007: Nvr better than mid div: 7 wk abs, h'cap bow. 7 26
4290 **GRAND FIVE 10** [7] 2-9-7 (73) R Hughes 8/1: 003208: Chsd ldrs till wknd qckly appr fnl 1f: op 6/1: 1 38
jockey reported the colt hated the grnd tho' he handled it well enough in 4076.
4154 **CALIBAN 20** [10] 2-8-5 (56)(1ow) K Darley 16/1: 05029: Al same pl: h'cap bow, see 4154 (seller). ¾ 21
4191 **SMOOTHIE 12** [12] 2-9-0 (66) J Fortune 8/1: -30540: In tch, eff 3f out, sn btn: 10th, up in trip. 3½ 24
3922 **CLASSIC MILLENNIUM 34** [17] 2-8-3 (55) R Brisland 33/1: -00000: Nvr a factor: 11th, up in trip. 3 8
4290 **THE FANCY MAN 10** [15] 2-8-12 (64)(vis) T Quinn 14/1: 060100: Al towards rear: 12th, back in trip. ½ 16
3949 **BAJAN BLUE 33** [3] 2-8-6 (58) J Carroll 16/1: 63330: Nvr dangerous: 13th, op 12/1, h'cap bow. ¾ 9
4084 **ESPANA 25** [8] 2-9-2 (68) Pat Eddery 7/2 FAV: 030520: Rdn, wide, in tch, btn ent straight & eased ¾ 18
fnl 1f: 14th, nicely bckd from 5/1: much btr 4084 (C/D fill nursery).
4235 **QUAZAR 14** [14] 2-9-1 (67) D O'Donohoe 10/1: -03050: Early ldr, wknd qckly 3f out: 18th, raced too freely. 0
4007 Christmas Morning 30 [11] 2-8-2 (54)(BL) Dale Gibson 20/1:
4084 Tenerife Flyer 25 [20] 2-8-5 (57) A Beech (3) 12/1:
1838 Golden Dragonfly 128 [6] 2-8-10 (62) J Bramhill 33/1: 4254 Kandymal 13 [19] 2-8-1 (53) P Hanagan (5) 16/1:
3632 Tony 51 [4] 2-8-1 (53) O Pears 40/1:
20 ran   Time 1m 53.1 (11.3)   (M Tabor)   N A Callaghan Newmarket, Suffolk

1355

WOLVERHAMPTON (Fibresand)   TUESDAY OCTOBER 17TH   Lefthand, Sharp Track

Official Going: STANDARD   Stalls: Inside, except 7f - Outside

4379   1.30 WILLIAM MED AUCT MDN DIV 1 2YO (F)   6f aw rnd   Going 30   -18 Slow
£1757   £502   £251

4246 **MOYNE PLEASURE** 14 [8] J A Osborne 2-9-0 S W Kelly (3) 11/4: 051: 2 b f Exit To Nowhere - Ilanga   hd   77a
(Common Grounds) Prom, rdn & short of room 1f out, drvn/styd on well cl home, just held: fin 2nd, plcd 1st:
jockey given 2-day whip ban: Ir 23,000gns purchase, first foal: dam 5/7f wnr: eff over 6f on fibresand.
--   **AFRICAN CZAR** [9] M L W Bell 2-9-0 M Fenton 10/1: 1D: 2 b c Inzar - African Grace (Fayruz)   78a
Prom, drvn/led over 1f out, all out to hold on nr fin: fin 1st, plcd 2nd: op 9/4: March foal, cost Ir 10,000gns:
first foal: dam unrcd: sire high class 6/7f performer: eff over a sharp 6f on fibresand: can find compensation.
4096 **NOSY BE** 25 [2] P J Makin 2-9-0 S Sanders 4/6 FAV: -5323: 2 b c Cyrano de Bergerac -   nk   76a
Blossomville (Petong) Dwelt, rdn chasing ldrs halfway, outpcd 2f out, drvn & styd on well inside last, nrst
fin: well bckd: AW bow: acts on fast & gd grnd, looks to be crying out for 7f+ now: see 4096, 3387.
3710 **TIMELESS FARRIER** 49 [6] B Smart 2-9-0 Paul E ddery 25/1: 66004: Led, hdd over 1f out, rdn/no   1   74$
extra when not much room nr fin: 7 week abs: AW bow: t-strap omitted: prob flattered: see 2039.
--   **ROBIN SHARP** [3] 2-9-0 P Doe 12/1: 5: In tch, eff wide halfway, btn 2f out: op 6/1, clr rem: 1   72a
First Trump colt, Jan foal: brother to a 6f wnr: dam a mdn: sire a top class 2yo performer: with W Jarvis.
4309 **WAIKIKI DANCER** 8 [4] D Sweeney 33/1: 0006: Chsd ldrs till halfway: AW bow, mod form prev.   5   55a
3853 **HURLINGHAM STAR** 41 [1] 2-9-0 J Fanning 66/1: 00667: Prom 4f: 6 wk abs, AW bow, mod form.   1¼   57$
4225 **LORD LIAM** 17 [7] 2-9-0 T G McLaughlin 6/1: 534568: Wide, al bhd: btr 3492, 3252 (firm & fast).   3   50a
3912 **PREMIER AMBITIONS** 36 [5] 2-9-0 F Norton 16/1: 009: Al bhd: op 12/1, AW bow: see 3520.   hd   49a
9 ran   Time 1m 15.7 (2.9)   (Berkeley Land Limited)   J A Osborne Lambourn, Berks

4380   2.00 RENAULT MASTER HCAP 3YO+ 0-75 (E)   6f aw rnd   Going 27   +03 Fast   [75]
£3038   £868   £434   3 yo rec 1 lb

4215 **SHOUF AL BADOU** 17 [5] B W Hills 3-9-7 (69) F Norton 11/4 FAV: 650601: 3 b c Sheikh Albadou -   76a
Millfit (Blushing Groom) Trckd ldrs, rdn/prog to lead inside last, styd on strongly for press, eased nr line: good
time: bckd, op 4/1: '99 wnr here at W'hampton (2, mdn & stakes, rtd 97a) & Doncaster (stakes, rtd 97): eff at
7f/1m, suited by this drop to 6f: acts on fast, hvy & loves fibresand: acts on a gall or sharp trck, loves W'hampton
(unbtn here from 3 starts): looks well h'capped & could win again in a similar contest.
3765 **MISTER TRICKY** 46 [10] P Mitchell 5-10-0 (75) J Quinn 10/1: 100002: 5 ch g Magic Ring - Splintering   2   76a
(Sharpo) Mid div, rdn & styd on fnl 1f, no impress on wnr: abs: acts on firm, gd/soft & both AWs: see 881.
3257 **RING DANCER** 68 [11] P J Makin 5-10-0 (75) S Sanders 7/1: 000103: 5 b g Polar Falcon - Ring   ¾   74a
Cycle (Auction Ring) Dwelt, rear, hdwy wide halfway, kept on fnl 1f, no threat: op 9/1: 10 wk abs: acts on firm,
gd/soft & fibresand: fine run despite being staid: can rate higher: see 3769.
4207 **PERIGEUX** 17 [6] K T Ivory 4-9-6 (67)(bl) C Carver (3) 20/1: 003004: Led 1f, drvn/briefly led again   ½   64a
over 1f out, no extra inside last: blinks reapp: see 2428.
4165 **DAYS OF GRACE** 20 [12] 5-9-9 (70) C Rutter 13/2: 142065: Towards rear/wide, late gains, nrst fin.   1   65a
3123 **BLACK ARMY** 74 [13] 5-9-6 (67) F Lynch 16/1: -05156: Chsd ldrs halfway, nvr able to chall: abs.   nk   61a
4136 **QUIET VENTURE** 23 [8] 6-10-0 (75)(tvi) R Winston 50/1: 410007: Towards rear/wide, mod late hdwy.   nk   68a
678 **TELECASTER** 215 [3] 4-9-13 (74)(bl) D Sweeney 13/2: 211528: Led after 1f till over 1f out, fdd: nk   66a
op 5/1, 7 month abs: showed up well for a long way, shld prove sharper for this in similar: see 622 (C/D).
4069 **ACE OF PARKES** 27 [7] 4-9-9 (70) O Pears 25/1: 030009: Chsd ldrs 4f: AW bow: op 1245.   2½   55a
4331 **CASTLE SEMPILL** 6 [2] 3-9-10 (72)(vis) R Studholme 9/1: 040360: Chsd ldrs 4f: 10th: qck reapp.   2½   50a
3569 **SOMESESSION** 55 [4] 3-9-13 (75) P Hanagan (5) 10/1: 001000: Al towards rear: 11th: op 8/1,   hd   52a
7 wk abs: prev with Ms J Morgan, now with R A Fahey: AW bow today: see 3349.
4069 **SUMTHINELSE** 27 [1] 3-9-11 (73) T G McLaughlin 7/1: 460300: Al outpcd fnl 1f: 12th: btr 3771 (7f).   nk   49a
*3774 **RUSSIAN ROMEO** 45 [9] 5-9-11 (72)(bl) M Fenton 5/1: 023510: Bhd: 13th, something amiss?   1¼   45a
13 ran   Time 1m 14.4 (1.6)   (Hilal Salem)   B W Hills Lambourn, Berks

4381   2.30 WILLIAM MED AUCT MDN DIV 2 2YO (F)   6f aw rnd   Going 30   -18 Slow
£1750   £500   £250

3830 **TUMBLEWEED TENOR** 42 [2] B J Meehan 2-9-0 D R McCabe 11/4: -52031: 2 b g Mujadil - Princess Carmen 75a
(Arokar) Cl up, drvn/duelled with rnr up fnl 1f, narrowly preveiled, all out: op 7/2: 6 wk abs: AW bow:
eff between 5/7f on firm & fibresand: likes a sharp trk: runs well fresh.
4090 **A C AZURE** 25 [4] P D Evans 2-9-0 T G McLaughlin 10/1: -65302: 2 br g Dolphin Street - Kelvedon   1   72a
(General Assembly) Prom, led 2f out, joined & duelled with wnr fnl 1f, just held cl home: prob handles
gd grnd & fibresand: return to 7f+ & h'cap company should suit: see 3866, 3508.
4188 **MYSTERI DANCER** 18 [7] R J O'Sullivan 2-9-0 P Doe 2/1 FAV: 0223: 2 b g Rudimentary - Mystery   1¼   69a
Ship (Decoy Boy) Chsd ldrs, kept on onepace fnl 2f: AW bow: btr 4188, 3832 (firm & soft).
4253 **FLY BOY FLY** 14 [8] M Johnston 2-9-0 K Darley 11/4: -4644: Rdn & towards rear/wide, mod late   2½   62a
hdwy, nvr a threat: AW bow: handles gd, soft & prob fibresand: should improve when returning to 7f+: see 2628.
4247 **BETTER OFF** 14 [6] 2-9-0 R Fitzpatrick 33/1: 55: Prom 3f: see 4247 (5f).   1¾   58a
--   **HANDSOME BADSHA** [3] 2-9-0 (t) S W Kelly (3) 16/1: 6: Nvr on terms with ldrs: Petardia colt,   2½   51a
April foal, cost 7,500gns: half brother to a 5f juv wnr: dam a Irish 9f wnr: with J Osborne.
3679 **LAI SEE** 50 [1] 2-9-0 J Quinn 7/1: 225557: Led 4f, fdd: op 5/1, 7 wk abs: visor omitted on AW bow.   3½   42a
4187 **FAST FORTUNE** 18 [5] 2-8-9 J Tate 11/1: 08: Chsd ldrs 4f: op 8/1: AW bow: btr 4187 (soft).   5   25a
--   **THE TUBE** [9] 2-8-9 A Nicholls 25/1: 9: Slowly away & al bhd: Royal Abjar filly, March foal, cost   4   15a
Ir8,000gns: a first foal: dam a mdn: sire a high class miler abroad: with A Reid.
9 ran   Time 1m 15.7 (2.9)   (The Seventh Tumbleweed Partnership)   B J Meehan Upper Lambourn, Berks

4382   3.00 KANGOO HCAP 3YO 0-75 (E)   1m1f79y aw   Going 30   -08 Slow   [81]
£2843   £875   £437   £218

*4251 **FARAWAY LOOK** 14 [2] J R Fanshawe 3-9-4 (71) D Harrison 1/1 FAV: 42011: 3 br c Distant View -   83a
Summer Trip (L'Emigrant) Al prom, led over 3f out & sn cruised clr, eased down fnl 1f: val for 5L+: well
bckd, op 6/4: recent wnr here at W'hampton (C/D h'cap, first win): eff between 7/9.5f should get further: acts on
fibresand & handles gd: likes a sharp trk, esp W'hampton: progressive colt, plenty in hand here, can win again.

4313 **SHALBEBLUE 8** [11] B Ellison 3-8-5 (58)(vis) D Sweeney 16/1: 004042: 3 b g Shalford - Alberjas   1¾   60a
(Sure Blade) Mid div, rdn/chsd wnr over 1f out, kept on tho' flattered by margin of defeat: AW bow: eff around
9/10f on firm & fibresand: eff in a visor.

4046 **FISHER ISLAND 28** [5] R Hollinshead 3-7-12 (51) P M Quinn (3) 16/1: 401053: 3 b f Sri Pekan -   1½   50a
Liberty Song (Last Tycoon) Towards rear, kept on fnl 2f, nvr a threat: op 14/1: see 2685.

4173 **SHAMSAN 20** [12] M Johnston 3-9-0 (67)(bl) J Fanning 8/1: 223034: Cl up, briefly led 4f out, sn no   2   62a
impress: clr rem: op 6/1: see 4173, 3093.

4251 **ABSINTHER 14** [3] J Carroll 11/4: 312525: Mid div, btn 3f out: op 2/1: btr 4251, 3591.   6   43a

4306 **SLANEYSIDE 8** [9] 3-8-4 (57) G Bardwell 33/1: 010006: Rear, little hdwy: btr 3741 (3 rnr stks, 12f).   2½   35a

4256 **CHIEF OF JUSTICE 14** [1] 3-9-5 (72) S W Kelly (3) 14/1: 113007: Al twds rear: op 10/1: btr 640 (12f).   3½   43a

3810 **NOBLE SPLENDOUR 44** [13] 3-8-9 (62) K Darley 12/1: 334508: Chsd ldrs over 3f out, sn wknd: abs.   2   29a

2411 **SWISS ALPS 104** [6] 3-7-11 (49)(bl) (1ow) Dale Gibson 33/1: -00009: Led 5f, fdd: abs: see 2411.   1½   14a

4248 **MISS WORLD 14** [8] 3-8-9 (62) J Quinn 33/1: 050000: Al bhd: 10th: btr 213 (1m, t-strap).   18   0a

4360 **ARIZONA LADY 3** [7] 3-9-0 (67) R Winston 10/1: 500240: Prom 5f: 11th: quick reapp: btr 4360, 4228.   5   0a
11 ran   Time 2m 01.6 (3.4)   (Cheveley Park Stud)   J R Fanshawe Newmarket, Suffolk

---

4383   3.30 TRAFIC MDN AUCT DIV 1 2YO (E)   7f aw rnd   Going 30   +04 Fast
    £2219   £634   £317

4095 **ASWHATILLDOIS 25** [1] D J S Cosgrove 2-8-1 C Rutter 20/1: 0501: 2 b f Blues Traveller - Reasonably   66a
French (Reasonable) Made all, pressed & held on well fnl 1f, rdn out: gd juv time: apprec step up to 7f, 1m
shld suit: acts on fibresand & eff forcing the pace: gd AW bow, open to further improvement.

--   **FOREIGN AFFAIRS** [9] Sir Mark Prescott 2-8-12 S Sanders 8/15 FAV: 2: 2 ch c Hernando - Entente   ½   75a
Cordiale (Affirmed) Slowly away, sn tracking ldrs, rdn/chsd wnr fnl 2f, styd on well, al just held: hvly bckd at odds
on: Jan foal, cost 20,000gns: brother to useful 10f performer Bien Entendu: sire top class 12f performer: eff
at 7f, crying out for 1m+: acts on fibresand: clr of rem here, sure to rate higher & relish 1m+.

3940 **CELTIC MISSION 34** [7] M Johnston 2-8-12 K Darley 3/1: 053: 2 ch g Cossene - Norfolk Lavender   5   65a
(Ascot Knight) Prom, no impress over 1f out: op 2/1: AW bow: btr 3940, 3840 (fm).

4137 **NOON GUN 22** [5] W R Muir 2-8-10 D Harrison (7): 44: Chsd ldrs, outpcd fnl 2f: op 5/1, AW bow: ½   62a
this longer 7f trip will suit: fin well clr of rem here: see 4137.

--   **BUDDELIEA** [4] 2-8-1 P M Quinn (3) 40/1: 5: Slowly away, nvr on terms: Pivotal filly, March foal,   11   36a
cost 5,000gns: dam plcd in Listed comp in Ireland: sire a high class sprinter: with J S Moore.

4267 **AMIGO 13** [3] 2-8-12 J Fanning 10/1: 066: In tch 4f: AW bow: btr 4267, 3867.   ½   46a

3976 **KALUKI 32** [6] 2-8-8 S W Kelly (3) 20/1: 332207: Prom 3f: AW bow: btr 3732, 3582.   1¾   39a

4209 **ELYSIAN FIELDS 17** [2] 2-8-7 M Fenton 33/1: 08: Al bhd: AW bow, longer 7f trip.   14   17a

4164 **PHARMACYS PET 20** [8] A Nicholls 40/1: -00069: Prom 2f, sn struggling: AW bow, mod form.   20   0a
9 ran   Time 1m 28.00 (1.8)   (The Cosgrove Group)   D J S Cosgrove Newmarket, Suffolk

---

4384   4.00 WALKERS SELLER 3YO (G)   7f aw rnd   Going 30   -29 Slow
    £1939   £554   £277

4272 **VALENTINES VISION 13** [4] N P Littmoden 3-9-0 J Tate 6/1: 0-0341: 3 b g Distincly North - Sharp   50a
Anne (Belfort) Dwelt, trcking ldrs halfway, drvn/chall & narrow lead fnl 1f, just prevailed, all out: bought in for
2,600gns: first win: rtd 63 in '99 (auction mdn): eff at 7f, tried 9f: acts on firm & both AWs: likes a sharp trk.

4328 **STOP THE TRAFFIC 6** [12] C N Allen 3-8-9 (t) J Quinn 12/1: 560002: 3 b f College Chapel - Miss   hd   44a
Bagatelle (Mummy's Pet) Held up, prog/rdn & narrow lead over 1f out, hdd inside last, kept on well for press, just
held: quick reapp: clr rem: back to form on return to fibresand but a mdn after 23: see 397, 286.

4223 **VILLA ROMANA 17** [6] W M Brisbourne 3-8-9 T G McLaughlin 7/4: -06503: 3 b f Komaite - Keep   3½   37a
Quiet (Reprimand) Prom, rdn over 1f out, no extra inside last: bckd, op 9/4: acts on fast, soft & fibresand.

2900 **GRAND BAHAMIAN 84** [2] J Noseda 3-9-5 (BL) K Darley 5/4 FAV: 010P04: Trckd ldrs, drvn/btn over   1½   44a
1f out: first time blinks, well bckd: 12 wk abs, AW bow: btr 840 (g/s, mdn, made all).

4087 **MARON 26** [1] 3-9-5 J Carroll 9/1: 100005: Led after 3f till over 1f out, fdd: btr 2440 (fast).   1   42a

4293 **CONSIDERATION 11** [8] 3-8-9 J Lowe 16/1: 420006: Chsd ldrs halfway, wknd over 1f out: btr 2640.   1   30a

4361 **KERRIDGE CHAPEL 3** [10] 3-8-9 (bl) Martin Dwyer 50/1: 006007: Chsd ldrs 5f: mod form.   7   16a

4142 **PETRIE 22** [7] 3-9-0 Jonjo Fowle 33/1: 006008: Al bhd: see 2291, 42.   1¾   18a

3775 **SANDOWN CLANTINO 45** [11] 3-8-9 Dean McKeown 50/1: -0009: Dwelt, al bhd: 6 wk abs, AW bow.   2   9a

3964 **SKI FREE 33** [5] 3-8-9 S Sanders 40/1: -60000: Led 3f, sn btn: 10th: mod form.   9   0a

3670 Croeso Adref 51 [3] 3-9-0 D Mernagh (3) 20/1:   4081 Fay King 26 [9] 3-9-0 F Norton 50/1:
12 ran   Time 1m 30.3 (4.1)   (Alan Miller & Mrs Maggie McClean)   N P Littmoden Newmarket, Suffolk

---

4385   4.30 TRAFIC MDN AUCT DIV 2 2YO (E)   7f aw rnd   Going 30   -31 Slow
    £2219   £634   £317

4225 **MONTE MAYOR GOLF 17** [3] D Haydn Jones 2-8-1 F Norton 33/1: 506001: 2 b f Case Law - Nishiki   71a
(Brogan) Led 1f, remained prom, rdn/led again inside last, styd on well, rdn out: unplcd/mod form prev:
eff at 7f, 1m could suit: acts on fibresand & a sharp trck.

4332 **SYLVAN GIRL 6** [4] C N Allen 2-8-7 Martin Dwyer 7/4: 040052: 2 ch f Case Law - Nordic Living   2½   72a
(Nordico) Prom, led halfway & clr over 1f out, wknd/hdd inside last & no extra: well bckd, op 5/2: quick reapp:
confirmed improv of latest: handles fast, gd/soft & both AWs: return to 6f could suit: see 4332 (stks).

3678 **GAMITAS 50** [1] A P Jarvis 2-8-1 J Quinn 11/1: 03: 2 b f Dolphin Street - Driftholme (Safawan)   hd   65a
Twds rear, styd on well fnl 1f, not reach wnr: abs: AW bow: eff at 7f, return to 1m should suit: acts on fibresand.

4083 **BASINET 26** [6] D W Barker 2-8-10 F Lynch 11/10 FAV: 034: Prom, onepce fnl 2f: op 4/5: AW bow.   1½   71a

3866 **NUGGET 40** [8] 2-8-12 J Fanning 8/1: 05: Slowly away, in tch halfway, outpcd fnl 3f: clr rem: abs.   1   71a

3867 **FLYING FAISAL 40** [7] 2-8-12 S W Kelly (3) 6/1: 06: Led after 1f till halfway, btn 2f out: op 12/1, abs.   7   58a

3911 **SANAPTA 36** [2] 2-8-1 P Doe (7): 07: Al bhd: longer 7f trip, mod form.   2   42a

--   **TEMPER TANTRUM** [9] 2-8-6 A Nicholls 14/1: 8: Slowly away, al bhd: Pursuit Of Love gelding,   14   25a
March foal: cost 4,500gns: dam unraced: fin 7f 2yo wnr: with A Reid.

--   **SILK ON SONG** [5] 2-8-10 Paul Eddery 10/1: 9: Al bhd: op 5/1: Hazaam colt, May foal, 15,000gns   6   17a
2yo: half brother to a wnr abroad: dam a lightly rcd mdn: with B Smart.
9 ran   Time 1m 30.5 (4.3)   (Mrs E M Haydn Jones)   D Haydn Jones Efail Isaf, Rhondda C Taff

WOLVERHAMPTON (Fibresand) TUESDAY OCTOBER 17TH Lefthand, Sharp Track

4386

5.0 RENAULT HCAP 3YO+ 0-60 (F) **1m4f aw** **Going 30** **-17 Slow** [59]
£2530 £723 £361   3 yo rec 7 lb

4026 **MYSTERIUM 31** [12] N P Littmoden 6-9-5 (50) T G McLaughlin 7/4 FAV: 100031: 6 gr g Mystiko - Way **55a**
To Go (Troy) Held up, prog wide fnl 4f & led 2f out, hdd inside last, styd on gamely to lead again line, all out:
bckd, op 9/4: earlier scored here at W'hampton (h'cap), Windsor (h'cap) & Newmarket (lady riders h'cap, rtd 56):
'99 Yarmouth wnr (rtd 44) & W'hampton (h'caps, rtd 53a): eff at 9/12f on fast, gd & fibresand: best without a vis.
4046 **SHARP BELLINE 28** [8] J L Harris 3-9-0 (52) S Sanders 10/1: 404262: 3 b g Robellino - Moon shd **56a**
Watch (Night Shift) Prom, led 3f out till 2f out, drvn/narrow lead again inside last, hdd line: well clr rem: styd
longer 12f trip: remains a mdn but shown enough to find similar: see 4021 (mdn h'cap).
4176 **STITCH IN TIME 20** [5] G C Bravery 4-9-4 (49) A Nicholls 8/1: 433323: 4 ch g Inchinor - Late 6 **44a**
Matinee (Red Sunset) Keen/prom, no impress fnl 2f: see 4176, 3499.
4258 **ALDWYCH ARROW 14** [10] M A Buckley 5-9-5 (50) A Culhane 5/1: 060254: Prom, onepce/held fnl 2f. hd **44a**
4074 **PAARL ROCK 27** [6] 5-9-1 (46) (vis) G Gibbons (7) 10/1: 441605: Led 9f: btr 3524 (10f, made all). 9 **30a**
3915 **ARBENIG 36** [9] 5-9-3 (48) D Sweeney 12/1: 204026: Chsd ldr, btn 3f out: btr 3915, 1732 (1m, clmr). hd **31a**
3603 **SWINGING THE BLUES 53** [3] 6-9-9 (54) (vis) F Lynch 16/1: 010007: Al rear: abs, AW bow: vis reapp. 8 **28a**
4228 **SACREMENTUM 17** [7] 5-9-9 (54) S W Kelly (3) 14/1: 424F68: Rear, btn 3f out: see 2295, 381 & 326. 2 **25a**
4226 **FALCON SPIRIT 17** [1] 4-9-3 (48) (bl) J Carroll 7/1: 004059: Al rear: blinks reapp: see 4226, 2836. ¾ **18a**
1934 **NO LANGUAGE PLEASE 124** [4] 6-9-10 (55) J Lowe 14/1: 130: Rear, eff 4f out, no impress: 10th: 7 **15a**
op 9/1, AW bow, 4 month abs: better on turf earlier, see 1934, 1647 (claimer).
1857} **Stakis Casinos Boy 496** [11] 6-9-4 (49) F Norton 25/1:4258 **Moonlight Monty 14** [2] 4-9-9 (54) R Winston 16/1:
12 ran Time 2m 39.2 (5.6)   (Alcester Associates)   N P Littmoden Newmarket, Suffolk

YARMOUTH TUESDAY OCTOBER 17TH Lefthand, Flat, Fair Track

Official Going SOFT. Stalls: Inside, except Straight course - Far side

4387

1.50 RANWORTH MDN DIV 1 3YO (D) **7f str** **Soft 107** **-02 Slow**
£3360 £1034 £517 £258 Raced stands side

3696 **IN THE ARENA 50** [12] B W Hills 3-9-0 Pat Eddery 9/1: 434001: 3 ch g Cadeaux Genereux - **80**
Tajfah (Shadeed) Led, pushed clr appr fnl 1f, eased down nr fin: 7 wk abs: well btn both juv starts: eff forcing
the pace over an easy 7f, stays 1m: acts on gd grnd, suited by soft: runs well fresh: hurdles type.
971 **AKHIRA 181** [4] S P C Woods 3-8-9 R Mullen 9/2: 45-02: 3 b f Emperor Jones - Fakhira (Jareer) 3½ **69**
Towards rear, prog to go 2nd ent fnl 2f, hard rdn, onepce: op 7/2, 6 month abs: v promising debut 4th last
term (val sales stks, rtd 90), well below that since: eff over a stiff 7f on gd grnd, prob handles soft.
-- **THERE WITH ME** [2] J H M Gosden 3-8-9 R Hills 9/2: 3: 3 b f Distant View - Breeze Lass (It's ½ **68**
Freezing) Held up, prog 2f out, pressed rnr up ent fnl 1f till nr fin: pulled well clr of rem on debut: $65,000
filly, dam 5f wnr: gets 7f & prob handles soft grnd.
4038 **SINCERITY 29** [6] J R Fanshawe 3-8-9 M Hills 7/2 FAV: -02304: Cl up, no extra fnl 2f: best 2464 (gd). 8 **53**
4177 **DOUBLE FAULT 20** [3] 3-8-9 (bl) A Daly 40/1: 000045: Chsd ldrs, fdd ent fnl 2f: stiff task, jumps rnr. 2 **49$**
1263 **PEKANESE 158** [10] B Marcus 5/1: 6206: Chsd ldrs, hung left/btn 2f out: op 7/2: btr 1012. shd **54**
-- **LOUEST** [8] 3-9-0 D Holland 6/1: 7: Went right start, in tch till 2f out: op 4/1 on debut: 1¼ **52**
350,000gns Gone West colt: dam a useful 9/10f wnr in France: G Wragg & shld be capable of better.
4273 **ASSURANCE 13** [9] 3-9-0 W Supple 33/1: 508: Chsd ldrs, wknd qckly 2f out: stiff task. 8 **38**
4207 **RUN FOR GLORY 17** [7] 3-9-0 N Pollard 40/1: 0-09: Al bhd: beat 1 home sole juv start: with D Elsworth. 4 **30**
-- **PETITE GALERIE** [5] 3-8-9 T Williams 14/1: 0: Sn handy, wknd rapidly ent fnl 3f: 10th, debut: 2½ **20**
17,000gns Pips Pride half-sister to useful chaser Chief's Song & a couple of winning sprinters: with T Mills.
3796 **MISTY BOY 44** [1] 3-9-0 G Carter 40/1: 60-000: Bhd after halfway: 11th, 6 wk abs, stiff task. 5 **15**
11 ran Time 1m 30.3 (7.7)   (Maktoum Al Maktoum)   B W Hills Lambourn, Berks

4388

2.20 RANWORTH MDN DIV 2 3YO (D) **7f str** **Soft 107** **+01 Fast**
£3341 £1028 £514 £257 Raced stands side

4273 **RUSSIAN RHAPSODY 13** [2] M A Jarvis 3-8-9 P Robinson 4/1: 542221: 3 b f Cosmonaut - **80**
Hannah's Music (Music Boy) Led, incrsd pace 2f out, clr after, rdn out: nicely bckd, fair time, enterprising
ride: unrcd juv: eff forcing the pace at 7f, prob stys 1m: acts on gd, suited by soft grnd, prob any track.
4126 **FREDDY FLINTSTONE 23** [10] R Hannon 3-9-0 R Hughes 4/1: 234302: 3 b c Bigstone - Daring Ditty 5 **75**
(Daring March) Bhd, prog ent fnl 2f rdn dist, kept on for 2nd but no ch wnr: op 9/4: acts on firm grnd,
prob handles soft: will apprec a return to 1m & h'cap company: see 1183.
4274 **MAC BE LUCKY 13** [9] J Noseda 3-9-0 J Weaver 15/8 FAV: 002023: 3 b c Magic Ring - Take Heart shd **75**
(Electric) Waited with, eff 2f out, briefly short of room, kept on, nvr dangerous: nicely bckd: given
an uninspired ride by the usually astute J Weaver: see 4274 (led), 3477.
4093 **CONISTON MILL 25** [1] W R Muir 3-8-9 J P Spencer 20/1: 34: Prom, eff ent fnl 2f, same pace. hd **69**
4273 **DEFIANT 13** [3] 3-9-0 P D'Arcy 40/1: 005: Dwelt, chsd ldrs till fdd appr fnl 1f: Indian Ridge colt. 2 **70**
4273 **MUCH ADO 13** [8] 3-9-0 J Fortune 20/1: 06: Hmpd after 2f, rear, nvr got in it: Mujtahid filly, nds further? 3 **59**
3977 **GALLANT 32** [4] 3-9-0 Pat Eddery 7/2: 0-347: Chsd ldrs, rdn appr fnl 1f, no impress, eased: backed. hd **64**
4202} **PUSSIE WILLOW 381** [6] 3-8-9 P Dobbs (5) 16/1: 20-8: In tch till ent fnl 2f: op 12/1: reapp: rnr up nk **58**
first of 2 juv starts (fill mdn, rtd 88): eff at 5f poss gets 6f: acts on fast grnd, poss gd/soft: with P Cole.
3343 **CHICANERY 65** [5] 3-9-0 Kristin Stubbs (7) 50/1: -69: Handy 4f: 9 week abs. 2 **59**
4004 **SWING CITY 31** [7] 3-8-9 M Tebbutt 66/1: 030000: Al towards rear: 10th, stiff task. 10 **38**
1155 **FIORA 165** [11] 3-8-9 R Price 50/1: -00: Nvr on terms: 11th, 5 month abs: Sri Pekan filly. nk **37**
11 ran Time 1m 30.0 (7.4)   (Magno Pulse Ltd)   M A Jarvis Newmarket, Suffolk

1358

4389   2.50 EBF WICKHAMPTON NOV STKS 2YO (D)   7f str   Soft 107   -12 Sow
£3786   £1165   £582   £291   Raced stands side

4243 **LAGUDIN** 16 [6] L M Cumani 2-9-5 J P Spencer 11/2: 121: 2 b c Eagle Eyed - Liaison (Blushing   93
Groom) Made all, pshd out to hold rnr-up fnl 1f: op 4/1: earlier won debut at Newmarket (mdn): half-brother
to wnrs between 1m & 12f, dam 10f wnr: eff at 7f, stays 1m & should get at least 10f next term: acts on gd & soft
grnd, handles hvy, stiff/gall track: suited forcing the pace: useful, progressive colt.
3999 **MUTHAABER** 31 [1] J H M Gosden 2-8-12 R Hills 2/5 FAV: -52: 2 b c Machiavellian - Raheefa   ¾ 83
(Riverman) Trckd wnr throughout, niggled appr fnl 1f, styd on but al held: well bckd from 8/13: clr rem
& ran well tho' defeat not expected after eyecatching debut: handles firm & soft grnd, probably needs 1m.
-- **HOUSEPARTY** [4] Sir Michael Stoute 2-8-9 Pat Eddery 6/1: 3: 2 b c Grand Lodge - Special   9 65+
Display (Welsh Pageant) Prom when jinked violently right after 2f, unable to go with front pair 2f out, pshd out
out to keep 3rd: op 4/1: IR 100,000gns brother to a 7f juv, dam a winning juv: likely to leave this well bhd in time.
-- **ALMAYDAN** [3] Sir Michael Stoute 2-8-9 W Supple 20/1: 4: Held up, hmpd after 2f, improved   ¾ 64
halfway, no extra 2f out: op 14/1, stablemate 3rd: Marju colt, dam useful 10/12f performer: bred for 10f+.
-- **BANSTEAD** [2] T Williams 2-8-9 Pat Eddery nk/2: 5: Handy, outpcd appr fnl 2f: debut: 42,000gns Known   nk 63
Fact colt: dam & half brother wnrs in the States, sire a miler: with T Mills.
-- **PRINCE ALBERT** [5] 2-8-9 S Whitworth 50/1: 6: Dwelt & badly hmpd more than once after 2f, left   3½ 57
bhd appr fnl 2f: 3,400gns Rock City gldg, half brother to a wng juv sprinter, dam a decent maiden: forget this.
-- **REDNAP** [7] 2-8-9 G Hind 16/1: 7: Bmpd after 2f, bhd: op 12/1: IR 45,000gns Red Ransom first foal.   3 51
7 ran   Time 1m 30.9 (8.3)   (Miss G Gatto Roissard)   L M Cumani Newmarket, Suffolk

---

4390   3.20 MAUTBY COND STKS 2YO (C)   6f   Soft 107   -11 Slow
£5779   £2192   £1096   £498   Raced stands side

3693 **SIR FRANCIS** 50 [8] J Noseda 2-9-2 Pat Eddery 7/4 FAV: 061321: 2 b g Common Grounds - Red Note   98
(Rusticaro) Qckly grabbed stands rail, made all, clr appr fnl 1f, easily: well bckd from 11/4, 7 wk abs, jockey
given 4 day ban for irresp. riding: earlier won at Brighton (2, mdn & nursery): eff at 5f, best at 6f: acts on
fast & soft, poss not hvy: likes Brighton & forcing the pace: goes v well fresh & can carry big weights: useful
gelding, 4th consecutive wnr to make all down stands rail.
4157 **TRILLIE** 21 [4] D R C Elsworth 2-9-2 T Quinn 13/2: -11602: 2 b f Never So Bold - Trull (Lomond)   4 88
Prom, wide, drvn ent fnl 2f, kept on for 2nd but no ch wnr: op 5/1: prob ran to best: eff at 6f, will apprec
a return to 7f: acts on fast & soft grnd: see 3591.
4203 **MATLOCK** 17 [6] P F I Cole 2-9-2 J Fortune 5/2: -143: 2 b c Barathea - Palio Flyer (Slip Anchor)   ¾ 86
Chsd ldrs, shaken up appr fnl 1f, kept on same pace: prob not far off best tho' will apprec a return to 7f+:
acts on fast, handles soft: see 2921 (made all).
3425 **TEREED ELHAWA** 60 [9] E A L Dunlop 2-8-11 G Carter 6/1: 63144: Rcd in 2nd, onepce dist: 9 wk abs.   ½ 80
3567 **SHUSH** 55 [5] 2-9-2 P Robinson 7/1: 601005: Chsd ldrs, no extra appr fnl 1f: 8 wk abs, op 11/2, see 2773.   2 79
3895 **MISDEMEANOR** 38 [1] 2-8-6 R Havlin 100/1: 056: Nvr troubled ldrs: stiff task & poss flattered.   3½ 60
4281 **DUNKIRK SPIRIT** 11 [3] 2-8-11 R Ffrench 66/1: 007: Dwelt, al towards rear: stiff task, needs sells.   nk 64
-- **AMWELL STAR** [10] 2-8-7(1ow) S Whitworth 50/1: 8: Nvr on terms: highly tried on debut: 2½ 54
Silver Buck half-sister to a cple of wnrs in the States: dam 7f wnr, sire a dirt performer in the USA.
-- **FRIENDLY HOSTESS** [11] 2-8-6 (BL) A Daly 100/1: 9: Dwelt, sn struggling: blnkd for debut: 18 33
800gns Environment Friend half-sister to 3 wnrs, dam 7f/10f wnr: with J Gilbert.
4277 **ZANGOOEY** 12 [7] 2-8-11 M Tebbutt 66/1: 00: Al bhd: 10th: Polar Falcon gelding.   nk 37
4042 **BEANBOY** 28 [2] 2-8-11 P McCabe 100/1: 60: Bhd from halfway: 11th, needs sellers.   hd 36
11 ran   Time 1m 17.5 (7.1)   (L P Calvente)   J Noseda Newmarket, Suffolk

---

4391   3.50 MARTHAM SELL HCAP 3-4YO 0-60 (G)   1m3f101y   Soft 107   -08 Slow   [58]
£2012   £575   £287   3 yo rec 6 lb

4208 **THOMAS HENRY** 17 [6] J S Moore 4-8-9 (39) N Farmer (7) 6/1: 646351: 4 br g Petardia - Hitopah   44
(Bustino) Trckd ldrs, trav well, led ent fnl 3f, pshd clr towards fin: bght in for 4250gns: '99 wnr at Lingfield
(mdn, rtd 63a & 70): rtd 78 in '98 (visor): eff at 10/12f: acts on firm, soft grnd & equitrack, any trk.
3935 **GAME TUFTY** 34 [4] P Howling 4-9-2 (46) R Mullen 11/2: 000622: 4 b g Sirgame - Melancolia   4 46
(Legend Of France) Towards rear, improved ent straight & chsd wnr 2f out, onepace under press inside
last: tchd 8/1: eff at 1m/10f, stays 11.5f: goes on gd & soft grnd: see 1210.
4176 **LUNAR LORD** 20 [13] J S Moore 4-8-1 (31) T Williams 5/1 FAV: 244033: 4 b g Elmaamul - Cache   nk 30
(Bustino) Cl up, led ent straight till bef 2f out, onepce till kept on towards fin: shorter-priced stablemate
of wnr, clr rem: ran nr to best: see 2254, 1465.
4186 **PROUD CAVALIER** 18 [5] K Bell 4-7-13 (29) A Mackay 25/1: 004004: Keen bhd ldrs, shaken up 3f   3½ 24
out, no impress: moderate tho' will prob apprec a drop back in trip.
4041 **SILKEN LADY** 28 [7] 4-7-10 (26)(7oh) G Baker (5) 33/1: 360505: Mid div, chsd ldrs 3f out, sn onepace.   2½ 18
3827 **RUNAWAY STAR** 43 [15] 3-8-4 (40) L Newton 16/1: 665006: Held up, prog & ch ent str, fdd 2f out.   2½ 29
4292 **LADY MUCK** 11 [10] 4-9-0 (44) Craig Williams 33/1: 00-007: Nvr better than mid div: unplcd in '99   5 27
(h'cap, rtd 50): juv wnr at Epsom (auct mdn, rtd 73): eff at 7f/1m: acts on firm & gd/soft grnd, with/without
blnks: best held up: nicely h'capped if returning to form: with D Ffrench Davis.
4029 **INDIANA SPRINGS** 29 [1] 3-8-7 (43) D Holland 10/1: 603538: Held up, brief eff 3f out: tchd 14/1.   6 20
3921 **SOBER AS A JUDGE** 35 [11] 3-7-13 (35) R Ffrench 16/1: 300009: Nvr on terms: lngr trip, see 2413.   5 7
3773 **FLY LIKE A BIRD** 45 [9] 4-7-13 (29) J Mackay(5) 8/1: 400550: In tch till appr fnl 2f: 6 wk abs, see 2075.   ½ 0
4066 **GREEN MAGICAL** 27 [8] 4-9-1 (45) J P Spencer 6/1: 304-00: Led till ent str, sn btn: 15th, op 3/1, lngr trip.   0
4248 **Edifice** 14 [2] 4-10-0 (58) B Marcus 14/1:   2423 **Chilli** 104 [3] 3-8-9 (45)(vis) P Robinson 16/1:
4229 **Http Flyer** 15 [14] 3-8-5 (40)(BL)(1ow) Pat Eddery 14/1: 2651 **Te Anau** 95 [12] 3-8-1 (37) N Pollard 25/1:
15 ran   Time 2m 36.0 (13.2)   (J S Moore)   J S Moore East Garston, Berks

---

4392   4.20 TOTE EXACTA HCAP 3YO+ 0-85 (D)   1m2f   Soft 107   +06 Fast   [83]
£8222   £2530   £1265   £632   3 yo rec 5 lb

4340 **IRON MOUNTAIN** 5 [14] N A Callaghan 5-9-1 (70) L Newman (3) 8/1: 305301: 5 b g Scenic - Merlannah   78
(Shy Groom) Towards rear, smooth prog appr fnl 2f, pshd into lead dist, readily: tchd 12/1, gd time, qk reapp:
earlier won at Newmarket (h'cap): '99 Goodwood wnr (amat h'cap, rtd 75): '98 wnr here at Yarmouth, Brighton,

Beverley & Leicester (h'caps, rtd 73): eff at 1m/11f on firm & soft, any track, likes Yarmouth: best without blnks.

4282} **GENEROUS DIANA** 375 [5] H R A Cecil 4-9-1 (70) T Quinn 7/1: 4221-2: 4 ch f Generous -   **5 71**
Lypharitissima (Lightning) Cl up, led appr fnl 2f till bef 1f out, onepace: op 5/1 on belated reappr, h'cap bow:
won fnl '99 start at Lingfield (mdn, rtd 71, K Mahdi): eff at 7/9f, stays 10f: acts on fast & soft, sharp/undul
tracks: best up with the pace: significant she is still in training & may find a race before seasons end.

4197 **THUNDERING SURF** 18 [11] J R Jenkins 3-9-9 (83) Craig Williams 4/1: 013543: 3 b c Lugana Beach -   **2 81**
Thunder Bug (Secreto) Mid div, shaken up 3f out, imprvd 2f out, short of room dist & not rch ldrs: bckd, tho' op
3/1: again given plenty to do & will apprec a more positive ride: see 4197, 2499 (fast).

1343 **EASY TO LOVE** 152 [9] H R A Cecil 4-9-10 (79) W Ryan 25/1: 5-304: Cl up, led appr fnl 3f till   ¾ 76
bef 2f out, no extra: stalemate 2ND, 5 month abs, h'cap bow: shade btr 1054.

4306 **RINGSIDE JACK** 8 [7] 4-9-1 (70)(vis) W Supple 20/1: 400105: Trckd ldrs, chall 3f out till onepce 2f out. ½ 66

4282 **CHEMS TRUCE** 11 [17] 3-9-4 (78) B Marcus 9/1: 454436: Bhd, pushed along ent staight, mod prog. ½ 73

4300 **ANNADAWI** 10 [12] 5-9-13 (82) G Baker (5) 14/1: 331027: Held up, prog 3f out, chsd ldrs 2f out,   ½ 76
rdn bef fnl 1f sn held & not much room: op 8/1, top-weight: poss worth another chance, see 4300, 4085.

4275 **AL AZHAR** 12 [4] 6-9-10 (79) T Williams 33/1: -50668: Patiently rdn, shaken up ent fnl 3f,   ½ 72
not the clearest of runs & styd on without threatening: nicely h'capped, see 757.

3794 **RUM PUNCH** 45 [3] 3-9-3 (77)(t) Pat Eddery 12/1: -00209: Chsd ldrs, rdn & btn 2f out: op 8/1. 2½ 66

1785 **LADY ROCKSTAR** 131 [15] 5-9-2 (71) P Robinson 20/1: 020000: Mid div, outpcd 2f out: 10th, op 14/1. ¾ 59

4217 **ITS MAGIC** 17 [1] 4-8-10 (65)(bl) R Hughes 25/1: 206600: Al rear: 11th, up in trip, see 3018, 2758. 1¼ 51

4038 **FINAL DIVIDEND** 29 [10] 4-8-12 (67) M Tebbutt 33/1: -45000: Handy till wknd appr fnl 2f: 12th. 2 50

*4197 **SHRIVAR** 18 [16] 3-9-6 (80)(vis) M Henry 3/1 FAV: 042110: Al bhd: 13th, well bckd from 5/1:   shd 63
better than this: progressive earlier, had enough for the season? see 4197.

1977 **Salix Dancer** 123 [8] 3-9-1 (75) S Whitworth 40/1:   968 **Williamshakespeare** 181 [2] 4-9-9 (78) J P Spencer 20/1:
2666 **Bali Batik** 95 [13] 3-9-7 (81) D Holland 16/1:

16 ran   Time 2m 14.3 (10.1)   (Gallagher Equine Ltd)   N A Callaghan Newmarket, Suffolk

---

4393   **4.50 BILLOCKBY NURSERY HCAP 2YO 0-85 (E)   1m str   Soft 107 -36 Slow   [84]**
£2926   £836   £418   Raced stands side

4191 **PORT MORESBY** 18 [7] N A Callaghan 2-9-0 (70) L Newman (3) 20/1: 010001: 2 b c Tagula - Santana   76
Lady (Blakeney) Dwelt, chsd ldrs, hard rdn appr fnl 1f, kept on gamely to lead cl home: slow time: earlier
won at Beverley (mdn): eff at 7.5f/1m, likely to get further next term: acts on gd/soft & soft grnd, stiff
or easy track: tried blnks & t-strap, better without.

4230 **REVIEWER** 15 [6] J H M Gosden 2-9-0 (70)(bl) J Fortune 5/1: 60452: 2 b c Sadler's Wells -   nk 75
Clandestina (Secretariat) Cl up, led appr fnl 1f, under press inside last & worn down nr fin: bckd: suited
by the return to 1m: acts on soft grnd: shld win similar.

4163 **DARDANUS** 20 [10] E A L Dunlop 2-9-2 (72) G Carter 13/8 FAV: 4043: 2 ch c Komaite - Dance On A   ¾ 75
Cloud (Capote) Slow away, struggling halfway, kept on appr fnl 1f, nvr nrr: well bckd from 5/2 on h'cap bow:
acts on gd/soft & soft grnd but is already in need of 10f+.

4191 **SANDLES** 18 [12] S C Williams 2-8-12 (68) T Quinn 12/1: 440054: Towards rear, imprvd to chse ldrs   nk 70
2f out, onepce till kept on cl home: pulled clr of rem & ran to best: acts on fast, soft grnd & fibresand.

3968 **CHEVENING LODGE** 33 [8] 2-7-11 (53) M Henry 16/1: 460035: Led till 2f out, no extra: stays 1m   7 43
but could do with a drop back in trip & prob faster grnd, see 3968.

3901 **FLUTED** 38 [3] 2-8-9 (65) Craig Williams 14/1: 303406: Nvr a factor: up in trip, see 3444. 2 51

3592 **ORIGINAL SINNER** 54 [5] 2-8-9 (64)(1ow) J P Spencer 11/2: 64657: Chsd ldrs, fdd ent fnl 2f: 8 wk abs. 5 43

3968 **GROVE DANCER** 33 [11] 2-8-8 (64) Pat Eddery 20/1: 134008: In tch till appr fnl 1f: op 14/1, see 1612. 5 34

3922 **RICHENDA** 35 [9] 2-9-5 (75) R Hughes 14/1: 066009: Wide & al towards rear, eased ins last: tchd 20/1. ¼ 44

4230 **DON ALFRED** 15 [2] 2-9-6 (76) P Dobbs 8/1: 50330: In tch till 2f out: 10th, see 3779. 5 37

4188 **DREAM MAGIC** 18 [1] 2-9-7 (77) P Robinson 14/1: 0640: Rcd alone far side 2f, al bhd: 11th, op 10/1. 2½ 34

4172 **ABBY GOA** 20 [4] 2-9-1 (71)(bl) W Ryan 12/1: 45030: Bhd from halfway: last, lngr trip on h'cap bow. 16 3

12 ran   Time 1m 46.5 (11.4)   (Martin Moore)   N A Callaghan Newmarket, Suffolk

---

LONGCHAMP   SUNDAY OCTOBER 15TH   Righthand, Stiff, Galloping Track

Official Going   SOFT

4394   **2.20 GR 2 PRIX DU CONSEIL DE PARIS 3YO+   1m4f   Soft**
£28818   £11527   £5784   £2882

3929 **CRIMSON QUEST** 35 [3] A Fabre 3-8-8 O Peslier 13/10 FAV: 120221: 3 ch c Rainbow Quest - Bex   117
(Explodent) Trkd ldr, went on 2f out, styd on well, rdn out: earlier won in Listed company & 8L rnr-up to
Arc wnr Sinndar: stays 12f well on gd & soft grnd: proving tough & smart.

1547} **SLEW THE RED** 509 [2] A Fabre 3-8-8 T Jarnet 17/10: 24-212: 3 b c Red Ransom - Great Lady Slew   2 114
(Seattle Slew) In tch, hdwy to chase stablemate over 1f out, kept on same pace: stays 12f on soft grnd.

*2572 **FOLIE DANSE** 98 [4] Y de Nicolay 3-8-7 D Bonilla 54/10: 152513: 3 b f Petit Loup - Folle Envie   2½ 110
(Un Desperado) Held up, eff over 2f out, onepace over 1f out: ran to form of 2572 (Gr3) after 3 month abs.

*4128 **KIND REGARDS** 21 [1] M Johnston 3-8-5 Craig Williams 17/10: 111514: Set pace till 2f out, no   5 103
extra: big step up in class after impressive h'cap win in 4128.

3849 **HOLDING COURT** 42 [5] 3-9-1 P Robinson 2/1: 111655: Prom, rdn & wknd over 3f out, t.o.: 6 wk abs: 15 99
something surely amiss: now thrice below impressive 6L French Derby winning form of 1752.

5 ran   Time 2m 34.4   (Sultan Al Kabeer)   A Fabre France

4395   **2.55 GR 1 PRIX DE LA FORET 3YO+   7f   Soft**
£48031   £19212   £9606   £4803

4111 **INDIAN LODGE** 22 [9] Mrs A J Perrett 4-9-2 Pat Eddery 36/10: 130101: 4 b c Grand Lodge - Repetitious   124
(Northfields) Cl-up, led over 1f out, qcknd clr fnl 1f, readily: earlier scored at Newmarket (Gr 3, reapp) &
Sandown (Gr 2): '99 scorer at Newbury, Yarmouth & Newmarket (2, List, rtd 112): eff over 7/9f & handles fast,
revels in soft & hvy grnd: likes a stiff trk, esp Newmarket: runs well fresh: tough, progressive & high-class.

3847 **DANSILI** 42 [5] A Fabre 4-9-2 O Peslier 8/5 FAV: 112262: 4 b c Danehill - Hasili (Kahyasi)   2½ 120
Hld up, eff 2f out, styd on to chase wnr ins last, no impress: 6 wk abs: not disgraced but optimum trip is 1m.

LONGCHAMP   SUNDAY OCTOBER 15TH   Righthand, Stiff, Galloping Track

4259 **SUGARFOOT** 14 [3] N Tinkler 6-9-2 J Reid 15/1: 100533: 6 ch h Thatching - Norpella (Northfields)   2   117
Prom, onepcd over 1f out: smart run in the highest grade & would relish a return to List/Gr 3 company.
4125 **TOMBA** 21 [11] M A Jarvis 6-9-2 P Robinson 42/1: 350307: Bhd, some late gains: close to best.   3   113
3784 **BOLD EDGE** 43 [2] 5-9-2 R Hughes 30/1: 034108: Led till over 1f out, no extra: 6 wk abs, btr 3212.   ½   112
4111 **GOLDEN SILCA** 22 [10] 4-8-12 Craig Williams 24/1: 541059: Nvr a factor: see 4111, best 3554 (Gr 3).   ¾   107
2571 **TRANS ISLAND** 99 [8] 5-9-2 K Darley 64/10: -22140: Handy, wknd qckly well over 1f out: 3 month   0
abs & a rare below par run: does like this grnd: see 2571, 1847.
11 ran   Time 1m 22.3   (S Cohn & Sir Eric Parker)   Mrs A J Perrett Pulborough, W Sussex

CAPANNELLE   SUNDAY OCTOBER 15TH   Righthand, Flat, Galloping Track

Official Going HEAVY.

4396	3.30 GR 2 PREMIO LYDIA TESIO 3YO+ FILLIES 1m2f Heavy
	£85172 £38667 £21440 3 yo rec 5 lb

*2851 **CLAXON** 85 [14] J L Dunlop 4-9-0 T Quinn : 15-211: 4 b f Caerleon - Bulaxie (Bustino)   107
Led after 2f, made rest, styd on well fnl 1f, rdn out: 3 month abs since scoring at Newbury (Listed): '99 wnr
at Kempton & Goodwood (List, rtd 109): suited by 10f on firm, hvy & any trk: runs well fresh & loves to dominate:
useful & game, will reportedly now be retired.
--   **USTIMONA** [1] H Blume 3-8-9 A Boschert : 2: 3 b f Mondrian - Well Known (Knoigsstuhl)   3   103
*2857 **ABITARA** 85 [2] A Wohler 4-9-0 J Weaver : 111113: 4 ch f Rainbow Quest - Arastou (Surumu)   ½   102
In tch, eff over 2f out, kept on for press ins last, no threat: needs 12f as in 2857.
13 ran   Time 2m 7.2   (Hesmonds Stud)   J L Dunlop Arundel, W Sussex

CURRAGH   SUNDAY OCTOBER 15TH   Righthand, Galloping Track

Official Going YIELDING/SOFT.

4397	3.00 GR 3 BERESFORD STKS 2YO 1m Soft
	£32500 £9500 £4500

4127 **TURNBERRY ISLE** 21 [3] A P O'Brien 2-9-0 M J Kinane 4/11 FAV: -1121: 2 ch c Deputy Minister - Blush   112
With Pride (Blushing Groom) Cl-up, eff to lead dist, pushed clr, v cmftbly: earlier scored at Gowran (mdn),
Ascot (stks) & ½L rnr-up in Gr 2 Royal Lodge: full brother to a 9f juv wnr: stays 1m well, further sure to suit
next term: smart & improving juv, sure to win more Gr races.
4237 **SLIGO BAY** 15 [1] A P O'Brien 2-9-0 J A Heffernan 4/1: -2132: 2 b c Sadler's Wells - Angelic Song   4   101
(Halo) Set pace, collared dist, not pace of stable-mate: useful, would apprec Listed company: see 4237.
--   **VINNIE ROE** [4] D K Weld 2-9-0 P J Smullen 11/2: -13: 2 b c Definite Article - Kayu (Tap On Wood)   shd   101
In tch, eff 2f out, onepace fnl 1f: Leopardstown scorer on debut: stays 1m on soft: open to improvement.
6 ran   Time 1m 46.4   (Mrs John Magnier)   A P O'Brien Ballydoyle, Co Tipperary

4398	4.00 LISTED WATERFORD STKS 3YO+ 6f Soft
	£19500 £5700 £2700 3 yo rec 1 lb

4266 **COBOURG LODGE** 14 [3] J T Gorman 4-8-12 P Shanahan 7/1: 344621: 4 b g Unblest - Rachel Pringle   109
(Doulab) Rear, prog 2f out, styd on well to lead cl home, drvn out: op 5/1: eff at 6/7f on soft grnd: useful.
--   **ANNA ELISE** [8] J A Flynn 4-8-9 J P Spencer 10/1: 410102: 4 b f Nucleon - Tormented (Alleged)   hd   105
Set pace & clr 4f, worn down cl home: op 7/1: earlier won here at The Curragh (3, h'caps): eff at 6f on gd & soft.
--   **TIGER ROYAL** [6] D K Weld 4-8-12 (bl) E Ahern 8/1: 433213: 4 gr g Royal Academy - Lady Redford   nk   107
(Bold Lad) Held up, imprvd 2f out, ran on under press & nrst fin: not btn far in a tight fin: recent wnr here
at The Curragh (5f h'cap): eff at 5/6f on soft grnd: wears blnks: useful.
4198 **AREYDHA** 16 [5] M R Channon 3-8-8 M J Kinane 6/1: 0-0024: Prom till no extra fnl 1f: fin 6th.   0
11 ran   Time 1m 17.9   (Andrews Syndicate)   J T Gorman The Curragh, Co Kildare

WOODBINE   SUNDAY OCTOBER 15TH   -

Official Going FIRM.

4399	8.02 GR 1 E P TAYLOR STKS 3YO+ FILLIES 1m2f Firm
	£126582 £42194 £23207 3 yo rec 5 lb

--   **FLY FOR AVIE** [5] D Bell 5-8-11 T Kabel 81/10: -1: 5 br m Lord Avie - Fly For Baby (Arctic Tern)   117
4263 **LADY UPSTAGE** 14 [8] B W Hills 3-8-5 M Hills 41/20: 251032: 3 b f Alzao - She's The Tops (Shernazar)   nse   115
Chsd ldrs, prog to chall dist, just btn in a v cl fin: fine run, smart filly: acts on firm & gd/soft: see 4263.
3829) **INNUENDO** 403 [7] USA 5-8-11 L Dettori 2/1: 2214-3: 5 b m Caerleon - Infamy (Shirley Heights)   nse   116
6 ran   Time 2m 2.78   (I Dalos)   D Bell Canada

4400	9.40 GR 1 CANADIAN INTERNATIONAL 3YO+ 1m4f Firm
	£379747 £126582 £69620

4055 **MUTAFAWEQ** 29 Saeed bin Suroor 4-9-0 L Dettori 4/1: 301031: 4 b h Silver Hawk - The Caretaker   122
(Caerleon) Mid-div, prog to lead 1½f out, hdd ins fnl 1f, rallied to regain lead on line, all-out: earlier won
at Dusseldorf (Gr 1): '99 Doncaster (stks, reapp), R Ascot (Gr 2) & Doncaster wnr (Gr 1 St Leger, rtd 125): '98
Newmarket wnr: eff at 12/14f on gd & firm, handles gd/soft: runs well fresh: high-class, globe-trotting performer.

-- **WILLIAMS NEWS** T Amoss 5-9-0 P Husbands 13/1: 121432: 5 b g Alleged - Wooden Crown (His Majesty) Rear, switched ent str & prog, led ins fnl 1f till collared on line: eff at 12f on firm: high-class.   *nse* **121**
3849 **DALIAPOUR** 42 Sir Michael Stoute 4-9-0 J Murtagh 5/4 FAV: -11343: 4 b h Sadler's Wells - Dalara (Doyoun) Nvr far away, went on 2f out till 1½f out, not pace of front 2 cl home: 6 wk abs: can rate higher.   2¾ **117**
3931 **MURGHEM** 35 M Johnston 5-9-0 D Holland 96/10: 112146: Trkd ldr till fdd ent str: 6th: btr 3483.   4¾ **111**
12 ran   Time 2m 27.62   (Godolphin)   Saeed bin Suroor Newmarket

Official Going   HEAVY.

4401 2.10 GR 3 PRIX DES RESERVOIRS 2YO FILLIES   1m   Heavy
£21134 £7685 £3842

*3990 **PERFECT PLUM** 32 [9] Sir Mark Prescott 2-8-9 G Duffield 61/10: 321011: 2 b f Darshaan - Damascene (Scenic) Trkd ldr till went on 2½f out, held on well despite drifting left, drvn out: earlier won at Newcastle & Ayr (nursery h'caps): eff at 1m, mid-dists will suit in '01: acts on firm, loves gd/soft & hvy grnd: handles stiff/gall trks: gd weight carrier who likes to run up with the pace: v useful & progressive mud lover.   **105**
4260 **ASCENSION** 16 [2] M R Channon 2-9-0 C Asmussen 17/10 FAV: -11162: 2 ch f Night Shift - Outeniqua (Bold Lad) Rear, switched to stands side & hdwy 1½f out, fin well but not rch wnr: stays 1m on hvy: see 4260.   1 **108**
-- **LINEA DOMBRA** [3] D Smaga 2-8-9 O Peslier 31/10: -4113: 2 ch f Zafonic - Canaletto (Iron Duke) Mid-div, prog 2f out, chsd wnr ent fnl 1f, lost 2nd cl home: eff at 1m on hvy grnd: useful filly.   ½ **102**
4159 **LADY LAHAR** 21 [6] M R Channon 2-9-0 J Murtagh 81/10: 134104: Chsd ldrs, onepcd fnl 1f: s/mate 2nd.   hd **107**
4096 **LUNEVISION** 25 [7] 2-8-9 D Boeuf 19/1: 3238: Led till 2½f out, wknd into last: highly tried.   20 **67**
8 ran   Time 1m 50.3   (Sir Edmund Loder)   Sir Mark Prescott Newmarket

Official Going   HEAVY. Stalls: Str Course - Stands Side; Round Course - Inside.

4402 2.00 EBF MDN 2YO (D)   6f str   Heavy 182 -14 Slow
£3334 £1026 £513 £256   Winner & 9th raced stands side - rem raced far side.

3974 **ARJAY** 33 [14] Andrew Turnell 2-9-0 R Thomas (7) 11/2: -5621: 2 b g Shaamit - Jenny's Call (Petong) Led duo stands side, rdn/led overall over 1f out, sn clr, pushed out: Apr foal, dam mod: eff arnd 6f & clrly relishes soft/hvy grnd: acts on a stiff/gall trk: improving, shld win again on testing grnd.   **87**
4216 **ROSALIA** 18 [9] T D Easterby 2-8-9 K Darley 4/1: -46362: 2 b f Red Ransom - Normandy Belle (Fit To Fight) Trkd ldr far side, outpcd over 2f out, rallied ins last but no ch with wnr: handles hvy & 7f suits.   5 **72**
4188 **ATLANTIC MYSTERY** 19 [6] M Johnston 2-8-9 D Holland 7/1: 353: 2 ch f Cadeaux Genereux - Nottash (Royal Academy) Front rank far side, went on appr fnl 1f, sn hdd, not pace of wnr: handles hvy: see 4001.   hd **72**
4082 **MASTER FELLOW** 27 [13] J G Given 2-9-0 A Culhane 20/1: 64: Well bhd far side, gd late hdwy under hands & heels, nvr nrr: handles hvy: looks sure to relish a step up to 7f & one to keep in mind: see 4082.   2½ **71+**
3958 **ALS ME TRAINER** 34 [2] 2-9-0 D Mernagh (3) 50/1: -405: Led far side, hdd appr fnl 1f, wknd: op 20/1.   1 **68**
4082 **EXCEPTIONAL PADDY** 27 [4] 2-9-0 S W Kelly 3/1: 36: Prom far side, chall ldr over 1f out, sn btn: well bckd & better expected after a promising debut in 4082 (soft).   2½ **62**
4083 **EGYPT** 27 [11] 2-9-0 G Duffield 10/1: 07: Chsd ldrs far side, rdn/onepcd fnl 2f: see 4083.   4 **53**
-- **NANCYS BOY** [12] 2-9-0 R Winston 50/1: 8: Al bhd far side: Perpendicular Apr foal, dam mod hdler, sire mid-dist performer: shld apprec further next year for J Hetherton.   2½ **48**
4082 **GEM BIEN** 27 [10] 2-9-0 P Fessey 16/1: 59: Prom stands side, wknd qckly over 1f out: btr 4082 (soft).   3 **42**
4283 **KNIGHT CROSSING** 12 [1] 2-9-0 W Supple 20/1: 50: Trkd ldrs far side, wknd fnl 2f, 10th: btr 4283.   8 **27**
4252 **DIABOLO** 15 [5] 2-9-0 T Lucas 33/1: 000: Al well bhd far side, 11th: see 4082.   1½ **24**
4083 **FOLLOW FREDDY** 27 [3] 2-9-0 J Fanning 14/1: 000: In tch far side, fdd fnl 2f, 12th: see 4083, 3245.   ½ **23**
4252 **Statosilver** 15 [7] 2-9-0 J Carroll 33/1:   -- **Prince Jack** [8] 2-9-0 C Teague 66/1:
14 ran   Time 1m 23.08 (11.78)   (Dr John Hollowood)   Andrew Turnell Sandhutton, N Yorks

4403 2.30 BETSMART FILLIES MDN 2YO (D)   7f str   Heavy 182 -41 Slow
£3315 £1020 £510 £255   Raced in 2 groups - no significant advantage.

4158 **SHAANARA** 22 [5] Andrew Turnell 2-8-11 P Fessey 6/1: 601: 2 b f Darshaan - Mochara (Last Fandango) Cl-up far side, rdn to lead just ins last, styd on well for press, asserted cl-home, drvn out: op 4/1: 130,000gns May foal, half sister to a 7f wnr: eff around a stiff/gall 7f, apprec this v hvy grnd: tough & imprvg filly.   **82**
4035 **FOLLOW A DREAM** 30 [1] Sir Michael Stoute 2-8-11 F Lynch 7/4 FAV: 632: 2 b f Gone West - Dance A Dream (Sadler's Wells) Led far side, hdd ins last, no extra fnl 50yds: hvly bckd: eff at 7f on soft/hvy, win sn.   1¾ **78**
4322 **THEATRE LADY** 8 [15] M Johnston 2-8-11 D Holland 10/1: 43: 2 b f King's Theatre - Littlepace (Indian King) Made all stands side, drvn & held by far side fnl 1f: 8L clr rem: imprvd on this drop to 7f on hvy.   1½ **76**
4216 **ELLA TINO** 18 [14] J A Glover 2-8-11 W Supple 7/1: 654: In tch stands side, drvn/no extra over 2f out.   8 **64**
4131 **MICKLOW MAGIC** 24 [6] 2-8-11 L Newton 9/2: 225: Front rank stands side, wknd qckly fnl 2f: op 7/2: up in trip & prob not get home over 7f on hvy: btr 4131 (5f, gd/soft).   3 **59**
4312 **ALLELUIA** 9 [8] 2-8-11 G Duffield 9/2: 36: Prom stands side, fdd fnl 2f: tchd 7/1: shade btr 4312.   shd **59**
4322 **DANCE QUEEN** 8 [11] 2-8-11 T Williams 33/1: 060067: Keen/prom stands side, wknd fnl 2f: stiff task.   8 **40**
4172 **LA TRAVIATA** 21 [3] 2-8-11 K Darley 20/1: 008: Dwelt, sn chasing ldrs far side, lost tch fnl 3f: op 12/1.   ½ **39**
3776 **SORAYAS QUEST** 46 [12] 2-8-11 A Culhane 20/1: 049: Al outpcd on stands side: abs: btr 3776 (gd/soft).2 **36**
4281 **TOP QUALITY** 12 [10] 2-8-11 R Winston 20/1: 500: Mid-div at best stands side, 10th: btr 3308 (firm).   10 **21**
3957 **Mud N Bert** 34 [2] 2-8-11 J Bramhill 50/1:   4303 **Rose Of America** 4 [4] 2-8-11 C Lowther 50/1:
4281 **High Society Lady** 12 [9] 2-8-11 (bl) J McAuley 66/1: 3949 **Royal Musical** 35 [13] 2-8-11 D Mernagh (3) 33/1:
14 ran   Time 1m 39.77 (15.67)   (Dr John Hollowood)   Andrew Turnell Sandhutton, N Yorks

---

4404   3.05 NORTHERN HCAP 3YO+ 0-60 (F)   1m2f32y   Heavy 182 -12 Slow   **[60]**
£3090   £883   £441   3 yo rec 5 lb

4221 **KONKER** 18 [6] Mrs M Reveley 5-9-6 (52) A Culhane 5/1 JT FAV: 6-0031: 5 ch g Selkirk - Helens **58**
Dreamgirl (Caerleon) Mid-div, hdwy over 2f out, styd on for strong press to lead ins last, rdn out: unplcd in 2 '99
starts for G M Moore (rtd 60): '98 Newbury wnr (clmr, rtd 78, W Haggas): eff arnd 10/11f on gd, hvy & a stiff/gall trk.

4280 **DARK VICTOR** 13 [19] D Shaw 4-9-2 (48)(BL) N Callan 9/1: 010662: 4 b g Cadeaux Genereux - 1¾ **51**
Dimmer (Kalaglow) In tch, smooth hdwy to chall 2f out, rdn & kept on ins last, no ch with wnr: gd eff in
first time blnks, likes gd/soft & hvy & could find similar: see 1050.

4275 **SUSANS DOWRY** 13 [7] Andrew Turnell 4-8-8 (40) P Fessey 20/1: 000403: 4 b f Efisio - Adjusting 2½ **39**
(Busted) Waited with, hdwy 3f out, led appr fnl 1f, hdd dist, sn btn: clr rem: likes soft & hvy grnd: see 3827.

*4306 **LOVE KISS** 9 [14] W Storey 5-9-9 (55)(6ex) T Williams 5/1 JT FAV: 006414: Cl-up, led over 2f out, 5 **48**
hdd appr fnl 1f, fdd: op 3/1: shade btr 4306.

4229 **SMARTER CHARTER** 16 [2] 7-9-5 (51) Kristin Stubbs (7) 9/1: 306445: Late hdwy, nvr dngrs: see 4229. ½ **43**

4046 **KIERCHEM** 29 [13] 9-8-7 (39) T Hamilton (7) 16/1: 043036: Rear, mod late hdwy, no threat to ldrs: 6 **23**
may apprec a return to further now: both wins at Ripon: see 4046, 2099.

4306 **ZAMAT** 9 [10] 4-9-1 (47) R Winston 25/1: 0-0407: Mid-div, hdwy 3f out, lost tch appr fnl 1f: see 3780. 1¼ **29**

4282 **CAPTAIN BRADY** 12 [8] 5-9-4 (50) A McGlone 12/1: 136008: In tch, hmpd after 1f, bhd fnl 3f: see 3826. 9 **22**

4135 **TAKER CHANCE** 24 [15] 4-8-6 (38) A Robertson (7) 20/1: 000009: Dsptd lead, went on 3f out, hdd 1 **8**
2f out & qckly lost tch: see 2970 (1m, fast).

3603 **TURTLE** 54 [18] 4-8-9 (41) D Mernagh (3) 25/1: 040-00: Prom, dropped rear 4f out, no ch after: 4 **6**
10th: 8 wk abs: '99 Pontefract wnr (sell, rtd 54, M Johnston): plcd twice in '98 (mdns, rtd 74): eff arnd
10f on fast & gd/soft, poss handles soft & fibresand: likes to race up with/force the pace: with W Storey.

3465 **COSMIC SONG** 60 [3] 3-8-9 (46) V Halliday 11/2: 446050: Al rear, 11th: btr 1722. ½ **10**

4275 **ANGEL DUST** 13 [11] 4-8-8 (40) J Fanning 20/1: -5600: Led to 3f out, wknd, t.o. in 12th: h'cap bow. 12 **0**

4174 **DILETIA** 21 [20] 3-9-5 (56)(bl) K Darley 11/2: 604140: Cl-up, wknd rapidly fnl 2f, 13th: btr 4029 (sell). 7 **1**

4105 **GRAND SLAM GB** 25 [9] 5-10-0 (60) W Supple 12/1: 42-400: Lost tch halfway, 14th: bckd: likes fast. 9 **0**

3288 **Rimatara** 68 [16] 4-8-9 (41) T Lucas 25/1:   4221 **Haikal** 18 [1] 3-9-6 (57) P Bradley (5) 33/1:

4256 **Roman Emperor** 15 [12] 3-8-6 (43)(bl) G Duffield 16/1:

2785 **Birth Of The Blues** 90 [17] 4-9-3 (49)(BL) A Daly 20/1:

3191 **Landican Lad** 72 [4] 3-9-3 (54) F Lynch 20/1:
19 ran   Time 2m 26.3 (19.8)   (J & M Leisure/Unos Restaurant)   Mrs M Reveley Lingdale, N Yorks

---

4405   3.35 TOTALBET.COM HCAP 3YO+ 0-95 (C)   6f str   Heavy 182 +09 Fast   **[87]**
£7117   £2190   £1095   £547   3 yo rec 1 lb   2 groups - no significant advantage.

4377 **COLLEGE MAID** 2 [1] J S Goldie 3-8-5 (64)(1ow) A McGlone 20/1: 400201: 3 b f College Chapel - Maid **70**
Of Mourne (Fairy King) Cl-up far side, led over 2f out, hdd appr fnl 1f, rallied gamely to lead again ins last,
drvn out: best time of day: ran 48hrs ago: earlier won at Ripon, Catterick & Ayr (h'caps): '99 Musselburgh
wnr (mdn auct, rtd 74 at best): eff at 5/6f on firm & gd, likes hvy & any trk: v tough & genuine filly.

4069 **DOWNLAND** 28 [3] G Wragg 4-9-6 (79)(bl) D Holland 9/2 FAV: -06022: 4 b c Common Grounds - ½ **83**
Boldabsa (Persian Bold) Trkd ldrs far side, hdwy to lead over 1f out, hdd ins last, no extra c-home:
acts on firm & hvy grnd, shld go one better sn: see 4069, 1173.

4287 **ROYAL ROMEO** 12 [20] T D Easterby 3-8-11 (71) K Darley 14/1: 000503: 3 ch g Timeless Times - 1¾ **71**
Farinara (Dragonara Palace) Cl-up stands side, led that group appr fnl 1f, styd on but no ch with front 2
on far side: won race on stands side, encouraging: see 2663, 1768.

4301 **BON AMI** 11 [2] A Berry 4-9-12 (85) P Bradley (5) 8/1: 400004: Chsd ldrs far side, rdn over 2f out, ¾ **83**
no extra appr fnl 1f: well bckd: see 4301, 1004.

4044 **REX IS OKAY** 29 [18] 4-8-6 (65) L Newton 20/1: 260005: Led stands side, hdd 1f out, wknd: on a fair mark.5 **53**

*4327 **RYEFIELD** 8 [11] 5-8-10 (69)(7ex) J Carroll 12/1: 263316: Dwelt, hdwy from rear stands side over 6 **45**
2f out, rdn/btn appr fnl 1f: carried 7lb pen for scoring in 4327 (Ayr).

4257 **BABY BARRY** 15 [8] 3-9-5 (79) J Fanning 40/1: 350007: Prom far side, wknd over 1f out: btr 3335 (fast). 1 **52**

4302 **MISTER MAL** 11 [10] 4-9-4 (77) G Duffield 13/2: 020658: Cl-up far side, rdn/dropped away appr fnl 1f: 4 **42**
nicely bckd & better expected with connections in his favour: shld be front-run: see 3785, 3250.

4287 **SHAROURA** 12 [16] 4-8-12 (71) R Winston 8/1: 200039: Handy stands side, wknd fnl 2f: btr 4287 (soft). 1¼ **33**

4301 **FIRST MAITE** 11 [15] 7-9-10 (83) N Callan 20/1: 000000: Towards rear stands side, nvr dangerous: 10th. 1¼ **42**

2616 **PIPS SONG** 97 [7] 5-9-9 (82) J Lowe 16/1: 103000: Dwelt, nvr dangerous far side, 11th: long abs. ½ **40**

4015 **MUNGO PARK** 32 [19] 6-9-8 (81) A Culhane 20/1: 510000: Mid-dist stands side, rdn/lost tch fnl 2f, 12th. nk **39**

4301 **JUWWI** 11 [4] 6-9-13 (86) M Searle 9/2 FAV: 7 **32**
4/1: 000400: Dwelt, al rear, 13th: habitual slow starter.

4287 **DAY BOY** 12 [6] 4-8-9 (68) A Nicholls 8/1: 304440: Al rear far side, 14th: flattered 4287. 1 **12**

4287 **GET STUCK IN** 12 [9] 4-9-1 (74) C Lowther 14/1: 002300: Sn clr ldr far side, hdd/wknd 2f out, 17th. **0**

4287 **Technician** 12 [14] 5-8-7 (66)(bl) W Supple 20/1:   4327 **Peppiatt** 8 [5] 6-8-0 (59) T Williams 33/1:
4257 **First Musical** 15 [17] 4-9-3 (76) D Mernagh (3) 20/1:   4302 **Sulu** 11 [12] 4-8-5 (64) T Lucas 25/1:
4302 **Unshaken** 11 [13] 6-8-6 (65) F Lynch 16/1:
20 ran   Time 1m 21.7 (10.4)   (S Bruce)   J S Goldie Uplawmoor, E Renfrews

---

4406   4.10 MINDKEY CLAIM HCAP 3YO+ 0-60 (F)   1m rnd   Heavy 182 -63 Slow   **[54]**
£2922   £835   £417   3 yo rec 3 lb

4324 **GINNER MORRIS** 8 [3] J Hetherton 5-9-1 (41)(bl) W Supple 8/1: 5-0041: 5 b g Emarati - Just Run **47**
(Runnett) Front rank, rdn to lead over 2f out, styd on strongly ins last, rdn out: 1st win: recently plcd
over hdles (mdn, rtd 77h): unplcd in '99 (rtd 46 & 26a, h'caps, C Booth): plcd in '98 (rtd 50 & 46a):
eff around 1m/10f on gd/soft, hvy & equitrack: handles a sharp or stiff/gall trk.

4365 **KING TUT** 2 [7] J G Given 4-9-8 (48) D McGaffin (5) 7/1: 204007: 4 ch g Anshan - Fahrenheit 3½ **48**
(Mount Hagen) Chsd ldrs, rdn to improve 2f out, styd on, no ch with wnr: nicely bckd, clr rem: gd eff: see 1907.

2366 **UP IN FLAMES** 107 [16] Mrs G S Rees 9-8-12 (38)(f) J Carroll 20/1: 203563: 9 b g Nashamaa - Bella 5 **30**
Lucia (Camden Town) Bhd, imprvd 3f out, styd on but no ch with ldrs: not disgraced after long abs: see 1546.

2479 **ZECHARIAH** 103 [11] J L Eyre 4-8-12 (38) R Cody Boutcher (7) 20/1: 564004: Led, hdd 2f out, sn btn. hd **30**

3671 **CITY BANK DUDLEY** 52 [18] 3-9-1 (44) C Teague 40/1: 464005: Late hdwy from rear, no threat: 7 wk abs. 6 **28**

3480 **TIME TO WYN** 60 [8] 4-9-0 (40) D Mernagh (3) 12/1: 0-0056: Cl-up, rdn/btn fnl 2f: abs: btr 3480 (10f). 2 **21**

NEWCASTLE WEDNESDAY OCTOBER 18TH Lefthand, Galloping Track, Stiff Track

4306 **AMRON 9** [2] 13-8-12 (38) J Bramhill 20/1: 060007: In tch, late hdwy, no threat: 13yo: drop in trip. ½ **18**
4275 **TO THE LAST MAN 13** [20] 4-9-10 (50) D Holland 25/1: 6-0008: Mid-div at best: top weight: see 4275. ½ **29**
4256 **FRENCH MASTER 15** [13] 3-8-11 (40)(vis) Iona Wands 20/1: 000609: Nvr dngrs: op 14/1: see 4256, 806. 7 **10**
4275 **DIAMOND FLAME 13** [12] 6-9-5 (45)(BL) R Lappin 33/1: 400000: Lost tch fnl 2f, 10th: blnkd (prev visored). 4 **10**
2538 **I CANT REMEMBER 100** [4] 6-9-3 (43) N Callan 12/1: 603400: Nvr a threat, 11th: abs: drop in trip. *hd* **8**
3963 **FLOORSOTHEFOREST 34** [14] 4-9-2 (42) C Lowther 16/1: 050000: Al towards rear, 12th: see 2094. *1* **5**
4293 **BLACKPOOL MAMMAS 12** [1] 3-9-5 (48) P Fitzsimons (5) 12/1: 660600: Sn struggling, 13th: btr 1061. *6* **2**
2816 **ALABAMY SOUND 89** [10] 4-9-5 (45) K Darley 12/1: -40400: Cl-up, wknd rapidly fnl 2f, 15th: 3 month abs. **0**
3871 **MOROCCO 41** [9] 11-9-5 (45) S W Kelly (3) 8/1: 06-030: Al rear, 16th: op 5/1, 6 wk abs: btr 3871 (7f, gd). **0**
2820 **FOIST 89** [6] 8-9-2 (42) T Lucas 10/1: 502600: In tch, hung badly right & lost tch fnl 3f, 17th: **0**
op 6/1 after 3 month abs: best around 6/7f: see 2820, 587.
4232 **SWYNFORD ELEGANCE 16** [5] 3-9-1 (44) T Williams 6/1 FAV: 000240: Handy, lost tch fnl 2f, t.o. **0**
in 19th: nicely bckd & a disapp run here: much btr 4232, 3971.
3603 **Woore Lass 54** [15] 4-9-5 (45) Kin Tinkler 20/1: 3702 **Glen Vale Walk 51** [19] 3-9-2 (45) G Duffield 16/1:
4276 **Petara 13** [17] 5-8-12 (38) F Lynch 20/1:
20 ran Time 1m 58.6 (19.6) (Formulated Polymer Products Ltd) J Hetherton Malton, N Yorks

4407 **4.40 BETSMART HCAP 3YO+ 0-70 (E) 5f str Heavy 182 +04 Fast** **[70]**
£2999 £923 £461 £230 2 groups - no significant advantage.

1840 **REGAL SONG 130** [16] T J Etherington 4-9-5 (61) J Fanning 20/1: W50301: 4 b g Anita's Prince - Song **67**
Bearn (Song) Cl-up stands side, led that group 2f out, led overall ins last, rdn clr: gd time, 4 month abs, drop
in trip: '99 Hamilton wnr (auct mdn, rtd 63): plcd fnl 2 '98 starts (nurs, rtd 65): eff at 5/6f, has tried 7f:
acts on fast & fibresand, likes gd/soft & hvy: eff with/without blnks & clrly goes v well fresh.
4295 **MUKARRAB 12** [2] D W Chapman 6-8-6 (48) A Culhane 6/1: 445002: 6 br g Dayjur - Mahassin (Biscay) *2* **49**
Far side, led that group ins last, styd on but no ch with wnr: op 8/1: on a wng mark, likes soft: could win sn.
4307 **ROBIN HOOD 9** [9] Miss L A Perratt 3-8-10 (52) R Winston 14/1: 102003: 3 b g Komaite - Plough Hill ½ **52**
(North Briton) Towards rear far side, rdn & styd on well fnl 2f, nvr nrr: gd eff, likes easy grnd: see 3825, 3536.
4327 **JACKERIN 8** [6] Miss J F Craze 5-8-0 (42)(bl) T Williams 11/1: 000204: Led far side, hdd ins last, *2½* **36**
sn btn: twice below 3964 (6f, fast grnd).
3653 **DOMINELLE 53** [7] 8-8-8 (50) P Fessey 16/1: 061005: Mid-div, rdn/imprvd over 2f out, btn fnl 1f: ¾ **43**
6 wk abs: best on faster grnd, as in 2969 (6f, fast).
4136 **BUNDY 24** [18] 4-9-10 (66) A Nicholls 20/1: 003006: Rear, hdwy when short of room 2f out & appr fnl ¾ **58**
1f, styd on, nvr nrr: top weight: shade unlucky & sure to relish a return to 6f (all wins at that trip).
4220 **LUCKY COVE 18** [5] 4-8-8 (50)(bl) Kim Tinkler 8/1: 000047: Sn outpcd far side, late hdwy, nvr *nk* **42**
dangerous: tchd 11/1: flattered 4220 (stks, gd/soft).
4220 **JAILHOUSE ROCKET 18** [19] 3-9-8 (64) G Duffield 10/1: 000008: Cl-up stands side, btn fnl 2f: op 8/1. ½ **55**
4307 **BENNOCHY 9** [20] 3-8-4 (46) J Bramhill 25/1: 460009: Mid-div stands side, drvn/lost tch appr fnl 1f. *3* **30**
4310 **PICCOLO CATIVO 9** [11] 5-8-4 (46) Angela Hartley (7) 25/1: 104000: Prom to halfway, sn bhd, ¾ **28**
fin 10th: prob unsuited by this big drop in trip: see 1066 (7.5f).
3377 **SHARP EDGE BOY 63** [1] 4-8-8 (50) W Supple 8/1: 000200: Chsd ldrs far side, wknd fnl 2f, 11th: abs. *shd* **32**
4220 **PLUM FIRST 18** [4] 10-8-6 (48) Iona Wands 33/1: 56-600: Nvr dangerous, fin 12th: 10yo: see 4043. *2* **25**
4185 **BRANSTON PICKLE 20** [3] 3-9-6 (62) D Holland 9/2 FAV: 012000: Trkd ldrs, wknd qckly appr fnl 1f, *shd* **39**
13th: can do much better & likes soft grnd, seems to have gone off the boil: btr 3825.
4295 **TANCRED TIMES 12** [14] 5-9-1 (57) F Lynch 8/1: 260620: Led stands side, hdd 2f out, qckly wknd, 14th. *5* **24**
4294 **MUTASAWWAR 12** [12] 6-8-6 (48) P Fitzsimons (5) 10/1: 022200: Mid-div stands side, wknd rapidly *1½* **12**
appr fnl 2f, 15th: much btr 4155 (fibresand, 6f).
3966 **Sounds Ace 34** [17] 4-8-1 (43)(bl) D Mernagh (3) 33/14327 **Oriel Star 8** [13] 4-8-2 (44) J McAuley 16/1:
*1806 **Pleasure 131** [15] 5-9-0 (56)(hbl) N Callan 16/1: 4255 **Jeminar 15** [8] 3-8-6 (48) T Lucas 25/1:
4327 **Golden Biff 8** [10] 4-8-4 (46) R Lappin 25/1:
20 ran Time 1m 07.12 (8.92) (Mrs Y Brierley) T J Etherington Norton, N Yorks

NOTTINGHAM WEDNESDAY OCTOBER 18TH Lefthand, Galloping Track

Official Going SOFT (HEAVY in places). Stalls: 6f - Stands' side: Remainder - inside (Stands' side dolled out at 3f).

4408 **1.50 ROSELAND GROUP MDN DIV 1 3YO (D) 1m2f Heavy 157 +03 Fast**
£3445 £1060 £530 £265

4081 **TIKRAM 27** [6] H R A Cecil 3-9-0 T Quinn 5/2: -031: 3 ch c Lycius - Black Fighter (Secretariat) **90**
Held up in tch, eff appr fnl 2f, ran on to lead ent fnl 1f & rdn, kept on strongly: bckd, best time of day: unrcd
juv, brother to 12f wnr Taming: eff at 10f, 12f will suit: acts on soft & hvy grnd, gall trk: going the right way.
4081 **SECOND AFFAIR 27** [9] C F Wall 3-8-9 R Mullen 4/1: 32422: 3 b f Pursuit Of Love - Startino *3* **80**
(Bustino) Wide, in tch, smooth prog to lead ent fnl 3f rdn & hdd dist, no extra: acts on fast & hvy grnd.
-- **YA TARRA** [3] Saeed bin Suroor 3-8-9 L Dettori 6/4 FAV: 3: 3 ch f Unbridled - Snow Bride *1½* **78**
(Blushing Groom) Led till 3f out, ev ch till fdd ins last: bckd tho' op 4/5 on debut, clr rem: half-sister to top-
class Lammtarra: stays 10f on hvy tho' will prob apprec a faster surface: held big race entries & better expected.
3818 **SHATTERED SILENCE 44** [7] R Charlton 3-8-9 (VIS) R Hughes 10/1: 033334: Held up, closed appr *6* **70**
straight, wknd qckly 2f out: op 7/1, 6 wk abs, visored: best 2531 (gd).
3838 **DE TRAMUNTANA 43** [1] 3-8-9 J Fortune 16/1: 242505: Held up, rdn 3f out, no impress: 6 wk abs. *2½* **67**
4133 **SEOMRA HOCHT 24** [8] 3-9-0 Dean McKeown 33/1: 046: Al bhd: stiff task, see 4133. ½ **71**
4141 **HOLY ISLAND 23** [2] 3-8-9 J P Spencer 15/2: 37: Prom till 4f out: btr 4141 (soft). *19* **46**
4089 **ROYAL TEMPTATION 26** [5] 3-9-0 O Pears 50/1: 5048: Al bhd: stiff task. *1¼* **49**
4119 **STRAWMAN 24** [4] 3-9-0 Pat Eddery 50/1: 00659: Well plcd, wknd ent straight: stiffish task, see 704. *1¼* **47**
9 ran Time 2m 17.7 (15.4) (Buckram Oak Holdings) H R A Cecil Newmarket, Suffolk

4409 2.20 MIDLANDS SELL HCAP 3YO 0-60 (G) 1m6f Heavy 157 -28 Slow [65]
£1817 £519 £259

4178 **DANGEROUS DEPLOY** 20 [5] D R C Elsworth 3-9-6 (57) T Quinn 7/4 FAV: 550051: 3 b g Deploy - 60
Emily Mou (Cadeaux Genereux) Led after 4f till 4f out, hard rdn 2f out, regained lead dist, styd on grimly:
bckd, sold to Miss K George for 7,800gns: clrly relished this step up to 14f on hvy grnd & drop in grade.
3963 **GYPSY SONG** 34 [3] J A Glover 3-8-2 (39) O Pears 7/2: 050052: 3 b g Turtle Island - Kate 1¼ 39
Labelle (Teenoso) Dwelt, keen, prog appr fnl 2f, edged left ins last, kept on for 2nd: eff at 14f on hvy grnd.
4150 **BEE GEE 22** [4] M Blanshard 3-7-12 (35) Dale Gibson 6/1: 500433: 3 b f Beveled - Bunny Gee 1¼ 33
(Last Tycoon) Well plcd, led 4f out till bef 2f out, onepce ins last: stys 14f: handles hvy grnd & equitrack.
3664 **WEST END DANCER** 52 [6] P S McEntee 3-7-11 (34)(VIS)(1ow)(2oh) J Quinn 6/1: 033004: Held up, nk 31
drvn to chse ldrs 3f out & ch till no extra 1f out: visored, hdles rnr 3 weeks ago: stys 14f on hvy grnd.
3917 **HIGH BEAUTY** 36 [2] 3-7-10 (33)(2oh) G Baker (5) 8/1: 000065: Held up, prog ent straight & 5 25
led appr fnl 2f till bef fnl 1f, wknd: hdles fit, stiffish task, longer trip.
4193 **SALIENT POINT** 19 [1] 3-9-7 (58)(t) R Hughes 13/2: 4000P6: Early ldr, wknd 4f out, t.o.: top-weight. dist 0
6 ran Time 3m 24.2 (25.9) (Del & Jake Partnership) D R C Elsworth Whitsbury, Hants

4410 2.50 ROOF TOP NOV AUCT STKS 2YO (F) 6f Heavy 157 -63 Slow
£2878 £822 £411

4098 **OPEN WARFARE** 26 [1] M Quinn 2-8-11 F Norton 10/1: 500301: 2 b f General Monash - Pipe 78
Opener (Prince Sabo) Chsd ldrs, led appr fnl 1f, drvn out: tchd 12/1, slow time: earlier won at Haydock
(fill mdn): eff up with/forcing the pace at 5/6f: acts on fast & hvy grnd, gall trks: back to form.
-- **STORNOWAY** [7] G C Bravery 2-8-5 L Newman (2) 20/1: 2: 2 b f Catrail - Heavenly Waters 3½ 65
(Celestial Storm) Dwelt, imprvd after halfway, rdn 2f out, chsd wnr ins last, onepce: well clr rem on debut:
7,800gns filly, dam a winning styer: eff at 6f, get further next term: handles hvy grnd.
-- **SO TEMPTING** [11] J R Fanshawe 2-8-11 D Harrison 4/1: 3: 2 b c So Factual - Persuasion 6 59
(Batshoof) Dwelt, rear, styd on thro' tired horses ins last: bckd from 8/1: cost 10,000gns, dam 10/12f wnr.
*4137 **CANTERLOUPE 23** [2] P J Makin 2-8-11 S Sanders 9/4 FAV: 14: Front rank, pulled hard, ev ch till ¾ 57
wknd appr fnl 1f: bckd tho' op 5/4: raced much too freely in these testing conditions: see 4137.
3911 **LIGHT OF FASHION** 37 [5] Paul Eddery 25/1: 005: Nvr better than mid div: stiff task. 2½ 47
-- **DASH OF MAGIC** [4] 2-8-3 J Quinn 40/1: 6: Dwelt, nvr trbld ldrs: 2,600gns Magic Ring filly. 1¾ 40
4253 **DIAMOND JAYNE 15** [10] 2-8-4 R Fitzpatrick 40/1: 007: Nvr on terms: 2,600gns Royal Abjar 2½ 36
half sister to a decent 6f juv wnr: with J Hetherton.
-- **AMOROUS SARITA** [6] 2-8-6 P Doe 12/1: 8: Prom till hung left & wknd qckly 2f out: op 8/1: 2 34
9,000gns Pursuit Of Love filly: half-sister to sev wnrs up to mid dists, dam 7f/12f wnr: with P Harris.
-- **COLONEL KURTZ** [8] 2-8-11 M Fenton 25/1: 9: Al rear: 5,000gns colt: stoutly bred. hd 39
4247 **TICCATOO 15** [9] 2-8-7 Pat Eddery 16/1: 020040: Led till 2f out, sn btn: 10th, op 12/1, stiffish task. ¾ 34
*4252 **BINT ROYAL 15** [12] 2-8-10 C O Pears 4/1: 010: Trkd ldrs, lost plce appr fnl 2f: btr 4252 (5f). shd 36
3639 **MULSANNE 53** [3] 2-8-9 S Righton 66/1: -00000: Sn struggling: last, 8 week abs, new stable. 26 6
12 ran Time 1m 24.0 (13.2) (Open Warfare Partners) M Quinn Sparsholt, Oxon

4411 3.25 FREETHCARTWRIGHT HCAP 3YO+ 0-80 (D) 6f Heavy 157 +02 Fast [79]
£4452 £1370 £685 £342 3 yo rec 1 lb

*4204 **SLUMBERING 18** [7] B A Pearce 4-9-3 (68) O Urbina 12/1: 400511: 4 b g Thatching - Bedspread 74
(Seattle Dancer) Trkd ldrs, went on & edged left 1f out, ran on well for pressure: fair time: recent Sandown
wnr (h'cap): unplcd in 3 '99 starts (h'caps, rtd 83, B Meehan): '98 York wnr (mdn, rtd 89): eff at 6/7f, stays
a stiff 1m: acts on gd & hvy grnd, any trk: best up with/forcing the pace: eff with/without blnks: in fine form.
4293 **AMBER BROWN 12** [8] K T Ivory 4-8-6 (57)(bl) C Carver 20/1: 400602: 4 b f Thowra - High ½ 61
Velocity (Frimley Park) Tried to make all, under press & hung left appr fnl 1f, hdd dist, rallied: op 16/1:
a bold attempt, suited by soft & hvy grnd: see 1542.
3569 **CD FLYER 56** [4] M R Channon 3-9-9 (75) Craig Williams 9/1: 633003: 3 ch g Grand Lodge - 1¾ 75
Pretext (Polish President) Bhd, prog 2f out, chsd ldrs & carried left inside last, no extra nr fin: op 7/1, 8 wk abs:
gd run: acts on fast & hvy grnd: see 852.
4377 **PREMIUM PRINCESS 2** [9] J J Quinn 5-9-7 (72) J Fortune 11/2 FAV: 410234: Held up, imprvd 2f out, nk 71
drvn bef fnl 1f, unable to chall: bckd, ran 48hrs ago: acts on firm & hvy grnd: see 3975 (C/D).
4233 **CHARMING LOTTE 16** [16] 3-8-12 (64)(vis) C Rutter 20/1: 513035: Bhd, prog ent fnl 2f & bmpd, nvr dngrs. 1 60
4107 **THE GAY FOX 25** [2] 6-9-8 (73)(tbl) R Hughes 9/1: 100466: Mid div, chsd ldrs 2f out, sn onepce for press. 3 62
4121 **COMPRADORE 24** [5] 5-9-1 (66) D Sweeney 16/1: 003037: Towards rear, prog to trck ldrs 2f out, ¾ 53
sn shaken up, fdd fnl 1f: back in trip, see 1467 (7f, class stakes).
+4207 **CARLTON 18** [15] 6-10-0 (79) T Quinn 6/1: 005618: Nvr a factor tho' stying on fin: btr 4207 (clmr). ¾ 64
4287 **MANTLES PRIDE 12** [6] 5-9-9 (74)(bl) J Reid 6/1: 000229: Nvr nr ldrs: btr 4287, 1514. hd 59
4010 **FRANCPORT 32** [1] 4-9-6 (71) G Carter 7/1: 306000: Al bhd: 10th, op 12/1: see 824. 3½ 49
4295 **DIAMOND DECORUM 12** [14] 4-9-1 (66)(t) R Fitzpatrick 12/1: 060000: Sn prom, rdn & btn 2f out: 13th. 0
4167} Hidden Fort 384 [11] 3-10-0 (80) Pat Eddery 20/1: 4377 Classy Cleo 2 [13] 5-9-9 (74) Joanna Badger(7) 20/1:
4294 Present Chance 12 [10] 6-8-4 (55)(bl) J Quinn 25/1:
14 ran Time 1m 20.1 (9.3) (Mrs Christine Painting) B A Pearce Newchapel, Surrey

4412 3.55 ROSELAND GROUP MDN DIV 2 3YO (D) 1m2f Heavy 157 -11 Slow
£3445 £1060 £530 £265

-- **EATON PLACE** [9] H R A Cecil 3-8-9 T Quinn 2/1 JT FAV: 1: 3 b f Zafonic - One Way Street (Habitat) 83
Led after 3f, rdn appr fnl 2f & sn hdd, rallied well to regain lead inside last: drfter from 4/5 on debut:
related to sev decent wnrs: eff over a gd 10f, get 12f on this evidence: acts on hvy grnd & runs fresh.
4205 **BRADY BOYS 18** [2] J H M Gosden 3-9-0 J Fortune 12/1: 02: 3 b g Cozzene - Elvia (Roberto) 2 84
Early ldr, rdn to lead again 2f out, onepce & hdd inside last: tchd 16/1, 12L clr of 3rd: blnks omitted today:
stazys 10f on hvy grnd: shld win a maiden.
-- **DAILY TONIC** [7] Mrs A J Perrett 3-9-0 Pat Eddery 2/1 JT FAV: 3: 3 ch c Sanglamore - Woodwardia 12 70
(El Gran Senor) Chsd ldrs, eff 4f out, btn 2f out: bckd, rather green on debut: bred to apprec this 10f trip.
4205 **GENERAL ALARM 18** [4] J R Fanshawe 3-9-0 D Harrison 3/1: 04: Keen in rear, rdn 2f out, nvr nr ldrs: nk 69

op 6/1: better expected from this Warning half brother to sev wnrs.
3914 **SCENTED AIR 37** [1] 3-8-9 Dean McKeown 16/1: 05: Dwelt, handy till 4f out: stiffish task. *5* **59**
3914 **FLIGHT REFUND 37** [6] 3-9-0 P M Quinn (3) 50/1: 00-006: Al bhd: flattered, no worthwhile form. *9* **55$**
2585 **BOP 98** [5] 3-8-9 N Pollard 20/1: 07: Unruly in stalls, trckd ldrs till 4f out: 14 week abs. *10* **40**
1725 **TARRIFA 135** [8] 3-8-9 F Norton 66/1: 0-08: Chsd ldrs till halfway: over 4 month abs: no form. *2½* **37**
8 ran Time 2m 19.1 (16.8) (H R H Prince Fahd Salman) H R A Cecil Newmarket, Suffolk

4413

4.30 NOTTS CLASS STKS 3YO+ 0-60 (F) 1m2f Heavy 157 -05 Slow
£2903 £829 £414 3 yo rec 5 lb

*4169 **COUGHLANS GIFT 21** [9] J C Fox 4-9-0 R Smith (5) 8/1: U05011: 4 ch f Alnasr Alwasheeek - Superfrost (Tickled Pink) Held up, stdy wide prog ent str to lead bef 2f out, edged left und press ins last but styd on well: recent Salisbury wnr (appr h'cap): '99 wnr at Bath (h'cap, rtd 60 & 54a): plcd in '98 (rtd 57): prev eff at 7f/1m, now suited by 10f: acts on gd & hvy grnd, prob equitrack, any trk: runs well fresh: in fine form. **62**
*4311 **CAUTIOUS JOE 9** [14] R A Fahey 3-8-13 P Hanagan (5) 11/4 FAV: 030112: 3 b f First Trump - Jomel Amou (Ela Mana Mou) Well plcd, chall 2f out, sn drvn, slightly checked 1f out, kept on: bckd to land the hat-trick, lost little in defeat: eff at 1m/10f: progressive, see 4311. *¾* **64**
3951 **TYPHOON GINGER 35** [6] G Woodward 5-9-0 J P Spencer 5/1: 662053: 5 ch m Archway - Pallas Viking (Viking) Patiently rdn, clsd on bit 3f out, rdn 2f out, styd on but held: bckd from 8/1, clr rem: 10f on this grnd stretches stamina to limit tho' fine run at the weights: handles firm & hvy grnd: still a mdn: see 1070. *2* **57**
4118 **HAVANA 24** [2] Mrs A J Perrett 4-9-0 T Ashley 20/1: 233004: Mid div, not much room 4f out & switched, styd on but no impress on ldrs: see 2627, 1343. *5* **51**
4374 **RUTLAND CHANTRY 2** [13] 6-9-3 (BL) J Fortune 4/1: 053425: Cl up, led appr fnl 3f till bef 2f out, sn no extra: blnkd, tchd 11/2: ran better than this 48hrs ago: see 601. *nk* **53**
4088 **VICTORY ROLL 27** [1] 4-9-3 S Drowne 33/1: -02606: Nvr better than mid div: stiffish task at the weights. *6* **46**
4074 **BACHELORS PAD 28** [7] 6-9-5 I Mongan (5) 16/1: 461007: Al mid div: op 12/1, top-weight. *½* **47**
4178 **ICE CRYSTAL 20** [11] 3-8-12 C Rutter 16/1: 400608: Dwelt, chsd ldrs till 3f out: tchd 20/1. *hd* **45**
3383 **ABLE MILLENIUM 63** [16] 4-9-3 (BL) R Price 25/1: 0-0009: Keen in rear, improved halfway till 3f out. *5* **39**
4311 **HEATHYARDS LAD 9** [12] 3-8-12 Pat Eddery 16/1: 345040: In tch till 3f out: 10th, stiffish task. *nk* **38**
4311 **MARTELLO 9** [10] 4-9-3 C Haddon (7) 13/2: 05-420: Led till after halfway, sn btn: 11th, op 9/2, lngr trip. *2½* **35**
3755 **Red Canyon 48** [8] 3-8-12 M Fenton 16/1: 3915 **Red Delirium 37** [5] 4-9-3 L Newman (3) 14/1:
51 **Sweet Patoopie 338** [3] 6-9-0 C Carver (3) 50/1: 4148} **Cabcharge Blue 385** [4] 8-9-0 R Mullen 50/1:
15 ran Time 2m 18.5 (16.2) (Mrs J A Cleary) J C Fox Collingbourne Ducis, Wilts

4414

5.05 SPONSORSHIP HCAP 3YO 0-75 (E) 1m54y rnd Heavy 157 -26 Slow **[81]**
£3172 £976 £488 £244

4175 **DIGITAL 21** [4] M R Channon 3-9-7 (74) Craig Williams 11/1: 423021: 3 ch g Safawan - Heavenly Goddess (Soviet Star) Towards rear, prog 2f out, ran on strgly ins last to lead fnl 100y, rdn out: jt top weight: 1st win, unrcd juv: eff at 1m, will get further: acts on fast, suited by soft & hvy grnd, prob any trk. **82**
2906 **MY RETREAT 85** [7] B W Hills 3-9-0 (67) Pat Eddery 7/1: 005052: 3 b c Hermitage - My Jessica Ann (Native Rythm) Led, under press appr fnl 1f, worn down towards fin: op 5/1, clr rem, 12 week abs: fine run, blinkers omitted: suited by hvy grnd: see 884. *1¾* **72**
4173 **COLLEGE ROCK 21** [14] R Brotherton 3-8-10 (63)(vis) L Newman (3) 14/1: 304243: 3 ch c Rock Hopper - Sea Aura (Roi Soleil) Cl up & ev ch till rdn & same pace fnl 1f: tough: acts on firm & hvy grnd. *3* **63**
4126 **OMNIHEAT 24** [5] M J Ryan 3-9-4 (71) P Robinson 16/1: 000504: Rear, prog & not much room ent fnl 2f, styd on for press inside last: see 3317, 1649. *½* **70**
4232 **ROYAL CAVALIER 16** [1] 3-8-13 (66) P M Quinn (3) 12/1: 006405: Bhd ldrs, not much room 3f out till 2f out, same pace: tchd 16/1, see 2250, 720. *2* **62**
4208 **KELBURNE 18** [13] 3-7-10 (49)(1oh) P Hanagan (2) 25/1: 400006: Chsd ldrs, fdd fnl 1f: back in trip. *1½* **43**
4292 **HUGS DANCER 12** [3] 3-8-13 (66) Dean McKeown 6/1: 334037: Al mid div: tchd 12/1: see 4292. *nk* **59**
4004 **STORMSWELL 32** [15] 3-7-11 (50) G Baker (5) 10/1: 304048: Mid div, lost pl 3f out, mod fnl 1f rally. *hd* **43**
*4093 **ALMIDDINA 26** [11] 3-9-6 (73) T Quinn 2/1 FAV: 4019: Chsd ldrs, rdn & btn ent fnl 2f, eased cl-home: bckd tho' op 5/4: unsuited by return to 1m on h'cap bow?: see 4093. *hd* **65**
4038 **KNOCKTOPHER ABBEY 30** [12] 3-9-7 (74) G Hind 16/1: 536500: Chsd ldrs till appr fnl 2f: 10th. *1½* **64**
4234 **STRATTON 16** [6] 3-8-11 (64) R Mullen 12/1: 6-4030: Dwelt, nvr on terms: 11th on h'cap bow. *16* **34**
4031 **Tea For Texas 30** [8] 3-7-10 (49)(4oh) D Kinsella (7) 25/1:
3658 **Time Vally 52** [10] 3-9-2 (69) P Doe 20/1: 4038 **Jazzy Millennium 30** [9] 3-8-10 (63) Cheryl Nosworthy(7) 33/1:
14 ran Time 1m 54.0 (14.6) (W G R Wightman) M R Channon West Isley, Berks

BRIGHTON THURSDAY OCTOBER 19TH Lefthand, Very Sharp, Undulating Track

Official Going: SOFT Stalls: Inside, except 10f/12f - Outside

4415

2.20 TAX FREE MED AUCT MDN 2YO (E) 7f rnd Soft 107 +04 Fast
£3157 £902 £451 Majority raced centre - stands side

4189 **FATHER THAMES 20** [15] J R Fanshawe 2-9-0 D Harrison 11/4 FAV: 31: 2 b c Bishop Of Cashel - Mistress Thames (Sharpo) Al prom, rdn/led over 2f out, asserted inside last, pushed out nr fin: bckd, op 4/1: gd time: confirmed promise of debut: April foal, half brother to a 10f wnr abroad, dam a mdn: apprec step up to 7f, 1m shld suit: acts on soft grnd & a sharp/undulating trck: clearly going the right way. **89**
4172 **LUCEFER 22** [12] G C H Chung 2-9-0 M Henry 5/1: -02022: 2 b g Lycius - Maharani (Red Ransom) Chsd ldrs, rdn/prog to chall 2f out, no impress inside last: op 9/2: shown enough to win, try headgear? *3½* **83**
3901 **KAI ONE 40** [10] R Hannon 2-9-0 P Fitzsimons (5) 100/30: 32333: 2 b c Puissance - Kind Of Shy (Kind Of Hush) Prom, rdn/chall 2f out, no impress fnl 1f: op 4/1, 6 week abs: acts on firm & soft: see 3901. *2* **80**
4184 **EMPORIO 21** [1] L M Cumani 2-9-0 J P Spencer 8/1: 04: Led till over 2f out, outpcd fnl 2f: op 5/1. *3½* **75**
4172 **KELLS 22** [4] 2-9-0 A Clark 50/1: 005: Dwelt, rear, in tch/remained far side fnl 3f, held 2f out. *1½* **73**
4219 **OOMPH 19** [2] 2-8-9 M Tebbutt 7/2: 4366: Prom, rdn/wknd 2f out, eased nr fin: see 4219, 3938. *3* **64**
-- **ULTIMATE CHOICE** [14] 2-9-0 D Holland 9/1: 7: Keen/prom 5f: Petong colt, April foal, cost 21,000gns: half brother to sprint h'capper Friar Tuck & a useful 6/7f juv wnr Kaibo: dam a 2yo wnr. *1½* **67**
4267 **DETACHING 15** [6] 2-8-9 W Ryan 20/1: 08: Al towards rear: see 4267. *1½* **60**

3760 **ANKASAMEN 48** [5] 2-8-9 R Mullen 33/1: -009: Al rear: 7 wk abs: see 3358.   ½   59
2209 **MUTAMADEE 115** [9] 2-9-0 J Reid 25/1: 00: Rear, nvr a factor: 10th: 4 month abs: see 2209.   1   63
4189 **Brief Contact 20** [7] 2-9-0 I Mongan (5) 33/1:   --   **Skimmer** [13] 2-9-0 P Doe 25/1:
4095 **Les Girls 27** [3] 2-8-9 Paul Eddery 50/1: U
13 ran   Time 1m 27.00 (7.2)   (Mrs Denis Haynes)   J R Fanshawe Newmarket, Suffolk

---

4416   **2.50 TAX FREE NURSERY HCAP 2YO 0-75 (E)**   **7f rnd**   **Soft 107**   **-16 Slow**   **[82]**
       £3031   £866   £433   Raced centre - stands side

3867 **SAORSIE 42** [2] J C Fox 2-7-12 (52) D Kinsella (7) 25/1: -00001: 2 b g Emperor Jones - Exclusive   58
Lottery (Presidium) Bhd, hdwy fnl 3f & led dist, styd on well dispite carrying head high, rdn out: 6 wk abs:
unplcd prev: eff over a sharp/undulating 7f on soft: runs well fresh.
2459 **JARV 104** [9] J Akehurst 2-8-5 (56)(3ow) G Carter 20/1: -0002: 2 b f Inzar - Conditional Sale   1¾   62
(Petorius) Bhd, hdwy to chall dist, not pace of wnr nr fin: abs, h'cap bow: eff at 7f on soft: lightly raced.
4191 **CHAWENG BEACH 20** [4] R Hannon 2-8-13 (67) P Fitzsimons (5) 12/1: 451103: 2 ro f Chaddleworth -   1¾   68
Swallow Bay (Penmarric) Chsd ldrs, kept on onepce fnl 2f: acts on firm & soft grnd: see 3830 (firm).
3973 **PACKIN EM IN 34** [1] N Hamilton 2-8-6 (60) D Harrison 20/1: 0044: Led after 1f, rdn/clr 2f out,   nk   60
hdd dist & no extra: op 14/1, h'cap bow: stays a sharp 7f, improved last twice on soft grnd: see 3973.
4076 **SEL 28** [7] 2-8-8 (62)(bl) D Holland 14/1: 125105: Rdn/chsd ldr 2f out, fdd fnl 1f: acts on firm & soft.   ½   61
-4305 **GALY BAY 10** [14] 2-9-7 (75) I Mongan (5) 7/4 FAV: 33326: Chsd ldrs, rdn/btn over 1f out: hvly bckd.   ½   73
4034 **UNDERCOVER GIRL 31** [2] 2-8-3 (57) P Doe 20/1: 5007: Handy halfway, wknd 2f out: h'cap bow.   shd   55
4254 **APRIL LEE 16** [16] 2-8-11 (65)(e) J Reid 16/1: 520308: Led 1f, prom 5f: btr 4116 (1m).   nk   62
*4030 **LADY KINVARRAH 31** [15] 2-9-5 (73) A Clark 6/1: 060319: Held up, eff when hmpd & lost plce over   1½   68
2f out, mod late gains: no luck in running, prob worth another look after 4030 (6f, gd/soft).
4288 **FADHAH 13** [8] 2-9-1 (69) J P Spencer 14/1: 5200: Towards rear, rdn/no room over 2f out, sn   1   63
held: 10th: op 10/1: h'cap bow: prob closer with a clr run here: see 2290 (fast).
4154 **MENAS ERN 23** [6] 2-7-12 (52) G Bardwell 20/1: 00040: Al towards rear: 11th: h'cap bow.   1¼   44
4117 **BEE J GEE 25** [18] 2-8-11 (65) T G McLaughlin 14/1: 60040: Chsd ldrs 5f: 12th: op 10/1: flattered 4117.   nk   56
4191 **MISS TRESS 20** [5] 2-9-3 (71) P Dobbs (5) 14/1: -46400: Al towards rear: 13th: op 10/1: see 2259.   ½   61
2687 **Physical Force 96** [12] 2-8-1 (55) A Polli (3) 12/1:   4096 **Safinaz 27** [10] 2-7-8 (51) D R McCabe 12/1:
4269 **Empress Of Austria 15** [13] 2-8-6 (60)(t) M Tebbutt 12/1:4171 **Vine Court 22** [17] 2-8-1 (55) R Mullen 14/1:
17 ran   Time 1m 28.4 (8.6)   (Lord Mutton Racing Partnership)   J C Fox Collingbourne Ducis, Wilts

---

4417   **3.20 EBF TAX FREE MDN DIV I 2YO (D)**   **1m rnd**   **Soft 107**   **+02 Fast**
       £2886   £888   £444   £222   Raced centre - stands side

3940 **TUDOR REEF 36** [7] J Noseda 2-9-0 J P Spencer 6/1: -04641: 2 b c Mujadil - Exciting (Mill Reef)   91
Made all, readily pulled clr fnl 2f despite drifting badly left, pushed out inside last, easily: val for 9L+:gd
time: apprec this step up to 1m, further could suit in time: handles firm grnd, greatly improved on soft today:
plenty in hand here, looks one to note if reappearing soon in similar conditions.
4230 **ENGLISH HARBOUR 17** [9] B W Hills 2-8-9 D Holland 2/1 FAV: -00422: 2 ch f Sabrehill - Water   7   76
Woo (Tom Rolfe) Rdn/chsd wnr 2f out, no impress: bckd, op 5/2: caught a tartar here: see 4230.
4116 **MIDNIGHT CREEK 25** [3] Mrs A J Perrett 2-9-0 W Ryan 7/1: 523: 2 b c Tragic Role - Greek Night Out   3   77
(Ela Mana Mou) Prom, outpcd fnl 2f: op 5/1: prob handles gd/soft & soft grnd: see 4116 (C/D).
-- **DISTILLERY** [4] P F I Cole 2-9-0 G Carter 4/1: 4: Rear, hdwy 3f out, no impress fnl 2f: op 4/1:   1   76
Mister Baileys colt, March foal, cost $50,000: dam a sprinter abroad: sire high class juv, subs won 2,000 Guineas.
3940 **SINJAREE 36** [8] 2-9-0 J Reid 10/1: 05: Chsd ldrs 6f: see 3940.   nk   75
-- **TENDERFOOT** [1] 2-8-9 G Bardwell 7/1: 6: Prom 6f: Be My Chief filly, March foal, cost 13,000gns: 13   55
sister to smart 1m/10f performer Whitefoot: dam a mid dist 4yo wnr: shld apprec further next term: with J Pearce.
-- **BUZ KIRI** [6] 2-9-0 M Tebbutt 25/1: Sn bhd: Gulch colt, Jan foal, cost $25,000, dam a wng miler.   hd   59
3999 **STAR GLADE 33** [2] 2-8-9 D R McCabe 33/1: -08: Al bhd: well bhd on debut prev.   2½   50
3985 **IRISH VERSE 34** [5] 2-8-9 R Havlin 4/1: -69: Slowly away, keen/held up, well bhd fnl 2f: op 7/4.   dist   0
9 ran   Time 1m 40.4 (8.4)   (B E Nielsen)   J Noseda Newmarket, Suffolk

---

4418   **3.50 EBF TAX FREE MDN DIV II 2YO (D)**   **1m rnd**   **Soft 107**   **-33 Slow**
       £2886   £888   £444   £222   Raced centre - stands side

4341 **AMONG WOMEN 7** [3] N A Callaghan 2-8-9 D Harrison 4/1: 001: 2 b f Common Grounds - Key West   74
(Highest Honor) Led/dsptd lead till went on over 2f out, held on well fnl 1f, rdn out: op 7/2:
apprec this step up to 1m: acts on soft grnd & a sharp/undulating trk: going the right way.
4297 **ART EXPERT 12** [1] P F I Cole 2-9-0 D Holland 11/10 FAV: 022: 2 b c Pursuit Of Love - Celtic   ½   77
Wing (Midyan) Rear, hdwy to chall fnl 1f, rdn/held nr fin: hvly bckd, tchd 2/1: acts on soft & hvy: see 4297.
-- **MODEL QUEEN** [6] B W Hills 2-8-9 R Havlin 4/1: 3: 2 ch f Kingmambo - Model Bride (Blushing Groom)   1   70
Keen/trckd ldrs, not much room 2f out till 1f out, styd on well cl home, not pace to chall: op 3/1: closer
here with a clr run at a crucial stage: March foal, half sister to 2 winning milers: dam a 6f wnr.
4189 **FAR SOUTH TRADER 20** [2] R J O'Sullivan 2-9-0 R Havlin 50/1: 04: Led halfway till over 2f out,   1   73
no extra fnl 1f: styd longer 1m trip, handles soft grnd: left debut bhd, bred to apprec mid dists next term.
4062 **ALFANO 29** [8] 2-9-0 M Henry 20/1: 55: Led after 1f till halfway, no extra fnl 2f: see 4062.   hd   73
4268 **SUNGIO 15** [4] 2-9-0 J P Spencer 12/1: 066: Towards rear, eff 2f out, little hdwy: op 10/1: see 4268.   nk   72
4209 **LONG DAY 19** [7] 2-9-0 P Dobbs (5) 6/1: 07: Trkd ldrs 6f: longer 1m trip: see 4209.   7   57
-- **DON RUBINI** [5] 2-9-0 Paul Eddery 14/1: 8: Al rear: Emarati colt, April foal, cost 18,000gns: 14   42
half brother to 1m h'cap wnr Warring: dam a 6f wnr: with B Smart.
8 ran   Time 1m 43.2 (11.2)   (Gallagher Equine Ltd)   N A Callaghan Newmarket, Suffolk

---

4419   **4.20 BRIGHTWELLS SELL HCAP 3YO+ 0-60 (F)**   **1m2f**   **Soft 107**   **-27 Slow**   **[60]**
       £2394   £684   £342   3 yo rec 5 lb   Raced across track final 3f

*4324 **RED CAFE 9** [15] P D Evans 4-8-12 (44)(6ex) J Bramhill 7/1: 240011: 4 ch f Perugino - Test Case   49
(Busted) Towards rear, hdwy halfway & drvn ahead over 1f out, styd on well inside last: no bid: earlier scored at
Ayr (seller) first win: missed '99: plcd in '98 (rtd 63 at best, seller): eff at 6f prev, now suited by 9/10f:
acts on fast, likes soft/hvy, any track: enjoys mid grade: in fine form at present.
4208 **ZIDAC 19** [4] P J Makin 8-10-0 (60) A Clark 7/2 FAV: 002622: 8 b g Statoblest - Sule Skerry (Scottish   2   62

BRIGHTON
THURSDAY OCTOBER 19TH **Lefthand, Very Sharp, Undulating Track**

Rifle) Chsd ldrs, rdn/chsd wnr fnl 1f, al held: bckd: topweight: see 1509 (C/D).

4334 **WAIKIKI BEACH 8** [8] G L Moore 9-8-10 (42)(bl) R Brisland (5) 25/1: 620603: 9 ch g Fighting Fit -   2 42
Running Melody (Rheingold) In tch, hdwy halfway & led 4f out till over 1f out, no extra inside last: clr rem: blinks
reapp: acts on firm, soft & both AWs: see 3490, 136 (AW).

3915 **BECKON 38** [3] B R Johnson 4-8-8 (40) G Gibbons (7) 10/1: 506104: Mid div, rdn/prog to chall   7 33
4f out, wknd over 1f out: op 12/1: prefer a faster surface: see 3737 (C/D, firm).

14] **TREVERRICK 1075** [5] 5-9-9 (55)(t) R Mullen 33/1: 5063/5: Rear, late hdwy, no threat: long abs: shd 48
mod form over timber 99/00 (T R George, rtd 51h, nov h'cap): ex Irish, '97 wnr on the level at Cork (mdn): eff
at 9f, tried 12f: acts on soft grnd: with R Cowell.

4208 **OSCIETRA 19** [2] 4-8-12 (44) P Dobbs (5) 6/1: 600306: Rear, mod late gains: see 1096.   6 31
4311 **SOCIETY KING 10** [18] 5-9-0 (46) Darren Williams (5) 33/1: 000-07: Chsd ldr 6f, fdd: unplcd in   hd 32
'99 (rtd 50a, claimer): plcd on reapp in '98 (rtd 71, mdn): stys a sharp 7f, handles soft grnd.

4208 **KINNINO 19** [1] 6-8-10 (42) I Mongan (5) 13/2: 144668: In tch, btn 2f out: see 4208, 3737 & 3111.   2½ 26
3823 **ESPERTO 45** [19] 7-8-5 (37) G Bardwell 12/1: 044009: Prom 7f: op 10/1, 6 wk abs: see 1546.   5 16
3816 **JOHN STEED 45** [13] 3-8-7 (44) Paul Eddery 20/1: -04000: Bhd, mod late hdwy: 10th: 6 week abs.   3 20
4229 **COY DEBUTANTE 17** [14] 6-8-8 (40) J Reid 16/1: 3-0000: Mid div, btn 3f out: 11th: see 1364.   ½ 15
3691 **DISTANT FLAME 52** [12] 3-7-13 (36) P Doe 33/1: 005600: Mid div, btn 3f out: 12th: abs: see 3691.   4 7
4334 **MASSEY 8** [17] 4-8-8 (40)(vis) D Harrison 16/1: 000000: Led 6f: 17th: vis reapp: see 752 (AW, 12f).   0
2331 Leonie Samual 110 [9] 5-8-12 (44) G Carter 14/1: 4274 **Mercede** 15 [20] 3-8-2 (35)(4ow) D R McCabe 25/1:
4176 Rock On Robin 22 [16] 3-7-13 (36) A Polli (3) 40/1:1572 **Mademoiselle Paris** 142 [7] 3-7-13 (36) S Righton 33/1:
4224 Darwells Folly 19 [10] 5-9-2 (48) D Holland (5) 12/1: 837] **Incepta** 556 [6] 5-9-8 (54) T G McLaughlin 33/1:
19 ran   Time 2m 11.2 (13.4)   (J E Abbey)   P D Evans Pandy, Gwent

---

4420	4.50 FRED B'DAY CLASS STKS 3YO+ 0-80 (D)	1m rnd	Soft 107	-14 Slow
	£3965 £1220 £610 £305 Majority raced centre - stands side			

4018 **NIGHT EMPRESS 33** [5] J R Fanshawe 3-8-8 D Harrison 12/1: 451501: 3 br f Emperor Jones - Night   78
Trader (Melyno) Al prom, led going easily over 3f out, drvn/pressed from over 1f out, held on well: earlier scored
at Yarmouth (h'cap): plcd twice '99 (rtd 84): eff at 7f/1m on firm & soft grnd, prob handles any track.

4340 **MAKE WAY 7** [3] B J Meehan 4-9-0 D R McCabe 4/1: 255032: 4 b g Red Ransom - Way Of The   1 82
World (Dance Of Life) Rear, drvn & styd on fnl 2f, not rch wnr: gd run: op 5/1: see 1528, 986.

4206 **KAREEB 19** [7] W R Muir 3-9-0 P Doe 14/1: 436103: 3 b g Green Desert - Braari (Gulch)   ¾ 81
Towards rear, hdwy to chase wnr over 2f out, drvn/no extra fnl 1f: op 12/1: acts on firm & soft: see 3998.

4121 **CEDAR MASTER 25** [15] R J O'Sullivan 3-8-11 (vis) D Holland 14/1: 032004: Prom, onepce fnl 2f: ¾ 77
acts on firm & soft grnd: see 3580, 1029.

*4177 **THREE OWLS 22** [2] 3-8-11 J P Spencer 5/4 FAV: 315: Chsd ldrs, onepce/held fnl 2f: hvly bckd.   2½ 73
3115 **DARE HUNTER 76** [4] 3-8-11 J Reid 16/1: 024006: Towards rear, hdwy/no room & lost plce over 2f   nk 72
out, no rch after: op 12/1: closer without interference: 11th: abs: see 1366, 1055.

4206 **SABREON 19** [12] 3-8-8 G Carter 10/1: -25067: Rear, eff 3f out, little hdwy: op 7/1: btr 2449 (10f).   1¼ 67
*4234 **ATLANTIC ACE 17** [9] 3-9-0 Paul Eddery 2/1: 0-18: Keen/held up, no impress fnl 3f: btr 4234 (mdn).   3½ 68
4212 **PRINCE SLAYER 19** [14] 4-9-0 (BL) I Mongan (5) 10/1: 000009: Prom, rdn/btn over 2f out: blnks.   1¼ 66
4274 **GROVE LODGE 15** [11] 3-8-11 A Clark 50/1: 000600: Al rear: 10th: see 1024.   5 56$
3426 **CARENS HERO 62** [10] 3-8-11 (BL) W Ryan 12/1: 326153: 8 ch g Diesis - Last Bird (Sea Bird II)   shd 56
Slowly away/rear, prog/chsd wnr 3f out, no impress fnl 2f: well clr of rem: see 4229.

4206 **RESOUNDING 19** [13] 3-8-8 R Mullen 8/1: 324650: Prom 5f: 14th: visor omitted: see 3178, 2614.   5 48
4335 **Kafil 8** [1] 6-9-0 R Brisland (5) 50/1:   4169 **Max 22** [6] 5-9-0 D Kinsella (7) 66/1:
4276 **Frontier Flight 14** [8] 10-9-0 Darren Williams (5) 100/1:
15 ran   Time 1m 41.7 (9.7)   (The Woodman Racing Syndicate)   J R Fanshawe Newmarket, Suffolk

---

4421	5.20 SKI & SNOWBOARD APPR HCAP 3YO+ 0-80 (E)	1m3f196y	Soft 107	-07 Slow	[75]
	£2779 £794 £397 3 yo rec 7 lb Winner raced alone far side				

3049 **GOT ONE TOO 80** [1] E J O'Neill 3-7-10 (50) D Glennon (3) 20/1: 000101: 3 ch g Green Tune -   57
Gloria Mundi (Saint Cyrien) Made all & clr over 2f out, in command fnl 1f, pushed out: op 12/1, 12 wk abs: prev
with D Sasse & earlier scored at Folkestone (h'cap, first win): unplcd in '99 (rtd 62 at best, blinkd on debut):
loves to dominate at 12f: acts on gd & soft: eff with/without a t-strap: runs well fresh: likes a sharp/undul trk.

4299 **KADOUN 12** [6] L M Cumani 3-9-10 (78) G Sparkes 1/1 FAV: 244322: 3 b c Doyoun - Kumta (Priolo)   3½ 79
Held up, rdn & kept on fnl 2f, no impress on wnr: well bckd: return to 12f+ should suit: see 4299 (14f).

4280 **LANCER 14** [3] J Pearce 3-8-8 (55)(vis) C Catlin 5/1: 326153: 8 ch g Diesis - Last Bird (Sea Bird II)   1¾ 54
Slowly away/rear, prog/chsd wnr 3f out, no impress fnl 2f: well clr of rem: see 4229.

4166 **GALAPINO 22** [7] Jamie Poulton 7-7-10 (43)(1oh) D Kinsella (5) 16/1: 520004: Chsd ldrs, btn 3f out.   10 30
4271 **DAUNTED 15** [2] 4-8-8 (55)(bl) G Hannon 7/1: -00205: Trckd ldrs 10f: op 20/1: btr 4101 (AW).   3½ 41
1281 **SINGLE CURRENCY 159** [4] 4-8-8 (55) N Farmer (7) 50/1: 3-006: Chsd wnr 6f, sn btn: 5 month abs,   8 33
h'cap bow: prev with P Cole, now with P Butler: see 832.

1030 **LIGHTNING STAR 176** [5] 5-10-0 (75)(bl) W Hutchinson (3) 10/1: 036/47: Chsd ldrs 1m: op 6/1:   5 48
jmps fit: rtd 101h at best, h'cap): blinks reapp today: see 1030.

3122 **BOLD PRECEDENT 76** [8] 3-9-4 (72) Darren Williams 7/1: -43408: Chsd wnr halfway till 3f out, sn   hd 45
btn/eased: op 4/1, 11 wk abs: see 2265, 4524.

4208 **ZURS 19** [9] 7-9-0 (61) D McGaffin 20/1: 000-09: Slowly away, rear, struggling 3f out: see 4208.   2½ 32
9 ran   Time 2m 41.8 (13.6)   (Christopher P Ranson)   E J O'Neill Newmarket, Suffolk

---

NEWCASTLE
THURSDAY OCTOBER 19TH **Lefthand, Galloping Track, Stiff Track**

Official Going   HEAVY Stalls: Str Course - Stands Side; Round Course - Inside; 10f - Far Side.

4422	2.05 BETSMART.CO.UK MDN 2YO (D)	1m rnd	Heavy 215	+01 Fast
	£3435 £1057 £528 £264			

4281 **TOMASINO 13** [2] M Johnston 2-9-0 K Darley 7/2: 461: 2 br c Celtic Swing - Bustinetta (Bustino)   83
Chsd wnr, rdn into lead appr fnl 2f, styd on well, drvn out: half brother to a 1m/14f wnr, dam 11f wnr: eff over
a stiff/gall 1m, mid-dists will suit next term: goes v well on hvy: open to improvement further.

3760 **ALAKANANDA 48** [1] Sir Mark Prescott 2-8-9 G Duffield 10/11 FAV: -22: 2 b f Hernando - Alouette   1 76

NEWCASTLE THURSDAY OCTOBER 19TH Lefthand, Galloping Track, Stiff Track

(Darshaan) Settled last, imprvd over 2f out, chsd wnr fnl 1f but no impress: 5L clr rem, nicely bckd: 7 wk abs:
stays 7f/1m: acts on gd & hvy, the former may reportedly suit best: see 3760.

3906 **MORSHID** 40 [3] M R Channon 2-9-0 A Culhane 2/1: 033: 2 b c Gulch - Possessive Dancer (Shareef 5 73
Dancer) Led early, remained with ldr, led again over 2f out, sn hdd, fdd fnl 1f: op 6/4 after 6 wk abs:
poss not quite get home in these v testing conditions: btr 3906 (gd).

4158 **CARRACA** 23 [4] J D Bethell 2-9-0 (BL) J Carroll 25/1: -004: Dwelt, led after 1f, hdd appr fnl 2f, 9 58
grad wknd: op 14/1: 1st time blnks: 55,000 gns 1st foal, dam related to a high-class mid-dist performer.

4 ran   Time 1m 56.1 (17.1)   (P D Savill)   M Johnston Middleham, N Yorks

4423 2.35 SPIRIT NURSERY HCAP 2YO 0-75 (E) 5f str Heavy 215 +01 Fast [78]
£2751 £786 £393   2 groups - no significant advantage.

4338 **TIME MAITE** 7 [16] M W Easterby 2-9-4 (68) P Hanagan (5) 7/2 FAV: 531301: 2 b g Komaite - Martini 76
Time (Ardoon) Slow to start, sn prom stands side, led that group appr fnl 1f, led overall well ins last, rdn clr:
tchd 9/2, quick reapp: earlier won here at Newcastle (clmr) & Haydock (nurs): suited by 5/6f on gd & hvy, poss
handles fibresand: likes a stiff or gall trk & racing up with/forcing the pace: tough.

4235 **PATRICIAN FOX** 17 [3] J J Quinn 2-8-5 (55) N Kennedy 20/1: 432602: 2 b f Nicolotte - Peace Mission 2½ 56
(Dunbeath) Prom far side, led that group ins last, styd on but no threat: handles fast & hvy: consistent, see 2120.

3955 **MAGNANIMOUS** 36 [1] N Tinkler 2-8-0 (50) (vis) Kim Tinkler 14/1: 000003: 2 ch g Presidium - Mayor nk 50
(Laxton) Led far side to halfway, rall well fnl 1f: 1st time in the frame over a stiff 5f on hvy, shld apprec 6f.

4131 **DISPOL CHIEFTAN** 25 [11] S E Kettlewell 2-9-6 (70) F Lynch 14/1: 550304: Led stands side, hdd appr hd 70
fnl 1f, held well ins last: handles fast & hvy: see 3710 (mdn).

4202 **KARITSA** 19 [4] W Supple 13/2: 2-9-2 (66) 510345: Cl-up far side, led that group over 2f out, shd 66
hdd ins last, wknd: op 11/2: see 4202, 2668.

3958 **GARRISON** 35 [10] 2-8-5 (55) D Mernagh (3) 25/1: 0406: Bhd far side, hdwy halfway, no extra 2½ 49
appr fnl 1f: h'cap bow: rtd higher 3958, 3801.

*4333 **PAT THE BUILDER** 8 [15] 2-8-13 (63) (6ex) N Callan 10/1: 404617: Front rank stands side, rdn/wknd 1¾ 53
appr fnl 1f: not handle hvy: better on the A/W in 4333 (sell, equitrack).

+4305 **PHARAOH HATSHEPSUT** 10 [9] 2-8-11 (61) (6ex) G Baker (5) 6/1: 045018: Chsd ldrs stands side, ½ 50
wknd qckly over 1f out: op 5/1: much better on similar grnd in 4305 (6f).

3743 **RENEE** 49 [8] 2-8-9 (59) J Mackay 7/1: 355069: Handy throughout, lost tch over 1f out: 7 wk hd 48
abs: 1st try on hvy: much better on debut in 2034 (fills mdn, fast).

4103 **BOLLIN TOBY** 26 [5] 2-8-5 (55) (bl) O Pears 25/1: 000650: Sn outpcd far side, nvr a factor, 10th. nk 43

4303 **SHATIN PLAYBOY** 10 [12] 2-9-1 (65) K Darley 10/1: 44020: In tch stands side till halfway, sn well 0
bhd, 15th: prob unsuited by drop back to the minimum trip: much btr 4303 (7f mdn).

4305 Thornton Diva 10 [6] 2-9-7 (71) (t) A Culhane 25/1: 3987 **Milliken Park** 34 [13] 2-9-4 (68) G Duffield 14/1:
4235 Naughty Knight 17 [2] 2-8-4 (53) (1ow) J Carroll 14/1: 4252 **Trudie** 16 [7] 2-8-9 (59) V Halliday 16/1:
4235 Beau Sauvage 17 [14] 2-8-10 (60) J Fanning (5):
16 ran   Time 1m 08.88 (10.68)   (Tom Beston & Bernard Bargh)   M W Easterby Sheriff Hutton, N Yorks

4424 3.05 NEWCASTLE HCAP 3YO+ 0-65 (F) 2m Heavy 215 -04 Slow [63]
£2233 £638 £319   3 yo rec 10lb

4245 **YOURE SPECIAL** 16 [10] P C Haslam 3-8-13 (58) (VIS) Dean McKeown 10/1: 000601: 3 b g Northern 65
Flagship - Pillow Mint (Stagedoor) Trkd ldrs, went on after halfway, qcknd clr 4f out, held on well, drvn out:
back to form in 1st time visor: early this year won on the AW at W'hampton (mdn, rtd 82a): rnr-up in '99 (auct
mdn, rtd 81): eff at 1m, clrly suited by this step up to 2m: acts on gd, hvy & fibresand: handles a sharp or
stiff/gall trk: clrly relished this step up in trip & the fitting of headgear: enterprising D McKeown ride.

4231 **BOLD CARDOWAN** 17 [9] John Berry 4-8-0 (35) J Mackay (5) 6/1: 000402: 4 b g Persian Bold - 3½ 38
Moving Trend (Be My Guest) In tch, imprvd 5f out, chsd wnr appr fnl 2f, closing at fin but line came too sn:
op 5/1: blnks omitted: prob ran to best with conditions in his favour & has slipped down the weights: see 876.

3618 **LUCKY JUDGE** 55 [11] W W Haigh 3-9-6 (65) F Lynch 14/1: 464233: 3 b g Saddlers' Hall - Lady Lydia 5 64
(Ela Mana Mou) Hdwy from rear 5f out, styd on well but nvr nrr: not disgraced after a 8 wk abs: stays 2m on hvy.

4258 **ROBBO** 16 [1] Mrs M Reveley 6-9-4 (53) (bl) A Culhane 5/2 FAV: 0/6-64: Towards rear, prog over 6f 1¾ 51
out, styd on but nvr nrr: nicely bckd, 17L clr of rem: sharper now for a jumps campaign: see 4258.

4325 **EXALTED** 9 [6] 7-10-0 (63) G Duffield 9/1: 0-1565: Mid-div, fdd final 2f: top weight: unproven beyond 13f. 17 47

3774] **THORNTOUN HOUSE** 766 [3] 7-7-10 (31) (vis) (6oh) G Baker (5) 33/1: 4000/6: Cl-up, ev ch till wknd 4 12
qckly fnl 3f: long abs: prolific chase wnr in 99/00, scoring at Perth (2, nov & h'cap) & Ayr (3 nov h'caps,
rtd 113c, 2½m/3m1f, fast, likes hvy, visored): only modest Flat form when last seen back in '98.

4099 **NEEDWOOD TRIDENT** 27 [12] 3-7-10 (41) (6oh) P M Quinn (3) 10/1: 042047: Al towards rear, t.o. 23 6

4258 **REVENGE** 16 [4] 4-9-8 (57) (bl) K Darley 14/1: 4-0028: Chsd ldrs, rdn/lost tch fnl 5f, t.o.: btr 4258. 2½ 20

4258 **TOP OF THE CHARTS** 16 [2] 4-8-3 (38) (bl) W Supple 6/1: 501049: Al in rear, t.o. fnl 5f: see 4258. dist 0

4258 **MRS JODI** 16 [7] 4-8-12 (47) P Hanagan (5) 16/1: 300-00: Cl-up, wknd rapidly fnl 5f, t.o. in 10th. 11 0

4222 **PRETTY OBVIOUS** 19 [5] 4-9-6 (55) T Eaves (7) 12/1: 611-00: Al struggling, t.o. in 11th: '99 wnr dist 0
at Catterick (sell), Newcastle & Nottingham (h'caps, rtd 60): '98 rnr-up (nurs, rtd 57, R Fahey): prev suited
by 2m on any grnd/trk: eff without blnks.

4371 **AMSARA** 3 [8] 4-7-10 (31) (bl) (6oh) D Mernagh (3) 33/1: 000200: Led 1m, qckly wknd, t.o. in 12th. 10 0
12 ran   Time 4m 00.57 (35.07)   (Les Buckley)   P C Haslam Middleham, N Yorks

4425 3.35 BETSMART.CO.UK HCAP 3YO+ 0-70 (E) 6f str Heavy 215 -02 Slow [66]
£2905 £830 £415   3 yo rec 1 lb   Flip start - draw meaningless.

-4377 **BOWLERS BOY** 3 [9] J J Quinn 7-9-4 (56) K Darley 3/1 FAV: 403521: 7 ch g Risk Me - Snow Wonder 62
(Music Boy) Mid-div stands side, imprvd to chall over 1f out, led ins last, strongly prsd cl-home, all out: nicely
bckd, quick reapp: earlier won at Carlisle (appr h'cap) & Hamilton (amat h'cap): plcd in '99 (1st time blnks,
h'cap, rtd 49): '98 wnr at Pontefract (2 h'caps) & Redcar (stks, rtd 76): suited by 5/6f: acts on fast, loves
gd/soft & hvy, poss handles f/sand: dislikes blnks: loves stiff finishes: esp Pontefract: v tough.

4220 **SUPERFRILLS** 19 [19] Miss L C Siddall 7-7-10 (34) G Baker (5) 20/1: 400502: 7 b m Superpower - Pod's hd 39
Daughter (Tender King) Front rank stands side, led that group over 2f out, overall ldr dist, hdd ins last, rall &
not btn far: clr rem: best run for some time in these v testing conds: eff at 5/6f, likes hvy: well h'capped.

4327 **MISTER WESTSOUND** 9 [17] Miss L A Perratt 8-7-12 (36) (bl) N Kennedy 7/1: 000063: 8 b g Cyrano de 5 31
Bergerac - Captivate (Mansingh) Slow to start stands side, rear, gd late hdwy, nvr nrr: often loses ch at the start.

4294 **TANCRED ARMS** 13 [7] D W Barker 4-8-9 (47) (vis) F Lynch 14/1: 030044: Led far side, clr 2f out, nk 42

1369

hdd dist, wknd: op 10/1: see 4294, 3312.

4387 **MISTY BOY** 2 [1] 3-8-7 (46)(BL) G Faulkner (0) 14/1: 0-0005: Mid-div far side, imprvd 2f out, kept on but no ch with ldrs: pulled well clr of rem: 1st time blnks, ran 48hrs ago: see 1494.	1	39
4327 **HIGH ESTEEM** 9 [18] 4-8-10 (48) Dean McKeown 40/1: 000506: Chsd ldrs, wknd fnl 2f: see 1421 (AW).	9	25
4407 **SHARP EDGE BOY** 1 [4] 4-8-12 (50) W Supple 16/1: 002007: Handy far side, wknd fnl 2f: ran yesterday.	7	12
1734 **VICE PRESIDENTIAL** 136 [5] 5-8-4 (41)(1ow) J Fanning 20/1: 450408: Led stands side, hdd over 2f out, nk 4 wknd qckly sn after: over 4 month abs & prob just sharper for this: see 1734, 32.	nk	4
4293 **SHINING STAR** 13 [2] 3-9-6 (59) S W Kelly (3) 8/1: 050439: Dwelt, sn mid-div far side, rdn/btn fnl 2f.	nk	21
4293 **ENCOUNTER** 13 [3] 4-9-0 (52) T Williams 10/1: 605450: Al bhd far side, 10th: btr 4293 (gd/soft).	3	8
4307 **ABLE AYR** 10 [16] 3-9-7 (60) A Culhane 33/1: 000000: Cl-up stands side, wknd fnl 2f, 11th: see 1768.	11	0
4307 **MAROMITO** 10 [13] 3-9-11 (64) H Bastiman 16/1: 000200: Prom stands side 4f, fdd, 12th: top weight.	¾	0
4327 **PANDJOJOE** 9 [11] 4-9-1 (53) P Hanagan (5) 9/2: 060030: In tch stands side, wknd from halfway, 13th.	5	0
4327 **BIFF EM** 9 [12] 6-7-10 (34) J Mackay (5) 12/1: 000050: Al rear stands side, 17th: op 10/1: see 4327.		0
3970 *Fantasy Adventurer* 35 [14] 3-8-3 (42) O Pears 33/1: 3380 **Pups Pride** 64 [6] 3-8-4 (43)(BL) G Duffield 20/1:		
3605 *Souperlicad* 55 [10] 9-8-5 (43) Kim Tinkler 25/1: 4156 **Aljazir** 23 [8] 3-8-13 (52) A Mackay 33/1:		
2093 *La Tortuga* 120 [15] 3-9-10 (63) J Carroll 33/1:		
19 ran Time 1m 24.3 (13.0) (Bowlers Racing) J J Quinn Settrington, N Yorks		

4426 4.05 GOSFORTH PARK HCAP DIV 1 3YO+ 0-60 (F)   7f str   Heavy 215 -03 Slow   [60]
£1834   £524   £262   3 yo rec 2 lb   Raced stand side - high numbers held big advantage.

4217 **ONLY FOR GOLD** 19 [12] A Berry 5-9-5 (51) J Carroll 8/1: 200561: 5 b g Presidium - Calvanne Miss (Martinmas) Towards rear, gd hdwy over 3f out, grabbed stands rail & led appr fnl 2f, styd on strongly & drvn out: op 5/1: plcd numerous times in '99 (h'caps, rtd 67): 4th of 29 on best '98 run (val h'cap, rtd 77), prev term won at Chester & Beverley (stks, rtd 90): eff at 7f/1m on fast, hvy & any trk: likes to race up with/force the pace & runs well fresh: best without a visor: confidence boosting first win in 3 years.	56	
3711 **SKYERS FLYER** 51 [14] Ronald Thompson 6-8-3 (32)(3ow) R Fitzpatrick 16/1: 000602: 6 b m Magical Wonder - Siwana (Dom Racine) Waited wth, hdwy over 3f out, chsd wnr appr fnl 1f, held well ins last: 6L clr rem & a gd eff after 7 wk abs: eff at 5/7f on fast & hvy: well h'capped & worth a look in a sell h'cap: see 1421.	2½	36
4406 **FOIST** 1 [3] M W Easterby 8-8-10 (42) J Fanning 14/1: 026003: 8 b g Efisio - When The Saints (Bay Express) Towards rear, prog 3f out, ev ch till hung right & fdd fnl 1f: unplcd yesterday: see 4406, 2820.	6	35
3192 **BY THE GRASS** 73 [7] N Tinkler 4-7-10 (28)(1oh) Kim Tinkler 25/1: 000604: Hdwy from rear over 3f out, rdn/btn appr fnl 1f: 10 wk abs: prev win with D Enrico Incisa: see 1132.	4	15
4327 **MAGIC MILL** 9 [13] 7-9-13 (59) A Culhane 13/2: 400005: Led, hdd appr fnl 2f, lost tch over 1f out: fin well clr rem: well h'capped if returning to best: see 844.	5	39
4310 **FALLS OMONESS** 10 [6] 6-9-1 (47) W Supple 8/1: 002006: Hmpd after 1f, rear, eff over 3f out, sn well bhd, t.o.: all wins at 1m+: see 3777, 2062.	27	2
3652 **MYBOTYE** 54 [4] 7-9-10 (56)(t) D Mernagh 12/1: 101007: Rear, brief eff halfway, sn lost tch: t.o.: 8 wk abs: thrice below 1681 (class stks).	2½	7
4311 **GREEN GOD** 10 [3] 4-9-9 (55) G Duffield 10/1: 054008: Mid-div, wknd halfway, t.o.: btr 3753 (firm).	1½	4
4310 **BODFARI ANNA** 10 [5] 4-9-10 (56)(vis) G Baker (5) 8/1: 300209: Dwelt, al rear, t.o. halfway: btr 4136.	2½	2
4228 **MAI TAI** 19 [2] 5-8-8 (40)(vis) P Hanagan (5) 14/1: 625000: Prom, lost tch halfway, t.o., 10th: see 867.	2	0
3593 **CALLING THE SHOTS** 56 [1] 3-9-4 (52) T Williams 9/1: 004240: Trkd ldrs, wknd rapidly after halfway, t.o. in 11th: op 6/1, 8 wk abs: jockey referred to Jockey Club for irresponsible riding: btr 3593, 2719 (gd/firm).	4	0
3939 **RIOS DIAMOND** 36 [9] 3-8-13 (47) G Faulkner (3) 11/1: 340030: Mid-div, wknd rapidly 2f, t.o. in 12th.	12	0
4046 **PENG** 30 [11] 3-8-11 (45) O Pears 25/1: 000000: T.o from halfway, 13th.	23	0
1760 **VICTORIOUS** 134 [8] 4-10-0 (60) K Darley 10/1: 100500: Chsd ldrs, rdn halfway, wknd rapidly fnl 3f, t.o. in 14th: much better expected after 4 month abs under top weight: much btr 908.	2	0
14 ran Time 1m 39.39 (15.29) (Mr John Milner & Mrs Stephen Milner) A Berry Cockerham, Lancs		

4427 4.35 XMAS FESTIVAL HCAP 3YO+ 0-75 (E)   1m2f32y   Heavy 215 -04 Slow   [73]
£2870   £820   £410   3 yo rec 5 lb   Flip start.

4282 **ARCHIE BABE** 13 [9] J J Quinn 4-10-0 (73) K Darley 13/2: 500301: 4 ch g Archway - Frenshan Manor (Le Johnstan) Front rank, went on over 4f out, strongly prsd 2f out, styd on strongly & drvn clr well ins last: earlier won at Pontefract (2, h'cap & class stks) & here at Newcastle (h'cap): '99 wnr again at Pontefract & Redcar (2, h'caps, rtd 70): '98 Thirsk wnr (auct mdn, rtd 75): suited by 10/12f on firm, hvy & any trk, likes a stiff/gall one: eff weight carrier: most tough & genuine & an excellent eff in these conditions under 10-0.	80	
4324 **ACE OF TRUMPS** 9 [5] J Hetherton 4-7-10 (44)(t)(4oh) N Kennedy 9/1: 435232: 4 ch g First Trump - Elle Reef (Shareef Dancer) Prom, chall over 2f out, rdn/btn fnl 1f: consistent, capable of landing a sell h'cap.	2½	44
4300 **ROLLER** 12 [6] J G Given 4-9-12 (71) G Baker (5) 9/2: 036063: 4 b g Bluebird - Tight Spin (High Top) Mid-div, hdwy over 2f out, no extra appr fnl 1f: op 3/1, 11L clr rem: poss not quite get home over 10f on hvy.	1¾	71
4169 **DOUBLE RED** 22 [4] M L W Bell 3-8-13 (63) J Mackay (5) 11/8 FAV: 300164: Mid-div, imprvd over 2f out, wknd rapidly appr fnl 1f: nicely bckd: unproven on hvy: btr 4067 (soft grnd).	11	51
4324 **HUTCHIES LADY** 9 [3] 8-7-10 (41)(4oh) J McAuley 9/1: 310025: Nvr dngrs, lost tch fnl 2f: see 4324.	½	28
3524 **STERLING HIGH** 59 [8] 5-7-10 (41)(t)(9oh) Clare Roche (7) 25/1: 000006: Sn struggling, t.o.: 8 wk abs.	16	12
*4275 **SKYERS A KITE** 14 [7] 5-9-7 (66) T Williams 13/2: 215517: Led, hdd appr fnl 4f, wknd, t.o.: btr 4275.	15	22
3827 **KATIE KOMAITE** 45 [1] 7-7-10 (41)(7oh) A Mackay 11/1: 352208: Al well bhd, t.o.: 6 wk abs: btr 3531.	5	0
8 ran Time 2m 28.4 (21.9) (Mrs K Mapp) J J Quinn Settrington, N Yorks		

4428 5.05 GOSFORTH PARK HCAP DIV 2 3YO+ 0-60 (F)   7f str   Heavy 215 00 Slow   [60]
£1834   £524   £262   3 yo rec 2 lb   2 groups - no significant advantage.

4217 **ORIOLE** 19 [13] Don Enrico Incisa 7-8-11 (43) Kim Tinkler 14/1: 004001: 7 b g Mazilier - Odilese (Mummy's Pet) Held up stands side, eff over 3f out, styd on strongly for press to lead ins last, drvn out: '99 rnr-up (h'cap, rtd 51 at best), prev term won at Carlisle & Redcar (h'caps, rtd 49): eff at 7f/1m on firm & hvy grnd: acts on a stiff/gall trk & eff with/without visor: took advantage of a handy mark today.	50	
3871 **SAND HAWK** 42 [3] D Shaw 5-9-3 (49)(bl) N Callan 4/1: 410622: 5 ch g Polar Falcon - Ghassanah (Pas de Seul) Cl-up far side, led that group 2f out, held overall lead appr fnl 1f, hdd well ins last, no extra: op 5/2 & a gd eff fnl 1f: acts on fast, hvy & fibresand: see 3871, 3440.	2½	52
4324 **AMBUSHED** 9 [9] P Monteith 4-9-10 (56) F Lynch 7/1: 521063: 4 b g Indian Ridge - Surprise Move (Simply Great) Led stands side, hdd appr fnl 1f, sn no extra: beat at 1m/9f on firm & gd/soft, handles hvy.	2	56
4066 **KNOBBLEENEEZE** 29 [4] M R Channon 10-8-9 (41)(vis) A Culhane 8/1: 600004: Cl-up far side, ev ch	2½	37

NEWCASTLE THURSDAY OCTOBER 19TH Lefthand, Galloping Track, Stiff Track

appr fnl 1f, wknd ins last: 8L clr rem: see 3294 (appr h'cap).

4257 **LANDING CRAFT** 16 [5] 6-9-5 (51) D Nolan (7) 9/1: 000005: Handy far side, rdn/lost tch appr fnl 1f.   8   37

3399 **FOREST QUEEN** 64 [1] 3-7-13 (33) T Williams 33/1: 000006: Led far side, hdd over 2f out, sn lost   5   12
tch: 9 wk abs, big drop in trip: see 3217.

3671 **ST PACOKISE** 53 [14] 3-8-13 (47) D Mernagh (3) 20/1: 4-0057: Handy stands side, wknd qckly over   6   18
1f out: 8 wk abs: see 3671, 3326.

4220 **MILLSEC** 19 [12] 3-9-5 (53) O Pears 20/1: 62-008: Mid-div at best stands side: rnr-up on fnl   4   18
of 4 '99 starts (sell nurs, h'cap bow, rtd 67 at best): eff around a sharp 5f on gd.

4033 **LYNTON LAD** 31 [11] 8-9-9 (55) W Supple 8/1: 100509: Handy stands side, wknd rapidly over 1f out.   5   13

4310 **SWYNFORD WELCOME** 10 [2] 4-8-12 (44) G Duffield 16/1: 100000: In tch far side, fdd fnl 2f, t.o., 10th.   1¼   0

4300 **JORROCKS** 12 [8] 6-9-13 (59) K Darley 3/1 FAV: -26000: Prom stands side, wknd rapidly fnl 2f,   15   0
fin 11th: nicely bckd under top weight & capable of better: see 2882 (reapp, 7.5f).

3966 **SILK ST BRIDGET** 35 [7] 3-8-4 (38) G Baker (5) 12/1: 000600: Mid-div, lost tch after halfway, 13th: op 10/1.   0

4041 **Danny Deever** 30 [6] 4-7-10 (28) (1oh) A Mackay 33/1: 3574 **Top Of The Class** 57 [10] 3-9-11 (59) R Lappin 20/1:
14 ran   Time 1m 39.14 (15.04)   (Don Enrico Incisa)   Don Enrico Incisa Coverham, N Yorks

---

BATH THURSDAY OCTOBER 19TH Lefthand, Turning Track with Uphill Finish

Official Going   GOOD/SOFT. Stalls: Straight course - far side: Round course - inside.

4429   2.0 END OF SEASON AUCT MDN DIV 1 2YO (E)   1m rnd   Soft 113   -15 Slow
£2320   £714   £357   £178

--   **PRINCE SHAAMAAL** [2] K Bell 2-9-0 A Nicholls 20/1: 1: 2 b c Shaamit - Prince Alaska (Northern   88
State) Led, hard rdn & hung right appr fnl 1f, held on gamely: bckd from 6/1 on debut: 6,000gns first foal,
dam unrcd: eff forcing the pace at 1m, bred to get 10f+: acts on soft grnd & a turning trck & runs well fresh.

--   **POST BOX** [15] R Charlton 2-9-0 C Rutter 20/1: 2: 2 b c Quest For Fame - Crowning Ambition   nk   87
(Chief's Crown) In tch, prog appr fnl 1f, rdn, edged left & chall inside last, held nr fin: op 12/1, debut:
half-brother to sev wnrs up to 12f, dam 7f wnr: eff at 1m, get at least 10f next term: acts on soft grnd.

4163 **OVAMBO** 22 [5] P J Makin 2-9-0 S Sanders 7/4 FAV: 33: 2 b c Namaqualand - Razana (Kahyasi)   2   83
Prom, chsd wnr 2f out, rdn 1f out, onepce: nicely bckd: prob ran to form of debut, acts on gd/soft & soft grnd.

--   **INVINCIBLE** [8] J R Fanshawe 2-8-9 O Urbina 7/1: 4: Mid div, chsd ldrs 4th ent fnl 1f, no dngr: 2   74
op 5/1, clr rem: Slip Anchor half-sister to fair 6/7f juv Icicle, dam 7f juv wnr: bred to apprec 10f+, handles soft.

4209 **TIBBIE** 19 [4] B J Makin 2-8-9 G Hind 33/1: 05: Chsd ldrs, outpcd appr fnl 1f: v stoutly bred, Slip Anchor filly.   6   64

4281 **MY PLACE** 13 [6] 2-8-9 M Hills 4/1: 3046: Well plcd, briefly short of room fnl 2f, fdd appr fnl 1f.   ½   63

4163 **INDEFINITE STAY** 22 [7] 2-9-0 R Hughes 50/1: 07: Nvr nr ldrs: 9,600gns half-brother to sev wnrs.   ½   67

4154 **DIVEBOMB** 23 [1] 2-8-9 S Carson (3) 66/1: 0008: Chsd ldrs till 2f out: v stiff task, flattered.   2   58$

--   **ASHA FALLS** [12] 2-9-0 D Sweeney 50/1: -9: Nvr a factor: 3,000gns sprint bred River Falls colt.   hd   62

3949 **NIGHT ON THE TOWN** 36 [13] 2-9-0 J Bosley (7) 50/1: 00: In tch till 2f out: 10th.   1¼   60

3766 **LADY SHARP SHOT** 48 [11] 2-8-9 Pat Eddery 4/1: 50: Nvr in it, btn halfway, eased fnl 1f: abs, btr 3766.   0

--   **Songs Of Praise** [9] 2-9-0 R Perham 16/1:   4079 **Da Wolf** 28 [16] 2-9-0 Martin Dwyer 50/1:

--   **Nosmokewithoutfire** [3] 2-8-9 R Studholme (3) 66/1:   3420 **Flipside** 63 [14] 2-9-0 T Quinn 50/1:
15 ran   Time 1m 48.5 (10.2)   (The Upshire Racing Partnership)   K Bell Lambourn, Berks

4430   2.30 END OF SEASON AUCT MDN DIV 2 2YO (E)   1m rnd   Soft 113   -32 Slow
£2320   £714   £357   £178

3969 **FLYING LYRIC** 35 [7] S P C Woods 2-9-0 J Fortune 7/2 FAV: 41: 2 b c Definite Article - Lyric Junction   88
(Classic Secret) Rear, prog appr fnl 3f, pshd into lead 1f out, styd on strgly: nicely bckd from 5/1, slow time:
30,000gns colt, dam unrcd: eff at 1m, mid dists are going to suit: acts on soft, prob handles fast, turning track.

3999 **COSMOCRAT** 33 [6] B J Meehan 2-9-0 S Clancy (7) 33/1: -02: 2 b c Cosmonaut - Bella Coola   2½   83
(Northern State) Prom, eff & ev ch appr fnl 1f, styd on but not as well as wnr: first foal, dam modest,
sire unrcd: apprec step up to 1m on soft grnd.

4281 **PRECISO** 13 [16] Mrs A J Perrett 2-9-0 S Sanders 15/2: 203: 2 b c Definite Article - Symphony   3   77
(Cyrano de Bergerac) Well plcd, led bef halfway till appr fnl 1f, same pace: op 6/1: better, tho' still below debut.

--   **FLAMME DE LA VIE** [13] G A Butler 2-9-0 J Quinn 16/1: 4: Bhd, kept on appr fnl 1f, nrst fin: nk   76+
9,000gns half brother to sprinter Paradise Lane, dam 6/7f wnr: promising debut, shld win similar.

3766 **GREENHOPE** 48 [9] 2-9-0 Pat Eddery 10/1: 05: Rear, kept on ent fnl 2f, nvr dngrs: 7 week abs.   nk   75

4279 **ISLAND QUEEN** 14 [12] 2-8-9 R Hughes 5/1: 43256: Cl up, ch 2f out, sn onepcd & eased in last.   hd   70

--   **MOSCA** [10] 2-8-9 Craig Williams 6/1: 7: Al around same plc: debut: Most Welcome half-sister   hd   69
to useful mid dist/styer Eilean Shona, dam won over 2m: will apprec mid-dists next term: with J Fanshawe.

3363 **GILDED DANCER** 65 [1] 2-9-0 Martin Dwyer 9/2: 3638: Rear, eff 3f out, nvr nr to chall: 9 week abs.   nk   73

--   **GOLD STANDARD** [3] 2-9-0 T Quinn 7/1: 9: Bhd, eff/no room thro'out fnl 2f, no ch after: IR 32,000   nk   72
gns half brother sev wnrs up to 12f: dam useful in the States, sire a miler: 10f shld suit: worth another chance.

--   **LYCHEEL** [11] 2-9-0 B Marcus 20/1: 0: Dwelt, nvr on terms, 10th: 40,000gns Lycius half-brother   2½   67
to wnrs at 6f & 1m, dam & sire milers: with W Muir.

--   **URBAN MYTH** [2] 2-9-0 M Hills 14/1: 0: Rear, bdly hmpd & snatched up 2f out, no ch after: 11th: ½   66
half brother to 1m/10f wnr Francesca's Folly: dam 7f/1m wnr, sire high-class mid-dist performer: with J Hills.

4249 **Definite Return** 16 [5] 2-8-9 Joanna Badger (7) 66/1: 3577 **Impero** 57 [4] 2-9-0 S Drowne 66/1:

--   **Jennifer Jenkins** [14] 2-9-0 D Sweeney 40/1:   --   **Kitty Bankes** [15] 2-8-9 A Daly 40/1:

--   **Oh Jamila** [8] 2-8-9 S Carson (3) 33/1:
16 ran   Time 1m 49.9 (11.6)   (Mrs Marian Borsberry)   S P C Woods Newmarket, Suffolk

4431   3.0 LAST CHANCE SELLER 2YO (G)   5f161y rnd   Soft 113   -17 Slow
£1911   £546   £273

4025 **IVANS BRIDE** 33 [16] G G Margarson 2-8-7 N Pollard 33/1: 624001: 2 b f Inzar - Sweet Nature   57
(Classic Secret) Slow away, sn pshd along, imprvd appr fnl 2f, rdn ins last & got up towards fin: no bid:
stays 7f but clearly suited by this drop to 5.5f: acts on gd & soft grnd, turning track.

4289 **MISS INFORM** 13 [14] D R C Elsworth 2-8-7 T Quinn 14/1: 500002: 2 b f So Factual - As Sharp   ¾   55
As (Handsome Sailor) Cl up, led halfway, under press 1f out, worn down well inside last: gd run,

eff at 5/5.5f on gd/soft & soft grnd.

3491 **SOOTY TIME 61** [13] J S Moore 2-8-12 J Bosley (7) 25/1: 623403: 2 ch g Timeless Times -   ½ 58
Gymcrak Gem (Don't Foget Me) Mid div, prog to chse ldr 2f out, kept on for press, held towards fin: clr rem,
9 wk abs: handles fast & soft grnd: see 3204.

4171 **BALI ROYAL 22** [12] J M Bradley 2-8-7 J Tate 6/1: 000024: Front rank & ev ch till no extra appr fnl 1f.   3½ 45

4097 **GOLDEN BEACH 27** [10] 2-8-7 S Whitworth 12/1: 005205: Towards rear, mod late hdwy, nvr a threat.   2½ 39

4269 **BEE KING 15** [3] 2-8-12 S Drowne 9/4 FAV: 033206: Mid div, prog 2f out, wknd dist: nicely bckd   hd 44
tho' op 13/8: capable of better, see 4170.

4333 **SONG N DANCE 8** [15] 2-8-7 Martin Dwyer 16/1: 056047: Prom, wide, no extra fnl 2f: see 4333 (AW).   1¼ 35

4190 **QUATREDIL 20** [6] 2-8-7 L Newman (3) 7/1: 04068: Al mid div: op 12/1: see 2748.   ½ 34

4333 **QUIZZICAL LADY 8** [8] 2-8-12 F Norton 10/1: 003059: Front rank, chall 3f out, btn 2f out, eased fnl 1f.   ¾ 37

2507 **SHARP VISION 103** [7] 2-8-7 J Quinn 33/1: 00: Nvr better than mid div: 10th, 15 wk abs.   shd 32

3815 **MISTY BELLE 45** [11] 2-8-7 B Marcus 8/1: 34D000: Led/dsptd lead till halfway, lost pl: tchd 14/1, abs.   0

3443 Turbo Blue 62 [4] 2-8-7 G Hind 20/1:   4190 Delphyllia 20 [18] 2-8-8(1ow) S Sanders 25/1:
4171 Savanna Miss 22 [9] 2-8-7 D Sweeney 33/1:   4336 Alfalfa 7 [2] 2-8-12 S Carson (3) 33/1:
4138 Sunny Stroka 24 [5] 2-8-7 C Rutter 66/1:   3661 Fire Belle 53 [17] 2-8-7 A Nicholls 50/1:
4244 Fire Princess 16 [1] 2-8-7 Dale Gibson 14/1:
18 ran   Time 1m 16.5 (7.4)   (K Reveley)   G G Margarson Newmarket, Suffolk

---

4432   3.30 CAUDA EQUINA HCAP 3YO+ 0-75 (E)   5f rnd   Soft 113   +15 Fast   [75]
    £3630   £1117   £558   £279

4287 **MR STYLISH 13** [19] I A Balding 4-9-9 (70)(tvi) Martin Dwyer 12/1: 330101: 4 b g Mazilier - Moore   76
Stylish (Moorestyle) Slightly hmpd start & bhd, gd wide prog ent fnl 2f, led 1f out & sn clr, pushed out: fast
time: earlier won at Beverley (mdn): plcd sev times in '99 (h'caps, rtd 71): eff at 5/6f: acts on firm & hvy
grnd, any trck: best in a t-strap & visor: improving.

4185 **ULYSSES DAUGHTER 21** [17] G A Butler 3-9-11 (72)(t) Pat Eddery 4/1 FAV: 421542: 3 ch f College   ½ 76
Chapel - Trysinger (Try My Best) Held up, not much room 2f out & swtchd, picked up well for press ins last, post
came too soon: prob unlucky, clr rem: acts on fast & soft grnd but needs a return to 6f: see 3820 (here).

4285 **THREAT 13** [13] S C Williams 4-9-11 (72)(t) T Quinn 7/1: 513503: 4 br g Zafonic - Prophecy   2½ 71
(Warning) Rear, gd progress on rail appr fnl 1f, kept but no ch with front 2: gd run, acts on firm & soft grnd.

3920 **DIAMOND GEEZER 37** [18] R Hannon 4-9-7 (68) L Newman (3) 16/1: 240004: Wide, in tch,   ¾ 65
eff appr fnl 1f, kept on but not pce of ldrs: see 113.

4156 **TREASURE TOUCH 23** [6] 6-9-7 (68) Joanna Badger (7) 25/1: 404005: Chsd ldrs, outpcd 2f out,   ½ 64
late rally: handles soft, acts on firm, gd/soft & fibresand: see 3080.

2761 **KHALIK 92** [2] 6-9-7 (68)(t) S Whitworth 12/1: 140036: Bhd till ran on strgly fnl 1f, nvr nrr: 3 mth abs.   shd 64

4285 **BOND BOY 13** [14] 3-9-13 (74) J Bosley (7) 33/1: 451007: Cl up, led briefly appr fnl 1f, no extra.   shd 70

4270 **QUEEN OF THE MAY 15** [15] 3-9-9 (70) S Drowne 10/1: 006058: Nvr out of mid div: see 4270, 1098.   nk 65

4285 **BARRINGER 13** [9] 3-10-0 (75) Craig Williams 25/1: 300009: Trkd ldrs, not clr run 2f out, onepace.   nk 69

4207 **ANSELLMAN 19** [7] 10-9-0 (61)(bl) R Hughes 16/1: 332050: Early ldr, fdd appr fnl 1f: 10th, see 2788.   1¼ 52

4285 **POLLY GOLIGHTLY 13** [11] 7-9-10 (71)(bl) Dale Gibson 25/1: 301100: Well plcd, led bef halfway   ½ 61
till appr fnl 2f, btn dist: 11th: see 4107.

*4295 **CHORUS 13** [20] 3-9-11 (72) G Hind 11/1: 160010: Wide & nvr a factor: 13th: see 4295.   0

4285 **WHIZZ KID 13** [1] 6-9-5 (66) Claire Bryan (5) 8/1: 050260: Prom, ev ch 2f out, wknd: 17th, see 1391.   0

4023 **CAROLS CHOICE 33** [13] 3-8-13 (60) A McGlone 20/1: 235620: Led after 2f till dist, btn: 18th, mdn.   0

3920 Mousehole 37 [12] 8-9-7 (68) J Quinn 20/1:   4204 Easter Ogil 19 [10] 5-9-12 (73) Leanne Masterton(7) 20/1:
3280 Kissing Time 69 [4] 3-9-12 (73)(BL) S Carson (3) 20/1:   4185 Brandon Rock 21 [8] 3-9-6 (67) J Fortune 20/1:
4015 Speed On 33 [3] 7-10-0 (75) C Rutter 14/1:   3747 Endymion 49 [5] 3-8-13 (60) A Nicholls 50/1:
20 ran   Time 1m 05.2 (4.9)   (T J W Burton)   I A Balding Kingsclere, Hants

---

4433   4.0 DOUBLEPRINT HCAP 3YO+ 0-70 (E)   1m3f144y   Soft 113   -22 Slow   [70]
    £3669   £1129   £564   £282   3 yo rec 7 lb

4232 **LADY TWO K 17** [15] J Mackie 3-9-4 (67) A Nicholls 10/1: -04601: 3 b f Grand Lodge - Princess   73
Pavlova (Sadler's Wells) Bhd, improved 3f out, rdn to lead appr fnl 1f, held on gamely: op 16/1: unrcd
juv: clearly suited by this step up to 11.5f & should stay further: acts on soft grnd & a turning track.

4166 **GEMINI GUEST 22** [8] G G Margarson 4-9-2 (58) S Sanders 16/1: 503002: 4 ch g Waajib - Aldhabyih   nk 63
(General Assembly) Prom, wide prog to chall appr fnl 1f, styd on for press but al just held: tchd 25/1, clr
rem: gd run: acts on fast & soft grnd, eff at 10/12f: see 2667.

1122 **POLAR PROSPECT 896** [14] P J Hobbs 7-9-4 (60) T Quinn 7/2 FAV: 213/3: 7 b g Polar Falcon -   5 59
Littlemisstrouble (My Gallant) Held up, prog 3f out to chse ldrs 2f out, onepce inside last: abs: last ran in
98/99, hdles wnr at Sandown (val h'cap, 2m1f/2m4f, fast & hvy, rtd 136h): ran once on the level in '98 (plcd, rtd
61): '97 wnr at Redcar (h'cap, rtd 60): 3 ch g at Banbury: eff at 1m/12f, acts on firm & hvy grnd.

4088 **SPEED VENTURE 28** [10] S P C Woods 3-9-3 (66) S Drowne 16/1: 550404: Bhd, late prog, nvr dngrs: nk 64
op 12/1: handles gd/soft & soft grnd: see 3014, 1640.

4228 **BILLY BATHWICK 19** [3] 3-9-1 (64) J Stack 16/1: 032445: Led & clr appr fnl 3f, sn drvn, hdd &   3½ 58
btn bef fnl 1f: longer trip, eff at 1m/10f: see 2278.

3870 **CALLAS 42** [2] 3-9-1 (64) S Carson (3) 12/1: -00566: Chsd ldrs till fdd ent fnl 2f: op 8/1, abs, longer trip.   1 57

4280 **MORGANS ORCHARD 14** [6] 4-9-4 (60) N Pollard 8/1: 326007: Well plcd till wknd qckly 2f out: 7 44
needs faster grnd: see 3541, 607.

3402 **LEGAL LUNCH 64** [13] 5-10-0 (70)(vis) F Norton 10/1: 356158: Nvr a factor: top-weight, vis reapplied.   4 49

4208 **KYLKENNY 19** [11] 5-8-13 (55) R Hughes 14/1: 055-09: In tch till 3f out, ran wide: longer trip.   shd 34

3125 **LA FAY 76** [17] 3-9-2 (65)(t) B Marcus 9/1: -00000: Nvr troubled ldrs: 10th: 11 wk abs, see 1200.   4 39

4040 **SELVORINE 31** [12] 3-8-13 (62) J Fortune 8/1: -5060: In tch 3f out, eased: 11th, op 6/1, h'cap bow.   3½ 32

4108 **VARIETY 26** [1] 3-9-2 (65) O Urbina 10/1: 03630: Prom till 3f out: 15th, op 12/1, see 4108.   0

3353 Ignite 66 [4] 3-9-0 (63) A Beech (3) 20/1:   4126 Zulu Dawn 25 [19] 4-9-13 (69) M Hills 25/1:
4280 Two Socks 14 [20] 7-9-9 (65) L Newman (3) 16/1:   3858 Spirit Of Tenby 43 [18] 3-9-2 (65) Pat Eddery 20/1:
815 Grosvenor Flyer 199 [9] 4-9-10 (66) C Rutter 33/1:   4123 After The Blue 25 [5] 3-9-7 (70) Craig Williams 14/1:
4166 Bandore 22 [16] 6-9-4 (60)(t) J Quinn 50/1:   3424 Alnajashee 63 [7] 4-9-2 (58) D Sweeney 33/1:
20 ran   Time 2m 40.5 (15.5)   (Gwen K Dot.Com)   J Mackie Church Broughton, Derbys

4434
4.30 BON VOYAGE MDN 3YO (D)   1m3f144y   Soft 113   -17 Slow
£4033   £1241   £620   £310

4205 **MANIATIS** 19 [10] P F I Cole 3-9-0 D Sweeney 11/10 FAV: 0321: 3 b c Slip Anchor - Tamassos 93
(Dance In Time) Easily made all, came clr appr fnl 1f: well bckd: unrcd juv: eff forcing the pace at 10/11.5f,
14f + will suit: acts on soft grnd, stiff/gall & turning track: quick h'cap follow-up?

4141 **FLAME OF TRUTH** 24 [7] J H M Gosden 3-8-9 J Fortune 11/2: 3222: 3 b f Rainbow Quest - River 10 76
Lullaby (Riverman) Mid div, prog to trck wnr 5f out, eff over 2f out, same pace: op 9/2: btr 4141, 3818.

4205 **HIGH BARN** 19 [19] J R Fanshawe 3-8-9 O Urbina 10/1: 043: 3 b f Shirley Heights - Mountain 3½ 71
Lodge (Blakeney) Prom, outpcd 3f out, kept on onepce for 3rd: op 8/1: nds a drop in grade, see 4205.

1093 **MY LAST BEAN** 170 [18] B Smart 3-9-0 S Drowne 16/1: 54: Handy, eff 4f out, sn onepce: long abs. 1½ 74

3907 **SUMMER DREAMS** 40 [9] 3-8-9 M Hills 11/2: 235: Mid div, prog 4f out, no extra 3f out: 6 wk abs. nk 68

4205 **COLETTE** 15 [8] 3-8-9 A McGlone 33/1: 0-06: Chsd ldrs, wknd 2f out: needs a drop in grade. 2½ 64

3818 **ANEEFAH** 45 [4] 3-8-9 (BL) R Perham 10/1: 57: Dwelt & reluctant, nrst at fin: 6 wk abs, blnkd. 5 57

-- **SADLERS WALTZ** [6] 3-9-0 B Marcus 66/1: 8: Nvr a factor: debut: In The Wings gldg out of a 6f wnr. 11 47

3517 **HIGH TOWER** 60 [1] 3-9-0 Pat Eddery 10/1: 449: Rcd in 2nd, wknd under press 4f out: 9 wk abs. 3 42

4536J **SHOOFHA** 357 [14] 3-8-9 Craig Williams 14/1: 0-0: In tch till 4f out: 10th: rtd 76 sole '99 start. 4 31

4141 **Vetority** 24 [11] 3-8-9 S Sanders 20/1: -- **Robellando** [2] 3-9-0 Martin Dwyer 14/1:

4081 **Gay Lover** 28 [20] 3-8-9 A Daly 14/1: 4175 **Cosmic Dancer** 22 [5] 3-9-0 R Studholme (3) 100/1:

4205 **Barnaby** 19 [13] 3-9-0 S Whitworth 100/1: 4099 **Topman** 27 [3] 3-9-0 C Rutter 100/1:

3517 **Bishops Blade** 60 [12] 3-9-0 A Nicholls 100/1: -- **Jam** [15] 3-8-9 R Hughes 33/1:

-- **Oloroso** [17] 3-9-0 L Newman (3) 50/1: -- **State Opening** [16] 3-8-9 S Carson (3) 66/1:

20 ran   Time 2m 40.0 (15)   (Athos Christodoulou)   P F I Cole Whatcombe, Oxon

4435
5.0 BACKEND HCAP 3YO 0-60 (F)   1m rnd   Soft 113   -33 Slow   [66]
£2289   £654   £327

4173 **DISTANT GUEST** 22 [14] G G Margarson 3-9-2 (54)(bl) J Quinn 16/1: 050001: 3 b c Distant Relative 60
- Teacher's Game (Mummy's Game) Held up, prog after halfway, hard rdn appr fnl 1f, led ins last, just held on:
first success, unplcd juv (mdn, rtd 76): eff over a turning 1m on gd & soft grnd: best in blnks, tried visor.

4310 **ARMENIA** 10 [10] A G Newcombe 3-9-0 (52) J Fortune 9/1: 000002: 3 ch f Arazi - Atlantic Flyer nk 57
(Storm Bird) Bhd, shaken up 3f out, improved 2f out, drvn inside last, ran on, too late: just btn, clr rem:
back to form: acts on soft/hvy grnd & fibresand: eff at 1m, return to 7f will suit: see 415.

4174 **KOSMIC LADY** 22 [12] G A Butler 3-9-1 (53)(t) Pat Eddery 7/1: 00003: 3 b f Cosmonaut - Ktolo 4 50
(Tolomeo) Cl up, led ent fnl 3f, sn rdn, hdd below dist & no extra: clr rem: stays 1m on soft grnd.

4310 **BAJAN BROKER** 10 [6] E Stanners 3-9-7 (59) J Bosley (7) 20/1: 405604: Held up, prog halfway, 5 47
chsd ldrs appr fnl 2f till fdd appr fnl 1f: op 16/1, top-weight, return to 7f will suit: see 2111.

4274 **PURSUIT OF DREAMS** 15 [16] J Pearce 3-9-1 (53) Dale Gibson 16/1: 0005: Rear, went past btn horses appr fnl 1f. ½ 40

4143 **LIVELY FELIX** 24 [7] 3-9-0 (52) C Rutter 9/1: 004056: Chsd ldrs till 3f out: needs sells, see 3696. 5 30

3383 **LION GUEST** 64 [11] 3-8-13 (51) G Hind 16/1: 405007: Rear, mod late hdwy: abs, stablemate wnr. 3½ 23

4291 **PRINISHA** 13 [8] 3-9-3 (55) A McGlone 16/1: 220008: Chsd ldrs, wknd 2f out: see 2491. nk 26

3739 **SANGRA** 50 [2] 3-9-6 (58)(bl) R Hughes 3/1 FAV: 425029: Led till appr fnl 2f, sn btn, eased fnl 2½ 25
1f: tchd 4/1, 7 week abs, 2nd time blnks: needs fast grnd?: see 3739 (firm).

3476 **WADENHOE** 61 [3] 3-8-10 (48) S Carson 20/1: -60000: Bhd fnl 3f: 10th, 9 wk abs, new stable. 3½ 9

3885 **RIBBON LAKE** 41 [9] 3-9-3 (55) L Newman (3) 25/1: 000500: Prom 4f; 11th, 6 wk abs, see 1672. 2½ 12

4232 **BINT HABIBI** 17 [4] 3-9-1 (53) T Quinn 7/1: 530300: Mid div till 3f out: 12th, see 4004, 2914. 7 0

3970 **SLAM BID** 35 [5] 3-8-12 (50) J Stack 9/1: 563000: Prom 4f: 13th, op 6/1, new stable, btr 3266. 1¾ 0

2025 **Northern Times** 123 [1] 3-9-4 (56) D Sweeney 20/1: 4368 **Miss Flirtatious** 3 [13] 3-8-11 (49)(bl) F Norton 16/1:

15 ran   Time 1m 50.0 (11.7)   (John Guest)   G G Margarson Newmarket, Suffolk

4436
5.30 SAFFIE JOSEPH HCAP 3YO+ 0-70 (E)   1m2f46y   Soft 113   -22 Slow   [68]
£2970   £914   £457   £228   3 yo rec 5 lb

3986 **GREYFIELD** 34 [17] M R Channon 4-9-10 (64) Craig Williams 6/1: 454401: 4 b g Persian Bold - Noble 69
Dust (Dust Commander) Patiently rdn, gd hdwy 2f out, led dist, held on well under press: recent hdles rnr,
Mar '00 wnr at Wincanton (mdn, 2m, soft, rtd 125h): '99 Flat wnr at Folkestone, Beverley (ddht) & Chester (h'caps,
rtd 76): eff at 10/12f, poss stays 14f: acts on firm & soft grnd, any trck: nicely h'capped.

4374 **WILEMMGEO** 3 [14] P D Evans 3-8-13 (58) Joanna Badger (7) 10/1: 141102: 3 b f Emarati - Floral nk 61
Spark (Forzando) Held up, prog 3f out, hard rdn appr fnl 1f & ev ch, kept on, just held: tchd 16/1: back to
form, qck reappr: has had a fine season, see 4232.

4142 **MOORLANDS AGAIN** 24 [5] D Burchell 5-9-8 (62) R Price 25/1: 504543: 5 b g Then Again - Sandford nk 64
Springs (Robellino) Early ldr, again 3f out till 1f out, styd on: clr rem, game run: stays 10f on soft grnd.

4291 **IL DESTINO** 3 [9] B W Hills 5-9-2 (56) R Hughes 5/1 FAV: 003034: Mid div, chsd ldrs briefly 2f out. 4 52

3683 **SHEER FACE** 52 [15] 6-9-7 (61) Martin Dwyer 12/1: 501225: In tch, rdn 2f out, kept on same pace: abs. 1¾ 55

4123 **KISTY** 25 [10] 3-9-6 (65) S Whitworth 25/1: 333666: Rear, prog 3f out, sn rdn & no further impress. 1¼ 57

4310 **LADY JONES** 10 [7] 3-8-8 (53) J Fortune 14/1: 300567: Ran in snatches, onepce fnl 3f: see 4310. nk 44

4291 **THIHN** 13 [18] 5-9-10 (64) A Beech (3) 11/2: 231228: Rear, wide prog halfway, rdn & btn appr fnl 2f. 1¼ 53

4160 **BELLA BELLISIMO** 23 [13] 3-9-10 (69) S Drowne 10/1: 060409: Nvr a factor: 10th, see 874. 2½ 54

4221 **QUEENS PAGEANT** 19 [12] 6-10-0 (68) B Marcus 16/1: 303260: Nvr on terms: 10th, top-weight. 2½ 49

4168 **FORT SUMTER** 22 [2] 4-9-4 (58) J Bosley (7) 10/1: 00-620: Prom till wknd qckly appr fnl 2f: 15th, btr 4168. 0

4330 **SHOTACROSS THE BOW** 8 [4] 3-9-6 (65) Pat Eddery 10/1: 230300: Early ldr, wknd 3f out: 18th, 0
tchd 14/1: prob needs faster grnd, see 4228, 3140.

*3868 **ARTFUL DANE** 42 [11] 8-9-5 (59)(bl) S Sanders 11/2: 300110: Cl up, led after 3f till appr fnl 3f, sn btn: 0
20th, 6 wk abs: unsuited by step up to 10f on testing grnd?: see 3868 (1m, seller).

4174 **Cool Spice** 22 [11] 3-8-10 (55) D Sweeney 33/1: 3390 **No Mercy** 64 [16] 4-9-12 (66)(VIS) T Quinn 20/1:

4366 **Constant** 3 [20] 3-8-10 (55) F Norton 25/1: 3794 **Lovers Leap** 47 [3] 4-9-12 (66) C Rutter 25/1:

3810 **Harmony Hall** 46 [19] 6-9-6 (60) J Tate 20/1: 4334 **Supersonic** 8 [4] 4-9-8 (62)(t) S Carson (3) 25/1:

3636 **Sweet Angeline** 54 [6] 3-9-9 (68) G Hind 14/1:

20 ran   Time 2m 19.5 (13.5)   (Paulton Bloodstock)   M R Channon West Isley, Berks

WOLVERHAMPTON (Fibresand)   FRIDAY OCTOBER 20TH   LH, Oval, Sharp Track

Official Going   STANDARD   Stalls: Inside.

4437
1.35 PENDEFORD HCAP DIV 1 3YO+ 0-60 (F)   1m100y   Going 27 +02 Fast   [60]
£1792   £512   £256   3 yo rec 3 lb

4363 **GROESFAEN LAD** 6 [6] P S McEntee 3-9-9 (58)(vis) G Faulkner (3) 7/1: 063531: 3 b g Casteddu - Curious   65a
Feeling (Nishapour) Trkd ldrs, led going well 3f out, rdn over 1f out, styd on strongly, rdn out: op 5/1, first
win: qk reapp: plcd a couple of times prev this term: rnr-up thrice in '99 for B Palling (rtd 83): eff at 5f,
suited by 7/8.5f now: acts on firm, gd/soft & fibresand: sharpened up by recent fitting of a visor.
4033 **GOLDEN TOUCH** 32 [3] H J Collingridge 8-9-4 (50) S Whitworth 3/1: 600/62: 8 ch h Elmaamul - Tour   ¾ 55a
D'Argent (Halo) Prom, rdn to chall 2f out, not pace of wnr ins last: pulled 9L clr rem: op 5/1, gd run.
4363 **ROBBIES DREAM** 6 [9] R M H Cowell 4-9-7 (53)(t) S W Kelly (3) 13/8 FAV: 012123: 4 ch g Balla Cove -   9 43a
Royal Golden (Digamist) Dwelt, sn in mid-div, eff halfway, late hdwy but no threat to ldrs: qck reapp: btr 3499.
*4363 **BURNING TRUTH** 6 [7] Mrs A Duffield 5-9-6 (66)(6ex) L Enstone (7) 6/1: 020014: Twrds rear, rdn   ½ 55a
halfway, styd on late but no impress on ldrs: op 7/2, qk reapp: stiffish task under 10-6: btr 4363.
*4122 **HEATHYARDS JAKE** 26 [4] 4-8-13 (45) D Sweeney 12/1: 040015: In tch, eff 3f out, rdn/no extra   ¾ 33a
over 2f out: op 8/1, A/W return: much better on turf in 4122 (seller, gd/soft).
3770 **COMEOUTOFTHEFOG** 48 [12] 5-9-2 (48) R Lake (7) 16/1: 015006: Chsd ldrs, rdn/wknd fnl 2f: 7 wk abs. 1½ 33a
4143 **RIDGECREST** 25 [13] 3-9-2 (51)(t) Joanna Badger (7) 16/1: 450537: Led early, remnd cl-up, drvn/fdd   ½ 35a
over 2f out: well btn 5th over timber (2m juv nov, hdles bow, rtd 54h) since 4143.
4102 **SELLINGERS ROUND** 28 [11] 4-9-6 (52) I Mongan (5) 25/1: 633008: Led to 3f out, sn rdn & lost tch.   4 30a
3498 **INDIAN SWINGER** 62 [8] 4-9-0 (46) T Williams 25/1: 300039: Al rear: 9 wk abs: btr 3498 (9.4f).   6 16a
4406 **CITY BANK DUDLEY** 2 [2] 3-8-9 (44) R Lappin 33/1: 640050: Mid-div, wknd from halfway, 10th: qck reapp.5 7a
3188 **Karakul** 74 [5] 4-8-13 (45) P Dobbs (5) 16/1:   4365 **Gablesea** 4 [10] 6-9-3 (49)(bl) J Bosley (7) 20/1:
12 ran   Time 1m 48.3 (2.1)   (John Harris And Mrs Sian Harris)   P S McEntee Newmarket

4438
2.05 TIPTON MDN 2YO (D)   1m1f79y   Going 27 +06 Fast
£2737   £782   £391

4076 **BOUND** 29 [3] B W Hills 2-9-0 A Beech (3) 4/7 FAV: 000361: 2 b c Kris - Tender Moment   81a
(Caerleon) Made all, rdn & easily went clr fnl 2f, unchall/val 20L+: AW bow, best time of day: plcd once from
3 prev starts half-brother to wnrs over 1m/10f: apprec step up to 9.4f on fibresand, handles fast & soft:
further will suit: won v convincingly here in a gd time against some modest sorts.
-- **KESTLE IMP** [2] R M H Cowell 2-8-9 I Mongan (5) 16/1: 2: 2 b f Imp Society - Dark Truffle (Deploy)   16 53a
Sn well outpcd, rdn & gd late hdwy but no ch with easy wnr: Mar 1st foal, dam modest: sire multiple dirt wnr
in the USA: took a long time for the penny to drop here: shld do better.
3909 **MARREL** 39 [1] B Hanbury 2-9-0 O Urbina 8/1: 003: 2 b g Shareef Dancer - Upper Caen (High Top)   ½ 57a
Twrds rear, outpcd mid-race, styd on for press fnl 2f: op 6/1: no turf form prev: will apprec 10f + h'caps.
3449 **ANN SUMMERS** 63 [6] B J Meehan 2-8-9 P Doe 11/1: -04: Cl-up, rdn 4f out, wknd fnl 2f: 9 wk abs,   1¾ 49a
AW bow, op 10/1: big step up in trip & shld apprec mid-dists in time: see 3449 (6f, firm).
4152 **COPCOURT ROYALE** 24 [5] 2-8-9 S Whitworth 25/1: 65: Al twrds rear: up in trip: see 4152.   1¼ 47a
4230 **NARJIS FLOWER** 18 [8] 2-8-9 J Fanning 16/1: 06: Prom, lost tch appr fnl 2f: AW bow: see 4230.   1½ 44a
3958 **ROYAL WANDERER** 36 [4] 2-9-0 L Enstone (7) 25/1: 007: With ldr 4f, fdd fnl 3f: AW bow, up in trip.   nk 49a
-- **BEAUCHAMP PILOT** [7] 2-9-0 S W Kelly (3) 8: V slow to start, sn in tch, hdwy 3f out, sn   2½ 45a
wknd qckly: debut: Mar foal, dam 9f wnr in Ireland: sire high-class at 7f: with G A Butler.
8 ran   Time 2m 00.2 (2.0)   (Ray Richards)   B W Hills Lambourn, Berks

4439
2.35 NURSERY HCAP 2YO 0-75 (E)   1m100y a   Going 27 -26 Slow   [79]
£2772   £792   £396

4254 **FORUM FINALE** 17 [10] M Johnston 2-8-12 (63) J Fanning 7/1: 25001: 2 b f Silver Hawk - Silk Masque   68a
(Woodman) Cl-up, rdn 2f out, closed in rivals ins last, drvn out to get up nr fin: AW bow: earlier rnr-up
on debut (5-rnr fillies stks): dam a 6f juv wnr: eff at 6/8.5f on soft & fibresand, stiff or sharp trk.
4235 **THOMAS SMYTHE** 18 [11] N P Littmoden 2-9-5 (70) D Sweeney 3/1 FAV: 226322: 2 ch c College   nk 74a
Chapel - Red Barons Lady (Electric) Trkd ldrs, went on over 1f out, hung right & tried to pull himself up ins last,
collared nr fin: threw away a clr winning opportunity here, prob needs headgear: eff at 6/8.5f on gd, soft & f/sand.
*3837 **KUMAKAWA** 45 [2] M J Polglase 2-8-5 (53) P Doe 7/1: 000013: 2 ch g Dancing Spree - Maria Cappuccini 2 53a
(Siberian Express) Chsd ldrs, sltly outpcd over 2f out, styd on again fnl 1f: 6 wk abs, new stable: prev with
J G Given: eff at 1m/8.5f on firm grnd & fibresand, further may suit: see 3837.
1602 **TIRANA** 142 [6] D Shaw 2-7-12 (49) J McAuley 25/1: -0004: Led early, remnd with ldrs, drvn/kept on   ¾ 48a
onpcd fnl 2f: v long abs & 1st time in the frame on A/W bow, mod turf form prev: stays a sharp 8.5f on fibresand.
4350 **COUNTRYWIDE PRIDE** 7 [3] 2-9-4 (69) S W Kelly 7/2: 304605: Mid-div, gd hdwy appr fnl 2f, rdn &   ¾ 67a
no impress appr fnl 1f: op 5/1: 5L clr rem, qck reapp: generally consistent form: handles fast, gd & fibresand.
4157 **EARLY WISH** 24 [13] 2-9-7 (72) A Beech (3) 6/1: -63306: Twrds rear, eff halfway, kept on fnl 2f   5 62a
under a v quiet ride, nvr plcd to chall: top-weight: shld be capable of better: see 2583.
3729 **IZZET MUZZY** 51 [8] 2-8-4 (55)(VIS) T Williams 25/1: 546007: Led after 1f till appr fnl 2f: abs, vis.   hd 45a
4250 **NO NAME CITY** 17 [1] 2-8-13 (64) S Whitworth 11/1: 0038: In tch, fdd fnl 2f: h'cap bow: see 4250.   1¾ 51a
4373 **TAMILIA** 4 [9] 2-8-3 (54) R Fitzpatrick 16/1: -00049: Al in rear: AW bow: qck reapp: btr 4383 (soft).   6 31a
4132 **GAZETTE IT TONIGHT** 26 [12] 2-8-2 (53) P Bradley (5) 12/1: 331400: Al bhd, 10th: btr 3615 (sell, fast).   2½ 26a
3910 **Degree Of Power** 39 [4] 2-8-1 (52) G Bardwell 25/1:   4227 **No Surrender** 20 [7] 2-7-12 (49) Claire Bryan (5) 25/1:
4230 **Sir Edward Burrow** 18 [5] 2-8-8 (59) J Stack 14/1:
13 ran   Time 1m 50.7 (4.1)   (Mrs Jacqueline Conroy)   M Johnston Middleham, N Yorks

4440
3.05 PENDEFORD HCAP DIV 2 3YO+ 0-60 (F)   1m100y   Going 27 -13 Slow   [60]
£1785   £510   £256   3 yo rec 3 lb

4018 **SOUHAITE** 34 [4] W R Muir 4-8-10 (42) S W Kelly (3) 7/1: 000101: 4 b g Salse - Parannda (Bold Lad)   50a
Made all, rdn & in command appr fnl 1f, eased nr fin, val 5/6f: op 4/1: earlier won at Leicester & Chepstow
(h'caps): '99 Southwell wnr (h'cap, 1st win, rtd 45a): eff between 7f & 12f, has tried 2m: acts on firm, gd &
fibresand: acts on any trk & runs well fresh: best forcing the pace, without t-strap: tough, win again.
4310 **BOBBYDAZZLE** 11 [9] C A Dwyer 5-9-10 (56) O Urbina 14/1: 340402: 5 ch m Rock Hopper - Billie Blue   3½ 56a

(Ballad Rock) Hdwy from rear appr fnl 2f, styd on well but no threat to wnr: op 10/1, 5L clr rem, top-weight.
3839 **SAMARA SONG 45** [7] Ian Williams 7-9-1 (47) R Fitzpatrick 7/1: 040403: 7 ch g Savahra Sound - Hosting (Thatching) Prom, rdn & kept on onepacd appr fnl 1f: on a fair mark: see 3839, 1003. *5* **39a**
3856 **VICTORIET 44** [12] A T Murphy 3-8-12 (47) J Fanning 20/1: 444404: Trkd wnr, rdn/no extra appr fnl 1f: 6 wk abs: stays a sharp 8.5f on fibresand?: see 1435. *1¾* **35a**
4335 **HEVER GOLF GLORY 9** [2] 6-9-6 (52) T Williams 6/1: 000335: Chsd ldrs, fdd fnl 2f: btr 4335 (equitrk). *¾* **38a**
4174 **MISTY MAGIC 23** [13] 3-9-4 (53) P Doe 6/1: 263006: Late gains from rear, nvr a threat: see 2013. *3* **34a**
2554 **LEES FIRST STEP 102** [5] 3-9-2 (51) S Whitworth 25/1: 0-0007: Mid-div at best: 9 wk jumps abs (p.u. in a 2m juv nov hdle, broke blood vessel): see 1292. *3½* **27a**
4328 **ARZILLO 9** [3] 4-9-2 (48) Claire Bryan (5) 14/1: 002608: Nvr a factor: btr 3939 (7f, firm grnd). *1¼* **21a**
3279 **GAELIC FORAY 70** [6] 4-8-13 (45) I Mongan (5) 25/1: 035309: Dwelt, al bhd, 10th: 10 wk abs: see 2759. *1¼* **15a**
4251 **ADRIFT 17** [11] 3-9-8 (57)(t) A Beech (3) 11/2: 002030: Dwelt, nvr in it: op 7/2, btr 4251 (9.4f). *½* **25a**
4033 **DANIELLA RIDGE 32** [1] 4-9-7 (53) P Dobbs (5) 5/2 FAV: 002540: Prom, fdd appr fnl 2f, 11th: stewards considered running, reportedly was 'nvr travelling' on a/w bow: btr 4033. *3* **16a**
1884 **ROI DE DANSE 129** [10] 5-9-0 (46) T G McLaughlin 14/1: 025000: Lost tch halfway, t.o. last: abs. *15* **0a**
12 ran Time 1m 49.6 (3.4) (J Bernstein) W R Muir Lambourn, Berks

4441 **3.35 PENKRIDGE MED AUCT MDN 2YO (F) 5f aw Going 27 -11 Slow**
£2226 £636 £318

4202 **ROXANNE MILL 20** [7] M D I Usher 2-8-9 I Mongan (5) 4/1: 034631: 2 b f Cyrano De Bergerac - It Must Be Millie (Reprimand) Led, styd on strongly fnl 1f, rdn out: dam a dual 5f 3yo wnr: eff arnd 5f, 6f may suit in time: acts on fast, soft & fibresand: loves to force the pace: consistent, deserved 1st win. **72a**
4030 **GEMTASTIC 32** [8] P D Evans 2-8-9 Joanna Badger (7) 20/1: 033202: 2 b f Tagula - Its So Easy (Shaadi) Cl-up, styd on but not pace of wnr fnl 1f: eff at 5f on firm, gd/soft & fibresand: deserves to go one better. *2* **65a**
4225 **SMIRFYS PARTY 20** [6] B A McMahon 2-9-0 T G McLaughlin 13/8 FAV: 625533: 2 ch c Clantime - Party Scenes (Most Welcome) In tch, hdwy appr fnl 1f, no extra ins last: gamble from 4/1: shade btr 4225 (6f). *2* **65a**
4269 **WINTER DOLPHIN 16** [9] I A Wood 2-8-9 J Fanning 12/1: 06604: In tch, styd on well, fnl 1f, not pace to chall ldrs: op 7/1, AW bow: poss stays 5f on fibresand. *½* **59a**
4288 **CHISPA 14** [10] 2-8-9 P Doe 8/1: 0005: Wide/prom, no extra fnl 1f: AW/h'cap bow: see 1454. *1* **56a**
4345 **TROUBADOUR GIRL 7** [1] 2-8-9 D Sweeney 5/1: 000306: Al outpcd: qck reapp: btr 3757 (6f sell, firm). *5* **45a**
4247 **PIDDINGTON FLYER 17** [2] 2-9-0 S Clancy (7) 7/1: 67: Sn outpcd: op 5/1, see 4257. *½* **49a**
-- **TUNEFUL MELODY** [3] 2-8-9 G Parkin 16/1: 8: V slow to start, al rear: op 10/1: half-sister to a 6f juv wnr. *¾* **42a**
4171 **ALICIAN SUNHILL 23** [4] 2-8-9 (bl) T Williams 25/1: 304439: Rear, lost tch halfway: jockey referred to Jockey Club for irresponsible riding (2nd time in 2 days): see 4171 (soft). *nk* **42a**
4131 **ANTHONY ROYLE 26** [5] 2-9-0 (BL) P Bradley (5) 16/1: 655000: Prom, wknd rapidly fnl 3f, 10th. *5* **37a**
10 ran Time 1m 02.1 (1.9) (The Goodracing Partnership) M D I Usher Kingston Lisle, Oxon

4442 **4.05 TETTENHALL HCAP DIV 1 3YO+ 0-60 (F) 6f aw Going 27 -21 Slow** **[59]**
£1799 £514 £257 3 yo rec 1 lb

4153 **PUPPET PLAY 24** [13] E J Alston 5-9-6 (51) S W Kelly (3) 5/2 FAV: 321021: 5 ch m Broken Hearted - Fantoccini (Taufan) Mid-div, imprvd appr fnl 2f, ran on to lead fnl 50y, drvn out: earlier won at Pontefract (fills h'cap) & Ripon (h'cap): rnr-up on turf in native Ireland & on sand in '99 (rtd 52a, AW mdn): likes to race up with/force the pace over 6f/1m, stays 9f: acts on firm, fast, both AWs & any trk: best without blnks: tough. **54a**
1913 **ALJAZ 128** [11] Miss Gay Kelleway 10-9-1 (46) D Sweeney 20/1: 646402: 10 b g Al Nasr - Santa Linda (Sir Ivor) In tch, hdwy to chall well ins last, not btn far: 4 month abs & a gd run: h'capped to win. *nk* **48a**
4293 **PALO BLANCO 14** [4] Andrew Reid 9-9-8 (53) S Whitworth 4/1: 440163: 9 b m Precocious - Linpac Mapleleaf (Dominion) Sn outpcd, strong run appr fnl 1f, closing at fin: in gd form: see 4156. *hd* **55a**
4257 **PALACEGATE TOUCH 17** [9] A Berry 10-9-10 (55)(bl) D Allan (7) 16/1: 000034: Front rank, narrow lead appr fnl 1f, hdd well ins last, hung left & no extra: ran to best: flattered 4257, see 1139. *nk* **56a**
3966 **TWO STEP 36** [6] 4-8-12 (43)(t) O Urbina 4/1: 050325: Cl-up, chall over 1f out, held well ins last: jockey received a caution for whip misuse: remains in gd form, acts on fast, gd & fibresand: see 3613. *nk* **43a**
4407 **SOUNDS ACE 2** [7] 4-8-12 (43)(bl) J Fanning 33/1: 006006: Prom, drvn/onepcd fnl 1f: ran 48hrs ago. *1½* **39a**
3956 **HOUT BAY 37** [1] 3-9-8 (54) P Dobbs (5) 10/1: 300547: Dwelt, sn in tch, no extra over 1f out: op 7/1. *½* **49a**
4223 **CAPPELLINA 20** [2] 3-9-7 (53) P Doe 10/1: 042008: Al twrds rear: btr 3279 (7f, firm). *1* **45a**
4155 **PETITE DANSEUSE 24** [8] 6-8-13 (44) Joanna Badger (7) 14/1: 546009: Nvr a factor: op 10/1: see 3578. *¾* **34a**
909 **IM SOPHIE 189** [3] 3-10-0 (60) R Price 14/1: 2-450: Prom, rdn/wknd appr fnl 1f, 10th: 6 month abs, new stable: top-weight on h'cap bow: prev with T D Barron, sharper next time for D Burchell: see 740. *1½* **47a**
4087 **YOUNG IBNR 29** [10] 5-9-5 (50) L Newton 12/1: 001500: Led to over 1f out, fdd, 11th: btr 3180. *½* **36a**
4358 **SAMWAR 6** [5] 8-9-11 (56)(vis) R Fitzpatrick 9/1: 32635P: Al struggling, p.u. lame 1f out: qck reapp. **0a**
12 ran Time 1m 15.7 (2.9) (Mrs F D McAuley) E J Alston Longton, Lancs

4443 **4.35 SHIFNAL MDN HCAP 3YO+ 0-70 (E) 1m4f aw Going 27 -45 Slow** **[62]**
£2716 £776 £388 3 yo rec 7 lb

4100 **LUNA FLIGHT 28** [8] M Johnston 3-8-4 (45) J Fanning 9/1: -5561: 3 b f Ela Mana Mou - Lotus Moon (Shareef Dancer) Waited with, imprvd over 5f out, led 2f out, sn clr, eased fnl 50y, val 7/8L: op 7/1, h'cap bow: unplcd in 3 mdns prev (rtd 65 on debut): mid-dist bred: eff over a sharp 12f on fibresand: apprec drop in grade. **53a**
4329 **TUFTY HOPPER 9** [12] P Howling 3-9-8 (63)(VIS) G Faulkner (3) 4/1 FAV: 332662: 3 b g Rock Hopper - Melancolia (Legend Of France) Chsd ldr, outpcd 5f out, rdn & ran on well fnl 1f, no ch with wnr: not disgraced in 1st time visor: consistently plcd but still a mdn after 21 starts: see see 3954. *5* **62a**
3835 **FLAVIA 45** [3] R W Armstrong 3-8-8 (47)(2ow)(bl) R Price 16/1: 66053: 3 b f Lahib - Gustavia (Red Sunset) Trkd ldrs, went on 3f out, hdd 2f out, no extra appr fnl 1f: eff at 12f on fibresand: see 2770. *hd* **48a**
4360 **BUSY BUSY BEE 6** [4] N P Littmoden 3-9-0 (55) T G McLaughlin 12/1: -50464: Twrds rear, prom halfway, rdn & onepcd appr fnl 2f: qck reapp: clr rem: stays 7/12f, handles fibresand. *1½* **51a**
4386 **FALCON SPIRIT 3** [11] 4-9-0 (48)(bl) S W Kelly (3) 5/1: 040505: In tch, drvn/wknd fnl 2f: qck reapp. *3½* **39a**
4313 **BOOMSHADOW 11** [5] 3-8-1 (42) Joanna Badger (7) 33/1: 600056: Mid-div at best: up in trip, see 570. *2* **30a**
4329 **LE CAVALIER 9** [6] 3-9-5 (60)(bl) G Bardwell 7/1: 650007: Keen/led to over 3f out, fdd: btr 752. *¾* **47a**
4229 **NORTHERN ECHO 18** [7] 3-8-9 (50) T Williams 9/2: 006208: Cl-up, rdn/wknd fnl 3f: op 7/2: btr 3606. *shd* **37a**
4205 **BOLD GUEST 20** [9] 3-10-0 (69) S Whitworth 11/2: 033409: Mid-div, lost tch fnl 2f: top-weight. *13* **40a**
4208 **CHARLIES QUEST 20** [2] 4-8-11 (45) I Mongan (5) 20/1: 006-00: Chsd ldrs, wknd qckly over 3f out, 10th: unplcd in 3 '99 turf mdns (tried 1m/10f, rtd 59 at best). *¾* **15a**

WOLVERHAMPTON (Fibresand)   FRIDAY OCTOBER 20TH   LH, Oval, Sharp Track

4150 **Pursuivant 24** [1] 6-8-3 (37)(1ow)(bl) R Fitzpatrick 25/1 **36 Pure Brief 245** [10] 3-8-6 (47) P Doe 16/1:
12 ran   Time 2m 42.3 (8.7)   (J Godfrey)   M Johnston Middleham, N Yorks

4444	5.05 TETTENHALL HCAP DIV 2 3YO+ 0-60 (F) 6f aw Going 27 -01 Slow	[59]
	£1799 £514 £257 3 yo rec 1 lb	

4425 **PUPS PRIDE 1** [3] R A Fahey 3-8-12 (44)(bl) R Havlin 11/1: 034001: 3 b g Efisio - Moogie (Young   **51a**
Generation) Sn outpcd, rdn/imprvd 2f out, styd on to lead ins last, rdn out: ran 24hrs ago: little mdn/nurs
form in '99: eff at 6f, stays an easy 1m: acts on gd/soft, fibresand & in blnks/visor.
4365 **FEATHERSTONE LANE 4** [11] Miss L C Siddall 9-9-7 (52) D Sweeney 16/1: 343502: 9 b g Siberian   2½ **52a**
Express - Try Gloria (Try My Best) Mid-div, gd hdwy 3f out, ev ch till no extra fnl 1f: qck reapp: likes W'hampton.
3964 **JANICELAND 36** [1] M Wigham 3-9-9 (55) J Stack 10/3 JT FAV: 105533: 3 b f Foxhound - Rebecca's   2½ **49a**
Girl (Nashamaa) Led early, remnd in tch, ev ch till not qckn ins last: op 11/4: shade btr 3964 (gd/firm).
4327 **YOUNG BIGWIG 10** [10] D W Chapman 6-9-10 (55) G Parkin 10/3 JT FAV: 403004: Prom, rdn to chall   1¼ **46a**
appr fnl 1f, no impress fnl 1f: op 5/1: see 3774, 425.
4294 **MARENGO 14** [5] 6-9-11 (56) P Fitzpatrick 9/1: 000105: Sn rdn in rear, gd hdwy appr fnl 1f, drvn   1 **44a**
& btn sn after: op 6/1: twice below 4155 (Southwell).
3275 **PURPLE FLING 70** [8] 9-10-0 (59) T G McLaughlin 7/1: -00236: Handy, rdn into lead appr fnl 1f,   hd **47a**
hdd just ins last, wknd: top-weight & just sharper for this after a 10 wk abs: see 3275 (C/D), 82.
3975 **KILBRANNAN SOUND 35** [6] 3-9-8 (54) L Newton 12/1: 000007: Lost tch halfway: see 1219.   5 **30a**
4156 **BANGLED 24** [2] 3-9-4 (50) P Doe 9/2: 030428: Mid-div, wknd qckly appr fnl 1f: much btr 4156.   hd **26a**
677 **DAYNABEE 218** [7] 5-8-13 (44) R Lake 16/1: 463549: Mid-div, btn fnl 3f: 7 month abs & prob   ½ **19a**
better for race: may apprec a return to 7f: see 567, 391.
4223 **ZARAGOSSA 20** [4] 4-9-7 (52) Iona Wands 20/1: 500600: Led after 1f, hdd over 1f out, wknd, 10th.   nk **26a**
4192 Believing 21 [13] 3-9-6 (52) P Dobbs (5) 12/1:   4407 Plum First 2 [1] 10-8-12 (43) C Teague 33/1:
12 ran   Time 1m 14.5 (1.7)   (The Slurping Toads)   R A Fahey Butterwick, W Yorks

---

DONCASTER   FRIDAY OCTOBER 20TH   Lefthand, Flat, Galloping Track

Official Going: GOOD (GD/SOFT PLCS)   Stalls: Straight Course - Stands side, Rnd course - Inside, Rnd 1m - Outside

4445	1.30 EBF FILL MDN 2YO (D) 1m rnd Good/Soft 78 -17 Slow	
	£4371 £1345 £672 £336	

-- **QUICK TO PLEASE** [20] H R A Cecil 2-8-11 T Quinn 13/8 FAV: 1: 2 b f Danzig - Razyana (His   **98+**
Majesty) Sn cl up, led over 1f out & qckd clr, impressive: hvly bckd: May foal, full sister to top class
sprinter Danehill & useful 7f performer Shibboleth: eff at 1m, will get further: acts on gd/soft grnd &
a gall trck: runs well fresh: excellent debut, potentially high-class with a turn of foot, keep on your side.
3836 **KAZANA 45** [19] S P C Woods 2-8-11 J Carroll 50/1: 42: 2 b f Salse - Sea Ballad (Bering)   5 **85**
Led, rdn/hdd over 1f out, kept on onepace: abs: rarely meet one so smart: eff at 1m, further suit: win a race.
3853 **ZANZIBAR 44** [5] M L W Bell 2-8-11 R Mullen 10/1: 523: 2 b f In The Wings - Isle Of Spice (Diesis)   shd **85**
Trckd ldrs, not much room 2f out & 1f out, styd on well inside last, no threat to wnr: op 12/1, 6 wk abs: acts on
gd & gd/soft grnd: not get the run of the race: should find a race & shld win a less competitive mdn: see 3853.
-- **CHARMER VENTURE** [21] M R Perham 40/1: -4: Towards rear/wide halfway, styd   ¾ **84+**
on strongly under hands & heels riding fnl 2f, nrst fin: stablemate of rnr up: Zilzal filly, April foal: half sister
to 12f stable wnr Angels Venture: dam unrcd: eff at 1m, mid dists look sure to suit next term: acts on gd/soft grnd:
most eyecatching late headway here, looks sure to improve & should find a race.
-- **MARANI** [16] 2-8-11 L Dettori 8/1: 5: Chsd ldrs halfway, kept on fnl 2f, nvr pace to threaten: op 6/1:   ½ **83+**
Ashkalani filly, March foal: half sister to a 1m juv wnr abroad: dam 11f wnr: mid dists suit: improve plenty.
3752 **KAZEEM 50** [25] 2-8-11 M Hills 12/1: 66: In tch, onepace fnl 2f: abs, wants mid-dists.   shd **83**
-- **ASAREER** [10] 2-8-11 W Supple 9/1: -7: Prom, rdn/onepce fnl 2f: op 8/1: Gone West filly, Feb foal,   ¾ **82**
cost $650,000: dam a juv wnr in US: sire top class 1m/9f performer, this 1m trip should suit: with M Tregonning.
4019 **SILVER GREY LADY 34** [18] 2-8-11 Paul Eddery 12/1: 38: Prom halfway, rdn/no extra over 1f out.   hd **81**
3786 **ROSE PEEL 48** [17] 2-8-11 A Culhane 20/1: 09: Rcd keenly, mid div, mod late hdwy under minimal   nk **80+**
press, no threat to ldrs: not given a hard time, will improve: see 3786 (7f).
-- **HIGH SPOT** [22] 2-8-11 C Rutter 40/1: -0: In tch halfway, kept on onepce fnl 2f, nvr a threat: 10th: 1 **78**
Shirley Heights first foal: dam eff at 1m/10f: looks sure to relish mid dists.
-- **NATIVE FORCE** [9] 2-8-11 R Havlin 20/1: 0: Mid div, nvr pace to chall: 11th: Indian Ridge filly,   nk **77**
Feb foal, a first foal: dam mod form at 1m/12f: sire a high class sprinter: with J H M Gosden.
-- **MADELINE BASSETT** [12] 2-8-11 E Ahern 33/1: 0: Dwelt, towards rear, late gains fnl 3f, nrst fin: nk **76**
Kahyasi filly, May foal, cost Ir 19,000gns: half sister to a smart 6f juv wnr Compton Arrow: dam a 7f 2yo wnr in
Ireland: looks sure to apprec mid dists next term & should repay this kind intro for G Butler.
-- **MATTHIOLA** [13] 2-8-11 J P Spencer 16/1: 0: Chsd ldrs 5f: 13th: op 20/1: Ela Mana Mou filly,   1 **74**
Feb foal: dam a top class 12f performer, dam lightly rcd abroad: mid dists will suit next term for L Cumani.
-- **LAILANI** [2] 2-8-11 Martin Dwyer 33/1: 0: Hmpd & lost plce/dropped towards rear after 1f, no   shd **74**
impress on ldrs: Unfuwain filly, Feb foal, half sister to wnrs at 1m/12f: dam a mid dist mdn: sure to need 10f+.
-- **SPRING SYMPHONY** [14] 2-8-11 F Lynch 9/1: 0: Mid div, btn 2f out: 15th: Darshaan filly, Feb   nk **73**
foal: half sister to a 10f wnr: dam unrcd: half sister to high class mid dists performer Spectrum: sire a French
Derby wnr: sure to relish mid dists next term for Sir Michael Stoute.
-- **LUCILLE** [24] 2-8-11 C Lowther 20/1: 0: Dwelt, towards rear, no impress fnl 3f: 16th: Sadlers Wells   1½ **70**
filly, May foal: half sister to smart mid dist performer Lucido: dam a 6f Irish wnr: likely to improve over further.
-- **SUNSTONE** [7] 2-8-11 R ffrench 40/1: 0: Unruly start, in tch halfway, outprod fnl 3f: 17th: Caerleon   hd **69**
filly, April foal: dam a mdn styer: sire top class 10/12f performer: mid dists look sure to suit next term.
-- **Royal Kiss** [1] 2-8-11 G Carter 16/1:   -- **Scheherazade** [15] 2-8-11 G Sparkes (7) 33/1:
-- **Eastern Jewel** [11] 2-8-11 T Ashley 50/1:   -- **Hyde Hall** [23] 2-8-11 A McGlone 16/1:
-- **Distant Decree** [8] 2-8-11 J Weaver 40/1:   -- **Dream Time** [4] 2-8-11 D Harrison 16/1:
3829 **Tennessee Waltz 45** [3] 2-8-11 M Tebbutt 50/1:   -- **Red Crystal** [6] 2-8-11 O Pears 40/1: F
25 ran   Time 1m 43.66 (7.56)   (K Abdulla)   H R A Cecil Newmarket, Suffolk

---

4446   **2.0 EBF OCTOBER MDN DIV 1 2YO (D)**   **7f str**   **Good/Soft 78**   **-15 Slow**
£3477   £1070   £535   £267   Raced across track, no advantage

4184 **HARMONY ROW 22** [22]   E A L Dunlop 2-9-0 G Carter 5/1 JT FAV: 31: 2 ch c Barathea - Little Change
(Grundy) Al prom, rdn & styd on well to lead inside last, pushed out cl home: op 4/1: confirmed promise of debut
prev: half brother to 5 wnrs, sire a top class miler: eff at 7f, 1m shuld suit: acts on gd & gd/soft grnd:
handles a stiff/gall trck: looks a useful prospect & should win more races.   **90**

--   **TRAMWAY** [16]   H R A Cecil 2-9-0 T Quinn 10/1: 2: 2 ch c Lycius - Black Fighter (Secretariat)
Prom, rdn/led over 3f out till inside last, not pace of wnr: Feb foal, brother to 3yo mid dist performer Taming:
dam a 1m wnr: eff at 7f, 1m will suit: acts on gd/soft grnd & a gall trck: encouraging intro, can find a mdn.   2   **85**

4036 **SERGE LIFAR 32** [18]   R Hannon 2-9-0 J Weaver 5/1 JT FAV: 33: 2 b c Shirley Heights - Ballet
(Sharrood) Trkd ldrs, kept on fnl 2f under hands & heels: bckd, clr rem: return to 1m+ will see a win.   ½   **84**

4167 **HAASIL 23** [15]   J L Dunlop 2-9-0 W Supple 12/1: 34: Sn trckd ldrs, rdn & onepce fnl 2f: op 8/1:
left debut bhd (last of 3): eff at 7f on gd/soft grnd, 1m should suit: see 4167.   4   **76**

4163 **NORTH POINT 23** [14]   2-9-0 E Ahern 50/1: 005: Chsd ldrs, rdn halfway, kept on onepce fnl 2f.   2   **72**

3962 **IRISH STREAM 36** [6]   2-9-0 C Rutter 13/2: 326: Keen/held up, kept on fnl 2f, nvr a threat to ldrs:
1m+ & h'cap company now look in order: kind ride: just btr 3962, 3608.   1¾   **69**

1859 **RED RIVER REBEL 131** [9]   2-9-0 O Pears 100/1: -67: Chsd ldrs 5f: 4 mth abs: see 1859 (6f).   2½   **64**

4341 **ATLANTIC EAGLE 8** [12]   2-9-0 R Ffrench 16/1: 08: Prom 5f: see 4341 (6f).   ¾   **63**

4183 **MACDUNE 22** [2]   2-9-0 M Tebbutt 16/1: 09: Trkd ldrs 5f, fdd: see 4183.   hd   **62**

--   **ROUE** [8]   2-9-0 (t) F Lynch 14/1: 0: Rdn/bhd early, late gains, nvr a threat to ldrs: 10th: Efisio
colt, Feb foal, cost 100,000gns: half brother to 7f juv wnr Iftiraas: dam a 5f juv wnr.   2   **58**

3909 **OCEAN ROAD 39** [7]   2-9-0 T Ashley 50/1: 060: Prom, hung left/fdd fnl 3f: 11th: btr 3909 (fast).   hd   **57**

--   **RIBBON OF LIGHT** [5]   2-9-0 M Hills 7/1: 0: Trkd ldrs 5f: 12th: op 7/2: Spectrum filly, March foal,
cost 100,000gns: half sister to a 7f 3yo Listed wnr: dam unrcd: sire top class 1m/10f performer: shld apprec 1m+.   hd   **56**

--   **DAVID WYNNE** [20]   2-9-0 J P Spencer 20/1: 0: Keen/rear, little hdwy: 13th: Dolphin Street colt,
March foal, cost 14,000gns: a first foal: dam a 5f juv wnr: with L Cumani.   ½   **55**

4161 **RIPCORD 24** [10]   2-9-0 L Dettori 12/1: 00: Trkd ldrs, fdd over 2f out: op 16/1: 14th: see 4161.   1¼   **52**

--   **RAHEIBB** [21]   2-9-0 A McGlone 33/1: 0: In tch, outpcd fnl 3f: 15th: Lion Cavern colt, March foal, a first
foal: dam useful 6f/1m wnr: sire a smart 6/7f performer: with A Stewart.   ½   **51**

4184 **Cassius 22** [19] 2-9-0 D Harrison 16/1:   --   **Guru** [3] 2-9-0 Martin Dwyer 33/1:

3999 **Doc Davis 34** [11] 2-9-0 J Carroll 50/1:   --   **Lafayette** [1] 2-9-0 R Mullen 33/1:

--   **Mutawaqed** [13] 2-9-0 R Perham 25/1:   4253 **Grand Houdini 17** [4] 2-9-0 T Lucas 66/1:

--   **Ridge And Furrow** [17] 2-9-0 A Culhane 66/1:

22 ran   Time 1m 29.73 (6.53)   (The Right Angle Club)   E A L Dunlop Newmarket, Suffolk

---

4447   **2.30 EBF OCTOBER MDN DIV 2 2YO (D)**   **7f str**   **Good/Soft 74**   **-08 Slow**
£3477   £1070   £535   £267   Majority raced towards centre

--   **ALDEBARAN** [10]   H R A Cecil 2-9-0 T Quinn 5/2 FAV: 1: 2 b c Mr Prospector - Chimes Of Freedom
(Private Account) Dwelt, sn handy rdn/prog to lead over 1f out, styd on well inside last, drvn out: hvly bckd: Feb
foal: half brother to 2 US wnrs: dam a high class performer between 6f/1m: eff at 7f, 1m will suit: acts on gd/sft
grnd & a gall trk: runs well fresh: useful debut, type to rate higher & win races in higher class.   **93+**

2521 **TAKE TO TASK 103** [18]   M Johnston 2-9-0 J Weaver 11/1: -222: 2 b c Conquistador Cielo - Tash
(Never Bend) Al prom, rdn & styd on for press fnl 2f, not pce of wnr: abs: acts on gd & gd/soft: deserves a race.   2   **88**

3840 **POLISH OFF 45** [16]   B W Hills 2-9-0 M Hills 4/1: 543: 2 b c Polish Precedent - Lovely Lyca (Night
Shift) Al prom, rdn & kept on for press fnl 2f, not pace of wnr: well bckd, clr rem, abs: handles firm & gd/soft.   2½   **83**

4163 **SPANISH SPUR 23** [6]   J H M Gosden 2-9-0 L Dettori 5/1: 254: Led/dsptd lead till over 1f out, no
extra inside last: dropped in trip: see 3906 (1m).   4   **75**

4281 **LORD PROTECTOR 14** [12]   2-9-0 J Weaver 8/1: -425: Led/dsptd lead till over 1f out, fdd: btr 4281.   ½   **74**

--   **COLLARD** [17]   2-9-0 C Rutter 16/1: 6: Slowly away, styd on well fnl 3f, nrst fin: op 12/1:
Wolfhound filly, April foal, dam a 1m wnr: sire high class 5/7f performer: eyecatching late headway, will improve.   1¼   **66+**

4188 **EASTERN BREEZE 21** [1]   2-9-0 A Culhane 20/1: 37: Mid div, nvr pace to chall: btr 4188 (6f, soft).   nk   **70**

--   **SAMAWI** [19]   2-9-0 W Supple 20/1: 8: Trkd ldrs 5f: Pennekamp colt, May foal, dam unrcd: sire
top class juvenile/miler: with M Tregoning.   2½   **65**

--   **MAGIC TO DO** [22]   2-9-0 C Lowther 50/1: 9: Dwelt, nvr on terms with ldrs: Spectrum colt, March
foal, cost Ir 30,000gns: half brother to a 6f juv wnr: dam lightly rcd: with R F Johnson Houghton.   2   **61**

--   **CUT RATE** [21]   2-9-0 J P Spencer 16/1: 0: Dwelt, towards rear, mod hdwy fnl 3f: 10th: Diesis colt,
Jan foal: half brother to 6f juv wnr Magnasonic: dam a 7f juv wnr: sire a top class juv: with Mrs A J Perrett.   4   **53**

3705 **BLIND SPOT 53** [8]   2-9-0 M Tebbutt 50/1: -00: Chsd ldrs 4f: abs: 11th: see 3705.   1   **51**

3766 **SOUTHERN DANCER 49** [14]   2-9-0 P M Quinn 33/1: 00: Mid div at best: 12th: 7 week abs.   1¼   **48**

4267 **TAFFRAIL 16** [16]   2-9-0 Paul Eddery 50/1: 00: Mid div at best: 13th: bred to apprec mid-dists.   nk   **47**

4252 **MAMCAZMA 17** [20]   2-9-0 J Lowe 66/1: 060: Mid div, btn 2f out: 14th: longer 7f trip.   ½   **46**

--   **DANIAVI** [1]   2-9-0 F Lynch 12/1: 0: Dwelt, al towards rear: 20th: Kris colt, Feb foal: half brother
to a 7f wnr: dam unrcd: sire a top class miler: with Sir Michael Stoute.   **0**

4137 **Raptor 25** [15] 2-9-0 J Carroll 50/1:   --   **Perestroika** [7] 2-9-0 G Carter 33/1:

--   **Anshan Squaw** [3] 2-8-9 Martin Dwyer 40/1:   --   **Abyssinian Wolf** [13] 2-9-0 D Harrison 20/1:

4209 **Miss Devious 20** [2] 2-8-9 J Mackay (5) 50/1:   --   **She Wadi Wadi** [4] 2-8-9 R Mullen 33/1:

21 ran   Time 1m 28.93 (5.73)   (Niarchos Family)   H R A Cecil Newmarket, Suffolk

---

4448   **3.00 WESTWOODSIDE HCAP 3YO 0-80 (D)**   **1m2f60y**   **Good/Soft 78**   **+07 Fast**   **[86]**
£5892   £1813   £906   £453

4280 **SCHEMING 15** [17]   W M Brisbourne 3-8-7 (65) R Mullen 16/1: 16001: 3 br g Machiavellian -
Alusha (Soviet Star) Held up, rdn/hdwy over 2f out & drvn/styd on to lead well ins last: bckd at long odds: gd
time: earlier made a winning debut at Haydock (mdn): eff at 10/12f on fast & gd/soft, gall trk: runs well fresh.   **71**

4291 **RED LION FR 14** [15]   B J Meehan 3-8-3 (61) D R McCabe 7/1: 000642: 3 ch g Lion Cavern -
Mahogany River (Irish River) Unruly stalls, slowly away & rear, hmpd halfway, rdn/hdwy fnl 3f & led ins
last, drvn/hdd towards fin: clr rem: mdn, but shone towards fin to win similar: see 4291.   nk   **66**

4197 **KING SPINNER 21** [10]   A P Jarvis 3-9-5 (77) E Ahern 33/1: 51-003: 3 b g Mujadil - Money Spinner
(Teenoso) Chsd ldrs, rdn fnl 4f, onepce/held over 1f out: eff at 1m/10f: lightly raced this term: see 1366.   4   **76**

DONCASTER **FRIDAY OCTOBER 20TH Lefthand, Flat, Galloping Track**

4206 **COOLING OFF 20** [3] G Wragg 3-9-0 (72) G Carter 20/1: -03504: Trckd ldrs, led 3f out till just inside last, no extra: bold eff over longer 10f trip: handles gd & gd/soft grnd: see 3350 (mdn). *shd* **71**
4280 **MERRYVALE MAN 15** [2] 3-8-13 (71) P Hanagan (5) 25/1: 020505: Chsd ldrs, onepce fnl 3f: see 4280. *2* **67**
4206 **TRIPLE SHARP 20** [20] 3-9-6 (78) J P Spencer 10/1: 4106: Rear, drvn/mod gains fnl 3f, no threat. *1* **73**
4197 **ECSTASY 21** [4] 3-9-5 (77) J Mackay (5) 14/1: -01307: Mid div, mod hdwy fnl 3f: btr 1439 (fast). *5* **65**
4067 **CAPRICCIO 30** [16] 3-9-3 (75) J Weaver 9/1: 352528: Handy, led over 3f out, sn hdd, btn over 1f out. *½* **62**
3907 **MARENKA 41** [1] 3-8-13 (71) C Rutter 20/1: 42359: Held up, mod hdwy fnl 3f: 6 wk abs: h'cap bow. *1* **57**
*4256 **BOLLIN NELLIE 17** [8] 3-8-7 (65) J Carroll 5/1 FAV: 216210: Prom, btn 2f out: 10th: hvly bckd. *shd* **51**
4092 **KAIPOI 28** [19] 3-9-7 (79) A Culhane 20/1: 502060: Rear, eff 3f out, no impress: 11th: btr 1225 (12f). *5* **58**
4300 **EYELETS ECHO 13** [7] 3-8-6 (64)(vis) Paul Eddery 20/1: 150600: Chsd ldrs 7f: 12th: see 4300, 2776. *2½* **39**
4118 **ADAMAS 26** [13] 3-8-11 (69) R Thomas (7) 25/1: 043U00: Rear, no impress: 13th: btr 3606 (fm). *½* **43**
4061 **ASTRONAUT 30** [9] 3-9-0 (72)(vis) T Quinn 8/1: 122640: Prom, btn 2f out: 15th: bckd: btr 4061. **0**
4284 **STRASBOURG 14** [6] 3-9-6 (78) Kim Tinkler 33/1: 000060: Led till over 3f out, sn btn: 18th: see 2330. **0**
*4108 **Tycoons Last 27** [18] 3-8-3 (61) G Baker (5) 16/1: 3606 **Clear Prospect 56** [5] 3-8-5 (63) R Ffrench 25/1:
4205 **Roboastar 20** [11] 3-9-3 (75) Martin Dwyer 14/1: 3265 **Green Wilderness 71** [14] 3-9-3 (75) D Harrison 11/1:
4605} **Approbation 350** [12] 3-9-0 (72) W Supple 40/1:
20 ran Time 2m 13.67 (7.27) (Christopher Chell) W M Brisbourne Great Ness, Shropshire

4449

3.30 DBS YEARLING STAKES 2YO (B) 6f Good/Soft 78 -17 Slow
£18910 £3782 £1891 £945 Raced across the track

-4219 **ZIETUNZEEN 20** [22] A Berry 2-8-6 C Lowther 11/10 FAV: 551521: 2 b f Zieten - Hawksbill Special (Taufan) Al prom, rdn/led inside last, just held on for press cl home: hvly bckd tho' op 8/11: earlier won at Nottingham (auct mdn), subs fine rnr up in val Redcar 2yo trophy (rtd 98): suited by 6f on firm & gd/soft: useful. **86**
*4281 **THE BYSTANDER 14** [15] N P Littmoden 2-8-6 T Quinn 11/2: 012: 2 b f Bin Ajwaad - Dilwara (Lashkari) Chsd ldrs, rdn/outpcd halfway, drvn & styd on well fnl 1f, just held: bckd: eff at 6f, crying out for return to 7f+: lightly raced & looks worth following with a return to further: see 4281 (1m). *shd* **85**
3959 **NIFTY ALICE 36** [21] A Berry 2-8-6 J Bramhill 12/1: 100103: 2 ch f First Trump - Nifty Fifty (Runnett) Led stands side, rdn/hung left over 2f out, hdd inside last & no extra: longer priced stablemate of wnr: eff at 5/6f. *1½* **81**
4305 **SECOND VENTURE 11** [19] J R Weymes 2-8-11 L Dettori 20/1: 032444: Chsd ldrs, rdn & styd on fnl 2f, not pace to chall: fine eff here but (officially rtd 68) treat rating with caution: win a race on this. *shd* **86$**
3714 **LAUREL DAWN 52** [10] 2-8-11 J Weaver 12/1: 121345: Chsd ldrs 5f: stablemate of wnr: 8 wk abs. *1¾* **82**
4252 **SIAMO DISPERATI 17** [14] 2-8-11 A Culhane 33/1: -30026: Chsd ldrs onepce fnl 2f: see 4252, 1764. *1½* **78$**
4187 **KINGSCROSS 21** [17] 2-8-11 M Hills 50/1: 07: Chsd ldrs till over 1f out: left debut bhd: Kings Signet colt, April foal, cost 6,800gns: dam a winning sprinter: with Major D N Chappell. *1¼* **75**
4137 **YOUNG TERN 25** [16] 2-8-11 A Daly 66/1: 0008: In tch, nvr pace to chall: see 2454 (mdn). *hd* **74$**
3814 **ARRAN MIST 47** [20] 2-8-6 F Lynch 50/1: -03069: Chsd ldrs, nvr on terms: abs: see 1294, 1130 (mdn). *1* **67$**
4098 **LITTLE CALLIAN 28** [1] 2-8-6 D Harrison 25/1: 436250: Led 4f, fdd: 10th: btr 3942 (5f, fast). *½* **65**
3814 **TOPOS GUEST 47** [2] 2-8-6 V Halliday 50/1: -540: Chsd ldr till over 1f out: 7 wk abs: see 3096. *1¼* **62**
3950 **MARE OF WETWANG 37** [11] 2-8-6 Paul Eddery 100/1: 600000: Mid div at best: plating form prev. *1¾* **58$**
4235 **GONE TOO FAR 18** [8] 2-8-11 C Rutter 33/1: -02160: In tch halfway, sn btn: 13th: btr 3776 (7f, g/s). *1* **61**
4373 **ST NICHOLAS 4** [6] 2-8-11 M Tebbutt 66/1: 00050: Al bhd: 14th: qck reapp: see 3029 (7f). *½* **59$**
4298 **MAMMAS TONIGHT 13** [9] 2-9-3 G Carter 9/1: 400440: In tch halfway, sn btn: 15th: stablemate of wnr. *1* **61**
4030 **White Star Lady 32** [7] 2-8-6 W Supple 33/1: 4244 **Mr Tod 17** [3] 2-8-11 P McCabe 100/1:
4209 **Polyphonic 20** [12] 2-8-6 P Fessey 100/1: 4084 **Pentagon Lady 29** [18] 2-8-6 R Cody Boutcher 100/1:
3704 **Galaxy Returns 53** [5] 2-8-11 J Carroll 50/1: 4219 **Majestic Quest 20** [13] 2-8-11 J P Spencer 25/1:
3942 **Minnies Mystery 37** [4] 2-8-6 R Mullen 66/1:
22 ran Time 1m 16.49 (5.69) (Chris & Antonia Deuters) A Berry Cockerham, Lancs

4450

4.00 TEN TO FOLLOW NURSERY HCAP 2YO 0-90 (D) 1m rnd Good/Soft 78 -15 Slow [92]
£5050 £1554 £777 £388

4254 **BORDERS BELLE 17** [1] J D Bethell 2-8-8 (72) Paul Eddery 20/1: 320601: 2 b f Pursuit Of Love - Sheryl Lynn (Miller's Mate) Dwelt/rear, swtchd/hdwy over 2f out, drvn & strong run fnl 1f to lead on line, all out: 1st win: apprec return to 1m: acts on firm & soft grnd: likes a sharp/gall trk: deserved this first success. **78**
4350 **KINGS CREST 7** [10] S C Williams 2-7-12 (62) J Mackay (5) 11/2: 641452: 2 b g Deploy - Classic Beauty (Fairy King) Trkd ldrs, drvn/led over 1f out, hdd line: fine run: likes gd/soft: see 4350, 4132. *shd* **67**
4350 **DOMINAITE 7** [12] M W Easterby 2-9-2 (80) T Quinn 3/1 FAV: 132323: 2 b g Komaite - Fairy Kingdom (Prince Sabo) Trckd ldrs, rdn/led 2f out till over 1f out, no extra inside last: hvly bckd, v consistent: see 4350. *1¾* **82**
3690 **JOHNSONS POINT 53** [8] B W Hills 2-9-2 (80) M Hills 9/1: 2104: Chsd ldrs, efft over 2f out, kept on inside last: 8 wk abs: stays 1m & further will suit: acts on fast & gd/soft: see 3412 (mdn, 7f). *1¼* **79**
*3906 **ELMONJED 41** [6] 2-9-7 (85) W Supple 11/2: -00215: Trckd ldrs, led over 2f out, sn hdd & no extra inside last: bckd: 6 wk abs: acts on gd & gd/soft: see 3906. *hd* **83**
4350 **SISTER CELESTINE 7** [3] 2-8-10 (74) Martin Dwyer 9/1: 24146: Chsd ldrs, onepace fnl 2f: nicely bckd. *2* **68**
*4084 **CYNARA 29** [5] 2-8-2 (66) G Baker (5) 11/1: 215517: Outpcd/towards rear early, mod gains fnl 2f. *shd* **60**
4279 **DUSTY CARPET 15** [11] 2-9-1 (79) J Carroll 11/1: 643038: Led till over 2f out, sn held: btr 4279 (sft). *½* **72**
4323 **BALL GAMES 10** [7] 2-7-13 (63) J Bramhill 20/1: 646049: Keen/mid div, btn 2f out: btr 4323 (hvy). *8* **44**
*3617 **SMART DANCER 56** [4] 2-9-0 (78) J Weaver 9/1: 504410: Keen, al towards rear: 10th: 8 wk abs: much better on fast grnd in 3617 (7f). *8* **47**
*4323 **ORIENTAL MIST 10** [2] 2-8-10 (74)(6ex) D Mernagh (3) 12/1: 446010: Trkd ldrs, btn 2f out, eased: 11th. *5* **33**
4028 **KENNYTHORPE BOPPY 32** [9] 2-7-12(2ow)(62) C Rutter 25/1: -5050: Dwelt, al rear, 12th: h'cap bow. *8* **9**
12 ran Time 1m 43.53 (7.43) (M J Dawson) J D Bethell Middleham, N Yorks

4451

4.30 THORNE HCAP 3YO+ 0-85 (D) 1m6f132y Good/Soft 78 -09 Slow [84]
£4660 £1434 £717 £358 3 yo rec 9 lb

3565 **LOOP THE LOUP 58** [17] Mrs M Reveley 4-9-13 (83) A Culhane 14/1: 500001: 4 b g Petit Loup - Mithi Al Gamar (Blushing Groom) Held up, rdn/prog fnl 3f & led inside last, styd on well, drvn out: op 12/1: 2 month abs: rtd 86h over timber last season (M Hammond): trained by J Dunlop on the level in '99, scored at Lingfield (auction mdn), Salisbury & York (h'caps, rtd 99): stays 15f on firm, likes & hvy, any trk: runs well fresh: well h'capped. **88**
4139 **PALUA 25** [5] Mrs A J Bowlby 3-8-11 (76) Paul Eddery 16/1: 332432: 3 b c Sri Pekan - Reticent Bride (Shy Groom) Mid div, rdn/prog to lead inside last, sn hdd & no extra: op 12/1: remains in fine form. *1¼* **78**
4040 **GUARD DUTY 32** [8] M P Tregoning 3-8-11 (76)(t) A Daly 14/1: -62453: 3 b g Deploy - Hymne d'Amour *1¼* **76**

(Dixieland Band) Mid div, drvn & styd on well fnl 3f, not rch front pair: fine run in t-strap: stays 14f: see 2249.
4213 **HAMBLEDEN 20** [6] M A Jarvis 3-9-3 (82) M Tebbutt 14/1: 320104: Trckd ldrs, led 2f out, hdd ins last & no extra: op 12/1: see 3948. *hd* **81**
4162 **REFLEX BLUE 24** [11] 3-8-11 (76)(BL) T Quinn 25/1: 236405: Rear, rdn/prog to press ldrs 2f out, held inside last: blinks, imprvd effort: prob stays 14f, handles firm & gd/soft grnd: see 1198. *2½* **71**
3518 **DOODLE BUG 61** [2] 3-8-5 (70) O Pears 16/1: 0-3536: Chsd ldrs, rdn/onepce fnl 3f: 2 month abs. *nk* **64**
2498 **PULAU PINANG 104** [4] 4-9-8 (78)(t) E Ahern 12/1: -22107: Held up, mod hdwy fnl 3f: 3 mth abs. *nk* **71**
4370 **MR FORTYWINKS 4** [14] 6-8-6 (62) R Cody Boutcher (5) 12/1: 134148: Cl up, rdn/ch 2f out, wknd. *1* **54**
4213 **BOULDER 20** [10] 3-8-9 (73)(1ow) J P Spencer 6/1: 454449: Held up, eff 3f out, no impress, eased nr fin: fin lame: op 5/1: blinks omitted after latest: see 4213, 3870. *3½* **61**
*3313 **TROILUS 69** [15] 3-9-1 (80) L Dettori 100/30 FAV: 032210: Mid div, eff 3f out, sn btn: 10th: hvly bckd, tchd 5/1: 10 wk abs/h'cap bow: not handle gd/soft? blinks omitted after 3313 (12f, fast, mdn). *2½* **63**
3978} **FULLOPEP 398** [16] 6-8-7 (63) D Harrison 20/1: 34/2-0: Led over 3f out till 2f out, wknd: 12th: Flat reapp, 8 mth jumps abs, won 2 nov chases in '99/00 at Sedgefield, (eff at 2m/2m5f, fast & gd/soft, rtd 119c): rnr up sole Flat start in '99 (h'cap, rtd 63): back in '97 scored at Catterick (mdn, rtd 63+): eff at 12f/2m on fast & gd grnd. **0**
2856 **FIORI 90** [1] 4-9-12 (82) P Goode (3) 11/1: 413220: Led 11f, wknd: 15th: op 9/1, abs: btr 2164 (5 rnr hcap). **0**
2176 **Ledgendry Line 117** [3] 7-7-13 (55) P Fessey 20/1: 4162 **The Woodstock Lady 24** [9] 3-9-5 (84) M Hills 16/1:
4039 **Bow Strada 32** [13] 3-9-6 (85) R Mullen 25/1: 4370 **Rainbow Spirit 4** [7] 3-7-11 (62) D Mernagh (2) 11/1:
3725 **Nichol Fifty 51** [12] 6-9-4 (74) J Carroll 14/1:
17 ran Time 3m 15.66 (12.66) (ANd Mrs J D Cotton) Mrs M Reveley Lingdale, N Yorks

4452

5.00 AUTUMN APPR HCAP 3YO 0-70 (E) 7f str Good/Soft 78 -04 Slow [76]
£3211 £988 £494 £247 Raced across the track

4156 **PRINTSMITH 24** [22] J Norton 3-8-3 (51) P Hanagan (3) 25/1: 603001: 3 br f Petardia - Black And Blaze (Taufan) Chsd ldrs, prog to lead over 1f out, styd on well inside last, rdn out: earlier scored at Warwick (fill h'cap, rtd 58): '99 Catterick scorer (sell, rtd 61): suited by sharp/gall 7f on fast, likes gd/soft & any trk. **56**
4307 **CRYFIELD 11** [15] N Tinkler 3-9-1 (63)(vis) J Mackay 7/1: 006242: 3 b g Efisio - Ciboure (Norwick) Rear, styd on well from over 2f out & ch inside last, not pace of wnr cl home: op 11/2: eff at 6/7f: see 4270, 2243. *¾* **66**
*4192 **DIAMOND OLIVIA 21** [6] John Berry 3-9-0 (62) D Mernagh 7/1: 625013: 3 b f Beveled - Queen Of The Quorn (Governor General) In tch, rdn/prog to lead over 1f out, sn hdd & onepce ins last: op 11/2: see 4192. *3½* **58**
4294 **BROMPTON BARRAGE 14** [18] R Hannon 3-8-1 (49) R Smith (3) 20/1: 000004: Chsd ldrs, onepace fnl 2f. *1* **43**
4294 **AIR MAIL 14** [3] 3-8-12 (60) Sarah Robinson (7) 16/1: 010205: Chse ldr, rdn/briefly led over 1f out, sn hdd/fdd: see 4192, 3770 (AW claimer). *¾* **53**
3771 **OSCAR PEPPER 48** [14] 3-8-12 (60) M Worrell (5) 8/1: 303626: Rear, kept on fnl 2f, nrst fin: 7 wk abs. *nk* **52**
3345 **NOBLE PASAO 67** [11] 3-9-7 (69) R Thomas (5) 16/1: 531337: Chsd ldrs, onepace fnl 2f: 2 month abs. *¾* **60**
4156 **AISLE 24** [4] 3-8-7 (55)(tbl) R Brisland (3) 50/1: 050008: Led, drvn/hdd over 1f out, fdd: see 128. *½* **45**
*4136 **YENALED 26** [8] 3-9-2 (64) G Baker 4/1 FAV: 622519: In tch 5f: hvly bckd, op 11/2: btr 4136. *shd* **54**
4270 **OCEAN RAIN 16** [7] 3-9-6 (68) G Hannon (5) 16/1: 403460: Cl up 5f: 10th: blinks omitted: see 954. *2* **54**
4287 **SANTIBURI LAD 14** [1] 3-9-7 (69) Mark Flynn (7) 25/1: 1200: Chsd ldrs 5f: 11th: btr 4233, 3462 (5/6f). *½* **54**
4233 **STEALTHY TIMES 18** [21] 3-8-12 (60) P Goode 20/1: 540000: Prom, wknd 2f out: 12th: see 1138 (AW). *¾* **44**
540 **Modem 245** [20] 3-8-6 (54) Darren Williams (3) 50/1:
4192 **Bishopstone Man 21** [17] 3-9-6 (68) W Hutchinson (5) 16/1:
4065 **Polar Lady 30** [5] 3-8-12 (60) D McGaffin (3) 9/1: 4294 **Kebabs 14** [13] 3-8-6 (54) R Cody Boutcher (5) 20/1:
4088 **Borderline 29** [10] 3-8-10 (58) G Sparkes (5) 33/1:
4004 **Highly Sociable 34** [2] 3-8-4 (52) Jonjo Fowle (3) 50/1:
4044 **Scafell 31** [9] 3-8-10 (58)(BL) Clare Roche (5) 25/1:
4248 **Myttons Again 17** [16] 3-9-7 (69)(bl) C McCavish (7) 16/1:
4425 **Aljazir 1** [19] 3-8-4 (52) Barry Smith (5) 33/1:
21 ran Time 1m 28.95 (5.75) (Ecosse Racing) J Norton High Hoyland, S Yorks

NEWBURY FRIDAY OCTOBER 20TH Lefthand, Flat, Galloping Track

Official Going SOFT. Stalls: Straight Course - Centre: 2m - outside.

4453

2.10 ALL LEISURE NURSERY HCAP 2YO 0-85 (D) 7f str Good/Soft 68 -11 Slow [88]
£4602 £1416 £708 £354

4191 **LOOKING FOR LOVE 21** [16] J G Portman 2-8-13 (73) L Newman (3) 9/1: 332321: 2 b f Tagula - Mousseux (Jareer) Nvr far away stands side, led appr fnl 2f, kept on well under press: deserved first success, plcd last 6 starts: eff at 7f, stays 1m: acts on fast, likes soft grnd & any trck: tough. **79**
4254 **PASITHEA 17** [7] T D Easterby 2-9-3 (77) K Darley 8/1: 310222: 2 b f Celtic Swing - Midnight Reward (Night Shift) Prom centre, rdn, edged right & ev ch appr fnl 1f, held towards fin: op 10/1: consistent. *¾* **81**
4191 **DANE DANCING 21** [1] J H M Gosden 2-8-6 (66) J Fortune 25/1: -50003: 2 b f Danehill - My Ballerina (Sir Ivor) Rear centre, prog 2f out, und press dist, drftd right, not pce to chall: op 16/1, stays 7f on gd/soft. *1¼* **67**
4345 **EXTRA GUEST 7** [9] M R Channon 2-8-11 (71) Craig Williams 11/2: 223344: Prom centre, chall ent fnl 1f, sn same pace: h'cap bow, tchd 13/2: styd longer 7f trip: see 2029. *shd* **72**
4338 **SABO ROSE 8** [2] 2-9-7 (81) P Robinson 7/2 FAV: 3135: Dwelt centre, swtchd & hdwy halfway, rdn & no impress: nicely bckd, clr rem: ran well up in trip, see 4338, 4082. *¾* **80**
4219 **STRUMPET 20** [5] 2-9-2 (76) J Reid 14/1: 163006: Chsd ldr centre, no extra appr fnl 1f: reportedly 'hung under press': see 3630, 2227. *4* **67**
4254 **MONTANA MISS 17** [8] 2-9-4 (78) N Callan 14/1: 411637: Led in centre till appr fnl 2f, grad wknd. *hd* **69**
4332 **MAGICAL FLUTE 9** [15] 2-9-3 (77) S Drowne 10/1: 031328: Nvr a factor stands side: op 8/1, st/mate 4th: faster grnd possibly suits, see 4332, 2784. *1½* **65**
4098 **SECURON DANCER 28** [4] 2-8-4 (64) F Norton 33/1: 40609: Nvr on terms centre: longer trip. *½* **51**
3852 **SHARP ACT 44** [10] 2-8-8 (68) R Hills 20/1: -00550: Sn handy in centre, wknd qckly appr fnl 1f: 10th. *¾* **53**
3760 **TRILLIONAIRE 49** [6] 2-9-2 (76) R Hughes 14/1: 0640: Trckd ldrs centre, lost pl appr fnl 2f: 11th, op 10/1. *½* **60**
3299 **MAINE LOBSTER 70** [3] 2-9-1 (75) Pat Eddery 12/1: -03250: Slow away centre, al bhd: 12th, 10 wk abs. *1¾* **56**
2714 **PIVOTABLE 95** [14] 2-8-13 (73) S Sanders 20/1: -32500: Al bhd stands side: 15th, 3 mth abs, h'cap bow. **0**
3888 **Forever My Lord 42** [13] 2-9-3 (77) J Quinn 14/1: 4289 **Miss Beetee 14** [11] 2-8-5 (65) A Nicholls 20/1:
15 ran Time 1m 29.83 (5.53) (Out To Grass Partnership) J G Portman Compton, Berks

NEWBURY FRIDAY OCTOBER 20TH Lefthand, Flat, Galloping Track

4454 **2.40 GR 3 CORNWALLIS STKS 2YO (A) 5f Good/Soft 68 +10 Fast**
£16950 £6497 £3248 £1553

+4247 **DANEHURST 17** [2] Sir Mark Prescott 2-8-7 G Duffield 7/2 FAV: 111: 2 b f Danehill - Miswaki Belle (Miswaki) Cl up centre, rdn to lead 1f out, sn clr, readily: well bckd, fast time: unbtn, hat-trick landed after wins at Warwick (fill mdn) & Wolverhampton (nov stakes, rtd 103a): eff at 5f, will get 6f: acts on fast, gd/soft grnd & fibresand, sharp or gall tracks: runs well fresh: smart & progressive filly with a turn of foot. **109**
*4138 **FROMSONG 25** [17] B R Millman 2-8-12 B Marcus 11/2: 512: 2 b c Fayruz - Lindas Delight (Batshoof) Overall ldr stands side, hdd ent fnl 2f, rallied for 2nd but no ch wnr: tchd 13/2: progressive colt, fine run in this higher grade: acts on gd/soft & soft grnd: win a Listed/Gr race at 6f: see 4138. *2½* **106**
3959 **RED MILLENNIUM 36** [1] A Berry 2-8-7 F Norton 20/1: 113423: 2 b f Tagula - Lovely Me (Vision) Sn led centre & briefly overall appr fnl 1f, kept on: tough filly, ran to best: see 3959, 2664. *nk* **100**
4051 **KACHINA DOLL 27** [15] M R Channon 2-8-7 Craig Williams 20/1: 040344: Outpcd stands side till kept on appr fnl 1f, nvr nrr: op 33/1: gd run, acts on fast & gd/soft: return to 6f should suit: see 2996, 1437. *2* **94**
*4009 **ALSHADIYAH 34** [13] 2-8-7 R Hills 15/2: 1315: Rear, some late hdwy for press, nvr dangerous: bckd from 9/1: not disgraced but was clearly unsuited by the drop bck to 5f, sure to rate higher at 6f+. *½* **92**
4051 **JACK SPRATT 35** [11] 2-8-12 L Newman 25/1: 101126: Front rank & every ch till fdd und press fnl 1f. *¾* **95**
4179 **AMELIA 22** [14] 2-8-7 D O'Donohoe 50/1: 431127: Trckd ldrs stands side, drvn/swtchd 2f out, onepace. *hd* **89**
3797 **SILLA 47** [4] 2-8-7 Pat Eddery 16/1: 311208: In tch centre, rdn & onepce fnl 2f: 7 week abs, btr 3797. *shd* **89**
3900 **TARAS EMPEROR 41** [3] 2-8-12 J Fortune 14/1: 105009: In tch centre, unable to qckn ent fnl 2f. *hd* **93**
*3767 **KINGS BALLET 49** [12] 2-8-12 S Sanders 12/1: 010: Outpcd till styd on inside last: 10th, 7 wk abs. *2½* **87**
3900 **THE TRADER 41** [10] 2-8-12 Dale Gibson 20/1: 211340: Al mid div: 11th, 6 wk abs, btr 3900, 3446 (fast). *hd* **86**
3965 **GREENWOOD 36** [9] 2-8-12 J Tate 25/1: 120: Nvr a factor: 12th, stiffish task, see 3047 (6f, fast). *shd* **86**
4219 **SECRET INDEX 20** [8] 2-8-7 D Holland 33/1: 446000: In tch till wknd 2f out: 13th, stiff task, tchd 33/1. *¾* **79**
3862 **REEL BUDDY 44** [5] 2-8-12 R Hughes 12/1: 001120: Mid div, outpcd 2f out: 14th, 6 wk abs: capable of much better on fast grnd, see 3862, 3714. *1* **81**
*3959 **VICIOUS DANCER 36** [16] 2-8-12 J Quinn 12/1: -06110: Speed 2f: 15th, much btr 3959 (beat this 3rd). *½* **80**
+3795 **PALACE AFFAIR 47** [7] 2-8-7 (bl) S Drowne 10/1: W510: Sn in rear: 16th, 7 wk abs: looks talented but temperamental: rated much higher on fast grnd in 3795 (6f fill mdn, made all). *1½* **72**
3900 **ROMANTIC MYTH 41** [6] 2-8-10 K Darley 8/1: 116450: Cl up, eff & btn bef 2f out: 17th, 6 wk abs. *½* **74**
17 ran Time 1m 03.18 (2.88) (Cheveley Park Stud) Sir Mark Prescott Newmarket, Suffolk

4455 **3.10 GR 3 HORRIS HILL STKS 2YO (A) 7f str Good/Soft 68 +01 Fast**
£21000 £8050 £4025 £1925

*4068 **CLEARING 30** [6] J H M Gosden 2-8-9 J Fortune 9/2: 2211: 2 b c Zafonic - Bright Spells (Alleged) In tch, shkn up 3f out, hdwy to lead 1f out, rdn clr: bckd, fair time: earlier won at Chester (mdn): dam 10f wnr: eff at 7f, 1m suit & shld get 10f: acts on fast & soft: smart & fast improving juvenile with a future. **110**
4127 **PRIZEMAN 26** [9] R Hannon 2-8-9 K Darley 4/1 JT FAV: -1142: 2 b c Prized - Shuttle (Conquistador Cielo) In tch, clsd halfway, led 2f out, rdn & hdd 1f out, no ch with wnr: tough & useful, win another Listed. *3½* **103**
-- **FRENCHMANS BAY** [5] R Charlton 2-8-9 S Drowne 9/2: 3: 2 b c Polar Falcon - River Fantasy (Irish River) Hld up trav well, prog & ev ch appr fnl 1f, sn rdn, kept on onepace: well bckd, highly tried on debut: 42,000gns colt: dam modest: eff at 7f on gd/sft grnd: impressive debut, lks a v useful prospect for next term. *shd* **103+**
*4314 **POTARO 16** [3] B J Meehan 2-8-12 Pat Eddery 9/1: 353114: Led till 2f out, onepce und press: tchd 11/1: confirmed his recent improvement & stays 7f: see 4314. *½* **105**
*4028 **CAFETERIA BAY 32** [1] 2-8-9 N Callan 25/1: 1315: Chsd ldrs, no extra fnl 1f: gd run up in class. *nk* **101**
4196 **TRIPLE BLUE 21** [2] 2-8-9 J Reid 20/1: 453406: Nvr nr ldrs: stablemate 2nd: much btr 3996 (fm). *1½* **98**
*2269 **PRIORS LODGE 113** [7] 2-8-9 R Hughes 9/2: 17: V Slow away, al rear: 4 mnth abs, stablemate 2nd must be worth another chance after 2269 (beat this winner on fast grnd, mdn). *nk* **97**
4196 **IMPERIAL DANCER 21** [8] 2-8-9 Craig Williams 4/1 JT FAV: 513258: Bhd, brief eff 2f out, eased ins last: surely something amiss, see 4196, 3700. *½* **96**
3862 **IMPERIAL MEASURE 44** [4] 2-8-9 G Hind 14/1: 502139: Cl-up till lost pl 2f out: 6 wk abs: longer trip. *5* **86**
9 ran Time 1m 29.02 (4.72) (K Abdulla) J H M Gosden Manton, Wilts

4456 **3.40 SCHRODERS RATED HCAP 3YO+ 0-110 (B) 6f Good/Soft 68 -20 Slow [114]**
£9709 £3682 £1841 £837 3 yo rec 1 lb

4317 **GAELIC STORM 12** [1] M Johnston 6-9-7 (107) D Holland 5/2 FAV: 540121: 6 b g Shavian - Shannon Princess (Connaught) Towards rear, gd prog 2f out, led dist, rdn clr: well bckd: earlier won at Klampenborg & Redcar (stks): '99 wnr at Goodwood (stakes), Sweden (2, incl List) & Newmarket (List, rtd 114): won this race in '98 (rtd 114): eff at 6/7f on firm, suited by gd & soft, any trck: smart, 15 wins from 60 starts. **115**
4195 **GREY EMINENCE 21** [7] R Hannon 3-8-4 (91)(2oh) L Newman (3) 12/1: 221202: 3 gr c Indian Ridge - Rahaam (Secreto) Well plcd, rdn to lead briefly appr fnl 1f, kept on for 2nd but no ch with wnr: coped admirably with the step back in trip: eff at 6/7f, stays a stiff 1m: tough sort: see 3343. *2½* **93**
4339 **BLUE VELVET 8** [4] K T Ivory 3-8-5 (92)(1oh) C Carver (3) 14/1: 623063: 3 gr f Formidable - Sweet Whisper (Petong) Rear, gd prog appr fnl 2f, rdn bef dist, kept on same pace: op 11/1: ran nr to best: see 2568. *½* **92**
*4112 **DUKE OF MODENA 27** [2] G B Balding 3-8-13 (100) S Drowne 5/1: 144614: Held up, prog to chase ldrs appr fnl 1f, onepce inside last: op 7/2: fair run but is best at 7f: see 4112. *1½* **97**
4339 **SHEER VIKING 8** [12] 4-8-9 (95) J Reid 7/1: 050405: Trckd ldrs going well, led appr fnl 2f, sn rdn, hdd/fdd bef fnl 1f: clr rem, tchd 7/1: better at 5f & needs a longer lead, see 1182, 702. *1½* **88**
4346 **YORKIES BOY 7** [14] 5-9-6 (106)(bl) K Darley 20/1: 104006: Sn led, hdd appr fnl 2f, no extra: qk reapp. *3* **92**
3920 **TRAVESTY OF LAW 38** [9] 3-7-11 (84)(9oh) D Glennon (7) 33/1: 325547: Hld up, hdwy appr fnl 2f, sn btn. *4* **60**
4346 **MONKSTON POINT 7** [11] 4-9-7 (107)(vis) Pat Eddery 20/1: 300008: Speed till 2f out: jt top-weight. *1½* **80**
4346 **LADY BOXER 7** [13] 4-8-0 (86)(7oh) A Mackay 12/1: 101109: Dwelt, nvr a factor: bckd despite 7lbs o/h. *nk* **58**
4339 **ALPEN WOLF 8** [8] 5-8-1 (87)(6oh) S Carson (3) 33/1: 130000: Chsd ldrs till after halfway: 10th, stiff task. *¾* **57**
4129 **KATHOLOGY 26** [6] 3-8-7 (94) N Pollard 16/1: 002000: Early ldr, btn appr fnl 2f: 11th, see 1219. *18* **34**
4073 **BOLD EFFORT 14** [3] 8-7-9 (81)(12oh)(bl) D O'Donohoe 66/1: 010000: Al rear: 12th, stiff task: see 3516. *12* **0**
4339 **MELON PLACE 8** [10] 3-8-0 (87)(6oh) N Callan 66/1: 31-0U0: Struggling halfway: 13th, stiff task. *8* **0**
4339 **CANDLERIGGS 8** [5] 4-8-2 (88)(5oh) R Hughes 4/1 FAV: 05-120: Chsd ldrs, eff & btn appr fnl 2f, virt p.u. fnl 1f: 14th, bckd despite 5lbs 'wrong': reportedly lost his action & is prob best caught fresh: see 3791. *4* **0**
14 ran Time 1m 15.01 (4.41) (H C Racing Club) M Johnston Middleham, N Yorks

---

4457   **4.10 VODAFONE COND STKS 2YO (C)**   **1m str** Good/Soft 68 -17 Slow
£6612 £2508 £1254 £570

4184 **ALDWYCH 22** [7] R Charlton 2-8-11 Pat Eddery 6/1: 01: 2 ch c In The Wings - Arderelle (Pharly) **99**
Hmpd start, in tch going well, pld out & smooth prog to lead dist, pshd out, v cmftbly: half-brother to sev wnrs,
incl useful mid-dist/styr Spout, dam 10f wnr: apprec step up to 1m on gd/sft, shld get 12f next term: looks useful.
4203 **BLACK KNIGHT 20** [2] S P C Woods 2-9-0 R Hughes 4/1: 116632: 2 b c Contract Law - Another Move 2½ **95**
(Farm Walk) Chsd ldrs, led bef 2f out, rdn/hdd dist, no ch wnr: bckd tho' op 9/4: cght a tartar, see 4203, 2514.
-- **WINGS OF SOUL** [11] P F I Cole 2-8-8 J Fortune 4/1: 3: 2 b c Thunder Gulch - Party Cited 1 **87+**
(Alleged) Trckd ldrs, rdn, ch & slightly hmpd ent fnl 2f, kept on: clr rem on debut: $90,000 brother to
a winning miler, dam useful 1m/10f wnr: eff at 1m on gd/soft, will stay further: promising intro, win races.
*3458 **ROSIS BOY 63** [9] J L Dunlop 2-9-0 K Darley 3/1 FAV: 214: Towards rear, prog 2f out, sn slightly 5 **83**
checked & no extra: 9 wk abs, bckd: btr 3458, 2563 (fast & gd).
3999 **LEARNED LAD 34** [5] 2-8-11 D Holland 11/2: -05: In tch, nvr pce to chall: op 4/1, already nds 10f. 1 **78**
4161 **PRIZE DANCER 24** [6] 2-8-11 P Robinson 16/1: 0406: Went right start, nvr troubled ldrs: stiffish task. 3 **72**
-- **INVITATION** [3] 2-8-8 S Sanders 33/1: 7: Wide, nvr a threat: stablemate of 5th & 6th, debut: 2 **65**
4,800gns Bin Ajwaad colt, dam lightly rcd, sire a miler: with D Elsworth.
-- **ST MATTHEW** [1] 2-8-8 R Hills 8/1: 8: Wide, struggling halfway: $130,000 Lear Fan colt, dam unrcd. 6 **55**
-- **RAZZAMATAZZ** [4] 2-8-8 G Duffield 50/1: 9: 4l bhd: 1,500gns Alhijaz colt, dam 6f juv wnr. ½ **55**
4203 **FATHER SEAMUS 20** [8] 2-8-11 P Fitzimons (5) 100/1: 000000: Keen, prsd ldr till appr fnl 2f: 10th. 3 **51**
3799 **BRENDAS DELIGHT 47** [10] 2-8-6 S Carson (3) 100/1: 0000: Led till appr fnl 2f, sn btn & fin v tired: 11th. 8 **34**
11 ran   Time 1m 43.43 (6.63)   (Lady Rothschild)   R Charlton Beckhampton, Wilts

---

4458   **4.40 VODAFONE HCAP 3YO+ 0-90 (C)**   **2m** Good/Soft 68 -22 Slow   **[86]**
£7280 £2240 £1120 £560   3 yo rec 10lb

*4299 **DISTANT PROSPECT 13** [9] I A Balding 3-8-11 (79) K Darley 9/2 JT FAV: 354111: 3 b c Namaquland - **84**
Ukraine's Affair (The Minstrel) Towards rear, improved ent straight, led 2f out, rdn out: nicely bckd tho'
op 3/1: qck hat-trick landed after wins at Bath (mdn h'cap) & York (h'cap): plcd juv (rtd 73): eff at
13f/2m: acts on fast & hvy grnd, any track: progressive young stayer.
4166 **MANE FRAME 23** [12] H Morrison 5-8-8 (66) R Hughes 11/2: 210662: 5 b g Unfuwain - Moviegoer 1¼ **69**
(Pharly) Patiently rdn, last ent straight, switched & kept on well ent fnl 2f, chsd wnr inside last, no
impress nr fin: tchd 8/1: gd run but was asked to make up too much grnd: see 1711.
3905 **FIRST BALLOT 41** [5] D R C Elsworth 4-9-11 (83) D Holland 14/1: 000363: 4 b g Perugino - Election 2 **84**
Special (Chief Singer) Mid div, clsd ent str, same pace appr fnl 1f: abs, rtd 91/4, acts on firm & gd/soft.
4299 **NIGHT VENTURE 13** [10] B W Hills 4-9-11 (83) J Reid 16/1: 030444: Mid div, rdn 3f out, styd on hd **84**
late: op 12/1: styd longer 2m trip, see 4014, 1031.
4162 **SOLITARY 24** [1] 3-9-3 (85)(bl) Pat Eddery 12/1: -22105: Led till 2f out, fdd inside last: op 8/1: 1¾ **84**
a long way clr of rem & a bold attempt over much longer trip: rtd to 12 or 14f likely to suit: see 3701 (mdn).
1980} **SADLERS REALM 493** [7] 7-8-12 (70) J Fortune 9/2 JT FAV: 3/10-6: Mid div, some prog 3f out, 16 **55**
btn bef fnl 1f: bckd from 8/1 on reapp: landed first of just 2 '99 starts, at Haydock (h'cap, rtd 74): also won
over hdles at Chepstow (h'cap, 2m/2m4.5f, gd & hvy, rtd 126h): eff at 14f, shld get 2m: acts on fast & hvy.
4299 **NICELY 13** [4] 4-8-4 (60)(2ow) R Hills 12/1: 500007: Nvr nr ldrs & not much rm 2f out: op 8/1: won 1¾ **45**
this last term off a 13lbs higher mark: see 1527.
4115 **BRAVE TORNADO 27** [13] 9-9-5 (77) S Carson (3) 7/1: 245308: Wide, in tch till 3f out: see 1052, 917. 7 **54**
4213 **BOX BUILDER 20** [15] 3-9-0 (82) S Drowne 14/1: 514409: Handy till lost pl 3f out: op 10/1, nds faster grnd? 4 **55**
101 **HENRY ISLAND 331** [8] 7-9-8 (80) F Norton 12/1: /300-0: Nvr a factor: 10th, bckd, jumps fit, rnr 5 **48**
up both starts this term: dual 99/00 wnr at Huntingdon (2m/2m5.5f, fast & gd/soft, rtd 107h): see 101.
4075 **CHIEF WALLAH 29** [14] 4-8-1 (58)(1ow) N Pollard 20/1: 042600: Struggling halfway: 11th, best 3501 (fm).1¾ **26**
*4193 **DISTANT COUSIN 21** [11] 3-9-3 (85) W Ryan 11/2: 2310: Chsd ldrs, wknd qckly appr fnl 3f: 13th: 20 **34**
op 4/1 on h'cap bow: longer trip: see 4193.
901} **Ballet High 553** [3] 7-8-12 (70) G Duffield 33/1:   4162 **Eighty Two 24** [2] 4-9-12 (84) N Callan 25/1:
4061 **Blue Style 30** [6] 4-8-4 (62)(t) M Henry 14/1:
15 ran   Time 3m 41.73 (15.73)   (The Rae Smiths And Pauline Gale)   I A Balding Kingsclere, Hants

---

4459   **5.10 M ROONEY HCAP 3YO+ 0-65 (F)**   **5f34y** Good/Soft 68 -31 Slow   **[65]**
£3458 £1064 £532 £266   Raced centre-stands side, high no's prob favoured

4295 **FRAMPANT 14** [15] M Quinn 3-8-13 (50) F Norton 33/1: 306001: 3 ch f Fraam - Potent (Posen) **55**
In tch centre, hdwy appr fnl 1f, ran on strongly for press to lead fnl strides: '99 Windsor wnr (fill auct mdn,
rtd 72): eff at 5/6f: acts on gd/soft & soft grnd, handles firm, any track: back to form, as is the stable.
4295 **ABSOLUTE FANTASY 14** [10] E A Wheeler 4-9-11 (62)(bl) S Carson (3) 14/1: 205102: 4 b f Beveled - ½ **65**
Sharp Venita (Sharp Edge) Chsd ldrs centre, rdn appr fnl 1f, ran on to lead inside last, hdd nr fin: gd run.
4327 **GARNOCK VALLEY 10** [25] A Berry 10-9-4 (55) R Hughes 6/1 JT FAV: 013043: 10 b g Dowsing - nk **57**
Sunley Sinner (Try My Best) Outpcd stands side & plenty to do till ran on strgly und press ins last, too late:
op 9/2: game 10yo, prob better at 6f nowadays tho' won this race last term off a 9lbs lower mark: see 2819.
4295 **WAFFS FOLLY 14** [11] D J S ffrench Davis 5-9-3 (54) Craig Williams 14/1: 353244: Front rank ½ **54**
centre & led briefly inside last, onepce for press towards fin: op 10/1: tough: see 1082.
4027 **MARY JANE 32** [12] 5-8-11 (48) Pat Eddery 6/1 JT FAV: 000065: Cl up centre, led halfway till 1¼ **44**
appr fnl 1f, no extra inside last: op 9/2: well h'capped: see 4027, 844.
4293 **BORDER GLEN 14** [18] 4-9-4 (55) A Nicholls 8/1: 064336: Unable to go pace stands side till fnl 1f hdwy. nk **50**
4294 **HARVEYS FUTURE 14** [1] 6-9-0 (51) A Polli (3) 12/1: 2W0627: Cl up towards far side till onepce fnl 1f. shd **46**
4307 **TICK TOCK 11** [7] 3-8-9 (46)(vis) A Mackay 14/1: 400638: Towards rear centre, some late prog. nk **40**
4295 **POLAR MIST 14** [5] 5-9-5 (56)(tbl) Dean McKeown 14/1: 606039: Led centre/overall till halfway, fdd fnl 1f. ½ **48**
4270 **RISKY REEF 16** [21] 3-10-0 (65) K Darley 8/1: 455040: Rcd stands side, nvr on terms: 10th, top-weight. ¾ **54**
4380 **PERIGEUX 3** [14] 4-9-4 (55)(bl) C Carver (3) 25/1: 030040: Chse ldrs in centre, wknd ins last: 11th. shd **44**
3536 **DAZZLING QUINTET 59** [22] 4-8-8 (45) C Catlin (7) 25/1: 210000: Speed stands side, no ch with nk **33**
far side appr fnl 1f: 12th: best 1923 (firm).
4295 **KILCULLEN LAD 14** [23] 6-9-9 (60)(vis) P Fitzsimons (5) 16/1: 350500: Nvr a factor stands side: 13th. 1 **45**
4407 **MUTASAWWAR 2** [24] 6-8-11 (48) D Holland 14/1: 222000: Nvr dangerous stands side: 14th, qk reapp. ½ **32**
4065 **BEDEVILLED 30** [16] 5-10-0 (65) J Fortune 9/1: 016030: Nvr in it: 19th, op 7/1: see 3441. **0**

NEWBURY   FRIDAY OCTOBER 20TH   Lefthand, Flat, Galloping Track

4270 **ABSENT FRIENDS 16** [13] 3-9-11 (62) D O'Donohoe 12/1: 005300: Al towards rear: 22nd, see 4185.   0
4295 **Knockemback Nellie 14** [8] 4-9-3 (54)(bl) Dale Gibson 16/1:
3536 **Off Hire 59** [3] 4-9-3 (54)(vis) L Newman (3) 20/1:
4294 **On The Trail 14** [19] 3-9-0 (51) W Ryan 20/1:   4207 **Madame Jones 20** [17] 5-8-12 (49)(bl) J Reid 50/1:
4295 **White Summit 14** [20] 3-8-9 (46) N Callan 33/1:   4295 **Clan Chief 14** [6] 7-9-7 (58) J Quinn 16/1:
3765 **Reachforyourpocket 49** [4] 5-8-10 (47) S Drowne 25/14293 **Sunset Harbour 14** [9] 7-8-6 (43) M Henry 25/1:
4311 **Regalo 11** [2] 5-8-12 (49)(bl) Sophie Mitchell 50/1:
25 ran   Time 1m 05.16 (4.86)   (The Frampant Fellows)   M Quinn Sparsholt, Oxon

DONCASTER   SATURDAY OCTOBER 21ST   Lefthand, Flat, Galloping Track

Official Going: SOFT. Stalls: Straight Course - Stands' side, Round course - Inside, Round 1m - Outside

4460   2.10 JOCK MURRAY NURSERY HCAP 2YO 0-95 (C)   7f str   Soft 103   -18 Slow   [96]
£6844   £2106   £1053   £526   Raced centre - stands side

4267 **MODRIK 17** [15] R W Armstrong 2-9-3 (85) W Supple 9/2 FAV: -03421: 2 ch c Dixieland Band - Seattle   91
Summer (Seattle Slew) Al prom, led over 2f out, styd on well fnl 1f, rdn out: hvly bckd on h'cap bow, first win:
eff at 7f, stays 1m: acts on fast & soft grnd, sharp/undul or stiff/gall trck: progressive colt.
4179 **MY LUCY LOCKET 23** [2] R Hannon 2-8-11 (79) L Newman (3) 20/1: 210502: 2 b f Mujadil - First Nadia   1   82
(Auction Ring) Al prom, rdn & styd on fnl 1f, not pce of wnr: styd longer 7f trip well: see 2665 (5f).
4070 **LA NOTTE 31** [5] W Jarvis 2-8-12 (80) M Tebbutt 11/2: 3133: 2 b f Factual - Miss Mirror (Magic   shd   83
Mirror) Prom, rdn/ch 1f out, no extra fnl 1f: acts on firm & soft grnd: see 4070.
*4336 **NOSE THE TRADE 9** [6] J A Osborne 2-8-4 (72) J Quinn 11/2: 514: Chsd ldrs, no impress fnl 1f: 1½   73
op 7/2, h'cap bow: acts on gd & soft grnd: clr of rem here: see 4336 (seller).
4350 **DIVINE WIND 8** [12] 2-7-10 (64) K Dalgleish (5) 14/1: 002005: Held up, prog/chsd ldrs over 1f out,   7   55
wknd inside last: bckd from 25/1: btr 4350 (6f).
4214 **AUNT RUBY 21** [8] 2-8-2 (70) A Beech (3) 12/1: 02606: Chsd ldrs 5f: btr 3649 (6f).   1¼   59
4345 **PAULAS PRIDE 8** [1] 2-8-11 (79) A Polli (3) 12/1: 006167: Chsd ldrs till over 1f out: see 4345, 4117.   shd   68
4104 **CHANTAIGNE 28** [13] 2-8-1 (69) D Mernagh (3) 20/1: 0538: Led till over 2f out, wknd: see 4104.   hd   57
3906 **DOMINION PRINCE 42** [3] 2-8-2 (70) Craig Williams 33/1: -00009: Mid div at best: abs: see 3162.   nk   57
4035 **SHIRLEY FONG 33** [7] 2-8-1 (68)(1ow) M Tebbutt 11/2: 0600: Held up, rdn halfway, no impress: 10th.   1½   54
3879 **PEREGIAN 44** [14] 2-9-7 (89) K Darley 9/1: 110350: Led/dsptd lead 5f: 11th: abs: btr 3879, 2928.   1½   72
-4279 **FAZZANI 16** [9] 2-8-7 (75) P Hanagan (5) 5/1: 121220: Well bhd from over 2f out, t.o.: 14th: 0
jockey reported filly lost her action: see 4279, 3706 (claimer).
4191 **Numerate 22** [10] 2-8-7 (75) J Mackay (3) 20/1:   4277 **Takaroa 16** [4] 2-9-5 (87) J Reid 16/1:
14 ran   Time 1m 13.64 (8.44)   (Hamdan Al Maktoum)   R W Armstrong Newmarket, Suffolk

4461   2.40 THEHORSESMOUTH CLAIMER 3-5YO (E)   7f str   Soft 103   -34 Slow
£3786   £1165   £582   £291   3 yo rec 2 lb   Raced across track

4411 **MANTLES PRIDE 3** [14] J A Glover 5-8-13 (bl) K Darley 7/2 JT FAV: 002201: 5 br g Petong - State   65
Romance (Free State) Al prom, prog to lead over 1f out, styd on well ins last, rdn out: bckd, qck reapp: earlier
won here at Doncaster (h'cap): '99 wnr at Carlise, Redcar & Haydock (h'caps, rtd 84): plcd in '98 (rtd 86): eff
at 6f/1m, suited by 7f: acts on firm, soft & any trk, likes Doncaster: runs well fresh & eff in blnks/visor:
tough & genuine gelding, well suited by drop to claiming grade.
4215 **CHAMPAGNE RIDER 21** [3] K McAuliffe 4-9-7 J Reid 10/1: 000402: 4 b c Presidium - Petitesse   1   71
(Petong) Chsd ldrs, rdn & styd on fnl 1f, not pace of wnr: op 12/1, top weight: see 1173.
4192 **STRAND OF GOLD 22** [18] R Hannon 3-8-7 (bl) L Newman (3) 25/1: 500003: 3 b g Lugana Beach -   2½   55
Miss Display (Touch Paper) Al prom, kept on onepce fnl 2f: stays 7f: acts on fast & soft: see 1220 & 1181 (mdn).
4232 **JAMESTOWN 19** [6] C Smith 3-9-1 Dean McKeown 12/1: 461404: Led, rdn/hdd over 1f out, no extra.   2   60
4044 **CUSIN 32** [2] 4-9-7 T Hamilton (7) 16/1: 005205: Chsd ldrs, no impress fnl 1f: see 926.   2½   60
4340 **REDSWAN 9** [22] 5-8-11 (t) J Murtagh 7/2 JT FAV: 331506: Trkd ldrs, hung left/btn over 1f out.   1½   48
4302 **TUMBLEWEED RIVER 14** [13] 4-8-13 R Hughes 5/1: 000207: In tch 5f: btr 4204.   nk   49
3951 **DIHATJUM 38** [19] 3-8-7 J Carroll 16/1: 123308: Prom 5f: op 12/1: btr 3196 (firm).   ½   44
3992 **ZIRCONI 36** [15] 4-8-13 A Culhane 8/1: 033009: Held up, eff 3f out, sn btn: vis omitted: see 2704.   ¾   47
--   **LOCH AILORT 1** [1] 4-8-4 (VIS) O Pears 50/1: 0: Prom 5f: 10: visor, debut: cost 2,000gns as a 3yo.   ¾   37
4327 **Boadicea The Red 11** [21] 3-8-0 D Mernagh (3) 33/1: 3970 **Ballets Russes 37** [12] 3-8-4 J Quinn 66/1:
3964 **Czar Wars 37** [8] 5-8-9 (bl) K Dalgleish (5) 40/1:   4224 **Santandre 21** [11] 4-8-13 P M Quinn (3) 66/1:
3966 **Indian Dance 37** [17] 4-8-13 A Beech (3) 50/1:   2612 **Patsy Culsyth 100** [9] 5-8-3 Kim Tinkler 33/1:
3251 **Defiance 72** [7] 5-8-8 Michael Doyle (7) 100/1:   4156 **Thatcham 25** [10] 4-8-12 (bl) M J Kinane 12/1:
--   **Jack The Knife 16** [16] 4-8-11 C Teague 40/1:   4218 **Sealed By Fate 21** [20] 5-8-9 R Winston 50/1:
4425 **Sharp Edge Boy 2** [5] 4-8-9 W Supple 33/1:   3253 **Castrato 72** [4] 4-8-9 A Polli (3) 100/1:
22 ran   Time 1m 32.76 (9.56)   (Mrs Janis Macpherson)   J A Glover Carburton, Notts

4462   3.10 LISTED DONCASTER STKS 2YO (A)   6f   Soft 103   -04 Slow
£12701   £3908   £1954   £977   Raced stands side

3700 **SHAARD 54** [6] B W Hills 2-8-9 (bl) W Supple 6/1: -1341: 2 b c Anabaa - Braari (Gulch)   108
Chsd ldrs halfway, drvn/styd on well fnl 1f to lead line, all out: 8 wk abs: earlier won on debut at Bath (mdn):
eff at 6/7f on fast & soft: handles a sharp/gall trck: suited by blnks: runs well fresh: progressive, useful colt.
4058 **DOWN TO THE WOODS 34** [2] M Johnston 2-8-9 K Darley 9/2 CO FAV: 15142: 2 ch c Woodman -   shd   107
Riviera Wonder (Batonnier) Al prom, led 1f out, sn drvn/strongly pressed, collared on line: nicely bckd: acts on
firm & soft grnd: fine run, v useful colt, shld win more races: see 4058, 3895 (C/D).
3700 **PICCOLO PLAYER 54** [5] R Hannon 2-8-9 L Newman 3/1 CO FAV: 141123: 2 b g Piccolo - The Frog Lady   3½   100
(Al Hareb) Narrow lead halfway till 1f out, no extra fnl 1f: abs: acts on fast & soft: ahd of this wnr in 3700 (gd).
3900 **ZILCH 42** [4] R Hannon 2-8-9 R Hughes 9/2 CO FAV: 24234: Held up, rdn/no room over 1f out,   2   96
kept on ins last, no threat: 6 wk abs, stablemate of 3rd: closer with a clr run tho' wld not have troubled front
pair: acts on firm & soft grnd: see 3900 (Gr 2).
3105 **CEEPIO 79** [7] 2-8-9 M J Kinane 9/2 CO FAV: -3135: Led 3f, btn over 1f out: abs: btr 3105, 2819.   1¾   93
*4214 **CAUSTIC WIT 21** [8] 2-8-9 J Reid 9/2 CO FAV: 501216: Cl up 4f: bckd: btr 4214 (h'cap, fast).   1   91

1382

4219 **PROMISED** 21 [3] 2-8-4 (VIS) G Duffield 33/1: 000407: Mid div, btn over 1f out: visor: btr 4009 (g/s).   nk   85
4286 **BYO** 15 [1] 2-8-9 R Mullen 33/1: 435648: Held up, rdn/btn 2f out: see 3264, 2483.   1¼   87
*4283 **STARBECK** 15 [10] 2-8-5(1ow) D Harrison 16/1: -419: Dwelt/rear, no impress: up in grade after 4283.   hd   82
4283 **ORIENTOR** 15 [9] 2-8-9 A Culhane 20/1: 320: Al bhd: 10th: mdn, highly tried: see 4283, 3958.   nk   85
10 ran   Time 1m 17.21 (6.4)   (Hamdan Al Maktoum)   B W Hills Lambourn, Berks

---

4463   3.45 GR 1 RACING POST TROPHY 2YO (A)   1m rnd   Soft 103   -19 Slow
£105000 £40250 £20125 £9625

3946 **DILSHAAN** 38 [9] Sir Michael Stoute 2-9-0 J Murtagh 14/1: 21: 2 b c Darshaan - Avila (Ajdal)   116
Dwelt, hdwy over 2f out, strong run to lead fnl 100y, pushed clr cl home: 190,000gns Feb foal, half brother to
a wnr abroad: sire high class at 12f: apprec step up to 1m, mid dists look sure to suit in '01: acts on fast,
clearly relishes soft: handles a stiff/gall trk: most progressive, a v smart mid-dist prospect for next term.
*4161 **TAMBURLAINE** 25 [10] R Hannon 2-9-0 R Hughes 11/4: -2212: 2 b c Royal Academy - Well Bought   2½   111
(Auction Maybe) Rear, hdwy to lead over 2f out, rdn & clr dist, overhauled by wnr fnl 100y: hvly bckd: acts on
firm & soft grnd: v useful colt, lkd all over the wnr & prob didn't quite get home in these testing conditions.
4058 **BONNARD** 34 [5] A P O'Brien 2-9-0 G Duffield 25/1: 132203: 2 b c Nureyev - Utr (Mr Prospector)   ¾   110
In tch, kept on fnl 2f, not pace to chall: clr of rem: back to form with blnks omitted: stays 1m on fast & soft.
4058 **DARWIN** 34 [6] A P O'Brien 2-9-0 P J Scallan 11/1: 164: Cl up, rdn/briefly led 3f out, sn hdd & no   5   103
impress fnl 2f: shorter priced stablemate of 3rd: this longer 1m trip will suit: see 4058, 1624.
4354 **FREUD** 7 [8] 2-9-0 M J Kinane 2/1 FAV: -255: Trckd ldrs, rdn/no impress when no room over 1f out: ¾   102
hvly bckd stablemate of 3rd & 4th: this longer 1m trip should suit, poss too sn after 4354 (gd grnd, 7f).
4237 **DAYGLOW DANCER** 21 [7] 2-9-0 K Darley 33/1: 425226: Chsd ldrs, btn 2f out: see 4237, 4072.   ½   101
4196 **GRANDERA** 22 [2] 2-9-0 D Harrison 5/1: -5127: Trckd ldrs, no impress/hmpd over 1f out: bckd: 1¾   99
this longer 1m trip will suit next term: see 4196, 3909 (7f).
4320 **CD EUROPE** 13 [4] 2-9-0 Craig Williams 9/1: -11248: Trckd ldrs, btn/hmpd over 1f out: fcd too   shd   99
freely today & reportedly struck into: btr 4320.
4196 **CAUVERY** 22 [3] 2-9-0 K Darley 25/1: 210309: Held up, eff 2f out, sn btn: needs a drop in grade.   2½   95
*3879 **SNOWSTORM** 44 [1] 2-9-0 R Mullen 20/1: 261210: Led, rdn/hdd 3f out, sn btn: 10th: 6 wk abs.   2   92
10 ran   Time 1m 45.87 (9.77)   (Saeed Suhail)   Sir Michael Stoute Newmarket, Suffolk

---

4464   4.15 TEN TO FOLLOW HCAP 3YO+ 0-100 (C)   1m4f   Soft 103   +03 Fast   [91]
£14820 £4560 £2280 £1140   3 yo rec 7 lb

4160 **NORCROFT JOY** 25 [8] N A Callaghan 5-8-7 (70) G Duffield 9/1: 104551: 5 b m Rock Hopper -   76
Greenhills Joy (Radetzky) In tch, hdwy halfway, rdn to lead 1f out, rdn out: gd time: earlier scored at
Beverley (h'cap): '99 Warwick & Doncaster wnr (h'caps, rtd 77, M Ryan): '98 wnr at Yarmouth, Hamilton &
Beverley (h'caps, rtd 71): eff at 10f, suited by 12/14f on fast, soft & gd: likely Beverley: can go well fresh.
4061 **CAPRIOLO** 31 [10] R Hannon 4-8-12 (75)(bl) R Hughes 16/1: 163132: 4 ch g Priolo - Carroll's   1¾   78
Canyon (Hatim) Led 1f, rdn/led again over 2f out, hdd 1f out, kept on well: clr rem, fine effort: see 4061, 3725.
3131 **MICHELE MARIESCHI** 78 [3] P F I Cole 3-8-12 (82) J Carroll 40/1: -50003: 3 b g Alzao - Escape   6   79
Path (Wolver Hollow) Led after 1f, keen, hdd 3f out, kept on for press, no threat to front pair: abs: prob stays 12f.
-- **DHAUDELOUP** [14] R A Fahey 5-8-4 (67) J Quinn 2/1 FAV: 3160/4: Mid div, rdn/prog to chse ldrs   3   61
over 2f out, no impress fnl 1f: hvly bckd on Flat reapp: 6 month jmps abs, 99/00 Chepstow wnr (h'cap, rtd 119h,
eff at 2m on gd & hvy): won on the level in native France back in '98: eff at 12f on gd/soft grnd.
4282 **MCGILLYCUDDY REEKS** 15 [1] 9-8-5 (68) Kim Tinkler 20/1: 056455: Rear, kept on fnl 3f, no threat.   1   61
3379 **HUNTERS TWEED** 66 [7] 4-8-3 (66) Craig Williams 20/1: 020666: Rear, mod hdwy fnl 3f: 10 wk abs.   ¾   58
3986 **KENNET** 36 [5] 5-8-9 (72) A Beech 15/1: 113657: Chsd ldrs 10f: see 3518.   1¼   63
3454 **WILCUMA** 64 [16] 9-9-5 (82) A Clark 20/1: 553038: Rear, mod hdwy fnl 3f: abs: see 845, 380.   5   68
4342 **MARDANI** 9 [11] 5-9-10 (87) M J Kinane 11/1: 662639: Towards rear, mod hdwy: prefer faster grnd.   1   72
4299 **SPRING PURSUIT** 14 [2] 4-9-0 (77) P Fitzsimons 66/1: 000330: Chsd ldrs 9f: 10th: btr 4299.   1½   60
4160 **FOREST HEATH** 25 [4] 3-8-12 (82) J Reid 10/1: -21220: Chsd ldrs 9f: 12th: btr 2755 (C/D, fast).   0
4221 **KATHRYNS PET** 21 [15] 7-9-7 (84) A Culhane 7/1: 1-6120: Rear, nvr any impress: 14th: btr 4221, 1411.   0
4276 **CANFORD** 16 [18] 3-9-3 (87) K Darley 10/1: 355520: Held up, eff 4f out, sn btn: 19th: see 3541, 1588.   0
4092 **Warning Reef** 29 [11] 7-8-4 (67) W Supple 14/1:   4276 **Montecristo** 16 [6] 7-9-8 (85) J Mackay (5) 12/1:
4433 **Billy Bathwick** 2 [13] 3-7-10 (66)(2oh) K Dalgleish (5) 50/1:
4101 **Tate Venture** 29 [12] 3-7-10 (66)(1oh) Dale Gibson 40/1:
4212 **Weet A Minute** 21 [17] 7-9-3 (80) D Sweeney 33/1:   874 **Bawsian** 193 [9] 5-9-8 (85) D Harrison 33/1:
19 ran   Time 2m 41.84 (12.04)   (Norcroft Park Stud)   N A Callaghan Newmarket, Suffolk

---

4465   4.45 RACINGPOST COND STKS 3YO+ (B)   7f   Soft 103   -02 Slow
£11163 £3435 £1717 £858   3 yo rec 2 lb   Raced centre - stands side

4347 **UMISTIM** 8 [10] R Hannon 3-9-2 R Hughes 7/4 JT FAV: 520201: 3 ch c Inchinor - Simply Sooty   115
(Absalom) Trckd ldr, prog to chall over 1f out, led ins last, styd on well, drvn out: hvly bckd: earlier won at
Newmarket (reapp, Gr 3): '99 wnr at Windsor (stks) & Newbury (2, mdn & Gr 3, rtd 112): suited by 7f/1m, tried 9f:
acts on firm grnd, relishes gd/soft & soft grnd: likes to race with/force the pace on any trk: smart & genuine.
3878 **CAYMAN SUNSET** 44 [12] E A L Dunlop 3-8-12 G Duffield 4/1: 1642: 3 ch f Night Shift - Robinia   nk   100
(Roberto) Chsd ldrs, styd on well fnl 1½f despite flashing tail, not btn far: op 11/4, abs: acts on fast & soft.
+4301 **FURTHER OUTLOOK** 14 [9] D Nicholls 6-8-9 R Winston 7/4 JT FAV: 300313: 6 gr g Zilzal - Future   1¼   103
Bright (Lyphard's Wish) Led, drvn & strongly prsd from over 1f out & hdd ins last, no extra: well clr of rem:
hvly bckd: fine run over 7f trip, prob just best at 5/6f: see 4301 (h'cap).
4300 **ADELPHI BOY** 14 [13] M C Chapman 4-9-2 A Culhane 9/2: 002104: Mid div, mod hdwy, no threat.   8   98$
4278 **ADJUTANT** 16 [3] 5-8-12 M Tebbutt 40/1: 600265: Chsd ldrs 5f: see 4142, 1286 (h'cap).   7   84
*4287 **LOOK HERE NOW** 15 [8] 3-8-10 K Dalgleish 10/1: 000016: Chsd ldrs 5f: btr 4287 (6f).   ½   83$
-- **RED BLAZER NZ** [15] 7-8-9 S Righton 100/1: 0-7: Al towards rear: Flat reapp, 5 month jumps abs   7   70
(mod form): wnr on the level & over hdles in native NZ prev.
4220 **TIME TO FLY** 21 [14] 7-8-9 (bl) D Sweeney 200/1: 060008: Prom 5f: blnks reapp: see 2525 (5f).   2½   66$
4324 **HOT POTATO** 11 [6] 4-8-9 J Carroll 100/1: 206059: Al bhd: imposs task.   3½   61$
4566} **HI FALUTIN** 357 [11] 4-8-4 J Quinn 200/1: 0-0: Dwelt, al bhd: 10th: reapp, no form.   ¾   40
4308 **TIME FOR THE CLAN** 12 [2] 3-8-7 O Pears 100/1: 500000: 11th: plater.   11   35
4308 **THE CASTIGATOR** 12 [4] 3-8-7 D Mernagh 200/1: 000050: Chsd ldrs, bhd 3f out: 12th: see 4276, 1905.   7   25
12 ran   Time 1m 30.53 (7.33)   (Mrs S Joint)   R Hannon East Everleigh, Wilts

DONCASTER   SATURDAY OCTOBER 21ST   Lefthand, Flat, Galloping Track

| 4466 | 5.15 MAGIC RTD HCAP 3YO+ 0-100 (B) | 5f | Soft 103 | +04 Fast | [107] |

£9657   £3663   £1831   £832   Raced across track

*4339 **DANCING MYSTERY** 9 [1] E A Wheeler 6-9-7 (100) S Carson (3) 13/2: 011211: 6 b g Beveled - **105**
Batchworth Dancer (Ballacashtal) Trkd ldr far side, rdn to lead dist, styd on well despite hanging badly right ins
last, rdn out: gd time: earlier scored at Salisbury, Ascot, Yarmouth & Newmarket (2, h'caps): '99 Lingfield,
Southwell (rtd 82a), Warwick (h'caps) & Redcar wnr (stks, rtd 78): '98 Windsor & Goodwood wnr (h'caps, rtd 57 &
74a): stays 6f, suited by 5f on fast, soft & both AWs: goes on any trk & runs well fresh, with/without blnks:
remarkably tough, useful & prog gelding, a magnificent record in ultra competitive h'caps of late.

3727 **NOW LOOK HERE** 52 [4] B A McMahon 4-8-13 (92) K Dalgleish (5) 11/1: 200502: 4 b g Reprimand - 1 **94**
Where's Carol (Anfield) Dwelt & bhd far side, styd on well for press fnl 2f, not rch wnr: op 14/1, abs: see 1337.
4339 **WHISTLER** 9 [13] R Hannon 3-8-10 (89) R Hughes 8/1: 412153: 3 ch g Selkirk - French Gift shd **91**
(Cadeaux Genereux) Led stands side, rdn & styd on well fnl 1f: remains in fine form: acts on firm & soft grnd.
4339 **AMARANTH** 9 [21] J L Eyre 4-8-10 (89) K Darley 9/1: 650144: Prom stands side, ev ch dist, held nr fin. hd **90**
4339 **DELEGATE** 9 [11] 7-8-9 (88) J Murtagh 8/1: 202005: Bhd, kept on fnl 2f despite hanging left: see 3861. ¾ **88**
3861 **SINGSONG** 45 [14] 3-8-7 (86) D Harry (7) 33/1: 330006: Cl up 4f stands side: 6 wk abs: see 1047. ½ **85**
4339 **NIGHT FLIGHT** 9 [9] 6-8-12 (91) J Reid 7/1: 012037: In tch, no impress over 1f out: see 3543 (6f). ½ **89**
4301 **LAGO DI VARANO** 14 [20] 8-8-8 (87)(bl) Dean McKeown 11/1: 002658: Chsd ldrs 4f: btr 3183 (6f). shd **85**
3920 **AMBITIOUS** 39 [10] 5-8-11 (90) C Catlin (7) 20/1: 101009: Prom 4f stands side: btr 3176 (fast). 1½ **85**
*4285 **NINEACRES** 15 [2] 9-8-8 (87)(bl) P Fitzsimons (5) 9/2-FAV: 302210: Chsd ldrs 3f: 10th: btr 4285. ½ **81**
4339 **AFAAN** 9 [6] 7-8-8 (87)(bl) T G McLaughlin 16/1: 005000: Led till over 1f out, fdd: see 113. 4 **73**
4339 **GUINEA HUNTER** 9 [7] 4-9-6 (99) J Carroll 10/1: 503500: Bhd 2f out: 12th: op 8/1: btr 4102, 2859. **0**
4356} **Light The Rocket** 373 [15] 4-9-2 (95) P McCabe 33/1: 4129 **Caxton Lad** 27 [18] 3-8-9 (88) A Clark 12/1:
4301 **Pips Magic** 14 [3] 4-8-7 (86)(7oh) J Quinn (5) 25/1: 4129 **Saphire** 27 [8] 4-8-7 (86)(1oh) A Culhane 25/1:
4339 **Hammer And Sickle** 9 [16] 3-8-7 (86)(1oh) J Fanning 25/1:
4301 **Loch Inch** 14 [12] 3-8-7 (86)(bl)(4oh) R Winston 50/1:
18 ran   Time 1m 03.17 (4.97)   (Austin Stroud & Co Ltd)   E A Wheeler Whitchurch On Thames, Oxon

NEWBURY   SATURDAY OCTOBER 21ST   Lefthand, Flat, Galloping Track

Official Going   HEAVY. Stalls: Straight Course - Stands' side: Round Course - Inside

| 4467 | 1.30 LISTED RADLEY STKS 2YO (A) | 7f str | Soft/Heavy 128 | +06 Fast |

£13520   £4160   £2080   £1040

-- **RELISH THE THOUGHT** 2 [2] B W Hills 2-8-8 M Hills 10/1: 1: 2 b f Sadler's Wells - Viz (Kris S) **105**
Shkn up in rear, hdwy 2f out, led 1f out, rdn & styd on well: smart debut: gd time: dam 1m 2yo wnr: eff at 7f,
shld apprec mid-dists next term: acts on soft/hvy grnd & runs well fresh: may develop into a Classic prospect.
*4063 **BLUSHING BRIDE** 31 [10] J Noseda 2-8-8 Pat Eddery 2/1 FAV: -112: 2 b f Distant Relative - Dime ½ **103**
Bag (High Line) Bhd & ran in snatches, prog & short of room 2f out, sn switched & rdn, ran on ins last, not btn
far: nicely bckd, poss unlucky: jockey given 3 day irresp riding ban: imprvd again, acts on gd & soft/hvyd.
*4034 **LIPICA** 33 [4] K R Burke 2-8-8 J P Spencer 8/1: 313: 2 b f Night Shift - Top Knot (High Top) 1¼ **101**
In tch, gd prog to lead ent fnl 2f, rdn dist, sn hdd, onepce towards fin: pulled well clr of rem: improving,
useful filly: clearly handles soft/hvy grnd tho' reportedly prefers fast: see also 4034.
4009 **DANCE ON** 35 [8] Sir Michael Stoute 2-8-8 L Dettori 6/1: 061034: Held up, prog & not much room 7 **89**
2f out, sn no ch with ldrs: worth another try at 7f on better grnd, see 3027.
4210 **NAFISAH** 21 [7] 2-8-8 R Hills 4/1: -22125: Led till ent fnl 2f, no extra: goes on soft, much btr 4210 (fast). ½ **88**
4315 **SIPTITZ HEIGHTS** 14 [3] 2-8-8 E Ahern 50/1: 105056: Chsd ldrs, fdd ent fnl 2f: stiffish task, lngr trip. 3½ **82**
4209 **CIELITO LINDO** 21 [11] 2-8-8 J Fortune 9/1: 27: Mid div, eff 3f out, no impress: much btr 4209 (6f, fast). 4 **75**
4110 **SHAHIRAH** 28 [1] 2-8-8 T Quinn 6/1: 108: Prom, rdn & btn appr fnl 2f: see 3359 (7f fast grnd fill mdn). 3 **70**
4034 **RECIPROCAL** 33 [5] 2-8-8 N Pollard 40/1: 0049: Well plcd, wknd qckly 3f out: stiff task. 5 **62**
4219 **MUSIC MAID** 21 [6] 2-8-8 A Nicholls 40/1: 300010: Bhd from halfway, hmpd 2f out: 10th, highly tried. 1 **60**
-- **LA SAYIDA** [9] 2-8-8 Paul Eddery 25/1: 0: Sn struggling: 11th, highly tried on debut: 11 **44**
April foal: dam a smart high-class mid-dist performer: reportedly not handle this testing grnd: with B Smart.
11 ran   Time 1m 32.85 (8.55)   (Maktoum Al Maktoum)   B W Hills Lambourn, Berks

| 4468 | 2.00 CAPEL CURE SHARP NURSERY HCAP 2YO (B) | 6f | Soft/Heavy 128 | +11 Fast | [97] |

£22230   £6840   £3420   £1710

4338 **RASOUM** 9 [4] E A L Dunlop 2-9-7 (90) T Quinn 12/1: 313001: 2 gr c Miswaki - Bel Ray (Restivo) **104**
Held up, prog after halfway, pushed into lead bef fnl 1f & easily qcknd clr despite running v green: fast time:
earlier won at Newmarket (nov): eff at 6f, will stay 7f: acts on fast & gd, revls in soft/hvy grnd: goes on
any trk & has a fine turn of foot: runs well fresh, gd weight carrier: v useful, looks Listed class.
4286 **PRINCE PYRAMUS** 15 [12] C Grant 2-8-12 (81) F Lynch 16/1: -44122: 2 b c Pyramus - Rekindled 9 **81**
Flame (King's Lake) Prom, chall 2f out, styd on for 2nd but sn outpcd by wnr: op 12/1: ran to best.
*4001 **SPY MASTER** 35 [21] Sir Michael Stoute 2-8-12 (81)(vis) Pat Eddery 12/1: 023413: 2 b c Green ¾ **79**
Desert - Obsessive (Seeking The Gold) Chsd ldrs, eff 2f out, unable to qckn: not disgraced bck in h'cap comp.
4338 **FOREVER TIMES** 9 [10] T D Easterby 2-8-4 (73) T Williams 16/1: 033004: Towards rear, rdn appr shd **71**
fnl 1f, styd on, nvr dangerous: well apprec a return to 7f: see 3860, 3346.
4289 **PIQUET** 15 [13] 2-7-10 (65)(2oh) G Baker (5) 33/1: -0455: Towards rear, improved appr fnl 2f, shd **63**
rdn & onepce 1f out, styd on nr fin: prob ran to best on h'cap bow: see 4289.
4127 **RUSSIAN WHISPERS** 27 [14] 2-9-6 (89)(VIS) J P Spencer 16/1: -3506: Led till bef fnl 1f, onepce: vis. hd **86**
4305 **JOINT INSTRUCTION** 12 [8] 2-8-4 (73) Martin Dwyer 25/1: 011007: Prom, chall 2f out, sn no extra. nk **69**
4338 **BLAKESHALL BOY** 9 [15] 2-8-7 (76) S Drowne 33/1: 353008: Chsd ldrs till 2f out: see 3228. 1 **75**
4332 **LILLEMAN** 10 [7] 2-9-0 (83)(BL) E Ahern 20/1: 502239: Rear, switched & brief eff 2f out: tried blnks. nk **75**
4338 **ADWEB** 9 [20] 2-7-12 (67) M Henry 13/2: 004100: Al mid div: 10th, tchd 9/1: had this wnr bhd in 4338. 1¾ **56**
*4131 **YNYSMON** 27 [17] 2-8-8 (79) C Lowther 20/1: 504010: Cl up, fdd appr fnl 1f: 11th: btr 4131 (5f). ¾ **64**
*4338 **IDLE POWER** 9 [18] 2-9-6 (89) B Marcus 9/1: 516610: Handy till 2f out: 12th, see 4338 (made all on gd). 1¾ **73**
4214 **ZHITOMIR** 21 [9] 2-9-3 (86) P Doe 11/1: 061230: Trckd ldrs & ch till wknd qckly appr fnl 1f: 12th. shd **70**

1384

4214 **FACTUAL LAD** 21 [6] 2-9-7 (90) L Dettori 20/1: 310600: Mid div, no extra 2f out: 14th, jt top-weight.   *hd*   73
4179 **VENDOME** 23 [16] 2-9-0 (83) J Weaver 14/1: 312230: Nvr troubled ldrs: 16th, tchd 20/1: longer trip.   0
3888 **FAIR PRINCESS** 43 [3] 2-8-13 (82) M Hills 6/1 FAV: 062220: Nvr a factor in 20th: tchd 9/1: btr 3888 (fm).   0
3614 Proletariat 57 [13] 2-9-3 (86) C Rutter 20/1:   4267 **Artifact** 17 [11] 2-7-10 (65)(2oh) G Bardwell 33/1:
4214 Pashmeena 21 [24] 2-8-10 (79) J Fortune 20/1:   4345 **El Maximo** 3 [19] 2-8-5 (74)(tbl) S W Kelly (3) 20/1:
4214 Our Destiny 21 [1] 2-8-8 (77) N Callan 33/1:   4235 **Piccolo Rose** 19 [22] 2-7-11 (65)(1ow) A Nicholls 33/1:
3015 Pairing 83 [23] 2-9-1 (84) G Carter 16/1:
23 ran   Time 1m 18.6 (7)   (Khalid Ali)   E A L Dunlop Newmarket, Suffolk

---

4469   2.30 GR 3 ST SIMON STKS 3YO+ (A)   1m4f   Soft/Heavy 128   -12 Slow
        £21000   £8050   £4025   £1925   3 yo rec 7 lb

*4194 **WELLBEING** 22 [5] H R A Cecil 3-8-7 T Quinn 4/7 FAV: -11511: 3 b c Sadler's Wells - Charming Life (Sir   115
Tristram) Trkd ldrs, led 1f out, ran on strgly, pshd out cl home: hvly bckd: earlier won at Newmarket (3, mdn,
stks & List): also 13L 5th in the Derby: eff at 12f, likely to get 14f: acts on fast & soft/hvy, stiff/gall trks,
likes Newmarket: runs well fresh: stays in training & can develop into a high-class mid-dist performer next term.
3898 **MARIENBARD** 42 [3] M A Jarvis 3-8-7 L Dettori 13/2: 111262: 3 b c Caerleon - Marienbard   1¼   112
(Darshaan) Handy, prog to lead 2f out till 1f out, styd on: 6 wk abs: v useful: acts on fast & soft/hvy grnd.
3565 **BOREAS** 59 [2] L M Cumani 5-9-0 J P Spencer 10/1: 43/123: 5b g In The Wings - Ramur (Top Ville)   ¾   111
Led till 2f out, kept on till no extra inside last: op 7/1, clr rem, 8 wk abs: v useful run, acts on fast & soft/hvy.
+4011 **ISLAND HOUSE** 35 [4] G Wragg 4-9-0 D Holland 11/2: 115414: Keen, held up, mod hdwy 3f out, sn   7   104
left bhd by front 3: longer 12f trip, much btr 4011 (11f gd/soft).
4109 **NADOUR AL BAHR** 28 [7] 5-9-0 T Williams 50/1: 235/65: Held up in tch, imprvd 5f out till wknd 2f out.   4   100
4109 **HAPPY CHANGE** 28 [6] 6-9-0 M Hills 11/1: 015326: Prom, chsd ldr halfway till ent straight: btr 3640.   17   85
4239 **KING O THE MANA** 21 [1] 3-8-7 J Fortune 14/1: 132347: Prom, not much room halfway & drpd rear,   30   60
rallied to chall 3f out, sn wknd: see 3892, 1089.
7 ran   Time 2m 46.1 (16.8)   (Exors Of The Late Lord Howard de Walden)   H R A Cecil Newmarket, Suffolk

---

4470   3.00 EBF MDN DIV 1 2YO (D)   6f   Soft/Heavy 128   -07 Slow
        £5102   £1570   £785   £392

4137 **MUNIR** 26 [4] B W Hills 2-9-0 R Hills 4/1 JT FAV: 31: 2 ch c Indian Ridge - Al Bahathri (Blushing Groom)   93+
Trkd ldrs, briefly short of room ent fnl 2f, switched to lead dist, cmftbly pld clr: left debut well bhd: half-brother
to wnrs btwn 6f & 1m, dam high class sprinter/miler: eff at 6f, 7f is going to suit: acts on soft/hvy grnd, gall trk.
-- **FUNNY VALENTINE** [11] T G Mills 2-9-0 T Williams 9/1: 2: 2 ch c Cadeaux Genereux - Aunt   3½   84
Hester (Caerleon) Prom, led 2f out, sn rdn & hdd, styd on but no ch with wnr: debut: IR 55,000gns half brother
to sev wnrs, dam 5f winning juv: eff at 6f on soft/hvy grnd: shld win a maiden.
3973 **HIRAETH** 36 [18] B Palling 2-8-9 T Quinn 10/1: 323: 2 b f Petong - Floppie (Law Society)   nk   78
Prom & ev ch till onepce fnl 1f: tchd 14/1, clr rem: acts on firm & soft/hvy grnd: consistent.
-- **STANDS TO REASON** [5] Lg Cottrell 2-9-0 A Daly 30/1: 4: Dwelt & well off the pace till hands/heels   4   73
hdwy appr fnl 1f, nvr plcd to chall: 9,600gns Hernando gldg out of a 5/6f wng juv: handles soft/hvy grnd, shld
apprec 1m+ next term: most eye-catching & one to keep in mind next term.
4341 **CHANTRESS LORELEI** 9 [15] 2-8-9 W Ryan 14/1: 05: Prom, eff 2f out, onepace: see 4341.   ¾   66
-- **FIRST STEPS** [6] Paul Eddery 33/1: 6: Prom, rdn appr fnl 2f, fdd: 7,800gns half-sister   1¼   63
to wnrs between 6f & 11f: some promise here, likely to apprec faster grnd: with B Smart.
3980 **GLORIOUS QUEST** 36 [14] 2-9-0 P Robinson 4/1 JT FAV: -37: Led till ent fnl 2f, fdd: op 5/2: much   hd   68
better on firm grnd debut in 3980.
4289 **SUNLEY SCENT** 15 [13] 2-8-9 S Drowne 7/1: 08: Handy, wknd dist: tchd 14/1: see 4289.   2   58
-- **PERFIDIOUS** [7] 2-9-0 S Sanders 16/1: 9: Al mid div on debut: March foal: dam a 7f wnr, from a   2½   57
v gd family: sire a top-class miler: with Sir Mark Prescott & likely to improve considerably.
4124 **CHALOM** 27 [16] 2-9-0 J Fortune 14/1: -060: Well plcd till wknd qckly till ent fnl 2f: 10th, btr 4124.   ¾   55
-- **LUCKY HETTIE** [3] 2-8-9 C Rutter 33/1: 0: In tch till 2f out: fin 11th: 19,500gns Apr foal: 4   42
hal sister to a wnr in the USA: dam a wnr in the States: bred to apprec 1m+ next term: with C Egerton.
4163 **CREDENZA MOMENT** 24 [10] 2-9-0 R Smith (5) 33/1: 000: Nvr trbld ldrs: 12th: May foal, with R Hannon.   1   45
-- **JAYCAT** [9] 2-8-9 E Ahern 20/1: 0: Nvr a factor: 13th, tchd 33/1: 11,000gns April foal: half   shd   40
sister to a wng juv in France: sire a high-class 6/7f performer: with G Butler.
-- **INSPECTOR BLUE** [17] 2-9-0 Martin Dwyer 14/1: 0: Al bhd: 14th: first foal, dam useful at 5/7f.   1¾   41
4341 **AFGHAN** 9 [8] 2-9-0 (t) L Dettori 11/2: 00: Sn struggling: 16th, tchd 7/1: see 4341.   0
-- **Valeureux** [19] 2-9-0 D Holland 33/1:   4268 **Golfagent** 17 [1] 2-9-0 M Hills 33/1:
-- **Brand New Day** [12] 2-9-0 J Weaver 33/1:
18 ran   Time 1m 19.71 (8.11)   (Hamdan Al Maktoum)   B W Hills Lambourn, Berks

---

4471   3.30 EBF MDN DIV 2 2YO (D)   6f   Soft/Heavy 128   -02 Slow
        £5102   £1570   £785   £392

-- **PRIME VERSION** [16] P F I Cole 2-9-0 J Fortune 12/1: 1: 2 b c Primo Dominie - Cashew (Sharrood)   93
Shkn up somewhat early, imprvd halfway, led ent fnl 2f, kept on strngy, pshd out: tchd 16/1: 70,000gns half brother to
wng sprint juv Pistachio, dam a miler: eff at 6f, get at least 7f: acts on soft/hvy grnd & runs well fresh: promising.
4341 **SMIRK** 9 [1] D R C Elsworth 2-9-0 T Quinn 6/1: -602: 2 ch c Selkirk - Elfin Laughter (Alzao)   2   87
In tch, improved 2f out, drvn to chall bef fnl 1f, onepace fnl 100y: op 8/1, well clr rem: much better run,
clearly relished this soft/hvy grnd: should get 1m next term & win a maiden.
1782 **SANTA ISOBEL** 135 [4] I A Balding 2-8-9 Pat Eddery 7/1: 33: 2 ch f Nashwan - Atlantic Record   6   70
(Slip Anchor) Towards rear, went past btn horses appr fnl 1f, no ch with front 2: tchd 10/1, over 4 mth abs:
bred for 1m+ next term & crying out for longer trips: handles fast 7 soft/hvy grnd: see 1782.
3044 **FAITHFUL WARRIOR** 82 [8] B W Hills 2-9-0 M Hills 10/1: -454: Early ldr, hmpd 2f out, kept on same   2½   69
pace for 4th: op 7/1, 12 wk abs: better on faster grnd prev starts.
4183 **ASTRAL PRINCE** 23 [6] 2-9-0 W Ryan 20/1: 005: Chsd ldrs, kept on onepace fnl 2f: rtd higher 4183.   2½   63
-- **MAID FOR FREEDOM** [3] 2-8-9 E Ahern 33/1: 6: Nvr better than mid div: 37,000gns April foal: ¾   56
sister to a Listed wnr in the States, dam wnr in the States: stoutly bred, with G Butler.
-- **COMPTON CHICK** [2] 2-8-9 (t) J P Spencer 20/1: 7: Rear, went thro' btn horses appr fnl 1f: hd   56
t-strap, debut, op 14/1, stablemate 6th: half-sister a wng miler: dam multiple wnr in the US: will improve.
-- **IKBAL** [14] 2-9-0 R Hills 11/10 FAV: 8: Mid div, prog to chse ldrs appr fnl 2f, sn rdn, fdd: nicely   ½   60
bckd tho' op 4/6: Indian Ridge first foal, dam useful sprint juv: better expected & worth another ch on faster grnd.

-- **GILDA** [7] 2-8-9 G Carter 12/1: 9: Al around same pl: op 8/1: stablemate 4th: IR 13,000gns Mar foal: dam unrcd, sire 1m Franch juv wnr: with B Hills. *nk* **54**
3047 **REVERIE 82** [19] 2-9-0 J Weaver 33/1: 000: Keen, sn led, hdd ent fnl 2f, tired badly ins last: 10th, 12 wk abs: much too free on this testing surface: see 2494. *nk* **58**
3958 **PLEINMONT POINT 37** [13] 2-9-0 J Bramhill 50/1: -460: Handy till 2f out: 11th, see 3958, 3812. *1* **55**
4188 **WORTH A GAMBLE 22** [12] 2-9-0 G Baker (5) 50/1: -000: In tch till halfway: 12th, highly tried. *2* **50**
4137 **HIGH PASTURE 26** [18] 2-8-9 S Drowne 14/1: 60: Nvr troubled ldrs: 13th, see 4137. *nk* **44**
-- **City Player** [17] 2-9-0 S Sanders 16/1: 4289 **Caposo 15** [15] 2-8-9 F Norton 20/1:
-- **True Note** [10] 2-9-0 N Pollard 25/1: 4289 **Choralli 15** [9] 2-8-9 D Holland 20/1:
3980 **Tropical River 36** [5] 2-9-0 J Stack 50/1: 3484 **Royal Enclosure 63** [11] 2-9-0 (BL) D R McCabe 50/1:
19 ran Time 1m 19.41 (7.81) (Richard Green (Fine Paintings)) P F I Cole Whatcombe, Oxon

4472

4.05 MITSUBISHI RTD HCAP 3YO+ 0-100 (B) 1m1f Soft/Heavy 128 -23 Slow [104]
£9477 £3594 £1797 £817 3 yo rec 4 lb

*4308 **CORNELIUS 12** [9] P F I Cole 3-9-3 (97) J Fortune 7/2 FAV: 204011: 3 b c Barathea - Rainbow Mountain (Rainbow Quest) Made all, styd on well, drvn out: tchd 9/2, game eff: recent Ayr wnr (stks): '99 wnr at York (debut, mdn), subs 3rd in Gr 3 Coventry at R Ascot (rtd 106+): eff at 1m/10f: acts on fast, all 3 wins on soft/hvy grnd: loves to force the pace, stiff or gall track: v useful, in-form colt. **103**
3131 **HIGHLAND REEL 78** [2] D R C Elsworth 3-8-10 (90) N Pollard 10/1: 033102: 3 ch c Selkirk - Taj Victory (Final Straw) Prom, chsd wnr 2f out, kept on but al being held: op 8/1, 11 week abs: settled better & bounced back to form: see 3131, 3048. *1* **93**
4278 **SWAN KNIGHT 9** [11] J L Dunlop 4-9-5 (95) Pat Eddery 8/1: 601003: 4 b c Sadler's Wells - Shannkara (Akarad) Well plcd, rdn 2f out, unable to qckn: eff at 1m/9f: acts on fast, suited by soft/hvy grnd. *1½* **96**
4212 **ATLANTIC RHAPSODY 21** [8] M Johnston 3-9-3 (97) P Robinson 5/1: 546204: Waited with, hdwy & put head to one side 1f out, not trble ldrs: gd run, but has cost his supporters dearly since May: see 1535. *1* **96**
4392 **ANNADAWI 4** [4] 5-8-6 (83)(1oh) G Baker (5) 12/1: 310205: Rear, prog to chase ldrs ent fnl 2f, no extra & edged left inside last: qck reapp: better giving weight to lesser rivals?: see 4300. *2½* **77**
3998 **TROUBLE MOUNTAIN 35** [5] 3-9-1 (95) M Hills 16/1: 650006: Held up, closed ent straight, wknd dist: op 10/1: poss failed to see out this longer 9f trip on testing grnd: see 969. *2½* **86**
4337 **ISSEY ROSE 9** [1] 3-8-10 (90) T Williams 25/1: -00007: Chsd ldrs, eff & btn appr fnl 2f: see 3726. *6* **73**
4348 **MADAM ALISON 8** [7] 4-8-7 (83) R Smith (5) 16/1: 150308: Nvr troubled ldrs: see 4160, 2890. *3* **62**
4347 **ANNAPURNA 8** [6] 4-9-7 (97)(BL) D Holland 20/1: 400409: Al towards rear: blnkd, top-weight. *12* **62**
3896 **LUXOR 42** [12] 3-8-8 (88) T Quinn 11/2: 421000: Well plcd till 3f out: 10th, 6 wk abs, see 2135 (fast). *4* **48**
4276 **BARTON SANDS 16** [13] 3-8-8 (88) J P Spencer 5/1: 21260: Trckd ldrs, wknd appr fnl 3f: 11th, op 7/2: needs faster grnd by the looks of things: see 4276, 4197, 1242 (firm). *7* **39**
11 ran Time 2m 02.57 (13.57) (Sir George Meyrick) P F I Cole Whatcombe, Oxon

4473

4.35 NEWBURY HCAP 3YO+ 0-100 (C) 1m2f Soft/Heavy 128 -31 Slow [94]
£7182 £2210 £1105 £552 3 yo rec 5 lb

4197 **BONAGUIL 22** [17] C F Wall 3-9-6 (91) G Baker (5) 8/1: 420231: 3 b g Septieme Ciel - Chateaubrook (Alleged) Waited with, gd prog 3f out, led ent fnl 2f, edged left, rdn out: op 6/1, slow time: plcd sev times since won first 3 this term, at Lingfield (mdn auct, rtd 77a), Sandown & Kempton (h'caps): unplcd in '99 & gelded: eff at 9/10f: acts on firm, soft/hvy grnd & equitrack, any trk: runs well fresh: useful, tough & progressive **96**
4282 **GENTLEMAN VENTURE 15** [10] J Akehurst 4-8-12 (78) P Doe 16/1: 513062: 4 b g Polar Falcon - Our Shirley (Shirley Heights) Nvr far away, led appr fnl 2f, sn hdd, styd on well, not btn far: op 12/1: back to form over this testing 10f, acts on firm & soft/hvy grnd: see 3402 (12f). *½* **81**
*4340 **SCENE 9** [18] N P Littmoden 5-8-12 (78) T Quinn 4/1: 000413: 5 b m Scenic - Avebury Ring (Auction Ring) In tch, prog to dispute 2nd appr fnl 1f, no extra & eased cl home: bckd, tchd 5/1, qckish reapp: finishing the season in gd heart: see 4340 (1m). *1¾* **79**
1575] **ZYDECO 873** [4] Mrs A J Perrett 5-9-3 (83) W Ryan 20/1: 2-24/4: Held up, styd on for press appr fnl 1f, nvr nr ldrs: 2 yr Flat abs: plcd over hdles in 99/00 (2m, soft, rtd 104h, prob best without blnks/vis, M Pipe): rnr-up in '98 (mdn, rtd 96$ & 92) & '97 (mdn, rtd 88, J Dunlop): eff at 10/12f: acts on fast & soft/hvy. *1* **82**
4282 **SAGAPONACK 15** [14] 4-8-7 (73) O Urbina 20/1: 514005: Bhd, went past btn horses fnl 2f: op 14/1. *5* **65**
4160 **CHIEF CASHIER 25** [1] 5-8-11 (77) P Dobbs (5) 14/1: 146006: Prom, fdd 2f out: see 2552. *3½* **64**
4113 **CROWN LODGE 28** [15] 3-9-1 (86) J P Spencer 15/2: 215057: Nvr better than mid div: op 6/1, lngr trip. *¾* **72**
4206 **PIPSSALIO 21** [12] 3-8-8 (79) M Henry 7/2 FAV: 140148: Ran in snatches, nvr a factor: bckd from 9/2: had conditions in his favour, clry not his form: see 1528. *2½* **62**
*3997 **KOMISTAR 35** [6] 5-9-7 (87) P Robinson 8/1: 000319: Led till appr fnl 2f, sn lost place: suited by faster grnd: see 3997 (beat this wnr on firm grnd). *1* **69**
4282 **ADMIRALS PLACE 15** [5] 4-8-4 (69)(1ow) G Carter 10/1: 053220: Handy till appr fnl 2f: 10th. *¾* **51**
*4175 **CORK HARBOUR 24** [3] 4-8-9 (75) F Norton 14/1: 63-10: Mid div till wknd qckly 3f out: 11th, h'cap bow. *8* **46**
4061 **SOVEREIGNS COURT 31** [2] 7-8-7 (73) S Sanders 10/1: 301620: Al towards rear: 12th, see 4061, 1666. *4* **39**
3339 **IMPERIAL ROCKET 69** [8] 3-9-0 (85) J Fortune 12/1: 002200: Chsd ldrs till 4f out: 13th, 10 wk abs. *6* **44**
2471 **TURAATH 106** [16] 4-9-10 (90) R Studholme (3) 20/1: 1-0020: Cl up 5f: 14th, op 14/1, new stable. *dist* **0**
14 ran Time 2m 18.74 (15.94) (Mrs R M S Neave) C F Wall Newmarket, Suffolk

4474

5.00 VINEYARD AT STOCKCROSS MDN 3YO (D) 1m2f Soft/Heavy 128 -41 Slow
£5174 £1592 £796 £398

-- **MUBTAKER** [9] M P Tregoning 3-9-0 R Hills 4/1: 2-1: 3 ch c Silver Hawk - Gazayil (Irish River) Trkd ldrs, led on bit 2f out, sn settled matters, v easily: nicely bckd tho' op 5/2 on Brit bow: rnr-up for D Loder in France sole '99 start (mdn): eff at 10f, will get 12f: acts on gd, relishes soft/hvy, gall trk: runs well fresh. **100**
-- **PETERSHAM** [5] L M Cumani 3-9-0 J P Spencer 16/1: 2: 3 b c Petardia - Hayhurst (Sandhurst Prince) Early ldr & ev ch till easily outpcd by wnr appr fnl 1f: op 12/1 on debut, caught a tartar: by a sprinter/ miler out of a winning hdlr: prob stys 10f on soft/hvy: will not always meet one as useful, can win a mdn. *8* **88**
1692 **DEXTROUS 140** [6] H R A Cecil 3-9-0 T Quinn 11/8 FAV: -33: 3 gr c Machiavellian - Heavenly Cause (Grey Dawn II) Held up, prog to press ldrs 3f out, sn no extra: well bckd from 2/1, 5 month abs: unsuited by step up to 10f on testing grnd?: see 1692 (1m, fast). *9* **78**
3870 **ARDUINE 44** [8] J H M Gosden 3-8-9 J Fortune 8/1: 303304: Sn led, rdn 3f out, hdd & btn 2f out. *2½* **70**
2231 **POWERLINE 115** [13] 3-8-9 P Dobbs (5) 16/1: -06345: Chsd ldrs till ent straight: 4 mth abs, stiff task. *½* **69**
4040 **STORM WIZARD 33** [12] 3-9-0 S Drowne 20/1: 422006: Nvr nr ldrs: see 1193. *14* **58**

NEWBURY SATURDAY OCTOBER 21ST Lefthand, Flat, Galloping Track

4040 **POLAR STAR 33** [11] 3-9-0 S Sanders 16/1: -04507: Pulled hard & chsd ldrs till ent straight: op 12/1. *7* **49**
-- **MAVURA** [7] 3-8-9 R Perham 12/1: 8: Nvr in it, btn 4f out: tchd 16/1, stablemate wnr: Bering filly. *1½* **42**
4205 **ISLAND PRINCESS 21** [10] 3-8-9 P Robinson 14/1: -50409: Prom 5f: stiff task, see 4040, 1045. *2½* **39**
4274 **COUNTESS COLDUNELL 17** [4] 3-8-9 Pat Eddery 16/1: 60: Al bhd: 10th. *1¾* **37**
4205 **Poli Knight 21** [3] 3-8-9 M Hills 25/1: -- **I Bite** [2] 3-9-0 G Baker (5) 50/1:
12 ran Time 2m 19.66 (16.86) (Hamdan Al Maktoum) M P Tregoning Lambourn, Berks

YARMOUTH SUNDAY OCTOBER 22ND Lefthand, Flat, Fair Track

Official Going HEAVY. Stalls: Str Course - Stands Side; Rem - Inside.

4475 1.45 NOGDAM END FILLIES MDN DIV 1 2YO (D) 1m str Heavy 131 -38 Slow
£3233 £995 £497 £248

4158 **HEAVENLY WHISPER 26** [12] M L W Bell 2-8-11 M Fenton 13/2: 01: 2 b f Halling - Rock The Boat (Slip Anchor) Made all, prsd appr fnl 1f, rdn clr ins last: 55,000gns half sister to a decent German sprinter: eff arnd 1m, further will suit next term: acts on hvy grnd & a fair trk: lightly raced & can rate more highly in '01. **87**
4183 **RANIN 24** [6] E A L Dunlop 2-8-11 R Hills 11/4: 352: 2 b f Unfuwain - Nafhaat (Roberto) *2½* **82**
Dsptd lead, ev ch appr fnl 1f, sn hung right & no extra: bckd from 5/1: up in trip, stays 7f/1m, mid-dists shld suit next term: handles firm & hvy grnd: win a mdn: see 4183, 3748.
4216 **BYLAW 22** [2] J H M Gosden 2-8-11 J Fortune 12/1: 203: 2 b f Lear Fan - Byre Bird (Diesis) *1½* **80**
Chsd ldrs, rdn/onepace fnl 1f: improved at 1m: acts on fast & hvy: shld win a race: see 3359.
3752 **DEAR DAUGHTER 52** [4] Sir Michael Stoute 2-8-11 F Lynch 2/1 FAV: 34: Cl-up, eff when short of room appr fnl 1f, sn held: nicely bckd after 7 wk abs: up in trip: rated higher on fast grnd in 752. *½* **79**
4020 **ROSIE 36** [5] 2-8-11 D Harrison 12/1: 55: Towards rear, prog appr fnl 2f, onepcd fnl 1f: clr rem: poss stays 1m on hvy, mid-dist bred & will be seen to best effect next term: see 4020. *nk* **79**
-- **LATE SUMMER** [9] 2-8-11 T Quinn 4/1: 6: Prom, eff when hmpd appr fnl 1f, no ch after: mkt drifter on debut: Feb foal, half sister to a couple of useful 6/7f juv scorers, dam landed sole juv start: with H Cecil shld improve & may be seen to better effect on a sounder surface. *5* **71**
3962 **OUR EMILY 38** [10] 2-8-11 N Callan 40/1: 07: In tch, fdd appr fnl 1f: see 3962. *1½* **69**
4184 **SMASHING TIME 24** [8] 2-8-11 M Hills 11/1: 08: Handy, lost tch appr fnl 1f: op 8/1: see 4184. *½* **68**
3940 **OLYMPIC PRIDE 39** [1] 2-8-11 J Mackay (5) 50/1: 09: Prom, rdn/wknd qckly appr fnl 1f: 14,000 gns Up And At 'Em filly, dam a mdn: with C N Allen. *2½* **64**
-- **LADY INCH** [7] 2-8-11 Paul Eddery 33/1: 0: Very green, al towards rear, 10th: op 20/1: 3,700 gns Mar filly, dam won at 12f/2m, also over timber: shld apprec much further than this in time for B Smart. *1¾* **62**
4349 **BEZZA 9** [3] 2-8-11 S Sanders 50/1: 00: Al rear, 11th: stoutly bred. *shd* **62**
11 ran Time 1m 48.6 (13.5) (Dhg Partnership) M L W Bell Newmarket

4476 2.15 FAMILY FUNDAY HCAP 3YO+ 0-75 (E) 1m6f Heavy 131 -13 Slow [74]
£2905 £830 £415 3 yo rec 9 lb

*4006 **COCO LOCO 36** [2] J Pearce 3-8-6 (61) T Quinn 11/4 FAV: 650211: 3 b f Bin Ajwaad - Mainly Me (Huntingdale) Mid-div, gd hdwy to lead appr fnl 1f, rdn clr ins last: recent wnr at Catterick (1st win, h'cap): unplcd in a mdn sole '99 start (rtd 63): suited by 14f/2m: acts on gd, hvy & a sharp or easy trk: on the up-grade since stepped up to staying trips, could complete a hat-trick. **68**
4334 **PENALTA 11** [10] M Wigham 4-7-12 (44) J Quinn 13/2: 003102: 4 ch g Cosmonaut - Targuette (Targowice) V keen, led after 3f, hdd appr fnl 2f, ev ch until not pace of wnr ins last: op 5/1: gd run up in trip, eff at 12/14f on soft & hvy, handles fast: see 4176. *4* **47**
3994 **ENFILADE 36** [11] B Hanbury 4-9-13 (73)(t) R Hills 8/1: 016503: 4 b g Deploy - Bargouzine (Hotfoot) *4* **72**
Trkd ldr, rdn to lead appr fnl 2f, hdd over 1f out, fdd: not disgraced under top weight: likes Haydock.
4256 **BAHAMAS 19** [1] Sir Mark Prescott 3-9-3 (72)(bl) G Duffield 5/1: 110624: Cl-up, rdn/btn appr fnl 2f: drifted from 2/1 & prob not quite get home over 14f on hvy: btr 4256 (12f, soft). *4* **67**
4174 **ALZITA 25** [4] 3-7-10 (51)(1oh) J Mackay (5) 33/1: -03005: V keen towards rear, late hdwy but no threat to ldrs: big step up in trip & sell h'caps may suit over this dist: see 2024. *hd* **46**
1582 **COURT OF JUSTICE 145** [8] 4-9-8 (68) P Dobbs (5) 25/1: 0-506: Hdwy from rear halfway, lost tch appr fnl 2f: h'cap bow, 5 month abs: up in trip: just sharper for this: see 1582, 1054. *7* **55**
3914 **COLLINE DE FEU 41** [5] 3-8-7 (62) F Norton 33/1: 0407: Bhd, eff 3f out, wknd qckly fnl 2f: 6 wk abs, h'cap bow: big step up in trip: see 3914. *8* **39**
4222 **DAME FONTEYN 22** [6] 3-8-6 (61) M Fenton 9/1: 261308: Dwelt, rear, imprvd 3f out, wknd rapidly fnl 2f. *14* **23**
2856 **PRASLIN ISLAND 92** [7] 4-8-3 (49) N Callan 12/1: 1D5039: Sn rdn in tch, wknd qckly fnl 3f: long abs. *8* **0**
*4178 **FINAL LAP 24** [3] 4-8-8 (54) M Hills 7/1: 000010: Al twrds rear, t.o., 10th: up in trip, btr 4178 (gd). *20* **0**
3755 **ZINCALO 52** [9] 4-8-4 (50) P Robinson 25/1: 336000: Led early, wknd rapidly halfway, t.o. 11th. *dist* **0**
11 ran Time 3m 18.0 (20.2) (Mr & Mrs J Matthews) J Pearce Newmarket

4477 2.45 NOGDAM END FILLIES MDN DIV 2 2YO (D) 1m str Heavy 131 -05 Slow
£3233 £995 £497 £248

-- **AUTUMN RHYTHM** [3] H R A Cecil 2-8-11 (t) T Quinn 5/4 FAV: 1: 2 b f Hernando - Fextal (Alleged) Cl-up, imprvd over 1f out & sn led, rdn & rdly qcknd clr, cmftbly: nicely bckd on debut: Apr foal, half sister to 10f wnr Dynamism: sire top-class at mid-dists: eff arnd an easy 1m, mid-dists look sure to suit next term: runs well fresh on hvy grnd: wears a t-strap: op to plenty of improvement & shld be one to follow as a 3yo. **98+**
-- **PERFECT PIROUETTE** [1] M L W Bell 2-8-11 J Mackay (5) 25/1: 2: 2 b f Warning - Prancing Ballerina (Nijinsky) Dwelt & sn outpcd, rdn/styd on fnl 2f, no ch with impress wnr: 66,000 gns Apr foal, half sister to a wnr in Japan, dam scored in the US: stays an easy 1m on hvy: caught a tartar here & shld win races. *8* **81**
4309 **WESTERN EDGE 13** [11] J H M Gosden 2-8-11 J Fortune 25/1: 563: 2 b f Woodman - Star Pastures (Northfields) Prom, led briefly appr fnl 1f, no extra well ins last: imprvd in defeat: stays 1m on hvy, win a mdn. *½* **80**
4216 **STARRY LADY 22** [6] M R Channon 2-8-11 S Drowne 4/1: 24: Led, hdd appr fnl 1f, sn onepace: tchd 11/2, up in trip: rtd higher on debut in 4216 (7f, gd/soft). *nk* **80**
4183 **DRAGNET 24** [9] 2-8-11 F Lynch 3/1: 65: Unruly start, towards rear, imprvd over 3f out, no extra appr dist: tchd 4/1: up in trip/softer grnd: much btr on debut in 4183 (7f, gd). *5* **72**
-- **LAROUSSE** [10] 2-8-11 G Faulkner (3) 33/1: 6: Cl-up, rdn/no extra appr fnl 2f: Unfuwain Mar *¾* **71**

1st foal, dam useful in France: with S C Williams, will apprec 10f+ in time.
3910 **POLAR ROCK 41** [7] 2-8-11 M Fenton 25/1: 07: Rear, switched/eff appr fnl 1f, no impress: 6 wk abs. ¾ 70
-- **KARPASIANA** [2] 2-8-11 P Robinson 14/1: 8: Handy, wknd qckly appr fnl 1f: 75,000 gns Woodman ½ 69
filly, dam French 1m2f Listed wnr: with M A Jarvis, prob capable of imprvment.
-- **CRESSIDA** [4] 2-8-11 G Duffield 14/1: 9: Chsd ldrs, wknd fnl 3f: Feb foal, half sister to a 3½ 64
1m juv scorer: dam won over 7f as a 2yo: with Sir M Prescott, sharper for this.
-- **EMBRACE ME** [8] 2-8-11 G Carter 16/1: 0: V keen, al towards rear, 10th: Nashwan filly, half 8 52
sister to a French 1m wnr, dam scored over 7f as a juv: with E Dunlop.
4184 **Jennash 24** [5] 2-8-11 D Holland 40/1: -- **Astrolove** [12] 2-8-11 S Sanders 33/1:
12 ran Time 1m 46.0 (10.9) (Niarchos Family) H R A Cecil Newmarket

4478

3.15 GT YARMOUTH HCAP 3YO 0-85 (D) 1m str Heavy 131 00 Slow [90]
£3997 £1230 £615 £307 Winner, rnr-up & 7th raced centre trk.

4080 **JAWLA 31** [1] J H M Gosden 3-9-7 (83) J Fortune 7/1: 211051: 3 ch f Wolfhound - Majmu (Al Nasr) 94
Led centre group, led overall appr fnl 2f, hung right appr fnl 1f but sn clr, rdn out: earlier won at Catterick (fill auct mdn) & Doncaster (fills h'cap): well btn sole '99 start: eff at 7f, now suited by 1m & 10f could suit: acts on fast, likes hvy: can go well when fresh: excellent weight carrying run, shld follow up in similar grnd.
3854 **CATALONIA 46** [2] M L W Bell 3-8-4 (66) R Mullen 20/1: 5-W502: 3 ch f Catrail - Shakanda (Shernazar) 7 65
Dwelt, rear centre group, imprvd over 3f out, kept on but not pace of wnr: ran to near best after 6 wk abs: stays 7f/1m on soft & hvy grnd: see 3289.
*4274 **HINDAAM 18** [4] E A L Dunlop 3-9-0 (76) R Hills 1/1 FAV: 513: 3 b c Thunder Gulch - Party Cited *shd* 75
(Alleged) Prom stands side, hung left appr fnl 2f, rdn/btn over 1f out: clr rem: nicely bckd tho' op 4/5 & shade better expected on this h'cap bow: acts on soft & hvy: see 4274 (7.7f mdn, soft).
3793 **DESERT FURY 50** [6] B Hanbury 3-9-2 (78) W Ryan 14/1: 604654: Rear stands side, hung left/mod 4 71
late gains, no threat: 7 wk abs: rtd higher 3793 (fast grnd).
4121 **SPORTY MO 28** [7] 3-8-12 (74)(vis) N Callan 14/1: 131005: Led stands side, hdd appr fnl 2f, fdd: btr 894. *1* 65
4292 **TAKE MANHATTAN 16** [8] 3-8-7 (69) S Drowne 6/1: 664026: Prom, wknd fnl 2f: unproven on hvy grnd. *8* 50
4340 **TAKE FLITE 10** [3] 3-8-11 (73) Martin Dwyer 8/1: 031607: Handy centre, wknd/eased appr fnl 2f: op 7/1. *6* 46
2808} **SIOUX CHEF 460** [5] 3-8-10 (72) G Duffield 10/1: 41-8: Lost tch halfway, eased/t.o.: big step up *dist* 0
in trip on reapp/new stable: won 2nd of 2 '99 starts for M Channon, at Bath (auct fills mdn, rtd 78): sister to a high-class juv sprinter: eff around 5/7f on firm, bred to appr further in time: with J Osborne.
8 ran Time 1m 45.6 (10.5) (Hamdan Al Maktoum) J H M Gosden Manton, wilts

4479

3.50 SOMERTON MDN 2YO (D) 6f Heavy 131 -14 Slow
£4225 £1300 £650 £325

-- **SUAVE NATIVE** [4] A C Stewart 2-9-0 D Harrison 16/1: 1: 2 ch c Shuailaan - Courtly Courier (Raise A 96+
Native) Cl-up, led appr fnl 1f, pshd out, rdly: May foal, half brother to 2 wnrs in the States: dam unrcd: eff arnd 6f on hvy: runs well fresh on an easy trk: fine debut: win again, esp when sent over further.
-- **MATRON** [16] L M Cumani 2-8-9 G Sparkes (7) 12/1: 2: 2 b f Dr Devious - Matrona (Woodman) *2* 85
Towards rear, rdn/imprvd 2f out, styd on fnl 1f, no ch with wnr: 20,000 gns Mar first foal, dam unrcd: sire Derby wnr: eff at 6f, 7f+ will suit: acts on hvy: fine debut, will races, esp over further.
4209 **RED CARNATION 22** [17] M A Jarvis 2-8-9 P Robinson 11/8 FAV: 33: 2 b f Polar Falcon - Red *2* 80
Bouquet (Reference Point) Cl-up, hung left appr fnl 1f, no extra ins last: nicely bckd tho' op 10/11: handles fast & hvy: rtd higher on debut in 4209 (gd/firm grnd).
-- **HEADLAND** [5] J M P Eustace 2-9-0 J Tate 25/1: 4: Prom, rdn/fdd appr fnl 1f: 30,000gns Distant *4* 76
View colt, dam won in the States: may apprec 7f next time & shld improve.
3940 **ZOZARHARRY 39** [6] 2-9-0 G Carter 33/1: 005: Led, hdd appr fnl 1f, wknd: showed little on faster *1* 74
grnd prev, much imprvd in testing conds here, handles hvy: see 3215.
4209 **EMERALD PALM 22** [12] 2-8-9 D Holland 6/1: 66: Keen/rear, late gains: rtd higher 4209 (fast grnd). 2½ 64
4341 **PICO 10** [7] 2-8-9 T Quinn 9/1: 07: Keen/prom, wknd qckly appr fnl 1f: 38,000 gns Feb foal, half *hd* 64
sister to a couple of 2yo wnrs, dam scored over 5f: with C E Brittain.
4341 **SCOTTYS FUTURE 10** [15] 2-9-0 R Mullen 25/1: 08: Dwelt, al towards rear: Namaqualand colt. 1¾ 65
4283 **TONTO OREILLY 16** [2] 2-9-0 Paul Eddery 14/1: 09: Prom, wknd qckly appr fnl 1f: needs sells. 1¼ 62
4189 **SEARCH AND DESTROY 23** [9] 2-9-0 G Duffield 33/1: 000: Mid-div, fdd fnl 2f, 10th: see 4082. *1* 60
-- **LATENSAANI** [14] 2-9-0 F Norton 14/1: 0: Dwelt, al outpcd, 14th: 18,000 gns Shaamit colt. 0
-- **SHANNON FLYER** [11] 2-9-0 M Hills 6/1: 0: Bhd, eff over 3f out, sn lost tch, 15th: mid-dist bred. 0
4042 **Kentucky Bound 33** [10] 2-9-0 A McGlone 33/1: 4312 **Blue Pool 13** [3] 2-8-9 S Whitworth 25/1:
-- **Gompas Pal** [8] 2-9-0 N Callan 33/1:
15 ran Time 1m 19.1 (8.7) (Roy Clemons) A C Stewart Newmarket

4480

4.25 SEA PALLING HCAP 3YO+ 0-85 (D) 6f Heavy 131 +03 Fast [80]
£3981 £1225 £612 £306 3 yo rec 1 lb

4204 **BINTANG TIMOR 22** [16] W J Musson 6-8-10 (62) J Fortune 5/1: 000001: 6 ch g Mt Livermore - Frisky 66
Kitten (Isopach) Switched left leaving stalls, towards rear, gd hdwy appr fnl 1f, styd on strongly to lead fnl strides, drvn out: best time of day: '99 wnr at Newmarket (appr h'cap) & here at Yarmouth (h'cap, rtd 73 at best): '98 Leicester wnr (h'cap, rtd 72): suited by 6/7f on firm & hvy grnd: acts on a stiff/gall or easy trk, likes Yarmouth: best held up for a late run: took advantage of a handy mark today.
2961 **BREVITY 86** [9] E J O'Neill 5-8-0 (52) J Quinn 25/1: -00002: 5 b g Tenby - Rive (Riverman) *hd* 55
V keen, led, hdd dist, rallied to lead again fnl 50yds, hdd fnl strides: gd run for new stable after a long abs, prev with D Sasse: acts on firm & hvy grnd: returning to a wng mark: see 1953.
4432 **KHALIK 3** [5] Miss Gay Kelleway 6-9-2 (68)(tbl) S Whitworth 9/2 FAV: 400363: 6 b g Lear Fan - Silver ¾ 70
Dollar (Shirley Heights) Cl-up, led 1f out, hdd fnl 50yds, sn held: qck reapp: see 4432, 1092.
4185 **BUDELLI 24** [11] M R Channon 3-9-13 (80) S Drowne 7/1: 502004: Prom, sltly outpcd 2f out, late 1½ 79
hdwy, no ch with ldrs: prob best when dominating: see 1399 (mdn, gd grnd).
4425 **SHINING STAR 3** [7] 3-8-6 (59) S W Kelly (3) 9/1: 504305: Prom, rdn/grad wknd ins last: qck reapp. 1½ 55
4037 **CHIQUITA 34** [3] 3-9-13 (80) P Dobbs (5) 7/1: 002106: Late gains from rear, no dngr: btr 3698 (gd). *hd* 76
4185 **BOANERGES 24** [6] 3-9-11 (78) D Holland 7/1: 060407: Held up, imprvd over 2f out, fdd fnl 1f: see 4185. ¾ 72
2899 **SURVEYOR 89** [4] 5-9-2 (68) Martin Dwyer 14/1: -00008: Nvr a factor after 3 month abs: see 1851. 2½ 57
4207 **POWER PACKED 22** [12] 3-9-11 (78)(BL) P Robinson 16/1: -56009: V keen towards rear, lost tch fnl 2½ 62
2f: rcd far to freely in 1st time blnks, unproven at 6f: see 1847.

YARMOUTH SUNDAY OCTOBER 22ND Lefthand, Flat, Fair Track

4301 **IVORY DAWN 15** [14] 6-9-11 (77) C Carver (3) 12/1: 020000: Nvr dangerous, fin 10th: unproven on hvy. *2* **57**
4215 **LOCHARATI 22** [10] 3-9-9 (76) J Tate 14/1: 200000: Led, hdd over 1f out, wknd qckly, 11th. *½* **55**
4357 **Temeraire 8** [13] 5-10-0 (80) G Duffield 16/1: 4357 **Ravishing 8** [15] 3-9-5 (72) M Hills 16/1:
13 ran Time 1m 18.1 (7.7) (Goodey & Broughton) W J Musson Newmarket

4481 **5.00 COME RACING MDN 3YO+ (D) 1m3f101y Heavy 131 00 Slow**
£3094 £952 £476 £238 3 yo rec 6 lb

4392 **EASY TO LOVE 5** [12] H R A Cecil 4-9-1 T Quinn 2/1 FAV: 5-3041: 4 b f Diesis - La Sky (Law Society) **82**
Cl-up, short of room & swtchd appr fnl 1f, led dist, rdn clr: tchd 11/4, qck reapp: unplcd sole '99 start (mdn, rtd 83): eff at 10f, apprec this step up to 11/5f & further could suit: acts on fast, improved on hvy.
1428 **YOUHADYOURWARNING 153** [11] E A L Dunlop 3-8-9 G Carter 7/2: 3-32: 3 b f Warning - Youm Jadeed *4* **75**
(Sadler's Wells) Mid-div, rdn/imprvd appr fnl 1f, kept on but not pace of wnr: 3 month abs, new stable: prev with S Bin Suroor: up in trip & stys 11.5f well: handles hvy & just sharper for this: see 1428.
4119 **MACHRIE BAY 28** [3] J L Dunlop 3-9-0 S Sanders 5/1: -32523: 3 b c Emarati - Fleeting Rainbow *¾* **79**
(Rainbow Quest) Prom, eff/no room 2f out, styd on but no ch with wnr: clr rem: consistent, see 4119.
4275 **CARRIE CAN CAN 17** [7] J G Given 3-8-9 G Baker (5) 20/1: 653054: Towards rear, imprvd appr fnl 3f, *3½* **69$**
hung left/no extra appr fnl 1f: up in trip & seemingly imprvd but prob flattered (offic only 59): see 4275, 3116.
4141 **BROKEN SPECTRE 27** [5] 3-8-9 J Fortune 14/1: 05: Towards rear, eff & sltly hmpd over 3f out, *1½* **67**
switched & mod late gains, no danger: op 10/1, up in trip: see 4141 (10f mdn).
3586 **FIRST IMPRESSION 59** [1] 5-9-6 P Doe 10/1: -20206: Led, drvn/hdd appr fnl 1f, wknd: 8 wk abs *shd* **72**
& poss just sharper for this when returning to h'cap company: see 3353, 2263.
4040 **PRIDE OF INDIA 34** [6] 3-9-0 D Harrison 25/1: 0-07: Mod late gains, nvr dangerous: mod prev form. *2½* **68**
-- **JEDEYDD** [13] 3-9-0 W Ryan 11/2: 8: Cl-up, went on appr fnl 1f, sn hdd, wknd qckly: Shareef *1½* **65**
Dancer gldg, with B Hanbury: showed up well for a long way here, sharper for this debut.
3626 **WODHILL FOLLY 57** [4] 3-8-9 J Quinn 20/1: 69: Nvr a factor after 8 wk abs: up in trip: see 3626. *¾* **59**
1509 **JOEY TRIBBIANI 149** [2] 3-9-0 Martin Dwyer 50/1: 4-0000: Rear, eff/no room 3f out, sn btn: 10th: abs. *7* **54**
4285} **WESTERN RIDGE 379** [9] 3-9-0 S W Kelly (3) 15/2: 45-0: Nvr dangerous, no room/wknd qckly 2f out, **0**
12th: op 5/1 on reapp: up in trip: ran twice in '99, fin 4th & 5th in List company (rtd 91 at best): half brother to a useful 9f wnr: handles fast & bred to apprec 1m+: capable of better.
4374 **Caunton 6** [10] 3-8-9 F Norton 50/1: 1199 **Waseyla 167** [8] 3-8-9 R Mullen 33/1:
13 ran Time 2m 37.9 (15.1) (Lordship Stud) H R A Cecil Newmarket

LINGFIELD (Mixed) MONDAY OCTOBER 23RD Lefthand, Sharp, Undulating Track

Official Going Turf - HEAVY, AW - STANDARD. Stalls: Turf - Stands Side, AW - Inside.

4482 **2.20 LEISURE CLUB HCAP 3YO 0-70 (E) 1m2f aw Going 29 -01 Slow [77]**
£2940 £840 £420

4291 **FAIR LADY 17** [3] B W Hills 3-9-6 (69) W Ryan 11/4 FAV: 304201: 3 b f Machiavellian - Just Cause **75a**
(Law Society) Chsd ldrs, hdwy when no room 2f out, switched & qcknd to lead dist, styd on strongly under hands-&-heels riding: earlier scored at W'hampton (mdn), subs rnr-up on turf (rtd 78): rtd 80 in '99 (rnr-up, mdn): eff at 1m/11f on firm, soft & both AWs: likes a sharp trk, prob handles any: runs well fresh: looks on a fair mark.
*3970 **SNATCH 39** [1] M L W Bell 3-7-10 (45) J Mackay (5) 9/2: 640012: 3 b f Elmaamul - Tarkhana (Dancing *1¾* **47a**
Brave) Keen, rear, hdwy/chsd ldrs 2f out, chsd wnr ins last, kept on: op 3/1: AW bow: acts on fast & equitrack.
4330 **SASH 12** [4] S Dow 3-8-1 (50) A Nicholls 8/1: 050003: 3 b f Sabrehill - Lady Nash (Nashwan) *3½* **47a**
Dwelt, keen/held up, kept on fnl 3f, no threat to front pair: eff at 9/10f, 12f may suit: handles firm & equitrack.
4248 **CORUSCATING 20** [12] Sir Mark Prescott 3-9-0 (63) G Duffield 7/1: 041004: Chsd ldrs 9f: op 5/1. *2½* **56a**
3310 **MONKEY BUSINESS 72** [10] 3-9-0 (63) D Harrison 9/1: -06005: Led after 2f till 4f out, fdd fnl 1f: abs. *2* **53a**
3944 **SEEKING UTOPIA 40** [14] 3-8-9 (58) R Mullen 20/1: P03306: In tch wide, rdn/btn over 2f out: abs. *4* **42a**
4294 **MAGIC EAGLE 17** [11] 3-7-11 (46) J Quinn 14/1: 000007: Led over 4f out, drvn/hdd over 1f out, fdd. *nk* **29a**
4360 **BAILEYS ON LINE 9** [6] 3-8-2 (51) R Ffrench 10/1: 002308: Trkd ldrs, btn 3f out: btr 2920, 2425 (turf). *hd* **33a**
3907 **AMRITSAR 44** [8] 3-9-7 (70) Paul Eddery 10/1: 323369: Led 2f, prom 7f: abs, AW bow: btr 2175. *1* **51a**
4102 **INNKEEPER 31** [9] 3-8-13 (62) D Holland 14/1: 066400: Slowly away, wide, al rear: 10th: AW bow. *3* **39a**
2362 **Quids Inn 112** [2] 3-7-12 (47) M Henry 20/1: 4306 **Count On Thunder 14** [13] 3-7-10 (45)(5oh) G Baker (5) 20/1:
4174 **Culminate 26** [5] 3-7-10 (45)(3oh) A Polli (2) 33/1:
13 ran Time 2m 05.80 (3.0) (Maktoum Al Maktoum) B W Hills Lambourn, Berks.

4483 **2.50 WILLOW MDN 2YO (D) 7f str Soft 119 -01 Slow**
£3549 £1092 £546 £273 Raced centre - stands side

-- **ASIAN HEIGHTS** [17] G Wragg 2-8-11 D Holland 13/2: 1: 2 b c Hernando - Miss Rinjani (Shirley **86+**
Heights) Sn handy, chall fnl 2f, narrowly asserted ins last, pushed out cl home: tchd 10/1: Mar foal, half-brother to useful 10f wnr St Expedit: dam a 7f juv wnr, sire top-class at 12f: eff at 7f, 1m+ will suit: acts on soft grnd & a sharp/undul trk: runs well fresh: well regarded, potentially useful mid-dist prospect, shld rate more highly.
3940 **WANNABE AROUND 40** [14] T G Mills 2-8-11 T Williams 7/1: 632: 2 b c Primo Dominie - Noble *½* **84**
Peregrine (Lomond) Led after 2f, duelled with wnr fnl 2f, just hdd ins lat, kept on well: well clr of rem, op 5/1, 6 wk abs: acts on firm & soft grnd: now quals for h'caps, shown enough to find a race.
4063 **UNSIGNED 33** [18] J R Fanshawe 2-8-11 D Harrison 7/4 FAV: 043: 2 b c Cozzene - Striata (Gone West) *16* **62**
Prom, rdn/outpcd by front pair from over 2f out: hvly bckd from 3/1: rtd higher 4063, 3799.
-- **SILVAANI** [8] Miss Gay Kelleway 2-8-11 J Quinn 25/1: 4: Led 2f, remained prom 5f: April foal, *1¾* **60**
cost IR 25,000gns: dam a US mdn: sire a smart performer at 7f/1m: showed gd speed & faster grnd shld suit.
4188 **DOWNPOUR 24** [16] 2-8-11 G Duffield 33/1: 005: Mid-div, no impress fnl 3f: h'cap comapny will suit. *1½* **58**
4184 **HARLEQUIN 25** [13] 2-8-11 F Lynch 9/4: 06: Mid-div, mod late gains, no threat: hvly bckd, tchd 7/2. *½* **57**
1573 **MOON MASTER 146** [2] 2-8-11 J P Spencer 16/1: 47: Rear, mod gains fnl 2f: abs: btr 1573 (6f, g/f). *1¼* **55**
4415 **BRIEF CONTACT 4** [9] 2-8-11 J Fanning 33/1: 008: Chsd ldrs to halfway: qck reapp: see 4189 (6f). *7* **45**
-- **MEDRAAR** [7] 2-8-11 G Carter 14/1: 9: Hmpd start, sn chsd ldrs mid-div, no ch fnl 3f: op 8/1: *hd* **44**
jockey reported colt was hanging thro'out: Mar first foal: dam a 1m wnr: with J Dunlop & worth another chance.
4183 **CAQUI DOR 25** [3] 2-8-11 Paul Eddery 20/1: -000: Hmpd start, al towards rear: 10th, op 14/1: *1¼* **42**
likely to apprec 1m+ & h'cap company for J Dunlop next term.

-- **SOARING PHOENIX** [6] 2-8-11 S Sanders 12/1: 0: Al rear: 11th: St Jovite colt, Jan foal: dam a   ½ 41
7f juv wnr: likely to appre 1m+ in time for B W Hills.
4389 **PRINCE ALBERT** 6 [12] 2-8-11 S Whitworth 33/1: 60: Al towards rear: 12th: qck reapp: see 4389.   hd 40
4345 **DARK SOCIETY** 10 [5] 2-8-11 B Marcus 16/1: 400: Went left start, in tch 4f: 13th: btr 4345, 4083 (6f).   ½ 39
-- **ADJAWAR** [15] 2-8-11 W Ryan 12/1: 0: Al rear: 14th: mkt drifter, op 6/1: Ashkalani colt, Feb foal: 3½ 34
half-brother to wnrs btwn 1m/11f abroad: dam a 1m wnr: improve over further in time for Sir Michael Stoute.
-- **Lanoso** [10] 2-8-11 L Newman (3) 33/1:   4140 **The Doctor** 28 [1] 2-8-11 D Sweeney 33/1:
-- **Variegation** [11] 2-8-11 R Mullen 25/1:   4349 **Firewire** 10 [4] 2-8-11 P Doe 33/1:
18 ran   Time 1m 28.8 (8.4) Flag Start   (J L C Pearce)   G Wragg Newmarket.

4484   **3.20 CEDAR FILLIES MDN 2YO (D)**   **7f str**   **Soft 119**   **-51 Slow**
             £3510   £1080   £540   £270

-- **NEVER END** [7] B W Hills 2-8-11 W Ryan 11/2: 1: 2 b f Alzao - Eternal (Kris)   83
Chsd ldr, led appr fnl 1f, rdn out: slow time: half-sister to wnrs up to 12f: eff at 7f on soft, 1m+ will suit.
-- **GOLDEN SPARROW** [14] J L Dunlop 2-8-11 Paul Eddery 14/1: 2: 2 ch f Elmaamul - Moon Spin (Night   1¾ 80
Shift) In tch, shkn up halfway, kept on to go 2nd ins last but unable to chall: 5,000gns half-sister to decent styr
Rosa Canina & a 1m wnr: dam 1m/12f wnr: eff at 7f but bred to apprec 10f+: handles soft grnd: find similar.
3980 **CELTIC MISS** 38 [12] J L Dunlop 2-8-11 G Carter 6/1: -03: 2 b f Celtic Swing - Regent Miss (Vice   2½ 76
Regent) Chsd ldrs, rdn ent fnl 2f, onepace ins last: tchd 10/1, stablemate 2nd: imprvd on soft, bred for mid-dists.
-- **MOREOVER** [11] Sir Mark Prescott 2-8-11 G Duffield 6/1: 4: Handy till no extra fnl 1f: Caerleon   2 73
sister to smart 1m/12f wnr Overbury: dam 1m juv wnr: decent pedigree, shld do better over 10f+ next term.
-- **KARMINIYA** [5] 2-8-11 F Lynch 11/4 FAV: 5: In tch, niggled halfway, nvr any impress on ldrs: 1¼ 71
drifter from 6/4: Primo Dominie filly, dam useful up to 11f: with Sir M Stoute, may do better on faster grnd.
-- **REMARKABLE** [9] 2-8-11 D Holland 4/1: 6: Al mid-div: tchd 5/1: half-sister to top-class juv wnr   ½ 70
First Trump: dam styd 12f, from a gd family: with G Wragg & worth another chance on faster grnd.
4183 **LOOSE CHIPPINS** 25 [6] 2-8-11 S Whitworth 33/1: 07: Bhd, moderate late hdwy: half-sister to sev wnrs.   1 69
-- **AMACITA** [10] 2-8-11 S Drowne 33/1: 8: Dwelt, nvr nr ldrs: 2,500gns half-sister to a 1m/10f wnr.   ½ 68
-- **GABI** [8] 2-8-11 P Doe 33/1: 9: Sn in a 3L lead, no extra ent fnl 2f & sn hdd, btn: Gabitat sister   7 58
to 7f/10f wnr Multi Franchise, dam & sire sprinters: with B Gubby.
-- **SNAKE GODDESS** [4] 2-8-11 J Fanning 33/1: 0: Nvr in it: 10th: 10,000gns Primo Dominie first foal.   4 52
3388 **Formal Party** 68 [2] 2-8-11 C Rutter 12/1:   -- **Lara Falana** [3] 2-8-11 (t) J P Spencer 14/1:
-- **Its Your Bid** [13] 2-8-11 A Clark 25/1:   4209 **Summer Key** 23 [1] 2-8-11 S Sanders 50/1:
14 ran   Time 1m 32.30 (11.9)   (K Abdulla)   B W Hills Lambourn, Berks.

4485   **3.50 ARENA LEISURE COND STKS 2YO (D)**   **5f**   **Soft 119**   **+01 Fast**
             £3474   £1069   £534   £267

+4367 **CLARION** 7 [1] Sir Mark Prescott 2-9-2 G Duffield 10/11 FAV: 213111: 2 ch c First Trump - Area Girl   90
(Jareer) Trkd ldrs, shkn up 2f out, rdn & edged left bef dist, sn led, drvn out nr fin: well bckd, fair time,
qck reapp: earlier won at Yarmouth (mdn), Sandown (nursery), W'hampton (clmr) & Southwell (nurs, rtd 92a):
acts on firm, soft grnd & fibresand: can carry big weights: v tough & progressive & well placed.
4179 **MILLYS LASS** 25 [4] M R Channon 2-8-6 S Drowne 7/2: 302502: 2 b f Mind Games - Millie's Lady   ½ 77
(Common Grounds) Chsd ldrs, switched & hdwy to chase wnr ins last, kept on but held: not btn far, tchd 11/4:
ran to beat at the weights: well worth another try at 6f: see 1176.
4305 **BARON CROCODILE** 14 [3] A Berry 2-8-11 C Lowther 10/1: 402103: 2 b g Puissance - Glow Again   1½ 78
(The Brianstan) Led till appr fnl 1f, onepace under press: prob ran to beat at the weights: see 4096.
3862 **DOUBLE FANTASY** 47 [5] B Smart 2-8-11 Paul Eddery 3/1: 06104: 2 b g Clup & ev ch till no extra fnl 1f: ¾ 77
well bckd, tchd 4/1, 7 wk abs: poss handles soft, btr 3621 (firm).
3418 **BARBERELLO** 67 [2] 2-8-6 R Havlin 25/1: 05: Dwelt, in tch, left bhd appr fnl 1f: stiff task, 10 wk abs.   13 52
5 ran   Time 1m 02.7 (5.9)   (Neil Greig)   Sir Mark Prescott Newmarket.

4486   **4.20 CARVERY HCAP 3YO+ 0-70 (E)**   **1m4f aw**   **Going 29**   **-02 Slow**   [64]
             £2884   £824   £412   3 yo rec 7 lb

4208 **FIFE AND DRUM** 23 [11] J Akehurst 3-9-0 (57) S Sanders 14/1: 001001: 3 b g Rahy - Fife (Lomond)   63a
Nvr far away, went on 3f out, clr 1f out, drvn ins last: wng AW bow: prev won at Nottingham (mdn h'cap, rtd 58, 1st
time blnks): unplcd juv (rtd 69): eff at 10/12f: acts on gd grnd & equitrack, sharp or gall trks, with/without blnks.
3858 **FUSUL** 47 [10] G L Moore 4-9-13 (63)(t) I Mongan (5) 11/2: 302502: 4 ch g Miswaki - Silent Turn   1¾ 66a
(Silent Cal) Clup, rdn 5f out, onepace till kept on appr fnl 1f: 7 wk abs, t-strap: gd run, see 835, 441 (C/D).
1934 **TWICE** 130 [8] G L Moore 4-9-3 (53)(t) D Holland 20/1: 0-0053: 4 b g Rainbow Quest - Bolas (Unfuwain)   ¾ 55a
Wide, rear, struggling halfway, rallied 2f out & ran on strongly ins last, nvr nrr: stablemate 2nd, AW bow, 4
month abs: eff at 12f on equitrack & likely to get further on this evidence: at right end of h'cap.
4248 **COMPATRIOT** 20 [12] P S Felgate 4-9-1 (61) G Duffield 16/1: 361064: In tch wide, rdn 4f out, nvr   3½ 58a
pace to chall: worth another try over this 12f trip: acts on firm, soft & fibresand, prob equitrack: see 3769.
4186 **TAJAR** 24 [17] 8-8-7 (43) S Whitworth 7/1: 030025: In tch, prog to chase ldrs 3f out, sn onepace: 1 39a
tchd 12/1: flattered in non h'cap company last time, see 4186, 2109.
3753 **BROWNING** 53 [1] 5-10-0 (64) D Harrison 4/1: 00-206: Led till 3f out, fdd appr fnl 1f: nicely bckd.   1¾ 58a
3915 **ORDAINED** 42 [9] 7-7-11 (33) J Quinn 16/1: 260067: Nvr better than mid-div: op 12/1, 6 wk abs.   11 15a
*4443 **LUNA FLIGHT** 3 [13] 3-8-8 (51)(6ex) J Fanning 11/4 FAV: -55618: Nvr troubled ldrs: poss better on   nk 32a
fibresand tho' this may have come too soon after Friday's win in 4443 (mdn h'cap).
4245 **ABLE NATIVE** 20 [4] 3-9-5 (62) R Price 11/1: 004069: Chsd ldrs, lost pl 3f out, eased: btr 2217 (C/D).   ½ 42a
3917 **SLIEVE BLOOM** 41 [5] 3-8-6 (49) L Carter 14/1: 050030: Bhd from halfway: 10th, 6 wk abs, see 3917.   3½ 24a
4329 **DANDES RAMBO** 12 [7] 4-8-3 (46)(BL) P Doe 14/1: 042650: Chsd ldrs till after halfway: 11th, blnkd.   A 20a
3858 **TULSA** 47 [6] 6-8-2 (38)(bl) P Bradley 25 10/1: 552000: Wide, nvr in it: 13th, op 16/1, jumps rnr since 3858.   0a
*4391 **THOMAS HENRY** 6 [16] 4-8-6 (42)(6ex) N Farmer (7) 8/1: 463510: Well plcd till 4f out: 14th, tchd 10/1,   0a
qck reapp with a penalty after 4391 (soft).
4291 **Fifth Edition** 17 [15] 4-8-10 (46) R Mullen 20/1:   3735 **Forest Dream** 54 [2] 5-8-1 (37) J Tate 20/1:
4363 **Castlebridge** 9 [3] 3-8-12 (55)(vis) G Baker (5) 33/1:   4331 **Grand Musica** 12 [14] 7-8-6 (42)(bl) R Brisland(5) 40/1:
17 ran   Time 2m 32.91 (3.71)   (Last Order's Partnership)   J Akehurst Epsom, Surrey.

LINGFIELD (Mixed)   MONDAY OCTOBER 23RD   Lefthand, Sharp, Undulating Track

4487   4.50 BY TRAIN CLASS STKS 3YO+ 0-65 (E)   7f aw rnd   Going 29   +03 Fast
£2968   £848   £424   3 yo rec 2 lb

4330 **PENGAMON** 12 [2] M Wigham 8-9-0 J Stack 7/4 FAV: 021241: 8 gr g Efisio - Dolly Bevan (Another | | 65a
Realm) Well plcd, led bef fnl 1f, rdn clr, pshd out cl-home: nicely bckd, fair time: earlier won at Doncaster
(h'cap): '99 wnr here at Lingfield (h'cap, rtd 57a, D Thom): missed '98, '97 wnr again at Lingfield (h'cap, rtd
77a & 76): eff at 7f/1m: acts on fast, gd/soft grnd, equitrack/Lingfield specialist: has a decent turn of foot.
4294 **KAYO GEE** 17 [3] L Montague Hall 4-8-11 (bl) N Callan 25/1: 000002: 4 b f Komaite - Darling Miss | 1¼ | 57a
Daisy (Tina's Pet) Outpcd & carr head high, hard rdn 2f out, strong burst fnl 1f, nrst fin: gd run at the
weights, blnks reapplied: eff at 5f, clrly gets a sharp 7f: suited by equitrack, handles soft, see 1543, 146.
*4368 **STAND BY** 7 [5] B A Pearce 3-8-11 G Baker (5) 6/1: 330013: 3 b f Missed Flight - Ma Rivale | 1¾ | 56a
(Last Tycoon) Dwelt, in tch, chsd ldrs ent straight, styd on for 3rd but no impression: qck reapp: acts on
fibresand, handles equitrack: stays 7f, poss just best at 6f: see 4368.
4066 **BUTRINTO** 33 [8] B R Johnson 6-9-0 I Mongan (5) 6/1: 322054: In tch, hdwy 2f out, sn rdn & onepace. | ½ | 56a
4331 **SUPERCHIEF** 12 [9] 5-9-0 (tbl) S Carson (3) 14/1: 000235: Pressed ldr & ev ch till fdd appr fnl 1f. | 2½ | 51a
107 **VASARI** 334 [1] 6-9-0 R Mullen (5): 0060-6: Chsd ldrs till ent fnl 2f: plcd on sand & turf in early | 2 | 47a
'99 for W Musson (h'caps, rtd 67a & 70): rtd 75 for M Channon in '98, sole win in '96 at Chester (mdn, rtd 100):
eff at 6/7f: acts on firm & soft grnd, without blnks: now with J Poulton.
4328 **ANNIE APPLE** 12 [13] 4-8-13 D Harrison 10/1: 014237: Nvr better than mid-div: bckd: flattered 4328. | nk | 45a
*4331 **TALARIA** 12 [7] 4-9-1 S Drowne 100/30: 056118: Set gd clip till hdd appr fnl 1f, wknd qckly: | nk | 46a
nicely bckd, new stable: much btr 4331 (clmr, uncontested lead).
4160 **SOUTH SEA PEARL** 27 [4] 3-8-9 D Holland 7/1: 223609: Prom till ran wide 2f out: op 5/1 on AW bow: | 2 | 38a
big drop in trip, stays 12f: see 3416, 3185.
3769 **SPOT** 51 [10] 3-8-9 S Whitworth 16/1: 034000: In tch till halfway: 10th, 7 wk abs: btr 2604 (6f, f/sand). | 6 | 28a
3045 **Shannons Dream** 84 [6] 4-8-11 J Mackay (5) 66/1:   3235} **Millionformerthyr** 441 [12] 4-8-11 A Nicholls 66/1:
*4255 **Betty Bathwick** 20 [14] 3-8-11 G Duffield 14/1:   4143 **Inviramental** 28 [15] 4-9-0 S Sanders 33/1:
14 ran   Time 1m 24.65 (1.85)   (Miss Arabella Smallman)   M Wigham Newmarket.

DEAUVILLE   WEDNESDAY OCTOBER 18TH   Righthand, Galloping Track

Official Going   HEAVY

4488   1.25 LISTED PRIX ZEDDAAN 2YO   6f   Heavy
£13449   £4611   £3458

-- **SIGN OF NIKE** [1] D Richardson 2-9-2 Stephen Davies : -1: 2 b c Mistertopogigo - Infanta Maria | | 102
(King Of Spain) -:
4210 **NASMATT** 18 [4] M R Channon 2-8-8 C Asmussen : -33142: 2 b f Danehill - Society Lady (Mr Prospector) snk | | 93
Keen/cl-up, chall ldr apr fnl 1f, hdd ins last, rallied cl-home, not btn far: ran to best: acts on firm & hvy.
-- **BROWNISE** [3] France 2-8-8 O Peslier : 3: 2 b f Tabasco Cat - Life At The Top (Habitat) | 3 | 86
5 ran   Time 1m 16.6   (Stall Silvester)   D Richardson Germany

---

LONGCHAMP   THURSDAY OCTOBER 19TH   Righthand, Stiff, Galloping Track

Official Going   HEAVY

4489   2.05 LISTED PRIX CASIMIR 3YO FILLIES   1m1f   Heavy
£13449   £4611   £3458

-- **TERRE VIERGE** [4] E Lellouche 3-9-0 A Junk : 1: 3 b f Common Grounds - Divine Madness (Carwhite) | | 92
4197 **MUSCHANA** 20 [11] J L Dunlop 3-9-0 D Bonilla : 103152: 3 ch f Deploy - Youthful (Green Dancer) | 1 | 90
Led, strongly pressed well ins last, hdd fnl 50y: gd run upped in grade: acts on fast & hvy: see 3425 (h'cap).
4113 **GRANTED** 26 [7] M L W Bell 3-9-0 F Sanchez : 432103: 3 b f Cadeaux Genereux - Germane (Distant | hd | 90
Relative) Dwelt, sn prom, drvn over 1f out, held well ins last: ran to best, acts on fast & hvy grnd: see 3793.
11 ran   Time 1m 58.6   (Ecurie Ferdane)   E Lellouche France

---

BORDEAUX   FRIDAY OCTOBER 20TH   -

Official Going   VERY SOFT

4490   2.20 GR 3 PRIX ANDRE BABION 3YO+   1m1f110y   Soft
£21134   £7685   £3842   3 yo rec 4 lb

4064 **RIGHT WING** 30 [10] J L Dunlop 6-9-0 (bl) G Mosse : 221321: 6 b h In The Wings - Nekhbet (Artaius) | | 114
Held up, rdn/imprvd appr fnl 2f, strong run to lead ins last, pshd out: earlier won Listed races at Kempton
& York, also plcd numerous times: '99 wnr at Doncaster (reapp, Lincoln h'cap, rtd 107) & Nottingham (stks):
'98 wnr again at Doncaster (rtd h'cap, rtd 102): suited by coming as late as poss over 1m/10f on any grnd,
likes an easy surface: acts on any trk, likes Doncaster: eff in blnks/visor & runs well fresh: v tough & smart.
-- **ABOU SAFIAN** [11] Mlle V Dissaux 4-8-10 A Junk : -15612: 4 ch c Bluebird - Kind Of Cute (Prince | 2 | 104
Sabo) In tch, imprvd over 1f out, styd on, no ch with wnr: recent Longchamp h'cap wnr: eff at 9.5f on hvy.
-- **CUT QUARTZ** [3] R Gibson 3-8-7 (bl) O Peslier : 631413: 3 b c Johann Quatz - Cutlass (Sure Blade) | snk | 105
Front rank, went on 2f out, hdd ins last, no extra: dual wnr prev this term: eff blnkd over 9.5f on hvy grnd.
11 ran   Time 2m 01.2   (The Earl Cadogan)   J L Dunlop Arundel, W Sussex

SAINT-CLOUD   SATURDAY OCTOBER 21ST   Lefthand, Galloping Track

Official Going   HEAVY

4491   **2.55 LISTED PRIX LE FABULEUX 3YO   1m2f   Heavy**
£13449   £3458   £2305

4347 **INGLENOOK 8** [1] J L Dunlop 3-9-2 O Peslier : 110441: 3 b c Cadeaux Genereux - Spring (Sadler's   **111**
Wells) Cl-up, swtchd to chall over 1f out, sn led, idled ins last, drvn out to hold on: earlier won at Kempton
(2, mdn & List): eff at 1m/10f: acts on fast, likes gd/soft & hvy grnd: acts on a gall or flat/easy trk:
useful colt, back to best today with conditions in his favour.
945   **CAZOULIAS 190** [2] Mme N Rossio 3-8-11 G Mosse : 32: 3 b g Rasi Brasak - Cazouls (Gairloch)   snk   105
--   **MIRIO** [5] France 3-8-11 T Jarnet : 3: 3 ch c Priolo - Mira Monte (Baillamont)   ¾   103
9 ran   Time 2m 16.0   (Seymour Cohn)   J L Dunlop Arundel, W Sussex

SAN SIRO   SUNDAY OCTOBER 22ND   Righthand, Stiff, Galloping Track

Official Going   HEAVY

4492   **2.00 GR 1 GRAN CRITERIUM 2YO   1m   Heavy**
£62705   £29949   £18657   £9332

4296 **COUNT DUBOIS 15** [6] W J Haggas 2-8-11 B Marcus : -12331: 2 b c Zafonic - Madame Dubois (Legend   **112**
Of France) Trkd ldrs, led 2f out, styd on strongly, drvn out: recent 7L 3rd to high-class juv Nayef (1st time
blnks): earlier won at Haydock (debut, mdn) & subs tried visor: half-brother to 3 wnrs at up to 12f, dam useful
stayer: eff at 7f/1m, 10f+ lks sure to suit next term: acts on gd/soft, likes hvy & a stiff/gall trk: eff in
blnks/visor, career best run today without: v smart, can win more Gr races as a 3yo.
4320 **KINGS COUNTY 14** [7] A P O'Brien 2-8-11 M J Kinane : -1222: 2 b c Fairy King - Kardelle (Kalaglow)   nk   111
Waited with, drvn/imprvd 2f out, ev ch when hung in bhd wnr ent fnl 1f, styd on & not btn far: much better
expected but poss not totally happy in these v testing conds: rtd higher & a v smart eff in 4320 (soft).
*3787 **SPETTRO 50** [4] P F I Cole 2-8-11 L Dettori : 51113: 2 b c Spectrum - Overruled (Last Tycoon)   ½   110
Led, hdd 2f out, rdn & rall well ins last: 7 wk abs: winning run ended but produced a career best performance
here: acts on fast, likes gd/soft & hvy grnd: win more races next term when upped in dist: see 3787.
*4243 **SOPRAN GLAUMIX 21** [1] B Grizzetti 2-8-11 M Demuro : 211114: Trkd ldrs, drvn/no extra appr fnl   2   106
1f: not disgraced upped to Gr 1 company: stays a stiff 1m on hvy grnd.
*3946 **ATTACHE 39** [2] 2-8-11 K Darley : -2115: Mid-div, drvn & not pace of ldrs appr fnl 1f: reportedly   ¾   105
coughed during race: poss styd this longer 1m trip: acts on fast, handles hvy: see 3946.
6 ran   Time 1m 44.7   (Wentworth Racing (Pty) Ltd)   W J Haggas Newmarket

4493   **3.00 GR 1 GRAN PREMIO DEL JOCKEY CLUB 3YO+   1m4f   Heavy**
£106053   £53840   £31556   3 yo rec 7 lb

*4147 **GOLDEN SNAKE 28** [10] J L Dunlop 4-9-4 Pat Eddery 13/10: 0-4511: 4 b h Danzig - Dubian (High Line)   **120**
Cl-up, went on over 1f out, styd on strongly when prsd over 1f out, drvn out: recent wnr at Cologne (Gr 1):
'99 wnr at Newmarket (List) & Chantilly (Gr 1, rtd 119, B W Hills): '98 Doncaster wnr (mdn, rtd 93+): eff at
9/12f on fast, likes soft & hvy & a stiff/gall trk: runs well fresh: tough & high-class, credit to connections.
4263 **REVE DOSCAR 21** [5] Mme M Bollack Badel 3-8-9 L Dettori 4/5 FAV: 143262: 3 gr f Highest Honor -   ½   117
Numidie (Baillamont) Mid-div, gd hdwy over 1f out, sn chall wnr, not qckn well ins last: clr rem: most tough,
smart & consistent filly: deserves another win in Gr company: see 4263.
--   **MONTALBAN** [1] A Lowe 4-9-4 D Vargiu 121/10: 651163: 4 ch c Mondrian - Majestic Image (Niniski)   3½   114
In tch, rdn/prog over 1f out, styd on but no ch with front 2: German raider: eff at 12f on hvy grnd.
10 ran   Time 2m 34.9   (The National Stud)   J L Dunlop Arundel, W Sussex

LONGCHAMP   SUNDAY OCTOBER 22ND   Righthand, Stiff, Galloping Track

Official Going   HEAVY

4494   **2.15 GR 1 PRIX ROYAL-OAK 3YO+   1m7f110y Heavy**
£38425   £15370   £7685   £3842   3 yo rec 9 lb

*1456 **AMILYNX 154** [3] A Fabre 4-9-4 O Peslier 13/10 FAV: -20111: 4 gr c Linamix - Amen (Alydar)   **123**
Chsd ldrs, led going well 2f out, rdn & pulled clr ins last: defied a 5 month abs: earlier won twice here at
Longchamp (Gr 3 & Gr 2): '99 wnr again at Longchamp (2, incl this race, rtd 123): suited by 2m: acts on gd,
loves gd/soft & hvy grnd: Longchamp specialist: runs v well fresh: tough & high-class stayer.
*4264 **SAN SEBASTIAN 21** [7] J L Dunlop 6-9-4 (bl) D Bonilla 11/1: 643612: 6 ch g Niniski - Top Of The   5   119
League (High Top) Front rank, led briefly 2f out, styd on appr fnl 1f but not pace of wnr: fine run over a trip
which is the bare minimum these days: reportedly may go hdlg this winter & would be an exciting prospect.
4264 **TAJOUN 21** [11] A de Royer Dupre 6-9-4 G Mosse 38/10: -14363: 6 b g General Holme - Taeesha (Mill   1   118
Reef) Twrds rear, imprvd to dspt 2nd 2f out, drvn/no extra fnl 1f: v consistent styr: see 3851.
4236 **CHIANG MAI 22** [2] A P O'Brien 3-8-6 J P Spencer 58/1: -10164: Chsd ldrs, drvn appr fnl 2f, no extra   ½   114
appr fnl 1f: up in trip & best run to date: stays 15.5f & likes easy grnd: see 4236, 4057.
4239 **RIDDLESDOWN 22** [1] 3-8-9 R Hughes 194/10: 001125: Bhd, late hdwy: needs drop in grade: see 4239.   3   114
4351 **ROYAL REBEL 8** [4] 4-9-4 (bl) J Reid 25/2: 211326: Cl-up, dropped rear over 4f out, brief eff 2f out,   nk   114
sn btn: capable of better but is unproven on grnd this testing: see 4351, 4264 (gd grnd).
*3851 **ORCHESTRA STALL 47** [9] 8-9-4 T Thulliez 15/2: 1/6118: Nvr a factor, 8th: btr 3851 (g/s).   3   111
11 ran   Time 3m 33.4   (J-L Lagardere)   A Fabre France

LONGCHAMP
SUNDAY OCTOBER 22ND **Righthand, Stiff, Galloping Track**

4495 **2.45 GR 3 PRIX DU PETIT COUVERT 2YO+** **5f** **Heavy**
£21134 £7685 £3842

4129 **REPERTORY** 28 [6] M S Saunders 7-9-10 R Hughes 34/1: 001001: 7 b g Anshan - Susie's Baby (Balidar) 112
Sn clr ldr, ran on strongly for press, drvn out for a surprise win: earlier won at Epsom (h'cap) & plcd in List
company: plcd 3 times in '99 (incl in this race, rtd 106): '98 wnr again at Epsom (h'cap, rtd 106) & The Curragh
(List h'cap) & again 3rd in this race: all wins at 5f: acts on firm, hvy & any trk, likes Epsom: has run well
fresh, eff weight carrier: loves to front-run: smart & v speedy, career best performance today.
4125 **LINCOLN DANCER** 28 [3] M A Jarvis 3-9-10 O Peslier 29/10: 012002: 3 b c Turtle Island - Double Grange *1* 109
(Double Schwartz) Twrds rear, rdn halfway, ran on strongly fnl 1f, closing at fin: best at 6f, see 4125.
2997 **EL GRAN LODE** 85 [5] Diego Lowther 5-9-10 F Diaz 44/10: 031213: 5 ch h Lode - La Pastoral (Cinco 2½ 103
Grande) Chsd wnr, rdn & kept on onepcd fnl 1f: Swedish raider: twice a wnr since 2997 (val 7f h'cap).
4261 **PERRYSTON VIEW** 21 [2] J A Glover 8-10-3 (bl) J Reid 4/1: 055646: Prom, eff halfway, ev ch till 4 101
fdd ins fnl 1f, fin 6th: stiffish task under burden of 10-3: unproven on hvy: see 4261 (Gr 1), 1566 (Gr 2).
8 ran Time 59.4 (M S Saunders) M S Saunders Haydon, Somerset

REDCAR
TUESDAY OCTOBER 24TH **Lefthand, Flat, Galloping Track**

Official Going SOFT (GOOD/SOFT in places). Stalls: Straight Course - Stands' side: Remainder Inside.

4496 **1.55 GIVES YOU MORE MED AUCT MDN 2YO (F)** **5f** **Good/Soft 60 -04 Slow**
£2404 £687 £343

4288 **HOW DO I KNOW** 18 [3] G A Butler 2-8-9 K Darley 1/1 FAV: -0221: 2 gr f Petong - Glenfield 82
Portion (Mummy's Pet) Cl up, shaken up 2f out, led 1f out & rdn, ran on well: well bckd: sister to 10/12f performer
I Cant Remember: eff at 5/6f, shld get further in time: acts on gd & gd/soft grnd, sharp or gall track.
-- **SOPHIELU** [5] M Johnston 2-8-9 J Fanning 6/1: 2: 2 ch f Rudimentary - Aquaglow (Caerleon) ¾ 78
Pressed ldr, led 2f out till 1f out, held towards fin: well clr of rem on debut: 20,000gns half-sister to
sev wnrs up to 12f, dam 7f/1m wnr, sire a miler: bred to apprec 1m+ in time, clearly eff at 5f on gd/soft.
-- **EAGLERIDER** [9] J G Given 2-9-0 Dean McKeown 10/1: 3: 2 b c Eagle Eyed - What A Summer 10 58
(What Luck) Led till 2f out, no extra: debut: lr 12,000gns half brother to sev wnrs: dam high-class in US.
4252 **DIAMOND ZOE** 21 [2] J L Eyre 2-8-9 Joanna Badger (7) 20/1: 44: Bhd, mod hdwy under a weak ride. 1½ 49
3143 **GOGS GIFT** 80 [7] 2-9-0 R Winston 12/1: 05: Chsd ldrs, fdd ent fnl 2f: abs, uninspired gamble from 33/1.nk 53
4131 **TALISKER BAY** 30 [11] 2-9-0 J Stack 6/1: 05536: Handy till rdn & btn 2f out: much btr 4131, 3714. nk 52
3776 **TARAS TIPPLE** 52 [4] 2-9-0 O Pears 50/1: 07: Nvr troubled ldrs: 7 wk abs, 5,000gns College 3½ 44
Chapel home to a 7f wnr: gelding with J Quinn.
3223 **FATHERS FOOTSTEPS** 76 [6] 2-9-0 M Fenton 50/1: 00008: Struggling after halfway: 11 wk abs.; ¾ 42
2277 **TUSCAN FLYER** 117 [1] 2-9-0 J Carroll 14/1: -0509: Mid div, wknd appr fnl 2f: 4 month abs, plater. 1¼ 39
4252 **LAST TIME** 21 [8] 2-8-9 G Parkin 25/1: 00: Nvr in it: 10th. ¾ 32
-- **Pawn In Life** [12] 2-9-0 P Fessey 20/1: -- **Time Marches On** [1] 2-9-0 A Culhane 33/1:
12 ran Time 59.7 (3.2) (Manny Bernstein Racing Ltd) G A Butler Blewbury, Oxon

---

4497 **2.25 DIGITAL SERVICE CLAIMER 3YO+ (F)** **1m3f** **Soft Inapplicable**
£2373 £678 £339 3 yo rec 6 lb

-- **BLENHEIM TERRACE** [7] W H Tinning 7-8-7 A Culhane 20/1: 0414/1: 7 b g Rambo Dancer - Boulevard 42
Girl (Nicholas Bill) Chsd ldrs, closed appr fnl 2f, rdn dist & ran on to lead inside last, just held on: op 33/1:
well btn in nov hdles last yr (reportedly choked): last seen on the Flat over 3 yrs ago, scored at Musselburgh
(h'cap, rtd 55, C Booth): eff at 10/12f: acts on firm & soft grnd, sharp or gall track: runs well fresh.
4406 **I CANT REMEMBER** 6 [6] S R Bowring 6-8-9 Dean McKeown 14/1: 034002: 6 gr g Petong - Glenfield hd 43
Portion (Mummy's Pet) Early ldr, again 2f out, rdn & hdd inside last, rallied, just failed: op 10/1, qk reapp.
4256 **ROOM TO ROOM MAGIC** 21 [11] B Palling 3-8-2 K Dalgleish (5) 14/1: 025203: 3 ch f Casteddu - 1 40
Bellatrix (Persian Bold) Led after 3f, hdd 2f out, kept till no extra fnl 50y: stiff task: stays 11f on fast & soft.
4413 **BACHELORS PAD** 6 [12] Miss S J Wilton 6-9-5 M Tebbutt 6/1: 610004: Mid-div, shkn up ent str, kept ¾ 50
on bef fnl 1f, unable to chall: qck reapp: acts on firm, soft grnd & fibresand: see 3430.
*4041 **FIELD OF VISION** 35 [14] 10-8-11 G Duffield 3/1 FAV: 222415: In tch, eff appr fnl 2f, styd on 1½ 40
without threatening: op 9/2: clr rem, stiff task at the weights: see 4041 (seller).
3480 **ROCK SCENE** 66 [1] 8-8-13 F Lynch 9/1: 541006: Rear, mod late hdwy: 9 wk abs, op 7/1, stiff task. 4 36
3808 **THREE CHERRIES** 51 [5] 4-8-4 P Fessey 25/1: 554507: Chsd ldrs, wknd ent fnl 2f: 7 wk abs, stiff task. 2 24
3574 **NILOUPHAR** 62 [9] 3-7-10 P M Quinn (3) 25/1: -00008: Nvr troubled ldrs: 9 wk abs, longer trip. 4 17
*3247 **MITHRAIC** 76 [13] 8-8-9 P Hanagan (5) 14/1: 3-5619: Mid div, wknd qckly appr fnl 1f: abs, jmps rnr. hd 24
3026 **DIVINE HOSTESS** 452 [10] 3-7-10 J McAuley 50/1: -040-0: Al towards rear: 10th, reapp aft'lng pcd bow, mod. 1 14
4304 **MANSTAR** 15 [2] 3-8-5 N Kennedy 11/2: 000630: Chsd ldrs till 3f out: 11th: flattered last time. nk 22
4419 **TREVERRICK** 5 [16] 5-8-9 (t) Dale Gibson 9/2: 063/50: Held up, brief eff 3f out: 12th: see 4419. 4 15
943 **Anniversary Day** 190 [8] 4-8-9 O Pears 33/1: 2537 **Manx Shadow** 106 [3] 3-8-10 R Ffrench 33/1:
14 ran Time 2m 27.3 (11.8) (W H Tinning) W H Tinning Thornton-le-Clay, W Yorks

---

4498 **3.00 WATCH THIS RACE HCAP 3YO+ 0-85 (D)** **7f str** **Good/Soft 60 -33 Slow** [85]
£4680 £1440 £720 £360 3 yo rec 2 lb

4432 **TREASURE TOUCH** 5 [10] P D Evans 6-8-11 (68) Joanna Badger (7) 20/1: 040051: 6 b g Treasure Kay - 72
Bally Pourri (Law Society) Chsd ldrs, rdn appr fnl 1f, kept on strongly to lead fnl stride: qk reapp, slow time:
earlier won at Catterick (2, claimer & h'cap, D Nicholls), Carlisle (2, claimer & sell) & Leicester (h'cap):
'99 rnr up (rtd 60): suited by 6/7.5f on firm, gd/soft & fibresand: handles any trk, without blnks: tough.
4405 **REX IS OKAY** 6 [2] S R Bowring 4-8-8 (65) Dean McKeown 14/1: 600052: 4 ch g Mazilier - Cocked shd 68
Hat Girl (Ballacashtal) Tried to make all, rdn fnl 1f, hdd post: qck reapp & back to form: nicely h'capped.
*4310 **NATALIE JAY** 15 [12] M R Channon 4-9-0 (71) Pat Eddery 5/1 FAV: 063313: 4 b f Ballacashtal - Falls ½ 73
Of Lora (Scottish Rifle) Held up, gd prog/edged left ent fnl 2f, chall 1f out, hard rdn, held nr fin: best at 1m.
4452 **AISLE 4** [15] S R Bowring 3-7-10 (55)(tbl) J Bramhill 25/1: 500004: Well plcd, rdn appr fnl 1f, ½ 56

1393

unable to qckn: qck reapp, ran to best: acts on gd/soft, soft & fibresand, handles firm: both wins at 6f.

4018	DANDY REGENT 38 [16] 6-7-13 (56) K Dalgleish (5) 12/1: 040035: In tch, eff 2f out, kept on same pace.	3	51
4218	ROYAL REPRIMAND 24 [1] 5-7-11 (54)(1ow)(3oh) P Fessey 20/1: 243236: Chsd ldrs, onepce appr fnl 1f.	1	47
4405	ROYAL ROMEO 6 [8] 3-8-12 (71) K Darley 6/1: 005037: Al same pl: qck reapp, better at 6f, see 1768.	nk	63
4232	GLENDAMAH 22 [9] 3-7-11 (55)(1ow) Dale Gibson 25/1: -00008: Chsd ldrs, no extra fnl 2f: blnks off.	½	47
4224	REDOUBTABLE 24 [17] 9-8-8 (65) A Culhane 14/1: 305049: In tch, onepce appr fnl 1f: see 2994.	½	55
4302	PETERS IMP 17 [13] 5-9-2 (73) J Carroll 16/1: 433600: Nvr troubled ldrs: 10th, see 2999.	nk	62
4365	ROYAL WAVE 8 [4] 4-7-10 (53)(3oh) P M Quinn (3) 16/1: 00-030: Held up, imprvd 2f out, sn wknd: 11th.	½	41
*4428	ORIOLE 5 [5] 7-7-10 (53)(6ex)(4oh) Kim Tinkler 15/2: 040010: Al bhd: 12th, bckd from 14/1, qk reapp,	½	40
	stiff task, 4lbs o/h despite penalty: see 4428.		
4215	DONNAS DOUBLE 24 [7] 5-8-12 (69) A Beech (3) 6/1: 402400: Chsd ldrs, rdn & btn 2f out: 13th.	½	55
4380	BLACK ARMY 7 [11] 5-8-5 (62) F Lynch 12/1: 051560: In tch, wknd appr fnl 1f: 14th, up in trip,	½	47
	4-day whip ban: see 4380.		
4302	TAFFS WELL 17 [3] 7-8-7 (64) J Fanning 10/1: 000000: Handy till 2f out: 15th, op 8/1, see 715.	shd	49
3992	TIPPERARY SUNSET 39 [6] 6-8-6 (63)(bl) T Williams 14/1: D41400: Dwelt, al bhd: 16th, qck reapp.	2½	43
4257	KINAN 21 [14] 4-9-11 (82) A Nicholls 10/1: 036060: Nvr on terms: 17th, top-weight, see 3992, 2431.	1¾	59

17 ran   Time 1m 28.3 (6.5)   (David Oxley & James Mitchell)   P D Evans Pandy, Gwent

---

4499   3.35 COME HOME HCAP 3YO+ 0-75 (E)   1m str   Good/Soft 60   +07 Fast   [71]
£4030   £1240   £620   £310   3 yo rec 3 lb

4273	LUCKY GITANO 20 [3] J L Dunlop 4-9-13 (70) Pat Eddery 8/1: 024641: 4 b g Lucky Guest - April Wind		78
	(Windjammer) Towards rear & trav well, imprvd halfway, barged thro' appr fnl 1f, sn led, cmftly: gd time, first win:		
	fearless jockey given another ban for irresponsible ride: '99 rnr up (mdn auct, rtd 87): '98 rnr up (mdn		
	auct, rtd 76): eff at 1m/10f: acts on firm & gd/soft grnd: can run well fresh & carry big weights.		
4094	ABAJANY 32 [5] M R Channon 6-9-11 (68) M Tebbutt 12/1: 000002: 6 b g Akarad - Miss Ivory	2	70
	Coast (Sir Ivor) Bhd, rdn & ran on appr fnl 1f, nrst fin: op 10/1: back to form & v handily weighted now.		
4404	DARK VICTOR 6 [13] D Shaw 4-8-5 (48)(bl) R Winston 5/1 FAV: 106623: 4 b g Cadeaux Genereux -	¾	48
	Dimmer (Kalaglow) Prom, rdn appr fnl 1f, looked held when bmpd dist, rallied for 3rd: op 4/1, qck		
	reapp: eff at 1m but will apprec a return to 10f: see 4404, 1050.		
4302	RYMERS RASCAL 17 [4] E J Alston 8-9-10 (67) M Fenton 11/2: 303144: Bhd ldrs, chall 1f out,	½	66
	sn rdn & onepce: op 4/1: consistent, see 4217 (C/D).		
4311	SOPHOMORE 15 [16] 6-8-9 (52) K Dalgleish (5) 16/1: 020555: Cl up, led appr fnl 2f till 1f out, no extra.	nk	50
4217	MEHMAAS 24 [11] 4-8-8 (51)(vis) P Fessey 33/1: 530406: Chsd ldrs, rdn & onepce fnl 1f: see 1920.	2	45
4217	CAUTION 24 [15] 6-8-12 (55) K Darley 6/1: 233347: Prom, drvn fnl 2f, no impress: see 2561, 645.	2	45
3534	MR PERRY 63 [1] 4-7-11 (40) Dale Gibson 33/1: 060008: Al around same pl: 9 wk abs: op 20/1.	shd	30
4217	PENNYS PRIDE 24 [7] 5-9-12 (69) A Culhane 12/1: 230309: Held up, prog 2f out, rdn & hmpd bef	½	58
	fnl 1f, no extra: mdn: see 1892, 759.		
4217	TARRADALE 24 [8] 6-8-1 (44) J McAuley 33/1: 0-0000: Chsd ldrs, led briefly appr fnl 1f, wknd: 10th:	hd	32
	thrice rnr up in '99 (h'cap, rtd 48, claimer, rtd 50): '98 wnr at Hamilton (h'cap, rtd 39 & 43a): eff at		
	1m/10f, tried 12f: acts on firm, hvy grnd & equitrack: with C Booth.		
*4406	GINNER MORRIS 6 [20] 5-8-1 (44)(bl) P Hanagan (5) 7/1: -00410: Chsd ldrs 4f: 14th, too sn after 4406?	0	
3616	INITIATIVE 60 [2] 4-8-4 (45)(2ow)(BL) J Fanning 20/1: -00030: Led till 3f out, sn btn: 15th, blnkd, tchd 40/1.	0	
4404	Kierchem 6 [10] 9-7-10 (39) T Hamilton (7) 33/1: 4426 By The Glass 5 [12] 4-7-10 (39)(12oh) Kim Tinkler 33/1:		
3839	Italian Symphony 49 [18] 6-8-12 (55)(vis) Melissa Scherer (7) 25/1:		
3288	Noble Cyrano 74 [9] 5-8-7 (50) G Duffield 33/1:		
4366	Thieves Welcome 8 [17] 3-9-0 (60) A Beech (3) 33/1: 2420 Almazhar 111 [6] 5-8-13 (56)(vis) J Carroll 14/1:		
3250	Northgate 76 [19] 4-8-4 (47)(bl) T Williams 20/1:		

19 ran   Time 1m 39.0 (4.2)   (Anamoine Ltd)   J L Dunlop Arundel, W Sussex

---

4500   4.10 RACING CHANNEL NOV STKS 2YO (D)   7f str   Good/Soft 60   -09 Slow
£3510   £1080   £540   £270

4124	LANESBOROUGH 30 [5] G A Butler 2-8-12 K Darley 7/2: 51: 2 ch c Irish River - Hot Option		89
	(Exploded) Bhd ldrs, shaken up 2f out, rdn ent fnl 1f, qcknd to lead fnl 100y, readily: drifter from 9/4: highly		
	tried on debut (Ascot): half brother to a useful wnr in the States, dam a miler: eff at 7f, 1m is going to		
	suit: acts on gd/soft grnd, gall trck: potentially useful, improving colt.		
*4172	MUTARASED 27 [4] J L Dunlop 2-9-5 Pat Eddery 11/10 FAV: 012: 2 b c Storm Cat - Sajjaya (Blushing	1	92
	Groom) Well plcd, led ent fnl 1f, sn rdn & hdd, not pce to repel wnr towards fin: nicely bckd: acts on gd/soft & soft.		
4028	TEEHEE 36 [1] B Palling 2-8-12 M Fenton 20/1: 5533: 2 b c Anita's Prince - Regal Charmer (Royal	¾	83
	And Regal) Bhd, hard rdn & hdd 1f out, onepce nr fin: prob ran to best: return to mdn comp will suit: see 4028.		
4390	MATLOCK 7 [2] P F I Cole 2-9-5 J Carroll 11/2: -1434: Well plcd & ev ch till no extra inside last.	¾	88
2474	BLUE PLANET 109 [6] 2-9-5 G Duffield 4/1: 135: Held up, eff 2f out, styd on inside last, no threat.	¾	86
4230	HEATHYARDS GUEST 22 [7] 2-8-12 A Culhane 25/1: 0246: Chsd ldrs, fdd appr fnl 2f: stiffish task.	11	59
2014	SPUR OF GOLD 128 [3] 2-8-7 R Winston 100/1: -667: Bhd from halfway: 4 month abs, imposs task.	18	24

7 ran   Time 1m 26.6 (4.8)   (Mr & Mrs J Amerman)   G A Butler Blewbury, Oxon

---

4501   4.45 7 DAYS CLASS STKS 3YO+ 0-65 (E)   1m2f   Soft   Inapplicable
£2873   £884   £442   £221   3 yo rec 5 lb

4160	ANGUS G 28 [7] Mrs M Reveley 8-9-3 A Culhane 5/1: -00001: 8 br g Chief Singer - Horton Line (High		68
	Line) Rear, eff 3f out, prog appr fnl 1f, sn rdn, kept on grimly to lead bef fnl 1f, ran on: tchd 7/1: rnr-up in '99 (h'cap,		
	rtd 92): last won in '97 at Newmarket & York (h'caps, rtd 94): eff at 10/12f: acts on firm & soft grnd, gall trks.		
*4436	GREYFIELD 5 [4] M R Channon 4-9-5 Pat Eddery 1/1 FAV: 544012: 4 b g Persian Bold - Noble Dust	hd	69
	(Dust Commander) Held up, prog appr straight, drvn to lead bef fnl 1f, ran on, collared late:		
	well bckd, qck reapp: game attempt giving weight: in-form & versatile: see 4436.		
4306	SPREE VISION 15 [8] P Monteith 4-9-3 J Carroll 16/1: 650023: 4 b g Suave Dancer - Regent's Folly	2½	63$
	(Touching Wood) Waited with, eff & hmpd ent fnl 1f, no impress on ldrs till kept on well fnl 1f: op 12/1,		
	stiff task at the weights & prob flattered: eff at 10/12f: jumps rnr since 4306, see 1908.		
4374	WILTON 8 [6] Miss S J Wilton 5-9-3 M Tebbutt 4/1: 010054: Handy, led 3f out till appr fnl 1f, onepce.	1¾	60
4234	DENA 22 [2] 3-8-9 K Darley 5/1: 5-025: Bhd ldrs, short of room 3f out, sn rdn, no impress: op 4/1,	1	55
	clr rem: unsuited by return to 10f?: see 4234 (1m mdn).		
2883	BOLD AMUSEMENT 92 [5] 10-9-3 O Pears 8/1: 200166: Al bhd, brief eff 3f out; 3 mth abs, see 2518.	5	51

REDCAR TUESDAY OCTOBER 24TH Lefthand, Flat, Galloping Track

4131} **MISS ALL ALONE 392** [9] 5-9-0 G Duffield 50/1: 5400-7: Well plcd & ch till fdd 2f out: reapp, v stiff task: '99 rnr up (auction mdn, rtd 51a, plcd on turf, h'cap, rtd 45 at best): eff at 7f/1m: acts on fibresand, gd & hvy grnd, poss best with blnks or visor now, not worn today: has tried hdles: maiden. **7 38**
4437 **CITY BANK DUDLEY 4** [1] 3-8-12 C Teague 100/1: 400508: Led till 3f out, sn btn: stiff task, qk reapp. **6 32**
4300 **DISPOL ROCK 17** [3] 4-9-3 M Fenton 16/1: -00009: Sn struggling: see 4300. **4 26**
9 ran Time 2m 11.4 (9.1) (W Ginzel) Mrs M Reveley Lingdale, N Yorks

4502 **5.20 NTL NURSERY HCAP 2YO 0-75 (E) 6f Good/Soft 60 -02 Slow [75]**
£2925 £900 £450 £225

3175 **DIAMOND MAX 79** [3] P D Evans 2-9-0 (61) Joanna Badger (7) 11/2: 414551: 2 b c Nicolotte - Kawther (Tap On Wood) Bhd ldrs, rdn appr fnl 1f, sn led & qckly went clr despite edging right: 11 wk abs: earlier won at Nottingham (seller, made all): eff at 5/6f, tried 7f & should stay in time: acts on gd/soft & hvy grnd, prob any track: runs well fresh, qck follow-up likely **75**
4373 **DARWIN TOWER 8** [4] B W Murray 2-8-2 (49)(VIS) K Dalgleish (5) 5/1: 000022: 2 gr c Bin Ajwaad - Floria Tosca (Petong) Well plcd & ev ch till outpcd by wnr appr fnl 1f: drifter from 3/1, visored: flattered in mdn auction comp last time (blnkd): see 4373. **7 51**
4369 **CO DOT UK 8** [2] K A Ryan 2-9-4 (65)(bl) F Lynch 11/2: 502023: 2 b g Distant Relative - Cubist (Tate Gallery) Led, rdn & hdd appr fnl 1f, no extra: back in trip, 2nd time blnks: see 4369 (AW seller). **½ 65**
3767 **MISS BEADY 53** [6] Don Enrico Incisa 2-9-1 (62) Kim Tinkler 25/1: 055004: Chsd ldrs, onepce fnl 2f. **2½ 56**
4369 **PREMIER BOY 8** [9] 2-8-10 (57)(tVIS) J Bramhill 25/1: 004065: Towards rear, went past btn horses fnl 1f: visord on h'cap bow: needs further. **nk 50**
4372 **ALIS IMAGES 8** [10] 2-8-11 (58) J Carroll 14/1: 033556: Chsd ldrs, fdd appr fnl 1f: see 2377 (fm). **1¾ 48**
4249 **EL UNO 21** [11] 2-8-12 (59) A Culhane 16/1: 006507: Nvr dangerous: back in trip, needs sellers. **2 43**
4252 **CLOONDESH 21** [5] 2-8-7 (54) P Hanagan (5) 11/2: 5008: Nvr troubled ldrs: h'cap bow, longer trip. **¾ 36**
4283 **AMY DEE 18** [8] 2-8-7 (54) P M Quinn (3) 16/1: 6009: Dwelt, nvr a factor: h'cap bow. **½ 35**
3184 **KOMALUNA 78** [7] 2-8-3 (50) P Fessey 12/1: -00000: Al rear: 10th, tchd 16/1, 11 wk abs, h'cap bow. **1 28**
*4235 **SPICE ISLAND 22** [1] 2-9-7 (68) K Darley 7/2 FAV: 530010: Chsd ldrs till halfway: 11th, nicely bckd, top weight: went up a staggering 15lbs for 4235. **2 40**
4312 **ARONA 15** [12] 2-9-1 (62) Dean McKeown 20/1: 0050: In tch 3f: 12th, h'cap bow, bck in trip. **8 18**
12 ran Time 1m 12.6 (3.7) (Diamond Racing Ltd) P D Evans Pandy, Gwent

NOTTINGHAM TUESDAY OCTOBER 24TH Lefthand, Galloping Track

Official Going Rnd Crse - SOFT (HVY PLCS) 5f Crse - GD/SFT (SFT PLCS) Stalls: Str - Stands side, Rem - Inside

4503 **2.05 ROSELAND GROUP MDN 2YO (D) 5f Good/Soft Inapplicable**
£4563 £1404 £702 £351 High numbers favoured

4283 **NIGHT GYPSY 18** [15] T D Easterby 2-8-9 T Quinn 10/1: 3201: 2 b f Mind Games - Ocean Grove (Fairy King) Held up, hdwy over 1f out, led ins last, pushed out: op 7/1: eff at 5f, stays 6f well: acts on gd & soft grnd & on a stiff/gall trk: made most of fav high draw. **76**
4341 **PRIDE IN ME 12** [12] E A L Dunlop 2-8-9 J Reid 6/4 FAV: 02: 2 ch f Indian Ridge - Easy Option (Prince Sabo) Chsd ldrs, swtchd/rdn to chall fnl 1f, not pace of wnr: hvly bckd: acts on gd/soft, apprec drop to 5f. **1¼ 72**
-- **MR MAHOOSE** [17] W J Haggas 2-9-0 S Drowne 20/1: 3: 2 b c Rakeen - Golden Hen (Native Prospector) Dwelt, rdn & styd on from over 1f out, nvr nrr: op 14/1: March foal, half brother to a 2yo US wnr: dam a mdn: eff at 5f, 6f will suit: acts on gd/soft grnd: encouraging intro. **1¼ 74**
3614 **FLYING PETREL 60** [16] M Johnston 2-8-9 D Holland 14/1: -04: Chsd ldrs, no impress fnl 1f: 2 mth abs: prob handles fast & gd/soft grnd: see 3614 (6f). **2½ 64**
4253 **THE SCAFFOLDER 21** [8] 2-9-0 R Hughes 10/1: 65: Dwelt, chsd ldrs halfway, kept on for press fnl 1f, no threat: bckd at long odds, op 33/1: handles gd/soft grnd: see 4253. **nk 68**
4288 **SYRINGA 18** [5] 2-8-9 J Fortune 7/2: 66: Prom, rdn/briefly led 1f out, sn no extra: well bckd. **hd 62**
4289 **BEENABOUTABIT 18** [14] 2-8-9 P Doe 12/1: 027: Prom 4f: btr 4289 (G/S). **¾ 61**
3955 **YORKER 41** [4] 2-9-0 J Tate 66/1: 008: Swtchd right start & towards rear, kept on fnl 2f under min press: 6 wk abs: given a v kind ride: now qual for h'caps & shld apprec 6f+: one to keep in mind: see 3500. **nk 65+**
4137 **EAST OF JAVA 29** [3] 2-9-0 N Callan 20/1: 0309: Prom till over 1f out: btr 3973. **¾ 64**
3513 **TWILIGHT MISTRESS 65** [9] 2-8-9 L Newman (3) 20/1: -00430: Led 4f, fdd: 10th: 2 mth abs, bckd. **1 57**
3223 **ALBURACK 76** [6] 2-9-0 G Hind 25/1: 000: Chsd ldrs 3f: 11th: 11 wk abs: see 1774. **3 56**
4187 **SO SOBER 25** [10] 2-9-0 R Mullen 11/2: 420620: Chsd ldrs 3f: 15th: btr 4187. **0**
-- **Croeso Croeso** [7] 2-8-9 A Mackay 50/1: -- **Sheriff Song** [13] 2-9-0 T Lucas 50/1:
-- **Greycoat** [11] 2-9-0 J Quinn 50/1: -- **Swallow Magic** [2] 2-9-0 G Carter 50/1:
-- **Rinka Blue** [1] 2-8-9 G Faulkner (0) 66/1:
17 ran Time 1m 05.00 (6.5) (T G Holdcroft) T D Easterby Great Habton, N Yorks

4504 **2.40 OATH MDN 2YO (D) 1m54y rnd Heavy 167 -25 Slow**
£5239 £1612 £806 £403

4158 **RANDOM QUEST 28** [2] P F I Cole 2-9-0 R Hughes 2/1 FAV: 01: 2 b c Rainbow Quest - Anne Bonny (Ajdal) Led after 1f, styd on strongly fnl 2f, rdn out: 90,000gns purchase, half brother to a 13f wnr: apprec step up to 1m, mid dists looks sure to suit next term: acts on hvy grnd & a gall trk: can rate more highly. **83**
3705 **STAGING POST 57** [10] H R A Cecil 2-9-0 T Quinn 9/4: -32: 2 b c Pleasant Colony - Interim (Sadler's Wells) Led 1f, remained prom, rdn & kept on fnl 2f, not pace of wnr: clr rem, bckd tho' op 5/4, 8 wk abs: acts on gd/soft & hvy grnd: stays 1m, mid dists sure to suit: see 3705. **1¼ 80**
4163 **MAGZAA 27** [3] J L Dunlop 2-9-0 D Harrison 20/1: -003: 2 gr c Marju - Labibeh (Lyphard) Chsd ldrs, rdn & kept on fnl 2f, no threat to front pair: eff at 1m on hvy grnd: mid dists h'caps will suit, improve. **4 74+**
4350 **HOMELIFE 11** [18] P W D'Arcy 2-9-0 J Quinn 12/1: 066204: Held up, keen, kept on onepce fnl 2f, nvr threat: acts on gd & hvy: see 4290 (h'cap). **½ 73**
-- **TENDER TRAP** [7] 2-9-0 T Williams 16/1: 5: Held up, mod hdwy fnl 3f, nvr threat to ldrs: Sadler's Wells colt: May foal, cost IR 190,000gns: half brother to a French mid dist wnr: dam a mdn: sire a top class 1m/12f performer: sure to relish mid dists for T Mills. **¾ 72**
-- **SALTRIO** [4] 2-9-0 J Fortune 6/1: 6: Slowly away/rear, kept on fnl 2f, nvr threat: Slip Anchor **3½ 67**

colt, Feb foal: dam a 5f/1m wnr: sires progeny often thorough stayers, sure to improve when tackling further.

-- **UNDENIABLE** [5] 2-9-0 A McGlone 33/1: 7: Slowly away/bhd, no room over 2f out, late gains, no 2½ 63
threat: Unfuwain gelding, March foal, cost 13,000gns: dam a 7f 2yo wnr: sire top class at 12f: improve over further.

-- **ROUTE BARREE** [1] 2-9-0 P Doe 50/1: 8: Chsd ldrs 6f: Exit To Nowhere colt, dam a 2yo wnr abroad. shd 63

4082 **DIWAN** 33 [12] 2-9-0 R Price 33/1: 09: Held up, eff 3f out, no impress: see 4082 (6f). 1¾ 61

4249 **TWILIGHT DANCER** 21 [6] 2-8-9 D Holland 40/1: 650: Prom 6f: 10th: btr 3867 (gd). 2 53

-- **FARCE** [15] 2-8-9 Paul Eddery 50/1: 0: Slowly away, al rear: 11th: Kings Theatre filly, April foal, 4 47
cost 10,500gns: dam unrcd: with B Smart.

4349 **False Promise** 11 [9] 2-9-0 G Carter 33/1: -- **Camzo** [14] 2-9-0 R Havlin 25/1:

-- **Baderna** [13] 2-9-0 S Drowne 25/1: -- **Greenborough** [11] 2-9-0 D Sweeney 33/1:

4283 **Illustrious Duke** 18 [17] 2-9-0 A Mackay 100/1: -- **Not Fade Away** [8] 2-9-0 J Reid 20/1:

17 ran   Time 1m 55.3 (15.9)   (The Blandford Partnership)   P F I Cole Whatcombe, Oxon

---

4505   3.15 RENAULT VANS MDN 3YO (D)   1m54y rnd   Heavy 167 -11 Slow
£4615   £1420   £710   £355

1188 **SAWWAAH** 170 [4] E A L Dunlop 3-9-0 G Carter 1/2 FAV: 32-61: 3 b c Marju - Just A Mirage (Green 88
Desert) Outpcd early, prog to lead over 1f out, pulled clr fnl 1f under hands & heels riding: hvly bckd, 6 month
abs: plcd both '99 starts (rtd 100, mdn): eff at 1m, 10f will suit: acts on firm & hvy grnd, stiff/gall trk:
runs well fresh: useful colt, can rate more highly, esp over further.

3813 **BRANDY COVE** 51 [3] B Smart 3-9-0 Paul Eddery 20/1: -02: 3 b c Lugana Beach - Tender Moment 9 75
(Caerleon) Chsd ldrs halfway, rdn & kept on fnl 2f, no ch wth facile wnr: 7 wk abs: prob handles hvy grnd.

4387 **LOUEST** 7 [2] G Wragg 3-9-0 D Holland 9/1: 03: 3 b c Gone West - La Carene (Kenmare) 3 71
Chsd ldrs, rdn & onepcd 3f, no threat: op 6/1, qck reapp: bred to apprec longer 1m trip: see 4387.

4118 **WOOLFE** 30 [7] J H M Gosden 3-8-9 (VIS) J Fortune 6/1: 33204: Led, clr 3f out, sn rdn & hdd over 5 59
1f out, fdd: op 4/1, first time visor: btr 3474, 3190 (gd).

-- **FRAZERS LAD** [1] 3-9-0 R Lappin 50/1: 5: Dwelt, nvr a factor: debut, with A Bailey. 1¾ 62

-- **BELLE AMOUR** [9] 3-8-9 Martin Dwyer 7/1: 6: Slowly away, rear, nvr factor: debut, with M Tregoning. 3 53

4434 **OLOROSO** 5 [8] 3-9-0 L Newman 33/1: 07: Prom 5f: qck reapp. hd 57

4367} **TAXI FOR ROBBO** 375 [6] 3-8-9 D Sweeney 100/1: 0360-8: Chsd ldrs 5f: reapp: plcd in '99 19 31
(rtd 43, sell, J L Eyre): eff at 5f on gd grnd: prev with J Eyre, now with I Wood.

4361 **BATTLE GREEN LAD** 10 [5] 3-9-0 J Edmunds 100/1: -09: Keen/trckd ldrs 5f: no form. 24 9

9 ran   Time 1m 54.2 (14.8)   (Hamdan Al Maktoum)   E A L Dunlop Newmarket, Suffolk

---

4506   3.50 TOTE PLACEPOT HCAP 3YO + 0-90 (C)   1m54y rnd   Heavy 167 -03 Slow   [86]
£7442   £2290   £1145   £572   3 yo rec 3 lb

*4300 **GREENAWAY BAY** 17 [17] K R Burke 6-8-5 (63) G Baker (5) 6/1: 63-511: 6 ch g Green Dancer - 69
Raise 'N Dance (Raise A Native) Rcd keenly in rear, prog to lead dist, styd on well, rdn out: op 5/1: recent
York wnr (h'cap): '99 Brighton wnr (h'cap, rtd 59): plcd form in '98 for W Musson (rtd 62 & 59a): eff at 1m/10f on
firm & hvy grnd, any trk: can go well fresh: in great form, heads now for the valuable Autumn h'cap at Newmarket.

4300 **ROUTE SIXTY SIX** 17 [10] Jedd O'Keeffe 4-8-1 (59) G Sparkes (7) 6/1: 232232: 4 b f Brief Truce - 2 61
Lyphards Goddess (Lyphard's Special) Rear, rdn & styd on fnl 2f, not rch wnr: see 4300, 3011.

4340 **SCOTTISH SPICE** 12 [16] I A Balding 3-9-6 (81) Martin Dwyer 14/1: 06D203: 3 b f Selkirk - Dilwara hd 82
(Lashkari) Trckd ldrs, rdn/ch over 1f out, not pace of wnr inside last: acts on firm & hvy grnd: see 4206, 912.

4204 **CAD ORO** 24 [12] G B Balding 7-8-8 (66) S Carson (3) 6/1: 030204: Held up, kept on fnl 2f, no threat. 2½ 63

4436 **THIHN** 5 [1] 5-8-6 (64) S Drowne 14/1: 312205: Held up, rdn/prog & ch over 1f out, no extra inside 1¼ 59
last: op 10/1: qck reapp: see 4291, 4044 & 3951.

4300 **CHINA RED** 17 [13] 6-9-0 (72) D Holland 20/1: 010006: Led 6f, no extra: see 3404 (claimer). hd 66

4348 **MELODIAN** 11 [11] 5-9-1 (73) (bl) D Mernagh (3) 11/2 FAV: 013227: Chsd ldr 7f: see 4044 (Beverley). 2 64

4292 **PRINCE DU SOLEIL** 18 [3] 4-8-7 (65) J Fortune 11/1: 000048: Held up, smooth prog to trck ldrs ½ 55
over 2f out, kept on well: did not find as much as looked likely: see 4292.

4427 **ROLLER** 5 [7] 4-8-13 (71) J Reid 7/1: 360639: Prom till over 1f out: quick reapp: see 1007. 1¾ 59

4348 **CHAPEL ROYALE** 11 [8] 3-9-5 (80) D McGaffin (5) 12/1: 033000: Held up, eff 3f out, no impress: 10th. 1¼ 66

3826 **Pips Way** 50 [9] 3-9-5 (80) N Callan 16/1: *4233 **Pipadash** 22 [15] 3-9-0 (75) J P Spencer 25/1:

4340 **Fredora** 12 [2] 5-9-9 (81) D Sweeney 33/1: 2858 **So Precious** 94 [14] 3-9-10 (85) T Quinn 25/1:

4363 **Shaanxi Romance** 10 [6] 5-7-11 (55)(vis)(1ow)(7oh) J Quinn 50/1348 **Caliwag** 159 [5] 4-8-10 (68) O Urbina 50/1:

4126 **Adobe** 30 [4] 5-9-8 (80) T G McLaughlin 20/1:

17 ran   Time 1m 53.5 (14.1)   (Asterlane Ltd)   K R Burke Newmarket, Suffolk

---

4507   4.25 COME RACING SELLER 2YO (G)   1m54y rnd   Heavy 167 -63 Slow
£1985   £567   £283

3837 **SPIRIT OF TEXAS** 49 [12] K McAuliffe 2-8-11 (t) N Callan 16/1: 000001: 2 b g Namaqualand - Have 68
A Flutter (Auction Ring) Mid div, prog fnl 3f, led over 1f out, styd on well, drvn out: 7 wk abs: bt in for
7,000gns: first win, blinks ommitted: eff over a gall 1m on hvy grnd: eff in a t-strap: suited by sell grade.

4369 **TATTY THE TANK** 8 [4] M C Pipe 2-8-11 A McGlone 16/1: 02: 2 b c Tragic Role - Springfield Girl 1¼ 65
(Royal Vulcan) Led, rdn/hdd over 1f out, kept on for press: turf bow, eff at 1m on hvy grnd.

3690 **MEDIA BUYER** 57 [1] B J Meehan 2-8-11 (bl) D R McCabe 3/1 FAV: 032003: 2 b g Green Dancer - 2 62
California Rush (Forty Niner) Al prom, rdn fnl 3f & ev ch ins last, drvn & no extra nr fin: jockey given a whip ban
& referred to Portman Square: op 7/4, abs, clr of rem: stays 1m, acts on gd & hvy: eff in blnks: see 2791.

2972 **TONY DANCER** 88 [10] K Bell 2-8-11 L Newman (3) 14/1: 004: Prom 6f: op 33/1: abs: see 2635. 10 47

*4431 **IVANS BRIDE** 5 [7] 2-8-11 N Pollard 9/1: 240015: Mid div, btn 2f out: op 6/1: btr 4431 (5f). shd 47

4187 **PERTEMPS REVEREND** 25 [9] G Faulkner (3) 7/1: 06: Chsd ldrs 6f: longer 1m trip. 2½ 43

3950 **MASTER COOL** 41 [13] 2-8-11 D Holland 16/1: 445507: Mid div, btn 2f out: 6 wk abs: see 1679. shd 43

4369 **CHANCE REMARK** 8 [14] 2-8-6 J Quinn 33/1: 05: Slowly away/rear, mod hdwy: no form. 2 35

4332 **DARK DOLORES** 13 [16] 2-8-6 S Drowne 10/1: -0009: Al towards rear: longer 1m trip, no form. shd 35

4336 **JUNIOR BRIEF** 12 [6] 2-8-11 J Reid 25/1: 000000: Keen/trckd ldrs 6f: 10th: longer 1m trip, no form. 3 36

4336 **FARAUDE** 12 [15] 2-8-6 Martin Dwyer 7/2: 040: Al bhd: 13th: bckd, op 5/1: see 4190. 0

4431 **Turbo Blue** 5 [3] 2-8-6 G Hind 16/1: 4154 **Only When Provoked** 28 [11] 2-8-11 R Havlin 50/1:

4190 **Oso Neet** 25 [8] 2-8-11 R Smith (5) 33/1: 4225 **Chesters Boy** 24 [2] 2-8-11 (bl) T G McLaughlin 50/1:

15 ran   Time 1m 58.5 (19.1)   (The Tri Nations Syndicate)   K McAuliffe Lambourn, Berks

4508	5.00 WAREHOUSE HCAP 3YO+ 0-60 (F)　　2m　　Heavy 167　+04 Fast	[60]
	£2878　　£822　　£411　　3 yo rec 10lb	

*4424 **YOURE SPECIAL** 5 [12]　P C Haslam 3-9-8 (64)(6ex) P Goode (3)　11/2: 006011: 3 b g Northern Flagship - 　71
Pillow Mint (Stagedoor Johnny) Led bef halfway, clr over 3f out, rdn out: qck reapp, best time of day: 6lb pen
for recent Newcastle win (h'cap): earlier scored at W'hampton (AW mdn, rtd 82a): suited by 2m, shld stay further:
acts on gd, hvy & fibresand, sharp or gall trck: decisive wnr, hat-trick on the cards.

3978 **ALCAYDE** 39 [14]　J Akehurst 5-9-4 (50) J Fortune 33/1: 053502: 5 ch g Alhijaz - Lucky Flinders 　5　51
(Free State) Held up, rdn & kept on fnl 3f, no threat: stays 2m: handles fast & hvy grnd: well h'capped: see 1373.

4256 **GRACILIS** 21 [4]　W W Haigh 3-8-7 (49) D Holland 20/1: -40053: 3 b g Caerleon - Grace Note (Top 　2½　48
Ville) Dwelt, sn prom, rdn/no impress fnl 2f: op 33/1: prob styd longer 2m trip: handles hvy: cld find a race.

*4075 **SAMARARDO** 33 [11]　N P Littmoden 3-9-1 (57) R Hughes　5/1 JT FAV: 464214: In tch 4f out, kept 　1½　55
on onepace for press fnl 3f: remains in gd form tho' just btr 4075.

4376 **MARTHA REILLY** 8 [7]　4-8-11 (43) A Mackay 14/1: 003155: Chsd ldrs 3f out, no impress: op 9/1. 　2　39
4229 **SECRET DROP** 22 [8]　4-9-4 (50)(e) J Reid 20/1: 004336: Chsd ldrs 5f out, btn 3f out: clr rem, lngr trip. 　½　45
4258 **FAIRTOTO** 21 [2]　4-8-13 (45) D Sweeney 14/1: 003-37: Held up, no impress throughout: btr 4258. 　15　29
4231 **MY LEGAL EAGLE** 22 [1]　6-8-7 (39) P Doe 9/1: 040648: Mid div, btn 3f out: see 1023. 　1　22
*4166 **TE DEUM** 27 [9]　3-9-1 (57) R Smith (5)　10/1: -05019: Mid div, btn 3f out: op 7/1: btr 4168 (14f). 　17　18
3657 **SUPLIZI** 58 [15]　9-8-10 (42) G Hind 33/1: 606000: Trckd ldrs, btn 4f out: 10th: abs, longer 2m trip. 　2　11
4376 **BLACK ICE BOY** 8 [3]　9-8-10 (42)(vis) T Quinn 10/1: 600230: Led 4f, btn 4f out, sn eased: 10th: btr 4376. 4　7
4139 **CANDLE SMILE** 29 [10]　8-10-0 (60)(vis) L Vickers (7)　20/1: -65360: Trkd ldrs, btn 4f out: 12th: see 3295. 10　17
*4376 **SHERIFF** 8 [6]　9-9-11 (57)(6ex) S Whitworth　5/1 JT FAV: 034110: Mid div, btn 4f out: 13th: btr 4376. 　3　11
2173 **DUTCH DYANE** 122 [17]　7-8-11 (43) S Carson (3)　10/1: 3-5300: Prom, struggling halfway & eased 　20　0
fnl 2f: 14th: 4 month abs: see 1394.
4376 **Irelands Eye** 8 [13] 5-8-8 (40)(vis) G Bardwell 20/1:　　1264] **Backwoods** 893 [16] 7-9-4 (50) T G McLaughlin 33/1:
211 **Vantage Point** 308 [5] 4-9-3 (49) N Callan 33/1:
17 ran　　　Time 3m 50.2 (26.0)　　　(Les Buckley)　　　P C Haslam Middleham, N Yorks

4509	5.30 CONFERENCE HCAP 3YO 0-65 (F)　　1m2f　　Heavy 167　-00 Slow	[71]
	£2991　　£854　　£427	

4436 **LADY JONES** 5 [11]　J Pearce 3-8-8 (51) J Fortune　3/1 FAV: 005601: 3 b f Emperor Jones - So 　57
Beguiling (Woodman) Held up, prog to lead over 2f out & sn in command, readily: qck reapp: earlier scored at
Haydock (h'cap): '99 Brighton wnr (sell, rtd 61 at best): eff at 1m/10f on fast, relishes soft & hvy grnd:
acts on a gall or sharp/undul trk: seems best held up.

4370 **SATIRE** 8 [9]　T J Etherington 3-8-0 (40)(3ow) J Tate 33/1: -50002: 3 br f Terimon - Salchow (Niniski) 　5　43
Held up, rdn & kept on fnl 2f, no threat to wnr: eff at 10f, handles hvy grnd: lightly rcd & mod form prev.

4334 **GOLDEN ROD** 13 [3]　P W Harris 3-8-4 (47) P Doe 8/1: 460003: 3 ch g Rainbows For Life - Noble Form 　7　40
(Double Form) Led 7f, sn no impress: see 1743, 1608.

3612 **LEEN** 60 [10]　M J Polglase 3-8-1 (44) Martin Dwyer 14/1: 060204: Chsd ldrs 1m: abs, prev with C Cox. 　2½　34
3819 **MEMPHIS TEENS** 90 [12]　3-9-7 (64) S Whitworth 12/1: 30305: Held up, rdn/mod gains fnl 2f: abs. 　2½　43
4448 **TYCOONS LAST** 4 [13]　3-9-4 (61) T G McLaughlin 7/1: 304106: Chsd ldrs 1m: qck reapp: btr 4108. 　1¼　47
3806 **THE LONELY WIGEON** 51 [15]　3-7-10 (39)(4oh) G Baker (5)　20/1: 050657: Dwelt, held up, little 　6　19
hdwy: 7 wk abs: longer 10f trip, t-strap ommitted.

4404 **COSMIC SONG** 6 [1]　3-8-3 (46) J Quinn 20/1: 460508: Chsd ldrs 1m: qck reapp: btr 1722 (9f, g/s). 　shd　26
3255 **STAFFORD KING** 75 [2]　3-8-5 (48) R Brisland (5)　9/1: 006409: Held up, no impress: op 7/1, 11 wk 　6　22
abs: eff at 10/12f on firm & hvy grnd: btr 2656, 1002.

3971 **CHILWORTH** 40 [4]　3-8-5 (48) A Daly 10/1: 003000: Prom 7f: 10th: 6 wk abs: btr 2026 (7f, firm). 　2　20
*4313 **CENTAUR SPIRIT** 15 [6]　3-9-1 (58) R Havlin 11/2: 040010: Trkd ldrs, wknd over 2f out: 11th: op 4/1. 　2　28
3530 **Bosscat** 64 [16] 3-8-12 (55)(bl) N Callan 20/1:　　4361 **Northern Trio** 10 [5] 3-8-0 (43) A Mackay 33/1:
3827 **Dee Diamond** 50 [8] 3-7-10 (39)(5oh) D Mernagh (1)　14/1:
14 ran　　　Time 2m 19.00 (16.7)　　　(Mrs Jean Routledge)　　　J Pearce Newmarket, Suffolk

Official Going　　SOFT Stalls: Str Course - Stands Side, Rem - Inside

4510	2.05 NEWPORT CLAIMER 3YO+ (F)　　1m6f　　Soft 110　-52 Slow	
	£2289　　£654　　£327　　3 yo rec 9 lb	

3731 **ACEBO LYONS** 56 [4]　A P Jarvis 5-8-13 D Holland　11/4 FAV: 403201: 5 b m Waajib - Etage (Ile de Bourbon) 　39
Held up, rdn/hdwy fnl 2f to lead ins last, drvn out: bckd: 8 wk abs: earlier scored at Doncaster (lady rdrs
h'cap, rtd 60): rnr-up in '99 (rtd 57, h'cap, unplcd on sand, rtd 20a): '98 Haydock wnr (stks, rtd 70): eff
at 10/14f on fast & soft: best without vis: runs best when fresh, likes a stiff/gall trck: can rate higher.

4280 **TURGENEV** 20 [12]　R Bastiman 11-8-10 J Fortune 5/1: 664002: 11 b g Sadler's Wells - Tilia 　½　34
(Dschingis Khan) Chsd ldrs, rdn & kept on fnl 2f, not pace of wnr: tough 11yo: see 576.

4409 **HIGH BEAUTY** 7 [3]　M J Ryan 3-7-10 G Baker (5)　16/1: 000653: 3 br f High Kicker - Tendresse 　1¾　27
(Tender King) Dwelt, held up, styd on fnl 2f, not able to chall: op 14/1, clr rem: eff at 14f on soft: mdn.

4149 **BLOWING AWAY** 29 [6]　J Pearce 6-8-11 G Bardwell 14/1: 503104: Chsd ldrs, onepace fnl 3f: op 12/1. 　4　29
4391 **SILKEN LADY** 8 [9]　4-8-7 J Tate 25/1: 605055: Held up, prog/lead over 2f out, hdd ins last, fdd. 　1½　24
4100 **CARAMELLE** 33 [11]　4-8-9 I Mongan (5)　33/1: 0006: Prom, saddle slipped early, & outpcd, late gains 　5　21
wide: some promise here in the circumstances: see 3189.

2076 **DJAIS** 126 [5]　11-9-2 (vis) R Havlin 7/2: /6-127: Held up, rdn 3f out: op 9/2, jumps fit. 　5　23
recent Huntingdon wnr (h'cap, rtd 88h, eff at 2m6f/3m2f on firm & gd/soft): see 2076, 1802 (AW clmr).

4151 **MARIANA** 33 [1]　5-8-7 D McGaffin (1)　25/1: 303008: Led over 4f out, hdd/btn 2f out: flattered 3247. 　½　13
4178 **KATIES CRACKER** 27 [8]　5-8-5 S Carson 25/1: 046409: Led 9f: rcnt jumps rnr (unplcd, rtd 57h). 　4　7
4149 **MISCHIEF** 29 [10]　4-8-10 (vis) G Hannon (7)　33/1: 165000: Chsd ldrs 12f: 10th: see 2827 (firm). 　3½　9
4176 **Bamboozle** 28 [2] 4-8-11 J Quinn 16/1:　　4041 **Cool Vibes** 36 [1] 5-8-10 (vis) K Darley 12/1:
3406 **Italian Rose** 69 [7] 5-8-9 S Righton 14/1:

13 ran Time 3m 20.5 (22.7) (Terence P Lyons II) A P Jarvis Aston Upthorpe, Oxon

---

4511 2.40 LOUND NURSERY HCAP 2YO 0-85 (D) 5f43y Soft 110 -07 Slow [92]
£3510 £1080 £540 £270 Majority racing centre favoured

4338 **Y TO KMAN** 13 [1] R Hannon 2-9-7 (85) R Hughes 5/4 FAV: 124061: 2 b c Mujadil - Hazar (Thatching) 92
Made all, rdn/clr 1f out, styd on strongly fnl 1f under hands & heels riding: well bckd: earlier scored at Kempton
(mdn, debut): stays 6f, apprec return to 5f: acts on gd & soft grnd, prob handles fast: gd weight carrier, likes
to force the pace: handles a stiff/gall or easy trk: useful.
4219 **PRINCESS OF GARDA** 25 [4] Mrs G S Rees 2-9-4 (82) K Darley 9/1: 454002: 2 b f Komaite - Malcesine 3½ 82
(Auction Ring) Chsd wnr, no impress over 1f out: acts on fast & soft grnd: see 2248 (made all).
-4367 **AMEN CORNER** 9 [2] M Johnston 2-9-1 (79) M Hills 11/2: 135023: 2 ch c Mt Livermore - For All 1½ 76
Seasons (Crafty Prospector) Chsd ldrs, rdn & onepace fnl 2f: acts on fast, fibresand & handles soft: see 4367.
4179 **RED RYDING HOOD** 7 [5] C A Dwyer 2-8-12 (76) D Holland 7/2: 232054: Led race racing stands side, 1¼ 70
no impress on ldrs in centre over 1f out: return to faster grnd may suit: btr 4179, 3630 & 3394.
4209 **MAY PRINCESS** 25 [3] 2-8-5 (69) R Winston 20/1: 0005: Nvr on terms: h'cap bow, dropped in trip. 4 55
4131 **LADY ROCK** 31 [6] 2-8-4 (68) J Quinn 11/1: 046366: Al near: flattered 3500 (firm). hd 53
4214 **XALOC BAY** 25 [8] N Callan 13/2: -22007: Dwelt, in tch stands side 3f: op 11/2: btr 2700 (6f) nk 61
7 ran Time 1m 06.2 (6.1) (The Cayman 'A' Team) R Hannon East Everleigh, Wilts

---

4512 3.15 STH NORFOLK MDN 2YO (D) 1m str Soft 110 -19 Slow
£3932 £1210 £605 £302 Raced towards centre

4349 **CAUGHNAWAGA** 12 [2] H R A Cecil 2-9-0 T Quinn 4/6 FAV: 61: 2 b c Indian Ridge - Wakria (Sadler's 96 +
Wells) Trkd ldrs, pushed along & prog to lead over 1f out, styd on well ins last, pushed out: hvly bckd: confirmed
promise of debut: dam a Listed wnr in France: eff at 1m, shld stay further: acts on gd & soft grnd, stiff/gall
or fair trk: useful colt, type to rate higher next term.
3121 **CANADA** 82 [3] B W Hills 2-9-0 M Hills 9/2: 422: 2 b c Ezzoud - Chancel (Al Nasr) ¾ 92
Chsd ldrs, rdn/ch over 1f out, kept on well ins last, not pace of wnr: 3/1, 12 wk abs: styd longer 1m trip
well, 10f will suit next term: acts on fast & soft grnd: useful, can win a mdn: see 3121, 2563.
-- **YORK CLIFF** [10] J H M Gosden 2-9-0 J Fortune 14/1: 3: 2 b c Marju - Azm (Unfuwain) nk 91 +
Led, rdn/hdd over 1f out, kept on well ins last: mkt deb: op 8/1: Marju colt, Apr foal: dam a mdn: sire a top-class 1m/12f
performer: eff at 1m, mid-dists looks sure to suit: acts on soft: encouraging intro, will win races on this evidence.
4281 **MA JOLIE** 19 [4] H Akbary 2-8-9 J Stack 7/1: 034: Al prom, rdn/ch over 1f out, no impress ins last: 2½ 82
clr rem: confirmed improvement of 4281, now qual for h'caps & shld find a race.
2599 **DUCS DREAM** 105 [5] R Winston 66/1: 45: Mid-div, eff 4f out, btn over 1f out: 3 month abs. 5 80
-- **BLUSHING PRINCE** [8] 2-9-0 J Weaver 20/1: 6: Held up, rdn/mod gains fnl 2f: Priolo colt, Mar ½ 79
foal, cost 15,000 gns: first foal: dam a 3yo wnr abroad: sire a top-class miler: with J Noseda.
4161 **LAZEEM** 17 [17] 2-9-0 G Carter 20/1: 07: Held up, mod late gains: op 8/1: see 4161. 1¼ 75
-- **CAREL** [16] 2-9-0 M Fenton 20/1: 8: Held up, eff 3f out, no impress: Polish Precedent colt, Apr 5 70
foal: half brother to a 2m wnr: dam a 12f wnr: looks sure to relish mid/staying dists in time, with M Bell.
4341 **PUZZLE** 13 [9] 2-9-0 (t) A Clark 66/1: 9: Held up, eff 3f out, no impress: well bhd on debut 2½ 66
prev: half brother to smart 6f wnr Efisio, dam a 6f/1m wnr: with Lady Herries.
4161 **RANVILLE** 29 [13] 2-9-0 G Hind 50/1: 00: In tch halfway, sn btn: 10th: mod form so far. shd 66
3840 **DANCE IN THE DAY** 50 [14] W Ryan 50/1: 00: Chsd ldrs 6f: 11th: 7 wk abs, stablemate of 7th. 1 65
-- **SHOW THE WAY** [7] 2-9-0 J Quinn 50/1: 0: Dwelt, al towards rear: 12th: Hernando colt, Apr foal, hd 64
cost IR6,000gns: dam a 12f wnr: sire a top-class 12f performer: sure to relish mid-dists in time: with A Jarvis.
3940 **Crossways** 42 [6] 2-9-0 R Mullen 50/1: 3665 **Grandma Griffiths** 59 [15] 2-8-9 W Supple 66/1:
3999 **Masque Tonnerre** 39 [12] 2-9-0 P Robinson 25/1: 4336 **High Tempo** 13 [11] 2-9-0 Darren Williams (5) 66/1:
-- **Pachinco** [1] 2-9-0 D Holland 50/1:
17 ran Time 1m 45.4 (10.3) (Lady Harrison) H R A Cecil Newmarket, suffolk

---

4513 3.50 TOTE HCAP 3YO+ 0-80 (D) 7f str Soft 110 +09 Fast [77]
£7637 £2350 £1175 £587 3 yo rec 2 lb Raced towards centre

*4365 **SHARP GOSSIP** 9 [6] J A R Toller 4-8-7 (56) S Whitworth 6/1: 002211: 4 b g College Chapel - Idle 62
Gossip (Runnett) Trkd ldrs, led over 1f out, held on well fnl 1f, rdn out: best time of day: recent Southwell wnr
(appr h'cap, rtd 63a, 1st success): ex-Irish mdn, dual '99 rnr-up: eff at 6f, suited to 7f/1m, may get further:
acts on fast, soft & fibresand: likes a sharp/fair trk: without blnks: nicely h'capped, shld land hat-trick.
4428 **SAND HAWK** 6 [11] D Shaw 5-8-0 (49)(bl) T Williams 8/1: 106222: 5 ch g Polar Falcon - Ghassanah nk 53
(Pas de Seul) Held up, prog/ch fnl 1f, just held cl-home: qk reapp, clr rem: consistent, deserves another race.
4414 **OMNIHEAT** 7 [12] M J Ryan 3-9-6 (71)(bl) P Robinson 16/1: 005043: 3 b f Ezzoud - Lady Bequick 4 69
(Sharpen Up) Held up, rdn & kept on fnl 2f, no threat to front pair: back on a wng mark: btr 1649 (10f).
4136 **JEFFREY ANOTHERRED** 31 [14] M Dods 6-9-2 (65) F Lynch 7/1: 042044: Chsd ldrs halfway, rdn & kept hd 62
on from over 1f out, nvr able to chall: ar fair mark at present, likes Ayr/Doncaster: see 3708, 2163.
4293 **AKEBONO** 19 [5] 4-8-4 (53) D R McCabe 25/1: 100005: Hmpd/towards rear early, kept on fnl 2f, hd 49
no threat: return to soft may suit 5/6f: see 3436 (5f).
4204 **SARSON** 25 [17] 4-9-7 (70) R Hughes 11/1: 000046: Trkd ldrs, onepace fnl 2f: see 4204, 1676. ½ 65
4080 **CLOTTED CREAM** 34 [2] 3-9-12 (77) S Sanders 8/1: 000:Chsd ldrs 6f: op 8/1: btr 4080, 1500. ¾ 71
4287 **ALMASI** 19 [1] 8-9-10 (73) G Baker (5) 12/1: 022508: Held up, eff 2f out, no impress: see 1531. ½ 66
4126 **DOLPHINELLE** 31 [7] 4-9-0 (63) O Urbina 25/1: 160009: Held up, rdn 3f out, no impress: see 1926. shd 56
3839 **PRIME OFFER** 50 [8] 4-9-2 (65) K Darley 16/1: 410-50: Led after 2f till over 1f out: 10th, btr 3839 (frm). nk 57
4487 **BETTY BATHWICK** 2 [3] 3-8-12 (63) D Holland 33/1: -00100: Prom till over 1f out: 11th: quick reapp. ½ 54
4215 **PROSPECTORS COVE** 25 [9] 7-9-7 (70) T Quinn 4/1 FAV: 623600: Al rear: 12th: btr 1611 (C/D, g/s). 2½ 57
3623 **THE THIRD CURATE** 61 [4] 5-7-13 (48) J Quinn 12/1: 001100: Led 1f, prom 5f: 13th: op 8/1: abs. 2½ 31
4270 **CAPE COAST** 21 [13] 3-9-5 (70) S Carson (3) 9/1: 112630: Al rear: 15th: see 4080, 3854. 0
4204 **Fallachan** 25 [16] 4-9-6 (69) Darren Williams (5) 20/1: 4215 **Kamareyah** 25 [15] 3-9-8 (73) W Supple 20/1:
4340 **Infotec** 13 [10] 3-9-5 (70) J Stack 20/1:
17 ran Time 1m 29.7 (7.1) (Buckingham Thoroughbreds I) J A R Toller Newmarket, Suffolk

---

1398

YARMOUTH WEDNESDAY OCTOBER 25TH Lefthand, Flat, Fair Track

4514 4.25 EBF HERRINGFLEET MDN 2YO (D) 7f str Soft 110 -14 Slow
£4160 £1280 £640 £320 Raced towards centre

3840 **HALLAND 50** [4] G Wragg 2-9-0 D Holland 15/2: 661: 2 ch c Halling - Northshiel (Northfields) 89+
Al prom, styd on well fnl 2f under hands & heels riding to lead nr line, shade readily: op 8/1: 7 wk abs: Feb foal,
cost 140,000gns, half brother to sev wnrs abroad, dam a 7f wnr: eff at 7f, 1m will suit: acts on firm & soft,
stiff/gall or fair track: runs well fresh: progressive colt, given a fine ride here & can rate more highly.
-- **CONTINUATION** [11] J H M Gosden 2-9-0 J Fortune 10/1: 2: 2 b c Sadler's Wells - Sequel (Law nk 86
Society) Held up, prog to lead ins last, hdd nr line: mkt drifter, op 9/2: Apr foal, cost 180,000gns: brother to
a smart 2yo Irish performer Family Tradition: dam a mdn: sire top-class performer at 1m/12f: eff at 7f, 1m+ will
suit: acts on soft grnd: most encouraging intro, can improve & find a similar contest.
-- **SEA STAR** [9] H R A Cecil 2-9-0 T Quinn 1/2 FAV: 3: 2 b c Distant Relative - Storm Card (Zalazl) 2 83
Trkd ldrs, rdn/ch over 1f out, no pace of front pair ins last: hvly bckd at odds-on: Mar first foal: dam
unrcd: sire top-class 1m performer: eff at 7f on soft, 1m will suit: well regarded & can rate higher.
-- **PIETRO SIENA** [7] E A L Dunlop 2-9-0 G Carter 14/1: 4: Prom, led over 2f out, hdd ins last & no 3 79
extra: op 8/1: Gone West colt, Mar foal: half brother to a wnr abroad: dam a Gr3 Irish & Gr2 US wnr:
eff at 7f, 1m shld suit: acts on soft grnd: encouraging intro.
-- **RAINY RIVER** [2] J H M Gosden 2-9-0 J Fortune 33/1: 5: Held up, kept on fnl 3f, no threat to ldrs: Irish River filly, 1 73
May first foal, cost 100,000IR gns: dam unrcd: sire a top class juv & 1m performer: come on for this.
-- **NIYABAH** [15] 2-8-9 W Supple 7/1: 6: Held up, eff 2f out, no impress on ldrs: clr rem: op 5/1: 1¼ 71
Nashwan filly, Feb foal: sister to wnrs btwn 7f/10f: dam a 6f juv wnr: mid-dists will suit.
-- **SERENGETI BRIDE** [13] 2-8-9 M Tebbutt 33/1: 7: Held up, mod gains fnl 2f: Lion Cavern filly, 6 62
half sister to smart 10f wnr Winter Romance: dam a 7f/1m wnr: shld appreci 1m+, with E Dunlop.
3985 **NEVER PROMISE 40** [12] 2-8-9 M Hills 11/1: -08: Chsd ldrs till over 1f out: op 8/1: 6 wk abs. shd 62
4267 **JAMIE MY BOY 21** [5] 2-9-0 N Callan 50/1: 409: Prom 5f: now qual for h'caps. nk 66
-- **BLUE AWAY** [3] 2-9-0 R Mullen 50/1: 0: Slowly away, al rear: 10th: Blues Traveller gldg, Apr foal, 1 65
cost 34,000 gns: half brother to a 5f 2yo wnr: dam plcd at 1m as a 2yo: with C Wall.
-- **ROMAN HIDEAWAY** [16] 2-9-0 S Sanders 25/1: 0: Al rear: 11th: Hernando colt, cost 82,000 IR gns: ½ 64
dam a 7f French wnr, sire top-class 12f performer: with Sir M Prescott.
-- **TROTTERS FUTURE** [8] 2-9-0 R Hughes 33/1: 0: Al towards rear: 12th: longer priced stablemate ½ 63
of 6th: Emperor Jones colt, Apr foal, cost 20,000 gns: brother to a 7f juv wnr: dam unrcd.
4268 **GOLDEN BRIEF 21** [10] 2-9-0 Darren Williams (5) 50/1: 00: Led 4f, sn btn: 13th: mod form. ½ 62
4341 **Rateeba 13** [1] 2-8-9 A McGlone 50/1: 4183 **Winning Pleasure 27** [14] 2-9-0 J Quinn 50/1:
4267 **Anonymity 21** [6] 2-9-0 F Lynch 20/1:
16 ran Time 1m 31.3 (8.7) (Mollers Racing) G Wragg Newmarket, Suffolk

4515 5.00 CLASSIFIED STKS 3YO+ 0-85 (C) 1m2f21y Soft 110 -01 Slow
£6597 £2030 £1015 £507 3 yo rec 5 lb

4392 **GENEROUS DIANA 8** [3] H R A Cecil 4-8-13 T Quinn 2/1 FAV: 221-21: 4 ch f Generous - Lypharitissima 78
(Lightning) Trkd ldrs, no room over 1f out, rdn & styd on well ins last to lead nr line: well bckd: '99 wnr at
Lingfield (mdn, rtd 71, K Mahdi): eff at 7f, now suited by 10f, may get further: acts on fast & soft grnd, sharp/
undul or fair trk: proving tough & progressive.
4392 **THUNDERING SURF 8** [6] J R Jenkins 3-9-0 J Fortune 11/4: 135432: 3 b c Lugana Beach - Thunder hd 83
Bug (Secreto) Held up, hdwy fnl 3f & rdn/led ins last, hdd nr line: bckd, better ride: acts on fast & soft.
4212 **PINCHINCHA 25** [4] D Morris 6-9-8 K Darley 9/2: 421533: 6 b g Priolo - Western Heights (Shirley 1¾ 84
Heights) Trkd ldrs, rdn/led over 2f out, hdd & no extra in last: clr rem: acts on firm & soft: v tough.
4342 **SOLO FLIGHT 13** [1] B W Hills 3-9-0 M Hills 7/1: -21004: Held up, eff 3f out, no impress: see 1466 (mdn). 4 77
4212 **CULZEAN 25** [5] 4-9-5 R Hughes 6/1: 362005: Held up, eff 2f out, sn btn: btr 2287 (fast). hd 76
4115 **RIVERTOWN 32** [2] 6-9-2 W Ryan 20/1: 435606: Led after 1f till over 2f out, fdd: see 3230, 2630. ½ 72
4465 **THE CASTIGATOR 4** [8] 3-8-11 M Fenton 150/1: 000507: In tch 7f: quick reapp, impossible task. dist 0
4465 **TIME FOR THE CLAN 4** [7] 3-8-11 M Tebbutt 150/1: 000000: Prom 5f: quick reapp: poorly plcd again. 9 0
8 ran Time 2m 15.4 (11.2) (Greenfield Stud) H R A Cecil Newmarket, Suffolk

MUSSELBURGH THURSDAY OCTOBER 26TH Righthand, Sharp Track

Official Going SOFT (GOOD/SOFT places). Stalls: 5f - Stands Side; Rem - Inside.

4516 1.55 LINKS PAVILION HCAP 3YO+ 0-75 (E) 5f Soft 91 -15 Slow [74]
£2779 £794 £397

4459 **GARNOCK VALLEY 6** [5] A Berry 10-8-9 (55) D Holland 9/2 JT FAV: 130431: 10 b g Dowsing - Sunley 61
Sinner (Try My Best) Rdn bhd, hdwy 2f out, switched right & styd on to lead ins last, rdn clr: qck reapp:
earlier won at Southwell (2, h'cap & seller, rtd 66a): '99 scorer at W'hampton, Lingfield (clmr), Southwell (2)
& Newbury (h'cap, rtd 52 & 68a): '98 Musselburgh wnr: eff over 5/7f on fast, likes soft & AWs: eff with/without
blnks & runs well fresh under big weights: handles any trk, likes a sharp one, esp Southwell: v tough 10yo.
+4307 **PRIME RECREATION 17** [8] P S Felgate 3-9-3 (63) Dale Gibson 9/2 JT FAV: 000612: 3 b g Primo 3 63
Dominie - Night Transaction (Tina's Pet) Chsd ldrs, hdwy to lead over 1f out till ins last, no pace of wnr: op 3/1.
4405 **GET STUCK IN 8** [2] Miss L A Perratt 4-10-0 (74) C Lowther 5/1: 023003: 4 b g Up And At'Em - Shoka ¾ 72
(Kaldoun) Set pace till over 1f out, no extra: clr of rem under a big weight & all 3 wins at 6f: see 4010.
4407 **ROBIN HOOD 8** [13] Miss L A Perratt 3-8-5 (51) R Winston 11/2: 020034: Slow away, switched left 3 43
start & bhd, some late gains: see 4407.
4407 **TANCRED TIMES 8** [11] 5-8-11 (57) F Lynch 12/1: 606205: Prom, wknd over 1f out: op 8/1: btr 4295. ½ 48
4407 **BRANSTON PICKLE 8** [10] 3-9-2 (62) K Darley 6/1: 120006: In tch, rdn & btn appr fnl 1f: see 4407. 1¾ 49
*3781 **UPPER CHAMBER 54** [9] 4-7-10 (42)(4oh) P Hanagan (1) 12/1: 000517: Prom, wknd over 1f out: 8 3½ 22
wk abs: btr 3781 (mdn h'cap, gd/soft).
4010 **SABRE LADY 40** [4] 3-9-10 (70) J Carroll 25/1: 000008: Al rdn & bhd: abs: see 1219 (gd/firm). nk 49
4307 **SHATIN BEAUTY 17** [12] 3-8-0 (46) G Baker (5) 20/1: 000009: Chsd ldrs till wknd 2f out: out of sorts. 4 17
4307 **MARIA FROM CAPLAW 17** [1] 3-7-10 (42)(4oh) K Dalgleish (5) 50/1: 500-00: Al bhd: 10th. shd 13

3825 **Shalarise** 52 [7] 3-8-4 (50)(bl) G Duffield 33/1: 4327 **Johayro** 16 [6] 7-8-12 (58) A Culhane 14/1:
4327 **Pallium** 16 [3] 12-7-10 (42)(t)(17oh) J McAuley 66/1:
13 ran   Time 1m 02.8 (5.3)   (Robert Aird)   A Berry Cockerham, Lancs.

4517   2.25 WEIGHING MED AUCT MDN 2YO (E)   7f30y str   Soft 91   -35 Slow
£2842   £812   £406

4402 **GEM BIEN** 8 [2] Andrew Turnell 2-9-0 P Fessey 25/1: 501: 2 b c Bien Bien - Easter Gem (Jade Hunter)   76
Cl-up, led 2f out, styd on for press ins last, drvn out: Mar first foal: imprvd for step up to 7f on soft grnd.
-4422 **ALAKANANDA** 7 [5] Sir Mark Prescott 2-8-9 G Duffield 4/7 FAV: -222: 2 b f Hernando - Alouette   nk   70
(Darshaan) Cl-up, eff to chall dist, kept on, just held: well bckd at odds on & 3rd successive rnr-up placing.
4403 **ROSE OF AMERICA** 8 [12] Miss L A Perratt 2-8-9 C Lowther 50/1: 503: 2 ch f Brief Truce - Kilcoy   ½   69
(Secreto) Went left start, in tch, effort & switched left over 1f out, kept on ins last, just held: much improved
over this easy 7f on soft grnd: win a modest race on this form, see 4303.
4281 **FOXES LAIR** 20 [3] M Dods 2-9-0 J Fanning 9/2: 54: Set pace till 2f out, kept on same pace for   shd   74
press, not btn far: stays 7f on soft grnd: see 4281.
4423 **SHATIN PLAYBOY** 7 [7] 2-9-0 F Lynch 14/1: 440205: Chsd ldrs, rdn & onepace over 1f out: stablemate   ¾   72$
of 3rd, op 10/1: has had chances & prob flattered by this rating: see 4423, 4303.
3776 **GARDOR** 54 [8] 2-9-0 J Carroll 8/1: 44426: Keen cl-up, ev ch appr fnl 1f, no extra: clr of rem   1   70
after 7 wk abs, op 6/1: ran to form of 3776.
-- **BELSTANE BADGER** [11] 2-8-9 R Lappin 33/1: 7: Bmpd start, nvr a factor on debut: op 14/1:   5   57
Jan foal: half-sister to a 7f juv wnr.
-- **BELSTANE FOX** [9] 2-8-9 R Winston 50/1: 8: Slow away & al bhd on debut: Apr foal: with I Semple.   6   48
4402 **NANCYS BOY** 8 [4] 2-9-0 A Culhane 33/1: 09: Al bhd: see 4402.   5   46
4281 **CYBER SANTA** 20 [1] 2-9-0 O Pears 25/1: 500: Slow away, al bhd in 10th: twice below 3952 (debut).   3   42
-- **SHOOT AWAY** [10] 2-8-9 Dale Gibson 7/1: 0: Slow away, sn in tch till wknd over 2f out: 1½   35
11th on debut: op 4/1: Apr foal: bred to apprec 1m+ in time.
-- **BRAVO** [8] 2-9-0 Dean McKeown 25/1: 0: Slow away, al bhd: fin last on debut: brother to a 6f wnr.   1½   38
12 ran   Time 1m 34.0 (9.1)   (Mrs Claire Hollowood)   Andrew Turnell Sandhutton, N.Yorks.

4518   2.55 STEWARDS HCAP DIV 1 3YO+ 0-70 (E)   7f30y rnd   Soft 91   -31 Slow   [68]
£2268   £648   £324   3 yo rec 2 lb

4358 **LADY OF WINDSOR** 12 [4] I Semple 3-9-2 (58)(bl) R Winston 6/1: 604041: 3 ch f Woods Of Windsor -   63
North Lady (Northfields) Made all, clr well over 2f out, kept on: op 3/1, well rdn: earlier won here at
Musselburgh (class stks, first win): plcd in '99 (rtd 74): suited by 7f/1m on firm, soft & fibresand: handles
any trk, likes Musselburgh: eff in blnks/a visor: reportedly in season & trainer describes her as a "madam".
4425 **ENCOUNTER** 7 [5] J Hetherton 4-8-12 (52) O Pears 10/1: 054502: 4 b g Primo Dominie - Dancing Spirit 2½   53
(Ahonoora) Chsd ldrs, eff 2f out, kept on to take 2nd fnl 1f, no threat to wnr: gave wnr too much rope & prev
thought best on faster grnd, tho' clearly handles soft: see 3144 (ladies sell h'cap).
4324 **PHILAGAIN** 16 [8] Miss L A Perratt 3-7-13 (41) N Kennedy 16/1: 304003: 3 b f Ardkinglass - Andalucia   1¼   40
(Rheingold) In tch, eff 2f out, onepace: handles soft, acts on fast: see 2205.
*4426 **ONLY FOR GOLD** 7 [1] A Berry 5-9-3 (57)(6ex) J Carroll 7/4 FAV: 005614: Chsd wnr, rdn & onepace   ½   55
over 1f out: ran to form of 4426.
4327 **JACMAR** 16 [3] 5-8-5 (45) F Lynch 14/1: 000005: Bhd, late gains: op 8/1, all 6 wins at Hamilton.   2   40
4405 **RYEFIELD** 8 [7] 5-9-12 (66) Dean McKeown 5/2: 633166: In tch, wknd over 1f out: nicely bckd.   3   57
3375 **POWER GAME** 71 [2] 7-7-10 (38)(10oh) J McAuley 50/1: 040007: Al bhd: 10 wk abs: see 2046, 1685.   2   24
4428 **FOREST QUEEN** 7 [6] 3-7-10 (38)(5oh) D Mernagh (3) 25/1: 000068: Al bhd: see 4428.   2   23
8 ran   Time 1m 33.7 (8.8)   (Raeburn Brick Ltd)   I Semple Carluke, S.Lanarkshire.

4519   3.25 ROCKAVON BAR MDN 3YO (D)   1m rnd   Soft 91   +17 Fast
£2726   £779   £389

2581 **AURA OF GRACE** 106 [3] M Johnston 3-8-9 D Holland 4/1: 0-6501: 3 b f Southern Halo - Avarice   72
(Manila) Cl-up, led 3f out, sn clr, easily: best time of day, op 5/2: over 3 month abs & unplcd for R Armstrong
earlier: stays 1m on soft: runs well fresh: expect his smart trainer to extract further improvement.
4366 **FOR HEAVENS SAKE** 10 [4] C W Thornton 3-9-0 Dean McKeown 7/1: 323562: 3 b g Rambo Dancer -   10   59
Angel Fire (Nashwan) Cl-up, eff to go 2nd 3f out, no impress on wnr: stiff task back in trip: mdn after 16.
4387 **THERE WITH ME** 9 [2] J H M Gosden 3-8-9 K Darley 4/11 FAV: 33: 3 b f Distant View - Breeze   2   51
Lass (It's Freezing) In tch, rdn & bhd well over 1f out: well bckd at odds on & better expected after debut.
4255 **SCHATZI** 23 [4] D Moffatt 3-8-9 (vis) J Fanning 25/1: 200054: In tch, wknd 3f out: needs sell h'caps.   20   21
4133 **LUBOHENRIK** 32 [5] 3-8-9 R Winston 50/1: 00-005: Led till 3f out, wknd: poor.   8   9
-- **IAMATMEWHITZEND** [1] 3-8-9 R Lappin 50/1: 6: Slow away, al bhd, no ch on debut: op 12/1.   dist   0
6 ran   Time 1m 43.4 (5.9)   (R N Bracher)   M Johnston Middleham, N.Yorks.

4520   3.55 ROSEBERY HALL HCAP DIV 1 3YO+ 0-65 (F)   1m1f   Soft 91   -01 Slow   [61]
£1788   £511   £255   3 yo rec 4 lb

4428 **AMBUSHED** 7 [1] P Monteith 4-9-7 (54) R Winston 5/1: 210631: 4 b g Indian Ridge - Surprise Move   58
(Simply Great) Led after 1f, made rest, kept on for press fnl 1f: earlier scored at Southwell (appr mdn h'cap,
with M Johnston, rtd 36a) & Hamilton (h'cap): eff over 1m/9f on firm, hvy & fibresand: prob handles any trk
& effective with/without blnks: best dominating: in form & proving tough.
4374 **KIDZ PLAY** 10 [5] J S Goldie 4-9-10 (57) A Culhane 11/4 JT FAV: 014P32: 4 b g Rudimentary - Saka   2   58
Saka (Camden Town) Cl-up, eff over 2f out, no extra for press well ins last: nicely bckd under top-weight.
4324 **GO THUNDER** 16 [8] D A Nolan 6-8-10 (43)(t) Iona Wands 11/1: 531403: 6 b g Nordico - Moving Off   3   40
(Henbit) Led 1f, hmpd over 4f out but kept on to chall 2f out, sn no extra: op 8/1: win a sell h'cap: see 3823.
3951 **SWYNFORD PLEASURE** 43 [6] J Hetherton 4-9-1 (48) O Pears 5/1: 003044: Chsd ldrs, rdn & no impress   3   41
fnl 2f: 6 wk abs, btr 2180 (firm), 2094.
3603 **A DAY ON THE DUB** 62 [7] 7-8-12 (45) J Fanning 11/4 JT FAV: 400505: Slow away, al bhd: unplcd   3   34
hdle rnr since 3603.
4374 **RIVERSDALE** 10 [2] 4-9-6 (53) J Carroll 11/1: 020-06: Al bhd: see 4374.   5   36
4404 **LANDICAN LAD** 8 [4] 3-9-3 (54) K Dalgleish (5) 50/1: 050007: Chsd ldrs, wknd over 3f out, t.o.   dist   0

MUSSELBURGH THURSDAY OCTOBER 26TH Righthand, Sharp Track

4428 **TOP OF THE CLASS** 7 [3] 3-9-8 (59) (BL) R Lappin 50/1: 030008: Al bhd: tried blnks: see 1710. 3 0
8 ran Time 1m 59.0 (8.3) (Allan W Melville) P Monteith Rosewell, Midlothian.

4521 4.25 OFFICIAL HCAP 3YO+ 0-60 (F) 1m5f Soft 91 [54]
£2310 £660 £330 3 yo rec 8 lb

1936 **CRAIGARY** 133 [10] D A Nolan 9-7-10 (22) (5oh) G Baker (5) 33/1: 6-0501: 9 b g Dunbeath - Velvet Pearl 26
(Record Token) Cl-up, styd on to lead 2f out, rdn on ins last: modest recent chase form, rtd 79c: rnr-up over
hdles in 99/00 (rtd 87h, stays 2m6.5f on firm & gd/soft, with Mrs A Duffield): modest Flat form in '99, '97 wnr at
Hamilton (sell h'cap, rtd 42): eff over 12/13f on firm & gd, likes soft & hvy: eff with/without blnks on any trk.
4134 **NORTHERN MOTTO** 32 [7] J S Goldie 7-9-0 (40) (VIS) K Dalgleish (5) 7/1: 436002: 7 b g Mtoto - Soulful 1½ 42
(Zino) Keen in lead, hdd 2f out, no extra: op 5/1, clr of rem in first time visor: has slipped to a handy mark.
4299 **TOTEM DANCER** 19 [9] J L Eyre 7-9-11 (51) D Holland 9/2: 063003: 7 b m Mtoto - Ballad Opera 5 48
(Sadler's Wells) In tch, lost pl over 5f out, some late gains: btr 3783, 1087.
4427 **HUTCHIES LADY** 7 [2] J S Goldie 8-8-11 (37) Joanna Badger (7) 6/1: 100254: Held up, eff over ½ 33
2f out, sn no extra: btr 4324 (9f, seller), 3805.
4306 **OCEAN DRIVE** 17 [8] 4-9-4 (44) C Lowther 14/1: 424005: Al bhd: see 3963. 3½ 36
4370 **ONE LIFE TO LIVE** 10 [4] 7-8-11 (37) (vis) T Williams 25/1: 40/056: In tch, btn over 2f out: see 4370. 1½ 28
4222 **HAPPY DAYS** 26 [6] 5-8-8 (34) J Bramhill 10/1: 524407: In tch, btn 3f out: well btn in a recent nov hdle. ¾ 24
4382 **SLANEYSIDE** 9 [5] 3-9-9 (57) G Duffield 20/1: 100068: Prom, wknd over 2f out: btr 3741 (gd/firm). 1 46
3805 **PRINCE NICHOLAS** 53 [11] 5-9-13 (53) Dean McKeown 11/2: 404069: Prom, wknd over 2f out: 8 wk abs.2½ 39
4256 **LENNY THE LION** 23 [1] 3-9-1 (49) A Culhane 7/2 FAV: 530000: Bhd, short of room over 2f out, no 1 34
impression: 10th: see 2332.
4324 **PHILMIST** 16 [3] 8-8-4 (30) (bl) R Winston 20/1: -00000: Al bhd: 11th: see 1361. 4 11
11 ran Time 3m 0.6 (James A Cringan) D A Nolan Newmains, N Lanarkshire.

4522 4.55 STEWARDS HCAP DIV 2 3YO+ 0-70 (E) 7f30y Soft 91 -49 Slow [68]
£2257 £645 £322 3 yo rec 2 lb

4327 **GAY BREEZE** 16 [6] P S Felgate 7-9-11 (65) K Darley 7/2: 000221: 7 b g Dominion - Judy's Dowry 69
(Dragonara Palace) Handy, hdwy to lead ins last, drvn out: top-weight: trained by D Nicholls in '99, plcd
sev times (h'caps, rtd 81): '98 wnr at Nottingham, Doncaster & Haydock (h'caps, rtd 80): winning form over
5/7f & acts on firm, hvy & fibresand: handles any track.
4407 **PICCOLO CATIVO** 8 [3] Mrs G S Rees 5-8-4 (44) G Duffield 13/2: 040002: 5 b m Komaite - Malcesine ¾ 46
(Auction Ring) Cl-up, led 4f out till ins last, not btn far: back on a fair mark & likes soft: see 1066.
4425 **MISTER WESTSOUND** 7 [7] Miss L A Perratt 8-7-10 (36) (bl) N Kennedy 9/2: 000633: 8 b g Cyrano nk 38
de Bergerac - Captivate (Mansingh) Slow away, held up, effort over 2f out, no extra ins last: see 4425.
4426 **BODFARI ANNA** 7 [2] J L Eyre 4-9-2 (56) (vis) D Holland 6/1: 002004: Bhd, kept on late, nrst fin: op 4/1. 2 55
4327 **SMOKEY FROM CAPLAW** 16 [5] 6-8-7 (46) (1ow) A Culhane 25/1: 000-05: Cl-up, rdn & outpcd 2f out, 2 43
sn short of room & no impression: op 12/1.
4425 **BIFF EM** 7 [8] 6-7-12 (38) (2ow) (3oh) Dale Gibson 10/1: 000506: Keen, handy, wknd over 1f out: op 7/1. ½ 33
4136 **MAMMAS BOY** 32 [4] 5-8-12 (52) C Lowther 3/1 FAV: 460167: Al bhd: twice below 3745 (fast grnd, 1m) 5 40
4327 **DOUBTLESS RISK** 16 [1] 3-7-10 (38) (8oh) J McAuley 33/1: 00-008: Led till 4f out, wknd 3f out: modest. 5 19
8 ran Time 1m 35.0 (10.1) (E Rollinson) P S Felgate Grimston, Leics.

4523 5.25 ROSEBERY HALL HCAP DIV 2 3YO+ 0-65 (F) 1m1f Soft 91 -20 Slow [61]
£1778 £508 £254 3 yo rec 4 lb

4427 **ACE OF TRUMPS** 7 [2] J Hetherton 4-8-10 (43) (t) N Kennedy 3/1: 352321: 4 ch g First Trump - 47
Elle Reef (Shareef Dancer) Handy, styd on to lead over 2f out, kept on for press ins last: well bckd &
deserved win after numerous plcd efforts: earlier scored at Hamilton (clmr) & here at Musselburgh (sell h'cap,
rtd 55): '99 scorer at Nottingham (sell h'cap) & Warwick (clmr, with W Haggas, rtd 70): eff over 7f/10f on firm,
hvy & any trk, likes Musselburgh: best in a t-strap, with/without blnks/visor: proving v tough.
4406 **TIME TO WYN** 8 [6] J G FitzGerald 4-8-7 (40) J Carroll 8/1: -00562: 4 b g Timeless Times - Wyn 2 41
Bank (Green God) Chsd ldrs, rdn & outpcd over 2f out, kept on late: acts on firm & soft: on a handy mark.
3731 **MARGARETS DANCER** 57 [9] J L Eyre 5-9-1 (48) (t) D Holland 8/1: 006103: 5 b g Rambo Dancer nk 49
- Cateryne (Ballymoss) Led till 3f out, sn rdn, kept on again ins last: abs: stays 9f, win another sell h'cap.
4363 **HOWARDS LAD** 12 [3] I Semple 3-9-6 (57) (bl) G Duffield 20/1: 200004: Slow away, bhd, effort 2f 2½ 54
out, btn when eased cl-home: blnks reapplied: acts on firm & soft: prob stays at least 1m: see 2396 (6f).
3741 **LITTLE JOHN** 56 [4] 4-9-13 (60) (BL) R Winston 12/1: 524235: Led 3f out till over 2f out, no 1 55
extra: 8 wk abs, tried blnks back in trip: see 1656.
4404 **LOVE KISS** 8 [1] 5-9-4 (51) T Williams 13/8 FAV: 064146: Chsd ldrs, switched left over 2f out, 3 42
sn wknd: well bckd: btr 4306.
4414 **STORMSWELL** 8 [5] 3-8-13 (50) R Winston 10/1: 040407: Al bhd: btr 4004 (7f). 2½ 37
4133 **FASTWAN** 32 [7] 4-7-10 (29) (vis) (9oh) K Dalgleish (5) 50/1: 000008: Cl-up, wknd over 2f out: see 4133. 5 9
4406 **AMRON** 8 [8] 13-8-0 (33) J Bramhill 16/1: 600009: Al bhd: 13yo now, see 846. 9 1
9 ran Time 2m 0.7 (10) (C D Barber-Lomax) J Hetherton Malton, N Yorks.

WINDSOR THURSDAY OCTOBER 26TH Sharp, figure eight track

Official Going HEAVY Stalls: Inside (Moved forwards 30 yards in 2nd & 3rd race).

4524 2.20 SENNHEISER FILLIES MDN 2YO (D) 1m67y rnd Heavy Inapplicable
£4166 £1282 £641 £320

-- **JUMAIREYAH** [8] L M Cumani 2-8-11 J P Spencer 12/1: -1: 2 b f Fairy King - Donya (Mill Reef) 80+
Dwelt, sn in tch, rdn/imprvd appr fnl 1f, styd on strongly to lead well inside last, drvn out: op 8/1: Feb foal,
half sister to a juv 6f wnr, also a 1m & 12f wnr: eff around 1m, further will suit next term: acts on hvy grnd
& runs v well fresh: acts on a sharp trck: improve over mid dists next term & can win more races.
-- **CARIOCA DREAM** [16] W J Haggas 2-8-11 P Robinson 14/1: -2: 2 b f Diesis - Highland Celidh ¾ 77+

(Scottish Reel) Dwelt, sn prom, ran green for press 2f out, styd on strongly inside last, closing at fin: March foal, half sister to a couple of 12f wnrs, dam scored over 1m/10f: eff over a sharp 1m on hvy grnd: encouraging debut, mid-dists sure to suit: will be winning next year.

4163 **ARAVONIAN 29** [14] R Hannon 2-8-11 R Hughes 6/1: -563: 2 ch f Night Shift - Age Of Reality (Alleged) Led to 4f out, remnd cl up, led again appr fnl 1f, hung badly left & caused interference just ins last, sn hdd, no extra: tchd 8/1, jockey received 3 day carless riding ban: handles gd/soft & hvy grnd: see 4035.	¾	75
-- **DOUBLE CROSSED** [15] H R A Cecil 2-8-11 T Quinn 5/4 FAV: -4: Dwelt, sn cl up, rdn appr fnl 3f, responding well for press when badly hmpd inside last, no ch after: well bckd tho' op 4/6 & looked unlucky not to get at least plcd here: April filly, half sister to a 12f wnr, dam scored over 10/12f: stys a sharp 1m on hvy: looks a sure-fire wnr over mid dists next year.	2	71 +
3910 **SHII TAKES GIRL 45** [9] 2-8-11 T Ashley 20/1: -305: Chsd ldrs, drvn 2f out, cl-up but lkd just held when hmpd ins last: clr rem, 6 wk abs: consistent form, stys 7f/1m on fast & hvy: apprec mid dists: see 3577.	nk	70
4322 **SWIFTMAR 16** [4] 2-8-11 J Fortune 20/1: -36: Dsptd lead, led 3f out, hdd appr fnl 1f, wknd, eased when btn: op 14/1: bred to relish mid-dists next year: see 4322.	3½	65
4034 **LADY ANGOLA 38** [13] 2-8-11 J Reid 10/1: -407: Chsd ldrs, rdn/onepcd appr fnl 1f: up in trip.	1¼	63
4403 **ALLELUIA 8** [2] 2-8-11 S Sanders 16/1: -368: Mid div, drvn/no response appr fnl 2f: up in trip.	1½	61
4349 **PLAY TIME 13** [6] 2-8-11 N Pollard 6/1: -09: Sn well bhd, plenty to do halfway, gd hdwy 2f out, no extra fnl 1f: tchd 12/1 & will come into her own over mid-dists next term: see 4349.	1¾	59
4163 **STAR OF WONDER 29** [12] 2-8-11 P Fitzsimons (5) 25/1: -00: Handy, rdn/lost tch fnl 2f, fin 10th.	2½	55
-- **LAURIESTON FLO** [10] 2-8-11 D McCabe 14/1: -0: Ran green in rear, mod late hdwy, 11th: op 10/1: 6,500gns Feb foal, half sister to a couple of wnrs, dam a mdn: with B J Meehan, learn from this.	¾	53
3953 **MASAKIRA 43** [11] 2-8-11 L Newman (3) 11/2: -40: Chsd ldrs, wknd qckly fnl 2f, fin 13th: v disappointing by prob not handle these testing conditions: much better on gd grnd on debut in 3953.		0

4309 Sitara 17 [6] 2-8-11 G Sparkes(7) 20/1:   4438 Ann Summers 6 [1] 2-8-11 Paul Eddery 33/1:
-- Memsahib [7] 2-8-11 D Cosgrave(7) 12/1:   4429 Nosmokewithoutfire 7 [3] 2-8-11 R Ffrench 33/1:
16 ran   Time 1m 50.2   (Sheikh Mohammed Obaid Al Maktoum)   L M Cumani Newmarket, Suffolk

---

4525   2.50 ALFINI NURSERY HCAP 2YO 0-85 (D)   6f   Heavy   Inapplicable   [88]
£3445   £1060   £530   £265   Stalls moved forwards 30 yards.

4323 **BARATHIKI 16** [6] P F I Cole 2-9-5 (79) I Mongan (5) 7/1: 146201: 2 gr f Barathea - Tagiki (Doyoun) Led/dsptd lead till hdd dist, rall strongly to get up nr fin, drvn out: drftd from 7/2: drop in trip: earlier won on debut at York (nov fill stakes, rtd 87 +): 30,000gns April foal, dam 7f juv wnr abroad: eff at 6f, stys 7f, poss nt 1m: acts on fast, hvy & a gall or sharp trk: bck to best & apprec drop in trip/omission of blnks.		83
*4372 **CAPTAIN GIBSON 10** [1] D J S ffrench Davis 2-9-4 (78)(6ex) T Quinn 7/2: 006212: 2 b g Beveled - Little Egret (Carwhite) Veered left start, al hanging left, veered badly left towards far rail over 2f out, drvn & ran on strongly against rail, led 1f out, styd on, hdd fnl strides: op 9/2 & would surely have won today if keeping a straight course: acts on gd & hvy grnd: see 4372.	nk	81
4269 **LAW BREAKER 22** [5] J Cullinan 2-8-3 (62) J Quinn 12/1: 405303: 2 ch c Case Law - Revelette (Runnett) Front rank, outpcd 2f out, rall strongly inside last, not btn far: ran to best, eff at 6f on fast & hvy.	½	64
4338 **AINTNECESSARILYSO 14** [7] D R C Elsworth 2-8-10 (70) R Hughes 5/1: 023004: Led/dsptd lead, drvn/hdd dist, held well inside last: clr rem: handles fast & hvy grnd: ran to nr best: see 3852, 3387 (mdns).	nk	71
4187 **BELLA PAVLINA 27** [3] A Nicholls 2-7-13 (59) A Nicholls 10/1: -0065: Dwelt, bhd, rdn/prog 2f out, no extra appr fnl 1f: tchd 14/1 on h'cap debut: rtd higher 4095 (gd soft).	2½	54
2468 **YOUNG JACK 111** [4] 2-8-8 (68) J Fortune 9/1: -52356: Prom, drvn/wknd appr fnl 1f: nr 4 month abs & poss just sharper for this run: see 2057 (7f, fast).	3	55
4341 **FOREST DANCER 14** [2] 2-9-7 (81) L Newman (3) 13/8 FAV: -3507: Reared start, sn prom, drvn/wknd qckly over 1f out: well bckd, h'cap bow: top weight: not handle hvy? better 4341 (gd).	2	63
4416 **PACKIN EM IN 7** [8] 2-8-0 (60) P Doe 10/1: -00448: Slow to start, sn handy, wknd fnl 2f: qck reapp.	3	35

8 ran   Time 1m 15.6   (Axom Barathiki Partnership)   P F I Cole Whatcombe, Oxon

---

4526   3.20 SERVISPAK MDN 3YO+ (D)   6f   Heavy   Inapplicable
£3006   £925   £462   £231   3yo rec 1lb   Stalls moved forwards 30 yards.

3933} **DEEP BLUE 407** [4] Dr J D Scargill 3-8-13 J Lowe 4/1: 3220-1: 3 b c Lake Coniston - Billie Blue (Ballad Rock) Front rank, rdn/improved appr fnl 2f, grabbed far rail & led appr fnl 1f, drvn out: tchd 5/1 on belated reapp: rnr up twice as a juv in '99 (mdns, rtd 86 at best): half brother to a smart 5/7f wnr & a juv 1m wnr: eff around 5/6f on firm & hvy grnd: runs esp well fresh & on any trk: can rate higher.		56
4273 **TIME BOMB 22** [11] B R Millman 3-8-8 R Havlin 16/1: 000002: 3 b f Great Commotion - Play For Time (Comedy Star) Front rank, slightly outpcd 2f out, rallied & styd on well inside last, no impress on wnr: op 8/1 & first time in the frame on her 11th career start: stys a sharp 6f on hvy grnd: see 1525.	1¼	47
4293 **MASTER LUKE 20** [9] G L Moore 3-8-13 (bl) I Mongan (5) 9/2: 002023: 3 b g Contract Law - Flying Wind (Forzando) Disputed lead, rdn & wandered over 2f out, ev ch until no extra inside last: acts on fast & hvy: better off in sell h'caps: see 4293 (C/D, gd/soft).	nk	51
4364 **FFYNNON GOLD 10** [6] J G Portman 3-8-8 L Newman (3) 20/1: 006044: Dsptd lead, went on over 3f out, hdd appr fnl 1f, wknd inside last: stys 6f on hvy, needs sellrs: mod form prev.	2	41
1773 **BETHESDA 141** [15] 3-8-8 (t) T Quinn 15/8 FAV: 65-505: Outpcd, rdn 3f out, styd on late, nvr dangerous: nicely bckd tho' op 5/4: long abs: has twice disappointed in testing grnd: see 877.	1¾	38
-- **VANITY** [3] 3-8-8 S Drowne 10/1: 6: Dwelt, bhd, chasing ldrs halfway, drvn/fdd appr fnl 1f: debut: half sister to a decent 6f/1m wnr: Thatching filly, with G B Balding.	5	26
4292 **REGENT 20** [14] 5-9-0 A Mackay 66/1: 000007: Dwelt, sn outpcd, late gains: mod Flat/hdles form.	hd	31
4294 **LADY JEANNIE 20** [8] 3-8-8 J Mackay (5) 33/1: 06008: Led till halfway, lost tch fnl 2f: lks modest.	shd	26
3914 **HERRING GREEN 45** [2] 3-8-13 S Carson 33/1: -00009: Prom, rdn & wknd qckly fnl 2f: 6 wk abs: big drop in trip, mod form.	2	26
3820 **CURRENCY 52** [12] 3-8-13 P Fitzsimons (5) 12/1: 60: Mid div, drpd rear halfway, 10th: 7 wk abs.	4	16
4388 **CHICANERY 9** [13] 3-8-13 Kristin Stubbs (7) 33/1: -600: Al outpcd, fin 11th: see 3343.	1	13
3872 **CYMMERIAD O GYMRU 49** [7] 5-9-0 N Callan 50/1: 00: 00m, drvn, wknd qckly fnl 2f, 12th: 7 wk abs.	½	12

4273 Bold Byzantium 22 [5] 4-9-0 D R McCabe 33/1:   3256 Red White And Blue 77 [10] 3-8-8 Martin Dwyer 50/1:
-- Almutan Star [1] 5-8-9 S Whitworth 16/1:
15 ran   Time 1m 14.4   (R A Dalton)   Dr J D Scargill Newmarket, Suffolk

4527 **3.50 JHF HCAP 3YO+ 0-90 (C) 5f Heavy Inapplicable [90]**
£7247 £2230 £1115 £557 Majority raced towards far side

4466 **NINEACRES 5** [20] J M Bradley 9-9-11 (87)(bl) P Fitzsimons (5) 11/1: 022101: 9 b g Sayf El Arab - Mayor (Laxton) Prom stands side, led halfway, drvn & held on well fnl 1f: op 8/1, qck reapp: earlier won at Bath (2), W'hampton, Southwell (rtd 58a), Windsor, Cheptstow & York (h'caps): '99 W'hampton wnr (clmr, rtd 59a & 42): eff at 5/6f, stays 7f: acts on firm, soft & both AWs: goes on any trk: wears blnks or visor: best up with or forcing the pace: most tough & progressive 9yo, a credit to connections. **91**
4411 **CARLTON 8** [10] D R C Elsworth 6-9-3 (79) T Quinn 12/1: 056102: 6 ch g Thatching - Hooray Lady (Ahonoora) Towards rear far side, hdwy over 1f out, fin fast but just failed in an exciting fin: see 4207 (clmr). ½ **82**
4198 **LIVELY LADY 27** [16] J R Jenkins 4-9-7 (83)(bl) J Fortune 20/1: 300003: 4 b f Beveled - In The Papers (Aragon) Dwelt, rear far side, prog to lead that group 1f out, edged left ins last, not btn far: op 14/1: jockey reportedly given 3 day careless riding ban: blnks reapplied: see 1013 (visor). *shd* **86**
4466 **AMBITIOUS 5** [1] K T Ivory 5-10-0 (90) C Catlin(7) 16/1: 010004: Prom far side, kept on fnl 1f: top-weight. *1* **90**
4405 **JUWWI 8** [4] 6-9-10 (86) Darren Williams (5) 16/1: 004005: Slowly away, rear, kept on far side fnl 2f, nrst fin: longer priced stablemate of wnr: slipping to a handy mark for next term: see 1337 (6f, firm). ½ **85**
+3419 **SUSSEX LAD 70** [6] 3-9-0 (76) P Dobbs (5) 25/1: 064616: Al prom far side, onepace inside last: 10 wk abs: acts on firm & hvy grnd: see 3419. *shd* **75**
4165 **SUPREME ANGEL 29** [2] 5-8-1 (63) A Nicholls 16/1: 500007: Rear far side, keeping on fnl 1f when hmpd, no impress after: poss plcd with a clr run, worth another chance: see 1264. *hd* **62**
+4377 **JAMES STARK 10** [13] 3-9-10 (86)(bl)(7ex) J Weaver 3/1 FAV: 615318: Mid div far side, not pace to chall: hvly bckd under a 7lb pen: see 4377. ¾ **82**
4432 **QUEEN OF THE MAY 7** [3] 3-8-8 (70) T A O'Sullivan (5) 20/1: 060509: Al mid div far side: see 4270. ½ **65**
4010 **SMOKIN BEAU 40** [18] 3-9-6 (82) R Hughes 14/1: 110000: Cl up stands side 2f, swtchd/rcd far side & led that group halfway, no impress fnl 1f: 10th, 6 wk abs: trailblazer, may have gone cl if staying stands side. *nk* **76**
4165 **RAILROADER 29** [5] 3-9-3 (79) S Drowne 20/1: 020000: Rear far side, mod gains: 11th: see 1220. ½ **72**
4432 **CHORUS 7** [8] 3-8-10 (72) G Hind 25/1: 600100: Chsd ldrs far side 4f, btn/eased fnl 1f: 12th: btr 4295. ¾ **62**
4456 **TRAVESTY OF LAW 6** [19] 3-9-8 (84) D Glennon (7) 25/1: 255400: Led overall stands side, hdd halfway & sn held: 13th: qck reapp: see 1849. *1* **71**
*4407 **REGAL SONG 8** [9] 4-8-6 (68)(7ex) R Ffrench 7/1: 503010: Prom far side 3f: 14th: op 5/1: btr 4407. *shd* **55**
4107 **EASTERN TRUMPETER 33** [14] 4-9-4 (80) L Newman (3) 10/1: 030040: Prom far side 4f: 16th: op 8/1. **0**
1178 **EXORCET 172** [11] 3-9-10 (86) Martin Dwyer 12/1: 00-100: Prom far side 3f: 18th: abs: btr 909 (mdn). **0**
-4301 **CARD GAMES 19** [7] 3-9-8 (84) T Lucas 5/1: 005020: Al rear: 19th: op 13/2: more expected after 4301. **0**
4466 **Caxton Lad 5** [12] 3-9-12 (88) A Clark 16/1: 4185 **Poppys Song 28** [15] 3-8-9 (71) C Rutter 20/1:
4486} **Elegant Lady 369** [17] 4-9-6 (82) W Ryan 14/1:
20 ran Time 1m 02.1 (J M Bradley) J M Bradley Sedbury, Gloucs

4528 **4.20 QUALITY SELLER 3YO (G) 1m2f Heavy Inapplicable**
£1907 £545 £272 Raced centre - stands side in straight

4178 **WOODYATES 28** [8] D R C Elsworth 3-8-9 L Branch(1) 6/1: 605001: 3 b f Naheez - Night Mission (Night Shift) Trckd ldrs, led 2f out, styd on well fnl 1f, rdn out: no bid, t-strap ommitted: first win: eff at 10f, tried 12f: acts on hvy grnd: apprec drop to selling grade. **45**
4313 **ARIALA 17** [1] K R Burke 3-8-9 N Callan 7/2 JT FAV: 600302: 3 b f Arazi - Kashtala (Lord Gayle) Mid div, rdn & styd on fnl 2f, post came too sn: op 7/4: acts on soft & hvy grnd: see 4208 h'cap). ½ **43**
4420 **GROVE LODGE 7** [6] S Woodman 3-9-0 S Whitworth 12/1: 006003: 3 b c Donna's Red - Shanuke (Contract Law) Rear, hdwy/ch 2f out, onepce inside last: op 10/1: styd longer 10f trip: handles hvy grnd. 1½ **46**
3915 **WISHFUL THINKER 45** [9] N Tinkler 3-9-6 J Reid 13/2: 301204: Trckd ldrs, fdd fnl 1f: 6 wk abs: acts on firm & hvy grnd: see 2989 (mdn seller). *nk* **51$**
4387 **DOUBLE FAULT 9** [4] 3-8-9 (bl) A Daly 16/1: 000455: Led 2f, btn over 1f out: see 4177, 1024. *hd* **40**
4419 **JOHN STEED 7** [10] 3-9-0 Paul Eddery 12/1: 040006: Chsd ldrs 6f, btn 2f out: see 2264. *4* **39**
4313 **OK TWIGGY 17** [7] 3-8-9 D Kinsella (7) 16/1: -67: Rear, eff 3f out, little hdwy: see 4313. *nk* **33**
4304 **INDY CARR 17** [12] 3-9-1 A Clark 7/2 JT FAV: 001068: Keen, led after 2f, hdd/btn 2f out: op 9/2. 1¾ **37**
-- **KEALAKEKUA BAY** [3] 3-9-0 I Mongan (5) 7/1: -9: Twds rear, eff 3f out, sn btn: debut, with G L Moore. 1½ **34**
4391 **INDIANA SPRINGS 9** [5] 3-9-0 J Weaver 10/1: 035300: Rear, eff 3f out, sn btn: 10th: op 8/1. 1½ **32**
4081 **SUPER STORY 35** [11] 3-8-9 T Quinn 33/1: 0-00: Mid div, btn/eased over 2f out: 11th: no form. *13* **7**
11 ran Time 2m 19.0 (D R C Elsworth) D R C Elsworth Whitsbury, Hants

4529 **4.50 STRATEGIC HCAP 3YO 0-80 (D) 1m3f35y Heavy Inapplicable [81]**
£3848 £1184 £592 £296 Raced stands side in straight

4213 **THREE LIONS 26** [7] R F Johnson Houghton 3-9-5 (72) J Reid 11/2: 164101: 3 ch g Jupiter Island - Super Sol (Rolfe) Trkd ldr, led 4f out, pulled clr under hands & heels riding, eased down inside last: val for 8L+: earlier won at Beverley (class stks) & Kempton (h'cap): unplcd in '99 (rtd 67): eff btwn 10/14f, 2m cld suit: acts on fast & gd, much imprvd on hvy: handles a stiff or sharp trk: can force the pace: progressive 3yo. **83**
4291 **DICKIE DEADEYE 20** [5] G B Balding 3-9-4 (71) P Dobbs (5) 11/4: 560152: 3 b g Distant Relative - Accuracy (Gunner B) Rear, hdwy/chsd wnr over 2f out, btn/hung left fnl 1f: well bckd: longer 12f trip. *4* **73**
4160 **NEVER DISS MISS 30** [3] W Jarvis 3-9-6 (73) D McGaffin (5) 9/1: 132503: 3 b f Owington - Pennine Pink (Pennine Walk) Handy 4f out, onepce/btn fnl 2f: op 6/1: see 1448. 1½ **73**
3977 **SIMPLY SENSATIONAL 41** [1] P F I Cole 3-9-6 (73) J Fortune 5/2 FAV: -4434: Chsd wnr over 3f out till over 2f out, sn btn: hvly bckd, clr rem, h'cap bow, 6 wk abs: longer 12f trip may suit: see 3477. *2* **70**
*2712 **SECOND PAIGE 101** [4] 3-9-7 (74) J Weaver 4/1: 022115: Handy 4f out, wknd fnl 2f: bckd: abs. *10* **57**
4474 **STORM WIZARD 5** [6] 3-9-5 (72) S Drowne 12/1: 220066: Sn rdn along, bhd 5f out, t.o.: op 8/1. *24* **25**
1640 **NO PASS NO HONOR 147** [2] 3-8-0 (53) P Doe 20/1: 00-657: Led 1m, sn btn, t.o.: 5 month abs. 2½ **3**
7 ran Time 2m 38.1 (Jim Short) R F Johnson Houghton Blewbury, Oxon

NEWMARKET FRIDAY OCTOBER 27TH Righthand, Stiff, Galloping Track

Official Going SOFT Stalls: 12f/2m - Far Side, Rem - Stands Side

4530 **2.00 GEORGE COLLING MDN 2YO (D) 6f str Good/Soft 71 -42 Slow**
£4589 £1412 £706 £353 Raced stands side

4268 **HERETIC 23** [10] J R Fanshawe 2-9-0 D Harrison 7/1: 61: 2 b c Bishop Of Cashel - Barford Lady (Stanford) Led/dsptd lead thro'out, rdn fnl 2f & styd on well ins last to lead nr line: confirmed promise of debut: suited by drop to 6f, 7f will suit: acts on gd/soft grnd, handles soft: likes a stiff/gall trk: clearly going the right way, looks potentially useful & shld win more races. **93**
-- **FUTURE FLIGHT** [2] B W Hills 2-8-9 M Hills 5/1 FAV: 2: 2 b f Polar Falcon - My Branch (Distant Relative) Al prom, led halfway, rdn/duelled with wnr ins last, hdd nr fin, just held: nicely bckd tho' op 7/2: Apr first foal: dam smart at 6/1m: eff at 6f, 7f will suit: acts on gd/soft: will improve & win races. *hd* **87+**
-- **ZIBET** [3] E A L Dunlop 2-8-9 L Dettori 11/2: 3: 2 b f Kris - Zonda (Fabulous Dancer) Dwelt, sn chsd ldrs, rdn/ch over 1f out, kept on onepace ins last: bckd tho' op 4/1: Kris filly, Apr foal: half sister to smart 6/7f wnr Zoning: dam a 6f wnr: eff at 6f, 7f shld suit: acts on gd/soft grnd: encouraging intro. *2½* **80**
-- **MORE MODERN** [8] R Charlton 2-9-0 S Drowne 10/1: 4: Chsd ldrs, pushed along bef halfway, kept on well fnl 1f, not able to chall: op 9/2: Mt Livermore colt, Mar first foal: eff at 6f, further suit: improve. *2* **80+**
4379 **ROBIN SHARP 10** [18] 2-9-0 J Quinn 25/1: 55: Chsd ldrs, ch 2f out, onepace/held ins last: turf debut: prob handles gd/soft & fibresand: see 4379. *1½* **76**
-- **ON GUARD** [11] 2-9-0 M Tebbutt 9/1: 6: Dwelt, towards rear, kept on fnl 3f, nvr pace to threaten: Sabrehill colt, Feb first foal: dam a 7f 3yo wnr: sire a top-class performer at 10f: will improve over further. *½* **74**
3187 **VITESSE 81** [7] 2-8-9 S Sanders 33/1: 07: Chsd ldrs, no impress fnl 2f: 12 wk abs. *1½* **65**
4341 **ILLUSIONIST 15** [17] 2-9-0 G Carter 16/1: 408: Held up, eff halfway, no impress: op 12/1, see 1367. *¾* **68**
4341 **STREET LIFE 15** [13] 2-9-0 P Robinson 12/1: 09: Chsd ldrs till over 1f out: bckd, op 33/1. *hd* **67**
-- **CHAMLANG** [12] 2-8-9 S Whitworth 40/1: 0: Towards rear, mod hdwy halfway: 10th: with N Graham. *2½* **55**
-- **GENTLE MAGIC** [5] 2-8-9 G Hind 33/1: 0: Prom, outpcd halfway: 11th: cheaply bought Feb foal. *1½* **52**
-- **ABBOT** [14] 2-9-0 D R McCabe 25/1: -0: Prom 4f: 12th: 8,000gns Apr foal, with B Meehan. *1½* **53**
-- **AGNES FOR RANSOM** [6] 2-8-9 J Reid 9/1: 0: Dwelt, nvr on terms: 13th: op 5/1: Red Ransom filly, Apr foal, cost Ffr320,000: half sister to top-class 2yo Seattle Rhyme: dam a 7f wnr: bred to be useful. *nk* **47**
4189 **BEIDERBECKE 28** [4] 2-9-0 J P Spencer 25/1: -060: Al towards rear: 14th: needs h'caps: see 3980. **0**
-- **WA NAAM** [15] 2-9-0 R Hills 10/1: 0: Held up, eff halfway, no impress: 15th: op 6/1: May foal. **0**
-- **ONE MIND** [1] 2-9-0 R Hughes 9/1: 0: Prom 3f: 19th: op 5/1: Mind Games colt, 40000gns Mar foal. **0**
-- **Dovedon Supreme** [9] 2-8-9 J Stack 40/1: -- **York Whine** [16] 2-8-9 R Mullen 40/1:
4390 **Dunkirk Spirit 10** [21] 2-9-0 R Ffrench 50/1: -- **Killarney** [19] 2-8-9 L Newman (3) 25/1:
20 ran Time 1m 17.57 (6.77) (Barford Bloodstock) J R Fanshawe Newmarket

4531 **2.30 LAWDIRECT COND STKS 2YO (C) 1m str Good/Soft 71 -31 Slow**
£5707 £2164 £1082 £492 Raced centre - stands side

*3972 **WELSH BORDER 42** [10] H R A Cecil 2-8-13 T Quinn 9/4: 11: 2 ch c Zafonic - Welsh Daylight (Welsh Pageant) Chsd ldr, rdn & duelled with rnr-up from over 1f out, narrowly asserted well ins last, hands & heels: well bckd, abs: earlier scored at Nottingham (debut, mdn): eff at 1m, brother to a 10f wnr & that trip shld suit: acts on soft & likes a stiff/gall trk: runs well fresh: progressive, type to improve again. **91+**
4277 **TURKU 22** [4] M Johnston 2-8-13 K Darley 8/1: 132: 2 b c Polar Falcon - Princess Zepoli (Persepolis) Led, rdn/duelled with wnr from over 1f out, drvn/kept on tho' just held nr fin: op 6/1: styd longer 1m trip well. *hd* **90**
4349 **XTRA 14** [2] L M Cumani 2-8-11 J P Spencer 9/1: 03: 2 b c Sadler's Wells - Oriental Mystique (Kris) Held up, rdn & kept on well fnl 2f: op 7/1: stays 1m on gd/soft: crying out for 10f+ & type to win in 2001. *1¼* **85**
-- **CARNIVAL DANCER** [3] Sir Michael Stoute 2-8-11 L Dettori 4/5 FAV: 4: Trkd ldrs, rdn/no impress over 1f out: hvly bckd: Sadler's Wells colt, Jan first foal: dam a smart 6f wnr: sire top-class at 1m/12f: stays 1m, mid-dists will suit next term: handles gd/soft grnd: clearly well reagarded, will learn from this. *2½* **80**
-- **PUTRA SANDHURST** [9] 2-8-11 P Robinson 12/1: 5: Held up, rdn/outpcd halfway, kept on fnl 2f under minimal press, no threat: Royal Academy colt, Apr foal, cost 120,000 gns: dam a French 12f wnr: stays 1m, mid-dists sure to suit: educational debut, will do much better next term. *½* **79+**
4349 **ONLYTIME WILL TELL 14** [5] 2-8-11 S Drowne 66/1: 06: Held up, eff 3f out, no impress: well clr rem. *3* **73**
4344 **SCARROTTOO 14** [8] 2-8-11 G Carter 66/1: 67: Dwelt/held up, eff 3f out, sn btn/eased over 1f out. *14* **52**
4483 **PRINCE ALBERT 4** [1] 2-8-11 S Whitworth 66/1: 608: Chsd ldrs 6f: longer 1m trip, highly tried. *1½* **49**
-- **TROUBLE NEXT DOOR** [6] 2-8-11 R Mullen 33/1: 9: Prom 5f: Persian Bold colt, May foal, half brother to a 12f wnr: dam a 10/12f wnr: mid-dists will suit in time, with N Littmoden. *16* **25**
-- **SONIQUE** [7] 2-8-6 Martin Dwyer 66/1: 0: Bhd 3f out: 10th: Shaamit filly, Apr foal, cheaply bought. *5* **10**
10 ran Time 1m 44.64 (8.14) (K Abdulla) H R A Cecil Newmarket, Suffolk

4532 **3.05 LISTED JAMES SEYMOUR STKS 3YO+ (A) 1m2f str Good/Soft 71 -03 Slow**
£13224 £5016 £2508 £1140 3 yo rec 5 lb Raced towards centre

4308 **ISLAND SOUND 18** [11] D R C Elsworth 3-8-9 T Quinn 20/1: 253441: 3 b g Turtle Island - Ballet (Sharrood) Made all, drvn clr over 1f out, styd on strongly ins last under hands & heels riding: '99 wnr at Salisbury (mdn) & Newbury (stks, rtd 105): eff at 1m, improved at 10f: handles hvy grnd, loves gd/soft & soft: likes a stiff/gall trk: eff forcing the pace: smart & much improved today. **111**
4212 **MAN OMYSTERY 27** [10] J Noseda 3-8-9 D Holland 2/1 FAV: 242642: 3 b c Diesis - Eurostorm (Storm Bird) Held up, rdn & prog to chase wnr ins last, no impress: hvly bckd: ran to form: see 4212 (h'cap), 1041 & 789. *5* **104**
*2630 **EXPLODE 106** [3] R Charlton 3-8-9 R Hughes 11/2: 3113: 3 b c Zafonic - Didicoy (Danzig) Chsd wnr, rdn/no impress over 1f out: bckd: 3 month abs: up in grade: lightly raced, btr 2630 (made all). *1½* **102**
4347 **DUCK ROW 14** [8] J A R Toller 5-9-0 S Whitworth 6/1: 232034: Held up, eff 3f out, kept on onepace: all 3 wins at 1m: see 4347, 1847 & 1489 (1m). *1¾* **100**
4337 **DIAMOND WHITE 15** [9] 5-8-9 K Darley 7/1: 533055: Held up, eff over 2f out, mod hdwy: see 3984, 967. *1* **94**
4180 **SOVIET FLASH 29** [5] 3-8-9 J Reid 14/1: 41-246: Prom, fdd over 1f out: op 8/1: btr 4180, 3893 (1m). *1½* **97**
4259 **CRIMSON TIDE 26** [1] 6-9-0 M Hills 25/1: /35007: Keen, chsd ldrs halfway, btn 1f out: btr 3291 (1m). *2½* **93**
4017 **CAPE GRACE 41** [2] 4-8-13 J P Spencer 16/1: 524028: Held up, bhd 2f out: abs: btr 4017 (C/D, gd). *13* **78**
2148} **EL DIVINO 495** [7] 5-9-4 L Dettori 20/1: 150069: Held up, eff 3f out, no impress: German raider, earlier this term won at Hamburg (Listed): twice a wnr in native land in '99: suited by 1m on gd & soft grnd. *2½* **79**
*3782 **POLAR RED 55** [4] 3-8-9 P Robinson 6/1: 431110: Hld up, eff 3f out, sn btn: 10th, abs, amiss? *3½* **70**
2851 **ELMUTABAKI 97** [6] 4-9-0 R Hills 14/1: 0-5060: Chsd ldrs 1m, 11th: op 12/1, abs: btr 1247 (14f, fm). *5* **63**

11 ran   Time 2m 09.47 (7.37)   (Mrs Michael Meredith)   D R C Elsworth Whitsbury, Hants

4533

3.40 LISTED RTD HCAP 3YO+ 0-105 (A) 2m Good/Soft 71 +10 Fast   [112]
£13108 £4972 £2486 £1130 3 yo rec 10lb

4128 **ROMANTIC AFFAIR** 33 [7] J L Dunlop 3-8-10 (104) T Quinn 3/1 FAV: 142121: 3 ch g Persian Bold - Broken 112+
Romance (Ela Mana Mou) Held up, prog/led over 2f out & sn clr, styd on strongly ins last under hands & heels riding.
eased nr fin: hvly bckd, fast time: earlier scored at Sandown, Salisbury & Doncaster (h'caps): '99 Newcastle wnr
(auct mdn, rtd 74): eff at 12f/14f, well suited by this step up to 2m, may get further: acts on firm & soft, loves
a stiff/gall trk: v useful gldg, continues to progress & Group staying prizes look well within his grasp next term,
but would also be a leading player if allowed to take his chance in next week's November H'cap.
*4115 **MBELE** 34 [1] W R Muir 3-8-5 (99) Martin Dwyer 9/2: 321612: 3 b c Mtoto - Majestic Image (Niniski) 6 100
Prom, rdn & kept on fnl 2f, no ch with wnr: sound run but caught a tartar here: see 4115.
4130 **CEPHALONIA** 33 [4] J L Dunlop 3-8-4 (98) W Supple 20/1: 161003: 3 b f Slip Anchor - Cephira (Abdos) 1½ 98
Led, hdd over 2f out & sn no impress: usful & lightly raced: see 2594 (15f, fast).
4343 **RADAS DAUGHTER** 14 [10] I A Balding 4-9-7 (105) K Darley 11/2: 100204: Held up, prog over 2f out, 1½ 104
no impress over 1f out: bckd, tchd 16/1: clr of rem: longer 2m trip: see 3863, 2502.
4353 **EASTWELL HALL** 13 [13] 5-8-7 (91)(6oh) L Newman 14/1: 515205: Held up, rdn/no impress fnl 4f. 7 83
*1824 **FOLLOW LAMMTARRA** 140 [3] 3-7-11 (91)(2oh) D Mernagh 20/1: 3616: Chsd ldrs 14f: abs, h'cap bow. ½ 82
4162 **BE THANKFULL** 14 [5] 4-8-8 (92) S Sanders 16/1: 536037: Prom 14f: btr 4162 (12f, gd). 1¾ 81
4115 **BUSY LIZZIE** 34 [9] 3-8-2 (96) R Ffrench 10/1: 251168: Prom, btn 3f out: op 8/1: btr 3961. 12 76
*4134 **COVER UP** 33 [12] 3-8-2 (96) J Quinn 8/1: 030019: Held up, rdn/btn 4f out: op 6/1: btr 4134. 2½ 74
4458 **NICELY** 7 [6] 4-8-7 (91)(31oh)(BL) M Hills 50/1: 000000: Bhd 4f out: 10th: blnks: see 1527. hd 69
3877 **EILEAN SHONA** 50 [11] 4-9-0 (98) L Dettori 9/2: 054500: Held up, eff 5f out, sn btn: 11th: bckd, 7 69
7 wk abs: won this race last term off a 7lb lower mark: has struggled for form this term: see 1222.
4342 **HELENS DAY** 15 [8] 4-8-7 (91)(6oh) R Hills 7/1: 21014P: Bhd when p.u./dismounted ins last, sadly died. 0
12 ran   Time 3m 32.53 (9.73)   (The Earl Cadogan)   J L Dunlop Arundel, W Sussex

4534

4.15 EBF FILLIES HCAP 3YO+ 0-80 (D) 1m4f Good/Soft 71 -28 Slow   [69]
£6942 £2136 £1068 £534 3 yo rec 7 lb

4213 **ALPHA ROSE** 27 [9] M L W Bell 3-9-9 (71) A Beech (3) 9/1: 142101: 3 ch f Inchinor - Philgwyn (Milford) 79
Twrds rear, gd hdwy appr fnl 3f, led over 2f out, sn clr, rdn out: op 5/1: earlier won at Musselburgh, Ayr (stks),
Lingfield & Brighton (2 fills h'caps): unplcd for R Williams in '99 (rtd 68): suited by 10/14f, has tried 2m:
acts on firm/fast & equitrack, career best run today on gd/soft: acts on a sharp/undul or gall trk: tough & v prog.
4448 **COOLING OFF** 7 [12] G Wragg 3-9-10 (72) D Holland 6/1: 035042: 3 b f Brief Truce - Lovers' 5 73
Parlour (Beldale Flutter) Front rank, went on over 3f out, hdd appr fnl 2f, sn not pace of wnr: quick reapp:
up in trip, stays 10/12f on gd & gd/soft, shown enough to win a race: see 4448, 3350.
4271 **SHARP SPICE** 23 [8] D J Coakley 4-9-5 (60) W Supple 14/1: 031403: 4 b f Lugana Beach - Ewar Empress 3 57
(Persian Bold) Waited with, rdn/ran on well fnl 2f, nvr nrr: generally consistent recent turf form: see 3858.
*4510 **ACEBO LYONS** 2 [4] A P Jarvis 5-9-6 (61)(6ex) L Dettori 6/1: 032014: Bhd, imprvd appr fnl 2f, ½ 57
drvn/no extra over 1f out: nicely bckd: landed a poor claimer 2 days ago in 4510.
3979 **MA VIE** 42 [11] 3-9-0 (62)(vis) D Harrison 7/2 FAV: 020225: Led, hdd appr fnl 3f, wknd appr fnl 1f: hd 58
nicely bckd after 6 wk abs: up in trip & poss not quite get home over a stiff 12f: btr 3979 (10f stks, soft).
4413 **TYPHOON GINGER** 9 [13] 5-9-0 (55) N Callan 11/1: 620536: Bhd, eff over 2f out, wknd appr fnl 1f 6 44
1f out: op 8/1: remains a mdn after 20 starts: see 4413.
4486 **ORDAINED** 4 [10] 7-8-1 (42) Martin Dwyer 20/1: 600607: Bhd, prog 3f out, wknd qckly fnl 2f: qck reapp. ½ 30
4061 **BLESS THE BRIDE** 37 [6] 3-9-10 (72) T Quinn 5/1: -10058: Prom, rdn/lost tch fnl 3f: nicely bckd: 5 54
back on a wng mark & may apprec a drop back to 10f: see 1094.
4374 **SOPHALA** 11 [3] 3-9-5 (67) R Mullen 8/1: 001349: Twrds rear, eff halfway, fdd fnl 3f: btr 4374, 4174. 2 46
4409 **WEST END DANCER** 9 [1] 3-7-10 (44)(12oh) K Dalgleish 9/1: 330040: Nvr a factor, 10th: stiff task. 16 16
4437 **Karakul** 7 [7] 4-8-10 (51) S Drowne (5)   4474 **Powerline** 6 [5] 3-9-10 (72) R Hughes 16/1:
4443 **Flavia** 7 [2] 3-7-11 (45)(bl) J Mackay (5) 16/1:
13 ran   Time 2m 40.64 (11.84)   (Richard I Morris Jr)   M L W Bell Newmarket

4535

4.45 ROYSTON COND STKS 2-3YO (C) 6f str Good/Soft 71 -07 Slow
£6356 £2411 £1205 £548 2 yo rec 20lb

4456 **GREY EMINENCE** 7 [6] R Hannon 3-9-10 L Newman (3) 9/2: 212021: 3 gr c Indian Ridge - Rahaam (Secreto) 102
Cl-up, went on appr fnl 1f, went clr despite edging right, rdn out: op 7/2: quick reapp: earlier won at Ascot
(mdn), rnr-up 5 of his 6 other starts: rtd 82 when 5th sole juv start: brother to useful 6/7f wnr Cassandra Go:
dam 7f wnr: eff at 6/7f, stays 1m: acts on fast, soft & a stiff/gall or easy trk: tough, useful & improving.
4346 **MOLLY BROWN** 14 [1] R Hannon 3-9-5 J Carroll 4/1: 220302: 3 b f Rudimentary - Sinking (Midyan) 3 90
Led till over 1f out, not pace of wnr fnl 1f: op 7/1: useful: see 4346, 3768.
4398 **AREYDHA** 12 [3] M R Channon 3-9-5 L Dettori 4/1: -00243: 3 b f Cadeaux Genereux - Elaine's Honor 2 85
(Chief's Crown) Cl-up, ev ch until drvn/onepcd over 1f out: op 3/1: rtd higher 4198 (fills rtd h'cap, gd, C/D).
*4341 **AJWAA** 15 [10] M P Tregoning 2-8-8 R Hills 6/4 FAV: 214: Prom, drvn 2f out, no extra appr fnl 1f: 2½ 89
hvly bckd tho' op 1/1: came home best of the 2yos: not one more highly when returning to faster grnd: btr 4341.
*4364 **SHERINGHAM** 11 [7] 3-9-2 S Sanders 10/1: 15: Dwelt, sn rdn in rear, late gains for press, no 1 74
danger: turf bow: shade better on debut in 4364 (AW med auct mdn).
4037 **LA CAPRICE** 39 [8] 3-9-5 G Carter 25/1: 201006: Handy, drvn/fdd fnl 2f: btr 2934 (5f h'cap, fast). 3½ 69
4390 **TRILLIE** 10 [2] 2-8-3 J Quinn 10/1: 116022: In tch, drvn/fdd fnl 2f: btr 4390 (soft). ½ 72
4515 **THE CASTIGATOR** 2 [4] 3-9-7 D Mernagh (3) 100/1: 005008: Al in rear 48hrs ago, v stiff task. 12 45$
4515 **TIME FOR THE CLAN** 2 [11] 3-9-7 Dean McKeown 100/1: 000000: Lost tch halfway: quick reapp. 1¾ 43$
4359 **IN TOUCH** 13 [5] 2-8-0 R Ffrench 66/1: -000: Al struggling, 10th: poor form. 11 22
3675 **TOBYTOO** 61 [9] 2-8-5 J Stack 100/1: 000000: Al well bhd, t.o. in 11th: 9 wk abs, imposs task. 16 0
11 ran   Time 1m 15.5 (4.7)   (Jeffen Racing)   R Hannon East Everleigh, Wilts

4536   5.20 AVENUE APPR HCAP 3YO 0-70 (E)   1m str   Good/Soft 71   -14 Slow   [76]
£3653   £1124   £562   £281

*4310 **EVE 18** [5] M L W Bell 3-9-6 (68) J Mackay 9/4 FAV: 300111: 3 b f Rainbow Quest - Fade (Persepolis)   73
Twrds rear, imprvd after halfway, styd on strongly despiting edging right appr fnl 1f, led ins last, drvn out:
well bckd to complete hat-trick: earlier won at Brighton (class stks) & Leicester (fills h'cap): uncrd juv:
suited by 1m, poss stays 10f: handles firm, loves gd/soft & hvy grnd: handles any trk: progressive in the mud.

3856 **HARMONIC 51** [7] D R C Elsworth 3-9-6 (68) R Thomas (5) 16/1: 220242: 3 b f Shadeed - Running   ½   72
Melody (Rheingold) Front rank, drvn ot chall ins last, kept on, not btn far: abs: acts on firm & gd/soft.

3095 **AL AWAALAH 86** [2] M Salaman 3-7-11 (45) G Sparkes (2) 33/1: 00003: 3 b f Mukaddamah - Zippy Zoe 2½   45
(Rousillon) Front rank, went on appr fnl 3f, hung right appr fnl 1f, hdd ins last, wknd fnl 50yds: 3 month abs
& 1st time in the frame today: stays a stiff/gall 1m on gd/soft: shown enough to land a sell h'cap: see 1436.

4168 **GRUINART 30** [20] H Morrison 3-9-5 (67) N Esler (5) 16/1: 140004: Prom, drvn 2f out, no extra fnl 1f.   ½   66
4452 **DIAMOND OLIVIA 7** [24] 3-9-0 (62) K Dalgleish 7/1: 250135: Towards rear, gd hdwy over 2f out,   nk   61
hung left/onepcd fnl 2f: quick reapp: prob ran to form of win in 4192 (7f).

4251 **MUST BE MAGIC 24** [8] 3-9-5 (67) G Baker 16/1: 431006: Waited with, imprvd appr fnl 1f, styd on   ¾   65
but nvr dangerous: op 10/1: visor omitted: see 2795 (mdn h'cap, 1st time visor).

4452 **MODEM 7** [6] 3-8-6 (54) Darren Williams (3) 33/1: 136407: Trkd ldrs, rdn to improve 2f out,   1½   49
no extra over 1f out: quick reapp: see 540 (AW).

4452 **CRYFIELD 7** [22] 3-9-1 (63)(vis) R Cody Boutcher (3) 13/2: 062428: Mid-div at best: quick reapp.   ¾   57
4334 **NUTMEG 16** [21] 3-7-12 (46) D Glennon (5) 25/1: 006609: Cl-up, chall over 2f out, fdd fnl 1f: op 16/1.   ½   39
4391 **RUNAWAY STAR 10** [13] 3-7-10 (44)(4oh) Clare Roche (5) 33/1: 650060: Late hdwy, nvr dngrs, fin 10th. 3½   32
4452 **BROMPTON BARRAGE 7** [4] 3-8-1 (49) R Smith 16/1: 000040: Rear, mod late gains, 11th: quick reapp. ¾   36
4406 **SWYNFORD ELEGANCE 9** [12] 3-7-10 (44) Michael Doyle (5) 16/1: 002400: Dwelt, in tch 6f, sn btn, 12th. ½   30
4280 **SHERZABAD 22** [16] 3-7-11 (45) Jonjo Fowle (3) 20/1: -00000: Nvr a factor, 13th: drop in trip.   1   29
3163 **REGARDEZ MOI 83** [9] 3-8-0 (48) A Hall (7) 50/1: 630000: Led to halfway, lost tch fnl 2f, 14th: 12 wk abs.1¼   30
4436 **KISTY 8** [1] 3-9-3 (65) P Dobbs 20/1: 336660: Nvr dangerous, 15th.   ½   46
4414 **HUGS DANCER 9** [14] 3-9-4 (66) S Finnamore (3) 11/1: 340300: In tch, wknd fnl 3f, 16th: tchd 14/1. hd   47
4391 **Sober As A Judge 10** [18] 3-7-10 (44)(9oh) C Catlin (3) 33/1:
2025 **The Jam Saheb 131** [3] 3-7-11 (45) N Farmer (4) 50/1:
4045 **Hint Of Magic 38** [10] 3-9-3 (65)(t) P Bradley 25/1:   4300 **Welsh Ploy 20** [19] 3-9-7 (69) P Hanagan 33/1:
4232 **Alawar 25** [15] 3-8-7 (55)(t) G Hannon (3) 20/1:   4426 **Rios Diamond 8** [11] 3-7-13 (47) Joanna Badger (3) 25/1:
4435 **Wadenhoe 8** [17] 3-8-0 (48) N Carter (5) 25/1:   3971 **Summer Cherry 43** [23] 3-8-10 (58) D Meah (5) 16/1:
24 ran   Time 1m 43.3 (6.8)   (Lady Carolyn Warren)   M L W Bell Newmarket

---

BRIGHTON   FRIDAY OCTOBER 27TH   Lefthand, V Sharp, Undulating Track

Official Going   SOFT (GOOD/SOFT PLACES). Stalls - Inside, except 10f & 12f - Outside.

4537   2.25 EBF PILTDOWN MDN 2YO (D)   6f rnd   Heavy Inapplicable
£3693   £1136   £568   £284   Raced towards stands side

3795 **ECSTATIC 54** [3] R Hannon 2-8-9 J Fortune 4/11 FAV: -24331: 2 ch f Nashwan - Divine Quest   88+
(Kris) Led/dsptd lead throughout, easily drew clr fnl 2f: val for 8L+: hvly bckd, abs: eff at 6f, stays a
7f: acts on fast & hvy, any trk: runs well fresh: can rate more highly & win more races.

4189 **SINGLE TRACK MIND 28** [5] N Hamilton 2-9-0 S Rehman 10/1: 052: 2 b c Mind Games - Compact   2½   76
Disc (Royal Academy) Prom, rdn/chsd wnr over 1f out, drifted left & no impress: op 14/1, clr rem: handles hvy.

-- **CEDAR TREBLE** [4] R J O'Sullivan 2-9-0 P Doe 25/1: 3: 2 b c Emperor Jones - Tjakka (Little   9   58
Missouri) In tch 4f: March run, cost 2000gns: dam unrcd: bred for 7f+.

4381 **HANDSOME BADSHA 10** [10] J A Osborne 2-9-0 J Weaver 20/1: 64: Held up, mod hdwy 2f out.   shd   57
4187 **KILMEENA STAR 28** [7] N Hamilton 2-9-0 S Carson (3) 16/1: 05: Led 5f out till 2f out, sn btn: see 4187. 2   54
2209 **HIDDEN LAKE 123** [2] 2-9-0 A Nicholls 20/1: 506: Prom 3f: 4 mth abs: btr 1844 (fast).   4   46
4268 **MISS POLLY 23** [9] 2-8-9 I Mongan (4) 20/1: 007: Al rear: see 4035 (7f).   ½   40
4172 **BUNKUM 30** [8] 2-9-0 M Fenton 25/1: 008: In tch 3f: dropped in trip: see 4172.   hd   40
4402 **EGYPT 9** [6] 2-9-0 G Duffield 10/1: 009: Struggling halfway: mod form.   1½   41
3911 **PERTEMPS BOYCOTT 46** [1] 2-9-0 T G McLaughlin 20/1: 00: Al bhd: 10th: abs: no form.   3   35
10 ran   Time 1m 15.7 (7.9)   (Exors Of The Late Lord Howard de Walden)   R Hannon East Everleigh, Wilts

4538   2.55 INDEPENDENT NURSERY HCAP 2YO 0-85 (D)   1m rnd   Heavy Inapplicable   [87]
£3536   £1088   £544   £272   Raced across track final 3f

*4378 **LEATHERBACK 11** [3] N A Callaghan 2-8-0 (59)(6ex) T Williams 11/2: 000011: 2 b g Turtle Island - Phyllode   66
(Pharly) In tch, prog to lead over 1f out, styd on well, rdn out: earlier landed a Pontefract nursery h'cap (1st
win): eff at 1m, 10f shld suit: loves soft/hvy grnd: handles a stiff or sharp/undul trk: progressive type.

3922 **MERIDEN MIST 45** [9] P W Harris 2-8-13 (72) C Rutter 10/1: 140542: 2 b f Distinctly North - Bring On The 4   72
Choir (Chief Singer) Rear, not much room 3f out, rdn/styd on fnl 2f, no threat: abs: stays 1m, handles firm & hvy.

*4416 **SAORSIE 8** [5] J C Fox 2-7-13 (58)(6ex) R Dinsella (7) 8/1: 000013: 2 b g Emperor Jones - Exclusive   1   57
Lottery (Presidium) Rear, prog/ch over 1f out, no extra ins last: stays 1m, poss just best at 7f for now: see 4416.

4416 **JARV 8** [6] J Akehurst 2-7-11 (56)(1ow) P Doe 6/1: -00024: In tch, prog/led over 2f out till over 1f out, fdd. 1½   54
4350 **TEMPLES TIME 14** [7] 2-9-1 (74) J Fortune 11/2: 436105: Led 2f, btn/hung left over 1f out: btr 4116 (g/s).1   70
4416 **SEL 8** [1] 2-8-3 (62)(bl) R Brisland (5) 14/1: 251056: Led 6f out till over 2f out, fdd: btr 4416, 3733 (7f). 6   49
4378 **BORDER EDGE 11** [11] 2-7-10 (55)(2ow) A Nicholls 33/1: 050067: Prom 6f: needs sells: see 1236.   3   40
4453 **STRUMPET 7** [4] 2-9-3 (76) S Carson (3) 14/1: 630068: Prom 5f: op 12/1: btr 3630 (6f, fast).   3½   54
*4438 **BOUND 7** [2] 2-9-7 (80)(6ex) G Duffield 7/2 FAV: 003619: Prom till over 1f out: bckd: btr 4438 (AW).   ¾   57
4267 **TOKEN 23** [8] 2-9-0 (59) A Daly 11/2: -0430: Chsd ldrs 5f: 10th: h'cap bow: btr 4267, 4036 (mdns).   4   51
3729 **PILGRIM GOOSE 58** [10] 2-7-10 (55)(2oh) G Bardwell 33/1: 0000: Slowly away, al rear: 11th: abs.   nk   25
11 ran   Time 1m 44.60 (12.6)   (M Tabor)   N A Callaghan Newmarket

BRIGHTON   FRIDAY OCTOBER 27TH   Lefthand, V Sharp, Undulating Track

4539   3.30 SPORTSADVISER MDN 2YO (D)   1m2f   Heavy   Inapplicable
£2873   £884   £442   £221   Raced centre - stands side fnl 3f

4140 **COMPTON COMMANDER 32** [6] G A Butler 2-9-0 M Fenton 5/2: 031: 2 ch c Barathea - Triode (Sharpen Up) **85**
Chsd ldrs, rdn fnl 4f, led 1f out, styd on strongly ins last to assert, pushed out: eff at 10f, 12f shld suit:
acts on soft & hvy grnd: likes a sharp/undul trk: going the right way.

4417 **ENGLISH HARBOUR 8** [8] B W Hills 2-8-9 G Duffield 9/4: 004222: 2 ch f Sabrehill - Water Woo   3½ **76**
(Tom Rolfe) Handy, led over 2f out, hdd 1f out & no extra ins last: bckd: clr rem: acts on soft & hvy: see 4230.

-- **POLISH FLAME** [7] P W Harris 2-9-0 G Bardwell 10/1: 3: 2 b c Blushing Flame - Lady Emm (Emarati)   5 **76**
Towards rear, mod late gains, no threat: op 8/1: Apr first foal: dam unrcd: 10f+ shld suit in time.

4114 **LUMIERE DESPOIR 34** [4] S Dow 2-8-9 P Doe 14/1: 04: Cl-up, wknd fnl 2f: op 8/1: longer 10f trip.   5 **66**

4418 **ART EXPERT 8** [3] 2-9-0 (BL) J Fortune 7/4 FAV: 0225: Led till over 2f out, wknd: blnks, nicely bckd: 2 **69**
this longer 10f trip may suit next term tho' much btr 4418, 4297 (1m).

4507 **OSO NEET 3** [2] 2-9-0 (BL) P Fitzsimons 25/1: 600006: Sn bhd: qck reapp, blnks: longer trip.   dist **0**

4184 **ROYAL SATIN 29** [5] 2-9-0 A Clark 25/1: 007: T.o. halfway: longer 10f trip, no form.   22 **0**
7 ran   Time 2m 14.9 (17.1)   (E Penser)   G A Butler Blewbury, Oxon

4540   4.05 COURAGE BEST HCAP 3YO 0-85 (D)   1m2f   Heavy   Inapplicable   [88]
£3705   £1140   £570   £285   Raced across track fnl 3f

*4374 **SUCH FLAIR 11** [5] J Noseda 3-8-12 (72)(6ex) J Weaver 4/6 FAV: -30411: 3 b f Kingmambo - Lady   **75**
Fairfax (Sharrood) Al cl-up, rdn/narrow lead over 2f out, drifted left & styd on gamely to prevail on line, all out:
bckd: 6lb pen for recent Pontefract win (h'cap, 1st win): unplcd sole '99 start (rtd 79, fills mdn): well suited
by step up to 10f last twice, may get further: likes soft & hvy grnd: handles a sharp or stiff/undul trk.

3870 **GUARDED SECRET 50** [3] P J Makin 3-9-1 (75) A Clark 2/1: 022102: 3 ro g Mystiko - Fen Dance   shd **77**
(Trojan Fen) In tch, rdn/strong chall fnl 2f, drvn ins last, just held: 7 wk abs: acts on firm & hvy: see 3390.

3870 **SALZGITTER 50** [4] H Candy 3-8-12 (72) C Rutter 6/1: 330603: 3 b f Salse - Anna Of Brunswick   12 **64**
(Rainbow Quest) Led halfway, btn 2f out: op 4/1, 7 wk abs: btr 1343 (gd, mdn).

4174 **BUXTEDS FIRST 30** [2] G L Moore 3-7-10 (56)(9oh) R Brisland (5) 20/1: 033004: Well bhd 3f out.   dist **0**
4 ran   Time Not taken (due to poor visibility)   (Sanford R Robertson)   J Noseda Newmarket, Suffolk

NEWMARKET   SATURDAY OCTOBER 28TH   Righthand, Stiff, Galloping Track

Official Going   SOFT. Stalls: Stands' side

4541   2.00 EBF BALATON LODGE FILLIES MDN 2YO (D)   7f str   Soft 118   -32 Slow
£4862   £1496   £748   £374   Raced towards centre

-- **GOOD STANDING** [16] B W Hills 2-8-11 M Hills 13/2: 0: 2 b f Distant View - Storm Dove (Storm Bird)   **88+**
Held up, prog 3f out, led ins fnl 1f, styd on well, rdn out: bckd from 10/1: Jan foal, half sister to a 7f plcd
juv: dam a 6f juv wnr, sire top class at 1m: eff at 7f, 1m will suit: acts on soft grnd & a stiff/gall track:
runs well fresh: reportedly held in some regard & a nice prospect for 2001.

4184 **TOFFEE NOSED 30** [1] B W Hills 2-8-11 J Carroll 8/1: 42: 2 ch f Selkirk - Ever Welcome (Be My   1¼ **84**
Guest) Led till ins last, kept on: stablemate of wnr: acts on gd & soft, 1m should suit: see 4184.

4268 **VILLA CARLOTTA 24** [22] J L Dunlop 2-8-11 P Doe 33/1: 303: 2 ch f Rainbow Quest - Subya   ¾ **82+**
(Night Shift) Dwelt, not much room 2f out, styd on well fnl 1f, not rch front pair: acts on gd & soft grnd:
promising, not much luck today: now qual for h'caps & will relish 1m+ next term: see 4020.

4268 **COMO 24** [5] R Charlton 2-8-11 R Hughes 9/1: 44D: Chsd ldrs, rdn & onepce ins last: fin 4th,   nk **81**
subs disqual & plcd last: jockey referred to Portman Square for not keep straight from the stalls: see 4268.

-- **PANNA** [6] 2-8-11 D Holland 16/1: 4: Held up, kept on fnl 2f, nrst fin: fin 5th, plcd 4th: nk **80+**
Apr foal, half sister to high class mid dist performer Pentire: dam a smart mid dist performer: eff at 7f, will
relish step up to 1m+ next term: handles soft grnd: eye-catching, improve over further & one to keep in mind.

-- **ZOUDIE** [15] 2-8-11 J Fortune 10/1: 5: Pushed along rear, kept on strongly fnl 2f, nrst fin: op   ¾ **78+**
10/1: April foal, half sister to sev wnrs, incl useful 1m performer Grannys Pet: dam a 6f 2yo wnr: eff at 7f,
sure to relish 1m+: most encouraging intro, will improve on this for J Noseda.

3748 **PUFFIN 58** [14] 2-8-11 K Darley 33/1: -566: Held up, eff over 2f out, kept on onepace: 8 wk abs.   1 **76**

4445 **LAILANI 8** [17] 2-8-11 J Reid 33/1: 07: Nvr plcd to chall, styd on late: sure to improve.   ¾ **74+**

-- **LONDONNET** [12] 2-8-11 T Quinn 33/8 FAV: 8: Chsd ldrs, rdn/onepce fnl 2f: hvly bckd tho' op 11/8:   ½ **73**
May foal, cost IR 40,000gns: half sister to a 7f juv wnr: dam a 12f wnr: 1m+ will suit: better expected.

-- **SALEYMA** [7] 2-8-11 L Dettori 12/1: 9: Chsd ldrs, no impress fnl 2f: op 10/1: Mtoto filly, Feb foal: nk **72**
sister to a 7f juv wnr: dam a mid dist wnr, sire top class at 10/12f: sure to improve over mid-dists next term.

-- **LAKE KINNERET** [13] 2-8-11 F Lynch 10/1: 0: Held up, kept on fnl 2f, no threat: 10th, op 6/1: May   1½ **69**
foal, half sister to a 5f juv wnr: dam a smart 1m/10f performer: with Sir M Stoute, likely to improve on better grnd.

-- **ISHAAM** [11] 2-8-11 W Supple 14/1: 0: Hmpd start, rear, mod hdwy: 11th: Feb foal, cost 160,000   4 **61**
gns: half sister to a 3yo wnr abroad: dam a 2yo wnr abroad: with Sir M Stoute, forget this.

-- **ASHNAYA** [10] 2-8-11 D Harrison 50/1: -0: Held up, nvr a factor: 12th: Ashkalani filly, April foal: shd **61**
cost 22,000gns: half sister to a 1m juv wnr: dam a smart 12f wnr: looks sure to improve over further for J Dunlop.

4312 **KRISTINEAU 19** [9] 2-8-11 R Mullen 50/1: 00: Prom 5f: 13th: see 4312.   1 **59**

4445 **ROYAL KISS 8** [3] 2-8-11 G Carter 40/1: 00: Chsd ldrs 5f: 14th: no form prev.   ¾ **57**

4034 **CHAFAYA 40** [2] 2-8-11 R Hills 4/1: 30: Chsd ldr 4f, btn/hmpd 2f out: 18th: op 3/1, abs.   **0**

-- **Rock Concert** [8] 2-8-11 C Rutter 40/1:   4445 **Tennessee Waltz 8** [18] 2-8-11 W Ryan 50/1:
3910 **Relative Delight 47** [20] 2-8-11 N Callan 50/1:   -- **Belle Rouge** [4] 2-8-11 A McGlone 50/1:
4477 **Cressida 6** [23] 2-8-11 G Duffield 40/1:   2588 **Bonella 108** [19] 2-8-11 G Bardwell 50/1:
22 ran   Time 1m 33.7 (10.5)   (K Abdulla)   B W Hills Lambourn, Berks

---

4542   **2.30 NGK SPARK PLUGS SELLER 2YO (E)**   1m str   Soft 118   -41 Slow
£3575   £1100   £550   £275   Raced stands side

4290 **POLISH PADDY** 22 [10] R Hannon 2-8-11 (BL) L Newman (3) 7/1: 446001: 2 b c Priolo - Polish   **66**
Widow (Polish Precedent) Made all, styd on well fnl 2f, rdn out: bt in for 9,000gns, galvanised by first time blnks
& forcing tactics: eff at 1m, tried 10f: acts on fast & soft, likes a stiff/gall trck: apprec sell grade.
4290 **LOOK FIRST** 22 [16] A P Jarvis 2-9-0 N Callan 7/2 FAV: 23102: 2 b c Namaqualand - Be Prepared   1¾   **65**
(Be My Guest) Prom, rdn/chsd wnr fnl 2f, kept on, held nr fin: op 5/2, 5L clr rem: stays 1m: acts on fast & soft.
-- **JOSH MOR** [8] G L Moore 2-8-11 J Mongan (5) 50/1: 3: 2 b g Chaddleworth - Little Morston   5   **55**
(Morston) Rear, styd on for press fnl 2f, nvr nrr: May foal, dam unrcd: eff at 1m on soft, 10f+ shld suit.
4336 **SUGAR ROLO** 16 [4] D Morris 2-8-6 R Winston 20/1: 540304: Chsd ldrs 6f: btr 4154 (AW).   2½   **46**
4333 **CARRICK LADY** 17 [6] 2-8-6 D Kinsella (7) 40/1: 00005: Held up, eff 3f out, no impress: see 4333.   ½   **45$**
4161 **BOY BAND** 32 [7] 2-8-11 A Culhane 4/1: 06: Chsd wnr 5f, sn btn: see 4161.   3   **46**
4138 **PHURTIVE** 33 [1] 2-8-11 R Mullen 16/1: 007: Towards rear, mod hdwy: mod form.   1¾   **44**
4369 **MINUS FOUR** 12 [12] 2-8-11 Dean McKeown 50/1: 008: Prom till halfway: longer 1m trip, no form.   10   **29**
4429 **DIVEBOMB** 9 [3] 2-8-7 (BL) (1ow) J Reid 9/1: 00009: Prom 6f: tried in blnks: mod form.   1   **24**
4068 **RACINGFORYOU LASS** 38 [2] 2-8-6 P Doe 50/1: 00: Prom 4f: 10th: longer 1m trip.   1½   **21**
4393 **GROVE DANCER** 11 [14] 2-8-9 (BL) T Quinn 7/1: 340000: Chsd ldrs 6f, btn/eased 1f out: 11th.   1½   **22**
-- **TREMOR** [11] 2-8-11 J Fortune 14/1: 0: Chsd ldrs 5f: 12th: 7,000gns purchase: with W Muir.   ½   **23**
4336 **THE WALL** 16 [9] 2-8-6 J Quinn 50/1: 000000: Bhd halfway: 13th: longer 1m trip, mod form.   nk   **17**
4309 **BALANOU** 19 [5] 2-8-6 G Carter 13/2: 00: Chsd ldrs 5f: 14th: longer 1m trip: rtd higher 4309 (7f).   5   **10**
4336 Inzarmoud 16 [13] 2-8-6 B Reilly (7) 50/1:   4336 Treble Red 16 [15] 2-8-6 S Drowne 20/1:
16 ran   Time 1m 49.18 (12.68)   (Denis Barry)   R Hannon East Everleigh, Wilts

---

4543   **3.05 LISTED ZETLAND STKS 2YO (A)**   1m2f   Soft 118   -28 Slow
£12528   £4752   £2376   £1080   Raced towards centre

*4375 **WORTHILY** 12 [2] M R Channon 2-9-2 J Reid 8/1: 051211: 2 b c Northern Spur - Worth's Girl (Devil's   **98**
Bag) Prom, went on ins fnl 1f, styd on well, rdn out: op 6/1: earlier won at Kempton (mdn) & Pontefract (List):
eff at 1m, suited by this step up to 10f, 12f+ shld suit: acts on soft & a stiff/gall trk: useful, progressive
colt, can rate higher in Group company next term.
*4140 **CAPAL GARMON** 33 [3] J H M Gosden 2-8-11 J Fortune 3/1 JT FAV: 4312: 2 b c Caerleon - Elevate   1¼   **90**
(Ela Mana Mou) Led/dsptd lead till over 1f out, kept on for press inside last: nicely bckd tho' op 7/4: suited
by 10f, shdl stay 12f next term: useful colt: see 4140 (mdn).
*4350 **REGATTA POINT** 15 [5] A P Jarvis 2-8-11 K Darley 6/1: -02113: 2 b c Goldmark - Flashing Raven   ½   **89**
(Maelstrom Lake) Held up, rdn/outpcd over 2f out, rallied ins last, not able to chall: bckd from 10/1: stays
10f on gd & soft grnd, handles fast: progressive colt: see 4350 (h'cap).
4375 **RATHKENNY** 12 [6] J G Given 2-8-11 Dean McKeown 16/1: 641624: Trckd ldrs, led over 1f out,   ½   **88**
hdd inside last & no extra: 6L clr rem: also bhd this wnr in 4375.
-- **CHICAGO BULLS** [4] 2-8-11 R Mullen 50/1: -45: Dwelt, rcd keenly in rear, eff 3f out, sn no   6   **80**
impress: British debut, 4th of 5 on recent Italian debut (1m): longer 10f trip today.
4267 **PARK HALL** 24 [1] 2-8-11 R Hughes 40/1: 46: Led 5f, wknd inside last: clr rem: longer 10f trip.   5   **73**
*3766 **MORSHDI** 57 [8] 2-8-11 L Dettori 4/1: 517: Held up, eff over 3f out, sn btn: bckd, abs: btr 3766.   3½   **69**
4296 **LUNAR CRYSTAL** 21 [9] 2-9-0 T Quinn 3/1 JT FAV: -148: Held up, eff 3f out, sn btn: hvly bckd tho'   16   **54**
op 5/2: longer 10f trip: btr 4296, 4124 (7f/1m).
3680 **KINGS OF EUROPE** 61 [7] 2-8-11 M Hills 14/1: 429: Chsd ldrs 7f: abs: btr 3680, 3298 (firm & fast).   9   **39**
9 ran   Time 2m 16.79 (14.69)   (Salem Suhail)   M R Channon West Isley, Berks

---

4544   **3.35 LISTED MARSHALL STKS 3YO+ (A)**   1m2f   Soft 118   +03 Fast
£14210   £5390   £2695   £1225   3 yo rec 3 lb   Raced centre - stands side

*4347 **ALBARAHIN** 15 [2] M P Tregoning 5-9-1 R Hills 8/11 FAV: 121211: 5 b h Silver Hawk - My Dear Lady   **119**
(Mr Prospector) Trkd ldr going well, led over 2f out, clr fnl 1f, readily: val for 5L+, hvly bckd, gd time:
earlier won at Sandown (reapp, stks), Goodwood & here at Newmarket (List), also rnr up in Gr 2 company: '99 wnr
at Leicester (reapp), Sandown & Newbury (h'caps, rtd 105): acts on fast, hvy & any trk, loves a stiff/
gall one: gd weight carrier, runs fresh: tough, smart & genuine performer, can win in Group company.
3918 **ROSSE** 46 [1] G Wragg 3-8-4 K Darley 16/1: 151362: 3 ch f Kris - Nuryana (Nureyev)   4   **102**
Held up, prog to chse wnr over 1f out, no impress: 6 wk abs: apprec return to 1m: acts on firm & soft grnd.
4352 **WARNINGFORD** 14 [11] J R Fanshawe 6-9-1 O Urbina 12/1: 631503: 6 b h Warning - Barford Lady   ½   **109**
(Stanford) Held up, kept on fnl 2f, no threat: all wins at 7f: see 3995 (7f).
4355 **COMPTON BOLTER** 14 [5] G A Butler 3-8-9 (t) L Dettori 7/2: 045104: Trckd ldrs, outpcd fnl 2f: bckd.   3   **102**
4347 **HASTY WORDS** 15 [4] 4-8-10 M Hills 33/1: 640405: Led 5f, wknd inside last: clr rem: see 4347.   hd   **99**
4078 **BEDAZZLING** 37 [6] 3-8-4 D Harrison 8/1: 014046: Held up, eff 3f out, no impress: see 4078, 2597.   6   **87**
4323} **GOODWOOD BLIZZARD** 384 [10] 3-8-4 G Carter 25/1: 2132-7: Prom 6f: belated reapp: '99 wnr at   6   **78**
Salisbury (fill auct mdn) & Ascot (auct stks), subs rnr up in a Gr 3 (rtd 99): suited by 7f/1m, may get further:
acts on firm & gd grnd: likes a stiff/gall trck, prob handles any: with J Dunlop.
4142 **GLEN ROSIE** 33 [3] 3-8-4 G Duffield 50/1: 240068: Held up, btn 3f out: btr 913.   4   **72**
4274 **DANZIG WITHWOLVES** 24 [12] 3-8-4 T Quinn 20/1: 449: Chsd ldrs 6f, wkly tried after 4274, 2938.   5   **65**
4302 **KUWAIT DAWN** 21 [8] 4-8-7 S Drowne 200/1: 060000: Prom 5f: 10th: highly tried.   3½   **60**
4456 **LADY BOXER** 8 [7] 4-8-7 A Mackay 100/1: 011000: Held up, btn 3f out: 11th: btr 4069 (6f, Chester).   7   **50**
11 ran   Time 1m 45.72 (9.22)   (Hamdan Al Maktoum)   M P Tregoning Lambourn, Berks

---

4545   **4.05 LADBROKE AUTUMN HCAP 3YO+ 0-100 (C)**   1m str   Soft 118   +03 Fast   **[99]**
£23200   £8800   £4400   £2000   3 yo rec 3 lb   Majority racing centre favoured

*4506 **GREENAWAY BAY** 4 [13] K R Burke 6-7-11 (68)(5ex) C Catlin (7) 8/1: 3-5111: 6 ch g Green Dancer -   **77**
Raise 'N Dance (Raise A Native) Held up, smooth prog to lead ins last, rdn out: gd time, qck reapp:
recent Nottingham wnr, earlier scored at York (h'caps): '99 Brighton wnr (h'cap, rtd 59): plcd sev times in '98
(rtd 62 & 59a, W Musson): eff at 1m/10f on firm, loves soft/hvy grnd: handles any trk, likes a stiff/gall one:
has run well fresh: most progressive gelding, winning run may not have ended.
4472 **ATLANTIC RHAPSODY** 7 [2] M Johnston 3-9-8 (96) R Hughes 16/1: 462042: 3 b g Machiavellian - First   1¾   **101**

Waltz (Green Dancer) Held up, rdn & styd on fnl 2f, not rch wnr: op 20/1: acts on firm & soft: useful: see 1535.
3945 **NIMELLO 45** [9] P F I Cole 4-8-11 (82) J Fortune 16/1: 100043: 4 b c Kingmambo - Zakota (Polish Precedent) Trkd ldrs trav well, went on over 1f out, hdd ins last & no extra: 6 wk abs: acts on firm, clearly loves soft & hvy grnd: back on a handy mark: see 1042 (hvy). ½ 86
4199 **BOLD KING 29** [14] J W Hills 5-9-4 (89) D Harrison 25/1: 000164: Held up, hdwy/no room over 1f out, kept on inside last, not able to chall: loves soft grnd: not much luck today, see 4077 (stks). 1 91
4348 **LAGOON 15** [10] 3-9-5 (93) D Holland 8/1: 003145: Trckd ldrs, not much room over 1f out, onepace inside last: op 6/1: acts on firm & soft grnd: see 4199 (C/D). 1¼ 93
4473 **SCENE 7** [16] 5-8-7 (78) T Quinn 8/1: 004136: Trckd ldrs, onepce inside last: bckd: see 4340 (C/D). hd 77
4348 **ATAVUS 15** [30] 3-8-5 (79) J Mackay (5) 25/1: 500007: Chsd ldrs 6f: see 2858, 1183. 1¾ 76
4284 **GREAT NEWS 22** [21] 5-9-1 (86) P Hanagan (5) 12/1: 011128: Keen/trckd ldrs, led over 2f out till over 1f out, fdd: op 10/1: rcd too freely today: btr 4284, 4102. 1 82
4126 **JUST NICK 34** [11] 6-8-2 (73) P Doe 25/1: 521109: Prom, outpcd fnl 2f: just btr 2707 (firm). 1 68
*4348 **ELGHANI 15** [20] 3-9-6 (94) R Hills 6/1 FAV: 01210: Led main group 5f, fdd: 10th: btr 4348 (C/D). 2½ 85
4506 **PIPS WAY 4** [25] 3-8-6 (80) N Callan 50/1: 315400: Chsd ldrs 6f: 11th: qck reapp: btr 2581. ¾ 70
4357 **PRINCE BABAR 14** [4] 9-8-10 (81) J Reid 25/1: 501650: Chsd ldrs stands side, led that group over 1f out, no impress on ldrs in centre: 12th: first home on unfav stands side: worth a qck reapp: see 3785 (7f). ¾ 70+
4506 **MELODIAN 4** [18] 5-8-2 (73)(bl) D Mernagh (3) 25/1: 132200: Led overall twds stands side 5f: 13th. 4 56
4348 **TORNADO PRINCE 15** [19] 5-9-0 (85) R Winston 20/1: 420100: Held up, eff 2f out, no impress: 14th. 1 67
4348 **SILK ST JOHN 15** [8] 6-9-1 (86) G Duffield 33/1: 000500: Trckd ldrs 6f: 15th: btr 1836. ½ 67
4340 **TOPTON 16** [15] 6-8-2 (73)(bl) R Mullen 33/1: 060040: Mid div at best: 16th: btr 2899 (7f, firm). 1¼ 52
4357 **CAPTAIN SCOTT 14** [24] 6-9-5 (90)(t) L Dettori 9/1: 400-0P: Held up in tch, lost place/eased 3f out, p.u/dismounted inside last: reportedly suffered a slight knock: see 4357. 0
4348 **Sir Ferbet 15** [29] 3-8-13 (87) M Hills 16/1:
4348 **Salty Jack 15** [26] 6-8-13 (84) W Supple 25/1:
4506 **Chapel Royale 4** [3] 3-8-6 (80) S Drowne 50/1:
4420 **Kareeb 9** [27] 3-8-6 (80) G Baker (5) 40/1:
4340 **Pentagon Lad 16** [12] 4-8-0 (71) K Dalgleish (5) 50/1:
4284 **Tony Tie 22** [23] 4-9-5 (90) A Culhane 33/1:
*4302 **I Cried For You 21** [5] 5-9-2 (87) Dean McKeown 14/1:
*4278 **Big Future 23** [6] 3-9-6 (94) W Ryan 20/1:
4472 **Swan Knight 7** [28] 4-9-10 (95) J Carroll 25/1:
*4113 **Riberac 35** [22] 4-9-10 (95) K Darley 16/1:
4206 **Beading 28** [17] 3-7-11 (71)(t) M Henry 33/1:
4206 **Colne Valley Amy 28** [1] 3-7-11 (71) R Brisland(5) 66/1:
29 ran Time 1m 45.73 (9.23) (Asterlane Ltd) K R Burke Newmarket, Suffolk

4546 **4.40 LISTED MONTROSE FILLIES STKS 2YO (A) 1m str Soft 118 -07 Slow**
£12354 £4686 £2343 £1065 Raced towards centre

*4104 **LA VITA E BELLA 35** [2] C F Wall 2-8-8 R Mullen 20/1: 0211: 2 b g Definite Article - Coolrain Lady (Common Grounds) Held up, prog to lead dist, styd on strongly, rdn out: recent Haydock wnr (fill mdn): eff at 1m, mid dists shld suit next term: acts gd/soft & soft, untried on faster: likes a stiff/gall trk: useful & progressive filly: will reporetdly be aimed at one of the European Guineas next term. 96
3876 **ESYOUEFFCEE 51** [1] M W Easterby 2-8-8 T Lucas 20/1: 2102: 2 b f Alzao - Familiar (Diesis) Held up racing keenly, prog & ch over 1f out, kept on well, not btn far: 7 wk abs: acts on fast & soft grnd. ½ 94
-4467 **BLUSHING BRIDE 7** [7] J Noseda 2-8-8 D Holland 2/1 FAV: -1123: 2 b f Distant Relative - Dime Bag (High Line) Held up, prog dist, kept on well ins last for press: btn under 1L, hvly bckd: stays 1m. hd 93
4114 **INCHIRI 35** [3] G A Butler 2-8-8 J Reid 14/1: 54: Held up, rdn/outpcd over 2f out, kept on inside last, no threat to front trio: stays 1m: handles gd & soft grnd: should find at least a mdn: see 4114. 3½ 88
4157 **LOVE EVERLASTING 32** [4] 2-8-8 K Darley 12/1: 342125: Prom, ch over 1f out, fdd: op 14/1: longer 1m trip: acts on fast & soft grnd: return to h'caps could suit: see 4157, 3953. 1¾ 86
3876 **ELREHAAN 51** [8] 2-8-8 R Hills 14/1: 2106: Chsd ldrs till over 1f out: 7 wk abs: btr 3308 (firm). 5 79
*4309 **GONCHAROVA 19** [5] 2-8-8 L Dettori 11/4: 17: Led, hdd over 1f out, sn btn: well bckd tho' op 7/4: better expected after 4309 (debut), but this was much tougher. 3½ 74
4356 **GOT TO GO 14** [9] 2-8-8 M Hills 5/1: -108: Prom till over 1f out: longer 1m trip: see 4288 (6f). 2½ 70
*4312 **PEARL BRIGHT 19** [6] 2-8-8 T Quinn 12/1: 219: Bolted to start, prom 6f: op 16/1: btr 4312 (7f). 14 50
9 ran Time 1m 46.51 (10.01) (Ettore Landi) C F Wall Newmarket, Suffolk

4547 **5.15 BURROUGH GREEN HCAP 3YO+ 0-85 (D) 7f str Soft 118 -31 Slow [85]**
£5837 £1796 £898 £449 3 yo rec 2 lb Raced towards centre

3992 **WEETMANS WEIGH 43** [2] R Hollinshead 7-8-5 (62) N Callan 7/1: 406501: 7 b h Archway - Indian Sand (Indian King) Held up, prog to lead over 1f out, held on gamely inside last, all out: 6 wk abs: '99 wnr at Southwell & W'hampton (h'caps, rtd 96a & 80): '98 W'hampton, Newcastle & Newmarket wnr (h'caps, rtd 78 & 86a): eff at 7f/ 8.5f on firm & soft, loves fibresand: handles any trk, loves a sharp one: gd weight carrier: runs well fresh. 67
*4480 **BINTANG TIMOR 6** [7] W J Musson 6-8-9 (66) J Fortune 4/1 FAV: 000012: 6 ch g Mt Livermore - Frisky Kitten (Isopach) Held up, rdn & styd on well from 1f out, just held: well bckd: qck reapp: see 4480. nk 70
4330 **COMPTON ARROW 17** [3] G A Butler 4-8-13 (70) L Dettori 14/1: 000053: 4 b g Petardia - Impressive Lady (Mr Fluorocarbon) Held up, rdn & kept on fnl 2f, nrst fin: op 8/1, btn under 1L: tumbled down the h'cap this term, fine run here with t-strap omitted: can find a race: see 1810, 1450. ½ 73
4357 **GIFT OF GOLD 14** [14] A Bailey 5-9-6 (77) D Harrison 11/1: 500604: Held up, no room over 2f out, kept on inside last: sound run in the circumstances: see 1483. 1½ 78
3089 **FAIR IMPRESSION 87** [6] 3-9-8 (81) J Reid 12/1: 001105: Held up, kept on onepce fnl 2f: op 9/1, abs. 1 81
4357 **INTRICATE WEB 14** [4] 4-8-11 (68)(bl) W Supple 25/1: 530006: Chsd ldrs, rdn/led & hung right over 2f out, hdd over 1f out & fdd: blnks reapp: see 2241 (fast). 1¾ 66
*4461 **MANTLES PRIDE 7** [20] 5-9-2 (73)(bl) D Holland 6/1: 022017: Chsd ldrs 6f: see 4461 (clmr). 1¾ 69
4513 **SARSON 3** [19] 4-8-13 (70) R Hughes 12/1: 000468: Led 1f, ch over 1f out when hmpd, eased inside last: op 10/1, qck reapp: closer to placed horses if ridden out to the line: see 4204, 1676. shd 66
3885 **ONE DINAR 50** [9] 5-8-6 (61)(2ow) S Drowne 16/1: 360329: Held up, eff 2f out, no impress: abs. 1¼ 57
4478 **DESERT FURY 6** [10] 3-9-3 (76) W Ryan 16/1: 046540: Held up, eff 2f out, no impress: 10th. 4 64
4302 **A TOUCH OF FROST 21** [11] 5-9-10 (81)(bl) K Darley 6/1: 0-1400: Chsd ldrs 5f: 11th: bckd, op 9/1. 2½ 65
4340 **PACIFIC ALLIANCE 16** [1] 4-9-8 (79) Dean McKeown 12/1: 311100: Held up, nvr able to chall: 12th. nk 62
4206 **DANDILUM 28** [21] 3-9-5 (78) G Hind 33/1: 4W0200: Struggling over 2f out: 13th: btr 3977. ¾ 60
*4411 **SLUMBERING 10** [24] 4-9-2 (73) O Urbina 6/1: 005110: Held up, rdn 3f out, sn btn: 14th: btr 4411. 1¼ 53
4215 **GOODENOUGH MOVER 28** [12] 4-9-8 (79) T Quinn 12/1: 114200: Briefly led 3f out, sn btn: 20th: op 10/1. 0
4405 **Pips Song 10** [13] 5-9-8 (79) J Lowe 25/1:
4185 **Second Generation 30** [17] 3-7-10 (55)(5oh) Karen Peippo(7) 33/1:
4038 **Silk Daisy 40** [25] 4-8-9 (66) A McGlone 20/1:
4405 **Baby Barry 10** [18] 3-9-2 (75) A Mackay 25/1:

4480 **Ravishing 6** [22] 3-8-9 (68) P Hanagan (5) 25/1: 4357 **Norfolk Reed 14** [16] 3-9-8 (81)(vis) L Newman (3) 16/1: 812} **Sharp Pearl 569** [23] 7-8-0 (57) P Doe 33/1:
22 ran Time 1m 33.63 (10.43) (Ed Weetman (Haulage & Storage) Ltd) R Hollinshead Upper Longdon, Staffs

WOLVERHAMPTON (Fibresand) SATURDAY OCTOBER 28TH LH, Oval, Sharp Track

Official Going STANDARD. Stalls: 7f - Outside; Rem - Inside.

4548 7.00 LASSO MED AUCT MDN 2YO (F) 6f aw rnd Going 43 -05 Slow
£2261 £646 £323

4372 **TRAVEL TARDIA 12** [4] I A Wood 2-9-0 M Tebbutt 2/1 FAV: 021: 2 br c Petardia - Annie's Travels (Mac's Imp) Chsd ldrs, led over 3f out, clr dist, pshd out, eased cl-home, val 4/5L: nicely bckd: 8,500gns first foal, dam unrcd: sire high-class miler: eff arnd 6f on soft, fibresand & any trk: going the right way. 85a

3974 **IN SPIRIT 43** [2] D J S Cosgrove 2-9-0 J Quinn 6/1: 02: 2 b c Distinctly North - June Goddess (Junius) In tch, sltly outpcd 3f out, rdn & late hdwy fnl 1f, no threat to wnr: tchd 8/1 after 6 wk abs: improved form on this switch to AW, stays a sharp 6f on fibresand: see 3974. 2½ 74a

4253 **LADY LENOR 25** [11] Mrs G S Rees 2-8-9 Angela Hartley (7) 6/1: -023: 2 b f Presidium - Sparkling Roberta (Kind Of Hush) Cl-up, ev ch till rdn/no extra fnl 1f: op 4/1: AW debut: up in trip & prob not quite get home over 6f on fibresand: btr 4253 (5f, soft). 1 66a

3852 **REAP 52** [10] J Pearce 2-9-0 (VIS) G Bardwell 33/1: 064: Sn outpcd, rdn/hdwy appr fnl 1f, styd on well but nvr nrr: 7 wk abs, first time visor: needs a step up in trip: see 3000. 3½ 63a

4415 **ULTIMATE CHOICE 9** [1] 2-9-0 J Fanning 6/1: 05: Led till over 3f out, fdd fnl 1f: op 3/1, btr 4415 (7f). 2½ 57a

4362 **MRS TIGGYWINKLE 14** [9] M Fenton 9/1: 006026: Handy, rdn/wknd fnl 2f: big drop in trip & prob ran to form of 4362 (8.5f fillies seller). ¾ 51a

3973 **LIFFORD LADY 43** [7] P Fessey 33/1: 00067: Al outpcd, nvr dngrs: 6 wk abs, modest form. 3½ 43a

4471 **CITY PLAYER 7** [8] 2-9-0 S Sanders 9/2: 08: Sn struggling: qck reapp: 26,000gns Mar foal, half-brother to a useful 6f juv wnr: dam won in the USA: with Sir M Prescott. 2 43a

4131 **NIGHT OF NIGHTS 34** [13] M Fenton 20/1: 09: Mid-div, lost tch fnl 2f: up in trip: see 4131. 10 18a

3911 **DOLPHIN BEECH 47** [5] 2-8-9 A Clark 33/1: 00: Chsd ldrs, rdn & lost tch from halfway, 10th: 7 wk abs. 1½ 15a

-- **BEAT THE RING** [3] 2-9-0 D R McCabe 12/1: -0: V slow to start, al well bhd, 11th: tchd 20/1: 10,000gns Mar foal, half-brother to sev wnrs, dam 5f 2yo scorer: with G Brown. 2½ 15a

4138 **DUSKY SWALLOW 33** [12] 2-9-0 (VIS) O Pears 33/1: 00: Prom 3f, wknd rapidly, t.o. in 12th: visored. 8 0a

12 ran Time 1m 15.7 (2.9) (Neardown Stables) I A Wood Upper Lambourn, Berks.

4549 7.30 COUNTRY CLAIMER 3YO+ (F) 1m4f aw Going 43 -27 Slow
£2240 £640 £320 3 yo rec 7 lb

4334 **FAILED TO HIT 17** [2] N P Littmoden 7-9-8 (vis) S Sanders 1/1 FAV: 263151: 7 b g Warrshan - Missed Again (High Top) Made all, pushed clr appr fnl 1f, easily: val 8/10L+: earlier won twice here at W'hampton (clmr & h'cap): '99 wnr again at W'hampton (h'cap) & Lingfield (clmr, rtd 74a), prev term won at Lingfield (3, h'caps & ltd stks) & W'hamton (3, clmr & h'caps, rtd 68a): suited by forcing the pace around 12f, has been furthest: handles fast grnd, AW/sharp trk specialist, loves W'hampton/Lingfield: suited by blnks/visor: v tough front rnr. 72a

4226 **TOUJOURS RIVIERA 28** [8] J Pearce 10-9-4 G Baker (5) 4/1: 151262: 10 ch g Rainbow Quest - Miss Beaulieu (Northfields) In tch, eff 4f out, rdn & styd on to take 2nd 2f out, chsd wnr in vain fnl 1f, no threat: 6L clr rem, op 5/2: best in sell/claim grade these days: see 3775. 6 56a

3631} **MOONRAKING 427** [12] Miss S J Wilton 7-8-12 (bl) R Lake (7) 12/1: 0050-3: 7 gr g Rusticaro - Lunaire (Try My Best) Sn well bhd, hdwy appr halfway, sn prom, drvn/no extra fnl 2f: recent unplcd hdles rnr (h'cap & sell, rtd 68a), prev term won at Ludlow & Hereford (sell h'caps, rtd 92h, 2m/2m1f, firm & gd/soft, blnks, sharp trks): '99 Flat wnr at Southwell (2, appr clmr for T Etherington & clmr, rtd 69a at best): '98 wnr again at Southwell (2, h'caps, rtd 70a): stays 14f, best at 10/12f on soft & gd/soft, loves fibresand/Southwell: eff with/without blnks. 6 42a

4371 **PENNYS FROM HEAVEN 12** [9] D Nicholls 6-9-10 O Pears 8/1: 304044: Prom, drvn/grad wknd fnl 3f: op 5/1, had rest well covered: better off in h'caps: see 4149 (amat h'cap, 2m). 2½ 50a

4391 **GAME TUFTY 11** [5] 4-9-4 J Quinn 9/1: 006225: Bhd, eff 4f out, drvn/lost tch fnl 2f: op 6/1 & capable of better tho' still disappointing: better off fnl 4391 (11.5f sell h'cap, soft). 25 19a

4041 **GO WITH THE WIND 39** [10] 7-8-12 R Winston 12/1: -03206: In tch, rdn/fdd fnl 4f: btr 3633 (14f, fast). nk 13a

4391 **LUNAR LORD 11** [6] 4-8-12 N Farmer (7) 14/1: 440337: Prom, lost tch fnl 4f: op 10/1: btr 4391 (soft). 1¼ 11a

4371 **BAMBOO GARDEN 12** [1] 4-9-3 (bl) M Fenton 12/1: 350-08: Front rank, wknd rapidly fnl 3f: early '99 Southwell wnr (sell h'cap, rtd 61a): well btn in 3 '98 turf starts: eff at 1m, has tried 10/12f: acts on fibresand & sharp trks: off in blnks, has prev tried a visor. 3½ 12a

4370 **BEAUCHAMP NYX 12** [4] 4-8-11 S Righton 50/1: 06-009: Al in rear: see 4141. 1½ 4a

4360 **DIZZY TILLY 14** [11] 6-9-5 (BL) K Dalgleish (5) 25/1: 060000: Prom 1m, wknd qckly, t.o., 10th: blnkd. 14 0a

2181 **EXECUTIVE PROFILES 125** [3] 5-8-3 T Williams 50/1: 00: Pulled hard & saddle slipped early stages, no ch from halfway, t.o. in 11th: no form on Flat debut recently for Miss K George, now with C N Kellett. 4 0a

11 ran Time 2m 42.0 (8.4) (M C S D Racing Ltd) N P Littmoden Newmarket.

4550 8.00 INTERCLASS HCAP 3YO+ 0-70 (E) 7f aw rnd Going 43 -11 Slow [66]
£2957 £845 £422 3 yo rec 2 lb

4192 **DIAMOND RACHAEL 29** [9] Mrs N Macauley 3-9-9 (63)(vis) R Fitzpatrick 20/1: 012001: 3 b f Shalford - Brown Foam (Horage) Hdwy from rear hdwy, went on appr fnl 1f & sn clr, drvn out: earlier won here at W'hampton (mdn, rtd 63a) & Leicester (fill h'cap, rtd 65): no form on turf in '99 tho' plcd on sand (rtd 63a, mdn): eff at 6/7f, has tried 1m: acts on fast grnd & fibresand, sharp or stiff/gall trk: eff in a visor & back to best today. 67a

-4358 **TEOFILIO 14** [6] A J McNae 6-10-0 (66)(bl) K Dalgleish (5) 2/1 FAV: 540222: 6 ch h Night Shift - Rivoltade (Sir Ivor) Dwelt/outpcd, rcd wide & gd hdwy appr fnl 2f, styd on fnl 1f but no threat to wnr: bckd. 1¼ 67a

4426 **VICTORIOUS 9** [12] R A Fahey 4-9-11 (63) S Sanders 11/1: 005003: 4 ch g Formidable - Careful Dancer (Gorytus) Dwelt, sn well bhd, imprvd halfway, styd on well but nvr nrr: op 7/1, clr trm: see 4426. shd 64a

*4153 **MOONLIGHT SONG 32** [4] W Jarvis 3-9-12 (66) M Tebbutt 9/1: 222014: Prom, drvn/kept on onepace appr fnl 1f: op 4/1: rtd higher 4153 (Southwell). 4 60a

4358 **AUBRIETA 14** [5] 4-9-10 (62)(bl) Dean McKeown 16/1: 114005: Handy, drvn & grad wknd appr fnl 1f: both wins this term have come in clmrs & will appr a return to that grade, see 1913. nk 56a

1410

4224 **ROYAL CASCADE** 28 [10] 6-9-8 (60)(bl) L Newton 12/1: 015026: Mid-div, drvn/onepcd fnl 3f: op 10/1. **3** **49a**

4307 **RYTHM N TIME** 19 [1] 3-9-8 (62) P Doe 20/1: 660057: Led, hdd appr fnl 1f, sn lost tch: set off too **1½** **49a**
fast today & is unproven at 7f: btr 3056 (class stks, 5f, gd/soft).

4363 **PIPPAS PRIDE** 14 [7] 5-9-4 (56) D R McCabe 25/1: 023608: Prom, wknd qckly fnl 2f: likes Southwell. **1** **41a**

*4437 **GROESFAEN LAD** 8 [8] 3-9-11 (65)(vis) G Faulkner 8/1: 635319: Mid-div at best, btn fnl 2f: much **5** **42a**
better when racing up with the pace over 8.5f in 4437.

*4293 **BOUND TO PLEASE** 22 [3] 5-9-11 (63) A Clark 3/1: 13-110: Sn outpcd, nvr dngrs, 10th: op 2/1 & **3½** **34a**
much better expected on this hat-trick bid, something amiss?: much btr 4293 (6f, gd/soft).

4010 **Persian Fayre** 42 [9] 8-9-9 (61) R Winston 25/1:   4287 **La Piazza** 22 [2] 4-10-0 (66) F Lynch 25/1:
12 ran   Time 1m 30.0 (3.8)   (Diamond Racing Ltd)   Mrs N Macauley Sproxton, Leics.

4551	8.30 SIX GUN MDN 3YO+ (D)	1m100y aw rnd Going 43 -14 Slow		
	£2899 £892 £446 £223	3 yo rec 3 lb		

4292 **IPANEMA BEACH** 22 [8] J W Hills 3-8-9 M Tebbutt 4/1: -03601: 3 ch f Lion Cavern - Girl From Ipanema **69a**
(Salse) Trkd ldrs, went on halfway, rdn clr over 1f out, rdn out, flashed tail nr fin: op 3/1: AW bow: rtd 72
when unplcd on sole juv start: dam 7f/1m wnr: eff around 1m/8.5f: handles fast grnd, imprvd today on fibresand.

4273 **SUMMER JAZZ** 24 [10] P J Makin 3-8-9 S Sanders 1/1 FAV: 52: 3 b f Alhijaz - Salvezza (Superpower) **1** **65a**
In tch, imprvd 3f out, styd on fnl 1f but no threat to wnr: nicely bckd, 5L clr rem: eff at 8.5f on fibresand.

4505 **FRAZERS LAD** 4 [1] A Bailey 3-9-0 R Lappin 12/1: 53: 3 b g Whittingham - Loch Tain (Lochnager) **5** **60a**
Handy, drvn 2f out, sn no extra: qck reapp & prob ran to form of debut in 4505 (hvy grnd).

4443 **LE CAVALIER** 8 [13] C N Allen 3-9-0 (bl) G Bardwell 8/1: 500004: Mid-div, rdn & kept on onepcd **1** **58$**
fnl 2f: prob unsuited by this big drop in trip & treat rating with caution (offic only 54): see 395, 240.

4361 **CRISTOFORO** 14 [6] 3-9-0 J Stack 7/1: -05: Prom, rdn/lost tch appr fnl 1f: up in trip: see 4361. **nk** **58a**

-- **MEMAMEDA** [4] 4-8-12 F Lynch 14/1: 6: Dwelt, nvr dngrs: belated debut: with K A Ryan. **9** **40a**

1546 **MERCHANT PRINCE** 152 [11] 5-9-0 M Fenton 33/1: 500007: Led after 2f till halfway, wknd: 5 month abs. **5** **38$**

3914 **REPLACEMENT PET** 47 [9] 3-8-9 (BL) K Dalgleish (5) 10/1: 4008: Dwelt, mid-div at best: 7 wk abs, **3** **28a**
blnkd on AW bow: best turf form when 4th on debut in 3146.

4255 **LAKESIDE LADY** 25 [11] 3-8-9 R Winston 16/1: 009: Al outpcd: up in trip, modest form. **shd** **28a**

3606} **MARTINEZ** 427 [2] 4-9-3 Dean McKeown 12/1: 0-0: Sn struggling, fin 10th: big step up in trip on **5** **26a**
reapp: well btn on sole '99 juv start (5f mdn, gd grnd, rtd 37).

3206 **GOLDFAW** 81 [7] 3-9-0 J Fanning 50/1: -00000: Led early, wknd rapidly halfway, t.o. in 11th: poor. **25** **0a**

-- **AMERTON HEATH** [12] 7-8-12 J Bosley (7) 33/1: 0: Al in rear, t.o. in 12th: Flat debut, poor hdlr. **nk** **0a**
12 ran   Time 1m 51.1 (4.9)   (J W Hills)   J W Hills Upper Lambourn, Berks

---

4552	9.00 SELL NURSERY HCAP 2YO 0-65 (G)	1m100y aw rnd Going 43 -27 Slow	[67]
	£1848 £528 £264		

*4362 **JEZADIL** 14 [5] P S McEntee 2-9-6 (59) G Faulkner 11/4 FAV: 434011: 2 b f Mujadil - Tender Times **67a**
(Tender King) Cl-up, led over 2f out, drvn clr despite flashing tail appr fnl 1f, styd on strongly under hands
& heels last, cosily: new stable, btn in for 8,200 gns: recent wnr for M Dods here at W'hampton (fill slr,
first win): plcd on turf once prev (rtd 60, clmr): eff around 8.5f, has tried 10f: acts on fast & soft, likes
fibresand/W'hampton & racing up with/forcing the pace: in fine form, could complete an AW hat-trick.

4336 **FINN MCCOOL** 16 [10] R A Fahey 2-9-6 (59) J Quinn 4/1: -6102: 2 b g Blues Traveller - Schonbein **3½** **59a**
(Persian Heights) Mid-div, imprvd after halfway, chsd wnr appr fnl 1f, styd on but nvr dngrs: stays 8.5f.

4362 **EMMA CLARE** 14 [1] J A Osborne 2-8-13 (52) T Williams 10/1: 410063: 2 b f Namaqualand - **nk** **52a**
Medicosma (The Minstrel) Prom, outpcd halfway, styd on well in last: op 7/1, apprec mid-dists next term.

4416 **MENAS ERN** 9 [3] S Dow 2-8-12 (51) P Doe 8/1: 000404: Mid-div, eff 3f out, kept on onepcd fnl 2f: **2½** **47a**
up in trip, rtd higher 4154 (7f, AW bow).

3837 **I GOT RHYTHM** 53 [7] 2-8-7 (46) S Sanders 9/1: 004005: Sn rdn/rear, late hdwy for press: 7 wk abs. **½** **41a**

4502 **CO DOT UK** 4 [8] 2-9-7 (60)(bl) F Lynch 4/1: 020236: Front rank, led after 3f, hdd over 2f out, **nk** **55a**
wknd qckly: qck reapp: longer 8.5f trip & prob not get home: btr 4502 (6f), 4369 (7f).

4336 **MISS DAMINA** 16 [4] 2-9-1 (54) R Ffrench 10/1: 040407: Late gains from rear, nvr dngrs: see 4097. **4** **42a**

4362 **SUSIE THE FLOOSIE** 14 [9] 2-8-5 (44) M Tebbutt 25/1: 00008: Al outpcd: looks modest. **3** **27a**

4439 **NO SURRENDER** 8 [2] 2-8-4 (43) O Pears 33/1: 60009: Led to 5f out, lost tch halfway: see 2057. **½** **25a**

4362 **RED FANFARE** 16 [6] 2-8-11 (50) J Fanning 10/1: 000250: Well bhd halfway, 10th: op 8/1, btr 4025. **2** **29a**
10 ran   Time 1m 52.2 (6.0)   (John Harris & Mrs Sian Harris)   P S McEntee Newmarket.

4553	9.30 WILD WEST HCAP 3YO+ 0-60 (F)	6f aw rnd Good 43 +13 Fast	[60]
	£2590 £740 £370	3 yo rec 1 lb	

4442 **PALACEGATE TOUCH** 8 [2] A Berry 10-9-9 (55) D Allan (7) 12/1: 000341: 10 gr g Petong - Dancing Chimes **61a**
(London Bells) Sltly outpcd early, rdn/imprvd 2f out, ran on strongly to lead ins last, drvn out: fast time, op
9/1: earlier this term won here at W'hampton (amat clmr): '99 scorer at Lingfield (2 clmrs, rtd 75a & 62) &
prev term again at Lingfield (clmr, rtd 78a), Warwick, Hamilton & Catterick (2, clmr/sllr, rtd 60): eff at 5/6f,
stays 7f on firm, gd/soft & both AWs: handles any trk, with/without blnks/visor: tough veteran (29 wins from 156).

*4444 **PUPS PRIDE** 8 [10] R A Fahey 3-9-4 (51)(bl) S Sanders 3/1 FAV: 340012: 3 b g Efisio - Moogie **1¾** **52a**
(Young Generation) Sn outpcd, rallied 2f out, styd on well ins last but not ch with wnr: wants 7f now?

4444 **PURPLE FLING** 8 [6] A J McNae 9-9-10 (56) K Dalgleish (5) 10/1: 002363: 9 ch g Music Boy - Divine **shd** **57a**
Fling (Imperial Fling) Mid-div, imprvd over 2f out, kept on ins last: op 7/1: see 3275, 82.

4444 **JANICELAND** 8 [4] M Wigham 3-9-7 (54) M Fenton 6/1: 055334: Trkd ldrs, drvn/no extra ins fnl 1f. **1½** **52a**

4405 **TECHNICIAN** 10 [7] 5-9-5 (51)(bl) P Doe 8/1: 220005: Front rank, led briefly 2f out, wknd: op 5/1/ **1** **46a**

4444 **YOUNG BIGWIG** 8 [5] 6-9-7 (53) J Quinn 9/1: 030046: Led over 3f out, hdd ins last, wknd. **¾** **46a**

4442 **HOUT BAY** 8 [11] 3-9-5 (52) R Winston 14/1: 005407: Front rank, chall ldr 2f out, wknd qckly fnl 1f. **1** **43a**

4442 **PALO BLANCO** 8 [9] 9-9-8 (54) G Baker (5) 8/1: 401638: In tch, wknd fnl 2f: ahd of this wnr in 4442. **1½** **42a**

4444 **FEATHERSTONE LANE** 8 [3] 9-9-8 (54) Dean McKeown 8/1: 435029: Al wellbhd: much btr 4444 (C/D). **5** **32a**

4407 **DOMINELLE** 10 [12] 8-9-3 (49) P Fessey 16/1: 610050: Prom 4f, sn lost tch, 10th: btr 2969 (gd/firm). **½** **26a**

4459 **BORDER GLEN** 8 [13] 4-9-9 (55)(bl) M Tebbutt 8/1: 643360: Mid-div, lost tch over 2f out, fin 11th. **shd** **32a**

3272 **COST AUDITING** 78 [1] 3-9-5 (52) R Studholme (3) 25/1: -50000: Led, hdd halfway, sn btn, 12th: abs. **1¾** **25a**

4442 **CAPPELLINA** 8 [8] 3-9-3 (50) A Clark 16/1: 420000: Mid-div, no room over 2f out & sn lost tch, 13th. **7** **8a**
13 ran   Time 1m 14.6 (1.8)   (A B Parr)   A Berry Cockerham, Lancs.

LEOPARDSTOWN
SATURDAY OCTOBER 28TH   Lefthand, Galloping Track

Official Going   HEAVY

4554
2.00 IRISH BUSINESS EBF MDN 2YO   1m   Heavy
£11050   £3250   £1530

--   **GALILEO** A P O'Brien 2-9-2 M J Kinane 1/1 FAV: 1: 2 b c Sadler's Wells - Urban Sea   **107+**
(Miswaki) Chsd ldrs, hdwy to lead over 1f out, soon pulled well clr, easily: op 2/5: half-brother to Irish Oaks
runner-up Melikah: dam Arc winner: eff at 1m, mid-dists sure to suit next term: acts on hvy & a gall trk: runs
well fresh: most impressive debut, well regarded by powerful stable & looks a Classic horse for next year.
--   **TARAZA** J Oxx 2-8-11 J Murtagh 5/2: -02: 2 b f Darshaan - Tarziyana (Danzig)   14   77
Led/dsptd lead till over 1f out, no chance with easy wnr: op 3/1.
4058   **AMERICAN GOTHIC 41** C O'Brien 2-9-2 F M Berry 12/1: -003: 2 b c Shirley Heights - Hocus   3½   77
(High Top) Mid-div, mod late hdwy, no impress on front pair: op 8/1: bred to apprec mid-dists next term.
16 ran   Time 1m 48.2   (Mrs John Magnier)   A P O'Brien Ballydoyle, Co Tipperary

4555
3.30 EBF AGRICULTURE HCAP 3YO+   6f   Heavy   **[114]**
£19500   £5700   £2700   3 yo rec 1 lb

*4456   **GAELIC STORM 8** M Johnston 6-9-12 (112) J Murtagh 1/1 FAV: 401211: 6 b g Shavian - Shannon Princess   118
(Connaught) Chsd ldrs, rdn/prog to lead over 1f out, styd on well, rdn out: earlier won at Klampenborg, Redcar (stks)
& Newbury (rtd h'cap): '99 wnr at Goodwood (stks), Sweden (2, incl List) & Newmarket (List, rtd 114): '98 Newbury
wnr (rtd h'cap, rtd 114): eff at 6/7f on firm, loves gd & hvy, any track: tough & smart, at the top of his form.
4398   **TIGER ROYAL 13** D K Weld 4-9-2 (102)(bl) P J Smullen 4/1: 332132: 4 gr g Royal Academy - Lady   1   105
Redford (Bold Lad) Hld up, hdwy when short of room & switched over 1f out, styd on ins last: well clr rem.
--   **EVEAM** N Meade 3-7-12 (85) M C Hussey (3) 14/1: 340203: 3 b f Mujadil - Christoph's Girl (Efisio)   7   73
Cl up, rdn/outpcd fnl 2f: op 8/1.
10 ran   Time 1m 17.7   (H C Racing Club)   M Johnston Middleham, N Yorks

SAINT CLOUD
SUNDAY OCTOBER 29TH   Lefthand, Galloping Track

Official Going   VERY SOFT

4556
1.35 GR 1 CRITERIUM DE SAINT-CLOUD 2YO   1m2f   Soft
£38425   £15370   £8780   £3842

--   **SAGACITY** A Fabre 2-9-0 O Peslier 24/10: -11: 2 br c Highest Honor - Saganeca (Sagace)   110
Prom, chall appr fnl 1f, led ins last, pshd out: recent debut scorer: half-brother to Arc wnr Sagamix: eff
at 10f, 12f will suit: acts on soft: shld be a force in the top mid-dists races in 2001.
+3867   **REDUIT 52** G A Butler 2-9-0 L Dettori 74/10: -4412: 2 ch c Lion Cavern - Soolaimon (Shareef Dancer)   1   108
Chsd ldrs, hdwy to lead over 1f out, hdd ins last, no extra for press: 7 wk abs: improved plenty
in defeat stepped up to 10f on soft grnd, acts on fast: useful & progressive colt who shld win Gr races next year.
4397   **SLIGO BAY 14** A P O'Brien 2-9-0 M J Kinane 21/10 JT FAV: -21323: 2 b c Sadler's Wells - Angelic   3   103
Song (Halo) Front rank, ev ch over 1f out, kept on onepcd fnl 1f: reportedly unsuited by steady pace: btr 4397.
--   **BLUE STELLER** F Head 2-9-0 D Bonilla 25/2: -24: Twrds rear, outpcd 4f out, rdn & styd on late,   1   101
no threat to ldrs: will apprec mid-dists next year on this showing: handles soft grnd.
2091   **LEOPARD SPOT 130** 2-9-0 (BL) J Murtagh 21/10 JT FAV: 352225: Mid-div at best: blnkd: stable-mate   shd   101
of 3rd, also reportedly unsuited by slow pace: rnr-up thrice (7f/1m mdns, gd/soft & hvy) since 2091.
*4322   **SAMARA MIDDLE EAST 19** 2-8-10 J Reid 63/10: 616: Set steady pace, hdd over 1f out, fdd.   ¾   96
4260   **WINTER SOLSTICE 28** 2-8-10 O Doleuze 36/10: -1207: Nvr a factor: rtd higher 4260, 3934.   snk   96
--   **CRIQUETOT** 2-8-10 C Asmussen 9/1: -118: Al last: dual wnr in minor company prev.   ½   95
8 ran   Time 2m 17.8   (J-L Lagardere)   A Fabre France

LEOPARDSTOWN
MONDAY OCTOBER 30TH   Lefthand, Galloping Track

Official Going   HEAVY

4557
2.00 GR 3 KILLAVULLAN STKS 2YO   7f   Heavy
£29250   £8550   £4050   £1350

--   **PERIGEE MOON [7]** A P O'Brien 2-8-10 M J Kinane 4/1: -11: 2 ch c Hennessy - Lovlier Linda (Vigors)   104
Chsd ldrs, gd hdwy to lead 1f out, pshd out, cosily: recent debut wnr at The Curragh (mdn, by 2½L): eff at
6/7f, 1m shld suit next term: acts on soft, hvy & a gall or stiff trk: useful & unbeaten, win more races as a 3yo.
--   **DR BRENDLER [4]** J C Hayden 2-8-10 W J O'Connor 16/1: -532: 2 b c Distant View - Lady Of Vision   1   100
(Vision) Twrds rear, rdn/imprvd 3f out, led over 1f out, sn hdd, styd on but not pace of wnr: clr rem: recently
plcd in a mdn at The Curragh: eff arnd 7f on gd/soft & hvy: much imprvd here in testing conds.
--   **LOVE ME TRUE [10]** A P O'Brien 2-8-7 J A Heffernan 25/1: -263: 2 ch f Kingmambo - Lassie's Lady   4½   90
(Alydar) Settled last, rdn 3f out, styd on strongly fnl 2f, nvr nrr: s-mate of wnr, relish a step up in trip.
--   **LETHAL AGENDA [11]** D K Weld 2-8-10 P J Smullen 2/1 FAV: -14: Chsd ldrs, eff over 3f out, drvn &   1½   91
no impress ins fnl 1f: better expected after recent mdn success at Cork (7f, soft, made all, won by 3½L).
12 ran   Time 1m 38.6   (Mrs John Magnier)   A P O'Brien Ballydoyle, Co Tipperary

LEOPARDSTOWN   MONDAY OCTOBER 30TH   Lefthand, Galloping Track

4558   3.30 LISTED TRIGO STKS 3YO+   1m2f   Heavy
£19500   £5700   £2700   3 yo rec 5 lb

3556 **JAMMAAL 71** [5] D K Weld 3-9-3 (bl) P J Smullen 9/4 FAV: 124321: 3 b c Robellino - Navajo Love Song   110
(Dancing Brave) Prom, led 3f out, clr appr fnl 1f, eased fnl 50y, val 6L+: 8 wk abs: rnr-up in a Galway List
race on most recent start: earlier won at Cork (stks) & The Curragh (List): juv wnr at Leopardstown (mdn, Gr 1 3rd,
rtd 104): eff at 1m, suited by 10f: acts on fast, loves soft & hvy grnd: v tough & useful.
947 **GOLOVIN 197** [11] M J Grassick 3-8-10 E Ahern 14/1: 1-432: 3 b c Bering - Guilinn (Last Tycoon)   4   94
Mid-div, imprvd over 2f out, styd on, no impress on wnr: recent 3rd at The Curragh (stks): eff at 1m/10f,
has tried 12f & that trip shld suit in time: acts on hvy grnd: see 947.
-- **TARWILA** [10] J Oxx 3-8-8(1ow) J Murtagh 5/1: 152013: 3 ch f In The Wings - Tarwiya (Dominion)   nk   92
Rear, rdn/late gains, no dngr: prev won at Cork (mdn), Curragh (stks) & Naas (h'cap): stays 9/12f on fast & hvy.
12 ran   Time 2m 23.2   (Hamdan Al Maktoum)   D K Weld Curragh, Co Kildare

---

MUSSELBURGH   WEDNESDAY NOVEMBER 1ST   Righthand, Sharp Track

Official Going   GOOD TO SOFT (SOFT In Places). Stalls: 5f & 2m - Stands Side; Rem - Inside.

4559   1.10 EBF MED AUCT MDN DIV 1 2YO (E)   7f30y rnd   Soft 114   -25 Slow
£2323   £715   £357   £178

4283 **ALBUHERA 26** [6] M Johnston 2-9-0 D Holland 7/2: 261: 2 b c Desert Style - Morning Welcome   87
(Be My Guest) Chsd ldrs, slightly outpcd halfway, styd on well to lead well in last, going away: cost IR 12,000gns:
brother to French/Irish 2,000 Guineas wnr Bachir: eff at 7f, 1m will suit next term: acts on gd, should win more races next term, esp over further.
3029 **ECCLESIASTICAL 93** [3] J R Fanshawe 2-9-0 T Quinn 1/1 FAV: 02: 2 b c Bishop Of Cashel - Rachael   nk   86
Tennessee (Matsadoon) Front rank, led appr fnl 1f, not pace to repel wnr cl home: clr rem, well bckd after long
abs: eff over a sharp 7f on soft, can win over 1m+ next term: see 3029.
4309 **VINCENTIA 23** [2] C Smith 2-8-9 M Fenton 13/2: 0443: 2 ch f Komaite - Vatersay (Far North)   3½   75
Prom, chall ldr halfway, sn led, hdd appr fnl 1f, not pace of front 2: op 7/2: shade btr 4309.
4517 **NANCYS BOY 6** [1] J Hetherton 2-9-0 R Winston 100/1: 004: Led, rdn/hdd appr fnl 2f, grad wknd: 2½   76
quick reapp & imprvd today for forcing tactics: see 4402.
4471 **COMPTON CHICK 11** [5] 2-8-9 (t) K Darley 5/1: 05: Mid-div, rdn over 3f out, lost tch appr fnl 2f: 8   59
nicely bckd & better expected up in trip: see 4471 (6f).
4517 **ROSE OF AMERICA 6** [8] 2-8-9 C Lowther 10/1: 5036: Dwelt/rear, eff halfway, wknd qckly appr fnl   9   47
2f: op 6/1, quick reapp: rtd higher over C/D in 4517.
4373 **ARCHIRONDEL 16** [4] 2-9-0 Dean McKeown 100/1: 007: Bhd, gd hdwy bef halfway, rdn/lost tch fnl 3f.   6   44
4303 **MEIKLE PRINCE 23** [7] 2-9-0 K Dalgleish (5) 100/1: 038: Al bhd: see 4303.   2½   41
8 ran   Time 1m 34.9 (10.0)   (D J & F A Jackson)   M Johnston Middleham, N Yorks

4560   1.35 LINKS PAVILION HCAP 3YO+ 0-70 (E)   1m4f   Soft 114   -01 Slow   [64]
£4238   £1304   £652   £326   3 yo rec 6 lb

4229 **CLARINCH CLAYMORE 30** [1] J M Jefferson 4-9-1 (51) P Hanagan (5) 7/1: 300421: 4 b g Sabrehill -   56
Salu (Ardross) Mid-div, imprvd to lead over 1f out, styd on strongly, drvn out: jockey reportedly given a 3 day
whip ban: '99 wnr at Beverley (amat h'cap, rtd 55 at best): prev term rtd 60 at best (auct mdn): eff at 1m/12f
on fast, soft & fibresand: acts on any trk: in gd heart in testing conditions, deserved this.
1238 **TWEED 174** [13] Jedd O'Keeffe 3-8-13 (55) G Duffield 33/1: 0-0042: 3 ch g Barathea - In Perpetuity   3½   55
(Great Nephew) Held up, gd hdwy 3f out, ev ch appr fnl 1f, not pace of wnr ins last: ddhtd for 2nd: op 20/1,
long abs: eff over 12f on soft: prev with R Charlton, promising run for new stable: shld win a sell h'cap.
4521 **OCEAN DRIVE 6** [7] Miss L A Perratt 4-8-8 (44) K Dalgleish (5) 20/1: 240052: 4 b g Dolphin Street -   dht   44
Blonde Goddess (Godswalk) Chsd ldrs, gd hdwy to lead appr fnl 1f, hdd over 1f out, kept on onepace fnl 1f:
ddhtd for 2nd: op 14/1, quick reapp: acts on fast & soft grnd: well h'capped: see 3379, 846.
4421 **LANCER 13** [6] J Pearce 8-9-3 (53)(vis) T Quinn 5/1 FAV: 261534: Towards rear, imprvd over 3f out,   ¾   52
ev ch appr fnl 1f, held ins last: clr rem: consistent recent form: see 4421, 4229.
3590 **COSMIC CASE 69** [9] 5-8-8 (44) D Holland 16/1: 211345: Hdwy from rear appr fnl 2f, styd on but nvr   4   38
dngrs: op 10/1: recent rnr-up over timber (h'cap hdle), rtd 83h, stays 2m on firm & gd/soft): see 3590, 2392.
4371 **KILCREGGAN 16** [2] 6-9-0 (50) A Culhane 12/1: 033006: Late gains, nvr dangerous: needs further.   3   40
4404 **SMARTER CHARTER 14** [12] 7-9-0 (50) Kristin Stubbs (7) 8/1: 064457: Mid-div, imprvd 3f out,   nk   40
lost tch fnl 2f: tchd 12/1: twice below 4229.
3951 **KESTRAL 49** [15] 4-9-6 (56) R Ffrench 8/1: 321238: Prom, drvn 3f out, sn fdd: 7 wk abs, up in   5   40
trip: unproven at 12f & on grnd softer than gd: see 3731 (10f), 3603.
4520 **A DAY ON THE DUB 6** [3] 7-8-9 (45) J Fanning 14/1: 005059: Handy, chall 3f out, sn wknd: qck reapp.   2½   25
4370 **EVENING SCENT 16** [5] 4-9-10 (60) Dean McKeown 14/1: 411560: Cl-up, drvn/lost tch fnl 3f: 10th,   ½   39
top weight: much btr 4280 (appr h'cap).
4501 **SPREE VISION 8** [14] 4-9-3 (53) K Darley 8/1: 500230: Nvr a threat, fin 11th: flattered 4501.   2½   29
*4497 **BLENHEIM TERRACE 8** [10] 7-8-9 (45)(6ex) M Fenton 10/1: 414/10: Rear, eff over 3f out, sn lost   3   16
tch, 12th: better expected after a fine come-back in 4497 (11f clmr).
4521 **SLANEYSIDE 6** [4] 3-9-1 (57)(BL) R Winston 33/1: 000600: Led to over 3f out, wknd qckly, 13th: blnkd.   8   18
4280 **FIVE OF WANDS 27** [16] 3-9-8 (64) J Fortune 11/2: -23020: Handy, wknd rapidly fnl 3f, 14th: btr 4280.   2½   22
4404 **Grand Slam Gb 14** [11] 5-9-5 (55) S W Kelly (3) 14/1: 4523 **Howards Lad 6** [8] 3-9-1 (57) R Lappin 33/1:
16 ran   Time 2m 44.4 (13.8)   (John Donald)   J M Jefferson Norton, N Yorks

4561 2.05 SELL NURSERY HCAP 2YO 0-65 (F) 5f str Soft 114 -26 Slow [70]
£2268 £648 £324

4336 **BOWFELL** 20 [7] C Smith 2-9-2 (58) M Fenton 12/1: 0601: 2 b f Afflora - April City (Lidhame) **62**
Cl-up, imprvd into lead just ins last, drvn out: no bid: mkt drifter, 1st win: failed to make the frame in 6/7f
mdns/sells prev: suited by this drop back to a sharp 5f: acts on gd grnd & enjoys sell grade.
4446 **GRAND HOUDINI** 12 [5] M W Easterby 2-8-13 (55) J Fortune 7/2: 0502: 2 b g Primo Dominie - Cole ½ **57**
Slaw (Absalom) Dwelt, sn chasing ldrs, switched/imprvd appr fnl 1f, just btn in a cl fin: tchd 5/1 & benefitted
for this big drop in grade: stays a sharp 5f on soft: see 4253.
4423 **GARRISON** 13 [4] Miss L A Perratt 2-8-11 (53) A Mackay 11/2: 04063: 2 b f College Chapel - Milain 1 **52**
(Unfuwain) Cl-up, rdn appr fnl 1f, kept on but not pace of ldrs fnl 1f: tchd 7/1: stays 5f on soft: see 3079.
4333 **BRANSTON GEM** 21 [9] M Johnston 2-9-7 (63) K Darley 6/1: 005024: Front rank, led 3f out, drvn, hung 1 **60**
left & hdd just ins last, fdd: top weight, jockey received a 2 day careless riding ban: handles soft & equitrack.
4359 **OLYS GILL** 18 [8] 2-7-10 (38)(1oh) K Dalgleish (5) 14/1: 000005: Led after 1f, hdd bef halfway, 2 **30**
fdd appr fnl 1f: mod prev form, see 3592.
4362 **SLIPPER ROSE** 18 [2] 2-8-3 (45) P M Quinn (3) 20/1: 000506: Mid-div at best: big drop in trip. shd **37**
-4423 **PATRICIAN FOX** 13 [3] 2-9-1 (57) D Holland 5/2 FAV: 326027: Handy, imprvd appr fnl 1f, ev ch when 1¼ **46**
badly hmpd & snatched up ins last, no ch after: nicely bckd tho' op 2/1: most unlucky, deserves comp: see 4423.
4470 **GOLFAGENT** 11 [10] 2-8-10 (52) A Culhane 9/1: -0008: Mid-div, eff over 2f out, sn btn: h'cap bow. 1 **38**
4359 **TUPGILL TIPPLE** 18 [1] 2-8-6 (48) R Winston 20/1: 340059: Sn outpcd: see 4359. 1¾ **30**
4246 **EMMA THOMAS** 29 [6] 2-8-2 (44) D Mernagh (3) 20/1: 000300: Led early, remained with ldrs, 5 **16**
lost tch halfway, fin 10th: see 4025, 2539.
10 ran Time 1m 04.5 (7.0) (Mr & Mrs T I Gourley) C Smith Temple Bruer, Lincs

4562 2.40 EBF MED AUCT MDN DIV 2 2YO (E) 7f30y rnd Soft 114 -17 Slow
£2307 £710 £355 £177

3999 **MAYVILLE THUNDER** 46 [7] G A Butler 2-9-0 K Darley 1/1 FAV: -31: 2 ch c Zilzal - Mountain Lodge **78**
(Blakeney) Settled rear, imprvd over 3f out, sn cl-up, kept on strongly to lead ins last, rdn out: well bckd tho'
op 4/6, 7 wk abs: 75,000gns Apr foal, half brother to sev wnrs, incl useful styr Compton Ace: dam smart styr:
eff at 7f, 1m + sure to suit: acts on firm, soft & a gall or sharp trk: rate more highly over 1m/10f next year.
4410 **SO TEMPTING** 14 [5] J R Fanshawe 2-9-0 T Quinn 9/1: 32: 2 b c So Factual - Persuasion (Batshoof) ¾ **76**
Cl-up, hdwy to lead 2f out, rdn/hdd dist, hung right & no extra fnl 50yds: op 11/2 & left debut run bhd:
eff at 7f on soft, 1m+ will suit next term: see 4410.
-- **SKY TO SEA** [3] M J Grassick 2-9-0 E Ahern 9/2: -43: 2 b c Adieu Au Roi - Urban Sky (Groom Dancer) shd **76**
Mid-div, prog appr fnl 2f, ev ch till no extra well ins last: clr rem, op 7/2: 6 month abs: Irish raider, 4th
on sole prev start back in May (5f mdn, gd/soft): full brother to 9f wnr: dam scored over 10f in France: eff
at 7f on soft: fine run after a long abs, shld win races next term.
4450 **BALL GAMES** 12 [1] D Moffatt 2-9-0 J Fanning 50/1: 460404: Towards rear, imprvd 3f out, ev ch 3½ **70$**
until hung left & wknd over 1f out: treat rating with caution (offic only 61): see 4323.
4471 **GILDA** 11 [6] 2-9-0 A Culhane 8/1: 05: Led, drvn/hdd appr fnl 2f, wknd: op 6/1: up in trip: see 4471. 2½ **62**
4349 **RAPT** 19 [4] 2-9-0 J Fortune 8/1: 06: Cl-up, chall ldr 3f out, fdd fnl 2f: op 12/1: IR 47,000gns colt, nk **66**
half brother to numerous wnrs, incl a smart 1m wnr (styd 10f): with W Jarvis, do better over further next year.
4517 **SHATIN PLAYBOY** 6 [5] 2-9-0 R Winston 14/1: 402057: Nvr dangerous: quick reapp: flattered 4517. nk **66**
4253 **STORMY CREST** 29 [8] 2-9-0 M Fenton 40/1: 08: Handy, wknd rapidly halfway: big step up in trip. 14 **46**
8 ran Time 1m 34.7 (9.8) (Jan H Stenbeck) G A Butler Blewbury, Oxon

4563 3.10 TOTE BOOKMAKERS HCAP 3YO+ 0-90 (C) 2m Soft 114 +02 Fast [90]
£13910 £4280 £2140 £1070 3 yo rec 9 lb

*4508 **YOURE SPECIAL** 5 [5] P C Haslam 3-7-11 (68)(6ex) G Baker (5) 11/4 FAV: 060111: 3 b g Northern **79**
Flagship - Pillow Mind (Stagedoor Johnny) Front rank, smooth hdwy to go on appr fnl 3f, pushed clr fnl 2f, rdly:
nicely bckd, gd time: hat-trick landed, earlier won at Newcastle & Nottingham (h'caps): earlier scored at
W'hampton (AW mdn, rtd 82a): much imprvd since tried over 2m, even further shld suit: acts on gd hvy & f/sand:
handles a sharp or gall trk: v prog stayer, can extend wng run on the sand this winter.
4458 **MANE FRAME** 12 [10] H Morrison 3-8-8 (70) J Fortune 9/2: 106622: 5 b g Unfuwain - Moviegoer (Pharly) 8 **72**
Towards rear, imprvd from halfway, chsd wnr in vain fnl 2f but no impress: ran to best against a prog rival.
3993 **BHUTAN** 47 [3] Mrs M Reveley 5-8-8 (70) A Culhane 10/1: 012423: 5 b g Polish Patriot - Bustinetta 2½ **70**
(Bustino) Settled rear, hdwy appr fnl 5f, ev ch fnl 3f, styd on: not pace of wnr appr fnl 2f: op 7/1: recent hdles wnr
at Kelso (h'cap, rtd 126h, 2m, firm & soft, any trk): consistent form: see 3993.
4464 **MONTECRISTO** 11 [1] R Guest 7-9-6 (82) D Holland 14/1: 545304: Rear, gd hdwy over 3f out, styd on 1½ **80**
but nvr nrr: only 2nd try at 2m & prob stays: see 1030 (12f).
4353 **PRAIRIE FALCON** 18 [2] 6-9-7 (83) K Darley 4/1: 400165: Handy, drvn/no extra appr fnl 2f: btr 4071. ½ **80**
4353 **WAVE OF OPTIMISM** 18 [9] 5-10-0 (90) T Quinn 9/1: 100026: Towards rear, imprvd over 4f out, ev ch 3 **84**
till wknd appr fnl 2f: rtd higher when a fine rnr-up in the Cesarewitch in 4353 (2m2f, gd grnd).
4424 **EXALTED** 13 [7] 7-7-13 (61) Dale Gibson 33/1: -15657: Bhd, imprvd after 1m, wknd fnl 3f: see 4424. 5 **51**
3961 **VANISHING DANCER** 48 [4] 3-7-11 (68) P Hanagan (2) 33/1: 331208: Mid-div, eff over 5f out, drvn 4 **54**
& lost tch appr fnl 3f: 7 wk abs & unproven beyond 14f: twice well below 3637 (14f fast grnd), 2651.
4521 **NORTHERN MOTTO** 6 [6] 7-7-10 (58)(vis)(18oh) K Dalgleish (5) 50/1: 360029: Led, drvn/hdd appr shd **44**
fnl 3f, wknd qckly: stiff task from 18lbs o/h: quick reapp: btr 4521 (13f).
4353 **FLETCHER** 18 [8] 6-8-3 (65) J Fanning 12/1: 102000: Handy, rdn & wknd rapidly fnl 5f, fin 10th. 12 **41**
10 ran Time 3m 40.4 (17.9) (Les Buckley) P C Haslam Middleham, N Yorks

4564 3.45 EBF PACEPADDOCKS MDN 2YO (D) 1m rnd Soft 114 -24 Slow
£3526 £1085 £542 £271

4383 **CELTIC MISSION** 15 [5] M Johnston 2-9-0 D Holland 11/10 FAV: 0531: 2 ch g Cozzene - Norfolk **82**
Lavender (Ascot Knight) Mid-div going well, gd hdwy to lead 2f out, pushed clr, cmftbly: val for 8L+, hvly bckd:
cost 20,000gns, dam & sire milers: eff at 7f, apprec this step up to 1m, 10f+ will suit next term: acts on
soft, poss handles fibresand: plenty in hand here, imprv further over mid-dists next year.
4418 **SUNGIO** 13 [3] L M Cumani 2-9-0 S W Kelly (3) 5/1: 0662: 2 b c Halling - Time Or Never (Dowsing) 6 **72**

MUSSELBURGH

WEDNESDAY NOVEMBER 1ST **Righthand, Sharp Track**

Cl-up, chall over 3f out, not pace of cmftble wnr appr fnl 1f: op 3/1: prob stays a sharp 1m on soft: see 4268.

-- **DR KNOCK** [1] M J Grassick 2-9-0 E Ahern 5/2: -0403: 2 b g Dr Devious - Fuchsia Belle (Vision) 3½ 67
Twrds rear, imprvg when short of room over 2f out, switched over 1f out, sn no extra: Irish raider, 4th at best
from 3 mdn starts prev (7.5f, soft grnd): half brother to a couple of mid-dists wnrs, dam scored over 1m/10f.

4446 **RIDGE AND FURROW** 12 [4] T P Tate 2-9-0 A Culhane 50/1: 04: Prom, hung left for press appr fnl 2½ 63
2f, fdd: jockey received a 2 day careless riding ban: IR 6,500gns gldg, sire smart at 7f/1m: with T P Tate.

2639 **KILBARCHAN** 110 [2] 2-8-9 G Duffield 10/1: 355: Handy, losing tch when hmpd appr fnl 2f: long abs, 6 49
up in trip: 1st try on soft: rtd higher on debut in 2234 (6f).

-- **HOWARDS DREAM** [6] 2-9-0 R Winston 2/1: 6: Dwelt, rear, gd hdwy when sltly hmpd halfway, ½ 53
drvn/lost tch appr fnl 2f: 29,000gns Kings Theatre filly: dam won over 5f, sire top-class at 12f: with I Semple.

3706 **NETTLES** 65 [7] 2-9-0 K Dalgleish (5) 33/1: 006207: Led, drvn/hdd over 2f out, wknd qckly: 9 wk abs. 2½ 49
7 ran   Time 1m 48.6 (11.1)   (C H Racing Partnership)   M Johnston Middleham, N Yorks

---

4565   4.15 THEHORSESMOUTH HCAP 3YO+ 0-70 (E)   1m rnd   Soft 114   +08 Fast   [70]
£3052   £872   £436   3 yo rec 2 lb

4414 **MY RETREAT** 14 [3] B W Hills 3-9-12 (70) A Culhane 5/1 FAV: 050521: 3 b c Hermitage - My Jessica 76
Ann (Native Rythm) Prom, prog to lead 2f out, drvn clr ins last, eased nr fin: best time of day: earlier won at
Warwick (mdn): in '99 rnr-up at Brighton (mdn auct, soft grnd) with L Cumani): eff at 7f/1m: acts on firm, loves
gd/soft & hvy grnd: acts on a sharp or turning trk & runs well fresh: mud lover, in fine form.

4506 **THIHN** 8 [12] J L Spearing 5-9-8 (64) K Darley 9/1: 122052: 5 ch g Machiavellian - Hasana (Private 2½ 66
Account) Towards rear, imprvd appr fnl 3f, styd on fnl 2f but no ch with wnr: ran to best: see 4291, 4044.

4452 **YENALED** 12 [4] J S Goldie 3-9-6 (64) T Quinn 6/1: 225103: 3 gr g Rambo Dancer - Fancy Flight 1¾ 63
(Arctic Tern) Hdwy from rear over 3f out, rdn appr fnl 1f, sn no extra: likes Musselburgh, acts on firm & soft.

4414 **ROYAL CAVALIER** 14 [2] R Hollinshead 3-9-6 (64) D Holland 10/1: 064054: Towards rear, effort hd 63
when short of room over 2f out, switched/styd on late, nvr dangerous: see 4414, 2250.

*4523 **AMBUSHED** 6 [5] 4-9-5 (61)(6ex) R Winston 8/1: 106315: Led till over 2f out, sn rdn, fdd: quick 56
reapp, op 6/1: prob ran to form of 9f success here in 4520.

4513 **JEFFREY ANOTHERRED** 7 [13] 6-9-9 (65) F Lynch 10/1: 420446: Handy, drvn/onepcd fnl 2f: qck reapp. ½ 59
4310 **VENTO DEL ORENO** 23 [6] 3-9-4 (62) S W Kelly (3) 9/1: 004257: Waited wth, imprvd after halfway, 1½ 53
styd on but no threat to ldrs: twice below 4173 (class stks).

*4523 **ACE OF TRUMPS** 6 [1] 4-9-7 (49)(t)(6ex) N Kennedy 12/1: 523218: In tch, eff 4f out, lost tch ½ 39
fnl 2f: quick reapp: rtd higher 4523 (9f).

4405 **DAY BOY** 14 [11] 4-9-10 (66) K Dalgleish (5) 12/1: 044409: Sn struggling, nvr dangerous: up in trip. ¾ 55
4310 **YOUNG ROSEIN** 23 [8] 4-9-2 (58) G Duffield 12/1: 113030: Mid-div, rdn/lost tch fnl 3f, 10th: btr 4310. 3½ 41
4513 **PROSPECTORS COVE** 7 [7] 7-10-0 (70) J Fortune 7/1: 236000: Dwelt, al bhd, 13th: top weight, qck reapp. 0
4452 **Noble Pasao** 12 [9] 3-9-10 (68) R Thomas (7) 20/1:   4522 **Mammas Boy** 6 [14] 5-8-10 (52) C Lowther 14/1:
4518 **Ryefield** 6 [10] 5-9-10 (66) Dean McKeown 16/1:
14 ran   Time 1m 46.0 (8.5)   (Ms A Soltesova)   B W Hills Lambourn, Berks

---

DONCASTER

FRIDAY NOVEMBER 3RD **Lefthand, Flat, Galloping Track**

Official Going   HEAVY (SOFT places). Stalls: Str Crse - Stands Side; Rdn Crse - Inside; Rnd 1m - Outside.

4566   12.30 EBF CISWO MDN DIV 1 2YO (D)   7f str   Heavy 145   -08 Slow
£3331   £1025   £512   £256   Field raced up centre of course

-- **JUNGLE LION** [16] H R A Cecil 2-9-0 (t) T Quinn 7/1: -1: 2 ch c Lion Cavern - Star Ridge (Storm 99+
Bird) Made virtually all, styd on strongly despite drifting to far rail fnl 1f, pushed out, decisively: fair juv time,
wore a t-strap on debut, op 5/1: Feb foal, related to numerous wnrs, inc smart miler On The Ridge: sire a smart
6/7f performer: eff over a stiff 7f, 1m+ will suit next term: acts on hvy grnd & on a gall trk, runs well fresh:
wears a t-strap: most favourable racecourse box, should rate more highly & win more races next term.

-- **LURINA** [5] J H M Gosden 2-8-9 R Havlin 14/1: -2: 2 b f Lure - Alligatrix (Alleged) 3½ 86+
Trkd ldrs, chsd wnr fnl 1f, kept on well but not pace of wnr: 3L clr 3rd, debut: Feb foal, half-sister to sev wnrs,
incl smart mid-dist wnr Croco Rouge: dam a smart 7f winning juv, sire a top-class miler in the USA: eff at 7f on
hvy grnd, 1m+ will suit next term: beat all but impressive wnr today & looks nailed on to go one better.

4447 **EASTERN BREEZE** 14 [1] P W Harris 2-9-0 A Culhane 20/1: -303: 2 b c Sri Pekan - Elegant Bloom 3 85+
(Be My Guest) Rear, swiched & hdwy 2f out, fin well but too late: eye-catching, one to keep a close eye on in
h'caps over 1m+ next term: acts on soft & hvy grnd, untried on faster: also eye-catching on debut in 4188.

4483 **WANNABE AROUND** 11 [15] T G Mills 2-9-0 K Darley 11/8 FAV: -6324: Trkd ldrs, onepcd fnl 1f: hvly nk 84
bckd from 2/1: handles firm & hvy grnd: rtd higher 4483.

4445 **HIGH SPOT** 14 [2] 2-8-9 C Rutter 16/1: -05: Chsd ldrs, eff 2f out, no impress fnl 1f: flashed tail: nk 78
bred for mid-dists next term & shld improve once qual for h'caps: see 4445 (1m here, debut).

4483 **HARLEQUIN** 11 [12] 2-9-0 L Newman (3) 16/1: -066: Chsd ldrs, kept on under press, not pace to ½ 82
chall: runs as tho' 1m+ will suit next term, now quals for h'caps: see 4184 (debut).

4514 **WINNING PLEASURE** 9 [13] 2-9-0 N Callan 66/1: -007: Chsd ldrs till left bhd fnl 2f: IR 20,000gns 3 77
Feb foal: half-brother to numerous wnrs, incl sprint h'capper Proud Native: sire a high-class miler: with
A Jarvis & shld be capable of better.

4475 **ROSIE** 12 [8] 2-8-9 Paul Eddery 16/1: -558: Nvr better than mid-div: h'cap qual run, 3½ 66
bred for mid-dists next term & will be seen to much better effect over further in h'caps: see 4475.

4504 **UNDENIABLE** 10 [4] 2-9-0 G Carter 20/1: -09: Rdn in mid-div: shld benefit from faster grnd. 5 63
4446 **RAHEIBB** 14 [14] 2-9-0 A McGlone 33/1: -00: Slowly away, nvr a factor in 10th: see 4446 (C/D). hd 63
4297 **FIND THE KING** 27 [17] 2-9-0 J Weaver 33/1: -40: Prom 5f, wknd into 11th: shld do better on faster 2 59
grnd & over further: see 4297 (1m, debut).

4163 **SKI WELLS** 37 [11] 2-9-0 M Tebbutt 25/1: -00: Slowly away, nvr a factor: fin 12th: lost all chance shd 59
at the start & prob not suited by these v testing conditions: mid-dist bred, see 4163.

-- **HONEST OBSESSION** [9] 2-9-0 J Reid 10/1: -0: Slowly away, al bhd, fin 15th on debut: Feb foal, 0
bred in the purple: dam a smart mid-dist performer, sire a top-class performer over mid-dists: bred to apprec
mid-dists next term: with B Hills & can leave this bhd on better grnd.

-- **MOSTABSHIR** [7] 2-9-0 J Fortune 7/1: -0: Mid-div till outpcd fnl 2f: fin 16th, debut: Mar foal, dam a 0
6f wnr: sire a top-class mid-dist performer: J Gosden colt, shld apprec better grnd.

-- **HYDERABAD** [18] 2-9-0 M Hills 8/1: -0: Slowly away, al bhd & fin 17th on debut: May foal, half brother to smart mid-dist performers Prolix & Bad Bertrich Again: dam won over 6f as a 2yo: with B Hills.   0
4484 **Moreover 11** [6] 2-8-9 G Duffield 20/1:   -- **Olivers Trail** [3] 2-9-0 Dean McKeown 66/1:
4446 **Red River Rebel 14** [10] 2-9-0 O Pears 50/1:
18 ran   Time 1m 33.97 (10.77)   (Buckram Oak Holdings)   H R A Cecil Newmarket.

4567   1.00 EBF CISWO MDN DIV 2 2YO (D)   7f str   Heavy 145   -21 Slow
£3331   £1025   £512   £256   Field raced up centre of course

3999 **CHANCELLOR 48** [13] B W Hills 2-9-0 M Hills 11/4 FAV: -01: 2 b f Halling - Isticanna (Far North)   91 +
Dwelt, recovered to chase ldrs, imprvd to lead ent fnl 1f, pulled away ins last, rdn out: hvly bckd from 4/1, 7 wk abs: improved for eye-catching debut: 190,000gns half-brother to sev wnrs both here & abroad: dam a sprint winning 2yo, sire a top-class mid-dist performer: eff over a stiff 7f on hvy grnd, will stay 1m+: runs well fresh & handles a gall trk: improving, exciting prospect for next term.

4470 **AFGHAN 13** [12] J H M Gosden 2-9-0 (t) R Havlin 20/1: -002: 2 ch c Hennessy - Affirm The Gold   2½   85+
(Golden Act) Rcd keenly in bhd ldrs, went after wnr 1f out, styd on well but al held: 4L clr 3rd: much imprvd effort, eff over a stiff 7f on hvy grnd, 1m sure to suit: wears a t-strap: must win a mdn judged on this.

-- **A BIT SPECIAL** [1] H R A Cecil 2-8-9 T Quinn 7/2: -3: 2 b f Rahy - Speedybird (Danehill)   4   73
Set pace till ent fnl 1f, no extra: well bckd tho' drifted from 2/1 on debut: Feb foal, dam a 7f wnr: sire smart over 1m in the USA: eff at 7f, 1m will suit: handles hvy grnd, tho' will prob improve on a faster surface: encouraging debut & shld win in mdn grade.

4530 **STREET LIFE 7** [7] W J Musson 2-9-0 P McCabe 20/1: -004: Rcd keenly in bhd ldrs, onepace fnl   3½   72
1½f: Mar foal, cost 17,500gns: sire a high-class 6/7f performer: eff over a stiff 7f on hvy grnd, may benefit from 1m: now quals for h'caps & clearly has ability.

-- **SECURITY COUNCIL** [17] 2-9-0 R Hughes 13/2: -5: Chsd ldrs, no impress fnl 1½f, drifted left: op   1¾   70+
4/1, debut, longer priced stablemate of wnr: Feb foal, half-brother to a couple of wnrs, incl useful 7f performer Valentine Song: dam a 10f wnr in France, sire a top-class miler: sure to benefit from this & improve.

-- **CLOCHE CALL** [2] 2-8-9 M Tebbutt 20/1: -6: Front rank, ev ch 1½f out, fdd ins last on debut: Feb   ½   64
foal, cost 6,000gns: half-sister to sev wnrs, incl smart stayer Merit: dam from a gd mid-dist family, sire a top-class sprinter: with W Jarvis & ran well for a long way here: will relish 10f+ next term.

4447 **SHE WADI WADI 14** [16] 2-8-9 R Mullen 50/1: -07: Slowly away, recovered to chase ldrs, lost pl   ¾   62
halfway, rallied late but ch had gone: May foal, sister to 5f juv wnr Alfailak: dam a 7f wnr, sire a top-class miler: with A Stewart & showed some promise here, shld learn plenty from this.

4035 **SHADED MEMOIR 46** [8] 2-8-9 J Fortune 16/1: -608: Front rank 4½f, fdd: 7 wk abs, s/mate of 2nd.   hd   62
-- **INCHDURA** [8] 2-9-0 S Drowne 14/1: -9: Chsd ldrs till outpcd halfway, no ch after on debut: Feb   ¾   65
foal, cost 40,000gns: related to 5f juv wnr Cote Soleil: dam a 7f scorer, sire high-class over 7f: R Charlton colt.

4235 **WEET A WHILE 32** [15] 2-9-0 N Callan 66/1: 005000: Chsd ldrs till lost pl 2f out, rallied cl-home: nk   64$
fin 10th: highly tried, btn off 62 in a nurs h'cap in 4235.

4484 **REMARKABLE 11** [14] 2-8-9 J Quinn 14/1: -60: Slowly away, modest late hdwy, nvr dngrs in 11th: ½   58
some promise & shld do much better on faster grnd: see 4484.

-- **SHAANDAR** [18] 2-9-0 G Carter 16/1: -0: Al bhd stands side, some late hdwy: fin 12th on debut: ¾   62+
Mar foal, cost 100,000gns: half-brother to sev wnrs, notably smart stayer Rain Rider: dam won over 10f, hails from a v smart family: sire a smart mid-dist performer: bred in the purple & will relish mid-dists next term: with J Dunlop & looks sure to leave this bhd.

4477 **LAROUSSE 12** [4] 2-8-9 K Darley 20/1: -60: Chsd ldrs till wknd over 2f out: fin 13th: see 4477.   8   42
-- **SENATORS ALIBI** [5] 2-9-0 G Duffield 14/1: -0: Speed to halfway, sn bhd: fin 14th, debut, op 10/1:   ½   46
Mar foal, cost 115,000gns: dam unrcd but related to a decent mid-dist performer: sire top-class over mid-dists: with Sir M Prescott & likely to be a different proposition over mid-dists next term: v green today.

4483 **Variegation 11** [3] 2-9-0 Paul Eddery 50/1:   4447 **Miss Devious 14** [10] 2-8-9 S Sanders 66/1:
4297 **Canovas Kingdom 27** [11] 2-9-0 Dale Gibson 100/1:   4470 **Brand New Day 13** [9] 2-9-0 J Weaver 66/1:
18 ran   Time 1m 34.84 (11.64)   (W J Gredley)   B W Hills Lambourn, Berks.

4568   1.30 AUKER RHODES COND STKS 3YO+ (C)   1m6f132y   Heavy 145   -09 Slow
£6922   £2130   £1065   £532   3yo rec 8lb

4351 **JARDINES LOOKOUT 20** [10] A P Jarvis 3-8-9 N Callan 11/8 FAV: 21D151: 3 b g Fourstars Allstar -   107
Foolish Flight (Fool's Holme) In tch, imprvd 3f out, sn ent fnl 1f, drvn out: hvly bckd: earlier won at Salisbury (mdn) & Newmarket (rtd h'cap) & also controversially disq at York (val h'cap): eff arnd 14.6f, further will suit: acts on fast & hvy, any trk, loves a gall one: v progressive, shld win List/Group staying races in 2001.

4329 **DESTINATION 23** [2] C A Cyzer 3-8-6 G Carter 33/1: 445322: 3 ch g Deploy - Veuve (Tirol)   ¾   102$
Cl-up, chall 3f out, led brief dist, rdn/no extra well ins last: excellent run at the weights (offic only 74), but treat rating with caution: clearly enjoys hvy & shld win a mdn: see 4329 (mdn h'cap), 4193 (mdn).

4162 **DOLLAR BIRD 38** [9] J L Dunlop 3-8-1 R Ffrench 11/2: 200203: 3 b f Kris - High Spirited (Shirley   1¾   95
Heights) Prom, chall 5f out, led over 3f out till dist, sn onepcd: handles firm & hvy grnd, ran to best here.

3565 **YORKSHIRE 72** [1] P F I Cole 6-9-0 J Fortune 5/1: 5/5304: In tch, imprvd 3f out, ev ch till not   1¼   99
qckn fnl 1f: 10 wk abs, op 7/2, 7L clr rem: prob best at 2m+ & a sounder surface: see 3171.

4397} **SPUNKIE 384** [4] 7-9-0 J Reid 12/1: 0210-5: Led till over 3f out, fdd: belated reapp: in '99 won at   7   90
Newbury (h'cap, rtd 90): prev term scored at Salisbury (mdn, debut) & Ascot (h'cap), subs 3rd in the Cesarewitch (h'cap, rtd 87): 96/97 Fontwell bmpr wnr: eff at 14f/2m, stays 2m2f well: acts on fast & hvy grnd, handles any trk, likes a stiff/gall one: best to force the pace & can go well fresh: spot on for a hdles campaign.

1216 **JOLLY SHARP 178** [8] 3-8-9 T Quinn 11/4: 4-166: Chsd ldrs, drvn & wknd appr fnl 2f: 6 month abs,   12   78
well bckd: prob not stay this extended 14f trip: unproven on hvy: see 1216, 1017.

4508 **BLACK ICE BOY 10** [3] 9-9-0 Dean McKeown 100/1: 002307: Trkd ldr, rdn 5f out & sn lost tch, t.o.   10   60$
3838 **LUCKY UNO 59** [5] 4-9-0 M Fenton 200/1: -00608: Slow to start, al bhd, t.o.: 8 wk abs, up in trip.   22   30
4535 **THE CASTIGATOR 7** [7] 3-8-6 G Pears 200/1: 050009: Al bhd: qck reapp: imposs task.   8   18
4275 **MARTIAL EAGLE 29** [6] 4-9-0 Kim Tinkler 100/1: 0/1-00: Held up, rdn halfway, sn lost tch, t.o. in   1½   17
last: ex-Irish, '99 Cork wnr on sole start (14f mdn, 4 rnrs, fast grnd): now with N Tinkler.
10 ran   Time 3m 25.56 (22.56)   (Ambrose Turnbull)   A P Jarvis Aston Upthorpe, Oxon.

DONCASTER   FRIDAY NOVEMBER 3RD   Lefthand, Flat, Galloping Track

4569   **2.00 BWD RENSBURG MED AUCT MDN 2YO (E)   1m str   Heavy 145   -23 Slow**
£3997   £1230   £615   £307   Field raced up centre of course

4484 **GOLDEN SPARROW 11** [7] J L Dunlop 2-8-9 T Quinn 7/1: -21: 2 ch f Elmaamul - Moon Spin (Night Shift) **87+**
Nvr far away, forged ahd cl-home, rdn out: nicely bckd: Feb foal, half-sister to useful stayer Rosa Canina & 1m wnr The Thruster: dam scored over 1m/12f, sire a top-class mid-dist performer: apprec this step up to 1m, mid-dists will suit next term: clrly revels in testing conditions, handles a gall trk: progressive filly.

3420 **POLE STAR 78** [1] J R Fanshawe 2-9-0 J Fanning 7/2: -32: 2 br c Polar Falcon - Ellie Ardensky (Slip Anchor) Nvr far away, went on 3f out till worn down cl-home: well bckd, 11 wk abs, pulled 8L clr 3rd: eff over a stiff 1m, 10f+ will suit next term: acts on fast, relishes hvy grnd: looks nailed on for similar, see 3420. *nk* **91**

-- **STAPLOY** [23] B W Hills 2-8-9 M Hills 9/2: -3: 2 b f Deploy - Balliasta (Lyphard) *8* **72+**
Waited with, imprvd 2f out, kept on fnl 1f but no ch with front 2: debut, op 5/2: Mar foal, half-sister to 7f winning 2yo Kilting: sire a high-class mid-dist performer, dam lightly rcd & related to a top-class mid-dist wnr: likely to benefit from mid-dists next term: sure to learn from this & improve.

-- **GUMPTION** [12] J L Dunlop 2-9-0 S Sanders 33/1: -4: Dwelt, imprvd halfway, kept on fnl 1f but nvr dngrs: debut, longer priced stablemate of wnr: 20,000gns Apr foal: half-brother to 1m wnr Hazy Heights: dam scored over 6f, sire a top-class mid-dist performer: ran as tho' mid-dists will suit next term: sure to improve. *3½* **72**

4429 **POST BOX 15** [13] 2-9-0 R Hughes 5/2 FAV: -25: Trkd ldrs racing keenly, left bhd 3f out, no ch after: hvly bckd: much better clrly expected: poss not handles these v testing conditions?: btr 4429. *hd* **72**

4484 **CELTIC MISS 11** [9] 2-8-9 G Carter 16/1: -036: Front rank 6½f, fdd: longer priced stablemate of wnr: much closer to today's wnr in 4484. *1* **65**

3972 **TOMMY LORNE 49** [3] 2-9-0 G Duffield 20/1: -637: Rear, imprvd to chase ldrs halfway, btn 2f out: 7 wk abs: longer priced stablemate of wnr & 4th: rtd higher 3972. *1* **68**

4402 **MASTER FELLOW 16** [4] 2-9-0 Dean McKeown 33/1: -648: Chsd ldrs 6½f, fdd: btr 4402. *1¼* **66**

-- **ANOTHER DIAMOND** [22] 2-8-9 R Winston 40/1: -9: Rear, late hdwy despite drifting left, nvr dngrs on debut: Apr foal, half-sister to a couple of sprint wnrs: dam a 5f winning 2yo, sire a top-class juv performer. *1¼* **59**

-- **LITZINSKY** [5] 2-9-0 A Culhane 66/1: -0: Unruly before race, slowly away, imprvd halfway, btn 2f out: 10th, debut: Mar foal, half-brother to mid-dist wnr Blenheim Terrace: dam a 1m winning 2yo, sire a top-class mid-dist performer: with C Booth. *nk* **63**

4446 **LAFAYETTE 14** [18] 2-9-0 R Mullen 66/1: -00: Nvr better than mid-div, fin 11th: Feb foal, cost IR 40,000gns: sire a decent juv performer: with A Stewart. *1* **61**

-- **BISQUE** [20] 2-8-9 S Drowne 25/1: -0: Well bhd, some late hdwy but nvr dngrs in 12th: debut: Feb foal, dam related to a couple of 2yo wnrs: sire a high-class 7f performer: with R Charlton. *½* **55**

4116 **MARSHAL BOND 40** [11] 2-9-0 Paul Eddery 33/1: -6200: Chsd ldrs till left bhd halfway: fin 13th, 6 wk abs: btr 3952 (gd grnd). *hd* **60**

3912 **BROUGHTONS FLUSH 53** [17] 2-9-0 P McCabe 66/1: -00: Rear, imprvd 2f out, sn btn: fin 14th, abs. *½* **59**

4415 **EMPORIO 15** [2] 2-9-0 G Sparkes (7) 14/1: -040: Led till 3f out, fdd into 15th: btr 4415. *nk* **58**

4445 **Eastern Jewel 14** [14] 2-8-9 T Ashley 50/1:
4430 **Flamme De La Vie 15** [8] 2-9-0 J Quinn 14/1:
4496 **Diamond Zoe 10** [15] 2-8-9 R Fitzpatrick 100/1:
-- **Perfectly Honest** [21] 2-8-9 M Tebbutt 33/1:
4514 **Trotters Future 9** [19] 2-9-0 A McGlone 50/1:
-- **Fortune Found** [24] 2-8-9 (t) J Reid 100/1:
-- **Noble Arc** [10] 2-9-0 D Mernagh (3) 100/1:

22 ran   Time 1m 49.94 (13.44)   (J Dunlop)   J L Dunlop Arundel, W.Sussex.

4570   **2.30 CPL PRODUCTS HCAP 3YO+ 0-80 (D)   5f str   Heavy 145   +24 Fast   [80]**
£4485   £1380   £690   £345   Field raced accross the course

4516 **GET STUCK IN 8** [22] Miss L A Perratt 4-9-7 (73) K Dalgleish (5) 12/1: 230031: 4 b g Up And At 'Em - Shoka (Kaldoun) Trkd ldrs, drvn ahd over 1f out, edged right & pulled clr ins last: best time of day: deserved this, plcd numerous times this term: '99 wnr at Hamilton (class stks), Ripon & York (h'caps, rtd 87): rnr-up 7 times in '98 (rtd 94$ at best): eff at 5/6f: acts on fast, loves soft & hvy grnd: handles any trk: tried blnks, best without: likes to race with/force the pace: gd weight carrier: tough & genuine performer. **83**

4527 **REGAL SONG 8** [13] T J Etherington 4-9-1 (67)(bl) J Fanning 20/1: 030102: 4 b g Anita's Prince - Song Beam (Song) Prom, ch over 1f out, not pace of wnr ins last: blnks reapplied & back to form after 4527. *3* **70**

4432 **BOND BOY 15** [1] B Smart 3-9-4 (70) M Tebbutt 14/1: 510003: 3 b c Piccolo - Arabellajill (Aragon) In tch, drvn & styd on fnl 2f, no threat to wnr: acts on fast & hvy grnd: see 2519 (mdn). *1¼* **70**

4432 **POLLY GOLIGHTLY 15** [16] M Blanshard 7-9-4 (70)(bl) Dale Gibson 20/1: 011004: Al prom, kept on onepace for press fnl 2f: tough: see 4107. *¾* **68**

4411 **CLASSY CLEO 16** [18] 5-9-6 (72) J Bramhill 25/1: 030405: Rear, styd on fnl 2f, nvr dngrs: see 64. *1¼* **67**

+4270 **TOLDYA 30** [21] 3-9-2 (68) N Callan 7/1: 132416: Rdn/chsd ldrs halfway, kept on fnl 1f, nvr pace to chall: eff at 5f, prob better over 6f: see 4270 (6f). *nk* **62**

4285 **PTARMIGAN RIDGE 28** [9] 4-9-12 (78) C Lowther 33/1: -10007: Nvr pace to chall: s/mate of wnr. *1½* **69**

4287 **SHARP HAT 28** [8] 6-9-7 (73) A Culhane 16/1: 230308: Prom till over 1f out: see 2721. *½* **63**

4377 **TORRENT 18** [2] 5-9-4 (70)(bl) Lynsey Hanna (7) 20/1: 103009: Trkd ldrs halfway, btn over 1f out. *1½* **57**

*4405 **COLLEGE MAID 16** [5] 3-9-4 (70) A McGlone 12/1: 002010: Chsd ldrs 4f: 10th, op 8/1: btr 4405 (6f). *¾* **55**

4527 **QUEEN OF THE MAY 8** [12] 3-9-3 (69) T A O'Sullivan (5) 8/1: 605000: Mid-div, nvr able to chall: fin 11th, gamble from 20/1: not handle hvy? btr 4270, 1098. *½* **53**

4285 **NIFTY MAJOR 28** [3] 3-9-6 (72) J Weaver 25/1: 05R300: Led 3f, sn btn: 12th: btr 3960, 1219. *¾* **54**

3569 **ELVINGTON BOY 72** [20] 3-9-11 (77) T Lucas 25/1: 252200: Prom 3f: 13th: 10 wk abs: btr 3569, 3161. *1¼* **56**

4405 **SHAROURA 16** [6] 4-9-3 (69) A Nicholls 14/1: 000300: Cl-up 3f: 14th, op 8/1: btr 4287 (6f, soft). *1* **45**

4285 **BODFARI KOMAITE 28** [19] 4-9-6 (72) R Winston 16/1: 340000: Al outpcd: 15th: btr 1662. *¾* **46**

-4432 **ULYSSES DAUGHTER 15** [15] 3-9-10 (76) K Darley 3/1 FAV: 215420: Dwelt, chsd ldrs halfway, rdn/btn over 1f out: 18th: hvly bckd: more expected after unlucky effort in 4432. **0**

4165 **Russian Fox 37** [10] 3-9-13 (79) R Hughes 20/1:
4120 **Red Typhoon 40** [14] 3-9-5 (71) S Sanders 25/1:
4480 **Boanerges 12** [7] 3-9-11 (77) G Duffield 16/1:
4432 **Kissing Time 15** [4] 3-9-4 (70) I Mongan (3) 25/1:
4285 **Harryana 28** [17] 3-9-8 (74) M Hills 33/1:

21 ran   Time 1m 04.26 (6.06)   (David R Sutherland)   Miss L A Perratt Ayr, Strathclyde.

4571 3.00 RJB MINING FILL COND STKS 3YO+ (C) 1m2f60y Heavy 145 -08 Slow
£7020 £2160 £1080 £540 3yo rec 4lb

*4515 **GENEROUS DIANA 9** [5] H R A Cecil 4-9-4 T Quinn 9/4 FAV: 21-211: 4 ch f Generous - Lypharitissima (Lightning) Front rank, imprvd to lead 2f out, drifted left appr fnl 1f, styd on strongly, drvn out: hvly bckd: recent Yarmouth wnr (class stks, overcame trouble in running): '99 wnr at Lingfield (mdn, rtd 71, K Mahdi): eff at 7f, suited by 10f & may get further: acts on fast & hvy grnd & prob any trk: tough & progressive. 90

4408 **YA TARRA 16** [7] Saeed bin Suroor 3-8-8 J Carroll 14/1: -32: 3 ch f Unbridled - Snow Bride (Blushing Groom) Mid-div, short of room 4f out, prog to chase wnr when slightly short of room ins last, kept on & not btn far: gd effort on only 2nd career start in hvy grnd: win a race: see 4408. 1 82

4534 **TYPHOON GINGER 7** [10] G Woodward 5-8-12 P Fessey 100/1: 205363: 5 ch m Archway - Pallas Viking (Viking) Towards rear, gd hdwy appr fnl 3f, chall appr fnl 1f, no extra ins last: remarkable effort at the weights by this mdn: treat rating with caution (offic only 55): see 4413. 2 79$

3019 **FARRFESHEENA 96** [3] Saeed bin Suroor 3-8-8 (t) J Reid 9/2: 5-24: In tch, rdn into lead 4f out, hdd over 2f out, wknd over 1f out: 3 month abs, op 3/1, 4L clr rem: better expected on this step up to 10f & poss not handle this v testing grnd: much better in 3019 (fast grnd, fill mdn, reappl). 2 76

*3432 **GWENEIRA 77** [4] K Darley 3-8-12 K Darley 8/1: -15: Dwelt, sn prom, sltly outpcd 4f out, rallied to lead 2f out, sn hdd & fdd: 20L clr rem, 11 wk abs: not quite get home in v hvy grnd: btr 3432 (debut, gd grnd). 4 74

-- **WHIZZ** [1] 3-8-5 S Drowne 20/1: -6: Dwelt, rear, nvr a factor on debut: mid-dist bred filly, prob not handle these v testing conditions: with R Charlton. 20 37

*4481 **EASY TO LOVE 12** [8] 4-9-2 A McGlone 10/1: -30417: Prom, ev ch till wknd rapidly fnl 3f: v disapp here, handled hvy grnd well in 4481 (11.5f mdn). 9 31

3375 **LAUND VIEW LADY 79** [11] 3-8-8 O Pears 150/1: 600008: Al outpcd: recent well btn 4th over timber (2m juv nov hdle, rtd 70h, hvy grnd): v stiff task at these weights: see 1351 (seller). shd 27

3808 **PARISIENNE HILL 61** [12] 4-8-12 K Dalgleish (5) 200/1: 000009: Al rear, t.o.: abs, impossible task. 5 20

4014 **ORIGINAL SPIN 48** [9] 3-8-8 (vis) G Carter 8/1: 112200: Prom, rdn over 3f out, wknd rapidly, 10th: 7 wk abs: much better expected, something clearly amiss: see shd 3467 (bl first time): see 2272. 11 5

*4412 **EATON PLACE 16** [2] 3-8-12 W Ryan 9/1: -10: Sn led, hdd 4f out, qckly lost tch, t.o. in 11th: longer priced s/mate of wnr: surely something amiss here, handled hvy grnd well on debut in 4412 (mdn). 10 0

*3350 **ALWAYS VIGILANT 81** [6] 3-8-12 R Hughes 8/1: -0310: Led early, wknd radily over 2f out, virtually p.u. fnl 1f: fin last: much btr on gd grnd in 3350 (1m, mdn). dist 0

12 ran Time 2m 22.22 (15.82) (Greenfield Stud) H R A Cecil Newmarket.

4572 3.30 DRANSFIELD COND STKS 2YO (C) 1m str Heavy 145 -13 Slow
£6084 £1872 £936 £468 Field raced up centre of course

+4417 **TUDOR REEF 15** [5] J Noseda 2-9-1 J Weaver 2/1: 046411: 2 b c Mujadil - Exciting (Mill Reef) Made all, hung left appr fnl 2f, just held on in a driving fin: swtg, bckd from 11/4: recent easy wnr at Brighton (mdn): half-brother to sev wnrs, incl smart miler Almushtarak: eff arnd 1m, further dist suit: handles firm, much imprvd recently on soft & hvy: most progressive & useful: reportedly hds for a Gr 3 in France. 101

4463 **DAYGLOW DANCER 13** [6] M R Channon 2-9-1 J Reid 11/10 FAV: 252262: 2 b c Fraam - Fading (Pharly) Trkd wnr thr'out, chall strongly fnl 1f, just btn in a driving fin: hvly bckd, 16L clr rem: lost nothing in defeat. ½ 100

-- **LORD JOSHUA** [4] G A Butler 2-8-8 K Darley 14/1: -3: 2 b c King's Theatre - Lady Joshua (Royal Academy) Slow to start, sn in tch, hung left & fdd fnl 2f: op 10/1: Mar first foal: dam plcd as a juv, sire top-class mid-dist performer: shld apprec further next term & will improve. 16 71

-- **GEORGE STUBBS** [1] P F I Cole 2-8-8 J Fortune 5/1: -4: Towards rear, rdn 3f out, sn under press & wknd qckly: op 11/4, debut: 32,000gns purchase: dam a dual wnr in the USA: may do better on faster grnd. shd 71

4249 **DENISE BEST 31** [3] 2-8-6 Mark Flynn (6) 16/1: -02405: Cl-up, rdn & lost tch halfway: btr 4072 (soft). 6 60

4390 **ZANGOOEY 17** [2] 2-8-11 R Winston 66/1: -006: Al last, t.o. halfway: highly tried: little form. dist 0

6 ran Time 1m 49.17 (12.67) (B E Nielson) J Noseda Newmarket.

4573 4.00 LADY RIDERS HCAP 3YO+ 0-80 (E) 1m str Heavy 145 -39 Slow
£4680 £1440 £720 £360 3yo rec 2lb Field raced up centre of course [54]

4498 **NATALIE JAY 10** [4] M R Channon 4-11-3 (71) Miss L Bates (7) 12/1: 633131: 4 b f Ballacashtal - Falls Of Lora (Scottish Rifle) V slowly away, hdwy halfway, led 1f out, held on well under hands-&-heels riding: earlier scored at Salisbury & Leicester (fill h'caps): '99 wnr again at Salisbury (same fill h'cap, rtd 69 & 68a): suited by 1m/10f: acts on fast & equitrack, loves soft & hvy grnd: handles any trk, likes Salisbury & a stiff fin: gd weight carrier: runs well for an amateur: progressive, memorable wnr on first public ride for Leeanne Bates. 83

*4545 **GREENAWAY BAY 6** [7] K R Burke 6-11-0 (68) (5ex) Miss K Warnett (7) 5/2 FAV: -51112: 6 ch g Green Dancer - Raise 'N Dance (Raise A Native) Chsd ldrs, prog to lead over 3f out, hdd 1f out, kept on well ins last: 7L clr 3rd, hvly bckd under a 5lb pen: tough & progressive, lost little in defeat: see 4545. ¾ 77

4386 **SWINGING THE BLUES 17** [15] C A Dwyer 6-9-12 (52)(vis) Miss Michelle Saunders(7) 33/1: 100003: 6 b g 7 50 Bluebird - Winsong Melody (Music Maestro) Towards rear, kept on fnl 2f, no threat to front pair: acts on firm & soft, prob hvy: return to 10f+ shld suit: see 2199 (10f, fast).

*4536 **EVE 7** [6] M L W Bell 3-10-12 (68) Mrs S Bosley 3/1: 001114: Dwelt, chsd ldrs halfway, rdn & kept on fnl 2f, no threat to front pair: op 9/2: a real mudlark: see 4536. shd 66

4365 **BENBYAS 18** [8] 3-9-12 (54)(bl) Miss Diana Jones 16/1: 004305: Trkd ldrs halfway, kept on onepace fnl 2f: op 10/1, blnks reapplied: acts on gd & hvy grnd: see 1723 (mdn, 6f). 1 50

4499 **MR PERRY 10** [10] 4-9-3 (43)(3oh) Mrs S Moore (5) 33/1: 600006: Chsd ldrs, rdn/no extra fnl 2f. 2½ 35

4520 **KIDZ PLAY 8** [12] 4-10-3 (57) Mrs C Williams 7/1: 14P327: Led after 2f till 3f out, fdd: bckd from 14/1. 6 40

4499 **PENNYS PRIDE 10** [9] 5-11-1 (69) Miss P Robson 16/1: 303008: Chsd ldrs, nvr able to chall. 1 50

3573 **DISTINCTIVE DREAM 72** [21] 6-10-6 (60) Miss A L Hutchinson(5) 33/1: 000209: Towards rear, mod hdwy 3f out, no impress: 10 wk abs: see 1250, 598. 4 35

4536 **GRUINART 7** [18] 3-10-11 (67) Miss E Ramsden 12/1: 400040: Mid-div at best: 10th: btr 2025 (firm). nk 41

4046 **MR SPEAKER 45** [16] 7-10-1 (55) Miss H Webster (5) 33/1: 500000: Chsd ldrs 5f: 11th, 6 wk abs. ½ 28

4452 **MYTTONS AGAIN 14** [1] 3-10-11 (67)(bl) Miss Bridget Gatehouse(3) 25/1: 640000: Prom till over 2f out, wknd into 12th: btr 3593 (7f, fast). ¾ 39

4506 **CAD ORO 10** [20] 7-10-12 (66) Miss D J Jones 8/1: 302040: Mid-div, rdn over 3f out, btn: 13th: nicely h'capped, more expected on this fav'd hvy grnd: see 1058, 817. 0

4282 **Tap 28** [17] 3-11-2 (72) Miss L J Harwood (7) 16/1: -- **Mon Prefere** [19] 5-11-7 (75) Miss E Folkes (5) 33/1:

DONCASTER   FRIDAY NOVEMBER 3RD   Lefthand, Flat, Galloping Track

4523 Margarets Dancer 8 [14] 5-9-8 (48)(t) Miss A Deniel 20/1:
4375] Mr Nevermind 739 [10] 10-9-3 (43)(5oh) Miss S Cassidy (1) 50/1:
4420 Atlantic Ace 15 [5] 3-11-5 (75) Mrs V Smart (5) 25/1:   3440 **Princess Ria 77** [11] 3-10-4 (60) Miss J Ellis (5) 33/1:
4451} Manufan 380 [13] 5-9-6 (46)(t) Miss H Garrett (7) 33/1:
20 ran   Time 1m 51.22 (14.72)   (Peter Jolliffe)   M R Channon West Isley, Berks.

DONCASTER   SATURDAY NOVEMBER 4TH   Lefthand, Flat, Galloping Track

Official Going   HEAVY. Stalls: Str - Stands; Rnd - Inside; Rnd 1m - Outside.

4574

12.20 FURNITURE APPR HCAP 3YO+ 0-90 (E)   7f str   Heavy 130   -25 Slow   [90]
£3916   £1205   £602   £301   3yo rec 1lb   Field raced in 2 Groups

*4499 **LUCKY GITANO 11** [6] J L Dunlop 4-9-1 (77) A Beech 6/1 FAV: 246411: 4 b g Lucky Guest   86
- Afwind Wind (Windjammer) Switched right after start, hld up, gd hdwy over 2f out to lead ins last, rdn clr:
recently won cmftbly at Redcar (h'cap, first win): rnr-up in '99 (rtd 87): eff at 7f/1m, stays 10f & handles
firm, likes gd/soft, hvy & a gall trk: can run well fresh under big weights: fast improving.

4545 **TOPTON 7** [16] P Howling 6-8-10 (72)(bl) J Banks (7) 16/1: 600402: 6 b g Royal Academy - Circo   4   74
(High Top) Hld up, gd hdwy to lead over 2f out, hdd & not pace of wnr ins last: acts on fm, hvy & both a/w's.

*4498 **TREASURE TOUCH 11** [1] P D Evans 6-8-9 (71) Joanna Badger (5) 12/1: 400513: 6 b g Treasure   1¼   71
Kay - Bally Pourri (Law Society) Chsd ldr far side, led that small group 1f out, not pace of near side group:
fine run: acts on firm, hvy & fibresand: see 4498.

4013 **DURAID 49** [18] Denys Smith 8-9-12 (88) A Nicholls 12/1: 165644: Cl up, outpcd 2f out, rallied   nk   88
ins last: 7 wk abs: acts on firm & hvy: v tough 8yo, see 2648.

*4388 **RUSSIAN RHAPSODY 18** [17] 3-9-1 (78) Lindsey Rutty (7) 14/1: 422215: In tch, kept on late.   shd   78

4461 **CHAMPAGNE RIDER 14** [8] 4-8-10 (72) G Gibbons (7) 9/1: 004026: Switched right after start, sn   1½   70
in tch, onepace fnl 2f: bckd from 9/1: proved he stays 7f in 4461.

4547 **GIFT OF GOLD 7** [2] 5-9-2 (78) I Mongan (3) 10/1: 006047: Led far side till wknd over 1f out.   ½   75

4405 **MISTER MAL 17** [15] 4-8-13 (75) D Mernagh 14/1: 206508: Handy, no impress fnl 2f: see 4405.   nk   71

4547 **BABY BARRY 7** [11] 3-8-9 (72) C Poste (7) 33/1: 000009: In tch, kept & no impress fnl 2f.   nk   67

*4527 **NINEACRES 9** [12] 9-10-1 (91)(bl) P Fitzsimons (3) 12/1: 221010: With ldrs, rdn 2f out,   1¼   85
wknd fnl 1f: 10th, big weight: not stay 7f: most tough & progressive over 5/6f earlier, see 4527.

4527 **JUWWI 9** [21] 6-9-8 (84) Darren Williams (5) 14/1: 040050: Nvr a factor: 11th, best at 5/6f.   hd   77

4527 **SUSSEX LAD 9** [5] 3-8-12 (75) P Dobbs (3) 20/1: 646160: Switched left start, in tch, wknd over 1f   1   66
out: 12th: not stay 7f? btr 4527, 3419 (6f).

4405 **DOWNLAND 17** [20] 4-9-7 (83)(bl) P M Quinn 10/1: 060220: Cl up, wknd 2f out: 18th, now with S Williams.   0

4527 **CARD GAMES 9** [13] 3-9-7 (84) P Hanagan (3) 10/1: 050200: Led till over 2f out: 21st, btr 4301 (6f).   0

4357 **Royal Result 21** [14] 7-9-9 (85) Clare Roche (7) 14/1: 4545 **Tony Tie 7** [10] 4-9-12 (88) Dawn Rankin (7) 25/1:
4465 **Look Here Now 14** [19] 3-8-13 (76) G Baker (3) 20/1: 4547 **Fair Impression 7** [7] 3-9-3 (80) J Mackay (3) 14/1:
4380 **Somesession 18** [4] 3-8-11 (74) B McHugh (7) 33/1: 4165 **Mersey Mirage 38** [22] 3-9-10 (87) L Newman 12/1:
4506 **Adobe 11** [9] 5-9-4 (80) K Dalgleish (3) 25/1:   1385} **Bring Sweets 536** [3] 4-10-0 (90) S Carson 25/1:
22 ran   Time 1m 34.03 (10.83)   (Anamoine Ltd)   J L Dunlop Arundel, W Sussex

4575

12.50 EBF AUTUMN MDN DIV 1 2YO (D)   6f str   Heavy 130   -26 Slow
£3363   £1035   £517   £258   Field raced centre to far side

4462 **ZILCH 14** [1] R Hannon 2-9-0 L Newman 15/8 FAV: 242341: 2 ch c Zilzal - Bunty Boo (Noalto)   103
Trkd ldrs, prog to lead dist, styd on strongly, pushed out: hvly bckd: deserved win, plcd sev times, notably
nk 2nd in Gr 2 Gimcrack at York: eff at 5/6f on firm & hvy grnd, 7f will suit next term: handles a gall trk,
runs well fresh: v useful juv who shld win in Listed company next term.

-- **LA PASSIONE** [4] H R A Cecil 2-8-9 T Quinn 3/1: -2: 2 ch f Gulch - Larking (Green Forest)   1½   93+
Mid-div, prog 2f out, ev ch dist, kept on under hands-&-heels riding, not pace of wnr: nicely bckd on debut: Jan
foal, cost $280,000: dam lightly rcd but related to a high-class performer: sire a top-class performer in the US:
eff at 6f on hvy grnd, 7f/1m will suit in '01: handles a gall trk: potentially smart filly, will win her mdn.

-- **INCHCAPE** [12] R Charlton 2-9-0 S Drowne 10/1: -3: 2 b c Indian Ridge - Inchmurrin (Lomond)   1¾   94+
Chsd ldrs, slightly bmpd 1½f out, ran on nicely under hands-&-heels riding: drifted from 5/1, clr of 4th on
debut: Apr foal, half brother to smart 6/7f performer Inchinor: dam a high-class 5f/1m wnr, sire a high-class
sprinter: eff at 6f, 7f looks sure to suit: handles hvy grnd & a gall trk: lks nailed on to win a mdn.

-- **CHICANE** [10] L M Cumani 2-9-0 S W Kelly (3) 33/1: -4: Unruly start, chsd ldrs, slightly outpcd   7   79
2f out, styd on late, no ch with front 3: debut: Mar foal, half brother to a couple of wnrs, incl 7f juv scorer:
dam a 7f winning 2yo: sure to apprec 7f/1m next term: handles hvy: sure to improve on this promising debut.

-- **GOLDEN HIND** [9] 2-8-9 G Duffield 20/1: -5: Front rank, losing place when switched 1½f out,   ¾   72
no impress fnl 1f: Apr first foal: dam from a gd staying family: sire a top-class performer in the USA: likely
to apprec 7f/1m+ in '01: with Sir M Prescott & sure to improve.

4496 **EAGLERIDER 11** [20] 2-9-0 Dean McKeown 40/1: -36: Chsd ldrs, drifted left & fdd fnl 1½f: see 4496.   ½   76

-- **QUINTA LAD** [13] 2-9-0 J Edmunds 66/1: -7: Chsd ldrs 4f, hung left & wknd: Feb first foal: dam   ¾   74
a sprint wnr: sire a high-class miler: with J Balding.

4446 **RIPCORD 15** [21] 2-9-0 J Carroll 25/1: -008: Rear, styd on fnl 2f, nvr plcd to chall: back in   2   69+
trip: eye-catching h'cap qual run: one to keep in mind next season over further: see 4161 (debut, 1m).

4479 **SCOTTYS FUTURE 13** [22] 2-9-0 R Mullen 50/1: -009: Rear, styd on fnl 1½f, nvr nrr: some promise   nk   68
& will do better in h'caps over further next term.

4183 **COLLECTIVITY 19** [2-8-9] M Hills 10/1: -00: Chsd ldrs till outpcd halfway, no ch after: fin 10th.   hd   63

4479 **TONTO OREILLY 13** [19] 2-9-0 Paul Eddery 50/1: -000: Held up, some late gains, nvr dngrs in 11th.   shd   68

-- **SECRET SENTIMENT** [15] 2-8-9 G Carter 20/1: -0: Slowly away, al bhnd on debut: fin 12th: May foal,   1½   60
half sister to sev mid-dist scorers: sire a top-class miler: bred to apprec 1m+: shld improve on faster grnd.

4138 **POYLE PICKLE 40** [18] 2-8-9 M Tebbutt 50/1: -00: Speed till halfway: fin 13th, 6 wk abs.   1   57

-- **UNDERWOOD FERN** [8] 2-9-0 W Ryan 9/1: -0: Chsd ldrs 4f, wknd into 14th: debut: Feb foal, half brother to sev wnrs: dam a 10f wnr in France: sire a smart 7f/1m performer.   shd   62

-- **GINA** [5] 2-8-9 R Winston 33/1: -0: Set pace till 1½f out, fdd into 16th: debut: IR 6,000gns   0
Apr foal: half sister to a 7f/1m wnr: dam unrcd, related to a decent performer: sire a smart miler: J Glover
filly, ran well for a long way here.

4470 **Perfidious** 14 [2] 2-9-0 S Sanders 20/1: 4503 **Sheriff Song** 11 [16] 2-9-0 T Lucas 50/1:
-- **Ash** [17] 2-8-9 G Sparkes (7) 20/1: 4410 **Colonel Kurtz** 17 [3] 2-9-0 Dale Gibson 66/1:
4496 **Gogs Gift** 11 [11] 2-9-0 A Culhane 66/1: 4537 **Pertemps Boycott** 8 [6] 2-9-0 J Tate 50/1:
21 ran Time 1m 20.17 (9.37) (Mary Mayall, Linda Corbett, Julie Martin) R Hannon East Everleigh, Wilts

---

4576

1.25 EBF AUTUMN MDN DIV 2 2YO (D) 6f str Heavy 130 -21 Slow
£3347 £1030 £515 £257 Field raced across the course

4288 **OREANA** 29 [18] J L Dunlop 2-8-9 W Supple 12/1: -051: 2 b f Anabaa - Lavinia Fontana (Sharpo) **96**
Clr stands side, overall ldr over 2f out, pushed clr fnl 1f, cmftbly: Feb foal, dam a mud loving top-class sprinter:
eff at 6f, shld stay further: clearly relished hvy: type to improve further & win good races on similar grnd.
4479 **MATRON** 13 [20] L M Cumani 2-8-9 G Sparkes (7) 15/2: -22: 2 b f Dr Devious - Matrona (Woodman) **5 88+**
Bhd, styd on well over 1f out, nrst fin: op 6/1: eye-catching late hdwy from the rear over inadequate trip:
one to keep on your side over 7f/1m+ next term: see 4479.
4462 **ORIENTOR** 14 [3] J S Goldie 2-8-9 A Culhane 7/1: -3203: 2 b c Inchinor - Orient (Bay Express) **¾ 90**
Chsd ldr far side, led that group over 1f out, onepace: op 5/1: acts on hvy & shown enough to win a race.
4496 **SOPHIELU** 11 [5] M Johnston 2-8-9 K Darley 9/2: -24: Led far side till over 1f out, no extra: **1½ 82**
bckd from 6/1: clr of rem & ran well: stays 6f on hvy: shld win a race: see 4496.
4470 **FUNNY VALENTINE** 14 [11] 2-9-0 S Finnamore (5) 5/1: -25: In tch, wknd 2f out: btr 4470. **7 74**
-- **MOTTO** [9] 2-8-9 T Quinn 4/1 FAV: -6: Sn bhd, mod late gains: well bckd on debut: Mtoto Feb **2 65**
foal: half sister to a 7f juv wnr: dam 1m juv/Gr 3 mid-dists scorer: bred to relish mid-dists next term.
4470 **FIRST STEPS** 14 [4] 2-8-9 Paul Eddery 33/1: -67: In tch, btn over 2f out: see 4470. **¾ 63**
-- **GENTLE NIGHT** [15] 2-8-9 M Hills 8/1: -8: Slow away, nvr a factor: op 5/1 on debut: Zafonic **1 61**
Apr foal: half sister to a Gr 3 juv wnr Land Of Dreams: dam Molecomb wnr: speedily bred.
4447 **BLIND SPOT** 15 [16] 2-9-0 G Carter 33/1: -009: Cl up, wknd over 2f out: see 3705. **3 60**
4470 **JAYCAT** 14 [8] 2-8-9 J Quinn 50/1: -00: Chsd ldr stands side till over 2f out: 10th. **½ 54**
4514 **ROMAN HIDEAWAY** 10 [10] 2-9-0 S Sanders 25/1: -00: Al bhd: 11th, see 4514. **¾ 58**
-- **MAGDALEON** [12] 2-8-9 C Rutter 14/1: -0: Nvr dangrs on debut: 12th: Lion Cavern Mar first foal: **nk 52**
bred to apprec 1m+ next term: with R Charlton.

-- **College Queen** [1] 2-8-9 V Halliday 66/1: 4512 **Grandma Griffiths** 10 [22] 2-8-9 S W Kelly(3) 66/1:
-- **Hornby Boy** [21] 2-9-0 R Winston 66/1: 4449 **Minnies Mystery** 15 [19] 2-8-9 G Baker(5) 50/1:
4503 **Greycoat** 11 [2] 2-9-0 D Holland 66/1: -- **Picture Palace** [13] 2-9-0 G Duffield 20/1:
4530 **Chamlang** 8 [6] 2-8-9 S Whitworth 33/1: 1260 **Bolingbroke Castle** 176 [17] 2-9-0 J Carroll 20/1:
-- **Laund View Leona** [14] 2-8-9 O Pears 50/1:
21 ran Time 1m 19.9 (9.1) (Cyril Humpris) J L Dunlop Arundel, W Sussex

---

4577

1.55 BOC SUREFLOW NURSERY HCAP 2YO 0-85 (D) 7f str Heavy 130 -41 Slow [88]
£4777 £1470 £735 £367 Split into 3 groups - centre/far side favoured

*4538 **LEATHERBACK** 8 [7] N A Callaghan 2-8-8 (68) C Catlin (7) 10/3 FAV: 000111: 2 b g Turtle Island **74**
- Phyllode (Pharly) Chsd ldrs centre, strong run fnl 1f to lead near line, drvn out: hvly bckd: completed
hat-trick after wins at Pontefract & Brighton (nursery h'caps): eff at 7f/1m, will stay 10f next term: loves
soft & hvy grnd: handles a stiff or sharp/undul trk: fast improving mudlark.
4269 **CHURCH MICE** 31 [2] W H Tinning 2-9-2 (76)(vis) J McAuley 20/1: 364132: 2 br f Petardia - Negria **1 79**
(Al Hareb) Prom far side, went on 2½f out & kicked for home, worn down near line: prev trained by M Bell &
fine first run for new connections: stays 7f & a real mudlark: enterprising tactics nearly paid off: see 4269.
*4502 **DIAMOND MAX** 11 [10] P D Evans 2-8-13 (73) Joanna Badger (5) 7/1: 145513: 2 b c Nicolotte - **½ 75**
Kawther (Tap On Wood) Chsd ldrs centre, went with wnr 2f out, styd on well & not btn far: stays 7f: see 4502.
4336 **WATTNO ELJOHN** 23 [3] D W P Arbuthnot 2-8-5 (65) J Quinn 20/1: 163534: Waited with far side, prog **1 64**
2f out, fin v fast but too late: fine run in this better grade: acts on fast & hvy: see 4336 (seller).
4453 **EXTRA GUEST** 15 [22] 2-8-13 (73) Kim Tinkler 16/1: 233445: Al prom on stands rail, ran on well **2½ 66**
fnl 1f, no ch with centre/far side: fine run from what was prob the worst of the draw: now with N Tinkler.
3913 **MUJALINA** 54 [20] 2-8-8 (68) G Duffield 25/1: 100006: Prom stands rail, onepcd 1f: 8 wk abs: **2½ 55**
not disgraced from unfav draw: see 3913 (first time blnks).
4191 **DODONA** 36 [21] C Rutter 25/1: 400407: Chsd ldrs stands side, drifted to centre halfway, **3 45**
onepcd fnl 1½f: eye-catching in 3976.
4450 **DOMINAITE** 15 [13] 2-9-7 (81) T Quinn 6/1: 323238: Disputing lead centre, ch 2f out, fdd fnl 1f: **nk 60**
top-weight: see 4450, 4350 (1m).
4281 **CERALBI** 29 [11] 2-8-8 (68) P M Quinn (3) 33/1: 622009: Nvr a factor in centre: best 388 (fast grnd). **1½ 44**
4416 **APRIL LEE** 16 [19] 2-8-2 (62)(ec) G Baker(5) 25/1: 203000: Prom 4f stands side: fin 10th: btr 4116 (1m). **½ 37**
4416 **GALY BAY** 16 [14] 2-9-4 (78) J Carroll 20/1: 333260: Chsd ldrs 5f far side, wknd into 11th: nicely bckd. **2½ 47**
4453 **DANE DANCING** 15 [15] 2-8-6 (66) W Supple 10/1: 500030: Speed 5f centre: fin 12th: btr 4453 (gd/soft). **2 29**
4338 **JOHNNY REB** 23 [8] 2-9-3 (77)(t) L Newman 33/1: 260500: Rcd far side, left bhd halfway: 13th. **1 37**
4336 **JETHAME** 23 [5] 2-8-5 (65)(bl) D R McCabe 20/1: 353320: Made most till over 2f out, wknd into 14th: **nk 24**
prob meant off too fast in these testing conditions: see 4336 (gd grnd).
*4254 **CLASSY ACT** 32 [17] 2-9-3 (77) G Carter 10/1: 301610: Nvr a factor in centre: 20th: see 4254. **0**
4350 **BOUCHRA** 22 [16] 2-8-13 (73) J Mackay (5) 10/1: 220360: Speed 4f centre: fin 21st: btr 4157 (gd). **0**
4477 **WESTERN EDGE** 13 [18] 2-9-1 (75) K Darley 10/1: -5630: Nvr a factor in centre: fin last: h'cap bow **0**
& better expected: see 4477 (1m).
4449 **Siamo Disperati** 15 [4] 2-8-11 (71) A Culhane 25/1: 4449 **Young Tern** 15 [9] 2-8-6 (66) A Daly 20/1:
4338 **Serviceable** 23 [12] 2-9-4 (78) J Tate 25/1: *4410 **Open Warfare** 17 [1] 2-9-3 (77) S Drowne 20/1:
3824 **Emissary** 61 [14] 2-8-3 (63) K Dalgleish (5) 20/1:
22 ran Time 1m 35.21 (12.01) (M Tabor) N A Callaghan Newmarket

---

4578

2.25 LISTED CIU SERLBY STKS 3YO+ (A) 1m4f Heavy 130 +09 Fast
£14235 £4380 £2190 £1095 3yo rec 6lb

4469 **BOREAS** 14 [3] L M Cumani 5-8-13 K Darley 5/6 FAV: 3/1231: 5 b g In The Wings - Reamur (Top Ville) **112**
Trkd ldr, led 1m out, pushed clr over 2f out, easily: val 14L, hvly bckd: gd time: earlier won at York (rtd
h'cap) '99 & 2nd in Tote Ebor h'cap: missed '99, '98 wnr at Ripon (mdn, rtd 87): eff at 12/14f on fast & hvy,
likes a gall trk: runs well fresh: smart & improving.
4162 **ZILARATOR** 39 [1] W J Haggas 4-8-13 T Quinn 9/2: 616152: 4 b g Zilzal - Allegedly (Sir Ivor) **13 97**
Keen to post, sn led for 4f, lost plc over 5f out, plugged on for 2nd ins last: loves the mud but this was

1420

a step up in class: see 4162 (h'cap), 4039.

*4474 **MUBTAKER** 14 [2] M P Tregoning 3-8-7 W Supple 5/2: 2-13: 3 ch c Silver Hawk - Gazayil   ½   96
(Irish River) Handy, chsd wnr over 5f out, rdn over 3f out, sn outpcd & lost 2nd ins last: lngr trip, see 4474.

4148 **COOL INVESTMENT** 41 [4] M Johnston 3-8-12 D Holland 16/1: 135104: Handy, rdn over 4f out,   *dist*   0
sn btn, t.o.: stiff task: see 3850.

4 ran   Time 2m 44.36 (14.56)   (Aston House Stud)   L M Cumani Newmarket

---

4579	**3.00 PERTEMPS HCAP 3YO+ 0-95 (C)** **2m110y** **Heavy 130** **-15 Slow**	**[95]**
	£8736 £2688 £1344 £672 3yo rec 9lb	

*4476 **COCO LOCO** 13 [3] J Pearce 3-7-10 (72)(2oh) G Baker (5) 5/2-FAV: 502111: 3 b f Bin Ajwaad -   85
Mainly Me (Huntingdale) Waited with, smooth hdwy to lead on bit 3f out, sn clr, v easily: hvly bckd: completed
qck hat-trick after wins at Catterick & Yarmouth (h'caps): eff at 14f/2m, shld stay further: acts on gd, revels
in soft or hvy grnd: handles a gall or sharp trk: fast improving filly who is a confirmed mudlover.

4451 **MR FORTYWINKS** 15 [7] J L Eyre 6-7-10 (63)(2oh) K Dalgleish (5) 8/1: 341402: 6 ch g Fool's Holme -   12   62
Dream On (Absalom) Rear, hdwy to chase wnr fnl 2f, no impress: nicely bckd: fair run, stays 2m: see 4370.

2130} **SECRET STYLE** 502 [6] R Hollinshead 5-8-8 (75) P M Quinn (3) 33/1: 0041-3: 5 b g Shirley Heights -   1½   73
Rosie Potts (Shareef Dancer) Held up, prog over 3f out, no impress fnl 2f: belated reapp: '99 Nottingham wnr
(clmr, with E Dunlop, rtd 78), subs won in Jersey: ex-German, won at Dusseldorf (11f mdn): eff at 2m on gd &
fast grnd, prob handles hvy: can run well fresh: best prev in blnks: fitter next time.

4374 **ASPIRANT DANCER** 19 [4] M L W Bell 5-8-0 (67) J Mackay (5) 20/1: 16-004: In tch, left bhnd fnl 2f.   2½   63

4071 **JASEUR** 45 [10] G Duffield 7/1: 060245: Set pace 6f, wknd 3f out: cl 2nd in a nov hdle   7   59
at Aintree 2 wks ago: see 3511.

4091 **RUM POINTER** 43 [12] 4-10-0 (95) P Dobbs (5) 12/1: 005546: Rcd wide back str, came back to main   2   83
group, then went wide again, lost pl ent str, rallied late: 6 wk abs, top-weight: strange tactics, jockey seemed
not to be able to make up his mind where he wanted to go & subs gave up many lengths: flattered 4091.

4353 **WEET FOR ME** 21 [14] 4-8-10 (77) N Callan 25/1: 016307: Front rank, led after 6f till 3f out, fdd.   shd   65

4353 **BRIDIES PRIDE** 21 [1] 4-8-5 (72) Jonjo Fowle (5) 12/1: 0-2408: In tch, btn 4f out: unable to dominate.   25   40

4353 **ROYAL EXPRESSION** 21 [2] 8-8-3 (70) W Supple 25/1: 630009: AI areal, t.o.: see 1052 (C/D).   9   31

4353 **TURNPOLE** 21 [9] 9-8-8 (75) A Culhane 7/1: 641400: Taken far side back str, v wide home bend, sn   1¼   35
btn & t.o.: fin 10th: tactics did not pay off: see 2600 (fast grnd).

4231 **GIVE AN INCH** 33 [5] 5-8-0 (67) P Hanagan (5) 11/2: 001100: Nvr a factor in 11th: btr 3993.   3½   24

4451 **PULAU PINANG** 15 [13] 4-8-9 (76)(t) K Darley 10/1: 221000: Prom, dsptd lead halfway till 4f out,   *dist*   0
wknd qckly & virtually p.u. fnl 1f: reportedly fin lame: see 1440 (13f fast grnd).

12 ran   Time 3m 52.83 (24.03)   (Mr & Mrs J Matthews)   J Pearce Newmarket

---

4580	**3.35 TOTE NOVEMBER HCAP 3YO+ (B)** **1m4f** **Heavy 130** **+10 Fast**	**[100]**
	£23627 £7270 £3635 £1817 3yo rec 6lb	

3858 **BATSWING** 59 [14] B Ellison 5-8-8 (80) R Winston 14/1: 120021: 5 b g Batshoof - Magic Milly   86
(Simply Great) Chsd ldrs, hdwy to laed over 1f out, drvn out: fast time: rnr-up in a h'cap hdle 34 days ago
(rtd 108h, 2m): earlier won at Chester (h'cap): plcd in '99 (rtd 75 for B Millman): 98/99 Taunton mdn hdle
wnr (rtd 104h, 2m3.5f, soft): stays 12f well on fast, likes gd grnd & hvy: handles any trk, with/without blnks.

4353 **CARLYS QUEST** 21 [2] J Neville 6-9-0 (86)(tvi) S Drowne 9/1: 040552: 6 ch g Primo Dominie - Tuppy   1¼   90
(Sharpen Up) Handy, short of room over 2f out, kept on over 1f out, nvr get to wnr: v tough, rnr-up in
this race off 78 & 79 prev 2 seasons: see 4353, 1373.

*4342 **SEREN HILL** 23 [10] G A Butler 4-9-7 (93)(8ex) K Darley 12/1: 200113: 4 ch f Sabrehill   2   95
- Seren Quest (Rainbow Quest) Hld up, eff over 3f out, kept on over 1f out: in grand form: see 4342.

4299 **NOWELL HOUSE** 28 [19] M W Easterby 4-8-6 (78) P Hanagan (5) 25/1: 001104: Hld up, gd hdwy over   shd   80
7f out, led on bit over 2f out till over 1f out, onepace: acts on fast & hvy: see 4221.

4342 **KUSTER** 23 [11] 4-9-1 (87) S W Kelly (3) 20/1: -42405: Hnady, onepace fnl 2f: prob stays 12f on hvy.   2½   86

2092 **CAPTAIN MILLER** 136 [7] 4-8-6 (78) J Mackay (5) 11/2: 0-1206: In tch, eff 3f out, onepace: well   1¼   76
bckd: not disgraced: see 1187.

4448 **CAPRICCIO** 15 [6] 3-7-11 (75) G Baker (5) 10/1: 525207: Hld up, eff over 3f out, late gains: uninspired   ¾   72
gamble from 50/1 in the morning: mdn who is unproven over 12f on hvy grnd: btr 4067.

4464 **MCGILLYCUDDY REEKS** 14 [9] 9-7-10 (68) Kim Tinkler 25/1: 564558: In tch, rdn & onepace fnl 2f.   6   59

4464 **HUNTERS TWEED** 14 [1] 4-7-10 (68)(BL)(2oh) C Catlin (7) 40/1: 206669: Keen, led till over 3f out,   ½   58
wknd 2f out: blnks: see 4464.

4300 **DEE PEE TEE CEE** 28 [8] 6-8-2 (74) Dale Gibson 25/1: -00000: In tch, rdn & outpcd over 3f out: 10th.   1½   62

4392 **SHRIVAR** 18 [4] 3-8-2 (80)(vis) M Henry 25/1: 421100: Keen, bhd, eff 3f out, hung left 2f out,   1   67
no impress: 11th: twice below 4197 (gd grnd).

2354 **BATHWICK BABE** 125 [15] 3-7-11 (75) A Nicholls 66/1: 00-20: Keen, bhd, no danger: 12th, long abs.   2½   59

4464 **DHAUDELOUP** 14 [20] 5-7-10 (68)(1oh) K Dalgleish (5) 7/1: 160/40: Keen bhd, hdwy over 4f out, wknd   0
over 2f out: 13th: see 4464.

*4213 **THARI** 35 [3] 3-9-10 (102) W Supple 14/1: -06310: With ldr, led over 3f out till over   0
2f out, wknd: 14th: not handle hvy? btr 4213 (14f, fast grnd).

4342 **FLOSSY** 23 [21] 4-9-8 (94) D Holland 11/4 FAV: 233120: Hld up, plenty to do, eff over 3f out, sn   0
no impress: fin 15th: hvly bckd to repeat last year's head win in this race (offic rtd 82, same grnd): btr 4342.

--   **El Emel** 16 [16] 3-8-12 (90) Martin Dwyer 16/1:

4464 **Warning Reef** 14 [17] 7-7-10 (68)(1oh) P M Quinn (3) 40/1:

4464 **Bawsian** 14 [13] 5-8-13 (85) D Mernagh (3) 33/1:   4464 **Kathryns Pet** 14 [5] 7-8-12 (84) A Culhane 25/1:

3599 **White House** 72 [18] 3-8-1 (79) J Quinn 11/1:

20 ran   Time 1m 18.45 (7.65)   (Ashley Carr)   B Ellison Lanchester, County Durham

---

4581	**4.10 LISTED WENTWORTH STKS 3YO+ (A)** **6f str** **Heavy 130** **+01 Fast**	
	£14950 £4600 £2300 £1150 3 raced far side	

4346 **ANDREYEV** 22 [5] R Hannon 6-9-0 K Darley 5/2: 413621: 6 ch c Presidium - Missish (Mummy's Pet)   111
Handy, hdwy to lead over 1f out, drvn to assert ins last: well bckd: earlier won here at Doncaster (Listed,
reapp) & York (rtd h'cap): twice rnr-up in '99 (rtd 109, Gr 3), subs gelded & had a wind op: rtd 117 at best
in '98: eff at 7f, best at 6f on soft & hvy grnd, acts on fast: handles any trk, with/without blnks: runs
well fresh: smart & tough: fitting winning end of the season for Champion Jockey Kevin Darley.

4465 **FURTHER OUTLOOK** 14 [7] D Nicholls 6-8-11 R Winston 5/1: 003132: 6 gr g Zilzal - Future Bright   2½   103

(Lyphard's Wish) Led, hung right & hdd over 1f out, onepace: v tough & useful: see 4465.

*4555 **GAELIC STORM** 7 [4] M Johnston 6-8-11 D Holland 5/4 FAV: 012113: 6 b g Shavian - Shannon Princess (Connaught) Chsd ldrs, rdn over 2f out, onepace over 1f out: well bckd: been busy, better than this.	1¼	101
4466 **NOW LOOK HERE** 14 [8] B A McMahon 4-8-11 S Sanders 14/1: 005024: Slow away, sn in tch, hmpd & onepace over 1f out: better off in h'caps: see 4466.	3	94
4357 **BOLDLY GOES** 21 [11] 4-8-11 (bl) J Fanning 33/1: 140065: With ldr, wknd 2f out: stiff task, see 4357.	2	90$
4129 **SEE YOU LATER** 41 [1] 3-8-6 W Supple 16/1: 001206: Led far side, no ch over 1f out: abs, see 3874 (gd).	½	84
4456 **MONKSTON POINT** 15 [9] 4-9-0 J Quinn 20/1: 000007: Al bhd: capable of better, see 4125, 1529.	shd	92
*4257 **BOOMERANG BLADE** 32 [3] 4-8-6 A Clark 25/1: 660518: Al bhd, far side: stiff task, see 4257.	4	76
4043 **DON PUCCINI** 46 [10] 3-8-11 Paul Eddery 50/1: 1-5009: Al bhd: abs, prob not handle hvy.	2	77
4456 **YORKIES BOY** 15 [2] 5-9-0 (bl) J Carroll 20/1: 040060: Cl up far side, wknd 2f out: 10th, btr 4456.	6	68
3120 **PERUGIA** 92 [6] 3-8-6 N Callan 50/1: 0-0400: Al bhd, t.o.: last, needs h'caps, see 3120.	26	10

11 ran   Time 1m 18.45 (7.65)   (J Palmer-Brown)   R Hannon East Everleigh, Wilts

A To Z Index

With the A To Z Index, you can see at a glance where each horse performed best, and pinpoint it's optimum distance, going and track preferences.

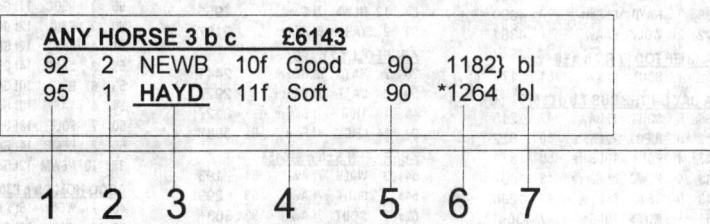

```
ANY HORSE 3 b c      £6143
92   2   NEWB   10f   Good      90   1182} bl
95   1   HAYD   11f   Soft      90   *1264 bl
```

        1   2   3   4   5   6   7

The first line in **_bold type and underlined_** provides the horse's name, age, sex and total prize money won last season (win and place).

1 Superform performance rating in that race.
 a = all weather rating
 Each time a horse runs, Superform's experienced handicappers
 award a rating which indicates the "worth" of the performance.
 The Scale used is 0-140, as used by the official handicappers.

2 Finishing position.   F=fell   U=unseated   R=refused.
 B=brought down   P=pulled up

3 Track name. **Bold underlined** type indicates a win

4 Distance of the race and state of the ground on the day.

5 If the race is a handicap, the official rating going into the race (the
 rating the horse ran off) is shown here. This figure also includes
 any pounds out of the handicap.   For example a horse rated
 officially 80 may be allotted 7-3 in a handicap. However the race
 conditions state that the minimum weight to be carried is 7-10.
 Thus the horse is said to be 7lbs out of the handicap and in effect
 runs off an official mark of 87.

6 The race reference number * indicates a win } indicates last season.

7 Any headgear worn.   bl=blinkers BL=blinkers worn for first time
 vis=visor   VIS=visor worn for first time t=tongue strap

A B MY BOY 2 ch c £0
44 6 BRIG 5f Gd/Sft 891
46 7 BRIG 5f Gd/Fm 1124
18 9 LING 6f Good 1396
44 6 GOOD 6f Gd/Sft 1634
0 17 BRIG 7f Soft 4172

A BIT SPECIAL 2 b f £512
73 3 DONC 7f Heavy 4567

A BOB LIGHT 3 br f £0
39 12 MUSS 8f Gd/Fm 62 1434
47 6 LEIC 8f Gd/Sft 1731
36 5 PONT 8f Good 1865

A C AZURE 2 br c £1096
62 6 CHES 7f Gd/Fm 3508
69 5 THIR 8f Gd/Fm 3614
72 3 CHEP 7f Good 3866
39 7 HAYD 6f Soft 73 4090
72a 2 WOLV 6f Aw 4381

A CHEF TOO FAR 7 b g £0
0a 13 SOUT 8f Aw 51 177 t

A DAY ON THE DUB 7 b g £3576
36a 5 SOUT 12f Aw 47 215
42 6 RIPO 12f Soft 50 822
47 4 PONT 10f Soft 50 871
43 4 NEWC 8f Heavy 48 1007
43 9 REDC 8f Firm 47 1296
51 1 NOTT 10f Gd/Sft 47 1364*
49 4 PONT 10f Soft 51 1705
33 13 BEVE 10f Firm 51 1921
31 7 NEWC 10f Gd/Fm 50 2309
41 5 HAYD 11f Gd/Fm 50 2453
30 11 NEWC 9f Firm 47 3603
34 5 MUSS 9f Soft 45 4520
25 9 MUSS 12f Soft 45 4560

A TEEN 2 ch c £0
32a 7 WOLV 6f Aw 2077

A TOUCH OF FROST 5 gr m £5220
85 1 THIR 7f Gd/Sft 1716* bl
83 4 SAND 7f Gd/Fm 84 1989 bl
62 8 YORK 7f Gd/Fm 83 4302 bl
65 11 NEWM 7f Soft 81 4547 bl

AA YOUKNOWNOTHING 4 b c £5739
51a 12 WOLV 5f Aw 72 40
60a 3 SOUT 5f Aw 71 VIS
61a 3 WOLV 5f Aw 60 139 vis
62a 4 LING 5f Aw 62 205 vis
71a 1 LING 5f Aw 62 235* tvi
63a 6 WOLV 5f Aw 272 tvi
71a 2 LING 5f Aw 67 403 tvi
56a 7 LING 5f Aw 69 506 tvi
66a 4 LING 5f Aw 69 631 tvi
65 2 MUSS 5f Gd/Sft 62 798 tvi
60 3 WARW 5f Heavy 65 1005 tvi
0 18 BEVE 5f Firm 65 1278 tvi

ABAJANY 6 b g £1240
68 8 WIND 8f Good 77 3642
73 8 YORK 8f Good 75 3810
50 7 HAMI 8f Gd/Sft 75 3826
60 7 KEMP 8f Soft 72 4038
0 12 HAYD 8f Soft 72 4094
70 2 REDC 8f Gd/Sft 68 4499

ABBAJABBA 4 b c £23733
49a 9 SOUT 7f Aw 64 35
64 3 NOTT 6f Good 62 787
76 1 HAMI 6f Good 63 844*
80 1 EPSO 6f Heavy 74 1028+
80 3 HAMI 6f Gd/Fm 79 1192
83 1 AYR 6f Good 3366*
83 2 HAYD 6f Gd/Sft 79 4107
0 12 SALI 6f Gd/Fm 79 4165
80 4 YORK 6f Heavy 81 4301

ABBOT 2 b g £0

53 12 NEWM 6f Gd/Sft 4530

ABBY GOA 2 b f £820
65 4 LEIC 7f Gd/Fm 2916
71 5 BATH 6f Firm 3205
67 7 LING 7f Firm 3833
70 3 BRIG 7f Gd/Fm 4172 BL
3 12 YARM 8f Soft 71 4393 bl

ABCO BOY 3 b c £0
47 8 THIR 6f Gd/Sft 1354
22 10 PONT 6f Good 1500
0 14 DONC 6f Gd/Fm 48 2315
37 6 REDC 5f Gd/Fm 43 2864 BL
0 14 MUSS 7f Good 41 3103 bl
0 17 THIR 6f Gd/Fm 41 3124 bl

ABDERIAN 3 b c £3216
93 5 DONC 8f Good 735
87 13 NEWM 7f Good 955
99 2 YARM 6f Gd/Fm 2197

ABERFOLLY 2 b f £0
26 7 HAYD 6f Gd/Fm 2441
39 6 CATT 7f Gd/Fm 2927
45 7 THIR 7f Good 3127
0 14 LEIC 8f Firm 51 3837

ABERKEEN 5 ch g £10456
54a 3 WOLV 7f Aw 54 193
54a 2 SOUT 7f Aw 53 299
62a 5 SOUT 7f Aw 53 368+
64a 2 SOUT 7f Aw 59 476
62a 2 WOLV 8f Aw 59 521
67 1 SOUT 7f Good 59 803*
68 2 THIR 7f Gd/Fm 65 1158
0 15 DONC 7f Gd/Fm 66 1840
0 22 YORK 7f Good 66 3809

ABERNANT LADY 3 gr f £0
0 12 SALI 8f Firm 2024
21 5 CHEP 10f Gd/Fm 2449
0a 10 WOLV 9f Aw 3272

ABITARA 4 ch f £36143
106 1 NEWM 12f Gd/Fm 2857*
102 3 CAPA 10f Heavy 4396

ABLE AYR 3 ch c £0
60 11 DONC 6f Gd/Sft 76 1074
68 7 HAMI 6f Gd/Fm 76 1192
0 14 YORK 7f Gd/Fm 79 1308
70 5 NEWC 6f Heavy 74 1768
55 8 RIPO 5f Aw 72 2101
64 10 AYR 7f Good 72 2163
57 12 HAYD 6f Gd/Fm 69 2444
52 11 PONT 6f Gd/Fm 69 2559
59 9 CARL 5f Firm 63 3572
50 9 RIPO 6f Good 63 3698
45 11 AYR 5f Heavy 60 4307
0 11 NEWC 6f Heavy 60 4425

ABLE MILLENIUM 4 ch g £368
58a 3 WOLV 8f Aw 133
43a 8 WOLV 7f Aw 57 193
50a 7 SOUT 8f Aw 55 326
27a 10 WOLV 9f Aw 1388
44 10 YARM 10f Gd/Fm 3383
39 9 NOTT 10f Heavy 4413 BL

ABLE NATIVE 3 b f £4085
56a 7 WOLV 7f Aw 70 1390
65 2 BRIG 10f Good 68 1649
70a 1 LING 12f Aw 65 2217*
58 7 WIND 12f Good 70 2712 BL
53 12 ASCO 12f Gd/Fm 67 3014 bl
49 4 SAND 14f Good 63 3472 bl
0a 11 LING 12f Aw 63 4101 bl
55a 6 WOLV 12f Aw 67 4245 bl
42a 9 LING 12f Aw 62 4486

ABLE PETE 4 b c £2312
19a 8 LING 10f Aw 44 100

19a 9 SOUT 8f Aw 39 326
36a 5 SOUT 11f Aw 40 390
7a 9 SOUT 11f Aw 33 560
40a 2 SOUT 12f Aw 38 590
38a 1 WOLV 12f Aw 33 608*
33a 4 SOUT 12f Aw 40 682
35a 6 SOUT 11f Aw 39 1306
28 8 PONT 10f Soft 37 1705
18 12 NEWM 12f Firm 32 1852
22 10 WIND 12f Gd/Fm 29 2887
10a 10 LING 10f Aw 35 3828

ABLE SEAMAN 3 b g £4248
0 17 WIND 10f Gd/Fm 1200
72 1 LING 10f Soft 1287
54 5 SOUT 7f Soft 1607
64 3 REDC 10f Good 62 1895
55 3 REDC 11f Gd/Fm 2146
60 3 BRIG 12f Gd/Sft 64 2425
61 4 EPSO 12f Gd/Fm 62 2793
59 3 SAND 14f Gd/Fm 62 2936
53 6 BRIG 12f Gd/Fm 60 3244
54 4 YARM 10f Gd/Fm 3383
50 7 FOLK 16f Gd/Fm 58 3588 VIS
58 2 KEMP 14f Gd/Fm 54 3800 vis
37 10 NEWM 12f Good 4178 vis

ABOO HOM 6 b g £3055
43a 7 WOLV 16f Aw 55 141 t
50a 3 WOLV 16f Aw 49 194 t
53a 1 SOUT 16f Aw 49 253* t
56a 4 SOUT 16f Aw 55 284

ABOU SAFIAN 4 ch c £7685
104 2 BORD 10f Soft 4490

ABOVE BOARD 5 b g £2146
40a 5 WOLV 8f Aw 39
32a 5 SOUT 8f Aw 35 85
46a 6 SOUT 8f Aw 201
42a 5 SOUT 7f Aw 249
39a 8 SOUT 7f Aw 53 282
19a 7 SOUT 7f Aw 32 297
49a 8 SOUT 6f Aw 389 bl
59a 2 SOUT 6f Aw 472 bl
59a 2 SOUT 6f Aw 558 bl
18a 10 SOUT 7f Aw 46 598 bl
54a 3 SOUT 6f Aw 685 bl
54a 3 SOUT 6f Aw 740 bl
0 16 PONT 6f Gd/Sft 1105 bl
45a 6 SOUT 6f Aw 56 1422 bl
2 11 GOOD 5f Gd/Sft 37 1487 bl

ABRACADABJAR 2 b c £0
62 8 LING 6f Firm 3577
39 5 EPSO 9f Good 3853
0 16 BRIG 7f Soft 4172

ABSCOND 3 b f £4007
98 5 CHES 11f Gd/Fm 1223
88 1 BEVE 10f Good 1447*
96 7 ASCO 12f Good 2112
83 8 NEWC 10f Firm 2339

ABSENT FRIENDS 3 b c £1112
0 16 WIND 5f Gd/Sft 68 1098
63 4 WARW 5f Gd/Sft 1712
50 9 CHEP 6f Gd/Fm 65 2489
36a 7 WOLV 6f Aw 65 2603
54 5 PONT 5f Soft 61 4087
63 3 NEWM 5f Good 61 4185
0 14 LING 6f Soft 59 4270
0 16 NEWB 5f Gd/Sft 62 4459

ABSINTHER 3 b c £6635
42 11 HAYD 6f Soft 64 1494
61 2 MUSS 8f Gd/Fm 60 2205
55 7 NEWC 8f Good 61 2524
51 10 NEWC 7f Good 60 3033
50 5 CARL 7f Firm 3196 VIS

56	3	AYR	7f Good		3364	
57	1	**MUSS**	9f Gd/Fm		3591*	
56	2	HAMI	9f Soft	54	3806	
51	5	REDC	10f Gd/Sft	55	4221	
60a	2	WOLV	9f Aw	55	4251	
43a	5	WOLV	9f Aw	60	4382	

ABSOLUTE FANTASY 4 b f £15994

46a	4	LING	8f Aw		109	BL
29a	6	LING	8f Aw		265	bl
47a	2	LING	6f Aw		399	bl
25a	6	SOUT	6f Aw		472	bl
20a	8	LING	6f Aw	44	628	bl
48	2	LEIC	7f Good		790	bl
25	8	FOLK	6f Soft	45	958	bl
49	1	**BRIG**	6f Firm	44	1211*	bl
48	4	BRIG	6f Gd/Sft	48	1464	bl
41	7	BRIG	7f Good	48	1652	bl
50	3	BRIG	6f Gd/Fm	48	1932	bl
41	4	SALI	6f Gd/Fm	48	2230	bl
51	2	BRIG	5f Soft	48	2428	bl
39	8	WIND	6f Good	51	2716	bl
52	2	BRIG	5f Firm		2905	bl
44	4	WIND	6f Gd/Fm	50	3046	bl
52	2	BRIG	6f Gd/Fm	50	3243	bl
54	1	**NEWB**	6f Firm	50	3455*	bl
58	2	BRIG	5f Firm		3562	bl
46	7	FOLK	5f Gd/Fm		3587	bl
53	5	SALI	5f Firm	55	3747	bl
61	1	**GOOD**	5f Soft	56	4065*	bl
46	17	WIND	5f Gd/Sft	62	4295	bl
65	2	NEWB	5f Gd/Sft	62	4459	bl

ABSOLUTE MAJORITY 5 ch g £2883

36a	4	SOUT	7f Aw		130
48a	4	LING	7f Aw		156
39a	7	SOUT	8f Aw	55	176
50a	2	WOLV	9f Aw		259
42a	5	SOUT	11f Aw	50	324
55a	1	**SOUT**	12f Aw		344*
52a	3	SOUT	12f Aw	51	590
47a	5	SOUT	12f Aw	51	641

ABSTRACT 4 b f £638

0	23	REDC	6f Gd/Sft	37	1578	
42	7	CATT	7f Gd/Sft		1818	
23	10	HAMI	6f Gd/Fm	34	1941	vis
17	8	HAMI	5f Gd/Fm	34	2233	bl
36a	3	WOLV	8f Aw	36	2601	
50	4	CARL	7f Firm		2824	vis
0	24	REDC	8f Gd/Fm	31	2861	vis
0	12	REDC	8f Firm		2994	vis
0	12	REDC	8f Firm		3330	vis

ABTAAL 10 b g £2262

46a	6	WOLV	7f Aw		1038	vis
46a	8	WOLV	7f Good	55	1235	vis
52a	1	**SOUT**	7f Aw		1305*	vis
54a	3	SOUT	6f Aw	58	1421	vis
37a	6	SOUT	8f Aw		1505	vis
21	10	SOUT	7f Soft		1601	vis
48a	8	SOUT	7f Aw	57	1801	vis
35a	6	SOUT	7f Aw	55	2122	vis
32a	7	SOUT	8f Aw	53	2379	vis
32a	6	SOUT	8f Aw		2816	vis
39a	7	WOLV	7f Aw		3770	vis
0a	11	WOLV	7f Aw		4224	vis

ABU CAMP 5 b g £0

42a	6	LING	8f Aw		264	t

ABUZAID 3 b c £9076

69	16	NEWM	7f Good	87	954
0	19	NEWM	7f Gd/Fm	85	1153
67	9	NEWM	8f Firm	81	1853
82	1	**SALI**	10f Gd/Fm	78	2270*
79	5	HAYD	12f Gd/Fm	84	2702
85	3	DONC	10f Gd/Fm	84	3159
85	2	REDC	11f Firm	84	3329

84	4	RIPO	10f Gd/Fm	85	3713

ABYSSINIAN WOLF 2 ch c £0

0	19	DONC	7f Gd/Sft		4447

ACADEMIC ACCURACY 2 b f £0

81	7	ASCO	7f Good		2091
61	6	WIND	6f Gd/Fm		2886

ACADEMIC GOLD 2 ch c £537

75	3	NOTT	8f Good		3523

ACADEMIC RECORD 2 b c £0

53	7	CHES	7f Firm		3169
37	8	CHES	10f Gd/Fm		3508
48	5	HAMI	5f Soft		3801

ACAMANI 3 £0

110	6	BADE	12f V		3849

ACANTHUS 4 ch c £1694

75	3	FRAU	12f Good		1903

ACCEPTING 3 b c £645

79	6	NEWM	10f Good		957
82	4	CHES	12f Gd/Fm	83	1225

ACCOUNTING 4 b f £0

32	10	BATH	12f Good	67	1091

ACCYSTAN 5 ch g £3336

20a	12	SOUT	11f Aw	69	390
47a	6	WOLV	9f Aw	69	447
57a	2	SOUT	12f Aw		498
46a	7	SOUT	11f Aw	59	561
56a	1	**SOUT**	12f Aw	50	642*
46a	6	SOUT	12f Aw	56	671
55a	3	SOUT	11f Aw	55	742
57a	3	SOUT	11f Aw	55	1306
51a	5	SOUT	16f Aw	55	1416
38	9	CATT	14f Soft	54	1683
35	8	HAMI	12f Gd/Fm	50	1908

ACE OF PARKES 4 b c £589

83	5	CHES	5f Firm	85	1245
69	11	YORK	5f Gd/Fm	84	1983
76	6	CHES	5f Gd/Fm	82	2247
91	5	CHES	7f Gd/Fm		2670
55	9	WARW	6f Gd/Fm	80	2845
48	9	HAYD	6f Gd/Fm		3283
78	3	AYR	6f Good		3366
52	15	CARL	5f Firm		3572
0	28	AYR	6f Gd/Sft	76	4010
59	8	CHES	6f Soft		4069
55a	9	WOLV	6f Aw	70	4380

ACE OF TRUMPS 4 b g £10909

0a	16	SOUT	8f Aw		45	tbl
55	1	**MUSS**	9f Gd/Sft	50	795*	t
0	13	HAMI	9f Good	55	846	t
12	11	WARW	11f Heavy	55	889	t
37	9	DONC	10f Gd/Sft	53	1050	t
40	7	PONT	8f Gd/Fm	53	1101	t
53	1	**HAMI**	9f		1195*	t
52	2	HAMI	11f Gd/Fm	51	1361	t
0	12	MUSS	9f Firm	51	1689	t
36	3	REDC	10f Gd/Fm		2143	t
0	11	BEVE	7f Gd/Fm	49	2479	t
38	7	HAMI	9f Gd/Fm		2642	t
40	2	HAMI	9f Gd/Fm		2780	t
43	5	AYR	11f Firm		2875	t
37	6	AYR	9f Gd/Fm	41	3141	t
26	4	HAMI	9f Gd/Fm		3375	t
35	3	HAMI	8f Gd/Sft	38	3534	t
30	5	HAMI	11f Soft	37	3805	t
37	2	HAMI	9f Gd/Fm		3823	t
45	3	AYR	9f Heavy		4324	t
44	2	NEWC	10f Heavy	41	4427	t
47	1	**MUSS**	9f Soft	43	4523*	t
39	8	MUSS	8f Soft	49	4565	t

ACEBO LYONS 5 b m £7149

22a	9	WOLV	12f Aw	49	170	vis
60	1	**DONC**	10f Gd/Fm	56	705*	

58	6	LEIC	10f Good	62	793	
55	6	NOTT	10f Gd/Sft	59	1370	
61	5	YARM	10f Gd/Sft	59	1615	
48	8	NEWM	12f Firm		1852	
56	4	NEWC	16f Gd/Fm	57	2273	
47	7	CHEP	12f Gd/Fm	55	2656	
54	3	PONT	12f Gd/Fm	55	2829	
57	2	KEMP	12f Gd/Fm	54	3073	
0	18	YORK	10f Gd/Fm	57	3731	
39	1	**YARM**	14f Soft		4510*	
57	4	NEWM	12f Gd/Sft	61	4534	

ACHILLES SKY 4 b c £6114

75	1	**SOUT**	12f Good	71	805*	
65	10	NEWM	12f Firm	77	1187	
51	11	HAYD	14f Gd/Sft	77	1536	
75	2	YORK	12f Firm		1984	
75	3	NEWC	10f Gd/Fm		2314	
47	8	EPSO	12f Gd/Sft	75	2626	
65	7	EPSO	10f Gd/Fm		3403	
0	13	YARM	10f Firm	74	3941	VIS

ACHILLES SPIRIT 2 b c £5903

70	11	WIND	6f Gd/Fm		1876
80	1	**EPSO**	6f Gd/Sft		2628*
82	3	GOOD	7f Firm	78	3149
69	6	NEWC	8f Gd/Sft	81	3704
53	8	YORK	7f Soft	80	4279

ACHILLES SUN 2 b c £511

0	U	SAND	7f Gd/Fm		2494
68	4	ASCO	7f Good		2677
73	10	GOOD	7f Firm		3154
55	8	NEWC	7f Gd/Sft		3705
62a	7	WOLV	8f Aw		4022
0	17	LING	6f Soft	65	4269

ACHILLES WINGS 4 b c £3060

70a	3	LING	10f Aw		629
48a	4	WOLV	8f Aw		661
60	4	NOTT	8f Good		784
69	2	DONC	10f Gd/Sft	65	1050
42	10	NEWM	10f Gd/Fm	65	1150
71	2	NEWB	13f Gd/Sft	69	1594
42	12	NEWB	13f Gd/Fm	69	1784

ACID TEST 5 ch g £1227

51a	8	LING	7f Aw	65	525	
43a	6	LING	8f Aw	62	596	
46a	6	LING	6f Aw	58	691	
66	3	CATT	7f Gd/Fm	68	780	
0	16	THIR	6f Gd/Sft	68	1356	BL
50	12	CATT	7f Soft	66	1680	
55	7	LEIC	8f Firm	64	2027	
64	3	THIR	7f Gd/Fm	64	2063	
52	12	CARL	8f Gd/Fm	62	2242	
0	15	DONC	8f Gd/Fm	65	2349	
63	7	CATT	8f Gd/Fm	65	2420	
59	5	CATT	7f Gd/Fm		2437	
47	8	BEVE	7f Good	62	2882	
54	6	CATT	7f Gd/Fm	60	3200	VIS
57	7	CHEP	7f Good	58	3871	
27	10	CHES	10f Soft	56	4074	

ACORN CATCHER 2 b f £4740

35	13	WARW	5f Soft		812
65	1	**LEIC**	5f Gd/Fm		2507*
60	3	LEIC	6f Gd/Fm	64	2773
52	8	BATH	5f Firm		3204
45	7	LING	5f Firm	59	3491
63a	1	**WOLV**	5f Aw		4227*
63a	3	WOLV	6f Aw		4359

ACQUITTAL 8 b g £855

0	15	HAYD	11f Soft	35	1819	
31	11	NEWM	12f Firm	35	1852	vis
32	4	RIPO	12f Gd/Fm	35	2109	vis
34	4	BEVE	12f Gd/Fm	37	2482	vis
52	5	CHES	12f Good		2667	

33	3	NOTT	14f Gd/Fm	35	3002	vis
29	8	THIR	16f Gd/Fm	35	3348	vis
24	7	BEVE	12f Gd/Fm	31	3674	vis
29	6	WARW	16f Gd/Fm	38	3916	vis

ACROBATIC 3 br c £5661

99	6	NEWM	7f Good		955
100	2	NEWM	7f Firm		1186
100	2	NOTT	8f Good		1872

ACT OF REFORM 2 b c £7496

62	5	LING	6f Firm		2760
84a	1	**WOLV**	7f Aw		3497*
82	4	BATH	8f Gd/Fm	83	3817
86	3	AYR	8f Soft	83	3990
85a	1	**SOUT**	8f Aw		4152*

ACTION JACKSON 8 ch g £0

0a	12	SOUT	16f Aw	33	737	t
29	5	WARW	13f Gd/Fm	33	2843	
21	8	NOTT	14f Gd/Fm	29	3002	
10	7	BRIG	12f Gd/Fm	28	3260	

ACTIVIST 2 ch c £0

58	8	AYR	7f Soft		3962

ACTUALLY 3 b f £0

31a	8	SOUT	8f Aw		48	
0a	10	WOLV	8f Aw		80	BL
0	14	BRIG	10f Firm	40	3530	
0	8	YARM	11f Firm		3917	

ADAMAS 3 b f £5131

102	7	YORK	10f Gd/Fm		1309
62	4	THIR	8f Gd/Sft		1717
71	1	**BEVE**	8f Firm		2222*
58	12	NEWM	8f Gd/Fm	86	2614
60	8	NOTT	8f Gd/Fm	82	3005
71	4	REDC	11f Firm	73	3329
72	3	NEWC	12f Firm	72	3606
0	U	LEIC	10f Firm	71	3842
0	16	BRIG	10f Gd/Sft	71	4118
43	13	DONC	10f Gd/Sft	69	4448

ADAWAR 3 b c £5885

72	5	PONT	10f Soft		873
71	6	DONC	10f Gd/Sft		1054
78	2	REDC	10f Gd/Sft		1582
80	1	**BEVE**	7f Firm		1922*
80	3	NEWC	8f Gd/Fm	79	2311
75	6	BATH	10f Gd/Sft	80	2552

ADDICKS ADDICTS 3 b c £0

21a	8	LING	5f Aw		487

ADDITION 4 b f £352

43	9	CHEP	7f Gd/Fm	58	1799
0	15	BATH	5f Gd/Sft	56	2555
53	4	SALI	7f Gd/Fm	53	2978
41	6	BATH	8f Firm	53	3207
39	12	CHEP	7f Good	52	3871

ADELPHI BOY 4 ch c £15329

77a	9	SOUT	8f Aw	90	251
97a	3	WOLV	8f Aw	90	448
102	1	**WOLV**	9f Aw		480*
95a	4	SOUT	7f Aw		539
70	6	THIR	8f Good	72	1160
0	17	YORK	12f Gd/Fm	70	1307
0	21	YORK	6f Good	70	3543
71	2	LEIC	7f Firm	70	3839
73	1	**YARM**	8f Firm	67	3936*
27	15	YORK	9f Heavy	71	4300
98	4	DONC	7f Soft		4465

ADILABAD 3 b c £46433

109	5	NEWM	8f Gd/Sft		981
116	1	**GOOD**	8f Firm		3150*
117	1	**WIND**	10f Gd/Fm		3641*
109	3	LONG	10f Good		4238

ADIOS 2 b c £0

82	5	NEWM	7f Good		3608

ADIRPOUR 6 gr g £2901

29a	8	SOUT	8f Aw		50
32a	6	SOUT	8f Aw	37	85
46a	7	WOLV	8f Aw		138
35a	3	SOUT	11f Aw		178
19a	9	WOLV	12f Aw		231
23a	9	SOUT	8f Aw		252
35a	6	SOUT	12f Aw		344
27a	5	WOLV	9f Aw		360
30a	8	WOLV	9f Aw		433
42a	4	SOUT	12f Aw		498
54a	1	**SOUT**	12f Aw		556*
16a	5	WOLV	12f Aw		626
37a	4	SOUT	11f Aw		670
34a	7	WOLV	12f Aw		710
27	8	RIPO	12f Soft	39	822
42a	3	SOUT	8f Aw		869
32a	7	WOLV	12f Aw		1039
21a	8	SOUT	12f Aw		1203
0a	14	SOUT	7f Aw		1305
45a	4	SOUT	11f Aw		1417
33	3	LEIC	8f Gd/Sft		1732
41a	6	SOUT	11f Aw		1978
0a	11	SOUT	11f Aw		2119

ADJAWAR 2 b c £0

34	14	LING	7f Soft		4483

ADJOURNMENT 2 b c £6882

66	7	GOOD	6f Gd/Sft		1472
87	1	**SAND**	7f Gd/Fm		1988*
77	6	SAND	7f Good		2474
90	2	THIR	7f Gd/Fm		2966
88	4	KEMP	7f Gd/Fm		3361
74	11	BATH	8f Gd/Fm	85	3817

ADJUTANT 5 b g £23255

94	3	KEMP	7f Good	92	725
82	15	NEWM	8f Gd/Sft	93	966
95	3	KEMP	8f Gd/Sft	93	1077
96	1	**LING**	7f Soft	93	1286*
100	2	DONC	7f Good	97	1514
83	10	HAYD	7f Gd/Sft		1834
98	6	NEWB	7f Firm		2809
90	8	GOOD	7f Firm		3155
88	7	YORK	10f Gd/Fm	97	3563
91	2	BATH	8f Soft		4142
84	6	YORK	7f Soft	95	4278
84	5	DONC	7f Soft		4465

ADMIRALS FLAME 9 b g £2765

52	7	WIND	8f Gd/Fm	56	1201
60	1	**NOTT**	8f Soft	55	1646*
62	3	WIND	8f Gd/Fm	60	2367
58	3	WIND	8f Soft	60	2546
0	13	LEIC	8f Gd/Fm		4032

ADMIRALS PLACE 4 ch c £15633

57a	5	LING	10f Aw	58	220
64a	1	**LING**	10f Aw		268*
67a	2	LING	10f Aw	65	400
65a	2	LING	10f Aw	65	575
63	3	LEIC	10f Good	64	793
68	1	**FOLK**	10f Soft	64	965*
69	4	DONC	10f Gd/Sft	67	1070
69	2	NEWB	10f Good	67	1375
55a	8	LING	12f Aw	65	1677
66	5	EPSO	10f Gd/Fm		3403
67	3	KEMP	10f Gd/Fm	67	3794
70	2	CHES	10f Soft	67	4074
71	2	YORK	10f Soft	67	4282
51	10	NEWB	10f Sft/Hv	69	4473

ADMIRALS SECRET 11 ch g £2404

43	5	BRIG	12f Gd/Fm	50	1128
42	7	PONT	12f Good	47	1499
51	1	**YARM**	11f Gd/Sft	48	1614*
40	9	NEWM	12f Firm	51	1852
36	6	KEMP	12f Gd/Fm	50	2081
42	10	SALI	12f Good	49	2689

ADOBE 5 b g £40956

30a	8	WOLV	8f Aw	49	38	t
55a	1	**WOLV**	7f Aw	47	754*	
45a	9	SOUT	7f Aw	55	867	
58a	2	WOLV	8f Aw	55	921	
58a	4	WOLV	7f Aw		1038	
54	2	HAMI	8f Firm	49	1243	
54	1	**HAMI**	8f Gd/Fm	49	1360*	
66	1	**HAMI**	8f Gd/Fm		1940*	
68	1	**BATH**	8f Firm	59	1998*	
66	1	**GOOD**	8f Gd/Fm	59	2126+	
72	3	GOOD	7f Good	72	2303	
69	3	GOOD	8f Gd/Fm	66	2356	
67	4	YORK	8f Gd/Fm	68	2645	
71	1	**DONC**	8f Gd/Fm	68	2758*	
73	2	NOTT	8f Gd/Fm	72	3115	
77	1	**THIR**	8f Gd/Fm	72	3147*	
82	1	**HAYD**	8f Gd/Fm	77	3325*	
76	7	YORK	8f Firm	91	3597	
81	5	WIND	8f Good	83	3642	
65	11	GOOD	9f Good	82	3883	
67	8	ASCO	8f Gd/Sft	81	4126	
0	17	NOTT	8f Heavy	80	4506	
0	21	DONC	7f Heavy	80	4574	

ADORABLE 4 b f £0

0a	11	LING	6f Aw		484

ADORNMENT 4 b f £0

0a	12	WOLV	8f Aw		136

ADRIANA 3 b f £4745

37	8	KEMP	6f Good		729
32	13	WARW	8f Heavy		884
43	10	WIND	10f Firm		1293
39	8	YARM	10f Gd/Sft	42	1615
44	1	**LING**	11f Firm	39	1914*
5a	7	LING	12f Aw	43	2217
46	1	**BRIG**	10f Firm	42	2908*
36	4	BRIG	10f Gd/Fm	46	3263
0	14	FOLK	12f Gd/Fm	49	3586

ADRIFT 3 ch f £1448

61	8	NEWM	7f Gd/Fm		1155	
65	7	BEVE	10f Good		1447	
65	2	SALI	10f Good		3289	
0	20	GOOD	8f Good	62	3885	
50a	3	WOLV	9f Aw	59	4251	t
25a	10	WOLV	8f Aw	57	4440	t

ADULATION 6 ch g £0

44	10	NEWC	7f Soft		759	
32	15	CARL	9f Firm	60	1254	
0	12	CARL	9f Firm		2282	
0	16	BEVE	7f Gd/Fm	55	2479	BL

ADWEB 2 b f £4943

50	13	WIND	6f Gd/Fm		1876
45	8	BEVE	5f Gd/Sft		3055
58	4	SAND	5f Gd/Fm		3942
64	1	**SAND**	5f Soft	60	4202*
66	7	NEWM	6f Good		4338
56	10	NEWB	6f Stft/Hvy	67	4468

AEGEAN DREAM 4 b f £26331

78	2	WIND	10f Gd/Fm		747
79	3	WIND	12f Good	78	853
72	4	BATH	12f Good	78	1091
75	4	KEMP	10f Soft	78	1528
79	3	NEWB	10f Gd/Fm	76	1785
80	3	KEMP	9f Gd/Fm	79	2262
82	1	**NEWB**	9f Firm	78	2853*
88	1	**GOOD**	9f Gd/Fm	81	3089*
86	7	SAND	8f Good		3469
88	4	NEWB	10f Good	87	3997
78	13	NEWM	9f Gd/Fm	87	4212

AEGEAN FLAME 4 ch f £0

53	6	LING	7f Gd/Sft		838
45	12	BRIG	7f Firm	65	1213

AEGEAN FLOWER 3 b g £1311

0	14	NEWB	8f Good		1377	
47	4	LING	7f Good		1675	BL
59	8	SALI	7f Gd/Fm		1886	bl
44	10	SALI	8f Gd/Fm	57	2264	bl
14	10	FOLK	12f Good	52	2624	bl
0	13	EPSO	9f Good	52	2795	bl
50	3	SALI	7f Gd/Fm	49	2980	bl
47	4	SALI	7f Gd/Fm	49	3294	bl
0	15	BATH	8f Firm	49	3623	bl
46	3	YARM	8f Gd/Fm	48	3971	bl

AEGEAN WIND 3 b c £0

68	5	KEMP	12f Gd/Fm		1929
65	9	SALI	10f Gd/Fm		2265
47	7	YARM	14f Firm	67	2902
46	12	SALI	14f Gd/Fm	67	3424

AESKULAP 3 b c £15484

106	2	DORT	14f Heavy		4265

AFAAN 7 ch h £5066

78a	4	WOLV	5f Aw	80	64	bl
82a	3	LING	6f Aw	80	113	bl
82a	3	WOLV	6f Aw	81	191	bl
64a	8	LING	6f Aw	81	223	bl
85	19	NEWM	5f Gd/Fm		1172	bl
94	6	YORK	5f Firm	95	1324	bl
93	4	GOOD	6f Gd/Sft		1453	
66	11	EPSO	5f Good	96	1849	bl
99	2	YARM	6f Gd/Fm		1952	
0	15	NEWC	5f Gd/Fm	94	2310	bl
102	4	NEWM	5f Good		2960	bl
83	12	GOOD	5f Good		3059	bl
59	19	EPSO	5f Good	93	3687	bl
85	7	YARM	5f Firm	90	3920	
94	5	YARM	6f Firm		3937	
0	16	NEWM	5f Good		4182	
84	9	NEWM	5f Good	90	4339	bl
73	11	DONC	5f Soft	87	4466	bl

AFFARATI 2 b c £7154

77	2	PONT	5f Gd/Fm		1102
79	1	PONT	6f Good		1497*
82	6	BEVE	5f Gd/Sft		1761
67	7	PONT	6f Gd/Fm	80	2557
75	5	REDC	7f Good		2991
56	10	YORK	7f Good	74	3542

AFFIANCED 2 b f £16250

101	1	CURR	7f Good		3555*	BL
0	7	CURR	7f Gd/Fm		3845	bl

AFFIRMED SUCCESS 6 b g £46414

119	3	WOOD	8f Firm		3933

AFGHAN 2 ch c £1025

73	12	NEWM	6f Good		4341	t
0	15	NEWB	6f Stf/Hvy		4470	t
85	2	DONC	7f Heavy		4567	t

AFRICA 3 b f £5113

61a	1	SOUT	7f Aw	56	1202*
45	6	RIPO	8f Good		1596
40	7	CARL	7f Firm	54	2017
47a	4	SOUT	7f Aw		2633
52	1	BEVE	7f Firm		2731*
40	6	CARL	8f Gd/Fm	51	3082
39	8	BEVE	8f Good		3393
42	4	BEVE	7f Gd/Fm		3671

AFRICAN CZAR 2 b c £502

78a	D	WOLV	6f Aw		4379

AFRICAN PETE 3 b c £696

53	6	SALI	8f Good	65	1345
56	7	SALI	7f Gd/Fm	63	1889
62	2	BATH	10f Firm	60	2332
55	6	WIND	10f Good		2372
55	6	BEVE	10f Good		2884
50	7	BRIG	10f Firm	61	3530

0	18	YARM	8f Gd/Fm	59	3971	BL

AFTER EIGHT 5 b g £0

15a	10	WOLV	8f Aw		322

AFTER THE BLUE 3 b c £12992

46	16	NEWM	10f Good		957
59	9	KEMP	8f Gd/Sft		1080
49	6	BATH	8f Gd/Sft	62	1671
65	4	GOOD	10f Gd/Sft	62	1812
64	1	NOTT	10f Good		2012*
65	2	NEWC	12f Gd/Fm	62	2272
67	2	SALI	12f Gd/Sft	62	2470
67	4	KEMP	12f Gd/Fm	65	2872
67	5	ASCO	12f Gd/Fm	66	3014
79	1	SALI	12f Gd/Fm	66	3290*
73	2	EPSO	12f Gd/Fm	72	3417
76	2	NEWB	10f Firm	75	3453
68	7	THIR	12f Gd/Sft	75	3778
61	10	CATT	12f Soft	74	4003
60	4	BRIG	12f Gd/Fm	73	4123
0	18	BATH	12f Soft	70	4433

AFTERJACKO 4 ch c £45965

84	5	NEWM	14f Gd/Fm	83	968
88	1	SALI	14f Firm	83	1180*
91	2	YORK	14f Firm	88	1329
91	7	ASCO	12f Good	91	2069
77	14	NEWC	16f Firm	91	2336
89	5	GOOD	14f Gd/Fm	89	3058
88	6	ASCO	16f Gd/Fm	89	3302
92	4	YORK	14f Gd/Fm	89	3565
98	2	DONC	15f Firm	91	3890
101	1	NEWB	13f Firm	95	3994*

AGENT LE BLANC 5 b g £0

0	P	CHEP	18f Gd/Fm	70	2490
0	8	SAND	14f Gd/Fm	70	2923

AGENT MULDER 6 b g £3235

67	2	WARW	7f Soft		816	bl
73	3	PONT	6f Heavy	71	941	bl
64	3	DONC	6f Gd/Sft		1068	bl
61	8	NEWB	6f Gd/Sft	70	1591	bl
55	2	SAND	5f Soft		4207	bl

AGILE DANCER 2 ch f £0

0	16	NEWB	5f Good		1782
0	17	LING	5f Gd/Fm		2214
59	5	BRIG	7f Firm		3558
0	27	NEWM	7f Good		4336

AGIOTAGE 4 br c £5946

0a	10	SOUT	16f Aw	73	253
0	19	WIND	12f Gd/Fm	70	748
0	15	FOLK	15f Soft	60	963
57	1	MUSS	9f Firm	50	2049*
35a	6	LING	10f Aw	51	2186
57	1	MUSS	8f Firm	54	2378*
53	5	BRIG	8f Gd/Fm	57	2726
55	6	RIPO	9f Gd/Fm	57	3011
54	4	NOTT	10f Good	57	3524
56	4	MUSS	8f Gd/Fm	57	3745
0	13	BEVE	8f Good	55	3951

AGNES FOR RANSOM 2 b f £0

47	13	NEWM	6f Gd/Sft		4530

AGNES WORLD 5 br h £126750

120	2	ASCO	5f Good		2065
120	1	NEWM	6f Gd/Fm		2615*

AGO 2 ch f £0

39	8	REDC	10f Gd/Fm		2990

AGOL LACK 4 ch c £49953

113	2	LONG	10f Good		2072
117	1	DEAU	10f Good		3370*
117	1	MAIS	10f Good		4050*

AGRIPPINA 3 b f £0

100	13	NEWM	8f Firm		1185
102	8	YORK	10f Gd/Fm		1309

AGUA CABALLO 3 b g £0

24a	10	SOUT	7f Aw	64	416
53a	7	LING	7f Aw	59	488
47a	5	WOLV	8f Aw	54	566

AHOUOD 4 b f £1684

37a	4	SOUT	7f Aw		367
44a	2	WOLV	9f Aw		446
43a	2	WOLV	8f Aw		490
35a	5	SOUT	8f Aw	43	585
40	6	HAYD	7f Gd/Sft	50	811
36	9	WARW	11f Soft	48	1065
33a	4	LING	10f Aw	41	1265
25	10	FOLK	10f Gd/Fm	44	2296
34	8	WARW	11f Good	44	2463
23a	6	WOLV	8f Aw	38	2601
0	15	WIND	12f Gd/Fm	39	3049

AHRAAR 2 b c £0

81	11	NEWM	8f Good		4349

AILINCALA 2 b f £0

0	U	NEWM	6f Gd/Fm		2285
57	8	NEWM	6f Gd/Fm		2618
77	5	WARW	7f Gd/Fm		3910
58	6	BRIG	7f Soft		4172

AINTNECESSARILYSO 2 ch c £2033

82	8	NEWB	6f Gd/Fm		1403	
75	8	NEWB	6f Gd/Fm		1943	
76	6	SALI	7f Gd/Fm		2269	
80	7	GOOD	5f Gd/Fm		3064	
79	2	SALI	8f Gd/Fm		3387	
73	3	EPSO	8f Good		3852	
59	7	BATH	8f Soft		4138	BL
65	12	NEWM	6f Good	72	4338	
71	4	WIND	6f Heavy	70	4525	

AIR DEFENCE 3 br c £15891

92	2	NEWM	10f Good		957
90	1	CHES	10f Gd/Fm		1218*
93	9	NEWM	10f Gd/Fm	96	2596
80	15	YORK	12f Good	94	3541
94	2	DONC	10f Firm	90	3899
88	8	NEWM	9f Gd/Fm	94	4212

AIR MAIL 3 b f £7160

64a	2	SOUT	8f Aw		415	
75a	1	LING	7f Aw		651*	
41	17	WIND	6f Good	77	852	
75a	5	LING	8f Aw	77	1259	
0a	12	SOUT	8f Aw	75	1504	
54	8	CHES	7f Gd/Fm	74	2250	BL
47	10	CHEP	10f Gd/Fm	74	2450	VIS
29	8	LEIC	7f Gd/Fm		3218	vis
57a	1	WOLV	7f Aw		3770*	
50	8	LEIC	8f Gd/Sft		4032	
60	2	LING	7f Soft	60	4192	
0	16	WIND	6f Gd/Sft	56	4294	
53	5	DONC	7f Gd/Sft	60	4452	

AIR MARSHALL 3 ch c £189970

110	2	HAYD	12f Gd/Fm		2503
111	2	GOOD	12f Gd/Fm		3061
117	1	YORK	12f Good		3540*
117	2	DONC	15f Firm		3898

AIR OF ESTEEM 4 b g £1606

68	3	THIR	8f Gd/Sft	69	1718	
60	5	HAYD	11f Gd/Stt	69	1790	
58a	7	SOUT	8f Aw	69	2121	
65	4	LEIC	7f Gd/Fm		2508	
62a	5	SOUT	8f Aw		2946	VIS
67a	2	WOLV	8f Aw	63	3499	

AIR SHAKUR 5 b g £0

103	5	ASCO	12f Gd/Fm		2998

AIRA FORCE 3 ch g £1140

81a	2	LING	5f Aw	81	774
62	12	CHES	5f Gd/Fm	81	1219
60	13	EPSO	5f Good	80	3855
0	28	NEWM	5f Good	74	4185

AIRLINE 3 £0
| 106 | 7 | LONG | 10f Good | | 4263 | |

AISLE 3 b c £1882
36a	6	SOUT	8f Aw	61	128	
30a	9	WOLV	7f Aw	59	188	
58a	5	WOLV	7f Aw	57	257	BL
59a	2	SOUT	6f Aw	57	331	bl
59a	2	SOUT	6f Aw	56	365	bl
45a	5	SOUT	7f Aw	60	416	bl
50a	5	WOLV	6f Aw	60	479	
32	8	NOTT	6f Good	61	785	
59	5	WARW	7f Heavy	60	887	bl
0	14	NOTT	5f Good	59	1412	bl
0	16	BEVE	8f Sft/Hvy	57	4045	
0a	15	SOUT	6f Aw	57	4156	tbl
45	10	DONC	7f Gd/Sft	55	4452	tbl
56	4	REDC	7f Gd/Sft	55	4498	tbl

AIWIN 3 b c £1577
0	20	THIR	6f Soft		909	
68a	4	WOLV	9f Aw		1388	t
65	5	HAYD	8f Gd/Fm		1837	
68a	3	SOUT	8f Aw		1977	t
39	9	WIND	10f Good		2372	t
51a	5	SOUT	11f Aw	69	2945	
63a	3	WOLV	9f Aw		3272	t
52a	2	WOLV	9f Aw		3498	tBL

AIX EN PROVENCE 5 b g £0
40a	10	LING	10f Aw		1	
31a	7	LING	8f Aw		92	
49	5	YARM	7f Firm		3921	

AJDAR 9 b g £0
0a	11	SOUT	14f Aw		124	
14a	10	SOUT	12f Aw	42	215	
6a	10	SOUT	12f Aw	37	641	

AJJAE 4 b c £0
31a	10	WOLV	9f Aw	41	67	bl
20	10	HAMI	9f Gd/Fm		1191	bl
0	15	HAMI	11f Gd/Fm	39	1361	bl
0	14	AYR	8f Gd/Fm	36	1658	bl

AJNAD 6 b g £1023
44a	10	SOUT	7f Aw	74	282	
52a	8	SOUT	6f Aw	72	342	
52a	8	SOUT	6f Aw	72	386	
49a	7	SOUT	6f Aw	69	454	
62a	5	SOUT	6f Aw	65	499	
40	11	NOTT	6f Firm	57	1273	
57	6	PONT	5f Good		1868	
46	6	YARM	6f Gd/Fm	55	1953	
0	17	NEWM	6f Gd/Fm	56	2961	bl
53	4	GOOD	5f Gd/Fm	55	3091	bl
50	7	NOTT	5f Good		3113	bl
54a	3	SOUT	6f Aw	58	4156	
0	23	YORK	6f Soft		4287	bl

AJWAA 2 ch c £9461
87	2	GOOD	6f Good		3881	
96	1	NEWM	6f Good		4341*	
89	4	NEWM	6f Gd/Sft		4535	

AJYAAL 3 b c £672
0	9	SOUT	6f Soft		1605	
31	11	SALI	6f Gd/Fm		2977	BL
70	3	YARM	6f Firm		3919	t
0	19	NEWM	5f Good	70	4185	tbl

AKALIM 7 b g £0
0	17	GOOD	7f Gd/Sft	68	1483	
56	5	CHEP	7f Gd/Sft	66	1799	
55	10	CHEP	7f Good	66	1969	
0	14	BRIG	7f Gd/Sft	63	4121	

AKATIB 2 b f £0
| 0 | 16 | DONC | 5f Good | | 730 | |
| 47 | 8 | REDC | 5f Gd/Fm | | 1558 | |

AKBAR 4 b c £40147
99	1	DIEL	12f Good		1119*	
99	1	FRAU	12f Good		1903*	
98	11	ASCO	12f Good	103	2069	
97	6	HAYD	12f Gd/Fm	99	2502	
98	4	GOOD	10f Gd/Fm	97	3060	
99	1	DIEL	16f Good		3553*	
102	1	DIEL	12f Good		4148*	

AKEBONO 4 ch g £0
39	10	SAND	5f Good	63	3436	
51	11	KEMP	7f Gd/Fm	62	3796	
0	13	LING	7f Good	60	4102	bl
48	9	WIND	6f Gd/Sft	56	4293	bl
49	5	YARM	7f Soft	53	4513	

AKEED 3 ch c £4455
111	4	MAIS	7f Heavy		9	
79	5	NEWM	10f Gd/Fm		1151	
76	5	BATH	8f Soft		4142	
0	19	NEWM	12f Good	95	4342	

AKER WOOD 2 b f £1338
67	7	GOOD	6f Gd/Fm		1957	
80	2	KEMP	7f Gd/Sft		2583	
78	7	GOOD	7f Good		3108	
78	5	YORK	7f Good	82	3542	
0	16	DONC	7f Firm	82	3901	
0	22	NEWM	7f Good	82	4157	

AKHIRA 3 b f £1034
| 80 | 10 | NEWM | 7f Gd/Sft | | 971 | |
| 69 | 2 | YARM | 7f Soft | | 4387 | |

AL AWAALAH 3 b f £562
34	8	BATH	8f Gd/Fm		1436	
50	10	WIND	10f Good		1725	
44	8	WARW	8f Good		2464	
0	15	LEIC	8f Gd/Fm	50	3095	
45	3	NEWM	8f Gd/Sft	45	4536	

AL AZHAR 6 b g £0
88	5	NEWC	10f Soft	94	757	
61	13	YORK	10f Gd/Fm	92	3563	
75	6	KEMP	12f Soft		4039	
69	6	YORK	10f Soft		4275	
72	8	YARM	10f Soft	79	4392	

AL GHABRAA 3 ch f £0
74	6	KEMP	8f Soft		995	
91	5	AYR	8f Gd/Fm		1630	
70	8	NEWB	9f Firm	88	2853	
75	7	THIR	8f Gd/Fm	83	3147	
39	10	SAND	10f Good	78	3471	

AL IHSAS 2 b f £13746
| 91 | 2 | BATH | 6f Gd/Sft | | 1667 | |
| 99 | 2 | ASCO | 5f Good | | 2088 | |

AL KING SLAYER 3 b c £756
| 6a | 8 | SOUT | 8f Aw | | 415 | |
| 75 | 2 | FOLK | 7f Soft | | 961 | |

AL MABROOK 5 b g £3786
63a	5	LING	7f Aw	66	59	
38a	7	LING	8f Aw	66	97	
0a	16	SOUT	7f Aw	62	216	
62a	1	WOLV	9f Aw	58	270*	
40a	8	WOLV	9f Aw	61	469	
29a	8	WOLV	12f Aw	60	554	
29	8	BEVE	8f Gd/Fm	55	3054	
40	10	HAYD	8f Good	56	3288	
50	3	THIR	8f Gd/Fm	49	3344	
45	5	REDC	11f Gd/Fm	50	3636	
46	7	YORK	9f Good		3808	
0	16	AYR	11f Soft	49	3963	
40a	5	SOUT	11f Aw		4151	BL
38a	11	LING	9f Aw		4331	bl
52a	4	WOLV	8f Aw	53	4363	bl

AL MUALLIM 6 b g £10571
99	3	KEMP	6f Good	97	728	
80	16	NEWM	7f Gd/Sft	97	966	
72	7	KEMP	6f Soft		1016	
0	25	ASCO	6f Good	95	2151	
0	18	NEWC	6f Firm	93	2334	
82	9	AYR	7f Firm	89	2878	t
86	4	ASCO	6f Gd/Fm	89	2954	t
77	11	GOOD	8f Firm	89	3152	t
91	1	EPSO	7f Gd/Fm	87	3414*	t
68	13	YORK	8f Firm	91	3597	t
0	20	DONC	7f Gd/Fm	90	3880	t
82	10	AYR	6f Gd/Sft	90	4012	t
80	13	ASCO	7f Good	90	4112	t
87	4	YORK	7f Soft	89	4278	t
83	10	NEWM	7f Good	88	4357	t

AL RABEH 8 ch g £0
| 22a | 6 | LING | 16f Aw | | 402 | |

AL TOWD 3 b c £729
87	11	HAYD	8f Gd/Sft	94	810	
93	5	BATH	10f Good		1089	
89	4	SALI	12f Good		1347	
78	6	NEWM	10f Good		4017	
0	17	NEWM	12f Good	89	4342	

ALABAMA JACKS 4 ch c £0
| 108 | 2 | CAPA | 8f Heavy | | 11 | |

ALABAMA WURLEY 3 b f £1939
52	8	SOUT	10f Good	65	807	
0	19	DONC	8f Gd/Sft	63	1053	
7a	9	WOLV	8f Aw		1234	
46	10	NOTT	8f Gd/Sft	60	1365	VIS
48	6	YARM	8f Gd/Sft	56	1610	
42	9	SALI	7f Gd/Fm	52	1889	
26	12	NOTT	8f Gd/Fm	49	2187	
47	1	YARM	7f Gd/Fm		2413*	vis
35	8	BEVE	7f Firm		2731	vis
41	4	YARM	8f Good	46	3236	vis
25	9	NEWM	8f Good		3456	vis
0	11	NEWM	7f Good		3612	

ALABAMY SOUND 4 ch f £188
44	4	HAMI	9f Gd/Fm		1195	
32	9	NOTT	8f Good		1407	
34	4	LEIC	8f Gd/Sft		1732	
24a	8	SOUT	8f Aw		2816	
0	14	NEWC	8f Heavy	45	4406	

ALAGAZAM 2 ch g £0
64	12	WIND	6f Good		1876	
58	7	LING	7f Good		2653	
58	8	BEVE	7f Gd/Sft		3051	

ALAKANANDA 2 b f £3189
76	2	EPSO	7f Good		3760	
76	2	NEWC	8f Heavy		4422	
70	2	MUSS	7f Soft		4517	

ALAKDAR 6 ch g £0
| 28a | 6 | WOLV | 16f Aw | 46 | 190 | |

ALAMEIN 7 ch g £3821
47	8	CARL	9f Firm	55	1254	
0	15	PONT	12f Good	51	1499	t
30	11	RIPO	8f Gd/Fm	46	2099	t
7	12	NEWC	10f Gd/Fm	46	2309	t
40	2	HAMI	9f Gd/Fm		2642	t
33	3	HAMI	9f Gd/Fm		2780	t
37	10	RIPO	9f Gd/Fm	47	3011	t
41	1	HAMI	9f Gd/Sft		3375*	t
29	10	HAMI	8f Gd/Sft	43	3534	t
46	4	RIPO	8f Gd/Fm		3711	t
0	19	YORK	9f Good		3808	t

ALASAN 3 b c £0
| 51 | 9 | NEWM | 8f Good | | 956 | |
| 52 | 12 | WARW | 7f Gd/Sft | | 1708 | |

ALASTAIR SMELLIE 4 ch c £499
82	10	NEWM	8f Gd/Fm	89	1173	
0	14	YORK	6f Firm	90	1337	
80	5	PONT	6f Soft	86	1702	
59	14	EPSO	8f Good	83	1851	
75	4	EPSO	6f Gd/Sft	80	2432	
65	14	GOOD	6f Firm	80	3152	

47	20	RIPO	6f Gd/Fm	76	3464	
0	19	DONC	7f Gd/Fm	73	3880	
49	18	AYR	6f Gd/Sft	73	4010	

ALAWAR 3 ch c £669

59	7	WIND	6f Good	72	852	t
43	9	KEMP	6f Soft	70	994	t
0	28	NEWM	8f Firm	68	1183	t
60	4	HAYD	7f Gd/Sft	63	1793	t
50	4	DONC	8f Gd/Fm	61	2579	t
56	4	GOOD	7f Soft	58	4080	t
43	5	PONT	8f Soft	57	4232	t
0	21	NEWM	8f Gd/Sft	55	4536	t

ALAZAN 5 ch g £0

0	11	LING	8f Gd/Fm	52	2185
0	14	SAND	10f Gd/Fm	46	2527
0	7	NEWB	10f Firm		2709

ALBANECK 2 gr c £1333

66	7	HAYD	5f Gd/Sft	1835
68	6	RIPO	5f Gd/Fm	2100
68	4	BEVE	5f Gd/Fm	2480
70	2	RIPO	5f Gd/Fm	2835

ALBARAHIN 5 b h £96924

112	2	SAND	10f Good	107	2475
115	1	SAND	9f Good		3230*
116	2	WIND	10f Good		3641
118	1	GOOD	10f Soft		4064*
118	2	LONG	10f Good		4238
119	1	NEWM	9f Good		4347*
119	1	NEWM	8f Soft		4544*

ALBARDEN 3 ch c £0

52	5	REDC	10f Firm		1295
0	5	NEWC	12f Heavy		1767
42	10	BEVE	10f Gd/Fm	54	2518
36	7	BEVE	10f Good	49	2879
37	6	NEWC	14f Good	44	3249

ALBARSHA 3 br f £0

62	5	BATH	10f Soft	4141

ALBASHOOSH 2 b c £1692

0	13	NEWB	7f Firm	2708
77	3	CHEP	8f Gd/Fm	3680
83	2	YARM	7f Firm	3940

ALBEMINE 11 b g £0

0a	13	WOLV	16f Aw	40	66

ALBERGO 3 b g £634

47a	5	WOLV	9f Aw		395
50	9	SOUT	10f Gd/Sft		858
0	16	WIND	12f Heavy	50	937
55a	2	WOLV	8f Aw		1234
39	8	LEIC	8f Gd/Sft		1572
33	9	SALI	10f Gd/Fm		2981
40	4	WIND	12f Good		3351
0	11	BATH	12f Firm		3624 VIS
0	12	LEIC	10f Gd/Sft		4029

ALBERICH 5 b g £4740

92a	1	LING	12f Aw		27+
78a	5	LING	12f Aw	95	508
0	19	NEWM	12f Gd/Sft	95	968
92	5	NEWM	12f Firm	93	1187
93	4	YORK	12f Gd/Fm	92	1307

ALBERKINNIE 5 b m £5929

18a	8	SOUT	12f Aw	31	211
22a	7	WOLV	9f Aw	27	305
27a	2	LING	12f Aw	29	377
12a	5	LING	13f Aw	26	458
15a	3	WOLV	14f Aw	25	520
19a	3	WOLV	14f Aw	22	608
27a	2	SOUT	8f Aw	24	692
47	1	NOTT	10f Gd/Sft	44	1086*
18	10	BRIG	12f Firm	38	1209
32	9	YARM	11f Gd/Sft	47	1614
0	26	NEWM	12f Firm	45	1852

ALBERT THE BEAR 7 b g £2990

32	14	HAMI	6f Gd/Fm	62	1192	
54	6	BATH	6f Gd/Fm	61	1438	
51	12	CARL	5f Gd/Sft	59	1724	vis
43	8	PONT	6f Good	59	1869	vis
58	3	CARL	6f Firm	56	2015	vis
47	9	NEWC	6f Gd/Fm	57	2275	vis
20	7	HAMI	6f Firm		2396	vis
59	2	PONT	6f Gd/Fm	57	2559	vis
23	6	PONT	6f Gd/Fm		2833	vis
0	14	PONT	5f Firm	58	3502	vis
41	8	LING	7f Good	57	4102	vis
40	6	PONT	5f Soft	55	4377	vis

ALBINONA 3 b f £524

46	6	BRIG	10f Firm	1210
37a	2	LING	12f Aw	1540
19a	5	LING	12f Aw	2181
0a	8	LING	13f Aw	2323

ALBUHERA 2 b f £4043

85	2	NEWM	7f Good	4020
63	6	YORK	6f Soft	4283
87	1	MUSS	7f Soft	4559*

ALBURACK 2 b c £0

62	7	YARM	6f Good	1774
44	10	PONT	6f Gd/Fm	3223
56	11	NOTT	5f Gd/Sft	4503

ALCAYDE 5 ch g £1267

0	13	NEWB	12f Good	74	1373
31	7	SAND	10f Soft	68	1570
18	5	SAND	10f Gd/Fm	63	2937
55	3	SALI	14f Gd/Fm	55	3424
53	5	KEMP	14f Gd/Fm	55	3800
0	11	NOTT	16f Soft	55	3978
51	2	NOTT	16f Heavy	50	4508

ALCONLEIGH 5 ch g £0

0	12	SOUT	6f Good	43	802

ALCOVE 9 ch g £0

47	10	LEIC	10f Good	60	793	
0	18	GOOD	9f Gd/Sft	55	1807	
40	7	BATH	8f Firm	50	2331	BL
30	11	PONT	10f Gd/Fm	46	2556	bl
0	13	NEWM	8f Gd/Fm	46	2802	bl
24	10	WIND	12f Good	43	3186	bl

ALDEBARAN 2 b c £3477

93	1	DONC	7f Gd/Fm	4447*

ALDWYCH 2 ch c £6612

78	8	NEWM	7f Good	4184
99	1	NEWB	8f Gd/Sft	4457*

ALDWYCH ARROW 5 b m £964

49	7	RIPO	10f Gd/Fm	60	2836
39	8	RIPO	12f Gd/Fm	58	3013
0	17	HAYD	12f Good	53	3284
32	11	BEVE	12f Gd/Fm	47	3674
36	6	HAMI	12f Gd/Sft	41	3827
35	7	HAYD	14f Gd/Sft	48	4105
38	2	REDC	14f Gd/Sft	37	4222
30	5	CART	16f Soft	37	4258
44a	4	WOLV	12f Aw	50	4386

ALEANBH 5 ch g £0

38a	6	WOLV	8f Aw		39
0a	13	SOUT	12f Aw	35	215
37a	7	WOLV	8f Aw		229
2a	9	WOLV	9f Aw	29	306

ALEGRIA 4 b f £6418

82	7	YORK	6f Firm	90	1337	
91	1	WIND	6f Good		1728*	
82	9	ASCO	6f Good	91	2151	BL
89	6	DONC	5f Gd/Fm	90	2348	bl
0	22	GOOD	6f Good	90	3152	bl
79	1	PONT	6f Firm		3503	
67	10	HAYD	6f Heavy		3768	bl

ALEXANDER STAR 2 b f £767

61	4	YARM	6f Gd/Fm	1954

77	3	BATH	5f Gd/Fm		3815
38	10	BATH	6f Soft		4137

ALEXANDRINE 3 b f £12756

61	1	YARM	10f Gd/Fm	52	1955*
65	1	MUSS	12f Gd/Fm	58	2202*
60	4	LING	11f Firm	64	2321
59	1	CARL	12f Firm		2826*
72	1	AYR	13f Firm		2876*
56	4	LEIC	12f Gd/Fm		3336
72	3	THIR	12f Gd/Sft	72	3778
72a	4	WOLV	12f Aw	72	4245

ALFAHAAL 7 b h £0

0	12	NOTT	6f Firm	46	1273	
47	8	NOTT	6f Gd/Sft		1368	
0	13	YARM	7f Gd/Sft	45	1611	
0	27	NEWM	6f Gd/Fm	45	1690	
0	13	YARM	6f Gd/Fm	40	1953	
11	8	BRIG	7f Gd/Fm	36	2728	
11	10	NEWM	8f Gd/Fm		3117	
0	17	CHEP	8f Good		3868	VIS

ALFAHAD 7 b g £0

63	8	HAMI	11f Good		848	
0	16	HAMI	11f Gd/Fm	38	1361	
0a	12	SOUT	14f Aw	38	1501	VIS

ALFAILAK 3 b c £0

80	7	HAYD	6f Gd/Fm		2458	
98	5	NEWB	6f Firm		2847	
0	30	GOOD	6f Gd/Fm	101	3152	
70	6	YARM	6f Gd/Fm		3667	
65	8	LEIC	5f Firm		3841	VIS

ALFALFA 2 b g £0

0	13	LING	7f Soft	4267
0	22	NEWM	7f Good	4336
0	15	BATH	6f Soft	4431

ALFANO 2 b c £0

73	5	GOOD	8f Soft	4062
73	5	BRIG	8f Soft	4418

ALFASEL 2 b c £0

59	9	SAND	7f Gd/Fm	2494
77	6	KEMP	7f Firm	2867

ALFIE BOY 4 b g £0

91	9	YORK	8f Firm	100	1327

ALFIE LEE 3 ch c £0

0	23	NEWM	6f Gd/Fm	93	1694	
89	7	SAND	5f Gd/Fm		1987	
84	5	YARM	6f Gd/Fm		2197	
68	8	YARM	6f Firm	89	2900	
67	7	DONC	6f Good		3158	t
72	5	YARM	6f Gd/Fm		3667	tBL

ALFINI 3 ch c £0

0	P	NEWM	8f Gd/Fm	1171

ALHAWA 7 ch h £2864

84	2	NEWM	12f Gd/Sft	79	968
83	5	YORK	14f Firm	83	1329
0	B	ASCO	20f Good	83	2092
79	9	NEWC	16f Firm	83	2336
77	4	NEWM	15f Good	83	3025
60	8	NEWM	16f Firm	81	3295
0	29	NEWM	18f Good	79	4353

ALHESN 5 b g £8645

42a	10	LING	16f Aw	69	6
70a	1	WOLV	16f Aw	65	135*
71a	5	WOLV	16f Aw	71	141
67a	4	WOLV	13f Firm	69	296
72a	1	WOLV	16f Aw	67	348*
71a	3	LING	16f Aw	70	424
71a	2	LING	16f Aw	70	548
65a	3	WOLV	16f Aw	70	627
40	6	MUSS	16f Gd/Sft	45	797

ALHUFOOF 3 b f £2262

101	4	NEWM	7f Good	953
90	9	LING	7f Gd/Sft	1283

92	4	YARM	6f Gd/Fm		3667		
85	6	YARM	6f Firm		3937		

ALHUWBILL 5 b g £662

31	6	LING	7f Good	42	1672		
16	13	GOOD	9f Gd/Sft	36	1807		
31	7	GOOD	7f Good	48	2303	BL	
36	4	SALI	6f Good	38	2690		
36	3	SALI	7f Gd/Fm	37	3294		
26	7	SALI	10f Gd/Fm	37	4168		

ALI OOP 3 b c £321

0	6	RIPO	10f Gd/Fm		3185	
53	4	RIPO	12f Good		3701	
41	8	MUSS	12f Gd/Fm		4133	

ALICIAN SUNHILL 2 br f £1042

61	8	MUSS	5f Gd/Fm		1146	
60	3	HAMI	6f Good		1359	
48	8	CATT	5f Good		1659	
54	4	MUSS	5f Gd/Fm		3589	
54	4	HAMI	5f Soft	55	3802	
49	3	BRIG	5f Soft		4171	BL
42a	9	WOLV	5f Aw		4441	bl

ALIGN 4 gr f £0

0	14	HAMI	8f Gd/Fm	50	1190	
0a	14	SOUT	7f Aw	50	1801	

ALINGA 2 b f £10198

64	5	LEIC	5f Gd/Sft		1737	
79	1	**AYR**	6f Good		2137*	
92	3	NEWM	6f Firm		2344	
87	7	NEWM	6f Good		2565	
92	2	HAYD	6f Gd/Fm		3320	
86	1	**HAMI**	6f Gd/Fm		3533*	
72	8	AYR	6f Gd/Sft		4009	
95	9	NEWM	7f Good		4356	

ALIS IMAGES 2 b f £804

54a	6	WOLV	5f Good		1236	
57	6	CATT	5f Good		1659	
57	7	PONT	5f Good		2174	
60	3	MUSS	7f Firm		2377	
63	3	HAMI	6f Gd/Fm		2778	
57	5	CATT	7f Gd/Fm	62	2928	
48	5	PONT	6f Soft		4372	
48	6	REDC	6f Gd/Sft	58	4502	

ALJAARIF 6 ch h £12100

103a	2	LING	10f Aw		690

ALJABR 4 gr c £94475

122	1	**NEWB**	8f Gd/Fm		1402+
119	4	ASCO	8f Good		2064
114	5	GOOD	8f Gd/Fm		3087

ALJAWF 3 gr c £9792

80	7	CHES	6f Gd/Fm	85	1220	
82	6	NEWB	6f Gd/Fm	84	1406	
95	1	**RIPO**	6f Gd/Fm	84	2101*	
72	12	NEWM	6f Good	92	2568	
80	7	YARM	6f Firm	92	2900	VIS
92	2	NEWB	7f Gd/Fm	91	3481	

ALJAZ 10 b g £2414

63a	2	SOUT	6f Aw	62	44
63a	3	WOLV	6f Aw	67	175
65a	4	SOUT	6f Aw		279
54a	8	LING	5f Aw	66	403
63a	2	LING	5f Aw		440
51a	8	SOUT	6f Aw	64	499
42a	6	WOLV	5f Aw	62	614
53a	4	LING	6f Aw	59	691
41a	6	WOLV	6f Aw		1137
40a	4	LING	7f Aw		1741
31a	7	LING	6f Aw		1913
48a	2	WOLV	6f Aw	46	4442

ALJAZIR 3 b c £714

22	11	NOTT	6f Good	59	785
61	2	WARW	7f Heavy	57	887
43	12	CARL	8f Firm	60	1255

55	5	THIR	8f Good	60	1387	
41	10	SAND	7f Soft	58	1569	
54	5	CHES	7f Gd/Fm	57	2250	
34	12	LEIC	8f Gd/Fm	57	2512	
0	14	HAYD	7f Gd/Sft	55	3269	
0a	13	SOUT	6f Aw	52	4156	
0	18	NEWC	6f Heavy	52	4425	
0	21	DONC	7f Gd/Sft	52	4452	

ALJOHONCHA 2 b f £0

19	10	LEIC	7f Gd/Fm		2916

ALL BLEEVABLE 3 b g £0

0	15	NOTT	8f Good		784
0	11	SOUT	10f Gd/Sft		858

ALL GOOD THINGS 3 b c £339

75	4	GOOD	10f Soft		4081

ALL GRAIN 2 b f £0

70	6	LING	7f Firm		3833

ALL MINE 3 ch g £0

25a	6	SOUT	7f Aw		283	
27a	8	SOUT	7f Aw		330	
41a	6	SOUT	7f Aw		417	t
35a	5	SOUT	6f Aw		472	tBL
0	14	HAYD	8f Gd/Sft		3266	
31	8	THIR	5f Gd/Sft	35	3781	

ALL ON MY OWN 5 ch g £1166

53	3	CATT	14f Good		1660	
34a	8	SOUT	11f Aw		1978	
35	6	BEVE	12f Firm		2219	
34	2	MUSS	16f Gd/Sft		2536	
0a	15	SOUT	16f Aw	35	2951	VIS

ALL ROSES 3 b f £0

33a	7	SOUT	7f Aw		88

ALL THE GEARS 3 b c £2547

83	5	NEWM	8f Firm	85	1183
86	3	YORK	8f Firm	85	1341
0	23	ASCO	8f Good	86	2117
84	2	HAYD	7f Gd/Fm		2443

ALL THE LUCK 3 ch f £0

68	6	YARM	8f Good		1771

ALL THE WAY 4 b c £141296

113	1	**KRAN**	10f Good		1230*

ALLEGRESSE 3 b f £749

80	3	WIND	8f Good		745	
58	5	PONT	10f Gd/Sft	77	1104	
54	8	PONT	10f Good	75	1866	
52	4	CHEP	10f Gd/Fm	71	2493	BL

ALLELUIA 2 b f £494

68	3	LEIC	7f Heavy		4312
59	6	NEWC	7f Heavy		4403
61	8	WIND	8f Heavy		4524

ALLEZ LA CLASSE 2 b f £0

0	8	CURR	7f Gd/Fm		3845

ALLOTROPE 5 b g £0

26	8	NOTT	14f Gd/Fm	60	2681	
42	7	REDC	16f Firm	55	3331	
0	11	PONT	17f Good	48	3501	
0	12	MUSS	16f Gd/Fm	41	3742	bl

ALLRIGHTHEN 4 b g £0

0	15	BEVE	8f Heavy		973

ALLTHEDOTCOMS 2 ch c £321

50	8	FOLK	7f Good		2619
67	6	EPSO	7f Good		2791
60	6	YARM	7f Good		3029
26	7	FOLK	7f Gd/Fm	66	3444
47	11	LING	7f Firm	59	3830

ALLURING 3 b f £7200

0	10	CURR	8f Gd/Sft		1626
106	3	CURR	10f Yldg		2404
99	5	CURR	10f Gd/Fm		3068

ALMAMZAR 10 b g £488

0a	16	SOUT	14f Aw	58	37

17a	5	SOUT	14f Aw	43	89	
15a	7	SOUT	16f Aw	43	253	
26a	5	SOUT	16f Aw	28	284	
26a	4	SOUT	16f Aw	35	428	
18a	4	SOUT	16f Aw	28	502	
0a	7	SOUT	16f Aw	23	542	
31	9	NEWC	16f Soft	38	760	t
0	13	PONT	22f Heavy	31	940	t

ALMASHROUK 3 b c £390

56	6	DONC	6f Good		731	
72	6	LING	7f Gd/Sft		839	
82	4	NEWM	6f Good		956	
45	14	NOTT	6f Firm		1266	
66	6	FOLK	5f Gd/Fm		2294	
47	5	NEWM	6f Gd/Fm		3319	
36	10	GOOD	7f Soft	66	4080	
58	8	BRIG	6f Gd/Sft	66	4120	
0	30	NEWM	5f Good	66	4185	BL
0	18	LING	6f Soft	62	4270	

ALMASI 8 b m £3909

69	5	KEMP	6f Soft	74	1531
74	3	DONC	6f Gd/Fm	74	1842
72	4	DONC	6f Good		2580
62	8	ASCO	7f Gd/Fm	73	2999
73	2	YARM	7f Gd/Fm	73	3384
75	2	GOOD	7f Good		3662
70	5	BRIG	7f Gd/Sft	74	4121
58	10	YORK	6f Soft		4287
66	8	YARM	7f Soft	73	4513

ALMATY 7 b h £0

85	11	DONC	5f Gd/Fm	100	702
80	10	CHES	5f Firm	99	1245
84	9	EPSO	5f Firm	97	1849

ALMAYDAN 2 b c £291

64	4	YARM	7f Soft		4389

ALMAZHAR 5 b g £22845

64a	3	SOUT	7f Aw	64	35	
73a	1	**WOLV**	7f Aw	64	79*	
75a	2	SOUT	6f Aw	70	129	
77a	1	**WOLV**	7f Aw	70	143*	
78a	2	SOUT	6f Aw	74	183	
69a	6	SOUT	8f Aw	74	216	
79a	2	SOUT	8f Aw	78	251	
81a	2	SOUT	7f Aw	78	282	
52	3	MUSS	7f Gd/Fm	49	1148	
49	5	BEVE	7f Firm	51	1275	
53	4	MUSS	7f Gd/Fm	51	1431	
54	2	AYR	7f Gd/Fm	51	1631	vis
57	1	**AYR**	8f Gd/Fm	51	1658*	
53	8	CATT	7f Gd/Fm	56	2420	vis
0	18	REDC	8f Gd/Sft	56	4499	vis

ALMERINA 5 b m £0

39a	9	WOLV	8f Aw	66	1037
0	16	WIND	8f Gd/Fm	66	1201
0	16	REDC	7f Firm	66	1297

ALMIDDINA 3 b f £4510

75	4	NEWB	8f Good		1376
58	8	LING	7f Firm		3834
74	1	**HAYD**	7f Soft		4093*
65	9	NOTT	8f Heavy	73	4414

ALMINSTAR 4 b f £0

0	18	BATH	10f Gd/Sft	37	1666
20	9	WARW	12f Gd/Fm	37	2255

ALMOST FREE 3 b c £4597

91	1	**NEWC**	12f Heavy		1009*
84	4	YORK	14f Gd/Fm		1311

ALMUSHTARAK 7 b h £6900

114	3	SAND	8f Heavy		1043
109	6	NEWB	8f Gd/Fm		1402
108	9	GOOD	8f Gd/Fm		3087
102	6	YORK	10f Good		3539
101	9	ASCO	8f Good		4111

ALMUTAN STAR 5 b m £0
```
75 14 NEWM 10f Good        4355

0  15 WIND  6f Heavy       4526
```

ALMUTAWAKEL 5 b h £48193
```
120c5 GULF 10f Fast          21
```

ALNAAMI 3 b c £0
```
0  13 NEWM 10f Gd/Fm       1697
```

ALNAHAAM 2 ch c £1160
```
65  6 NEWM  6f Gd/Fm       2854
89  2 DONC  7f Gd/Fm       3156
```

ALNAHIGHER 2 b f £830
```
43  6 SAND  5f Heavy       1046
64  5 CARL  5f Firm        1252
61a 2 SOUT  6f Aw          1503
0  11 THIR  7f Gd/Fm       2057
```

ALNAJASHEE 4 b c £6325
```
62a 1 SOUT 12f Aw    55  339* t
52a 4 SOUT 11f Aw    55  390  t
48a 6 SOUT 16f Aw    66  502  t
0a  9 SOUT 12f Aw    64  682  t
0  16 WARW 11f Gd/Fm 58 2033  t
61  1 SALI 14f Gd/Fm 58 2268* t
42  7 NOTT 14f Gd/Fm 61 2681  t
0  15 SALI 14f Gd/Fm 60 3424  t
0  20 BATH 12f Soft  58 4433
```

ALOWMDAH 2 b c £0
```
78 10 NEWM  6f Good        4341
```

ALPATHAR 3 ch f £2838
```
55  1 THIR  7f Soft         930*
53  6 NEWC  8f Gd/Sft 60   1477
52  6 HAYD  7f Gd/Sft 58   1793
54  4 CARL  7f Firm   56   2017
45  8 MUSS  8f Gd/Fm  55   2205
38 12 NEWC  7f Good   52   3033
```

ALPEN WOLF 5 ch g £17417
```
76  3 BRIG  6f Gd/Fm  77   1126
79  1 BATH  5f Gd/Fm       1441*
61  7 BRIG  5f Good   82   1650
81  2 BATH  5f Firm   78   1999
85  1 WARW  6f Gd/Fm       2035*
72 10 NEWC  6f Firm   85   2334
89  1 NEWB  6f Firm   85   2813*
89  3 EPSO  6f Gd/Fm  88   3414
81  8 NEWB  6f Firm   88   3981
0  25 ASCO  8f Good   88   4112
77 13 NEWM  5f Good   90   4339
57 10 NEWB  6f Gd/Sft 87   4456
```

ALPENGLOW 4 b f £3180
```
91  3 ASCO  8f Gd/Fm       3340
87 11 ASCO  8f Good  100   4113
```

ALPHA HEIGHTS 3 b f £0
```
0  20 SALI  7f Good   73   1348
50  8 WARW 11f Heavy  68   1521
38  5 NEWB 12f Gd/Fm  63   1948
43  8 WIND 10f Gd/Fm  55   2206
0  13 WIND 12f Good   50   2887
```

ALPHA ROSE 3 ch f £23508
```
61  5 KEMP  6f Good         729
46a 5 LING  5f Aw           883
62  4 REDC 10f Firm   60   1299
59  1 MUSS 14f Gd/Fm       1433*
58  1 AYR  13f Gd/Fm       1657*
63  2 YARM 14f Gd/Fm  56   1949
39a 5 SOUT 12f Aw     53   2123
53  3 MUSS 16f Firm   60   2373
61a 1 LING 12f Aw     53   2593*
65  1 BRIG 12f Firm   60   2893*
60  4 MUSS 12f Good   65   3102
70  2 BRIG 12f Firm   65   3560
71  1 BRIG 12f Firm   65   3735*
69  7 NEWM 14f Gd/Fm  73   4213
79  1 NEWM 12f Gd/Sft 71   4534*
```

ALPHACALL 2 b f £0
```
59  4 REDC  5f Firm        1294
65  5 RIPO  5f Soft        2539
37  8 BEVE  7f Gd/Fm       3409
```

ALPHAEUS 2 b g £4625
```
67  5 PONT  6f Gd/Fm       3223
76  5 FOLK  6f Gd/Fm       3443
80  1 BEVE  8f Gd/Fm       3675*
81a 2 SOUT  8f Aw          4152
```

ALPHILDA 3 gr f £1310
```
73 12 NEWM  7f Good   82    954
70  8 SALI  8f Firm   80   1178
74  3 WIND  8f Firm   77   1289
69  4 NEWM  7f Firm   77   1855
52 12 GOOD  7f Gd/Fm  76   2128
76  3 LEIC  7f Gd/Fm  74   2918
67  9 NEWM  7f Gd/Fm  74   3163
21 14 SALI  7f Firm   74   3750
```

ALPINE HIDEAWAY 7 b g £0
```
41a 6 LING 12f Aw     50   4334
```

ALPINE PANTHER 7 b g £0
```
33 10 HAYD 14f Gd/Sft 58   1536
42  8 REDC 14f Gd/Sft 53   4222
```

ALQAWAASER 3 b c £235
```
74  5 ASCO  8f Good        2679
68  6 SALI  8f Gd/Fm  70   2980
64  4 SALI 10f Gd/Fm  68   3390
63  5 BATH 13f Gd/Fm  66   3819
0  18 GOOD 10f Soft   62   4067
```

ALQUID NOVI 2 ch f £425
```
78  3 NOTT  6f Good        2010
65  4 PONT  5f Good        2361
53  8 CHEP  6f Gd/Fm       2972
44  9 WARW  7f Gd/Fm  65   3913
0a 11 LING  6f Aw          4332
```

ALRASSAAM 4 b c £61683
```
94  7 SAND 10f Heavy       1057
100 4 SAN   8f Good        1460
116 1 CURR  9f Good        2410*
74  8 DEAU 10f Good        3370
```

ALRIGHT POPS 4 b f £0
```
14  8 WARW  7f Soft         816
```

ALRISHA 3 b f £10268
```
65  7 SALI 10f Gd/Fm       2265
78  2 KEMP 12f Gd/Fm       2751
77  1 NEWM 15f Good        3023*
84  2 KEMP 16f Gd/Fm  80   3360
86  4 YORK 14f Firm   81   3599
84  3 NEWB 16f Firm   83   3986
38 15 ASCO 16f Good   83   4115
```

ALS ALIBI 7 b g £4123
```
38 10 HAYD 12f Gd/Fm  70    809
56 14 NEWM 12f Gd/Sft 67    968
48 11 NEWB 12f Good   62   1373
65a 2 SOUT 11f Aw          2119
71a 1 SOUT 12f Aw          2298*
40a 4 SOUT 11f Aw          2381
59  2 BEVE 12f Gd/Sft 58   3053
31 13 HAYD 12f Good   58   3284
```

ALS ME TRAINER 2 b g £281
```
71  4 REDC  7f Gd/Fm       3635
0  12 AYR   6f Soft        3958
68  5 NEWC  6f Heavy       4402
```

ALSHADIYAH 2 gr f £17627
```
95  1 LING  6f Firm        3492*
98  3 SALI  6f Firm        3749
97  1 AYR   6i Gd/Sft      4009*
92  5 NEWB  5f Gd/Sft      4454
```

ALSHAKR 3 b f £72490
```
101 1 NEWM  7f Gd/Sft       971*
110 3 LONG  8f V           1319
109 1 NEWM  8f Gd/Fm       2597*
110 2 NEWM  8f Gd/Fm       4211
73 13 NEWM 10f Good        4355
```

ALSYATI 2 ch c £0
```
74  6 KEMP  7f Gd/Fm       3790
72  7 WARW  7f Gd/Fm       3909
```

ALTARA 3 b f £315
```
63  4 CHEP  7f Gd/Fm       2491
59  6 SAND  8f Gd/Fm       2938
0  12 LING  7f Firm        3834
```

ALTAY 3 b c £9324
```
0  22 REDC  8f Firm   62   1296
56  3 REDC 14f Gd/Sft 58   1581
50  6 REDC 10f Good   55   1895
56  3 BEVE 12f Gd/Fm  55   2482
55  5 HAMI 12f Gd/Fm  55   2783
61  1 RIPO 10f Good   51   3702*
60  1 EPSO  9f Good   57   3856*
39  7 PONT  8f Soft   61   4232
```

ALUSTAR 3 b f £0
```
0a  P SOUT  5f Aw     66    870
0   U CATT  5f Gd/Fm  66   2418
0  16 THIR  5f Gd/Fm  66   3349
```

ALVA GLEN 3 b c £44756
```
96  6 NEWM  9f Gd/Sft       980
68  9 EPSO 10f Gd/Fm  98   1831
102 1 YORK 10f Firm   94   2004*
104 2 HAYD 12f Gd/Fm 100   2502
107 3 GOOD 12f Gd/Fm 103   3088
105 6 YORK 14f Gd/Fm 103   3565
111 1 GOOD 14f Good        3645*
99  6 KEMP 12f Gd/Fm       3792
79  8 NEWM 16f Good        4351
```

ALVARO 3 ch g £750
```
52  6 YARM 10f Gd/Fm       3383
73  4 DONC 10f Firm        3889
40a 8 SOUT 16f Aw     58   4149
33 11 CATT 12f Soft   58   4256
```

ALWAYS ALIGHT 6 ch g £6500
```
71 15 KEMP  6f Good   90    728
92  1 WIND  6f Heavy        935*
87  5 ASCO  7f Gd/Sft 91   1110
85  7 SAND  8f Soft   91   1567
64 22 AYR   6f Gd/Sft 90   4012
```

ALWAYS VIGILANT 3 b f £3548
```
0  11 BATH 10f Good        1093
76  3 DONC  8f Gd/Fm       2611
91  1 WIND  8f Good        3350*
0  12 DONC 10f Heavy       4571
```

ALYZIG 3 £0
```
111 5 LONG 11f V           1317
```

ALZITA 3 b f £547
```
63  7 SALI  8f Firm        2024
67  3 YARM  8f Gd/Fm       2198
33  8 YARM  8f Gd/Fm  59   3970
43  8 BRIG 10f Soft   54   4174
46  5 YARM 14f Heavy  51   4476
```

AMACITA 2 b f £0
```
68  8 LING  7f Soft        4484
```

AMALIA 4 b f £37639
```
0   4 SAIN 10f Hldng        665
97  4 EPSO 10f Heavy  98   1031
105 1 YORK 10f Firm   98   1342*
107 3 EPSO 12f Good  103   1850
100 4 KEMP 10f Good        2260
106 1 NEWC 10f Firm        2339*
105 4 AYR  10f Gd/Fm       2720
```

AMAMACKEMMUSH 2 b g £2725
```
66 11 MUSS  5f Gd/Fm       1429
76  2 RIPO  5f Gd/Fm       2100
73  2 PONT  5f Good        2361
60  3 CHES  5f Gd/Fm       2668
61  5 THIR  5f Gd/Fm  69   3145
```

61	2	MUSS	5f Gd/Fm			3589
43	9	MUSS	5f Gd/Fm	65		3743
53a	7	WOLV	5f Aw			4227
62a	4	WOLV	6f Aw			4246

AMANCIO 9 b g £2494

69	2	GOOD	14f Gd/Fm	68		1959
62	3	GOOD	14f Good	69		2305
69	4	SALI	14f Gd/Sft	69		4166

AMARANTH 4 b c £13818

75a	7	LING	5f Aw	80		631	t
52	19	DONC	5f Gd/Fm	80		702	t
69	7	THIR	5f Soft			905	t
53	14	THIR	6f Good	77		1383	t
80	1	AYR	6f Gd/Fm	74		1654*	
78	2	MUSS	5f Firm	74		1687	t
77	6	YORK	5f Gd/Fm	84		1983	
83	5	RIPO	6f Gd/Fm	83		3183	
80	8	RIPO	6f Gd/Fm	83		3464	
87	1	NEWM	5f Gd/Fm	82		3631*	
89	4	NEWM	5f Good	90		4339	
90	4	DONC	5f Soft	89		4466	

AMARO 4 b f £420

32a	5	WOLV	6f Aw	45		226
38a	5	SOUT	7f Aw			247
35a	6	SOUT	6f Aw	42		280
37a	3	LING	6f Aw			399
16a	6	LING	7f Aw	39		439
0	15	LEIC	6f Gd/Fm	42		2777
34	7	BEVE	5f Gd/Fm	43		3653
35	9	THIR	5f Gd/Sft	41		3781
34	8	YARM	6f Gd/Fm	40		3966

AMARONE 2 b g £0

0	16	NEWB	6f Gd/Fm			1943
37	6	LING	5f Firm			2324
0	16	NEWM	6f Gd/Fm			3162
0	18	LING	6f Soft			4190 BL

AMAZED 3 ch f £1068

59	4	LEIC	5f Gd/Fm			2919
64	2	RIPO	5f Gd/Fm			3462
0	13	LING	5f Gd/Fm	65		3759
45	12	PONT	5f Soft	63		4087

AMAZING FACT 5 b g £208

28a	7	WOLV	8f Aw			136
24a	3	WOLV	12f Aw	30		607
9a	6	SOUT	14f Aw			668
0	16	RIPO	12f Soft	27		822
33	11	BRIG	10f Firm			1331 BL
14	7	BRIG	12f Good			1647 bl

AMBASSADOR LADY 2 b f £0

0	18	WIND	6f Gd/Fm			3047
53	6	LING	6f Firm			3492
39	11	LING	7f Firm			3833

AMBER BROWN 4 b f £8762

47	9	WIND	6f Gd/Fm	58		746
61	1	THIR	6f Soft	55		910*
42	9	NOTT	6f Gd/Fm	60		1082
50	10	REDC	7f Firm	59		1297
65	1	LING	7f Soft	58		1542* BL
63	4	LING	6f Good	62		1676 bl
46	9	SALI	6f Gd/Fm	62		2230 bl
43	12	WIND	6f Gd/Fm	62		2371 bl
48	6	LING	7f Good	60		4102
49	11	WIND	6f Gd/Sft	59		4293 bl
61	2	NOTT	6f Heavy	57		4411 bl

AMBER FORT 7 gr g £6820

73	3	WARW	8f Soft	72		817 bl
73	6	NEWC	7f Heavy	72		1011 bl
73	5	THIR	7f Good	73		1158 bl
70	4	SALI	7f Good	73		1348 bl
69	7	GOOD	7f Gd/Sft	73		1483 bl
69	5	BRIG	7f Good	72		1652 bl
62	5	LING	8f Gd/Fm			2215 vis
62	5	LEIC	7f Gd/Fm			2508 vis
69	3	YORK	7f Good	66		2694 bl
71	4	AYR	7f Firm	70		2878 bl
67	5	YARM	7f Gd/Fm	70		3384 bl
55	12	YORK	7f Good	69		3809 bl
63	9	LING	8f Firm	69		3831 bl
71	4	AYR	7f Soft	69		3992 bl
67	4	BRIG	7f Gd/Sft	68		4121 bl
68	10	SALI	6f Gd/Sft	77		4165 bl
69	3	YORK	7f Heavy	68		4302 bl

AMBER GO GO 3 ch f £0

0	16	MUSS	5f Gd/Fm	42		1143
0	15	REDC	14f Gd/Sft	42		1581
0	13	CATT	12f Gd/Fm	40		2746

AMBER REGENT 5 ch g £0

0a	13	SOUT	8f Aw			45
0a	7	WOLV	15f Aw			117 VIS

AMBER ROSE 2 ch f £856

73	3	YORK	6f Firm			2005

AMBER TIDE 2 ch f £883

79	3	SAND	5f Heavy			1046
82	4	GOOD	6f Gd/Sft			1486
0	11	PONT	8f Soft			4082

AMBERSONG 2 ch c £0

63	7	CHEP	7f Good			3866
13	7	YORK	8f Heavy			4297

AMBIDEXTROUS 8 b h £545

10a	10	SOUT	12f Aw	35		211
40a	2	WOLV	12f Aw			231
12a	10	WOLV	16f Aw	30		318
23a	4	WOLV	12f Aw	28		410
40a	5	WOLV	12f Aw			581
0	16	DONC	12f Gd/Fm	53		699
13a	5	WOLV	12f Aw	33		723
38	4	BEVE	12f Firm			2219

AMBITIOUS 5 b m £27517

66	8	DONC	5f Gd/Fm	78		702
85	1	THIR	5f Soft			905*
34	11	BATH	5f Good			1090
84	4	CHES	5f Firm	84		1245
79	11	YORK	5f Firm	83		1324
75a	1	SOUT	5f Aw	62		1976*
84	4	NEWC	5f Gd/Fm	83		2310
89	1	SAND	5f Gd/Fm	83		2473*
81	7	ASCO	5f Good	88		2676
91	1	NEWB	5f Gd/Fm	87		3176*
72	13	RIPO	6f Gd/Fm	90		3464
76	12	YARM	5f Firm	90		3920
85	2	DONC	5f Soft	90		4466
90	4	WIND	5f Heavy	90		4527

AMBUSHED 4 b g £11665

36a	9	LING	7f Aw			225
31a	8	LING	10f Aw			238
2a	10	WOLV	9f Aw			259
0a	11	SOUT	12f Aw	30		413
34a	1	SOUT	8f Aw	25		585* BL
17a	7	SOUT	6f Aw	27		602 bl
65	5	AYR	6f Good			3366
36	2	NEWC	9f Firm	38		3603
56	1	HAMI	8f Gd/Sft	48		3826*
0	24	REDC	8f Gd/Sft	56		4217
40	6	AYR	9f Heavy			4324
56	3	NEWC	7f Heavy	56		4428
58	1	MUSS	9f Soft	54		4520*
56	5	MUSS	8f Soft	61		4565

AMEERAT 2 b f £20120

99	1	GOOD	7f Good			3108*
103	2	DONC	8f Gd/Fm			3876
103	6	NEWM	7f Good			4356

AMELIA 2 b f £28100

51a	4	SOUT	7f Aw			1302
61	2	LEIC	5f Soft			1549
57	3	BEVE	5f Firm			1918
62	3	BEVE	5f Firm			2730
67	4	SAND	5f Gd/Fm			2933
68	3	SAND	5f Good	70		3228
79a	1	WOLV	6f Aw			3496*
79	1	LING	5f Good	71		4098*
80	2	NEWM	5f Good	78		4179
89	7	NEWB	5f Gd/Sft			4454

AMELIA JESS 3 ch f £2720

48a	2	SOUT	7f Aw			330	
43a	3	SOUT	7f Aw			417	
51a	1	SOUT	8f Aw	46		429*	t
36a	5	WOLV	9f Aw			481	t
49a	4	SOUT	8f Aw			514	t
47a	5	SOUT	8f Aw	54		540	t

AMELIAS FIELD 3 b f £705

78	4	GOOD	9f Gd/Sft			1481
69	9	GOOD	8f Gd/Sft			1811
69	4	SALI	8f Firm			2024

AMELLNAA 3 gr f £4771

85	1	NOTT	10f Gd/Fm			3006*

AMEN CORNER 2 ch c £6044

72	4	HAMI	6f Gd/Fm			2234
80	1	AYR	6f Gd/Fm			2717*
82	3	NEWM	6f Gd/Fm			2959
76	5	NEWB	7f Gd/Fm	82		3486
54	7	YORK	8f Soft	75		4286
83a	2	SOUT	6f Aw	79		4367
76	3	YARM	5f Soft	79		4511

AMERICA 3 ch f £49952

112	1	LONG	9f Heavy			1114*
97	6	LONG	10f Gd/Sft			1457
112	1	LONG	10f Good			2224*
103	8	LONG	10f Good			4263

AMERICAN COUSIN 5 b g £7952

37	9	MUSS	5f Gd/Sft	59		798
42	15	BEVE	5f Firm	57		1278
47	7	CATT	5f Good	54		1662
37	11	HAMI	6f Gd/Fm	51		1941
39	9	CARL	6f Firm	51		2015
43	8	BEVE	5f Firm	48		2732
46	7	SAND	5f Gd/Fm	48		2925
45	5	CATT	5f Gd/Fm	47		3203
40	9	NEWC	6f Firm	47		3605
51	1	SALI	5f Firm	47		3747*
53	1	CHEP	5f Good	46		3872*
62	1	YARM	6f Gd/Fm	57		3966*
53	9	LEIC	5f Gd/Fm	59		4027

AMERICAN GOTHIC 2 £1530

0	7	CURR	7f Gd/Fm			4058
77	3	LEOP	8f Heavy			4554

AMERTON HEATH 7 b m £0

0a	12	WOLV	8f Aw			4551

AMETHYST 3 b f £56250

110	1	LEOP	7f Soft			948*
104	8	NEWM	8f Gd/Fm			1185
112	2	CURR	8f Gd/Sft			1626
81	9	ASCO	8f Good			2150
0	7	CURR	12f Gd/Fm			2739

AMEZOLA 4 gr c £0

0	15	KEMP	12f Gd/Sft	81		1076	t
71	6	KEMP	16f Soft	79		1527	t
61	6	KEMP	14f Aw			1928	t
0	11	PONT	18f Firm	70		2176	t
51	11	SAND	16f Gd/Fm	65		2498	tBL

AMICA BELLA 3 b f £0

0	17	SAND	10f Soft			4205

AMICABLE 2 b f £1987

85	4	NEWB	6f Firm			3980
90	2	NEWM	7f Good			4184

AMIGO 2 b c £0

66	7	CHEP	8f Good			3867

78	6	LING	7f Soft		4267
46a	6	WOLV	7f Aw		4383

AMILYNX 4 gr c £96830

117	2	SAIN	10f Hldng		665
122	1	**LONG**	16f Heavy		1116*
123	1	**LONG**	16f Gd/Sft		1456*
123	1	**LONG**	16f Heavy		4494*

AMINGTON GIRL 5 b m £0

13a	6	WOLV	9f Aw		259	vis

AMIR ZAMAN 2 ch c £0

70	10	YARM	7f Firm	3940
0	22	NEWM	12f Good	4158

AMIS ANGEL 2 b f £7077

79	2	NOTT	5f Gd/Sft	1642
80	1	**PONT**	5f Firm	3500*
94	6	YORK	8f Firm	3596
63	11	DONC	8f Gd/Fm	3876
65	16	NEWM	7f Good	4356

AMITGE 6 ch m £0

57	5	BATH	12f Firm	2943
29	9	BRIG	7f Gd/Fm	3259

AMJAD 3 ch c £1227

78	5	LEIC	8f Good		789	
80	9	NEWB	8f Good		1377	
70	4	BEVE	7f Firm		1922	
68	5	WARW	8f Good		2465	
62	5	NEWB	12f Firm		2710	
63	7	ASCO	10f Gd/Fm	69	2955	
56	7	LEIC	10f Gd/Fm	65	3337	BL
76	2	LING	6f Firm		3579	bl
53	9	LING	6f Firm	63	3759	bl
62	12	NEWM	7f Gd/Fm	70	4215	bl
64a	6	LING	8f Aw	68	4330	bl

AMNERIS 3 b f £2289

80	2	KEMP	10f Firm		2258	
66	3	NEWB	12f Firm		2710	
66	4	CHEP	12f Good		3869	BL
23	8	BRIG	12f Gd/Sft	68	4123	bl

AMONG ISLANDS 9 b m £0

0a	10	WOLV	12f Aw	32	607

AMONG WOMEN 2 b f £2886

59	8	LING	6f Soft	4189
61	17	NEWM	6f Good	4341
74	1	**BRIG**	8f Soft	4418*

AMONITA 2 b f £76849

113	1	**LONG**	8f Good	4260*

AMORAS 3 b f £6056

72	4	BRIG	8f Gd/Fm		1125
56	8	YARM	8f Gd/Sft	73	1610
63	7	BATH	8f Firm	71	2330
71	4	CHEP	8f Good	68	2661
72	2	SALI	7f Gd/Fm	68	2978
58	5	BRIG	7f Gd/Fm		3259
72	1	**WIND**	8f Good	70	3643*

AMOROUS SARITA 2 b f £0

34	8	NOTT	6f Heavy	4410

AMPULLA 2 b c £0

61	7	BATH	6f Gd/Sft	2550

AMRAK AJEEB 8 b h £7044

65	7	NEWB	10f Good	67	1375
69	3	WIND	10f Good		1729
75	1	**CHEP**	10f Good	67	1973*
73	4	SAND	10f Gd/Fm	74	2527
75	3	KEMP	10f Gd/Fm	74	2750
67	8	NEWM	10f Gd/Fm	74	3166
73	2	LEIC	10f Firm	73	3842
60	17	NEWB	10f Firm	73	3997

AMRITSAR 3 ch c £3456

0	19	NEWM	8f Gd/Sft		972
75	5	DONC	7f Gd/Sft		1072
75	4	HAYD	7f Gd/Sft		1537
75	3	GOOD	10f Gd/Sft	71	1812

75	2	PONT	10f Firm	72	2175
72	3	BATH	12f Gd/Sft	74	2554
74	3	YARM	10f Gd/Fm		3381
69	6	GOOD	10f Good		3907
51a	9	LING	10f Aw	70	4482

AMRON 13 b g £0

28	8	HAMI	9f Good	50	846
0	18	NEWC	8f Heavy	48	1007
41	6	CARL	9f Firm	45	1254
0	12	MUSS	12f Gd/Fm	42	1432
23	10	AYR	11f Good	41	2139
9	7	AYR	10f Heavy	38	4306
18	7	NEWC	8f Heavy	38	4406
1	9	MUSS	9f Soft	33	4523

AMSARA 4 b f £772

0a	12	SOUT	11f Aw	39	324	
6a	6	SOUT	12f Aw	33	412	
0a	9	WOLV	16f Aw	28	492	
0a	9	WOLV	12f Aw	28	607	BL
0	12	PONT	22f Heavy	37	940	
2a	8	SOUT	14f Aw	28	1501	
26	2	MUSS	12f Gd/Sft	25	2537	
0a	13	SOUT	14f Aw	38	4371	
0	12	NEWC	16f Heavy	31	4424	bl

AMULETTE 2 ch f £0

0	12	KEMP	7f Soft	4034

AMWELL STAR 2 gr f £0

54	8	YARM	6f Soft	4390

AMY DEE 2 b f £0

69	6	REDC	6f Good		1893
0	15	YORK	6f Good		2692
35	10	YORK	6f Soft		4283
35	9	REDC	6f Gd/Sft	54	4502

AMY G 2 b f £0

0	14	YORK	6f Good	3812
50	6	BEVE	5f Good	3955

AN JOLIEN 3 b f £0

60	4	WARW	7f Heavy	60	887	
0	19	WIND	6f Firm	60	1289	
0	18	YARM	7f Gd/Sft	58	1611	bl
0	17	CHEP	7f Good	57	3873	bl
0	16	CATT	7f Soft	54	4004	
0	18	BRIG	10f Soft	50	4174	

AN LU ABU 4 b g £0

0a	13	LING	7f Aw	54	162	
0a	13	WOLV	8f Aw	50	227	
29a	7	SOUT	8f Aw		252	VIS
27a	9	WOLV	12f Aw		295	vis

AN SMEARDUBH 4 b f £0

0a	7	SOUT	12f Aw		603	
33	14	WIND	12f Gd/Fm	49	748	
20	6	PONT	10f Good	40	1496	
0	8	MUSS	12f Gd/Fm	36	2202	
20	6	HAMI	12f Gd/Sft	31	3531	BL
16	11	YARM	14f Gd/Fm	36	3664	bl

ANALYSER 2 ch c £430

76	4	NEWM	7f Good	4020
81	9	NEWM	6f Good	4341

ANALYTICAL 4 b c £426

0	15	KEMP	7f Good	75	725	
49	12	ASCO	8f Gd/Sft	72	1113	
62	8	GOOD	8f Gd/Fm	69	2126	
62	3	CATT	7f Gd/Fm		2437	
30	8	FOLK	7f Gd/Fm	65	3041	VIS

ANALYZE 2 b c £2487

69	12	NEWB	7f Gd/Fm		1403
70	3	LEIC	6f Gd/Sft		1573
74	5	GOOD	8f Gd/Sft		1809
50	7	NEWM	7f Gd/Fm	71	2962
74	2	NEWB	7f Gd/Fm	66	3486

ANASTASIA VENTURE 3 b f £2306

77	5	WIND	8f Gd/Fm	745

76	3	DONC	10f Gd/Sft		1051
66a	2	WOLV	9f Aw		1388
60	4	ASCO	8f Gd/Fm		3019
56	5	REDC	9f Firm		3326
44a	3	LING	12f Aw		3835
0	9	YARM	10f Firm		3935	VIS

ANCHOR VENTURE 7 b g £0

0a	16	SOUT	8f Aw	38	83	
0a	13	SOUT	8f Aw		199	BL
0a	11	SOUT	8f Aw	26	297	
0a	12	SOUT	8f Aw	40	340	
0a	10	WOLV	9f Aw	28	568	

ANCIENT ALMU 4 ch g £0

0a	12	SOUT	11f Aw	54	561	
0a	12	WOLV	12f Aw	54	608	BL

ANDREYEV 6 ch g £59492

109	1	**DONC**	6f Good		734*
86	10	NEWB	5f Soft	108	914
90	10	NEWM	6f Good		952
103	5	GOOD	6f Gd/Sft		1453
94	8	LING	6f Good		1674
105	4	NEWB	6f Firm	105	2706
111	1	**YORK**	6f Gd/Fm	105	3727*
105	3	NEWB	5f Firm		3982
102	6	NEWM	5f Good		4182
109	2	NEWM	6f Good		4346
111	1	**DONC**	6f Heavy		4581*

ANDROMEDAS WAY 2 b f £214

74	6	GOOD	6f Gd/Fm		1957
68	4	CATT	6f Gd/Fm		2419
39	10	WIND	6f Gd/Fm		2886
52	12	LING	7f Firm	67	3830
0	14	GOOD	8f Soft	60	4076

ANDROMEDES 3 b c £11415

81	4	NEWB	11f Soft		916
88	3	NEWM	12f Gd/Fm		1696
82	1	**WARW**	12f Gd/Fm		2038*
90	7	NEWM	15f Gd/Fm		2594
73	6	NEWM	10f Good	82	3024
84	1	**RIPO**	10f Gd/Fm	80	3713*

ANDYS ELECTIVE 3 b c £3829

65	3	DONC	7f Good		717	
60	6	BRIG	8f Gd/Sft		894	
42	10	SALI	8f Good	66	1345	
50a	5	LING	7f Aw		1745	
64	1	**BRIG**	7f Firm	60	2044*	VIS
60	8	EPSO	7f Good	65	2794	vis
56	7	KEMP	7f Gd/Fm	65	3076	vis
52	8	LING	8f Firm	65	3580	vis

ANEEFAH 3 b f £0

72	5	BATH	12f Gd/Fm		3818
57	7	BATH	12f Soft		4434	BL

ANEES 3 b c £339754

122£	1	**GULF**	9f Fast		19*	vis

ANEMOS 5 ch g £11808

80a	1	**LING**	10f Aw	71	160*
78a	2	LING	10f Aw	75	244
77a	3	LING	10f Aw	78	374
68a	4	LING	10f Aw	78	442
77a	2	LING	10f Aw	76	632
68	6	NOTT	10f Good	71	786
70	3	WIND	8f Gd/Fm	69	1201
70	4	KEMP	10f Firm	87	1926
57	8	WIND	8f Good	70	2367

ANGE DHONOR 5 b g £325

56	6	SALI	14f Firm	58	1180
51	8	WIND	12f Good	58	1730
56	4	SAND	14f Gd/Fm	56	1991
38	10	CHEP	18f Gd/Fm	55	2490

ANGEL DUST 4 b f £0

41	5	NEWC	12f Good	3034
46	6	BEVE	12f Gd/Fm	3672

27	11	YORK	10f Soft		4275	
0	12	NEWC	10f Heavy	40	4404	

ANGEL HILL 5 ch m £7180

0	17	THIR	6f Soft	67	910	
38	8	NEWC	5f Heavy	64	1008	
51	8	THIR	5f Good	61	1162	
45	7	NEWC	5f Gd/Sft	58	1479	
50	6	DONC	6f Gd/Fm	55	1842	bl
55	1	**NEWC**	6f Gd/Fm	52	2275*	
41	11	NEWC	5f Good	55	2525	VIS
38	11	LEIC	6f Gd/Fm	55	2777	vis
53	4	BEVE	7f Gd/Fm	54	3652	
49	12	LEIC	7f Firm	54	3839	
60	1	**CATT**	7f Soft	53	4004*	
61a	4	SOUT	7f Aw	61	4153	
50a	7	WOLV	8f Aw	61	4248	

ANGEL LANE 3 b f £327

36	12	BEVE	10f Good	53	1448	
42	7	NOTT	8f Good	48	2013	
42	4	PONT	8f Firm	46	2180	
33	8	YARM	8f Firm	43	2767	
0	15	WIND	8f Gd/Sft		4292	

ANGELAS HUSBAND 2 b c £372

70	6	THIR	5f Good		1161	
57	8	HAMI	5f Gd/Fm		1359	
55	9	AYR	6f Gd/Fm		1628	
58	3	MUSS	5f Gd/Fm		2200	BL
65	3	CARL	5f Firm		3193	bl
49	9	MUSS	5f Gd/Fm		3589	VIS
0	14	BEVE	7f Good	56	3950	vis
12a	12	WOLV	6f Aw		4359	

ANGELAS PET 3 ch f £0

31a	6	LING	6f Aw	48	165	
43a	6	LING	6f Aw		221	
55	6	SALI	6f Gd/Sft		2472	
1	6	SALI	8f Gd/Fm		3289	
1	11	SALI	6f Gd/Fm	49	3419	

ANGELLO 3 ch c £0

16a	9	LING	8f Aw		103

ANGELS VENTURE 4 ch c £2680

76	10	NEWM	12f Gd/Sft	82	968	
77	7	SALI	14f Firm	81	1180	
76	11	SALI	12f Good	80	1350	t
73	4	NEWM	12f Gd/Fm	77	2131	t
70	3	LEIC	12f Gd/Fm	74	2917	tvl
72	2	LEIC	12f Gd/Fm		3336	tvi
61	6	EPSO	12f Good	70	3686	tvi
60a	4	LING	12f Aw		4101	t

ANGIE BABY 4 b f £292

65	4	WIND	5f Gd/Fm		1881

ANGIE MARINIE 4 b f £0

63	10	CHES	12f Firm	64	1251
54	6	CHES	10f Gd/Sft	62	1777
20	7	CHES	12f Good		2667

ANGIES QUEST 3 b f £1650

72	2	NOTT	8f Gd/Fm		2188
69	4	THIR	8f Gd/Sft	78	3777

ANGIOLINI 3 ch c £0

0	17	NEWM	8f Gd/Sft		972

ANGUS G 8 br g £2873

61	8	HAYD	14f Gd/Fm	83	3323
101	18	YORK	12f Good	80	3541
55	10	YORK	14f Good	75	3811
60	8	NEWM	10f Good	68	4160
68	1	**REDC**	10f Soft		4501*

ANGUS THE BOLD 4 b g £0

25	12	NOTT	6f Gd/Fm	45	2192	
0	14	CHES	8f Good	40	2673	
16	11	CHEP	7f Gd/Fm	32	2974	VIS
21	6	YARM	8f Good	31	3236	vis
0a	11	WOLV	12f Aw	28	3494	

ANIMAL CRACKER 2 gr f £4767

69	8	ASCO	5f Gd/Sft		1107
78	5	NEWB	5f Good		1372
84	1	**NEWB**	5f Gd/Sft		1589*
77	5	NEWB	6f Gd/Fm		1944
84	5	SAND	5f Gd/Fm		2529

ANKASAMEN 2 b f £0

0	11	KEMP	6f Gd/Fm		3358
33	9	EPSO	7f Good		3760
59	9	BRIG	7f Soft		4415

ANN SUMMERS 2 b f £0

39	10	NEWB	6f Firm		3449
49a	4	WOLV	9f Aw		4438
0	14	WIND	8f Heavy		4524

ANNA ELISE 4 b f £5700

105	2	CURR	6f Soft		4398

ANNADAWI 5 b g £21160

32a	4	WOLV	7f Aw		173	
46a	4	WOLV	8f Aw		229	
42a	4	WOLV	8f Aw		308	
37a	4	WOLV	9f Aw		378	
1a	7	SOUT	11f Aw	40	474	BL
22a	5	WOLV	9f Aw		490	tbl
41a	4	WOLV	9f Aw		531	VIS
41	6	LEIC	7f Gd/Sft	52	834	
56	3	PONT	8f Heavy		942	
44	2	WARW	11f Heavy	37	1003	
44	2	WARW	11f Soft	42	1065	
47	2	NOTT	10f Gd/Sft	44	1370	
49	1	**LEIC**	10f Gd/Sft	45	1575*	
40	7	BEVE	10f Firm	50	2220	
53	2	PONT	10f Good	50	2366	
52	2	PONT	10f Gd/Fm	47	2556	
37	3	HAMI	11f Gd/Fm	47	2638	
49	6	DONC	10f Gd/Fm	51	3159	
50	3	HAYD	11f Gd/Sft	50	3480	
40	3	YORK	10f Good	49	3731	
73	1	**PONT**	10f Soft	72	4085*	
49	7	NEWM	10f Good	55	4160	
83	2	YORK	9f Heavy	79	4300	
76	7	YARM	10f Soft	82	4392	
77	5	NEWB	9f Sft/Hvy	83	4472	

ANNAKAYE 3 b f £0

0	14	BEVE	7f Good		1444
34	7	BEVE	7f Firm		1922
46	5	THIR	7f Gd/Fm		2058
12a	10	SOUT	5f Aw	36	2632
31	5	REDC	5f Gd/Fm	33	2864
0	15	CARL	6f Aw	35	3194

ANNANDALE 4 ch f £848

21a	9	SOUT	7f Aw		249
0a	11	WOLV	9f Aw	41	306
35a	2	SOUT	8f Aw	35	1803

ANNAPURNA 4 b f £10829

79	8	KEMP	10f Soft		1014	
100	2	NEWM	9f Gd/Fm		1154	
100	3	GOOD	10f Gd/Sft		1482	
89	4	NEWB	10f Gd/Sft		1592	
62	9	EPSO	9f Gd/Sft		1825	
98	4	ASCO	8f Good	98	4113	
87	11	NEWM	9f Good		4347	
62	9	NEWB	9f Sft/Hvy	97	4472	BL

ANNATTO 2 b f £4251

77	2	RIPO	6f Gd/Fm		3009
70	4	SALI	6f Gd/Fm		3387
85	2	LING	7f Firm		3829
91	3	NEWB	7f Firm		3985
83	12	NEWM	7f Good		4158

ANNE MCCOL 2 b f £0

41	8	BATH	5f Firm		3621
0	17	WARW	7f Gd/Fm		3910

ANNE SOPHIE 2 ch f £0

41	7	LEIC	6f Gd/Fm		3096

49	9	KEMP	6f Gd/Fm		3358	
0	13	LING	5f Good		4096	

ANNELIINA 4 b f £0

10a	9	WOLV	8f Aw		409	
9a	7	WOLV	9f Aw		578	t
28a	10	WOLV	7f Aw	45	635	
28	12	BATH	13f Gd/Fm	58	1440	

ANNESPRIDE 3 b f £0

12	5	CATT	7f Soft		1682	
34	5	REDC	8f Good		2159	
0	14	NEWC	8f Good	51	2524	t

ANNETTE VALLON 3 b f £7107

85	2	HAYD	8f Gd/Sft		808
79	1	**FOLK**	5f Gd/Fm		2294*
86	3	NEWM	5f Good	83	2569
89	2	NEWM	5f Gd/Fm	85	2859

ANNIE APPLE 4 ch f £3454

40a	7	LING	5f Aw	54	147	
39a	7	LING	8f Aw	51	594	
32a	9	LING	6f Aw	48	691	
37	10	WARW	7f Soft	52	1066	
47	5	BRIG	7f Gd/Sft	50	1336	
43	8	CHEP	7f Gd/Sft	49	1794	
47	4	BRIG	7f Gd/Fm	49	1930	vis
34	5	EPSO	8f Gd/Sft		2433	vis
23	7	BRIG	7f Gd/Fm	47	2728	vis
34	9	EPSO	8f Gd/Fm		3404	
45	1	**BRIG**	7f Firm		3559*	
41	8	BRIG	8f Firm		3736	
45	2	BATH	8f Gd/Fm	43	3816	
54a	1	LING	7f Aw		4328	
45a	7	LING	7f Aw		4487	

ANNIE RUAN 2 b f £749

0	15	BATH	6f Gd/Sft		1667
72	5	LEIC	7f Good		2029
72	4	FOLK	6f Gd/Fm		3443
75	4	BATH	5f Firm		3621
0	14	LING	5f Good	73	4098

ANNIEIRWIN 4 ch f £18050

100	1	**LEOP**	9f Good		2071*
101	4	CURR	10f Good		3556

ANNIJAZ 3 b f £8141

60a	5	LING	7f Aw	68	773	
0	15	WIND	10f Good		850	
8	11	BEVE	8f Heavy		973	
0	16	BRIG	6f Firm	58	1211	
46	4	SALI	7f Good		1349	
40a	6	LING	6f Aw	51	1742	
47	3	SALI	8f Firm	51	2025	
47	3	LING	6f Gd/Fm	48	2591	
22	12	BRIG	7f Gd/Fm	48	2729	
57	1	**EPSO**	7f Good	48	2794*	
49	7	YARM	7f Good	56	3030	
57	3	LING	7f Gd/Fm	56	3279	
47	5	BRIG	8f Firm	56	3561	
60	2	EPSO	7f Good	56	3765	
55	3	BEVE	7f Sft/Hvy	59	4044	
57	4	LING	7f Soft	59	4192	

ANNIVERSARY DAY 4 ch g £0

0	13	PONT	10f Heavy	47	943
0	13	REDC	11f Soft		4497

ANNO DOMINI 4 b c £0

49	9	SALI	7f Gd/Fm		1884
62	10	CHEP	5f Gd/Fm	80	2451

ANNS MILL 3 b f £0

0	15	BRIG	10f Gd/Sft	60	892
51	4	BRIG	7f Firm		1212
42	7	SALI	7f Good		1349
34	12	BRIG	7f Gd/Fm	52	1930
39	7	NOTT	8f Gd/Fm	48	2187
22	8	YARM	7f Gd/Fm		2413

ANONYMITY 2 ch c £0

ANOTHER (continued)

58	10	LING	7f Soft		4267
0	16	YARM	7f Soft		4514

ANOTHER ARTHUR 4 b c £0

36	6	MUSS	16f Gd/Fm		1145

ANOTHER BEVELED 5 ch g £0

0a	14	LING	10f Aw	45	2212
42	4	SALI	12f Good	43	2689
U	U	CHEP	12f Gd/Fm	43	2971

ANOTHER DIAMOND 2 b f £0

59	9	DONC	8f Heavy		4569

ANOTHER MONK 9 b g £9581

52a	1	LING	16f Aw	48	6	
19a	8	WOLV	16f Aw	49	141	
43a	4	LING	13f Aw	49	317	
47a	1	LING	16f Aw		402*	VIS
35a	4	LING	13f Aw	46	458	vis
48a	1	LING	13f Aw	41	835*	
51	1	WIND	10f Gd/Sft	44	1100*	
52a	2	LING	12f Aw	48	1677	
39	10	WIND	12f Good	49	1730	

ANOTHER NIGHTMARE 8 b m £2115

36a	7	LING	5f Aw	48	57
43a	4	WOLV	5f Aw	47	116
32a	9	WOLV	5f Aw	47	139
45a	3	LING	6f Aw	45	154
49a	1	LING	6f Aw	44	262*

ANOTHER RAINBOW 4 br f £216

51a	5	LING	13f Aw	63	167
40a	10	LING	10f Aw	58	224
5a	8	SOUT	11f Aw		248
46a	3	WOLV	12f Aw		295
29a	5	WOLV	12f Aw		347

ANOTHER SECRET 2 b f £658

77	4	NEWB	6f Gd/Fm		3449
66	7	KEMP	7f Gd/Fm		3789
72	4	LING	6f Soft		4189
56	9	WIND	6f Gd/Fm		4289

ANOTHER TIME 8 ch g £5714

76	7	NEWM	10f Gd/Fm	86	1170
81	5	REDC	10f Gd/Sft	83	1561
67	13	EPSO	10f Good	82	1845
78	4	RIPO	10f Gd/Fm	79	2102
79	3	NEWM	10f Gd/Fm	77	3166
72	5	LEIC	10f Gd/Fm	78	3337
82	2	NEWM	10f Gd/Fm	83	3628
75	10	YARM	10f Firm	83	3941

ANOTHER VICTIM 6 ch g £904

20	11	DONC	6f Gd/Sft		1073
0	14	REDC	6f Firm		1298
53	3	BRIG	6f Gd/Sft		1508
41	8	SALI	7f Gd/Fm		1884
35	7	CHEP	6f Good	42	1971
34	8	NOTT	6f Gd/Fm	39	2192
40	2	BATH	5f Gd/Sft	37	2555
18	10	DONC	5f Gd/Fm	37	2753

ANSAR 4 b c £20000

91	2	CHES	19f Gd/Fm	87	1222
86	10	NEWC	16f Firm	91	2336
87	8	NEWM	18f Good	91	4353

ANSELLAD 3 b c £2130

73	9	LING	6f Gd/Sft	90	1285
77	7	ASCO	5f Good	86	2168
84	2	BATH	5f Firm	82	2787
81	5	GOOD	5f Good	84	3135
66	15	EPSO	5f Good	83	3687
63	10	CHES	5f Soft	82	4073

ANSELLMAN 10 gr g £5337

27	13	DONC	6f Gd/Sft		1068	bl
65	2	REDC	6f Firm		1298	bl
47	5	CATT	6f Good		1664	bl
60	4	PONT	5f Good		1868	bl
58	7	HAMI	6f Firm	63	2097	bl
41	12	NEWC	5f Firm	60	2340	bl
63	1	BATH	5f Firm		2788*	bl
55	4	CATT	5f Gd/Fm		2931	bl
59	5	LEIC	5f Gd/Fm	64	3214	bl
62	3	NEWM	5f Gd/Fm	63	3631	bl
62	3	EPSO	6f Good		3689	bl
65	2	SAND	5f Gd/Fm		3947	bl
0	14	HAYD	5f Gd/Sft	65	4107	bl
51	5	SAND	5f Soft		4207	bl
52	10	BATH	5f Soft	61	4432	bl

ANSHAAM 3 b c £0

84	6	NEWM	12f Gd/Fm		1168

ANSHAN SQUAW 2 b f £0

0	18	DONC	7f Gd/Sft		4447

ANSTAND 5 b g £0

30	11	WIND	6f Gd/Fm	66	746	
0	25	ASCO	8f Gd/Sft	63	1113	
54	6	LING	7f Soft	58	1542	
0	13	CHEP	7f Gd/Sft	55	1799	
0	17	CHEP	7f Gd/Fm	52	2974	
0	14	KEMP	7f Gd/Fm	50	3362	
40	7	LING	6f Firm	50	3493	bl
34	11	SALI	7f Gd/Fm	45	3747	
0	13	YARM	6f Gd/Fm	43	3964	bl

ANTHEMION 3 ch c £6850

45	12	DONC	7f Good	70	736
64a	3	SOUT	6f Aw	66	1205
71a	1	WOLV	7f Aw	65	1390*
72	1	HAYD	7f Gd/Sft	65	1793*
65	4	REDC	7f Gd/Fm	71	2145

ANTHONY MON AMOUR 5 b g £11530

0	23	THIR	5f Good	62	1162	
0a	14	SOUT	6f Aw	66	1504	
55	4	CATT	6f Gd/Sft	59	1815	t
66	1	CATT	5f Aw	56	2418+	t
55	7	YORK	5f Gd/Fm	63	2644	
74	1	PONT	5f Gd/Fm	66	2830*	t
71	3	BATH	6f Firm	72	2944	t
67	5	NEWB	5f Gd/Fm	73	3176	t
71	6	RIPO	6f Gd/Fm	73	3464	
65	7	EPSO	5f Good	72	3687	
0	17	DONC	5f Firm	72	3894	
62	13	AYR	5f Soft	71	3960	t
0	19	YORK	5f Soft	69	4285	t

ANTHONY ROYLE 2 ch c £236

54	6	CHES	5f Good		2664	
64	6	THIR	7f Gd/Fm		2966	
64	5	HAYD	6f Good		3286	
45	5	RIPO	5f Good		3463	
73	8	RIPO	5f Gd/Fm		3714	
63	10	MUSS	5f Gd/Sft		4131	
37a	10	WOLV	5f Aw		4441	BL

ANTICLES 3 ch c £0

92	6	CLAI	12f Good		3718
93	10	NEWM	10f Good	98	4197

ANTIGONEL 3 b f £370

60	7	LING	7f Gd/Sft		839
58	3	NOTT	8f Heavy	57	1024
45	7	BRIG	8f Soft	58	1511
0	14	CHEP	7f Gd/Sft	58	1799

ANTINNAZ 4 ch f £0

82	9	MAIS	6f Heavy		820

ANTIPODES 2 gr f £0

68	9	NEWM	7f Gd/Fm		3459

ANTONIAS DILEMMA 2 ch f £4657

53	8	WARW	5f Heavy		886
77	1	LING	5f Firm		2324*
77	3	GOOD	5f Good	77	3109

ANTONIAS DOUBLE 5 ch m £5891

50a	5	WOLV	5f Aw	69	751
0	17	THIR	5f Gd/Sft	75	1357
66	12	RIPO	5f Good	74	1861
68	11	YORK	5f Gd/Fm	74	1980
75	3	NEWC	5f Gd/Fm	73	2310
61	9	SAND	5f Gd/Fm	70	2473
54	13	YORK	5f Gd/Fm	73	2644
75	2	NEWC	5f Gd/Fm	71	2987
54	17	GOOD	5f Gd/Fm	71	3091
73	3	NEWB	5f Gd/Fm	73	3485
0	19	DONC	5f Firm	73	3894

ANTONIO CANOVA 4 ch c £14296

73	3	THIR	6f Gd/Fm	72	1356
64	9	WIND	6f Gd/Fm	73	2054
62	11	YORK	7f Good	73	2694
76	1	NEWM	6f Gd/Fm	70	2961*
78	2	YORK	6f Good	75	3543

ANUGRAHA 7 gr g £0

19a	9	SOUT	12f Aw		387

ANYHOW 3 b f £2199

65	7	LEIC	7f Good		794
63	4	NOTT	8f Soft		1643
67	1	LING	7f Good	62	2591*
35	14	NEWM	7f Gd/Fm	69	3163
38a	7	WOLV	8f Aw	70	3274
53	12	LING	7f Soft	69	4192

ANZARI 3 b c £20900

96	3	CURR	7f Soft		1120
105	1	LEOP	8f Gd/Fm		1316*

APACHE POINT 3 ch c £0

72	14	NEWM	7f Gd/Sft		983

APADI 4 ch c £0

80a	6	LING	12f Aw		27
76a	8	LING	10f Aw		55
52a	9	LING	10f Aw		157
0	19	SALI	7f Good	74	1348
33	13	NEWB	7f Gd/Fm	10	1590

APLESTEDE 3 b f £287

69	10	GOOD	8f Gd/Fm		1811
37	13	WIND	8f Gd/Fm		2211
51	4	YARM	7f Firm		2770

APLOY 3 b f £9695

67	6	BRIG	7f Gd/Fm		1125	
62	4	LING	8f Gd/Fm		2215	
66	4	LEIC	8f Gd/Fm	66	2512	
62	5	LEIC	7f Gd/Fm	65	2775	
71	1	SALI	7f Gd/Fm	65	2978*	
74	2	KEMP	7f Gd/Fm	68	3362	
76	2	SALI	7f Firm	73	3750	VIS
71	6	KEMP	8f Soft	76	4038	
73	8	NEWM	7f Firm	76	4215	

APOLLO BAY 4 b c £3867

70a	1	WOLV	12f Aw	67	407*	bl
0a	5	WOLV	12f Aw		679	

APOLLO RED 11 ch g £9134

73a	7	LING	8f Aw	82	7
62a	8	LING	7f Aw		104
58a	1	LING	7f Aw		156*
72a	3	LING	7f Aw	72	239
65a	1	LING	8f Aw		316*
72a	2	LING	7f Aw		398
62a	6	LING	7f Aw	70	462
77a	1	LING	7f Aw	68	503*
62a	1	LING	7f Aw		571*
34	11	NEWM	7f Gd/Fm	52	2347
59a	4	LING	7f Aw		2759

APOLLO VICTORIA 3 b c £4280

107	2	GOWR	9f Gd/Fm		818	
103	4	LING	11f Gd/Sft		1284	VIS
0	8	CURR	10f Gd/Sft		1627	BL
99	5	CURR	10f Good		3556	
92	6	LEOP	10f Good		3925	

APORTO 2 ch c £3612

35	8	CATT	5f Firm		2435
0	13	BEVE	5f Firm		2730

59	3	NEWC	6f Gd/Fm		2983	
29	13	NEWC	7f Good	58	3246	
52	4	THIR	7f Gd/Fm		3615	
57	1	**CATT**	7f Soft	51	4007*	
40	7	MUSS	8f Gd/Sft	56	4132	
48	4	PONT	6f Soft	56	4235	
0a	13	SOUT	6f Aw	60	4367	

APPELLATION 2 b c £9403

74	6	WIND	5f Good		2368
88	4	WIND	5f Gd/Fm		3044
95	1	**GOOD**	6f Good		3881*
95	1	**GOOD**	6f Soft		4079*

APPLE TOWN 3 br f £13535

77	3	THIR	12f Good		1386
71	2	CATT	12f Good		1661
75	1	**BRIG**	12f Gd/Fm		3241+
83	1	**HAYD**	12f Soft	76	4092*
83	4	YORK	12f Soft		4276

APPLES AND PEARS 4 b f £0

6a	12	WOLV	5f Aw	51	291
41a	5	LING	5f Aw	51	312
18a	9	SOUT	6f Aw	47	425
35	14	REDC	5f Gd/Sft	51	1133
42	7	HAMI	5f Gd/Fm	47	1358
27	7	CATT	6f Good		1664
14	12	CARL	6f Gd/Fm		2240
43	4	WARW	5f Good		3694
38	5	THIR	5f Gd/Sft	38	3781

APPROACHABLE 5 b g £5715

60a	2	SOUT	8f Aw		45	
54a	4	SOUT	8f Aw		138	
45a	7	SOUT	8f Aw		197	VIS
55a	2	SOUT	8f Aw		252	
26a	5	WOLV	9f Aw		259	
46a	4	WOLV	8f Aw		322	
47a	4	WOLV	8f Aw		393	
48a	2	SOUT	11f Aw		455	
47a	3	SOUT	12f Aw		530	
44a	2	WOLV	12f Aw		626	
31a	4	SOUT	11f Aw		672	
46a	2	WOLV	12f Aw		710	
52a	2	SOUT	11f Aw		866	
33a	5	WOLV	12f Aw		1039	
45a	4	SOUT	12f Aw		1203	
43a	2	WOLV	12f Aw		1389	
43a	2	SOUT	11f Aw		1415	
0	14	BEVE	10f Firm	40	1921	
46a	2	LING	10f Aw	43	2212	
43a	3	SOUT	8f Aw	43	2380	
47a	3	SOUT	12f Aw	47	2634	
33a	6	WOLV	8f Aw	47	3499	

APPROBATION 3 ch c £0

0	20	DONC	10f Gd/Sft	72	4448

APPROVED QUALITY 7 b m £0

0a	9	SOUT	12f Aw	40	590

APPYABO 5 ch g £2464

47a	7	LING	10f Aw		1	
28a	8	LING	10f Aw		111	
10a	7	LING	10f Aw	35	167	
19a	7	SOUT	11f Aw		248	
37a	2	WOLV	12f Aw		347	
32a	1	**LING**	13f Aw	28	458*	
33a	3	LING	13f Aw		524	
18a	6	WOLV	13f Aw	31	608	
40a	5	LING	12f Aw		650	
10a	7	LING	13f Aw	33	835	
14a	7	LING	12f Aw		2181	BL

APRIL ACE 4 ch g £0

0a	13	LING	10f Aw	57	842
0	29	ASCO	10f Gd/Sft	57	1113
41	10	HAMI	8f Firm	57	1243
42	8	BRIG	8f Firm	55	1330

0	20	DONC	7f Gd/Fm	52	1840	
0	15	BATH	8f Firm	48	1998	

APRIL LEE 2 b f £2218

50a	6	SOUT	5f Aw		865	E
57a	7	SOUT	5f Aw		1304	e
62	5	BRIG	5f Gd/Sft		1463	e
61	5	FOLK	7f Gd/Fm		2290	e
74	2	WARW	7f Good		2459	e
64	5	LING	6f Good		2588	e
72	2	YARM	7f Good		3029	e
53	8	NEWB	7f Gd/Fm	70	3175	e
66	3	BRIG	8f Gd/Sft		4116	e
60	9	CATT	5f Soft	65	4254	e
62	8	BRIG	7f Soft	65	4416	e
37	10	DONC	7f Heavy	62	4577	ec

APRIL STAR 3 ch f £0

44	9	SALI	11f Gd/Fm		2232
55	5	SALI	6f Gd/Sft		2472
43	7	YARM	7f Firm		2770
0	18	GOOD	10f Good	49	3663
0	14	LEIC	10f Heavy		4313

APRIL STOCK 5 ch m £7150

71	5	EPSO	10f Heavy	73	1031	
80	1	**CHEP**	12f Heavy	73	1555*	t
64	14	ASCO	12f Good	78	2069	t

APRILS COMAIT 3 br f £832

44a	3	SOUT	5f Aw		217	
30a	6	LING	5f Aw	45	269	
32a	8	SOUT	6f Aw		426	
36a	5	WOLV	5f Aw		659	
43a	3	SOUT	5f Aw		696	
50	3	CATT	5f Gd/Fm		777	
31	10	MUSS	5f Gd/Sft	52	901	
51	9	BEVE	5f Firm		1280	
36	8	CATT	5f Gd/Fm	49	1817	BL
45	5	MUSS	5f Firm	47	2047	bl
44	6	MUSS	5f Firm	47	2374	bl
25	8	NOTT	5f Firm		2680	bl
12	12	RIPO	5f Gd/Fm	45	2839	bl
0	12	THIR	8f Gd/Fm	45	2964	

APTITUDE 3 br c £103659

121e	2	CHUR	10f Dirt		1226

AQUADAM 3 b g £0

25	10	LEIC	8f Gd/Fm		3094
24a	8	WOLV	9f Aw		3498
20	11	LEIC	10f Gd/Sft		4029

AQUARIUS 2 b c £0

78	5	NEWB	7f Firm		2708

AQUATIC KING 5 b g £0

0a	15	SOUT	12f Aw	42	70

AQUAVITA 6 b m £2248

10a	9	SOUT	14f Aw	40	1501
33a	3	SOUT	14f Aw		1975
0a	5	LING	13f Aw		2323
33a	4	WOLV	16f Aw	33	2606
23	4	LING	16f Firm	33	2763
33a	1	**SOUT**	16f Aw	28	2951*
18a	6	WOLV	15f Gd/Fm	33	3276

AQUIRE NOT DESIRE 4 ch g £0

68	5	GOOD	8f Soft		4077
42	8	NEWM	12f Good		4178

ARAB GOLD 5 b g £4242

10a	11	LING	10f Aw		110	
27a	10	LING	7f Aw		156	
34a	10	WOLV	7f Aw		379	VIS
0a	11	WOLV	7f Aw		449	vis
56a	3	LING	7f Aw		507	
25a	12	LING	6f Aw	37	543	
53a	3	WOLV	5f Aw		624	
40a	1	**LING**	6f Aw	36	634*	
45a	4	SOUT	5f Aw		653	
34a	4	SOUT	5f Aw	40	674	

44a	8	WOLV	5f Aw		1237	
49	6	BRIG	6f Gd/Sft		1508	
33a	8	LING	7f Aw		1739	
39a	3	SOUT	5f Aw	39	1806	BL
37	4	HAMI	5f Firm		2095	bl
0	14	LING	5f Gd/Fm	38	2184	
0	18	BATH	5f Gd/Sft	36	2555	bl
43	3	BATH	5f Firm		2788	
20	10	BATH	6f Firm	43	2944	
50	2	BATH	6f Firm		3208	vis
36	6	LING	6f Firm	44	3578	vis

ARABELLA GIRL 3 ch f £0

0a	16	SOUT	8f Aw	55	2380

ARABESQUE 3 b f £24389

93	3	NEWM	7f Gd/Sft		971
91	1	**SALI**	6f Firm		1175*
93	4	NOTT	6f Good		1410
89	11	NEWM	6f Gd/Fm	94	1694
98	4	ASCO	8f Good	93	2167
101	1	**PONT**	6f Firm		3503*
87	13	NEWM	6f Good		4346

ARABIAN MOON 4 ch c £16240

0	13	KEMP	12f Gd/Sft	87	1076
91	3	YORK	12f Good		1307
75	5	YORK	14f Gd/Fm	89	1982
89	1	**PONT**	10f Firm		2178+
91	3	HAYD	12f Gd/Fm	89	2502
85	4	SAND	12f Good	90	2937

ARABIAN WATERS 2 b f £0

0	12	WIND	6f Good		3187
58	7	FOLK	7f Gd/Fm		3583

ARAGANT 4 b g £0

31	12	BRIG	10f Firm		1210	
21	11	LEIC	8f Gd/Fm		1731	
30	9	BRIG	10f Gd/Fm		1933	BL
0	10	FOLK	12f Gd/Fm	40	2295	
30	9	WARW	8f Good		2460	
30	6	BRIG	12f Firm	34	2904	

ARANA 5 b m £0

8a	9	LING	10f Aw		110	
19a	8	LING	10f Aw		163	BL
0	12	LEIC	8f Gd/Sft		1731	
0	11	LEIC	6f Firm	38	2031	
0	11	SAND	11f Good	50	2530	bl
0	6	WIND	12f Soft		2547	bl
16	12	WIND	12f Gd/Fm	28	2887	bl
0	7	CATT	16f Gd/Fm		3199	
0	15	WARW	16f Gd/Fm	38	3916	

ARANUI 3 b c £500

28a	13	SOUT	5f Aw		34	
54	8	DONC	8f Gd/Fm		2611	t
56	3	RIPO	9f Gd/Fm		2838	t
55	5	RIPO	10f Gd/Fm		3185	t
25a	9	WOLV	8f Aw	55	4021	

ARANYI 3 gr c £14049

82	5	NEWM	10f Gd/Sft	84	979	
77	4	THIR	12f Good		1386	
83	1	**RIPO**	9f Good		1863*	
78	3	RIPO	8f Gd/Fm	82	2108	
83	3	CHEP	8f Gd/Fm	80	2661	
84	3	BRIG	8f Firm	80	2906	
91	1	**RIPO**	9f Gd/Fm	83	3182*	
78	6	HAMI	9f Gd/Sft	90	3535	
90	5	NEWM	8f Good		4199	

ARAVONIAN 2 ch f £641

72	5	KEMP	7f Soft		4035
63	6	SALI	8f Gd/Sft		4163
75	3	WIND	8f Heavy		4524

ARAWAK PRINCE 4 ch g £0

0a	12	LING	10f Aw	83	632	BL

ARBENIG 5 b m £3873

25a	10	WOLV	7f Good	50	1235

50 3 BATH 8f Gd/Fm 48 1442
39 1 **LEIC** 8f Gd/Sft 1732*
0 12 CHEP 7f Gd/Fm 55 1794
42 5 BATH 8f Firm 49 2331
50 2 CHEP 8f Gd/Fm 48 2658
45 7 GOOD 9f Good 50 3110
34 4 CHEP 8f Gd/Fm 50 3251
40 8 BATH 8f Firm 49 3623
50 2 WARW 11f Gd/Fm 47 3915
31a 6 WOLV 12f Aw 48 4386

ARC 6 b g £10434
65a 2 WOLV 8f Aw 62 38
51a 4 WOLV 9f Aw 64 119
68a 2 WOLV 8f Aw 64 551
67a 4 WOLV 9f Aw 69 611
70a 2 WOLV 9f Aw 68 681
66a 4 WOLV 8f Aw 70 718
65 1 **MUSS** 8f Gd/Sft 60 899*
60 2 PONT 8f Heavy 942
38 10 BEVE 8f Firm 65 1279
69 1 **CARL** 8f Gd/Sft 64 1721*
63 11 CARL 8f Gd/Fm 67 2242

ARC EN CIEL 2 b c £313
66 9 NEWB 7f Firm 2708
80 6 NEWB 7f Gd/Fm 3484
64 4 EPSO 9f Good 3853
0 17 WIND 10f Gd/Sft 74 4290

ARCADIAN CHIEF 3 b g £0
0 15 NOTT 6f Good 45 785
45 5 BRIG 5f Firm 43 1334
27 5 BRIG 5f Soft 42 1512
35 7 LING 5f Gd/Fm 44 2184
0 19 BATH 5f Gd/Sft 41 2555
0 12 LEIC 7f Gd/Fm 3332
0 18 LING 6f Firm 44 3759

ARCHDUKE FERDINAND 2 ch c £1086
80 9 ASCO 7f Good 2091
95 1 **GOOD** 7f Firm 3154*
98 5 GOOD 8f Good 3882

ARCHELLO 6 b m £3831
0a 13 SOUT 8f Aw 43 85
53 1 **CARL** 6f Firm 43 1258*
30 9 DONC 7f Good 52 1519
43 8 DONC 6f Gd/Fm 52 1842
32 13 CARL 6f Firm 51 2015
27 7 WARW 8f Gd/Fm 49 2257
48 3 PONT 6f Good 49 2364
28 10 PONT 8f Gd/Fm 47 2561

ARCHIE BABE 4 ch g £15486
48 6 RIPO 12f Soft 67 825
58 5 PONT 10f Heavy 67 943
40 12 NEWM 10f Gd/Fm 66 1150
70 1 **PONT** 12f Good 63 1499*
61 7 THIR 12f Gd/Sft 68 1715
77 1 **NEWC** 10f Heavy 67 1769*
67 9 CATT 12f Gd/Sft 73 1816
79 1 **PONT** 10f Gd/Fm 2562*
56 8 NEWM 10f Good 79 3024
80 2 PONT 12f Gd/Fm 79 3224
69 5 PONT 12f Firm 80 3504
56 9 YORK 12f Gd/Fm 80 3725
0 17 DONC 10f Firm 78 3899
75 3 CATT 12f Soft 76 4003
52 8 YORK 10f Soft 74 4282
80 1 **NEWC** 10f Heavy 73 4427*

ARCHIRONDEL 2 b c £0
37 8 CATT 5f Soft 4252
0 8 PONT 6f Soft 4373
44 7 MUSS 7f Soft 4559

ARCTIC CHAR 4 br f £15665
88 14 NEWM 7f Gd/Sft 98 966
99 1 **HAYD** 7f Gd/Fm 1163*

93 7 HAYD 7f Gd/Sft 1834
96 6 GOOD 7f Gd/Fm 3132

ARCTIC HIGH 3 b f £1973
45a 3 WOLV 7f Aw 493
70a 2 WOLV 9f Aw 610
62a 3 WOLV 8f Aw 658
50 11 WIND 8f Gd/Fm 62 744
61a 3 WOLV 9f Aw 62 1040
22a 8 LING 7f Aw 1745
42 8 BRIG 10f Firm 2041
0 16 BATH 12f Gd/Sft 50 2554
20 14 YARM 8f Gd/Fm 44 3971
45 8 GOOD 7f Soft 60 4080

ARCTIC OWL 6 b g £162400
114 3 SAND 16f Soft 1565
114 7 ASCO 20f Good 2114
116 1 **ASCO** 12f Gd/Fm 3306*
119 1 **CURR** 14f Good 4055*

ARDANZA 3 b f £2330
73 2 SALI 10f Good 1343
57 4 NEWM 12f Gd/Fm 2963
66 6 SAND 10f Good 3432
65 5 THIR 8f Gd/Sft 74 3977
65 2 BRIG 8f Soft 4177

ARDARROCH PRINCE 9 b g £0
32 8 REDC 16f Gd/Fm 55 2866
5 10 CARL 14f Gd/Fm 50 3084

ARDENT 6 b g £4171
51a 2 LING 10f Aw 47 23
53a 2 LING 10f Aw 50 100
12a 10 LING 10f Aw 51 161
45a 6 LING 10f Aw 51 203 HD
28a 6 LING 12f Aw 50 332 hd
46 4 BRIG 8f Gd/Fm 49 1129
42 8 BATH 8f Gd/Fm 48 1442
29 11 EPSO 10f Good 46 2790
31 9 KEMP 8f Gd/Fm 44 3078
40 5 BRIG 8f Firm 42 3527
46 1 **BRIG** 10f Firm 42 3557*
43 3 BRIG 10f Firm 42 3737
51a 4 LING 12f AW 4186

ARDUINE 3 ch f £3468
82 3 WIND 10f Gd/Fm 1200
83 3 NEWB 10f Gd/Fm 1404
0 10 CHAN 11f Gd/Sft 1901
80 3 ASCO 8f Gd/Fm 3019
70 3 EPSO 9f Gd/Fm 3413
67 8 CHEP 10f Good 78 3870
70 4 NEWB 10f Sft/Hv 4474

AREION 5 b g £38710
114 1 **HAMB** 6f Soft 2403*

AREISH 7 b m £16341
51a 2 WOLV 9f Aw 51 67
31a 10 SOUT 11f Aw 50 131
43a 5 WOLV 9f Aw 50 271
56a 1 **WOLV** 9f Aw 50 305*
54a 1 **WOLV** 9f Aw 48 349*
58a 1 **WOLV** 9f Aw 54 447*
56a 2 WOLV 9f Aw 55 529
60a 1 **WOLV** 9f Aw 55 611*
57a 3 WOLV 9f Aw 59 681
50a 5 WOLV 9f Aw 59 749
48a 6 SOUT 8f Aw 58 2121
34a 8 SOUT 8f Aw 57 2379
34 9 HAYD 11f Good 48 3285
39a 7 WOLV 9f Aw 55 4228

ARETHA 3 ch f £13000
98 2 LEOP 7f Soft 948
96 4 CURR 7f Soft 1122 BL
108 4 LEOP 6f Good 3373
109 3 LEOP 5f Good 3923 bl

ARETINO 3 ch c £2588

0 18 NEWM 7f Good 92 954
73 5 LING 8f Gd/Sft 1262
73 8 KEMP 6f Gd/Fm 85 1925
78 5 KEMP 7f Firm 80 2261
10 16 SAND 10f Gd/Fm 79 2495
60 9 YARM 7f Firm 77 2768
76 2 FOLK 7f Gd/Fm 75 3041
74 6 EPSO 7f Gd/Fm 75 3414
75 4 RIPO 6f Good 76 3698

AREYDHA 3 b f £4909
88 10 NEWM 7f Good 955
92 7 DUSS 8f Good 1229
94 2 NEWM 6f Good 93 4198
0 4 CURR 6f Soft 4398
85 3 NEWM 6f Gd/Fm 4535

ARGENT FACILE 3 b c £10883
81 2 FOLK 5f Soft 959 t
86 2 SAND 5f Heavy 82 1047 t
74 9 CHES 8f Gd/Fm 86 1219 t
90 2 LEIC 6f Gd/Fm 1576 t
90 2 WIND 6f Good 1728 t
91 3 ASCO 5f Good 89 2168 t
75 10 NEWM 6f Good 90 2568 t
35 5 KEMP 5f Gd/Fm 3077 t
83 5 YARM 5f Gd/Fm 89 3668

ARGENTAN 3 b c £8549
90 2 NEWB 8f Good 1377
85 2 HAYD 7f Gd/Sft 1789
80 13 ASCO 8f Good 86 2117 VIS
86 1 **DONC** 8f Gd/Fm 2611*
87 4 NEWM 10f Gd/Fm 86 2858 BL
85 4 ASCO 8f Gd/Fm 86 3338 bl

ARHAAFF 2 b f £1616
83 2 NEWM 6f Gd/Fm 1691

ARIALA 3 b f £995
63 6 WIND 8f Heavy 934
40 7 PONT 10f Gd/Sft 1103
42 7 LEIC 12f Gd/Sft 1738
55 3 SAND 10f Soft 53 4208
9 7 LEIC 10f Heavy 4313
43 2 WIND 10f Heavy 4528

ARIES FIRECRACKER 2 b c £0
39 12 REDC 5f Gd/Sft 1131
33 11 AYR 6f Gd/Fm 1628
20 9 AYR 6f Gd/Fm 1653
22 11 CATT 7f Gd/Fm 2927
0 14 CATT 7f Good 3438 BL

ARISTAEUS 2 b c £0
6 9 REDC 7f Gd/Fm 3635

ARISTOCRAT 3 b c £235
84 4 WIND 10f Good 850
64 13 YORK 10f Gd/Fm 83 1310

ARISTOTLE 3 b c £5764
117 D LONG 11f Heavy 1026
102 10 EPSO 12f Good 1848

ARIUS 4 ch c £0
42 12 DONC 6f Gd/Sft 1068
0 17 WIND 6f Gd/Sft 1423
0 15 BEVE 7f Gd/Sft 55 1760 bl
39 6 BATH 8f Firm 48 2331 t
0 13 CHEP 8f Gd/Fm 45 2658 t

ARIZONA LADY 3 ch f £9684
70 1 **MUSS** 9f Gd/Sft 902*
0 12 PONT 10f Gd/Sft 68 1104
61 7 MUSS 9f Firm 68 2049
62 3 AYR 9f Good 68 2166
70 2 HAMI 8f Gd/Fm 68 2235
67 1 **HAMI** 9f Firm 63 2397*
61 5 HAMI 9f Gd/Fm 68 2799
70 7 AYR 8f Good 68 3365
41 11 MUSS 8f Gd/Sft 4135
67a 2 WOLV 9f Aw 65 4228

ARJAN 5 gr m £0 (continued)

60a	4	WOLV	12f Aw	67	4360
0a	11	WOLV	9f Aw	67	4382

ARJAN 5 gr m £0

26a	7	WOLV	5f Aw		639
0	16	THIR	5f Soft	73	926

ARJAY 2 b c £4324

48	5	RIPO	6f Good		1859
60	6	AYR	7f Good		3363
78	2	NOTT	6f Soft		3974
87	1	NEWC	6f Heavy		4402*

ARKADIAN HERO 5 ch g £134295

109	4	NEWM	6f Good		952
103	4	NEWM	5f Gd/Fm		1172
108	4	YORK	6f Firm		1338
115	1	NEWM	7f Firm		2343+
114	6	GOOD	8f Gd/Fm		3087
120	1	NEWB	7f Firm		3452+
120	2	WOOD	8f Firm		3933

ARM AND A LEG 5 ch g £0

0a	11	WOLV	9f Aw	50	749

ARMAGNAC 2 b c £10191

61	6	NEWM	5f Gd/Fm		1169
85	4	EPSO	6f Good		1846
58	12	ASCO	6f Good		2067
92	4	NEWM	6f Gd/Fm		2598
80	2	PONT	6f Gd/Fm		2828
72	5	HAYD	6f Gd/Sft		3268
77	5	NEWM	8f Gd/Fm		3458
92	1	AYR	6f Soft		3958*
90	2	AYR	6f Soft	88	3987
82	8	NEWM	6f Gd/Fm	90	4214
76	14	NEWM	6f Good	89	4338

ARMEN 3 b c £2434

83	2	KEMP	12f Gd/Fm		1929
82	2	SALI	14f Good		2691
61	14	HAYD	14f Soft	80	3783

ARMENIA 3 ch f £5412

53a	2	LING	8f Aw		265
72a	1	SOUT	8f Aw		415*
62a	4	LING	10f Aw	69	509
51a	3	LING	10f Aw		545
51a	4	LING	10f Aw		882
38a	9	SOUT	8f Aw	58	1419
24a	8	WOLV	9f Aw	54	2080
53	7	HAYD	11f Good	58	3285
82	9	SALI	10f Gd/Fm		3389
0	19	YORK	10f Gd/Fm	60	3731
46	7	GOOD	10f Soft	55	4067
0	16	LEIC	8f Sft/Hvy	52	4310
57	2	BATH	8f Soft	52	4435

ARMIDA 2 b f £0

0	15	WIND	5f Gd/Sft		1424
29	11	NEWM	6f Gd/Fm		2854
31	11	BATH	6f Firm		3205
57	7	YARM	8f Gd/Fm		3665
0	15	LING	7f Firm	53	3830
0	27	NEWM	6f Good		4345

AROB PETE 3 b c £0

52a	8	LING	10f Aw		240
0a	9	WOLV	8f Aw		395
67	6	WIND	10f Good		1725
50	8	BATH	10f Firm	60	2332
32	8	EPSO	9f Good	57	2795

AROGANT PRINCE 3 ch g £8747

47	9	WIND	5f Gd/Sft	56	1098
54	4	BRIG	5f Firm	56	1211
54	3	BRIG	5f Firm	52	1334
62	1	WIND	5f Gd/Sft	59	1427*
39	6	BRIG	5f Good	59	1650
53	7	GOOD	6f Gd/Fm	62	1961
48	11	LING	5f Gd/Fm	60	2184
42	10	SAND	5f Gd/Fm	59	2478
53	4	KEMP	5f Gd/Sft	59	2586
45	12	GOOD	5f Gd/Fm	61	3135
55	3	WIND	5f Good	55	3191
47	8	EPSO	6f Gd/Fm	55	3405
41	13	SALI	6f Firm	54	3747
44	11	GOOD	5f Good	53	3908

ARONA 2 b f £0

50	7	NOTT	6f Soft		3974
60	10	REDC	7f Gd/Sft		4216
61	5	LEIC	7f Heavy		4312
18	12	REDC	6f Gd/Sft	62	4502

ARPEGGIO 5 b g £12596

0a	12	SOUT	6f Aw	75	645
54	11	CATT	7f Gd/Fm	73	780
60	9	THIR	5f Gd/Sft	68	1714
67	4	WIND	6f Good	64	2371
67	1	CATT	7f Gd/Fm		2437*
0	16	DONC	7f Gd/Fm	70	2612
65	3	REDC	7f Firm	69	3328
77	1	LING	8f Firm	69	3831*
77	3	DONC	7f Gd/Fm	75	3880
75	7	AYR	7f Soft	75	3992
60	16	NEWM	7f Gd/Fm	76	4215
70	9	NEWM	7f Good	75	4357 BL

ARPELLO 3 b f £0

43a	8	WOLV	5f Aw		77
24a	11	WOLV	6f Aw		118
35a	10	LING	7f Aw		164

ARRAN MIST 2 b f £328

46	9	REDC	5f Gd/Sft		1130
65	3	REDC	5f Firm		1294
54	7	RIPO	6f Gd/Fm		3466
50	6	YORK	6f Good		3814
67	9	DONC	5f Gd/Sft		4449

ARROGANT 3 b g £340

31a	11	LING	7f Aw		94
40	3	BRIG	10f Firm	37	2908
4	10	BRIG	10f Gd/Fm	40	3244

ART EXPERT 2 b c £2940

67	10	NEWM	8f Good		4161
77	2	YORK	8f Heavy		4297
77	2	BRIG	8f Soft		4418
69	5	BRIG	10f Heavy		4539 BL

ARTAX 5 br h £344578

124a1		GULF	6f Fast		17*

ARTERXERXES 7 b g £2701

0a	14	SOUT	8f Aw	79	49
79	3	CHES	8f Firm	75	1250
52	14	KEMP	8f Gd/Fm	75	1926
0	20	DONC	8f Gd/Fm	75	2349
72	4	KEMP	8f Gd/Fm	73	3078
74	4	YORK	8f Good	72	3810

ARTFUL DANE 8 b g £5408

48	8	NOTT	8f Good		1407 bl
44	5	LEIC	8f Gd/Fm		1731
30	7	BATH	8f Firm	43	1998 bl
40	3	BATH	8f Firm	42	2331 bl
0	17	RIPO	10f Soft		2538 bl
31	7	NEWM	8f Gd/Fm		3117 vis
54	1	RIPO	8f Gd/Fm		3711* bl
60	1	CHEP	8f Good		3868* bl
0	13	BATH	10f Soft	59	4436 bl

ARTHUR K 3 ch g £607

48	6	KEMP	12f Gd/Fm		1929
70	4	SALI	14f Good		2691
47	8	HAYD	12f Gd/Fm		3324
45	3	CARL	17f Gd/Fm	45	3575

ARTHURS KINGDOM 4 b g £1287

39	11	LEIC	12f Good	63	791
58	3	HAMI	13f Gd/Fm	59	1363 vis
41	11	YARM	11f Gd/Sft	59	1614
57	4	HAMI	13f Gd/Fm	58	1936
48	4	BRIG	12f Gd/Sft	58	2425
50	6	LING	10f Good	58	2655
57	3	WARW	13f Gd/Fm	56	2843

ARTHURS QUAY 3 gr g £0

17a	6	SOUT	7f Aw		741

ARTIC COURIER 9 gr g £6566

46a	1	WOLV	12f Aw		581*
51a	1	WOLV	12f Aw		626*
49a	4	WOLV	12f Aw		710
46a	4	WOLV	12f Aw		1039
48	1	WIND	12f Gd/Fm	45	2887*
45	4	FOLK	12f Gd/Fm		3447
32	11	FOLK	12f Gd/Fm	47	3586

ARTIFACT 2 b f £450

70	3	LEIC	6f Gd/Fm		3096
0	11	WIND	6f Good		3187
69	7	LING	7f Soft		4267
0	18	NEWB	6f Sft/Hvy	65	4468

ARTYFACTUAL 3 ch c £0

0	12	LING	6f Firm		3579
46	9	BATH	6f Gd/Fm		3820
32	5	BRIG	8f Soft		4177

ARZILLO 4 b g £1398

32	13	WIND	6f Firm	55	854
54	3	BRIG	6f Firm	53	1211
50	4	NOTT	8f Good	53	1414
0	13	REDC	8f Gd/Sft	53	1578
47	4	CHEP	6f Good	51	1971
27	13	WARW	7f Gd/Fm	49	2840
45	3	THIR	7f Gd/Fm	48	3129
0	19	THIR	8f Gd/Fm	48	3144
45	5	SALI	7f Gd/Fm	49	3294
34	8	BEVE	10f Gd/Fm	47	3656 BL
30	9	BATH	8f Gd/Fm	47	3816 bl
54	2	YARM	7f Firm	48	3939
26	6	BEVE	7f Sft/Hvy	44	4044
46a	7	LING	7f Aw		4328
21a	8	WOLV	8f Aw	48	4440

AS GOOD AS IT GETS 2 b f £0

0	17	WARW	8f Soft		4281

ASAAL 3 b c £0

92	5	NEWB	8f Soft	98	912
76	6	ASCO	6f Gd/Sft		1111
83	9	HAYD	8f Gd/Sft	96	1534
83	9	NEWB	7f Firm	92	3981

ASAKIR 5 ch h £0

95	8	ASCO	8f Good		2675
96	9	ASCO	10f Gd/Fm	105	2995

ASAREER 2 b f £0

82	7	DONC	8f Gd/Sft		4445

ASCARI 4 br g £1682

46	8	CHEP	10f Good	62	1973
63	2	NEWM	8f Gd/Fm	62	2130
60	7	SAND	10f Gd/Fm	64	2527
61	3	BEVE	10f Good		2884
46	8	NEWM	10f Gd/Fm	61	3314
54	8	BRIG	8f Firm	60	3527
41	12	LEIC	8f Gd/Sft		4033 BL

ASCENSION 2 ch f £41455

102	1	NEWB	6f Firm		2850*
108	1	DEAU	7f Gd/Fm		3722*
102	6	LONG	8f Good		4260
108	2	DEAU	8f Heavy		4401

ASCENSIONNA 4 b f £3599

94	3	MAIS	11f Heavy		122

ASH 2 b f £0

0	18	DONC	6f Heavy		4575

ASH BOLD 3 ch c £0

44a	7	LING	7f Aw		164
0	16	PONT	8f Soft	51	4232
38a	8	SOUT	6f Aw		4364

ASH HAB 2 b c £0

81 7 NEWM 7f Firm 2346
57 11 KEMP 7f Firm 2867
0 12 KEMP 8f Gd/Fm 3799

ASH MOON 2 ch f £13248
83 1 HAYD 5f Gd/Sft 1538*
85 1 CARL 6f Firm 2014*
80 9 NEWM 6f Firm 2344
94 3 HAYD 6f Gd/Fm 3320
92 7 YORK 6f Firm 3596
94 2 AYR 6f Gd/Sft 4009
79 10 NEWM 6f Good 4345

ASHA FALLS 2 ch c £0
62 9 BATH 8f Soft 4429

ASHGAR 4 ch c £3663
92 7 HAYD 12f Heavy 987
101 5 ASCO 16f Gd/Sft 1109
100 6 CHES 13f Firm 1247
106 4 LONG 16f Gd/Sft 1456
88 11 ASCO 20f Good 2114 VIS
71 4 NEWB 16f Firm 100 2705 vis
70 8 ASCO 16f Gd/Fm 96 3302
90 6 NEWB 13f Gd/Fm 3483
58 6 NEWM 14f Good 90 4016

ASHKAAL 2 b c £0
48 12 SALI 8f Gd/Sft 4163
55 9 YORK 8f Soft 4281

ASHLEEN 3 ch f £275
58 4 SALI 6f Gd/Sft 2472
64 7 SALI 6f Soft 2977
39 9 CHEP 7f Gd/Fm 3256
0 16 LING 7f Firm 3834 t

ASHLEIGH BAKER 5 b m £7562
36 6 BRIG 12f Firm 51 1332
43 4 LEIC 12f Soft 49 1551
40 7 HAMI 9f Gd/Fm 46 1939
39 3 MUSS 12f Gd/Fm 43 2202
27 7 PONT 10f Good 43 2366
48 1 MUSS 12f Gd/Sft 43 2537*
45 6 CHES 10f Gd/Fm 48 2671
52 1 HAMI 12f Gd/Fm 48 2783*
51 2 MUSS 12f Good 51 3102
52 4 RIPO 12f Gd/Fm 51 3181
51 4 CHES 16f Gd/Sft 51 3511
26 12 YORK 10f Good 50 3731
41 5 HAYD 14f Gd/Sft 49 4105
40 6 REDC 14f Gd/Sft 48 4222

ASHLINN 2 ch f £5577
90 2 NEWM 6f Gd/Fm 2285
90 1 NEWM 7f Gd/Fm 3459*
86 7 NEWM 7f Gd/Fm 4210
86 14 NEWM 7f Good 4356

ASHNAYA 2 b f £0
61 13 NEWM 7f Soft 4541

ASHOVER AMBER 4 b f £1173
69a 4 SOUT 6f Aw 68 280
64a 5 LING 5f Aw 68 506
71a 2 WOLV 5f Aw 67 609
64a 3 SOUT 5f Aw 70 673
58a 4 SOUT 6f Aw 738

ASHVILLE LAD 3 b g £0
0 19 PONT 8f Firm 3506

ASIAN HEIGHTS 2 b c £3549
86 1 LING 7f Soft 4483*

ASKHAM 2 b c £2282
89 3 ASCO 7f Gd/Sft 4124

ASLY 3 b r c £18350
92 2 NEWM 8f Gd/Fm 1692
89 1 YORK 8f Firm 2006*
105 1 ASCO 10f Gd/Fm 3017*
95 8 YORK 9f Gd/Fm 3726
78 7 BATH 8f Soft 4142

ASPEN GEM 6 b m £0

25 8 MUSS 16f Gd/Sft 34 797 t

ASPIRANT DANCER 5 b g £672
63 9 NEWM 10f Good 71 4160
47 7 PONT 10f Soft 70 4374
63 4 DONC 17f Heavy 67 4579

ASPIRING DIVA 2 b f £4035
89 3 MAIS 7f Good 4049

ASSURANCE 3 b c £0
50 5 YARM 7f Firm 2770
0 13 LING 8f Soft 4273
38 8 YARM 7f Soft 4387

ASSURED PHYSIQUE 3 b c £595
55 7 KEMP 9f Gd/Sft 74 1075
64 5 NOTT 8f Good 1407
69 3 YARM 11f Good 67 1770
64 6 SAND 11f Good 67 1967 t
62 6 NEWM 8f Gd/Fm 67 2130 VIS
51 5 NOTT 8f Gd/Fm 2682 tvi
60 5 YARM 7f Good 64 3030 tvi
53 6 BRIG 10f Firm 62 3530 tvi
37 7 FOLK 10f Gd/Fm 62 3585 tvi
58a 4 LING 8f Aw 3756
54 6 BEVE 8f Good 58 3951
13 10 BEVE 10f Sft/Hv 58 4046

ASTAIREDOTCOM 2 b f £3288
56 4 BRIG 5f Firm 1208
50 5 HAYD 5f Soft 1492
36 11 YORK 6f Gd/Fm 1981 VIS
52 4 LEIC 6f Gd/Fm 54 3216
43 7 SAND 7f Good 53 3468
57 2 LING 6f Soft 4190
69a 1 WOLV 6f Aw 4359*

ASTER FIELDS 2 b f £0
41 9 WARW 5f Heavy 886
68 6 BEVE 5f Gd/Sft 1759
44 8 REDC 5f Gd/Fm 2142
49 5 HAMI 5f Soft 54 3802

ASTON MARA 3 b c £0
45 7 HAYD 11f Heavy 86 990
66 8 CHES 12f Gd/Fm 83 1225 BL
55 7 AYR 11f Gd/Fm 70 1633 bl
37 16 ASCO 16f Good 70 2173 bl
0a 7 SOUT 12f Aw 60 2382 bl
44 8 NEWC 14f Good 55 3249

ASTONISHED 4 ch g £36594
113 1 EPSO 5f Good 1091849*
107 4 SAND 5f Gd/Fm 2496
104 7 DONC 5f Gd/Fm 3874
108 2 NEWM 5f Good 4182

ASTRAC 9 b g £4761
77a 3 LING 7f Aw 104
85a 3 SOUT 6f Aw 84 129
61a 5 SOUT 6f Aw 84 183
85a 1 WOLV 6f Aw 406+
85a 3 WOLV 6f Aw 83 532
67a 10 SOUT 7f Aw 83 687
0 16 KEMP 6f Good 84 728
43 7 WARW 7f Soft 816
0 15 NEWB 6f Gd/Sft 78 1591
0 18 SALI 6f Gd/Fm 73 1887
0 21 GOOD 6f Gd/Fm 67 2355
55 7 KEMP 7f Gd/Fm 60 3796
51 10 GOOD 5f Soft 58 4065
42 13 WIND 6f Gd/Sft 55 4293

ASTRAL PRINCE 2 ch c £0
67 11 ASCO 7f Gd/Fm 2956
79 13 NEWM 7f Good 4183
63 5 NEWB 6f Sft/Hvy 4471

ASTRAL RHYTHM 5 b g £0
0a 15 SOUT 17f Aw 45 75

ASTROLOVE 2 ch f £0
0 12 YARM 8f Heavy 4477

ASTRONAUT 3 b g £5725
44 8 KEMP 7f Soft 1018
61 4 PONT 6f Gd/Sft 1105
75a 1 WOLV 9f Aw 1388*
78 2 CHEP 10f Gd/Fm 75 2450
74 2 PONT 10f Gd/Fm 2562
64 6 HAYD 12f Gd/Sft 76 3270
69 4 GOOD 12f Soft 4061 VIS
0 14 DONC 10f Good 72 4448 vis

ASTURIAN LADY 3 b f £0
0 12 NEWM 8f Firm 94 1853

ASWHATILLDOIS 2 b f £2219
46 11 LING 6f Firm 3832
57 5 WARW 15f Gd/Fm 3911
59 8 LING 5f Good 4095
66a 1 WOLV 7f Aw 4383*

AT LARGE 6 b g £8018
59 8 SAND 5f Gd/Fm 70 763
61 6 PONT 6f Heavy 68 941
72 1 WIND 6f Gd/Fm 66 1196*
61 7 BEVE 5f Firm 66 1278
76 1 LEIC 6f Soft 69 1545*
0 12 WIND 6f Gd/Fm 76 2207
0 7 NEWM 5f Good 76 2569
0 16 YORK 6f Good 76 2697
38 10 NEWM 6f Gd/Fm 75 3119
51 14 YORK 7f Good 3809
70 9 AYR 7f Soft 72 3992

ATACAT 4 b h £2250
99 3 LEOP 9f Good 2071

ATALYA 3 ch g £2395
43a 6 WOLV 6f Aw 118
54a 7 WOLV 8f Aw 171
75a 2 WOLV 9f Aw 319
65a 4 WOLV 6f Aw 610
37a 5 WOLV 8f Aw 661
65 2 WARW 8f Gd/Fm 2846
54 8 SALI 10f Gd/Fm 67 3390
40 11 WARW 7f Good 3696
0a 12 WOLV 8f Aw 65 4021

ATAMANA 2 b f £2430
85 2 GOOD 6f Good 3661
83 2 BEVE 7f Good 3953

ATAVUS 3 b c £19389
81 4 KEMP 9f Good 727
86 1 NEWM 8f Firm 79 1183*
80 8 GOOD 9f Gd/Sft 85 1452
86 3 NEWM 8f Gd/Fm 85 2858
82 5 NEWM 8f Good 85 3022
74 8 SAND 8f Good 85 3435
0 14 NEWB 8f Firm 83 3998
76 12 NEWM 9f Gd/Fm 85 4212
74 7 NEWM 8f Good 81 4348
76 7 NEWM 8f Soft 79 4545

ATEMME 2 b f £590
0 16 WIND 5f Gd/Fm 3044
64 3 NOTT 5f Gd/Fm 3114
37 7 LING 5f Firm 3576
0 R LEIC 6f Gd/Sft 65 4030
0 15 BATH 6f Soft 4137 BL
0 21 WIND 10f Gd/Sft 65 4290 bl

ATHLETIC SAM 2 b c £0
0 27 NEWM 8f Good 4349

ATLANTIC ACE 3 b c £2912
78 1 PONT 8f Soft 4234*
68 8 BRIG 8f Soft 4420
0 18 DONC 8f Heavy 75 4573

ATLANTIC CHARTER 4 b c £0
0 17 NEWC 10f Soft 70 757
62 6 PONT 8f Gd/Sft 67 875
57 5 HAMI 8f Gd/Fm 65 1190
32 5 NEWC 10f Heavy 63 1769

ATLANTIC EAGLE 2 b c £0 *(continued)*

```
35  14 AYR   11f Soft   60  3963
34   9 CHES  10f Soft   60  4074
```

ATLANTIC EAGLE 2 b c £0
```
71  13 NEWM  6f Good         4341
63   8 DONC  7f Gd/Sft       4446
```

ATLANTIC MYSTERY 2 ch f £985
```
67   3 CATT  6f Soft         4001
65   5 LING  6f Soft         4188
72   3 NEWC  6f Heavy        4402
```

ATLANTIC RHAPSODY 3 b c £73932
```
91a  1 SOUT  8f Aw       694*     BL
84   7 HAYD  8f Gd/Sft 88 810  bl
88   4 CHES  8f Gd/Sft 86 1215
90   4 GOOD  9f Gd/Sft 86 1452
95   1 HAYD  8f Gd/Sft 86 1535*
96   2 EPSO  7f Gd/Sft 92 1826
97   5 ASCO  8f Good   95 2117
93   6 SAND  10f Good  95 2475
89  11 NEWM  10f Gd/Fm 95 2596 bl
97   5 GOOD  8f Good   95 3107
95   4 GOOD  7f Gd/Fm  94 3130
98   2 DONC  8f Firm   95 3897
80  19 NEWM  9f Gd/Sft 95 4212
96   4 NEWB  9f Sft/Hvy 97 4472
101  2 NEWM  8f Soft   96 4545
```

ATLANTIC VIKING 5 b g £1089
```
78  14 RIPO  5f Good   88 1861
0   16 YORK  5f Good   88 1980
80   7 NEWC  5f Gd/Fm  86 2310 bl
82   4 AYR   5f Gd/Fm  84 2721 bl
80   9 ASCO  5f Good   84 3016 bl
83   4 RIPO  6f Gd/Fm  82 3183 bl
58  18 RIPO  6f Gd/Fm  82 3464 bl
```

ATLANTIS PRINCE 2 ch c £95397
```
82   1 EPSO  7f Good       2791*
101  1 NEWM  7f Gd/Fm      3164*
105  1 GOOD  8f Good       3882*
112  1 ASCO  8f Gd/Sft     4127*
```

ATMOSPHERIC 2 ch c £51119
```
89   1 PONT  5f Gd/Sft     1102*
92   2 NOTT  6f Gd/Sft     1367
102  1 EPSO  6f Good       1846*
67  10 GOOD  7f Gd/Fm      3086
106  1 YORK  6f Heavy      4298* BL
```

ATTACHE 2 ch c £9648
```
87   2 CHES  7f Gd/Fm      3508
85   1 REDC  7f Gd/Fm      3635*
104  1 SAND  7f Gd/Fm      3946*
105  5 SAN   8f Heavy      4492
```

ATTACKER 3 b g £0
```
0    9 HAYD  12f Gd/Fm     3324
50   6 NEWC  8f Soft       3707
0   11 YORK  10f Good      3813
0   19 KEMP  12f Soft      4040
0   13 PONT  17f Soft  57  4231 t
```

ATTO 6 b g £0
```
50   9 WARW  8f Good       2465
45   6 SALI  10f Gd/Fm     2981
64   9 BATH  12f Gd/Fm     3818
```

ATTORNEY 2 ch c £2945
```
60   9 GOOD  6f Gd/Sft     1472
82   2 HAYD  8f Gd/Sft     1835
88   2 KEMP  6f Soft       2082
84   2 CHEP  5f Gd/Fm      3252
```

ATYLAN BOY 3 b c £5262
```
45   9 WIND  8f Heavy  72  933
0   15 SALI  8f Good   69  1345
67   3 SAND  7f Soft   65  1569 BL
78a  1 LING  7f Aw         1745*
58   5 REDC  7f Gd/Fm  67  2145
77a  2 SOUT  7f Aw     76  2300
67   4 EPSO  7f Good   67  2794
```

AUBERGADE 4 gr f £5764 *(first entries continued)*
```
58   6 KEMP  7f Gd/Fm  67  3076
61   8 NEWM  7f Gd/Sft 67  3163 bl
0   12 BEVE  8f Sft/Hvy 65 4045
55   5 BRIG  8f Soft       4173 bl
```

AUBERGADE 4 gr f £5764
```
107  3 DEAU  14f Gd/Sft    3070
```

AUBRIETA 4 b f £8432
```
59a  1 LING  6f Aw          25* bl
47a  7 WOLV  6f Aw     56  466  bl
53a  5 LING  7f Aw     54  525  bl
54a  2 LING  6f Aw     52  628  bl
33   8 NOTT  6f Good   50  787  bl
54a  4 WOLV  6f Aw     54  923  bl
42a  5 WOLV  8f Aw     54  1037
44   7 LEIC  8f Gd/Sft 48  1734 bl
63a  1 LING  7f Aw         1739* bl
63a  1 LING  6f Aw         1913* bl
47   4 NOTT  6f Gd/Fm  53  2193 bl
0   13 HAYD  7f Gd/Fm  53  2442 bl
50a  8 WOLV  6f Aw     64  4358 bl
56a  5 WOLV  7f Aw     62  4550 bl
```

AUCHONVILLERS 3 b c £3835
```
83   1 NOTT  8f Good       784*
83   7 DONC  8f Gd/Sft     1069
63  20 ASCO  8f Good   83  2117
```

AUCTIONEERS CO UK 2 br c £352
```
75   3 BATH  6f Firm       2784
0a   P WOLV  6f Aw         3496
```

AUDACIEUSE 3 £0
```
106  6 LONG  10f Good      4263
```

AUDACITY 4 b g £0
```
56   5 SAND  10f Soft      1588
12  18 NEWM  12f Firm  37  1852
0   12 WARW  16f Gd/Fm 34  2037
16a  8 LING  12f Aw        3835
```

AUENKLANG 3 b c £33795
```
119  1 NEWB  6f Firm       2847+ VIS
116  2 ASCO  6f Gd/Fm      3303
88  11 HAYD  8f Gd/Sft     3784 vis
```

AUNT DORIS 3 b f £1312
```
46   6 BRIG  7f Soft       1467
41   9 WIND  6f Gd/Fm  62  1877
50  12 WARW  5f Gd/Fm  58  2252
54   4 LEIC  6f Gd/Fm  54  2511
55   2 LEIC  6f Gd/Fm  54  2777
53   5 BRIG  6f Gd/Fm  56  3243
```

AUNT RUBY 2 ch f £1320
```
55  10 KEMP  6f Gd/Fm      2748
75   2 GOOD  6f Good       3649
61   6 BEVE  7f Good       3952
63  10 NEWM  6f Gd/Fm  73  4214
59   6 DONC  7f Soft   70  4460
```

AUNT SUSAN 2 b f £0
```
0a  13 WOLV  6f Aw         3496
```

AUNTY ROSE 3 b f £3850
```
102  3 NEWM  7f Good       953
98  15 NEWM  8f Firm       1185
89  11 NEWM  8f Good       4180
```

AURA OF GRACE 3 b f £2726
```
72   6 NEWB  8f Good       1376
83   5 LEIC  7f Gd/Sft     1733
0   13 KEMP  9f Gd/Sft 75  2581
72   1 MUSS  8f Soft       4519+
```

AURATUM 3 ch f £1205
```
0    P LING  7f Gd/Sft     1283
92   4 HAYD  6f Gd/Sft     1833
```

AURIGNY 5 b m £524
```
80a  5 WOLV  5f Aw     83  191
77a  5 LING  6f Aw     83  223
58a  9 WOLV  6f Aw     80  258
63a  8 LING  5f Gd/Sft 77  506
63  11 LING  5f Gd/Sft 83  1264
```

AURIGNY 5 b m £524 *(continued)*
```
75   6 LING  5f Good   78  1398
68   4 BRIG  5f Good   76  1650
0   13 NOTT  5f Good   74  1871
67   4 LING  5f Firm   71  2326 VIS
60   8 CHEP  5f Gd/Fm  71  2451 vis
59   9 NEWM  8f Good   69  2569
```

AUTONOMY 3 b c £7845
```
101  3 NEWM  10f Firm      3300
108  2 YORK  9f Gd/Sft     3726
86  12 NEWM  8f Good       4180
```

AUTUMN COVER 8 gr g £0
```
0   16 LING  8f Gd/Fm  68  3831
21a 11 WOLV  9f Aw     60  4228
```

AUTUMN LEAVES 4 b f £0
```
12a  9 WOLV  8f Aw         133
36a  6 WOLV  8f Aw         229
25a  7 WOLV  8f Aw         308
7a  10 SOUT  12f Aw        387
```

AUTUMN RAIN 3 br c £5046
```
84   2 RIPO  8f Soft       826
75  12 NEWM  10f Gd/Sft 84 979
74   1 LING  7f Gd/Sft     1263*
79   3 NOTT  8f Soft   82  1645
51  10 NEWC  7f Soft   80  3708
```

AUTUMN RHYTHM 2 b f £3233
```
98   1 YARM  8f Heavy      4477* t
```

AUTUMNAL 2 b f £49019
```
83   3 WIND  8f Gd/Sft     1424
80   1 HAYD  5f Gd/Sft     1835*
98   1 ASCO  5f Good       2152*
101  2 ASCO  6f Gd/Fm      2996
104  3 YORK  8f Gd/Fm      3596
107  4 NEWM  6f Good       4159
99   8 NEWM  7f Good       4356
```

AVANTI 4 gr c £0
```
0   27 NEWM  8f Good   72  4340
```

AVERHAM STAR 5 ch g £0
```
0   16 HAYD  11f Soft  26  1819 vis
60   9 NOTT  8f Gd/Fm      2188
10  12 HAYD  11f Gd/Fm 37  2453
24   6 NOTT  10f Gd/Fm 36  3007
18   8 PONT  10f Gd/Fm 37  3220
31a  7 WOLV  9f Aw         3498
27  10 NOTT  10f Good  38  3524 bl
34  11 WARW  11f Good      3691 vis
```

AVERY RING 2 b c £1873
```
77   6 NEWB  5f Gd/Fm      1782
77   2 WIND  5f Good       2711
73   3 WIND  6f Gd/Fm      3047
70   4 KEMP  6f Gd/Fm      3358
64   7 LING  8f Firm       3577
```

AVONDALE GIRL 4 ch f £1175
```
39a  9 SOUT  5f Aw         214
54a  7 WOLV  5f Aw         272
44a  8 WOLV  5f Aw         379
33a  8 SOUT  6f Aw     55  425
35a  5 WOLV  5f Aw         639
60   7 THIR  6f Soft   70  910
63   8 REDC  5f Gd/Sft 68  1133
41   7 REDC  6f Firm       1298
55   6 NEWC  5f Gd/Fm  66  1479
40   3 NEWC  5f Heavy      1766
63   2 PONT  5f Good       1868
```

AVORADO 2 b c £1920
```
85   2 GALW  7f Good       3072
```

AWAKE 3 ch c £33381
```
98   D MAIS  6f Heavy      99
84  10 DONC  6f Good       734
93   4 HAYD  5f Heavy      988
98   2 LING  6f Gd/Sft 98  1285
92   7 HAYD  6f Gd/Fm      1534
97   3 CHEP  5f Gd/Fm  97  2451
```

NEWB
100	1	NEWB	6f Firm	97	2706*	
94	4	ASCO	6f Gd/Fm		3303	
85	9	SAND	5f Good	99	3473	
90	11	NEWM	5f Good	99	4339	

AWAY WIN 2 b f £0
64	5	KEMP	7f Firm		2259
64	9	CHEP	8f Gd/Fm		3678

AWESOME VENTURE 10 b g £0
0a	13	SOUT	8f Aw		252
22a	8	SOUT	11f Aw	35	325
15a	8	SOUT	7f Aw	39	599

AWTAAN 3 b f £2834
42	4	FOLK	12f Soft		964
72	1	LING	14f Firm		3489*

AYMARA 3 b f £6034
73	4	ASCO	8f Good		2679
80	2	HAYD	11f Gd/Sft		3265
73	2	CHES	12f Gd/Fm		3429
83	1	MUSS	12f Gd/Sft		4133*
74	13	NEWM	12f Good		4343

AZAAN 3 ch c £2874
85	2	SAND	10f Good		3232
85	2	NEWM	8f Gd/Fm		3626

AZIRA 3 ch f £0
46a	6	LING	6f Aw		5
0	12	LING	6f Gd/Fm		2183
47	8	KEMP	5f Gd/Sft	60	2586
26	6	BRIG	5f Firm		2905
3	10	BRIG	5f Firm		3562

AZIZ PRESENTING 2 br f £8439
85	2	SAND	5f Heavy		1046
79	7	ASCO	5f Gd/Sft		1107
81	1	SALI	5f Firm		2020*
78	12	ASCO	5f Good		2088
91	2	SALI	6f Gd/Sft		2469
91	3	CHES	5f Good		2664

AZIZZI 8 ch g £0
0	14	NEWM	5f Gd/Sft	90	3788
0	20	DONC	5f Gd/Fm	90	3861
84	9	NEWM	5f Good	88	4015

AZKABAN 2 ch c £3001
84	3	LEIC	7f Gd/Fm		3333
90	2	KEMP	8f Gd/Fm		3790
75	5	YARM	8f Gd/Fm		3969
90	10	NEWM	7f Good		4158

AZOUZ PASHA 4 b c £2251
105	5	KEMP	10f Soft		1014
110	5	NEWM	10f Gd/Fm		1174 vis
105	3	WIND	12f Good		3640
106	4	DONC	12f Firm		3892

AZTEC FLYER 7 b g £0
0	14	SOUT	16f Gd/Sft	50	860

AZUR 3 b f £0
0	22	NEWM	8f Firm	83	1183
62	9	DONC	10f Gd/Fm	82	2610
49	7	HAYD	12f Gd/Sft	77	3270
62	8	KEMP	8f Gd/Fm	70	3793 VIS
41	9	GOOD	12f Soft		4061 vis

AZZAN 4 b c £0
51a	6	WOLV	9f Aw		189
40a	8	WOLV	8f Aw	60	255 t
0	18	WARW	11f Heavy	55	890 t

B W LEADER 3 b c £0
43	8	BEVE	5f Good		3956 t

BAAJIL 5 b g £1798
61a	1	LING	10f Aw		3*
50a	4	LING	10f Aw		163
59a	6	LING	10f Aw	60	220
49a	8	LING	12f Aw	59	290
25a	9	LING	10f Aw	57	400
18a	10	WOLV	9f Aw	54	637
0a	11	LING	10f Aw	51	842
7a	12	LING	8f Aw	46	1915

BAARIDD 2 b c £25502
90	1	GOOD	5f Gd/Sft		1454*
105	2	ASCO	7f Good		2091
97	5	GOOD	7f Gd/Fm		3086
105	1	RIPO	6f Good		3700*
105	6	NEWM	6f Good		4181

BABA AU RHUM 8 b g £0
52	8	LEIC	8f Gd/Fm	63	3334
45	11	GOOD	8f Good	63	3644

BABY BARRY 3 b c £9226
83	7	NEWM	7f Good	84	954
70	12	CHES	5f Gd/Fm	83	1220
84	3	NOTT	6f Good		1409
81	4	YORK	6f Firm	83	2003
85	3	CHES	5f Gd/Fm	83	2247
69	11	NEWM	6f Good	85	2568
85	3	GOOD	5f Gd/Fm	85	3135
85	3	LEIC	6f Gd/Fm	85	3335
85	5	NEWM	7f Gd/Fm	85	3629
0	21	DONC	6f Gd/Fm	85	3861 vis
63	8	HAYD	7f Gd/Sft	84	4106
57	10	CATT	6f Soft		4257
52	7	NEWC	6f Heavy	79	4405
0	19	NEWM	7f Soft	75	4547
67	9	DONC	7f Heavy	72	4574

BABY BUNTING 2 b f £952
75	4	NEWM	5f Gd/Sft		970
67	4	HAYD	5f Gd/Fm		1166
72	4	WIND	6f Good		3638

BABY MAYBE 2 b f £0
62	7	HAYD	6f Gd/Fm		2454
0	11	HAYD	5f Soft		3767
38	5	BEVE	5f Sft/Hvy		4042

BABY ROCKET 3 b c £0
34a	4	WOLV	5f Aw		120

BACCHUS 6 b g £13338
68	2	REDC	9f Gd/Sft	62	1583
69	3	BEVE	10f Firm	67	1921
72	2	BEVE	10f Firm	67	2220
70	2	BEVE	10f Firm	67	2481
76	1	CHES	10f Gd/Fm	69	2671* VIS
71	5	NEWM	10f Good	75	3024 vis
67	6	EPSO	10f Gd/Fm		3403
45	12	YORK	9f Good		3808 vis
72	2	REDC	8f Gd/Sft	70	4217 vis
32	14	YORK	9f Heavy	72	4300 vis

BACCURA 2 b c £7686
60	13	NEWB	5f Gd/Fm		1782
76	2	REDC	5f Good		2142
84	1	PONT	6f Gd/Fm		2828*
89	2	GOOD	6f Gd/Fm	87	3062

BACH 3 b c £42070
109	1	LEOP	8f Soft		947*
111	2	LEOP	10f Gd/Fm		1314
109	2	CHAN	9f V		1753

BACHELORS PAD 6 b g £14447
39a	8	SOUT	8f Aw	54	297
62a	2	SOUT	8f Aw	54	329
62a	1	WOLV	9f Aw		360*
65a	1	WOLV	9f Aw		433*
65a	2	WOLV	9f Aw		517
58a	1	WOLV	9f Aw		553*
59a	4	SOUT	12f Aw	64	671
60	1	SOUT	11f Gd/Sft	54	855*
63a	4	SOUT	11f Aw	62	1306
59	2	SOUT	10f Soft	58	1598
56	3	HAYD	11f Soft	58	1819
48	4	KEMP	10f Gd/Fm	58	2081
47	6	NEWC	10f Gd/Fm	58	2309
61	1	CHES	12f Gd/Fm	56	3430*
45	8	GOOD	12f Good	60	3887
50	7	CHES	10f Soft	59	4074
47	7	NOTT	10f Heavy		4413
50	4	REDC	11f Soft		4497

BACHIR 3 b c £273637
112ε	2	NAD	9f Dirt		765
120	1	LONG	8f V		1318*
120	1	CURR	8f Gd/Sft		1623*
115	6	ASCO	8f Good		2066
109	5	GOOD	8f Good		3647

BACK PASS 2 b f £0
80	9	NEWM	7f Good		3020

BACKEND CHARLIE 6 b g £0
31	9	THIR	12f Gd/Sft		1353
0	10	REDC	14f Gd/Fm	30	2156

BACKWOODS 7 ch g £0
0	16	NOTT	16f Heavy	50	4508

BAD AS I WANNA BE 2 ch c £92128
75	11	NEWB	6f Gd/Fm		1403
109	1	WIND	5f Gd/Fm		3044*
119	1	DEAU	6f Gd/Sft		3550*
105	4	LONG	7f Gd/Sft		4054
108	4	NEWM	6f Good		4181

BADAAWAH 3 ch f £1076
67	2	SALI	7f Gd/Fm		3423
51	5	EPSO	9f Good		3764

BADERNA 2 b c £0
0	14	NOTT	8f Heavy		4504

BADR RAINBOW 3 b c £4894
87	3	ASCO	10f Gd/Fm		2957
76	1	HAYD	8f Gd/Sft		3477*

BADRINATH 6 b g £1416
0a	11	LING	10f Aw	45	102
23a	6	WOLV	9f Aw		360
36a	3	LING	10f Aw	38	620
38a	2	LING	10f Aw		775
32	12	PONT	10f Soft	58	871
27	14	BRIG	10f Firm		1331
50	2	YARM	8f Good	48	1772
47	5	NEWM	8f Gd/Fm	51	2130
0	19	DONC	8f Gd/Fm	51	2349

BAHAMAS 3 b c £10196
64	1	REDC	10f Good	58	1895*
65	2	NOTT	10f Good		2012
58a	3	SOUT	12f Aw	63	2382
64	3	FOLK	12f Good	63	2624 BL
70a	1	SOUT	12f Aw	60	2815* bl
71a	1	SOUT	11f Aw	66	2945* bl
68	7	EPSO	12f Good	70	3858 bl
59	6	CHES	10f Soft	68	4074 bl
72	2	CATT	12f Soft	67	4256 bl
67	4	YARM	14f Heavy	72	4476 bl

BAHAMIAN PIRATE 5 ch g £99899
49	12	THIR	5f Good	62	1162
69	1	CARL	6f Firm	62	1257*
75a	1	SOUT	6f Aw	58	2385*
78	2	NEWM	5f Good	74	2569
75	2	LING	6f Firm	70	2761
78	2	NEWM	6f Gd/Fm	76	2961
87	1	NEWM	6f Firm	78	3297*
87	3	RIPO	6f Gd/Fm	84	3464
74	13	KEMP	6f Gd/Fm	86	3791
94	1	AYR	6f Gd/Sft	86	4012*
92	5	NEWM	7f Good	93	4195
111	1	NEWM	6f Good		4346*

BAHAMIAN PRINCE 3 b c £0
39a	7	LING	8f Aw		221
20a	9	LING	8f Aw		265
46a	6	WOLV	9f Aw		319 VIS
27a	7	SOUT	8f Aw	38	429 BL

BAHRAIN 4 ch c £4099
51	4	FOLK	7f Soft		961
59	8	WIND	8f Gd/Fm	64	1201 t

30	11	NOTT	10f Gd/Sft	64	1364	t
58	8	WIND	10f Good	61	1729	t
45	6	REDC	8f Gd/Fm	58	2147	t
56	2	CARL	7f Firm		3197	
56a	3	WOLV	8f Aw	57	3769	
60a	1	**WOLV**	8f Aw	57	4021*	
32a	10	WOLV	8f Aw	61	4248	

BAILAMOS 2 ch c £0

29	8	GOOD	8f Good		3906	

BAILEYS CREAM 2 ch f £4177

55	9	PONT	6f Firm		2174	
75	2	AYR	7f Firm		2873	
84	1	**AYR**	7f Good		3363*	
83	8	ASCO	8f Good		4110	

BAILEYS ON LINE 3 b f £1532

0	15	NEWM	7f Gd/Sft		971	
16	8	SOUT	6f Soft		1605	
55	9	YARM	7f Gd/Fm		1951	
54	2	BRIG	12f Gd/Sft	51	2425	
53	3	YARM	14f Firm	55	2902	
17a	9	WOLV	12f Aw	55	4360	
33a	8	LING	10f Aw	51	4482	

BAILEYS PRIZE 3 ch c £18826

69a	2	WOLV	8f Aw		920	
64	7	DONC	8f Gd/Sft	73	1053	
79	1	**REDC**	10f Firm	70	1299*	
80	4	BEVE	10f Good	76	1448	
70	6	HAYD	11f Soft	73	1491	
82	2	LEIC	10f Gd/Sft	76	1735	
82	2	GOOD	10f Gd/Sft	76	1812	
82	2	GOOD	10f Gd/Fm	76	1958	
79	3	REDC	10f Gd/Fm	79	2157	
83	1	**NEWM**	10f Gd/Fm	79	2805*	
80	4	RIPO	12f Gd/Fm	83	3013	
73	7	NEWM	10f Gd/Fm	82	3628	

BAILEYS WHIRLWIND 3 b f £5200

82	5	NEWM	7f Firm		1186	
86	14	NEWM	6f Gd/Fm	93	1694	
92	3	YARM	6f Gd/Fm		2197	
91	4	NEWM	6f Good	92	2568	
87	4	YARM	7f Firm		2769	
92	4	LEIC	6f Gd/Fm	92	3335	
91	4	YORK	6f Gd/Fm	92	3727	
76	6	GOOD	7f Good	91	3902	
80	12	NEWM	7f Good	90	4195	

BAILLIESTON 2 ch g £5012

81	3	HAYD	6f Gd/Sft		3478	
83	3	HAYD	7f Soft		3786	
82	5	AYR	8f Gd/Sft		4008	
81	1	**AYR**	7f Heavy		4303*	
50	9	PONT	8f Soft		4375	

BAISSE DARGENT 4 b c £4070

48a	3	LING	13f Aw	52	317	
52a	2	LING	16f Aw	50	424	
52a	3	LING	16f Aw	52	548	
54	2	PONT	17f Good	50	1867	
54	4	PONT	18f Firm	53	2176	
47	8	FOLK	16f Good	52	2622	
45	3	YARM	16f Good	50	3026	

BAJAN BELLE 3 b f £2227

46	16	WIND	6f Good	78	852	
63a	8	WOLV	6f Aw	75	1138	
70	4	WIND	6f Firm	75	1289	
6	16	SAND	7f Soft	73	1569	
66	3	NEWM	7f Firm	72	1855	
63	8	AYR	7f Gd/Fm	70	2719	
43	11	NEWC	6f Good	68	3037	
59	2	CARL	7f Firm		3196	
59	2	BEVE	7f Gd/Fm		3671	
54	5	HAMI	6f Soft	62	3803	
39	11	MUSS	7f Gd/Sft	60	4136	
0	13	LING	6f Soft	57	4270	

BAJAN BLUE 2 b f £1584

38	6	NEWC	6f Good		3032	
60	3	EPSO	6f Gd/Fm		3400	
57	3	BEVE	7f Gd/Fm		3655	
50	3	BEVE	7f Good		3949	
9	13	PONT	8f Soft	58	4378	

BAJAN BROKER 3 br f £326

48	10	NEWM	8f Gd/Fm		1692	
53	4	RIPO	10f Gd/Fm		2111	
55	10	NOTT	10f Gd/Fm	69	2685	
60	5	NOTT	10f Good	64	3524	
39	6	EPSO	9f Good		3764	
0	15	LEIC	8f Sft/Hvy	59	4310	
47	4	BATH	8f Soft	59	4435	

BAJAN SUNSET 3 ch c £1980

51	9	NOTT	8f Gd/Sft		1084	
41	6	YORK	10f Gd/Fm		1985	
52	2	LEIC	8f Gd/Fm	49	2512	
52	2	SALI	8f Gd/Fm	51	2980	
27	10	PONT	8f Gd/Fm	51	3226	
4	15	EPSO	10f Good	51	3762	
0	16	LEIC	8f Gd/Sft		4033	

BALACLAVA 5 b g £0

0	13	BRIG	7f Firm	36	1336	

BALADEUR 2 b c £2250

84	3	LEOP	6f Yldg		1756	

BALANITA 5 b g £850

52a	9	LING	7f Aw	60	28	
0	24	WIND	6f Gd/Fm	72	1196	
55	9	WIND	6f Gd/Fm	68	2207	
53	2	FOLK	6f Gd/Fm		2292	BL
42	5	BATH	6f Firm		2329	bl
40	4	NOTT	6f Gd/Fm		2680	bl
48	3	BRIG	8f Gd/Sft		4122	
19	11	LEIC	8f Sft/Hvy		4311	

BALANOU 2 b f £0

61	9	LEIC	7f Sft/Hvy		4309	
10	14	NEWM	8f Soft		4542	

BALDAQUIN 3 b c £4231

79	15	NEWM	8f Gd/Sft		972	
70	4	REDC	10f Firm		1295	
85	1	**GOOD**	10f Gd/Sft		1640*	
88	5	ASCO	12f Good	85	2116	
0	11	DONC	10f Gd/Fm	85	2610	

BALFOUR 3 b c £8670

62	1	**WARW**	7f Heavy	57	887*	
55	5	DONC	8f Gd/Sft	61	1053	
53	6	HAYD	6f Soft	61	1494	
46	12	NEWB	7f Gd/Fm	60	1787	VIS
61	3	REDC	6f Good	60	1891	
58	4	SAND	5f Gd/Fm	60	2934	
64	3	LING	6f Firm	60	3280	
67	1	**LING**	8f Firm	61	3580*	vis
52	9	LING	7f Firm	67	3758	vis

BALI BATIK 3 b g £5498

76	4	LING	7f Gd/Sft		839	
81	3	DONC	7f Gd/Sft		1072	
82	1	**LING**	7f Gd/Sft		1261*	
70	14	GOOD	9f Gd/Sft	84	1452	
80	4	REDC	10f Gd/Fm	82	2157	
79	4	CHES	10f Good	81	2666	
0	16	YARM	10f Soft	81	4392	

BALI ROYAL 2 b f £1240

73	2	NOTT	5f Gd/Sft		1641	
63	8	CHEP	6f Gd/Sft		1798	
61	7	CHEP	6f Gd/Fm		2488	
49	8	LING	5f Firm	66	3491	
0	14	LEIC	6f Gd/Sft	63	4030	
55	2	BRIG	5f Soft		4171	
45	4	BATH	6f Soft		4431	

BALI STAR 5 b g £1680

50	2	SOUT	6f Good	50	802	
27	9	FOLK	6f Soft	50	958	
42	7	BATH	6f Gd/Fm	50	1438	
40	10	CHEP	7f Gd/Sft	49	1794	
35	12	CHEP	6f Good	49	1971	
47	2	SALI	6f Good	46	2690	

BALIDARE 3 b f £0

16	9	FOLK	7f Soft		961	
31	8	BRIG	5f Firm	46	1334	
0	11	WARW	7f Gd/Fm	42	2036	
1	12	SALI	6f Gd/Fm	41	3293	
31	8	BRIG	5f Firm		3562	
36	9	SALI	5f Firm	47	3747	
0	16	GOOD	5f Good	53	3908	

BALL GAMES 2 b c £724

75	6	RIPO	5f Soft		821	
71	4	NEWC	5f Gd/Sft		1475	
59	6	AYR	6f Gd/Fm		2717	
44	8	HAYD	5f Gd/Sft	67	3264	
64	4	AYR	8f Heavy	63	4323	
44	9	DONC	8f Gd/Sft	63	4450	
70	4	MUSS	7f Soft		4562	

BALLA DAIRE 5 br g £0

23a	5	LING	13f Aw		483	bl

BALLADEER 2 b c £225

74	9	SAND	7f Gd/Fm		2921	
82	4	SALI	7f Gd/Fm		3420	

BALLADONIA 4 b f £1114

88	6	GOOD	12f Gd/Fm	96	3134	
92	5	SALI	10f Gd/Fm		3389	
92	4	NEWC	10f Good	92	3703	
95	5	YARM	10f Firm		3918	
85	8	NEWM	12f Good	93	4162	

BALLET HIGH 7 b g £0

0	13	NEWB	16f Gd/Sft	70	4458	

BALLET MASTER 4 ch c £0

65	9	WARW	7f Heavy		1004	

BALLETS RUSSES 3 b f £638

50	4	YARM	5f Gd/Sft		1609	
50	3	WARW	7f Gd/Fm	50	2036	
6	13	LEIC	6f Gd/Fm	50	2511	
35	9	YARM	7f Good	50	3030	
0	8	YARM	6f Gd/Fm	49	3386	
0	15	BRIG	8f Firm	49	3561	
24	6	YARM	8f Gd/Fm	44	3970	
0	12	DONC	7f Soft		4461	

BALLINA LAD 4 b c £0

0a	12	SOUT	6f Aw		2118	
0	18	NOTT	6f Gd/Fm		2680	
43	5	CATT	6f Gd/Fm		2744	
36	14	THIR	6f Gd/Fm	47	3144	
39	6	NEWC	6f Firm	43	3605	
39	8	YARM	6f Gd/Fm	43	3964	

BALLISTIC BOY 3 ch c £400

43	9	NOTT	8f Gd/Sft	64	1085	
54	8	HAMI	8f Gd/Fm	62	1360	
59	3	AYR	9f Gd/Fm		1632	
30	10	HAYD	8f Soft	58	1822	

BALLY CYRANO 3 b c £0

0a	17	SOUT	5f Aw	57	1806	BL
0a	14	SOUT	6f Aw	51	2297	VIS
0	15	HAYD	8f Gd/Sft		3266	vis
24	11	BEVE	5f Gd/Fm		3651	tbl

BALLY PRIDE 3 ch c £8012

104	4	HAYD	6f Gd/Sft	104	1534	
95	9	YORK	6f Firm	103	2003	
103	3	CHES	7f Gd/Fm		2670	
91	5	ASCO	6f Gd/Fm		3303	

BALLYCROY RIVER 4 b c £0

25a	9	WOLV	8f Aw		393	
0a	8	SOUT	16f Aw	45	542	
0a	11	SOUT	8f Aw	45	585	

BALLYKISSANN 5 ch g £0

29 7 BATH 10f Gd/Sft 36 1666 bl

29	7	BATH	10f Gd/Sft	36	1666	bl
0	13	BATH	8f Firm	43	1998	bl
21	10	WARW	8f Good	36	2460	
18	11	CHEP	8f Gd/Fm	36	2658	VIS

BALLYMORRIS BOY 4 b c £708

39a	7	LING	7f Aw		8	
26a	5	SOUT	7f Aw	42	75	
49a	3	LING	7f Aw		156	
51a	4	LING	7f Aw		225	
48a	3	WOLV	7f Aw		274	
28a	4	WOLV	7f Aw		310	
42a	6	LING	10f Aw		375	
42a	8	LING	7f Aw		398	BL
43a	3	LING	8f Aw		505	
21a	10	WOLV	8f Aw		550	
44a	5	SOUT	12f Aw		603	

BALMAINE 2 b f £0

55	10	SALI	7f Firm		3752

BALSOX 4 b c £0

0	10	EPSO	12f Heavy	79	1030

BAMBOO GARDEN 4 b c £0

0a	16	SOUT	14f Aw	57	4371	bl
12a	8	WOLV	12f Aw		4549	bl

BAMBOOZLE 4 b f £0

0	11	WIND	8f Gd/Sft		1428
70	5	SALI	10f Gd/Fm		2265
49	11	SALI	14f Good		2691
0	16	FOLK	12f Gd/Fm	65	3586
0a	9	WOLV	15f Aw		4024
27	6	BRIG	12f Soft	45	4176
0	11	YARM	14f Soft		4510

BANAFSAJYH 3 b f £10308

77	1	NOTT	6f Firm		1266*
0	22	NEWM	6f Gd/Fm	79	1694
75	4	LING	6f Gd/Fm	77	2216
71	8	NEWM	7f Gd/Fm	77	2855
82	1	LING	6f Firm	75	3280*

BANBURY 6 b g £0

92	8	NEWM	12f Gd/Sft	94	968	t

BANCO SUIVI 3 b f £10416

88	2	KEMP	11f Soft		1017
63	7	LING	11f Gd/Sft		1282
88	2	DONC	10f Gd/Fm		2317
80	3	HAYD	11f Gd/Fm		2703
86	1	DONC	12f Gd/Fm		3157*
86	3	NEWM	14f Good	84	4016
76	8	NEWM	12f Good	84	4342

BANDANNA 3 gr f £8115

82	13	NEWM	7f Good		953
0	16	LING	6f Gd/Sft	90	1285
75	6	ASCO	5f Good	84	2168
78	5	CHEP	5f Gd/Fm	81	2451
84	1	BATH	5f Firm	79	2787*
71	6	KEMP	6f Firm		2869
83	3	BATH	6f Gd/Fm	84	3209
82	5	BATH	6f Gd/Fm	84	3516
80	4	KEMP	6f Gd/Sft	82	4037

BANDARELLO 2 b f £0

59	6	CHEP	5f Gd/Fm		3252

BANDBOX 5 ch g £8725

68a	1	SOUT	7f Aw		511*	
65a	2	SOUT	7f Aw	65	598	
56a	7	SOUT	7f Aw	66	687	
54	8	LING	7f Gd/Fm		838	
64	7	WIND	6f Gd/Fm	64	1196	
61	3	NOTT	6f Gd/Fm		1368	bl
0	13	NEWB	6f Gd/Fm	63	1591	
61	6	CHEP	7f Gd/Sft	63	1794	
58	7	WIND	6f Gd/Fm	62	2054	
63	3	BATH	6f Firm		2329	
0	15	WIND	8f Soft	61	2546	
56	6	LEIC	6f Gd/Fm	61	2777	
62	2	CHEP	5f Gd/Fm	60	2976	
68	3	LEIC	6f Gd/Fm		3097	
59	6	CHEP	6f Gd/Fm	62	3257	
67	1	FOLK	6f Gd/Fm		3587*	
68	2	CHEP	5f Good	63	3872	
68	5	NEWM	5f Good	67	4015	
64	5	BRIG	6f Gd/Sft	67	4120	

BANDIDA 6 ch m £0

30	7	HAMI	5f Firm	38	1244
19	6	NEWC	5f Heavy		1766
18	10	HAMI	5f Gd/Fm	35	1910
40	7	CARL	5f Firm		2822
22	9	AYR	7f Gd/Fm	31	3138
4	10	MUSS	8f Gd/Fm	28	3745

BANDIDO 3 b g £0

0	14	CHEP	8f Good		3868

BANDLER CHING 3 b c £7242

66	5	WARW	11f Gd/Fm	71	2842
72	2	FOLK	9f Gd/Fm	68	3043
76	1	LEIC	10f Gd/Fm	68	3217*
74	3	EPSO	10f Gd/Fm	75	3415
76	4	YARM	10f Firm	75	3941
62	13	NEWM	10f Good	75	4197

BANDOLERA BOY 3 b c £0

0a	14	SOUT	8f Aw		36	
20a	10	LING	7f Aw		53	BL

BANDORE 6 ch g £0

0	20	SALI	14f Gd/Sft	65	4166	
0	19	BATH	12f Soft	60	4433	t

BANGALORE 4 ch c £73822

84	3	KEMP	16f Soft	81	997
91	1	CHES	19f Gd/Fm	86	1222*
89	7	ASCO	20f Good	90	2092
94	1	NEWB	16f Firm	90	3986*

BANGLED 3 ch c £1004

40	12	HAYD	6f Soft	63	1494
43a	8	LING	6f Aw	58	1742
0	16	LING	5f Gd/Fm	53	2184
0	13	CHEP	6f Gd/Fm	48	2489
47a	3	WOLV	5f Aw	50	2603
28	9	EPSO	6f Gd/Fm	45	3405
43	4	YARM	6f Gd/Fm	43	3964
48a	2	SOUT	4f Aw	47	4156
26a	8	WOLV	6f Aw	50	4444

BANITA 2 b f £0

46	8	WARW	7f Good		2459
42	9	WARW	15f Gd/Fm		3912

BANIYAR 3 ch c £5251

89	4	KEMP	11f Soft		1017
85	1	HAMI	11f Gd/Fm		1193*
104	5	ASCO	12f Good		2148

BANJO BAY 2 b c £1090

76	5	NEWM	5f Soft		984
65	3	CHES	5f Gd/Fm		1221
64	10	ASCO	5f Good		2152
69	5	HAYD	5f Gd/Sft	73	3475
58	10	DONC	7f Firm	70	3901

BANK BUSTER 3 b g £0

0	10	THIR	12f Good		1386	
0	16	RIPO	8f Good		1596	
0	11	HAMI	9f Gd/Fm		2236	BL

BANK ON HIM 5 b g £0

59a	6	LING	10f Aw	75	442

BANNERET 7 b g £3651

38a	4	WOLV	12f Aw		231	
56a	2	WOLV	12f Aw		307	VIS
54a	1	WOLV	12f Aw		347*	vis
21a	7	WOLV	12f Aw	56	437	vis
46a	5	SOUT	12f Aw		498	vis
48a	3	WOLV	12f Aw		581	vis
48a	2	WOLV	12f Aw		1039	
26a	6	SOUT	12f Aw		1203	
38a	4	SOUT	14f Aw	40	1301	
33a	6	SOUT	16f Aw	40	1416	vis

BANNINGHAM BLIZ 2 ch f £1615

36	10	DONC	5f Good		730	
32	11	REDC	5f Gd/Sft		1131	
57	6	THIR	5f Good		1381	
50	5	PONT	5f Soft		1704	
49	4	REDC	7f Gd/Fm		2155	
50	3	YARM	6f Firm		2388	
48	8	PONT	6f Gd/Fm	63	2557	BL
52	2	YARM	7f Firm		2898	bl
50	2	YARM	6f Good		3028	bl
52	3	LEIC	6f Gd/Fm	52	3216	VIS

BANNISTER 2 ch c £75146

98	2	GOOD	6f Gd/Sft		1809
100	2	NEWM	6f Gd/Fm		3162
107	1	YORK	6f Gd/Fm		3566*
78	10	NEWM	6f Good		4181

BANSTEAD 2 b c £0

63	5	YARM	5f Firm		4389

BANYUMANIK 4 b c £7685

112	2	CHAN	8f Soft		1619

BANZHAF 7 ch g £14620

100	2	JAGE	9f Good		1323

BAPTISMAL ROCK 6 ch g £0

45a	7	WOLV	5f Aw	55	40
32a	8	SOUT	6f Aw	53	246
47a	5	WOLV	6f Aw	50	445
30a	11	WOLV	6f Aw	47	622

BARABASCHI 4 b c £7187

70	2	CHEP	8f Heavy		1552
77	2	GOOD	8f Gd/Fm	72	2126
73	6	NEWM	8f Gd/Fm	75	2564
68	1	AYR	8f Gd/Fm		3139*
75	2	BATH	8f Firm	74	3514
63	16	DONC	7f Gd/Fm	74	3880
66	16	ASCO	7f Good	79	4112

BARAGUEY 6 ch g £0

72	9	SAND	8f Heavy	85	1042
41	13	CHES	10f Gd/Fm	80	1217

BARAKANA 2 b c £4475

66	3	NEWB	5f Soft		911	
76	3	YORK	6f Firm		1328	
77	2	KEMP	6f Firm		1526	
76	6	SAND	7f Gd/Fm		1988	
81	3	BRIG	7f Firm	80	2894	BL
75	5	EPSO	7f Aw		3412	bl
69	10	DONC	8f Gd/Fm	79	3879	bl
61	7	BRIG	7f Soft		4172	bl

BARAKULA 3 b f £0

55	8	NEWM	10f Good		4017

BARANN 4 ch c £0

0a	12	WOLV	8f Aw		39
0a	15	SOUT	12f Aw	30	215
0a	10	SOUT	12f Aw	27	338
0a	11	LING	13f Aw	26	460
0	12	NOTT	14f Aw	18	3002

BARANOVA 2 b f £3887

84	5	NEWM	7f Good		3607
85	1	LEIC	8f Firm		3836*

BARATHEA GUEST 3 b c £78604

115	1	NEWM	7f Good		950*
117	3	NEWM	8f Gd/Fm		1171
115	4	CURR	8f Gd/Sft		1623
106	8	EPSO	12f Good		1848
112	5	MUNI	10f Soft		3071
109	5	YORK	10f Good		3539
110	5	DONC	8f Gd/Fm		3875
115	4	LONG	8f Good		4259
113	3	SAN	8f Soft		4319
72	15	NEWM	10f Good		4355

BARATHEASTAR 2 ch f £0

BARA... (continued)

84	5	KEMP	7f Gd/Fm	3789	
89	6	NEWM	7f Gd/Fm	4210	

BARATHIKI 2 gr f £14990

88	1	YORK	6f Gd/Fm	1312*	
75	6	HAYD	6f Gd/Fm	2500	
81	2	SALI	7f Gd/Sft	4167	
51	8	AYR	7f Heavy	81	4323	BL
83	1	WIND	6f Heavy	79	4525*

BARBA PAPA 6 b h £41900

95	1	ASCO	20f Good	82	2092* t
97	3	NEWM	18f Good	91	4353 t

BARBASON 8 ch g £7417

60a	3	LING	8f Aw	93	
68a	1	LING	10f Aw	163*	
63a	3	LING	8f Aw	66	210
55a	7	LING	10f Aw	66	224
56a	2	LING	10f Aw	335	
50a	5	LING	10f Aw	63	374
44a	5	WOLV	8f Aw	477	
70	1	GOOD	9f Gd/Sft	65	1807*
42a	5	LING	10f Aw	57	2186
59	5	WIND	10f Soft	70	2544
67	3	BRIG	8f Firm	2895	
70	4	LING	10f Firm	3281	

BARBERELLO 2 b f £0

12	9	SALI	7f Gd/Fm	3418	
52	5	LING	5f Soft	4485	

BARBOLA 5 ch g £5764

113	3	LONG	10f Hldng	819	

BARCELONA 3 b c £11831

57a	3	WOLV	12f Aw	752	
76	1	NOTT	14f Gd/Fm	68	1270*
80	1	KEMP	14f Gd/Fm	1928*	
73	6	ASCO	16f Good	79	2173
80	3	NOTT	14f Good	3522	
84	1	NEWC	14f Soft	78	3709*

BARDEN LADY 3 b f £0

64	8	NOTT	8f Gd/Fm	1269	
36	9	SOUT	7f Soft	1607	
0	12	WIND	6f Gd/Fm	60	2885

BAREFOOTED FLYER 2 ch f £1464

61	9	DONC	5f Gd/Fm	1048	
66	2	NOTT	6f Good	1408	
63	4	PONT	6f Soft	1700	
57a	3	SOUT	6f Aw	1974	
51	9	YARM	7f Firm	65	3922

BARITONE 6 b g £3044

0a	13	WOLV	6f Aw	44	232 vis
30a	7	SOUT	6f Aw	44	246 vis
30a	4	LING	6f Aw	38	358 vis
38a	3	LING	5f Aw	38	371 vis
35a	4	SOUT	6f Aw	38	425 vis
45a	1	WOLV	5f Aw	38	445* vis
42a	5	LING	6f Aw	44	543 vis
41a	3	WOLV	5f Aw	44	564 vis
31a	6	LING	6f Aw	43	628 vis
0	13	DONC	5f Gd/Fm	39	2753 vis
0	18	REDC	6f Firm	36	3312 vis
40	8	AYR	6f Good	3366 vis	

BARKING MAD 2 b c £27530

87	3	NEWM	5f Soft	984	
90	1	YORK	6f Firm	1328*	
96	6	ASCO	6f Good	2067	
95	1	THIR	7f Gd/Fm	2966*	
101	3	SAND	7f Good	3470	
102	6	DONC	7f Firm	3891	
89	7	REDC	6f Gd/Sft	4219	

BARNABY 3 b g £0

0	16	SAND	10f Soft	4205	
0	15	BATH	12f Soft	4434	

BARNEY KNOWS 5 b g £0

59	5	MUSS	12f Gd/Sft	4133	

BARNIE RUBBLE 4 ch c £1500

72	6	HAYD	7f Gd/Sft	1537	
67	4	WARW	7f Gd/Sft	1708	
76	2	AYR	7f Good	2140	

BARNINGHAM 2 b c £231

61	6	NEWC	7f Good	2521	
63	4	REDC	7f Gd/Fm	2862	
72	5	BEVE	7f Good	3397	

BARON CROCODILE 2 b c £6974

77	2	WIND	5f Good	849	
80	2	WARW	5f Heavy	1001	
59	4	CHES	5f Gd/Fm	1221	
72	5	BATH	5f Firm	1993	
66	8	LING	5f Gd/Fm	2214	
76	2	MUSS	5f Gd/Sft	2532	
72	4	THIR	5f Good	3143	
51	7	BATH	5f Gd/Fm	3513	BL
74	2	RIPO	5f Good	3710	
80	1	LING	5f Good	4096*	
58	8	AYR	6f Heavy	80	4305
78	3	LING	5f Soft	4485	

BARON DE PICHON 4 b c £4263

71a	1	SOUT	8f Aw	2950*	
55a	10	WOLV	8f Aw	83	3495
0	14	NEWM	7f Good	4018	
71a	1	WOLV	7f Aw	4224*	
69a	4	SOUT	8f Aw	73	4365

BAROSSA VALLEY 9 b g £0

0a	14	SOUT	8f Aw	58	85
0a	15	SOUT	14f Aw	124	
0	19	GOOD	9f Gd/Sft	41	1807

BARR BEACON 4 br c £0

38a	7	LING	6f Aw	313	

BARRETTSTOWN 5 ch g £948

66	2	WIND	10f Gd/Fm	3045	

BARRIER REEF 3 b c £14620

110	2	TABY	12f Good	3931	

BARRIER RIDGE 6 ch g £0

37a	6	SOUT	8f Aw	50	
6a	10	LING	10f Aw	43	102

BARRINGER 3 b c £2365

86	4	DONC	6f Good	90	716
85	1	WIND	6f Heavy	935	
87	3	SAND	5f Heavy	88	1047
0	21	GOOD	6f Good	87	3646
59	12	HAYD	5f Gd/Sft	85	3788
0	13	HAYD	5f Gd/Sft	82	4107
66	12	YORK	5f Soft	79	4285
69	9	BATH	5f Firm	75	4432

BARROW 3 br c £4694

55	7	WIND	12f Heavy	70	937
59	9	WIND	12f Firm	66	1292
72	1	NEWC	16f Gd/Fm	65	2273*
74	2	CHEP	16f Gd/Fm	78	2659
66	6	REDC	16f Firm	71	3331

BARRYS DOUBLE 3 br c £0

16a	8	SOUT	6f Aw	74	VIS
52a	4	SOUT	8f Aw	181	vis
2a	10	SOUT	8f Aw	57	213 vis
44a	4	SOUT	7f Aw	283	
38	11	SALI	8f Firm	55	3753
0	16	GOOD	8f Good	55	3885
0	11	BATH	8f Soft	48	4143 vis

BARTEX 6 b h £3842

107	3	SAIN	8f Hldng	861	

BARTON LEA 3 b f £0

19a	10	SOUT	8f Aw	86	
25a	9	SOUT	8f Aw	198	

BARTON MISS 3 ch f £0

0	17	NOTT	6f Firm	1266	

BARTON SANDS 3 b c £6732

85	2	NOTT	8f Gd/Sft	1084	
83	1	HAMI	9f Firm	1242*	
90	2	NEWM	10f Good	85	4197
69	6	YORK	12f Soft	4276	
39	11	NEWB	9f Sft/Hvy	88	4472

BASE LINE 2 b c £0

29	9	LING	6f Firm	2760	

BASHER JACK 4 b c £0

17a	7	WOLV	12f Aw	47	522 t
22	7	LEIC	12f Good	40	791 t

BASHKIR 3 b c £6650

93	5	LEOP	8f Gd/Fm	1316	bl
100	2	LEOP	7f Good	2070	bl

BASIC INSTINCT 3 ch f £0

30a	9	WOLV	6f Aw	118	
38a	7	WOLV	7f Aw	192	
14a	8	SOUT	7f Aw	281	
31a	8	WOLV	6f Aw	549	
27a	4	SOUT	7f Aw	688	
0	10	NOTT	8f Good	783	

BASINET 2 b c £515

0	16	HAYD	6f Gd/Sft	3268	
75	3	PONT	6f Soft	4083	
71a	4	WOLV	7f Aw	4385	

BASMAN 6 b g £0

87	6	DONC	10f Gd/Fm	1841	
0	17	YORK	12f Firm	88	2002
67	5	WIND	12f Soft	2547	
55	7	BEVE	8f Gd/Sft	78	3054

BATALEUR 7 b g £0

38a	6	SOUT	6f Aw	42	499
47	5	NOTT	6f Good	52	787
45	4	WARW	5f Heavy	51	1005
38	8	DONC	6f Gd/Sft	1068	
0	21	REDC	6f Firm	1298	
33	7	HAMI	5f Gd/Fm	45	1910
0	17	NOTT	6f Gd/Fm	42	2193

BATCHWORTH BELLE 5 b m £4955

85a	2	LING	5f Aw	82	506
89	3	DONC	6f Gd/Fm	93	702
0	R	KEMP	5f Soft	93	1013

BATCHWORTH BREEZE 2 ch f £0

47	9	WIND	5f Gd/Fm	2545	
11	12	WIND	6f Gd/Fm	2886	

BATCHWORTH LOCK 2 b g £0

0	15	NEWB	5f Gd/Fm	1782	
55	8	WIND	5f Gd/Fm	2711	
55	10	WIND	5f Gd/Fm	3044	

BATHWICK BABE 3 b f £1248

75	2	GOOD	12f Gd/Fm	2354	
59	12	DONC	12f Heavy	75	4580

BATHWICK DREAM 3 b f £0

0	11	SALI	7f Gd/Fm	3423	

BATOUTOFTHEBLUE 7 br g £4591

46	1	MUSS	16f Gd/Sft	42	797*
38	3	CARL	14f Firm	46	2016
45	4	MUSS	16f Gd/Fm	46	2203
48a	10	WOLV	16f Aw	65	2606

BATSWING 5 b g £35043

58	7	DONC	12f Gd/Fm	68	699
52	7	PONT	10f Soft	66	871
70	2	CHES	12f Firm	63	1251
55	8	NEWB	12f Good	63	1373
74	1	CHES	10f Gd/Sft	66	1777*
77	2	YORK	12f Firm	73	2002
66	14	GOOD	14f Gd/Fm	77	3058
0	17	YORK	12f Good	76	3541
81	2	EPSO	12f Good	75	3858
86	1	DONC	12f Heavy	80	4580+

BATTLE GREEN LAD 3 b g £0

0a	10	WOLV	7f Aw	4361	
9	9	NOTT	8f Heavy	4505	

BATTLE WARNING 5 b g £1244
57	2	LEIC	10f Good	55	793
0	15	RIPO	8f Good	58	1598
0	31	NEWM	12f Firm	56	1852

BATWINK 3 b f £0
0	14	SAND	10f Good		2531
27	8	NEWB	12f Firm		2710
32	8	KEMP	8f Firm		2871
27	10	LING	10f Firm		3281
0	5	NEWB	12f Gd/Fm		3487

BAUGET JOUETTE 3 gr f £0
| 0a | 13 | LING | 7f Aw | | 155 |

BAWSIAN 5 b g £522
85	4	PONT	10f Soft		874
0	19	DONC	12f Soft	85	4464
0	18	DONC	12f Heavy	85	4580

BAY OF BENGAL 4 ch f £2185
0	11	THIR	12f Gd/Sft		1353
45	3	HAMI	9f Gd/Fm	43	1939
43	2	HAMI	9f Gd/Fm		2236
16	8	MUSS	12f Gd/Sft	43	2537
35	6	HAMI	9f Gd/Fm	43	2799
0	15	YARM	10f Good		3031
38	3	LING	10f Firm		3490
23	8	BEVE	10f Gd/Fm	46	3676
40	4	YORK	9f Good		3808
0	14	PONT	10f Soft		4088
0	14	MUSS	8f Gd/Sft		4135

BAY OF ISLANDS 8 b g £84159
0	18	NEWM	12f Gd/Sft	94	968	
92	8	CHES	13f Firm		1247	vis
90	3	YORK	14f Gd/Fm	90	1982	vis
97	1	NEWC	16f Firm	90	2336*	vis
98	3	YORK	14f Good	97	2695	vis
84	16	YORK	14f Gd/Fm	97	3565	vis
99	3	DONC	15f Firm	97	3890	vis

BAY VIEW 5 b m £625
74	3	LEIC	10f Gd/Sft		833
0	21	NEWM	12f Gd/Sft	70	968
0	18	GOOD	9f Good	68	3110
28	14	NEWM	8f Gd/Fm	65	3317
0	22	YORK	8f Good	58	3810
61	5	LING	8f Soft		4274

BAYARD LADY 4 b f £0
0a	11	SOUT	8f Aw		45	
29	7	MUSS	9f Gd/Sft	40	795	
0	14	PONT	10f Soft	38	871	
0	6	BEVE	8f Heavy		973	t
0	20	DONC	7f Good	34	1519	BL
0	18	REDC	7f Gd/Sft		1559	t
14	5	HAMI	5f Gd/Fm	27	2233	
25	9	HAMI	5f Gd/Fm	37	2796	
0	14	REDC	7f Gd/Fm		2994	
34	6	LEIC	6f Gd/Fm		3097	

BAYONET 4 b f £3560
42	10	BATH	6f Gd/Fm	56	1438
52	2	LEIC	6f Gd/Sft	51	1734
55	1	CHEP	6f Good	51	1971*
44	7	SALI	6f Gd/Fm	56	2230
0	12	LEIC	6f Gd/Fm	56	2777

BAYRAMI 2 ch f £0
20a	7	WOLV	5f Aw		722
44	5	NOTT	5f Gd/Sft		1083
14a	8	SOUT	5f Aw		1206
1	11	NEWC	6f Gd/Fm		1476
20	9	CATT	6f Soft		1679
57	4	LEIC	5f Gd/Fm		2507
51	4	LEIC	5f Gd/Fm		2772
0	11	BATH	5f Firm		3204

BAYSWATER 3 b f £6224
| 57 | 14 | NEWB | 10f Gd/Fm | | 1404 |
| 72 | 2 | BATH | 12f Firm | | 2327 |

70	2	CATT	14f Gd/Fm		2930	
75	1	CHES	12f Gd/Fm		3429+	
67	5	RIPO	16f Gd/Fm	72	3715	BL

BAYTOWN RHAPSODY 3 b f £7863
49a	3	SOUT	8f Aw		303
56a	2	WOLV	7f Aw	49	346
58a	1	WOLV	6f Aw	47	397*
53a	3	LING	7f Aw		459
62a	1	SOUT	6f Aw	55	515*
57a	3	WOLV	6f Aw	62	638
57a	1	SOUT	7f Aw		688*
0a	11	WOLV	6f Aw	60	1233

BE GONE 5 ch g £4567
84a	3	LING	12f Aw	85	151
69a	8	SOUT	12f Aw	85	200
87a	1	WOLV	16f Aw	82	296*
79a	3	LING	12f Aw	86	508
0a	7	WOLV	16f Aw	85	664
82	11	ASCO	20f Good	88	2092

BE MY TINKER 2 ch f £2249
59	6	WIND	5f Good		2711
64	2	BATH	6f Firm		2939
64	2	NOTT	5f Gd/Fm		3114

BE MY WISH 5 b m £5928
68a	4	LING	8f Aw	70	7	
59a	5	WOLV	8f Aw	70	78	bl
54	3	YARM	7f Gd/Sft	52	1611	
57	2	YARM	6f Gd/Fm	54	1953	
58	2	NOTT	6f Gd/Fm	56	2192	
54	5	YARM	7f Firm	56	2391	
66	1	NEWM	6f Good	59	3613*	bl
56	8	SALI	7f Firm	59	3750	bl
49	8	NEWM	7f Good		4018	bl

BE THANKFULL 4 gr f £3279
82	5	KEMP	12f Firm	85	2263
80	3	NEWM	10f Gd/Fm	85	2805
96	6	NEWB	12f Gd/Fm		3177
87	11	YARM	10f Firm		3918
93	3	NEWM	12f Good	92	4162
81	7	NEWM	16f Gd/Sft	92	4533

BE THE CHIEF 4 ch c £0
| 8 | 11 | LEIC | 8f Gd/Sft | | 1732 | |
| 0a | 11 | WOLV | 8f Aw | 60 | 4248 | VIS |

BE VALIANT 6 gr g £0
| 11a | 6 | WOLV | 15f Aw | | 468 |
| 0a | 10 | WOLV | 9f Aw | | 553 |

BE WARNED 9 b g £4214
0a	13	SOUT	8f Aw	78	251	bl
52a	4	WOLV	12f Aw		307	vis
48a	7	WOLV	12f Aw	65	407	vis
55a	5	SOUT	8f Aw	63	496	vis
55a	9	SOUT	8f Aw		600	vis
63a	1	SOUT	8f Aw		686*	vis
61a	2	WOLV	8f Aw		707	vis
42a	7	SOUT	11f Aw		866	vis
0a	11	SOUT	8f Aw	60	1207	vis
60a	1	SOUT	11f Aw		4150*	vis
50a	7	SOUT	12f Aw		4366	vis

BEACH BABY 3 ch f £0
35a	9	LING	7f Aw		164
12a	7	LING	10f Aw		204
0a	12	LING	10f Aw		240
45	7	WIND	8f Gd/Fm		745
30	8	LING	7f Gd/Sft	38	841
0	12	FOLK	7f Soft		962
55	9	WARW	8f Soft		1062
0	16	WIND	10f Gd/Sft		1423
18	7	LING	5f Soft	42	1543
29	10	SALI	7f Gd/Fm		1884

BEACON OF LIGHT 2 b f £0
| 0 | 15 | THIR | 5f Soft | | 928 |
| 42 | 7 | NEWC | 6f Gd/Fm | | 2312 |

| 42 | 8 | BEVE | 7f Gd/Fm | | 2513 |
| 0 | 16 | LEIC | 8f Firm | 42 | 3837 |

BEACONS A LIGHT 2 b g £0
| 0 | 16 | BATH | 5f Firm | | 3204 |
| 0 | 14 | FOLK | 7f Gd/Fm | | 3582 |

BEADING 3 b f £8467
73	13	NEWM	7f Gd/Sft		971	
64	7	CHES	7f Gd/Fm		1224	
63	2	CATT	7f Gd/Fm		2437	t
62	5	CHEP	7f Gd/Fm	66	2974	t
70	1	NEWM	8f Gd/Fm	65	3317*	t
71	4	SALI	7f Firm	71	3750	t
71	3	SAND	8f Soft	71	4206	t
0	28	NEWM	8f Soft	71	4545	t

BEANBOY 2 ch c £0
| 38 | 6 | BEVE | 5f Stt/Hvy | | 4042 |
| 36 | 11 | YARM | 6f Soft | | 4390 |

BEAT ALL 4 b c £77100
0	W	CHES	10f Firm		1248
104	5	SAND	10f Soft		1587
116	3	ASCO	10f Good		2089
114	2	AYR	10f Gd/Fm		2720
116	4	ASCO	12f Gd/Fm		2998
106	5	ASCO	12f Good		4109

BEAT HOLLOW 3 b c £247166
112	1	NEWM	10f Gd/Fm		1151*
120	3	EPSO	12f Good		1848
120	1	LONG	10f Good		2225*

BEAT IT 2 b f £0
| 0 | 13 | BEVE | 5f Good | | 3955 |

BEAT THE RING 2 br c £0
| 15a | 11 | WOLV | 6f Aw | | 4548 |

BEAU CHEVALIER 4 b c £0
| 0 | 14 | THIR | 7f Gd/Fm | 52 | 3129 |

BEAU DUCHESS 3 ch f £0
62	8	NEWM	10f Firm		1857
52	6	PONT	12f Good		2179
67	7	SAND	10f Good		2531

BEAU SAUVAGE 2 b c £0
0	15	HAYD	6f Gd/Sft		3268
50	8	HAYD	6f Gd/Fm		3478
64	5	REDC	7f Gd/Fm		3635
0	17	PONT	6f Soft	63	4235
0	16	NEWC	5f Heavy	60	4423

BEAUCHAMP MAGIC 5 b g £9852
18a	8	LING	12f Aw	40	115
37a	1	WOLV	16f Aw	33	141*
32a	6	WOLV	16f Aw	36	194
17a	12	LING	16f Aw	61	285
37a	4	WOLV	16f Aw	36	318
17a	8	SOUT	16f Aw	36	428
32a	5	WOLV	16f Aw	36	494
32a	4	WOLV	16f Aw	33	577
28a	3	LING	16f Aw	31	649
25	7	FOLK	16f Good	29	2622
31	1	BRIG	12f Firm	25	2904*
37a	1	WOLV	15f Gd/Fm	30	3276*
33	1	THIR	16f Gd/Fm	30	3348*
29	6	LING	16f Firm	31	3755

BEAUCHAMP NYX 4 b f £0
29a	6	SOUT	12f Aw		84
43	9	BATH	10f Soft		4141
0a	8	SOUT	14f Aw	38	4370
4a	9	WOLV	12f Aw		4549

BEAUCHAMP PILOT 2 ch g £0
| 45a | 8 | WOLV | 9f Aw | | 4438 |

BEAUMONT 10 br g £0
| 18a | 9 | LING | 16f Aw | 55 | 285 |

BEAUTIFUL BUSINESS 2 b f £587
41	10	SALI	6f Gd/Fm		1883
50	3	REDC	7f Gd/Fm		2155
52	3	BEVE	7f Gd/Fm		2513

40 5 YARM 7f Firm   2898 VIS

BEAUTY ROSE 3 ch f £456

| 64 | 3 | REDC | 9f Firm | | 3326 | |

BEBE DE CHAM 3 b f £376

33a	8	LING	7f Aw	73	617	
50	10	DONC	7f Good	73	736	
48	6	THIR	8f Soft		925	
0	24	ASCO	8f Gd/Sft	70	1113	
51	7	HAYD	8f Soft	67	1822	
0	18	REDC	6f Good	67	1891	VIS
36	6	REDC	7f Gd/Fm	62	2145	
0	6	RIPO	12f Soft	56	2540	
41	6	CARL	9f Firm	56	2825	
27	12	LEIC	8f Gd/Fm	48	3095	
0	14	RIPO	10f Good	48	3702	

BECKETT 2 b c £119100

| 110 | 3 | CURR | 7f Good | | 3719 | |
| 118 | 1 | **CURR** | 7f Gd/Sft | | 4058* | |

BECKON 4 ch f £6495

53a	1	LING	10f Aw		111*	
52a	3	LING	10f Aw	51	203	
51a	5	LING	12f Aw	51	290	
49a	4	LING	10f Aw		335	
40a	5	LING	12f Aw	54	377	
28	7	BRIG	12f Gd/Fm		1934	
52a	1	**LING**	10f Aw	47	2212*	
42a	5	LING	12f Aw	53	2593	
31	8	WIND	8f Good	38	3188	
35	6	LING	10f Firm	36	3581	
42	1	**BRIG**	10f Firm	36	3737*	
36	8	WARW	11f Gd/Fm	40	3915	
33	4	BRIG	10f Soft	40	4419	

BECKY SIMMONS 2 b f £13509

81	1	**HAMI**	5f Gd/Fm		1906*	
84	1	**SALI**	6f Good		2687*	
88	1	**REDC**	6f Firm	80	3327*	
77	5	CHES	6f Gd/Sft		3425	
76	11	DONC	7f Gd/Fm	86	3860	
78	10	NEWM	7f Good	85	4157	

BEDARA 3 b f £5045

83	1	**WARW**	11f Soft		814*	
88	4	LING	11f Gd/Sft		1282	
82	6	ASCO	12f Gd/Sft		4130	
62	12	NEWM	10f Good		4337	

BEDAZZLING 3 gr f £11122

86	11	NEWM	7f Good		953	
104	1	**LEIC**	7f Gd/Sft		1733*	
105	4	NEWM	8f Gd/Fm		2597	
84	8	SAND	8f Good		3469	
105	4	GOOD	7f Soft		4078	
87	6	NEWM	8f Soft		4544	

BEDEVILLED 5 ch g £9061

68a	2	SOUT	6f Aw	67	342	
63a	7	WOLV	5f Aw	67	394	
71a	2	WOLV	5f Aw	67	614	
63a	5	WOLV	5f Aw	70	678	
73	1	**NEWC**	5f Soft	67	758+	
60	15	THIR	5f Soft	75	926	
0	W	NEWC	5f Heavy	74	1008	
0	22	DONC	6f Gd/Sft	74	1074	
62	2	CATT	6f Good		1664	
64	7	HAYD	5f Gd/Fm	69	2701	
43	7	NEWC	5f Gd/Fm	67	2987	
66	1	**CATT**	5f Good		3441*	
57	6	NEWM	5f Gd/Sft	65	3631	
56	9	HAMI	5f Gd/Sft	65	3825	
64	3	GOOD	5f Soft	63	4065	
0	15	NEWB	5f Gd/Sft	65	4459	

BEDEY 3 b c £7685

78	4	WARW	8f Good		2465	
84	2	ASCO	8f Good		2679	
83	2	WIND	10f Good		3189	

BEDFORD FALLS 2 b f £0

| 17 | 9 | WIND | 5f Good | | 1727 | |

BEDOUIN QUEEN 3 ch f £940

56a	7	LING	8f Aw	71	2	
47a	9	LING	8f Aw	71	54	
49a	5	LING	7f Aw		164	BL
27a	7	LING	8f Aw		264	bl
38	11	NOTT	8f Gd/Sft	68	1085	
59	6	NOTT	8f Good	63	1414	
20	10	NEWB	10f Gd/Sft		1593	
34	13	NOTT	8f Gd/Fm	58	2187	
47	2	CHEP	8f Gd/Fm		2448	
26	12	BATH	8f Gd/Fm	50	3816	
19	8	LEIC	10f Gd/Sft		4029	
28	3	LEIC	10f Heavy		4313	

BEE GEE 3 b f £2790

35	7	NOTT	8f Gd/Sft	44	1365	
40a	1	**LING**	12f Aw		1540*	
40	4	LING	11f Firm	40	1914	
38a	3	LING	12f Aw	41	2217	
33	8	CHEP	16f Gd/Fm	47	2659	
39	5	BRIG	10f Firm	39	2908	
28	8	BEVE	12f Gd/Sft	39	3050	
21	8	BRIG	12f Gd/Sft	39	3260	
41	4	LEIC	10f Gd/Sft		4029	
46a	3	SOUT	11f Aw		4150	
33	3	NOTT	14f Heavy	35	4409	

BEE J GEE 2 b c £0

50	6	SAND	5f Good		1962	
59	12	LING	5f Gd/Fm		2214	
58	9	WARW	7f Good		3692	
69	4	BRIG	8f Gd/Sft		4117	
56	12	BRIG	7f Soft	65	4416	

BEE KING 2 ch c £2214

0	13	BATH	5f Good		1088	
59	10	DONC	6f Gd/Fm		1838	
61	8	CARL	6f Gd/Fm		2239	
63	9	YORK	7f Gd/Fm		3730	VIS
60	3	NOTT	6f Soft	59	3976	
60	3	HAYD	6f Soft	59	4090	
62	2	BRIG	6f Soft	60	4170	
56	8	LING	6f Soft	61	4269	
44	6	BATH	6f Soft		4431	

BEE ONE 2 b f £1865

70	5	SAND	5f Good		1568	
78	4	NEWB	5f Gd/Fm		1782	
87	8	ASCO	5f Good		2088	
89	4	GOOD	6f Gd/Fm		3090	
92	5	CURR	6f Yldg		3720	
86	2	BATH	5f Gd/Fm		3815	

BEEKEEPER 2 b c £0

| 85 | 5 | LEIC | 7f Firm | | 3840 | |
| 97 | 5 | NEWM | 7f Good | | 4158 | |

BEENABOUTABIT 2 b f £895

57	9	LING	5f Good		4095	
70	2	WIND	6f Gd/Sft		4289	
61	7	NOTT	5f Gd/Sft		4503	

BEGORRAT 6 ch g £0

| 42 | 12 | DONC | 10f Gd/Fm | 60 | 705 | vis |

BEGUILE 6 b g £3307

52a	2	LING	7f Aw	44	439	
47a	4	LING	8f Aw	48	503	
52a	1	**WOLV**	7f Aw	48	635*	
14	12	WIND	6f Gd/Fm	51	746	t
37a	6	LING	10f Aw	50	842	t
48	3	BRIG	8f Gd/Fm	48	1129	t
29	10	YARM	8f Good	48	1772	t
0	16	NEWM	8f Gd/Fm	48	2802	t

BEHARI 6 b g £0

| 20a | 8 | SOUT | 12f Aw | | 387 | |

BEHRENS 6 br h £731707

| 124a | 2 | NAD | 10f Dirt | | 769 | bl |

BEIDERBECKE 2 ch c £0

63	10	NEWB	6f Firm		3980	
65	6	LING	6f Soft		4189	
0	14	NEWM	6f Gd/Sft		4530	

BEL TEMPO 2 b f £0

| 0 | 7 | BRIG | 6f Firm | | 3525 | |
| 40 | 12 | LING | 7f Firm | | 3829 | |

BELANDO 2 b g £0

44	14	CARL	5f Firm		1252	
0	15	HAYD	5f Gd/Sft		1488	
0a	16	SOUT	7f Aw		4369	

BELIEVING 3 b f £0

60a	4	WOLV	5f Aw	74	751	
66	6	BRIG	6f Gd/Fm	76	1126	
53	14	NEWB	7f Gd/Fm	73	1405	
55	9	WIND	6f Gd/Fm	70	3046	
38	11	EPSO	6f Gd/Fm	66	3405	
47	11	SALI	7f Firm	62	3750	
0	17	LING	7f Soft	57	4192	
0a	11	WOLV	6f Aw	52	4444	

BELINDA 3 ch f £3177

44a	7	WOLV	8f Aw		920	
48a	4	SOUT	8f Aw		1204	
38	8	SOUT	7f Soft		1607	
65a	1	**SOUT**	8f Aw		1977*	
51	9	SALI	8f Gd/Fm	62	2264	
28a	10	SOUT	8f Aw	66	2634	
60a	3	SOUT	11f Aw	65	2945	
27	11	EPSO	10f Good	55	3762	
34a	11	SOUT	7f Aw	63	4153	

BELLA BELLISIMO 3 b f £430

52	7	PONT	10f Soft		874	
71	1	YORK	7f Gd/Fm	83	1308	
72	6	THIR	8f Gd/Fm	80	2062	
63	7	BEVE	8f Gd/Fm	76	2515	
70	4	KEMP	10f Gd/Fm	72	3794	
57	11	NEWM	10f Good	71	4160	
54	9	BATH	10f Soft	69	4436	

BELLA LAMBADA 3 ch f £5642

| 76 | 6 | NEWM | 7f Gd/Fm | | 1155 | |
| 85 | 1 | **YORK** | 10f Gd/Fm | | 1985* | |

BELLA PAVLINA 2 ch f £0

51	12	KEMP	6f Gd/Fm		3795	
60	7	LING	5f Good		4095	
57	6	LING	5f Soft		4187	
54	5	WIND	6f Heavy	59	4525	

BELLAS GATE BOY 8 b g £332

1a	12	WOLV	8f Aw	48	676	
0	13	BEVE	7f Firm	59	1275	
34	14	WARW	8f Heavy	57	1520	
50	3	LING	7f Good	54	1672	
45	9	BRIG	7f Gd/Fm	53	1930	
45	5	YARM	10f Firm	51	2387	

BELLE AMOUR 3 b f £0

| 53 | 6 | NOTT | 8f Heavy | | 4505 | |

BELLE DANCER 6 b m £0

| 0 | 15 | CHEP | 8f Gd/Fm | 29 | 3251 | |

BELLE OF HEARTS 4 gr f £0

0a	13	SOUT	8f Aw	39	692	
0	12	DONC	6f Gd/Sft		1073	
0	20	PONT	8f Gd/Sft	39	1101	
10	10	CATT	7f Gd/Sft		1818	
0	18	NOTT	6f Gd/Fm	33	2192	

BELLE ROUGE 2 b f £0

| 0 | 20 | NEWM | 7f Soft | | 4541 | |

BELLINO EMPRESARIO 2 b g £0

| 47 | 10 | WARW | 7f Good | | 3692 | |
| 45 | 7 | KEMP | 8f Soft | | 4036 | |

BELLS ARE RINGING 3 b f £750

| 94 | 4 | LEOP | 7f Soft | | 948 | |
| 0 | 13 | CURR | 8f Gd/Sft | | 1626 | |

BELLS BEACH 2 ch f £520
```
0   8  THIR  6f Gd/Sft       1713
35a 3  WOLV  6f Aw           2079
45a 4  SOUT  5f Aw           2384
23a 10 SOUT  6f Aw       52  2948
```

BELSTANE BADGER 2 b f £0
```
57  7  MUSS  7f Soft         4517
```

BELSTANE FOX 2 ch f £0
```
48  8  MUSS  7f Soft         4517
```

BELTANE 2 b c £0
```
40  9  WIND  6f Good         3638
0   15 WARW  7f Gd/Fm        3909
```

BEN EWAR 6 b h £6724
```
109 3  CHAN  12f Gd/Sft      1902
0   P  MAIS  13f Soft        2737
```

BENATOM 7 gr g £0
```
77  13 CHES  19f Gd/Fm   96  1222
```

BENBYAS 3 b g £3810
```
41  9  THIR  8f Good     60  1387
47  6  RIPO  8f Good     57  1600  VIS
60  1  CARL  6f Gd/Sft       1723*  vis
45  8  THIR  8f Gd/Fm    63  2060  vis
40  9  BEVE  8f Gd/Fm    59  2515  vis
43  4  BEVE  8f Sft/Hvy  57  4045  BL
49  3  PONT  8f Soft     55  4232  bl
41a 10 SOUT  8f Aw       54  4365  vis
50  5  DONC  8f Heavy    54  4573  bl
```

BENEDICTINE 2 b c £1426
```
79  2  HAYD  5f Soft         3767
```

BENEVOLENCE 2 b f £336
```
49  9  NEWM  6f Gd/Fm        2618
37  4  NOTT  6f Gd/Fm        3003
73  6  NEWM  7f Firm         3298
```

BENJAMIN 2 b c £0
```
0   14 WIND  5f Good         849
0   13 LING  7f Gd/Fm        2182
30  10 SALI  6f Good         2687
```

BENNOCHY 3 ch c £2797
```
58  1  CATT  5f Gd/Fm        777*
0   14 THIR  5f Gd/Sft   61  1357
56  5  CATT  5f Gd/Sft   59  1817
52  7  MUSS  5f Firm     57  2047
55  4  CATT  6f Gd/Fm    55  2440
53  5  HAMI  6f Gd/Fm    55  2779
49  4  DONC  5f Gd/Fm    54  3161
51  6  CATT  5f Good         3441
43  10 MUSS  5f Gd/Fm    53  3594
0   13 LEIC  6f Gd/Sft       4031
34  9  AYR   5f Heavy    46  4307
30  9  NEWC  5f Heavy    46  4407
```

BENOUI SPRINGS 3 br c £281
```
52  4  NEWC  7f Firm         3604
```

BENTICO 11 b g £657
```
26a 7  SOUT  8f Aw           646  vis
44a 4  SOUT  8f Aw           684  vis
50a 2  WOLV  8f Aw           750  vis
35a 4  WOLV  9f Aw           922  vis
0a  13 SOUT  12f Aw          1203 vis
```

BENTYHEATH LANE 3 b c £0
```
28  9  LEIC  8f Soft         1548
0   11 CHES  16f Soft    60  4071
```

BENVOLIO 3 br g £0
```
0   7  PONT  12f Firm        2179
```

BENZOE 10 b g £8501
```
53  5  THIR  5f Gd/Sft   57  1714
0   12 PONT  6f Good     57  1869
49  6  CATT  7f Gd/Fm    53  2418
58  1  HAYD  5f Gd/Fm    52  2701*
53  5  AYR   6f Gd/Fm    57  2877
52  3  THIR  6f Gd/Sft   57  3123
0   13 HAMI  6f Gd/Sft   57  3377
56  4  THIR  5f Gd/Fm    57  3619
53  6  CHEP  5f Good     56  3872
```

BERBERIS 4 b c £0
```
28  8  NOTT  8f Good     45  1414
0   18 CHEP  7f Gd/Sft   41  1799
0   14 BATH  8f Firm     43  1998
0   12 WARW  12f Gd/Fm   35  2255
0   16 CHEP  7f Gd/Fm    32  2974  BL
```

BEREZINA 2 b f £2779
```
67  5  PONT  5f Heavy        938
50  6  THIR  5f Good         1385
67  4  HAYD  6f Gd/Fm        2454
47  8  PONT  6f Good         2828
65  1  REDC  8f Gd/Fm        2990*
0   14 REDC  6f Firm     69  3327
59  8  BEVE  5f Good     69  3394
50  15 CATT  7f Soft     67  4007
```

BERGAMO 4 b c £0
```
0   15 CATT  14f Gd/Fm   74  779
62  8  HAMI  13f Good    70  845   bl
0   14 KEMP  12f Gd/Sft  65  1076  bl
36  5  CARL  12f Firm        1253  bl
49  7  CATT  14f Soft    58  1683
```

BERGEN 5 b g £0
```
62  8  DONC  7f Good     74  1514
69  5  CHES  8f Gd/Sft   72  1778
0   15 BEVE  5f Gd/Fm    70  3653
33  11 AYR   8f Gd/Sft   67  4013
```

BERINES SON 3 b c £59559
```
114 1  LONG  8f Heavy        1025*
118 2  LONG  8f V            1318
97  6  CHAN  9f V            1753
```

BERISKAIO 3 b c £3842
```
110 3  LONG  9f Good         1379
```

BERKELEY DIDO 3 b f £0
```
15a 8  WOLV  7f Aw       54  346  BL
16a 8  LING  8f Aw       51  419  VIS
```

BERKELEY HALL 3 b f £3098
```
35  10 WARW  7f Heavy    58  887
17a 11 WOLV  9f Aw       56  1040
61  1  NOTT  6f Firm     56  1273*  BL
66  2  CATT  6f Good     63  1665  bl
43  6  PONT  8f Gd/Fm        3225  bl
47  13 CHEP  7f Good     65  3871
```

BERLIN 2 b c £62780
```
104 1  CURR  6f Good         2400*
95  3  CURR  6f Good         2738
96  5  CURR  7f Gd/Sft       4058
```

BERMUDA GRASS 2 £2305
```
101 4  LONG  9f Good         4237
```

BERNARDO BELLOTTO 5 b g £736
```
41a 7  SOUT  6f Aw       57  386
47a 7  SOUT  7f Aw       55  867
17  13 THIR  7f Soft     55  908   bl
0   15 REDC  7f Gd/Sft       1132
38  8  BEVE  7f Gd/Sft   48  1760
28  8  MUSS  7f Firm         2046  bl
43  2  WARW  7f Gd/Fm    40  2479
```

BERNARDON 4 b c £6452
```
108 3  HOPP  8f Good         2573
```

BERNSTEIN 3 b c £82500
```
55  26 NEWM  8f Gd/Fm        1171
111 1  ASCO  6f Gd/Fm        3303*
90  11 YORK  5f Firm         3598  VIS
115 3  CORK  7f Soft         4266*
```

BERTOLINI 4 b c £175976
```
112r2  NAD   6f Dirt         766   vis
115 3  ASCO  6f Good         2065  vis
107 6  NEWM  6f Gd/Fm        2615  vis
118 2  YORK  5f Firm         3598  vis
102 7  LONG  5f Good         4261  bl
```

BERTY BOY 4 ch g £0

BERZOUD 3 b f £4274
```
58  9  NOTT  8f Gd/Fm        1268
75  2  WIND  8f Soft         2548
69  1  REDC  9f Firm         3326*
```

BESCABY BLUE 3 b f £1168
```
23a 12 SOUT  8f Aw       65  125
54a 2  WOLV  6f Aw           228
46a 6  LING  7f Aw       60  287
45a 6  SOUT  8f Aw       58  365
52a 2  SOUT  7f Aw           417  BL
```

BEST BOND 3 ch c £1040
```
0   13 KEMP  6f Soft     68  994
68  3  WIND  5f Gd/Sft   66  1098
48  8  RIPO  6f Good     67  1600
49  10 KEMP  6f Gd/Fm    66  1925  BL
49  9  BRIG  7f Firm     66  2044
60  5  BEVE  5f Firm     64  2223
42  6  WIND  6f Soft     62  2549
40  9  SAND  5f Gd/Fm    60  2934
47  6  DONC  5f Gd/Fm    56  3161  VIS
57  3  CARL  6f Firm     56  3194  vis
0   12 BEVE  7f Gd/Fm    56  3652  vis
53  6  THIR  5f Gd/Sft   55  3781  vis
38a 10 SOUT  8f Aw       55  4156  vis
```

BEST EVER 3 ch c £1054
```
0   22 RIPO  10f Soft    59  827
35  16 DONC  8f Gd/Sft   56  1053
38  11 NEWC  8f Gd/Sft   52  1477
52  2  THIR  8f Gd/Sft   51  1718
50  5  BEVE  10f Firm    51  1921
15  13 BEVE  8f Firm     53  2735
```

BEST GUEST 2 b c £0
```
69  8  YORK  7f Gd/Fm        3730
47  9  PONT  8f Soft         4086
54  9  LING  6f Soft         4188
```

BEST KEPT SECRET 9 b g £0
```
14  8  MUSS  10f Gd/Sft  35  798
```

BEST MUSIC METROFM 3 b c £0
```
0a  11 WOLV  8f Aw           273
0a  9  WOLV  9f Aw           319
```

BEST OF THE BESTS 3 ch c £194418
```
113 3  YORK  10f Firm        1326
114 4  EPSO  12f Good        1848
110 4  LONG  10f Good        2225
119 1  DEAU  10f Gd/Fm       3374*
119 3  LEOP  10f Good        3925
119 3  ASCO  8f Good         4111
```

BEST PORT 4 b g £5105
```
26a 7  SOUT  12f Aw      35  641
24a 8  WOLV  12f Aw          1039
30  3  REDC  14f Gd/Sft  36  1563
35  4  CATT  12f Gd/Sft  35  1816
33  3  NOTT  14f Good    32  2008
39  7  CARL  12f Firm    46  2279
27  7  HAMI  13f Gd/Fm   32  2643
29  2  NOTT  14f Gd/Fm   29  3002
35  1  BEVE  16f Gd/Fm   31  3406*
38  2  RIPO  16f Gd/Fm   38  3715
29  7  CATT  16f Soft    38  4006
26  9  REDC  14f Gd/Sft  37  4222
33a 5  SOUT  14f Aw      38  4371
```

BEST QUEST 5 b g £7840
```
64a 2  LING  7f Aw       64  59   t
48a 9  LING  7f Aw       64  162  t
0a  14 SOUT  7f Aw       62  216
61a 3  SOUT  7f Aw       60  246  t
70a 1  LING  6f Aw           313*  t
70a 2  SOUT  6f Aw       66  386  t
70a 3  LING  5f Aw       66  403  t
68a 3  SOUT  8f Aw       66  425  t
```

68a	3	SOUT	6f Aw	66	454	t
63a	5	LING	7f Aw	68	462	t
63a	8	WOLV	6f Aw	68	532	t
68a	2	LING	7f Aw		571	t
66a	2	LING	7f Aw		616	t
0a	7	SOUT	7f Aw		693	t

BET ME BEST 4 ch c £60976

112ε3		NAD	6f Dirt	766	BL

BETACHANCE DOT COM 3 b f £0

0	19	WIND	10f Gd/Fm		1200
43	8	NEWM	10f Gd/Fm		2135
0	12	SALI	14f Good		2691
0	14	BEVE	16f Good	51	2879

BETASITO 2 b c £3578

85	2	SAN	8f Heavy		4242

BETCHWORTH SAND 4 ch g £0

0a	11	LING	7f Aw		8
0	14	LING	7f Gd/Sft		1263
42	6	SAND	10f Soft		1588
28	10	WIND	8f Good	49	2367
0	15	LING	6f Firm	44	3578
11a	11	LING	10f Aw	39	3828 BL

BETHANIA 2 gr f £0

0	24	NEWM	6f Good		4341

BETHESDA 3 gr f £292

59	6	PONT	6f Soft		877
63	4	YARM	6f Good		1773
38	5	WIND	6f Heavy		4526 t

BETTER MOMENT 3 b g £584

64	4	PONT	12f Gd/Fm		2560
48	7	HAYD	12f Gd/Fm		3324
64	4	BEVE	10f Gd/Fm		3672

BETTER OFF 2 ch g £0

54a	5	WOLV	5f Aw		4247
58a	5	WOLV	6f Aw		4381

BETTINA BLUE 3 b f £0

53a	5	LING	6f Aw		5
53	6	WIND	8f Gd/Fm		745
57	6	BRIG	6f Firm	63	1211
49	10	LING	6f Good	60	2654
0	16	EPSO	7f Good	60	2794
41	14	LING	7f Firm	56	3279
50	7	FOLK	5f Gd/Fm		3584
47	6	LING	6f Firm	52	3759
0	20	WIND	6f Gd/Sft	52	4293

BETTY BATHWICK 3 b f £2310

0	12	BRIG	8f Firm	56	3561
0	12	CHEP	7f Good	51	3873
64	1	CATT	6f Soft		4255*
0a	13	LING	7f Aw		4487
54	11	YARM	7f Soft	63	4513

BETTYJOE 3 ch f £0

42	8	MUSS	7f Gd/Fm	55	1149
30	10	HAYD	6f Soft	51	1494
20	13	RIPO	6f Good	51	1600

BEVEL BLUE 2 b c £0

56	9	WIND	6f Gd/Fm		3047
0	12	LING	5f Good		4095
0	14	LING	5f Soft		4187

BEVELED CRYSTAL 6 ro m £0

31a	9	LING	6f Aw		25
0a	13	LING	6f Aw	30	148 BL

BEVELED HAWTHORN 5 b m £0

26a	4	WOLV	6f Aw	32	563
0a	12	SOUT	5f Aw	38	673
0	W	MUSS	5f Gd/Sft	35	798

BEVELENA 4 ch f £0

0	17	REDC	5f Gd/Sft	77	1133
61	9	LING	5f Good	75	1398
0	16	NEWB	6f Gd/Sft	73	1591
0	15	NOTT	5f Good	69	1871 BL

BEVERLEY MACCA 2 ch f £6248

76a	2	SOUT	5f Aw		865
70	2	WARW	5f Heavy		1000
76a	1	WOLV	5f Aw		1136*
80	1	REDC	5f Firm		1294*
78	4	REDC	5f Gd/Sft		1558
56	7	WIND	5f Good		2368

BEVERLEY MONKEY 4 b f £0

1a	11	WOLV	6f Aw		436
13a	9	LING	7f Aw	36	503
25	12	BRIG	6f Gd/Sft	39	1464
8	9	CATT	6f Good		1664
3	6	FOLK	6f Gd/Fm		2292

BEWARE 5 br g £2586

51a	3	SOUT	6f Aw		30
34a	8	WOLV	6f Aw		134
50a	3	SOUT	7f Aw		247
46a	6	SOUT	6f Aw		279
44a	6	SOUT	7f Aw	53	368
55a	1	SOUT	6f Aw		559* BL
48a	5	WOLV	6f Aw	55	622 bl
48	4	DONC	6f Gd/Sft		1073
52	5	GOOD	5f Gd/Sft	65	1487
59	4	CARL	5f Gd/Fm	62	1724
0	12	BATH	6f Firm	60	1999

BEWILDERED 3 br f £2539

14a	9	SOUT	6f Aw	62	365
25a	9	WOLV	8f Aw	54	495
13a	7	WOLV	6f Aw	48	706
36a	3	WOLV	9f Aw	42	1040
0	15	PONT	10f Good	53	1496
0	15	HAYD	7f Gd/Sft	46	1793 BL
0	16	REDC	8f Good	49	1892
33	6	CARL	7f Firm	44	2017
24	7	THIR	6f Gd/Fm	40	2060
29	3	REDC	8f Gd/Fm	40	2147 bl
22	11	LEIC	8f Gd/Fm	41	2512 bl
41a	1	WOLV	8f Aw	36	2601* bl

BEYOND CALCULATION 6 ch g £1016

65	5	BEVE	5f Firm	65	1278
66	1	NOTT	6f Gd/Sft		1368*
55	5	BRIG	5f Good	66	1650
54	10	SALI	6f Gd/Fm	65	1887
70	1	WIND	6f Gd/Fm	64	2207*
54	6	EPSO	6f Gd/Sft	69	2631
69	4	WARW	6f Gd/Fm	69	2845
69	4	CHEP	5f Gd/Fm	68	3257
71	2	BEVE	5f Gd/Fm	68	3653
66	10	KEMP	6f Gd/Fm	71	3791
57	13	BATH	6f Gd/Fm	71	3821
64	10	WIND	5f Gd/Sft	70	4295

BEYOND THE CLOUDS 4 b g £15489

4	8	NEWC	6f Soft		756 vis
0	14	NEWC	8f Heavy	51	1007 vis
52	3	HAMI	6f Gd/Fm	48	1358 vis
34	6	GOOD	5f Gd/Sft	48	1487 vis
55	1	HAMI	5f Gd/Fm	50	1910*
57	4	NEWC	5f Good	56	2525
62	1	WIND	5f Good	55	2716*
62	4	SAND	5f Gd/Fm	61	2925
65	2	WIND	5f Good	61	3191
70	1	BEVE	5f Gd/Fm	65	3653*
63	9	YARM	5f Firm	70	3920

BEYOND THE WAVES 4 b g £15369

108	3	LONG	9f Heavy		1114
108	2	LONG	13f Good		4236

BEZZA 2 ch f £0

0	28	NEWM	8f Good		4349
62	11	YARM	8f Heavy		4475

BEZZAAF 3 b f £4316

88	1	WIND	10f Gd/Fm		1200*
100	5	GOOD	10f Gd/Sft		1469

0	P	NEWB	10f Gd/Fm		1945
80	7	ASCO	10f Good		2169
58	10	NEWM	10f Good	93	3024
83	5	HAYD	11f Gd/Sft	89	4108

BHUTAN 5 b g £13817

69	1	HAMI	13f Gd/Fm	65	1194*
58	6	YORK	12f Firm	68	2002
55	9	CARL	12f Firm	68	2279
62	7	RIPO	9f Gd/Fm	66	3011
70	1	CATT	14f Gd/Fm	66	3201*
74	2	MUSS	14f Gd/Fm	70	3590
71	4	HAYD	14f Soft	72	3783
72	2	AYR	17f Soft	71	3993
70	3	MUSS	16f Soft	70	4563

BHUTAN PRINCE 3 b c £3501

85a	1	LING	6f Aw		5*

BIANCHI 2 b f £624

76	4	ASCO	6f Gd/Fm		2952

BIBLE BOX 2 b f £0

60	7	LEIC	6f Firm		2029

BICTON PARK 6 b g £0

0a	11	WOLV	7f Aw		61
0a	13	SOUT	6f Aw	35	83
0a	12	SOUT	8f Aw		195
0a	11	WOLV	8f Aw	34	432
0	12	WIND	5f Good	38	2716

BID FOR FAME 3 b c £4689

75	5	LEIC	10f Gd/Sft		833
86	3	NEWM	12f Good		951
76	8	LING	11f Gd/Sft		1284
85	1	PONT	12f Firm		2179*
87	3	NEWB	13f Firm	85	2852
82	7	GOOD	14f Firm	86	3153

BID ME WELCOME 4 b c £10416

0	15	NEWM	12f Firm	81	1187
62	10	NOTT	14f Good	80	1411
75	5	NEWB	13f Gd/Fm	77	1784
76	2	WARW	16f Gd/Fm	74	2256
72	3	HAYD	14f Gd/Fm	74	2455
80	1	NEWB	16f Firm	75	2812*
73	5	NEWM	16f Good	80	3295
80	2	NEWM	15f Good	79	3611
72	11	DONC	15f Firm	80	3890
80	6	NEWB	16f Firm	80	3986
80	3	ASCO	16f Gd/Fm	79	4115
0	24	NEWM	18f Good	80	4353

BIEN ENTENDU 3 b c £6434

98	1	NEWM	10f Good		957*
101	3	NEWB	10f Good		2709

BIENNALE 4 b c £11567

102	4	HAYD	12f Heavy		987
106	4	SAND	16f Soft		1565
104	5	NEWC	16f Firm	104	2336
105	3	ASCO	16f Gd/Fm	104	3302
107	5	YORK	14f Gd/Fm	104	3565
105	2	HAYD	14f Soft		4091

BIFF EM 6 ch g £1563

35	5	MUSS	5f Gd/Fm	40	1143
16	13	CARL	6f Firm	40	1257
40	3	HAMI	5f Gd/Fm	39	1358
35	9	CARL	5f Gd/Sft	39	1724
32	4	HAMI	5f Gd/Fm	39	1910
37	5	HAMI	5f Gd/Fm	37	2233
36	6	NEWC	5f Firm	39	2340
31	5	CATT	7f Good	40	3440
32	9	HAMI	5f Gd/Sft	40	3536
31	10	NEWC	6f Firm	40	3605
23	12	HAMI	5f Gd/Sft	37	3825
33	5	AYR	6f Heavy	43	4327
0	14	NEWC	6f Heavy	34	4425
33	6	MUSS	7f Soft	38	4522

BIG AL 4 b c £578

49 2 HAYD 11f Soft 49 1819

BIG BEN 6 ch g £2159
67a 3 LING 7f Aw 68 28
66a 5 LING 7f Aw 68 58
69a 1 LING 8f Aw 93*
54a 8 LING 8f Aw 68 169

BIG CHIEF 4 ch c £0
0 18 PONT 10f Soft 40 871 t

BIG E 3 ch g £0
22a 4 LING 12f Aw 1540 VIS
39a 5 SOUT 11f Aw 1978 vis

BIG FUTURE 3 b c £21938
77 1 KEMP 7f Soft 1018*
81 4 NEWB 8f Gd/Fm 1786
90 1 LING 7f Firm 79 2325*
89 5 SAND 8f Aw 2495
89 3 NEWB 7f Gd/Fm 89 3481
87 3 GOOD 7f Good 85 3902
80 12 ASCO 7f Good 90 4112
95 1 YORK 7f Soft 90 4278*
0 25 NEWM 8f Soft 94 4545

BIG ISSUE 3 b c £0
37a 9 LING 7f Aw 60 654

BIG JAG 7 br g £445372
114ε3 GULF 6f Fast 17
121ε1 NAD 6f Dirt 766*

BIG JOHN 2 ch c £267
72 4 AYR 6f Gd/Fm 1628
60 7 YORK 6f Firm 2005

BIG MOMENT 2 ch c £1570
96 2 NEWM 7f Good 4183

BIGGLES 3 b g £266
74 4 RIPO 8f Gd/Fm 2104
68 9 NEWM 10f Gd/Fm 2617

BIGWIG 7 ch g £0
30a 5 LING 13f Aw 46 219 bl
26a 5 LING 16f Aw 44 649 bl

BIJA 5 b g £0
0a 11 WOLV 8f Aw 42 254
0a 8 SOUT 12f Aw 25 339
0a 13 WOLV 9f Aw 32 405
0a 10 LING 13f Aw 24 458

BIJAN 2 b f £4014
74 5 HAYD 5f Gd/Sft 1488
74 3 DONC 6f Gd/Fm 1844
75 1 CARL 5f Firm 2277*
0 13 CURR 6f Yldg 3720
77 4 DONC 6f Firm 3895

BILLADDIE 7 b g £0
33a 10 LING 12f Aw 68 4271

BILLICHANG 4 b c £7635
0a 13 LING 10f Aw 50 102
53a 1 LING 8f Aw 238*
54a 2 WOLV 8f Aw 322
57a 3 LING 10f Aw 335
52a 3 WOLV 8f Aw 393
57a 3 WOLV 9f Aw 433
48a 3 WOLV 8f Aw 517 BL
41a 4 WOLV 8f Aw 550
31a 4 WOLV 12f Aw 626
47a 2 LING 12f Aw 650
35a 6 WOLV 9f Aw 710
47a 1 LING 10f Aw 775*
25a 8 LING 10f Aw 49 842
0 33 NEWM 12f Firm 40 1852
32a 4 LING 12f Aw 2181
32a 4 LING 10f Aw 2587
42a 5 WOLV 9f Aw 3498
40a 4 WOLV 12f Aw 43 3773 bl
45a 2 LING 10f Aw 43 3828 bl
0a 15 LING 12f Aw 46 4334 bl

BILLIE H 2 ch f £2775

62 7 WIND 5f Gd/Fm 1197
41a 9 SOUT 5f Aw 1304
56 7 NEWM 5f Gd/Fm 2599
60 6 BRIG 7f Gd/Fm 3239
67 1 BRIG 7f Firm 3558*
53 10 LING 7f Firm 64 3830

BILLY BATHWICK 3 ch c £6169
65 5 SOUT 7f Good 804
64 5 WARW 8f Heavy 884
72 5 FOLK 7f Soft 962 BL
68 2 PONT 6f Gd/Sft 1105 bl
56 8 NOTT 6f Firm 1266 bl
68 1 CARL 6f Firm 2278*
59 7 LEIC 7f Gd/Fm 2508
46 9 BATH 6f Firm 68 2944
0 14 NEWM 6f Gd/Fm 68 2961
64 3 KEMP 6f Gd/Fm 64 3357
65 2 EPSO 10f Good 3762
63 4 NOTT 10f Soft 3979
54a 4 WOLV 9f Aw 64 4228
58 5 BATH 12f Soft 64 4433
0 16 DONC 12f Soft 66 4464

BILLYJO 2 b g £0
44a 6 LING 5f Aw 1740
42 6 WIND 6f Gd/Fm 2052
54 4 BATH 6f Gd/Sft 2551
49 4 YARM 7f Firm 2898 BL
51a 5 WOLV 7f Aw 4025 bl

BILLYS BLUNDER 3 b f £1347
47a 9 SOUT 5f Aw 179 t
34a 7 SOUT 5f Aw 217 tVl
51a 3 SOUT 6f Aw 426
52a 2 WOLV 7f Aw 493 t
36a 7 WOLV 54 534 t
36a 4 WOLV 8f Aw 52 638 t
43a 4 WOLV 9f Aw 659 vis
37a 5 SOUT 5f Aw 46 870 tvi
38a 4 SOUT 7f Aw 43 1202 tvi
0 15 REDC 6f Gd/Sft 42 1578 tvi
0a 13 SOUT 8f Aw 42 1804 tvi

BIMBOLA 6 br m £119472
116 2 SHA 12f Gd/Fm 185

BIN ALMOOJID 4 b c £0
0a 9 WOLV 15f Aw 468 BL

BINA RIDGE 3 b f £5330
99 1 GOOD 9f Gd/Sft 1481*
96 5 DONC 10f Gd/Fm 1841

BINT ALJOOD 3 b f £0
25a 11 SOUT 7f Aw 58 1506

BINT HABIBI 3 b f £6092
36 8 HAYD 8f Soft 62 1822
49 1 CHEP 7f Good 1972*
43 6 CARL 8f Gd/Fm 57 2281
42 6 CHEP 8f Gd/Fm 2448
50 3 EPSO 7f Good 50 2794
56 1 LEIC 8f Gd/Fm 2914*
55 5 NEWM 8f Gd/Fm 50 3317
51 3 BRIG 8f Firm 56 3561
34 12 EPSO 7f Good 58 3854
54 3 CATT 8f Soft 54 4004
0 14 PONT 8f Soft 54 4232
0 12 BATH 8f Soft 53 4435

BINT ROYAL 2 ch f £2730
44 8 BEVE 5f Good 3955
68 1 CATT 5f Soft 4252*
36 11 NOTT 6f Heavy 4410

BINTALREEF 3 ch f £0
83 18 NEWM 8f Firm 1185

BINTANG TIMOR 6 ch g £10421
56 7 LEIC 7f Gd/Sft 70 834
70 3 NOTT 6f Firm 70 1273
71 4 GOOD 7f Gd/Sft 71 1483

70 6 LING 6f Good 71 1676
73 2 GOOD 7f Gd/Sft 71 1810
68 5 CHEP 7f Good 71 1969
66 9 WIND 6f Good 72 2371
51 16 YORK 7f Good 72 2694
40 13 NEWM 6f Gd/Fm 70 2961
0 13 NEWM 6f Firm 68 3297
0 15 SAND 7f Soft 65 4204
66 1 YARM 6f Heavy 62 4480*
70 2 NEWM 7f Soft 66 4547

BIRCHWOOD SUN 10 b g £1013
51 3 NEWC 6f Soft 756 vis
52 3 LEIC 7f Good 790 vis
48 4 PONT 6f Soft 872 vis
24 10 REDC 7f Gd/Sft 1132 vis
47 3 HAMI 6f Gd/Fm 2798 vis
38 13 THIR 6f Gd/Fm 47 3144 vis

BIRDSAND 3 ch f £0
58 6 LING 6f Gd/Fm 1263
56 7 WARW 7f Gd/Sft 1708
55 6 NOTT 8f Good 59 2013
31 6 CARL 8f Firm 2283

BIRDSONG 3 b f £8933
26 9 NEWM 7f Gd/Fm 1155
0 15 NEWM 10f Gd/Fm 1697
66 1 NEWC 6f Firm 2313*
65 3 YARM 6f Gd/Fm 64 3386
70 1 LING 6f Firm 65 3759*
53 7 NOTT 6f Soft 48 3975

BIRTH OF THE BLUES 4 ch c £0
37 8 SAND 8f Heavy 67 1058
59 10 WIND 8f Gd/Fm 65 1201
0 15 BATH 10f Gd/Sft 63 1666
46 7 WIND 8f Gd/Fm 60 2051
57 5 SALI 10f Gd/Fm 60 2270 VIS
31 5 SALI 8f Gd/Sft 57 2467 vis
39 7 BATH 12f Firm 2785 vis
0 18 NEWC 10f Heavy 49 4404 BL

BISHOPS BLADE 3 b g £0
52 8 NEWB 8f Aw 3179
4 9 BATH 12f Gd/Fm 3517
0 17 BATH 12f Soft 4434

BISHOPS COURT 6 ch g £6148
99 11 NEWM 6f Gd/Fm 1172 t
105 5 EPSO 5f Good 110 1849 t
109 1 SAND 5f Gd/Fm 1987+ t

BISHOPS SECRET 2 b c £0
0 14 LEIC 6f Firm 2029
28 9 FOLK 7f Good 2620
25 10 AYR 8f Soft 3957
53 5 NEWM 7f Good 4336 BL

BISHOPSTONE MAN 3 b c £5478
66 4 WARW 7f Soft 68 1061
49 7 LING 7f Good 1397
0 14 BATH 8f Gd/Sft 65 1671
64 3 SALI 7f Gd/Fm 62 1889
45 5 WARW 8f Gd/Fm 64 2257
68 1 LEIC 8f Gd/Fm 64 2512*
43 13 KEMP 8f Gd/Fm 67 2752
68 2 LEIC 8f Gd/Fm 67 3095
59 8 CHEP 8f Firm 67 3254
53 9 LING 8f Firm 69 3580
72 3 LING 6f Firm 69 3759
62 5 EPSO 7f Good 67 3854
59 7 YARM 6f Firm 70 3939
66 6 LING 7f Soft 69 4192
0 14 DONC 7f Gd/Sft 68 4452

BISHOPSTONE POND 4 b f £0
0a 10 SOUT 16f Aw 33 737

BISQUE 2 ch f £0
55 12 DONC 8f Heavy 4569

BISQUET DE BOUCHE 6 ch m £0

0   17 BEVE 16f Firm   36 1276

BITTER SWEET 4 gr f £837
0a   8 WOLV 9f Aw   446
25a 4 WOLV 9f Aw   490
48   8 WIND 10f Gd/Sft 54 1100
52   3 NOTT 10f Gd/Fm   54 1272
37   5 PONT 10f Good   52 1496
43   4 LEIC 10f Gd/Sft 52 1575
38   9 WARW 11f Good   49 2463
0   15 SALI 12f Good   44 2689 VIS
38   5 WIND 10f Gd/Fm   3045 vis
26   7 CARL 8f Firm   40 3192 vis
36   6 GOOD 10f Good   39 3663
54   6 PONT 10f Soft   4088
29   7 SALI 10f Gd/Sft 37 4169

BITTY MARY 3 ch f £0
44   7 SOUT 10f Good   55 807
33   8 REDC 14f Gd/Sft 50 1581
0   14 BEVE 12f Gd/Sft 50 1758
0   13 PONT 12f Good   46 2362 VIS
29   5 CARL 9f Firm   38 2825 vis
26   6 RIPO 10f Gd/Fm   34 3008 tvi
23   9 THIR 12f Gd/Fm   45 3125 tvi
10   8 CARL 12f Firm   3570 vis
17   7 CATT 14f Soft   4002 BL

BLACK ARMY 5 b g £2400
66a 3 SOUT 6f Aw   74   44
60a 8 SOUT 6f Aw   73 129
56 12 NOTT 5f Good   70 1412
38   5 NOTT 6f Gd/Fm   2680
55   1 CATT 6f Gd/Fm   2744*
56   5 THIR 6f Gd/Fm   63 3123
61a 6 WOLV 6f Aw   67 4380
47 14 REDC 7f Gd/Sft   62 4498

BLACK ICE BOY 9 b g £1888
0a   P WOLV 16f Aw   33 141 vis
23a 5 SOUT 16f Aw   31 542 vis
24 12 NEWC 16f Soft   44 760 vis
7   11 PONT 17f Soft   42 876 vis
8   8 PONT 22f Heavy   42 940 vis
0   18 BEVE 16f Firm   38 1276 vis
18a 7 SOUT 16f Aw   40 1416 vis
46   4 PONT 17f Soft   47 1701 vis
35 11 PONT 17f Good   44 1867 vis
21a 6 SOUT 16f Aw   28 2951 vis
23 10 PONT 17f Firm   34 3501 vis
88   7 HAYD 14f Soft   4091 vis
39   2 PONT 17f Soft   39 4231 vis
37   3 PONT 18f Soft   42 4376 vis
7   11 NOTT 16f Heavy   42 4508 vis
60   7 DONC 15f Heavy   4568

BLACK JACK GIRL 3 br f £0
0   12 RIPO 10f Gd/Fm   3012

BLACK KNIGHT 2 b c £11187
80   3 SAND 7f Gd/Fm   1988
87   1 FOLK 7f Gd/Fm   2290*
88   1 BEVE 7f Gd/Fm   2514*
79   6 ASCO 7f Gd/Fm   3015
85   6 DONC 8f Gd/Fm   88 3879
95   3 SAND 8f Soft   4203
95   2 NEWB 8f Gd/Sft   4457

BLACK MARK 6 b g £0
26   6 PONT 10f Soft   1699
0a 10 SOUT 11f Aw   2119

BLACK MINNALOUSHE 2 b c £26050
103 1 CURR 6f Gd/Sft   4060*

BLACK ROCKET 4 br f £2696
33a 8 LING 7f Aw   8
49a 6 LING 10f Aw   56
31a 7 LING 12f Aw   48 115
54a 1 WOLV 8f Aw   133*
37a 7 WOLV 8f Aw   53 233

---

0   12 FOLK 10f Gd/Fm   53 2296
0   13 BEVE 10f Gd/Fm   50 2518

BLACK SAINT 3 br g £0
21a 6 WOLV 7f Aw   4361

BLACK SILK 4 b c £9077
91   1 GOOD 8f Gd/Sft   1635*
96   6 ASCO 8f Good   90 2090
96   3 GOOD 7f Good   94 3648
93   4 DONC 8f Firm   94 3897
83 15 ASCO 7f Aw   94 4112

BLACK WEASEL 5 b g £1093
36a 5 WOLV 9f Aw   40   67
54a 2 SOUT 14f Aw   124
38a 4 WOLV 16f Aw   37 141
12   7 CATT 16f Gd/Fm   40 2436
37a 5 WOLV 16f Aw   40 2606
36   6 CHES 16f Gd/Fm   45 2672
41a 2 WOLV 15f Gd/Fm   35 3276
39   5 CHES 16f Gd/Fm   40 3511
40   5 AYR   17f Soft   46 3993
41   5 CHES 16f Gd/Fm   47 4071

BLACKFOOT 4 br g £0
17a 12 WOLV 5f Aw   65 139 bl
33a 9 WOLV 5f Aw   272

BLACKHEATH 4 ch c £0
49   8 KEMP 6f Soft   1016
83 10 NEWM 6f Firm   95 1182
69   8 NEWB 6f Firm   92 2706 BL
71   8 NEWM 6f Gd/Fm   88 2961
75   8 NEWM 6f Gd/Fm   88 3119

BLACKPOOL MAMMAS 3 b f £4246
30a 9 WOLV 5f Aw   659
69   1 WARW 7f Soft   813*
49 10 WIND 8f Good   68 852
69   2 WARW 7f Soft   65 1061
35 15 CARL 8f Firm   65 1255
43 11 SALI 8f Good   65 1345
65   6 WARW 7f Gd/Sft   66 1710
0   16 SALI 7f Gd/Fm   65 1889
57   6 CHES 7f Gd/Sft   63 2250
28   6 NOTT 8f Gd/Fm   3004
0   17 CHEP 7f Good   59 3871
37   6 LEIC 8f Gd/Sft   4031
0   19 WIND 8f Gd/Sft   52 4293
2   13 NEWC 8f Heavy   48 4406

BLAIR 3 b g £0
25a 9 SOUT 8f Aw   328
29a 7 SOUT 8f Aw   453
61   4 CATT 12f Good   1661
35   9 AYR   11f Good   51 2139
32   7 PONT 12f Good   45 2362
34   5 RIPO 10f Soft   2538
32   7 HAMI 11f Gd/Fm   45 2638
31   5 RIPO 10f Gd/Fm   37 3008
0   14 CARL 8f Gd/Fm   37 3082

BLAKESET 5 ch g £8316
79a 1 LING 7f Aw   74 106* bl
82a 2 SOUT 6f Aw   78 180 bl
59a 10 LING 6f Aw   78 223 bl
82a 5 LING 8f Good   82 337 bl
65a 5 WOLV 8f Aw   82 580 bl
84a 1 WOLV 7f Aw   677* bl
51 11 KEMP 7f Good   74 725 bl
52   9 PONT 6f Heavy   73 941
0   15 THIR 7f Good   71 1158
0   14 BEVE 8f Firm   68 1279
59   6 THIR 6f Good   64 1383
45 10 THIR 6f Gd/Fm   62 3123
49 15 LEIC 7f Firm   58 3839 bl
65   1 YARM 7f Firm   58 3939* bl

BLAKESHALL BOY 2 b c £12199
78   3 BRIG 5f Gd/Sft   891

---

70   4 NEWM 5f Soft   985
79   1 BRIG 5f Gd/Fm   1124*
75   4 PONT 6f Good   1497
68 10 LING 6f Good   81 2589
77   3 KEMP 5f Firm   78 2868
79   2 MUSS 5f Good   76 3101
82   1 SAND 5f Good   76 3228*
79   3 NOTT 6f Good   80 3519
78   5 BEVE 5f Gd/Fm   80 3673
79   3 YORK 6f Good   79 3807
72   9 LING 5f Good   80 4098
0   16 NEWM 6f Good   78 4338
69   8 NEWB 6f Stt/Hvy 76 4468

BLAKESHALL JOE 2 ch c £0
45a 5 WOLV 5f Aw   722

BLAKEY 4 b g £0
0   17 BRIG 6f Firm   47 1211
0   16 NOTT 8f Good   43 1414
0   20 CHEP 6f Good   39 1971
28   8 BEVE 5f Firm   35 2223 BL
0   17 BATH 5f Gd/Sft   33 2555 bl
12   5 RIPO 6f Gd/Fm   32 2839 bl
0   12 THIR 7f Gd/Fm   30 3129 bl

BLAYNEY DANCER 3 b c £746
35a 7 LING 8f Aw   150
31a 7 LING 8f Aw   40 419
39a 3 LING 10f Aw   42 461
23a 6 LING 10f Aw   43 597
59a 5 LING 10f Aw   629
0   15 WIND 12f Heavy   45 937
14   9 YARM 14f Firm   46 2902
34   3 BRIG 12f Gd/Fm   39 3260
35   8 FOLK 16f Gd/Fm   43 3448
11a 7 LING 16f Aw   40 4099

BLAZING BILLY 5 ch g £0
0a 12 LING 7f Aw   33 439

BLAZING IMP 7 ch g £0
18   9 NEWC 5f Heavy   1766
13   8 HAMI 5f Firm   2095

BLAZING PEBBLES 3 ch f £0
9a   9 SOUT 5f Aw   74
25a 7 WOLV 5f Aw   145
31a 10 WOLV 7f Aw   192
16a 8 LING 7f Aw   38 287
0a 11 SOUT 7f Aw   330
0a 11 SOUT 6f Aw   426 BL
32a 8 LING 8f Aw   507
11   8 NOTT 8f Good   783
0   12 NOTT 6f Gd/Sft   1081
29   9 NEWM 10f Firm   1857

BLAZING ROCK 3 b g £0
0a 14 SOUT 6f Aw   74
0a 11 LING 8f Aw   150
0   5 WOLV 9f Aw   382 E

BLENHEIM TERRACE 7 b g £2373
42   1 REDC 11f Soft   4497*
16 12 MUSS 12f Soft   45 4560

BLESS 3 ch f £4689
37 10 BRIG 10f Gd/Sft 54 892
46   7 WIND 12f Gd/Sft   1096
42a 6 LING 10f Aw   53 1265
22   9 BRIG 12f Firm   49 1332
31   9 LING 11f Firm   43 1911
45   3 WIND 10f Gd/Fm   44 2206 VIS
44   3 FOLK 10f Gd/Fm   42 2296 vis
0   18 BRIG 10f Gd/Fm   45 2727 vis
36   9 SALI 12f Gd/Fm   44 3290 vis

BLESS THE BRIDE 3 b f £2821
76   1 BATH 10f Good   72 1094*
67   8 WIND 12f Gd/Sft 74 1425
67   8 WIND 12f Gd/Fm   74 2210
62   5 GOOD 12f Soft   4061

BLESSINGINDISGUISE 7 b g £4284

54	8	NEWM	12f Gd/Sft	72	4534	
73	5	NEWC	5f Soft	77	758	bl
67	11	THIR	5f Soft	76	926	bl
75	2	THIR	5f Good	74	1162	bl
74	8	YORK	5f Firm	76	1324	bl
74	6	NEWC	5f Gd/Fm	76	2310	bl
79	2	YORK	5f Gd/Fm	76	2644	bl
52	8	NEWC	5f Gd/Fm	78	2987	bl
0	19	BEVE	5f Good	78	3398	bl
0	20	DONC	5f Firm	76	3894	bl
0	14	YORK	5f Soft	74	4285	bl

BLEU DALTAIR 3 £7685

103	5	DEAU	10f V	2736
110	2	LONG	10f Gd/Sft	4053

BLIND SPOT 2 ch c £0

54	9	NEWC	7f Gd/Sft	3705
51	11	DONC	7f Gd/Sft	4447
60	9	DONC	6f Heavy	4576

BLINDING MISSION 3 b f £651

60	9	NEWM	8f Gd/Fm		1692
77	3	KEMP	9f Gd/Fm		2086
36	9	KEMP	9f Firm	70	2262
53	6	SAND	8f Good		3474
36	12	NOTT	10f Soft		3979
53a	5	LING	16f Aw	65	4099

BLIXEN 2 b f £2250

98	3	CURR	7f Gd/Fm	3067

BLOOD ORANGE 6 ch g £0

19	10	THIR	7f Gd/Fm	35	3129

BLOODY MARY 3 ch f £3640

38	10	BRIG	8f Gd/Sft		894
69	1	SALI	8f Gd/Fm		3289*
55	11	WIND	8f Good	67	3643
60	10	SAND	8f Gd/Fm	65	3944
0	13	WIND	10f Gd/Sft	62	4291

BLOOM 2 b f £0

62	5	HAYD	5f Gd/Fm		1166
50	11	CARL	5f Firm		2277
40	10	HAMI	5f Gd/Sft		3376
0	11	THIR	7f Gd/Fm		3615
0	17	LEIC	8f Firm	45	3837

BLOOMING AMAZING 6 b g £256

54a	3	SOUT	8f Aw	54	176	
45a	10	SOUT	7f Aw	59	216	
25a	10	WOLV	9f Aw	54	306	
44a	7	SOUT	7f Aw	54	368	
48a	6	SOUT	8f Aw		452	
26a	8	SOUT	8f Aw	50	497	BL
49	5	LEIC	7f Good		790	
45	10	THIR	8f Soft	62	907	
47	5	PONT	8f Gd/Sft	56	1101	
25	12	RIPO	8f Good		1858	
50	5	BEVE	7f Firm	54	1920	

BLOSSOM WHISPERS 3 b f £2653

50	12	SAND	10f Heavy		1045
64	6	SAND	10f Gd/Fm		1992
69	4	GOOD	12f Gd/Fm		2354
67	3	CHEP	16f Gd/Fm	70	2659
72	2	NEWM	15f Good		3023
56	3	BRIG	12f Gd/Fm		3241
54	8	FOLK	16f Gd/Fm	65	3588

BLOW ME A KISS 5 ch m £0

0a	15	SOUT	11f Aw	52	131

BLOWING AWAY 6 b m £2689

28a	7	SOUT	11f Aw	40	325
0a	10	SOUT	12f Aw	40	413
0	13	BRIG	12f Firm	38	1209
24	5	HAYD	11f Soft	30	1819
20	9	FOLK	16f Good	28	2622
24	3	WIND	12f Good	24	2887
26	1	BRIG	12f Gd/Fm	28	3260*
0a	11	SOUT	16f Aw	29	4149
29	4	YARM	14f Soft		4510

BLU AIR FORCE 3 b c £36204

112	2	MAIS	7f Heavy		9
112	1	LONG	7f Good		1617*
102	10	ASCO	7f Good		2087

BLUE 4 b c £30855

88	1	DONC	10f Gd/Sft		1054*
88	5	NEWM	12f Gd/Fm		1695
95	1	ASCO	10f Good	90	2170*
79	13	SAND	10f Good	94	2475
88	15	NEWB	10f Firm	95	3997

BLUE ACE 7 gr g £281

66	5	THIR	6f Soft		927
55	12	NEWM	6f Good		952
85	8	WARW	7f Heavy		1004
48	9	SALI	7f Good	65	1348
47	6	REDC	9f Gd/Sft	60	1583
34	6	CHEP	8f Gd/Fm	55	2492
42	6	WIND	10f Soft	55	2544
47	4	WARW	7f Gd/Fm	49	2840
39	6	NOTT	8f Gd/Fm	49	3115
31	10	SALI	7f Gd/Fm	49	3294

BLUE AWAY 2 b g £0

65	10	YARM	7f Soft		4514

BLUE CAVALIER 3 b c £0

48a	6	SOUT	8f Aw		86
16a	11	WOLV	8f Aw		171
0a	11	SOUT	7f Aw		278
29	7	LEIC	12f Gd/Sft	47	1571
40a	4	SOUT	12f Aw	41	2123
39	7	CHEP	18f Gd/Fm	51	2452

BLUE DOVE 3 b f £0

60	12	SALI	6f Firm		1181
40	11	NEWB	6f Gd/Fm		1783
0	14	LING	7f Good	54	2591
0	17	LING	6f Firm	50	3759

BLUE FALCON 2 b c £0

45	8	LEIC	7f Gd/Fm	2916
58	6	THIR	6f Gd/Sft	3143
0	13	RIPO	6f Good	3697

BLUE FOREST 2 b c £4533

84	1	NEWC	5f Soft	755*
84	2	HAMI	6f Gd/Sft	3533

BLUE GODDESS 2 b f £106146

97	1	CHEP	6f Gd/Sft	1798*
96	1	WIND	6f Good	2714*
107	1	CURR	6f Yldg	3720*

BLUE GOLD 3 b c £66037

86	4	EPSO	10f Heavy		1029
101	2	SALI	10f Firm	93	1177
85	11	GOOD	9f Gd/Fm	96	1452
98	1	SAND	10f Good	95	1965*
98	2	DONC	10f Gd/Fm		2351
93	10	NEWM	10f Gd/Fm	98	2596
103	1	GOOD	12f Gd/Fm	97	3088*
103	2	WIND	12f Good		3640
108	3	SOUT	12f Firm		3892

BLUE HAWAII 3 ch c £917

56	2	RIPO	10f Soft	54	827	
0	10	DONC	15f Gd/Sft	55	1071	
25a	7	WOLV	12f Good	55	1238	t

BLUE HAWK 3 ch c £0

7	8	THIR	8f Gd/Fm	1352
59	8	LEIC	10f Gd/Fm	2774
58	6	HAYD	12f Gd/Fm	3324
41	8	BEVE	7f Gd/Fm	3670

BLUE HOLLY 3 b f £6128

69	5	CHES	5f Gd/Fm	76	1219
76	2	THIR	5f Good	75	1384
0	24	NEWM	6f Gd/Sft	79	1694
83	1	CHEP	5f Gd/Sft	76	1795*
69	11	ASCO	5f Good	84	2168
69	9	HAYD	5f Gd/Sft	83	3788
0	15	YARM	5f Firm	81	3920
0	22	NEWM	5f Good	79	4185
0	17	PONT	5f Soft	77	4377

BLUE KITE 5 ch g £15043

66a	3	SOUT	6f Aw	66	47
69a	2	LING	7f Aw	66	107
62a	6	WOLV	7f Aw	70	143
76a	1	SOUT	6f Aw	69	212*
80a	1	WOLV	6f Aw	72	258*
77a	6	WOLV	6f Aw	78	320
76a	6	WOLV	5f Aw	79	394
66a	9	WOLV	5f Aw	79	435
79a	3	WOLV	5f Aw	79	491
77a	4	LING	7f Aw	78	525
75a	5	WOLV	5f Aw	79	579
85a	1	SOUT	6f Aw	78	645*
72a	11	WOLV	6f Aw	84	660
0	14	HAMI	6f Good	59	844
63	2	WIND	6f Gd/Fm	59	1196
55	4	NOTT	8f Firm	59	1273
54	6	NEWM	6f Good	61	3613
0	17	NEWM	5f Good	61	4015
0	16	WIND	6f Gd/Sft	58	4293

BLUE LADY 2 b f £6401

57	7	WARW	5f Heavy		886
71	6	NEWM	5f Gd/Sft		970
54a	5	WOLV	5f Good		1236
65	10	NEWM	7f Good		3020
60	6	BATH	6f Firm		3205
61a	3	WOLV	6f Aw		3496
49a	3	WOLV	7f Aw		3772
54	6	WARW	15f Gd/Fm		3912
70a	1	WOLV	6f Aw		4244*
67a	2	WOLV	6f Aw		4359

BLUE LEGEND 3 b f £0

36	8	HAMI	9f Gd/Fm	48	1939
42	4	MUSS	8f Gd/Fm	44	2205
17	5	MUSS	9f Gd/Sft	42	2534
9	6	HAMI	9f Soft	42	3806

BLUE LINE ANGEL 4 b g £0

0a	15	SOUT	8f Aw	48	85

BLUE LINE LADY 3 b f £0

42	7	CATT	5f Gd/Fm		777	
0	15	REDC	7f Firm	56	1297	
43	5	RIPO	8f Good	52	1600	BL
44	7	HAYD	7f Gd/Sft	52	1793	bl
0	16	RIPO	8f Gd/Fm	48	2099	bl
0	12	CARL	8f Firm	48	2281	bl
32	9	REDC	6f Gd/Fm	41	2864	
35	5	THIR	6f Gd/Fm	38	3144	
0	11	PONT	6f Soft		4233	

BLUE MOON 3 £0

105	9	LONG	8f V	1319

BLUE MOUNTAIN 3 ch g £39626

84	5	NEWM	7f Gd/Sft		983
86	2	WIND	8f Gd/Sft		1099
91	2	GOOD	7f Gd/Sft		1638
88	1	KEMP	6f Gd/Fm	84	1925*
95	1	GOOD	6f Good	88	2355*
76	15	GOOD	8f Firm	93	3152
96	2	RIPO	6f Gd/Fm	92	3464
91	8	GOOD	6f Good	95	3646
99	1	GOOD	7f Good		3884*
107	3	NEWB	7f Firm		3995
106	5	NEWM	7f Good		4352

BLUE ORLEANS 2 b g £320

66a	3	WOLV	5f Aw		1136
44a	11	SOUT	5f Aw		1418
59	8	BATH	5f Firm		1993
39	7	SALI	7f Gd/Sft	65	2468

BLUE PLANET 2 b c £4859

```
47a  6  WOLV  7f  Aw      65  3273
0    14  LING  7f  Firm    59  3830
51   6  YARM  8f  Gd/Fm   59  3968
```

BLUE PLANET 2 b c £4859

```
85   1  HAMI  6f  Gd/Fm       2234*
89   3  SAND  7f  Good        2474
86   5  REDC  7f  Gd/Sft      4500
```

BLUE POOL 2 b f £0

```
29   8  LEIC  7f  Heavy       4312
0    14  YARM  6f  Heavy      4479
```

BLUE REIGNS 2 b c £32822

```
70   5  WARW  5f  Heavy       1522
80   1  SAND  5f  Gd/Fm       2933*
91   1  DONC  6f  Firm        3888*
90   2  NEWM  6f  Good    88  4338
```

BLUE SAPPHIRE 3 b f £699

```
31a  11  SOUT  5f  Aw             34
40   6  NOTT  6f  Gd/Sft      1081
0    18  REDC  6f  Firm       1298
19   11  CARL  6f  Gd/Fm      2240
30   9  MUSS  5f  Firm    39  2374
63   3  CATT  7f  Gd/Fm       2745
23   6  THIR  8f  Gd/Fm   36  2964
36   3  NEWC  7f  Good    39  3033
9    11  CARL  8f  Gd/Fm   39  3082
23   10  AYR   7f  Good        3364
```

BLUE SNAKE 4 br c £5824

```
113a 1  NAD   8f  Dirt        666*
93a  9  NAD   8f  Dirt        764
```

BLUE STAR 4 b c £24121

```
77a  5  WOLV  6f  Aw      84  258
84a  2  WOLV  7f  Aw      80  364
82a  4  LING  7f  Aw      81  423   vis
88a  1  WOLV  6f  Aw      81  435*  vis
85a  5  WOLV  6f  Aw      85  532   vis
92a  1  WOLV  6f  Aw      85  660*  vis
94a  2  SOUT  7f  Aw      91  687   vis
77   2  LING  7f  Gd/Sft      838   vis
50   12  EPSO  6f  Heavy   75  1028  vis
70   9  DONC  6f  Gd/Sft  75  1074  vis
63   9  CHES  8f  Firm    74  1250  vis
0    23  YORK  6f  Good    72  3543  vis
0    19  NEWM  6f  Gd/Fm   68  4215  vis
```

BLUE STELLER 2 £3842

```
101  4  SAIN  10f Soft        4556
```

BLUE STREAK 3 ch c £630

```
86   7  NEWM  8f  Gd/Sft      972
62   8  WIND  8f  Gd/Sft      1099
68   4  BEVE  7f  Good        1444
68   4  YARM  7f  Good    70  3238
62   6  EPSO  9f  Gd/Fm   70  3401
46a  8  WOLV  8f  Aw      68  4021  VIS
```

BLUE STREET 4 b c £4482

```
54   8  LING  10f Gd/Sft      1281
62   8  WARW  7f  Heavy       1525
62   6  WARW  7f  Gd/Sft      1708
0    13  WARW  11f Good    60  2463
60   2  RIPO  8f  Gd/Sft      2836
60   3  NEWM  12f Gd/Fm   59  3122
56   1  BEVE  12f Good        3399*
50   6  GOOD  12f Good    59  3657
43   8  CATT  12f Soft    55  4003
43   10  NEWM  10f Good   52  4160
```

BLUE STYLE 4 ch g £12725

```
33a  6  WOLV  8f  Aw          750
66   1  BRIG  12f Gd/Sft      893*
65   2  EPSO  12f Heavy   62  1030   t
68   1  KEMP  12f Gd/Sft  60  1076*  t
57   9  NEWB  12f Good    66  1373   t
52   10  LING  11f Good   66  1743   t
49   8  GOOD  12f Soft        4061   t
0    15  NEWB  16f Gd/Sft  62  4458  t
```

BLUE SUGAR 3 ch c £23197

```
77   4  KEMP  10f Soft        998
88   2  HAYD  7f  Soft        1820
88   2  NEWM  8f  Gd/Fm   85  2858
93   2  SALI  8f  Gd/Fm       3421
93   1  NEWM  10f Gd/Fm   89  3628*
```

BLUE VELVET 3 gr f £20896

```
83   6  NEWM  6f  Gd/Sft  86  982
59   10  LING  8f  Gd/Sft  86  1285
75   10  NEWB  6f  Gd/Fm   83  1406
79   10  NEWM  8f  Gd/Fm   81  1694
59   15  YORK  6f  Firm    80  2003
86   1  SAND  5f  Gd/Fm   79  2478*
91   1  NEWM  6f  Good    85  2568*
90   6  GOOD  7f  Gd/Fm   90  3130
84   5  LEIC  6f  Gd/Fm   90  3335
87   7  YORK  6f  Gd/Fm   91  3727
78   6  HAYD  6f  Heavy       3768
93   2  YARM  6f  Firm        3937
88   3  KEMP  6f  Gd/Sft  89  4037
87   10  ASCO  5f  Gd/Fm   92  4129
89   6  NEWM  5f  Good    92  4339
92   3  NEWB  6f  Gd/Sft  92  4456
```

BLUEBEL 2 b g £0

```
53   5  BRIG  5f  Gd/Sft      891
0    17  BATH  6f  Gd/Sft     1667
45   4  YARM  6f  Firm        2388
```

BLUEBELL WOOD 3 ch f £10142

```
71a  1  LING  10f Aw          240*
74a  1  LING  10f Aw      67  461*
82a  1  LING  10f Aw      73  509*
79a  4  WOLV  9f  Aw      82  625
74   12  EPSO  12f Gd/Sft     1828
64   12  ASCO  12f Good    85  2116
```

BLUEBERRY FOREST 2 br c £26965

```
84   1  DONC  6f  Good        1513*
98   2  NEWB  6f  Gd/Fm       1944
98   2  SAND  7f  Good        2474
95   2  NEWB  7f  Firm        2848
85   6  ASCO  8f  Gd/Fm       3304
96   1  AYR   7f  Soft        3991*
90   3  SAN   8f  Heavy       4243
```

BLUEGRASS MOUNTAIN 3 b c £572

```
0    11  BEVE  7f  Heavy   70  976
0a   15  SOUT  8f  Aw      66  1205
40   9  THIR  6f  Gd/Sft      1354
0    25  REDC  6f  Gd/Sft  60  1578
55   3  CHES  6f  Gd/Sft      1780  BL
0    17  BEVE  5f  Firm    55  2223  bl
```

BLUEMAMBA 3 b f £129219

```
107  3  MAIS  7f  Soft        946
112  1  LONG  8f  V          1319*
107  3  ASCO  8f  Good        2150
```

BLUEPRINT 5 b g £50325

```
115  1  NEWM  12f Gd/Fm       1152*
117  3  ASCO  12f Good        2149
```

BLUES WHISPERER 3 b c £0

```
0    14  WIND  10f Good        850
0    13  BATH  10f Good        1093
0    11  BATH  8f  Gd/Sft  53  1671
21   10  SALI  8f  Firm    49  2025
```

BLUNDELL LANE 5 ch g £4676

```
30a  11  WOLV  6f  Aw      67  175   vis
26a  10  WOLV  6f  Aw      63  226   vis
77   1  BRIG  6f  Gd/Fm   67  1126*
59   8  GOOD  6f  Gd/Sft  76  1471
55   12  AYR   6f  Gd/Fm   76  1654
62   6  SAND  5f  Good         1966  vis
49   14  CHES  5f  Gd/Fm   72  2247
65   4  KEMP  6f  Gd/Fm        2747  vis
38   7  BRIG  7f  Gd/Fm        3259
43   8  BATH  6f  Gd/Fm   64  3516
```

```
60   4  BRIG  5f  Firm    61  3734
```

BLUSHING BRIDE 2 b f £17028

```
82   1  EPSO  7f  Good         3760*
93   1  GOOD  7f  Soft         4063*
103  2  NEWB  7f  Sft/Hvy      4467
93   3  NEWM  8f  Soft         4546
```

BLUSHING GRENADIER 8 ch g £7162

```
52a  3  WOLV  8f  Aw      51  38    bl
51a  4  WOLV  8f  Aw          136   bl
37a  9  WOLV  7f  Aw      51  193   bl
50a  3  WOLV  8f  Aw          256
48a  3  SOUT  7f  Aw          341
57a  4  SOUT  8f  Aw          389
53a  3  WOLV  6f  Aw          406   bl
53a  3  SOUT  8f  Aw          475
48a  7  WOLV  8f  Aw          533   bl
54a  1  SOUT  6f  Aw      50  602*  bl
44a  6  SOUT  5f  Aw      54  674   bl
44   6  PONT  6f  Soft        872   bl
36   6  DONC  6f  Gd/Sft      1073  bl
44a  7  WOLV  5f  Aw          1237  bl
51   2  LEIC  6f  Soft    50  1545  bl
45   1  CATT  6f  Good        1663* bl
38   7  HAYD  6f  Gd/Fm       3283  bl
38   8  WARW  5f  Good        3694  bl
53a  2  WOLV  8f  Aw          3770  bl
46a  7  WOLV  7f  Aw          4224  bl
```

BLUSHING PRINCE 2 b c £0

```
79   6  YARM  8f  Gd/Fm       4512
```

BLUSHING SPUR 2 b g £2240

```
38   5  NOTT  6f  Gd/Sft      1367
0    11  SOUT  6f  Soft       1602
65a  2  SOUT  7f  Aw          2383
53   5  ASCO  6f  Good    68  2678
64   2  CATT  6f  Soft    60  4007
59   3  PONT  6f  Soft    63  4235
56a  6  SOUT  6f  Aw      73  4367
```

BLUSIENKA 3 b f £5248

```
91   4  DONC  8f  Good        735
99   3  KEMP  8f  Soft        995
99   5  LONG  10f Gd/Sft      1457
69   4  NEWC  8f  Gd/Fm       2274
76   10  SALI  10f Soft       3389
74   3  AYR   8f  Heavy       4308
```

BOADICEA THE RED 3 gr f £361

```
71a  3  LING  6f  Aw      71  222
55   3  THIR  6f  Gd/Sft      3780
0a   13  SOUT  6f  Aw      65  4153
0    17  AYR   6f  Heavy   60  4327
0    11  DONC  7f  Soft       4461
```

BOANERGES 3 br c £10275

```
0    19  PONT  6f  Aw      81  875
54   9  WARW  7f  Soft    79  1061
69   7  NEWB  6f  Gd/Sft  75  1591
80   1  GOOD  6f  Gd/Fm   72  1961*
81   1  NEWM  5f  Gd/Fm   77  2288*
79   3  HAYD  6f  Gd/Fm   79  2504
70   9  ASCO  6f  Gd/Fm   80  2954
71   6  GOOD  6f  Gd/Fm   79  3136
57   11  RIPO  6f  Good    80  3698
78   4  LEIC  5f  Gd/Sft  79  4027
75   10  NEWM  5f  Good    79  4185
72   7  YARM  6f  Gd/Fm   78  4480
0    19  DONC  5f  Heavy   77  4570
```

BOAST 3 ch f £13694

```
95   6  LING  7f  Gd/Sft      1283
99   3  LEIC  7f  Gd/Sft      1733
94   5  YORK  6f  Firm    97  2003
98   1  NEWM  6f  Gd/Fm       2289*
78   16  ASCO  6f  Gd/Fm   97  2997
98   3  ASCO  6f  Gd/Fm   97  3301
97   4  PONT  6f  Firm        3503
```


BOASTED 3 b f £0

0	14	LEIC	10f Gd/Sft		4029	t
0	16	NEWM	12f Good		4178	t

BOATER 6 b g £335

58	3	BATH	10f Gd/Sft	60	1666	
50	6	CHEP	10f Good	60	1973	

BOBANVI 2 b f £266

50a	5	SOUT	5f Aw		856	
49	4	NOTT	5f Heavy		1019	
24	8	NEWC	6f Gd/Sft		1476	
36	9	NEWC	6f Gd/Fm		2312	
50a	3	SOUT	7f Aw		2949	
39	6	SAND	7f Good	47	3468	
35	5	LEIC	8f Firm	41	3837	
44	5	AYR	8f Soft		3957	
54	6	AYR	8f Heavy	56	4323	

BOBBYDAZZLE 5 ch m £3733

53a	3	WOLV	8f Aw	58	78	ebl
59a	2	SOUT	8f Aw	56	384	ebl
46a	4	WOLV	8f Aw		477	ebl
44a	4	WOLV	8f Aw		707	ebl
30	13	ASCO	8f Gd/Sft	56	1113	
52	3	YARM	8f Firm	52	2767	
46	4	YARM	10f Good	52	3031	
44	9	GOOD	8f Good	52	3885	
51	4	YARM	8f Firm	52	3936	
0	14	LEIC	8f Sft/Hvy	52	4310	
56a	2	WOLV	8f Aw	56	4440	

BOBONA 4 b c £2265

31a	1	SOUT	11f Aw		178*	
13a	9	WOLV	12f Aw	32	410	
28a	2	WOLV	16f Aw	30	492	
6a	6	WOLV	12f Aw	30	522	
15a	5	SOUT	12f Aw	33	642	
0a	14	SOUT	14f Aw	32	1301	
26a	6	SOUT	11f Aw		1415	

BOBS BUSTER 4 b c £0

9a	9	WOLV	9f Aw		292	
40a	5	SOUT	8f Aw		322	
20a	5	SOUT	8f Aw		366	

BOCA CHICA 3 gr f £0

9	7	CHEP	12f Gd/Fm		3681	
0a	12	WOLV	12f Aw	35	3773	

BODFARI ANNA 4 br f £8772

40a	3	SOUT	6f Aw	43	604	vis
3a	9	SOUT	6f Aw	43	697	vis
33a	5	WOLV	7f Aw	43	754	bl
46	4	HAYD	7f Gd/Sft	46	811	vis
29a	5	WOLV	6f Aw	40	1233	bl
12a	9	SOUT	7f Aw	38	1506	bl
52	1	SOUT	7f Soft	46	1606*	vis
40	9	BEVE	7f Gd/Sft	52	1760	vis
31	8	CARL	7f Firm	51	2282	vis
53	3	HAYD	7f Gd/Fm	51	2442	vis
57	1	CHES	8f Gd/Fm	52	2673*	vis
54	4	CARL	7f Firm	52	2823	vis
52	3	CARL	7f Gd/Fm	59	3083	vis
34	11	HAYD	8f Good	59	3288	vis
47	7	CATT	7f Soft	57	4004	vis
56	2	MUSS	7f Gd/Sft	55	4136	vis
28	11	LEIC	8f Sft/Hvy	54	4310	vis
2	9	NEWC	7f Heavy	54	4426	vis
55	4	MUSS	7f Soft	54	4522	vis

BODFARI JET 3 b g £0

0a	12	SOUT	6f Aw	54	1422	
0	21	RIPO	6f Good	54	1600	

BODFARI KOMAITE 4 b c £12795

0	W	NEWC	7f Aw	61	1008	
69	2	BEVE	5f Firm	61	1278	
64	1	THIR	5f Gd/Sft	61	1357*	
73	1	CATT	5f Good	67	1662*	
73	3	CHES	5f Gd/Fm	72	3512	

74	4	EPSO	5f Good	73	3687	
69	7	DONC	5f Firm	73	3894	
58	7	CHES	5f Soft	74	4073	
66	10	YORK	5f Soft	74	4285	
46	15	DONC	5f Heavy	72	4570	

BODFARI MILLENNIUM 2 b g £0

51	9	THIR	7f Gd/Fm		3128	

BODFARI PRIDE 5 b g £12035

0a	15	SOUT	6f Aw	73	645	
44	11	PONT	6f Heavy	73	941	
0	17	CHES	8f Firm	69	1250	
68	1	GOOD	6f Gd/Sft	64	1636*	
79	1	CHES	5f Gd/Sft	70	1781*	
66	6	HAYD	6f Gd/Sft	70	1792	
77	2	EPSO	6f Gd/Sft	76	2631	
54	13	YORK	6f Good	76	2697	
68	16	AYR	5f Soft	78	3960	
78	2	CHES	5f Soft	78	4073	
77	2	CATT	6f Soft		4257	

BODFARI QUARRY 4 b f £9181

81a	1	WOLV	12f Aw	75	81*	t
88a	1	SOUT	12f Aw	80	200*	t
70a	6	LING	12f Aw	85	237	t

BODFARI SIGNET 4 ch c £0

11a	10	WOLV	8f Aw		136	bl
0	20	DONC	10f Gd/Fm	54	705	
0	12	PONT	8f Heavy		942	
37	7	HAMI	8f Gd/Fm	50	1190	
32	9	BATH	8f Gd/Fm	46	1442	bl
0	14	WARW	11f Gd/Sft	42	1707	bl
28	11	RIPO	8f Good		1858	bl
8	7	BRIG	8f Firm		2040	bl
38	6	HAMI	9f Gd/Fm		2236	bl
0	20	RIPO	10f Soft		2538	bl
20	8	LEIC	7f Gd/Fm		3332	tVl

BODFARI TIMES 4 ch f £0

35a	10	WOLV	5f Aw	55	518	
0	15	NOTT	5f Good	48	1412	t
0	15	LEIC	6f Gd/Sft	42	1734	t
0	19	CHEP	6f Gd/Fm	42	1971	
0	17	WARW	6f Gd/Fm	36	2252	
0	15	HAYD	5f Gd/Fm	38	2505	
15	10	MUSS	7f Good	32	3103	

BOGUS DREAMS 3 ch c £3500

94	5	KEMP	8f Soft		996	
100	3	GOOD	10f Gd/Sft		1451	

BOGUS MIX 3 gr f £0

62	13	NEWB	10f Gd/Fm		1404	
52	5	GOOD	12f Gd/Fm		1808	
62	5	BRIG	8f Soft		2426	

BOGUS PENNY 2 b f £2973

76	4	NEWM	6f Good		1856	
81	2	FOLK	7f Gd/Fm		3583	
89	2	WARW	7f Gd/Fm		3910	
74	8	NEWM	6f Good	79	4157	

BOHEMIAN SPIRIT 2 b g £0

48	5	KEMP	5f Good		724	
67	4	LEIC	5f Gd/Sft		828	
45	10	BATH	5f Good		1088	

BOILING POINT 4 b f £0

0	17	LING	8f Soft		4273	

BOIRA 2 b f £0

85	6	NEWM	7f Good		3020	

BOIS DE CITRON 2 b f £4773

83	3	NEWM	6f Firm		1856	
73	4	NEWM	6f Gd/Fm		2285	
89	1	LEIC	5f Gd/Fm		3092*	
91	7	NEWB	5f Gd/Fm		3482	
84	6	AYR	6f Gd/Sft		4009	

BOISDALE 2 b c £10037

49	9	CHEP	6f Gd/Fm		2972	
54	10	LEIC	6f Gd/Fm		3215	

69	6	SALI	6f Gd/Fm		3387	
67	4	LING	7f Firm	66	3830	
48	15	DONC	7f Firm	66	3901	
78	1	CHES	7f Soft	65	4070*	
80	1	LING	7f Soft	72	4191*	

BOISMORAND 4 ch f £2948

89	3	YORK	10f Good		1325	

BOKAY 3 b f £0

0	12	DONC	6f Good		731	
0	13	LEIC	7f Good		794	
0	14	LING	6f Good		1399	

BOLD AMUSEMENT 10 ch g £4022

66	2	HAMI	8f Good		847	
46	11	REDC	9f Gd/Sft	66	1583	
55	8	MUSS	12f Firm	65	2048	
64	1	BEVE	10f Gd/Fm	60	2518*	
54	6	BEVE	10f Good	63	2883	
51	6	REDC	10f Soft		4501	

BOLD ARISTOCRAT 9 b g £0

0a	15	SOUT	7f Aw	56	1801	
0	20	NOTT	6f Gd/Fm		2680	
45a	4	SOUT	7f Aw		2819	
0	17	RIPO	5f Gd/Fm	45	3180	
0a	14	SOUT	6f Aw	46	4156	

BOLD BAHAMIAN 3 b c £0

65	6	SOUT	10f Gd/Sft		858	
49a	4	LING	13f AW		4193	
56a	4	LING	6f Aw	60	4329	

BOLD BYZANTIUM 4 b f £0

1	7	BRIG	8f Soft		4177	
0	14	LING	8f Soft		4273	
0	13	WIND	9f Heavy		4526	

BOLD CARDOWAN 4 br c £848

36	7	PONT	17f Soft	49	876	
42	10	NOTT	14f Heavy	46	1023	
27	10	HAMI	13f Gd/Fm	44	1194	
31	11	RIPO	14f Good	43	1597	
35	4	NEWC	14f Good	40	3249	BL
10	9	PONT	17f Soft	38	4231	bl
37	2	NEWC	16f Heavy	35	4424	

BOLD CONQUEROR 4 br f £0

0	11	WARW	11f Heavy		1523	

BOLD EDGE 5 ch g £61531

80a	5	NAD	6f Dirt		766	
115	3	YORK	6f Firm		1338	
117	4	ASCO	6f Good		2115	
120	1	DEAU	7f Good		3212*	
84	12	HAYD	6f Gd/Sft		3784	
112	8	LONG	7f Soft		4395	

BOLD EFFORT 8 b g £21202

20a	12	LING	6f Aw	95	223	bl
68a	12	WOLV	6f Aw	92	320	bl
68a	4	LING	6f Aw		376	bl
0a	12	WOLV	6f Aw	83	435	bl
0a	13	WOLV	6f Aw	80	532	bl
81a	1	LING	5f Aw	70	774*	bl
0a	9	LING	6f Aw	80	881	bl
0	24	NEWM	6f Gd/Fm	80	1173	bl
72	5	LING	5f Good	75	1398	bl
76	2	NEWB	6f Gd/Sft	73	1591	bl
82	1	SALI	6f Gd/Fm	76	1887*	bl
70	8	WIND	6f Good	80	2207	bl
67	5	EPSO	6f Gd/Fm	80	2631	bl
0	26	GOOD	8f Firm	80	3152	bl
81	1	BATH	6f Gd/Fm	78	3516*	bl
75	9	DONC	6f Gd/Sft	81	3861	bl
42	11	CHES	5f Soft	81	4073	bl
0	12	NEWB	6f Gd/Sft	81	4456	bl

BOLD EMMA 3 b f £0

0a	11	SOUT	5f Aw		127	
58	10	LING	6f Gd/Fm		2183	
55	6	FOLK	7f Good		2621	

BOLD EWAR (continued)

0	14	THIR	6f Gd/Fm	60	3124
0	20	LING	6f Firm	54	3578
27	8	LEIC	6f Gd/Sft		4031

BOLD EWAR 3 ch c £11063

63a	4	LING	8f Aw		26	
76a	1	SOUT	8f Aw	70	125*	bl
53a	5	LING	8f Aw	76	401	bl
72a	3	SOUT	8f Aw	75	601	bl
81	2	NEWM	10f Gd/Sft	75	979	bl
73	5	NEWB	12f Gd/Fm	79	1400	bl
47	10	EPSO	10f Gd/Sft	79	1831	bl
75	5	NEWM	10f Gd/Fm	76	2287	bl
77	2	BEVE	8f Gd/Fm	74	2515	bl
75	7	NEWM	8f Gd/Fm	76	2858	bl
83	1	BRIG	8f Gd/Fm	75	3261*	bl
77	5	ASCO	8f Gd/Fm	80	3338	bl
58	10	GOOD	9f Good	80	3658	bl
67	9	NEWB	8f Firm	79	3998	bl
65	6	ASCO	8f Gd/Sft	78	4126	bl
0	19	NEWM	8f Good	77	4340	bl

BOLD FELICITER 4 ch f £0

0	15	NOTT	14f Good	34	2008	vis

BOLD GUEST 3 ch c £1282

80	11	NEWM	8f Gd/Sft		972
68	3	REDC	7f Gd/Sft		1134
71	3	BATH	10f Gd/Sft		1668
73	4	WIND	10f Gd/Fm	75	2053
59	9	SAND	10f Soft		4205
40a	9	WOLV	12f Aw	69	4443

BOLD HUNTER 6 b g £0

27a	9	LING	8f Aw	47	336
28a	5	WOLV	12f Aw	42	522

BOLD KING 5 br g £35839

94	1	ASCO	7f Gd/Sft	86	1110*
62	13	YORK	8f Firm	94	1327
89	3	NEWB	7f Gd/Fm	94	1946
0	17	ASCO	7f Gd/Fm	93	2997
58	14	CHES	8f Gd/Fm	92	3510
92	1	GOOD	8f Soft		4077*
85	6	NEWM	8f Good		4199
91	4	NEWM	8f Soft	89	4545

BOLD MCLAUGHLAN 2 b c £233

73	8	DONC	5f Gd/Fm		700
65	11	DONC	5f Gd/Sft		1067
60	8	HAMI	5f Gd/Fm		1189
52	6	MUSS	5f Gd/Sft		2532
65	5	THIR	5f Gd/Fm		3143
67	4	THIR	5f Gd/Fm		3346
47	8	MUSS	5f Gd/Fm	65	3743

BOLD PRECEDENT 3 b c £1080

73	4	WIND	10f Gd/Fm		2056
78	3	SALI	10f Gd/Fm		2265
70	4	PONT	10f Gd/Sft		2832
69	7	NEWM	12f Gd/Fm	75	3122
45	8	BRIG	12f Soft	72	4421

BOLD RAIDER 3 b c £7768

64	1	NOTT	8f Heavy	60	1024*
67	2	BATH	8f Gd/Sft	62	1671
52	3	HAYD	8f Soft	62	1822
70	4	GOOD	8f Good	67	3885
70	3	KEMP	8f Soft	67	4038
64	5	HAYD	8f Soft	67	4094
70	1	WIND	8f Gd/Sft		4292*

BOLD SABOTEUR 3 b c £0

42	9	BATH	6f Gd/Fm	55	1438
41	7	GOOD	7f Gd/Sft		1638
0	15	BRIG	6f Gd/Sft		3243
0	17	LING	6f Firm	46	3493

BOLD STATE 3 b c £7965

66	10	NEWM	10f Gd/Fm	73	979
58	8	PONT	12f Gd/Sft	70	1106
61	8	BEVE	10f Good	66	1448

BOLD STATE (continued)

67	1	NOTT	8f Good	63	2013*	
65	1	HAMI	8f Firm		2093*	
67	2	MUSS	9f Gd/Sft	66	2534	
72	2	BRIG	8f Firm		2895	
57	5	BRIG	8f Gd/Fm	70	3261	

BOLD WILLY 3 b c £0

0	10	PONT	12f Gd/Sft	55	1106
0	14	LEIC	8f Gd/Sft		1572

BOLDER ALEXANDER 3 b c £0

31	9	WARW	12f Soft	69	815	
0	18	WIND	12f Firm	52	1292	
0	14	CHES	10f Gd/Fm		2245	
4	12	CHEP	12f Gd/Fm	49	2656	bl
0	F	RIPO	10f Gd/Fm	40	3008	bl
0	11	BRIG	10f Gd/Fm	40	3244	bl

BOLDLY CLIFF 6 br h £3027

10a	8	LING	8f Aw		93	
53a	1	LING	5f Aw	45	166*	bl
56a	2	LING	5f Aw	54	372	bl
38a	10	LING	5f Aw	56	506	bl
51	4	LING	5f Gd/Fm	56	2184	bl

BOLDLY GOES 4 b c £11155

0a	11	LING	10f Aw		690	
70	10	RIPO	6f Gd/Sft	87	824	
74	6	BEVE	7f Heavy		977	
71	12	NEWM	6f Gd/Fm	80	1173	
78	4	THIR	6f Good	77	1383	
77	3	DONC	6f Good		1517	
83	1	YORK	6f Firm	78	2000*	BL
72	7	NEWC	6f Firm	82	2334	bl
59	14	YORK	6f Good	82	2697	bl
81	6	RIPO	6f Gd/Fm	81	3183	bl
79	7	RIPO	6f Gd/Fm	81	3464	bl
89	1	NEWC	7f Soft	80	3708*	bl
85	4	HAYD	7f Soft	86	3785	bl
80	10	DONC	7f Gd/Fm	86	3880	bl
81	10	NEWM	7f Gd/Fm	86	4215	bl
83	6	NEWM	7f Good	85	4357	bl
90	5	DONC	6f Heavy		4581	bl

BOLEYN CASTLE 3 ch c £0

71	12	HAYD	5f Heavy		988
93	5	THIR	5f Good	97	1384
89	12	NEWM	6f Gd/Fm	95	1694
90	8	NEWM	5f Good	93	4015
0	19	NEWM	5f Good	91	4339

BOLHAM LADY 2 b f £0

25	7	BEVE	5f Stf/Hvy		4042
34a	10	WOLV	6f Aw		4225
36a	5	SOUT	7f Aw		4369

BOLINGBROKE CASTLE 2 ch c £0

75	5	LING	5f Gd/Sft		1260	t
0	20	DONC	6f Heavy		4576	

BOLLIN ANN 5 b m £4858

53	11	BEVE	5f Firm	60	1278
64	1	NEWC	5f Gd/Sft	58	1479*
56	7	DONC	6f Gd/Fm	65	1842
68	2	RIPO	5f Gd/Fm	64	2107
67	3	NEWC	5f Firm	66	2340
56	9	YORK	5f Gd/Fm	67	2644
54	6	BEVE	5f Gd/Sft		3056
56	8	BEVE	5f Good	65	3398
57	5	BEVE	5f Gd/Fm	63	3653
55	11	DONC	5f Firm	61	3894

BOLLIN NELLIE 3 ch f £8033

51	4	CATT	12f Gd/Fm	63	782
54	5	PONT	12f Gd/Sft	61	1106
52	7	REDC	10f Firm	52	1299
51	5	REDC	10f Good	54	1895
35	8	CARL	9f Firm	52	2825
53	2	RIPO	10f Gd/Fm	49	3008
54	1	HAYD	12f Good	50	3284*
49	6	NOTT	14f Good	53	3522

BOLLIN NELLIE (continued)

57	2	HAMI	12f Gd/Sft	52	3827
65	1	CATT	12f Soft	57	4256*
51	10	DONC	10f Gd/Sft	65	4448

BOLLIN RITA 4 b f £1938

0	16	RIPO	6f Soft	72	824	
0	18	THIR	6f Soft	72	910	
0	23	YORK	6f Firm	68	2000	
45	9	REDC	6f Gd/Fm	64	2158	
62	2	HAYD	5f Gd/Fm	59	2505	
0	16	HAYD	5f Gd/Sft	59	2701	
56	4	THIR	5f Gd/Fm	59	2969	
45	11	PONT	5f Gd/Fm	58	3222	
57	3	CARL	5f Firm	56	3572	bl
40	10	CATT	7f Soft	56	4004	bl

BOLLIN ROBERTA 4 b f £9181

53	5	THIR	7f Soft	60	908
62	2	MUSS	7f Gd/Fm	59	1148
56	8	BEVE	7f Firm	61	2221
61	5	HAYD	7f Gd/Fm	61	2442
61	3	PONT	8f Gd/Fm	60	2831
64	1	BEVE	8f Gd/Sft	60	3054*
69	2	RIPO	10f Gd/Fm	62	3465
69	2	BEVE	10f Gd/Fm	67	3676
55	5	AYR	10f Soft	68	3989

BOLLIN ROCK 3 b g £0

48	5	THIR	7f Gd/Fm		2965
47	6	BEVE	5f Gd/Fm		3651

BOLLIN THOMAS 2 b g £0

66	7	CATT	5f Gd/Fm		2926
68	7	HAYD	7f Good		3287
54	8	BEVE	8f Gd/Fm		3675
26	7	PONT	8f Soft	59	4378

BOLLIN TOBY 2 ch c £0

0	14	RIPO	6f Gd/Fm		3009	
64	7	THIR	5f Gd/Fm		3346	BL
51	11	CARL	5f Firm		3571	bl
55	6	CATT	6f Gd/Fm		4001	
50	5	HAYD	7f Gd/Sft		4103	
43	10	NEWC	5f Heavy	55	4423	bl

BOLSHOI BALLET 2 b c £3326

67	9	WIND	6f Gd/Fm		1876
74	3	FOLK	7f Gd/Fm		2290
73	3	NEWC	7f Gd/Fm		2985
72	2	BEVE	6f Gd/Fm		3675
73	2	BRIG	8f Gd/Sft		4117
73	4	PONT	8f Soft	73	4378

BOLSHOI GB 8 br g £532

102	9	NEWM	6f Gd/Fm		1172
44	8	SAND	5f Soft		1566
107	10	ASCO	5f Good		2065
93	3	ASCO	6f Good		2115
96	4	HAYD	6f Gd/Fm		2458

BOLT FROM THE BLUE 4 b g £0

14a	9	SOUT	12f Aw	51	68
0	16	PONT	12f Good	51	1499
34	8	CATT	14f Soft	49	1683
40	5	THIR	12f Gd/Fm	44	2061
34	6	HAMI	13f Gd/Fm	44	2238
33	9	BEVE	12f Gd/Fm	42	2482
31	6	REDC	11f Gd/Fm	36	3636
3	9	AYR	10f Heavy	38	4306

BOMB ALASKA 5 br g £9467

108	4	DONC	8f Gd/Fm		703
110	4	NEWM	9f Gd/Sft		967
110	3	SAND	10f Heavy		1057
103	4	GOOD	10f Gd/Sft		1482
98	8	HAYD	7f Gd/Fm		1834
59	24	ASCO	8f Good	109	2090
74	20	GOOD	8f Good	108	3107
100	6	NEWB	9f Firm		4000
93	16	NEWM	9f Gd/Fm	105	4212
97	9	NEWM	9f Good		4347

BOMBAY BINNY 2 b f £1075

51	7	REDC	5f	Gd/Sft		1131	
65	2	NEWC	5f	Heavy		1764	
46	7	HAMI	6f	Gd/Fm		1938	
37	5	BEVE	7f	Firm		2218	
45	5	HAYD	6f	Gd/Fm		2441	BL
41	5	NEWC	7f	Good	54	3246	
0	13	BEVE	7f	Good	47	3950	bl

BOMBELLINA 3 b f £0

49a	4	WOLV	6f	Aw		62	
16a	10	LING	8f	Aw		236	

BON AMI 4 b c £24028

91	9	DONC	6f	Good		734	
85	10	NEWM	6f	Good		952	
90	4	WARW	7f	Heavy		1004	
85	9	NEWM	6f	Firm	95	1182	
80	8	YORK	6f	Firm	90	1337	BL
70	12	YORK	6f	Gd/Fm	86	1983	
0	24	ASCO	6f	Good	86	2151	
86	3	GOOD	6f	Good	82	2355	
83	4	ASCO	6f	Good	84	2676	
78	6	AYR	6f	Firm	84	2877	
73	13	ASCO	5f	Gd/Fm	84	3016	
87	2	GOOD	6f	Good	84	3152	
90	4	RIPO	6f	Gd/Fm	89	3464	
72	17	YORK	6f	Good	89	3543	
65	21	AYR	6f	Gd/Sft	90	4012	
87	7	ASCO	5f	Gd/Sft	90	4129	
68	10	YORK	6f	Heavy	88	4301	
83	4	NEWC	6f	Heavy	85	4405	

BON GUEST 6 ch g £0

32a	10	LING	10f	Aw	58	2212	
14	10	LING	10f	Firm		3490	
0	16	WARW	11f	Gd/Fm	40	3915	
30a	4	WOLV	12f	Aw	54	4026	

BONAGUIL 3 b c £49948

77a	1	LING	8f	Aw		591*	
85	1	SAND	8f	Good	78	761*	
90	1	KEMP	9f	Gd/Sft	82	1075*	
89	3	YORK	10f	Gd/Fm	87	1310	
91	4	ASCO	12f	Good	87	2116	
90	2	HAYD	12f	Gd/Fm	87	2702	
71	8	HAYD	11f	Soft	87	3782	
90	2	NEWB	10f	Firm	87	3997	
93	3	NEWM	10f	Good	89	4197	
96	1	NEWB	10f	Sft/Hv	91	4473*	

BONANZA PEAK 7 b h £0

22a	9	WOLV	8f	Aw	54	254	VIS

BOND BOY 3 b c £4826

68	4	KEMP	6f	Good		729	
84	5	HAYD	5f	Gd/Sft		808	
71	1	BEVE	5f	Gd/Fm		2519*	
0	15	HAYD	6f	Gd/Sft	83	3788	
0	20	YORK	5f	Soft	80	4285	
70	7	BATH	5f	Soft	74	4432	
70	3	DONC	5f	Heavy	70	4570	

BOND DIAMOND 3 gr c £2872

67a	1	SOUT	7f	Aw		427*	
47a	7	SOUT	8f	Aw	69	473	
63a	5	LING	7f	Aw	70	617	
50	9	CATT	7f	Gd/Fm	68	780	
0	12	BEVE	7f	Heavy	63	976	
0	11	NOTT	6f	Gd/Sft		1368	
30	10	LING	7f	Good	53	2592	
54	3	BRIG	10f	Gd/Fm	53	2727	
21	12	BRIG	10f	Firm	49	2908	
0	13	BRIG	10f	Firm	54	3530	

BOND MILLENNIUM 2 ch c £0

43	11	WARW	15f	Gd/Fm		3912	
60	7	YORK	8f	Soft		4281	

BONDI BAY 3 b f £3410

55a	3	WOLV	7f	Aw		41	
64a	5	LING	8f	Aw		103	
55	2	NOTT	8f	Good		783	
0a	12	SOUT	8f	Aw		869	
53	1	BEVE	10f	Firm		1274*	
43	7	MUSS	8f	Gd/Fm	55	1434	
0	17	AYR	8f	Gd/Fm	55	1658	
41	5	MUSS	12f	Gd/Fm	53	2202	

BONDS GULLY 4 b c £902

55a	3	LING	7f	Aw		547	
58a	2	LING	10f	Aw	58	620	
51	8	WIND	12f	Gd/Fm	59	748	
52	4	BRIG	12f	Gd/Fm	55	1128	
50	4	BRIG	10f	Gd/Sft	53	1509	
35	10	NEWB	13f	Gd/Fm	52	1784	
49	4	WARW	12f	Gd/Fm	50	2255	

BONELLA 2 gr f £0

50	7	NEWM	6f	Gd/Fm		2285	
44	11	LING	6f	Good		2588	
0	22	NEWM	7f	Soft		4541	

BONELLI 4 ch c £0

34	6	LEIC	10f	Gd/Sft	46	1575	
18a	10	SOUT	11f	Aw		1978	

BONIFACIO 4 br c £209

45a	4	LING	10f	Aw		771	

BONNARD 2 b c £43556

104	3	NEWM	7f	Gd/Fm		2613	
105	2	GOOD	7f	Gd/Fm		3086	
110	2	CURR	7f	Good		3719	
0	8	CURR	7f	Gd/Sft		4058	BL
110	3	DONC	8f	Soft		4463	

BONNES NOUVELLES 4 b f £0

30a	5	SOUT	12f	Aw		84	

BONNET ROUGE 3 b c £7685

110	2	LONG	12f	Good		1380	
107	5	LONG	15f	Good		4239	

BONNIE DUNDEE 4 b f £0

11a	10	LING	8f	Aw	46	776	
0	16	BRIG	7f	Firm	46	1213	bl
37	5	SOUT	7f	Soft		1601	bl
22a	7	LING	7f	Aw		1741	bl
0	16	SALI	7f	Gd/Fm		1884	bl
10	7	BRIG	8f	Firm		2040	bl
33	4	FOLK	6f	Gd/Fm		2292	bl
30	5	BRIG	7f	Firm		2907	bl
24	6	LEIC	7f	Gd/Fm		3332	bl
16	6	BRIG	8f	Firm		3738	bl

BONNIE FLORA 4 b f £616

64	7	SALI	10f	Good		1343	
0	14	NEWB	10f	Gd/Fm	70	1785	
61	3	SALI	10f	Aw	63	2270	
0	U	LEIC	12f	Gd/Fm	62	2509	
41	10	SALI	12f	Gd/Fm	62	3392	
31	12	CHEP	10f	Gd/Fm	56	3683	
0a	11	WOLV	12f	Aw	53	4026	

BONNYELLA 2 b f £0

50	5	LEIC	5f	Gd/Fm		2772	
25	9	LING	6f	Firm		3757	
41a	9	WOLV	7f	Aw		4025	

BOOGY WOOGY 4 ch g £0

51	7	REDC	10f	Gd/Sft	62	4221	

BOOMERANG BLADE 4 b f £7139

79	11	DONC	6f	Good		734	
82	6	WIND	6f	Heavy		935	
82	6	WARW	7f	Heavy		1004	
82	2	GOOD	7f	Gd/Sft	80	1483	
80	2	THIR	5f	Good		1716	
79	6	GOOD	7f	Gd/Fm	81	2128	
81	6	HAYD	7f	Gd/Fm	81	2456	
74	5	HAYD	6f	Heavy		3768	
84	1	CATT	6f	Soft		4257*	
76	8	DONC	6f	Heavy		4581	

BOOMSHADOW 3 ch g £0

34a	6	LING	7f	Aw		570	
34	8	CATT	6f	Good	60	1665	
0	13	PONT	8f	Gd/Fm	55	3226	
0	17	THIR	8f	Gd/Sft		3775	t
21	5	LEIC	10f	Heavy		4313	t
30a	6	WOLV	12f	Aw	42	4443	

BOP 3 b f £0

60	7	KEMP	7f	Gd/Fm		2585	
40	7	NOTT	10f	Heavy		4412	

BORDER ARROW 5 ch g £38850

104	6	NEWM	12f	Gd/Fm		1152	
115	2	SAND	10f	Soft		1587	
119	3	EPSO	12f	Gd/Sft		1827	
92	7	SAND	10f	Gd/Fm		2497	
111	6	NEWM	10f	Good		4355	t

BORDER COMET 2 b c £1863

84	4	ASCO	7f	Gd/Fm		2956	
92	2	KEMP	7f	Gd/Fm		3799	

BORDER EDGE 2 b c £0

14a	11	WOLV	5f	Good		1236	
70	4	NOTT	6f	Good		1408	
57	7	NEWB	5f	Gd/Fm		1589	
55a	5	SOUT	7f	Aw		2383	
41a	7	WOLV	7f	Aw	64	3273	
0	18	WIND	10f	Gd/Sft	60	4290	VIS
34	6	PONT	8f	Soft	55	4378	
40	7	BRIG	8f	Heavy	55	4538	

BORDER GLEN 4 b c £3023

61a	3	LING	8f	Aw	61	96	bl
68a	3	SOUT	8f	Aw		197	
60a	4	WOLV	8f	Aw	61	233	bl
56a	3	WOLV	9f	Aw		292	bl
15a	6	LING	10f	Aw	59	546	bl
59a	2	LING	8f	Aw	57	596	bl
83a	6	LING	7f	Aw		630	vis
24a	3	LING	7f	Aw	62	879	bl
7a	12	WOLV	7f	Aw		1038	bl
45	5	LING	8f	Firm	53	2761	bl
48	7	GOOD	5f	Gd/Fm	51	3091	bl
33	7	SALI	6f	Gd/Fm	50	3419	bl
43	5	LING	6f	Firm	50	3493	bl
71	3	BATH	5f	Firm		3622	vis
35a	7	LING	8f	Aw		3756	vis
80	6	LEIC	5f	Firm		3841	vis
53	4	GOOD	5f	Soft	54	4065	bl
57	3	SAND	5f	Soft		4207	bl
56	3	WIND	6f	Gd/Sft	54	4293	bl
50	6	NEWB	5f	Gd/Sft	54	4459	
32a	11	WOLV	6f	Aw	55	4553	bl

BORDER RUN 3 b g £1013

65	5	WIND	8f	Gd/Fm	68	744	
51	16	RIPO	10f	Soft	68	827	
0	19	WIND	12f	Heavy	65	937	BL
61	3	WIND	12f	Firm	59	1292	
30a	6	LING	10f	Aw	63	1544	
43	9	SAND	11f	Good	61	1967	
63	3	NEWM	10f	Gd/Fm		2284	
31a	7	WOLV	12f	Aw	59	4026	bl

BORDER SUBJECT 3 b c £10071

88	6	NEWM	8f	Gd/Sft		972	
72	9	NEWB	8f	Good		1376	
90	1	CHEP	7f	Gd/Fm		3256*	t
92	1	WIND	8f	Good	87	3642*	
0	20	ASCO	7f	Good	92	4112	

BORDER TERRIER 2 b c £967

37	7	CATT	7f	Gd/Fm		2927	
56	4	THIR	7f	Gd/Fm		3127	
64	2	NEWC	8f	Soft		3706	
43	7	AYR	8f	Soft		3957	

BORDERLINE 3 ch c £0

60	7	WIND	10f	Heavy		936	
47	9	RIPO	10f	Good		3711	

BORDERS BELLE 2 b f £6939 (and preceding)

93	7	DONC	8f Firm		3893	
0	11	PONT	10f Soft		4088	
0	17	DONC	8f Gd/Sft	58	4452	

BORDERS BELLE 2 b f £6939

61	4	NEWC	6f Firm		2333	
76	3	PONT	6f Gd/Fm		2828	
75	2	CHES	7f Firm		3169	
59	9	NEWC	8f Gd/Sft	79	3704	
71	6	DONC	7f Firm	76	3901	
71	7	CATT	7f Soft	74	4254	
78	1	**DONC**	8f Gd/Sft	72	4450*	

BOREAS 5 b g £64129

89	1	**YORK**	12f Gd/Fm	82	2647*	
102	2	YORK	14f Gd/Fm	95	3565	
111	3	NEWB	12f Stt/Hv		4469	
112	1	**DONC**	12f Heavy		4578*	

BORGIA GER 6 b m £326853

118	5	GULF	11f Good		18	
107	8	TOKY	12f Firm		123	
120	1	**SHA**	12f Gd/Fm		185*	

BORN FREE 4 ch f £0

| 13a | 8 | WOLV | 8f Aw | | 133 | |

BORN SOMETHING 2 £0

| 104 | 5 | LONG | 8f Good | | 4260 | |

BORN TO RULE 3 ch c £0

60	11	WARW	6f Heavy		888	
0	15	WIND	5f Gd/Sft	69	1098	
47	11	BRIG	5f Firm	66	1334	BL
69	5	FOLK	5f Gd/Fm		2294	
43	11	SAND	5f Gd/Fm	62	2478	
54	10	BATH	5f Gd/Sft	62	2555	
53	8	WIND	6f Gd/Fm	57	2885	
43	11	CHEP	5f Gd/Fm	57	2976	
39	8	BRIG	7f Gd/Fm	55	3242	

BORN WILD 2 b f £0

| 0 | 12 | BEVE | 7f Good | | 3953 | |

BOSRA BADGER 2 ch c £0

0	21	WIND	6f Gd/Fm		1876	
0	19	LING	5f Gd/Fm		2214	
41	11	FOLK	6f Gd/Fm		3443	
24	12	LING	6f Firm		3757	
66	5	LING	5f Good		4095	
59	8	LING	5f Soft		4187	

BOSS TWEED 3 b g £7857

31a	11	SOUT	7f Aw	57	31	
66a	1	**SOUT**	8f Aw		303*	
67a	1	**LING**	8f Aw	58	355*	
48a	4	SOUT	8f Aw		385	
45a	3	SOUT	11f Aw		670	t
67	1	**RIPO**	10f Soft	59	827*	
37	9	PONT	10f Gd/Sft		1104	
60	5	PONT	10f Soft	66	1705	
9a	10	SOUT	11f Aw	62	2945	
61	3	BEVE	8f Stt/Hvy	65	4045	
51	10	PONT	10f Soft		4088	t
46	7	YORK	10f Soft		4275	t

BOSSCAT 3 b c £0

0	19	WARW	11f Good	65	2463	
60	5	FOLK	7f Good		2621	
57	10	LEIC	10f Gd/Fm		2774	
0	11	BRIG	10f Firm	59	3530	BL
0	12	NOTT	10f Heavy	55	4509	bl

BOSSY SPICE 3 br f £0

50	9	BATH	13f Gd/Fm	63	1440	
42	10	LEIC	12f Gd/Sft	52	1736	
0	13	NOTT	14f Good	41	2008	
0	14	BATH	10f Firm	36	2332	

BOTTELINO JOE 3 b c £0

32	14	WARW	7f Heavy	63	887	
48	10	SALI	7f Good		1349	BL
0	14	BRIG	7f Gd/Fm	56	3242	
42a	7	WOLV	7f Aw	57	3771	

| 0 | 13 | CHEP | 7f Good | 50 | 3873 | |

BOUCHRA 2 ch f £5645

74	2	REDC	7f Gd/Fm		3635	
76	3	EPSO	6f Good		3852	
44	9	BEVE	5f Good		3955	
74	3	NEWM	7f Good	71	4157	
70	6	NEWM	8f Good	73	4350	
0	16	DONC	7f Heavy	73	4577	

BOULDER 3 b c £1908

67	6	LEIC	12f Gd/Sft		1738	
77	4	SALI	10f Gd/Fm		2265	
74	5	KEMP	12f Gd/Sft		2751	
70	4	PONT	10f Gd/Fm	77	3220	
74	4	CHEP	10f Good	74	3870	
72	4	NEWM	14f Gd/Fm	73	4213	BL
61	9	DONC	15f Gd/Sft	73	4451	

BOUNCING BOWDLER 2 b c £79309

79	3	RIPO	5f Soft		821	
79	2	MUSS	5f Gd/Sft		898	
90	2	HAMI	5f Gd/Fm		1189	
90	1	**RIPO**	5f Good		1595*	
102	2	BEVE	5f Gd/Sft		1761	
106	2	ASCO	5f Good		2113	
106	2	GOOD	5f Gd/Fm		3133	
106	1	**YORK**	5f Gd/Fm		3567*	
109	1	**NEWB**	6f Firm		3996*	

BOUND 2 b c £3804

47	10	SAND	7f Gd/Fm		2494	
0	14	NEWB	7f Firm		2708	
73	10	SAND	7f Gd/Fm		2921	
74	3	BATH	8f Gd/Fm	74	3817	
74	6	GOOD	8f Soft	75	4076	
81a	1	**WOLV**	9f Aw		4438*	
57	9	BRIG	8f Heavy	80	4538	

BOUND FOR PLEASURE 4 gr c £2614:

77	2	NEWB	8f Firm	75	2707	t
75	3	GOOD	9f Good	75	3110	t
86	1	**GOOD**	9f Good	75	3644*	t
92	1	**DONC**	10f Firm	86	3899*	t
57	24	NEWM	9f Gd/Fm	80	4212	t

BOUND TO PLEASE 5 b g £6611

61a	1	**SOUT**	7f Aw	48	69*	
55a	3	SOUT	8f Aw	55	177	
64a	3	SOUT	7f Aw	55	299*	
52	1	**WIND**	6f Gd/Sft	48	4293*	
34a	10	WOLV	7f Aw	63	4550	

BOURGAINVILLE 2 b c £9276

90	1	**SALI**	7f Gd/Fm		3420*	
97	1	**KEMP**	7f Gd/Fm		3790*	
89	10	NEWM	7f Good		4196	

BOURGEOIS 3 ch c £10758

108	3	CHAN	13f Good		2398	
99	4	CHAN	15f Soft		3065	
102	2	DEAU	15f Soft		3545	
103	5	LONG	15f Soft		3848	BL

BOURKAN 3 gr c £270

62	8	HAYD	11f Gd/Sft		1539	
57	7	HAYD	14f Soft		1824	
71	4	RIPO	10f Gd/Fm		3185	

BOUTRON 3 b c £51873

111	2	LONG	11f Heavy		1026	
111	2	LONG	9f Good		1379	
110	4	LONG	10f Good		2225	
111	1	**CHAN**	9f Soft		2913*	

BOW PEEP 5 br m £4287

56	1	**MUSS**	5f Gd/Sft	46	798*	bl
57	2	THIR	6f Soft	55	910	bl
54	4	HAMI	5f Firm	57	1244	bl
0	17	DONC	6f Gd/Fm	56	1842	bl
52	8	CARL	5f Firm	55	3572	bl
34	15	PONT	5f Soft	53	4087	bl

BOW STRADA 3 ch c £0

79	5	WIND	10f Gd/Fm		1198	
74	7	KEMP	12f Soft		4039	
0	15	DONC	10f Gd/Sft	85	4451	

BOWCLIFFE 9 b g £7999

42a	8	WOLV	9f Aw	73	270	
69a	4	WOLV	9f Aw	68	447	
61a	3	WOLV	9f Aw	68	469	
57a	6	WOLV	8f Aw	67	521	
39	8	PONT	10f Soft	57	871	
60	2	REDC	8f Firm	54	1300	
61	2	MUSS	9f Firm	56	2049	
62	1	**CARL**	8f Firm		2283*	
0	14	DONC	8f Gd/Fm	63	2349	
49	10	AYR	9f Gd/Fm	61	3141	
62	1	**REDC**	8f Firm		3330*	
0	16	YORK	9f Good		3808	

BOWCLIFFE GRANGE 8 b g £1041

45a	2	LING	5f Aw	43	57	
28a	8	LING	5f Aw	43	91	
23a	10	WOLV	5f Aw	45	139	
20a	8	LING	5f Aw	44	166	
15a	9	LING	5f Aw	42	372	
31a	9	WOLV	5f Aw	39	445	
35	3	MUSS	5f Gd/Sft	39	798	
0	13	HAMI	5f Firm	38	1244	
0a	16	SOUT	5f Aw	35	1806	
28	6	MUSS	5f Gd/Sft	36	2535	
26	9	RIPO	5f Gd/Fm	33	3180	bl
24	8	CATT	5f Gd/Fm	33	3203	bl
30	5	MUSS	5f Firm	30	3594	

BOWFELL 2 b f £2268

46	10	PONT	6f Firm		2174	
67	6	NOTT	6f Gd/Fm		2683	
38	10	NEWM	7f Gd/Fm		4336	
62	1	**MUSS**	5f Soft	58	4561*	

BOWLERS BOY 7 ch g £14223

37	7	SOUT	7f Good	50	803	
0	W	NEWC	5f Heavy	49	1008	
53	2	BATH	5f Good	49	1092	
49	4	LEIC	6f Soft		1545	
57	1	**CARL**	5f Gd/Sft	52	1724*	
57	2	CATT	6f Gd/Sft	52	1815	
57	1	**HAMI**	6f Gd/Fm	57	1941*	
38	5	HAMI	6f Firm		2396	
57	4	PONT	6f Gd/Fm	57	2559	
39	11	HAMI	6f Gd/Sft	57	3377	
56	3	PONT	5f Soft		4087	
46	5	WIND	6f Gd/Sft	57	4294	
57	2	PONT	5f Soft		4377	
62	1	**NEWC**	6f Heavy	56	4425*	

BOX BUILDER 3 ch c £6892

88	3	NEWB	11f Soft		916	
84	3	SALI	12f Firm		1179	
76	5	YORK	14f Gd/Fm		1311	
85	1	**SAND**	14f Good		2477*	
86	4	GOOD	14f Firm	85	3153	
74	4	AYR	15f Soft	85	3961	
79	8	NEWM	14f Gd/Fm	84	4213	
54	4	NEWB	16f Gd/Sft	82	4458	

BOX CAR 3 b c £4246

35a	6	LING	8f Aw	56	54	
58a	2	LING	10f Aw		204	
67a	5	LING	10f Aw		240	
60a	3	LING	10f Aw	59	315	
67	2	WIND	12f Heavy		937	
68	2	WIND	12f Gd/Fm	65	1199	
36	9	GOOD	12f Gd/Sft	67	1637	
42	14	SAND	10f Gd/Fm	67	2499	
57	6	WIND	12f Good	64	2712	
44	11	GOOD	9f Good	61	3110	
50	8	EPSO	10f Good	60	3762	
35	7	WIND	12f Gd/Sft	56	4123	

BOXBERRY 3 b f £263

41	4	BRIG	5f Gd/Fm	41	1932
17	12	MUSS	5f Firm	39	2374
0	11	LING	7f Good	39	2592

BOY BAND 2 b c £0

59	11	NEWM	8f Good		4161
46	6	NEWM	8f Soft		4542

BRADY BOYS 3 b g £1060

44	11	SAND	10f Soft	4205	BL
84	2	NOTT	10f Heavy	4412	

BRAHMS 3 br c £0

96a	7	GULF	9f Fast	19	vis

BRAINWAVE 2 b f £300

68	4	LING	5f Soft	4187

BRAITHWELL 2 b c £0

60	9	CARL	5f Firm		2277
64	7	BEVE	5f Gd/Fm		2480
26	7	BEVE	5f Good		2880
0	16	PONT	6f Soft	62	4235

BRAM STOKER 2 ch c £38509

84	2	BRIG	5f Gd/Sft		891
98	1	DONC	6f Gd/Sft		1048*
97	1	NOTT	6f Gd/Sft		1367*
104	2	ASCO	6f Good		2067
99	3	NEWM	6f Gd/Fm		2595
100	3	MAIS	6f V		3066
96	3	DONC	6f Firm		3895
107	3	NEWB	6f Firm		3996
102	7	NEWM	6f Good		4181

BRAMBLE BEAR 6 b m £9560

49a	4	LING	5f Aw	52	403
49a	6	LING	5f Aw	51	543
46a	6	LING	5f Aw	49	631
47a	2	LING	5f Aw	47	691
48	6	SAND	5f Gd/Fm	52	763
39	7	BRIG	5f Gd/Sft	51	897
37	7	BATH	5f Good	49	1092
51	1	BRIG	5f Gd/Sft	47	1464*
27	9	GOOD	6f Gd/Sft	54	1636
48	4	LEIC	6f Firm	50	2031
36	8	SALI	6f Aw	50	2230
48	3	LING	6f Good	49	2654
49	3	WIND	6f Gd/Fm	49	3046
51	2	SALI	6f Aw	49	3293
51	3	LING	6f Firm	50	3493
44	6	BATH	6f Firm	50	3821
60	1	BRIG	6f Gd/Sft	50	4120*
0	15	WIND	6f Gd/Sft	59	4293

BRAMBLES WAY 11 ch g £0

0	8	AYR	11f Firm	2875

BRANCASTER 4 br c £2332

108	5	NEWM	9f Gd/Sft	967
100	2	EPSO	10f Gd/Sft	2630

BRAND NEW DAY 2 b c £0

0	18	NEWB	6f Sft/Hvy	4470
0	18	DONC	7f Heavy	4567

BRANDON MAGIC 7 ch g £370

0a	13	SOUT	8f Aw	62	418
14a	10	SOUT	8f Aw	55	497
48	3	AYR	8f Gd/Fm	47	1658
21	8	RIPO	10f Good	47	1860
44	5	MUSS	9f Firm	47	2049
18a	5	SOUT	12f Aw		2298
42	7	MUSS	8f Gd/Sft	45	2533 bl
32	5	CARL	8f Firm	42	3192

BRANDON ROCK 3 b c £0

59	11	NEWM	6f Gd/Sft	76	982
0	29	NEWM	5f Good	73	4185
0	18	BATH	5f Soft	67	4432

BRANDON WIZZARD 2 b c £1259

76	6	NEWM	6f Gd/Fm		3162
0	14	CURR	6f Yldg		3720 t

77	2	BEVE	5f Good	3955

BRANDONVILLE 7 b h £0

0a	15	SOUT	7f Aw	44	69
14a	10	SOUT	8f Aw	44	83
18a	9	WOLV	8f Aw	38	255 t
9a	7	SOUT	7f Aw	36	299 t
28	9	HAMI	8f Gd/Fm	48	1190 t
32	9	WARW	8f Heavy	42	1520 t
27	5	NOTT	8f Soft	42	1646 t

BRANDY COVE 3 b c £1420

54	10	YORK	10f Good	3813
75	2	NOTT	8f Heavy	4505

BRANICKI 2 b f £6061

86	3	CHEP	8f Gd/Fm	3678
87	1	NEWM	8f Good	4019*

BRANSTON FIZZ 3 b f £7127

67a	3	LING	6f Aw		5
60	4	THIR	6f Soft		909
59	7	WARW	8f Soft		1062
0	15	BEVE	5f Firm		1280
68a	1	SOUT	6f Aw		2947*
60	7	BATH	5f Firm	68	3209
75	1	YARM	7f Gd/Fm	65	3666*
64	15	DONC	7f Gd/Fm	75	3880
54	14	AYR	6f Gd/Fm	68	4010

BRANSTON GEM 2 br f £530

60	9	BATH	5f Firm		3205
55	8	REDC	5f Gd/Fm		3632
63	5	LING	5f Good		4096
40a	11	WOLV	5f Aw		4227
60a	2	LING	5f Aw		4333
60	4	MUSS	5f Soft		4561

BRANSTON LUCY 3 b f £5151

46a	9	WOLV	6f Aw	59	1138
0	17	NOTT	5f Good	59	1412
49	8	MUSS	5f Firm	57	2047 hBL
57	2	MUSS	5f Firm	55	2374
60	1	MUSS	5f Gd/Sft	55	2535*
62	2	CATT	5f Gd/Fm		2931
61	2	NOTT	5f Gd/Fm		3113
60a	4	WOLV	5f Aw	60	3271
58	3	CATT	5f Good		3441
0	27	NEWM	5f Good	59	4185
37	9	WIND	6f Gd/Sft	59	4294
42a	9	WOLV	6f Aw	57	4358

BRANSTON PICKLE 3 ch c £8438

80a	1	WOLV	6f Aw		62*
84a	2	WOLV	6f Aw	80	275
54a	10	WOLV	6f Aw	83	435
48	11	THIR	5f Soft		905
0a	11	SOUT	6f Aw	82	1504
47	7	CHES	6f Gd/Sft		1780
48	10	AYR	5f Good	72	2165 BL
0	15	PONT	5f Gd/Fm	67	3222
58	8	MUSS	5f Gd/Fm	62	3594 bl
63	1	HAMI	5f Gd/Sft	59	3825*
62	2	GOOD	5f Good	59	3908
0	18	AYR	5f Soft	59	3960
59	11	NEWM	5f Good	63	4185
39	13	NEWC	5f Heavy	62	4407
49	6	MUSS	5f Soft	62	4516

BRATBY 4 b c £0

0a	8	SOUT	12f Aw	47	682
0	14	PONT	6f Soft		872
0a	12	SOUT	7f Aw	42	1979

BRATHAY MAJIC 6 ch m £0

0a	16	SOUT	8f Aw	50

BRAVADO 2 b c £10251

85a	1	WOLV	6f Aw	2077*
102	1	DONC	6f Gd/Fm	2352*
97	4	NEWM	6f Gd/Fm	2595
97	3	NEWB	6f Firm	2850

BRAVE BURT 3 ch c £1116

80	9	HAYD	5f Heavy		988
90	3	HAYD	6f Gd/Fm		1164
87	8	THIR	5f Good	94	1384
85	8	YORK	6f Firm	91	2003

BRAVE EDGE 9 b g £9115

64	12	KEMP	7f Good	91	725
88	3	WIND	6f Heavy		935
91	3	WARW	7f Firm		1004
78	8	THIR	6f Good	85	1383
84	2	NEWB	6f Gd/Sft	83	1590
85	3	LING	6f Good	83	1676
76	11	KEMP	7f Firm	84	2261
84	4	SAND	5f Gd/Fm	84	2473
85	2	CHEP	6f Gd/Fm		2660
84	3	NEWB	6f Firm	84	2813
0	28	GOOD	6f Firm	84	3152

BRAVE KNIGHT 3 b c £630

50	3	BEVE	10f Gd/Fm	3677
62	6	AYR	8f Heavy	4308

BRAVE TORNADO 9 ch g £15129

75	1	NEWB	16f Soft	68	917*
80	2	KEMP	16f Soft	76	997
80	2	DONC	17f Gd/Sft	77	1052
80	4	KEMP	16f Soft	80	1527
78	5	CHEP	18f Gd/Sft	79	1800
80	3	SAND	16f Gd/Fm	78	2498
72	7	ASCO	16f Good	78	4115
53	8	NEWB	16f Gd/Sft	77	4458

BRAVE VISION 4 b g £0

0a	14	LING	7f Aw	44	28 bl

BRAVO 2 b c £0

38	12	MUSS	7f Soft	4517

BRAVURA 2 ch g £0

0	12	WIND	5f Gd/Fm		3044
0	16	SAND	5f Gd/Fm		3942
59	8	LING	5f Good		4096
0	16	LING	6f Soft	60	4269

BRAZILIAN MOOD 4 b c £2879

74a	1	LING	10f Aw		56*
30a	11	WOLV	8f Aw	76	137
64	5	SAND	10f Good	70	1965
40	9	NEWC	10f Gd/Fm	68	2309

BREAD WINNER 4 b c £2197

54a	4	LING	7f Aw	56	504
56a	2	WOLV	9f Aw	54	568 VIS
59a	2	WOLV	9f Aw	56	637 vis
59a	2	WOLV	9f Aw	57	675 vis
55a	3	WOLV	8f Aw	56	707 vis
52	4	WIND	8f Good	56	854 vis

BREAK THE GLASS 3 b c £3048

76	3	LING	7f Gd/Sft		840
78	2	LING	7f Gd/Sft		1261
82	3	HAYD	11f Soft	80	1491
62	3	BRIG	8f Soft		4177

BREAK THE RULES 8 b g £0

9a	7	SOUT	14f Aw		668
28	7	CHES	12f Gd/Fm	56	3430

BREAKFAST BAY 2 b f £5009

76	3	SALI	7f Good	2686
82	1	FOLK	7f Gd/Fm	3583*
80	14	NEWM	7f Good	4158

BREAKIN GLASS 3 b f £299

53	5	CHES	10f Gd/Fm		1218
44	5	HAYD	7f Gd/Fm		2443
47	4	THIR	7f Gd/Fm		2965
0	16	HAMI	8f Gd/Sft	40	3534 BL

BREAKING NEWS 2 b c £1435

79	3	LING	6f Firm	3832
69	8	SAND	6f Gd/Fm	3942
79	2	LING	6f Soft	4189

BREAKWATER 3 b f £899

BREATHLESS DREAMS 3 ch c £0 is preceded by:

74	4	NOTT	8f Gd/Fm		1268
63	5	GOOD	7f Gd/Sft		1468
64	3	CHEP	7f Gd/Fm		2491

BREATHLESS DREAMS 3 ch c £0

57	5	KEMP	10f Soft		998
71	8	YORK	10f Gd/Fm	82	1310
0	12	RIPO	8f Good	78	1598

BRECONGILL LAD 8 b g £20822

75	3	THIR	5f Soft	74	926
62	16	WIND	6f Gd/Fm	74	1196
76	3	REDC	5f Gd/Sft	72	1580
77	2	CATT	5f Good	72	1662
78	2	RIPO	5f Good	76	1861
67	12	YORK	6f Firm	77	2000
60	12	YORK	5f Gd/Fm	77	2644
77	3	PONT	5f Gd/Fm	77	2830
85	1	**NEWC**	5f Gd/Fm	77	2987*
85	2	NEWB	5f Gd/Fm	82	3176
75	10	HAYD	5f Gd/Fm	84	3322
87	2	NEWB	5f Gd/Fm	84	3485
85	3	YORK	6f Good	84	3543
76	11	DONC	6f Gd/Fm	87	3861
0	19	YORK	6f Heavy	87	4301

BREEZE HOME 4 b g £757

67	5	LEIC	10f Gd/Fm		2774
72	4	YARM	10f Gd/Fm		3381
62	D	LING	11f Firm		3754
0	13	WARW	16f Gd/Fm	69	3916

BREEZY LOUISE 3 b f £2268

69	1	**FOLK**	5f Soft		959*	BL
59	8	CHES	6f Gd/Fm	68	1220	bl
59	6	BRIG	5f Firm	68	1334	bl
49	6	BATH	5f Gd/Sft		1670	
56	8	CHEP	5f Gd/Sft	66	1795	bl
33	9	BRIG	5f Gd/Fm	63	1932	bl
0	15	PONT	6f Soft		4233	bl

BREMRIDGE 3 ch c £0

49	5	BRIG	10f Soft		1466
45	8	EPSO	10f Gd/Fm		3403
0	17	LEIC	11f Firm	70	3842

BRENDAS DELIGHT 2 b f £0

47	9	GOOD	6f Good		2357
0	16	NEWB	7f Firm		2708
0	15	KEMP	8f Gd/Fm		3799
34	11	NEWB	8f Gd/Sft		4457

BREVITY 5 b g £1225

52	7	YARM	6f Gd/Fm	61	1953	t
46	13	WIND	6f Gd/Fm	61	2054	t
41	10	NEWM	7f Firm	57	2347	t
0	16	NEWM	6f Gd/Fm	56	2961	t
55	2	YARM	6f Heavy	52	4480	

BREW 4 b c £0

36	12	BATH	5f Good	60	1092
51	6	CHEP	6f Good	57	1971
43	10	LING	5f Gd/Fm	54	2184
40	7	LING	5f Firm	51	2326
5	7	SAND	5f Good		3229
42	7	BEVE	5f Gd/Fm		3651

BREYDON 7 ch g £0

13	10	MUSS	16f Gd/Fm	34	797
26	8	MUSS	14f Gd/Sft	37	903
27	8	MUSS	16f Gd/Fm		1145

BRIANS BLUE 5 ch g £0

17a	9	WOLV	5f Aw		753

BRIDAL WHITE 4 b f £0

4a	9	WOLV	8f Aw	43	676
20	10	SOUT	10f Gd/Fm	40	859
0	10	WARW	11f Heavy	40	889
0	13	YARM	7f Good	38	3030

BRIDIES PRIDE 9 b g £2976

72	2	NEWB	16f Soft	68	917
74	4	KEMP	16f Soft	72	997

0	20	NEWM	18f Good	79	4353
40	8	DONC	17f Heavy	72	4579

BRIEF CALL 3 b f £0

0a	13	WOLV	5f Aw	54	445
25a	6	LING	5f Aw		487
0a	13	WOLV	5f Aw		1036
42	8	BATH	5f Gd/Sft		1670

BRIEF CONTACT 2 b g £0

55	10	LING	6f Soft		4189
0	11	BRIG	7f Soft		4415
45	8	LING	7f Soft		4483

BRIEF KEY 2 b f £0

0	12	REDC	7f Gd/Sft		4216

BRIEF STAR 2 b f £378

43	8	DONC	5f Gd/Sft		730
49	3	MUSS	5f Gd/Sft		796
58	5	REDC	5f Gd/Sft		1130
42a	8	SOUT	5f Aw		1304
0	26	NEWM	6f Good		4345

BRIERY MEC 5 b g £6834

31	10	WARW	11f Heavy	43	890
46	1	**BRIG**	10f Gd/Sft	41	1509*
41	5	NEWM	12f Firm	47	1852
34	9	SALI	10f Gd/Fm	48	2270
42	3	LING	10f Good	46	2655
48	1	**NEWM**	10f Gd/Fm	45	2958*

BRIG OTURK 3 ch g £657

74	4	LING	10f Gd/Sft		1281
51	3	BRIG	10f Good		3262
46a	4	LING	12f Aw		3835

BRIGHT BLADE 4 b c £0

34a	7	LING	8f Aw		109
5	11	CHEP	12f Gd/Fm	40	2656
0	12	SALI	14f Gd/Fm	38	2982

BRIGHT BLUE 4 b g £0

0	10	LEIC	7f Gd/Fm		3332
0	16	WARW	11f Good		3691

BRIGHT HOPE 4 b f £0

40	9	NEWM	10f Gd/Fm	82	2287

BRIGHT QUESTION 3 ch c £0

44	9	WARW	8f Good		2464

BRIGMOUR 4 gr f £0

0	14	RIPO	8f Soft		826
18	10	BEVE	8f Heavy		973
0	10	BEVE	8f Good		1447
23	5	CATT	7f Soft		1681
0	8	REDC	10f Gd/Fm		2143
0	13	RIPO	8f Gd/Fm		2834
24	11	REDC	9f Gd/Fm		2865
0	11	CARL	10f Gd/Fm		3081

BRILLIANCY 5 b g £430

44a	3	LING	12f Aw	267	t
27	5	BRIG	12f Gd/Sft	893	t
32	5	BEVE	8f Heavy	973	t
0	16	NOTT	14f Good	37	2008 t

BRILLIANT RED 7 b g £23587

104a	1	**LING**	10f Aw		55*	t
79	14	KEMP	8f Gd/Sft	102	1077	t
87	10	YORK	8f Firm	102	1327	t
95	9	ASCO	10f Good	100	2170	t
103	3	SAND	10f Good	100	2475	t
100	6	ASCO	10f Gd/Fm	102	2995	t
106	2	BATH	10f Good		3515	t
97	12	NEWB	10f Firm	102	3997	t
95	10	NEWM	9f Gd/Fm	102	4212	t
72	17	NEWM	8f Good	100	4348	t

BRILLIANTRIO 2 ch f £6955

80	1	**NEWC**	7f Gd/Fm		2985*
46	9	BEVE	7f Gd/Fm		3409
70	6	PONT	8f Soft	79	4084

BRILLYANT DANCER 2 b f £0

61	10	THIR	5f Gd/Fm		3614

62	9	REDC	7f Gd/Sft		4216

BRIMSTONE 5 ch g £0

50a	11	LING	6f Aw	68	113	
48a	8	LING	7f Aw	60	162	
47a	6	LING	8f Aw	56	210	
41a	9	LING	10f Aw		268	
51	9	SAND	5f Gd/Fm	58	2925	
43	9	NEWM	6f Gd/Fm	53	3457	
40	10	YARM	6f Gd/Fm	48	3964	VIS

BRING PLENTY 2 b f £13000

60	11	BATH	6f Gd/Sft		1667	
94	1	**GOOD**	6f Gd/Fm		1957*	
94	3	SAND	6f Gd/Fm		2935	
101	2	NEWM	7f Gd/Fm		3316	
101	4	DONC	8f Gd/Fm		3876	
94	10	LONG	8f Good		4260	BL

BRING SWEETS 4 b c £0

0	22	DONC	7f Heavy	90	4574

BRIONEY 3 ch f £367

60	8	WIND	8f Gd/Fm		1428 t
59	8	WIND	8f Soft		2548 t
71	4	NOTT	10f Gd/Fm		3006 t

BRISBANE ROAD 3 b c £4646

58	4	BATH	8f Gd/Fm		1435 t
59	5	PONT	10f Good	62	1866 t
66	1	**BATH**	12f Gd/Sft	60	2554* t
70	2	NOTT	14f Good	68	3522 t
61	11	HAYD	14f Soft	70	3783 t
53	10	SAND	14f Gd/Fm	70	3948 t

BRITANNIA 3 b f £0

93	5	GOOD	10f Gd/Sft		1469

BRITTAS BAY 2 b f £0

34	7	BRIG	5f Firm		2039

BRITTAS BLUES 3 b f £1497

50	7	THIR	8f Gd/Sft		1354
47	3	NEWC	6f Gd/Fm		2313
43	4	CATT	6f Gd/Fm		2421
41	5	THIR	6f Gd/Fm	50	3124
26	10	SALI	6f Gd/Fm	50	3419
47	3	HAMI	9f Soft	47	3806
26	5	AYR	10f Heavy	46	4306

BROADWAY LEGEND 3 b f £6224

86	1	**HAYD**	11f Gd/Fm		1165*
84	8	NEWB	10f Good		1374
67	9	ASCO	8f Good	87	2167
87	2	DONC	10f Good	85	2610
70	10	NEWC	10f Good	85	3703

BROCHE 3 b c £9078

92	20	NEWM	8f Gd/Fm		1171
111	1	**DONC**	10f Good		1515*
111	5	CHAN	12f V		1752
90	12	EPSO	12f Good		1848

BROCKHALL LAD 2 b g £0

0	11	PONT	5f Good		2361
0	12	DONC	6f Gd/Fm		2608

BROCTUNE GOLD 9 b g £0

41	5	AYR	8f Gd/Fm	42	1658
0	15	RIPO	8f Gd/Fm	42	2099
36	4	AYR	7f Gd/Fm	40	3138
0	13	CATT	7f Gd/Fm	40	3200
35	5	THIR	8f Gd/Fm	38	3344
16	9	MUSS	8f Gd/Fm	36	3745

BROCTUNE LINE 6 ch g £0

9	11	WARW	15f Heavy	36	1524

BROKE ROAD 4 b g £0

36	10	YARM	10f Gd/Sft	48	1615

BROKEN SPECTRE 3 b f £0

58	7	BATH	10f Soft		4141
67	5	YARM	11f Heavy		4481

BROKENBOROUGH 3 ch c £0

0	17	BRIG	10f Gd/Sft	63	892

BROMEIGAN 3 b f £0

50	5	WARW	12f Soft	58	1064
0	12	NOTT	14f Gd/Fm	58	1270
46	11	WIND	10f Good		1725
57	7	NOTT	8f Gd/Fm		2188
44	6	EPSO	10f Gd/Sft		2627
18	8	BRIG	10f Gd/Fm	47	3244

BROMPTON BARRAGE 3 b c £247

69	9	NEWM	7f Good	75	954	
50	9	BRIG	7f Gd/Fm		1125	
45	8	LING	7f Good		1397	t
0	18	SALI	7f Gd/Fm	65	1889	t
0	14	SALI	8f Gd/Fm.	60	2264	BL
0	21	WIND	6f Gd/Sft	54	4294	
43	4	DONC	7f Gd/Sft	49	4452	
36	11	NEWM	8f Gd/Sft	49	4536	

BRONZINO 5 ch g £0

0	16	PONT	10f Soft	54	4374	vis

BROOKFURLONG 4 br f £0

0	7	BRIG	8f Soft	4175

BROTHER TOM 3 b c £0

0	20	LEIC	6f Gd/Sft	4031

BROUGHTON BELLE 4 b f £0

1a	10	SOUT	8f Aw	25	298
4a	8	LING	7f Aw	28	438
0a	9	SOUT	8f Aw	24	585
0	13	AYR	8f Good	18	2136
0	16	YARM	8f Good	18	3236

BROUGHTON MAGIC 5 ch g £2326

28a	5	SOUT	7f Aw	35	368
45a	1	SOUT	8f Aw	33	497*
23a	9	WOLV	8f Aw	43	583
17a	10	SOUT	8f Aw	43	647
0a	14	SOUT	8f Aw	41	2379

BROUGHTON STORM 2 ch g £0

23	10	WIND	5f Good	2368
43	11	NEWM	7f Gd/Fm	2599
39	6	NEWM	7f Firm	3296
0	14	WIND	5f Good	3639

BROUGHTONS FLUSH 2 b g £0

26	13	WARW	15f Gd/Fm	3912
59	14	DONC	8f Heavy	4569

BROUGHTONS LURE 6 ch m £1037

19a	5	WOLV	16f Aw	38	66
36a	2	SOUT	12f Aw	33	215
33a	2	SOUT	12f Aw	34	339
9a	8	SOUT	16f Aw	34	502
12a	8	SOUT	12f Aw	35	590

BROUGHTONS MILL 5 gr g £1046

8a	11	SOUT	8f Aw	44	418
12a	8	WOLV	9f Aw	39	568
38	4	LEIC	10f Soft	39	1568
42	2	WARW	11f Gd/Sft	39	1707
41	3	AYR	13f Good	42	2141
35	6	WARW	11f Good	42	2463
31	9	HAYD	12f Good	40	3284
15a	6	WOLV	12f Aw	30	3494

BROUGHTONS MOTTO 2 b f £2233

0	16	WIND	5f Gd/Fm		1197
68a	1	SOUT	5f Aw		1304*
64	4	LING	6f Good		1673
63	6	LING	6f Good	64	2589

BROUGHTONS TURMOIL 11 b g £187(

67a	1	WOLV	7f Aw	65*
58a	3	SOUT	7f Aw	130
27a	12	SOUT	6f Aw	201

BROWN HOLLY 2 br c £0

0	14	SAND	5f Gd/Fm	3942
0	15	LING	5f Soft	4187

BROWNING 5 b g £941

62	3	SALI	10f Gd/Fm	57	3390
42	12	SALI	8f Firm	60	3753
58a	6	LING	12f Aw	64	4486

BROWNISE 2 b f £3458

86	3	DEAU	6f Heavy	4488

BROWNS DELIGHT 3 b f £3305

48a	7	LING	7f Aw	63	112	
45a	4	LING	7f Aw	63	287	
53a	4	LING	10f Aw		523	
44a	4	LING	10f Aw	57	597	VIS
40a	8	LING	7f Aw	55	654	vis
45	9	BRIG	8f Soft	60	1511	
48	6	NOTT	8f Good	54	1873	
45	5	BRIG	8f Firm	52	2043	
28	8	LING	8f Good	48	2591	
37	11	BRIG	10f Gd/Fm	48	2727	
28	9	YARM	10f Good	45	3031	
46	2	YARM	8f Good	45	3236	
52	4	EPSO	8f Gd/Fm		3404	
47	1	BATH	12f Firm		3624*	

BROWNS FLIGHT 4 b f £0

0	17	WARW	11f Soft	48	1065	
0	17	LING	16f Good	45	1394	
42	7	NEWM	8f Gd/Fm	40	2130	t
23	12	PONT	8f Gd/Fm	45	2561	t

BROWSER 2 b c £2056

64	10	KEMP	6f Gd/Fm	1924
68	3	LING	7f Good	2653
83a	1	WOLV	8f Aw	4249*
70	8	PONT	8f Soft	4375

BRUNNHILDE 2 ch f £0

63	11	WIND	5f Gd/Sft	1424
45	11	LEIC	6f Firm	2029
66	5	HAYD	8f Gd/Sft	4104

BRUTAL FANTASY 6 b g £5329

52a	7	SOUT	6f Aw	68	44
30a	12	LING	6f Aw	68	113
65a	2	LING	5f Aw	63	205
60a	5	LING	5f Aw	65	235
67a	2	LING	6f Aw	65	262
70a	1	LING	6f Aw		288*
66a	4	LING	5f Aw	71	312
52a	8	LING	6f Aw	70	358
80a	3	LING	6f Aw		376
40a	11	LING	7f Aw	69	462
56a	6	LING	6f Aw	67	506
43a	9	LING	7f Aw	67	525
49	11	SAND	7f Gd/Fm	66	763
40	13	LING	5f Gd/Sft	64	1264
55	7	PONT	5f Good		1868
0a	13	WOLV	5f Aw	62	2078

BRYNA 3 b f £0

0a	13	LING	10f Aw	240	VIS
0a	8	LING	8f Aw	373	vis

BRYNKIR 6 b g £0

0a	11	WOLV	12f Aw	49	608	BL
0	17	WARW	16f Gd/Sft	39	1711	
0	13	BATH	17f Firm	37	1996	

BUCKMINSTER 3 br c £3406

85	3	WIND	10f Good		850
88	1	REDC	10f Firm		1295*
61	15	ASCO	12f Good	87	2116
70	6	HAYD	12f Gd/Fm	87	2702

BUCKS BOY 7 b g £144578

128	3	GULF	12f Good	20

BUDDELIEA 2 b f £0

36a	5	WOLV	7f Aw	4383

BUDELLI 3 b c £8411

71	3	KEMP	6f Good		729
69	6	LING	6f Gd/Sft		837
75	2	NOTT	5f Heavy		1021
81	3	SALI	6f Firm		1181
81	1	LING	6f Good		1399*
80	2	KEMP	6f Gd/Fm	78	1925
77	5	PONT	6f Firm		2177
0	16	GOOD	7f Gd/Fm	80	3130
80	2	RIPO	6f Good	78	3698
0	15	KEMP	6f Gd/Sft	80	4037
77	8	NEWM	5f Good	80	4185
79	4	YARM	6f Heavy	80	4480

BUDROYALE 7 b g £418928

124 2	2	GULF	10f Fast	21

BUGGY RIDE 3 b c £8839

68a	2	LING	7f Aw		164	
75a	4	LING	7f Aw		206	
76a	2	LING	6f Aw		221	
74a	2	LING	10f Aw		240	
83a	1	LING	8f Aw		265*	vis
87a	1	LING	8f Aw	75	401*	vis
88a	6	LING	10f Aw		690	vis
0	17	CHES	8f Gd/Fm	87	1215	

BULA ROSE 2 ch f £2971

63	5	LING	6f Soft		1541
61	2	REDC	7f Good		1890
60	3	THIR	6f Good		2059
59	1	REDC	7f Gd/Fm		2155*
59	4	NEWC	7f Good	58	3246
38	9	BEVE	7f Gd/Fm	58	3411
29	17	CATT	7f Soft	58	4007

BULAWAYO 3 b c £3301

47a	6	SOUT	6f Aw		46
72a	1	WOLV	7f Aw	72	362*
68a	4	WOLV	7f Aw	72	534
0	16	DONC	7f Good	70	736
64a	4	SOUT	6f Aw	70	1205
73	6	NOTT	6f Good		1409
55	5	PONT	6f Gd/Fm		3225
0	18	RIPO	6f Good	64	3698

BULLSEFIA 2 gr c £1840

75	3	NEWM	6f Gd/Fm	2854
86	2	WARW	6f Gd/Fm	3909

BUNDY 4 b c £15745

62	1	NOTT	6f Good	56	787*
51	5	HAMI	6f Firm		1239
58	3	DONC	7f Good	60	1519
66	1	PONT	6f Good	60	1869*
67	1	PONT	6f Gd/Fm	64	2559*
55	7	NEWM	6f Good	67	2961
0	15	BEVE	5f Good	67	3398
67	3	YORK	7f Good	68	3809
57	10	AYR	6f Gd/Sft	66	4010
52	8	MUSS	7f Gd/Sft	67	4136
58	6	NEWC	5f Heavy	66	4407

BUNKUM 2 b c £0

0	16	LEIC	7f Firm	3840
55	10	BRIG	7f Soft	4172
44	8	BRIG	6f Heavy	4537

BUNTY 4 b f £303

22a	6	LING	7f Aw	38	58	
27a	4	SOUT	8f Aw	35	297	E
0a	10	SOUT	8f Aw	36	384	
21a	6	SOUT	8f Aw	38	513	
0	14	DONC	12f Gd/Fm	50	699	
32	4	LEIC	8f Gd/Sft	48	831	
0	16	THIR	8f Soft	48	907	
0	27	REDC	8f Firm	45	1300	
0	12	BEVE	8f Good		3393	
35	7	EPSO	10f Good		3857	

BURCOT GIRL 3 b f £389

10	9	RIPO	10f Gd/Fm		2105	
0	17	CHEP	6f Gd/Fm	43	2489	
0	15	WARW	7f Gd/Fm	40	2840	BL
36	3	NOTT	8f Gd/Fm		3004	
10	11	LEIC	8f Gd/Fm		3094	
0	15	BRIG	7f Firm		3559	

BURGUNDIAN RED 3 b c £0

BURGUNDY 3 b g £3497

32	11	SOUT	7f Good		804	
66	7	DONC	7f Gd/Sft		1072	
60	7	HAYD	7f Gd/Sft		1537	
80	1	**SALI**	7f Gd/Fm		3423*	

BURN PARK 3 ch f £0

0	12	NEWT	8f Good	57	1873
0	16	BATH	10f Firm	52	2332

BURNING 8 b g £584

0	16	WARW	11f Heavy	51	890	
0	18	DONC	10f Gd/Sft	48	1050	
0	15	NOTT	10f Gd/Sft	46	1364	
0	15	LEIC	8f Firm	40	2032	
0	15	PONT	10f Gd/Fm	34	2556	bl
7a	9	SOUT	8f Aw		2950	
54	3	LEIC	12f Gd/Fm		3336	bl
16	12	REDC	11f Gd/Fm	36	3636	bl

BURNING DAYLIGHT 3 b g £0

0	17	NEWM	10f Gd/Fm		1697
58	5	PONT	12f Firm		2179
46	7	YARM	11f Firm		2897

BURNING SUNSET 3 ch f £8915

91	3	SAND	10f Heavy		1045	
80	9	NEWB	10f Good		1374	
91	2	NEWM	10f Gd/Fm		1697	
91	2	SAND	9f Gd/Fm	86	1990	
88	3	PONT	10f Good		2365	
73	1	**LING**	7f Firm		3834*	t

BURNING TRUTH 6 ch g £4884

59	6	HAMI	8f Gd/Fm	63	1907
46	13	NEWM	8f Good	62	2564
64	2	RIPO	9f Gd/Fm	60	3011
47	10	NOTT	10f Soft		3979
51	9	REDC	8f Gd/Sft	62	4217
65a	1	**WOLV**	8f Aw	60	4363*
55a	4	**WOLV**	8f Aw	66	4437

BUSTLE 2 ch f £0

0	16	YARM	7f Firm		3940
50	12	WIND	6f Gd/Sft		4289

BUSTLING RIO 4 b g £25918

61a	2	SOUT	14f Aw	55	37
61a	1	**SOUT**	16f Aw	55	51*
68a	1	**SOUT**	16f Aw	61	428*
58a	5	WOLV	16f Aw	67	482
55	8	DONC	18f Good	64	714
45	10	DONC	17f Gd/Sft	60	1052
63	1	**PONT**	18f Firm	55	2176*
69	1	**BEVE**	16f Gd/Fm	60	2516*
67	1	**DONC**	17f Gd/Fm	65	2607*
62	5	GOOD	20f Gd/Fm	67	3085
70	1	**BEVE**	16f Good	65	3395*
72	3	PONT	17f Firm	71	3501

BUSTOPHER JONES 6 b g £0

39	8	NOTT	14f Gd/Sft	49	1087

BUSY BUSY BEE 3 gr f £0

51a	5	WOLV	9f Aw		3272
0a	11	LING	12f Aw		3835
47a	4	WOLV	9f Aw	57	4251
31a	6	WOLV	12f Aw	55	4360
51a	4	WOLV	12f Aw	55	4443

BUSY LIZZIE 3 b f £14494

77	2	FOLK	12f Soft		964
66	11	SALI	12f Firm		1179
67	6	GOOD	12f Gd/Sft	80	1637
78	2	KEMP	14f Gd/Sft	73	2584
79	5	HAYD	14f Gd/Fm	79	3323
90	1	**CHES**	16f Gd/Fm	79	3511*
96	1	**AYR**	15f Soft	90	3961*
92	6	ASCO	16f Good	97	4115
76	8	NEWM	16f Gd/Sft	96	4533

BUTRINTO 6 ch g £8478

56a	8	LING	8f Aw	71	7
37a	5	WOLV	8f Aw		256	
0a	12	SOUT	16f Aw		327	vis
23a	6	WOLV	7f Aw		391	bl
55	1	**BRIG**	7f Firm	46	1213*	
58	1	**BRIG**	7f Firm	52	1335*	
52	4	BRIG	8f Gd/Sft	52	1462	
53	9	KEMP	8f Gd/Fm	60	1926	
59	2	BRIG	7f Gd/Fm	59	2728	
58	3	ASCO	7f Gd/Fm	62	2999	
65	2	BRIG	7f Gd/Fm		3259	
63	2	BRIG	8f Firm		3736	
53	11	LING	8f Firm	63	3831	
57	5	GOOD	8f Soft	62	4066	
56a	4	LING	7f Aw		4487	

BUTTERSCOTCH 4 b c £1128

0a	11	SOUT	11f Aw		248
0a	15	SOUT	8f Aw	42	1207
48	3	PONT	10f Soft	49	1705
48	3	THIR	12f Gd/Fm	49	2061
46	5	BEVE	10f Gd/Fm	47	2518
39	7	CHES	8f Gd/Fm	48	2671
36	10	REDC	10f Firm	45	3310

BUTTERWICK CHIEF 3 b g £259

62	9	HAYD	11f Gd/Sft		1539	
68	4	RIPO	8f Soft		2543	
0	18	PONT	8f Firm		3506	
0	16	HAMI	12f Gd/Fm	49	3827	BL

BUXTEDS FIRST 3 gr f £1321

53	11	WIND	8f Firm		1099
49	3	BRIG	8f Soft	55	1511
52	3	LING	9f Firm	52	1917
9a	8	LING	12f Aw	51	2217
0	14	BRIG	10f Soft	54	4174
0	4	BRIG	10f Heavy	56	4540

BUY A VOWEL 2 b c £0

77	7	NEWB	7f Firm		2708
66	6	BEVE	7f Gd/Sft		3051
51	10	NEWC	7f Gd/Sft		3705
62	10	NEWM	8f Good	70	4350

BUYING A DREAM 3 ch c £1085

79	3	HAYD	8f Gd/Sft	77	810
0	14	BEVE	10f Good	77	1448

BUZ KIRI 2 b c £0

59	7	BRIG	8f Soft		4417

BUZZ THE AGENT 5 b g £1077

36	2	BEVE	10f Gd/Sft	36	3052	tbl
28	7	RIPO	12f Gd/Fm	38	3181	tbl
0	17	THIR	8f Gd/Fm	33	3344	bl
30	6	CATT	12f Good	43	3437	tbl

BY DEFINITION 2 b f £0

50	11	DONC	6f Gd/Fm		1838
0	14	LING	7f Gd/Fm		2182

BY THE GLASS 4 b c £0

32	6	REDC	7f Gd/Sft		1132
39	7	REDC	7f Gd/Sft		1559
46	9	HAYD	7f Gd/Fm		2704
31	7	RIPO	8f Gd/Fm		2834
23	6	THIR	8f Gd/Fm	30	2970
11	8	CARL	8f Firm		3192
15	4	NEWC	7f Heavy	28	4426
0	14	NEWC	8f Gd/Sft	39	4499

BYLAW 2 b f £1841

91	2	KEMP	8f Gd/Fm		3359
71	7	REDC	7f Gd/Sft		4216
80	3	YARM	8f Heavy		4475

BYO 2 gr c £11067

59	9	DONC	6f Gd/Fm		1838
79	1	**RIPO**	5f Gd/Fm		2100*
76	5	CHES	5f Gd/Fm		2248
93	1	**BEVE**	5f Gd/Fm		2483*
99	2	CHES	5f Good		2664
83	4	YARM	5f Good		3027
100	3	HAYD	5f Gd/Sft	99	3264
93	5	YORK	5f Gd/Fm		3567
85	6	RIPO	5f Gd/Fm		3714
79	4	YORK	6f Soft	89	4286
87	8	DONC	6f Soft		4462

BYZANTIUM GB 6 b g £1481

64	5	NEWM	8f Gd/Sft	68	3118
65	4	LING	9f Firm	68	3488
68	3	LING	8f Firm	67	3831
0	14	KEMP	8f Soft	67	4038

C HARRY 6 ch g £4057

44a	11	SOUT	7f Aw	65	35	
61a	4	WOLV	7f Aw	62	79	
67a	1	**SOUT**	7f Aw		130*	
61a	3	WOLV	7f Aw		142	
56a	8	SOUT	8f Aw	65	216	
63a	3	WOLV	6f Aw	64	226	
51a	5	SOUT	6f Aw	64	250	
63a	2	WOLV	7f Aw		274	
63a	5	WOLV	8f Aw	65	323	
60a	4	WOLV	7f Aw	64	364	
57a	2	WOLV	7f Aw		391	
53a	6	WOLV	7f Aw		449	
53a	5	SOUT	7f Aw		667	
51a	7	WOLV	8f Aw		677	
49a	5	SOUT	7f Aw	54	867	
29a	10	WOLV	8f Aw		1038	
0a	12	WOLV	8f Aw	49	1393	
25a	6	SOUT	8f Aw	46	2379	

CABALLE 3 ch f £7479

80	2	PONT	10f Soft		873
79	3	SALI	10f Good		1344
78	3	YARM	8f Good		1771
69	2	REDC	8f Gd/Fm		2159
78	2	THIR	8f Gd/Fm		3126
78	1	**BRIG**	10f Gd/Fm		3262*
79	3	BEVE	12f Gd/Fm		3654
0	18	NEWM	10f Good	80	4197

CABARET QUEST 4 ch c £1840

41	12	WIND	8f Good	62	854
21	9	WARW	11f Heavy	60	1003
0	16	NOTT	10f Gd/Sft	55	1364
22	9	LEIC	8f Firm	50	2032
37	6	SALI	8f Gd/Sft	45	2467
24	8	WIND	8f Soft	45	2546
42	3	REDC	8f Gd/Fm	41	2861
41	3	LEIC	10f Gd/Fm	42	3093
38	6	BRIG	8f Firm	42	3527
43	2	BATH	8f Firm	42	3623

CABCHARGE BLUE 8 b m £0

0	15	NOTT	10f Heavy		4413

CABRIAC 3 b c £1184

83	2	NEWC	7f Soft		759

CACOPHONY 3 b c £1907

60a	3	LING	7f Aw		94	
38a	8	LING	7f Aw	59	149	E
48a	3	LING	6f Aw		207	
50a	3	WOLV	6f Aw		228	
51a	5	LING	7f Aw	55	242	
51a	4	WOLV	6f Aw	54	397	
49a	6	LING	7f Aw	50	488	
51a	2	SOUT	7f Aw		541	
47a	2	SOUT	8f Aw		684	VIS
0	13	NOTT	10f Heavy	48	1022	
0a	15	SOUT	11f Aw		4150	

CAD ORO 7 ch g £2820

52	9	WARW	8f Soft	66	817
57	3	SAND	8f Heavy	65	1058
0	12	CHEP	7f Gd/Sft	65	1799
66	2	CHEP	7f Good	65	1969
56	8	SAND	7f Soft	66	4204
63	4	NOTT	8f Heavy	66	4506

0	13	DONC	8f Heavy	66	4573	

CADEAUX CHER 6 ch g £21170
81	2	DONC	6f Good	76	716	
83	2	NEWM	6f Gd/Fm	78	1173	
61	11	GOOD	8f Gd/Sft	81	1471	
0	14	SALI	6f Gd/Fm	81	1887	
70	8	YORK	6f Good	80	2697	
84	1	**WARW**	6f Gd/Fm	78	2845*	
0	15	ASCO	6f Gd/Fm	81	2954	
80	7	GOOD	6f Firm	85	3152	
83	5	RIPO	6f Gd/Fm	83	3464	
72	12	GOOD	6f Gd/Fm	83	3646	
82	5	KEMP	6f Gd/Fm	82	3791	
80	5	DONC	6f Gd/Fm	82	3861	

CADILLAC JUKEBOX 5 b g £217
0	14	CATT	14f Gd/Fm	65	779
45	4	CARL	12f Firm		1253

CAERDYDD FACH 4 b f £296
0	13	YARM	11f Gd/Sft	31	1614
25	4	YARM	8f Good	30	1772
15	7	YARM	8f Gd/Fm		2411
20a	7	LING	10f Aw		2587
20	7	YARM	10f Good		3234
0a	15	LING	7f Aw		4328

CAERNARFON BAY 5 ch g £1027
54a	2	LING	10f Aw	50	160
42a	9	LING	10f Aw	56	203
45a	10	LING	12f Aw	56	290
31	13	WIND	12f Gd/Fm	47	748

CAEROSA 5 b m £0
36a	4	WOLV	12f Aw	42	43	bl
0a	13	SOUT	12f Aw	42	68	bl
0a	13	WOLV	16f Aw	40	141	bl

CAFE GRANDE 2 b c £2871
85	2	NEWM	7f Good	4344

CAFE OPERA 3 b f £4668
90	8	ASCO	8f Gd/Sft		1108
83	5	WIND	8f Good		3350
81	1	**NEWC**	8f Soft		3707*
81	8	ASCO	8f Good	86	4113

CAFETERIA BAY 2 ch c £8740
87	1	**YARM**	6f Gd/Fm	3385*
88	3	DONC	7f Gd/Fm	3859
88	1	**LEIC**	7f Gd/Sft	4028*
101	5	NEWB	7f Gd/Sft	4455

CAFFE LATTE 4 £33263
118	4	GULF	11f Good	18

CAIR PARAVEL 3 b c £6861
84	5	KEMP	6f Soft	85	994	
88	3	NEWM	7f Gd/Fm	84	1153	
75	11	YORK	7f Gd/Fm	86	1308	
0	25	ASCO	8f Good	86	2117	
83	7	HAYD	7f Gd/Fm	84	2456	BL
88	1	**SALI**	8f Good	82	2688*	
82	9	NEWM	8f Gd/Fm	88	2858	
77	9	EPSO	7f Gd/Fm	87	3414	bl
77	11	NEWM	7f Good	86	4195	bl

CAIRN DHU 6 ch g £426
38a	2	LING	7f Aw		159
30a	10	SOUT	6f Aw		201
0	13	PONT	6f Soft		872
0	20	REDC	7f Gd/Sft		1132
0	20	RIPO	8f Gd/Fm	32	2099
21	9	AYR	8f Good	32	2136
35	7	CATT	6f Gd/Fm		2744
26	5	CARL	6f Gd/Fm		3080
10	13	THIR	8f Gd/Fm	32	3344
0	13	BEVE	12f Sft/Hv		4041

CAITANO 6 b g £297742
118	2	NAD	12f Good	767	bl
110	3	CAPA	10f Good	1321	bl

CAJOLE 4 ch f £0

13	14	HAYD	7f Gd/Sft	58	811	

CALANDA 2 b f £0
62	6	BATH	5f Firm	3621

CALANDRELLA 7 b m £656
18a	7	LING	5f Aw	30	371
15a	7	WOLV	5f Aw	27	563
0	18	BATH	6f Gd/Fm	40	1438
0	16	GOOD	5f Gd/Fm	38	2124
30	6	NOTT	6f Gd/Fm	38	2193
39	3	BRIG	5f Soft	36	2428
34	3	BATH	5f Gd/Sft	36	2555
15	12	CHEP	5f Gd/Fm	38	2976
26	8	NEWB	6f Firm	41	3455
34	10	SALI	5f Firm	45	3747
26	11	HAMI	5f Gd/Sft	37	3825
0	21	GOOD	5f Soft	37	4065

CALCAVELLA 4 b f £1819
63	4	DONC	7f Gd/Fm	62	2320
56	7	DONC	7f Gd/Fm	62	2612
58	5	KEMP	7f Gd/Fm	62	2749
49	9	ASCO	7f Good	61	2999
59	4	LING	7f Firm	61	3279
63	2	BEVE	8f Good	61	3652
62	5	YORK	7f Good	62	3809

CALCUTTA 4 b c £2529
0	20	KEMP	8f Soft	99	1015	
73	6	EPSO	9f Gd/Sft	97	1829	
45	26	ASCO	8f Good	97	2090	
94	6	SAND	8f Gd/Fm	95	2528	
96	3	KEMP	8f Firm	94	2870	
71	19	GOOD	8f Good	94	3107	
83	8	YORK	8f Firm	94	3597	BL

CALDEY ISLAND 3 b c £0
0	17	WARW	7f Soft	69	1061
42	10	LEIC	6f Soft	65	1545
0	15	LEIC	7f Firm	60	2026
31	13	BATH	8f Firm	53	2331
31	12	LEIC	8f Gd/Fm	50	2506
0	12	PONT	8f Good	45	3226
42	5	NEWM	8f Gd/Fm		3456
45	7	BEVE	7f Gd/Fm		3670
35	5	YARM	8f Gd/Fm	39	3971
0a	14	LING	7f Aw		4328

CALDIZ 3 b c £0
50	6	LING	9f Firm	1912	t
74	6	SALI	10f Gd/Fm	2265	t
0	6	BRIG	12f Gd/Fm	3241	t
39	4	CHEP	8f Good	3868	t
0	8	YARM	10f Firm	3935	t
0	11	LEIC	10f Heavy	4313	t

CALEBS BOY 3 b c £0
0	15	CHEP	7f Good	1972
0	10	WARW	11f Gd/Fm	2253

CALEDONIAN EXPRESS 5 b m £0
22a	9	LING	8f Aw	53	776

CALIBAN 2 ch c £552
47	7	YARM	6f Gd/Fm		3385
69	5	YARM	8f Gd/Fm		3665
26	8	YARM	8f Gd/Fm		3969
55a	2	SOUT	7f Aw		4154
21	9	PONT	8f Soft	56	4378

CALICO 3 b f £0
0	10	WARW	11f Heavy	68	1002
38	8	PONT	12f Gd/Fm	64	2829
0	14	NOTT	16f Gd/Fm	54	3112

CALIFORNIA SON 4 ch g £0
0	U	WARW	11f Gd/Sft	36	1707
35	8	NOTT	16f Gd/Fm		2191
17	8	WARW	13f Gd/Fm	32	2843

CALIWAG 4 b c £0
74	7	SALI	6f Firm	1181
0	12	SALI	7f Good	71	1348

0	16	NOTT	8f Heavy	68	4506	

CALKO 3 ch g £10279
63a	1	**SOUT**	6f Aw		74*	bl
46a	5	LING	6f Aw	60	165	bl
52a	3	SOUT	6f Aw		300	bl
66a	1	**SOUT**	7f Aw		330*	bl
66a	1	**SOUT**	8f Aw		385*	bl
68a	1	**SOUT**	8f Aw	62	540*	bl
37a	7	WOLV	8f Aw	67	613	bl
0	13	NOTT	8f Gd/Sft	61	1085	bl
28	13	MUSS	8f Gd/Fm	59	1434	bl

CALLAS 3 b f £0
65	11	NEWB	8f Good		1377
56	13	NEWB	7f Gd/Fm	75	1787
67	5	SALI	6f Gd/Fm		2977
65	6	CHEP	10f Good	66	3870
57	6	BATH	12f Soft	64	4433

CALLDAT SEVENTEEN 4 b c £4997
80a	7	LING	10f Aw		55	
0	20	EPSO	10f Heavy	77	1031	
82	2	NOTT	10f Gd/Fm		1271	
70	4	BEVE	8f Good	77	1445	
71	6	NOTT	10f Gd/Fm	77	2190	
70	7	NEWM	8f Good	74	2564	
59	6	NEWB	9f Firm	72	2853	
31	13	ASCO	10f Good	73	3018	
50	6	BRIG	10f Firm	68	3557	
70	1	**NOTT**	10f Soft		3979*	t
0	R	NEWM	10f Good	74	4160	t
56	9	YORK	9f Heavy	74	4300	tVI

CALLING DOT COM 2 ch c £0
42	7	NOTT	6f Soft	3973

CALLING THE SHOTS 3 b c £1564
0	15	HAMI	5f Firm	53	1244	
41	7	NEWC	8f Gd/Sft	49	1477	
32	7	CARL	9f Gd/Sft	46	1722	
34	8	RIPO	8f Gd/Fm	43	2099	
50	4	NEWC	8f Good	50	2524	
52	2	AYR	7f Gd/Fm	49	2719	VIS
52	4	MUSS	7f Gd/Fm	52	3593	vis
0	11	NEWC	7f Heavy	52	4426	

CALLMEMRWOO 2 ch g £0
37	12	WARW	15f Gd/Fm	3912
0	13	PONT	6f Soft	4083

CALUKI 3 b c £15896
105	3	CAPA	8f Soft	1118

CAMAIR CRUSADER 6 br g £748
31	4	MUSS	10f Aw	34	795	
36	5	RIPO	12f Soft	34	822	
33	5	HAMI	12f Firm	34	1241	
34	3	HAMI	11f Gd/Fm	34	1361	
32	5	RIPO	13f Gd/Fm	33	2109	
15	6	CARL	17f Gd/Fm	33	2244	
0	13	NEWC	12f Good		3247	

CAMARADERIE 4 b g £1031
47	3	NEWC	10f Heavy	48	1769
48	3	AYR	11f Gd/Fm	48	2139
43	7	HAYD	12f Good	48	3284

CAMBERLEY 3 b c £43911
76	3	DONC	6f Good		731
91	2	NEWM	7f Good	82	954
91	2	CHES	8f Gd/Fm	86	1215
95	1	**GOOD**	7f Gd/Sft	88	1470*
83	13	GOOD	7f Gd/Fm	93	3130
93	6	ASCO	7f Good	93	4112

CAMBIADO 2 ch c £345
50	9	SALI	6f Good	2687
74	3	WARW	15f Gd/Fm	3911

CAMEROSA 4 b c £0
0a	13	WOLV	8f Aw	39	
0a	11	WOLV	7f Aw	142	BL

CAMZO 2 ch c £0

0   13 NOTT 8f Heavy   4504

CANADA 2 b c £2995
90 4   NEWM 7f Good   2563
92 2   NEWM 7f Gd/Fm   3121
92 2   YARM 8f Soft   4512

CANADIAN APPROVAL 4 ch f £10446
77a 1   LING 8f Aw   72   336*
19a 11 WOLV 8f Aw   76   580
49a 4   WOLV 8f Aw   750
53a 4   SOUT 11f Aw   866
0   10 EPSO 9f Heavy   1033
50a 10 LING 10f Aw   70   1265
48a 2   SOUT 8f Aw   1505
53a 1   SOUT 11f Aw   1978*
61a 1   SOUT 11f Aw   2119*
34a 4   SOUT 12f Aw   2298
8   8   WIND 8f Good   51 2713
63a 1   WOLV 9f Aw   3498*
61a 6   LING 8f Aw   3756 BL

CANCUN CARIBE 3 ch g £602
29a 9   LING 10f Aw   629
68a 4   WOLV 8f Aw   708
73 3   KEMP 7f Soft   1018
0   17 WIND 10f Gd/Sft 73 4291

CANDICE 2 br f £9455
80 3   YARM 7f Firm   2390
91 8   NEWM 7f Good   3020
94 1   CHEP 8f Gd/Fm   3678*
102 3   DONC 8f Gd/Fm   3876

CANDLE SMILE 8 b g £387
63 6   NEWM 16f Firm 75 3295
57 5   WARW 16f Good 70 3695
61 3   NOTT 16f Soft 63 3978
54 6   BATH 17f Soft 63 4139 VIS
17 12 NOTT 16f Heavy 60 4508 vis

CANDLERIGGS 4 ch c £19317
91 1   KEMP 6f Gd/Fm 84 3791*
93 2   NEWM 5f Good   90 4339
0   14 NEWB 6f Gd/Sft 88 4456

CANDOTHAT 2 b c £7215
69 7   DONC 6f Good   1513
70 6   KEMP 6f Gd/Fm   1924
80 1   PONT 5f Good   2361*
81 5   SALI 6f Good   2687
84 1   MUSS 5f Good   80 3101*
80 5   SAND 5f Good   83 3431
50 9   RIPO 6f Gd/Fm   3712
37 11 AYR   6f Soft   81 3987
70 11 NEWM 5f Good   80 4179

CANFORD 3 b c £8391
88 1   SAND 10f Soft   1588*
82 3   SALI 10f Gd/Fm   1885
94 5   NEWM 15f Gd/Fm   2594
85 5   YORK 12f Good 85 3541
73 5   HAYD 12f Soft 85 4092
87 2   YORK 12f Soft   4276
0   13 DONC 12f Soft 87 4464

CANNY CHIFTANE 4 b g £369
55a 3   SOUT 12f Aw   510

CANNY HILL 3 ch g £378
62a 4   SOUT 8f Aw   198
62a 3   SOUT 8f Aw   453
34 12 HAMI 9f Good   68 846
0   13 HAYD 7f Gd/Sft 63 3269
54 5   AYR   9f Soft   3988
0   13 REDC 10f Gd/Sft 53 4221
28 7   AYR   11f Heavy   4304

CANOPY 2 b f £0
73 5   ASCO 6f Gd/Fm   2952
78 9   NEWM 7f Good   4183

CANOVAS HEART 11 b g £0
0   P   YORK 7f Heavy 80 4302

CANOVAS KINGDOM 2 ch c £0
49 10 PONT 6f Soft   4082
55 5   YORK 8f Heavy   4297
0   17 DONC 7f Heavy   4567

CANTERBURY 5 b g £2259
81 3   DIEL 12f Good   1119

CANTERLOUPE 2 b f £2918
75 1   BATH 6f Soft   4137*
57 4   NOTT 6f Heavy   4410

CANTGETYOURBREATH 4 ch g £1574
30a 9   WOLV 8f Aw   138 bl
35a 5   WOLV 7f Aw   44   193 bl
55a 1   SOUT 6f Aw   199* bl
38a 7   WOLV 6f Aw   54   351 bl
52a 10 SOUT 6f Aw   389 bl
27a 10 WOLV 7f Aw   449 bl
11a 12 WOLV 7f Aw   48   754 bl

CANTINA 6 b m £26422
72a 2   LING 7f Aw   66   162
56a 9   LING 7f Aw   70   239
0a 15 LING 7f Aw   70   337
72 1   BEVE 7f Firm 66 1275*
72 4   CATT 7f Soft 72 1680
73 3   GOOD 7f Gd/Fm 72 2128
82 1   CARL 7f Gd/Fm 72 3083*
88 1   CHES 8f Firm 78 3170+
96 1   CHES 8f Gd/Fm 88 3427*
81 7   CHES 8f Gd/Fm 88 3510
81 11 DONC 7f Gd/Fm   3878

CAP COZ 3 b f £7685
112 2   LONG 7f Good   2226 BL

CAPA 3 b c £1328
85 4   NEWM 12f Good   951
70 5   CHEP 12f Heavy   1554
71 2   WARW 12f Gd/Fm   2038

CAPACOOSTIC 3 ch f £975
0a 14 SOUT 8f Aw   198
0   15 REDC 6f Good   49 1891
25 10 NOTT 8f Gd/Fm 44 2187
45 2   LEIC 8f Gd/Fm 42 2506
34 7   BEVE 8f Firm   45 2735
0a 11 SOUT 11f Aw   45 2945
23 9   LEIC 8f Sft/Hvy 45 4310

CAPAL GARMON 2 b c £9271
79 4   KEMP 7f Gd/Fm   3790
90 3   YARM 8f Gd/Fm   3969
88 1   BATH 10f Soft   4140*
90 2   NEWM 10f Soft   4543

CAPE COAST 3 b c £16274
34a 10 WOLV 6f Aw   549
28 12 NOTT 6f Good   70 785 BL
62 1   NOTT 6f Gd/Sft   1081*
52 6   BRIG 7f Firm   1212
71 3   WIND 6f Gd/Sft   1423
36 11 SALI 7f Gd/Fm   1884
45 4   PONT 6f Good   2833
57 2   HAYD 6f Gd/Fm   3283
68 1   EPSO 6f Good   3689*
71 1   EPSO 6f Good   66 3854*
69 2   GOOD 7f Soft   70 4080
66 6   BRIG 6f Gd/Sft 70 4120
69 3   LING 6f Soft   70 4270
0   14 YARM 7f Soft   70 4513

CAPE COD 2 b f £788
71 4   SALI 7f Gd/Fm   3292
63 10 CHEP 8f Gd/Fm   3678
59 3   NOTT 6f Soft   3974

CAPE GRACE 4 b f £24257
90 6   KEMP 10f Soft   1014
104 1   NEWM 9f Gd/Fm   1154*
104 5   SAIN 11f Good   1378
0   8   CURR 10f Yldg   2404

93 5   NEWB 10f Firm   2851
101 2   CHEP 10f Gd/Fm   2975
102 4   DEAU 10f Good   3370
82 12 YORK 12f Firm   3595 VIS
102 2   NEWM 10f Good   4017
78 8   NEWM 10f Gd/Sft   4532

CAPE LODGE 3 b f £0
60 6   WIND 8f Gd/Sft   1428
71 5   CHEP 10f Gd/Sft   1796

CAPE ROSE 2 b f £0
78 5   KEMP 7f Gd/Fm   3074
70 7   LING 7f Firm   3829

CAPE SOCIETY 2 ch f £0
0   17 WIND 6f Gd/Sft   4288

CAPE TOWN 3 gr c £69275
110 1   NEWM 7f Gd/Sft 105 969*
101 12 NEWM 8f Gd/Fm   1171
117 3   CURR 8f Gd/Sft   1623
107 11 ASCO 8f Good   2066
109 2   NEWB 7f Firm   3452
117 3   GOOD 8f Good   3647
117 3   DONC 8f Gd/Fm   3875
112 3   NEWM 7f Good   4352

CAPERCAILLIE 5 ch g £0
0   14 YARM 10f Gd/Sft 34 1615
14a 6   SOUT 11f Aw   2381
26a 4   SOUT 12f Aw   2636
0a 14 SOUT 16f Aw   30 2951

CAPITAL LAD 2 b c £330
69 8   NEWB 7f Gd/Fm   3484
73 4   EPSO 6f Good   3852
45a 6   WOLV 8f Aw   4249

CAPITALIST 4 br g £0
42a 6   SOUT 16f Aw   327

CAPOSO 2 gr f £0
60 7   WIND 6f Gd/Sft   4289
0   15 NEWB 6f Sft/Hvy   4471

CAPPELLINA 3 b f £975
62 7   CHEP 10f Gd/Sft   1796
42 10 WIND 10f Gd/Fm 58 2206
53 4   SAND 8f Gd/Fm   2920
56 2   LING 7f Firm   53 3279
50 7   LING 6f Firm   3759
48a 7   WOLV 6f Aw   56   4223
45a 8   WOLV 6f Aw   53   4442
8a 13 WOLV 7f Aw   50   4553

CAPPUCINO LADY 3 b f £0
23a 8   LING 6f Aw   221
5a 10 LING 6f Aw   40   242
28a 5   LING 5f Aw   357
0a 9   LING 7f Aw   459
0   19 WIND 6f Gd/Sft   1423
0   12 LING 7f Good   43 2591
44 5   SALI 8f Gd/Fm   3421
48 9   LEIC 5f Firm   3841
0   18 GOOD 5f Soft   38 4065

CAPRI 5 ch g £10437
115 2   HAYD 12f Heavy   987
0   9   CHES 13f Firm   1247
107 2   HAYD 12f Gd/Sft   3479

CAPRICCIO 3 gr g £4305
76 4   SALI 7f Gd/Fm   1886
75 3   WIND 8f Gd/Fm   2211
80 5   BATH 10f Gd/Sft   2553
75 2   HAYD 11f Gd/Sft 75 3267
71 5   HAMI 11f Gd/Sft 75 3379
75 2   GOOD 10f Soft 74 4067
62 8   DONC 10f Gd/Sft 75 4448
72 7   DONC 12f Heavy 75 4580

CAPRICE 3 gr f £0
0a 12 SOUT 7f Aw   278
28a 11 WOLV 6f Aw   549

CAPRICHO 3 gr g £29368
79	2	HAYD	7f Gd/Sft		1537	
84	1	AYR	7f Good		2140*	
85	1	NEWM	7f Gd/Fm	74	2855*	
87	2	GOOD	7f Gd/Fm	84	3130	
82	9	YORK	6f Good	86	3543	
0	16	KEMP	6f Gd/Fm	86	3791	
92	1	NEWM	7f Good	86	4195*	

CAPRIOLO 4 ch c £17620
70	6	NEWB	10f Good	71	1375	
62	7	SALI	10f Gd/Fm	71	2270	
63	9	SAND	10f Gd/Fm	70	2527	
69	1	CHES	12f Good		2667*	bl
69	6	CHES	12f Firm	72	3173	bl
67	3	CHES	12f Gd/Fm	71	3430	bl
77	1	YORK	12f Gd/Fm	70	3725*	bl
77	3	GOOD	12f Soft		4061	bl
78	2	DONC	12f Soft	75	4464	bl

CAPTAIN BOYCOTT 3 b g £0
| 0 | 13 | LING | 7f Gd/Sft | | 839 | |

CAPTAIN BRADY 5 ch g £5296
55	1	HAMI	11f Gd/Sft	51	3379*	
53	3	RIPO	10f Gd/Fm	53	3713	
42	6	HAMI	8f Gd/Sft	52	3826	
41	8	AYR	11f Soft	52	3963	
0	13	YORK	10f Soft	52	4282	
22	8	NEWC	10f Heavy	50	4404	

CAPTAIN CRUSOE 2 b g £0
| 0 | 22 | NEWM | 8f Good | | 4349 | |

CAPTAIN GIBSON 2 b c £4114
23	5	KEMP	6f Gd/Fm		2083	
0	12	GOOD	6f Good		2357	VIS
50	8	BRIG	7f Gd/Fm		3239	
73	6	WIND	6f Good		3638	
71	2	LING	6f Soft	68	4269	
78	1	PONT	6f Soft		4372*	
81	2	WIND	6f Heavy	78	4525	

CAPTAIN KOZANDO 2 b g £2510
57	5	YORK	8f Gd/Fm		3729	
64	2	WARW	15f Gd/Fm		3912	
67	1	PONT	6f Soft		4373*	

CAPTAIN LOGAN 5 b g £0
| 27a | 10 | LING | 8f Aw | 65 | 96 | |
| 0a | 14 | SOUT | 8f Aw | 50 | 418 | tBL |

CAPTAIN MCCLOY 5 ch g £3673
32a	5	LING	10f Aw	44	100	bl
37a	7	LING	10f Aw	42	209	
34	6	BRIG	10f Gd/Sft	40	1509	
42	3	WARW	11f Gd/Fm	40	2033	bl
44	3	SALI	8f Gd/Sft	43	2467	bl
43	3	EPSO	10f Good	42	2790	bl
33	11	NEWM	10f Gd/Fm	42	2958	bl
44	1	WIND	10f Good	41	3356*	bl
33	12	LEIC	10f Firm	45	3842	bl

CAPTAIN MILLER 4 b c £13313
76	1	KEMP	16f Soft	67	997*	
80	2	NEWM	12f Firm	74	1187	
70	13	ASCO	20f Good	78	2092	
76	6	DONC	12f Heavy	78	4580	

CAPTAIN SCOTT 6 b g £0
| 83 | 12 | NEWM | 7f Good | 90 | 4357 | t |
| 0 | P | NEWM | 8f Soft | 90 | 4545 | t |

CAPTAINS FOLLY 2 b f £0
0	13	CATT	5f Good		1659	
37	8	BEVE	5f Firm		1918	
54	5	LEIC	5f Gd/Fm		2507	
45	7	HAMI	5f Gd/Sft		3376	
0	13	THIR	7f Gd/Fm		3615	

CAPTAINS LOG 5 b g £22353
69	4	NEWC	10f Soft	72	757	
76	2	EPSO	10f Heavy	72	1031	
63	5	NEWM	10f Gd/Fm	72	1150	
80	1	WIND	10f Good	75	1729*	
82	1	YORK	12f Gd/Fm		1984*	
81	4	NEWM	10f Gd/Fm	80	2287	
80	1	NEWC	12f Good		2523*	
83	5	ASCO	12f Good	80	2674	
53	9	NEWM	10f Good	81	3024	
78	4	NEWM	10f Gd/Fm	81	3628	
83	2	EPSO	10f Good		3857	

CAPTIVATING 5 b m £0
11a	7	SOUT	8f Aw	38	513	
9a	10	SOUT	11f Aw	31	1306	
21	9	WARW	16f Gd/Fm	28	2037	
29	7	PONT	17f Firm	34	3501	
0	22	EPSO	12f Good	43	3858	

CAQUI DOR 2 b c £0
0	19	NEWB	7f Firm		3999	
0	14	NEWM	7f Good		4183	
42	10	LING	7f Soft		4483	

CARAMBO 5 b m £297
1a	12	WOLV	8f Aw	75	78	
39a	7	SOUT	6f Aw	70	180	
46a	10	LING	6f Aw	64	239	
40a	6	SOUT	6f Aw	60	384	
45a	4	SOUT	6f Aw		414	bl
51a	3	LING	6f Aw		484	bl
40a	11	LING	6f Aw	52	543	bl

CARAMELLE 4 ch f £0
49	7	WIND	10f Good		3189	
0	13	BATH	12f Gd/Fm		3818	
0a	11	LING	10f Aw		4100	
21	6	YARM	14f Soft		4510	

CARBON COPY 2 ch f £434
| 73 | 3 | HAYD | 6f Gd/Sft | | 3268 | |
| 69 | 5 | AYR | 6f Soft | | 3958 | |

CARD GAMES 3 b f £19719
0	21	DONC	6f Good	88	716	
0	15	RIPO	6f Soft	84	824	
0	14	PONT	6f Heavy	80	941	
82	1	REDC	5f Gd/Sft	75	1133*	
83	2	YORK	7f Gd/Fm	80	1308	
64	9	HAYD	6f Gd/Fm	83	2504	
71	14	YORK	6f Good	82	3543	
84	5	AYR	6f Gd/Sft	82	4010	
59	9	HAYD	7f Gd/Sft	82	4106	
86	2	YORK	6f Heavy	82	4301	
0	17	WIND	5f Heavy	84	4527	
0	14	DONC	7f Heavy	84	4574	

CARDIFF ARMS 6 b g £4056
98	2	ASCO	8f Gd/Fm		1112	
97	8	WIND	8f Firm		1291	
79	8	SAND	8f Soft	97	1567	
85	5	EPSO	9f Gd/Sft	97	1829	
55	20	ASCO	8f Good	97	2090	
90	5	YORK	10f Good	95	2696	
94	4	ASCO	10f Gd/Fm	94	2995	

CARDINAL FAIR 3 b f £319
0a	10	SOUT	6f Aw		74	
44a	5	WOLV	7f Aw		192	
38a	4	WOLV	8f Aw		350	
27a	8	SOUT	7f Aw		417	BL
34a	7	SOUT	8f Aw	43	555	
51a	3	WOLV	8f Aw		636	
43a	5	WOLV	8f Aw		708	

CARDINAL VENTURE 2 b c £299
| 65 | 10 | DONC | 7f Good | | 3156 | |
| 73 | 4 | AYR | 6f Soft | | 3958 | |

CAREFULLY 2 ch c £0
0	14	KEMP	6f Gd/Fm		1924	
47	13	HAYD	6f Gd/Fm		2454	
55	6	SALI	7f Gd/Fm		3418	

CAREL 2 b c £0
| 70 | 8 | YARM | 8f Soft | | 4512 | |

CARELESS 3 b f £8768
56	4	BEVE	7f Heavy	57	976	
43	10	DONC	8f Gd/Sft	57	1053	
55	4	CARL	8f Firm	56	1255	
57	2	BEVE	10f Gd/Fm	55	2484	BL
44	7	CHES	10f Good	58	2666	bl
67	1	NEWM	10f Good		3021*	bl

CARELLA BOY 3 br g £0
| 0 | 6 | NEWC | 12f Good | | 3034 | |

CARENS HERO 3 ch c £3107
89	3	KEMP	8f Gd/Fm		1080	
77	1	BATH	8f Gd/Fm		1436*	
75	7	LING	9f Good	86	1744	
82	4	FOLK	10f Gd/Fm		3042	
64	6	CHES	10f Gd/Fm	82	3426	
56	11	BRIG	8f Soft		4420	BL

CAREQUICK 4 ch f £544
0a	13	SOUT	11f Aw	45	131	
51a	5	SOUT	8f Aw		197	
40a	3	WOLV	8f Aw	39	233	
40a	3	WOLV	6f Aw	40	352	
35a	5	LING	7f Aw	39	438	
30a	6	WOLV	7f Aw	37	583	

CAREW CASTLE 3 b g £484
71	5	LING	6f Gd/Sft		837	
62	5	NOTT	5f Heavy		1021	
0	15	NOTT	6f Firm		1266	
49	10	HAYD	7f Gd/Sft	63	3269	
0	16	LING	7f Soft	60	4192	
53a	2	SOUT	8f Aw		4368	VIS

CARHUE LASS 6 b m £2431
| 104 | 3 | BATH | 5f Good | | 1090 | |
| 86 | 17 | NEWM | 5f Gd/Fm | | 1172 | |

CARIBBEAN MONARCH 5 b g £11054
94	4	NEWM	7f Gd/Sft	92	966	
94	3	ASCO	7f Gd/Sft	92	1110	
96	2	YORK	8f Firm	93	1327	
107	1	ASCO	8f Good	96	2090*	
110	1	SAND	8f Gd/Fm	102	2528*	
92	12	ASCO	7f Gd/Fm	105	2997	
106	8	GOOD	8f Good	109	3107	

CARIBBEAN SUMMER 3 b g £0
| 0 | 12 | NEWC | 12f Good | | 3247 | |
| 9 | 9 | CARL | 12f Firm | | 3570 | |

CARIBBEANDRIFTWOOD 2 ch f £5662
82	2	KEMP	7f Firm		2259	
84	1	KEMP	7f Gd/Sft		2583*	
80	9	SAND	7f Gd/Fm		2935	
76	5	NEWC	8f Gd/Sft	87	3704	

CARINTHIA 5 br m £2691
38	12	HAYD	7f Gd/Fm	64	811	
43	9	WIND	8f Gd/Fm	60	1201	
62	2	BRIG	8f Soft	56	1511	
0	13	REDC	8f Good	61	1892	
62	2	NEWM	8f Gd/Fm	60	2804	
61	3	LING	7f Good	63	4102	

CARIOCA DREAM 2 b f £1282
| 77 | 2 | WIND | 8f Heavy | | 4524 | |

CARK 2 b c £3046
68	1	CARL	8f Gd/Sft		1719*	
74	4	RIPO	5f Gd/Fm		2100	
67	5	REDC	6f Firm	69	3327	
50	11	HAYD	5f Gd/Sft	67	3475	

CARLISLE BAY 6 b g £0
| 0 | 12 | NEWC | 6f Soft | | 756 | BL |

CARLTON 6 ch g £15494
70a	1	SOUT	6f Aw	54	44*	
69a	2	SOUT	7f Aw	60	69	
70a	1	WOLV	6f Aw		76*	
90	4	WIND	6f Heavy		935	
76	2	EPSO	6f Heavy	73	1028	
45	17	ASCO	8f Gd/Sft	79	1113	

CARLOW (cont.)

67	7	NEWB	7f Gd/Sft	76	1590	
76	2	KEMP	7f Firm	75	2261	
77	4	LING	6f Firm	77	2761	
67	3	ASCO	7f Gd/Fm	77	2999	
66	10	NEWM	7f Gd/Fm	77	3315	
75	5	KEMP	7f Gd/Fm	75	3796	
70	6	NEWM	7f Firm	75	3981	
75	1	**SAND**	5f Soft		4207+	
64	8	NOTT	6f Heavy	79	4411	
82	2	WIND	5f Heavy	79	4527	

CARLYS QUEST 6 ch g £17789

80	3	HAYD	12f Heavy	82	991	tvi
89	1	**NEWB**	12f Good	82	1373*	tvi
91	3	NEWM	12f Gd/Fm		1695	tvi
82	3	ASCO	12f Good	90	2069	tvi
86	11	ASCO	12f Good	90	2674	tvi
89	4	NEWB	13f Firm	89	2852	tvi
80	7	ASCO	12f Gd/Fm	88	3001	vis
73	5	PONT	12f Gd/Fm	87	3224	tvi
87	5	NEWM	18f Good	86	4353	tvi
90	2	DONC	12f Heavy	86	4580	tvi

CARMARTHEN 4 ch g £221

49a	4	LING	6f Aw		25	
46a	4	LING	5f Aw	47	57	
42a	4	LING	5f Aw	47	235	
25a	8	WOLV	5f Aw	45	291	
25	10	MUSS	5f Gd/Sft	52	798	
24a	4	WOLV	8f Aw		1036	
35	11	BEVE	5f Firm	48	2223	
29	8	CATT	6f Gd/Fm		2421	
25	9	DONC	5f Gd/Fm	44	2753	t
0	11	THIR	8f Gd/Fm	44	2970	
31	12	RIPO	5f Gd/Fm	40	3180	tVI
6	11	LEIC	5f Gd/Fm	40	3214	tvi

CARNAGE 3 b c £925

39	10	EPSO	9f Heavy		1032
28	8	LEIC	8f Gd/Sft		1732
48	2	WIND	6f Soft	45	2549
49	6	WIND	6f Gd/Fm	53	2885
0	13	LING	8f Firm	53	3580

CARNBREA DANCER 3 b f £1254

76	5	NEWM	10f Good		957
72	2	YARM	14f Gd/Fm		2194
65	4	NEWM	15f Good		3023

CARNIVAL DANCER 2 b c £492

80	4	NEWM	8f Gd/Sft		4531

CARNIVAL LAD 2 ch c £2636

73	2	YARM	6f Soft		1612
75	5	YARM	6f Good		1774
72a	3	WOLV	7f Aw		3497
79a	2	WOLV	8f Aw		4022

CARNOT 2 b c £2763

61	8	LING	6f Good		2588
61	5	CARL	6f Gd/Fm		3079
76	1	**BRIG**	7f Gd/Fm		3239*
0	21	DONC	6f Firm		3888
39	10	AYR	8f Heavy	75	4323

CAROLES DOVE 4 b f £0

56	9	HAYD	5f Gd/Fm		808
37	9	WARW	8f Soft		1063
23	10	NOTT	6f Gd/Fm		1368
28	9	WARW	15f Heavy	42	1524

CAROLS CHOICE 3 ch f £4427

44a	4	WOLV	7f Aw		493	
62a	2	WOLV	6f Aw		549	
32	9	NOTT	6f Good	65	785	
61a	3	SOUT	7f Aw	63	870	BL
62a	3	WOLV	6f Aw	63	1138	
65a	2	WOLV	6f Aw	63	1391	
60	3	CHEP	5f Gd/Sft	62	1795	
58a	5	WOLV	5f Aw	65	2078	
50	6	KEMP	5f Gd/Sft	61	2586	
66a	2	WOLV	6f Aw	64	4023	
0	14	BATH	5f Soft	60	4432	

CAROUSING 3 b c £10801

92	1	**PONT**	10f Soft		1703*	
94	5	YORK	10f Firm	93	2004	
57	20	SAND	10f Good	93	2475	
72	9	HAYD	11f Soft	92	3782	
80	1	AYR	9f Soft		3988*	BL
70	13	NEWM	12f Good	90	4162	bl
53	4	AYR	11f Heavy		4304	bl
0	15	NEWM	12f Good	86	4342	

CARPET LADY 2 b f £2023

70	3	WIND	6f Good		2714
73	3	ASCO	6f Gd/Fm		3342
70	9	KEMP	6f Gd/Fm		3795
59	5	SAND	5f Soft	72	4202

CARPET PRINCESS 2 gr f £448

68	4	WIND	6f Good		2369
43	9	WIND	6f Gd/Fm		2886

CARRABAN 2 b f £2295

72	5	NEWM	5f Gd/Sft		970
0	W	HAYD	5f Gd/Fm		1166
69	3	NOTT	6f Gd/Fm		1367
60	3	BRIG	6f Good		1507
72	6	AYR	7f Gd/Fm	73	2718
72a	3	WOLV	7f Aw	68	3273
70a	3	WOLV	8f Aw		4022
62	12	WIND	10f Gd/Sft	70	4290

CARRACA 2 b c £264

0	16	NEWM	10f Gd/Fm		1691	
0	26	NEWM	7f Good		4158	
58	4	NEWC	8f Heavy		4422	BL

CARRADIUM 4 b g £0

51	6	PONT	8f Firm		3506
48	7	MUSS	12f Gd/Sft		4133

CARRICK LADY 2 ch f £0

26	8	LING	6f Firm		3278	
0	12	WIND	5f Good		3639	
25	8	BRIG	5f Soft		4171	
34a	10	LING	5f Aw		4333	BL
45	5	NEWM	8f Soft		4542	

CARRIE CAN CAN 3 b f £1268

60	6	NOTT	8f Gd/Fm		3116
49	5	PONT	8f Firm		3506
62	3	YORK	10f Good		3813
54	8	NOTT	10f Soft		3979
57	5	YORK	10f Soft		4275
69	4	YARM	11f Heavy		4481

CARRIE POOTER 4 b f £20991

75a	1	**SOUT**	6f Aw	69	698*	
61	6	THIR	6f Soft	70	910	bl
53	8	NOTT	6f Gd/Sft	69	1082	
55	1	REDC	7f Firm	67	1297	
46	10	SOUT	7f Soft	65	1606	
47	13	DONC	6f Gd/Fm	63	1842	
45	10	CARL	6f Firm	60	2015	
69	1	**PONT**	6f Good	57	2364+	bl
70	1	**THIR**	6f Gd/Fm	65	2969*	bl
77	1	**HAMI**	6f Soft	70	3803*	bl

CARRY THE FLAG 5 b g £119444

120	3	KRAN	10f Firm		657

CARTMEL PARK 4 ch g £4746

63	12	DONC	5f Gd/Fm	80	702	
76	5	THIR	5f Soft		905	
72	13	YORK	5f Firm	78	1324	
59	12	CATT	5f Good	76	1662	
83a	1	**WOLV**	5f Aw	74	2078+	
70	8	AYR	5f Gd/Fm	78	2721	
78	3	CATT	5f Gd/Fm	78	2929	vis
0	14	HAYD	5f Gd/Fm	78	3322	vis
29	14	CHES	5f Good	78	3512	vis
73	4	BATH	5f Firm		3622	vis
57	8	CHES	5f Soft	74	4073	
0	12	SAND	5f Soft		4207	BL

CARTMEL PRINCE 2 b c £840

73	6	HAMI	5f Good		843
57	9	HAMI	5f Gd/Fm		1189
46	7	HAYD	5f Soft		1492
58	2	HAMI	5f Gd/Fm		1937
43	7	CATT	5f Gd/Fm		2435
53	7	AYR	7f Gd/Fm	58	2718

CARUSOS 2 b f £325

62	10	MUSS	5f Soft		1429
39	8	REDC	6f Gd/Sft		1577
62	3	BRIG	5f Firm		2039
44	6	CATT	6f Gd/Fm		2419
0	15	BEVE	5f Gd/Sft		3055

CASAMASA 4 b c £13200

112	2	NEWM	12f Gd/Fm		1152

CASCINA BICOCCA 3 b f £5465

87	3	SAN	10f Heavy		1227

CASE THE JOINT 2 b c £0

0	15	LING	5f Good		4095

CASH 2 b g £0

0	17	AYR	6f Soft		3958

CASHAPLENTY 7 ch g £0

44a	4	WOLV	12f Aw	45	260	
21a	9	SOUT	12f Aw	43	370	t

CASHDOWN 2 b g £0

0	15	LING	7f Soft		4267

CASHEL PALACE 2 b c £0

0	10	LEOP	6f Good		3372
77	13	NEWM	7f Good		4196
88	10	NEWM	7f Good		4354

CASHIKI 4 ch f £4254

42a	8	LING	10f Aw	47	23	
36a	9	WOLV	6f Aw	46	67	
41	6	SOUT	10f Gd/Sft	46	859	
33	8	WARW	11f Soft	43	1065	
47	2	THIR	12f Gd/Sft		1353	
24	8	WARW	11f Gd/Sft	38	1707	
36	2	NOTT	14f Good	35	2008	
32	6	FOLK	12f Gd/Fm	35	2295	
35	1	**MUSS**	16f Gd/Sft		2536*	
26	7	LING	16f Firm	40	2763	
31	4	BEVE	16f Gd/Fm	35	3406	

CASHMERE LADY 8 b m £8185

76a	1	LING	12f Aw		27	
39	10	DONC	12f Gd/Fm	56	699	
61	1	**RIPO**	12f Soft	54	825*	
63	1	**HAYD**	12f Gd/Fm	61	2446*	
61	10	ASCO	12f Good	63	2674	
63	2	PONT	12f Gd/Fm	63	2829	
56	7	RIPO	12f Gd/Fm	63	3013	
55	6	PONT	12f Gd/Fm	63	3224	
53	8	THIR	12f Gd/Sft	62	3778	
43	12	CATT	12f Soft	60	4003	

CASHNEEM 2 b c £3500

65	4	LING	7f Good		2653
77	1	**MUSS**	7f Good		3100*
82	2	BEVE	7f Gd/Fm		3409
81	7	GOOD	8f Soft	83	4076

CASPIAN 2 b f £4865

77	2	SAND	7f Good		1988
70	1	**DONC**	7f Gd/Fm		2316*
48	13	YORK	7f Good	75	3542

CASSANDRA 4 b f £1965

53	2	SOUT	10f Gd/Sft	50	859
44	5	NOTT	10f Gd/Fm	52	1272
39	8	MUSS	12f Gd/Sft	52	1432
55	2	PONT	10f Good	52	1496
37	15	NEWM	8f Gd/Fm	55	1690
30	9	PONT	10f Gd/Fm	55	3220
50	4	BEVE	10f Gd/Fm	53	3676

31	11	YORK	10f Gd/Fm	53	3731
22	9	PONT	10f Soft	49	4374

CASSANDRA GO 4 gr f £54843
109	1	BATH	5f Good		1090+
107	2	LEOP	5f Yldg		1757
111	6	ASCO	5f Good		2065
109	2	YORK	6f Gd/Fm		2646
110	1	GOOD	5f Gd/Fm		3059*

CASSIUS 2 b g £0
79	5	NEWM	7f Good		4184
0	16	DONC	7f Gd/Sft		4446

CASTANEA SATIVA 3 b f £0
0	20	RIPO	10f Soft	62	827
48	4	BEVE	12f Heavy	59	978
31	5	MUSS	14f Gd/Fm		1433 BL
26	11	REDC	14f Gd/Sft	56	1581

CASTIYA 3 £0
107	7	LONG	8f V		1319

CASTLE BEAU 5 ch g £0
42	10	LEIC	7f Good		790
0	11	PONT	6f Gd/Fm		1105
34	11	BATH	6f Gd/Fm	48	1438
28	8	LEIC	6f Gd/Sft	44	1734
0	15	CHEP	6f Good	44	1971
22	11	BATH	8f Firm	40	2331
0	11	BATH	12f Firm		2785

CASTLE FRIEND 5 b g £0
0a	8	SOUT	8f Aw	51	669

CASTLE SECRET 14 b g £0
0a	15	SOUT	14f Aw	47	37
0a	11	SOUT	16f Aw	35	470

CASTLE SEMPILL 3 b c £20882
65a	4	LING	8f Aw	69	54 VIS
63a	3	LING	7f Aw	66	149 vis
69a	1	LING	6f Gd/Fm	64	222* vis
73a	1	LING	5f Aw	67	269* vis
76a	2	LING	6f Aw	70	444 vis
78a	1	WOLV	6f Aw	70	479* vis
75a	3	LING	6f Aw	77	592 vis
51a	5	SOUT	6f Aw	77	689 vis
76	1	WIND	6f Good	73	852*
0	12	KEMP	6f Soft	77	994
67	6	YARM	6f Firm	76	2900
0	18	GOOD	7f Gd/Fm	76	3130
66	9	LING	6f Gd/Fm	75	3280 vis
68	4	YARM	6f Gd/Fm	73	3668 vis
0	16	YARM	5f Firm	71	3920 vis
70a	3	WOLV	7f Aw		4224 vis
52a	6	LING	7f Aw		4331 vis
50a	10	WOLV	6f Aw	72	4380 vis

CASTLEBAR 3 b g £2769
66a	1	SOUT	6f Aw		472*
57	12	WARW	6f Heavy		888
0	20	WARW	7f Soft	67	1061

CASTLEBRIDGE 3 b g £7285
12a	10	LING	8f Aw		103
34a	8	LING	8f Aw		150
23a	9	LING	8f Aw		236
17a	9	SOUT	8f Aw		303
65a	1	WOLV	8f Aw		350* VIS
71a	1	WOLV	8f Aw		481* vis
46a	6	WOLV	8f Aw	72	551 vis
75	1	WARW	11f Heavy	69	1002* vis
74	5	NEWB	10f Good	75	1375 vis
76	3	WARW	11f Heavy	75	1521 vis
33	11	CHEP	10f Good	75	1973 vis
51	4	CHEP	8f Gd/Fm		2448 vis
38	5	CHEP	12f Gd/Fm		3681 vis
47	11	NOTT	10f Soft		3979 vis
0	16	SALI	10f Gd/Sft	62	4169 vis
15a	9	WOLV	8f Aw	60	4363 vis
0a	16	LING	12f Aw	55	4486 vis

CASTLES BURNING 6 b g £1939
54a	1	LING	8f Aw		4272*

CASTLETOWN COUNT 8 b g £0
36	6	NEWC	16f Soft	38	760

CASTRATO 4 b g £0
0a	8	WOLV	9f Aw		378
0a	8	WOLV	9f Aw		578
0	15	LEIC	7f Good		790
0	12	NOTT	6f Gd/Fm		2680
0	11	CHEP	7f Gd/Fm		3253
0	22	DONC	7f Soft		4461

CAT THIEF 4 ch c £1253012
127ε1		GULF	10f Fast		21* bl

CATALAN BAY 2 b f £0
33	9	REDC	5f Gd/Sft		1558
0	12	RIPO	6f Gd/Fm		3009
21	8	BEVE	5f Good		3408
13	11	RIPO	5f Gd/Fm		3710
36	9	CATT	6f Soft		4001
0	12	MUSS	5f Gd/Sft		4131

CATALONIA 3 ch f £1230
0	W	SALI	8f Good		3289
63	5	SAND	8f Good		3474
50	10	EPSO	7f Good	69	3854
65	2	YARM	8f Heavy	66	4478

CATAMARAN 5 ch g £301
70	4	KEMP	7f Soft		1018
70	5	SALI	7f Good	73	1348
59	7	LING	7f Good	72	1672
0	16	KEMP	8f Gd/Fm	70	1926
0	15	GOOD	8f Good	67	3885 BL
39	8	BRIG	12f Soft	64	4176 bl

CATCH THE CHRON 2 b f £4498
60	2	HAYD	5f Soft		1492
51	7	PONT	6f Good		1864
34	4	BEVE	5f Good		2880
31	9	LEIC	6f Gd/Fm	55	3216
69	1	HAMI	5f Gd/Sft		3376*
58	6	HAMI	5f Good	65	3802
68	2	HAYD	5f Soft	65	4090
10	11	PONT	5f Gd/Fm	68	4235

CATCHTHEBATCH 4 b g £0
8a	12	WOLV	6f Aw	65	175
47a	8	LING	6f Aw	60	371
35a	14	LING	6f Aw	55	543
52a	5	LING	5f Aw	55	631 BL
0	18	BATH	5f Good	54	1092 bl

CATCHY WORD 3 ch c £17450
103	2	NEWM	7f Gd/Sft	105	969
97	6	CAPA	8f Good		1118
92	5	EPSO	7f Gd/Sft		1830
99	4	NEWB	7f Firm		2809
0	20	ASCO	8f Gd/Fm	104	2997
91	8	NEWM	7f Gd/Fm	100	3315 VIS
101	3	EPSO	10f Good		3684
103	1	NEWM	10f Good		4017*

CATEEL BAY 2 b f £0
53	6	NEWC	7f Gd/Sft		3705
50	10	YORK	8f Soft		4281

CATELLA 4 ch f £179334
106	2	SAN	12f Gd/Fm		2074
116	3	DUSS	12f Good		2911
117	2	BADE	12f V		3849
104	3	COLO	12f Soft		4147

CATSTREET 2 b c £0
0	28	NEWM	6f Good		4341

CATZ 3 £750
97	4	LEOP	8f Gd/Fm		1316

CAUDA EQUINA 6 gr g £16785
58	16	DONC	6f Gd/Fm	81	702
80	2	THIR	5f Soft		905
61	9	EPSO	6f Heavy	80	1028
66	17	NEWM	6f Gd/Fm	80	1173
73	5	BATH	5f Gd/Fm		1441
74	6	NEWB	6f Gd/Sft	79	1591
64	11	SALI	6f Gd/Fm	76	1887
76	4	BATH	6f Firm	76	1999
74	3	SALI	5f Gd/Fm	75	2266
72	8	GOOD	6f Good	75	2355
77	2	EPSO	6f Gd/Sft	75	2432
67	7	DONC	6f Gd/Fm		2580
75	4	YORK	6f Good	75	2697
63	8	KEMP	6f Firm		2869
0	17	ASCO	7f Gd/Fm	75	2999
73	4	NEWB	5f Gd/Fm	75	3176
70	6	BATH	5f Firm	75	3209
63	5	SALI	6f Gd/Fm	74	3419
77	2	BATH	6f Gd/Fm	74	3516
80	1	BATH	5f Firm		3622*
81	1	GOOD	7f Good		3662*
82	3	BATH	6f Gd/Fm	81	3821
71	10	GOOD	8f Good	81	3904
80	5	SALI	6f Gd/Sft	82	4165
73	7	CATT	6f Soft		4257
62	9	YORK	6f Heavy	81	4301
0	22	NEWM	7f Good	79	4357

CAUGHNAWAGA 2 b c £3932
87	6	NEWM	8f Good		4349
96	1	YARM	8f Soft		4512*

CAUNTON 3 b f £0
77	8	NEWM	10f Firm		1184
0	10	LEIC	12f Gd/Sft	65	1571
0	15	YARM	10f Gd/Fm	60	1955
21	12	PONT	10f Soft	54	4374
0	12	YARM	11f Heavy		4481

CAUSTIC WIT 2 b c £18619
83	5	NEWM	6f Gd/Fm		1691
57	11	ASCO	5f Good		2152
101	1	DONC	6f Gd/Fm		2608*
95	2	NEWM	6f Gd/Fm	89	3165
99	6	NEWM	6f Gd/Fm	92	4214*
91	6	DONC	6f Soft		4462

CAUTION 6 b m £5970
53a	6	SOUT	8f Aw	67	645
0	17	DONC	6f Gd/Fm	1ow	716
56	6	RIPO	6f Soft	66	824
55	8	THIR	5f Soft	66	910
40	13	NOTT	6f Gd/Sft	63	1082
0	15	PONT	6f Good	57	1869
51	4	YARM	7f Firm	52	2391
54	2	PONT	5f Good	52	2561
53	2	CHES	6f Gd/Fm	52	2673
43	5	PONT	5f Good	52	2831
57	2	WIND	8f Good	54	3188
55	3	NEWM	6f Gd/Fm	54	3317
56	3	WIND	8f Good	55	3643
54	3	THIR	8f Gd/Sft	56	3777
54	4	REDC	8f Gd/Sft	55	4217
45	7	REDC	8f Gd/Sft	55	4499

CAUTIONARY 3 b f £0
66	9	PONT	6f Good	81	2364
65	6	RIPO	6f Gd/Fm	77	3010
59	8	HAMI	6f Soft	74	3803

CAUTIOUS JOE 3 b f £7383
72a	7	SOUT	5f Aw	78	202
33a	10	WOLV	6f Aw	78	275
56	10	NEWC	5f Gd/Sft	74	1479
51	8	CHES	5f Gd/Sft	70	1781
67	3	MUSS	5f Firm	76	2047
64	5	CARL	5f Firm	66	2280
63	5	LEIC	6f Gd/Fm	66	2511
57	8	YORK	7f Good	65	2694
61	3	CARL	7f Firm		3573
0	19	YORK	8f Good	62	3810
59	1	LEIC	8f Gd/Sft		4032*

64 1 LEIC 8f Sft/Hvy 4311*

64	1	**LEIC**	8f Sft/Hvy			4311*	
64	2	NOTT	10f Heavy			4413	

CAUVERY 2 ch c £5255

84	2	WIND	6f Gd/Fm			1876	
87	1	**NEWC**	7f Gd/Fm			2271*	
92	7	GOOD	7f Gd/Fm			3086	
102	3	SAND	7f Gd/Fm			3946	
99	7	NEWM	7f Good			4196	
95	9	DONC	8f Soft			4463	

CAVANIA 3 ch f £935

71	3	CHEP	10f Gd/Fm			2449	
68	4	SAND	10f Gd/Fm			2924	
0	16	KEMP	12f Soft			4040	

CAVERNARA 2 b f £552

59	4	PONT	6f Good			1864	
55	5	THIR	7f Gd/Fm			3347	
64a	4	WOLV	7f Aw			3497	

CAVERSFIELD 5 ch g £277

47a	7	LING	8f Aw	56		336	
0	14	WARW	8f Soft	53		1066	
39	7	BRIG	8f Firm	50		1330	
39	7	LING	7f Soft	47		1542	
41	6	SOUT	7f Soft			1603	
32	9	RIPO	8f Gd/Fm	41		2099	
38	3	FOLK	6f Gd/Fm			2292	
23	11	BRIG	7f Gd/Fm	38		2729	
40a	9	LING	7f Aw			4328	

CAXTON LAD 3 b c £2668

88a	1	**SOUT**	5f Aw	78		202*	
86	9	ASCO	5f Gd/Sft	91		4129	
0	14	DONC	5f Soft	88		4466	
0	18	WIND	5f Heavy	88		4527	

CAYMAN EXPRESSO 2 b f £516

62	6	SAND	5f Gd/Fm			1986	
71	3	SALI	5f Gd/Fm			2227	
77	5	SAND	5f Gd/Fm			2526	
79	12	NEWB	5f Firm			2849	

CAYMAN SUNSET 3 ch f £8734

80	1	**KEMP**	7f Gd/Sft			2585*	
95	6	SAND	8f Good			3469	
100	4	DONC	8f Good			3878	
100	2	DONC	7f Soft			4465	

CAYOKE 3 b c £21134

110	1	**CHAN**	8f Gd/Sft			1900*	

CAZOULIAS 3 b g £6916

101	3	MAIS	7f Soft			945	
105	2	SAIN	10f Heavy			4491	

CD EUROPE 2 ch c £73032

94	1	**GOOD**	6f Gd/Sft			1472*	
107	1	**ASCO**	6f Good			2067*	
109	2	DONC	7f Firm			3891	
108	4	LONG	8f Soft			4320	
99	8	DONC	8f Soft			4463	

CD FLYER 3 ch c £2530

0	14	SAND	5f Gd/Fm	79		763	
67	6	WIND	6f Good	77		852	
74	4	KEMP	6f Soft	75		994	
75	4	WIND	5f Gd/Sft	74		1098	
67	6	AYR	5f Good			2165	
78	3	DONC	6f Gd/Fm	73		2577	
76	3	WIND	6f Gd/Fm	74		2885	
72	8	GOOD	7f Gd/Fm			3130	
67	9	YORK	5f Gd/Fm	76		3569	
75	3	NOTT	6f Heavy	75		4411	

CEARNACH 2 b c £1294

0	13	GOOD	6f Good			2357	
42	11	BATH	6f Gd/Sft			2550	
69	5	SALI	6f Good			3387	
67	4	DONC	7f Firm	66		3901	
69	3	GOOD	8f Soft	67		4076	
0	21	NEWM	8f Good	67		4350	

CEDAR BILL 2 ch c £262

---

54 5 LING 5f Gd/Sft 836

54	5	LING	5f Gd/Sft		836	
52	9	BRIG	5f Gd/Sft		1463	
48	4	GOOD	6f Gd/Sft		1634	

CEDAR BOSS 3 gr g £0

14a	7	LING	6f Aw		153	

CEDAR CHIEF 3 b c £0

0	14	WIND	12f Heavy	45	937	

CEDAR DU LIBAN 2 b g £0

0	16	DONC	6f Firm		3888	bl

CEDAR FLAG 6 br g £3450

47a	7	LING	10f Aw		56	
36a	6	LING	12f Aw		101	
34a	9	LING	7f Aw		156	
31a	3	LING	16f Aw	38	285	
42a	2	SOUT	12f Aw	38	370	
38a	4	LING	16f Aw	41	424	
38a	3	SOUT	14f Aw	41	502	
49a	1	**SOUT**	12f Aw	40	682*	
17a	12	LING	13f Aw	47	835	
35	8	BRIG	12f Firm	45	1209	
41	4	WARW	11f Gd/Sft	40	1707	
30	11	WARW	11f Gd/Fm	41	2033	
19	7	EPSO	12f Gd/Sft	43	2626	

CEDAR GROVE 3 b c £587

0	14	DONC	10f Gd/Sft		1054	
0	15	NEWB	10f Gd/Fm		1404	
64	4	NEWM	12f Gd/Fm		1696	
39	9	SALI	12f Gd/Fm	62	2470	
52	4	YARM	14f Firm	55	2902	
44	9	NOTT	16f Gd/Fm	55	3112	

CEDAR GUVNOR 3 b c £0

43a	6	LING	6f Aw	57	2	
35a	7	LING	8f Aw	57	54	

CEDAR JENEVA 2 b f £0

29	9	WIND	5f Heavy		932	
0	U	BRIG	5f Gd/Fm		1124	
38	8	WARW	5f Gd/Sft		1706	
42	10	LING	7f Firm		3833	

CEDAR LIGHT 3 b c £340

34	11	KEMP	6f Good		729	
0	12	KEMP	8f Gd/Sft		1080	
35a	10	LING	6f Aw	52	1742	
0	17	CHEP	6f Good	52	1971	
41	3	BRIG	6f Gd/Fm	47	2896	
37	5	BRIG	7f Gd/Fm	45	3242	
28a	9	LING	10f Aw	43	3828	

CEDAR LORD 3 b c £0

60	6	WIND	10f Heavy		936	
50	7	BRIG	10f Gd/Fm		1127	
16	7	BRIG	8f Gd/Fm	58	2726	
0	20	WIND	10f Gd/Fm		3045	
0	18	BRIG	7f Gd/Fm	52	3242	BL

CEDAR MASTER 3 b c £2945

93	7	NEWM	7f Good		955	
66	5	EPSO	10f Heavy		1029	
83	5	NOTT	8f Good		1872	
78	6	ASCO	8f Good		2171	bl
77	11	SAND	8f Gd/Fm	85	2528	bl
76	3	WARW	8f Gd/Fm		2844	bl
79	2	LING	8f Firm	78	3580	VIS
69	7	LING	7f Firm	78	3758	vis
67	11	BRIG	8f Gd/Sft	80	4121	vis
77	4	BRIG	8f Soft		4420	vis

CEDAR PRINCE 3 b c £0

0	14	WIND	8f Heavy	81	933	
16	12	KEMP	9f Gd/Sft	79	1075	bl
48	9	LING	8f Good	75	1744	bl
63	6	LING	8f Gd/Fm	70	2185	bl
0	11	KEMP	8f Gd/Sft	66	2749	bl
58	10	SAND	8f Gd/Fm	66	2922	bl
56	9	KEMP	7f Gd/Fm	64	3362	bl
53	8	BRIG	10f Gd/Fm	64	3530	VIS

---

31 12 EPSO 10f Good 60 3762 vis

31	12	EPSO	10f Good	60	3762	vis	
0	14	LING	7f Soft	56	4192	vis	

CEDAR RANGERS 2 b c £4023

73	5	LING	5f Gd/Fm			2214	
80	1	**LING**	6f Good			2652*	
57	9	GOOD	6f Good	78		3886	

CEDAR TREBLE 2 b c £568

58	3	BRIG	6f Heavy			4537	

CEDAR TSAR 2 b c £7224

57	6	BRIG	5f Firm			1208	
66	2	LING	6f Good			1396	
32	9	LING	6f Good			1673	
61	2	YARM	7f Gd/Fm			1950	
69a	1	**SOUT**	7f Aw			2301*	
65	3	PONT	6f Gd/Fm	62		2557	
68	3	AYR	7f Gd/Fm	65		2718	
61	3	AYR	8f Gd/Fm	62		2874	
82a	1	**SOUT**	6f Aw		69	2948*	
0	15	REDC	6f Firm	65		3327	
33	7	RIPO	6f Gd/Fm	62		3712	
0a	12	WOLV	6f Aw			4244	
19a	12	SOUT	7f Aw			4369	

CEDAR WELLS 4 b c £0

20a	9	WOLV	9f Aw	61		681	
0	15	SOUT	7f Good	57		803	
46	6	BRIG	7f Firm	53		1336	
0	19	CHEP	7f Gd/Stt	51		1794	
0	12	BEVE	7f Gd/Fm	48		2479	
26	6	BRIG	7f Gd/Fm	44		2728	
36	4	BRIG	7f Firm			2907	BL

CEEPIO 2 b c £9783

93	3	NEWB	6f Gd/Fm			1943	
101	1	**NOTT**	6f Gd/Fm			2189*	
104	3	GOOD	6f Good			3105	
93	5	DONC	6f Soft			4462	

CEINWEN 5 ch m £0

0a	9	WOLV	8f Aw			920	
0	11	FOLK	7f Soft			961	
13	9	BRIG	7f Firm			1333	

CELANDINE 7 b m £0

41	9	BEVE	7f Gd/Fm	46		2221	
24	13	DONC	7f Gd/Fm	46		2320	
34	9	DONC	7f Gd/Fm	43		2612	
37	6	WARW	7f Gd/Fm	41		2840	

CELEBES 3 b c £892

63a	3	LING	8f Aw			591	
64a	4	WOLV	9f Aw		69	709	
68	6	SOUT	8f Gd/Sft	74		857	
68	4	DONC	8f Gd/Sft	72		1053	
0	24	NEWM	8f Firm	70		1183	
33	10	BEVE	10f Good	67		1448	
50	12	WIND	8f Good	62		1726	VIS
46	8	CHEP	7f Good			1972	vis

CELEBRATION TOWN 3 b c £29370

73	1	**SOUT**	8f Gd/Sft	67		857*	
59	9	YORK	8f Firm	72		1341	
77	1	**SAND**	7f Soft	72	1569*	
76	6	SAND	7f Gd/Fm	76		2495	
87	1	**NEWM**	7f Gd/Fm	76	3163*	
87	2	HAYD	7f Gd/Sft	83		4106	
91	1	**YORK**	8f Gd/Sft	86	4284*	

CELEBRE BLU 3 b c £1819

38	6	HAMI	9f Firm			1242	
52	3	THIR	7f Gd/Fm			1351	
74	3	REDC	6f Gd/Sft			1562	
71	3	HAYD	7f Gd/Fm			1789	
22	9	REDC	7f Gd/Fm	72		2145	
56	8	BEVE	8f Gd/Fm	70		2515	
59	7	BEVE	7f Firm	66		2733	
55	3	BEVE	7f Gd/Fm			3670	
42a	6	WOLV	8f Aw		60	3769	
35	9	PONT	8f Soft		60	4232	

CELERIC 8 b g £4830
115	3	ASCO	16f Gd/Sft		1109
90	7	YORK	14f Firm		1339
98	9	ASCO	20f Good		2114

CELERITY 2 b f £0
19	11	NEWB	6f Firm		3449
43	6	DONC	6f Firm		3895
30a	9	WOLV	8f Aw		4022
41a	7	SOUT	6f Aw	60	4367

CELESTIAL KEY 10 br g £3166
48a	2	SOUT	8f Aw		452
3a	10	LING	8f Aw		574
49a	7	SOUT	8f Aw		600
62	2	MUSS	9f Gd/Sft	60	795
62	1	FRAU	9f Good		1904*

CELESTIAL POWER 2 b f £0
| 31 | 10 | CHES | 5f Firm | | 1249 |
| 0 | 9 | HAYD | 5f Gd/Sft | | 1835 |

CELESTIAL WELCOME 5 b m £8437
77	6	NEWC	10f Gd/Sft	85	757
83	1	HAYD	11f Heavy		986*
64	13	YORK	12f Gd/Fm	85	1307
69	12	REDC	10f Gd/Sft	83	1561
68	8	YORK	12f Firm	81	2002
66	12	HAYD	12f Gd/Fm	79	2502
64	13	HAYD	14f Soft	76	3783

CELLO SOLO 3 b c £394
| 71 | 3 | LING | 8f Soft | | 4274 |

CELOTTI 2 b f £3860
73	3	NOTT	6f Gd/Fm		2189
70	5	CHEP	6f Gd/Fm		2488
73a	1	SOUT	5f Aw		2818*
73	7	GOOD	5f Good	78	3109
77	2	BEVE	5f Good	75	3394
43	10	AYR	6f Soft	77	3987
0	14	NEWM	5f Good	77	4179

CELTIC BAY 3 b f £0
70	6	CHEP	10f Gd/Sft		1796
50	6	GOOD	12f Gd/Fm		2354
70	6	WIND	10f Gd/Fm		2889
53	6	SALI	8f Gd/Fm	66	3422
54	5	CHEP	10f Gd/Fm	62	3683

CELTIC EXIT 6 b h £11163
66	5	ASCO	8f Gd/Sft	73	1113 t
80	1	GOOD	7f Gd/Sft	73	1810* t
74	5	SAND	7f Gd/Fm	78	1989 t

CELTIC FLING 4 b f £0
| 50 | 9 | THIR | 8f Soft | 77 | 931 |

CELTIC ISLAND 2 b f £20150
86	2	SAND	5f Gd/Fm		762
88	1	PONT	5f Heavy		938*
82	2	SALI	5f Firm		1176
88	2	YORK	6f Gd/Fm		1312
76	8	ASCO	7f Good		2091
93	1	SALI	7f Gd/Fm		2267*
96	4	SAND	8f Good		2935
84	8	GOOD	8f Good		3882
81	16	NEWM	7f Good	96	4157

CELTIC LEGEND 2 b f £0
0	12	REDC	5f Gd/Sft		1130
26	9	RIPO	6f Good		1859
13	10	NEWC	6f Firm		2333

CELTIC MISS 2 b f £540
57	11	NEWB	6f Firm		3980
76	3	LING	7f Soft		4484
65	6	DONC	8f Heavy		4569

CELTIC MISSION 2 ch g £3843
76	7	LEIC	7f Gd/Fm		3840
80	5	YARM	7f Firm		3940
65a	3	WOLV	7f Aw		4383
82	1	MUSS	8f Soft		4564*

CELTIC SEAL 4 br f £0

45a	5	WOLV	5f Aw		272
36a	7	WOLV	5f Aw		379
25a	8	WOLV	5f Aw		639	BL

CELTIC SILENCE 2 b c £27300
| 97 | 1 | AYR | 6f Gd/Fm | | 1653* |
| 106 | 1 | ASCO | 7f Good | | 2091* |

CELTIC SPRING 2 b c £0
| 21 | 12 | NEWC | 7f Gd/Sft | | 3705 |

CELTIC VENTURE 5 ch g £2362
42a	8	LING	5f Aw	55	57
36a	9	LING	5f Aw	55	91
27a	6	LING	6f Aw	51	263
42a	6	WOLV	5f Aw		1237
48	1	BRIG	7f Firm		2907*
32	12	BRIG	6f Gd/Fm	51	3243
40	8	BRIG	7f Firm		3559
34	6	BRIG	8f Firm		3736

CELTS DAWN 2 b f £0
| 66 | 7 | NOTT | 6f Gd/Fm | | 2683 |

CENTAUR SPIRIT 3 b c £1974
25	7	RIPO	10f Gd/Fm		2105
47	4	NOTT	8f Gd/Fm		3004
26	12	HAYD	8f Gd/Fm		3266
30	7	LEIC	10f Gd/Sft		4029
43	1	LEIC	10f Heavy		4313*
28	11	NOTT	10f Heavy	58	4509

CENTER STAGE 3 ch c £0
| 63 | 6 | WIND | 8f Good | | 3350 |

CENTRAL COAST 4 b c £0
0	17	SALI	6f Gd/Fm	83	1887
0	16	NEWC	5f Gd/Fm	81	2310
55	15	YORK	6f Good	79	2697
0	18	ASCO	6f Gd/Fm	80	2954

CENTURY STAR 2 b c £0
0	17	DONC	5f Good		730
41	8	LEIC	5f Gd/Sft		828
52	6	BEVE	7f Good		3949
0	12	LING	6f Soft		4190	BL

CEPHALONIA 3 b f £30117
85	1	PONT	12f Gd/Sft	75	1106*
94	1	NEWB	12f Gd/Fm	85	1400*
80	6	HAYD	12f Gd/Sft	93	1832
99	1	NEWM	15f Good		2594*
97	7	DONC	15f Gd/Sft		3863
51	11	ASCO	12f Gd/Sft		4130
98	3	NEWM	16f Gd/Sft	98	4533

CERALBI 2 b c £2015
74	6	CATT	6f Gd/Fm		2926
72	2	NEWC	6f Good		3032
70	2	THIR	7f Gd/Fm		3347
0	19	DONC	6f Firm		3888
52	13	YORK	8f Soft		4281
44	9	DONC	7f Heavy	68	4577

CERTAIN JUSTICE 2 gr c £12222
| 96 | 1 | NEWM | 5f Soft | | 984* |
| 108 | 1 | WIND | 5f Firm | | 1290* |

CERTAINLY SO 2 ch f £0
| 0 | 13 | WIND | 5f Gd/Fm | | 2209 |
| 66 | 7 | KEMP | 7f Soft | | 4034 |

CEZZARO 2 ch c £550
80	5	NEWM	6f Gd/Fm		2132
79	7	YORK	7f Gd/Fm		2649
80	3	CHES	7f Firm		3169
46	16	NEWC	8f Gd/Sft	82	3704
83	15	NEWM	7f Good		4158	VIS

CHAFAYA 2 ch f £467
| 77 | 3 | KEMP | 7f Soft | | 4034 |
| 0 | 16 | NEWM | 7f Soft | | 4541 |

CHAGALL 3 ch c £7700
| 109 | 2 | NEWM | 7f Firm | | 2343 |
| 99 | 7 | NEWM | 8f Good | | 4180 |

CHAGUARAMAS 2 b f £13378
85	1	WIND	6f Gd/Fm		2209*
87	1	BATH	5f Firm		2940*
94	5	NEWM	7f Gd/Fm		3316
96	4	GOOD	7f Good		3659
98	2	GOOD	8f Good		3882
85	8	NEWM	7f Gd/Fm		4210

CHAHAYA TIMOR 8 b g £583
41a	4	WOLV	15f Aw		174
57a	3	SOUT	16f Aw		327
48a	3	WOLV	15f Aw		363

CHAI YO 10 b g £0
| 0 | 19 | SAND | 10f Soft | 70 | 4208 |

CHAIN 3 b c £0
| 58 | 8 | HAYD | 11f Gd/Sft | | 3265 |

CHAIRMAN BOBBY 2 ch g £411
72	3	CARL	5f Firm		3571
45	8	YORK	6f Good		3814
54a	5	WOLV	6f Aw		4225

CHAKA ZULU 3 b g £13839
44	1	BATH	10f Firm	40	2332*
45	3	NOTT	10f Gd/Fm	44	2685
52	1	CATT	12f Gd/Fm	44	2746*
61	1	NEWC	12f Good	52	3036*
57	3	NEWM	12f Gd/Fm	52	3167
69	1	NEWC	12f Firm	65	3606*
69	2	MUSS	12f Gd/Fm		3741
35a	9	WOLV	12f Aw		4245

CHAKRA 6 gr g £8432
25a	7	LING	6f Aw	41	358
24a	6	LING	5f Aw	41	372
63a	5	LING	6f Aw		440
26a	9	LING	5f Aw		484
23a	6	WOLV	5f Aw	36	564
37a	1	LING	6f Aw	32	628*
19	9	NOTT	6f Good	40	787
31	6	BRIG	5f Gd/Sft	43	897
37a	8	WOLV	6f Aw		1137
28	9	HAMI	5f Firm	38	1244
27	10	NOTT	5f Good	38	1412
22	11	BRIG	5f Gd/Sft	35	1464
39	2	GOOD	6f Gd/Fm	38	2124
48	1	FOLK	6f Gd/Fm		2291*
47	3	BRIG	7f Gd/Fm	47	2729
32	8	BATH	6f Firm	47	2944
49	2	AYR	7f Gd/Fm	47	3138
51	1	BRIG	6f Gd/Fm	45	3243*
42	6	LING	6f Firm		3493
54	6	EPSO	6f Good		3689
48	5	BRIG	5f Gd/Fm	50	3734
49	5	YARM	6f Gd/Fm	50	3966
0	17	GOOD	5f Soft	50	4065

CHALCEDONY 4 ch g £10680
73a	1	SOUT	11f Aw	66	343*
73a	2	LING	12f Aw	71	508
72a	4	SOUT	11f Aw	71	512
48a	7	LING	12f Aw	69	633
55	4	RIPO	12f Soft	58	825
38	9	PONT	10f Soft	58	871
60a	3	SOUT	12f Aw		1203
35	6	SAND	14f Good	55	3472
51	2	GOOD	12f Good	51	3887
60a	1	LING	12f AW		4186*
27a	13	SOUT	12f Aw		4366

CHALLENOR 2 ch c £0
57	6	YARM	5f Firm		2901
0	15	CHEP	8f Good		3867
0	18	YORK	8f Soft		4281

CHALOM 2 b c £0
53	16	NEWB	7f Firm		3999
81	6	ASCO	7f Gd/Sft		4124
55	10	NEWB	6f Sft/Hvy		4470

CHALUZ 6 b g £1104
51a	2	SOUT	7f Aw	50	75	t
38a	5	WOLV	7f Aw	51	187	t
47a	5	WOLV	6f Aw	51	232	t
48a	4	SOUT	7f Aw		247	t
50a	2	WOLV	7f Aw		310	tVl
41a	5	SOUT	7f Aw		341	t
42a	5	LING	6f Aw		484	vis
36a	5	WOLV	8f Aw		550	t
41a	4	SOUT	6f Aw	45	602	t
35a	5	SOUT	8f Aw		686	t

CHAMBOLLE MUSIGNY 4 b f £328
41a	3	WOLV	9f Aw	44	359	
20a	7	SOUT	12f Aw		387	
16a	7	SOUT	8f Aw	42	430	
2a	8	SOUT	8f Aw		453	bl

CHAMELEON 4 b f £4798
78a	1	WOLV	7f Aw		478*	
58	9	NEWM	6f Gd/Fm	76	2961	
70	5	HAYD	7f Soft	74	3785	
73	2	AYR	10f Soft	72	3989	
61	6	HAYD	11f Gd/Sft	72	4108	
44	10	WIND	8f Gd/Sft		4292	

CHAMELI 5 b m £0
0a	16	SOUT	11f Aw		178	

CHAMLANG 2 b f £0
55	10	NEWM	6f Gd/Sft		4530	
0	19	DONC	6f Heavy		4576	

CHAMPAGNE GB 4 b g £2609
39a	8	WOLV	9f Aw	62	516	
39a	5	SOUT	7f Aw	57	648	
0	15	SOUT	11f Gd/Sft	62	855	
57a	3	WOLV	7f Aw		1038	BL
0	14	WARW	11f Soft	59	1065	bl
63a	1	WOLV	8f Aw	55	1393*	bl
0	18	NEWM	8f Gd/Fm	56	1690	bl
39a	13	SOUT	8f Aw	63	2121	bl
43	4	WIND	8f Soft	53	2546	bl

CHAMPAGNE N DREAMS 8 b m £0
0	U	BEVE	7f Firm	56	1275	
41	6	CATT	7f Soft		1681	
45	7	BEVE	7f Firm	55	1920	
42	6	PONT	8f Firm	53	2180	
0	13	BEVE	7f Gd/Fm	50	2479	
21	11	BEVE	8f Gd/Fm	46	3407	
38	5	THIR	8f Gd/Sft		3775	
18a	8	LING	8f Aw		4272	

CHAMPAGNE RIDER 4 b c £1552
73	18	NEWM	6f Gd/Fm	88	1173	
76	9	GOOD	7f Gd/Sft	87	1483	
0	15	GOOD	7f Gd/Sft	85	1810	
72	12	KEMP	7f Firm	82	2261	
68	14	GOOD	6f Good	82	2355	
75	6	EPSO	6f Gd/Sft	82	2431	
72	8	LEIC	7f Gd/Fm	78	2775	
66	11	ASCO	6f Gd/Fm	80	2954	
0	29	GOOD	6f Firm	78	3152	
71	4	HAYD	8f Soft	73	4094	
0	25	NEWM	7f Gd/Fm	72	4215	BL
71	2	DONC	7f Soft		4461	
70	6	DONC	7f Heavy	72	4574	

CHAMPFIS 3 b c £2058
63	4	NEWC	8f Soft		2337	
73	2	CATT	7f Soft		4005	
66	5	REDC	8f Gd/Sft	72	4217	
63	2	CATT	6f Soft		4255	

CHAMPION LODGE 3 b c £17623
97	2	NEWM	8f Gd/Sft		972	
95	1	NEWM	8f Firm		1188*	
97	1	THIR	8f Good		1382*	
93	7	NEWM	10f Firm		1854	
82	9	RIPO	8f Good	97	3699	
0	15	NEWB	8f Firm	95	3998	

CHANCE REMARK 2 ch f £0
13a	10	SOUT	7f Aw		4369	
35	8	NOTT	8f Heavy		4507	

CHANCELLOR 2 b f £3331
74	9	NEWB	7f Firm		3999	
91	1	DONC	7f Heavy		4567*	

CHANCERY 4 ch g £724
55	3	NEWM	12f Gd/Fm		3313	

CHANCY DEAL 3 b f £0
6a	8	SOUT	8f Aw		694	
0	11	LEIC	10f Gd/Sft		833	

CHANGE OF IMAGE 2 b f £200
50	6	LING	6f Good		1673	
64	4	SALI	6f Gd/Fm		1883	
33a	11	SOUT	5f Aw		2120	

CHANGING SCENE 2 b c £4075
69	9	ASCO	7f Gd/Fm		2956	
81	5	NEWB	7f Gd/Fm		3484	
86	1	EPSO	9f Good		3853*	
0	P	YORK	7f Soft	86	4279	

CHANTAIGNE 2 ch f £685
38	8	CHES	5f Firm		1249	
62	5	AYR	7f Soft		3962	
72	3	HAYD	8f Gd/Sft		4104	
57	8	DONC	7f Soft	69	4460	

CHANTRESS LORELEI 2 b f £0
61	18	NEWM	6f Good		4341	
66	5	NEWB	6f Sft/Hvy		4470	

CHAPEL ROYALE 3 gr c £13358
76	5	RIPO	9f Soft		823	
56	7	PONT	10f Gd/Sft	83	1104	
78	7	EPSO	7f Gd/Sft	80	1826	
81	2	WIND	8f Gd/Fm		1879	
0	27	ASCO	8f Good	78	2117	
80	3	BEVE	8f Gd/Fm	78	2515	
82	1	NEWM	8f Gd/Fm	78	2614*	
74	10	NEWM	8f Gd/Fm	83	2858	
78	7	WIND	8f Good	82	3642	
70	11	KEMP	8f Gd/Fm	81	3793	
81	3	GOOD	9f Good	81	3883	
93	3	GOOD	8f Soft		4077	
0	33	NEWM	9f Gd/Fm	85	4212	
72	11	NEWM	8f Gd/Fm	81	4348	
66	10	NOTT	8f Heavy	80	4506	
0	20	NEWM	8f Soft	80	4545	

CHARENTE 2 ch c £398
44	5	NOTT	6f Gd/Fm		2189	
75	8	NEWB	6f Firm		2808	
64	9	SALI	6f Gd/Fm		3387	
70	3	WIND	10f Gd/Sft	68	4290	

CHARGE 4 gr c £7614
64a	1	LING	6f Aw		95*	t
56a	6	LING	6f Aw	69	223	t
54a	7	WOLV	6f Aw	65	258	t
51a	7	LING	6f Aw	62	403	t
64a	2	LING	6f Aw	59	543	t
60a	2	LING	6f Aw	59	573	t
77a	1	LING	6f Aw	62	691*	t
71a	5	LING	6f Aw	77	881	t
60	14	WIND	6f Gd/Fm	70	1196	t
45	8	BRIG	5f Good	67	1650	tBL
57	5	LING	5f Firm	64	2326	t
21	11	LING	6f Firm	61	2761	t

CHARITY CRUSADER 9 b g £0
27	12	HAMI	12f Firm	47	1241	bl
0	13	THIR	12f Gd/Sft		1353	bl
14	5	REDC	14f Firm		3311	bl

CHARLATAN 2 b c £0
42	11	NEWM	7f Good		2563	

CHARLEM 3 br f £650
44a	6	WOLV	8f Aw		920	
39a	6	WOLV	9f Aw	46	1040	
28a	6	SOUT	12f Aw	44	2123	VIS
9	11	BEVE	10f Gd/Fm	42	2484	vis
41a	2	WOLV	8f Aw	40	2601	vis
19	9	EPSO	9f Good	45	2795	vis
0	21	REDC	8f Gd/Fm	37	2861	vis
0	12	YARM	10f Good	44	3031	BL

CHARLIE BIGTIME 10 b g £0
0a	8	WOLV	12f Aw	32	607	bl

CHARLIE PARKES 2 ch c £5379
82	2	NEWC	5f Soft		755	
94	2	CHES	5f Gd/Sft		1214	
85	2	NEWC	5f Gd/Sft		1475	

CHARLIE SILLETT 8 ch g £0
0	13	LEIC	6f Soft	65	1545	
25	8	LEIC	8f Gd/Sft		1731	
0	20	NOTT	6f Gd/Fm	51	2192	VIS

CHARLIES QUEST 4 b g £0
0	18	SAND	10f Soft	51	4208	
15a	10	WOLV	6f Aw	45	4443	

CHARLOTTE RUSSE 3 b f £0
0a	15	SOUT	8f Aw		48	VIS
0	14	HAYD	11f Gd/Fm	40	3480	

CHARLOTTEVALENTINA 3 ch f £3848
0	14	EPSO	6f Heavy	83	1028	
85	2	CHES	6f Gd/Fm	80	1220	
62	9	BATH	5f Gd/Fm		1441	
21		YORK	6f Firm	82	2003	
66	14	KEMP	6f Gd/Fm	80	3791	
66	5	CHES	6f Soft		4069	

CHARLTON IMP 7 b m £0
0	18	PONT	8f Aw	35	2561	
24	10	CHEP	7f Gd/Fm		3253	

CHARMED 2 ch c £0
0	14	BEVE	5f Firm		2730	
0	14	YORK	6f Good		3814	
44	11	WARW	15f Gd/Fm		3911	

CHARMER VENTURE 2 ch f £336
84	4	DONC	8f Gd/Sft		4445	

CHARMING ADMIRAL 7 b g £5544
17a	8	SOUT	16f Aw	46	737	bl
52	1	PONT	17f Soft	48	876*	bl
56	2	PONT	22f Heavy	53	940	bl
43	13	HAYD	14f Gd/Fm	56	1167	bl
46	10	RIPO	16f Good	56	1597	bl
57	3	PONT	17f Soft	56	1701	bl
23a	9	SOUT	16f Aw	42	2951	bl
56	3	AYR	17f Soft	56	3993	bl
26	9	PONT	18f Soft	54	4376	VIS

CHARMING LOTTE 3 b f £4680
46	15	DONC	7f Good	76	736	vis
60	13	CHES	6f Gd/Fm	75	1220	vis
0	21	NEWB	7f Gd/Fm	72	1405	vis
61	5	REDC	6f Gd/Sft		1579	vis
65	1	CHES	6f Gd/Sft		1780*	vis
67	3	HAMI	6f Gd/Sft	66	3377	vis
0	13	RIPO	6f Good	67	3698	vis
62	3	PONT	6f Soft		4233	vis
60	5	NOTT	6f Heavy	64	4411	vis

CHARTER FLIGHT 4 b g £214
58a	7	WOLV	9f Aw	46	383	
55a	4	SOUT	8f Aw	65	473	
48a	7	WOLV	9f Aw	63	611	
42	11	NOTT	10f Good	58	786	
26	7	SAND	8f Heavy	55	1058	
0	17	NOTT	10f Gd/Fm	50	1272	

CHARTERHOUSE 3 b c £0
68	13	WIND	10f Gd/Fm		1200	
42	5	NEWM	12f Gd/Fm		1696	

CHARTLEYS PRINCESS 2 b f £864
57	5	CATT	5f Good		1659	
69	3	MUSS	5f Firm		2045	

67	3	RIPO	5f Soft			2539	
65	5	BEVE	5f Good	68		3394	
63	7	BEVE	5f Gd/Fm	66		3673	
0	23	NEWM	6f Good			4345	

CHARTWELL 3 ch g £0

29a	7	LING	6f Aw		527
21a	6	LING	8f Aw		595
0	14	LING	6f Firm		3579

CHASE THE BLUES 3 b c £0

31	6	CATT	6f Gd/Fm		2421
53	5	LING	5f Good		2590
70	7	NEWM	7f Gd/Fm		2860
33	14	NEWM	8f Gd/Fm	70	3118
0	18	LING	6f Firm	65	3493

CHASETOWN CAILIN 5 b m £0

20a	6	SOUT	7f Aw	36	739	
19a	8	SOUT	8f Aw	31	1419	t

CHASKA 5 b m £0

0a	9	WOLV	16f Aw	38	66

CHATER FLAIR 3 b c £4426

72	7	NEWM	12f Good		951
56	4	BRIG	10f Firm		2041
60	1	EPSO	12f Gd/Sft	55	2429*
60	7	KEMP	12f Firm	61	2872
48	8	KEMP	14f Gd/Fm	59	3800

CHAUNTRY GOLD 2 b g £5001

55	14	WIND	6f Gd/Fm		1876
64	9	WIND	8f Gd/Fm		2209
78	3	NEWM	7f Gd/Fm		2599
72	2	BRIG	5f Firm		2903 BL
77	1	NEWM	7f Firm		3296*

CHAWENG BEACH 2 ro f £12722

52	13	WIND	6f Gd/Fm		1197
62	1	LING	6f Good		1396*
56	6	SALI	6f Good		2687
53	4	BRIG	6f Gd/Fm	57	3258
52	5	WIND	6f Gd/Fm	60	3354
66	1	EPSO	7f Good	58	3690*
68	1	LING	7f Firm	62	3830*
58	9	LING	7f Soft	49	4191
68	3	BRIG	7f Soft	67	4416

CHAYANEES ARENA 5 b m £0

0a	15	SOUT	12f Aw	28	211

CHEEK TO CHEEK 6 b m £1719

53	5	BATH	12f Good	65	1091
57	5	BATH	13f Gd/Fm	63	1440
60	2	SAND	14f Gd/Fm	59	1991
43	5	YARM	14f Gd/Fm	59	2416
60	4	FOLK	16f Good	59	2622
48	3	LING	16f Firm	58	2763
19	7	NEWM	15f Good	59	3025

CHEERFUL GROOM 9 ch g £0

0a	11	WOLV	8f Aw	33	675
29a	7	WOLV	8f Aw		750

CHELONIA 3 b f £770

65	8	BATH	8f Gd/Sft		1669
72	5	KEMP	9f Gd/Fm		2086
62	6	NOTT	10f Gd/Fm	69	2685
66	3	NEWB	10f Gd/Fm	66	3178
51	7	BEVE	10f Gd/Fm	66	3676
0	19	LEIC	7f Firm	65	3839

CHELSEA MANOR 4 b c £40729

115	2	LONG	10f Hldng	819
115	3	LONG	11f Heavy	1115
116	3	LONG	9f Gd/Sft	1458
115	2	DEAU	8f V	2571
111	4	MAIS	10f Good	4050

CHEMCAST 7 ch g £2148

48a	1	LING	5f Aw	45	57*	bl
17a	12	WOLV	5f Aw	48	116	bl
40a	7	LING	6f Aw	47	154	bl
44a	5	LING	5f Aw	46	371	bl

CHEMICALATTRACTION 2 b c £238

43	8	NEWC	5f Soft		755
56	8	NEWC	7f Gd/Fm		2985
64	4	THIR	7f Gd/Fm		3347
57	7	THIR	7f Gd/Fm		3617
0	20	DONC	7f Firm	64	3901
50	10	CATT	7f Soft	60	4007

CHEMS TRUCE 3 b c £5004

91	3	NEWB	8f Soft	90	912	
83	8	SAND	8f Heavy	90	1055	
0	18	GOOD	9f Gd/Sft	89	1452	
0	24	ASCO	8f Good	87	2117	BL
80	3	SALI	8f Good	83	2688	
83	4	NEWM	10f Gd/Fm	82	3166	
76	5	NEWB	11f Firm	82	3451	
76	4	EPSO	10f Good		3857	
78	4	GOOD	10f Soft	79	4067	
80	3	YORK	10f Soft	78	4282	
73	6	YARM	10f Gd/Fm	78	4392	

CHERISH ME 4 b f £7164

69a	1	WOLV	6f Aw		63*
83a	1	WOLV	6f Aw	70	175+
80a	2	WOLV	6f Aw	79	320

CHEROKEE FLIGHT 6 b g £0

34	11	NOTT	10f Gd/Fm	54	1272

CHERRY FLYER 2 b f £0

62	6	WARW	5f Gd/Sft	1706

CHESHIRE 3 b g £13449

109	1	DEAU	10f Good	3369*

CHESTER HOUSE 5 b h £134940

121e4	GULF	10f Fast	21

CHESTERS BOY 3 ch g £0

55	10	LEIC	7f Gd/Fm		3333
44	6	REDC	7f Gd/Fm		3635
0	18	LEIC	7f Firm		3840
0a	13	WOLV	6f Aw		4225 BL
0	15	NOTT	8f Heavy		4507 bl

CHEVENING LODGE 2 ch c £733

56	4	WIND	5f Gd/Sft		1095
54	6	LEIC	5f Soft		1550
47	7	RIPO	6f Good		1859
57	8	NOTT	5f Good		2009
51	3	YARM	8f Gd/Fm	53	3968
43	5	YARM	8f Soft	53	4393

CHEWIT 8 gr g £1570

97a	3	WOLV	8f Aw	100	137
72a	5	LING	8f Aw		208
83	6	NEWM	7f Gd/Sft	83	966
0	16	GOOD	7f Gd/Sft	83	1483
71	4	GOOD	8f Gd/Sft		1635
67	10	GOOD	7f Gd/Sft	81	1810
0	R	GOOD	7f Good	76	2303

CHEZ BONITO 3 br f £3076

37	5	SOUT	10f Good		806
45	2	HAMI	9f Gd/Fm		1195
26	11	SOUT	7f Soft		1607
40	5	WIND	10f Gd/Fm	43	2206
43	4	FOLK	10f Gd/Fm	42	2296
34	8	BEVE	10f Gd/Fm	40	2484
39	8	BRIG	10f Firm	42	2908
34	5	BRIG	10f Firm	41	3530
39	4	CHEP	12f Gd/Fm		3681
47	1	YARM	11f Firm		3917*
0	14	SALI	10f Gd/Sft	46	4169

CHEZ CHERIE 3 ch f £12877

103	9	NEWM	8f Firm	1185
92	4	NEWB	10f Gd/Fm	1945
101	4	NEWC	10f Firm	2339
103	3	HAYD	12f Gd/Fm	2501
105	2	NEWM	12f Gd/Fm	2857

CHIANG MAI 3 b f £75252

106	1	LEOP	9f Soft	14*

103	1	CURR	8f Yldg		863*
0	8	CURR	8f Gd/Sft		1626
108	1	CURR	11f Gd/Sft		4057*
103	6	LONG	13f Good		4236
114	4	LONG	16f Heavy		4494

CHIANTI 2 b c £23875

91	1	YORK	6f Firm	2005*
100	1	YORK	7f Good	2693*
94	6	GOOD	7f Gd/Fm	3086
105	3	DONC	7f Firm	3891
105	7	NEWM	7f Good	4354

CHIARO 3 b f £0

0	19	CHEP	7f Good	1972
0	13	SALI	7f Gd/Fm	2232

CHICAGO BEAR 4 ch c £0

19a	5	SOUT	11f Aw	369	tbl

CHICAGO BLUES 3 b f £0

41a	6	SOUT	8f Aw	48	125

CHICAGO BULLS 2 b c £0

80	5	NEWM	10f Soft	4543

CHICANE 2 ch c £258

79	4	DONC	6f Heavy	4575

CHICANERY 3 b g £0

32	6	ASCO	7f Gd/Fm	3343
59	9	YARM	7f Soft	4388
13	11	WIND	6f Heavy	4526

CHICARA 2 ch f £595

68	3	HAYD	7f Gd/Fm	1166
45	8	WARW	5f Gd/Fm	2034

CHICKASAW TRAIL 2 ch f £0

40	8	BEVE	7f Gd/Sft	3057
49	8	WARW	7f Good	3692
59	7	BEVE	7f Good	3953

CHIEF CASHIER 5 b g £7490

78	5	WIND	10f Gd/Fm		747
54	10	EPSO	10f Heavy	79	1031
61	12	NEWB	12f Good	79	1373
67	7	EPSO	10f Good	76	1845
82	1	BATH	10f Gd/Sft	74	2552*
79	4	KEMP	10f Gd/Fm	79	2750
79	6	GOOD	10f Gd/Fm	80	3060
59	9	ASCO	10f Gd/Fm	80	3339
53	15	NEWM	10f Good	79	4160
64	6	NEWB	10f Sft/Hv	77	4473

CHIEF JUSTICE 3 b c £0

8a	8	SOUT	7f Aw	283
17a	8	WOLV	8f Aw	350
0a	4	WOLV	9f Aw	382

CHIEF MONARCH 6 b g £9694

72	2	NEWC	10f Soft	70	757
71	5	PONT	8f Soft	72	875
39	11	NEWC	8f Heavy	72	1007
74	2	AYR	10f Gd/Fm	72	1656
74	3	EPSO	10f Good	75	1845
54	12	YORK	12f Firm	76	2002

CHIEF OF JUSTICE 3 b c £5266

65a	1	SOUT	11f Aw	58	537*
72a	1	WOLV	12f Aw	63	640*
69	3	CATT	12f Gd/Fm	67	782
2	8	DONC	15f Gd/Sft	69	1071
0	13	CATT	12f Soft	68	4256
43a	7	WOLV	9f Aw	72	4382

CHIEF SEATTLE 3 br c £130675

115e2	GULF	9f Fast	19

CHIEF WALLAH 4 b c £1456

56	10	SALI	14f Good		2691
60	4	BRIG	12f Gd/Fm		3241
59	2	PONT	17f Firm	57	3501
40a	6	LING	12f Aw		3835
0	12	GOOD	16f Soft	59	4075
25	11	NEWB	16f Gd/Sft	58	4458

CHIEF WARDANCE 3 ch g £633

65	5	HAYD	11f Gd/Sft		3265	
72	3	BEVE	10f Gd/Fm		3672	
65	10	LEIC	10f Firm		3838	

CHIKO 3 b c £0

0a	12	SOUT	7f Aw	65	31	vis
0	16	LEIC	8f Gd/Fm	65	3095	
0	14	PONT	8f Gd/Fm	65	3226	BL

CHILDRENS CHOICE 9 b m £3162

40a	2	WOLV	16f Aw	38	66	
32a	6	WOLV	16f Aw	42	141	
40a	3	WOLV	15f Aw	41	277	
49a	1	**WOLV**	15f Aw		363*	vis
42a	3	WOLV	16f Aw	46	492	vis
31a	4	WOLV	16f Aw	44	576	vis
11	9	BRIG	12f Good		1647	vis
32	8	NOTT	14f Good	40	2008	
5	10	BRIG	12f Firm	36	2904	
20	11	NOTT	14f Gd/Fm	36	3002	vis

CHILI PEPPER 3 b f £2619

39a	6	WOLV	8f Aw		636	
58a	1	**WOLV**	6f Aw	53	706*	
19	16	WARW	7f Heavy	53	887	bl
53a	3	WOLV	7f Aw	58	1390	
18	14	RIPO	6f Good	51	1600	
33a	9	SOUT	6f Aw	58	4155	

CHILLI 3 br c £2751

53a	3	LING	5f Aw	54	419	
53a	3	WOLV	8f Aw	54	566	
54a	2	LING	10f Aw	54	597	
52	3	BRIG	10f Gd/Sft	54	892	
50	3	NOTT	10f Heavy	53	1022	
33	12	YARM	11f Gd/Sft	53	1614	
51a	3	SOUT	8f Aw	54	1804	VIS
41	5	YARM	14f Gd/Fm	50	1949	
30a	7	LING	10f Aw	49	2212	vis
44	5	BRIG	10f Gd/Sft		2423	vis
0	13	YARM	11f Soft	45	4391	vis

CHILLI BOY 2 gr g £0

33a	7	SOUT	5f Aw		1302	
33	8	RIPO	6f Gd/Fm		3009	
52	7	CATT	7f Good		3438	

CHILLIAN 4 b c £0

23a	8	SOUT	5f Aw	36	674	
20a	5	SOUT	6f Aw	30	1422	
27	12	REDC	7f Gd/Sft		1559	
9	11	NEWC	6f Gd/Fm	41	2275	
29	10	CARL	5f Firm		2822	
0	16	REDC	7f Gd/Fm		2994	
48	9	BEVE	5f Gd/Sft		3056	
0	16	RIPO	5f Gd/Fm	25	3180	

CHILWORTH 3 ch c £1107

41a	11	LING	7f Aw	71	488	
15a	8	LING	7f Aw		570	
51	5	WARW	7f Soft		813	
42	6	KEMP	9f Soft	60	999	BL
0	21	NEWB	7f Gd/Fm	57	1787	bl
56	4	SALI	7f Gd/Fm	57	1889	VIS
56	2	LEIC	7f Firm	50	2026	vis
36	7	LING	7f Good	56	2591	vis
0	15	EPSO	7f Good	56	2794	
32	11	KEMP	8f Gd/Fm	55	3078	vis
56	3	LEIC	7f Gd/Sft		3218	bl
44	7	CHEP	7f Good	52	3873	
25	15	YARM	8f Gd/Fm	52	3971	vis
20	10	NOTT	10f Heavy	48	4509	

CHIMES AT MIDNIGHT 3 b c £63750

104	3	CURR	10f Gd/Fm		3068	
106	3	CURR	14f Yldg		3721	BL
115	3	DONC	15f Firm		3898	bl
106	6	CURR	14f Good		4055	bl
110	2	CURR	11f Gd/Sft		4057	bl

CHIMNEY DUST 3 b c £0

| 77 | 14 | NEWM | 7f Gd/Fm | 85 | 1153 | |
| 75 | 8 | CATT | 7f Soft | 84 | 1680 | |

CHIN UP 3 b f £0

| 0 | 18 | BEVE | 5f Firm | | 1280 | |
| 43a | 7 | SOUT | 7f Aw | 60 | 1506 | |

CHINA CASTLE 7 b g £12976

91a	2	LING	12f Aw		27	
89a	5	WOLV	8f Aw	100	137	
80a	4	LING	10f Aw		157	
75a	7	LING	12f Aw	97	356	
89a	6	WOLV	8f Aw		448	
64a	6	LING	12f Aw	90	508	
90a	2	SOUT	11f Aw	85	605	
91a	1	**LING**	12f Aw	85	633*	

CHINA FAIN 2 b f £0

| 1 | 6 | CHEP | 6f Gd/Fm | | 2447 | |

CHINA RED 6 br g £2834

88	7	JAGE	9f Good		1323	
65	7	EPSO	9f Gd/Sft	86	1829	
61	10	GOOD	9f Good	84	2356	
68	9	GOOD	9f Good	80	3110	
77	1	**EPSO**	9f Gd/Fm		3404*	
71	12	DONC	7f Gd/Fm	78	3880	
56	10	MUSS	8f Gd/Fm	76	4136	
71	7	YORK	9f Heavy	74	4300	
66	6	NOTT	8f Heavy	72	4506	

CHINA VISIT 3 b c £182927

120a	1	**NAD**	9f Dirt		765*	
110a	6	CHUR	10f Dirt		1226	
107	10	ASCO	8f Good		2066	

CHINABERRY 6 b m £1044

11a	9	SOUT	7f Aw	44	299	
30a	4	SOUT	8f Aw	42	1303	
0a	11	SOUT	8f Aw	42	1419	
33	11	CATT	7f Soft	48	1680	
44	2	CARL	8f Firm	44	3192	
40	5	MUSS	8f Gd/Fm	45	3746	

CHINATOWN 3 br c £3255

| 98 | 5 | NEWM | 9f Gd/Sft | | 980 | |
| 102 | 3 | ASCO | 10f Good | | 2169 | |

CHIPPEWA 6 b m £0

| 25 | 9 | BRIG | 12f Soft | 48 | 4176 | t |

CHIQUITA 3 ch f £7370

78	5	NEWM	6f Gd/Sft	80	982	
78	11	NEWM	7f Gd/Fm	80	1153	
67	11	NEWB	6f Gd/Fm	78	1406	
63	8	SAND	7f Soft	76	1569	
79	2	LING	6f Firm	74	3280	
81	1	**RIPO**	6f Good	76	3698*	
0	14	KEMP	6f Gd/Sft	80	4037	
76	6	YARM	6f Heavy	80	4480	

CHISPA 2 b f £0

55	8	GOOD	5f Gd/Sft		1454	
0	15	LING	5f Gd/Fm		2214	
70	7	WIND	5f Gd/Fm		4288	
56a	5	WOLV	5f Aw		4441	

CHIST 5 br g £1176

| 89 | 4 | AYR | 11f Gd/Sft | | 4011 | |

CHOC ICE 2 b f £17675

| 94 | 3 | CHAN | 8f Good | | 3934 | |
| 107 | 3 | LONG | 8f Good | | 4260 | |

CHOCOLATE FOG 2 b f £0

50	9	YARM	6f Good		1774	
62	5	WARW	5f Gd/Fm		2034	
57	7	YARM	7f Firm		2390	
33	5	NOTT	6f Gd/Fm		3003	
22a	7	WOLV	7f Aw		3497	tVl

CHOCOLATE ICE 7 b g £0

| 0 | 13 | WARW | 13f Gd/Fm | 46 | 2843 | |

CHOCSTAW 3 b c £2566

69	7	NEWM	8f Gd/Fm		1692	
50	10	DONC	8f Gd/Fm		2611	
60	5	BATH	12f Gd/Fm		3517	
53	4	CATT	12f Soft	60	4256	
65a	1	**SOUT**	12f Aw		4366*	

CHOK DI 4 b g £219

49a	4	WOLV	6f Aw		273	
26a	7	SOUT	6f Aw	44	425	
36a	8	WOLV	5f Aw	44	445	
16	12	MUSS	9f Gd/Sft	38	795	
0	16	REDC	7f Gd/Sft		1132	
0	15	REDC	6f Firm		1298	BL
36	11	MUSS	6f Gd/Fm		1430	bl
14	11	REDC	6f Gd/Sft	33	1578	bl
14	10	NEWC	5f Heavy		1766	bl
0	15	HAMI	5f Gd/Fm	33	1910	bl

CHOOKIE HEITON 2 br g £1075

| 77 | 2 | HAMI | 5f Gd/Fm | | 2639 | |

CHORALLI 2 ch f £0

| 49 | 13 | WIND | 8f Gd/Sft | | 4289 | |
| 0 | 17 | NEWB | 6f Sft/Hvy | | 4471 | |

CHORUS 3 b f £10638

76	2	WARW	6f Heavy		888	
0	14	WIND	5f Gd/Sft	75	1098	
63	9	SALI	6f Firm	77	1178	
69	6	WIND	5f Gd/Fm	73	1427	
63	3	BATH	5f Gd/Fm		1670	
66	2	WIND	6f Gd/Fm	70	1877	
64a	3	SOUT	6f Aw		2299	
70	2	LEIC	5f Gd/Fm		2919	
73	1	**SAND**	5f Good		3229*	VIS
69	5	SALI	5f Firm	75	3747	vis
67	7	GOOD	5f Good	72	3908	vis
0	23	KEMP	6f Gd/Sft	70	4037	vis
72	1	**WIND**	5f Gd/Sft	67	4295*	
62	12	WIND	5f Heavy	72	4527	

CHORUS GIRL 2 ch f £888

52	5	THIR	5f Soft		928	
53	4	BEVE	5f Good		1443	
51	3	CATT	6f Soft		1679	
44	8	YORK	5f Gd/Fm		1981	
47	4	NEWC	6f Gd/Fm		2312	
47	6	BEVE	7f Gd/Fm		2513	
45	5	CATT	7f Gd/Fm		2927	
33	10	THIR	7f Gd/Fm		3128	
46	8	CATT	7f Good		3438	

CHOTO MATE 4 ch c £14711

0	W	WIND	6f Heavy		935	
78	10	GOOD	8f Gd/Sft	89	1450	
83	4	WIND	6f Good		1728	
91	1	**SAND**	7f Gd/Fm	86	1989*	
83	14	NEWM	8f Gd/Fm	90	2616	
88	7	KEMP	8f Firm	90	2870	
71	13	NEWM	7f Gd/Fm	89	3315	
75	8	HAYD	6f Heavy		3768	
76	12	NEWM	8f Good	86	4348	

CHRISMAS CAROL 4 b f £0

| 32a | 8 | LING | 7f Aw | 44 | 59 | |

CHRISS LITTLE LAD 3 ch c £536

67	2	BATH	8f Gd/Fm		1435	
49	7	BATH	8f Gd/Sft	63	1671	
57	7	SALI	8f Gd/Fm	65	2264	
0a	5	SOUT	8f Aw		2816	

CHRISTENSEN 4 ch f £0

| 0a | 11 | SOUT | 8f Aw | 49 | 604 | |
| 29 | 9 | MUSS | 5f Gd/Sft | 49 | 901 | |

CHRISTIANSTED 5 ch g £6347

71	6	DONC	12f Good		732	
82	1	**MUSS**	16f Firm	78	1686*	
80	7	NEWC	16f Gd/Fm	82	2336	
81	5	SAND	16f Gd/Fm	81	2498	

68 7 GOOD 20f Gd/Fm 81 3085
70 11 NEWM 18f Good 79 4353

CHRISTMAS MORNING 2 b g £0
50 7 YORK 6f Gd/Fm 1981
55 9 PONT 5f Good 2361
0 12 BEVE 5f Firm 2730
48 9 CATT 7f Soft 56 4007
0 16 PONT 8f Soft 54 4378 BL

CHRISTOPHERSSISTER 3 br f £3019
64a 2 SOUT 5f Aw 34
51a 7 SOUT 5f Aw 179
65a 1 **SOUT** 6f Aw 426*
42a 7 WOLV 6f Aw 68 479
0 14 NOTT 6f Aw 67 785
0a 13 SOUT 6f Aw 2118
62 4 CARL 5f Firm 64 2280
44 10 NEWC 6f Good 62 2525
26a 13 SOUT 5f Aw 55 2632 BL
43 13 CARL 7f Firm 60 2823
30 12 RIPO 6f Gd/Fm 55 3010
42 6 CARL 5f Aw 53 3194
39 7 AYR 5f Heavy 47 4307 t

CHRYSOLITE 5 ch g £0
0 11 PONT 10f Soft 1699 tbl
38 10 SAND 10f Soft 44 4208

CHURCH BELLE 2 gr f £809
62 8 WIND 5f Gd/Fm 1197
65 2 BRIG 5f Gd/Sft 1463
53 7 LING 6f Good 1673
41 8 KEMP 6f Gd/Fm 62 3075
62 6 DONC 7f Good 61 3860
51 6 YARM 7f Firm 58 3922
0 18 NEWM 7f Good 71 4157 t

CHURCH FARM FLYER 3 b f £9061
31a 6 SOUT 8f Aw 36
48a 3 SOUT 8f Aw 88
57a 1 **LING** 8f Aw 150*
62a 1 **WOLV** 8f Aw 52 188*
66a 2 WOLV 7f Aw 60 294
53a 3 LING 8f Aw 65 401
59a 6 WOLV 8f Aw 65 534
62a 3 WOLV 8f Aw 62 613
62a 2 WOLV 9f Aw 62 625
56 4 SOUT 10f Good 58 807

CHURCH MICE 2 br f £10539
69 2 WARW 5f Soft 1059
60 4 NOTT 5f Aw 1267
71a 2 SOUT 5f Aw 1418 VIS
75 1 **LEIC** 5f Soft 1550* vis
73 5 LING 6f Good 74 2589 vis
75a 3 SOUT 6f Aw 76 2948 vis
71 6 GOOD 7f Firm 73 3149 vis
66a 4 WOLV 7f Aw 73 3273 vis
75 1 **HAYD** 6f Soft 70 4090* vis
75 3 LING 6f Soft 75 4269 vis
79 2 DONC 7f Heavy 76 4577 vis

CHURCHILLS SHADOW 6 b g £263
42a 3 WOLV 7f Aw 49 187
46a 5 LING 8f Aw 316
24a 11 LING 8f Aw 48 336
0a 12 LING 8f Aw 45 776
28 14 LEIC 8f Gd/Fm 53 3334

CHURLISH CHARM 5 b g £48155
104 7 NEWM 12f Gd/Fm 1152
113 3 YORK 14f Firm 1339
118 2 SAND 16f Soft 1565
107 3 CURR 14f Yldg 2405
111 6 GOOD 16f Good 3106
111 1 **SALI** 14f Firm 3751*
113 2 DONC 18f Good 3877
118 4 LONG 20f Good 4264
90 6 NEWM 16f Good 4351

CIBENZE 3 b f £2739
49 10 NOTT 6f Gd/Sft 68 1082
57 6 WIND 6f Firm 65 1289
69 4 NEWB 7f Gd/Fm 65 1405
69 2 NEWB 7f Gd/Fm 65 1787
59 6 SALI 7f Gd/Fm 65 1889
54 7 BRIG 7f Firm 67 2044
67 2 HAYD 8f Gd/Fm 66 2699
51 6 EPSO 9f Good 66 2795
63 8 LEIC 8f Gd/Fm 66 2918
53 8 NEWM 7f Gd/Fm 65 3460

CICATRIX 6 ch g £0
6a 6 SOUT 8f Aw 366

CIEL DE REVE 6 b g £0
0a 16 SOUT 8f Aw 55 85
0a 16 WIND 6f Aw 45 568 VIS
0 21 WIND 10f Gd/Sft 42 1100
0 11 CATT 12f Gd/Fm 3202 tBL

CIELITO LINDO 2 b f £1735
89 2 NEWM 6f Gd/Fm 4209
75 7 NEWB 7f Sft/Hvy 4467

CINCINNATI 2 ch c £0
0 14 NOTT 6f Good 3520

CINDER HILLS 5 ch m £878
62 2 NEWC 16f Soft 60 760

CINDESTI 4 b c £0
50 7 SOUT 16f Gd/Sft 56 860
44 9 DONC 17f Gd/Sft 56 1052
32 14 NOTT 14f Gd/Sft 53 1087
0 14 NOTT 14f Good 49 1411 BL
23 10 GOOD 16f Soft 43 4075
26a 10 WOLV 12f Aw 55 4245 bl

CINEMA POINT 3 b g £545
19a 8 LING 10f Aw 42 315
38a 2 SOUT 8f Aw 38 429
0 16 BEVE 10f Firm 1274
49a 4 SOUT 11f Aw 1502
0 14 BRIG 8f Firm 2040 BL

CINNAMON COURT 3 b f £3965
76 1 **LEIC** 7f Good 794*
70 11 NEWM 7f Good 78 954
0 20 NEWB 7f Gd/Fm 76 1405
0 16 WIND 8f Good 74 1726
48 10 BATH 8f Firm 70 2330
0 11 LEIC 7f Gd/Fm 2508

CIRCLE OF LIGHT 3 b f £11224
94 3 ASCO 8f Gd/Sft 1108
100 2 NEWB 10f Good 1374
100 3 NEWB 10f Gd/Fm 1945
96 3 SAND 8f Good 2476
0 8 NEWB 12f Gd/Fm 3177
96 4 BATH 8f Gd/Fm 3515
89 7 EPSO 7f Good 3763

CIRCLE OF WOLVES 2 ch c £0
66 9 KEMP 6f Gd/Fm 1924
63 10 LING 7f Gd/Fm 2182

CIRCLET 2 ch f £0
41 9 WIND 6f Good 3187

CIRCUIT LIFE 2 ch g £2922
69 8 DONC 5f Gd/Sft 1067
52a 5 SOUT 5f Aw 1503
60 3 RIPO 6f Good 1859
47 9 RIPO 6f Gd/Fm 2106
54 6 PONT 5f Gd/Fm 63 2557
59 6 REDC 7f Good 2862
51 6 REDC 7f Gd/Fm 58 2991 BL
57 2 LEIC 6f Gd/Fm 55 3216
54 3 RIPO 6f Good 3697
51 4 BEVE 7f Good 55 3950
48 3 MUSS 8f Gd/Sft 54 4132
55 3 AYR 8f Heavy 56 4323

CIRCUS DANCE 3 b c £48031

113 3 CHAN 12f V 1752

CIRCUS PARADE 3 b c £610
58 5 GOOD 9f Gd/Fm 2129
52 9 BATH 10f Gd/Sft 2553
83 3 WIND 10f Gd/Fm 2889
70 6 REDC 11f Firm 79 3329
59a 5 LING 10f Aw 4100 t

CIRO 3 ch c £279536
112 3 LONG 11f V 864
116 1 **LONG** 11f V 1317*
111 6 CHAN 12f V 1752
116 3 CURR 12f Good 2409
119 1 **ARLI** 10f Yldg 3549*

CIROS PEARL 6 b m £0
22 8 CHEP 18f Gd/Fm 36 2452

CITRUS 2 b f £0
45 11 THIR 5f Soft 928
41a 4 SOUT 6f Aw 1420
26 7 REDC 7f Gd/Fm 2155

CITRUS MAGIC 3 b c £1078
69 4 LING 9f Firm 1912
64 8 SAND 10f Good 2531
69 7 WIND 10f Gd/Fm 2889
61 7 SALI 12f Gd/Fm 65 3290
62a 2 LING 13f AW 4193
58a 3 LING 16f Aw 60 4329

CITY BANK DUDLEY 3 b g £623
0 13 BEVE 7f Good 1444
36 3 REDC 6f Gd/Fm 2154
41 6 CARL 6f Firm 2278
54 4 BEVE 10f Good 2884
34 6 THIR 8f Gd/Fm 45 2964
39 4 CARL 8f Gd/Fm 45 3082
46 7 BEVE 8f Good 3393
43 7 BEVE 7f Gd/Fm 3671
28 5 NEWC 8f Heavy 44 4406
7a 10 WOLV 8f Aw 44 4437
32 8 REDC 10f Soft 4501

CITY FLYER 3 br c £3029
62a 5 WOLV 9f Aw 610
0 16 DONC 10f Gd/Fm 62 701
44 11 BEVE 10f Good 59 1448 t
0 13 NEWC 8f Gd/Sft 55 2524
41 6 BEVE 7f Aw 2731 t
0 16 BEVE 7f Good 50 2882 t
54 1 **CARL** 8f Gd/Fm 45 3082*
40 12 CATT 7f Gd/Fm 51 3200
0 12 HAYD 8f Good 51 3288
47 9 LEIC 8f Gd/Sft 4032 VIS

CITY GAMBLER 6 b m £2925
47 5 NOTT 10f Gd/Sft 50 1364
41 10 BRIG 10f Gd/Fm 48 2727
43 7 WIND 8f Gd/Fm 48 2890
51 1 **YARM** 10f Good 46 3031+
31 9 WIND 12f Good 51 3186
2 9 LEIC 10f Gd/Fm 53 3337

CITY GUILD 4 b g £0
36 11 LEIC 10f Soft 56 1546
0 19 WARW 11f Gd/Fm 50 2033
0 17 WARW 11f Good 44 2463

CITY OF LONDON 2 ch c £0
56 6 NOTT 6f Soft 3974

CITY PLAYER 2 ch c £0
0 14 NEWB 6f Sft/Hvy 4471
43a 8 WOLV 6f Aw 4548

CITY PRINCESS 3 b f £0
0a 15 SOUT 7f Aw 61 31

CITY PURSUIT 4 b g £0
0 19 WARW 11f Heavy 56 890
0 18 NOTT 10f Gd/Fm 56 1272
0a P WOLV 12f Aw 1389

CITY REACH 4 b c £11594

CITY STANDARD continued

54a	3	LING	7f Aw		8	
57a	2	WOLV	7f Aw	54	187	
35a	4	WOLV	7f Aw		293	
61a	1	**SOUT**	7f Aw		367*	VIS
54a	3	SOUT	7f Aw	60	471	vis
14	15	LING	7f Soft	62	1542	vis
44a	5	SOUT	6f Aw		2118	vis
54	1	**BRIG**	5f Firm		2905*	vis
34	13	BRIG	6f Gd/Fm	59	3243	vis
52	3	BRIG	5f Firm		3562	vis
53a	3	WOLV	6f Aw	56	4023	vis
68a	1	**WOLV**	6f Aw	56	4223*	vis
70a	1	**WOLV**	6f Aw	64	4358+	vis

CITY STANDARD 4 b c £0

| 31 | 13 | KEMP | 14f Good | 74 | 726 | |
| 0a | 8 | SOUT | 14f Aw | 70 | 868 | |

CIVIL LIBERTY 7 b g £547

65a	4	SOUT	8f Aw	65	251	t
60a	5	WOLV	9f Aw	65	309	t
0a	P	SOUT	11f Aw	64	474	t

CLADANTOM 4 b f £0

1a	12	WOLV	8f Aw		138	
39a	6	LING	7f Aw		156	
16a	10	SOUT	7f Aw		341	
0	15	CATT	7f Gd/Fm	58	780	
18	11	MUSS	7f Gd/Fm	52	1149	
0	16	THIR	7f Gd/Sft		1351	
0	14	REDC	7f Gd/Sft		1559	BL

CLAIM GEBAL CLAIM 4 b c £4196

21	11	MUSS	8f Gd/Sft	38	2533	
33	8	HAMI	9f Gd/Fm		2642	
39	1	**HAMI**	9f Gd/Fm		2780*	
42	6	AYR	11f Firm		2875	
31	7	AYR	9f Gd/Fm	39	3141	
38	3	HAMI	9f Gd/Sft		3375	
42	2	HAMI	8f Gd/Sft		3534	
39	3	MUSS	8f Gd/Fm	38	3746	
33	4	HAMI	9f Gd/Sft		3823	

CLAN CHIEF 7 b g £797

0	13	LING	5f Gd/Fm	65	2184	
61	2	FOLK	5f Good	60	2623	
44	8	LING	6f Firm	60	2761	
36	9	NEWB	6f Firm	60	3455	
57	5	WIND	5f Gd/Sft	58	4295	
0	22	NEWB	5f Gd/Sft	58	4459	

CLANBROAD 2 ch c £6844

60	4	BATH	6f Firm		2328	
80	1	**LEIC**	6f Gd/Fm		3215*	
78	4	BATH	6f Firm		3620	
58	14	DONC	7f Aw	76	3901	
78	1	**LING**	6f Soft		4190*	

CLANSINGE 2 ch f £4921

56	5	HAMI	5f Firm		1240	
57	3	HAYD	5f Soft		1492	
69	1	**BEVE**	5f Firm		1918*	
65	3	CHES	5f Good	70	2665	
58	4	AYR	6f Firm	68	2874	
44	9	HAYD	5f Gd/Sft	67	3264	
45	10	BEVE	5f Good	67	3394	
59	6	BEVE	5f Gd/Fm	62	3673	
50	7	HAMI	5f Soft	59	3802	
59	2	LING	5f Good		4097	
58	3	LING	6f Soft		4190	BL
44a	6	WOLV	6f Aw		4244	bl
0a	15	SOUT	6f Aw	62	4367	bl

CLANSMAN 3 ch g £0

0	13	WIND	5f Gd/Sft	65	1427	
49	9	CHEP	5f Gd/Sft	60	1795	
0	13	BATH	6f Firm	56	1994	
42	7	DONC	5f Gd/Fm	51	3161	
0	15	WARW	5f Good		3694	BL
26	10	PONT	6f Soft		4233	

| 11 | 9 | LEIC | 10f Heavy | | 4313 | |

CLARA BLUE 4 gr f £0

27a	9	LING	5f Aw	42	57	
0a	10	LING	7f Aw	37	504	
15	6	FOLK	6f Gd/Fm		2291	
0	11	WIND	5f Good	39	2716	
0	13	SAND	5f Gd/Fm		3947	

CLARANET 3 ch f £16905

81a	3	WOLV	9f Aw		662	
77	3	DONC	8f Gd/Fm		704	
75	1	**WIND**	8f Heavy		934*	
102	11	NEWM	8f Firm		1185	
13	14	NEWB	10f Good		1374	
51	9	EPSO	7f Gd/Sft		1830	
104	2	GOOD	7f Good		3104	
91	5	ASCO	6f Gd/Fm	95	3301	
99	4	SAND	8f Good		3469	
95	6	GOOD	7f Soft		4078	

CLARENDON 4 ch c £4725

78	7	NEWM	12f Gd/Sft	77	968	
71	9	KEMP	12f Gd/Sft	77	1076	
71	6	NEWB	13f Gd/Fm	77	1784	
81	2	CHEP	10f Good	77	1973	
79	3	SALI	10f Gd/Fm	80	2270	
77	3	SAND	10f Gd/Fm	80	2937	
65	9	DONC	10f Gd/Fm	79	3159	
79	3	YORK	12f Gd/Fm	77	3725	
53	14	NEWB	13f Firm	77	3994	

CLARINCH CLAYMORE 4 b g £5759

36a	7	SOUT	11f Aw	52	131	
51a	2	SOUT	11f Aw	48	324	
50a	3	SOUT	12f Aw	48	413	
40a	8	SOUT	16f Aw	50	470	
0	16	LEIC	10f Firm	52	3842	
48	4	AYR	11f Soft	52	3963	
51	2	PONT	12f Soft	49	4229	
56	5	**MUSS**	12f Soft	51	4560*	

CLARION 2 ch c £18746

74a	2	SOUT	5f Aw		2818	
85	1	**YARM**	5f Firm		2901*	
85	2	SAND	5f Good	81	3228	
86	1	**SAND**	5f Good	81	3431*	
85	3	BEVE	5f Gd/Fm	85	3673	
88a	1	**WOLV**	6f Aw		4246*	
92a	1	**SOUT**	5f Aw	85	4367*	
90	1	**LING**	5f Soft		4485*	

CLASSIC COLOURS 7 ch g £0

9	9	WARW	11f Heavy		1523	t
27	7	NOTT	10f Good	34	2007	
21	8	CHEP	12f Gd/Fm	36	2656	
0	13	NOTT	14f Gd/Fm	31	3002	

CLASSIC CONKERS 6 b g £3890

13	7	SALI	12f Gd/Fm	34	1888	
42	1	**WARW**	12f Good	41	2466*	
14	5	DONC	17f Gd/Fm	38	2607	
35	11	SALI	12f Good	43	2689	
43	2	WIND	12f Good	38	3186	
38	4	CHES	12f Gd/Fm	43	3430	
32	9	GOOD	12f Good	43	3887	

CLASSIC DEFENCE 7 b g £688

46	3	LEIC	12f Gd/Fm		2776	
30	7	CATT	12f Good		3202	
43	3	CHEP	12f Gd/Fm		3681	
40	5	WARW	11f Gd/Fm	41	3915	

CLASSIC EAGLE 7 b g £221

43	8	NOTT	10f Gd/Fm	56	1272	
0	14	YARM	11f Gd/Sft	55	1614	
0	12	FOLK	16f Good	50	2622	
29	10	NEWM	8f Gd/Fm	50	2802	
29	5	PONT	10f Gd/Fm	42	3220	
41	4	BEVE	8f Gd/Fm	42	3407	VIS
33	10	GOOD	9f Good	47	3644	vis

0	14	BRIG	10f Firm	40	3737	vis
33a	5	SOUT	16f Aw	39	4149	
0a	11	SOUT	14f Aw	40	4370	

CLASSIC LORD 3 b c £1438

55	8	MUSS	8f Gd/Sft	59	800	
35	12	BATH	10f Good	57	1094	
28	12	BEVE	12f Good	54	1446	bl
50	3	HAMI	8f Gd/Fm	49	1907	
0	U	HAMI	9f Firm	49	2094	
51	2	REDC	10f Gd/Sft	50	2160	
28	9	CARL	8f Firm	50	2281	

CLASSIC MILLENNIUM 2 b f £0

66	9	SAND	5f Gd/Fm		2526	
56	9	KEMP	5f Gd/Fm		2748	
0	13	LING	8f Firm		3577	
44	10	YARM	7f Firm	59	3922	
8	11	PONT	5f Soft	55	4378	

CLASSIC REFERENDUM 6 ch g £0

0a	12	WOLV	16f Aw	57	66	
0a	11	WOLV	16f Aw	50	190	
0	13	NOTT	14f Good	57	788	
0	11	FOLK	15f Soft	52	963	
19	14	BRIG	12f Gd/Fm	47	1128	bl

CLASSY ACT 2 ch f £9760

69	2	REDC	6f Gd/Sft		1577	
68	3	HAMI	6f Gd/Fm		1633	
0	17	YORK	8f Good		2692	
75	1	**HAMI**	6f Gd/Sft	69	3824*	
71	6	**CATT**	7f Soft	73	4007	
78	1	**CATT**	7f Soft	73	4254*	
0	15	DONC	7f Heavy	77	4577	

CLASSY CLEO 5 b m £14469

93a	3	WOLV	5f Aw	93	64	
97a	2	LING	6f Aw	93	223	
95a	4	WOLV	6f Aw	95	320	
77a	2	LING	6f Aw		376	
95a	3	WOLV	5f Aw	94	394	
88a	9	LING	7f Aw	93	423	
86a	7	WOLV	6f Aw	93	435	
87a	9	WOLV	6f Aw	93	532	
0	16	DONC	6f Good	86	716	
78	7	CHES	5f Firm	85	1245	
59	14	GOOD	6f Gd/Sft	83	1471	
75	4	CHES	5f Gd/Sft	80	1781	
73	6	BATH	5f Firm	78	1999	
66	4	WARW	6f Gd/Fm		2035	
57	12	CHES	5f Gd/Fm	76	2247	
0	18	THIR	6f Gd/Fm	73	3123	
74	1	**CHES**	5f Gd/Fm	69	3512*	
61	8	BEVE	5f Gd/Fm	74	3653	
62	11	BATH	5f Gd/Fm	74	3821	
0	3	CHES	5f Soft	74	4073	
0	17	YORK	5f Soft		4287	
60	4	PONT	5f Soft	74	4377	
0	13	NOTT	6f Heavy	74	4411	
67	5	DONC	5f Heavy	72	4570	

CLASSY IRISH 3 ch c £1417

79	6	NEWM	8f Gd/Fm		1692	
79	2	SALI	10f Gd/Fm		2265	
68	4	PONT	10f Gd/Fm		2558	
71	6	NOTT	8f Soft		3977	

CLAUDIUS TERTIUS 3 b c £1103

0a	16	SOUT	8f Aw	49	1205	
43	9	YARM	10f Gd/Sft	47	1615	
24	9	BEVE	12f Gd/Sft	47	1758	
43a	3	WOLV	9f Aw	41	2080	
56	4	NEWM	8f Gd/Fm		2345	
45	2	YARM	8f Gd/Fm		2411	
15	12	CARL	8f Gd/Fm	46	3082	
0	26	YORK	9f Good		3808	

CLAXON 4 b f £106858

| 105 | 2 | NEWC | 10f Firm | | 2339 | |

104	1	NEWB	10f Firm		2851*
107	1	CAPA	10f Heavy		4396*

CLEAR AMBITION 2 ch g £0
79	7	NEWB	7f Gd/Fm		3484
78	8	KEMP	8f Gd/Fm		3799
71	9	WARW	7f Good		3909
0	15	YORK	8f Soft		4281

CLEAR CRYSTAL 3 b f £0
41	6	THIR	7f Soft		930	
0	15	BRIG	6f Firm	62	1211	VIS
24a	7	SOUT	8f Aw	58	1803	
47	6	WARW	7f Gd/Fm	52	2036	
41	6	NEWB	10f Firm	51	2811	t
25	7	FOLK	7f Good	50	3043	
42	6	YARM	7f Gd/Fm	47	3666	
42	6	HAMI	6f Soft	50	3803	
31	10	YARM	7f Firm	46	3939	

CLEAR MOON 3 b c £0
45	5	THIR	7f Soft		929	
29	8	AYR	9f Gd/Fm		1632	
48	5	CATT	7f Gd/Sft		1818	
38	5	CATT	7f Gd/Fm	49	2438	
24	8	HAMI	6f Gd/Fm	46	2779	BL
0	12	MUSS	7f Good	42	3103	bl
0	R	AYR	6f Good		3366	bl
0	R	MUSS	7f Gd/Fm	45	3593	bl
0	20	AYR	5f Heavy	41	4307	

CLEAR NIGHT 4 b c £1780
0a	12	WOLV	8f Aw	55	38	
53a	2	SOUT	8f Aw	48	83	
45a	4	SOUT	8f Aw	52	496	
55a	2	WOLV	7f Aw	50	583	
57a	2	SOUT	8f Aw	53	648	t

CLEAR PROSPECT 3 b c £0
0	15	YORK	10f Gd/Fm	84	1310
48	7	NEWC	10f Gd/Sft		1480
68	4	PONT	10f Firm	75	2175
0	10	HAYD	12f Gd/Sft	72	3270
63	4	NEWC	12f Firm	66	3606
0	17	DONC	10f Gd/Sft	63	4448

CLEARING 2 b c £26985
87	2	SALI	7f Gd/Fm		2269
93	2	CHEP	7f Good		3866
89	1	CHES	7f Soft		4068*
110	1	NEWB	7f Gd/Sft		4455*

CLEF OF SILVER 5 b g £0
75	8	WIND	6f Good	80	2371
62	9	KEMP	6f Firm		2869

CLEPSYDRA 3 b f £6957
77	2	DONC	10f Gd/Sft		1051	
81	2	HAYD	12f Soft		1493	
73	3	PONT	12f Firm		2179	
53	5	CHEP	10f Gd/Fm	74	2493	
80	1	EPSO	12f Gd/Fm		3416*	
56	11	GOOD	10f Soft	78	4067	BL

CLEVER GIRL 3 b f £3499
82	4	RIPO	9f Soft		823	
68	12	YORK	8f Firm	86	1341	
89	D	NOTT	8f Soft	83	1645	
77	8	HAYD	8f Gd/Sft	88	1836	
79	9	HAYD	7f Gd/Fm	86	2456	
70	8	NEWM	8f Gd/Fm	86	2614	
77	4	RIPO	9f Gd/Fm	83	3182	
79	3	HAMI	9f Gd/Sft	80	3535	
68	9	HAYD	7f Soft	79	3785	BL
73	5	HAMI	8f Gd/Sft	79	3826	bl
0	13	HAYD	8f Soft	76	4094	
0	18	REDC	8f Gd/Fm	74	4217	
59	8	YORK	9f Heavy	70	4300	

CLICK ON 2 b c £0
83	6	NEWM	6f Good		4341

CLIFTON WOOD 5 b g £0
38	6	LING	9f Good	53	1395	
23	10	BATH	8f Firm	49	1998	
0	19	WARW	8f Good	43	2460	
0	19	CHEP	8f Gd/Fm	43	2658	

CLIMBING ROSE 2 b f £496
75	5	SALI	7f Firm		3748
80	3	LEIC	8f Sft/Hvy		4309

CLIPPER 3 b f £3080
101	3	NEWM	10f Firm		1184	
87	9	EPSO	12f Gd/Sft		1828	
82	8	ASCO	12f Good		2112	BL
94	8	YORK	12f Firm		3595	
94	8	DONC	15f Gd/Fm		3863	
62	8	ASCO	12f Gd/Sft		4130	

CLOCHE CALL 2 b f £0
64	6	DONC	7f Heavy		4567

CLOG DANCE 3 b f £8728
91	2	DONC	8f Gd/Fm		704
105	2	NEWM	10f Firm		1184
86	10	EPSO	12f Gd/Sft		1828
86	2	EPSO	10f Gd/Sft		2434

CLOHAMON 5 b g £0
28	6	HAMI	5f Gd/Fm	37	1910
20	8	MUSS	7f Good	34	3103
23	5	HAMI	8f Gd/Sft	31	3380
21	7	HAMI	8f Gd/Sft	30	3534

CLONOE 6 b g £3195
57a	2	LING	10f Aw		268	
30a	4	WOLV	9f Aw	36	306	
0a	11	WOLV	10f Aw	42	431	
40a	4	LING	8f Aw		505	
52a	1	LING	8f Aw		574*	
0a	11	LING	10f Aw	44	620	
26a	10	WOLV	7f Aw	51	754	
18	14	BATH	8f Firm	43	2331	t
38	5	KEMP	8f Gd/Fm	43	2752	t
41	3	YARM	7f Good	41	3030	
35	5	FOLK	7f Gd/Fm	41	3445	t
36	8	EPSO	7f Good	41	3765	t

CLOONDESH 2 b g £0
58	5	RIPO	5f Good		1595
56	10	CARL	5f Firm		2277
38	7	CATT	5f Soft		4252
36	8	REDC	6f Gd/Sft	54	4502

CLOPTON GREEN 3 b g £1767
54a	3	SOUT	6f Aw		46	
25a	12	WOLV	5f Aw		118	
41a	6	WOLV	5f Aw		145	t
12a	11	SOUT	6f Aw	48	331	
44a	3	LING	5f Aw		487	BL
45a	3	LING	5f Aw	45	526	bl
49a	3	LING	5f Aw		619	bl
47a	5	LING	5f Aw	58	652	bl
49a	2	SOUT	5f Aw		696	bl
52	7	NEWM	5f Good	55	4185	
42	8	AYR	5f Heavy	52	4307	

CLOTH OF GOLD 3 b c £0
77	8	KEMP	11f Soft		1017

CLOTTED CREAM 3 grf £7071
70	3	LING	7f Gd/Sft		1261
78	1	PONT	6f Good		1500*
81	2	PONT	6f Good	75	2364
75	3	GOOD	7f Soft	77	4080
71	7	YARM	7f Soft	77	4513

CLOUD HOPPING 3 ch c £4329
80	6	NEWM	10f Gd/Fm		2617
84	1	SAND	10f Gd/Fm		2924*
66	16	NEWM	10f Good		4197

CLOUD INSPECTOR 9 b g £433
31a	2	LING	13f Aw	30	460
19a	4	WOLV	16f Aw	30	492
15a	6	SOUT	16f Aw	30	542

CLOUDY 2 b f £0
81	5	NEWM	6f Gd/Fm		2598
65	6	ASCO	6f Gd/Fm		2952
78	7	NEWM	7f Good		3607

CO DOT UK 2 b g £7034
73	5	HAMI	5f Good		843	
81	3	THIR	5f Good		1161	
62	10	YORK	6f Firm		1328	
77	1	SOUT	6f Soft		1602*	
69	3	MUSS	7f Gd/Fm		2201	
73	4	PONT	7f Good		2363	
68	5	BEVE	7f Gd/Fm		2514	
24	11	NEWC	8f Gd/Sft	73	3704	
63	2	AYR	8f Soft		3957	
40a	10	SOUT	7f Aw		4154	
60a	2	SOUT	7f Aw		4369	BL
65	3	REDC	8f Gd/Sft	65	4502	bl
55a	6	WOLV	8f Aw	60	4552	bl

COASTAL BLUFF 8 gr g £9877
78	5	LING	5f Gd/Sft	79	1264
61	7	DONC	6f Good		1517
79	2	LING	6f Good	77	1676
83	1	NOTT	5f Good	78	1871*
69	12	NEWC	5f Gd/Fm	82	2310
106	2	NEWM	5f Gd/Fm		2960
0	25	GOOD	6f Firm	81	3152
99	4	NOTT	5f Good		3521
71	14	EPSO	5f Good	87	3687
91	4	LEIC	5f Firm		3841
91	4	NEWM	5f Gd/Fm	89	4015
99	7	NEWM	5f Good		4182
85	10	NEWM	5f Gd/Fm	92	4339

COASTGUARDS HERO 7 ch g £531
43a	2	LING	16f Aw		402
0a	9	LING	13f Aw	39	458

COBOURG LODGE 4 b c £29000
114	2	CORK	7f Soft		4266
109	1	CURR	6f Soft		4398*

COCCOLONA 2 b f £231
65	4	AYR	6f Good		2137
39	14	LING	7f Good		2653
68	6	KEMP	7f Soft		4034
54	11	LING	6f Soft	68	4269

COCHITI 6 b m £0
0a	14	LING	16f Aw	37	285	t
5a	5	SOUT	13f Aw	23	339	t
6a	5	WOLV	15f Aw		468	t
13a	8	WOLV	12f Aw		581	tbl

COCO 3 ch f £7026
90	1	NOTT	8f Gd/Fm		1268*
98	4	LEIC	7f Gd/Sft		1733
103	3	ASCO	8f Good	95	2167
99	7	GOOD	7f Good		3104

COCO DE MER 3 ch c £0
0	23	THIR	5f Soft	89	926
66	8	SAND	5f Heavy	85	1047
59	10	THIR	5f Good	80	1384
44	9	CHES	6f Good	75	2663
37	10	BEVE	5f Gd/Sft		3056
0	17	PONT	5f Good	64	3502
51	14	THIR	5f Gd/Fm	64	3619

COCO GIRL 4 ch f £630
38a	4	LING	13f Aw	52	219
41a	2	LING	13f Aw		483
2a	8	LING	16f Aw	42	649
0a	7	LING	13f Aw		2323

COCO LOCO 3 b f £15037
58	6	WARW	8f Heavy		884
74	7	SAND	10f Heavy		1045
50	11	REDC	10f Firm	65	1299
54	6	NOTT	10f Good	60	2007
50	5	WARW	12f Gd/Fm	56	2255

CODICIL (continued)

46	10	NEWM	12f Gd/Fm	53	3167
53	2	CATT	16f Good	48	3442
60	1	**CATT**	16f Soft	52	4006*
68	1	**YARM**	14f Heavy	61	4476*
85	1	**DONC**	17f Heavy	72	4579*

CODICIL 4 ch f £3307

22	11	PONT	8f Gd/Sft	52	1101
0	14	PONT	10f Good	48	1496
32	3	PONT	10f Soft		1699
30	4	RIPO	8f Good		1858
39	1	**AYR**	7f Gd/Fm	36	3138*
28	11	THIR	8f Gd/Fm	39	3344
35	12	YARM	7f Firm		3921

COEUR DE LA MER 3 b f £1045

83	3	PONT	10f Soft	1703

COHIBA 7 b g £0

39a	6	WOLV	12f Aw	42	260	BL
1a	7	WOLV	12f Aw	38	408	bl
0	15	NOTT	14f Gd/Sft	42	1087	

COIS CUAIN 3 b f £1800

86	3	THE	7f Soft	770
100	4	LEOP	8f Gd/Fm	1315

COL WOODY 4 ch g £348

3a	8	WOLV	12f Aw		710	
39	7	FOLK	10f Soft	60	965	bl
44	3	WARW	11f Heavy		1523	

COLD CLIMATE 5 b g £557

60	5	EPSO	6f Heavy	60	1028	
49	15	WIND	6f Gd/Fm	60	1196	
47	10	GOOD	7f Gd/Sft	59	1483	
53	9	KEMP	7f Firm	57	2261	
56	4	EPSO	7f Gd/Sft	57	2431	
38	8	EPSO	8f Gd/Sft	55	2631	vis
48	5	NEWM	6f Firm	55	3297	vis

COLD ENCOUNTER 5 ch g £0

21	14	CHEP	10f Gd/Fm	60	3683	
0	15	GOOD	12f Good	60	3887	vis

COLERIDGE 12 gr g £0

2a	9	SOUT	16f Aw	46	502	bl
32a	8	WOLV	16f Aw	42	577	bl
10a	10	SOUT	16f Aw	35	644	bl

COLETTE 3 b f £0

62	8	SAND	10f Soft	4205
64	6	BATH	12f Soft	4434

COLEY 3 ch f £259

51a	3	LING	6f Aw	51	443	BL
29a	5	SOUT	6f Aw	51	515	bl
47a	6	LING	7f Aw	51	654	bl
40	9	LING	7f Gd/Sft		841	
33a	7	LING	8f Aw		4272	

COLIN COOK 2 b c £0

21	12	CATT	6f Soft	4001

COLLARD 2 ch f £0

66	6	DONC	7f Gd/Sft	4447

COLLECTIVITY 2 b f £0

75	12	NEWM	7f Good	4183
63	10	DONC	6f Heavy	4575

COLLEGE BLUE 4 b f £2957

51a	2	WOLV	6f Aw		273	
33a	8	LING	8f Aw		353	
21a	7	WOLV	7f Aw		396	
58a	1	LING	6f Aw		484*	
44a	13	LING	6f Aw	60	543	
36a	7	LING	6f Aw	58	628	
36a	5	LING	6f Aw		653	BL

COLLEGE DEAN 4 ch c £0

19	6	NEWC	6f Soft		756
49	7	HAMI	8f Good		847
27	8	HAMI	8f Gd/Fm		1191
14	7	HAMI	11f Soft	36	3805
10	9	AYR	9f Heavy		4324

COLLEGE FACT 2 b c £0

56	8	YARM	6f Good	1774

COLLEGE GALLERY 3 b c £0

37a	12	SOUT	5f Aw		34	
37a	9	LING	7f Aw		94	
0	17	SALI	6f Firm		1175	
0	18	NOTT	8f Gd/Sft	45	1365	
17a	9	SOUT	6f Aw		2299	BL

COLLEGE KING 4 b c £0

0	28	REDC	8f Gd/Fm	55	1300
0	13	REDC	9f Gd/Sft	52	1583

COLLEGE MAID 3 b f £24512

53	2	CATT	5f Gd/Fm	56	777
43	9	MUSS	5f Gd/Fm	56	1143
46	8	HAMI	5f Firm	56	1244
55	2	HAYD	6f Soft	53	1494
61	1	**RIPO**	6f Good	53	1600*
68	1	**CATT**	6f Good	59	1665*
67	2	CATT	5f Gd/Sft	62	1817
64	5	REDC	6f Good	65	1891
46	9	THIR	6f Gd/Fm	65	2060
67	1	**AYR**	5f Good	65	2165*
56	8	NEWC	5f Firm	69	2340
56	9	NEWC	5f Good	69	2525
58	5	CHES	6f Good	69	2663
48	8	RIPO	6f Gd/Fm	68	3010
57	12	CARL	5f Firm	67	3572
65	4	HAMI	6f Soft	67	3803
0	26	AYR	5f Soft	66	3960
54	12	AYR	6f Gd/Sft	67	4010
66	2	AYR	5f Heavy	64	4307
44	10	PONT	5f Soft	64	4377
70	1	**NEWC**	6f Heavy	64	4405*
55	10	DONC	5f Heavy	70	4570

COLLEGE PRINCESS 6 b m £0

28	4	BEVE	8f Heavy		973
33	7	NOTT	10f Gd/Sft	44	1086

COLLEGE QUEEN 2 b f £0

0	13	DONC	6f Heavy	4576

COLLEGE ROCK 3 ch c £7460

47a	10	LING	7f Aw	61	488	
48a	4	LING	10f Aw		545	
55	2	SOUT	10f Good		806	
48	6	BRIG	10f Gd/Sft	57	892	vis
54	3	BRIG	10f Firm		1210	vis
50	7	BRIG	10f Firm		1331	vis
43	6	LEIC	8f Gd/Sft		1572	BL
45	4	NOTT	8f Gd/Fm	48	2187	vis
57	1	**CHEP**	8f Gd/Fm		2448*	vis
44a	4	WOLV	9f Aw		2602	vis
55	6	BRIG	10f Firm	55	2908	vis
57	1	**LEIC**	8f Gd/Fm		3094*	vis
61	3	BRIG	8f Gd/Fm	61	3261	vis
48	7	KEMP	9f Gd/Fm	55	3357	vis
52	4	BRIG	10f Firm	59	3530	vis
66	2	LEIC	8f Gd/Sft		4032	vis
63	4	BRIG	8f Soft		4173	vis
63	3	NOTT	8f Heavy	63	4414	vis

COLLEGE STAR 2 b c £0

0	13	RIPO	6f Gd/Fm	3009
57	5	CATT	6f Soft	4001
19a	7	SOUT	8f Aw	4152

COLLIERS TREASURE 3 b f £0

0	13	BATH	10f Soft	4141

COLLINE DE FEU 3 ch f £306

64	12	WIND	10f Gd/Fm		1200
69	4	LEIC	12f Gd/Fm		1738
45	9	WARW	8f Gd/Fm		3914
39	7	YARM	14f Heavy	62	4476

COLLISION 3 ch f £0

54	6	SALI	7f Gd/Fm	2232
51	10	WIND	8f Soft	2548

COLLISION TIME 3 b f £0

42	12	CHEP	5f Gd/Sft	62	1795	
47	9	PONT	5f Good		1868	
27	11	CARL	6f Gd/Fm	52	2243	
46	8	MUSS	5f Firm	52	2374	vis
0	16	CARL	6f Firm	48	3194	vis

COLNE VALLEY AMY 3 b f £15189

50	2	BRIG	7f Firm	50	2044
56	1	**SALI**	8f Gd/Fm	50	2264*
66	1	**SALI**	8f Gd/Sft	58	2467*
50	4	LING	7f Good	55	2591
67	3	BRIG	8f Firm	64	2906
67	2	BRIG	10f Gd/Fm	65	3263
59	5	SALI	8f Gd/Fm	65	3422
71	1	**SAND**	8f Gd/Fm	67	3944*
55	10	SAND	8f Soft	71	4206
0	29	NEWM	8f Soft	71	4545

COLOMBE DOR 3 gr g £1927

47a	6	SOUT	8f Aw	59	213	
59a	2	WOLV	8f Aw	55	311	
59a	2	LING	10f Aw	58	461	
33a	6	SOUT	11f Aw		586	BL
30	11	RIPO	8f Good		1596	
42	7	CARL	17f Gd/Fm	54	2244	
42	7	PONT	10f Gd/Sft	51	2556	
43	3	BEVE	12f Gd/Sft	47	3050	
45a	4	SOUT	11f Aw		4151	

COLONEL CUSTER 5 ch g £3761

44a	5	LING	10f Aw		3	
0a	14	SOUT	11f Aw	58	131	
0a	14	SOUT	12f Aw	53	211	
50a	1	**WOLV**	12f Aw		231*	
46a	3	SOUT	12f Aw		344	
54a	1	**WOLV**	12f Aw	48	408*	VIS
17a	9	WOLV	12f Aw	55	489	vis
4a	11	WOLV	12f Aw	53	607	vis
37a	5	WOLV	12f Aw		710	BL
27	7	SOUT	11f Gd/Sft	42	855	
35a	6	WOLV	12f Aw		1039	
38a	5	SOUT	12f Aw		1203	bl
17	10	WARW	11f Gd/Sft	34	1707	bl
25a	4	SOUT	7f Aw	37	2122	
27	10	BATH	12f Firm		2785	vis
56a	6	WOLV	6f Aw		3275	vis
47a	10	WOLV	7f Aw		3770	vis
36	7	CHEP	8f Good		3868	
36a	7	SOUT	11f Aw		4151	

COLONEL KURTZ 2 b c £0

39	6	NOTT	6f Heavy	4410
0	19	DONC	6f Heavy	4575

COLONEL NORTH 4 b g £0

65a	6	LING	10f Aw	73	22
65a	4	LING	10f Aw	70	90
42a	7	LING	10f Aw		163
32a	8	LING	13f Aw	63	317
56	7	NOTT	10f Gd/Fm		1271
66	10	WIND	10f Firm		1288
56	6	WIND	8f Gd/Fm	69	2051
59	6	DONC	8f Gd/Fm	65	2349
43	5	YARM	8f Gd/Fm		2411
38a	5	LING	10f Aw		2764
55	4	BRIG	8f Firm	57	3527
51	5	BRIG	8f Firm		3736
50	7	GOOD	8f Good	56	3885
42a	6	WOLV	8f Aw	54	4363

COLONEL SAM 4 b c £636

17a	10	SOUT	6f Aw		558	
31a	8	WOLV	7f Aw	47	635	bl
18a	10	SOUT	5f Aw	43	673	tbl
0	18	NOTT	6f Aw	50	787	tbl
39	8	THIR	5f Gd/Sft	48	1357	tbl
43	5	NOTT	5f Good	45	1412	tbl

24	12	CARL	6f Firm	43	2015	tbl
0	15	BEVE	5f Firm	42	2223	tbl
40	4	DONC	6f Gd/Fm	42	2315	tbl
0	14	RIPO	8f Soft	40	2542	tbl
0	R	WARW	7f Gd/Fm	40	2840	tbl
36	3	THIR	6f Gd/Fm	40	3124	bl
0	18	HAYD	8f Good	40	3288	bl

COLONIAL RULE 3 b c £0
85	7	BATH	10f Good		1089
78	7	NEWB	12f Gd/Fm	90	1400
57	8	HAYD	12f Gd/Sft	86	1832
72	6	SALI	12f Gd/Sft	80	2470 BL
0	16	NEWM	14f Gd/Fm	75	4213

COLORFUL AMBITION 10 b g £0
37a	5	SOUT	16f Aw	327

COLOUR KEY 6 b g £0
0	13	KEMP	12f Firm	48	2872
0	18	WIND	12f Gd/Fm	42	3049

COLOUR SERGEANT 2 ch c £642
70	3	KEMP	5f Good	724

COLUMBINE 2 b f £5766
82	1	DONC	5f Gd/Fm	2756*
82	3	CHES	6f Gd/Fm	3425
69a	3	WOLV	5f Aw	4247

COLUMBUS 3 b c £0
63	7	HAYD	14f Gd/Fm	78	3323 bl
63	6	BEVE	16f Good	78	3395 bl

COLWAY RITZ 6 b g £14859
59	11	NEWC	10f Soft	75	757
77	3	BEVE	8f Firm	74	1279
72	6	REDC	10f Gd/Sft	76	1561
81	1	RIPO	10f Good	75	1860*
83	1	RIPO	10f Gd/Fm	78	2102*
86	2	REDC	10f Gd/Fm	84	2157
57	17	YORK	10f Good	83	2696
84	2	THIR	8f Gd/Fm	84	3147
82	4	BEVE	10f Gd/Fm	84	3410
82	5	RIPO	10f Gd/Fm	84	3713
79	8	DONC	10f Firm	83	3899
0	16	REDC	8f Gd/Sft	81	4217

COMANCHE QUEEN 3 ch f £0
0	17	NOTT	8f Gd/Sft	52	1085
0	10	HAMI	9f Gd/Fm		1195
0	11	BEVE	12f Gd/Sft	42	3050
2	12	CATT	14f Gd/Fm	46	3201
15	9	BEVE	10f Good	43	3396 BL

COMBINED VENTURE 4 b c £0
0a	10	WOLV	12f Aw	33	3494 t

COME ON MURGY 3 b f £3969
54a	1	WOLV	7f Aw		192*
53a	3	LING	8f Aw		236
55a	1	SOUT	7f Aw		283*
43a	4	SOUT	6f Aw		300
51a	4	SOUT	7f Aw		330
49a	4	WOLV	7f Aw	55	346
29a	7	WOLV	7f Aw	51	450
40a	5	SOUT	7f Aw		589 bl
42a	4	WOLV	6f Aw	48	706 bl
48a	3	SOUT	7f Aw		741

COME ON PEKAN 2 b c £2265
85	2	HAYD	7f Soft	3786
89	4	ASCO	7f Gd/Sft	4124

COMEONMOM 4 b c £5824
113ε	3	NAD	10f Dirt	655

COMEOUTOFTHEFOG 5 b g £3100
60a	2	LING	7f Aw	57	239
58a	5	LING	8f Aw	60	336
54a	7	LING	7f Aw		398
51a	1	WOLV	7f Aw		567*
34a	5	WOLV	8f Aw		612
31a	9	WOLV	7f Aw		677
45a	8	WOLV	7f Aw		3770

33a	6	WOLV	8f Aw	48	4437

COMEUPPANCE 2 b g £0
37	6	MUSS	7f Firm	2377
19	8	CARL	6f Gd/Fm	3079
57	6	THIR	7f Gd/Fm	3617

COMEX FLYER 3 ch g £2052
53	4	THIR	7f Soft		929
47	10	CARL	8f Firm	60	1255
45	6	MUSS	8f Gd/Fm	57	1434
44	7	REDC	11f Gd/Sft	57	1560
0	13	CARL	6f Gd/Sft		1723 BL
55	1	CATT	7f Gd/Sft		1818*
0	11	THIR	6f Gd/Fm	56	2060
46	8	BEVE	6f Firm	56	2733
34	9	CARL	6f Firm	54	3194

COMING UP ROSES 3 b f £0
0	11	THIR	6f Good	1354
0a	16	SOUT	8f Aw	1505

COMMANDER 4 b c £398
59	5	NOTT	8f Good		784
0	17	WIND	8f Gd/Fm	65	1201
60	3	BRIG	7f Soft		1467 t
11	14	KEMP	7f Firm	60	2261 tVI

COMMANDER COLLINS 4 b c £19455
108	4	SAND	10f Heavy	1057
111	3	NEWM	12f Good	2566
111	3	LONG	12f Good	3927
108	4	ASCO	12f Good	4109
100	5	BELM	12f Firm	4316

COMMON CAUSE 4 b f £854
73	4	NOTT	10f Gd/Fm		1271
76	4	NEWB	10f Gd/Fm	77	1785
58	5	SALI	12f Firm	75	2023
73	5	LEIC	12f Gd/Fm	75	2509
35	8	NEWM	15f Gd/Fm	73	2856

COMMON CONSENT 4 b f £6691
48	7	WIND	12f Good	54	1730
44	6	BRIG	10f Firm		2041
56	1	FOLK	10f Gd/Fm	52	2296*
37	10	KEMP	8f Gd/Fm	55	2752
56	4	WIND	8f Gd/Fm	55	2890
56	2	GOOD	9f Gd/Fm	55	3089
28	9	SALI	8f Good	56	3422
47	6	EPSO	9f Good	56	3685
46	11	GOOD	8f Good	56	3885
0	15	BRIG	10f Gd/Sft	54	4118

COMMON PLACE 3 b c £21275
70a	5	WOLV	8f Aw	79	495
75a	6	WOLV	9f Aw	79	625
88	1	KEMP	9f Good		727*
90	1	KEMP	9f Soft	85	999*
94	3	SALI	10f Firm	89	1177
94	2	HARD	11f Soft	90	1491
96	1	SAND	9f Gd/Fm	90	1990*
93	4	ASCO	10f Gd/Fm		3017

COMMONBIRD 3 b f £0
35	8	NOTT	6f Gd/Sft		1081
42	5	BRIG	7f Firm		1212
15	8	BRIG	7f Firm		1333
31	8	BRIG	5f Soft	40	2428

COMMONWOOD 3 b c £0
65	4	WIND	8f Good	63	1726
53	8	SALI	8f Firm	64	2025
40	13	LEIC	8f Gd/Fm	64	2506
47	7	LEIC	10f Gd/Fm	62	3217
28a	10	WOLV	8f Aw	58	3769
25a	6	WOLV	12f Aw	53	4026
27	11	BRIG	10f Soft	46	4174

COMO 2 b f £646
79	4	LING	7f Soft	4268
81	D	NEWM	7f Soft	4541

COMPANION 2 b f £274

70	4	LING	8f Firm	3577
75	6	HAYD	8f Soft	3766
70a	4	WOLV	8f Aw	4022

COMPATRIOT 4 b c £5182
67	2	NOTT	8f Good	64	1414
63	4	LEIC	8f Soft	66	1547
61	6	LEIC	8f Firm	65	2027
51	12	BEVE	7f Firm	64	2221
63	2	WIND	8f Soft	62	2546
52a	5	SOUT	8f Aw	62	2817
62	3	WIND	10f Gd/Fm	62	3045
57	6	WIND	12f Good	62	3353
62a	1	WOLV	8f Aw	57	3769*
32	11	LEIC	8f Gd/Sft		4032
54a	6	WOLV	8f Aw	62	4248
58a	4	LING	12f Aw	61	4486

COMPRADORE 5 b m £10664
50	8	WARW	8f Soft	62	817
60	3	NOTT	6f Gd/Sft	60	1082
64	2	BRIG	7f Firm	60	1213
68	1	SALI	7f Good	61	1348*
68	1	BRIG	7f Soft		1467*
53	11	NEWB	7f Gd/Sft	74	1590
67	3	LING	8f Gd/Fm		2215
56	12	YORK	7f Good	68	2694
57	10	GOOD	8f Gd/Fm	66	3063
65	3	NEWM	7f Gd/Fm	65	3460
57	8	KEMP	7f Gd/Fm	65	3796
65	3	BRIG	7f Gd/Sft	65	4121
53	7	NOTT	6f Heavy	66	4411

COMPTON ACE 4 ch c £25366
115	2	NEWB	10f Gd/Sft	1592 t
118	3	ASCO	20f Good	2114 t

COMPTON AMBER 4 b f £0
0a	12	SOUT	6f Aw	47	87
0a	11	WOLV	7f Aw	41	187

COMPTON ANGEL 4 b f £0
66a	5	LING	10f Aw	74	161

COMPTON ARROW 4 b f £898
0	24	DONC	8f Good	97	733
0	14	GOOD	8f Gd/Sft	92	1450 t
0	13	GOOD	7f Gd/Sft	88	1810 tBL
44	12	GOOD	8f Gd/Fm	84	2356 t
54	14	NEWB	7f Firm	79	3981 t
58	10	ASCO	8f Gd/Sft	75	4126 t
69a	5	LING	8f Aw	72	4330 t
73	3	NEWM	7f Soft	70	4547

COMPTON AVIATOR 4 ch c £1785
0	16	DONC	10f Firm	80	3899
79	7	NEWB	16f Firm	80	3986 t
38	14	ASCO	16f Good	78	4115 t
58a	1	LING	7f Aw		4328* t

COMPTON BANKER 3 br c £60154
60	11	LING	6f Gd/Sft		837
74	5	GOOD	6f Gd/Sft	80	1636
84	1	ASCO	5f Good	77	2168*
78	9	GOOD	6f Good	82	2355
89	2	ASCO	5f Gd/Fm	82	3016
79	4	GOOD	6f Gd/Fm	82	3136
92	4	YORK	5f Gd/Fm	88	3569
96	1	DONC	6f Gd/Fm	89	3861*
95	12	NEWM	5f Good		4182

COMPTON BOLTER 3 b c £21113
112	3	MAIS	7f Heavy		9
102ε	8	NAD	9f Dirt		765
112	6	NEWM	8f Gd/Fm		1171
108	9	ASCO	8f Good		2066
107	4	DEAU	10f V		2736
99	5	ARLI	10f Yldg		3549 BL
108	1	NEWB	9f Firm		4000* t
110	7	NEWM	10f Good		4355 t
102	4	NEWM	8f Soft		4544 t

COMPTON CHICK 2 b f £0
56	7	NEWB	6f Sft/Hvy		4471	t
59	5	MUSS	7f Soft		4559	t

COMPTON COMMANDER 2 ch c £3391
73	8	ASCO	7f Gd/Fm		2956
79	3	BATH	10f Soft		4140
85	1	BRIG	10f Heavy		4539*

CONCIERGE 3 b c £0
55	7	NEWM	8f Gd/Fm		2134
26a	7	SOUT	8f Aw		2950
0	15	LEIC	8f Gd/Fm		3094
0a	14	SOUT	11f Aw		4150

CONCINO 3 b c £426
28	11	MUSS	8f Gd/Sft	42	800
53	3	CATT	14f Gd/Fm		2930
9	10	CATT	14f Gd/Fm	47	3201
43	9	PONT	8f Firm		3506
26	7	BEVE	10f Gd/Fm	38	3656
0	13	YORK	10f Good		3813
41a	6	SOUT	14f Aw	47	4371

CONDOR HERO 3 b g £647
68	3	THIR	7f Gd/Fm		2058
53	6	WARW	6f Good		2462

CONEY KITTY 2 ch f £29950
92	2	CURR	5f Gd/Sft		1621
94	4	CURR	7f Gd/Sft		4240
100	1	CORK	6f Gd/Sft		4315*

CONFLICT 4 b c £91463
109ε	1	NAD	8f Dirt		764*

CONFRONTER 11 ch g £235
61a	6	LING	10f Aw	63	23	
53a	4	LING	10f Aw	60	161	e
56a	5	LING	10f Aw	58	209	
43a	11	LING	12f Aw	55	290	
22a	7	LING	12f Aw	53	486	
31a	9	LING	10f Aw	49	618	
24	9	BRIG	10f Gd/Sft	40	1509	

CONGENIALITY 2 b f £285
63	10	YORK	7f Gd/Fm		2649
50	9	NEWC	6f Good		3245
52	4	BEVE	7f Gd/Fm		3655
0	13	CATT	7f Soft	58	4254

CONISTON 2 b g £0
0a	14	SOUT	5f Aw		1418

CONISTON MILL 3 b f £903
60	3	HAYD	7f Soft		4093
69	4	YARM	7f Soft		4388

CONNECT 3 b c £2124
75	7	NEWM	7f Firm		1186	
0	15	LING	6f Gd/Sft	90	1285	
74	20	NEWM	6f Gd/Fm	86	1694	
0	18	YORK	5f Gd/Fm	83	1980	
74	4	ASCO	5f Good	78	2168	VIS
79	3	NEWM	5f Gd/Fm	78	2288	vis
59	9	BATH	5f Firm	79	2787	BL
77	5	YARM	6f Firm	79	2900	
74	6	DONC	5f Gd/Fm	78	3894	
69	13	NEWM	5f Good	77	4185	

CONORA 7 b g £0
21a	10	WOLV	7f Aw		142

CONORMARA 3 br c £11150
112	2	LEOP	6f Good		3373
109	3	CORK	7f Soft		4266

CONQUERING LOVE 2 b c £0
65	10	NEWM	7f Good		3608
60	9	DONC	8f Good		3864
0	14	BRIG	7f Soft		4172

CONSIDERATION 3 ch f £1957
29	10	CARL	6f Gd/Sft		1723
57	2	HAMI	5f Firm		2096
40	4	MUSS	5f Gd/Fm		2204

51	4	CARL	6f Firm		2278
61	2	HAMI	5f Firm		2640
0	18	RIPO	6f Gd/Fm	51	2839
0	12	BATH	8f Soft	48	4143
0	18	WIND	6f Gd/Fm	48	4293
30a	6	WOLV	7f Aw		4384

CONSORT 7 b h £555
58a	7	LING	10f Aw	75	161	
82a	3	LING	8f Aw		208	
45a	11	LING	7f Aw	72	239	
46a	12	LING	8f Aw	70	336	
0a	13	LING	10f Aw	66	632	t
0	17	WIND	8f Good	65	854	
0	22	ASCO	8f Gd/Fm	60	1113	
54	4	WIND	9f Gd/Fm	60	1201	
38	12	REDC	8f Firm	56	1300	
0	22	NEWM	8f Gd/Fm	54	1690	

CONSPICUOUS 10 b g £0
78	8	KEMP	12f Gd/Sft	82	1076
80	6	NEWB	12f Good	82	1373
76	6	LING	9f Good	80	1744
62	6	GOOD	12f Gd/Fm	78	2127

CONSPIRACY THEORY 2 b f £580
31	6	NEWC	6f Gd/Sft		1476
54	3	MUSS	5f Firm		1684
43	4	HAMI	5f Gd/Fm		1937
35	6	THIR	6f Gd/Fm		2059
19	4	HAMI	6f Firm		2394
19a	8	SOUT	7f Aw		2949
0	13	CATT	7f Good		3438
22	11	BEVE	8f Gd/Fm		3675
0	12	YORK	6f Good		3814

CONSPIRE 2 b f £1044
86	3	SAND	8f Good		3433
78	4	HAYD	8f Soft		3766

CONSTANT 3 b c £0
69	8	NEWM	10f Gd/Sft	75	979
68	5	CHES	12f Gd/Fm	73	1225
59	9	WIND	12f Gd/Fm	70	1425
25	10	WIND	12f Good	67	3353
55	9	BATH	13f Gd/Fm	64	3819
45	5	BRIG	12f Gd/Sft	59	4123
27a	11	SOUT	12f Aw		4366
0	16	BATH	10f Soft	55	4436

CONSULTANT 4 b g £1517
46a	11	WOLV	5f Aw	65	40
32a	10	WOLV	5f Aw	60	175
39a	10	WOLV	6f Aw	56	232
46a	8	SOUT	8f Aw	58	251
54a	3	WOLV	8f Aw	56	254
55a	2	WOLV	9f Aw	51	306
26a	8	WOLV	8f Aw	54	381
26a	7	WOLV	8f Aw	54	411
55a	2	LING	10f Aw	52	842
19	9	SAND	8f Heavy	53	1058
0	15	BRIG	7f Firm	48	1213
43a	6	WOLV	8f Aw	54	1393
0	23	NEWM	8f Gd/Fm	43	1690
0	17	LEIC	8f Firm	38	2032
0a	15	SOUT	8f Aw	54	4365

CONTACT 3 br g £0
76	11	CHES	8f Gd/Fm	93	3510
71	8	RIPO	10f Gd/Fm	88	3713
0	14	GOOD	8f Good	83	3904
77	6	NEWM	7f Gd/Fm	78	4215

CONTINUATION 2 b c £1280
86	2	YARM	7f Soft		4514

CONTRABAND 2 b c £0
81	10	NEWM	7f Good		4183

CONTRARY MARY 5 b m £11024
38	10	WIND	6f Gd/Fm	59	746
0	11	FOLK	6f Soft	57	958

52	5	LING	7f Soft	55	1542
60	1	SALI	6f Gd/Fm	53	2230*
63	2	WIND	6f Good	59	2371
60	2	EPSO	7f Gd/Sft	58	2431
55	7	SALI	6f Good	63	2690
67	1	EPSO	7f Good	62	3765*
60	4	LING	7f Good	66	4102

CONWY CASTLE 3 b c £2857
66	5	SAND	8f Gd/Fm		2938
80	5	LEIC	10f Firm		3838
86	1	BRIG	12f Gd/Sft		4119+

COOL AFFAIR 5 ch g £0
35	11	CATT	7f Gd/Fm	45	3200
19	15	THIR	8f Gd/Fm	45	3344

COOL INVESTMENT 3 b c £24916
94	2	RIPO	9f Soft		823
85	6	YORK	10f Firm		1340
89	4	EPSO	10f Gd/Sft	92	1831
92	1	WIND	12f Soft		2547*
92	3	ASCO	12f Gd/Fm	91	3001
69	5	NEWM	15f Good	91	3611
92	1	LUCE	15f Heavy		3850*
0	8	DIEL	12f Good		4148
0	4	DONC	12f Heavy		4578

COOL JUDGE 3 b g £0
20a	8	SOUT	6f Aw		181

COOL LOCATION 3 b f £0
0a	15	SOUT	8f Aw		36	BL
13	10	LING	11f Firm	35	1911	
0	7	BRIG	10f Gd/Sft		2423	
5	6	WIND	12f Good		2715	
0	15	NOTT	16f Gd/Fm	37	3112	

COOL PROSPECT 5 b g £10191
0a	12	SOUT	8f Aw	58	345	VIS
44a	5	WOLV	7f Aw	50	582	
35a	7	LING	10f Aw	50	618	
45a	5	WOLV	8f Aw	46	675	
32a	4	WOLV	7f Aw	46	711	
52	1	MUSS	5f Gd/Fm	47	1143*	bl
33	11	HAMI	6f Firm		1239	bl
51	4	THIR	6f Gd/Sft	52	1356	bl
54	2	THIR	5f Gd/Sft	52	1714	bl
57	3	RIPO	6f Gd/Fm	54	2107	bl
57	2	REDC	6f Gd/Fm	54	2158	
58	2	HAYD	6f Gd/Fm	54	2444	
54	7	YORK	7f Good	60	2694	
42	11	THIR	6f Gd/Fm	60	3123	vis
49a	3	WOLV	5f Aw	48	3271	bl
0	15	PONT	5f Firm	59	3502	
53	6	THIR	7f Good	59	3619	

COOL SPICE 3 b f £290
55	10	WIND	8f Gd/Fm		3048
68	4	CHEP	7f Gd/Fm		3256
50	6	WARW	7f Good		3696
48	5	LEIC	8f Gd/Sft		4033
50	7	BRIG	10f Soft	60	4174
0	14	BATH	10f Soft	55	4436

COOL TEMPER 4 b g £1117
71	5	WARW	7f Soft		1060	
74	5	LING	7f Soft	78	1286	
74	5	NEWB	8f Gd/Sft	76	1590	
74	7	DONC	7f Gd/Fm	76	1840	
62a	5	SOUT	8f Aw	74	2634	t
72	4	ASCO	8f Good	73	3018	
70	4	LEIC	8f Gd/Fm	73	3334	
0	19	KEMP	10f Gd/Fm	72	3794	
0	25	NEWM	8f Good	70	4340	

COOL VIBES 5 br g £293
43a	8	WOLV	8f Aw	68	1037	
0	16	NOTT	10f Gd/Sft	68	1370	
33	7	RIPO	8f Good		1858	VIS
34	12	BATH	8f Firm	53	2331	vis

(continued)

0a	11	WOLV	12f Aw	47	3773	vis
31	3	BEVE	12f Sft/Hv		4041	vis
0	12	YARM	14f Soft		4510	vis

COOLING OFF 3 b f £3043

60	7	WIND	8f Gd/Fm		3048
78	3	WIND	8f Good		3350
63	5	WARW	8f Gd/Fm		3914
63	7	SAND	8f Soft	75	4206
71	4	DONC	10f Gd/Sft	72	4448
73	2	NEWM	12f Gd/Sft	72	4534

COPCOURT ROYALE 2 b f £0

25a	8	SOUT	8f Aw		4152
47a	5	WOLV	9f Aw		4438

COPPELIUS 2 b f £0

60	11	CHEP	8f Gd/Fm		3678

COPPER COOKIE 5 ch m £0

0a	8	WOLV	15f Aw	35	277

COPPER SHELL 6 ch g £0

35a	7	LING	12f Aw	69	237
0a	9	WOLV	12f Aw	67	437 t

COPPLESTONE 4 b g £8635

64	7	DONC	10f Gd/Sft	76	1070
78	2	BRIG	8f Firm	74	1330
67	4	GOOD	8f Gd/Sft	74	1473
74	4	LING	9f Good	76	1744
59	11	GOOD	8f Gd/Fm	75	2126
69	4	YARM	10f Firm	73	2387
69	3	BRIG	8f Gd/Fm	72	2726
74	2	LING	9f Firm	71	3488
74	2	EPSO	9f Good	72	3685
74	2	LING	8f Firm	72	3831
52	12	YARM	7f Firm	72	3939

COPY CAT 2 b f £0

70	4	WIND	5f Gd/Fm		1197
0	12	BATH	6f Gd/Sft		1667
27	12	FOLK	6f Gd/Fm		3443

COPYFORCE BOY 4 ch g £209

21a	10	LING	10f Aw		314 t
28a	4	LING	8f Aw		615 t

COPYFORCE GIRL 4 b f £8813

58	1	BRIG	12f Gd/Fm		1934* t
62	3	EPSO	12f Gd/Sft	58	2429 t
60	2	EPSO	12f Gd/Sft	58	2626 t
64	2	SAND	14f Gd/Fm	60	2923 t
63	2	SAND	14f Good	62	3231 t
56	6	SAND	16f Good	62	3434 t
65	2	BRIG	12f Firm	63	3735 t

CORAL SHELLS 3 b f £0

43	8	BRIG	8f Soft	57	1511
41	8	SAND	10f Soft	57	1585
39	7	BRIG	8f Firm	52	2043
0	12	SALI	8f Gd/Fm	52	2264
0	16	WIND	12f Gd/Fm	49	3049
24	6	BRIG	10f Gd/Fm	45	3263 BL
34	8	BRIG	7f Firm		3739 bl
0	15	YARM	7f Firm		3921 bl
0	13	YARM	8f Gd/Fm	38	3970 bl

CORAL WATERS 4 b f £0

0a	10	SOUT	7f Aw		247 BL

CORBLETS 3 b f £5082

56a	3	LING	5f Aw		883
67	2	WIND	5f Gd/Sft	65	1098
68	2	WIND	5f Gd/Fm	66	1427
54	5	BRIG	6f Good		1651
56	7	KEMP	6f Gd/Fm	68	1925
59	11	WARW	5f Gd/Fm	66	2252
52	8	SAND	5f Gd/Fm	60	2478
60	3	KEMP	5f Gd/Fm	64	2586
54	6	WIND	5f Good	62	2716
57	3	FOLK	5f Firm		3584
41	12	EPSO	5f Good	59	3855
55	6	GOOD	5f Soft	57	4065

CORETTA 6 b m £130675

118	2	GULF	11f Good		18

CORINIUM 3 br f £23133

108	1	GOOD	8f Gd/Sft		1485*
105	6	EPSO	12f Gd/Sft		1828

CORK HARBOUR 4 ch g £3282

77	1	BRIG	8f Soft		4175*
46	11	NEWB	10f Sft/Hv	75	4473

CORN DOLLY 4 ch f £3486

48a	4	LING	6f Aw		95
54a	1	LING	7f Aw		225*
54a	2	LING	6f Aw	49	263
49a	5	LING	7f Aw	51	503
0	18	REDC	7f Firm	49	1297
0	17	CHEP	7f Gd/Sft	47	1794
36	10	NOTT	6f Gd/Fm	43	2192
18	13	PONT	8f Gd/Fm	41	2561 BL
26	5	BRIG	7f Gd/Fm	41	2728 bl

CORNDAVON 4 b f £26130

68	2	FOLK	5f Soft		960
63	9	WIND	8f Gd/Fm	66	1196
66	4	REDC	7f Firm	66	1297
40	7	BRIG	7f Soft		1467
81	1	DONC	6f Gd/Fm	66	1842*
80	2	WARW	6f Good		2035
87	1	NEWC	6f Firm	80	2334*

CORNELIUS 3 b c £22661

101	2	DONC	10f Good		1515
100	5	NEWM	10f Firm		1854
97	12	ASCO	8f Good	102	2117
109	2	SAND	8f Good		2476
100	7	NEWM	10f Gd/Fm	100	2596
98	4	GOOD	8f Firm		3150
91	12	NEWM	10f Good	100	4197
101	1	AYR	8f Heavy		4308*
103	1	NEWB	9f Sft/Hvy	97	4472*

CORNER HOUSE 3 gr f £780

83	3	NEWM	6f Good		956

CORNISH ECLIPSE 3 b c £0

5	6	BATH	6f Firm		2329
25a	10	WOLV	6f Aw		3275
0	18	CHEP	8f Good		3868

CORRIDOR CREEPER 3 ch c £7800

73	7	LING	6f Gd/Sft	88	1285
87	3	NEWM	6f Gd/Fm	86	1694
82	7	YORK	6f Firm	87	2003
76	8	ASCO	8f Good	86	2168
82	6	CHEP	5f Gd/Fm	86	2451 BL
86	3	ASCO	5f Good	84	2676 t
78	8	EPSO	5f Good	86	3687
0	17	YARM	5f Firm	84	3920 t

CORSECAN 5 ch g £0

0	13	BRIG	7f Gd/Sft	38	896
0	17	BRIG	10f Firm		1210
18a	8	LING	7f Aw		1741

CORUNNA 3 b c £13817

75	3	CHES	6f Gd/Fm	73	1220
73	3	DONC	5f Good		1516
79	1	MUSS	5f Firm		1688*
73	3	RIPO	6f Gd/Fm	76	2101
78	1	LING	6f Gd/Fm	76	2216*
71	6	HAYD	6f Gd/Fm	79	2504
74	6	BATH	5f Firm	79	2787
59	11	GOOD	6f Gd/Fm	79	3136
0	15	RIPO	6f Good	77	3698

CORUSCATING 3 gr g £3316

42	8	BRIG	8f Gd/Fm	66	3261
66	4	EPSO	10f Good	66	3762
68a	1	LING	10f Aw		4100*
33	11	BRIG	8f Soft		4173
40a	9	WOLV	8f Aw	65	4248
56a	4	LING	10f Aw	63	4482

COSI FAN TUTTE 2 b c £955

91	3	NEWM	7f Good		2563

COSMIC BUZZ 3 ch c £386

50	17	RIPO	10f Soft	68	827
38	7	WARW	12f Soft	64	1064
0	14	WIND	12f Firm	58	1292
0	18	WARW	11f Gd/Sft	51	1707 VIS
34	7	CHEP	16f Gd/Fm	47	2659
0	4	CHEP	16f Gd/Fm	53	2973

COSMIC CASE 5 b m £7060

35	5	MUSS	9f Gd/Sft	39	795 vis
0	16	PONT	10f Soft	44	871 vis
36	4	HAMI	12f Firm	37	1241 vis
18	10	MUSS	12f Firm	36	1432 vis
29	7	HAMI	13f Gd/Fm	33	1936
37	4	MUSS	12f Firm	40	2048
33	2	MUSS	12f Gd/Sft	33	2202
38	1	MUSS	16f Firm	37	2373*
39	1	HAMI	12f Firm	37	2392*
40	3	HAMI	13f Gd/Fm	37	2643
34	4	MUSS	14f Gd/Fm	46	3590
38	5	MUSS	12f Soft	44	4560

COSMIC DANCER 3 b g £0

0	18	WARW	8f Gd/Fm		3914
6	6	BRIG	8f Soft		4175
0	14	BATH	12f Soft		4434

COSMIC MILLENNIUM 2 b c £3575

78	6	SALI	7f Good		2686
84	1	CHES	7f Firm		3169*

COSMIC PEARL 2 b f £0

0	11	WARW	7f Good		3692
44	5	LEIC	8f Firm		3836
10	10	BRIG	8f Gd/Fm		4117

COSMIC RANGER 2 b c £0

70	10	NEWM	6f Gd/Fm		3162
68	5	KEMP	6f Gd/Fm		3358
0	18	DONC	6f Firm		3888
58	6	BRIG	8f Gd/Sft		4117

COSMIC SONG 3 b f £3723

53a	5	SOUT	8f Aw		86
32a	5	SOUT	7f Aw		281
0a	6	WOLV	9f Aw		481
47	3	MUSS	8f Gd/Sft	45	800
40	5	MUSS	8f Gd/Fm	45	1434
51	1	CARL	9f Gd/Sft	45	1722*
50	4	REDC	10f Good	50	1895
22	4	AYR	9f Good	53	2166
45	6	LEIC	8f Gd/Fm	53	2506
36	8	CARL	8f Firm	53	3082
29	5	RIPO	10f Gd/Fm	49	3465
10	11	NEWC	10f Heavy	46	4404
26	8	NOTT	10f Heavy	46	4509

COSMO JACK 4 b g £820

33	9	BRIG	8f Gd/Sft	50	1462 vis
71	2	HAYD	12f Gd/Sft		1788 vis
63	5	NOTT	10f Gd/Fm	68	2190 vis
0	13	SALI	12f Good	65	2689 vis
23	11	SALI	10f Gd/Fm		2981 vis
7	12	BRIG	12f Gd/Fm	60	3260 vis
38a	7	WOLV	12f Aw	50	3773 vis

COSMOCRAT 2 b g £714

57	14	NEWB	7f Firm		3999
83	2	BATH	8f Soft		4430

COSMOGRAPHE 3 b c £0

106	9	CHAN	12f V		1752

COST AUDITING 3 ch f £0

41	5	LING	7f Good		1675
0	12	WIND	6f Soft	57	2549
30	11	LEIC	8f Gd/Fm	50	3095
32a	7	WOLV	9f Aw		3272
25a	12	WOLV	6f Aw	52	4553

COTE SOLEIL 3 ch c £1874

90	3	RIPO	9f Soft		823	
85	3	BEVE	7f Heavy		977	
0	16	CHES	8f Gd/Fm	88	1215	
80	11	HAYD	8f Gd/Sft	86	1535	
77	16	ASCO	8f Good	84	2117	BL
85	4	HAYD	7f Gd/Fm	84	2456	
75	9	SAND	7f Gd/Fm	82	2922	
64	10	HAYD	8f Gd/Sft	81	3325	
0	23	NEWM	7f Gd/Fm	79	4215	

COTTAM LILLY 3 b f £0
31	8	BEVE	5f Gd/Fm		3651
0	13	THIR	6f Gd/Sft		3780
31	10	CATT	12f Soft	46	4256

COTTON HOUSE 3 b f £45032
100	1	LEIC	6f Gd/Sft		1576*
92	5	HAYD	6f Gd/Sft		1833
101	1	YORK	6f Firm	95	2003*
96	5	SAND	5f Gd/Fm		2496
91	6	YORK	8f Heavy		2646

COTTONTAIL 2 b c £0
41	8	YORK	6f Firm		2005
54	11	YORK	7f Gd/Fm		2649
25	6	YORK	8f Heavy		4297

COUGHLANS GIFT 4 ch f £5006
54a	5	LING	8f Aw	61	210	
51a	7	LING	10f Aw		268	
0	14	WIND	8f Gd/Fm	61	1201	
0	13	NOTT	10f Gd/Sft	61	1370	
0	24	NEWM	10f Soft	57	1570	
50	5	SALI	8f Gd/Sft	53	2467	
32	12	SALI	10f Gd/Fm	51	3390	
55	1	SALI	10f Gd/Sft	49	4169*	
62	1	NOTT	10f Heavy		4413*	

COULD BE EXPENSIVE 3 b c £0
32a	6	SOUT	6f Aw	47	331	BL
28a	6	WOLV	6f Aw	44	397	
36a	4	SOUT	8f Aw	40	555	bl
0	15	YARM	8f Good	45	1772	
36	10	LEIC	10f Gd/Fm		2510	bl

COULTHARD 7 ch g £0
55	7	HAYD	12f Heavy	86	991

COUNT CALYPSO 2 ch c £315
0	18	NEWB	5f Gd/Fm		1782
53	9	BATH	5f Firm		1993
61	10	LING	5f Gd/Fm		2214
65a	3	SOUT	5f Aw		2818
40	7	SAND	5f Gd/Fm	67	3431

COUNT DE MONEY 5 b g £13487
47a	5	WOLV	12f Aw	57	43	
61a	2	SOUT	11f Aw	54	126	
63a	2	SOUT	14f Aw	57	182	
67a	1	SOUT	12f Aw	57	211*	
70a	2	WOLV	15f Aw	65	277	
72a	3	SOUT	12f Aw	70	370	
68a	1	SOUT	12f Aw		498*	
60a	2	SOUT	12f Aw		556	
76a	1	WOLV	12f Aw		679*	t
77a	1	SOUT	14f Aw	72	868*	t

COUNT DUBOIS 2 b c £116491
90	1	HAYD	6f Gd/Sft		3478*	
93	2	EPSO	7f Good		3688	
108	3	NEWM	7f Good		4158	VIS
105	3	ASCO	8f Heavy		4296	BL
112	1	SAN	8f Heavy		4492*	

COUNT FREDERICK 4 b g £0
0	12	WARW	11f Heavy	47	889
0	22	NEWM	12f Firm	45	1852
23a	6	LING	10f Aw	42	2212

COUNT ON THUNDER 3 ch c £0
55	5	REDC	11f Gd/Sft	62	1560
54	6	NOTT	10f Good		2012

40	5	BRIG	12f Gd/Sft	56	2425	
0	18	HAMI	12f Gd/Sft	51	3827	
55	6	MUSS	12f Gd/Sft		4133	
0	13	AYR	10f Heavy	45	4306	
0a	12	LING	10f Aw	45	4482	

COUNT TIROL 3 b c £0
31	11	NOTT	8f Good	63	2013
0	16	SALI	8f Gd/Fm	60	2264
0	12	BRIG	10f Firm	53	3530

COUNT TONY 6 ch g £0
0	16	SOUT	16f Gd/Sft	60	860

COUNTESS BANKES 2 b f £1831
54a	4	SOUT	5f Aw		801	
61a	4	SOUT	5f Aw		856*	
50	6	NOTT	5f Heavy		1019	VIS

COUNTESS COLDUNELL 3 b f £0
60	6	LING	8f Soft		4274
37	10	NEWB	10f Sft/Hv		4474

COUNTESS PARKER 4 ch f £0
31	7	LEIC	8f Gd/Sft		1731
0	15	WIND	8f Good	60	2367
0	11	LEIC	7f Gd/Fm	52	2775
30	10	THIR	6f Gd/Fm	52	2969
0	12	THIR	8f Gd/Fm	48	3124
0	15	BRIG	8f Firm	44	3527

COUNTRY BUMPKIN 4 ch g £0
0	12	NOTT	8f Gd/Fm		2188

COUNTRYSIDE FRIEND 3 ch c £1
0	2	NEWM	8f Gd/Fm		1156

COUNTRYWIDE PRIDE 2 ch c £952
45	7	KEMP	5f Gd/Sft		1079
62	4	FOLK	7f Good		2620
70	3	WARW	7f Good		2841
51	11	NEWB	7f Gd/Fm	75	3175
70	4	NEWM	8f Good	69	3609
58	6	EPSO	7f Good		3690
65	7	NEWM	8f Good	69	4350
67a	5	WOLV	8f Aw	69	4439

COURAGE UNDER FIRE 5 b g £0
29	10	PONT	10f Heavy	51	943	
0	18	BRIG	12f Gd/Fm	48	1128	VIS
25	10	NEWB	12f Gd/Sft	45	1594	

COURT CHAMPAGNE 4 b f £0
39	9	NOTT	8f Good		784
0	13	WARW	11f Heavy	44	889
28	6	BATH	12f Good	46	1091
1	10	BRIG	12f Firm	40	1332
5	10	NOTT	10f Good	33	2011
12	10	CHEP	18f Gd/Fm	28	2452

COURT EXPRESS 6 b g £6733
80	1	BEVE	8f Firm	75	1279*
69	6	BEVE	8f Good	79	1445
81	2	AYR	8f Good		2138
75	10	CARL	8f Gd/Fm	79	2242
70	5	NEWC	10f Good	80	2522
80	3	RIPO	10f Gd/Fm	78	2836
60	12	DONC	10f Gd/Fm	79	3159
77	4	REDC	8f Firm	79	3309
78	4	RIPO	8f Good	77	3699
64	21	NEWM	9f Gd/Fm	81	4212

COURT FLIRT 3 b f £0
5	9	NOTT	8f Good		783

COURT HOUSE 6 b g £0
5a	11	WOLV	8f Aw		322
0	20	REDC	7f Gd/Fm		2994

COURT OF APPEAL 3 ch c £5089
71	11	NEWM	8f Firm		1188
89	1	KEMP	8f Soft		1532*
66	8	NEWM	10f Gd/Fm	90	2287
66	8	HAYD	8f Soft	85	4094
83	4	YORK	10f Soft	82	4282

COURT OF JUSTICE 4 b c £0

73	5	DONC	10f Gd/Sft		1054
49	7	REDC	10f Gd/Sft		1582
55	6	YARM	14f Heavy	68	4476

COURT ONE 2 b c £0
39	13	NEWB	6f Gd/Fm		1403
0	14	KEMP	7f Firm		2867
15	7	WIND	6f Good		3352

COURT SHAREEF 5 b g £30955
65	1	WIND	12f Good	54	1730*
62	3	WIND	10f Gd/Fm	60	1878
73	1	GOOD	12f Gd/Fm	63	2127*
78	1	CARL	12f Firm	67	2279+
72	9	HAYD	12f Gd/Fm	77	2502
78	2	LEIC	12f Gd/Fm	77	2917
65	15	GOOD	14f Gd/Fm	77	3058

COURTEOUS 5 b g £0
116	7	GULF	12f Good		20

COURTING 3 gr f £36442
93	3	ASCO	8f Good		2171
100	1	BORD	8f Good		2487*
102	2	ASCO	8f Good		3340
107	1	YARM	10f Firm		3918+

COURTLEDGE 5 b g £0
0a	15	SOUT	14f Aw	42	1301

COURTNEY GYM 5 ch g £0
0a	13	LING	6f Aw		313	
4a	10	WOLV	7f Aw		391	bl
12	10	BRIG	7f Soft	35	2427	bl
16	8	BRIG	6f Firm	28	2896	bl

COUTURE 3 ch f £1050
72	2	PONT	8f Gd/Fm		3221
55	5	EPSO	9f Gd/Fm		3413
62	5	GOOD	10f Soft		4081
0	18	WIND	5f Gd/Sft	65	4295

COVENT GARDEN 2 b c £0
78	7	LING	7f Soft		4268

COVER UP 3 b c £13361
91	1	WIND	10f Good		850*	
67	14	ASCO	12f Good	92	2116	
93	3	GOOD	14f Firm	92	3153	
82	11	YORK	14f Gd/Fm	92	3599	VIS
89	7	DONC	15f Firm	91	3890	
95	1	MUSS	16f Gd/Sft	89	4134*	
74	9	NEWM	16f Gd/Sft	96	4533	

COWBOYS AND ANGELS 3 b c £9440
69a	3	WOLV	9f Aw		610
70a	3	WOLV	8f Aw		708
74	6	LEIC	10f Gd/Fm		833
38	13	BATH	10f Good	69	1094
71	1	SALI	7f Good		1349*
40	9	LEIC	8f Gd/Sft		1572
73	2	SALI	8f Firm	70	2025
70	4	SALI	8f Gd/Fm	70	2264
74	1	AYR	7f Gd/Fm	70	2719*
75	2	KEMP	7f Gd/Fm	74	3076
68	12	NEWM	7f Gd/Fm	76	3629
65	6	CHES	6f Soft		4069

COY DEBUTANTE 6 ch m £0
18	10	NOTT	10f Gd/Sft	49	1364
32	16	WIND	12f Good	49	1730
0	14	PONT	12f Soft	45	4229
15	11	BRIG	10f Soft	40	4419

COYOTE 2 b f £247
66	4	LEIC	7f Heavy		4312

COZZIE 2 ch f £8846
59a	3	SOUT	5f Aw		856
70	7	NEWM	5f Gd/Sft		970
65	5	MUSS	5f Gd/Fm		1429
65	1	MUSS	5f Firm		1684*
65a	1	LING	5f Aw		1916*
51	6	CHES	5f Good	63	2665
50	6	MUSS	5f Good	60	3101

CRACK (continued)

59	1	**BEVE**	5f Good	56	3394*
59	4	BEVE	5f Gd/Fm	60	3673
52	6	GOOD	6f Good	60	3886

CRACK DANCER 3 b f £0
| 34a | 9 | SOUT | 7f Aw | 59 | 31 |

CRACK ON CHERYL 6 b m £0
| 0a | 9 | WOLV | 9f Aw | | 378 |
| 0 | 13 | SALI | 10f Good | | 1343 |

CRACKLE 4 gr f £268
| 80a | 4 | LING | 12f Aw | | 27 |

CRACOW 3 b c £22843
87	4	NEWM	10f Gd/Sft	83	979
86	3	CHES	10f Gd/Fm		1218
87	1	**BRIG**	12f Gd/Sft		1510*
89	14	EPSO	12f Good		1848
86	5	GOOD	12f Gd/Fm	87	3088
90	2	NEWB	11f Firm	86	3451
91	1	**YORK**	12f Gd/Fm	88	3728*
80	9	NEWB	13f Firm	90	3994
0	16	NEWM	12f Good	90	4342

CRAFTY PICK 3 b f £310
49	7	KEMP	6f Good		729
0	16	LING	7f Gd/Sft		840
48	11	WIND	6f Gd/Sft		1423
51	3	LEIC	6f Gd/Sft	50	1734
54	4	SALI	7f Gd/Fm		1884

CRAIGARY 9 b g £2310
19	9	MUSS	16f Gd/Fm		1145
20	5	CARL	12f Gd/Sft		1720
0	14	HAMI	13f Gd/Fm	26	1936 bl
26	1	**MUSS**	13f Soft	22	4521*

CRAIGSTEEL 5 b h £91463
| 120 | 2 | BELM | 12f Firm | | 4316 |

CRASH CALL LADY 4 b f £825
26a	4	SOUT	14f Aw	51	89
34a	3	WOLV	15f Aw		117
36a	2	WOLV	16f Aw	38	190
0a	11	SOUT	16f Aw	35	284
17a	11	WOLV	16f Aw	37	318

CRAZY LARRYS 2 ch c £13340
88	1	**NEWC**	7f Good		2521*
102	2	NEWM	7f Gd/Fm		3164
102	1	**KEMP**	6f Gd/Fm		3361*

CREAM TEASE 3 b f £12057
34	12	NEWB	10f Good		1374
42	13	ASCO	8f Good	87	2167 BL
75	7	NEWM	7f Gd/Fm	80	2855
62	7	BATH	8f Firm	76	3207
78	1	**SALI**	7f Firm	73	3750+

CREDENZA MOMENT 2 b c £0
0	14	LEIC	7f Firm		3840
0	15	SALI	8f Gd/Sft		4163
45	12	NEWB	6f Sft/Hvy		4470

CREDIBILITY 2 ch f £430
| 69 | 3 | MUSS | 5f Good | | 3098 |

CREME DE CASSIS 4 ch f £0
| 34a | 5 | WOLV | 15f Aw | | 174 |
| 20a | 7 | LING | 13f Aw | 39 | 460 |

CRESSET 4 ch c £7871
41a	6	LING	10f Aw		238
34a	8	SOUT	12f Aw	54	338
61a	2	SOUT	12f Aw		387 BL
61a	1	**WOLV**	12f Aw	54	410* bl
57a	2	WOLV	12f Aw	52	437 bl
63a	1	**SOUT**	12f Aw	52	456* bl
64a	2	SOUT	16f Aw	64	502
65a	2	SOUT	14f Aw	63	868 bl
0	11	PONT	22f Heavy	60	940 bl
16	9	HAMI	13f Gd/Fm	56	1363 bl
0	7	CARL	14f Firm	50	2827

CRESSIDA 2 ch f £0
| 64 | 9 | YARM | 8f Heavy | | 4477 |
| 0 | 21 | NEWM | 7f Soft | | 4541 |

CRETAN GIFT 9 ch g £31813
100 e7		WOLV	6f Aw	105	660 vis
102	3	DONC	6f Good		734 vis
94	5	NEWB	5f Soft	99	914 vis
111	1	**NEWM**	6f Good		952* vis
104	1	DONC	7f Gd/Sft		1049 vis
105	6	NEWM	6f Firm	109	1182 vis
111	5	YARM	6f Gd/Fm		1952 vis
107	7	ASCO	6f Good		2115 vis
101	7	ASCO	6f Good	108	2151 vis
108	2	NEWC	6f Firm		2335 vis
108	3	NEWB	6f Firm		2847 vis
107	4	CHES	6f Firm		3172 vis
111	4	YARM	6f Good		3235 vis
108	5	LEOP	6f Good		3373 bl
109	5	NEWM	6f Good		3610 vis
98	8	HAYD	6f Gd/Sft		3784 vis
94	11	ASCO	6f Gd/Sft		4125 vis
102	8	NEWM	5f Good		4182
104	4	NEWM	6f Good		4346 vis

CRICKETERS CLUB 2 b c £0
0	14	HAYD	5f Gd/Sft		1488
0	12	KEMP	6f Gd/Fm		3358
0	15	LING	8f Firm		3577

CRILLON 4 br c £34582
104	2	LONG	12f Heavy		1034
109	2	SAIN	12f Soft		1461
111	2	LONG	12f Good		3927

CRIMPLENE 3 ch f £417290
101 e6		NAD	9f Dirt		765
103	3	NEWB	7f Soft		913
105	3	CAPA	8f Heavy		1117
114	1	**DUSS**	8f Good		1229*
116	1	**CURR**	8f Gd/Sft		1626*
121	1	**ASCO**	8f Good		2150*
120	1	**GOOD**	10f Firm		3151*
113	4	DEAU	8f Gd/Fm		3544
108	8	ASCO	8f Good		4111

CRIMSON GLORY 4 ch f £3989
71a	1	**WOLV**	8f Aw		409*
70a	2	LING	8f Aw	70	463
31a	9	SOUT	8f Aw	70	513

CRIMSON QUEST 3 ch c £61862
114	2	CHAN	11f V		1231
104	7	LONG	10f Good		2225
108	2	CLAI	12f Good		3718
117	2	LONG	12f Good		3929
117	1	**LONG**	12f Soft		4394*

CRIMSON RIDGE 2 b f £1567
67	3	NOTT	5f Good		2009
67	6	DONC	5f Gd/Fm		2756
52	4	LEIC	5f Good		3092
71	2	THIR	5f Gd/Fm		3346

CRIMSON TIDE 6 b h £2563
108	3	SALI	8f Gd/Fm		3291
101	5	WIND	10f Good		3641
104	7	LONG	8f Good		4259
93	7	NEWM	10f Gd/Fm		4532

CRIPSEY BROOK 2 ch c £340
81	4	GOOD	6f Gd/Sft		1472
76	5	WIND	6f Gd/Fm		1876
50	12	LING	7f Good		2653

CRIQUETOT 2 £0
| 95 | 8 | SAIN | 10f Soft | | 4556 |

CRISOS IL MONACO 5 b h £93772
| 114 | 2 | CAPA | 10f Good | | 1321 |

CRISS CROSS 3 b c £8461
78	2	WARW	8f Heavy		884
71	1	HAYD	7f Heavy		992
75	2	WARW	7f Soft		1060
74	4	LING	7f Gd/Sft		1261
74	5	NEWB	6f Gd/Fm		1783
63	4	BRIG	6f Firm	75	2042
76	1	**KEMP**	6f Gd/Sft		2582*
62	5	NEWM	7f Gd/Fm		3318

CRISTOFORO 3 b g £0
| 10a | 9 | WOLV | 7f Aw | | 4361 |
| 58a | 5 | WOLV | 8f Aw | | 4551 |

CROESO ADREF 3 ch f £4170
43a	3	LING	7f Aw		155
47a	1	**WOLV**	7f Aw	42	257*
51a	2	LING	7f Aw	48	287
45a	3	LING	8f Aw	50	355
39a	6	LING	7f Aw		459
41a	4	SOUT	7f Aw		589
45	3	SOUT	10f Good	46	807
45a	4	LING	10f Aw		882
0a	9	WOLV	8f Aw		1234 BL
0	12	NOTT	8f Gd/Sft	44	1365
29	7	CARL	6f Firm	42	3194
34	10	BEVE	7f Aw		3670
0a	11	WOLV	7f Aw		4384

CROESO CARIAD 3 b f £20625
100	5	NEWM	7f Good		953
96	8	SAN	11f Good		1459
107	4	ASCO	12f Good		2112
107	2	NEWM	8f Gd/Fm		2597

CROESO CROESO 2 b f £0
| 0 | 13 | NOTT | 5f Gd/Fm | | 4503 |

CROFT SANDS 7 ch g £0
| 0a | 12 | SOUT | 8f Aw | | 45 |
| 0a | 11 | LING | 13f Aw | 35 | 168 |

CROMABOO COUNTESS 3 b f £0
| 25a | 7 | WOLV | 7f Aw | | 41 |
| 0 | 17 | LEIC | 10f Gd/Sft | | 4029 |

CROMER PIER 5 b g £0
| 15 | 10 | LEIC | 12f Good | 38 | 791 |

CROOKFORD WATER 3 b c £258
44	10	NOTT	10f Good		2012
41	4	WARW	12f Gd/Fm		2253
32a	3	SOUT	12f Aw		2636 tvl

CROSBY DONJOHN 3 ch c £1080
31a	10	SOUT	8f Aw	63	128 BL
63a	2	WOLV	7f Aw	56	188 bl
33a	6	WOLV	7f Aw	60	294 bl
45a	7	SOUT	6f Aw	60	365 bl

CROSS DALL 3 b f £3197
56a	3	LING	7f Aw	53	VIS
40	3	PONT	12f Heavy		939 e
57	1	**WIND**	12f Gd/Sft		1096*
27a	8	WOLV	12f Good	57	1238
52	11	WIND	12f Firm	60	1292
55	5	WIND	12f Good	55	1730 e
44	8	LING	11f Firm	55	1911 vis
53	4	SALI	14f Gd/Fm	54	2982

CROSS FINGERS 2 ch f £0
| 22a | 6 | LING | 5f Aw | | 1916 |
| 6 | 9 | REDC | 7f Gd/Fm | | 2155 |

CROSS LUGANA 4 b f £0
25	8	FOLK	7f Soft		962
56	10	CHEP	10f Gd/Sft		1796
18	11	WARW	12f Gd/Fm	50	2254

CROSSWAYS 2 b c £0
| 0 | 17 | YARM | 7f Firm | | 3940 |
| 0 | 13 | YARM | 8f Soft | | 4512 |

CROWDED AVENUE 8 b g £2737
43a	9	LING	7f Aw		104
77	9	MUSS	5f Firm	85	1687
71	3	SAND	5f Good		1966
80	2	SALI	5f Gd/Fm	80	2266 VIS
73	8	BRIG	5f Firm	80	3734 vis
52	10	SAND	5f Gd/Fm		3947 vis
0	13	SAND	5f Soft		4207 vis

CROWN LODGE 3 ch f £5219
82	2	CHEP	8f Heavy		1556
90	1	HAYD	8f Gd/Sft		1837*
89	5	ASCO	8f Gd/Fm		3340
80	7	NEWC	10f Good	90	3703
86	5	ASCO	8f Good	87	4113
72	7	NEWB	10f Stt/Hv	86	4473

CROWN MINT 3 gr c £675
23a	8	LING	8f Aw		103
53	2	LING	11f Firm	51	1914
16	11	WARW	12f Gd/Fm	52	2255
30	10	CHEP	12f Good	52	2656

CRUAGH EXPRESS 4 b g £5590
53	5	YARM	10f Good	54	1775	
46	6	NOTT	10f Good	53	2011	
0	15	NEWM	8f Gd/Fm	51	2802	bl
33a	8	WOLV	8f Aw	47	3499	
50a	1	LING	10f Aw	43	3828*	bl
53	1	GOOD	8f Soft	50	4066*	bl
50	6	WIND	10f Gd/Sft	53	4291	
54a	3	LING	8f Aw	53	4330	bl

CRUISE 3 ch c £4571
55a	5	LING	7f Aw		94
72a	1	LING	6f Aw		153*
0	14	BRIG	7f Firm	68	1213
58	5	HAYD	6f Soft	65	1494
51	11	SALI	7f Gd/Fm	63	1889
0	14	CHEP	12f Gd/Fm	60	2974
64	1	BRIG	7f Firm		3739*
54	7	EPSO	12f Good	62	3854
22	14	BRIG	8f Soft		4173

CRUISE AHEAD 4 b g £0
| 37a | 7 | LING | 10f Aw | | 110 |

CRUSTY LILY 4 gr f £1780
0	13	BATH	6f Gd/Fm	43	1438
42	4	BEVE	7f Firm	42	2221
45	2	YARM	6f Gd/Fm	42	2415
0	18	DONC	7f Gd/Fm	42	2612
18	10	BRIG	6f Gd/Fm	45	2728
38	6	THIR	6f Gd/Fm	45	2969
36	6	THIR	6f Gd/Fm	47	3123
45	3	CHEP	6f Gd/Fm	43	3257
24	9	SALI	6f Gd/Fm	46	3419
41	5	CHEP	5f Good	44	3872
42	6	YARM	6f Gd/Fm	44	3964

CRUZ SANTA 7 b m £1075
| 35 | 2 | CATT | 16f Gd/Fm | 33 | 2436 |

CRYFIELD 3 b g £9217
31	9	DONC	7f Good		717	
49	5	LEIC	6f Gd/Sft		830	
0	18	THIR	6f Soft		909	
51a	2	SOUT	6f Aw	51	1205	
40a	7	SOUT	5f Aw	52	1422	
59	1	REDC	6f Gd/Sft	51	1578*	
59	3	HAYD	7f Gd/Sft	57	1793	
62	1	CARL	6f Aw	58	2243*	
48	11	HAYD	7f Gd/Sft	63	3269	
0	14	NEWC	6f Firm	63	3605	
56	6	RIPO	6f Good	63	3698	
62	2	LING	6f Soft	64	4270	VIS
61	4	AYR	5f Heavy	61	4307	vis
66	2	DONC	7f Gd/Sft	63	4452	vis
57	8	NEWM	6f Gd/Sft	63	4536	vis

CRYHAVOC 6 b g £19758
81	6	DONC	6f Good	88	716
62	13	RIPO	6f Soft	86	824
0	13	PONT	5f Heavy	83	941
83	3	CHES	5f Firm	82	1245
79	7	YORK	5f Firm	81	1324
82	3	GOOD	6f Gd/Sft	82	1471
87	2	REDC	5f Gd/Sft	82	1580
65	14	MUSS	5f Firm	82	1687

90	2	DONC	5f Gd/Fm	85	2348
94	1	EPSO	6f Gd/Sft	85	2432*
83	10	ASCO	5f Good	93	2676
96	2	ASCO	6f Gd/Fm	93	2954
89	8	ASCO	5f Gd/Fm	93	3016
73	16	GOOD	6f Firm	91	3152
88	10	RIPO	6f Gd/Fm	93	3464
0	20	YORK	6f Good	93	3543
89	6	YORK	6f Gd/Fm	92	3727
79	13	DONC	6f Gd/Fm	91	3861
73	15	AYR	6f Gd/Sft	92	4012

CRYSTAL CANYON 3 ch f £0
| 51 | 7 | WARW | 8f Gd/Sft | | 1712 |

CRYSTAL CASTLE 2 b c £21134
| 103 | 1 | DEAU | 6f Gd/Fm | | 3210* |

CRYSTAL CHANDELIER 2 ch f £0
| 36 | 9 | THIR | 6f Gd/Fm | | 3143 |
| 37 | 8 | CATT | 6f Soft | | 4001 |

CRYSTAL CREEK 4 b c £0
0	17	KEMP	8f Soft	86	1015
65	6	GOOD	8f Gd/Sft		1635
73	8	NOTT	10f Gd/Fm	82	2190
60	12	KEMP	10f Gd/Fm	78	2750
60	13	NEWM	8f Good	75	4340

CRYSTAL DASS 3 b f £13832
109	4	LONG	8f Heavy		1025	bl
107	3	CHAN	8f Soft		1900	bl
109	2	CHAN	9f Soft		2913	bl

CRYSTAL FLITE 3 b f £1148
68	7	NEWM	10f Gd/Sft	72	979
44	11	SALI	10f Firm	70	1177
67	2	CHES	12f Gd/Fm	66	2246
29	6	CHES	12f Good		2667
42	11	WIND	12f Gd/Fm	65	3049
54	5	SALI	12f Gd/Fm	60	3392
56	5	SALI	14f Gd/Sft	57	4166

CRYSTAL LASS 4 b f £250
63a	4	SOUT	7f Aw	71	33	bl
0a	14	SOUT	8f Aw	69	251	bl
50a	5	SOUT	8f Aw	66	513	bl
37	7	SOUT	7f Soft	52	1606	
0	15	REDC	8f Good	47	1892	
42	5	DONC	5f Gd/Fm	42	2320	
29	13	DONC	7f Gd/Fm	41	2612	
36	5	THIR	6f Gd/Fm	40	2969	
0	15	THIR	6f Gd/Fm	47	3123	
40	4	REDC	6f Firm	39	3312	
0	17	NEWC	7f Firm	40	3605	
44a	7	SOUT	7f Aw	60	4153	

CRYSTAL MUSIC 2 b f £125913
105	1	NEWM	7f Gd/Fm		2806*
100	1	SAND	8f Good		3433*
111	3	ASCO	8f Good		4110*

CUBISM 4 b c £9655
99	7	YORK	6f Firm		1338	
97	3	YARM	6f Gd/Fm		1952	t
103	5	NEWB	6f Firm	103	2706	t
103	3	GOOD	6f Firm	103	3152	t
80	8	NEWM	6f Good		3610	t
0	18	NEWM	5f Good	104	4339	

CUIGIU 3 b c £2001
53a	4	WOLV	6f Aw		118	
28a	10	WOLV	8f Aw		171	
42a	7	SOUT	8f Aw		328	
29a	5	SOUT	7f Aw		741	BL
51	4	LEIC	6f Gd/Sft		830	
55	2	THIR	7f Soft		930	
45	12	DONC	8f Gd/Sft	63	1053	
54	5	HAMI	9f Firm		1242	
46a	4	SOUT	8f Aw	50	1804	
32a	7	SOUT	7f Aw	50	1979	
46	8	NOTT	8f Gd/Fm	58	2187	

54	2	LEIC	8f Gd/Fm		2914
56	3	RIPO	10f Gd/Fm	54	3008
23	14	BATH	8f Gd/Fm	53	3816
30	12	YARM	8f Gd/Fm	53	3971

CULMINATE 3 ch g £0
0	17	WIND	8f Good		3048
22	9	NEWB	9f Gd/Fm		3179
62	11	NEWM	8f Gd/Fm		3626
0	20	BRIG	10f Soft	52	4174
0a	13	LING	10f Aw	45	4482

CULTURED PEARL 3 b f £536
76	3	NOTT	8f Gd/Fm		1268	
56a	6	WOLV	9f Aw		1388	
46	10	BRIG	10f Good	73	1649	
54	7	NEWM	7f Firm	70	1855	
46	11	EPSO	7f Good	66	3854	
0a	13	WOLV	8f Aw	60	4021	BL

CULZEAN 4 b c £13542
86	5	DONC	6f Gd/Fm	85	733	
81	3	HAYD	11f Heavy		986	
78	6	KEMP	8f Gd/Sft	83	1077	
73	7	CHES	10f Gd/Fm	83	1217	BL
68	11	GOOD	8f Gd/Sft	80	1450	bl
80	4	WIND	10f Gd/Fm	78	1878	
86	1	NEWM	10f Gd/Fm	78	2287*	
83	2	WARW	8f Gd/Fm		2844	
75	10	GOOD	10f Gd/Fm	83	3060	
85	3	LEIC	10f Gd/Fm	83	3337	
79	6	NEWM	10f Gd/Fm	84	3628	
87	2	DONC	10f Gd/Fm		3865	
79	13	NEWB	10f Firm	84	3997	
71	17	NEWM	9f Gd/Fm	84	4212	
76	5	YARM	19f Soft		4515	

CUMBRIAN CASPER 2 b g £0
| 22 | 4 | NOTT | 5f Heavy | | 1020 |

CUMBRIAN HARMONY 2 b f £5573
50	9	NEWC	5f Heavy		1006
73	2	MUSS	5f Gd/Fm		1429
67	3	REDC	6f Gd/Sft		1577
49	7	DONC	6f Gd/Fm		1844
67	5	CARL	5f Firm		2277
57	5	YORK	5f Good	67	2698
67	2	CARL	5f Firm		2821
72	1	NEWC	6f Good		3032*
51	9	NEWC	7f Good	69	3246
53	13	DONC	7f Gd/Fm	69	3860

CUMBRIAN PRINCESS 3 gr f £0
0	27	NEWB	7f Gd/Fm	61	1405
0	13	WARW	7f Gd/Sft	59	1710
0	16	HAYD	7f Gd/Sft	59	1793
48	6	WIND	10f Gd/Fm	53	2206
29	8	NEWB	10f Firm	51	2811
30	5	BRIG	10f Gd/Fm	45	3263
0	19	CHEP	7f Good	42	3871

CUPBOARD LOVER 4 ch g £6781
57	6	NOTT	14f Good	64	788
53a	5	SOUT	14f Aw	60	868
52	6	NOTT	14f Good	58	1411
50	6	KEMP	12f Gd/Fm	55	1927
49	3	NOTT	12f Good	52	2681
57	1	CHEP	12f Gd/Fm	50	3255*
57	4	BATH	13f Gd/Fm	60	3518
58a	1	WOLV	12f Aw	48	4026*
59a	4	WOLV	12f Aw	62	4226
63a	2	LING	12f Aw	60	4334

CUPERCOY 2 £3362
| 100 | 4 | MAIS | 6f V | | 3066 |

CUPIDS CHARM 3 b f £8427
45	9	PONT	6f Soft		877
50	8	PONT	6f Gd/Sft		1105
73	1	BRIG	5f Firm	65	1334*
56	7	WIND	6f Gd/Fm	71	1877

77	1	CARL	5f Firm	71	2280*
67	6	NEWM	6f Gd/Fm	78	2804
69	8	LING	6f Firm	77	3280
55	8	BRIG	5f Firm	76	3528
76	4	NEWM	7f Gd/Fm	75	4215

CUPIDS DART 3 ch g £2806

55a	3	WOLV	8f Aw		80
49a	6	SOUT	8f Aw		198
58a	5	LING	6f Aw		334
64a	2	LING	8f Aw		373
64a	3	LING	7f Aw		421
54a	5	LING	5f Aw		507
66a	2	LING	8f Aw		615
58a	3	LING	7f Aw		651
27a	7	WOLV	8f Aw		1234
53	9	LEIC	7f Firm	65	2026
0	14	NEWM	8f Gd/Fm		2134
32	5	YARM	7f Gd/Fm		2413 bl
0	13	LEIC	8f Firm		2914 bl
49a	4	LING	10f Aw	57	3828
29a	8	LING	10f Aw		4100

CURRENCY 3 b c £0

59	6	BATH	6f Gd/Fm		3820
16	10	WIND	6f Heavy		4526

CURTSEY 2 b f £0

32	11	BATH	6f Soft	4138

CURULE 3 br c £30488

111ε3		NAD	9f Dirt	765
110ε7		CHUR	10f Dirt	1226

CUSIN 4 ch c £3465

72	7	THIR	5f Soft	74	926
61	10	THIR	7f Good	73	1158
73	3	DONC	7f Gd/Fm	71	1840
63	11	YORK	9f Firm	72	2001
66	5	LING	8f Gd/Fm	72	2185
51	10	CATT	7f Gd/Fm	71	2420
53	15	YORK	7f Good	70	2694
56	9	NEWC	7f Gd/Fm	67	2986
60	5	CARL	7f Firm		3573
64	2	YORK	7f Good	63	3809
38	8	BEVE	7f Stt/Hvy	64	4044
60	5	DONC	7f Soft		4461

CUT QUARTZ 3 b c £3842

105	3	BORD	10f Soft	4490 bl

CUT RATE 2 c £0

53	10	DONC	7f Gd/Sft	4447

CUTE CAROLINE 4 ch f £1536

47	3	HAMI	8f Gd/Fm	52	1190
47	5	HAMI	8f Firm	52	1243
39	11	AYR	8f Gd/Fm	50	1658
26a	6	SOUT	8f Aw	50	1803
46	2	REDC	8f Gd/Fm	47	2147 BL
46	3	MUSS	8f Aw	46	2378 bl
19a	8	WOLV	8f Aw	45	2601 VIS
34	9	HAMI	9f Gd/Fm	46	2799 vis
32	7	HAMI	8f Gd/Sft	44	3380 vis
49	4	MUSS	7f Gd/Fm		3744 vis

CYBER BABE 3 b f £11251

47a	7	LING	7f Aw		53 vis
3a	9	WOLV	8f Aw		80 vis
53	7	LING	7f Gd/Sft	60	841
50a	2	WOLV	9f Aw	45	1040
51a	1	WOLV	9f Aw		1141*
18a	10	SOUT	8f Aw	55	1303
35	11	NOTT	8f Gd/Fm	56	2187
48	2	BRIG	10f Gd/Sft		2423
56	1	BRIG	10f Gd/Fm	52	2727*
58	3	BATH	12f Firm		3206
62	1	SALI	12f Gd/Fm	56	3392*
45	7	YORK	12f Gd/Fm	63	3725
29a	10	SOUT	12f Aw		4366

CYBER SANTA 2 b c £0

65	5	BEVE	7f Good	3952
0	20	YORK	8f Soft	4281
42	10	MUSS	7f Soft	4517

CYBERTECHNOLOGY 6 b g £8946

35	12	THIR	8f Soft	64	907
0	17	NEWC	8f Aw	62	1007
39	8	BEVE	8f Firm	60	1279
38	10	REDC	9f Gd/Sft	57	1583
55	3	HAMI	8f Gd/Fm		1940
60	1	BEVE	10f Firm	53	2220*
56	6	BEVE	10f Gd/Fm	58	2518
62	1	AYR	8f Gd/Fm	58	3141*
56	8	AYR	10f Good	62	3368
52	6	BEVE	10f Gd/Fm	62	3410
50	10	BEVE	8f Good	61	3951

CYCLONE CONNIE 2 ch f £2252

87	2	GOOD	6f Gd/Fm	1957
87	3	ASCO	6f Good	2172

CYMBAL MELODY 4 b f £0

0a	9	WOLV	15f Aw	39	277
12a	5	WOLV	15f Aw		363
0a	7	WOLV	15f Aw		468
0a	6	WOLV	15f Aw	24	492

CYMMERIAD O GYMRU 5 b g £0

0	16	BATH	8f Firm	50	3623
0	15	CHEP	5f Good	43	3872
12	12	WIND	8f Heavy		4526

CYNARA 2 b f £6390

55	8	REDC	6f Good		1893
57	5	CARL	6f Gd/Fm		2239
58	2	CATT	7f Gd/Fm		2927
62	1	NEWC	7f Gd/Fm	54	3246*
58	5	BEVE	7f Gd/Fm	60	3411
57	5	YARM	7f Firm	62	3922
69	1	PONT	8f Soft	62	4084*
60	7	DONC	8f Gd/Sft	66	4450

CYPRESS CREEK 3 b f £0

44	11	WIND	12f Gd/Fm	60	1199
0	16	WIND	12f Firm	56	1292
27	7	NOTT	10f Soft	51	1644
0	13	YARM	10f Gd/Fm	47	1955
0	16	NEWM	8f Gd/Fm		2134 VIS

CYRAN PARK 4 b c £263

31	9	CATT	7f Gd/Fm		778
42	4	REDC	7f Gd/Sft		1132
37	8	CARL	6f Firm	53	1257
39	11	REDC	8f Firm	48	1296
31	7	PONT	8f Good		1498
40	4	THIR	8f Gd/Sft	42	1718 BL
6	14	BEVE	8f Aw	42	1920 bl
0	14	REDC	7f Firm	42	3328 VIS
0	15	HAMI	8f Gd/Sft	38	3534
0	17	NEWC	9f Firm	38	3603
0	14	RIPO	8f Gd/Fm		3711 vis

CYRAZY 2 b f £650

68	3	LEIC	5f Soft	1550
0	19	NEWB	5f Firm	2849
62	4	NOTT	5f Gd/Fm	3114

CZAR WARS 5 b g £3072

53a	5	SOUT	5f Aw		71 bl
35a	8	WOLV	5f Aw	45	116 bl
41a	4	SOUT	6f Heavy		199 bl
44a	4	SOUT	6f Aw	43	212 bl
0a	11	SOUT	6f Aw	42	246 bl
0	17	LEIC	7f Good		790 bl
31	10	REDC	7f Gd/Sft		1559
40a	3	SOUT	7f Aw	41	2297 bl
27a	4	SOUT	7f Aw	41	2637 bl
31	6	THIR	6f Gd/Fm	34	3144 bl
53	1	HAYD	6f Gd/Fm		3283* bl
41	3	LING	6f Firm	41	3578 bl
38	7	YARM	6f Gd/Fm	42	3964 bl

0	13	DONC	7f Soft		4461 bl

D W MCCEE 4 b g £0

0	16	NOTT	6f Good	52	787
0	16	WARW	8f Soft	47	1066
0a	12	SOUT	7f Aw	42	1801
0	15	BATH	8f Firm	40	2331 VIS

DA BOSS 5 ch g £0

0	16	SOUT	11f Gd/Fm	60	855
0	17	WIND	10f Gd/Sft	54	1100
0a	14	SOUT	12f Aw		1203

DA VINCI 2 b c £5893

74	1	PONT	5f Soft		1704*
52	7	BATH	5f Firm		1995
49	11	THIR	5f Gd/Fm	75	3145
79	1	HAMI	5f Soft	70	3802*
66	6	SAND	5f Soft	79	4202

DA WOLF 2 ch c £0

52	6	GOOD	5f Firm	4079
0	13	BATH	8f Soft	4429

DAAWE 9 b h £22150

86a	1	SOUT	6f Aw	70	499* bl
82a	1	WOLV	6f Aw	76	532* bl
98a	1	WOLV	5f Aw	86	579+ bl
84a	6	SOUT	6f Aw	86	587 bl
98a	3	WOLV	6f Aw	96	660 bl
55	11	DONC	6f Good	69	716 bl
65	6	KEMP	5f Soft	68	1013 bl
74	1	DONC	6f Gd/Sft	68	1074* bl
0	15	THIR	6f Good	73	1162 bl
28	9	CHES	5f Gd/Sft	72	1781 bl
69	5	HAYD	5f Gd/Sft	72	1792 bl
71	7	RIPO	5f Good	72	1861 bl
71	5	YORK	6f Good	72	2697 bl
65	14	DONC	5f Firm	72	3894
64	10	AYR	5f Soft	72	3960 bl
46	20	AYR	6f Gd/Sft	72	4010 bl
61	5	REDC	5f Gd/Sft		4220 bl
65	8	YORK	5f Soft	70	4285 bl
0	18	PONT	5f Soft	68	4377 bl

DABUS 5 b g £0

56	14	YORK	10f Gd/Fm	92	3563
0	13	DONC	10f Gd/Fm		3865

DACCORD 3 ch c £8343

80a	1	LING	6f Aw		221*
86a	1	LING	5f Aw	78	234*
73a	5	WOLV	6f Aw	80	275
87a	3	LING	6f Aw	85	444
77	5	GOOD	6f Gd/Fm	80	1961
58	11	LING	6f Gd/Fm	79	2216
72	6	SAND	5f Aw	80	2478
76	4	DONC	5f Firm	76	3894
81	2	NEWM	5f Good	76	4185
76	4	YORK	5f Soft	76	4285

DAHLIDYA 5 b m £16214

36a	5	SOUT	6f Aw		30
44a	3	SOUT	6f Aw	45	87
59a	1	SOUT	6f Aw	54	180*
51a	2	SOUT	7f Aw	57	216
64a	3	SOUT	7f Aw	62	282
59a	4	SOUT	6f Aw	62	342
51a	6	WOLV	7f Aw	62	364
57a	1	WOLV	6f Aw		436*
67a	1	SOUT	6f Aw		475*
0a	12	WOLV	6f Aw	67	532
65a	1	SOUT	6f Aw		538*
53a	5	SOUT	6f Aw	69	557
42a	9	SOUT	6f Aw	62	645
56a	3	WOLV	7f Aw		677
66a	1	SOUT	6f Aw	60	697*
66a	3	SOUT	7f Aw	65	739
65a	3	WOLV	6f Aw	65	923
37a	11	WOLV	7f Good	65	1235

31	7	NOTT	6f Firm	41	1273
49a	9	SOUT	6f Aw	65	1504
15	10	DONC	7f Good	38	1519
56a	7	WOLV	6f Aw	64	4023
0a	14	SOUT	7f Aw	63	4153
52a	7	WOLV	6f Aw	61	4358

DAILY TONIC 3 ch c £530
70	3	NOTT	10f Heavy		4412

DAINTY DISH 4 ch f £0
32a	5	SOUT	6f Aw		32 BL

DAJAM VU 3 ch f £0
0	12	SALI	10f Good		1344
0	12	CHEP	10f Gd/Sft		1796
53	8	BATH	10f Gd/Sft		2553
21	7	BATH	12f Firm	46	3206

DAKHIRA 2 b f £0
60	6	CHEP	7f Good		3866

DAKISI ROYALE 3 ch f £0
35a	5	LING	6f Aw	49	4 vis
9a	7	WOLV	8f Aw		80
41	6	NOTT	8f Gd/Fm	47	2187
0	15	WARW	8f Good	47	2460
0	14	THIR	8f Gd/Fm	42	2964

DAKOTA SIOUX 3 ch f £20551
51	3	CATT	6f Soft		1678
53	6	NEWC	8f Firm		2337
0	17	PONT	8f Gd/Fm	56	2561
60	1	NEWC	7f Good	51	3033* BL
61	1	HAYD	7f Gd/Sft	57	3269* bl
50	8	CARL	8f Firm	61	3574 VIS
72	1	HAYD	7f Gd/Sft	67	4106* bl
32	10	YORK	7f Heavy	74	4302 bl

DALAMPOUR 3 b c £57258
82	7	NEWB	12f Gd/Fm		1404
96	1	NEWM	12f Gd/Fm		1696*
109	1	ASCO	16f Good		2068*
112	3	YORK	12f Good		3540
111	5	DONC	15f Firm		3898

DALBY OF YORK 4 ch g £0
52	6	WIND	12f Gd/Sft		1096

DALIAPOUR 4 b c £370378
119	1	CHES	13f Firm		1247+
121	1	EPSO	12f Gd/Sft		1827*
119	3	ASCO	12f Gd/Fm		2998
115	4	BADE	12f V		3849
117	3	WOOD	12f Firm		4400

DALLACHIO 9 ch g £0
4a	8	WOLV	16f Aw	44	66 t
25a	5	SOUT	14f Aw	34	1501 t

DALWHINNIE 7 b m £0
0a	8	SOUT	14f Aw	41	182
19a	4	WOLV	16f Aw	35	190 bl
13a	6	SOUT	16f Aw	30	535 bl

DALYAN 3 b c £0
41	8	PONT	10f Gd/Sft	70	1104
41	12	THIR	8f Good	68	1387
54	4	REDC	11f Gd/Fm		2146
54	7	BEVE	12f Gd/Fm	60	2482
47	5	RIPO	12f Soft	60	2540
39	10	BEVE	12f Gd/Fm	53	3674
7	9	BEVE	10f Stt/Hv	47	4046

DAM ELHANAH 2 b f £756
69	2	MUSS	5f Gd/Sft		796
63	4	MUSS	5f Gd/Sft		898
61	5	THIR	5f Good		1381

DAMAGES 2 b f £0
0	19	WIND	6f Gd/Sft		4288

DAMALIS 4 b f £26281
83	4	DONC	5f Good	89	702
92	6	BATH	5f Good		1090
97	1	CHES	5f Firm	88	1245*
0	17	YORK	5f Firm	94	1324
87	8	EPSO	5f Good	96	1849
98	1	CHES	5f Gd/Fm	93	2247*
0	19	ASCO	5f Gd/Fm	98	3016
98	3	CHES	5f Firm		3172
96	5	PONT	6f Firm		3503
0	18	ASCO	5f Gd/Sft	98	4129

DAMASQUINER 3 b f £2579
22a	6	LING	6f Aw		153
31a	4	LING	8f Aw	45	355
58a	1	LING	7f Aw		459*
39a	6	LING	7f Aw		547
54a	3	LING	8f Aw		595
53a	5	LING	7f Aw	56	654
41a	6	LING	7f Aw	54	773

DAME FONTEYN 3 b f £4629
0	P	MUSS	12f Gd/Sft		799
47	2	PONT	12f Heavy		939
58	2	PONT	12f Gd/Sft	55	1106
51	6	NOTT	14f Gd/Fm	52	1270
63	1	REDC	14f Gd/Sft	58	1581*
48	3	NEWC	12f Heavy		1767
45	10	REDC	14f Gd/Sft	63	4222
23	8	YARM	14f Heavy	61	4476

DAME HATTIE 5 b m £0
68	5	RIPO	10f Good		1599
65	5	HAYD	14f Soft		1824
59	6	DONC	12f Gd/Fm		3157

DAME JUDE 4 ch f £0
34	11	BATH	5f Good	57	1092
38	11	BRIG	7f Firm	57	1213
45	8	BRIG	6f Gd/Sft	53	1464

DANAKIL 5 b g £9289
65a	5	SOUT	8f Aw	69	326
60a	6	WOLV	9f Aw	67	383
48a	6	WOLV	8f Aw	66	432
66a	3	WOLV	9f Aw	64	521
46a	5	WOLV	8f Aw	64	551 VIS
69a	1	WOLV	9f Aw	64	681*
54a	6	WOLV	9f Aw	68	718
68	4	WIND	8f Gd/Fm	63	1201*
65	2	GOOD	8f Gd/Sft	66	1473
61	7	THIR	8f Gd/Sft	68	1718

DANAKIM 3 b c £772
42a	9	WOLV	8f Aw	78	566
32a	9	SOUT	8f Aw	78	601
42a	8	SOUT	8f Aw	68	698
57	2	CATT	6f Gd/Fm		781 BL
68	4	NOTT	5f Heavy		1021 bl
15	10	CATT	6f Good	65	1665
57	5	CARL	5f Firm		2822
15a	9	SOUT	6f Aw		2947
0	17	THIR	5f Gd/Fm	59	3619 bl
0	22	REDC	5f Gd/Sft		4220
0	12	CATT	6f Soft		4257

DANAMALA 4 b f £1436
71	2	WARW	8f Soft		1063
67	4	SAND	7f Soft	72	1564

DANANEYEV 4 br c £13449
109	1	MAIS	6f Heavy		820*

DANCE DIRECTOR 3 b c £6437
75	4	HAYD	11f Gd/Sft		3265
83	2	YORK	10f Good		3813
89	1	KEMP	12f Soft		4040*

DANCE IN THE DAY 2 b c £0
0	13	LEIC	7f Firm		3840
65	11	YARM	8f Soft		4512

DANCE IN TUNE 3 ch c £0
76	5	FOLK	10f Gd/Fm		3042
0a	11	WOLV	9f Aw	83	3495

DANCE LITTLE LADY 3 b f £3315
63a	6	WOLV	5f Aw		77
48a	4	WOLV	5f Aw		145
0	21	REDC	6f Gd/Sft	57	1578
56	1	REDC	6f Good	52	1891*
47	6	CARL	6f Gd/Fm	56	2243
0	11	BEVE	5f Firm	55	2732
0a	15	SOUT	6f Aw	54	4155

DANCE MELODY 6 b m £0
0	12	CARL	8f Firm	32	3574

DANCE OF LOVE 3 b f £0
100	5	LEOP	8f Gd/Fm		1315 t

DANCE ON 2 ch f £12810
89	1	LEIC	5f Gd/Sft		1737*
89	7	ASCO	5f Good		2088
86	6	NEWM	6f Good		2344
96	1	YARM	5f Good		3027*
94	8	NEWB	5f Gd/Fm		3482
96	3	AYR	8f Gd/Sft		4009
89	4	NEWB	7f Sft/Hvy		4467

DANCE ON THE TOP 2 ch c £8053
69	6	DONC	6f Good		1513
87	1	KEMP	7f Firm		2867*
89	2	GOOD	7f Gd/Sft	84	3149
55	15	NEWC	8f Gd/Sft	88	3704
0	21	NEWM	7f Good		4158

DANCE QUEEN 2 b f £0
65	6	PONT	5f Heavy		938
0	11	MUSS	5f Gd/Fm		1146
0	12	REDC	6f Gd/Sft		1577
61	6	CATT	7f Gd/Sft		2417
0	11	AYR	7f Good		3363
30	8	THIR	6f Good		3615
50	6	AYR	8f Heavy		4322
40	7	NEWC	7f Heavy		4403

DANCE TO THE BEAT 5 b m £0
0a	11	SOUT	11f Aw	45	325 bl

DANCE WEST 3 b c £5403
64	7	KEMP	7f Soft		1012
83	7	NEWM	8f Firm		1188
85	4	NEWM	8f Gd/Fm		1692
81	2	SAND	7f Good		1963
85	1	YARM	7f Firm		2770*
82	8	NEWM	7f Gd/Fm	85	3629

DANCE WITH ME 2 b g £0
0	11	WIND	5f Heavy		932
0	13	NOTT	6f Good		1408
48	4	YARM	7f Gd/Fm		1950 BL

DANCEABOUT 3 b f £77942
88	1	GOOD	7f Gd/Sft		1468*
101	5	ASCO	7f Good		2087
106	3	NEWM	8f Gd/Fm		2597
105	1	GOOD	7f Good		3104*
108	2	CURR	8f Gd/Fm		3846
108	1	NEWM	8f Gd/Fm		4211*

DANCEMMA 3 ch f £1220
62	7	LING	6f Gd/Sft		837
66	11	WIND	5f Gd/Sft	76	1098
43	13	NOTT	6f Firm		1266
64	2	WARW	8f Gd/Sft		1712
64	5	CHEP	5f Gd/Sft	69	1795
0	15	CHEP	6f Gd/Fm	66	2489
0	11	SALI	6f Good		2690
39a	8	SOUT	6f Aw	66	2820
56	4	FOLK	5f Gd/Fm		3584
0	16	NOTT	6f Soft	59	3595
38	8	BRIG	8f Soft		4173
35	8	WIND	6f Gd/Sft	55	4294

DANCING BAY 3 b c £18933
88	1	NEWC	7f Soft		759*
89	1	PONT	10f Gd/Sft	80	1104*
72	10	YORK	10f Gd/Fm	88	1310
84	4	PONT	10f Soft	88	4085
92	1	AYR	13f Heavy	87	4325*

DANCING DERVISH 5 b g £0

39 7 WARW 11f Heavy 52 889 vis
0 12 WARW 13f Gd/Fm 50 2843 vis

DANCING DREAMS 3 b g £0
0 19 NEWM 8f Firm 1188

DANCING EMPRESS 3 b f £8295
76a 2 WOLV 5f Aw 77
80a 1 **SOUT** 5f Aw 179*
68 7 WARW 6f Heavy 888
81a 1 **WOLV** 6f Aw 75 1138*
78 2 CHEP 6f Heavy 74 1557
72 4 NEWC 6f Heavy 74 1768
58a 10 WOLV 5f Aw 80 2078
76 6 DONC 6f Gd/Fm 77 2577
0 15 GOOD 6f Good 76 3904
52 10 KEMP 6f Gd/Sft 73 4037 BL
0 18 NEWM 6f Gd/Fm 73 4185 bl

DANCING JACK 7 ch g £0
6a 10 LING 5f Aw 38 57
21a 7 LING 7f Aw 42 107
32a 7 LING 7f Aw 159
36a 6 LING 6f Aw 43 235
11a 5 LING 6f Aw 30 263
0a 11 LING 6f Aw 313
50 7 BATH 5f 3622
0 12 SAND 5f Gd/Fm 3947

DANCING KING 4 b c £0
0 12 MUSS 12f Gd/Sft 4133

DANCING KRIS 7 b g £0
69 7 DONC 8f Gd/Fm 703
0 35 NEWM 9f Gd/Fm 95 4212 BL

DANCING LAWYER 9 b g £0
0a 11 WOLV 7f Aw 43 582
25 8 MUSS 9f Gd/Sft 39 795
0 13 SOUT 11f Gd/Sft 36 855

DANCING LILY 3 ch f £538
35 11 WIND 6f Firm 52 1289
25 8 GOOD 5f Gd/Fm 49 1487
67 7 WARW 7f Gd/Sft 73 1710
0 13 WIND 6f Gd/Fm 50 1877
43 2 LING 7f Good 43 2592
42 8 SALI 8f Gd/Fm 47 2980
37 5 SALI 8f Gd/Fm 43 3293
48 7 SALI 7f Gd/Fm 3423
0 16 LING 8f Firm 53 3580

DANCING MAESTRO 4 gr c £3355
74 10 SAND 5f Gd/Fm 2496
101 6 NEWM 6f Gd/Fm 2960
103 3 YARM 6f Good 3235
101 2 YARM 6f Gd/Fm 3667
89 8 DONC 5f Gd/Fm 3874
88 15 NEWM 6f Good 4346

DANCING MARY 3 gr f £1211
51a 3 SOUT 8f Aw 500
34a 7 LING 10f Aw 523
48a 3 SOUT 12f Aw 643
51 5 CATT 12f Gd/Fm 65 782
44 7 BEVE 12f Heavy 60 978
56 4 BATH 12f Firm 1997
51 3 WARW 12f Gd/Fm 55 2254
45 6 PONT 12f Gd/Fm 54 2829
35a 9 SOUT 14f Aw 47 4371

DANCING MASTER 2 b c £1204
80 3 KEMP 7f Gd/Fm 3790

DANCING MILLY 2 ch f £0
0 U BATH 6f Gd/Sft 2550
32 6 BATH 6f Firm 2939
0 17 BATH 5f Gd/Fm 3204

DANCING MIRAGE 3 ch f £1001
77 6 GOOD 10f Gd/Fm 87 1958
76 3 SAND 8f Gd/Fm 3945
0 20 NEWM 10f Good 81 4197

DANCING MYSTERY 6 b g £64735

77a 7 WOLV 5f Aw 80 64
0 22 WIND 5f Gd/Fm 80 1196
70 7 LING 5f Gd/Sft 75 1264
76 3 BATH 5f Gd/Fm 1441
70 3 BRIG 5f Good 73 1650
68 5 SALI 5f Firm 75 2022
80 1 **SALI** 5f Gd/Fm 73 2266+
79 7 GOOD 6f Good 80 2355
81 3 SAND 5f Gd/Fm 80 2925
61 17 GOOD 6f Gd/Fm 80 3152
84 1 **ASCO** 5f Gd/Fm 80 3341*
80 4 BRIG 5f Firm 83 3528
75 9 EPSO 5f Good 83 3687
91 1 **YARM** 5f Firm 82 3920*
96 1 **NEWM** 5f Good 88 4015*
98 2 ASCO 5f Gd/Sft 94 4129
102 1 **NEWM** 5f Good 96 4339*
105 1 **DONC** 5f Soft 1004466*

DANCING PENNEY 2 b f £5501
48 5 MUSS 5f Gd/Sft 796
36 13 THIR 5f Soft 928
57 8 THIR 5f Good 1381 BL
60 1 **CATT** 5f Gd/Fm 2435* bl
58a 2 WOLV 5f Aw 2605 bl
60 2 NEWC 6f Gd/Fm 2983
62 1 **REDC** 6f Firm 3307*
60 6 BEVE 5f Good 66 3394
51 6 RIPO 6f Gd/Fm 60 3712
46 12 CATT 5f Soft 59 4007
61a 3 WOLV 6f Aw 4246
60a 4 WOLV 6f Aw 4359

DANCING RIDGE 3 b c £0
29 13 HAYD 6f Soft 54 1494
31 7 CATT 6f Good 54 1665
30 10 CARL 5f Firm 49 2280

DANCING SEA 4 b f £167
42a 4 LING 8f Aw 114

DANCING TSAR 2 b c £0
60 6 BATH 6f Soft 4138

DANCING VENTURE 2 b f £1705
76 5 GOOD 6f Gd/Fm 1957
63 4 FOLK 7f Gd/Fm 3039
60 3 REDC 7f Firm 3308
71 2 YARM 8f Gd/Fm 66 3968
43 7 AYR 8f Heavy 70 4323

DANDES RAMBO 3 gr g £2402
61 5 SAND 8f Heavy 1041
44 6 LEIC 12f Gd/Sft 58 1571
54 3 SAND 11f Good 54 1967
46 6 YARM 14f Gd/Fm 54 2195
23 13 BATH 12f Gd/Sft 53 2554
50 4 BATH 12f Firm 48 3206
49 2 NEWM 10f Gd/Fm 48 3314
41 6 CHEP 10f Gd/Fm 51 3683
42a 5 LING 16f Aw 50 4329
20a 11 LING 12f Aw 46 4486 BL

DANDILUM 3 b c £1609
85 4 NEWM 7f Gd/Sft 983
0 W NEWM 8f Gd/Fm 1692
62 9 LING 7f Firm 3834
79 2 NOTT 8f Soft 3977
58 12 SAND 8f Soft 80 4206
60 13 NEWM 7f Soft 78 4547

DANDY NIGHT 3 b f £9651
82 7 LEIC 7f Gd/Sft 1733
99 1 **YARM** 6f Gd/Fm 2197*
101 3 NEWM 6f Gd/Fm 2289
87 8 YORK 6f Gd/Fm 2646
95 6 PONT 6f Firm 3503
91 8 YARM 6f Firm 3937
93 6 NEWM 6f Good 4198

DANDY REGENT 6 b g £6508

54 1 **LEIC** 7f Good 790*
44 7 PONT 6f Soft 872
65 1 **THIR** 7f Gd/Sft 1351*
0 12 YARM 7f Gd/Fm 60 1611
40 9 THIR 7f Gd/Fm 60 2063
56 4 LEIC 7f Gd/Fm 58 2775
0 13 THIR 6f Gd/Fm 55 3123
29 9 NEWM 7f Gd/Fm 3318
53 3 NEWM 7f Good 4018
51 5 REDC 7f Gd/Sft 56 4498

DANE DANCING 2 b f £708
63 5 ASCO 6f Gd/Fm 3342
73 7 KEMP 6f Gd/Fm 3795
72 8 YARM 6f Firm 3938
63 7 LING 7f Soft 68 4191
67 3 NEWB 7f Gd/Fm 66 4453
29 12 DONC 7f Heavy 4577

DANE FLYER 2 b c £0
85 7 ASCO 6f Gd/Fm 3000
49 10 SALI 6f Gd/Fm 3387 t
58 8 BATH 6f Soft 4138

DANE FRIENDLY 4 b c £11366
101 3 SAN 8f Good 1460

DANEGOLD 8 b g £1961
49 9 DONC 18f Good 63 714
59 3 SALI 14f Firm 60 1180
53 5 THIR 16f Gd/Sft 60 1355
58 4 BATH 17f Firm 1996
38 11 ASCO 16f Good 58 2173
55 7 SAND 16f Gd/Fm 57 2498
50 8 ASCO 16f Gd/Fm 56 2953
54 4 SAND 14f Good 57 3231
40 6 KEMP 16f Gd/Fm 55 3360
52 3 SAND 16f Good 3434
51 8 YARM 14f Gd/Fm 55 3664
0 9 BATH 17f Soft 51 4139

DANEHURST 2 b f £23567
81 1 **WARW** 5f Gd/Fm 2034*
103?1 **WOLV** 5f Aw 4247+
109 1 **NEWB** 5f Gd/Fm 4454+

DANES LADY 4 b f £321
66 4 NEWM 6f Firm 70 3297
0 22 YORK 8f Soft 4287
57 18 NEWM 7f Good 68 4357

DANESTAR 5 b m £0
19a 9 WOLV 8f Aw 42 233
26a 6 WOLV 8f Aw 308 VIS

DANGER BABY 10 ch g £4347
0a 10 WOLV 16f Aw 51 194 bl
49 6 CHEP 18f Gd/Sft 51 1800 bl
49 2 WARW 16f Gd/Fm 48 2037
41 5 MUSS 16f Gd/Fm 48 2203
49 2 CHEP 18f Gd/Fm 49 2452 bl
49 1 **FOLK** 16f Good 46 2622* bl
40 6 FOLK 15f Gd/Fm 49 3040 bl

DANGER OVER 3 b c £49953
108 1 **MAIS** 7f Soft 945*
109 2 DEAU 6f V 2574
109 2 DEAU 6f Gd/Sft 3724
111 1 **CHAN** 6f Good 4052*

DANGERMAN 5 ch g £281
30a 3 SOUT 8f Aw 38 340 t
5a 9 SOUT 11f Aw 38 390 t

DANGEROUS DEPLOY 3 b g £1817
67 5 NEWM 10f Good 3021
58 5 WIND 8f Good 3190
43 9 SALI 7f Gd/Fm 3423
63 8 GOOD 10f Soft 60 4067
64 5 NEWM 12f Good 4178
60 1 **NOTT** 14f Heavy 57 4409*

DANGEROUS FORTUNE 4 b c £0
73 6 KEMP 8f Soft 81 1015

73	7	HAYD	8f Gd/Sft	81	1836	
72	8	GOOD	8f Gd/Fm	79	3063	
66	10	KEMP	7f Gd/Fm	76	3796	
0	24	NEWM	8f Good	73	4340	

DANGEROUS LADY 3 ch f £0
| 16a | 8 | LING | 8f Aw | | 544 | |
| 13a | 6 | SOUT | 11f Aw | | 670 | |

DANGEROUS MIND 4 b f £29753
| 105 | 1 | MAIS | 11f Heavy | | 122* | |
| 100 | 2 | SAN | 12f Gd/Fm | | 2073 | |

DANIAVI 2 ch c £0
| 0 | 15 | DONC | 7f Gd/Sft | | 4447 | |

DANIEL DERONDA 6 b g £0
| 0 | 13 | NOTT | 10f Gd/Sft | 58 | 1364 | |
| 0 | 17 | WIND | 12f Good | 58 | 1730 | BL |

DANIELLA RIDGE 4 b f £1353
0	13	NEWB	10f Gd/Fm	68	1785	
0	12	KEMP	9f Gd/Sft	63	2581	
20	8	BATH	10f Firm	63	2789	BL
58	2	SALI	8f Gd/Fm	56	3422	
50	5	SALI	8f Firm	56	3753	
50	4	LEIC	8f Gd/Sft		4033	
16a	11	WOLV	8f Aw	53	4440	

DANIELLES LAD 4 b c £16634
78a	8	WOLV	5f Aw	85	64	
83	7	WIND	6f Heavy		935	
87	4	KEMP	5f Soft	88	1013	
82	7	NEWM	6f Gd/Fm	87	1173	
94	1	GOOD	6f Gd/Sft	86	1471*	
97	1	KEMP	6f Soft	92	1531*	
80	13	ASCO	6f Good	96	2151	
95	4	CHEP	5f Gd/Fm	96	2451	
76	18	GOOD	6f Firm	96	3152	
94	6	YORK	6f Good	95	3543	
89	8	YORK	6f Gd/Sft	95	3727	
92	6	AYR	6f Gd/Sft	95	4012	
0	14	SALI	6f Gd/Sft	94	4165	

DANISH RHAPSODY 7 b g £6900
| 110 | 3 | CHES | 13f Firm | | 1247 | |

DANITY FAIR 2 b f £0
48a	4	SOUT	5f Aw		2120	
22a	9	SOUT	6f Aw		2635	
15	11	RIPO	6f Gd/Fm		3009	

DANIYSHA 3 b f £6121
77	4	CHES	7f Gd/Fm		1224	
80	3	GOOD	7f Gd/Sft		1468	
76	1	CHEP	7f Gd/Fm		2491*	
61	11	ASCO	7f Gd/Fm	76	2999	
70	6	CHEP	8f Gd/Fm	76	3254	
74	3	YARM	7f Gd/Fm	74	3666	

DANKA 6 gr g £0
39a	7	WOLV	9f Aw	44	67	
0a	14	SOUT	14f Aw		124	
21a	5	WOLV	16f Aw	38	190	
0a	8	WOLV	16f Aw	34	492	vis
0	20	SAND	10f Soft	38	4208	

DANNI 7 ch m £0
| 0a | 12 | WOLV | 6f Aw | | 1137 | |
| 21a | 10 | SOUT | 8f Aw | | 1505 | |

DANNY DEEVER 4 b c £0
0a	10	SOUT	16f Aw	52	51	
0	14	BEVE	12f Sft/Hv		4041	
0	13	NEWC	7f Heavy	28	4428	

DANO MAST 4 b c £7310
| 108 | 3 | TABY | 12f Good | | 3931 | |

DANSILI 4 b c £157264
120	1	SAIN	8f Hldng		861*	
121	1	SAIN	8f Hldng		1123*	
123	2	ASCO	8f Good		2064	
123	2	GOOD	8f Gd/Fm		3087	
112	6	LONG	8f Soft		3847	
120	2	LONG	7f Soft		4395	

DANZA MONTANA 2 ch f £0
| 74 | 7 | NEWB | 5f Good | | 1372 | |
| 62 | 8 | NEWM | 6f Firm | | 1856 | |

DANZAS 6 b g £4281
29a	6	WOLV	8f Aw	40	255	bl
38a	7	WOLV	7f Aw	41	323	bl
33a	6	WOLV	8f Aw		393	bl
31a	4	WOLV	9f Aw	38	404	bl
29a	6	LING	7f Aw	36	504	bl
14a	7	WOLV	9f Aw	33	568	bl
27a	6	WOLV	9f Aw	33	582	bl
47	1	BRIG	7f Gd/Sft	40	896*	bl
32	8	WARW	8f Soft	44	1066	bl
47	3	BRIG	8f Firm	44	1330	bl
47	2	BRIG	8f Gd/Sft	44	1462	bl
42	6	WARW	8f Heavy	45	1520	bl
45	2	RIPO	8f Gd/Fm	45	2099	bl
44	5	WARW	8f Good	47	2460	bl
35	7	CHEP	8f Gd/Fm	47	2658	bl
43	4	THIR	8f Gd/Sft	45	2970	bl
44	6	BRIG	7f Firm		3559	bl
43	6	CHEP	7f Good	44	3871	bl
42	5	YARM	7f Aw	44	3939	bl
34	7	BRIG	8f Gd/Sft		4122	bl
51a	6	WOLV	7f Aw		4224	bl

DANZIG FLYER 5 b g £0
| 0 | 12 | HAYD | 11f Soft | 38 | 1819 | |
| 0a | 8 | SOUT | 14f Aw | | 1975 | |

DANZIG WITHWOLVES 3 b f £522
74	4	SAND	8f Gd/Fm		2938	
65	4	LING	8f Soft		4274	
65	9	NEWM	8f Sort		4544	

DANZIGAWAY 4 b f £35208
114	1	SAIN	8f Heavy		10*	
111	2	DEAU	8f Gd/Sft		3069	
105	6	LONG	8f Good		4259	

DANZIGEUSE 3 b f £277
25	18	WIND	8f Good	64	852	
49	8	KEMP	7f Gd/Fm	61	3076	
47	4	YARM	6f Gd/Fm	56	3386	
30	10	CARL	7f Firm		3573	
0	14	LEIC	6f Gd/Sft		4031	

DANZINO 5 b g £0
0a	10	SOUT	12f Aw		2298	vis
0a	13	WOLV	9f Aw	85	3495	BL
0a	P	WOLV	12f Aw	85	4226	vis

DAPHNES DOLL 5 b m £2281
48a	4	LING	8f Aw	49	147	
54a	1	LING	10f Aw	48	209*	
26a	7	WOLV	9f Aw	53	270	
20a	10	LING	10f Aw	53	400	
35a	8	LING	8f Aw	51	776	
46	7	CHEP	7f Gd/Sft	50	1794	
16	10	WARW	8f Gd/Fm	48	2257	
48	3	SALI	8f Gd/Fm	48	2467	
0	18	REDC	8f Gd/Fm	47	2861	

DARAKIYLA 3 b f £3842
| 101 | 3 | SAIN | 11f Heavy | | 1313 | |

DARARIYNA 3 b f £10621
80	2	HAYD	11f Gd/Sft		1539	
79	2	GOOD	12f Gd/Sft		1808	
83	1	CHES	13f Gd/Fm		2249*	
75	5	SAND	14f Gd/Sft	82	2936	
82	1	BEVE	12f Gd/Fm		3654*	
57	14	DONC	12f Firm	84	3896	
73	5	YORK	12f Soft		4276	

DARAYDAN 8 b g £0
| 30 | 19 | ASCO | 20f Good | 84 | 2092 | |

DARCY DANCER 3 b c £0
0	11	WARW	11f Heavy	63	1521	
44	8	WARW	12f Gd/Fm	58	2254	BL
26	9	WIND	12f Good	54	2712	

(continued)
| 0 | 17 | NOTT | 16f Gd/Sft | 49 | 3112 | |

DARCY ROAD DANCER 3 b g £0
| 55 | 7 | LING | 9f Firm | | 2322 | |
| 0 | 8 | KEMP | 12f Gd/Fm | | 2751 | |

DARDANUS 2 ch c £988
64	4	BEVE	7f Gd/Fm		3057	
0	14	CHEP	8f Good		3867	
79	4	SALI	8f Gd/Sft		4163	
75	3	YARM	8f Soft	72	4393	

DARE 5 b g £7920
57a	3	WOLV	12f Aw	54	43	
42a	12	WOLV	9f Aw	54	67	
64a	1	SOUT	8f Aw	57	83*	vis
45a	9	SOUT	11f Aw	63	131	vis
45a	10	LING	8f Aw	63	210	vis
48a	8	LING	10f Aw	63	224	
61a	3	SOUT	8f Aw	61	251	BL
67a	2	WOLV	9f Aw	61	309	bl
65a	2	WOLV	9f Aw	61	349	bl
32a	10	WOLV	9f Aw	64	405	bl
40a	7	WOLV	12f Aw	64	489	vis
35a	9	WOLV	9f Aw	62	611	bl
64a	3	WOLV	9f Aw	62	637	bl
56a	5	WOLV	9f Aw	63	681	vis
44	8	HAMI	8f Gd/Fm	61	1190	vis
61	7	CHES	12f Firm	61	1251	vis
57	3	SAND	10f Soft	58	1570	vis
47	8	BATH	10f Gd/Sft	58	1666	vis
56	4	CHES	10f Gd/Sft	58	1777	vis
51	6	HAYD	11f Soft	58	1819	vis
44a	11	SOUT	8f Aw	63	2121	vis

DARE HUNTER 3 ch c £2616
73	9	SAND	8f Heavy	88	1055	
83	2	NOTT	8f Gd/Sft		1366	
80	4	SAND	9f Gd/Sft	85	1990	
66	11	KEMP	10f Gd/Fm	83	2750	
66	8	NOTT	8f Gd/Sft	80	3115	
72	6	BRIG	8f Soft		4420	

DARGO 6 b g £0
| 45a | 6 | WOLV | 16f Aw | 60 | 380 | |

DARING MISS 4 b f £98944
110	1	CHAN	12f Gd/Sft		1902*	
116	2	SAIN	12f Good		2406	
115	2	DEAU	13f Gd/Sft		3723	
115	7	LONG	12f Good		4262	

DARK ALBATROSS 4 b f £0
| 7a | 11 | WOLV | 8f Aw | 76 | 78 | |

DARK DOLORES 2 b f £0
0	17	NEWB	6f Firm		3980	
48	11	BRIG	7f Soft		4172	
0a	13	LING	6f Aw		4332	
35	9	NOTT	8f Heavy		4507	

DARK FINISH 2 b f £355
| 59 | 4 | HAYD | 5f Soft | | 3767 | |

DARK MENACE 8 br g £4572
48a	7	SOUT	7f Aw		130	bl
52a	1	LING	7f Aw		159*	bl
42a	9	LING	7f Aw		243	bl
30a	8	LING	7f Aw		547	bl
38a	8	LING	7f Aw		616	bl
38a	6	SOUT	7f Aw	45	867	bl
30	12	BRIG	7f Firm	49	1336	bl
53	1	BRIG	8f Gd/Sft	49	1462*	bl
38	8	YARM	8f Good	51	1772	bl
18a	11	YARM	8f Aw	43	2122	bl
28	9	GOOD	7f Good	51	2303	bl
51	2	BRIG	8f Firm		2892	bl

DARK SHADOWS 5 b g £4760
60	5	NEWC	12f Heavy		1009	
77	3	HAMI	11f Gd/Fm		1193	
59	6	REDC	10f Gd/Sft		1582	
56	3	NEWC	10f Good	62	2522	

61	1	**RIPO**	12f Gd/Fm	58	3181*		
43	11	REDC	14f Gd/Sft	62	4222		

DARK SOCIETY 2 b c £257
74	4	PONT	6f Soft		4083
74	13	NEWM	6f Good		4345
39	13	LING	7f Soft		4483

DARK VICTOR 4 b g £5639
49a	4	WOLV	9f Aw		578	
33a	8	SOUT	12f Aw		643	
46a	5	SOUT	6f Aw		685	
35	7	THIR	8f Soft	50	907	
54	1	**DONC**	10f Gd/Sft	47	1050*	
35	13	LEIC	10f Firm	54	3842	
48	6	AYR	11f Soft	54	3963	
44	6	YORK	12f Soft	50	4280	
51	2	NEWC	10f Heavy	48	4404	BL
48	3	REDC	8f Gd/Sft	48	4499	bl

DARLING COREY 4 b f £0
| 49 | 12 | LEIC | 10f Good | 72 | 793 |

DARVAN 3 b g £0
| 0 | 9 | CATT | 12f Gd/Fm | 54 | 782 | t |

DARWELLS FOLLY 5 ch g £337
44	3	CHEP	8f Good		3868	vis
34	13	YARM	7f Firm		3921	vis
0	16	LING	7f Good	56	4102	tvi
40a	8	WOLV	7f Aw		4224	vis
0	18	BRIG	10f Soft	48	4419	

DARWIN 2 b c £16525
100	1	**CURR**	6f Gd/Sft		1624*
89	6	CURR	7f Gd/Sft		4058
103	4	DONC	8f Soft		4463

DARWIN TOWER 2 gr c £1420
60	11	HAYD	5f Gd/Sft		1488	
0	12	THIR	6f Gd/Fm		2057	
65	10	YORK	6f Good		2692	
0	15	RIPO	6f Good		3466	
47	9	YORK	6f Good		3812	
37	13	CATT	7f Soft	52	4007	
65	2	PONT	6f Soft		4373	BL
51	2	REDC	6f Gd/Sft	49	4502	VIS

DARYABAD 8 b g £15099
69a	1	**LING**	7f Aw	64	28*	bl
58a	6	LING	7f Aw	69	162	bl
33	9	LEIC	8f Firm	49	2027	
34	7	NEWM	7f Aw	47	2347	bl
45	3	DONC	8f Gd/Fm	45	2612	bl
40	8	NEWM	8f Gd/Fm	45	2802	bl
51	1	**YARM**	7f Good	44	3030*	bl
52	3	YARM	7f Good	50	3238	bl
55	1	**YARM**	7f Good	50	3384*	bl
55	3	KEMP	7f Gd/Sft	53	3796	bl
54	3	YARM	8f Soft	54	3936	bl
67a	6	LING	8f Aw	69	4335	bl

DASH OF MAGIC 2 b f £0
| 40 | 6 | NOTT | 6f Heavy | | 4410 |

DASHIBA 4 gr f £7397
90	3	SAND	10f Good	91	1965
84	11	ASCO	10f Good	92	2170
98	6	NEWC	10f Firm		2339
86	6	ASCO	12f Gd/Fm	92	3001
95	2	SALI	10f Gd/Fm		3389
90	5	YORK	10f Gd/Fm	90	3563
91	7	NEWB	10f Good	92	3997
74	14	ASCO	8f Good	92	4113

DASHING BLUE 7 ch g £0
0	22	YORK	5f Firm	107	1324	
97	6	SAND	5f Gd/Fm		2496	
57	9	NEWB	6f Firm	100	2706	
0	17	ASCO	5f Gd/Fm	105	3016	
65	11	SAND	5f Good	97	3473	
65	18	EPSO	5f Good	93	3687	BL

DASHING CHIEF 5 b g £283

| 39a | 3 | LING | 12f Aw | | 2181 | t |

DATIN STAR 2 ch f £213
42	6	WARW	7f Gd/Fm		2251	
38	11	LING	7f Good		2653	
52	6	WARW	7f Gd/Fm		2841	
61	4	BRIG	7f Firm		3558	
52	8	LING	7f Firm	58	3830	
0	12	PONT	6f Soft	55	4235	

DATO STAR 9 br g £0
| 77 | 12 | CHES | 19f Gd/Fm | 92 | 1222 | t |

DATURA 3 b f £3556
51a	8	LING	8f Aw	74	54	
55	14	NEWM	7f Good	70	954	
45	6	AYR	9f Gd/Fm		1632	VIS
52	4	NOTT	10f Good		2012	
60	1	**LEIC**	8f Gd/Fm	56	2506*	
60	3	HAMI	8f Good		2781	

DAUNTED 4 b g £880
66a	8	LING	10f Aw		157	bl
59a	7	LING	10f Aw	76	244	bl
0a	11	LING	12f Aw	72	332	bl
68a	2	LING	12f Aw		4101	bl
44a	7	LING	12f Aw	67	4271	bl
41	5	BRIG	12f Soft	55	4421	bl

DAUNTING ASSEMBLY 5 ch m £0
| 0 | 10 | BEVE | 10f Gd/Fm | | 3672 |

DAVEYS PANACEA 3 ch f £2315
54	2	CARL	6f Firm		2278
45	5	HAMI	6f Gd/Fm		2640
61	3	LEIC	6f Gd/Sft		2919
60	3	RIPO	5f Gd/Fm		3462
61	3	BEVE	5f Good		3651
45	7	THIR	6f Gd/Sft		3780
41	7	BEVE	5f Good		3956

DAVEYSFIRE 2 b f £309
30	6	HAMI	5f Gd/Fm		1937
28	3	HAMI	6f Firm		2394
0	12	AYR	8f Soft		3957

DAVID USA 4 ch c £30488
| 108a | 3 | SUFF | 9f Fast | | 1749 |

DAVID WYNNE 2 b c £0
| 55 | 13 | DONC | 7f Gd/Sft | | 4446 |

DAVIDE UMBRO 3 b c £57166
| 112 | 1 | **CAPA** | 8f Soft | | 1118* |

DAVIS ROCK 6 ch m £8922
49a	5	WOLV	8f Aw	58	38	
46a	5	SOUT	8f Aw	55	176	
63a	1	**SOUT**	7f Aw		249*	
63a	1	**SOUT**	7f Aw		341*	
32a	9	SOUT	8f Aw	62	497	
68a	1	**SOUT**	8f Aw	60	601*	
43a	6	SOUT	8f Aw	65	669	
56a	6	SOUT	8f Aw	65	687	
48	2	CHEP	7f Good	47	3873	
41	6	CATT	7f Soft	49	4004	
44	4	LEIC	8f Stt/Hvy	49	4310	

DAWARI 2 b c £1478
81	7	DONC	8f Gd/Fm		3864
92	3	NEWM	8f Good		4161
92	4	NEWM	8f Good		4349

DAWN 3 b f £1353
71	3	REDC	5f Gd/Sft	70	1133
58	6	BEVE	5f Firm		1280
0	17	NEWC	5f Gd/Sft	70	1479
63	3	WARW	5f Gd/Sft		1712
61	6	NEWM	5f Gd/Fm	66	2288
0	21	YORK	6f Soft		4287

DAWN ROMANCE 2 b f £0
47	5	BRIG	6f Good		1648
64	7	WIND	6f Gd/Fm		1876
58	5	WARW	7f Good		2459
67	7	NEWB	7f Firm		2810

49	6	MUSS	7f Good		3100
59	6	NOTT	6f Good		3520
54	6	YORK	8f Gd/Fm		3729

DAWN TRAVELLER 3 b f £0
52	10	WARW	7f Gd/Sft		1708
0	13	SAND	10f Good		2531
45	5	ASCO	7f Gd/Sft		3343
0	15	PONT	8f Firm		3506
22	10	YARM	8f Gd/Fm	43	3971

DAWNS DANCER 3 b f £454
0	20	NEWM	7f Aw		1082
51	6	NEWM	7f Good	66	1855
60	3	BRIG	7f Firm	62	2044
53	7	LING	7f Firm	62	2325

DAY BOY 4 b g £1897
67	3	THIR	7f Soft	69	908
66	7	THIR	7f Good	69	1158
67	4	AYR	7f Gd/Fm	68	1631
64	6	CARL	7f Gd/Fm	68	2241
72	4	YORK	7f Soft		4287
12	14	NEWC	6f Heavy	68	4405
55	9	MUSS	6f Soft	66	4565

DAY JOURNEY 3 b c £1740
104	3	LEIC	7f Gd/Sft		829
97	4	KEMP	7f Soft		1016
101	6	YORK	7f Gd/Fm	104	1308

DAY STAR 4 b f £0
| 41a | 10 | LING | 6f Aw | 67 | 358 |

DAYGLOW DANCER 2 b c £23712
77	1	**NOTT**	5f Heavy		1020*
85	3	KEMP	6f Gd/Fm		2083
91	2	PONT	6f Good		2363
95	4	SAND	7f Good		3470
97	2	DEAU	7f Gd/Fm		3716
99	5	LONG	8f Good		3926
94	2	CHES	8f Good		4072
103	2	LONG	9f Good		4237
101	6	DONC	8f Soft		4463
100	2	DONC	8f Heavy		4572

DAYLAMI 6 gr g £626506
| 136 | 1 | **GULF** | 12f Good | | 20* |

DAYLILY 3 ch f £3537
25	11	PONT	6f Soft		877
0	15	THIR	6f Soft		909
69	6	DONC	7f Gd/Sft		1072
34	8	PONT	8f Good	65	1495
61	3	NEWC	6f Heavy	62	1768
62	3	PONT	7f Good		1868
62	2	NEWC	6f Gd/Fm		2313
61	3	BEVE	5f Gd/Fm		2519
47	5	BEVE	5f Gd/Fm		3651
35	9	THIR	6f Gd/Sft		3780
55	3	CATT	5f Soft		4255
50	6	AYR	5f Heavy	56	4307

DAYNABEE 5 b m £3264
41a	5	LING	7f Aw	44	28	
43a	4	LING	7f Aw	44	58	
47a	2	LING	7f Aw	44	106	
40a	5	LING	8f Aw	46	148	
48a	2	WOLV	6f Aw	46	232	
36a	5	WOLV	6f Aw	46	351	
55a	1	**WOLV**	7f Aw		391*	
49a	5	WOLV	7f Aw		449	
51a	4	SOUT	6f Aw		511	
34a	6	WOLV	8f Aw		550	
47a	3	WOLV	7f Aw		567	
37a	5	SOUT	6f Aw	45	604	
48a	4	WOLV	7f Aw		677	
19a	9	WOLV	6f Aw	44	4444	

DAYS OF GRACE 5 gr m £20626
| 62a | 2 | WOLV | 7f Aw | 61 | 121 |
| 58a | 4 | SOUT | 6f Aw | 62 | 180 |

59a 2 LING 7f Aw 243

59a	2	LING	7f Aw		243	
66a	1	**SOUT**	6f Aw	61	280*	
64a	2	LING	6f Aw	64	358	
66a	3	SOUT	6f Aw	64	388	
67a	1	**WOLV**	6f Aw	64	466*	
62a	3	SOUT	6f Aw	67	557	
68a	2	WOLV	6f Aw	67	622	
56	2	WIND	6f Gd/Fm	54	746	
35	11	NOTT	6f Gd/Sft	56	1082	
35	11	CHEP	7f Gd/Sft	56	1799	
50	5	SALI	6f Good	55	2690	
54	3	SALI	7f Gd/Fm	53	2978	
62	1	**SALI**	6f Gd/Fm	52	3293*	
64	1	**LING**	6f Firm	59	3493*	
64	4	FOLK	6f Firm		3587	
70a	2	WOLV	6f Aw	68	3774	
45	10	NOTT	6f Soft	63	3975	
74	6	SALI	6f Aw	77	4165	
65a	5	WOLV	6f Aw	70	4380	

DAYS OF THUNDER 12 ch g £0

0a	10	WOLV	12f Aw		626

DAZZLING DAISY 3 b f £444

62	4	NOTT	8f Gd/Fm		3116
42	4	BRIG	10f Gd/Fm		3262
0	14	NEWM	8f Gd/Fm		3626
40	6	YARM	8f Gd/Fm	47	3971
0	12	BRIG	12f Soft	44	4176

DAZZLING QUINTET 4 ch f £3859

40	6	MUSS	8f Gd/Fm	46	1143
38	7	NOTT	5f Good	45	1412
47	2	CARL	5f Gd/Sft	43	1724
49	1	**BEVE**	5f Firm	43	1923*
35	10	NEWC	5f Good	49	2525
0	16	BEVE	5f Firm	48	2732
35	10	HAMI	5f Gd/Sft	47	3536
33	12	NEWB	5f Gd/Sft	45	4459

DE TRAMUNTANA 3 b f £4150

83	2	CHES	10f Gd/Fm		1218
59	4	BATH	10f Gd/Sft		1668
80	2	SAND	10f Good		2531
55	5	RIPO	10f Gd/Fm		3012
52	11	LEIC	10f Firm		3838
67	5	NOTT	10f Heavy		4408

DEAD AIM 6 b g £0

33	11	HAYD	11f Gd/Fm	60	2453
38	6	BEVE	12f Gd/Sft	55	3053

DEADLY NIGHTSHADE 4 b f £0

84	10	BATH	5f Good		1090
0	23	YORK	5f Firm	100	1324

DEADLY SERIOUS 4 ch c £1009

42a	4	LING	6f Aw		399
63a	3	WOLV	7f Aw		478
56a	3	SOUT	6f Aw		558
42a	8	LING	6f Aw	56	691
0	15	SALI	6f Firm		1175
50	7	WIND	5f Gd/Fm		1881

DEAR DAUGHTER 2 ch f £1021

86	3	SALI	7f Firm		3752
79	4	YARM	8f Heavy		4475

DEAR GIRL 3 b f £642

78	3	LEIC	10f Firm		3838

DEAR PICKLES 2 b f £1140

68	6	FOLK	6f Gd/Fm		3443
75	2	WIND	6f Good		3638
70	8	KEMP	7f Soft		4035
64a	4	WOLV	6f Aw		4225

DEAR PRUDENCE 4 b f £0

11	11	WIND	12f Good	48	853
0	16	FOLK	15f Soft	43	963

DEBBIES WARNING 4 b c £608

83a	9	WOLV	8f Aw	100	663	t
93	6	DONC	8f Gd/Fm		703	t

91	4	GOOD	6f Gd/Sft	92	1471	
75	9	EPSO	6f Good	92	1851	
90	7	SAND	8f Gd/Fm	91	2528	
94	6	NEWM	7f Gd/Fm	91	2616	
17	22	YORK	10f Good	91	2696	
77	16	GOOD	8f Good	90	3107	
102	5	GOOD	7f Gd/Fm		3132	
0	15	NEWM	7f Gd/Fm	90	3315	
0	16	YORK	6f Heavy	87	4301	
73	15	NEWM	7f Good	83	4357	t

DEBRIEF 2 b g £0

0	12	SALI	7f Gd/Fm		3388

DEBS SON 3 b g £0

59	6	RIPO	10f Soft	62	827
18	6	CARL	12f Firm		1253
43	6	REDC	14f Gd/Sft	57	1581
0	10	HAYD	16f Gd/Sft	53	3476

DECARCHY 3 b c £1739

91	5	DONC	8f Gd/Sft		1069
80	3	DONC	10f Good		1515

DECEITFUL 2 ch g £3398

64	1	**BRIG**	5f Firm		2039*
62	3	NEWC	6f Gd/Fm		2312
57	4	CHEP	6f Gd/Fm		2447

DECEIVES THE EYE 2 b c £2076

57a	3	WOLV	5f Aw		722	
50	4	LING	5f Gd/Sft		836	BL
39a	5	SOUT	6f Aw		1420	
38	7	CATT	6f Soft		1679	
60a	1	**WOLV**	6f Aw		2079*	
45a	6	SOUT	7f Aw		2301	

DECISION MAID 3 b f £1398

94	7	NEWM	7f Good		953
99	4	GOOD	8f Gd/Sft		1485
93	7	ASCO	8f Good		2150

DEE DIAMOND 3 b f £0

51	8	PONT	10f Soft		873
0	17	NEWC	8f Gd/Sft	53	1477
42	7	LING	11f Firm	48	1914
39	5	WIND	12f Good	44	2370
30	8	NOTT	16f Gd/Fm	40	3112
27	11	HAMI	12f Gd/Sft	38	3827
0	14	NOTT	12f Heavy	39	4509

DEE PEE TEE CEE 6 b g £0

29	11	HAYD	12f Heavy	86	991
66	10	RIPO	8f Good	84	3699
0	15	HAYD	8f Soft	82	4094
34	16	YORK	9f Heavy	79	4300
62	10	DONC	12f Heavy	74	4580

DEEP BLUE 3 b c £3006

56	1	**WIND**	6f Heavy		4526*

DEEP SPACE 5 br g £17330

101	6	NEWM	6f Good		952
103	3	GOOD	6f Gd/Sft		1453
97	5	LING	6f Good		1674
104	4	ASCO	6f Good	105	2151
104	3	NEWC	6f Good		2335
94	10	GOOD	6f Gd/Fm	105	3152
105	1	**YARM**	6f Gd/Fm		3667*
105	3	YARM	6f Gd/Fm		3937

DEEP WATER 6 b g £868

72	2	HAMI	11f Good		848
53	7	HAYD	14f Gd/Sft	70	1536

DEFIANCE 5 b g £0

0a	11	SOUT	6f Aw	35	1422
21	9	REDC	6f Gd/Sft	35	1578
48	10	PONT	5f Good		1868
0	18	NOTT	6f Gd/Fm	32	2193
34	8	NOTT	8f Gd/Fm		2682
25	7	WARW	7f Gd/Fm	33	2840
0	10	CHEP	8f Gd/Fm	30	3251
0	17	DONC	7f Soft		4461

DEFIANT 3 b c £0

0	20	NEWM	7f Good		4018
61	7	LING	8f Soft		4273
70	5	YARM	7f Soft		4388

DEFINITE GUEST 2 gr c £282

64	6	YARM	6f Gd/Fm		2414
69	12	YARM	7f Firm		3940
62	4	CHES	7f Soft		4068
0	13	LING	6f Soft	68	4269

DEFINITE RETURN 2 ch f £0

36	7	LING	6f Good		4097
42a	4	WOLV	8f Aw		4249
0	12	BATH	8f Soft		4430

DEGREE OF POWER 2 b f £273

52	4	WARW	5f Soft		1059
61	11	NEWM	6f Good		3607
0	15	WARW	7f Gd/Fm		3910
0a	11	WOLV	8f Aw	52	4439

DEHOUSH 4 ch c £8388

111	1	**NEWB**	10f Gd/Sft		1592*
102	10	SAND	10f Good	107	2475
107	3	NEWB	10f Firm		2851
104	7	HAYD	11f Gd/Fm		3321

DEIDAMIA 2 b f £600

60	4	NEWB	5f Gd/Fm		3174
67	7	PONT	5f Firm		3500
65	4	BEVE	5f Good		3955
46	8	SAND	5f Soft	64	4202

DEKELSMARY 5 b m £0

24a	8	SOUT	6f Aw	44	212	t
25a	6	SOUT	7f Aw	41	304	t
16a	11	WOLV	6f Aw	41	352	t

DEL MAR SHOW 3 b c £13415

104	3	ARLI	10f Firm		2912

DELAMERE 3 b f £7225

67	6	LING	7f Gd/Sft		1261
82	4	GOOD	8f Gd/Sft		1811
77	3	KEMP	10f Firm		2258
81	1	**AYR**	10f Gd/Fm		2722*
84	2	NEWB	10f Gd/Fm	82	3178
82	4	KEMP	12f Gd/Sft	83	3798

DELCIANA 5 b m £0

0a	16	SOUT	12f Aw	32	70
12a	7	WOLV	15f Aw		174
0a	14	SOUT	11f Aw		178

DELEGATE 7 ch g £13998

92	8	NEWM	6f Firm	100	1182
92	6	YORK	6f Firm	95	1337
87	4	EPSO	6f Good	92	1851
93	2	NEWB	7f Gd/Fm	92	1946
0	28	ASCO	6f Good	92	2151
91	2	DONC	6f Gd/Fm	88	3861
75	14	AYR	6f Gd/Sft	88	4012
75	15	NEWM	5f Good	90	4339
88	5	DONC	5f Soft	88	4466

DELIGHT OF DAWN 8 b m £645

40a	6	LING	7f Aw	45	59	bl
44a	2	LING	8f Aw	43	147	bl

DELPHYLLIA 2 b f £0

57	9	NEWM	5f Gd/Sft		970
53	12	WIND	5f Gd/Fm		1197
67	7	BATH	5f Gd/Fm		3815
0	15	LING	5f Good	63	4098
0	14	LING	6f Soft		4190
0	13	BATH	6f Soft		4431

DELTA GEORGIA 4 ch f £0

0	15	WARW	11f Heavy	47	890
27	10	BRIG	8f Gd/Sft	45	1462
25	12	REDC	6f Gd/Fm	45	1578

DELTA SOLEIL 8 b h £0

45	10	LING	7f Gd/Fm		838
0	15	NOTT	6f Firm	66	1273

DELTA SONG (continued)

43	12	BATH	6f Gd/Fm	63	1438
46	10	YARM	6f Gd/Fm	60	1953
0	16	WIND	6f Gd/Fm	60	2054 VIS
25	9	NOTT	6f Gd/Fm		2680

DELTA SONG 2 b f £14696

64	1	LING	6f Firm		3278*
80	2	FOLK	6f Good	74	3446
85	1	EPSO	6f Good	74	3761*
89	1	GOOD	6f Good	81	3886*
84	2	SALI	6f Gd/Sft		4164

DEMOCRACY 4 ch c £611

54a	11	LING	7f Aw	78	162	bl
36a	13	WOLV	6f Aw	75	258	bl
0a	13	LING	7f Aw	70	337	bl
50a	5	WOLV	8f Aw	65	381	bl
50a	3	WOLV	8f Aw		477	bl
41a	7	WOLV	8f Aw	60	521	bl
50a	7	WOLV	8f Aw	58	583	bl
0	11	WARW	7f Soft		816	bl
0	20	BATH	5f Good	70	1092	bl
46	10	SALI	7f Good	64	1348	
51	11	CHEP	7f Gd/Sft	60	1794	
56	5	SALI	7f Firm		1884	
38	3	BRIG	8f Firm		2040	
44	4	BATH	8f Firm	50	2331	
34	10	CHEP	8f Gd/Fm	50	2658	
49	4	BRIG	7f Gd/Fm	50	2729	
5	9	BATH	8f Firm	46	2942	
0	12	BRIG	8f Firm	45	3527	

DEMOLITION JO 5 gr m £4911

46a	8	SOUT	6f Aw	65	47	vis
0	16	HAMI	6f Good	74	844	vis
73	6	DONC	6f Gd/Sft	74	1074	vis
62	9	HAMI	6f Good	74	1192	vis
0	16	CHES	8f Firm	74	1250	vis
0	17	THIR	6f Gd/Fm	72	3123	BL
94	6	CHES	6f Firm		3172	vis
0	15	HAYD	5f Gd/Fm	72	3322	vis
71	2	CHES	8f Firm	73	3510	vis
61	7	HAMI	6f Soft	71	3803	vis

DEMOPHILOS 2 b c £5102

97	1	NEWM	7f Aw		4183*

DENA 3 b f £896

58	10	KEMP	12f Soft		4040
65	2	PONT	8f Soft		4234
55	5	REDC	10f Soft		4501

DENARIUS SECUNDUS 3 ch c £0

61	7	WARW	8f Good		2465	
64	9	WIND	10f Gd/Fm		2889	
0	12	SALI	8f Good		3423	
44	10	GOOD	8f Soft	55	4066	BL

DENBRAE 8 b g £0

0	12	BRIG	7f Gd/Sft	51	896

DENISE BEST 2 ch f £2897

24	7	MUSS	8f Gd/Fm		3740
76	2	AYR	7f Soft		3991
83	4	CHES	8f Soft		4072
8a	8	WOLV	8f Aw		4249
60	5	DONC	8f Heavy		4572

DENNIS BERGKAMP 3 b c £0

0a	13	SOUT	9f Aw		328
0a	8	WOLV	9f Aw		395
0	12	DONC	10f Gd/Fm		3865
76	8	HAYD	14f Soft		4091

DENNIS EL MENACE 2 b c £3215

47	11	DONC	5f Good		730
64a	4	SOUT	5f Aw		1418
72	6	HAYD	5f Gd/Sft		1488
55a	4	SOUT	7f Aw		2383
71	3	SALI	7f Gd/Sft	70	2468
78	2	NEWM	7f Gd/Fm	72	2962
68	11	GOOD	7f Firm	77	3149
79	3	NEWM	8f Good	77	3609 BL

DENNIS OUR MENACE 2 b c £1449

53	10	SALI	7f Gd/Fm		2269
80	3	NEWB	7f Firm		2708
80	3	NEWM	8f Gd/Fm		3458
0	20	NEWM	8f Good	83	4350

DENS JOY 4 b g £11219

48a	5	WOLV	9f Aw		189
68a	3	SOUT	12f Aw		301
35a	8	SOUT	11f Aw	62	390
47	8	SOUT	10f Gd/Sft	59	859
59	1	WIND	8f Gd/Sft	56	1097*
50	9	REDC	7f Firm	58	1297
43	9	YARM	7f Gd/Sft	58	1611
61	1	LING	9f Firm	57	1917*
64	2	WIND	8f Gd/Fm	63	2051
0	13	NEWM	8f Gd/Fm	63	2130
46	10	KEMP	9f Gd/Sft	65	2581
56	5	ASCO	8f Gd/Fm	63	2999
62	4	GOOD	9f Gd/Fm	63	3089
54	7	LEIC	8f Gd/Fm	63	3334
63	2	WIND	8f Good	62	3643
55	10	LING	8f Gd/Fm	64	3831
40	13	WIND	8f Gd/Sft		4292

DENSIM BLUE 2 b c £5285

68	10	DONC	5f Gd/Fm		700
78	2	MUSS	5f Gd/Fm		1146
71	4	HAMI	5f Gd/Fm		1189
78	1	BRIG	5f Gd/Sft		1463*
80	4	BATH	5f Firm		1995
69	5	DONC	5f Gd/Fm	80	2575
76	2	BRIG	6f Gd/Fm	76	3258
74	4	WARW	15f Good	76	3693
71	7	LING	5f Good	75	4098

DENTON LADY 3 br f £402

37	6	MUSS	9f Gd/Sft	47	795	
42	7	MUSS	9f Gd/Sft	51	899	
16a	10	SOUT	7f Aw	44	1202	
32	10	HAMI	11f Gd/Fm	44	1361	
42	3	MUSS	8f Gd/Fm	44	1434	bl
20	13	REDC	7f Gd/Sft	44	1559	bl
26	10	REDC	6f Gd/Sft	42	1578	bl
6	10	MUSS	7f Firm		2046	bl

DEREKS PRIDE 2 b f £0

0a	15	SOUT	7f Aw		4369

DERIVATIVE 2 b c £1500

102	4	CURR	7f Good		3719

DERRYQUIN 5 b g £17019

0	18	WIND	6f Gd/Fm	52	1196	bl
58	1	REDC	8f Firm	52	1296*	bl
52	12	NEWM	8f Gd/Sft	58	1690	bl
60	2	LEIC	8f Firm	58	2027	bl
0	16	DONC	8f Gd/Fm	60	2349	
59	4	NEWM	8f Gd/Fm	60	2802	bl
51	8	NEWM	8f Gd/Sft	58	3118	bl
67	1	LEIC	8f Gd/Fm	56	3334+	bl
75	1	REDC	8f Gd/Fm	64	3454+	bl
0	19	ASCO	8f Gd/Fm	73	4126	bl

DESAMO 3 br c £3923

77	3	LING	7f Gd/Sft		839
78	3	NEWB	8f Gd/Fm		1783
77	1	REDC	6f Gd/Sft		2154*

DESARU 4 br c £0

95	10	NEWM	9f Gd/Sft		967
96	9	NEWM	7f Firm		2343
85	11	NEWB	6f Firm		2847

DESERT CHARM 3 b f £0

0	12	BEVE	12f Heavy	42	978

DESERT FIGHTER 9 b g £7392

51	10	DONC	10f Gd/Fm	64	705
37	11	PONT	10f Soft	63	871
57	1	THIR	12f Gd/Sft		1353*
0	11	CATT	12f Gd/Sft	57	1816
57	2	HAYD	12f Gd/Fm		2457
61	1	CATT	12f Gd/Fm		2742*
62	2	THIR	12f Gd/Fm	60	3148

DESERT FURY 3 b c £2074

94	3	KEMP	6f Soft		1016
72	11	LING	6f Gd/Sft	100	1285
86	18	NEWM	6f Gd/Fm	97	1694
0	20	YORK	6f Firm	94	2003
82	6	YORK	8f Gd/Fm	90	2648
82	8	NEWM	6f Gd/Fm	87	2858
77	4	KEMP	7f Gd/Fm	84	3076
55	6	EPSO	10f Gd/Fm	82	3415
76	5	KEMP	8f Gd/Fm	80	3793
71	4	YARM	8f Heavy	78	4478
64	10	NEWM	7f Soft	76	4547

DESERT INVADER 9 br g £0

0a	15	SOUT	7f Aw	43	867
24a	9	SOUT	7f Aw		1305
15a	8	SOUT	6f Aw	41	1421
18a	10	SOUT	7f Aw	36	1801
18a	5	SOUT	6f Aw	32	2122
7a	12	SOUT	6f Aw	29	2385

DESERT ISLAND DISC 3 b f £4030

62	6	DONC	8f Gd/Sft	69	1053
64	5	NOTT	8f Good	67	1414
70	1	WARW	11f Heavy	66	1521*

DESERT KNIGHT 4 b c £8174

106	3	DONC	8f Gd/Fm		703
108	1	WARW	7f Heavy		1004*
93	5	HAYD	7f Gd/Fm		1163

DESERT MAGIC 4 b f £24250

106	1	CURR	7f Soft		1122*
106	2	CORK	6f Good		1232
90	9	ASCO	6f Gd/Fm	105	3301

DESERT MUSIC 4 b f £0

22	7	HAMI	12f Gd/Fm		1362
47	5	CATT	12f Good		1661
45	5	PONT	12f Gd/Fm		2560
32	5	NEWC	12f Good	46	3036
3	12	NEWC	14f Good	46	3249
30	7	REDC	11f Gd/Fm	36	3636

DESERT NORTH 3 b g £0

0	13	LING	6f Gd/Sft		837
69	11	SALI	6f Firm		1181

DESERT RAGE 3 b c £880

86	5	NEWM	8f Firm		1188
82	3	GOOD	8f Gd/Sft		1449

DESERT RECRUIT 4 b c £610

40	5	CATT	14f Gd/Fm	46	779
41	5	PONT	10f Soft	44	871
45	3	CATT	14f Soft	42	1683
39	6	CATT	12f Gd/Sft	42	1816
45	6	HAMI	13f Gd/Fm	44	1936
32	5	MUSS	14f Firm	44	2050

DESERT SAFARI 3 b f £7944

29	15	HAYD	7f Gd/Sft	74	811
72	5	WARW	6f Heavy		888
68a	4	WOLV	6f Aw	71	1138
57	8	YORK	8f Firm	70	1341
35	14	SAND	7f Soft	69	1569
73	1	CARL	7f Gd/Fm	67	2017*
75	1	CATT	7f Gd/Fm	71	2438*
74	3	HAYD	8f Gd/Fm	75	2699
73	6	LEIC	7f Gd/Sft	75	2918
46	7	THIR	8f Gd/Fm	74	3345
42	10	HAYD	7f Gd/Sft	72	4106

DESERT SPA 5 b g £7972

33a	8	SOUT	12f Aw	54	68
54a	2	WOLV	12f Aw	49	170
54a	1	WOLV	12f Aw	51	261*
60a	1	WOLV	12f Aw	55	464*

28	8	BRIG	12f Gd/Fm	45	1128	
60a	1	**WOLV**	12f Aw		1389*	
0	13	WIND	10f Soft	45	2544	
60a	2	WOLV	10f Aw	60	4026	
45a	7	WOLV	12f Aw	61	4245	

DESERT VALENTINE 5 b g £4560
27	11	HAYD	7f Gd/Fm	45	2442
44	2	CHEP	12f Gd/Fm	42	2971
41	5	SALI	14f Gd/Fm	43	3424
55	1	**GOOD**	11f Good	50	3887*
0	13	SALI	14f Gd/Fm	54	4166

DESIRE ME 2 b f £0
41	5	FOLK	5f Gd/Fm	3038
48	7	BATH	5f Gd/Fm	3204
38	5	LING	6f Firm	3757

DESIRES GOLD 5 br g £0
12a	11	WOLV	12f Aw	40	43
0a	10	SOUT	8f Aw	35	297

DESRAYA 3 b c £14968
0	7	THIR	12f Soft		924	
49	6	THIR	8f Good	62	1387	BL
39	9	RIPO	8f Good	59	1600	bl
56	2	THIR	6f Gd/Fm	54	2060	bl
51	3	CARL	6f Gd/Fm	54	2243	bl
61	1	**RIPO**	6f Soft	56	2541*	bl
76	1	**HAMI**	6f Gd/Fm	63	2779*	bl
78	1	**RIPO**	6f Gd/Fm	71	3010+	bl
73	8	YORK	5f Gd/Fm	77	3569	bl
0	22	AYR	6f Gd/Sft	77	4010	bl

DESTINATION 3 ch g £4876
45a	5	LING	10f Aw		771
79	2	WIND	10f Heavy		936
81	4	BATH	10f Good		1093
80	4	WIND	12f Gd/Sft	79	1425
78	5	GOOD	12f Gd/Fm	79	1637
61a	3	LING	13f AW		4193
67a	2	LING	16f Aw	65	4329
102	2	DONC	15f Heavy		4568

DETACHING 2 b f £0
58	9	LING	7f Soft	4267
60	8	BRIG	7f Soft	4415

DETECTIVE 4 ch c £0
27	5	PONT	6f Gd/Fm		2833	
52	7	NEWM	6f Gd/Fm	59	3119	
36	10	NEWM	6f Gd/Fm	55	3457	
40	14	WIND	5f Gd/Sft	51	4295	BL

DETROIT CITY 5 b g £1364
41	4	MUSS	6f Gd/Fm	43	1148
45	2	MUSS	7f Firm		1685
32	9	RIPO	8f Good		1858
38	2	MUSS	7f Firm		2046
0	16	CARL	8f Good		2240
37	4	BEVE	7f Gd/Fm	41	2479
18	14	CARL	7f Firm	41	2823
0	13	BEVE	7f Good		2882
0	11	BEVE	8f Good		3393
25	7	MUSS	8f Aw	35	3746

DEUCE OF TRUMPS 2 b c £4266
84	3	HAYD	8f Soft	3766
79	5	PONT	8f Soft	4086
83	1	**PONT**	10f Soft	4230*

DEVIL LEADER 3 ch f £6359
70	7	DONC	10f Gd/Sft		1051
69	5	SALI	10f Good		1343
74	3	RIPO	8f Gd/Fm		2104
72	2	BRIG	8f Soft		2426
72	1	**WARW**	8f Gd/Fm		2846*
64	4	DONC	8f Gd/Sft	74	3160

DEVILS NIGHT 5 b g £0
15a	8	SOUT	11f Aw	196
8a	8	SOUT	16f Aw	327

DEVON HEIGHTS 3 ch f £3842
110	3	CHAN	8f V	1754

DEXTROUS 3 gr c £1596
85	3	NEWM	8f Gd/Fm	1692
78	3	NEWB	10f Sft/Hvy	4474

DHAUDELOUP 5 ch g £1140
61	4	DONC	12f Soft	67	4464
0	13	DONC	12f Heavy	68	4580

DI CANIO 2 ch c £0
32	9	CATT	6f Gd/Fm	2926

DI MOI OUI 3 b f £42268
110	1	**CHAN**	9f Good	2401*
111	1	**DEAU**	10f Gd/Fm	3546*
109	5	LONG	10f Good	4263

DIABLENEYEV 5 b g £2305
112	4	LONG	7f Good	2226	bl

DIABLO DANCER 4 b c £2635
30	12	KEMP	14f Good	72	726	
60	5	WARW	15f Heavy	70	885	
65	1	**WARW**	11f Soft	62	1065*	VIS
59	7	NOTT	10f Gd/Sft	64	1370	vis

DIABOLO 2 b c £0
58	7	PONT	6f Soft	4082
35	10	CATT	5f Soft	4252
24	11	NEWC	6f Heavy	4402

DIAMOND 4 b f £322
55	11	SALI	10f Gd/Fm	2265
71	4	DONC	12f Gd/Fm	3157

DIAMOND CROWN 9 ch g £907
0	14	MUSS	12f Gd/Fm	36	1432
35	2	CATT	14f Gd/Sft		1814
24	10	HAMI	13f Gd/Fm	32	1936
19	10	HAMI	13f Gd/Fm	32	2643
17	4	MUSS	16f Good	28	3099

DIAMOND DECORUM 4 ch g £8489
60	6	WARW	5f Heavy	68	1005	
71	1	**THIR**	6f Gd/Sft	66	1356*	
67	8	YORK	6f Firm	70	2000	
67	6	WIND	6f Gd/Fm	70	2054	
53	11	CATT	6f Gd/Fm	70	2929	
52	10	GOOD	6f Gd/Fm	70	3136	
0	19	WIND	6f Gd/Sft	68	4295	
0	11	NOTT	6f Heavy	66	4411	t

DIAMOND FLAME 6 b g £408
55a	8	WOLV	9f Aw	78	681	
45	11	WIND	12f Gd/Fm	59	748	
28	9	FOLK	10f Soft	55	965	
48	4	BEVE	10f Good	52	2883	
45	8	HAYD	11f Good	50	3285	
43	7	HAYD	11f Gd/Sft	47	3480	
25a	10	WOLV	9f Aw	58	4228	
10	13	YORK	10f Soft		4275	VIS
10	10	NEWC	8f Heavy	45	4406	BL

DIAMOND GEEZER 4 br c £16162
58a	2	WOLV	6f Aw		76
61a	1	LING	6f Aw	57	113*
66a	2	LING	6f Aw	60	148
69a	3	LING	6f Aw	66	223
40a	5	LING	6f Aw		288
45	12	SAND	5f Gd/Fm	63	763
68a	2	LING	6f Aw	67	881
61	4	BATH	5f Good	62	1092
64	4	WIND	6f Gd/Fm	62	1196
64	3	BATH	6f Gd/Fm	62	1438
48	3	GOOD	6f Gd/Sft	62	1636
55	6	WIND	6f Gd/Fm	63	2207
68	1	**WIND**	6f Good	63	2371*
67	4	WIND	5f Good	69	2716
71	2	SAND	6f Gd/Fm	67	2925
68	2	NEWM	6f Gd/Fm	67	3119
71	4	ASCO	5f Gd/Fm	69	3341
47	12	NEWM	5f Gd/Fm	70	3631
63	7	SALI	5f Firm	70	3747
63	8	YARM	5f Firm	69	3920
65	4	BATH	5f Soft	68	4432

DIAMOND GEORGIA 3 ch f £0
0a	11	SOUT	5f Aw		179	E
27a	9	LING	7f Aw	49	287	e
26a	5	LING	8f Aw	44	355	VIS
11a	10	SOUT	8f Aw	40	429	vis
23	8	CATT	12f Gd/Fm	50	782	
0	18	BRIG	10f Gd/Sft	45	892	
5	6	YARM	16f Gd/Sft		1613	

DIAMOND ISLE 3 b f £0
40a	6	WOLV	5f Aw		42

DIAMOND JAYNE 2 ch f £0
0	15	BEVE	5f Good	3955
0	11	CATT	5f Soft	4253
36	7	NOTT	6f Heavy	4410

DIAMOND KISS 3 b f £0
58	8	WIND	10f Good		850
60	11	SAND	10f Heavy		1045
0	15	SALI	7f Gd/Fm	58	1889
41	6	CHEP	8f Gd/Sft	52	2658

DIAMOND LOOK 3 b c £3947
84	1	**LING**	7f Gd/Sft		839*
88	3	NEWM	7f Good	82	954
68	12	GOOD	7f Gd/Sft	84	1470

DIAMOND MAX 2 b c £6266
56	7	WIND	5f Good		849
67	4	THIR	5f Good		928
66	1	**NOTT**	5f Heavy		1019*
58	4	CHES	5f Good	66	2665
61	5	LEIC	5f Gd/Fm	65	2915
55	5	NEWB	7f Gd/Sft	65	3175
75	1	**REDC**	6f Gd/Sft	61	4502*
75	3	DONC	7f Heavy	73	4577

DIAMOND MILLENNIUM 2 b c £849
55	5	WIND	5f Good		849	
18a	7	SOUT	8f Aw		1206	
38	5	CATT	6f Soft		1679	
39	3	BRIG	6f Gd/Fm		1931	
46	3	WIND	6f Gd/Fm		2052	
43	3	YARM	5f Gd/Fm		2196	
44	6	LEIC	5f Gd/Fm		2507	VIS

DIAMOND MURPHY 2 gr f £0
0	14	THIR	6f Good	1381
42a	8	WOLV	7f Aw	4025

DIAMOND OLIVIA 3 b f £5265
56	3	WARW	7f Heavy	53	887
56	4	NOTT	8f Heavy	55	1024
39a	7	SOUT	7f Aw	53	1202
53	6	EPSO	7f Good	55	2794
56	2	NEWC	7f Good		3033
50	5	THIR	8f Gd/Fm	56	3345
39	9	BRIG	8f Firm	55	3561
61	1	**LING**	7f Soft	53	4192*
58	3	DONC	8f Gd/Sft	62	4452
61	5	NEWM	8f Gd/Sft	62	4536

DIAMOND PROMISE 3 b f £2789
45a	5	WOLV	6f Aw		228
52a	2	LING	6f Aw		357
23a	7	SOUT	6f Aw	55	515
53	4	NOTT	6f Gd/Sft		1081
58	1	**BATH**	5f Gd/Sft		1670*
0	14	SALI	6f Gd/Fm	59	2230
0	16	BATH	5f Gd/Sft	58	2555
0	23	WIND	5f Gd/Sft	66	4295

DIAMOND RACHAEL 3 b f £13334
63a	3	SOUT	5f Aw		127	VIS
67a	4	SOUT	5f Aw		179	vis
44a	7	SOUT	6f Aw	63	331	vis
63a	1	**WOLV**	6f Aw		549*	vis
65a	2	WOLV	6f Aw	64	638	vis
59a	3	SOUT	6f Aw	65	689	vis

55a	6	SOUT	5f Aw	65	870	
52a	6	WOLV	7f Aw	64	1390	vis
52	7	LEIC	6f Gd/Fm	62	2511	vis
65	1	**LEIC**	7f Gd/Fm	58	2918*	vis
65	2	DONC	8f Gd/Fm	63	3160	vis
42	9	YARM	7f Gd/Fm	66	3666	vis
0	15	LING	7f Soft	65	4192	vis
67a	1	**WOLV**	7f Aw	63	4550*	vis

DIAMOND ROAD 3 b c £2514

70	3	GOOD	8f Gd/Fm		1960
73	3	GOOD	9f Gd/Fm		2129
76	2	GOOD	10f Good		2308
71	6	KEMP	12f Gd/Fm		2751
40	13	ASCO	12f Gd/Fm	74	3014
57	7	GOOD	10f Good		3907

DIAMOND VANESSA 3 b f £0

37a	8	SOUT	6f Aw		46
45a	10	SOUT	5f Aw		179
40a	5	SOUT	7f Aw		417
22	10	SOUT	10f Good		806
0	16	NOTT	8f Heavy	46	1024 t

DIAMOND WHITE 5 b m £69107

110	8	NEWM	9f Gd/Sft	967
113	2	SAND	10f Heavy	1057
106	3	NEWM	8f Gd/Fm	1154
104	4	CAPA	10f Gd/Fm	1321
108	5	LONG	10f Gd/Fm	1458
103	6	SAND	10f Soft	1587
91	4	CHEP	10f Gd/Fm	2975
104	5	GOOD	10f Firm	3151
102	3	NEWB	11f Firm	3984
108	3	GOOD	10f Soft	4064
97	9	LONG	10f Good	4263
94	5	NEWM	10f Good	4337
94	5	NEWM	10f Gd/Sft	4532

DIAMOND ZOE 2 b f £210

44	4	CATT	5f Soft	4252
49	4	REDC	5f Gd/Sft	4496
0	18	DONC	8f Heavy	4569

DIANEME 3 b f £2906

68	3	RIPO	8f Soft		826
61	8	DONC	10f Gd/Sft		1051
64	4	THIR	8f Gd/Sft		1352
44	5	RIPO	10f Gd/Fm		2111
51	10	DONC	6f Gd/Fm	60	2577
29	10	RIPO	8f Aw	56	2839
61	2	THIR	7f Gd/Fm		3146
0	13	NEWM	8f Gd/Fm		3456
50	3	NEWC	7f Firm		3604
0	14	BEVE	8f Good	56	3951
60	4	CATT	7f Soft		4005
0	11	PONT	8f Gd/Fm	54	4232

DICKIE DEADEYE 3 b g £3287

62	7	WARW	8f Heavy		884
76	5	KEMP	8f Soft		1532
64	6	WIND	8f Gd/Fm		2211
59	5	SALI	8f Good	72	2688
59	6	SALI	10f Gd/Fm	69	3390
52	9	GOOD	10f Soft	65	4067
70	1	**SALI**	10f Gd/Sft	65	4168*
59	5	WIND	10f Gd/Sft	61	4291
73	2	WIND	11f Heavy	71	4529

DID YOU MISS ME 3 ch f £0

49	7	PONT	6f Good	1500
62	5	YARM	6f Good	1773

DIETRICH 2 br f £1750

86	4	ASCO	5f Good	2152
98	8	NEWM	6f Good	4159

DIFFERENTIAL 3 b c £580

92	5	HAYD	6f Gd/Fm		2458
85	5	NEWM	5f Gd/Fm	97	2859
88	4	DONC	6f Gd/Fm		3158

DIGITAL 3 ch g £6434

75	4	WIND	8f Gd/Fm		3048
78	2	CHEP	7f Gd/Fm		3256
75	3	NEWM	8f Gd/Fm		3626
55	11	NEWB	8f Firm	77	3998
77	2	BRIG	8f Soft		4175
82	1	**NOTT**	8f Heavy	74	4414*

DIGITAL IMAGE 3 b c £0

71	6	LEIC	7f Good	90	792
71	15	NEWM	7f Good	87	954
0	15	CHES	8f Gd/Fm	83	1215
53	8	CHES	7f Gd/Sft	78	1778

DIGNIFY 3 b f £17139

105	4	SAN	11f Good	1459
96	5	ASCO	12f Gd/Fm	3305

DIGON DA 4 ch g £0

0	18	WIND	8f Gd/Fm	70	1201
51	12	WIND	10f Firm		1288

DIHATJUM 3 b g £6017

64	3	CARL	8f Firm	63	1255
66	2	CATT	7f Gd/Fm	63	2438
63	4	BEVE	8f Good	66	2733
52	7	BEVE	7f Good	66	2882
66	1	**CARL**	7f Firm		3196*
63	2	BEVE	8f Good		3393
59	3	BEVE	8f Gd/Fm		3671
53	3	RIPO	8f Good		3711
53	7	BEVE	8f Good	60	3951
44	8	DONC	7f Soft		4461

DIKTAT 5 br g £247492

120	2	TOKY	8f Firm	1755
116	3	LONG	8f Soft	3847
114	6	ASCO	8f Good	4111

DIL 5 b g £7685

92a	5	WOLV	5f Aw	95	64
75a	7	WOLV	8f Aw	93	137
90a	3	SOUT	7f Aw	91	216
81a	9	WOLV	6f Aw	91	320
93a	1	**WOLV**	5f Aw	89	394+
86a	8	WOLV	5f Aw	95	435
83a	9	WOLV	5f Aw	92	579
84a	8	WOLV	6f Aw	91	660
38	12	NOTT	6f Good	63	787
0	20	BEVE	5f Firm	60	1278

DILETIA 3 b f £2051

57	10	LING	7f Gd/Sft		840	
60	4	NOTT	8f Gd/Sft	67	1085	
57	5	SALI	8f Good	65	1345	
54	6	BRIG	10f Good	62	1649	BL
53	7	CARL	8f Firm	59	3574	
54	4	BATH	10f Gd/Fm	56	3816	bl
56	1	**LEIC**	10f Gd/Fm		4029*	bl
55	4	BRIG	10f Soft	60	4174	bl
1	13	NEWC	10f Heavy	56	4404	bl

DILETTO 4 b f £2509

2a	9	SOUT	11f Aw		248
26a	8	WOLV	12f Aw		295
32a	6	WOLV	8f Aw		322
0a	12	WOLV	8f Aw		550
44a	2	WOLV	7f Aw		567
25a	6	SOUT	8f Aw	37	584
38	1	**CATT**	7f Gd/Fm		778*
31	7	REDC	7f Gd/Sft		1132
47	6	THIR	11f Gd/Sft		1351
30	8	AYR	8f Good	37	2136
46	9	CATT	7f Gd/Fm		2437

DILKUSHA 5 b g £1948

69a	6	LING	8f Aw	77	7
50	11	SAND	8f Gd/Fm	77	1989
73	8	KEMP	7f Firm	76	2261
76	4	EPSO	7f Good		2792
75	3	FOLK	7f Gd/Fm	76	3041
64	5	BATH	8f Firm	76	3207
70	4	LING	7f Gd/Fm	76	3758
72	8	DONC	7f Gd/Fm	76	3880

DILLY 2 br f £5942

60	2	WARW	7f Gd/Fm		2841
60	4	SALI	7f Gd/Fm		3418
70	3	WARW	7f Good		3692
76	1	**YARM**	7f Firm	66	3922*

DILSAA 3 ch c £355

77	5	HAYD	8f Gd/Sft	79	810	
68	8	NEWB	8f Gd/Fm		1786	
62	7	KEMP	9f Gd/Fm	75	2085	
51	8	YARM	8f Gd/Fm	72	2412	BL
66	6	LEIC	7f Gd/Fm	69	2775	
62	4	NEWM	8f Gd/Fm	65	3163	
59	6	HAYD	7f Gd/Sft	65	3269	
43a	9	LING	8f Aw	62	4335	

DILSHAAN 2 b c £106512

92	2	SAND	7f Gd/Fm		3946
116	1	**DONC**	8f Soft		4463*

DIM DOT 2 b c £0

0	14	LING	5f Good	4095
49a	8	LING	5f Aw	4333

DIM OFAN 4 b f £4130

57a	6	LING	8f Aw	62	147	
56a	4	WOLV	8f Aw	60	271	
66a	1	**SOUT**	8f Aw	60	326*	
11a	11	SOUT	8f Aw	65	384	
40a	6	SOUT	8f Aw	65	430	BL
18a	11	WOLV	9f Aw	64	637	
0	15	BEVE	7f Aw	62	2221	
50	7	RIPO	8f Aw	58	2542	bl
53	4	WIND	10f Gd/Fm		3045	
39	8	CHEP	12f Gd/Fm	54	3255	
25	11	SALI	10f Gd/Sft	52	4169	

DIM SUMS 2 b g £84580

71a	2	SOUT	5f Aw		801
76a	1	**SOUT**	6f Aw		1503*
95	1	**PONT**	6f Gd/Fm	79	2557*
105	1	**NEWM**	6f Gd/Fm	91	3165*
104	1	**REDC**	6f Gd/Fm		4219*

DIMMING OF THE DAY 3 ch f £2345

63a	1	**WOLV**	5f Aw	42*	bl
63a	3	WOLV	5f Aw	120	
54a	3	WOLV	5f Aw	145	
0	11	NEWC	5f Soft	756	bl

DINAR 5 b g £8059

42	3	WARW	11f Heavy	41	890
27	11	WARW	11f Soft	41	1065
43	2	NOTT	10f Good	40	1646
45	8	DONC	7f Gd/Fm	48	1840
48	2	BATH	8f Firm	43	1998
45	7	NOTT	10f Gd/Fm	52	2190
55	1	**WIND**	8f Good	46	2367*
62	1	**WIND**	8f Soft	54	2546*

DINKY 3 ch f £0

18a	7	LING	6f Aw		24
0a	11	LING	7f Aw		53
0a	15	SOUT	8f Aw		1505
27	8	PONT	8f Good		1865
6	10	PONT	12f Good	33	2362
0	13	LEIC	10f Good		2510
32	8	WIND	12f Gd/Fm	36	2887
37	8	NEWM	10f Good		3021
0	12	BEVE	12f Gd/Sft	31	3050
31	7	YARM	11f Firm		3917

DINOFELIS 2 b c £0

55	10	DONC	8f Gd/Fm	3864
54	5	KEMP	8f Soft	4036
64	7	SALI	8f Gd/Sft	4163

DINOS GIRL 3 ch f £0

0	15	MUSS	5f Gd/Fm	42	1143

DION DEE 4 ch f £4870

42a	8	LING	10f	Aw		314	
20a	7	LING	12f	Aw		457	
46a	3	WOLV	12f	Aw		565	
21a	9	SOUT	12f	Aw		643	
32	12	WIND	12f	Gd/Fm	45	748	
40	3	BRIG	10f	Gd/Sft	42	1509	
36	6	LING	11f	Good	43	1743	
44	1	NOTT	10f	Gd/Fm	39	2011*	
33	8	FOLK	10f	Gd/Fm	46	2296	
48	2	FOLK	10f	Gd/Fm	46	2625	
45	5	EPSO	10f	Good	46	2790	
46	6	WIND	10f	Gd/Fm		3045	
46	4	SALI	12f	Gd/Fm	49	3392	
17	15	EPSO	12f	Good	47	3858	

DIPLOMAT 4 b c £0

0a	12	SOUT	8f	Aw	80	49	

DIRECT DEAL 4 b c £1907

72	7	WIND	10f	Gd/Fm		747	t
0	16	KEMP	12f	Gd/Sft	77	1076	
48	12	BRIG	8f	Firm	73	1330	t
38	11	BATH	10f	Gd/Sft	68	1666	
38	12	WIND	10f	Gd/Fm	65	1878	
45	8	SALI	10f	Gd/Fm	58	2270	BL
50	1	WIND	12f	Good		2715*	t
32	10	WIND	12f	Gd/Fm	53	3049	t

DIRECT REACTION 3 b c £11138

60a	5	LING	7f	Aw	72	149	
62a	3	SOUT	8f	Aw		198	
71a	3	LING	8f	Aw		264	
58a	5	SOUT	7f	Aw		278	VIS
70a	1	LING	6f	Aw		399*	vis
71a	4	LING	6f	Aw	75	444	vis
77a	1	LING	7f	Aw	69	488*	vis
79a	1	LING	7f	Aw	73	617*	vis
61	4	CARL	7f	Firm		3196	vis
66	2	NEWM	7f	Gd/Fm		3318	vis
57	8	LING	6f	Firm	67	3759	vis
52a	10	WOLV	7f	Aw	79	3771	vis

DISGLAIR 2 b f £0

23a	11	SOUT	5f	Aw		865	
49	7	REDC	5f	Firm		1294	
4	10	NEWC	6f	Gd/Sft		1476	

DISPOL CHIEFTAN 2 b c £474

67	8	MUSS	5f	Gd/Sft		898	
65	5	REDC	5f	Firm		1131	
62	5	REDC	5f	Firm		1294	
57	11	THIR	5f	Gd/Fm		3346	
72	3	RIPO	5f	Good		3710	t
68	7	MUSS	5f	Gd/Sft		4131	t
70	4	NEWC	5f	Heavy	70	4423	

DISPOL FOXTROT 2 ch f £537

0	15	RIPO	6f	Good		3697	
45	4	HAMI	8f	Gd/Fm		3822	
39	6	AYR	8f	Soft		3957	
50a	3	WOLV	8f	Aw		4362	

DISPOL JAZZ 3 ch f £627

65	3	MUSS	7f	Gd/Sft		900	
59	7	MUSS	8f	Gd/Fm		1144	
0	13	REDC	10f	Gd/Fm	68	1299	
20	13	RIPO	8f	Good		1596	
23	8	RIPO	8f	Gd/Fm		2834	

DISPOL LAIRD 2 ch c £0

71	5	NEWC	5f	Soft		755	
60	8	REDC	5f	Gd/Sft		1130	
50	8	REDC	7f	Gd/Fm		2862	

DISPOL MISS CHIEF 3 ch f £0

0	14	REDC	14f	Gd/Sft	48	1581	

DISPOL ROCK 4 b g £0

62	10	NEWC	10f	Soft	74	757	
23	15	DONC	10f	Gd/Sft	72	1070	
49	10	YORK	9f	Heavy	69	4300	

26	9	REDC	10f	Soft		4501	

DISTANT COUSIN 3 b c £4488

80	2	LING	11f	Firm		3754	
80	3	KEMP	12f	Soft		4040	
80a	1	LING	13f	AW		4193*	
33	12	NEWB	16f	Gd/Sft	85	4458	

DISTANT DAWN 2 b f £627

59	4	WARW	5f	Heavy		1000	
0	12	NOTT	6f	Good		1413	
57	2	CHEP	6f	Heavy		1553	
42	6	BRIG	7f	Gd/Fm		2723	
45	9	BATH	5f	Firm		3204	VIS
23	10	SALI	7f	Gd/Fm		3388	vis
47	4	LING	6f	Firm		3757	vis

DISTANT DECREE 2 ch f £0

0	22	DONC	8f	Gd/Sft		4445	

DISTANT FLAME 3 b f £0

0	15	LING	6f	Gd/Sft		837	
50	7	FOLK	7f	Soft		962	
0	19	NEWB	7f	Gd/Fm	54	1787	BL
0	16	DONC	6f	Gd/Fm	50	2315	bl
36	5	NEWM	8f	Gd/Fm		3117	
32	6	NEWM	8f	Gd/Fm		3456	
32	10	WARW	11f	Good		3691	
7	12	BRIG	10f	Soft	36	4419	

DISTANT GUEST 3 b c £4010

65	2	WARW	7f	Soft		813	
41	11	WARW	7f	Heavy	65	887	
66	2	LING	7f	Good		1397	BL
59	4	BRIG	7f	Soft		1467	bl
0	14	LEIC	7f	Firm	67	2026	bl
56	5	PONT	8f	Gd/Sft	65	3226	bl
47	9	HAMI	8f	Gd/Sft	65	3380	bl
39	7	YARM	8f	Gd/Fm	60	3970	VIS
36	9	BRIG	8f	Soft		4173	bl
60	1	BATH	8f	Soft	54	4435*	bl

DISTANT KING 7 b g £0

0a	10	WOLV	6f	Aw		82	
0	18	WARW	5f	Heavy	36	1005	
19	12	CARL	5f	Firm		1256	
0	27	REDC	8f	Good	33	1296	
0	15	DONC	7f	Good	36	1519	
0	11	PONT	5f	Good		1868	
19	8	HAMI	5f	Gd/Fm	33	1910	
25	8	HAMI	5f	Gd/Fm	33	1941	
0	13	CARL	7f	Firm	31	2282	
0	14	DONC	6f	Gd/Sft		2580	
44	10	HAYD	7f	Gd/Fm		2704	
50	6	CARL	5f	Firm		2822	
32	8	REDC	9f	Gd/Fm		2865	
46	10	REDC	10f	Gd/Sft		2994	
50	8	BEVE	5f	Gd/Sft		3056	
82	10	NOTT	5f	Good		3521	
82	5	BEVE	5f	Sft/Hvy		4043	
57	10	REDC	7f	Gd/Sft		4218	
0	11	CATT	6f	Soft		4257	

DISTANT MUSIC 3 b c £71900

113	2	NEWM	7f	Good		950	
111	8	NEWM	8f	Gd/Fm		1171	
120	1	DONC	8f	Gd/Fm		3875*	
120	3	NEWM	10f	Good		4355	

DISTANT PROSPECT 3 b c £20177

71	2	BATH	10f	Good	68	1094	
74	3	WIND	12f	Gd/Sft	69	1425	
62	5	LEIC	12f	Gd/Sft	69	1571	
72	4	SALI	12f	Gd/Sft	71	2470	
77	1	BATH	13f	Gd/Fm	69	3819*	
80	1	YORK	14f	Heavy	74	4299*	
83	1	NEWB	16f	Gd/Sft	79	4458*	

DISTANT STORM 7 ch g £545

52	4	DONC	18f	Good	54	714	bl
50	10	SALI	14f	Firm	57	1180	bl

57	7	CHES	16f	Gd/Fm	51	3511	bl

DISTILLERY 2 ch c £222

76	4	BRIG	8f	Soft		4417	

DISTINCTIVE DREAM 6 b g £9026

57a	6	WOLV	8f	Aw	74	254	
62a	2	SOUT	6f	Aw		389	
62a	1	WOLV	7f	Aw		449*	
61a	5	LING	7f	Gd/Sft	65	504	
64a	3	SOUT	7f	Aw	66	539	
65a	4	SOUT	7f	Aw	63	587	
67a	1	SOUT	7f	Aw	63	598*	
43a	7	WOLV	7f	Aw	67	721	
67a	3	SOUT	7f	Aw		738	
62	6	WARW	8f	Soft	72	817	
68	7	DONC	6f	Gd/Sft	70	1074	
72	2	HAMI	6f	Gd/Fm	70	1192	
69	6	CHES	8f	Firm	70	1250	
59	13	AYR	7f	Gd/Fm	71	1631	
64	8	AYR	6f	Gd/Fm	71	1654	
44	9	CHES	7f	Gd/Sft	71	1778	
63	4	HAMI	8f	Firm		1905	
0	19	NEWC	6f	Firm	67	2334	
61	5	YARM	6f	Gd/Fm	67	2415	
52	10	HAMI	6f	Gd/Sft	64	2641	
47	10	CHES	6f	Gd/Sft	64	2673	
54	8	HAMI	8f	Gd/Fm	64	2796	vis
65a	2	WOLV	6f	Aw		3275	
57	7	CARL	7f	Firm		3573	
35	9	DONC	8f	Heavy	60	4573	

DISTINCTIVE MANNA 2 b g £0

0	13	PONT	5f	Firm		3500	
0	14	THIR	5f	Gd/Fm		3615	

DISTINCTLY BLU 3 b f £13386

45a	6	SOUT	5f	Aw		740	
61	1	MUSS	5f	Gd/Sft	57	901*	
58a	6	WOLV	6f	Aw	63	1138	
66	2	REDC	6f	Good	63	1891	
53	5	THIR	6f	Gd/Fm	63	2060	
68	2	CATT	6f	Gd/Fm	65	2440	
73	1	CHES	5f	Good	66	2663+	
63	8	CATT	5f	Gd/Fm	73	2929	
54	13	THIR	5f	Gd/Fm	72	3349	

DISTINCTLY CHIC 2 b f £4215

67	6	WIND	5f	Gd/Fm		1197	
75	1	HAMI	5f	Gd/Fm		1359*	
79	2	AYR	6f	Gd/Fm		1628	

DISTINCTLY DANCER 2 b c £3842

101	3	CHAN	5f	Hldng		2485	

DISTINCTLY EAST 3 b c £560

55	8	DONC	7f	Good	75	736	
61	4	PONT	10f	Gd/Sft	72	1104	
58	10	YARM	10f	Good	69	1775	
63	5	NEWM	8f	Firm		2345	VIS
27	6	YARM	8f	Gd/Fm		2411	vis

DISTINCTLY WELL 3 b g £2377

69	2	HAMI	9f	Good	67	846	
72	3	WIND	12f	Heavy	70	937	
0	10	CHES	12f	Gd/Fm	70	1225	
72	2	WARW	11f	Heavy	70	1521	
62	6	CHES	10f	Gd/Sft		1779	

DIVA 3 b f £4796

44	6	REDC	7f	Gd/Sft		1135	
49	11	NOTT	6f	Firm		1266	
60a	3	WOLV	9f	Aw		1388	
62a	2	LING	7f	Aw		1745	
64a	2	WOLV	9f	Aw	61	2080	
69	1	BEVE	10f	Gd/Fm	64	2484*	
55a	4	LING	12f	Aw	69	2651	

DIVAS ROBE 2 b f £0

60	6	KEMP	7f	Firm		2259	
72	6	NEWB	7f	Firm		2810	

DIVE 3 b c £0

37a	8	WOLV	12f Aw	54	1142

DIVEBOMB 2 b f £0
0	18	WIND	5f Gd/Sft		1424
34	9	SOUT	6f Soft		1602
0a	11	SOUT	7f Aw		4154
58	8	BATH	8f Soft		4429
24	9	NEWM	8f Soft		4542 BL

DIVERS PEARL 3 b f £10911
78	2	LING	6f Gd/Sft		837
80a	1	WOLV	7f Aw		1035*
77	3	REDC	7f Firm	76	1297
57	8	SALI	8f Good	77	2688
82	1	THIR	8f Gd/Sft	75	3777*
57	13	SAND	8f Soft	81	4206

DIVIDE AND RULE 6 b g £0
0a	15	SOUT	5f Aw		71
26a	11	WOLV	6f Aw		132
26a	10	WOLV	6f Aw		272
0a	12	WOLV	8f Aw		322

DIVINATION 5 ch m £5167
107	2	SAIN	15f Heavy		140

DIVINE APPEAL 5 b m £0
0	18	NEWM	12f Gd/Fm	82	1187
60	6	AYR	10f Gd/Fm	75	1656
32	7	NEWC	10f Heavy	75	1769
0	14	HAMI	12f Gd/Fm	69	1908
0	14	CATT	16f Soft	55	4006

DIVINE HOSTESS 3 br f £0
14	10	REDC	11f Soft		4497

DIVINE MISS P 7 ch m £0
51a	10	WOLV	5f Aw	70	40
0a	13	SOUT	5f Aw		71

DIVINE PROSPECT 3 br f £2299
72	6	DONC	10f Gd/Fm	74	701
65	5	KEMP	9f Gd/Sft	74	1075
70	6	WIND	12f Gd/Sft	72	1425
70	4	AYR	11f Gd/Fm	72	1633
44	11	SALI	8f Gd/Sft	69	2467
71	2	KEMP	9f Gd/Sft	69	2581
64	3	NEWB	10f Firm	67	2811
57	5	YORK	12f Gd/Fm	70	3725
0	14	BRIG	10f Gd/Sft	70	4118
40	11	WIND	8f Gd/Sft		4292

DIVINE WIND 2 ch f £6601
72	1	DONC	5f Good		730*
70	4	THIR	5f Soft		904
69	7	DONC	5f Gd/Sft		1067
74	3	RIPO	5f Gd/Fm		2100
85	3	DONC	5f Gd/Fm		2318
77	4	HAYD	6f Gd/Fm		2500
0	21	NEWB	5f Firm		2849
56	7	HAYD	5f Gd/Fm	75	3264
57	7	WARW	15f Good	72	3693
0	16	DONC	7f Gd/Fm	72	3860
68	2	LEIC	6f Gd/Sft	65	4030
0	20	NEWM	7f Good	71	4157
56	13	NEWM	8f Good	68	4350
55	5	DONC	7f Soft	64	4460

DIVORCE ACTION 4 b c £2940
0a	14	LING	12f Aw	65	290
63	2	NOTT	10f Gd/Sft	60	1364
64	5	WIND	10f Gd/Sft	63	1878
0	9	GOOD	9f Good	63	2304
42	11	KEMP	8f Gd/Fm	61	2752
49	5	SALI	10f Gd/Fm		2981
61	1	WARW	11f Good		3691*

DIVULGE 3 b c £4455
83	5	NEWM	8f Gd/Fm		1692
93	1	GOOD	8f Gd/Fm		1960*
85	4	DONC	8f Gd/Fm		2757
62	11	GOOD	9f Good	90	3658
0	18	SAND	8f Soft	86	4206

DIWAN 2 b c £0
50	9	PONT	6f Soft		4082
61	9	NOTT	8f Heavy		4504

DIXIE FLYER 3 b f £215
0a	12	SOUT	7f Aw		330
0a	3	WOLV	9f Aw		382 BL

DIXIELAKE 3 b f £5771
83	1	CHEP	8f Heavy		1556*
80	3	SALI	7f Gd/Fm		2228
82	3	KEMP	9f Gd/Sft	80	2581
0	17	SAND	8f Soft	81	4206

DIXIES DARTS 2 b g £0
59	9	LING	6f Firm		3832
0	24	NEWM	6f Good		4345

DIZZIE LIZZIE 3 b f £0
57	8	KEMP	9f Gd/Fm		2086
48	8	FOLK	7f Gd/Fm		2293
0	11	LING	6f Firm		3579

DIZZY KNIGHT 3 b f £312
62	4	NEWM	6f Gd/Fm		3319
46	13	NOTT	8f Soft		3977
15	9	CATT	6f Soft		4255

DIZZY TILLY 6 b m £3867
0	15	WIND	12f Gd/Fm	50	748
28	9	WIND	12f Good	46	853
22	13	NOTT	14f Heavy	44	1023
51	4	WIND	12f Gd/Fm		1880
44	3	SALI	12f Firm	46	2023
31a	3	WOLV	12f Aw	40	2075
27	8	KEMP	9f Firm	51	2262
49	1	WIND	12f Good	44	2370*
32	8	WIND	10f Soft	50	2544
35	6	BATH	12f Aw	50	2789
0	13	WIND	12f Gd/Fm	49	3049
0	11	WIND	12f Good	46	3353
0a	11	WOLV	12f Aw	45	4360
0a	10	WOLV	12f Aw		4549 BL

DJAIS 11 ch g £2815
74a	1	SOUT	16f Aw		1802* vis
73a	2	WOLV	16f Aw		2076
23	7	YARM	14f Soft		4510 vis

DJIBOUTI 3 b c £24839
104	2	COLO	8f Good		1322

DOBAANDI SECRET 4 b g £0
11a	8	WOLV	15f Aw		363

DOBERMAN 5 br g £4867
30a	8	WOLV	12f Aw	46	43 vis
41a	4	LING	10f Aw		111 vis
39a	4	WOLV	8f Aw	42	254 vis
13a	11	WOLV	9f Aw	38	305
37a	3	SOUT	8f Aw	39	345 bl
40a	5	WOLV	7f Aw		396 bl
6a	9	WOLV	8f Aw	38	411 vis
35a	3	WOLV	8f Aw	38	431 bl
49a	1	WOLV	8f Aw		550* bl
24a	7	SOUT	7f Aw	45	599 bl
35a	8	WOLV	8f Aw	43	675 bl
44	2	MUSS	8f Firm	42	2378 vis
46	2	WARW	7f Gd/Fm	44	2840 vis
46	2	CHEP	8f Gd/Fm	46	3251 vis
22a	10	WOLV	8f Aw	42	3499 vis
42	7	BRIG	10f Firm	46	3737 vis

DOC DAVIS 2 ch c £0
0	20	NEWB	7f Firm		3999
0	18	DONC	7f Gd/Sft		4446

DOC RYANS 6 b g £0
64a	5	SOUT	16f Aw	75	253

DOCKLANDS ROLLER 2 b g £0
23	9	NEWC	6f Gd/Sft		1476
56	5	REDC	7f Good		1890
27	8	REDC	7f Gd/Fm		2155

DOCKSIDER 5 ch g £387262
122	3	GULF	8f Good		16
122	1	SHA	8f Gd/Fm		184*

DOCTOR DENNIS 3 b c £9963
41	9	BRIG	8f Gd/Sft		894 bl
0	15	WARW	7f Soft	67	1061 bl
60	12	WIND	6f Gd/Fm	67	1196
64	2	WIND	6f Gd/Sft		1423
60	1	BRIG	6f Gd/Sft		1508*
61	2	BRIG	6f Firm	60	2042
51	7	WIND	6f Gd/Sft	60	2207
69	1	WIND	6f Soft	60	2549*
67a	2	WOLV	6f Aw	66	2603
69	2	WIND	6f Gd/Fm	67	2885
71	4	LING	6f Firm	69	3280
71	4	LING	6f Firm	69	3759
70	2	BRIG	6f Gd/Sft	69	4120
55	11	LING	6f Soft	70	4270

DOCTOR JOHN 3 ch g £220
0	13	DONC	10f Gd/Sft		1054
68	7	THIR	12f Good		1386
65	4	PONT	12f Firm		2179
58a	4	SOUT	12f Aw	60	2815

DOCTOR SPIN 4 b c £11639
108	1	NEWM	6f Firm	98	1182*
108	5	YORK	6f Firm		1338
0	23	ASCO	6f Good	105	2151
105	2	YARM	6f Good		3235

DODONA 2 b f £587
72	4	KEMP	7f Gd/Sft		2583
53	9	KEMP	7f Gd/Fm		3074
51	9	LING	8f Firm		3577
66	4	NOTT	6f Soft	67	3976
54	10	LING	7f Soft	66	4191
45	7	DONC	7f Heavy	65	4577

DOJIMA MUTEKI 10 b h £0
0	22	ASCO	5f Good		2065

DOLFINESSE 3 ch f £2319
0	14	NOTT	8f Gd/Sft	58	1365
42	5	RIPO	8f Good		1596
46	2	PONT	8f Good		1865 VIS
49	3	CARL	7f Firm	50	2017 vis
46	4	NEWM	8f Gd/Fm		2134 vis
27	10	CARL	8f Firm	49	2281 vis
41	6	BEVE	8f Firm	46	2735 vis
44	2	NOTT	8f Gd/Fm		3004 vis
17	10	CARL	8f Gd/Fm	46	3082 vis
37	6	HAYD	8f Gd/Sft		3266 vis
29	7	YARM	8f Gd/Fm	39	3971 vis

DOLLAR BIRD 3 b f £12447
90	3	NEWM	10f Gd/Sft	86	979
96	2	LING	11f Gd/Sft		1282
89	6	EPSO	12f Gd/Sft		1828
86	9	HAYD	12f Gd/Fm		2501
97	2	GOOD	14f Firm	95	3153
73	15	NEWM	12f Good	96	4162
95	3	DONC	15f Heavy		4568

DOLPHIN BEECH 2 b f £0
38	12	WARW	15f Gd/Fm		3911
15a	10	WOLV	6f Aw		4548

DOLPHINELLE 4 b c £8354
38a	6	WOLV	6f Aw	82	bl
52a	5	LING	7f Aw	60	107 bl
49a	4	WOLV	7f Aw	57	187 VIS
61a	1	LING	6f Aw	55	263*
48a	11	LING	7f Aw	59	337
56a	4	LING	5f Aw	58	372
43a	5	SOUT	6f Aw		414
54a	4	LING	7f Aw		484
54a	4	LING	7f Aw		547
55a	3	LING	6f Aw	54	634
41a	7	LING	6f Aw	54	691
53a	3	WOLV	7f Aw	53	754

43a 4 LING 7f Aw 53 879
53 7 BRIG 8f Gd/Fm 64 1129
65 3 LING 7f Soft 62 1542
66 1 NEWB 7f Gd/Sft 62 1590*
63 6 KEMP 8f Gd/Fm 64 1926
47 15 NEWM 8f Good 64 2564
44 11 ASCO 8f Gd/Fm 67 3338
52 11 ASCO 8f Gd/Sft 70 4126
56 9 YARM 7f Soft 63 4513

DOLYDILLE 4 b f £29400
107 2 LEOP 10f Good 3924
111 1 CURR 10f Gd/Sft 4241*

DOM MIGUEL 3 b c £0
52 7 SOUT 7f Good 804
17 10 CATT 7f Soft 1681
0 12 BATH 10f Firm 53 2332
25 7 EPSO 8f Good 48 2795
0 12 BRIG 7f Gd/Fm 44 3242
0 11 EPSO 9f Good 49 3856
31 6 BRIG 12f Gd/Sft 4119
0a 12 LING 12f AW 4186

DOM SHADEED 5 b g £4368
53 1 KEMP 8f Gd/Fm 50 2752*

DOMINAITE 2 b g £16415
47 10 REDC 5f Gd/Sft 1131
56 10 CARL 5f Firm 1252
73 3 THIR 5f Good 1381
71 2 PONT 5f Soft 1704
75 1 REDC 7f Gd/Fm 71 2991*
76 3 NEWC 7f Good 74 3246
80 2 YORK 7f Good 75 3542
80 3 NEWC 8f Gd/Sft 76 3704
82 2 NEWM 8f Good 80 4350
82 3 DONC 8f Gd/Sft 80 4450
60 8 DONC 7f Heavy 81 4577

DOMINANT DUCHESS 6 b m £53165
88 1 YORK 14f Firm 82 1329*
99 1 ASCO 22f Good 2153*
94 1 ASCO 16f Gd/Fm 92 3302*
82 9 DONC 18f Gd/Fm 3877
0 19 NEWM 18f Good 96 4353

DOMINELLE 8 b m £1977
0 15 CARL 6f Firm 57 1258
0 17 THIR 6f Gd/Sft 57 1356
38 12 DONC 6f Gd/Fm 53 1842
49 4 BEVE 5f Firm 53 1923
43 10 WARW 6f Gd/Fm 49 2252
46 4 BEVE 5f Gd/Fm 48 2517
36 8 NEWC 6f Good 48 2525
44 6 BEVE 5f Firm 46 2732
51 1 THIR 6f Gd/Fm 46 2969*
40 11 REDC 6f Good 51 3312
0 17 BEVE 5f Gd/Sft 51 3653
43 5 NEWC 5f Heavy 50 4407
26a 10 WOLV 6f Aw 49 4553

DOMINION PRINCE 2 b c £0
73 9 NEWM 6f Gd/Fm 3162
0 13 SALI 6f Gd/Fm 3387
70 7 KEMP 7f Gd/Fm 3790
51 7 GOOD 8f Good 3906
57 9 DONC 7f Soft 70 4460

DOMINIQUE 2 ch f £404
61 10 BATH 6f Gd/Fm 1667
77 3 BATH 5f Firm 1993

DOMINO FLYER 7 b g £0
14a 9 SOUT 11f Aw 59 126
0a 12 SOUT 8f Aw 56 497
37a 4 SOUT 8f Aw 869
26a 9 WOLV 8f Aw 49 1393 BL

DOMINUS 2 b c £10938
91 2 NEWM 5f Soft 984
92 2 ASCO 5f Gd/Sft 1107

97 1 NEWM 6f Gd/Fm 2598*
97 6 GOOD 6f Good 3105
92 5 KEMP 6f Gd/Fm 3797
99 8 DONC 7f Firm 3891

DON ALFRED 2 b c £1195
78 5 NEWM 7f Good 2563
74 7 DONC 7f Gd/Fm 3156
77 3 THIR 8f Gd/Sft 3779
70 3 PONT 10f Soft 4230
37 10 YARM 8f Soft 76 4393

DON BOSCO 4 ch c £3087
0 10 LING 7f Soft 72 1286
64 10 AYR 7f Gd/Fm 70 1631
56 8 YARM 6f Gd/Fm 68 1953
55 9 RIPO 5f Gd/Fm 68 2107 BL
54 3 YARM 7f Firm 63 2899
34 11 YARM 7f Good 63 3030
43 8 REDC 8f Firm 3330
53 1 LING 10f Firm 3490*
53a 9 LING 12f Aw 4101
57a 2 LING 8f Aw 55 4335

DON FAYRUZ 8 b g £0
3a 11 WOLV 8f Aw 138

DON PUCCINI 3 ch c £0
102 5 SAND 5f Gd/Fm 1987
86 10 NEWB 6f Firm 2847
46 10 BEVE 5f Sft/Hvy 4043
77 9 DONC 6f Heavy 4581

DON QUIXOTE 4 b c £0
37 8 BRIG 6f Firm 47 1211
33 6 REDC 6f Gd/Sft 45 1578
27 10 LEIC 6f Gd/Sft 45 1734 BL
34 7 BATH 6f Firm 40 1994 bl
31 7 BEVE 5f Firm 38 2223
22 9 THIR 7f Good 36 3129

DON RUBINI 2 b c £0
42 8 BRIG 8f Soft 4418

DONATUS 4 b c £852
71a 2 LING 10f Aw 629
62 7 NEWB 13f Firm 70 3994

DONE AND DUSTED 4 ch f £4089
55a 7 LING 7f Aw 68 29
53a 6 LING 7f Aw 66 107
39a 8 WOLV 8f Aw 63 175
66a 1 WOLV 7f Aw 59 226*
41a 10 SOUT 8f Aw 65 246
60a 6 WOLV 8f Aw 64 466
63a 3 LING 8f Aw 63 503
68a 1 WOLV 7f Aw 62 583*
49a 5 WOLV 7f Aw 67 711
62a 6 WOLV 8f Aw 67 921
53 10 BRIG 8f Firm 70 1330

DONE WELL 8 b g £0
0 15 MUSS 9f Gd/Sft 40 795
11 10 MUSS 14f Gd/Sft 37 903
14 7 MUSS 12f Gd/Fm 41 1147 t
21 7 HAMI 12f Firm 27 1241 t
16 9 HAMI 11f Gd/Fm 17 1361 t
18 9 MUSS 9f Firm 28 1689 t
32 7 HAMI 8f Firm 1940 t

DONNA DOUGHNUT 2 ch f £0
39 10 GOOD 6f Good 2357
27a 5 WOLV 5f Aw 2605

DONNAS DOUBLE 5 ch g £19216
51 10 PONT 8f Soft 67 875
56 5 NEWC 7f Heavy 65 1011
55 6 HAMI 8f Firm 64 1243
62 3 RIPO 8f Good 62 1598
61 5 NEWC 8f Gd/Fm 64 2311
67 2 NEWC 10f Good 64 2522
69 1 YORK 7f Good 63 2694*
0 14 CHES 8f Firm 70 3170

69 3 NEWC 7f Good 70 3250
68 4 HAMI 9f Gd/Sft 70 3535
30 11 NEWC 7f Soft 69 3708
73 2 YORK 8f Good 69 3810
70 4 DONC 10f Firm 69 3899
58 14 NEWM 7f Gd/Fm 69 4215
55 13 REDC 8f Gd/Sft 69 4498

DONNINI 3 ch g £0
44 8 NOTT 8f Soft 1643

DONOSTIA 4 b f £0
93 2 MULH 17f V 13

DONT SURRENDER 3 b c £6087
84 9 NEWM 6f Gd/Sft 91 982
93 2 SALI 6f Firm 90 1178
95 3 HAYD 6f Gd/Sft 94 1534
71 13 NEWM 6f Good 94 2568
76 13 YORK 6f Gd/Fm 94 3727
78 7 HAYD 7f Gd/Sft 92 4106

DONT WORRY BOUT ME 3 b c £4359
55a 7 LING 8f Aw 67 158
32a 9 LING 10f Aw 62 315
61a 1 LING 12f Aw 457* VIS
56 6 LING 11f Firm 62 2321
64a 2 LING 12f Aw 62 2651 vis
48 6 BRIG 12f Gd/Fm 62 2725 vis
55 2 BRIG 10f Gd/Fm 54 3244 vis
40 8 RIPO 10f Good 57 3702 vis
15a 12 WOLV 9f Aw 62 4228 vis
0a 16 LING 12f Aw 55 4334 vis

DONTBESOBOLD 3 b g £1933
53a 7 SOUT 7f Aw 278
59a 4 SOUT 8f Aw 328
59a 3 WOLV 9f Aw 395
32a 6 SOUT 11f Aw 58 536
47a 6 WOLV 12f Aw 565
59a 2 WOLV 8f Aw 661
62 4 HAMI 8f Good 847
64 4 WARW 11f Heavy 63 1002
21 11 PONT 10f Gd/Sft 63 1104 VIS
56 5 NEWC 8f Gd/Sft 62 1477 vis
0 12 REDC 9f Gd/Sft 62 1583 vis
61 2 CATT 7f Soft 1682 vis
52 8 HAYD 7f Gd/Sft 61 1793 vis
46a 6 SOUT 8f Aw 63 1979 vis
0 15 HAYD 7f Gd/Sft 60 3269 vis

DOODLE BUG 3 b f £1082
79 3 WARW 11f Soft 814
61 5 DONC 12f Gd/Fm 3157
72 3 BATH 13f Gd/Fm 70 3518
64 6 DONC 15f Gd/Sft 70 4451

DORA CARRINGTON 2 b f £50241
78 1 PONT 6f Firm 2174*
108 1 NEWM 6f Good 2565*
103 3 LEOP 6f Good 3372

DORANFIELD LADY 5 b m £0
0a 7 WOLV 9f Aw 378
17a 8 WOLV 8f Aw 465
28a 5 WOLV 9f Aw 531
4a 6 SOUT 11f Aw 672

DORCHESTER 3 b c £3650
0 28 NEWM 6f Gd/Fm 100 1694
0 18 YORK 6f Gd/Fm 96 2003
78 9 ASCO 5f Gd/Fm 92 2168
0 14 DONC 5f Gd/Sft 92 2348
83 5 ASCO 5f Gd/Fm 86 3016 BL
87 3 SAND 5f Gd/Fm 86 3473
71 14 DONC 8f Gd/Fm 86 3861

DORISSIO 4 b f £1964
65 3 HAYD 7f Gd/Sft 64 811
62 3 HAMI 8f Good 847
64 3 WIND 8f Gd/Sft 64 1097
61 6 BATH 8f Gd/Fm 64 1442

DOROTHEA SHARP 3 b f £0 — continued section (top)

54	9	BEVE	8f Good	63	3951	
64	3	GOOD	8f Soft	63	4066	
0	13	SAND	7f Soft	64	4204	
0	18	YORK	9f Heavy	64	4300	

DOROTHEA SHARP 3 b f £0

0	16	SOUT	7f Gd/Sft	53	857	
45a	5	WOLV	7f Aw		1035	
35a	7	LING	10f Aw	53	1265	
23	9	BRIG	10f Good	49	1649	
0	11	NOTT	8f Good	54	1873	VIS
0a	9	LING	12f Aw	41	2217	vis

DOROTHY ALLEN 4 b f £0

0a	12	LING	7f Aw		8	
10a	8	LING	8f Aw	40	152	
0a	11	SOUT	8f Aw	33	340	

DOUBLE ACTION 6 br g £1984

57a	4	WOLV	7f Aw		623	
54	13	PONT	8f Soft	67	875	
57	4	NEWC	7f Heavy	64	1011	
57	7	REDC	8f Firm	63	1300	
54	5	RIPO	8f Good	61	1598	
63	3	CATT	7f Soft	61	1680	bl
66	2	PONT	6f Good	61	1869	bl
53	6	CARL	6f Firm	61	2015	bl
61	6	HAYD	6f Gd/Fm	64	2444	bl
43	12	PONT	6f Gd/Fm	64	2559	bl
61	6	YORK	6f Good	64	2697	bl
44	12	HAMI	6f Gd/Sft	63	3377	bl
53	11	NEWC	6f Firm	63	3605	bl
58	6	NEWC	7f Soft	62	3708	bl
69	6	YORK	6f Soft		4287	
50	7	AYR	6f Heavy	60	4327	

DOUBLE BANGER 3 b c £4649

73a	1	**LING**	10f Aw		204*	
76a	3	LING	10f Aw		420	
69	3	DONC	15f Gd/Sft	77	1071	

DOUBLE BID 3 b g £1286

72	2	THIR	8f Gd/Sft		1717	
42	7	PONT	10f Gd/Fm		2558	
27	9	RIPO	10f Gd/Fm		3012	

DOUBLE BLADE 5 b g £9228

61	2	DONC	12f Gd/Fm	59	699	
54	10	HAYD	14f Gd/Fm	62	1167	
67	1	**DONC**	12f Gd/Fm	60	2755*	
69	1	**REDC**	11f Gd/Fm	64	3636*	

DOUBLE BOUNCE 10 b g £868

53	10	NEWM	6f Firm	70	3297	
64	3	FOLK	6f Gd/Fm		3587	
0	16	LEIC	7f Firm	62	3839	

DOUBLE BREW 2 ch c £6643

62	3	KEMP	6f Soft		1526	
87	4	GOOD	6f Gd/Sft		1809	
87	2	KEMP	6f Gd/Fm		2083	
81	2	GOOD	6f Good		2357	
72	5	SAND	5f Gd/Fm		2933	
81	4	DONC	6f Firm		3888	
79	6	NEWM	5f Good	80	4179	

DOUBLE CROSSED 2 b f £320

| 71 | 4 | WIND | 8f Heavy | | 4524 | |

DOUBLE DESTINY 4 b g £744

0	14	NOTT	10f Gd/Sft	60	1370	
41	7	YARM	7f Gd/Sft	55	1611	BL
39	8	LEIC	8f Firm	52	2027	bl
37a	8	SOUT	8f Aw	48	2385	bl
49	3	KEMP	7f Gd/Fm	48	2749	bl
35	9	CHEP	7f Gd/Fm	48	2974	bl
38	8	KEMP	8f Gd/Fm	48	3078	bl

DOUBLE DIGIT 2 b f £0

8	8	HAYD	5f Soft		1492	
39	9	CATT	7f Good		3438	
0	12	RIPO	6f Good		3697	
0	19	BEVE	7f Good		3955	

DOUBLE ECLIPSE 8 b h £4884

| 109 | 2 | NEWM | 12f Firm | | 2341 | |

DOUBLE ENTRY 3 b c £0

2	9	CARL	9f Gd/Sft	45	1722	
0	14	AYR	8f Good	33	2136	
0	14	CARL	6f Gd/Fm		2240	

DOUBLE FANTASY 2 b f £3770

56	20	ASCO	5f Good		2088	
6	6	THIR	5f Good		3346	
85	1	**BATH**	5f Firm		3621*	
0	20	DONC	6f Gd/Fm		3862	
77	4	LING	5f Soft		4485	

DOUBLE FAULT 3 br f £843

53	5	NOTT	8f Heavy	55	1024	
0a	11	SOUT	7f Aw	54	1202	
25	15	NEWC	8f Gd/Sft	54	1477	
52	3	RIPO	8f Good		1596	BL
47	3	CATT	7f Gd/Sft		1818	bl
21	10	CARL	7f Firm	50	2017	bl
0	15	YARM	8f Good	47	3236	
32	11	YARM	7f Firm		3921	bl
0	7	YARM	10f Firm		3935	bl
47	4	BRIG	8f Soft		4177	bl
49	5	YARM	7f Soft		4387	bl
40	5	WIND	10f Heavy		4528	bl

DOUBLE GUN 3 b c £0

32	15	WARW	6f Heavy		888	
57	6	NOTT	6f Firm		1266	
65	5	WARW	7f Heavy		1525	
65	7	SALI	7f Gd/Fm		1886	

DOUBLE HEART 4 b c £14794

101	3	SAIN	10f Hldng		665	
115	3	SAIN	8f Hldng		1123	
115	4	LONG	10f Gd/Sft		1458	

DOUBLE HONOUR 2 gr c £4879

77	2	NEWC	7f Good		2271	
65	4	BEVE	7f Good		2881	
84	1	**HAMI**	8f Gd/Fm		3822*	

DOUBLE KAY 2 gr g £0

| 55 | 9 | THIR | 5f Good | | 1381 | |
| 43 | 5 | MUSS | 5f Firm | | 1684 | |

DOUBLE M 3 ch c £0

55	10	SALI	5f Firm	80	2022	
65	6	BATH	5f Firm		3622	
46a	11	WOLV	6f Aw	70	4023	bl

DOUBLE MARCH 7 b g £0

53	13	WIND	6f Gd/Fm	62	1196	
56	5	NOTT	5f Gd/Sft		1368	
0	11	NEWB	6f Gd/Sft	58	1591	BL
48	11	SAND	5f Gd/Fm	57	2925	

DOUBLE O 6 b g £1282

74a	3	LING	5f Aw	73	91	bl
67a	7	SOUT	6f Aw	73	129	bl
66a	4	WOLV	6f Aw	73	678	bl
54	8	BRIG	5f Gd/Sft	70	897	bl
22	7	FOLK	5f Soft		960	bl
65a	3	WOLV	5f Aw	72	1140	bl
62a	5	SOUT	6f Aw	70	1504	bl

DOUBLE OSCAR 7 ch g £6426

82a	10	WOLV	6f Aw	93	660	bl
48	18	DONC	6f Gd/Fm	74	702	bl
0	17	THIR	6f Good	72	1162	
67	5	THIR	5f Gd/Sft	70	1357	
66	6	REDC	5f Gd/Sft	69	1580	
70	3	PONT	6f Good	67	1869	
73	2	YORK	5f Gd/Fm	67	1980	
74	1	**NEWC**	5f Firm	70	2340*	
66	7	PONT	5f Gd/Fm	73	2830	bl
58	9	GOOD	6f Gd/Fm	73	3136	bl
52	15	RIPO	6f Gd/Fm	72	3464	

DOUBLE PING 2 ch f £0

| 54 | 10 | THIR | 5f Gd/Fm | | 3346 | |

| 41 | 5 | RIPO | 6f Good | | 3697 | |
| 0 | 13 | PONT | 6f Soft | | 4082 | |

DOUBLE PLATINUM 3 b f £3575

70	3	YARM	5f Gd/Sft		1609	
71	6	YARM	7f Gd/Fm		1951	
76	2	NEWM	6f Gd/Fm		2807	
76	2	NEWM	6f Gd/Fm		3319	
71	3	LING	6f Firm		3579	

DOUBLE RED 3 b f £4794

64	2	SOUT	10f Good	62	807	
57	3	BEVE	12f Heavy	62	978	
40	10	BEVE	12f Good	62	1446	
48	9	EPSO	10f Good	60	3762	
65	1	**GOOD**	10f Soft	56	4067*	
55	6	SALI	10f Gd/Sft	62	4169	
51	4	NEWC	10f Heavy	63	4427	

DOUBLE ROCK 4 b f £901

49	5	YARM	11f Firm		2897	
38	4	NEWM	12f Gd/Fm		3313	
42	2	WIND	12f Good		3351	

DOUBLE RUSH 8 b g £4518

0a	9	SOUT	14f Aw	58	182	
24a	6	LING	16f Aw	52	285	
44	1	**NOTT**	14f Good	36	788*	t
44	2	SOUT	16f Gd/Sft	42	860	t
45	3	NOTT	14f Heavy	44	1023	t
38	4	WARW	16f Gd/Sft	44	1711	t
38	7	WARW	16f Firm	42	2256	t

DOUBLE SPLENDOUR 10 b g £1120

0	16	THIR	6f Good	82	1383	
75	11	DONC	7f Gd/Fm	80	1840	
0	20	YORK	6f Firm	77	2000	
55	7	HAYD	7f Good	73	2704	
59	6	NEWM	6f Firm	71	3297	
68	2	NEWM	6f Good	73	3613	
37	16	YORK	7f Good	69	3809	

DOUBLE STYLE 3 ch c £0

| 0 | 13 | PONT | 8f Good | | 1865 | |

DOUBLE VISION 3 ch c £0

| 20a | 6 | WOLV | 8f Aw | | 80 | |
| 0a | 14 | SOUT | 8f Aw | 50 | 125 | |

DOUBTLESS RISK 3 b f £0

0	13	MUSS	7f Good	42	3103	
0	22	AYR	6f Heavy	36	4327	
19	8	MUSS	7f Soft	38	4522	

DOVEBRACE 7 b g £10585

40	3	BRIG	8f Gd/Sft	58	1462	
43	2	BRIG	8f Firm		2040	
49	1	**AYR**	8f Good	38	2136*	
47	2	CARL	8f Firm	43	2282	
54	1	**CATT**	7f Gd/Fm	48	2420*	
46	6	HAYD	7f Gd/Fm	48	2442	
45	6	CHES	8f Gd/Fm	53	2673	
55	6	AYR	7f Firm	53	2878	
55	2	BATH	8f Good	53	2942	
54	3	AYR	9f Gd/Fm	53	3141	
46	8	CHES	8f Firm	53	3170	
42	11	BEVE	7f Gd/Fm	55	3652	

DOVEDON SUPREME 2 b f £0

| 0 | 17 | NEWM | 6f Gd/Sft | | 4530 | |

DOVES DOMINION 3 b c £0

55	5	LING	7f Gd/Fm	58	841	
38	14	DONC	8f Gd/Sft	56	1053	
44	9	NOTT	8f Gd/Sft	56	1365	
11a	11	SOUT	8f Aw	53	2379	
61	5	NEWB	10f Firm		2709	
51	5	LEIC	12f Gd/Fm	52	2776	VIS
37	5	LEIC	8f Soft		3094	vis
24	8	CHEP	8f Gd/Fm	53	3251	vis

DOWN TO THE WOODS 2 ch c £20875

| 96 | 1 | **DONC** | 6f Gd/Fm | | 1844* | |
| 101 | 5 | CURR | 7f Good | | 3719 | |

102 1 **DONC** 6f Firm 3895*
104 4 CURR 7f Gd/Sft 4058
107 2 DONC 6f Soft 4462

DOWNLAND 4 b c £3564
78 8 NEWM 6f Gd/Fm 83 1173
77 6 GOOD 6f Gd/Sft 82 1471
61 11 YORK 6f Good 80 2697
81 2 CHES 6f Soft 4069 BL
83 2 NEWC 6f Heavy 79 4405 bl
0 13 DONC 7f Heavy 83 4574 bl

DOWNPOUR 2 b g £0
42 7 CHES 7f Soft 4068
0 12 LING 6f Soft 4188
58 5 LING 7f Soft 4483

DR BRENDLER 2 b c £8550
100 2 LEOP 7f Heavy 4557

DR COOL 3 b c £428
71a 3 LING 8f Aw 103
0 13 KEMP 8f Gd/Sft 1080
55 5 WARW 11f Heavy 56 1521
56 4 WIND 12f Good 56 1730
44 10 WARW 11f Good 56 2463 VIS
0 15 NEWM 12f Gd/Fm 54 3167 BL
23 9 AYR 17f Soft 62 3993 bl

DR DUKE 3 b c £0
39a 5 SOUT 8f Aw 36
32a 5 LING 10f Aw 204
48a 4 LING 8f Aw 241 BL
5a 11 LING 10f Aw 47 315
35a 6 SOUT 8f Aw 43 429 bl
40a 4 WOLV 9f Aw 481 bl
0a 9 SOUT 11f Aw 42 536 E
27 12 BEVE 10f Firm 1274 bl
43 6 NOTT 8f Gd/Sft 51 1365 bl

DR EDGAR 8 b g £0
10a 10 WOLV 12f Aw 55 170
42a 4 SOUT 12f Aw 48 413 vis
0a 10 WOLV 12f Aw 46 489 vis

DR GORDON 2 b c £0
0 13 KEMP 8f Gd/Fm 3799

DR GREENFIELD 2 ch c £0
83 8 NEWM 8f Good 4349

DR KNOCK 2 b g £542
67 3 MUSS 8f Soft 4564

DR MARTENS 6 b g £0
17 10 FOLK 10f Soft 51 965
39 9 NOTT 10f Gd/Sft 48 1370
24 9 WIND 8f Soft 45 2546 BL
32 9 BRIG 8f Firm 41 3527

DR STRANGELOVE 2 ch c £0
82 5 NEWM 7f Firm 3298
90 6 YORK 7f Gd/Fm 3730

DRAGNET 2 ch f £0
84 6 NEWM 7f Good 4183
72 5 YARM 8f Heavy 4477

DRAGON STAR 3 b f £0
54a 6 SOUT 8f Aw 34
46a 5 LING 6f Aw 57 105
46a 6 LING 7f Aw 56 617

DRAMA CLASS 3 ch f £7274
90 2 PONT 10f Good 2365
90 1 **BATH** 10f Gd/Sft 2553*
93 3 CHEP 10f Gd/Fm 2975
94 5 ASCO 12f Gd/Fm 4130
101 6 NEWM 12f Good 4343

DRAMA CRITIC 4 b c £33537
119 3 BELM 11f Fast 3932

DRAMA PREMIERE 2 br f £0
65 9 NEWM 6f Gd/Fm 4209
62 16 NEWM 6f Good 4341

DRAMATIC QUEST 3 b c £0

---

101 5 DONC 8f Firm 3893

DREAM CARRIER 12 b g £0
12a 10 WOLV 8f Aw 44 255
20a 9 SOUT 11f Aw 37 325
0a 7 SOUT 12f Aw 30 412
19a 9 WOLV 8f Aw 25 675
0a 11 SOUT 7f Aw 28 1979
0a 9 SOUT 8f Aw 36 2302 bl

DREAM MAGIC 2 b g £268
72 9 HAYD 7f Soft 3786
78 6 YARM 7f Firm 3940
76 4 LING 6f Soft 4188
34 11 YARM 8f Soft 77 4393

DREAM ON ME 4 b f £1724
50a 4 WOLV 7f Aw 65
52a 3 WOLV 8f Aw 138
39a 5 WOLV 8f Aw 60 172
35a 8 WOLV 8f Aw 53 227
50a 1 **WOLV** 12f Aw 295*
0 6 SALI 12f Firm 50 2023

DREAM POWER 5 ch h £0
0 5 TABY 12f Good 3931

DREAM QUEST 3 ch f £15308
90 1 **SAND** 10f Heavy 1045*
95 3 LING 11f Gd/Sft 1282
94 3 SALI 10f Gd/Fm 3389 t
97 2 LONG 12f Soft 4321

DREAM TIME 2 b f £0
0 23 DONC 8f Gd/Sft 4445

DREAM WELL 5 b g £24096
118 5 GULF 12f Good 20 bl

DREAMIE BATTLE 2 br f £1303
52 3 NOTT 6f Gd/Fm 3003
73 3 HAYD 7f Good 3287
58 5 BEVE 8f Good 3675
61 7 DONC 7f Firm 68 3901
65 5 CHES 5f Soft 65 4070

DREAMS DESIRE 2 b f £7549
82 1 **DONC** 5f Gd/Sft 1067*
90 1 **THIR** 5f Good 1385*
62 16 ASCO 5f Good 2088

DRESS CODE 2 b f £7992
67 3 KEMP 5f Good 1079
79 1 **CHES** 5f Firm 1249*
77 7 EPSO 6f Good 1846
77 10 NEWM 6f Firm 2344
84 4 YARM 6f Gd/Fm 3965
88 7 NEWM 7f Good 4158

DRESS REHEARSAL 2 b c £0
69 9 NEWM 7f Good 3608

DRIPPING IN GOLD 2 ch f £318
59 3 LING 5f Gd/Sft 836
45 7 WARW 5f Soft 1059
47 9 LING 5f Gd/Sft 1260
0 12 LING 6f Good 1396

DRIVE ASSURED 6 gr g £0
3a 7 WOLV 12f Aw 1389 t

DROWNED IN BUBBLY 4 b c £0
0a 11 SOUT 16f Aw 52 51

DRURIDGE BAY 4 b g £0
0 17 WARW 11f Heavy 44 889
0 18 WIND 10f Gd/Sft 41 1100
12 7 SOUT 10f Soft 41 1608
0 14 YARM 8f Good 36 1772
0 11 LEIC 8f Firm 33 2032
0a 11 SOUT 7f Aw 30 2637 BL

DRYING GRASS MOON 4 b f £0
51a 4 WOLV 12f Aw 519

DUBAI MILLENNIUM 4 b c £2386694
128ε 1 **NAD** 10f Dirt 655*
134ε 1 **NAD** 10f Dirt 769*

---

133 1 **ASCO** 10f Good 2089*

DUBAI NURSE 6 ch m £215
23 7 MUSS 5f Gd/Sft 39 901
54 4 MUSS 5f Firm 1688
45 6 DONC 5f Gd/Fm 1843 BL
0 13 HAMI 5f Gd/Fm 35 1910 bl
8a 12 SOUT 5f Aw 35 2632
26 7 CATT 5f Gd/Fm 2931 VIS

DUBAI SEVEN STARS 2 ch f £1577
71 4 WARW 5f Heavy 1522
91 5 ASCO 7f Good 2091
85 2 LING 8f Firm 3577
90 2 CHEP 8f Good 3867
84 5 NEWM 7f Good 84 4157

DUBAI TWO THOUSAND 3 b c £0
92 6 LING 11f Gd/Fm 1284
92 7 ASCO 16f Good 2068

DUCHAMP 3 b c £10584
82 5 SALI 10f Firm 84 1177
84 4 YORK 10f Gd/Fm 83 1310
67 7 GOOD 12f Gd/Sft 83 1637
87 2 SALI 12f Gd/Fm 83 2231
87 1 **NEWB** 13f Firm 83 2852*
88 5 YORK 14f Firm 88 3599
38 12 YORK 14f Good 86 3811 VIS
70 10 NEWB 13f Firm 85 3994

DUCHCOV 2 ch f £656
93 3 NEWM 7f Good 2806

DUCIE 3 b f £0
57 13 NEWM 5f Gd/Sft 69 1098
57 8 HAYD 6f Soft 67 1494
45 8 WIND 6f Gd/Fm 64 1877

DUCK OVER 4 b f £0
41a 9 LING 10f Aw 56

DUCK ROW 5 ch g £42056
106 1 HAYD 8f Gd/Sft 1489*
110 2 EPSO 9f Good 1847
109 2 GOOD 8f Gd/Fm 2359
108 3 ASCO 8f Good 2675
109 2 CURR 8f Good 3554
103 7 NEWM 9f Gd/Fm 108 4212
106 3 NEWM 9f Good 4347
100 4 NEWM 10f Gd/Fm 4532

DUCS DREAM 2 b c £392
64 4 NEWM 7f Gd/Fm 2599
80 5 YARM 8f Soft 4512

DUELLO 9 b g £5330
56 3 BRIG 12f Gd/Sft 54 1465
51 3 SALI 12f Gd/Fm 54 1888
47 3 HAYD 12f Gd/Fm 2457 vis
54 1 **BATH** 12f Firm 2785* vis
51 1 **FOLK** 12f Gd/Fm 3447* vis

DUEMILA 3 b g £0
60 10 WIND 10f Gd/Fm 2889
0 16 WIND 8f Gd/Fm 3048
34 7 EPSO 9f Good 3764

DUKE OF MODENA 3 ch c £81401
87 1 **KEMP** 6f Soft 79 994*
93 1 **SALI** 6f Firm 85 1178*
91 5 GOOD 7f Gd/Sft 92 1470
98 1 **NEWB** 7f Gd/Fm 92 1946+
97 4 SAND 7f Gd/Fm 94 2495
94 4 ASCO 7f Gd/Fm 96 2997
89 6 NEWB 7f Gd/Fm 95 3481
101 1 **ASCO** 7f Gd/Fm 95 4112*
97 4 NEWB 6f Gd/Sft 100 4456

DULCIFICATION 2 b c £217
63 7 MUSS 5f Good 898
62 4 HAMI 5f Firm 1240

DULZIE 3 b f £737
49a 2 SOUT 7f Aw 589
51a 4 LING 7f Aw 53 654

37a 6 SOUT 8f Aw 53 1303
54 5 AYR 9f Gd/Fm 1632
48 5 HAMI 11f Gd/Fm 1909
0 15 LING 10f Firm 55 3581
15 10 LEIC 10f Gd/Sft 4029

DUMARAN 2 b c £0
0 17 NEWB 6f Gd/Fm 1943

DUN DISTINCTLY 3 b g £860
42a 7 WOLV 7f Aw 54 188
39a 4 SOUT 8f Aw 48 451
48a 2 SOUT 11f Aw 45 536
28 6 CATT 12f Gd/Fm 50 782
39 5 PONT 12f Heavy 939 VIS
33a 6 WOLV 12f Good 47 1238

DUNKELD CHAMP 3 br c £0
0 15 NEWC 7f Soft 759
0 8 MUSS 8f Gd/Fm 1144
15 8 HAMI 12f Gd/Fm 1362

DUNKELLIN HOUSE 3 gr g £0
47a 8 SOUT 5f Aw 60 870
39 10 CARL 5f Firm 1256
0 13 BEVE 5f Firm 54 2732

DUNKIRK SPIRIT 2 b c £0
63 7 NEWM 6f Gd/Fm 3627
54 11 YORK 8f Soft 4281
64 7 YARM 6f Soft 4390
0 19 NEWM 6f Gd/Sft 4530

DURAID 8 ch g £19680
76 4 THIR 8f Good 76 1160
78 2 BEVE 8f Good 78 1445
84 1 CATT 7f Soft 78 1680*
80 4 NEWC 8f Gd/Fm 82 2311
88 1 YORK 8f Gd/Fm 82 2648+
86 6 THIR 8f Gd/Fm 88 3147
85 5 YORK 8f Firm 91 3597
83 6 RIPO 8f Good 87 3699
83 4 AYR 8f Gd/Sft 89 4013
88 4 DONC 7f Heavy 88 4574

DURHAM 9 ch g £2714
42 14 LING 16f Good 60 1394
58 1 NOTT 14f Good 56 2008* bl
49 5 YARM 14f Good 58 3233 bl
54 7 YARM 14f Gd/Fm 56 3664 bl
56 3 KEMP 14f Gd/Fm 54 3800 bl

DURHAM FLYER 5 b g £0
23a 10 LING 10f Aw 43 23

DURLSTON BAY 3 b c £504
67 3 LEIC 12f Gd/Sft 832
49 10 WIND 10f Heavy 936
60 8 NOTT 14f Gd/Fm 66 1270
52 7 FOLK 12f Good 60 2624
48 7 SALI 14f Gd/Fm 55 2982

DUSKY SWALLOW 2 b f £0
0 12 BATH 6f Soft 4138
0a 12 WOLV 6f Aw 4548 VIS

DUSKY VIRGIN 3 b f £8201
0 26 NEWB 7f Gd/Fm 61 1405
49 7 BRIG 6f Good 1651
51 4 BRIG 8f Gd/Fm 55 2726
46 9 BRIG 10f Firm 55 2908
51 2 BRIG 8f Gd/Fm 51 3261
60 1 EPSO 9f Gd/Fm 51 3401*
57 2 BRIG 8f Firm 55 3561
54 3 BRIG 7f Firm 3739
59 2 EPSO 9f Good 58 3856
55 8 SAND 8f Gd/Fm 58 3944

DUSTY CARPET 2 ch c £2836
66 6 YARM 6f Good 1774
87 4 NEWM 7f Firm 2346
87 6 NEWM 6f Gd/Fm 2598
74 4 NEWM 7f Gd/Fm 81 2962
86 3 CHES 6f Gd/Fm 80 3428

64 9 NEWM 6f Gd/Fm 80 3630
80 3 YORK 7f Soft 79 4279
72 8 DONC 8f Gd/Sft 79 4450

DUSTY DEMOCRAT 2 b c £527
61a 2 WOLV 5f Aw 722
23 8 MUSS 8f Gd/Fm 3740
40a 12 WOLV 7f Aw 4025 VIS
0 18 SALI 8f Gd/Sft 4163

DUSTY PRINCESS 2 gr f £0
41a 10 SOUT 5f Aw 1418
30 6 THIR 6f Gd/Sft 1713
0 16 RIPO 6f Good 3697 BL

DUSTY SHOES 3 b f £877
62 3 SALI 8f Gd/Fm 3289
72 4 GOOD 10f Good 3907

DUTCH DYANE 7 b m £429
40 5 LING 16f Good 40 1394
43 3 WARW 15f Heavy 40 1524
34 8 ASCO 16f Good 47 2173
0 14 NOTT 16f Heavy 43 4508

DUTCH HARRIER 3 ch c £17310
102 2 ASCO 16f Good 2068
103 4 CURR 14f Yldg 2405
101 3 LEOP 14f Good 2909

DUTCH LAD 5 b g £0
0a 10 SOUT 11f Aw 75 302
0 12 BRIG 12f Gd/Sft 893 BL

DYNAMIC DREAM 3 b f £2265
95 3 DONC 8f Gd/Fm 2578
85 5 NEWM 10f Firm 3300
81 4 GOOD 9f Good 87 3658

DYNAMISM 5 b g £0
71a 9 LING 10f Aw 55 VIS
68a 6 SOUT 11f Aw 80 200
0a 11 SOUT 11f Aw 75 302

E B PEARL 4 ch f £3824
18a 7 SOUT 6f Aw 45 557
37a 6 SOUT 6f Aw 45 602
33a 5 SOUT 6f Aw 40 673
43a 1 WOLV 5f Aw 38 751*
0 20 REDC 5f Gd/Sft 48 1133
32 6 CARL 6f Firm 41 1257
17 12 NEWC 5f Gd/Sft 39 1479
36 5 AYR 5f Gd/Fm 39 1629
37a 5 SOUT 5f Aw 44 1806
18a 10 SOUT 7f Aw 42 2122
28 13 WARW 5f Gd/Fm 36 2252
32a 4 SOUT 5f Aw 40 2632
35 2 THIR 6f Gd/Fm 34 3144
34 6 MUSS 5f Gd/Fm 35 3594

EAGALITY 2 b f £0
30 7 SAND 5f Firm 1986
41 11 KEMP 7f Gd/Sft 2583
33 12 KEMP 6f Gd/Fm 2748
50 6 EPSO 6f Gd/Fm 3400 BL
56 7 BATH 8f Firm 3620 bl
0 15 LEIC 8f Firm 54 3837

EAGER ANGEL 2 b f £0
37 5 LEIC 5f Gd/Fm 3092
65 8 PONT 5f Firm 3500
0 15 YORK 6f Good 3814

EAGLERIDER 2 b c £343
58 3 REDC 5f Gd/Sft 4496
76 6 DONC 6f Heavy 4575

EAGLES CACHE 2 b c £4084
65 4 LEIC 5f Soft 1550
71 3 DONC 6f Gd/Fm 1838
68 6 HAYD 6f Gd/Fm 2454
72 2 LING 7f Good 2653
58 6 PONT 6f Gd/Fm 2828
70 2 RIPO 6f Good 3466
77 3 WARW 15f Good 75 3693

0 17 DONC 6f Firm 3888
77 2 CHES 7f Soft 4068
50a 5 WOLV 8f Aw 4250

EAGLES CROSS 5 b h £2259
86 2 DIEL 16f Good 3553

EAGLET 2 b c £0
0 10 HAYD 6f Soft 1823
44 9 REDC 5f Gd/Fm 2142
0 12 NEWC 6f Firm 2333
73 5 NEWC 7f Good 2521
62 4 CATT 7f Gd/Fm 2741
74 5 THIR 7f Gd/Fm 2966
59 5 BEVE 7f Gd/Sft 3057
0 15 NEWC 7f Good 70 3246
36 8 RIPO 8f Gd/Fm 66 3712

EARL GREY 2 b c £6988
75 1 LEIC 6f Gd/Sft 1573*
99 4 ASCO 6f Good 2067
98 6 NEWM 7f Gd/Fm 2613
93 6 NEWM 7f Good 4158

EARLENE 3 b f £0
80 6 CHEP 10f Gd/Fm 2975 t

EARLEY SESSION 3 b c £0
24a 8 WOLV 7f Aw 41
40 8 BATH 6f Gd/Fm 51 1438
19 7 FOLK 6f Gd/Fm 2292
0 14 CHEP 8f Gd/Fm 40 3251 VIS
0a 11 LING 8f Aw 4272

EARLY MORNING MIST 2 b f £7312
73 3 CATT 6f Gd/Fm 2926
84 1 ASCO 6f Gd/Fm 3342*

EARLY WARNING 5 b h £7195
104ε 2 BELM 9f Dirt 1616

EARLY WISH 2 ch f £1460
58 6 SAND 5f Soft 1568
76 3 PONT 6f Firm 2174
73 3 KEMP 7f Gd/Sft 2583
68 12 NEWM 7f Good 76 4157
62a 6 WOLV 8f Aw 72 4439

EASAAR 4 b c £243902
113 2 NAD 9f Good 768
83 8 SAND 10f Soft 1587
79 19 ASCO 8f Good 114 2090

EAST CAPE 3 b c £5813
80 4 WIND 10f Gd/Fm 1200
80 2 CARL 9f Firm 2019
81 1 WIND 8f Gd/Fm 2211*
61 9 NEWM 8f Gd/Fm 79 2614

EAST OF JAVA 2 b c £495
56 8 FOLK 6f Aw 3443
76 3 NOTT 6f Soft 3973
53 9 BATH 6f Soft 4137
64 9 NOTT 5f Gd/Sft 4503

EAST ROSE 4 b f £0
31 11 SAND 10f Soft 1588

EASTER BONNET 2 ch f £0
4 9 HAYD 5f Soft 1492

EASTER ISLAND 2 b f £1884
43 11 WIND 5f Good 849
0 17 WIND 5f Gd/Fm 1197
50 7 GOOD 6f Gd/Sft 1486
51 9 SALI 6f Good 1883
19 14 GOOD 6f Good 61 3886
59 1 BRIG 5f Soft 4171*
49a 7 LING 5f Aw 4333

EASTER OGIL 5 ch g £8801
83 5 KEMP 7f Good 82 725
59 10 PONT 6f Heavy 82 941 vis
72 11 ASCO 8f Gd/Sft 81 1110 vis
60 6 LING 7f Soft 80 1286 vis
73 4 BATH 6f Gd/Fm 1441 vis
82 1 DONC 6f Good 1517* vis

EASTERN (continued)

80	2	PONT	6f Soft	80	1702	vis
77	5	SALI	6f Gd/Fm	80	1887	vis
73	7	BATH	6f Firm	80	1999	vis
73	7	KEMP	6f Firm		2869	vis
59	13	ASCO	7f Gd/Fm	78	2999	vis
76	4	BATH	6f Gd/Fm	78	3516	vis
55	15	BATH	6f Gd/Fm	77	3821	vis
57	11	SAND	7f Soft	75	4204	vis
0	16	BATH	5f Soft	73	4432	vis

EASTERN BREEZE 2 b c £1048
79	3	LING	6f Soft		4188
70	7	DONC	7f Gd/Sft		4447
85	3	DONC	7f Heavy		4566

EASTERN CHAMP 4 ch c £1791
52a	11	LING	8f Aw	73	7	t
57	11	PONT	8f Soft	73	875	t
74a	2	LING	8f Aw	71	1259	t
44	9	EPSO	9f Gd/Sft	71	1829	t
55	6	LING	8f Gd/Fm		2215	t
72a	3	SOUT	8f Aw	72	2817	t
63	4	BRIG	8f Firm		2895	t
48	6	REDC	8f Firm		3330	t
59	6	BRIG	10f Firm	60	3737	t
65a	5	SOUT	8f Aw	72	4365	.t

EASTERN JEWEL 2 b f £0
0	20	DONC	8f Gd/Sft		4445
0	16	DONC	8f Heavy		4569

EASTERN LILAC 2 b f £0
0	11	REDC	7f Gd/Sft		4216

EASTERN PROMISE 2 gr f £3992
74	2	NOTT	5f Gd/Sft		1083
66	4	NOTT	5f Gd/Sft		1642
71	1	MUSS	5f Firm		2045*
65	4	DONC	5f Gd/Fm	74	2575
54	10	THIR	5f Gd/Fm	70	3145

EASTERN PROPHETS 7 b g £3491
55	3	CARL	6f Firm	59	1258	vis
53	10	MUSS	7f Gd/Fm	59	1431	vis
34	14	CARL	6f Firm	57	2015	vis
49	7	NOTT	6f Gd/Fm	54	2192	bl
44	7	HAMI	5f Firm	54	2395	vis
51	4	BEVE	5f Firm	51	2732	vis
47	4	HAMI	5f Firm	51	2796	vis
0	12	REDC	6f Firm	51	3312	bl
54	1	NEWC	6f Firm	49	3605*	vis
41	8	YARM	7f Firm	53	3939	vis

EASTERN PURPLE 5 b g £45490
97	8	DONC	6f Good		734	
105	3	THIR	6f Soft		927	
107	7	NEWM	6f Gd/Fm		1172	
30	9	SAND	5f Soft		1566	bl
114	5	ASCO	5f Good		2065	
109	6	ASCO	5f Gd/Fm	112	3016	
117	2	GOOD	5f Gd/Fm		3059	
113	1	LEOP	6f Good		3373*	
104	8	YORK	5f Firm		3598	
104	6	HAYD	6f Gd/Sft		3784	
112	2	NEWB	5f Firm		3982	

EASTERN RAINBOW 4 b c £1171
0	16	DONC	10f Gd/Fm	44	705	
0	11	RIPO	12f Soft	40	825	
36	2	REDC	6f Gd/Sft	33	1578	bl
36	3	HAMI	5f Gd/Fm	38	1910	bl
34	6	NOTT	6f Gd/Fm	38	2192	bl
41	5	DONC	5f Gd/Fm	38	2753	bl

EASTERN RED 2 b f £1678
42	9	DONC	5f Good		730	
48	5	THIR	5f Soft		904	
53	6	PONT	6f Good		1864	
53	2	REDC	7f Gd/Fm		2155	
35	10	NEWC	6f Gd/Fm		2312	BL
48a	5	SOUT	6f Aw	54	2948	

51	4	HAMI	5f Gd/Fm		3376	
35	6	RIPO	6f Good		3697	
48	2	LEIC	8f Firm	46	3837	
48	3	BEVE	7f Good	46	3950	
49a	3	WOLV	8f Aw		4249	

EASTERN SPICE 3 b c £12994
45	10	WIND	8f Heavy	77	933
79	2	WIND	8f Good	75	1726
81	1	GOOD	9f Gd/Fm		2129*
79	3	BATH	8f Firm	77	2330
73	8	NEWM	8f Good	77	2564
81	1	BATH	8f Firm	77	2942*
58	15	GOOD	9f Good	83	3110
51	10	EPSO	9f Good	81	3685

EASTERN TRUMPETER 4 b c £44654
68a	1	WOLV	5f Aw	61	491*
63a	4	WOLV	5f Aw	66	579
72a	1	WOLV	5f Aw	66	678*
49	9	SAND	5f Gd/Fm	63	763
9	12	NEWC	5f Heavy	62	1008
0	15	BATH	5f Good	62	1092
71a	2	WOLV	5f Aw	71	1140
67	1	CARL	5f Firm		1256*
67	1	LING	5f Good	62	1398+
73	1	REDC	5f Gd/Sft	66	1580+
74	1	RIPO	5f Good	70	1861+
73	3	SALI	5f Firm	73	2022
63	8	CHES	5f Firm	73	2247
77	2	CHEP	5f Firm	73	2451
80	1	YORK	5f Gd/Fm	73	2644*
75	8	GOOD	5f Good	79	3091
81	3	NEWB	5f Gd/Fm	79	3176
73	7	HAYD	5f Gd/Sft	81	3788
73	11	AYR	5f Soft	81	3960
82	4	HAYD	5f Gd/Sft	80	4107
0	15	WIND	5f Heavy	80	4527

EASTWAYS 3 ch c £12056
89	7	NEWM	6f Gd/Sft	93	982
91	10	NEWM	7f Gd/Fm	93	1153
91	3	LING	6f Gd/Sft	91	1285
84	9	YORK	7f Gd/Fm	91	1308
81	9	GOOD	7f Gd/Sft	91	1470
81	17	NEWM	6f Gd/Fm	89	1694
0	17	NEWC	6f Firm		2334
73	7	HAYD	6f Gd/Fm	84	2504
79	4	NEWB	7f Firm	81	2814
86	2	NEWM	8f Good	81	3022
86	2	NEWM	10f Gd/Fm	83	3166
85	4	ASCO	10f Gd/Fm	83	3339
81	7	DONC	10f Firm	84	3899

EASTWELL HALL 5 b g £5994
75	5	KEMP	16f Soft	81	1527	
83	1	CHEP	18f Gd/Sft	78	1800*	
86	5	ASCO	20f Good	83	2092	
86	2	YARM	18f Gd/Fm	83	3967	
64	17	NEWM	18f Good	84	4353	
83	5	NEWM	16f Gd/Sft	91	4533	

EASTWELL MANOR 2 b c £0
53	7	SAND	7f Good		3470
73	10	KEMP	8f Gd/Fm		3799

EASTWELL MINSTREL 5 ch g £0
0a	15	SOUT	6f Aw	40	2297	
0	14	PONT	17f Firm	40	3501	BL

EASTWOOD DRIFTER 3 ch c £4260
68	3	BRIG	8f Gd/Sft		894	
50	10	BATH	10f Good	68	1094	
65	3	PONT	8f Good	66	1495	
66	6	GOOD	10f Gd/Sft	66	1812	
65	2	WIND	10f Gd/Fm	64	2053	
47	6	MUSS	9f Firm		2376	BL
64	2	LEIC	10f Gd/Fm	62	3217	
59	5	BEVE	12f Gd/Fm	63	3674	

58	7	NOTT	10f Soft		3979	
60a	3	LING	16f Aw	63	4099	
33a	9	LING	13f AW		4193	

EASY DOLLAR 8 ch g £0
96	6	LING	6f Good		1674	bl
0	27	ASCO	6f Good	89	2151	bl
80	7	NEWB	6f Firm	89	2813	bl
76	10	ASCO	6f Gd/Fm	89	2954	bl
90	5	GOOD	7f Firm		3155	vis
85	5	NEWM	7f Gd/Fm	86	3315	bl
77	9	GOOD	6f Good	84	3646	bl
0	17	KEMP	6f Gd/Fm	83	3791	bl
76	5	GOOD	7f Good	95	3902	vis
80	12	NEWM	5f Good	90	4339	bl

EASY ENIGMA 2 ch c £0
74	8	NEWB	7f Firm		2708
76	5	CHES	7f Firm		3169

EASY FREE 2 b f £0
57	8	HAYD	5f Gd/Sft		1538
38	10	THIR	7f Gd/Fm		3617
42	10	THIR	7f Gd/Sft		3776

EASY TO LOVE 4 b f £4473
78	3	DONC	10f Gd/Sft		1054
63	8	SALI	10f Good		1343
76	4	YARM	10f Soft	79	4392
82	1	YARM	11f Heavy		4481*
31	7	DONC	10f Heavy		4571

EATON PLACE 3 b f £3445
83	1	NOTT	10f Heavy		4412*
0	11	DONC	10f Heavy		4571

EAU ROUGE 2 ch f £2040
74	7	NOTT	5f Gd/Sft		1641
73	2	SALI	6f Gd/Fm		1883
70	2	CARL	6f Gd/Fm		2239

EBBA 3 ch f £2454
86	7	THIR	5f Good	92	1384
90	4	AYR	8f Gd/Fm		1630
56	11	ASCO	8f Good	88	2167
86	3	NEWM	7f Good	85	2567
56	5	WARW	8f Gd/Fm		2844

EBULLIENCE 2 b f £4159
62	10	WIND	5f Good		1197
78	1	SALI	6f Gd/Fm		1883*
78	2	LING	6f Good	75	2589
55	10	WIND	6f Good	79	3354
78	3	BATH	6f Firm		3620

ECCENTRICITY 2 b f £0
0	13	BATH	5f Firm		3204
19	11	FOLK	7f Gd/Fm		3582

ECCLESIASTICAL 2 b c £715
46	10	YARM	7f Good		3029
86	2	MUSS	7f Soft		4559

ECKSCLUSIVE STORY 2 ch f £241
39	15	CARL	5f Firm		1252	
60	4	PONT	5f Soft		1704	
57	4	MUSS	7f Firm		2377	
32	7	LEIC	6f Gd/Fm	64	2773	
43	6	NEWC	7f Firm		2983	
56	4	CATT	7f Good		3438	
21	11	RIPO	6f Good		3697	VIS

ECLECTIC 4 b f £0
0	13	SOUT	10f Gd/Sft	42	859

ECOLOGY 2 b c £15977
94	2	NEWB	6f Gd/Fm		1403
88	1	RIPO	6f Good		1859*
99	1	KEMP	6f Gd/Fm		2083*
102	1	DONC	7f Gd/Fm		2576*
90	8	GOOD	7f Gd/Fm		3086
92	9	GOOD	8f Good		3882

ECSTASY 3 b f £4791
71	9	NEWM	10f Gd/Sft	78	979
79	1	BATH	10f Gd/Fm		1439*

79 3 SAND 9f Gd/Fm 78 1990
76 8 NEWM 10f Good 78 4197
65 7 DONC 10f Gd/Sft 77 4448

ECSTATIC 2 ch f £6916
81 2 SAND 5f Soft 1568
88 4 NEWM 6f Gd/Fm 2618
87 3 NEWM 7f Good 3607
91 3 KEMP 6f Gd/Fm 3795
88 1 **BRIG** 6f Heavy 4537*

ECTON PARK 4 ch c £0
111£5 NAD 10f Dirt 769

ECUDAMAH 4 ch c £4752
67a 1 WOLV 5f Aw 60 40*
70a 2 LING 5f Aw 67 91
58a 4 WOLV 5f Aw 67 139
64a 6 LING 5f Aw 68 205
43a 11 WOLV 5f Aw 67 1140
0 14 BATH 6f Gd/Fm 60 1438
33 9 GOOD 5f Gd/Sft 60 1487 t
55 6 WIND 5f Gd/Fm 1881
38a 4 LING 6f Aw 1913 BL
38 11 WARW 7f Gd/Fm 58 2840
59 3 CHEP 5f Gd/Fm 58 2976 bl
59 3 NOTT 5f Gd/Fm 3113 bl
54 7 SAND 5f Good 59 3436 bl
37 12 LING 6f Firm 59 3578 bl
0 18 CHEP 5f Good 3872 bl
34 12 BRIG 6f Gd/Sft 4120 VIS
48 4 SAND 5f Soft 4207 vis
49 7 WIND 5f Gd/Sft 52 4293 vis

EDDIE ROYALE 2 b g £0
48 9 REDC 6f Gd/Sft 1131
63a 5 SOUT 5f Aw 1418
49 7 NEWC 5f Aw 2333

EDDYS LAD 2 b c £1378
75 2 REDC 7f Gd/Fm 2862
77 3 CATT 7f Gd/Fm 3198

EDEIFF 3 b f £624
50 6 BATH 10f Gd/Fm 1439
43 8 RIPO 8f Good 1596
30a 5 LING 7f Aw 1741
0 19 SALI 7f Good 1884
28 5 LEIC 8f Gd/Fm 3094 t
47 5 YARM 8f Good 53 3236 t
47 2 YARM 10f Gd/Fm 3382 t

EDHKERINI 3 ch f £586
76 3 HAYD 12f Soft 1493

EDIFICE 4 ch c £0
68 5 YARM 10f Gd/Fm 70 2199
59 6 RIPO 10f Gd/Fm 69 2836
0 13 SALI 10f Gd/Fm 67 3390
0 14 NOTT 10f Soft 3979
0a 10 WOLV 8f Aw 60 4248 BL
0 12 YARM 11f Soft 58 4391

EDIPO RE 8 b g £0
0 12 NOTT 14f Good 65 1411
34 10 WARW 15f Heavy 51 1524

EDMO HEIGHTS 4 ch c £0
0 13 BEVE 8f Firm 59 1279
0 17 BEVE 10f Firm 56 1921
25 8 NEWC 10f Gd/Fm 52 2309
43 10 BEVE 12f Gd/Fm 52 2482 BL
3 10 BEVE 10f Good 42 2883 bl

EFFERVESCE 2 b f £4670
72 4 HAYD 5f Gd/Sft 1538
58 6 PONT 6f Firm 2174
62 8 HAYD 6f Gd/Fm 2500
73 1 **HAYD** 5f Gd/Sft 67 3264*
77 2 HAYD 5f Gd/Sft 71 3475
77 9 AYR 5f Soft 3959
70 10 NEWM 5f Good 75 4179

EFFERVESCENT 3 b f £5322

72 8 NEWB 7f Soft 915
75 2 SALI 6f Firm 1175
70 3 PONT 6f Good 1500
64 4 SALI 7f Gd/Fm 2232
55 1 **CATT** 6f Gd/Fm 2421*
70 3 RIPO 6f Good 72 3010
53 12 SALI 7f Firm 72 3750
0 22 KEMP 6f Gd/Sft 71 4037

EFIDIUM 2 b c £0
67 5 THIR 5f Gd/Fm 3346
70 7 CARL 5f Firm 3571
52 7 CATT 6f Soft 4001
25a 10 SOUT 6f Aw 62 4367

EGYPT 2 b c £0
41 11 PONT 6f Soft 4083
53 7 NEWC 6f Heavy 4402
41 9 BRIG 6f Heavy 4537

EGYPTBAND 3 b f £380404
123 1 **CHAN** 11f Gd/Sft 1901*
118 3 LONG 12f Good 3928
127 2 LONG 12f Good 4262

El El 5 b g £1103
23a 9 LING 10f Aw 40 224
14a 7 SOUT 11f Aw 35 324
34a 2 WOLV 9f Aw 33 404
28a 4 WOLV 8f Aw 34 432 BL
23a 6 WOLV 8f Aw 612
38a 6 LING 12f Aw 650
44 2 BRIG 12f Gd/Sft 893
52 4 BRIG 10f Firm 1210
0 15 BRIG 10f Firm 1331
42 5 BRIG 10f Firm 1933
23a 8 LING 10f Aw 2587
15 10 YARM 10f Firm 2765

EIGHT 4 ch c £1025
42 14 WIND 8f Good 68 854
63 3 GOOD 9f Gd/Sft 64 1807
58 5 NOTT 10f Good 64 2007
58 4 WIND 10f Good 2372 VIS
53 10 NEWM 10f Gd/Fm 62 2958 vis
55 3 YARM 10f Good 3383 vis
48 11 GOOD 10f Good 59 3663 vis
23 9 BATH 8f Soft 56 4143 vis
0a 11 WOLV 8f Aw 54 4363 BL

EIGHTY TWO 4 br c £0
58 16 NEWM 12f Good 87 4162
0 14 NEWB 16f Gd/Sft 84 4458

EILEAN SHONA 4 b f £4250
83 10 CHES 19f Gd/Fm 97 1222
102 5 SAND 16f Soft 1565
95 4 ASCO 22f Good 2153
96 5 ASCO 16f Gd/Fm 97 3302
97 7 DONC 18f Gd/Fm 3877
69 11 NEWM 16f Gd/Sft 98 4533

EJDER 4 b f £0
0 17 SALI 6f Firm 1181
0 12 WIND 8f Gd/Sft 1428
0 14 LING 6f Gd/Fm 2183
0a 14 SOUT 6f Aw 47 4155

EJTITHAAB 3 ch c £1417
84 4 NEWM 10f Good 957
93 4 NEWM 10f Good 1168
74 9 NEWB 10f Gd/Fm 1404
0 29 ASCO 8f Good 90 2117 BL
77 3 WARW 8f Good 2464
59 9 RIPO 10f Gd/Fm 80 3713

EKRAAR 3 b c £66891
112 3 NEWM 8f Gd/Sft 981 bl
113 4 LONG 8f V 1318 bl
116 1 **NEWB** 10f Firm 2709*
117 1 **HAYD** 11f Gd/Fm 3321*
120 1 **GOOD** 10f Good 3903+

EL ACTOR 2 ch g £0
79 17 NEWM 6f Good 4345

EL CURIOSO 3 b c £7725
83 11 NEWM 10f Gd/Sft 92 979
95 1 **LING** 8f Gd/Sft 1262*
94 6 HAYD 8f Gd/Sft 94 1535
86 8 NEWM 8f Firm 94 1853
92 3 SALI 8f Gd/Fm 92 2229
75 8 YORK 8f Gd/Fm 92 2648 BL
79 7 NEWM 8f Good 4199
76 15 NEWM 8f Good 88 4348

EL DIVINO 5 b h £0
79 9 NEWM 10f Gd/Sft 4532

EL EMEL 3 b g £0
0 16 DONC 12f Heavy 90 4580

EL EMPERADOR 3 b c £715
69 5 BEVE 7f Firm 1922
75 4 WIND 8f Gd/Fm 2211
52 5 PONT 10f Gd/Fm 2562
75 3 LING 8f Soft 4273

EL GIZA 2 ch c £0
0 25 NEWM 6f Good 4341

EL GRAN LODE 5 ch h £3842
93 8 ASCO 7f Gd/Fm 100 2997
103 3 LONG 5f Heavy 4495

EL GRAN PAPA 3 b c £101923
85 2 SALI 6f Firm 1181
88 1 **NEWB** 8f Good 1786*
96 1 **ASCO** 8f Good 85 2117*
80 12 SAND 8f Gd/Fm 94 2495
104 2 ASCO 8f Gd/Fm 96 2997
88 10 GOOD 8f Good 94 3107
109 1 **DONC** 8f Firm 3893*
106 3 NEWM 8f Good 4180

EL HAMRA 2 gr c £4237
57a 5 WOLV 5f Aw 1136
55 9 NOTT 6f Good 1413
71a 3 WOLV 6f Aw 2077
69 3 LEIC 5f Good 2916
71a 3 WOLV 7f Aw 68 3273
71 5 WARW 7f Good 3692
70a 2 WOLV 8f Aw 3772
70 3 BEVE 7f Good 3952
75a 1 **WOLV** 8f Aw 4250*

EL KARIM 4 ch c £0
23 10 CARL 12f Gd/Fm 3081 t
31 5 LEIC 12f Gd/Fm 3336 t

EL MAXIMO 2 b c £4619
63 6 REDC 5f Gd/Sft 1130
71 3 NOTT 6f Good 1408
72 2 DONC 6f Gd/Fm 1838
69 6 BATH 5f Firm 1993
75 1 **FOLK** 7f Good 2620*
63 5 NEWM 7f Gd/Fm 77 2962
76 2 FOLK 9f Good 73 3444 tBL
74 4 NEWM 6f Gd/Fm 74 4214 tbl
68 19 NEWM 6f Good 4345 tbl
0 20 NEWB 6f Sft/Hvy 74 4468 tbl

EL SALIDA 4 b g £201
43a 4 SOUT 7f Aw 73
66 7 NEWC 10f Soft 75 757
64 7 BEVE 10f Heavy 73 975
44 17 CARL 8f Gd/Fm 70 2242
47 12 NEWC 9f Firm 65 3603

EL UNO 2 ch c £0
4 8 PONT 5f Soft 1698 BL
65 11 THIR 6f Good 3614
61 6 THIR 7f Gd/Sft 3776
57 5 BEVE 7f Good 3950
36a 7 WOLV 8f Aw 4249
43 7 REDC 6f Gd/Sft 59 4502

EL ZITO 3 b g £13528

```
69a  3  SOUT  8f Gd/Sft       86
67  14  WIND  10f Gd/Fm      1200
79   2  BRIG  10f Soft       1466
86   1  CHES  10f Gd/Sft     1779*
84   1  BEVE  12f Firm    80 1919*
63  13  ASCO  12f Good    87 2116
84   3  CHES  10f Good    83 2666
88   3  FOLK  10f Gd/Fm      3042
43   9  HAYD  12f Gd/Sft  83 3270
 0  15  YARM  10f Firm    86 3941

ELA ARISTOKRATI 8 b h £530
74   6  DONC  10f Gd/Fm      2351
56   4  NEWM  12f Gd/Fm      2803

ELA ATHENA 4 gr f £167381
 80 10  NEWM  12f Gd/Fm      1152
105  4  CURR  10f Yldg       2404
110  1  HAYD  12f Gd/Fm      2501+
116  2  GOOD  10f Firm       3151
108  5  YORK  12f Gd/Fm      3564
116  2  BELM  11f Fast       3932
114  3  BELM  12f Firm       4316

ELA DARLIN MOU 2 gr f £0
60   9  LING  7f Gd/Fm       2182
64   8  SALI  7f Firm        3752
56  12  NEWB  6f Firm        3980

ELAANDO 5 b g £0
51   8  WIND  12f Good    70 3186
32   7  SAND  14f Good    64 3472

ELAFLAAK 3 b f £0
85  10  ASCO  6f Gd/Fm   103 3301

ELAINES REBECCA 2 ch f £550
60   6  MUSS  5f Gd/Fm        898
55   2  NOTT  5f Heavy       1019
37   9  CHES  5f Firm        1249
50   6  HAMI  5f Gd/Fm       1359

ELBA MAGIC 5 b m £0
26a  8  WOLV  8f Aw           707
 0  12  SOUT  10f Gd/Sft  60  859 VIS
 0  11  LING  9f Good     58 1395
 0  15  LEIC  10f Aw      55 2027
 0  14  YARM  8f Firm     51 2767
 0  14  YARM  10f Good    46 3031 vis

ELBADER 2 b c £9000
81   3  CURR  6f Good        2400
 0   9  CURR  7f Gd/Sft      4058 bl

ELEANOR J 2 ch f £0
49a  4  WOLV  5f Aw           722
48a  6  SOUT  5f Aw           856
12  10  LING  6f Good        1396
30   7  THIR  6f Aw          1713 VIS

ELEGANT DANCE 6 ch m £320
36a  8  LING  7f Aw      56   58
19a 11  LING  7f Aw      56  106
20a  6  LING  7f Aw      49  879
49   4  BRIG  6f Gd/Fm   54 1126
0a  13  WOLV  6f Aw      43 1391

ELEGANT ESCORT 3 b c £2794
73a  1  SOUT  8f Aw           198*
64   6  HAYD  11f Gd/Sft  85 3267
57  12  RIPO  8f Good     82 3699

ELEGANT LADY 4 ch f £0
 0  20  WIND  5f Heavy    82 4527

ELEGIA PRIMA 3 ch f £1479
53   7  BATH  10f Good    63 1094
60   4  BATH  13f Gd/Fm   63 1440
60   2  HAYD  14f Soft    60 1821
19  10  WARW  15f Good    60 2461
51   6  BATH  17f Firm    58 2941

ELENII 4 b f £0
0a  10  SOUT  11f Aw           196
0a   8  LING  13f Aw           483 BL

ELGHANI 3 br c £15060
```

```
78   9  NEWM  7f Gd/Sft        983
91   1  WIND  8f Gd/Sft       1099*
94   2  THIR  8f Good         1382
96   1  NEWM  8f Good     90  4348*
85  10  NEWM  8f Soft     94  4545

ELGRIA 2 b c £681
82   3  GOOD  6f Gd/Sft       1472

ELITE HOPE 8 ch m £2033
62a  2  WOLV  6f Aw            132
50a  4  WOLV  7f Aw            142
55a  1  WOLV  7f Aw            274*
25a  8  WOLV  7f Aw            396

ELJOHAR 3 ch c £828
84   3  ASCO  8f Good         2679 t

ELLA TINO 2 b f £255
64   6  PONT  8f Soft         4086
74   5  REDC  7f Gd/Sft       4216
64   4  NEWC  7f Heavy        4403

ELLAS PAL 2 ch f £2404
75a  1  WOLV  6f Aw           4225*

ELLE DANZIG 5 b m £76711
115  1  CAPA  10f Heavy         12*
101  7  SAND  10f Soft        1587
112  4  MUNI  10f Soft        3071

ELLENDUNE GIRL 2 b f £315
50   9  SALI  5f Good         2227
60   5  WIND  5f Good         2711
39  10  BEVE  5f Gd/Sft       3055
64   4  BATH  6f Aw           3513
 0  16  LEIC  6f Gd/Sft    63 4030
67  15  NEWM  6f Good         4345

ELLENS ACADEMY 5 b g £3293
50  13  KEMP  7f Good      79  725
77   4  DONC  6f Gd/Sft   77 1074
91   3  BEVE  5f Firm        1277 bl
81   8  HAYD  5f Gd/Sft   82 1533 bl
82   3  YORK  6f Firm     80 2000 bl
72   9  NEWC  5f Gd/Fm    80 2310 bl
76   4  KEMP  6f Firm        2869
67  15  NEWM  7f Gd/Fm    80 4215
 0  17  NEWM  5f Good      90 4339 bl

ELLENS LAD 6 b g £70170
65  20  DONC  5f Gd/Fm    95  702
92   5  KEMP  5f Soft     95 1013
89   7  NEWM  6f Firm     95 1182
99   1  YORK  5f Firm     92 1324*
98   5  HAYD  5f Gd/Sft   97 1533
88  13  YORK  5f Gd/Fm    97 1980
102  1  DONC  5f Gd/Fm    96 2348+
106  1  ASCO  5f Good    100 2676*
101  7  GOOD  5f Gd/Fm      3059
99   5  NOTT  5f Good        3521
97  10  DONC  6f Gd/Fm   104 3861
110  1  ASCO  5f Gd/Sft  103 4129*

ELLIEBERRY 2 ch f £0
 0  12  CATT  5f Soft        4253

ELLPEEDEE 3 b g £0
 0  14  MUSS  8f Gd/Sft   54  800
59   6  THIR  6f Soft         909 t
49   5  NOTT  6f Gd/Sft      1081 t
46   6  MUSS  5f Gd/Fm       1430 t
48   7  BATH  5f Gd/Sft      1670 t
33  10  CATT  5f Gd/Fm    50 1817 t
32  11  MUSS  5f Firm      48 2374

ELLWAY HEIGHTS 3 b g £322
56   7  NEWB  9f Gd/Fm       3179
56   6  EPSO  9f Gd/Fm       3413
60   4  EPSO  9f Good        3764
55   5  BEVE  12f Good    60 3954

ELLWAY PRINCE 5 b g £10040
48a  8  LING  7f Aw       64   29 vis
49a  8  LING  6f Aw       61  113 vis
```

```
55a  4  LING  5f Aw       58  166 vis
49a  7  LING  5f Aw       56  205 vis
41a 10  LING  6f Aw           313 vis
55a  2  WOLV  8f Aw            393
52a  2  SOUT  8f Aw       50  418
35a  6  WOLV  9f Aw       52  469
52a  2  SOUT  9f Aw       52  497
39a  5  LING  8f Aw       52  596
0a  14  SOUT  8f Aw       51  647
64a  1  LING  8f Aw       48  776+
64a  1  LING  10f Aw      54  842*
66a  4  LING  8f Aw       65 1259
53   3  REDC  8f Firm     48 1300
51   2  KEMP  8f Gd/Fm    49 2752
48   4  ASCO  7f Gd/Fm    53 2999
38  10  NEWM  8f Gd/Fm    51 3118
 0  13  YARM  7f Good     51 3238

ELLWAY QUEEN 3 b f £3055
65   8  NEWM  10f Gd/Fm      2617
68   6  NEWM  7f Gd/Fm       2860
77   1  NOTT  8f Gd/Fm       3116*
57   9  YARM  7f Gd/Fm    76 3384

ELMHURST BOY 4 b c £20744
88a  2  LING  8f Aw            208 BL
84a  1  LING  7f Aw       78  239* vis
78a  5  LING  8f Aw       82  463 vis
83a  4  LING  8f Aw       82  485 vis
88a  5  LING  7f Aw            630 vis
74   6  EPSO  6f Heavy    76 1028
72   6  ASCO  7f Gd/Sft   76 1110
59  11  GOOD  7f Gd/Fm    75 1483
79   1  BRIG  7f Good     75 1652*
57  12  EPSO  6f Good     78 1851
79   3  SAND  7f Gd/Fm    78 1989
69   7  EPSO  7f Gd/Sft   78 2431
76   4  NEWB  8f Gd/Fm    78 2707 vis
80   5  KEMP  8f Firm     83 2870 vis
80   2  GOOD  8f Good     78 3063 vis
73   7  NEWM  7f Gd/Fm    80 3315 vis
76   7  EPSO  8f Gd/Fm    80 3414 vis
86   1  KEMP  10f Gd/Fm   79 3794*
71   5  EPSO  10f Good       3857
108  5  GOOD  10f Soft       4064
 0  23  ASCO  8f Gd/Sft   84 4126

ELMONJED 2 b c £5588
73   8  SALI  7f              2269
79   7  SAND  7f Gd/Fm        2921
86   2  GOOD  7f Good         3650
84   1  GOOD  8f Good         3906*
83   5  DONC  8f Gd/Sft   85 4450

ELMS SCHOOLGIRL 4 ch f £2180
65   2  BRIG  12f Firm     64 1332
44  12  NEWB  10f Gd/Fm    68 1785
64   6  YARM  10f Gd/Fm    67 2199
57   7  EPSO  12f Gd/Sft   67 2429
25   6  BRIG  12f Firm     65 2893
60   4  LEIC  10f Gd/Fm    65 3093
57   5  LEIC  10f Gd/Fm       3219
60   2  YARM  14f Gd/Fm    60 3664
66  15  YARM  10f Firm        3918

ELMS SCHOOLPREFECT 3 b f £0
 0   9  BRIG  12f Gd/Sft   50 2425
 0  19  BRIG  10f Gd/Fm    45 2727

ELMUTABAKI 4 b c £0
104  5  CHES  13f Firm        1247
106  7  HAYD  12f Gd/Fm   108 2502
81   6  NEWB  10f Firm        2851
63  11  NEWM  10f Gd/Sft      4532

ELNAHAAR 2 b c £9452
86   1  SALI  7f              2686*
98   1  CHES  8f Soft         4072*

ELREHAAN 2 b f £4146
```

ELSIE BAMFORD etc. — racing form index

93	2	NEWM	7f Gd/Fm		2806	
85	1	**REDC**	7f Firm		3308*	
93	7	DONC	8f Gd/Fm		3876	
79	6	NEWM	8f Soft		4546	

ELSAAMRI 2 b c £843

70	4	CHEP	7f Good		3866	
86	3	LING	7f Soft		4268	

ELSAS PRIDE 5 b g £0

44	3	AYR	8f Gd/Fm		3139	

ELSIE BAMFORD 4 b f £13220

0a	14	SOUT	12f Aw	45	70	
27a	6	SOUT	12f Aw	42	215	
38	3	HAMI	13f Gd/Fm	38	1194	
16a	8	SOUT	14f Aw	38	1301	
39	4	MUSS	12f Gd/Fm	38	1432	
41	3	PONT	12f Good	38	1499	
44	1	**WARW**	15f Heavy	38	1524*	
49	1	**CATT**	14f Soft	41	1683*	
50	2	LEIC	12f Gd/Sft	47	1736	
51	3	HAMI	13f Gd/Fm	51	1936	
52	3	BATH	17f Firm	51	1996	
51	3	HAMI	13f Gd/Fm	50	2098	
51	3	NEWC	16f Gd/Fm	51	2273	
49	3	CATT	16f Gd/Fm	51	2436	
51	4	HAMI	13f Gd/Fm	51	2643	
51	3	HAMI	13f Gd/Fm	50	2801	
53	2	BATH	17f Firm	49	2941	
46	5	FOLK	15f Gd/Fm	50	3040	

ELSIE PLUNKETT 2 b f £61246

57	5	HAYD	5f Heavy		989	
87	1	**SAND**	5f Heavy		1046*	
92	1	**NOTT**	5f Firm		1267*	
92	1	**NEWB**	5f Good		1372*	
92	3	SAND	5f Soft		1586	
90	2	NEWB	5f Firm		2849	
96	4	GOOD	5f Gd/Fm		3133	
94	4	DONC	5f Gd/Fm		3862	
96	3	AYR	5f Soft		3959	
69	10	REDC	5f Gd/Sft		4219	

ELTARS 3 ch c £0

8a	7	SOUT	6f Aw		472	
22a	9	SOUT	6f Aw		558	
46	8	WARW	5f Gd/Sft		1712	BL
0	17	NOTT	6f Gd/Fm	45	2192	
0	19	YARM	8f Gd/Fm	40	3971	

ELTON LEDGER 11 b g £4688

47a	6	SOUT	7f Aw	67	33	vis
65a	2	SOUT	6f Aw		279	
65a	1	**SOUT**	6f Aw		389*	vis
66a	2	SOUT	6f Aw		475	vis
58a	2	SOUT	6f Aw		538	vis
54a	2	SOUT	6f Aw		559	vis
50a	7	SOUT	5f Aw	61	674	vis
57a	3	SOUT	6f Aw	61	698	vis
59a	5	SOUT	6f Aw		738	vis
43	7	SOUT	6f Good	48	802	vis
51a	7	SOUT	7f Gd/Fm	59	1801	vis
44a	6	SOUT	6f Aw		2118	vis
45a	4	SOUT	8f Aw	57	2302	vis
43a	7	SOUT	6f Aw	54	2385	vis
28	11	NOTT	6f Gd/Fm		2680	vis

ELVINGTON BOY 3 ch c £5337

53	10	NEWC	5f Soft	74	758	
64	8	BEVE	5f Firm	69	1278	
67	3	RIPO	6f Good	66	1600	
69	2	AYR	5f Good	68	2165	
52	5	RIPO	6f Soft	71	2541	
75	2	RIPO	5f Gd/Fm	70	3010	
79	2	DONC	5f Gd/Fm	74	3161	
58	15	YORK	5f Gd/Fm	74	3569	
56	13	DONC	5f Heavy	77	4570	

ELVIS REIGNS 4 b g £0

0	15	NEWC	10f Soft	85	757	
0	17	THIR	8f Good	80	1160	
0	16	RIPO	8f Good	73	1598	
53	7	YORK	12f Firm	65	2002	
44	11	CARL	12f Good	60	2279	
23	9	RIPO	12f Gd/Fm	54	3013	

ELYSIAN FIELDS 2 br f £0

54	13	NEWM	6f Gd/Fm		4209	
17a	8	WOLV	7f Aw		4383	

EMALI 3 b c £3496

62	2	NEWM	8f Firm		2345	
65	2	NOTT	10f Gd/Fm	63	2685	
41	9	NEWM	10f Good		3021	
60	4	YARM	10f Good		3234	
57	3	YARM	10f Gd/Fm		3382	
34	10	BRIG	10f Firm	62	3557	VIS
57	3	BATH	8f Gd/Fm	56	3816	
57	2	YARM	11f Firm		3917	
45	5	LEIC	10f Gd/Sft		4029	
0	12	LEIC	10f Heavy		4313	

EMANS JOY 3 b f £5703

67	3	YARM	6f Good		1773	
58	5	FOLK	7f Gd/Fm		2293	
62	1	**WARW**	6f Good		2462*	
62	4	YARM	7f Good	65	3030	
62	5	LING	7f Firm	65	3279	
64	3	SAND	8f Gd/Fm	63	3944	
0	17	WIND	8f Gd/Fm		4292	

EMBODY 5 b h £20302

106	2	SAN	8f Good		1460	

EMBRACE ME 2 ch f £0

52	10	YARM	8f Heavy		4477	

EMBRACED 3 b f £14963

106	1	**ASCO**	8f Gd/Sft		1108*	
107	6	YORK	10f Gd/Fm		1309	
98	10	NEWM	8f Gd/Fm		2597	

EMBRYONIC 8 b g £1262

60	7	HAMI	13f Good	66	845	
54	9	MUSS	14f Gd/Sft	66	903	
57	6	DONC	17f Gd/Sft	61	1052	
71	8	CHES	19f Gd/Fm	82	1222	
54	6	AYR	15f Good	60	3367	
60	2	THIR	16f Gd/Fm	60	3618	
32	9	MUSS	16f Gd/Fm	58	3742	
0	15	CATT	16f Soft	60	4006	

EMERALD IMP 3 ch f £0

21a	6	WOLV	9f Aw		720	
30	11	BRIG	7f Firm	55	2044	
0	16	SALI	6f Gd/Fm	55	2230	

EMERALD PALM 2 b f £0

78	6	NEWM	6f Gd/Fm		4209	
64	6	YARM	6f Heavy		4479	

EMERALD PEACE 3 b f £7790

89	9	GOOD	5f Gd/Fm		3059	
73	13	YORK	5f Firm		3598	
101	1	**LEIC**	5f Firm		3841+	
97	6	NEWB	5f Firm		3982	
95	4	NEWM	5f Good		4182	

EMERGING MARKET 8 b g £2416

83	7	KEMP	6f Good	90	728	
82	9	NEWM	6f Gd/Fm	84	1173	
71	11	ASCO	6f Good	86	2151	
78	5	NEWC	7f Good	84	2338	
86	2	RIPO	6f Gd/Fm	82	3183	
75	8	NEWB	7f Gd/Fm	84	3481	
77	13	DONC	7f Gd/Fm	84	3880	

EMINENCE 2 b c £8073

94	3	NEWM	6f Gd/Fm		3162	
105	2	YORK	7f Good		3537	
0	R	NEWM	7f Good		4158	

EMINENCE GRISE 5 b g £24172

85	8	NEWM	12f Firm	92	1187	
97	2	YORK	14f Gd/Fm	92	1982	
97	1	**YORK**	14f Good	95	2695*	
90	11	GOOD	14f Gd/Fm	95	3058	
96	7	YORK	14f Gd/Fm	95	3565	
96	4	DONC	15f Firm	95	3890	

EMISSARY 2 gr c £1337

51	6	CHES	5f Gd/Fm		1221	
51	6	SOUT	6f Soft		1602	
67	4	HAYD	5f Gd/Sft		1976	
53	9	PONT	5f Firm	68	2557	
66	2	AYR	6f Firm	65	2874	
64	4	HAYD	5f Gd/Fm	67	3264	
58	5	HAMI	6f Gd/Sft	65	3824	
0	22	DONC	7f Heavy	63	4577	

EMLEY 4 b f £0

44	6	CATT	7f Gd/Sft		1818	
35	13	BEVE	5f Firm	50	2223	
42	7	DONC	5f Gd/Fm	50	2315	
22	14	PONT	8f Gd/Fm	46	2561	
37	5	THIR	7f Gd/Fm	43	3129	

EMMA AMOUR 3 br f £0

52a	5	WOLV	6f Aw		62	
0	23	REDC	5f Gd/Sft	65	1133	
0	16	NEWC	5f Gd/Sft	60	1479	
0	14	CATT	6f Gd/Fm	53	1815	
30	10	MUSS	5f Firm	49	2047	BL
32	7	THIR	6f Gd/Fm	44	3124	
33	8	THIR	6f Gd/Fm	41	3619	
0	17	BEVE	5f Good		3956	

EMMA CLARE 2 b f £4427

38	8	LING	6f Good		1673	
48	8	SALI	6f Gd/Fm		1882	
61	7	LING	7f Gd/Fm		2182	
63	2	THIR	7f Gd/Fm		3128	
52	4	FOLK	7f Gd/Fm	62	3444	
59	1	**MUSS**	8f Gd/Fm		3740*	
37	11	PONT	8f Soft	62	4084	
0	14	WIND	10f Gd/Sft	60	4290	BL
47a	6	WOLV	8f Aw		4362	bl
52a	3	WOLV	8f Aw	52	4552	

EMMA LYNE 4 b f £0

0a	12	LING	6f Aw	47	691	
0	17	BRIG	7f Gd/Sft	45	896	
0	17	BRIG	10f Firm		1331	

EMMA THOMAS 2 b f £281

62	7	RIPO	5f Soft		2539	
44	9	BEVE	5f Gd/Sft		3055	
31	8	RIPO	6f Good		3697	
26	11	BEVE	7f Good	44	3950	
48a	3	WOLV	7f Aw		4025	
11a	9	WOLV	6f Aw		4246	
16	10	MUSS	5f Gd/Fm	44	4561	

EMMAJOUN 5 b m £966

43a	3	SOUT	6f Aw		32	
44a	6	WOLV	6f Aw		134	
50a	2	LING	7f Aw		156	
39a	5	SOUT	6f Aw		199	
8a	7	WOLV	7f Aw		276	VIS
42a	3	LING	6f Aw		354	
26a	4	WOLV	7f Aw		391	

EMMAS HOPE 3 b f £0

31a	5	LING	6f Aw		207	BL
13a	9	LING	6f Aw	35	242	bl
12	8	WARW	11f Gd/Fm		2253	
0	12	LEIC	10f Gd/Fm		2510	
19	8	CHES	12f Good		2667	

EMMAS SUNSET 4 ch f £0

0	10	BEVE	10f Gd/Fm		3677	

EMMS 2 gr c £15365

84	2	NEWM	5f Soft		985	
89	3	YORK	7f Gd/Fm		2649	
94	1	**NEWM**	7f Firm		3298*	

| 95 | 2 | NEWC | 8f Gd/Sft | 90 | 3704 |
| 79 | 8 | ASCO | 8f Gd/Sft | | 4127 |

EMPEROR NAHEEM 5 b g £1439

79a	2	LING	6f Aw	76	113	
71a	3	WOLV	6f Aw		134	
48a	11	LING	6f Aw	78	223	bl

EMPERORS FOLLY 2 b c £0

| 41 | 8 | BRIG | 8f Gd/Sft | | 4116 |

EMPERORS GOLD 5 gr g £209

27a	8	SOUT	11f Aw		178
39a	3	WOLV	9f Aw	44	306
25a	6	SOUT	11f Aw	42	390
32a	4	WOLV	9f Aw	38	516
40a	5	WOLV	9f Aw		553
26a	5	LING	10f Aw	33	618
0a	13	LING	12f Aw		650

EMPIRE DREAM 3 b c £2403

62	4	REDC	10f Gd/Sft		1582
73	2	BEVE	8f Firm		2222
73	2	PONT	12f Gd/Fm		2560
64	10	ASCO	12f Gd/Fm	75	3014
0	12	REDC	10f Firm	73	3310
0	16	CATT	12f Soft	70	4256

EMPIRE STATE 5 b g £0

| 40a | 6 | WOLV | 9f Aw | 44 | 305 |
| 14a | 9 | WOLV | 12f Aw | 42 | 464 |

EMPORIO 2 b c £0

75	10	NEWM	7f Good		4184
75	4	BRIG	7f Soft		4415
58	15	DONC	8f Heavy		4569

EMPRESS OF AUSTRIA 2 ch f £554

58	3	LEIC	5f Gd/Fm		3092	
41	12	LING	6f Gd/Fm		3832	
61	6	LING	5f Good		4095	t
59	7	LING	6f Soft	63	4269	t
0	16	BRIG	7f Soft	60	4416	t

EN GRISAILLE 4 gr f £0

29a	9	LING	10f Aw	48	1265
44	7	YARM	10f Gd/Sft	46	1615
26	9	YARM	10f Gd/Fm	44	2199
0	14	SALI	10f Gd/Sft	41	4168

ENCHANTING 2 b f £0

| 50 | 10 | ASCO | 7f Good | | 4114 |

ENCORE DU CRISTAL 3 b f £0

| 0 | 18 | NEWM | 8f Gd/Sft | | 972 |

ENCOUNTER 4 br c £10870

0a	13	SOUT	7f Aw		130
47	4	NOTT	6f Good	51	787
28	10	DONC	6f Gd/Sft		1068
45	7	MUSS	7f Gd/Fm	50	1149
48	4	HAMI	6f Firm		1239
40	10	THIR	7f Gd/Sft		1351
37	11	AYR	7f Gd/Fm	46	1631
26	8	MUSS	7f Firm		1685
42	5	CATT	6f Gd/Fm	43	2420
43	2	HAMI	6f Gd/Fm	43	2641
49	1	HAMI	6f Gd/Fm	41	2796*
52	1	CATT	7f Gd/Sft	50	2932*
34	7	THIR	6f Gd/Fm	47	3123
54	1	THIR	6f Gd/Fm	51	3144*
46	6	REDC	7f Firm	53	3328
32	10	REDC	6f Gd/Sft	53	3634
52	5	YARM	6f Gd/Fm	52	3964
51	4	BRIG	6f Gd/Sft	52	4120
52	5	WIND	6f Gd/Sft	52	4293
8	10	NEWC	6f Heavy	52	4425
53	2	MUSS	7f Soft	52	4518

ENCYCLOPEDIA 2 b f £0

55	5	BEVE	5f Gd/Fm		3408
0	10	HAYD	5f Soft		3767
56	5	BEVE	5f Good		3955

END OF STORY 4 b c £0

0a	10	LING	10f Aw		111
0	14	LING	7f Gd/Sft		838
20	9	GOOD	7f Good		3662
0	11	KEMP	14f Gd/Fm	44	3800

END OF THE DAY 4 br g £0

| 0 | 19 | PONT | 10f Soft | | 4088 |

ENDEAVOUR TO DO 3 ch c £0

| 30 | 8 | FOLK | 7f Good | | 2621 |

ENDLESS HALL 4 b c £120985

| 117 | 1 | SAN | 12f Gd/Fm | | 2074* |
| 121 | 1 | AYR | 10f Gd/Fm | | 2720+ |

ENDLESS SUMMER 2 b c £98612

96	1	NEWB	6f Firm		2808*
113	1	GOOD	6f Good		3105*
110	2	DEAU	6f Gd/Sft		3550
114	2	NEWM	6f Good		4181

ENDORSEMENT 4 b f £380

90	10	ASCO	20f Good		2114
90	8	HAYD	12f Gd/Sft		2501
93	6	NEWM	12f Gd/Sft		2857

ENDYMION 3 ch f £440

47	11	SALI	6f Firm	77	1178
0	14	WIND	6f Gd/Fm	72	1877
0	14	WIND	6f Gd/Fm	68	2207
61	3	CHEP	6f Good	63	2489
41	9	WIND	5f Good	62	2716
61	4	WIND	6f Gd/Sft	62	2885
55	6	SALI	6f Gd/Fm	62	3293
0	17	SALI	5f Firm	61	3747
0	20	BATH	5f Soft	60	4432

ENFILADE 4 b c £11569

67	5	HAYD	12f Gd/Sft	75	809	t
72	8	CHES	12f Firm	73	1251	t
78	1	HAYD	14f Gd/Sft	71	1536*	t
67	6	SALI	14f Gd/Fm	78	2268	t
43	5	KEMP	14f Gd/Fm	77	2584	t
52	13	NEWB	13f Firm	75	3994	t
72	3	YARM	14f Heavy	73	4476	t

ENGLISH HARBOUR 2 ch f £3255

75	8	GOOD	7f Good		3108
69	6	NEWM	7f Gd/Fm		3459
75	4	PONT	8f Soft		4086
77	2	PONT	10f Soft		4230
76	2	BRIG	8f Soft		4417
76	2	BRIG	10f Heavy		4539

ENRICH 2 b f £4500

| 103 | 3 | CURR | 7f Gd/Sft | | 4240 |

ENTAIL 3 b f £1669

80	5	NEWM	7f Good		1155
74	3	WIND	8f Gd/Fm		3048
63	4	ASCO	7f Gd/Fm		3343
56	3	BRIG	8f Soft		4175

ENTHUSED 2 b f £86314

91	1	NEWM	6f Gd/Fm		2285*
106	2	NEWM	6f Good		2565
110	1	ASCO	6f Gd/Sft		2996*
114	1	YORK	6f Firm		3596*
103	6	NEWM	6f Good		4159

ENTISAR 3 br c £7222

| 94 | 3 | NEWM | 10f Gd/Fm | | 1151 |
| 91 | 1 | GOOD | 10f Gd/Sft | | 1455* |

ENTITY 3 ch c £12925

60	7	DONC	10f Gd/Fm	72	701	
54	15	RIPO	10f Soft	70	827	
43	9	BEVE	7f Heavy	67	976	
65	3	DONC	8f Gd/Sft	64	1053	
0	14	THIR	8f Good	64	1387	
49	7	THIR	7f Gd/Fm	64	2063	BL
27	7	REDC	7f Gd/Fm	64	2145	bl
49	5	MUSS	8f Firm	61	2378	
45	7	MUSS	7f Good	57	3103	
49	7	THIR	7f Gd/Fm	57	3129	

60	1	HAMI	8f Gd/Sft	54	3380*
66	2	RIPO	10f Good	60	3702
64	1	HAMI	9f Soft	60	3806*
73	1	BEVE	8f Stt/Hvy	63	4045*
0	12	PONT	8f Soft	72	4232

ENTROPY 4 b f £4760

25a	9	LING	7f Aw	49	107
41a	5	LING	8f Aw	43	147
12a	11	WOLV	8f Aw	43	193
9a	11	LING	8f Aw		316
16	9	BRIG	7f Firm	36	1335
38	2	BRIG	6f Gd/Sft	36	1464
49a	3	LING	8f Aw		1739
22	10	LEIC	8f Firm	38	2027
48	5	GOOD	7f Gd/Fm	49	2128
47	1	BATH	8f Firm	43	2331*
32	9	WIND	8f Good	49	2367
51	3	BATH	8f Firm		2786
44	6	LING	7f Firm	48	3279
0	12	BATH	8f Firm	47	3623

ENVY 4 gr f £0

0a	13	WOLV	8f Aw		229
2a	9	WOLV	8f Aw		273
0a	13	SOUT	6f Aw		389

ENZELI 5 b g £28750

114	2	LEOP	14f Good		1620	
112	8	ASCO	20f Good		2114	
121	1	DONC	18f Gd/Fm		3877+	BL
118	5	LONG	20f Good		4264	bl

EPERNAY 4 b f £2651

72a	1	SOUT	8f Aw		453*
61a	5	SOUT	8f Aw	72	601
26	7	WIND	8f Gd/Sft	70	1097
0	17	YARM	7f Gd/Sft	67	1611

EPIC PURSUIT 2 b c £1360

| 80 | 2 | GOWR | 7f Gd/Sft | | 1896 |

EPITRE 3 b c £62440

111	4	LONG	11f V		1317
111	2	CHAN	13f Good		2398
115	1	LONG	15f Soft		3848*
115	1	LONG	15f Good		4239*

EPONA 3 ch f £0

43a	9	SOUT	5f Aw		127
33a	6	SOUT	6f Aw		181
0	24	REDC	6f Gd/Sft	42	1578
0	14	PONT	8f Good		1865

EPWORTH 6 b m £0

| 0a | 11 | WOLV | 12f Aw | 39 | 464 |

EQUAL BALANCE 2 ch c £281

0	21	NEWB	7f Firm		3999	
0	16	SALI	8f Gd/Sft		4163	
47a	3	SOUT	7f Aw		4369	VIS

EQUERRY USA 2 br c £21134

| 111 | 1 | LONG | 8f Good | | 3926* |

EREBUS 3 b c £267

0	16	WARW	8f Heavy		884
60	6	LING	10f Gd/Sft		1281
68	3	BATH	8f Gd/Fm		1436
62	4	REDC	9f Gd/Fm	67	2160
28	9	FOLK	7f Good		2621

ERIN ANAM CARA 3 ch f £295

38	7	LEIC	8f Gd/Sft		1572	
34	8	NEWM	8f Good		2134	
37a	7	WOLV	8f Aw	53	2601	
44	9	WIND	12f Gd/Fm	50	2887	
26	5	WIND	12f Good		3351	
33	3	YARM	10f Firm		3935	BL
0	16	LEIC	10f Heavy		4313	bl

ERITHS CHILL WIND 4 b f £380

51a	4	LING	10f Aw	49	23	
40a	4	LING	10f Aw	48	100	
44a	4	WOLV	9f Aw	46	305	BL

40a 3 LING 12f Aw 48 377 bl

ERRACHT 2 gr f £3870
84	2	PONT	5f Heavy		938	
82	1	**BEVE**	5f Gd/Sft		3055*	
39	6	CATT	6f Good	82	3439	
71a	2	WOLV	6f Aw		4246	

ERRO CODIGO 5 b g £738
25a	11	SOUT	7f Aw	64	33
35a	10	WOLV	5f Aw	60	116
52a	3	SOUT	5f Aw	55	180
45a	4	WOLV	6f Aw	53	226
38a	6	SOUT	6f Aw	53	250

ERTLON 10 b g £3281
0a	12	LING	10f Aw	54	842
0	15	DONC	10f Gd/Sft	55	1050
0	15	YARM	7f Gd/Sft	50	1611
30	7	NOTT	8f Soft	50	1646
44	6	YARM	10f Good	50	1775
0	20	WARW	11f Gd/Fm	44	2033
42	3	WARW	8f Good	42	2460
32	5	YARM	10f Firm		2765
39	5	BRIG	7f Firm		3559
52	1	**BRIG**	8f Firm		3736*
52	2	CHEP	8f Good		3868
44	9	YARM	7f Firm		3921
27a	9	LING	8f Aw		4272

ERUPT 7 b g £7224
37a	7	WOLV	9f Aw	41	60
34a	6	SOUT	7f Aw	41	69
39a	2	SOUT	8f Aw	38	647
22a	8	SOUT	8f Aw		684
49	4	BEVE	7f Firm	51	1275
53	2	THIR	7f Gd/Sft		1351
55	1	**MUSS**	7f Gd/Fm	50	1431*
58	1	**SOUT**	7f Soft		1601*
59	3	CHEP	7f Gd/Sft	59	1799
41	11	CHEP	7f Good	55	1969
41	12	NEWM	7f Firm	59	2347
46	12	DONC	7f Good	57	2612
0	16	NOTT	6f Gd/Fm		2680	vis
52	4	WARW	11f Good		3691
45	11	LEIC	10f Firm	54	3842
54	7	LEIC	8f Gd/Sft		4032

ESCALADE 3 b c £0
42	12	LEIC	7f Firm	63	2026

ESHER COMMON 2 b c £3991
81	5	LEIC	7f Gd/Fm		3333
90	1	**HAYD**	7f Soft		3786*

ESHTIAAL 6 br g £862
65a	3	LING	12f Aw	70	52	bl
68a	2	LING	12f Aw		101	bl
58a	4	LING	13f Aw	65	167	bl
23a	10	WOLV	12f Aw	60	407	bl

ESPADA 4 b c £35800
84	6	DONC	8f Good	85	733
90	2	KEMP	8f Soft	85	1015
92	1	**KEMP**	8f Gd/Sft	85	1077*
40	25	ASCO	8f Good	91	2090
86	9	SAND	8f Gd/Fm	91	2528
82	8	CHES	8f Gd/Fm	90	3510
71	9	AYR	8f Good	89	4013
73	15	NEWM	7f Good	87	4195	VIS

ESPANA 2 gr f £1496
64	7	HAYD	6f Gd/Fm		2500
70	3	KEMP	6f Gd/Fm		2748
45	7	WIND	6f Good		3187
61	5	NEWM	8f Good	69	3609
71	2	PONT	8f Soft	65	4084
18	14	PONT	8f Soft	68	4378

ESPERE DOR 3 b c £0
5a	12	WOLV	8f Aw		171
5a	10	WOLV	8f Aw		273

35a	9	WOLV	6f Aw		549
0a	10	WOLV	8f Aw		707
34a	9	WOLV	9f Aw		720
0	11	WARW	11f Heavy	44	1002
0	13	NOTT	14f Gd/Sft		1369
0a	11	WOLV	9f Aw	47	2080
0	6	DONC	10f Gd/Fm		2317
0	12	LEIC	7f Gd/Fm		2508
22	10	NOTT	8f Gd/Fm		2682
0	13	HAYD	7f Gd/Fm		2704
0	18	CHEP	7f Gd/Fm	43	2974
0	18	NEWC	7f Good	39	3033

ESPERTO 7 b g £2390
5a	8	WOLV	9f Aw		922
23	10	PONT	8f Gd/Sft	47	1101
45	9	BRIG	10f Firm		1210
36	6	HAMI	11f Gd/Fm	44	1361
41	1	**LEIC**	10f Soft	37	1546*
0	11	RIPO	10f Soft		2538
39	4	YARM	10f Firm		2765
36	4	AYR	11f Firm		2875
24	9	YARM	10f Good		3234
22	7	HAMI	9f Gd/Sft		3823
16	9	BRIG	10f Gd/Fm	37	4419

ESSENCE 2 b f £0
0	16	LEIC	6f Firm		2029
33a	8	SOUT	7f Aw		2383
41a	6	SOUT	7f Aw		2949
0	18	LEIC	8f Firm	45	3837

ESSIE 3 b f £0
0	17	WARW	11f Gd/Sft	54	1707	bl

ESTABELLA 3 ch f £6759
55	2	MUSS	12f Gd/Sft		799
64	1	**BEVE**	12f Heavy	55	978*
59a	3	WOLV	12f Aw	63	1142
35	13	BEVE	12f Good	63	1446
54	5	YARM	11f Good	60	1770
48	5	BRIG	10f Firm		2041	VIS
45a	5	LING	12f Aw	60	2217
49a	4	LING	12f Aw	57	2593	BL
42	9	YARM	10f Gd/Fm		3383	vis
59a	1	**LING**	16f Aw	51	4099*

ESTABLISHED 3 b g £6880
30a	8	LING	13f Aw	55	835
39	5	WIND	12f Heavy	45	937
0	13	NOTT	14f Gd/Fm	45	1270
38	3	LING	11f Firm	37	1914	BL
30	5	BRIG	12f Gd/Fm	40	1935	BL
36	5	FOLK	12f Aw	38	2295
0a	9	SOUT	12f Aw	35	2815	bl
45	1	**NOTT**	16f Gd/Fm	37	3112*
48	3	FOLK	16f Gd/Fm	43	3588
48	1	**LING**	16f Firm	43	3755*
48	3	WARW	16f Gd/Fm	51	3916

ESTABLISHMENT 3 b c £3816
68	6	WIND	8f Gd/Fm	72	744
67	4	BRIG	10f Gd/Sft	70	892
50	11	BATH	10f Good	68	1094
68a	2	LING	10f Aw	65	1544
70	1	**BRIG**	12f Gd/Fm	65	1935*
65	5	LING	11f Firm	70	2321
34a	6	LING	12f Aw	67	2651
54	6	EPSO	12f Gd/Fm	65	3417
44	6	BRIG	12f Firm	65	3560	BL

ESTACADO 4 b f £0
45	5	GOOD	16f Soft	48	4075
0	11	PONT	18f Soft	44	4376	vis

ESTIHAN 2 b f £0
71	6	LING	7f Firm		3829

ESTOPPED 5 b g £0
3a	10	LING	10f Aw	46	22
11a	9	LING	12f Aw		101

0a	14	SOUT	11f Aw		248	BL

ESTUARY 5 ch g £1282
58a	2	LING	12f Aw		457
46a	3	LING	10f Aw		771
43	10	LING	10f Gd/Sft		1281	t
0	16	NEWM	8f Gd/Fm	53	2130

ESYOUEFFCEE 2 b f £9659
86	2	BEVE	7f Good		3397
94	1	**BEVE**	7f Gd/Fm		3655*
89	8	DONC	8f Gd/Fm		3876
94	2	NEWM	8f Soft		4546

ETBASH 3 b c £3765
86	2	LUCE	15f Heavy		3850

ETERNAL SPRING 3 b c £12480
102	1	**EPSO**	10f Heavy		1029*
93	5	LING	11f Gd/Sft		1284

ETHMAAR 3 b c £1377
88	4	NEWM	10f Firm		1151
96	5	DONC	12f Firm	97	3896
94	9	NEWM	10f Good	97	4197
88	6	NEWM	12f Good	96	4342

ETIENNE LADY 3 gr f £4065
56	6	YARM	6f Good		1773
78	1	**NEWM**	6f Gd/Fm		3319*

ETISALAT 5 b g £15028
47a	1	**LING**	10f Aw	42	100*
0a	12	SOUT	8f Aw	46	176
53a	3	WOLV	8f Aw		322
58a	1	**WOLV**	9f Aw	49	405*
56a	2	WOLV	8f Aw	54	432
47a	6	WOLV	9f Aw	58	568
57a	3	WOLV	9f Aw	57	749
51	1	**MUSS**	7f Gd/Fm	46	1149*
52	1	**HAMI**	8f Gd/Fm	46	1190*
58	1	**CARL**	9f Firm	52	1254*
62	3	HAMI	8f Gd/Fm	63	1360
28	14	LEIC	8f Firm	61	2027
49	12	NEWM	8f Gd/Fm	61	2130
20	11	YARM	8f Gd/Fm	59	2412
44	12	NEWM	8f Good	59	2564

EUCALYPTUS 3 ch c £0
54	11	LING	7f Gd/Sft		1261

EUGEN 5 b g £635
89	3	KLAM	6f Good		3213

EURIBOR 2 b c £7685
101	2	DEAU	6f Gd/Fm		3210

EURO DANDY 3 b c £0
6a	8	SOUT	8f Aw		385

EURO IMPORT 2 ch g £0
0	15	DONC	5f Good		730
32	10	BEVE	5f Heavy		974
35	8	RIPO	6f Good		1859

EURO VENTURE 5 b g £14520
50a	10	SOUT	6f Aw	71	645
0	11	CATT	7f Gd/Fm	76	780
60	13	THIR	5f Soft	74	926
0	13	THIR	7f Good	72	1158
65	6	THIR	8f Gd/Sft	69	1356
64	7	AYR	6f Gd/Fm	69	1654
63	9	YORK	6f Firm		2000
71	1	**REDC**	6f Gd/Fm	66	2158*
65	6	NEWC	6f Firm	70	2334
77	1	**BEVE**	5f Gd/Fm	70	2517*
78	4	YORK	5f Good	77	2644
69	4	NEWC	5f Gd/Fm	77	2987
63	8	THIR	6f Gd/Fm	77	3123
0	15	LEIC	5f Gd/Sft	76	4027

EUROLINK APACHE 5 b g £960
61a	2	WOLV	12f Aw		519
49a	4	WOLV	12f Aw		565
60	9	SALI	12f Good	63	1350
58	5	RIPO	16f Good	61	1597

58 6 NOTT 16f Gd/Fm   2191 BL

EUROLINK ARTEMIS 3 b f £4278

84	4	NEWB	7f Soft			915	
81	3	GOOD	9f Gd/Sft			1481	
64	5	WIND	8f Soft			2548	
73	1	LEIC	10f Gd/Fm			2774*	
62	4	RIPO	10f Gd/Fm	75		3465	
0	13	GOOD	10f Soft	73		4067	

EUROLINK MAYFLY 3 b f £0

| 0 | 12 | LING | 7f Gd/Sft | | | 839 | |

EUROLINK MOUSSAKA 5 b g £0

| 39 | 5 | CARL | 8f Firm | | | 2283 | |
| 0 | 15 | RIPO | 8f Soft | 55 | | 2542 | |

EUROLINK RAINDANCE 3 b f £13335

106	3	NEWM	7f Gd/Fm	109		969	
94	4	CAPA	8f Heavy			1117	
102	2	GOOD	8f Gd/Sft			1485	
105	2	NEWB	10f Gd/Fm			1945	

EUROLINK SUNDANCE 2 ch f £6347

64	9	GOOD	6f Gd/Fm			1957	
79	1	GOOD	6f Good			2357*	
79	3	LING	6f Good	79		2589	
78	4	GOOD	5f Good			3109	
78	3	EPSO	6f Good	80		3761	

EUROLINK ZANTE 4 b g £0

| 65 | 5 | WIND | 8f Good | | | 3350 | |
| 59 | 8 | LING | 8f Soft | | | 4273 | |

EUROPRIME GAMES 2 b c £0

| 57 | 8 | YORK | 6f Soft | | | 4283 | |

EVANDER 5 ch g £0

65	8	HAYD	12f Gd/Sft	84		809	
86	6	ASCO	12f Good	84		2674	
77	5	NEWM	15f Good	84		3025	

EVE 3 b f £12904

73	4	KEMP	8f Soft			1532	
74	2	WIND	8f Gd/Fm			2211	
72	3	BRIG	8f Soft			2426	
58	4	THIR	12f Gd/Fm	72		2967	
66	3	LING	10f Firm			3281	
57	12	GOOD	10f Good	68		3663	
62	7	SAND	8f Gd/Fm	66		3944	
65	1	BRIG	8f Soft			4173*	
70	1	LEIC	8f Sft/Hvy	64		4310*	
73	1	NEWM	8f Gd/Sft	68		4536*	
66	4	DONC	8f Heavy	64		4573	

EVEAM 3 b f £2700

| 73 | 3 | LEOP | 6f Heavy | 85 | | 4555 | |

EVENING CHORUS 5 b g £0

| 28 | 11 | CARL | 17f Gd/Fm | 60 | | 2244 | tvi |

EVENING SCENT 4 b f £19716

45	6	NOTT	14f Heavy	47		1023	
0a	14	SOUT	11f Aw	40		1306	
47	3	SOUT	12f Soft	48		1604	
48	2	CATT	12f Gd/Sft	45		1816	
34	7	HAMI	12f Gd/Fm	45		1908	
50	1	HAMI	13f Gd/Fm	45		1936*	
47	6	MUSS	12f Firm	54		2048	
48	4	CATT	16f Soft	50		4006	
55	1	HAYD	14f Gd/Sft	48		4105*	
61	1	YORK	12f Soft	55		4280*	
46	5	YORK	14f Heavy	55		4299	
21a	6	SOUT	14f Aw	51		4370	
39	10	MUSS	12f Soft	60		4560	

EVENTUALITY 4 b f £6417

65	5	BRIG	7f Firm	69		1213	
36	15	GOOD	6f Gd/Sft	68		1471	
0	15	DONC	6f Gd/Fm	65		1842	
68	1	LING	6f Good	61		2654*	
72	2	WARW	6f Gd/Fm	67		2845	
54	12	ASCO	7f Gd/Fm	70		2999	
58	7	NEWM	6f Gd/Fm	70		3613	
52	9	NOTT	6f Soft	69		3975	

EVER IN LOVE 3 b f £3458

| 102 | 3 | DEAU | 8f Gd/Sft | | | 3551 | |

EVER REVIE 3 b f £1918

39	8	NOTT	10f Heavy	56		1022	
31	11	THIR	8f Good	53		1387	bl
51	1	SOUT	7f Soft			1603*	bl
43	4	HAYD	8f Soft	55		1822	
29a	11	SOUT	6f Aw			2118	bl
18a	9	SOUT	8f Aw			2816	bl
0	11	BEVE	7f Sft/Hvy	51		4044	

EVERBOLD 3 b f £0

21	7	LEIC	7f Gd/Fm			3332	
0	16	NEWM	7f Good			3612	
25	11	LEIC	6f Gd/Sft			4031	

EVEREST 3 ch c £32830

87	2	LEIC	8f Good			789	
74	3	MUSS	9f Gd/Sft			902	
88	2	SAND	8f Heavy	82		1055	
87	1	THIR	8f Gd/Sft			1352*	
88	1	PONT	8f Firm	84		3505*	
90	1	GOOD	9f Good	85		3658*	
82	5	HAYD	11f Soft	89		3782	
0	15	SAND	8f Soft	89		4206	

EVERGREEN 3 ch f £5217

74	3	LEIC	7f Good			794	
62	5	THIR	8f Soft	76		931	
56	9	WARW	11f Heavy	74		1521	
70	4	BRIG	10f Good	74		1649	
64	7	NOTT	8f Good	72		1873	
0	14	SALI	8f Gd/Sft	70		2467	
69	2	EPSO	9f Good	67		2795	t
73	1	SALI	8f Gd/Fm	67		2980*	
67	6	NEWM	8f Gd/Fm	71		3317	
66	9	SAND	8f Gd/Fm	71		3944	t

EVERLASTING LOVE 3 b f £0

100	5	NEWM	10f Firm			1184	
109	5	YORK	10f Gd/Fm			1309	
86	6	EPSO	9f Gd/Sft			1825	
72	16	ASCO	7f Good			2087	

EVERMOORE 2 b f £284

17	10	NOTT	5f Heavy			1019	
61	4	BATH	5f Good			1088	
55	6	SALI	6f Gd/Sft			2469	
50	4	LEIC	6f Gd/Fm	64		2773	
46	7	SALI	7f Gd/Fm			3420	
31	15	NEWM	7f Good			4336	

EVERY RIGHT 2 b c £0

| 54 | 10 | PONT | 6f Gd/Fm | | | 2828 | |

EVEZIO RUFO 8 b g £11787

37a	5	SOUT	12f Aw	42		211	
38a	4	WOLV	12f Aw	40		261	vis
24a	4	SOUT	11f Aw	40		324	
31a	5	SOUT	12f Aw	38		413	
48a	1	WOLV	12f Aw	38		437*	bl
35a	3	WOLV	12f Aw	41		489	bl
52a	1	WOLV	12f Aw	46		562*	bl
46a	4	SOUT	12f Aw	46		590	vis
32a	5	WOLV	12f Aw	46		607	bl
56a	1	SOUT	12f Aw	50		683*	vis
61a	1	WOLV	12f Aw	54		723*	bl
46a	5	LING	13f Aw	60		835	vis
46	1	BRIG	12f Gd/Fm	41		1128*	vis
25	8	HAMI	13f Gd/Fm	45		1363	vis

EVIL EMPIRE 4 ch f £2788

| 105 | 3 | NEWM | 12f Gd/Fm | | | 2857 | |

EVIYRN 4 b g £0

45a	8	WOLV	8f Aw			920	
31	6	BRIG	12f Gd/Sft			1510	
54	10	BATH	12f Gd/Fm			3818	

EX GRATIA 4 b g £0

| 50 | 16 | NEWM | 10f Gd/Fm | 88 | | 1170 | |
| 79 | 5 | DONC | 10f Gd/Fm | 88 | | 2350 | |

EXALT 4 b c £0

| 0a | 15 | SOUT | 11f Aw | 60 | | 1306 | BL |

EXALTED 7 b g £10676

65	1	HAMI	13f Good	60		845*	
63	5	HAYD	14f Gd/Fm	65		1167	
54	6	AYR	13f Heavy	63		4325	
46	5	NEWC	14f Heavy	63		4424	
51	7	MUSS	16f Soft	61		4563	

EXCEPTIONAL PADDY 2 b c £517

| 77 | 3 | PONT | 6f Soft | | | 4082 | |
| 62 | 6 | NEWC | 6f Heavy | | | 4402 | |

EXCLUSION ZONE 3 ch g £2257

| 69a | 1 | LING | 12f Aw | | | 3835* | |

EXEAT 4 br c £4653

103	2	HAYD	8f Gd/Sft			1489	
91	11	ASCO	8f Good	105		2090	vis
0	17	NEWM	7f Gd/Fm	103		2616	vis
77	6	GOOD	7f Good			3884	
92	3	REDC	7f Gd/Sft			4218	

EXECUTIVE GHOST 3 gr g £336

0	16	YARM	8f Good			1771	
47	7	RIPO	5f Gd/Fm			3462	
66	4	YARM	6f Firm			3919	
0	14	BRIG	6f Gd/Sft	69		4120	
0	15	LING	6f Soft	66		4270	

EXECUTIVE ORDER 3 b c £2356

87	4	NEWM	8f Firm			1188	
87	2	NEWM	10f Gd/Fm			2135	
79	4	SAND	10f Good			2531	

EXECUTIVE PROFILES 5 ch m £0

| 2a | 9 | LING | 12f Aw | | | 2181 | |
| 0a | 11 | WOLV | 12f Aw | | | 4549 | |

EXECUTIVE WISH 3 b f £0

22a	7	SOUT	6f Aw			2299	
26a	7	WOLV	6f Aw			2604	
35	9	LING	8f Aw			3579	
0	16	YARM	7f Soft			3921	

EXELLENT ADVENTURE 2 ch c £0

0	W	NOTT	5f Heavy			1020	
34a	6	SOUT	6f Aw			1420	
48	6	HAYD	5f Soft			1492	
33a	5	SOUT	6f Aw			1805	

EXHIBITION GIRL 3 ch f £0

75	5	DONC	10f Gd/Sft			1051	
39	7	RIPO	9f Good			1863	
0	14	WIND	8f Soft			2548	

EXILE 3 b c £7362

69	2	LING	11f Firm	66		2321	
69	5	SAND	10f Gd/Fm	68		2499	
70	2	KEMP	12f Good	67		2872	
74	1	KEMP	12f Gd/Fm	69		3073*	
74	2	SALI	12f Gd/Fm	69		3290	

EXORCET 3 b f £3822

80	1	THIR	6f Soft			909*	
53	12	SALI	6f Firm	88		1178	
0	16	WIND	5f Heavy	86		4527	

EXOTIC FAN 2 b f £1353

70	4	YARM	7f Firm			2390	
66	7	SALI	7f Gd/Fm			3292	
71	2	HAMI	8f Gd/Sft			3822	
66	13	WIND	10f Gd/Sft	74		4290	

EXPEDIENT 3 ch c £0

| 0 | 15 | LEIC | 8f Good | | | 789 | |
| 22 | 10 | NOTT | 10f Heavy | 51 | | 1022 | |

EXPLODE 3 b c £13358

62	3	NOTT	8f Good			784	
91	1	SALI	10f Gd/Fm			2265*	
106	1	EPSO	10f Gd/Fm			2630*	
102	3	NEWM	10f Gd/Sft			4532	

EXPLOSIVE 2 b g £0

| 45 | 9 | FOLK | 7f Good | | | 2619 | |

70 8 NEWM 7f Firm 3298

EXTRA GUEST 2 b f £15297

71	4	WARW	5f Heavy		886	
79	3	PONT	5f Heavy		938	
72	2	NOTT	6f Good		1413	
64	6	HAYD	5f Gd/Sft		1538	
73	2	LEIC	6f Firm		2029	
72	2	CARL	5f Firm		2277	
72	2	BEVE	5f Gd/Fm		2480	
74	4	YORK	6f Good		2692	
78	2	DONC	6f Gd/Fm		2756	
75	2	SAND	5f Gd/Fm		2933	
73	2	MUSS	5f Good		3098	
73	3	FOLK	6f Firm		3443	
69	3	BRIG	6f Firm		3525	
92	4	NEWM	6f Good		4345	
72	4	NEWB	7f Gd/Fm	71	4453	
66	5	DONC	7f Heavy	73	4577	

EXUDE 3 br f £0

39a	6	SOUT	8f Aw		48
35a	5	SOUT	7f Aw		88
21a	8	LING	8f Aw		236

EYE OF GOLD 2 b f £0

83	5	KEMP	6f Gd/Fm		3795

EYECATCHER 3 b c £321

69	4	LING	7f Firm		3834

EYELETS ECHO 3 b c £3607

77	9	DONC	8f Good		735	
0	13	LING	7f Gd/Sft		840	
40	7	PONT	8f Good	70	1495	
69	1	NEWC	9f Gd/Fm	66	2276*	
64	5	REDC	11f Gd/Fm	70	2863	
59	11	NEWM	12f Gd/Fm	69	3167	
64	6	GOOD	10f Soft	67	4067	
35	13	YORK	9f Heavy	66	4300	VIS
39	12	DONC	10f Gd/Sft	64	4448	vis

EYES DONT LIE 2 b c £242

57	9	MUSS	5f Good		1146	
62	4	HAMI	5f Gd/Fm		1359	
50	8	AYR	6f Good		1653	
0	16	NEWC	7f Good	59	3246	
53	8	AYR	7f Good		3363	VIS
38	6	MUSS	8f Gd/Fm		3740	BL
23	9	AYR	8f Heavy	56	4323	

F ZERO 3 b c £2717

68a	1	LING	8f Aw		615*
51	13	DONC	10f Gd/Fm	76	701

FABERGER 4 b c £78032

116	1	DEAU	8f V		2571*
118	1	SAN	8f Soft		4319*

FABI 5 br g £0

0	15	RIPO	14f Good		3711

FACE D FACTS 2 b f £6602

77	5	NOTT	5f Gd/Sft		1641
77	1	LING	5f Gd/Fm		2214*
78	3	WIND	5f Good		2368
56	9	WIND	6f Gd/Fm	78	3354
75	2	RIPO	6f Gd/Fm	74	3712
70	4	GOOD	6f Good	74	3886
74	3	NEWM	6f Good	73	4338

FACILE TIGRE 5 gr g £2600

57a	4	WOLV	5f Aw	60	146
52a	4	WOLV	6f Aw	57	175
42a	6	SOUT	6f Aw	56	212
41a	6	WOLV	6f Aw	56	226
49a	8	WOLV	7f Aw	53	323
41a	6	WOLV	6f Aw		436
24a	10	LING	6f Aw		484
21a	11	SOUT	6f Aw	43	642
37a	7	LING	6f Aw	43	634
0	18	HAMI	5f Firm	49	1244
47	5	HAMI	5f Gd/Fm	49	1358

36	10	MUSS	5f Gd/Fm		1430	
32	6	HAMI	5f Firm		2095	
44	7	CARL	6f Gd/Fm		2240	
44	5	HAMI	5f Gd/Fm	47	2395	
41	5	MUSS	5f Gd/Sft	44	2535	
36	7	HAMI	6f Gd/Fm	44	2641	
52	3	AYR	5f Gd/Fm	52	2721	
31	8	HAMI	6f Firm		2798	
23	11	AYR	6f Firm	52	2877	
39	9	AYR	6f Good		3366	
51	2	HAMI	5f Gd/Sft	49	3536	
50	3	MUSS	5f Gd/Sft	49	3594	
45	6	HAMI	5f Gd/Sft	51	3825	
0	23	AYR	5f Soft	52	3960	
45	9	WIND	5f Gd/Sft	50	4295	

FACT OR FICTION 3 b f £0

23	5	RIPO	8f Soft		2543

FACTUAL LAD 2 b c £6342

75	2	KEMP	5f Good		724	
73	3	WIND	5f Good		849	
72	3	WARW	5f Heavy		1001	
88	2	CHEP	6f Gd/Sft		1798	
84	3	KEMP	6f Gd/Fm		2082	
88	1	CHEP	6f Gd/Fm		2488*	
64	9	NEWB	6f Firm		2808	
92	6	DONC	6f Good		3862	
0	18	NEWM	6f Gd/Fm	92	4214	
73	14	NEWB	6f Sft/Hvy	90	4468	

FADHAH 2 b f £711

73	5	NEWM	6f Firm		1856
70	2	FOLK	7f Good		2290
0	16	WIND	6f Gd/Fm		4288
63	10	BRIG	7f Soft	69	4416

FAERIE REALM 2 b f £0

78	5	LEIC	7f Sft/Hvy		4309

FAGIN 3 b c £0

33	13	WIND	12f Gd/Sft	75	1425

FAHAN 3 b f £0

0	11	GOOD	10f Gd/Sft	72	1812	
55	5	WIND	8f Good	66	2713	
47	5	FOLK	9f Gd/Fm	62	3043	
31	5	NEWC	12f Firm	59	3606	BL
0a	12	WOLV	8f Aw	55	3769	
0a	10	LING	16f Aw	48	4099	

FAHS 8 b g £15918

81a	3	LING	10f Aw	78	160
82a	1	LING	13f Aw	78	219*
82a	2	LING	12f Aw	78	332
63a	5	LING	12f Aw	80	441
65	7	WARW	12f Good	73	2466
74	1	YARM	11f Firm	69	2771*
76	2	REDC	9f Gd/Fm		2865
82	1	NEWM	12f Gd/Fm	75	3122*
84	1	LEIC	12f Gd/Fm		3336*
77	5	SAND	10f Good	85	3471
72	11	YARM	10f Good	82	3941
78	11	NEWB	10f Good	82	3997
78a	3	LING	12f Aw	80	4271

FAILED TO HIT 7 b g £16647

70a	5	LING	10f Aw	70	23	vis
65a	1	LING	12f Aw		101*	vis
64a	5	WOLV	14f Aw	74	135	vis
62a	2	LING	10f Aw		163	vis
67a	2	LING	10f Aw	66	220	vis
63a	4	LING	12f Aw	67	245	vis
71a	2	SOUT	11f Aw	66	302	vis
64a	3	SOUT	11f Aw	66	343	vis
68a	2	WOLV	12f Aw	68	407	vis
38a	8	LING	12f Aw	67	441	vis
61a	1	WOLV	12f Aw		530*	vis
62a	6	LING	12f Aw	74	572	vis
49a	3	LING	12f Aw		650	vis

69a	4	SOUT	12f Aw	68	695	vis
62a	3	WOLV	12f Aw	65	723	vis
56a	6	SOUT	14f Aw	65	868	vis
59a	5	WOLV	9f Aw	62	3495	vis
55a	2	WOLV	15f Aw		4024	vis
56a	6	LING	12f Aw		4101	vis
52a	3	LING	12f AW		4186	vis
63a	1	WOLV	12f Aw	54	4245*	vis
51a	5	LING	12f Aw	55	4334	vis
72a	1	WOLV	12f Aw		4549*	vis

FAIR FINNISH 6 b g £0

46	9	NOTT	16f Gd/Fm		2191

FAIR IMPRESSION 3 ch f £7926

56	9	KEMP	7f Soft		1012
0	15	NEWB	7f Gd/Fm	75	1405
82	1	BRIG	8f Soft		2426*
78	1	HAYD	7f Gd/Fm		2704*
49	9	GOOD	9f Gd/Fm	84	3089
81	5	NEWM	7f Soft		4547
0	18	DONC	7f Heavy	80	4574

FAIR LADY 3 b f £8021

76a	1	WOLV	9f Aw		467*
78	6	CHEP	10f Gd/Fm	78	2450
78	3	REDC	11f Gd/Fm	77	2863
61	11	DONC	10f Gd/Fm	78	3159
68	4	CHES	10f Gd/Fm		3426
71	2	MUSS	8f Gd/Sft		4135
62	8	WIND	10f Gd/Fm	71	4291
75a	1	LING	10f Aw	69	4482*

FAIR PRINCESS 2 b f £16593

82	2	NEWB	5f Good		1372
81	2	HAYD	5f Gd/Sft		1538
77	3	ASCO	5f Good		2088
65	6	WIND	5f Soft		2545
83	3	SAND	5f Good	82	3431
80	2	BATH	5f Firm		3621
84	2	DONC	6f Firm		3888
0	16	NEWB	6f Stt/Hvy	82	4468

FAIR QUESTION 2 b c £5675

88	1	NEWM	7f Good		3608*
104	4	NEWB	8f Firm		3983

FAIR STEP 2 ch f £812

57	2	CATT	5f Gd/Fm		2435
52	3	LEIC	5f Gd/Fm		2772
39	8	NEWC	5f Good		2983
50	5	RIPO	5f Gd/Fm		3710

FAIR WARNING 4 b c £6217

83	5	EPSO	12f Heavy	92	1030
0	15	YORK	12f Gd/Fm	92	1307
73	7	GOOD	12f Gd/Fm	96	3134
91	1	NEWB	12f Gd/Fm		3487*
71	13	DONC	12f Firm	90	3896
85	5	NEWM	12f Good	90	4342

FAIRFIELD BAY 4 b g £0

0	20	WIND	12f Gd/Fm	42	748	
18	11	FOLK	7f Soft		962	BL
0	12	PONT	8f Good		1498	bl
0	12	LEIC	8f Gd/Sft		1732	E
9a	8	LING	6f Aw		1913	

FAIRGAME MAN 2 ch c £7729

72	3	PONT	5f Good		2361
79	1	CARL	5f Firm		2821*
90	1	CHES	6f Firm	75	3168*
86	3	RIPO	6f Gd/Fm		3463
74	11	AYR	5f Good		3959

FAIRLY SURE 7 b m £0

0	11	BRIG	8f Soft	33	1511
10	7	KEMP	12f Gd/Fm	32	2081

FAIRTOTO 4 b g £430

45	5	CATT	16f Gd/Fm	45	4258
29	7	NOTT	16f Heavy	45	4508

FAIRY GEM 3 b f £1162

70 7 KEMP 8f Soft 995
97 4 LING 7f Gd/Sft 1283
82 6 LEIC 7f Gd/Sft 1733
50 6 SAND 8f Good 2476
86 7 NEWM 6f Gd/Fm 3120
0 R GOOD 7f Good 92 3648 VIS

FAIRY GODMOTHER 4 b f £8292
108 2 NEWM 9f Gd/Sft 967
73 5 NEWM 9f Gd/Fm 1154

FAIRY KING PRAWN 4 b g £581037
121 1 TOKY 8f Firm 1755*

FAIRY PRINCE 7 b g £4287
0 12 NOTT 6f Gd/Sft 1368
56 4 PONT 6f Good 57 1869
55 5 GOOD 6f Good 57 2124
62 1 NOTT 6f Gd/Fm 56 2192*
56 12 GOOD 6f Good 64 2355
0 13 PONT 6f Good 60 2559
61 4 NOTT 5f Gd/Fm 60 3113 BL
60 4 NEWB 6f Firm 60 3455
61 3 BEVE 5f Gd/Fm 60 3653 bl
0 14 LEIC 5f Gd/Sft 62 4027 bl
0 21 WIND 5f Gd/Sft 62 4295 bl

FAIRY QUEEN 4 b f £10457
108 4 CAPA 10f Heavy 12

FAIRYTIME 4 b f £0
0 14 BRIG 6f Gd/Fm 40 1211 BL
0 17 SALI 6f Gd/Fm 35 2230 bl
26 8 BRIG 6f Gd/Fm 33 3243
42 9 FOLK 6f Gd/Fm 3587
48a 5 LING 7f Aw 4328 t

FAIT LE JOJO 3 b c £21891
80 4 WIND 10f Gd/Fm 747
79 5 WIND 12f Gd/Fm 80 1199
78 4 REDC 11f Gd/Sft 79 1560
80 1 SALI 14f Firm 77 2021*
82 1 GOOD 14f Good 80 2305*
83 3 NEWM 16f Gd/Fm 84 2600
81 5 GOOD 14f Firm 82 3153
83 1 NEWM 15f Good 81 3611*

FAITH AGAIN 4 b f £0
36 8 NOTT 14f Good 45 788
30 8 BATH 17f Firm 40 2941

FAITHFUL WARRIOR 2 ch c £786
75 4 NEWB 6f Firm 2808
86 5 WIND 5f Gd/Fm 3044
69 4 NEWB 6f Stt/Hvy 4471

FAL N ME 3 b f £0
0a 7 WOLV 5f Aw 42

FALCON GOA 2 b f £10685
52 10 DONC 5f Gd/Sft 1067
69 4 DONC 6f Good 1513
76 1 PONT 5f Soft 1698*
76 6 ASCO 5f Good 2152
76a 2 WOLV 6f Aw 3496

FALCON SPIRIT 4 b g £310
50 8 RIPO 10f Gd/Fm 62 2836
49 9 RIPO 12f Gd/Fm 60 3181
50 4 REDC 11f Gd/Fm 51 3636 bl
20 7 BEVE 10f Stt/Hv 51 4046 VIS
50a 5 WOLV 12f Aw 53 4226 vis
18a 9 WOLV 12f Aw 48 4386 bl
39a 5 WOLV 12f Aw 48 4443 bl

FALCONIDAE 3 ch c £9247
78 10 NEWB 8f Good 1377
77 5 NEWB 8f Gd/Fm 1786
84 1 BATH 8f Firm 77 2330*
84 2 SAND 7f Gd/Fm 81 2922
75 7 CHEP 6f Gd/Fm 82 3254
0 U NEWB 8f Firm 82 3998
69 8 SAND 8f Soft 82 4206

FALL HABIT 3 b f £7685

107 2 DEAU 10f Good 3211

FALLACHAN 4 ch c £3382
0 16 THIR 8f Good 84 1160
85 4 HAYD 8f Soft 82 1490
77 4 EPSO 9f Gd/Sft 82 1829
60 15 CARL 8f Gd/Fm 80 2242
76 3 YARM 7f Firm 78 2768
46 13 NEWM 8f Gd/Fm 78 3118
55 11 HAYD 7f Soft 75 3785
63 7 SAND 7f Soft 72 4204
0 15 YARM 7f Soft 69 4513

FALLS OMONESS 6 b m £5470
50 2 THIR 8f Soft 47 931
5 14 HAMI 8f Firm 51 1243
28 8 PONT 10f Good 51 1496
51 2 THIR 8f Gd/Fm 49 2062
41 9 DONC 8f Gd/Fm 49 2349
37 10 HAMI 9f Gd/Fm 49 2799
35 7 HAYD 8f Good 47 3288
24 14 THIR 8f Gd/Fm 47 3344
48 2 THIR 8f Gd/Sft 47 3777
43 7 REDC 8f Gd/Sft 53 4217
22 10 LEIC 8f Stt/Hvy 47 4310
2 6 NEWC 7f Heavy 47 4426

FALSE PROMISE 2 b c £0
59 12 LEIC 7f Firm 3840
0 23 NEWM 8f Good 4349
0 12 NOTT 8f Heavy 4504

FAME AT LAST 3 b f £2200
100 4 CHES 11f Gd/Fm 1223
90 7 HAYD 12f Gd/Fm 2501
91 7 NEWM 10f Good 4337

FAMOUS 7 b g £670
42a 4 LING 10f Aw 44 22
32a 5 LING 10f Aw 53 90
35a 7 LING 10f Aw 42 203
43a 2 LING 10f Aw 42 224
11a 10 WOLV 12f Aw 42 261
31a 9 LING 12f Aw 42 290
40 7 WIND 12f Gd/Fm 48 748
34 5 SAND 8f Heavy 53 1058
0 14 WIND 10f Gd/Sft 42 1100 bl
0 15 SALI 12f Good 48 1350
14 8 SALI 12f Gd/Fm ,39 1888
28 11 SAND 10f Gd/Fm 46 2527
21 13 BRIG 10f Gd/Fm 35 2727 bl
0 17 WIND 12f Gd/Fm 37 3049 bl
67 8 KEMP 12f Soft 4039 bl
61 7 GOOD 12f Soft 4061 bl
26 6 SALI 10f Gd/Sft 36 4168 bl

FAN TC GEM 4 b f £0
15a 9 WOLV 6f Aw 63
32a 6 SOUT 7f Aw 247
0a 12 SOUT 8f Aw 47 297
29a 7 SOUT 7f Aw 341
29a 7 SOUT 7f Aw 367

FANAAR 3 ch c £15885
102 1 NEWM 8f Gd/Sft 972*
109 8 ASCO 8f Good 2066
111 1 SAND 8f Good 2476*
100 3 YORK 9f Gd/Fm 3726

FANCY A FORTUNE 6 b g £0
37a 5 SOUT 7f Aw 48 299 bl
35a 7 SOUT 8f Aw 48 340 bl
31a 7 WOLV 8f Aw 44 432 bl

FANDANGO DREAM 4 ch c £3284
26 9 SOUT 11f Gd/Sft 43 855
34 4 BRIG 12f Firm 38 1209
27 5 LEIC 12f Soft 34 1551
22 7 NEWM 12f Firm 31 1852
28 4 NOTT 14f Good 28 2008
36 4 CHEP 18f Gd/Fm 38 2490 vis

39 1 CHEP 12f Gd/Fm 36 2656*
38 3 EPSO 12f Good 37 2793
29 5 CHEP 12f Gd/Fm 38 2971
35 5 FOLK 16f Gd/Fm 38 3448
33 8 LING 16f Firm 37 3755

FANFARE 3 b f £19408
57 7 WIND 8f Heavy 934
70 1 WIND 12f Firm 63 1292*
77 1 SAND 10f Soft 72 1585*
66 8 SAND 11f Good 75 1967
83 2 WIND 12f Gd/Fm 75 2210
91 4 NEWM 15f Gd/Fm 2594
84 1 GOOD 14f Firm 81 3153*
84 6 YORK 14f Soft 85 3599
65 10 NEWM 14f Gd/Fm 83 4213

FANNY PARNELL 4 b f £651
0a 14 SOUT 8f Aw 50
26a 8 SOUT 7f Aw 367
54a 2 SOUT 7f Aw 427
22a 8 SOUT 6f Aw 53 697

FANTAIL 6 b g £0
0 17 WIND 10f Good 83 1729
73 8 SAND 11f Good 78 2530
68 8 NEWM 12f Gd/Fm 75 3122
60 6 PONT 12f Good 75 3224
56 6 SAND 10f Good 70 3471 vis

FANTASIA GIRL 3 b f £18665
101 2 YORK 12f Firm 3595
100 8 LEOP 12f Good 3924 BL
100 2 CURR 10f Gd/Sft 4241 bl

FANTASTIC FANTASY 3 b f £13344
73 1 SOUT 10f Good 67 807*
76 1 YARM 11f Good 71 1770*
72 6 RIPO 12f Gd/Fm 75 2110
77 2 REDC 10f Gd/Fm 75 2863
80 1 NOTT 14f Good 76 3522*
60 11 SAND 14f Gd/Fm 80 3948

FANTASTIC LIGHT 4 b c £1164573
124 1 NAD 12f Good 767*
120 2 EPSO 12f Gd/Sft 1827
116 5 SAND 10f Gd/Fm 2497
124 2 ASCO 12f Gd/Fm 2998
124 1 BELM 11f Fast 3932*
115 4 BELM 12f Gd/Fm 4316

FANTASY ADVENTURER 3 b g £695
0 16 NOTT 6f Good 69 785
0 13 SOUT 7f Gd/Sft 65 857
0 18 CARL 8f Firm 60 1255
53 4 REDC 6f Good 53 1891
40 8 CARL 5f Firm 53 2280
52 4 RIPO 6f Soft 53 2541
30 9 HAMI 6f Gd/Fm 52 2779
35 10 THIR 6f Gd/Fm 52 3124
32 9 MUSS 7f Gd/Fm 50 3593
0 18 YARM 8f Gd/Fm 47 3970
0 15 NEWC 6f Heavy 42 4425

FANTASY BELIEVER 2 b g £7864
82 3 HAYD 5f Heavy 989
73 2 REDC 5f Firm 1294
76 4 HAYD 5f Gd/Sft 1488
84 2 HAMI 5f Gd/Fm 1906
85 2 WIND 5f Gd/Fm 2055
79 1 MUSS 5f Gd/Sft 2532*
79 6 KEMP 5f Firm 86 2868
77 9 BEVE 5f Gd/Fm 81 3673
78 2 HAMI 5f Soft 3801
0 16 NEWM 6f Gd/Fm 77 4214

FANTASY HILL 4 b c £35051
78 5 NEWB 16f Soft 91 917
93 3 CHES 19f Gd/Fm 90 1222
94 4 NEWC 16f Firm 93 2336
91 8 YORK 14f Good 96 2695

CHES (continued)

99	1	**CHES** 19f Firm	95	3171*	BL
95	4	ASCO 16f Gd/Fm	95	3302	bl

FANTASY PARK 3 b c £3945

89	1	**BATH** 10f Good		1093*

FANTASY RIDGE 2 ch f £3815

91	1	**SALI** 7f Gd/Fm		3292*
94	5	GOOD 7f Good		3659
93	10	NEWM 7f Good		4356

FANTAZIA 4 b f £6529

94	2	YORK 10f Firm		1325
98	5	NEWM 12f Gd/Fm		2857
75	23	NEWM 9f Gd/Fm	95	4212

FAR AHEAD 8 b g £0

34	11	DONC 12f Good	82	1518
71	7	DONC 12f Gd/Fm	78	1839
0	13	YORK 12f Firm	74	2002

FAR CRY 5 b g £63800

120	2	ASCO 20f Good		2114
118	2	GOOD 16f Good		3106

FAR SOUTH TRADER 2 gr c £222

0	15	LING 6f Soft		4189
73	4	BRIG 8f Soft		4418

FARAUDE 2 b f £469

50	7	LING 6f Soft		4190
50	4	NEWM 7f Good		4336
0	11	NOTT 8f Heavy		4507

FARAWAY JOHN 2 b c £0

0	19	LING 6f Good		4097

FARAWAY LOOK 3 br c £6666

67	4	WIND 8f Good		3350
59	2	WARW 7f Good		3696
65	7	NOTT 8f Soft		3977
71a	1	**WOLV** 9f Aw	64	4251*
83a	1	**WOLV** 9f Aw	71	4382*

FARAWAY MOON 4 gr f £728

38a	8	LING 6f Aw		25
51a	2	LING 8f Aw		109

FARCE 2 b f £0

47	11	NOTT 8f Heavy		4504

FAREHAM 2 b f £0

42	7	LING 6f Firm		3492
31	8	REDC 7f Gd/Fm		3635
0	16	LING 6f Good		4096	BL

FARFALA 4 gr f £16521

90	5	YORK 10f Firm		1325
100	2	NEWB 12f Gd/Fm		3177
102	3	DEAU 10f Gd/Fm		3547
95	7	YORK 12f Firm		3595
75	14	YARM 10f Firm		3918

FARHA 2 b f £5819

75	3	YARM 10f Firm		2901
77	2	ASCO 6f Gd/Fm		3342
79	1	**NOTT** 6f Soft		3973*

FARMOST 7 ch g £8697

89a	1	**LING** 10f Aw	85	90*

FARRFESHEENA 3 ch f £2605

105	2	ASCO 8f Gd/Fm		3019	t
76	4	DONC 10f Heavy		4571	t

FARRIERS GAMBLE 4 ch f £0

42	5	FOLK 7f Soft		961
55	8	SALI 6f Gd/Fm		2977
42	12	SALI 5f Firm	55	3747
23	5	YARM 6f Firm		3919
0	16	YARM 6f Gd/Fm	50	3964	BL

FAS 4 ch g £509

35a	6	SOUT 7f Aw		367	bl
15a	7	SOUT 8f Aw	34	497	bl
23a	5	SOUT 8f Aw	32	584	bl
0	16	MUSS 9f Gd/Sft	29	795	bl
14	4	REDC 8f Gd/Fm		2147	VIS
0	15	CARL 7f Firm	27	2282	vis

45	7	NOTT 8f Gd/Fm		2682	vis
33	7	REDC 9f Gd/Fm		2865	vis
0	18	REDC 7f Gd/Fm		2994	vis
45	8	CARL 8f Gd/Fm		3081
1	7	BEVE 12f Good		3399
19	4	THIR 8f Gd/Fm		3616	vis

FASHION 3 b f £6720

74	1	**LING** 10f Firm		3281*
75	1	**BEVE** 10f Good	71	3396*

FAST BUCK 2 b g £0

48	9	REDC 5f Firm		1294
38	10	SOUT 6f Soft		1602
40	11	DONC 6f Gd/Fm		1844	BL
50	5	NEWC 6f Gd/Fm		2312
33	13	NEWM 7f Gd/Fm		2599
25	9	CATT 7f Gd/Fm		2927

FAST FOIL 2 b f £2670

78	3	SAND 5f Soft		1568
78	2	DONC 6f Gd/Fm		1844
55	6	BATH 6f Firm		2328
76	3	ASCO 6f Good	76	2678
59	9	NEWB 7f Gd/Fm	77	3175

FAST FORTUNE 2 ch f £0

56	7	LING 5f Soft		4187
25a	8	WOLV 6f Aw		4381

FAST FORWARD FRED 9 gr g £1356

46	8	CHEP 18f Gd/Sft	52	1800
0	11	WARW 16f Gd/Fm	52	2037
52	3	FOLK 15f Gd/Fm	52	3040
47	5	SAND 16f Good	52	3434
52	2	BATH 17f Firm	52	3625
49	4	LING 16f Firm	50	3755

FAST TRACK 3 b c £2948

100	3	YORK 10f Firm		1340
97	6	NEWM 10f Firm		1854

FASTBEAT RACING 3 b f £0

0	9	NOTT 10f Gd/Fm		3006
0	13	LEIC 7f Gd/Fm		3332

FASTESTBARBERALIVE 5 b g £0

0a	9	LING 8f Aw		264

FASTINA 2 b f £1666

66	4	LEIC 6f Firm		2029
74	3	GOOD 7f Good		2306
92	7	NEWM 7f Gd/Fm		3316
74	3	REDC 7f Gd/Fm		3635
70	4	CHEP 8f Good		3867
66	5	PONT 8f Soft	73	4084

FASTRACK TIME 3 ch g £0

0	18	CHEP 6f Good	68	1971
0	14	LEIC 6f Gd/Fm	63	2777
36a	10	WOLV 5f Aw	57	3271
39	9	THIR 5f Gd/Fm	50	3619
30	13	THIR 5f Gd/Sft	45	3781	VIS
0	14	YARM 5f Gd/Fm	42	3964

FASTWAN 4 ch g £0

0	7	NEWC 12f Good		2523
0	12	HAYD 7f Gd/Fm		2704
0	27	REDC 8f Gd/Fm	28	2861
0	19	REDC 7f Gd/Fm		2994
20	5	AYR 7f Gd/Fm	25	3138
0	9	CARL 8f Firm		3192
14	10	HAMI 9f Gd/Sft		3375
0	11	HAMI 9f Gd/Sft		3823
0	12	AYR 9f Soft		3988
0	11	MUSS 12f Gd/Sft		4133	VIS
9	8	MUSS 9f Soft	29	4523	vis

FATEHALKHAIR 8 ch g £8645

49a	4	SOUT 12f Aw	63	456
52	8	CATT 14f Gd/Fm	63	779
63	2	DONC 12f Gd/Fm	60	1839
64	3	YORK 12f Firm	62	2002
66	1	**THIR** 12f Gd/Fm	62	2061*

63	5	CARL 12f Firm	67	2279
62	10	YORK 12f Good	66	3541
64	4	THIR 12f Gd/Sft	64	3778

FATH 3 b c £8695

96	16	NEWM 8f Gd/Fm		1171
105	6	ASCO 7f Good		2087
111	1	**DONC** 6f Gd/Fm		3158*	t
108	4	NEWM 6f Good		3610	t

FATHER JUNINHO 3 b c £15229

89	7	SAND 8f Heavy	92	1055
86	6	SALI 10f Firm	90	1177
90	5	GOOD 9f Gd/Sft	88	1452
96	2	EPSO 10f Gd/Sft	88	1831
93	3	YORK 10f Firm	90	2004
96	3	NEWM 10f Gd/Fm	90	2596
90	5	GOOD 10f Gd/Fm	93	3131
92	4	NEWB 11f Firm	92	3451
86	11	YORK 12f Good	92	3541	VIS
88	4	DONC 12f Firm	89	3896
85	5	NEWB 13f Firm	89	3994

FATHER SEAMUS 2 b c £313

31	10	LING 6f Good		1673
0	11	GOOD 6f Good		2357
57	11	NEWB 7f Gd/Fm		2708
68	7	KEMP 7f Firm		2867
48	3	BRIG 7f Gd/Fm		3240
64	8	GOOD 7f Soft		4063
67	7	SAND 8f Soft		4203
51	10	NEWB 8f Gd/Sft		4457

FATHER TED 3 b c £0

0	14	SALI 6f Firm		1181
0	16	LING 7f Gd/Sft		1263
0	12	SALI 7f Gd/Fm		1886
0	12	SALI 8f Gd/Fm	47	2980
0	17	BRIG 12f Gd/Fm	40	3242

FATHER THAMES 2 b c £3689

78	3	LING 6f Soft		4189
89	1	**BRIG** 7f Soft		4415*

FATHERS FOOTSTEPS 2 ch c £0

0a	13	SOUT 5f Aw		1418
6	9	PONT 5f Soft		1704
0	17	BEVE 6f Good		2730
0	11	PONT 6f Gd/Fm		3223
42	8	REDC 5f Gd/Sft		4496

FAUTE DE MIEUX 5 ch g £7130

54a	8	LING 5f Aw	68	205
48a	6	SOUT 5f Aw	64	673	BL
0	11	LING 7f Gd/Sft		838
80	1	**FOLK** 5f Soft		960*
0	14	WARW 5f Heavy	71	1005
74	3	WIND 5f Gd/Fm		1881
74	3	LING 5f Firm	74	2326
79	2	SAND 5f Gd/Fm	74	2473
58	14	ASCO 5f Good	78	2676

FAVORISIO 3 br g £5577

82a	1	**WOLV** 9f Aw		610*
86a	1	**WOLV** 9f Aw	73	709*
45	6	HAYD 11f Heavy	83	990
50	9	PONT 8f Good	82	1495
0	22	REDC 8f Gd/Sft	77	4217
0	20	YORK 9f Heavy	69	4300

FAY 3 ch f £0

67	6	WARW 11f Soft		814
27	5	FOLK 12f Soft		964
67	6	SALI 10f Good		1343

FAY KING 3 ch g £0

0	11	GOOD 10f Soft		4081
0a	12	WOLV 7f Aw		4384

FAYRWAY RHYTHM 3 b c £5437

77	4	LEIC 10f Gd/Sft		833
79	4	WARW 12f Soft	79	1064
80	5	WIND 12f Gd/Sft	80	1425

82	1	**CARL**	9f Firm		2019*	
74	8	SAND	10f Gd/Fm	80	2499	
79a	3	WOLV	8f Aw	79	3274	

FAYZ SLIPPER 2 b f £672
57	7	PONT	5f Heavy		938
45	8	REDC	5f Gd/Sft		1131
42	10	THIR	5f Good		1381
50	4	HAYD	5f Soft		1492
54	2	BEVE	5f Firm		1918
55	4	CATT	5f Gd/Fm		2435
47	5	CHES	5f Good	56	2665
45	5	NEWC	5f Gd/Sft		2983
49	5	HAMI	5f Gd/Sft		3376

FAZENDA 2 b f £0
48a	7	WOLV	6f Aw		3496

FAZZANI 2 b f £12742
67	9	WIND	5f Gd/Sft		1424
78	4	SAND	5f Soft		1568
71	4	SALI	6f Gd/Fm		1882
73	4	LING	7f Gd/Fm		2182
82	3	SALI	7f Gd/Fm		2267
55	7	BRIG	7f Firm	75	2894
63	1	**THIR**	7f Gd/Fm		3128*
68	2	SALI	7f Gd/Fm		3388
69	1	**NEWC**	8f Soft		3706*
75	2	AYR	8f Soft	68	3990
76	2	YORK	7f Soft	73	4279
0	12	DONC	7f Soft	75	4460

FEARBY CROSS 4 b c £13112
76	1	**SAND**	5f Gd/Fm	70	763*
75	3	DONC	6f Gd/Sft	74	1074
73	4	LING	5f Good		1398
81	1	**NEWB**	6f Gd/Sft	75	1591*
69	11	NEWM	5f Good	80	2569
0	22	YORK	6f Good	80	3543
77	7	GOOD	6f Good	79	3904
77	8	AYR	5f Gd/Sft	80	4010
0	15	YORK	6f Heavy	78	4301

FEARSOME FACTOR 5 b g £2473
21a	8	WOLV	9f Aw	80	172	
0a	7	WOLV	12f Aw		307	
53a	4	WOLV	9f Aw		360	
32a	10	WOLV	9f Aw		393	bl
52a	2	SOUT	16f Aw	52	542	
57a	1	**WOLV**	16f Aw	52	577*	

FEAST OF ROMANCE 3 b c £10439
77a	1	SOUT	6f Aw		46*	
70a	3	SOUT	6f Aw	72	202	
80a	1	**WOLV**	6f Aw	72	275*	
60a	6	SOUT	7f Aw	79	416	
74a	5	WOLV	7f Aw	79	534	
68	6	CHES	6f Gd/Fm	73	1220	
0	18	NEWB	6f Gd/Fm	71	1406	
56	6	BRIG	6f Good		1651	
0	14	REDC	6f Good	65	1891	
60	3	LING	6f Gd/Fm	61	2216	BL
41	12	SAND	5f Gd/Fm	61	2478	bl
56	9	WIND	6f Gd/Fm	60	2885	bl
58	4	CARL	6f Firm	58	3194	
43	9	NEWM	7f Good		3612	
54	9	CHES	6f Soft		4069	

FEATHER N LACE 4 b f £2812
64	2	SALI	7f Good	62	1348
65a	2	LING	8f Aw	64	1915
61	4	NEWM	8f Firm	64	2342
42	10	YARM	8f Aw	64	2767

FEATHERSTONE LANE 9 b g £7310
47a	4	WOLV	6f Aw		82
53a	5	WOLV	6f Aw		132
34a	8	WOLV	6f Aw	48	232
38a	4	WOLV	5f Aw	44	291
44a	4	WOLV	6f Aw		406
53a	2	WOLV	6f Aw		436
43a	5	LING	6f Aw	45	634
53a	2	LING	6f Aw		653
48a	2	WOLV	7f Aw	44	754
51a	2	WOLV	6f Aw	47	923
44a	3	WOLV	6f Aw		1139
55a	1	**WOLV**	7f Good	50	1235*
47a	6	SOUT	7f Aw	54	1801
47a	3	SOUT	7f Aw	54	1979
56a	3	SOUT	6f Aw		2118
38a	6	SOUT	6f Aw	53	2297
56a	3	SOUT	6f Aw		2819
62a	4	WOLV	6f Aw		3275
50a	3	WOLV	6f Aw		3770
50a	5	SOUT	6f Aw	53	4155
36a	11	SOUT	8f Aw	52	4365
52a	2	WOLV	6f Aw	52	4444
32a	9	WOLV	6f Aw	54	4553

FEATHERTIME 4 b f £1299
46	5	HAYD	7f Gd/Sft	54	811
51	3	THIR	8f Soft	54	931
55	3	DONC	10f Gd/Sft	54	1050

FEDINA 2 br f f £10020
92	2	SAN	8f Gd/Sft		4145

FEE MAIL 4 b f £5440
66	3	WIND	12f Gd/Fm	65	748
64	3	BATH	12f Good	65	1091
70	1	**CARL**	12f Firm		1253*
71	2	BATH	13f Gd/Fm	68	1440
0	13	NEWB	13f Gd/Sft	68	1594

FEEL NO FEAR 7 b m £503
55a	2	LING	10f Aw		3
37a	6	LING	8f Aw		93
36	6	BRIG	8f Firm	48	2043

FEEL THE STEEL 3 b f £0
0	12	NEWM	8f Gd/Fm		3456
0	10	YARM	10f Gd/Fm		3935

FEMME FATALE 3 b f £6502
99	4	NEWM	6f Gd/Fm		3120
94	1	**YARM**	6f Firm		3937*
0	15	NEWM	5f Good		4182

FENCERS QUEST 7 ch g £0
36a	10	WOLV	7f Aw		65

FENWICKS PRIDE 2 b g £11496
57	5	DONC	5f Good		730	
76	3	MUSS	5f Gd/Sft		898	
72	3	REDC	5f Gd/Sft		1131	
78	2	DONC	5f Gd/Fm	75	2575	
72	6	THIR	5f Gd/Fm	81	3145	
73	6	HAYD	5f Gd/Sft	77	3475	
76	1	**RIPO**	5f Gd/Fm		3710*	
76	8	DONC	6f Firm		3888	
64	5	HAYD	6f Soft	74	4090	
83	1	**YORK**	6f Soft	75	4286*	VIS

FERNDOWN 2 b f £276
41	4	THIR	6f Gd/Fm		2968
44	6	REDC	7f Firm		3308
0	14	RIPO	6f Gd/Fm		3466
49	10	CARL	5f Firm		3571

FERNS MEMORY 5 ch m £0
0a	12	LING	13f Aw	22	460	
28a	7	LING	7f Aw		570	BL

FERNY FACTORS 4 ch c £0
0a	8	SOUT	12f Aw	49	683
0	22	DONC	12f Gd/Fm	55	699
0	17	WARW	11f Heavy	55	890
0	15	NOTT	10f Gd/Fm	52	1272
23	10	PONT	10f Soft		1699
0	19	RIPO	10f Soft		2538

FERNY HILL 6 b g £0
74a	7	SOUT	12f Aw	90	200

FERZAO 3 b c £8287
93	3	WIND	8f Good		851	
92	1	**WIND**	10f Gd/Fm		1198*	
94	5	GOOD	10f Gd/Sft		1451	
70	17	SAND	10f Good	95	2475	
69	13	NEWM	8f Gd/Fm	93	2858	
89	4	NEWM	8f Good		4199	t
76	14	NEWM	8f Good	88	4348	t

FESTINO 2 b f £0
37a	10	SOUT	5f Aw		865
52	4	NOTT	5f Gd/Sft		1083

FESTIVE AFFAIR 2 b c £0
50	8	BATH	5f Gd/Fm		3513
0	20	REDC	6f Gd/Sft		4219

FFIFFIFFER 2 b c £0
69	4	NEWC	8f Firm		3601
51	9	THIR	7f Gd/Sft		3776

FFYNNON GOLD 3 b f £231
65	12	GOOD	8f Gd/Sft		1811
3	11	SALI	8f Firm		2024
0	11	WIND	8f Soft		2548
14	9	BRIG	10f Gd/Fm	58	3263
43	12	WARW	8f Gd/Fm		3914
60	6	LING	8f Soft		4273
41	10	WIND	6f Gd/Sft	50	4293
53a	4	SOUT	6f Aw		4364
41	4	WIND	6f Heavy		4526

FIAMMA ROYALE 2 b f £7814
76	4	WARW	5f Soft		812
80	2	WIND	5f Gd/Fm		1197
77	2	WARW	5f Heavy		1522
79	5	EPSO	6f Good		1846
78	2	WARW	5f Firm		2034
80	4	KEMP	5f Firm	83	2868
72	2	BATH	6f Firm		3205
0	12	CURR	6f Yldg		3720
70	1	**SAND**	5f Gd/Fm		3942*

FIDDLERS MOLL 2 b f £233
76	4	KEMP	7f Soft		4035
68	13	NEWM	8f Good		4349

FIDDLERS ROCK 5 b g £0
0	14	PONT	5f Soft	70	4377

FIELD MASTER 3 ch c £4638
69a	2	CAGN	10f Aw		606
75a	1	**LING**	10f Aw		771*
0	8	KEMP	9f Soft	75	999
52	7	GOOD	10f Gd/Fm	72	1958
56	9	BATH	8f Firm	68	2330
61	5	EPSO	12f Gd/Sft	68	2429
42	10	WIND	10f Soft	65	2544
55	9	EPSO	10f Good	63	2790
0	12	KEMP	12f Firm	62	2872
23	7	SAND	8f Good	54	3227

FIELD OF HOPE 5 ch m £119472
116	2	SHA	8f Gd/Fm		184

FIELD OF VISION 10 b g £9116
37	9	DONC	12f Gd/Fm	53	699	
53	2	MUSS	14f Gd/Sft	51	903	
47	4	MUSS	12f Gd/Fm	53	1147	
54	3	HAMI	12f Firm	53	1241	bl
56	2	CATT	14f Good		1660	
54	1	**CARL**	12f Gd/Sft		1720*	
50	4	HAMI	13f Firm	50	2098	
38	5	BEVE	12f Firm		2219	
47	2	HAMI	11f Gd/Fm		2800	
45	2	CATT	12f Firm		3202	
41	2	CARL	12f Firm		3570	
41	4	HAMI	11f Soft		3804	
42	1	**BEVE**	12f Sft/Hv		4041*	
40	5	REDC	11f Soft		4497	

FIELDGATE FLYER 5 b m £0
0a	8	WOLV	15f Aw		174

FIENNES 2 b c £594

```
73   5  WIND 5f Heavy        932
66   7  WIND 5f Good        1727
45a  6  WOLV 6f Aw          2077
72   3  BEVE 5f Gd/Fm       2480 t
47   6  YORK 5f Good     69 2698 t
47  10  NEWM 8f Good     69 3609
```

FIERY WATERS 4 b g £0
```
47  11  WIND 12f Good    58 1730
42   7  WARW 15f Good    55 2461
44   6  NEWM 12f Gd/Fm   49 3122
0   19  HAYD 12f Good    49 3284
0   14  BEVE 10f Sft/Hv  42 4046
29   8  SALI 10f Gd/Sft  42 4169 BL
```

FIFE AND DRUM 3 b c £5852
```
47  14  RIPO 10f Soft    62  827
47   9  WIND 12f Gd/Sft     1096
33   9  BEVE 12f Good    55 1446
58   1  NOTT 10f Good    50 2007* BL
53   7  FOLK 12f Gd/Fm   58 2295 bl
45   5  SAND 10f Soft    57 4208
63a  1  LING 12f Aw      57 4486*
```

FIFTEEN REDS 5 b g £860
```
45a  2  SOUT 16f Aw      43  253 vis
18a  6  WOLV 16f Aw      44  348 vis
19  10  CARL 17f Firm    44 3575
```

FIFTH EDITION 4 b f £0
```
39  12  KEMP 8f Gd/Fm    59 2752
38  10  YARM 10f Good    57 3031
0   14  WIND 10f Gd/Sft  51 4291
0a  14  LING 12f Aw      46 4486
```

FIGURA 2 b f £2893
```
60   6  FOLK 7f Gd/Fm       2290
82   1  FOLK 7f Good        2619*
88   6  SAND 7f Gd/Fm       2935
80   4  ASCO 7f Gd/Fm       3015
76  10  NEWM 7f Gd/Fm       4210
```

FILIAL 7 b g £0
```
19a  9  SOUT 11f Aw      57  742
```

FILLE DE BUCHERON 2 b f £935
```
88   2  LING 7f Firm        3833
```

FILLE DE DAUPHIN 2 b f £0
```
30  10  REDC 5f Gd/Fm       3632
39   8  BEVE 7f Good        3949
0   12  YORK 6f Soft        4283
0a  14  SOUT 7f Aw          4369
```

FILM SCRIPT 3 b f £43541
```
76   6  KEMP 11f Soft       1017
94   1  SALI 12f Firm       1179*
98   1  LING 11f Gd/Sft     1282*
102  3  ASCO 12f Good    96 2116
100  6  HAYD 12f Gd/Fm      2501
102  1  CHEP 10f Gd/Fm      2975*
101  3  NEWB 12f Gd/Fm      3177
102  5  DONC 15f Gd/Fm      3863
97   4  ASCO 12f Gd/Fm      4130 VIS
```

FINAL DIVIDEND 4 b c £0
```
0a  13  SOUT 8f Aw       74   49
74   4  DONC 10f Gd/Fm   74  705
69   5  LING 7f Good     74 1672
0   13  LING 8f Firm     73 3831
55  11  KEMP 8f Soft     70 4038
50  12  YARM 10f Soft    67 4392
```

FINAL KISS 3 b c £0
```
0   13  FOLK 7f Soft         961
0    F  SALI 7f Gd/Fm    52 1889 t
```

FINAL LAP 4 b c £5021
```
63a  5  LING 10f Aw         56
0   18  WIND 10f Good    74 1729
53  14  NEWM 8f Good     70 2564
59   9  REDC 10f Firm    67 3310
53   9  KEMP 12f Gd/Fm   63 3794
47   9  CATT 12f Soft    59 4003
```

```
57   1  NEWM 12f Good       4178*
0   10  YARM 14f Heavy   54 4476
```

FINAL PURSUIT 2 b f £3562
```
44   7  SALI 5f Firm        1176
94   1  BATH 6f Gd/Sft      1667*
58  19  ASCO 5f Good        2088
0   21  DONC 6f Gd/Fm       3862
87  12  NEWM 6f Good        4159
```

FINAL SETTLEMENT 5 b g £15692
```
65   1  KEMP 14f Good    61  726*
66   6  KEMP 16f Soft    65  997
64   5  NEWB 12f Good    65 1373
67   3  KEMP 12f Gd/Fm   65 1927
64   4  KEMP 12f Firm    65 2263
68   1  NEWM 15f Gd/Fm   65 2856*
62   4  NEWM 15f Good    68 3611
40   8  CHES 16f Soft    67 4071
```

FINCH 3 b f £0
```
13a  9  LING 8f Aw       49  419
3a   8  SOUT 11f Aw      44  536
```

FIND THE KING 2 b c £513
```
62   4  YORK 8f Heavy       4297
59  11  DONC 7f Heavy       4566
```

FINE FEATHER 2 b f £595
```
68   3  GOWR 7f Gd/Sft      1896
```

FINE MELODY 3 b f £6126
```
51a  3  WOLV 6f Aw           434
65a  1  LING 7f Aw           570*
73a  1  LING 7f Aw       65  773*
76   4  CHEP 5f Gd/Sft   80 1795
57  10  RIPO 6f Gd/Fm    79 2101
42  11  HAYD 6f Gd/Fm    77 2504
0   20  YORK 6f Soft        4287
```

FINERY 3 ch g £5822
```
55a  6  WOLV 7f Aw           362
68a  4  WOLV 8f Aw           409
66a  2  LING 10f Aw          545
66a  4  LING 10f Aw          629
54  10  NOTT 14f Gd/Fm   65 1270
64a  1  SOUT 11f Aw         1502*
46  10  YARM 11f Good    60 1770
26a  9  SOUT 11f Aw         2119
63   2  NEWM 10f Gd/Fm      2284 VIS
53   3  MUSS 9f Gd/Sft   60 2534 vis
26  12  BEVE 8f Firm     60 2735 vis
28  12  NEWM 10f Good       3021 vis
53   3  NEWM 8f Gd/Fm       3456
53   4  NEWM 7f Good        3612
38   9  YARM 7f Firm     52 3939
0   21  NEWM 7f Good        4018 vis
```

FINISHED ARTICLE 3 b c £6185
```
72   4  KEMP 7f Soft        1012
84   6  NEWB 10f Gd/Fm      1404
80   3  RIPO 10f Good       1599
69   5  SALI 10f Gd/Fm      1885
78   2  WIND 8f Good        3190
78   1  EPSO 9f Gd/Fm       3413*
51  13  KEMP 8f Gd/Fm    79 3793
0   21  NEWM 8f Good     78 4340
```

FINLAYS FOLLY 3 b g £0
```
0   13  SALI 7f Gd/Fm       3423
0   15  LEIC 10f Gd/Fm      3838
```

FINMAR 2 b c £550
```
49   5  AYR 6f Good         3137
67   9  THIR 6f Gd/Fm       3614
73   9  DONC 6f Good        3888
66   4  AYR 7f Soft         3991
```

FINN MCCOOL 2 b g £2498
```
46   6  THIR 7f Good        3615
59a  1  WOLV 7f Aw          4025*
49   9  NEWM 7f Good        4336
59a  2  WOLV 8f Aw       59 4552
```

FIONN DE COOL 9 b g £428
```
0   15  CHEP 7f Gd/Fm    49 1799
34   9  SALI 8f Gd/Sft   48 2467
44   5  BATH 8f Firm     45 2942
42   3  SAND 8f Good     45 3227
20  14  SALI 8f Firm     45 3753
```

FIORA 3 b f £0
```
0   10  NEWM 7f Gd/Fm       1155
37  11  YARM 7f Soft        4388
```

FIORI 4 b c £13841
```
58a  6  SOUT 11f Aw      80  302
81a  2  WOLV 16f Aw      78  380
75   8  NEWC 10f Soft    84  757
57  12  BEVE 10f Heavy   83  975
80   6  YORK 12f Gd/Fm   80 1307
78   4  DONC 12f Good    78 1518
73   4  YORK 12f Firm    78 2002
82   1  AYR 15f Good     77 2164*
83   3  DONC 15f Gd/Fm   82 2319
83   2  NEWM 16f Gd/Fm   82 2600
83   3  NEWM 15f Gd/Fm   82 2856
0   12  DONC 15f Gd/Sft  82 4451
```

FIRE BELLE 2 ch f £0
```
14   8  KEMP 5f Gd/Fm       2082
11  13  CHEP 6f Gd/Fm       2488
38   5  GOOD 6f Good        3661
0   17  BATH 6f Soft        4431
```

FIRE DOME 8 ch g £56379
```
50a  8  WOLV 7f Aw           677
82   3  NEWC 5f Soft     83  758
67   3  DONC 6f Gd/Sft      1073
68   1  REDC 6f Firm        1298*
80   1  WIND 6f Gd/Sft      1423*
82   1  LING 6f Good     75 1676*
88   1  EPSO 6f Gd/Fm    80 1851*
69   9  YORK 6f Gd/Fm    84 1983
80   7  NEWB 6f Firm     91 2706
93   1  SALI 6f Gd/Sft   87 4165+
92   3  YORK 6f Heavy    89 4301
74  16  NEWM 5f Good     90 4339
```

FIRE PRINCESS 2 b f £0
```
49a  5  SOUT 5f Aw           801
30a  9  WOLV 6f Aw          4244
0   18  BATH 6f Soft        4431
```

FIRECREST 3 b f £51154
```
62   7  WIND 10f Good        850
75   1  LEIC 12f Gd/Sft  63 1571*
85   1  LEIC 12f Gd/Sft  69 1736*
90   1  NEWB 12f Gd/Fm   82 1948*
100  1  SALI 12f Gd/Fm   90 2231+
100  4  NEWM 12f Gd/Fm      2857
107  1  YORK 12f Firm       3595*
107  4  HANN 12f Good       3930
104  4  NEWM 12f Good       4343
```

FIREWIRE 2 b c £0
```
0   20  NEWM 8f Good        4349
0   18  LING 7f Soft        4483
```

FIREWORK 2 b c £5012
```
86   2  NEWM 5f Gd/Fm       1169
86   2  YORK 6f Firm        1328
72   3  YORK 6f Soft        4283
65a  9  LING 6f Aw          4332
```

FIRST BACK 3 b c £4766
```
64   4  NEWC 10f Gd/Sft     1480
0   15  BEVE 12f Gd/Sft  57 1758
49   7  CATT 12f Gd/Fm   56 2746
53   3  AYR 11f Gd/Fm    52 3140
0    9  HAYD 16f Gd/Sft  50 3476
57   1  BEVE 10f Gd/Fm      3677*
```

FIRST BALLOT 4 b g £2777
```
65  14  CHES 19f Gd/Fm   90 1222
86  10  ASCO 12f Good    90 2069
```

81 12 NEWC 16f Firm 90 2336
86 3 KEMP 12f Gd/Fm 85 3798
83 6 GOOD 16f Good 84 3905
83 3 NEWB 16f Gd/Sft 83 4458

FIRST CUT 4 b f £0
41a 8 LING 10f Aw 56

FIRST DEGREE 2 br f £0
53 10 WIND 6f Gd/Fm 2209
30 12 WIND 5f Good 2711
53 9 LING 5f Soft 4187
55 5 AYR 8f Heavy 57 4323

FIRST DRAW 3 b f £1110
48 13 NEWB 7f Gd/Fm 68 1405
68 2 YARM 6f Gd/Fm 66 3386
52 13 GOOD 5f Good 68 3908 t
65 9 NEWM 5f Good 68 4185

FIRST FANTASY 4 b f £22187
0 14 EPSO 10f Heavy 83 1031
86 5 NEWM 10f Gd/Fm 86 1170
84 1 WARW 11f Gd/Fm 1709*
74 8 SAND 10f Good 86 1965
99 5 NEWC 10f Firm 2339
68 13 YORK 10f Good 86 2696
96 1 SALI 10f Gd/Fm 3389*
97 7 YARM 10f Firm 3918
90 6 NEWM 9f Gd/Fm 93 4212
96 6 NEWM 10f Good 4337

FIRST GOLD 11 gr g £0
30a 9 WOLV 6f Aw 1137
3 10 CARL 7f Firm 27 2282

FIRST IMPRESSION 5 b g £2134
71 2 KEMP 12f Firm 69 2263
55 9 NEWB 13f Firm 70 2852
72 2 WIND 12f Good 70 3353
48 12 FOLK 12f Gd/Fm 70 3586
72 6 YARM 11f Heavy 4481

FIRST LEGACY 4 ch f £0
0 11 SOUT 10f Gd/Sft 40 859
0 14 RIPO 8f Gd/Fm 33 2099
26 7 CARL 6f Firm 2278
0 14 RIPO 10f Soft 2538
25 6 CARL 12f Firm 2826
35 10 BEVE 8f Good 3393

FIRST MAGNITUDE 4 ch c £63401
115 1 LONG 12f Heavy 1034*
115 1 SAIN 12f Soft 1461*
117 2 CHAN 12f Gd/Sft 1902

FIRST MAITE 7 b g £13784
91a 1 SOUT 7f Aw 84 35* bl
87a 5 SOUT 8f Aw 90 49 bl
87a 4 SOUT 8f Aw 90 129 bl
70a 12 SOUT 8f Aw 90 216 bl
90a 4 WOLV 6f Aw 89 435 bl
81a 10 WOLV 6f Aw 88 532 bl
78a 8 SOUT 7f Aw 88 539
87a 3 WOLV 5f Aw 88 579 bl
91a 2 WOLV 6f Aw 87 660 bl
88a 4 SOUT 7f Aw 87 687 bl
101 4 DONC 6f Good 734 bl
93 6 NEWB 5f Soft 102 914 bl
98 5 NEWM 6f Firm 100 1182 bl
94 10 HAYD 5f Gd/Sft 98 1533 bl
75 11 EPSO 6f Good 96 1851 bl
95 3 YORK 6f Gd/Fm 96 1983 vis
97 4 HAYD 7f Gd/Fm 95 2456 vis
85 11 ASCO 5f Gd/Fm 95 3016 vis
78 12 RIPO 8f Gd/Fm 95 3183 vis
80 7 LEIC 5f Firm 3841 bl
86 8 ASCO 5f Gd/Sft 90 4129 bl
71 17 NEWM 7f Good 90 4195 bl
0 20 YORK 6f Heavy 4301 tvi
42 10 NEWC 6f Heavy 83 4405

FIRST MANASSAS 3 b c £0
57 9 CHES 12f Gd/Fm 84 1225
69 8 NEWB 12f Gd/Fm 84 1400
76 6 EPSO 10f Gd/Sft 82 1831

FIRST MEETING 2 b f £1046
67 2 BEVE 7f Firm 2218
53 5 MUSS 7f Good 3100
49 9 NEWC 8f Soft 3706
59 4 CATT 6f Soft 4001

FIRST MUSICAL 4 ch f £0
76 8 RIPO 6f Soft 92 824
84 5 BEVE 5f Firm 1277
0 13 YORK 6f Firm 91 1337
0 25 AYR 6f Gd/Sft 86 4012
68 5 CATT 6f Soft 4257
0 18 NEWC 6f Heavy 86 4405

FIRST OFFICER 3 b c £8807
60 10 WIND 10f Good 850
85 2 DONC 10f Gd/Sft 1054
87 1 HAYD 11f Gd/Sft 1539*
59 7 HAYD 10f Gd/Sft 87 1832
83 6 YORK 12f Gd/Fm 87 2647
86 3 SAND 14f Good 86 3231
88 2 NEWB 16f Firm 86 3986
72 10 ASCO 16f Good 86 4115

FIRST SIGHT 2 ch g £872
60 2 CARL 5f Gd/Sft 1719
35 13 YORK 6f Firm 1981
18 9 NEWC 6f Gd/Fm 2983 VIS

FIRST STEPS 2 b f £0
63 6 NEWB 6f Sft/Hvy 4470
63 7 DONC 6f Heavy 4576

FIRST TRUTH 3 b c £4141
88 6 DONC 8f Good 735
91 4 HAYD 8f Gd/Sft 90 810
94 2 HAYD 11f Heavy 89 990
81 7 CHES 12f Gd/Fm 92 1225
65 4 CHES 13f Gd/Fm 95 3509
80 6 HAYD 11f Soft 92 3782
81 5 AYR 8f Gd/Sft 88 4013

FIRST VENTURE 3 b c £5312
78a 2 LING 7f Aw 74 617
74 2 DONC 7f Good 72 736
73 3 SOUT 7f Good 804 bl
53 12 WIND 6f Good 73 852 bl
0 17 CHES 8f Firm 72 3170
60 4 RIPO 5f Gd/Fm 3462 bl
59 4 BEVE 5f Gd/Fm 3651 VIS
59 2 THIR 6f Gd/Fm 3780 vis
0 20 GOOD 5f Soft 60 4065 vis
49 8 LING 6f Soft 54 4270 vis
72a 2 SOUT 6f Aw 4364 vis

FISHER ISLAND 3 b f £4152
42a 6 WOLV 9f Aw 54 709
50a 3 WOLV 8f Aw 920
49a 4 WOLV 9f Aw 51 1040
46a 4 WOLV 12f Aw 51 1142
47 9 LEIC 10f Gd/Sft 53 1735
51 4 REDC 8f Good 53 1892
42 7 REDC 9f Gd/Fm 51 2160
54 1 NOTT 10f Gd/Fm 49 2685*
43 8 BEVE 10f Good 53 3396
32 5 BEVE 10f Sft/Hv 53 4046
50a 3 WOLV 9f Aw 51 4382

FISHERMANS COVE 5 b g £0
0 11 MUSS 14f Gd/Sft 63 903

FIVE OF WANDS 3 b f £4085
69 2 DONC 12f Good 2353
71 3 SALI 14f Good 2691
0 21 EPSO 12f Good 70 3858
65 2 YORK 12f Soft 60 4280
22 14 MUSS 12f Soft 64 4560

FIZZLE 3 ch c £1596
53 5 AYR 7f Good 2140
56 7 NEWC 8f Firm 2337
72 2 NEWC 8f Good 2520

FLAG FEN 9 b g £651
0 15 NEWM 10f Gd/Fm 68 1150
62 6 NOTT 8f Good 1407
65 2 NOTT 10f Good 1875
50 7 WIND 10f Good 2372
48 6 NEWM 10f Gd/Fm 63 2805
36 8 NOTT 10f Gd/Fm 60 3007
0 18 EPSO 12f Good 57 3858

FLAK JACKET 5 b g £26236
0 22 THIR 5f Good 77 1162
0 17 THIR 6f Good 75 1383
0 18 HAYD 5f Gd/Sft 72 1533
16 10 CHES 7f Gd/Sft 68 1778
70 2 DONC 5f Gd/Fm 62 2753 t
74 1 PONT 6f Gd/Fm 2833* t
74 1 CATT 5f Gd/Fm 68 2929+ t
71 1 GOOD 6f Gd/Fm 62 3136* t
76 3 ASCO 5f Gd/Fm 73 3341 t
66 12 YORK 6f Good 75 3543 t
51 11 HAYD 5f Gd/Sft 75 3788
63 13 NEWM 5f Good 74 4015
0 17 HAYD 5f Gd/Sft 73 4107
0 17 YORK 5f Soft 71 4285

FLAMBE 2 b c £340
49a 4 WOLV 5f Good 1236
54 3 BEVE 5f Good 2880
55 7 THIR 5f Gd/Fm 3143

FLAME OF TRUTH 3 b f £4509
66 3 BATH 12f Gd/Fm 3517
77 2 BATH 12f Gd/Fm 3818
78 2 BATH 10f Soft 4141
76 2 BATH 12f Soft 4434

FLAME TOWER 5 ch g £0
0a 13 WOLV 8f Aw 58 38 t
14a 8 WOLV 12f Aw 54 81 t

FLAMEBIRD 3 b g £0
38 7 NEWB 7f Gd/Fm 1947
40 10 WARW 8f Good 2465
61 5 NOTT 8f Aw 3116
0 14 CHEP 7f Good 55 3873

FLAMENCO RED 3 b f £9746
80 4 LING 8f Firm 2762
87 2 CHEP 12f Gd/Fm 87 3254
45 1 THIR 8f Gd/Fm 3616*
76 8 NEWC 10f Good 88 3703
89 3 NEWM 8f Good 4199

FLAMME DE LA VIE 2 b g £178
76 4 BATH 8f Soft 4430
0 17 DONC 8f Heavy 4569

FLANDERS 4 b f £6264
100 1 BEVE 5f Firm 1277*
103 12 ASCO 5f Good 2065
72 7 CHES 5f Gd/Fm 2669
92 7 ASCO 6f Gd/Fm 101 3301

FLAPDOODLE 2 b f £0
40 10 WIND 5f Good 2711
0 14 BATH 6f Soft 4137

FLASH BACK 2 b c £0
58 9 NEWM 6f Gd/Fm 2854

FLASH OF LIGHT 2 b f £0
63 9 SALI 7f Gd/Fm 3292
66 8 SALI 7f Firm 3748

FLASHFEET 10 b g £0
0a 11 WOLV 8f Aw 136
26a 10 LING 7f Aw 398
20a 10 SOUT 8f Aw 452
7a 9 WOLV 9f Aw 517
3a 9 SOUT 11f Aw 29 561

0a	12	SOUT	8f Aw	36	647
22a	4	WOLV	9f Aw	28	749
21a	6	WOLV	9f Aw		922
22a	10	SOUT	7f Aw		1305
29a	7	SOUT	8f Aw		1505
40	4	LING	7f Good	45	1672
29	12	CHEP	7f Good	47	1969
41	6	GOOD	7f Good	48	2303
0	14	WARW	8f Good	36	2460
14	13	KEMP	8f Gd/Fm	42	3078
4	9	CHEP	8f Gd/Fm	34	3251
23	8	SALI	7f Gd/Fm	35	3294

FLASHTALKIN FLOOD 6 ch g £884

0	14	REDC	9f Gd/Sft	49	1583
0	13	HAYD	11f Soft	49	1819
39	4	RIPO	8f Gd/Fm	42	2099
0	17	REDC	8f Gd/Fm	41	2861
39	2	BEVE	8f Gd/Fm	38	3407
0	13	PONT	12f Soft	38	4229

FLAVIA 3 b f £388

45	6	YARM	7f Firm		2770
48a	6	WOLV	9f Aw		3272
39	7	SAND	8f Good		3474
37a	5	LING	12f Aw		3835 BL
48a	3	WOLV	12f Aw	47	4443 bl
0	13	NEWM	12f Gd/Sft	45	4534 bl

FLAVIAN 4 b f £6380

89	8	BATH	5f Good		1090
89	7	NOTT	6f Good		1410
96	1	YARM	7f Firm		2389+
97	8	GOOD	7f Good		3104
89	8	DONC	7f Gd/Fm		3878

FLAWLY 3 b f £11527

106	2	CHAN	12f Gd/Sft		1748
103	3	DEAU	13f Hldng		2572

FLAXEN PRIDE 5 ch m £0

32	8	REDC	8f Firm	40	1300
0	13	MUSS	8f Firm	39	1689
0	18	REDC	8f Good	38	1892

FLEDGLING 3 b f £4173

57	5	PONT	6f Good		1500
82	1	HAYD	7f Gd/Sft		1789*

FLEETING FANCY 3 b f £693

56	9	LING	6f Good		1399
51	3	WIND	6f Gd/Fm	56	1877
41	10	WIND	6f Good	57	2371
36	7	WIND	6f Soft	57	2549
47	5	NEWM	6f Gd/Fm	56	2804
43	7	SALI	7f Gd/Fm	55	2978
50	4	SALI	8f Gd/Fm	53	3293
27	11	BRIG	8f Firm	51	3561
33	11	LING	8f Firm	51	3759

FLEETING FOOTSTEPS 8 b h £0

0a	9	SOUT	12f Aw	30	339

FLETCHER 6 b g £18462

35a	7	SOUT	14f Aw	69	182
51	10	CATT	14f Gd/Fm	65	779
36	7	WARW	15f Heavy	60	885
48	8	WIND	12f Gd/Sft		1096
48	10	SALI	12f Good	50	1350
53	2	HAYD	14f Gd/Sft	50	1536
56	2	NEWM	12f Firm	53	1852
57	3	ASCO	16f Good	55	2173
57	2	MUSS	14f Firm	56	2375
59	1	SALI	12f Good	55	2689*
64	1	SAND	14f Gd/Fm	58	2923*
62	5	SAND	14f Good	63	3231
68	1	SALI	14f Gd/Fm	63	3424*
58	12	HAYD	14f Soft	68	3783
68	2	SAND	14f Gd/Fm	66	3948
57	2	SALI	14f Gd/Fm	66	4166
61	14	NEWM	18f Gd/Fm	79	4353

41	10	MUSS	16f Soft	65	4563

FLICKER 5 b m £0

0a	12	WOLV	9f Aw		433

FLIGHT ETERNAL 3 ch c £0

0a	11	SOUT	8f Aw		48

FLIGHT FOR FREEDOM 5 b m £0

5a	7	SOUT	12f Aw		556

FLIGHT OF DREAMS 3 b f £2787

0	8	PONT	12f Heavy		939
0	12	LING	6f Good	42	2654
28	6	BRIG	6f Firm	35	2896 BL
43	1	BRIG	7f Gd/Fm	32	3242*
41	3	CHEP	7f Good	41	3873
43	4	YARM	7f Firm	46	3939

FLIGHT OF FANCY 2 b f £6633

96	2	NEWM	7f Good		3020
102	1	SALI	7f Firm		3748*

FLIGHT REFUND 3 ch g £0

0a	13	SOUT	8f Aw		198
0	12	NOTT	8f Gd/Sft		1084
0	15	WARW	8f Gd/Fm		3914
55	6	NOTT	10f Heavy		4412

FLIGHT SEQUENCE 4 b f £5493

62	6	KEMP	7f Soft		1012
74	8	KEMP	8f Gd/Fm	76	1926
78	2	KEMP	9f Firm	75	2262
60	9	KEMP	8f Gd/Fm	76	2581
75	1	EPSO	10f Gd/Fm		3403* VIS
74	6	EPSO	12f Gd/Fm	75	3858 vis

FLINT 2 b g £2619

53	7	PONT	5f Soft		1704
61	5	PONT	5f Good		2361
67	4	BEVE	5f Firm		2730
70	1	BEVE	5f Good		2880*
70	5	MUSS	5f Good	74	3101
52	11	REDC	6f Firm	73	3327

FLINT RIVER 2 b c £6901

88	2	SALI	5f Good		1346
85	2	WIND	5f Good		1727
78	10	ASCO	5f Good		2113
82	2	PONT	5f Firm		3500
85	1	WARW	15f Gd/Fm		3911*
75	9	NEWM	6f Gd/Fm	84	4214

FLINTSTONE 3 b c £0

50	10	NOTT	8f Gd/Sft		1084
0	12	CARL	14f Gd/Fm	57	3084 VIS
0	14	BEVE	12f Gd/Fm	52	3674

FLIPSIDE 2 b c £0

41	8	SALI	7f Gd/Fm		3420
0	15	BATH	8f Soft		4429

FLIQUET BAY 3 b c £1864

58	4	WIND	12f Heavy	60	937
57	2	WIND	12f Gd/Sft		1096 BL
39	11	NOTT	14f Gd/Fm	60	1270 bl
59	3	WIND	12f Gd/Sft	56	2210 bl
26	9	CHEP	16f Gd/Fm	55	2659 bl
57	3	NEWM	12f Good		4178 bl

FLIT ABOUT 2 ch f £8492

79	2	CHEP	6f Gd/Fm		2488
80	3	KEMP	7f Gd/Fm		3074
58a	2	WOLV	7f Aw		3497
80	1	BATH	8f Gd/Fm	77	3817*
67	7	PONT	8f Soft	80	4084

FLITE OF ARABY 3 b c £718

64	3	BATH	12f Firm		1997
62	4	DONC	12f Gd/Fm	64	2755
51	6	LEIC	12f Gd/Fm		3219

FLITE OF LIFE 4 gr c £1871

52a	10	LING	7f Aw	65	28
39a	5	LING	8f Aw	61	97
68a	1	SOUT	8f Aw	57	177*
61a	6	SOUT	8f Aw	65	251

31a	9	WOLV	8f Aw	65	381
0	12	LEIC	7f Good		790

FLITWICK 3 b c £5787

45	8	EPSO	9f Heavy		1032
83	1	RIPO	10f Good		1599*
79	6	DONC	10f Gd/Fm	85	2610
85	2	LEIC	8f Gd/Fm	82	3334

FLOATING CHARGE 6 b g £18675

85a	2	WOLV	8f Aw	77	580
0a	U	SOUT	7f Aw	84	687
69	8	KEMP	8f Gd/Sft	77	1077
53	8	WIND	8f Good	76	3355
79	1	KEMP	7f Gd/Fm	74	3796*
82	1	NEWB	7f Firm	77	3981+
74	4	YORK	8f Soft	81	4284

FLOATING EMBER 3 b f £3918

0	12	MUSS	8f Gd/Sft	45	800
26	8	MUSS	8f Gd/Fm	39	1434
39	1	PONT	10f Soft		1699*
0	12	YARM	10f Gd/Fm	45	1955
37	3	PONT	12f Good	38	2362

FLOORSOTHEFOREST 4 ch g £1843

52	6	HAMI	8f Good		847
32	5	HAMI	9f Gd/Fm		1191
56	5	HAMI	9f Gd/Fm	60	1360
58	2	MUSS	9f Firm	57	1689
26	6	NEWC	10f Heavy	57	1769
52	5	HAMI	9f Gd/Fm		1940
58	2	HAMI	9f Firm	57	2094
39	7	NEWC	8f Gd/Fm	56	2311
25	7	MUSS	8f Firm	53	2378
42	7	HAMI	8f Firm	58	2397
39	5	HAMI	9f Gd/Fm		2781
0	14	HAMI	9f Gd/Fm	56	2799
0	12	HAMI	9f Gd/Sft		3823
33	10	AYR	11f Soft	50	3963
5	12	NEWC	8f Heavy	42	4406

FLOOT 2 b c £477

66	8	GOOD	8f Gd/Sft		1472
60	8	CHEP	6f Gd/Fm		2488
55	10	LING	8f Firm		3577
67	3	LING	7f Soft	65	4191

FLORA DREAMBIRD 6 b m £0

20a	6	WOLV	15f Aw		174
0a	9	SOUT	16f Aw	33	284 bl
23a	7	SOUT	16f Aw		327 bl
18a	5	LING	16f Aw		402 tbl
16a	6	LING	13f Aw		483 bl
5a	6	LING	16f Aw	28	649 bl
0	9	PONT	22f Heavy	31	940 bl

FLORIDA 2 b f £0

0	12	LEIC	6f Gd/Fm		3215
50	9	LING	7f Firm		3829
0	14	KEMP	7f Soft		4034

FLOSSY 4 b f £35001

70	14	NEWM	10f Gd/Fm	86	1170
85	4	NEWM	12f Gd/Fm		1695
82	4	YORK	12f Gd/Fm	85	2647
88	1	CHES	12f Firm	84	3173*
86	11	YORK	14f Gd/Fm	91	3565
90	2	NEWC	10f Good	86	3703
89	3	AYR	13f Gd/Sft	89	4014
87	3	ASCO	12f Gd/Sft	88	4128
95	1	NEWM	12f Good	89	4162+
100	2	NEWM	12f Good	94	4342
0	15	DONC	12f Heavy	94	4580

FLOTSAM 4 ch c £0

0	8	SALI	14f Firm		3751

FLOW BEAU 3 b f £192

59	4	REDC	7f Gd/Sft		1134
53	6	BEVE	7f Good		1444
40	6	RIPO	9f Good		1863

0	15	RIPO	10f Good		50	3702	
24	13	YARM	8f Gd/Fm		47	3971	BL
40a	7	SOUT	14f Aw		47	4371	bl

FLOWER OCANNIE 5 b m £0
52	12	CATT	14f Gd/Fm	54	779

FLOWING RIO 2 b f £5096
0	13	THIR	5f Good		1381
75	1	**HAMI**	6f Gd/Fm		1938*
71	5	PONT	6f Gd/Fm	78	2557
75	3	REDC	7f Gd/Fm	74	2991
64	3	THIR	7f Gd/Fm		3127
0	18	DONC	6f Gd/Fm	72	3860
69a	2	WOLV	6f Aw		4244

FLOWINGTON 3 b f £4813
90	5	NEWB	6f Good		1371
0	29	NEWM	6f Gd/Fm	94	1694
84	4	YARM	6f Gd/Fm		2197
92	2	NEWM	6f Gd/Fm		2289
91	6	YORK	6f Gd/Fm		2646
96	3	NEWM	6f Gd/Fm		3120
72	12	PONT	6f Firm		3503
89	4	YARM	6f Firm		3937

FLOWLINE RIVER 2 b f £0
22	8	LEIC	5f Gd/Fm		2772
0a	11	SOUT	7f Aw		2949
0	18	BATH	5f Firm		3204

FLUME 3 br f £535
62	3	BEVE	7f Gd/Sft		1763

FLUMMOX 2 b c £4103
84	1	**WARW**	5f Heavy		1522*
89	3	CATT	5f Gd/Sft		1813
63	4	WIND	5f Gd/Fm		2055
79	4	PONT	6f Gd/Fm	86	2557

FLUSH 5 b m £0
0a	14	SOUT	7f Aw	60	69	
23a	9	LING	10f Aw	52	160	
33a	5	WOLV	12f Aw	45	520	
0	13	NOTT	10f Gd/Fm	55	1272	
22a	10	SOUT	8f Aw	42	1419	

FLUTED 2 ch c £1334
73	4	FOLK	7f Gd/Fm		2290
58	10	CHEP	6f Gd/Fm		2488
68	3	BRIG	5f Firm		2903
69	7	GOOD	7f Firm	72	3149
69	3	FOLK	7f Gd/Fm	69	3444
61	4	GOOD	7f Good		3660
54	12	DONC	7f Gd/Fm	68	3901
51	6	YARM	8f Soft	65	4393

FLUXUS 3 b c £5465
83	3	SAN	10f Heavy		1228

FLY BOY FLY 2 b c £529
75	4	EPSO	6f Gd/Sft		2628
74	6	EPSO	5f Good		3760
75	4	CATT	5f Soft		4253
62a	4	WOLV	6f Aw		4381

FLY FOR AVIE 5 br m £126582
117	1	**WOOD**	10f Firm		4399*

FLY HOME 5 br m £0
0a	13	SOUT	14f Aw		124

FLY LIKE A BIRD 4 ch f £0
0	13	LEIC	12f Gd/Sft	55	1736
37a	4	WOLV	12f Aw	47	2075
26a	9	WOLV	16f Aw	40	2606
23	7	WARW	13f Gd/Fm	37	2843
27	5	NOTT	14f Gd/Fm	37	3002
28a	5	WOLV	12f Aw	34	3773
0	10	YARM	11f Soft	29	4391

FLY LIKE THE WIND 3 br f £4840
70	2	BEVE	5f Firm		1280
72	4	DONC	5f Good		1516
75	3	FOLK	5f Gd/Fm		2294
73	1	**LING**	5f Good		2590*

48	17	GOOD	5f Gd/Fm		73	3135
0	24	NEWM	5f Good		73	4185

FLY MORE 3 ch g £3546
49	4	SOUT	6f Soft		1605
70	5	SALI	7f Gd/Fm		1886
54	5	WARW	6f Good		2462
71	1	**RIPO**	6f Gd/Fm	64	2839*
66	5	RIPO	6f Gd/Fm	71	3010
67	5	GOOD	7f Good	70	3908

FLY TO THE STARS 6 b g £8646
102	7	NAD	9f Good		768
100	5	EPSO	9f Good		1847
116	4	LONG	8f Soft		3847

FLY WITH ME 2 b c £0
74	6	YARM	8f Gd/Fm		3969
75	10	LING	7f Soft		4268

FLYING BACK 3 b g £652
67	4	NEWB	7f Good		1947
72	4	KEMP	7f Gd/Sft		2585
28	11	HAYD	8f Gd/Fm		3266

FLYING CARPET 3 b f £8419
61	6	NEWC	7f Soft		759
53	7	PONT	6f Soft		877
47	11	REDC	7f Firm	58	1297
56	3	NEWC	8f Gd/Fm	58	1477
68	1	**BEVE**	8f Gd/Fm	59	2515*
71	3	NEWM	8f Good	66	3022
56	7	THIR	8f Good	68	3777

FLYING EAGLE 9 b g £0
33	8	CHES	12f Gd/Fm	75	3430

FLYING FAISAL 2 b c £0
63	9	CHEP	6f Good		3867
57a	6	WOLV	7f Aw		4385

FLYING GREEN 7 ch g £0
0a	12	WOLV	9f Aw		922 bl

FLYING HIGH 5 b g £258
43a	7	WOLV	7f Aw		61	bl
53a	6	SOUT	8f Aw		389	
27a	4	SOUT	7f Aw	35	476	
9a	10	WOLV	8f Aw	33	583	
30a	3	SOUT	8f Aw	33	585	
17a	8	SOUT	8f Aw		646	
5	14	REDC	8f Firm	31	1300	bl
34a	5	SOUT	8f Aw		1505	bl

FLYING LYRIC 2 b c £2598
80	4	YARM	8f Gd/Fm		3969
88	1	**BATH**	8f Soft		4430*

FLYING MEMORY 4 b f £0
0	14	BRIG	7f Gd/Fm	37	2728
0	13	THIR	8f Gd/Fm	33	3124

FLYING MILLIE 2 b f £4504
87	1	**WIND**	5f Gd/Sft		1424*
90	6	ASCO	5f Good		2088
82	7	ASCO	6f Gd/Fm		2996

FLYING OFFICER 4 ch c £525
97	4	YARM	6f Gd/Fm		1952

FLYING PENNANT 7 ch h £6236
34	5	BRIG	7f Gd/Sft	42	896	bl
31	5	BRIG	7f Firm	40	1335	bl
38	3	SOUT	7f Soft		1601	bl
31	8	BRIG	7f Gd/Fm	38	1930	bl
38	6	BEVE	7f Firm	39	2221	bl
41	1	**BRIG**	7f Soft	36	2427*	bl
0	17	DONC	7f Gd/Fm	44	2612	bl
36	3	BRIG	7f Gd/Fm	41	2728	bl
36	6	CHEP	7f Gd/Fm	41	2974	bl
46	3	FOLK	7f Gd/Fm	42r	3445	bl
34	10	EPSO	7f Good	44	3765	bl
39	5	CHEP	7f Good	44	3873	bl

FLYING PETREL 2 b f £351
62	8	THIR	6f Gd/Fm		3614
64	4	NOTT	5f Gd/Sft		4503

FLYING ROMANCE 2 b f £404
54	8	RIPO	5f Gd/Fm		2100	
60	5	PONT	5f Good		2360	
46	5	HAMI	6f Gd/Fm		2778	
61	3	CARL	5f Firm		3193	
58	7	YORK	6f Good		3812	
61	4	CATT	7f Soft	60	4007	
39	10	CATT	7f Soft	60	4254	

FLYING RUN 3 b f £348
38	8	WIND	8f Heavy	62	933	
0a	14	SOUT	7f Aw	59	1202	
0	12	WARW	7f Gd/Sft	57	1710	
0	13	SALI	8f Gd/Fm	50	2264	BL
38	10	LEIC	8f Gd/Fm	47	2512	bl
29	7	BRIG	7f Gd/Fm	42	3242	
35	3	BRIG	10f Firm	39	3530	
31	7	EPSO	10f Good	41	3762	
23a	10	LING	13f AW		4193	

FLYING TACKLE 2 ch c £0
0	13	BEVE	5f Gd/Fm		2480
46	10	YORK	5f Gd/Fm		3812
44	11	BEVE	5f Good		3955

FLYING TRAPEZE 2 ch c £0
0	27	NEWM	6f Good		4341

FLYING TREATY 3 br c £2333
74	5	YARM	8f Good		1771
77	2	GOOD	9f Gd/Fm		2129
73	3	NEWC	8f Good		2337
0	7	EPSO	10f Gd/Fm	75	3415

FLYING TURK 2 ch c £2372
69	3	SOUT	6f Soft		1602	
47	12	LEIC	6f Firm		2029	
73	4	HAYD	6f Gd/Sft		3268	
73	4	NEWB	7f Gd/Fm	78	3486	
77	6	DONC	6f Firm		3888	
62	6	HAYD	6f Firm	76	4090	t
56	12	LING	6f Soft	75	4269	

FLYOVER 3 b f £8971
0	12	BATH	8f Gd/Sft	63	1671	
49	11	SALI	8f Firm	58	2025	
54	5	SALI	8f Gd/Fm	54	2980	BL
60	1	**BATH**	12f Firm	54	3206*	
56	6	SALI	12f Gd/Fm	59	3290	
63	1	**EPSO**	10f Good	57	3762*	
62	4	BRIG	10f Gd/Sft	62	4118	

FOCUSED ATTRACTION 2 b c £267
59	6	WIND	5f Firm		1290
79	5	KEMP	5f Gd/Fm		2082
79	4	WIND	5f Good		2368
35	13	GOOD	6f Good	76	3886

FOIST 8 b g £930
51a	9	SOUT	6f Aw	60	587	
45a	10	SOUT	7f Aw	56	867	
41	6	BEVE	7f Firm	52	1275	
39a	5	SOUT	6f Aw	49	1421	
0	14	BEVE	7f Gd/Sft	48	1760	
40a	2	SOUT	6f Aw	46	2385	
38	6	HAMI	6f Gd/Fm	44	2641	
23a	7	SOUT	6f Aw	46	2820	
0	16	NEWC	8f Heavy	42	4406	
35	3	NEWC	7f Heavy	42	4426	

FOLAANN 2 ch c £0
54	11	LING	7f Soft		4267

FOLEY MILLENNIUM 2 ch c £7976
58	5	BRIG	6f Gd/Sft		1507
59	5	BRIG	5f Firm		2039
80	1	**HAYD**	6f Gd/Fm		2441*
83	3	SALI	6f Good		2687
65	4	NEWM	6f Gd/Fm		2959
86	1	**NEWB**	5f Gd/Fm		3174*
84	3	HAYD	6f Good		3286
82	5	BATH	6f Firm		3620

52	8	EPSO	6f Good	84	3761	

FOLIE DANSE 3 b f £46130

109	2	LONG	10f Gd/Sft		1457
110	5	CHAN	11f Gd/Sft		1901
110	1	**DEAU**	13f Hldng		2572*
110	3	LONG	12f Soft		4394

FOLK DANCE 3 b f £0

25a	6	WOLV	7f Aw		493
0a	11	WOLV	9f Aw		610
28a	7	LING	7f Aw		651

FOLLOW A DREAM 2 b f £1487

76	6	KEMP	7f Gd/Fm		3359
78	3	KEMP	7f Soft		4035
78	2	NEWC	7f Heavy		4403

FOLLOW FREDDY 2 ch g £0

0	11	NEWC	6f Good		3245
66	7	PONT	6f Soft		4083
23	12	NEWC	6f Heavy		4402

FOLLOW LAMMTARRA 3 ch g £4847

84	3	THIR	14f Good		1157
76	6	NOTT	14f Gd/Sft		1369
84	1	**HAYD**	14f Soft		1824*
82	6	NEWM	16f Gd/Sft	91	4533

FOLLOW SUIT 3 ch c £0

0	13	NEWB	6f Gd/Fm	81	1406
77	7	NEWM	7f Gd/Fm	79	3629

FOLLOW YOUR STAR 2 ch c £0

78	6	NEWB	7f Firm		2708	
85	6	NEWM	7f Gd/Fm		3121	
61	7	CHES	6f Gd/Fm		3508	
73	7	GOOD	6f Good	82	3886	
53	7	BRIG	6f Soft	77	4170	VIS

FOLLOWEROFFASHION 3 b c £0

0	17	KEMP	12f Soft		4040
0	13	SAND	10f Soft		4205

FOODBROKER FANCY 2 ch f £8066

86	2	SAND	5f Gd		1986
80	4	ASCO	6f Good		2172
81	1	**NEWM**	6f Gd/Fm		2854*
77	7	NEWM	6f Gd/Fm	86	3165
85	2	GOOD	7f Good	79	3660

FOOL ON THE HILL 3 b c £1702

79	4	KEMP	6f Good		1080
77	2	NEWB	7f Gd/Fm		1947
58	8	LING	8f Soft		4274

FOOLS PARADISE 3 ch g £0

0a	11	LING	8f Aw		26
0a	6	LING	10f Aw		771
50a	6	SOUT	11f Aw		1502
0	14	BRIG	10f Gd/Fm		1933
8a	8	LING	12f Aw		2181

FOOTPRINTS 3 b f £7546

76	1	**WARW**	7f Heavy		888*
0	10	WARW	7f Soft	76	1061
63	10	NEWB	7f Gd/Fm	75	1405
76	2	WARW	7f Gd/Sft	73	1710
64	7	PONT	6f Good	75	2364
65	1	**LEIC**	7f Gd/Fm		3218*
73	6	SAND	8f Gd/Fm	75	3944
0	14	HAYD	8f Soft	75	4094
0	25	NEWM	7f Good	72	4357

FOR HEAVENS SAKE 3 b c £4341

53a	4	SOUT	6f Aw		46	
59a	6	SOUT	5f Aw		127	
51a	6	WOLV	7f Aw	61	188	
61a	4	WOLV	7f Aw	59	257	
61a	3	WOLV	8f Aw	59	311	
61a	2	WOLV	8f Aw		636	
58	6	MUSS	8f Gd/Sft	60	800	
45	9	HAYD	7f Gd/Sft	58	3269	
60	2	MUSS	7f Gd/Sft	56	3593	
55	3	MUSS	7f Gd/Fm		3744	BL

62a	2	WOLV	8f Aw	60	3769	
61	3	BEVE	12f Good	60	3954	
45a	5	LING	12f AW		4186	
49a	6	SOUT	12f Aw		4366	
59	2	MUSS	8f Soft		4519	

FOR LOVE 4 b g £0

0a	12	LING	12f Aw		2181

FOR PLEASURE 5 b h £753

61	2	FRAU	9f Good		1904

FOR YOUR EYES ONLY 6 b g £0

61	17	KEMP	8f Gd/Sft	99	1077	bl
0	31	NEWM	8f Gd/Fm	95	4212	bl

FORBEARING 3 b c £73718

88a	1	**LING**	8f Aw		103*
95a	1	**WOLV**	8f Aw		171*
84	8	BATH	10f Good		1089
86	7	GOOD	9f Gd/Sft	90	1452
104	1	**EPSO**	10f Gd/Sft	88	1831*
103	1	**GOOD**	10f Gd/Fm	94	1958*
108	1	**SALI**	10f Gd/Sft		2471*
111	2	NEWM	10f Gd/Fm	105	2596
113	2	HAYD	11f Gd/Fm		3321
114	3	WIND	10f Good		3641
111	2	AYR	11f Gd/Sft		4011

FOREIGN AFFAIRS 2 ch c £634

75a	2	WOLV	7f Aw		4383

FOREIGN EDITOR 4 ch c £18890

36a	4	SOUT	7f Aw	49	75
58a	1	**WOLV**	7f Aw	46	193*
71a	1	**WOLV**	6f Aw	52	232*
67a	D	SOUT	6f Aw	58	250
80a	1	**WOLV**	6f Aw	65	364*
78a	1	**LING**	7f Aw	73	423*
77a	3	LING	7f Aw	76	462
78a	3	SOUT	8f Aw	76	645
65	2	CATT	7f Gd/Fm	61	780
37	11	SOUT	7f Good	61	803
49	9	CARL	6f Firm	65	1257
33	16	PONT	5f Soft	64	4087

FOREIGN SECRETARY 3 b c £6107

92	1	**NEWB**	8f Good		1377*
95	2	PONT	10f Soft		1703
97	6	ASCO	12f Good	95	2116
80	10	GOOD	10f Gd/Fm	94	3131
59	9	NEWM	10f Good		4017

FOREON 3 b f £0

0a	11	LING	8f Aw		103

FOREST DANCER 2 b c £619

75	3	LING	6f Good		2652
64	5	BATH	6f Soft		4138
82	7	NEWM	6f Good		4341
63	7	WIND	6f Heavy	81	4525

FOREST DREAM 5 b m £2671

60a	2	WOLV	12f Aw	55	43	
55a	4	WOLV	12f Aw	60	81	
0a	13	LING	10f Aw	60	203	
47a	8	LING	10f Aw		268	
0a	10	LING	12f Aw	55	332	
0a	10	WOLV	12f Aw	48	407	t
32	13	BRIG	12f Gd/Fm	58	1128	
32	7	BRIG	12f Firm	53	1332	
39	8	BRIG	10f Gd/Sft	53	1509	
51	2	YARM	10f Firm	47	1615	
47	3	YARM	10f Good	47	1775	
0	15	WARW	11f Gd/Fm	47	2033	
3	7	WIND	12f Good	46	2370	
44	2	LING	11f Firm	45	3282	
43	7	LING	10f Firm	45	3581	
35	4	BRIG	12f Firm	43	3735	
0a	15	LING	12f Aw	37	4486	

FOREST ECHO 6 gr g £0

0a	13	SOUT	16f Aw		327

FOREST FIRE 5 b m £2810

85	2	KEMP	12f Gd/Sft	80	1076
78	7	YORK	10f Firm		1325
81	7	NEWM	12f Gd/Fm		1695
83	3	GOOD	14f Gd/Fm	83	1959
68	6	LEIC	12f Gd/Fm	83	2509

FOREST FRIENDLY 3 b f £0

69	10	NEWM	10f Good		957
64	13	GOOD	8f Gd/Sft		1811
64	5	RIPO	8f Gd/Fm	77	2108
51	7	HAMI	9f Gd/Sft	73	3535
0	15	LEIC	10f Firm	68	3842

FOREST HEATH 3 gr g £8218

78	2	NOTT	8f Soft		1643
77	1	**GOOD**	10f Good		2308*
80	2	DONC	12f Gd/Fm	75	2755
82	2	NEWM	10f Good	78	4160
0	11	DONC	12f Soft	82	4464

FOREST KITTEN 2 b f £0

15	9	NOTT	5f Good		1870

FOREST LIGHT 2 gr f £0

50	15	NEWB	6f Firm		3980
0	23	NEWM	7f Good		4158

FOREST MOON 2 b f £1865

63	6	WIND	5f Heavy		932
50	6	WARW	5f Soft		1059
0	16	BATH	6f Gd/Sft		1667
57	1	**WIND**	5f Gd/Fm		2052*
0	13	LEIC	6f Gd/Sft	56	4030
51a	10	LING	6f Aw		4332

FOREST QUEEN 3 b f £0

0	22	REDC	6f Gd/Fm	57	1133
0	15	HAMI	6f Gd/Fm	64	1192
0	17	NEWC	7f Good	54	3033
27	11	LEIC	10f Gd/Fm	54	3217
33	10	HAYD	11f Good	54	3285
0	8	BEVE	12f Good	54	3399
12	6	NEWC	7f Heavy	33	4428
23	8	MUSS	7f Soft	38	4518

FOREST ROBIN 7 ch g £0

45a	4	LING	10f Aw		3	
38a	8	WOLV	9f Aw	52	60	vis
0a	12	SOUT	11f Aw		178	

FOREVER FABULOUS 2 b c £0

47	6	REDC	6f Firm		3307
27	10	LING	6f Firm		3757
34a	10	WOLV	6f Aw		4244

FOREVER MY LORD 2 b c £21671

67	6	WARW	5f Heavy		1522
76	7	CHEP	6f Gd/Sft		1798
76	1	**NEWM**	7f Gd/Fm		2599*
76	1	**NEWM**	7f Gd/Fm	69	2962*
81	1	**GOOD**	7f Firm	75	3149*
68	7	NEWC	8f Gd/Sft	81	3704
62	14	DONC	6f Firm		3888
0	14	NEWM	7f Gd/Sft	77	4453

FOREVER TIMES 2 b f £12420

76	3	HAYD	6f Gd/Fm		2500
69	6	YORK	6f Good		2692
79	2	THIR	6f Gd/Fm		2968
72	2	THIR	6f Gd/Fm		3143
77	1	**THIR**	5f Gd/Fm		3346*
70	8	BEVE	5f Gd/Fm	73	3673
77	3	DONC	7f Gd/Fm	73	3860
76	3	AYR	7f Soft		3991
71	7	NEWM	7f Good	76	4157
70	10	NEWM	6f Gd/Fm	75	4338
71	4	NEWB	6f Sft/Hvy	73	4468

FORGOTTEN TIMES 6 ch m £14368

70	2	BRIG	5f Gd/Sft	64	897	
29	13	KEMP	5f Soft		1013	
65	6	LING	5f Gd/Sft	67	1264	vis

FORMAL (continued)

70	2	GOOD	5f Gd/Sft	66	1487	vis
66	2	BRIG	5f Good	66	1650	vis
73	1	**LING**	5f Gd/Fm	69	2184*	vis
65	2	BATH	6f Firm		2329	vis
64	10	NEWM	5f Good	74	2569	vis
71	6	GOOD	5f Gd/Fm	74	3091	vis
64	9	ASCO	5f Gd/Fm	73	3341	vis
58	13	EPSO	5f Good	72	3687	vis
73	3	BRIG	5f Firm	72	3734	vis
76	1	**EPSO**	5f Good	72	3855*	vis
67	9	GOOD	6f Good	76	3904	vis
63	10	HAYD	5f Gd/Sft	74	4107	vis

FORMAL BID 3 br c £0

59	8	WARW	8f Good		2465
63	11	NEWM	7f Gd/Fm	74	2855
51	6	LEIC	10f Gd/Fm	70	3093

FORMAL PARTY 2 ch f £397

61	6	LEIC	6f Firm	2029
58	6	REDC	6f Gd/Sft	2628
61	3	REDC	6f Gd/Fm	2990
28	9	SALI	7f Gd/Fm	3388
0	11	LING	7f Soft	4484

FORMIDABLE FLAME 7 ch g £0

0	12	CHEP	18f Gd/Fm	40	2490

FORMULA VENETTA 2 ch c £0

29	8	NEWC	6f Gd/Fm	2333
50	5	DONC	7f Gd/Fm	2576
62	7	THIR	7f Gd/Fm	2966
70	6	BEVE	7f Good	3397

FORT KNOX 9 b g £0

23a	6	LING	8f Aw		574	bl
22	6	BRIG	8f Gd/Fm	46	2726	bl
0	11	NEWM	8f Gd/Fm		3117	bl

FORT SUMTER 4 b c £601

45a	6	WOLV	8f Aw	58	4021
57	2	SALI	10f Gd/Sft	56	4168
0	11	BATH	10f Soft	58	4436

FORTHECHOP 3 b c £337

8a	2	SOUT	8f Aw		36
39a	6	SOUT	7f Aw		88
40a	4	SOUT	7f Aw		281
42a	5	SOUT	7f Aw		330
35a	4	SOUT	8f Aw	41	429
41a	3	SOUT	8f Aw	40	555
25a	7	SOUT	8f Aw		684
20	9	BEVE	10f Gd/Fm	40	3656

FORTUNA 2 b c £0

17a	8	SOUT	6f Aw	1974
58a	5	WOLV	6f Aw	2077
24	9	HAYD	6f Gd/Fm	2441

FORTUNE COOKIE 4 ch f £0

16a	10	LING	10f Aw	56

FORTUNE FOUND 2 b f £0

0	21	DONC	8f Heavy	4569	t

FORTUNE HOPPER 6 gr g £0

26	8	CATT	12f Gd/Fm	3202

FORTUNE POINT 2 ch c £1542

81	4	HAYD	7f Soft	3786
83	2	HAYD	7f Gd/Sft	4103

FORTY FORTE 4 b g £20667

71a	1	**LING**	10f Aw	68	22*
64a	3	WOLV	9f Aw	65	67
72a	2	LING	8f Aw	70	97
48a	9	WOLV	7f Aw	72	143
64a	5	LING	10f Aw	71	244
69a	6	LING	10f Aw	70	337
74a	1	**LING**	10f Aw	69	400*
65a	6	LING	10f Aw	72	463
73a	2	LING	10f Aw	71	546
69a	4	LING	12f Aw	72	572
71a	4	LING	10f Aw	72	632
76	1	**NOTT**	10f Good	71	786*

FORUM (continued)

59	5	HAMI	9f Good	74	846
74	3	EPSO	10f Heavy	74	1031
63	8	CHES	10f Gd/Fm	74	1217

FORUM CHRIS 3 ch g £8861

70	7	THIR	12f Good		1157
70	4	HAMI	12f Gd/Fm		1362
68	3	NEWC	10f Gd/Sft		1480
68	3	HAYD	14f Soft	69	1821
73	1	**HAMI**	13f Gd/Fm	66	2238*
81	1	**MUSS**	14f Firm	72	2375*

FORUM FINALE 2 b f £3892

72	2	PONT	6f Soft		1700
64	5	YORK	6f Firm		2005
57	8	PONT	8f Soft		4086
62	8	CATT	7f Soft	66	4254
68a	1	**WOLV**	8f Aw	63	4439*

FORWOOD 2 b c £16498

98	1	**NEWB**	6f Gd/Fm		1943*
99	1	**ASCO**	7f Good		2677*
98	4	ASCO	8f Gd/Fm		3304
101	3	NEWM	7f Good		4196

FORZA FIGLIO 7 b g £3558

72	10	WIND	10f Good	77	1729	
74	3	KEMP	12f Gd/Fm	75	2085	
70	3	DONC	10f Gd/Fm	75	2350	
74	4	GOOD	9f Good	74	3110	
74	4	EPSO	10f Gd/Fm	74	3403	
58	12	KEMP	10f Gd/Fm	74	3794	bl
0	20	NEWM	8f Good	73	4340	

FOSTON FOX 3 b f £200

36a	6	LING	7f Aw		94	
37a	4	LING	10f Aw		204	
0a	10	SOUT	8f Aw		303	
30	5	MUSS	12f Gd/Sft		799	
37	8	NOTT	8f Gd/Sft	47	1365	
38	7	RIPO	8f Good		1596	BL
44	6	REDC	8f Good	49	1892	bl
35	7	DONC	7f Gd/Fm	44	2320	bl
27	9	LEIC	8f Gd/Fm		3094	bl
40	5	HAYD	8f Gd/Sft		3266	bl
22	7	NEWM	8f Gd/Fm		3456	bl
41	4	YARM	6f Gd/Fm	40	3966	bl
38	8	PONT	6f Soft		4233	bl

FOSTON SECOND 3 ch f £1252

37	4	REDC	11f Gd/Fm		2989
31	2	NEWC	12f Good		3247
32	4	REDC	14f Gd/Fm	40	3637
33	2	HAMI	12f Soft		3804
0	9	CATT	14f Soft		4002

FOUETTE 2 b f £0

0	24	NEWM	8f Good	4349

FOUND AT LAST 4 b g £5156

51a	3	WOLV	6f Aw		273	
40a	11	WOLV	7f Aw	53	323	
36a	7	WOLV	5f Aw		624	
54	3	CATT	6f Aw		781	
49	5	NOTT	6f Firm	56	1273	
7a	11	SOUT	6f Aw	47	1421	
50	2	CATT	7f Gd/Sft		1818	
52	2	DONC	6f Gd/Fm	50	2315	
52	2	CATT	8f Gd/Fm		2421	
43	4	RIPO	6f Gd/Fm	51	2839	
50	3	MUSS	7f Good	51	3103	
45	5	HAMI	8f Gd/Sft	51	3377	BL
67	2	BEVE	5f Gd/Fm		3651	
58	2	MUSS	7f Gd/Fm		3744	
62	9	YARM	6f Firm		3937	
58	11	YORK	6f Soft		4287	

FOUNDRY LANE 9 b g £8714

70	4	HAYD	14f Gd/Fm	74	1536
73	2	HAYD	16f Gd/Sft	72	1791
77	1	**HAYD**	14f Gd/Fm	74	2455*

(continued)

74	3	BEVE	16f Good	76	3395
71	3	HAYD	14f Gd/Sft	75	4105

FOUR EAGLES 2 b c £0

88	5	NEWM	8f Good	4349

FOUR LEGS GOOD 2 b f £0

48	8	ASCO	6f Gd/Fm		2952
0	12	HAYD	8f Soft		3766
73	7	WARW	7f Gd/Fm		3910
39	9	MUSS	8f Gd/Sft	64	4132

FOUR MEN 3 b c £2819

0	13	MUSS	8f Gd/Sft	49	800
0	14	RIPO	8f Good		1858
36	7	HAMI	9f Gd/Fm		2236
0	13	LEIC	7f Gd/Fm		2508
45	6	PONT	10f Gd/Fm		2562
46	6	NOTT	8f Gd/Fm		2682
41	11	WARW	7f Gd/Fm		2704
51	6	WARW	8f Gd/Fm		2844
38	5	REDC	9f Gd/Fm		2865
31	6	REDC	11f Gd/Fm		2989
66	5	CARL	8f Gd/Fm		3081
40	3	AYR	10f Gd/Fm		3142
44	7	REDC	8f Firm		3330
37	2	THIR	8f Gd/Fm		3616
40	11	BEVE	7f Gd/Fm		3670
70	6	REDC	7f Gd/Sft		4218
43	9	AYR	8f Heavy		4308

FOURDANED 7 b g £0

21a	5	LING	12f Aw	39	52	
9	10	BRIG	12f Good		1647	
0	28	ASCO	8f Gd/Fm	53	2999	bl
0	12	LING	10f Firm		3490	

FOURTH TIME LUCKY 4 b c £0

14a	10	SOUT	8f Aw		195
15a	9	SOUT	7f Aw		247
26	11	BEVE	7f Firm	39	2221
28	6	RIPO	8f Gd/Fm		2834
25	10	REDC	8f Firm		3330

FOX COTTAGE 2 ch f £0

0	16	LING	6f Firm	3832
50	10	LING	5f Good	4096
0	17	WIND	8f Gd/Sft	4289

FOX STAR 3 b f £411

37a	7	LING	8f Aw		26	BL
32a	10	LING	7f Aw		94	bl
42a	6	LING	6f Aw		313	
39	10	WARW	8f Soft		1062	bl
38	7	BRIG	7f Firm		1212	
23	13	BRIG	10f Firm		1331	
15a	5	LING	12f Aw		1540	
43	3	BRIG	7f Gd/Fm	44	1930	bl
0	17	NEWM	7f Firm	44	2347	bl
0	22	ASCO	7f Gd/Fm	60	2999	bl
19	11	BRIG	7f Gd/Fm	42	3242	bl
0	13	EPSO	9f Good	52	3856	bl

FOXDALE 3 ch f £0

42	5	CATT	6f Gd/Fm		781
43	9	NOTT	5f Heavy		1021
0	17	SALI	7f Good		1349
22	11	BRIG	6f Firm	44	2896

FOXES LAIR 2 b g £0

70	5	YORK	8f Soft	4281
74	4	MUSS	7f Soft	4517

FOXKEY 3 ch f £0

52a	6	LING	5f Aw	67	234	BL
31a	6	SOUT	7f Aw		281	

FOXS IDEA 3 b f £5242

77a	1	**WOLV**	7f Aw	70	294*
77a	3	SOUT	7f Aw	76	416
76a	3	WOLV	8f Aw	76	495
0	23	DONC	8f Gd/Sft	73	1053
71	5	NEWB	7f Gd/Fm	70	1405

54	9	SAND	7f Soft	69	1569	
65	5	NOTT	8f Good	68	2013	
47	4	NEWM	10f Gd/Fm		2284	
61	3	WIND	6f Soft	64	2549	
15	13	WIND	8f Good	63	3355	
0	19	LEIC	8f Gd/Sft		4033	

FOXY ALPHA 3 ch f £0

27	9	PONT	6f Good		1500	
34	5	CATT	5f Soft		1678	
20	8	CARL	8f Firm	40	2281	
16	11	BEVE	8f Firm	40	2735	

FOXY BROWN 3 b f £807

59a	2	WOLV	5f Aw		120
67a	3	SOUT	5f Aw		179
55a	4	SOUT	6f Aw	63	331

FRAMPANT 3 ch f £5118

53a	4	SOUT	6f Aw	68	689
60a	3	LING	7f Aw	65	773
0	16	WARW	7f Soft	67	1061
50	10	WIND	6f Firm	65	1289
0	17	NEWB	6f Gd/Fm	65	1406
56	4	BRIG	6f Good		1651
59	4	CHES	6f Gd/Sft		1780
59	3	CARL	6f Firm	60	2280
35	14	SAND	5f Gd/Fm	60	2478
50	6	WIND	5f Good	58	3191
42	9	HAMI	6f Soft	56	3803
0	20	WIND	5f Firm	54	4295
55	1	**NEWB**	5f Gd/Sft	50	4459*

FRANCESCO GUARDI 3 b c £20750

106	1	**DONC**	10f Firm		3889*
110	2	NEWB	11f Good		3984

FRANCHETTI 4 b f £0

0	16	HAYD	14f Gd/Fm	80	1167

FRANCPORT 4 b c £7923

67	5	DONC	6f Good	72	716
77	1	**RIPO**	6f Soft	70	824*
61	9	THIR	6f Good	77	1383
59	7	KEMP	6f Soft	77	1531
67	11	YORK	6f Firm	76	2000
75	3	REDC	6f Gd/Fm	74	2158
64	9	NEWC	6f Firm	75	2334
72	6	DONC	6f Good		2580
53	12	GOOD	6f Gd/Fm	75	3136
59	13	AYR	6f Gd/Sft	73	4010
49	10	NOTT	6f Heavy	71	4411

FRANGY 3 b f £8171

73	3	CHEP	12f Heavy		1554
79	1	**DONC**	12f Gd/Fm		2609*
79	1	**BATH**	12f Firm		2943*
72	5	HAYD	12f Gd/Sft	78	3270
54	14	YORK	14f Firm	81	3599

FRANICA 2 b f £8769

74	2	WARW	5f Soft		812
77	2	WARW	5f Heavy		886
77	2	HAYD	5f Heavy		989
78	2	DONC	5f Gd/Sft		1067
47	7	CHES	5f Firm		1249
77	1	**MUSS**	5f Gd/Fm		1429*
79	5	BEVE	5f Gd/Sft		1759
77	2	AYR	5f Good		2162
79	2	PONT	6f Gd/Fm	74	2557
79	4	CHES	5f Firm	78	3168
75	7	REDC	6f Firm		3327
0	19	NEWM	7f Good	77	4157

FRANKLIN D 4 ch c £1327

46a	3	LING	7f Aw	46	58
46a	2	LING	7f Aw	45	438
54a	3	LING	7f Aw		570
44a	4	WOLV	7f Aw	45	754
22a	12	WOLV	8f Aw	45	923
45a	4	SOUT	7f Aw	44	1801

21a	7	LING	8f Aw	44	1915	
8	11	BRIG	7f Gd/Fm	45	2728	vis

FRANKLIN LAKES 5 ch g £1098

44a	5	LING	8f Aw		93	vis
36a	7	LING	7f Aw		156	vis
37a	8	LING	7f Aw		225	vis
33a	3	SOUT	8f Aw	35	298	bl
21a	7	SOUT	8f Aw	34	418	tbl
37a	5	SOUT	8f Aw		452	tbl
39a	4	SOUT	7f Aw		501	tbl
23a	6	SOUT	8f Aw	32	585	tbl
24	10	NOTT	6f Gd/Fm		2680	
0	14	WARW	7f Gd/Fm	33	2840	bl
38	2	LEIC	5f Gd/Fm	37	3214	bl
25	10	LING	6f Firm	40	3493	bl
31	8	LING	6f Firm	40	3578	bl

FRATERNITY 3 b c £292

72	4	NEWC	12f Heavy		1009
72	7	WIND	12f Gd/Sft	77	1425

FRAZERS LAD 3 b g £446

62	5	NOTT	8f Heavy		4505
60a	3	WOLV	8f Aw		4551

FREDDY FLINTSTONE 3 b c £6202

74	12	NEWM	7f Gd/Sft		983
76	4	NEWM	8f Firm	75	1183
75	7	GOOD	10f Gd/Sft	76	1812
76	8	NEWM	10f Gd/Fm	76	2596
82	2	SAND	8f Gd/Fm		2938
80	3	NEWB	9f Gd/Fm		3179
78	4	NEWB	8f Firm	81	3481
82	3	NEWB	8f Firm	80	3998
0	16	ASCO	8f Gd/Sft	83	4126
75	2	YARM	7f Soft		4388

FREDORA 5 ch m £13715

73	5	HAYD	11f Heavy		986
52	14	NEWM	10f Gd/Fm	82	1150
75	9	WIND	10f Good	79	1729
83	2	WIND	10f Gd/Fm	79	1878
74	4	KEMP	9f Gd/Fm	76	2085
85	1	**KEMP**	9f Firm	80	2262*
79	8	SAND	8f Gd/Fm	83	2528
86	1	**EPSO**	9f Gd/Sft	83	2629*
84	4	NEWB	9f Firm	86	2853
79	7	GOOD	9f Gd/Fm	86	3089
82	4	SALI	8f Gd/Fm	85	3422
80	5	WIND	8f Good	84	3643
84	2	SAND	8f Gd/Fm		3945
71	6	HAYD	8f Soft	83	4094
76	8	NEWM	8f Good		4199
0	23	NEWM	8f Good	83	4340
0	13	NOTT	8f Heavy	81	4506

FREE 5 ch g £2730

0	12	BEVE	16f Firm	58	1276
0	14	RIPO	16f Good	54	1597
58	1	**NEWC**	14f Good	50	3249*
45	10	SAND	16f Good	54	3434

FREE KEVIN 4 b g £580

61	3	NEWC	9f Good		3248
0	25	YORK	9f Good		3808
38	9	MUSS	12f Gd/Sft		4133
0	15	AYR	10f Heavy	42	4306

FREE OPTION 5 ch g £17351

96	3	YORK	8f Firm	94	1327
48	22	ASCO	8f Good	94	2090

97	3	HAYD	7f Gd/Fm	94	2456
97	1	**KEMP**	8f Firm	94	2870*
84	10	ASCO	7f Gd/Fm	94	2997
97	3	NEWM	7f Gd/Fm	96	3315
91	6	YORK	8f Firm	96	3597
93	7	GOOD	8f Good		3883
93	7	NEWM	7f Gd/Fm	96	4195

FREE RIDER 3 b c £5407

106	2	NEWM	7f Good		955
96	15	NEWM	8f Gd/Fm		1171
87	15	GOOD	7f Gd/Sft	106	1470
108	3	NEWM	7f Gd/Fm		1693
97	9	ASCO	7f Good		2087

FREE TO SPEAK 8 ch h £5800

105	2	LEOP	9f Good		2071	bl
103	4	CURR	8f Gd/Fm		2740	

FREE WILL 3 ch c £834

46	5	RIPO	9f Good		1863
70	6	BATH	10f Gd/Sft		2553
74	3	PONT	10f Gd/Fm		2832
74	4	PONT	10f Gd/Fm		3221

FREECOM NET 2 b c £0

0	U	NEWB	7f Firm		2708
72	7	YORK	7f Gd/Fm		3730

FREEDOM NOW 2 b c £0

85	7	NEWM	7f Good		4183

FREEDOM QUEST 5 b g £13641

61	4	LEIC	10f Good	62	793	
61	4	MUSS	14f Gd/Sft	62	903	
63	3	MUSS	12f Gd/Fm	62	1147	
55	4	THIR	16f Gd/Sft	62	1355	
59	6	MUSS	12f Gd/Fm	62	1432	
57	4	CATT	14f Soft	60	1683	
61	2	RIPO	10f Good	58	1860	
52	5	BEVE	10f Firm	59	2220	
56a	2	SOUT	8f Aw	53	2379	
63	1	**NEWC**	10f Good	58	2522*	
60	4	CHES	10f Gd/Fm	60	2671	
52	8	DONC	10f Gd/Fm	60	3159	
56	7	AYR	10f Good	60	3368	
59	4	HAMI	11f Gd/Fm	60	3379	
61	2	REDC	11f Gd/Fm	59	3636	
49	15	YORK	8f Good	61	3810	
56	5	CHES	10f Soft	60	4074	
47	3	AYR	10f Heavy	59	4306	

FREEFOURINTERNET 2 b c £3429

90	3	NEWM	7f Gd/Fm		3164
90	5	NEWB	7f Firm		3450
92	2	DONC	9f Gd/Fm		3895

FREEFOURRACING 2 b f £37959

100	1	**BEVE**	5f Gd/Sft		1759*
100	1	**WIND**	6f Good		2369*
84	8	NEWM	6f Good		2565
105	1	**GOOD**	7f Good		3659*

FREETOWN 4 b c £1205

64	6	HAMI	13f Gd/Fm	67	1194
73	2	NEWC	17f Gd/Sft	67	1478

FRENCH BRAMBLE 2 ch f £0

57a	6	SOUT	5f Aw		1304	
49a	7	SOUT	5f Aw		1418	
51	8	PONT	5f Good		2360	
44	9	PONT	6f Gd/Fm		2828	
56	6	REDC	6f Gd/Fm		2990	
67	4	NEWC	6f Good		3245	BL
62	4	REDC	5f Gd/Fm		3632	bl
38a	8	WOLV	6f Aw		4225	bl

FRENCH CONNECTION 5 b g £617

37a	6	SOUT	8f Aw	50	298	
48a	2	SOUT	7f Aw		341	bl
14a	9	SOUT	7f Aw	48	471	
0a	9	WOLV	9f Aw	48	516	bl
20	11	NOTT	10f Gd/Fm	48	3111	VIS

FRENCH EMPIRE 2 b c £0

0	10	YORK	6f Gd/Fm		3566	

FRENCH FANCY 3 gr f £3674

28a	7	LING	7f Aw		421	
46a	4	LING	6f Aw		443	BL
47a	5	LING	7f Aw	47	488	bl
43a	3	SOUT	6f Aw	46	515	bl
15a	7	LING	8f Aw		574	bl
43a	4	LING	7f Aw	49	617	bl
43a	2	LING	7f Aw	44	773	bl
44	4	LING	7f Gd/Sft	46	841	bl
35	10	WIND	8f Heavy		934	bl
37	7	BRIG	7f Firm	45	1336	bl
45	4	BRIG	6f Gd/Sft		1508	bl
50a	1	LING	6f Aw	45	1742*	bl
25a	9	LING	8f Aw	51	1915	bl
35	8	GOOD	6f Gd/Fm	45	2124	bl
33	9	BRIG	5f Soft	42	2428	bl
29	5	LING	7f Good	42	2591	
0	16	LEIC	7f Gd/Fm	42	2777	

FRENCH FELLOW 3 b c £24539

114	2	THIR	8f Soft		925	
95	17	NEWM	8f Gd/Fm		1171	
110	1	DONC	8f Gd/Fm		2578*	
112	3	HAYD	11f Gd/Fm		3321	
109	4	YORK	12f Good		3540	

FRENCH GINGER 9 ch m £0

0a	11	SOUT	8f Aw		50	t
16a	7	WOLV	9f Aw		292	

FRENCH GRIT 8 b g £621

47a	2	LING	5f Aw	46	166	
47a	5	LING	6f Aw	48	205	
0a	13	SOUT	6f Aw	48	246	
35a	6	WOLV	6f Aw	47	351	VIS
24a	9	WOLV	7f Aw		567	vis
46a	7	LING	7f Aw		616	
20a	10	LING	6f Aw	40	691	
43	6	DONC	6f Gd/Sft		1068	
23a	10	WOLV	6f Aw		1139	
37	8	REDC	6f Firm		1298	
28	9	CATT	6f Good		1663	
0	15	HAMI	6f Gd/Fm	42	1941	

FRENCH HORN 3 b g £9138

57	8	WIND	8f Gd/Fm	66	744	
64	3	KEMP	9f Soft	66	999	
77	1	DONC	8f Gd/Sft	66	1053*	
85	1	CHEP	8f Heavy		1552*	
0	22	ASCO	8f Good	86	2117	
77	7	KEMP	8f Gd/Fm	83	3793	
75	7	NEWB	8f Firm	82	3998	

FRENCH LIEUTENANT 3 b c £2332

86	6	NEWM	7f Gd/Fm	85	1153	
89	2	GOOD	8f Gd/Sft		1635	
57	21	ASCO	8f Good	87	2117	

FRENCH MASTER 3 b g £4778

40a	4	SOUT	8f Aw		36	vis
52a	3	SOUT	8f Aw		385	BL
53a	3	SOUT	8f Aw	57	429	bl
58a	3	SOUT	11f Aw	58	537	bl
57	1	SOUT	10f Good		806*	vis
38	9	BEVE	10f Firm		1274	vis
46	3	NOTT	10f Soft	58	1644	
44	3	HAMI	11f Gd/Fm		1909	vis
53	2	NEWC	9f Gd/Fm	53	2276	vis
0	13	PONT	10f Gd/Fm	54	2556	
44	7	RIPO	10f Gd/Fm	53	3008	vis
0	11	NEWC	12f Good		3247	vis
30	6	HAMI	9f Gd/Sft		3375	vis
30	9	CATT	12f Soft	45	4256	vis
10	9	NEWC	8f Heavy	40	4406	vis

FRENCH SPICE 4 b f £15455

32a	6	LING	10f Aw		95	

(FRENCH SPICE continued)

48a	1	WOLV	8f Aw	40	227*	
57a	1	WOLV	9f Aw	46	306*	
58a	1	WOLV	9f Aw	46	359*	
72a	1	WOLV	9f Aw	57	469+	
72a	1	WOLV	8f Aw		477+	
76a	1	WOLV	12f Aw	62	489*	
82a	1	SOUT	12f Aw		510*	
61a	4	WOLV	12f Aw	80	562	

FRENCHMANS BAY 2 b c £4025

103	3	NEWB	7f Gd/Sft		4455	

FRESHWATER PEARL 2 b f £16250

97	1	LEOP	6f Gd/Fm		2399*	

FREUD 2 b c £0

111	5	NEWM	7f Good		4354	
102	5	DONC	8f Soft		4463	

FRIAR TUCK 5 ch g £23285

0	14	AYR	7f Gd/Fm	68	1631	
68	7	HAMI	6f Gd/Fm		1905	
70	1	YORK	6f Firm	65	2000*	
63	8	AYR	7f Good	69	2163	
70	3	NEWC	6f Firm	69	2334	
55	10	YORK	6f Good	70	2697	
77	1	CARL	5f Firm		2822*	
80	1	AYR	6f Firm	75	2877*	
83	3	RIPO	6f Gd/Fm	82	3183	
61	16	RIPO	6f Gd/Fm	81	3464	
62	16	AYR	6f Gd/Sft	81	4010	
55	14	YORK	6f Heavy	80	4301	

FRIENDLY HOSTESS 2 gr f £0

33	9	YARM	6f Soft		4390	BL

FRILLY FRONT 4 ch f £16685

42a	4	WOLV	6f Aw		76	
58a	1	WOLV	5f Aw	54	116*	
50a	8	WOLV	5f Aw	58	191	
0a	P	WOLV	5f Aw	57	291	
62a	1	LING	5f Aw	57	403*	
69a	1	LING	5f Aw	60	506*	
44a	11	WOLV	5f Aw	68	579	
79a	1	LING	5f Aw	68	631*	
66a	6	LING	5f Aw	78	774	
46	12	REDC	5f Gd/Sft	61	1133	
48	11	THIR	5f Good	61	1162	
39	11	NEWC	5f Gd/Sft	59	1479	
56	5	CARL	5f Gd/Sft	57	1724	
0	12	CATT	6f Gd/Sft	57	1815	
39	10	NEWC	5f Firm	56	2340	
51	4	YARM	6f Gd/Fm	56	2415	
72a	2	LING	5f Aw		2650	
44	8	PONT	5f Aw	54	3502	

FRISCO BAY 2 b c £0

58	5	PONT	5f Gd/Sft		1102	

FRISKY FOX 6 b m £0

0a	11	WOLV	16f Aw	40	66	

FROMSONG 2 b c £9405

76	5	SALI	5f Good		1346	
103	1	BATH	6f Soft		4138*	
106	2	NEWB	5f Gd/Sft		4454	

FRONTIER 3 b c £14911

90	5	WIND	8f Good		851	
85	3	WIND	10f Gd/Fm		1198	
88	3	HAYD	11f Gd/Sft	88	3267	
68	6	NEWB	10f Firm	88	3453	
86	4	NEWB	8f Gd/Fm	86	3998	
92	1	SAND	8f Soft	86	4206*	

FRONTIER FLIGHT 10 b g £0

5a	6	SOUT	12f Aw	28	70	
0a	9	WOLV	14f Aw	31	190	
28a	7	SOUT	14f Aw		1975	
0	13	YORK	12f Soft		4276	
0	15	BRIG	8f Soft		4420	

FROSTED AIRE 4 ch g £0

0	10	NEWC	6f Soft		756	
0	16	PONT	6f Soft		872	

FROZEN SEA 9 ch g £0

0	12	BRIG	12f Gd/Sft	32	1465	
1a	11	LING	12f Aw		2181	t
26a	6	LING	10f Aw		2587	t
27	7	BRIG	12f Firm	30	2904	t

FRUIT PUNCH 2 b f £0

86	5	NEWM	7f Good		3020	
67	5	HAYD	7f Good		3287	
66	8	YORK	6f Gd/Fm		3568	
52	12	DONC	8f Gd/Fm	70	3879	

FRUITS OF LOVE 5 b h £129387

112	9	TOKY	12f Firm		123	
122	1	ASCO	12f Good		2149+	vis
121	3	BADE	12f V		3849	vis

FUEGIAN 5 ch g £3906

57	2	WIND	8f Gd/Fm	55	1201	
45	11	KEMP	8f Gd/Fm	56	1926	vis
58	1	WIND	8f Gd/Fm	56	2051*	
32	12	WIND	8f Good	59	2367	
0	P	BRIG	8f Gd/Fm	59	2726	vis
30	14	WIND	8f Good	59	3188	
0	17	SALI	8f Firm	57	3753	
30	13	GOOD	8f Soft	66	4066	vis

FUERO REAL 5 b g £2314

24a	10	LING	10f Aw	40	209	
34a	5	LING	13f Aw	38	460	
48	3	BRIG	10f Firm		1331	
39	1	BRIG	12f Gd/Sft	35	1465*	
0	12	BATH	10f Gd/Sft	44	1666	

FUJIYAMA CREST 8 b g £2383

0	19	LING	16f Good	72	1394	vis
63	7	CHEP	18f Gd/Fm	69	1800	
56	7	BATH	17f Firm	62	1996	
62	1	NOTT	16f Gd/Fm		2191*	
53	5	NOTT	14f Gd/Fm	59	2681	

FULHAM 4 ch c £1050

48a	4	LING	7f Aw		616	BL
56a	2	LING	10f Aw		771	bl
24a	8	LING	10f Aw	50	880	bl
19a	10	LING	12f Aw	48	1677	bl
40	4	EPSO	9f Gd/Sft		2433	bl
0	10	WIND	12f Good		2715	bl
22	11	EPSO	9f Gd/Fm		3404	

FULL AHEAD 3 b c £6089

81	3	DONC	10f Good		713	
77	3	NOTT	10f Gd/Fm		1271	
74	2	HAMI	12f Gd/Fm		1362	
81	2	YARM	11f Good	77	1770	
85	1	REDC	14f Gd/Fm		2144*	
92	6	NEWM	15f Gd/Fm		2594	
62	11	NEWM	14f Gd/Fm	84	4213	
0	27	NEWM	18f Good	91	4353	

FULL CIRCUIT 4 ch g £0

0	16	PONT	8f Good		1498	

FULL EGALITE 4 gr g £3707

9	15	BRIG	12f Gd/Fm	52	1128	
40	7	BRIG	10f Gd/Sft	47	1509	
0	21	NEWM	12f Firm	43	1852	
44a	1	LING	12f Aw		2181*	BL
41a	2	LING	13f Aw		2323	bl
0	15	NEWM	10f Gd/Fm	43	2958	
16	10	BRIG	12f Gd/Fm	40	3260	bl
50	2	FOLK	12f Gd/Fm		3447	bl
59	3	WARW	11f Good		3691	bl
60a	5	LING	12f Aw		4101	bl
63a	D	LING	12f AW		4186	bl
51a	3	LING	12f Aw	51	4334	bl

FULL FLOW 3 b c £16029

99	4	NEWM	7f Gd/Sft	104	969	
104	4	YORK	7f Gd/Fm	103	1308	
93	12	GOOD	8f Good	103	3107	

104	1	BATH	8f Gd/Fm		3515+
114	2	NEWB	9f Firm		4000
99	8	NEWM	8f Good		4180

FULL SPATE 5 ch g £11459

65	3	EPSO	6f Heavy	64	1028
61	6	HAMI	6f Gd/Fm	65	1192
49	12	THIR	6f Gd/Sft	65	1356
63	3	CHEP	7f Good	64	1969
62	5	WIND	6f Gd/Fm	64	2054
60	4	WIND	6f Gd/Fm	63	2207
69	1	HAYD	6f Gd/Fm	63	2444*
50	12	YORK	6f Good	70	2697
70	3	AYR	6f Firm	70	2877
55	9	THIR	6f Gd/Fm	70	3123
69	4	NEWM	6f Gd/Fm	71	3457
62	10	GOOD	6f Good	70	3646

FULLOPEP 6 b g £0

| 0 | 11 | DONC | 15f Gd/Sft | 63 | 4451 |

FULLY INVESTED 2 b f £3542

| 88 | 1 | LING | 7f Soft | | 4267* |

FUNNY GIRL 3 b f £1350

91	5	ASCO	8f Gd/Sft		1108
90	6	ASCO	10f Good		2169
81	2	NEWB	10f Good		3179
75	5	SAND	10f Good		3432
70	6	THIR	8f Gd/Sft	80	3777

FUNNY VALENTINE 2 ch c £1570

| 84 | 2 | NEWB | 6f Sft/Hvy | | 4470 |
| 74 | 5 | DONC | 6f Heavy | | 4576 |

FURNESS 3 b g £3819

60a	2	SOUT	12f Aw	54	2815
57	5	NEWM	12f Gd/Fm	58	3167
54	2	HAYD	16f Gd/Sft	54	3476
41a	5	WOLV	15f Aw		4024
62a	1	SOUT	14f Aw	53	4370*

FURTHER OUTLOOK 6 gr g £59592

78	15	DONC	5f Gd/Fm	99	702
84	11	NEWM	6f Firm	98	1182
90	8	CHES	5f Firm	98	1245
0	20	YORK	5f Firm	96	1324
95	5	YORK	6f Firm	96	1337
97	3	HAYD	5f Gd/Sft	94	1533
97	2	EPSO	6f Good	95	1851
96	5	YORK	5f Gd/Fm	95	1980
98	3	ASCO	5f Gd/Fm	96	3016
92	6	GOOD	6f Firm	96	3152
95	4	HAYD	5f Gd/Fm	97	3322
88	12	RIPO	6f Gd/Fm	97	3464
98	3	YORK	6f Gd/Fm	97	3727
0	16	DONC	6f Gd/Fm	97	3861
91	9	AYR	6f Gd/Sft	97	4012
100	3	ASCO	5f Gd/Sft	96	4129
105	1	YORK	6f Heavy	97	4301+
103	3	DONC	7f Soft		4465
103	2	DONC	6f Heavy		4581

FUSAICHI PEGASUS 3 b c £541585

| 125¢ | 1 | CHUR | 10f Dirt | | 1226* |

FUSUL 4 ch c £8784

37a	7	LING	8f Aw	50	96
42a	4	LING	10f Aw	45	203
55a	1	LING	12f Aw		267*
63a	1	LING	12f Aw	53	441*
55a	3	LING	12f Aw	57	486
36a	11	LING	10f Aw	63	632
65a	2	LING	13f Aw	61	835
35	5	LING	9f Firm	63	3488
44	12	EPSO	12f Good	63	3858
66a	2	LING	12f Aw	63	4486 t

FUTURE COUP 4 b g £437

47	10	CARL	9f Firm	59	1254
36	9	NOTT	10f Gd/Fm	59	1364
30	13	LEIC	8f Firm	56	2027

50a	4	SOUT	8f Aw	53	2380	
0a	13	SOUT	8f Aw	53	2634	
43a	5	SOUT	8f Aw		2816	
55	3	BEVE	8f Good		3393	BL
28	12	HAMI	8f Gd/Sft	48	3534	bl
46	4	THIR	8f Gd/Sft		3775	bl
43	9	WARW	11f Gd/Fm	48	3915	VIS

FUTURE FLIGHT 2 b f £1412

| 87 | 2 | NEWM | 6f Gd/Fm | | 4530 |

FUTURE PROSPECT 6 b g £1408

63	2	BEVE	7f Firm	62	1920
61	5	HAMI	9f Firm	62	2094
49	5	MUSS	9f Firm		2376
44	13	HAMI	9f Gd/Fm	62	2799
47	8	YORK	9f Good		3808
0	11	BEVE	8f Good	55	3951

GABI 2 ch f £0

| 58 | 9 | LING | 7f Soft | | 4484 |

GABIDIA 3 br f £1125

61	6	WARW	8f Soft		1063
57	4	SOUT	7f Soft		1607
51	8	CARL	7f Firm	65	2017
38a	6	SOUT	7f Aw		2633
58	3	NEWM	10f Good		3021

GABLESEA 6 b g £4620

0a	13	WOLV	8f Aw		477	
46a	2	WOLV	9f Aw	46	569	
43a	4	WOLV	9f Aw	46	637	
44a	6	WOLV	9f Aw	46	675	
53	1	WARW	11f Heavy	46	890*	
37	12	WARW	11f Soft	53	1065	
55	2	HAMI	8f Gd/Fm	53	1190	
49	8	NOTT	10f Gd/Sft	55	1370	
46	5	REDC	10f Gd/Sft	55	1583	
39	8	CHES	10f Gd/Sft	55	1777	
43	9	NEWM	8f Gd/Fm	51	2130	
32	8	HAYD	11f Gd/Fm	49	2453	
42	4	CHES	8f Gd/Sft	45	2673	VIS
27	6	LEIC	8f Sft/Hvy		4311	vis
37a	9	SOUT	8f Aw	49	4365	
0a	12	WOLV	8f Aw	49	4437	bl

GAD YAKOUN 7 ch g £0

0	16	REDC	6f Firm		1298	
0	12	SOUT	7f Soft		1601	
0a	12	WOLV	7f Aw	31	2122	
38	8	CARL	6f Gd/Fm		2240	
29	7	HAYD	5f Gd/Fm	38	2505	
0	18	HAYD	5f Gd/Fm	45	2701	
0	11	WARW	5f Good		3694	
0	15	CHES	6f Soft		4069	t
0	16	REDC	5f Gd/Sft		4220	t

GADGE 9 br g £610

45a	3	SOUT	8f Aw	50	83
50a	4	LING	7f Aw	50	106
43a	10	WOLV	7f Aw	49	193
28a	9	WOLV	8f Aw	47	227
25a	8	SOUT	8f Aw	45	298
32a	8	LING	8f Aw		316
42a	3	WOLV	7f Aw		391
38a	8	WOLV	8f Aw		449
26a	7	SOUT	6f Aw	37	604
27	11	CATT	7f Gd/Fm		778

GAELIC FORAY 4 b f £669

10a	7	LING	10f Aw		775
0	13	BRIG	10f Firm		1210
36a	3	LING	7f Aw		1741
26a	5	LING	6f Aw		1913
51a	3	LING	7f Aw		2759
34	10	LING	7f Firm	45	3279
15a	9	WOLV	8f Aw	45	4440

GAELIC STORM 6 b g £61511

| 90 | 9 | LING | 6f Good | | 1674 |

107	6	YARM	6f Gd/Fm		1952	
110	5	ASCO	6f Good		2115	
71	11	NEWC	6f Firm		2335	
98	4	CHES	7f Gd/Fm		2670	
97	6	NEWB	6f Firm		2847	
107	1	KLAM	6f Good		3213*	
101	5	EPSO	7f Good		3763	
108	4	AYR	6f Gd/Sft	107	4012	
104	7	ASCO	7f Good	107	4112	
108	1	REDC	7f Gd/Fm		4218*	
108	2	MUNI	7f Soft		4317	
115	1	NEWB	6f Gd/Sft		1074456*	
118	1	LEOP	6f Heavy		1124555*	
101	3	DONC	6f Heavy		4581	

GAIN TIME 3 b g £0

| 44a | 10 | SOUT | 7f Aw | 69 | 31 | bl |

GALANTA 2 b c £13000

| 98 | 4 | CURR | 6f Yldg | | 3720 |

GALAPAGOS GIRL 2 b f £5932

78	1	WIND	6f Gd/Fm		2886*
80	2	HAYD	6f Good		3286
78	10	DONC	6f Good		3862

GALAPINO 7 b g £1115

48	5	SAND	16f Heavy	55	1044	
51	4	LING	16f Good	51	1394	
44	8	NEWB	13f Gd/Fm	52	1784	
37	5	SAND	14f Gd/Fm	50	1991	
33	9	ASCO	20f Good	58	2092	
35	5	KEMP	16f Gd/Fm	48	3360	
45	2	SAND	16f Good	47	3434	bl
0	12	LING	16f Firm	48	3755	bl
40	8	GOOD	16f Soft	48	4075	bl
0	16	SALI	14f Gd/Sft	48	4166	bl
32	4	BRIG	12f Soft	43	4421	

GALAXY RETURNS 2 ch c £4323

65	7	HAYD	5f Gd/Sft		1488
70	2	CARL	6f Firm		2014
64	6	WARW	7f Good		2459
70	1	CARL	6f Gd/Fm		3079*
55	7	BEVE	7f Gd/Fm	72	3411
49	10	NEWC	6f Gd/Sft	69	3704
0	20	DONC	6f Gd/Sft		4449

GALI 4 gr c £0

42	7	WIND	8f Good	48	2367	
0	15	BRIG	10f Gd/Fm	45	2727	
33	9	WIND	10f Gd/Fm		3045	VIS
27	11	WIND	10f Good	41	3188	

GALILEO 2 b c £11050

| 107 | 1 | LEOP | 8f Heavy | | 4554* |

GALLA PLACIDIA 2 b f £0

| 78 | 6 | KEMP | 8f Gd/Fm | | 3799 |
| 66a | 5 | WOLV | 8f Aw | | 4022 |

GALLANT 3 b c £876

80	3	NEWC	8f Soft		3707
73	4	NOTT	8f Soft		3977
64	7	YARM	7f Good		4388

GALLANT FELLOW 5 ch g £0

26a	11	LING	6f Aw		25
34a	5	LING	10f Aw		111
35a	8	LING	7f Aw		156

GALLEON BEACH 3 b c £2307

87	3	EPSO	10f Heavy		1029
66	8	CHES	12f Gd/Fm		1216
0	P	YORK	12f Gd/Fm	95	2647

GALLERY GOD 4 ch c £22675

81	9	NEWM	12f Gd/Sft	84	968
78	6	NEWM	12f Firm	84	1187
85	3	GOOD	14f Gd/Sft	83	1484
88	1	THIR	12f Gd/Sft	80	1715*
94	2	ASCO	12f Good	86	2069
93	2	ASCO	12f Gd/Fm	91	3001

GALLITO CASTAO 2 b c £2700

95 3 CURR 5f Gd/Sft 1621

GALLOWAY BOY 3 ch c £2250
68 13 HAYD 5f Heavy 988
98 3 FAIR 6f Firm 3548 t

GALTEE 8 b h £3012
94 2 DIEL 12f Good 1119

GALY BAY 2 b f £2609
64 3 LEIC 5f Gd/Sft 828
67 3 PONT 6f Good 1497
71 3 HAYD 7f Gd/Sft 4103
79 2 AYR 6f Heavy 75 4305
73 6 BRIG 7f Soft 75 4416
47 11 DONC 7f Heavy 78 4577

GAME MAGIC 2 b c £810
74 4 WIND 5f Good 849
75 4 LING 5f Gd/Fm 2214
65 3 NEWM 7f Firm 3296

GAME N GIFTED 2 b c £3856
88 2 NEWB 5f Gd/Sft 1589
84 1 NOTT 5f Good 2009*
98 5 YORK 6f Gd/Fm 3566
84 8 KEMP 6f Gd/Fm 3797

GAME TUFTY 4 b g £1165
0 19 WARW 11f Soft 63 1065
47 8 BRIG 10f Firm 1210
26 8 NEWM 8f Gd/Fm 3117
41 6 WARW 11f Good 3691
43 2 YARM 10f Firm 3935
46 2 YARM 11f Soft 46 4391
19a 5 WOLV 12f Aw 4549

GAMITAS 2 b f £317
66 7 CHEP 8f Gd/Fm 3678
65a 3 WOLV 7f Aw 4385

GARBO 5 b m £0
0a 16 SOUT 12f Aw 40 68

GARDEN IN THE RAIN 3 b f £3170
89 3 BORD 8f Good 2487

GARDEN OF EDEN 2 b f £0
49 6 LEIC 7f Heavy 4312

GARDEN SOCIETY 3 ch c £7066
96 1 THIR 12f Good 1157*
90 3 YORK 14f Gd/Fm 1311
101 3 DONC 10f Gd/Fm 1841
92 6 NEWM 10f Firm 3300

GARDOR 2 b c £1979
68 4 PONT 6f Gd/Fm 2828
71 4 NEWC 7f Gd/Fm 2985
66 4 NOTT 6f Good 3520
70 2 THIR 7f Gd/Sft 3776
70 6 MUSS 7f Soft 4517

GARDRUM 2 ch c £0
0 R YORK 6f Soft 4283

GARGALHADA FINAL 3 b c £8699
94 1 LEIC 10f Gd/Sft 833*
101 2 NEWM 12f Gd/Fm 1168
92 5 LONG 12f Good 1380
105 6 GOOD 10f Soft 4064
104 2 AYR 8f Heavy 4308

GARGOYLE GIRL 3 b f £1012
0 15 NEWC 8f Heavy 58 1007
43 6 AYR 11f Gd/Fm 53 1633
46 4 AYR 13f Good 48 2141
46 4 PONT 12f Good 47 2362
54 5 HAYD 12f Gd/Fm 57 2446
35 5 HAMI 12f Gd/Fm 47 2638
22 5 THIR 12f Gd/Fm 50 2967
48 4 AYR 11f Gd/Fm 50 3140
45 4 REDC 10f Firm 47 3310
44 3 HAMI 8f Gd/Sft 47 3380

GARNOCK VALLEY 10 b g £15974
67a 1 SOUT 6f Aw 62 47*

60a 5 SOUT 6f Aw 67 180
68a 2 SOUT 6f Aw 67 218
76a 1 SOUT 6f Aw 67 250*
60a 6 SOUT 6f Aw 74 342
72a 4 SOUT 6f Aw 74 499
0 12 WARW 5f Heavy 52 1005
42 10 HAMI 5f Firm 52 1244
68a 3 SOUT 6f Aw 73 1504
46 6 AYR 5f Gd/Fm 50 1629
49 2 NOTT 6f Gd/Fm 48 2193
37 5 CARL 7f Firm 48 2282
56 2 MUSS 5f Gd/Sft 52 2535
42 10 BEVE 5f Firm 52 2732
66a 1 SOUT 6f Aw 2819*
56 3 HAMI 5f Gd/Sft 56 3536
52 8 AYR 5f Soft 56 3960
54 4 AYR 6f Heavy 55 4327
57 3 NEWB 5f Gd/Sft 55 4459
61 1 MUSS 5f Soft 55 4516*

GARRISON 2 b f £562
17 7 CARL 5f Gd/Fm 3079
57 4 HAMI 5f Soft 3801
57 7 AYR 6f Soft 3958
49 6 NEWC 5f Heavy 55 4423
52 3 MUSS 5f Soft 53 4561

GARTH POOL 3 b c £5903
51a 5 SOUT 5f Aw 740
79a 1 WOLV 5f Aw 1036+
88a 1 SOUT 6f Aw 72 1205*
5 11 NEWC 6f Gd/Fm 77 1768
56 8 HAMI 5f Firm 73 2395
68 2 PONT 6f Gd/Fm 3225

GASCON 4 b g £1502
60 8 SALI 6f Firm 1175
68 2 SOUT 6f Soft 1605
55 4 SAND 5f Good 3229
0 14 NEWM 6f Good 72 3613
57 8 BATH 6f Gd/Fm 65 3821

GATHERING CLOUD 4 b f £0
0a 15 SOUT 8f Aw 45

GAVEL 3 b g £0
0 20 BRIG 10f Gd/Sft 66 892
50 9 SALI 7f Good 1349 BL
26 12 RIPO 8f Good 1596 bl
0 17 NEWM 8f Gd/Fm 2134

GAY BREEZE 7 b g £5379
77 3 THIR 5f Soft 905
0 18 DONC 6f Gd/Sft 79 1074
77 3 THIR 5f Gd/Sft 77 1357
75 5 REDC 5f Gd/Fm 77 1580
64 10 NOTT 5f Good 77 1871
0 17 NEWC 5f Gd/Fm 75 2310
69 6 HAYD 7f Gd/Sft 73 2701
63 12 GOOD 5f Soft 71 3091
56 11 BEVE 5f Good 69 3398
57 7 YARM 5f Gd/Fm 66 3668
65a 2 WOLV 6f Aw 63 4223
66 2 AYR 6f Heavy 63 4327
69 1 MUSS 7f Soft 65 4522*

GAY CHALLENGER 2 b g £318
39 5 NEWM 6f Gd/Fm 2959
42 10 NEWM 7f Gd/Fm 3121
85 4 YARM 7f Good 3237
0 19 DONC 7f Firm 71 3901
50 9 GOOD 8f Soft 63 4076
51 9 WIND 10f Gd/Sft 56 4290

GAY HEROINE 2 b f £1302
83 2 SAND 6f Gd/Fm 3943

GAY LOVER 3 gr f £0
38 8 GOOD 10f Soft 4081
0 13 BATH 12f Soft 4434

GAYE CHARM 3 ch g £0

47 9 NEWM 8f Firm 2345
53 6 KEMP 8f Firm 2871
39 10 NEWM 10f Good 3021
14 12 YARM 8f Gd/Fm 52 3970

GAZETTE IT TONIGHT 2 b f £6551
52 5 HAMI 5f Gd/Fm 1359
58 5 PONT 5f Soft 1698
46 6 YORK 6f Gd/Fm 1981
55 3 CATT 5f Gd/Fm 2435
43a 3 WOLV 5f Aw 2605
59 1 CATT 7f Gd/Fm 2927*
58 3 THIR 7f Gd/Fm 3128
57 3 CATT 7f Good 3438
63 1 THIR 7f Gd/Fm 3615*
63 4 CHES 7f Soft 61 4070
34 10 MUSS 8f Gd/Sft 61 4132
26a 10 WOLV 8f Aw 53 4439

GDANSK 3 b c £9806
62 4 MUSS 7f Gd/Sft 900
43 10 WARW 7f Good 69 1061
76 2 PONT 6f Good 1500
72 1 WARW 5f Gd/Sft 1712*
60 8 AYR 5f Good 76 2165
62 7 SAND 5f Gd/Fm 75 2467
64 4 CHES 5f Good 75 2663
36 12 PONT 5f Gd/Fm 72 2830
0 16 GOOD 5f Gd/Fm 75 3136
62 2 WARW 5f Good 3694
68 1 REDC 5f Gd/Sft 4220*
45 15 AYR 5f Heavy 66 4307

GEE BEE BOY 6 ch g £436
0a 13 LING 10f Aw 50 2212
43 6 FOLK 16f Good 45 2622
42 3 BRIG 10f Firm 41 3557

GEEFORCE 4 ch f £0
0a 12 WOLV 8f Aw 44 233

GEEGEE EMMARR 7 b m £0
0a 12 SOUT 12f Aw 35 211
0a 12 SOUT 8f Aw 34 298
0a 8 WOLV 16f Aw 37 348
6a 9 WOLV 15f Aw 363

GEETEE 3 b g £0
0 7 KEMP 12f Gd/Fm 1929

GEETEE EIGHTYFIVE 2 b c £0
0 11 LING 5f Gd/Sft 1260
61 12 NEWB 5f Gd/Fm 1782

GEM BIEN 2 b c £2842
60 5 PONT 6f Soft 4082
42 9 NEWC 6f Heavy 4402
76 1 MUSS 7f Soft 4517*

GEM OF WISDOM 3 gr c £0
41a 8 SOUT 5f Aw 55 72 vis
40a 8 SOUT 5f Aw 62 202 vis
0a 11 SOUT 5f Aw 300 vis

GEMINI GUEST 4 ch c £1738
0 30 ASCO 8f Gd/Sft 78 1113
68 5 NOTT 10f Gd/Fm 1271
62 7 NEWB 13f Gd/Sft 72 1594
62 3 CHES 12f Good 2667
46 8 LEIC 12f Gd/Fm 3219
51 9 SALI 14f Gd/Sft 62 4166
63 2 BATH 12f Soft 58 4433

GEMTASTIC 2 b f £2015
46 6 CHES 5f Gd/Sft 1776
59 8 CHES 5f Gd/Fm 2248
54 3 BATH 5f Firm 3204
55 3 HAMI 5f Gd/Sft 3376
58 2 WIND 5f Good 3639
47 11 LEIC 6f Gd/Sft 58 4030
65a 2 WOLV 5f Aw 4441

GENERAL ALARM 3 b c £265
70 7 SAND 10f Soft 4205

69 4 NOTT 10f Heavy 4412

GENERAL DOMINION 3 b g £0

49	8	MUSS	9f Gd/Sft		902
61	8	THIR	7f Good		1159
44	5	REDC	10f Firm		1295
55	4	REDC	6f Gd/Sft	57	1578
41	7	CARL	6f Gd/Fm	57	2243
0	19	REDC	5f Soft		4220

GENERAL HAWK 2 b c £412

82	3	REDC	6f Good		1893

GENERAL JACKSON 3 ch c £1001

64	12	NEWB	8f Good		1376
75	4	SAND	8f Soft		1584
73	3	NEWB	7f Gd/Fm		1947
58	10	SAND	10f Good		2531
46	7	GOOD	10f Soft		4081

GENERAL JANE 2 ch f f £547

53	3	WARW	5f Soft		1059
23	7	GOOD	6f Gd/Sft		1634

GENERAL KLAIRE 5 b m £5809

72a	5	SOUT	6f Aw	75	47
68a	6	WOLV	7f Aw	75	79
69a	5	SOUT	6f Aw	73	129
64a	3	SOUT	6f Aw	73	183
50a	7	SOUT	6f Aw	71	388
58a	1	**SOUT**	7f Aw		501*
64a	3	SOUT	7f Aw	67	588
52a	6	SOUT	7f Aw	66	647
57a	4	SOUT	7f Aw	64	739
31	11	HAYD	7f Gd/Sft	49	811
6	14	PONT	5f Gd/Sft	45	1101
69a	1	**SOUT**	7f Aw	62	2637*
53a	4	WOLV	7f Aw		3770
62a	6	SOUT	7f Aw	68	4153

GENERAL SONG 6 b g £0

0a	12	SOUT	7f Aw		1305

GENERATE 4 b f £11250

64a	1	**WOLV**	9f Aw		578*
49a	6	SOUT	7f Aw		667
58	D	BEVE	10f Heavy	56	975
57a	1	**SOUT**	11f Aw	51	1306*
42	12	YORK	12f Gd/Fm	62	1307
59	2	SAND	10f Soft	57	1570
63	1	**PONT**	10f Soft	57	1705*
44a	5	WOLV	12f Aw	57	2075

GENEROSA 7 b m £0

0	U	ASCO	20f Good	70	2092

GENEROUS DIANA 4 ch f £16147

71	2	YARM	10f Soft	70	4392
78	1	YARM	19f Soft		4515*
90	1	**DONC**	10f Heavy		4571*

GENEROUS TERMS 5 ch g £0

70	8	NEWB	13f Gd/Fm		1401
90	6	THIR	12f Gd/Sft	96	1715 t

GENEROUS WAYS 5 ch g £10578

53a	4	WOLV	16f Aw	60	627
20	11	KEMP	14f Good	60	726
44	5	MUSS	12f Gd/Sft	57	1147
55	4	BEVE	16f Firm	56	1276
44	11	NEWC	16f Gd/Sft	53	1478
59	1	**ASCO**	16f Good	52	2173*
49	11	ASCO	16f Gd/Fm	58	2953
65	2	NEWM	16f Firm	56	3295
58	2	REDC	16f Firm	56	3331
33	6	MUSS	14f Gd/Fm	58	3590

GENIUS 5 b g £966

0a	14	SOUT	8f Aw		45
27a	11	WOLV	7f Aw		65
0a	12	SOUT	8f Aw	52	177
58a	4	SOUT	6f Aw		201
8a	10	WOLV	8f Aw	54	233
43a	2	SOUT	7f Aw		247
53a	2	SOUT	8f Aw	52	298
25a	7	SOUT	8f Aw	52	329
19a	13	WOLV	9f Aw	53	404
44a	4	SOUT	8f Aw		452
0a	11	SOUT	8f Aw		646
29a	5	WOLV	9f Aw		922
0a	11	WOLV	12f Aw		1039

GENSCHER 4 b g £0

37	9	HAMI	12f Gd/Fm	55	1908

GENTLE ANNE 3 b f £277

45a	3	SOUT	8f Aw		36
45a	4	SOUT	7f Aw		88
49a	5	SOUT	8f Aw		198
48a	4	SOUT	8f Aw		303
46a	4	SOUT	11f Aw	47	537
31a	5	SOUT	11f Aw		586

GENTLE MAGIC 2 b f £0

52	11	NEWM	6f Gd/Sft		4530

GENTLE NIGHT 2 b f £0

61	8	DONC	6f Heavy		4576

GENTLEMAN VENTURE 4 b c £24129

78	3	NEWM	12f Gd/Sft	76	968
75	6	KEMP	12f Gd/Sft	77	1076
78	4	NEWB	10f Good	77	1375
78	2	EPSO	12f Good	78	1845
77	5	HAYD	12f Gd/Fm	78	2502
73	5	ASCO	12f Gd/Fm	79	3001
82	1	**EPSO**	12f Gd/Fm	75	3402+
80	3	GOOD	12f Good	81	3657
77	14	NEWB	10f Firm	81	3997
72	6	YORK	10f Soft	80	4282
81	2	NEWB	10f Sft/Hv	78	4473

GENUINE JOHN 7 b g £1379

26a	9	SOUT	8f Aw	40	85
24a	6	SOUT	11f Aw	40	131
37a	3	SOUT	12f Aw	36	215
36a	3	WOLV	12f Aw	36	522
36a	2	SOUT	11f Aw	36	561
34	4	SOUT	11f Gd/Sft	40	855
34	5	HAMI	11f Gd/Fm	36	1361
25	10	BEVE	10f Firm	38	1921
28	5	CATT	12f Gd/Fm	34	2422
40	3	RIPO	10f Soft		2538
12	9	BEVE	10f Good	36	2883
0	12	BEVE	12f Gd/Sft	36	3053
47	7	BEVE	12f Gd/Fm		3654
0	13	BEVE	12f Gd/Fm	30	3674
0	12	YORK	12f Soft		4276

GEORGE STUBBS 2 b c £468

71	4	DONC	8f Heavy		4572

GEORGES WAY 2 b c £0

59	7	KEMP	6f Gd/Fm		3358
40	8	CHES	7f Soft		4068

GERONIMO 3 b c £3571

63a	7	WOLV	5f Aw		77
70a	2	SOUT	6f Aw		2299
71a	1	**WOLV**	6f Aw		2604*
38	6	RIPO	9f Gd/Fm	70	3182
45a	6	WOLV	8f Aw	70	3274
53a	6	WOLV	7f Aw		3770

GET A LIFE 7 gr m £200

0	15	PONT	6f Soft		872
42	5	THIR	7f Soft		930
0	15	CARL	6f Firm	39	1257
25	5	CATT	6f Good		1663
21	9	CATT	6f Gd/Fm		2744
29	4	RIPO	7f Gd/Fm		2834

GET IT SORTED 2 ch f £0

0	5	BRIG	5f Firm		2891
0	U	NOTT	12f Gd/Fm		3114

GET STUCK IN 4 b c £10667

55	7	HAMI	6f Good	85	844
80	6	NEWM	6f Gd/Fm	84	1173
0	16	YORK	5f Firm	83	1324
72	5	EPSO	6f Good	81	1851
77	4	NEWC	6f Firm	79	2334
77	4	HAMI	5f Firm	79	2395
0	23	YORK	6f Good	79	2697
0	23	GOOD	6f Firm	78	3152
49	7	AYR	6f Good		3366
72	2	AYR	5f Good	72	3960
76	3	AYR	5f Gd/Sft	72	4010
46	16	YORK	6f Soft		4287
0	15	NEWC	6f Heavy	74	4405
72	3	MUSS	5f Soft	74	4516
83	1	**DONC**	5f Heavy	73	4570+

GET THE POINT 6 b g £0

43	6	WARW	15f Heavy	53	885

GHAAZI 4 ch c £3031

53a	4	LING	7f Aw		8
53a	3	SOUT	7f Aw		73
57a	1	**LING**	8f Aw		109*
56a	4	WOLV	8f Aw	60	227 BL
43a	7	LING	8f Aw	58	463 bl
28a	8	WOLV	8f Aw		750
7a	8	LING	7f Aw	54	879 bl
34	8	BRIG	7f Firm	50	1335
0	13	BRIG	8f Gd/Sft	50	1462

GHADIR 2 b f £0

53	7	NEWC	7f Gd/Fm		2985
58	8	CHEP	7f Good		3866

GHAY 2 b f £0

74	7	LEIC	7f Sft/Hvy		4309

GHAYTH 2 b c £23255

87	6	ASCO	6f Gd/Fm		3000
106	1	**YORK**	6f Gd/Fm		3568*
105	3	DONC	6f Gd/Fm		3891
82	9	NEWM	6f Good		4181

GHAZAL 2 b f £7054

92	2	KEMP	6f Gd/Fm		3795
101	1	**NEWM**	6f Gd/Fm		4209*

GHOST OF A CHANCE 2 b c £0

0	11	LING	6f Good		4097
0	13	LING	6f Soft		4190
0	26	NEWM	7f Good		4336

GHOST PATH 5 gr m £0

0a	10	LING	16f Aw		402
0a	7	WOLV	16f Aw	20	492

GHUTAH 6 ch g £0

0a	12	SOUT	8f Aw		646 bl
0a	9	SOUT	14f Aw		668 bl
25	8	BEVE	8f Heavy		973

GIANNI 2 ch c £0

0	22	DONC	6f Gd/Fm		3862

GIANTS CAUSEWAY 3 ch c £1483950

120	1	**CURR**	7f Yldg		862*
120	2	NEWM	8f Gd/Sft		1171
119	2	CURR	8f Gd/Sft		1623
120	1	**ASCO**	8f Good		2066*
126	1	**SAND**	10f Gd/Fm		2497+
126	1	**GOOD**	8f Gd/Fm		3087+
126	1	**YORK**	10f Good		3539+
124	1	**LEOP**	10f Good		3925*
125	2	ASCO	8f Good		4111

GIBNEYS FLYER 2 br f £2828

55	6	RIPO	6f Gd/Fm		3009
70	1	**CARL**	5f Firm		3193*
56	7	REDC	5f Gd/Fm		3632
0	P	HAMI	5f Soft		3801

GIFT OF GOLD 5 ch g £14022

0a	13	SOUT	7f Aw	64	216
57a	4	WOLV	7f Aw	59	323
51a	5	WOLV	9f Aw	57	383
46	11	LEIC	7f Gd/Sft	81	834

0	15	CHES	8f Firm		79	1250
86	1	**GOOD**	7f Gd/Sft		77	1483*
85	3	GOOD	7f Gd/Sft		84	1810
80	7	AYR	7f Good		84	2163
85	9	NEWM	7f Gd/Fm		84	2616
80	5	CHES	8f Gd/Fm		83	3510
74	7	HAYD	7f Soft		82	3785
0	26	AYR	6f Gd/Sft		82	4010
69	6	YORK	7f Heavy		80	4302 BL
0	24	NEWM	7f Good		78	4357 bl
78	4	NEWM	7f Soft		77	4547
75	7	DONC	7f Heavy		78	4574

GIKO 6 b g £300

39	8	EPSO	9f Heavy			1033
0	26	ASCO	8f Gd/Sft		65	1113
52	12	NEWB	10f Good		60	1375
52	6	LEIC	8f Soft		57	1547
58	5	WIND	10f Good		57	1729 BL
55	6	WIND	10f Gd/Fm		57	1878 bl
40	10	KEMP	9f Gd/Fm		57	2085 bl
17	14	KEMP	8f Gd/Fm		53	2752 bl
0	16	WIND	10f Good			3045 t
0	20	GOOD	9f Good		51	3110 tbl
44	3	SALI	10f Gd/Sft		46	4169
12	12	LEIC	8f Sft/Hvy			4311

GILDA 2 b f £0

54	9	NEWB	6f Sft/Hvy		4471
62	5	MUSS	7f Soft		4562

GILDED DANCER 2 b c £1012

81	3	LING	5f Gd/Sft		1260
82	6	GOOD	7f Firm		3154
81	3	AYR	7f Good		3363
73	8	BATH	8f Soft		4430

GILDERSLEVE 5 ch m £0

0a	11	WOLV	9f Aw		259

GILFOOT BREEZE 3 b g £0

0a	13	SOUT	8f Aw		48
18a	7	SOUT	11f Aw	35	537
47a	4	SOUT	11f Aw		586 BL
0a	7	SOUT	11f Aw		672 bl

GILLS DIAMOND 2 ch f £624

66	3	HAYD	6f Soft		1823
62	5	BEVE	5f Gd/Sft		3055
56	9	RIPO	6f Gd/Fm		3466
14	10	WIND	5f Good		3639
52a	3	WOLV	5f Aw		4227
19a	11	SOUT	6f Aw	60	4367

GILT TRIP 2 b c £0

43	14	LING	6f Firm		3832
0	13	BATH	8f Soft		4138
0a	12	WOLV	6f Aw		4225

GILWILL 5 b g £0

0a	8	WOLV	9f Aw		553
20a	10	WOLV	7f Aw		677

GIMCO 3 b c £5488

70	4	WARW	8f Heavy		884
75	3	LING	10f Gd/Sft		1281
75	2	NEWC	10f Gd/Sft		1480
75	2	RIPO	12f Gd/Fm		2103
77a	1	**SOUT**	12f Aw	73	2382*
55	6	FOLK	9f Gd/Fm	75	3043

GIN PALACE 2 b c £0

85	6	GOOD	7f Soft		4063

GINA 2 b f £0

0	15	DONC	6f Heavy		4575

GINGKO 3 b g £564

77	4	DONC	7f Gd/Sft		1072
57	4	WARW	8f Good		2464
57a	4	SOUT	6f Aw		2947
67	6	NEWM	7f Gd/Fm	68	3629
57	12	LING	8f Firm	68	3831

GINISKI PARK 4 b f £0

0a	13	SOUT	8f Aw		195
2a	8	WOLV	7f Aw		276

GINNER MORRIS 5 b g £2922

43	7	WARW	11f Heavy	45	890
0	15	PONT	8f Good		1498
39	4	AYR	9f Heavy		4324 BL
47	1	**NEWC**	8f Heavy	41	4406* bl
0	11	REDC	8f Gd/Sft	44	4499 bl

GINNY WOSSERNAME 6 br m £0

6	9	FOLK	10f Good	32	2625
20	8	SALI	7f Gd/Fm	33	2978

GINOLAS MAGIC 3 b c £0

94	7	COLO	8f Good		1322

GIRARE 4 b c £0

46a	6	LING	10f Aw		629

GIRL BAND 2 b f £0

0	11	WIND	8f Gd/Fm		3047
46	6	WIND	6f Good		3187
75	8	KEMP	7f Gd/Fm		3359
56	9	SALI	7f Firm		3752 VIS

GIRL FRIDAY 2 ch f £0

28	11	CATT	6f Soft		4001

GIRLIE SET 5 b m £0

6a	10	SOUT	8f Aw	62	329

GIRLS BEST FRIEND 3 b f £0

70	9	MAIS	6f Heavy		99
14	13	NEWB	10f Good		1374
59	5	CHEP	10f Gd/Fm		1797
61a	6	SOUT	7f Aw	82	2300
55	12	HAYD	7f Soft	80	3785
76	9	ASCO	7f Good	82	4112 t
20	17	YORK	7f Heavy	76	4302 t
0	21	NEWM	8f Good	76	4348 tBL

GIULIA MURIEL 4 ch f £0

0a	9	SOUT	11f Aw		1417
0	15	YARM	10f Gd/Sft	42	1615 VIS
0a	14	SOUT	7f Aw	30	1979

GIVE AN INCH 5 b m £7511

63	8	NEWC	16f Soft	69	760
34	9	PONT	17f Soft	66	876
50	14	HAYD	14f Gd/Fm	63	1167
52	10	NEWC	17f Gd/Sft	60	1478
54	7	RIPO	16f Good	60	1597
61	1	**PONT**	17f Soft	58	1701*
69	1	**AYR**	17f Soft	60	3993*
0	11	PONT	17f Soft	70	4231
24	1	DONC	17f Heavy	67	4579

GIVE AND TAKE 7 ch g £0

33	12	LING	16f Good	45	1394

GIVE BACK CALAIS 2 b c £10482

94	3	GOOD	6f Gd/Sft		1809
100	2	ASCO	5f Good		2152
96	3	SAND	5f Gd/Fm		2529
85	5	NEWB	6f Firm		3980

GIVE NOTICE 3 b c £14020

68	10	LEIC	8f Good		789
62	6	REDC	10f Firm	64	1299
75	1	**YARM**	14f Gd/Fm	62	1949*
86	1	**HAYD**	14f Gd/Fm	72	2445*
86	1	**KEMP**	14f Gd/Sft	77	2584*
82	13	GOOD	14f Gd/Fm	88	3058
60	13	YORK	14f Firm	86	3599

GIVE THE SLIP 3 b c £165952

85	3	WIND	8f Gd/Sft		1099
94	1	**WIND**	10f Firm		1293*
98	2	GOOD	9f Gd/Sft	90	1452
105	1	**ASCO**	12f Good	95	2116+
108	4	GOOD	12f Gd/Fm		3061
110	1	**YORK**	14f Gd/Fm		1013565*

GLAD MASTER 3 b c £3669

0	7	CURR	8f Gd/Sft		1623
107	2	NEWB	7f Firm		2809

GLADIATORIAL 8 b g £0

0a	7	WOLV	12f Aw		530

GLASTONBURY 4 b g £334

0a	10	SOUT	6f Aw	48	425
26a	8	LING	7f Aw	42	503
32a	4	WOLV	5f Aw	37	564
0a	8	WOLV	5f Aw	37	614 BL
38a	9	WOLV	5f Aw		1237 VIS
0	19	YARM	7f Gd/Sft	44	1611
42a	5	LING	7f Aw		1739
0	13	YARM	8f Good	44	1772
35a	3	LING	6f Aw		1913
0	20	LING	5f Gd/Fm	38	2184
9	8	YARM	6f Gd/Fm	35	2415
25a	6	LING	5f Aw		2650

GLEAMING BLADE 2 ch c £5624

82	2	KEMP	7f Firm		2867
91	1	**LEIC**	7f Gd/Fm		3333*
99	4	SAND	7f Gd/Fm		3946

GLEDSWOOD 3 ch f £4602

84	3	NEWB	8f Firm		1377
80	2	YORK	8f Firm		2006
77	2	BEVE	10f Gd/Fm		3672
66	6	LEIC	10f Firm		3838
65	3	WARW	8f Gd/Fm		3914
46	4	BRIG	8f Soft		4175 VIS

GLEN ROSIE 3 ch f £10355

104	2	LING	8f Good		913
100	8	NEWM	8f Gd/Fm		2597
79	7	CHEP	10f Gd/Fm		2975
68	6	BATH	8f Soft		4142
72	8	NEWM	8f Soft		4544

GLEN VALE WALK 3 ch g £2415

40	8	WARW	7f Heavy	62	887
40	15	DONC	8f Gd/Sft	60	1053
0	16	CARL	8f Firm	57	1255
0	18	NEWC	8f Gd/Sft	52	1477
39	4	CARL	8f Firm	47	2281
36	8	NOTT	10f Gd/Fm	45	2685
44	2	CARL	8f Gd/Fm	42	3082
0	6	REDC	10f Firm	44	3310
35	9	HAYD	11f Gd/Sft	47	3480
21	11	RIPO	10f Good	46	3702
0	19	NEWC	8f Heavy	45	4406

GLENDALE RIDGE 5 b g £1062

64	4	LING	8f Gd/Sft		1263
64	4	SAND	10f Soft		1588
66	4	GOOD	9f Gd/Fm		2129
0	13	WIND	8f Soft	66	2546
42	7	NEWB	7f Firm	66	2814
0	17	GOOD	9f Good	64	3110
0	17	LING	8f Firm	60	3831
50	4	GOOD	8f Soft	53	4066
41	12	WIND	6f Gd/Sft	52	4293

GLENDAMAH 3 b c £0

64	10	AYR	7f Firm	76	2878
46	10	REDC	10f Good	71	3328
0	15	BEVE	8f Sft/Hvy	66	4045
27	11	PONT	8f Soft	60	4232 BL
47	8	REDC	7f Gd/Sft	55	4498

GLENHURICH 3 b f £349

60	4	PONT	8f Firm		3506
46	5	NEWC	7f Firm		3604

GLENQUOICH 3 ch c £0

45	5	HAYD	8f Gd/Sft		3477

GLENROCK 3 ch c £4077

79	8	CHES	8f Gd/Fm	92	1215
87	6	HAYD	8f Gd/Fm	91	1534
88	5	NEWM	6f Gd/Fm	88	1694
67	16	YORK	6f Firm	88	2003
89	2	NEWM	6f Good	87	2568
81	8	ASCO	6f Gd/Fm	89	2954

GLENWHARGEN 3 b f £2458 (top of column 1, preceded by three lines)

78	14	GOOD	7f Gd/Fm	89	3130
74	6	LEIC	6f Gd/Fm	87	3335
62	8	CATT	6f Soft		4257

GLENWHARGEN 3 b f £2458

50a	4	SOUT	8f Aw		48
43a	5	LING	8f Aw		236
56a	1	**LING**	10f Aw		286*
50a	3	WOLV	8f Aw		350

GLOBAL DRAW 4 ch g £0

33	9	NOTT	14f Good	37	1874
0	13	WARW	16f Gd/Fm	28	2037

GLOBAL EXPLORER 2 b c £0

20	10	WIND	5f Good		1727
0	11	PONT	5f Firm		3500
63	6	REDC	5f Gd/Fm		3632
51	7	HAMI	6f Gd/Sft	62	3824
49	8	NOTT	6f Soft	62	3976

GLORIOUS QUEST 2 ch c £844

88	3	NEWB	6f Firm		3980
68	7	NEWB	6f Sft/Hvy		4470

GLORY DAYS 2 ch c £3542

88	1	**KEMP**	5f Gd/Sft		1079*

GLORY OF LOVE 5 b g £0

13a	10	WOLV	12f Aw		295

GLORY QUEST 3 b c £9157

84	2	FOLK	7f Soft		962
76	2	EPSO	9f Heavy		1032
82	3	NEWB	8f Good		1376
88	4	GOOD	7f Gd/Sft		1638
82	2	KEMP	8f Gd/Fm	80	3793
82	2	GOOD	10f Good		3907
79	1	**LING**	8f Soft		4273*

GLOW 4 br f £1247

0a	10	WOLV	12f Aw		1039
45a	3	SOUT	11f Aw		1417
52	5	SOUT	12f Soft	54	1604
47a	2	SOUT	14f Aw		1975
47	4	REDC	14f Gd/Fm		2144
37	9	CHEP	18f Gd/Fm	51	2490

GLOWING 5 ro m £10418

77	2	DONC	6f Gd/Fm	74	1842
0	15	WIND	6f Gd/Fm	75	2054
79	2	GOOD	6f Good		2355
76	4	NOTT	5f Gd/Fm	76	2684
80	1	**NEWM**	6f Gd/Fm	76	2804*
81	5	GOOD	6f Good	81	3904
73	7	NEWM	6f Good		4198

GLYNDEBOURNE 3 b c £187150

118	1	**CURR**	10f Soft		1899*
118	2	CURR	12f Good		2409

GO FOR IT SWEETIE 7 b m £0

21	7	REDC	14f Gd/Fm		3633 t

GO MAN 6 b g £0

0a	9	LING	12f Aw		267
0a	14	SOUT	12f Aw		301

GO SALLY GO 4 b f £0

0a	11	SOUT	6f Aw		32
5a	8	SOUT	7f Aw		73
23	9	BATH	5f Gd/Sft	30	2555
0	11	THIR	6f Gd/Fm	28	3124

GO THUNDER 6 b g £3213

29	9	MUSS	9f Gd/Sft	43	795 t
24	9	MUSS	7f Gd/Fm	38	1149 t
0	17	HAMI	6f Firm		1239 t
31	5	HAMI	9f Gd/Sft		3375 t
32	3	MUSS	8f Gd/Sft	30	3745 t
36	1	**HAMI**	9f Gd/Sft		3823* t
59	4	AYR	9f Soft		3988 t
23	8	AYR	9f Heavy		4324 t
40	3	MUSS	9f Soft	43	4520 t

GO TOO MOOR 7 b g £0

0a	12	SOUT	14f Aw		124

GO WITH THE WIND 7 b h £1077

33	7	CATT	12f Gd/Fm		2742
31	3	REDC	14f Firm		3311
46	2	REDC	14f Gd/Fm		3633
24	7	BEVE	12f Sft/Hv		4041
13a	6	WOLV	12f Aw		4549

GODMERSHAM PARK 8 b g £6557

23a	10	SOUT	8f Aw		45
49a	3	WOLV	8f Aw		136
36a	2	SOUT	8f Aw	50	177
45a	5	WOLV	8f Aw	48	233
48a	2	SOUT	8f Aw	47	345
42a	3	WOLV	8f Aw	47	411
39a	4	SOUT	7f Aw	47	471
36a	4	SOUT	8f Aw	47	497
50a	1	**SOUT**	8f Aw	45	648*
45a	4	WOLV	8f Aw	50	676
36a	7	WOLV	8f Aw	49	749
41a	9	SOUT	8f Aw	48	1207
45	1	**RIPO**	8f Good		1858*
37a	4	SOUT	8f Aw	47	2379

GOES A TREAT 4 b f £0

0a	13	WOLV	6f Aw	73	435
0a	12	WOLV	7f Aw	65	582

GOGGLES 2 b c £163486

89	4	NEWB	6f Gd/Fm		1943
98	1	**GOOD**	6f Gd/Fm		3064*
100	1	**DONC**	6f Gd/Fm		3862*

GOGS GIFT 2 b g £0

53	8	THIR	5f Gd/Fm		3143
53	5	REDC	5f Gd/Sft		4496
0	20	DONC	6f Heavy		4575

GOING GLOBAL 3 ch c £27768

96	1	**RIPO**	9f Soft		823*
107	3	SAND	10f Heavy		1056
108	2	LING	11f Gd/Sft		1284
89	13	EPSO	12f Good		1848
102	6	ASCO	12f Good		2148
94	9	GOOD	12f Gd/Fm		3061
97	4	GOOD	14f Good		3645
102	10	DONC	15f Firm		3898 VIS
91	5	NEWM	12f Good		4194 t

GOING HOME 3 b g £0

0	17	BEVE	5f Firm	53	2732
0	15	CARL	8f Gd/Fm	48	3082 bl

GOLAN 2 b c £3877

98	1	**CHEP**	7f Good		3866*

GOLCONDA 4 br f £8246

88	3	NEWM	10f Gd/Fm	86	1170
83	4	YORK	10f Gd/Fm	87	1342
77	8	EPSO	10f Good	87	1845
69	7	PONT	10f Firm		2178
76	10	YORK	10f Good	86	2696 VIS
85	1	**FOLK**	10f Gd/Fm		3042*
78	6	NEWC	10f Good	87	3703
79	11	NEWM	9f Gd/Fm	87	4212

GOLD ACADEMY 4 b c £4532

103	6	SAND	10f Heavy		1057
109	6	ASCO	12f Good		2149
112	6	SAND	10f Gd/Fm		2497
105	2	EPSO	10f Good		3684
95	4	GOOD	10f Good		3903
101	11	NEWM	10f Good		4355

GOLD AIR 2 b f £5359

0	18	WIND	5f Gd/Fm		1197
82	1	**SAND**	5f Soft		1568*
72	15	ASCO	5f Good		2088
80	2	WIND	5f Good		2368
55	8	ASCO	6f Good	82	2678
50	9	KEMP	6f Gd/Fm	80	3075
33	9	HAYD	6f Soft	75	4090 BL
40a	8	SOUT	6f Aw	69	4367

GOLD BLADE 11 ch g £3500

36a	4	SOUT	12f Aw	45	412
0	15	DONC	10f Gd/Fm	47	705
35	8	YARM	10f Gd/Fm	45	2199
39	5	PONT	10f Gd/Fm	43	2556
32	4	HAMI	11f Gd/Fm	43	2638
35	6	NEWM	10f Gd/Fm	40	2958
47	1	**BEVE**	10f Gd/Sft	40	3052*
0	12	BRIG	10f Firm	47	3737

GOLD EDGE 6 ch m £0

21a	7	LING	6f Aw	34	148
6a	10	SOUT	6f Aw	43	218
0a	8	SOUT	7f Aw	31	471
22a	5	WOLV	5f Aw	28	564 BL
24a	9	WOLV	6f Aw	38	622 bl
20	6	BRIG	7f Firm		1335
22	10	BRIG	6f Gd/Sft	34	1464
24	7	BRIG	5f Gd/Fm	32	1932
0	18	GOOD	6f Gd/Fm		2124
12a	10	SOUT	6f Aw	30	2385
27	4	BATH	5f Gd/Sft	30	2555

GOLD KRIEK 3 b g £0

40a	8	LING	7f Aw		164
55a	8	LING	7f Aw		206
23	8	FOLK	12f Good	46	2624
40	7	BRIG	10f Firm	41	2908
31	7	BEVE	12f Gd/Sft	43	3050

GOLD LANCE 7 ch g £0

52	5	BRIG	7f Firm		1210
36	6	BRIG	12f Gd/Sft	42	1465
21	11	WARW	11f Gd/Fm	40	1707
3	9	EPSO	12f Gd/Fm	43	2626
22	7	CHEP	12f Gd/Fm	34	2971

GOLD MILLENIUM 6 gr g £6780

31	11	GOOD	9f Gd/Sft	42	1807
42	4	NEWB	10f Gd/Fm	42	1942
46	1	**WARW**	12f Gd/Fm	40	2255*
45	3	WARW	15f Good	45	2461
39	6	SALI	14f Gd/Fm	46	2982
41	3	WIND	12f Gd/Fm	44	3186
45	1	**FOLK**	16f Gd/Fm	44	3448*
49	2	LING	16f Firm	43	3755
42	5	WARW	16f Good	49	3916

GOLD QUEST 3 ch c £7618

79	5	WIND	10f Gd/Fm		1200
79	2	BRIG	12f Gd/Sft		1510 t
71	3	SALI	14f Firm	81	2021 t
76	3	SAND	14f Good		2477 t
86	1	**YARM**	11f Firm		2897*
85	3	RIPO	12f Gd/Fm	86	3467
0	18	NEWM	12f Good	85	4162

GOLD RIDER 3 b c £0

49	8	BRIG	7f Firm		1212
53	7	BATH	8f Gd/Fm		1436
0	11	BATH	15f Gd/Sft		1670
0	16	CHEP	6f Good	50	1971
21	9	WIND	6f Soft	46	2549
0	12	BRIG	7f Gd/Fm	46	2728 BL

GOLD ROUND 3 b f £24976

107	3	LONG	8f Heavy		1027
108	1	**SAIN**	11f Heavy		1313*
80	11	EPSO	12f Gd/Sft		1828
102	7	LONG	15f Good		4239

GOLD STANDARD 2 ch c £0

72	9	BATH	8f Soft		4430

GOLD STATUETTE 2 ch c £252

75	7	SALI	7f Gd/Fm		2269
81	6	YORK	7f Good		2649
77	4	BEVE	7f Gd/Sft		3051
58	11	NEWC	8f Gd/Fm	78	3704

GOLDAMIX 3 gr f £31700

102	4	LONG	10f Gd/Sft		1457

113 3 CHAN 11f Gd/Sft 1901

GOLDBRIDGE 5 b g £0
37 4 FOLK 15f Gd/Fm 40 3040
37 4 WARW 16f Gd/Fm 40 3916

GOLDEN ACE 7 ch g £0
37 4 LEIC 12f Good 39 791 tbl
27 5 RIPO 12f Soft 37 825 tbl
18 8 FOLK 15f Soft 36 963 tbl
0 22 YORK 9f Good 3808 tbl
0 11 BEVE 12f Stf/Hv 4041 tbl

GOLDEN BEACH 2 b f £630
61 10 WIND 6f Gd/Fm 1876
46 10 KEMP 7f Gd/Sft 2583
58 12 SALI 7f Gd/Fm 3292
50 5 FOLK 7f Gd/Fm 3582
48 2 BRIG 7f Firm 3733
0 13 LING 6f Good 4097
39 5 BATH 6f Soft 4431

GOLDEN BIFF 4 ch c £0
41a 6 WOLV 6f Aw 76
20 14 THIR 7f Soft 60 908
42 6 HAMI 6f Firm 1239
44 7 CATT 6f Firm 1681
0 14 HAMI 6f Gd/Fm 50 1941
0 23 AYR 6f Heavy 46 4327
0 20 NEWC 5f Heavy 46 4407

GOLDEN BRIEF 2 ch g £0
0 17 LING 7f Soft 4268
62 13 YARM 7f Soft 4514

GOLDEN CHANCE 3 b c £7819
78 3 THIR 8f Gd/Sft 1352
75 2 BEVE 8f Gd/Sft 1763
79 2 BEVE 7f Firm 1922
81 1 **REDC** 8f Gd/Fm 2159*
80 3 CHEP 10f Gd/Fm 78 2450
64 8 CHES 10f Good 78 2666
77 4 ASCO 10f Gd/Fm 78 2955
79 2 AYR 10f Gd/Fm 3142
63 6 REDC 8f Firm 78 3309

GOLDEN CHIMES 5 ch g £4153
68 1 **CARL** 14f Firm 60 2016*
67 6 PONT 18f Firm 67 2176
59 8 CARL 12f Firm 67 2279
38 6 CARL 14f Firm 63 2827

GOLDEN DRAGONFLY 2 ch c £0
63 12 DONC 5f Gd/Fm 700
62 10 RIPO 5f Soft 821
68 6 DONC 6f Gd/Fm 1838
0 18 PONT 8f Soft 62 4378

GOLDEN FORTUNA 2 b f £0
75 7 NEWM 7f Gd/Fm 3459

GOLDEN GROOVE 4 ch f £0
0 10 CATT 12f Gd/Fm 3202 BL

GOLDEN HAWK 5 ch g £0
25a 5 WOLV 12f Aw 50 4026

GOLDEN HIND 2 ch f £0
72 5 DONC 6f Heavy 4575

GOLDEN INDIGO 3 ch c £25795
109 2 CAPA 8f Soft 1118

GOLDEN LEGEND 3 b c £328
81 4 DONC 8f Gd/Fm 704
69 7 LING 7f Gd/Sft 840
0 18 NEWM 6f Gd/Sft 74 982

GOLDEN LOCKET 3 ch f £305
70 4 LEIC 7f Good 794
70 8 NEWB 7f Gd/Fm 72 1405
50 11 YARM 8f Gd/Sft 70 1610

GOLDEN LYRIC 5 ch g £3243
44a 3 WOLV 9f Aw 40 60
13a 8 LING 10f Aw 40 102
0a 15 SOUT 11f Aw 40 126

21a 7 WOLV 12f Aw 38 260
36a 4 SOUT 11f Aw 455
50a 2 WOLV 9f Aw 553
42a 2 WOLV 8f Aw 612
48a 1 **SOUT** 8f Aw 646*

GOLDEN MIRACLE 3 b c £7039
60 9 DONC 7f Good 83 736
0 16 CHES 6f Gd/Fm 82 1220
0 12 NEWC 6f Heavy 80 1768 BL
79 1 **REDC** 7f Gd/Fm 75 2145*
0 16 GOOD 6f Good 79 2355
80 2 RIPO 6f Soft 78 2541

GOLDEN MISSILE 5 ch g £289157
124 3 GULF 10f Fast 21 bl

GOLDEN NEEDLE 2 b f £222
48a 4 SOUT 8f Aw 4152

GOLDEN OSCAR 3 ch g £643
0 13 NOTT 8f Gd/Sft 1084
47 7 THIR 8f Gd/Sft 1352
72 3 THIR 8f Gd/Sft 1717
47 7 RIPO 8f Gd/Fm 2104

GOLDEN POUND 8 b g £1129
45 4 SALI 5f Firm 48 2022
40 5 LING 5f Gd/Fm 46 2184
44 4 EPSO 6f Gd/Sft 48 2631
38 7 LEIC 6f Gd/Fm 45 2777
36 4 SALI 5f Gd/Fm 46 3419

GOLDEN RETRIEVER 3 b c £0
75 10 NEWM 7f Gd/Sft 983
58 10 KEMP 8f Gd/Sft 1080
46 9 SALI 8f Good 70 1345
0 15 SALI 8f Firm 67 2025
0 11 SALI 8f Gd/Fm 62 2980

GOLDEN ROD 3 ch c £845
53 10 DONC 10f Gd/Fm 71 701
0 17 WIND 12f Firm 69 1292
65 3 SOUT 10f Soft 65 1608
64 4 LING 11f Good 66 1743
59 6 HAYD 14f Gd/Fm 64 2445
44 9 BEVE 16f Good 60 2879
0 14 SALI 14f Gd/Fm 57 3424
21a 11 LING 12f Aw 52 4334
40 3 NOTT 10f Heavy 47 4509

GOLDEN SILCA 4 ch f £71875
88 8 NAD 9f Good 768
113 4 NEWB 8f Gd/Fm 1402
112 1 **EPSO** 9f Gd/Sft 1825*
88 8 ASCO 8f Good 2064
103 5 NEWM 8f Gd/Fm 2597
114 4 GOOD 8f Good 3087
114 1 **CURR** 8f Good 3554*
109 7 LONG 8f Soft 3847
112 5 ASCO 8f Good 4111
107 9 LONG 7f Soft 4395

GOLDEN SNAKE 4 b c £206827
116 4 CURR 11f Gd/Sft 1625
110 5 MAIS 10f Good 4050
117 1 **COLO** 12f Soft 4147*
120 1 **SAN** 12f Heavy 4493*

GOLDEN SPARROW 2 ch f £5077
80 2 LING 7f Soft 4484
87 1 **DONC** 8f Heavy 4569*

GOLDEN TOUCH 8 ch h £512
49 6 LEIC 8f Gd/Sft 4033
55a 2 WOLV 8f Aw 50 4437

GOLDEN WAY 3 ch f £13721
63 6 WIND 8f Soft 2548
85 1 **HAYD** 11f Gd/Sft 3265*
88 1 **AYR** 10f Soft 80 3989*
83 2 PONT 10f Soft 83 4085
84 12 NEWM 12f Good 4343

GOLDEN WHISPER 2 b g £743

69 4 DONC 5f Gd/Sft 1067
0 14 WIND 5f Gd/Fm 1197
61 3 PONT 5f Soft 1704
38 9 SALI 7f Gd/Sft 66 2468
50 6 KEMP 6f Gd/Fm 64 3075

GOLDEN WINGS 2 b f £0
57 10 NEWB 7f Firm 2810
63 12 NEWB 7f Firm 3786
37 9 BEVE 7f Good 3953 BL

GOLDENGIRLMICHELLE 5 b m £0
18a 7 WOLV 16f Aw 26 577

GOLDFAW 3 ch c £0
0 14 SALI 6f Firm 1175
0 20 SALI 7f Good 1349
0 15 BATH 10f Firm 42 2332 BL
0 8 BATH 12f Firm 45 3206
0a 11 WOLV 8f Aw 4551

GOLDFINCH 3 b f £0
51 10 WIND 8f Gd/Fm 1428
62 8 YARM 8f Good 1771
24a 14 SOUT 8f Aw 60 2380
57 5 YARM 8f Firm 58 2767

GOLDIE 2 b f £13781
80 1 **BATH** 6f Firm 3205*
79 2 BATH 6f Firm 3620
82 3 NEWM 6f Good 4345

GOLFAGENT 2 b g £0
0 19 NEWB 6f Firm 3980
67 12 LING 7f Soft 4268
0 17 NEWB 6f Sft/Hvy 4470
38 8 MUSS 5f Soft 52 4561

GOLGOTHA 2 gr f £0
48 9 HAMI 5f Gd/Fm 1906
47a 5 SOUT 5f Aw 2120
43 7 LEIC 5f Gd/Fm 2507
44 8 HAMI 6f Gd/Sft 3376
52 5 MUSS 5f Gd/Fm 3589

GOLOVIN 3 b c £6450
94 4 LEOP 8f Soft 947
94 2 LEOP 10f Heavy 4558

GOMPAS PAL 2 b c £0
0 15 YARM 6f Heavy 4479

GONCHAROVA 2 b f £3224
90 1 **LEIC** 7f Sft/Hvy 4309*
74 7 NEWM 8f Soft 4546

GONE TOO FAR 2 b g £4110
62 7 NEWC 6f Good 3245
71 2 THIR 7f Gd/Fm 3617
71 1 **THIR** 7f Gd/Sft 3776*
58 6 PONT 6f Soft 71 4235
61 13 DONC 6f Gd/Sft 4449

GONE WITH THE WIND 2 br f £0
0 14 NEWB 6f Firm 1782
0 13 WIND 6f Good 3187
51 9 NEWB 6f Firm 3449

GOOD EVANS ABOVE 3 br f £0
37 6 THIR 7f Soft 929
13 14 REDC 8f Gd/Sft 1132
0a 11 WOLV 8f Aw 1234 BL

GOOD FRIDAY 3 b f £0
61 6 WIND 8f Heavy 69 933
64 5 WIND 12f Firm 67 1292
56 6 NEWB 13f Gd/Fm 65 1594
0 U SAND 11f Good 63 1967
63 6 CHEP 8f Gd/Fm 63 2661
58 7 SALI 8f Gd/Fm 61 2980

GOOD STANDING 2 b f £4862
88 1 **NEWM** 7f Soft 4541*

GOOD TIMING 2 bl g £260
74 6 PONT 5f Firm 3500
63 3 PONT 6f Soft 4373

GOOD WHIT SON 4 b c £0
0a	14	LING	6f Aw		25	
35a	7	LING	6f Aw		95	
12a	8	WOLV	6f Aw		273	
0a	10	LING	7f Aw	35	439	

GOODBYE GOLDSTONE 4 b c £0
66	11	WIND	10f Firm		1288
71	5	EPSO	10f Good	75	1845
20	8	GOOD	12f Gd/Fm	71	2127
58	6	EPSO	12f Gd/Sft	70	2626
29	9	EPSO	12f Gd/Sft	67	3402

GOODENOUGH MOVER 4 ch g £17124
0	16	WIND	8f Good	50	854
54	1	CHEP	7f Gd/Sft	45	1799*
67	1	CHEP	7f Good	51	1969*
70	1	CHEP	8f Gd/Fm	64	2492*
78	1	SALI	6f Good	70	2690*
73	4	FOLK	7f Gd/Fm	77	3041
79	2	NEWB	7f Firm	77	3981
75	9	NEWM	7f Firm	79	4215
0	15	NEWM	7f Soft	79	4547

GOODGOLLYMISSMOLLY 2 b f £0
56	9	SALI	7f Firm	3748
49	8	PONT	6f Soft	4082

GOODIE TWOSUES 2 b f £57742
93	1	GOOD	6f Gd/Sft	1486*
93	3	NEWB	6f Gd/Fm	1944
94	4	NEWM	6f Firm	2344
92	5	NEWM	6f Good	2565
93	6	NEWM	7f Firm	3316
92	1	NEWM	6f Good	4345*

GOODWOOD BLIZZARD 3 ch f £0
78	7	NEWM	8f Soft	4544

GORDONS FRIEND 2 ch c £0
53	6	CATT	7f Good	3438
0	14	RIPO	6f Good	3697
38	11	YORK	6f Good	3812
38a	3	SOUT	7f Aw	4154

GORETSKI 7 b g £0
62	8	NEWC	5f Soft	75	758
68	10	THIR	5f Soft	74	926
0	14	NEWC	5f Heavy	73	1008
60	9	THIR	5f Good	73	1162
0	18	THIR	5f Gd/Sft	69	1357
38	11	KEMP	6f Soft	67	1531
62	6	WIND	5f Gd/Sft	64	4295
49	7	PONT	5f Soft	64	4377

GORSE 5 b g £46888
112	3	NEWM	6f Good	952
110	6	CURR	6f Gd/Sft	1622
115	2	HAMB	6f Soft	2403
114	1	DEAU	6f V	2574*
115	3	DEAU	7f Good	3212

GOT ALOT ON 2 b g £0
0	16	BEVE	5f Firm		2730
0	18	HAYD	6f Gd/Sft		3268
59	8	RIPO	6f Gd/Fm		3466
52	6	NOTT	6f Soft	62	3976

GOT ONE TOO 3 ch c £5684
0	17	NEWM	10f Gd/Fm	66	1150	t
27	7	NOTT	8f Soft	60	1645	t
33	9	WIND	8f Gd/Fm	52	2051	t
51	1	FOLK	12f Good	46	2624*	t
0	14	WIND	12f Gd/Fm	52	3049	t
57	1	BRIG	12f Soft	50	4421*	

GOT TO GO 2 b f £2918
90	1	WIND	6f Gd/Fm	4288*
100	7	NEWM	7f Good	4356
70	8	NEWM	8f Soft	4546

GOTHIC REVIVAL 3 b c £298
79	4	DONC	8f Gd/Fm		2611
66	5	NEWC	9f Gd/Fm	82	2988

GRACE 6 br m £848
48	4	SOUT	6f Good	50	802	
48	4	THIR	6f Soft	50	910	
36	6	FOLK	6f Soft	50	958	
39	6	NOTT	6f Gd/Sft	49	1082	
33	4	CHEP	6f Heavy	47	1557	
32	8	SOUT	7f Soft	47	1606	
34	6	BEVE	5f Firm	43	1923	Vls
37	6	LEIC	6f Gd/Fm	43	2031	vis
41	4	GOOD	6f Gd/Fm	43	2124	
41	6	DONC	6f Gd/Fm	42	2320	
0	17	LEIC	6f Gd/Fm	42	2777	

GRACE AND POWER 3 b f £0
51	11	WIND	8f Heavy	83	933
49	10	KEMP	8f Gd/Sft	80	1075

GRACEFUL EMPEROR 2 b g £0
36	8	PONT	6f Soft	1704
0	13	NEWC	7f Gd/Fm	2985

GRACILIS 3 b g £810
65	4	NEWC	8f Good		2520
69	8	HAYD	11f Gd/Fm		2703
26	10	RIPO	10f Gd/Fm		3012
44	5	CATT	12f Soft	54	4256
48	3	NOTT	16f Heavy	49	4508

GRACIOUS AIR 2 b f £0
50	7	HAYD	8f Gd/Sft	4104

GRACIOUS GIFT 4 ch f £0
78	14	NEWM	6f Gd/Fm	89	1173
53	16	GOOD	6f Gd/Fm	88	1471
0	26	ASCO	6f Good	85	2151

GRAF PHILIPP 5 b g £59028
107	2	KRAN	10f Good	656

GRAIG PARK 2 b c £0
0	13	HAYD	6f Gd/Fm	3268
0	12	WARW	7f Good	3692

GRAIN STORM 2 b f £0
46	12	HAYD	6f Gd/Sft	3268
46	8	EPSO	7f Gd/Sft	3412
73	5	LING	7f Firm	3833

GRALMANO 5 b g £39129
90a	1	WOLV	8f Aw	85	551*
92a	4	WOLV	8f Aw	90	663
68	5	CHES	10f Gd/Fm	71	1217
72	2	BEVE	9f Gd/Sft	70	1762
72	5	YORK	9f Firm	72	2001
77	1	REDC	10f Gd/Fm	72	2157*
74	6	GOOD	9f Good	78	2304
71	4	DONC	8f Gd/Fm	75	2758
80	1	RIPO	9f Gd/Fm	75	3011*
85	1	DONC	10f Gd/Fm	80	3159*
76	13	YORK	12f Good	85	3541
76	6	RIPO	10f Gd/Fm	85	3713

GRAMPAS 3 br c £6510
78	2	NEWM	7f Gd/Fm	2860
96	1	NEWB	9f Gd/Fm	3179*
95	6	BATH	9f Good	3515
93	4	NEWM	10f Good	4017

GRAND AMBITION 4 b g £0
60	5	THIR	8f Gd/Sft		1352	
0	14	HAYD	8f Gd/Sft	83	1490	
72	5	RIPO	10f Gd/Fm	75	2102	
71	7	HAYD	11f Gd/Fm		2703	
41	9	CARL	8f Gd/Fm		3081	
52	7	PONT	10f Gd/Fm	9	3220	
28	11	YORK	12f Gd/Fm	62	3725	t

GRAND BAHAMIAN 3 gr c £2697
43	11	NEWC	7f Good		759
83	1	LING	7f Gd/Sft		840*
0	17	NEWM	10f Good	85	954
0	P	NOTT	8f Soft	82	1645
57	10	YARM	6f Firm	82	2900
44a	4	WOLV	7f Aw		4384 BL

GRAND CRU 9 ch g £6812
44a	4	SOUT	14f Aw	47	37	vis
56a	1	SOUT	14f Aw		124*	vis
53a	4	SOUT	16f Aw		327	e
55a	2	SOUT	12f Aw	50	412	vis
53a	3	SOUT	16f Aw	50	470	vis
25a	7	SOUT	16f Aw	50	502	vis
23a	7	SOUT	16f Aw	50	535	vis
30	8	SOUT	16f Gd/Sft	37	860	BL
49	1	WARW	15f Heavy	44	885*	bl
39	4	FOLK	15f Soft	43	963	bl
39	6	SAND	16f Heavy	47	1044	bl
36	12	HAYD	14f Gd/Fm	47	1167	bl
24	12	AYR	11f Soft	44	3963	
33a	8	SOUT	14f Aw	44	4371	vis

GRAND ESTATE 5 b g £3058
47a	4	WOLV	5f Aw	56	614
0a	14	SOUT	6f Aw	56	645
44a	7	SOUT	6f Aw	52	697
44a	3	WOLV	5f Aw		753
56	8	SOUT	6f Good	64	802
46a	3	SOUT	7f Aw	45	867
49	10	MUSS	5f Gd/Fm	63	1143
0	23	THIR	6f Gd/Sft	61	1356
53	5	CATT	6f Gd/Sft	58	1815
54	4	HAMI	6f Firm	55	2097
49	5	NOTT	6f Gd/Sft	55	2193
57	2	NEWC	6f Gd/Fm	55	2275
54	3	HAMI	6f Firm	55	2396
54	5	HAYD	6f Gd/Sft	55	2444
46	9	HAMI	6f Good	57	2641
56	3	NEWC	6f Good	56	3037
57	4	THIR	6f Gd/Sft	56	3144
50	8	PONT	5f Gd/Fm	56	3222
43	13	NEWC	6f Good	57	3605
34a	7	SOUT	6f Aw	45	4155

GRAND FINALE 3 b c £38020
101	1	GOWR	9f Gd/Sft	818*
110	1	LEOP	10f Soft	949*
110	1	LEOP	12f Good	3371*

GRAND FIVE 2 b c £3064
74	2	LEIC	6f Gd/Fm		1573
73	11	ASCO	7f Good		2091
65	8	SALI	6f Gd/Fm		3387
72	3	HAMI	6f Gd/Sft	72	3824
74	2	GOOD	8f Soft	71	4076
67	10	WIND	10f Gd/Fm	73	4290
38	8	PONT	8f Soft	73	4378

GRAND HOUDINI 2 b g £648
0	14	PONT	6f Soft		4083
57	5	CATT	5f Soft		4253
0	21	DONC	7f Gd/Sft		4446
57	2	MUSS	5f Soft	55	4561

GRAND JURY 3 ch c £0
35a	1	LING	10f Aw	240

GRAND MUSICA 7 b g £0
0	16	BRIG	7f Gd/Sft	55	4121	bl
0a	14	LING	7f Aw		4331	tbl
0a	11	LING	12f Aw	42	4486	bl

GRAND ORO 3 ch c £0
70	12	NEWM	8f Firm	1188

GRAND SLAM GB 5 b g £215
42	4	CARL	12f Firm		2826
39	12	HAYD	14f Gd/Sft	60	4105
0	14	NEWC	10f Heavy	60	4404
0	15	MUSS	12f Soft	55	4560

GRAND VIEW 4 ch c £2183
48a	6	SOUT	7f Aw	66	599
63a	1	LING	6f Aw		653*
61a	3	LING	6f Aw	63	691
61	9	DONC	5f Firm	66	3894
55	4	YARM	7f Firm		3921

GRANDERA 2 ch c £11535					
83	5	DONC	6f Gd/Fm		2608
100	1	WARW	7f Gd/Fm		3909*
103	2	NEWM	7f Good		4196
99	7	DONC	8f Soft		4463

GRANDMA GRIFFITHS 2 b f £0					
46	8	YARM	8f Gd/Fm		3665
0	14	YARM	8f Soft		4512
0	14	DONC	8f Heavy		4576

GRANDMA ULLA 3 b f £0					
57	10	WARW	6f Heavy		888
21	11	KEMP	6f Soft	69	994
43	9	WARW	7f Gd/Sft	64	1710
44	11	BRIG	7f Gd/Fm	59	1930
50	7	KEMP	9f Firm	59	2262
28	14	WIND	10f Gd/Fm		3045
42	9	LING	7f Firm	52	3279

GRANITE CITY 3 ro c £3844					
0	11	MUSS	7f Soft	51	1148
40	8	HAMI	5f Gd/Fm	47	1358
9	10	AYR	5f Gd/Fm	43	1629
31	7	MUSS	7f Firm		2046
34	7	MUSS	8f Gd/Fm	40	2205
49	3	CATT	7f Gd/Fm	48	2438
40	9	AYR	7f Gd/Fm	49	2719
53	2	THIR	8f Gd/Fm	49	2964
53	1	MUSS	7f Good	48	3103*
47	6	MUSS	7f Gd/Sft	54	3593
45	6	MUSS	8f Gd/Fm	54	3746

GRANNY RICH 6 ch m £0					
31	9	GOOD	16f Soft	41	4075
0	26	NEWM	18f Good	79	4353

GRANNYS PET 6 ch g £16593					
105	3	DONC	7f Gd/Fm		1049
108	1	LEIC	7f Gd/Sft		1574*
95	6	YARM	7f Firm		2389
96	8	NEWB	7f Firm		2809
85	5	GOOD	7f Good		3884
104	3	NEWM	7f Good	100	4195
104	2	YORK	7f Soft	100	4278

GRANNYS RELUCTANCE 4 br f £0					
38a	6	WOLV	8f Aw	50	38
29a	9	SOUT	7f Aw	50	69

GRANTED 3 b f £27094					
77	3	HAYD	11f Gd/Fm		1165
68	3	AYR	10f Gd/Fm		1655	VIS
77	2	KEMP	8f Gd/Fm	73	2084
76	1	HAMI	8f Gd/Fm	73	2235*
82	1	DONC	8f Gd/Fm	76	2579*
79	4	WIND	8f Good	82	2713
77	3	NEWC	9f Gd/Fm	81	2988
82	2	HAMI	9f Gd/Sft	81	3535
87	1	KEMP	8f Gd/Fm	81	3793*
77	10	ASCO	8f Good	86	4113
90	3	LONG	9f Heavy		4489

GRANTLEY 3 b c £0					
0	11	BEVE	7f Good		1444
48	7	BEVE	10f Good	53	3396
15	9	REDC	14f Gd/Fm	48	3637
0	15	HAMI	12f Gd/Sft	45	3827
40	6	LEIC	10f Gd/Fm		4029	VIS

GRASSLANDIK 4 b c £1271					
30a	9	WOLV	6f Aw	56	175
53a	2	WOLV	6f Aw	52	226
48a	3	SOUT	6f Aw	52	250
42a	5	SOUT	6f Aw	53	454
50a	3	WOLV	6f Aw	52	622
53	5	WIND	6f Gd/Fm	56	746
0	17	HAMI	6f Good	55	844
42a	7	WOLV	6f Aw	51	923
40a	8	SOUT	6f Aw	49	1422
36a	5	SOUT	6f Aw	47	2297	BL

26a	6	SOUT	6f Aw	44	2820	bl
50	8	CHEP	7f Good	53	3871

GRAY PASTEL 6 gr g £0					
17	10	HAYD	12f Gd/Fm		2457	vis

GREAT CRAIC 3 b m £0					
13a	7	SOUT	7f Aw		283

GREAT HOPPER 5 b m £0					
23	7	REDC	14f Gd/Sft	36	1563
15	7	CARL	12f Gd/Sft		1720

GREAT MANOEUVRE 2 b f £0					
55	5	FOLK	7f Gd/Fm		3039

GREAT NEWS 5 b g £34362					
60	12	DONC	8f Good	83	715
69	9	PONT	8f Soft	83	875
44	18	ASCO	8f Gd/Sft	80	1113
67	14	NEWB	10f Good	77	1375
56	8	KEMP	10f Soft	73	1528
59	7	CHES	10f Gd/Fm	70	1777
75	1	AYR	7f Soft	67	3992*
79	1	AYR	8f Gd/Sft	67	4013*
85	1	LING	7f Good	73	4102*
85	2	YORK	8f Soft	83	4284
82	8	NEWM	8f Soft	86	4545

GREAT RICHES 3 b g £0					
0	11	LEIC	12f Gd/Sft	45	1571
0	16	CARL	8f Gd/Fm	39	3082

GREAT WHITE 3 gr c £0					
34a	10	SOUT	5f Aw	66	72
0	19	WIND	6f Good	66	852
30	6	FOLK	5f Soft		960

GRECIAN HALO 2 b f £0					
54	6	FOLK	7f Gd/Fm		3039
55	8	FOLK	7f Gd/Fm		3583
0	18	WIND	6f Gd/Sft		4288

GREEK DANCE 5 b g £223864					
118	2	LONG	11f Heavy		1115
121	2	CURR	11f Gd/Sft		1625
111	5	ASCO	12f Good		2149
121	1	MUNI	10f Soft		3071*
121	2	LEOP	10f Good		3925
101	10	NEWM	10f Good		4355

GREEK DREAM 2 ch f £0					
75	6	BATH	6f Gd/Sft		1667

GREEN BOPPER 7 b g £9547					
59a	5	SOUT	11f Aw	72	302
71a	2	SOUT	11f Aw	70	474
71a	3	SOUT	11f Aw	70	512
70a	4	SOUT	11f Aw	71	605
73a	2	SOUT	12f Aw	70	671
74a	1	SOUT	12f Aw	70	695*
54	7	HAYD	12f Gd/Sft	68	809
65	5	DONC	12f Gd/Fm	67	1839
61	5	HAMI	12f Gd/Fm	67	1908
39	8	BEVE	10f Good	63	2883
44	7	PONT	12f Gd/Fm	60	3224

GREEN CARD 6 b g £9803					
84	4	ASCO	8f Gd/Sft		1112
88	6	YORK	8f Firm	92	1327
83	3	HAYD	7f Soft		1820
67	16	ASCO	8f Good	90	2090	BL
82	4	WIND	12f Soft		2547	vis
87	1	DONC	10f Gd/Fm		3865*
71	6	SAND	8f Gd/Fm		3945

GREEN CASKET 3 b c £0					
73	6	KEMP	8f Gd/Sft		1080

GREEN GINGER 4 ch c £0					
59	16	YORK	6f Firm	75	2000
0	13	REDC	6f Gd/Fm	70	2158
0	15	PONT	6f Gd/Fm	65	2559	VIS
0	16	NEWC	6f Firm	60	3605	vis
0	17	LEIC	7f Firm	55	3839	vis

GREEN GOD 4 b c £248

48	10	LING	7f Soft	68	1542
65	5	CHEP	7f Gd/Sft	65	1794
54	10	GOOD	8f Gd/Fm	65	2126
0	20	DONC	7f Gd/Fm	63	2612
58	5	KEMP	7f Gd/Fm	60	3362
55	4	SALI	8f Firm	58	3753
26	12	LEIC	8f Gd/Sft		4032
0	15	LEIC	8f Sft/Hvy		4311	VIS
4	8	NEWC	7f Heavy	55	4426

GREEN MAGICAL 4 ch f £0					
16	14	GOOD	8f Soft	48	4066
0	11	YARM	11f Soft	45	4391

GREEN MINSTREL 2 b f £21134					
106	1	CHAN	8f Good		3934*
102	8	LONG	8f Good		4260

GREEN POWER 6 b g £0					
0	15	RIPO	12f Soft	48	822

GREEN PURSUIT 4 b g £672					
46a	7	SOUT	6f Aw		538
49	8	LING	8f Gd/Fm		2215
52	2	LEIC	7f Gd/Fm		3332
25a	12	WOLV	7f Aw		3770

GREEN TAMBOURINE 2 b f £3841					
86	1	HAYD	6f Gd/Fm		2500*
83	6	ASCO	6f Gd/Fm		2996

GREEN TURTLE CAY 4 b g £0					
0	12	BRIG	8f Gd/Fm	60	1129
0	12	LING	9f Good	60	1395
0	22	LEIC	6f Gd/Sft	53	1734
0a	11	LING	7f Aw		2759

GREEN WILDERNESS 3 b f £1130					
73	6	KEMP	10f Firm		2258
73	2	PONT	10f Gd/Fm		2558
56	6	HAYD	11f Gd/Sft		3265
0	19	DONC	10f Gd/Sft	75	4448

GREENAWAY BAY 6 ch g £45771					
49	5	NEWC	9f Firm	58	3603
64	1	YORK	9f Good	57	4300*
69	1	NOTT	8f Heavy	63	4506*
77	1	NEWM	8f Soft	68	4545*
77	2	DONC	8f Heavy	66	4573

GREENBOROUGH 2 b c £0					
0	15	NOTT	6f Heavy		4504

GREENGROOM 2 £2305					
100	4	LONG	8f Good		3926
99	5	LONG	8f Soft		4320

GREENHOPE 2 b c £0					
73	10	HAYD	8f Soft		3766
75	5	BATH	8f Soft		4430

GREENLEES 2 b f £0					
0	16	CHEP	8f Good		3867
0a	14	SOUT	7f Aw		4154

GREENSTONE 4 b f £0					
46a	9	LING	12f Aw	77	52

GREENWOOD 2 ch c £6216					
77	1	WIND	6f Gd/Fm		3047*
93	2	YARM	6f Gd/Fm		3965
86	12	NEWB	5f Gd/Sft		4454

GREGORIAN 3 b c £0					
0	8	CURR	8f Gd/Sft		1623

GREMLIN ONE 3 ch g £0					
12	7	CARL	6f Gd/Fm		3080
43	6	CARL	7f Firm		3196

GRENADIER 3 b c £530					
72	5	EPSO	9f Heavy		1032
86	4	SAND	8f Heavy		1041
52	12	SAND	7f Soft	73	1569

GREY BIRD 3 ro f £0					
0a	12	SOUT	12f Aw		643

GREY BUTTONS 5 gr m £0					
0	13	LEIC	12f Good	39	791

```
10  9  BRIG  12f Gd/Sft       893  t
 0  14 FOLK  15f Soft   39    963
 0  12 BRIG  12f Good         1647
```

GREY COSSACK 3 gr g £3547
```
72  6  HAYD  5f Gd/Sft        808  VIS
63  3  PONT  6f Gd/Sft        1105
75  4  PONT  6f Good          1500
78  1  REDC  6f Gd/Sft        1562*
52  12 RIPO  6f Good    76    1600
```

GREY EMINENCE 3 gr c £22975
```
82  2  NEWB  8f Good          1376
89  2  SAND  8f Soft          1584
89  2  HAYD  8f Gd/Sft        1837
84  1  ASCO  7f Gd/Fm         3343*
87  2  KEMP  6f Gd/Sft  88    4037
83  9  NEWM  7f Good    88    4195
93  2  NEWB  8f Gd/Sft  91    4456
102 1  NEWM  6f Gd/Sft        4535*
```

GREY FLYER 3 gr g £6907
```
54a 4  LING  6f Aw     61     4
58a 2  LING  6f Aw            207
64a 1  LING  6f Aw     55     242*
66a 2  LING  5f Aw     61     269
36a 8  LING  5f Aw     63     526
50a 5  LING  5f Aw     63     592
43  10 BRIG  5f Firm   60     1334
56  3  CATT  6f Good   57     1665
47  9  MUSS  5f Firm   56     2047
59  1  MUSS  5f Firm   55     2374*
```

GREY IMPERIAL 2 gr c £0
```
50  9  THIR  7f Gd/Fm         3617
62  11 LEIC  7f Firm          3840
```

GREY PRINCESS 4 gr f £0
```
42  9  BRIG  5f Firm    78    1650
36  11 SALI  5f Firm    75    2022
```

GREY STRIKE 4 gr c £0
```
0  19  PONT  8f Gd/Sft  40    1101
```

GREYCOAT 2 ch g £0
```
0  15  NOTT  5f Gd/Sft        4503
0  17  DONC  6f Heavy         4576
```

GREYFIELD 4 b c £7406
```
56  4  YORK  12f Gd/Fm        1984
72  5  SAND  11f Good   73    2530
70  7  NEWB  13f Firm   73    2852
72  4  CHES  12f Firm   71    3173
61  5  NEWM  12f Gd/Fm  71    3461
68  4  GOOD  12f Good         3657
66  4  YORK  14f Good   70    3811
65  9  NEWB  16f Good   68    3986
69  1  BATH  10f Soft   64    4436*
69  2  REDC  10f Soft         4501
```

GRIEF 7 ch g £0
```
21  10 BRIG  12f Gd/Sft       893
30  11 FOLK  10f Soft   65    965  bl
38  8  EPSO  12f Heavy  65    1030 bl
40  11 BRIG  12f Gd/Fm  60    1128
```

GROESFAEN LAD 3 b c £2911
```
0  15  WIND  8f Gd/Fm   75    744
70  4  SOUT  7f Gd/Sft  72    857
64  7  BRIG  7f Gd/Fm         1125
11a 10 SOUT  6f Aw            2947
56  6  LEIC  8f Aw      68    3095
58a 3  WOLV  8f Aw      59    4021
41a 5  WOLV  9f Aw      59    4251
58a 3  WOLV  8f Aw      58    4363 VIS
65a 1  WOLV  8f Aw      58    4437* vis
42a 9  WOLV  7f Aw      65    4550 vis
```

GROESFAEN LADY 4 b f £0
```
43a 4  SOUT  6f Aw             30
0a  14 SOUT  5f Aw             71
34a 9  WOLV  5f Aw      48     116
```

GROOMS GOLD 8 ch g £1434
```
0a  12 SOUT  12f Aw    47     70
0a  11 SOUT  11f Aw    44     324
35a 4  SOUT  11f Aw           369  bl
34a 2  LING  13f Aw    30     458
34a 2  WOLV  16f Aw    30     494
0a  12 SOUT  16f Aw    32     644  VIS
0a  11 SOUT  16f Aw    29     737  vis
23  8  HAMI  12f Firm   29    1241 vis
29  2  BRIG  12f Gd/Sft 26    1465 vis
20  10 WARW  16f Gd/Fm  28    2037 vis
3a  4  LING  13f Aw            2323 vis
19  10 FOLK  16f Good    30   2622 vis
21  6  WIND  12f Gd/Fm   24   2887 vis
19  6  NOTT  14f Gd/Fm   24   3002 bl
```

GROSVENOR FLYER 4 ch c £0
```
26  14 KEMP  14f Good   73    726
44  7  WARW  12f Soft   71    815
0  17  BATH  12f Soft   66    4433
```

GROVE DANCER 2 b f £4102
```
70  1  YARM  6f Gd/Sft         1612*
69  3  YARM  6f Gd/Fm          1954
66  4  NEWM  7f Firm    70     3299
51  13 DONC  7f Firm    68     3901
59  7  YARM  6f Gd/Fm   68     3968
34  8  YARM  8f Soft    64     4393
22  11 NEWM  8f Soft           4542 BL
```

GROVE LODGE 3 b c £272
```
38  10 KEMP  6f Good           729
63  9  LING  7f Gd/Sft         840
45  8  NOTT  8f Heavy    53    1024
42  7  BRIG  6f Firm     50    1211
32  8  BRIG  8f Gd/Fm    47    2044
25  10 LING  7f Firm     58    2325
41  10 WIND  8f Good           3350
47  6  GOOD  10f Soft          4081
57  9  LING  8f Soft           4274
56  10 BRIG  8f Soft           4420
46  3  WIND  10f Heavy         4528
```

GRUB STREET 4 b c £3425
```
0  14  NEWC  7f Soft           759
53  1  THIR  8f Gd/Sft   50    1718*
```

GRUINART 3 br c £4277
```
71  8  LEIC  8f Good           789
65  9  LING  6f Gd/Sft         837
64  4  SALI  8f Good     67    1345
67  3  WIND  8f Good     65    1726
75  1  SALI  8f Firm     66    2025*
71  4  HAMI  8f Gd/Fm    72    2235
57  12 SAND  10f Gd/Fm   72    2499
54  7  WIND  8f Good     71    3355
0  15  SALI  10f Gd/Sft  69    4168
66  4  NEWM  8f Gd/Sft   67    4536
41  10 DONC  8f Heavy    67    4573
```

GRYFFINDOR 2 b c £2892
```
89  3  NEWM  7f Firm           2346
94  7  NEWM  8f Gd/Fm          2613
87  2  ASCO  7f Gd/Fm          2956
```

GUARANDA 2 b f £1700
```
79  5  LING  7f Firm           3829
79  2  NEWM  8f Good           4019
```

GUARD DUTY 3 b g £2250
```
71  6  WIND  10f Good          850
80  2  WARW  12f Soft    79    1064
67  4  CHES  13f Gd/Fm         2249 BL
76  5  KEMP  12f Soft          4040
76  3  DONC  15f Gd/Sft  76    4451 t
```

GUARDED SECRET 3 ch c £5644
```
70  10 NEWB  8f Good           1376
69a 2  SOUT  8f Aw             1977
69  2  LING  9f Firm           2322
77  1  SALI  10f Gd/Fm   69    3390*
71  7  CHEP  10f Good    75    3870
```

(continued)
```
77  2  BRIG  10f Heavy   75    4540
```

GUARDIA 2 ch f £1196
```
64  7  NEWM  6f Firm            1856
80  2  LEIC  8f Firm            3836
```

GUDLAGE 4 b c £0
```
0  14  NEWM  7f Gd/Fm    91    2133
0  18  SAND  8f Gd/Fm    88    2528 t
```

GUEST ENVOY 5 b m £12820
```
24a 8  WOLV  8f Aw              322
37a 3  WOLV  7f Aw              396
53a 2  SOUT  7f Aw              501
51a 2  SOUT  7f Aw              511
49a 1  SOUT  6f Aw      43      557*
40a 4  SOUT  6f Aw      49      588
47a 4  SOUT  6f Aw      49      697
54a 1  SOUT  7f Aw      49      739*
50  1  HAYD  7f Gd/Sft  42      811*
55a 2  SOUT  7f Aw      52      867
41  6  WARW  8f Soft    49      1066
46a 7  WOLV  6f Aw      54      1391
49a 5  SOUT  8f Aw      54      1419
43a 5  SOUT  8f Aw      54      1506
39  5  SOUT  7f Aw      49      1606
22  10 WIND  8f Soft    48      2546
38a 5  SOUT  7f Aw      52      2637
42  4  NEWM  6f Gd/Fm   48      2804
39  6  YARM  7f Good    47      3238
30  12 NEWM  7f Firm    50      3297
34  7  YARM  7f Gd/Fm   45      3384
39  5  YARM  7f Gd/Fm   44      3666
```

GUEST OF HONOUR 4 gr f £0
```
6  16  HAYD  7f Gd/Sft  58      811
```

GUILLAMOU CITY 3 £26829
```
107 6  LONG  10f Good           2225
107 3  ARLI  10f Yldg           3549
```

GUILSBOROUGH 5 br g £7654
```
62a 6  LING  8f Aw      69      96
53a 8  WOLV  7f Aw      69      143
72a 1  SOUT  8f Aw      65      2121*
78a 1  SOUT  8f Aw      71      2302*
81a 1  SOUT  8f Aw      75      2634*
0  12  WIND  10f Gd/Sft 55      4291
```

GUINEA HUNTER 4 b c £23397
```
91  7  DONC  5f Gd/Fm   101     702
95  1  HAYD  6f Gd/Fm           1164*
97  9  HAYD  5f Gd/Sft  100     1533
85  7  YORK  6f Gd/Fm   98      1983
101 1  NEWM  5f Gd/Fm   96      2859+
78  17 RIPO  6f Gd/Fm   100     3464
91  11 YORK  6f Good     100    3543
97  5  YORK  6f Gd/Fm   99      3727 BL
0  17  DONC  6f Gd/Fm   98      3861 bl
101 3  AYR   6f Gd/Sft  100     4012 bl
102 5  ASCO  5f Gd/Sft  100     4129 bl
95  8  NEWM  5f Good     100    4339 bl
0  12  DONC  5f Soft            4466
```

GULCHIE 2 ch c £3271
```
80  1  REDC  7f Gd/Fm           2862*
86  4  NOTT  8f Good            3523
```

GULF SHAADI 8 b g £761
```
72a 9  SOUT  8f Aw      83      49
56a 9  LING  8f Aw      80      169
49a 8  WOLV  9f Aw      75      611
71  4  WARW  8f Soft    73      817
66  7  BRIG  8f Gd/Sft  73      895
67  5  BRIG  8f Gd/Fm   70      1129
71  4  BRIG  7f Firm    70      1213
53  9  BRIG  8f Firm    68      1330
81  5  LING  8f Firm            2762
66  3  SAND  8f Gd/Fm           2920
63  6  LING  10f Firm           3281
53  10 BRIG  7f Gd/Fm   65      4121
```

GULFSTREAM PARK 2 b f £5465
| 91 | 3 | SAN | 8f Gd/Fm | | 2486 | |

GUMPTION 2 b g £307
| 72 | 4 | DONC | 8f Heavy | | 4569 | |

GUNBOAT DIPLOMACY GB 5 br g £23
0	16	LEIC	10f Soft	33	1546	
0	15	HAMI	13f Gd/Fm	28	1936	
42	1	**REDC**	10f Gd/Fm		2143*	
29	5	NOTT	10f Gd/Fm	40	3007	
34	7	NEWC	12f Good		3247	
29	10	REDC	11f Gd/Fm	37	3636	

GUNNER SAM 4 ch c £0
51a	6	SOUT	6f Aw		30	
22a	11	WOLV	6f Aw		76	
49a	6	SOUT	7f Aw		130	
56a	5	SOUT	6f Aw		201	BL
0a	12	SOUT	6f Aw	52	246	bl
39a	7	WOLV	5f Aw	52	291	
33a	8	SOUT	7f Aw	48	368	
20	13	REDC	7f Gd/Sft		1132	
0	18	NOTT	6f Firm	54	1273	
0	20	LEIC	6f Gd/Sft	47	1734	
10a	10	LING	8f Aw		4272	

GURU 2 b c £0
| 0 | 17 | DONC | 7f Gd/Fm | | 4446 | |

GUTTERIDGE 10 b g £206
| 42a | 4 | SOUT | 12f Aw | | 84 | |

GWENDOLINE 3 b f £6322
71	2	WARW	7f Gd/Sft		1708	
80	1	**SALI**	7f Gd/Fm		2232*	
83	2	NEWM	8f Gd/Fm	80	3118	
73	7	NEWM	7f Gd/Fm	84	3460	

GWENEIRA 3 gr f £4309
| 84 | 1 | **SAND** | 10f Good | | 3432* | |
| 74 | 5 | DONC | 10f Heavy | | 4571 | |

GYMCRAK FIREBIRD 3 ch f £0
53a	4	SOUT	7f Aw	55	31	
55a	6	WOLV	8f Aw		171	
28	13	NOTT	8f Aw	55	1024	
0a	12	SOUT	7f Aw	55	1202	
40	9	CATT	12f Gd/Fm	50	2746	
17	10	THIR	12f Gd/Fm	46	3125	
27a	9	SOUT	11f Aw		4150	BL

GYMCRAK FLYER 9 b m £0
0	15	THIR	8f Soft	53	907	
0	19	REDC	8f Firm	52	1300	
0	16	LEIC	8f Firm	50	2027	vis
29	9	PONT	8f Gd/Fm	47	2561	
42	9	CARL	7f Firm	47	2823	vis
37	5	CARL	8f Firm	40	3574	vis
18	10	MUSS	8f Gd/Fm	40	3746	vis

GYPSY 4 b c £1128
64a	3	WOLV	9f Aw	68	270	
39a	5	LING	10f Aw		335	
58a	4	WOLV	12f Aw	65	407	
53a	4	SOUT	10f Aw		510	BL
68	3	PONT	10f Soft	68	871	
65	7	DONC	10f Gd/Fm	68	1050	
49	5	NOTT	10f Good		1875	
59	6	NEWM	10f Good	65	4160	

GYPSY SONG 3 b g £519
0	16	NOTT	6f Firm		1266	
33	10	CATT	6f Good		1663	
44a	5	SOUT	7f Aw		2633	
37a	7	WOLV	8f Aw	51	3499	
31a	9	WOLV	12f Aw	48	3773	
38	5	AYR	11f Soft	42	3963	
39	2	NOTT	14f Heavy	39	4409	

HAAFEL 3 ch c £0
| 52 | 8 | THIR | 12f Good | | 1386 | |

HAASIL 2 b c £839
| 64 | 3 | SALI | 7f Gd/Sft | | 4167 | |

| 76 | 4 | DONC | 7f Gd/Sft | | 4446 | |

HABIBA 3 b f £0
0	22	WIND	10f Gd/Fm		1200	BL
0	14	WIND	10f Firm		1293	bl
27	11	YARM	7f Firm		1951	

HADATH 3 br c £16684
0	17	WARW	8f Heavy		884	
0	7	HAYD	11f Gd/Fm		986	
74	5	YORK	8f Firm	75	1341	VIS
60	6	PONT	8f Good	75	1495	vis
80	1	**THIR**	7f Gd/Fm		2058*	
78	2	NEWC	8f Good	75	2524	
82	1	**BEVE**	7f Firm	77	2733*	
83	2	NOTT	8f Gd/Fm	82	3005	
83	3	THIR	8f Gd/Fm	83	3147	
0	14	NEWM	7f Gd/Fm	83	3629	
0	25	AYR	6f Gd/Sft	83	4010	

HADEQA 4 ch g £0
38	11	CHES	10f Gd/Fm	63	2671	
21	16	RIPO	9f Gd/Fm	60	3011	
0	15	CHES	8f Firm	54	3170	
0	13	BATH	8f Gd/Fm	48	3623	bl
0	15	GOOD	8f Soft	43	4066	bl

HADLEIGH 4 b c £876
0	21	ASCO	8f Gd/Sft	72	1113	
56	14	ASCO	10f Good	73	2170	
0	14	WIND	8f Soft	68	2546	
0	12	LEIC	7f Gd/Fm	68	2775	
66	2	YARM	10f Good		3234	VIS
57	8	NOTT	10f Good	63	3524	vis
53	8	GOOD	8f Good	60	3885	vis

HAIKAL 3 b c £301
66	8	LEIC	6f Gd/Sft		829	
41	8	FOLK	7f Soft		961	
62	4	NEWC	8f Gd/Sft	65	1477	
59	5	MUSS	8f Gd/Fm	64	2205	BL
0	14	REDC	10f Gd/Sft	62	4221	
0	16	NEWC	10f Heavy	57	4404	

HAIL SHEEVA 3 ch f £0
| 0 | 11 | LING | 10f Firm | | 3490 | |

HAIL THE CHIEF 3 b c £14021
69	4	GOOD	8f Gd/Fm		1960	
69	3	FOLK	7f Gd/Fm		2293	
51	6	WIND	8f Soft	70	2546	
51	12	EPSO	7f Good	70	2794	
72	1	**FOLK**	7f Gd/Fm	68	3041*	
71	1	**BRIG**	7f Gd/Fm		3259*	
72	2	EPSO	8f Good	71	3854	
65	6	BRIG	7f Gd/Sft	72	4121	
76a	2	LING	8f Aw	72	4330	

HAITHEM 3 b c £0
48	14	DONC	10f Gd/Fm	74	701	
49	6	PONT	10f Gd/Sft		1103	
47	10	CATT	7f Gd/Fm		2437	
26a	12	SOUT	12f Aw		4366	

HAKEEM 5 ch g £5674
0	19	THIR	6f Gd/Sft	61	1356	
61	2	RIPO	8f Good	59	1598	
62	2	THIR	10f Gd/Fm	61	2063	
49	13	CARL	8f Gd/Fm	61	2242	
62	3	DONC	8f Good	62	2349	
63	3	YORK	8f Gd/Fm	62	2645	
47	14	YORK	7f Good	62	2694	
45	10	NEWC	8f Good	62	2986	
36	10	LEIC	8f Gd/Sft		4032	

HAL HOO YAROOM 7 b h £1593
| 58 | 3 | LING | 16f Good | 57 | 1394 | |
| 60 | 2 | BATH | 17f Gd/Fm | 58 | 1996 | |

HALAWAN 2 b c £1666
| 88 | 2 | NEWB | 7f Firm | | 3999 | |

HALCYON DAZE 2 ch f £1230
| 77 | 8 | NEWM | 7f Good | | 3607 | |

| 75 | 4 | REDC | 7f Gd/Sft | | 4216 | |
| 83 | 2 | LEIC | 7f Heavy | | 4312 | |

HALCYON MAGIC 2 b g £3462
0	17	KEMP	6f Gd/Fm		1924	
0	20	LING	5f Gd/Fm		2214	
50a	4	SOUT	5f Aw		2384	
60	5	KEMP	5f Firm	64	2868	
53	5	KEMP	6f Gd/Fm	60	3075	
75	2	NOTT	6f Good		3520	
49	6	RIPO	5f Gd/Fm		3710	
74	2	YORK	6f Good		3812	
70	2	WARW	15f Gd/Fm		3911	
45	7	PONT	6f Soft		4372	

HALF MOON BAY 3 b c £0
60	6	NEWM	5f Gd/Fm	92	2859	
66	16	YORK	5f Gd/Fm	90	3569	
0	16	NEWM	5f Gd/Fm	85	4015	
0	23	YORK	5f Soft	80	4285	

HALF TIDE 6 ch g £7475
42a	3	LING	10f Aw	42	220	
1a	8	LING	12f Aw	50	245	
34	6	GOOD	9f Gd/Sft	39	1807	
43	2	EPSO	12f Gd/Sft	39	2429	
48	1	**EPSO**	12f Gd/Sft	43	2626*	
25	9	EPSO	12f Good	42	2793	
43	5	WIND	12f Good	47	3353	
39	8	GOOD	12f Good	51	3657	
45	5	EPSO	12f Gd/Fm	45	3858	
41	7	SAND	10f Soft	44	4208	
48a	1	**SOUT**	14f Aw	43	4371*	

HALF TONE 8 gr h £1070
0	15	SAND	5f Gd/Fm	46	763	bl
17	10	FOLK	6f Soft	43	958	bl
39	5	BRIG	6f Gd/Sft	40	1464	bl
41	3	GOOD	5f Gd/Sft	40	1487	bl
23a	13	SOUT	5f Aw	55	1806	bl
41	3	GOOD	6f Gd/Fm	41	2124	bl
41	2	NEWM	7f Firm	41	2347	bl
36	5	BRIG	7f Soft	41	2427	bl
32	11	BATH	5f Gd/Sft	41	2555	bl
28	8	FOLK	5f Good	41	2623	bl
29	10	BRIG	5f Gd/Fm	37	3243	bl

HALHOO LAMMTARRA 3 ch c £0
68	11	NEWB	8f Good		1376	
49	10	KEMP	8f Soft		1532	
69	5	GOOD	10f Gd/Fm	73	1958	
63	5	PONT	10f Firm	70	2175	

HALLAND 2 ch c £4160
62	6	YARM	6f Gd/Fm		3385	
80	6	LEIC	7f Firm		3840	
89	1	**YARM**	7f Soft		4514*	

HALLAND PARK GIRL 3 b f £5258
95	6	NEWM	7f Good		953	
99	14	NEWM	6f Gd/Fm		1185	
103	2	NOTT	6f Good		1410	
87	9	YORK	6f Gd/Fm		2646	
87	8	NEWB	6f Firm		2847	BL
89	7	GOOD	7f Firm		3155	

HALLIANA 2 b f £0
| 26 | 6 | NOTT | 6f Gd/Fm | | 2189 | |

HALMAHERA 5 b g £8127
103	5	DONC	6f Good		734	
108	2	MAIS	6f Heavy		820	
99	8	NEWM	6f Good		952	
108	5	NEWM	5f Gd/Fm		1172	
99	6	KEMP	5f Soft		1529	
87	19	ASCO	6f Good	108	2151	
101	4	NEWB	6f Firm		2847	
99	9	GOOD	6f Firm	106	3152	
101	3	NOTT	5f Good		3521	

HALMANERROR 10 gr g £2164
| 48 | 6 | LEIC | 7f Good | | 790 | |

88	5	WARW	7f Heavy		1004	
47	3	REDC	7f Gd/Sft		1132	
56	3	BRIG	6f Gd/Sft	55	1464	
58	2	GOOD	6f Gd/Sft	55	1636	
56	4	CHEP	7f Gd/Sft	56	1794	
57	6	GOOD	6f Good	57	2355	
49	8	CHEP	7f Good	57	3873	

HAMADEENAH 2 ch f £5227

82	1	NEWM	6f Gd/Fm	3627*	
88	5	NEWB	7f Gd/Fm	3985	
43	11	ASCO	7f Good	4114	

HAMASKING 2 b f £2299

51	6	PONT	5f Gd/Sft	1102	
53	6	REDC	7f Firm	1294	
60	1	CATT	6f Soft	1679*	
36	11	PONT	6f Gd/Fm	61	2557

HAMATARA 2 ch g £5941

65	4	NEWB	5f Soft		911	
65	10	DONC	6f Gd/Sft		1048	
68	4	SOUT	6f Soft		1602	t
75	1	LEIC	5f Gd/Fm	69	2915*	t
75	2	GOOD	5f Good	74	3109	t
61	6	NOTT	6f Good	75	3519	t

HAMBLEDEN 3 b c £9109

40	10	NOTT	8f Good	784	
66	3	WARW	11f Heavy	65	1002
79a	1	WOLV	12f Good	65	1238*
56	8	GOOD	12f Gd/Sft	75	1637
74	3	KEMP	14f Gd/Fm	1928	
81	2	NOTT	14f Gd/Fm	74	2681
41	9	NEWM	15f Good	81	3025
83	1	SAND	14f Gd/Fm	80	3948*
0	17	NEWM	14f Gd/Sft	83	4213
81	4	DONC	15f Gd/Sft	82	4451

HAMBLETON HIGHLITE 2 ch g £4496

80	1	HAMI	5f Firm		1240*	
82	3	NEWC	6f Gd/Sft		1475	
70	7	BEVE	5f Gd/Sft		1761	
84	4	YORK	5f Good	85	2698	BL
61	4	HAMI	5f Gd/Fm		2797	bl
68	7	CHES	6f Firm	80	3168	
54a	3	WOLV	6f Aw		4244	VIS

HAMERKOP 5 br m £236

12a	1	LING	13f Aw		483	e
44	4	YARM	14f Gd/Fm		2194	
11	9	NEWM	8f Gd/Fm		3117	
52	10	NEWM	10f Good		4017	

HAMISH G 3 ch g £0

30	10	REDC	9f Gd/Fm	3326	
40	12	PONT	8f Firm	3506	

HAMLYN 3 br c £780

83	6	NEWM	7f Gd/Fm		983	
80	4	GOOD	8f Gd/Sft		1449	
67	6	SALI	7f Gd/Fm		1886	
74	4	NEWM	7f Gd/Fm		2860	BL
61	7	SAND	8f Gd/Fm		2938	bl
0	16	SAND	8f Soft	74	4206	

HAMMER AND SICKLE 3 b c £0

0	17	ASCO	5f Gd/Sft	95	4129
77	14	NEWM	5f Good	90	4339
0	17	DONC	5f Soft	86	4466

HAMMOCK 2 b c £0

0	14	WIND	6f Gd/Fm		2209	
68	5	FOLK	7f Good		2619	
66	5	EPSO	7f Good		2791	
0	18	LING	7f Soft	65	4191	VIS

HANAS PRIDE 4 gr f £0

0a	8	SOUT	6f Aw	2819	

HAND CHIME 3 ch g £22126

0	16	LING	6f Gd/Fm	837	
63	1	CATT	7f Soft	1682*	
70	1	CARL	8f Firm	62	2281*

71	2	SALI	8f Gd/Sft	68	2467	
67	3	NOTT	8f Gd/Fm		2682	
80	1	KEMP	7f Gd/Fm	70	3076*	
81	1	PONT	6f Gd/Fm		3225*	
86a	1	WOLV	7f Aw	80	3771*	

HANDSOME BADSHA 2 b c £284

51a	6	WOLV	6f Aw		4381	t
57	4	BRIG	6f Heavy		4537	

HANDSOME BEAU 5 ch g £0

3a	12	SOUT	8f Aw	50	bl
38a	7	WOLV	9f Aw	274	bl

HANDSOME LAD 2 ch c £0

27	6	NEWC	5f Heavy	1764	
26	10	RIPO	6f Gd/Fm	2100	

HANDSOME RIDGE 6 ch g £33557

117	2	CAPA	10f Heavy	12	
104	6	SAND	8f Heavy	1043	

HANGOVER SQUARE 6 ch h £5848

99	3	JAGE	9f Good	1323	

HANNAH BURDETT 3 ch f £680

71	3	NEWM	7f Gd/Fm	2860	
50	5	THIR	7f Gd/Fm	3146	

HANNIBAL LAD 4 ch g £48583

62a	2	WOLV	9f Aw	60	233
71a	1	WOLV	9f Aw	62	309*
63a	5	WOLV	9f Aw	68	349
71a	2	WOLV	9f Aw	67	381
72a	3	WOLV	9f Aw	70	447
75a	1	SOUT	11f Aw	70	512*
80a	1	SOUT	11f Aw	74	605*
80a	3	SOUT	12f Aw	78	671
74a	5	SOUT	12f Aw	78	695
53	9	CHES	10f Gd/Fm	64	1217
68	4	CHES	12f Firm	64	1251
68	2	DONC	12f Good	64	1518
69	1	SOUT	12f Soft	64	1604*
75	1	DONC	12f Gd/Fm	67	1839*
72	4	GOOD	12f Gd/Fm	75	2127
77	4	HAYD	12f Gd/Fm	76	2502
82	1	ASCO	12f Good	76	2674*
85	3	DONC	12f Gd/Fm	82	2755
84	5	CHES	12f Firm	84	3173
73	5	NEWB	13f Firm	83	3454
81	6	DONC	12f Firm	83	3896
78	5	AYR	13f Heavy	82	4325

HANOI 3 b f £0

30	8	LEIC	8f Soft		1548	BL
61	5	YARM	8f Gd/Fm		2198	bl
0	15	SAND	10f Good		2531	
0	12	YARM	8f Firm	49	2767	bl
26	7	YARM	10f Gd/Fm		3382	bl
0	15	NEWM	7f Good		3612	bl

HANOVER HOUSE 3 br c £2824

0	3	LUCE	15f Heavy	3850	

HAPPY CHANGE 6 ch g £26607

106	3	NEWM	10f Gd/Fm	1174	
103	8	HAYD	11f Gd/Fm	3321	
108	1	WIND	12f Good	3640*	
103	5	KEMP	12f Gd/Fm	3792	
109	3	CURR	11f Gd/Sft	4057	
109	2	ASCO	12f Good	4109	
85	6	NEWB	12f Sft/Hv	4469	

HAPPY DAYS 5 b g £3246

16a	7	WOLV	16f Aw	42	552
21	10	NEWC	16f Soft	38	760
15	8	PONT	17f Soft	41	876
35	4	HAMI	13f Gd/Fm	37	1194
35	2	HAMI	13f Gd/Fm	35	1363
31	6	RIPO	16f Good	35	1597
38	2	HAMI	13f Gd/Fm	35	1936
31	5	HAMI	13f Firm	35	2098
41	2	HAMI	13f Gd/Fm	38	2643

34	4	CARL	14f Gd/Fm	39	3084
34	4	AYR	15f Good	38	3367
0	12	REDC	14f Gd/Sft	38	4222
24	7	MUSS	13f Soft	34	4521

HAPPY DIAMOND 3 b c £59832

88	3	LEIC	6f Gd/Sft	1576	
0	23	YORK	6f Firm	84	2003
87	2	DONC	10f Gd/Fm	81	2350
94	D	NEWC	10f Good	89	2522
96	1	DONC	10f Gd/Fm	89	2610*
100	1	ASCO	10f Gd/Fm	94	2995*
109	1	GOOD	10f Gd/Fm	101	3131*

HAPPY GO LUCKY 6 ch m £1944

53	10	BATH	13f Gd/Fm	67	1440
50	6	SALI	12f Gd/Fm	64	1888
64	2	SALI	12f Firm	64	2023
63	3	SALI	14f Gd/Fm	64	2268
0	12	GOOD	12f Soft	4061	

HAPPY HOOLIGAN 3 b c £928

45	9	NEWC	7f Soft	759	
72	5	RIPO	8f Soft	826	
72	3	BEVE	7f Heavy	72	976
72	3	HAMI	9f Firm	1242	

HAPPY LADY 4 b f £420

39a	3	WOLV	9f Aw	446	
24a	6	WOLV	9f Aw	578	

HARD DAYS NIGHT 3 b c £1612

0	12	WIND	8f Heavy	59	933
0	14	BATH	10f Good	50	1094
0	16	BATH	10f Gd/Sft	46	1671
38	6	LING	11f Firm	40	1911
44	4	YARM	14f Gd/Fm	43	2195
33	6	FOLK	12f Good	41	2624
37	2	BEVE	16f Good	36	2879
18	13	NOTT	16f Gd/Fm	38	3112
44	2	FOLK	16f Gd/Fm	45	3448
44	4	FOLK	16f Gd/Fm	43	3588
0a	9	LING	16f Aw	41	4099

HARD LINES 4 b c £3215

41	16	ASCO	8f Gd/Sft	75	1113	
65	10	DONC	7f Gd/Fm	70	1840	
51	8	BATH	8f Firm	68	1998	
0	16	WIND	8f Good	65	2367	
45a	4	WOLV	9f Aw		3498	
61	1	BATH	8f Gd/Fm	55	3816*	
63	3	LEIC	8f Gd/Sft		4032	
53	3	LEIC	8f Sft/Hvy		4311	

HARD TO CASH 2 b c £0

29	7	YARM	7f Firm	2898	
44	4	YARM	6f Good	3028	
0	24	NEWM	7f Good	4336	

HARD TO CATCH 2 b c £4167

58	5	NEWB	5f Soft		911	
59	3	NOTT	5f Heavy		1019	
70	4	YARM	6f Gd/Sft		1612	
65	6	GOOD	6f Good		2357	
53	7	SAND	5f Good	67	3228	
74	1	LING	5f Firm		3576*	BL
77	7	RIPO	6f Gd/Fm		3714	bl
0	12	LING	5f Good	76	4098	bl
83a	6	LING	5f Good		4332	bl

HARD TO FOLLOW 5 b m £0

0	19	PONT	8f Gd/Fm	27	2561
18	9	BATH	12f Firm	2785	
30	7	SALI	12f Firm	2981	

HARD TO KNOW 2 b c £647

62	4	LING	6f Firm	2760	
0	14	NEWM	6f Gd/Fm	3162	
75	4	NEWM	6f Gd/Fm	3627	

HARD TO LAY 2 br f £1930

67	2	PONT	5f Soft	1698	
59	5	PONT	6f Good	1864	

HARPOON LOUIE 10 b g £0 (continued)

56	7	PONT	5f Good		2361
44	8	WARW	7f Gd/Fm		2841
57	2	BRIG	7f Gd/Fm		3240
60	3	FOLK	7f Gd/Fm		3582

HAREEBA 3 ch f £432

75	4	GOOD	7f Gd/Sft		1468
51	11	WARW	7f Gd/Sft		1708
34	10	SALI	7f Gd/Fm		3423

HARIK 6 b m £7900

66a	3	LING	12f Aw	72	332
79a	1	**LING**	16f Aw	70	424*
82a	1	**LING**	16f Aw	78	548*
81a	2	WOLV	16f Aw	81	664

HARISHON 4 b c £9600

95	2	FRAU	12f Good		1903
90	3	DIEL	16f Good		3553
95	3	DIEL	12f Good		4148

HARIYMI 5 gr h £0

70	12	SALI	12f Good	79	1350

HARLEQUIN 2 b c £0

77	9	NEWM	7f Good		4184
57	6	LING	7f Soft		4483
82	6	DONC	7f Heavy		4566

HARLEQUIN DANCER 4 b c £0

0	15	BEVE	8f Firm	82	1279	
49	7	BEVE	8f Good	79	1445	
35	8	DONC	8f Gd/Fm	73	2758	
44	11	HAYD	11f Good	65	3285	
0	14	CHES	10f Soft	58	4074	vis

HARMONIC 3 b f £6679

45	6	BRIG	7f Firm		1333
49	13	SAND	7f Soft	75	1569
74	2	SALI	7f Gd/Fm		1886
72	2	SALI	7f Gd/Fm		2232
68	2	FOLK	7f Good		2621
48	15	ASCO	7f Gd/Fm	71	2999
72	2	ASCO	7f Gd/Fm		3343
68	4	EPSO	9f Good	69	3856
72	2	NEWM	8f Gd/Fm	68	4536

HARMONIC WAY 5 ch g £77623

86	6	KEMP	6f Soft		1016
101	4	NEWM	6f Firm	101	1182
106	2	YORK	6f Firm	101	1337
112	1	**ASCO**	6f Good	102	2151*
100	6	NEWC	6f Firm		2335
105	2	NEWB	6f Firm		2847
100	9	YORK	5f Firm		3598
107	4	HAYD	6f Gd/Sft		3784
112	6	ASCO	6f Gd/Sft		4125
100	10	NEWM	6f Good		4346

HARMONIZE 3 b f £392

17	4	NEWC	6f Gd/Fm		2313

HARMONY HALL 6 ch g £8300

53	4	CHEP	10f Good	60	1973
61	4	GOOD	8f Gd/Fm	60	2126
65	2	DONC	8f Gd/Fm	59	2349
67	2	CHEP	8f Gd/Fm	63	2492
66	2	YORK	8f Firm	63	2645
61	7	BATH	8f Firm	65	2942
50	8	BATH	8f Firm	65	3207
61	3	LING	9f Firm	62	3488
0	17	YORK	8f Good	62	3810
0	18	BATH	10f Soft	60	4436

HARMONY ROW 2 ch c £4259

87	3	NEWM	7f Good		4184
90	1	**DONC**	7f Gd/Fm		4446*

HARNAGE 5 b g £0

0	14	LEIC	10f Soft	27	1546

HAROLDON 11 ch g £0

21	12	WARW	11f Heavy	40	890
40	6	WARW	11f Heavy		1523

HARPOON LOUIE 10 b g £0

45a	4	LING	8f Aw		93

HARRIER 2 b c £10567

68	3	PONT	5f Gd/Sft		1102
69	3	PONT	5f Soft		1698
56	10	PONT	5f Good		2361
77	1	**THIR**	7f Gd/Fm		3127*
87	1	**BEVE**	7f Gd/Fm		3409*
97	1	**AYR**	8f Gd/Sft		4008*

HARRY JUNIOR 2 b c £524

25	6	DONC	5f Good		712	
30	7	LING	8f Good		1396	t
40	5	YARM	7f Gd/Fm		1950	
52	2	YARM	5f Gd/Fm		2196	VIS
0	W	YARM	6f Firm		2388	BL
0	8	YARM	7f Firm		2898	vis
9	11	LEIC	6f Gd/Fm	53	3216	

HARRY TASTERS 3 ch c £0

54	12	LING	7f Gd/Sft		1263
56	12	WIND	7f Gd/Sft		1423
44	10	RIPO	8f Good		1596

HARRYANA 3 b f £0

0	22	YORK	5f Soft	78	4285
0	21	DONC	5f Heavy	74	4570

HARVEY LEADER 5 b g £372

49a	3	WOLV	8f Aw		661
64	9	YARM	8f Gd/Fm		1771
56	10	LING	8f Soft		4273

HARVEY WHITE 8 br g £928

0a	12	WOLV	12f Aw	37	261	
39a	2	WOLV	16f Aw	37	318	VIS
33a	3	LING	16f Aw		402	BL

HARVEYS FUTURE 6 b g £2179

43	3	NOTT	5f Good	43	1412	
44	2	HAMI	5f Gd/Fm	44	1910	
0	W	YARM	6f Gd/Fm	46	2415	
0	19	LEIC	5f Gd/Sft	47	4027	BL
39	6	SAND	5f Soft		4207	
49	2	WIND	5f Gd/Fm	46	4294	
46	7	NEWB	5f Gd/Sft	51	4459	

HARVY 3 ch c £0

0	17	LING	7f Gd/Sft		1261
0	13	SALI	7f Gd/Fm		1886
0	12	SALI	6f Gd/Fm		2977

HASTA LA VISTA 10 b g £9954

48	1	**MUSS**	14f Gd/Sft	43	903*	vis
36	11	NOTT	14f Gd/Sft	49	1087	vis
51	2	CATT	14f Soft	47	1683	vis
51	1	**CATT**	12f Gd/Sft	47	1816*	vis
48	4	THIR	12f Gd/Fm	50	2061	vis
46	3	CATT	12f Gd/Fm	50	2422	vis
48	5	HAMI	13f Gd/Fm	50	2643	bl
0a	12	SOUT	16f Aw	38	2951	vis
35	8	CATT	14f Gd/Fm	48	3201	vis
39	7	HAMI	12f Gd/Sft	45	3827	vis
42	3	CATT	16f Soft	43	4006	vis
22	8	CATT	16f Soft	41	4258	vis

HASTY PRINCE 2 ch c £0

78	6	LEIC	7f Good		3333

HASTY WORDS 4 b f £18790

104	1	**DONC**	8f Gd/Fm		703*
106	6	NEWM	9f Gd/Sft		967
98	4	NEWM	9f Gd/Fm		1154
51	11	ASCO	8f Good		2064
102	4	NEWM	8f Gd/Fm		4211
97	8	NEWM	8f Good		4347
99	5	NEWM	8f Soft		4544

HATA 2 ch f £352

87	4	NEWB	6f Gd/Fm		1403

HATAAB 3 ch c £21229

111	1	**YORK**	10f Firm		1340*
111	2	KEMP	10f Firm		2260
100	7	GOOD	12f Gd/Fm		3061
105	4	NEWM	12f Good		4194

HATHA ANNA 3 b c £0

95	5	YORK	10f Firm		1340
109	6	EPSO	12f Good		1848
92	7	ASCO	12f Good		2148

HATHEETHAH 3 b f £280

57	9	WIND	8f Gd/Fm		1428
80	5	NEWM	10f Firm		1857
60	5	SALI	7f Gd/Fm		2232
61	4	SALI	8f Gd/Fm		3289

HATHNI KHOUND 4 b f £0

25a	9	LING	10f Aw		238
48	6	WARW	11f Heavy	50	890
38	7	WARW	11f Soft	48	1065
0a	11	SOUT	16f Aw	31	1416
0	18	WARW	11f Gd/Fm	45	2033
0	16	SALI	10f Gd/Sft	40	4168

HAULAGE MAN 2 ch g £0

63	6	REDC	5f Gd/Sft		1131
64	6	HAMI	5f Firm		1240

HAUNT THE ZOO 5 b m £8825

48a	1	**SOUT**	6f Aw	40	87*
54a	1	**LING**	6f Aw	47	148*
41a	7	WOLV	7f Aw	53	193
55a	3	SOUT	6f Aw	54	280
39a	7	SOUT	6f Aw	54	342
17a	7	WOLV	7f Aw	53	739
34	15	REDC	5f Gd/Sft	50	1133
36a	7	WOLV	6f Aw	51	1233
35	8	NOTT	6f Firm	45	1273
58a	1	**SOUT**	7f Aw	49	1506*
0	13	BEVE	6f Gd/Sft	42	1760
38	3	LEIC	6f Firm	39	2031
0	19	NEWM	7f Good		4018
61a	3	SOUT	7f Aw	60	4153
61a	2	SOUT	8f Aw	60	4365

HAVANA 4 b f £2723

72	4	SALI	10f Good		1343	
73	2	EPSO	10f Gd/Sft		2627	
67	3	BATH	12f Firm		2943	
65	3	EPSO	12f Gd/Fm		3416	
58	10	BATH	13f Gd/Fm	70	3819	BL
52	7	BRIG	10f Gd/Sft	63	4118	
51	4	NOTT	10f Heavy		4413	

HAVENT MADE IT YET 3 ch f £0

0	15	YARM	8f Gd/Sft	48	1610	
0a	12	SOUT	8f Aw	35	1804	VIS
0a	10	LING	12f Aw	40	2217	

HAWK 2 b c £2058

84	3	NEWM	5f Gd/Fm		1169	
85	3	GOOD	5f Gd/Sft		1454	
93	3	WIND	5f Gd/Fm		3044	t

HAWKES RUN 2 b g £878

78	6	GOOD	8f Gd/Sft		1472
72	6	SAND	7f Gd/Fm		2494
73	4	BRIG	7f Gd/Fm		3239
73	5	GOOD	8f Soft	73	4076
73a	2	WOLV	8f Aw		4250

HAWKSBILL HENRY 6 ch g £7038

36a	7	LING	10f Aw	60	100
0a	11	LING	10f Aw	58	209
52a	7	LING	12f Aw	54	290
56a	1	**LING**	12f Aw	49	332*
54a	1	LING	12f Aw	53	441
62a	1	**LING**	12f Aw	53	486*
38a	7	LING	12f Aw	61	572
60a	3	LING	12f Aw	61	621
39	6	WIND	12f Gd/Fm	46	748
0	23	NEWM	12f Firm	40	1852

HAYA YA KEFAAH 8 b g £2310

8a	8	WOLV	12f Aw	47	608
0	15	DONC	12f Gd/Fm	50	699

51 1 **RIPO** 12f Soft 47 822*
0   16 YORK 14f Firm 59 1329
25 9 HAYD 12f Gd/Sft   1788 VIS
0   14 WARW 11f Gd/Fm 49 2033 vis
0   11 WARW 13f Gd/Fm 47 2843

HAYAAIN 7 b h £466
66 3 PONT 17f Soft 65 876
57 10 BEVE 16f Firm 68 1276
0   16 WARW 16f Gd/Sft 65 1711

HAYDN JAMES 6 ch g £0
51a 6 LING 10f Aw   1 vis
43 4 CHEP 12f Gd/Fm 51 2971

HAYLEYS AFFAIR 2 b f £0
75 5 LING 7f Soft   4267

HAYMAKER 4 b c £3589
64a 3 WOLV 8f Aw   39
71a 1 **SOUT** 7f Aw   73*
70a 3 SOUT 6f Aw   67 212

HAYSTACKS 4 b c £848
34 10 HAMI 8f Gd/Fm 56 1190 vis
54 4 HAMI 12f Gd/Fm 53 2783 vis
53 2 NEWC 12f Good 53 3036 vis
44 5 NEWC 14f Good 53 3249 vis

HAZIRAAN 3 b c £518
56 7 NOTT 8f Soft   1643
77 3 RIPO 8f Soft   2543
46 7 LEIC 8f Gd/Fm   3094
45 12 CATT 7f Good   62 3440
44a 7 WOLV 8f Aw   57 4021

HAZY HEIGHTS 3 b f £3182
75 6 NEWB 7f Soft   915
57 8 KEMP 8f Gd/Sft   1080
0   16 NEWB 10f Gd/Fm   1404
48 8 NOTT 8f Good   58 2013
42 8 SALI 8f Gd/Fm 52 2264
46 4 LING 7f Good   48 2592
42 3 BRIG 7f Gd/Fm 47 3242
51 1 **BRIG** 8f Firm 45 3561*

HEAD IN THE CLOUDS 2 b f £2310
81 5 SALI 7f Firm   3752
94 3 ASCO 7f Good   4114

HEAD SCRATCHER 2 ch g £388
60 3 MUSS 5f Gd/Fm   3589
57 10 AYR   6f Soft   3958

HEADLAND 2 b c £325
76 4 YARM 6f Heavy   4479

HEALEY 2 ch c £10964
83 1 RIPO 6f Gd/Fm   3184*
94 1 RIPO 6f Gd/Fm   3463*
81 4 DONC 7f Gd/Fm   3859
85 3 YORK 6f Heavy   4298

HEATHER VALLEY 4 ch f £216
6a 10 SOUT 6f Aw   44 2297
32a 5 WOLV 8f Aw   39 2601
41 5 WARW 7f Gd/Fm 44 2840
40 4 THIR 7f Gd/Fm 44 3129
0   11 BRIG 8f Firm   42 3527

HEATHERHILL LASS 5 b m £307
0   4 AYR   10f Heavy   4230

HEATHYARDS GUEST 2 ch c £1233
59 7 LEIC 7f Gd/Fm   2916
78 2 BEVE 7f Good   3949
65 4 PONT 10f Soft   4230
59 6 REDC 7f Gd/Sft   4500

HEATHYARDS JAKE 4 b c £7588
67a 2 WOLV 8f Aw   39
44a 6 WOLV 9f Aw   60 119
58a 2 WOLV 8f Aw   133
60a 2 WOLV 9f Aw   189
58a 1 **WOLV** 8f Aw   229*
58a 4 WOLV 9f Aw   63 270
47a 5 WOLV 9f Aw   57 306

31a 4 SOUT 8f Aw   366
27a 7 WOLV 9f Aw   433
32a 8 WOLV 9f Aw   553
42a 6 WOLV 9f Aw   51 637
42a 6 SOUT 8f Aw   684
41a 5 WOLV 8f Aw   750
25a 7 WOLV 9f Aw   922
29a 9 SOUT 8f Aw   45 2380
37 5 RIPO 8f Gd/Fm   2834
50a 4 SOUT 8f Aw   2950
37 9 THIR 8f Gd/Fm 45 3344
41 4 HAMI 8f Gd/Sft 45 3534
40 7 WARW 11f Good   3691
38 7 THIR 8f Gd/Fm   3775
52 1 **BRIG** 8f Gd/Sft 4122*
33a 5 WOLV 8f Aw   45 4437

HEATHYARDS LAD 3 b c £2634
60a 5 WOLV 7f Aw   77 294
62a 4 WOLV 9f Aw   73 392
51a 7 WOLV 8f Aw   49 495
65 6 HAYD 8f Gd/Sft 69 810
63 3 SOUT 7f Gd/Sft 62 857
63 2 BEVE 7f Heavy 62 976
48 5 NOTT 8f Gd/Sft 63 1085
47 6 NOTT 8f Soft   63 1646
59 5 HAYD 7f Gd/Sft 63 1793
54 5 LEIC 8f Gd/Fm 61 2506
41 9 BEVE 8f Firm   59 2735
44 11 NEWC 7f Good   56 3033
57 3 HAYD 7f Gd/Sft 56 3269
51 4 THIR 8f Gd/Fm 53 3345
57 5 LEIC 8f Gd/Sft   4032
24a 10 WOLV 8f Aw   64 4251
44 4 LEIC 8f Sft/Hvy   4311
38 10 NOTT 10f Heavy   4413

HEATHYARDS MATE 3 b c £8959
58a 2 SOUT 8f Aw   36
71a 1 **SOUT** 8f Aw   48*
74a 1 **SOUT** 8f Aw 65 128*
75a 4 WOLV 8f Aw   171
72a 3 SOUT 8f Aw   75 213
54a 8 SOUT 7f Aw   74 416
67a 4 WOLV 8f Aw   72 566
61a 2 SOUT 11f Aw   586
67a 1 **SOUT** 8f Aw   741*
0   17 DONC 8f Gd/Sft 69 1053
45 10 NOTT 8f Good   2013
47 6 LEIC 10f Gd/Fm   2510
25a 6 WOLV 9f Aw   2602
42 3 LEIC 8f Gd/Fm   3094

HEATHYARDS SIGNET 2 b g £0
36 5 CHES 5f Gd/Fm   2668
37 6 LEIC 5f Gd/Fm   3092
43 13 THIR 5f Gd/Fm   3346

HEATHYARDSBLESSING 3 b c £0
78 8 HAYD 6f Gd/Fm   2458

HEAVENLY MISS 6 b m £3531
46a 5 WOLV 5f Aw   51 40   bl
46a 4 SOUT 6f Aw   49 87   bl
45a 5 WOLV 5f Aw   49 116   bl
15a 9 SOUT 6f Aw   47 218   bl
47 4 NOTT 6f Gd/Sft 49 1082 bl
58 1 **HAMI** 5f Firm 49 1244* bl
41a 4 WOLV 6f Aw   45 1391 bl
30a 10 SOUT 5f Aw   45 1806 bl
40 14 DONC 6f Gd/Fm 57 1842 bl
38 11 NOTT 6f Gd/Fm 56 2193 bl
36 14 BATH 6f Gd/Fm 54 3821 bl
38 8 NOTT 6f Soft   54 3975 bl
0   12 LEIC 7f Gd/Sft 52 4027 bl

HEAVENLY WHISPER 2 b f £3233
84 11 NEWM 7f Good   4158
87 1 **YARM** 8f Heavy   4475*

HEFIN 3 ch c £310
48 11 KEMP 8f Soft   1532
0   12 YARM 8f Good   1771
49 7 LING 9f Firm   1912
48 4 FOLK 10f Gd/Fm 55 3585

HEIRESS OF MEATH 5 ch m £394
31a 3 LING 10f Aw   38 1265
0   12 BRIG 8f Soft   28 1511
13a 9 LING 7f Aw   1739
29 4 BRIG 8f Firm   33 2043
0   13 FOLK 10f Gd/Fm 33 2296
18 7 BATH 10f Firm 34 2789

HEJAZIAH 2 b f £32628
91 2 GOOD 6f Gd/Sft   1486
98 3 BEVE 5f Firm   1759
98 1 **ASCO** 6f Good   2172*
101 1 **SAN** 8f Gd/Fm   2486*

HELALI MANOR 2 b f £0
15 9 RIPO 6f Gd/Fm   3714
0   6 DONC 7f Gd/Fm   3859
29 11 CATT 5f Soft   4252

HELEN ALBADOU 3 b f £2352
71 1 **NOTT** 5f Heavy   1021*
0   8 WIND 5f Gd/Fm   1881

HELENS DAY 4 ch f £13807
82 2 YORK 10f Gd/Fm   1985
82 1 HAYD 11f Gd/Fm   2703
85 1 **NEWC** 12f Good   3034*
81 11 YORK 12f Firm   3595
84 1 **AYR** 13f Gd/Sft 78 4014*
84 4 NEWM 12f Good   85 4342
0   P NEWM 16f Gd/Sft 91 4533

HELLO HOLLY 3 b f £351
52 6 PONT 8f Firm   58 2180
44 11 LEIC 7f Gd/Fm 52 2918
45 3 PONT 8f Gd/Fm 49 3226
35 9 CARL 8f Firm   49 3574
29 14 CHEP 7f Good   47 3871

HELLO SAILOR 3 ch f £0
12 8 AYR   7f Good   2140
14 5 NEWC 6f Gd/Fm   2313

HELLO VEGAS 3 b c £0
63 13 NEWB 8f Good   1376
65 4 HAYD 8f Gd/Sft   1837
0   P RIPO 10f Gd/Fm   2111

HELLOFABUNDLE 2 b g £596
0   15 NEWB 7f Firm   2708
54 3 SALI 6f Gd/Fm   2979
49 9 EPSO 5f Gd/Fm   3412

HELVETIUS 4 b c £1095
81 5 LEIC 12f Firm   2028
68 4 NEWB 10f Firm   2709
69 6 SAND 14f Good   88 3231

HEMINGWAY 2 b c £28272
106 1 **GALW** 7f Good   3072*
113 1 **YORK** 7f Good   3537*

HENRIETTA HOLMES 4 gr f £0
53a 4 LING 10f Aw   1
41a 6 LING 12f Aw   60 52
50a 5 LING 13f Aw   55 168   e
0   9 SALI 14f Gd/Fm 60 2268

HENRY HALL 4 b c £26482
83 6 DONC 5f Gd/Fm 92 702
75 14 THIR 5f Soft   90 926
81 6 CHES 5f Firm   87 1245
84 9 YORK 5f Firm   87 1324
78 13 HAYD 5f Gd/Sft 86 1533 VIS
87 3 RIPO 5f Good   85 1861
94 1 **YORK** 5f Gd/Fm 85 1980*
97 1 **NEWC** 5f Gd/Fm 90 2310*
84 9 DONC 5f Gd/Fm 90 2348
80 16 ASCO 5f Gd/Fm 95 3016

83	11	EPSO	5f Good	94	3687		
0	22	DONC	6f Gd/Fm	94	3861		

HENRY HEALD 5 b g £0

0	16	SALI	8f Gd/Sft	70	2467	
21a	9	LING	7f Aw		2759	
24	10	EPSO	9f Gd/Fm		3404	BL
0	15	CHEP	10f Gd/Fm	43	3683	bl

HENRY ISLAND 7 ch h £0

14a	10	LING	12f Aw		101	
47	10	NEWB	16f Gd/Fm	80	4458	

HENRY PEARSON 2 ch c £0

56	8	HAYD	6f Gd/Sft	3268
75	5	HAYD	6f Gd/Fm	3478
59	10	PONT	6f Good	4083

HENRY THE HAWK 9 b g £915

37	4	NEWC	6f Soft		756	
26	12	HAMI	5f Firm	43	1244	bl
36	10	CARL	5f Gd/Sft	41	1724	bl
42	5	NEWC	5f Heavy		1766	bl
0	12	BATH	6f Firm	41	1994	vis
49	2	HAMI	6f Gd/Fm		2798	
38	11	THIR	6f Gd/Fm	45	3144	

HENRY TUN 2 b c £0

70	6	MUSS	5f Gd/Fm	1429
46	8	DONC	6f Gd/Fm	1844

HER OWN WAY 3 b f £924

85	3	NEWM	8f Firm	1188

HERACLES 4 b g £6641

72	6	HAMI	11f Gd/Fm		1193	
69	3	CATT	12f Good		1661	
84	4	HAYD	11f Gd/Fm		2703	
78	1	CATT	14f Gd/Fm		2930*	
17	11	CHES	12f Firm	75	3173	
61	9	HAMI	11f Gd/Sft	75	3379	
104	6	HAYD	14f Soft		4091	
71	2	MUSS	10f Gd/Sft	70	4134	
67	4	AYR	13f Heavy	70	4325	

HERBSHAN DANCER 6 b g £1320

62	5	LING	10f Soft		1287
52	6	SAND	10f Soft		1588
0	29	NEWM	12f Firm	35	1852
47	2	SALI	14f Gd/Fm	46	2268
45	5	SALI	14f Gd/Fm	48	2982
0	P	ASCO	16f Gd/Fm	91	3302

HERCULANO 3 b c £15369

106	3	LONG	12f Good	1380
112	2	MAIS	13f Soft	2737

HERETIC 2 b c £4589

79	6	LING	7f Soft	4268
93	1	NEWM	6f Gd/Sft	4530*

HERITAGE 6 b g £845

66	6	YORK	14f Gd/Fm	83	1982	
64	13	ASCO	10f Good	75	2170	
65	6	DONC	12f Gd/Fm	70	2755	
67	2	AYR	13f Firm		2876	VIS

HERITAGE PARK 3 gr c £0

74	5	SALI	6f Firm	81	1178
62	9	KEMP	6f Gd/Fm	79	1925

HERMITS HIDEAWAY 3 b g £1129

41	5	CATT	6f Gd/Fm	2421
51	3	HAMI	6f Gd/Fm	2640
57	3	THIR	7f Gd/Fm	2965

HERNANDITA 2 b f £992

69	8	NEWB	7f Firm	3999
82	2	LEIC	7f Sft/Hvy	4309

HEROS FATAL 6 ch h £82600

87	3	ASCO	20f Good	82	2092
69	13	NEWC	16f Firm	82	2336
92	1	NEWM	18f Good	83	4353*

HERR TRIGGER 9 gr g £0

63a	5	LING	10f Aw	69	22	ebl
33	8	NEWM	10f Gd/Fm	52	1150	bl
41	7	YARM	10f Gd/Fm	48	2199	bl
21a	9	LING	10f Aw		2587	ebl

HERRING GREEN 3 b g £0

0	13	WIND	10f Gd/Fm	2056
0	11	SAND	10f Good	2531
52	7	CHEP	7f Gd/Fm	3256
0	17	WARW	8f Gd/Fm	3914
26	9	WIND	6f Heavy	4526

HERSELF 3 b f £331

62	8	SAND	10f Heavy		1045
53	7	LING	10f Soft		1287
46	6	CATT	12f Good		1661
26	8	YARM	14f Gd/Fm	48	1949
46	3	CARL	17f Gd/Fm	48	2244
56	5	CHEP	18f Gd/Fm	60	2490
35	6	CATT	16f Good	47	3442
0	12	PONT	17f Soft	51	4231

HESIODE 3 gr c £18252

110	3	CHAN	11f V		1231	
105	10	CHAN	12f V		1752	
107	3	DEAU	10f V		2736	BL
109	3	DEAU	10f Gd/Fm		3374	
105	9	LONG	12f Good		4262	bl

HETRA HAWK 4 ch g £0

7a	9	SOUT	8f Aw	42	496

HETRA HEIGHTS 5 b m £7484

28a	6	WOLV	16f Aw	37	482
45a	1	WOLV	16f Aw	37	576*
50a	1	SOUT	16f Aw	44	644*
0	10	PONT	22f Heavy	38	940
51a	3	SOUT	16f Aw	50	1416
27	9	PONT	16f Aw	35	1867
31	5	FOLK	16f Good	30	2622
31	1	FOLK	15f Gd/Fm	28	3040*

HETRA REEF 2 b c £0

48	11	WARW	7f Gd/Fm	2459
0	15	WARW	15f Gd/Fm	3911
0	18	NEWM	7f Gd/Fm	4336

HEVER GOLF GLORY 6 b g £1580

50a	10	SOUT	7f Aw	71	35	
42a	8	WOLV	9f Aw	69	119	
53a	7	LING	8f Aw	65	210	
50a	7	WOLV	8f Aw	62	255	
54a	4	WOLV	9f Aw	59	383	
40a	5	WOLV	9f Aw	59	405	
36a	9	WOLV	8f Aw		477	BL
50a	3	LING	10f Aw	53	842	
32	9	CARL	9f Firm	41	1254	
31	3	LEIC	10f Gd/Sft	37	1575	
28	8	YARM	10f Good	37	1775	
22	12	BEVE	10f Firm	38	1921	
31	5	LEIC	8f Firm	33	2027	
30	6	REDC	8f Gd/Fm	32	2861	VIS
21	9	BEVE	10f Gd/Sft	35	3052	vis
14	9	BEVE	8f Gd/Fm	37	3407	vis
28	9	NOTT	10f Good	38	3524	
29	3	HAMI	9f Gd/Sft		3823	
52a	3	LING	8f Aw	52	4335	
38a	5	WOLV	8f Aw	52	4440	

HI BUDDY 3 br c £0

48a	8	SOUT	8f Aw	63	125	bl

HI FALUTIN 4 b f £0

40	10	DONC	7f Soft	4465

HI MUJTAHID 6 ch g £675

18a	11	WOLV	6f Aw		1139
9	10	BRIG	7f Firm	30	1335
23	8	SOUT	7f Soft		1601
39	2	BRIG	7f Firm		2907
0	9	THIR	8f Gd/Fm	30	2970
31	8	CHEP	8f Good		3868
27	8	BRIG	8f Gd/Sft		4122
49a	4	LING	7f Aw		4331

HI NICKY 4 ch f £304

0	21	REDC	5f Gd/Sft	70	1133
0	18	PONT	10f Good	66	1496
0	13	CATT	7f Soft	60	1680
45	7	THIR	8f Gd/Fm	54	2062
0	23	REDC	8f Gd/Fm	50	2861
46	7	REDC	7f Gd/Fm		2994
65	4	CARL	10f Gd/Fm		3081
54	8	MUSS	8f Gd/Sft		4135

HIBAAT 4 ch c £0

19a	9	SOUT	6f Aw	64	180
0a	16	SOUT	8f Aw	58	251
29a	9	SOUT	12f Aw		301
11a	9	SOUT	16f Aw		327
34a	4	SOUT	7f Aw		511
0a	15	SOUT	8f Aw		600
20a	4	SOUT	12f Aw	40	683
0	24	DONC	12f Gd/Fm	50	699
0a	15	SOUT	16f Aw	33	737
0	P	PONT	22f Heavy	43	940

HIBERNATE 6 ch g £7302

41a	7	LING	12f Aw	77	422	
46a	8	LING	12f Aw	75	508	VIS
62	11	DONC	12f Gd/Fm	80	699	
47	9	HAYD	12f Gd/Sft	78	809	
44	14	HAMI	13f Good	75	845	
12	12	HAYD	12f Heavy	70	991	
69	4	DONC	10f Gd/Sft	70	1050	
74	2	EPSO	9f Gd/Sft	69	1829	
61	7	SAND	10f Good	69	1965	
5		CARL	12f Firm	73	2279	
57	13	HAYD	12f Gd/Fm	76	2502	
51	12	GOOD	9f Good	71	3110	
46	8	EPSO	12f Gd/Fm	75	3402	
39	8	EPSO	12f Good	65	3686	vis
37	10	YORK	10f Soft		4275	

HICKLETON DANCER 3 b g £0

38	6	CATT	7f Soft	4005
0a	9	SOUT	6f Aw	4368

HICKLETON DREAM 3 b f £0

36	11	PONT	8f Firm	3506
32	5	BEVE	10f Good	3677
19	6	PONT	8f Soft	4234

HIDALGUIA 3 b f £45149

109	2	LONG	9f Heavy	1114
109	3	LONG	10f Gd/Sft	1457
110	1	DEAU	10f Good	3211*
112	4	LONG	10f Good	4263

HIDDEN BRAVE 3 b c £4793

78	1	HAMI	11f Gd/Fm		848*
88	6	NEWM	12f Gd/Fm		1695
88	2	SALI	14f Firm	88	2021

HIDDEN ENEMY 4 b c £0

29a	6	SOUT	7f Aw		73
32	8	WARW	11f Heavy	65	1003
0	17	DONC	10f Gd/Sft	65	1050

HIDDEN FORT 3 ch c £0

0	12	NOTT	6f Heavy	80	4411

HIDDEN LAKE 2 b c £0

66	5	DONC	6f Gd/Fm	1844
0	15	WIND	6f Gd/Fm	2209
46	6	BRIG	6f Heavy	4537

HIDDEN MEANING 2 ch f £645

78	3	GOOD	6f Good	3661
77	8	NEWB	7f Firm	3985

HIDDNAH 3 ch f £10429

98	2	ASCO	10f Gd/Fm	3017
100	3	YORK	12f Firm	3595
102	6	DONC	15f Gd/Fm	3863
97	3	NEWM	12f Good	4194
92	6	LONG	12f Soft	4321

HIGH BARN 3 b f £941

59	9	KEMP	12f Soft		4040
73	4	SAND	10f Soft		4205
71	3	BATH	12f Soft		4434

HIGH BEAUTY 3 br f £327

0a	11	SOUT	12f Aw		643
39	4	NOTT	8f Good		783
18	8	BEVE	12f Heavy	47	978
29	4	NOTT	10f Soft	42	1644
30	8	NOTT	10f Good	45	2011
18	9	PONT	12f Good	38	2362
40	5	LEIC	10f Gd/Fm		2510
12	9	YARM	10f Firm		2765
30	11	WIND	10f Gd/Fm	38	2887
50	7	NEWM	10f Good		3021
20	9	BEVE	12f Gd/Sft	35	3050 BL
35	6	YARM	11f Firm		3917
25	5	NOTT	14f Heavy	33	4409
27	3	YARM	14f Soft		4510

HIGH CAPACITY 3 b f £0

39	10	RIPO	10f Soft	47	827
28	6	BEVE	12f Heavy	44	978
0a	12	WOLV	12f Aw	40	1142 bl

HIGH CARRY 5 b m £711

50	3	HAMI	5f Firm	53	1244
49	4	NEWC	5f Gd/Sft	52	1479

HIGH DRAMA 3 b c £0

74	8	WIND	10f Gd/Fm		1200
69	12	NEWB	10f Gd/Fm		1404
0	14	NEWM	10f Gd/Fm		1697
45	8	WIND	10f Good		2372
0	16	WARW	11f Good	65	2463 BL

HIGH ESTEEM 4 b c £2261

59a	1	SOUT	6f Aw	53	1421*
45	9	CATT	6f Gd/Sft	54	1815
37a	9	SOUT	6f Aw	50	1976
40	14	HAYD	5f Gd/Fm	53	2701
51	5	HAYD	6f Gd/Fm		3283
0	21	AYR	6f Heavy	48	4327
25	6	NEWC	6f Heavy	44	4425

HIGH PASTURE 2 b f £0

60	6	BATH	6f Soft		4137
44	13	NEWB	6f Sft/Hvy		4471

HIGH POLICY 4 ch g £3738

70a	1	WOLV	12f Aw		519*
0	15	YORK	14f Firm	83	1329
30	6	LEIC	12f Gd/Fm		3336
0a	12	LING	12f Aw		4101
59a	2	WOLV	12f Aw	56	4245 VIS
60a	3	SOUT	14f Aw	57	4371

HIGH RISE 5 b h £481733

120	3	TOKY	12f Firm		123
116	3	NAD	12f Good		767

HIGH SHOT 10 b g £3591

58a	2	LING	10f Aw		110
58a	2	LING	10f Aw	56	209
55a	3	LING	10f Aw		268
55a	3	LING	10f Aw		375
49a	1	LING	8f Aw		505* t
36a	4	LING	8f Aw		574 t
0	15	WARW	11f Gd/Fm	56	3915
23	8	BEVE	10f Stt/Hv	56	4046

HIGH SOCIETY LADY 2 ch f £0

36a	10	SOUT	5f Aw		2120
0	14	CARL	5f Firm		2277
17a	10	SOUT	6f Aw		2635
53	7	REDC	7f Gd/Fm		2862
15	10	RIPO	6f Gd/Fm		3009
39	8	THIR	7f Gd/Fm		3347
50	7	BEVE	8f Gd/Fm		3675
37	10	BEVE	7f Good	52	3950
48	12	YORK	8f Soft		4281 BL

HIGH SPOT 2 b f £0

78	10	DONC	8f Gd/Sft		4445
78	5	DONC	7f Heavy		4566

HIGH SUN 4 b c £0

44	4	PONT	8f Heavy		942
32	7	NEWC	8f Heavy	60	1007
0	21	REDC	8f Firm	58	1300
38	9	PONT	8f Good		1498
45	7	BEVE	7f Gd/Sft	54	1760
42	8	BEVE	7f Firm	54	1920
44	5	RIPO	8f Soft	50	2542
0	14	NEWM	8f Gd/Fm	50	2802 bl
33	7	NEWM	10f Gd/Fm	47	3314
56	5	RIPO	8f Gd/Fm		3711
42	5	LEIC	10f Firm	44	3842
0	16	YORK	10f Soft		4275

HIGH TEMPO 2 b c £0

22	10	BRIG	8f Gd/Sft		4116 t
0	25	NEWM	7f Good		4336
0	16	YARM	8f Good		4512

HIGH TOPPER 3 b c £21993

74	2	MUSS	9f Gd/Sft		902
75	5	HAYD	11f Gd/Sft		1539
75	2	BEVE	12f Firm	74	1919
75	4	RIPO	12f Gd/Fm	74	2110
70	4	CATT	12f Gd/Fm	74	2422
78	1	CHES	16f Gd/Fm	73	2672*
82	1	CHEP	16f Gd/Fm	78	2973*
79	6	GOOD	14f Firm	81	3153
74	4	KEMP	16f Gd/Fm	80	3360
64	5	NEWC	14f Soft	79	3709 BL
70	6	AYR	17f Soft	77	3993

HIGH TOWER 3 b c £712

82	4	BATH	10f Gd/Sft		2553
67	4	BATH	12f Gd/Fm		3517
42	9	BATH	12f Soft		4434

HIGH WALDEN 3 b f £18700

108	5	NEWM	8f Firm		1185
111	3	YORK	10f Gd/Fm		1309
111	2	EPSO	9f Gd/Sft		1825
0	W	ASCO	10f Good		2169
111	4	GOOD	10f Firm		3151

HIGH YIELD 3 ch c £78405

113t	3	GULF	9f Fast		19

HIGHCAL 3 gr c £5240

0	18	BEVE	10f Firm		1274
0	13	BEVE	12f Gd/Sft	50	1758
26	8	PONT	12f Good	42	2362
43	7	PONT	10f Gd/Fm		2833
43	1	RIPO	10f Gd/Fm	36	3008*
47	1	BRIG	10f Firm	40	3530*
0	11	BEVE	10f Sft/Hv	48	4046

HIGHFIELD FIZZ 8 b m £7606

0	13	NEWC	16f Soft	45	760
0	13	SOUT	16f Gd/Sft	43	860
0	P	PONT	22f Heavy	43	940
36	9	BEVE	16f Firm	42	1276
0	13	NEWC	17f Gd/Sft	46	1478
42	1	REDC	14f Gd/Sft	37	1563*
41	6	PONT	11f Good	42	1867
23	7	MUSS	16f Gd/Fm	41	2203
38	6	BEVE	16f Gd/Fm	40	2516
33	3	NEWC	14f Soft	37	3249
35	4	REDC	16f Firm	37	3331
38	1	AYR	15f Good	37	3367*
38	3	MUSS	14f Gd/Fm	42	3590
21	10	CATT	16f Soft	40	4066
37	7	MUSS	16f Gd/Sft	51	4134
25	7	REDC	14f Gd/Sft	35	4222

HIGHFIELDER 4 br c £506

2a	10	LING	7f Aw		8 vis

32a	4	LING	12f Aw	46	52
0a	12	SOUT	8f Aw	42	83 vis
56a	3	LING	12f Aw		101
30a	9	LING	13f Aw	53	168
40a	6	LING	10f Aw	47	224 BL
27a	5	SOUT	12f Aw	44	412
11a	5	WOLV	9f Aw		446 vis
45a	4	LING	8f Aw		544 bl

HIGHLAND FLIGHT 2 gr f £237

0	18	LING	6f Good		2588
59	4	RIPO	5f Gd/Fm		3710
57	7	SAND	5f Gd/Fm		3942
0	29	NEWM	6f Good		4345

HIGHLAND GOLD 3 ch c £2641

71	3	YORK	8f Firm		2006
59	5	HAMI	8f Gd/Fm	70	2235
44	7	HAYD	11f Gd/Sft	66	3267
54	8	AYR	8f Good		3365
49	8	HAMI	8f Gd/Sft	65	3380
54	4	HAMI	9f Soft	60	3806
16	9	AYR	11f Heavy		4304
55	2	AYR	10f Heavy		4326

HIGHLAND REEL 3 ch c £10222

88	3	SAND	8f Heavy		1041
84	7	NEWB	8f Good		1377
87	3	SAND	8f Soft		1584
85	3	BATH	10f Gd/Sft		2553
86	1	WIND	8f Gd/Fm		3048*
79	7	GOOD	10f Gd/Fm	87	3131
93	2	NEWB	9f Sft/Hvy	90	4472

HIGHLY FANCIED 4 b f £0

0	21	THIR	6f Soft	48	910
0	15	CARL	6f Firm	44	1258
16	9	AYR	5f Gd/Fm	40	1629

HIGHLY PLEASED 5 b g £0

42	11	WIND	6f Good	60	854
49	10	GOOD	8f Good	58	3885

HIGHLY PRIZED 6 b g £5125

57a	5	LING	16f Aw	69	6
59a	4	LING	16f Aw		101
62a	3	LING	13f Aw	58	168
63a	1	WOLV	15f Aw	57	277*
56a	6	WOLV	16f Aw	63	318
45a	7	LING	16f Aw	62	424
52	11	SALI	14f Gd/Fm	69	2982
54	9	SALI	14f Gd/Fm	64	3424
60	1	CHEP	12f Gd/Fm		3681*
36	13	SAND	14f Gd/Fm	57	3948
40a	7	LING	12f Aw	53	4334

HIGHLY SOCIABLE 3 b f £0

34	11	CATT	7f Soft	57	4004
0	18	DONC	7f Gd/Sft	52	4452

HIGHTORI 3 b c £21134

113	1	LONG	10f Gd/Sft		4053*
121	5	LONG	12f Good		4262

HILL COUNTRY 2 b c £22298

68	10	ASCO	7f Gd/Fm		2956
97	1	KEMP	8f Gd/Fm		3799*
107	3	ASCO	8f Gd/Sft		4127
107	2	ASCO	8f Heavy		4296

HILL FARM BLUES 7 b m £3185

70	4	HAYD	12f Gd/Sft	78	809
53	5	HAYD	14f Heavy	76	991
54	13	NEWM	12f Firm	74	1187
58	8	HAYD	16f Gd/Sft	69	1791
58	8	BATH	17f Firm	65	1996
62	2	NEWM	15f Good	60	3025
58	4	NEWM	11f Good	61	3295

HILL FARM DANCER 9 ch m £8278

0a	R	SOUT	12f Aw	30	68
31a	4	WOLV	15f Aw		117
0a	13	SOUT	12f Aw	30	211

30a	3	WOLV	12f Aw		231	
27a	5	WOLV	12f Aw	30	261	
30a	5	WOLV	16f Aw	30	318	
29a	2	WOLV	12f Aw	29	408	
32a	3	WOLV	16f Aw	30	494	
34a	1	**WOLV**	12f Aw	30	520*	
42a	4	WOLV	12f Aw		581	
34a	3	WOLV	12f Aw		626	
34	5	MUSS	14f Gd/Sft	37	903	
47a	1	**WOLV**	12f Aw		1039*	
38	1	**HAMI**	12f Firm	33	1241*	
34a	4	WOLV	12f Aw		1389	
37	5	HAMI	13f Gd/Fm	38	1936	
39	2	MUSS	14f Firm	38	2050	

HILL MAGIC 5 br g £2390

67	10	WIND	6f Heavy		935	
77	11	NEWM	6f Gd/Fm	85	1173	
61	12	GOOD	6f Gd/Sft	82	1471	
72	9	HAYD	6f Gd/Fm	79	2444	
0	20	GOOD	6f Good	76	3646	
76	2	KEMP	7f Gd/Fm	73	3796	
68	7	NEWB	7f Firm	74	3981	

HILL STORM 4 b c £210

23a	3	WOLV	15f Aw		468	
0a	10	WOLV	12f Aw		710	t

HILL WELCOME 2 ch f £792

57	3	BATH	6f Firm	2939	
60	4	PONT	6f Soft	4082	
30a	11	WOLV	6f Aw	4225	

HILLSWICK 9 ch g £0

29	5	BATH	17f Soft	37	4139

HILLTOP WARNING 3 b c £5730

0	12	LING	6f Gd/Sft		837	
78	1	**NEWB**	7f Gd/Fm		1947*	
79	5	SAND	7f Gd/Fm	79	2922	
74	4	SAND	8f Good	79	3227	
63	8	LING	7f Firm	77	3758	BL
76	3	NEWM	7f Gd/Fm	74	4215	

HILTON HEAD 2 b f £2730

82	1	**CATT**	5f Soft	4253*	

HIMSELF 5 b h £6868

89	4	EPSO	10f Good	90	1845
94	3	ASCO	10f Gd/Fm	92	2995
91	4	YORK	10f Gd/Fm	91	3563

HINDAAM 3 b c £3176

72	5	NOTT	8f Soft	3977	
77	1	**LING**	8f Soft	4274*	
75	3	YARM	8f Heavy	76	4478

HINDI 4 b c £970

55	8	NOTT	10f Good	66	786	
65	2	FOLK	10f Soft	63	965	
0	13	DONC	10f Gd/Sft	65	1050	
50	8	NOTT	10f Gd/Sft	65	1364	BL

HINT OF MAGIC 3 b c £536

79	4	DONC	10f Good		713	
79	4	PONT	10f Soft		873	
0	19	NEWB	10f Good	78	1375	
0	17	KEMP	8f Gd/Fm	75	3793	
18	7	BEVE	8f Sft/Hvy	70	4045	t
0	19	NEWM	8f Gd/Sft	65	4536	t

HIRAETH 2 b f £2314

78	3	BATH	5f Firm	3621	
72	2	NOTT	6f Soft	3973	
78	3	NEWB	5f Stt/Hvy	4470	

HIRAPOUR 4 b g £2250

102	3	LEOP	14f Good		1620	
74	17	ASCO	12f Good	99	2069	BL

HISAR 7 br g £0

0	16	SALI	10f Gd/Fm	65	3390

HISTORIC 4 b c £1065

62	8	NEWB	16f Soft	82	917
78	3	HAYD	14f Gd/Fm	79	1167

65	10	KEMP	16f Soft	77	1527	BL
73	8	ASCO	20f Good	75	2092	bl

HIT THE TRAIL 2 b f £242

72	4	PONT	5f Heavy	938	

HO LENG 5 ch g £18233

105	3	NEWM	6f Firm	103	1182
89	11	YORK	8f Firm	104	1327
105	3	NEWB	6f Firm	104	2706
83	19	GOOD	6f Firm	104	3152
108	2	NEWM	7f Gd/Fm	105	3315
107	3	YORK	7f Firm		3600
109	3	NEWM	6f Good		3610
106	4	DONC	6f Gd/Fm	107	3861
104	5	NEWB	7f Firm		3995
94	10	NEWM	8f Good		4180

HO PANG YAU 2 b c £1055

39	7	AYR	6f Gd/Fm	2717	
69	5	AYR	7f Firm	2873	
67	2	MUSS	8f Gd/Fm	3740	
62	6	AYR	8f Gd/Fm	4008	

HOBART JUNCTION 5 ch g £0

53	9	KEMP	12f Gd/Fm	65	3073

HOBB ALWAHTAN 3 ch c £0

79	5	NEWB	8f Good	1376	

HOBO 2 b g £234

35	13	DONC	5f Gd/Fm	700	
57	7	AYR	7f Good	3363	
52	9	YORK	8f Good	3729	
67	4	BEVE	7f Good	3952	

HOH GEM 4 b c £4847

0	13	WARW	11f Heavy	40	890
48a	1	**SOUT**	8f Aw	40	1207*
44a	4	WOLV	8f Aw	40	1393
49	1	**WARW**	8f Heavy	44	1520*
44	11	NEWM	8f Gd/Fm	49	1690
54a	2	SOUT	8f Aw	49	2302
16	12	WIND	8f Soft	49	2546
43	4	NOTT	10f Gd/Fm	47	3111
33	6	CHES	12f Gd/Fm	47	3430
29	10	SALI	10f Gd/Stt	44	4168
25	7	LEIC	8f Sft/Hvy		4311

HOH HOH SEVEN 4 b g £732

0	12	KEMP	7f Soft		1012
55	3	SALI	7f Good	57	1348
54	5	LEIC	8f Soft	57	1547
46	7	CHEP	7f Good	56	1969
0	17	LING	7f Good	54	4102
0a	13	LING	16f Aw	50	4329

HOLBECK 2 b f £0

34	6	CATT	6f Soft	1679	
30	5	HAMI	5f Gd/Fm	1937	
12	5	YARM	5f Gd/Fm	2196	

HOLDING COURT 3 b c £268001

108	1	**HAYD**	11f Heavy	97	990*
116	1	**LONG**	12f Good		1380*
123	1	**CHAN**	12f V		1752*
112	6	CURR	12f Good		2409
111	5	BADE	12f V		3849
99	5	LONG	12f Soft		4394

HOLLY BLUE 4 ch f £0

65	19	ASCO	7f Gd/Sft	94	1110
31	30	ASCO	6f Gd/Fm	93	2090

HOLY ISLAND 3 b b f £608

72	3	BATH	10f Soft	4141	
46	7	NOTT	10f Heavy	4408	

HOMBRE 5 ch g £319

40	4	CARL	14f Firm	58	2016
39	6	HAMI	11f Gd/Fm	51	2638
19	9	CARL	14f Gd/Fm	43	3084

HOME COUNTIES 11 ch g £380

40	9	HAMI	13f Good	55	845	t
47	7	DONC	17f Gd/Sft	52	1052	t
42	7	HAYD	14f Gd/Fm	48	1167	
0	14	NEWC	17f Gd/Sft	46	1478	
35	6	BEVE	12f Gd/Fm	41	3674	t
43	4	AYR	17f Soft	46	3993	t

HOME FORCE 3 b c £1951

58	10	LING	7f Gd/Fm		839
54	10	WIND	12f Gd/Fm	67	1199
57	6	YARM	11f Good	64	1770
58	1	**WARW**	11f Gd/Fm		2253*

HOMELIFE 2 b c £1199

64	6	NEWM	5f Soft		984
70	4	NOTT	6f Good		1413
64	7	SAND	7f Gd/Fm		1988
62	6	NEWM	7f Gd/Fm		2599
62	6	LING	7f Soft	66	4191
70	2	WIND	10f Gd/Sft	66	4290
58	8	NEWM	8f Good	63	4350
73	4	NOTT	8f Heavy		4504

HOMER 3 b c £4750

107	2	LEOP	9f Soft		14

HOMESTEAD 6 ch g £2285

56a	1	**SOUT**	12f Aw	52	70*
56a	4	LING	12f Aw	56	290

HONEST BORDERER 5 b g £11680

69	6	ASCO	8f Gd/Sft	77	1113
82	1	**LING**	8f Gd/Fm	77	2185*
78	4	YARM	7f Firm	80	2768
81	3	RIPO	8f Good	80	3699
78	4	ASCO	8f Gd/Sft	80	4126
0	29	NEWM	8f Good	80	4340

HONEST OBSESSION 2 b c £0

0	13	DONC	7f Heavy		4566

HONEST VILLAIN 3 b c £0

0	13	BATH	13f Gd/Fm	60	3819

HONEST WARNING 3 b c £1723

78	4	LING	6f Gd/Fm		2183
71	2	THIR	7f Gd/Fm		2965
70	4	LING	6f Firm		3579
66	5	LING	7f Firm		3834
50	12	LING	8f Soft		4273

HONESTY FAIR 3 b f £37940

72	4	REDC	5f Gd/Sft	72	1133
79	1	**BEVE**	5f Firm		1280*
85	1	**THIR**	5f Good	72	1384*
79	8	REDC	5f Gd/Sft	85	1580
71	9	NOTT	5f Good	84	1871
60	16	ASCO	5f Good	84	2168
77	4	HAYD	5f Gd/Fm	82	2504
76	6	NOTT	5f Gd/Fm	81	2684
74	6	THIR	5f Gd/Fm	80	3349
87	1	**YORK**	5f Gd/Fm	80	3569*
94	1	**NEWM**	6f Good	84	4198*

HONEY HOUSE 4 gr f £0

23a	7	SOUT	7f Aw		73	
0a	9	WOLV	12f Aw		752	t
11a	7	SOUT	6f Aw		2819	
7a	11	SOUT	8f Aw		2946	

HONG KONG 3 b g £0

38	10	MUSS	8f Gd/Sft	47	800	tbl
31	16	REDC	8f Firm	47	1296	tbl
24	13	NEWC	8f Gd/Sft	47	1477	tbl
16	10	SOUT	7f Soft		1603	tbl

HONOURS LIST 2 b c £69897

96	1	**GOWR**	7f Gd/Sft		1896*
111	1	**CURR**	6f Good		2408*
113	2	LONG	7f Gd/Sft		4054
110	3	LONG	8f Soft		4320

HOPEFUL 3 b f £0

42	8	WIND	10f Gd/Fm		2056

HOPEFUL HENRY 4 ch g £0

0a	11	LING	6f Aw		95
45	6	SAND	5f Good		3229

0	13	LING	6f Firm	3579	
51	8	SAND	5f Gd/Fm	3947	
0	17	WIND	6f Gd/Sft	48	4293

HOPEFUL LIGHT 3 b c £39224

101	4	NEWB	6f Good	1371	
66	8	EPSO	7f Gd/Sft	1830	
101	1	SALI	7f Gd/Fm	2228*	
110	1	SALI	8f Gd/Fm	3291*	
104	4	YORK	9f Gd/Fm	3726	
112	1	NEWM	8f Good	4180*	

HOPGROVE 2 b f £445

56	6	NEWC	5f Soft	755
35a	6	SOUT	5f Aw	1302
19	10	BEVE	5f Good	1443
55	3	THIR	5f Gd/Sft	1713
50	5	BEVE	5f Firm	1918
43	9	YORK	6f Gd/Fm	1981

HORMUZ 4 b c £3455

29	12	BRIG	8f Gd/Sft	82	895
0	16	BEVE	8f Firm	77	1279
35	9	RIPO	10f Good	72	1860
34	10	CHEP	10f Good	72	1973
37	8	WARW	8f Gd/Fm	62	2257
53	7	BEVE	10f Gd/Fm	57	2518
57	1	RIPO	8f Gd/Fm	2834*	
55	8	RIPO	9f Gd/Fm	61	3011
55	5	YARM	10f Gd/Fm	3383	
56	5	BATH	8f Firm	60	3623
59	2	THIR	8f Gd/Sft	3775	
42	6	CHEP	8f Good	3868	

HORNBEAM 6 b g £17055

68	15	DONC	8f Good	88	733	t
91	2	WIND	8f Heavy	935		
94	2	ASCO	7f Gd/Sft	90	1110	
86	4	LING	8f Gd/Fm	1262		
97	1	PONT	6f Soft	93	1702*	
47	27	ASCO	8f Good	100	2090	

HORNBY BOY 2 b g £0

0	15	DONC	6f Heavy	4576

HORTA 3 b c £0

10	14	LEIC	10f Gd/Fm	63	3217

HORTON DANCER 3 b g £645

42a	6	WOLV	12f Aw	752		
59	7	SOUT	10f Gd/Sft	858		
33a	9	WOLV	12f Aw	55	1142	VIS
48	4	BEVE	10f Firm	1274		vis
35	8	BEVE	12f Gd/Sft	49	1758	vis
27	10	WARW	12f Gd/Sft	49	2254	vis
52	3	CATT	14f Gd/Fm	2439		
0	17	BEVE	16f Good	46	2879	
50	3	BEVE	12f Good	3399		
29	5	REDC	14f Gd/Fm	43	3637	

HOSSRUM 2 br c £505

78	6	NEWM	6f Gd/Fm	2132
53	7	FOLK	7f Good	2620
77	3	BEVE	7f Gd/Sft	3051

HOT ICE 3 b f £0

36a	10	SOUT	5f Aw	53	870
0a	13	SOUT	7f Aw	48	1202
19	12	BRIG	5f Firm	52	1334

HOT LEGS 4 b f £384

13a	10	WOLV	6f Aw	63		
15a	9	WOLV	6f Aw	44	121	
31a	5	WOLV	6f Aw	39	352	
41a	4	WOLV	6f Aw	379		BL
38a	5	WOLV	6f Aw	434		bl
36a	5	SOUT	6f Aw	475		
20a	8	WOLV	7f Aw	567		bl
32a	3	WOLV	6f Aw	37	751	
32	10	PONT	6f Soft	872		bl
0a	12	WOLV	6f Aw	37	1391	bl
0a	16	SOUT	7f Aw	33	2122	bl

HOT PANTS 2 ch f £815

56	11	WIND	5f Gd/Fm	1197	
74	5	NEWB	5f Gd/Fm	1782	
73	3	YARM	5f Firm	2766	
66	9	WIND	5f Gd/Fm	3044	
68	6	GOOD	5f Good	73	3109
72	4	LING	5f Firm	3277	

HOT POTATO 4 b c £1105

30a	5	SOUT	7f Aw	73		
14a	9	SOUT	8f Aw	37	298	
31a	4	SOUT	12f Aw	37	338	
12a	6	WOLV	9f Aw	490		
7a	8	SOUT	11f Aw	30	560	
29	7	BEVE	8f Heavy	973		
38	5	HAMI	9f Gd/Fm	1195		
18	7	HAMI	11f Gd/Fm	27	1361	
38	2	PONT	10f Soft	1699		
0	16	RIPO	8f Good	1858		
18	6	HAMI	9f Gd/Sft	3823		
60	9	REDC	7f Gd/Sft	4218		vis
36	5	AYR	9f Heavy	4324		
61	9	DONC	7f Soft	4465		

HOT TIN ROOF 4 b f £60480

98	2	THIR	6f Soft	927
102	1	LING	7f Gd/Sft	1283*
108	1	NOTT	6f Good	1410+
107	2	LING	6f Good	1674
107	3	HAYD	7f Gd/Sft	1834
103	6	NEWM	7f Firm	2343
111	1	YORK	6f Gd/Fm	2646*
110	4	DEAU	7f Good	3212
92	8	PONT	6f Firm	3503

HOTELGENIE DOT COM 2 b f £66795

85	1	SAND	7f Good	2474*
95	2	SAND	7f Gd/Fm	2935
103	2	CURR	7f Gd/Sft	3845
104	3	ASCO	8f Good	4110

HOTELIERS PRIDE 3 b g £0

0	13	NEWB	8f Good	1377	
59	5	BATH	12f Firm	1997	
0	16	SALI	12f Good	60	2689
49a	5	WOLV	15f Gd/Fm	55	3276

HOTSPUR STREET 8 b g £0

0a	10	SOUT	12f Aw	38	412	bl

HOUNDS OF LOVE 3 b f £843

0	16	NEWM	7f Gd/Sft	971
38a	3	WOLV	8f Aw	1234
45a	3	SOUT	11f Aw	1415
23a	3	LING	12f Aw	1540

HOUSE OF DREAMS 8 b g £3495

21	10	NEWC	12f Good	3247	
48	1	REDC	14f Gd/Fm	3633*	
48	2	CATT	16f Soft	46	4006
48	3	REDC	14f Gd/Sft	48	4222

HOUSEPARTY 2 b c £582

65	3	YARM	7f Soft	4389

HOUT BAY 3 ch c £1096

42	6	CATT	6f Gd/Fm	781	
46	4	THIR	7f Soft	930	
36a	5	WOLV	5f Aw	1036	
66	3	THIR	6f Soft	1354	
63	8	DONC	5f Good	1516	
33	10	NEWC	6f Heavy	63	1768
22	5	MUSS	7f Gd/Fm	3744	
56	4	BEVE	7f Good	3956	
49a	7	WOLV	6f Aw	54	4442
43a	7	WOLV	6f Aw	52	4553

HOW DO I KNOW 2 gr f £3866

76	8	GOOD	6f Gd/Fm	3090
82	2	LING	5f Good	4095
80	2	WIND	5f Good	4288
82	1	REDC	5f Gd/Sft	4496*

HOW HIGH 5 b g £0

0	17	SALI	10f Gd/Sft	35	4169

HOWABOYS QUEST 3 b c £0

26	8	LEIC	12f Gd/Sft	832
41	8	CATT	7f Gd/Sft	1818
41	6	AYR	7f Good	2140

HOWARDS DREAM 2 b f £0

53	6	MUSS	8f Soft	4564

HOWARDS LAD 3 b c £3144

55	13	HAMI	6f Gd/Fm	78	1192	
59	9	THIR	5f Good	73	1384	
0	15	AYR	6f Gd/Fm	68	1654	BL
45	9	HAMI	6f Firm	62	2097	
54	5	CARL	6f Gd/Fm	62	2243	vis
58	1	HAMI	6f Firm	2396*		bl
44	12	HAMI	6f Gd/Fm	64	2641	bl
61	2	HAMI	6f Gd/Fm	60	2779	bl
39	9	RIPO	6f Good	60	3010	bl
39	10	CARL	6f Firm	60	3194	bl
41	8	MUSS	7f Gd/Fm	59	3593	vis
13a	8	WOLV	8f Aw	57	4363	
54	4	MUSS	9f Soft	57	4523	bl
0	16	MUSS	12f Soft	57	4560	

HOXTON SQUARE 3 ch f £644

33a	7	WOLV	6f Aw	549	
61a	2	WOLV	7f Aw	1035	
43a	11	WOLV		63	1138
0	12	LING	6f Good	68	3280
40	8	YARM	7f Gd/Fm	63	3666
0	13	NOTT	6f Soft	58	3975
0a	15	SOUT	7f Aw	53	4153

HTTP FLYER 3 b f £0

31	10	NEWM	8f Gd/Sft	2134		
49	7	NEWM	8f Gd/Fm	2345		
44	7	SAND	8f Gd/Fm	2920		
0	16	PONT	12f Soft	45	4229	
0	14	YARM	11f Soft	40	4391	BL

HUDOOD 5 ch h £2042

93	5	EPSO	12f Good	92	1850
84	10	ASCO	10f Good	91	2170
83	11	SAND	10f Good	91	2475
95	D	NEWM	10f Gd/Fm	89	2805
91	9	GOOD	10f Gd/Fm	94	3060
93	5	ASCO	10f Gd/Fm	94	3339
90	3	NEWM	10f Gd/Fm	92	3628

HUGS DANCER 3 b g £2642

75	3	ASCO	7f Gd/Fm	3343	
66	3	PONT	8f Firm	3506	
67	4	YORK	10f Good	3813	
0	12	PONT	10f Soft	4088	
67	3	WIND	8f Gd/Sft	4292	
59	7	NOTT	8f Heavy	66	4414
47	16	NEWM	8f Gd/Sft	66	4536

HUGWITY 8 ch g £18114

68a	6	LING	8f Aw	208	
66a	8	LING	10f Aw	85	244
80a	1	LING	10f Aw	333*	
83a	1	LING	10f Aw	375*	
85a	2	LING	12f Aw	82	422
94a	4	WOLV	9f Aw	480	
71a	4	LING	10f Aw	83	546
84a	3	LING	10f Aw	593	
68a	8	LING	10f Aw	83	632
85a	7	LING	10f Aw	690	
69	3	DONC	12f Gd/Fm	70	699
71	3	BRIG	8f Gd/Sft	70	895
58	6	NEWM	10f Gd/Fm	70	1150
70	2	BEVE	7f Firm	70	1259
75	1	NOTT	8f Good	1407*	
71	4	RIPO	8f Good	75	1598
42	12	BATH	8f Firm	75	1998
52	1	YARM	8f Gd/Fm	2411*	

52 5 SAND 8f Gd/Fm 2920
60 3 YARM 10f Good 3234
56 6 EPSO 9f Gd/Fm 3404
50 6 RIPO 8f Gd/Fm 3711

HULLBANK 10 b g £5701
57 1 **CATT** 14f Good 1660*
59 4 NOTT 16f Gd/Fm 2191
46 5 CATT 16f Gd/Fm 65 2436
50 1 **REDC** 14f Firm 3311*
55a 2 SOUT 14f Aw 51 4371

HUMES LAW 2 b c £3327
56 7 HAYD 5f Heavy 989
75 4 REDC 5f Gd/Fm 2142
30 6 PONT 6f Good 2363
76 1 **BEVE** 5f Firm 2730*
56 11 NEWM 6f Gd/Fm 79 3165
70 7 HAYD 5f Gd/Sft 75 3475
58 10 BEVE 6f Good 72 3673
68 18 NEWM 6f Good 4345

HUNAN SCHOLAR 5 b g £0
19a 11 LING 7f Aw 225
6a 9 SOUT 7f Aw 44 476
23a 11 WOLV 7f Aw 41 635
0 17 NOTT 6f Good 44 787
0 19 YARM 8f Good 39 1772 t
0 18 LEIC 8f Firm 33 2032 tbl
0 13 BRIG 7f Gd/Fm 3559
0 8 BRIG 8f Firm 3738
0 16 CHEP 8f Good 3868 bl

HUNT HILL 5 b g £0
0 15 PONT 17f Soft 58 876

HUNTERS TWEED 4 ch c £2719
36 11 HAYD 12f Gd/Sft 72 809
72 2 HAMI 13f Gd/Fm 69 1194
50 8 DONC 12f Good 72 1518
72 2 NEWC 12f Good 2523
45 7 NEWM 15f Gd/Fm 73 2856
63 6 RIPO 12f Gd/Fm 70 3181
61 6 HAMI 11f Gd/Sft 70 3379
58 6 DONC 12f Soft 66 4464
58 9 DONC 12f Heavy 68 4580 BL

HUNTING LION 3 b c £34050
95 8 NEWM 7f Gd/Sft 108 969
94 7 NEWB 6f Good 1371
107 1 **NEWM** 6f Gd/Fm 1041694*
109 3 ASCO 7f Good 2087

HUNTING TIGER 3 ch c £2170
63 7 LEIC 7f Good 88 792
62 14 NEWM 6f Gd/Sft 87 982
58 10 SALI 6f Firm 85 1178
62 12 NEWB 6f Gd/Fm 82 1406
56 8 GOOD 6f Gd/Fm 78 1961
0 16 WIND 6f Gd/Fm 73 2207
61 5 KEMP 5f Gd/Sft 68 2586
73 2 NEWB 5f Firm 68 2813
53 7 SAND 6f Gd/Fm 64 2934
39 10 NEWM 6f Good 64 2961

HUREYA 2 b f £348
71 5 KEMP 7f Gd/Sft 2583
79 4 KEMP 7f Soft 3074

HURGILL DANCER 6 b g £808
41a 3 LING 10f Aw 39 100
34a 4 LING 13f Aw 39 168
41a 3 LING 12f Aw 39 290
39a 4 WOLV 12f Aw 40 464
13a 7 WOLV 12f Aw 40 607
32 6 BRIG 12f Firm 38 1209
34 6 BRIG 10f Gd/Fm 36 2727 BL

HURLINGHAM STAR 2 b c £0
14 7 BRIG 5f Gd/Sft 891
0 12 FOLK 7f Gd/Fm 2290 VIS
16 6 FOLK 5f Gd/Fm 3038

14 6 EPSO 9f Good 3853
57a 7 WOLV 6f Aw 4379

HURRICANE FLOYD 2 b f £12856
90 2 YORK 7f Gd/Fm 2649
110 1 **NEWM** 6f Gd/Fm 3162*
104 4 YORK 6f Gd/Fm 3566
95 7 NEWB 6f Firm 3996

HURRICANE STORM 3 b g £0
13 8 NEWB 7f Gd/Fm 1947

HUTCHIES LADY 8 b m £4084
34 3 CARL 8f Gd/Fm 32 3574
38 1 **HAMI** 11f Soft 32 3805*
0 12 CATT 16f Soft 38 4258
34 10 YORK 12f Soft 43 4280
37 2 AYR 9f Heavy 4324
28 5 NEWC 10f Heavy 41 4427
33 4 MUSS 13f Soft 37 4521

HUTOON 3 b c £0
57 6 HAMI 12f Gd/Fm 1362
49 9 CHEP 10f Good 75 1973
42 9 DONC 8f Gd/Fm 70 2579
26 12 BRIG 8f Soft 4173

HWISPRIAN 2 b f £0
65 8 CHEP 8f Firm 3678
67 10 NEWB 7f Firm 3999

HYDE HALL 2 b f £0
0 21 DONC 8f Gd/Sft 4445

HYDE PARK 6 b g £2912
0a 15 SOUT 7f Aw 68 687
0 14 THIR 8f Soft 60 907
0 14 CATT 7f Soft 58 1680
0 16 THIR 7f Gd/Fm 54 2063
53 1 **CARL** 8f Firm 48 3192*
40 8 CATT 7f Good 48 3440
35 11 YARM 7f Firm 51 3939 t

HYDERABAD 2 ch c £0
0 15 DONC 7f Heavy 4566

HYMN 3 b c £39029
94 2 NEWM 8f Firm 1188
90 1 **SAND** 8f Soft 1584*
101 1 **ASCO** 8f Good 2171*
105 2 ARLI 10f Firm 2912

HYPERACTIVE 4 b c £1452
51 12 GOOD 7f Gd/Sft 70 1483
71 2 DONC 7f Gd/Fm 68 1840
67 7 NEWM 7f Gd/Fm 70 2133
58 8 SALI 8f Good 70 2690
56 10 YARM 7f Good 69 3238
58 14 LEIC 7f Firm 67 3839
62a 4 WOLV 6f Aw 65 4023 BL
31a 12 WOLV 6f Aw 64 4358

HYPERSONIC 3 b c £0
35 14 WARW 8f Heavy 884
0 20 NEWM 8f Firm 80 1183
0 13 KEMP 6f Gd/Fm 77 1925

HYPNOTIZE 3 b f £5720
96 6 NEWM 10f Firm 1184
87 7 EPSO 9f Gd/Fm 1825
105 2 NEWC 8f Gd/Fm 2274
96 7 ASCO 8f Good 2675
93 10 GOOD 7f Good 3104

I BITE 3 b c £0
0 12 NEWB 10f Sft/Hv 4474

I CANT REMEMBER 6 br g £1595
42a 6 SOUT 16f Aw 54 428
36a 5 SOUT 16f Aw 54 502
51a 2 WOLV 12f Aw 530
41a 4 SOUT 12f Aw 556
54 5 DONC 12f Gd/Fm 60 699
56 4 NOTT 14f Good 60 788
0 11 SOUT 16f Gd/Sft 57 860
51 5 THIR 12f Gd/Sft 1353

36 15 NEWM 12f Firm 54 1852
46 6 NOTT 14f Good 50 2008
43 7 RIPO 12f Gd/Fm 50 2109
40 3 BEVE 12f Firm 2219 t
47 4 HAYD 12f Gd/Fm 2457 t
26 9 RIPO 10f Soft 2538 t
8 11 NEWC 8f Heavy 43 4406
43 2 REDC 11f Soft 4497

I CRIED FOR YOU 5 b g £28791
74 1 **LING** 7f Gd/Sft 838*
66 3 NEWC 7f Heavy 73 1011
79 2 CHES 8f Firm 73 1250
81 1 **DONC** 7f Gd/Fm 75 1840*
82 2 NEWM 8f Good 79 2564
68 10 CHES 8f Firm 82 3170
81 7 AYR 7f Gd/Fm 82 4010
83 4 ASCO 7f Good 82 4112
88 1 **YORK** 7f Heavy 82 4302*
0 24 NEWM 8f Soft 87 4545

I GOT RHYTHM 2 gr f £0
0 12 MUSS 5f Gd/Fm 1146
38 10 REDC 5f Good 1294
51 4 NEWC 6f Gd/Sft 1476
0 16 PONT 6f Good 1864
37 9 LEIC 8f Firm 50 3837
41a 5 WOLV 8f Aw 46 4552

I PROMISE YOU 3 b c £7936
72 1 **LEIC** 7f Good 70 792*
66 10 NEWM 7f Good 73 954
53 17 NEWM 8f Firm 73 1183
67 10 EPSO 7f Gd/Sft 72 1826
72 3 REDC 7f Gd/Fm 70 2145
69 5 LING 7f Good 72 2325

I RECALL 9 b g £0
33 9 WARW 11f Heavy 42 890 tvi

I T CONSULTANT 2 b c £0
41 9 YORK 6f Good 3814

I TINA 4 b f £226
58 6 WIND 12f Good 69 853
22 11 BATH 12f Good 67 1091
59 4 LEIC 12f Gd/Fm 3219
0 13 SALI 14f Gd/Fm 62 3424
55 5 BRIG 10f Gd/Sft 58 4118
0 30 NEWM 18f Good 79 4353 VIS

IAMATMEWHITZEND 3 ch f £0
0 6 MUSS 8f Soft 4519

ICE 4 b c £13503
81 5 BEVE 8f Good 90 1445 vis
93 1 **LING** 9f Good 88 1744* vis
86 6 HAYD 8f Gd/Sft 94 1836 vis
95 1 **YORK** 9f Firm 90 2001+ vis
92 4 PONT 10f Firm 2178 vis
87 4 DONC 10f Gd/Fm 2351 vis
73 14 SAND 8f Gd/Fm 95 2528 vis
86 7 YORK 8f Gd/Fm 95 2648 vis
67 10 AYR 8f Gd/Sft 93 4013 vis

ICE AGE 6 gr g £0
21a 8 SOUT 6f Aw 53 218 bl
27a 9 SOUT 6f Aw 53 250 bl
49a 5 SOUT 6f Aw 279 bl
20a 9 SOUT 6f Aw 51 386 bl
45a 7 WOLV 5f Aw 51 445 bl
0a 11 SOUT 6f Aw 47 499 bl
38a 11 WOLV 5f Aw 533 bl

ICE CRYSTAL 3 b c £273
69 8 LEIC 10f Gd/Sft 833
78 7 KEMP 11f Soft 1017
84 4 SALI 12f Good 1179
58 8 SALI 14f Good 2691
64 9 NEWM 12f Gd/Fm 70 3167
63 6 CHEP 12f Good 3869
58 7 NEWM 12f Good 4178

45 8 NOTT 10f Heavy 4413

ICE MAIDEN 2 b f £6083
85 1 NEWM 5f Gd/Sft 970*
88 3 KEMP 7f Gd/Fm 3361
76 4 FOLK 5f Gd/Fm 3446
0 21 DONC 7f Gd/Fm 81 3860

ICE PACK 4 gr f £857
26a 6 SOUT 12f Aw 556
0a 10 SOUT 14f Aw 668
22 11 HAMI 12f Firm 39 1241
39 8 AYR 13f Gd/Fm 1657
33 3 REDC 16f Good 1894
30 4 CARL 17f Gd/Fm 32 2244
31 3 BEVE 16f Firm 30 2734
29 6 REDC 14f Gd/Fm 3633
8 10 PONT 17f Soft 38 4231
0a 10 SOUT 14f Aw 45 4370

ICE PRINCE 2 b c £0
0 13 HAYD 8f Soft 3766
70 11 WARW 7f Gd/Fm 3909
66a 6 WOLV 8f Aw 4022

ICEALION 2 b g £0
45 11 DONC 5f Gd/Sft 1048

ICHI BEAU 6 b g £4589
33a 4 WOLV 12f Aw 40 489
46a 1 WOLV 12f Aw 40 554*
53a 1 SOUT 12f Aw 47 641*
49a 3 SOUT 12f Aw 53 683
0a 8 WOLV 12f Aw 53 723

ICICLE 3 br f £7000
103 10 NEWM 8f Firm 1185
106 3 EPSO 9f Gd/Sft 1825
104 5 NEWM 7f Firm 2343
102 4 ASCO 6f Gd/Fm 105 3301
88 9 DONC 7f Gd/Fm 3878

ICICLE QUEEN 3 ch f £0
0a 9 SOUT 8f Aw 453

ICON 3 b f £0
69 11 NEWB 7f Soft 915
61 9 BATH 10f Good 1093
29 11 BEVE 5f Good 3956
20a 8 WOLV 9f Aw 55 4251 t
0a 18 LING 12f Aw 55 4334 t

IDLE POWER 2 b c £11878
81 2 LING 5f Gd/Sft 1260
61 5 SOUT 6f Soft 1602
89 1 KEMP 5f Gd/Fm 2082*
78 6 DONC 6f Gd/Fm 2318
83 6 YARM 6f Gd/Fm 3965
90 1 NEWM 6f Good 84 4338*
73 12 NEWB 6f Sft/Hvy 89 4468

IDOLIZE 3 ch f £6425
72 16 GOOD 9f Gd/Sft 89 1452
92 1 CHEP 10f Gd/Fm 1797*
56 8 NEWB 10f Gd/Fm 1945
0 7 LEOP 10f Good 3924
74 10 NEWM 10f Good 4337

IF BY CHANCE 2 ch c £913
55 11 WARW 5f Soft 812
68 4 KEMP 5f Soft 993
70a 2 WOLV 5f Good 1236
53 8 KEMP 5f Firm 71 2868
60 5 SAND 5f Good 66 3228
53 5 LING 5f Firm 62 3491

IFFAH 2 ch f £1140
81 6 GOOD 7f Good 3108
77 2 BEVE 5f Gd/Fm 3655

IFTIRAAS 3 b f £54714
111 1 NEWB 7f Soft 913*
109 5 LONG 8f V 1319
94 6 ASCO 8f Good 2150
99 9 NEWM 8f Gd/Fm 2597

109 3 DEAU 8f Gd/Sft 3069
113 1 CURR 8f Soft 3846*

IFTITAH 4 ch c £32843
108a 2 NAD 8f Dirt 764
103 4 WIND 8f Firm 1291
93 3 YARM 7f Firm 2389

IGMAN 3 b c £0
0 8 LONG 8f Soft 3847

IGNITE 3 b c £0
63 9 KEMP 10f Gd/Fm 73 2750
64 3 ASCO 12f Gd/Fm 68 3014
56 8 WIND 12f Good 66 3353
0 13 BATH 12f Soft 63 4433

IHTIMAAM 8 b g £0
0a 12 LING 10f Aw 268
0a 13 LING 12f AW 4186

IKBAL 2 ch c £0
60 8 NEWB 6f Sft/Hvy 4471

IL CAPITANO 3 ch c £0
91 7 CHES 12f Gd/Fm 1216
97 5 ASCO 16f Good 2068
81 10 GOOD 12f Gd/Fm 95 3088
88 7 YORK 14f Firm 89 3599 BL
71 5 AYR 15f Soft 86 3961

IL CAVALIERE 5 b g £1194
72 3 REDC 8f Gd/Fm 2159
58 7 DONC 8f Gd/Fm 2611
81 4 AYR 10f Gd/Fm 2722
65 7 YORK 14f Good 75 3811
69 3 MUSS 12f Gd/Sft 4133

IL DESTINO 5 b g £1071
56 6 BATH 10f Gd/Sft 62 1666
49 5 SALI 12f Gd/Fm 61 1888
47 8 WARW 12f Good 60 2466
37 8 NOTT 10f Gd/Fm 55 3111 BL
57 3 PONT 10f Gd/Fm 55 3220
30 13 GOOD 12f Good 55 3887
57 3 WIND 10f Gd/Sft 54 4291
52 4 BATH 10f Soft 56 4436

IL PRINCIPE 6 b g £756
67a 2 SOUT 14f Aw 65 89 e
46a 4 SOUT 14f Aw 124 e
0 16 NEWC 10f Soft 80 757
64 11 HAMI 13f Good 80 845
64 7 NEWB 16f Soft 80 917
0 15 NOTT 14f Good 75 1411
55 9 NEWB 13f Gd/Fm 70 1784
33 8 DONC 15f Gd/Fm 65 2319
35 10 NEWM 12f Gd/Fm 62 3122
21 8 SAND 14f Good 54 3472
38 4 REDC 14f Gd/Fm 3633
22 9 CATT 16f Soft 40 4006

ILE DISTINCT 6 b g £1492
61 2 THIR 12f Gd/Fm 60 2061
44 9 BEVE 10f Firm 60 2220
45 4 HAMI 11f Gd/Fm 60 2782
36a 8 SOUT 11f Aw 4150 bl

ILE MICHEL 3 b c £0
76 13 NEWM 8f Good 88 4348

ILEWIN JANINE 9 b m £0
0a 10 SOUT 12f Aw 498

ILISSUS 4 b c £0
29a 10 LING 10f Aw 238
17a 11 LING 10f Aw 314
0 17 EPSO 10f Heavy 75 1031
0 16 GOOD 8f Soft 65 4066
0 16 GOOD 8f Soft 4274 VIS

ILJASOOR 3 b c £0
77 6 BATH 10f Good 1093

ILLUSIONIST 2 b c £260
58 4 NOTT 6f Gd/Sft 1367
0 20 NEWM 6f Good 4341

68 8 NEWM 6f Gd/Sft 4530

ILLUSIVE 3 b c £17324
71a 2 LING 6f Aw 65 2 bl
73a 1 SOUT 5f Aw 65 72* bl
71a 4 WOLV 6f Aw 71 275 bl
79a 1 LING 8f Aw 71 444* bl
82a 1 LING 5f Aw 71 592* bl
83a 2 LING 5f Aw 81 652 bl
34 15 NEWM 6f Gd/Sft 71 982 bl
71 3 NEWB 6f Gd/Fm 70 1406 bl
67 5 WIND 5f Gd/Sft 70 1427 bl
64 5 KEMP 6f Gd/Fm 71 1925 bl
70 3 BATH 5f Firm 70 2787 bl
71 3 YARM 6f Firm 70 2900 bl
74 2 SAND 5f Gd/Fm 70 2934 bl
47 16 GOOD 5f Gd/Fm 71 3135 bl
0 23 KEMP 6f Aw 74 3791 bl
38 17 BATH 6f Gd/Fm 74 3821 bl

ILLUSTRIOUS DUKE 2 b c £0
0 16 WARW 7f Gd/Fm 3909
0 11 YORK 6f Soft 4283
0 16 NOTT 8f Heavy 4504

IM A CHARACTER 2 br f £0
59 7 KEMP 7f Firm 2259
30 8 FOLK 7f Good 2620
43a 5 SOUT 7f Aw 2949

IM LULU 2 b g £0
39 13 LING 6f Firm 3832
71 6 KEMP 7f Soft 4035
60 12 WIND 6f Gd/Sft 4288

IM SOPHIE 3 ch f £211
48a 4 SOUT 5f Aw 740
55 5 THIR 8f Soft 909
47a 10 WOLV 6f Aw 60 4442

IMAD 10 b g £4079
45a 3 SOUT 16f Aw 49 737 t
42 4 SOUT 16f Gd/Sft 46 860 t
50 1 PONT 22f Heavy 46 940* t
43 10 PONT 17f Good 51 1867 t

IMAGINE 2 b f £50250
94 3 CURR 7f Good 3555
95 6 CURR 7f Gd/Fm 3845
101 4 ASCO 8f Good 4110
108 1 CURR 7f Gd/Sft 4240*
109 2 NEWM 7f Good 4356

IMARI 3 b f £6503
26a 12 WOLV 7f Aw 192
53a 2 SOUT 8f Aw 303
31a 5 SOUT 8f Aw 385
0 11 BRIG 7f Firm 60 1335
60 1 YARM 8f Good 55 1772*
64 3 YARM 10f Gd/Fm 61 1955
65 2 WIND 10f Gd/Fm 63 2206
53 6 PONT 8f Gd/Fm 63 2561
62 3 BRIG 10f Gd/Fm 63 3263
63 1 YARM 10f Gd/Fm 63 3382*
30 13 SALI 10f Gd/Sft 63 4169

IMBACKAGAIN 5 b g £3852
18a 9 WOLV 8f Aw 136 t
5a 12 WOLV 7f Aw 41 193 t
24a 6 SOUT 8f Aw 36 297
39a 3 SOUT 8f Aw 366
24a 9 WOLV 9f Aw 433
28a 8 SOUT 8f Aw 452
0a 13 SOUT 11f Aw 33 561
47 2 BRIG 7f Firm 47 1336
0 14 DONC 7f Good 48 1519
48 2 BRIG 7f Gd/Fm 47 1930
38a 1 SOUT 7f Aw 30 2122*
43 4 NEWM 7f Firm 48 2347
43 6 BRIG 7f Soft 48 2427

IMMACULATE CHARLIE 2 ch f £1320

IMP (continued)

49	3	CHEP	6f Heavy		1553
47	2	WIND	6f Gd/Fm		2052
0	12	BATH	6f Gd/Sft		2550
49	4	SAND	8f Good		3433
0	7	EPSO	9f Good		3853

IMPALDI 5 b m £2302

27	8	MUSS	5f Gd/Fm	38	1143
0	14	HAMI	5f Gd/Fm	36	1910
22	5	HAMI	5f Firm		2095
26	10	NEWC	5f Gd/Fm	42	2275
31	7	NEWC	5f Firm	38	2340
6a	11	SOUT	5f Aw	32	2632
47	2	CATT	6f Gd/Fm		2744
36	3	NEWC	5f Good		3035
41	3	THIR	6f Gd/Fm	40	3144
36	7	RIPO	5f Gd/Fm	40	3180
53	3	THIR	6f Gd/Sft		3780

IMPEACHMENT 3 b c £52829

115ε3		CHUR	10f Dirt	1226

IMPERIAL BEAUTY 4 b f £10725

90	4	SAND	5f Soft	1566
112	4	ASCO	5f Good	2065

IMPERIAL DANCER 2 b c £32082

58	4	KEMP	5f Good		724
89	2	WIND	5f Heavy		932
84	1	WARW	5f Heavy		1001*
86	3	BATH	5f Firm		1995
83	10	ASCO	5f Good		2067
89	2	DONC	7f Gd/Fm		2576
90	4	NEWB	7f Firm		2848
95	5	ASCO	8f Gd/Fm		3304
104	1	YORK	7f Good	95	3542*
99	3	RIPO	6f Good		3700
103	2	CURR	8f Gd/Sft		4060
101	5	NEWM	7f Good		4196
96	8	NEWB	7f Gd/Sft		4455

IMPERIAL HONEY 5 b m £0

14a	10	SOUT	6f Aw	32

IMPERIAL MEASURE 2 b c £38881

77	1	WIND	5f Gd/Sft		1095*
70	5	SALI	6f Gd/Sft		2469
0	18	NEWB	5f Firm		2849
85	2	KEMP	6f Gd/Fm	79	3075
91	1	NOTT	6f Good	82	3519*
96	3	DONC	6f Good		3862
86	9	NEWB	7f Gd/Sft		4455

IMPERIAL ROCKET 3 b c £5549

89	4	NEWB	8f Soft	92	912
89	6	BATH	10f Good		1089
88	7	YORK	10f Gd/Fm	90	1310
50	11	EPSO	10f Gd/Sft	87	1831
85	2	KEMP	10f Gd/Fm	84	2750
87	2	ASCO	10f Gd/Fm	84	2955
77	8	ASCO	10f Gd/Fm	86	3339
44	13	NEWB	10f Sft/Hv	85	4473

IMPERIALIST 3 b f £2983

79	5	KEMP	6f Gd/Sft		1078	
49	9	NEWM	7f Gd/Fm		1693	
66	9	SAND	5f Gd/Fm		1987	
77	7	NEWM	6f Gd/Fm		2289	
83	2	CHES	5f Good	82	2663	BL
67	8	BATH	5f Firm	82	2787	bl
64	14	GOOD	5f Gd/Fm	83	3135	bl
69	10	BATH	6f Gd/Fm	80	3821	bl
66	4	CHES	6f Soft		4069	bl
64	9	LING	6f Soft	74	4270	bl

IMPERO 2 b c £0

57	5	WARW	7f Gd/Fm		2251
63	7	FOLK	7f Good		2619
0	11	LING	8f Gd/Fm		3577
0	13	BATH	8f Soft		4430

IMPISH LAD 2 b g £1974

67	11	DONC	5f Gd/Fm		700	
62	5	BEVE	5f Heavy		974	
64a	2	SOUT	6f Aw		1420	
62	3	REDC	7f Good		1890	BL
47	6	REDC	7f Gd/Fm		2155	
58a	3	SOUT	7f Aw		2301	bl
63	2	BEVE	5f Gd/Fm		2513	bl
62	3	CATT	6f Gd/Fm		2927	bl
41	9	THIR	7f Gd/Fm		3127	bl

IMPORTUNE 3 b c £0

0a	12	SOUT	8f Aw	86

IMPREVUE 6 ch m £5395

60a	1	LING	10f Aw		1*	bl
61a	4	LING	10f Aw	62	160	bl
59	6	EPSO	12f Good	63	2793	
57	3	BRIG	12f Firm	63	2893	bl
57	1	YARM	10f Gd/Fm		3383*	bl
0	12	BRIG	10f Gd/Sft	60	4118	bl

IMPREZA 2 b f £222

21	8	CATT	5f Soft		1679	
35	4	THIR	6f Gd/Sft		1713	VIS
25	7	REDC	7f Good		1890	vis
0	15	REDC	7f Gd/Fm		4216	vis
28	10	CATT	5f Soft		4253	vis
0a	11	WOLV	8f Aw		4362	

IMPULSIVE AIR 8 b g £1984

25a	5	WOLV	9f Aw	46	569
13	13	MUSS	9f Gd/Sft	46	795
34	7	HAMI	9f Gd/Fm		1195
44	2	HAMI	8f Gd/Fm	43	1360
41	7	RIPO	8f Good	50	1598
33	8	HAMI	9f Gd/Fm		2799
44	4	AYR	9f Gd/Fm	43	3141
45	3	AYR	10f Good	44	3368
32	7	HAMI	11f Gd/Sft	44	3379
34	7	NEWC	9f Firm	45	3603
34	13	YORK	9f Good		3808
42	7	AYR	9f Soft		3988
0	20	REDC	8f Gd/Sft	53	4217

IN A TWINKLING 3 b f £0

0	22	NEWB	7f Gd/Sft	68	1405
51	10	GOOD	10f Gd/Sft	65	1812
56	6	SALI	10f Gd/Fm	60	2270
0	18	BRIG	10f Gd/Sft	61	4118

IN GOOD FAITH 8 b g £0

0	13	PONT	10f Soft	4088

IN SEQUENCE 3 gr f £0

53	7	LEIC	5f Gd/Fm		2919
27	10	BRIG	7f Firm		3739
0	18	NOTT	6f Soft	54	3975

IN SPIRIT 2 b c £646

50	8	NOTT	6f Soft	3974
74a	2	WOLV	6f Aw	4548

IN THE ARENA 3 ch c £4665

72	4	DONC	6f Good		731
73	3	WARW	7f Soft	74	1061
71	4	PONT	8f Good	74	1495
52	8	DONC	8f Gd/Fm	72	2579
32	12	WARW	7f Good		3696
80	1	YARM	7f Soft		4387*

IN THE STOCKS 6 b m £3384

44	10	WIND	10f Gd/Sft	52	1100
44	9	WIND	12f Good	52	1730
44	6	WARW	12f Good	50	2466
48	2	WIND	12f Gd/Fm	46	2887
38	9	LING	10f Firm	47	3581
50	1	WARW	11f Gd/Fm	45	3915*
41	5	SALI	10f Gd/Sft	46	4168

IN THE WOODS 2 br f £15452

93	1	SALI	6f Gd/Fm		1882*
95	1	NEWM	6f Firm		2344*
80	8	ASCO	6f Gd/Fm		2996

IN TOUCH 2 ch f £0

0	14	LING	6f Soft	4189
38a	11	WOLV	6f Aw	4359
22	10	NEWM	6f Gd/Sft	4535

INAAQ 3 ch f £11642

90	1	NEWM	10f Gd/Fm		2617*
107	4	LONG	13f Good		4236
108	3	NEWM	12f Good		4343

INCA STAR 3 b c £9136

62	5	DONC	10f Good		713
73	6	NOTT	8f Gd/Sft		1084
79	1	HAMI	12f Gd/Fm		1362*
84	2	WIND	12f Gd/Sft	79	1425
86	1	RIPO	12f Good	82	1862*
0	P	ASCO	12f Good	85	2116

INCEPTA 5 b g £0

0	19	BRIG	10f Soft	54	4419

INCH PERFECT 5 b g £30255

63a	1	WOLV	12f Aw	57	43*
73	1	THIR	8f Soft	65	907*
71	3	NEWM	10f Gd/Fm	70	1150
82	1	YORK	12f Gd/Fm	73	1307*
80	3	REDC	10f Gd/Sft	79	1561
88	1	YORK	14f Gd/Sft	82	1982*
53	21	YORK	12f Good	87	2696
82	12	YORK	14f Gd/Fm	87	3565
76	8	YORK	14f Good	86	3811

INCH PINCHER 3 ch c £541

0a	14	SOUT	7f Aw	64	31	
62a	2	LING	7f Aw		53	
41a	5	LING	8f Aw		150	
35a	7	SOUT	7f Aw		281	
43a	5	LING	7f Gd/Fm		459	BL
53a	5	LING	6f Aw		527	bl

INCHALONG 5 b m £0

32a	9	SOUT	6f Aw	57	44	vis
34a	6	LING	6f Aw	57	97	vis
42	12	CATT	7f Gd/Fm	64	780	vis
49	10	HAYD	7f Gd/Fm	64	811	vis
41	11	NOTT	6f Soft	62	3975	vis

INCHCAPE 2 b c £517

94	3	DONC	6f Heavy	4575

INCHDURA 2 ch c £0

65	9	DONC	7f Heavy	4567

INCHING CLOSER 3 b c £8723

71	8	NEWM	8f Firm	78	1183
0	20	GOOD	9f Gd/Sft	79	1452
82	1	AYR	10f Gd/Fm		1655*
82	3	LEIC	10f Firm		2030
83	3	WIND	12f Good	79	2712
84	3	ASCO	12f Gd/Fm	81	3014

INCHINNAN 3 b f £6363

68	2	BRIG	8f Gd/Sft		894
69	1	EPSO	9f Heavy		1033*
70	3	PONT	10f Good	68	1496
66	2	NOTT	8f Gd/Fm		2682
66	6	GOOD	9f Good	70	3110

INCHIRI 2 b f £1065

87	5	ASCO	10f Good	4114
88	4	NEWM	8f Soft	4546

INCHLONAIG 3 ch c £0

100	11	EPSO	12f Good	1848

INCLINATION 6 b m £0

0	15	NEWC	16f Soft	40	760

INCREDULOUS 3 ch f £6049

92	2	CHES	7f Gd/Fm		1224
34	4	BEVE	7f Gd/Sft		1763
87	1	NOTT	8f Gd/Fm		2188*
74	7	NEWM	7f Good	85	2567
103	4	GOOD	7f Good		3104
87	8	EPSO	7f Good		3763

INDEFINITE STAY 2 b g £0
| 0 | 14 | SALI | 8f Gd/Sft | | 4163 |
| 67 | 7 | BATH | 8f Soft | | 4429 |

INDEPENDENCE 2 b f £470
| 82 | 3 | LING | 7f Firm | | 3829 |
| 76 | 7 | ASCO | 7f Good | | 4114 |

INDIAN BAZAAR 4 ch c £3326
0	14	BRIG	8f Gd/Sft	40	1462
38	3	REDC	6f Gd/Sft	40	1578
41	2	CHEP	6f Good	40	1971
28	9	GOOD	6f Gd/Fm	40	2124
46	1	BEVE	5f Firm	42	2223*
35	7	BRIG	5f Soft	41	2428
34	13	BATH	5f Gd/Sft	47	2555
45	5	BEVE	5f Firm	47	2732
44	6	CHEP	5f Gd/Fm	47	2976
34	10	THIR	5f Gd/Fm	46	3619
37	7	CHEP	5f Good	44	3872

INDIAN BLAZE 6 ch g £1463
71a	3	WOLV	7f Aw	67	143
66a	4	SOUT	7f Aw	69	216
84	7	DONC	8f Good	86	733
66	12	KEMP	8f Soft	85	1015
64	17	ASCO	7f Gd/Sft	85	1110
0	19	KEMP	6f Gd/Fm	83	3791
0	17	KEMP	8f Soft	80	4038
54	16	NEWM	8f Good	75	4340

INDIAN DANCE 4 ch c £390
0	16	CATT	7f Gd/Fm	56	780	t
0a	14	SOUT	8f Aw	48	1207	t
35	10	REDC	6f Good		1298	t
14	10	CATT	6f Good		1664	
30	7	RIPO	8f Gd/Fm	38	2099	t
51	3	CATT	6f Good		2421	t
0	15	YARM	6f Gd/Fm	43	3966	
0	15	DONC	7f Soft		4461	

INDIAN DANEHILL 4 b c £116261
119	1	LONG	10f Hldng		819*
120	1	LONG	11f Heavy		1115*
118	2	LONG	9f Gd/Sft		1458
116	4	LEOP	10f Good		3925
116	5	NEWM	10f Good		4355

INDIAN DRIVE 3 b c £0
| 77 | 6 | SALI | 6f Firm | | 1181 |
| 59 | 5 | NEWB | 7f Gd/Fm | | 1947 |

INDIAN FILE 2 ch c £0
| 0 | 17 | NEWB | 7f Firm | | 3999 |

INDIAN GIVER 2 ch f £0
| 54 | 10 | SAND | 5f Gd/Fm | | 3942 |
| 61 | 11 | WIND | 6f Gd/Sft | | 4288 |

INDIAN LODGE 4 b c £206321
116	1	NEWM	9f Gd/Sft		967*
118	1	SAND	8f Heavy		1043*
117	3	NEWB	8f Gd/Sft		1402
99	7	ASCO	8f Good		2064
121	1	LONG	8f Soft		3847*
113	7	ASCO	8f Good		4111
124	1	LONG	7f Soft		4395*

INDIAN MUSIC 3 b c £1835
39	14	WARW	6f Heavy		888	
65	9	AYR	6f Gd/Fm	74	1654	
66	4	RIPO	6f Gd/Fm	72	2101	
65	5	HAYD	6f Gd/Fm	70	2504	
71	5	DONC	6f Gd/Fm	70	2577	BL
66	5	AYR	7f Gd/Fm	70	2719	bl
66	3	CARL	5f Firm		2822	bl
68	2	LEIC	6f Gd/Fm		3097	bl
60	6	HAMI	6f Gd/Sft	68	3377	
62	11	CARL	5f Firm	68	3572	
62	4	HAMI	5f Gd/Sft	65	3825	bl
41	19	AYR	6f Gd/Sft	66	4010	

INDIAN NECTAR 7 b m £5357
30	8	BRIG	12f Firm	56	1332
53	4	NOTT	10f Good		1875
55	2	WARW	11f Gd/Sft	53	2033
0	11	FOLK	10f Gd/Fm	53	2296
51	5	CHEP	12f Gd/Fm	55	2656
55	2	BATH	10f Gd/Fm	55	2789
51	3	NOTT	10f Gd/Fm	55	3007
42	6	NEWM	10f Gd/Fm	55	3314
56	4	LING	10f Firm	54	3581
59	1	CHEP	10f Gd/Fm	54	3683*
31	13	EPSO	12f Good	59	3858

INDIAN PLUME 4 b c £12300
0	22	DONC	8f Good	78	715
81	1	MUSS	7f Gd/Sft		900*
62	14	ASCO	7f Gd/Sft	78	1110
55	14	THIR	8f Good	78	1160
81	1	RIPO	8f Good	76	1598*
78	7	GOOD	8f Gd/Fm	82	2356
37	20	YORK	7f Good	81	2694
82	3	BEVE	8f Gd/Sft	79	3054
69	5	HAMI	9f Gd/Sft	80	3535
82	2	RIPO	8f Good	80	3699
72	7	MUSS	7f Gd/Sft	80	4136

INDIAN PROSPECTOR 3 b c £7685
| 108 | 2 | CHAN | 8f Gd/Sft | | 1900 |

INDIAN ROPE TRICK 4 ch c £0
0	13	PONT	12f Good	50	1499
0	11	HAMI	13f Gd/Fm	47	1936
17	10	BEVE	12f Gd/Sft	44	3053	t

INDIAN SPARK 6 ch g £51053
70	8	DONC	6f Good	78	716
77	4	THIR	5f Soft		905
89	1	NEWC	5f Heavy	78	1008*
83	5	HAMI	6f Gd/Fm	86	1192
0	21	YORK	5f Firm	86	1324
93	1	HAYD	5f Gd/Sft	85	1533*
102	1	YORK	6f Gd/Fm	91	1983+
98	8	ASCO	6f Good	99	2151
105	2	NEWC	6f Gd/Fm	100	2310
99	7	NEWC	6f Firm		2335
110	1	CHES	5f Gd/Fm		2669*
54	13	HAYD	6f Gd/Sft		3784

INDIAN SUN 3 ch c £1718
75	4	LEIC	7f Good	81	792	
78	6	KEMP	6f Soft	80	994	
67	11	NEWM	8f Firm	79	1183	
61	7	THIR	8f Good	78	1387	
77	2	NEWC	8f Firm	76	1765	
0	13	KEMP	8f Soft	76	4038	BL

INDIAN SWINGER 4 ch c £2014
39a	9	WOLV	7f Aw	64	582
0a	13	SOUT	8f Aw		600
33a	5	SOUT	8f Aw		646
57a	2	SOUT	7f Aw		667
52a	2	SOUT	8f Aw		686
0a	11	LING	8f Aw	52	776
27a	7	SOUT	8f Aw		869
47a	3	WOLV	8f Aw	49	1393
44a	3	SOUT	8f Aw		1505
35a	7	SOUT	11f Aw		1978
26	7	WIND	8f Soft	46	2546
13	11	YARM	10f Firm		2765
46a	3	WOLV	9f Aw		3498
16a	9	WOLV	8f Aw	46	4437

INDIAN WARRIOR 4 b c £1226
46a	7	WOLV	7f Aw	62	364
55a	6	LING	7f Aw	58	503
54a	6	LING	7f Aw	58	525
46a	6	LING	8f Aw	55	594
43	11	LEIC	10f Good	62	793
39	7	PONT	8f Heavy		942
25	11	BRIG	8f Gd/Fm	57	1129
6	9	LING	9f Good	53	1395
36	6	YARM	6f Gd/Fm	49	2415
35	9	KEMP	7f Gd/Fm	47	2749
47	2	YARM	7f Good	45	3030
38	8	YARM	7f Good	47	3238
0	13	YARM	6f Gd/Fm	47	3966
28	6	WIND	6f Gd/Sft	45	4294	BL

INDIANA JONES 3 b c £0
0	11	LING	7f Gd/Sft		840
43	7	FOLK	7f Soft		961
0	13	DONC	7f Gd/Sft		1072
0a	16	SOUT	6f Aw	50	4156

INDIANA PRINCESS 7 b m £2169
68	2	MUSS	16f Gd/Sft	65	797
64	6	MUSS	14f Gd/Sft	69	903
63	3	THIR	16f Gd/Sft	69	1355
65	5	MUSS	16f Firm	68	1686

INDIANA SPRINGS 3 b c £562
0a	9	WOLV	7f Aw	50	346	
12a	7	SOUT	8f Aw		415	
34a	5	SOUT	11f Aw	38	537	VIS
28a	4	WOLV	12f Aw	44	640	vis
57	8	SOUT	10f Gd/Sft		858	vis
42	7	BEVE	10f Firm		1274	vis
42	6	LING	11f Aw	45	1914	vis
0	13	BEVE	12f Gd/Sft	43	3050	vis
42	3	WIND	12f Good		3351	
43	5	WARW	11f Good		3691	
49	3	LEIC	10f Gd/Sft		4029	
20	8	YARM	11f Soft	43	4391	
32	10	WIND	10f Heavy		4528	

INDIGENOUS 7 br g £425666
| 120 | 2 | TOKY | 12f Firm | | 123 |
| 104e | 8 | NAD | 10f Dirt | | 769 |

INDIGO BAY 4 b c £7106
71a	2	LING	12f Aw	66	52	
36a	12	LING	12f Aw	66	115	
42a	8	LING	13f Aw	68	167	
55a	4	LING	12f Aw	66	285	VIS
44a	5	LING	12f Aw	64	332	vis
65a	1	LING	13f Aw		524*	vis
44	13	DONC	12f Gd/Fm	65	699	vis
36	8	RIPO	12f Soft	63	825	vis
0	17	NOTT	14f Gd/Sft	58	1087	
0	18	PONT	12f Good	53	1499	
26	7	CATT	12f Gd/Fm	48	2422	vis
25	7	HAMI	11f Gd/Fm	44	2782	tbl
37	5	HAMI	11f Gd/Fm		2800	tbl
42	1	MUSS	12f Good	38	3102*	tbl
23	7	YARM	14f Good	43	3233	tbl
42	3	BEVE	12f Gd/Fm	41	3674	bl
28	13	CATT	12f Soft	46	4003	bl
60a	2	SOUT	11f Aw		4150	bl

INDIUM 6 b g £5380
51a	4	SOUT	8f Aw	66	648
31	18	DONC	8f Good	79	715
78	4	PONT	8f Soft	78	875
69	9	KEMP	8f Gd/Sft	78	1077
81	1	NEWB	10f Good	76	1375*
72	14	WIND	10f Good	79	1729
75	5	KEMP	9f Gd/Fm	79	2085
50	19	SAND	10f Good	79	2475
49	18	NEWM	8f Good	78	2564
69	11	KEMP	8f Firm	83	2870
0	21	YORK	8f Good	77	3810
65	8	YARM	8f Firm	79	3936

INDUCEMENT 4 ch c £5831
75	4	NEWM	10f Gd/Fm	83	2805
86	1	LEIC	10f Gd/Fm	81	3337*
82	5	NEWM	10f Gd/Fm	86	3628
83	1	PONT	10f Soft	85	4085

INDY CARR 3 b f £2133

```
47   6   MUSS  7f Gd/Sft        900
53  10   THIR  8f Good      74  1387
65   4   NEWC  8f Heavy    70  1765
55   6   PONT 10f Firm     66  2175
49   6   HAYD  8f Gd/Fm    62  2699
52   8   NEWC  7f Good     59  3033
50   8   HAYD  7f Gd/Sft   59  3269
40   8   AYR   7f Good         3364
22a 12   WOLV  6f Aw       53  3774
37   1   CATT 14f Soft        4002*
0   13   REDC 14f Gd/Sft  50  4222
31   6   AYR  11f Heavy        4304
37   8   WIND 10f Heavy        4528
```

INFORAPENNY 3 b g £33124
```
83   1   PONT 10f Soft          873*
101  2   CHES 11f Gd/Fm        1223
104  3   GOOD 10f Gd/Stt       1469
91   5   NEWW 10f Gd/Fm        1945
109  3   CURR 12f Gd/Fm        2739
95   7   DEAU 14f Gd/Sft       3070
78  10   DONC 15f Gd/Fm        3863
```

INFOTEC 3 b c £4912
```
69   7   KEMP  6f Soft     74   994
79   1   WARW  7f Soft     72  1061*
0   13   SALI  7f Good     78  1348
68   5   NOTT  8f Soft     77  1645
74   3   THIR  7f Gd/Sft       1716
0   19   DONC  7f Gd/Fm    75  1840
0   28   NEWM  8f Good     73  4340
0   17   YARM  7f Soft     70  4513
```

INGLEMOTTE MISS 2 ch f £0
```
5    5   HAMI  5f Gd/Sft       3822
```

INGLENOOK 3 b c £36462
```
91   5   NEWM  8f Gd/Sft        972
99   1   KEMP  8f Gd/Sft       1080*
107  1   KEMP  8f Soft         1530*
112  7   ASCO  8f Good         2066
111  4   HAYD 11f Gd/Fm        3321
107  4   NEWM  9f Good         4347
111  1   SAIN 10f Heavy        4491*
```

INHERIT THE EARTH 6 b m £0
```
0    8   MUSS 16f Gd/Sft       2536
```

INIGO JONES 4 b g £7137
```
95   1   HAYD 12f Gd/Sft   88   809*
82   4   HAYD 12f Heavy    94   991
95   5   YORK 12f Gd/Fm    94  1307
93   6   NEWC 16f Firm     93  2336
78  17   YORK 14f Gd/Fm    93  3565
```

INITIATIVE 4 ch c £1119
```
0   15   HAYD  8f Soft     87  1490
0   15   YORK  9f Firm     80  2001
31   7   NEWC 10f Good     74  2522
19   3   THIR  8f Good         3616
0   12   REDC  8f Gd/Sft   45  4499 BL
```

INJAAZ 2 ch f £3821
```
44  14   YORK  6f Good         2692
83   1   LEIC  6f Gd/Fm        3096*
84   2   NOTT  6f Good     80  3519
82   7   DONC  7f Gd/Fm    84  3860
75  11   NEWM  7f Good     83  4157
```

INKWELL 6 b g £416
```
33a  4   LING 10f Aw       38   224 bl
34a  5   WOLV 12f Aw       36   260 bl
35a  2   WOLV 12f Aw       32   608 bl
22a  5   SOUT 12f Aw       46   683 bl
9a   9   LING 10f Aw            775 bl
0   16   WARW 11f Soft     40  1065 bl
0   11   BRIG 12f Gd/Sft   33  1465
0   14   BATH 10f Gd/Sft   36  1666 tbl
```

INNES 4 b f £218
```
50a  4   SOUT 12f Aw            301
```

INNIT 2 b f £114990
```
65   3   WARW  5f Heavy        1000
85   2   DONC  5f Gd/Sft       1048
87   1   HAMI  5f Gd/Fm        1189*
83   3   THIR  5f Good         1385
96   5   CURR  5f Gd/Sft       1621
91   4   BEVE  5f Good         1759
86   3   GOOD  6f Good         2307
85   4   SALI  6f Good         2687
84   9   NEWB  5f Firm         2849
0    8   CURR  6f Yldg         3720
99   2   SALI  6f Firm         3749
93   1   DONC  7f Gd/Fm    85  3860*
98   1   MAIS  7f Good         4049*
100  1   SAN   8f Gd/Sft       4145*
103  1   SAN   8f Soft         4318*
```

INNKEEPER 3 b c £1322
```
67   5   KEMP  7f Soft         1012
73   2   LING  7f Gd/Sft       1263
58   9   WARW  7f Heavy        1525
66  15   ASCO  6f Good         2115
70   6   LING  7f Firm     75  2325
70   6   SALI  6f Gd/Fm        2977
59   4   WIND  8f Good         3190
0   14   LING  7f Good     66  4102
39a 10   LING 10f Aw       62  4482
```

INNUENDO 5 b m £23207
```
116  3   WOOD 10f Firm         4399
```

INOURHEARTS 4 b f £0
```
81  11   GOOD  5f Gd/Fm        3059
```

INSHEEN 2 b g £0
```
0   11   BATH  5f Good         1088
55   5   LING  6f Good         1673
0   19   WIND  6f Gd/Fm        1876
```

INSIGHTFUL 3 b g £7503
```
87a  1   LING  7f Aw            108*
89a  2   LING  7f Aw            206
67   5   SAND  8f Good     80   761
58  11   SALI  7f Good     77  1348
76   2   SAND  7f Soft     74  1569
70   6   NEWB  7f Gd/Fm    74  1787
76   4   SAND  8f Good     76  1964
73   4   LING  7f Firm     75  2325 BL
34  12   GOOD  8f Gd/Fm    74  3063 bl
46   6   SAND  8f Good     74  3227
67   4   BRIG  8f Gd/Fm    74  3261
0   16   KEMP  8f Gd/Fm    70  3793
0   15   GOOD 10f Soft     66  4067
0    P   LEIC 10f Heavy        4313
```

INSPECTOR BLUE 2 ch c £0
```
41  14   NEWB  6f Sft/Hvy       4470
```

INSPECTOR GENERAL 2 b c £14848
```
84   1   NEWB  5f Soft          911*
97   1   THIR  5f Good         1161*
100  1   SALI  6f Gd/Sft       4164*
87  12   NEWM  6f Good         4345
```

INTENSITY 4 b c £1192
```
78   5   DONC 10f Gd/Sft   78  1070
79   3   NEWB 12f Good     78  1373
74   7   REDC 10f Gd/Sft   78  1561
51  14   EPSO 10f Good     78  1845
```

INTERLUDE 3 b f £46543
```
108  3   ASCO 12f Good         2112
103  4   HAYD 12f Gd/Fm        2501
109  1   DEAU 14f Gd/Sft       3070*
107  6   YORK 12f Gd/Fm        3564
90   9   DONC 15f Gd/Fm        3863
```

INTERNAL AFFAIR 5 b g £11160
```
64a  6   WOLV  9f Aw       65    60
67a  2   SOUT  8f Aw            197
33a  8   WOLV  9f Aw       65   230
65a  1   WOLV  8f Aw            256*
53a  8   SOUT  8f Aw       62   345
65a  1   WOLV  8f Aw            393*
62a  4   WOLV  9f Aw            433
66a  1   WOLV  8f Aw       62   521*
62a  3   WOLV  8f Aw       68   580
65a  5   SOUT  8f Aw            600
67a  1   SOUT  8f Aw       64   647*
63a  5   WOLV  8f Aw       68   718
44   6   THIR  8f Soft     49   907
54a  6   WOLV  8f Aw       68  1037
```

INTO THE CLOUDS 4 br f £0
```
0   11   WIND 10f Gd/Fm        2056
```

INTRICATE WEB 4 b g £6516
```
49a  6   WOLV  7f Aw            623
0   13   WARW  8f Soft     68   817
0   20   NEWC  7f Heavy    68  1011
52   6   THIR  7f Gd/Fm    66  2063
71   1   CARL  7f Gd/Fm    66  2241*
70   3   LEIC  7f Gd/Fm        2508
69   3   DONC  8f Gd/Fm    71  2758
69   7   ASCO  8f Gd/Fm    71  3018
68   5   CHES  8f Firm     71  3170
73   3   AYR   8f Good         3365
53   6   REDC  8f Gd/Fm    70  3634
51  12   ASCO  8f Gd/Sft   70  4126 VIS
62  13   NEWM  7f Good     69  4357
66   6   NEWM  7f Soft     68  4547 bl
```

INTRUM MORSHAAN 3 b f £3990
```
61   9   GOOD 10f Gd/Sft   71  1812
70   2   HAYD 12f Gd/Fm    70  2446
83   1   HAYD 16f Gd/Sft   71  3476*
81   7   HAYD 14f Soft     84  3783
72   6   HAYD 14f Gd/Sft   82  4105
```

INVADER 4 b c £5426
```
91a  5   WOLV  8f Aw       90   663
99a  5   LING 10f Aw            690
62  15   KEMP  8f Soft     90  1015
80   9   YORK  9f Firm     85  2001
85   2   DONC  8f Gd/Fm        2611 VIS
83   1   SAND  8f Gd/Fm        2938* vis
66   7   DONC 10f Gd/Fm        3865 vis
74   5   SAND  8f Gd/Fm        3945 vis
```

INVER GOLD 3 ch c £10550
```
77a  2   LING  8f Aw             26
70a  4   LING  8f Aw            103
75a  1   SOUT  7f Aw            278*
75a  3   WOLV  8f Aw       74   921
74   9   GOOD  9f Gd/Sft   79  1452
71   8   LEIC 10f Gd/Sft   77  1735
71a  4   SOUT  7f Aw       74  2300
77   3   GOOD 10f Gd/Fm    75  2358
56  10   CHES 10f Good     75  2666
78a  1   WOLV  8f Aw       73  3274*
```

INVESTMENT FORCE 2 b c £1004
```
41a  8   LING  6f Good         1740
59   9   REDC  6f Good         1893
68   5   EPSO  6f Gd/Sft       2628
73   2   BEVE  7f Gd/Sft       3069
61   8   NEWM  8f Good     78  3609
30  12   MUSS  8f Gd/Sft   72  4132
```

INVESTOR RELATIONS 2 b g £0
```
68   6   KEMP  6f Gd/Fm        3358
68   9   NOTT  6f Good         3520
47   9   NOTT  6f Soft         3974
```

INVINCIBLE 2 b f £178
```
74   4   BATH 10f Good         4429
```

INVINCIBLE SPIRIT 3 b c £2000
```
105  4   NEWB  7f Firm         3995
104  6   NEWM  7f Good         4352
```

INVIRAMENTAL 4 b c £551
```
43a  4   WOLV  7f Aw       48   193 BL
50a  2   WOLV  6f Aw       46   352 bl
60a  5   LING  7f Aw            421 bl
```

INVISIBLE FORCE 3 b c £5144 (continued)

0	13	BATH	8f Soft	46	4143
0a	14	LING	7f Aw		4487

INVISIBLE FORCE 3 b c £5144

23	6	HAYD	7f Heavy		992	
0	14	HAMI	5f Firm	47	1244	
34a	4	LING	6f Aw	42	1742	
33	6	CATT	5f Gd/Sft	42	1817	
25a	6	WOLV	9f Aw	40	2080	
48	1	CARL	9f Firm	38	2825*	BL
45	3	BEVE	10f Good	45	2883	bl
28a	4	SOUT	11f Aw	45	2945	bl
47	4	NEWM	12f Gd/Fm	48	3167	bl
47	4	BEVE	10f Good	45	3396	VIS
45	3	HAMI	11f Soft	45	3805	vis

INVITATION 2 b c £0

65	7	NEWB	8f Gd/Sft	4457

INZACURE 2 b c £3636

56	8	WIND	5f Good		849
48a	9	SOUT	5f Aw		1418
56	5	MUSS	7f Firm		2377
62	1	BRIG	6f Soft	58	4170*

INZARMOOD 2 b f £0

15a	10	WOLV	6f Aw	4246
0	19	NEWM	7f Good	4336
0	15	NEWM	8f Soft	4542

INZARS BEST 2 br c £7685

97	2	SAIN	7f Gd/Sft	4314

IONIAN SPRING 5 b g £0

0	15	WIND	10f Good	79	1729
70	12	NEWM	10f Gd/Fm	77	2133
73	7	YORK	8f Good	74	3810

IORANA 4 ch g £1580

75	2	SALI	10f Gd/Fm	2981
76	2	LING	14f Firm	3489

IPANEMA BEACH 3 ch f £3499

54	8	HAYD	7f Gd/Sft		1537
67	3	SAND	8f Good		3474
64	6	KEMP	8f Gd/Fm	69	3793
0	18	WIND	8f Gd/Sft		4292
69a	1	WOLV	8f Aw		4551*

IPLEDGEALLEGIANCE 4 b c £1055

95	3	NEWC	10f Soft	93	757
50	13	EPSO	10f Heavy	95	1031
92	7	ASCO	10f Good	95	2170
91	9	SAND	10f Good	95	2475
77	8	NEWM	10f Gd/Fm	93	3628
0	19	DONC	10f Firm	92	3899

IRANOO 3 b c £0

30	8	HAMI	8f Gd/Fm	1940	t
32	11	HAMI	9f Gd/Fm	2642	t
24	7	REDC	11f Gd/Fm	2989	t
24	4	CATT	16f Gd/Fm	3199	t
30	5	CARL	12f Firm	3570	t
11	8	HAMI	9f Gd/Fm	3823	t
13	8	CATT	14f Soft	4002	t

IRELANDS EYE 5 b g £2355

2a	8	SOUT	16f Aw	54	51	
54	3	NOTT	14f Gd/Sft	54	1087	
56	3	BEVE	16f Firm	56	1276	
53	2	WARW	16f Gd/Sft	54	1711	
47	8	BEVE	16f Gd/Fm	53	2516	
48	6	PONT	17f Soft	52	3501	
39	6	CARL	17f Soft	52	3575	
29	8	CATT	16f Soft	46	4006	
41	3	PONT	17f Soft	42	4231	
22	6	PONT	18f Soft	47	4376	VIS
0	15	NOTT	16f Heavy	40	4508	vis

IRIDANOS 4 b c £9798

109	2	SAIN	8f Hldng	861
108	4	LONG	7f Good	1617

IRIDESCENT 2 b f £510

56	4	HAYD	6f Good	3286

IRISH CREAM 4 b f £4760

48a	2	WOLV	12f Aw	44	464	
27a	7	SOUT	12f Aw	49	590	
45a	1	SOUT	14f Aw		668*	vis
30	10	NOTT	14f Good	40	788	vis
38a	6	WOLV	16f Aw	44	918	vis
41a	2	WOLV	12f Aw		1389	vis
24	6	LEIC	12f Soft	32	1551	vis
41a	2	WOLV	12f Aw	40	2075	vis
8a	11	WOLV	15f Gd/Fm	42	3276	vis
42a	2	WOLV	12f Aw	41	3773	vis

IRISH DANCER 3 ch f £7526

30a	4	WOLV	8f Aw		80	BL
37	10	LING	7f Gd/Sft	49	841	
22a	7	WOLV	9f Aw		1141	
47	3	LING	11f Firm	45	1911	
56	1	PONT	12f Good	45	2362*	
56	1	RIPO	12f Soft	51	2540*	
40	9	PONT	10f Gd/Fm	68	2829	
44	7	RIPO	10f Good	60	3702	

IRISH DISTINCTION 2 b c £0

77	5	AYR	6f Gd/Fm	1653

IRISH MELODY 4 ch f £0

13a	10	LING	7f Aw	159	
7a	6	WOLV	7f Aw	173	bl
0a	12	LING	10f Aw	238	
19a	7	LING	8f Aw	544	t

IRISH STREAM 2 ch c £2110

84	3	NEWM	7f Good	3608
82	2	AYR	7f Soft	3962
69	6	DONC	7f Gd/Sft	4446

IRISH VERSE 2 ch f £250

82	6	NEWB	7f Firm	3985
0	9	BRIG	8f Soft	4417

IRON DRAGON 2 b c £270

55	6	RIPO	6f Gd/Fm	2106	t
69	4	YARM	6f Gd/Fm	2414	t
57	6	LING	6f Good	2652	t

IRON HORSE 8 b g £29861

106	3	KRAN	10f Good	656

IRON MAN 8 b g £0

47a	7	SOUT	7f Aw	60	282
0a	9	SOUT	8f Aw	55	473
14a	8	SOUT	8f Aw	48	648

IRON MASK 2 b c £42268

105	2	CHAN	5f Hldng	2485
105	2	MAIS	6f V	3066
111	1	CHAN	6f Good	3843*
108	5	LONG	5f Good	4261

IRON MOUNTAIN 5 b g £22554

72	3	ASCO	8f Gd/Sft	72	1113
74	5	WIND	10f Firm		1288
72	3	GOOD	8f Gd/Sft	72	1450
72	4	AYR	10f Gd/Fm	72	1656
52	12	YORK	9f Firm	70	2001
73	1	NEWM	8f Good	68	2564*
55	4	NOTT	8f Gd/Fm		2682
74	3	NEWM	8f Gd/Fm	73	2802
68	5	GOOD	9f Good	72	3644
73	3	AYR	9f Soft		3988
67	7	NEWM	8f Gd/Fm	70	4340
78	1	YARM	10f Soft	70	4392*

IRSAL 6 ch g £784

16a	5	SOUT	12f Aw	30	70	
0a	10	WOLV	16f Aw	30	190	
31a	3	SOUT	11f Aw	33	325	
0a	9	SOUT	11f Aw	29	413	
32a	2	SOUT	11f Aw	30	560	bl
7a	8	SOUT	11f Aw	34	742	bl
13	14	RIPO	12f Soft	35	822	bl
0	11	SOUT	11f Gd/Sft	36	855	bl
0	16	MUSS	9f Firm	28	1689	bl

IS WONDERFUL 2 ch c £0

0	26	NEWM	8f Good	4349

ISABELLA R 3 ch f £832

63a	2	WOLV	7f Aw		41
17a	11	WOLV	7f Aw	63	188

ISADORA 3 b f £4182

87	1	CHEP	12f Good	3869*

ISHAAM 2 ch f £0

61	12	NEWM	7f Soft	4541

ISHIGURU 2 b c £2276

94	2	NEWM	6f Good	4341

ISIT IZZY 8 b m £336

24	10	NOTT	6f Firm	38	1273	
33	3	RIPO	8f Gd/Fm	35	2099	
0	15	PONT	8f Gd/Fm	37	2561	
22	9	CHEP	8f Gd/Fm	37	2658	VIS

ISLA 3 b f £0

33	7	SOUT	10f Good		806
39	5	WIND	8f Heavy		934
0a	8	SOUT	12f Aw	48	2382

ISLAND ESCAPE 4 b f £0

19	9	WIND	8f Firm	50	2890
0	21	WIND	10f Gd/Fm		3045 bl

ISLAND HOUSE 4 ch c £64846

117	1	NEWM	10f Gd/Fm	1174*
113	1	GOOD	10f Gd/Sft	1482*
114	1	KEMP	10f Firm	2260+
108	5	AYR	10f Gd/Fm	2720
102	4	WIND	10f Good	3641
116	1	AYR	11f Gd/Sft	4011+
104	4	NEWB	12f Sft/Hv	4469

ISLAND PRINCESS 3 b f £312

82	5	SAND	10f Heavy		1045
67	9	NEWB	10f Gd/Fm	79	3178
74	4	KEMP	12f Soft		4040
46	10	SAND	10f Soft		4205
39	5	NEWB	10f Sft/Hv		4474

ISLAND QUEEN 2 b f £1651

70	4	WARW	5f Gd/Sft		1706
79	3	LING	7f Gd/Fm		2182
79	2	KEMP	7f Soft		4034
69	5	YORK	7f Soft	80	4279
70	6	BATH	8f Soft		4430

ISLAND SANDS 4 b c £7685

114	2	DEAU	8f Gd/Fm	3717

ISLAND SOUND 3 b g £22695

108	2	NEWM	9f Gd/Sft	980
103	5	CHES	10f Good	1246
99	3	CURR	10f Gd/Sft	1627
102	4	NEWB	9f Firm	4000
73	4	AYR	8f Heavy	4308
111	1	NEWM	10f Gd/Sft	4532*

ISLAND THYMES 3 br g £418

61	3	WARW	7f Soft		813
41	7	WARW	7f Heavy	58	887
0	15	WIND	10f Gd/Sft	56	1100

ISLE OF SODOR 4 b f £0

0	14	CATT	7f Gd/Fm	55	780
43	8	HAYD	7f Gd/Sft	55	811
6	5	LEIC	8f Gd/Sft	55	831
0	15	AYR	8f Gd/Fm	45	1658
20	12	HAMI	9f Gd/Fm	40	1939

ISSARA 3 b g £0

0	16	WIND	8f Gd/Sft		1099 BL
0	12	LING	11f Firm	35	1911

ISSEY ROSE 3 b f £0

95	16	NEWM	8f Firm		1185
91	7	YORK	9f Gd/Fm		3726
88	9	ASCO	8f Good	94	4113
72	11	NEWM	10f Good		4337
73	7	NEWB	9f Sft/Hvy	90	4472

ISTIHSAAN 2 b c £0

| 69 | 5 | CHEP | 7f Good | | 3866 | |
| 76 | 6 | ASCO | 8f Heavy | | 4296 | |

IT CAN BE DONE 3 ch c £5575

0	12	RIPO	8f Soft		826	
51	9	PONT	6f Gd/Sft		1105	
74	7	BEVE	7f Good		1444	
70	2	SOUT	7f Soft		1607	
65	1	NOTT	8f Soft	60	1645*	
46	6	RIPO	8f Gd/Fm	67	2108	
30	13	HAYD	11f Gd/Fm	66	2453	
0	13	CHES	8f Gd/Fm	65	2673	
52	6	BEVE	10f Good		2884	
40	13	LEIC	8f Gd/Fm	64	3095	
0	10	CHES	16f Gd/Fm	60	3511	

IT GIRL 2 b f £1578

75	2	GOOD	7f Good		2306	
66	4	KEMP	6f Gd/Fm		2748	
66	6	SALI	7f Gd/Fm		3292	
67	5	GOOD	7f Good	74	3660	
52	8	PONT	8f Soft	67	4084	

ITALIAN AFFAIR 2 ch f £3711

0	7	CHES	5f Gd/Fm		1214	
64	2	MUSS	5f Firm		1684	
59	7	HAMI	5f Gd/Fm		1906	
62	2	MUSS	5f Gd/Fm		2200	
64	1	YARM	6f Firm		2388*	
48	7	CHES	5f Good	66	2665	
0	5	AYR	5f Firm	60	2874	
0	13	CATT	7f Gd/Fm		2927	
59	4	MUSS	5f Good		3101	
48	6	CHES	6f Firm	60	3168	
45	7	LEIC	5f Gd/Fm	60	3216	
47	10	MUSS	5f Gd/Fm		3589	

ITALIAN ROSE 5 ch m £2035

0	17	NEWM	8f Gd/Fm	38	2130	
25	6	WARW	13f Gd/Fm	35	2843	
29	1	NOTT	14f Gd/Fm	28	3002*	
0	9	BEVE	16f Gd/Fm	32	3406	
0	13	YARM	14f Soft		4510	

ITALIAN SYMPHONY 6 b g £13296

85a	8	SOUT	8f Aw	95	49	vis
95a	5	LING	10f Aw		55	vis
82a	4	WOLV	8f Aw	92	137	vis
88a	3	LING	10f Aw		157	vis
77a	4	WOLV	9f Aw	90	172	vis
88a	4	LING	8f Aw		208	vis
95a	1	SOUT	7f Aw	88	216*	vis
83a	5	WOLV	9f Aw	91	230	vis
75a	9	LING	10f Aw	95	244	vis
85a	5	WOLV	8f Aw		321	vis
87a	10	LING	7f Aw	93	423	vis
92a	5	WOLV	8f Aw		448	vis
80a	7	LING	8f Aw	91	485	vis
83a	7	SOUT	7f Aw	90	539	vis
60	4	BRIG	8f Firm	58	1330	vis
57	5	MUSS	7f Gd/Fm	58	1431	vis
53	5	BRIG	8f Gd/Sft	58	1462	vis
50	7	BRIG	7f Gd/Fm	57	1930	vis
51	5	BATH	8f Firm	57	1998	vis
49	6	CARL	7f Gd/Fm	55	2241	vis
52	3	CARL	8f Firm		2283	
49	5	CATT	7f Gd/Fm	53	2932	vis
56	1	YARM	8f Good	52	3238*	vis
53	6	AYR	8f Good	58	3365	vis
48	5	BATH	8f Gd/Fm	56	3514	vis
51	7	BEVE	8f Good	56	3652	vis
45	8	MUSS	8f Gd/Fm	56	3746	vis
56	7	LEIC	7f Firm	55	3839	vis
0	15	REDC	8f Gd/Sft	55	4499	vis

ITCH 5 b g £5878

38a	2	SOUT	6f Aw	40	250	
43a	1	SOUT	7f Aw	38	304*	
45a	3	SOUT	7f Aw	43	368	
50a	1	SOUT	7f Aw	43	471*	
47a	4	WOLV	7f Aw	50	582	
52a	2	SOUT	7f Aw	50	599	
0a	11	SOUT	8f Aw	50	647	
44a	8	SOUT	7f Aw	53	867	

ITHADTOBEYOU 5 ch m £1828

49a	2	LING	7f Aw	49	879	
50a	2	WOLV	6f Aw		1139	
52a	3	LING	8f Aw	50	1259	
40	8	BRIG	7f Firm	50	1336	
26	13	LEIC	6f Gd/Sft	48	1734	
40	5	LING	6f Firm	43	3578	
28a	9	WOLV	6f Aw	50	3774	t

ITIS ITIS 2 b c £0

| 54 | 7 | REDC | 5f Gd/Sft | | 1558 | |
| 0 | 19 | YORK | 8f Gd/Fm | | 3729 | |

ITS ALLOWED 3 b f £0

73	10	YORK	7f Gd/Fm	83	1308	
66	7	RIPO	6f Gd/Fm	82	2101	
69	5	PONT	6f Good	79	2364	
66	9	YORK	7f Good	75	2694	
70	7	NEWC	7f Gd/Fm	72	2986	
59	10	YORK	7f Good	71	3809	
47	12	NOTT	6f Soft	69	3975	

ITS ANOTHER GIFT 3 b f £424

31	8	CATT	6f Gd/Fm		781	
56	3	MUSS	5f Gd/Sft	60	901	BL
43a	10	WOLV	6f Aw	59	1138	bl
51	5	CARL	5f Firm		1256	bl
55	5	THIR	6f Gd/Sft		1354	bl

ITS ECCO BOY 2 ch c £506

65	7	NOTT	6f Good		3520	
73	4	WARW	15f Gd/Fm		3911	
69	4	YORK	6f Soft		4283	

ITS MAGIC 4 b g £2180

0	17	PONT	8f Soft	73	875	bl
56	6	DONC	8f Gd/Fm	71	2758	
73	2	ASCO	8f Gd/Fm	69	3018	bl
61	9	NEWM	8f Gd/Fm	69	3118	bl
64	6	LEIC	8f Gd/Fm	72	3334	bl
63	6	SALI	8f Firm	70	3753	bl
51	13	REDC	8f Gd/Sft	68	4217	bl
51	11	YARM	10f Soft	65	4392	bl

ITS OUR SECRET 4 ch c £1200

67	2	BEVE	8f Firm	63	1279	
64	4	BATH	8f Gd/Fm	66	1442	
50	14	NEWM	8f Gd/Fm	66	1690	
9	13	PONT	8f Gd/Fm	65	2831	
58	5	NOTT	8f Gd/Fm	63	3115	
33	10	FOLK	7f Gd/Fm	63	3445	
42	11	LEIC	8f Gd/Sft		4033	
56a	4	LING	8f Aw	57	4335	

ITS SMEE AGAIN 2 ch f £2789

64	4	NOTT	5f Good		1870	
64	4	WARW	5f Gd/Fm		2034	
60	4	BATH	6f Firm		2784	
45	6	FOLK	7f Gd/Fm	65	3444	
59	1	RIPO	6f Good		3697*	
33	16	CATT	7f Soft	61	4007	

ITS YOUR BID 2 b f £0

| 0 | 13 | LING | 7f Soft | | 4484 | |

ITSAKINDOFMAGIC 2 b f £0

| 23 | 8 | REDC | 7f Good | | 1890 | |
| 0 | 12 | THIR | 7f Gd/Fm | | 3615 | |

ITSANOTHERGIRL 4 b f £6731

35a	9	SOUT	8f Aw	67	384	
52	9	HAYD	7f Gd/Sft	67	811	
70	1	THIR	8f Soft	65	931*	
70	2	NEWC	8f Heavy	70	1007	
71	2	NOTT	10f Gd/Sft	70	1086	
67	9	YORK	12f Gd/Fm	70	1307	

ITSGOTTABDUN 3 b c £4870

57a	3	LING	5f Aw	61	234	
62a	4	LING	6f Aw	61	269	
59a	4	LING	6f Aw		334	
43a	7	LING	6f Aw		373	
42a	6	WOLV	6f Aw	58	479	VIS
60a	1	LING	6f Aw		527*	bl
48a	4	LING	6f Aw	60	592	bl
55a	2	LING	5f Aw		619	bl
59a	3	LING	7f Aw	60	654	bl
37	6	NOTT	6f Good	60	785	bl
54	6	LING	7f Gd/Sft	60	841	bl
56	4	BATH	6f Gd/Fm		1670	bl
51a	3	LING	6f Aw	58	1742	bl
46	9	LING	6f Gd/Fm	60	2216	bl
31	10	WIND	6f Soft	57	2549	bl
55a	2	LING	7f Aw		2759	

IVANS BRIDE 2 b f £3141

38	8	SAND	5f Heavy		1046	
60	6	NOTT	6f Good		1408	
61	4	REDC	6f Gd/Sft		1577	
40	8	NEWM	7f Gd/Fm	64	2962	
47	6	LEIC	6f Gd/Fm	58	3216	
55	2	SAND	7f Good	54	3468	
14	4	BRIG	7f Firm		3733	
45	9	BEVE	7f Good	56	3950	
41a	10	WOLV	7f Aw		4025	
57	1	BATH	6f Soft		4431*	
47	5	NOTT	8f Heavy		4507	

IVORS INVESTMENT 4 ch f £0

42	7	HAYD	7f Gd/Fm	48	2442	
0	16	REDC	8f Gd/Fm	46	2861	
0	16	LEIC	6f Gd/Sft		4031	
0a	12	WOLV	7f Aw		4224	

IVORY DAWN 6 b m £15009

50	13	DONC	6f Good	70	716	
52	7	LING	7f Gd/Fm		838	
70	2	BRIG	6f Gd/Fm	66	1126	
70	2	THIR	6f Gd/Fm	68	1356	
70	4	GOOD	6f Gd/Fm	70	1636	
58	13	YORK	6f Firm	70	2000	
74	3	WIND	6f Gd/Fm	70	2054	
67	10	GOOD	6f Good	73	2355	
78	1	LING	6f Firm	72	2761*	
71	5	NEWM	6f Gd/Fm	79	2961	
65	7	WIND	6f Gd/Fm	77	3046	
70	7	ASCO	5f Gd/Fm	76	3341	
76	3	NEWM	6f Gd/Fm	76	3457	
60	14	GOOD	6f Good	76	3646	
81	2	KEMP	6f Gd/Fm	76	3791	
73	8	GOOD	6f Good	79	3904	
77	7	NEWM	5f Good	79	4015	
62	8	YORK	6f Heavy	78	4301	
57	10	YARM	6f Heavy	77	4480	

IVORYS GUEST 3 gr g £0

| 0a | 11 | LING | 8f Aw | | 236 | |

IVORYS JOY 5 b m £59748

87a	1	WOLV	5f Aw	80	64+	
0a	13	SOUT	6f Aw	86	129	
75	5	DONC	5f Gd/Fm	82	702	
79	6	THIR	5f Soft	80	926	
66	9	KEMP	5f Soft	79	1013	
78	3	LING	5f Gd/Sft	77	1264	
86	1	BRIG	5f Good	77	1650+	
86	6	YORK	5f Gd/Fm	86	1980	
72	13	NEWC	5f Gd/Fm	86	2310	
88	4	DONC	5f Gd/Fm	86	2348	
84	5	ASCO	5f Good	87	2676	
84	7	ASCO	5f Good	87	3016	
94	1	HAYD	5f Gd/Fm	86	3322*	
97	2	EPSO	5f Good	93	3687	
108	1	NEWB	5f Firm		3982+	

96 9 NEWM 5f Good   4182

IYAVAYA 3 b f £0
72 7 LEIC 6f Gd/Sft   829
81 12 EPSO 7f Gd/Sft 92 1826
84 7 ASCO 8f Good   88 2167
0   R WARW 8f Gd/Fm   2844

IZZET MUZZY 2 ch c £0
63 5 LEIC 5f Gd/Sft   828
68 8 DONC 5f Gd/Sft   1048
56 5 LEIC 5f Gd/Sft   1573
46a 5 SOUT 6f Aw   1974
69 4 CATT 7f Gd/Fm   2417
57 6 CATT 7f Gd/Fm   2741
27 10 LEIC 8f Gd/Fm   64 3216
29 14 YORK 8f Gd/Fm   3729
45a 7 WOLV 8f Aw   55 4439 VIS

J R STEVENSON 4 ch c £0
82 15 NEWM 10f Gd/Fm 100 1170
95 7 YORK 10f Firm   98 1342
87 11 REDC 10f Gd/Sft 97 1561
84 6 DONC 10f Gd/Fm 95 2350
89 5 YORK 12f Gd/Fm 92 2647
58 11 ASCO 10f Gd/Fm 91 3339
0 13 GOOD 9f Good   89 3883 vis

JABUKA 3 b f £4653
76 4 YARM 7f Gd/Fm   1951
67 3 NEWM 6f Gd/Fm   3319
65 2 BRIG 7f Firm   3529
59 1 MUSS 7f Gd/Fm   3744*

JACANA 2 ch f £1570
85 2 NEWB 6f Firm   3449
80 5 NEWM 6f Gd/Fm   4209

JACK DAWSON 3 b c £11305
47 8 WIND 6f Good   64 852
45 8 BRIG 7f Firm   61 1213
37 9 NOTT 8f Good   58 1414
0   W REDC 10f Good   54 1895
57 2 BRIG 12f Gd/Fm 54 1935
48 5 WIND 10f Gd/Fm 54 2053
46 9 BATH 10f Gd/Fm 57 2332
64 1 CHEP 16f Gd/Fm 54 2659*
64 2 CHEP 16f Gd/Fm 62 2973
67 2 NOTT 16f Gd/Fm 62 3112
64 3 HAYD 16f Gd/Sft 65 3476
70 1 REDC 14f Gd/Fm 63 3637*
70 2 WARW 16f Gd/Fm 68 3916
0 12 CHES 16f Soft   68 4071
39 12 NEWM 14f Gd/Fm 70 4213

JACK SPRATT 2 b c £16021
50 10 LING 5f Gd/Sft   1260
85 8 NEWB 5f Gd/Sft   1589
75 3 WIND 5f Gd/Fm   2055
78 1 CHEP 5f Gd/Fm   2657*
76 8 GOOD 5f Good   82 3109
85 1 LING 5f Firm   78 3491*
90 1 CHEP 5f Gd/Fm   84 3679*
98 2 CHAN 5f Good   4051
95 6 NEWB 5f Gd/Sft   4454

JACK THE KNIFE 4 b g £0
0 19 DONC 7f Soft   4461

JACK TO A KING 5 b g £6220
43a 7 WOLV 5f Aw   51 116 tBL
47a 6 SOUT 5f Aw   214 tbl
52a 1 WOLV 5f Aw   46 291* tbl
47a 5 LING 5f Aw   50 372 tbl
52a 2 WOLV 5f Aw   50 445 tbl
44a 7 WOLV 5f Aw   52 518 tbl
54a 2 WOLV 5f Aw   52 564 tbl
59a 1 WOLV 5f Aw   51 609* bl
60a 2 SOUT 5f Aw   57 674 bl
25 13 NOTT 6f Gd/Fm 46 2192 bl
28 11 NEWC 5f Firm   46 2340 tbl

0 19 NEWC 5f Good   43 2525 tbl
0 12 BEVE 5f Gd/Sft   3056 tbl
45a 9 WOLV 5f Aw   61 3271 bl
42a 8 SOUT 6f Aw   58 4155 bl
0 15 REDC 5f Gd/Fm   4220
36a 11 WOLV 6f Aw   56 4358

JACKERIN 5 b g £840
41 6 MUSS 5f Gd/Fm 52 798 bl
42 5 WARW 5f Heavy 49 1005 bl
44 5 DONC 6f Gd/Sft   1068 bl
47 4 MUSS 5f Gd/Fm 49 1143 bl
51 4 REDC 6f Firm   1298 bl
43 7 THIR 5f Gd/Sft 48 1357 bl
40 6 REDC 7f Gd/Sft   1559 bl
32 6 CATT 6f Good   1663 vis
43 4 NEWC 5f Heavy   1766
32a 8 SOUT 5f Aw   45 1976
39 8 REDC 6f Firm   45 3312 t
0 16 HAMI 5f Gd/Sft 43 3536
44 2 YARM 6f Gd/Fm 40 3964 vis
17 13 AYR   6f Heavy 42 4327 tvi
36 4 NEWC 5f Heavy 42 4407 bl

JACKIES BABY 4 b c £2687
67a 9 WOLV 5f Aw   80 394
75a 4 WOLV 5f Aw   77 491
61a 9 LING 5f Aw   77 506
64a 10 WOLV 5f Aw   76 579
61a 8 WOLV 5f Aw   74 1140
83 4 THIR 5f Good   85 1162
84 5 YORK 5f Firm   84 1324
85 4 MUSS 5f Firm   84 1687
75 10 EPSO 5f Gd/Fm 96 1849
67 10 BATH 6f Gd/Fm 84 1999
80 4 CHES 5f Gd/Fm 82 2247
46 13 BATH 5f Firm   82 3209
61 12 NOTT 5f Good   3521

JACKS BIRTHDAY 2 b c £0
37 8 KEMP 5f Soft   993
55 5 KEMP 5f Gd/Sft   1079
63 11 KEMP 6f Firm   1924
0 15 LING 6f Good   2588

JACMAR 5 br g £9063
46 2 MUSS 7f Gd/Fm 42 1149
35 6 HAMI 5f Firm   42 1244
34 4 CARL 6f Firm   42 1258
49 1 HAMI 5f Gd/Fm 44 1358*
0 12 DONC 7f Good   48 1519
48 5 AYR   6f Gd/Fm 49 1654
52 2 HAMI 6f Gd/Fm 48 1941
51 1 HAMI 6f Firm   48 2097*
0 11 CARL 7f Firm   56 2282
50 3 HAMI 6f Gd/Fm 51 2641
43 7 HAMI 6f Gd/Fm 51 2796
27 10 NEWC 6f Good   51 3037
36 13 HAMI 5f Gd/Sft 50 3825
0 22 AYR   5f Soft   52 3960
0 24 AYR   6f Heavy 48 4327
40 5 MUSS 7f Soft   45 4518

JACOBINA 5 b m £0
18 14 NEWC 6f Good   52 3037
0 13 REDC 6f Firm   49 3312 t
0 16 BEVE 5f Gd/Fm 45 3653

JADE TIGER 4 ch c £0
41a 8 WOLV 9f Aw   62 349
48a 4 WOLV 9f Aw   57 469
19a 10 WOLV 12f Aw   54 520
31a 6 WOLV 12f Aw   51 607

JAHMHOOR 3 b g £0
79 14 NEWM 8f Gd/Sft   972
66 6 BEVE 7f Good   1444
73 5 RIPO 8f Gd/Fm   2104
63 7 YARM 7f Good   72 3238

58 5 SALI 7f Gd/Fm 3423 t

JAILHOUSE ROCKET 3 gr c £0
0 26 NEWM 6f Gd/Fm 92 1694
0 19 YORK 7f Firm   89 2003
63 14 ASCO 5f Good   84 2168
0 20 GOOD 6f Good   79 2355
39 11 CHES 5f Good   74 2663
50 9 REDC 5f Gd/Sft   4220
55 8 NEWC 5f Heavy 64 4407

JALAD 3 b c £2984
102 2 DONC 8f Gd/Fm   1069 t
0 14 HAYD 8f Gd/Fm 104 1535 t
102 4 DONC 8f Firm   3893 t
0 19 NEWM 10f Good   99 4197 t
90 8 NEWM 8f Good   97 4348 tBL

JALISCO 3 b f £11373
85 1 LEIC 10f Firm   3838*
98 2 ASCO 12f Gd/Sft   4130
72 14 NEWM 12f Good   4343

JALONS STAR 2 b g £0
28 5 DONC 7f Gd/Fm   3859
0 14 YARM 7f Firm   3940
66 6 YORK 7f Soft   4277
45 6 PONT 6f Soft   4373

JALOUSIE 2 b f £0
74 16 NEWM 7f Good   4158

JAM 3 b f £0
0 18 BATH 12f Soft   4434

JAMADYAN 3 b c £1030
69 6 KEMP 8f Soft   996
83 4 SALI 7f Gd/Fm   2228
81 6 DONC 8f Gd/Fm   3158
68 8 PONT 8f Firm   89 3505
0   9 PONT 10f Soft   82 4085
0 19 YORK 10f Soft   4275

JAMAICAN FLIGHT 7 b h £6275
65a 5 SOUT 14f Aw   72 37
69a 3 SOUT 16f Aw   68 253
66a 3 WOLV 16f Aw   68 296
63a 4 WOLV 16f Aw   67 348
68a 4 SOUT 14f Aw   66 470
77 3 DONC 18f Good   75 714
75 2 SOUT 12f Good   75 805
28 12 WARW 15f Heavy 76 885 VIS
72 4 SAND 16f Heavy 75 1044
67 8 HAYD 14f Gd/Fm 73 1167
69 7 YORK 14f Firm   71 1329
48 6 PONT 17f Soft   71 1701
71 5 PONT 18f Firm   70 2176
62 5 WARW 15f Good   67 2461
54 4 CHES 12f Good   2667
60 4 ASCO 16f Gd/Fm 60 2953
61 2 CHES 12f Gd/Fm 59 3430
57 3 THIR 16f Gd/Fm 59 3618

JAMAIEL 3 b f £1205
72 3 LEIC 12f Gd/Sft   1738
69 6 NEWM 10f Gd/Fm   2135
36 3 YARM 11f Firm   2386

JAMES DEE 4 b c £4498
59a 9 LING 7f Aw   76 462
80a 2 SOUT 6f Aw   75 587
80a 2 SOUT 6f Aw   78 645
65 2 NOTT 6f Good   61 787
54 6 BRIG 7f Gd/Sft 64 896
63 2 NOTT 6f Gd/Sft   1368
44 10 CHEP 7f Gd/Sft 64 1799
52 9 WARW 7f Gd/Fm 63 2840
60 4 BRIG 7f Gd/Fm   3243

JAMES STARK 3 b c £21842
84a 1 SOUT 5f Aw   34* bl
85a 1 LING 6f Aw   80 105* bl
80a 6 SOUT 5f Aw   85 202 bl

57a 9 WOLV 6f Aw 85 275 VIS

57a	9	WOLV	6f Aw	85	275	VIS
0	17	NEWM	6f Gd/Sft	83	982	
74	8	WIND	6f Gd/Sft	79	1098	
57	13	WIND	6f Firm	76	1289	vis
74	2	BATH	5f Gd/Sft		1670	vis
66	7	CHEP	5f Gd/Sft	74	1795	vis
74	3	GOOD	5f Gd/Sft	74	1961	vis
74	4	NEWM	5f Gd/Fm	74	2288	vis
76	2	SAND	5f Aw	74	2478	vis
71	4	BATH	5f Firm	74	2787	vis
69	4	RIPO	6f Gd/Fm	74	3010	
74	5	LING	6f Firm	73	3280	vis
70	6	YORK	5f Gd/Fm	72	3569	bl
79	1	**GOOD**	5f Good	71	3908*	bl
77	5	NEWM	5f Good	78	4185	bl
79	3	YORK	5f Soft	78	4285	bl
85	1	**PONT**	5f Soft	79	4377+	bl
82	8	WIND	5f Heavy	86	4527	bl

JAMESTOWN 3 b c £3348

0	19	YORK	8f Firm	75	1341
72	4	LEIC	7f Firm	72	2026
56	6	HAYD	7f Gd/Fm		2704
70	1	**BEVE**	7f Gd/Fm		3671*
65	4	NEWM	7f Good		4018
47	8	PONT	8f Soft	70	4232
60	4	DONC	7f Soft		4461

JAMIE MY BOY 2 b g £327

57	4	GOOD	7f Good	3650
73	8	LING	7f Soft	4267
66	9	YARM	7f Soft	4514

JAMILA 2 b f £2750

0	14	NEWM	7f Aw	1691
77a	2	SOUT	6f Aw	1974
72	2	WARW	7f Gd/Fm	2251
64	9	NEWM	6f Good	2565
75a	2	WOLV	7f Aw	3497
0	15	REDC	6f Gd/Sft	4219 BL

JAMMAAL 3 b c £71775

104	2	THE	7f Soft	770	BL
104	2	LEOP	8f Gd/Fm	1316	
107	1	**CURR**	10f Gd/Sft	1627*	BL
104	2	CURR	9f Good	2410	bl
103	4	CURR	10f Gd/Sft	3068	bl
110	3	CURR	10f Good	3556	bl
110	1	**LEOP**	10f Heavy	4558*	bl

JAMMIE DODGER 4 b g £3544

28	10	MUSS	9f Gd/Sft	44	795
0	17	RIPO	12f Soft	44	822
23	9	PONT	10f Soft	37	1705
39	2	RIPO	8f Good		1858
26	10	RIPO	8f Gd/Fm	37	2099
40	1	**MUSS**	8f Gd/Sft	35	2533*
0	U	RIPO	8f Good		2834
35	11	RIPO	9f Gd/Fm	47	3011
60	6	CARL	8f Gd/Fm		3081
34	8	THIR	8f Gd/Fm	41	3344
30	15	YORK	9f Good		3808

JAMORIN DANCER 5 b g £1568

0a	12	SOUT	12f Aw	51	68
25a	8	SOUT	11f Aw	51	126
49a	1	**SOUT**	11f Aw	46	325*
39a	8	SOUT	12f Aw	52	370
30a	8	WOLV	12f Aw	48	410

JAMPET 4 b c £0

0	14	LEIC	7f Gd/Fm	2508	
0	12	SALI	10f Gd/Fm	2981	bl

JANE ANN 4 ch f £0

0	15	NEWM	14f Heavy	46	1023
0	R	CHEP	12f Gd/Fm	42	2971
0	9	YARM	14f Good	42	3233

JANET 3 b f £2951

74	1	**WIND**	10f Gd/Fm	2056*

JANETTE PARKES 3 ch f £0

44	4	CATT	7f Soft	1682

JANICELAND 3 b f £4208

62a	5	SOUT	5f Aw	34	
39a	4	SOUT	6f Aw	74	
66a	1	**WOLV**	5f Aw	120*	
55a	1	**LING**	6f Aw	443*	
30a	7	LING	5f Aw	487	VIS
25a	5	SOUT	6f Aw	559	
48a	5	LING	5f Aw	619	
62	3	YARM	6f Gd/Fm	60	3964
49a	3	WOLV	6f Aw	55	4444
52a	4	WOLV	6f Aw	54	4553

JANMO 2 ch f £0

41	10	NOTT	6f Good	1413

JARDINES LOOKOUT 3 b g £37367

82	5	SALI	12f Firm		1179
87	3	NOTT	14f Gd/Sft		1369
67	6	HAYD	14f Soft		1824
84	2	REDC	14f Gd/Fm		2144
92	1	**SALI**	14f Good		2691*
93	2	GOOD	14f Gd/Fm	90	3058
102	D	YORK	14f Firm	92	3599
105	1	**NEWM**	14f Good	100	4016+
102	5	NEWM	16f Good		4351
107	1	**DONC**	15f Heavy		4568*

JARN 3 b c £11618

106	1	**NEWB**	6f Good	1371*	t
94	8	NEWM	7f Gd/Fm	1693	t
104	2	YARM	7f Firm	2389	t
97	6	EPSO	7f Good	3763	t

JARV 2 b f £1138

0	16	WIND	5f Gd/Sft		1424
58	7	SALI	6f Gd/Fm		1883
41	10	WARW	7f Good		2459
62	2	BRIG	7f Soft	56	4416
54	4	BRIG	8f Heavy	56	4538

JASEUR 7 b g £1942

62	9	ASCO	16f Gd/Sft		1109	BL
82	7	HAYD	16f Gd/Sft	92	1791	vis
75	7	YORK	14f Gd/Fm	92	1982	vis
73	6	WARW	16f Gd/Fm	80	2256	vis
48	10	HAYD	14f Gd/Fm	75	3323	vis
72	2	CHES	16f Gd/Fm	70	3511	bl
69	4	CHES	16f Soft	70	4071	bl
59	5	DONC	17f Heavy	69	4579	

JASMICK 2 ch f £0

58	7	BATH	5f Firm	1993

JATHAAB 3 b c £0

81	5	DONC	10f Gd/Fm	79	701
70	8	WIND	12f Gd/Fm	80	1199

JATHAABEH 3 ch f £22600

90	1	**NEWM**	8f Gd/Fm		1692*
62	18	ASCO	7f Good		2087
94	1	**NEWM**	8f Gd/Fm	89	2858*
80	18	NEWM	9f Gd/Fm	93	4212

JATO DANCER 5 b m £233

0a	11	SOUT	7f Aw		130
9a	9	WOLV	7f Aw		142
0a	13	SOUT	11f Aw		178
25a	5	WOLV	9f Aw	33	359
16a	7	WOLV	9f Aw	35	404
0a	11	SOUT	8f Aw		452
7a	8	WOLV	9f Aw		517
14a	7	WOLV	12f Aw		581
15a	5	WOLV	8f Aw	22	676
43	4	THIR	12f Gd/Sft		1353
16a	9	SOUT	11f Aw		1415
49	6	HAYD	12f Gd/Sft		1788
0a	9	SOUT	11f Aw		2381
12	8	CATT	7f Gd/Fm	25	2932
34	6	CATT	12f Gd/Fm		3202

JAVA SHRINE 9 b g £2841

76a	3	LING	10f Aw	73	23	bl
74a	2	LING	10f Aw	73	90	bl
48a	6	LING	10f Aw	73	160	bl
59a	7	WOLV	9f Aw	73	230	bl
63a	1	**WOLV**	12f Aw		307*	bl
36a	6	WOLV	12f Aw		347	bl

JAVELIN 4 ch g £0

58a	5	WOLV	8f Aw		658
59a	4	WOLV	9f Aw		720
0	13	LEIC	10f Gd/Sft		833
34	6	SAND	8f Heavy	59	1058
16	12	NOTT	8f Good	55	1414
0a	11	WOLV	8f Aw	51	4021

JAWAH 6 br g £0

68	8	KEMP	16f Soft	78	1527	
0	12	CHEP	18f Gd/Sft	75	1800	vis
51	7	KEMP	14f Gd/Fm		1928	
0	8	GOOD	20f Gd/Fm	65	3085	

JAWHARI 6 b g £2808

56a	7	WOLV	5f Aw	63	491
69a	1	**WOLV**	5f Aw	63	518*
52a	7	WOLV	5f Aw	66	564
47	9	NEWC	5f Soft	64	758

JAWLA 3 ch f £13412

80	3	CHES	7f Gd/Fm		1224
84	2	GOOD	7f Gd/Sft		1468
80	1	**CATT**	7f Gd/Sft		2745*
84	1	**DONC**	8f Gd/Fm	80	3160*
71	12	WIND	8f Good	84	3643
79	5	GOOD	7f Soft	83	4080
94	1	**YARM**	8f Heavy	83	4478*

JAWRJIK 2 b c £0

0	11	PONT	8f Soft	4086
0	19	YORK	8f Soft	4281

JAY AND A 5 br m £0

66	10	DONC	8f Good	79	716

JAY DEES GIRL 3 ch f £0

0a	11	WOLV	9f Aw	3498

JAY OWE TWO 6 b g £0

0	13	RIPO	8f Good	1858

JAYCAT 2 ch f £0

40	13	NEWB	6f Stt/Hvy	4470
54	10	DONC	6f Heavy	4576

JAYNES PRINCESS 3 b f £0

26	8	BATH	8f Gd/Fm	1435

JAYPEECEE 4 b g £0

28	10	HAMI	6f Good	64	844	
29	9	REDC	7f Gd/Sft		1132	
43	9	THIR	7f Gd/Sft		1351	
48	4	LEIC	6f Gd/Sft	48	1734	VIS
46	5	CARL	6f Gd/Fm		2240	vis
41	8	DONC	7f Gd/Fm	48	2612	vis
0	16	HAMI	6f Gd/Sft	46	3377	vis

JAZZ NIGHT 3 b g £0

34	8	REDC	9f Firm	3326	
22a	5	WOLV	7f Aw	4361	BL

JAZZ TRACK 6 b g £0

47a	6	WOLV	16f Aw	65	552	bl
20a	9	SOUT	16f Aw	60	737	t
16	10	PONT	17f Soft	50	876	tbl

JAZZNIC 4 b f £2743

16a	5	WOLV	7f Aw		173	
46a	6	LING	7f Aw		421	
10a	10	LING	8f Aw		505	
59a	1	**LING**	5f Aw		883*	
0a	11	WOLV	6f Aw		1137	
6	11	NEWC	5f Heavy		1766	
0	19	BATH	6f Firm	50	1994	VIS

JAZZY MILLENNIUM 3 ch c £507

74	8	SALI	6f Firm	1181

JEANNIES GIRL 2 b f £0 — *(continued)*

71 3 LING 6f Good 1399
66 5 GOOD 8f Gd/Fm 1960
44 11 KEMP 7f Gd/Fm 70 3076
0 19 KEMP 8f Soft 67 4038
0 14 NOTT 8f Heavy 63 4414

JEANNIES GIRL 2 b f £0
23 11 CHES 5f Firm 1249
24 9 BEVE 5f Good 1443
20 7 YARM 6f Firm 2388 BL
54 8 HAYD 6f Gd/Fm 2454
0 12 CATT 7f Good 3438
0 13 LEIC 8f Firm 40 3837 bl

JEDEYDD 3 b g £0
65 8 YARM 11f Heavy 4481

JEDI KNIGHT 6 b g £2610
0 18 THIR 8f Good 88 1160
89 2 YORK 9f Firm 86 2001
62 18 YORK 10f Good 89 2696

JEED 3 b f £533
91 8 LING 7f Gd/Sft 1283
84 4 NEWM 6f Gd/Fm 2289

JEFFREY ANOTHERRED 6 b g £3635
0 18 THIR 8f Good 76 1383
0 21 DONC 7f Gd/Fm 75 1840
0 18 YORK 8f Firm 73 2000
66 6 AYR 7f Good 70 2163
39 18 YORK 7f Good 69 2694
67 4 CHES 8f Firm 66 3170
67 2 NEWC 7f Soft 66 3708
53 11 YORK 7f Good 66 3809
63 4 MUSS 7f Gd/Sft 66 4136
62 4 YARM 7f Soft 66 4513
59 6 MUSS 8f Soft 66 4565

JELBA 2 b f £1185
23 5 PONT 6f Soft 1700
84 3 NEWM 6f Gd/Fm 2132
87 5 NEWM 6f Firm 2344
55 12 DONC 8f Gd/Fm 3876
84 5 YARM 8f Good 3938
85 4 NEWM 6f Gd/Fm 4209

JELLYBEEN 4 ch f £0
25a 9 LING 13f Aw 54 460

JEMIMA 3 b f £2737
95 9 NEWM 7f Good 953
93 19 NEWM 6f Gd/Fm 104 1694
87 13 YORK 6f Firm 102 2003
86 11 DONC 5f Gd/Fm 99 2348
91 6 NEWM 6f Gd/Fm 96 2568
88 9 NEWM 6f Gd/Fm 3120
99 3 PONT 6f Firm 3503 BL
94 6 YORK 7f Firm 3600 bl

JEMINAR 3 b f £0
0 11 CATT 6f Soft 4255
0 19 NEWC 5f Heavy 48 4407

JENIN 3 b f £0
0 20 NOTT 6f Firm 1266
9 10 WARW 7f Gd/Fm 37 2036
0 13 MUSS 5f Firm 30 2374

JENKO 3 b g £0
0 17 LEIC 7f Firm 53 2026
0 13 LING 7f Good 46 2591 BL
13 14 NEWM 10f Good 3021

JENNASH 2 b f £0
0 13 NEWM 7f Good 4184
0 11 YARM 8f Heavy 4477

JENNELLE 6 b m £0
62a 6 SOUT 6f Aw 70 47 e

JENNIFER JENKINS 2 b f £0
0 14 BATH 8f Soft 4430

JENNY WEST 3 ch f £0
0a 12 SOUT 6f Aw 74
0a 15 SOUT 6f Aw 127

0a 12 SOUT 6f Aw 426

JENSENS TALE 3 b c £0
38 7 LEIC 6f Gd/Sft 830
0 13 LEIC 8f Gd/Sft 1572
0 16 LEIC 6f Gd/Sft 46 1734 BL
16 9 WARW 11f Gd/Fm 2253
0 12 LEIC 8f Gd/Sft 2914
20 7 YARM 8f Good 31 3236
0 12 BEVE 10f Gd/Sft 28 3656

JENTZEN 2 b c £4117
90 4 ASCO 6f Gd/Fm 3000
92 1 SALI 6f Gd/Fm 3387*

JEPAJE 3 b g £1106
56a 4 LING 6f Aw 62 105
41a 7 WOLV 6f Aw 118
35 9 CARL 6f Gd/Sft 1723
0 14 HAYD 7f Gd/Sft 60 1793
42 11 BATH 6f Firm 55 1994 BL
35a 6 WOLV 6f Aw 53 2603 bl
51 4 HAMI 6f Gd/Fm 50 2779 bl
47 4 HAMI 8f Gd/Fm 50 2798 bl
47 5 MUSS 7f Good 50 3103 bl
30 8 CARL 6f Aw 50 3194 bl
57 2 AYR 7f Good 3364
59 5 HAYD 7f Soft 4093

JESSINCA 4 b f £10073
40a 3 SOUT 8f Aw 46 430
52a 1 SOUT 8f Aw 44 513*
36a 5 SOUT 7f Aw 50 588
53a 1 WOLV 8f Aw 48 675*
29a 10 SOUT 8f Aw 54 692
28 8 WOLV 9f Aw 51 749
34 7 WIND 10f Gd/Sft 40 1100
44 1 BRIG 8f Soft 38 1511*
39 4 BATH 10f Gd/Sft 43 1666
44 2 YARM 8f Firm 43 2767
47 2 NEWM 8f Gd/Fm 45 3317
0 11 BATH 10f Firm 47 3623
34 8 SALI 8f Aw 47 3753

JETHAME 2 ch f £3312
57 7 GOOD 5f Gd/Sft 1454
67 7 BATH 6f Gd/Sft 1667
70 3 WIND 5f Soft 2545
70 5 NEWB 7f Firm 2810
69 3 YARM 7f Good 3029
68 3 WIND 6f Good 69 3354
64 2 NEWM 7f Good 4336 BL
24 14 DONC 7f Heavy 65 4577 bl

JETSTREAM FLYER 2 b f £0
0 12 LING 10f Good 4189

JEUNE PREMIER 3 ch c £0
70 5 WIND 10f Heavy 936
0 14 KEMP 11f Soft 1017
54 10 WIND 12f Gd/Sft 68 1425
57 5 SAND 10f Soft 68 1585
34 10 SAND 11f Good 62 1967
45 10 WIND 12f Gd/Fm 62 2210
0 12 BEVE 16f Good 56 2879
35 10 BEVE 12f Gd/Sft 56 3050 BL
9 6 YARM 10f Firm 3935 VIS

JEWEL FIGHTER 6 br m £0
19 8 LING 10f Firm 3490
7a 5 SOUT 11f Aw 4151
21 10 SALI 10f Firm 38 4169

JEWELLERY BOX 2 b f £0
51 5 WARW 5f Soft 1059
0a 12 SOUT 5f Aw 1304
18 5 LEIC 5f Soft 1549
2 6 MUSS 5f Firm 1684

JEZADIL 2 b f £4786
25 7 NEWC 6f Gd/Sft 1476
51 6 PONT 5f Soft 1704

61 4 HAMI 6f Gd/Fm 2778
59 4 THIR 7f Gd/Fm 3128
57 3 NEWC 8f Soft 3706
50 4 AYR 8f Soft 3957
49 11 WIND 10f Gd/Sft 56 4290
63a 1 WOLV 8f Aw 4362*
67a 1 WOLV 8f Aw 59 4552*

JEZEBEL 3 b f £16764
101 2 KEMP 6f Gd/Sft 1078
97 5 NOTT 6f Good 1410
101 3 YORK 8f Good 2646
100 2 NEWM 6f Gd/Sft 3120
100 2 PONT 8f Firm 3503
105 3 CHAN 6f Good 4052

JIBEREEN 8 b g £3876
41a 8 SOUT 8f Aw 197
0a 15 SOUT 8f Aw 76 251
62a 4 SOUT 11f Aw 73 343
70a 2 SOUT 12f Aw 70 456
56a 7 SOUT 11f Aw 70 512
48a 4 WOLV 12f Aw 530
66a 3 SOUT 8f Aw 68 647
59a 1 SOUT 11f Aw 866*
30a 9 SOUT 12f Aw 1203
50 8 NEWM 8f Gd/Fm 50 1690
44 8 NEWM 8f Gd/Fm 50 2130
47a 4 SOUT 8f Aw 2816
27a 8 SOUT 11f Aw 4151

JIEMCE 3 b g £0
0 12 EPSO 9f Good 55 3856

JILA 5 ch h £1747
109e 3 NAD 8f Dirt 666

JIM AND TONIC 6 ch g £686072
115 9 GULF 8f Good 16
126 1 SHA 10f Gd/Fm 186*
121 2 KRAN 10f Firm 657

JIMAL 3 b c £0
0 15 KEMP 8f Gd/Sft 1080
69 5 WIND 8f Gd/Fm 2211
65 6 KEMP 7f Gd/Sft 2585

JIMGAREEN 3 br f £0
30 7 AYR 9f Gd/Fm 1632
60 6 HAMI 9f Gd/Fm 62 1939
44 4 HAMI 8f Firm 2093
39 5 NEWC 9f Gd/Fm 60 2276 BL
0 10 HAMI 11f Gd/Fm 56 2638 bl
0 15 HAMI 9f Gd/Fm 56 2799
20 6 AYR 11f Gd/Fm 50 3140

JIMMY SWIFT 5 b g £0
39 4 WARW 11f Heavy 1523
33 7 WIND 12f Gd/Fm 1880

JINAAN 2 ch f £0
78 6 KEMP 6f Gd/Fm 3795

JO MELL 7 b g £18620
0a 12 SOUT 7f Aw 88 687
90 1 BEVE 7f Heavy 977*
84 10 ASCO 7f Gd/Sft 92 1110
97 1 BEVE 8f Soft 91 1445*
98 2 SAND 8f Soft 94 1567
66 18 ASCO 8f Good 96 2090
63 10 NEWC 7f Firm 96 2338

JOCKO GLASSES 3 ch c £8446
54 10 NOTT 6f Firm 1266
70 5 WIND 10f Good 1725
75 1 PONT 10f Firm 67 2175*
84 1 WARW 11f Gd/Fm 74 2842*

JODEEKA 3 ch f £2899
60 5 PONT 6f Soft 877
76 1 DONC 5f Good 1516*
59 5 WIND 5f Firm 1881
69 7 NEWM 5f Gd/Fm 74 2288

JOE TAYLOR 2 b c £0

51	11	SAND	5f Gd/Fm		3942

JOEBERTEDY 3 b c £0

0	18	WARW	8f Heavy		884
0	14	PONT	6f Gd/Sft		1105
0	12	PONT	6f Good		1500
0a	11	SOUT	6f Aw		2947

JOELY GREEN 3 b c £7628

69a	1	WOLV	7f Aw		41*	
16a	14	SOUT	8f Aw	68	128	
67a	2	LING	8f Aw	68	266	
64a	3	WOLV	8f Aw	68	294	
54a	4	LING	8f Aw	68	401	
58a	5	LING	10f Aw		420	vis
51a	8	WOLV	7f Aw	65	1390	
0	18	WIND	8f Good	62	1726	
57	7	SAND	11f Good	62	1967	
41	9	PONT	10f Firm	57	2175	
61	1	LING	11f Firm	57	2321*	BL
53	6	CHEP	16f Gd/Fm	61	2659	bl

JOEY TRIBBIANI 3 b c £0

0	21	NEWM	7f Good	71	954
0	26	NEWM	8f Firm	67	1183
39	12	BRIG	10f Gd/Sft	62	1509
54	10	YARM	11f Heavy		4481

JOHAYRO 7 b g £7936

0	18	DONC	6f Good	65	716	
61	4	MUSS	5f Gd/Sft	65	798	
37	11	THIR	7f Soft	63	908	
60	5	MUSS	7f Gd/Fm	61	1149	
44	12	HAMI	6f Gd/Fm	61	1192	
0	22	THIR	6f Gd/Sft	60	1356	
58	7	MUSS	7f Gd/Fm	60	1431	vis
45	8	AYR	5f Gd/Fm	58	1629	
48	10	MUSS	5f Firm	58	1687	vis
56	2	HAMI	6f Firm	55	2097	
43	4	HAMI	5f Gd/Fm	55	2233	
55	3	HAMI	5f Firm	55	2395	
42	13	HAYD	5f Gd/Fm	56	2444	
36	13	HAMI	6f Gd/Fm	56	2641	
49	7	AYR	5f Gd/Fm	56	2721	bl
58	1	REDC	6f Firm	53	3312*	
58	2	MUSS	5f Gd/Fm	56	3594	
58	2	THIR	5f Gd/Fm	56	3619	
0	25	AYR	6f Heavy	58	4327	
0	12	MUSS	5f Soft	58	4516	

JOHN BOWDLER MUSIC 5 b g £436

65a	2	SOUT	6f Aw		201

JOHN COMPANY 3 ch c £1082

52a	5	WOLV	6f Aw		118	t
25a	7	WOLV	7f Aw	64	294	t
54a	3	SOUT	6f Aw	58	365	tVI
57a	2	LING	7f Aw		459	tvi

JOHN FERNELEY 5 b g £83726

95a	3	WOLV	8f Aw	90	663	
99	1	DONC	8f Good	90	733*	
104	2	ASCO	8f Good	95	2090	
104	4	GOOD	8f Good	101	3107	
101	4	YORK	8f Firm	102	3597	bl
103	3	NEWM	8f Good	100	4348	

JOHN FOLEY 2 b c £2564

67	8	WARW	5f Soft		812	
54	9	THIR	5f Soft		928	
67a	2	WOLV	5f Aw		1136	
58a	5	SOUT	5f Aw		1302	
67a	2	LING	6f Aw		1740	
61a	4	WOLV	6f Aw		2077	
58a	2	SOUT	7f Aw		2301	
62	2	WARW	6f Firm		2388	VIS
45	6	BATH	5f Gd/Sft		2551	BL

JOHN OGROATS 2 b c £275

57	4	NEWC	7f Gd/Fm		2271

JOHN STEED 3 b g £222

36	11	SALI	8f Gd/Fm	52	2264	
44	4	BATH	12f Gd/Sft	49	2554	
35	13	GOOD	10f Good	47	3663	
29	10	BATH	10f Good	47	3816	
20	10	BRIG	10f Soft	44	4419	
39	6	WIND	10f Heavy		4528	

JOHNNIE THE JOKER 9 gr g £0

8a	10	SOUT	12f Aw	48		70	bl

JOHNNY OSCAR 3 b g £1558

73	4	SAND	10f Gd/Fm		1992	
75	3	GOOD	10f Good		2308	
78	3	DONC	12f Gd/Fm		2609	
60	10	HAYD	14f Gd/Sft	77	4105	

JOHNNY REB 2 b c £2772

81	2	WIND	5f Gd/Sft		1426	
82	6	NEWM	6f Gd/Fm		1691	
65	9	ASCO	5f Good		2152	
77	5	EPSO	6f Good	83	3761	t
0	17	NEWM	6f Good	79	4338	t
37	13	DONC	7f Heavy	77	4577	t

JOHNNY STACCATO 6 b g £0

0	14	HAMI	6f Firm		1239	
0	18	WIND	6f Firm		1423	
21	10	BRIG	6f Gd/Sft		1508	
0	15	CARL	6f Gd/Fm		2240	VIS
24	7	BATH	6f Gd/Sft	28	2555	vis
6	12	HAYD	6f Gd/Fm		3283	

JOHNS CALL 9 ch h £274390

121	1	BELM	12f Firm		4316*

JOHNSONS POINT 2 ch f £5992

81	2	KEMP	7f Gd/Fm		3074
81	1	EPSO	7f Gd/Fm		3412*
60	8	EPSO	7f Good	82	3690
79	4	DONC	8f Gd/Sft	80	4450

JOHNSTONS DIAMOND 2 b g £266

61	4	AYR	5f Firm		3137
65	8	CARL	5f Firm		3571
50	6	CHES	7f Soft		4068

JOHNSTONS FANFAN 4 b g £0

0	16	THIR	8f Gd/Sft		3775

JOHS BROTHER 4 ch c £0

0	14	MUSS	5f Gd/Sft	31	2535
14	12	HAMI	6f Gd/Fm		2798
0	23	REDC	7f Gd/Fm		2994
0	19	RIPO	5f Gd/Fm	28	3180

JOIN THE PARADE 4 b f £1200

30a	10	LING	12f Aw	58	115
51	7	WARW	11f Gd/Fm	58	2033
56	3	YARM	10f Firm	56	2387
54	8	KEMP	12f Firm	57	2872
58	2	YARM	10f Good	56	3031
43	9	NEWM	10f Gd/Fm	60	3314
41	9	BRIG	10f Firm	60	3557
49	7	SAND	14f Gd/Fm	58	3948

JOINT INSTRUCTION 2 b c £12264

72	4	WARW	5f Heavy		1001
70	5	BATH	5f Good		1088
75	2	CARL	5f Firm		1252
77	1	BRIG	6f Gd/Sft		1507*
73	5	YARM	6f Gd/Fm		1612
70	2	YORK	6f Gd/Fm		1981
48	8	NEWC	6f Good		2312
70	2	CHEP	6f Gd/Fm		2447
53	12	NEWM	7f Gd/Fm		2599
70	1	WARW	15f Good	65	3693*
77	1	HAMI	6f Gd/Sft	71	3824*
69	7	CATT	7f Soft	75	4007
16	12	AYR	6f Heavy	75	4305
69	7	NEWB	6f Sft/Hvy	73	4468

JOKEL 5 ch m £0

0a	13	WOLV	6f Aw		680

JOLI ECLIPSE 3 b f £0

0	15	WIND	8f Gd/Fm		3048
0	14	BATH	12f Gd/Fm		3818
0	8	PONT	8f Soft		4234

JOLI FLYERS 6 gr g £2530

21	10	FOLK	15f Soft	44	963
0	19	WIND	10f Gd/Sft	41	1100
38	1	LEIC	12f Soft	37	1551*
0	11	SALI	12f Gd/Fm	42	1888

JOLI SADDLERS 4 b f £0

38	8	WIND	12f Good	52	853	
36	10	NOTT	14f Gd/Sft	48	1087	
21	15	LING	16f Good	44	1394	BL
26	9	EPSO	12f Gd/Sft	38	2429	VIS

JOLLANDS 2 b c £321

45	8	LING	6f Firm		2760
74	3	SALI	7f Gd/Fm		3388
0	17	LEIC	7f Firm		3840

JOLLY SHARP 3 ch c £4387

95	1	KEMP	11f Soft		1017*
99	6	CHES	12f Gd/Fm		1216
78	6	DONC	16f Heavy		4568

JONA HOLLEY 7 b g £0

0	17	HAMI	9f Good	51	846	bl
41	6	PONT	8f Heavy		942	bl

JONATHANS GIRL 5 b m £208

29a	5	LING	6f Aw	39	358
16a	7	LING	7f Aw	35	438
51a	4	LING	5f Aw		507
14a	12	WOLV	6f Aw		680
27a	4	WOLV	5f Aw		1036
0	17	WIND	6f Gd/Fm	45	1196
25	10	LING	7f Good	42	1672
32	9	SALI	5f Firm	48	2022
20	6	SALI	5f Good	31	2230
26	8	LING	6f Good	36	2654
0	13	BRIG	7f Gd/Fm	30	2728

JONLOZ 3 ch c £3215

40a	4	SOUT	7f Aw	49	128	
0a	12	SOUT	8f Aw		198	
11a	5	SOUT	8f Aw	43	451	
18a	4	SOUT	7f Aw		541	
41	5	NOTT	8f Good		783	
58	6	PONT	10f Soft		873	
21	6	PONT	12f Heavy		939	
28	8	BEVE	8f Firm	40	2735	
44	1	BEVE	12f Gd/Sft	37	3050*	
50	2	RIPO	12f Gd/Fm		3181	
0	11	PONT	12f Soft	50	4229	

JOONDEY 3 b c £6476

0	18	NEWM	8f Firm		1188
78	3	CHEP	8f Heavy		1556
78	2	WIND	10f Good		1725
76	5	SAND	10f Good		2531
78	2	RIPO	9f Good		2838
80a	1	WOLV	9f Aw		3272*
81a	2	WOLV	9f Aw	80	3495

JOPLIN 2 ch c £0

91	6	YORK	5f Good		3567
93	6	DONC	5f Firm		3900
94	8	NEWM	6f Good		4181

JORDANS RIDGE 4 b g £642

41	7	AYR	15f Good	49	3367
50	2	CARL	17f Firm	49	3575

JORROCKS 6 b g £1392

64	2	BEVE	7f Good	59	2882
58	6	NEWC	7f Gd/Fm	59	2986
56	7	YORK	7f Good	63	3809
12	17	YORK	9f Heavy	62	4300
0	11	NEWC	7f Soft	59	4428

JOSEPH VERNET 3 b g £0

60	6	PONT	10f Gd/Fm		2832
0	17	PONT	10f Soft	63	4374

JOSH MOR 2 b g £550
| 55 | 3 | NEWM | 8f Soft | | 4542 |

JOSR ALGARHOUD 4 b c £21134
| 116 | 1 | LONG | 7f Good | | 2226* |
| 112 | 8 | GOOD | 8f Gd/Fm | | 3087 |

JOURNALIST 3 b f £0
| 75 | 6 | YARM | 7f Firm | | 2769 |

JOYRENA 3 ch f £0
| 0a | 11 | WOLV | 8f Aw | | 80 |

JUBILEE SCHOLAR 7 b g £0
18a	10	LING	10f Aw	54	100	bl
0a	P	LING	10f Aw	49	209	bl
0a	10	LING	10f Aw		375	bl
0a	12	LING	10f Aw	43	618	bl

JUDIAM 3 b f £4641
65a	4	LING	5f Aw	74	652
55	5	FOLK	5f Soft		959
55	11	CHES	5f Gd/Fm	71	1219
61	8	WIND	5f Gd/Sft	68	1427
0	13	REDC	6f Good	66	1891
60	5	NEWM	5f Gd/Fm	64	2288
65	1	KEMP	5f Gd/Sft	62	2586*
54	8	SAND	5f Good	67	2934
54	9	NEWM	5f Good	67	3631
54	15	GOOD	5f Soft	66	4065
0	26	NEWM	5f Good	66	4185

JUDICIOUS 3 b c £9077
59	8	WIND	10f Heavy		936
70	3	PONT	10f Good	68	1866
51	8	DONC	10f Gd/Fm	70	2610
76	1	LEIC	8f Gd/Fm	70	3095*
67	6	LING	8f Firm	76	3580
80	2	PONT	8f Soft	76	4232
79	2	NEWM	8f Good	76	4340

JULIA TITUS 3 ch f £0
58	8	WIND	8f Gd/Fm		3048
0	16	CATT	12f Soft	60	4043
0	19	NEWM	10f Good	56	4160

JULIES GIFT 3 ch f £0
| 15 | 8 | BEVE | 10f Gd/Fm | | 3672 |
| 0 | 14 | YORK | 10f Good | | 3813 |

JULIES JEWEL 5 ch g £0
| 0a | P | SOUT | 8f Aw | 52 | 176 |

JULIUS 3 b f £27245
67	1	NOTT	10f Good		1875*
75	2	YARM	10f Gd/Fm	70	1955
80	1	MUSS	12f Gd/Fm	70	2048*
80	1	RIPO	10f Gd/Fm		2111*
88	1	CHES	12f Gd/Fm	80	2246*
82	1	NEWC	10f Gd/Fm		2314*
89	7	ASCO	12f Good	87	2674
87	4	NEWM	10f Good	87	3024
74	10	YORK	10f Good	87	3563
86	5	YARM	10f Firm	86	3941
90	1	NEWM	10f Good	85	4160*
57	7	YORK	12f Soft		4276

JUMAIREYAH 2 b f f £4166
| 80 | 1 | WIND | 8f Heavy | | 4524* |

JUMBO JET 3 b c £207
75	4	LING	7f Gd/Sft		840
79	8	NEWM	8f Gd/Sft		983	t
68	5	WIND	8f Gd/Sft		1099	t
36	5	RIPO	10f Gd/Fm		2105	t
0	11	WIND	6f Gd/Fm	73	2885

JUMBOS FLYER 3 ch c £2772
13a	8	WOLV	8f Aw	63	613
59	5	CARL	8f Firm	60	1255
61	2	MUSS	9f Gd/Fm	60	1434
60	4	CARL	9f Gd/Fm	61	1722
50	6	HAMI	8f Gd/Fm		1940
62	2	CARL	8f Firm	59	2281
54	8	NEWC	8f Good	61	2524

49	9	BEVE	7f Firm	61	2733
54	3	THIR	12f Gd/Fm	61	2967
46	7	CARL	8f Gd/Fm	60	3082

JUMP 3 b c £876
63a	2	SOUT	8f Aw		328
47a	6	LING	8f Aw		373
35	12	BRIG	10f Gd/Fm	62	892
41a	9	WOLV	9f Aw	60	1040
52	4	MUSS	8f Gd/Fm	57	1434
38a	7	SOUT	8f Aw		1804
15	7	BRIG	12f Gd/Fm	55	1935
0	16	BATH	8f Firm	48	2331	BL
4	13	LEIC	10f Gd/Fm	44	3217

JUNGLE LION 2 ch c £3331
| 99 | 1 | DONC | 7f Heavy | | 4566* | t |

JUNGLE MOON 2 b f £0
| 0 | 10 | CURR | 7f Gd/Fm | | 3845 |

JUNIKAY 6 b g £20497
37	11	WARW	11f Heavy	55	890
52	2	BRIG	9f Gd/Fm	51	1129
60	1	NOTT	10f Gd/Fm	51	1272*
64	1	LING	9f Good	57	1395*
63	3	LING	11f Good	62	1743
66	2	KEMP	9f Gd/Fm	61	2085
60	8	SAND	10f Gd/Fm	66	2527
66	4	EPSO	10f Good	66	2790
73	1	GOOD	9f Good	65	3110*
68	4	SAND	10f Good	72	3471
70	3	EPSO	9f Good	72	3685
71	10	NEWB	10f Firm	73	3997

JUNIOR BRIEF 2 b g £0
0	15	NEWB	10f Gd/Fm		1943
31a	10	SOUT	7f Aw		2383
30a	7	SOUT	6f Aw		2635
45	8	CHES	7f Firm		3169	BL
45	9	BATH	5f Gd/Fm		3513
0	15	CURR	6f Yldg		3720	bl
49	7	NEWM	7f Good		4336
36	10	NOTT	8f Heavy		4507

JUNIPER 2 b c £13750
| 106 | 3 | YORK | 6f Gd/Fm | | 3566 |

JUNO BEACH 4 ch f £949
69	3	CHES	12f Gd/Fm		3429
74	4	BATH	12f Gd/Fm		3818
33a	7	LING	13f AW		4193

JUNO MARLOWE 4 b f £2420
61	16	KEMP	8f Gd/Sft	96	1077
90	7	YORK	8f Firm	95	1327
72	8	EPSO	9f Gd/Sft		1825
95	2	NEWM	7f Gd/Fm	94	2133
92	12	NEWM	7f Gd/Fm	95	2616
0	19	ASCO	7f Gd/Fm	95	2997
81	9	RIPO	6f Gd/Fm	94	3183

JUST A STROLL 5 ch g £0
0a	10	WOLV	9f Aw		259	VIS
0a	10	WOLV	16f Aw	25	492
0	13	CHEP	8f Gd/Fm	27	3251

JUST AS YOU ARE 2 b f £0
59	9	RIPO	5f Soft		2539	t
62	7	DONC	5f Gd/Fm		2756
45	9	HAYD	6f Gd/Sft		3268	BL
38	10	HAMI	5f Soft	57	3802	tbl

JUST BREMNER 3 b c £0
63a	4	SOUT	8f Aw	62	125
41	10	RIPO	8f Soft	62	2542
29	11	PONT	8f Gd/Fm	59	3226

JUST DISSIDENT 8 b g £366
43a	11	LING	7f Aw	57	28
56a	4	LING	7f Aw	57	91
52a	4	LING	7f Aw	57	107
53a	4	LING	6f Aw	57	148
51a	5	LING	5f Aw	57	166

54a	4	LING	5f Aw	55	371
37a	7	SOUT	6f Aw		414
35a	8	WOLV	5f Aw	54	609
0	17	REDC	6f Firm		1298
49	5	MUSS	5f Gd/Fm		1430
35	5	BATH	6f Gd/Fm	40	1994
35	10	CARL	6f Gd/Fm		2240
0	12	MUSS	5f Gd/Sft	38	2535
44	4	CATT	6f Gd/Fm		2744
50	5	CATT	5f Gd/Fm		2931

JUST FOR YOU 4 b c £0
34a	8	WOLV	8f Aw		39
34a	6	WOLV	6f Aw		273
0a	6	WOLV	7f Aw		293

JUST FOR YOU JANE 4 b f £337
0	13	EPSO	6f Heavy	63	1028
0a	12	WOLV	6f Aw	55	1233	bl
43	9	CHEP	6f Good	53	1971	bl
34	4	FOLK	6f Gd/Fm		2291	bl
36	3	BRIG	7f Firm		2907
32	7	EPSO	9f Gd/Fm		3404
27	7	BRIG	8f Firm		3736

JUST GIFTED 4 b c £8023
70	2	PONT	12f Good	65	1499
0	8	THIR	12f Gd/Sft	68	1715
62	6	DONC	12f Gd/Fm	65	1839
67	2	NEWM	12f Gd/Fm	65	2131
67	2	NEWM	12f Gd/Fm	65	2286
68	2	SAND	11f Good	66	2530
64	7	CHES	12f Firm	68	3173
64	3	PONT	12f Firm	67	3504
57	6	YORK	14f Good	66	3811
61	4	YORK	12f Soft	64	4280
30	11	PONT	10f Soft	61	4374

JUST GOOD FRIENDS 3 b g £0
0	17	REDC	7f Gd/Sft		1132
0	19	REDC	8f Gd/Sft		1559
27	6	MUSS	7f Firm		2046
21	6	REDC	10f Gd/Fm		2143
0	12	RIPO	8f Gd/Fm		2834
0	13	THIR	8f Gd/Fm	28	2964	BL

JUST GRAND 6 b g £0
| 42 | 8 | SALI | 14f Gd/Fm | 74 | 2268 |

JUST IN TIME 5 b g £19501
97a	1	LING	10f Aw	88	546*
99a	4	LING	10f Aw		690
92	1	PONT	10f Soft		874*
92	4	NEWM	10f Gd/Fm	91	1170
80	9	EPSO	10f Good	91	1845
91	3	PONT	10f Firm		2178
72	14	SAND	10f Good	90	2475
94	5	GOOD	12f Gd/Fm	90	3134
87	7	ASCO	10f Gd/Fm	92	3339
90	4	YARM	10f Gd/Fm		3669
87	4	KEMP	12f Soft		4039

JUST LOUI 6 gr g £0
| 73a | 6 | LING | 7f Aw | 78 | 28 |
| 20a | 12 | WOLV | 7f Aw | 76 | 143 | vis |

JUST MAC 3 br c £370
69a	3	LING	6f Aw		221
37a	10	SOUT	7f Aw		278
51a	6	LING	6f Aw		334	BL
45a	7	SOUT	6f Aw		558
44	6	WARW	7f Soft		813
41	7	FOLK	5f Soft		959
36	9	NOTT	6f Gd/Fm	49	2187
28	7	YARM	7f Gd/Fm		2413

JUST MIDAS 2 b c £0
17a	8	WOLV	7f Aw		3497
69	12	WARW	7f Gd/Fm		3909
60	8	BRIG	7f Soft		4172

JUST MISSED 2 b c £500

51	7	PONT	5f Soft		1698	
36	12	YORK	6f Gd/Fm		1981	
52	5	THIR	7f Gd/Fm		3127	
0	13	RIPO	6f Gd/Fm		3466	
57	5	NEWC	8f Soft		3706	
53	3	AYR	8f Soft		3957	

JUST MURPHY 2 b g £806

65	6	CARL	5f Firm	1252	
64	9	CARL	5f Firm	3571	
68	3	YORK	6f Good	3814	

JUST NICK 6 b g £18685

61	3	GOOD	8f Gd/Sft	64	1473	
62	6	GOOD	7f Gd/Sft	64	1810	
61	5	NEWM	7f Gd/Fm	63	2133	
67	2	GOOD	8f Good	63	2303	
71	1	GOOD	8f Gd/Fm	62	2356*	
74	1	NEWB	8f Firm	68	2707*	
0	17	ASCO	8f Gd/Sft	73	4126	
68	9	NEWM	8f Soft	73	4545	

JUST ON THE MARKET 3 ch f £0

0	13	CATT	5f Gd/Sft	63	1817
37a	10	SOUT	5f Aw	63	1976
0a	15	SOUT	8f Aw	57	2379
0a	15	SOUT	5f Aw	57	2632

JUST THE JOB TOO 3 b g £2362

0a	13	SOUT	8f Aw		179
33a	8	SOUT	8f Aw		198
54a	6	SOUT	7f Aw		278
50a	4	LING	8f Aw	52	419
56a	1	SOUT	8f Aw	52	555*
45	12	RIPO	10f Soft	55	827
44	6	BEVE	7f Heavy	52	976
33a	8	SOUT	8f Aw	55	1804
12a	8	SOUT	11f Aw	52	2945

JUST TRY ME 6 b g £0

0	13	BRIG	8f Firm	2040	t

JUST WHATEVER 3 ch f £0

4	6	AYR	8f Gd/Fm	3139

JUST WIZ 4 b c £10740

80a	1	LING	10f Aw	73	23*	bl
80a	3	WOLV	9f Aw	77	119	bl
86a	1	LING	10f Aw	79	161*	bl
0a	11	LING	10f Aw	84	244	bl
68a	5	LING	10f Aw	84	442	bl
65a	5	LING	10f Aw	79	546	vis
58a	3	WOLV	8f Aw		750	bl
0	16	WARW	11f Heavy	60	889	bl
39	11	WIND	12f Gd/Sft		1096	bl
56	2	BRIG	10f Firm		1210	
52	2	BRIG	10f Firm		1331	
49	2	BRIG	10f Gd/Sft		1933	
72a	1	WOLV	9f Aw	66	4228*	

JUST WOODY 2 br c £1045

84	3	CHES	6f Gd/Fm	3507	
0	16	AYR	6f Soft	3958	

JUSTALORD 2 b g £7429

54	6	DONC	5f Good	730	
71a	1	LING	5f Aw	878*	
63	6	CHES	5f Good	1214	
73	1	THIR	5f Good	1381*	
77	5	BATH	5f Firm	1995	
68	2	FOLK	5f Gd/Fm	3038	
56	4	BRIG	5f Soft	4171	
65a	2	WOLV	5f Aw	4227	

JUSTELLA 2 b f £3412

60	6	BATH	5f Good	1088	
56	6	CHES	5f Firm	1249	
63	7	MUSS	5f Gd/Fm	1429	
72	1	GOOD	6f Gd/Sft	1634*	

JUSTINIA 2 b f £550

53	7	BRIG	5f Gd/Fm	1463	
67	3	DONC	7f Gd/Fm	2316	

66	5	YARM	7f Firm		2390
47	7	BEVE	7f Gd/Sft		3057
46	8	YARM	7f Firm	59	3922

JUVWWI 6 ch g £51429

80a	2	WOLV	5f Aw	75	64
85a	1	SOUT	6f Aw	79	129*
77a	5	SOUT	8f Aw	84	180
80a	3	SOUT	7f Aw	84	216
80a	3	WOLV	6f Aw	83	258
84a	3	WOLV	6f Aw	83	320
83a	5	LING	7f Aw	83	423
86a	3	WOLV	6f Aw	83	435
85a	2	LING	7f Aw	83	462
87a	2	WOLV	8f Aw	84	532
76a	8	WOLV	6f Aw	84	579
82a	6	WOLV	6f Aw	84	660
84	11	KEMP	6f Good	77	728
84	1	WIND	6f Gd/Fm	77	746*
77	5	RIPO	6f Soft	82	824
94	1	THIR	5f Soft	82	926*
84	4	PONT	6f Heavy	88	941
91	4	YORK	5f Firm	90	1324
97	1	YORK	6f Firm	90	1337*
96	5	THIR	6f Good	96	1383
83	8	EPSO	6f Good	96	1851
90	5	YORK	6f Gd/Fm	96	1983
84	10	ASCO	6f Good	96	2151
79	13	NEWC	6f Firm	96	2334
92	7	DONC	5f Gd/Fm	95	2348
90	7	CHEP	5f Gd/Fm	95	2451
83	9	NEWB	6f Firm	94	2813
90	7	ASCO	6f Gd/Fm	94	2954
70	20	GOOD	6f Firm	94	3152
86	7	RIPO	6f Gd/Fm	92	3183
77	13	AYR	6f Gd/Sft	90	4012
79	13	ASCO	5f Gd/Sft	90	4129
88	4	SALI	6f Gd/Sft	88	4165
61	13	YORK	6f Heavy	86	4301
32	13	NEWC	6f Heavy	86	4405
85	5	WIND	5f Heavy	86	4527
77	11	DONC	7f Heavy	84	4574

K ACE THE JOINT 3 ch g £286

0a	16	SOUT	8f Aw		36	BL
32a	11	WOLV	7f Aw		192	
15a	9	SOUT	7f Aw		281	
40a	6	WOLV	5f Aw		659	
53	3	NOTT	6f Gd/Sft		1081	
33	11	NOTT	8f Gd/Sft	53	1365	

KABOOL 5 b g £144508

116	4	SHA	10f Gd/Fm	186	
110	4	NAD	9f Good	768	
112	4	LONG	11f Heavy	1115	
107	3	DEAU	10f Good	3370	
118	1	LONG	8f Good	4259*	
85	9	NEWM	7f Good	4352	

KACHINA DOLL 2 br f £22984

73	3	DONC	5f Good	730	
71	7	WARW	5f Soft	812	
51	8	NEWC	5f Heavy	1006	
83	1	WIND	5f Gd/Fm	1197*	
87	1	BATH	5f Gd/Fm	1437*	
74	8	ASCO	5f Good	2152	
85	5	DONC	5f Gd/Fm	2318	
89	2	DONC	5f Gd/Fm	2352	
86	7	NEWB	5f Firm	2849	
99	3	ASCO	6f Gd/Fm	2996	
95	3	NEWB	5f Gd/Fm	3482	
0	9	CURR	6f Yldg	3720	
88	4	KEMP	6f Gd/Fm	3797	
86	7	DONC	5f Firm	3900	
95	3	CHAN	5f Good	4051	
94	4	NEWB	5f Gd/Sft	4454	

KADINSKY 3 b g £0

59	12	NEWM	8f Gd/Fm	3626	
64	5	YORK	10f Good	3813	
55	11	NOTT	8f Soft	3977	

KADOUN 3 b c £5773

81	2	CHEP	12f Heavy		1554	
69	4	KEMP	12f Gd/Fm		1929	
77	4	DONC	12f Gd/Fm		2609	
74	3	NEWM	15f Good		3023	
80	2	YORK	14f Heavy	76	4299	
79	2	BRIG	12f Soft	78	4421	

KAFEZAH 2 br f £815

85	4	KEMP	7f Gd/Fm	3789	
86	4	YARM	6f Firm	3938	

KAFI 4 b c £0

0	17	THIR	8f Soft	62	907	
42	9	NOTT	10f Good	55	2007	VIS
39	6	WARW	12f Gd/Fm	49	2255	vis
0	14	CHEP	18f Gd/Fm	46	2490	vis

KAFIL 6 b g £1841

55a	3	LING	10f Aw		1	
36a	6	LING	10f Aw	55	100	
48a	5	LING	8f Aw	53	169	
47a	6	LING	10f Aw	51	209	
20a	10	LING	10f Aw	51	220	
47a	2	WOLV	8f Aw	47	254	
29a	6	WOLV	9f Aw	47	404	
21a	7	WOLV	8f Aw	46	676	
23	10	BRIG	7f Firm	36	1336	BL
19	12	GOOD	9f Gd/Sft	36	1807	
40	10	LING	8f Gd/Fm		2215	
46a	3	LING	10f Aw	36	2764	bl
0	17	WIND	10f Gd/Fm		3045	bl
39	6	KEMP	8f Gd/Fm	42	3078	bl
36	8	GOOD	9f Good	47	3644	
76	3	GOOD	7f Good		3662	
62	7	SAND	8f Aw		3945	
67	6	GOOD	8f Soft		4077	
47a	7	LING	8f Aw	49	4335	bl
0	13	BRIG	8f Soft		4420	

KAGOSHIMA 5 b g £10910

29	12	NOTT	14f Gd/Sft	49	1087	
47	2	BEVE	16f Firm	47	1276	VIS
47	3	NEWC	17f Gd/Sft	44	1478	vis
53	1	PONT	17f Good	45	1867*	vis
59	2	PONT	18f Good	53	2176	vis
61	1	BEVE	16f Firm	58	2734*	vis
49	12	ASCO	16f Gd/Fm	62	2953	vis

KAHAL 6 b g £0

0	5	WOOD	8f Firm	3933	

KAHTAN 5 b g £10500

110	4	NEWM	12f Gd/Fm	1152	
105	4	YORK	14f Firm	1339	
105	6	ASCO	22f Good	2153	
104	4	CURR	14f Yldg	3721	

KAHYASI MOLL 3 b f £0

4a	8	WOLV	8f Aw	80	
15a	6	LING	10f Aw	204	
17a	9	LING	12f Aw	457	

KAI ONE 2 b c £4668

91	3	GOOD	6f Gd/Fm		3064
85	2	LEIC	6f Gd/Fm		3215
77	3	GOOD	6f Good		3649
83	3	DONC	7f Firm	81	3901
80	3	BRIG	7f Soft		4415

KAIAPOI 3 ch c £11467

75	1	DONC	10f Gd/Fm	67	701*
78	1	CHES	12f Gd/Fm	73	1225*
0	U	HAYD	14f Soft	80	1821
81	3	RIPO	12f Gd/Fm	80	2110
76	5	HAYD	14f Gd/Fm	80	2445
63	9	CHES	10f Good	80	2666
81	2	CHES	10f Gd/Fm	79	3426

79 8 YORK 14f Firm 81 3599
59 6 HAYD 12f Soft 81 4092
58 11 DONC 10f Gd/Sft 79 4448

KAID 5 b g £0
36a 5 WOLV 16f Aw 38 194
34a 4 WOLV 15f Aw 36 277 VIS
52a 6 SOUT 12f Aw 301
10a 7 LING 16f Aw 35 649

KAILAN SCAMP 7 gr m £0
0 9 BEVE 10f Gd/Fm 3677
21 5 BEVE 12f Sft/Hv 4041 t
0 14 YORK 10f Soft 4275 t

KALA SUNRISE 7 ch h £6405
46 14 DONC 8f Good 77 715
70 7 PONT 8f Soft 76 875
75 3 THIR 8f Good 74 1160
72 3 CARL 8f Firm 2018
70 5 DONC 8f Gd/Fm 74 2349
64 9 YORK 8f Gd/Fm 73 2645
80 1 CARL 8f Good 3081*

KALAHARI FERRARI 4 ch g £0
0 13 NOTT 8f Good 50 1414
0 17 WARW 8f Good 45 2460

KALANISI 4 b c £490380
117 2 WIND 8f Firm 1291
122 1 ASCO 8f Good 2064+
125 2 SAND 10f Gd/Fm 2497
125 2 YORK 10f Good 3539
125 1 NEWM 10f Good 4355*

KALAR 11 b g £2938
21a 9 LING 5f Aw 37 371 bl
0a 12 WOLV 5f Aw 33 445 bl
20a 5 WOLV 5f Aw 29 563 bl
11a 11 SOUT 5f Aw 38 673 bl
26 11 MUSS 5f Gd/Fm 40 1143 bl
39 4 HAMI 5f Gd/Fm 40 1358 bl
45 1 HAMI 5f Gd/Fm 39 2233* bl
13 13 CATT 5f Gd/Fm 45 2418 bl
0 16 NEWC 5f Good 47 2525 bl
0 23 THIR 6f Gd/Fm 45 3144 bl
0 17 HAMI 5f Gd/Sft 43 3536 bl

KALEMAAT 3 ch f £1615
63 5 PONT 10f Gd/Fm 2558
79 4 SAND 10f Good 3432
79 2 RIPO 12f Good 3701

KALINDI 3 ch f £15151
69 10 HAYD 5f Heavy 988
65 7 KEMP 6f Gd/Sft 1078
91 6 NOTT 5f Good 3521
86 9 YORK 6f Gd/Fm 94 3727
104 1 DONC 7f Gd/Fm 3878*
92 8 NEWB 7f Firm 3995
91 10 ASCO 6f Gd/Sft 4125

KALLISTO 3 b c £210544
111 1 CAPA 12f Gd/Fm 1618*

KALUANA COURT 4 b f £0
0 15 SALI 10f Gd/Sft 33 4169

KALUGA 2 ch f £0
59 8 HAYD 5f Gd/Sft 1488
42 11 PONT 6f Good 1864

KALUKI 2 ch c £4124
62 6 WIND 5f Good 849
72 3 BATH 5f Good 1088
69 3 BRIG 5f Gd/Sft 1463
63 4 BRIG 6f Good 1648
75 2 FOLK 7f Good 2619
0 20 NEWB 5f Firm 2849
70 3 MUSS 7f Good 3100
70 3 SAND 7f Good 72 3468
69 2 FOLK 7f Gd/Fm 3582
68 2 BRIG 6f Firm 3732
58 7 NOTT 6f Soft 70 3976

39a 7 WOLV 7f Aw 4383

KALYPSO KATIE 3 gr f £98700
114 1 YORK 10f Gd/Fm 1309*
116 2 EPSO 12f Gd/Sft 1828
107 5 CURR 12f Gd/Fm 2739

KAMA SUTRA 2 b c £569
93 4 NEWM 6f Good 4341

KAMARAZI 3 ch c £0
82a 7 LING 7f Aw 630
67a 8 LING 8f Aw 78 1259
57 8 GOOD 8f Gd/Sft 73 1473
60 9 WIND 8f Good 68 1726
42 4 BRIG 8f Firm 2040

KAMAREYAH 3 b f £0
0 30 NEWM 6f Gd/Fm 85 1694
77 7 KEMP 7f Firm 80 2261
73 7 NEWM 7f Gd/Sft 78 3163
0 21 NEWM 7f Gd/Fm 76 4215
0 16 YARM 7f Soft 73 4513

KANAKA CREEK 3 ch f £4003
74 2 PONT 8f Soft 877
73 1 WARW 8f Soft 1063*
85 6 AYR 8f Gd/Fm 1630

KANDYMAL 2 ch f £0
48 7 DONC 5f Good 730
63 6 HAMI 5f Gd/Fm 1906
52 8 PONT 5f Good 2361
44 6 HAMI 6f Gd/Fm 2778
54 6 CATT 7f Soft 55 4254
0 19 PONT 8f Good 53 4378

KANZ WOOD 4 ch c £6328
65 1 GOOD 8f Gd/Sft 62 1473*
50 8 LING 9f Good 68 1744
61 7 GOOD 8f Gd/Fm 67 2126
51 4 CHEP 8f Gd/Fm 66 2492

KARA SEA 3 ch f £3624
63a 1 SOUT 8f Aw 500*
39a 8 WOLV 7f Aw 623
59 4 NOTT 10f Gd/Fm 64 2685
68a 2 SOUT 11f Aw 64 2945
42a 10 LING 12f Aw 4101 VIS
41a 7 WOLV 12f Aw 68 4360

KARAJAN 3 b c £218
75 7 NEWM 10f Gd/Fm 2617
59a 4 WOLV 9f Aw 3272
66 7 LEIC 10f Firm 3838
36a 9 LING 16f Aw 65 4329

KARAKUL 4 ch f £0
0a 10 WOLV 9f Aw 65 172
5a 12 WOLV 8f Aw 61 254
20 9 NOTT 10f Aw 2682
15 10 WIND 8f Gd/Fm 61 2890
0 18 WIND 8f Good 58 3188
0a 11 WOLV 8f Aw 45 4437
0 11 NEWM 12f Gd/Sft 51 4534

KARALIYFA 3 gr f £3500
84 6 LING 11f Gd/Sft 1282
75 1 RIPO 9f Gd/Fm 2838*
82 7 DONC 10f Gd/Fm 85 3159

KARAMEG 4 b f £6555
0 14 GOOD 7f Gd/Sft 79 1483
78 4 DONC 7f Gd/Fm 78 1840
83 2 YORK 7f Good 78 2694
86 2 NEWC 7f Gd/Fm 84 2986
68 11 NEWM 7f Gd/Sft 85 3315
83 5 SALI 7f Firm 85 3750
0 14 AYR 5f Soft 84 3992
0 17 YORK 6f Heavy 82 4301

KARASTA 2 b f £59615
100 1 NEWM 7f Good 3607*
107 1 DONC 8f Gd/Fm 3876*
107 2 LONG 8f Good 4260

KAREEB 3 b c £11511
81 6 NEWM 8f Firm 83 1183
83 5 YORK 7f Gd/Fm 83 1308
0 30 ASCO 8f Good 82 2117
68 8 NEWC 7f Firm 80 2338
80 3 SALI 8f Gd/Fm 2977 BL
77 4 NEWM 6f Gd/Fm 77 3119 bl
77 3 CHEP 7f Gd/Fm 3256 bl
74 6 KEMP 7f Gd/Fm 77 3796 bl
80 1 NEWB 8f Firm 76 3998*
66 9 SAND 8f Soft 80 4206
81 3 BRIG 8f Soft 4420
0 21 NEWM 8f Soft 80 4545

KARINS LAD 3 b g £0
0 5 DONC 10f Gd/Fm 2317
0 16 LEIC 10f Good 3838

KARITSA 2 b f £6386
77 2 LEIC 5f Gd/Sft 1737
57 5 NOTT 5f Good 1870
72 1 CHES 5f Gd/Fm 2668*
66 8 HAYD 5f Gd/Sft 74 3475
67 3 RIPO 6f Gd/Fm 71 3712
63 4 SAND 5f Soft 68 4202
66 5 NEWC 5f Heavy 4423

KARMINIYA 2 b f £0
71 5 LING 7f Soft 4484

KAROWNA 4 ch f £547
66 4 HAYD 16f Gd/Sft 68 1791
0 16 NEWC 16f Firm 82 2336

KARPASIANA 2 ch f £0
69 8 YARM 8f Heavy 4477

KASHRA 3 b f £4446
97 4 BATH 5f Good 1090
70 8 NOTT 6f Good 1410
64 12 HAYD 6f Gd/Sft 97 1534
79 13 ASCO 6f Gd/Fm 95 2954
94 2 GOOD 7f Firm 3155
86 10 PONT 6f Firm 3503
87 6 GOOD 7f Good 93 3648
88 6 DONC 6f Gd/Fm 91 3861

KASS ALHAWA 7 b g £9497
56a 1 WOLV 8f Aw 50 38*
30a 8 SOUT 8f Aw 54 176
55a 2 SOUT 8f Aw 54 326
14a 9 WOLV 8f Aw 55 569
29a 6 WOLV 8f Aw 54 676
69 2 THIR 7f Soft 67 908
68 4 MUSS 8f Gd/Fm 1144
51 7 REDC 10f Soft 1579
59 5 BEVE 9f Gd/Sft 69 1762
66 4 BEVE 7f Firm 68 1920
70 2 BEVE 7f Firm 67 2221
54 4 BEVE 8f Gd/Fm 67 2481
50 4 REDC 9f Aw 2865
66 2 REDC 7f Gd/Fm 2994
70 2 BEVE 8f Gd/Sft 67 3054
65 5 CATT 7f Good 68 3440
63 8 BEVE 7f Gd/Fm 68 3652 bl
56 4 BEVE 7f Stt/Hvy 67 4044
48 9 WIND 8f Gd/Fm 4292

KASTAWAY 4 b f £0
89 7 BATH 5f Good 1090
90 6 EPSO 5f Good 98 1849

KATHAKALI 3 b c £12350
68a 2 LING 10f Aw 60 315
74a 1 LING 8f Aw 373*
77a 1 LING 10f Aw 420*
77a 1 LING 10f Aw 73 880*
48 9 KEMP 9f Gd/Sft 70 1075
58 10 WIND 12f Firm 65 1292
68a 7 LING 12f Aw 77 1677
46 9 WIND 10f Gd/Fm 64 1878

49	9	WIND	12f Gd/Fm	60	2210
61	5	CHEP	10f Gd/Fm	60	2450
49	9	NOTT	10f Gd/Fm	59	2685
50	9	ASCO	12f Gd/Fm	60	3014
32	13	CHEP	10f Gd/Fm	58	3683

KATHANN 2 ch f £0

0	14	PONT	6f Gd/Fm		2828
0	11	DONC	7f Gd/Fm		3156
53	7	BEVE	7f Good		3952

KATHERINE SEYMOUR 2 b f £20500

106	2	CURR	7f Gd/Sft		4240
106	D	NEWM	7f Good		4356

KATHIR 3 ch c £14939

72	12	NEWM	8f Firm	85	1183
83	3	NEWC	8f Heavy	84	1765
87	2	GOOD	9f Good	83	2304
88	1	WARW	8f Gd/Fm		2844*
81	5	HAYD	8f Gd/Fm	87	3325
89	2	GOOD	9f Good	85	3658
83	5	NEWB	8f Firm	88	3998
0	20	ASCO	8f Gd/Sft	87	4126

KATHMANDU 3 br c £7012

108	3	CLAI	12f Good		3718
116	4	LONG	12f Good		3929 bl

KATHOLOGY 3 b c £28435

76a	2	SOUT	6f Aw		46
78a	3	WOLV	5f Aw		77
88	2	NEWM	6f Gd/Sft	84	982
89	1	SAND	5f Heavy	84	1047+
94	1	CHES	5f Gd/Fm	89	1219*
94	4	NEWM	6f Gd/Fm	93	1694
44	17	ASCO	5f Good	94	2168
81	15	ASCO	5f Gd/Fm	94	3016
97	2	YORK	5f Gd/Fm	91	3569
89	9	NEWB	5f Firm		3982
82	14	ASCO	5f Gd/Sft	94	4129
34	11	NEWB	6f Gd/Sft	94	4456

KATHRYNS PET 7 b m £7409

59	6	HAYD	12f Gd/Sft	73	809
78	1	NOTT	14f Good	73	1411*
84	2	REDC	10f Gd/Sft	79	4221
0	12	DONC	12f Soft	84	4464
0	19	DONC	12f Heavy	84	4580

KATIE HAWK 6 b m £0

0	13	THIR	7f Gd/Fm	24	3129

KATIE JANE 5 b m £0

29a	9	WOLV	8f Aw		39
7a	5	SOUT	12f Aw		84
0a	8	WOLV	12f Aw		144

KATIE KING 3 ch f £0

7a	1	LING	6f Aw		443
15a	8	LING	6f Aw		527
0	12	NEWM	8f Gd/Fm		2134
12	8	BRIG	12f Firm	33	2904
12	9	RIPO	10f Gd/Fm	29	3008 BL

KATIE KOMAITE 7 b m £3052

39	4	WARW	11f Heavy	39	890 vis
22	13	WARW	11f Soft	39	1065 vis
26	7	MUSS	12f Gd/Fm	38	1432 vis
29	7	PONT	10f Soft	36	1705 vis
37	2	HAYD	11f Gd/Fm	37	2453
35	3	HAMI	11f Gd/Fm	38	2782
33	5	RIPO	12f Gd/Fm	39	3181
36	2	HAYD	11f Gd/Sft	38	3480
36	2	HAMI	12f Gd/Sft	35	3531
26	9	HAMI	12f Gd/Fm	35	3827
0	8	NEWC	10f Heavy	41	4427

KATIES CRACKER 5 b m £0

23a	6	LING	16f Aw	37	6
2a	11	LING	12f Aw		101
14a	7	LING	13f Aw	35	168
8a	10	WOLV	12f Aw		231

0a	13	LING	16f Aw	37	285
0a	7	WOLV	16f Aw	37	348
18a	4	WOLV	15f Aw		468
10a	6	LING	13f Aw		524
19a	4	SOUT	14f Aw		668
0	13	NEWM	12f Good		4178
7	9	YARM	14f Soft		4510

KATIES DOLPHIN 2 ch f £1543

45	6	REDC	6f Gd/Sft		1577
67	2	HAMI	6f Gd/Fm		1938
69	3	CARL	5f Firm		2277
51	7	NEWC	7f Good		2521
61	5	CHES	6f Firm	67	3168
54	6	HAYD	6f Gd/Sft		3478
28	9	PONT	6f Soft	62	4235 BL

KATIES VALENTINE 3 b f £1388

55a	4	LING	6f Aw		5
46a	5	WOLV	7f Aw		41
55	3	HAYD	6f Soft	55	1494
52	2	CARL	6f Gd/Sft		1723
50	8	REDC	6f Good	56	1891 VIS
0	11	AYR	8f Good	56	2136
25a	10	WOLV	8f Aw	54	2601 vis

KATIYKHA 4 b f £52000

109	1	ASCO	12f Good	100	2069*
109	1	CURR	14f Yldg		3721*
0	7	CURR	14f Good		4055

KATIYMANN 8 ch g £0

22	12	LEIC	10f Soft	43	1546 t
22	10	HAMI	12f Gd/Fm	41	1908 tVl
0	P	MUSS	12f Firm	41	2048 tBL

KATIYPOUR 3 ch c £1879

68	8	NEWM	8f Gd/Fm		1692
76	2	SAND	10f Gd/Fm		1992
72	3	PONT	10f Gd/Fm		2558
57	13	GOOD	9f Good	79	3110
0	14	SAND	10f Soft		4205

KATTEGAT 4 b c £1070

87	3	NEWB	16f Gd/Fm	92	917
0	32	NEWM	18f Good	90	4353

KATUN 7 b h £7685

108	2	LONG	16f Heavy		1116

KATY IVORY 3 b f £0

38a	5	LING	7f Aw		651

KATY NOWAITEE 4 b f £98486

94	1	DONC	8f Good	84	715*
104	1	NEWM	9f Gd/Fm	92	4212*
105	1	NEWM	10f Good		4337*

KAURI 2 b f £0

45	11	DONC	6f Gd/Fm		2608

KAYF TARA 6 b g £200100

125	1	YORK	14f Firm		1339*
122	1	ASCO	20f Good		2114*

KAYO 5 b g £27927

81a	3	LING	8f Aw	80	7
0a	11	SOUT	8f Aw	80	49
69a	8	WOLV	7f Aw	82	258
59a	8	WOLV	7f Aw	80	364
62a	11	LING	7f Aw	78	423
95	2	YORK	6f Gd/Fm	93	1983
94	3	NEWM	7f Gd/Fm	93	2133
103	1	NEWC	7f Firm	94	2338*
100	2	HAYD	7f Gd/Fm	97	2456
101	2	NEWB	8f Firm	99	2706
82	12	NEWM	7f Gd/Fm	100	3315
95	3	CHES	8f Gd/Sft	100	3427
99	5	YORK	6f Good	100	3543
85	10	YORK	7f Firm		3600
98	4	GOOD	7f Good	100	3902
77	18	AYR	6f Gd/Sft	99	4012
89	7	YORK	6f Heavy	98	4301
54a	12	SOUT	8f Aw	75	4365

KAYO GEE 4 b f £1264

22a	13	LING	6f Aw	80	113 bl
28a	8	WOLV	5f Aw	78	146 bl
59a	6	LING	5f Aw	74	312 bl
35a	7	LING	5f Aw	70	774 bl
61	3	LING	5f Soft	63	1543 VIS
58	7	LING	6f Good	61	1676 vis
0	13	KEMP	7f Gd/Fm	60	2749 vis
0	15	WIND	6f Gd/Fm	59	3046 vis
45	12	GOOD	5f Soft	56	4065 vis
0	20	WIND	6f Gd/Sft	52	4294 vis
57a	2	LING	7f Aw		4487 bl

KAZANA 2 b f £1644

50	4	LEIC	8f Firm		3836
85	2	DONC	8f Gd/Sft		4445

KAZEEM 2 b f £0

73	6	SALI	7f Aw		3752
83	6	DONC	8f Gd/Fm		4445

KAZZOUD 4 b f £0

0a	9	WOLV	12f Aw		111
7a	7	WOLV	12f Aw		144

KEALAKEKUA BAY 3 ch g £0

34	9	WIND	10f Heavy		4528

KEATS 2 b c £9675

103	4	ASCO	5f Good		2113
100	2	CORK	6f Gd/Sft		4315

KEBABS 3 b f £634

75	5	DONC	7f Good	83	736
74	5	LEIC	7f Gd/Sft	82	834
60	13	NEWM	6f Gd/Sft	80	982
68a	7	WOLV	6f Aw	76	1138
0	19	NEWB	7f Gd/Fm	75	1405
65	3	BRIG	6f Good		1651
0	12	WIND	6f Gd/Fm	67	1877 BL
43	5	LEIC	6f Good		3097
44	8	SALI	6f Gd/Fm	62	3419
52	4	PONT	5f Soft	58	4087
0	19	WIND	6f Gd/Sft	57	4294
0	16	DONC	7f Gd/Sft	54	4452

KEE RING 4 ch c £0

53	6	BRIG	7f Firm	58	1213
51	7	BRIG	6f Gd/Sft	56	1464 BL
47	6	GOOD	6f Gd/Sft	56	1636 bl
41	11	CHEP	6f Good	53	1971 bl
71	6	LING	6f Gd/Fm		2183 bl
43	7	YARM	6f Gd/Sft	56	2415 bl
33	9	BRIG	6f Firm	48	2896 bl

KEEN DANCER 6 ch g £0

46	6	HAYD	12f Gd/Fm		2457 tbl
50	6	BATH	11f Aw		2943 bl

KEEN HANDS 4 ch g £13470

65a	4	SOUT	7f Aw	69	35 vis
50a	8	LING	7f Aw	68	106 vis
69a	2	WOLV	6f Aw	68	175 vis
66a	4	SOUT	6f Aw	68	218 vis
75a	1	SOUT	6f Aw	68	246* vis
62a	10	LING	7f Aw	74	337 vis
74a	4	SOUT	6f Aw	74	388 vis
79a	1	SOUT	6f Aw	74	454* vis
76a	7	WOLV	6f Aw	79	532 vis
75a	5	SOUT	7f Aw	79	539 vis
59a	8	SOUT	7f Aw	78	645 vis
64a	5	WOLV	5f Aw	76	721 vis
66a	5	WOLV	5f Aw	74	1140 vis
80a	1	SOUT	5f Aw	72	1504* vis
63a	8	WOLV	5f Aw	80	2078 vis
65	4	BATH	6f Firm		2329 vis
55	7	NEWC	5f Good	64	2525 vis
40	9	LING	6f Firm	62	2761 vis
35	6	CARL	7f Firm		3197 vis
0	22	WIND	6f Gd/Sft	56	4293 vis

KEEN WATERS 6 b m £0

1a	8	LING	16f Aw	37	285	bl
8a	9	LING	12f Aw	37	377	

KEEP DREAMING 2 b f £0

43a	8	SOUT	5f Aw		865
39	8	RIPO	5f Good		1595
29	7	BEVE	7f Firm		2218
34	6	BEVE	5f Gd/Fm		2483

KEEP IKIS 6 ch m £12249

47	1	**RIPO**	16f Good	40	1597*
47	4	PONT	17f Good	46	1867
51	3	PONT	18f Firm	46	2176
56	1	**CATT**	16f Gd/Fm	50	2436*
56	5	BEVE	16f Firm	56	2734
62	1	**PONT**	17f Firm	56	3501*

KEEP TAPPING 3 b c £628

78	3	WARW	6f Heavy		888

KEEP THE PEACE 2 br c £0

78	9	NEWB	6f Gd/Fm		1403
0	19	KEMP	6f Gd/Fm		1924

KEEPSAKE 6 b m £0

0a	9	WOLV	16f Aw	28	576	bl

KELBURNE 3 b c £643

63	5	AYR	10f Gd/Fm		1655
70	4	CARL	9f Firm		2019
35	4	DONC	12f Gd/Fm		2353
53	8	REDC	10f Firm	59	3310
0	14	BEVE	10f Gd/Fm	55	3656
45	8	LEIC	10f Firm	52	3842
0	17	SAND	10f Soft	51	4208
43	6	NOTT	8f Heavy	49	4414

KELETI 2 b c £0

69	5	HAMI	5f Gd/Fm		1906
68	6	REDC	5f Gd/Fm		2142

KELLING HALL 3 b c £0

0	11	NOTT	8f Gd/Sft		1084
35	10	LEIC	10f Soft	50	1546
0	13	WARW	8f Good	45	2460

KELLS 2 b c £0

63	10	SALI	7f Good		2686
58	9	BRIG	7f Soft		4172
73	5	BRIG	7f Soft		4415

KELSO MAGIC 3 ch f £0

69	11	HAYD	5f Heavy		988	
59	8	KEMP	6f Gd/Sft		1078	
40	14	NEWM	6f Good	93	2568	
55	7	LEIC	6f Gd/Fm	88	3335	BL

KELTECH GOLD 3 b c £10760

61	8	WARW	8f Heavy		884
67	2	DONC	8f Gd/Fm	64	1053
71	1	**BATH**	8f Gd/Sft	65	1671*
72	5	CHEP	8f Gd/Fm	71	2661
77	1	**CHEP**	8f Gd/Fm	71	3254*
0	15	KEMP	8f Gd/Fm	71	3793

KELTECH STAR 4 b f £0

44	6	NOTT	10f Gd/Fm	54	1272	
32	7	PONT	10f Good	54	1496	
0	18	HAMI	13f Gd/Fm	50	1936	
30	5	BRIG	12f Firm	45	2893	VIS

KELTIC BARD 3 b c £7772

69	9	NEWM	8f Firm	77	1183
0	14	RIPO	8f Good	76	1598
67	7	NEWM	8f Firm	73	1853
68	5	DONC	10f Gd/Fm	71	2610
74	1	**FOLK**	9f Gd/Fm	68	3043*
74	2	LING	11f Firm		3281
82	1	**FOLK**	10f Gd/Fm	75	3585*
37a	10	WOLV	12f Aw	85	4226

KENNET 5 b g £11080

64a	5	SOUT	11f Aw	67	512
63a	6	SOUT	11f Aw	66	605
48	11	ASCO	8f Gd/Sft	69	1113
58	13	NEWB	10f Good	67	1375
64	7	WIND	10f Good	65	1729
49	8	KEMP	9f Gd/Fm	63	2085 BL
63	2	WIND	10f Good		2372
51	10	SAND	10f Gd/Fm	60	2527 VIS
48a	2	LING	10f Aw		2764 vis
64	2	WIND	12f Gd/Fm	60	3049
63	3	LEIC	12f Gd/Fm		3219
68	1	**WIND**	12f Good	62	3353*
73	1	**BATH**	13f Gd/Fm	68	3518*
73	3	EPSO	12f Good	72	3686
71	6	DONC	15f Firm	72	3890
72	5	NEWB	16f Firm	72	3986
63	7	DONC	12f Soft	72	4464

KENNYTHORPE BOPPY 2 ch g £0

58	5	BEVE	7f Gd/Fm		3409
54	8	BEVE	5f Gd/Fm		3675
58	5	LEIC	7f Gd/Sft		4028
9	12	DONC	8f Gd/Sft	2ow	4450

KENT 5 b g £6279

38a	5	SOUT	12f Aw	43	68
45a	1	**SOUT**	16f Aw	39	284*
51a	2	SOUT	16f Aw	45	428
52a	1	**SOUT**	16f Aw	45	502*
36a	6	SOUT	16f Aw	53	644
46a	4	SOUT	16f Aw	51	737
32	7	FOLK	15f Soft	45	963

KENTISH ROCK 5 b g £0

0a	11	LING	10f Aw		375	
12a	4	LING	7f Aw		571	BL
25	5	LING	14f Good		3489	
0a	16	LING	12f AW		4186	

KENTUCKY BOUND 2 b c £0

69	7	KEMP	5f Gd/Fm		2082
24	8	BEVE	5f Sft/Hvy		4042
0	13	YARM	6f Heavy		4479

KERMIYANA 3 b f £19500

103	1	**LEOP**	8f Gd/Fm		2570*
90	5	CURR	8f Gd/Fm		2740

KERRICH 3 ch f £0

0	14	SALI	7f Gd/Fm		2232
0	14	WARW	7f Good		3696
26	10	BATH	8f Gd/Fm		3820

KERRIDGE CHAPEL 3 b f £0

32a	10	WOLV	5f Aw		77	
0	19	WARW	5f Gd/Fm	49	2252	
0	16	HAYD	5f Gd/Fm	44	2505	
33	6	CATT	5f Gd/Fm		2931	bl
9	13	CATT	5f Gd/Fm	36	3203	bl
32	8	RIPO	5f Gd/Fm		3462	bl
40	6	BEVE	7f Gd/Fm		3671	bl
0	16	WARW	8f Gd/Fm		3914	
13a	7	WOLV	7f Aw		4361	bl
16a	7	WOLV	7f Aw		4384	bl

KERRYGOLD 4 ch c £3842

113	2	LING	10f Good		2072

KESTLE IMP 2 b f £782

53a	2	WOLV	9f Aw		4438

KESTRAL 4 ch c £8143

35a	5	WOLV	7f Aw	41	635	
0a	10	WOLV	9f Aw	38	749	
41	6	MUSS	7f Gd/Fm	42	1149	
25	10	CARL	6f Firm	42	1257	t
27	6	MUSS	8f Firm	40	2378	t
37	2	PONT	10f Gd/Fm		2831	
38	3	BEVE	7f Good	36	2882	
42	2	AYR	8f Gd/Fm	37	3141	
49	1	**NEWC**	9f Firm	42	3603*	
50	2	YORK	10f Gd/Fm	48	3731	
57	3	BEVE	8f Good	56	3951	
40	8	MUSS	10f Aw	54	4560	

KEW GARDENS 3 ch c £3765

94	2	KEMP	10f Soft		998
89	3	NEWB	12f Gd/Fm	88	1400
81	11	ASCO	16f Good		2068
55	13	NEWM	14f Gd/Fm	88	4213
0	14	NEWM	12f Aw	86	4342

KEWARRA 6 b g £324

46	7	RIPO	10f Good	72	1860
50	7	HAYD	10f Gd/Fm		2457
65	3	CHEP	12f Gd/Fm	68	2656

KEY 4 b f £0

0	15	REDC	6f Firm	55	3312
41	9	EPSO	5f Good	52	3855

KEZ 4 b g £793

36a	10	LING	10f Aw	68	842	
59	7	NOTT	8f Good		1407	
57	2	BRIG	12f Gd/Fm		1934	
37	12	EPSO	12f Gd/Sft	58	2429	VIS
53	4	BRIG	12f Gd/Fm		2725	

KHABAR 7 b g £0

33	10	CATT	7f Gd/Fm	51	780

KHALED 5 b g £705

7a	11	WOLV	9f Aw		360
66	3	NEWM	8f Gd/Fm	66	3118
25	12	WIND	8f Good	68	3355
0	15	LING	8f Good	67	3831
24a	12	LING	8f Aw	65	4330

KHALIK 6 br g £5216

36a	9	SOUT	6f Aw	64	47	t
65	3	SAND	6f Good	64	763	t
70	1	**BATH**	5f Gd/Fm	64	1092*	t
69	4	LING	5f Gd/Sft	70	1264	t
55	7	GOOD	6f Gd/Sft	69	1636	t
66	7	WIND	6f Gd/Fm	69	2371	t
68	3	LING	6f Firm	68	2761	tbl
64	6	BATH	5f Soft	68	4432	t
70	3	YARM	6f Heavy	68	4480	tbl

KHASAYL 3 b f £7685

107	2	CHAN	6f Good		4052
99	8	LONG	5f Good		4261

KHATANI 5 b g £389

85	6	CHES	19f Firm	98	3171

KHATTAFF 5 ch g £0

41a	5	WOLV	8f Aw		229	bl

KHAYSAR 2 b c £700

80	3	CURR	7f Good		2407

KHAYYAM 2 b c £308

67	8	YORK	6f Firm		1328
70	4	HAYD	8f Gd/Sft		4103

KHITAAM 2 b c £2607

90	2	KEMP	7f Gd/Fm		3361
96	4	YORK	7f Gd/Fm		3730

KHUCHN 4 b c £4032

39	9	LEIC	12f Good	62	791	
35	10	PONT	10f Soft	60	871	
57	5	BEVE	10f Heavy	60	975	
0	19	NEWC	8f Heavy	56	1007	
53	5	NOTT	10f Gd/Sft	54	1370	
52	2	LEIC	10f Gd/Sft	52	1575	
40	6	BEVE	9f Gd/Sft	52	1762	t
47	5	RIPO	10f Good	52	1860	
51	4	BEVE	10f Firm	49	2220	
50	2	BEVE	10f Gd/Fm	49	2518	
49	2	BEVE	10f Gd/Fm	48	2883	
0	P	BEVE	10f Gd/Sft	48	3053	

KHULAN 2 b f £23385

106	1	**NEWM**	6f Gd/Fm		2618*
105	2	YORK	6f Firm		3596
84	13	NEWM	6f Good		4159

KI CHI SAGA 8 ch g £767

22a	10	WOLV	12f Aw	49	43	bl
39a	4	SOUT	12f Aw	49	70	bl
41a	4	LING	12f Aw	43	115	bl
7a	9	LING	13f Aw	38	167	bl

46a 2 LING 13f Aw 46 219 bl
11a 11 WOLV 12f Aw 231 bl
14a 6 LING 13f Aw 37 317 bl
0a 9 LING 16f Aw 402 bl
0a 7 LING 13f Aw 30 458 bl
25a 4 LING 10f Aw 775 bl
20a 4 LING 13f Aw 33 835 bl
0a 11 SOUT 14f Aw 32 1301 bl
10a 10 SOUT 11f Aw 1415 bl
20 6 BRIG 12f Good 1647 tbl
0a 14 LING 13f Aw 2181 tvi
18a 3 LING 13f Aw 2323 tbl
10a 11 LING 10f Aw 2587 t

KIDNAPPED 4 b g £0
1a 11 LING 7f Aw 49 59
39a 7 WOLV 8f Aw 133
0a 10 SOUT 8f Aw 43 345
0 18 BRIG 6f Firm 49 1211 BL

KIDOLOGY 4 b g £0
0 9 NEWC 10f Heavy 44 1769 t

KIDZ PLAY 4 b g £6519
43 7 MUSS 7f Gd/Fm 54 1148
58 1 **MUSS** 9f Firm 53 1689*
56 4 HAMI 8f Gd/Fm 1940
36 13 CARL 12f Firm 57 2279
51 4 HAMI 8f Gd/Fm 2781
50 10 AYR 10f Good 57 3368
28 14 YORK 10f Gd/Fm 54 3731
58 1 **AYR** 11f Soft 51 3963*
41 4 AYR 10f Heavy 57 4306
0 P AYR 13f Heavy 57 4325
58 3 PONT 10f Soft 57 4374
58 2 MUSS 9f Soft 57 4520
40 7 DONC 8f Heavy 57 4573

KIER PARK 3 b c £8800
114 2 NEWM 5f Gd/Fm 1172

KIERCHEM 9 b g £3612
37 2 BEVE 8f Heavy 973
35 8 PONT 8f Good 1498
24 10 HAYD 11f Soft 37 1819
37 1 RIPO 8f Gd/Fm 34 2099*
30 4 PONT 10f Good 2366
33 6 PONT 10f Gd/Fm 38 2556
29 12 REDC 8f Gd/Fm 37 2861
45 11 REDC 7f Gd/Fm 2994
33 4 THIR 8f Gd/Fm 35 3344
38 3 CATT 12f Good 43 3437
0 12 CATT 16f Soft 44 4006
32 3 BEVE 10f Sft/Hv 44 4046
23 6 NEWC 10f Heavy 39 4404
0 13 REDC 8f Gd/Sft 39 4499

KIFTSGATE 3 ch c £11851
86 6 NEWM 10f Gd/Fm 1697
88 1 **SAND** 10f Good 2531*
94 2 NEWB 12f Gd/Fm 3487
94 2 YORK 12f Gd/Fm 93 3728

KIGEMA 3 ch f £3638
51a 5 LING 7f Aw 53
48a 7 LING 7f Aw 155
49a 6 WOLV 7f Aw 192
52a 1 **LING** 8f Aw 241*
38a 4 LING 10f Aw 286
18a 6 WOLV 8f Aw 53 311
52a 2 LING 8f Aw 595
57a 2 LING 7f Aw 51 654
30a 6 SOUT 8f Aw 686

KILBARCHAN 2 ch f £583
69 3 HAMI 6f Gd/Fm 2234
55 5 HAMI 5f Gd/Fm 2639
49 5 MUSS 8f Soft 4564

KILBRANNAN SOUND 3 b f £677
74 4 CHES 5f Gd/Fm 78 1219

72 5 NOTT 6f Good 1409
57 9 RIPO 6f Gd/Fm 75 2101
34 12 HAYD 6f Gd/Fm 73 2504
39 10 CHES 5f Good 73 2663
48 10 BATH 5f Firm 70 2787
35 9 CARL 7f Firm 3573
0 14 NOTT 6f Soft 59 3975
30a 7 WOLV 6f Aw 54 4444

KILCREGGAN 6 b g £866
53 8 LEIC 10f Good 60 793
55 3 MUSS 14f Gd/Fm 1433
53 3 AYR 13f Gd/Fm 1657
52 7 NOTT 14f Gd/Fm 53 1874
35a 10 SOUT 14f Aw 51 4371
40 6 MUSS 12f Soft 50 4560

KILCULLEN LAD 6 b g £3398
0 14 LING 5f Gd/Sft 70 1264
69 5 BATH 6f Gd/Fm 70 1438 vis
73 2 SALI 6f Gd/Fm 70 1887 vis
73 3 BATH 6f Firm 70 1999 vis
61 10 LING 5f Firm 72 2326 vis
60 10 SAND 6f Gd/Fm 72 2473 vis
53 6 LING 6f Firm 69 2761 vis
60 10 GOOD 5f Gd/Fm 67 3091 vis
63 3 SALI 6f Gd/Fm 64 3419 vis
57 5 FOLK 6f Gd/Fm 3587 vis
38 16 BATH 6f Gd/Fm 64 3821 vis
61 5 GOOD 5f Soft 63 4065 vis
49 15 WIND 5f Gd/Sft 62 4295 vis
45 13 NEWB 5f Gd/Sft 60 4459 vis

KILDARE CHILLER 6 ch g £0
0 19 GOOD 8f Good 55 3885

KILLARNEY 2 gr f £0
0 20 NEWM 6f Gd/Sft 4530

KILLARNEY JAZZ 5 b g £2668
60a 4 WOLV 9f Aw 63 67
35a 8 SOUT 11f Aw 62 302 tbl
49a 8 SOUT 8f Aw 62 340 tbl
60a 3 WOLV 8f Aw 58 432 bl
39a 8 WOLV 8f Aw 477 bl
59a 1 **SOUT** 8f Aw 869* vis
54a 5 SOUT 8f Aw 56 1207 vis
29 5 SOUT 7f Soft 1601 vis
59a 2 SOUT 7f Aw 55 2122 bl
46a 5 SOUT 8f Aw 59 2379 vis
31a 8 SOUT 7f Aw 59 2637 vis

KILMEENA LAD 4 b c £8313
68a 7 LING 6f Aw 79 113
75a 4 LING 6f Aw 79 223
76a 4 LING 7f Aw 77 336
84a 1 **LING** 7f Aw 76 462*
0 27 ASCO 8f Gd/Sft 72 1113
0 18 SALI 7f Good 70 1348
0 14 NEWB 6f Gd/Sft 68 1591
61 5 BATH 6f Firm 65 1999
0 17 GOOD 6f Gd/Fm 65 2124
27 15 WIND 6f Good 62 2371 BL
51 7 BATH 6f Gd/Fm 58 3821
54 7 YARM 6f Gd/Fm 58 3966
55 2 LING 7f Good 55 4102
30 12 WIND 6f Gd/Sft 56 4294

KILMEENA STAR 2 b c £0
56 10 LING 5f Soft 4187
54 5 BRIG 6f Heavy 4537

KIMOE WARRIOR 2 ch c £0
63 5 HAYD 6f Soft 1823
0 18 YORK 6f Good 2692
0 12 HAYD 6f Gd/Sft 3478
54 5 CHES 7f Soft 4068
0 16 YORK 8f Soft 4281

KINAN 4 b c £8407
78 13 NEWM 7f Gd/Fm 85 2133

87 1 **EPSO** 7f Gd/Sft 81 2431*
0 15 NEWM 7f Gd/Fm 86 2616
71 12 ASCO 6f Gd/Fm 86 2954
84 3 HAYD 7f Soft 85 3785
86 6 AYR 7f Soft 85 3992
78 11 ASCO 7f Good 85 4112
71 6 CATT 6f Soft 4257
59 17 REDC 7f Gd/Sft 82 4498

KIND EMPEROR 3 br c £3251
75a 3 SOUT 5f Aw 34
46a 4 SOUT 6f Aw 472
63a 4 SOUT 6f Aw 70 673
79 2 DONC 6f Good 731
75 5 LEIC 6f Gd/Sft 829
68 3 THIR 6f Soft 909
55 7 EPSO 9f Heavy 1032
0 17 YORK 7f Gd/Fm 80 1308
59 9 DONC 6f Good 1516
35 4 REDC 6f Gd/Fm 2154
0 R CHEP 6f Gd/Fm 68 2489 VIS
35a 9 SOUT 6f Aw 68 2820
44 2 NEWC 5f Good 3035
49 8 THIR 6f Gd/Fm 63 3124
0 21 WIND 6f Gd/Sft 57 4293

KIND REGARDS 3 b f £77534
64 18 NEWM 8f Firm 86 1183
74 5 NOTT 8f Gd/Sft 1366
84 2 EPSO 9f Gd/Sft 82 2629
82 5 NEWM 8f Gd/Fm 82 2858
83 4 NEWC 7f Gd/Fm 82 2986
83 5 GOOD 7f Gd/Fm 82 3130
88 1 **BEVE** 10f Gd/Fm 82 3410*
95 1 **HAMI** 9f Gd/Sft 85 3535*
100 1 **NEWC** 10f Good 88 3703*
91 5 GOOD 10f Good 3903
107 1 **ASCO** 12f Gd/Sft 96 4128*
103 4 LONG 12f Soft 4394

KIND SIR 4 b c £0
43 8 WARW 12f Soft 73 815

KING ADAM 4 b c £9290
113 1 **DONC** 10f Gd/Fm 1841*
111 5 ASCO 10f Good 2089
99 4 CURR 9f Good 2410
101 6 NEWM 9f Good 4347

KING CAREW 2 b c £4565
92 2 ASCO 7f Gd/Sft 4124
93 5 ASCO 8f Heavy 4296

KING CHARLEMAGNE 2 b c £24840
100 2 YORK 6f Gd/Fm 3568
104 1 **NEWM** 7f Good 4196*

KING CUGAT 3 b c £48780
120 2 ARLI 10f Yldg 3549

KING FLYER 4 b c £25380
39a 6 LING 13f Aw 55 835 t
0 11 NEWM 12f Firm 66 1187 t
62 5 NOTT 14f Good 62 1874 t
64 2 BRIG 12f Gd/Fm 2725 t
65 1 **NEWM** 15f Good 60 3025* t
69 1 **SAND** 14f Good 65 3231* t
70 2 SAND 14f Good 69 3472 t
72 2 GOOD 16f Good 70 3905 t
73 1 **YARM** 18f Gd/Fm 70 3967* t

KING FOR A DAY 4 b c £3151
34 12 WIND 12f Good 47 1730 vis
0 12 NOTT 14f Good 47 1874 vis
38 4 REDC 14f Gd/Fm 39 2156
42 1 **YARM** 14f Firm 38 2902* vis
42 4 THIR 16f Gd/Fm 43 3348 vis
40 4 SAND 16f Good 43 3434 vis
42 10 NOTT 16f Soft 42 3978 vis

KING HALO 5 b h £144787
119 3 TOKY 8f Firm 1755

1548

KING O THE MANA 3 b c £31599
83	8	DONC	8f Good		735	
98	4	THIR	8f Soft		925	
106	1	**BATH**	10f Good		1089*	
105	3	LING	11f Gd/Sft		1284	
108	2	DONC	12f Firm		3892	
108	3	ASCO	12f Good		4109	
112	4	LONG	15f Good		4239	
60	7	NEWB	12f Sft/Hv		4469	

KING OF INDIA 2 ch g £0
61	8	KEMP	7f Firm		2867	

KING OF MOMMUR 5 b g £1017
47	3	NEWB	13f Gd/Sft	46	1594	
47	4	ASCO	16f Good	47	2173	

KING OF PERU 7 br h £8495
84a	5	WOLV	4f Aw	84	660	vis
68	5	SAND	5f Gd/Sft	71	763	vis
49	6	HAMI	6f Good	70	844	vis
65	4	BRIG	5f Gd/Sft	70	897	vis
76a	4	WOLV	5f Aw	83	1140	vis
74	2	WIND	5f Good		1881	vis
72	2	SAND	5f Good		1966	vis
50	13	WIND	6f Good	71	2371	vis
74	1	**CATT**	5f Gd/Fm		2931*	
69	1	**KEMP**	5f Gd/Fm		3077*	
60	4	HAYD	6f Gd/Fm		3283	
72	2	CATT	5f Good		3441	
71	4	EPSO	6f Good		3689	

KING OF SPAIN 3 ch c £595
63	3	HAYD	8f Gd/Sft		3477	

KING OF THE WEST 4 ch g £0
44	9	SAND	10f Soft		1588	
0	7	SAND	14f Good		2477	

KING OF TRUTH 2 b g £0
43a	6	SOUT	5f Aw		2818	

KING OF TUNES 8 b h £0
55a	4	LING	10f Aw	56	102	
42a	6	SOUT	8f Aw	55	177	

KING PRIAM 5 b g £44088
82a	1	**SOUT**	8f Aw	74	49*	bl
88a	1	**WOLV**	8f Aw	80	137+	bl
94a	1	**WOLV**	8f Aw	86	172*	bl
83a	5	SOUT	12f Aw	92	200	bl
98a	2	WOLV	8f Aw	93	230	bl
100a	3	WOLV	8f Aw		321	bl
101a	1	**WOLV**	8f Aw		448*	bl
100a	3	WOLV	8f Aw		480	bl
95a	6	WOLV	8f Aw	99	663	bl
96	2	DONC	8f Good	89	733	bl
103	9	NEWM	9f Gd/Sft		967	bl
66	14	KEMP	8f Soft	92	1015	bl
76	8	SAND	10f Heavy		1057	bl
95	5	JAGE	9f Good		1323	bl
49	9	SAND	8f Soft	92	1567	bl
75	13	ASCO	8f Good	92	2090	bl

KING SILCA 3 b g £6922
75	2	WARW	7f Heavy		1525	
78	1	**WARW**	7f Gd/Sft		1708*	
77	3	WARW	6f Gd/Fm		2035	
74	8	SAND	7f Gd/Fm	79	2495	
55	9	YARM	6f Firm	78	2900	
76	3	EPSO	7f Good	76	3854	

KING SPINNER 3 b c £906
57	8	NOTT	8f Gd/Sft		1366	
68	14	NEWM	10f Good	82	4197	
76	3	DONC	10f Gd/Sft	77	4448	

KING TUT 4 ch c £2563
48	2	SOUT	7f Soft		1603	
50	2	HAMI	8f Gd/Fm	48	1907	
36	11	WARW	11f Good	49	2463	
49	4	REDC	10f Gd/Fm	49	2861	
37	7	NOTT	10f Gd/Fm	49	3007	
37a	8	SOUT	8f Aw	48	4365	
48	2	NEWC	8f Heavy	48	4406	

KING UNO 6 b g £0
0	20	NOTT	6f Good	60	787	
41	9	HAMI	8f Good		847	

KINGCHIP BOY 11 b g £247
41a	7	SOUT	7f Aw	63	33	vis
24a	11	WOLV	9f Aw	63	60	bl
0a	14	SOUT	8f Aw	59	177	bl
51a	3	SOUT	7f Aw		249	
40a	7	SOUT	8f Aw	54	298	
44a	7	SOUT	8f Aw	52	345	
35a	9	SOUT	8f Aw	50	418	vis
34a	5	SOUT	8f Aw	46	497	vis
19a	6	WOLV	9f Aw	43	569	
0a	14	SOUT	8f Aw		600	
14a	10	SOUT	8f Aw		646	bl

KINGDOM OF GOLD 3 b c £1375
79	11	ASCO	8f Good	81	2117	
82	4	GOOD	10f Gd/Fm	81	2358	
82	4	SAND	10f Gd/Fm	81	2499	

KINGFISHER EVE 2 b f £0
0	13	BEVE	8f Gd/Fm		3675	

KINGFISHER GOLD 4 b g £0
0	26	REDC	8f Firm	46	1300	

KINGFISHERS BONNET 4 b f £3730
28a	7	WOLV	8f Aw		707	
47	1	**WARW**	11f Heavy	42	889*	
51	3	WARW	11f Soft	50	1065	
50	5	SALI	12f Good	50	1350	
42	4	PONT	10f Good	50	1496	
34	8	BATH	10f Gd/Sft	52	1666	
40	3	CHEP	10f Gd/Fm	50	2493	
35	8	CHES	10f Gd/Fm	48	2671	
25	7	LEIC	10f Gd/Fm	46	3093	

KINGS BALLET 2 b c £4634
68	8	NEWB	5f Gd/Fm		1782	
84	1	**HAYD**	5f Soft		3767*	
87	10	NEWB	5f Gd/Sft		4454	

KINGS BEST 3 b c £181700
115	2	NEWM	8f Gd/Sft		981	
127	1	**NEWM**	8f Gd/Fm		1171+	
0	P	CURR	12f Good		2409	

KINGS CAY 9 b g £0
17a	7	WOLV	12f Aw		347	vis
33a	4	WOLV	15f Aw		363	vis
0a	12	WOLV	12f Aw	35	607	vis

KINGS CHAMBERS 4 ch g £587
0a	12	WOLV	6f Aw		63	bl
0a	9	SOUT	11f Aw		196	bl
11a	10	SOUT	7f Aw		367	bl
0a	15	SOUT	8f Aw		646	bl
0	14	DONC	6f Gd/Sft		1073	bl
29	5	BEVE	12f Good		3399	
35	5	REDC	14f Gd/Fm		3633	t
33	2	WARW	12f Stt/Hv		4041	t

KINGS COUNTY 2 b c £106973
110	2	CURR	7f Gd/Sft		4058	
115	2	LONG	8f Soft		4320	
111	2	SAN	8f Heavy		4492	

KINGS CREST 2 b c £7019
0	12	WIND	5f Heavy		932	
53	6	WIND	5f Gd/Sft		1095	
36a	6	SOUT	6f Aw		1974	
47	4	YARM	8f Gd/Fm	50	3968	
63	1	**MUSS**	8f Gd/Sft	54	4132+	
63	4	WIND	10f Gd/Sft	62	4290	
64	5	NEWM	8f Good	63	4350	
67	2	DONC	8f Gd/Sft	62	4450	

KINGS GINGER 3 ch g £1182
38a	9	SOUT	7f Aw		278	
29a	7	SOUT	9f Aw	62	392	
55a	3	SOUT	8f Aw	56	540	
45a	4	WOLV	8f Aw	56	613	
0	13	WIND	8f Heavy	67	933	
42a	3	WOLV	8f Aw		1141	
32a	8	SOUT	11f Aw		1415	
0	12	LEIC	8f Gd/Sft		1572	VIS
0	16	NOTT	8f Gd/Fm	49	2187	vis

KINGS IRONBRIDGE 2 b c £24564
96	2	NEWB	6f Gd/Fm		1943	
100	1	**NEWM**	7f Firm		2346*	
100	5	NEWM	7f Gd/Fm		2613	
105	1	**SAND**	7f Good		3470*	
99	8	NEWM	7f Good		4354	

KINGS MILL 3 b c £26539
94	1	**SOUT**	10f Gd/Sft		858*	
94	1	**NEWM**	10f Gd/Sft	86	979*	
99	1	**YORK**	10f Gd/Fm	92	1310*	
95	8	ASCO	12f Good	98	2116	
99	5	SAND	10f Good	98	2475	
107	5	HAYD	11f Gd/Fm		3321	

KINGS OF EUROPE 2 b c £1395
84	4	NEWM	7f Firm		3298	
80	2	CHEP	8f Gd/Fm		3680	
39	9	NEWM	10f Soft		4543	

KINGS SECRET 2 ch c £1751
89	3	LEIC	7f Firm		3840	
92	2	KEMP	8f Soft		4036	

KINGS SIGNAL 2 b c £0
58	8	SALI	8f Gd/Sft		4163	

KINGS TO OPEN 3 b c £0
49a	7	WOLV	7f Aw		1035	
45	6	SOUT	7f Soft		1607	
50	7	LING	11f Firm	53	1911	
39	9	WARW	11f Good		3691	
0	14	WARW	11f Gd/Fm	47	3915	BL

KINGS VIEW 3 b c £0
55	11	RIPO	8f Soft		826	
64	4	YARM	11f Firm	64	2771	
47	7	LEIC	12f Gd/Fm		3219	

KINGS WELCOME 2 b c £5006
70	3	REDC	7f Gd/Fm		2862	
78	1	**THIR**	7f Gd/Fm		3347*	
93	3	HAYD	8f Soft		3787	

KINGSALSA 4 br c £231461
111	3	NAD	9f Good		768	
116	2	SAIN	8f Hldng		1123	
115	1	**CHAN**	8f Soft		1619*	
117	3	DEAU	8f V		2571	
117	3	DEAU	8f Gd/Fm		3544	
117	2	LONG	8f Soft		3847	
117	2	LONG	8f Good		4259	

KINGSCLERE 3 b c £20145
111	1	**KEMP**	8f Gd/Fm		996*	
101	5	CHES	12f Gd/Fm		1216	
0	15	EPSO	12f Good		1848	
71	5	ASCO	12f Gd/Fm		3306	
0	9	WIND	10f Good		3641	

KINGSCROSS 2 ch c £0
0	12	LING	5f Soft		4187	
75	7	DONC	6f Gd/Sft		4449	

KINGSDON 3 b c £2917
95	6	SAND	8f Heavy	95	1055	
91	3	THIR	8f Good		1382	
0	13	HAYD	8f Gd/Sft	94	1535	
92	3	ASCO	12f Good	92	2117	t
85	6	NEWM	8f Gd/Fm	92	2614	t
83	5	NEWM	10f Gd/Fm	92	3421	t
87	4	SALI	8f Gd/Fm		3782	t
86	4	HAYD	11f Soft	87	4199	t
77	9	NEWM	8f Good		4199	t
83	5	NEWM	8f Gd/Fm	85	4340	tVI

KINGSTON VENTURE 4 b g £0

84 7 KEMP 16f Soft 93 1527

KINNESCASH 7 ch g £3125
56 7 EPSO 12f Heavy 82 1030
68 10 CHEP 18f Gd/Sft 79 1800
78 2 NEWB 16f Firm 76 2705

KINNINO 6 b g £6902
43a 2 LING 10f Aw 111
21a 8 LING 10f Aw 38 220
44a 1 **WOLV** 8f Aw 42 254*
39a 3 WOLV 9f Aw 44 405
40a 4 WOLV 8f Aw 44 431
10a 9 LING 8f Aw 43 596 bl
34a 3 LING 10f Aw 41 2212 bl
40 2 EPSO 10f Good 38 2790
44 1 **NOTT** 10f Gd/Fm 41 3111*
41 4 WIND 10f Good 43 3356
43 4 BRIG 10f Firm 43 3737
37 6 GOOD 8f Soft 43 4066
40 6 SAND 10f Soft 43 4208
26 8 BRIG 10f Soft 42 4419

KINSAILE 3 ro f £0
56 8 LING 6f Good 1399
41 10 NEWB 6f Gd/Fm 1783
33 13 SAND 5f Gd/Fm 55 2478

KINSMAN 3 b c £8951
67a 3 WOLV 7f Aw 68 534
58 7 DONC 7f Good 68 736
40 14 WIND 6f Good 67 852 bl
55 6 WARW 7f Soft 65 1061
64 2 BRIG 7f Firm 1467 vis
65a 3 LING 7f Aw 1745 vis
68 1 **BRIG** 6f Firm 63 2042* vis
51 6 CATT 8f Gd/Fm 67 2440 vis
53 10 EPSO 7f Good 67 2794 vis
68 1 **EPSO** 6f Gd/Fm 66 3405* vis
53 7 EPSO 6f Good 3689 vis
0 19 LING 6f Soft 68 4270 vis

KIPPANOUR 8 b g £0
0a 14 SOUT 16f Aw 40 644 bl
23 5 PONT 22f Heavy 35 940 bl
0 10 PONT 18f Soft 28 4376

KIRISNIPPA 5 b g £9920
40a 6 SOUT 8f Aw 56 176
3a 11 WOLV 8f Aw 52 233 VIS
39a 5 SOUT 11f Aw 48 325
52a 1 **SOUT** 11f Aw 42 390*
44a 3 SOUT 12f Aw 48 456
54a 1 **SOUT** 11f Aw 51 474*
53a 6 SOUT 11f Aw 57 512
23a 10 SOUT 11f Aw 55 560
47a 5 SOUT 11f Aw 53 671
52 3 BRIG 12f Gd/Fm 51 1128
54 2 BRIG 12f Firm 51 1209
51 7 SALI 12f Good 51 1350
54 4 NEWB 13f Gd/Fm 52 1784
0 15 YORK 12f Firm 56 2002
52 3 SAND 11f Good 52 2530
49 5 BRIG 12f Good 51 2725
29 9 WIND 12f Gd/Fm 50 3049
42 4 CHEP 12f Gd/Fm 50 3255
48 2 BATH 13f Gd/Fm 45 3518
0 12 KEMP 14f Gd/Fm 45 3800

KIRIWINA 2 ch f £0
22 9 SAND 5f Heavy 1046
56 6 SALI 6f Gd/Fm 1882
33 10 FOLK 5f Gd/Fm 2290
0 16 LING 7f Firm 51 3830
0 15 LING 6f Good 4097

KIRKBYS TREASURE 2 br c £537
41 8 HAYD 5f Gd/Sft 1835
73 3 HAMI 5f Gd/Fm 2639
39 6 RIPO 5f Gd/Fm 2835

63 6 NEWC 6f Good 3245
71 5 CARL 5f Firm 3571
29 9 AYR 6f Heavy 66 4305

KIROVSKI 3 b c £42454
73 2 SAND 8f Good 68 1964
80 1 **CARL** 8f Gd/Fm 70 2242+
85 1 **NEWM** 8f Good 76 3022*
90 1 **ASCO** 8f Gd/Fm 84 3338*
88 3 ASCO 8f Gd/Sft 90 4126

KIRSCH 3 ch f £5680
66a 2 LING 6f Aw 64 4
59a 3 LING 6f Aw 62
69a 3 LING 6f Aw 66 269 VIS
71a 1 **WOLV** 5f Aw 66 361* vis
61a 5 LING 6f Aw 70 444 vis
59a 6 LING 6f Aw 70 526 vis
32 13 BRIG 5f Firm 66 1334
24 8 CHES 6f Gd/Sft 1780 vis
56 5 WARW 7f Gd/Fm 58 2036 vis
56 3 LEIC 6f Gd/Fm 56 2511 vis
53 7 LEIC 7f Gd/Fm 56 2918 vis
34 6 YARM 6f Gd/Fm 55 3386 vis
0 16 LING 6f Firm 53 3759 vis
0 18 AYR 5f Heavy 50 4307 vis

KIRTHAR 2 b c £900
85 2 LING 6f Firm 3492
82 6 GOOD 6f Good 3881

KISS CURL 2 ch f £0
0 15 KEMP 7f Soft 4034
0 19 WIND 6f Gd/Sft 4289

KISS ME KATE 4 b f £0
50 16 NEWB 10f Good 67 1375

KISSED BY MOONLITE 4 gr f £0
0 27 ASCO 7f Gd/Fm 53 2999
0 6 CATT 16f Gd/Fm 3199
5a 12 SOUT 11f Aw 4150

KISSING TIME 3 b f £0
0 16 NEWB 7f Gd/Fm 78 1405
71 5 WIND 10f Gd/Fm 75 2885
63 10 LING 6f Firm 75 3280
0 17 BATH 5f Firm 73 4432 BL
0 20 DONC 5f Heavy 70 4570

KISTY 3 b f £1717
61 8 BATH 10f Good 72 1094
69 3 LEIC 12f Gd/Sft 70 1571
70 3 BEVE 12f Firm 70 1919
70 3 HAYD 14f Gd/Fm 71 2445
53 6 BATH 12f Gd/Fm 3517
48 6 BRIG 12f Gd/Sft 68 4123
57 6 BATH 10f Soft 65 4436
46 15 NEWM 8f Gd/Sft 65 4536

KITTY BANKES 2 b f £0
0 15 BATH 8f Soft 4430

KIVOTOS 2 gr c £0
58 6 GOOD 8f Good 3906
73 4 BRIG 8f Gd/Sft 4116

KNAVES ASH 9 ch g £554
0 14 PONT 8f Heavy 942
22 12 HAMI 8f Gd/Fm 52 1190
35 15 REDC 8f Firm 49 1296
34 9 HAYD 11f Soft 46 1819
44 3 CHES 10f Gd/Fm 2245
34 6 HAMI 9f Firm 43 2397
32 7 HAYD 11f Gd/Fm 43 2453
39 8 MUSS 8f Gd/Sft 43 2533
34 4 AYR 7f Gd/Fm 40 3138
31 10 CATT 7f Gd/Fm 40 3200
35 4 HAYD 8f Good 40 3288

KNIGHT CROSSING 2 b c £0
64 5 YORK 6f Soft 4283
27 10 NEWC 6f Heavy 4402

KNIGHTS EMPEROR 3 b c £308

81 4 LEIC 8f Good 789
74 11 NEWM 7f Gd/Sft 983
0 16 YORK 8f Firm 74 1341
57 6 WARW 11f Gd/Fm 71 2842
0 12 LEIC 10f Firm 3838 BL

KNIGHTS RETURN 3 ch c £0
2a 10 WOLV 9f Aw 37 1040
0 14 NOTT 14f Good 41 2008
27 5 WARW 11f Gd/Fm 2253

KNOBBLEENEEZE 10 ch g £3841
0 12 BEVE 7f Firm 47 1275 vis
32 8 BRIG 8f Gd/Sft 45 1462 vis
35 8 LING 7f Soft 45 1542 vis
44 3 BRIG 7f Good 45 1652
30 7 CHEP 7f Gd/Sft 42 1799
18 12 LEIC 8f Firm 44 2027
37 5 CHES 8f Good 41 2673 vis
43 2 BRIG 7f Gd/Fm 41 2729 vis
35 4 CHEP 7f Gd/Fm 39 2974 vis
42 1 **SALI** 7f Gd/Fm 41 3294* vis
31 6 FOLK 7f Gd/Fm 41 3445 vis
33 7 SALI 8f Firm 44 3753 vis
33 11 CHEP 7f Gd/Fm 44 3873 vis
20 13 YARM 7f Firm 43 3939 vis
31 11 GOOD 8f Soft 42 4066 vis
37 4 NEWC 7f Heavy 41 4428 vis

KNOCK 2 b c £7274
63 4 BRIG 6f Gd/Sft 1507
80 1 **BRIG** 6f Good 1648*
71 5 YARM 6f Gd/Fm 1954
80 2 NEWM 6f Gd/Fm 2959
80 4 NEWM 6f Gd/Fm 80 3165
79 3 GOOD 7f Good 80 3660
65 11 DONC 7f Firm 79 3901
72 4 BRIG 6f Soft 78 4170

KNOCKEMBACK NELLIE 4 b f £7457
24 11 BRIG 5f Gd/Sft 65 897
0 19 BATH 6f Good 63 1092
58 7 WIND 6f Gd/Sft 1423 BL
67 1 **LING** 5f Soft 60 1543* bl
68 2 BRIG 5f Gd/Fm 64 1932 bl
67 4 **SAND** 5f Good 1966* bl
0 14 WARW 5f Gd/Fm 66 2252 bl
48 11 HAYD 5f Gd/Fm 66 2505 bl
51 5 BATH 5f Firm 2788 bl
52 13 GOOD 5f Gd/Fm 63 3091 bl
46 9 SAND 5f Good 60 3436 bl
56 5 EPSO 6f Good 3689 bl
51 6 WIND 5f Gd/Sft 55 4295 bl
0 17 NEWB 5f Gd/Sft 54 4459 bl

KNOCKHOLT 4 b g £10156
82 12 NEWM 12f Firm 98 1187
71 8 ASCO 22f Good 2153
98 1 **NEWB** 16f Firm 95 2705*
91 7 ASCO 16f Gd/Fm 3302
88 12 DONC 15f Firm 97 3890

KNOCKTOPHER ABBEY 3 ch c £997
82 5 EPSO 7f Gd/Sft 82 1826
64 3 SAND 7f Gd/Fm 82 2495
65 5 EPSO 7f Good 2792
77 3 CHEP 8f Gd/Fm 78 3254
68 6 BATH 8f Gd/Fm 78 3514
75 5 LING 8f Firm 77 3831
59 12 KEMP 8f Soft 75 4038
64 10 NOTT 8f Heavy 74 4414

KNOTTY HILL 8 b g £0
0 19 NEWC 6f Firm 50 3605

KOCAL 4 b g £516
43a 2 SOUT 8f Aw 45 584
32a 5 SOUT 8f Aw 45 647
36 9 WIND 10f Gd/Sft 43 1100
36 8 REDC 8f Firm 40 1296

(continued)

	19	DONC	7f Good	38	1519	
0a	15	SOUT	8f Aw	43	2121	
0a	16	SOUT	8f Aw	40	2379	BL

KOINCIDENTAL 3 b f £0

68	7	NOTT	8f Gd/Fm		1268	
0	15	GOOD	8f Gd/Sft		1811	
52	9	WIND	8f Gd/Fm		2211	
31	11	LING	7f Good	58	2591	
48	5	EPSO	10f Good	53	3762	
33	5	YARM	8f Gd/Fm	50	3970	
0	12	BRIG	10f Soft	47	4174	

KOMALUNA 2 ch c £0

65	7	REDC	6f Good		1893	
56	9	RIPO	5f Gd/Fm		2100	
0	12	BEVE	5f Gd/Fm		2480	
30	8	RIPO	6f Gd/Fm		3184	t
28	10	REDC	6f Gd/Sft	50	4502	

KOMASEPH 8 b g £219

35a	3	SOUT	6f Aw	35	602	bl
28a	6	SOUT	6f Aw	41	697	bl
0	16	PONT	8f Gd/Sft	38	1101	
31a	6	SOUT	7f Aw		1305	
30a	4	SOUT	6f Aw	35	1421	
20a	9	SOUT	8f Aw	34	1806	
18	9	NOTT	6f Gd/Fm	33	2193	
44a	7	WOLV	6f Aw		3275	t
0	17	YARM	7f Firm		3921	t

KOMENA 2 b f £5208

66	4	WIND	5f Good		2711	
76	2	LEIC	6f Gd/Fm		3096	
86	1	**BRIG**	6f Firm		3525*	
87	4	DONC	7f Gd/Fm	85	3860	
0	17	NEWM	7f Good	87	4157	

KOMISTAR 5 ch g £46542

48	12	EPSO	10f Heavy	88	1031	
87	2	CHEP	10f Gd/Sft		1797	
84	8	ASCO	10f Good	88	2170	
75	11	YORK	10f Good		2696	
77	7	NEWM	10f Good	86	3024	
81	3	PONT	12f Gd/Fm	84	3224	
87	1	**NEWB**	10f Firm	83	3997*	
69	9	NEWB	10f Sft/Hv	87	4473	

KOMPLIMENT 2 ch c £8471

62	5	NEWM	5f Soft		985	
85	1	**CHES**	5f Gd/Fm		1221*	
84	3	WIND	5f Gd/Sft		1426	
63	11	ASCO	5f Good		2113	

KONA GOLD 6 b g £132530

121£2	GULF	6f Fast		17	

KONKER 5 ch g £3947

48	11	AYR	10f Good	57	3368	
43	10	NEWC	9f Firm	57	3603	
50	3	REDC	10f Gd/Sft	53	4221	
58	1	**NEWC**	10f Heavy	52	4404*	

KOOKABURRA 3 b c £23495

99	1	**DONC**	8f Gd/Fm		704*	
0	13	CHES	8f Gd/Fm	95	1215	
85	4	KEMP	8f Soft		1530	
100	6	NEWM	7f Gd/Fm		1693	
98	3	ASCO	8f Good	93	2117	
100	4	NEWM	10f Gd/Fm	96	2596	
106	1	**NEWB**	10f Firm	97	3453*	
102	2	DONC	10f Firm		3889	

KOOL JULES 4 b f £0

0a	13	SOUT	11f Aw		248	
0a	10	WOLV	8f Aw		308	
19a	6	SOUT	7f Aw		427	
0a	10	SOUT	8f Aw	29	585	BL
7	9	YARM	8f Good	25	1772	t

KOORI 2 b f £0

10	12	GOOD	8f Good	3881	

KORASOUN 3 b c £6175

104	2	CURR	10f Gd/Sft		1627	
92	10	CURR	12f Good		2409	

KOSEVO 6 b g £3349

30a	9	SOUT	5f Aw	53	673	vis
30a	7	SOUT	6f Aw	53	698	vis
44	10	SOUT	6f Good	56	802	vis
3	15	THIR	7f Soft	53	908	vis
33	13	THIR	6f Gd/Sft	50	1356	vis
47	5	NOTT	5f Good	53	1871	vis
50a	2	SOUT	5f Aw	50	1976	vis
32	10	RIPO	5f Gd/Fm	48	2107	vis
0a	11	SOUT	6f Aw	50	2297	vis
30	10	CATT	5f Aw	47	2418	vis
0	20	NEWC	5f Good	47	2525	vis
33	13	HAYD	5f Gd/Fm	45	2701	vis
28	10	LEIC	5f Gd/Fm	42	2777	bl
0	19	THIR	6f Gd/Fm	47	3123	bl
38	3	LEIC	5f Gd/Fm	39	3214	bl
36	10	BEVE	5f Good	48	3398	bl
0	12	NEWM	6f Good	43	3613	bl
24	10	BEVE	5f Gd/Fm	43	3653	bl
35a	6	WOLV	6f Aw	49	3774	bl
43	1	**YARM**	6f Gd/Fm	38	3964*	bl
0a	11	SOUT	6f Aw	47	4155	bl

KOSMIC LADY 3 b f £327

65	14	NEWB	7f Soft		915	
63	9	SAND	10f Heavy		1045	
50	7	WARW	8f Gd/Fm		3914	
43	9	BRIG	10f Soft	55	4174	
50	3	BATH	8f Soft	53	4435	t

KPOLO 5 b g £0

22a	8	SOUT	12f Aw	84	

KRANTOR 3 ch c £5589

75	6	KEMP	8f Soft		1532	
81	2	GOOD	8f Gd/Fm		1960	
94	1	**EPSO**	10f Gd/Sft		2434*	
65	5	ASCO	10f Gd/Fm		3017	
87	5	NEWM	10f Good		4017	

KRISPIN 3 ch c £7252

76	6	LEIC	8f Good		789	
0	15	NEWM	7f Gd/Sft		983	
83	3	NOTT	8f Gd/Sft		1084	
79	3	RIPO	10f Gd/Fm	78	2102	
80	1	**PONT**	10f Gd/Fm		2558*	
69	11	GOOD	8f Gd/Fm	84	3063	
87	2	YARM	10f Firm	81	3941	
53	12	YORK	10f Soft	85	4282	

KRISTINEAU 2 ch f £0

20	10	LEIC	7f Heavy		4312	
59	14	NEWM	7f Soft		4541	

KRYSTAL MAX 7 b g £8611

79a	4	LING	6f Aw	78	113	
79a	2	WOLV	5f Aw	78	146	
30a	11	SOUT	5f Aw		214	
73a	2	WOLV	5f Aw		272	
77a	5	WOLV	6f Aw	78	320	
70a	1	LING	6f Aw		354*	
70a	1	**LING**	5f Aw		2650*	
74a	1	**LING**	7f Aw		2759*	

KUMAIT 6 b g £1052

84	4	NEWB	7f Gd/Fm	101	1946	
79	7	YARM	7f Firm		2389	
92	6	HAYD	6f Gd/Fm		2458	
79	9	GOOD	7f Firm		3155	
71	6	CHES	7f Gd/Fm	90	3427	

KUMAKAWA 2 ch c £2335

45	13	CARL	5f Firm		1252	
45	9	DONC	5f Good		1844	
41	10	REDC	7f Gd/Fm		2862	VIS
32	10	RIPO	6f Good		3697	
53	1	**LEIC**	8f Firm	47	3837*	
53a	3	WOLV	8f Aw	53	4439	

KUMATOUR 5 b h £5085

102	3	THIR	12f Gd/Sft	100	1715	
92	11	NEWC	16f Firm	100	2336	
70	6	ASCO	12f Gd/Fm		3306	

KUMON EILEEN 4 ch f £0

30a	9	LING	10f Aw		314	
14a	7	LING	12f Aw	40	377	

KUNDALILA 2 b f £287

0	13	NEWC	6f Good		3245	
59	4	BEVE	8f Gd/Fm		3675	
57	8	BEVE	7f Good		3953	
0	14	CATT	7f Gd/Fm	61	4254	

KURANDA 2 gr f £0

56	6	YARM	8f Gd/Fm		3665	

KUSTER 4 b c £2551

88	4	WIND	8f Good		851	
88	2	WIND	10f Gd/Fm		1198	
87	4	KEMP	12f Soft		4039	
78	7	NEWM	12f Good	87	4342	
86	5	DONC	12f Heavy	87	4580	

KUSTOM KIT KEVIN 4 b c £4137

47a	3	SOUT	12f Aw		387	
61a	2	SOUT	8f Aw		453	
57a	2	SOUT	8f Aw		500	
23a	10	SOUT	11f Aw	53	561	
57a	1	**SOUT**	8f Aw	53	584*	
35a	8	SOUT	8f Aw	59	647	
0	19	WARW	8f Soft	53	1066	
0	17	NOTT	10f Gd/Sft	47	1370	
41	7	NEWM	8f Gd/Fm	40	1690	t
42	3	LEIC	8f Firm	40	2027	t
25	9	HAYD	11f Gd/Fm	42	2453	t
29	15	DONC	7f Gd/Fm	42	2612	t
0	22	REDC	8f Gd/Fm	40	2861	t
20	12	THIR	8f Gd/Fm	39	3344	BL
0	17	LEIC	8f Gd/Sft		4033	

KUT O ISLAND 2 br c £0

65	11	KEMP	8f Gd/Fm		3799	
0	25	NEWM	7f Good		4158	t

KUTUB 3 b c £87414

118	1	**LONG**	11f V		864*	
115	2	LONG	11f V		1317	
112	4	CHAN	12f V		1752	BL
117	2	DEAU	10f Gd/Fm		3374	
117	3	MAIS	10f Good		4050	

KUUIPO 3 b f £848

34	7	THIR	7f Soft		930	
0a	16	SOUT	7f Aw	54	1202	VIS
0	20	REDC	8f Aw	54	1300	t
54	6	NEWC	10f Gd/Sft		1480	t
54	7	HAYD	12f Gd/Sft		1788	
47	2	NOTT	10f Good	48	2007	t
43	6	BEVE	10f Gd/Fm	40	2484	t
42	5	PONT	12f Gd/Fm	46	2829	t
27	7	PONT	8f Gd/Fm	42	3226	t
39	4	HAYD	11f Gd/Fm	40	3480	t

KUWAIT DAWN 4 b f £0

0	20	DONC	8f Good	90	733	
0	17	NEWM	7f Gd/Sft	86	966	
52	10	EPSO	9f Gd/Sft		1825	
73	6	NEWM	10f Gd/Fm	82	2287	
48	8	LEIC	12f Gd/Fm	77	2509	
14	6	KEMP	9f Gd/Sft	77	2581	VIS
27	13	YORK	7f Heavy	73	4302	
60	10	NEWM	8f Soft		4544	

KUWAIT FLAVOUR 4 b c £384

56a	6	WOLV	7f Aw		478	
49	8	WIND	8f Gd/Fm		3350	
74	4	NEWM	8f Gd/Fm		3626	
57	5	WARW	7f Good		3696	
63	8	LEIC	10f Firm		3838	

KUWAIT MILLENNIUM 3 b c £293

75	5	THIR	12f Good		1157	
71	4	CHEP	12f Heavy		1554	
70	5	SAND	10f Gd/Fm		1992	

KUWAIT ROSE 4 b c £6219

39a	6	WOLV	6f Aw		63	
68a	2	SOUT	7f Aw		73	
44a	6	SOUT	6f Aw	65	218	
54	4	WARW	8f Soft	60	1066	
73	5	LING	7f Gd/Sft		1261	
64	4	FOLK	7f Gd/Fm		2293	
32	9	YARM	8f Gd/Fm	65	2415	
66	2	WARW	6f Good		2462	
69	5	KEMP	6f Gd/Fm		2747	
57	8	NEWM	6f Gd/Fm	65	3457	
67	1	WARW	7f Good		3696*	
44	15	YORK	7f Gd/Fm	69	3809	
0	13	BRIG	7f Gd/Sft	70	4121	

KUWAIT SAND 4 b c £558

36a	7	WOLV	6f Aw		63	
55a	3	LING	6f Aw		95	
42a	7	WOLV	5f Aw	55	139	

KUWAIT THUNDER 4 ch c £940

33a	11	SOUT	7f Aw	57	368	vis
30a	7	WOLV	8f Aw	51	431	
34a	4	WOLV	12f Aw	45	520	
30a	4	WOLV	12f Aw	40	607	
34	9	DONC	10f Gd/Fm	46	705	
37	6	HAMI	8f Gd/Fm	43	1360	vis
0	16	DONC	7f Good	40	1519	
37	7	AYR	8f Gd/Fm	40	1658	vis
24	5	REDC	8f Gd/Fm	37	2147	vis
30	9	MUSS	8f Gd/Sft	35	2533	vis
31	5	REDC	8f Gd/Fm	32	2861	vis
23	7	THIR	8f Gd/Fm	32	2970	vis
33	2	HAMI	8f Gd/Sft	31	3380	vis
23	6	HAMI	8f Gd/Sft	31	3534	vis

KUWAIT TROOPER 3 b c £27039

57a	6	LING	8f Aw		103	
16a	8	LING	10f Aw		204	t
68a	4	LING	10f Aw		240	
66	1	MUSS	12f Gd/Sft		799*	
26	12	WIND	12f Heavy	65	937	
63	3	WIND	12f Gd/Fm	62	1199	
93	1	YORK	14f Gd/Fm		1311*	
90	8	ASCO	16f Good		2068	
105	5	GOOD	12f Gd/Fm		3061	
105	2	GOOD	14f Good		3645	
106	2	KEMP	12f Gd/Fm		3792	BL
97	11	DONC	15f Firm		3898	bl

KWAHERI 2 b f £342

0	W	SAND	5f Gd/Fm		762	
0	18	KEMP	6f Gd/Fm		1924	
75	4	NEWB	7f Firm		2810	
58	11	SALI	7f Gd/Fm		3292	

KYLKENNY 5 b g £0

50	9	SAND	10f Soft	55	4208	
34	9	BATH	12f Soft	55	4433	

KYLLACHY 2 b c £5366

86	1	CHEP	5f Gd/Fm		3252*	
86	2	BEVE	5f Sft/Hvy		4042	
88	2	SAND	5f Soft	85	4202	

L A TOUCH 7 b m £269

0	14	BEVE	5f Firm	49	2732	
50	3	WARW	7f Gd/Fm	49	2840	
32	6	FOLK	7f Gd/Fm	51	3041	
43	8	LING	7f Firm	51	3279	
43	6	YARM	7f Gd/Fm	51	3384	
23	14	LING	6f Firm	49	3493	
0	20	NEWC	6f Firm	49	3605	

L S LOWRY 4 b c £0

0a	12	LING	12f Aw	77	4271	

LA BIRBA 3 b f £0

6	8	WARW	7f Soft		813	
27	11	NOTT	6f Gd/Sft		1081	bl

LA CAPRICE 3 ch f £8656

65	10	CHES	5f Gd/Fm	78	1219	
76	3	THIR	5f Good	77	1384	
76	2	DONC	6f Good		1517	
51	12	KEMP	6f Gd/Fm	76	1925	
76	2	NEWM	5f Gd/Fm	75	2288	
68	7	EPSO	5f Gd/Sft	75	2432	
81	1	SAND	5f Gd/Fm	76	2934*	
78	7	YORK	5f Gd/Fm	81	3569	
0	18	KEMP	6f Gd/Fm	81	4037	
69	6	NEWM	6f Gd/Fm		4535	

LA CHATELAINE 6 b m £0

0	11	BRIG	12f Gd/Sft		893	

LA CINECITTA 4 ch f £0

0	14	SOUT	11f Gd/Sft	39	855	
0a	11	SOUT	11f Aw		1415	
22	6	LEIC	8f Gd/Sft		1732	
27	10	REDC	9f Gd/Fm		2865	
33	5	CATT	12f Gd/Fm		3202	
0	10	REDC	14f Gd/Fm		3633	

LA DOYENNE 6 ch m £0

48a	6	LING	5f Aw	58	91	

LA FAY 3 b f £0

0	15	WIND	10f Gd/Fm		1200	
61	7	YARM	10f Gd/Fm	70	1955	
0	8	WIND	12f Good	68	2370	
38	11	THIR	12f Gd/Fm	68	3125	t
39	10	BATH	12f Soft	65	4433	t

LA FOSCARINA 2 ch f £0

17	12	HAYD	5f Heavy		989	

LA GANDILIE 3 gr f £3842

103	3	CHAN	9f Good		2401	

LA MONDOTTE 2 b f £0

68	5	BATH	10f Soft		4140	

LA NOTTE 2 b f £5208

76	3	YARM	6f Gd/Fm		3385	
78	1	LING	6f Firm		3832*	
83	3	CHES	7f Soft	79	4070	
83	3	DONC	7f Soft	80	4460	

LA PASSIONE 2 ch f £1035

93	2	DONC	6f Heavy		4575	

LA PETITE FLAMECHE 5 b m £0

0	15	WARW	11f Gd/Sft	43	1707	

LA PIAZZA 4 ch f £1848

0	25	NEWM	6f Gd/Fm	82	1173	
52a	9	WOLV	6f Aw	69	1391	
79	7	YORK	6f Firm	80	2000	
0	13	WIND	6f Gd/Fm	79	2207	
76	2	KEMP	6f Gd/Fm		2747	
76	3	NEWM	6f Gd/Fm	78	2804	
66	3	CATT	5f Gd/Fm		2931	
70	6	BATH	6f Gd/Fm	77	3516	
69	6	YARM	5f Gd/Fm	75	3668	
58	9	YORK	6f Soft		4287	
0a	12	WOLV	7f Aw	66	4550	

LA SAYIDA 2 b f £0

44	11	NEWB	7f Sft/Hvy		4467	

LA SPEZIANA 3 b f £12120

73	1	NEWB	7f Gd/Fm	62	1405*	
80	1	SAND	7f Soft	68	1564*	
75	3	BATH	8f Gd/Sft	74	1671	

LA SYLPHIDE GB 3 ch f £798

62	3	NEWC	8f Good		2520	
52	6	RIPO	10f Gd/Fm		3012	
33	14	PONT	8f Firm		3506	

LA TORTUGA 3 b g £251

69a	4	LING	7f Aw		108	
67a	5	WOLV	8f Aw		171	BL
62a	8	WOLV	7f Aw	75	188	bl

0	19	WARW	7f Soft	75	1061	
61	7	HAYD	6f Soft	70	1494	
43	6	CHES	6f Gd/Sft		1780	
46	6	HAMI	11f Gd/Fm		1909	
0	W	HAMI	8f Firm		2093	
0	19	NEWC	6f Heavy	63	4425	

LA TRAVIATA 2 b f £0

0	11	KEMP	7f Soft		4034	
0	18	BRIG	7f Soft		4172	
39	8	NEWC	7f Heavy		4403	

LA VIDA LOCA 2 ch f £17935

95	2	LEOP	6f Gd/Fm		2399	
98	5	LEOP	6f Good		3372	
99	4	CURR	7f Gd/Fm		3845	
104	4	LONG	8f Good		4260	

LA VITA E BELLA 2 b f £17682

68	7	KEMP	7f Gd/Sft		2583	
81	2	HAYD	8f Soft		3766	
87	1	HAYD	8f Gd/Sft		4104*	
96	1	NEWM	8f Soft		4546*	

LAA JADEED 5 b g £0

11a	7	SOUT	7f Aw	41	476	
11a	7	WOLV	9f Aw	38	569	
29a	5	WOLV	9f Aw	35	637	
7a	7	SOUT	12f Aw	38	683	
0a	6	WOLV	12f Aw	33	723	
0	14	BEVE	7f Firm	39	2221	BL
26	9	BEVE	10f Gd/Fm	37	2518	bl
0	14	NOTT	14f Gd/Fm	30	3002	

LABRETT 3 b c £6591

83	7	HAYD	5f Heavy		988	bl
69	9	SAND	5f Heavy	90	1047	bl
75	10	CHES	6f Gd/Fm	85	1220	
64	13	GOOD	7f Gd/Sft	81	1470	
77	4	KEMP	6f Gd/Fm	77	1925	bl
76	4	PONT	6f Firm		2177	bl
8	6	LING	6f Gd/Fm	77	2216	bl
78	1	KEMP	6f Gd/Fm		2747*	
77	1	BATH	6f Firm		3208*	bl
71	4	NEWM	5f Gd/Fm	77	3631	bl
0	18	DONC	6f Firm	76	3894	bl
54	8	KEMP	6f Gd/Sft	73	4037	bl
63	14	NEWM	5f Good	73	4185	bl
66	7	LING	6f Soft	72	4270	bl

LACE WING 3 ch f £3243

89	1	SALI	10f Good		1344*	
83	6	NEWB	10f Gd/Fm		1945	

LADY ABAI 3 b f £0

61	8	CHEP	10f Gd/Sft		1796	
0	12	LEIC	10f Gd/Fm		2774	
0	12	BATH	12f Gd/Fm		3818	

LADY AMBITION 2 b f £0

46	12	CARL	5f Gd/Fm		1252	
55	5	CATT	5f Gd/Fm		2741	
12	9	BEVE	5f Good		2880	
48	6	HAMI	5f Gd/Sft		3376	

LADY ANGHARAD 4 b f £68577

83	1	NOTT	10f Gd/Fm		1271*	
87	1	LEIC	10f Firm		2030*	
90	1	SAND	10f Good	84	2475*	
75	9	NEWC	10f Good	89	3703	
73	20	NEWM	8f Gd/Fm	89	4212	

LADY ANGOLA 2 ch f £375

85	4	NEWM	7f Good		3607	
61	10	KEMP	7f Soft		4034	
63	7	WIND	8f Heavy		4524	

LADY BALLA CALM 4 b f £0

0a	13	LING	6f Aw		25	
0a	9	LING	8f Aw		109	
6a	8	LING	6f Aw	25	263	
10a	8	LING	5f Aw	28	372	
0a	11	LING	7f Aw	23	439	

LADY BEAR 2 b f £14328

71	6	YORK	6f Gd/Fm		1312	
68	3	PONT	6f Good		1864	
58a	3	SOUT	7f Aw		2383	
69	4	AYR	7f Gd/Fm	67	2718	
65	4	REDC	6f Gd/Fm	64	2991	VIS
74	1	MUSS	7f Gd/Fm	64	3592*	vis
66	9	DONC	8f Gd/Sft	72	3879	vis
78	2	MUSS	8f Gd/Sft	72	4132	
81	1	YORK	7f Soft	76	4279*	

LADY BENSON 7 b m £217

62	4	HAMI	11f Good		848	t
24	7	FOLK	12f Soft		964	t

LADY BOXER 4 b f £30920

0	14	AYR	6f Gd/Fm	74	1654
0	18	HAYD	6f Gd/Fm	70	2444
0	17	CHES	8f Gd/Fm	63	2673
0	16	CHES	8f Firm	63	3170
45	8	HAMI	6f Gd/Fm	56	3377
74	1	CHES	8f Gd/Fm	68	3510*
62	10	HAYD	7f Soft	63	3785
82	1	AYR	6f Gd/Sft	74	4010*
88	1	CHES	6f Soft		4069*
92	11	NEWM	6f Good		4346
58	9	NEWB	6f Gd/Sft	86	4456
50	11	NEWM	8f Soft		4544

LADY BREANNE 4 b f £354

34a	6	LING	7f Aw		8
47a	3	LING	8f Aw		109
39a	6	LING	8f Aw	50	152
44	10	CHEP	6f Good	55	1971
43	9	GOOD	7f Gd/Fm	55	2128
38	9	YARM	8f Firm	50	2767

LADY CAROLINE 4 b f £0

0a	12	LING	7f Aw		159	BL
0	16	CHEP	8f Gd/Fm	42	2658	

LADY COLDUNELL 4 b f £2212

30	13	HAMI	13f Good	60	845	BL
53	3	EPSO	12f Gd/Fm	58	3402	
57	2	NEWC	14f Soft	54	3709	

LADY CYRANO 3 b f £1436

40a	3	SOUT	7f Aw		283	
27a	6	SOUT	7f Aw		330	
46a	2	SOUT	8f Aw		514	
12a	12	SOUT	8f Aw	41	555	BL
23a	6	SOUT	7f Aw		688	
0	16	NOTT	8f Gd/Sft	51	1365	
48	2	WARW	7f Gd/Fm	47	2036	
17	10	YARM	7f Gd/Fm		2413	
0	15	LEIC	7f Gd/Fm		2914	
14	9	LEIC	7f Gd/Fm		3332	
23	12	LEIC	6f Gd/Sft		4031	vis
3a	8	SOUT	6f Aw		4368	vis

LADY DEALER 5 b m £0

0	25	WIND	6f Gd/Fm	45	1196
0	8	LING	5f Soft	35	1543
0	U	SALI	7f Gd/Fm		1884
0	9	BRIG	8f Soft		4175
0	15	LING	6f Soft		4274
0a	15	LING	7f Aw		4331

LADY DONATELLA 3 b f £660

52	6	YARM	10f Good	60	3031
53	2	BEVE	12f Good		3399
44	7	BEVE	12f Good	53	3954

LADY EBERSPACHER 2 b f £1865

51	9	WIND	5f Good		849
75	4	GOOD	5f Gd/Fm		1454
75	2	SALI	5f Gd/Fm		2227
66	4	CHEP	5f Gd/Fm		2657
75	4	BATH	5f Gd/Fm		3815
0	11	LING	5f Soft		4187

LADY FEARLESS 3 b f £0

19a	8	SOUT	6f Aw		2947
0	18	CHEP	7f Good	45	3873
39	6	AYR	9f Soft		3988
0	14	PONT	17f Soft	49	4231

LADY FLORA 4 b f £0

37	10	PONT	8f Firm		3506
5	9	HAMI	9f Gd/Sft		3823

LADY GEORGIA 4 gr f £0

39a	9	WOLV	8f Aw	85	78

LADY HELEN 3 b f £8196

53	9	DONC	8f Gd/Fm	66	2320
62	5	NEWC	8f Good	62	2524
71	1	HAYD	8f Gd/Fm	62	2699*
59	10	NEWM	8f Gd/Fm	70	2855
75	1	NEWC	8f Gd/Fm	70	2988*
60	7	DONC	8f Gd/Fm	75	3160
59	10	NEWM	8f Gd/Fm	74	3317
50	7	CHES	10f Gd/Fm	74	3426

LADY IN LOVE 2 b f £0

37	12	DONC	6f Gd/Fm		1838	
0	11	NEWC	7f Gd/Fm		2985	BL

LADY IN THE NIGHT 2 ch f £258

61	4	SALI	5f Gd/Fm		2227
0	17	WIND	6f Good		3187
38	11	GOOD	6f Good		3881

LADY IN WAITING 5 b m £0

105	5	SAND	10f Soft		1587
106	5	CURR	10f Yldg		2404

LADY INCH 2 b f £0

62	10	YARM	8f Heavy		4475

LADY IONA 4 ch f £0

11a	7	SOUT	12f Aw	32	339

LADY IRENE 4 br f £0

9a	8	WOLV	16f Aw	36	194	
0a	12	SOUT	11f Aw		248	BL
0	11	LEIC	12f Gd/Sft	42	1736	

LADY JAZZ 5 b m £0

27	10	SALI	7f Gd/Fm	53	2978	t

LADY JEANNIE 3 b f £0

52	11	LING	7f Gd/Sft		1263
52	6	GOOD	7f Gd/Sft		1638
0	16	LING	6f Gd/Fm		2183
19	13	WIND	6f Gd/Sft	47	4294
26	8	WIND	6f Heavy		4526

LADY JO 4 ch f £2898

61a	6	LING	12f Aw	62	290
39a	6	LING	10f Aw	60	400
55	6	NEWB	10f Gd/Fm	60	1785
43	7	BRIG	10f Firm		2041
52	6	KEMP	9f Gd/Sft	56	2581
41	7	NEWB	9f Firm	58	2853
47	5	YARM	10f Good	54	3031
59	1	LING	11f Firm	54	3282*
42	6	NEWM	12f Gd/Fm	57	3461
56	9	FOLK	12f Gd/Fm	60	3586
25a	10	LING	12f Aw	54	4334

LADY JONES 3 b f £6413

0	16	NOTT	8f Gd/Sft	53	1085
59	1	HAYD	8f Soft	50	1822*
56	3	BRIG	8f Firm	59	2043
38	9	HAYD	8f Gd/Fm	58	2699
42	11	WIND	10f Gd/Fm		3045
50	5	EPSO	9f Good	54	3856
38	6	LEIC	8f Sft/Hvy	53	4310
44	7	BATH	10f Soft	53	4436
57	1	NOTT	10f Heavy	51	4509*

LADY KINVARRAH 2 b f £3244

64	10	WIND	5f Gd/Sft		1424
64	6	LEIC	5f Gd/Sft		1737
68	7	WIND	5f Gd/Sft		2209
68	3	FOLK	7f Good		2619
73	1	LEIC	6f Gd/Sft	69	4030*

68	9	BRIG	7f Soft	73	4416

LADY LAHAR 2 b f £42494

93	1	CHEP	6f Good		1968*
101	3	NEWM	6f Good		2565
97	4	NEWM	7f Gd/Fm		3316
109	1	CURR	7f Good		3719*
94	10	NEWM	6f Good		4159
107	4	DEAU	8f Heavy		4401

LADY LAUREATE 2 b f £0

39	10	WARW	15f Gd/Fm		3912
65	5	BRIG	8f Gd/Sft		4116
21a	6	WOLV	8f Aw		4250
0	21	NEWM	6f Good		4345

LADY LAUREN 4 b f £0

6a	10	WOLV	8f Aw		133

LADY LAZARUS 4 ch f £0

0	16	THIR	8f Soft	49	931

LADY LENOR 2 b f £1163

21	12	CARL	5f Firm		3571
77	2	CATT	5f Soft		4253
66a	3	WOLV	6f Aw		4548

LADY LIFFEY 2 ch f £0

45	8	SAND	5f Gd/Fm		2933
0	14	BATH	5f Firm		3204

LADY LOVE 3 b f £1620

63	5	MUSS	8f Gd/Fm		1144	
47	14	MUSS	7f Gd/Fm	67	1431	
64	2	REDC	7f Gd/Sft		1579	BL
56	9	NEWC	7f Good	64	3033	
28	9	REDC	8f Firm		3330	
60	2	NEWC	6f Good	58	3605	

LADY LUCHA 3 ch f £3358

75	12	NEWM	8f Gd/Fm		972
67	2	BATH	8f Gd/Fm		1436
72	1	RIPO	10f Gd/Fm		2105*
69	4	WIND	12f Good	72	2370

LADY MILETRIAN 2 b f £1320

76	5	NEWM	6f Gd/Fm		2618
80	2	NEWM	6f Gd/Fm		2854
42	8	WIND	6f Good		3187

LADY MUCK 4 b f £0

0	15	LEIC	8f Gd/Sft		4033
0	14	WIND	8f Gd/Sft		4292
27	7	YARM	11f Soft	44	4391

LADY NAIRN 4 b f £0

0a	11	WOLV	6f Aw		63	
15a	9	SOUT	6f Aw	47	280	
7a	9	WOLV	7f Aw		391	t

LADY NOOR 3 b f £0

0	20	WIND	6f Good	70	852
0	20	WIND	7f Gd/Fm	68	1196
0	23	NEWB	7f Gd/Sft	64	1405
0	12	NEWB	6f Gd/Sft	60	1591
37	5	WIND	6f Soft	55	2549
39	9	LING	7f Soft	52	4192
0	18	WIND	6f Gd/Sft	52	4294

LADY ODDJOB 4 gr f £0

19a	10	SOUT	8f Aw	50	176	bl

LADY OF BILSTON 3 b f £430

58a	3	WOLV	7f Aw		362
54a	4	WOLV	9f Aw		467

LADY OF CHAD 3 b f £49952

114	1	LONG	8f Heavy		1027*
105	8	LONG	8f V		1319
109	7	CHAN	11f Gd/Sft		1901
117	1	DEAU	8f Gd/Fm		3069*
100	6	NEWM	8f Gd/Fm		4211

LADY OF KILDARE 2 b f £21300

91	2	NAAS	6f Yldg		1750
81	8	SAND	7f Gd/Fm		2935
100	1	CURR	6f Good		3844*

LADY OF THE NIGHT 4 b m £770
```
50a  2  LING  10f Aw         238
0a  11  LING  12f Aw         267
20a 10  LING  7f Aw     47   438  t
```

LADY OF WINDSOR 3 ch f £7306
```
51  5  MUSS  7f Gd/Sft        900  vis
71  1  MUSS  8f Gd/Fm       1144*  vis
2  11  NOTT  8f Good         1407  vis
71  2  CARL  7f Firm    69   2017  vis
67  3  CARL  8f Gd/Fm   70   2241  vis
53  8  HAYD  8f Gd/Fm   69   2699  vis
52  9  AYR   6f Firm    67   2877  vis
54  6  CARL  8f Gd/Fm   67   3083  vis
56  7  HAMI  6f Gd/Sft  65   3377  bl
59  4  CARL  7f Firm         3573  vis
28 14  MUSS  7f Gd/Sft  62   4136  bl
56a 4  WOLV  6f Aw      60   4358  bl
63  1  MUSS  7f Soft    58   4518* bl
```

LADY PAHIA 2 ch f £336
```
90  4  KEMP  7f Gd/Fm            3359
```

LADY QUINTA 4 ch f £0
```
29a 7  LING  10f Aw         375
40a 5  LING  8f Aw         505  bl
```

LADY RACHEL 5 b m £1015
```
47a 3  WOLV  16f Aw      46   318
27a 7  SOUT  16f Aw      46   428
47a 2  SOUT  16f Aw      45   737  BL
40  5  SOUT  16f Gd/Sft  45   860  bl
39  7  NOTT  14f Heavy   42  1023  bl
```

LADY ROCK 2 b f £1187
```
54  7  CATT  5f Good          1659
56  8  HAMI  5f Gd/Fm         1906
63  4  RIPO  5f Gd/Fm         2835
54  6  MUSS  5f Good          3098
77  3  PONT  5f Firm          3500
64  6  MUSS  5f Gd/Sft        4131
53  6  YARM  5f Soft     68   4511
```

LADY ROCKSTAR 5 b m £609
```
69  7  LEIC  10f Good    75   793
74  2  BEVE  10f Heavy   74   975
67  7  WIND  10f Firm        1288
0  17  NEWB  10f Good    74  1375
64  7  NEWB  10f Gd/Fm   74  1785
59 10  YARM  10f Soft    71  4392
```

LADY SANDROVITCH 3 b f £250
```
45a 4  WOLV  5f Aw            42
47a 3  SOUT  6f Aw           181
43a 7  WOLV  7f Aw      49   257
37a 6  SOUT  6f Aw           426
32 11  DONC  5f Gd/Fm   47  3161
0  16  REDC  6f Firm    42  3312
```

LADY SANTANA 3 b f £0
```
62  5  WIND  12f Gd/Fm  67   748
```

LADY SHARP SHOT 2 b f £0
```
76  5  HAYD  8f Soft         3766
0  11  BATH  8f Firm         4429
```

LADY STALKER 3 b f £657
```
34 10  WIND  6f Gd/Fm   58  1877
29  9  CATT  5f Gd/Fm   54  2743
39 10  RIPO  6f Firm    54  2896
46  3  EPSO  6f Gd/Fm   47  3405
29 12  LING  6f Firm    47  3759
0  15  GOOD  5f Good    50  3908
```

LADY TILLY 3 b f £0
```
0a 12  SOUT  7f Aw      47  1506
42  5  REDC  7f Gd/Sft       1559
46  4  CATT  7f Gd/Sft       1818
53  4  CATT  7f Gd/Fm        2745
0  26  REDC  8f Gd/Fm   46  2861
0  11  THIR  8f Firm    46  2964
19 10  MUSS  7f Gd/Fm   45  3593
```

LADY TWO K 3 b f £3980

```
60  8  NOTT  8f Gd/Fm        1268
73  4  HAYD  11f Gd/Sft      1539
54  6  DONC  8f Gd/Fm        2611
0  13  PONT  8f Soft    72  4232
73  1  BATH  12f Soft   67  4433*
```

LADY UPSTAGE 3 b f £136743
```
103 1  KEMP  8f Soft          995*
113 2  YORK  10f Gd/Fm       1309
107 5  EPSO  12f Gd/Sft      1828
111 1  CURR  10f Yldg        2404*
102 7  GOOD  10f Firm        3151
115 3  LONG  10f Good        4263
115 2  WOOD  10f Firm        4399
```

LADY VETTORI 3 b f £4612
```
108 2  MAIS  7f Soft          946
```

LADY VIENNA 3 ch f £278
```
30  5  NOTT  10f Soft    50  1644
26  8  BRIG  10f Gd/Fm       1933
38  3  WARW  11f Gd/Fm       2253  VIS
29  8  LEIC  10f Gd/Fm       2510  vis
34  7  LEIC  8f Gd/Fm        2914
```

LADY WARD 2 b f £593
```
59  8  NOTT  6f Gd/Fm        2683
72  3  WIND  6f Good         3187
60  6  RIPO  6f Gd/Fm        3466
64  5  WARW  15f Good    70  3693
0  17  DONC  7f Gd/Fm    70  3860
```

LADY WYN 5 ch m £0
```
0  16  BRIG  10f Firm        1210
0  11  BRIG  12f Good        1647
0  13  WARW  11f Gd/Sft  25  1707
```

LADYCAKE 4 gr f £0
```
26  8  BATH  5f Good     43  1092
22  8  BATH  5f Firm         2788
0  14  CHEP  5f Gd/Fm    40  2976
0  14  WARW  5f Good         3694
```

LADYS HEART 5 b m £0
```
0a 12  WARW  7f Aw      48   75
```

LADYWELL BLAISE 3 b f £6939
```
50a 5  LING  6f Aw           221
62a 3  SOUT  7f Aw           278
69a 1  LING  6f Aw           334*
58a 4  WOLV  6f Aw      67   450
53a 6  LING  6f Aw      67   592
59  4  WARW  7f Soft         813
41 11  SALI  7f Good        1349
41a 6  LING  7f Aw          1745
37 13  WARW  11f Gd/Fm  55  2033
58  1  DONC  7f Gd/Fm   53  2320*
60  2  YARM  7f Firm    59  2391
0  12  KEMP  7f Gd/Fm   60  2749
28 12  KEMP  7f Gd/Fm   60  3076
53  7  LING  7f Firm    60  3279
37 13  LING  6f Firm    58  3493
0  15  LING  7f Gd/Fm   56  3759
0  13  KEMP  7f Gd/Fm   56  3796
45 10  GOOD  5f Good    53  3908
35  9  GOOD  7f Soft    59  4080
57  8  BATH  8f Soft        4142
```

LAFAYETTE 2 b c £0
```
0  19  DONC  7f Gd/Sft       4446
61 11  DONC  8f Heavy        4569
```

LAFFAH 5 b g £30966
```
60  1  CHEP  18f Gd/Fm  54  2490*  t
61  3  FOLK  16f Good   60  2622   t
58  4  NEWM  15f Gd/Fm  60  2856   t
65  1  BATH  17f Firm   60  2941*  t
67  1  GOOD  20f Gd/Fm  61  3085*  t
59  8  SAND  16f Good   67  3434   t
70  1  GOOD  16f Good   66  3905*  t
0  21  NEWM  18f Good   79  4353   t
```

LAFITE 4 b f £15544

```
75  9  NEWM  10f Gd/Fm  86  1170   t
95  1  YORK  10f Firm       1325*  t
78 11  EPSO  10f Good   91  1845   t
```

LAFLEUR 3 ch f £0
```
71  9  KEMP  11f Soft        1017
69  9  SALI  12f Firm        1179
48 12  WIND  12f Gd/Sft  68  1425
54  7  BRIG  10f Good    68  1649
53  9  NOTT  8f Good     63  1873  VIS
```

LAGGAN MINSTREL 2 b c £0
```
72  8  SALI  7f Good         2686
31 11  CHES  7f Soft         4068
```

LAGO 2 b c £0
```
52  8  CHEP  8f Gd/Fm        3680
```

LAGO DI COMO 3 b c £2756
```
73a 3  LING  10f Aw          240
26a 10 LING  10f Aw      65  315
60  4  LING  11f Firm    58  1911
69  1  LING  9f Firm         2322*
38 12  CHES  10f Good    71  2666
9  12  EPSO  9f Good     67  3685
```

LAGO DI LEVICO 3 ch c £1939
```
60  1  NOTT  8f Good          783*
57  5  BRIG  10f Gd/Sft  62  892
52  4  LEIC  8f Gd/Sft       1731
40  6  BRIG  8f Firm         2040
0   8  BRIG  8f Gd/Fm    54  2726
19  8  FOLK  9f Gd/Fm    50  3043
0  15  CHEP  7f Good     49  3873
```

LAGO DI VARANO 8 b g £37320
```
62 13  DONC  5f Soft     81  702   vis
72  6  NEWC  5f Soft     81  758   vis
73  3  THIR  5f Soft         905   vis
71  8  THIR  7f Good     77  1158  vis
76  3  THIR  6f Good     75  1383  bl
71  5  DONC  6f Good         1517  bl
73  3  CHES  5f Gd/Sft   75  1781  bl
80  1  HAYD  5f Gd/Sft   75  1792+ bl
82  5  RIPO  5f Good     81  1861  bl
73 12  YORK  5f Gd/Fm    82  1980  bl
82  5  DONC  5f Gd/Fm    82  2348  bl
84  3  SAND  5f Gd/Fm    81  2473  bl
69 10  YORK  5f Gd/Fm    81  2644  bl
79  7  YORK  6f Good     83  2697  bl
87  1  RIPO  6f Gd/Fm    82  3183+ bl
87  2  SAND  5f Good     86  3473  bl
79 10  YORK  6f Good     86  3543  bl
75 12  DONC  6f Gd/Fm    86  3861  bl
90  2  AYR   6f Gd/Sft   86  4012  bl
87  6  ASCO  5f Gd/Fm    90  4129  bl
87  5  YORK  6f Heavy    88  4301  bl
85  8  DONC  5f Soft     87  4466  bl
```

LAGOON 3 ch c £11316
```
96  5  NEWM  7f Gd/Fm    96  1153
95  4  GOOD  7f Gd/Sft   95  1470
94  7  SAND  7f Gd/Fm    95  2495
0  15  GOOD  7f Gd/Fm    94  3130
84  8  RIPO  8f Good     92  3699
92  3  AYR   7f Soft     89  3992
95  1  NEWM  8f Good         4199*
95  4  NEWM  8f Gd/Fm    93  4348
93  5  NEWM  8f Soft     93  4545
```

LAGUDIN 2 b c £19396
```
88  1  NEWM  7f Good          4020*
93  2  SAN   8f Heavy         4243
93  1  YARM  7f Soft          4389*
```

LAGUNA BAY 6 b m £0
```
0  18  LING  16f Firm    40  3755
```

LAHAAY 3 ch c £1091
```
59  9  WARW  8f Heavy         884
48  7  BRIG  7f Firm         1333
68  4  CHES  7f Gd/Fm    70  2250
```

LAHAN 3 b f £146925 ... (continued from previous)

56 5 DONC 8f Gd/Fm 70 2579
70 3 LEIC 10f Gd/Fm 69 3217
67 6 WARW 8f Gd/Fm 3914
0 13 BEVE 8f Sft/Hvy 70 4045

LAHAN 3 b f £146925
102 4 NEWB 7f Soft 913
120 1 **NEWM** 8f Firm 1185*

LAI SEE 2 b c £3716
52 10 GOOD 6f Gd/Sft 1472
57 11 CHEP 6f Gd/Sft 1798
65 8 KEMP 6f Firm 1924
80 2 LING 5f Gd/Fm 2214
78 2 PONT 5f Good 2360
79 2 KEMP 5f Firm 79 2868
74 5 GOOD 5f Good 78 3109
66 5 BATH 5f Good 3513
65 5 CHEP 5f Gd/Fm 73 3679 VIS
42a 7 WOLV 6f Aw 4381

LAILANI 2 b f £0
74 14 DONC 8f Gd/Sft 4445
74 7 NEWM 7f Soft 4541

LAJADHAL 11 gr g £0
0 13 FOLK 16f Good 28 2622
0 7 BATH 17f Firm 30 3625

LAKE ARIA 7 b g £0
28a 8 WOLV 7f Aw 61
0a 10 SOUT 6f Aw 32 87 bl
0a 11 SOUT 12f Aw 301 bl

LAKE DOMINION 11 b g £0
8a 6 SOUT 14f Aw 124
8a 7 LING 16f Aw 37 285 bl

LAKE KINNERET 2 b f £0
69 11 NEWM 7f Soft 4541

LAKE MILLSTATT 5 b m £0
35a 10 WOLV 8f Aw 72 137

LAKE SUNBEAM 4 b c £6803
68a 4 LING 8f Aw 92
73a 5 LING 12f Aw 77 151
70 5 GOOD 8f Gd/Sft 1635
67 6 LEIC 10f Firm 2030
70 1 **EPSO** 9f Gd/Sft 2433*
69 1 **SAND** 8f Gd/Fm 2920*
72 3 SALI 10f Gd/Fm 2981
72 2 EPSO 9f Gd/Fm 3404
46 9 YORK 9f Good 3808

LAKELAND PADDY 3 b c £6899
71 3 WIND 6f Good 73 852
75 3 KEMP 6f Soft 73 994
65 6 SALI 6f Firm 76 1178
68 4 SAND 7f Soft 74 1569
79 1 **NEWB** 6f Gd/Fm 1783*
68 7 NEWM 6f Good 80 3297
69 9 CHES 8f Gd/Fm 78 3510
0 17 KEMP 6f Gd/Sft 4037
56 12 LING 6f Soft 72 4270

LAKESIDE LADY 3 b f £0
0 14 BEVE 5f Good 3956
22 7 CATT 6f Soft 4255
28a 9 WOLV 8f Aw 4551

LAKOTA BRAVE 6 ch g £3060
51 6 SAND 8f Gd/Fm 2920
61 4 NEWM 8f Gd/Fm 3318 t
75a 1 **LING** 8f Aw 3756* t
59 6 GOOD 8f Good 62 3885 t

LALA SALAMA 4 br f £0
0 15 WIND 8f Gd/Fm 55 1201
0 10 LING 9f Good 52 1395
29 10 CHEP 10f Gd/Fm 47 3683
43 4 WARW 11f Gd/Fm 43 3915
3a 10 SOUT 11f Aw 4151

LAMBAY RULES 2 b c £0
74 7 NEWM 7f Firm 3298

---

70 9 NEWM 8f Good 4161

LAMBRINI LAD 5 b g £0
0a 9 SOUT 12f Aw 38 412

LAMBSON KATOOSHA 5 b m £0
0a 15 SOUT 8f Aw 50

LAMEH 3 ch f £804
89 3 NEWM 7f Gd/Fm 1155

LAMENT 4 b f £0
30a 8 SOUT 6f Aw 30
41a 8 WOLV 7f Aw 65 VIS
0 17 WARW 8f Soft 58 1066
56 4 WIND 6f Gd/Sft 1423

LAMERIE 4 b c £716
99a 4 LING 10f Aw 55

LAMMAS 3 b c £2250
89 3 LEOP 10f Soft 949

LAMMOSKI 3 ch c £263
22a 10 SOUT 5f Aw 46
3a 11 SOUT 6f Aw 74
0a 12 SOUT 5f Aw 179
42a 5 SOUT 5f Aw 217 VIS
30a 8 SOUT 5f Aw 300 vis
10a 10 SOUT 6f Aw 44 331
29a 9 SOUT 6f Aw 426 tBL
43a 5 SOUT 5f Aw 696 bl
50 10 DONC 6f Good 731
34 10 CATT 5f Gd/Fm 777
50 5 DONC 5f Gd/Fm 1843
38 12 BEVE 5f Firm 52 2223
36 10 DONC 6f Gd/Fm 52 2315 tbl
0 11 LEIC 10f Gd/Fm 2510
35 4 BEVE 12f Gd/Sft 40 3050
0 11 BEVE 16f Gd/Sft 35 3406
31 3 CATT 14f Soft 4002

LANCE FEATHER 2 b c £0
60 6 THIR 7f Gd/Fm 3347
53 8 THIR 7f Gd/Fm 3617
0 12 PONT 8f Soft 4086

LANCER 8 ch g £11412
31a 8 SOUT 14f Aw 47 37 vis
57 6 DONC 12f Gd/Fm 65 699 vis
67 1 **WARW** 12f Soft 63 815* vis
67 6 NEWM 12f Gd/Sft 66 968 vis
49 6 MUSS 12f Gd/Fm 66 1147 vis
46 11 YORK 12f Firm 66 2002 bl
54 6 NEWM 12f Gd/Fm 66 2131 vis
55 5 NEWM 12f Gd/Fm 65 2286
47 8 EPSO 12f Good 62 2793 vis
60 3 AYR 13f Firm 2876 vis
44 2 HAMI 12f Soft 3804 vis
48 6 GOOD 16f Soft 53 4075 vis
54 1 **PONT** 12f Soft 49 4229* vis
51 5 YORK 12f Soft 55 4280 vis
54 3 BRIG 12f Soft 55 4421 vis
52 4 MUSS 12f Soft 53 4560 vis

LANCRESS PRINCESS 3 b f £0
0a 12 LING 8f Aw 236
0a 5 WOLV 9f Aw 467

LAND AHEAD 3 ch f £7746
76 3 YARM 7f Gd/Fm 1951
87 1 **CHEP** 10f Gd/Fm 2449*
84 2 NOTT 10f Gd/Fm 3006
80 3 SAND 10f Good 3432
77 2 NEWC 8f Soft 3707
70 12 SAND 8f Gd/Fm 83 3944

LAND GIRL 2 b f £0
26 8 HAYD 6f Gd/Fm 2441

LANDFALL LIL 3 b f £0
20a 8 WOLV 6f Aw 62
11a 11 SOUT 7f Aw 88
24 9 HAMI 6f Gd/Fm 2798
0 13 AYR 7f Gd/Fm 49 3138

LANDICAN LAD 3 b c £0
45 11 SALI 6f Firm 1175
63 7 LING 6f Good 1399
42 5 SOUT 6f Good 1605
34 9 CHES 7f Gd/Fm 62 2250
22 10 WIND 5f Good 58 3191
0 19 NEWC 10f Heavy 54 4404
0 7 MUSS 9f Soft 54 4520

LANDICAN LANE 4 b g £0
9a 11 LING 12f Aw 50 52
12a 9 LING 6f Aw 43 262
4a 9 LING 12f Aw 50 332
0 17 WIND 12f Gd/Fm 43 748 bl
0 18 WARW 11f Soft 39 1065 bl
0 13 BATH 10f Gd/Sft 36 1666
10 14 GOOD 9f Gd/Sft 34 1807
0 15 BRIG 7f Gd/Fm 32 1930
0 19 NEWM 7f Firm 36 2347
0 U GOOD 9f Good 47 3644

LANDING CRAFT 6 ch g £1022
33 13 NOTT 8f Aw 60 787
38 11 THIR 8f Soft 57 907
53 3 NEWC 8f Heavy 54 1007
56 2 WARW 8f Soft 54 1066
35 11 HAMI 8f Gd/Fm 54 1243
50 7 CATT 8f Gd/Sft 56 1815
32a 11 SOUT 8f Aw 54 2380
0 12 LING 7f Good 54 4102
61 9 CATT 6f Soft 4257
37 5 NEWC 7f Heavy 51 4428

LANELLE 3 b f £0
75 8 SALI 12f Firm 1179
60 9 SALI 10f Good 1343

LANESBOROUGH 2 ch c £3510
87 5 ASCO 6f Firm 4124
89 1 **REDC** 7f Gd/Sft 4500*

LANGUAGE OF LOVE 4 br f £0
45a 5 WOLV 7f Aw 54 121

LANNTANSA 3 b c £869
58 7 PONT 10f Soft 873
57 6 NEWC 12f Heavy 1009
71 2 RIPO 10f Gd/Fm 2105

LANOSO 2 b c £0
0 15 LING 7f Soft 4483

LANTIC BAY 3 b f £0
23 7 WIND 12f Good 3351
34 4 BATH 12f Firm 3624
16 9 LEIC 10f Gd/Sft 4029

LANZLO 3 b c £888
66 2 BATH 12f Gd/Sft 61 2554
56 5 WIND 12f Good 61 2712

LAPWING 2 b c £10987
77 4 CATT 6f Gd/Fm 2926
75 1 **AYR** 6f Gd/Fm 3137*
81 1 **WARW** 7f Gd/Fm 78 3913*
84 6 CHES 7f Soft 84 4070

LARA FALANA 2 b f £0
0 12 LING 7f Soft 4484 t

LARAS DELIGHT 5 b m £0
5 7 BRIG 12f Gd/Sft 1510
50 7 BATH 12f Firm 2327
35 6 BATH 12f Firm 2785

LARAZA 3 ch f £1156
63 5 HAYD 7f Good 1165
61 5 BRIG 10f Good 66 1649 BL
0 19 REDC 8f Good 64 1892 bl
57 7 BRIG 8f Firm 62 3527
61 5 YORK 8f Good 3810
60 2 YARM 8f Gd/Fm 59 3970
59 3 LING 7f Soft 60 4192

LARGESSE 6 b g £16935
110 1 **DONC** 12f Good 732+

87	9	HAYD	12f Heavy		987	
110	3	NEWM	12f Gd/Fm		1152	
100	5	YORK	14f Firm		1339	

LARIMAR BAY 4 b c £0
0	12	FOLK	7f Soft		961	
0	15	BATH	6f Firm	40	1994	

LARITA 3 ch f £540
83	D	NEWM	7f Gd/Fm	81	1855	
82	4	KEMP	8f Gd/Fm	83	2084	
63	7	SALI	8f Good	83	2688	

LAROUSSE 2 ch f £0
71	6	YARM	8f Heavy		4477	
42	13	DONC	7f Heavy		4567	

LAS LLANADAS 2 b f £0
35	5	THIR	6f Gd/Fm		2968	
48	6	MUSS	5f Gd/Fm		3589	

LAS RAMBLAS 3 b c £3606
76	10	NEWM	6f Gd/Sft	85	982	
81	9	NEWM	7f Gd/Fm	82	1153	
50	13	LING	6f Gd/Sft	80	1285	
78	7	NEWM	6f Gd/Fm	79	1694	
78	4	GOOD	6f Gd/Fm	80	1961	
80	2	KEMP	6f Firm		2869	
81	3	NEWM	6f Gd/Fm	80	2961	VIS
64	9	NEWM	6f Firm	80	3297	vis
72	5	NEWM	5f Gd/Fm	79	3631	vis
69	12	KEMP	6f Gd/Fm	78	3791	
0	21	KEMP	6f Gd/Sft	76	4037	
0	27	NEWM	7f Good	73	4357	BL

LAST IMPRESSION 2 b f £3582
71	1	HAMI	5f Gd/Fm		1937*	
77	4	AYR	5f Good		2162	
77	2	HAMI	6f Gd/Fm		2237	

LAST OF THE MICE 2 b c £0
59	6	BEVE	8f Gd/Fm		3675	

LAST RESORT 3 ch f £80008
92	4	NEWM	7f Gd/Sft		971	
99	1	CHES	7f Gd/Fm		1224*	
100	3	GOOD	8f Gd/Sft		1485	
100	6	NEWM	8f Good		2597	
103	3	GOOD	7f Good		3104	
100	4	YORK	7f Firm		3600	
100	3	DONC	7f Gd/Fm		3878	
106	3	GOOD	7f Soft		4078	
115	1	NEWM	7f Good		4352*	

LAST SYMPHONY 3 b c £4004
80	13	NEWM	8f Gd/Sft		972	
73	6	THIR	7f Good		1159	
81	1	HAYD	7f Gd/Sft		1537*	

LAST TIME 2 b f £0
31	9	CATT	5f Soft		4252	
32	10	REDC	5f Gd/Sft		4496	

LASTMAN 5 b g £3780
66	5	HAMI	11f Good		848	
59	2	NEWC	12f Heavy		1767	
57	2	CARL	17f Gd/Fm	56	2244	
49	10	BEVE	16f Gd/Fm	59	2516	
59	2	CHES	16f Soft	55	4071	

LASTOFTHECASH 4 b g £0
46a	8	WOLV	7f Aw		478	
25a	6	WOLV	7f Aw		531	

LASTOFTHEWHALLEYS 2 b f £2892
39a	7	SOUT	5f Aw		856	
0	14	THIR	5f Soft		928	
62	1	THIR	6f Gd/Sft		1713*	
40	6	REDC	7f Good		1890	
0a	9	SOUT	7f Aw		2949	
35	9	THIR	7f Gd/Fm		3615	

LATALOMNE 6 ch g £0
38a	10	WOLV	8f Aw	92	580	
90	8	DONC	8f Good	92	733	
81	5	AYR	10f Gd/Fm	90	1656	

26	32	ASCO	8f Good	90	2090	VIS
75	7	NEWC	7f Firm	86	2338	

LATCH LIFTER 4 b c £0
18a	12	LING	7f Aw		225	

LATE ARRIVAL 3 b c £2241
50	4	NOTT	10f Heavy	58	1022	
61	2	REDC	10f Firm	56	1299	
45	8	YARM	11f Good	57	1770	
41	11	NOTT	10f Good		2012	BL
42	11	YARM	10f Gd/Fm		3383	
58	2	NEWM	7f Good		3612	VIS
47	3	YARM	8f Gd/Fm	56	3970	

LATE AT NIGHT 2 b g £660
48	8	THIR	7f Gd/Fm		2057	
55	12	CARL	5f Firm		2277	
29a	8	SOUT	6f Aw		2635	
57	4	NEWC	6f Gd/Fm		2983	BL
56	2	REDC	6f Firm		3307	bl
42	5	CATT	6f Good	57	3439	bl
36a	11	WOLV	5f Aw		4227	bl

LATE NIGHT LADY 3 b f £0
0a	9	LING	6f Aw		24	

LATE NIGHT OUT 5 b g £37413
85a	6	NAD	8f Dirt		764	
105	1	CHES	7f Gd/Fm		2670+	
109	2	SALI	8f Good		3291	
110	1	YORK	7f Firm		3600*	
98	7	NEWB	7f Firm		3995	
0	7	CORK	7f Soft		4266	

LATE SUMMER 2 b f £0
71	6	YARM	8f Heavy		4475	

LATENSAANI 2 b c £0
0	11	YARM	6f Heavy		4479	

LATIN BAY 5 b g £566
0	19	WIND	12f Good	45	1730	
26	11	NOTT	14f Good	40	2008	
43a	2	LING	12f Aw		2181	

LATINO BAY 3 ch c £2233
52	7	LEIC	7f Firm	58	2026	
41	6	LING	7f Good	56	2592	
19a	8	WOLV	9f Aw		3272	
0	14	NEWM	7f Good		3612	
32a	8	WOLV	12f Aw	48	3773	
44a	1	WOLV	7f Aw		4361*	

LATOUR 3 b f £3422
76	2	WIND	8f Gd/Sft		1428	
78	3	BATH	8f Gd/Sft		1669	
77	2	RIPO	8f Soft		2543	
39	9	WARW	11f Gd/Fm	78	2842	
42	9	EPSO	10f Gd/Fm		3403	BL
32	11	BATH	10f Soft		4141	

LAUDABLE LAD 2 b g £0
0	15	SAND	5f Gd/Fm		3942	
25	9	BRIG	8f Gd/Sft		4117	
0	28	NEWM	7f Good		4336	BL

LAUND VIEW LADY 3 b f £0
39	8	THIR	7f Gd/Sft		1351	
30	6	CATT	6f Good		1664	
35	9	CARL	7f Firm	54	2017	
0a	12	SOUT	6f Aw	47	2297	
9	12	PONT	8f Gd/Fm	45	2831	
17	8	HAMI	9f Gd/Sft		3375	
27	8	DONC	10f Heavy		4571	

LAUND VIEW LEONA 2 ch f £0
0	21	DONC	6f Heavy		4576	

LAUNFAL 3 gr c £785
0	19	NEWM	6f Gd/Sft	95	982	
88	4	SALI	8f Firm	92	1178	
76	11	GOOD	7f Gd/Fm	91	1470	

LAUREL DAWN 2 gr c £13909
67	4	REDC	5f Gd/Sft		1130	
73	8	MUSS	5f Gd/Fm		1429	

76a	1	LING	5f Aw		1740*	
79	2	CHES	5f Gd/Fm		2248	
81	1	YORK	5f Good	76	2698*	
82	3	THIR	5f Gd/Fm	82	3145	
83	4	RIPO	5f Gd/Fm		3714	
82	5	DONC	6f Gd/Sft		4449	

LAURIESTON FLO 2 b f £0
53	11	WIND	8f Heavy		4524	

LAUTREC 4 b c £0
0a	12	LING	10f Aw		56	
33a	5	LING	8f Aw		544	
0a	9	WOLV	12f Aw	45	608	BL

LAVANTER 2 b c £0
0	14	NEWM	7f Good		4184	

LAW BREAKER 2 ch c £1088
46	7	SAND	5f Good		1962	
55	4	HAMI	6f Gd/Fm		2237	
0	14	LING	6f Good		2588	
65a	5	WOLV	6f Aw		3496	
64	3	WARW	15f Gd/Fm		3912	
0	19	LING	6f Soft	62	4269	
64	3	WIND	6f Heavy	62	4525	

LAW COMMISSION 10 ch g £4551
66	6	WIND	6f Gd/Fm	66	1196	
56	10	WIND	6f Gd/Fm	66	2054	
66	1	BATH	6f Firm		2329*	
65	4	KEMP	7f Gd/Fm	65	2749	
65	2	SALI	8f Good	65	3294	
55	7	NEWB	6f Firm	65	3455	
62	7	LING	6f Good	66	3831	

LAWNETT 4 b m £0
40a	8	WOLV	9f Aw	58	271	
42a	5	WOLV	12f Aw	55	437	
50	6	CATT	14f Gd/Fm	58	779	
38	7	PONT	10f Heavy	56	943	
36	13	CARL	9f Firm	53	1254	
38	5	HAMI	13f Gd/Fm	53	1363	
0	14	CARL	12f Firm	47	2279	
21	9	CATT	14f Gd/Fm	40	3201	

LAY DOWN SALLY 2 ch f £218
56	7	SALI	6f Good		2687	
62	9	KEMP	7f Soft		4034	
50	8	LING	6f Soft		4188	
54a	4	SOUT	6f Aw	60	4367	

LAYAN 3 b f £2506
48	5	CATT	6f Good		777	
45	6	MUSS	5f Gd/Sft	56	901	
61	6	DONC	5f Good		1516	
41	10	BEVE	5f Firm	53	2223	
53	3	MUSS	5f Firm	53	2374	
51	4	REDC	5f Gd/Fm	54	2864	
62a	2	SOUT	6f Aw		2947	
42	9	DONC	5f Gd/Fm	54	3161	
56	3	RIPO	6f Good	55	3698	
35	6	BEVE	5f Good		3956	
57	3	NOTT	6f Soft	56	3975	
53	4	CATT	6f Soft		4255	
57a	3	SOUT	6f Aw		4364	

LAZEEM 2 b c £0
81	7	NEWM	8f Good		4161	
77	7	YARM	8f Soft		4512	

LAZZAZ 2 b c £268
47	7	SALI	7f Gd/Fm		3391	
74	4	CHEP	8f Gd/Fm		3680	

LE CAVALIER 3 b c £4091
66a	4	SOUT	8f Aw		86	
48a	7	SOUT	8f Aw	60	125	
65a	2	LING	10f Aw		240	
39a	7	LING	10f Aw	61	315	bl
62a	2	WOLV	9f Aw		395	
62a	2	WOLV	12f Aw		565	
62a	2	SOUT	12f Aw		603	

LE ... (continued)

62a	2	SOUT	12f Aw		643	
64a	2	WOLV	12f Aw		752	
18	6	MUSS	12f Gd/Sft		799	
54a	5	WOLV	12f Aw	65	1142	
42	10	REDC	10f Firm	54	1299	
0a	13	LING	12f Aw	65	4271	t
16a	11	LING	16f Aw	64	4329	
47a	7	WOLV	12f Aw	60	4443	bl
58a	4	WOLV	8f Aw		4551	bl

LE FANTASME 2 b c £0

44	8	KEMP	8f Soft	4036

LE FOLLIE 3 ch f £0

52	7	SALI	6f Gd/Sft	2472
47	6	WIND	8f Good	3190

LE GRAND GOUSIER 6 ch g £0

0	17	WARW	11f Gd/Fm	45	3915	bl

LE KHOUMF 9 ch g £2446

57	1	SOUT	16f Gd/Sft	50	860*
50	12	SALI	14f Firm	57	1180

LE LOUP 3 b c £329

51	9	BRIG	6f Gd/Sft	62	1464
44	10	BATH	8f Gd/Fm	62	1671
56	4	CHEP	7f Good		1972
48	3	CHEP	8f Gd/Fm		2448
42	4	CHEP	8f Gd/Fm	56	2658
38	4	LEIC	8f Aw		3094
0a	14	LING	10f Aw	48	3828

LE MERIDIEN 2 ch f £788

55	8	PONT	6f Firm		2174
75	4	HAYD	6f Good		2700
64	4	MUSS	5f Good		3098
53	10	REDC	6f Firm	67	3327
59	4	HAMI	6f Gd/Sft	63	3824
0	15	LEIC	6f Gd/Sft	60	4030

LE NOMADE 3 b c £3842

100	3	CHAN	15f Soft	3065

LE PIN 3 ch f £0

24	9	BEVE	12f Heavy	60	978

LE ROI CHIC 4 b c £3842

111	3	CHAN	8f Soft	1619

LE SAUVAGE 5 b g £0

20a	9	SOUT	14f Aw	47	37
9	8	MUSS	16f Gd/Fm	26	3742

LE TETEU 7 b g £0

52	7	LING	16f Good	55	1394

LE TINTORET 7 b g £13832

112	2	LONG	16f Gd/Sft	1456
106	5	DEAU	15f Gd/Sft	3552
112	4	LONG	16f Gd/Sft	3851
115	7	LONG	20f Good	4264

LEA VALLEY EXPRESS 3 b f £0

54a	5	LING	6f Aw		24	vis
0	18	WARW	7f Heavy	54	887	vis
21	9	BRIG	8f Gd/Sft		1508	tvi
0a	14	LING	6f Aw	50	1742	vis
18a	10	SOUT	8f Aw	50	1804	vis
0	9	WIND	12f Good		2715	
0	11	LEIC	8f Gd/Fm		2914	vis

LEADING SPIRIT 8 b g £0

0a	R	WOLV	12f Aw		626
0	18	SALI	14f Gd/Sft	65	4166

LEANADIS ROSE 2 b f £0

32	5	BEVE	7f Gd/Fm	3655
39	6	LEIC	8f Firm	3836
28	9	CATT	5f Soft	4253

LEAPING CHARLIE 4 b c £0

0	15	HAMI	5f Gd/Fm	59	3825
50a	5	SOUT	6f Aw	57	4156
39	8	PONT	5f Soft	57	4377

LEAR SPEAR 5 b h £159830

118	3	SHA	10f Gd/Fm	186
118ε	2	NAD	10f Dirt	655
103ε	9	NAD	10f Dirt	769
115	3	YORK	10f Good	3539
110	1	DONC	12f Firm	3892*

LEARNED LAD 2 ch c £0

75	7	NEWB	7f Firm	3999
78	5	NEWB	8f Gd/Sft	4457

LEATHERBACK 2 b g £11511

48	8	RIPO	6f Gd/Fm		2106
57	12	NEWM	6f Gd/Fm		3162
51	9	PONT	8f Gd/Fm		3223
58	12	NEWM	8f Good		4161
59	1	PONT	8f Soft	53	4378*
66	1	BRIG	8f Heavy	59	4538*
74	1	DONC	7f Heavy	48	4577*

LEAVE US LEAP 4 b c £3842

111	3	DEAU	8f Gd/Fm	3717

LEDGENDRY LINE 7 b g £2872

59	5	NEWC	10f Soft	60	760
56	6	HAYD	14f Gd/Fm	60	1167
55	4	NEWC	17f Gd/Sft	58	1478
58	1	PONT	17f Soft	55	1701*
57	5	PONT	17f Good	57	1867
55	7	PONT	18f Firm	57	2176
0	13	DONC	15f Gd/Sft	55	4451

LEEN 3 b f £708

53a	8	WOLV	16f Aw	70	275	
16a	11	SOUT	7f Aw	66	416	
0	16	NOTT	6f Gd/Sft	68	1082	
0	24	NEWB	7f Gd/Fm	63	1405	
44	7	CHEP	7f Good		1972	
46	6	SALI	8f Gd/Fm	53	2264	
0	12	CHEP	8f Gd/Fm	50	2658	VIS
44	2	LEIC	7f Gd/Sft		3218	
29	7	NEWM	7f Good		3612	
34	4	NOTT	10f Heavy	44	4509	

LEEROY 3 b c £830

78	2	LING	10f Gd/Sft	840
61	8	KEMP	7f Soft	1012
45	7	FOLK	7f Good	2621
45	5	LEIC	7f Good	3218
38	12	NEWM	7f Good	4018

LEES FIRST STEP 3 b f £0

50	13	WIND	12f Firm	64	1292
47	7	WARW	12f Gd/Fm	60	2254
38	10	BATH	12f Gd/Sft	55	2554
27a	7	WOLV	8f Aw	51	4440

LEGACY OF LOVE 4 b f £776

0	11	REDC	8f Gd/Fm	62	1892	
58	2	HAMI	8f Gd/Fm		2781	
31	15	RIPO	9f Gd/Fm	60	3011	
44	4	BEVE	12f Good		3399	VIS
32	6	CARL	12f Firm		3570	vis

LEGAL ISSUE 8 b h £2585

55a	4	WOLV	8f Aw	56	38
58a	3	SOUT	7f Aw	56	69
ε2a	1	SOUT	11f Aw	55	131*
45a	8	WOLV	12f Aw	63	170
61a	4	SOUT	12f Aw	63	200
0	18	PONT	10f Heavy	66	943

LEGAL JOUSTING 3 b c £14400

105	2	LEOP	8f Soft		947	
104	2	CURR	7f Soft		1120	BL
107	6	CURR	8f Gd/Sft		1623	

LEGAL LUNCH 5 b g £14479

71a	3	LING	16f Aw	68	6	vis
52a	3	SOUT	14f Aw	68	89	vis
67	4	KEMP	14f Good	67	726	vis
69	2	WARW	12f Soft	67	815	vis
53	16	NEWM	12f Gd/Sft	68	968	vis
67	5	KEMP	12f Gd/Sft	68	1076	vis
70	3	BRIG	12f Firm	68	1209	vis
72	1	DONC	12f Good	68	1518+	BL
72	3	DONC	12f Gd/Fm	71	1839	bl
58	5	GOOD	12f Gd/Fm	71	2127	bl
64	6	DONC	15f Gd/Fm	71	2319	vis
72	1	EPSO	12f Good	69	2793+	bl
65	5	EPSO	12f Gd/Fm	71	3402	bl
49	8	BATH	12f Gd/Sft	70	4433	vis

LEGAL SET 4 b c £6064

70	2	WIND	8f Good	68	854	
53	9	ASCO	8f Gd/Sft	70	1113	
9	14	BRIG	8f Firm	70	1330	
70	3	WIND	8f Gd/Fm	70	2051	
75	3	CARL	8f Good	70	2242	
66	6	EPSO	9f Gd/Sft	72	2629	VIS
68	7	KEMP	8f Gd/Fm	72	3078	vis
73	2	WIND	8f Good	70	3355	
74	3	WIND	8f Good	74	3642	
60	10	YARM	8f Firm	74	3936	
49a	10	LING	8f Aw	73	4330	

LEGAL TENDER 3 b g £0

0	19	NOTT	6f Good	1266
14	9	BATH	8f Gd/Fm	1436
45	8	CHEP	8f Heavy	1556

LEGAL VENTURE 4 ch g £1051

31a	13	WOLV	5f Aw	59	40	vis
28a	11	WOLV	5f Aw	55	116	bl
0a	U	LING	5f Aw	52	166	bl
29a	10	WOLV	6f Aw	52	291	
26a	9	WOLV	6f Aw	47	352	vis
52a	3	WOLV	6f Aw		379	bl
51a	4	LING	5f Aw		440	bl
36a	10	WOLV	6f Aw	47	445	bl
47a	2	WOLV	5f Aw		639	bl
44a	7	WOLV	5f Aw		753	bl
47	4	KEMP	5f Gd/Fm		3077	bl
34	6	LEIC	5f Aw	43	3214	bl
38	7	BRIG	5f Firm		3562	bl

LEGAL WORD 2 b c £0

0	12	KEMP	7f Firm	2867

LEGEND 4 b f £723

63	2	LEIC	12f Soft	64	1551
0	10	NOTT	14f Good	67	1874

LEGENDAIRE 3 gr c £2082

57a	2	LING	8f Aw	55	355
64a	2	LING	7f Aw	58	488
62a	4	LING	8f Aw		591
58	3	BRIG	7f Firm		1333
50	6	BRIG	7f Firm	60	2044
35a	6	LING	10f Aw		2213
55	8	NEWM	7f Gd/Fm		2860

LEGENDARY LOVER 6 b g £394

53	5	WARW	11f Heavy	53	890	
54	3	WIND	12f Good	52	1730	vis
0	15	SALI	14f Gd/Sft	53	4166	

LEGGIT 2 b f £560

0	13	WIND	6f Good	3044	t
63	7	BATH	6f Firm	3205	t
73	9	KEMP	7f Gd/Fm	3359	t
37	5	WIND	5f Good	3639	
58	2	LING	6f Firm	3757	

LEGGY LADY 4 b f £436

48a	4	LING	16f Aw	50	6
35	8	BATH	13f Gd/Fm	47	1440
44	5	BATH	17f Firm	46	1996
44	3	LING	16f Firm	43	3755
17a	8	LING	16f Aw	43	4329

LEGS BE FRENDLY 5 b g £364

0	W	NEWC	5f Heavy	65	1008	
66	3	MUSS	5f Gd/Fm	65	1143	
64	5	AYR	5f Gd/Sft	66	2721	bl
0	11	BEVE	5f Gd/Sft		3056	bl
45	14	PONT	5f Soft	64	4087	

56a 4 WOLV 6f Aw 62 4223

LEILA 5 b m £218
47	8	WIND	10f	Good		3189
34	4	LING	14f	Firm		3489
61	8	BATH	12f	Gd/Fm		3818

LEMARATE 3 b c £0
66	9	NEWM	8f	Gd/Fm		3626
43	12	SAND	10f	Soft		4205

LEMON BRIDGE 5 b g £0
57	5	WARW	12f	Soft	77	815
73	5	KEMP	12f	Gd/Fm	75	3798

LEMON STRIP 4 ch f £844
43a	4	SOUT	6f	Aw		32
47a	2	WOLV	6f	Aw		63
39a	4	WOLV	7f	Aw	47	121
38a	4	WOLV	5f	Aw	47	139
22a	9	WOLV	7f	Aw	45	187
22a	6	WOLV	5f	Aw		1036
0a	13	WOLV	6f	Aw	39	1233
0	21	LEIC	6f	Gd/Sft	38	1734 BL

LEND A HAND 5 b h £81207
121	4	GULF	8f	Good		16
100a	6	NAD	6f	Dirt		766
121	1	YORK	6f	Firm		1338*
113	3	ASCO	6f	Good		2115
113	5	NEWM	6f	Gd/Fm		2615
119	2	DEAU	7f	Good		3212

LENNEL 2 b g £566
62	6	CARL	6f	Gd/Fm		2239
70	3	AYR	6f	Gd/Fm		2717
70	5	AYR	7f	Good		3363
69	5	AYR	6f	Soft	72	3987
55	5	AYR	6f	Heavy	70	4305

LENNOX 4 b c £0
11	7	LEIC	12f	Gd/Fm		2776

LENNY THE LION 3 b c £348
31	11	BRIG	10f	Gd/Sft	57	892
52	5	BRIG	10f	Gd/Sft	54	1509
56	5	WIND	12f	Gd/Fm	54	2210
54	3	BATH	10f	Firm	54	2332 BL
0	8	BRIG	12f	Gd/Sft	54	2425 bl
40	9	BEVE	12f	Good	54	3954
41	7	CATT	12f	Soft	52	4256
34	10	MUSS	13f	Soft	49	4521

LEOFRIC 5 b g £2048
44a	4	SOUT	6f	Aw		50 bl
36a	10	SOUT	7f	Aw		130
48a	3	SOUT	7f	Aw		693 bl
48	5	WARW	7f	Soft		816 bl
17	8	FOLK	10f	Soft	45	965 bl
42	3	BEVE	8f	Heavy		973 bl
39	3	WARW	8f	Soft	44	1066 bl
38	7	CARL	9f	Firm	44	1254 bl
45	3	PONT	8f	Good		1498 bl
0	11	SOUT	10f	Soft	42	1608 bl
40	6	AYR	8f	Gd/Fm	42	1658 bl
40	3	BEVE	7f	Gd/Sft	43	1760 bl
0	13	LEIC	8f	Firm	41	2032 bl
16a	3	SOUT	7f	Aw	40	2122 bl
16a	10	SOUT	9f	Aw	37	2380
28	7	EPSO	9f	Gd/Sft		2433 bl

LEONATO 8 b g £0
68	9	YORK	14f	Good	87	3811 t
57	5	NEWM	14f	Good	82	4016 t

LEONIE SAMUAL 5 b m £2756
45	4	LEIC	7f	Good		790
35	3	FOLK	6f	Soft	42	958
46	1	PONT	8f	Gd/Sft	42	1101*
34	8	LEIC	10f	Soft	45	1546
31	9	BATH	8f	Firm	45	2331
0	14	BRIG	10f	Soft	44	4419

LEOPARD SPOT 2 b c £3750

99	3	ASCO	7f	Good		2091
101	5	SAIN	10f	Soft		4556 BL

LEOZIAN 2 b c £5063
90	2	LING	5f	Firm		3277
83	11	DONC	5f	Firm		3900
73	4	LING	5f	Good		4096
82	1	LING	5f	Soft		4187+
82a	7	LING	6f	Aw		4332

LERMONTOV 3 br c £1050
100	4	LEOP	10f	Good		3924
0	8	CURR	14f	Good		4055
77	11	ASCO	8f	Good		4111
89	12	NEWM	10f	Good		4355

LES GIRLS 2 b f £0
0	18	LING	6f	Firm		3832
0	16	LING	5f	Good		4095
0	U	BRIG	7f	Soft		4415

LET ALONE 3 b f £6955
73	7	NEWB	7f	Soft		915
81	1	BATH	8f	Gd/Sft		1669*
42	10	GOOD	10f	Gd/Fm	81	2358
53	10	ASCO	10f	Good	79	2955

LETHAL AGENDA 2 ch c £1350
91	4	LEOP	7f	Heavy		4557

LETS REFLECT 3 b f £275
64	5	PONT	10f	Gd/Fm		2832
64	4	RIPO	10f	Gd/Fm		3012
45	7	BEVE	10f	Gd/Fm		3672
55	5	CATT	7f	Soft		4005
15	7	PONT	5f	Gd/Fm		4234

LETTRE PERSANNE 3 gr f £0
24	6	YARM	7f	Gd/Fm		2413

LEVEL BEST 2 ch g £0
0	12	SALI	6f	Gd/Fm		3387

LEVEL HEADED 5 b m £13104
42a	5	LING	6f	Aw	25	BL
0a	11	WOLV	8f	Aw	133	bl
54	8	WARW	7f	Gd/Sft		1708
35	3	NOTT	10f	Good	36	2011
31	5	LEIC	8f	Firm	36	2032
18a	9	LING	10f	Aw	39	2212
33	4	RIPO	10f	Soft		2538
34	4	LING	10f	Good	39	2655
41	1	BATH	10f	Firm	36	2789*
38	3	YARM	10f	Good	40	3031
37	4	BRIG	10f	Gd/Fm	40	3244
49	1	LING	10f	Firm	40	3581*
31	11	BRIG	10f	Firm	45	3737
58	1	BEVE	10f	Sft/Hv	44	4046*
59	1	BRIG	10f	Gd/Sft	50	4118*
45	8	REDC	10f	Gd/Sft	58	4221

LEVENDI 3 ch g £0
55	8	NEWC	5f	Sft/Hvy		4043
0	11	REDC	7f	Gd/Sft		4218
60	7	AYR	8f	Heavy		4308

LEVER TO HEAVEN 4 b f £3599
97	3	MAIS	6f	Heavy		98

LIBERTY BOUND 2 b f £247
59	4	NOTT	6f	Soft		3974
61	8	MUSS	5f	Gd/Fm		4131
0	21	REDC	6f	Gd/Sft		4219

LICENCE TO THRILL 3 ch f £13260
77a	2	LING	6f	Aw		5
70a	5	WOLV	5f	Aw		47
74a	1	LING	5f	Aw		507*
78a	1	LING	5f	Aw	70	652*
63	12	WIND	5f	Gd/Sft	75	1098
79	2	ASCO	5f	Good	75	2168
40	16	CHES	5f	Gd/Fm	72	2247
65	7	GOOD	5f	Gd/Fm	77	3135

LIDAKIYA 3 b f £22051
76	4	DONC	10f	Gd/Sft		1051

85	1	THIR	12f	Good		1386*
88	1	NEWB	10f	Gd/Fm	79	1785*
93	2	GOOD	12f	Gd/Fm	84	2127
96	1	PONT	12f	Firm	92	3504*
75	12	NEWC	10f	Good	101	3703

LIFE IS LIFE 4 b f £17825
104	3	HAYD	12f	Heavy		987
113	2	CHES	13f	Firm		1247
112	5	ASCO	20f	Good		2114
91	8	NEWM	12f	Gd/Fm		2857

LIFE OF RILEY 6 ch g £0
0	15	NEWC	16f	Firm	100	2336 t

LIFFORD LADY 2 b f £0
32	8	LEIC	6f	Gd/Fm		3096
54	11	SALI	7f	Good		3752
0	14	WARW	7f	Gd/Fm		3910
40	6	NOTT	6f	Soft		3973
43a	7	WOLV	6f	Aw		4548

LIFT THE OFFER 5 ch g £0
55a	7	SOUT	6f	Aw	71	212
40a	9	SOUT	7f	Aw	68	282
30a	12	SOUT	7f	Aw	62	368

LIGHT BREEZE 4 b f £0
32a	7	LING	5f	Aw	43	91
23a	8	LING	6f	Aw	37	148

LIGHT EVIDENCE 2 ch f £0
45	8	WIND	5f	Good		1727
53	5	LING	6f	Good		4097
43	8	LING	6f	Soft		4190
50a	5	LING	5f	Aw		4333

LIGHT OF ARAGON 2 b f £0
0	15	PONT	6f	Good		1864
0	12	PONT	6f	Firm		2174
33	10	THIR	7f	Gd/Fm		3127
33	7	THIR	7f	Gd/Fm		3615
31	6	BEVE	7f	Good	39	3950
34a	9	WOLV	8f	Aw		4362

LIGHT OF FASHION 2 b f £0
55	8	BATH	8f	Gd/Fm		3620
45	9	WARW	15f	Gd/Fm		3911
47	5	NOTT	6f	Heavy		4410

LIGHT PROGRAMME 6 b g £0
63a	9	WOLV	8f	Aw	73	921
39	12	DONC	10f	Gd/Sft	69	1070

LIGHT THE ROCKET 4 ch c £0
0	13	DONC	5f	Soft	95	4466

LIGHTNING ARROW 4 br c £32469
85	11	HAYD	12f	Heavy		987
108	2	NEWB	13f	Gd/Fm		1401
101	4	LEIC	12f	Firm		2028
109	1	NEWM	12f	Gd/Fm		2803+
110	2	GOOD	12f	Gd/Fm	108	3134
109	2	CHES	12f	Gd/Fm	108	3509
111	2	SALI	14f	Firm		3751

LIGHTNING STAR 5 b g £828
73	4	EPSO	12f	Heavy	77	1030
48	7	BRIG	12f	Soft	75	4421 bl

LIGNE GAGNANTE 4 b c £20623
65	6	HAYD	12f	Heavy	90	991
76	10	YORK	12f	Gd/Fm	90	1307
95	2	EPSO	12f	Good		1850
94	2	YORK	12f	Gd/Fm	92	2647
96	3	GOOD	12f	Gd/Fm	96	3134
94	9	YORK	14f	Gd/Fm	94	3565

LIKE BLAZES 2 ch f £0
0	13	KEMP	7f	Soft		4034

LILANITA 5 b m £1478
49a	3	SOUT	8f	Aw		45
45a	2	WOLV	8f	Aw		136
27a	7	WOLV	7f	Aw	47	187
46a	3	WOLV	8f	Aw	45	227
45a	2	WOLV	8f	Aw	45	255

22a	8	WOLV	9f Aw	45	306	VIS
27a	8	WOLV	9f Aw	47	404	
5a	10	WOLV	8f Aw	47	432	BL
10a	11	SOUT	7f Aw	44	598	
16	13	WIND	8f Good	40	3188	vis
39	6	YORK	9f Good		3808	

LILIUM 2 b f £16330

95	1	WARW	7f Gd/Fm		3910*
100	1	NEWM	7f Gd/Fm		4210*
85	15	NEWM	7f Good		4356

LILLAN 3 b f £1080

63	6	WIND	8f Gd/Sft		1099	
54	4	GOOD	10f Gd/Sft		1640	
40	4	GOOD	10f Good		2308	t
0a	W	WOLV	8f Aw	62	2601	BL
51a	4	WOLV	8f Aw	62	3769	t
64a	3	LING	12f Aw		4101	t
45a	6	LING	12f Aw	64	4271	t

LILLEMAN 3 b c £2300

88	5	GOOD	6f Gd/Fm		3064
81	7	YORK	6f Gd/Fm		3568
82	2	PONT	6f Soft		4082
72a	2	WOLV	6f Aw		4225
82a	3	LING	6f Aw		4332	t
75	9	NEWB	6f Sft/Hvy	83	4468	BL

LILS JESSY 2 b f £20330

73	5	YORK	6f Gd/Fm		1312
87	1	YARM	7f Firm		2390*
73	10	SAND	7f Good		2935
91	1	CHES	7f Gd/Fm	78	3428*
92	1	DONC	7f Firm	85	3901*
96	3	NEWM	7f Gd/Fm		4210
89	12	NEWM	7f Good		4356

LIMBO DANCER 2 ch f £0

42	6	NOTT	5f Gd/Sft		1083
0	14	MUSS	5f Gd/Fm		1429
10a	9	SOUT	6f Aw		1974
5	12	CATT	6f Gd/Fm		2927
22a	11	WOLV	6f Aw		4244

LIMBURG 2 b c £0

59	14	NEWB	6f Gd/Fm	1943
48	7	WARW	7f Gd/Fm	2841
0	14	HAYD	6f Gd/Sft	3268

LIMELIGHTING 4 b f £53368

97	1	MAIS	11f Heavy	122
88	4	YORK	10f Firm	1325
101	5	HAYD	12f Gd/Fm	2501
98	4	NEWB	12f Gd/Fm	3177
107	1	DEAU	10f Gd/Fm	3547*
96	9	LONG	13f Good	4236

LINCOLN DANCER 3 b c £59035

102	4	KEMP	8f Soft	996
105	10	NEWM	8f Gd/Fm	1171
115	1	HAYD	6f Gd/Sft	1051534*
119	2	NEWM	6f Gd/Fm	2615
102	7	HAYD	6f Gd/Sft	3784
97	9	ASCO	6f Gd/Sft	4125
109	2	LONG	5f Heavy	4495

LINCOLN DEAN 4 b g £3870

37	7	HAMI	8f Firm	48	1243
41	8	AYR	8f Gd/Fm	45	1658
19	9	MUSS	9f Firm	43	2049
40	3	HAMI	9f Firm	40	2397
42	2	HAMI	9f Gd/Fm	40	2799
34	9	AYR	9f Gd/Fm	43	3141
39	4	NEWC	9f Firm	43	3603

LINCONNU 5 ch g £0

0	12	LING	10f Soft	1287	bl

LINDEN GRACE 3 b f £7020

85	1	NEWC	8f Gd/Fm	80	2311*
0	P	BEVE	8f Gd/Fm	84	2515

LINEA DOMBRA 2 ch f £3842

102	3	DEAU	8f Heavy	4401

LINEA G 6 ch m £0

53	6	HAYD	12f Gd/Fm	64	2446
4	12	HAYD	12f Gd/Fm	62	3323
47a	5	SOUT	12f Aw		4366

LINGUISTIC DANCER 5 ch m £2758

44a	1	LING	10f Aw	38	1265*

LINKSMAN 5 b g £0

0a	12	SOUT	6f Aw	32
0a	16	SOUT	5f Aw	71

LION CUB 4 b g £0

0a	17	SOUT	12f Aw	44	68
27a	5	WOLV	12f Aw		144	BL

LION DOR 4 b c £565

61	3	FRAU	9f Good	1904

LION GUEST 3 ch c £0

63	4	WIND	10f Firm		1293
0	17	WIND	8f Good	68	1726
50	5	CARL	8f Firm	63	2281
0	14	YARM	7f Good	60	3030	BL
0	12	YARM	10f Gd/Fm		3383	t
23	7	BATH	8f Soft	51	4435

LION IN THE COURSE 2 b c £903

78	4	HAYD	6f Gd/Sft	3478
74	3	THIR	7f Gd/Fm	3617
77	7	DONC	6f Firm	3888

LION OF JUDAH 3 b c £0

62	5	CHEP	8f Heavy	1556

LION SONG 2 b c £0

0	14	DONC	5f Good	730
51	12	WARW	5f Soft	812

LIONARDO 4 b c £0

53	9	YARM	8f Gd/Fm	75	2412

LIONEL ANDROS 2 b c £0

0	13	CHEP	6f Gd/Sft	1798
61	5	BATH	6f Firm	2328

LIONESS 4 b f £0

0	12	WARW	8f Soft	72	817	
13	13	FOLK	10f Soft	68	965	
24	12	BRIG	10f Firm		1331	
32	7	BRIG	10f Gd/Fm		1933	
0	18	CHEP	8f Gd/Fm	38	2658	
0	15	THIR	6f Gd/Fm	34	3124	BL
0	22	THIR	8f Gd/Fm	34	3144	BL

LIONS DOMANE 3 b g £3471

50a	8	SOUT	5f Aw		127	
50a	2	WOLV	7f Aw	47	257	
28a	6	WOLV	7f Aw	48	346	
40	8	HAMI	8f Gd/Fm	47	1907	
38	6	DONC	6f Gd/Fm	44	2315	
49	1	THIR	7f Gd/Fm	41	3129*	
27	11	SALI	7f Gd/Fm	47	3294	

LIPICA 2 b f £6117

92	3	YORK	7f Gd/Fm	3730
85	1	KEMP	7f Soft	4034*
101	3	NEWB	7f Sft/Hvy	4467

LISA B 3 b f £546

50a	7	SOUT	7f Aw	60	31	bl
50a	7	SOUT	5f Aw	60	72	bl
53a	2	WOLV	5f Aw		533	bl
37a	7	WOLV	5f Aw	52	609	bl
0	14	SALI	7f Good		1349	vis
48	8	WIND	6f Gd/Sft		1423	
35	9	BATH	5f Gd/Sft		1670	bl
33a	9	LING	6f Aw	50	1742	bl

LISAS PRINCESS 7 b m £0

33a	11	WOLV	12f Aw	62	394
3a	12	WOLV	6f Aw	38	466
7a	10	LING	7f Aw	36	503

LITE A CANDLE 3 b f £0

0	15	LING	7f Gd/Sft	839

44	10	SALI	6f Firm		1175
0	14	NEWB	8f Good		1376
0	12	LING	7f Good	50	2592

LITERARY SOCIETY 7 ch h £1210

82	15	NEWM	6f Gd/Fm	93	1173
0	12	YORK	6f Firm	92	1337
69	7	WIND	6f Good		1728
88	4	KEMP	6f Gd/Fm	86	3791

LITIGIOUS 3 b f £2351

70	2	YARM	8f Gd/Fm		2198	
64	2	CHES	8f Good		2662	
32	9	HAYD	8f Gd/Sft		3266	
0	14	BRIG	7f Firm	52	3561	
33	4	YARM	8f Gd/Fm	45	3970	VIS
0a	12	LING	7f Aw		4331	vis

LITTLE AMIN 4 b c £8008

31	10	WARW	12f Soft	77	815
33	10	HAYD	12f Heavy	75	991
62	11	CHES	12f Firm	73	1251
76	1	BEVE	9f Gd/Sft	71	1762*
72	6	ASCO	10f Good	75	2170
78	3	GOOD	9f Good	75	2304
78	2	BEVE	10f Gd/Fm	77	3410
74	6	WIND	9f Gd/Fm	77	3642
75	6	GOOD	9f Good	77	3883
73	5	PONT	10f Soft	77	4085
70	14	NEWM	9f Gd/Fm	80	4212

LITTLE BRAVE 5 b g £7752

79a	2	SOUT	16f Aw	75	51	
73a	4	WOLV	16f Aw	78	135	
59	4	PONT	17f Soft	59	876	
37	6	PONT	22f Heavy	59	940	
51	9	HAYD	14f Gd/Fm	58	1167	
53	5	CHEP	18f Gd/Fm	56	2452	
64	1	LING	16f Firm	54	2763*	
60	4	NEWB	16f Firm	60	2812	
59	3	ASCO	16f Good	58	2953	
60	3	NEWM	16f Firm	58	3295	
57	3	FOLK	16f Gd/Fm	59	3448	
41	6	WARW	16f Good	58	3695	

LITTLE CALLIAN 2 ch f £1843

47	6	GOOD	7f Gd/Fm		2306
42	10	LING	6f Good		2588
66	4	WIND	6f Gd/Fm		2886
66	3	BATH	6f Firm		3205
48	6	EPSO	6f Good	69	3761
64	2	SAND	5f Gd/Fm		3942
62	5	LING	5f Good	65	4098
65	10	DONC	6f Gd/Sft		4449

LITTLE CHAPEL 4 b f £210

58	4	CATT	6f Soft		1678
28	9	CATT	7f Gd/Sft		1818
0	19	NOTT	6f Gd/Fm	50	2192
0	16	PONT	8f Gd/Fm	45	2561
0	18	LEIC	7f Aw		4032

LITTLE CHRISTIAN 3 b c £0

43a	5	SOUT	8f Aw	303
0a	13	SOUT	7f Aw	330
30a	7	SOUT	7f Aw	385

LITTLE DOCKER 3 b c £1834

70	3	REDC	10f Firm		1295
63	5	NEWC	10f Gd/Sft		1480
68	4	BEVE	12f Firm	69	1919
71	2	NEWC	16f Gd/Fm	69	2273

LITTLE FINTLOCH 7 b m £0

0a	8	WOLV	12f Aw	519

LITTLE FIREFLY 2 b c £6235

97	3	ASCO	5f Good	2088
99	5	CURR	7f Gd/Fm	3845

LITTLE FOX 5 br m £0

20a	7	SOUT	16f Aw	60	51

LITTLE IBNR 9 b g £741

LITTLE JOHN 4 b c £5031 (continued)

38a	8	WOLV	6f Aw		436	vis
49a	4	WOLV	7f Aw		449	vis
53a	3	WOLV	6f Aw		465	vis
40a	10	WOLV	5f Aw		533	vis
37a	6	SOUT	6f Aw		538	vis
50a	2	SOUT	6f Aw	48	604	vis
21a	11	WOLV	6f Aw		680	vis

LITTLE JOHN 4 b c £5031

59	3	AYR	10f Gd/Fm	58	1656	
59	4	HAMI	12f Gd/Fm	58	1908	
59	3	MUSS	9f Firm		2376	
59	2	HAMI	12f Firm	58	2392	
53	5	HAMI	9f Gd/Fm		2642	
62	2	HAMI	12f Gd/Fm	59	2783	VIS
46	4	HAMI	11f Gd/Fm		2800	vis
60	2	AYR	8f Gd/Fm		3139	vis
0	3	MUSS	12f Gd/Fm		3741	vis
55	5	MUSS	9f Soft	60	4523	BL

LITTLE LES 4 b g £0

61	6	AYR	10f Gd/Fm		1655
31	7	AYR	7f Good		2140
23	6	MUSS	5f Gd/Fm		2204
40	4	AYR	8f Gd/Fm		3139
0	13	HAMI	8f Gd/Sft	40	3380
18	6	MUSS	8f Gd/Fm	30	3745

LITTLE LOTTIE 4 gr f £0

0a	12	WOLV	8f Aw	229
0a	15	SOUT	12f Aw	301
0	12	PONT	10f Soft	1699

LITTLE MOUSE 2 b f £0

0	17	WIND	5f Gd/Sft	1424
0	13	REDC	6f Gd/Sft	1577
49	9	NOTT	5f Good	2009
27	4	YARM	5f Gd/Fm	2196

LITTLE PILGRIM 7 b g £0

16a	9	LING	8f Aw	92

LITTLE PIPPIN 4 ch f £581

87	4	NEWM	12f Gd/Sft	85	968
79	6	GOOD	14f Gd/Sft	85	1484

LITTLE PIXIE 2 ch f £0

8	10	YORK	7f Soft	4277

LITTLE ROCK 4 b c £73603

113	1	SAND	10f Heavy	1057+
106	6	CHAN	12f Gd/Sft	1902
116	1	NEWM	12f Good	2566*
112	3	ASCO	12f Gd/Fm	3306
115	4	DEAU	13f Gd/Sft	3723
107	5	CURR	14f Good	4055

LITTLE TARA 3 b f £0

45	8	WIND	8f Gd/Fm		745
9	11	NOTT	10f Heavy	39	1022
0	14	CHEP	7f Good		1972
0a	13	LING	10f Aw		2587
0	11	CHEP	12f Gd/Fm	35	2971
0	11	CHEP	8f Gd/Fm	34	3251

LITTLE TASK 2 b c £5057

67	3	CARL	6f Gd/Fm		2239	
36	8	NEWC	7f Good		2521	
70	2	AYR	6f Gd/Fm		2717	
72	4	AYR	7f Firm		2873	
70	2	AYR	8f Gd/Fm		3137	
0	6	CHES	7f Gd/Fm	72	3428	
50	12	YORK	7f Good	73	3542	
59	6	NEWC	8f Soft		3706	
35	8	AYR	8f Soft		3957	
60a	1	SOUT	7f Aw		4369*	BL

LITTLE TUMBLER 5 b m £1645

0a	14	LING	10f Aw	47	100
44	6	GOOD	9f Gd/Sft	47	1807
46	6	KEMP	9f Firm	48	2262
45	5	BRIG	10f Gd/Fm	46	2727
15	15	WIND	8f Good	46	3188

47	2	BRIG	10f Firm	45	3557
48	2	BRIG	10f Firm	45	3737

LITTLE WHITE HEART 5 ch m £0

0a	9	LING	8f Aw	93

LITTLEFEATHER 3 b f £11543

98	5	NEWC	6f Firm	2335
108	1	NEWM	6f Gd/Fm	3120*
74	9	ASCO	6f Good	3303
105	2	NEWM	6f Good	3610
93	7	DONC	7f Gd/Fm	3878
89	8	GOOD	7f Soft	4078

LITTLEPACEPADDOCKS 3 b f £37506

98	3	AYR	8f Gd/Fm	1630
107	1	NEWB	10f Gd/Fm	1945*
108	4	CURR	12f Gd/Fm	2739
107	2	ASCO	12f Gd/Fm	3305
100	8	DONC	15f Gd/Fm	3898
109	2	NEWM	12f Good	4343

LITZINSKY 2 b g £0

63	10	DONC	8f Heavy	4569

LIVADIYA 4 b f £0

98	5	CURR	8f Gd/Fm	3846

LIVE IN LOVER 2 b g £0

0	16	RIPO	6f Gd/Fm	3466
0	17	YORK	7f Gd/Fm	3729
14	7	PONT	6f Soft	4373

LIVE THE DREAM 2 b f £0

45	8	CATT	7f Gd/Fm	2417
49	7	HAYD	7f Gd/Fm	2700
56	4	MUSS	7f Good	3100

LIVE TO TELL 4 ch f £0

5a	11	WOLV	6f Aw	51	226

LIVELY FELIX 3 b g £325

0	14	WIND	8f Gd/Fm		3048
42	9	WIND	8f Good		3350
57	4	WARW	7f Good		3696
36	11	YARM	8f Gd/Fm	58	3971
40	5	BATH	8f Soft	55	4143
30	6	BATH	8f Soft	52	4435

LIVELY JACQ 4 ch f £0

34a	9	LING	7f Aw	57	29	
49a	4	WOLV	6f Aw		132	VIS
32a	6	WOLV	5f Aw	51	187	vis
43a	6	WOLV	6f Aw	48	232	vis
42a	4	WOLV	7f Aw		274	

LIVELY LADY 4 b f £11486

80	4	KEMP	6f Good	81	728	vis
88	1	KEMP	5f Soft	81	1013*	vis
70	21	NEWM	6f Gd/Fm	90	1173	vis
90	3	KEMP	6f Soft	89	1531	vis
90	3	WIND	6f Good		1728	vis
72	14	SAND	5f Gd/Fm	90	2473	vis
73	11	ASCO	5f Good	88	2676	BL
0	13	SALI	6f Gd/Sft	88	4165	vis
76	8	NEWM	6f Good	86	4198	vis
86	3	WIND	5f Heavy	83	4527	bl

LIVELY MILLIE 3 b f £271

41	14	WIND	8f Good	56	1726	
46	7	WARW	10f Gd/Fm	52	2036	
0	14	CHEP	6f Gd/Fm	48	2489	VIS
43	4	NEWM	8f Gd/Fm		3456	
42	5	BEVE	7f Gd/Fm		3670	

LIVIUS 6 b g £17306

85	3	NEWM	12f Firm	80	1187
77	4	YORK	14f Gd/Fm	83	1982
88	1	GOOD	12f Good	83	3657*
86	6	ASCO	12f Gd/Sft	88	4128
0	18	NEWM	12f Good	88	4342

LIZZEY LETTI 2 ch f £0

46	8	YARM	7f Firm	2390

LIZZIE SIMMONDS 3 b f £2986

49	4	CATT	5f Gd/Fm	777	t

47	5	MUSS	5f Gd/Sft	56	901	t
54	5	WIND	5f Gd/Sft	54	1098	t
0	13	BEVE	5f Firm		1280	t
59	1	CATT	5f Gd/Sft	53	1817*	
52	6	MUSS	5f Aw	57	2047	
52	5	CATT	6f Gd/Fm	57	2440	
58	3	BEVE	5f Firm	57	2732	
0	16	PONT	5f Firm	58	3502	
51	5	HAMI	5f Gd/Sft	57	3825	
0	17	NEWM	5f Good	56	4185	
37	14	AYR	5f Heavy	55	4307	

LOBLITE LEADER 3 b c £0

0	18	RIPO	10f Soft	60	827
0	15	REDC	10f Firm	56	1299
33	9	REDC	14f Gd/Sft	50	1581
0	4	NEWC	12f Heavy		1767
0a	10	SOUT	12f Aw	40	2815

LOBUCHE 5 b g £0

0a	13	SOUT	12f Aw	34	70	
26	10	THIR	12f Gd/Sft		1353	t

LOCH AILORT 4 b f £0

37	10	DONC	7f Soft	4461	VIS

LOCH DIAMOND 3 ch f £0

49	11	BEVE	5f Firm	1280
41	9	WARW	5f Gd/Sft	1712

LOCH INCH 3 ch c £0

68	9	SALI	8f Gd/Fm	90	2229	
0	21	YORK	6f Heavy	87	4301	bl
0	18	DONC	5f Soft	86	4466	bl

LOCH LAIRD 5 b g £0

77	5	GOOD	6f Gd/Sft	79	1471	
63	10	LING	6f Good	78	1676	
73	7	SALI	6f Gd/Fm	77	1887	
0	18	WIND	6f Gd/Fm	77	2054	
64	13	GOOD	6f Gd/Fm	76	2355	VIS
65	9	GOOD	8f Gd/Fm	74	3063	
58	6	SALI	6f Gd/Fm	70	3419	

LOCH SOUND 4 b g £0

0	13	BEVE	10f Gd/Fm	32	3656

LOCHARATI 3 ch c £5120

89	1	LING	6f Gd/Sft		837*
26	8	ASCO	6f Gd/Sft		1111
87	2	NOTT	6f Good		1409
0	17	YORK	6f Firm	87	2003
65	10	NEWM	8f Gd/Fm	85	2614
72	14	DONC	7f Gd/Fm	82	3880
0	22	NEWM	12f Gd/Fm	79	4215
55	11	YARM	6f Heavy	76	4480

LOCHLASS 6 b m £0

0a	13	WOLV	9f Aw	29	305	bl

LOCHSPRITE 2 ch f £1318

56	8	LING	6f Firm	3832
74	2	BATH	6f Soft	4137
71	3	CATT	6f Soft	4253

LOCOMBE HILL 4 b c £3725

96	3	GOOD	12f Gd/Sft		1474
35	10	YORK	14f Gd/Fm	95	1982
83	5	SALI	10f Gd/Sft		2471
62	11	GOOD	10f Gd/Fm	85	3060
63	8	SAND	10f Good	82	3471
74	4	KEMP	8f Gd/Fm	77	4038
64	9	SAND	7f Soft	77	4204

LOCOMOTION 4 ch c £272

62a	10	SOUT	8f Aw	74	49	
29a	10	WOLV	6f Aw	73	143	t
0a	9	WOLV	9f Aw		360	
39a	7	WOLV	7f Aw		449	
50a	3	SOUT	7f Aw		501	
42a	5	WOLV	8f Aw		567	
43a	10	SOUT	8f Aw		600	

LODEN BLUE 3 b f £0

0	24	RIPO	10f Soft	45	827

LOGANLEA 6 br m £0
0a 10 SOUT 8f Aw 46 648

LOGIC LANE 2 ch c £8798
74 9 NEWB 6f Gd/Fm 1943
89 1 GOOD 6f Good 2307*
87 2 DONC 6f Gd/Fm 2754
83 8 GOOD 7f Firm 88 3149

LOKOMOTIV 4 b c £5001
49 6 BEVE 10f Firm 54 1921
35 10 BEVE 10f Firm 54 2220
33 7 WIND 10f Soft 49 2544 bl
23 7 YARM 10f Firm 2765
42 1 AYR 11f Firm 2875* bl
17 11 CHEP 12f Gd/Fm 40 3255 bl
41 5 BRIG 10f Firm 3526 bl
46 2 BATH 12f Firm 3624 bl
29a 6 WOLV 12f Aw 37 3773 bl
49 1 YARM 10f Firm 3935* bl
20a 10 SOUT 11f Aw 4150 bl

LOMOND DANCER 3 b c £0
0 11 PONT 8f Good 65 1495
59 5 LING 11f Firm 60 1914
46 7 WARW 12f Gd/Fm 54 2255
40 12 PONT 10f Gd/Fm 57 2556
28 11 BRIG 10f Firm 54 2908
28 9 BRIG 10f Firm 49 3530
30 9 RIPO 10f Good 3702
5a 8 LING 16f Aw 44 4099

LONDON EYE 2 b f £4079
51 7 WIND 5f Heavy 932
51 6 BRIG 5f Gd/Fm 1124
34a 10 SOUT 5f Aw 1304
52 3 LING 6f Good 1396 BL
50 3 GOOD 6f Gd/Sft 1634 bl
55 2 BRIG 5f Firm 2039 bl
61 7 LING 5f Firm 2214 bl
33a 7 SOUT 5f Aw 2384 bl
64 1 BRIG 5f Firm 2891* bl
49 6 BRIG 6f Gd/Fm 65 3258
61 4 LING 5f Firm 3491 bl
55 4 EPSO 6f Good 61 3761 bl
0 15 YARM 7f Firm 60 3922 bl
49 5 BRIG 6f Soft 58 4170 bl

LONDONER 2 ch c £11333
94 1 NEWM 6f Firm 2563*
98 1 YARM 7f Good 3237*
101 4 GOOD 8f Good 3882

LONDONNET 2 b f £0
73 8 NEWM 7f Soft 4541

LONE PIPER 5 b g £3284
99a 4 WOLV 6f Aw 97 660
0 17 KEMP 6f Good 97 728
21 NEWM 6f Gd/Sft 95 966
46 9 YARM 6f Gd/Fm 1952 t
72 9 CHEP 5f Gd/Fm 87 2451 VIS
72 9 ASCO 5f Good 82 2676 tvi
0 16 ASCO 6f Gd/Fm 80 2954 tvi
0 27 GOOD 6f Firm 87 3152 tvi
76 3 KEMP 6f Gd/Fm 3791
59 13 YARM 5f Firm 75 3920
0 19 YORK 6f Soft 4287

LONER 2 b g £9781
73 8 NEWM 6f Gd/Fm 2598
73 4 YARM 5f Firm 2901
82 6 WIND 5f Gd/Fm 3044
77 2 CHES 7f Good 3428
80 1 GOOD 7f Good 72 3660*
64 5 EPSO 7f Good 72 3690
72 8 DONC 8f Gd/Fm 80 3879
84 7 AYR 8f Soft 80 3987
0 14 NEWM 6f Gd/Fm 78 4214
0 19 NEWM 6f Gd/Fm 76 4338

LONG DAY 2 b f £0
56 12 NEWM 6f Gd/Fm 4209
57 7 BRIG 8f Soft 4418

LONG WEEKEND 2 b c £296
65 7 NEWM 6f Gd/Fm 2854
59 5 LEIC 6f Gd/Fm 3215
65 4 THIR 7f Gd/Fm 3617
0 14 LING 7f Soft 64 4191

LONGCHAMP DU LAC 2 b c £0
39 8 HAYD 6f Gd/Fm 2700
0 11 HAYD 6f Gd/Sft 3478

LONGUEVILLE LEGEND 2 b f £5600
102 4 LEOP 7f Good 3372

LOOK FIRST 2 b c £4137
63 2 BRIG 7f Gd/Sft 2424
62 3 BRIG 7f Gd/Fm 2723
65 1 BRIG 7f Gd/Fm 3240*
60 8 WIND 10f Gd/Sft 65 4290
65 2 NEWM 8f Soft 4542

LOOK HERE NOW 3 gr c £12401
83 1 DONC 6f Good 731*
83 5 HAYD 6f Gd/Fm 1164
56 15 CHES 5f Gd/Fm 81 2247
50 17 YORK 7f Good 78 2694
65 11 RIPO 6f Gd/Fm 81 3183
0 14 CHES 6f Soft 4069
80 1 YORK 6f Soft 4287*
83 6 DONC 7f Soft 4465
0 17 DONC 7f Heavy 76 4574

LOOKING FOR LOVE 2 b f £7750
65 8 WIND 6f Gd/Fm 2209
66 3 LING 6f Good 2588
73 3 WIND 6f Gd/Fm 2886
64 3 BRIG 7f Gd/Fm 3239
73 2 WARW 7f Good 3692
71 3 PONT 8f Soft 69 4084
74 2 LING 7f Soft 72 4191
79 1 NEWB 7f Gd/Sft 73 4453*

LOOP THE LOUP 4 b g £4660
77 5 DONC 12f Good 732
23 14 HAYD 12f Heavy 98 991
85 8 YORK 12f Gd/Fm 95 2647
75 16 GOOD 14f Gd/Fm 92 3058
81 14 YORK 14f Gd/Fm 92 3565
88 1 DONC 15f Gd/Sft 83 4451*

LOOSE CHIPPINS 2 b f £0
0 17 NEWM 7f Good 4183
69 7 LING 7f Soft 4484

LORD ADVOCATE 12 br g £0
0 13 HAMI 13f Gd/Fm 37 1194 vis
10 13 HAMI 12f Firm 32 1241 vis
8 10 MUSS 9f Firm 28 1689 vis
32 6 HAMI 12f Gd/Fm 41 1908 vis
0 13 HAMI 12f Gd/Fm 26 1936 vis
30 6 HAMI 13f Firm 35 2098 vis
29 6 HAMI 13f Gd/Fm 33 2801 vis
23 8 HAMI 13f Gd/Sft 40 3378 vis
15 5 HAMI 12f Gd/Sft 20 3827 vis
75 6 AYR 11f Gd/Sft 54 4011 vis

LORD ALASKA 3 b c £11930
0 20 WIND 10f Gd/Fm 1200
50 9 WIND 10f Firm 1293
63 5 BATH 10f Soft 1668
34 12 BATH 12f Gd/Sft 60 2554
63 1 FOLK 16f Gd/Fm 55 3588*
64 1 MUSS 16f Gd/Fm 55 3742*
69 1 WARW 16f Gd/Fm 64 3916*
75 2 NEWM 14f Gd/Fm 70 4213

LORD BERGERAC 4 b c £0
40a 10 SOUT 6f Aw 59 602 bl
25 10 BRIG 7f Firm 3559

LORD EFISIO 2 b c £0
0 9 YORK 6f Firm 2005

LORD EUROLINK 6 b g £16005
47a 7 LING 12f Aw 76 245
73a 3 LING 10f Aw 333 VIS
36a 11 LING 10f Aw 70 400 vis
0a 5 WOLV 12f Aw 530 E
36a 3 LING 8f Aw 574 tvi
52a 1 WOLV 8f Aw 612* tvi
64a 1 SOUT 8f Aw 684* tvi
68a 1 WOLV 8f Aw 62 718* tvi
59 7 WARW 8f Soft 70 817 tvi
68a 4 WOLV 8f Aw 67 921 tvi
66a 4 WOLV 8f Aw 67 1037 tvi
61 6 CHES 10f Gd/Fm 67 1217 tvi
65 4 NOTT 10f Gd/Sft 67 1364
64 5 LING 10f Firm 3281
44a 9 WOLV 9f Aw 67 3495 vis
66 1 YORK 9f Good 3808* vis
66 2 AYR 9f Soft 3988 vis
68 3 YORK 10f Soft 4275 vis
43 6 AYR 10f Heavy 69 4306 vis

LORD FLASHEART 3 b c £141210
114 2 LONG 11f V 864
115 1 CHAN 11f V 1231*
116 2 CHAN 12f V 1752

LORD GIZZMO 3 ch c £0
17 9 KEMP 8f Firm 2871
60 6 WIND 10f Good 3189
42 7 BATH 12f Gd/Fm 3517
0 15 BRIG 10f Soft 48 4174

LORD HARLEY 3 b c £7317
51a 4 LING 8f Aw 236
58a 2 LING 8f Aw 52 419
55a 2 WOLV 7f Aw 52 450
62a 1 WOLV 8f Aw 56 613*
70a 1 WOLV 9f Aw 60 1040*
57 5 BATH 8f Gd/Fm 60 1442

LORD HIGH ADMIRAL 12 b g £2627
56a 4 SOUT 5f Aw 71 vis
57a 1 SOUT 5f Aw 50 673* vis
56 4 SAND 5f Gd/Fm 55 763 vis
31 8 DONC 6f Gd/Sft 1073 vis
41 11 NOTT 5f Good 54 1412 vis
54a 4 SOUT 5f Aw 58 1806 vis
44 6 HAYD 5f Gd/Fm 52 2505 vis
32 8 HAYD 6f Gd/Fm 3283 vis

LORD JIM 8 b g £0
88 5 NEWB 10f Gd/Sft 1592

LORD JOSHUA 2 b c £936
71 3 DONC 8f Heavy 4572

LORD KINTYRE 5 b g £40874
100 2 NEWB 5f Soft 95 914
109 4 NEWM 5f Gd/Fm 1172
99 4 KEMP 5f Soft 1529
111 8 ASCO 5f Good 2065
108 2 SAND 5f Gd/Fm 2496
107 1 NEWM 5f Gd/Fm 2960+
114 1 NOTT 5f Good 3521+
112 1 DONC 5f Gd/Fm 3874*
102 5 NEWB 5f Firm 3982

LORD LAMB 8 gr g £2290
92 2 HAYD 12f Heavy 90 991

LORD LIAM 2 b c £819
68 5 CHEP 6f Gd/Fm 3252
76 3 LING 6f Firm 3492
78 4 EPSO 7f Good 3688
75 5 EPSO 7f Good 3760
52a 6 WOLV 6f Aw 4225
50a 8 WOLV 6f Aw 4379

LORD OMNI 3 ch c £2827
54 6 NEWC 6f Heavy 70 1768
72 1 THIR 6f Gd/Fm 67 2060*

66	5	BEVE	7f Firm	71	2733	t

LORD PACAL 3 b c £21406

0	19	NEWM	7f Good	92	954
82	13	NEWM	7f Gd/Fm	89	1153
54	13	GOOD	6f Gd/Sft	77	1471
79	8	EPSO	7f Gd/Sft	81	1826
84	2	DONC	6f Gd/Fm	79	2577
81	2	EPSO	7f Good		2792
85	1	**YARM**	6f Firm	80	2900*
83	4	YORK	6f Good	83	3543
90	1	**NEWM**	7f Gd/Sft	83	3629*
77	12	AYR	6f Gd/Sft	88	4012
90	2	NEWM	7f Good	87	4357

LORD PROTECTOR 2 b c £2693

83	4	NEWB	7f Firm	3999
83	2	YORK	8f Soft	4281
74	5	DONC	7f Gd/Sft	4447

LORD YASMIN 3 b c £6743

77a	1	**SOUT**	6f Aw		685*
57	11	CHES	6f Gd/Fm	68	1220
66	3	WIND	5f Gd/Sft	66	1427
73	1	**BRIG**	6f Good		1651*
41a	8	SOUT	7f Aw	75	2300

LORDOFENCHANTMENT 3 ch c £292£

39	11	DONC	7f Good	63	736	
57	5	BEVE	7f Heavy	60	976	
61	2	RIPO	6f Good	58	1600	vis
62	2	NEWC	6f Heavy	58	1768	
59	7	REDC	6f Good	61	1891	
47	5	RIPO	6f Soft	62	2541	
53	5	AYR	7f Good		3364	vis
55	2	BEVE	7f Gd/Fm		3670	
52	4	LEIC	6f Gd/Sft		4031	
0	13	PONT	6f Soft		4233	vis

LOST AT SEA 2 b c £4533

75	8	NEWM	6f Gd/Fm		1691	
85	2	YORK	6f Firm		2005	
65	7	LING	6f Good		2588	
81	1	**YARM**	7f Good		3029*	
90	7	YORK	6f Gd/Fm		3566	t
87	5	WARW	7f Gd/Fm	90	3913	t

LOST IN HOOK 3 b f £624

81a	3	LING	5f Aw	83	652	
52	10	SAND	5f Heavy	83	1047	
72	7	CHES	5f Gd/Fm	80	1219	
52	11	AYR	5f Good	77	2165	
0	20	LEIC	5f Gd/Sft	73	4027	
17	11	SAND	5f Soft		4207	VIS

LOST IN LUCCA 4 b f £0

51a	4	SOUT	12f Aw	52	68

LOST SPIRIT 4 b g £16446

46a	7	WOLV	12f Aw	63	81
54a	6	LING	12f Aw	63	115
42a	6	WOLV	12f Aw	57	170
0a	11	SOUT	12f Aw	52	211
49a	1	**LING**	12f Aw	45	290*
56a	2	LING	13f Aw	51	317
16a	10	SOUT	12f Aw	47	370
56a	2	LING	12f Aw	54	441
46a	5	WOLV	12f Aw	54	464
35a	9	LING	12f Aw	66	508
19a	6	SOUT	12f Aw	52	682
2a	7	WOLV	12f Aw	50	723
19a	9	LING	13f Aw	46	835
36	3	WARW	11f Heavy	41	889
19	5	WARW	11f Heavy	37	1003
9	11	BRIG	12f Firm	38	1209
52	6	THIR	12f Gd/Sft		1353
40	4	CARL	12f Aw		1720
7a	10	LING	12f Aw		2181
33	1	**WARW**	13f Gd/Fm	30	2843*
36	1	**BEVE**	12f Gd/Sft	32	3053*

33	3	CHEP	12f Gd/Fm	38	3255	
37	5	HAMI	13f Gd/Sft	39	3378	
42	2	CATT	12f Good	43	3437	
40	1	**FOLK**	12f Gd/Fm	38	3586*	
9	16	EPSO	12f Good	43	3858	
35a	9	LING	12f AW		4186	

LOST THE PLOT 5 b m £0

58	7	SALI	14f Good	2691

LOTS OF LOVE 2 b c £3137

88	1	**NEWC**	7f Gd/Sft		3705*
79	4	LEIC	7f Gd/Sft		4028

LOTS OF MAGIC 4 b c £0

101	6	DONC	6f Good	734
105	8	ASCO	6f Good	2115
103	8	NEWM	7f Firm	2343
92	7	NEWB	7f Firm	2809

LOUEST 3 br c £710

52	7	YARM	7f Soft	4387
71	3	NOTT	11f Heavy	4505

LOUGH BOW 2 b g £0

66	7	BEVE	7f Good	3397
47	10	BEVE	8f Gd/Fm	3675

LOUGH SWILLY 4 b c £0

42	10	WIND	8f Good	60	854
0	28	ASCO	8f Gd/Sft	56	1113
0	16	CHEP	7f Gd/Fm	51	1799
50	7	LING	8f Gd/Fm		2215
0	13	SALI	6f Good	46	2690

LOUP CERVIER 3 b g £487

0	15	LING	7f Gd/Sft		840
52	9	SALI	6f Firm		1175
47	11	LING	6f Good		1399
0	16	NEWB	7f Gd/Sft	56	1787
0a	1	SOUT	6f Aw		2118
36	11	BATH	10f Firm	50	2332
47	3	LEIC	8f Gd/Fm	46	2506
46	4	BEVE	8f Firm	47	2735
47	4	BRIG	10f Firm	47	2908
31	8	LEIC	10f Gd/Fm	47	3217
11	13	EPSO	10f Good	45	3762
0	17	EPSO	12f Good	52	3858
0a	13	LING	16f Aw		4099

LOUS WISH 3 b c £4440

62a	3	SOUT	8f Aw		328	BL
62a	1	**WOLV**	7f Aw	54	346*	bl
65a	2	SOUT	7f Aw	60	416	bl
49a	6	WOLV	7f Aw	65	450	bl
65a	3	WOLV	6f Aw	65	479	bl
46a	6	SOUT	8f Aw	65	540	bl
44a	7	WOLV	8f Aw	65	566	bl
0	20	YORK	8f Firm	63	1341	bl
30	10	PONT	8f Good	63	1495	
0	18	NEWM	8f Gd/Fm		2134	bl
24a	8	SOUT	7f Aw		2633	
42a	9	SOUT	8f Aw		2946	
31	10	NEWM	7f Good		3612	bl
17a	14	SOUT	8f Aw	56	4365	bl

LOVE 2 b c £0

65	5	AYR	5f Gd/Fm	1628
0	17	BEVE	5f Good	3955
70	5	MUSS	5f Gd/Sft	4131

LOVE BITTEN 3 b g £5516

0	14	LEIC	8f Good		789
0	14	LING	7f Gd/Sft		840
68	8	DONC	10f Gd/Sft		1054
70	4	NOTT	14f Gd/Fm	68	1270
66	5	BEVE	12f Good	67	1446
68	2	AYR	11f Gd/Fm	67	1633
67	1	**AYR**	13f Good	67	2141*
70	3	YARM	14f Gd/Fm	67	2195
66	4	CARL	12f Firm	67	2279
56	11	BEVE	12f Gd/Sft	69	2482

LOVE DIAMONDS 4 b g £2205

32a	10	LING	8f Aw	72	97	
71a	2	SOUT	11f Aw	69	390	
6a	9	SOUT	11f Aw	69	474	
21a	6	WOLV	12f Aw	69	562	
0	17	NEWM	10f Gd/Fm	49	2958	
0	16	WIND	8f Good	45	3188	VIS
34	9	LEIC	10f Firm	41	3842	
42	3	WARW	11f Gd/Fm	40	3915	
58a	3	SOUT	11f Aw		4151	
57a	2	SOUT	11f Aw		4366	

LOVE DIVINE 3 b f £286985

114	1	**GOOD**	10f Gd/Sft		1469*
121	1	**EPSO**	12f Gd/Sft		1828*
119	2	YORK	12f Gd/Fm		3564
115	4	LONG	12f Good		3928
115	4	NEWM	10f Gd/Sft		4355

LOVE EVERLASTING 2 b f £13838

68	3	RIPO	6f Gd/Fm		3009
88	4	YORK	6f Gd/Fm		3568
93	2	YORK	7f Gd/Fm		3730
85	1	**BEVE**	7f Good		3953*
91	2	NEWM	7f Good	88	4157
86	5	NEWM	8f Soft		4546

LOVE IN VAIN 3 b f £532

28a	7	WOLV	9f Aw	610
37a	3	SOUT	7f Aw	688
41a	3	LING	10f Aw	882

LOVE KISS 5 b g £5137

39	9	REDC	9f Gd/Sft	55	1583	
0	13	THIR	7f Gd/Fm	50	2063	
47	2	RIPO	8f Soft	44	2542	
18	15	CARL	7f Firm	44	2823	
0	15	REDC	7f Gd/Fm		2994	t
37	6	NEWC	9f Firm	47	3603	
71	4	CATT	6f Soft		4257	
51	1	**AYR**	10f Heavy	45	4306*	
48	4	NEWC	10f Heavy		4404	
42	6	MUSS	9f Soft	51	4523	

LOVE LADY 2 b f £1015

72	4	RIPO	6f Gd/Fm		2106
59	4	CARL	6f Gd/Fm		2239
70	3	CATT	6f Gd/Fm		2419
45	7	EPSO	6f Good	67	3761

LOVE LANE 3 b c £1096

81	3	LEIC	7f Good	80	792

LOVE LETTERS 3 ch f £0

73	15	NEWM	7f Gd/Fm	82	1153

LOVE ME TRUE 2 ch f £4050

90	3	LEOP	7f Heavy	4557

LOVE THING 2 b f £4371

61	6	HAYD	5f Gd/Sft		1835	
33	12	BEVE	5f Gd/Sft		3055	
70	1	**RIPO**	6f Gd/Fm		3466*	VIS
54	11	NEWM	6f Gd/Fm	74	3630	vis
76	9	NEWM	6f Good		4345	BL

LOVE TUNE 2 b f £4046

65	5	WIND	5f Gd/Fm		1197
62a	3	SOUT	5f Aw		1304
50	6	HAMI	6f Gd/Fm		1938
63	2	CHES	5f Good	62	2665
65	2	CHES	6f Firm	64	3168
69	2	HAYD	5f Gd/Sft	67	3264
49	12	HAYD	5f Gd/Sft	69	3475
67	16	NEWM	6f Good		4345

LOVE YOU TOO 3 ch f £791

79	12	NEWM	7f Good		955
82	4	NEWM	7f Firm		1186
36	14	ASCO	8f Good	88	2167
70	5	REDC	8f Firm	82	3309
69	8	WIND	8f Gd/Fm	79	3643
50	14	NEWM	10f Good	75	4160

LOVERS LEAP 4 b g £0
56	13	KEMP	8f Soft	81	1015	
75	7	CHES	8f Firm	80	1250	
75	6	NEWB	7f Gd/Sft	78	1590	
55	13	CHEP	7f Good	77	1969	VIS
70	7	KEMP	10f Gd/Fm	75	2750	
39	8	LEIC	10f Gd/Fm	72	3337	
55	11	KEMP	10f Gd/Fm	70	3794	
0	17	BATH	10f Soft	66	4436	

LOVES DESIGN 3 b c £696
75	3	DONC	7f Good	75	736	
58	9	WIND	6f Good	75	852	vis
69	8	NEWM	6f Gd/Sft	75	982	vis
0	16	NEWB	6f Gd/Fm	74	1406	vis
45	9	NEWC	6f Heavy	71	1768	vis

LOYAL TARTARE 3 £0
| 101 | 5 | CHAN | 9f V | | 1753 | |

LOYAL TOAST 5 b g £1639
42a	2	SOUT	11f Aw		670	
12a	7	SOUT	11f Aw	37	742	
22	11	RIPO	12f Soft	37	822	
32	3	HAMI	9f Gd/Fm		1191	
42	8	THIR	12f Gd/Sft		1353	
27	5	PONT	10f Soft		1699	
25	8	HAMI	13f Gd/Fm	30	1936	
0	5	NEWC	12f Good		2523	
29	3	HAMI	12f Gd/Fm	28	2783	
42	3	CARL	12f Firm		2826	
9	6	MUSS	16f Good	30	3099	
15	7	REDC	14f Firm		3311	
0a	15	SOUT	16f Aw	33	4149	

LOYAL TYCOON 2 br c £6345
88	3	NEWM	6f Gd/Fm		2598	
86	1	LEIC	7f Gd/Fm		2916*	
87	6	SAND	7f Good		3470	
87	2	GOOD	7f Soft		4063	
21	9	YORK	7f Soft		4277	

LUANSHYA 4 b f £1909
70	4	DONC	7f Good	71	1514	
70	5	CATT	7f Soft	71	1680	
69	4	DONC	6f Gd/Fm	70	1842	
60	10	YORK	6f Firm	69	2000	
60	9	AYR	7f Good	68	2163	
59	9	LEIC	7f Gd/Fm	66	2775	
64	3	THIR	6f Gd/Fm	66	2969	
59	4	THIR	6f Gd/Fm	65	3123	
0	P	NEWM	6f Firm	65	3297	

LUBOHENRIK 3 b f £0
0	14	MUSS	8f Gd/Fm	43	3745	
0	13	MUSS	12f Gd/Sft		4133	
9	5	MUSS	8f Soft		4519	

LUCAYAN BEACH 6 gr g £242
0a	13	LING	7f Aw	60	29	
57a	2	LING	8f Aw		92	
0	17	BATH	10f Gd/Fm	60	1666	
35	9	BATH	8f Firm	55	1998	
0	17	SALI	8f Gd/Sft	50	2467	
19	8	KEMP	6f Gd/Fm		2747	

LUCAYAN CHIEF 2 b c £11908
78	5	KEMP	7f Firm		2867	
90	1	BEVE	7f Gd/Sft		3051*	
96	3	NEWB	7f Soft		3450	
96	2	HAYD	8f Soft		3787	
96	3	CHAN	8f Soft		4144	

LUCEFER 2 b g £2877
6	12	THIR	7f Gd/Fm		3617	
83	2	NEWC	7f Gd/Sft		3705	
62	9	CHEP	7f Good		3866	
83	2	BRIG	7f Soft		4172	
83	2	BRIG	7f Soft		4415	

LUCIDO 4 b c £4862
109	5	NEWM	12f Gd/Fm		1152	
108	4	CHAN	12f Gd/Sft		1902	
75	6	NEWM	12f Good		2566	

LUCILLE 2 b f £0
| 70 | 16 | DONC | 8f Gd/Sft | | 4445 | |

LUCKS LUVLY 2 ch f £0
| 0 | 14 | HAYD | 5f Soft | | 3767 | |

LUCKY ARCHER 7 b g £0
| 61 | 8 | CHEP | 7f Good | 71 | 1969 | |
| 56 | 9 | LING | 8f Gd/Fm | 70 | 2185 | |

LUCKY ARROW 3 b f £0
| 68 | 10 | NEWB | 10f Gd/Fm | | 1404 | |

LUCKY BEA 7 b g £0
| 37a | 11 | LING | 7f Aw | | 4328 | |

LUCKY BREAK 2 ch c £0
53	11	WIND	6f Gd/Fm		3047	
69	7	SALI	6f Gd/Fm		3387	
60	13	NEWB	6f Firm		3980	

LUCKY CHRYSTAL 2 b c £0
| 67 | 5 | YARM | 7f Good | | 3029 | |

LUCKY COVE 4 gr c £233
0	22	DONC	6f Good	64	716	
68	7	HAYD	5f Gd/Sft		808	
0a	16	SOUT	6f Aw	59	1422	
0	11	THIR	5f Gd/Sft	59	1714	
0	12	PONT	5f Good		1868	
0	14	DONC	5f Gd/Fm	50	2753	
0	19	RIPO	6f Gd/Fm	50	2839	
25	10	BEVE	5f Gd/Fm		3651	
63	4	REDC	5f Gd/Sft		4220	BL
42	7	NEWC	5f Heavy	50	4407	bl

LUCKY DREAM 6 b g £19213
111	5	CHAN	12f Gd/Sft		1902	
108	1	CHAN	15f Good		2402*	
111	3	MAIS	13f Soft		2737	

LUCKY GITANO 4 b c £10044
49	13	DONC	10f Gd/Sft	81	1070	
73	13	WIND	10f Good	78	1729	
76	2	NEWC	10f Gd/Fm		2314	
65	4	PONT	10f Gd/Fm		2562	
70	6	LING	8f Firm	73	3831	
71	4	LING	8f Soft		4273	
78	1	REDC	8f Gd/Sft	70	4499*	
86	1	DONC	7f Heavy	77	4574*	

LUCKY HETTIE 2 b f £0
| 42 | 11 | NEWB | 6f Sft/Hvy | | 4470 | |

LUCKY JUDGE 3 b c £2136
58	5	MUSS	9f Gd/Fm		902	
47	7	HAMI	11f Gd/Fm		1193	
66	4	HAMI	11f Gd/Fm		1909	
54	6	CATT	12f Gd/Fm	60	2746	
55	4	BEVE	16f Good	60	2879	
55	2	NEWC	14f Gd/Fm	57	3249	
63	3	THIR	16f Gd/Fm	65	3618	
63	3	NEWC	16f Heavy	65	4424	

LUCKY LADY 3 ch f £7078
85	2	HAYD	11f Gd/Fm		1165	
89	1	CHEP	12f Good		1970*	
90	2	WIND	12f Soft		2547	

LUCKY MELODY 3 b c £0
0a	11	SOUT	8f Aw		303	
10a	8	LING	8f Aw	45	355	
25a	8	SOUT	8f Aw	38	555	VIS
0a	8	SOUT	7f Aw		688	

LUCKY NEMO 4 b c £0
| 24a | 6 | SOUT | 11f Aw | | 178 | |

LUCKY RASCAL 4 b g £0
| 20a | 6 | WOLV | 6f Aw | | 434 | |

LUCKY STAR 3 b f £5365
63a	6	LING	7f Aw		206	
62a	1	LING	7f Aw	57	287*	
57a	3	WOLV	7f Aw	61	450	
62a	1	WOLV	8f Aw		636*	
53a	4	LING	7f Aw		1745	
52	7	BATH	12f Firm		1997	e
44	10	LEIC	8f Gd/Fm	55	2506	

LUCKY SWEEP 3 ch c £0
| 69 | 5 | KEMP | 7f Soft | | 1018 | |
| 54 | 8 | THIR | 8f Good | 72 | 1387 | |

LUCKY UNO 4 b c £0
0	15	PONT	6f Gd/Sft		1105	
0	18	BEVE	5f Firm	40	2223	
37	6	BEVE	10f Gd/Fm		3677	
0	17	LEIC	10f Firm		3838	BL
30	8	DONC	15f Heavy		4568	

LUCKYS SON 3 gr g £4818
0	11	LING	7f Gd/Sft		839	
0	13	YARM	8f Good		1771	
25	8	RIPO	10f Gd/Fm		2105	
24	14	LEIC	8f Gd/Fm	49	2512	
42	2	BRIG	8f Firm	42	2896	
47	1	THIR	6f Gd/Fm	42	3124*	
41	6	EPSO	6f Gd/Fm	48	3405	
0	14	LING	6f Firm	47	3759	

LUCY MARIELLA 4 b f £0
| 48 | 10 | BRIG | 8f Gd/Fm | 66 | 1126 | |
| 11 | 14 | NEWB | 7f Gd/Sft | 64 | 1590 | t |

LUCY TUFTY 9 b m £0
| 0 | 34 | NEWM | 12f Firm | 33 | 1852 | |

LUDERE 5 ch g £1806
| 45 | 4 | LEIC | 12f Gd/Fm | | 2776 | |
| 36 | 1 | CATT | 16f Gd/Fm | | 3199* | |

LUGANA LADY 4 b f £0
| 0a | 13 | WOLV | 16f Aw | 36 | 194 | VIS |

LULLABY 3 b f £5710
71	3	WIND	8f Heavy		934	
67	4	WARW	8f Soft		1062	
51	10	YARM	8f Gd/Sft	70	1610	
65	1	NEWM	10f Gd/Sft		2284*	
63	2	CHES	12f Good		2667	
29	10	PONT	12f Gd/Fm	67	2829	
58	5	REDC	11f Firm	66	3329	

LUMIERE DESPOIR 2 br f £221
| 56 | 9 | ASCO | 7f Good | | 4114 | |
| 66 | 4 | BRIG | 10f Heavy | | 4539 | |

LUMIERE DU SOLEIL 2 b f £0
61	5	RIPO	6f Gd/Fm		3466	
52	7	NEWC	7f Gd/Sft		3705	
58	6	AYR	7f Soft		3962	

LUNA FLIGHT 3 b f £2716
65	5	SAND	10f Good		3232	
38	5	CHES	12f Gd/Fm		3429	
42a	6	LING	10f Aw		4100	
53a	1	WOLV	12f Aw	45	4443*	
32a	8	LING	12f Aw	51	4486	

LUNAJAZ 3 ch g £0
39a	5	LING	8f Aw		241	
18a	7	LING	8f Aw	42	355	
24a	7	LING	7f Aw		459	
9	10	BRIG	7f Firm		1212	VIS
0	13	BRIG	10f Gd/Fm		1933	

LUNALUX 3 b f £1358
41	8	YARM	6f Good		1773	
41	2	HAMI	8f Gd/Fm		2095	
54	4	MUSS	5f Firm	55	2374	
47	7	REDC	5f Gd/Fm	54	2864	
45	10	RIPO	5f Gd/Fm	53	3180	vis
55	5	FOLK	5f Gd/Fm		3584	vis
52	2	LEIC	6f Gd/Sft		4031	BL
45	6	PONT	5f Soft		4233	bl

LUNAR CRYSTAL 2 b c £13072
93	1	ASCO	7f Gd/Sft		4124*	
103	4	ASCO	8f Heavy		4296	
54	8	NEWM	10f Soft		4543	

LUNAR LEO 2 b g £5292

75	4	DONC	6f Gd/Fm		1844	
87	1	**WARW**	7f Good		2459*	
85	3	NEWM	7f Gd/Fm	83	2962	
81	6	YORK	7f Good	85	3542	
85	3	GOOD	6f Good	85	3886	
85	5	NEWM	6f Good		4345	t

LUNAR LORD 4 b c £2750

0a	12	WOLV	12f Aw	41	489	
0	16	BRIG	12f Firm	38	1209	
32	4	BRIG	12f Gd/Sft	32	1465	
35	2	LEIC	10f Soft	32	1546	
0	13	NOTT	14f Good	37	1874	
37	2	WARW	12f Gd/Fm	37	2254	
38	2	CHEP	12f Soft	37	2656	
38	4	BRIG	12f Firm	38	2904	
28	4	BRIG	12f Gd/Fm	37	3260	
28	8	HAMI	12f Gd/Sft	35	3827	
30	3	BRIG	12f Soft	31	4176	
30	3	YARM	11f Soft	31	4391	
11a	7	WOLV	12f Aw		4549	

LUNASALT 2 b c £17291

100	3	DEAU	6f Gd/Fm		3210
100	1	**DEAU**	7f Gd/Fm		3716*

LUNCH PARTY 8 b g £2923

56	4	MUSS	8f Gd/Sft	59	899
14	12	MUSS	7f Gd/Sft	58	1149
54	6	CATT	7f Gd/Fm	56	2420
60	1	**CATT**	7f Gd/Fm	54	3200*
40	9	MUSS	7f Gd/Sft	59	4136

LUNEVISION 2 b f £2446

71	3	KEMP	6f Gd/Fm	3358
76	2	NEWM	6f Gd/Fm	3627
69	3	LING	5f Good	4096
67	8	DEAU	8f Heavy	4401

LURINA 2 b f £1025

86	2	DONC	7f Heavy	4566

LUSONG 3 ch c £2691

65a	2	LING	5f Aw		289
63a	2	LING	6f Aw		334
51a	6	WOLV	6f Aw		549
58	3	NOTT	6f Good	62	785
59	4	WIND	6f Good	62	852
51	10	BRIG	6f Firm	62	1211
56	5	CHEP	6f Good	61	1971
53	5	CHEP	7f Gd/Fm	59	2489
0	13	CHEP	7f Gd/Fm	58	2974

LUTINE BELL 5 b g £0

12a	7	WOLV	15f Aw		363
0a	10	LING	13f Aw	28	460

LUVADUCK 4 b f £0

0	10	NOTT	10f Gd/Sft	70	1086	
0	15	SOUT	7f Soft	68	1606	
0	13	WIND	8f Gd/Fm	63	2051	VIS

LUVLY TIMES 2 ch g £0

46	12	THIR	5f Gd/Fm	928
36	9	NOTT	5f Heavy	1019

LUXOR 3 ch c £6262

81	4	DONC	10f Gd/Sft		1054	
80	2	REDC	10f Firm		1295	
92	1	**NEWM**	10f Gd/Fm		2135*	
0	8	NEWM	10f Gd/Fm	92	2805	
84	7	DONC	12f Firm	90	3896	
48	10	NEWB	9f Stt/Hvy	88	4472	

LV GIRL 4 ch f £0

44a	7	WOLV	7f Aw	51	635
0a	12	SOUT	8f Aw	48	692

LYCHEEL 2 ch c £0

67	10	BATH	8f Soft	4430

LYCIAN 5 b g £11821

54	6	BRIG	8f Gd/Fm	59	1129
53	7	BATH	8f Gd/Fm	58	1442
57	3	YARM	10f Gd/Fm	56	2199
57	4	BRIG	10f Gd/Fm	57	2727
51	7	NEWM	8f Gd/Fm	57	3118
62	1	**LEIC**	10f Firm	56	3842*
65	1	**YARM**	10f Firm	56	3941*
62	4	NEWM	10f Good	64	4160

LYCIAT SPARKLE 2 b g £0

5	10	NEWM	6f Soft	4372

LYCITUS 3 b c £21134

114	1	**CHAN**	13f Good	2398*	bl
114	5	**LONG**	12f Good	3929	bl

LYDIAS LOOK 3 b f £2958

31a	5	SOUT	8f Aw		415
47a	4	SOUT	6f Aw		558
54a	1	**SOUT**	5f Aw		740*
48a	9	SOUT	5f Aw	63	870
41a	8	SOUT	7f Aw	61	1202
24a	10	SOUT	6f Aw	58	2820
43	10	THIR	5f Gd/Fm	58	3349
0	17	CHEP	5f Good	52	3872

LYMOND 5 b h f1581

95	3	DUSS	8f Good	2910

LYNA 2 b f £0

75	7	KEMP	7f Gd/Fm	3359

LYNTON LAD 8 b g £3341

36	6	WARW	7f Soft		816
43	6	NEWC	8f Heavy	65	1007
41	10	BEVE	7f Firm	62	1275
47	10	HAYD	7f Gd/Fm	59	2442
60	1	**PONT**	7f Gd/Fm	55	2831*
0	25	ASCO	7f Gd/Fm	59	2999
34	13	CHES	8f Firm	59	3170
54	5	HAMI	8f Gd/Sft	59	3534
0	14	LEIC	8f Gd/Fm		4033
13	9	NEWC	7f Heavy	55	4428

LYONETTE 2 b f £3055

88	1	**LING**	7f Firm	3829*

LYRICAL LEGACY 3 ch f £0

0	12	LING	7f Gd/Sft	49	841	
30	10	NOTT	6f Gd/Sft		1081	VIS
0	16	HAMI	5f Gd/Fm	42	1910	vis

LYSANDERS QUEST 2 br c £342

82	4	NEWB	7f Gd/Fm	3484
92	5	SAND	7f Gd/Fm	3946
70	6	SAND	8f Soft	4203

LYSANDROS 6 b h £0

68a	5	WOLV	12f Aw	76	407

MA JOLIE 2 ch f £1440

58	8	PONT	6f Soft	4083
76	3	YORK	8f Soft	4281
82	4	YARM	8f Soft	4512

MA VIE 3 b f £3306

44	8	REDC	8f Gd/Fm	66	2147	
62	2	WARW	11f Good	62	2463	
53	7	YARM	10f Good	63	3031	
63	2	GOOD	10f Good	61	3663	VIS
59	2	NOTT	10f Soft		3979	vis
58	5	NEWM	12f Gd/Sft	62	4534	vis

MA YORAM 3 gr c £1190

107	5	NEWM	7f Good	950
104	4	ASCO	6f Gd/Sft	1111
100	8	CURR	6f Gd/Sft	1622

MAAS 5 br g £952

55a	2	LING	6f Aw		25
54a	6	LING	7f Aw	60	106

MABROOKAH 4 b f £0

45a	5	LING	8f Aw		109
60	10	NEWM	8f Gd/Fm		3626
52	6	YARM	7f Firm	62	3939
0	17	BRIG	10f Gd/Sft	59	4118
0	16	LING	8f Soft		4273

MABSHUSH 4 b g £0

42	8	AYR	10f Gd/Fm	1655
0	9	REDC	10f Gd/Fm	2143

MAC BE LUCKY 3 b c £2492

68	10	HAYD	8f Gd/Sft	75	810
59	7	DONC	10f Gd/Fm	73	2610
75	2	HAYD	8f Gd/Sft		3477
0	12	GOOD	10f Soft	75	4067
75	2	LING	8f Soft		4274
75	3	YARM	7f Soft		4388

MAC HALL 3 b c £2863

78	6	NEWM	12f Good	951

MACARA 2 b f £11793

97	3	SAN	8f Soft	4318

MACDUNE 2 b c £0

84	8	NEWM	7f Good	4183
62	9	DONC	8f Gd/Sft	4446

MACHALINI 7 b g £0

53a	5	SOUT	16f Aw	60	2951	t
21a	10	WOLV	15f Gd/Fm	54	3276	t

MACHE 3 b g £0

21	10	NOTT	10f Good	47	2007
12	8	BEVE	16f Gd/Fm	40	3406

MACHIAVELLI 6 b g £0

57a	5	LING	16f Aw	69	285	bl
47a	8	WOLV	16f Aw	65	482	bl
10a	8	LING	13f Aw		524	bl

MACHRIE BAY 3 b c £2868

87	3	SOUT	10f Gd/Sft	858
85	2	NEWC	12f Heavy	1009
68	5	CHEP	12f Good	3869
79	2	BRIG	12f Gd/Sft	4119
79	3	YARM	11f Heavy	4481

MACHUDI 3 b f £0

57	6	SOUT	7f Good		804
0	19	WARW	8f Heavy		884
42a	6	SOUT	7f Aw	55	1202
30a	10	WOLV	7f Aw	52	1390

MACKEM BEAT 2 ch f £0

25	10	BRIG	5f Gd/Sft	1463
43	5	GOOD	6f Gd/Sft	1634
13a	5	WOLV	6f Aw	2079
0a	8	SOUT	5f Aw	2384
0	7	FOLK	7f Gd/Fm	3039

MACS DREAM 5 b g £0

0	12	WARW	8f Good		2464	t
0	21	DONC	7f Gd/Fm	44	2612	t
27	12	CHEP	7f Gd/Fm	44	2974	t
68	5	WIND	10f Good		3189	t
49	7	WARW	7f Good		3696	t
72	5	REDC	10f Gd/Sft		4218	t
58a	9	LING	7f Aw		4331	t

MAD HABIT 2 b c £0

0	15	KEMP	7f Firm	2867
0	14	KEMP	8f Gd/Fm	3799
45	8	BATH	10f Soft	4140

MADAM ALISON 4 b f £10579

80	3	SAND	7f Soft	80	1564	
82	1	**WIND**	8f Gd/Fm		1879*	
78	3	NEWM	8f Firm	80	2342	
84	1	**WIND**	8f Gd/Fm	80	2890*	
79	5	LEIC	8f Gd/Fm	83	3334	
60	13	SALI	7f Firm	83	3750	
84	3	NEWM	10f Good	82	4160	
75	10	NEWM	8f Good	84	4348	
62	8	NEWB	9f Sft/Hvy	83	4472	

MADAME BUTTERFLY 2 b f £0

0	15	WIND	6f Gd/Fm	3047

MADAME GENEREUX 3 ch f £272

61	4	PONT	6f Soft	877
38	5	HAYD	7f Heavy	992

35	6	CARL	6f Gd/Sft		1723
37	9	LEIC	6f Gd/Fm	57	2511
0	16	THIR	6f Gd/Fm	53	3124

MADAME JONES 5 ch m £0

30a	8	WOLV	6f Aw		76	
24a	10	WOLV	7f Aw	55	121	
0a	12	LING	6f Aw	49	148	
52	10	CHEP	6f Gd/Fm	65	3257	
38	11	CHES	6f Gd/Fm	59	3512	
63	5	BATH	5f Firm		3622	
49	9	SALI	7f Firm	56	3750	
44	9	CHEP	7f Good	53	3873	
37	7	SAND	5f Soft		4207	BL
0	20	NEWB	5f Gd/Sft	59	4459	bl

MADAME ROUX 2 b f £0

64	4	CATT	5f Good		1659
35	12	PONT	6f Gd/Fm		2828
57	9	SAND	6f Gd/Fm		3942

MADELINE BASSETT 2 b f £0

76	12	DONC	8f Gd/Sft		4445

MADEMOISELLE PARIS 3 gr f £198

38a	10	SOUT	5f Aw		34	BL
48a	4	SOUT	5f Aw	49	72	
9a	11	SOUT	8f Aw	47	128	
19a	10	WOLV	7f Aw	50	188	
0	13	NOTT	6f Gd/Sft		1081	
33a	5	SOUT	7f Aw	44	1202	
17a	9	SOUT	8f Aw	49	1303	
0a	15	SOUT	8f Aw	41	1422	
13	11	LEIC	8f Gd/Sft		1572	
0	17	BRIG	10f Soft	36	4419	

MADIES PRIDE 2 b f £217

68	4	RIPO	5f Soft		2539
39	7	CARL	5f Firm		2821
33	10	RIPO	5f Gd/Fm		3710

MADMUN 6 ch g £0

74	5	WIND	6f Good	74	2371
73	5	DONC	6f Gd/Fm		2580

MADRASEE 2 b f £2796

72	3	WIND	6f Gd/Fm		2209
69	6	CHEP	6f Gd/Fm		2488
71	3	WIND	5f Good		2711
72	8	WIND	5f Gd/Fm		3044
73	3	LING	5f Firm		3277
73	2	LING	5f Firm	71	3491
52	12	NOTT	6f Soft	73	3976
71	4	LING	5f Good	73	4098
67	5	LING	6f Gd/Fm	71	4269

MADURESE 3 b c £938

54	4	BRIG	7f Firm		1333
71	7	ASCO	8f Good		2679
66	3	EPSO	9f Good		3764
0	14	BEVE	8f Sft/Hvy	66	4045

MAEANDER 3 ch f £3842

101	3	CHAN	12f Gd/Sft		1748

MAGDALEON 2 b f £0

52	12	DONC	6f Heavy		4576

MAGELTA 3 b c £1200

32	10	KEMP	6f Soft	79	994
0	16	YORK	7f Gd/Fm	79	1308
76	2	GOOD	6f Gd/Fm	75	1961
57	10	EPSO	7f Gd/Sft	75	2431
72	7	SAND	7f Gd/Fm	75	2922
62	9	KEMP	6f Gd/Fm	75	3076

MAGENKO 3 ch c £630

47	2	YARM	16f Gd/Sft		1613
31a	6	SOUT	14f Aw		1975
28	10	CARL	17f Gd/Fm	50	2244

MAGGIE FLYNN 2 b f £0

34a	9	WOLV	6f Aw		4225

MAGIC AIR 2 b f £0

0	16	LING	8f Firm		3577

MAGIC BABE 3 b f £5656

47a	8	LING	6f Aw	55	634	
56	2	BRIG	6f Firm	55	1211	
48	4	BRIG	8f Soft	55	1511	
60	1	NEWB	7f Gd/Fm	55	1787*	
60	2	GOOD	7f Gd/Fm	58	2128	
59	4	EPSO	7f Good	59	2794	
53	5	SALI	7f Gd/Fm	59	2978	
0	11	FOLK	7f Gd/Fm	59	3445	
0	14	LING	8f Firm	59	3580	
0	11	GOOD	7f Soft	60	4080	

MAGIC BOX 2 b c £5061

77	6	DONC	5f Gd/Fm		700
82	4	NEWM	5f Soft		984
76	4	KEMP	5f Gd/Fm		1924
75	3	NEWC	7f Gd/Fm		2271
70	4	KEMP	5f Gd/Fm	76	3075
81	1	YARM	8f Gd/Fm		3665*

MAGIC COMBINATION 7 b g £5540

67	4	EPSO	12f Gd/Sft	64	2429
63	5	NEWM	14f Gd/Fm	66	2856
72	1	SAND	14f Good	65	3472*
71	5	HAYD	14f Soft	73	3783
56	8	HAYD	14f Gd/Sft	71	4105
0	12	YORK	14f Heavy	69	4299

MAGIC EAGLE 3 b g £0

66	6	NEWM	6f Good		956
63	7	KEMP	8f Gd/Sft		1080
0	17	LING	7f Gd/Fm		1263
0	18	NEWB	7f Gd/Fm	62	1787
0	14	YARM	6f Gd/Fm	58	3966
0	23	WIND	6f Gd/Sft	52	4294
29a	7	LING	10f Aw	46	4482

MAGIC FLUTE 4 ch f £868

69	2	NOTT	8f Good		1407	
0	15	KEMP	8f Gd/Fm	70	1926	
64	6	NEWM	8f Firm	68	2342	
43	8	LEIC	7f Gd/Fm		2508	
0	16	KEMP	7f Gd/Fm	65	2749	t
0	15	SALI	10f Gd/Fm	63	3390	

MAGIC GEM 2 gr c £0

0	17	WIND	6f Firm		2209
71	5	LING	5f Firm		3277
54	5	FOLK	5f Gd/Fm		3446
32	9	EPSO	6f Good	67	3761

MAGIC GLOW 4 b f £0

0a	3	SOUT	6f Aw		32

MAGIC HARP 2 b f £0

59	13	WIND	6f Gd/Sft		4288

MAGIC LAWYER 2 b f £0

0	17	LING	6f Soft		4190
33a	7	WOLV	6f Aw		4244

MAGIC MILL 7 b h £464

65	4	HAMI	6f Good	67	844
41	10	NEWC	7f Heavy	67	1011
54	8	HAMI	6f Gd/Fm	65	1192
0	13	AYR	7f Soft	63	3992
41	10	AYR	6f Heavy	59	4327
39	5	NEWC	7f Heavy	59	4426

MAGIC OF LOVE 3 b f £9472

98	3	NOTT	6f Good		1410
90	3	EPSO	7f Gd/Sft		1830
86	10	ASCO	6f Good		2115
100	4	YORK	6f Gd/Fm		2646
94	6	ASCO	6f Gd/Fm	99	3301
88	9	PONT	6f Firm		3503
83	10	NEWM	6f Good	99	4198

MAGIC OF YOU 2 b f £2931

69	1	MUSS	7f Firm		2377*	
69	3	CATT	7f Gd/Fm		2741	
27	14	NEWC	7f Good	70	3246	
0	14	YARM	7f Gd/Fm	68	3922	VIS

MAGIC POWERS 5 ch g £0

47	9	NEWB	7f Gd/Sft	61	1590	
0	13	NEWM	7f Firm	56	2347	
0	13	SALI	8f Gd/Sft	56	2467	VIS

MAGIC RAINBOW 5 b g £52061

90a	1	LING	7f Aw		630*
83a	9	WOLV	6f Aw	93	660
82	6	KEMP	6f Good	87	728
0	18	NEWM	7f Gd/Sft	86	966
60	14	YORK	6f Gd/Fm	84	1983
78	6	ASCO	5f Good	81	2676
77	5	ASCO	5f Good	80	2954
87	1	ASCO	5f Gd/Fm	82	3016*
83	5	SAND	5f Good	86	3473
80	7	DONC	5f Gd/Fm	86	3861

MAGIC SISTER 3 ch f £395

34	7	CATT	6f Gd/Fm		781
51	3	THIR	7f Soft		930
42a	7	WOLV	7f Aw		1038
33	8	CARL	6f Gd/Sft		1723

MAGIC SUNSET 3 b f £2198

69	9	WIND	10f Gd/Fm		1200	
40	11	BEVE	12f Good	65	1446	
39	11	WIND	10f Gd/Fm	60	2206	VIS
47a	1	WOLV	9f Aw		2602*	vis

MAGIC SYMBOL 3 gr f £0

0	17	GOOD	8f Gd/Sft		1811	
69	8	KEMP	10f Firm		2258	
51	5	EPSO	10f Gd/Fm		2627	
46	6	LEIC	10f Gd/Fm	60	3217	
0	13	GOOD	8f Good	55	3885	VIS
0	16	BRIG	10f Soft	50	4174	vis

MAGIC TO DO 2 b c £0

61	9	DONC	7f Gd/Sft		4447

MAGIC WATERS 2 b g £0

68	7	YORK	6f Firm		1328

MAGICAL BAILIWICK 4 ch g £3695

52	10	SALI	10f Gd/Fm	70	2270	
0	19	SALI	12f Good	67	2689	
44	10	CHEP	6f Gd/Fm	60	2974	
23	10	WIND	8f Good	55	3355	
44	8	BATH	8f Gd/Fm	55	3514	BL
42	7	LEIC	10f Firm	49	3842	bl
47	2	GOOD	8f Soft	46	4066	bl
53	1	BATH	8f Soft	46	4143*	bl
63	6	WIND	8f Gd/Sft		4292	bl

MAGICAL FLUTE 2 ch f £5385

56	7	SALI	5f Gd/Fm		2227
77	3	SAND	5f Gd/Fm		2526
77	1	BATH	6f Firm		2784*
80	3	THIR	7f Gd/Fm		2966
83a	2	LING	6f Aw		4332
65	8	NEWB	7f Gd/Sft	77	4453

MAGICAL JACK 3 b c £0

0a	13	SOUT	5f Aw		127
24a	10	SOUT	8f Aw		198
0a	13	SOUT	7f Aw		278

MAGICAL RIVER 3 ch f £0

0	13	BRIG	7f Gd/Fm	52	3242
35	7	BRIG	8f Firm	47	3561
0	18	CHEP	7f Good	44	3871

MAGICAL SHOT 5 b g £0

52a	4	SOUT	8f Aw	60	83
0a	14	SOUT	11f Aw	60	126

MAGIQUE ETOILE 4 b f £3167

48a	3	LING	6f Aw		25	vis
50a	2	LING	8f Aw		114	
44a	7	LING	7f Aw	55	504	
0a	16	SOUT	7f Aw	50	867	vis
54	6	WIND	6f Gd/Sft		1423	
45a	2	LING	7f Aw		1741	
54	2	SALI	6f Gd/Fm	50	2230	

47	6	LING	6f Good	55	2654
44	6	SALI	7f Gd/Fm	55	2978
42	8	SALI	8f Gd/Sft	53	3293
50	4	GOOD	10f Good	51	3663

MAGNANIMOUS 2 ch g £393

53	10	REDC	5f Gd/Sft		1130
0	12	THIR	5f Good		1381
42	10	YORK	6f Gd/Fm		1981
0	11	YORK	6f Good		3814
50	7	BEVE	5f Good		3955 VIS
50	3	NEWC	5f Heavy	50	4423 vis

MAGNI MOMENT 5 b m £0

0	14	BATH	12f Firm		2785

MAGNUS 4 b g £3842

110	3	LONG	16f Heavy		1116

MAGNUSSON 2 b c £1982

91	3	ASCO	6f Gd/Fm		3000
83	2	AYR	7f Good		3363

MAGZAA 2 gr c £806

69	11	NEWB	7f Firm		3999
49	11	SALI	8f Gd/Sft		4163
74	3	NOTT	8f Heavy		4504

MAHFOOTH 3 ch c £12483

87	2	KEMP	8f Soft		1532
102	1	HAYD	7f Gd/Fm		2443*
108	2	YORK	7f Firm		3600

MAHLSTICK 2 b c £0

0	12	HAYD	5f Soft		3767
0	12	BATH	6f Soft		4137
0	13	LING	6f Soft		4188

MAI TAI 5 b m £8068

41a	7	SOUT	7f Aw	53	35 vis
52a	4	SOUT	7f Aw	53	69 vis
46a	3	WOLV	7f Aw	51	121 vis
56a	1	LING	8f Aw	50	147* vis
56a	4	LING	7f Aw	56	162 vis
56a	2	SOUT	7f Aw	55	304 vis
45a	5	SOUT	8f Aw	55	340 vis
49a	4	SOUT	8f Aw	55	384 vis
30a	9	SOUT	8f Aw	54	692 vis
57a	1	SOUT	7f Aw	52	867* vis
32	9	THIR	8f Soft	48	907 vis
59a	2	SOUT	8f Aw	56	2121
53a	5	SOUT	8f Aw	58	2380
35	6	RIPO	8f Soft	42	2542
44a	6	SOUT	8f Aw	58	2634 vis
52a	6	SOUT	8f Aw		2946 vis
42	2	CARL	8f Firm	39	3574 vis
35	5	MUSS	8f Gd/Fm	39	3745 vis
38a	8	SOUT	8f Aw	56	4153 vis
36a	8	WOLV	9f Aw	56	4228
0	10	NEWC	7f Heavy	40	4426 vis

MAID FOR FREEDOM 2 gr f £0

56	6	NEWB	6f Stt/Hvy		4471

MAID OF ARC 2 b f £4118

0	14	BATH	6f Gd/Sft		1667
66	2	THIR	7f Gd/Fm		2057
68	2	CATT	7f Gd/Fm		2417 t
49a	4	SOUT	6f Aw		2635 t
47	4	BRIG	5f Firm		2903 t
38	6	NEWM	7f Firm	63	3299 t
52	3	THIR	7f Good		3615
61	1	LING	6f Firm		3757*
53	5	GOOD	6f Soft		4079

MAID PLANS 4 br f £0

0a	11	SOUT	7f Aw		247
22a	5	WOLV	7f Aw		310
0a	10	WOLV	8f Aw		409
0a	12	WOLV	7f Aw		449
0a	9	WOLV	12f Aw	22	522

MAID TO DANCE 2 b f £0

71	5	NOTT	6f Gd/Fm		2683

20	12	THIR	6f Gd/Fm		3614
0	13	REDC	7f Gd/Sft		4216

MAID TO LOVE 3 ch f £2579

62a	2	LING	8f Aw	57	54 bl
63a	3	LING	8f Aw	60	158 bl
57a	4	LING	10f Aw	60	315
65a	2	SOUT	8f Aw		385 t
61a	2	LING	8f Aw		544
57a	5	WOLV	8f Aw	61	1138
0	20	REDC	7f Firm	62	1297
0a	13	SOUT	8f Aw	60	1419
0a	12	WOLV	9f Aw	57	2080

MAIDAAN 4 b c £25600

110	3	CURR	7f Good		4056
113	2	NEWM	7f Good		4352

MAIDEN AUNT 3 b f £838

52	5	BATH	8f Gd/Fm		1436
63	9	BATH	8f Gd/Sft		1669
43	12	WIND	8f Gd/Fm		2211
47	10	LING	10f Firm	57	3581
38	9	SALI	10f Gd/Sft	52	4169
52a	2	WOLV	12f Aw	49	4360

MAINE LOBSTER 2 ch f £1891

68	12	NEWB	6f Gd/Fm		1943
80	3	NEWM	6f Gd/Fm		2285
74	2	WIND	6f Gd/Fm		2886
72	5	NEWM	7f Firm	77	3299
56	12	NEWB	7f Gd/Sft	75	4453

MAITEAMIA 7 ch g £0

58	5	REDC	6f Firm		1298 bl
52a	5	WOLV	6f Aw		3275 bl

MAIYSHA 3 b f £0

0	14	LING	7f Gd/Sft		839
0	18	WIND	12f Heavy	55	937
0	19	WIND	12f Firm	53	1292
0	16	YARM	11f Gd/Sft	47	1614 BL

MAJESTIC 5 b g £375

69a	3	WOLV	16f Aw	68	552 tbl

MAJESTIC BAY 4 b c £30955

75	3	NEWC	12f Heavy		1009
55	8	YORK	14f Gd/Fm	84	1982 BL
77	1	YARM	14f Gd/Fm		2194*
74	3	KEMP	14f Gd/Sft	75	2584
81	1	REDC	16f Gd/Fm	75	2993*
81	4	HAYD	14f Gd/Fm	80	3323
86	1	HAYD	14f Soft	80	3783*
68	11	NEWB	13f Firm	85	3994
0	11	YORK	14f Heavy	84	4299

MAJESTIC PREMIUM 2 b f £0

30	8	HAYD	8f Gd/Sft		4104

MAJESTIC QUEST 2 b c £4705

69	4	GOOD	5f Gd/Sft		1639
74	2	NOTT	5f Good		1870
71	1	RIPO	5f Gd/Fm		2835*
25	11	YORK	6f Good	77	3807
0	19	REDC	6f Gd/Sft		4219
0	21	DONC	6f Gd/Sft		4449

MAJOR ATTRACTION 5 gr g £5782

21a	9	WOLV	8f Aw		229
0a	10	WOLV	9f Aw		292
6a	10	WOLV	12f Aw	34	410
2a	7	SOUT	8f Aw	31	496
34a	6	WOLV	9f Aw		553 VIS
6a	7	WOLV	12f Aw		626 BL
64	7	HAMI	11f Good		848
0	13	FOLK	15f Soft	40	963 bl
37	1	HAMI	11f Gd/Fm	29	1361*
28	7	LEIC	12f Soft	38	1551
28	11	HAMI	13f Gd/Fm	37	1936
32	8	CHES	10f Gd/Fm		2245
48	1	HAYD	12f Gd/Fm		2457*

MAJOR BART 3 gr c £0

24a	10	SOUT	6f Aw		685
43a	5	SOUT	6f Aw	50	1205
16	15	HAYD	6f Soft	50	1494
12	9	CATT	6f Good	50	1665
31a	7	SOUT	7f Aw		2633

MAJOR FORCE 4 b c £2250

114	3	LEOP	7f Stt/Hvy		15

MAJOR MORRIS 5 br g £0

0a	13	SOUT	8f Aw		197
32a	9	SOUT	8f Aw		279
0a	13	SOUT	11f Aw	37	390 t

MAJOR REBUKE 3 b c £1157

0	18	NEWM	7f Gd/Fm	86	1153
0	18	GOOD	7f Gd/Sft	83	1470
63	9	NEWB	8f Gd/Fm		1786
60	2	BATH	8f Firm		2786
49	9	NOTT	8f Gd/Fm	66	3115 VIS
54	7	NEWM	6f Gd/Fm	60	3457 vis
31	9	BRIG	7f Firm		3739 BL

MAJOR REVIEW 2 b f £0

69	9	GOOD	7f Good		3108

MAKAAREM 3 gr c £1260

104	4	NEWM	7f Gd/Fm		1693
80	15	ASCO	7f Good		2087

MAKARIM 4 ch c £0

53a	6	WOLV	16f Aw	77	135
61a	5	LING	12f Aw	72	237
0a	13	LING	10f Aw	72	244
57a	5	WOLV	8f Aw	64	380
21	10	BRIG	10f Gd/Fm		1933
55a	4	SOUT	12f Aw		4366

MAKASSEB 3 ch c £4230

75	12	HAYD	8f Gd/Sft	86	810
69	7	NOTT	8f Gd/Sft		1366
82	6	YORK	10f Firm	82	2004
78	7	GOOD	10f Gd/Fm	79	2358
68	4	NEWC	12f Good		2523
73	4	SAND	14f Gd/Fm	76	2936
46	8	HAYD	12f Gd/Sft	74	3270
75	1	RIPO	16f Gd/Fm	72	3715*
25	10	AYR	17f Soft		3993
0	14	YORK	14f Heavy	73	4299

MAKATI 6 b g £0

44a	4	WOLV	15f Aw		4024

MAKBOOLA 2 b f £5534

86	3	GOOD	6f Gd/Sft		1486
85	1	REDC	6f Good		1893*
90	2	WIND	6f Good		2369

MAKE A WISH 2 ch c £0

0	11	FOLK	7f Gd/Fm		2290

MAKE READY 6 b m £0

25a	9	SOUT	6f Aw	57	87

MAKE WAY 4 b c £7918

73	6	HAYD	11f Heavy		986
74	12	NEWM	10f Gd/Fm	86	1170
83	3	KEMP	10f Soft		1528
83	2	WIND	10f Good	80	1729
82	2	SAND	10f Good	80	1965
80	5	ASCO	10f Good	82	2170
81	6	GOOD	9f Good	82	2304 bl
70	15	NEWM	9f Gd/Fm	81	4212
81	3	NEWM	8f Good	80	4340
82	2	BRIG	8f Soft		4420

MAKNAAS 4 ch c £16829

52a	3	LING	13f Aw	47	167
52a	1	WOLV	16f Aw	47	194*
52a	4	SOUT	16f Aw	52	253
56a	1	LING	16f Aw	52	285*
49a	5	LING	16f Aw	53	424
66a	1	WOLV	16f Aw	53	482*
68a	1	WOLV	16f Aw	61	627*
78a	1	LING	16f Aw	67	649*

80a 1 WOLV 16f Aw 69 664*
0 14 PONT 17f Soft 66 876
0 13 WARW 16f Gd/Sft 60 1711

MALA MALA 2 b f £30300
103 3 CURR 7f Gd/Fm 3845
108 3 NEWM 6f Good 4159

MALAAH 4 gr c £0
36 10 BATH 5f Gd/Fm 55 1092 bl
40 11 BRIG 6f Firm 55 1211 bl
45 8 LING 5f Good 50 1398 bl
41 5 YARM 6f Gd/Fm 48 1953 bl
0 15 LING 5f Gd/Fm 46 2184 bl
0 15 NOTT 6f Gd/Fm 46 2193 bl
35 5 BRIG 6f Firm 42 2896 bl
46 6 BRIG 7f Gd/Fm 3259 bl
57 9 SAND 5f Gd/Fm 3947 bl
37 8 SAND 5f Soft 4207 bl

MALADERIE 6 b g £1778
46a 7 SOUT 6f Aw 61 47 BL
32 12 NEWC 5f Soft 60 758
39 9 THIR 7f Soft 58 908
47 12 BEVE 5f Firm 56 1278 vis
58 2 THIR 5f Gd/Sft 56 1357 vis
55 7 AYR 5f Firm 59 1629 vis
0 11 BATH 6f Firm 59 1999 vis
41 9 NEWC 5f Firm 57 2340 vis
44 11 DONC 7f Gd/Fm 55 2612 vis
22 13 NEWC 6f Good 53 3037 vis
43 9 PONT 5f Gd/Fm 53 3222
46 7 REDC 6f Firm 50 3312 vis
48 4 CARL 5f Firm 48 3572
36 12 NEWC 6f Firm 48 3605
40 11 WIND 5f Gd/Sft 47 4295

MALAKAL 4 b c £0
3a 11 LING 10f Aw 56
8a 8 WOLV 7f Aw 173
14a 9 WOLV 8f Aw 308
35 15 WIND 8f Good 65 854
34 10 DONC 10f Gd/Sft 60 1050
0 12 NOTT 10f Gd/Fm 55 1272
18 11 NEWB 13f Gd/Sft 50 1594
0a 13 SOUT 8f Aw 33 2380

MALARKEY 3 b g £1545
64 7 SALI 6f Firm 1175
61 5 NOTT 6f Firm 1266
69 5 LING 6f Good 1399
65 4 REDC 7f Gd/Sft 1579
66 5 WIND 8f Good 67 2367
67 3 FOLK 9f Gd/Fm 65 3043
64 2 LEIC 12f Gd/Fm 3219
58 5 EPSO 12f Gd/Fm 65 3417

MALCHIK 4 ch c £4734
38a 7 LING 10f Aw 47 22
28a 8 LING 10f Aw 110
37a 5 LING 7f Aw 159
30a 7 LING 10f Aw 38 220
42a 5 LING 7f Aw 46 239
48a 5 LING 10f Aw 333
49a 5 LING 7f Aw 375
55a 6 LING 7f Aw 398
36a 9 LING 8f Aw 53 463
30a 8 LING 7f Aw 42 504
38a 2 LING 8f Aw 574
21a 8 LING 10f Aw 38 618
39a 7 LING 12f Aw 650
39a 3 WOLV 8f Aw 38 675
45a 3 WOLV 12f Aw 710
32a 3 LING 10f Aw 775
55a 1 **WOLV** 9f Aw 922*
55a 2 WOLV 8f Aw 54 1037
47a 7 LING 8f Aw 56 1259
57a 2 WOLV 8f Aw 56 1393
26 6 YARM 11f Gd/Fm 37 1614

0 32 NEWM 12f Firm 34 1852
29a 10 LING 8f Aw 58 1915
28a 9 WOLV 15f Gd/Fm 57 3276
25a 8 WOLV 12f Fm 54 4026

MALHUB 2 br c £5086
91 1 NEWM 7f Good 4184*

MALIAN 4 b g £0
36 9 KEMP 14f Good 61 726
0 15 PONT 22f Heavy 59 940
0 16 NOTT 14f Gd/Sft 57 1087 VIS
25 5 WIND 12f Good 2715 BL

MALLEUS 3 ch c £10622
87 2 KEMP 9f Gd/Sft 80 1075
88 1 **YORK** 8f Firm 83 1341*
80 15 ASCO 8f Good 87 2117

MALLIA 7 b g £7541
63a 6 SOUT 6f Aw 75 44 bl
57a 11 SOUT 6f Aw 74 129 bl
67a 4 WOLV 6f Aw 72 258 bl
48a 11 WOLV 6f Aw 72 320 bl
60a 5 SOUT 6f Aw 69 386 bl
55a 5 WOLV 6f Aw 406 bl
69a 1 **WOLV** 6f Aw 465*
68a 6 WOLV 6f Aw 69 532
63a 4 SOUT 6f Aw 68 645
69a 1 **WOLV** 6f Aw 719*
66 4 RIPO 6f Soft 69 824
26 14 DONC 6f Gd/Sft 1068
66 4 HAMI 6f Gd/Fm 68 1192 bl
65a 4 SOUT 6f Aw 70 1504 bl
69 4 YORK 6f Firm 67 2000 bl
67 4 NEWC 6f Gd/Fm 67 2275 bl
53 11 NEWC 6f Firm 67 2334 bl
0 14 HAYD 6f Gd/Fm 67 2444 bl

MALWINA 4 ch f £2764
38a P SOUT 16f Aw 327
21a 7 WOLV 9f Aw 360
46a 5 WOLV 9f Aw 433
46a 1 **SOUT** 11f Aw 44 561*
46a 2 SOUT 12f Aw 44 642
45a 5 SOUT 11f Aw 866
42a 5 WOLV 12f Aw 1039

MAMCAZMA 2 b c £0
0 12 PONT 6f Soft 4083
38 6 CATT 5f Soft 4252
46 14 DONC 7f Gd/Sft 4447

MAMEHA 2 b f £610
60 7 ASCO 6f Gd/Fm 2952
87 3 WARW 7f Gd/Fm 3910
94 5 ASCO 8f Good 4110

MAMMAS BOY 5 b g £9275
27 10 SOUT 7f Good 49 803
23 11 REDC 7f Gd/Sft 1132
51 4 THIR 7f Gd/Sft 1351
55 1 **REDC** 7f Gd/Sft 1559*
55 1 **MUSS** 7f Firm 1685*
53 1 **MUSS** 7f Firm 2046*
44 11 HAYD 6f Gd/Fm 54 2444
46 10 CARL 7f Firm 53 2823
50 4 CATT 7f Gd/Fm 53 2932
45 6 CATT 7f Good 51 3440
42 7 NEWC 7f Soft 53 3708
54 1 **MUSS** 8f Gd/Fm 49 3745*
47 6 MUSS 7f Gd/Sft 52 4136
40 7 MUSS 7f Soft 52 4522
0 13 MUSS 8f Soft 52 4565

MAMMAS F C 4 ch f £0
37a 8 WOLV 5f Aw 52 563
37a 10 WOLV 6f Aw 52 622
38a 5 SOUT 5f Aw 46 674
35a 5 LING 5f Aw 46 691
0 F WIND 6f Gd/Fm 57 746

MAMMAS TONIGHT 2 ch c £15110
82a 1 **SOUT** 5f Aw 801*
87 3 HAMI 5f Good 843
80 3 NEWC 5f Heavy 1006
81 3 AYR 6f Gd/Fm 1628
101 1 **BEVE** 5f Gd/Sft 1761*
101 5 ASCO 5f Good 2113
98 4 SAND 5f Gd/Fm 2529
91 8 GOOD 6f Good 3105
73 9 YORK 6f Gd/Fm 3566
100 4 AYR 5f Soft 3959 BL
76 4 YORK 6f Heavy 4298 bl
61 15 DONC 6f Gd/Sft 4449

MAMORE GAP 2 b c £9531
74 2 WIND 5f Gd/Fm 743
70a 2 LING 5f Aw 878
77 3 EPSO 6f Gd/Sft 2628
80 1 **BRIG** 5f Firm 2903*
87 1 **NEWB** 7f Gd/Fm 77 3175*

MAMZUG 3 b c £5456
78 4 CHES 10f Gd/Fm 1218
76 1 **BATH** 6f Gd/Fm 1435*
76 4 NEWM 8f Gd/Fm 79 1853
81 2 DONC 8f Gd/Fm 78 2579
79 3 BEVE 7f Firm 78 2733
75 5 CHEP 8f Gd/Fm 80 3254

MAN OF DISTINCTION 2 b c £5419
81 5 NEWB 5f Gd/Sft 1589
84 1 **KEMP** 6f Gd/Fm 1924*
90 2 NEWB 6f Firm 2808

MAN OMYSTERY 3 b c £47102
90 1 **LEIC** 8f Good 789*
100 2 SAND 8f Heavy 1041
96 4 ASCO 8f Good 94 2117
102 2 YORK 10f Good 94 2696
105 6 LONG 10f Gd/Sft 4053
103 4 NEWM 10f Gd/Fm 102 4212
104 2 NEWM 10f Gd/Sft 4532

MANA DARGENT 3 b c £18492
68 2 DONC 7f Good 717
71 7 SOUT 8f Gd/Sft 78 857
72 4 THIR 8f Good 76 1387
59 5 NEWC 8f Heavy 74 1765
68 6 HAMI 8f Firm 73 2097
72 3 EPSO 7f Gd/Sft 71 2431
50 12 DONC 10f Good 71 2577
74 3 AYR 7f Firm 72 2878 BL
84 1 **ASCO** 12f Gd/Fm 72 3014*
80 3 KEMP 12f Gd/Fm 78 3073
87 2 EPSO 12f Gd/Sft 81 3402
88 3 YORK 14f Firm 81 3599
75 4 YORK 14f Gd/Fm 87 3728
78 6 AYR 13f Gd/Sft 85 4014

MANA MOU BAY 3 b c £2907
95 18 NEWM 8f Gd/Fm 1171
104 2 SALI 7f Gd/Fm 2228
81 4 SALI 10f Gd/Fm 2471
101 5 GOOD 8f Firm 3150
97 9 NEWM 8f Good 4180
81 9 YORK 7f Soft 100 4278

MANAGERIAL 3 b c £0
35 9 LING 10f Soft 1287

MANDOOB 3 b c £269
72 10 NEWM 8f Firm 1188
76 4 RIPO 10f Good 1599
70 5 LEIC 10f Firm 2030
74 6 SAND 10f Gd/Fm 75 2499

MANE FRAME 5 b g £10446
59 9 SALI 14f Firm 66 1180
49 9 NOTT 14f Good 65 1411
67 2 WARW 15f Heavy 62 1524
67 1 **WARW** 16f Gd/Sft 65 1711*

69	10	ASCO	20f Good	71	2092	
68	6	SAND	16f Gd/Fm	69	2498	
65	6	SALI	14f Gd/Sft	68	4166	
68	2	NEWB	16f Gd/Sft	66	4458	
72	2	MUSS	16f Soft	70	4563	

MANFUL 8 b g £3164

20a	7	SOUT	12f Aw	37	68	
25a	7	WOLV	16f Aw	32	194	bl
34a	1	**WOLV**	12f Aw	31	260*	bl
15a	8	WOLV	16f Aw	33	318	bl
17a	8	SOUT	12f Aw	32	641	vis
33a	3	SOUT	12f Aw	38	682	bl
37	10	SOUT	16f Gd/Sft	49	860	bl
30a	2	SOUT	14f Aw	31	1301	bl
25a	3	SOUT	14f Aw	30	1501	bl
34	6	WARW	16f Gd/Fm	46	1711	bl
35a	4	SOUT	14f Aw		1975	bl

MANGUS 6 b g £4023

56a	11	WOLV	5f Aw	76	64	
81a	1	**WOLV**	5f Aw	74	146+	
78a	4	WOLV	5f Aw	80	191	
73a	6	WOLV	5f Aw	79	579	
73a	5	LING	5f Aw	78	774	
36	13	BATH	5f Good	61	1092	
54	8	LING	5f Gd/Sft	61	1264	
45	12	LING	5f Gd/Fm	58	2184	
50	5	BRIG	5f Soft	55	2428	
41	10	BATH	5f Firm	53	3209	
27	9	BRIG	5f Firm		3562	
0	16	SALI	5f Firm	51	3747	

MANHATTAN 3 b c £0

78	10	GOOD	8f Gd/Fm		3087
0	7	LEOP	10f Good		3925
67	12	ASCO	8f Good		4111

MANIATIS 3 b c £5758

71	11	KEMP	11f Soft		1017
78	3	BRIG	12f Gd/Sft		4119
85	2	SAND	10f Soft		4205
93	1	**BATH**	12f Soft		4434*

MANICANI 2 ch c £0

65	11	YORK	6f Gd/Fm		3568

MANIKATO 6 b g £2814

32a	4	WOLV	7f Aw	37	635
23a	6	WOLV	9f Aw	35	749
36	1	**CHEP**	8f Gd/Fm	27	3251*
38	5	BRIG	10f Firm	38	3737

MANOLO 7 b g £0

15a	10	WOLV	6f Aw		406	
40a	7	WOLV	6f Aw		436	bl
15a	6	SOUT	6f Aw		559	
35a	9	SOUT	6f Aw	54	602	bl
0	16	HAMI	5f Firm	52	1244	bl

MANOR LAKE 2 b f £0

60	5	BATH	6f Soft		4137

MANORBIER 4 ch g £26160

40a	9	SOUT	4f Aw	70	342
59a	1	**WOLV**	5f Aw		533*
60a	4	WOLV	5f Aw	60	609
64a	1	**WOLV**	6f Aw		680*
79	1	**DONC**	6f Good	65	716*
83	2	RIPO	6f Soft	77	824
36	12	HAMI	6f Good	77	844
82	4	NEWM	6f Gd/Fm	82	1173
85	1	**THIR**	6f Good	82	1383*
107	4	CURR	6f Gd/Sft		1622
88	9	HAYD	7f Gd/Sft		1834
102	5	CHES	6f Firm		3172
95	10	YORK	5f Firm		3598

MANSA MUSA 5 br g £1326

0	18	DONC	10f Gd/Fm	70	705
44	10	BRIG	8f Gd/Sft	70	895
70	2	EPSO	9f Heavy		1033

51	9	BRIG	8f Gd/Fm	67	1129

MANSTAR 3 b c £426

57	5	RIPO	10f Soft	60	827	
42	8	HAMI	8f Good		847	
39	10	NOTT	8f Heavy	57	1024	
72	5	HAMI	11f Gd/Fm		1193	
58	7	BEVE	12f Good	62	1446	BL
27	8	AYR	11f Gd/Fm	62	1633	bl
33	10	HAYD	11f Gd/Fm	54	2453	VIS
37	8	HAMI	12f Gd/Sft	51	3531	vis
37	6	RIPO	10f Good	51	3702	
48	3	AYR	11f Heavy		4304	
22	11	REDC	11f Soft		4497	

MANTILLA 3 b f £1433

72a	4	WOLV	5f Aw		77
35a	8	SOUT	8f Aw		328
70a	2	WOLV	8f Aw		409
70a	3	WOLV	9f Aw		467

MANTLES PRIDE 5 b g £16013

0a	13	SOUT	7f Aw	82	687	bl
70	7	DONC	8f Good	82	715	bl
83	4	THIR	7f Good	82	1158	vis
87	1	**DONC**	7f Good	82	1514*	bl
78	8	GOOD	7f Gd/Sft	86	1810	bl
84	6	NEWM	7f Gd/Sft	86	2133	bl
72	9	NEWC	7f Firm	85	2338	bl
71	13	YORK	7f Good	84	2694	bl
82	5	AYR	7f Firm	83	2878	bl
72	9	CHES	8f Firm	83	3170	bl
61	9	NEWC	7f Soft	80	3708	bl
0	18	DONC	7f Gd/Fm	80	3880	bl
66	2	NEWM	7f Good		4018	bl
75	2	YORK	6f Soft		4287	bl
59	9	NOTT	6f Heavy	74	4411	bl
65	1	**DONC**	7f Soft		4461*	bl
69	7	NEWM	7f Firm	73	4547	bl

MANTUSIS 5 ch g £18770

85	3	NOTT	10f Good	83	786
88	2	HAYD	11f Heavy		986
89	1	**HAYD**	11f Gd/Sft	86	1790*
81	4	DONC	10f Gd/Fm	89	2350
57	20	YORK	10f Good		2696
92	1	**LEIC**	12f Gd/Fm	88	2917*
76	6	NEWB	11f Firm	92	3451
83	10	DONC	10f Firm	91	3899
69	14	NEWM	12f Good	90	4162

MANUFAN 5 b g £0

0	20	DONC	8f Heavy	46	4573	t

MANUKA TOO 2 ch f £0

38	10	WIND	6f Good		3187
64	5	YARM	6f Gd/Fm		3385
63	9	YARM	6f Firm		3938
0	13	LING	7f Soft	64	4191

MANX GYPSY 2 b f £213

49	4	DONC	5f Good		712
36	9	NEWC	5f Soft		755
0	8	MUSS	5f Gd/Sft		2532

MANX SHADOW 3 b f £0

0	8	REDC	11f Gd/Sft	54	1560
5	9	MUSS	12f Gd/Sft	45	2537
0	14	REDC	11f Soft		4497

MANXWOOD 3 b c £7988

46	9	WIND	8f Good	64	854
66a	1	**WOLV**	7f Aw		1038*
65a	4	WOLV	7f Aw	64	1235
70a	2	WOLV	7f Aw	65	1390
65	1	**WIND**	8f Good	60	1726*
54	10	NEWM	8f Gd/Fm	63	2130
0	18	ASCO	7f Gd/Fm	63	2999
73a	2	WOLV	8f Aw	70	3274
54a	8	WOLV	9f Aw	73	3495
66a	4	WOLV	7f Aw	73	3771

MANY HAPPY RETURNS 3 br f £0

0	13	SALI	6f Firm		1175
46	5	NEWB	10f Gd/Sft		1593
0	13	SALI	8f Firm	48	2025
15	12	SALI	10f Gd/Sft	45	4169

MANZONI 4 b c £3445

0	12	RIPO	12f Soft	54	825	
0	19	DONC	10f Gd/Sft	52	1050	
45	6	CARL	12f Firm	50	2279	
19	11	BEVE	12f Gd/Sft	48	3053	
38	10	HAYD	12f Good	48	3284	VIS
48	1	**MUSS**	14f Gd/Fm	43	3590*	
19	9	CHES	16f Soft	47	4071	

MAP BOY 2 b g £0

0	15	LING	6f Soft		4188

MAPLE 4 ch c £590

58a	7	LING	6f Aw	66	106	
51a	6	LING	8f Aw	62	169	
58a	3	LING	10f Aw	59	224	
52a	6	LING	10f Aw		268	
38a	7	WOLV	9f Aw	58	309	
46a	6	LING	7f Aw	58	616	VIS
49a	3	LING	6f Aw	58	653	vis

MARABAR 2 b f £447

60	6	LEIC	7f Gd/Fm		2916
81	3	BATH	6f Soft		4138

MARAH 3 ch f £0

73	6	NEWM	7f Firm		1186	
74	6	SAND	9f Gd/Fm	92	1990	
50	9	GOOD	10f Gd/Fm	87	2358	BL

MARAHA 3 ch f £2988

79	4	GOOD	10f Gd/Fm	81	1958	
78	3	LEIC	12f Gd/Fm	80	2509	
74	2	NEWC	14f Gd/Fm	78	2984	
58	5	SAND	14f Good	77	3472	
69	10	HAYD	14f Soft	75	3783	BL

MARAMBA 4 b f £0

80	9	MAIS	11f Heavy		122

MARANI 2 ch f £0

83	5	DONC	8f Gd/Sft		4445

MARCH KING 2 b c £18600

108	3	CURR	7f Gd/Sft		4058

MARCHING ORDERS 4 b g £0

0	18	EPSO	10f Heavy	88	1031	
56	12	CHES	10f Gd/Fm	85	1217	
0	12	HAYD	8f Soft	80	1490	
54	9	HAYD	11f Gd/Sft	75	1790	
0	18	NEWM	7f Firm		2347	VIS
36	10	BEVE	8f Gd/Fm	60	3407	bl

MARCIANO 4 b g £0

4a	8	LING	13f Aw	40	458
0	14	PONT	22f Heavy	40	940

MARCUS MAXIMUS 5 ch g £0

82	6	WIND	12f Good		3640

MARDANI 5 b g £13495

70a	8	LING	12f Aw	98	633	
0	16	NEWM	12f Firm	98	1187	
77	11	EPSO	12f Good	96	1850	
87	10	GOOD	14f Gd/Fm	92	3058	
87	2	NEWM	12f Gd/Fm	87	3461	
86	6	YORK	12f Good	87	3541	
85	6	THIR	12f Gd/Sft	86	3778	
87	2	NEWM	14f Good	85	4016	
83	6	DIEL	12f Good		4148	
87	3	NEWM	12f Good	87	4342	
72	9	DONC	12f Soft	87	4464	

MARE OF WETWANG 2 ch f £0

64	6	RIPO	5f Soft		2539
24	13	WIND	5f Good		2711
37	8	THIR	7f Gd/Fm		3127
34	7	RIPO	6f Good		3697
0	15	BEVE	7f Good	47	3950

58	12	DONC	6f Gd/Sft			4449	

MAREMMA 6 b m £0

| 41 | 8 | CATT | 14f Good | | | 1660 | |
| 18 | 6 | CATT | 14f Gd/Sft | | | 1814 | |

MARENGO 6 b g £14120

41a	5	SOUT	7f Aw	52	33	
46a	3	WOLV	6f Aw		76	
59a	7	WOLV	6f Aw		132	
58a	1	**SOUT**	6f Aw	52	183*	
36a	10	SOUT	6f Aw	57	212	
58a	3	WOLV	6f Aw	58	232	
35a	9	SOUT	6f Aw	58	246	
32a	8	SOUT	6f Aw	56	388	
50a	3	SOUT	6f Aw		559	
48a	7	SOUT	6f Aw	54	587	
46a	6	SOUT	6f Aw	54	604	
52a	2	WOLV	6f Aw		680	
56a	2	SOUT	6f Aw	52	698	
57	3	PONT	6f Soft		872	
52	2	FOLK	5f Firm	51	958	
60	1	**DONC**	6f Gd/Sft		1073*	
48	5	CARL	6f Firm	62	1258	
53	10	BEVE	5f Firm	59	1278	
62	4	NOTT	6f Gd/Sft		1368	
37a	10	SOUT	6f Aw	57	1422	vis
64	2	AYR	6f Gd/Fm	61	1654	
58a	4	SOUT	7f Aw	57	1801	
39a	8	SOUT	6f Aw		2118	
43	10	REDC	6f Gd/Fm	63	2158	
46	9	EPSO	7f Gd/Sft	62	2431	
0	21	YORK	6f Good	60	2697	
52	6	NEWC	6f Good	56	3037	
57	3	KEMP	5f Gd/Fm		3077	
55a	6	WOLV	5f Aw	57	3271	
54	5	BEVE	5f Good	56	3398	
51	7	CHES	5f Gd/Fm	56	3512	
30a	11	WOLV	6f Aw	54	3774	
43	11	HAYD	5f Gd/Sft	56	4107	
57a	1	**SOUT**	6f Aw	52	4155*	
29	15	WIND	6f Gd/Sft	59	4294	
44a	5	WOLV	6f Aw	56	4444	

MARENKA 3 b f £1759

74	4	CHEP	10f Gd/Sft		1796	
69	2	LEIC	10f Gd/Fm		2774	
72	3	NOTT	10f Gd/Fm		3006	
71	5	GOOD	10f Good		3907	
57	9	DONC	10f Gd/Sft	71	4448	

MARGARETS DANCER 5 b g £3281

35a	7	WOLV	8f Aw	48	38	t
28	7	RIPO	10f Soft		2538	t
37	7	PONT	8f Gd/Fm	48	2831	t
30	6	PONT	10f Gd/Fm	44	3220	t
49	1	**THIR**	8f Gd/Fm	44	3344*	t
29	9	YORK	10f Gd/Fm	48	3731	t
49	3	MUSS	9f Soft	48	4523	t
0	16	DONC	8f Heavy	48	4573	t

MARGARITA 2 b f £0

23	10	WARW	5f Heavy		886	
54	7	EPSO	6f Gd/Sft		2628	
36	11	WIND	6f Gd/Fm		2886	
53	5	SALI	7f Gd/Fm		3388	
31	8	LING	6f Firm		3757	BL

MARGAY 3 b f £17734

| 98 | 3 | LEOP | 7f Soft | | 948 | |
| 104 | 2 | DUSS | 8f Good | | 1229 | |

MARIA FROM CAPLAW 3 ch f £0

| 0 | 16 | AYR | 5f Heavy | 41 | 4307 | |
| 13 | 10 | MUSS | 5f Soft | 42 | 4516 | |

MARIANA 5 ch m £531

6a	7	WOLV	7f Aw		173	vis
30a	5	SOUT	7f Aw		367	BL
5a	9	LING	7f Aw	30	438	bl

29a	5	SOUT	7f Aw		501	bl
0a	11	LING	8f Aw		574	vis
0	14	BRIG	7f Firm	33	1336	
14	10	LEIC	8f Gd/Sft		1731	
25a	3	SOUT	11f Aw		2381	
24a	7	SOUT	16f Aw	32	2951	
30	3	NEWC	12f Good		3247	
16	7	CARL	12f Firm		3570	
4a	11	SOUT	11f Aw		4151	
13	8	YARM	14f Soft		4510	

MARIENBARD 3 b c £36848

86	1	**LEIC**	12f Gd/Sft		1738*	
96	1	**WIND**	12f Gd/Fm		2208*	
111	1	**HAYD**	12f Gd/Fm		2503*	
112	2	YORK	12f Good		3540	
109	6	DONC	15f Firm		3898	
112	2	NEWB	12f Sft/Hv		4469	

MARIGLIANO 7 b g £0

| 24 | 8 | LEIC | 8f Sft/Hvy | | 4311 | |

MARIKA 2 b f £0

| 49 | 5 | WIND | 6f Good | | 3187 | |

MARINE 2 b c £16173

78	5	GOOD	6f Gd/Sft		1472	
102	1	**GOOD**	6f Gd/Sft		1809*	
102	1	**NEWB**	6f Gd/Fm		1944*	
96	5	NEWM	6f Gd/Fm		2595	
93	5	NEWB	7f Firm		2848	
102	3	GOOD	8f Good		3882	BL
100	3	PONT	8f Soft		4375	bl

MARINO STREET 7 b m £7521

48	2	BEVE	5f Firm	46	1923	
55	1	**NOTT**	6f Gd/Fm	48	2193*	
59	1	**WARW**	5f Gd/Fm	54	2252*	
0	W	HAYD	5f Gd/Fm	58	2505	
56	5	NOTT	6f Gd/Fm	58	2684	
60	6	NOTT	6f Gd/Fm		3113	
56	6	PONT	6f Gd/Fm	58	3222	
60	2	NOTT	6f Soft	58	3975	
50	11	LEIC	5f Gd/Fm	58	4027	

MARITUN LAD 3 b g £3229

40a	6	WOLV	7f Aw		41	
59a	5	SOUT	5f Aw		127	
62a	4	LING	6f Aw	57	242	
64a	3	WOLV	6f Aw	58	397	VIS
62a	1	**WOLV**	5f Aw		624*	BL
51	6	CATT	7f Gd/Fm		777	bl
57a	4	SOUT	5f Aw	61	870	bl
48	13	CARL	5f Firm	58	3572	bl
49	8	GOOD	5f Good	54	3908	bl
54a	6	WOLV	6f Aw	60	4358	bl

MARJAANA 7 b m £0

| 26a | 9 | SOUT | 7f Aw | 58 | 33 | |
| 0 | 13 | SOUT | 7f Gd/Fm | | 778 | |

MARJEUNE 3 b f £2605

57	7	PONT	12f Gd/Fm	67	2829	
70	2	THIR	12f Gd/Fm	67	3125	
66	3	SALI	12f Gd/Fm	67	3290	
64	3	AYR	15f Soft	68	3961	
47	11	SALI	14f Gd/Sft	65	4166	

MARJORY POLLEY 3 ch f £0

47	8	GOOD	9f Gd/Sft		1481	BL
0	20	CHEP	7f Gd/Sft	55	1794	
0a	16	SOUT	6f Aw	48	2385	

MARJU GUEST 3 b f £1138

65a	2	WOLV	8f Aw		658	
63a	3	WOLV	9f Aw		720	
42	10	WARW	11f Heavy	69	1521	
49	9	SALI	8f Firm	65	2025	

MARK OF PROPHET 5 b g £555

| 71 | 4 | NEWM | 12f Firm | 70 | 1187 | |

MARK ONE 2 b f £1571

| 80 | 3 | SAND | 7f Gd/Fm | | 2921 | |

| 82 | 2 | CATT | 7f Gd/Fm | | 3198 | |
| 83 | 5 | CHEP | 8f Gd/Fm | | 3678 | |

MARKELLIS 4 b g £1861

46a	8	LING	10f Aw		1	
34a	6	SOUT	12f Aw	41	68	
25a	11	SOUT	8f Aw	41	85	
0a	8	SOUT	14f Aw		124	BL
27a	4	SOUT	11f Aw		178	
41a	1	**SOUT**	12f Aw	36	215*	
15a	8	WOLV	12f Aw	38	261	
51a	4	WOLV	12f Aw		295	
41a	5	SOUT	12f Aw		344	
0a	13	SOUT	12f Aw	42	370	
30a	5	SOUT	16f Aw	41	428	
31a	6	SOUT	11f Aw		455	
23a	7	WOLV	16f Aw	35	494	
14a	5	SOUT	14f Aw		668	
0a	P	SOUT	16f Aw	33	737	

MARKING TIME 2 b g £0

| 29a | 8 | SOUT | 5f Aw | | 1302 | |

MARKUSHA 2 b c £1870

60	4	PONT	5f Gd/Sft		1102	
62a	3	SOUT	6f Aw		1503	
68	7	THIR	6f Gd/Fm		3614	
69	3	AYR	6f Soft	71	3987	

MARLATARA 3 br f £1154

| 79 | 2 | CHES | 13f Gd/Fm | | 2249 | |

MARMADUKE 4 ch c £1194

59a	8	WOLV	7f Aw	77	79	
56a	7	LING	7f Aw		104	
56a	9	LING	8f Aw	70	1259	
67	3	CHEP	8f Heavy		1552	
56a	6	LING	8f Aw	65	1915	VIS
62	6	EPSO	12f Gd/Sft	70	2429	
53	7	LING	10f Good	70	2655	
49	3	BATH	12f Firm		2785	vis
53	4	CATT	14f Gd/Fm	56	3201	vis
45	10	FOLK	16f Gd/Fm	56	3448	vis

MARNIE 3 ch f £4880

0a	12	SOUT	8f Aw	53	1419	
0	14	YARM	8f Gd/Sft	53	1610	
41	6	WIND	6f Gd/Fm	50	1877	
41	8	CHEP	6f Good	47	1971	
50	2	CHEP	6f Gd/Fm	46	2489	
56	2	EPSO	7f Good	52	2794	
59	1	**BRIG**	6f Firm	52	2896*	
50	11	BRIG	6f Gd/Fm	53	3243	
45	10	LING	6f Soft	59	4270	

MAROMA 2 b f £292

75	5	GOOD	6f Gd/Sft		1486	
71	4	WIND	6f Gd/Fm		2209	
59	7	EPSO	7f Good		3760	

MAROMITO 3 b c £980

59	14	YORK	5f Gd/Fm	85	2644	
64	13	GOOD	5f Gd/Fm	80	3135	
60	11	THIR	5f Gd/Fm	75	3349	
0	12	BEVE	5f Gd/Fm	70	3653	
0	21	DONC	5f Firm	65	3894	
63	2	PONT	5f Soft	60	4087	
48	13	AYR	5f Heavy	64	4307	
0	12	NEWC	6f Aw	64	4425	

MARON 3 b c £4931

27	9	NOTT	6f Gd/Sft		1368	
23	6	CHES	6f Gd/Sft		1780	
55	3	THIR	6f Gd/Fm	55	2060	
60	2	CARL	5f Firm	55	2280	
61	1	**CATT**	6f Gd/Fm	56	2440*	
31	7	RIPO	6f Soft	56	2541	
48	9	THIR	5f Gd/Fm	61	3349	
44	9	BEVE	5f Gd/Fm	60	3653	
48	7	PONT	5f Soft	58	4087	
42a	5	WOLV	7f Aw		4384	

MARRAKECH 3 ch f £4237
73	4	NEWB	9f Gd/Fm		3179
91	1	**SAND**	8f Good		3474*
77	13	YARM	10f Firm		3918

MARREL 2 b g £391
0	15	HAYD	8f Soft		3766
0	13	WARW	7f Gd/Fm		3909
57a	3	WOLV	9f Aw		4438

MARSAD 6 ch g £6990
90	5	KEMP	6f Good	92	728
84	12	NEWM	7f Gd/Sft	92	966
80	13	NEWM	6f Gd/Fm	90	1173
83	7	GOOD	6f Good	88	1471
90	2	GOOD	6f Good	86	3646
0	15	KEMP	6f Gd/Fm	89	3791
77	11	AYR	6f Gd/Sft	86	4012
67	12	YORK	6f Heavy	88	4301

MARSEILLE EXPRESS 2 ch f £2950
87	3	NAAS	6f Yldg		1750
95	3	LEOP	6f Gd/Fm		2399

MARSH MARIGOLD 6 br m £0
35	8	WARW	16f Gd/Fm	50	2256

MARSHAL BOND 2 b c £939
61	6	WARW	7f Good		3692
71	2	BEVE	7f Good		3952
57	7	BRIG	8f Gd/Sft		4116
60	13	DONC	8f Heavy		4569

MARSHALL ST CYR 3 ch g £904
51a	5	SOUT	6f Aw		46
0	21	DONC	7f Good	75	736
47	13	WIND	6f Good	70	852
42	5	FOLK	7f Soft		960
57	6	WIND	5f Gd/Sft	59	1098
56	4	CATT	5f Gd/Sft	58	1817
59	2	MUSS	5f Firm	57	2047
47	8	LING	5f Gd/Fm	57	2184 BL
45	11	REDC	5f Gd/Fm	58	2864

MARTELLO 4 b c £983
52	4	BATH	8f Soft	60	4143
60	2	LEIC	8f Sft/Hvy		4311
35	11	NOTT	10f Heavy		4413

MARTHA P PERKINS 2 b f £0
40	8	RIPO	5f Gd/Fm		3710
74	5	BATH	5f Gd/Fm		3815
0	14	LING	5f Good		4096

MARTHA REILLY 4 ch f £5436
41a	9	LING	10f Aw		1
45a	3	SOUT	12f Aw	50	70
33a	4	SOUT	14f Aw	48	182
37a	6	SOUT	12f Aw	44	211
33	2	LING	16f Firm	33	2763
30	7	SAND	16f Good	37	3434
0	14	LING	16f Firm	31	3755
43	3	GOOD	16f Soft	41	4075
42	1	PONT	17f Soft	40	4231*
29	5	PONT	18f Soft	43	4376
39	5	NOTT	16f Heavy	43	4508

MARTIAL EAGLE 4 b g £0
0	17	YORK	10f Soft		4275
17	10	DONC	15f Heavy		4568

MARTIN 3 b c £0
34	7	NOTT	8f Good		783
0	19	BEVE	5f Firm	50	2223
0	15	REDC	5f Gd/Fm	44	2864

MARTINEZ 4 b g £0
26a	10	WOLV	8f Aw		4551

MARTINS PEARL 3 gr c £0
31	10	SOUT	7f Soft		1607
49	8	NEWB	6f Gd/Fm		1783

MARTINS SUNSET 2 ch c £500
64	9	NEWM	7f Firm		3298
69	9	LEIC	7f Firm		3840

85	3	GOOD	8f Soft		4062

MARTON MERE 4 ch g £5638
15a	9	SOUT	7f Aw	40	1979
13a	8	SOUT	8f Aw	36	2302
52	1	**BEVE**	7f Gd/Fm	47	2479*
0	20	REDC	8f Gd/Fm	52	2861
0	13	REDC	8f Gd/Fm		2994
52	5	REDC	8f Firm		3330
64	1	BEVE	8f Good		3393*
0	20	YORK	9f Good		3808
0	12	BEVE	8f Good	60	3951
0	16	BEVE	10f Sft/Hv	60	4046

MARVEL 3 b f £1748
0	15	SOUT	7f Gd/Sft	70	857
0	14	NOTT	8f Gd/Sft	65	1085
49	10	NEWC	8f Gd/Sft	60	1477
59	2	CARL	9f Gd/Sft	57	1722
37	9	REDC	10f Good	57	1895
58	3	HAMI	8f Gd/Fm	58	2235
56	6	NEWC	8f Good	58	2524
0	10	BEVE	8f Sft/Hvy	57	4045
34	6	PONT	8f Soft	55	4232

MARWELL MAGNUS 3 b c £0
0	18	SALI	6f Firm		1175
48	8	FOLK	5f Gd/Fm		2294
0	13	SALI	8f Gd/Fm	45	2980

MARY HAYDEN 2 ch f £0
30	10	THIR	7f Gd/Fm		2057
47	11	SALI	5f Gd/Fm		2227
34	5	BRIG	7f Gd/Sft		2424

MARY JANE 5 b m £0
38	11	NEWC	5f Soft	61	758
26	8	HAMI	6f Good	60	844
11	10	NEWC	5f Heavy	58	1008
0	21	THIR	6f Gd/Sft	56	1356
40	10	CATT	5f Soft	53	1680
40	9	DONC	6f Gd/Fm	50	1842
46	6	LEIC	5f Gd/Fm	48	4027
44	5	NEWB	5f Gd/Sft	48	4459

MASAKIRA 2 b f £285
78	4	BEVE	7f Good		3953
0	12	WIND	8f Heavy		4524

MASAMADAS 5 ch g £14605
85	2	NEWB	13f Firm	82	2852
90	1	**NEWB**	13f Firm	84	3454*
92	2	NEWB	13f Firm	88	3994

MASQUE TONNERRE 2 b c £0
64	13	NEWB	7f Firm		3999
0	15	YARM	8f Soft		4512

MASRORA 3 br f £824
73	4	SALI	10f Good		1344
74	5	BATH	8f Gd/Sft		1669
79	3	CHEP	12f Good		1970
70	7	KEMP	10f Firm		2258
24	14	BATH	12f Gd/Sft	74	2554
47	5	WARW	8f Gd/Fm		2846

MASSEY 4 br c £2730
65a	1	**WOLV**	12f Aw		752*
68	6	MUSS	10f Good		1144
0	21	NEWB	10f Good	68	1375
55	9	YARM	10f Good	65	1775
0	14	LEIC	8f Firm	60	2032
36a	7	LING	10f Aw		2764
0	11	NOTT	10f Gd/Fm	55	3007
41	10	WIND	8f Good	51	3188
22	11	MUSS	8f Gd/Fm	47	3745 VIS
44	9	CHEP	7f Good	47	3871 vis
0	15	YARM	6f Gd/Fm	42	3964 vis
0a	17	LING	12f Aw	57	4334
0	13	BRIG	10f Soft	40	4419 vis

MASTER BEVELED 10 b g £1753
60	3	HAYD	12f Gd/Sft	67	809 bl

52	10	WARW	11f Soft	65	1065 bl
57	3	AYR	11f Soft	60	3963
57	4	CHES	10f Soft	60	4074 vis
45	8	PONT	12f Soft	58	4229 vis

MASTER COOL 2 br c £0
44	4	CATT	6f Soft		1679
57	4	REDC	7f Good		1890
40a	5	SOUT	7f Aw		2301
53	5	BEVE	7f Gd/Fm		2513
40	8	BEVE	7f Good	50	3950
43	7	NOTT	8f Heavy		4507

MASTER COOPER 6 b c £0
68	5	MUSS	8f Gd/Sft		4135 bl

MASTER FELLOW 2 ch c £256
60	6	PONT	6f Soft		4082
71	4	NEWC	6f Heavy		4402
66	8	DONC	8f Heavy		4569

MASTER GATEMAKER 2 b c £444
60	7	YARM	8f Gd/Fm		3969
55a	3	SOUT	8f Aw		4152

MASTER GEORGE 3 b c £11477
80	1	**WIND**	10f Heavy		936*
72	6	WIND	12f Gd/Fm	80	1199
83	2	NEWB	12f Gd/Fm	80	1400
70	5	HAYD	12f Gd/Sft	82	1832
82	7	ASCO	12f Good	82	2116 VIS
81	4	NEWB	13f Firm	80	3994
81	3	NEWM	14f Gd/Fm	80	4213

MASTER HENRY 6 b g £3280
67	6	ASCO	8f Gd/Sft		1112
71	6	BEVE	5f Firm		1277
65	6	GOOD	8f Gd/Sft		1453
53	7	CHES	7f Gd/Sft	70	1778
68	1	**MUSS**	9f Firm		2376*
59	6	CATT	7f Gd/Fm		2437
57	5	BEVE	8f Gd/Fm	71	2481

MASTER HYDE 11 gr g £0
28	9	HAMI	12f Firm	40	1241

MASTER JONES 3 b c £1883
57a	4	LING	7f Aw		94
0a	12	LING	10f Aw		204
55a	2	LING	8f Aw		241
48a	3	SOUT	5f Aw		281
50a	3	LING	5f Aw		357
53a	2	LING	5f Aw		443
35a	5	LING	5f Aw		487 BL
50a	3	LING	6f Aw		527
28a	6	SOUT	7f Aw		589
45a	5	LING	8f Aw		595
0	13	LING	7f Gd/Sft	60	841

MASTER LODGE 5 ch g £0
53a	5	LING	10f Aw		1 t
13a	13	LING	12f Aw	53	115 t

MASTER LUKE 3 b g £1701
47	7	LING	5f Good		2590
33a	8	LING	7f Aw		2759
36	10	SALI	6f Gd/Fm		2977
50	2	BRIG	7f Gd/Fm	45	3242 BL
12	11	YARM	8f Gd/Fm	48	3970 bl
51	2	WIND	6f Gd/Sft	48	4293 bl
51	3	WIND	6f Heavy		4526 bl

MASTER MAC 5 br g £0
26a	10	LING	7f Aw		547
0a	13	LING	10f Aw	49	620
34	10	BRIG	8f Gd/Fm	54	1129

MASTER MILLFIELD 8 b g £0
0	P	BRIG	8f Firm	47	1330

MASTER SODEN 3 b c £0
62	5	REDC	10f Firm	61	1299

MASTERFUL 2 b c £288
83	4	DONC	6f Gd/Fm		2608

MASTERMIND 3 ch c £6911

77 24 NEWM 8f Gd/Fm 1171
99 4 YORK 10f Firm 1340
0 12 CHAN 12f V 1752
100 2 NEWM 10f Firm 3300
101 3 YORK 10f Gd/Fm 100 3563

MASTERPIECE USA 3 b c £1579
78 11 EPSO 7f Gd/Sft 85 1826
75 4 RIPO 8f Gd/Fm 83 2108
79 4 BEVE 8f Gd/Fm 80 2515
78 4 NOTT 8f Gd/Fm 79 3005

MATADI 2 b c £477
65 4 DONC 6f Gd/Fm 2754
76 5 BEVE 7f Gd/Sft 3051
70 9 YORK 6f Gd/Fm 3568

MATASHAWAQ 3 gr c £0
0 11 LING 7f Firm 3834 BL

MATERIAL WITNESS 3 b c £14028
90 2 NEWM 7f Gd/Sft 983
91 2 KEMP 8f Gd/Sft 1080
93 3 HAYD 8f Gd/Sft 88 1535
76 19 ASCO 8f Good 90 2117
79 2 WIND 8f Gd/Sft 3048
74 1 CATT 7f Soft 4005*

MATIN DE PRINTEMPS 6 ch h £5167
101 2 MAIS 6f Heavy 98

MATLOCK 2 b c £6222
88 1 SAND 7f Gd/Fm 2921*
88 4 SAND 8f Soft 4203
86 3 YARM 8f Soft 4390
88 4 REDC 7f Gd/Sft 4500

MATOAKA 2 b f £3437
89 2 KEMP 7f Gd/Sft 3789
91 4 ASCO 7f Good 4114

MATRON 2 b f £2330
85 2 YARM 6f Heavy 4479
88 2 DONC 6f Heavy 4576

MATTHIOLA 2 b f £0
74 13 DONC 6f Gd/Fm 4445

MAUERSCHWALBE 5 b m £0
34a 7 LING 10f Aw 333
0a 8 LING 16f Aw 402

MAULD SEGOISHA 2 br f £8204
56 13 YORK 6f Good 2692
0 17 HAYD 6f Gd/Sft 3268
83 2 HAYD 6f Gd/Sft 3478
83 2 DONC 7f Gd/Fm 77 3860

MAURI MOON 2 b f £12994
71 5 SAND 7f Gd/Fm 1986
92 1 NOTT 6f Gd/Fm 2683*
97 1 CHES 6f Gd/Fm 3425*

MAVIS 3 ch f £0
36 10 WARW 5f Gd/Sft 1712
52 7 FOLK 5f Good 2294
9 12 BATH 5f Firm 2788

MAVURA 3 b f £0
42 8 NEWB 10f Stt/Hv 4474

MAWDSLEY 3 b f £0
0 12 THIR 6f Gd/Sft 1354
25 6 THIR 7f Gd/Fm 3146

MAWHOOB 2 gr c £955
77 6 NEWM 7f Good 2563
80 4 DONC 7f Gd/Fm 3156
78 3 THIR 8f Good 3614

MAWINGO 7 b h £1173
59a 4 LING 8f Aw 62 169
42 16 NEWM 8f Good 62 2564
54 7 WIND 8f Good 60 3188
60 2 YARM 10f Gd/Fm 3383
20 9 LEIC 8f Stt/Hvy 4311

MAX 5 b g £428
53a 8 LING 8f Aw 208

24a 6 WOLV 8f Aw 256 bl
41a 9 LING 10f Aw 333
0 15 BRIG 12f Firm 38 1209
0 16 BRIG 10f Firm 1331
14 9 WARW 11f Gd/Sft 30 1707
43 3 EPSO 9f Gd/Sft 2433 t
16 10 LING 10f Good 38 2655 t
27 10 EPSO 10f Good 38 2790 t
31 6 EPSO 9f Gd/Fm 3404
40 7 GOOD 9f Good 47 3644
60 8 GOOD 7f Good 3662
43 10 GOOD 12f Soft 4061
33 5 SALI 10f Gd/Sft 37 4169
0 14 BRIG 8f Soft 4420

MAX THE MAN 3 b c £0
19 10 FOLK 7f Soft 962

MAY BALL 3 b f £27507
1 1 NEWM 8f Gd/Fm 1156*
89 2 GOOD 9f Gd/Sft 1481
73 4 YORK 10f Gd/Fm 1985
84 1 ASCO 8f Good 2679*
101 1 DEAU 8f Gd/Sft 3551*
103 3 NEWM 8f Gd/Fm 4211

MAY CONTESSA 3 b f £13717
94 1 NEWM 6f Good 956*
101 1 KEMP 6f Gd/Sft 1078*
97 3 LING 7f Gd/Sft 1283
94 8 GOOD 5f Gd/Fm 3059
70 13 PONT 5f Firm 3503

MAY KING MAYHEM 7 ch g £17042
25 6 LEIC 12f Good 42 791
31 5 YARM 11f Gd/Sft 40 1614 bl
50 1 LING 11f Good 43 1743* bl
45 1 NEWM 12f Firm 39 1852* bl
50 1 KEMP 12f Gd/Fm 47 2081* bl
50 1 NEWM 12f Gd/Fm 47 2286* bl
52 2 WARW 12f Good 54 2466 bl
45 8 SALI 12f Good 49 2689 bl

MAY PRINCESS 2 ch f £0
65 8 NEWM 7f Gd/Fm 3121
75 9 NEWM 7f Good 3607
64 10 NEWM 6f Good 4209
55 5 YARM 5f Soft 69 4511

MAY QUEEN MEGAN 7 gr m £0
37 4 LEIC 8f Firm 40 2032
33 6 FOLK 10f Gd/Fm 39 2296
28 5 PONT 8f Gd/Fm 36 2561

MAYARO 4 £2882
100 4 MAIS 13f Soft 2737

MAYARO BAY 4 b f £42749
89 11 NEWM 7f Gd/Sft 96 966
0 18 KEMP 8f Soft 96 1015
101 1 YORK 8f Firm 94 1327*
84 6 GOOD 8f Gd/Sft 1485
81 14 ASCO 8f Good 100 2090
100 3 NEWB 8f Firm 99 2707
47 22 GOOD 8f Good 99 3107
100 2 ASCO 8f Gd/Fm 99 3338
100 3 YORK 8f Gd/Fm 100 3597
102 1 DONC 8f Firm 99 3897*
82 15 ASCO 8f Gd/Sft 102 4126
99 5 NEWM 8f Gd/Fm 4211

MAYBEE 4 b f £617
56 3 THIR 8f Gd/Fm 3126
41 7 PONT 8f Firm 3506
0 14 LEIC 10f Firm 3838
0a 14 SOUT 11f Aw 4151

MAYBEN 3 ch c £0
54 5 PONT 10f Gd/Sft 1103
50 6 BEVE 12f Good 53 1446
37 7 PONT 12f Soft 48 4229
21 8 PONT 18f Soft 45 4376

MAYCOCKS BAY 2 b f £0
65 14 NEWM 6f Good 4341

MAYDORO 7 b m £548
27a 7 WOLV 6f Aw 1137
28a 8 WOLV 6f Aw 37 1391
20a 6 SOUT 6f Aw 32 1421
37 2 SOUT 7f Soft 1601
29 4 MUSS 7f Firm 1685
0 12 CHES 10f Gd/Fm 2245
27 10 HAMI 9f Gd/Fm 2642
25a 5 SOUT 8f Aw 2819

MAYLAN 5 br m £0
3a 11 LING 10f Aw 3
12a 8 LING 13f Aw 35 168
0 15 LING 7f Gd/Sft 838

MAYLANE 6 b g £5094
92 8 HAYD 12f Heavy 987
108 4 NEWB 13f Gd/Fm 1401
64 6 LEIC 12f Firm 2028
109 3 NEWM 12f Firm 2341
109 3 HAYD 12f Gd/Sft 3479
104 5 DONC 12f Firm 3892

MAYSBOYO 2 b g £406
52 3 NOTT 5f Heavy 1020
25 8 CHES 6f Good 1221
48 8 HAYD 6f Soft 1823
2 8 LEIC 6f Gd/Fm 64 2773
26a 10 WOLV 7f Aw 63 3273

MAYTIME 2 ch f £0
63 10 NEWM 6f Gd/Fm 1691
59 8 LEIC 6f Firm 2029
65 5 KEMP 6f Gd/Fm 2748
0 13 LING 7f Firm 67 3830
0 18 LEIC 8f Gd/Sft 64 4030

MAYVILLE THUNDER 2 ch c £3140
84 3 NEWB 7f Firm 3999
78 1 MUSS 7f Soft 4562*

MAZAARR 3 ch c £5336
68 6 NEWB 11f Soft 916
76 7 BATH 10f Good 1093
71 11 NEWB 10f Gd/Fm 1404
62 9 YARM 11f Good 74 1770
71 1 RIPO 12f Gd/Fm 67 2110*
68 4 HAYD 14f Gd/Fm 70 2445
69 3 CHEP 12f Gd/Fm 69 2973

MAZEED 7 ch g £0
0 14 PONT 10f Gd/Fm 57 2556 vis

MAZILLA 8 b m £0
0 15 CHEP 12f Gd/Fm 32 3255

MAZZELMO 7 gr m £0
24 11 DONC 18f Good 63 714 VIS
61 5 PONT 17f Soft 63 876
0 16 CHES 10f Gd/Fm 1222
44 7 NEWM 16f Firm 62 3295

MBELE 3 b c £24168
31 4 KEMP 14f Soft 1017
94 2 SALI 12f Firm 1179
89 1 NOTT 14f Gd/Sft 1369*
97 6 ASCO 16f Good 2068
98 1 ASCO 16f Gd/Fm 92 4115*
100 2 NEWM 16f Gd/Sft 99 4533

MCDAB 3 b c £6650
107 2 CURR 8f Gd/Fm 2740 t

MCGILLYCUDDY REEKS 9 b m £1854?
71 3 DONC 10f Gd/Fm 67 1070
72 2 YORK 12f Gd/Fm 67 1307
68 5 DONC 12f Good 70 1518
72 2 HAYD 11f Gd/Fm 70 1790
68 3 YORK 12f Good 1984
73 1 DONC 10f Gd/Fm 71 2350*
71 8 YORK 10f Good 79 2696
70 5 BEVE 10f Gd/Fm 73 3676

69 6 DONC 10f Firm 72 3899
60 4 PONT 10f Soft 4088
68 5 YORK 10f Soft 69 4282
61 5 DONC 12f Soft 68 4464
59 8 DONC 12f Heavy 68 4580

MCQUILLAN 3 b g £0
0a 13 SOUT 6f Aw 685
49 8 SOUT 7f Good 804
0a 13 WOLV 9f Aw 40 1040
0 16 BEVE 5f Good 3956

MEA CULPA 2 b f £0
60 5 RIPO 6f Gd/Fm 2106
45 12 HAYD 6f Gd/Fm 2454
38 11 BEVE 5f Gd/Sft 3055

MEADAAAR 3 ch c £3389
97 7 NEWM 7f Gd/Fm 1693
103 2 DONC 8f Gd/Fm 2578
103 5 YORK 7f Firm 3600
93 3 GOOD 7f Good 3884
103 5 NEWM 6f Good 4346

MEADOW LEADER 10 gr h £0
63a 5 LING 6f Aw 64 113

MEADOW SONG 2 b f £0
13 4 BRIG 7f Gd/Fm 3240
24 8 SALI 7f Gd/Fm 3388
0 18 LING 6f Good 4097

MEADOWSWEET 2 b f £0
39 10 LING 6f Soft 4190
40a 9 WOLV 6f Aw 4359

MEDAILLE MILITAIRE 8 gr h £0
0 11 NEWM 12f Good 4178

MEDELAI 4 b f £3143
39a 2 WOLV 16f Aw 37 194
25a 7 SOUT 16f Aw 41 284
45a 1 WOLV 16f Aw 41 318*
29a 7 WOLV 16f Aw 44 482
34 4 PONT 22f Heavy 38 940
13a 12 WOLV 16f Aw 43 2606

MEDIA BUYER 2 b c £2215
54 9 NEWM 5f Soft 984
60 8 NOTT 6f Good 1413
69 13 ASCO 7f Good 2091
74 3 EPSO 7f Gd/Sft 2430 BL
77 2 EPSO 7f Good 2791 bl
61 12 GOOD 7f Firm 80 3149
61 7 EPSO 7f Good 76 3690 bl
62 3 NOTT 8f Heavy 4507 bl

MEDIA MOGUL 2 b g £15914
85 1 BEVE 5f Heavy 974*
90 3 ASCO 5f Gd/Sft 1107
92 1 NEWC 5f Gd/Sft 1475*
105 2 NEWM 6f Gd/Fm 2595
96 6 YORK 6f Gd/Fm 3566

MEDIA PUZZLE 3 ch c £26250
112 3 CURR 10f Soft 1899
104 7 CURR 12f Good 2409
100 3 CURR 14f Yldg 3721 bl
113 4 DONC 15f Firm 3898 bl

MEDICEAN 3 ch c £138455
96 3 NEWM 8f Gd/Sft 972
97 1 SAND 8f Heavy 1041*
111 1 AYR 8f Firm 1630*
117 3 ASCO 8f Good 2066
83 14 YORK 10f Good 102 2696
120 3 GOOD 8f Good 3087
123 1 GOOD 8f Good 3647*
117 4 ASCO 8f Good 4111

MEDOOZA 3 b f £0
4a 8 LING 10f Aw 523
41 8 WIND 8f Heavy 934
62 10 SAND 10f Heavy 1045
0 15 BEVE 12f Good 52 1446

0 14 YARM 10f Gd/Fm 46 1955
0 15 BRIG 10f Gd/Fm 43 3242

MEDRAAR 2 b c £0
44 9 LING 7f Soft 4483

MEGA 4 b f £0
35a 5 SOUT 8f Aw 48 298
34a 4 SOUT 12f Aw 48 339
9a 8 SOUT 8f Aw 42 513 BL

MEGABYTE 6 b m £0
0 12 MUSS 8f Gd/Fm 36 3746

MEGS PEARL 4 gr f £1273
19a 11 WOLV 6f Aw 46 466 vis
0 R CHES 8f Good 2662
43 2 THIR 8f Gd/Fm 41 3124 BL
28 5 LEIC 7f Gd/Fm 3332 bl
0 18 AYR 6f Heavy 45 4327 vis

MEHMAAS 4 b c £6458
34 10 HAMI 8f Gd/Fm 72 1360
52 3 REDC 7f Gd/Sft 1559 vis
60 4 THIR 7f Gd/Sft 1716 vis
62 1 BEVE 7f Firm 60 1920* vis
40 12 THIR 7f Firm 62 2063 vis
0 13 BEVE 7f Firm 62 2221 vis
0 18 DONC 8f Gd/Fm 62 2349 vis
0 14 HAYD 7f Good 2704 vis
53 11 REDC 8f Gd/Fm 60 2861 vis
49 5 BEVE 8f Gd/Sft 58 3054 vis
53 3 REDC 8f Firm 55 3309 vis
29 11 REDC 7f Firm 55 3328 vis
53 4 REDC 8f Gd/Fm 53 3634 vis
0 15 REDC 8f Gd/Sft 54 4217 vis
45 6 REDC 8f Gd/Sft 51 4499 vis

MEIKLE PRINCE 2 b c £581
48 9 HAMI 5f Gd/Sft 3376
46 3 AYR 7f Heavy 4303
41 8 MUSS 7f Soft 4559

MEILLEUR 6 b g £3282
57a 2 SOUT 12f Aw 54 68
54a 4 WOLV 12f Aw 57 170
60a 2 SOUT 16f Aw 56 284
60a 3 WOLV 16f Aw 60 348
45a 6 WOLV 12f Aw 60 464
55 9 NOTT 14f Heavy 59 1023
56 6 LING 16f Good 57 1394
58 3 YARM 11f Gd/Sft 58 1614
38 16 NEWM 12f Firm 57 1852
58 2 SALI 12f Good 58 2689
52 6 KEMP 12f Gd/Fm 58 3073
55 4 GOOD 12f Good 57 3887
54a 3 SOUT 16f Aw 54 4149

MEIOSIS 3 b f £5226
104 1 NEWM 7f Gd/Fm 1155*
0 9 CURR 8f Gd/Sft 1626
97 5 YORK 6f Gd/Fm 2646 t

MELANZANA 3 b f £2977
81 4 NOTT 6f Good 1409
86 2 LING 6f Gd/Fm 85 2216
82 5 NEWM 6f Good 87 2568
80 6 GOOD 5f Gd/Fm 86 3135
0 16 HAYD 5f Gd/Fm 85 3322
64 7 KEMP 6f Gd/Sft 83 4037
0 24 NEWM 7f Gd/Sft 80 4215

MELBA 3 b f £0
49 13 SAND 10f Heavy 1045

MELIKAH 3 ch f £90965
106 1 NEWM 10f Firm 1184*
115 3 EPSO 12f Gd/Sft 1828
114 2 CURR 12f Gd/Fm 2739
115 5 LONG 12f Good 3928

MELLEDGAN 3 b f £338
52 6 FOLK 5f Gd/Fm 3584
49 4 THIR 6f Gd/Sft 3780

33 10 BEVE 5f Good 3956
0 12 LING 8f Soft 4274

MELLORS 7 b h £1121
63a 3 LING 8f Aw 62 594
63a 2 WOLV 8f Aw 63 718

MELLOW JAZZ 3 b f £446
66 8 WARW 6f Heavy 888
62 3 REDC 7f Gd/Sft 1579

MELLOW MISS 4 b f £869
53a 4 LING 8f Aw 54 96
49a 4 LING 8f Aw 52 152
38a 8 LING 10f Aw 50 203
49a 5 LING 8f Aw 264 bl
37a 6 LING 12f Aw 51 377
33a 8 SOUT 8f Aw 47 418
53 3 BRIG 7f Gd/Fm 52 896
54 3 WIND 10f Gd/Sft 52 1100
0 15 GOOD 9f Gd/Sft 52 1807 bl
31 8 NEWB 10f Gd/Fm 52 1942 bl
43 7 FOLK 10f Gd/Fm 49 2296 bl
39 6 FOLK 10f Good 46 2625 bl

MELODIAN 5 b g £20206
0a 8 SOUT 7f Aw 54 304 bl
58 2 SOUT 7f Good 54 803 bl
58 3 THIR 8f Soft 56 907 bl
63 1 NEWC 7f Heavy 56 1011* bl
50 7 ASCO 8f Gd/Sft 61 1113 bl
62 4 REDC 8f Firm 62 1296 bl
71 1 BEVE 7f Gd/Sft 62 1760* bl
59 13 DONC 8f Gd/Fm 68 1840 bl
53 9 BEVE 7f Firm 68 1920 bl
49 13 AYR 8f Good 68 2163 bl
24 19 YORK 7f Good 66 2694 bl
72 1 BEVE 7f Sft/Hvy 64 4044* bl
69 3 REDC 8f Gd/Sft 69 4217 bl
73 2 YORK 7f Heavy 70 4302 bl
73 2 NEWM 8f Good 70 4348 bl
64 7 NOTT 8f Heavy 73 4506 bl
56 13 NEWM 8f Soft 73 4545 bl

MELODY LADY 4 ch f £2744
15 13 PONT 10f Good 54 1496
0 12 CATT 12f Gd/Sft 52 1816
51 2 AYR 11f Good 48 2139
49 2 NEWC 10f Gd/Fm 48 2309
37 11 BEVE 10f Gd/Fm 50 2518
48 3 NEWC 12f Good 48 3036
45 5 HAYD 12f Good 48 3284
14a 8 WOLV 12f Aw 46 4360 t

MELOMANIA 8 b g £0
0a 10 WOLV 8f Aw 42 254
10a 9 WOLV 9f Aw 40 405

MELON PLACE 3 b c £0
57 7 BEVE 5f Sft/Hvy 4043
0 U NEWM 5f Good 90 4339
0 13 NEWB 6f Gd/Sft 87 4456

MELS BABY 7 br g £0
36 7 RIPO 12f Soft 55 825
28 11 BEVE 10f Heavy 51 975

MELVELLA 4 b f £0
24a 6 SOUT 12f Aw 387
19a 8 LING 12f Aw 457
17a 7 WOLV 12f Aw 565
0 15 NOTT 10f Gd/Sft 45 1370
0 30 NEWM 12f Firm 40 1852
18 8 NEWM 15f Good 53 3025

MEMAMEDA 4 b f £0
40a 6 WOLV 8f Aw 4551

MEMBERS WELCOME 7 b g £0
0a 13 SOUT 16f Aw 31 1416

MEMPHIS TEENS 3 b c £1101
69 3 WIND 10f Firm 1293
62 7 WIND 10f Good 1725

65	3	DONC	12f Gd/Fm		2353	
51	12	BATH	13f Gd/Fm	68	3819	
51	5	NOTT	10f Heavy	64	4509	

MEMSAHIB 2 b f £0

0	15	WIND	8f Heavy	4524

MEN OF WICKENBY 6 b g £0

20	8	HAMI	9f Gd/Fm	2236

MENAS ERN 2 b c £0

27	11	GOOD	6f Gd/Sft		1472
48	10	EPSO	7f Gd/Fm		3412
70	9	GOOD	7f Soft		4063
53a	4	SOUT	7f Aw		4154
44	11	BRIG	7f Soft	52	4416
47a	4	WOLV	8f Aw	51	4552

MENTAL PRESSURE 7 ch g £8349

48	3	NOTT	14f Good	45	788
51	2	NOTT	14f Good	64	1411
45	5	REDC	14f Gd/Sft	54	1563
59	2	BEVE	16f Gd/Fm	52	2516
61	1	REDC	16f Firm	57	3331*
60	3	RIPO	16f Gd/Fm	60	3715
58	4	NOTT	16f Soft	60	3978
60	3	MUSS	16f Gd/Sft	60	4134

MENTEITH 4 b c £0

24a	9	SOUT	11f Aw		866
0	16	NOTT	14f Heavy	42	1023

MENTIGA 3 b c £0

78	9	HAYD	8f Gd/Sft	85	810
83	5	WIND	8f Heavy	83	933
0	14	CHES	8f Gd/Fm	81	1215
66	6	NOTT	8f Soft	79	1645
70	7	CHEP	10f Gd/Fm	76	2450
55	6	SALI	8f Good	74	2688
59	8	EPSO	9f Good	71	3856
52	10	GOOD	10f Soft	68	4067

MEPHITIS 6 gr g £0

12a	7	WOLV	9f Aw	720	t

MER LOCK 2 b f £0

27	8	LING	8f Firm	3492

MER MADE 2 b f £0

48	5	WIND	5f Gd/Sft	1095
45a	8	WOLV	5f Good	1236
0	17	LING	7f Gd/Fm	2182

MERANTI 7 b g £0

0	13	SOUT	6f Good	40	802
41	7	HAMI	6f Firm		1239
9	9	CARL	6f Firm	37	1258

MERCEDE 3 b f £0

28a	10	WOLV	6f Aw		118
0	15	YARM	8f Gd/Fm	40	3970
41	11	LING	8f Soft		4274
0	15	BRIG	10f Soft	35	4419

MERCHANT PRINCE 4 b g £0

35a	5	WOLV	8f Aw		707
45	10	PONT	8f Aw		1105
26a	12	WOLV	5f Aw		1237	BL
29a	8	SOUT	8f Aw		1505
0	17	LEIC	10f Soft	40	1546	VIS
38a	7	WOLV	8f Aw		4551

MERIDEN MIST 2 b f £6830

63	5	NOTT	6f Good		1413
70	2	PONT	6f Good		1864
69	5	WIND	6f Gd/Fm		2209
73	4	LING	6f Good	73	2589
74	1	BRIG	7f Firm	72	2894*
75	4	GOOD	7f Firm	74	3149
49	8	NEWB	7f Gd/Fm	74	3486
74	5	LING	7f Good	74	3830
72	4	YARM	7f Firm	72	3922
72	2	BRIG	8f Heavy	74	4538

MERIDIANA 4 gr f £0

0	17	NOTT	10f Gd/Sft	63	1364

0	11	BRIG	10f Gd/Fm	1933

MERLY NOTTY 4 ch f £752

34	2	HAMI	9f Gd/Fm		1191
33	4	HAMI	11f Gd/Fm	34	1361
32	6	CATT	14f Soft	36	1683

MERRY 3 ch f £0

0	10	CATT	12f Gd/Fm	50	782	t

MERRY DANCE 2 ch f £427

38	10	LING	7f Good		2653
68	3	BRIG	7f Firm		3558
41	10	YORK	8f Gd/Fm		3729
52	10	LEIC	6f Gd/Sft	61	4030
46	7	BRIG	8f Gd/Sft		4117

MERRY MERLIN 3 b c £32929

93	9	NEWM	7f Good		955
110	1	CHES	10f Firm		1246*
92	7	GOOD	10f Gd/Sft		1451
106	5	ASCO	10f Good		2169
106	6	AYR	10f Gd/Fm		2720
114	3	GOOD	8f Firm		3150
101	6	WIND	10f Good		3641

MERRY PRINCE 5 b g £0

0	14	WIND	10f Soft	48	2544

MERRYVALE MAN 3 b c £8486

60a	2	SOUT	8f Aw	58	128
37a	11	WOLV	7f Aw	59	257
52a	5	SOUT	8f Aw	59	429
60a	3	SOUT	11f Aw	58	536
72a	1	SOUT	11f Aw		586*
69a	2	WOLV	12f Aw	69	640
69	1	CATT	12f Gd/Fm	65	782*
48	8	WIND	12f Heavy	68	937
74	2	DONC	15f Gd/Sft	68	1071
63	7	NOTT	14f Gd/Fm	68	1270
70	5	HAYD	14f Soft	74	1821
60	13	YORK	12f Soft	74	4280
67	5	DONC	10f Gd/Sft	71	4448

MERSEY MIRAGE 3 b c £12067

85	7	GOOD	7f Gd/Fm	86	3130
88	1	LEIC	6f Gd/Fm	85	3335*
88	4	NEWM	7f Gd/Fm	87	3629
90	3	SALI	6f Gd/Sft	87	4165
0	20	DONC	7f Heavy	87	4574

MERSEY SOUND 2 b c £1790

102	3	NEWB	8f Firm	3983

METEOR STRIKE 6 ch g £2776

1a	6	WOLV	12f Aw		307	t
53a	2	SOUT	12f Aw		344	t
62a	1	SOUT	11f Aw		369*	t
36a	6	LING	12f Aw	60	441	tbl
18	11	NEWC	10f Gd/Fm	56	2309	
49	3	CATT	12f Gd/Fm		2742	t
46	5	BRIG	12f Firm	50	2904	t
42	4	CATT	12f Gd/Fm		3202	t
0	U	BRIG	10f Firm	44	3737	t
8a	13	LING	10f Aw	45	3828	t

METRONOME 3 b f £9595

75	8	NEWM	8f Firm		1188
85	2	BEVE	10f Good		1447
84	2	CHEP	12f Good		1970
85	1	LEIC	12f Gd/Fm	82	2509*
97	5	YORK	12f Firm		3595
74	7	ASCO	12f Gd/Sft		4130

MEXICAN ROCK 4 b c £0

54	7	GOOD	7f Good	90	3902
67	11	NEWM	8f Good		4199
0	21	YORK	7f Heavy	80	4302
0	28	NEWM	7f Good	73	4357	t

MEZZORAMIO 8 ch g £1881

0	12	YARM	10f Gd/Sft	46	1615	
16	13	BEVE	7f Firm	46	1920	t
45	3	NEWM	8f Gd/Fm	46	2130	t

41	5	BEVE	7f Gd/Fm	46	2479	tvi
39	9	REDC	8f Gd/Fm	45	2861	t
47	2	YARM	7f Firm		2899	tvi
36	8	YARM	7f Good	44	3030	tvi
45	4	YARM	7f Gd/Fm	47	3384	vis

MI AMIGO 3 b c £5450

76	2	THIR	6f Soft		909
65	4	NOTT	6f Firm		1266
74	3	LEIC	8f Soft		1548
65	1	HAMI	6f Gd/Fm		2640*
0	14	RIPO	6f Good	74	3698
69	3	BRIG	6f Gd/Sft	69	4120

MI FAVORITA 2 b f £0

52	10	NEWM	6f Firm	1856

MI ODDS 4 b g £428

49a	3	SOUT	12f Aw		603
42a	7	SOUT	12f Aw		643
46a	5	WOLV	12f Aw		752
41	8	HAYD	12f Good	46	3284
43	6	YARM	14f Gd/Fm	45	3664
0	14	NOTT	16f Soft	43	3978
0a	11	LING	13f AW		4193

MICE DESIGN 3 b c £418

0	9	THIR	12f Good		1157
58	5	HAMI	12f Good		1362
49	4	YARM	16f Gd/Sft		1613
46	3	BRIG	12f Gd/Fm	52	1935

MICE IDEAS 4 ch g £9377

47a	1	SOUT	11f Aw		248*
50a	6	SOUT	12f Aw	54	370
28a	7	WOLV	12f Aw	50	464
34a	5	SOUT	16f Aw	48	535
50a	1	SOUT	11f Aw		670*
50a	2	SOUT	11f Aw	46	742
44	3	SOUT	11f Gd/Sft	46	855
44	6	YARM	10f Gd/Sft	44	1615
47	1	BEVE	10f Firm	43	1921*
43	6	WARW	11f Gd/Fm	49	2033
17	9	WARW	12f Good	45	2466

MICHELE MARIESCHI 3 b g £2280

80	5	SALI	12f Good		1347
0	15	HAYD	8f Gd/Sft	96	1535
0	11	NEWM	8f Firm	92	1853
73	9	GOOD	10f Gd/Fm	87	3131
79	3	DONC	12f Soft	82	4464

MICKLEY 3 b g £15737

76	2	CHES	12f Gd/Fm	75	1225	
75	5	HAYD	11f Soft	77	1491	
71	4	RIPO	12f Good	76	1862	
72	5	RIPO	12f Gd/Fm	72	2110	BL
74	3	NEWC	12f Gd/Fm	72	2272	bl
60	6	CHES	10f Good	71	2666	VIS
69	3	RIPO	12f Gd/Fm	70	2837	vis
76	1	THIR	12f Gd/Fm	70	2967*	vis
82	1	RIPO	12f Gd/Fm	76	3467*	vis
72	10	YORK	14f Firm	81	3599	
45	8	HAYD	12f Soft	82	4092	vis

MICKLOW MAGIC 2 b f £1924

63	2	REDC	6f Gd/Fm	2990
73	2	MUSS	5f Gd/Sft	4131
59	5	NEWC	7f Heavy	4403

MICKY DEE 4 ch g £0

0a	13	LING	10f Aw		56	
0a	11	LING	10f Aw		111	t
0a	12	LING	8f Aw		353	t
26a	7	LING	6f Aw		399	t
23a	7	LING	5f Aw		440	t
49a	6	LING	5f Aw		507	t
10a	11	SOUT	5f Aw		558	t
26a	6	LING	6f Aw		653	t

MIDDAY COWBOY 7 b g £0

0a	12	SOUT	14f Aw		668	bl

MIDDLEHAMPARKFLYER 2 b f £0 (preceding lines)

0	11	MUSS	16f Gd/Sft	34	797
14	6	CARL	12f Gd/Sft		1720

MIDDLEHAMPARKFLYER 2 b f £0

0	16	BEVE	5f Gd/Sft		3055
32	11	THIR	7f Gd/Fm		3128

MIDDLETHORPE 3 b g £17081

37	11	DONC	8f Gd/Sft	55	1053	
52	5	BEVE	10f Good	52	1448	
57	1	**BEVE**	12f Gd/Sft	51	1758*	
38	7	BEVE	12f Firm	56	1919	
57	3	RIPO	12f Soft	55	2540	
40a	2	SOUT	12f Aw	55	2815	
61	1	**YORK**	10f Gd/Fm	55	3731*	BL
57	3	EPSO	12f Good	55	3858	bl
60	1	**CHEP**	10f Good	55	3870*	bl
65	3	YORK	12f Soft	64	4280	bl
49	6	PONT	10f Soft	65	4374	bl

MIDHISH TWO 4 b c £0

57	13	WIND	10f Heavy		935	
55	18	ASCO	7f Gd/Sft	80	1110	
50	8	LING	7f Soft	76	1286	
0	16	SALI	6f Gd/Fm	72	1887	
64	8	WIND	8f Gd/Fm	72	2054	
53	8	EPSO	9f Gd/Fm	69	2629	
39	12	NEWM	6f Gd/Fm	67	2961	t
0	15	KEMP	7f Gd/Fm	64	3362	BL
50	6	FOLK	6f Gd/Fm		3587	bl
40	11	EPSO	5f Good	57	3855	VIS
53a	6	LING	7f Aw		4328	

MIDNIGHT ALLURE 3 b f £9961

60	2	NOTT	8f Heavy	58	1024	
71	1	**YARM**	8f Gd/Sft	59	1610*	
77	1	**NOTT**	8f Good	67	1873*	
68	6	KEMP	8f Gd/Fm	73	2084	
76	2	WIND	8f Gd/Fm	74	2713	t
76	3	DONC	8f Gd/Fm	76	3160	t
75	4	WIND	8f Good	77	3643	t
99	5	DONC	7f Gd/Fm		3878	t
73	13	ASCO	8f Good	90	4113	t

MIDNIGHT ARROW 2 b f £6011

89	1	**NEWM**	5f Gd/Fm		1169*
81	5	SAND	5f Soft		1586
84	10	ASCO	5f Good		2088
84	8	NEWM	6f Firm		2344
72	4	RIPO	6f Gd/Fm		3463
71	10	NEWM	6f Gd/Fm	89	3630
70	15	NEWM	7f Gd/Fm	83	4157

MIDNIGHT CREEK 2 b c £949

59	5	GOOD	8f Good		3906
71	2	BRIG	8f Gd/Sft		4116
77	3	BRIG	8f Soft		4417

MIDNIGHT ESCAPE 7 b g £7496

83	7	KEMP	5f Soft	87	1013
0	19	YORK	5f Firm	86	1324
82	4	KEMP	6f Soft	83	1531
82	5	LING	6f Good	82	1676
81	6	SAND	6f Gd/Fm	82	2473
83	1	**KEMP**	6f Firm		2869+
73	7	NEWB	5f Gd/Fm	82	3463
0	18	GOOD	6f Good	82	3646
0	17	SALI	6f Gd/Sft	81	4165

MIDNIGHT MAX 3 b c £0

5a	8	LING	10f Aw	42	1544
33	9	NOTT	8f Good	43	2013
18	13	LEIC	8f Gd/Fm	41	2512

MIDNIGHT VENTURE 2 b c £6547

72	9	DONC	5f Gd/Fm	700
81	3	WARW	5f Soft	812
54	11	MUSS	5f Gd/Sft	898
78	2	LING	8f Good	2652
75	2	CARL	5f Firm	3193
78	1	**GOOD**	6f Good	3649*

57	10	GOOD	6f Good	80	3886

MIDNIGHT WATCH 6 b g £4100

11a	11	LING	16f Aw	50	285	t
14a	7	LING	12f Aw	46	332	t
22a	8	LING	10f Aw		375	t
39a	1	**WOLV**	8f Aw	33	431*	
26a	3	SOUT	8f Aw	36	497	
42a	2	WOLV	8f Aw	40	676	
46a	2	WOLV	9f Aw	42	749	
18	10	HAMI	9f Good	42	846	
47a	2	SOUT	8f Aw	45	1207	
46a	2	SOUT	7f Aw	45	1979	
35a	5	SOUT	8f Aw	47	2302	

MIDSHIPMAN 2 b c £3217

49	11	RIPO	6f Gd/Fm	3466
67	5	LING	6f Firm	3832
79	1	**NOTT**	6f Soft	3974*

MIDYAN BLUE 10 ch g £3359

47	1	**MUSS**	16f Gd/Fm		1145*
56	4	MUSS	14f Gd/Fm		1433
44	3	CARL	12f Gd/Sft		1720
0	P	MUSS	14f Firm	42	2050

MIDYAN CALL 6 b g £0

102	3	CAPA	8f Heavy	11

MIGHTY MAGIC 5 b m £0

0	17	SALI	14f Gd/Fm	49	4166

MIGWAR 7 b g £2661

50a	8	LING	10f Aw	60	22	
53a	4	SOUT	11f Aw	56	126	
28a	9	SOUT	8f Aw		195	
58a	1	**LING**	10f Aw	54	224*	vis
37a	10	LING	10f Aw		268	vis
46a	6	WOLV	9f Aw	57	349	vis
34a	7	LING	10f Aw	57	400	vis
52a	3	SOUT	11f Aw		455	
23	9	LING	10f Firm		3490	
16a	12	LING	10f Aw	51	3828	
0a	10	WOLV	12f Aw	45	4026	BL

MIKE SIMMONS 4 b g £317

28	7	WARW	16f Gd/Fm	38	3916
29	4	BATH	17f Soft	37	4139

MIKE THE SPUD 3 b c £0

46a	5	WOLV	5f Aw	42
33a	6	SOUT	6f Aw	74

MIKES DOUBLE 6 br g £715

49a	5	WOLV	7f Aw		65	vis
0a	U	WOLV	6f Aw		134	vis
36a	4	WOLV	6f Aw		142	vis
26a	9	WOLV	6f Aw	41	232	vis
47a	5	WOLV	6f Aw		274	vis
46a	2	WOLV	6f Aw		396	vis
52a	3	WOLV	7f Aw		449	vis
27a	7	WOLV	8f Aw		550	vis
37a	5	WOLV	6f Aw	44	583	vis
31a	8	WOLV	6f Aw		680	vis
0	12	WARW	7f Soft		816	vis
0	13	DONC	6f Gd/Sft		1073	vis
0a	14	SOUT	6f Aw	37	1422	vis
0	11	SOUT	7f Soft		1603	vis
0	20	YARM	8f Good	34	1772	
0a	12	SOUT	11f Aw		4151	vis

MIKES WIFE 3 b f £0

0a	14	SOUT	8f Aw		48
0a	12	SOUT	7f Aw		2633
0	16	THIR	8f Gd/Fm	31	2964

MILA 3 b f £0

12	6	NEWM	12f Gd/Fm	1696

MILAD 5 b g £0

0a	16	SOUT	8f Aw	869

MILADY LILLIE 4 b f £1460

54	6	WIND	6f Gd/Fm	58	746
0	23	THIR	6f Soft	57	910

0	17	BRIG	7f Firm	55	1213	
51	7	REDC	7f Firm	55	1297	
53	2	BRIG	7f Good	53	1652	
0	15	SALI	6f Gd/Fm	53	1887	
52	4	THIR	7f Good	53	2063	
47	7	BRIG	7f Soft	53	2427	
47	6	BRIG	7f Gd/Fm	52	2729	
44	6	YARM	7f Firm	52	2899	BL
38	11	LING	7f Firm	50	3279	
40	9	EPSO	7f Good	48	3765	
42	6	YARM	6f Gd/Fm	45	3966	

MILDON 4 ch c £0

20	11	HAMI	13f Gd/Fm	45	1194	
0	15	RIPO	16f Good	37	1597	
53	6	REDC	9f Firm		3326	
29	9	THIR	8f Gd/Sft		3775	BL

MILETRIAN 3 b f £121750

89	17	NEWM	8f Firm	1185
110	4	YORK	10f Gd/Fm	1309
45	16	EPSO	12f Gd/Sft	1828
110	1	**ASCO**	12f Good	2112*
106	6	CURR	12f Gd/Fm	2739
103	6	ASCO	12f Gd/Fm	3305
111	4	YORK	12f Gd/Fm	3564
112	1	**DONC**	15f Gd/Fm	3863+

MILL AFRIQUE 4 b f £0

37	8	NOTT	10f Good	45	2007
15	7	MUSS	12f Gd/Fm	42	2202
0	12	AYR	9f Heavy		4324

MILL EMERALD 3 b f £322

64	6	THIR	12f Gd/Fm		1386	
66	4	HAYD	14f Soft		1824	
50	6	NEWC	16f Gd/Fm	65	2273	
0	12	CATT	12f Gd/Fm	58	2746	
4	8	REDC	11f Gd/Fm		2989	VIS

MILL END QUEST 5 b m £4624

25	14	NOTT	6f Gd/Sft	50	1082	
56	1	**THIR**	6f Gd/Fm	48	3123+	bl
42	10	CATT	10f Good	54	3203	bl
36	10	NEWM	5f Gd/Fm	56	3631	bl
39	5	BEVE	7f Sft/Hvy	55	4044	bl

MILLENARY 3 b c £292200

89	1	**NEWB**	11f Soft	916*
105	1	**CHES**	12f Gd/Fm	1216*
106	8	CHAN	12f V	1752
112	1	**GOOD**	12f Firm	3061*
119	1	**DONC**	15f Firm	3898*

MILLENIUM MOONBEAM 3 ch c £0

104	11	NEWM	8f Gd/Fm	1171
91	6	GOOD	10f Gd/Sft	1451
69	17	ASCO	7f Good	2087

MILLENIUM PRINCESS 2 b f £11510

92	1	**NEWM**	6f Firm	1856*
100	2	ASCO	6f Good	2172
83	6	SAND	5f Gd/Fm	2529
95	2	CHES	5f Gd/Fm	3425
92	4	SALI	6f Firm	3749

MILLENNIUM BUG 4 b f £0

0a	12	LING	10f Aw	4100

MILLENNIUM CADEAUX 2 ch g £0

82	5	NEWM	8f Good	4161

MILLENNIUM DASH 3 b f £4276

77	4	LEIC	10f Firm	3838
88	1	**BATH**	10f Soft	4141*
95	9	NEWM	12f Good	4343

MILLENNIUM DREAM 3 b c £0

33a	8	LING	7f Aw	421
31a	6	LING	8f Aw	591
0	16	LING	7f Gd/Sft	839

MILLENNIUM LADY 2 ch f £565

80	7	GOOD	6f Gd/Fm	3090
83	5	KEMP	7f Gd/Fm	3359

57   3   CHES   7f Soft   4068

MILLENNIUM MAGIC 2 b f £5449
91	1	**SAND**	5f Gd/Fm		762*
82	3	NEWB	5f Good		1372
78	4	NOTT	5f Gd/Sft		1641
80	2	SALI	5f Firm		2020
79	8	SAND	5f Gd/Fm		2529
66	14	NEWB	5f Firm		2849
67	8	WIND	6f Good	83	3354
0	18	DONC	6f Gd/Sft		3862
63	10	LING	6f Soft	76	4269

MILLENNIUM MINX 3 b f £0
0	15	LING	7f Firm		3834

MILLENNIUM SUMMIT 3 b c £217
52	4	RIPO	10f Gd/Fm		2105
58	6	LING	9f Firm		2322
68	4	LEIC	10f Gd/Fm		2774
43	7	NOTT	14f Good	72	3522
0	12	NEWM	12f Good		4178

MILLER TIME 3 b h £0
45a	5	WOLV	6f Aw		273
24a	10	SOUT	8f Aw		328
37a	9	WOLV	7f Aw		362
35a	4	SOUT	6f Aw	47	515
39	9	MUSS	8f Gd/Sft	44	800 BL
0	19	REDC	6f Firm		1298

MILLIGAN 5 b g £8579
86	1	**NEWC**	10f Soft	75	757*
63	16	YORK	10f Good	85	2696
88	2	KEMP	10f Gd/Fm	85	3794
0	26	NEWM	9f Gd/Fm	85	4212

MILLIKEN PARK 2 ch f £5705
59	6	AYR	6f Gd/Fm		1628
71	1	**HAMI**	6f Gd/Fm		2778*
72	2	REDC	6f Firm	67	3327
74	3	HAMI	6f Gd/Sft		3533
42	11	BEVE	5f Gd/Fm	71	3673
47	9	AYR	6f Soft	71	3987
0	13	NEWC	5f Heavy	68	4423

MILLIONFORMERTHYR 4 b f £0
0a	12	LING	7f Aw		4487

MILLIONS 3 b c £925
61	5	BATH	10f Good	61	1094
64	2	WIND	12f Good	61	1292
49	9	SAND	10f Soft	66	1585
0	11	YARM	11f Gd/Fm	66	1770 BL

MILLSEC 3 b f £0
0	17	CATT	7f Soft	59	4004
0	17	REDC	5f Gd/Sft		4220
18	8	NEWC	7f Heavy	53	4428

MILLTIDE 2 b f £2702
70	4	WIND	6f Gd/Fm		1876
67	1	**THIR**	6f Gd/Fm		2059*
43	6	NEWC	6f Gd/Fm		2312

MILLYS LASS 2 b f £13052
78	3	DONC	5f Gd/Fm		700
76	1	**LEIC**	5f Gd/Sft		828*
76	2	THIR	5f Soft		904
80	1	**NOTT**	5f Gd/Sft		1083*
77	3	SALI	5f Firm		1176
68	2	CHEP	5f Firm		2657
65	15	NEWB	5f Firm		2849
79	3	NEWB	5f Firm		3174
60	7	WIND	6f Good	75	3354
76	2	CHEP	5f Gd/Fm	75	3679
72	5	DONC	6f Firm		3888
76	7	NEWM	5f Good	77	4179
77	2	LING	5f Soft		4485

MILNES DREAM 4 b f £0
0a	16	SOUT	14f Aw		124

MIMANDI 3 b f £0
0	12	PONT	5f Gd/Sft		1105

52	6	REDC	6f Gd/Sft		1562
0	15	MUSS	5f Firm	43	2047 VIS
36	6	BEVE	5f Gd/Fm		2519
0	19	AYR	5f Heavy	41	4307

MIN MIRRI 2 b f £4864
79	4	GOOD	6f Gd/Fm		1957
79	5	ASCO	6f Good		2172
84	3	**NEWM**	7f Gd/Fm		3459
83	1	**THIR**	8f Gd/Sft		3779*
46	9	AYR	8f Soft	82	3990

MINALCO 4 ch f £0
0	13	CATT	14f Soft	35	1683
24	7	REDC	16f Gd/Fm	38	2866
0	11	CARL	14f Gd/Fm	29	3084
15	9	REDC	16f Gd/Fm	33	3331
13	8	REDC	14f Gd/Fm		3633

MINARDI 2 br c £189735
96	2	ASCO	6f Gd/Fm		3000
122	1	**LEOP**	6f Good		3372*
120	1	**NEWM**	6f Good		4181*

MIND OVER MATTER 2 b g £0
34a	9	SOUT	7f Aw		2383
49	11	SALI	7f Good		2686

MIND THE SILVER 3 gr g £2476
0	14	LING	7f Gd/Sft		1261
0	15	NEWB	6f Gd/Fm	65	1406
55	6	LING	6f Gd/Fm	61	2216
43	11	CHEP	6f Gd/Fm	59	2489
0	17	EPSO	7f Good	59	2794 VIS
55	4	LEIC	6f Gd/Fm	56	3095
39	10	LING	8f Firm	56	3580
0	15	SALI	8f Firm	56	3753
57	1	**YARM**	8f Gd/Fm	52	3971*

MINDAHRA 2 b f £0
0	13	HAYD	5f Soft		3767

MINDANAO 4 b f £2564
80	4	BEVE	10f Heavy	82	975
87	2	DONC	10f Gd/Sft	82	1070

MINE 2 b c £740
79	3	NEWM	6f Gd/Fm		3627
71	9	YARM	7f Firm		3940

MINETTA 5 ch m £6743
64	6	WIND	8f Gd/Fm		1879
70	5	THIR	8f Gd/Fm	75	2062
62	9	NEWM	8f Good	73	2564
60	8	WIND	8f Gd/Fm	71	2890
74	1	**BATH**	8f Firm	69	3207*
64	7	BATH	8f Gd/Fm	74	3514
0	13	YARM	8f Firm	74	3936

MINETTE 2 br f £0
60	6	LING	6f Firm		3832
62	6	PONT	6f Soft		4083
0	14	WIND	6f Gd/Sft		4289

MINGLING 3 b c £2230
81	3	PONT	10f Soft		873
80	5	YORK	10f Gd/Fm	80	1310
80	2	BATH	10f Gd/Fm		1439
76	3	KEMP	12f Gd/Fm		1929
75	6	REDC	10f Gd/Fm	79	2157
69	5	BEVE	8f Gd/Fm	77	2515 VIS

MINI LODGE 4 ch c £13538
37	8	BEVE	10f Gd/Fm	65	2481 VIS
67	1	**RIPO**	10f Gd/Fm	60	2836*
69	2	HAYD	11f Good	64	3285
69	2	RIPO	10f Gd/Fm	63	3713
72	3	DONC	10f Firm	69	3899 vis
74	2	HAYD	12f Soft	71	4092

MINIHAHA 2 ch f £0
67	15	NEWM	8f Good		4349

MINIME 2 b c £0
29	8	NOTT	5f Good		1870
31a	4	WOLV	6f Aw		2079

MINIMUS TIME 3 ch f £1800
23a	8	LING	6f Aw	42	242
57a	1	**LING**	5f Aw		357* BL
39a	4	LING	5f Aw		487 bl
44a	6	LING	5f Aw		619 bl
45	4	FOLK	5f Soft		959 bl
27	10	BATH	5f Gd/Sft		1670 bl
36	6	BRIG	5f Gd/Fm	40	1932 bl
15a	7	LING	5f Aw		2650 VIS
8	10	LEIC	5f Gd/Fm	40	3214 bl
0	14	SAND	5f Gd/Fm		3947

MINJARA 5 b g £299
55	5	BRIG	10f Gd/Fm		1331
35	5	MUSS	9f Firm	38	1689
28	9	YARM	10f Firm	41	2387
30	8	BRIG	10f Gd/Fm	35	2727
35	4	NEWM	10f Gd/Fm	36	2958
34	5	REDC	10f Firm	37	3310

MINKASH 3 b c £2430
86	7	CHES	8f Gd/Fm	93	1215
93	6	YORK	10f Gd/Fm	93	1310
93	4	DONC	10f Gd/Fm	92	2610
77	4	LEIC	12f Gd/Fm	92	2917
89	3	SALI	8f Gd/Fm		3421 BL
69	8	EPSO	9f Good	88	3685 bl
85	5	DONC	10f Firm	86	3899

MINNESOTA 4 b c £0
38	4	LING	10f Firm		3490 vis

MINNIES MYSTERY 2 gr f £0
0	13	SAND	6f Gd/Fm		3942
0	22	DONC	6f Gd/Sft		4449
0	16	DONC	6f Heavy		4576

MINSTREL GEM 3 b c £0
0	14	NOTT	6f Gd/Sft		1081
28	10	RIPO	8f Good		1858
23a	9	SOUT	7f Aw		2633
20	10	RIPO	10f Gd/Fm	41	3008
0	16	LEIC	10f Gd/Sft		4029

MINT LEAF 3 b c £0
0	16	SALI	6f Firm		1181
0	12	WIND	6f Gd/Sft	70	1427 t
38	12	EPSO	7f Gd/Sft	66	2431
6	8	NEWB	7f Firm	60	2814 t
36	9	LING	10f Firm		3281 t
15	15	BATH	8f Gd/Fm	46	3816 t
24	9	SAND	5f Soft		4207
0a	13	LING	7f Aw		4331

MINT ROYALE 2 ch f £0
61	8	HAYD	6f Gd/Fm		3320

MINTY 4 b c £0
0	13	THIR	8f Gd/Sft		3775
0	11	AYR	9f Soft		3988 VIS

MINUS FOUR 2 b c £0
0	14	MUSS	5f Gd/Sft		4131
23a	7	SOUT	7f Aw		4369
29	8	NEWM	8f Soft		4542

MINUSCOLO 2 b f £567
54	9	CHEP	6f Gd/Fm		2488
44	8	LEIC	6f Gd/Fm		3215
65	6	CARL	5f Firm		3571
65	3	SAND	6f Gd/Fm		3942
57	5	LEIC	6f Gd/Sft	62	4030

MIRAGGIO 4 b c £0
0a	12	WOLV	12f Aw	42	410
0	15	SOUT	16f Gd/Sft	42	860

MIRIO 3 ch c £2305
103	3	SAIN	10f Heavy		4491

MISALLIANCE 5 ch m £625
0	16	BEVE	7f Firm	51	1275 BL
20a	7	SOUT	11f Aw		1415
48a	3	SOUT	16f Aw		1802
54a	3	WOLV	16f Aw		2076

0a	7	SOUT	12f Aw		2298	

MISBEHAVE 3 b f £3280

77	4	HAYD	11f Heavy	93	990	
49	4	PONT	10f Soft		1703	
74	2	NEWM	10f Good		3021	

MISCHIEF 4 ch c £4474

0a	9	WOLV	16f Aw	55	348	
37a	5	LING	12f Aw		457	bl
46a	5	WOLV	12f Aw		519	
37a	6	SOUT	12f Aw		603	bl
39a	2	LING	16f Aw	39	649	VIS
41	10	DONC	18f Good	60	714	vis
54	3	WARW	12f Soft	57	815	vis
12	11	WARW	15f Heavy	57	885	vis
27	8	SAND	16f Heavy	53	1044	vis
37	10	HAMI	12f Firm	50	1241	vis
35	5	BRIG	12f Good		1647	
29	9	NOTT	14f Good	39	2008	vis
0a	6	LING	13f Aw		2323	
35	1	CARL	14f Firm	31	2827*	vis
18	6	YARM	14f Good	35	3233	vis
29	5	HAMI	12f Soft		3804	vis
0	17	HAMI	12f Gd/Sft	33	3827	vis
2a	10	SOUT	14f Aw	28	4149	vis
9	10	YARM	14f Soft		4510	vis

MISCONDUCT 6 gr m £2420

49	2	WIND	12f Good	48	2370
49	3	SALI	12f Good	49	2689
53	2	SALI	14f Gd/Fm	52	3424
53	4	KEMP	14f Gd/Fm	53	3800
32	11	GOOD	16f Soft	52	4075

MISDEMEANOR 2 b f £0

49	10	NEWC	6f Good		3245
45	5	DONC	6f Firm		3895
60	6	YARM	6f Soft		4390

MISE EN SCENE 2 b f £3542

61	8	NEWM	5f Gd/Sft		970
88	1	SAND	5f Gd/Fm		1986*
65	16	NEWB	5f Firm		2849
75	5	YARM	5f Good		3027
71	7	YARM	6f Gd/Fm		3965
41	10	SAND	5f Soft	78	4202

MISHKA 2 b g £438

62	7	WIND	5f Good		2711
58	8	KEMP	6f Gd/Fm		3358
74	3	FOLK	5f Gd/Fm		3446
63	5	GOOD	6f Good		3649

MISRAAH 3 ch c £13698

108	1	NEWM	7f Good		955*
75	25	NEWM	8f Gd/Fm		1171
108	4	NEWM	7f Firm		2343
108	4	NEWM	7f Good		4352

MISS ALL ALONE 5 ch m £0

38	7	REDC	10f Soft		4501

MISS AMBER NECTAR 3 b f £0

0	21	WIND	10f Gd/Fm		1200
0	11	SALI	10f Good		1343
0	11	WIND	8f Good		3350
0	7	CHEP	12f Good		3869

MISS ARCH 4 ch f £325

30	5	RIPO	12f Soft	36	822	
15	9	CATT	12f Gd/Fm		3202	
29	3	CARL	12f Firm		3570	
20	7	RIPO	16f Gd/Fm	38	3715	
13	9	BEVE	12f Stt/Hv		4041	
0a	15	SOUT	11f Aw		4151	VIS

MISS ASIA QUEST 3 ch f £0

63	8	WIND	10f Gd/Fm		2889

MISS BANANAS 5 b m £5202

41a	9	WOLV	5f Aw	57	40
20a	9	WOLV	6f Aw		82
0a	11	LING	6f Aw	51	154

22a	7	WOLV	6f Aw	46	226	
34a	6	SOUT	6f Aw	46	246	
20a	9	WOLV	6f Aw	41	351	
0	14	SOUT	6f Good	42	802	
49	1	PONT	6f Soft		872*	
34	5	FOLK	6f Soft	47	958	
40	7	WARW	5f Heavy	51	1005	
0	16	NOTT	6f Firm	48	1273	
44a	4	WOLV	5f Aw		1392	
26	7	LEIC	6f Soft	45	1545	
32	7	BEVE	5f Firm	45	1923	
24	11	CATT	5f Gd/Fm	42	2418	
23	11	HAMI	6f Gd/Fm	42	2641	
21	16	THIR	6f Gd/Fm	39	3144	
46	1	LEIC	5f Gd/Fm	39	3214+	
29	11	NEWM	5f Gd/Fm	50	3631	
0	16	HAMI	5f Gd/Sft	45	3825	
0	18	LEIC	5f Gd/Sft	47	4027	

MISS BEADY 2 b f £225

17	9	HAYD	5f Gd/Fm		1538	
0	12	PONT	6f Good		1864	
69	5	REDC	5f Gd/Fm		2142	
62	5	CATT	6f Gd/Fm		2419	
0	11	BEVE	5f Good		2880	BL
46	8	HAYD	6f Soft		3767	
56	4	REDC	6f Gd/Sft	62	4502	

MISS BEETEE 2 b f £867

63	4	GOOD	6f Good		3661
63	4	GOOD	6f Soft		4079
64	4	WIND	6f Gd/Sft		4289
0	15	NEWB	7f Gd/Sft	65	4453

MISS BERBERE 5 ch m £4306

106	3	SAIN	8f Heavy		10

MISS BRIEF 2 b f £4614

19	11	HAYD	5f Heavy		989
77	2	CHES	5f Firm		1249
75	4	MUSS	5f Gd/Fm		1429
62	4	CHES	5f Gd/Sft		1776
73	2	THIR	5f Gd/Fm	71	3145
44	8	CHES	6f Firm	71	3168
55	9	LING	5f Firm	73	3491
56	7	MUSS	5f Gd/Fm	70	3743

MISS CASH 3 b f £1135

23	4	PONT	10f Soft		1699
40	2	REDC	11f Gd/Fm		2989
40	4	BEVE	10f Gd/Fm		3677

MISS DAMINA 2 b f £264

60	12	WIND	5f Gd/Sft		1424
56	7	WARW	5f Gd/Fm		2034
0	11	WIND	5f Gd/Fm		3044
46	4	BRIG	6f Firm		3732
25	10	YARM	8f Gd/Fm	53	3968
58	4	LING	6f Good		4097
35	12	NEWM	7f Good		4336
42a	7	WOLV	8f Aw	54	4552

MISS DANGEROUS 5 b m £3469

0a	15	LING	7f Aw	49	28	
22a	8	LING	7f Aw	44	107	
30a	6	LING	7f Aw	40	166	BL
60a	1	LING	7f Aw		243*	bl
53a	3	LING	6f Aw		288	bl
26a	10	WOLV	5f Aw	49	352	bl
50a	3	LING	7f Aw	49	504	bl
42a	5	LING	7f Aw		547	bl
40a	5	LING	6f Aw	48	628	
26a	8	LING	6f Aw	48	881	bl
24	10	WARW	5f Heavy	49	1005	
30	8	BRIG	7f Gd/Fm		3259	
26	10	HAMI	6f Soft	48	3803	
31	7	HAMI	5f Gd/Sft	38	3825	

MISS DEVIOUS 2 ch f £0

0	15	NEWM	6f Gd/Fm		4209

0	20	DONC	7f Gd/Stt		4447
0	16	DONC	7f Heavy		4567

MISS DOMUCH 2 ch f £28729

69	2	LEIC	5f Soft		1550
69	3	SALI	6f Gd/Fm		1882
77	1	BATH	6f Firm		2939*
82	2	NEWB	5f Gd/Fm		3174
97	3	CURR	6f Yldg		3720

MISS DORDOGNE 3 br b f £7394

97	1	NEWM	7f Gd/Fm		971
77	5	NOTT	8f Gd/Fm		1269
86	2	GOOD	8f Gd/Sft		1811
82	1	CHES	8f Good		2662*

MISS EQUINOX 2 b f £4451

44	5	BEVE	5f Good		1443
59	7	DONC	6f Gd/Fm		1838
61	2	THIR	6f Good		2059
58	2	HAMI	6f Firm		2394
61	3	LEIC	5f Gd/Fm		2507
61	1	NEWC	6f Gd/Fm		2983*
60	3	LING	6f Firm		3278
56	2	RIPO	6f Good		3697
0	20	DONC	7f Gd/Fm	61	3860
56	5	CATT	5f Soft	57	4007
0	15	PONT	6f Soft	55	4235

MISS FARA 5 ch m £0

65	9	WIND	10f Firm		1288

MISS FIT 4 b f £0

0	18	HAMI	6f Good	76	844
74	5	THIR	5f Soft	75	926
0	16	THIR	5f Gd/Sft	74	1357
0	15	YORK	5f Gd/Fm	73	1980
57	8	REDC	6f Gd/Fm	71	2158
0	15	HAYD	6f Gd/Fm	69	2444
60	5	HAYD	5f Gd/Sft	63	2701
48	5	NEWC	5f Gd/Fm	61	2987
53	7	BEVE	5f Good	60	3398
49	10	CHES	5f Gd/Sft	60	3512

MISS FLIRTATIOUS 3 b f £242

46	12	WIND	6f Firm	64	1289	
0	12	SALI	7f Gd/Fm	62	1889	BL
0	13	LEIC	7f Firm	62	2026	bl
0	23	WIND	6f Gd/Sft	55	4293	
39a	3	SOUT	6f Aw		4368	
0	15	BATH	8f Soft	49	4435	bl

MISS GRAPETTE 4 b f £760

20	15	THIR	6f Soft	49	910
0	13	MUSS	5f Gd/Fm	45	1143
23	9	LEIC	6f Gd/Fm	40	1734
32	5	HAMI	5f Gd/Fm	40	1910
0a	13	SOUT	6f Aw	36	2297
37	2	MUSS	8f Gd/Sft	36	2533
31	7	AYR	7f Gd/Fm	37	3138
0	11	LEIC	7f Gd/Fm		3332
24	9	HAMI	8f Gd/Sft	37	3534
0	17	LEIC	6f Gd/Sft		4031

MISS HIT 5 b m £4827

73	1	BRIG	5f Gd/Sft	64	897*
60	7	GOOD	6f Gd/Fm	69	3136
72	2	ASCO	5f Gd/Fm	69	3341
57	15	YORK	6f Good	71	3543
67	5	BATH	6f Gd/Fm	71	3821
45	12	PONT	5f Soft	70	4377

MISS INFORM 2 b f £1143

69	3	GOOD	5f Gd/Sft		1639
60	5	SALI	6f Gd/Fm		1883
66	7	SAND	5f Gd/Fm		2526
53	7	KEMP	6f Gd/Fm	69	3075
0	12	LING	5f Good		4096
51	11	WIND	6f Gd/Fm		4289
55	2	BATH	6f Soft		4431

MISS KIRSTY 3 ch f £4465

MISS LACHINE (continued)

90	6	NEWM	7f Gd/Sft		971	
84	10	ASCO	8f Gd/Sft		1108	
87	1	GOOD	8f Gd/Sft		1811*	t
80	8	ASCO	8f Good	86	2167	t
0	26	NEWM	7f Good	86	4357	t

MISS LACROIX 5 b m £0

16	7	CATT	16f Good	33	3442

MISS LORILAW 3 b f £15395

89	3	KEMP	10f Soft		998
92	3	NEWM	12f Gd/Fm		1168
102	6	SAN	11f Good		1459
75	12	ASCO	16f Good		2068
103	1	NEWB	12f Gd/Fm		3177*
88	10	YORK	12f Firm		3595
95	8	NEWM	12f Good		4343

MISS MANETTE 3 br f £0

34	6	GOOD	10f Gd/Sft		1640
14	9	LING	9f Firm		1912
56	9	WIND	8f Soft		2548
11	10	BATH	8f Soft	53	4143

MISS MARPLE 3 b f £565

65	7	LING	6f Good	2183
58	3	WARW	6f Good	2462

MISS MONEY SPIDER 5 b m £638

0	15	WARW	8f Heavy	50	1520
0	18	CHEP	7f Gd/Sft	48	1794
28	11	DONC	7f Good	45	2320
21	12	WARW	7f Gd/Fm	42	2840
30	8	CHEP	7f Gd/Fm	42	2974
41	4	CHEP	7f Gd/Fm		3253
38	4	FOLK	7f Gd/Fm	40	3445
41	2	LING	6f Firm	40	3578

MISS MOSELLE 2 b f £678

71	3	FOLK	7f Gd/Fm	3583
0	11	KEMP	7f Soft	4035
80	7	NEWM	8f Good	4349

MISS ORAH 3 b f £1155

72	12	LING	7f Gd/Sft	1283
80	7	YARM	6f Gd/Fm	1952
91	3	YARM	7f Firm	2769

MISS PHANTINE 2 b f £0

0	12	DONC	7f Gd/Fm	3156
0	15	KEMP	7f Soft	4035

MISS PIN UP 11 gr m £0

37a	7	LING	16f Aw	60	6

MISS PIPPIN 4 ch f £0

37a	5	WOLV	6f Aw		63
35a	8	SOUT	6f Aw	54	87
26	9	BEVE	5f Gd/Fm		3651

MISS PITZ 2 b f £0

69	6	KEMP	7f Gd/Sft	2583
64	6	SALI	7f Gd/Fm	3420
58	9	LING	7f Firm	3833

MISS POLLY 2 b f £0

66	9	KEMP	7f Soft	4035
0	15	LING	7f Soft	4268
40	7	BRIG	6f Heavy	4537

MISS PROGRESSIVE 2 b f £4224

51	6	MUSS	5f Gd/Sft		796
47a	7	SOUT	5f Aw		865
0	13	HAYD	5f Gd/Sft		1488
44	11	CATT	5f Good		1659
46	8	HAMI	5f Gd/Fm		1938
52a	2	SOUT	7f Aw		2949
44	5	REDC	6f Firm		3307
54	1	SAND	7f Good	49	3468*
57	3	CATT	7f Soft		4007
25	11	CATT	7f Soft	56	4254

MISS REBECCA 2 b f £0

0	15	PONT	6f Soft	4082

MISS RIMEX 4 b f £0

68	5	GOOD	8f Gd/Sft	77	1473
65	9	RIPO	8f Good	77	1598
56	8	SALI	8f Gd/Fm	75	2229

MISS RIVIERA GOLF 3 b f £5103

87	7	NEWM	7f Gd/Sft	971
86	2	WIND	10f Gd/Fm	2889
85	8	SALI	10f Gd/Fm	3389
85	1	NOTT	8f Soft	3977*

MISS ROXANNE 3 b f £0

0a	12	SOUT	5f Aw	127
0a	12	LING	8f Aw	150
0	18	NOTT	6f Gd/Sft	1081

MISS SCARLETT 7 ch m £0

0a	10	LING	10f Aw	775
0	5	BRIG	8f Firm	2892

MISS SINCERE 3 b f £420

0a	12	SOUT	6f Aw	53	331	VIS
33a	4	LING	5f Aw		357	vis
43a	4	WOLV	5f Aw		624	
29a	8	WOLV	5f Aw		659	
46	4	MUSS	5f Gd/Sft	51	901	
32	7	MUSS	5f Firm		1688	

MISS SKICAP 3 b f £3175

69a	4	SOUT	5f Aw		34	
71a	2	SOUT	5f Aw		179	
70a	1	WOLV	6f Aw		228*	
54a	4	WOLV	5f Aw	72	361	
42a	8	WOLV	6f Aw	68	479	
0	15	NOTT	8f Gd/Sft	66	1085	BL

MISS SPRINGFIELD 3 b f £275

38	3	LING	7f Gd/Sft	39	841	
0	16	YARM	8f Good	39	1772	
37	4	WARW	7f Gd/Fm	38	2036	VIS
32	5	NEWM	8f Gd/Fm		2134	vis
15a	10	SOUT	7f Aw		2633	vis

MISS SUTTON 2 b f £0

49	5	LING	6f Firm	3278
47	4	WIND	5f Gd/Fm	3639
48a	4	WOLV	5f Aw	4025

MISS SWIFT 3 b f £0

0	17	LING	6f Good	1399
0	15	WIND	10f Good	1725

MISS TAKE 4 ch f £425

36a	10	WOLV	9f Aw	60	305	
25a	8	SOUT	6f Aw	55	384	
40a	4	SOUT	11f Aw	50	474	
43a	4	WOLV	9f Aw	50	529	
0a	12	WOLV	9f Aw	45	569	bl
22a	10	WOLV	9f Aw	42	675	
28	5	BRIG	12f Firm	38	1332	
31	7	BRIG	12f Gd/Sft	38	1465	

MISS TEAK 2 b f £834

90	4	NEWB	7f Firm	3985

MISS TOPOGINO 2 b f £0

28a	8	WOLV	5f Aw	1136
31	5	THIR	6f Gd/Sft	1713
36a	6	SOUT	5f Aw	2384
32	7	LEIC	5f Gd/Fm	2772

MISS TRESS 2 b f £653

68	4	KEMP	7f Firm		2259
71	6	HAYD	7f Soft		3786
75	4	SAND	8f Gd/Fm		3943
0	16	LING	7f Soft	74	4191
61	13	BRIG	7f Soft	71	4416

MISS VERITY 2 ch f £24410

66	6	DONC	5f Gd/Sft		1067
66a	2	SOUT	5f Aw		1304
73a	1	SOUT	5f Aw		2120*
70	2	HAMI	5f Gd/Fm		2797
68	4	LING	5f Good	69	4269
81	2	NEWM	6f Good		4345

MISS WORLD 3 b f £4898

65a	2	SOUT	7f Aw	60	31	t
62a	3	LING	8f Aw	60	54	t
67a	2	LING	8f Aw	62	158	t
72a	1	SOUT	8f Aw	64	213*	t
49a	5	LING	7f Aw		243	t
67a	4	LING	8f Aw	73	266	t
44a	7	WOLV	9f Aw		662	t
60a	5	WOLV	9f Aw	69	709	t
32	13	BRIG	10f Gd/Sft	62	892	t
2	12	NOTT	10f Heavy	57	1022	t
0a	13	WOLV	9f Aw	66	4248	
0a	10	WOLV	9f Aw	62	4382	

MISSED MAY 6 br m £0

0a	16	SOUT	10f Aw	30	211	tBL

MISSED THE BOAT b g £0

0a	12	WOLV	9f Aw	32	405

MISSILE TOE 7 b h £8544

0a	11	LING	10f Aw	43	100
65	5	EPSO	9f Heavy		1033
46	5	REDC	8f Firm	45	1300
45	4	NEWM	8f Gd/Fm	44	1690
51	1	NEWM	8f Gd/Fm	45	2130*
51	1	NEWC	10f Gd/Fm	45	2309*
47	6	YARM	8f Gd/Fm	57	2412
50	5	NEWM	8f Gd/Sft	51	2802
50	3	NOTT	10f Gd/Fm	50	3111
0	15	YORK	10f Gd/Fm	50	3731

MISSING A BIT 2 b g £250

51	4	CHEP	6f Heavy		1553	
45	4	BRIG	6f Gd/Fm		1931	BL
46	5	WIND	6f Gd/Fm		2052	bl
42	5	LEIC	6f Gd/Fm	46	3216	
43	4	SAND	7f Good	48	3468	

MISSING DRINK 2 ch c £0

0	13	YORK	6f Firm	1328
52	5	WIND	5f Gd/Fm	2055
54	11	WIND	6f Gd/Fm	2209
67	5	CATT	7f Gd/Fm	2417
53	9	BEVE	5f Firm	2730
43	9	YARM	7f Good	3029

MISSING YOU TOO 2 b f £0

69	6	WIND	6f Gd/Fm	1876
63	8	LING	7f Gd/Fm	2182

MISSOURI 2 b f £0

77	6	NEWM	7f Gd/Fm	3459

MIST OVER MEUGHER 3 gr f £0

18a	9	SOUT	8f Aw		48
22	9	RIPO	8f Good		1596
0a	11	SOUT	8f Aw	36	1804
10	9	MUSS	8f Gd/Fm	40	2205

MISTER BUCKET 2 ch c £0

72	4	FOLK	7f Good	2619

MISTER CLINTON 3 ch g £7677

38	4	NOTT	6f Good	47	785
61	1	BRIG	7f Firm		1333*
33	12	NEWC	8f Gd/Sft	52	1477
60	3	NEWB	7f Gd/Fm	52	1787
63	1	SALI	7f Gd/Fm	57	1889*
61	6	LEIC	7f Gd/Fm	66	2026
58	7	EPSO	7f Good	62	2794
62	4	SAND	7f Gd/Fm	62	2922

MISTER DOC 2 ch g £0

0	12	AYR	7f Good	3363

MISTER ERMYN 7 ch g £0

0	13	SALI	14f Good	2691	bl

MISTER GILL 3 ch c £0

0a	13	SOUT	6f Aw	56	331	t
26	10	AYR	13f Gd/Fm		1657	
30	10	BEVE	12f Gd/Sft	59	1758	
0	14	REDC	10f Good	55	1895	

MISTER HAVANA 3 br g £0

31a	9	LING	7f Aw	421
49	8	LING	9f Firm	1912

MISTER JOLSON 11 br g £593

59	4	SAND	5f Good		1966
42	5	BATH	6f Firm		3208
36	10	LING	6f Firm	53	3578
48	4	BATH	6f Gd/Fm	50	3821
0	13	CHEP	5f Good	50	3872

MISTER KICK 3 gr c £15370

103	2	CHAN	15f Soft	3065
107	2	LONG	15f Soft	3848

MISTER MAL 4 b c £6155

43	11	WARW	8f Soft	77	817
71	5	PONT	6f Heavy	77	941
59	13	DONC	6f Gd/Sft	75	1074
0	12	DONC	6f Gd/Fm		2580
78	1	NEWC	7f Good	71	3250+
57	12	CHES	8f Gd/Fm	77	3510
77	2	HAYD	7f Soft	77	3785
0	17	DONC	7f Gd/Fm	77	3880
77	6	AYR	6f Gd/Sft	77	4010
76	5	YORK	7f Heavy	78	4302
42	8	NEWC	6f Heavy	77	4405
71	8	DONC	8f Heavy	75	4574

MISTER MCGOLDRICK 3 b g £4374

69	7	YARM	10f Gd/Fm		3381
78	1	HAYD	11f Soft		4089*
61	14	YORK	12f Soft	75	4280

MISTER MIND 2 b c £0

47	7	RIPO	5f Good	1595
45	10	BEVE	5f Good	3955
0	30	NEWM	6f Good	4345

MISTER PQ 4 ch c £0

34	6	FOLK	15f Good		963
0	17	BRIG	12f Gd/Fm	42	1128
16	17	NEWM	12f Firm	40	1852
0a	13	SOUT	16f Aw	29	2951

MISTER RAIDER 8 ch g £0

39a	5	LING	5f Aw	42	57	bl
4a	11	WOLV	5f Aw	41	139	bl
7a	9	LING	5f Aw	41	166	bl
38a	8	LING	6f Aw		313	bl
32a	9	LING	7f Aw		398	bl
0	19	LING	5f Gd/Fm	38	2184	bl
0	15	CHEP	14f Aw	34	2974	bl
20	8	WIND	5f Good	38	3191	bl

MISTER RAMBO 5 b g £7663

60	12	DONC	6f Good	79	716	
83	1	WARW	8f Soft	79	817*	
70	8	KEMP	8f Soft	81	1015	
82	5	CHES	8f Firm	81	1250	
82	2	LING	7f Soft	81	1286	
73	8	GOOD	7f Gd/Sft	83	1483	
64	6	EPSO	9f Gd/Sft	82	1829	
67	10	ASCO	7f Gd/Fm	81	2999	
77	5	EPSO	7f Gd/Fm	79	3414	
74	5	GOOD	8f Good	78	3648	
73	8	LING	8f Firm	78	3831	bl
64	6	NEWM	7f Good		4018	bl
66	8	BRIG	7f Gd/Sft	74	4121	bl

MISTER SANDERS 2 ch c £0

50	8	REDC	5f Firm		1294
66	6	PONT	5f Good		2361
64	11	YORK	6f Good		2692
56	9	DONC	7f Firm	66	3901
47	14	CATT	7f Soft	63	4007

MISTER SUPERB 3 ch c £12099

79	3	SALI	6f Firm	82	1178
76	3	NEWB	6f Gd/Fm	82	1406
79	2	NEWB	6f Gd/Fm		1783
84	1	LING	6f Gd/Fm		2183*
78	8	DONC	6f Gd/Fm	82	2577
75	6	NEWB	6f Firm	83	2813
77	3	KEMP	7f Gd/Fm	81	3076

90	6	ASCO	6f Gd/Fm		3303
79	9	NEWM	7f Gd/Fm	83	3629
76	7	SALI	6f Gd/Sft	81	4165
72	14	NEWM	7f Good	80	4357

MISTER TRICKY 5 ch g £14397

69a	1	LING	7f Aw	62	58*
72a	1	LING	6f Aw	67	223*
67a	2	LING	6f Aw		288
54a	12	LING	7f Aw	70	337
79a	1	LING	6f Aw	70	881*
0	12	BRIG	6f Gd/Fm	67	1126
0	22	GOOD	6f Good	67	2355
42	13	EPSO	7f Good	64	3765
76a	2	WOLV	6f Aw	75	4380

MISTER WEBB 3 b c £218

67	5	SOUT	10f Gd/Sft		858
72	10	SALI	12f Firm		1179
44	11	CHEP	10f Gd/Fm	64	3683
62	4	BATH	13f Gd/Fm	64	3819
40	7	CATT	16f Soft	59	4258
17a	7	SOUT	14f Aw	59	4370

MISTER WESTSOUND 8 b g £1046

56	4	AYR	6f Gd/Fm	56	1654	bl
33	12	HAMI	6f Gd/Fm	56	1941	bl
28	11	HAMI	6f Firm	56	2097	bl
16	12	NEWC	6f Gd/Fm	56	2275	bl
0	16	HAYD	7f Gd/Fm	54	2442	bl
44	8	HAMI	6f Gd/Fm	52	2641	bl
18	11	HAMI	6f Good		2798	bl
34	10	AYR	7f Gd/Fm	45	3138	bl
0	14	HAMI	8f Gd/Sft	41	3534	bl
33	6	AYR	6f Heavy	36	4327	bl
31	3	NEWC	6f Heavy	36	4425	bl
38	3	MUSS	7f Soft	36	4522	bl

MISTRESS BANKES 4 b f £0

5	10	YARM	10f Good	3234
0	7	BRIG	10f Firm	3526

MISTY BELLE 2 gr f £2103

0	15	WIND	5f Gd/Fm		1197
74	3	WARW	5f Gd/Sft		1706
76	2	BATH	5f Firm		1993
69	3	LING	5f Gd/Fm		2214
56	D	BATH	6f Firm		2939
9	10	SAND	5f Good	70	3228
54	9	BATH	5f Good		3815
0	11	BATH	5f Soft		4431

MISTY BOY 3 br g £0

34	9	HAYD	6f Soft	54	1494	
0	14	KEMP	7f Gd/Fm	51	3796	
15	11	YARM	7f Soft		4387	
39	5	NEWC	6f Heavy	46	4425	BL

MISTY DIAMOND 2 b f £0

59	9	NEWM	6f Firm	1856
42	9	NEWM	6f Gd/Fm	2132
0a	8	SOUT	7f Aw	2301

MISTY EYED 2 gr f £56739

74	5	WIND	5f Gd/Sft	1424
89	1	WIND	5f Good	1727*
91	7	ASCO	5f Good	2113
95	1	WIND	5f Good	2368*
100	1	SAND	5f Gd/Fm	2529*
109	1	GOOD	5f Good	3133*
109	2	DONC	5f Firm	3900
101	5	NEWB	6f Firm	3996

MISTY MAGIC 3 b f £2198

43	7	NOTT	8f Gd/Sft	61	1085
43	11	NEWB	7f Gd/Fm	58	1405
54	4	WARW	7f Gd/Sft	54	1710
54	3	NOTT	8f Good	54	2013
55	2	SALI	8f Gd/Fm	53	2264
51	6	LEIC	8f Gd/Fm	55	2512
55	3	EPSO	9f Good	55	3856

37	9	YARM	8f Gd/Fm	55	3971
37	10	BRIG	10f Soft	54	4174
34a	6	WOLV	8f Aw	53	4440

MISTY MISS 3 b f £0

91	10	NEWM	7f Good	953
0	P	BATH	5f Good	1090

MITCHAM 4 br c £1050

83	20	NEWM	5f Gd/Fm		1172
100	4	LEOP	7f Good		2070
87	11	ASCO	6f Good		2115
99	7	GOOD	7f Gd/Fm		3132
87	7	NEWM	6f Good		3610
73	11	NEWB	5f Firm		3982 BL

MITCHELLS MAYHEM 3 b f £0

28	5	MUSS	5f Gd/Fm		2204
0a	8	LING	5f Aw		2650
0	14	REDC	5f Gd/Fm	35	2864

MITHRAIC 8 b g £1890

29	5	REDC	10f Gd/Fm	2143
35	6	CATT	12f Gd/Fm	2742
37	1	NEWC	12f Good	3247*
23	9	REDC	11f Soft	4497

MITIE ACCESS 4 ch f £0

0	13	BRIG	7f Firm	35	1335
0	11	YARM	8f Gd/Fm		2411 VIS

MIZHAR 4 b c £5050

0	22	NEWM	6f Gd/Fm	90	1173	
77	14	YORK	5f Firm	85	1324	
70	9	YORK	6f Gd/Fm	84	1983	
71	10	NEWC	5f Gd/Fm	80	2310	
62	8	BEVE	5f Gd/Fm	77	2517	
67	10	SAND	5f Gd/Fm	75	2925	
78	2	BEVE	5f Good	72	3398	BL
78	2	YARM	5f Gd/Fm	76	3668	bl
78	4	EPSO	5f Good	77	3855	bl

MIZOG 5 b m £0

0a	12	LING	12f Aw	267

MIZZEN MAST 2 gr c £7685

110	2	LONG	8f Good	3926

MJOLNIR 3 gr g £0

31a	6	SOUT	8f Aw	694	t
35	10	SOUT	7f Good	804	t

MOBO BACO 3 ch c £0

0	14	LING	6f Gd/Sft		837
72	4	FOLK	7f Soft		962
58	12	WIND	8f Gd/Sft		1099
59	6	LING	7f Good		1397
0	13	BATH	8f Gd/Sft	62	1671
42	13	CHEP	6f Good	59	1971
35	9	LING	5f Good	55	2591
46	9	SALI	8f Gd/Fm	51	2980
52	5	PONT	6f Soft		4233

MOBTAKER 2 b c £0

77	8	GOOD	7f Firm	3154

MODEL GROOM 4 b c £0

40	6	NEWM	6f Gd/Fm	3117
38	5	CHEP	8f Good	3868
37	4	BRIG	10f Gd/Sft	4122

MODEL QUEEN 2 ch f £444

70	3	BRIG	8f Soft	4418

MODEM 3 b c £2249

59a	1	SOUT	7f Aw		281*
54a	3	SOUT	8f Aw	56	451 VIS
46a	6	WOLV	8f Aw	58	495 vis
50a	4	SOUT	8f Aw	56	540 BL
0	13	DONC	7f Gd/Sft	54	4452
49	7	NEWM	8f Gd/Sft	54	4536

MODERN BRITISH 3 ch g £7109

94	1	GOOD	7f Gd/Sft	1638*
99	2	ASCO	8f Good	2171
97	5	SAND	8f Good	2476

MODEST HOPE 13 b g £0
0a	9	SOUT	11f Aw	24	324	
0a	7	SOUT	11f Aw		369	
0a	7	SOUT	12f Aw	20	413	
6a	9	SOUT	12f Aw		498	vis

MODESTY 2 b f £0
42	9	BATH	6f Firm		2328
0	14	NEWM	6f Gd/Fm		4209
0	28	NEWM	6f Good		4345

MODIGLIANI 2 b c £13350
101	3	ASCO	6f Good		2067	
99	4	CURR	7f Gd/Fm		3067	
102	2	CURR	6f Good		3844	BL

MODISH 3 b c £8112
| 97 | 2 | EPSO | 10f Heavy | 1029 |
| 91 | 2 | YORK | 14f Gd/Fm | 1311 |

MODRIK 2 ch c £8922
62	8	NEWM	6f Gd/Fm		2854
92	3	NEWM	7f Gd/Fm		3121
88	4	KEMP	8f Gd/Fm		3799
88	2	LING	7f Soft		4267
91	1	DONC	7f Soft	85	4460*

MODUS OPERANDI 4 b c £791
75a	6	LING	10f Aw		593
74a	4	LING	12f Aw	80	633
36	10	NEWM	10f Gd/Fm	80	2287
69	8	KEMP	10f Gd/Fm	75	2750
52	14	RIPO	9f Gd/Fm	71	3011
47	12	GOOD	9f Good	69	3644

MOGIN 7 ch m £0
0a	11	LING	10f Aw	43	203
0a	13	LING	12f Aw	40	290
28a	4	LING	12f Aw	41	377
29a	4	LING	13f Aw	30	460
15a	5	LING	10f Aw		775

MOGUL 6 b g £0
| 37 | 7 | CHEP | 7f Gd/Fm | 3253 |

MOLE CREEK 5 gr m £0
0	15	NEWB	13f Gd/Fm	82	1784
0	20	ASCO	12f Good	78	2069
60	7	HAYD	12f Gd/Fm	72	2446
51	10	KEMP	12f Firm	67	2872

MOLLY BROWN 3 b f £16429
0	17	NEWM	7f Gd/Fm	86	1153
82	4	NEWB	6f Gd/Fm	83	1406
64	7	NEWC	6f Heavy	83	1768
64	12	ASCO	5f Good	82	2168
86	1	DONC	6f Gd/Fm	80	2577*
86	2	HAYD	6f Heavy		3768
91	2	GOOD	6f Good	88	3904
0	16	KEMP	6f Gd/Sft		4037
89	3	NEWM	6f Good	90	4198
95	9	NEWM	6f Good		4346
90	2	NEWM	6f Gd/Sft		4535

MOLLY IRWIN 2 b f £2906
53	3	DONC	5f Good		712
62a	1	WOLV	5f Aw		722*
64	2	LING	5f Gd/Sft		836
33a	9	SOUT	5f Aw		856
0	11	LING	6f Good		1396
35	10	LING	5f Firm	55	3491
26	7	WIND	5f Good		3639
0	16	LING	6f Good		4097

MOLLY MALONE 3 gr f £0
60	6	GOOD	7f Gd/Sft		1468
0	16	GOOD	8f Gd/Sft		1811
59	9	LING	6f Gd/Fm		2183
0	20	LEIC	8f Sft/Hvy	63	4310

MOLLYTIME 4 ch f £0
11a	7	SOUT	11f Aw		196
2a	8	SOUT	8f Aw	25	584
2a	7	SOUT	12f Aw	34	642

| 0a | 11 | SOUT | 8f Aw | 24 | 692 | BL |

MOLOMO 3 b f £11400
| 109 | 2 | CURR | 10f Good | 3556 |

MOLY 4 b f £0
| 7a | 10 | SOUT | 12f Aw | 84 |

MOMENTOUS JONES 3 b g £0
| 47 | 7 | SALI | 10f Gd/Fm | 58 | 3390 |
| 46 | 8 | GOOD | 10f Good | 54 | 3663 |

MOMENTS IN TIME 2 b f £324
58	6	SALI	5f Gd/Fm		2227
66	4	EPSO	7f Gd/Sft		2430
62	6	FOLK	7f Good		2619
52	5	CHES	7f Gd/Fm	65	3428
39	7	FOLK	7f Gd/Fm		3582
0	19	LEIC	8f Firm	54	3837

MON POTE LE GITAN 3 ch c £0
| 108 | 6 | LONG | 8f V | 1318 |

MON PREFERE 5 ch g £0
| 0 | 15 | DONC | 8f Heavy | 75 | 4573 |

MON SECRET 2 b c £6283
69	8	RIPO	5f Soft		821
74	3	REDC	5f Gd/Sft		1130
78	2	RIPO	5f Good		1595
76	4	HAMI	5f Gd/Fm		1906
80	1	CARL	6f Gd/Fm		2239*
79	4	ASCO	6f Good	79	2678
57	10	NEWC	7f Good	79	3246
15	16	NEWM	6f Gd/Fm	78	4214
0	21	NEWM	6f Good	75	4338

MONACLE 6 b g £5447
37	3	WARW	12f Good	41	2466
35	4	CARL	14f Firm	39	2827
41	1	YARM	16f Good	36	3026*
44	2	YARM	14f Gd/Fm	41	3233
41	5	THIR	16f Gd/Fm	43	3348
42	4	YARM	14f Gd/Fm	42	3664
40a	2	SOUT	16f Aw	39	4149	e

MONACO 6 b g £0
19	9	HAMI	9f Gd/Fm		1191
25	7	MUSS	7f Firm		1685
0	15	HAMI	9f Gd/Fm	32	1907
21	9	MUSS	9f Gd/Fm		2046
32	9	HAMI	9f Gd/Fm		2642
25	7	AYR	11f Firm		2875
15	7	HAMI	12f Soft		3804	VIS

MONASH FREEWAY 2 ch c £0
0	13	KEMP	6f Gd/Fm	3358
0	14	LING	6f Aw	3577
0	13	CHEP	7f Good	3866

MONASH LADY 2 ch f £0
51	4	LING	6f Firm	3278
44	6	LING	7f Gd/Fm	4097
46	6	NEWM	7f Good	4336

MONASHEE MOUNTAIN 3 b c £48900
115	1	THE	7f Soft		770*	
115	1	CURR	7f Soft		1120*	
112	5	LONG	8f V		1318	
95	13	ASCO	7f Good		2087	
91	9	NEWM	6f Gd/Fm		2615	VIS

MONAWARA 3 b f £0
| 0 | 18 | GOOD | 8f Gd/Sft | 1811 |

MONDRAGON 10 b g £1192
47	2	MUSS	16f Gd/Fm	1145
28	5	REDC	16f Good	1894
53	2	NOTT	16f Gd/Fm	2191

MONDURU 3 b c £605
68	7	RIPO	8f Soft		826
73	3	KEMP	7f Soft		1012
58	5	CHEP	8f Heavy		1552
55	7	DONC	8f Gd/Fm	72	2579
0	17	GOOD	10f Soft	67	4067
0	16	WIND	10f Gd/Sft	61	4291

| 31a | 9 | SOUT | 12f Aw | 4366 |

MONICA 2 ch f £0
42	10	MUSS	5f Gd/Fm		1146
37	11	THIR	5f Good		1381
45	4	MUSS	5f Firm		1684
37	5	MUSS	5f Firm		2045
36	6	MUSS	5f Gd/Fm		2200
19	10	CATT	7f Gd/Fm		2927
26	9	MUSS	5f Good	57	3101

MONICA GELLER 2 b f £6773
42a	7	SOUT	8f Aw		2120	
44a	6	SOUT	7f Aw		2383	
58a	3	SOUT	6f Aw		2635	
58a	7	SOUT	6f Aw	67	2948	
59	3	NEWM	7f Firm	61	3299	
58	6	LING	7f Firm	59	3830	
61	2	YARM	7f Firm	59	3922	
64	1	GOOD	8f Soft	60	4076*	
70	6	NEWM	8f Good	71	4157	
60	6	YORK	7f Gd/Fm	73	4279	

MONICAS CHOICE 9 b g £0
| 40a | 5 | SOUT | 8f Aw | 195 |

MONKEY BUSINESS 3 b f £0
50	15	NEWM	10f Good		957
64	6	NEWM	8f Gd/Fm	69	1853
41	9	WIND	10f Gd/Fm	69	2888
53	11	REDC	10f Firm	66	3310
53a	5	LING	10f Aw	63	4482

MONKSTON POINT 4 b c £33248
101	1	NEWB	5f Soft	95	914+	vis
104	1	KEMP	6f Soft		1016*	vis
102	7	LONG	5f V		1320	vis
107	1	KEMP	5f Soft		1529*	vis
102	3	LEOP	5f Yldg		1757	BL
65	16	ASCO	5f Good		2115	vis
83	20	AYR	6f Gd/Sft	107	4012	vis
107	3	ASCO	6f Gd/Sft		4125	vis
96	12	NEWM	6f Good		4346	vis
80	8	NEWB	6f Gd/Sft	107	4456	vis
92	7	DONC	6f Heavy		4581	

MONO LADY 7 b m £5373
36a	10	WOLV	9f Aw	68	469	bl
66a	2	LING	12f Aw	65	528	bl
32a	8	LING	12f Aw	65	572	bl
69	4	NEWB	12f Good	68	1373	bl
63a	5	LING	12f Aw	66	1677	bl
70a	1	WOLV	12f Aw	65	2075*	bl
73	4	NEWM	12f Gd/Fm	73	2286	bl
65	4	HAYD	12f Gd/Fm	68	2446	bl
70	3	SALI	12f Gd/Fm	68	3392	bl
59a	5	WOLV	12f Aw	73	4360	bl

MONONGAHELA 6 b g £0
| 0 | 16 | CHEP | 12f Gd/Fm | 60 | 3255 |
| 0a | 10 | WOLV | 15f Aw | | 4024 |

MONSAJEM 5 ch g £10066
111	7	KRAN	10f Firm		657	
92	9	NAD	9f Good		768	
104	4	KEMP	10f Soft		1014	
104	3	CHES	10f Firm		1248	BL
88	5	GOOD	10f Gd/Sft		1482	bl
108	1	HAYD	12f Gd/Sft		3479*	
94	8	ASCO	12f Gd/Sft	108	4128	

MONSIEUR LE BLANC 2 b c £1120
80	6	CHEP	6f Gd/Sft		1798	
79	3	SAND	7f Gd/Fm		2494	
80	5	ASCO	7f Gd/Fm		3015	
72	6	CHEP	8f Gd/Fm		3680	
78	7	DONC	8f Gd/Fm	82	3879	BL

MONSIEUR RICK 3 b c £4006
63a	3	LING	8f Aw		373
55a	4	SOUT	8f Aw		453
78a	1	LING	10f Aw		523*

82a 4 LING 10f Aw   593

MONT ROCHER 5 b g £17291
115	3	DEAU	13f Gd/Sft		3723	
113	2	MAIS	10f Good		4050	bl

MONTALBAN 4 ch c £31556
| 114 | 3 | SAN | 12f Heavy | | 4493 |

MONTALCINO 4 b c £10592
93	5	GOOD	14f Gd/Sft	92	1484
91	4	THIR	12f Gd/Sft	92	1715
97	2	YORK	14f Good	90	3811
97	2	ASCO	16f Good	95	4115

MONTANA MISS 2 b f £6028
80	4	CHEP	6f Gd/Sft		1798
76	1	BEVE	7f Firm		2218*
81	1	CATT	7f Gd/Fm		2741*
55	6	BEVE	7f Gd/Fm		3409
79	3	CATT	7f Soft	78	4254
69	7	NEWB	7f Gd/Sft	78	4453

MONTE CARLO 3 b c £0
99	8	LONG	11f V		864
101	6	SAND	10f Heavy		1056

MONTE MAYOR GOLF 2 b f £2219
0	14	BATH	5f Good		1088
71	5	CHEP	6f Gd/Sft		1798
28	11	BATH	6f Firm		2328
38	6	SALI	7f Gd/Fm		3388
46	8	WARW	15f Gd/Fm		3911
39a	7	WOLV	6f Aw		4225
71a	1	WOLV	7f Aw		4385*

MONTECRISTO 7 br g £4596
91	3	EPSO	12f Heavy	88	1030
85	5	THIR	12f Gd/Sft	90	1715
85	5	NEWM	16f Gd/Fm	90	2600
81	4	PONT	12f Firm	88	3504
85	5	THIR	12f Gd/Sft	86	3778
81	3	YORK	12f Soft		4276
0	15	DONC	12f Soft	85	4464
80	4	MUSS	16f Soft	82	4563

MONTENDRE 13 b g £0
18	9	WARW	7f Soft		816
0	12	FOLK	6f Soft	50	958
0	13	WIND	6f Gd/Sft		1423
36	9	BATH	6f Firm	45	1994

MONTEV LADY 2 ch f £2510
34	9	EPSO	6f Gd/Sft		2628
63	1	BATH	5f Firm		3204*
56	4	CHEP	5f Gd/Fm	60	3679
40	11	NOTT	6f Soft	60	3976
65a	8	LING	6f Aw		4332

MONTICELLO 8 ch g £0
| 24 | 6 | CHEP | 12f Gd/Fm | | 3681 |

MONTINI 5 ch h £0
| 92 | 3 | MULH | 17f V | | 13 |

MONTJEU 4 b c £960911
119	4	TOKY	12f Firm		123
127	1	CURR	11f Gd/Sft		1625*
130	1	SAIN	12f Good		2406*
134	1	ASCO	12f Gd/Fm		2998+
123	1	LONG	12f Gd/Fm		3927*
121	4	LONG	12f Gd/Fm		4262
124	2	NEWM	10f Good		4355

MONUMENT 8 ch g £337
52	3	WIND	12f Gd/Fm		1880
34	9	CHEP	12f Gd/Fm	51	2656
18	12	WIND	12f Gd/Fm	46	3049

MOO AZ 3 b c £4319
| 90 | 1 | THIR | 8f Gd/Fm | | 3126* |

MOOCHA CHA MAN 4 b c £3132
52a	7	WOLV	6f Aw	62	622	
38	9	HAMI	6f Good	72	844	bl
58a	5	WOLV	6f Aw	59	923	bl
0	13	BATH	6f Firm	70	1999	
0	17	HAYD	5f Gd/Fm	67	2701	bl
47	11	PONT	5f Firm	62	3502	bl
47a	5	WOLV	6f Aw	59	3774	VIS
62a	1	WOLV	6f Aw	57	4023*	bl
54a	6	WOLV	6f Aw	62	4223	bl

MOON AT NIGHT 5 gr g £3359
70	1	BRIG	8f Gd/Fm	64	1129*
17	12	GOOD	8f Gd/Fm	69	1473
68	3	BATH	8f Firm	69	1998
60	9	WIND	8f Good	69	3188
62	7	KEMP	7f Gd/Fm	69	3362
55	12	KEMP	7f Gd/Fm	67	3796
19a	12	LING	8f Aw	65	4335

MOON COLONY 7 b g £0
0a	9	SOUT	14f Aw		124
49	9	WARW	16f Gd/Fm	60	3916
25	6	BEVE	12f Sft/Hv		4041

MOON DREAM 4 gr f £0
0	21	DONC	7f Good	39	1519
56	8	NOTT	8f Gd/Fm		2188
0	17	CATT	7f Gd/Fm	33	3200

MOON EMPEROR 3 b c £3588
88	1	RIPO	8f Soft		826*
96	8	NEWM	7f Good		955
91	5	ASCO	8f Good		2171
88	7	DONC	8f Firm	96	3897

MOON GLOW 4 b g £1467
69	4	REDC	8f Gd/Fm		2159
62	2	CARL	7f Firm		2824
62	7	REDC	10f Firm	67	3310
0	24	YORK	9f Good		3808

MOON GOD 3 b c £574
| 72 | 3 | LING | 7f Good | | 1675 |

MOON MASTER 2 b c £283
69	4	LEIC	6f Gd/Sft		1573
55	7	LING	7f Soft		4483

MOON OF ALABAMA 3 b f £0
35	11	WIND	8f Gd/Fm		3048
0	17	YARM	8f Gd/Fm	55	3970
0	12	GOOD	7f Soft	58	4080
0	19	BRIG	10f Soft		4174

MOON ROYALE 2 ch f £0
61	5	THIR	7f Gd/Fm		3776
34	10	CATT	6f Soft		4001

MOON SOLITAIRE 3 b c £77382
76	4	NEWC	7f Soft		759	
87	1	FOLK	7f Soft		962*	
79	3	NEWM	8f Firm	77	1183	
91	1	GOOD	9f Gd/Sft	79	1452*	
96	3	EPSO	10f Gd/Sft	89	1831	
89	10	ASCO	8f Good	91	2117	VIS
99	1	NEWM	10f Gd/Fm	91	2596*	
97	3	HAYD	11f Soft	97	3782	
99	3	NEWM	10f Good	97	3997	
91	11	NEWM	10f Good	98	4197	

MOONJAZ 3 ch c £643
| 84 | 3 | SAND | 10f Soft | | 4205 |

MOONLADY 3 b f £62097
111	1	HANN	12f Good		3930*
108	1	DORT	14f Heavy		4265*

MOONLIGHT DANCER 2 b c £3603
77	4	SALI	5f Good		1346
75	2	CHES	5f Gd/Sft		1776
78	2	KEMP	6f Gd/Fm		1924
78	7	ASCO	5f Good		2152
73	2	BRIG	5f Gd/Fm		2724
74	5	BRIG	7f Gd/Fm		3239
61	7	NEWB	7f Gd/Fm	76	3486
68	5	SAND	5f Gd/Fm		3942
0	18	LING	5f Soft	72	4269

MOONLIGHT FLIT 5 b m £0
37a	7	SOUT	8f Aw	47	85	
39a	5	LING	8f Aw	45	152	
15a	9	SOUT	8f Aw	45	177	VIS
32a	5	WOLV	8f Aw	42	254	

MOONLIGHT MONTY 4 ch c £663
56	D	CATT	14f Gd/Fm	53	779
0	11	CATT	16f Soft	56	4258
0a	12	WOLV	12f Aw	54	4386

MOONLIGHT SONG 3 b f £8841
45	9	LEIC	6f Gd/Sft		829
0	14	GOOD	7f Gd/Sft	70	1810
51	8	LEIC	6f Firm	65	2031
62a	1	SOUT	7f Aw		2633*
63	2	LEIC	7f Gd/Fm	80	2918
63	2	HAYD	7f Gd/Fm	61	3269
63	2	NEWM	7f Gd/Fm	61	3460
50	8	NEWM	6f Good	63	3613
67a	1	SOUT	7f Aw	63	4153*
60a	4	WOLV	7f Aw	60	4550

MOONRAKING 7 gr g £320
| 42a | 3 | WOLV | 12f Aw | | 4549 | bl |

MOONRIDGE 3 b f £0
0a	16	SOUT	7f Aw	62	1801	t
26a	11	SOUT	5f Aw	62	1976	tbl

MOONSHIFT 6 b g £0
0a	11	SOUT	12f Aw	28	68	tvi
28a	5	SOUT	11f Aw		178	tvi
3a	8	SOUT	12f Aw	28	215	tvi
41	6	YARM	10f Good		3234	tvi
34	6	NOTT	10f Good	38	3524	tvi

MOORLANDS AGAIN 5 b g £1503
51	6	NEWB	10f Firm		2709
68	5	CHEP	7f Gd/Fm		3256
79	5	BATH	8f Gd/Fm		3515
78	4	CHEP	7f Gd/Fm		3682
59	5	PONT	10f Soft		4088
86	4	BATH	8f Soft		4142
64	3	BATH	10f Good	62	4436

MOOSE MALLOY 3 ch g £0
0	12	SOUT	7f Gd/Sft	53	857
0	18	NEWB	10f Gd/Fm		1404
0	11	YARM	10f Gd/Sft	48	1615
0	12	BEVE	12f Gd/Sft	48	1758
0	16	NEWM	8f Gd/Fm		3626

MOOTAFAYILL 2 b c £4793
95	2	GOOD	8f Gd/Fm		3064
98	2	NEWB	6f Firm		3980
92	2	BATH	6f Soft		4138

MORE MODERN 2 ch c £353
| 80 | 4 | NEWM | 6f Gd/Sft | | 4530 |

MOREOVER 2 b f £270
73	4	LING	7f Soft		4484
0	16	DONC	7f Heavy		4566

MORGAN LE FAY 5 b m £3737
63	1	THIR	6f Gd/Sft		1354*
49	11	AYR	6f Gd/Fm	63	1654
0	18	YORK	7f Good	61	3809
55	5	NOTT	6f Soft	58	3975
56a	4	SOUT	6f Aw	57	4155

MORGANS ORCHARD 4 ch g £16069
61a	3	SOUT	12f Aw		84
65a	1	SOUT	12f Aw	57	338*
48a	5	SOUT	12f Aw	62	456
64a	2	WOLV	12f Aw	60	562
65a	1	WOLV	12f Aw	60	607*
58a	5	WOLV	16f Aw	60	627
59	5	HAMI	13f Good	60	845
60	2	NEWB	12f Good	59	1373
0	14	YORK	12f Firm	60	2002
63	2	CHES	12f Firm	60	3173
60	3	NEWM	12f Gd/Fm	60	3461
64	2	YORK	12f Good	61	3541
63	6	HAYD	14f Soft	65	3783

57	8	NEWB	13f Firm	65	3994
57	7	YORK	12f Soft	63	4280
44	7	BATH	12f Soft	60	4433

MORNING BREEZE 4 ch f £750

95	4	LEOP	14f Good		2909

MORNING LOVER 3 b c £4197

84	5	NEWM	12f Good		951
76	1	CATT	12f Good		1661*
55	4	NEWB	12f Gd/Fm	77	1948
76	3	HAYD	12f Gd/Fm	74	2702 t

MORNING SUIT 6 b g £0

34a	5	WOLV	16f Aw		2076

MORNINGS MINION 3 b g £5726

55	4	HAYD	7f Heavy		992
89	4	NEWB	8f Good		1377
84	1	WARW	8f Good		2464*
80	5	NEWB	7f Gd/Fm	85	3481
85	3	HAYD	7f Gd/Sft	83	4106
73	16	NEWM	7f Good	83	4357

MORNINGSIDE 3 b f £322

77	6	SALI	12f Good		1179
61	4	GOOD	12f Gd/Sft		1455
64	6	BATH	12f Firm	69	3206
0	15	WIND	10f Gd/Sft	65	4291

MOROCCO 11 b g £320

28	9	FOLK	7f Gd/Fm	50	3445
47	3	CHEP	7f Good	45	3871
0	15	NEWC	8f Heavy	45	4406

MORSHDI 2 b c £3066

79	5	ASCO	7f Good		2956
91	1	HAYD	8f Soft		3766*
69	7	NEWM	10f Soft		4543

MORSHID 2 b c £1186

69	7	CHEP	8f Good		3680
81	3	GOOD	8f Good		3906
73	3	NEWC	8f Heavy		4422

MOSAAHIM 2 b c £1368

89	2	NEWB	7f Good		3484
84	5	DONC	8f Gd/Fm		3864

MOSAIC TIMES 3 ch c £0

29a	7	SOUT	6f Aw		181
40a	6	SOUT	7f Aw		217
14a	9	SOUT	6f Aw		300

MOSAYTER 2 b c £392

92	4	NEWM	7f Good		4183

MOSCA 2 ch f £0

69	7	BATH	8f Soft		4430

MOSELLE 3 b f £14763

86	2	SOUT	10f Gd/Sft		858
101	12	NEWM	8f Firm		1185
90	1	YARM	8f Gd/Fm		2198*
103	3	NEWC	10f Firm		2339
101	6	GOOD	7f Good		3104
102	2	SAND	8f Good		3469
93	5	YORK	9f Gd/Fm		3726
100	3	YARM	10f Firm		3918
88	9	NEWM	8f Gd/Fm		4211

MOSQUERA 3 ch f £3842

107	3	DEAU	10f Good		3211

MOSS ROSE 4 ch f £0

0a	11	LING	10f Aw		1
0a	14	LING	10f Aw	45	102

MOSSY MOOR 3 ch f £10715

76	5	GOOD	9f Gd/Sft		1481
83	3	GOOD	8f Gd/Sft		1811
89	1	KEMP	8f Gd/Fm	83	2084*
76	7	NEWM	8f Gd/Sft	89	2614
90	4	KEMP	8f Firm	89	2870
94	2	SAND	8f Good	89	3435
88	6	DONC	8f Firm	93	3897
88	3	ASCO	8f Good	92	4113

MOST RESPECTFUL 7 ch g £380

39a	4	SOUT	7f Aw		249 t
48a	3	SOUT	7f Aw	53	304 t
32a	9	SOUT	7f Aw	51	368 t
15a	8	SOUT	7f Aw	48	476 t

MOST SAUCY 4 br f £816

77	3	NOTT	8f Gd/Fm	77	3115
0	14	SAND	7f Soft	79	4204
0	20	YORK	7f Heavy	78	4302

MOST STYLISH 3 ch f £1428

64	5	WIND	8f Heavy		934
64a	2	SOUT	8f Aw		1204
64	3	SOUT	7f Soft		1607
66	4	YARM	10f Gd/Fm	66	1955
64	4	BEVE	10f Gd/Fm	65	2484
38a	6	SOUT	11f Aw	64	2945
59	4	SALI	10f Gd/Sft	62	4169
0	15	PONT	10f Soft	62	4374

MOSTABSHIR 2 b c £0

0	14	DONC	7f Heavy		4566

MOT JUSTE 2 b f £3620

89	1	YARM	8f Gd/Fm		3969*

MOTET 6 b g £0

59	10	ASCO	16f Good	77	2173 bl

MOTHER CORRIGAN 4 gr f £7702

8	9	THIR	7f Soft		930
58	1	REDC	7f Firm	54	1297* VIS
37	9	HAMI	8f Gd/Fm	60	1360 vis
0	15	AYR	7f Gd/Fm	57	1631 vis
0	14	PONT	6f Good	57	1869 BL
0	11	REDC	6f Gd/Fm	55	2158 vis
46	8	NEWC	6f Gd/Fm	55	2275 vis
0	22	YORK	6f Good	54	2697 vis
20	12	NEWC	6f Good	51	3037 vis
33	9	REDC	7f Firm	51	3328 vis
0a	12	SOUT	7f Heav	48	4153 vis

MOTHER MOLLY 3 b f £440

67	3	CATT	7f Soft		4005

MOTTO 2 b f £0

65	6	DONC	6f Heavy		4576

MOUJEEDA 3 ch f £1077

65	5	LING	10f Gd/Sft		1281
74	9	NEWM	10f Gd/Fm		1697
65	4	NEWB	10f Firm	69	2811
69	3	THIR	12f Gd/Fm	68	3125
63	3	LING	11f Firm		3754

MOULOUYA 5 gr m £0

62	8	YORK	10f Firm		1325

MOUNT ABU 3 b c £58429

101	4	NEWM	7f Good		955
113	1	ASCO	6f Gd/Sft		1111*
112	1	LING	6f Good		1674*
111	6	LONG	7f Good		2226
105	3	DEAU	6f Gd/Sft		3724
111	1	GOOD	7f Soft		4078*
94	7	NEWM	7f Good		4352

MOUNT LOGAN 5 b h £0

34a	8	LING	13f AW		4193

MOUNT MCKINLEY 3 ch c £0

63	7	LING	7f Firm		3834
54	6	HAYD	7f Soft		4093

MOUNT PARK 3 b f £2404

1a	8	SOUT	6f Aw		472
0a	11	SOUT	8f Aw		869
30a	9	WOLV	7f Aw		1038
27a	10	SOUT	6f Aw	53	1205
24a	10	WOLV	6f Aw	48	1391 BL
38a	6	SOUT	8f Aw	48	1419 bl
0	13	SOUT	8f Soft	65	1606
0	13	THIR	8f Gd/Fm	58	2060 bl
0	12	REDC	8f Gd/Fm	58	2147 bl
0	15	BEVE	7f Gd/Fm	50	2479
22	11	LEIC	6f Gd/Fm	50	2511 bl
0	17	RIPO	6f Gd/Fm	44	2839
49	1	REDC	5f Gd/Fm	44	2864* bl
37	8	THIR	5f Good	50	2969 bl
44	5	DONC	5f Gd/Fm	50	3161 bl
0	17	THIR	5f Gd/Fm	55	3349 bl
23	13	CATT	7f Soft	49	4004 bl
0	24	WIND	6f Gd/Sft	47	4293 bl

MOUNT ROYALE 2 ch c £0

52	7	PONT	5f Gd/Sft		1102
0	13	DONC	7f Good		3156
0	11	HAYD	8f Soft		3766
42	10	NOTT	6f Soft	61	3976

MOUNT VERNON 4 b c £0

0a	9	WOLV	12f Aw		626 t

MOUNTAIN DANCER 3 b f £4785

77	6	BEVE	10f Good		1447
73	3	CARL	9f Firm		2019
71	1	DONC	12f Gd/Fm		2353*

MOUNTAIN GREENERY 2 b f £0

61	17	ASCO	5f Good		2088

MOUNTAIN MAGIC 5 b m £0

0a	11	WOLV	9f Aw	42	405 bl

MOUNTRATH ROCK 3 b f £2094

0	23	RIPO	10f Soft	60	827
0	11	BEVE	12f Heavy	58	978
0	13	BEVE	10f Firm		1274 VIS
51	4	NOTT	8f Gd/Sft	53	1365 vis
41	4	RIPO	8f Good		1596 vis
26	9	PONT	8f Good		1865 BL
51	1	NOTT	8f Gd/Fm	47	2187* vis
38	5	NOTT	8f Gd/Fm		3004 bl
29	6	LEIC	8f Gd/Fm		3094 bl
42	6	BATH	8f Gd/Fm	49	3816 vis
37	5	YARM	11f Firm		3917 vis

MOURAMARA 3 b f £28818

112	1	LONG	13f Good		4236*

MOUSEHOLE 8 b g £6388

62	12	THIR	5f Soft	75	926
58	10	KEMP	5f Soft	74	1013
0	21	THIR	5f Good	72	1162
50	10	LING	5f Good	70	1398
57	8	CATT	5f Good	67	1662
68	2	NOTT	5f Good	64	1871
54	8	SALI	5f Firm	64	2022
72	2	WIND	5f Good	66	2716
71	1	SAND	5f Gd/Fm	66	2925*
60	8	SAND	5f Good	70	3436
57	8	YARM	5f Good	70	3668
60	10	YARM	5f Firm	69	3920
0	15	BATH	5f Soft	68	4432

MOUTON 4 b f £0

45a	5	LING	10f Aw		314
22a	10	LING	8f Aw		353
28a	5	LING	6f Aw		399
0a	9	LING	7f Aw	45	439
10	13	WIND	10f Gd/Fm	55	746
0	16	BRIG	7f Gd/Sft	49	896
0	13	SALI	10f Good		1344
19	6	LING	5f Soft	37	1543
0	11	WIND	8f Gd/Fm	40	2051
23	11	GOOD	8f Gd/Fm	38	2124
29	8	GOOD	7f Good	48	2303

MOVING EXPERIENCE 3 b f £235

57	7	LING	7f Gd/Sft		1263
55	4	HAMI	8f Gd/Sft	62	3380
53	7	GOOD	10f Good	59	3663
53	6	LEIC	8f Gd/Sft		4032
35	7	BATH	8f Soft	56	4143

MOWASSEL 2 b c £19000

97	2	CURR	6f Good		2400

MOWBRAY 5 br g £5329

97 5 NEWB 13f Gd/Fm 1401
98 6 EPSO 12f Good 100 1850
96 9 ASCO 12f Good 99 2069
98 4 YORK 14f Good 97 2695
99 4 GOOD 14f Gd/Fm 97 3058
89 13 YORK 14f Gd/Fm 97 3565
100 3 SALI 14f Firm 3751 bl
89 13 DONC 15f Firm 98 3890
103 5 HAYD 14f Soft 4091 VIS
84 11 NEWM 12f Good 97 4342 bl

MOWELGA 6 ch g £13003
99 1 NEWM 12f Gd/Sft 93 968*
86 7 NEWB 13f Gd/Fm 1401
103 2 DONC 12f Firm 99 3896
77 9 ASCO 12f Gd/Sft 99 4128

MOY 5 ch m £2257
46a 2 WOLV 6f Aw 44 466 bl
23a 6 SOUT 6f Aw 46 557 bl
34a 8 WOLV 7f Aw 46 582 bl
35a 5 WOLV 5f Aw 46 614 bl
45a 3 WOLV 7f Aw 44 635 bl
19a 9 WOLV 7f Aw 680 bl
9a 10 WOLV 7f Aw 44 711 bl
30 2 MUSS 5f Gd/Sft 28 901 bl
25a 9 WOLV 6f Aw 42 1201 bl
33a 5 WOLV 6f Aw 40 1391 VIS
0 17 REDC 6f Gd/Sft 32 1578 vis
52 5 MUSS 5f Firm 1688 vis

MOYNE PLEASURE 2 b f £1757
26 11 NOTT 6f Soft 3973
72a 5 WOLV 6f Aw 4246
77a 1 WOLV 6f Aw 4379*

MOZART 2 b c £246850
101 1 CURR 7f Good 2407*
112 1 NEWM 7f Good 4158*
113 4 NEWM 7f Good 4354

MR ACADEMY 4 b c £5379
104 2 MAIS 15f Soft 1897

MR BERGERAC 9 b g £0
66a 5 SOUT 7f Aw 73 35
57a 5 WOLV 9f Aw 70 119
38a 6 WOLV 9f Aw 67 172 bl
0 B BATH 8f Gd/Fm 64 1442
20 11 GOOD 8f Gd/Sft 64 1473

MR BOUNTIFUL 2 b c £0
69 7 CARL 5f Firm 2277
0 16 YORK 6f Good 2692
59 8 NEWC 8f Good 3245

MR CHRISBI 3 b g £0
0 18 NOTT 6f Firm 1266
0 10 LEIC 8f Soft 1548

MR COMBUSTIBLE 2 b c £1220
77 7 NEWM 7f Good 2563
83 2 PONT 8f Good 4086

MR COSPECTOR 3 b c £4043
74 1 HAYD 7f Heavy 992*
59 9 DONC 8f Gd/Sft 71 1053
42 8 CARL 9f Gd/Sft 70 1722
67 4 HAYD 11f Soft 70 1819
40 10 PONT 10f Firm 67 2175
0 18 PONT 10f Soft 65 4374

MR CUBE 10 ch h £3088
23a 8 WOLV 8f Aw 42 254 bl
36a 9 LING 6f Aw 313 bl
25a 8 SOUT 7f Aw 341 bl
31a 6 WOLV 6f Aw 396 bl
27a 7 LING 7f Aw 36 503 bl
44 1 BRIG 7f Firm 39 1336* bl
40 7 WARW 8f Heavy 44 1520 bl
41 4 SOUT 7f Soft 1603 bl
39 3 MUSS 7f Good 1685 bl
35 5 RIPO 8f Good 1858 bl

35 5 RIPO 8f Gd/Fm 41 2099 bl
39 2 FOLK 6f Gd/Fm 2291 bl
39 4 WARW 8f Good 40 2460 bl
32 7 BRIG 7f Firm 2907 bl
35 8 THIR 6f Gd/Fm 40 3144 bl
24 11 BRIG 7f Firm 3559 bl
26 10 CHEP 8f Good 3868 bl
24 9 BRIG 8f Gd/Fm 4122 bl

MR ED 2 ch c £0
0 20 WIND 6f Gd/Fm 1876

MR FORTYWINKS 6 ch g £12757
62 2 HAMI 13f Good 60 845
54 9 HAMI 13f Gd/Fm 62 1194
53 4 HAMI 13f Gd/Fm 61 1363
60 1 NEWC 12f Heavy 1767*
61 3 RIPO 12f Gd/Fm 60 2109
60 4 DONC 15f Gd/Fm 60 2319
62 1 REDC 14f Gd/Sft 59 4222*
57a 4 SOUT 14f Aw 70 4370
54 8 DONC 15f Gd/Sft 62 4451
62 2 DONC 17f Heavy 63 4579

MR GEORGE SMITH 3 b c £3581
54a 3 LING 7f Aw 57 112
61a 1 LING 7f Aw 54 149*
65a 3 LING 6f Aw 60 242
0 15 WIND 8f Heavy 61 933

MR KIPLING 2 ch c £0
0 12 CHEP 7f Good 3866

MR MAHOOSE 2 b c £702
74 3 NOTT 5f Gd/Sft 4503

MR MAJICA 6 b g £0
25a 8 SOUT 8f Aw 686 bl
24a 9 SOUT 8f Aw 869 bl

MR MORIARTY 9 ch g £0
3a 7 SOUT 16f Aw 30 737 t
25 6 RIPO 12f Gd/Fm 30 2109 t

MR NEVERMIND 10 b g £0
0 17 DONC 8f Heavy 43 4573

MR PERRY 4 br c £1391
0 17 DONC 10f Gd/Fm 57 705
32 7 HAMI 9f Good 53 846
54 2 MUSS 8f Gd/Sft 53 899
56 3 MUSS 7f Good 54 1149 BL
28 11 HAMI 8f Gd/Fm 54 1190 bl
46 11 MUSS 7f Gd/Fm 54 1431 VIS
40 9 CATT 7f Soft 52 1680 bl
38 6 CATT 7f Good 50 2932
17 12 AYR 9f Gd/Fm 50 3141 vis
0 16 CATT 7f Good 45 3440 vis
33 8 HAMI 8f Gd/Sft 45 3534
30 8 REDC 8f Gd/Fm 43 4499
35 6 DONC 8f Heavy 43 4573

MR PERTEMPS 2 b c £1156
44 15 RIPO 5f Soft 821
48a 6 SOUT 6f Aw 1503
34 9 NEWC 7f Good 2521
50 2 HAMI 5f Soft 45 3802

MR PIANO MAN 2 gr g £450
75 3 PONT 5f Good 2360
64 9 DONC 6f Gd/Fm 2608
75 5 CATT 8f Good 2926
68 9 PONT 5f Firm 3500

MR ROUGH 9 b g £439
29a 7 SOUT 8f Aw 50
26a 5 SOUT 8f Aw 38 83 vis
53a 2 WOLV 8f Aw 138 vis
0a 11 SOUT 8f Aw 252 vis
15a 9 WOLV 8f Aw 322 vis

MR SPEAKER 7 ch g £0
35a 5 WOLV 8f Aw 48 431
0a 11 SOUT 8f Aw 48 496
23a 8 LING 10f Aw 43 620

0 20 LEIC 7f Firm 61 3839
0 12 BEVE 10f Sft/Hv 58 4046
28 11 DONC 8f Heavy 55 4573

MR SPECULATOR 7 ch g £565
47a 3 WOLV 15f Aw 174 tbl
0a 11 WOLV 12f Aw 47 260 tbl
40a 5 WOLV 15f Aw 47 277
49a 3 WOLV 12f Aw 307
39a 4 WOLV 12f Aw 347 bl
35a 6 WOLV 12f Aw 42 410 bl

MR SQUIGGLE 2 b c £0
57 8 AYR 6f Gd/Fm 1628
40a 6 SOUT 6f Aw 2635
40 6 THIR 8f Gd/Sft 3779

MR STICKYWICKET 3 b c £0
0a 14 SOUT 5f Aw 127
0a 12 WOLV 7f Aw 362
29a 8 SOUT 6f Aw 558
0a 11 SOUT 5f Aw 51 674
23a 6 SOUT 6f Aw 59 689
30a 7 SOUT 5f Aw 41 870 VIS
0 13 BEVE 7f Heavy 47 976 vis
60 6 REDC 7f Gd/Sft 1134 BL
0 15 THIR 7f Gd/Fm 32 3129
0 13 NEWM 7f Good 3612

MR STYLISH 4 b g £11286
0 19 DONC 6f Gd/Sft 71 1074
71 2 BATH 6f Gd/Fm 68 1438
71 3 GOOD 6f Gd/Fm 68 1636
71 3 CHEP 6f Good 70 1971
0 15 GOOD 6f Gd/Fm 70 2124
71 5 GOOD 6f Good 70 2355 VIS
44 9 LEIC 7f Gd/Fm 2508 vis
66 5 BATH 6f Firm 70 2944 t
61 3 BATH 6f Firm 3208 t
71 3 BATH 6f Gd/Fm 69 3516 tvi
54 9 NEWM 6f Good 69 3613 tvi
75 1 BEVE 6f Good 3956* tvi
72 7 YORK 6f Soft 4287 tvi
76 1 BATH 5f Soft 70 4432+ tvi

MR TOD 2 b g £0
0a 12 WOLV 7f Aw 3496
50a 6 WOLV 7f Aw 4025
0a 15 SOUT 7f Aw 4154
36a 8 WOLV 6f Aw 4244
0 17 DONC 6f Gd/Sft 4449

MR UPHILL 2 b g £0
0 14 WARW 15f Gd/Fm 3911
45a 6 SOUT 7f Aw 4154 VIS

MRS JODI 4 b f £0
31 10 CATT 16f Soft 52 4258
0 10 NEWC 16f Heavy 47 4424

MRS MITCHELL 2 ch f £0
24 6 YARM 6f Good 3028
47 7 MUSS 5f Gd/Fm 3589
39a 10 WOLV 5f Aw 4227
16a 9 SOUT 7f Aw 4369

MRS P 3 b f £0
93 16 NEWM 5f Gd/Fm 1172
0 9 LEOP 5f Yldg 1757
0 18 NEWM 5f Good 4182

MRS PERTEMPS 2 ch f £642
51 10 PONT 5f Good 2360
67 3 CARL 5f Firm 2821
72 4 BATH 5f Firm 3205

MRS TIGGYWINKLE 2 b f £542
49a 6 WOLV 5f Aw 1136
63a 4 SOUT 5f Aw 1304
44 10 CATT 5f Good 1659
46 7 MUSS 5f Good 62 3101
50 10 BATH 6f Firm 3205
48a 6 WOLV 6f Aw 4246

MU TADIL 8 ch g £0 (preceding entries)

		Course	Dist	Going		No.	
0	20	NEWM	6f	Good		4345	BL
51a	2	WOLV	8f	Aw		4362	
51a	6	WOLV	6f	Aw		4548	bl

MU TADIL 8 ch g £0

		Course	Dist	Going		No.	
0	15	SALI	14f	Firm	57	1180	
34	10	LING	16f	Good	40	1394	
41	9	CHEP	18f	Gd/Sft	51	1800	
27	10	BATH	17f	Firm	37	1996	
31	6	CHEP	18f	Gd/Fm	38	2490	
29	7	BATH	17f	Firm	37	2941	
23a	4	WOLV	15f	Gd/Fm	27	3276	
11	8	PONT	17f	Soft	38	4231	
20a	11	SOUT	14f	Aw	38	4371	

MUAKAAD 3 b c £31570

		Course	Dist	Going		No.	
105	3	LEOP	10f	Gd/Fm		1314	
0	14	CHAN	12f	V		1752	
109	3	CURR	8f	Good		3554	t
113	1	LEOP	10f	Good		3924*	tBL

MUBTAKER 3 ch c £7364

		Course	Dist	Going		No.	
100	1	NEWB	10f	Sft/Hv		4474*	
96	3	DONC	12f	Heavy		4578	

MUCH ADO 3 b f £0

		Course	Dist	Going		No.	
47	11	LING	8f	Soft		4273	
59	6	YARM	7f	Soft		4388	

MUCHANA YETU 3 b f £0

		Course	Dist	Going		No.	
61	8	SALI	10f	Firm	70	1177	
52	6	SAND	10f	Soft	68	1585	
59	9	LEIC	12f	Gd/Sft	68	1736	
57	6	WIND	12f	Gd/Fm	61	2210	
51	5	BATH	12f	Gd/Sft	59	2554	
51	8	SALI	12f	Gd/Fm	57	3290	
49	5	FOLK	16f	Gd/Fm	63	3588	
30	6	BATH	8f	Soft	48	4143	BL

MUCHEA 6 ch h £22398

		Course	Dist	Going		No.	
93	10	DONC	8f	Good	100	733	
103	2	NEWM	7f	Gd/Sft	100	966	
100	2	WARW	7f	Heavy		1004	
97	7	ASCO	7f	Gd/Sft	101	1110	
107	5	LONG	7f	Good		1617	VIS
102	4	HAYD	7f	Gd/Sft		1834	vis
76	17	ASCO	8f	Good	101	2090	vis
83	14	ASCO	7f	Gd/Fm	100	2997	vis
95	4	GOOD	7f	Firm		3155	vis
101	1	GOOD	7f	Good	96	3648*	
101	2	GOOD	7f	Good	98	3902	
84	18	ASCO	7f	Good	98	4112	
94	5	YORK	7f	Soft	100	4278	
96	8	NEWM	7f	Good	99	4357	

MUCHO GUSTO 2 b c £0

		Course	Dist	Going		No.	
0	12	LING	7f	Gd/Fm		2182	
48	5	CHEP	6f	Gd/Fm		2447	

MUD N BERT 2 b f £0

		Course	Dist	Going		No.	
0	12	THIR	7f	Gd/Fm		3127	
0	11	AYR	8f	Soft		3957	
0	11	NEWC	7f	Heavy		4403	

MUDAA EB 4 br c £7600

		Course	Dist	Going		No.	
107	2	CURR	9f	Gd/Sft		4059	

MUDDY WATER 4 b f £3169

		Course	Dist	Going		No.	
23a	9	LING	8f	Aw		353	
57	1	FOLK	6f	Soft	52	958*	
49	7	WARW	8f	Soft	60	1066	
46a	7	WOLV	7f	Good	48	1235	
48a	3	SOUT	8f	Aw	47	1303	
48a	2	SOUT	8f	Aw	47	1419	
46	5	SAND	10f	Soft	50	1570	
0	15	NEWM	8f	Gd/Fm	60	2130	
26a	7	SOUT	7f	Aw	48	2637	

MUFFIN MAN 3 b c £220

		Course	Dist	Going		No.	
0	17	WIND	8f	Gd/Fm	66	744	
0	15	WIND	6f	Firm	63	1289	
0	17	NEWB	7f	Gd/Fm	58	1787	
48	4	CHEP	6f	Gd/Fm	53	2489	
35	6	LING	7f	Good	53	2591	
41	7	EPSO	6f	Gd/Fm	49	3405	
50	4	BRIG	7f	Firm		3739	
30	12	EPSO	7f	Good	47	3765	

MUFFLED 3 ch f £5624

		Course	Dist	Going		No.	
41a	7	WOLV	9f	Aw		1388	
42	10	BRIG	7f	Firm	64	2044	
64	2	LEIC	6f	Gd/Fm	60	2511	
0	15	RIPO	6f	Gd/Fm	64	2839	
44	8	FOLK	6f	Gd/Fm		3587	
64	1	THIR	6f	Gd/Sft		3780*	

MUGHARREB 2 b c £1138

		Course	Dist	Going		No.	
94	3	NEWM	6f	Good		4341	

MUHTATHIR 5 ch h £225235

		Course	Dist	Going		No.	
118	4	SHA	8f	Good		184	
118c	3	NAD	8f	Dirt		764	
119	1	SAN	8f	Good		1460*	
113	6	ASCO	8f	Good		2064	
125	1	DEAU	8f	Gd/Fm		3544*	
119	5	WOOD	8f	Firm		3933	

MUJA FAREWELL 2 ch f £17196

		Course	Dist	Going		No.	
79	1	REDC	5f	Gd/Sft		1130*	
81	2	THIR	5f	Good		1385	
81	2	REDC	5f	Gd/Sft		1558	
83	1	WIND	5f	Good		2055*	
74	9	HAYD	5f	Gd/Sft	83	3475	
85	1	NEWM	5f	Good	81	4179*	

MUJAALED 3 b g £0

		Course	Dist	Going		No.	
6	12	BEVE	7f	Gd/Fm		3670	
0	10	YARM	11f	Firm		3917	

MUJADO 2 b f £8130

		Course	Dist	Going		No.	
93	2	NEWM	6f	Gd/Fm		2618	
94	2	ASCO	6f	Gd/Fm		2952	
91	1	WIND	6f	Good		3187*	
75	11	DONC	6f	Gd/Fm		3862	

MUJAGEM 4 br f £4040

		Course	Dist	Going		No.	
33	13	REDC	5f	Gd/Sft	48	1133	
47a	1	SOUT	8f	Aw	44	1303*	
47a	4	SOUT	8f	Aw	50	1419	
37	6	SOUT	7f	Soft	48	1606	
32a	10	SOUT	8f	Gd/Fm	47	2121	BL
49a	2	SOUT	5f	Aw	46	2632	bl
36	7	THIR	6f	Gd/Fm	45	2969	
0	14	HAMI	6f	Gd/Sft	43	3377	bl
38	3	HAMI	5f	Gd/Sft	40	3825	bl
46a	5	SOUT	5f	Aw	51	4153	bl

MUJAHID 4 b c £3850

		Course	Dist	Going		No.	
111	3	NEWM	9f	Gd/Fm		967	
105	5	SAND	8f	Heavy		1043	

MUJALIA 2 b c £0

		Course	Dist	Going		No.	
40	9	GOOD	5f	Gd/Sft		1454	
0	13	KEMP	7f	Firm		2867	
70	11	GOOD	7f	Firm		3154	
0	15	GOOD	8f	Soft	60	4076	
0	14	LING	6f	Soft		4188	

MUJALINA 2 b c £3615

		Course	Dist	Going		No.	
42	10	DONC	7f	Gd/Fm		1844	
67	2	MUSS	7f	Gd/Fm		2201	
72a	1	SOUT	7f	Aw		2383*	
92	8	NEWM	7f	Gd/Fm		2613	
55	7	BEVE	7f	Gd/Fm		3409	
0	18	DONC	7f	Firm	79	3901	
57	10	WARW	7f	Gd/Fm	79	3913	BL
55	6	DONC	7f	Heavy	68	4577	

MUJAS MAGIC 5 b m £8750

		Course	Dist	Going		No.	
48a	7	WOLV	7f	Aw	59	121	vis
64a	1	WOLV	7f	Aw	58	187*	vis
65a	2	SOUT	6f	Gd/Fm	63	280	vis
60a	4	SOUT	7f	Aw	63	299	vis
56a	4	SOUT	8f	Aw	63	430	vis
57a	7	SOUT	6f	Gd/Fm	63	499	vis
63a	2	SOUT	6f	Aw	61	557	vis
43a	7	SOUT	7f	Aw	61	588	vis
49a	5	SOUT	7f	Aw	62	739	vis
38a	10	WOLV	6f	Aw	61	1233	vis
27	8	LEIC	8f	Firm	50	2032	vis
45	5	NOTT	6f	Gd/Fm	48	2192	vis
30	12	DONC	7f	Gd/Fm	48	2320	vis
52	1	YARM	6f	Gd/Fm	48	2415*	vis
45	7	LING	6f	Good	52	2654	vis
41	9	LEIC	6f	Gd/Fm	52	2777	vis
51	2	NEWB	6f	Firm	51	3455	vis
35	12	PONT	5f	Firm	51	3502	vis
0	13	NEWM	6f	Good	51	3613	vis
40	8	NEWM	6f	Gd/Fm	51	3631	vis

MUJKARI 4 ch c £1275

		Course	Dist	Going		No.	
32a	9	WOLV	7f	Aw	41	323	vis
22a	8	WOLV	8f	Aw		393	vis
16a	9	LING	7f	Aw	37	504	vis
0	15	BRIG	7f	Firm	41	1335	vis
33	8	BRIG	7f	Soft	39	2427	vis
32	4	CHEP	8f	Gd/Fm	39	2658	vis
27	7	BRIG	7f	Gd/Fm	36	2729	vis
23	10	WARW	7f	Gd/Fm	36	2840	vis
40	2	CHEP	6f	Gd/Fm	36	2974	vis
26	3	CHEP	8f	Gd/Fm	38	3251	vis
31	7	THIR	8f	Gd/Fm	36	3344	vis
19	11	EPSO	7f	Good	36	3765	vis

MUJODA 3 b f £0

		Course	Dist	Going		No.	
0	17	NOTT	6f	Gd/Sft		1081	

MUKAABED 3 b c £1464

		Course	Dist	Going		No.	
81	2	FOLK	6f	Gd/Fm		2294	
79	3	NEWM	6f	Gd/Fm		2807	

MUKARRAB 6 br g £7768

		Course	Dist	Going		No.	
73a	9	WOLV	5f	Aw	85	64	
0a	16	SOUT	5f	Aw	83	129	
77a	6	WOLV	5f	Aw	81	191	
56a	10	WOLV	6f	Aw	79	258	
75a	4	WOLV	5f	Aw	76	394	
74a	3	LING	5f	Aw	75	506	
63a	6	WOLV	5f	Aw	74	1140	
40	11	HAMI	5f	Gd/Fm	50	1358	
53	1	THIR	5f	Gd/Sft	48	1714*	
33	11	CARL	6f	Firm	52	2015	
31	11	THIR	7f	Gd/Fm	52	2063	
52	4	NEWC	5f	Firm	52	2340	
51	4	HAYD	5f	Gd/Fm	51	2505	
51	4	HAYD	5f	Gd/Fm	51	2701	
47	5	CATT	5f	Gd/Fm	51	2743	
39	11	THIR	5f	Gd/Fm	51	3619	
44	8	WIND	5f	Gd/Sft	49	4295	
49	2	NEWC	5f	Heavy	48	4407	

MUKHALIF 4 ch c £7000

		Course	Dist	Going		No.	
90	9	CAPA	10f	Gd/Fm		1321	
101	4	ASCO	12f	Gd/Fm		3306	

MUKHLLES 7 b h £0

		Course	Dist	Going		No.	
0	17	DONC	12f	Gd/Fm	50	699	
42	7	LING	11f	Good	50	1743	
0	P	KEMP	12f	Gd/Fm	47	2081	

MULL OF KINTYRE 3 b c £33263

		Course	Dist	Going		No.	
108a	4	GULF	9f	Fast		19	

MULLAGH HILL LAD 7 b g £0

		Course	Dist	Going		No.	
19a	7	WOLV	8f	Aw		612	

MULLAGHMORE 4 b c £8272

		Course	Dist	Going		No.	
68a	1	LING	8f	Aw		353*	bl
51a	5	LING	10f	Aw	63	400	bl
71a	1	LING	10f	Aw	63	620*	bl
57a	5	LING	10f	Good	57	880	bl
44	5	LING	9f	Good	57	1395	bl
0	17	KEMP	8f	Gd/Fm	55	1926	bl
0	13	WIND	8f	Good	54	2367	VIS
38	12	BRIG	10f	Gd/Fm	52	2727	bl
46	5	WIND	8f	Good	47	3188	
51	1	BATH	8f	Firm	46	3623*	

52	3	SALI	8f Firm	52	3753	
44	8	BEVE	8f Good	52	3951	

MULLING IT OVER 2 b f £1146
71	3	LEIC	5f Gd/Sft		1737	
46	7	RIPO	6f Gd/Fm		2106	
47	7	CATT	7f Gd/Fm		2417	
39	11	YARM	7f Firm	57	3922	
48	3	AYR	6f Heavy	55	4305	

MULSANNE 2 b c £0
18	7	HAMI	6f Gd/Fm	2778
0	15	BATH	5f Firm	3204
0	11	SALI	7f Gd/Fm	3388
25	8	WIND	5f Good	3639
6	12	NOTT	6f Heavy	4410

MULTI FRANCHISE 7 ch g £0
15	8	LEIC	12f Good	38	791	
0	11	WIND	12f Gd/Fm		1880	vis

MUMBAI 4 b c £0
0a	10	SOUT	11f Aw	1417

MUMBLING 2 ch c £0
0	15	NEWM	7f Good	4183
0	18	NEWM	8f Good	4349

MUMMY NOSE BEST 4 b f £0
25a	10	LING	7f Aw	243

MUNADIL 2 ch c £1200
81	6	NEWM	8f Good	4161
92	3	NEWM	8f Good	4349

MUNASIB 5 br g £0
0a	13	SOUT	7f Aw	43	75	BL

MUNEEFA 3 b f £6608
79	2	YARM	7f Gd/Fm		1951	
75	2	SALI	6f Gd/Fm		2977	t
81	1	YARM	6f Firm		3919*	t

MUNGO DUFF 5 b g £0
0	9	LEIC	10f Gd/Sft	65	1575

MUNGO PARK 6 b g £20000
72	2	NEWC	5f Soft	71	758	
53	14	THIR	6f Gd/Sft	73	1356	
74	3	SALI	5f Firm	71	2022	
61	9	SALI	5f Gd/Fm	74	2266	
74	2	BEVE	5f Gd/Fm	73	2517	bl
76	2	NEWC	5f Good	73	2525	
76	2	HAYD	5f Gd/Fm	73	2701	bl
77	2	AYR	5f Firm	75	2877	bl
76	5	ASCO	5f Gd/Fm	77	3341	bl
84	1	BEVE	5f Good	77	3398*	
69	16	YORK	6f Good	83	3543	bl
0	18	DONC	6f Gd/Fm	83	3861	
74	12	NEWM	6f Good	83	4015	
39	12	NEWC	6f Heavy	81	4405	

MUNIR 2 ch c £5551
77	3	BATH	6f Soft	4137
93	1	NEWB	6f Sft/Hvy	4470*

MUNJIZ 4 b c £0
76	10	NEWM	6f Gd/Fm	2615

MUQTADI 2 b c £5532
91	2	NEWM	7f Firm	3298
87	1	GOOD	7f Good	3650*

MUQTARB 4 ch c £0
0	18	KEMP	6f Good	90	728	
75	8	NOTT	6f Good	85	1871	t

MURAWWI 3 b c £5865
107	1	NAAS	7f Yldg	1751*	bl
87	14	ASCO	7f Good	2087	bl

MURCHAN TYNE 7 ch m £472
49	9	NOTT	14f Good	58	788
42a	7	WOLV	16f Aw	55	918
49	5	DONC	10f Gd/Sft	50	1050
35a	7	SOUT	11f Aw	49	1306
50	4	WARW	15f Heavy	48	1524
48	3	LEIC	12f Gd/Sft	48	1736
22	7	DONC	15f Gd/Fm	49	2319
38	6	WARW	15f Good	49	2461
12	14	HAYD	12f Good	47	3284

MURGHEM 5 b g £152425
103c	2	SOUT	12f Aw	100	695	
96	2	DONC	12f Good		732	
94	4	NEWB	16f Soft	100	917	
106	2	GOOD	14f Gd/Sft	99	1484	
110	1	EPSO	12f Good	104	1850*	
113	1	LEIC	12f Firm		2028+	
113	1	NEWM	12f Firm		2341*	
114	1	GOOD	12f Gd/Fm	110	3134*	
115	2	ASCO	12f Good		3306	
113	1	NEWB	13f Gd/Fm		3483*	
108	4	TABY	12f Good		3931	
111	6	WOOD	12f Firm		4400	

MURJAN 3 ch c £0
61	5	LEIC	12f Gd/Sft		832
46	7	SOUT	12f Soft	75	1604
70	4	FOLK	9f Gd/Fm	70	3043
60	7	LING	11f Firm	70	3282

MURRENDI 2 b c £3069
79	5	SALI	7f Good		2686
75	8	SAND	7f Gd/Fm		2921
84	5	GOOD	7f Firm		3154
80	4	EPSO	7f Gd/Fm		3412
81	2	BATH	8f Gd/Fm	80	3817
80	3	PONT	8f Soft		4086

MURRON WALLACE 6 gr m £0
1a	7	WOLV	9f Aw	44	359
0a	12	WOLV	9f Aw	38	469
19a	10	SOUT	8f Aw		869
35	8	WARW	11f Good		3691
0	15	LEIC	8f Gd/Sft		4032

MUSADIF 2 ch c £0
0	R	THIR	8f Gd/Fm	3779

MUSALLIAH 3 ch f £273
71	7	GOOD	8f Gd/Sft		1811	
66	4	YARM	8f Gd/Fm		2198	
47	8	RIPO	10f Gd/Fm		3012	
0	14	SALI	10f Gd/Fm	65	3390	VIS

MUSALLY 3 ch c £3142
82	4	NOTT	8f Gd/Sft		1084
84	1	NEWC	10f Gd/Sft		1480*
70	8	GOOD	10f Gd/Fm	85	2358
57	15	KEMP	10f Gd/Fm	83	3794
55	7	PONT	10f Soft	80	4085

MUSALSE 5 b g £0
19a	8	WOLV	16f Aw	53	190
36a	7	WOLV	16f Aw	49	328
0	14	NEWC	16f Soft	40	760

MUSCHANA 3 ch f £15836
65	3	BRIG	10f Soft		1466
82	1	WIND	10f Gd/Fm	73	2053*
81	7	SAND	10f Gd/Fm	83	2499
82	3	GOOD	9f Gd/Fm	81	3089
90	1	EPSO	10f Gd/Fm	82	3415*
90	5	NEWM	10f Good	89	4197
90	2	LONG	9f Heavy		4489

MUSH 3 b c £3886
77	2	PONT	8f Firm		3506
76	1	WARW	8f Gd/Fm		3914*
0	26	NEWM	8f Good	76	4340

MUSIC MAID 2 b f £9184
56	6	SALI	6f Gd/Fm	1883
84	1	LING	7f Gd/Fm	2182*
78	3	SALI	6f Gd/Sft	2469
64	12	SAND	7f Gd/Fm	2935
57	9	ASCO	8f Gd/Fm	3304
85	1	EPSO	7f Good	3688*
68	11	REDC	6f Gd/Sft	4219
60	10	NEWB	7f Sft/Hvy	4467

MUSICAL FRUITS 3 b f £0
0	18	SALI	7f Good		1349
0	15	NOTT	10f Soft	33	1644

MUSICAL HEATH 3 b c £6723
78	4	KEMP	8f Firm		2871	t
78	2	NOTT	8f Gd/Fm		3116	t
77	2	EPSO	9f Gd/Fm		3413	t
79	1	EPSO	9f Good		3764*	t
67	8	AYR	8f Gd/Sft	78	4013	t

MUSICIAN 4 b f £7174
81	11	NEWM	12f Firm	94	1187
95	2	YORK	14f Good	94	2695

MUSKETRY 4 b c £0
0a	11	WOLV	16f Aw	36	194	BL
14a	6	LING	12f Aw		267	bl
7a	6	SOUT	11f Aw		369	bl

MUST BE MAGIC 3 b c £4699
54	14	NEWM	8f Firm	69	1183	
56	6	SAND	7f Soft	66	1569	
62	3	NOTT	10f Good	63	2007	
58a	4	LING	10f Aw	61	2186	
58	3	DONC	10f Good	61	2579	
66	1	EPSO	9f Good	61	2795*	VIS
0	13	HAYD	10f Gd/Fm	67	3288	vis
19a	11	WOLV	9f Aw	67	4251	vis
65	6	NEWM	8f Gd/Sft	67	4536	

MUSTANG 7 ch g £3199
43a	4	LING	7f Aw	46	59	
43a	5	LING	7f Aw	46	106	
43a	3	SOUT	8f Aw	44	209	
43a	3	SOUT	8f Aw		252	bl
24a	10	LING	8f Aw		316	bl
8a	12	WOLV	8f Aw	41	404	bl
41a	2	WOLV	8f Aw	41	431	bl
37a	5	WOLV	8f Aw		517	vis
0a	12	WOLV	9f Aw	41	675	vis
41	3	PONT	8f Gd/Sft	39	1101	vis
18	13	REDC	8f Firm	40	1300	vis
31	6	YARM	8f Good	40	1772	bl
44	1	BRIG	8f Firm		2040*	bl
0	11	WARW	8f Good	45	2460	vis
32a	5	LING	10f Aw		2587	bl
42	4	BRIG	8f Firm		2892	vis
20	5	CHEP	8f Gd/Fm	42	3251	vis
0	18	THIR	8f Gd/Fm	42	3344	vis
32	9	BRIG	7f Firm		3559	vis

MUTABARI 6 ch g £1744
46a	8	SOUT	7f Aw	59	35	vis
4a	10	LING	7f Aw	59	58	vis
50a	3	WOLV	8f Aw	54	255	
52a	4	SOUT	7f Aw	54	326	
57a	2	SOUT	7f Aw	53	368	
32a	5	WOLV	8f Aw	53	411	
47a	3	SOUT	7f Aw	55	476	vis
0a	11	SOUT	6f Aw	53	587	vis
44a	4	SOUT	7f Aw	53	599	
0a	13	SOUT	16f Aw	50	644	
27	10	LEIC	7f Gd/Sft	52	834	vis
38	4	PONT	8f Gd/Sft	44	1101	
41	7	REDC	8f Firm	43	1296	
28	6	LEIC	6f Soft	42	1545	
36	5	YARM	8f Good	42	1772	
24a	10	SOUT	7f Aw	50	1979	
0	16	BEVE	7f Aw	40	2221	
33	6	RIPO	10f Soft		2538	vis
25	8	YARM	7f Firm	40	2899	vis

MUTABASSIR 6 ch g £5439
58	6	BRIG	8f Firm	65	1330
54	5	BRIG	7f Soft		1467
58	4	CHEP	7f Gd/Sft	62	1799
61	3	LING	8f Gd/Fm	60	2185
52	8	GOOD	8f Gd/Fm	60	2356

(continued)

63	2	BRIG	8f Gd/Fm	59	2726
54	5	SAND	8f Good	62	3227
64	1	**BRIG**	8f Firm	60	3527*
65	5	GOOD	8f Good	65	3885
53	9	BRIG	7f Gd/Sft	64	4121

MUTADARRA 7 ch g £4907

45a	4	WOLV	9f Aw		292
6a	10	WOLV	9f Aw		360
0a	12	WOLV	9f Aw		477
34a	8	WOLV	16f Aw	52	576
55	11	NOTT	10f Gd/Sft	65	1370
53	2	WIND	12f Gd/Fm		1880
45	5	HAYD	12f Gd/Fm		2457
57	1	**WIND**	10f Soft	52	2544*
48	9	BRIG	12f Gd/Fm	54	2727
56	2	BATH	12f Firm		2785
26	11	GOOD	12f Good	59	3657
51	7	WARW	11f Gd/Fm	54	3915

MUTAFAWEQ 4 b c £470313

119	3	CURR	11f Gd/Sft		1625
111	7	ASCO	12f Good		2149
122	1	**DUSS**	12f Good		2911*
95	8	BADE	12f V		3849
108	3	CURR	14f Good		4055
122	1	**WOOD**	12f Firm		4400*

MUTAHADETH 6 ch g £2013

47a	4	SOUT	6f Aw	61	183	bl
39a	11	SOUT	6f Aw	61	212	bl
54a	3	LING	7f Aw		243	bl
55a	2	SOUT	8f Aw	57	297	bl
46a	5	SOUT	8f Aw	57	329	bl
48a	6	SOUT	7f Aw	58	418	bl
31a	7	SOUT	7f Aw	57	471	bl
53a	3	WOLV	7f Aw	55	583	bl
50a	4	SOUT	8f Aw	55	598	bl
51a	4	SOUT	8f Aw	54	647	bl
45a	4	SOUT	8f Aw	53	669	bl
30a	6	WOLV	7f Aw	52	721	bl
27	9	SOUT	7f Good	44	803	bl
50a	4	SOUT	7f Aw	50	867	bl
47a	4	SOUT	7f Aw	49	1207	bl
32a	7	WOLV	8f Aw	48	1393	bl

MUTAMADEE 2 ch c £0

0	12	WIND	6f Gd/Fm		2209
63	10	BRIG	7f Soft		4415

MUTAMAM 5 b g £75428

104	2	NEWM	10f Gd/Fm		1174
112	1	**GOOD**	12f Gd/Sft		1474*
112	4	ASCO	12f Good		2149
117	1	**KEMP**	12f Gd/Fm		3792+
118	1	**ASCO**	12f Good		4109*

MUTARASED 2 b c £4887

71	8	LEIC	7f Firm		3840
90	1	**BRIG**	7f Soft		4172*
92	2	REDC	7f Gd/Sft		4500

MUTASADER 3 b f £0

81	5	BEVE	10f Good		1447
59	9	CHEP	10f Gd/Sft		1796
58	6	BATH	10f Soft		4141

MUTASAWWAR 6 ch g £2852

44	5	BRIG	6f Gd/Sft		1508
42	7	CARL	5f Gd/Sft	45	1724
36	8	BATH	6f Firm	43	1994
32	9	CHEP	5f Gd/Fm	41	2976
36	4	LING	6f Firm	39	3493
92	8	NOTT	5f Good		3521
38	9	WARW	5f Good		3694
50	2	LEIC	5f Gd/Sft	48	4027
47	2	GOOD	5f Soft	43	4065
56a	2	SOUT	6f Aw	55	4155
24	11	WIND	5f Gd/Sft	49	4294
12	15	NEWC	5f Heavy	48	4407
32	14	NEWB	5f Gd/Sft	48	4459

MUTAWAQED 2 ch c £0

0	20	DONC	7f Gd/Sft		4446

MUTED GIFT 2 ch f £0

0	17	LING	6f Firm		3832

MUTHAABER 2 br c £1165

79	5	NEWB	7f Firm		3999
83	2	YARM	7f Soft		4389

MUWAKALL 3 b c £3713

60a	3	LING	8f Aw	65	266
65a	3	CAGN	10f Aw		606
88	4	BRIG	10f Gd/Fm		1127
81	5	NOTT	14f Gd/Sft		1369
79	5	EPSO	10f Gd/Sft	83	1831
81	3	KEMP	12f Firm	80	2263
71	3	EPSO	10f Gd/Sft		2434

MUYASSIR 5 b g £17010

69	8	WIND	10f Firm		1288
82	1	**KEMP**	8f Gd/Fm	74	1926*
84	1	**GOOD**	9f Good	79	2304*
84	3	NEWB	9f Firm	82	2853
80	5	GOOD	8f Gd/Fm	83	3063
75	5	EPSO	9f Good	83	3685

MY ALIBI 4 b f £18165

60a	1	**SOUT**	8f Aw	56	692*
58a	2	SOUT	7f Aw	56	739
22	6	WIND	8f Gd/Sft	56	1097
64a	1	**SOUT**	8f Aw		2118*
66a	2	SOUT	7f Aw	61	2637
69a	1	**SOUT**	6f Aw	61	2820*

MY AMERICAN BEAUTY 2 ch f £8597

46	6	NEWC	6f Firm		2333
66	8	DONC	6f Gd/Fm		2608
64	3	RIPO	6f Gd/Fm		2835
72	1	**YORK**	6f Good	65	3807*
59	7	AYR	6f Soft	70	3987
56	12	NEWM	6f Gd/Fm	69	4214

MY BOLD BOYO 5 b g £289

31a	10	LING	8f Aw	61	169	
54a	4	LING	10f Aw		268	bl
47a	4	LING	12f Aw	56	441	bl
30a	11	LING	10f Aw	54	618	bl
43	5	FOLK	10f Soft	60	965	
39	13	WIND	8f Gd/Fm	57	1201	
23	11	YARM	7f Aw	54	2899	bl
0	14	BATH	8f Firm	47	3623	bl

MY BROADSTAIRS JOY 4 b g £0

8a	11	SOUT	7f Aw		341

MY BROTHER 6 b g £3250

40	1	**GOOD**	6f Gd/Fm	38	2124*
33	5	NEWM	7f Firm	40	2347

MY DARLING DODO 4 b f £0

31a	9	WOLV	9f Aw	48	60
23a	8	WOLV	8f Aw	42	233
30a	7	WOLV	12f Aw		295

MY DESPERADO 7 b m £0

46a	6	SOUT	11f Aw	67	343

MY DILEMMA 4 b f £0

0a	10	WOLV	8f Aw	35	411

MY EMILY 4 b f £5671

72	2	LING	7f Good	72	1672
67	1	**SALI**	7f Gd/Fm		1884*
69	6	KEMP	7f Firm	72	2261
54	7	EPSO	6f Gd/Fm	70	2631
0	24	ASCO	7f Gd/Fm	68	2999
69	2	LING	6f Firm	65	3493
63	2	EPSO	6f Good		3689
54	6	SAND	6f Gd/Fm		3947
44	11	LING	7f Good	68	4102
63a	2	LING	7f Aw		4328

MY FRIEND JACK 2 b c £265

68	5	KEMP	5f Soft		993
49	9	BATH	5f Good		1088
64	6	SAND	5f Gd/Fm		2933
38	10	BATH	5f Gd/Fm		3513
62a	3	LING	5f Aw		4333

MY HANSEL 3 b f £16120

100	9	YORK	10f Gd/Fm		1309
98	1	**NEWC**	8f Gd/Fm		2274+
91	11	GOOD	7f Good		3104
74	9	SAND	8f Good		3469

MY LAST BEAN 3 gr g £310

79	5	BATH	10f Good		1093
74	4	BATH	12f Soft		4434

MY LEGAL EAGLE 6 b g £10359

41a	7	WOLV	12f Aw	53	43
39a	5	WOLV	12f Aw	47	81
39a	3	SOUT	11f Aw	41	126
43a	2	WOLV	16f Aw	41	141
26a	7	WOLV	16f Aw	42	170
42a	4	WOLV	16f Aw	42	194
17a	12	WOLV	16f Aw	42	318
38a	3	SOUT	16f Aw	40	428
45a	2	WOLV	16f Aw	40	482
39a	2	WOLV	12f Aw	38	522
42a	2	WOLV	16f Aw	40	552
57	2	NOTT	14f Good	53	788
59	2	WARW	15f Heavy	55	885
62	1	**NOTT**	14f Heavy	57	1023*
63	3	SAND	16f Heavy	62	1044
66	6	CHES	12f Firm	65	1251
0	14	YORK	15f Firm	65	1329
60	6	WARW	15f Heavy	64	1524
0	15	WARW	16f Gd/Sft	62	1711
52	8	CHES	16f Gd/Fm	60	3511
50	4	WARW	16f Good	63	3695
39	10	WARW	16f Good	51	3916
40	5	CHES	16f Soft	51	4071
31	4	PONT	17f Soft	41	4231
22	8	NOTT	16f Heavy	39	4508

MY LINE 3 b c £0

18	11	RIPO	10f Gd/Fm		3012
33	9	REDC	9f Firm		3326
39	13	PONT	8f Firm		3506
0	15	CATT	12f Soft	45	4256

MY LITTLE MAN 5 b g £0

0	19	GOOD	10f Good	48	3663
0	18	SALI	8f Firm	48	3753

MY LOVELY 2 b f £6059

62	1	**WIND**	5f Good		3639*
86	1	**BEVE**	5f Sft/Hvy		4042*

MY LUCY LOCKET 2 b f £9901

76	3	WARW	5f Heavy		1522
79	3	WIND	5f Good		1727
77	2	BATH	5f Firm		1995
85	1	**CHES**	5f Good	80	2665*
80	7	KEMP	5f Firm	89	2868
79	5	WIND	6f Good		3638
70	12	NEWM	6f Good	81	4179
82	2	DONC	7f Soft	79	4460

MY MAN FRIDAY 4 b c £0

25	11	WIND	8f Good	47	2367
35	7	CHEP	7f Aw	43	2974
33	6	SALI	7f Gd/Fm	39	3294

MY PETAL 4 gr f £0

0	12	LING	7f Gd/Sft		838	
0	16	BATH	6f Gd/Fm	64	1438	BL

MY PLACE 2 b f £1244

64	3	FOLK	5f Gd/Fm		3039
62	8	HAYD	7f Good		3287
75	4	YORK	8f Soft		4281
63	6	BATH	8f Soft		4429

MY PLEDGE 5 b m £5959

58	2	KEMP	12f Gd/Fm	55	1927

60	1	KEMP	12f Firm	56	2263*
49	9	SAND	11f Good	58	2530
60	3	WIND	12f Gd/Fm	58	3049
55	4	WIND	12f Good	58	3353
58	4	FOLK	12f Gd/Fm	58	3586
47	9	KEMP	14f Gd/Fm	58	3800 E

MY RETREAT 3 b c £7976

80	1	WARW	8f Heavy		884*
31	11	KEMP	9f Gd/Sft	82	1075
62	12	YORK	10f Gd/Fm	80	1310
68	5	AYR	11f Gd/Fm	77	1633
46	11	BATH	8f Firm	73	2330
58	5	BRIG	8f Firm	69	2906 BL
72	2	NOTT	8f Heavy	64	4414
76	1	MUSS	8f Soft	70	4565*

MY TESS 4 b f £17157

70a	1	WOLV	8f Aw	64	78*
72a	4	WOLV	7f Aw	70	143
66a	4	WOLV	9f Aw	70	309
65a	5	WOLV	7f Aw	70	364
73a	2	SOUT	8f Aw	68	430
75a	2	SOUT	8f Aw	70	513
75a	1	SOUT	7f Aw	70	588*
73a	3	WOLV	7f Aw	74	721
64	2	HAYD	7f Gd/Sft	61	811
51	4	THIR	8f Soft	63	931
67	2	NOTT	6f Gd/Sft	63	1082
66	5	REDC	7f Firm	67	1297
0	13	LEIC	8f Sft/Hvy	67	4310

MY TYSON 5 b g £1970

41a	6	SOUT	6f Aw	68	183
37a	12	SOUT	7f Aw	68	212
35a	9	SOUT	7f Aw		341
32a	8	WOLV	7f Aw	50	583
33a	7	LING	10f Aw	50	620
50a	1	WOLV	8f Aw	44	676*
47a	3	WOLV	8f Aw	49	718
25	6	HAMI	9f Good	44	846
0a	12	SOUT	8f Aw	49	1207
0	26	REDC	8f Firm	41	1296
31	10	MUSS	8f Gd/Fm	38	2533
28	10	CATT	6f Gd/Fm		2744 BL
0	21	THIR	6f Gd/Fm	34	3144 t

MY VERY OWN 2 ch c £2545

0	16	KEMP	6f Gd/Fm		1924
57a	6	WOLV	7f Aw		3497
72	2	YORK	7f Gd/Fm		3729
80a	2	WOLV	8f Aw		4249
0	16	NEWM	8f Good	79	4350

MYAHSMONT 5 ch g £0

26a	11	WOLV	9f Aw		1388

MYBOTYE 7 br g £4872

0a	16	SOUT	7f Aw	52	69 t
0a	12	WOLV	7f Aw	44	187 tbl
37	4	CATT	7f Gd/Fm		778 t
52	1	REDC	7f Gd/Sft		1132* t
43	9	MUSS	7f Gd/Fm	48	1431 t
60	1	CATT	7f Soft		1681* t
0	19	NOTT	6f Gd/Fm	58	2193 t
0	13	BEVE	7f Gd/Fm	58	3652 t
7	7	NEWC	7f Heavy	56	4426 t

MYHAT 2 ch f £5171

66	2	GOOD	6f Gd/Fm		1634
73	2	WIND	6f Gd/Fm		2209
72	3	WIND	6f Good		2369
82	2	WIND	6f Good		2714
70	6	NEWB	6f Gd/Fm	80	3175
82	5	SALI	6f Firm		3749
52	11	GOOD	6f Good	78	3886 BL
0	13	BRIG	7f Soft		4172
62	10	WIND	6f Gd/Sft		4288

MYLANIA 4 b f £0

50	6	YARM	7f Gd/Sft	62	1611
54	7	NOTT	10f Good	61	2011

MYNAH 3 b f f £18502

0	16	NEWM	8f Firm		1188
86	1	NEWM	10f Firm		1857*
89	2	PONT	10f Firm		2178
89	2	NEWM	10f Gd/Fm	89	2805
94	1	ASCO	10f Gd/Fm	89	3339*
85	5	NEWC	10f Good	93	3703

MYSTERI DANCER 2 b c £2063

57	7	EPSO	6f Gd/Fm		3400
82	2	LING	6f Firm		3832
82	2	LING	6f Soft		4188
69a	3	WOLV	6f Aw		4381

MYSTERIUM 6 gr g £18111

53a	1	WOLV	9f Aw	41	67*
49a	2	LING	10f Aw	47	102
41a	4	SOUT	11f Aw	50	131
34a	10	LING	10f Aw	49	203
51a	2	WOLV	9f Aw	47	305
53a	1	WOLV	9f Aw	49	383*
55a	2	WOLV	9f Aw	52	469
35a	4	WOLV	9f Aw	53	569
43a	7	WOLV	9f Aw	52	637
35	10	WARW	11f Gd/Fm	44	2033
31a	8	LING	10f Aw	51	2212
47	2	LING	10f Good	42	2655
40	5	YARM	11f Firm	42	2771
52	1	WIND	12f Gd/Fm	45	3049*
56	1	NEWM	12f Gd/Fm	52	3314*
43a	7	WOLV	9f Aw	58	3495
40	8	YORK	10f Gd/Fm	58	3731
42	10	EPSO	12f Good	58	3858
48a	3	WOLV	12f Aw	52	4026
55a	1	WOLV	12f Aw	50	4386*

MYSTIC GEM 4 ch g £0

0a	8	SOUT	12f Aw		556
0	13	NEWC	7f Soft		759
0a	10	WOLV	9f Aw		922

MYSTIC RIDGE 6 ch g £2235

38a	9	LING	8f Aw	66	96
0a	13	WOLV	6f Aw	62	175
57a	4	SOUT	8f Aw	60	329
65a	1	SOUT	7f Aw	58	476*
40	11	BRIG	8f Gd/Sft	73	895
0	20	ASCO	6f Gd/Sft	72	1113
70	4	LING	7f Soft	70	1542
0	13	CHEP	7f Gd/Sft	69	1794
52	8	EPSO	7f Gd/Sft	67	2431
49	6	LING	6f Firm	65	2761
45	12	KEMP	7f Gd/Fm	63	3362
23	12	MUSS	8f Gd/Fm	60	3745
58a	4	WOLV	8f Aw	64	4248

MYSTICAL STAR 3 b g £0

74	6	SAND	10f Good		2531

MYSTICAL WISDOM 3 b f £0

0a	13	WOLV	8f Aw		1234
24a	7	SOUT	11f Aw		1502
0	17	CHEP	7f Good		1972

MYSTIFY 3 b f £15572

90	1	REDC	7f Gd/Sft		1134*
91	5	GOOD	8f Gd/Sft		1485
101	2	ASCO	8f Good	90	2167
98	2	ASCO	8f Good	95	4113

MYTHICAL JINKS 2 b c £0

68	5	YARM	6f Gd/Fm		2414
79	6	SAND	7f Gd/Fm		2921
76	6	DONC	7f Gd/Fm		3156
70	8	DONC	7f Firm	79	3901

MYTHICAL KING 3 b c £8878

79	3	BATH	10f Gd/Fm		1439
79	3	LEIC	10f Gd/Sft	78	1735
85	1	GOOD	10f Gd/Sft	78	1812*
81	4	LEIC	10f Firm		2030
83	2	CHES	10f Good	81	2666
59	9	ASCO	10f Gd/Fm	83	2955
58	10	DONC	10f Gd/Fm		3865

MYTHOLOGICAL 3 £0

97	5	CURR	10f Soft		1899

MYTTONS AGAIN 3 b g £7204

68a	6	LING	8f Aw	77	158 bl
3a	11	SOUT	8f Aw	74	213
59a	4	SOUT	7f Aw	70	416
31a	7	WOLV	6f Aw	67	638
0	18	DONC	7f Good	75	736
68	2	LEIC	6f Gd/Sft		830 bl
73	6	CHES	8f Gd/Fm	75	1215 bl
54	6	REDC	7f Gd/Sft		1579
47	5	CHES	6f Gd/Fm		1780
44	10	CATT	7f Gd/Fm	64	2438
50	7	CHES	8f Gd/Fm	60	2673 bl
56	6	AYR	7f Gd/Fm	60	2719 bl
59	3	AYR	7f Gd/Fm	57	3138 bl
61	1	AYR	7f Good		3364* bl
71	1	MUSS	7f Gd/Fm	65	3593* bl
49	6	BRIG	7f Firm		3739 bl
69	4	EPSO	7f Good	70	3854 bl
59	7	AYR	8f Gd/Sft	70	4013 bl
47a	8	WOLV	8f Aw	65	4248
0	20	DONC	8f Gd/Sft	69	4452 bl
39	12	DONC	8f Heavy	67	4573 bl

MYTTONS MISTAKE 7 b g £6667

37a	8	LING	8f Aw	58	96
33	11	WARW	8f Soft	49	1066
50	2	NOTT	6f Firm	49	1273
48	2	BRIG	7f Firm	47	1335
47	4	DONC	7f Good	51	1519
51	2	CHEP	7f Gd/Sft	50	1799
57	1	WARW	8f Gd/Fm	51	2257*
52	3	CHEP	8f Gd/Fm	56	2492
51	6	KEMP	7f Gd/Fm	56	2749
50	6	KEMP	8f Gd/Fm	55	3362
48	6	CHEP	7f Good	54	3873

MYTTONS MOMENT 4 b g £218

56a	3	SOUT	8f Aw	51	85 bl
43a	4	WOLV	8f Aw	50	255 bl
43a	4	SOUT	11f Aw	50	324 bl
45a	5	WOLV	16f Aw	46	552 bl
23a	5	WOLV	12f Aw	47	562 bl
0	16	PONT	10f Gd/Fm	51	2556 bl

NABADHAAT 3 b f £433

79	4	WIND	8f Gd/Fm		745
63	10	NEWB	10f Gd/Fm	76	1785
59	4	BRIG	12f Gd/Sft		4119

NADDER 5 ch g £1295

42a	7	WOLV	7f Aw		65
26a	8	WOLV	8f Aw		229
45a	2	WOLV	7f Aw	50	276 BL
26a	5	WOLV	7f Aw		293 bl
0a	10	WOLV	7f Aw	48	364 bl
43a	3	WOLV	6f Aw		1137 bl
0	13	HAMI	6f Firm		1239 VIS
42a	2	SOUT	6f Aw	40	1422
0	16	REDC	6f Gd/Sft	32	1578
18a	7	SOUT	6f Aw	43	2297
20	11	CATT	6f Gd/Fm		2744 vis
0	18	YORK	10f Soft		4275

NADOUR AL BAHR 5 b h £0

97	6	ASCO	12f Good		4109
100	5	NEWB	12f Sft/Hv		4469

NAFISAH 2 ch f £10525

87	2	NEWM	7f Gd/Fm		3459
87	2	SALI	7f Firm		3752
92	1	KEMP	7f Soft		4035*

99	2	NEWM	7f Gd/Fm			4210
88	5	NEWB	7f Sft/Hvy			4467

NAFITH 4 ch c £4290

52a	3	WOLV	8f Aw			308
52a	2	WOLV	9f Aw			378
52a	1	**WOLV**	9f Aw			446*
52a	3	WOLV	9f Aw	51		516
48	7	WIND	8f Good	57		854
50	6	WIND	10f Gd/Sft	55		1100
18	12	NOTT	10f Gd/Sft	52		1364

NAILER 4 b c £0

55	6	LEIC	12f Gd/Sft		832
0	14	BEVE	16f Firm	58	1276
32	8	LEIC	12f Soft	50	1551

NAISSANT 7 b m £8436

45	5	HAMI	6f Good	56	844
39	10	HAMI	6f Gd/Fm	54	1192
35	8	BEVE	7f Firm	51	1275
47	6	HAMI	5f Gd/Fm	51	1358
46	3	NEWC	5f Gd/Sft	48	1479
43	9	AYR	7f Gd/Fm	48	1631
47	4	CARL	5f Gd/Sft	48	1724
48	2	BEVE	7f Gd/Sft	48	1760
43	5	HAMI	6f Firm	48	1941
48	3	HAMI	6f Firm	48	2097
41	5	CARL	7f Gd/Fm	47	2241
48	3	PONT	6f Good	49	2364
54	1	**HAMI**	6f Gd/Fm	48	2641*
54	2	HAMI	6f Gd/Fm	52	2796
40	9	THIR	6f Gd/Fm	54	2969
39	7	CARL	7f Gd/Fm	54	3083
46	3	CARL	7f Firm		3197
38	9	HAMI	6f Gd/Sft	53	3377
30	14	HAMI	5f Gd/Sft	52	3536

NAJ DE 2 ch c £0

82	5	GOOD	6f Good	3881

NAJEYBA 3 ch f £5075

67	1	**SOUT**	6f Soft		1605*
77	3	PONT	6f Firm		2177
80	4	DONC	6f Gd/Fm	77	2577
59	12	NEWM	7f Gd/Fm	77	3163
72	8	EPSO	7f Gd/Fm	77	3414
52	11	KEMP	6f Gd/Sft	75	4037
0	16	PONT	5f Soft	73	4377

NAJJAR 5 gr g £0

0	15	HAMI	8f Gd/Fm	57	1190

NAJJM 3 br c £5827

65	6	WARW	12f Soft	79	1064
70	5	RIPO	12f Good	77	1862
82	1	**RIPO**	12f Gd/Fm	73	3013*
74	4	NEWB	13f Firm	81	3454
81	5	GOOD	16f Good	81	3905

NAJMAT JUMAIRAH 3 b f £0

52	6	GOOD	9f Gd/Fm		2129
60	5	BATH	12f Firm		2327
62	9	HAYD	11f Gd/Fm		2703
27	13	BRIG	10f Firm	57	2908

NAKED OAT 5 b g £1943

29a	8	SOUT	9f Aw	64	329
36a	9	WOLV	9f Aw	60	469
39a	7	WOLV	9f Aw	56	516
34a	8	SOUT	11f Aw	56	561
31a	7	SOUT	8f Aw		686
0	13	PONT	8f Heavy		942
32	9	WARW	8f Soft	45	1066
52	1	**BRIG**	10f Gd/Fm		1933*
48	6	BRIG	10f Gd/Fm		2423
0	17	BRIG	10f Gd/Fm	52	2727
28	8	YARM	10f Good		3234
0	11	RIPO	8f Gd/Fm		3711
49	6	THIR	8f Gd/Fm		3775
36	6	BRIG	8f Gd/Sft		4122

NAKWA 2 b c £0

42	9	HAYD	5f Heavy	989
33	9	CHES	7f Firm	3169

NAMID 4 b c £127556

109	3	CURR	7f Yldg	862
110	1	**CORK**	6f Good	1232*
115	2	**CURR**	6f Gd/Sft	1622*
120	1	**LEOP**	5f Good	3923*
125	1	**LONG**	5f Good	4261*

NAMLLAMS 2 b c £0

61	7	AYR	6f Gd/Fm	1653
63	7	RIPO	5f Gd/Fm	2100
75	5	YORK	6f Good	2692

NANCYS BOY 2 b g £178

48	8	NEWC	6f Heavy	4402
46	9	MUSS	7f Soft	4517
76	4	MUSS	7f Soft	4559

NAPIER STAR 7 b m £432

44a	2	WOLV	6f Aw		1137	t
31a	6	WOLV	6f Aw	44	1233	t
0	12	HAMI	5f Gd/Fm	33	1910	t
34	4	HAMI	6f Gd/Fm	33	1941	t
19	15	THIR	6f Gd/Fm	33	3144	t
0	16	CATT	7f Gd/Fm	33	3200	t

NAPPER BLOSSOM 3 b f £0

0	14	WIND	8f Heavy		934
0	15	SALI	6f Gd/Fm		1181
0	14	SALI	7f Gd/Fm		1884
0	17	WIND	12f Gd/Fm	43	2887
0	18	BRIG	10f Firm	40	3737

NARJIS FLOWER 2 b f £0

6	8	PONT	10f Soft	4230
44a	6	WOLV	9f Aw	4438

NASHAAB 3 b c £525

73	5	NEWM	7f Gd/Fm	2860
69	5	WIND	8f Gd/Fm	3048
75	3	PONT	8f Gd/Fm	3221

NASHIRA 2 ch f £3376

82	3	BATH	6f Gd/Sft	1667
80	1	**BATH**	5f Firm	1993*
0	16	REDC	6f Gd/Sft	4219

NASMATT 2 b f £12590

90	3	GOOD	6f Gd/Fm	3090
94	3	YORK	6f Gd/Fm	3568
93	1	**YARM**	6f Firm	3938*
91	4	NEWM	7f Gd/Fm	4210
93	2	DEAU	6f Heavy	4488

NATALIE JAY 4 b f £13362

59	3	LEIC	8f Gd/Sft	65	831
0	13	THIR	8f Soft	64	931
63	4	KEMP	9f Gd/Sft	62	2581
63	3	WIND	8f Gd/Fm	62	2890
48	10	GOOD	9f Good	62	3110
70	1	**SALI**	8f Gd/Fm	62	3422*
62	7	WIND	8f Good	69	3643
67	6	SALI	7f Firm	69	3750
67	3	AYR	10f Soft	69	3989
68	3	BRIG	10f Gd/Sft	67	4118
73	1	**LEIC**	8f Sft/Hvy	67	4310*
73	3	REDC	7f Gd/Sft	71	4498
83	1	**DONC**	8f Heavy	71	4573*

NATION 2 b c £2086

85	2	NEWM	7f Good	3608
85	3	WARW	7f Gd/Fm	3909

NATIONAL ACADEMY 5 b h £7529

99	2	DIEL	12f Good	4148

NATIONAL ANTHEM 4 b c £29308

105	1	**NEWM**	10f Gd/Fm	96	1170*
106	4	ASCO	12f Good	103	2069
106	4	NEWM	12f Firm		2341
106	1	**EPSO**	10f Good		3684*
106	2	GOOD	10f Good		3903

NATIONAL DANCE 3 b g £4629

65a	1	**SOUT**	8f Aw		328*
67a	4	LING	10f Aw		420
69a	2	SOUT	8f Aw	67	540

NATIONAL PRINCESS 3 br f £0

64	13	NEWM	8f Firm	1188
54	6	LEIC	8f Soft	1548

NATIVE FORCE 2 b f £0

77	11	DONC	8f Gd/Sft	4445

NATIVE TITLE 2 b c £268

86	5	NEWM	7f Gd/Fm	3121
81	4	SALI	7f Gd/Fm	3391

NATSMAGIRL 3 b f £818

42a	5	SOUT	6f Aw	74		VIS
37a	8	WOLV	7f Aw		192	vis
45	5	CATT	6f Gd/Fm	51	1665	
23	10	CARL	6f Gd/Fm	48	2243	
31a	5	WOLV	6f Aw	45	2603	
39	6	NEWC	7f Good	44	3033	
47	2	CARL	6f Firm	44	3194	
49	4	AYR	7f Good		3364	
34	6	BRIG	8f Gd/Fm	46	3561	

NATURAL 3 b c £972

70	10	SALI	8f Good		1181
64	6	WARW	7f Heavy		1525
65	2	NOTT	8f Good	62	2013
56	7	NOTT	10f Gd/Fm	64	2685

NATURAL EIGHT 6 b g £4764

23a	6	SOUT	16f Aw	50	51
53a	1	**LING**	13f Aw	42	168*
39a	6	LING	16f Aw	51	424
53	3	KEMP	14f Good	52	726
52	3	FOLK	15f Soft	53	963
55	3	NOTT	14f Good	53	1411
54	5	NEWB	13f Gd/Sft	58	1594
0	B	ASCO	20f Good	59	2092

NAUGHTY KNIGHT 2 ch c £5093

0	12	WIND	5f Good		849
52	5	NOTT	5f Heavy		1019
47a	7	WOLV	5f Good		1236
67	1	**BEVE**	5f Good		1443*
65	1	**LEIC**	5f Soft		1549*
57	3	DONC	5f Gd/Fm	63	2575
47	5	LEIC	6f Gd/Fm	64	2773
21	9	CHES	6f Firm	60	3168
0	13	PONT	6f Soft	55	4235
0	14	NEWC	5f Heavy	53	4423

NAUTICAL LIGHT 3 b f £0

0	16	WIND	10f Good	850

NAUTICAL STAR 5 b g £0

84	13	NEWM	12f Gd/Sft	94	968
71	14	NEWM	12f Firm	94	1187
79	10	EPSO	12f Good	91	1850
54	7	NEWM	12f Gd/Fm	89	3461
40	9	EPSO	12f Good	86	3686
44	9	NEWM	12f Good		4178

NAUTICAL WARNING 5 b g £15639

78a	1	**LING**	8f Aw	69	96*	t
80a	2	WOLV	7f Aw	75	143	t
85a	1	**LING**	7f Aw	77	337*	t
82a	4	LING	7f Aw	83	462	t
0a	14	LING	10f Aw		690	t
0	14	WIND	6f Gd/Sft	55	4293	t

NAVAL AFFAIR 3 b f £2630

101	4	NEWM	10f Firm		1184
98	6	SAN	11f Good		1459
86	12	NEWM	10f Gd/Fm	101	2596
99	4	YARM	10f Firm		3918

NAVAN PROJECT 6 gr g £0

0	14	HAMI	9f Good	44	846
24	8	PONT	10f Soft		1699
30	6	HAMI	11f Gd/Fm		2800

NAVARRE SAMSON 5 b g £802
35 8 NEWB 16f Firm 69 2812
60 4 EPSO 12f Good 65 3686 t

NAVIASKY 5 b g £3110
68 14 DONC 8f Good 84 733
68 10 SAND 8f Heavy 83 1042
76 9 THIR 8f Good 81 1160
79 4 GOOD 8f Gd/Sft 80 1450
53 10 EPSO 9f Gd/Sft 80 1829
80 4 WIND 8f Gd/Fm 1879
78 6 GOOD 8f Gd/Fm 80 2126
77 6 GOOD 8f Gd/Fm 79 2356
77 3 EPSO 7f Good 2792
77 4 GOOD 8f Gd/Fm 78 3063
62 9 ASCO 8f Gd/Fm 78 3338

NAYEF 2 b c £22926
110 1 NEWB 8f Firm 3983*
119 1 ASCO 8f Heavy 4296*

NEARCTIC LADY 2 gr f £7354
68 4 SALI 5f Firm 2020
73 9 GOOD 6f Gd/Fm 3090
97 1 BATH 5f Gd/Fm 3815*
95a 1 LING 6f Aw 4332*

NEARLY A FOOL 2 b g £21895
91 1 DONC 5f Gd/Fm 700*
89 4 HAMI 5f Good 843
90 3 NEWM 5f Soft 985
82 3 CHES 5f Gd/Fm 1214
91 1 BATH 5f Firm 1995*
82 3 DONC 6f Gd/Fm 2352
89 3 LEIC 5f Gd/Fm 91 2915
90 3 WIND 6f Good 3352
97 3 YORK 5f Gd/Fm 3567
84 10 DONC 5f Firm 3900
95 2 YORK 6f Heavy 4298

NEEDWOOD BLADE 2 ch c £0
54 7 HAYD 5f Soft 3767
27 10 NOTT 6f Soft 3973

NEEDWOOD BRAVE 2 b c £0
0 14 HAYD 8f Soft 3766
72 8 WARW 7f Gd/Fm 3909
56 14 NEWM 8f Good 4161

NEEDWOOD MAESTRO 4 b g £3178
43 5 WARW 11f Heavy 1523
30 7 CATT 12f Gd/Sft 35 1816
0a 9 SOUT 12f Aw 2298 VIS
32 3 HAMI 12f Gd/Sft 32 3531 vis
41 1 HAMI 12f Soft 3804* vis

NEEDWOOD MERLIN 4 b c £0
5a 10 SOUT 8f Aw 50
22a 7 SOUT 12f Aw 84

NEEDWOOD MINSTREL 4 b c £0
22a 10 WOLV 6f Aw 132
15a 8 WOLV 7f Aw 391

NEEDWOOD MYSTIC 5 b m £3185
11a 10 SOUT 12f Aw 48 68
42 4 BRIG 12f Firm 48 1332
0 12 PONT 12f Good 48 1499
0 27 NEWM 12f Firm 45 1852
48 1 CATT 12f Gd/Fm 42 2422*
43 8 HAMI 13f Gd/Fm 48 2643
45 5 CATT 14f Gd/Fm 49 3201
40 10 FOLK 12f Gd/Fm 46 3586

NEEDWOOD SPIRIT 5 b g £2130
52 11 NOTT 14f Heavy 62 1023
62 2 HAYD 14f Gd/Fm 60 1167
54 11 LING 16f Good 62 1394
57 7 WARW 15f Heavy 62 1524
43 9 WARW 16f Gd/Sft 60 1711

NEEDWOOD TRIBESMAN 3 gr c £0
0 19 THIR 6f Soft 909
41a 10 WOLV 7f Aw 1035

55 10 BEVE 5f Firm 1280
31 10 RIPO 6f Good 53 1600
22 12 CARL 6f Firm 50 3194
0 17 LING 6f Aw 44 3578
0 20 YARM 8f Gd/Fm 38 3971

NEEDWOOD TRICKSTER 3 gr c £779
61 8 HAYD 5f Gd/Sft 808 t
71 3 NOTT 5f Heavy 1021 t
69 3 NOTT 6f Firm 1266
60 6 LEIC 5f Gd/Fm 2919
61 7 LING 6f Firm 67 3280
44 10 FOLK 6f Gd/Fm 3587
0 19 BEVE 5f Good 3956
50 6 PONT 5f Soft 60 4087

NEEDWOOD TRIDENT 3 b f £845
0 16 LEIC 7f Good 790
37 5 NOTT 10f Heavy 46 1022
0 17 BEVE 10f Firm 1274
33 7 NEWM 10f Gd/Fm 2284
37 4 NOTT 16f Gd/Fm 37 3112
41 2 THIR 16f Gd/Fm 39 3348
12 9 CARL 17f Firm 34 3575
30a 4 LING 16f Aw 40 4099
5 7 NEWC 16f Heavy 41 4424

NEEDWOOD TROOPER 3 br c £1289
67 4 BEVE 5f Firm 1280
51 4 DONC 5f Gd/Fm 1843
64 3 SAND 5f Good 3229

NEEDWOOD TRUFFLE 3 ch f £0
0 14 WIND 5f Gd/Sft 1f 1427
62 9 GOOD 5f Gd/Fm 75 3135
0 17 RIPO 6f Good 72 3698

NEEDWOOD TRUMP 3 br c £0
0a 10 SOUT 7f Aw 281

NEELA 4 ch f £0
39a 7 LING 6f Aw 25
0a 14 SOUT 7f Aw 53 867
30 12 LING 7f Soft 58 1542
36 11 GOOD 7f Gd/Fm 53 2128

NEERUAM STAR 2 b c £436
57 3 CARL 5f Gd/Sft 1719
0 P HAMI 5f Good 2639

NEGATIVE EQUITY 8 ch g £1517
35a 1 LING 13f Aw 30 460* bl
28a 4 LING 13f Aw 524 bl
5a 10 WOLV 16f Aw 40 576 bl

NEGRONI 3 br f £1130
57 3 WARW 8f Gd/Fm 2846
70 3 NOTT 8f Gd/Fm 3116
50 6 YARM 10f Gd/Fm 3382

NEIGES ETERNELLES 5 b m £0
0a 7 WOLV 16f Aw 74 296

NELSONS FLAGSHIP 2 b c £0
0 17 WIND 6f Gd/Fm 1876
64 8 ASCO 7f Gd/Fm 3015
51 10 KEMP 6f Gd/Fm 3358

NEPTUNE 4 b c £898
27a 8 SOUT 8f Aw 38 85
31a 3 SOUT 12f Aw 35 338
33a 3 WOLV 12f Aw 35 408
30a 2 WOLV 15f Aw 468

NERA ZILZAL 2 b f £0
65 6 LING 5f Firm 3277

NERO TIROL 4 br g £0
51a 7 WOLV 6f Aw 63 232 bl

NERONIAN 6 ch g £3909
28a 6 SOUT 8f Aw 45 vis
0a 14 SOUT 8f Aw 35 83 bl
43a 5 LING 10f Aw 110
11a 6 LING 13f Aw 35 167
19a 4 WOLV 12f Aw 32 554
29a 3 WOLV 8f Aw 30 676

0a 9 WOLV 9f Aw 29 749
37a 5 WOLV 6f Aw 1137
0 11 PONT 8f Good 1498
0 21 NEWM 8f Gd/Fm 38 1690
35 1 BRIG 7f Gd/Fm 33 1930*
22 9 NEWM 7f Firm 36 2347
34 3 BRIG 7f Soft 35 2427
25 9 BRIG 7f Gd/Fm 35 2729
0 22 NEWM 7f Good 4018
50a 5 LING 8f Aw 4272

NESYRED 4 b f £0
37a 8 SOUT 8f Aw 73 557
57a 10 SOUT 6f Aw 73 587
0a 13 SOUT 6f Aw 65 645

NETTA RUFINA 5 ch g £1493
58a 3 SOUT 16f Aw 59 51 vis
61a 2 WOLV 16f Aw 57 135 vis

NETTLES 2 br g £548
34 13 MUSS 5f Gd/Sft 898
0 11 REDC 5f Gd/Fm 1130
54 7 HAMI 5f Gd/Fm 1359 BL
37 7 THIR 6f Gd/Fm 2059 bl
48 6 CATT 7f Gd/Fm 2435
63 2 CATT 7f Good 3438
45 8 NEWC 8f Soft 3706
49 7 MUSS 8f Soft 4564

NEVER DISS MISS 3 b f £7530
64 5 WARW 7f Soft 73 1061
79 1 BEVE 10f Good 71 1448*
78 3 SAND 10f Soft 76 1585
77 2 CHES 10f Gd/Sft 1779
75 5 ASCO 10f Gd/Fm 76 2955
52 13 NEWM 10f Good 75 4160
73 3 WIND 11f Heavy 73 4529

NEVER END 2 b f £3510
83 1 LING 7f Soft 4484*

NEVER FEAR 2 b f £0
8 7 DONC 5f Good 712
0 10 NOTT 5f Good 1870

NEVER PROMISE 2 b f £0
82 7 NEWB 7f Firm 3985
62 8 YARM 7f Soft 4514

NEW ASSEMBLY 3 b f £15750
85 2 NOTT 8f Gd/Fm 1269
85 1 LING 9f Firm 1912*
88 1 NOTT 10f Gd/Fm 82 2190*
102 6 GOOD 10f Firm 3151
98 4 YORK 12f Firm 3595
97 4 NEWM 10f Good 4337

NEW EARTH MAIDEN 3 b f £0
0 11 LING 11f Firm 35 1911
0 14 PONT 12f Good 35 2362

NEW FORTUNE 3 ch f £0
64 8 BATH 10f Good 1093
67 4 WIND 10f Good 1725
41 10 BRIG 10f Good 63 3530
43 12 NEWM 10f Good 58 4160
0 19 YORK 12f Soft 58 4280

NEW IBERIA 3 gr c £1145
66 14 NEWM 8f Firm 1188
63 11 NEWM 8f Gd/Fm 1697
75 2 PONT 10f Gd/Fm 2832

NEW STORY 3 b f £0
110 6 CHAN 11f Gd/Sft 1901
109 6 DEAU 8f Gd/Fm 3544

NEW WONDER 2 b f £1518
61a 3 WOLV 5f Good 1236
57 9 HAYD 5f Gd/Sft 1488
74 4 REDC 6f Good 1893
70 2 RIPO 5f Soft 2539
59 7 THIR 5f Gd/Fm 71 3145
50 3 REDC 6f Firm 3307

NEWRYMAN 5 ch g £0
```
0   16  NEWC  7f Soft            759
10  8   DONC  5f Gd/Fm          1843
0a  12  SOUT  11f Aw            2381
```

NEXT CHAPTER 2 b f £0
```
57  7   KEMP  7f Gd/Fm          3074
```

NIAGARA 3 b c £592
```
74  12  NEWM  7f Gd/Fm    80   1153
63  11  YORK  8f Firm     78   1341
66  3   PONT  10f Gd/Fm        2562
67  6   AYR   10f Good    70   3368
46  10  RIPO  10f Good    68   3702
```

NICANDER 2 b c £0
```
75  12  NEWM  8f Good           4349
```

NICE BALANCE 5 b g £5002
```
0a  11  SOUT  7f Aw      40     69
30a 6   SOUT  8f Aw            252
40a 1   SOUT  8f Aw      35    298*
30a 4   SOUT  8f Aw      35    345
40a 3   SOUT  11f Aw     39    390
46a 1   SOUT  8f Aw      39    418*
32a 5   SOUT  8f Aw      44    473
31a 6   SOUT  8f Aw      44    497
32a 5   SOUT  11f Aw     43    561
34a 3   SOUT  8f Aw      40    648
0   24  REDC  8f Firm    37   1296
18  10  YARM  11f Gd/Sft 36   1614
0a  13  SOUT  7f Aw      39   1801
22a 4   SOUT  8f Aw      37   2121
8a  8   SOUT  11f Aw          2381
```

NICE ONE CLARE 4 b f £22724
```
87  5   ASCO  6f Good    89   2151
94  3   NEWM  7f Gd/Fm   89   2616
90  2   LING  8f Firm         2762
72  15  ASCO  7f Gd/Fm   90   2997
95  2   ASCO  7f Good    90   4112
```

NICELY 4 gr f £0
```
74  9   KEMP  16f Soft   85   1527
77  5   HAYD  16f Gd/Sft 82   1791
68  10  SAND  16f Gd/Fm  79   2498
65  7   CHES  16f Firm   75   2672
40  10  CHES  16f Soft   70   4071
52  7   YORK  14f Heavy  65   4299
44  7   NEWB  16f Gd/Sft 60   4458
69  10  NEWM  16f Gd/Sft 91   4533 BL
```

NICHOL FIFTY 6 b g £621
```
73  4   YORK  12f Gd/Fm  75   3725
0   17  DONC  15f Gd/Sft 74   4451
```

NICHOLAS MISTRESS 4 b f £0
```
22a 9   LING  8f Aw            316
27a 5   WOLV  7f Aw            391
19a 9   WOLV  8f Aw            550
27a 7   WOLV  7f Aw      38    582 vis
0a  11  WOLV  8f Aw      33    676
```

NICIARA 3 b c £5984
```
0a  12  SOUT  8f Aw             48
51a 3   SOUT  6f Aw             74
48a 3   SOUT  8f Aw      50    128
0a  P   SOUT  5f Aw            179
31a 8   SOUT  8f Aw      51    213
34a 7   SOUT  8f Aw            303
57a 5   SOUT  8f Aw            328 BL
47a 3   SOUT  8f Aw            415
49a 2   SOUT  8f Aw      48    451 bl
41a 4   SOUT  8f Aw            500 bl
41a 6   SOUT  11f Aw     49    537 bl
28a 10  SOUT  8f Aw      49    555 VIS
41a 5   SOUT  8f Aw            694 bl
40  7   DONC  10f Good         713
44  10  SOUT  10f Gd/Fm        858
40  4   PONT  12f Heavy        939
38  9   NOTT  14f Gd/Fm  45   1270
```

```
44  3   YARM  16f Gd/Sft       1613
41a 3   SOUT  12f Aw     41   2123 bl
51a 2   SOUT  12f Aw     48   2382 bl
49  3   DONC  17f Gd/Fm  57   2607 bl
45  2   BEVE  16f Firm   43   2734
45  2   BEVE  16f Good   46   2879
37  4   YARM  16f Good   44   3026 bl
37  7   NOTT  16f Gd/Fm  44   3112 bl
27  7   HAYD  16f Gd/Sft 46   3476 bl
22  7   PONT  18f Soft   40   4376
```

NICKLES 5 b g £2446
```
0   17  BATH  5f Good    53   1092
40  6   BATH  5f Firm         2788
49  4   CHEP  5f Gd/Fm   50   2976
35  8   LEIC  5f Gd/Fm   49   3214
55  1   WARW  5f Good         3694*
48  11  YARM  5f Firm    59   3920
42  8   PONT  5f Soft    54   4087
52  11  REDC  5f Gd/Sft       4220
```

NICKS JULE 3 ch f £0
```
28  7   SOUT  6f Soft         1605
0   17  YARM  10f Gd/Fm  52   1955
0   17  LEIC  10f Heavy       4313
```

NICOBAR 3 b c £57960
```
100 3   DONC  8f Good          735
108 1   CHES  8f Gd/Fm   100  1215*
102 6   GOOD  9f Gd/Sft  104  1452
112 11  EPSO  7f Gd/Fm        1830*
102 8   ASCO  7f Good         2087
108 5   ASCO  8f Good         2675
98  11  ASCO  7f Good    110  2997 t
112 1   EPSO  7f Good         3763+
97  9   NEWB  7f Firm         3995
```

NICOL 2 b f £0
```
8a  9   WOLV  6f Aw            3496
```

NICOLAI 3 b c £2447
```
0   13  DONC  8f Good          731
0   17  THIR  6f Soft          909
50  8   NOTT  5f Heavy        1021
33  9   LEIC  8f Gd/Fm    50  3095
45  4   KEMP  9f Gd/Fm    47  3357
51  1   BEVE  10f Gd/Fm   45  3656*
0   15  BEVE  10f Sft/Hv  52  4046
```

NIFTY ALICE 2 ch f £15362
```
75  1   MUSS  5f Gd/Sft       796*
79  2   THIR  6f Good        1161
76  4   THIR  5f Good        1385
75  4   CATT  5f Gd/Sft      1813
79  1   AYR   5f Good        2162*
82  8   NEWB  5f Firm        2849
42  10  MUSS  5f Good     82  3101
83  1   MUSS  5f Gd/Fm    79  3743*
81  8   AYR   5f Soft         3959
81  3   DONC  6f Gd/Sft       4449
```

NIFTY MAJOR 3 b g £3208
```
0   21  THIR  5f Soft     83  926
83  2   CHES  5f Gd/Fm    80  1219
60  11  THIR  5f Good     83  1384
72  11  MUSS  5f Firm     83  1687
62  9   AYR   5f Good     82  2165
64  7   CHES  5f Good     80  2663
58  15  GOOD  8f Gd/Fm    77  3135
71  5   CHES  5f Gd/Fm    74  3512
0   R   HAYD  5f Gd/Sft   72  3788
72  3   AYR   5f Soft     72  3960
0   18  YORK  5f Soft     72  4285
54  12  DONC  5f Heavy    72  4570
```

NIFTY NORMAN 6 b g £9893
```
56a 6   SOUT  5f Aw             71
60a 6   WOLV  5f Aw      70    139 BL
54a 5   SOUT  5f Aw            214 bl
75a 1   WOLV  5f Aw            272* bl
```

```
68a 3   SOUT  6f Aw            279
57a 2   WOLV  5f Aw            379 bl
58a 3   LING  5f Aw            440 bl
54a 6   WOLV  5f Aw            533 bl
51a 3   WOLV  5f Aw            639 bl
47a 4   WOLV  6f Aw            680 bl
53  6   NEWC  5f Heavy    62  1008
54a 3   WOLV  5f Aw            1392
25  8   NEWC  5f Heavy        1766 bl
59  6   RIPO  5f Good     59  1861
63a 1   SOUT  5f Aw      52  2297*
59  3   MUSS  5f Gd/Sft       2535
67  1   FOLK  5f Good     59  2623+
61  5   WIND  5f Good     65  2716
71a 3   SOUT  6f Aw      70  2820
0   16  HAYD  5f Gd/Sft   65  4107
0   15  PONT  5f Soft     63  4377
```

NIGELS CHOICE 8 gr g £0
```
0a  10  SOUT  16f Aw      42   284
16a 7   SOUT  11f Aw      39   390
```

NIGHT ADVENTURE 4 ch g £0
```
0   16  SOUT  7f Good     57  803
0   18  WIND  8f Good     51  854
29  12  BRIG  6f Firm     45  1211
0   11  DONC  6f Gd/Fm    41  2315
32  5   BRIG  7f Gd/Fm    36  2729
26  9   BRIG  6f Firm         2907
0   14  BRIG  7f Firm          3559
```

NIGHT AND DAY 3 ch f £2485
```
50a 3   WOLV  6f Aw            118
66a 2   SOUT  7f Aw            278
63a 2   WOLV  7f Aw            362
51a 3   SOUT  7f Aw            427
16a 11  WOLV  6f Aw            3275 tVl
47  5   YARM  6f Gd/Fm    61   3386
50  4   BRIG  8f Firm     58   3561 vis
45  9   BRIG  10f Firm    56   3737 tvi
29  4   YARM  10f Firm         3935 vis
41a 5   SOUT  11f Aw           4150
36a 6   WOLV  9f Aw       54   4251 t
```

NIGHT CITY 9 b g £12753
```
77a 1   LING  8f Aw            92*
60a 9   LING  10f Aw      80   161
74a 3   LING  13f Aw      78   219
82a 2   LING  12f Aw      78   237
62a 6   LING  12f Aw      75   245
28a 5   WOLV  12f Aw           307
82a 2   LING  10f Aw           333
74a 2   LING  10f Aw           375
52a 6   LING  12f Aw      78   422
36a 7   SOUT  12f Aw           498
65a 2   LING  13f Aw           524
66a 1   LING  12f Aw           650*
45  4   BRIG  12f Gd/Sft       893
44a 7   WOLV  8f Aw       61   1037
35a 6   WOLV  12f Aw           1389 VIS
49a 4   SOUT  11f Aw           1415
47  4   BRIG  12f Good         1647
48  1   CATT  14f Gd/Sft       1814*
47  5   WIND  12f Gd/Fm        1880
52  2   REDC  10f Gd/Fm        2143
53  2   WIND  10f Soft    49   2544
35  5   LING  16f Firm    49   2763
55  2   WIND  10f Aw      54   3356
```

NIGHT DIAMOND 3 b c £5972
```
0   11  BRIG  7f Gd/Fm         1125
61  9   WIND  6f Firm     75   1289
49  11  KEMP  6f Gd/Fm    72   1925
54  6   WIND  6f Soft     69   2549 tVl
61  10  WIND  6f Gd/Fm    66   2885 tvi
46  4   CARL  6f Gd/Fm         3080 tvi
52  2   HAYD  8f Gd/Sft        3266 t
54  4   BEVE  8f Good          3393 t
```

57 1 **GOOD** 10f Good 54 3663* t
48 10 LEIC 10f Firm 57 3842 t
42 4 BEVE 10f Sft/Hv 57 4046 t
56 3 BRIG 10f Soft 57 4174 t

NIGHT EMPRESS 3 br f £10026
75 2 LEIC 7f Good 794
78 4 NEWM 7f Gd/Fm 75 1153
71 5 SAND 7f Soft 76 1564
80 1 **YARM** 7f Firm 75 2391*
85 5 YARM 7f Good 2769
51 10 NEWM 7f Good 4018
78 1 **BRIG** 8f Soft 4420*

NIGHT FALL 2 ch f £4591
50 5 SAND 5f Gd/Fm 762
61 6 SALI 5f Good 1346
80 1 **GOOD** 7f Gd/Fm 2125*
81 4 SAND 7f Good 2474
73 10 GOOD 7f Firm 81 3149
64 6 NEWB 7f Gd/Fm 78 3486

NIGHT FLIGHT 6 gr g £27559
62a 13 WOLV 6f Aw 86 660
79 9 DONC 5f Gd/Fm 92 702
93 2 THIR 5f Soft 90 926
79 16 NEWM 5f Gd/Fm 91 1173
0 18 YORK 5f Firm 90 1324
90 6 HAYD 5f Gd/Sft 90 1533
77 14 YORK 5f Gd/Fm 89 1980
81 8 NEWC 5f Gd/Fm 88 2310
75 12 DONC 5f Gd/Fm 88 2348
94 1 **YORK** 6f Good 86 3543*
92 2 YORK 6f Gd/Fm 91 3727
0 23 AYR 6f Gd/Sft 93 4012
91 3 NEWM 5f Good 91 4339
89 7 DONC 5f Soft 91 4466

NIGHT GYPSY 2 b f £6222
70 3 BEVE 5f Good 3955
73 2 PONT 6f Soft 4083
51 9 YORK 6f Soft 4283
76 1 **NOTT** 5f Gd/Sft 4503*

NIGHT HAVEN 2 gr f £6735
67 2 NOTT 5f Gd/Fm 3003
68 2 BEVE 5f Gd/Fm 3408
76 1 **NEWC** 5f Firm 3602*
80 4 NEWM 5f Good 78 4179
80 5 NEWM 6f Good 80 4338

NIGHT MUSIC 3 br f £863
48 7 SAND 10f Soft 64 1585
64 5 GOOD 12f Gd/Fm 1956
60 3 WARW 12f Gd/Fm 60 2255
50 8 BATH 12f Gd/Sft 60 2554
58 3 SALI 14f Gd/Fm 58 2982
54 6 SALI 14f Gd/Fm 57 3424
45 8 WARW 16f Gd/Fm 56 3916

NIGHT OF GLASS 7 b g £495
82 7 WIND 8f Good 851 vis
80 4 BEVE 7f Heavy 977
66 13 THIR 8f Good 88 1160

NIGHT OF GLORY 5 b m £0
0 13 BEVE 8f Good 3393
0 27 YORK 9f Good 3808
0 10 BEVE 12f Sft/Hv 4041 BL

NIGHT OF NIGHTS 2 b f £0
60 9 MUSS 5f Gd/Fm 4131
18a 9 WOLV 6f Aw 4548

NIGHT OMEN 3 ch c £0
0 14 LEIC 10f Gd/Sft 833

NIGHT ON THE TOWN 2 b g £0
44 9 BEVE 7f Good 3949
60 10 BATH 8f Soft 4429

NIGHT PEOPLE 5 ch h £0
27 5 FOLK 6f Gd/Fm 2292

NIGHT SHIFTER 3 b f £0

0 14 KEMP 6f Soft 70 994
0 16 WIND 6f Gd/Fm 67 1877
46 7 WIND 8f Good 63 2713
54 10 SALI 8f Gd/Fm 63 2980
0 19 GOOD 9f Good 58 3110
0 17 LING 7f Firm 58 3279
0 24 WIND 6f Gd/Sft 51 4294

NIGHT SIGHT 3 b c £6320
50 8 NEWC 7f Soft 759
56 11 KEMP 8f Gd/Sft 1080
78 2 HAMI 9f Good 1242
84 2 GOOD 8f Gd/Sft 1449
85 3 NEWM 8f Firm 85 1853
78 2 THIR 7f Gd/Fm 2058
78 2 KEMP 7f Gd/Fm 2585

NIGHT STYLE 3 b c £3300
82 6 KRAN 10f Good 656
82a 7 NAD 9f Dirt 765
106 4 CHES 12f Gd/Fm 1216
92 4 CAPA 12f Gd/Fm 1618
103 7 AYR 10f Gd/Fm 2720

NIGHT VENTURE 4 b c £17559
89 1 **EPSO** 10f Heavy 83 1031*
72 10 CHES 10f Gd/Fm 89 1217
86 8 EPSO 12f Good 90 1850
66 16 SAND 10f Good 87 2475
70 10 NEWB 13f Firm 85 2852
87 3 CHES 8f Firm 85 3173
0 16 YORK 12f Good 85 3541
84 4 AYR 13f Gd/Sft 85 4014
80 4 YORK 14f Heavy 85 4299
83 4 NEWB 16f Gd/Sft 83 4458

NIGHTGLADE 4 b c £0
23 10 RIPO 12f Soft 38 822

NIGHTINGALE SONG 6 b m £0
36a 7 WOLV 6f Aw 82
29 7 GOOD 5f Gd/Sft 50 1487
44 4 LING 5f Soft 50 1543
23 13 GOOD 6f Gd/Fm 47 2124
0 11 WIND 6f Gd/Fm 47 3046
37 9 GOOD 5f Soft 43 4065

NIGRASINE 6 b g £10287
95 7 DONC 6f Good 734 bl
102 3 NEWM 7f Gd/Sft 100 966 bl
85 13 ASCO 7f Gd/Sft 100 1110 bl
101 4 YORK 6f Firm 100 1337 bl
92 5 DONC 7f Good 100 1514 bl
101 1 **YARM** 6f Gd/Fm 1952* bl
79 21 ASCO 6f Good 104 2151 bl
93 4 CHES 7f Good 99 3427 bl
85 10 YORK 6f Gd/Fm 95 3727 bl
75 16 AYR 6f Gd/Sft 95 4012 bl
87 8 NEWM 7f Good 91 4195 bl

NILOUPHAR 3 b f £0
14a 9 SOUT 7f Aw 40 1202 BL
22a 8 SOUT 7f Aw 44 1506 bl
50 7 NOTT 10f Gd/Fm 3006
20 10 CARL 8f Firm 38 3574
17 8 REDC 11f Soft 4497

NIMELLO 4 b c £14783
77 12 DONC 8f Good 88 733 BL
91 1 **SAND** 8f Heavy 85 1042*
68 12 YORK 8f Firm 90 1327
42 15 ASCO 8f Gd/Fm 89 3018
79 7 HAYD 8f Gd/Fm 87 3325 bl
79 4 SAND 8f Gd/Fm 3945
86 3 NEWM 8f Soft 82 4545

NINE TO FIVE 2 b f £5903
72 1 **DONC** 5f Good 712*
73 1 **LING** 5f Gd/Sft 836*
69 3 NOTT 5f Gd/Sft 1083
74 3 NOTT 5f Firm 1267

71 4 BATH 5f Gd/Fm 1437
39 4 LEIC 5f Soft 1549
33a 5 LING 5f Aw 1916
27 6 CHEP 5f Gd/Fm 65 3679
0 17 LEIC 6f Gd/Sft 59 4030
35 7 BRIG 5f Soft 4171

NINEACRES 9 b g £54941
57a 1 **WOLV** 6f Aw 134* bl
34a 9 LING 5f Aw 50 148 bl
57a 2 SOUT 5f Aw 214 bl
56a 3 LING 5f Aw 55 263 bl
56a 2 LING 6f Aw 313 bl
58a 2 LING 6f Aw 354 bl
42a 6 WOLV 6f Aw 406 bl
58a 1 **WOLV** 5f Aw 53 564* bl
56a 4 LING 6f Aw 56 634 bl
56a 4 SOUT 7f Aw 667 bl
39a 9 WOLV 6f Aw 56 754 bl
54 1 **SOUT** 6f Good 43 802* bl
55 3 BRIG 5f Gd/Sft 54 897 bl
37 7 FOLK 6f Soft 54 958 bl
47 5 BRIG 6f Gd/Fm 54 1126 bl
64 2 HAMI 6f Firm 1239 bl
56 2 CARL 6f Firm 53 1258 bl
60 1 **BATH** 6f Gd/Fm 56 1438* bl
47 12 SALI 6f Gd/Fm 59 1887 bl
66 1 **BATH** 6f Firm 59 1999* bl
70 1 **WIND** 6f Gd/Fm 65 2054* bl
62 11 GOOD 6f Good 69 2355 bl
70 3 YORK 6f Good 68 2697 bl
45 8 WARW 6f Gd/Fm 70 2845 bl
67 4 BATH 6f Firm 70 3209 bl
75 1 **CHEP** 6f Gd/Fm 70 3257* bl
75 3 GOOD 6f Gd/Fm 74 3646 bl
69 11 KEMP 6f Gd/Fm 75 3791 bl
81 2 AYR 6f Gd/Fm 74 4010 bl
81 2 SALI 6f Gd/Sft 78 4165 bl
88 1 **YORK** 5f Soft 78 4285* bl
81 10 DONC 5f Soft 87 4466 bl
91 1 **WIND** 5f Heavy 87 4527* bl
85 10 DONC 7f Heavy 91 4574 bl

NINETEENNINETYNINE 3 b c £0
31a 7 SOUT 8f Aw 694 VIS
0 18 LEIC 7f Firm 63 2026 vis
45 5 NEWC 8f Good 2520
17a 8 SOUT 12f Aw 52 2815

NINNOLO 3 b c £2749
76 5 THIR 12f Good 1386
74 3 WIND 10f Good 1725
26a 7 LING 10f Aw 2213
62 10 SAND 10f Gd/Fm 70 2499 t
57 5 YARM 14f Firm 66 2902 t
67 2 NEWM 12f Gd/Fm 62 3167 t
66 3 EPSO 12f Gd/Fm 65 3417 t

NIP IN SHARP 7 b h £0
46 12 DONC 8f Gd/Fm 2611
17 10 THIR 8f Gd/Fm 55 2970
0 15 BEVE 8f Good 50 3951

NISAN BIR 2 b c £241
63 9 DONC 6f Good 1513
67 4 DONC 6f Gd/Fm 1838
62 7 CARL 6f Gd/Fm 2239
63 5 AYR 7f Gd/Fm 63 2718
52 9 NEWC 7f Gd/Fm 2985
57 8 THIR 7f Gd/Sft 3776
40 12 BEVE 7f Good 58 3950

NISIBIS 4 b f £0
0a 12 SOUT 12f Aw 84
0a 9 WOLV 15f Aw 174

NISR 3 b c £5772
69 6 SAND 5f Heavy 86 1047
0 14 LING 6f Gd/Sft 84 1285

79 1 PONT 6f Firm   2177*
64 8 EPSO 7f Good   80 3854

NITE OWL MATE 3 b c £3434
59a 3 SOUT 6f Aw   472
65a 3 WOLV 6f Aw   549
52   7 DONC 6f Good   731
0   17 REDC 6f Good   64 1891
31a 9 SOUT 6f Aw   65 2300
75a 1 **WOLV** 6f Aw 62 2603* t
0   7 PONT 6f Gd/Fm   2833 t
0   15 REDC 7f Firm   55 3328
0   19 RIPO 6f Good   55 3698 t
19a 13 WOLV 6f Aw   70 3774 t
10a 13 WOLV 6f Aw   70 4023 tBL

NITE OWLER 6 b g £552
17a 9 SOUT 7f Aw   58 75
55a 2 WOLV 7f Aw   449
41a 6 WOLV 7f Aw   567
35a 9 SOUT 7f Aw   667
39a 7 WOLV 7f Aw   51 754

NITWITTY 6 b g £0
0   18 BATH 6f Firm   47 1994

NIYABAH 2 ch f £0
71   6 YARM 7f Soft   4514

NIZAAL 9 ch g £0
25   10 HAMI 8f Good   847

NO COMMITMENT 3 b g £0
15a 9 SOUT 8f Aw   36
27a 9 SOUT 8f Aw   50 125
5a   11 LING 10f Aw   204

NO DISS GRACE 2 b g £0
55   5 RIPO 6f Gd/Fm   3184

NO EXCUSE NEEDED 2 ch c £37280
82   1 **SAND** 7f Gd/Fm   2494*
108 1 **GOOD** 8f Gd/Fm   3086*
105 5 ASCO 8f Gd/Sft   4127

NO EXTRAS 10 b g £9114
72   1 **BRIG** 8f Firm   67 1330*
74   1 **NEWM** 8f Gd/Fm   70 1690*
62   6 KEMP 9f Gd/Fm   73 2085
63   8 GOOD 9f Good   73 2304
71   2 BRIG 10f Firm   3526
34   7 BRIG 8f Firm   3738

NO FRILLS 3 b f £655
66   6 SALI 10f Good   1344
64   3 RIPO 9f Good   1863

NO LANGUAGE PLEASE 6 ch g £2685
51   1 **BRIG** 12f Good   1647*
57   3 BRIG 12f Gd/Fm   1934
15a 10 WOLV 12f Aw   55 4386

NO MATTER WHAT 3 £0
109 5 LONG 7f Good   2226

NO MERCY 4 ch c £1326
65   5 WIND 8f Gd/Fm   69 2051 t
42   9 WARW 8f Gd/Fm   69 2257 t
68   2 WIND 10f Gd/Fm   66 2888
63   7 NEWM 10f Gd/Fm   68 3166
61   5 SALI 10f Gd/Fm   67 3390 BL
0   15 BATH 10f Soft   66 4436 VIS

NO NAME CITY 2 ch c £242
0   16 CHEP 6f Gd/Sft   1798
15   10 LING 7f Gd/Fm   2182
52a 3 WOLV 8f Aw   4250
51a 8 WOLV 8f Aw   64 4439

NO NO NORA 5 ch m £0
0a   13 WOLV 7f Aw   40 469
0a   12 SOUT 8f Aw   30 584

NO PASS NO HONOR 3 b c £0
59   6 LING 10f Soft   1287
59   5 GOOD 10f Gd/Sft   1640
3   7 WIND 11f Heavy   53 4529

NO REGRETS 3 b c £836
25a 10 LING 8f Aw   26
41a 5 LING 8f Aw   591
40a 7 LING 10f Aw   629
0   17 DONC 10f Gd/Fm   65 701
33   9 NEWB 10f Gd/Sft   1593
41   5 HAMI 8f Firm   2093
22   10 CHES 7f Gd/Fm   57 2250 BL
24   10 CHEP 8f Aw   2448
29   7 NOTT 8f Gd/Fm   3004
53   2 BRIG 10f Gd/Fm   3262
30   6 WIND 12f Good   3351
45   5 FOLK 10f Gd/Fm   55 3585
8   14 EPSO 10f Good   43 3762

NO SAM NO 2 b f £0
55   9 PONT 6f Soft   4083

NO SURRENDER 2 ch f £0
56   6 THIR 7f Gd/Fm   2057
27   9 AYR   8f Soft   3957
41a 8 WOLV 5f Aw   4227
0a   12 WOLV 8f Aw   49 4439
25a 9 WOLV 8f Aw   43 4552

NO TOMORROW 3 b f £0
64   6 SALI 8f Firm   2024 t
0   12 SALI 7f Gd/Fm   2232 t
0   13 WARW 7f Good   3696 t
0a   12 WOLV 12f Aw   49 4360 tbl

NOBALINO 6 ch g £3206
57a 3 LING 7f Aw   60 29   vis
68a 1 **LING** 7f Aw 60 59*   vis
67a 3 LING 7f Aw   66 106   vis
63a 5 LING 7f Aw   68 162   vis
45   10 NEWC 7f Heavy   62 1011 vis
54   5 MUSS 7f Gd/Fm   62 1148 vis
46   8 YARM 7f Gd/Sft 60 1611 vis

NOBBY BARNES 11 b g £2448
28   8 PONT 8f Good   1498
36   2 CARL 8f Gd/Sft   36 1721
37   3 RIPO 8f Good   1858
29   8 HAMI 9f Firm   36 2094
35   2 HAMI 9f Firm   34 2397
40   6 HAMI 9f Gd/Fm   2642
26   7 HAMI 8f Gd/Fm   36 2799
35   10 RIPO 8f Gd/Fm   3711
23   5 HAMI 9f Gd/Sft   3823

NOBELIST 5 b g £11066
99   6 WIND 8f Firm   1291
101 1 **REDC** 10f Gd/Sft 95 1561*
89   12 EPSO 10f Good   103 1845
88   12 YORK 10f Good   103 2696
93   8 ASCO 10f Gd/Fm   101 2995
89   8 YORK 10f Gd/Fm   99 3563 VIS
97   6 YORK 10f Good   3726 vis
86   9 NEWM 12f Good   96 4342 vis

NOBLE ARC 2 b c £0
0   22 DONC 8f Heavy   4569

NOBLE CALLING 3 b c £6541
68   3 BEVE 10f Good   63 1448
55   7 YARM 11f Good   64 1770
64   2 REDC 11f Gd/Fm   2146 BL
47   9 BATH 12f Gd/Sft 64 2554 bl
51   6 YARM 14f Firm   62 2902 bl
63   2 BEVE 10f Good   60 3396 bl
63   3 EPSO 10f Good   63 3762 VIS
67a 2 LING 10f Aw   4100 vis
66a 2 LING 10f Aw   65 4271 vis

NOBLE CHARGER 5 ch g £0
38   11 NOTT 8f Good   784
39   8 NOTT 5f Gd/Fm   3113 vis
16   6 YARM 8f Firm   3919 bl
15a 11 SOUT 11f Aw   4150

NOBLE CYRANO 5 ch g £7931

62a 2 SOUT 8f Aw   56 177
67a 1 **SOUT** 8f Aw   58 251*
32a 9 WOLV 9f Aw   64 309
41a 8 SOUT 8f Aw   67 473
47   9 NOTT 10f Good   58 786
48   4 HAMI 8f Gd/Fm   56 1190
0   14 HAYD 8f Good   54 3288
0   16 REDC 8f Gd/Sft   50 4499

NOBLE DOBLE 2 b c £4632
83   4 NEWM 6f Gd/Fm   2132
87   5 NEWM 7f Firm   2346
75   2 EPSO 7f Gd/Sft   2430
75   3 NEWB 10f Gd/Fm   79 3486
71   4 NEWC 8f Gd/Sft   77 3704
52   14 DONC 8f Gd/Fm   77 3879
71   5 WIND 10f Gd/Sft   73 4290

NOBLE INVESTMENT 6 b g £2272
36a 3 WOLV 7f Aw   310
13a 10 WOLV 9f Aw   47 383
50a 1 **SOUT** 8f Aw   452*
29a 6 SOUT 8f Aw   40 496
0a   F WOLV 9f Aw   553
22a 9 WOLV 8f Aw   750
0   15 WARW 11f Soft   46 1065
0a   14 SOUT 8f Aw   1505
0   16 WARW 11f Gd/Sft   40 1707

NOBLE PASAO 3 b c £6032
73a 2 WOLV 7f Aw   70 495
62a 6 WOLV 8f Aw   73 566
57a 8 WOLV 9f Aw   73 709
60   8 SOUT 7f Gd/Sft   70 857
68   3 BEVE 7f Firm   68 1275
56   10 HAYD 7f Gd/Sft   68 1793
65   5 BRIG 7f Gd/Fm   68 1930
64   5 CATT 7f Gd/Fm   66 2438
66   3 BEVE 8f Firm   65 2735
70   1 **THIR** 8f Gd/Fm 65 2970*
65   3 LEIC 8f Gd/Fm   65 3095
68   3 THIR 8f Gd/Fm   69 3345
60   7 DONC 7f Gd/Sft   69 4452
0   12 MUSS 8f Soft   68 4565

NOBLE PATRIOT 5 b g £9726
55a 2 WOLV 7f Aw   61
22a 8 WOLV 8f Aw   136
37a 3 WOLV 7f Aw   173
42a 4 WOLV 7f Aw   276
40a 5 WOLV 8f Aw   308
17a 7 SOUT 12f Aw   36 338
26a 5 WOLV 8f Aw   378
22a 9 WOLV 7f Aw   396 bl
36a 9 WOLV 7f Aw   449
40a 7 WOLV 8f Aw   567
44a 2 WOLV 5f Aw   1036
46a 5 WOLV 5f Aw   1237
40a 5 WOLV 5f Aw   1392
31a 3 SOUT 7f Aw   40 2122
32   4 BEVE 5f Firm   33 2223
41   1 **DONC** 6f Gd/Fm 33 2315*
48   1 **DONC** 6f Gd/Fm 39 2753*
49   1 **CATT** 5f Gd/Fm 44 3203*
49   4 MUSS 5f Gd/Fm   48 3594

NOBLE PURSUIT 3 b c £8979
81   4 SAND 8f Good   86 761
76   10 GOOD 9f Gd/Sft   85 1452
81   4 NOTT 8f Soft   85 1645
89   1 **RIPO** 8f Gd/Fm 83 2108*
65   14 SAND 7f Good   90 2495
91   3 LING 8f Good   2762
85   8 NEWM 8f Good   90 3022

NOBLE REEF 3 b c £676
52   9 CARL 8f Firm   63 1255
61   3 NOTT 10f Good   2012
62   3 BRIG 12f Gd/Fm   2725

0 20 YORK 10f Gd/Fm 60 3731
0a 15 SOUT 12f Aw 4366

NOBLE SPLENDOUR 3 ch c £2090
73 5 BRIG 7f Gd/Fm 1125
51 8 SALI 8f Good 70 1345
66 2 AYR 9f Gd/Fm 1632
66 3 RIPO 10f Gd/Fm 2111
67 3 NEWC 8f Good 65 2524
65 4 PONT 8f Gd/Fm 66 2831
54 5 NEWC 8f Soft 3707
0 24 YORK 10f Good 65 3810
29a 8 WOLV 9f Aw 62 4382

NOBLENOR 3 ch c £2496
79 1 **REDC** 7f Gd/Sft 1135*
71 6 NOTT 8f Gd/Sft 1366
0 18 NEWM 8f Good 79 4340

NOCCIOLA 4 ch f £0
51 9 LING 7f Gd/Sft 1261
52 6 THIR 6f Gd/Sft 1354
0a 11 SOUT 7f Aw 55 1801
0 15 LING 7f Firm 52 3279

NODS NEPHEW 3 b g £5830
53 4 CATT 6f Gd/Fm 781
64 1 **BEVE** 7f Heavy 59 976*
38a 8 WOLV 7f Aw 1038
55a 4 WOLV 7f Aw 64 1390
31a 7 SOUT 7f Aw 60 2300
43 10 BEVE 8f Gd/Fm 64 2515
69 1 **BEVE** 7f Gd/Fm 3670*
0 20 YORK 7f Good 3809
28 10 BEVE 7f Sft/Hvy 65 4044

NOIRIE 6 br g £2780
41 2 PONT 10f Heavy 42 943
38 3 WARW 11f Heavy 37 1003
25a 8 SOUT 11f Aw 42 1306
44 2 NEWC 10f Heavy 44 1769
0 18 BEVE 10f Firm 42 1921
17 8 BEVE 12f Gd/Sft 40 3053
23 9 NEWC 14f Good 40 3249
0 16 REDC 14f Gd/Sft 34 4222
0a 15 SOUT 14f Aw 38 4371

NOMINATOR LAD 6 b g £3758
57 14 PONT 8f Soft 79 875
59 11 THIR 8f Good 77 1160
58 13 CHES 8f Firm 77 1250
65a 4 SOUT 8f Aw 72 2634
68a 4 SOUT 8f Aw 72 2817
78 1 **HAYD** 11f Good 72 3285* BL
59a 6 WOLV 9f Aw 72 3495 bl
69 12 YORK 8f Good 76 3810 bl
57 6 PONT 10f Soft 76 4085
44 11 YORK 9f Heavy 74 4300 bl

NOMORE MR NICEGUY 6 b g £5519
73a 10 WOLV 8f Aw 97 663
66 16 DONC 8f Good 87 733
54 7 BEVE 7f Heavy 977
77 8 CHES 8f Firm 83 1250
76 7 THIR 6f Good 81 1383
81 2 CHES 7f Gd/Sft 79 1778
68 7 EPSO 8f Good 79 1851
75 4 AYR 8f Good 2138
61 11 CHES 5f Gd/Fm 79 2247
63 9 PONT 6f Gd/Fm 77 2559
71 6 CHES 8f Firm 75 3170
69 6 HAYD 8f Gd/Fm 79 3325
72 4 CHES 8f Gd/Sft 73 3510
71 6 YORK 7f Good 73 3809
71 3 CHES 6f Soft 4069
62 5 ASCO 8f Gd/Sft 73 4126
17 16 YORK 7f Good 70 4302
58 19 NEWM 7f Good 4357

NON VINTAGE 9 ch g £0

0a 11 SOUT 12f Aw 47 412
0 12 PONT 17f Soft 41 876

NOON GUN 2 ch c £224
66 4 BATH 6f Soft 4137
62a 4 WOLV 7f Aw 4383

NOOSHMAN 3 ch c £62812
85 1 THIR 7f Good 81 1158*
87 5 HAYD 8f Gd/Sft 85 1535
86 8 ASCO 8f Good 85 2117
99 1 **GOOD** 10f Gd/Fm 85 2358*
99 3 YORK 10f Good 93 2696
104 2 YORK 10f Gd/Fm 99 3563
97 9 NEWB 10f Firm 99 3997
107 2 NEWM 9f Gd/Fm 99 4212

NORCROFT JOY 5 b m £21310
70 5 NOTT 10f Gd/Sft 72 1086
60 12 YORK 14f Firm 72 1329
71 3 NOTT 14f Good 69 1874
70 3 NEWM 12f Gd/Fm 69 2131
70 3 NEWM 12f Gd/Fm 69 2286
75 1 **BEVE** 12f Gd/Fm 69 2482*
71 7 SALI 12f Good 75 2689
74 4 NEWM 12f Gd/Fm 74 3122
67 5 BEVE 10f Gd/Fm 74 3410
68 5 NEWM 10f Good 73 4160
76 1 **DONC** 7f Soft 70 4464*

NORCROFT LADY 2 b f £7814
86 1 YARM 6f Good 1774*
83 4 NEWB 6f Gd/Fm 1944
89 1 **LING** 6f Good 84 2589*
81 6 NEWB 6f Firm 2850
67 12 NEWM 6f Gd/Fm 90 3165
85 6 WARW 7f Gd/Fm 89 3913

NORDIC SABRE 2 b f £3055
59 6 YARM 5f Firm 2766
79 1 **MUSS** 5f Good 3098*
48 4 NEWC 5f Firm 3602

NORFOLK REED 3 b c £10648
85 4 LING 6f Gd/Sft 87 1285
84 5 NEWB 6f Gd/Fm 86 1406
85 8 NEWM 6f Gd/Fm 86 1694
80 9 SAND 7f Gd/Fm 86 2495
81 8 SAND 7f Gd/Fm 86 2922
0 17 GOOD 7f Gd/Fm 85 3130 BL
66 3 NEWM 7f Good 3612 VIS
83 1 **DONC** 7f Gd/Fm 79 3880* vis
0 17 NEWM 7f Gd/Fm 82 4215 vis
76 11 NEWM 7f Good 82 4357 vis
0 21 NEWM 7f Soft 81 4547 vis

NORTH ARDAR 10 b g £1111
22a 9 SOUT 8f Aw 50
19a 9 LING 10f Aw 46 100
34a 2 SOUT 11f Aw 178
41a 4 SOUT 12f Aw 41 215
31a 6 WOLV 12f Aw 231
15a 5 WOLV 12f Aw 36 408
16a 7 SOUT 11f Aw 455
15a 9 SOUT 8f Aw 646
0a 11 SOUT 12f Aw 1203
30 7 LEIC 10f Soft 40 1546
42 3 WARW 11f Gd/Sft 40 1707
44a 3 SOUT 11f Aw 1978
45a 5 SOUT 11f Aw 2119
6a 12 LING 10f Aw 2587

NORTH BY NORTH 2 b c £0
41 7 YARM 5f Firm 2901
37 14 NEWM 7f Good 4336

NORTH OF KALA 7 b g £3874
39 1 **SALI** 12f Gd/Fm 32 1888*
30 3 KEMP 12f Gd/Fm 30 2081
45 3 FOLK 12f Gd/Fm 42 2295
35 8 SALI 14f Gd/Fm 43 2982

---

30 10 GOOD 12f Good 48 3887

NORTH POINT 2 b c £0
80 8 DONC 8f Gd/Fm 3864
0 13 SALI 8f Gd/Sft 4163
72 5 DONC 7f Gd/Sft 4446

NORTHERN ACCORD 6 b g £215
32 6 PONT 10f Heavy 45 943 BL
35 10 PONT 12f Good 42 1499 bl
32 4 NEWC 10f Heavy 45 1769 bl
25 11 BEVE 10f Firm 38 1921 bl

NORTHERN CASTLE 2 b g £0
0 12 PONT 5f Firm 3500
0 18 YORK 5f Good 3729
0a 8 WOLV 8f Aw 4250

NORTHERN ECHO 3 b g £2057
64 7 NEWC 7f Soft 759
55 7 THIR 8f Soft 909
0 16 THIR 8f Good 65 1387
41 5 CARL 6f Gd/Fm 1723 BL
56 3 CARL 6f Firm 2278 bl
56 2 BEVE 7f Firm 2731 bl
39 9 CARL 8f Gd/Fm 56 3082 bl
42 8 HAYD 8f Gd/Sft 3266 bl
50 5 REDC 10f Firm 54 3310
53 2 NEWC 12f Firm 52 3606
27 9 PONT 12f Soft 52 4229
37a 8 WOLV 12f Aw 50 4443

NORTHERN FLEET 7 b g £300
63 4 GOOD 14f Gd/Fm 68 1959
62 5 SALI 14f Gd/Fm 66 2268
52 9 SALI 14f Gd/Fm 63 2982
25 12 FOLK 16f Gd/Fm 61 3448

NORTHERN LIFE 3 b f £0
12 0 WIND 10f Firm 1293
20 10 LEIC 8f Gd/Sft 1572
47 6 SALI 7f Gd/Fm 1884
32 10 CHEP 7f Good 1972
17 10 LING 7f Good 41 2591
29 6 BRIG 7f Firm 2907 VIS
0 12 LEIC 8f Gd/Fm 3094 vis

NORTHERN MOTTO 7 b g £4898
51 5 MUSS 16f Gd/Sft 53 797
7 13 PONT 17f Soft 53 876
51 7 BEVE 16f Firm 55 1276
42 9 NEWC 17f Gd/Sft 50 1478
52 3 MUSS 16f Firm 52 1686
52 3 MUSS 14f Gd/Fm 51 2050
51 3 MUSS 16f Gd/Fm 51 2203
47 4 MUSS 14f Firm 51 2375
47 4 CHES 16f Gd/Fm 50 2672
47 3 CHES 16f Gd/Fm 47 3511
37 6 MUSS 16f Gd/Fm 46 3742
38 7 AYR 17f Soft 46 3993
31 8 MUSS 16f Gd/Sft 49 4134
42 2 MUSS 13f Soft 40 4521 VIS
44 9 MUSS 16f Soft 46 4563 vis

NORTHERN SUN 6 b g £0
0a 12 WOLV 12f Aw 58 43

NORTHERN SVENGALI 4 b g £6891
76a 3 LING 5f Aw 78 631
49 15 DONC 6f Good 79 716
74 4 CATT 7f Gd/Fm 79 780
62 7 PONT 6f Heavy 77 941
0 21 DONC 6f Gd/Sft 75 1074
0 12 THIR 7f Good 75 1158
58 10 THIR 8f Gd/Sft 72 1356
65 4 AYR 7f Gd/Fm 68 1631
52 12 AYR 7f Good 66 2163
59 9 CATT 7f Gd/Fm 64 2420
59 4 LEIC 6f Good 61 2777
45 10 AYR 6f Firm 2877
58 5 GOOD 5f Gd/Fm 61 3091

39 12 CATT 5f Gd/Fm 60 3203
62 3 PONT 5f Gd/Fm 60 3222
0 14 BEVE 5f Good 60 3398
66 2 CARL 5f Firm 61 3572
69 1 **THIR** 5f Gd/Fm 61 3619*
67 5 EPSO 5f Good 67 3855
63 7 LEIC 5f Gd/Sft 67 4027

NORTHERN TIMES 3 ch c £3768
45a 5 SOUT 6f Aw 426
59a 1 **SOUT** 7f Aw 541*
42a 7 WOLV 8f Aw 636
60 1 **LING** 7f Gd/Sft 58 841*
32 11 WIND 12f Heavy 61 937
34 8 LEIC 12f Gd/Sft 61 1571
0 16 SALI 8f Firm 58 2025
0 14 BATH 8f Firm 56 4435

NORTHERN TRIO 3 b g £0
33a 7 SOUT 7f Aw 417
24 7 NOTT 6f Good 52 785
37 8 LEIC 6f Gd/Sft 830
0 19 WIND 12f Gd/Fm 49 3049
14 10 NEWM 8f Good 3456
53 6 GOOD 7f Soft 64 4080
0 14 PONT 6f Soft 4233
23a 4 WOLV 7f Aw 4361
0 13 NOTT 10f Heavy 43 4509

NORTHFIELDS DANCER 2 ch c £1570
62 7 SAND 5f Gd/Fm 2494
83 2 NEWB 7f Firm 2708
85 2 SAND 8f Gd/Fm 2921
66 8 ASCO 8f Gd/Fm 3304
89 2 NEWM 8f Good 85 3609
92 2 DONC 8f Gd/Fm 89 3879
88 1 **GOOD** 8f Soft 4062*
93 2 YORK 7f Soft 4277
84 5 PONT 8f Gd/Fm 4375

NORTHGATE 4 b g £6327
32a 8 WOLV 7f Aw 46 754 bl
40 5 MUSS 8f Gd/Sft 46 899 bl
40 4 HAMI 8f Firm 44 1243 bl
47 2 AYR 8f Gd/Fm 42 1658 bl
50 1 **BEVE** 7f Firm 46 2221* bl
48 4 RIPO 8f Soft 49 2542 bl
50 2 DONC 7f Gd/Fm 49 2612 bl
36 12 CARL 7f Firm 49 2823 bl
30 10 BEVE 7f Good 49 2882 bl
12 6 NEWC 7f Good 49 3250 bl
0 19 REDC 8f Gd/Sft 47 4499 bl

NORTON 3 ch c £1740
86 8 GOOD 10f Gd/Sft 1451
88 3 HAYD 12f Gd/Fm 90 1832
81 7 NEWM 10f Gd/Fm 90 2287

NOSE THE TRADE 2 b g £6623
67 5 LING 5f Soft 4187
73 1 **NEWM** 7f Good 4336*
73 4 DONC 7f Soft 72 4460

NOSEY NATIVE 7 b g £7364
15a 10 SOUT 16f Aw 37 470
0a 9 SOUT 12f Aw 37 642
42 3 LEIC 12f Good 42 791
45 2 NOTT 14f Heavy 41 1023
46 2 YARM 11f Gd/Sft 45 1614
37 6 NEWM 12f Firm 45 1852
46 2 RIPO 12f Gd/Fm 44 2109
31 4 DONC 17f Gd/Fm 45 2607
49 1 **YARM** 14f Good 44 3233*
50 1 **CATT** 12f Good 49 3437*

NOSMOKEWITHOUTFIRE 2 ch f £0
0 14 BATH 8f Soft 4429
0 16 WIND 8f Heavy 4524

NOSY BE 2 b c £1369
66 5 WIND 6f Gd/Fm 3047

75 3 SALI 6f Gd/Fm 3387
76 2 LING 5f Good 4096
76a 3 WOLV 6f Aw 4379

NOT FADE AWAY 2 b c £0
0 17 NOTT 8f Heavy 4504

NOT JUST A DREAM 2 b f £560
68 4 MUSS 5f Gd/Fm 1146
64 3 PONT 6f Soft 1700
5 10 CATT 7f Gd/Fm 2417
58 4 REDC 6f Gd/Fm 2990
58 6 MUSS 7f Gd/Fm 62 3592
29 13 NOTT 6f Soft 60 3976

NOTAGAINTHEN 4 b f £0
0 13 CHEP 12f Gd/Fm 43 3255
0 11 BATH 13f Gd/Fm 40 3518

NOTATION 6 b g £6675
0a 8 WOLV 16f Aw 17 494
2a 8 WOLV 12f Aw 23 520 bl
0a 9 SOUT 16f Aw 20 542 bl
22a 4 SOUT 11f Aw 29 561 bl
0a 10 WOLV 12f Aw 21 608 bl
0a 13 SOUT 14f Aw 31 1301
0a 12 SOUT 14f Aw 32 1416 bl
7 11 MUSS 9f Firm 28 1689 bl
23 4 MUSS 16f Gd/Sft 2536
0 11 HAMI 13f Gd/Fm 25 2643
22 8 BEVE 16f Firm 26 2734
6 5 BEVE 16f Gd/Fm 18 3406
26 9 PONT 17f Soft 33 3501
28 1 **HAMI** 12f Gd/Sft 24 3531*
28 1 **BEVE** 12f Gd/Fm 25 3674*
23 4 MUSS 16f Gd/Fm 26 3742
18 12 HAMI 17f Gd/Fm 30 3827
0a 13 SOUT 16f Aw 38 4149
0a 9 SOUT 14f Aw 38 4370

NOTEWORTHY 4 br f £0
0 16 SALI 14f Firm 65 1180
48 7 BATH 13f Gd/Fm 60 1440
31 11 WARW 14f Gd/Sft 54 1711
0 12 BATH 17f Firm 47 1996
17 9 BATH 14f Firm 41 2941
14 10 CHEP 12f Gd/Fm 35 3406
0 20 EPSO 12f Good 43 3858 VIS

NOTHING DAUNTED 3 ch c £1192
96 3 NEWM 6f Gd/Sft 93 982
83 5 CAPA 8f Soft 1118

NOTIONAL 4 b f £0
8a 10 WOLV 8f Aw 229 t
15a 11 LING 10f Aw 238 tBL

NOUF 4 b f £7421
44a 12 WOLV 8f Aw 90 663
57 8 DONC 12f Good 732
79 2 LEIC 8f Gd/Sft 80 831
0 16 NEWC 7f Heavy 78 1011
70 6 NEWM 10f Gd/Fm 1174
69 6 NEWM 7f Gd/Fm 1410
60 10 WIND 8f Good 72 3643
63 10 YORK 8f Good 68 3810
64 5 YARM 8f Firm 66 3936
71 1 **HAYD** 8f Soft 66 4094*
70 2 BRIG 10f Gd/Sft 66 4118
65 13 NEWM 7f Gd/Fm 74 4215
74 5 YORK 9f Heavy 74 4300
0 22 NEWM 8f Good 74 4340

NOUFARI 9 b g £11200
64a 1 **WOLV** 15f Aw 117*
74a 1 **WOLV** 16f Aw 174*
72a 5 WOLV 16f Aw 296
72a 1 **SOUT** 16f Aw 327*
73a 2 SOUT 16f Aw 1802
52 1 **REDC** 16f Good 1894*
76a 1 **WOLV** 16f Aw 2076*

NOUKARI 7 b g £29779
67a 3 SOUT 14f Aw 68 37
78a 1 **LING** 12f Aw 68 52*
80a 1 **LING** 12f Aw 73 115*
84a 1 **LING** 12f Aw 77 151*
71a 4 LING 12f Aw 81 237
82a 2 LING 12f Aw 81 245
58a 7 SOUT 11f Aw 82 302
75a 5 LING 12f Aw 82 356
66a 4 LING 12f Aw 80 422
75a 4 LING 12f Aw 78 486
71a 5 LING 16f Aw 76 548
63a 3 WOLV 12f Aw 679
72 2 DONC 10f Gd/Fm 70 705
74 1 **CATT** 14f Gd/Fm 70 779*
72 4 SOUT 12f Good 76 805
14 13 HAYD 12f Heavy 74 991
80 1 **CHES** 10f Gd/Fm 74 1217*
79 9 CHES 12f Firm 80 1251
80 2 CHES 10f Gd/Sft 78 1777
61 9 YORK 12f Firm 78 2002
59 12 CARL 12f Firm 78 2279
74 5 CHES 10f Gd/Fm 78 2671

NOVELLINI STAR 3 ch c £0
0a 7 LING 12f Aw 1540
45 8 BATH 12f Firm 2327

NOVELTY 5 b m £628
0 9 THIR 7f Soft 929
0 16 NEWM 7f Firm 36 2347
58 3 CHES 8f Good 2662

NOVERRE 2 b c £142970
109 1 **NEWM** 6f Gd/Fm 2595*
107 3 DEAU 6f Gd/Sft 3550
113 1 **DONC** 7f Firm 3891*
115 2 NEWM 7f Good 4354

NOW IS THE HOUR 4 ch g £841
33a 6 WOLV 6f Aw 680
49a 6 WOLV 5f Aw 753 BL
51a 2 WOLV 5f Aw 1237
24a 9 SOUT 6f Aw 43 1422
23a 7 SOUT 7f Aw 43 2122
29 3 BEVE 5f Firm 30 2223
10 6 RIPO 6f Gd/Fm 33 2839
27 5 RIPO 5f Gd/Fm 30 3180
46 6 BEVE 5f Good 3956

NOW LOOK HERE 4 b g £20733
106 2 DONC 6f Good 734
106 3 NEWB 5f Soft 102 914
97 3 HAYD 7f Gd/Fm 1163
106 3 YORK 6f Firm 104 1337
106 4 HAYD 5f Gd/Sft 104 1533
102 5 HAYD 7f Gd/Sft 1834
70 14 ASCO 6f Good 2115
99 2 HAYD 6f Firm 2458
94 7 NEWB 6f Firm 2847
0 18 ASCO 7f Gd/Fm 103 2997 BL
87 5 DONC 6f Good 3158
80 12 YORK 6f Gd/Fm 96 3727
94 2 DONC 5f Soft 92 4466
94 4 DONC 6f Heavy 4581

NOWELL HOUSE 4 ch g £12011
38 9 RIPO 12f Soft 68 825
47 8 PONT 10f Heavy 66 943
27 12 DONC 10f Gd/Sft 66 1050
51 11 CARL 9f Firm 63 1254
47 7 REDC 9f Gd/Sft 61 1583
69 1 **CATT** 12f Soft 60 4003*
78 1 **REDC** 10f Gd/Sft 72 4221*
39 9 YORK 14f Heavy 78 4299
80 4 DONC 12f Gd/Fm 78 4580

NOWHERE TO EXIT 4 b c £0
96 5 NEWB 13f Gd/Fm 3483

NOWT BUT TROUBLE 2 ch g £404					
71	6	MUSS	5f Gd/Fm		1146
73	3	MUSS	5f Gd/Fm		1429
63	5	MUSS	5f Gd/Sft		2532
56	9	REDC	6f Gd/Fm	68	3327
0	22	DONC	7f Firm	64	3901

NOWT FLASH 3 ch c £7106						
53a	2	SOUT	5f Aw		217	
35a	9	WOLV	7f Aw	54	257	
60a	1	**SOUT**	6f Aw		300*	
39a	8	SOUT	6f Aw	60	331	
46a	7	SOUT	6f Aw		426	
28a	6	SOUT	6f Aw	56	515	
63a	1	**SOUT**	7f Aw		589*	
51	7	BEVE	7f Heavy	60	976	
34a	5	WOLV	8f Aw		1234	
59	2	THIR	8f Good	57	1387	
60	2	NEWC	8f Gd/Sft	57	1477	
47	5	CATT	7f Soft		1681	
34	9	HAYD	8f Soft	61	1822	
44	11	NEWC	8f Good	60	2524	
55	4	AYR	7f Gd/Fm	58	2719	
0	14	NEWC	7f Good	56	3033	
40	4	LEIC	7f Gd/Fm		3218	
0	12	PONT	6f Soft		4233	
0a	14	SOUT	12f Aw		4366	

NUBILE 6 b m £418						
8a	7	SOUT	12f Aw	32	70	
4a	6	SOUT	12f Aw	31	413	bl
6a	10	WOLV	16f Aw	33	482	bl
0a	12	SOUT	14f Aw	31	1301	tbl
40	2	NOTT	14f Good	37	1874	tbl
25	5	WARW	16f Gd/Fm	28	2037	tbl
26	5	YARM	16f Good	34	3026	tbl
12	11	NEWC	14f Good	34	3249	tbl

NUCLEAR DEBATE 5 b g £211318				
116	1	**CHAN**	5f Gd/Sft	1747*
122	1	**ASCO**	5f Good	2065*
123	1	**YORK**	5f Firm	3598*

NUGGET 2 b g £0				
0	11	CHEP	7f Good	3866
71a	5	WOLV	7f Aw	4385

NUMERATE 2 b f £3366					
65	3	NOTT	6f Good		1413
74	1	**REDC**	6f Gd/Sft		1577*
0	15	LING	7f Soft	75	4191
0	13	DONC	7f Soft	75	4460

NUN LEFT 2 b f £7752					
70	3	WIND	5f Gd/Fm		1197
77	2	PONT	6f Firm		2174
72	4	CHEP	6f Gd/Fm		2488
72	2	BRIG	7f		3558
81	1	**WARW**	7f Good		3692*
78	2	WARW	7f Gd/Fm	77	3913
69	14	NEWM	7f Good	80	4157

NUNKIE GIRL 3 ch f £354					
68	13	NEWB	7f Soft		915
56	8	WARW	8f Soft		1062
74	6	GOOD	9f Gd/Sft		1481
10	12	WIND	10f Good		2372 BL
29	8	CHEP	7f Gd/Fm		3253 bl
37	3	BRIG	8f Firm		3736 bl

NUTMEG 3 ch f £0					
59	4	BRIG	8f Gd/Sft		894
56	7	CARL	8f Firm	65	1255
0	18	RIPO	6f Good	62	1600
51	6	YARM	10f Gd/Fm		1955
35	6	MUSS	12f Gd/Sft	55	2537
23a	9	LING	12f Aw	51	4334
39	9	NEWM	8f Gd/Sft	46	4536

NUTS IN MAY 3 b f £0					
0	13	SALI	8f Good	65	1345

NZAME 2 b c £0				
78	5	KEMP	7f Gd/Fm	3790
71	11	NEWM	7f Good	4184

OAKWELL ACE 4 b f £950						
0a	14	SOUT	7f Aw	41	75	
42	5	PONT	6f Soft		872	
36	8	PONT	8f Heavy		942	
21	9	PONT	8f Gd/Sft	40	1101	
43	5	THIR	7f Gd/Sft		1351	
49	2	REDC	7f Gd/Sft		1559	
39	5	REDC	8f Good	42	1892	
0	14	DONC	7f Gd/Fm	41	2320	
39	4	YARM	8f Firm	39	2767	
28	5	CARL	7f Gd/Fm	40	3083	vis

OARE KITE 5 b m £5778						
34a	6	LING	7f Aw		159	bl
34a	3	SOUT	8f Aw	39	384	
24a	5	SOUT	8f Aw	41	430	
31a	4	SOUT	8f Aw	39	513	bl
39a	2	SOUT	8f Aw	39	588	bl
31a	4	SOUT	8f Aw	40	692	bl
29a	6	WOLV	7f Aw	40	754	bl
38a	3	WOLV	6f Aw	37	1233	bl
39a	2	SOUT	7f Aw	38	1506	bl
0	11	SOUT	7f Soft	48	1606	bl
53	1	**LEIC**	6f Firm	46	2031*	bl
0	14	NOTT	6f Gd/Fm	52	2193	bl
0	13	LEIC	6f Gd/Fm	52	2777	bl
0	12	WIND	6f Gd/Fm	51	3046	bl
42	7	YARM	7f Gd/Fm	50	3666	bl
41	5	CATT	7f Soft	48	4004	bl

OARE PINTAIL 3 b f £217					
0	12	SALI	8f Good	67	1345
0	12	SALI	8f Good	63	2230
57	4	SALI	5f Firm	58	3747
47	12	GOOD	5f Good	58	3908

OBSERVATORY 3 ch c £295244				
108	2	NEWM	7f Gd/Fm	1693
115	1	**ASCO**	7f Good	2087*
121	1	**GOOD**	7f Gd/Fm	3132*
120	2	GOOD	8f Good	3647
126	1	**ASCO**	8f Good	4111*

OCCAM 6 ch g £0				
0a	11	WOLV	9f Aw	189

OCEAN DRIVE 4 b c £5272					
24	9	HAMI	9f Good	48	846
44	5	HAMI	13f Gd/Fm	47	1194
29	6	HAMI	13f Gd/Fm	45	1363
36	5	MUSS	12f Firm	43	2048
42	4	AYR	11f Good	43	2139
43	3	NEWC	10f Gd/Fm	43	2309
40	4	HAMI	12f Firm	41	2392
47	2	HAMI	11f Gd/Fm	42	2638
44	2	HAMI	11f Gd/Fm	42	2782
60	4	AYR	13f Firm		2876
41	5	RIPO	12f Gd/Fm	46	3013
46	4	AYR	10f Good	46	3368
49	2	HAMI	11f Gd/Sft	46	3379
43	4	HAMI	12f Gd/Fm	46	3531
40	7	AYR	11f Soft	49	3963
0	14	AYR	10f Heavy	47	4306
36	5	MUSS	13f Soft	44	4521
44	2	MUSS	12f Soft	44	4560

OCEAN LINE 5 b g £5389					
38a	2	WOLV	9f Aw	36	383
36a	3	WOLV	12f Aw	37	464
38a	2	WOLV	12f Aw	37	520
42a	2	LING	12f Aw	42	621
37a	7	WOLV	8f Aw	40	675
40	4	WIND	12f Gd/Fm	43	748
15	12	BRIG	12f Gd/Fm	40	1128
0	18	BRIG	10f Firm		1331

42a	1	**LING**	10f Aw		2587*
44	2	YARM	10f Firm		2765
33	10	NOTT	14f Gd/Fm	46	3002
46	3	FOLK	12f Gd/Fm		3447

OCEAN LOVE 2 b f £1284				
55	5	WARW	7f Gd/Fm	2841
66	2	MUSS	7f Good	3100
66	3	YARM	8f Gd/Fm	3665

OCEAN OF WISDOM 3 b c £0				
95	7	LONG	11f V	1317

OCEAN RAIN 3 ch c £1576						
52	14	DONC	7f Good	80	736	
78	5	NEWM	7f Good	77	954	VIS
49	12	CHES	8f Gd/Fm	76	1215	
68	7	NEWB	7f Gd/Fm	75	1787	vis
73	4	BATH	8f Firm	72	2330	vis
70	7	CHEP	8f Firm	72	2661	vis
70	3	NEWM	7f Gd/Fm	71	3163	
70	4	EPSO	9f Gd/Fm	70	3401	
65	6	LING	6f Soft	69	4270	BL
54	10	DONC	7f Gd/Sft	68	4452	

OCEAN ROAD 2 ch c £0				
58	8	KEMP	7f Gd/Fm	3790
73	6	WARW	7f Gd/Fm	3909
57	11	DONC	7f Gd/Sft	4446

OCEAN SONG 3 b f £1842						
52a	2	WOLV	7f Aw		531	
49a	4	SOUT	8f Aw		694	
67	6	LEIC	7f Good		794	
0	11	SOUT	7f Gd/Sft	69	857	
51	13	REDC	7f Firm	65	1297	BL
60	3	YARM	8f Gd/Sft	62	1610	bl
53	7	REDC	10f Good	60	1895	bl
50	7	NOTT	10f Good		2012	bl
56a	7	SOUT	12f Aw	27	2815	
33	12	NOTT	16f Gd/Fm	52	3112	

OCEAN TIDE 3 b g £0				
69	8	KEMP	12f Soft	4040
0	15	SAND	10f Soft	4205

OCEAN VIEW 4 ch f £0				
36	8	REDC	10f Gd/Sft	1582
33	8	RIPO	10f Good	1599

OCHOS RIOS 9 br g £0					
20a	6	SOUT	7f Aw	37	471

OCKER 6 br g £2039						
76a	4	SOUT	6f Aw	78	47	
75a	6	WOLV	5f Aw	78	64	
58a	12	SOUT	6f Aw	76	129	
36a	8	SOUT	6f Aw	74	180	
67	13	NEWM	6f Firm	96	1182	
84	11	HAYD	5f Gd/Sft	91	1533	
85	8	RIPO	5f Good	87	1861	
82	6	REDC	6f Gd/Fm	86	2158	
0	13	DONC	5f Gd/Fm	85	2348	BL
83	4	NEWM	5f Good	83	2569	
73	5	WARW	6f Gd/Fm	83	2845	
80	5	NEWM	6f Gd/Fm	82	3119	
68	10	RIPO	6f Gd/Fm	82	3183	
90	9	NOTT	5f Good		3521	
82	3	HAYD	6f Heavy		3768	

OCTANE 4 b c £23748					
34	12	HAMI	13f Good	60	845
34	10	BEVE	10f Heavy	52	975
45	3	HAMI	8f Firm	47	1243
52	1	**MUSS**	12f Gd/Fm	46	1432*
49	3	MUSS	9f Firm	49	1689
54	2	HAMI	12f Gd/Fm	49	1908
41	7	MUSS	12f Firm	49	2048
60	2	CARL	12f Firm	54	2279
61	1	**HAYD**	11f Gd/Fm	54	2453*
70	1	**SAND**	10f Gd/Fm	59	2527*
70	4	ASCO	12f Good	67	2674

70 5 DONC 10f Gd/Fm 70 3159

OCTAVIUS CAESAR 3 ch c £7508

80	3	SAND	10f Good		3232
86	1	BATH	12f Gd/Fm		3517*
83	2	BEVE	12f Gd/Fm		3654
77	6	NEWB	13f Firm	83	3994

ODDSANENDS 4 b c £3453

0a	15	SOUT	8f Aw	77	49
66a	2	WOLV	7f Aw		142
62a	2	SOUT	8f Aw		195
38a	8	SOUT	7f Aw	68	299
51a	5	SOUT	7f Aw	64	599
64a	1	SOUT	7f Aw		667*
0	13	SOUT	7f Good	65	803
39	10	THIR	7f Soft	62	908
0	19	REDC	7f Gd/Sft		1132 BL
42a	5	SOUT	7f Aw		1305
51	7	THIR	7f Gd/Sft		1351

ODYN DANCER 3 b f £3274

38a	7	SOUT	8f Aw		48
17a	10	SOUT	8f Aw	49	125
44a	3	LING	8f Aw		150
61a	6	LING	10f Aw		240
32a	6	LING	10f Aw	50	315
39a	6	LING	8f Aw	45	419
48a	2	SOUT	11f Aw	42	537
14	10	BEVE	12f Heavy	54	978
31a	6	WOLV	12f Aw	46	1142
25a	7	SOUT	12f Aw	46	2123
41a	4	LING	12f Aw	46	2217
46a	7	WOLV	16f Aw	52	2606
22	11	NOTT	16f Gd/Fm	39	3112
30a	3	WOLV	12f Aw	39	3494
41a	1	WOLV	12f Aw	35	3773*
0a	12	SOUT	16f Aw	43	4149

OFF HIRE 4 b g £8659

30a	7	SOUT	6f Aw		32	VIS
57a	3	SOUT	5f Aw		214	vis
57a	1	WOLV	5f Aw		379*	vis
53a	4	WOLV	5f Aw	55	518	vis
56a	2	WOLV	5f Aw	55	563	vis
59a	1	WOLV	5f Aw	54	614*	vis
37a	8	SOUT	5f Aw	58	673	vis
46	6	BATH	5f Good	53	1092	vis
49a	7	SOUT	5f Aw	58	1806	vis
55a	4	SOUT	5f Aw	58	1976	vis
52a	4	SOUT	6f Aw		2118	vis
55	1	BEVE	5f Firm	51	2732*	vis
55	5	SAND	5f Gd/Fm	57	2925	vis
52	6	CATT	5f Gd/Fm	55	3203	vis
50	7	HAMI	5f Gd/Sft	55	3536	vis
0	18	NEWB	5f Gd/Sft	54	4459	vis

OFFENBURG 3 b c £0

39a	5	LING	8f Aw	42	419	
27a	6	LING	12f Aw		457	
36a	6	LING	10f Aw		545	VIS

OGGI 9 gr g £0

41	10	GOOD	6f Gd/Sft	79	1636
41	14	WIND	6f Good	74	2371

OGILIA 3 b f £9867

74	14	EPSO	7f Gd/Fm	86	1826
76	7	KEMP	8f Gd/Fm	83	2084
71	4	SALI	8f Good	80	2688
73	6	NEWM	8f Good	77	3022
81	1	SAND	8f Good	75	3435*
64	8	GOOD	9f Good	80	3658
72	13	YORK	8f Good	80	3810
80	2	SAND	8f Gd/Fm	79	3944

OH JAMILA 2 b f £0

0	16	BATH	8f Soft		4430

OH NO NOT HIM 4 b c £0

0	12	AYR	10f Heavy	38	4306

OH SO DUSTY 2 b f £4920

59	6	WARW	5f Heavy		886	
89	1	NEWB	5f Gd/Fm		1782*	
82	11	ASCO	5f Good		2088	
85	4	DONC	5f Gd/Fm		2318	
75	4	WIND	6f Good		2714	
87	4	LEIC	5f Gd/Fm	91	2915	BL
71	6	YARM	5f Good		3027	bl

OK BABE 5 b m £0

0a	12	LING	10f Aw	55	102
23a	8	SOUT	8f Aw		195
0	15	KEMP	7f Gd/Fm	37	2749
0	11	YARM	6f Gd/Fm	32	3964

OK JOHN 5 b g £504

57a	3	LING	5f Aw	56	57	
49a	8	LING	6f Aw	57	154	
52a	3	SOUT	6f Aw		201	
43a	8	SOUT	6f Aw		279	
40a	6	LING	5f Aw	51	371	bl
22a	7	LING	7f Aw	49	439	bl

OK TWIGGY 3 b f £0

15	6	LEIC	10f Heavy		4313
33	7	WIND	10f Heavy		4528

OKAWANGO 2 b c £117195

103	1	CHAN	8f Soft		4144*
118	1	LONG	8f Soft		4320*

OLD FEATHERS 3 b c £3326

0	14	BEVE	7f Heavy	68	976
61	7	BEVE	10f Good	65	1448
55	6	BEVE	12f Firm	61	1919
23	12	BEVE	12f Gd/Fm	56	2482
34	8	BEVE	16f Good	50	2879
54	1	CATT	16f Good	47	3442*
52	3	MUSS	16f Gd/Fm	53	3742

OLD HUSH WING 7 b g £0

51	5	DONC	18f Good	55	714
49	6	SOUT	16f Gd/Sft	54	860
39	9	NOTT	14f Gd/Sft	50	1087
0	16	BEVE	16f Firm	51	1276
0	12	NEWC	17f Gd/Sft	48	1478
43	7	PONT	17f Good	45	1867
29	11	BEVE	16f Gd/Fm	41	2516
16	11	CATT	16f Soft	38	4258

OLD IRISH 7 gr g £0

0	13	CHEP	18f Gd/Sft	65	1800

OLD SCHOOL HOUSE 7 ch h £0

17	10	BATH	10f Gd/Sft	45	1666
38	5	FOLK	12f Gd/Fm		3447
0	15	LING	10f Firm	33	3755

OLDEN TIMES 2 b c £545

89	4	YORK	7f Gd/Fm		2649

OLENKA 2 gr f £2782

82	1	CATT	6f Gd/Fm		2419*

OLIVERS TRAIL 2 ch c £0

0	17	DONC	7f Heavy		4566

OLLIES CHUCKLE 5 b g £442

42	6	THIR	7f Soft	53	908
0	13	NEWC	8f Heavy	52	1007
33	11	REDC	8f Firm	50	1300
40	6	PONT	10f Soft	47	1705
34	6	RIPO	8f Good		1858
34	7	HAMI	9f Firm	41	2094
27	6	PONT	8f Gd/Fm	37	2831
22	10	WIND	10f Gd/Fm		3045
37	3	BEVE	8f Gd/Fm	37	3407
27	8	NEWC	9f Firm	39	3603

OLLY MAY 5 b m £0

0	15	BRIG	10f Firm		1210
17	9	LEIC	8f Gd/Sft		1732
0	18	SALI	7f Gd/Fm		1884
0	17	SALI	10f Gd/Sft	40	4168

OLOROSO 3 b g £0

0 19 BATH 12f Soft 4434
57 7 NOTT 8f Heavy 4505

OLYMPIC PRIDE 2 b f £0

0	15	YARM	7f Firm		3940
64	9	YARM	8f Heavy		4475

OLYS DREAM 2 ch f £0

66	5	MUSS	5f Gd/Sft		898
42	8	MUSS	5f Good		3098
48	6	BEVE	5f Gd/Fm		3408
47	8	MUSS	5f Gd/Fm		3589
46	8	LEIC	6f Gd/Sft	54	4030
39	7	AYR	6f Heavy	55	4305
12a	11	SOUT	7f Aw		4369

OLYS GILL 2 b f £268

52	4	NEWC	5f Heavy		1764
42a	9	SOUT	5f Aw		2120
0a	7	SOUT	7f Aw		2301
37	7	MUSS	7f Gd/Fm	49	3592
32	9	HAMI	5f Gd/Fm	45	3802
34a	7	WOLV	6f Aw		4246
47a	7	WOLV	6f Aw		4359
30	5	MUSS	5f Soft	38	4561

OLYS WHIT 2 ch g £218

47	4	CARL	7f Aw		1719	
42	6	CARL	6f Gd/Fm		3079	VIS

OMAHA CITY 6 b g £23051

79	12	GOOD	8f Gd/Sft	95	1450
80	10	ASCO	8f Good	93	2090
94	7	NEWM	7f Gd/Fm	92	2616
95	5	NEWB	7f Firm		2809
84	9	KEMP	8f Firm	91	2870
97	3	GOOD	8f Gd/Fm	92	3107
106	5	NEWB	7f Firm		3452
99	2	GOOD	7f Good	95	3648
100	1	GOOD	7f Gd/Fm	96	3902*
94	7	GOOD	7f Soft		4078
87	13	NEWM	7f Soft	99	4195

OMNIHEAT 3 b f £7649

77	3	WIND	8f Heavy	72	933	
77	2	BRIG	7f Gd/Fm		1125	
78	3	NEWB	7f Gd/Fm	73	1405	
77	1	BRIG	10f Good	74	1649*	BL
73	6	NEWB	8f Gd/Fm		1786	bl
77	5	WIND	8f Gd/Fm		1879	bl
77	4	NEWM	8f Good	80	3022	
33	9	DONC	8f Gd/Fm	80	3160	bl
70	7	NEWM	8f Gd/Fm	78	3317	
64	7	GOOD	9f Good	78	3658	
73	5	SAND	8f Gd/Fm	75	3944	bl
0	24	ASCO	8f Gd/Sft	74	4126	bl
70	4	NOTT	8f Heavy	71	4414	
69	3	YARM	7f Aw	71	4513	bl

ON CREDIT 3 ch g £0

52a	6	LING	8f Aw		26	bl

ON GUARD 2 b c £0

74	6	NEWM	6f Gd/Sft		4530

ON MY HONOUR 2 b f £0

0	13	KEMP	7f Soft		4035
48	11	LING	6f Soft		4188

ON PORPOISE 4 b g £2044

0a	11	SOUT	11f Aw	46	560
39	8	WARW	8f Heavy	43	1520
40	9	NEWM	8f Gd/Fm	41	1690
27	11	HAYD	11f Soft	41	1819
45	1	YARM	8f Good	38	3236*
36	7	BATH	8f Firm	44	3623

ON SHADE 3 ch f £0

52	9	DONC	7f Gd/Fm		1072
0	19	NEWC	8f Gd/Sft	50	1477
30	6	HAYD	8f Soft	45	1822

ON THE RIDGE 5 ch b £6138

106	2	NEWM	8f Good		4180

| 102 | 5 | NEWM | 9f Good | | 4347 | |

ON THE TRAIL 3 ch c £0
29	12	KEMP	6f Good		729	
0	21	WIND	6f Good	60	852	
36	7	WIND	6f Gd/Sft	55	4294	
0	19	NEWB	5f Gd/Sft	51	4459	

ON TILL MORNING 4 ch f £0
43	13	THIR	6f Soft	66	910	
47	11	NEWC	7f Heavy	65	1011	
0	17	REDC	7f Firm	62	1297	
47	7	PONT	6f Good	59	1869	
56	4	HAYD	7f Gd/Fm	55	2442	
38	9	BEVE	7f Good	55	2882	
38	8	CARL	7f Gd/Fm	55	3083	
0	11	MUSS	8f Gd/Fm	52	3746	

ON TIME 3 b c £1878
100	3	LEIC	7f Gd/Sft		1574	
91	5	DONC	8f Gd/Fm		2578	
83	4	GOOD	8f Soft		4077	

ONCE MORE FOR LUCK 9 b g £5952
58	9	CATT	14f Gd/Fm	70	779	
55	6	SOUT	11f Gd/Sft	67	855	
44	10	CATT	14f Soft	63	1683	
63	3	HAMI	12f Gd/Fm	60	1908	
67	1	**HAMI**	13f Firm	60	2098*	
65	2	HAMI	13f Gd/Fm	63	2238	
63	5	HAMI	12f Firm	66	2392	
67	2	HAMI	13f Gd/Sft	65	2801	
66	3	HAMI	13f Gd/Sft	66	3378	
56	9	NOTT	10f Soft		3979	
0	17	YORK	12f Soft	64	4280	

ONCE REMOVED 2 b f £2209
69	8	WIND	5f Gd/Sft		1424	
69	4	LEIC	5f Gd/Sft		1737	
69	4	BATH	5f Firm		1993	
63	7	LING	6f Good		2589	
70	2	BEVE	5f Firm		2730	
69	3	BATH	5f Firm		2940	
71	4	GOOD	7f Gd/Fm	70	3149	
52	8	SAND	5f Good	70	3228	
58	5	EPSO	6f Gd/Fm		3400	
0	20	WIND	6f Gd/Sft		4288	

ONE BELOVED 2 b f £1036
31	7	LING	6f Soft		1541	
0	16	WIND	6f Good		2209	
57	3	BATH	6f Firm		2328	
56	2	BATH	5f Gd/Sft		2551	
54	4	BRIG	7f Gd/Fm		2723	
26	5	BEVE	5f Good		2880	

ONE CHARMER 2 b c £0
50	9	LING	5f Firm		3277	
0	13	WIND	5f Good		3639	
0	13	LING	5f Good		4095	
35a	12	WOLV	5f Aw		4227	
0a	13	SOUT	7f Aw		4369	

ONE DINAR 5 b g £11412
64a	2	WOLV	8f Aw		477	
76a	1	**WOLV**	8f Aw	67	580*	
78a	2	SOUT	8f Aw	74	669	
52	8	DONC	8f Good	69	715	
79a	5	WOLV	8f Aw	78	921	
0	12	NEWC	8f Heavy	67	1007	
61	3	KEMP	8f Gd/Fm	64	2752	
54	6	BEVE	8f Gd/Sft	64	3054	
44	12	LEIC	8f Gd/Fm	62	3334	
78a	3	WOLV	9f Aw	78	3495	
64	2	GOOD	8f Good	60	3885	
57	9	NEWM	7f Soft	61	4547	

ONE DOMINO 3 ch c £2568
56	3	THIR	7f Soft		929	
50	11	CARL	8f Firm	63	1255	
51	8	NEWC	8f Gd/Sft	60	1477	

61	3	AYR	11f Gd/Fm	60	1633	VIS
61	2	BEVE	12f Gd/Sft	57	1758	vis
49	4	NEWC	12f Gd/Fm	60	2272	vis
52	8	BEVE	12f Gd/Fm	60	2482	vis
50	5	BEVE	14f Good	58	2879	vis

ONE IN THE EYE 7 br g £0
| 0 | 13 | LING | 11f Good | 44 | 1743 | |

ONE LIFE TO LIVE 7 gr g £0
22	9	CATT	16f Soft	43	4258	
20a	9	SOUT	14f Aw	38	4370	
28	6	MUSS	13f Soft	37	4521	vis

ONE MIND 2 b c £0
| 0 | 16 | NEWM | 6f Gd/Sft | | 4530 | |

ONE QUICK LION 4 b c £216
52a	7	WOLV	9f Aw	69	271	
51a	4	LING	8f Aw		353	
48a	8	SOUT	8f Aw	60	2121	
12a	8	SOUT	8f Aw	57	2817	

ONE WON ONE 6 b g £63466
108	1	**LEOP**	7f Sft/Hvy		15*	
107	5	CURR	7f Yldg		862	
97	5	DONC	7f Gd/Sft		1049	
106	3	CORK	6f Good		1232	
106	3	LEOP	8f Gd/Fm		1316	
114	1	**HAYD**	7f Gd/Sft		1834*	
111	3	LEOP	6f Good		3373	
106	2	FAIR	6f Firm		3548	
108	4	CURR	7f Good		4056	
110	2	GOOD	7f Soft		4078	

ONEFOURSEVEN 7 b g £439
13a	10	SOUT	16f Aw	60	502	
39a	9	WOLV	16f Aw	52	577	
25a	7	SOUT	16f Aw	45	644	
41	3	NEWC	16f Soft	40	760	
40	10	PONT	18f Firm	46	2176	

ONES ENOUGH 4 b c £2520
28	11	BRIG	7f Gd/Sft	57	896	
0	15	WARW	8f Soft	52	1066	
0	13	BRIG	8f Gd/Fm	47	1930	t
52	1	**BATH**	6f Firm	47	1994*	t
30	11	EPSO	7f Gd/Sft	52	2431	
37	9	SALI	6f Good	52	2690	t
51	4	BATH	6f Firm		3208	
0	12	BRIG	7f Firm		3559	t
0	15	LEIC	6f Gd/Sft		4031	tbl

ONKAPARINGA 2 b f £0
| 0 | 6 | BRIG | 8f Good | | 1648 | |

ONLY FOR GOLD 5 b g £5489
47a	6	SOUT	7f Aw	57	35	
49	6	CATT	7f Gd/Sft	57	780	
53	6	REDC	8f Firm	56	1300	
57	2	DONC	7f Good	54	1519	
56	3	CHES	7f Gd/Sft	57	1778	
37	10	THIR	7f Gd/Sft	57	2063	
57	2	CARL	7f Gd/Fm	57	2241	
0	12	HAYD	7f Gd/Fm	56	2442	
0	15	CHES	8f Gd/Sft	56	2673	
52	5	BEVE	7f Gd/Sft	54	3652	
46	6	REDC	8f Gd/Sft	54	4217	
56	1	**NEWC**	7f Heavy	51	4426*	
55	4	MUSS	7f Soft	54	4518	

ONLY ONE LEGEND 2 b c £5415
40	10	HAYD	5f Heavy		989	
74	3	CARL	5f Firm		1252	
76	3	NOTT	5f Gd/Sft		1642	
80	1	**DONC**	5f Gd/Fm	76	2575*	
71	9	NEWM	6f Gd/Fm	83	3165	
72	5	NOTT	6f Good	79	3519	
84	2	REDC	5f Gd/Fm		3632	

ONLY WHEN PROVOKED 2 b c £0
| 0 | 17 | CHEP | 6f Gd/Sft | | 1798 | |
| 32 | 7 | WIND | 6f Gd/Fm | | 2052 | VIS |

24	11	WARW	7f Gd/Fm		2841	vis
0a	12	SOUT	7f Aw		4154	
0	13	NOTT	8f Heavy		4507	

ONLY WORDS 3 ch c £0
48	6	BRIG	10f Soft		1466	
0	18	NEWM	10f Gd/Fm		1697	
58	8	WIND	8f Gd/Fm		2211	t
42	6	DONC	8f Gd/Fm	59	2579	t

ONLYMAN 3 ch c £4612
| 102 | 2 | MAIS | 7f Soft | | 945 | |
| 97 | 14 | NEWM | 8f Gd/Fm | | 1171 | |

ONLYONEUNITED 3 b f £0
| 37 | 10 | NOTT | 5f Heavy | | 1021 | |
| 0 | 15 | WIND | 5f Gd/Sft | 70 | 1427 | |

ONLYTIME WILL TELL 2 ch g £0
| 71 | 16 | NEWM | 8f Good | | 4349 | |
| 73 | 6 | NEWM | 8f Gd/Sft | | 4531 | |

ONYOUROWN 7 b g £0
| 0a | 6 | SOUT | 14f Aw | 75 | 89 | vis |

OOMPH 2 b f £901
84	4	KEMP	6f Gd/Sft		3795	
87	3	YARM	6f Firm		3938	
83	6	REDC	6f Gd/Sft		4219	
64	6	BRIG	7f Soft		4415	

OPEN ARMS 4 ch c £3423
0	11	HAYD	8f Gd/Fm	75	1490	
40	7	BEVE	9f Gd/Sft	72	1762	
57	7	NOTT	8f Gd/Fm	68	3115	
67	1	**BEVE**	8f Gd/Fm	65	3407*	
66	3	GOOD	9f Good	66	3644	
0	18	DONC	10f Good		3899	
0	18	NEWM	10f Good	65	4160	

OPEN GROUND 3 ch c £5090
38a	7	SOUT	8f Aw		86	
44a	6	LING	7f Aw		164	
51a	3	LING	10f Aw		204	
48a	9	LING	10f Aw		240	
31	8	SOUT	10f Good		806	
56	1	**PONT**	12f Heavy		939*	
11	6	DONC	15f Gd/Sft	52	1071	
54	1	**YARM**	16f Gd/Sft		1613*	
0	14	WARW	16f Gd/Fm	54	3916	
45	4	PONT	18f Soft	51	4376	

OPEN WARFARE 2 br f £10701
73	3	WARW	5f Heavy		886	
75	3	NEWM	5f Gd/Sft		970	
78	4	SAND	5f Heavy		1046	
79	1	**HAYD**	5f Gd/Fm		1166*	
74	3	BATH	5f Gd/Sft		1437	
58	5	PONT	6f Good		1497	
74	3	LING	6f Good		1673	
77	3	CHES	5f Gd/Fm		2248	
84	3	BEVE	5f Gd/Fm		2483	
63	5	WIND	6f Good		2714	
65	8	THIR	5f Gd/Fm	77	3145	
0	11	CURR	6f Yldg		3720	
68	3	HAMI	5f Soft		3801	
0	11	LING	5f Good	70	4098	
78	1	**NOTT**	6f Heavy		4410*	
0	21	DONC	7f Heavy	77	4577	

OPERATION ENVY 2 b c £211
62	4	BRIG	5f Gd/Fm		1124	
73	6	LING	5f Gd/Sft		1260	
56	8	BRIG	5f Gd/Sft		1463	
57a	4	LING	5f Aw		1740	
40	9	FOLK	7f Gd/Fm		2290	
49	9	LING	6f Good	59	2589	
30	8	BRIG	7f Firm	55	2894	
0	14	WIND	6f Good		3044	

OPPORTUNE 5 br g £0
| 31 | 5 | CARL | 14f Gd/Fm | 40 | 3084 | |
| 23 | 11 | HAYD | 12f Good | 40 | 3284 | |

OPTIMAITE 3 b c £10245
99	3	BATH	10f Good		1089	
101	1	SALI	12f Gd/Fm		1347+	
89	9	ASCO	16f Good		2068	
93	5	HAYD	12f Gd/Fm		2503	
82	10	GOOD	12f Gd/Fm		3061	
83	5	NEWB	10f Firm	100	3453	
84	7	HAYD	11f Soft	97	3782	
72	12	NEWB	13f Firm	92	3994	
83	6	NEWM	12f Good	87	4162	

OPTION 3 b f £0
61	5	LING	9f Firm		1912	
55	7	WIND	8f Gd/Fm		2211	
59	7	BATH	10f Gd/Sft		2553	
45	5	THIR	12f Gd/Fm	54	3125	
31	12	HAYD	12f Good	54	3284	
0	10	CARL	12f Firm		3570	VIS

ORANGE TREE LAD 2 b g £2282
68	9	RIPO	5f Soft		821	
75	5	THIR	5f Soft		928	
75	3	HAMI	5f Gd/Fm		1189	
75a	2	SOUT	5f Aw		1302	
44	7	NOTT	5f Good		1870	
63	7	DONC	5f Gd/Fm	76	2575	
7	11	NEWC	7f Good	70	3246	

ORANGERIE 2 b c £0
48a	7	SOUT	7f Aw		2383	
67	5	LING	6f Good		2652	
48	7	LING	6f Firm		2760	

ORANGETREE COUNTY 2 b f £0
| 33 | 6 | LING | 6f Soft | | 1541 | |

ORANGEVILLE 3 b c £1000
| 78 | 4 | KEMP | 9f Gd/Fm | | 2086 | |
| 78 | 3 | DONC | 10f Gd/Fm | | 2317 | |

ORANGINO 2 b c £0
| 0 | 13 | MUSS | 5f Gd/Sft | | 4131 | |
| 52 | 7 | CATT | 5f Soft | | 4253 | |

ORCHARD RAIDER 2 b c £5375
38	8	NOTT	5f Heavy		1019	
62a	2	SOUT	5f Aw		1206	
51	4	LING	6f Good		1396	t
67a	1	SOUT	6f Aw		1805*	
58	2	NEWC	6f Gd/Fm		2312	
49	9	NEWM	7f Gd/Fm		2599	
68a	2	SOUT	6f Aw	69	2948	
40a	9	WOLV	7f Aw	67	3273	

ORCHESTRA STALL 8 b g £46334
95	6	HAYD	12f Heavy		987	
116	1	ASCO	16f Gd/Sft		1109*	
116	1	LONG	16f Gd/Sft		3851*	
111	8	LONG	16f Heavy		4494	

ORDAINED 7 b m £7069
30a	4	LING	12f Aw	36	528	
21a	6	LING	10f Aw	33	618	
0a	11	LING	12f Aw		650	
0a	4	LING	12f Aw		772	
48	2	BRIG	12f Gd/Fm	44	1128	
43	3	BRIG	12f Firm	47	1332	
31	9	BRIG	12f Gd/Sft	47	1465	
39	7	NOTT	12f Good	44	2008	
39	4	WARW	15f Good	40	2461	
46	1	PONT	12f Gd/Fm	38	2829*	
48	2	SALI	14f Gd/Fm	44	2982	
46	2	NEWM	12f Gd/Fm	45	3122	
37	6	EPSO	12f Gd/Fm	47	3402	
44	8	FOLK	12f Gd/Fm	47	3586	
37	10	GOOD	12f Good	55	3657	
41	6	WARW	11f Gd/Fm	43	3915	
15a	7	LING	12f Aw	33	4486	
30	7	NEWM	12f Gd/Sft	42	4534	

OREANA 2 b f £3347
| 65 | 9 | NEWB | 6f Firm | | 3980 | |

| 76 | 5 | WIND | 6f Gd/Sft | | 4288 | |
| 96 | 1 | DONC | 6f Heavy | | 4576* | |

OREGON FLIGHT 2 ch f £0
| 44 | 7 | NEWC | 5f Soft | | 755 | |
| 49 | 8 | HAMI | 5f Good | | 843 | |

ORIEL STAR 4 b f £394
19a	11	WOLV	5f Aw	57	291	
33a	7	LING	5f Aw	57	312	vis
46	6	SOUT	6f Good	51	802	bl
50	3	BATH	5f Good	49	1092	vis
34	11	HAMI	5f Firm	49	1244	vis
39	10	THIR	5f Gd/Sft	50	1714	bl
40	6	RIPO	5f Gd/Fm	48	2107	bl
43	8	WARW	5f Gd/Fm	48	2252	vis
31	9	MUSS	5f Gd/Sft	45	2535	bl
25	9	WIND	5f Good	42	3191	vis
33	7	THIR	5f Gd/Fm	40	3619	vis
44	12	AYR	5f Soft	52	3960	
37	5	LEIC	6f Gd/Sft		4031	
29	8	AYR	6f Heavy	44	4327	
0	17	NEWC	5f Heavy	44	4407	

ORIENT EXPRESS 3 b g £894
74	13	NEWM	7f Gd/Sft		983	
73	7	NEWB	8f Good		1376	
58	9	KEMP	8f Soft		1532	
66	3	LING	9f Firm		2322	
44	13	SAND	10f Gd/Fm	68	2499	
60	3	EPSO	9f Good	64	2795	
36	12	KEMP	8f Soft	63	3078	
43	12	GOOD	8f Soft	62	4066	
50a	9	LING	8f Aw	60	4330	

ORIENTAL FASHION 4 b f £27187
| 110 | 1 | CAPA | 8f Heavy | | 11* | |

ORIENTAL MIST 2 gr c £5434
72	5	MUSS	5f Gd/Fm		1146	
79	4	AYR	6f Gd/Fm		1653	
85	3	HAMI	5f Gd/Fm		1906	
77	3	AYR	6f Good		2137	
81	7	ASCO	7f Gd/Fm		3015	
71	4	AYR	7f Good		3363	
66	4	HAMI	8f Gd/Sft		3532	
65	6	AYR	6f Soft	76	3987	
44	11	MUSS	8f Gd/Sft	73	4132	
72	1	AYR	8f Heavy	68	4323*	
33	11	DONC	8f Gd/Sft	74	4450	

ORIENTAL PRIDE 4 ch c £0
| 48 | 5 | BRIG | 12f Gd/Sft | | 1510 | |
| 0 | 12 | WIND | 12f Gd/Fm | | 1880 | |

ORIENTOR 2 b c £3139
75	3	AYR	6f Soft		3958	
92	2	YORK	6f Soft		4283	
85	10	DONC	6f Soft		4462	
90	3	DONC	6f Heavy		4576	

ORIGINAL SINNER 2 b g £0
67	6	EPSO	7f Gd/Sft		2430	
67	4	WARW	7f Gd/Fm		2841	
61	6	THIR	7f Gd/Fm		3127	
63	5	MUSS	7f Gd/Fm	67	3592	
43	7	YARM	8f Soft	64	4393	

ORIGINAL SPIN 3 b f £15646
72	2	WIND	8f Heavy		934	
84	1	LEIC	10f Gd/Sft	77	1735*	
86	1	NEWC	12f Gd/Fm	81	2272*	
82	2	RIPO	12f Gd/Fm	84	2837	
85	2	RIPO	12f Gd/Fm	85	3467	BL
0	9	AYR	13f Gd/Sft	86	4014	VIS
5	10	DONC	10f Heavy		4571	vis

ORIOLE 7 b g £1834
43a	5	SOUT	7f Aw	45	69	
0	16	NEWC	8f Heavy	51	1007	
0	18	REDC	8f Firm	49	1300	
0	17	DONC	7f Gd/Fm	48	1840	vis

36	10	BEVE	7f Firm	44	2221	
0	14	HAYD	7f Gd/Fm	44	2442	
58	4	REDC	7f Gd/Fm		2994	
32	8	REDC	8f Gd/Fm	47	3634	
0	17	REDC	8f Gd/Sft	53	4217	
50	1	NEWC	7f Heavy	43	4428*	
40	12	REDC	7f Gd/Sft	53	4498	

ORLANDO SUNRISE 3 ch f £0
47	9	WIND	10f Heavy		936	
70	6	NOTT	8f Gd/Fm		1268	
58	7	BEVE	7f Good		1444	
57	4	SALI	8f Firm	63	2025	
59	5	SALI	8f Gd/Fm	60	2264	

ORLANDO SUNSHINE 3 ch g £0
47	10	BATH	6f Firm	58	1994	
44	7	CHEP	6f Gd/Fm	54	2489	
34	7	NOTT	6f Gd/Fm		2680	BL
27	6	BATH	6f Firm		3208	bl

ORMELIE 5 b g £6673
82	7	NEWB	8f Firm	93	2707	
92	5	ASCO	10f Gd/Fm	93	2995	
93	3	ASCO	10f Gd/Fm	92	3339	
94	3	NEWB	11f Firm	92	3451	
81	10	DONC	12f Firm	92	3896	
95	2	NEWM	12f Good	91	4162	BL

ORO STREET 4 b c £3485
79a	2	SOUT	12f Aw		301	
70a	1	SOUT	12f Aw		387*	
53	6	WARW	12f Soft	74	815	

OSCAR PEPPER 3 b c £10079
65a	1	SOUT	6f Aw	53	331*	
71a	1	SOUT	6f Aw	59	365*	
70a	2	WOLV	7f Aw	68	534	
73a	2	SOUT	6f Aw	70	689	
51	9	CATT	7f Gd/Fm	66	2438	
51	3	PONT	6f Gd/Fm		2833	
53	7	NEWC	7f Good	60	3033	BL
60	3	CATT	6f Gd/Fm		3200	
49	6	NEWM	6f Gd/Fm	56	3457	
77a	2	WOLV	7f Aw	74	3771	
52	6	DONC	7f Gd/Sft	60	4452	

OSCIETRA 4 b f £300
39	10	WIND	12f Gd/Sft		1096	
52	5	BATH	10f Gd/Sft	57	1666	
49	5	CHEP	10f Good	56	1973	
52	5	KEMP	9f Firm	53	2262	
48	6	SAND	10f Gd/Fm	51	2527	VIS
23	7	WIND	10f Good	50	3356	
38	8	GOOD	8f Soft	46	4066	vis
43	3	SALI	10f Gd/Sft	46	4168	vis
35	13	SAND	10f Soft	44	4208	vis
31	6	BRIG	10f Soft	44	4419	

OSO NEET 2 b c £0
64	7	LING	5f Gd/Sft		1260	
71	6	NEWB	5f Gd/Sft		1589	
23	8	WIND	6f Good		2052	
36	10	LING	6f Good		4097	
43	11	LING	6f Soft		4190	
0	14	NOTT	8f Heavy		4507	
0	6	BRIG	10f Heavy		4539	BL

OSOOD 3 b c £0
87	6	NEWM	10f Gd/Sft	90	979	
79	6	CHES	12f Gd/Fm	90	1225	
65	10	DONC	10f Gd/Fm	87	2610	

OSTARA 3 b g £7244
43	11	HAYD	7f Gd/Sft	58	1793	
54	3	CHES	8f Gd/Fm	55	2250	
42	8	CHES	8f Gd/Fm	55	2673	
25	11	RIPO	10f Gd/Fm	55	2839	
51	5	REDC	10f Gd/Fm	54	2992	
65	1	HAYD	8f Gd/Sft		3266*	
65	1	THIR	8f Gd/Fm	59	3345*	

0 15 AYR 7f Soft 65 3992
0 11 REDC 10f Gd/Sft 65 4221

OSWALD 4 b g £0
9a 9 SOUT 8f Aw 38 345

OTAHUNA 4 b c £433
60 3 RIPO 12f Soft 60 825
0 14 DONC 10f Gd/Sft 60 1050

OTIME 3 b c £7229
72a 1 **LING** 6f Aw 24*
74a 3 LING 7f Aw 108
57a 7 LING 7f Aw 73 149
78a 1 **LING** 6f Aw 73 165* VIS
77a 4 SOUT 5f Aw 80 202 vis
66a 6 WOLV 6f Aw 77 275 vis
57a 7 SOUT 7f Aw 76 416 vis
77a 2 LING 6f Aw 74 592 vis
34 10 NOTT 6f Good 68 785 vis
58a 6 LING 6f Aw 75 881 vis
68a 6 LING 8f Aw 74 1259 vis
67 2 SALI 7f Gd/Fm 65 1889 BL
63 5 LEIC 7f Firm 65 2026 bl
0 13 EPSO 7f Good 67 2794 bl
52 12 NEWM 7f Gd/Fm 67 2855 bl
53a 10 LING 7f Aw 4328 bl

OTTERINGTON GIRL 4 b f £0
28 8 RIPO 8f Good 1858
0 13 REDC 8f Gd/Fm 30 2147

OUDALMUTEENA 5 b g £0
42a 7 LING 8f Aw 353 VIS
42 9 LEIC 7f Good 790
41 6 WARW 11f Heavy 53 889

OUR DESTINY 2 b c £4327
0 13 LEIC 6f Firm 2029
83 1 **HAYD** 6f Gd/Fm 2454*
86 3 NEWB 6f Firm 2808
78 6 NEWM 6f Gd/Fm 86 3165
68 3 NEWC 5f Firm 3602
0 13 NEWM 6f Gd/Fm 80 4214
0 21 NEWB 6f Sft/Hvy 77 4468

OUR EMILY 2 b f £0
51 9 AYR 7f Soft 3962
69 7 YARM 8f Heavy 4475

OUR FIRST LADY 3 b f £2339
72 11 ASCO 8f Gd/Sft 1108
74 2 YARM 6f Good 1773
69 2 BATH 6f Gd/Fm 3820
50a 11 LING 8f Aw 71 4335

OUR FRED 3 ch c £8964
75 4 WIND 5f Gd/Sft 77 1427
71 4 REDC 6f Gd/Sft 1562
59 9 SAND 5f Gd/Fm 75 2478
69 2 LING 5f Good 2590 BL
78 1 **LEIC** 5f Gd/Fm 2919* bl
82 1 **THIR** 5f Gd/Fm 75 3349+ bl
84 2 NEWM 5f Gd/Fm 82 3631 bl
67 14 YARM 5f Firm 84 3920 bl

OUR INDULGENCE 2 ch g £0
42 12 RIPO 6f Gd/Fm 3466
46 7 YORK 6f Good 3814
55 9 BEVE 7f Good 3952

OUR JACK 5 ch g £0
28a 4 WOLV 9f Aw 259
23a 7 SOUT 12f Aw 344

OUR LITTLE CRACKER 2 b f £0
38a 7 LING 5f Aw 1740
43 4 WIND 6f Gd/Fm 2052
46 4 BRIG 7f Gd/Sft 2424

OUR MEMOIRS 3 ch c £0
49 10 LING 6f Good 1399 t
29 12 NEWB 6f Gd/Fm 1783 t

OUR MONOGRAM 4 b g £7427
36 9 BRIG 12f Gd/Fm 53 1128
42 8 RIPO 16f Good 49 1597
40 7 ASCO 16f Good 47 2173
43 3 REDC 16f Gd/Fm 42 2866
48 1 **SAND** 16f Good 43 3434*
55 1 **BATH** 17f Firm 49 3625*
51 5 NOTT 16f Soft 54 3978
0 8 BATH 17f Soft 54 4139

OUR PEOPLE 6 ch g £3731
36a 9 LING 10f Aw 48 22
38a 5 LING 10f Aw 43 102
26a 5 WOLV 12f Aw 40 170
11a 9 SOUT 12f Aw 36 211 t
31a 3 WOLV 12f Aw 31 261 t
28a 5 WOLV 9f Aw 31 305 t
29a 3 WOLV 12f Aw 31 410 t
29a 3 LING 13f Aw 30 458 t
36a 1 **WOLV** 12f Aw 30 522* t
29a 3 WOLV 12f Aw 33 554 t
39a 2 WOLV 16f Aw 33 576 t
39a 2 WOLV 12f Aw 35 607 t
15a 9 SOUT 16f Aw 39 644 t

OUR SHELLBY 2 b f £0
0 11 BEVE 7f Good 3953
9 7 PONT 10f Soft 4230

OUR SOUSY 3 b f £4117
83 1 **BEVE** 10f Gd/Fm 3672*

OUT LIKE MAGIC 5 ch m £0
0a 12 LING 7f Aw 45 29

OUT OF AFRICA 3 b f £0
30 9 NEWB 7f Soft 913
79 14 GOOD 7f Gd/Sft 97 1470
81 6 HAYD 6f Gd/Sft 1833
48 11 NEWM 6f Good 90 4198

OUT OF MIND 5 br h £60976
111ε 2 SUFF 9f Fast 1749

OUT OF REACH 3 b f £32810
87 5 NEWB 7f Soft 913
99 2 AYR 8f Gd/Fm 1630
98 1 **NEWM** 7f Good 90 2567*
102 4 GOOD 7f Good 3104
111 1 **SAND** 8f Good 3469*
106 3 CURR 8f Gd/Fm 3846

OUT OF SIGHT 6 ch g £15468
67a 1 **SOUT** 7f Aw 60 75*
70a 2 SOUT 8f Aw 68 473
75a 1 **SOUT** 7f Aw 68 539*
53a 7 WOLV 8f Aw 77 580
76a 3 SOUT 7f Aw 74 687
49 12 REDC 8f Firm 60 1296
49 10 WARW 8f Heavy 59 1520
54 9 DONC 7f Gd/Fm 57 1840
48 7 DONC 8f Gd/Fm 55 2349
67 1 **NOTT** 8f Gd/Fm 2682*
57 4 NOTT 8f Gd/Fm 62 3115
58 3 WIND 8f Good 62 3355
61 4 NEWC 7f Soft 61 3708
50 8 LEIC 8f Gd/Sft 4033
0 22 ASCO 8f Gd/Sft 70 4126

OUT ON A PROMISE 8 b g £3214
37 8 FOLK 12f Gd/Fm 44 2295
37 7 BRIG 10f Gd/Fm 41 2727
46 1 **CHEP** 12f Gd/Fm 41 2971*
42 7 WIND 12f Gd/Fm 47 3049
42 4 SALI 14f Gd/Fm 44 3424
40 9 LING 16f Firm 44 3755

OUT RANKING 8 b m £846
65 2 CHEP 18f Gd/Fm 65 2490
59 5 BATH 17f Firm 65 2941

OUTPLACEMENT 5 b g £1907
15a 8 SOUT 11f Aw 455
30a 1 **SOUT** 16f Aw 25 535*
0a 11 SOUT 16f Aw 30 644

OUTRAGEOUSE 2 b g £270
23 10 BRIG 7f Gd/Fm 3239
68 4 YARM 8f Gd/Fm 3665

OUTSTANDING TALENT 3 gr f £699
45 6 SALI 7f Good 1349
0 20 REDC 6f Gd/Sft 52 1578
35 7 RIPO 6f Good 52 1600
47 2 CHEP 7f Good 1972
37 4 YARM 7f Gd/Fm 2413
36 7 BATH 8f Gd/Fm 45 3816
8 8 LEIC 10f Heavy 4313

OUZO 7 b g £666667
123 1 **KRAN** 10f Firm 657*

OVAMBO 2 b c £995
82 3 SALI 8f Gd/Sft 4163
83 3 BATH 8f Soft 4429

OVER THE MOON 6 ch m £6238
46a 5 WOLV 7f Aw 61
38a 6 WOLV 8f Aw 136
20a 7 SOUT 11f Aw 178
52a 1 **WOLV** 9f Aw 259* vis
10a 8 WOLV 9f Aw 360 vis
58a 1 **SOUT** 8f Aw 600* vis
0a 13 SOUT 8f Aw 57 647 BL
58a 1 **SOUT** 11f Aw 672*
55a 4 WOLV 9f Aw 61 681
38 7 DONC 10f Gd/Fm 45 705
15 9 BATH 12f Good 47 1091
23a 7 SOUT 12f Aw 1203
0 15 LEIC 10f Soft 38 1546
41a 4 SOUT 11f Aw 1978 vis
49a 3 SOUT 11f Aw 2119 vis
32a 6 SOUT 8f Aw 41 2380 vis
37a 6 WOLV 16f Aw 41 2606 vis
42a 7 SOUT 8f Aw 2946 vis

OVERSLEPT 3 br c £0
21a 8 SOUT 6f Aw 2299
24a 8 WOLV 6f Aw 2604
7a 9 WOLV 9f Aw 3272

OVERSMAN 7 b g £828
49 2 HAMI 12f Firm 47 1241
28a 8 SOUT 11f Aw 1417

OVERSPECT 2 b c £7556
90 3 SALI 7f Gd/Fm 3391
102 1 **DONC** 7f Gd/Fm 3859*
72 6 CHES 8f Soft 4072

OZAWA 3 gr c £0
44 12 THIR 6f Soft 909
0 15 LING 6f Good 1399
40 9 LEIC 8f Gd/Fm 51 2506
12 13 YARM 8f Good 46 3236 t

OZONE LAYER 2 b c £21134
106 1 **CHAN** 5f Hldng 2485*
95 5 MAIS 6f V 3066

PAARL ROCK 5 ch g £9806
18a 8 WOLV 8f Aw 47 411 VIS
14a 10 SOUT 8f Aw 42 584
0 12 WARW 8f Soft 45 1066
40 3 HAYD 11f Gd/Fm 41 2453 vis
50 2 CHES 10f Gd/Fm 48 2671 vis
54 1 **LEIC** 10f Gd/Fm 50 3093* vis
56 4 HAYD 11f Good 56 3285 vis
54 4 LEIC 10f Gd/Fm 54 3337 vis
58 1 **NOTT** 10f Good 55 3524* vis
54 6 LEIC 10f Firm 58 3842 vis
20 13 CHES 10f Soft 58 4074 vis
30a 5 WOLV 12f Aw 46 4386 vis

PACHINCO 2 ch c £0
0 17 YARM 8f Soft 4512

PACIFIC ALLIANCE 4 b c £20043
63a 3 LING 8f Aw 65 463
55a 4 LING 8f Aw 65 596

PACIFIC PLACE (continued)

54a	4	LING	10f Aw	63	880	bl
0	14	BEVE	7f Good	65	2882	bl
55	7	HAYD	8f Good	61	3288	
60	3	BRIG	8f Firm	59	3527	
67	1	**MUSS**	8f Gd/Fm	59	3746*	bl
79	1	**YORK**	8f Good	67	3810*	
81	1	**MUSS**	8f Gd/Sft		4135*	
58	17	NEWM	8f Good	80	4340	
62	12	NEWM	7f Soft	79	4547	

PACIFIC PLACE 3 gr c £4406

43	11	DONC	6f Good		731
55	2	BRIG	5f Firm	50	1334
46	4	BRIG	5f Soft		1512
55	2	DONC	5f Gd/Fm		1843
55	3	HAMI	5f Firm		2096
56	2	REDC	6f Gd/Fm		2154
59	2	CARL	6f Gd/Fm	56	2243
46	8	CHEP	6f Gd/Fm	60	2489
30	11	HAMI	6f Gd/Fm	60	2779
54	8	FOLK	6f Gd/Fm		3584
0	20	NEWM	5f Good	57	4185
0	17	LING	5f Soft	57	4270

PACINO 3 b c £68975

111	1	**COLO**	8f Good		1322*
109	3	CHAN	9f V		1753

PACK A PUNCH 3 b f £0

59a	4	SOUT	5f Aw		127
56a	6	SOUT	5f Aw		179
36	7	MUSS	5f Firm		1430
0	11	CATT	5f Gd/Sft	45	1817
0	13	MUSS	5f Firm	41	2047

PACKIN EM IN 2 b c £247

0	15	WIND	5f Gd/Fm		3044
47	8	GOOD	6f Good		3649
62	4	NOTT	6f Soft		3973
60	4	BRIG	7f Soft	60	4416
35	8	WIND	6f Heavy	60	4525

PADAUK 6 b g £0

0a	13	LING	16f Aw	56	6	bl
0a	8	LING	16f Aw	56	424	bl

PADDY MCGOON 5 ch g £0

54	6	BRIG	10f Firm		1331
36	11	BRIG	10f Gd/Sft	56	1509
53	4	BRIG	12f Gd/Fm		1934

PADDY MUL 3 ch c £530

0	19	RIPO	10f Soft	45	827	t
0	14	REDC	8f Firm		3330	t
34	3	MUSS	9f Gd/Fm		3591	t
36	11	YORK	9f Good		3808	t
29	4	CATT	14f Soft		4002	t
0	10	AYR	11f Heavy		4304	VIS

PADDYS RICE 9 ch g £0

21	13	WIND	10f Good		3045	
16	11	WIND	12f Good	41	3186	
23	6	BRIG	10f Firm		3526	
0	15	BRIG	10f Firm	35	3737	t

PADDYWACK 3 b c £9354

43a	6	SOUT	5f Aw	49	72	bl
0a	10	SOUT	8f Aw	47	128	bl
11a	9	SOUT	6f Aw	42	331	bl
32a	5	WOLV	7f Aw	42	346	bl
42a	2	SOUT	6f Aw	36	515	bl
43a	4	LING	5f Aw	45	526	bl
49a	1	**WOLV**	6f Aw	42	638*	bl
55a	1	**LING**	7f Aw	48	654*	bl
57a	2	WOLV	6f Aw	55	706	bl
57	2	NOTT	6f Good	55	785	bl
59a	2	SOUT	5f Aw	58	870	bl
0a	11	WOLV	7f Aw	60	1390	bl
34	11	RIPO	6f Good	58	1600	bl
62a	2	LING	6f Aw	60	1742	bl
37	12	REDC	6f Good	56	1891	bl
0a	U	WOLV	6f Aw	64	2603	bl
0	14	RIPO	6f Gd/Fm	55	3010	bl
16a	12	WOLV	6f Aw	64	4023	bl
56a	5	WOLV	6f Aw	62	4223	bl
0a	13	WOLV	6f Aw	60	4358	bl

PADHAMS GREEN 4 b c £12156

64	3	NEWM	8f Gd/Fm	62	1690	
53	6	NEWB	10f Gd/Fm	63	1942	
65	2	NEWM	7f Firm	63	2347	
69	1	**NEWM**	8f Gd/Fm	65	2802*	
66	5	BEVE	8f Gd/Fm	69	3407	
71	2	BRIG	7f Gd/Sft	69	4121	
83a	1	**WOLV**	8f Aw	67	4248*	
83a	1	**LING**	8f Aw	73	4335*	

PAGAN KING 4 b c £2118

70a	5	LING	8f Aw	74	96
58a	6	LING	10f Aw	71	161
50	9	BRIG	8f Gd/Sft	74	895
60	8	NEWB	7f Gd/Sft	72	1590
61	4	BRIG	8f Firm	73	3259
66	3	BATH	8f Gd/Fm	66	3514
69	2	KEMP	8f Soft	66	4038
0	14	REDC	8f Gd/Sft	67	4217

PAGAN PRINCE 3 br c £0

55	10	WIND	8f Gd/Fm		2211
73	5	NEWM	8f Gd/Fm		3626
65	6	LING	7f Firm		3834

PAGE NOUVELLE 2 b f £5801

88	3	GOOD	7f Good		3108
88	1	**BEVE**	6f Good		3397*
85	7	ASCO	8f Good		4110

PAGEANT 3 br f £6047

67	5	SAND	7f Soft	74	1569
76	1	**YARM**	6f Good		1773*
75	2	LEIC	7f Firm	72	2026
64	6	PONT	6f Good	75	2364
78	2	NEWM	7f Gd/Fm	75	2855
74	5	NOTT	8f Gd/Fm	76	3005
54	5	NEWM	7f Good		3612
60	5	NEWM	7f Good		4018
51a	8	LING	7f Aw		4331

PAGEBOY 11 b g £280

43a	6	WOLV	7f Aw		65
44a	6	WOLV	8f Aw		138
51a	4	LING	6f Aw		313 vis
33a	4	WOLV	6f Aw	39	351 vis
22a	5	SOUT	7f Aw	39	476 vis
40	3	CATT	7f Gd/Fm		778 vis

PAGLIACCI 2 ch c £404

83	4	NEWM	6f Gd/Fm		1691
82	5	ASCO	5f Good		2152

PAID UP 2 b g £225

70	4	PONT	5f Good		2360
59	6	BEVE	5f Firm		2730
63	8	THIR	5f Gd/Fm		3346

PAINTED ROOM 2 ch c £4156

93	2	NEWM	8f Good		4161
93	2	NEWM	8f Good		4349

PAIRING 2 ch g £3447

71	4	SAND	5f Good		1962
82	1	**LING**	5f Aw		2588*
62	9	ASCO	7f Gd/Fm		3015
0	23	NEWB	6f Sft/Hvy	84	4468

PAIRUMANI STAR 5 ch g £33528

86	9	NEWM	12f Firm	95	1187
103	1	**GOOD**	14f Gd/Sft	95	1484*
107	2	CHAN	15f Good		2402
107	1	**LEOP**	14f Good		2909*
107	4	DEAU	15f Gd/Sft		3552
73	9	NEWM	16f Good		4351

PAIYDA 2 b f £3542

88	1	**LING**	7f Soft		4268*

PALACE AFFAIR 2 ch f £4602

0	W	SALI	5f Firm		1176	
63	5	WIND	6f Good		3352	BL
104	1	**KEMP**	6f Gd/Fm		3795*	bl
72	16	NEWB	5f Gd/Sft		4454	bl

PALACE GREEN 4 ch f £0

23a	10	SOUT	6f Aw		30
45a	7	SOUT	5f Aw		71
0a	12	SOUT	7f Aw		130
44a	8	SOUT	6f Aw		201
0a	12	SOUT	6f Aw	53	250
9a	12	WOLV	6f Aw	48	351

PALACE ROYALE 4 b f £4750

101	2	LEOP	12f Good		3371

PALACEGATE JACK 9 gr g £4583

45a	5	LING	5f Aw	53	91	bl
54a	2	WOLV	5f Aw	52	191	bl
56a	2	LING	5f Aw	53	312	bl
52a	5	LING	5f Aw	56	403	bl
56a	3	WOLV	5f Aw		533	bl
54a	2	WOLV	5f Aw		753	bl
58a	3	WOLV	5f Aw		919	bl
41	8	MUSS	5f Gd/Fm		1430	bl
0	14	NEWC	5f Heavy		1766	bl
33	3	HAMI	5f Gd/Fm	41	2233	
20	15	NEWC	5f Good	41	2525	
48a	5	LING	5f Aw		2650	bl
59	4	CARL	5f Firm		2822	
60	5	BEVE	5f Gd/Sft		3056	
53	6	AYR	6f Good		3366	
81	11	NOTT	5f Good		3521	
86	5	LEIC	5f Firm		3841	
92	4	BEVE	5f Sft/Hvy		4043	
55	7	REDC	5f Gd/Sft		4220	

PALACEGATE TOUCH 10 gr g £7488

59a	3	WOLV	7f Aw		61	bl
64a	2	LING	8f Aw		92	bl
55a	5	SOUT	6f Aw		130	bl
58a	3	LING	6f Aw		313	bl
60a	4	LING	7f Aw		398	bl
52a	2	LING	6f Aw		484	bl
35a	7	LING	7f Aw		547	bl
40a	5	WOLV	6f Aw		680	bl
13	7	NEWC	6f Soft		756	bl
57a	1	**WOLV**	5f Aw		1139*	bl
45	3	CARL	5f Gd/Sft	45	1724	bl
33	11	CATT	6f Gd/Sft	45	1815	bl
41	7	HAMI	6f Gd/Fm	45	1941	bl
45	3	HAMI	5f Firm		2095	bl
0	13	CARL	6f Gd/Fm		2240	bl
44	3	HAYD	5f Gd/Fm	44	2505	bl
48	3	NOTT	6f Gd/Fm		2680	hbl
48	6	CATT	6f Gd/Fm		2744	bl
51	5	HAMI	6f Gd/Fm		2798	
51	8	REDC	7f Gd/Fm		2994	bl
43	9	THIR	6f Gd/Fm	49	3144	bl
41	4	CARL	7f Firm		3197	bl
39	8	HAMI	5f Gd/Sft	46	3536	bl
73	7	HAYD	6f Heavy		3768	
0	12	CHES	6f Soft		4069	
0	13	REDC	5f Gd/Sft		4220	
75	3	CATT	6f Soft		4257	
56a	4	WOLV	6f Aw	55	4442	bl
61a	1	**WOLV**	6f Aw	55	4553+	

PALAIS 5 b g £0

53a	7	SOUT	14f Aw	62	37	
32a	8	SOUT	11f Aw	56	324	
0a	11	SOUT	16f Aw	51	428	
20	8	SOUT	11f Gd/Sft	36	855	vis
9a	11	SOUT	11f Aw	36	1306	vis
0	14	NOTT	14f Good	37	1874	

PALANZO 2 b c £6991

93 2 NEWM 6f Gd/Fm 2132
99 1 **NEWB** 6f Firm 3980*
98 8 NEWM 7f Good 4196

PALATIAL 2 b f £37907
84 2 YARM 6f Good 1774
84 2 NOTT 6f Gd/Fm 2189
89 2 NOTT 6f Gd/Fm 2683
90 1 NEWM 7f Firm 82 3299*
96 1 **NEWB** 7f Firm 3985*
94 1 NEWM 7f Good 89 4157*

PALAWAN 4 br g £14310
71a 2 WOLV 7f Aw 478
71a 1 **WOLV** 7f Aw 531*
76a 1 **SOUT** 7f Aw 71 599*
73 2 KEMP 6f Gd/Fm 71 728
0 13 HAMI 6f Gd/Fm 74 844
76 3 WIND 6f Gd/Fm 73 1196
52 9 KEMP 6f Soft 74 1531
76 1 **WIND** 5f Gd/Fm 1881*
65 7 SALI 6f Aw 74 2266
71 6 SAND 5f Gd/Fm 73 2925
77 2 BATH 5f Firm 72 3209
75 5 NEWB 6f Firm 76 3485
76 3 DONC 5f Firm 75 3894
71 8 LEIC 5f Gd/Sft 76 4027
76 5 YORK 5f Soft 76 4285

PALERIA 4 ch f £0
0a 13 LING 7f Aw 68 28

PALLIUM 12 b g £0
11 12 HAMI 5f Gd/Fm 30 1358 tbl
0 13 MUSS 5f Gd/Fm 1430 tbl
20 7 HAMI 5f Firm 2095 tbl
5 10 HAMI 5f Gd/Fm 28 2233 t
12 10 MUSS 5f Gd/Sft 28 2535 tbl
0 19 AYR 6f Heavy 35 4327 tbl
0 13 MUSS 5f Soft 42 4516 t

PALMSTEAD BELLE 3 b f £0
61 8 CHES 5f Gd/Fm 73 1219 t
53 11 CHEP 5f Gd/Sft 70 1795 t
35 9 NOTT 5f Gd/Fm 3113
0 15 THIR 5f Gd/Fm 58 3349 t

PALO BLANCO 9 b m £7141
9a 10 SOUT 6f Aw 56 47
38a 3 WOLV 6f Aw 680
50a 3 WOLV 6f Aw 719
45a 4 LING 6f Aw 48 881
51 2 DONC 6f Gd/Sft 1068
50a 2 WOLV 6f Aw 47 1233
51a 3 WOLV 6f Aw 50 1391
47 3 CHEP 6f Heavy 53 1557
41a 2 LING 6f Aw 1913
42a 4 SOUT 6f Aw 50 2297
40a 6 SOUT 6f Aw 50 2385
56 2 LING 6f Good 50 2654
20 11 SALI 6f Gd/Fm 54 3293
50 4 LING 6f Firm 54 3578
37a 4 WOLV 6f Aw 48 3774
43 10 YARM 6f Gd/Fm 93 3966
53a 1 **SOUT** 6f Aw 47 4156*
55 6 WIND 6f Gd/Sft 57 4293
55a 3 WOLV 6f Aw 53 4442
42a 8 WOLV 6f Aw 54 4553

PALUA 3 b c £8212
76 3 BATH 10f Good 75 1094
73 4 BATH 10f Gd/Fm 1439
76 3 CHES 10f Gd/Sft 1779 BL
78 2 NEWB 12f Gd/Fm 75 1948 bl
68 10 ASCO 12f Good 75 2116 bl
78 3 KEMP 14f Gd/Fm 75 2872 bl
75 3 THIR 12f Gd/Fm 77 3148 bl
78 2 WARW 16f Good 76 3695
78 4 SAND 14f Gd/Fm 78 3948

77 3 BATH 17f Soft 77 4139
78 2 DONC 15f Gd/Sft 76 4451

PALVIC LADY 4 b f £0
0 19 BEVE 5f Firm 60 1278
0 12 BEVE 5f Firm 57 1923
43a 8 WOLV 5f Aw 52 3271
37a 7 SOUT 6f Aw 47 4156

PAMELA ANSHAN 3 b f £0
25 10 WARW 7f Gd/Sft 48 1710
0 16 YARM 10f Gd/Fm 45 1955
16 8 BRIG 10f Gd/Fm 40 3263
51 7 LING 6f Firm 3579
41 6 YARM 7f Firm 3921 VIS
42 9 LEIC 6f Gd/Sft 4031 vis
0 15 LING 8f Soft 4273 vis

PAMPERED QUEEN 6 b m £0
0 12 WIND 10f Good 3189

PAN JAMMER 2 b c £44842
82 4 NEWM 5f Gd/Fm 1169
91 1 **SALI** 5f Good 1346*
94 2 LEOP 6f Yldg 1756
105 3 ASCO 5f Good 2113
104 1 **CURR** 6f Good 2738*
103 4 GOOD 5f Good 3105
0 16 DONC 6f Gd/Fm 3862
99 6 NEWB 6f Firm 3996

PANDJOE 4 b c £520
13 15 NEWC 5f Soft 62 758
56 5 NEWC 5f Heavy 60 1008
55 5 THIR 6f Gd/Fm 58 1356
55 6 AYR 6f Gd/Fm 58 1654
47 8 CARL 6f Firm 58 2015
54 6 HAMI 5f Gd/Sft 57 3536
55 11 LEIC 7f Firm 56 3839
38 11 PONT 5f Soft 4087 BL
55 3 AYR 6f Heavy 53 4327
0 13 NEWC 6f Heavy 53 4425

PANG VALLEY GIRL 2 ch f £0
66 6 KEMP 7f Gd/Fm 3074

PANIS 2 b c £24976
105 3 LONG 8f Good 3926
105 1 LONG 9f Good 4237*

PANNA 2 b f £0
80 4 NEWM 7f Soft 4541

PANOORAS LORD 6 b g £0
8 12 HAMI 13f Gd/Fm 37 1194

PANSY 4 br f £0
9a 10 SOUT 7f Aw 55 599

PANTAR 5 b g £38934
84a 7 WOLV 8f Aw 448
74a 3 WOLV 8f Aw 85 551 BL
87a 2 WOLV 9f Aw 83 611 bl
92a 1 **WOLV** 9f Aw 662* bl
96 4 DONC 8f Good 94 733 bl
96 3 KEMP 8f Soft 93 1015 bl
90 6 JAGE 9f Good 1323
97 3 SAND 8f Soft 94 1567 bl
42 13 EPSO 9f Gd/Sft 94 1829 bl
50 21 ASCO 8f Good 94 2090 bl
95 2 KEMP 8f Firm 92 2870 bl
94 3 GOOD 10f Gd/Fm 92 3060
88 6 YORK 10f Gd/Fm 94 3563
99 1 **GOOD** 9f Good 93 3883*
80 22 NEWM 9f Gd/Fm 99 4212

PANTHER 10 ch g £0
0 14 BRIG 6f Gd/Fm 33 3243
0 13 WARW 5f Good 3694
25 11 CHEP 8f Good 3868

PAOLINI 3 b c £71439
104 3 CAPA 12f Gd/Fm 1618
109 7 BADE 12f V 3849

PAPABILE 3 b f £46855

90 2 NEWM 7f Gd/Fm 1155
89 4 HAYD 8f Gd/Sft 86 1535
91 1 **YARM** 8f Good 1771*
101 1 **ASCO** 8f Good 89 2167*
105 1 **ASCO** 8f Gd/Fm 3340*
103 4 CURR 8f Gd/Fm 3846
92 8 NEWM 8f Gd/Fm 4211

PAPAGENA 3 b f £1196
58a 5 SOUT 5f Aw 60 72
43a 6 LING 7f Aw 58 149
48a 4 SOUT 8f Aw 56 213 BL
42a 6 SOUT 8f Aw 300 bl
52a 2 WOLV 9f Aw 51 392 bl
49a 4 SOUT 11f Aw 53 536 bl
49a 3 WOLV 9f Aw 52 709 bl
0 14 THIR 8f Soft 62 931 bl
41a 7 WOLV 9f Aw 51 1040 bl
30 10 BEVE 10f Firm 1274 bl

PAPARAZZA 3 b f £0
51 5 SALI 8f Gd/Fm 3289
0 15 NEWM 8f Gd/Fm 3626
0 13 LEIC 10f Good 3838
0 15 PONT 12f Soft 49 4229

PAPE DIOUF 3 b c £3642
24a 10 SOUT 6f Aw 426
56a 1 **LING** 5f Aw 487* bl
55a 4 LING 5f Aw 527 bl
58a 1 **LING** 5f Aw 619* bl
40 9 CATT 5f Gd/Fm 777 bl
42 6 FOLK 5f Soft 959 bl
0 14 MUSS 5f Firm 1430 bl
0 14 MUSS 5f Firm 47 2047
26 11 CARL 5f Firm 47 2280
30 10 MUSS 5f Firm 42 2374
28 7 HAMI 6f Gd/Fm 44 2779
0a 13 SOUT 6f Aw 56 4155
0 17 AYR 5f Heavy 41 4307

PAPER MOON 3 b f £0
0 11 CURR 8f Gd/Sft 1626

PAPERWEIGHT 4 b f £1850
43a 4 WOLV 12f Aw 752
63a 2 LING 10f Aw 60 1265
65a 3 WOLV 9f Aw 1388
15 9 SOUT 10f Soft 65 1608
63a 3 LING 10f Aw 65 2186
57 4 WARW 11f Good 62 2463
41a 4 LING 10f Aw 2764
43 9 WIND 10f Aw 3189 BL

PAPI SPECIAL 3 b c £5330
0 9 PONT 12f Gd/Sft 72 1106 vis
32 9 NEWC 10f Gd/Sft 1480 vis
54 2 HAMI 11f Gd/Fm 1909 vis
55 4 HAMI 13f Gd/Fm 54 2238 vis
48 3 HAMI 13f Gd/Fm 54 2643 vis
58 1 **HAMI** 13f Gd/Fm 54 2801*
57 D NEWC 14f Good 56 3249
57 2 HAMI 13f Gd/Sft 56 3378
39 12 BEVE 12f Gd/Fm 58 3674 vis
45 10 HAMI 12f Gd/Sft 55 3827 vis
0 11 AYR 11f Heavy 4304 vis

PARA GLIDER 2 br c £0
83 5 LING 7f Soft 4268
88 11 NEWM 6f Good 4345

PARABLE 4 b c £5168
60a 5 SOUT 12f Aw 70 590
70a 1 **SOUT** 12f Aw 66 671*
75a 3 SOUT 12f Aw 72 695
58 9 NEWC 10f Soft 68 757
0 13 YORK 14f Firm 68 1329
0 8 REDC 14f Gd/Fm 65 1563
54 5 AYR 11f Good 60 2139 BL

PARADISE 3 b c £0

PARADISE GARDEN 3 b c £1989
63a	9	NAD	9f Dirt		765
89	3	DONC	8f Gd/Sft		1069
85	8	CHES	10f Firm		1246
73	4	THIR	8f Good		1382
77	9	YORK	8f Firm	92	3597
78	7	KEMP	12f Gd/Fm	89	3798
0	14	YORK	10f Soft	84	4282

PARADISE LANE 4 ch c £2270
83	2	KEMP	5f Soft	83	1013
53	12	CHES	5f Firm	84	1245
48	13	KEMP	6f Soft	83	1531
64	13	ASCO	5f Good	81	2676
56	19	GOOD	5f Gd/Fm	78	3093
0	13	LEIC	5f Gd/Sft	74	4027

PARADISE NAVY 11 b g £587
35	11	NEWB	13f Gd/Fm	58	1784	bl
45	9	BATH	17f Firm	55	1996	bl
33	8	BATH	13f Gd/Sft	50	3518	bl
40	3	WARW	16f Good	43	3695	bl
38	6	GOOD	14f Gd/Sst	48	3887	bl
35	7	NOTT	16f Soft	43	3978	bl
37a	9	SOUT	16f Aw	60	4149	bl

PARADISE YANGSHUO 3 b f £3422
0	14	BEVE	5f Firm		1280
0	11	PONT	6f Good		1500
46	4	MUSS	5f Firm	46	2047
49	1	MUSS	5f Gd/Fm		2204*
44	5	HAYD	5f Gd/Fm	49	2505
48	3	HAMI	6f Gd/Fm	47	2779
31	12	DONC	5f Gd/Fm	47	3161
30	14	HAMI	5f Gd/Sft	46	3825
34	10	LEIC	6f Gd/Sft		4031

PARAGON OF VIRTUE 3 ch c £3089
82	7	NEWM	7f Gd/Sft		983
85	2	THIR	8f Gd/Sft		1352
85	3	HAYD	8f Gd/Sft		1837
85	3	DONC	10f Gd/Fm	83	2610

PARDAN 6 b h £0
4a	6	WOLV	12f Aw	34	408
23a	5	LING	13f Aw		524
15a	7	WOLV	16f Aw	31	576

PARDY PET 3 ch f £0
41a	6	WOLV	6f Aw		62
0	19	SALI	7f Good		1349
0	12	THIR	6f Gd/Fm	45	2060	BL
52	8	EPSO	6f Gd/Sft	62	2432	
31	10	CHEP	6f Gd/Fm	40	2976	bl
41	5	EPSO	6f Gd/Fm	45	3405	bl
34	10	WARW	5f Good		3694	bl
0	14	GOOD	5f Good	50	3908	bl

PARISIAN LADY 5 b m £5658
49a	8	LING	7f Aw	56	28
58a	1	LING	8f Aw	53	152*
0a	15	SOUT	7f Aw	59	216
52a	6	WOLV	9f Aw	65	230
40a	6	WOLV	9f Aw	56	309
50a	3	LING	12f Aw	54	528
48a	4	LING	12f Aw	52	621
46	4	BATH	8f Firm	50	1998
48	2	CHEP	10f Gd/Fm	49	2493
43	8	EPSO	10f Good	49	2790
48	2	BRIG	12f Firm	49	2893
0	U	BRIG	10f Firm	47	3557
36	4	YORK	10f Gd/Sft	47	3731
40	8	SAND	10f Soft	45	4208

PARISIEN STAR 4 ch c £33422
80	4	LING	7f Soft	82	1286
74	8	GOOD	8f Gd/Sft	82	1450
78	4	KEMP	7f Firm	80	2261
73	5	EPSO	7f Gd/Sft	80	2431

86	1	GOOD	8f Gd/Fm	79	3063*
89	2	GOOD	8f Good	84	3107
86	4	WIND	8f Good	87	3642
83	8	GOOD	9f Good	87	3883

PARISIENNE HILL 4 b f £0
11	9	NOTT	10f Good	33	2011
14	8	BEVE	12f Firm		2219
0	7	MUSS	16f Good	20	3099
19	10	BEVE	12f Gd/Fm		3654
30	7	BEVE	10f Gd/Fm		3677
0	17	YORK	9f Good		3808
20	9	DONC	10f Heavy		4571

PARK HALL 2 b c £272
84	4	LING	7f Soft		4267
73	6	NEWM	10f Soft		4543

PARK ROYAL 5 b g £0
13a	8	SOUT	8f Aw	39	83
23a	6	SOUT	11f Aw	33	325
0a	8	SOUT	12f Aw	27	413
0	13	GOOD	12f Soft		4061

PARKER 3 b c £2928
73	2	NOTT	6f Firm		1266
73	4	NEWB	7f Gd/Fm	73	1787
69	6	CHEP	7f Good	73	1969
73	3	FOLK	7f Good		2621
71	5	CHEP	6f Gd/Fm	72	3257
67	3	LING	8f Firm	72	3580
73	2	WARW	8f Gd/Fm		3914

PARKERS PEACE 3 b c £0
47	9	MUSS	8f Gd/Fm	61	1434
48	7	YARM	10f Good	57	1775
43	5	WARW	12f Gd/Fm	53	2254

PARKSIDE 4 b g £1215
0	20	DONC	8f Good	79	715
77	5	SAND	8f Heavy	78	1042
0	13	HAYD	8f Soft	76	1490
74	3	LEIC	8f Soft	76	1547
59	7	SALI	8f Gd/Fm	75	2229
50	17	NEWM	8f Good	73	2564
0	26	ASCO	7f Gd/Fm	70	2999
61	9	AYR	10f Good	67	3368

PARKSIDE PROPHECY 2 ch c £0
64	6	BATH	6f Gd/Sft		2550

PARKSIDE PROSPECT 3 b f £3503
53a	2	SOUT	5f Aw	50	72
51a	3	LING	6f Aw	51	165
62a	1	LING	6f Aw		207*
47a	4	LING	6f Aw		288
57a	5	WOLV	5f Aw	52	397
40a	7	LING	5f Aw	58	526
29a	7	LING	7f Aw	54	617
37a	7	LING	6f Aw	51	1742
0	13	BRIG	7f Gd/Fm	52	2729
0	19	LING	6f Firm	49	3759	BL

PARKSIDE PURSUIT 2 b c £2860
77	7	NEWB	5f Gd/Fm		1782
74	11	NEWB	6f Gd/Fm		1943
77	1	REDC	5f Gd/Fm		2142*

PARLEZ MOI DAMOUR 5 gr m £0
27a	7	SOUT	8f Aw		195

PARTE PRIMA 4 b g £0
38	4	BRIG	10f Gd/Sft		2423	bl
5a	6	SOUT	12f Aw		2636	bl

PARTING SHOT 2 b c £0
66	9	YORK	6f Firm		1328

PARTY CHARMER 2 b f £4186
79	1	WARW	5f Soft		1059*
85	4	WIND	5f Firm		1290
86	9	ASCO	5f Good		2088
82	6	NEWM	7f Gd/Fm		3164
94	5	YORK	6f Firm		3596
60	9	AYR	5f Gd/Sft		4009

PARTY PLOY 2 b g £0
61	7	WIND	6f Gd/Fm		3047
70	8	NEWM	7f Good		3608
60a	8	WOLV	8f Aw		4022

PARVENUE 2 b f £3845
78	1	NOTT	6f Good		1408*
78	2	CATT	7f Gd/Fm		2741
87	4	NEWM	7f Good		3164

PAS DE MEMOIRES 5 b g £1665
106&	3	LING	10f Aw		55

PAS DE PROBLEME 4 ch c £10482
54	8	WARW	11f Heavy	59	890
64	1	WARW	11f Heavy	56	1003*
60	5	WARW	11f Soft	62	1065
64	3	NEWB	10f Good	62	1375
68	1	SAND	10f Soft	63	1570*
65	4	KEMP	12f Gd/Fm	65	1927
63	6	HAYD	11f Good	65	3285
30	15	NEWB	13f Firm	64	3994
53	8	CHES	10f Soft	64	4074
38	9	YORK	10f Soft	62	4282

PAS DE SURPRISE 2 b c £0
0	18	LING	7f Soft		4268

PAS FARIBOLE 3 b f £0
46	8	YARM	10f Gd/Fm		3381
0	14	LING	8f Soft		4274

PASADENA 3 b f £343
59	10	LEIC	7f Good		794
68	4	WIND	8f Heavy		934
52	13	WIND	8f Gd/Sft		1099
0	14	NOTT	8f Good	67	1414
38	12	WIND	10f Gd/Fm	63	2206
29	9	CHEP	8f Gd/Fm		2448	BL

PASHMEENA 2 b f £2152
84	2	NEWM	5f Gd/Sft		970
72	6	SALI	5f Firm		1176
91	3	KEMP	7f Gd/Fm		3359
81	5	DONC	7f Gd/Fm	80	3860
78	7	CHES	7f Soft	81	4070
75	7	NEWM	6f Gd/Fm	80	4214
0	19	NEWB	6f Sft/Hvy	79	4468

PASITHEA 2 b f £10911
55	4	RIPO	5f Gd/Fm		1595
62	5	BEVE	5f Gd/Fm		2480
78	3	YORK	6f Good		2692
68	3	NEWC	6f Good		3245
75	1	BEVE	7f Gd/Fm	69	3411*
56	11	DONC	8f Gd/Fm	74	3879
80	2	CHES	7f Soft	74	4070
78	2	CATT	7f Soft	75	4254
81	2	NEWB	7f Gd/Sft	77	4453

PASO DOBLE 2 b c £3844
51	7	LEIC	5f Gd/Sft		828
80	3	WIND	6f Gd/Fm		1876
69	4	WARW	7f Good		2459
76	2	NEWB	7f Gd/Fm	70	3175
76	2	SALI	7f Gd/Fm		3418
78	2	LING	7f Firm	75	3830

PASS THE REST 5 b g £0
56	6	NEWC	17f Gd/Sft	62	1478

PASSE PASSE 4 b f £0
32a	5	LING	8f Aw		114	BL
42a	8	LING	10f Aw	60	161	bl

PASSION FOR LIFE 4 br g £10822
88	1	KEMP	6f Good	83	728*
86	8	WIND	6f Heavy		935
60	10	KEMP	6f Good	88	1531
10	8	SAND	5f Good	88	3473
0	28	AYR	6f Gd/Sft	86	4012
77	8	SALI	6f Gd/Sft	84	4165

PASSIONS PLAYTHING 4 ch g £0
53a	6	LING	12f Aw	75	486

0	21	DONC	12f Gd/Fm	70	699
0	10	KEMP	10f Soft	70	1528 BL
23	13	WIND	10f Gd/Fm	64	1878 bl

PAT PINKNEY 2 b f £324
46	7	CHES	5f Gd/Sft		1776
42	5	CARL	6f Firm		2014
52	4	MUSS	5f Gd/Fm		2200
44	5	CATT	5f Gd/Fm		2435
53	4	CHES	5f Gd/Fm		2668
45	6	THIR	7f Gd/Fm		3128
39	11	HAMI	5f Gd/Sft		3376

PAT THE BUILDER 2 b c £1855
60	5	BRIG	5f Gd/Fm		1124
66	4	BRIG	5f Firm		2039
29	8	YARM	5f Firm		2766
60	4	FOLK	5f Firm		3038
54	6	BATH	5f Firm		3204
68a	1	LING	5f Aw		4333*
53	7	NEWC	5f Heavy	63	4423

PATACAKE PATACAKE 3 b f £0
64	7	RIPO	10f Soft	68	827
52	6	THIR	12f Soft		924

PATHAN 2 b c £7994
53	7	YARM	6f Gd/Fm		1954
70	5	LING	7f Gd/Fm		2182
76	1	LING	7f Good		2653*
76	4	BRIG	7f Firm	78	2894
81	2	NEWM	7f Firm	76	3299
78	3	BEVE	7f Gd/Fm	76	3411
81	2	NEWC	8f Firm		3601
82a	1	WOLV	8f Aw		3772*

PATRICIAN FOX 2 b f £2390
53	7	REDC	5f Gd/Sft		1130
48	8	NOTT	6f Good		1408
64	3	CATT	6f Good		1659
60	4	HAMI	6f Gd/Fm		1938
58a	3	SOUT	5f Aw		2120
57	2	BEVE	6f Good		2880
52	6	BEVE	5f Gd/Sft		3055
8	10	PONT	6f Soft	58	4235
56	2	NEWC	5f Heavy	55	4423
46	7	MUSS	5f Soft	57	4561

PATRINIA 4 ch f £0
15a	8	SOUT	6f Aw	36	604
0a	16	SOUT	8f Aw		646

PATRITA PARK 6 br m £0
18	10	PONT	10f Good	42	1496
39	6	LEIC	12f Gd/Fm	42	1736

PATSY CULSYTH 5 b m £2874
45	1	NEWC	6f Soft		756*
35	9	THIR	6f Soft	50	910
45	7	REDC	5f Gd/Sft	48	1133
45	3	SOUT	5f Gd/Fm	46	1606
40	6	CATT	6f Gd/Sft	46	1815
32	8	BEVE	5f Firm	46	1923
46	3	DONC	7f Gd/Fm	44	2320
0	19	DONC	7f Gd/Fm	44	2612
0	16	DONC	7f Gd/Sft		4461

PATSY STONE 4 b f £13197
57	5	WIND	8f Good	61	854
48	8	ASCO	8f Gd/Sft	61	1113
70	1	LEIC	8f Soft	60	1547*
70	1	CHEP	7f Gd/Sft	66	1794*
67	4	WIND	8f Gd/Fm	69	2051
66	4	DONC	8f Gd/Fm	69	2349
57	5	WIND	8f Soft	69	2546
67	3	WIND	8f Good	69	2713
71	2	WIND	8f Gd/Fm	68	2890
56	10	ASCO	8f Gd/Fm	68	3018

PATSYS DOUBLE 2 b c £26254
101	1	NEWB	6f Gd/Fm		1403*
97	1	SALI	6f Gd/Sft		2469*

103	1	NEWB	7f Firm		2848*
104	5	DONC	7f Firm		3891
103	3	NEWM	7f Good		4196

PAULAS PRIDE 2 ch f £1767
45	7	WIND	7f Firm		1290
49	10	LING	7f Firm		3829
57	6	WARW	15f Gd/Fm		3911
72	1	BRIG	8f Gd/Sft		4117*
84	6	NEWM	6f Good		4345
68	7	DONC	7f Soft	79	4460

PAULINES STAR 4 b f £0
0a	13	LING	7f Aw		8

PAWN BROKER 3 ch c £98511
110	1	NEWM	9f Gd/Sft		980*
113	2	SAND	10f Heavy		1056
114	2	YORK	10f Firm		1326
0	13	CHAN	12f V		1752
105	3	KEMP	12f Gd/Fm		3792
113	1	NEWB	11f Firm		3984*
114	2	NEWM	12f Good		4194

PAWN IN LIFE 2 b g £0
0	11	REDC	5f Gd/Sft		4496

PAWSICLE 4 b f £324
38a	3	WOLV	16f Aw	47	66
27a	9	WOLV	16f Aw	45	318

PAX 3 ch c £547
88	4	LEIC	6f Gd/Sft		829
64	11	WIND	6f Heavy		935
0	26	NEWM	6f Gd/Fm	89	1173

PAY HOMAGE 12 ch g £0
0	14	SALI	12f Good	45	2689
35	7	KEMP	12f Gd/Fm	40	3073
30	7	WIND	12f Good	40	3186

PAY THE SILVER 2 gr c £1521
63	11	NEWB	7f Gd/Fm		1782
73	4	YORK	6f Firm		2005
75	3	AYR	7f Good		2161
68	5	NEWC	7f Gd/Fm		2985
65	5	BRIG	6f Gd/Fm	72	3258
66	4	EPSO	7f Good	70	3690

PAYS DAMOUR 3 b c £21298
62	7	WARW	7f Gd/Fm	73	1061
78	2	WIND	6f Firm	72	1289
75	5	EPSO	7f Gd/Sft	77	1826
69	17	ASCO	8f Good	78	2117
80	1	HAYD	6f Gd/Fm	75	2504*
82	2	DONC	6f Gd/Fm		2580
84	1	EPSO	7f Good		2792*
85	3	KEMP	6f Firm		2869
80	9	DONC	7f Gd/Fm	85	3880
88	2	NEWM	7f Gd/Fm	84	4215
89	3	NEWM	7f Good	87	4357

PCS EUROCRUISER 4 b c £0
23	9	PONT	10f Soft		1699

PEACE BAND 2 b c £826
67	5	PONT	6f Gd/Fm		2828
71	4	YARM	6f Gd/Fm		3385
69	3	LING	5f Firm		3576
69	8	NEWM	5f Good	71	4179

PEACE PACT 4 b f £0
0a	7	SOUT	6f Aw		559 bl

PEACEFUL PARADISE 2 b f £21005
87	3	CHEP	6f Gd/Sft		1798
86	1	KEMP	7f Firm		2259*
93	5	SAND	7f Good		2935
105	1	NEWM	7f Gd/Sft		3316*
103	3	DEAU	7f Gd/Sft		3722

PEACEFUL PROMISE 3 b c £5163
88	3	NEWM	7f Gd/Sft		983
86	1	DONC	7f Gd/Sft		1072*

PEACHES 3 b f £872
0	17	NEWM	7f Gd/Sft		971

0	11	NOTT	8f Gd/Fm		1269
61a	2	WOLV	9f Aw		3272
33a	9	WOLV	8f Aw	62	3769

PEACOCK ALLEY 3 gr f £47228
78	5	CHES	7f Gd/Fm	77	1215
82	1	WARW	7f Heavy		1525*
85	1	EPSO	7f Gd/Sft	77	1826*
88	1	AYR	7f Good	83	2163+
90	3	SAND	8f Gd/Fm	86	2495
91	2	DONC	7f Gd/Fm	88	3880
92	3	ASCO	8f Good	90	4113

PEACOCK JEWEL 3 ch c £2365
102	2	NEWB	10f Firm		2709

PEARL BRIGHT 2 gr f £4146
84	2	NEWB	7f Gd/Fm		4035
85	1	LEIC	7f Heavy		4312*
50	9	NEWM	8f Soft		4546

PEARL BUTTON 4 b f £860
25a	9	LING	8f Aw	52	147
31a	9	LING	10f Aw	46	209
43a	2	LING	12f Aw		267
0a	11	LING	12f Aw	45	377

PEARLY BROOKS 2 b f £601
74	5	NEWB	6f Firm		3449
71	3	LING	5f Soft		4187

PEARTREE HOUSE 6 b g £38385
67a	9	SOUT	7f Aw	82	687
77	5	KEMP	7f Good	84	725
80	6	THIR	7f Good	82	1158
63	14	CHES	8f Firm	82	1250
81	3	GOOD	7f Gd/Sft	79	1483
83	1	AYR	8f Good		2138*
88	2	AYR	7f Good	86	2163
86	4	GOOD	9f Good	86	2304
90	4	GOOD	8f Gd/Fm	88	2356
89	8	NEWM	7f Gd/Fm	88	2616
86	6	ASCO	7f Gd/Fm	90	2997
88	6	GOOD	8f Good	88	3107
94	1	YORK	8f Firm	91	3597*
78	10	DONC	8f Firm	96	3897
0	26	ASCO	7f Good	90	4112
0	18	ASCO	8f Gd/Sft	96	4126

PEDRO JACK 3 b c £11469
78	3	BRIG	7f Gd/Fm		1125
81	1	WIND	6f Firm	74	1289*
76	7	NEWB	6f Gd/Fm	80	1406
79	6	NEWM	6f Gd/Fm	80	1694
65	10	CHEP	5f Gd/Sft	80	1795
80	3	KEMP	6f Gd/Fm	80	1925
76	5	BATH	5f Firm	80	2787 BL
83	2	YARM	6f Firm	80	2900 bl
83	2	LEIC	6f Gd/Fm	82	3335 bl
65	16	GOOD	6f Good	83	3646 bl
83	6	KEMP	6f Gd/Fm	83	3791
70	6	KEMP	6f Gd/Sft	82	4037

PEDRO PETE 3 ch g £28862
55a	4	LING	8f Aw		373
69a	1	LING	10f Aw	59	597*
53a	4	WOLV	8f Aw		636
69	3	SAND	8f Good	70	761
70	3	CHEP	10f Gd/Fm	68	2450
73	1	CHES	10f Good	68	2666*
77	1	ASCO	10f Gd/Fm	73	2955*
67	8	GOOD	10f Gd/Fm	77	3131
66	5	CHES	10f Gd/Fm	83	3426
65	10	KEMP	10f Gd/Fm	76	3794
80	1	YORK	10f Soft	75	4282*

PEEJAY HOBBS 2 ch g £0
53	13	RIPO	5f Soft		821
42	8	BEVE	5f Heavy		974

PEEP O DAY 9 b m £0
0	13	PONT	17f Firm	33	3501

PEGASUS BAY 9 b g £5230
53	1	**HAMI**	9f Gd/Fm		2236*
55	1	**HAMI**	9f Gd/Fm		2642*
39	7	HAMI	9f Gd/Sft		3375
45a	6	LING	12f AW		4186

PEGGYS ROSE 3 b f £3466
68	1	**LEIC**	6f Gd/Sft		830*
65	4	EPSO	9f Heavy		1033
0a	11	SOUT	6f Aw	66	1205
0	25	NEWB	7f Gd/Fm	65	1405
55	2	CHES	6f Gd/Sft		1780
19	11	CHES	7f Gd/Fm	60	2250
0	17	PONT	6f Soft		4233

PEGGYS SONG 2 b f £0
36	8	CATT	6f Gd/Fm	2926
24	7	BEVE	5f Gd/Fm	3408
0	14	REDC	5f Gd/Fm	4216

PEGNITZ 5 b g £3636
98	6	NAD	12f Good		767
105	4	NEWM	10f Gd/Fm		1174	BL
102	4	CHES	10f Firm		1248
107	3	NEWB	10f Gd/Sft		1592
96	4	NEWM	10f Firm		3300

PEKAN HEIGHTS 4 b c £3601
55	1	CHES	10f Gd/Fm		2245*	vis
36	7	DONC	17f Gd/Fm	70	2607	vis
66	4	SALI	10f Good		2981	bl
55	9	CHES	12f Firm	64	3173	bl

PEKANESE 3 b c £1210
70	6	LING	7f Gd/Sft	840
76	2	KEMP	7f Soft	1012
60	9	LING	10f Gd/Sft	1263
54	6	YARM	7f Soft	4387

PEKANOORA 2 b c £0
41	9	SALI	10f Gd/Fm	3420
63	5	NOTT	8f Soft	3972
0	17	SALI	8f Gd/Sft	4163

PEKANSKI 3 b f £0
94	7	LING	10f Gd/Sft		1283
86	6	SAND	8f Good	93	3435

PEKAY 7 b g £1007
24a	2	SOUT	12f Aw	70	682	
35	10	KEMP	14f Good	65	726	bl
58	3	PONT	10f Heavy	60	943	
52	5	WIND	12f Gd/Sft		1096	bl
55	3	LEIC	12f Soft	58	1551	bl
41	9	NEWB	13f Gd/Sft		1594	bl
0	17	SALI	12f Good	56	2689	

PELAGIA 2 b f £386
84	4	SALI	7f Firm	3752

PELIGRO 5 b g £0
0a	9	WOLV	9f Aw	553

PELLI 2 b f £266
27	10	NEWM	5f Gd/Fm		970
0	18	LING	12f Gd/Fm		2182
45	3	YARM	7f Firm		2898
34	7	NEWM	7f Firm		3296
34	8	LEIC	8f Firm	46	3837
37a	7	SOUT	7f Aw		4154

PEMBROKE STAR 4 b f £0
0	16	LING	7f Gd/Sft	1261
0	13	WIND	10f Good	3189
0	17	NEWM	8f Gd/Fm	3626

PEN FRIEND 6 b g £2787
52a	5	WOLV	16f Aw	54	577
51a	2	SOUT	14f Aw	54	668
57	2	DONC	18f Good	54	714

PENALTA 4 ch g £4022
20a	8	WOLV	8f Aw		661
40	8	SALI	10f Gd/Fm		2981
40	7	NEWM	7f Gd/Fm		3318
36	3	BEVE	10f Gd/Fm	37	3656

44	1	**BRIG**	12f Soft	37	4176*
0a	14	LING	12f Aw	45	4334
47	2	YARM	14f Heavy	44	4476

PENANG PEARL 4 b f £3328
62	10	SAND	8f Good	3469
89	2	GOOD	8f Soft	4077

PENDULUM 2 ro f £0
73	7	YARM	7f Firm	3940

PENG 3 ch c £0
0a	14	SOUT	6f Aw		685	t
0	13	RIPO	8f Soft		826	t
67	7	NOTT	8f Gd/Sft		1084	t
0	17	YORK	8f Firm	74	1341	t
0	17	RIPO	8f Good		1596	t
0	16	HAMI	8f Gd/Fm	63	1907	t
37	7	CARL	7f Aw		2282	
0	17	BEVE	10f Sft/Hv	51	4046	
0	13	NEWC	7f Heavy	45	4426	

PENGAMON 8 gr g £14599
53a	2	LING	7f Aw	48	29
54a	2	LING	7f Aw	48	58
57a	1	**LING**	7f Aw	52	107*
57a	2	LING	8f Aw	57	210
59a	3	WOLV	8f Aw	59	1037
51	9	GOOD	8f Gd/Fm	59	2126
57	2	HAYD	7f Gd/Sft	54	2442
64	1	**DONC**	7f Gd/Fm	54	2612*
66	2	KEMP	7f Gd/Fm	54	2749
61a	4	LING	8f Aw	64	4330
65a	1	**LING**	7f Aw		4487*

PENMAR 8 b g £0
51	6	BEVE	12f Gd/Fm	3654

PENNY FARTHING 2 b f £0
67	7	LEIC	7f Gd/Fm	3333
66	7	SALI	7f Firm	3752
64	10	KEMP	7f Soft	4035

PENNY LASS 2 b f £806
69	6	WIND	6f Gd/Fm	2209
71	3	YORK	6f Good	3812

PENNY MUIR 3 b f £0
41	8	SAND	10f Soft	1588
0	9	KEMP	12f Gd/Fm	2751

PENNYS FROM HEAVEN 6 gr g £6786
62	7	BRIG	12f Firm	70	1209
61	3	THIR	12f Gd/Sft		1353
27	10	DONC	12f Good	60	1518
57	2	AYR	13f Gd/Sft		1657
46	4	CATT	14f Gd/Sft		1814
58	1	**AYR**	11f Good	53	2139*
50	2	BEVE	12f Firm		2219
57	4	NEWC	10f Gd/Fm	58	2309
51	5	EPSO	12f Gd/Sft	56	2626
49	7	NEWM	10f Gd/Fm	55	2958
53	4	BEVE	10f Gd/Sft	55	3052
50	6	CATT	14f Gd/Fm	55	3201
49	4	CATT	12f Good	54	3437
52	3	YARM	14f Gd/Fm	52	3664
35	9	AYR	11f Soft	52	3963
51a	4	SOUT	16f Gd/Sft	52	4149
26	10	PONT	12f Soft	52	4229
48a	4	SOUT	14f Aw	49	4371
50a	4	WOLV	12f Aw		4549

PENNYS GOLD 3 b f £28819
111	2	CHAN	8f V	1754
115	1	**DEAU**	8f Gd/Fm	3717*
110	5	LONG	8f Good	4259

PENNYS PRIDE 5 b m £2832
73	3	NEWC	7f Soft		759
68	7	LEIC	10f Gd/Sft		833
73	2	NEWC	8f Heavy		1010
71	3	WARW	8f Soft		1062
54	9	HAYD	8f Good	73	1490

69	3	REDC	8f Good	70	1892
54	12	REDC	8f Gd/Sft	70	4217
58	9	REDC	8f Gd/Sft	69	4499
50	8	DONC	8f Heavy	69	4573

PENSHIEL 3 b c £7688
64	1	**BEVE**	12f Good	56	1446*
69	1	**LING**	11f Firm	60	1911*
77	2	YARM	14f Gd/Fm	68	2195
77	3	NEWB	16f Firm	75	2812
77	3	REDC	16f Gd/Fm	77	2993

PENSION FUND 6 b g £1884
82	3	CHES	12f Gd/Fm	80	1217
78	7	YORK	9f Firm	81	2001
52	19	YORK	10f Good	81	2696
67	10	CHES	8f Gd/Fm	78	3510
55	11	RIPO	8f Good	78	3699

PENTAGON LAD 4 ch c £15706
30	15	DONC	8f Good	67	715
59	5	HAMI	8f Good		847
70	1	**HAMI**	8f Firm	63	1243*
68	4	BEVE	8f Gd/Fm	69	1279
63	8	REDC	10f Gd/Sft	69	1561
61	6	RIPO	8f Good	69	1598
71	2	RIPO	10f Gd/Fm		2111
68	5	CARL	8f Gd/Fm	67	2242
74	1	**HAMI**	9f Gd/Fm	67	2799+
74	4	RIPO	9f Gd/Fm	74	3011
77	2	REDC	8f Firm	74	3309
71	6	REDC	8f Gd/Fm	76	3634
0	16	YORK	8f Good	75	3810
73	3	MUSS	8f Gd/Sft		4135
65	9	NEWM	8f Gd/Fm	72	4340
0	22	NEWM	8f Soft	71	4545

PENTAGON LADY 2 ch f £218
0	12	CATT	5f Good		1659
0	13	THIR	5f Good		2057
41	9	BEVE	5f Gd/Fm		2480
57	5	REDC	7f Gd/Fm		2862
57	4	REDC	7f Firm		3308
20	13	PONT	8f Soft	55	4084
0	19	DONC	6f Gd/Sft		4449

PENTAGONAL 3 b c £15349
75	9	NEWM	10f Good		957	
82	1	**LING**	10f Gd/Sft		1281*	
84	3	GOOD	12f Gd/Sft	80	1637	
88	1	**YORK**	12f Firm	82	2002*	VIS

PENTLAND 2 br c £0
0	15	NEWM	6f Gd/Fm	3162
74	5	NEWM	6f Gd/Fm	3627
75	8	YARM	7f Firm	3940
0	24	NEWM	7f Good	4158

PEONY 3 ch f £56485
109	1	**MAIS**	7f Soft	946*
111	2	LONG	8f V	1319
108	5	DEAU	8f Gd/Fm	3069
104	2	DEAU	8f Gd/Sft	3551

PEPE GALVEZ 3 br c £1871
75	7	WIND	8f Gd/Fm	1200
88	3	GOOD	12f Gd/Sft	1455
88	2	LEIC	12f Gd/Sft	1738

PEPETA 3 b f £306
65	6	WIND	8f Gd/Fm	69	1201
48	12	NEWB	7f Gd/Fm	67	1405
48	9	SOUT	7f Soft		1606
63	4	NOTT	8f Good	64	1873

PEPPERCORN 3 b f £292
20a	3	SOUT	7f Aw		88
20a	9	SOUT	8f Aw	47	128
34a	6	SOUT	8f Aw		385
19a	8	SOUT	8f Aw	40	429
55	9	WIND	8f Gd/Fm		3048
37	3	YARM	8f Good	40	3236

40	6	KEMP	9f Gd/Fm	43	3357
8	10	BEVE	10f Gd/Fm	39	3656
31	6	EPSO	10f Good	41	3762
36	4	YARM	11f Firm		3917
25	11	SALI	10f Gd/Sft	41	4168

PEPPERDINE 4 b c £4000

96	3	NEWM	6f Gd/Fm	93	1173	
99	5	LEOP	5f Yldg		1757	
0	22	ASCO	6f Good	95	2151	
79	15	DONC	6f Gd/Fm	95	3861	
0	24	AYR	6f Gd/Sft	95	4012	VIS

PEPPIATT 6 ch g £6090

42a	7	SOUT	7f Aw		667
59	3	SOUT	6f Good	60	802
57	4	THIR	5f Good	60	908
44	8	NEWC	7f Heavy	60	1011
61	3	AYR	6f Gd/Fm	59	1654
59	5	AYR	6f Good	60	2163
43	15	GOOD	6f Good	60	2355
47	8	PONT	6f Gd/Fm	59	2559
62	2	YORK	6f Good	59	2697
62	5	NEWC	7f Gd/Fm	61	2986
62	3	NEWM	6f Gd/Fm	61	3119
54	5	NEWC	7f Good	61	3250
0	21	AYR	5f Soft	61	3960
0	16	AYR	7f Soft	61	3992
52	13	YORK	6f Soft		4287
42	9	AYR	6f Heavy	59	4327
0	17	NEWC	6f Heavy	59	4405

PERADVENTURE 5 b g £0

56	6	SOUT	12f Soft	77	1604

PERCHANCER 4 ch c £11766

44a	11	WOLV	9f Aw	55	67
34a	6	SOUT	11f Aw	52	126
48a	3	WOLV	9f Aw	49	305
48a	2	WOLV	9f Aw	48	405
60a	1	WOLV	9f Aw	48	432*
60a	1	SOUT	8f Aw	54	496*
16a	10	WOLV	9f Aw	58	569
35	11	DONC	10f Gd/Fm	52	705
57	1	HAMI	9f Good	51	846*
57	3	MUSS	8f Gd/Sft		899
51	4	REDC	9f Gd/Sft	57	1583
55	4	HAMI	9f Firm	56	2094
30	8	HAMI	9f Firm	56	2397
49	3	HAMI	9f Gd/Fm	54	2799

PERCHINO 3 b g £0

45a	8	WOLV	7f Aw		362

PERCUSSION 3 ch c £348

54	10	DONC	7f Gd/Sft		1072
0	13	LING	7f Gd/Sft		1261
54	6	BATH	8f Gd/Fm		1436
53	4	SAND	11f Good	54	1967
44	7	YARM	14f Gd/Fm	54	2195
34	10	BEVE	12f Good	53	3954
17	12	YORK	10f Soft		4275

PERCY VERANCE 2 ch c £0

54	10	MUSS	5f Gd/Sft		898
0a	12	SOUT	5f Aw		1418
39	10	NEWC	8f Soft		3706

PEREGIAN 2 b c £11482

68	5	HAMI	5f Gd/Fm		1189
78	3	DONC	6f Good		1513
60	7	HAYD	6f Soft		1823
80	1	CATT	7f Gd/Fm		2417*
87	1	AYR	7f Gd/Fm	74	2718*
87	1	CATT	7f Gd/Fm	80	2928*
82	9	GOOD	7f Gd/Fm		3086
90	3	YORK	7f Good	87	3542
88	5	DONC	8f Gd/Fm	89	3879
72	11	DONC	7f Soft	89	4460

PERESTROIKA 2 ch c £0

0	17	DONC	7f Gd/Sft		4447

PERFECT LOVER 2 ch c £0

0	9	PONT	6f Soft		4373

PERFECT MOMENT 3 b f £12984

25	15	WIND	6f Good	57	852
36a	4	WOLV	9f Aw		1141
52	2	NOTT	8f Gd/Sft	52	1365
58	1	NOTT	10f Soft	53	1644*
63	1	PONT	8f Good		1865*
60a	1	WOLV	9f Aw	55	2080*
62	6	GOOD	9f Gd/Fm	65	3089
70	1	BRIG	10f Gd/Fm	65	3263*
63	9	EPSO	12f Good	70	3858
63	9	YARM	10f Firm	70	3941
75	1	BRIG	12f Gd/Sft	68	4123*

PERFECT PEACH 5 b m £3884

0	16	THIR	7f Good	69	1158
54	10	CHES	8f Firm	69	1250
64	8	REDC	7f Firm	69	1297
54	11	DONC	6f Gd/Fm	67	1842
63	4	THIR	8f Gd/Fm	65	2062
66	3	BEVE	7f Firm	65	2221
58	4	CATT	7f Gd/Fm		2437
56	6	ASCO	7f Gd/Fm	66	2999
68	2	REDC	7f Firm	66	3328
93	7	PONT	6f Firm		3503
65	6	BEVE	7f Gd/Fm	69	3652
98	4	DONC	5f Gd/Fm		3874
91	10	NEWM	5f Good		4182
97	6	NEWM	6f Good		4346

PERFECT PIROUETTE 2 b f £995

81	2	YARM	8f Heavy		4477

PERFECT PLUM 2 b f £57352

60	5	PONT	7f Firm		2174
85	2	YARM	7f Firm		2390
66	3	BEVE	7f Good		2881
76	2	NEWC	7f Good	74	3246
87	1	NEWC	8f Gd/Sft	76	3704*
89	9	DONC	8f Gd/Sft		3876
102	1	AYR	8f Soft	85	3990*
105	1	DEAU	8f Heavy		4401*

PERFECT SUNDAY 2 b c £5032

82	3	DONC	7f Gd/Fm		3156
99	2	NEWB	7f Good		3450
92	3	DONC	8f Firm		3864

PERFECTLY HONEST 2 b f £0

0	19	DONC	8f Heavy		4569

PERFIDIOUS 2 b c £0

57	9	NEWB	6f Sft/Hvy		4470
0	16	DONC	6f Heavy		4575

PERICLES 6 b g £0

0	14	BRIG	7f Gd/Sft	27	896	bl

PERIGEE MOON 2 ch c £29250

104	1	LEOP	7f Heavy		4557*

PERIGEUX 4 b c £2837

71	5	WIND	6f Gd/Sft		1423	
51	5	LEIC	6f Soft	62	1545	
49	9	YARM	6f Gd/Fm	62	1953	
52	7	GOOD	6f Gd/Fm	62	2124	
56	5	SALI	5f Gd/Fm	59	2266	bl
63	1	BRIG	5f Soft	59	2428*	bl
45	9	FOLK	5f Good	64	2623	bl
42	10	WIND	5f Good	63	2716	bl
0	15	SALI	5f Firm	62	3747	
60	3	SAND	5f Gd/Fm		3947	VIS
48	14	GOOD	5f Gd/Fm	60	4065	vis
0	15	SAND	5f Soft		4207	
64a	4	WOLV	6f Aw	67	4380	bl
44	11	NEWB	5f Gd/Sft	55	4459	bl

PERLE DE SAGESSE 3 b f £8883

65a	2	LING	6f Aw		24
63a	1	LING	7f Aw		53*

48a	7	LING	6f Aw	68	105
63a	1	LING	7f Aw		155*
47a	7	LING	7f Aw		243
56a	5	LING	7f Aw	62	287
52a	4	LING	7f Aw		459
44a	5	SOUT	8f Aw		514
52	3	BRIG	7f Firm		1212
41	8	SALI	7f Good		1349
52a	2	LING	7f Aw		1739
55	1	WIND	6f Gd/Fm	53	1877*
43	14	WIND	6f Gd/Fm	59	2054
36	8	WIND	6f Soft		2549
41	11	BRIG	6f Gd/Sft	58	4120

PERPETUAL PRIDE 3 b c £0

0a	7	SOUT	11f Aw		586

PERPETUO 3 b f £5071

59	3	REDC	10f Gd/Sft		1582
65	3	PONT	12f Gd/Fm		2560
58	6	LEIC	10f Gd/Fm		2774
63	2	HAMI	11f Soft	62	3805
67	1	BEVE	12f Good	62	3954*
0	15	NEWM	14f Gd/Fm	70	4213
38	10	PONT	10f Soft	66	4374

PERRYSTON VIEW 8 b h £59165

108	1	DONC	5f Gd/Fm	98	702+	bl
98	14	NEWM	5f Gd/Fm		1172	bl
104	5	YORK	5f Firm	107	1324	
116	1	SAND	5f Soft		1566+	
99	19	ASCO	5f Good		2065	bl
105	5	YORK	5f Firm		3598	
105	5	HAYD	5f Gd/Sft		3784	
109	6	DONC	5f Gd/Fm		3874	
108	4	LONG	5f Good		4261	bl
101	6	LONG	5f Heavy		4495	bl

PERSEUS WAY 2 b c £0

53	12	LING	7f Soft		4267

PERSIAN CAT 2 b f £3216

69	5	SALI	6f Gd/Fm		1882
70	1	THIR	6f Gd/Fm		2057*
61	4	MUSS	7f Gd/Fm		2201

PERSIAN FAYRE 8 b g £5369

34	14	NEWC	7f Heavy	61	1011
63	1	AYR	6f Gd/Fm	59	1631*
52	11	AYR	7f Good	64	2163
54	8	CATT	7f Gd/Fm		2437
59	8	AYR	7f Firm	63	2878
68	2	CARL	7f Firm		3573
56	8	YORK	7f Good	65	3809
0	29	AYR	6f Gd/Sft	63	4010
0a	11	WOLV	7f Aw	61	4550

PERSIAN FILLY 3 b f £10020

92	2	SAN	10f Heavy		1227

PERSIAN POINT 4 ch g £0

25	10	MUSS	7f Gd/Fm	41	1149
18	12	HAMI	8f Firm	41	1243
26	6	MUSS	14f Firm	36	2375

PERSIAN PRIDE 2 ch c £1604

57	10	KEMP	7f Firm		2867
81	4	LEIC	7f Gd/Fm		3333
93	2	DONC	8f Gd/Fm		3864
76	17	NEWM	7f Good		4158

PERSIAN PUNCH 7 ch g £115290

115	2	ASCO	16f Gd/Sft		1109
75	8	YORK	14f Firm		1339
114	1	SAND	16f Soft		1565*
115	6	ASCO	20f Good		2114
113	5	GOOD	16f Good		3106
115	1	DEAU	15f Gd/Sft		3552*
115	3	DONC	18f Gd/Fm		3877
119	2	LCNG	20f Good		4264
122	1	NEWM	16f Good		4351+

PERSIAN SPIRIT 2 b f £0

68	8	NEWB	7f Firm		2810
60	6	EPSO	7f Gd/Fm		3412
44	11	YORK	8f Gd/Fm		3729

PERSIAN WATERS 4 b c £3889

67	1	NOTT	16f Soft	62	3978*
68	2	GOOD	16f Soft	66	4075

PERSIANO 5 ch g £98150

89	8	NEWM	7f Gd/Sft	92	966
87	3	LING	8f Gd/Sft		1262
93	1	GOOD	8f Gd/Sft	18	1450*
100	3	ASCO	8f Good	92	2090
104	2	NEWM	7f Gd/Fm	96	2616
93	5	ASCO	8f Good	96	2997
103	1	GOOD	8f Gd/Sft	97	3107+
69	14	YORK	8f Firm	101	3597

PERSUADE 2 ch c £872

62	4	GOOD	7f Gd/Fm		2125	
78	4	SAND	7f Gd/Fm		2494	t
71	6	SALI	7f Gd/Fm		3391	t

PERTEMPS BOYCOTT 2 b g £0

0	13	WARW	15f Gd/Fm		3911
35	10	BRIG	6f Heavy		4537
0	21	DONC	6f Heavy		4575

PERTEMPS FC 3 b c £0

0	15	CHES	6f Gd/Fm	67	1220	
57	8	NOTT	5f Good	65	1412	
0	15	RIPO	6f Good	62	1600	
0	16	DONC	7f Gd/Fm	59	1840	
30	13	RIPO	6f Gd/Fm	59	3010	
44	8	THIR	5f Gd/Fm	55	3349	t
33	12	HAMI	5f Gd/Sft	52	3536	

PERTEMPS GILL 2 b f £263

39	7	NOTT	5f Heavy		1019
0	20	WIND	5f Gd/Fm		1197
40a	3	LING	5f Aw		1916
0	11	LING	7f Gd/Fm		2182
41	5	BATH	5f Gd/Sft		2551
47	4	BRIG	5f Firm		2891

PERTEMPS JACK 2 br g £315

7	6	BRIG	6f Gd/Fm		1931
9a	6	WOLV	6f Aw		2079
23	3	BRIG	7f Firm		3733

PERTEMPS JARDINE 2 b c £764

68	3	CHES	5f Gd/Sft		1776
65	4	MUSS	5f Gd/Sft		2532
59	5	RIPO	5f Good		2835
52	9	THIR	5f Gd/Fm	68	3145

PERTEMPS REVEREND 2 b g £0

0	13	LING	5f Soft		4187
43	6	NOTT	8f Heavy		4507

PERTEMPS STAR 3 b c £0

55a	7	SOUT	5f Aw		34
26a	9	SOUT	5f Aw	49	72
30	11	GOOD	5f Soft	40	4065
0	17	SAND	5f Soft		4207

PERTEMPS THATCHER 2 b f £836

49	4	RIPO	6f Good		1859
0	9	BEVE	7f Firm		2218
68	2	FOLK	7f Good		2620

PERUGIA 3 gr f £818

62	8	NEWM	7f Firm		1186
87	4	NEWM	7f Gd/Fm	92	2567
79	8	NEWM	6f Gd/Fm		3120
10	11	DONC	6f Heavy		4581

PERUGINO PEARL 3 b f £0

35	10	PONT	6f Soft		877
0a	12	WOLV	5f Aw		1036

PERUGINOS MALT 4 ch f £0

27a	6	LING	10f Aw		111
0	13	BATH	8f Gd/Fm	60	1442

PERUVIAN CHIEF 3 b c £16544

89a	1	LING	7f Aw	76	112*

84a	3	LING	7f Aw		206
81	9	NEWB	6f Gd/Fm	88	1406
89	5	HAYD	6f Gd/Sft	91	1534
88	2	NEWM	6f Gd/Fm	87	1694
75	12	YORK	6f Firm	89	2003
89	4	NEWC	7f Firm	88	2338
87	3	NEWM	6f Good	87	2568
88	3	ASCO	8f Gd/Sft	88	2954
82	6	NEWM	7f Gd/Fm	88	3315
84	8	YORK	6f Good	88	3543
79	10	EPSO	5f Good	88	3687
64	9	HAYD	6f Heavy		3768

PERUVIAN JADE 3 gr f £314

56a	6	LING	5f Aw	74	652
74	4	WARW	6f Heavy		888
68	8	NEWM	7f Good	74	954

PERUVIAN STAR 4 b c £0

34a	4	WOLV	7f Aw	73	721
59	5	LING	7f Gd/Sft		838
38a	13	WOLV	6f Aw	65	923
22	10	SAND	8f Heavy	58	1058
0	18	BRIG	5f Soft	55	1213
43a	5	WOLV	8f Aw	50	1393
32	10	YARM	7f Gd/Fm	47	1611
33	6	BATH	8f Firm	44	1998
29	11	WIND	10f Good		2372

PETALITE 2 gr f £0

67	6	SAND	5f Gd/Fm		2526
59	8	KEMP	6f Gd/Fm		2748

PETANE 5 b g £0

0	14	LING	11f Good	43	1743

PETARA 5 ch g £0

37	5	LING	10f Firm		3490	vis
32	11	WARW	11f Gd/Fm	39	3915	vis
51	8	YORK	12f Soft		4276	
0	20	NEWC	8f Heavy	38	4406	

PETARGA 5 b m £8378

65	9	BATH	6f Firm	76	1999
64	8	NEWB	6f Firm	74	2813
66	5	NEWM	6f Gd/Fm	71	3457
54	10	NEWM	6f Good	71	3613
74	1	BATH	6f Gd/Fm	68	3821*
78	1	LEIC	5f Gd/Sft	73	4027+
0	15	YORK	5f Soft	78	4285

PETER PERFECT 6 gr g £0

0	12	BEVE	12f Stt/Hv		4041
9	7	BRIG	12f Soft	30	4176

PETERS IMP 5 b g £16208

51a	5	WOLV	7f Aw		1038
60	8	MUSS	7f Gd/Fm	65	1431
66	2	CATT	7f Soft	62	1680
61	5	HAYD	8f Gd/Sft	65	1836
65	3	HAMI	6f Gd/Fm		1905
42	16	CARL	7f Gd/Fm	65	2242
67	1	WARW	7f Gd/Fm	64	2840*
75	1	ASCO	7f Gd/Fm	67	2999*
69	4	NEWC	7f Good	74	3250
75	3	HAYD	8f Gd/Fm	76	3325
75	3	CHES	8f Gd/Fm	75	3510
70	6	HAYD	7f Soft	75	3785
21	15	YORK	7f Heavy	75	4302
62	10	REDC	7f Gd/Sft	73	4498

PETERS PRINCESS 3 ch f £0

26	8	CATT	6f Soft		1678
29	9	RIPO	5f Gd/Fm		3462
0	16	THIR	5f Gd/Sft	24	3781

PETERSHAM 3 b c £1592

88	2	NEWB	10f Stt/Hv		4474

PETEURESQUE 3 ch c £6426

54	6	DONC	10f Good		713
73	2	REDC	10f Gd/Sft		1134
54	13	YORK	8f Firm	73	1341

0	17	RIPO	6f Good	70	1600
70	2	REDC	10f Gd/Fm	66	2992
66	8	NEWM	12f Gd/Fm	69	3167
74	1	REDC	10f Firm	69	3310*
34	14	CHEP	10f Good	75	3870

PETIT MARQUIS 3 b c £4258

91a	1	WOLV	8f Aw		708*
90	2	BEVE	7f Heavy		977
0	17	GOOD	9f Gd/Sft	92	1452
67	13	NEWM	10f Gd/Fm	90	2596

PETIT PALAIS 4 gr c £0

0a	14	SOUT	7f Aw		130	vis
0a	13	WOLV	8f Aw		138	bl

PETIT TOR 2 b f £5648

47	8	THIR	5f Soft		928
64	4	THIR	5f Good		1381
58	2	NEWC	6f Gd/Sft		1476
56	5	THIR	7f Gd/Fm		2057
60	2	HAYD	6f Gd/Fm		2441
55	6	CATT	7f Gd/Fm	61	2928
48	4	REDC	6f Firm		3307
60	1	CATT	7f Good		3438*
60	2	THIR	7f Gd/Fm		3615
60	8	BEVE	7f Good	56	3950
60	4	CATT	7f Soft	60	4254

PETITE DANSEUSE 6 b m £6704

27a	7	SOUT	6f Aw	39	87
30a	5	SOUT	6f Aw	40	246
30a	5	SOUT	6f Aw	36	280
26a	8	WOLV	6f Aw	38	466
22a	9	SOUT	6f Aw	42	499
37a	1	SOUT	6f Aw	33	604*
33a	4	SOUT	6f Aw	41	698
15a	6	WOLV	6f Aw	38	711
44a	1	WOLV	6f Aw	38	1233*
48a	1	SOUT	6f Aw	43	1422*
37a	6	SOUT	7f Aw	49	1506
0	16	DONC	6f Gd/Fm	44	1842
37	5	LEIC	6f Firm	40	2031
47a	2	SOUT	6f Aw	48	2297
38a	5	SOUT	6f Aw	48	2385
36a	4	SOUT	6f Aw	47	2820
37	6	REDC	6f Firm	39	3312
30	7	LING	6f Firm	38	3578
19a	10	SOUT	6f Aw	46	4155
34a	9	WOLV	6f Aw	44	4442

PETITE GALERIE 3 b f £0

20	10	YARM	7f Soft		4387

PETONGSKI 2 b g £7157

89	2	YORK	6f Good		2692
92	1	NEWC	6f Good		3245*
85	2	RIPO	6f Gd/Fm		3463
70	8	YORK	6f Good	90	3807
60	13	REDC	6f Gd/Sft		4219

PETOSKIN 8 b g £0

0a	10	WOLV	15f Aw	50	277

PETRA NOVA 4 ch f £0

0	13	NOTT	6f Gd/Fm		2680
0	16	RIPO	6f Gd/Fm	36	2839
25	6	THIR	7f Gd/Fm	32	3129
19	12	THIR	8f Gd/Sft		3775
50	8	REDC	5f Gd/Sft		4220 BL

PETRAIL 2 b f £0

55	10	RIPO	5f Soft		2539
53	7	BEVE	5f Firm		2730
66	4	BEVE	5f Gd/Sft		3055

PETRIE 3 ch g £1967

52a	3	WOLV	5f Aw		42
54a	2	SOUT	6f Aw		74
56a	2	SOUT	7f Aw		88
51a	5	SOUT	6f Aw		181
20a	6	LING	6f Aw	54	222

37	9	NOTT	6f Gd/Sft		1081	
52	3	SALI	7f Good		1349	
55	5	BATH	5f Gd/Sft		1670	
0	14	CHEP	6f Good	52	1971	
39	8	FOLK	6f Gd/Fm		2291	
32	10	CHEP	6f Gd/Fm	47	2489	
30	8	BRIG	7f Firm		2907	
0	11	BATH	12f Gd/Fm		3517	
48	6	CHEP	6f Gd/Fm		3682	
21	11	BRIG	8f Gd/Sft		4122	
44	10	BATH	8f Soft		4142	
18a	8	WOLV	7f Aw		4384	

PETRISK 3 b f £0
0	19	BRIG	10f Firm	1331	

PETROSELLI 3 b c £2882
110	4	LONG	11f V	864	
0	11	CHAN	12f V	1752	

PETROV 2 b c £300
68	10	LEIC	7f Firm	3840	
75	4	NOTT	8f Soft	3972	
0	15	BRIG	7f Soft	4172	

PETRUS 4 b c £585
0	17	KEMP	7f Good	87	725	
0	11	LING	7f Soft	85	1286	
61	10	DONC	7f Good	82	1514	
0	17	NEWM	7f Gd/Fm	79	2133	
68	5	YARM	8f Gd/Fm	74	2412	t
52	11	YARM	7f Firm	72	2768	t
65	8	ASCO	8f Gd/Fm	69	3018	t
65	8	GOOD	8f Gd/Fm	74	3136	t
49	13	LEIC	8f Gd/Fm	68	3334	t
66	4	LING	8f Firm	65	3831	

PETRUSHKA 3 ch f £371568
116	1	NEWM	7f Good	953+	
110	3	NEWM	8f Firm	1185	
113	4	EPSO	12f Gd/Sft	1828	
122	1	CURR	12f Gd/Fm	2739*	
122	1	YORK	12f Gd/Fm	3564*	
121	1	LONG	10f Good	4263*	

PETURA 4 br g £0
0	14	MUSS	9f Gd/Sft	48	795	VIS

PEYTO PRINCESS 2 b f £3142
74	3	NOTT	5f Gd/Sft		1641	
70	2	MUSS	5f Firm		2045	
70	2	BEVE	5f Gd/Sft		3055	
70	4	BEVE	5f Good	71	3394	
72	3	MUSS	5f Gd/Fm	70	3743	

PHANTOM FOOTSTEPS 3 gr g £0
0	8	PONT	12f Firm	2179	

PHANTOM RAIN 3 b f £4667
55	14	NEWM	10f Good		957	
81	2	BATH	10f Gd/Sft		2553	
78	5	ASCO	10f Gd/Fm		2957	
80	1	RIPO	10f Gd/Fm		3185*	
28	9	FOLK	10f Gd/Fm	75	3585	

PHANTOM STAR 3 b c £0
13a	8	LING	7f Aw	459	
39a	5	LING	10f Aw	545	
0	12	SOUT	10f Good	806	

PHARAOH HATSHEPSUT 2 b f £3973
51	4	MUSS	5f Gd/Sft		796	
43	12	MUSS	5f Gd/Sft		898	
65	7	MUSS	5f Gd/Fm		1146	
60	9	MUSS	5f Gd/Fm		1429	
57	4	MUSS	7f Gd/Fm	59	3592	
57	5	YORK	6f Good		3814	
37	8	MUSS	8f Gd/Sft	57	4132	
61	1	AYR	6f Heavy	55	4305*	
50	8	NEWC	5f Heavy	61	4423	

PHARAOHS HOUSE 3 b c £0
32	8	CATT	7f Soft		1681	
41	9	HAMI	6f Gd/Fm	49	1907	bl
35	10	CATT	12f Gd/Fm	46	2746	
40	5	REDC	11f Gd/Fm		2989	bl
36	5	BEVE	12f Gd/Sft	42	3050	bl
19	5	CATT	16f Gd/Fm		3199	bl

PHARMACYS PET 2 b f £0
59	7	GOOD	6f Good	2357	
6	13	KEMP	7f Gd/Sft	2583	
0	7	ASCO	6f Gd/Fm	3342	
57	6	SALI	6f Gd/Sft	4164	
0a	9	WOLV	7f Aw	4383	

PHAROAHS GOLD 2 b c £3143
81	4	DONC	6f Gd/Sft	1048	
73	4	CARL	5f Firm	1252	
80	1	NOTT	6f Good	1413*	
0	7	CURR	6f Good	2400	

PHASE EIGHT GIRL 4 b f £0
0	13	CATT	12f Gd/Sft	38	1816
30	7	BEVE	12f Firm		2219
4	7	MUSS	12f Gd/Sft	30	2537
4	6	BEVE	16f Gd/Fm	25	3406
0	10	MUSS	16f Gd/Fm	26	3742

PHEISTY 3 b f £7289
70	5	NOTT	8f Good	74	1873	
73	4	KEMP	9f Firm	72	2262	
74	1	YARM	10f Firm	72	2387*	
72	6	SALI	12f Good	74	2689	
71	5	NEWM	10f Gd/Fm	74	2958	
75	2	EPSO	10f Gd/Fm		3403	BL
68	6	GOOD	9f Good	74	3644	bl
69	6	KEMP	10f Gd/Fm	74	3794	bl
74	1	GOOD	12f Soft		4061*	

PHILAGAIN 3 b f £3815
59	4	AYR	10f Gd/Fm		1655	
26	11	HAMI	9f Gd/Fm	42	1939	
42	1	MUSS	8f Gd/Fm	40	2205*	
1	6	MUSS	9f Gd/Sft	42	2534	
44	3	AYR	7f Gd/Fm	45	2719	
29	12	HAMI	9f Gd/Fm	46	2799	
40	4	NEWC	7f Good	43	3033	
5	13	MUSS	8f Gd/Fm	43	3745	
10	10	AYR	9f Heavy		4324	
40	3	MUSS	7f Soft	41	4518	

PHILATELIC LADY 4 ch f £8193
72a	5	LING	10f Aw		593	
77	3	WIND	10f Gd/Fm		747	
81	3	SAND	8f Heavy	79	1042	
63	7	KEMP	10f Soft	79	1528	
91	3	EPSO	10f Gd/Sft		2630	
82	1	LING	9f Firm	78	3488*	
91	4	EPSO	10f Good		3684	

PHILIPPI 2 b c £528
50	8	SALI	7f Gd/Fm		3418	
61	3	BRIG	6f Firm		3732	BL
43	12	BEVE	5f Good		3955	bl
34	9	BRIG	6f Soft	62	4170	

PHILISTAR 7 ch h £3035
72a	1	LING	8f Aw		93	
58a	6	WOLV	8f Aw	75	137	
65a	5	LING	10f Aw	72	160	
65a	3	LING	10f Aw	70	244	
57a	3	SOUT	8f Aw		452	
53a	6	SOUT	8f Aw		600	
40a	10	LING	10f Aw	65	632	bl
39	9	BRIG	10f Firm		1331	
30	5	LEIC	8f Gd/Sft		1732	
27	12	RIPO	8f Gd/Fm	47	2099	bl
40	3	WARW	8f Gd/Fm	47	2257	bl
39	6	WARW	8f Good	43	2460	bl
0a	12	MUSS	8f Aw	60	2634	bl
17	7	DONC	8f Gd/Fm	50	2758	bl
0	12	NEWM	8f Gd/Fm		3117	bl
0	13	BRIG	8f Firm	40	3527	bl

PHILMIST 8 b m £0
0	15	HAMI	9f Good	47	846	bl
0	12	HAMI	11f Gd/Fm	45	1361	bl
0	16	HAMI	13f Gd/Fm	40	1936	bl
18	7	AYR	9f Heavy		4324	bl
11	11	MUSS	13f Soft	30	4521	bl

PHOEBE BUFFAY 3 b f £0
53	11	NEWM	8f Gd/Fm	77	2614
50	13	NEWM	7f Gd/Fm	75	2855
59	8	GOOD	9f Gd/Fm	72	3089

PHOEBE ROBINSON 2 b f £1574
0	12	KEMP	7f Soft	4035	
77	3	REDC	7f Gd/Sft	4216	
77	2	AYR	8f Heavy	4322	

PHOEBUS 2 b f £3390
69a	1	SOUT	7f Aw	63	31*	
58a	5	LING	7f Aw	68	112	
35	13	WARW	7f Heavy	64	887	
0a	13	SOUT	6f Aw	66	1205	
0	17	SALI	8f Gd/Fm	60	2264	t
56a	3	SOUT	7f Aw		2633	t
63a	3	SOUT	8f Aw		2950	t
0	12	CHEP	7f Gd/Fm		3253	t
44a	9	WOLV	7f Aw		3770	t
0	18	LEIC	6f Gd/Fm		4031	

PHURTIVE 2 b g £0
0	14	WARW	7f Gd/Fm	3909	
49	10	BATH	6f Soft	4138	
44	7	NEWM	8f Soft	4542	

PHYSICAL FORCE 2 b c £0
0	12	YORK	6f Firm		1328	
61	10	CHEP	6f Gd/Fm		1798	
48	8	SALI	6f Good		2687	
0	14	BRIG	7f Soft	55	4416	

PIAF 4 b f £0
0a	11	LING	16f Aw	46	6
30a	5	SOUT	11f Aw	42	131

PIANIST 6 ch g £0
0a	14	SOUT	16f Aw	50	1416

PIANO POWER 2 b c £0
0	14	AYR	8f Soft	3958	

PIC OF THE FIELD 2 ch f £224
18	5	WIND	6f Good	2369	

PICASSOS HERITAGE 4 gr g £317
0a	15	SOUT	8f Aw		869	
32a	3	WOLV	5f Aw		1036	
33a	11	WOLV	5f Aw		1237	
0	11	SOUT	7f Soft		1601	
0a	15	SOUT	7f Aw	37	2122	
0	19	NOTT	6f Gd/Fm		2680	
18	12	CATT	6f Gd/Fm		2744	VIS

PICCADILLY 5 ch m £1847
39	2	MUSS	12f Gd/Sft	37	1432
30	10	CATT	12f Gd/Sft	37	1816
22	8	RIPO	12f Gd/Sft	37	2109
33	4	MUSS	12f Gd/Fm	37	2202
24	6	HAMI	12f Gd/Fm	36	2783
18	5	MUSS	16f Good	34	3099

PICCALILLI 3 ch f £0
0	19	SALI	6f Firm		1175	
36	6	LING	7f Good		1675	
0	11	SALI	7f Gd/Fm		1886	
0	6	BRIG	8f Soft		2426	BL
0	11	EPSO	9f Good	45	2795	
18	7	BRIG	10f Gd/Fm	40	3263	
29	7	FOLK	12f Firm		3447	
29	7	BATH	12f Firm		3624	

PICCATA 3 b c £0
30a	7	SOUT	7f Aw	330	
45a	4	SOUT	7f Aw	417	

PICCLED 2 b c £3883
75	6	GOOD	5f Gd/Sft	1454	

78	1	**GOOD**	5f Gd/Sft			1639*	
72	9	GOOD	5f Gd/Fm			3133	

PICCOLITIA 2 ch f £0

66	11	KEMP	6f Gd/Fm			3795	

PICCOLO CATIVO 5 b m £2556

49	1	**WARW**	8f Soft	43	1066*	
35	9	REDC	8f Firm	49	1300	
41	9	NOTT	8f Soft	49	1646	
34	9	CATT	7f Soft	48	4004	
26	8	LEIC	8f Sft/Hvy	46	4310	
28	10	NEWC	8f Soft	46	4407	
46	2	MUSS	7f Soft	44	4522	

PICCOLO PLAYER 2 b c £28133

73	2	BATH	5f Good		1088	
93	1	WIND	6f Gd/Fm		1876*	
70	4	GOOD	6f Good		2307	
97	1	GOOD	6f Gd/Fm	85	3062*	
102	1	WIND	6f Good		3352*	
103	2	RIPO	6f Good		3700	
100	3	DONC	6f Soft		4462	

PICCOLO ROSE 2 b f £2548

66	5	BATH	5f Firm		3621	
38	9	HAYD	5f Soft		3767	
70	9	WARW	7f Gd/Fm		3910	
66	1	**LING**	6f Good		4097*	
0	14	PONT	6f Soft	69	4235	
0	22	NEWB	6f Sft/Hvy	65	4468	

PICKENS 8 b g £1848

0a	10	SOUT	12f Aw	60	642	
29a	9	SOUT	12f Aw	60	671	
35a	6	SOUT	11f Aw		866	
6a	10	SOUT	12f Aw		1203	
44a	1	**SOUT**	11f Aw		1415*	
44a	4	SOUT	11f Aw		2119	
33a	6	SOUT	11f Aw		4150	

PICKETT POINT 2 b g £0

32	10	WIND	5f Soft	2545	
42	7	EPSO	7f Good	2791	
0	17	LING	8f Firm	3577	

PICO 2 ch f £0

0	23	NEWM	6f Good	4341	
64	7	YARM	6f Heavy	4479	

PICOLETTE 3 ch f £0

51a	5	SOUT	7f Aw	56	31	
47a	6	SOUT	8f Aw	53	125	
30a	6	LING	8f Aw		150	

PICOT 3 b f £0

0	28	NEWM	7f Gd/Fm	83	4215	
0	29	NEWM	7f Good	78	4357	

PICTURE MEE 2 b f £0

48	8	PONT	6f Good		1864	
17	8	BEVE	7f Firm		2218	
41	7	NEWC	8f Good		2983	
41	7	NEWC	8f Soft		3706	
25	10	LEIC	8f Firm	41	3837	

PICTURE PALACE 2 ch c £0

0	18	DONC	6f Heavy	4576	

PICTURE PUZZLE 4 b f £8426

74	3	THIR	8f Good	72	2062	
76	2	NEWM	8f Firm	72	2342	
73	1	**BATH**	8f Firm		2786*	
73	2	CARL	8f Gd/Fm		3081	
48	12	NEWM	8f Gd/Fm	75	3317	

PIDDINGTON FLYER 2 ch g £0

50a	6	WOLV	5f Aw	4247	
49a	7	WOLV	5f Aw	4441	

PIERPOINT 5 ch g £3613

64	9	THIR	5f Soft	70	926	
50	14	DONC	6f Gd/Sft	69	1074	
53	12	THIR	5f Gd/Sft	67	1357	
67	1	**PONT**	5f Good		1868*	
54	9	CHES	5f Gd/Fm	66	2247	

62	7	PONT	6f Gd/Fm	66	2559	
61	5	NOTT	5f Gd/Fm		3113	
62	3	PONT	5f Firm	63	3502	bl
54	7	NEWM	5f Gd/Fm	63	3631	bl
0	15	NEWM	5f Good	61	4015	bl

PIES AR US 3 b g £540

53	4	RIPO	9f Good		1863	
58	6	PONT	10f Gd/Fm		2558	
50	4	CATT	14f Gd/Fm		2930	
0	13	REDC	10f Firm	55	3310	

PIETA 3 b f £0

35	9	KEMP	6f Good		729	
0	17	LING	6f Gd/Sft		837	
0	15	NEWB	8f Good		1376	
56	5	WARW	6f Gd/Sft		1712	
0	15	LING	6f Firm	50	3493	

PIETRO SIENA 2 b c £320

79	4	YARM	7f Soft	4514	

PIGGY BANK 4 b f £0

53a	6	WOLV	5f Aw	60	40	
0	20	THIR	6f Soft	60	910	
0	18	REDC	5f Gd/Sft	58	1133	
35	8	CATT	6f Gd/Fm	56	2743	
0	20	THIR	6f Gd/Fm	53	3123	

PILGRIM GOOSE 2 ch g £0

56	8	LING	7f Good		2653	
51	7	LEIC	6f Good		3215	
33	13	YORK	8f Gd/Fm		3729	
25	11	BRIG	8f Heavy	55	4538	

PILGRIM PRINCESS 2 b f £0

42	9	HAMI	5f Good		1359	
62	7	HAYD	5f Gd/Sft		1538	
54	5	AYR	5f Good		2162	
0	13	CARL	5f Firm		2277	BL

PILLAGER 3 b c £938

51	6	DONC	7f Good		717	
66	11	LEIC	8f Good		789	
64	2	NOTT	8f Gd/Sft	60	1085	
56	6	WARW	11f Heavy	63	1521	
58	4	BATH	8f Gd/Sft	63	1671	
57	5	WARW	11f Good	62	2463	
54	7	BATH	12f Gd/Sft	62	2554	
46	9	YORK	10f Gd/Fm	58	3731	

PILOTS HARBOUR 4 b c £0

0a	13	SOUT	8f Aw	55	648	
0a	8	SOUT	11f Aw		672	bl
31	6	CARL	14f Gd/Fm	50	3084	

PIMPINELLA 4 b f £0

0a	12	SOUT	12f Aw	36	215	eBL
0a	15	SOUT	8f Aw		252	ebl

PINCHANINCH 3 ch g £4889

48a	7	WOLV	9f Aw	43	709	BL
0	17	WIND	12f Heavy	62	937	bl
56	4	WARW	11f Heavy	56	1521	
60	2	WIND	12f Good	56	1730	
67	1	**BATH**	12f Firm		1997*	
68	2	FOLK	12f Good	66	2624	
64	4	KEMP	12f Gd/Fm	67	3073	
66	4	SALI	12f Gd/Fm	67	3290	
62	6	FOLK	16f Gd/Sft	65	3588	

PINCHINCHA 6 b g £40645

76	4	NOTT	10f Good	75	786	
57	6	EPSO	10f Heavy	75	1031	vis
78	2	NEWM	10f Good	75	1150	
78	3	WIND	10f Firm		1288	
75	4	SAND	10f Good	77	1965	
76	3	NOTT	10f Good	77	2190	
81	4	SAND	10f Good	79	2475	
83	2	NEWM	10f Good	77	3024	
82	1	**NEWM**	10f Gd/Fm	78	3166*	
81	5	NEWB	10f Firm	80	3997	
82	3	NEWM	9f Gd/Fm	80	4212	

84	3	YARM	19f Soft	4515	

PINE DANCE 3 b c £73171

108	1	**ARLI**	10f Firm	2912*	

PINE RIDGE LAD 10 gr h £0

21a	9	SOUT	12f Aw	47	215	bl
13a	10	SOUT	8f Aw		252	bl
25a	10	SOUT	11f Aw	43	325	bl

PING ALONG 3 b f £0

40	6	NEWB	7f Gd/Fm		1947	
37	10	SALI	7f Gd/Fm		2232	
56	5	CHEP	7f Good		2491	
0	12	CHEP	12f Gd/Fm	46	3255	

PINHEIROS DREAM 3 ch f £9153

70	5	SOUT	7f Gd/Sft	72	857	
66	9	NEWB	7f Gd/Fm	70	1405	
68	5	WIND	8f Good	68	1726	
52	9	YARM	10f Gd/Fm	68	1955	
66	3	WIND	10f Gd/Fm	68	2053	BL
64	1	**NEWM**	8f Firm		2345*	bl
51	11	LEIC	8f Gd/Fm	65	2506	bl
61	4	BRIG	8f Firm	63	2906	bl
48	6	BRIG	8f Gd/Fm	61	3261	bl
61	2	NEWM	8f Good		3456	
58	1	**NEWM**	7f Good		3612*	
49a	7	SOUT	8f Aw	58	4365	

PINK CHAMPAGNE 2 ch f £0

12	7	BATH	6f Firm	2939	
40	6	BRIG	6f Firm	3525	

PINK MOSAIC 4 b f £0

0	18	WARW	5f Gd/Fm	59	2252	
0	13	LING	6f Good	55	2654	

PINMOOR HILL 4 b g £0

0	15	RIPO	6f Good		826	
23	7	PONT	22f Heavy	46	940	
38	6	AYR	13f Good	45	2141	
10	9	PONT	10f Good	39	2366	

PIPADASH 3 b f £8712

99	2	HAYD	5f Heavy		988	
80	7	SAND	5f Heavy	98	1047	bl
0	27	NEWM	6f Gd/Fm	96	1694	
66	11	RIPO	6f Gd/Fm	94	2101	
74	8	HAYD	6f Gd/Fm	91	2504	
87	3	NEWM	5f Gd/Fm	87	2859	
70	13	RIPO	8f Gd/Fm	87	3183	
72	12	YORK	5f Gd/Fm	86	3569	
65	17	AYR	6f Gd/Sft	86	4012	
0	15	HAYD	5f Gd/Sft	82	4107	
75	1	**PONT**	6f Soft		4233*	
0	12	NOTT	8f Heavy	75	4506	

PIPADOR 4 ch c £0

45a	5	LING	10f Aw	238	
10a	9	WOLV	9f Aw	259	
5a	8	SOUT	11f Aw	670	

PIPALONG 4 b f £193210

112	1	**THIR**	5f Soft	927*	
110	1	**NEWM**	5f Gd/Fm	1172*	
112	2	YORK	6f Firm	1338	
115	1	**HAYD**	6f Gd/Sft	1833+	
79	12	ASCO	6f Good	2115	
116	3	NEWM	6f Gd/Fm	2615	
111	3	YORK	5f Firm	3598	
116	1	**HAYD**	5f Gd/Fm	3784*	
109	3	LONG	5f Good	4261	

PIPE DREAM 4 b g £1836

0a	12	LING	10f Aw	52	100	
0a	16	SOUT	8f Aw	45	177	
46a	1	LING	7f Aw		225	
50a	3	LING	8f Aw		265	
60a	3	LING	8f Aw		353	
47a	6	LING	7f Aw	56	438	
28a	8	WOLV	8f Aw	53	521	
27	7	DONC	7f Good	43	1519	

42a 5   LING   8f Aw   50   1915
28   11   NEWM   8f Gd/Fm   40   2130
39   4   KEMP   8f Gd/Fm   43   2752
42   3   KEMP   8f Gd/Fm   42   3078
38   5   WIND   8f Good   44   3355

PIPE MUSIC 5 b g £5457
48a 3   SOUT   14f Aw   124   vis
44a 6   SOUT   14f Aw   63   182   vis
61a 3   SOUT   16f Aw   60   284   bl
61a 2   WOLV   16f Aw   60   348   vis
50a 7   SOUT   16f Aw   60   470   bl
47a 5   WOLV   16f Aw   60   576   bl
0   13   CATT   14f Gd/Fm   43   779   bl
33   7   MUSS   14f Gd/Sft   38   903   bl
37   2   HAMI   13f Firm   35   2098   vis
61a 2   SOUT   14f Aw   57   2951   bl
41   1   CARL   14f Gd/Fm   37   3084*   bl

PIPED ABOARD 5 b g £1150
84   3   CHES   12f Firm   79   1251   vis
62   5   NOTT   12f Gd/Fm   2191   vis
68   11   HAYD   12f Gd/Fm   79   2502   bl
60   9   CHES   10f Gd/Fm   75   2671
66   6   RIPO   12f Gd/Fm   72   3013
51   10   CHES   12f Firm   69   3173
58   6   LEIC   10f Gd/Fm   66   3337

PIPIJI 5 gr m £0
8   11   CARL   6f Firm   37   1258
0   23   REDC   8f Firm   35   1296
12   9   CARL   7f Firm   33   2282
29a 4   WOLV   8f Aw   30   2601
18   8   THIR   8f Gd/Fm   30   2970
21   8   THIR   7f Gd/Fm   30   3129

PIPPAS PRIDE 5 ch g £10693
57a 1   SOUT   8f Aw   195*
63a 1   SOUT   7f Aw   247*
57a 3   SOUT   8f Aw   54   329
65a 1   SOUT   8f Aw   366*
58a 5   WOLV   8f Aw   65   521
65a 4   SOUT   8f Aw   600
65a 3   WOLV   7f Good   64   1235
42   5   PONT   8f Good   1498
39   10   NEWM   8f Gd/Fm   42   1690
21   13   RIPO   8f Gd/Fm   41   2099
37   3   BEVE   7f Gd/Fm   39   2479   t
35a 4   SOUT   8f Aw   64   2634   t
62a 2   SOUT   8f Aw   2816
60a 3   SOUT   8f Aw   2946
39a 6   WOLV   9f Aw   3498
0a   12   WOLV   8f Aw   60   4363
41a 8   WOLV   7f Aw   56   4550

PIPS BRAVE 4 b c £2960
50a 3   SOUT   8f Aw   51   473   bl
39a 6   SOUT   11f Aw   51   560   bl
22a 7   SOUT   8f Aw   51   648   bl
49   2   WARW   11f Heavy   44   890   bl
47   4   WARW   11f Soft   48   1065   bl
34   12   NOTT   10f Gd/Sft   47   1370   bl
32   9   LEIC   10f Soft   45   1546   bl
29   12   WARW   11f Gd/Fm   43   2033
45a 1   SOUT   11f Aw   2381*
42   5   WIND   12f Gd/Fm   44   2887
20   7   BRIG   10f Gd/Fm   42   3244
37   6   FOLK   8f Firm   3447
34   7   LING   16f Firm   37   3755

PIPS MAGIC 4 b c £7871
65   14   DONC   5f Gd/Fm   85   702
0   17   DONC   6f Gd/Sft   83   1074
69   13   THIR   6f Good   83   1162
62   11   THIR   6f Gd/Fm   80   1383
0   W   AYR   6f Gd/Fm   77   1654
64   14   YORK   6f Firm   77   2000
65   8   NEWC   6f Firm   75   2334

79   1   **DONC**   6f Gd/Fm   2580+
67   9   YORK   6f Good   79   2697
67   8   AYR   6f Firm   78   2877
82   1   **NEWC**   6f Good   78   3037*
74   8   RIPO   6f Gd/Fm   81   3183
71   13   HAYD   5f Gd/Fm   84   3322
76   11   RIPO   6f Gd/Fm   83   3464
81   7   YORK   6f Good   83   3543
0   21   DONC   7f Gd/Fm   83   3880
0   27   AYR   6f Gd/Sft   83   4012
69   17   ASCO   7f Good   83   4112
0   22   YORK   6f Heavy   81   4301
0   15   DONC   5f Soft   86   4466

PIPS SONG 5 ch g £10877
63a 9   SOUT   6f Aw   77   129
77a 2   WOLV   5f Aw   75   258
79a 4   WOLV   6f Aw   77   532
66   10   KEMP   6f Good   75   728
86   1   **PONT**   8f Heavy   74   941*
64a 8   SOUT   6f Aw   77   1504
83   3   PONT   5f Soft   85   1702
66   17   ASCO   6f Good   85   2151
0   18   NEWM   7f Gd/Fm   83   2616
40   11   NEWC   6f Heavy   82   4405
0   16   NEWM   7f Soft   79   4547

PIPS STAR 3 b f £9847
56a 3   WOLV   5f Aw   64   361
64a 2   LING   5f Aw   62   526
51a 6   LING   5f Aw   62   573
52a 2   WOLV   5f Aw   659
48a 4   SOUT   5f Aw   696
0   15   NEWC   5f Good   60   2340
0   18   NEWC   5f Good   54   2525
0   19   HAYD   5f Gd/Fm   52   2701
52   1   **DONC**   5f Gd/Fm   46   3161*
58   1   **CARL**   6f Firm   52   3194*
62   2   THIR   5f Gd/Fm   58   3349
49   7   PONT   5f Firm   57   3502

PIPS TANGO 3 ch f £0
0   24   THIR   6f Aw   40   3144
0   12   CHEP   8f Gd/Fm   40   3251
4   11   CATT   12f Good   53   3437

PIPS WAY 3 ch f £9766
74   6   KEMP   9f Good   727
62   9   CHES   8f Gd/Fm   76   1215
70   4   YARM   8f Gd/Sft   73   1610
80   1   **NEWC**   8f Heavy   73   1765*
77   4   HAMI   9f Gd/Fm   77   1939
70   3   CHES   12f Gd/Fm   79   2246
82   1   **KEMP**   9f Gd/Sft   77   2581*
80   5   CHES   10f Good   83   2666
76   4   HAMI   8f Gd/Sft   81   3826
0   11   NOTT   8f Heavy   80   4506
70   11   NEWM   8f Soft   80   4545

PIPSSALIO 3 b c £24691
67   2   WIND   8f Heavy   60   933
82   1   **SAND**   8f Heavy   75   1055*
69   4   BATH   10f Good   69   1094
0   14   YORK   10f Gd/Fm   78   1310
82   1   **KEMP**   10f Soft   76   1528+
78   4   SAND   8f Soft   79   4206
62   8   NEWB   10f Sft/Hv   79   4473

PIQUET 2 br f £0
66   8   NEWB   6f Firm   3980
62   4   LING   5f Good   4095
62   5   WIND   6f Gd/Sft   4289
63   5   NEWB   6f Sft/Hvy   65   4468

PIRANESI 4 ch g £0
70   21   YORK   14f Gd/Fm   95   3565   t

PIRATE OF PENZANCE 2 br c £24230
101 1   LEOP   6f Yldg   1756*
99   2   CURR   6f Good   2738

0   7   LEOP   6f Good   3372

PISCES LAD 4 b c £4158
58   1   **CATT**   6f Gd/Fm   781*
38   8   CARL   6f Firm   62   1258
58   2   MUSS   5f Gd/Fm   1430
33   8   CATT   6f Good   1663
41   9   HAMI   5f Gd/Fm   57   1910
0   11   MUSS   5f Gd/Sft   55   2535
34   8   CATT   6f Good   2744
50   2   RIPO   5f Gd/Fm   50   3180
41   9   PONT   5f Firm   3502
51   7   MUSS   5f Gd/Fm   53   3594
0   24   WIND   5f Gd/Sft   51   4295   BL

PIVOTABLE 2 ch c £1489
76   3   LING   6f Soft   1541
76   2   WARW   5f Gd/Sft   1706
73   5   REDC   6f Good   1893
16   7   WIND   6f Good   2714
0   13   NEWB   7f Gd/Sft   73   4453

PIX ME UP 3 b f £3403
27a 8   WOLV   9f Aw   610
56   7   HAYD   7f Heavy   67   811
39   10   BEVE   7f Heavy   65   976
34   8   BEVE   10f Firm   1274
53   1   **RIPO**   8f Good   1596*
58   2   HAYD   8f Soft   60   1822
48   4   PONT   8f Good   1865
42   9   BEVE   10f Gd/Fm   56   2484
45   9   RIPO   8f Soft   2542
45   5   HAYD   8f Gd/Fm   53   2699
48a 4   SOUT   8f Aw   2946
38   7   THIR   12f Gd/Fm   50   3125
31   4   MUSS   9f Gd/Fm   3591

PLAIN CHANT 3 b c £0
58   9   LEIC   10f Gd/Fm   2774
0   11   WIND   10f Good   3189
0   15   KEMP   12f Soft   4040

PLANET GIRL 2 b f £587
74   3   SALI   7f Gd/Fm   3292
54   11   CHEP   8f Good   3867

PLANTAGEANT 3 ch g £0
41a 8   SOUT   7f Aw   278

PLATINUM 2 b c £1952
79   3   SAN   8f Heavy   4242

PLAY TIME 2 b f £0
76   10   NEWM   8f Good   4349
59   9   WIND   8f Heavy   4524

PLAYACT 3 ch f £15754
99   4   SAIN   11f Heavy   1313
108 2   DEAU   13f Hldng   2572
108 3   LONG   13f Good   4236

PLAYINAROUND 3 ch f £0
0a   13   LING   6f Aw   52   1742
38   9   CHEP   7f Good   1972
32   9   CARL   6f Gd/Fm   2240
13   11   YARM   7f Gd/Fm   2413

PLAYMAKER 7 b g £0
0   15   AYR   8f Good   35   2136

PLAYONETOONEDOTCOM 2 b f £0
31   12   NEWM   7f Good   3607
0   13   WARW   7f Gd/Fm   3910
43   6   KEMP   8f Soft   4036
39   7   LEIC   7f Heavy   4312

PLAZZOTTA 3 b g £0
33   6   HAYD   8f Gd/Sft   3477
0   P   THIR   6f Gd/Sft   3780

PLEADING 7 b h £5850
61a 2   SOUT   6f Aw   59   454
59a 3   SOUT   6f Aw   59   499
61   3   LEIC   7f Gd/Fm   67   834
41   9   BEVE   8f Firm   66   1279
43   11   LING   7f Soft   64   1542   bl

57	5	THIR	8f Gd/Sft	61	1718	bl
0	16	BEVE	7f Gd/Sft	61	1760	
23	12	RIPO	8f Soft	58	2542	bl
59	6	KEMP	6f Gd/Fm		2747	bl
62	1	**NEWM**	7f Gd/Sft		3318*	VIS
50	9	BEVE	8f Gd/Fm	60	3652	vis
53	13	LEIC	7f Firm	60	3839	vis
0	18	LEIC	8f Gd/Sft		4033	vis

PLEASANT MOUNT 4 b c £5297

43	11	NEWC	16f Soft	63	760
70a	1	**WOLV**	16f Aw	63	918*
65	5	DONC	17f Gd/Sft	65	1052
45	9	HAYD	14f Gd/Sft	64	1536
63	3	AYR	15f Good	63	2164
49	12	BEVE	16f Gd/Fm	63	2516
65	2	REDC	16f Gd/Sft	62	2993
60	3	AYR	15f Good	63	3367

PLEASURE 5 ch m £2296

50	5	DONC	6f Gd/Sft		1073	bl
48a	4	WOLV	6f Aw	52	1233	bl
42a	6	WOLV	6f Aw	50	1391	
40a	4	SOUT	7f Aw	50	1506	bl
52a	1	**SOUT**	5f Aw	48	1806*	hbl
0	18	NEWC	8f Heavy	56	4407	hbl

PLEASURE CENTER 3 ch f £5238

92	1	**NOTT**	8f Gd/Fm		1269*
99	4	EPSO	9f Gd/Sft		1825
60	12	ASCO	8f Good	99	2167
98	5	SAND	8f Good		3469

PLEASURE DOME 2 b f £714

82	2	FOLK	6f Gd/Fm	3443
72	14	NEWM	6f Good	4345

PLEASURE PRINCESS 3 b f £0

14	7	CATT	6f Gd/Fm	42	2440

PLEASURE TIME 7 ch g £3094

0	19	THIR	5f Good	73	1162	vis
63	6	NOTT	5f Gd/Fm	72	1871	vis
63	7	CATT	5f Gd/Fm	69	2418	vis
46	8	DONC	5f Gd/Fm	65	2753	vis
68	1	**NOTT**	5f Gd/Fm		3113*	vis
63	6	SAND	5f Good	67	3436	vis
0	17	LEIC	5f Gd/Sft	66	4027	vis

PLEASURE TRICK 9 br g £0

6a	10	SOUT	8f Aw	46	496	
24a	9	SOUT	7f Aw	42	599	
27a	7	SOUT	8f Aw	42	647	
46a	5	SOUT	8f Aw		684	
31	8	CATT	7f Gd/Fm		778	vis
23	9	BEVE	8f Heavy		973	
36	5	REDC	7f Gd/Sft		1132	
0	15	THIR	7f Gd/Fm		1351	vis
20	10	THIR	8f Gd/Sft	38	1718	

PLEINMONT POINT 2 b c £403

73	4	YORK	6f Good	3812
65	6	AYR	6f Soft	3958
55	11	NEWB	6f Sft/Hvy	4471

PLUM FIRST 10 b g £0

73	6	BEVE	5f Sft/Hvy		4043
0	20	REDC	6f Gd/Sft		4220
25	12	NEWC	5f Heavy	48	4407
0a	12	WOLV	6f Aw	43	4444

PLURABELLE 3 b f £595

89	3	NAAS	7f Yldg	1751

PLURALIST 4 b c £8879

58a	1	**SOUT**	11f Aw		196*
71	2	SOUT	11f Gd/Sft	68	855
61	4	FOLK	10f Soft	68	965
64	1	**WARW**	11f Heavy		1523*
75a	1	**LING**	12f Aw	70	1677*
63	9	KEMP	12f Gd/Fm	73	1927

PLUTOCRAT 4 b g £4251

74	1	**MUSS**	12f Gd/Fm	69	1147*

71	8	YORK	14f Firm	74	1329

POCKET VENUS 2 b f £0

4	11	NEWB	7f Firm	2810
20	9	BATH	10f Soft	4140
0a	12	WOLV	8f Aw	4362

POCO A POCO 3 b f £3150

97	3	LEOP	7f Good	2070

POETIC 3 b f £6077

88	3	NEWB	7f Soft	915
88	2	NOTT	8f Gd/Fm	1268
72	1	**THIR**	8f Gd/Sft	1717*

POETRY IN MOTION 5 gr m £0

53	8	LING	5f Firm	64	2326
64	5	SAND	5f Gd/Fm	64	2473
73	9	SAND	5f Gd/Fm		2496
42	11	DONC	5f Gd/Fm	64	2753

POINT OF DISPUTE 5 b g £9325

80	4	SALI	6f Gd/Fm	79	1887	vis
81	5	REDC	6f Gd/Fm	80	2158	vis
86	1	**NEWM**	6f Gd/Fm	80	3119*	vis
79	3	LING	7f Firm	84	3758	vis

POKER POLKA 3 b f £0

0	24	DONC	8f Gd/Sft	72	1053

POLAR BEAUTY 3 b f £0

0	W	WARW	6f Good	2462

POLAR CHALLENGE 3 b c £12808

43	10	WARW	8f Heavy		884	
82	3	CHES	8f Gd/Fm	79	1215	
82	3	NEWB	8f Gd/Fm		1786	
78	5	SAND	8f Good	79	1964	
84	2	CARL	8f Gd/Fm	78	2242	
83	3	AYR	10f Gd/Fm		2722	
81	1	**WIND**	8f Good	79	3190*	t
52	11	EPSO	9f Good	82	3685	t
83	5	NEWM	8f Good	81	4348	t

POLAR CHARGE 3 b f £54887

106	2	SAN	11f Good	1459
107	3	LONG	12f Good	2224

POLAR DIAMOND 3 b f £448

72	9	NEWB	7f Soft		915
70	3	WARW	8f Soft		1063
34	12	SALI	6f Firm		1175
0a	14	SOUT	8f Aw	68	1419
0	13	NEWM	8f Gd/Fm		2134

POLAR ECLIPSE 7 ch h £0

45a	6	WOLV	9f Aw	50	67
0a	12	SOUT	11f Aw	48	131
0a	11	WOLV	9f Aw		292

POLAR FAIR 4 ch f £2801

65a	1	**WOLV**	8f Aw		39*
4a	10	WOLV	8f Aw	58	78
0a	14	LING	10f Aw	55	203

POLAR HAZE 3 ch g £1692

74	2	MUSS	5f Firm		1688
50	3	MUSS	5f Gd/Fm		2204
48	11	RIPO	6f Gd/Fm	72	3010
67	3	PONT	5f Gd/Fm		3225
47	6	NEWM	7f Good		3612
53	9	MUSS	8f Gd/Sft		4135

POLAR ICE 4 b c £0

66a	7	WOLV	7f Aw	83	79	
28a	11	WOLV	7f Aw	81	143	
31a	9	WOLV	9f Aw	78	270	
31a	9	WOLV	9f Aw	73	364	
25a	10	WOLV	9f Aw	68	611	
43a	7	LING	6f Aw	62	881	
21a	11	WOLV	7f Aw		1038	tVl
0	14	FOLK	7f Gd/Fm	65	3445	

POLAR LADY 3 ch f £1485

67	3	PONT	6f Soft		877	
64	5	SALI	6f Firm		1175	
0	11	BEVE	5f Firm	67	1923	VIS

57	4	BATH	6f Gd/Fm		3820
58	2	BEVE	5f Good		3956
58	8	GOOD	5f Soft	63	4065
0	15	DONC	7f Gd/Sft	60	4452

POLAR MIST 5 b g £5141

46a	10	WOLV	6f Aw	65	923	tbl
0	15	WARW	5f Heavy	58	1005	tbl
0	16	BEVE	5f Firm	56	1278	tbl
57	1	**GOOD**	5f Gd/Sft	52	1487*	tbl
52	8	CARL	5f Gd/Sft	56	1724	tbl
57a	6	SOUT	5f Aw	63	1976	tbl
32	14	GOOD	6f Gd/Fm	56	2124	tbl
58	2	BEVE	5f Firm	55	2732	tbl
48	10	ASCO	5f Gd/Fm	58	3341	tbl
51	6	PONT	5f Firm	58	3502	tbl
44	11	HAMI	5f Gd/Sft	58	3536	tbl
53a	6	WOLV	6f Aw	61	4023	tbl
48a	9	WOLV	6f Aw	59	4223	tbl
57	3	WIND	5f Gd/Sft	56	4295	tbl
48	9	NEWB	5f Gd/Sft	56	4459	tbl

POLAR PROSPECT 7 b g £564

59	3	BATH	12f Soft	60	4433

POLAR RED 3 ch g £35377

79	3	KEMP	9f Gd/Sft	73	1075
85	1	**HAYD**	11f Soft	75	1491*
84	2	GOOD	12f Gd/Sft	80	1637
81	4	SALI	10f Gd/Fm		1885
88	3	SAND	10f Gd/Fm	83	2499
91	1	**KEMP**	10f Gd/Fm	85	2750*
102	1	**HAYD**	11f Gd/Sft	91	3267*
104	1	**HAYD**	11f Soft		1003782*
70	10	NEWM	10f Gd/Fm		4532

POLAR REFRAIN 7 ch m £0

0a	12	SOUT	8f Aw	197

POLAR ROCK 2 ch f £0

67	11	WARW	7f Good	3910
70	7	YARM	8f Heavy	4477

POLAR STAR 3 b c £513

43	11	NEWM	8f Gd/Fm	1692
86	4	ASCO	10f Gd/Fm	2957
71	5	YARM	10f Gd/Fm	3381
70	7	KEMP	12f Soft	4040
49	7	NEWB	10f Sft/Hv	4474

POLE STAR 2 b c £1680

83	3	SALI	7f Gd/Fm	3420
91	2	DONC	8f Heavy	4569

POLES APART 4 b c £590

0	23	NEWM	6f Gd/Fm	85	1173	t
76	11	YORK	6f Firm	90	1337	t
64	13	YORK	6f Gd/Fm	84	1983	
75	13	NEWM	7f Gd/Fm	80	2616	
74	5	KEMP	6f Firm		2869	
74	4	NEWM	6f Gd/Fm	78	2961	VIS
57	9	NEWM	6f Gd/Fm	77	3119	vis
58	12	BEVE	5f Good	74	3398	BL

POLI KNIGHT 3 b f £633

82	5	NEWM	10f Gd/Fm	1697	
74	5	KEMP	10f Firm	2258	
69	3	EPSO	10f Gd/Sft	2627	t
67	6	SAND	10f Soft	4205	
0	11	NEWB	10f Sft/Hv	4474	

POLICASTRO 2 b c £0

65	8	GOOD	6f Good	3881

POLISH FALCON 4 b g £197

0a	8	LING	8f Aw	114
55a	4	WOLV	9f Aw	189

POLISH FLAME 2 b c £442

76	3	BRIG	10f Heavy	4539

POLISH GIRL 4 b f £0

28	11	LING	10f Soft		1287
0	11	SALI	10f Good		1344
0	20	CHEP	7f Gd/Sft	49	1799

POLISH OFF 2 b c £848

93	4	YORK	6f Gd/Fm		3568	
87	4	LEIC	7f Firm		3840	
83	3	DONC	7f Gd/Sft		4447	

POLISH PADDY 2 b c £4272

23	9	NEWB	5f Gd/Sft		1589	
67	6	LING	7f Gd/Fm		2182	
55	6	LING	7f Good		2653	
68	4	YARM	7f Good		3029	
58	4	CHES	7f Gd/Fm	68	3428	
63	6	BATH	8f Gd/Sft	65	3817	
48	11	GOOD	8f Soft	67	4076	
0	19	WIND	10f Gd/Sft	66	4290	
66	1	**NEWM**	8f Soft		4542*	BL

POLISH PILOT 5 b g £0

41a	8	SOUT	11f Aw		866
31a	6	SOUT	11f Aw		1417

POLISH SPIRIT 5 b g £34065

68	1	**WIND**	8f Good	59	854*
72	1	**PONT**	8f Heavy		942*
82	1	**SAND**	8f Heavy	68	1058*
82	1	**ASCO**	8f Gd/Sft	73	1113*
74	7	GOOD	8f Gd/Sft	81	1450
81	3	ASCO	10f Good	81	2170
61	13	SAND	8f Gd/Fm	81	2528
80	6	KEMP	8f Firm	81	2870
78	8	GOOD	10f Gd/Fm	80	3060
87	1	**SAND**	10f Good	80	3471*
83	5	GOOD	9f Good	84	3883

POLISHED UP 3 b f £481

50	6	NEWB	6f Gd/Fm		1783
0	15	LING	10f Good		2183
48	3	BEVE	10f Gd/Fm	47	2484
34	12	LING	10f Firm	47	3581

POLIZIANO 4 ch c £0

46a	6	WOLV	8f Aw		409
0	15	CATT	7f Good	68	3440
0	18	NEWC	9f Firm	68	3603
0	18	WARW	11f Gd/Fm	60	3915

POLLSTER 3 b c £300

81	10	NEWM	8f Gd/Fm		972	
0	16	WIND	10f Gd/Fm		1200	
82	4	GOOD	12f Gd/Fm		1956	
68	5	DONC	12f Gd/Fm		2609	VIS

POLLY GOLIGHTLY 7 ch m £19893

0	13	WARW	5f Heavy	65	1005	bl
52	10	THIR	5f Good	64	1162	bl
67	2	LING	5f Gd/Sft	64	1264	bl
69	2	LING	5f Good	65	1398	bl
64	12	HAYD	5f Gd/Sft	72	1533	bl
50	6	CHES	5f Gd/Sft	68	1781	bl
70	4	YORK	5f Gd/Fm	68	1980	bl
57	8	YORK	5f Gd/Fm	68	2644	bl
63	9	GOOD	5f Gd/Fm	67	3091	bl
50	10	NEWB	5f Gd/Fm	67	3176	bl
52	12	HAYD	5f Gd/Sft	65	3322	bl
61	4	CHES	5f Gd/Fm	62	3512	bl
63	3	HAYD	5f Gd/Sft	61	3788	bl
57	8	DONC	5f Firm	61	3894	bl
67	1	**CHES**	5f Soft	61	4073*	bl
74	1	**HAYD**	5f Gd/Sft	67	4107+	bl
10	6	YORK	5f Soft	72	4285	bl
61	11	BATH	5f Soft	71	4432	bl
68	4	DONC	5f Heavy	70	4570	bl

POLLY MILLS 4 b f £833

62a	8	SOUT	6f Aw	85	44	vis
62a	2	WOLV	6f Aw		134	bl
54a	7	SOUT	6f Aw		214	bl
50a	11	WOLV	6f Aw	75	258	vis
67a	3	WOLV	6f Aw		272	vis
57a	6	LING	6f Aw	70	358	bl
63a	5	WOLV	6f Aw	66	466	vis
53a	7	LING	7f Aw	65	525	bl
59a	9	LING	6f Aw	65	543	vis

POLLYOLLY 3 b f £0

9a	7	LING	5f Aw	46	234
22a	7	LING	5f Aw	43	269

POLMARA 3 b f £0

0	20	NEWM	8f Gd/Sft	972

POLO VENTURE 5 ch g £0

51	8	HAMI	13f Gd/Fm	58	1194
44	6	REDC	14f Gd/Sft	54	1563

POLONAISE 2 b f £223

69	4	BATH	6f Soft		4138
66	9	WIND	6f Gd/Sft		4288

POLRUAN 4 ch c £312

56	5	LEIC	10f Good	59	793	
53	6	WIND	8f Good	58	854	
47	4	WARW	11f Heavy	56	1003	t
43	12	WIND	8f Gd/Sft		4292	

POLWHELE 2 ch c £0

43	10	WARW	7f Good		2841
50	8	YARM	7f Good		3029
0	14	LEIC	7f Good		3333

POLYANDRY 2 b f £3842

98	D	CHAN	8f Good	3934

POLYPHONIC 2 b f £0

39	8	THIR	5f Good		1385
46	6	PONT	5f Soft		1698
61	5	NOTT	6f Good		2010
26	10	YORK	6f Good		3814
0	16	NEWM	6f Gd/Fm		4209
0	18	DONC	6f Gd/Sft		4449

POMFRET LAD 2 b c £15946

61	8	BATH	6f Gd/Fm		2550
99	1	**KEMP**	6f Gd/Fm		3358+
108	2	NEWB	6f Firm		3996
108	5	NEWM	6f Good		4181

POMPEII 3 b c £9354

81	2	DONC	10f Gd/Fm	75	701
80	1	**LEIC**	12f Gd/Sft		832*
81	1	**WARW**	12f Soft	80	1064*
73	6	NEWB	12f Gd/Fm	84	1400
55	15	YORK	14f Firm	83	3599
50a	8	WOLV	12f Aw	82	4226

PONTIKONISI 3 b c £0

43a	5	WOLV	5f Aw		145	BL
48a	4	LING	8f Aw		150	bl
51a	5	LING	7f Aw		155	VIS
39a	8	WOLV	7f Aw	50	257	bl
50	5	CHEP	7f Good		1972	
24	14	NOTT	8f Gd/Fm	50	2187	
0	11	CHEP	8f Gd/Fm		2448	bl
0	13	LEIC	8f Gd/Fm		3094	

POP SHOP 3 b c £0

52	14	NEWC	5f Soft	85	758	
61	9	THIR	5f Soft		905	
66	7	WIND	6f Firm	75	1289	
64	7	CHES	7f Gd/Fm	72	2250	
65	7	CATT	7f Gd/Fm	72	2438	
61	9	NEWM	7f Gd/Fm	69	2855	
48	7	RIPO	6f Gd/Fm	67	3010	
55	7	RIPO	6f Good	63	3698	
59	5	LING	6f Firm	63	3759	BL
54	9	YARM	6f Gd/Fm	63	3964	bl

POP THE CORK 3 ch c £3582

49a	9	WOLV	5f Aw		77
34a	8	SOUT	6f Aw		685
41a	8	SOUT	6f Aw		740
69	3	BEVE	5f Firm		1280
66	7	DONC	6f Good		1516
51	10	CATT	5f Good	63	1662
63	1	**MUSS**	5f Firm	60	2047*
53	7	AYR	5f Good	66	2165

(continued)

0	22	DONC	5f Firm	62	3894

POPPADAM 3 ch f £7725

73	6	NOTT	8f Gd/Fm		1269
72	5	NOTT	8f Gd/Sft		1428
80	2	NOTT	8f Good	73	1873
79	1	**THIR**	8f Gd/Fm	73	2062*

POPPAEA 2 b f £296

64	4	WIND	6f Good	3187

POPPYS CHOICE 2 b f £0

47	14	RIPO	5f Soft		821
52	6	THIR	5f Soft		928
4	11	BEVE	5f Good		1443
0	12	NEWC	6f Gd/Fm		2312

POPPYS SONG 3 b f £5463

68	7	WIND	5f Gd/Sft	72	1098
65	7	WIND	5f Gd/Sft	70	1427
71	2	WARW	5f Gd/Fm	69	2252
75	1	**NOTT**	5f Gd/Fm	71	2684*
73	4	GOOD	5f Gd/Fm	73	3135
68	10	DONC	5f Firm	73	3894
61	15	NEWM	5f Good	72	4185
0	19	WIND	5f Heavy	71	4527

PORAK 3 ch g £0

72	6	RIPO	8f Gd/Fm		2104
64	8	NOTT	8f Soft		3977
64	7	LING	8f Soft		4274

PORT MORESBY 2 b c £6189

62	10	NEWM	7f Good		2563	
78	7	NEWB	6f Firm		2808	
75	1	**BEVE**	7f Gd/Sft		3057*	
61	8	BEVE	7f Gd/Fm	81	3411	
65	13	DONC	7f Good		3888	tBL
55	12	LING	7f Soft	75	4191	t
76	1	**YARM**	8f Soft	70	4393*	

PORT OF CALL 5 ch g £0

48a	5	SOUT	6f Aw		558
43a	6	SOUT	6f Aw		685
47	7	NOTT	8f Good		784
0	12	SOUT	11f Gd/Sft	50	855
16	11	DONC	10f Gd/Sft	47	1050
0a	16	SOUT	8f Aw	47	1207

PORT ST CHARLES 3 b c £1904

80	2	KEMP	6f Gd/Fm		729
80	4	NEWM	6f Gd/Sft	78	982
77	5	LING	8f Good		2183
49	13	NEWM	7f Gd/Fm	77	3163
41	6	NEWM	8f Gd/Fm		3319

PORT VILA 3 b c £27649

110	3	NEWM	10f Firm		1854	
108	1	**ASCO**	10f Good		2169*	
109	3	AYR	10f Gd/Fm		2720	
99	5	WIND	12f Good		3640	
105	5	NEWB	11f Good		3984	t

PORTHILLY BUOY 5 ch g £0

0a	10	LING	10f Aw		629

PORTIA LADY 3 b f £0

21	14	NOTT	8f Heavy	51	1024	
0	16	BEVE	10f Good	52	1448	
45	5	BEVE	12f Gd/Fm	50	1919	bl
40	8	HAYD	12f Gd/Fm		2457	bl

PORTITE SOPHIE 9 b m £0

0a	13	SOUT	14f Aw		668

PORTLAND 3 ch c £370

60a	3	LING	7f Aw		164
0a	P	LING	10f Aw		204

PORTRACK JUNCTION 3 b c £0

24a	7	LING	5f Aw		688	BL
0	13	SOUT	10f Good		806	bl
0	14	BEVE	7f Gd/Fm	48	2479	
0	19	REDC	8f Gd/Fm	42	2861	
23	8	RIPO	10f Gd/Fm	38	3008	
34	8	REDC	16f Firm	48	3331	

0	12	PONT	17f Firm	49	3501
53	5	BEVE	12f Gd/Fm		3654
27	9	BEVE	12f Gd/Fm	36	3674
29	5	CATT	14f Soft		4002

POSITIVE AIR 5 b m £0

0a	13	SOUT	8f Aw	51	176
0	17	LEIC	6f Gd/Sft	44	1734

POST BOX 2 b c £714

87	2	BATH	8f Soft	4429
72	5	DONC	8f Heavy	4569

POT LUCK 3 b c £645

75	3	HAYD	14f Soft	1824
70	5	SAND	14f Good	2477
64	6	SALI	14f Good	2691

POTARO 2 b c £26706

84	5	NEWB	6f Gd/Fm		1943
84	3	SALI	7f Gd/Fm		2269
80	5	SAND	7f Gd/Fm		2921
84	3	NEWB	7f Gd/Fm	84	3175
93	1	WARW	15f Gd/Fm		3912*
104	1	SAIN	7f Gd/Sft		4314*
105	4	NEWB	7f Good		4455

POUNCE 2 ch f £4614

74	4	SAND	6f Gd/Fm	1988
72	4	CURR	6f Good	2400
64	4	BRIG	7f Soft	4172
61	6	WIND	5f Gd/Sft	4289

POUR NOUS 2 gr g £0

40	14	HAYD	6f Gd/Fm		2454
52	7	PONT	6f Gd/Fm		2828
0	10	THIR	7f Gd/Fm		3347
40	11	CATT	7f Soft	52	4007

POWDER 2 gr f £0

53	7	LEIC	5f Gd/Sft	1737
35	7	LING	6f Firm	3278
36a	9	LING	5f Aw	4333

POWDER RIVER 6 b h £0

55	9	KEMP	12f Firm	64	2872

POWER AND DEMAND 3 b c £784

47a	4	LING	5f Aw	51	234	
21a	7	WOLV	7f Aw	48	346	
49a	2	LING	5f Aw		487	BL
41a	5	LING	5f Aw	45	526	bl
49a	4	LING	5f Aw		619	bl
55a	3	WOLV	5f Aw		659	bl
41a	7	SOUT	6f Aw	52	1205	bl
36	9	BRIG	5f Firm	52	1334	bl
0	22	REDC	6f Gd/Sft	48	1578	bl
42a	5	LING	5f Aw	52	1742	bl
0	12	MUSS	5f Firm	44	2047	bl
0	20	BEVE	5f Good	44	2223	bl

POWER GAME 7 b g £0

21	9	MUSS	7f Firm		1685
32	4	MUSS	7f Firm		2046
0	8	HAMI	7f Firm		2396
0	28	REDC	8f Gd/Fm	28	2861
11	12	HAMI	9f Gd/Sft		3375
24	7	MUSS	7f Soft	36	4518

POWER HIT 4 b g £0

0	16	BRIG	12f Gd/Fm	56	1128	bl
0	13	BRIG	12f Gd/Sft	54	1465	

POWER PACKED 3 b c £0

81	5	SAND	5f Heavy	94	1047	
88	6	THIR	5f Good	93	1384	
64	13	HAYD	5f Gd/Fm	91	3788	
37	10	SAND	5f Soft		4207	
62	9	YARM	6f Heavy	78	4480	BL

POWERLINE 3 b f £1137

86	8	NEWM	7f Gd/Sft		971
70	6	BATH	8f Gd/Fm		1669
75	3	CHEP	10f Gd/Sft		1796
52	4	SALI	12f Gd/Fm	75	2231

69	5	NEWB	10f Sft/Hv		4474
0	12	NEWM	12f Gd/Sft	72	4534

POYLE PICKLE 2 b f £0

49	9	BATH	6f Soft	4138
57	13	DONC	6f Heavy	4575

PRAIRIE FALCON 6 b g £58967

72	6	NEWB	16f Soft	88	917
77	9	KEMP	16f Soft	87	997
87	4	CHES	19f Gd/Fm	85	1222
0	F	ASCO	20f Good	87	2092
82	9	SAND	16f Gd/Fm	87	2498
85	6	YORK	14f Good	88	2695
63	17	GOOD	14f Gd/Fm	84	3058
85	4	CHES	19f Firm	88	3171
83	10	YORK	14f Gd/Fm	84	3565
80	8	DONC	15f Firm	82	3890
83	1	CHES	16f Soft	78	4071*
82	6	NEWM	18f Good	82	4353
80	5	MUSS	16f Soft	83	4563

PRAIRIE WOLF 4 ch c £13672

84	3	CHEP	10f Gd/Sft		1797
89	4	ASCO	10f Good	90	2170
83	10	SAND	8f Gd/Fm	90	2528
92	2	GOOD	10f Gd/Fm	89	3060
65	12	YORK	10f Gd/Fm	90	3563
87	8	GOOD	9f Good	91	3883
92	2	NEWM	8f Good		4199

PRASLIN ISLAND 4 ch c £12319

67a	2	SOUT	12f Aw		84	
76a	1	WOLV	12f Aw		144*	
76a	2	LING	13f Aw	71	168	
82a	1	SOUT	14f Aw	70	182*	
83a	2	WOLV	16f Aw	80	296	
83a	3	WOLV	16f Aw	83	380	
46	12	NOTT	14f Good	60	788	
0	12	SOUT	16f Gd/Sft	15	860	bl
52	D	NOTT	14f Good	48	1874	
43	5	WARW	16f Gd/Fm	50	2256	
36	11	FOLK	16f Good	49	2622	
51	3	NEWM	15f Gd/Fm	51	2856	
0	9	YARM	14f Heavy	49	4476	

PRECIOUS LOVE 3 ch c £0

0	16	NEWM	7f Gd/Sft	983
64	8	DONC	7f Gd/Sft	1072
53	10	BEVE	7f Good	1444

PRECIOUS PENNY 2 b f £0

60	7	KEMP	6f Gd/Fm	2748
0	14	WIND	6f Good	3187

PRECIOUS POPPY 3 b f £2908

75	4	NEWM	10f Gd/Fm		2135
74	3	GOOD	12f Gd/Fm		2354
69	3	RIPO	10f Gd/Fm		3012 VIS
69	2	HAYD	11f Soft		4089

PRECIOUS YEARS 5 ch g £0

22a	8	SOUT	12f Aw	344

PRECISION 5 b g £0

0	12	NEWC	7f Soft		759
56	10	RIPO	8f Soft		826
0	16	NOTT	5f Good	54	1412
44	6	THIR	5f Gd/Sft	49	1714
0	17	NEWC	5f Good	47	2525
16	8	RIPO	5f Gd/Fm	43	2839
0	17	REDC	7f Gd/Fm		2994
15	13	CATT	7f Good	42	3440

PRECISO 2 b c £1357

86	2	GOOD	8f Soft	4062
56	8	YORK	8f Soft	4281
77	3	BATH	8f Soft	4430

PREDOMINANT 4 ch g £0

17a	10	WOLV	9f Aw	189
46a	4	LING	10f Aw	238
0a	10	LING	12f Aw	267

PREFERRED 2 b c £12284

83	7	NEWB	6f Gd/Fm		1403
76	1	NOTT	5f Good		1870*
91	1	ASCO	6f Good	78	2678*
91	3	NEWB	7f Firm		2848
81	9	KEMP	6f Gd/Fm		3797
0	17	REDC	6f Gd/Sft		4219

PREMIER AMBITIONS 2 b c £0

59	11	NOTT	6f Good	3520
53	8	WARW	15f Gd/Fm	3912
49a	9	WOLV	6f Aw	4379

PREMIER BARON 5 b g £37048

84	1	KEMP	7f Good	80	725+	
76	4	LEIC	7f Gd/Sft	83	834	
79	9	NEWM	7f Gd/Sft	83	966	
48	20	ASCO	7f Gd/Sft	82	1110	
68	6	KEMP	6f Soft	81	1531	BL
77	4	CHES	7f Gd/Sft	79	1778	
84	4	HAYD	7f Soft		1820	
76	4	YORK	7f Good	77	2694	
74	6	NEWM	6f Gd/Fm	77	3119	
85	1	NEWM	7f Gd/Fm	76	3315+	
69	11	YORK	8f Firm	71	3597	
79	11	DONC	7f Gd/Fm	85	3880	
0	23	ASCO	7f Good	84	4112	
85	4	NEWM	7f Good	85	4357	

PREMIER BOY 2 b g £234

0	12	NEWC	7f Gd/Fm		2985
33	9	RIPO	6f Good		3697
55	4	BEVE	7f Good		3949
22a	7	WOLV	8f Aw		4250 t
31a	6	SOUT	7f Aw		4369 t
50	5	REDC	6f Gd/Sft	57	4502 tVI

PREMIER FOIS 3 b f £0

56	5	LING	7f Good	1397

PREMIER LASS 2 b f £0

33a	7	SOUT	5f Aw	801
40	10	THIR	5f Soft	928
60	4	THIR	6f Gd/Fm	2059
25	6	BEVE	5f Good	2880

PREMIER LEAGUE 10 gr g £0

17a	8	LING	12f Aw	42	52
8a	9	WOLV	12f Aw		581

PREMIER PAS 3 b c £65332

111	2	LONG	8f Heavy		1025
118	2	LONG	10f Good		2225 BL
107	2	DEAU	10f V		2736 bl

PREMIER PRIZE 3 ch f £2350

91	6	ASCO	10f Gd/Sft	1108
92	3	NEWB	10f Good	1374
51	15	EPSO	12f Gd/Sft	1828

PREMIERE CREATION 3 ch f £10567

108	2	CHAN	9f Good	2401
108	4	DEAU	8f Gd/Fm	3069

PREMIERE FOULEE 5 ch m £0

4a	9	SOUT	12f Aw	37	70	
14a	8	WOLV	12f Aw	34	260	VIS
10a	6	WOLV	9f Aw	32	405	
7a	8	WOLV	12f Aw	29	464	
31	6	CHES	10f Gd/Fm		2245	
31	6	CHEP	12f Gd/Fm	36	2656	
27	4	WARW	10f Gd/Fm		2843	
4	9	BRIG	12f Firm	30	2904	bl

PREMIERE VALENTINO 3 b g £0

56	5	GOOD	12f Gd/Sft		1455
56	6	BATH	13f Gd/Fm		2327
0	13	BATH	13f Gd/Sft	52	3518 BL
0	13	LEIC	10f Gd/Sft		4029 bl

PREMIUM PRINCESS 5 b m £22421

51	9	SOUT	6f Good	61	802
41	11	THIR	6f Soft	60	910
0	15	NOTT	6f Gd/Fm	58	1082

0	19	NEWC	5f Gd/Sft	55	1479
50	5	DONC	6f Gd/Fm	52	1842
47	5	BEVE	5f Firm	52	1923
49	3	NOTT	6f Gd/Fm	50	2193
54	3	NEWC	5f Good	52	2525
53	3	NOTT	5f Gd/Fm	51	2684
46	6	PONT	5f Gd/Fm	51	2830
56	2	WIND	6f Gd/Fm	52	3046
53	4	PONT	5f Gd/Fm	52	3222
60	1	**SAND**	5f Good	55	3436*
63	1	**PONT**	5f Firm	55	3502*
68	4	GOOD	6f Good	68	3646
68	4	GOOD	6f Good	68	3894
73	1	**NOTT**	6f Soft	68	3975*
36a	10	SOUT	7f Aw	63	4153
72	2	YORK	5f Soft	71	4285
64	3	PONT	5f Soft	72	4377
71	4	NOTT	6f Heavy	72	4411

PREPOSITION 4 b g £3921

40a	2	SOUT	8f Aw	40	340
32a	4	WOLV	9f Aw	40	405
19a	5	LING	5f Aw	41	439
38a	2	SOUT	8f Aw	38	585
40a	4	SOUT	8f Aw		646
43a	1	**SOUT**	11f Aw	37	742*
34	7	RIPO	12f Soft	43	822
33a	10	SOUT	8f Aw	41	1207

PRESELI 3 b f £38950

113	1	**LEOP**	8f Gd/Fm		1315*
0	12	CURR	8f Gd/Sft		1626
115	2	CURR	10f Yldg		2404
0	9	CURR	12f Gd/Fm		2739

PRESELI MAGIC 4 gr f £0

41a	5	LING	6f Aw		95
47a	5	WOLV	6f Aw		134
16a	10	WOLV	7f Aw	43	187
15a	11	SOUT	7f Aw		199 BL

PRESENT CHANCE 6 ch g £0

48a	9	SOUT	5f Aw	64	674	bl
58	12	KEMP	6f Good	70	728	bl
47	12	RIPO	6f Soft	68	824	
0	17	NEWC	7f Heavy	65	1011	
32a	9	SOUT	6f Aw	60	1421	bl
44a	10	SOUT	6f Aw	60	1504	bl
40a	11	SOUT	7f Aw	56	1806	bl
58	5	PONT	5f Good		1868	bl
32a	10	SOUT	6f Aw		2118	bl
57	5	PONT	5f Gd/Fm		2559	bl
57	5	YORK	7f Good	58	2694	bl
49	6	NEWM	6f Gd/Fm	58	2961	bl
28	14	WIND	6f Gd/Sft	57	4294	bl
0	14	NOTT	6f Heavy	55	4411	bl

PRESENT LAUGHTER 4 b c £11248

87	4	KEMP	6f Good	85	725
89	1	**NEWM**	7f Gd/Sft	85	966*
81	9	ASCO	7f Gd/Sft	88	1110

PRESENTATION 3 b f £19988

97	2	KEMP	6f Soft		1016
93	3	KEMP	6f Gd/Fm		1078
97	2	HAYD	6f Gd/Sft	96	1534
84	6	SAND	6f Gd/Fm		1987
78	6	NEWM	6f Gd/Fm		2289
87	8	NEWM	6f Gd/Fm	94	2568
89	5	NEWM	6f Gd/Fm		3120
95	2	ASCO	6f Gd/Fm	92	3301
95	2	LEIC	5f Firm		3841
0	19	ASCO	5f Gd/Sft	94	4129

PRESENTOFAROSE 2 b f £3067

40	5	SAND	6f Good		1396
42	5	CHEP	6f Heavy		1553
33	9	SALI	6f Gd/Fm		1882
44	2	BRIG	6f Gd/Fm		1931

53	3	BRIG	7f Gd/Sft		2424
51	4	BEVE	7f Gd/Fm		2513
53	3	BRIG	5f Firm		2891
53	1	**YARM**	6f Good		3028*
12	7	BRIG	6f Gd/Fm	58	3258
0	17	LING	6f Good		4097

PRESIDENTS LADY 3 b f £642

0	12	LEIC	7f Good		794
0	12	WIND	8f Heavy		934
46a	2	SOUT	7f Aw		2633
0	13	BRIG	10f Soft	47	4174

PRESS AHEAD 5 b g £4463

24a	8	WOLV	6f Aw	82		bl
57a	1	**WOLV**	6f Aw	50	351*	
54a	5	WOLV	6f Aw		436	
49a	5	WOLV	5f Aw	56	609	bl
28a	10	WOLV	6f Aw		680	
62	1	**DONC**	6f Gd/Sft		1068*	VIS
52	6	REDC	6f Firm		1298	vis
34	11	LEIC	6f Soft	58	1545	vis
44	8	RIPO	5f Gd/Fm	55	2107	
38	10	NOTT	6f Gd/Fm	55	2193	
0	12	BEVE	5f Firm	51	2732	vis
0	15	RIPO	5f Gd/Fm	46	3180	vis
41	6	HAYD	6f Gd/Fm		3283	vis
0	12	WARW	5f Good		3694	
31a	11	WOLV	7f Aw		3770	vis
0	18	YARM	7f Firm		3921	tvi
0a	12	SOUT	6f Aw	48	4155	vis

PRESTO 3 b c £5184

43a	7	SOUT	6f Aw		46	
48	9	NOTT	8f Heavy	60	1024	
45a	5	WOLV	12f Good	57	1238	
59	1	**NEWB**	10f Gd/Sft		1593*	tBL
28	10	REDC	10f Good	55	1895	tbl
62	1	**LEIC**	10f Gd/Fm		2510*	tbl
63	7	EPSO	12f Good	68	2793	tbl
57	5	LEIC	10f Gd/Sft	67	3093	tbl

PRETENDING 3 b c £336

0	20	DONC	7f Good	60	736
39	6	NOTT	8f Gd/Sft	55	1085
62	5	LEIC	8f Soft		1548
53	3	CARL	6f Gd/Sft		1723
50	6	REDC	6f Good	52	1891
36	9	CARL	6f Good	53	2243
40	8	LEIC	8f Gd/Sft	50	2506

PRETRAIL 3 b c £7449

55	9	NOTT	6f Firm		1266
75	2	REDC	6f Gd/Sft		1562
76	1	**LING**	7f Good		1675*
66	18	ASCO	8f Good	80	2117
62	11	SAND	7f Gd/Fm		2495
77	2	SALI	8f Good	74	2688
77	3	KEMP	8f Gd/Fm	76	3793
75	7	NEWM	10f Good	76	4197

PRETTY FLY GUY 4 ch g £0

0a	11	SOUT	8f Aw		195
32a	4	SOUT	11f Aw		248
0a	11	SOUT	16f Aw		327
0a	12	SOUT	11f Aw	31	560

PRETTY GIRL 2 ch f £113600

104	2	NEWM	7f Good		4158

PRETTY OBVIOUS 4 ch f £0

0	15	REDC	14f Gd/Sft	57	4222
0	11	NEWC	16f Heavy	55	4424

PRICE OF PASSION 4 b f £0

0	15	LING	5f Gd/Sft	73	1264	
43	11	BATH	5f Gd/Fm		1441	vis
56	16	GOOD	5f Gd/Fm	70	3091	bl
69	4	WIND	5f Good	70	3191	vis
66	5	SAND	5f Good	67	3436	vis
0	16	DONC	5f Firm	68	3894	vis

PRICELESS SECOND 3 b c £4393

23a	5	WOLV	8f Aw	80		bl
54a	2	SOUT	6f Aw	181		bl
47a	4	SOUT	5f Aw	217		bl
58a	2	SOUT	7f Aw	281		
52a	3	SOUT	7f Aw	330		
58a	1	**SOUT**	7f Aw	417*		
53a	4	SOUT	6f Aw	426		
54a	3	SOUT	7f Aw	541		
58a	2	SOUT	7f Aw	688		VIS
61a	2	SOUT	7f Aw	741		vis
0	14	SOUT	7f Gd/Sft	56	857	vis
51a	6	SOUT	6f Aw	60	1205	vis
50a	4	SOUT	7f Aw		1305	

PRICKLY POPPY 2 b f £0

76	5	BEVE	7f Good		3953

PRIDDY FAIR 7 b m £659

32	3	MUSS	16f Gd/Sft		2536
33	4	HAMI	13f Gd/Fm	33	2801
9	8	CARL	14f Gd/Fm	33	3084

PRIDE IN ME 2 ch f £1404

65	15	NEWM	6f Good		4341
72	2	NOTT	5f Gd/Sft		4503

PRIDE OF BRIXTON 7 b h £8860

25a	9	WOLV	7f Aw		61
69a	1	**WOLV**	5f Aw		753*
65a	1	**WOLV**	5f Aw		919*
73a	1	**WOLV**	5f Aw	64	1140*
49	2	NOTT	5f Good	47	1412
44a	11	WOLV	5f Aw	73	2078
45	7	GOOD	5f Soft	49	4065
35	16	WIND	5f Gd/Sft	49	4295

PRIDE OF INDIA 3 b g £0

0	11	KEMP	12f Soft		4040
68	7	YARM	11f Heavy		4481

PRIDE OF PERU 3 b f £0

30	10	THIR	5f Gd/Fm	52	2060
35	8	CARL	6f Gd/Fm	52	2243
39	5	BEVE	7f Firm		2731
39	5	THIR	8f Gd/Fm	48	2964
17	11	CARL	6f Firm	43	3194
46	5	BEVE	5f Good		3956

PRIDE OKILMARNOCK 2 ch f £0

0	W	NOTT	6f Good		2010

PRIDEWAY 4 b f £3675

67a	4	WOLV	6f Aw	70	466
62a	4	SOUT	6f Aw	69	557
42a	7	WOLV	7f Aw		623
64a	6	WOLV	7f Good	65	1235
69a	1	**SOUT**	8f Aw	63	1419*
61a	3	SOUT	7f Aw	69	1506
60	7	LEIC	8f Soft	66	1547
51	6	CHES	7f Gd/Sft	60	1778
61	5	HAMI	6f Gd/Fm	62	1939
58	6	HAMI	9f Firm	60	2094
33	7	CHES	10f Gd/Fm		2245
47	8	BATH	8f Firm	58	2331
38	11	CHES	8f Gd/Fm	56	2673
34a	6	SOUT	8f Aw		2950
23	13	HAMI	8f Gd/Sft	52	3534

PRIESTLAW 3 ch c £11972

66	8	NEWM	9f Gd/Sft		980
89	2	SAN	10f Heavy		1228

PRIESTRIG BRAE 4 ch f £0

0	12	MUSS	17f Gd/Fm		2046
0	10	HAMI	9f Gd/Fm		2236

PRIM N PROPER 3 b f £0

68	12	NEWB	7f Soft		915
41	10	SALI	7f Gd/Fm		1886
45	8	SALI	6f Gd/Sft		2472

PRIMA 3 b f £0

48	5	CARL	6f Firm		2278

63 6 BRIG 8f Firm 74 2906

PRIMA VENTURE 2 b f £276
70 4 LING 6f Soft 1541

PRIMATICCIO 5 b g £0
29a 8 SOUT 16f Aw 51 644 VIS
9a 10 LING 16f Aw 51 649 vis
0a 14 SOUT 16f Aw 51 737 vis

PRIME MATCH 8 ch g £1269
95 2 KLAM 6f Good 3213

PRIME OFFER 4 b c £0
67 5 LEIC 7f Firm 65 3839
57 10 YARM 7f Soft 65 4513

PRIME RECREATION 3 b g £4235
47 11 HAYD 5f Gd/Sft 808
0 17 WIND 5f Gd/Sft 70 1098
0 18 NOTT 5f Good 66 1412
64 3 CATT 5f Gd/Sft 60 1817
50 7 KEMP 5f Gd/Sft 62 2586
0 16 PONT 5f Gd/Fm 62 3222
0 18 PONT 5f Firm 60 3502
53 7 THIR 5f Gd/Sft 55 3781
48 9 GOOD 5f Good 55 3908
54 6 NEWM 5f Good 55 4185
62 1 AYR 5f Heavy 54 4307+
63 2 MUSS 5f Soft 63 4516

PRIME SURPRISE 4 b f £0
0a 13 LING 7f Aw 156
15a 11 SOUT 8f Aw 197

PRIME TRUMP 2 b c £301
78 5 SALI 7f Gd/Fm 2269
79 4 SALI 7f Good 2686
73 8 DONC 7f Gd/Fm 3156

PRIME VERSION 2 b c £5102
93 1 NEWB 6f Sft/Hvy 4471*

PRIMEVAL 6 b g £0
12a 12 WOLV 8f Aw 50 3499

PRIMO VALENTINO 3 b c £8250
111 7 NEWM 8f Gd/Fm 1171
103 6 BADE 6f Gd/Sft 1746
114 4 NEWM 6f Gd/Fm 2615
96 9 LONG 5f Good 4261

PRIMO VENTURE 2 b f £0
63 6 YARM 7f Firm 2390
52 8 KEMP 8f Soft 2583
32 9 KEMP 8f Soft 4036

PRINCE ALBERT 2 ch g £0
57 6 YARM 7f Soft 4389
40 12 LING 7f Soft 4483
49 8 NEWM 8f Gd/Sft 4531

PRINCE ALEX 6 b g £34513
97 1 NEWM 10f Good 87 3024* t
102 1 YORK 10f Gd/Fm 93 3563+ t
97 8 NEWB 10f Firm 99 3997 t

PRINCE AMONG MEN 3 b c £6806
69 3 HAYD 11f Heavy 83 990
80 3 HAYD 11f Gd/Sft 1539
80 3 HAYD 11f Gd/Sft 80 1790
63 3 NEWB 12f Gd/Fm 1948
79 2 HAYD 14f Gd/Fm 79 2445
79 2 YORK 10f Soft 4275

PRINCE BABAR 9 b g £13280
82 2 PONT 8f Soft 78 875
82 4 KEMP 8f Soft 80 1015
79 4 ASCO 7f Gd/Sft 80 1110
77 5 GOOD 7f Gd/Sft 80 1483
11 11 HAYD 8f Gd/Sft 79 1836
82 1 HAYD 8f Soft 79 3785*
72 6 AYR 8f Gd/Sft 82 4013
79 5 NEWM 7f Good 81 4357
70 12 NEWM 8f Soft 81 4545

PRINCE CASPIAN 3 ch g £4531

79 1 **NOTT** 8f Soft 1643*
93 4 YARM 7f Firm 2389
77 9 EPSO 7f Good 3763
56 16 NEWB 7f Firm 92 3981
0 18 NEWM 8f Good 88 4348

PRINCE DANZIG 9 ch g £0
48a 5 LING 12f Aw 101
59a 6 LING 13f Aw 65 168

PRINCE DARKHAN 4 b c £276
55 9 LEIC 10f Good 63 793
41 10 NOTT 10f Gd/Fm 59 1272
47 8 KEMP 12f Gd/Fm 56 1927
35 4 YARM 14f Gd/Fm 50 2416
31 6 LING 16f Firm 45 2763
26 12 WARW 16f Gd/Fm 40 3916

PRINCE DU SOLEIL 4 b c £0
63 8 DONC 8f Gd/Fm 703
0 19 KEMP 8f Soft 90 1015
0 15 GOOD 8f Gd/Sft 85 1450
49 7 GOOD 8f Gd/Sft 1635
54 9 SAND 10f Good 75 3471
47 10 HAYD 8f Soft 70 4094
66 4 WIND 8f Gd/Sft 4292
55 8 NOTT 8f Heavy 65 4506

PRINCE ELMAR 3 b c £0
74 10 KEMP 11f Soft 1017
58 11 WIND 12f Gd/Sft 74 1425
0 13 WIND 10f Good 1725
61 7 LEIC 10f Gd/Fm 2774 t
0 13 SALI 10f Gd/Sft 62 4168
0 21 WIND 10f Gd/Sft 62 4291

PRINCE GRIGORI 2 ch c £262
64 9 WARW 5f Soft 812
73 4 NEWC 5f Heavy 1006
45 7 CHES 5f Soft 1221
35 8 NEWC 6f Good 3032

PRINCE HUSSAR 3 b c £0
0 10 CATT 6f Soft 4255

PRINCE JACK 2 b c £0
0 14 NEWC 6f Heavy 4402

PRINCE KINSKY 7 ch h £0
0 14 NEWB 13f Gd/Fm 57 1784

PRINCE MILLENNIUM 2 b c £936
59 5 CHES 5f Gd/Fm 1221
78 6 NEWB 6f Firm 2808
75 3 CHEP 6f Gd/Fm 2972
72 7 NEWM 8f Gd/Fm 78 3630
77 4 BATH 8f Gd/Fm 78 3817
68 11 NEWM 8f Good 77 4350

PRINCE NICHOLAS 5 ch g £3821
0 19 DONC 12f Gd/Fm 57 699
60 2 CATT 14f Gd/Fm 57 779
61 2 RIPO 12f Soft 57 825
61 4 HAMI 13f Good 61 845
62 4 DONC 17f Gd/Sft 62 1052
57 7 HAMI 13f Gd/Fm 62 1194
55 4 REDC 14f Gd/Sft 61 1563
35 12 HAMI 12f Gd/Fm 58 1908
44 6 HAMI 11f Soft 56 3805
39 9 MUSS 13f Soft 53 4521

PRINCE NICO 3 b g £0
26 11 NEWM 6f Good 956
36a d WOLV 5f Aw 1237
33a 7 WOLV 5f Aw 1392
27 7 REDC 6f Gd/Sft 40 1578
49a 6 SOUT 6f Aw 2299
57 5 BEVE 5f Gd/Fm 2519
56a 4 LING 5f Aw 2650

PRINCE NOR 2 b c £0
64 10 HAYD 5f Gd/Sft 1488
44a 5 SOUT 6f Aw 2635
26 8 BEVE 5f Soft 2880

PRINCE OF ARAGON 4 b c £0
20 10 WIND 8f Gd/Fm 40 2051

PRINCE OF BLUES 2 b c £4436
70 5 LEIC 6f Firm 2029
84 2 NEWC 6f Firm 2333
90 6 NEWM 6f Gd/Fm 2595
95 5 NEWB 6f Firm 2850
0 8 LEOP 6f Good 3372
89 1 **LING** 5f Good 4095*
85a 2 WOLV 5f Aw 4247
85a 4 LING 6f Aw 4332

PRINCE OF MY HEART 7 ch h £0
84 6 EPSO 10f Heavy 86 1031
79 6 NEWM 10f Gd/Fm 86 1170

PRINCE OF MYSTERY 3 b c £638
32 8 KEMP 9f Gd/Fm 54 3357
36 9 EPSO 9f Good 49 3856
0 17 YARM 8f Gd/Fm 47 3971
42a 2 WOLV 7f Aw 4361 BL

PRINCE OMID 3 b c £1227
62a 3 SOUT 8f Aw 694
77 4 SOUT 10f Gd/Sft 858
0 13 SALI 12f Good 72 1350
57 13 WIND 8f Good 70 1726 VIS
67 4 LEIC 8f Gd/Fm 67 2506
66 3 GOOD 10f Soft 4067
61 7 WIND 10f Gd/Sft 67 4291

PRINCE PROSPECT 4 b c £10064
70a 9 LING 6f Aw 88 223
76a 8 WOLV 6f Aw 85 320
85a 1 **LING** 6f Aw 376*
61a 10 LING 7f Aw 80 462
92a 2 LING 7f Aw 630
82 2 SAND 5f Gd/Fm 77 763
60 10 BATH 5f Gd/Fm 1441
67 7 REDC 6f Gd/Fm 80 2158
77 4 SALI 5f Gd/Fm 80 2266
62 9 BEVE 5f Gd/Fm 79 2517
74 8 SAND 5f Gd/Fm 78 2925
0 11 ASCO 5f Good 73 3341
0 11 NEWM 6f Good 73 3613
69 6 GOOD 7f Good 3662

PRINCE PYRAMUS 2 b c £13592
69 4 RIPO 6f Gd/Fm 3009
63 4 RIPO 6f Gd/Fm 3466
79 1 **BEVE** 5f Good 3955*
81 2 YORK 6f Soft 4286
81 2 NEWB 6f Sft/Hvy 81 4468

PRINCE SHAAMAAL 2 b c £2320
88 1 **BATH** 8f Soft 4429*

PRINCE SLAYER 4 b c £23958
67 10 LEIC 10f Gd/Sft 833
78 2 WIND 10f Firm 1288
56 9 KEMP 10f Soft 76 1528
83 1 **EPSO** 9f Gd/Fm 76 1829*
64 9 GOOD 8f Gd/Fm 82 2356
0 15 SAND 8f Gd/Fm 82 2528
77 8 YARM 10f Firm 80 3941
65 7 ASCO 8f Gd/Sft 78 4126
0 30 NEWM 9f Gd/Fm 80 4212
66 9 BRIG 8f Soft 4420 BL

PRINCELY DREAM 4 br c £294
76 15 HAYD 5f Gd/Fm 86 1533
69 10 YORK 6f Gd/Fm 84 1983
0 16 NEWC 6f Firm 82 2334
68 4 AYR 6f Good 3366
72 5 MUSS 7f Gd/Sft 75 4136
67 8 YORK 6f Soft 4287 BL

PRINCES STREET 2 b c £1100
78 2 KEMP 5f Soft 993

PRINCES THEATRE 2 b c £669
83 4 NEWM 7f Good 3608

83 4 WARW 7f Gd/Fm 3909

PRINCESS AURORA 3 ch f £0
0 17 WIND 6f Firm 58 1289
0 6 BRIG 5f Soft 58 1512
39 7 CATT 5f Gd/Sft 52 1817
0 18 LING 5f Gd/Fm 48 2184
0 15 THIR 5f Gd/Sft 43 3781

PRINCESS BELFORT 7 b m £0
21a 7 SOUT 6f Aw 45 vis

PRINCESS CHLOE 2 br f £2908
70 8 KEMP 6f Gd/Fm 3795
74 1 **WIND** 6f Gd/Sft 4289*

PRINCESS CLAUDIA 2 b f £819
67 9 YORK 7f Gd/Fm 2649
59 3 BEVE 7f Gd/Sft 3057
72 4 BEVE 7f Good 3397
46 10 PONT 8f Soft 63 4084

PRINCESS ELLEN 3 br f £129250
92 8 NEWM 7f Good 953
116 2 NEWM 8f Firm 1185
104 5 CURR 8f Gd/Sft 1626
115 2 ASCO 8f Good 2150
112 3 GOOD 10f Firm 3151

PRINCESS EMERALD 2 b f £0
28 8 EPSO 7f Gd/Sft 2430
25 9 LEIC 7f Heavy 4312

PRINCESS EMILY 2 b f £7146
42 10 NEWC 7f Gd/Fm 2985
62 3 BEVE 7f Good 3409
73 1 **YORK** 8f Gd/Fm 3729*
75 5 AYR 8f Soft 74 3990
43 12 PONT 8f Soft 74 4084

PRINCESS FOLEY 4 ch f £0
0a 11 WOLV 6f Aw 82
22a 9 WOLV 6f Aw 132

PRINCESS KALI 4 ch f £2855
29a 9 LING 6f Aw 8 bl
54a 1 **SOUT** 6f Aw 30* bl
37a 7 WOLV 6f Aw 76 bl
48a 6 SOUT 6f Aw 57 87 bl
59a 2 SOUT 6f Aw 130 bl
30a 5 WOLV 6f Aw 142 bl
47a 5 SOUT 8f Aw 54 177
49a 2 SOUT 8f Aw 199 bl

PRINCESS MO 4 b f £0
29a 10 LING 6f Aw 38 154
32a 5 LING 10f Aw 38 224
29a 8 LING 10f Aw 333
18 9 BRIG 7f Firm 30 1336
0 13 BRIG 8f Soft 30 1511
36a 6 LING 7f Aw 1739 bl
22 10 WIND 12f Gd/Fm 1880 bl

PRINCESS OF GARDA 2 b f £10525
0 U HAYD 5f Heavy 989
65 4 REDC 5f Gd/Sft 1131
66 3 HAMI 5f Firm 1240
78 1 **HAYD** 5f Gd/Sft 1488*
87 2 CATT 5f Gd/Sft 1813
91 1 **CHES** 5f Gd/Sft 2248*
85 4 CHES 5f Good 2664
84 5 HAYD 5f Gd/Sft 89 3264
80 4 RIPO 6f Gd/Fm 85 3712
73 12 DONC 6f Gd/Fm 3862
73 9 REDC 6f Gd/Sft 4219
82 2 YARM 5f Aw 82 4511

PRINCESS PENNY 2 ch f £2355
0 R WARW 5f Soft 1059
51a 3 SOUT 5f Aw 1206
19 8 LING 6f Good 1396
60a 1 **SOUT** 6f Aw 1420*
55a 3 SOUT 6f Aw 1805
31 5 BRIG 6f Gd/Fm 1931

2a 7 WOLV 6f Aw 2079

PRINCESS RIA 3 b f £0
0 12 SOUT 7f Soft 68 1606
48 11 CATT 7f Good 64 3440
0 19 DONC 8f Heavy 60 4573

PRINCESS SENORITA 5 gr m £0
0 12 WARW 11f Heavy 1523
0 12 WIND 10f Gd/Fm 2056
7 9 SAND 8f Aw 2920 t

PRINCESS SOPHIE 2 b f £0
0 14 AYR 8f Soft 3957

PRINCESS TITANIA 2 b f £1682
73 4 NOTT 6f Gd/Fm 2683
85 7 NEWM 7f Good 3020
70 2 REDC 7f Firm 3308
70 3 HAMI 8f Gd/Sft 3822

PRINCESS TOPAZ 6 b m £681
55 2 NOTT 16f Gd/Fm 2191
45 6 NOTT 14f Gd/Fm 63 2681
37 7 SAND 14f Gd/Fm 58 2923 BL
15 8 YARM 14f Good 50 3233

PRINCESS VICTORIA 3 b f £1619
62a 2 LING 6f Aw 59 165
33a 6 LING 6f Aw 207
53 3 NOTT 8f Good 783
58 3 LEIC 6f Gd/Sft 830
58 3 FOLK 5f Soft 959
31 9 BRIG 7f Firm 1212

PRINCIPAL BOY 7 br g £216
49a 3 SOUT 7f Aw 50
39a 8 SOUT 7f Aw 130
39a 4 SOUT 7f Aw 195
33a 6 SOUT 7f Aw 249
21a 10 SOUT 8f Aw 43 340
0 11 AYR 9f Heavy 4324

PRINCIPLE 3 b c £12704
73 4 CHES 10f Gd/Sft 1779
60a 3 LING 10f Aw 2213
80 1 **HAYD** 12f Gd/Fm 74 2702+
80 4 ASCO 12f Gd/Sft 77 3014
85 1 **HAYD** 12f Gd/Sft 78 3270+
72 12 YORK 14f Firm 84 3599

PRINCIPLE ACCOUNT 3 b c £0
0 P NEWM 8f Firm 76 1183

PRINISHA 3 gr f £2613
52 8 LING 7f Gd/Sft 1261
71 2 LEIC 8f Soft 1548
51 8 SALI 8f Firm 2024
67 2 CHEP 7f Gd/Fm 2491
71 2 CATT 7f Gd/Fm 2655
49 8 LEIC 8f Gd/Fm 65 3095
46 9 CHEP 10f Gd/Fm 63 3683
0 19 WIND 10f Gd/Sft 60 4291
26 8 BATH 8f Soft 54 4435

PRINTSMITH 3 br f £6745
0 14 CARL 6f Firm 58 1257
58 1 **WARW** 7f Gd/Sft 53 1710*
40 9 WARW 7f Gd/Fm 57 2036
30 6 HAMI 6f Firm 2396
36 10 RIPO 6f Gd/Fm 57 3010
48 3 LEIC 7f Gd/Fm 3332
43 8 CATT 7f Soft 54 4004
0a 12 SOUT 6f Aw 51 4156
56 1 **DONC** 7f Gd/Sft 51 4452*

PRIOLETTE 5 b m £0
0 R HAMI 12f Firm 35 1241

PRIORS LODGE 2 br c £3640
90 1 **SALI** 7f Gd/Fm 2269*
97 7 NEWB 7f Gd/Sft 4455

PRIORS MOOR 5 br g £0
20a 9 WOLV 9f Aw 42 305
6a 7 WOLV 12f Aw 37 608

18 7 LEIC 10f Gd/Sft 40 1575
12 11 LEIC 8f Firm 34 2027
0a 13 SOUT 8f Aw 30 2379

PRIORY GARDENS 6 b g £3395
35a 3 LING 4f Aw 40 262
31a 10 WOLV 7f Aw 41 323
20a 9 LING 6f Aw 39 358
35a 7 LING 6f Aw 484
0a 13 WOLV 8f Aw 550
16 10 NOTT 6f Good 40 787
48 4 WARW 7f Soft 816
35 4 BRIG 7f Gd/Sft 37 896
34 9 HAMI 7f Firm 1239
22 7 CARL 6f Firm 37 1257
35 3 CATT 6f Good 1663
35 5 MUSS 7f Firm 1685
37 4 BATH 6f Gd/Fm 39 1994
33 6 RIPO 8f Gd/Fm 39 2099
42 1 **CHEP** 8f Gd/Fm 38 2658*
30 10 BRIG 7f Gd/Fm 44 2729
41 3 CHEP 8f Gd/Fm 44 2974
19 6 CHEP 8f Gd/Fm 44 3251
28 10 BRIG 8f Gd/Sft 44 4122

PRIVATE SEAL 5 b g £301
23a 5 LING 6f Aw 33 262 t
40a 6 LING 8f Aw 316 t
23a 6 LING 13f Aw 30 460 t
0 14 BRIG 10f Firm 1210 t
13 7 BRIG 7f Firm 28 1335 t
44 4 NEWM 8f Gd/Fm 3117 t
11 10 NEWM 8f Gd/Fm 3318 t
27 7 LING 10f Firm 3490
27 5 BRIG 8f Firm 3738 t

PRIX STAR 5 ch c £4210
51a 4 LING 7f Aw 53 28 vis
48a 5 SOUT 6f Aw 58 44 vis
43a 5 WOLV 6f Aw 82 vis
54 10 WIND 6f Gd/Fm 58 1196
60 3 CARL 6f Firm 58 1257
53 2 CATT 7f Soft 1681
52 9 NOTT 6f Gd/Fm 58 2192
58 4 CATT 6f Gd/Fm 58 2420
41 10 PONT 6f Gd/Fm 56 2559
57 7 CARL 7f Firm 57 2823
46 7 NEWC 6f Good 54 3037
51 5 CATT 6f Gd/Fm 54 3200 vis
56 2 REDC 6f Firm 52 3312 vis
56 2 CATT 7f Good 52 3440 vis
54 3 NEWC 6f Gd/Fm 54 3440 vis
30 12 MUSS 7f Gd/Sft 55 4136 vis

PRIYA 2 b f £3009
60 4 KEMP 5f Gd/Sft 1079
72 6 WIND 5f Gd/Sft 1424
81 2 SAND 5f Gd/Fm 2526
81 2 KEMP 8f Gd/Fm 2748
81 4 NEWM 7f Gd/Fm 3459
69 10 KEMP 5f Gd/Fm 3795

PRIZE DANCER 2 ch c £329
74 7 SALI 7f Good 2686
77 4 GOOD 6f Gd/Fm 3906
80 8 NEWM 8f Gd/Fm 4161
72 6 NEWB 8f Gd/Sft 4457

PRIZEMAN 2 b c £34500
102 1 **YORK** 6f Good 2692*
101 1 **NEWB** 7f Firm 3450*
103 4 ASCO 8f Gd/Sft 4127
103 2 NEWB 8f Gd/Sft 4455

PROCEED WITH CARE 2 b c £7407
57 5 NEWC 5f Heavy 1764
96 1 **RIPO** 6f Gd/Fm 2106*
100 2 KEMP 6f Gd/Fm 3797
90 8 DONC 5f Firm 3900

82 5 YORK 6f Soft 100 4286

PRODIGAL SON 5 b g £2045
77a 2 WOLV 9f Aw 73 119
48a 8 LING 10f Aw 76 160
73 3 DONC 10f Gd/Fm 72 705
62 6 NOTT 10f Gd/Fm 1271
55 8 WIND 10f Gd/Fm 72 1878
69 3 EPSO 12f Gd/Sft 69 2626
55 9 NEWM 12f Gd/Fm 69 3122 bl

PROFOUND 4 b c £0
58 9 WARW 7f Gd/Sft 1708
0 18 LING 8f Soft 4274

PROLETARIAT 2 gr c £2842
80 2 SALI 6f Gd/Fm 2979
84 4 NEWM 6f Gd/Fm 3162
88 2 THIR 6f Gd/Fm 3614
0 17 NEWB 6f Sft/Hvy 86 4468

PROMISED 2 b f £4080
79 1 REDC 5f Gd/Sft 1131*
78 3 REDC 5f Gd/Sft 1558
67 7 BEVE 5f Gd/Sft 1759
76 7 HAYD 6f Gd/Fm 3320
0 7 CURR 6f Yldg 3720
92 4 AYR 6f Gd/Sft 4009
0 14 REDC 6f Gd/Sft 4219
85 7 DONC 6f Soft 4462 VIS

PROMISING LADY 3 b f £2134
90 7 ASCO 8f Gd/Sft 1108
86 6 NEWB 10f Good 1374
0 7 CURR 10f Gd/Sft 1627
86 2 WIND 12f Gd/Fm 2208
86 6 GOOD 12f Gd/Fm 88 3088
82 9 DONC 15f Firm 87 3890
78 8 ASCO 16f Good 85 4115

PROPER GENT 3 b c £0
0 25 RIPO 10f Soft 45 827
0 16 NOTT 6f Gd/Sft 1081
0 7 HAMI 9f Firm 1242

PROPER SQUIRE 3 b c £1154
78 6 BRIG 10f Gd/Sft 1127
72 2 BATH 10f Gd/Sft 1668
62 11 ASCO 12f Good 76 2116
49 11 BATH 12f Gd/Sft 73 2554

PROPERTY MAN 8 gr g £0
14a 8 SOUT 7f Aw 511 VIS

PROPERTY ZONE 2 b g £0
14 10 CATT 6f Gd/Sft 1679
24 8 THIR 6f Gd/Fm 2059
51 7 BEVE 7f Gd/Fm 2513

PROSPECTORS COVE 7 b g £5850
57a 3 LING 10f Aw 62 618
50 11 DONC 8f Good 72 715
32a 9 LING 10f Aw 62 842
60 8 BRIG 8f Gd/Sft 72 895
3 12 SAND 8f Heavy 70 1058
56 8 HAMI 8f Firm 68 1243
32a 10 WOLV 8f Aw 58 1393
70 1 YARM 7f Gd/Sft 65 1611*
55 13 KEMP 8f Gd/Fm 70 1926
67 4 YARM 8f Gd/Fm 70 2412
60 6 YARM 7f Firm 70 2768
63 6 NEWM 8f Gd/Fm 70 3118
71 2 YARM 7f Good 68 3238
67 3 YARM 7f Gd/Fm 68 3384
68 6 YARM 8f Firm 71 3936
64 11 NEWM 7f Gd/Fm 71 4215
57 12 YARM 7f Soft 70 4513
0 11 MUSS 8f Soft 4565

PROTARAS BAY 6 b g £0
0 14 WARW 11f Good 3691 vis

PROTECTOR 3 b c £2460
64 10 LING 6f Gd/Sft 837

60 4 REDC 7f Gd/Sft 1135
63 8 GOOD 10f Gd/Sft 66 1812
66 1 REDC 11f Gd/Fm 2146*

PROTOCOL 6 ch g £6886
27a 7 LING 12f Aw 52 52 t
38 7 DONC 12f Gd/Fm 52 699 t
44 7 NOTT 14f Good 52 788 t
50 2 PONT 17f Soft 48 876 t
45 3 PONT 22f Heavy 48 940 t
46 5 NOTT 14f Gd/Sft 49 1087 t
39 5 PONT 17f Soft 47 1701 t
42 9 NOTT 14f Gd/Sft 45 1874 t
37 4 WARW 12f Good 42 2466 t
41 2 DONC 17f Gd/Fm 42 2607 t
41 2 CARL 14f Firm 39 2827 t
37 3 CARL 14f Gd/Fm 40 3084 t
46 1 PONT 10f Gd/Sft 40 3220* t
38 8 PONT 17f Firm 44 3501 t
47 3 GOOD 12f Good 48 3887 t
43 5 PONT 12f Soft 45 4229 t
0 28 NEWM 18f Good 79 4353 t

PROUD BOAST 2 b f £14554
73 1 CHES 5f Gd/Sft 1776*
59 18 ASCO 5f Good 2088
87 2 HAYD 6f Gd/Fm 2500
85 3 DONC 5f Good 2756
93 1 THIR 5f Gd/Fm 85 3145+
93 5 NEWB 5f Gd/Fm 3482
93 2 RIPO 5f Gd/Fm 3714
85 6 AYR 5f Soft 3959

PROUD CAVALIER 4 b g £0
19 9 SOUT 7f Soft 1603
28 5 NOTT 10f Good 33 2011
7a 12 SOUT 8f Aw 29 2380
15a 10 LING 10f Aw 2587
48 4 BATH 12f Firm 2785
22 10 NOTT 10f Gd/Fm 46 3111
41a 8 LING 12f AW 4186
24 4 YARM 11f Soft 29 4391

PROUD CHIEF 3 ch c £2192
77 2 LEIC 7f Good 76 792
78 6 NEWM 7f Good 78 954
55 10 CHES 8f Gd/Fm 78 1215
45 10 GOOD 8f Gd/Sft 77 1473
54 16 EPSO 7f Gd/Sft 75 1826 VIS
57 12 SAND 7f Gd/Fm 72 2922
62 8 KEMP 7f Gd/Fm 69 3362 vis
0 14 NEWC 9f Firm 69 3603 vis

PROUD NATIVE 6 b g £30651
95 15 NEWM 6f Gd/Fm 1172
103 9 YORK 6f Firm 1338
108 2 SAND 5f Soft 1566
111 2 EPSO 5f Good 110 1849
89 21 ASCO 5f Good 2065
88 6 CHES 5f Gd/Fm 2669
110 2 DONC 6f Gd/Fm 3158
106 2 NOTT 5f Good 3521
101 3 BEVE 5f Sft/Hvy 4043
95 11 NEWM 5f Good 4182

PROUD REFLECTION 2 b c £0
76 5 GOOD 5f Gd/Sft 1454

PROVE 2 £0
98 9 LONG 8f Good 4260

PROVIDENT 2 b c £0
72 7 NEWB 6f Firm 3980
64 7 BATH 6f Soft 4137

PROVOSKY 4 ch g £0
85 12 ASCO 10f Good 94 2170 bl

PRUDENT 3 b f £0
43a 6 WOLV 8f Aw 658

PSALMIST 3 ch f £587
63 3 WARW 7f Heavy 1525

0 14 GOOD 8f Gd/Fm 1811
59 8 LING 6f Gd/Fm 2183
55 7 KEMP 9f Gd/Sft 63 2581
0a 9 WOLV 12f Aw 60 4026
35 8 BRIG 10f Gd/Sft 54 4118

PTAH 3 b c £2946
15a 9 WOLV 8f Aw 636
46 9 RIPO 10f Soft 52 827
52 4 PONT 12f Gd/Sft 55 1106
53 3 NOTT 14f Gd/Fm 50 1270
52 2 REDC 14f Gd/Sft 50 1581
54 3 RIPO 12f Good 57 1862
30 9 YARM 14f Gd/Fm 53 1949
0 15 HAYD 12f Good 56 3284
33 6 HAYD 16f Gd/Sft 50 3476
48a 2 LING 16f Aw 41 4099
22a 7 LING 16f Aw 45 4329

PTARMIGAN RIDGE 4 b c £6500
80 1 AYR 5f Soft 72 3960*
51 21 AYR 6f Gd/Sft 77 4010
66 12 HAYD 5f Gd/Sft 80 4107
0 21 YORK 5f Soft 79 4285
69 7 DONC 5f Heavy 4570

PUBLIC PURSE 6 b g £365854
116ε3 NAD 10f Dirt 769

PUDDING LANE 3 b f £597
65a 2 LING 7f Aw 94
67a 5 LING 7f Aw 206 VIS

PUERTO MADERO 6 b h £182927
116ε4 NAD 10f Dirt 769

PUFFIN 2 b f £0
70 5 SALI 7f Gd/Fm 3292
74 6 SALI 7f Firm 3748
76 6 NEWM 7f Soft 4541

PUIWEE 5 b m £0
0a 10 SOUT 11f Aw 455 bl
3a 8 SOUT 8f Aw 24 585 bl
0 13 LEIC 7f Good 790
0a 13 SOUT 8f Aw 1505

PULAU PINANG 4 ch f £6601
64a 2 LING 12f Aw 772
76 2 BATH 12f Good 68 1091
79 1 BATH 13f Gd/Fm 72 1440* t
78 8 SAND 16f Gd/Fm 80 2498 t
71 7 DONC 15f Gd/Sft 78 4451 t
0 12 DONC 17f Heavy 76 4579 t

PULAU TIOMAN 4 b c £60208
98 2 KEMP 7f Good 95 725
103 1 KEMP 8f Soft 97 1015*
107 2 KEMP 8f Gd/Sft 102 1077
108 2 HAYD 7f Gd/Sft 1834
108 2 ASCO 8f Good 2675
89 18 GOOD 8f Good 106 3107
103 3 BATH 8f Gd/Fm 3515
102 3 NEWB 9f Firm 4000
89 3 BATH 8f Soft 4142

PULSE 2 b c £0
60 9 GOOD 6f Good 3881

PUNCTUATE 3 b c £1995
82 8 HAYD 5f Heavy 988
67 12 LING 6f Gd/Sft 96 1285
84 8 HAYD 6f Gd/Sft 92 1534
87 9 NEWM 6f Gd/Fm 89 1694
81 3 CHEP 6f Gd/Fm 2660
78 4 HAYD 6f Heavy 3768

PUNISHMENT 9 b h £5473
74a 6 LING 10f Aw 157 tVl
81a 2 LING 10f Aw 81 374 t
77a 3 LING 10f Aw 82 442 t
71a 5 LING 12f Aw 80 572 t
75 5 PONT 10f Soft 874 t
72 13 NEWM 10f Gd/Fm 86 1170 t

PUPPET PLAY (column 1, continued)

71	7	NEWB	12f Good	79	1373	t
70	11	WIND	10f Good	75	1729	t
68	6	SAND	10f Good	75	1965	t
75	2	SALI	8f Gd/Fm	71	2229	t
73	4	EPSO	9f Gd/Sft	74	2629	t
71	6	ASCO	8f Gd/Fm	73	3018	t
58	7	BATH	13f Gd/Fm	72	3518	t

PUPPET PLAY 5 ch m £15703

38a	6	SOUT	7f Aw	55	75	
52a	4	WOLV	8f Aw		133	
49a	2	LING	7f Aw		225	
52a	2	WOLV	8f Aw		229	bl
48a	3	WOLV	7f Aw		293	bl
49a	3	WOLV	8f Aw	50	323	
34a	4	WOLV	8f Aw	49	411	
50a	2	WOLV	7f Aw	47	635	
26a	8	SOUT	8f Aw	49	692	
47	3	CARL	9f Firm	48	1254	
0	14	PONT	12f Good	48	1499	
46	4	HAMI	8f Gd/Fm	46	1907	
51	1	PONT	8f Gd/Fm	47	2561*	
56	3	CARL	7f Firm	53	2823	
58	2	CARL	7f Gd/Fm	53	3083	
62	1	REDC	11f Firm	56	3328*	
46	8	NEWC	7f Soft	62	3708	
51a	2	SOUT	7f Aw	49	4153	
54a	1	WOLV	6f Aw	51	4442*	

PUPS PRIDE 3 b c £3087

52	5	MUSS	8f Gd/Sft	53	800	
46	7	NOTT	8f Heavy	51	1024	
0	15	BEVE	10f Good	52	1448	
44	9	AYR	8f Gd/Fm	49	1658	
44a	3	SOUT	6f Aw	47	2385	VIS
42a	4	WOLV	6f Aw	47	2603	vis
27	10	HAMI	8f Gd/Sft	47	3380	
0	16	NEWC	6f Heavy	43	4425	BL
51a	1	WOLV	6f Aw	44	4444*	bl
52a	2	WOLV	6f Aw	51	4553	bl

PURE BRIEF 3 b c £384

37a	7	SOUT	8f Aw	62	128
38a	7	SOUT	8f Aw	57	213
46a	3	WOLV	7f Aw	52	392
14a	7	SOUT	11f Aw	49	536
0a	12	WOLV	12f Aw	47	4443

PURE COINCIDENCE 5 b g £3370

60a	10	WOLV	5f Aw	78	64	
75a	3	WOLV	5f Aw	75	678	
72	8	KEMP	5f Soft	81	1013	
64	20	NEWM	6f Gd/Fm	80	1173	
71	7	LING	5f Good	78	1398	
62	10	CHES	5f Gd/Fm	76	2247	
76	3	HAYD	5f Gd/Fm	73	2701	
73	7	CARL	5f Firm	75	3572	
74	4	AYR	5f Soft	74	3960	
76	3	LEIC	5f Gd/Sft	74	4027	VIS

PURE ELEGANCIA 4 b f £2624

54	14	NEWC	5f Good	72	2525
67	2	CARL	5f Firm		2822
69	4	CATT	5f Gd/Fm	70	2929
67	3	GOOD	5f Gd/Fm	68	3091
53	16	EPSO	5f Good	71	3687
47	9	BRIG	5f Firm	69	3734

PURE SHORES 2 b c £940

75	4	RIPO	6f Gd/Fm	3184
75	3	RIPO	6f Gd/Fm	3466
65	9	AYR	6f Soft	3958

PURNADAS ROAD 5 ch m £605

19a	10	LING	8f Aw	48	147	BL
12a	8	WOLV	6f Aw	41	226	bl
18a	6	WOLV	7f Aw		276	bl
6a	11	WOLV	7f Aw		567	
36	3	BRIG	8f Firm		2892	

36	6	CHEP	7f Gd/Fm		3253
32	3	BRIG	10f Firm		3526
0	13	LING	10f Firm	33	3581
29a	12	LING	7f Aw		4328

PURPLE DAWN 4 b f £0

6	10	LEIC	8f Firm	34	2032
0a	8	LING	12f Aw	32	2593

PURPLE FLAME 4 b f £0

46	10	KEMP	7f Gd/Fm	55	3362
0	18	GOOD	8f Good	51	3885

PURPLE FLING 9 ch g £3085

64a	1	WOLV	6f Aw		82*
54a	6	WOLV	6f Aw	63	175
0	16	BATH	5f Good	56	1092
0	14	NOTT	6f Firm	56	1273
53a	2	SOUT	6f Aw		2819
59a	3	WOLV	6f Aw		3275
47a	6	WOLV	6f Aw	59	4444
57a	3	WOLV	6f Aw	56	4553

PURPLE HEATHER 3 b f £12423

87	2	BRIG	10f Gd/Fm		1127	
87	5	LING	11f Gd/Sft		1282	
83	3	NEWM	10f Firm		1857	
83	9	ASCO	12f Good	87	2116	BL
85	2	ASCO	10f Gd/Fm		2957	bl
85	1	WIND	10f Good		3189*	bl
93	4	SALI	10f Gd/Fm		3389	bl
92	8	YARM	10f Firm		3918	bl
89	2	KEMP	12f Soft		4039	

PURSUIT OF DREAMS 3 ch c £0

0	13	LING	7f Firm		3834
54	12	NOTT	8f Soft		3977
56	10	LING	8f Soft		4274
40	5	BATH	8f Soft	53	4435

PURSUIT OF LIFE 2 b f £5465

92	3	SAN	8f Gd/Sft		4145

PURSUIVANT 6 b g £2218

0a	7	WOLV	9f Aw		446	
51	3	SOUT	7f Good	56	803	
44	4	HAMI	9f Good	54	846	
17	13	PONT	8f Gd/Sft	51	1101	bl
40	6	HAMI	8f Gd/Fm	51	1190	bl
0a	11	SOUT	8f Aw		1505	bl
46	3	YARM	8f Good	47	1772	bl
46	2	NOTT	10f Good	47	2011	bl
0	17	WARW	11f Gd/Fm	47	2033	bl
41	4	WARW	12f Gd/Fm	47	2254	bl
39	7	WARW	11f Good	47	2463	bl
29	11	HAMI	9f Gd/Fm	44	2799	bl
29	8	BEVE	10f Gd/Sft	42	3052	VIS
29a	7	SOUT	11f Aw		4150	vis
0a	11	WOLV	12f Aw	37	4443	bl

PUSSIE WILLOW 3 b f £0

58	8	YARM	7f Soft		4388

PUTRA PEKAN 2 b c £3747

48	10	NEWM	6f Gd/Fm		2598	
83	6	GOOD	6f Gd/Fm		3064	
88	1	CHES	7f Gd/Fm		3508*	BL
97	6	NEWB	8f Firm		3983	bl

PUTRA SANDHURST 2 b c £0

79	5	NEWM	8f Gd/Sft		4531

PUZZLE 2 b c £0

0	29	NEWM	6f Good		4341	t
66	9	YARM	8f Soft		4512	t

PUZZLEMENT 6 gr g £6273

76a	3	SOUT	11f Aw	75	302
76a	3	LING	12f Aw	75	356
77a	3	LING	12f Aw	75	422
63a	3	WOLV	12f Aw	75	562
76	1	LEIC	12f Good	70	791*
62	10	NEWB	12f Good	75	1373
42	9	DONC	12f Good	74	1518

70	5	KEMP	12f Gd/Fm	72	1927
69	5	KEMP	10f Gd/Fm	70	2750
57	14	DONC	10f Firm	69	3899
68	6	YARM	10f Firm	69	3941
63a	5	LING	12f Aw	73	4271

PYJAMA GIRL 3 gr f £323

47a	6	LING	6f Aw	65	4	
55a	3	SOUT	7f Aw	60	1202	
35	8	BRIG	6f Good		1651	
49	10	SALI	7f Gd/Fm	60	1889	
25a	9	WOLV	9f Aw	58	2080	
45	9	LEIC	8f Gd/Fm	54	2512	BL
31	9	LING	7f Good	54	2592	bl

PYRUS 2 b c £30500

101	1	CURR	5f Gd/Sft		1621*
108	2	GOOD	6f Good		3105
97	5	DEAU	8f Gd/Sft		3550

PYTHAGORAS 3 ch c £0

85	6	NEWB	8f Good		1377
0	32	ASCO	8f Good	85	2117
53	8	NEWC	8f Firm		2337

PYTHIOS 4 b c £8220

46	14	EPSO	9f Gd/Sft	100	1829	
107	4	ASCO	8f Good	100	2090	t
102	2	DONC	8f Gd/Fm	100	2757	t
94	15	GOOD	8f Good	106	3107	t
52	16	YORK	8f Firm	105	3597	tVI
0	27	NEWM	9f Gd/Fm	105	4212	t

QAMOUS 3 gr c £4082

93	3	NEWM	7f Firm		1186
91	8	HAYD	8f Gd/Sft	93	1535
93	3	EPSO	7f Gd/Sft	92	1826
0	26	ASCO	8f Good	93	2117

QILIN 5 b m £0

95	5	MAIS	6f Heavy		98

QUAKERESS 5 b m £4346

12a	9	SOUT	6f Aw		32	
3a	11	SOUT	8f Aw	36	83	
0a	11	SOUT	11f Aw	35	178	Et
33a	6	WOLV	12f Aw		295	et
0a	9	SOUT	12f Aw	26	338	et
21a	4	LING	16f Aw		402	te
31a	1	WOLV	15f Aw		468*	et
27a	1	WOLV	16f Aw	22	494*	
28a	3	WOLV	16f Aw	27	577	
20a	4	SOUT	16f Aw	28	644	
22a	5	SOUT	16f Aw	28	737	
27a	3	LING	13f Aw	33	835	
31a	2	WOLV	16f Aw	28	918	
19	9	BRIG	12f Firm	38	1209	
22	10	EPSO	12f Gd/Sft	38	2429	
0a	P	WOLV	16f Aw	33	2606	

QUALITAIR PRIDE 8 b m £3737

0a	11	SOUT	14f Aw	30	1501
39	1	NEWM	7f Gd/Fm	36	2347*
20a	8	SOUT	8f Aw	29	2380
35	11	NEWM	8f Good	48	2564
25	9	NEWM	8f Gd/Fm	42	2802
33	6	YARM	7f Good	39	3030
19	11	YARM	7f Good	47	3238
0	13	LING	6f Firm	38	3578
0	16	NEWM	7f Good		4018
0a	14	LING	12f AW		4186

QUALITAIR SURVIVOR 5 gr g £285

38a	4	SOUT	8f Aw	38	85	
21a	5	SOUT	11f Aw	38	126	
0	16	REDC	8f Firm	34	1300	
40	4	HAMI	8f Gd/Fm	43	1360	VIS
35	6	MUSS	9f Firm	39	1689	vis
29	8	BEVE	10f Firm	38	1921	vis
29	8	MUSS	9f Firm	38	2049	vis
0	12	NEWM	8f Gd/Fm	42	2802	

0	12	NOTT	10f Gd/Fm	38	3007	vis
33	4	MUSS	7f Good	35	3103	
0	19	REDC	6f Firm	34	3312	

QUALITY 7 b g £692

50	2	CHEP	12f Gd/Fm		3681

QUALITY TEAM 3 b c £27450

100	3	LEOP	9f Soft		14	tBL
113	1	CURR	14f Yldg		2405*	bl

QUANTUM LADY 2 b f £8851

70	4	SAND	5f Gd/Fm		762
75	1	BATH	5f Good		1088*
75	2	BATH	5f Gd/Fm		1437
75	2	LING	6f Good		1673
71	3	WARW	7f Gd/Fm		2251
52	6	ASCO	6f Good	74	2678
68	4	WIND	6f Good	73	3354
80	1	NOTT	6f Soft	68	3976*
0	B	LEIC	6f Gd/Sft	75	4030

QUARRELL 3 ch f £318

62	4	NEWB	12f Firm		2710

QUATREDIL 2 b f £225

41	11	KEMP	6f Gd/Fm		2748
69	4	LEIC	6f Good		3096
46	11	LING	5f Good		4096
49	6	LING	6f Soft		4190
34	8	BATH	6f Soft		4431

QUAZAR 2 b c £575

0	14	NEWC	6f Good		3245
67	3	BEVE	6f Good		3675
57	8	AYR	6f Soft		3958
54	5	PONT	6f Soft	67	4235
0	15	PONT	8f Soft	67	4378

QUEDEX 4 b c £16610

56a	6	WOLV	9f Aw	68	271
0a	14	SOUT	12f Aw	66	370
73	2	HAYD	12f Gd/Sft	68	809
47	8	WARW	15f Heavy	72	805
79	1	HAYD	14f Gd/Fm	72	1167*
85	4	GOOD	14f Gd/Sft	83	1484
81	9	ASCO	12f Good	82	2674
79	7	GOOD	14f Gd/Fm	82	3058
86	1	KEMP	16f Gd/Fm	80	3360*
83	8	NEWB	16f Firm	85	3986
82	7	NEWM	18f Good	85	4353

QUEEN FOR A DAY 3 b f £0

27a	7	LING	8f Aw		236
29a	5	LING	10f Aw		286
0	19	BEVE	10f Firm		1274

QUEEN MOLLY 3 b f £840

56	5	REDC	6f Gd/Sft	1562	t
54	2	CATT	6f Soft	1678	t
49	4	HAMI	5f Firm	2096	t

QUEEN OF FASHION 4 b f £956

48	7	WIND	10f Gd/Fm		2056
61	4	BATH	12f Firm		2327
68	3	SAND	8f Good		2924
60	7	SALI	12f Gd/Fm	68	3392
54	10	GOOD	10f Good	65	3663
45	11	BATH	13f Gd/Fm	61	3819
44	8	SALI	10f Gd/Sft	56	4168

QUEEN OF THE KEYS 4 b f £5512

34a	7	LING	7f Aw	40	59	
38a	3	LING	8f Aw	38	147	
33a	6	WOLV	8f Aw	39	233	
0a	12	WOLV	8f Aw	39	255	VIS
51a	3	LING	10f Aw		314	vis
23a	9	LING	10f Aw		375	vis
14a	8	LING	7f Aw	39	439	vis
0	14	BRIG	7f Firm	37	1335	
18	10	BRIG	8f Soft	37	1511	
38a	3	LING	10f Aw	37	1915	
40a	2	LING	10f Aw	40	2186	
41a	2	LING	12f Aw	41	2593	
50a	1	LING	10f Aw		2764*	
14	10	NOTT	10f Gd/Fm	37	3007	

QUEEN OF THE MAY 3 b f £7139

77a	1	LING	6f Aw	70	4*	
74a	3	LING	6f Aw	75	105	
83	1	WIND	5f Gd/Sft	75	1098*	
77	6	LING	6f Gd/Sft	81	1285	
76	5	ASCO	5f Good	81	2168	
78	4	SAND	5f Gd/Fm	80	2478	
73	7	BATH	5f Firm	79	2787	
64	11	GOOD	5f Gd/Fm	77	3135	
71	6	GOOD	5f Good	75	3908	
67	7	BRIG	6f Gd/Sft	73	4120	
68	5	LING	5f Soft	71	4270	
65	8	BATH	5f Soft	70	4432	
65	9	WIND	5f Heavy	70	4527	
53	11	DONC	5f Heavy	69	4570	

QUEEN SARABI 5 b m £328

0a	12	SOUT	6f Aw	56	587	
46a	3	SOUT	5f Aw	50	674	
0	16	THIR	6f Soft	56	910	
35	16	REDC	5f Gd/Sft	52	1133	bl

QUEEN SPAIN 2 b f £4525

70	7	YORK	6f Gd/Fm		1312
77	2	LING	6f Soft		1541
75	2	RIPO	6f Good		1859
73	2	GOOD	7f Gd/Fm		2125
73	2	CATT	6f Gd/Fm		2419
58	7	CHEP	6f Gd/Fm		2972

QUEENIE 2 b f £0

86	8	NEWM	7f Good		4158

QUEENS BENCH 3 ch f £617

89	4	NEWM	7f Good	87	954	t
80	8	YORK	7f Good	87	1308	
79	5	NEWM	7f Good	86	2567	
67	8	ASCO	10f Gd/Fm	83	2955	
65	6	DONC	8f Gd/Fm	79	3160	t
73	7	SALI	7f Firm	76	3750	
0	20	KEMP	6f Gd/Fm	85	4037	
52	12	SAND	7f Soft	72	4204	

QUEENS COLLEGE 2 b f £639

0	16	WIND	6f Gd/Fm		1876
70	5	WIND	5f Good		2368
61	2	BRIG	5f Firm		2891
54	6	WIND	6f Good	65	3354

QUEENS HAT 5 b m £0

5a	10	LING	10f Aw		110

QUEENS MUSICIAN 2 b c £1479

83	3	AYR	6f Gd/Fm		1653
75	3	NEWC	6f Firm		2333
71	7	DONC	6f Gd/Fm		2608
69	3	THIR	5f Gd/Fm		3346

QUEENS PAGEANT 6 ch g £7867

60a	7	WOLV	9f Aw	84	119
52	10	ASCO	8f Gd/Sft	70	1113
62	4	NOTT	8f Good		1407
65	4	WIND	8f Good	66	2367
63	6	YORK	8f Gd/Fm	66	2645
63	5	WIND	8f Gd/Fm	64	2890
70	1	WIND	10f Gd/Fm		3045*
62	7	WIND	12f Good	71	3353
68	8	YORK	12f Good	71	3541
71	3	BEVE	10f Gd/Fm	70	3676
59	12	DONC	10f Firm	70	3899
	3	PONT	10f Soft		4088
67	2	HAYD	11f Gd/Sft	69	4108
59	6	REDC	10f Gd/Fm	69	4221
49	10	BATH	10f Soft	68	4436

QUEENS SIGNET 4 ch f £0

0a	10	LING	6f Aw		95
0a	14	LING	6f Aw	30	148

QUEENS SONG 2 ch f £309

16a	8	LING	5f Aw		1916
56	3	BATH	5f Gd/Sft		2551
38	6	LEIC	5f Gd/Fm		2772
49	5	BATH	5f Firm		3204
39	6	LING	5f Good	53	3491
33	6	BRIG	5f Soft		4171

QUEENS STROLLER 9 b m £0

0	17	LEIC	8f Firm	33	2027
0a	10	LING	10f Aw	33	2186
0	12	BATH	12f Firm		2785
28	9	CHEP	7f Gd/Fm		3253

QUEENSMEAD 3 b f £0

35	10	BRIG	5f Gd/Sft	64	897	
51	7	NOTT	6f Firm		1266	
29	8	CHEP	6f Heavy	60	1557	
0	12	BATH	5f Gd/Fm		1670	
48	4	LING	5f Good		2590	t
44	8	REDC	5f Gd/Fm	51	2864	t

QUERCUS 2 ch c £0

0	15	WIND	5f Good		849

QUEZON CITY GER 3 br f £25806

115	2	DUSS	12f Good		2911

QUI WARRANTO 2 ch c £315

76	8	YORK	7f Gd/Fm		2649
78	4	HAYD	7f Good		3287
57	7	HAYD	6f Gd/Sft		3478
64	7	PONT	8f Soft		4086

QUICK TO PLEASE 2 b f £4371

98	1	DONC	8f Gd/Sft		4445*

QUICKTIME 3 ch f £0

48a	8	LING	7f Aw		155
20a	9	SOUT	7f Aw		330

QUIDS INN 3 br c £988

54	2	REDC	8f Firm	51	1296
37	10	MUSS	8f Gd/Fm	51	1434
33	11	BEVE	7f Good	54	1920
45	6	REDC	9f Gd/Fm	52	2160
19	12	PONT	12f Good	50	2362
0a	11	LING	10f Aw	47	4482

QUIESCENT 2 ch f £4441

0	13	WIND	5f Gd/Sft		1424
90	1	NOTT	5f Gd/Sft		1642*
88	3	YARM	5f Good		3027
92	6	NEWB	5f Gd/Fm		3482

QUIET ARCH 7 b g £0

0a	8	WOLV	12f Aw		626	
61	5	HAYD	12f Gd/Sft		1788	vis
35	11	HAMI	12f Gd/Fm	55	1908	vis

QUIET MISSION 9 ch g £0

13a	12	WOLV	6f Aw		132

QUIET READING 3 b g £1531

39	10	KEMP	7f Soft		1018
72	10	WIND	10f Gd/Fm		1200
66	3	SAND	10f Soft		1588
58	6	BATH	8f Firm		1997
60a	4	LING	10f Aw		2213
14	10	WIND	12f Good	60	2712
51a	5	WOLV	12f Aw	64	3494
60a	2	LING	12f Aw		3835
41a	6	LING	16f Aw	60	4099
58a	4	LING	12f Aw		4334

QUIET TRAVELLER 2 b c £0

46	10	AYR	6f Gd/Fm		1628
52	9	AYR	7f Good		3363
48	8	HAMI	8f Gd/Sft		3532
8	13	MUSS	8f Gd/Sft	54	4132

QUIET VENTURE 6 b g £2537

60	11	THIR	7f Good	75	1158
52	12	THIR	6f Good	72	1383
0	15	CATT	7f Soft		1680
54	7	CARL	6f Firm	65	2015

```
49   4  MUSS    9f Firm         2376 t
60   1  CARL    7f Firm         3197* tvi
52   8  REDC    7f Firm     64  3328 tvi
0   19  YORK    7f Good     61  3809 tvi
28  13  MUSS    7f Gd/Sft   59  4136 tvi
68a  7  WOLV    6f Aw       75  4380 tvi
```

QUIGLEYS POINT 4 b g £0
```
0   16  RIPO    8f Soft         826
0   14  NOTT   14f Gd/Sft       1369
0    P  CHES   16f Soft     46  4071
```

QUINK 2 ch g £17425
```
84   1  YARM    6f Gd/Fm        2414*
89   3  DONC    7f Gd/Fm        2576
93   1  AYR     6f Firm     85  2874*
95   3  KEMP    6f Gd/Fm    91  3075
85   5  YARM    6f Gd/Fm        3965
94   1  YORK    7f Soft         4277*
91   4  PONT    8f Soft         4375
```

QUINTA LAD 2 b g £0
```
74   7  DONC    6f Heavy        4575
```

QUINTRELL DOWNS 5 b g £15640
```
78a  3  WOLV   12f Aw       74  81
80a  2  SOUT   12f Aw       77  200
86a  1  SOUT   11f Aw       79  302*
92a  1  LING   12f Aw       85  356*
```

QUITE HAPPY 5 b m £6369
```
36   9  BRIG    5f Gd/Sft   55  897
59   3  CARL    5f Firm         1256
45   3  MUSS    5f Gd/Fm        1430
54   3  CATT    5f Good     54  1662
51   5  BRIG    5f Good     53  1932
54   3  LING    5f Gd/Fm    53  2184
47   6  LING    5f Firm     55  2326
54   4  MUSS    5f Gd/Sft   55  2535
53   2  BATH    5f Firm         2788
54   2  KEMP    5f Gd/Fm        3077
59   2  PONT    5f Gd/Fm    55  3222
62   2  PONT    5f Firm     58  3502
40a  8  WOLV    6f Aw       62  3774
58   4  SAND    5f Firm         3947
0   16  GOOD    5f Soft     62  4065
```

QUITTE LA FRANCE 2 b f £3146
```
89   1  REDC    7f Gd/Sft       4216*
```

QUIZZICAL LADY 2 b f £5273
```
70   7  DONC    5f Gd/Fm        700
72   5  RIPO    5f Soft         821
81   1  WARW    5f Heavy        1000*
81   6  ASCO    5f Gd/Fm        1107
65   8  YORK    6f Gd/Fm        1312
68   4  WIND    5f Gd/Sft       1426
66   8  BEVE    5f Gd/Fm        1759
69   6  LEIC    5f Gd/Fm    74  2915
64   4  BATH    5f Firm         2940
70   2  WIND    6f Good     70  3354
50   8  WARW   15f Good     70  3693
59   8  HAMI    5f Soft     70  3802
64   3  LING    6f Good         4097
48   9  LING    6f Soft         4190
55a  1  LING    5f Aw           4333
37   9  BATH    6f Soft         4431
```

QUWS 6 b g £5700
```
101  2  CURR   10f Soft         1121
```

RA RA RASPUTIN 5 b g £3646
```
34a  9  SOUT    6f Aw           30
50a  3  WOLV    7f Aw           65
37a  7  WOLV    7f Aw           142 bl
0a  11  SOUT    8f Aw       54  177
51a  1  WOLV    7f Aw           310*
49a  4  SOUT    7f Aw           341
54a  1  WOLV    7f Aw           396*
10a 10  SOUT    7f Aw       50  471
18a 11  WOLV    8f Aw           550
```
```
7a   8  WOLV    8f Aw           612
12a  8  WOLV    8f Aw       45  676
21a 12  WOLV    8f Aw           1139
0a  13  SOUT    7f Aw           1305
0   15  REDC    7f Gd/Sft       1559 bl
0a  14  SOUT    7f Aw       34  2122 bl
0   15  CHES   10f Gd/Fm        2245 VIS
```

RAASED 8 b g £0
```
0   21  REDC    8f Firm     42  1296 t
0   13  AYR     8f Gd/Fm    40  1658 tvi
10  10  REDC    8f Gd/Fm    38  2861 vis
32   6  THIR    8f Gd/Fm    36  3344 tvi
```

RACE LEADER 3 b c £14558
```
113  1  THIR    8f Soft         925+
86  22  NEWM    8f Gd/Fm        1171
93  12  ASCO    7f Good         2087
```

RACHEL GREEN 2 b f £260
```
60   6  NOTT    5f Good         2009
0   16  LING    6f Gd/Fm        2214
58   4  BRIG    6f Gd/Fm        2724
```

RACINA 2 ch f £8624
```
74   2  YARM    5f Firm         2766
83   1  BEVE    5f Gd/Fm        3408*
94   3  CHAN    6f Good         3843
90  11  NEWM    6f Good         4159
```

RACINGFORYOU LASS 2 b f £0
```
30  10  CHES    7f Soft         4068
21  10  NEWM    8f Soft         4542
```

RADAS DAUGHTER 4 br f £47217
```
93   7  YORK   12f Gd/Fm    94  1307
91   7  EPSO   12f Good     94  1850
59  18  ASCO   12f Good     94  2069
98   1  HAYD   12f Gd/Fm    91  2502*
94   7  NEWB   12f Good         3177
97   8  YORK   14f Gd/Fm    97  3565
105  2  DONC   15f Gd/Fm        3863
104  7  NEWM   12f Good         4343
104  4  NEWM   16f Gd/Sft  105  4533
```

RADICAL JACK 3 b c £0
```
0   17  CARL    8f Firm     49  1255
41  10  HAMI    5f Gd/Fm    49  1358
```

RADIO STAR 3 b c £5249
```
82   1  SAND    7f Good         1963*
82   3  DONC   10f Gd/Fm        3865
0   22  NEWM   10f Good     82  4197
```

RAED 7 b h £272
```
0a  12  LING   16f Aw       65  6
23a  6  WOLV   15f Aw           117
19a 11  SOUT   12f Aw       54  215
42a  3  SOUT   11f Aw           369
10a  6  SOUT   12f Aw       40  683
20   9  BRIG   10f Gd/Fm    53  3244
39   5  BRIG   10f Firm     45  3557
```

RAFTERS MUSIC 5 b g £12654
```
58a  1  SOUT    6f Aw       48  342*
61a  2  SOUT    6f Aw       54  388
68a  1  SOUT    6f Aw       58  425*
49a  6  SOUT    6f Aw       64  454
56a  8  SOUT    6f Aw       64  587
54   3  BRIG    7f Firm     52  1213
55   3  MUSS    7f Gd/Fm    52  1431
56   1  DONC    7f Good     52  1519*
52   3  AYR     7f Gd/Fm    52  1631
46  10  CATT    7f Good     56  3440
55   4  NEWC    6f Good     56  3605
```

RAGAMUFFIN 2 ch c £5289
```
71   4  NEWC    5f Soft         755
59   6  HAYD    5f Heavy        989
80   2  CHES    5f Gd/Fm        1221
85   1  REDC    5f Gd/Sft       1558*
```

RAGDALE HALL 3 b c £3609
```
85   5  NEWB   10f Gd/Fm        1404
```
```
82   1  WIND   10f Good         1725*
78   8  ASCO   12f Gd/Fm    85  3014
82   3  HAYD   12f Gd/Sft   83  3270
81   7  YARM   10f Firm     82  3941
0   17  NEWM   10f Good     80  4197 BL
```

RAGING TIMES 2 ch f £0
```
31a  7  SOUT    7f Aw           2949
37   6  LING    6f Firm         3278
0   12  LING    6f Good         4097
```

RAGLAN ACCOLADE 3 b f £0
```
0a  15  LING   12f Aw           2181
```

RAHEEN 7 b h £0
```
61a 11  LING   10f Aw           55
```

RAHEIBB 2 ch c £0
```
51  15  DONC    7f Gd/Sft       4446
63  10  DONC    7f Heavy        4566
```

RAILROADER 3 ch c £24362
```
73   6  WARW    6f Heavy        888
83   1  CHES    6f Gd/Fm    74  1220*
0   14  NEWB    6f Gd/Fm    80  1406
83   2  YORK    6f Firm     80  2003
78   8  HAYD    5f Gd/Fm    83  3322
72  11  GOOD    6f Good     83  3904
0   16  SALI    6f Gd/Sft   81  4165
72  11  WIND    5f Heavy    79  4527
```

RAIN IN SPAIN 4 b c £8812
```
87   3  DONC   12f Good         732
105  2  CHES   10f Firm         1248
100  4  DONC   10f Gd/Fm        1841
104  8  ASCO   12f Gd/Fm   105  2069
101  3  HAYD   12f Gd/Fm   104  2502
102  3  NEWM   12f Gd/Fm        2803
```

RAIN RAIN GO AWAY 4 ch c £12637
```
34a  8  LING    7f Aw           109
37a  4  LING    7f Aw           159
51a  3  LING    7f Aw           225
54a  3  WOLV    8f Aw           229
61a  1  WOLV    7f Aw           293*
43a  6  WOLV    7f Aw           477
69a  1  LING    7f Aw           547*
66a  4  LING    8f Aw       66  594
71a  3  WOLV    7f Aw           623
73a  1  WOLV    7f Aw       66  721*
76a  1  LING    7f Aw       70  879*
0   11  YARM    6f Gd/Fm    60  1953
68a  6  SOUT    8f Aw       79  2817
```

RAINBOW FRONTIER 6 b g £0
```
77  12  ASCO   20f Good     85  2092
```

RAINBOW HIGH 5 b g £28200
```
113  5  CHES   19f Gd/Fm   113  1222
115  4  GOOD   16f Good         3106
115  2  YORK   16f Good         3538
113  4  DONC   18f Gd/Fm        3877
115  3  NEWM   16f Good         4351
```

RAINBOW HILL 3 b c £4688
```
88   2  YARM    8f Good         1771
85   1  RIPO    8f Gd/Fm        2104*
81   7  NEWM    8f Good     85  3022
```

RAINBOW PRINCESS 2 b f £0
```
0    P  KEMP    6f Gd/Fm        2748
```

RAINBOW RAIN 6 b g £6457
```
62a  2  LING    7f Aw       60  28
59a  3  LING    7f Aw       62  107
51a  7  LING    7f Aw       62  162 E
55a  5  WOLV    8f Aw       60  227
60a  3  LING    7f Aw       58  337
47a  7  LING    7f Aw       58  462
60a  2  LING    7f Aw       58  504
58a  2  LING    7f Aw           547
58   9  LING    5f Gd/Sft   67  1264
54   9  SALI    6f Gd/Fm    65  1887
0   17  WIND    6f Gd/Fm    65  2054
```

62	2	BRIG	7f Soft	60	2427	
0	14	KEMP	7f Gd/Fm	62	2749	
43	10	YARM	7f Firm	62	2899	
53	9	BRIG	6f Gd/Fm	61	3243	t
60	2	BRIG	8f Firm	59	3527	t
0	R	EPSO	7f Good	59	3765	t
54	7	BRIG	7f Gd/Sft	61	4121	

RAINBOW RAVER 4 ch f £0

0	23	DONC	12f Gd/Fm	50	699
0	14	NOTT	10f Gd/Sft	44	1364
0	11	MUSS	12f Gd/Fm	44	1432
14	7	BEVE	10f Good	37	2883

RAINBOW RIVER 2 ch g £277

36	9	BEVE	5f Firm		1918
60	7	PONT	6f Gd/Fm		3223
60	5	CATT	7f Good		3438
59	3	LEIC	8f Firm	58	3837

RAINBOW SPIRIT 3 b g £3829

80	5	NEWB	11f Soft		916
81	7	SALI	12f Firm		1179
74	3	HAMI	12f Gd/Fm		1362
72	4	HAYD	14f Soft	73	1821
72	3	LING	11f Firm	71	2321
66	4	CHEP	16f Gd/Fm	71	2659
66	2	BRIG	12f Gd/Fm		3241
61	3	BRIG	12f Firm	65	3560
64	3	SALI	14f Gd/Sft	63	4166
56a	3	SOUT	14f Aw	62	4370
0	16	DONC	12f Gd/Sft	62	4451

RAINBOW STAR 6 b g £0

0	18	SALI	12f Good	65	2689

RAINBOW VIEW 4 b g £0

0	16	LEIC	8f Sft/Hvy	4311

RAINBOW WAYS 5 b g £61648

106	1	NEWM	12f Firm	98	1187*
112	2	YORK	14f Firm		1339
115	2	LEIC	12f Firm		2028
115	3	NEWC	16f Good	111	2336
106	4	NEWM	12f Good		2566
101	8	GOOD	16f Good		3106
98	4	NEWB	13f Gd/Fm		3483

RAINSTORM 5 b g £416

32	12	NEWM	10f Gd/Fm	42	2958
40	3	CARL	8f Firm	41	3192
40	5	AYR	10f Good	41	3368
23	7	CATT	12f Good	43	3437
0	13	BRIG	10f Firm	38	3737

RAINWORTH LADY 3 b f £519

0a	13	SOUT	7f Aw	56	31	
27a	5	WOLV	6f Aw	49	638	
32	9	PONT	8f Heavy		942	
0	20	NEWC	8f Gd/Sft	45	1477	
17	9	BEVE	12f Good	50	1919	
0a	6	SOUT	12f Aw	50	2382	BL
53	3	NEWC	10f Good		3034	
40	5	LEIC	10f Gd/Fm	44	3217	
0	P	BEVE	10f Good	43	3396	
52	8	PONT	10f Soft		4088	

RAINY RIVER 2 b f £0

73	5	YARM	7f Soft	4514

RAISAS GOLD 2 b f £0

39a	6	WOLV	5f Aw	722
40a	9	SOUT	5f Aw	865
39a	10	WOLV	5f Good	1236

RAISE A GLASS 2 ch c £0

0	15	LING	5f Good	4096

RAISE A PRINCE 7 b h £3641

97	5	HAYD	12f Heavy		987	t
95	6	ASCO	16f Gd/Sft		1109	t
92	6	NEWB	13f Gd/Fm		1401	t
72	12	EPSO	12f Good	96	1850	t
84	9	YORK	14f Good	92	2695	t

88	2	AYR	13f Gd/Sft	87	4014	t
84	5	ASCO	12f Gd/Sft	87	4128	t
88	3	AYR	13f Heavy	87	4325	t

RAJMATA 4 b f £0

16a	7	WOLV	6f Aw		273	vis
25a	6	LING	6f Aw		399	vis
0	R	LEIC	6f Aw	53	2031	vis

RAKE HEY 6 gr g £0

48	6	NOTT	10f Good		1875	
42a	4	LING	10f Aw	51	2212	tvi

RAKEEB 5 ch g £3347

71	1	DONC	12f Gd/Fm	60	699*	bl
55	4	CATT	14f Gd/Fm	60	779	bl
52	8	DONC	12f Gd/Fm	69	1839	bl

RAMADANZEN 3 b f £0

0	20	NEWB	10f Good	1404
0	13	CHEP	10f Gd/Sft	1796

RAMBAGH 2 b f £2014

72	4	GOOD	7f Good		2306
68	2	FOLK	7f Gd/Fm		3039
64	5	FOLK	7f Good		3583
69	4	GOOD	8f Soft	68	4076

RAMBLIN MAN 2 b c £611

44	10	BATH	5f Firm		1993
57	5	LING	5f Firm		2324
46	9	WIND	5f Good		2711
64	3	LEIC	6f Gd/Fm		3215
60	8	NOTT	6f Good		3520
44	8	GOOD	6f Good	62	3886

RAMBLING BEAR 7 ch h £13532

112	3	NEWM	5f Gd/Fm	1172
105	3	SAND	5f Soft	1566
109	4	ASCO	5f Good	2065
83	7	SAND	5f Good	2496
108	5	GOOD	5f Gd/Fm	3059
105	6	YORK	5f Firm	3598
107	3	DONC	5f Good	3874
99	7	NEWB	5f Firm	3982
93	13	NEWM	5f Good	4182

RAMBO NINE 3 b c £0

0	14	BEVE	12f Good	55	3954
0	13	LEIC	8f Sft/Hvy		4311

RAMBO WALTZER 8 b g £17768

62a	1	SOUT	8f Aw		45*
57a	1	SOUT	7f Aw		130
66a	1	SOUT	8f Aw		197*
68a	1	SOUT	8f Aw		252*
62a	1	WOLV	7f Aw		276*
54a	2	SOUT	8f Aw		366
66a	1	WOLV	9f Aw		517*
76a	2	WOLV	7f Aw		623
62a	6	WOLV	9f Aw	70	681
65a	1	SOUT	7f Aw		693*
68a	1	WOLV	8f Aw		750*
53	3	WARW	8f Heavy	54	1520
56	2	NEWM	8f Gd/Fm	54	1690
51	7	NOTT	10f Good		1875
44	9	HAYD	7f Gd/Fm	55	2442
72a	2	SOUT	8f Aw		2950
71a	4	WOLV	9f Aw	72	3495
63a	6	SOUT	8f Aw	71	4365

RAMBOLD 9 b m £0

25a	11	LING	7f Aw	50	107
19a	7	LING	6f Aw	43	263

RAMESES 2 b g £267

41	12	DONC	6f Good		1513
69	4	LING	5f Firm		2324 VIS
0	12	BEVE	5f Good		2880 vis
0	23	NEWM	7f Good		4336

RAMOOZ 7 b h £6955

103	4	HAYD	7f Gd/Fm	1163
109	3	EPSO	9f Good	1847

90	9	ASCO	8f Good	2064

RAMPANT 2 b c £1276

83	2	SALI	8f Gd/Sft	4163

RAMPART 3 b c £0

55	11	DONC	10f Gd/Sft	1054
32	5	AYR	8f Gd/Fm	3139

RAMRUMA 4 ch f £27800

60	11	NEWM	12f Gd/Fm	1152
116	3	YORK	12f Good	3564
96	3	ASCO	12f Gd/Sft	4130

RANDOM KINDNESS 7 b g £522

79a	4	LING	12f Aw	85	356
54a	7	LING	12f Aw	82	508
0a	7	WOLV	16f Aw	78	627

RANDOM QUEST 2 b c £5239

91	9	NEWM	7f Good	4158
83	1	NOTT	8f Heavy	4504*

RANDOM TASK 3 b c £7930

0	15	NEWM	7f Gd/Fm	78	3629	
66a	6	WOLV	7f Aw	80	3771	
73	1	KEMP	6f Gd/Sft	70	4037*	BL
17	18	YORK	7f Heavy	77	4302	bl

RANEEN NASHWAN 4 b c £0

77	6	WIND	10f Gd/Fm	747

RANIN 2 b f £1771

82	3	SALI	7f Firm	3748
85	5	NEWM	7f Good	4183
82	2	YARM	8f Heavy	4475

RANVILLE 2 ch c £0

57	13	NEWM	8f Good	4161
66	10	YARM	8f Soft	4512

RAPID DEPLOYMENT 3 b c £6068

52	7	BRIG	8f Gd/Sft		894
46	9	BATH	10f Gd/Sft	67	2552
63	2	WARW	11f Gd/Fm	62	2842
63	1	CARL	12f Firm	60	3195*
62	4	BEVE	12f Good	63	3954

RAPIDASH 3 gr c £0

34	11	NOTT	5f Heavy		1021 vis
0	17	BEVE	5f Firm		1280 vis
43	8	LING	5f Good		2590 vis
37	11	LEIC	5f Gd/Fm		2919 vis

RAPIER 6 b g £5624

81	4	HAYD	11f Heavy		986
67	9	DONC	10f Gd/Sft	82	1070
77	1	HAYD	12f Gd/Sft		1788*
81	3	ASCO	12f Good	78	2674
56	10	YORK	12f Gd/Fm	81	3725
56	8	AYR	13f Gd/Sft	80	4014

RAPT 2 b c £0

0	19	NEWM	8f Good	4349
66	6	MUSS	7f Soft	4562

RAPTOR 2 ch c £0

50	11	NEWB	7f Gd/Fm	3484
0	13	BATH	6f Soft	4137
0	16	DONC	7f Gd/Sft	4447

RARE GENIUS 4 ch c £1981

66	2	LEIC	12f Good	64	791
67	3	SALI	14f Firm	66	1180
66	5	PONT	12f Good	68	1499
66	8	NOTT	14f Good	67	1874
60	6	KEMP	12f Firm	65	2263

RARE OLD TIMES 2 b f £7308

69	5	SALI	5f Firm		1176
82	1	WIND	5f Gd/Sft		1426*
53	11	ASCO	6f Good		2067
70	6	SAND	5f Good	82	3431
51	9	YORK	6f Good	78	3807
66	8	LING	5f Good	72	4098

RARE TALENT 6 b g £20014

39	9	NOTT	10f Gd/Fm	56	1272

30 19 NEWM 12f Firm 56 1852
56 3 BEVE 10f Firm 53 2220
33 8 PONT 10f Good 53 2366
54 3 BEVE 10f Gd/Fm 53 2518
54 2 YARM 11f Firm 53 2771
51 6 EPSO 10f Good 53 2790
59 1 BEVE 10f Good 53 2883*
50 5 BEVE 10f Gd/Sft 58 3052
60 2 NOTT 10f Gd/Fm 59 3111
64 2 PONT 10f Gd/Fm 59 3220
58 4 NEWM 10f Gd/Fm 60 3314
67 1 EPSO 12f Good 62 3686*
57 11 DONC 10f Firm 66 3899

RASHAS REALM 2 ch f £2347
84 2 NEWM 6f Firm 1856
81 3 GOOD 6f Good 3881
60 7 LING 6f Soft 4189

RASHIK 6 ch h £273
72 5 SAND 9f Good 3230
57 9 BATH 8f Gd/Fm 72 3514
46 13 YORK 7f Good 65 3809

RASM 3 b c £11836
100 1 NEWM 10f Gd/Fm 1697*
107 2 ASCO 10f Good 2169
99 3 NEWM 12f Gd/Fm 2803

RASMALAI 3 b f £1971
71 10 NEWB 7f Soft 915
70 3 EPSO 9f Heavy 1032
59 10 SALI 10f Gd/Fm 2265
68 2 EPSO 9f Gd/Fm 67 3401
27 12 LEIC 8f Sft/Hvy 67 4310

RASOUM 2 gr c £28140
88 3 YARM 6f Good 1774
88 1 NEWM 6f Gd/Fm 2959*
93 3 YARM 6f Gd/Fm 3965
90 9 NEWM 5f Good 92 4179
89 8 NEWM 6f Good 91 4338
104 1 NEWB 6f Sft/Hvy 90 4468+

RASSENDYLL 2 b c £0
58 7 FOLK 7f Gd/Fm 2290

RATEEBA 2 b f £0
0 26 NEWM 6f Good 4341
0 14 YARM 7f Soft 4514

RATHBAWN PRINCE 8 ch g £1127
77 3 GOOD 16f Good 76 3905
44 13 ASCO 16f Good 76 4115 BL

RATHCLOGHEENDANCER 3 ch g £0
0a 10 WOLV 7f Aw 46 346

RATHER DIZZY 5 b g £0
6 12 WARW 8f Good 2465 VIS

RATHKENNY 2 b c £9082
60 5 RIPO 6f Gd/Fm 3009
65 6 PONT 6f Gd/Fm 3223
52 4 RIPO 6f Good 3697
62 1 AYR 8f Soft 3957*
62 6 WIND 10f Gd/Sft 65 4290
99 2 PONT 8f Soft 4375
88 4 NEWM 10f Soft 4543

RATHLEA 6 b h £0
49 10 HAYD 5f Gd/Sft 808
0 11 PONT 8f Heavy 942
0 20 THIR 5f Gd/Sft 38 3781
0 17 LING 8f Soft 4274

RATIFIED 3 b c £4162
47a 7 LING 8f Aw 103
52 2 BRIG 10f Gd/Sft 46 892
55 1 NOTT 10f Heavy 51 1022*
50a 4 LING 10f Aw 57 1544
49 8 NOTT 10f Good 2012
55 5 EPSO 9f Gd/Fm 57 3401
52 2 BEVE 10f Sft/Hv 54 4046
54 6 BRIG 8f Soft 4173

RATTLE 7 b g £0
0 12 HAMI 8f Gd/Sft 33 3380 t

RAVENSWOOD 3 b c £9771
78 4 WIND 12f Gd/Fm 78 1199 t
81 2 SALI 12f Good 78 1350 t
86 1 NEWB 13f Gd/Fm 78 1784* t
98 4 ASCO 16f Good 2068 t
87 12 GOOD 14f Gd/Fm 93 3058 t
0 25 NEWM 18f Good 91 4353 t

RAVINE 3 ch f £8500
68 11 GOOD 8f Gd/Sft 1811
70 4 SAND 7f Good 1963
71 1 WIND 6f Gd/Fm 68 2885*
76 1 NEWM 7f Gd/Fm 71 3460*
75 4 GOOD 7f Good 3662

RAVISHING 3 b f £7601
69 4 WARW 7f Soft 1060
81 1 NEWB 6f Gd/Fm 77 1406*
74 15 NEWM 6f Gd/Fm 81 1694
68 11 YORK 6f Firm 80 2003
49 13 KEMP 6f Gd/Sft 80 4037
47 9 PONT 6f Soft 4233
0 23 NEWM 7f Good 75 4357
0 13 YARM 6f Heavy 72 4480
0 20 NEWM 7f Soft 68 4547

RAW SILK 2 b g £0
45 8 NEWB 5f Gd/Sft 1589
0 21 KEMP 6f Gd/Fm 1924
65 6 NEWM 6f Gd/Fm 3627
41 9 YARM 8f Gd/Fm 62 3968

RAWI 7 ch g £861
55a 3 LING 10f Aw 110
0a 12 LING 10f Aw 45 203
15a 8 LING 13f Aw 43 460
20a 6 WOLV 12f Aw 43 489
0a 14 LING 12f Aw 650 bl
0 12 BRIG 8f Gd/Sft 30 1462
41 2 BRIG 12f Good 1647
14 5 DONC 17f Gd/Fm 38 2607

RAYIK 5 br g £22975
50a 12 LING 8f Aw 72 7
54a 6 WOLV 12f Aw 67 81
58a 7 LING 12f Aw 64 151
70a 1 LING 13f Aw 60 317*
67a 2 LING 12f Aw 66 356
72a 1 LING 12f Aw 67 422*
62a 4 LING 12f Aw 70 508
77a 1 LING 12f Aw 70 621*
79a 2 LING 12f Aw 76 633
0 12 WIND 10f Soft 60 2544
33 10 CHEP 12f Gd/Fm 55 2971
53 1 WIND 12f Good 47 3186*
31 7 EPSO 12f Gd/Fm 53 3402
54 3 FOLK 12f Gd/Fm 53 3586
38 9 SALI 10f Gd/Sft 53 4168

RAYPOUR 3 ch c £28400
115 4 CURR 12f Good 2409
106 6 ASCO 12f Gd/Fm 2998
109 6 LONG 12f Good 3929
96 10 LONG 12f Good 4262

RAYWARE BOY 4 b c £1251
47a 9 LING 8f Aw 65 210 bl
35a 10 SOUT 8f Aw 61 326 bl
0a 11 WOLV 8f Aw 55 1037 bl
22 10 PONT 8f Good 1498
50 5 CATT 14f Good 1660 bl
35 4 REDC 10f Gd/Fm 2143 bl
18a 5 SOUT 11f Aw 2381 bl
38 2 CATT 12f Gd/Fm 40 2422 bl
34 7 DONC 12f Gd/Fm 44 2755 bl
20 7 YARM 16f Good 39 3026 bl
36 4 HAYD 12f Good 39 3284 bl
15 10 CATT 12f Good 43 3437 bl
40a 3 WOLV 12f Aw 40 3773 bl

RAYYAAN 3 ch c £22150
84 1 SOUT 7f Good 804*
90 1 NEWM 7f Good 80 954*
93 1 NEWM 7f Gd/Fm 85 1153*
83 6 GOOD 7f Gd/Sft 90 1470
90 2 CHES 7f Gd/Fm 90 3427
73 19 ASCO 7f Good 90 4112
79 17 NEWM 7f Good 89 4357

RAZZAMATAZZ 2 b c £0
54 9 NEWB 8f Gd/Sft 4457

REACH THE TOP 3 b c £16394
92 1 GOOD 8f Gd/Sft 1449*
73 6 SAND 8f Good 2476
106 1 NEWM 10f Firm 3300*
103 4 KEMP 12f Gd/Fm 3792
107 4 NEWB 11f Firm 3984

REACHFORYOURPOCKET 5 b g £554
52a 4 LING 10f Aw 314
43a 6 LING 8f Aw 353
45a 1 LING 7f Aw 40 438*
47a 2 LING 7f Aw 44 503
0 18 WARW 8f Soft 45 1066
43 3 BRIG 7f Firm 43 1335
36 6 GOOD 8f Gd/Sft 48 1473
38 6 BRIG 7f Good 44 1652
0 18 DONC 7f Gd/Fm 48 1840
35 9 CHEP 7f Good 45 1969 VIS
21 9 LING 10f Good 42 2655
46 1 BRIG 7f Gd/Fm 42 2728*
33 8 WARW 7f Gd/Fm 43 2840
44 7 BRIG 6f Gd/Fm 48 3243
31 8 FOLK 7f Gd/Fm 48 3445
55 2 BRIG 7f Firm 3559
44 5 EPSO 7f Good 46 3765
0 23 NEWB 5f Gd/Sft 47 4459

READING RHONDA 4 b f £385
46a 5 WOLV 8f Aw 920
54 7 ASCO 8f Gd/Sft 1112
40 11 NEWB 10f Gd/Fm 58 1785
11a 11 LING 10f Aw 53 2186
39 9 FOLK 10f Gd/Fm 53 2296
44a 3 LING 12f Aw 47 2593
34 6 SAND 14f Gd/Fm 45 2923
18 7 KEMP 16f Gd/Fm 48 3360
0 14 LING 10f Firm 38 3581
16 6 BRIG 12f Firm 37 3735 t

READY TO ROCK 4 b g £5081
41a 3 SOUT 6f Aw 199
0a 12 WOLV 6f Aw 45 226
0a 11 SOUT 6f Aw 389
3a 9 SOUT 6f Aw 472
36a 6 LING 6f Aw 484 bl
34a 8 LING 6f Aw 40 543 bl
50a 1 LING 5f Aw 40 573* bl
49a 2 LING 5f Aw 48 631 bl
49a 2 SOUT 5f Aw 48 673 bl
48a 4 LING 5f Aw 51 774 bl

REAL ESTATE 6 b g £2725
70 3 CHEP 10f Good 70 1973
70 2 BATH 10f Gd/Sft 70 2552
56 10 SALI 14f Gd/Fm 70 2982
41 9 BATH 13f Gd/Fm 70 3518
54 11 WIND 10f Gd/Sft 68 4291

REAL TING 4 br g £0
28a 5 LING 6f Aw 30 154 vis
16a 8 SOUT 6f Aw 30 602 vis
14a 9 SOUT 6f Aw 28 2385 vis

REAP 2 b c £0
63 9 ASCO 6f Gd/Fm 3000
29 6 EPSO 6f Good 3852

63a 4 WOLV 6f Aw 4548 VIS

REBECCA JAY 4 b f £0
16a 10 WOLV 7f Aw   61

REBEL STORM 2 b c £3753
68 10 YORK 6f Gd/Fm 3568
86 1 YARM 7f Firm 3940*

RECIPROCAL 2 gr f £233
53 10 NEWB 7f Firm 2708
0 22 NEWB 5f Firm 2849
76 4 KEMP 7f Soft 4034
62 9 NEWB 7f Sft/Hvy 4467

RECOLETA 3 b f £0
17a 12 LING 7f Aw 94
40 10 SALI 10f Good 1343
46 6 NEWB 10f Gd/Sft 1593 BL

RECORD TIME 4 ch f £6142
0 19 THIR 6f Soft 61 910
54 9 REDC 5f Gd/Sft 60 1133
53 4 CARL 5f Firm 1256
41 8 NEWC 5f Gd/Sft 56 1479
63 1 NEWM 5f Good 54 2569+
44 6 NEWB 5f Gd/Fm 60 3485

RED APOLLO 4 gr g £208
31a 6 LING 8f Aw 544
38a 4 LING 7f Aw 570
0a 9 WOLV 8f Aw 612 bl
32 10 PONT 8f Heavy 942 VIS
9 12 PONT 8f Gd/Sft 40 1101 vis

RED BLAZER NZ 7 ch g £0
70 7 DONC 7f Soft 4465

RED BORDEAUX 5 b g £0
0 16 WIND 12f Gd/Fm 60 748
0 12 FOLK 15f Soft 54 963
44 5 BRIG 12f Firm 47 1209 BL
0 16 LING 16f Good 44 1394 bl
33 8 BRIG 12f Gd/Sft 44 1465 bl
0 13 LING 16f Firm 40 3755

RED CAFE 4 ch f £5946
51 3 WIND 8f Good 52 854
36 6 THIR 8f Soft 52 931
31 14 CARL 9f Firm 51 1254
28 12 WARW 11f Gd/Sft 49 1707
0 17 HAYD 11f Soft 49 1819 BL
32 4 BRIG 8f Firm 2040
40 2 WARW 8f Good 40 2460 bl
39 4 MUSS 8f Gd/Sft 40 2533 bl
28 11 LING 10f Firm 40 3581 VIS
34 10 YORK 9f Good 3808
40 1 AYR 9f Heavy 4324*
49 1 BRIG 10f Soft 44 4419*

RED CANYON 3 b c £7832
67 2 MUSS 8f Gd/Sft 61 800
65 4 KEMP 9f Gd/Sft 63 1075
61 4 WIND 12f Firm 63 1292
64 1 AYR 11f Gd/Fm 62 1633*
66 2 RIPO 12f Gd/Fm 63 2110
63 3 HAMI 13f Gd/Fm 63 2238
62 4 RIPO 12f Soft 65 2540
0 13 NEWM 10f Gd/Sft 63 2958
59 4 LEIC 10f Gd/Fm 62 3217
54 10 LING 16f Firm 62 3755
0 12 NOTT 10f Heavy 4413

RED CARNATION 2 b f £1517
85 3 NEWM 6f Gd/Fm 4209
80 3 YARM 6f Heavy 4479

RED CARPET 2 ch c £38589
78 2 YARM 6f Good 2414
83 5 YORK 7f Gd/Fm 2649
82 1 CHEP 6f Gd/Fm 2972*
97 1 NEWM 6f Gd/Fm 84 3630*
112 3 NEWM 6f Good 4181

RED CHARGER 4 ch g £0

0 16 CARL 6f Firm 66 1257
46 7 CHES 5f Gd/Sft 65 1781
41 12 HAYD 5f Gd/Sft 63 2505
0 19 YORK 6f Good 63 2697
48 13 THIR 5f Gd/Fm 61 3619
45 12 CHEP 5f Good 58 3872

RED CORAL 2 b f £6900
98 1 NAAS 6f Yldg 1750*

RED CRYSTAL 2 b f £0
0 F DONC 8f Gd/Sft 4445

RED DEER 2 ch c £303
70 9 SALI 7f Good 2686
60 9 NEWM 7f Gd/Fm 3121
68 4 THIR 8f Gd/Sft 3779

RED DELIRIUM 4 b c £1120
68 2 WIND 8f Gd/Fm 66 746
62 10 DONC 6f Gd/Sft 68 1074
0 13 BRIG 7f Firm 68 1213
57 7 SALI 7f Good 68 1348
56 13 NEWM 8f Gd/Fm 66 1690
51 12 WIND 6f Gd/Fm 64 2054 BL
48 10 WIND 6f Gd/Fm 64 2207 tbl
55 5 BATH 5f Gd/Sft 59 2555 t
42 7 BATH 6f Firm 56 2944 t
48 6 NEWB 6f Firm 55 3455
44 12 WARW 11f Gd/Fm 52 3915
0 13 NOTT 10f Heavy 4413

RED EMPRESS 3 b f £7394
83 2 NEWB 10f Gd/Fm 1404
76 6 NEWM 10f Firm 1857
80 1 RIPO 12f Gd/Fm 2103*
85 2 LEIC 12f Gd/Fm 84 2509
72 11 ASCO 12f Gd/Sft 85 3014

RED FANFARE 2 ch f £563
56 7 NOTT 5f Good 2009
49 10 SALI 5f Gd/Fm 2227
67 7 FOLK 6f Gd/Fm 3443
58 9 LING 7f Firm 66 3830
52a 2 WOLV 7f Aw 4025
43a 5 WOLV 8f Aw 4362
29a 10 WOLV 8f Aw 50 4552

RED KING 3 b c £0
9a 11 SOUT 8f Aw 36
39 6 SOUT 10f Good 806
15a 6 WOLV 8f Aw 1234 BL

RED LETTER 3 b f £3887
78 3 NOTT 8f Gd/Sft 1366
83 2 NEWM 8f Firm 82 1853
84 4 ASCO 8f Good 86 2167
76 7 EPSO 9f Gd/Sft 85 2629
81 3 SALI 8f Gd/Fm 83 3422
61 14 KEMP 10f Gd/Fm 82 3794 VIS

RED LION FR 3 ch g £1813
0 18 WIND 10f Gd/Fm 1200
0 12 NEWB 8f Good 1377
60 8 WIND 10f Good 1725
59 6 NOTT 10f Soft 3979
62 4 WIND 10f Gd/Sft 60 4291
66 2 DONC 10f Gd/Sft 61 4448

RED LION GB 4 ch g £0
82 9 YORK 6f Gd/Fm 93 1337
74 14 ASCO 6f Firm 92 2151
64 15 NEWC 6f Firm 89 2334
63 13 YARM 7f Gd/Fm 86 2768
0 15 NEWM 6f Gd/Fm 86 2961 BL
0 18 NEWM 5f Good 82 4015

RED MAGIC 2 b c £8675
91 2 NEWM 6f Gd/Fm 2598
97 1 ASCO 5f Gd/Fm 2956*
87 6 DEAU 6f Gd/Sft 3550

RED MILLENNIUM 2 b f £38926
72 1 MUSS 5f Gd/Sft 898*

75 2 NOTT 5f Firm 1267
92 1 NOTT 5f Gd/Sft 1641*
100 2 NEWC 5f Gd/Sft 1759
97 1 DONC 5f Gd/Fm 2318*
100 1 CHES 5f Good 2664*
96 3 GOOD 5f Gd/Fm 3133
89 4 CHAN 6f Good 3843
98 2 AYR 5f Soft 3959
100 3 NEWB 5f Gd/Sft 4454

RED MITTENS 3 ch f £0
33 7 CARL 6f Gd/Sft 1723
4 8 REDC 7f Gd/Fm 50 2145
40 6 MUSS 7f Good 44 3103
33 6 THIR 6f Gd/Fm 44 3124
31 7 MUSS 5f Gd/Fm 45 3593
0 18 THIR 5f Gd/Fm 40 3781

RED N SOCKS 3 ch c £10683
91 2 NEWM 8f Firm 85 1183
79 12 GOOD 9f Gd/Sft 90 1452
91 7 ASCO 8f Good 90 2117
94 1 LING 8f Firm 2762*
87 7 GOOD 8f Good 90 3107
79 10 YORK 8f Firm 93 3597
87 6 NEWB 8f Firm 93 3998
85 10 NEWM 7f Good 92 4195

RED OCARINA 2 ch f £0
0 10 BEVE 5f Good 2880
19 7 REDC 6f Firm 3307

RED RAJA 7 b h £0
28a 8 LING 16f Aw 54 6 VIS
36a 8 WOLV 16f Aw 50 918

RED RAMONA 5 b g £0
47 9 YORK 12f Gd/Sft 4276
0 22 NEWM 18f Good 85 4353

RED REVOLUTION 3 ch c £3483
72a 2 SOUT 5f Aw 127
80a 1 LING 5f Aw 289+
74 6 YORK 5f Good 79 2003
69 8 NEWM 5f Gd/Fm 78 2288
0 20 YORK 6f Good 77 2697
0 18 YARM 5f Firm 75 3920

RED RIVER REBEL 2 b c £0
47 6 RIPO 6f Good 1859
64 7 DONC 7f Gd/Sft 4446
0 18 DONC 7f Heavy 4566

RED ROSES 4 b f £460
13 10 RIPO 12f Soft 47 825
0 14 PONT 10f Heavy 42 943
0 12 SOUT 10f Firm 41 1608
48 8 HAYD 12f Gd/Sft 1788
14 7 REDC 10f Gd/Fm 2143
23 4 HAMI 11f Firm 2393
17 10 RIPO 10f Soft 2538 BL
17 7 HAMI 11f Gd/Fm 2800 bl
29 4 NEWC 12f Good 3247
21 3 HAMI 12f Gd/Sft 23 3827 t
24 4 BEVE 12f Sft/Hvy 4041

RED ROSIE 2 b f £0
68 14 NEWM 8f Good 4349

RED RYDING HOOD 2 ch f £8030
52 6 YARM 6f Gd/Fm 1954
71 3 REDC 5f Gd/Fm 2142
70 4 YARM 5f Firm 2766
77 2 YARM 5f Firm 2901
74 3 BEVE 5f Good 74 3394
76 2 NEWM 6f Gd/Fm 74 3630
56 15 DONC 5f Firm 3860
76 5 NEWM 5f Good 75 4179
70 4 YARM 5f Soft 76 4511

RED SEPTEMBER 3 b c £0
0 23 REDC 8f Firm 55 1300
41 6 CARL 9f Gd/Sft 51 1722

RED SONNY 3 ch g £1602
(continued from previous)

0a	9	SOUT	11f Aw	47	2945	BL
33	7	NEWC	14f Good	43	3249	bl

0	8	THIR	7f Soft		929
44	7	NOTT	6f Gd/Sft		1081
43a	4	WOLV	6f Aw		1137
24a	9	WOLV	5f Aw		1392
0	16	NOTT	10f Soft	53	1644
46a	2	SOUT	8f Aw	45	1804
48	3	PONT	8f Good		1865
44	6	AYR	8f Good	46	2136
47	2	NOTT	8f Gd/Fm	46	2187
11a	10	SOUT	8f Aw	46	2379

RED SYMPHONY 4 b f £1961

0a	13	SOUT	6f Aw	54	87	
44a	5	WOLV	5f Aw		919	
36	11	CARL	5f Firm		1256	
28	13	NEWC	5f Gd/Sft	52	1479	
22	8	CATT	6f Good		1664	
45	1	NEWC	5f Heavy		1766*	VIS
0	17	HAMI	5f Gd/Fm	51	1910	vis
0	15	HAMI	6f Gd/Sft	50	3377	vis
30	13	HAMI	5f Gd/Sft	50	3536	vis
38	9	HAMI	6f Gd/Fm	46	3825	BL
0	20	AYR	5f Soft	52	3960	bl
18	12	AYR	6f Heavy	43	4327	bl

RED THATCH 3 ch c £0

0	12	WIND	8f Good		3350
60	10	NOTT	8f Soft		3977

RED TYPHOON 3 ro f £1332

68	10	WIND	5f Gd/Sft	77	1098	
0	14	CHES	6f Gd/Fm	77	1220	
47	11	WIND	6f Gd/Fm	74	1877	
54	10	HAYD	5f Gd/Fm	69	2505	
71	2	KEMP	5f Gd/Sft	69	2586	
68	8	EPSO	7f Good	72	3855	t
50	17	AYR	5f Good	73	4010	t
50	13	BRIG	6f Gd/Sft	72	4120	t
0	18	DONC	5f Heavy	71	4570	

RED VENUS 4 ch f £631

54a	5	LING	7f Aw		616	bl
54a	3	SOUT	7f Aw		667	bl
56a	3	SOUT	8f Aw	56	692	bl
40a	7	LING	8f Aw	54	776	bl
0a	13	SOUT	7f Aw	55	867	bl
40a	5	SOUT	8f Aw	53	1303	bl

RED WHITE AND BLUE 3 b f £0

0	11	SALI	7f Gd/Fm		2232
0	12	WIND	8f Soft		2548
30	10	CHEP	7f Gd/Fm		3256
0	14	WIND	6f Heavy		4526

RED WOLF 4 ch g £1132

0a	12	WOLV	8f Aw	54	227
12a	9	SOUT	8f Aw	48	329
31	8	BEVE	7f Aw	42	2479
42	3	RIPO	8f Gd/Fm		2834
42	2	MUSS	7f Good	39	3103
12	10	YARM	8f Good	39	3236
22	7	MUSS	8f Gd/Fm	41	3745

REDHILL 3 b f £0

35	9	BEVE	10f Good		1447
48	6	BEVE	7f Firm		1922
61	5	NOTT	8f Gd/Fm		2188
59	7	NOTT	8f Gd/Fm		3116

REDNAP 2 b c £0

51	7	YARM	7f Soft		4389

REDOUBLE 4 b c £5487

0a	13	LING	10f Aw	57	209
43	7	WIND	10f Gd/Fm	54	1878
58	2	WARW	12f Gd/Fm	56	2255
60	2	EPSO	12f Good	58	2793
61	3	CATT	14f Gd/Fm	60	3201
60	3	SAND	14f Good	60	3472
63	2	BATH	13f Gd/Fm	60	3819
60	2	SALI	14f Gd/Sft	59	4166

REDOUBTABLE 9 b h £24358

70a	6	LING	6f Aw	72	113	
72a	3	LING	7f Aw	72	162	
63a	6	WOLV	6f Aw	72	258	
71a	4	LING	7f Aw	70	337	
80a	1	SOUT	6f Aw	70	388*	
80a	2	WOLV	6f Aw	76	435	
84a	1	LING	7f Aw	77	525*	
77a	4	WOLV	7f Aw	82	721	
77	3	RIPO	6f Soft	79	824	
81	2	PONT	6f Heavy	78	941	
60	12	NEWC	7f Heavy	78	1011	
80	1	WARW	7f Soft		1060*	
74	9	THIR	7f Good	85	1158	
0	19	THIR	6f Good	82	1383	
71	7	DONC	7f Good	80	1514	
67	14	DONC	7f Gd/Fm	78	1840	
0	21	YORK	6f Firm	76	2000	
75	3	AYR	7f Good	73	2163	
65	6	NEWC	7f Firm	74	2338	
0	17	HAYD	6f Gd/Fm	74	2444	
0	11	DONC	6f Gd/Fm		2580	
70	4	HAYD	7f Gd/Fm		2704	
70	1	REDC	7f Gd/Fm		2994*	
69	4	LEIC	6f Gd/Fm		3097	
65	3	BRIG	6f Gd/Fm		3259	
38	12	REDC	7f Firm	70	3328	bl
64	5	NEWC	7f Soft	68	3708	
47	13	SALI	8f Firm	68	3753	
70a	4	WOLV	7f Aw		4224	
55	9	REDC	7f Gd/Sft	65	4498	

REDS DESIRE 3 ch g £0

5	8	REDC	6f Gd/Sft		1562
0	13	NEWC	5f Heavy		1766
0	6	NEWC	8f Good		2520
0	13	REDC	5f Gd/Fm	35	2864
0	13	CARL	6f Firm		3194
0	19	THIR	5f Gd/Sft	29	3781

REDSWAN 5 ch g £8849

55	12	PONT	8f Soft	73	875	t
70	7	GOOD	7f Gd/Sft	73	1810	tbl
57	9	SAND	7f Gd/Fm	72	1989	tbl
51	14	NEWC	6f Firm	70	2334	t
54	14	DONC	7f Gd/Fm	68	2612	t
68	2	LEIC	7f Gd/Fm	68	2775	t
0	12	YARM	7f Good	66	3030	t
62	3	NEWM	7f Gd/Fm		3318	t
65	3	LEIC	7f Firm	62	3839	t
66	1	NEWM	7f Firm		4018*	t
69	5	NEWM	7f Gd/Fm	69	4215	t
52	14	NEWM	8f Good	70	4340	t
48	6	DONC	7f Soft		4461	t

REDUIT 2 ch c £20156

85	4	SAND	7f Gd/Fm		2921
89	4	YORK	7f Good		3537
97	1	CHEP	8f Good		3867*
108	2	SAIN	10f Soft		4556

REEDS RAINS 2 b f £4915

81	1	THIR	5f Soft		904*
81	4	THIR	5f Good		1161
84	4	YORK	6f Gd/Fm		1312
0	17	DONC	6f Gd/Fm		3862

REEL BUDDY 2 ch c £73437

70	6	YORK	6f Firm		1328
85	2	GOOD	6f Gd/Sft		1472
82	13	NEWB	5f Firm		2849
97	7	GOOD	5f Firm		3133
69	7	LING	5f Firm		3277
95	1	BATH	5f Gd/Fm		3513*
101	1	RIPO	5f Gd/Fm		3714*
101	2	DONC	6f Gd/Fm		3862
81	14	NEWB	5f Gd/Sft		4454

REEMATNA 3 b f £2035

70	4	WARW	11f Soft		814
70	2	LING	7f Good		1675
62a	4	SOUT	8f Aw		1977
48	6	WARW	8f Good		2464
58	3	THIR	7f Gd/Fm		3146
35	10	BRIG	10f Gd/Sft	62	4118

REFERENDUM 6 b g £7959

65a	12	WOLV	6f Aw	88	660	
0	20	DONC	6f Good	88	716	
53	12	PONT	6f Heavy	83	941	BL
70	15	YORK	5f Firm		1324	
66	14	HAYD	5f Gd/Sft	75	1533	
69	8	YORK	7f Gd/Fm	72	1980	
67	5	NEWC	6f Gd/Fm	69	2275	
72	5	NEWC	5f Firm	69	2340	
66	6	NEWM	5f Good	71	2569	
63	6	CATT	5f Gd/Fm	71	2743	
62	11	GOOD	5f Gd/Fm	70	3091	
76	2	GOOD	8f Gd/Fm	73	3136	
74	2	SALI	7f Good	73	3419	
74	3	SAND	5f Good	73	3436	
0	19	GOOD	6f Good	74	3646	
0	24	AYR	5f Soft	74	3960	

REFERRAL 2 ch c £2386

85	2	YARM	7f Good		3237
85	5	YORK	7f Good		3537
90	2	YARM	8f Gd/Fm		3969

REFLEX BLUE 3 b c £5580

80	4	WIND	10f Gd/Fm		1198	
85	4	NEWB	12f Gd/Fm	87	1400	
85	2	SALI	10f Gd/Fm		1885	
80	3	SALI	12f Gd/Fm	85	2231	
76	6	NEWM	15f Good	83	3025	
71	4	DONC	10f Good		3865	
0	17	NEWM	12f Gd/Fm	83	4162	
71	5	DONC	10f Gd/Sft	76	4451	BL

REFRACT 2 b c £0

81	11	NEWM	7f Good		4183

REGAL ACADEMY 6 b m £654

0	15	WIND	12f Gd/Fm	39	2887	bl
37	4	BRIG	10f Firm	37	3557	tbl
28	3	BRIG	12f Firm	35	3735	tbl

REGAL AIR 2 b f £2675

67a	3	SOUT	5f Aw		865
68	5	CHES	5f Firm		1249
61a	3	SOUT	5f Aw		1418
0	17	NEWB	5f Gd/Sft		2849
68	3	BEVE	5f Gd/Sft		3055
61	7	BEVE	5f Good	69	3394
70	2	BRIG	6f Firm		3525
70	2	NOTT	6f Soft	69	3976

REGAL CHARM 3 b f £0

52	9	SALI	10f Good		1344
0	6	CHEP	12f Heavy		1554

REGAL HOLLY 5 b m £0

40	10	NOTT	14f Gd/Sft		1369 bl

REGAL MISTRESS 2 b f £0

40	5	DONC	5f Good		712
37a	8	SOUT	5f Aw		856
46	7	BEVE	5f Heavy		974

REGAL PHILOSOPHER 4 b c £14010

85	6	WIND	8f Good		851
91	2	SAND	8f Heavy	88	1042
92	2	GOOD	8f Gd/Sft	88	1450
92	4	SAND	8f Soft	91	1567
85	10	YORK	9f Firm	91	2001
92	3	SAND	8f Gd/Fm	90	2528
86	5	YORK	8f Gd/Fm	90	2648

REGAL ROSE 2 b f £83512

99 1 **ASCO** 6f Gd/Fm   2952*
114 1 **NEWM** 6f Good   4159*

REGAL SONG 4 b c £7255
49a 3 SOUT 6f Aw   414
57a 2 SOUT 6f Aw   55   499
30a 10 SOUT 7f Aw   667
62 3 HAMI 6f Good   63   844 bl
0   W NEWC 5f Heavy   63 1008 bl
60 5 BATH 5f Good   63 1092 bl
0a 12 SOUT 6f Aw   56 1421 bl
61 3 LEIC 6f Soft   63 1545 bl
0   22 DONC 7f Gd/Fm   62 1840
67 1 NEWC 5f Heavy   61 4407*
55 14 WIND 5f Heavy   68 4527
70 2 DONC 5f Heavy   67 4570 bl

REGAL SPLENDOUR 7 ch g £0
33a 6 SOUT 8f Aw   47   83
0a 10 SOUT 11f Aw   47 126
33a 10 WOLV 8f Aw   477

REGAL VISION 3 b g £0
44 7 WIND 8f Good   3190
42 8 WARW 7f Good   3696
49 11 WARW 8f Gd/Fm   3914
47 5 BRIG 10f Soft   55   4174

REGALITY 4 ch f £0
12a 12 WOLV 9f Aw   53   60
0a 12 SOUT 11f Aw   46   126

REGALO 5 b g £0
0   25 WIND 6f Gd/Sft   55   4294
0   18 LEIC 8f Sft/Hvy   4311 BL
0   25 NEWB 5f Gd/Sft   49   4459 bl

REGARDEZ MOI 3 b f £581
0   14 WARW 7f Soft   64   1061
0   18 NEWB 7f Gd/Fm   62   1405
57 6 WIND 8f Good   58   1726
46 3 NEWM 8f Gd/Fm   2134
8   9 YARM 8f Gd/Fm   2411
22 13 NEWM 10f Good   3021
41 11 NEWM 7f Gd/Fm   53   3163
30 14 NEWM 8f Gd/Sft   48   4536

REGATTA POINT 2 b c £12855
0   12 LEIC 7f Aw   3333
75 2 YARM 8f Gd/Fm   3665
85 1 **SALI** 8f Gd/Fm   4163*
84 1 **NEWM** 8f Good 77 4350*
89 3 NEWM 10f Soft   4543

REGENT 5 ch g £0
17a 9 LING 8f Aw   47   594
0   13 WARW 11f Good   3691
0   16 CHEP 7f Good   47   3871
0   16 LEIC 8f Gd/Sft   4032
62 8 REDC 7f Gd/Sft   4218
0   16 WIND 8f Gd/Sft   4292
31 7 WIND 6f Heavy   4526

REGENT COURT 2 grf f £950
73 5 DONC 7f Gd/Fm   3156
65 4 CHES 7f Gd/Fm   3508
51 5 THIR 8f Gd/Sft   3779
74 3 AYR 7f Soft   3962
20 10 YORK 7f Soft   74   4279

REGGIE BUCK 6 b g £0
34 6 BEVE 16f Firm   37   1276
29 11 NOTT 14f Good   48   1411

REIMS 2 b c £0
72 9 DONC 7f Gd/Fm   3156
38 9 CHES 7f Soft   4068
0   22 YORK 8f Soft   4281

REINE DE LA CHASSE 8 ch m £0
0a 7 LING 12f Aw   27
12a 5 WOLV 15f Aw   117

REINHARDT 7 b g £0
0a 8 WOLV 12f Aw   26   522 t

REKEN 4 b c £0
20 9 FOLK 7f Soft   962
0   11 BRIG 8f Gd/Sft   36   1462
20 7 LEIC 8f Gd/Sft   1732
5   10 BRIG 8f Firm   2040

RELATIVE DELIGHT 2 b f £0
68 10 WARW 7f Gd/Fm   3910
0   19 NEWM 7f Soft   4541

RELISH THE THOUGHT 2 b f £13520
105 1 **NEWB** 7f Sft/Hvy   4467*

REMARKABLE 2 ch f £0
70 6 LING 7f Soft   4484
58 11 DONC 7f Heavy   4567

REMEMBER STAR 7 ch m £2018
27 4 WARW 16f Gd/Fm   28   2037
26 3 BRIG 12f Firm   25   2904
26 2 FOLK 12f Aw   25   3040
26 2 BRIG 12f Good   29   3260
27 5 LING 16f Firm   29   3755
21 4 BRIG 12f Soft   30   4176

RENAISSANCE LADY 4 ch f £15210
13 10 WARW 15f Heavy   48   885
40 7 LEIC 12f Gd/Sft 45   1736
50 1 **WARW** 16f Gd/Fm 42 2037*
55 1 **WARW** 16f Gd/Fm 48 2256*
56 1 **WARW** 15f Good 54 2461*
62 2 NEWB 16f Firm   56   2812
55 5 ASCO 16f Gd/Fm   56   2953
59 3 GOOD 20f Gd/Fm   58   3085
57 3 BATH 17f Firm   58   3625
58 4 GOOD 16f Good   58   3905

RENDITA 4 b f £277
38a 10 LING 8f Aw   59   1259
34 7 AYR 12f Good   49   2139
21 11 LING 10f Good   45   2655 BL
21 9 CHEP 8f Good   3868
50a 5 WOLV 7f Aw   4224
42a 3 LING 8f Aw   4272
50a 4 LING 7f Aw   4328 bl

RENDITION 3 b f £34303
85 1 **BRIG** 7f Gd/Fm   1125*
88 1 **YORK** 7f Gd/Fm 79 1308*
89 3 YORK 6f Firm   87   2003
85 10 GOOD 7f Gd/Fm   89   3130
90 3 SALI 7f Firm   89   3750
96 6 DONC 7f Gd/Fm   3878
87 6 ASCO 8f Good   89   4113

RENEE 2 b f £494
68 3 WARW 5f Gd/Fm   2034
66 5 NEWM 6f Gd/Fm   2285
61 5 YARM 5f Firm   2766
44 9 SAND 5f Good   65   3228
50 6 MUSS 5f Gd/Fm   62   3743
48 9 NEWC 5f Heavy   59   4423

RENZO 7 b h £34808
65 1 **SAND** 16f Heavy 60 1044*
73 1 **THIR** 16f Gd/Sft 67 1355*
73 3 KEMP 16f Soft   71   1527
18 18 ASCO 20f Good   71   2092
0   1 **SAND** 16f Gd/Fm 71 2498*
80 2 CHES 16f Gd/Fm   77   2672
75 7 ASCO 16f Gd/Fm   79   2953
73 3 KEMP 16f Gd/Fm   78   3360
71 10 NEWM 18f Good   79   4353

REPEAT PERFORMANCE 2 b c £1927
76 4 BRIG 5f Gd/Sft   891
77 2 BRIG 5f Gd/Fm   1124 t
74 4 YORK 6f Firm   1328 t
69 4 BRIG 5f Gd/Sft   1463 t
81 4 CHEP 6f Good   1968 t
47 10 BATH 6f Gd/Sft   2550 t
69 5 BRIG 7f Firm   71   2894 t
61a 5 WOLV 7f Aw   69   3273 t
53 7 SALI 7f Gd/Fm   3388 t
44 8 FOLK 7f Gd/Fm   3582 t

REPERTORY 7 b g £51059
97 7 NEWB 5f Soft   107 914
98 12 NEWM 5f Gd/Fm   1172
100 3 EPSO 5f Good   103 1849
104 2 SAND 5f Gd/Fm   1987
104 3 SAND 5f Gd/Fm   2496
95 5 CHES 5f Gd/Fm   2669
91 13 GOOD 6f Firm   105 3152
96 7 NOTT 5f Good   3521
107 1 **EPSO** 5f Good 1023687+
98 8 NEWB 5f Firm   3982
94 12 ASCO 5f Gd/Sft   105 4129
112 1 **LONG** 5f Heavy   4495*

REPLACEMENT PET 3 b f £307
54 4 THIR 7f Gd/Fm   3146
34 10 LING 6f Firm   3579
0   13 WARW 8f Gd/Fm   3914
28a 8 WOLV 8f Aw   4551 BL

REPTON 5 ch g £319
30a 9 WOLV 12f Aw   53   43
29a 7 SOUT 12f Aw   50   215
22a 9 WOLV 12f Aw   46   260
32 9 PONT 12f Good   40   1499
24 8 WARW 16f Gd/Sft 38   1711
30 3 YARM 14f Good   30   3233
35 5 BATH 13f Gd/Fm   40   3518

REPUBLICAN LADY 8 b m £239
0   16 NEWM 10f Gd/Fm   1697
46 4 WARW 12f Gd/Fm   2038
35 6 LEIC 12f Good   2776
2   6 BEVE 12f Good   3399
0a 16 SOUT 16f Aw   33   4149

REPULSE BAY 2 b c £2257
85 4 GOOD 7f Firm   3154
84 2 SALI 7f Gd/Fm   3391
84 3 AYR 8f Gd/Sft   4008

REQUEST 3 b f £2567
89 2 SAND 10f Heavy   1045
89 4 NEWB 10f Good   1374

REQUESTOR 5 br g £6369
31 13 THIR 8f Soft   62   907
65 1 **RIPO** 8f Soft 60   2542*
71 1 **HAMI** 8f Gd/Fm   2781*
67 6 RIPO 9f Gd/Fm   70   3011

RESEARCH MASTER 3 br c £0
0   14 BATH 8f Gd/Fm   60   1442
26 10 LING 11f Firm   55   1914
21a 10 WOLV 8f Aw   55   2080
0   16 CHEP 8f Gd/Fm   2448 BL

RESFA 6 b h £54306
118 3 SHA 8f Gd/Fm   184

RESILIENT 3 b c £851
46 12 KEMP 8f Soft   1532
64 6 NOTT 8f Soft   1643
69a 5 SOUT 6f Aw   2299
70a 2 WOLV 6f Aw   2604
57 10 NEWM 7f Gd/Fm   3163

RESIST THE FORCE 10 br g £5087
67a 1 **LING** 8f Aw   60   210*
59a 7 LING 7f Aw   67   239
38a 8 LING 8f Aw   67   596
81 2 BRIG 8f Gd/Sft   78   895
71 8 EPSO 6f Heavy   80   1028
53 11 BRIG 8f Gd/Fm   80   1126

RESONATE 2 b c £4750
104 2 CURR 7f Gd/Fm   3067

RESOUNDING 3 b f £3369
78 3 NOTT 8f Good   79   1873
80 2 NEWM 8f Gd/Fm   79   2614

80	4	NEWB	10f Gd/Fm	80	3178	
68	6	BEVE	10f Gd/Fm	80	3676	
76	5	SAND	8f Soft	79	4206	VIS
0	12	BRIG	8f Soft		4420	

RESPLENDENT FLYER 2 b c £305

0	14	WIND	6f Gd/Fm		3047
63	4	LEIC	6f Good		3215
56	7	GOOD	6f Good		3649

RESPLENDENT STAR 3 b c £1262

82	4	YORK	8f Firm	82	1341	BL
72	10	KEMP	8f Firm	82	2870	bl
64	11	LEIC	8f Gd/Fm	81	3334	bl
72	3	FOLK	10f Gd/Fm	78	3585	vis
72	5	GOOD	10f Soft	75	4067	vis
0	16	YORK	12f Soft	74	4280	vis

RETALIATOR 4 b f £1356

54	8	CATT	7f Gd/Fm	69	780
51	11	THIR	6f Gd/Sft	68	1356
64	2	CHES	5f Gd/Sft	63	1781
0	11	WIND	6f Gd/Fm	64	2207
57	7	CHES	6f Gd/Fm	64	2247
41	11	CATT	6f Gd/Fm		2437
0	6	CHES	7f Gd/Fm		2670

RETSKI 3 b g £0

| 43 | 13 | LING | 6f Good | | 1399 |
| 53 | 7 | NEWB | 6f Soft | | 1783 |

RETURN 3 b f £4179

| 82 | 1 | SAND | 10f Soft | | 4205* |

RETURN OF AMIN 6 ch g £3037

81	9	KEMP	6f Good	90	728	
68	11	RIPO	6f Soft	88	824	
75	9	WIND	6f Heavy		935	
71	12	ASCO	7f Gd/Sft	83	1110	
83	2	GOOD	8f Gd/Fm	80	1471	VIS
79	4	NEWB	6f Gd/Sft	80	1591	bl
77	9	LING	6f Good	80	1678	bl
0	24	GOOD	6f Firm	81	3152	bl
0	18	YORK	6f Heavy	79	4301	bl

REVE DOSCAR 3 gr f £184485

108	2	SAIN	11f V		944
111	1	LONG	10f Gd/Sft		1457*
111	4	CHAN	11f Gd/Sft		1901
108	3	DEAU	10f Gd/Fm		3546
118	2	LONG	12f Good		3928
119	2	LONG	10f Good		4263
117	2	SAN	12f Heavy		4493

REVE RUSSE 3 b f £0

| 96 | 6 | YORK | 12f Firm | | 3595 | VIS |

REVENGE 4 b g £860

50	8	HAYD	14f Soft		1824	
0	14	BATH	13f Gd/Fm	65	3819	BL
56	2	CATT	16f Soft	55	4258	bl
19	8	NEWC	16f Heavy	57	4424	bl

REVERIE 2 b c £0

47	11	SAND	7f Gd/Fm		2494
55	10	WIND	6f Gd/Fm		3047
58	10	NEWB	6f Stt/Hvy		4471

REVIEWER 2 b c £1098

69	6	HAYD	7f Good		3287	
49	9	CHEP	8f Gd/Fm		3680	BL
77	4	BATH	10f Soft		4140	
50	5	PONT	10f Soft		4230	bl
75	2	YARM	8f Soft	70	4393	bl

REVIVAL 3 b f £6105

77	1	SALI	10f Good		1343*
82	3	WARW	11f Gd/Sft		1709
74	7	GOOD	12f Good	83	3657
72	4	AYR	10f Soft	83	3989

REVOLVER 2 b g £0

47	11	LEIC	6f Gd/Fm		3215
61	7	WARW	15f Gd/Fm		3912
46	8	LING	6f Good		4097

REX IS OKAY 4 ch c £2756

52a	10	SOUT	8f Aw	70	251	
58a	6	SOUT	7f Aw	70	282	
63a	6	SOUT	8f Aw	67	388	bl
58a	6	WOLV	5f Aw	64	518	bl
60a	4	WOLV	7f Aw	64	583	bl
52	9	DONC	8f Good	70	715	bl
52	9	RIPO	6f Soft	69	824	bl
71	2	DONC	6f Gd/Sft	67	1074	bl
66	6	BEVE	8f Firm	70	1279	bl
52	10	THIR	6f Good	70	1383	bl
0	11	YARM	7f Gd/Sft	69	1611	bl
42	7	BEVE	7f Sft/Hvy	67	4044	
53	5	NEWC	6f Heavy	65	4405	
68	2	REDC	7f Gd/Sft	65	4498	

RHAGAAS 4 b c £60976

| 113 | 4 | NAD | 12f Good | | 767 | vis |
| 88 | 9 | NEWM | 12f Gd/Fm | | 1152 | vis |

RHENIUM 3 ch c £65321

114	1	LONG	11f Heavy		1026*
113	3	LONG	11f V		1317
113	3	LONG	10f Gd/Sft		2225
113	3	LONG	10f Gd/Sft		4053

RHIANN 4 b f £0

| 0 | 14 | LING | 7f Firm | | 3834 |
| 36 | 10 | BATH | 10f Soft | | 4141 |

RHODAMINE 3 b c £9938

52a	7	WOLV	9f Aw	70	625
52	9	DONC	10f Gd/Fm	69	701
62	8	RIPO	10f Soft	67	827
57	4	THIR	12f Soft		924
63	2	PONT	10f Gd/Sft	61	1104
62	6	BEVE	10f Good	64	1448
70	1	REDC	11f Gd/Sft	64	1560*
66	4	PONT	10f Good	68	1866
66	3	PONT	10f Firm	68	2175
53	4	MUSS	9f Gd/Sft	67	2534
39	11	CHES	10f Good	67	2666
65	4	HAYD	11f Gd/Sft	66	3267
61	4	RIPO	10f Good	65	3702
34	15	AYR	11f Soft	63	3963

RHYTHM BAND 4 gr c £731707

116	1	NAD	9f Good		768*
104	6	ASCO	10f Good		2089
102	7	WIND	10f Good		3641

RHYTHMICALL 3 b c £3750

80	9	NEWM	8f Firm		1188
84	1	BATH	10f Gd/Sft		1668*
80	6	PONT	10f Firm		2178

RIBBLE ASSEMBLY 5 ch g £0

| 0 | 13 | RIPO | 8f Gd/Fm | | 3711 |

RIBBLE PRINCESS 5 b m £356

13a	9	SOUT	12f Aw		344	
39a	7	WOLV	9f Aw	57	469	VIS
10a	7	WOLV	9f Aw	52	529	vis
27a	9	WOLV	7f Aw	44	635	vis
39	3	MUSS	9f Gd/Sft	38	795	
37	5	SOUT	10f Gd/Sft	40	859	
14	14	HAMI	12f Firm	38	1241	
0	15	MUSS	9f Firm	36	1689	
0	17	RIPO	8f Good		1858	BL

RIBBON LAKE 3 b f £0

0	18	WIND	6f Firm	72	1289
53	9	LING	7f Good	69	1672
0	12	SALI	8f Firm	65	2025
51	5	NEWB	10f Firm	60	2811
0	21	GOOD	8f Good	55	3885
12	11	BATH	8f Soft	55	4435

RIBBON OF LIGHT 2 b f £0

| 56 | 12 | DONC | 7f Gd/Sft | | 4446 |

RIBERAC 4 b f £43221

| 55 | 17 | DONC | 5f Gd/Fm | 80 | 702 |

(continued)

0	17	RIPO	6f Soft	77	824	
74	2	HAMI	5f Firm	73	2395	
59	12	SAND	5f Gd/Fm	73	2473	
40	10	EPSO	6f Gd/Sft	73	2631	
64	7	AYR	6f Firm	73	2877	
82	1	SAND	8f Good	71	3227*	
81	1	AYR	8f Good	71	3365*	
58	7	SALI	8f Good	73	3422	
91	1	EPSO	9f Good	79	3685*	
93	1	EPSO	10f Good		3857*	
77	10	GOOD	9f Good	84	3883	
97	1	ASCO	8f Good	89	4113*	
0	27	NEWM	8f Soft	95	4545	

RICCARTON 7 b h £0

| 51 | 4 | NOTT | 10f Gd/Sft | 50 | 1370 |

RICH GIFT 2 b c £3347

| 57 | 5 | NEWC | 7f Gd/Sft | | 3705 |
| 74 | 1 | PONT | 6f Soft | | 4083* |

RICH IN LOVE 6 b m £8148

0	14	THIR	7f Good	84	1158
77	11	LING	7f Gd/Sft		1283
82	2	LING	8f Gd/Fm	80	2185
80	3	YARM	7f Firm	80	2391
86	1	YARM	8f Gd/Fm	80	2412*
70	8	YARM	7f Firm	85	2768
0	19	ASCO	7f Gd/Fm	85	2999
83	5	ASCO	8f Good	85	3018
69	12	YORK	8f Firm	91	3597
69	10	SALI	7f Firm	84	3750
70	14	NEWM	7f Good	83	4195

RICH VEIN 3 b c £21615

66	4	MUSS	8f Gd/Sft	65	800	
71	2	SALI	8f Good	64	1345	
71a	1	LING	10f Aw	67	1544*	
79a	1	LING	10f Aw	70	2186*	VIS
77	2	SAND	10f Gd/Fm	70	2499	vis
83	1	SAND	10f Gd/Fm	74	2937*	vis
79	4	GOOD	10f Gd/Fm	80	3131	vis
83	7	YORK	10f Good	85	3541	vis
78	8	DONC	12f Firm	84	3896	vis
87	4	ASCO	12f Gd/Sft	88	4128	vis
74	10	NEWM	12f Good	86	4342	vis

RICHENDA 2 b f £0

64	13	NEWB	6f Gd/Fm		1943
61	7	NEWM	6f Gd/Fm		2618
85	6	GOOD	8f Good		3090
71	6	NEWB	6f Firm		3449
74	8	BATH	8f Gd/Fm	80	3817
72	7	YARM	7f Firm	80	3922
44	9	YARM	8f Soft	75	4393

RICKISON 3 b c £1600

| 90 | 2 | CORK | 10f Good | | 1898 |

RIDDLESDOWN 3 ch c £54039

98	2	BATH	10f Good		1089
94	2	SALI	12f Good		1347
102	1	HAYD	12f Gd/Sft	96	1832*
70	13	ASCO	16f Good		2068
97	9	GOOD	14f Gd/Fm	102	3058
107	1	YORK	14f Firm	98	3599*
112	1	HAYD	14f Soft		4091*
113	2	LONG	15f Good		4239
114	5	LONG	16f Heavy		4494

RIDE THE TIGER 3 ch c £3169

53a	1	WOLV	8f Aw		1234*
53a	3	LING	10f Aw	58	1544
51	6	SALI	8f Firm	58	2025
58a	2	WOLV	9f Aw		2602

RIDGE AND FURROW 2 ch g £271

| 0 | 22 | DONC | 8f Gd/Sft | | 4446 |
| 63 | 4 | MUSS | 8f Soft | | 4564 |

RIDGE RUNNER 2 b c £5055

| 86 | 2 | DONC | 6f Gd/Fm | | 2608 |

86 1 **RIPO** 6f Gd/Fm 3009*
78 5 RIPO 6f Gd/Fm 85 3712
82 9 NEWM 6f Good 85 4338

RIDGECREST 3 ch c £1447
34a 8 LING 6f Aw 59 4
58a 4 LING 7f Aw 53
60a 2 LING 8f Aw 150
50a 4 WOLV 7f Aw 192
56a 2 LING 8f Aw 236
40a 5 LING 10f Aw 57 315
26a 4 WOLV 7f Aw 567
49a 5 WOLV 8f Aw 636
0 12 LING 8f Firm 55 3580
45 5 BATH 8f Gd/Fm 51 3816 t
49 3 BATH 8f Soft 49 4143 t
35a 7 WOLV 8f Aw 51 4437 t

RIDGEWAY DAWN 2 ch f £9231
73 1 **SALI** 7f Gd/Fm 3418*
92 1 **KEMP** 7f Gd/Fm 3789*

RIDGEWAY LAD 2 ch g £432
82 3 HAYD 5f Gd/Sft 1488

RIDGEWOOD BAY 3 b g £1844
0 7 WARW 11f Soft 814
0 15 WIND 8f Gd/Sft 1099
29 8 NEWB 10f Gd/Sft 1593
0 18 NOTT 14f Good 41 2008
35a 1 **LING** 13f Aw 2323*
14a 7 LING 12f Aw 40 2593

RIDGEWOOD BELLE 2 b f £0
0 18 WIND 6f Gd/Sft 4289

RIFIFI 7 ch h £324
73a 7 WOLV 6f Aw 78 320
71a 8 LING 7f Aw 75 423
56a 8 LING 8f Aw 72 462
70a 3 LING 7f Aw 69 543
0 19 DONC 6f Good 73 716
0 19 HAYD 6f Gd/Fm 70 2444
0 16 CHES 6f Gd/Fm 63 2673 VIS
11 11 CHEP 6f Gd/Fm 60 3257 tvi
0 15 LING 7f Good 55 4102 t

RIGADOON 4 b g £1423
55 4 MUSS 16f Gd/Sft 59 797 bl
58 5 BEVE 16f Firm 59 1276 bl
0 12 RIPO 16f Good 56 1597 bl
51 4 CATT 16f Gd/Fm 55 2436 bl
49 6 THIR 16f Gd/Fm 53 3348 bl
53 2 MUSS 16f Gd/Fm 51 3742 bl

RIGHT WING 6 b g £88256
110 3 DONC 8f Good 104 733 vis
112 1 **KEMP** 10f Soft 1014* vis
115 2 GOOD 10f Soft 1482 vis
113 2 CURR 10f Soft 1899 BL
115 1 **YORK** 9f Gd/Fm 3726+ vis
100 3 GOOD 10f Good 3903 vis
114 2 GOOD 10f Soft 4064 vis
114 1 **BORD** 10f Soft 4490* bl

RIGHTY HO 6 b g £4764
42 7 NOTT 10f Gd/Fm 53 1272
46 8 PONT 12f Good 53 1499
38 12 HAMI 13f Gd/Fm 48 1936
44 2 CARL 12f Firm 2826
46 2 REDC 14f Firm 3311
43 1 **CARL** 12f Firm 3570*
37 2 NOTT 16f Soft 38 3978
38 5 REDC 14f Gd/Sft 41 4222
0 U YORK 10f Soft 4275

RIMATARA 4 ch c £0
0 15 DONC 10f Gd/Sft 1072
0 10 THIR 12f Good 1157
33 9 PONT 8f Gd/Fm 50 2831
0 17 HAYD 8f Good 48 3288
0 15 NEWC 10f Heavy 41 4404

RIMFAXI 2 ch g £0
40 7 NEWC 6f Good 3032

RING DANCER 5 b g £4252
66 19 NEWM 6f Gd/Fm 82 1173
59 10 GOOD 6f Gd/Sft 79 1471
0 19 WIND 6f Gd/Fm 76 2054
75 1 **BATH** 6f Firm 72 2944*
68 7 CHEP 6f Gd/Fm 75 3257
74a 3 WOLV 6f Aw 75 4380

RING MY MATE 3 ch c £325
56a 3 SOUT 8f Aw 48
59a 4 LING 7f Aw 164
0 15 SALI 8f Gd/Fm 62 2264
40 7 LING 7f Good 57 2592
35 10 BRIG 7f Gd/Fm 53 3242
0a 13 WOLV 8f Aw 60 3769
44a 6 SOUT 8f Aw 4364

RING OF LOVE 4 b f £3197
0a 12 SOUT 5f Aw 71
60a 4 WOLV 6f Aw 134
53a 5 WOLV 6f Aw 58 175
61a 1 **LING** 5f Aw 56 372*
61a 3 WOLV 6f Aw 60 445
55a 6 WOLV 6f Aw 60 491
58a 5 WOLV 5f Aw 60 518
60a 3 LING 5f Aw 60 573
0 14 BEVE 5f Firm 69 1923
57a 3 WOLV 5f Aw 59 2078
0 13 NEWC 5f Firm 66 2340
54 9 CATT 5f Gd/Fm 66 2418
49 9 HAYD 5f Gd/Fm 63 2505 vis
46a 7 SOUT 5f Aw 58 2632

RING THE CHIEF 8 b g £0
36a 9 WOLV 6f Aw 3275

RINGSIDE JACK 4 b c £8662
71 1 **BEVE** 10f Heavy 64 975*
43 13 NEWM 10f Gd/Fm 71 1150
60 6 RIPO 10f Good 70 1860
55 9 MUSS 12f Firm 68 2048
65 4 BEVE 10f Gd/Fm 65 2518
58 12 YORK 12f Good 65 3541 vis
44 8 YORK 12f Gd/Fm 65 3725 vis
71 1 **CHES** 10f Soft 63 4074* vis
34 10 AYR 10f Heavy 70 4306 vis
66 5 YARM 10f Soft 70 4392 vis

RINGWOOD 2 b c £250
77 6 DONC 6f Gd/Fm 2608
74 4 LING 6f Firm 3832
76 4 GOOD 8f Soft 4062

RINKA BLUE 2 b f £0
0 17 NOTT 5f Gd/Sft 4503

RIOJA 5 ch g £0
59 7 REDC 5f Gd/Fm 65 1580
26a 14 SOUT 6f Aw 63 2820
0 14 THIR 6f Aw 63 3123
48 10 HAMI 5f Gd/Sft 59 3825
31 11 AYR 5f Gd/Fm 55 4327

RIOS DIAMOND 3 b f £4015
24a 8 LING 6f Aw 24 VIS
33a 7 WOLV 6f Aw 62
43a 2 SOUT 7f Aw 41 1202
13a 9 SOUT 6f Aw 14 1804
41 5 WIND 6f Gd/Fm 50 1877
42 1 **WARW** 7f Gd/Fm 39 2036*
52 3 MUSS 8f Gd/Fm 51 2205
46 4 CATT 7f Gd/Fm 47 2438
38 9 LING 6f Firm 51 3493
38 8 BRIG 8f Aw 51 3561
46 3 YARM 7f Firm 48 3939
0 12 NEWC 7f Heavy 47 4426
0 22 NEWM 8f Gd/Sft 47 4536

RIPARIAN 3 b c £6185

75 3 NOTT 8f Soft 1643
72 1 **NEWC** 8f Good 2520*
71 4 REDC 10f Gd/Fm 73 2992
0 14 CATT 12f Soft 71 4003

RIPCORD 2 b c £0
54 15 NEWM 8f Good 4161
52 14 DONC 7f Gd/Sft 4446
69 8 DONC 6f Heavy 4575

RIPPLE 3 ch f £0
23 10 NEWC 10f Gd/Sft 1480
0 12 PONT 8f Good 1865

RIPSNORTER 11 ch g £0
0a 11 SOUT 8f Aw 2816
0 19 WIND 10f Gd/Fm 3045
0 18 SALI 10f Gd/Sft 33 4169

RISING PASSION 2 ch g £0
43 9 THIR 5f Gd/Fm 2057
0 15 CARL 5f Firm 2277
48 12 THIR 5f Gd/Fm 3346

RISING SPRAY 9 ch g £0
41 10 BATH 10f Gd/Fm 67 2552
58 7 KEMP 12f Gd/Fm 65 3073
54 7 SALI 14f Gd/Fm 59 3424
0 13 FOLK 12f Gd/Fm 59 3586
51 6 KEMP 14f Gd/Fm 55 3800
0 14 SALI 14f Gd/Sft 53 4166
0 18 WIND 10f Gd/Sft 53 4291

RISK FREE 3 ch c £7166
73a 2 LING 7f Aw 108
85a 4 LING 7f Aw 630
88a 2 WOLV 7f Aw 82 721
90a 1 **WOLV** 8f Aw 85 921*
82 4 NOTT 8f Gd/Sft 1366
65 10 NEWM 8f Aw 85 1853
56 9 LING 7f Firm 83 2325 BL

RISKY DREAM 3 ch f £0
0 14 CHEP 10f Gd/Fm 1796
0 20 CHEP 7f Good 1972

RISKY GEM 3 ch c £992
66a 2 SOUT 6f Aw 426
56a 4 WOLV 6f Aw 66 479
0 19 WARW 7f Heavy 59 887
0 15 NOTT 6f Gd/Sft 1081

RISKY LOVER 7 b m £0
1a 11 WOLV 9f Aw 33 404
0a 9 WOLV 16f Aw 25 494

RISKY REEF 3 ch g £218
61a 4 WOLV 6f Aw 549
63a 5 WOLV 7f Aw 623
62 5 BATH 6f Gd/Fm 3820
0 19 KEMP 6f Gd/Sft 70 4037
64 4 LING 6f Soft 65 4270
54 10 NEWB 5f Gd/Sft 65 4459

RISQUE SERMON 2 b g £4598
64 8 WIND 5f Soft 2545
79 1 **LING** 5f Firm 2760*
54 7 GOOD 6f Gd/Fm 80 3062
77 4 SAND 5f Good 78 3431
76 3 LING 6f Good 76 4098 t
0 22 NEWM 6f Good 4345 t

RITA MACKINTOSH 3 b f £263
16a 10 SOUT 8f Aw 48
45a 3 SOUT 8f Aw 514
12a 13 SOUT 8f Aw 48 555
28a 5 WOLV 9f Aw 1141 vis

RITAS ROCK APE 5 b m £10595
64 8 BATH 5f Gd/Fm 1441
0 12 NOTT 5f Good 76 1871
68 6 SALI 5f Firm 76 2022
56 10 SALI 5f Gd/Fm 73 2266
61 11 HAYD 5f Gd/Fm 70 2701
70 1 **CHEP** 5f Gd/Fm 68 2976*

RIVER (continued)

60	9	BATH	5f Firm	71	3209	
63	8	ASCO	5f Gd/Fm	71	3341	
71	2	BRIG	5f Firm	70	3528	
77	1	**BRIG**	5f Firm	70	3734*	
80	2	EPSO	5f Good	78	3855	

RIVER ALN 2 b f £2268

0a	8	WOLV	6f Aw		2079	
38	5	YARM	6f Firm		2388	BL
72	1	**BEVE**	7f Gd/Fm		2513*	bl

RIVER BANN 3 ch c £10251

88	2	DONC	10f Good		713
82	2	THIR	12f Soft		906
90	1	**WIND**	12f Gd/Fm	85	1199*
90	4	GOOD	12f Gd/Sft	89	1637

RIVER BLEST 4 b g £1130

51	5	BEVE	7f Gd/Sft	57	1760
0	13	HAMI	6f Gd/Fm	57	1941
25a	8	SOUT	6f Aw	53	2297
54	2	CATT	5f Gd/Fm	53	2932
0	15	CATT	5f Gd/Fm	53	3200
53	3	THIR	5f Gd/Sft	52	3781

RIVER CAPTAIN 7 ch g £0

0a	16	SOUT	11f Aw	57	131	
12a	11	SOUT	11f Aw	55	390	t
20a	6	SOUT	11f Aw	50	474	t
0a	11	SOUT	11f Aw	45	561	tBL
0a	13	SOUT	11f Aw	38	1306	

RIVER ENSIGN 7 br m £13460

45a	4	WOLV	8f Aw	53	78	
35a	10	SOUT	8f Aw	50	85	
43a	6	WOLV	8f Aw	48	227	
51a	2	WOLV	9f Aw	48	270	
51a	1	**WOLV**	9f Aw		292*	
48a	3	WOLV	9f Aw		360	
25a	7	WOLV	9f Aw	50	381	
23a	10	WOLV	6f Aw	49	466	
36a	4	WOLV	9f Aw		517	
51a	1	**WOLV**	9f Aw	47	529*	
43a	6	WOLV	9f Aw	51	611	
32a	8	WOLV	9f Aw	50	637	
51	1	**SOUT**	10f Gd/Sft	46	859*	
30	8	THIR	8f Soft	52	931	
52	3	FOLK	10f Soft	52	965	
43	6	NOTT	10f Gd/Sft	53	1086	
10a	11	WOLV	8f Aw	50	1393	
55	1	**SOUT**	10f Soft	52	1608*	
59	3	CHES	10f Gd/Sft	58	1777	

RIVER FRONTIER 5 b m £0

30	8	WARW	16f Gd/Fm	36	2037

RIVER OF FIRE 2 ch g £3856

49a	8	SOUT	5f Aw		1418	
61	1	**YARM**	7f Firm		2898*	
67	1	**LEIC**	6f Gd/Fm	60	3216*	VIS
46	5	FOLK	10f Gd/Fm	66	3444	vis
53	8	LING	7f Soft	63	4191	

RIVER RAVEN 2 b c £14741

89	2	REDC	6f Good		1893
84	1	**HAMI**	5f Gd/Fm		2639*
89	4	THIR	7f Gd/Fm		2966
97a	1	**WOLV**	7f Aw	88	3273*
93	2	CHES	6f Good		3507
93	4	REDC	6f Gd/Sft		4219

RIVER SOUNDS 3 b c £2250

101	3	LEOP	8f Soft		947

RIVER TERN 7 b g £1245

66	6	THIR	5f Gd/Sft	70	1357
58	9	CATT	5f Good	69	1662
66	6	MUSS	5f Firm	69	1687
62	10	YORK	5f Aw	67	1980
58	7	SALI	5f Firm	67	2022
51	11	SALI	5f Gd/Fm	66	2266
63	3	BEVE	5f Gd/Fm	64	2517
57	6	YORK	5f Gd/Fm	64	2644
36	11	PONT	5f Gd/Fm	63	2830
30	11	BATH	6f Firm	62	2944
42	11	LING	6f Firm	58	3493
46	12	THIR	5f Gd/Fm	58	3619
0	14	SALI	5f Firm	55	3747
46	9	CHEP	5f Good	54	3872
51	3	YARM	6f Gd/Fm	50	3966
49	5	LEIC	5f Gd/Sft	50	4027

RIVER TIMES 4 b c £11720

99a	2	WOLV	8f Aw	93	663	bl
79	13	DONC	8f Good	93	733	bl
92	4	YORK	8f Firm	91	1327	
88	8	ASCO	8f Good	91	2090	
85	8	HAYD	7f Gd/Fm	91	2456	
50	21	GOOD	8f Good	90	3107	bl

RIVERBLUE 4 b c £2755

57a	8	SOUT	7f Aw	81	33
53a	9	WOLV	9f Aw	77	271
48a	9	WOLV	9f Aw	70	349
53a	5	WOLV	9f Aw	63	469
66a	1	**WOLV**	9f Aw	60	568*
63a	5	WOLV	9f Aw	66	611
65a	3	SOUT	12f Aw	65	641
75	4	WARW	12f Soft	80	815
0	16	HAYD	8f Soft	78	4094

RIVERDANCE 4 ch c £0

13a	12	WOLV	7f Aw		65	vis
34a	8	WOLV	5f Aw	48	139	BL
33a	6	WOLV	7f Aw	43	193	bl
34a	5	WOLV	7f Aw		276	vis

RIVERS CURTAIN 3 £0

107	6	LONG	11f V		1317
78	5	CAPA	12f Gd/Fm		1618

RIVERSDALE 4 b c £0

11a	11	WOLV	8f Aw	53	38
30	8	PONT	10f Soft	53	4374
36	6	MUSS	9f Soft	53	4520

RIVERTOWN 6 b g £1734

89	4	EPSO	10f Gd/Sft		2630
103	3	SAND	9f Good		3230
93	5	BATH	8f Gd/Fm		3515
86	6	KEMP	12f Gd/Fm	90	3798
62	12	ASCO	16f Good	87	4115
72	6	YARM	19f Soft		4515

RIVIERA 6 ch h £253165

119	1	**WOOD**	8f Firm		3933*

RIYAFA 3 b f £34595

87	2	SALI	10f Good		1344
89	1	**HAYD**	12f Soft		1493*
83	5	PONT	10f Firm		2178
89	3	YORK	12f Good	87	3541
93	2	KEMP	12f Gd/Fm	90	3798
104	1	**ASCO**	12f Gd/Fm		4130*
103	5	NEWM	12f Good		4343

RIZERIE 2 gr f £10077

76	1	**GOOD**	7f Good		2306*
83	2	YORK	7f Good		2693
90	7	SAND	7f Gd/Fm		2935
99	3	NEWM	7f Gd/Fm		3316
78	9	NEWM	7f Firm		4210

ROB LEACH 3 b g £956

77	5	KEMP	8f Gd/Sft		1080
77	2	LING	10f Gd/Sft		1281
62	6	GOOD	8f Gd/Sft		1449
77	5	GOOD	10f Gd/Sft	75	1812
72	5	SAND	11f Good	75	1967

ROBANNA 5 b m £0

21a	9	LING	16f Aw	46	6

ROBBER RED 4 b c £0

0a	13	LING	10f Aw		268
29a	8	LING	8f Aw	48	336
14a	10	SOUT	8f Aw	43	418
41	10	BRIG	7f Gd/Fm	53	1930
0	14	BRIG	8f Firm	50	3527

ROBBIES DREAM 4 ch c £6442

39a	5	SOUT	6f Aw	50	698	
35	7	BRIG	7f Gd/Sft	47	896	
0	16	BRIG	7f Firm	44	1335	VIS
47a	1	**SOUT**	8f Aw	38	2380*	t
49a	2	SOUT	8f Aw	44	2634	t
55a	1	**WOLV**	8f Aw	48	3499*	t
56a	2	WOLV	8f Aw	53	4363	t
43a	3	WOLV	8f Aw	53	4437	t

ROBBO 6 b g £0

48	6	CATT	16f Soft	57	4258	bl
50	4	NEWC	16f Heavy	53	4424	bl

ROBELLANDO 3 b g £0

0	12	BATH	12f Soft		4434

ROBELLION 9 b g £2735

51	5	WARW	8f Heavy	54	1520
56	1	**LING**	7f Good	54	1672*
51	3	CARL	7f Firm	59	2282
0	23	ASCO	8f Gd/Fm	59	2999
32	7	CHEP	8f Gd/Fm	59	3251
38	11	LING	6f Firm	57	3578

ROBELLITA 6 b g £788

67a	2	WOLV	12f Aw	62	81
62a	6	LING	12f Aw	67	151
45a	7	SOUT	11f Aw	67	343
38a	9	SOUT	16f Gd/Fm	65	428
0	11	WARW	15f Good	60	2461

ROBERT THE BRUCE 5 ch g £0

65	6	HAMI	11f Good		848

ROBIN HOOD 3 b c £4559

51	7	MUSS	9f Gd/Sft		902
36	10	HAMI	11f Gd/Fm		1193
48	4	HAYD	6f Soft	50	1494
41	4	RIPO	6f Good	50	1600
46	4	CARL	6f Gd/Sft		1723
43	7	AYR	7f Gd/Fm	49	2719
43	6	HAMI	10f Gd/Fm	49	2779
52	1	**HAMI**	5f Gd/Sft	46	3536*
0	15	THIR	5f Gd/Fm	52	3619
52	2	HAMI	5f Gd/Sft	51	3825
42	16	NEWM	5f Good	55	4185
40	10	AYR	5f Heavy	52	4307
52	3	NEWC	5f Heavy	52	4407
43	4	MUSS	5f Soft	51	4516

ROBIN SHARP 2 ch c £0

72a	5	WOLV	6f Aw		4379
76	5	NEWM	6f Gd/Sft		4530

ROBO MAGIC 8 b g £0

61a	6	LING	7f Aw	73	29
56a	10	LING	6f Aw	71	113
0a	15	LING	7f Aw	69	162

ROBOASTAR 3 b c £0

76	5	SAND	10f Soft		4205
0	18	DONC	10f Gd/Sft	75	4448

ROBZELDA 4 b g £4897

75	3	DONC	8f Good	75	715	bl
77	2	MUSS	7f Gd/Sft		900	bl
74	5	THIR	8f Good	75	1160	bl
63	6	KEMP	10f Soft	75	1528	bl
74	4	REDC	10f Gd/Sft	75	1561	
73	4	HAYD	11f Gd/Sft	74	1790	
12	10	RIPO	10f Good	74	1860	bl
51	11	YORK	8f Gd/Fm	73	2645	bl
51	11	NEWC	7f Gd/Fm	70	2986	

ROCCIOSO 3 br c £0

33	12	NEWM	8f Gd/Fm		1692
16	8	BATH	12f Gd/Fm		3517

ROCHAMPBEAU 2 ch f £0

0	11	SALI	6f Gd/Fm		1882

ROCK AND SKIP 2 b c £0						
38	9	WIND	5f Good		2368	
0	16	LING	6f Good		2588	
0	13	LEIC	6f Gd/Fm		3215	
ROCK CONCERT 2 b f £0						
0	17	NEWM	7f Soft		4541	
ROCK FALCON 7 ch g £0						
41a	13	WOLV	8f Aw	93	663	bl
0a	14	SOUT	7f Aw	93	687	bl
0	21	DONC	8f Good	93	733	bl
0	19	RIPO	6f Soft	92	824	bl
0	R	MUSS	7f Firm		1685	
ROCK ISLAND LINE 6 b g £1633						
67a	2	SOUT	6f Aw		738	
24	12	THIR	7f Soft	56	908	
68a	2	WOLV	7f Good	64	1235	
58a	6	SOUT	8f Aw	67	1504	
59a	5	SOUT	8f Aw	67	2121	
54a	5	SOUT	8f Aw	66	2820	
ROCK ON ROBIN 3 br c £700						
19a	8	SOUT			36	vis
0	9	DONC	15f Gd/Sft	52	1071	vis
51	2	BEVE	10f Firm		1274	vis
27	6	NOTT	10f Soft	51	1644	vis
19	8	BEVE	12f Firm	51	1919	vis
22	6	WARW	11f Gd/Fm		2253	
0	13	BRIG	12f Soft	43	4176	
0	16	BRIG	12f Soft	36	4419	
ROCK SCENE 8 b g £3260						
40	2	WARW	11f Heavy	39	889	
29	8	DONC	10f Gd/Sft	44	1050	
40	6	WARW	11f Soft	44	1065	
40	5	LEIC	10f Soft	41	1546	
38	5	WARW	11f Gd/Fm	41	1707	
41	4	CHES	10f Gd/Fm		2245	
49	1	**RIPO**	10f Soft		2538*	
27	9	HAMI	9f Gd/Sft		3375	
0	11	HAYD	11f Gd/Sft	48	3480	
36	6	REDC	11f Soft		4497	
ROCKERLONG 2 b f £5715						
90	2	YARM	6f Firm		3938	
94	2	ASCO	7f Good		4114	
88	13	NEWM	7f Good		4356	
ROCKETTE 5 ch m £0						
0	19	BRIG	10f Firm	35	3737	
ROCKLANDS LANE 4 b c £0						
0	13	FOLK	6f Soft	44	958	
0	20	WARW	5f Heavy	44	1005	
0	19	WIND	6f Gd/Fm	45	1196	
ROCKY ISLAND 3 b g £0						
24	10	REDC	14f Gd/Fm	44	1581	
RODOSLOVNAYA 2 b f £0						
0	16	LING	7f Soft		4268	
ROFFEY SPINNEY 6 ch g £1198						
39	7	SOUT	7f Soft		1603	
0a	14	SOUT	6f Aw		2118	
48	2	NEWM	10f Gd/Fm	46	2958	
ROGER ROSS 5 b g £1850						
35a	6	LING	10f Aw		3	
18a	8	LING	8f Aw	49	97	bl
55a	1	**LING**	10f Aw	49	102*	
28a	7	LING	10f Aw	55	160	
0a	14	LING	10f Aw	55	209	
42a	5	LING	10f Aw	53	842	
31	9	GOOD	8f Gd/Sft	49	1473	
0	13	YARM	10f Gd/Fm	49	1615	
26	16	NEWM	10f Gd/Fm	45	1690	bl
43	7	LING	10f Firm		3281	
ROGHAN JOSH 2 b g £0						
29	10	THIR	5f Gd/Fm		3143	
0	18	BEVE	5f Good		3955	
ROGUE SPIRIT 4 b c £3449						
63	8	WIND	6f Gd/Fm	73	746	
43	14	RIPO	6f Soft	73	824	BL
45	7	EPSO	9f Heavy		1033	
67	4	WIND	8f Gd/Fm	67	1201	
48	10	BATH	8f Gd/Fm	68	1442	
62	7	GOOD	9f Gd/Sft	68	1807	
68	2	YARM	10f Gd/Fm	67	2199	
40	11	BATH	10f Gd/Sft	68	2552	
43	9	NOTT	10f Gd/Fm	68	3007	
47	9	LING	11f Firm	67	3282	
0	21	YORK	9f Good		3808	
66a	1	**LING**	12f Aw	60	4334*	
ROI DE DANSE 5 ch £6173						
19a	12	SOUT	7f Aw	52	35	
29a	6	LING	10f Aw	44	102	
50a	3	LING	10f Aw		163	
45a	1	**LING**	10f Aw	40	203*	
46a	2	WOLV	8f Aw	44	227	
31a	12	LING	12f Aw	46	290	
47a	3	WOLV	8f Aw	46	381	
38a	4	LING	10f Aw	46	400	
49a	2	WOLV	9f Aw	46	447	
48a	2	WOLV	8f Aw	46	516	
42a	5	WOLV	10f Aw	46	568	
32a	9	LING	10f Aw	56	632	
46a	2	LING	8f Aw	46	776	
36a	5	LING	7f Aw	47	879	
27	11	BEVE	7f Gd/Sft	42	1760	
0	12	SALI	7f Gd/Fm		1884	
0a	12	WOLV	8f Aw	46	4440	
ROISIN SPLENDOUR 5 ch m £0						
56a	12	LING	7f Aw	71	28	
37a	9	LING	8f Aw	69	97	
0a	14	LING	10f Aw	66	337	
ROISTERER 4 ch g £0						
0	11	KEMP	7f Soft		1012	
12	8	CARL	6f Gd/Fm		3080	
0a	12	WOLV	10f Aw		3275	
43	7	CATT	5f Good		3441	
26	11	THIR	5f Soft	35	3781	
ROLE MODEL 4 b f £0						
17a	5	WOLV	16f Aw	36	492	
5a	9	SOUT	16f Aw	33	1416	
ROLI ABI 5 b g £3599						
106	3	SAIN	15f Heavy		140	
ROLLER 4 b c £10844						
60a	3	WOLV	7f Aw	61	711	
68	2	THIR	8f Soft	61	907	
77	1	**NEWC**	8f Heavy	65	1007*	
73	2	SAND	8f Heavy	69	1058	
78	2	ASCO	8f Gd/Fm	70	1113	
68	10	REDC	10f Gd/Sft	77	1561	
74	4	HAYD	8f Firm	77	1836	
67	10	DONC	8f Gd/Fm	76	2349	
74	3	HAYD	8f Soft	74	4094	
67	6	MUSS	8f Gd/Sft		4135	
61	11	REDC	8f Gd/Fm	74	4217	
70	6	YORK	8f Heavy	72	4300	
71	3	NEWC	10f Heavy	71	4427	
59	9	NOTT	8f Heavy	74	4506	
ROLLESTON ROCKET 3 ch f £0						
0a	13	SOUT	6f Aw		74	
ROLLING HIGH 5 ch g £0						
0a	10	SOUT	11f Aw		248	t
0a	13	WOLV	9f Aw	30	569	t
ROLLING STONE 6 b h £0						
78	11	NEWM	10f Gd/Fm	90	1170	
ROLLY POLLY 2 b f £41307						
104	1	**MAIS**	6f V		3066*	
96	4	DEAU	6f Gd/Sft		3550	
ROMA 5 ch m £0						
0a	11	SOUT	12f Aw	45	70	
10	8	MUSS	12f Gd/Fm	45	1147	
0	13	MUSS	12f Gd/Fm	43	1432	
0	13	HAMI	12f Gd/Fm	41	1908	BL
16	6	MUSS	12f Gd/Fm	35	2202	bl
ROMAN CANDLE 4 b c £0						
49a	8	WOLV	12f Aw	70	407	
60a	5	LING	12f Aw	68	621	
ROMAN EMPEROR 3 ch £0						
0a	11	SOUT	5f Aw	49	870	
0	19	WARW	5f Heavy	49	1005	
31	8	CATT	12f Soft	45	4256	BL
0	17	NEWC	10f Heavy	43	4404	bl
ROMAN HIDEAWAY 2 b c £0						
64	11	YARM	7f Soft		4514	
58	11	DONC	6f Heavy		4576	
ROMAN KING 5 b g £4159						
80	6	HAMI	13f Gd/Fm	85	845	
73	10	KEMP	16f Soft	83	997	
70	3	NEWC	12f Good		2523	
77	4	RIPO	10f Gd/Fm	77	2836	
80	2	GOOD	9f Good	76	3110	
ROMAN REEL 9 ch g £0						
21a	10	LING	12f Aw	53	52	
14a	8	LING	12f Aw	50	332	
0a	11	WOLV	12f Aw	43	408	BL
12	8	BRIG	12f Good		1647	
0	16	NEWM	10f Gd/Fm	36	2958	t
0	11	BRIG	12f Gd/Fm	32	3260	tbl
ROMANECH 3 b c £0						
35a	8	WOLV	8f Aw		636	VIS
31a	5	SOUT	7f Aw		688	BL
ROMANTIC AFFAIR 3 ch g £70350						
60	8	DONC	8f Gd/Sft	71	1053	
77	2	BEVE	10f Good	71	1448	
83	1	**SAND**	11f Good	73	1967*	
94	1	**SALI**	12f Gd/Sft	82	2470*	
92	4	GOOD	12f Gd/Fm	91	3088	
99	2	YORK	14f Firm	91	3599	
107	1	**DONC**	15f Firm	98	3890*	
104	2	ASCO	12f Gd/Sft	102	4128	
112	1	**NEWM**	16f Gd/Sft	104	4533+	
ROMANTIC MYTH 2 b f £51011						
87	1	**RIPO**	5f Soft		821*	
97	1	**CHES**	5f Gd/Fm		1214*	
107	1	**ASCO**	5f Good		2088*	
97	6	NEWB	5f Firm		2849	
104	4	YORK	6f Firm		3596	
99	5	DONC	5f Firm		3900	
74	17	NEWM	5f Soft		4454	
ROMANTIC POET 2 b g £535						
80	3	WIND	5f Heavy		932	
75	5	WIND	5f Good		1727	
ROMANYLEI 3 gr f £29820						
103	2	HAYD	6f Gd/Fm		1833	
105	1	**ASCO**	6f Gd/Fm		1023301*	
ROMERO 4 b c £0						
0	W	SAND	16f Heavy	62	1044	
55	11	SALI	14f Firm	62	1180	
ROMNEY 3 ch g £0						
67	5	LEIC	12f Gd/Sft		1738	
44	8	PONT	10f Firm	58	2175	
RONNI PANCAKE 3 b f £2467						
48a	6	LING	7f Aw		53	
0	21	WIND	6f Gd/Fm	63	1196	
54	1	**LEIC**	8f Gd/Sft		1572*	
53	5	NOTT	10f Good		2012	
52	7	WIND	12f Gd/Fm	58	2210	
52	6	PONT	12f Good	58	2362	
40	9	WARW	13f Gd/Fm	56	2843	
34	10	LEIC	8f Gd/Fm	53	3095	
27	9	KEMP	9f Gd/Fm	50	3357	
0	17	BRIG	10f Soft	48	4174	

RONQUISTA DOR 6 b g £0
35a 6 WOLV 15f Aw 49 277 bl
6a 10 WOLV 12f Aw 49 464 bl
45a 4 LING 12f Aw 650
31 14 NEWM 12f Firm 48 1852
8 10 WARW 13f Gd/Fm 45 2843 bl
33a 6 SOUT 11f Aw 4151 bl

RONS PET 5 ch g £6204
74a 2 SOUT 7f Aw 72 33 t
68a 6 SOUT 8f Aw 72 49 tvi
59a 9 SOUT 7f Aw 72 216 t
75a 2 WOLV 7f Aw 70 323 tvi
73a 3 WOLV 7f Aw 70 364 tbl
75a 3 LING 7f Aw 398 tvi
76a 2 LING 8f Aw 72 485 tbl
76a 2 LING 7f Aw 72 525 tbl
74a 3 LING 10f Aw 75 575 tbl
72a 5 LING 7f Aw 75 594 tbl
61a 5 WOLV 7f Aw 677 tbl
59a 4 WOLV 6f Aw 719 t
46 8 THIR 7f Soft 62 908

RONS ROUND 6 ch g £0
30a 5 WOLV 9f Aw 292
37a 4 SOUT 12f Aw 344
0a 10 WOLV 12f Aw 51 408

ROO 3 b f £5594
79 7 NEWB 6f Soft 95 912
73 6 KEMP 6f Gd/Sft 1078
78 5 WIND 6f Good 1728
92 3 SALI 6f Gd/Fm 90 1887
92 2 RIPO 6f Gd/Fm 88 2101
94 2 HAYD 6f Gd/Fm 91 2504
85 5 NEWB 6f Firm 92 2813
87 11 GOOD 7f Gd/Fm 92 3130
57 11 HAYD 6f Heavy 3768

ROOFER 2 b f £3547
68 5 KEMP 6f Gd/Fm 1924
69 4 PONT 7f Aw 2174
84 2 SALI 7f Firm 3748
81 4 NEWM 7f Good 79 4157
78 5 CATT 7f Soft 79 4254
71 12 NEWM 8f Good 80 4350

ROOFTOP 4 b g £0
44a 6 SOUT 8f Aw 453
57a 5 SOUT 11f Aw 60 605
35a 9 SOUT 12f Aw 60 641
50 8 MUSS 8f Gd/Fm 64 899
29 8 NEWC 8f Heavy 59 1007 BL
37 9 RIPO 12f Gd/Fm 54 2109 vis
8 13 CARL 17f Gd/Fm 54 2244 vis
50 4 HAMI 9f Gd/Fm 2642 vis
33 6 HAMI 9f Gd/Fm 2780 vis
30 11 AYR 9f Gd/Fm 43 3141
0 12 RIPO 8f Gd/Fm 3711

ROOFTOP PROTEST 3 b g £5503
0 20 DONC 8f Gd/Sft 68 1053
42 3 HAMI 9f Gd/Fm 1195
59 1 HAMI 11f Gd/Fm 1909*
49 6 REDC 14f Gd/Fm 55 2156
46 2 HAMI 11f Firm 2393
33 3 CATT 16f Gd/Fm 3199 BL
45 2 HAMI 9f Gd/Sft 3375

ROOKIE 4 b g £0
15a 11 LING 10f Aw 47 220
29a 8 LING 8f Aw 265 BL
27a 4 LING 13f Aw 483

ROOM TO ROOM MAGIC 3 ch f £1441
45a 4 WOLV 9f Aw 395
49a 5 SOUT 8f Aw 453
47a 6 LING 10f Aw 523
0a 11 WOLV 12f Aw 52 1142
43 2 WARW 11f Gd/Fm 2253

42 5 PONT 12f Good 47 2362
40 2 WIND 12f Good 2715
0 12 CATT 12f Soft 45 4256
40 3 REDC 11f Soft 4497

RORKES DRIFT 2 ch f £526
76 3 CHEP 6f Good 1968
65 5 EPSO 7f Gd/Sft 2430

ROSAKER 3 b c £0
0 W WIND 10f Firm 1293

ROSALIA 2 b f £1832
64 4 BEVE 5f Gd/Fm 3408
64 6 THIR 6f Gd/Fm 3614
81 3 BEVE 7f Good 3953
72 6 REDC 7f Gd/Sft 4216
72 2 NEWC 6f Heavy 4402

ROSCIUS 3 b c £38275
109 1 GOOD 10f Gd/Fm 1451*
108 7 CHAN 12f V 1752
107 3 ASCO 12f Good 2148

ROSE ADAGIO 3 b f £0
79 5 NEWM 10f Gd/Fm 2617
46 8 GOOD 10f Good 3907

ROSE GYPSY 2 b f £2700
96 3 CURR 6f Good 3844

ROSE OF AMERICA 2 ch f £406
21 5 AYR 7f Heavy 4303
0 12 NEWC 7f Heavy 4403
69 3 MUSS 7f Soft 4517
47 6 MUSS 7f Soft 4559

ROSE OF HYMUS 3 ch f £0
0 14 NEWM 7f Gd/Sft 971
0 15 WIND 6f Gd/Sft 1423
0 17 CHEP 8f Gd/Fm 50 2658
18 11 YARM 8f Good 46 3236

ROSE OF MOONCOIN 4 b f £355
68 6 NEWM 9f Gd/Fm 1154
76 5 SAND 7f Soft 85 1564 BL
53 6 WARW 6f Gd/Fm 2035 bl
63 20 ASCO 6f Good 85 2151 bl
0 13 DONC 6f Gd/Fm 2580 bl

ROSE PEEL 2 b f £0
69 7 HAYD 7f Soft 3786
80 9 DONC 8f Gd/Sft 4445

ROSE TINA 3 b f £0
52 7 LEIC 8f Soft 1548
51 9 WIND 10f Good 1725
23 9 SALI 8f Firm 2024
0a 10 LING 16f Aw 44 4329

ROSEAU 4 b f £756
70a 2 WOLV 12f Aw 144

ROSELYN 2 b f £817
63 6 LING 6f Good 2588
61 4 CARL 6f Gd/Fm 3079
70 4 FOLK 7f Gd/Fm 3583
65 5 YORK 6f Good 71 3807
68 4 LEIC 6f Gd/Sft 69 4030

ROSES TREASURE 4 b f £0
17a 13 WOLV 5f Aw 50 116 ebl
22a 10 SOUT 5f Aw 214 ebl
26 11 WARW 5f Heavy 43 1005 vis
40 10 REDC 5f Gd/Sft 48 1133 vis
0 25 REDC 8f Firm 43 1296
33 5 NEWC 5f Gd/Sft 43 1479 bl
0 12 NEWC 5f Heavy 1766

ROSETTA 3 b f £0
15 8 BATH 8f Gd/Sft 55 1671
26 13 CHEP 7f Good 1972
0 13 CHEP 8f Gd/Fm 2448

ROSEUM 4 b f £842
86 6 NEWM 6f Good 3610
69 19 AYR 6f Gd/Sft 92 4012

87 4 NEWM 6f Good 90 4198
83 7 MUNI 7f Soft 4317

ROSHANI 3 b f £9899
80 2 KEMP 9f Good 727
74 1 NEWC 8f Heavy 1010*
0 19 NEWM 10f Firm 78 1183
71 6 BATH 8f Firm 76 2330
77 1 NEWB 10f Firm 74 2811*
29 10 GOOD 9f Gd/Fm 79 3089

ROSIE 2 ch f £0
69 5 NEWM 7f Good 4020
79 5 YARM 7f Heavy 4475
66 8 DONC 7f Heavy 4566

ROSIES ALL THE WAY 4 b f £0
0a 13 SOUT 11f Aw 43 560
0 17 PONT 12f Good 38 1499
0 12 CATT 14f Soft 34 1683 t

ROSIS BOY 2 b c £6545
92 2 NEWM 7f Good 2563
85 1 NEWM 8f Gd/Fm 3458*
83 4 NEWB 8f Gd/Sft 4457

ROSSE 3 ch f £17704
87 4 NEWM 7f Good 1155
88 1 YARM 7f Gd/Fm 1951*
90 5 ASCO 8f Good 87 2167
98 1 YARM 7f Firm 2769*
102 3 SAND 8f Good 3469
94 6 YARM 10f Firm 3918
102 2 NEWM 8f Soft 4544

ROSSELLI 4 b c £15280
76 4 THIR 6f Soft 927 t
106 6 NEWM 5f Gd/Fm 1172
62 7 SAND 5f Soft 1566
100 18 ASCO 5f Good 2065
105 2 CHES 5f Gd/Fm 2669
102 6 GOOD 5f Gd/Fm 3059
81 12 YORK 5f Firm 3598
98 3 LEIC 5f Firm 3841
108 1 BEVE 5f Stt/Hvy 4043* BL
0 17 NEWM 5f Good 4182 bl
88 10 NEWM 5f Good 4346 bl

ROSSINI 3 b c £6000
113 4 NEWM 6f Gd/Sft 981
114 3 CURR 6f Gd/Fm 1622
82 13 ASCO 6f Good 2115

ROSSLYN CHAPEL 3 b c £0
0 14 YARM 6f Gd/Fm 45 1953

ROSTROPOVICH 3 gr c £13564
103 3 LEOP 12f Good 3371
107 5 YORK 16f Good 3538
107 7 DONC 15f Firm 3898 VIS
107 4 CURR 14f Good 4055
113 3 LONG 15f Good 4239

ROTHERHITHE 4 ch g £354
49a 3 LING 8f Aw 114
23a 8 WOLV 9f Aw 189
49a 6 LING 7f Aw 225
30a 7 LING 8f Aw 265
0a 14 LING 6f Aw 313
0a 11 LING 7f Aw 40 438
41 7 EPSO 7f Good 2792
12 11 BRIG 7f Firm 2907

ROTOSTAR 4 ch f £0
0 2 SOUT 7f Aw 501

ROUE 2 b c £0
58 10 DONC 7f Gd/Sft 4446 t

ROUGE 5 ch m £12554
77a 2 WOLV 7f Aw 72 79
0a 15 SOUT 6f Aw 75 129
61a 3 SOUT 8f Aw 197
80a 1 SOUT 6f Aw 279*
79a 3 SOUT 6f Aw 79 386

80a	1	LING	7f Aw		398*	
37	6	WIND	8f Good	1ow	2713	
54	1	**WIND**	6f Gd/Fm	45	3046*	
0	P	FOLK	7f Gd/Fm	52	3445	
52	3	HAMI	6f Soft	52	3803	
53	2	CATT	7f Soft	52	4004	

ROUGE ETOILE 4 b f £2310

29	13	HAYD	7f Gd/Sft	73	811
51	10	THIR	6f Soft	67	910
42	14	REDC	7f Firm	60	1297
44	6	CHEP	7f Gd/Sft	55	1799
45	10	REDC	8f Good	55	1892
0	16	ASCO	7f Gd/Fm	53	2999
50	5	NEWM	7f Gd/Fm	52	3460
51	2	HAMI	6f Soft	49	3803
0	14	CATT	7f Soft	52	4004

ROUGH SHOOT 2 ch g £5157

77a	1	**SOUT**	5f Aw		1418*	hd
72	5	RIPO	5f Gd/Fm		2100	
75	3	MUSS	5f Good	73	3101	hd
78	2	BEVE	5f Good	74	3673	hd
59	7	YORK	6f Good	78	3807	hd

ROUSING THUNDER 3 b c £4961

72	7	SALI	10f Firm	78	1177	
80	2	RIPO	10f Gd/Fm	77	2102	
64	8	BEVE	10f Firm	77	2220	
76	1	**PONT**	10f Gd/Fm		2832*	
68	5	HAYD	11f Gd/Sft	79	3267	VIS

ROUTE BARREE 2 ch c £0

63	8	NOTT	8f Heavy		4504

ROUTE ONE 7 b g £321

26a	6	SOUT	12f Aw		2298
75	4	SAND	14f Good		2477
67	5	SALI	14f Good		2691
36	11	HAYD	14f Gd/Fm	69	3323
48	14	GOOD	10f Good	60	3663

ROUTE SIXTY SIX 4 b f £8413

0	23	DONC	8f Good	75	715	
18	13	BRIG	8f Gd/Sft	73	895	BL
61	9	RIPO	9f Gd/Fm	70	3011	
54	2	REDC	8f Firm		3330	
53	3	NEWC	9f Firm	56	3603	
59	2	BEVE	8f Good	56	3951	
59	2	HAYD	8f Soft	56	4094	
60	3	YORK	9f Heavy	59	4300	
61	2	NOTT	8f Heavy	59	4506	

ROVERETTO 5 b g £2316

74	6	THIR	12f Good		1157
68	2	NEWC	12f Good		3034
62	4	CATT	16f Good	65	3442
63	3	NEWC	14f Soft	65	3709
61	4	MUSS	16f Gd/Sft	64	4134

ROWAASI 3 gr f £1750

92	9	BATH	5f Good		1090
86	10	NEWC	6f Firm		2335
91	4	CHES	5f Gd/Fm		2669
76	10	NEWM	6f Gd/Fm		3120

ROWENAS GIRL 2 b f £0

0	12	NEWC	6f Gd/Sft		1476

ROWLANDSONS STUD 7 b g £371

38a	9	WOLV	7f Aw		65	t
20a	10	LING	6f Aw	38	148	t
28a	9	SOUT	6f Aw		199	t
22a	6	LING	6f Aw	33	262	t
0a	14	SOUT	6f Aw		389	t
37a	3	LING	6f Aw		571	t
26a	6	LING	6f Aw	30	634	t
33a	7	WOLV	6f Aw		680	t
19	9	BRIG	7f Gd/Sft	38	896	t
0	16	NOTT	6f Gd/Fm	33	2192	t

ROXANNE MILL 2 b f £3652

59	5	SALI	5f Aw		2227
76	7	WIND	5f Gd/Fm		3044
74	3	CHEP	5f Gd/Fm		3252
73	4	HAYD	5f Gd/Sft	70	3475
66	6	LING	5f Good	70	4098
69	3	SAND	5f Soft	69	4202
72a	1	**WOLV**	5f Aw		4441*

ROXY LABURNUM 2 b f £0

0	12	LING	5f Gd/Sft		1260
34	10	SALI	5f Good		1346
27a	9	LING	5f Aw		1740
22	10	SALI	6f Gd/Fm		1882

ROYAL ALIBI 6 b g £0

0a	13	SOUT	14f Aw	45	4370	t

ROYAL AMARETTO 6 b g £540

71	4	YORK	10f Soft		4275

ROYAL ANTHEM 5 b g £240964

131	2	GULF	12f Good		20

ROYAL ARROW FR 4 b c £0

0	16	PONT	8f Soft	82	875	
61	10	DONC	10f Gd/Sft	79	1070	
46	10	HAYD	8f Soft	73	1490	
46	10	PONT	6f Good	68	1869	
54	5	HAMI	6f Gd/Fm		1905	
35	5	CARL	7f Firm		3197	VIS

ROYAL ARTIST 4 b g £31523

66a	1	**LING**	7f Aw		8*	
74a	2	WOLV	7f Aw	68	711	
78a	1	**WOLV**	8f Aw	72	1037*	
76	2	MUSS	8f Gd/Fm		1144	
71	6	YORK	9f Firm	74	2001	
79	2	NEWC	7f Aw	74	2338	
87	1	**LEIC**	7f Gd/Fm	75	2775+	
93	1	**ASCO**	6f Gd/Fm	80	2954+	
70	14	NEWM	7f Good	90	3315	
79	11	YORK	8f Gd/Fm	91	3727	
85	8	ASCO	7f Good	90	4112	
85	7	NEWM	7f Good	88	4357	

ROYAL ASSAY 2 ch f £480

72	3	SALI	5f Firm		2020
49	7	WARW	7f Good		2459
71	4	LING	6f Good		2588

ROYAL AXMINSTER 5 b g £427

0	16	DONC	10f Gd/Sft	49	1050	BL
0	18	WIND	12f Good	45	1730	
39	4	SALI	12f Gd/Fm	45	1888	
34	7	CHEP	18f Gd/Fm	42	2490	
38	9	SALI	12f Good	43	2689	
41	3	CHEP	12f Gd/Fm	40	2971	

ROYAL CANARY 3 ch c £0

0	10	HAMI	11f Good		848	
15	8	THIR	7f Soft		930	
0	16	MUSS	5f Gd/Fm		1430	t
44	6	MUSS	5f Firm		1688	

ROYAL CASCADE 6 b g £4538

81a	3	SOUT	7f Aw	82	33	bl
79a	5	WOLV	7f Aw	83	79	bl
66a	10	SOUT	6f Aw	82	129	bl
61a	10	WOLV	8f Aw	80	320	bl
61a	6	WOLV	8f Aw	77	381	bl
61a	3	SOUT	7f Aw		511	bl
48a	8	WOLV	8f Aw	75	580	bl
68a	2	WOLV	7f Aw		677	bl
39a	11	WOLV	8f Aw	68	921	bl
42	2	CATT	8f Good		1663	bl
27	10	BEVE	7f Firm	46	1920	bl
64a	1	**WOLV**	6f Aw		3275*	bl
56a	5	WOLV	7f Aw		3770	bl
51a	8	WOLV	6f Aw	62	4023	bl
67a	2	WOLV	7f Aw		4224	bl
49a	6	WOLV	6f Aw	60	4550	bl

ROYAL CASTLE 6 b g £0

74	6	YORK	14f Firm	75	1329
71	5	KEMP	14f Gd/Fm		1928
70	9	PONT	18f Firm	74	2176
62	7	NEWM	16f Gd/Fm	72	2600 VIS

ROYAL CAVALIER 3 b g £6540

70a	2	SOUT	8f Aw		86
0a	7	SOUT	8f Aw		500
75a	3	WOLV	9f Aw	78	625
67a	4	WOLV	8f Aw		658
83a	1	**WOLV**	9f Aw		720*
63	13	NEWM	10f Gd/Sft	82	979
76	7	YORK	7f Gd/Fm	80	1308
74	10	HAYD	8f Gd/Sft	79	1535
67	6	PONT	10f Good	76	1866
74	2	CHES	8f Gd/Fm	73	2250
68	7	NOTT	8f Gd/Fm	75	3005
0	23	YORK	8f Good	73	3810
30	6	BEVE	8f Sft/Hvy	70	4045
68	4	HAYD	7f Gd/Sft	70	4106
41	10	PONT	8f Soft	68	4232
62	5	NOTT	8f Heavy	66	4414
63	4	MUSS	8f Soft	64	4565

ROYAL CZARINA 3 ch f £0

28a	7	SOUT	8f Aw		198
34a	8	WOLV	9f Aw		319
29a	7	SOUT	8f Aw		514
20	12	WIND	12f Good	55	3186
34	9	FOLK	15f Gd/Fm		3584

ROYAL DOLPHIN 4 b c £857

0a	15	SOUT	12f Aw	38	68	
0a	11	SOUT	11f Aw		455	t
26a	7	WOLV	9f Aw		553	BL
23a	4	SOUT	8f Aw	27	584	bl
39a	3	WOLV	8f Aw		612	bl
51a	3	SOUT	8f Aw		686	tbl
34a	4	WOLV	8f Aw		707	tbl
19	9	BEVE	12f Firm		2219	
59	4	DONC	10f Gd/Fm		2317	
0	21	RIPO	10f Soft		2538	
0	25	REDC	8f Gd/Fm	34	2861	
0a	16	SOUT	16f Aw	34	2951	bl

ROYAL EAGLE 3 b c £1604

84	7	DONC	8f Good		735
78	9	BATH	10f Good		1089
92	3	SALI	12f Good		1347
89	8	NEWM	15f Gd/Fm		2594
92	7	GOOD	12f Gd/Fm	94	3088
78	11	DONC	12f Firm	92	3896

ROYAL ENCLOSURE 2 b c £0

60	9	LEIC	7f Gd/Fm		3333	
64	10	NEWB	7f Gd/Fm		3484	
0	19	NEWB	6f Sft/Hvy		4471	BL

ROYAL EXPOSURE 3 b g £564

35	11	NEWM	10f Good		3021
36	2	LEIC	10f Heavy		4313

ROYAL EXPRESSION 8 b g £15349

50a	5	SOUT	16f Aw	70	51	
63a	2	WOLV	15f Aw		117	
26a	9	WOLV	16f Aw	62	141	VIS
64a	1	**WOLV**	16f Aw	58	190*	
50a	6	SOUT	16f Aw	66	253	
63a	3	WOLV	16f Aw	62	482	
67a	1	**WOLV**	16f Aw	60	552*	
68a	2	WOLV	16f Aw	65	627	
63a	3	WOLV	16f Aw	65	664	
73	1	**DONC**	18f Good	70	714*	
63	6	PONT	17f Soft	73	876	
74	3	DONC	17f Gd/Sft	73	1052	
70	9	CHES	19f Gd/Fm	82	1222	
0	18	YORK	12f Soft	72	4280	
0	23	NEWM	18f Good	79	4353	
31	9	DONC	17f Heavy	70	4579	

ROYAL FLAME 4 b f £3399

59a 4 LING 10f Aw 56
55a 3 WOLV 9f Aw 189
68a 1 **LING** 10f Aw 314* BL
39a 6 WOLV 9f Aw 58 359 bl

ROYAL FUSILIER 4 b c £0
0a F SOUT 8f Aw 50

ROYAL GENT 2 b g £0
0 16 YORK 8f Gd/Fm 3729

ROYAL GLEN 2 b f £530
55 3 NEWC 6f Good 3032
62 6 YORK 6f Good 3812

ROYAL HIGHLANDER 3 b c £0
97 5 NEWM 7f Gd/Sft 104 969

ROYAL HUSSAR 4 gr c £0
0a 12 LING 6f Aw 25

ROYAL INSULT 3 ch c £0
0 20 NEWM 7f Good 85 954
79 7 NEWM 8f Firm 84 1183
65 12 KEMP 8f Gd/Fm 83 3793
60 9 KEMP 6f Gd/Sft 80 4037

ROYAL IVY 3 ch f £6417
74a 2 LING 7f Aw 70 149
67a 2 LING 8f Aw 264
58a 3 WOLV 9f Aw 319
69a 1 **LING** 7f Aw 421*
61a 9 LING 7f Aw 71 488
0 16 SALI 8f Good 70 1345
64 5 NEWB 7f Gd/Fm 67 1787
66 4 GOOD 7f Gd/Fm 66 2128
69 2 LING 7f Firm 66 2325
58 10 YORK 7f Good 68 2694
58 11 SAND 7f Gd/Fm 67 2922
60 6 EPSO 7f Good 66 3854
49 11 LING 7f Soft 64 4192

ROYAL KINGDOM 3 b c £0
108 5 LONG 8f Heavy 1025
100 5 YORK 10f Firm 1326

ROYAL KISS 2 b f £0
0 18 DONC 5f Gd/Sft 4445
57 15 NEWM 7f Soft 4541

ROYAL MEASURE 4 b c £649
50 3 SALI 12f Good 48 1350
16 10 SALI 12f Gd/Fm 49 1888
45 7 BATH 13f Gd/Fm 49 3819
25 12 SALI 14f Gd/Sft 46 4166

ROYAL MINSTREL 3 ch c £7651
83 3 DONC 10f Gd/Fm 79 701
85 1 **THIR** 12f Soft 906*
76 4 HAYD 12f Gd/Fm 82 3270
78 5 RIPO 12f Gd/Fm 81 3467
85 2 AYR 15f Soft 80 3961
58 7 AYR 13f Gd/Sft 80 4014 BL
0 14 YORK 12f Soft 4276

ROYAL MOUNT 4 ch g £0
0a 12 WOLV 9f Aw 189
0a 13 LING 12f Aw 267

ROYAL MUSICAL 2 ch f £0
51 5 REDC 6f Gd/Sft 1577
0 14 PONT 6f Good 1864
42 11 PONT 5f Good 2360
45 7 BEVE 7f Good 3949
0 14 NEWC 7f Heavy 4403

ROYAL ORIGINE 4 b c £0
32a 9 LING 5f Aw 55 205 tBL
32a 8 SOUT 7f Aw 247 tbl
0a 12 LING 6f Aw 313 tbl
51a 7 SOUT 6f Aw 389 tbl
15a 10 WOLV 6f Aw 436 tbl

ROYAL PARTNERSHIP 4 b g £4498
0a P LING 7f Aw 264
44a 5 WOLV 8f Aw 393
49a 1 **SOUT** 11f Aw 455*

43a 4 WOLV 12f Aw 50 522
52a 11 SOUT 8f Aw 600
62a 2 SOUT 11f Aw 672
40 11 MUSS 9f Gd/Sft 57 795
51a 3 SOUT 11f Aw 866
0a 12 WOLV 8f Aw 50 1037
48a 5 SOUT 11f Aw 48 1306 VIS
59a 1 **SOUT** 11f Aw 1417* vis

ROYAL PASTIMES 3 b f £0
31 6 NOTT 8f Good 783
0 9 PONT 12f Heavy 939
0 5 REDC 11f Gd/Fm 2146
3a 11 WOLV 8f Aw 34 2601
0 10 CATT 14f Soft 4002

ROYAL PATRON 4 ch f £2144
71 2 WIND 12f Good 70 853
70 3 BATH 13f Gd/Fm 71 1440
70 5 SAND 14f Gd/Fm 71 1991
68 4 REDC 16f Gd/Fm 70 2866
60 6 BATH 13f Gd/Fm 69 3518
60 7 KEMP 14f Gd/Fm 68 3800

ROYAL PLUM 4 ch g £0
0 14 MUSS 12f Gd/Sft 4133

ROYAL REBEL 4 b c £140611
67 8 ASCO 16f Gd/Sft 1109
110 3 LEOP 14f Good 1620* bl
108 2 CURR 14f Yldg 2405 bl
110 2 LEOP 14f Good 2909 bl
118 1 **GOOD** 16f Good 3106* vis
118 1 **YORK** 16f Good 3538* vis
118 3 LONG 20f Good 4264 bl
118 2 NEWM 16f Good 4351 vis
114 6 LONG 16f Heavy 4494 bl

ROYAL REPRIMAND 5 b g £3665
33 7 NEWC 12f Heavy 1009
0 11 CATT 14f Soft 36 1683 vis
26 9 BEVE 10f Firm 38 1921 vis
17 7 REDC 8f Gd/Fm 33 2147 vis
25 7 REDC 8f Gd/Fm 28 2861
57 5 REDC 7f Gd/Sft 2994
28 2 THIR 9f Firm 29 3129
36 4 CATT 7f Gd/Fm 38 3200
53 3 REDC 8f Firm 3330
65 2 NEWC 7f Firm 3604
89 3 REDC 7f Gd/Sft 4218
47 6 REDC 7f Gd/Sft 54 4498

ROYAL RESULT 7 br g £10347
84 8 KEMP 6f Good 92 728
77 12 NEWM 6f Firm 95 1182
78 10 YORK 6f Firm 90 1337
88 3 EPSO 6f Good 87 1851
84 6 ASCO 6f Good 87 2151
89 4 GOOD 6f Good 87 2355
86 4 GOOD 6f Firm 88 3152
59 9 NEWB 7f Gd/Fm 88 3481
0 12 GOOD 6f Good 88 3904
87 5 AYR 6f Gd/Sft 88 4012
85 6 YORK 6f Heavy 88 4301
74 20 NEWM 7f Good 87 4357
0 15 DONC 7f Heavy 85 4574

ROYAL ROMEO 3 ch g £5907
0 16 THIR 5f Good 73 1162
76 1 **NEWC** 5f Good 70 1768*
70 6 BEVE 5f Good 76 2517
76 3 RIPO 6f Soft 76 2541
60 8 CHES 5f Good 76 2663
66 10 YORK 5f Gd/Fm 76 3569
64 8 RIPO 6f Good 76 3698
70 5 HAYD 7f Gd/Sft low 4106
52 15 YORK 6f Soft 4287
71 3 NEWC 6f Heavy 71 4405
63 7 REDC 7f Gd/Sft 71 4498

ROYAL SATIN 2 b c £0
34 10 NEWM 7f Firm 3298
0 15 NEWM 7f Good 4184
0 7 BRIG 10f Heavy 4539

ROYAL SIGNET 5 ch m £284
58 4 BATH 12f Firm 2943
28 5 CHEP 12f Gd/Fm 37 3255
0 12 BATH 13f Gd/Fm 43 3518

ROYAL SIX 7 b g £0
21a 11 SOUT 8f Aw 50 584
0a 11 SOUT 7f Aw 1305

ROYAL TARRAGON 4 b f £0
44 9 LING 7f Gd/Fm 838
56 10 KEMP 7f Soft 1012
0 13 LING 6f Gd/Fm 2183
0 14 NOTT 6f Gd/Fm 2680
24 9 SALI 7f Gd/Fm 42 2978
36 10 WARW 7f Good 3696

ROYAL TEMPTATION 3 b g £336
63 4 HAYD 11f Soft 4089
49 8 NOTT 10f Heavy 4408

ROYAL TRYST 3 ch c £9776
91 2 NEWM 10f Gd/Fm 2617
89 1 **YORK** 10f Good 3813*
90 3 KEMP 12f Soft 4039

ROYAL WANDERER 2 ch c £0
44 7 RIPO 6f Gd/Fm 3184
0 15 AYR 6f Soft 3958
49a 7 WOLV 9f Aw 4438

ROYAL WAVE 4 b c £281
0a 14 SOUT 8f Aw 58 176
29 14 CATT 7f Good 55 3440
48a 3 SOUT 8f Aw 50 4365
41 11 REDC 7f Gd/Sft 53 4498

ROYLE FAMILY 2 b c £0
62a 4 SOUT 5f Aw 856
41a 5 SOUT 5f Aw 1206
41a 4 LING 5f Aw 1916
53 5 MUSS 5f Gd/Fm 2200
41a 4 WOLV 5f Aw 2605
5 12 HAMI 5f Soft 51 3802

ROYMILLON 6 b h £0
78a 10 LING 10f Aw 690
66 9 BATH 8f Soft 4142

ROZARY 2 b f £0
17 7 LEIC 5f Gd/Fm 3092
15 10 LEIC 7f Gd/Fm 3333

ROZEL 3 ch f £13874
53 8 BEVE 5f Firm 1280
80 1 **YARM** 5f Gd/Fm 1609*
78 3 AYR 5f Good 2165
87 4 ASCO 5f Gd/Fm 86 3016
92 3 YORK 5f Gd/Fm 86 3569
93 2 COLO 5f Soft 4146

RUBY BABE 2 b f £0
60 6 BEVE 5f Gd/Fm 2480
0a 8 SOUT 5f Aw 2818
9 8 PONT 5f Soft 4372

RUBY ESTATE 9 b m £0
0 12 LEIC 12f Good 38 791
0 17 PONT 10f Heavy 42 943

RUBY LASER 4 b f £0
34 7 WIND 12f Good 47 853
36 6 NOTT 14f Gd/Sft 43 1087
25 7 SALI 14f Gd/Fm 46 2268

RUBY RAVEN 3 b f £290
54 4 NEWC 9f Good 3248
29 8 BEVE 10f Gd/Fm 3677

RUDCROFT 4 ch g £0
0 21 REDC 7f Gd/Sft 1132
0 15 THIR 12f Gd/Sft 1353

0 18 RIPO 8f Good 1858
0 18 RIPO 8f Good 1858
5 9 RIPO 6f Gd/Fm 32 2839
50 7 BEVE 5f Gd/Sft 3056
12 9 THIR 6f Gd/Fm 27 3124
0 17 REDC 6f Firm 27 3312
0 11 REDC 8f Firm 3330

RUDDER 2 ch c £1374
73 2 HAYD 6f Soft 1823

RUDE AWAKENING 6 b g £10668
40a 4 SOUT 6f Aw 46 250
59a 1 **LING** 6f Aw 44 358*
51a 3 LING 6f Aw 50 372
28a 9 SOUT 6f Aw 57 454
56a 3 LING 7f Aw 56 525
62a 1 **LING** 6f Aw 56 543*
37a 13 SOUT 6f Aw 60 2385
48 1 **CATT** 5f Gd/Fm 43 2743*
37 9 CATT 5f Gd/Fm 49 2929
48 5 BATH 5f Firm 3209
51 2 CHEP 6f Gd/Fm 47 3257
38 9 BEVE 5f Good 48 3398
49 4 CHEP 5f Gd/Fm 49 3872
46a 9 WOLV 6f Aw 60 4023
59a 3 SOUT 6f Aw 59 4155
48a 11 WOLV 6f Aw 59 4223

RUDETSKI 3 b g £3491
44 13 THIR 5f Soft 909
0 13 PONT 6f Gd/Sft 1105
59 6 PONT 6f Good 1500
42 5 HAYD 8f Soft 56 1822
36 6 HAMI 11f Gd/Fm 53 2782
54 1 **PONT** 8f Gd/Fm 49 3226*
55 2 BEVE 6f Sft/Hvy 55 4045

RUDIK 3 br c £0
92 5 ASCO 6f Gd/Sft 1111
93 7 NEWM 6f Good 99 2568
86 12 GOOD 6f Firm 99 3152 t

RUDIS PET 6 ch g £28500
115 1 **LEOP** 5f Yldg 1757*
95 20 ASCO 5f Good 2065 bl
116 3 GOOD 5f Gd/Sft 3059 bl
104 7 YORK 5f Firm 3598 bl
88 10 NEWB 5f Firm 3982 bl

RULE OF THUMB 3 ch g £2166
72 15 NEWM 7f Good 84 954
73 16 NEWM 7f Gd/Fm 82 1153
0 16 GOOD 7f Gd/Sft 81 1470
66 5 FOLK 7f Gd/Fm 75 3041
75 2 FOLK 7f Gd/Fm 70 3445
60 7 LING 8f Firm 70 3580
75 2 BATH 6f Gd/Fm 73 3821

RUM BABA 6 b g £0
32 5 REDC 16f Gd/Fm 42 2866
23 6 YARM 16f Good 39 3026 bl
34 5 PONT 17f Firm 35 3501 bl

RUM LAD 6 gr g £0
0 14 NOTT 6f Good 63 787
43 10 PONT 5f Gd/Fm 61 2830
0 21 THIR 6f Gd/Fm 58 3123

RUM LASS 3 gr f £0
0 15 BEVE 7f Heavy 62 976
0 16 BEVE 5f Firm 1280
0 14 RIPO 5f Gd/Fm 52 2839
0 14 RIPO 5f Gd/Fm 47 3180

RUM POINTER 4 b c £9842
13 15 HAYD 12f Heavy 94 991
83 7 CHES 19f Gd/Fm 91 1222
90 2 THIR 12f Gd/Sft 87 1715
93 1 **HAYD** 16f Gd/Sft 87 1791*
60 9 YORK 14f Gd/Fm 90 1982
71 18 YORK 14f Gd/Fm 94 3565
85 5 YORK 14f Good 93 3811

---

90 5 AYR 13f Gd/Sft 92 4014
104 4 HAYD 14f Soft 4091
83 6 DONC 17f Heavy 95 4579

RUM PUNCH 3 b c £2260
72 8 NEWB 8f Good 1376
67 8 KEMP 8f Soft 1532
78 2 PONT 10f Good 73 1866 t
0 16 KEMP 10f Gd/Fm 77 3794
66 9 YARM 10f Soft 77 4392 t

RUMORE CASTAGNA 2 ch g £10623
78 1 **NEWC** 5f Heavy 1764*
90 5 CHES 5f Good 2664
84 3 DONC 6f Gd/Fm 2754
83 9 DONC 6f Gd/Fm 3862

RUMPOLD 2 b c £6711
111 1 **ASCO** 6f Gd/Fm 3000*

RUN FOR GLORY 3 ch c £0
0 14 SAND 5f Soft 4207
30 9 YARM 7f Soft 4387

RUN MACHINE 3 ch c £0
16 10 GOOD 5f Gd/Sft 48 1487
25 9 LEIC 5f Gd/Fm 44 3214

RUN ON 2 b c £1376
70 4 BATH 6f Gd/Sft 2550
68 2 LEIC 5f Gd/Fm 3092
0 18 NEWB 6f Firm 3980

RUNAWAY BRIDE 2 b f £0
65 5 HAYD 5f Gd/Sft 1538
50 5 HAMI 6f Good 1938
0 11 BEVE 5f Firm 2730
0 16 BEVE 7f Good 54 3950

RUNAWAY STAR 3 ch f £0
35 6 PONT 8f Good 1865
36 6 NEWM 8f Gd/Fm 2134
46 5 NEWM 10f Gd/Fm 2284
43 7 NEWM 12f Gd/Fm 45 3167
0 14 HAMI 12f Gd/Sft 43 3827
29 6 YARM 11f Soft 40 4391
32 10 NEWM 8f Gd/Sft 44 4536

RUNIN CIRCLES 3 b g £0
0 22 DONC 8f Gd/Sft 57 1053
0 12 REDC 14f Gd/Sft 55 1581

RUNNING BEAR 6 ch g £0
0a 13 SOUT 8f Aw 30
47a 5 WOLV 8f Aw 138
38a 5 LING 7f Aw 156
25a 10 SOUT 8f Aw 197
17a 7 WOLV 9f Aw 259

RUNNING FOR ME 2 ch f £4675
48 6 LEIC 5f Gd/Sft 828
61a 1 **SOUT** 5f Aw 1206*
45 8 BEVE 5f Good 1443
56a 2 SOUT 6f Aw 1805
56a 2 WOLV 6f Aw 2079
44a 5 SOUT 5f Aw 2384
64a 1 **WOLV** 5f Aw 2605*
52a 8 SOUT 6f Aw 62 2948

RUNNING FREE 6 b g £0
17 9 REDC 16f Gd/Fm 51 2866
0 8 REDC 14f Firm 3311

RUNNING STAG 6 b g £494309
103a 2 LING 10f Aw 55
120 2 SHA 10f Gd/Fm 186
112a 2 NAD 8f Dirt 666
105a 7 NAD 10f Dirt 769
115a 1 **BELM** 9f Dirt 1616*
115a 1 **SUFF** 9f Fast 1749*

RUNNING TIMES 3 b c £1546
64a 5 WOLV 9f Aw 68 625
45 12 DONC 10f Gd/Fm 68 701
58 3 THIR 12f Soft 924
43 5 DONC 15f Gd/Sft 62 1071 BL

---

63 4 BEVE 12f Good 60 1446
61 3 REDC 11f Gd/Sft 60 1560

RUNNING WATER 7 b g £0
0 12 NOTT 14f Gd/Sft 1369

RUSH 7 b h £0
46a 6 LING 10f Aw 110 t

RUSHBY 2 b c £1595
71 6 DONC 5f Gd/Sft 1048
86 3 SALI 6f Good 1346
71 6 SAND 5f Soft 1586
77 2 SAND 5f Good 1962
44 11 WIND 5f Good 2711
57 6 LING 5f Firm 3576

RUSHCUTTER BAY 7 br h £31197
77 2 BATH 6f Gd/Fm 1441
77 6 WIND 6f Good 1728
0 11 NOTT 5f Good 77 1871
84 2 NEWM 6f Firm 77 3297
83 1 **NEWM** 6f Gd/Fm 77 3457*
73 11 GOOD 6f Good 82 3646
80 8 KEMP 6f Gd/Fm 82 3791
88 2 NEWM 6f Good 82 4015 vis
106 1 **NEWM** 5f Good 4182+ vis
105 3 NEWM 6f Good 4346

RUSHED 5 b g £216
38a 4 LING 12f Aw 457
34a 9 LING 10f Aw 650
5a 8 LING 10f Aw 33 2186

RUSHMORE 3 ch c £38627
82 1 **DONC** 7f Good 717*
64 15 NEWM 6f Firm 80 1183
61 11 YORK 10f Gd/Fm 78 1310
84a 1 **SOUT** 7f Aw 74 2300*
81 1 **SAND** 7f Gd/Fm 74 2495*
65 6 EPSO 7f Good 2792
87 1 **SAND** 6f Gd/Fm 79 2922*

RUSSIAN FOX 3 ch c £0
70 11 EPSO 6f Heavy 92 1028
82 8 NEWB 6f Good 1371
80 21 NEWM 6f Gd/Fm 92 1694
70 10 EPSO 6f Good 90 1851
0 16 GOOD 6f Good 87 3904
74 10 NEWB 7f Firm 87 3981
73 11 SALI 6f Gd/Sft 83 4165
0 17 DONC 5f Heavy 79 4570

RUSSIAN HOPE 5 ch g £72047
115 1 **SAIN** 10f Hldng 665*
106 4 SAIN 12f Soft 1461
116 1 **DEAU** 13f Gd/Sft 3723*
117 8 LONG 12f Good 4262

RUSSIAN MUSIC 7 b g £0
0 15 BEVE 7f Firm 65 1275 t
0 16 LEIC 8f Firm 58 2032
0 P LEIC 12f Gd/Fm 3336 t

RUSSIAN RHAPSODY 3 b f £6980
57 5 LEIC 5f Gd/Fm 2919
65 4 SALI 7f Good 3423
62 3 EPSO 9f Good 3764
73 2 HAYD 7f Soft 4093
73 2 LING 8f Soft 4273
80 1 **YARM** 7f Soft 4388*
78 5 DONC 7f Heavy 78 4574

RUSSIAN ROMEO 5 b g £8024
69a 3 WOLV 5f Aw 69 40 bl
45a 7 WOLV 5f Aw 69 146 bl
53a 6 SOUT 6f Aw 69 386 bl
12a 10 SOUT 6f Aw 454 bl
57a 5 SOUT 6f Aw 538 bl
65a 5 SOUT 6f Aw 65 587 bl
65a 3 SOUT 6f Aw 64 697 bl
64a 2 WOLV 6f Aw 719 bl
61 3 WARW 7f Soft 816 bl

66	2	DONC	6f Gd/Sft		1073	bl
66	2	CARL	6f Firm	60	1257	vis
42	8	LEIC	6f Soft	64	1545	bl
52	8	PONT	5f Good		1868	bl
66a	2	SOUT	6f Aw	65	2820	bl
56	3	HAYD	6f Gd/Fm		3283	bl
60	5	CARL	5f Firm	60	3572	bl
73a	1	WOLV	6f Aw	66	3774*	bl
45a	13	WOLV	6f Aw	72	4380	bl

RUSSIAN SILVER 3 ch f £689

46	8	WARW	12f Soft	72	1064
60	4	LING	9f Firm	68	1917
61	3	WARW	11f Good	63	2463

RUSSIAN WHISPERS 2 b c £983

83	3	DONC	6f Gd/Fm		2608
98	5	NEWB	8f Firm		3983
91	7	ASCO	8f Gd/Sft		4127
86	6	NEWB	6f Stt/Hvy	89	4468 VIS

RUTLAND CHANTRY 6 b g £3356

75a	2	SOUT	8f Aw	70	601
64a	5	SOUT	8f Aw	73	669
63	6	PONT	10f Soft	70	871
65	6	BEVE	10f Heavy	70	975
36	10	NEWC	10f Gd/Fm	67	2309
59	5	CHES	12f Gd/Fm	64	3430
60	3	CHES	10f Soft	61	4074
57	4	REDC	10f Gd/Sft	60	4221
62	2	PONT	10f Soft	59	4374
53	5	NOTT	10f Heavy		4413 BL

RYANS GOLD 2 b c £0

60	8	GOOD	6f Good		2357
59	14	NEWB	6f Firm		3980
79	6	NEWM	7f Good		4184
0	17	NEWM	8f Good	72	4350

RYEFIELD 5 b g £15230

32	13	HAMI	8f Firm	58	1243
0	R	AYR	8f Gd/Fm	56	1658
62	2	CARL	7f Firm	56	2823
62	1	AYR	7f Firm	57	2878*
61	4	AYR	8f Good	61	3365
63	2	REDC	8f Gd/Fm	61	3634
62	6	YORK	8f Good	62	3810
61	3	HAMI	8f Gd/Sft	62	3826
62	3	MUSS	7f Gd/Sft	61	4136
67	1	AYR	6f Heavy	62	4327*
45	6	NEWC	6f Heavy	69	4405
57	6	MUSS	7f Soft	66	4518
0	14	MUSS	8f Soft	66	4565

RYELAND 4 b f £478

52	3	WARW	12f Gd/Fm	2038

RYKA 5 ch g £0

0	13	NOTT	8f Good	784
67	9	LEIC	10f Gd/Sft	833
52	6	MUSS	9f Gd/Sft	902

RYMERS RASCAL 8 b g £13822

41	5	PONT	8f Heavy		942
57	6	MUSS	7f Gd/Fm	59	1431
57	3	BEVE	7f Firm	57	1920
59	4	AYR	7f Good	58	2163
61	2	CATT	7f Gd/Fm	58	2420
54	5	BEVE	7f Good	60	2882
62	3	CHES	8f Good	60	3170
56	8	CARL	7f Firm		3573
63	3	YORK	8f Good	60	3810
67	1	REDC	8f Gd/Sft	60	4217*
67	4	YORK	7f Heavy	67	4302
66	4	REDC	8f Gd/Fm	67	4499

RYTHM N TIME 3 b f £4104

68	9	CHES	6f Gd/Fm	77	1220
72	4	AYR	5f Good	74	2165
48	10	HAYD	6f Gd/Fm	73	2504
61	8	PONT	5f Gd/Fm	72	2830
70	1	BEVE	5f Gd/Sft		3056*
56	4	PONT	6f Gd/Fm		3225
69	4	THIR	5f Gd/Fm	70	3349
66	6	CARL	5f Firm	67	3572
62	6	HAYD	5f Gd/Sft	68	3788
0	16	LEIC	5f Gd/Sft	66	4027
0	25	NEWM	5f Good	66	4185
63	5	AYR	5f Heavy	66	4307
49a	7	WOLV	7f Aw	62	4550

S AND O P 6 b g £0

0	7	MUSS	16f Gd/Sft	2536

S W THREE 2 b f £1174

76	2	SALI	7f Gd/Sft	3292

SAAFEND FLYER 2 b c £0

0	15	WIND	6f Gd/Fm		1876
64	8	SAND	7f Good		1988
53	9	BRIG	7f Gd/Sft		3239
0	16	GOOD	8f Soft	59	4076
0	20	WIND	10f Gd/Sft	55	4290 t

SAAFEND ROCKET 2 b c £0

68	5	GOOD	5f Gd/Sft	1639
66	5	SAND	5f Good	1962
62	8	CHEP	5f Good	3252

SAANEN 3 b c £2491

60	3	CARL	9f Gd/Sft	60	1722
63	2	REDC	10f Good	60	1895
62	2	HAMI	8f Firm		2093
61	3	NEWC	9f Gd/Fm	63	2276

SABANA 2 b c £1272

77	8	NEWM	6f Gd/Fm		2132
79	2	BEVE	7f Good		2881
85	5	NEWM	7f Gd/Sft		3164
71	8	YORK	7f Good	83	3542

SABICA 3 b f £0

0a	8	SOUT	7f Aw		427
15a	7	SOUT	8f Aw	49	540

SABLE CLOAK 5 b m £0

0a	13	WOLV	9f Aw	922

SABO ROSE 2 b f £4396

76	3	LING	7f Firm		3833
80	1	PONT	6f Soft		4082*
82	3	NEWM	6f Good	81	4338
80	5	NEWB	6f Gd/Fm	81	4453

SABOT 7 b h £0

59a	4	WOLV	9f Aw	58	60
0a	12	LING	8f Aw	56	1259
45	4	BRIG	7f Firm	47	1335
0a	11	LING	10f Aw	54	2212
0	13	SAND	10f Gd/Fm	46	2527
0	13	GOOD	9f Good	47	3644
0	17	BRIG	10f Firm	46	3737

SABRE LADY 3 ch f £1911

83	3	CHES	5f Gd/Fm	81	1219
81	4	THIR	5f Good	84	1384
42	14	HAYD	6f Gd/Fm	83	2504
68	8	GOOD	5f Gd/Fm	80	3135
62	12	THIR	5f Gd/Fm	78	3349
42	12	HAMI	6f Soft	75	3803
0	24	AYR	6f Gd/Sft	75	4010
49	8	MUSS	5f Soft	70	4516

SABREON 3 b f £1204

86	2	CHEP	10f Gd/Fm		2449
83	5	NEWB	10f Gd/Fm	85	3178
0	14	GOOD	9f Good	85	3883
74	6	SAND	8f Soft	82	4206
67	7	BRIG	8f Soft		4420

SACHO 7 b h £0

59	9	DONC	12f Good	732

SACRED HEART 3 b f £0

0	13	SALI	7f Good		1349
12	10	LEIC	8f Gd/Sft		1732 t
32	11	CHEP	7f Good		1972 t
0	13	BATH	10f Firm	37	2332 t

SACRED SONG 3 b f £27230

101	1	NOTT	8f Good		1872*
101	2	YARM	10f Firm		3918
114	1	NEWM	12f Good		4343+

SACREMENTUM 5 b g £3382

57a	6	SOUT	8f Aw	62	326
56a	4	WOLV	8f Aw	60	381
31a	8	SOUT	6f Aw		414 bl
57a	2	WOLV	7f Aw	56	582
34a	7	LING	8f Aw	56	596
44	6	SOUT	7f Good	56	803
47	4	WARW	11f Heavy	54	889
35	14	WIND	12f Good	50	1730
49	2	LEIC	8f Firm	48	2032
48	4	FOLK	12f Gd/Fm	49	2295
48	4	EPSO	12f Gd/Sft	48	2626
48	2	NOTT	10f Gd/Fm	47	3007
45	4	BEVE	12f Gd/Sft	47	3053
0	F	BRIG	10f Firm	47	3557
43a	6	WOLV	9f Aw	56	4228
25a	8	WOLV	12f Aw	54	4386

SADAKA 3 ch f £3505

63	8	LEIC	7f Good		794
63	3	NOTT	8f Good		1407
66	4	NOTT	8f Good	67	2013
71	1	YARM	8f Firm	66	2767*

SADDLE MOUNTAIN 4 b f £197

43a	4	WOLV	8f Aw	39
22a	6	WOLV	12f Aw	144

SADDLERS QUEST 3 b c £41413

102	1	KEMP	10f Soft	998*
109	1	LING	11f Gd/Sft	1284*

SADLERS FLAG 3 b f £48030

104	3	SAIN	11f V	944
107	1	CHAN	12f Gd/Sft	1748*
108	2	LONG	12f Good	2224
109	2	DEAU	14f Gd/Sft	3070
109	6	LONG	12f Good	3928
104	5	LONG	13f Good	4236

SADLERS REALM 7 b g £0

54	6	NEWB	16f Gd/Sft	70	4458

SADLERS SECRET 5 b g £423

70	3	CHEP	18f Gd/Fm	70	2490 vis
61	10	ASCO	16f Gd/Fm	70	2953 vis

SADLERS SONG 3 b f £0

51	5	BEVE	12f Gd/Sft	53	1758
42	8	LING	11f Firm	53	1914
38	7	WIND	10f Gd/Fm	49	2206
42	5	CHEP	16f Gd/Fm	49	2659
24	11	BEVE	16f Good	44	2879
0	14	CATT	12f Soft	45	4256

SADLERS SWING 4 b c £0

58	7	LING	10f Gd/Sft	1281
50	7	SAND	10f Soft	1588

SADLERS WALTZ 3 b g £0

47	8	BATH	12f Soft	4434

SAFARANDO 3 B C £24986

64a	8	LING	7f Aw	72	488
80a	1	WOLV	7f Aw	72	534*
87a	1	WOLV	8f Aw	76	566*
87a	2	WOLV	8f Aw	86	613
90	1	DONC	7f Good	77	736*
101	1	HAYD	8f Gd/Sft	89	810*
106	6	NEWM	7f Good		950
106	2	KEMP	8f Soft		996

SAFARASIKNOW 3 ch c £0

45a	8	LING	6f Aw	60	2

SAFARI BLUES 3 b f £8333

84a	1	LING	8f Aw		26+
93a	1	LING	8f Aw	82	54*
73	5	NEWM	7f Firm	82	1855

69	8	KEMP	8f Gd/Fm	80	2084
73	5	KEMP	9f Gd/Sft	76	2581
78	2	NEWB	10f Firm	76	2811
75	6	NEWB	10f Gd/Fm	80	3178
73	6	WIND	8f Good	79	3643
74	3	EPSO	10f Good		3857
44	11	BRIG	10f Gd/Sft	73	4118

SAFE SHARP JO 5 ch g £0

0a	11	SOUT	8f Aw	39	298
0a	13	SOUT	11f Aw	39	325
13a	6	WOLV	15f Aw		363
18a	8	WOLV	8f Aw	49	432
3a	7	WOLV	12f Aw	32	554
0a	9	WOLV	16f Aw	30	918
0a	12	WOLV	12f Aw		1039 vis
0a	13	WOLV	6f Aw		1137 BL

SAFFRON 4 ch f £667

45	10	DONC	6f Gd/Fm	57	1842
0	14	THIR	7f Gd/Fm	54	2063
27a	11	SOUT	6f Aw	49	2385
0	11	LING	6f Good	49	2654
37	5	YARM	7f Firm	44	2899 BL
36	4	CARL	7f Aw	44	3083
43	3	HAYD	8f Good	42	3288
37	6	CARL	8f Firm	42	3574
40	4	MUSS	8f Gd/Fm	42	3746
0	16	YARM	8f Firm	48	3936

SAFFRON WALDEN 4 b c £3150

103	3	CURR	8f Gd/Fm		2740

SAFINAZ 2 gr f £0

63	8	YORK	6f Good		2692
56	6	LEIC	6f Gd/Fm		3096
50	5	NOTT	6f Soft		3973
51	9	LING	5f Good		4096
0	15	BRIG	7f Soft	55	4416

SAFRANINE 3 b f £0

35a	8	LING	7f Aw		630
0	15	YORK	7f Gd/Fm	94	1308
73	14	YORK	6f Firm	90	2003
45	13	HAYD	6f Gd/Fm	85	2504
59	8	DONC	8f Gd/Fm	80	3160

SAGACITY 2 br c £38425

110	1	SAIN	10f Soft		4556*

SAGAMIX 5 br g £36805

103	9	NAD	12f Good		767
109	4	EPSO	12f Gd/Sft		1827
117	3	SAIN	12f Good		2406

SAGAPONACK 4 b g £3176

42a	5	WOLV	9f Aw		578
74a	1	SOUT	12f Aw		643*
75a	4	SOUT	14f Aw	82	868
67	12	KEMP	12f Gd/Fm	80	1076
49	10	YORK	10f Soft	78	4282
65	5	NEWB	10f Sft/Hv	73	4473

SAGUARO 6 b g £4620

63a	2	SOUT	8f Aw		600
47	1	MUSS	7f Gd/Fm	42	1148*
0	14	YARM	7f Gd/Sft	45	1611
47	3	LEIC	7f Gd/Fm	47	2775

SAHARA SPIRIT 3 b c £6338

78	2	SAND	8f Good	76	761
78	2	SOUT	7f Gd/Sft	76	857
77	4	ASCO	8f Gd/Fm	78	1113
71	1	SOUT	7f Soft		1607*
0	31	ASCO	8f Good	78	2117

SAHAYB 3 b f £3997

61	8	YARM	7f Gd/Fm		1951
15	11	WARW	8f Good		2465
64	1	THIR	7f Gd/Fm		3146* bl
21	13	BRIG	8f Soft		4173 bl

SAHHAR 7 ch g £0

17	10	HAYD	11f Gd/Sft	35	3480

SAIFAN 11 ch g £1874

0	20	YARM	7f Gd/Sft	56	1611 vis
18	4	YARM	8f Gd/Fm		2411 vis
47	2	REDC	8f Gd/Fm	46	2861 vis
47	3	NEWM	8f Gd/Fm		3117 vis
52	2	YARM	7f Firm		3921 vis

SAIL ON BUN 4 gr f £0

0	14	CATT	16f Soft	42	4258

SAIL WITH THE WIND 3 b f £0

0	11	LEIC	10f Gd/Fm		2774
50	5	LING	10f Firm	49	3581
18	11	BRIG	12f Soft	47	4176
5a	10	WOLV	12f Aw	48	4360

SAILING 3 ch f £89399

95	2	NEWB	8f Soft	93	912
100	1	SAN	10f Heavy		1227*
105	4	GOOD	10f Gd/Fm		1469
105	1	SAN	12f Gd/Fm		2073*
98	7	NEWM	12f Gd/Fm		2857
112	1	ASCO	12f Gd/Fm		3305*

SAILING SHOES 4 b c £0

42	14	KEMP	5f Soft	87	1013
0	12	GOOD	7f Gd/Sft	84	1810
0	13	SALI	6f Gd/Fm	84	1887 BL
75	6	SALI	5f Gd/Fm	79	2266 bl
65	9	NEWB	5f Gd/Fm	78	3176 bl
72	6	BRIG	5f Firm	76	3734
57	9	CHES	5f Soft	74	4073

SAILORMAITE 9 ch g £0

0	14	LEIC	6f Soft	50	1545

SAINT CRYSTALGLASS 3 ch f £0

0	5	HAYD	11f Soft		4089

SAINT GEORGE 4 b c £551

0a	13	SOUT	6f Aw	47	1422
0	19	NEWM	8f Gd/Fm	42	1690
38	4	AYR	8f Good	37	2136
38a	2	LING	10f Aw		2587
34	4	WIND	12f Good		2715
22	8	YARM	10f Firm		2765
14a	7	WOLV	12f Aw	38	3494

SAINTLY THOUGHTS 5 b g £0

0	13	BEVE	16f Firm	68	1276

SAKAMOTO 2 b c £0

58	8	ASCO	7f Gd/Sft		4124
37	8	SAND	8f Soft		4203
58	5	NEWM	7f Soft		4344

SAKHAROV 11 b g £0

17a	7	SOUT	11f Aw		2119
0	15	RIPO	10f Soft		2538

SAKHEE 3 b c £373075

115	1	SAND	10f Heavy		1056*
117	1	YORK	10f Firm		1326*
126	2	EPSO	12f Good		1848
119	4	SAND	10f Gd/Fm		2497

SALABUE 3 b c £0

0	15	DONC	10f Gd/Sft		1054

SALEE 3 b f £10708

85	1	GOOD	10f Good		3907*
100	2	NEWM	10f Good		4337

SALEM 3 b c £643

0	13	NEWM	8f Gd/Fm		3626
73	3	LING	7f Firm		3834
62a	4	LING	10f Aw		4100
63a	5	LING	8f Aw	65	4335

SALEYMA 2 b f £0

72	9	NEWM	7f Soft		4541

SALFORD FLYER 4 b c £2180

79	2	KEMP	14f Good	76	726
56	7	SAND	16f Heavy	79	1044

SALIENT POINT 3 gr f £212

66	5	LING	7f Gd/Sft		840

75	7	NEWM	7f Gd/Fm		1155
56	11	NOTT	8f Gd/Fm		1268
65a	4	SOUT	8f Aw	67	1803
39	13	WIND	10f Gd/Fm	66	2206
50	10	EPSO	10f Good	63	3762
33a	7	LING	10f Aw		4100
0a	13	LING	13f AW		4193
0	6	NOTT	14f Heavy	58	4409 t

SALIGO 5 b m £1934

0	14	NEWC	10f Soft	75	757
40	12	THIR	8f Soft	72	931
0	18	NEWC	7f Heavy	68	1011
45	11	CHES	10f Gd/Fm	64	1217
64	3	REDC	9f Gd/Sft	60	1583
58	4	BEVE	9f Gd/Sft	60	1762
66	2	HAMI	9f Gd/Fm	62	1939

SALIM 3 b c £6186

86	1	THIR	7f Good		1159*
81	4	LEIC	6f Gd/Sft		1576
70	9	KEMP	9f Gd/Fm	84	2085
72	4	NEWC	9f Gd/Fm	81	2988
79	3	CHES	10f Gd/Fm	80	3426
0	14	KEMP	8f Gd/Fm	79	3793 VIS

SALIX DANCER 3 b g £696

79	3	KEMP	8f Soft		1532
0	11	YARM	8f Good		1771
27a	6	SOUT	8f Aw		1977
0	14	YARM	10f Soft	75	4392

SALLY ANN 3 b f £0

2a	13	SOUT	8f Aw		36

SALLY GARDENS 3 b f £0

22a	11	LING	8f Aw	65	54
24a	7	LING	8f Aw		241
0a	10	SOUT	8f Aw		300

SALMON LADDER 8 b h £3295

85	4	DONC	12f Good		732
100	7	GOOD	14f Gd/Sft	100	1484 bl
97	4	EPSO	12f Good	96	1850
72	16	ASCO	12f Good	95	2069

SALORY 4 b c £1233

12a	9	LING	10f Aw	48	102
45a	3	WOLV	9f Aw		378 t
69	10	NEWM	10f Gd/Fm		1697
20a	8	LING	8f Aw	44	1915
42	9	KEMP	8f Gd/Fm	55	2752 t
62	2	SAND	8f Gd/Fm		2920
30	10	KEMP	8f Gd/Fm	52	3078
0	13	KEMP	7f Gd/Fm	55	3362 BL
0	20	WIND	10f Gd/Sft	52	4291

SALOUP 2 b f £0

0	14	WIND	6f Gd/Sft		4288

SALSA 2 b c £580

69	5	BATH	6f Gd/Sft		2550
76	3	NOTT	6f Good		3520

SALSIFY 4 b c £0

0	6	LING	14f Firm		3489

SALSKA 9 b m £1703

0	12	PONT	17f Good	67	1867
35	14	ASCO	16f Gd/Fm	63	2173
57	5	NEWC	16f Gd/Fm	63	2273
59	4	BEVE	16f Firm	58	2734
60	2	REDC	16f Gd/Fm	58	2866
53	5	REDC	16f Gd/Fm	60	2993
38	10	REDC	16f Firm	59	3331
53	6	CHES	16f Gd/Fm	59	3511
44	6	RIPO	16f Gd/Fm	52	3715 vis
0	7	BATH	17f Soft	48	4139

SALTAIRE 2 b f £0

29	9	SAND	5f Gd/Fm		2933

SALTRIO 2 b c £0

67	6	NOTT	8f Heavy		4504

SALTWOOD 2 b f £4784

60 8 NEWB 6f Firm   3449
76 4 SALI 7f Firm   3748
79 1 **AYR**   7f Soft   3962*
72 9 NEWM 7f Good 78 4157
0   14 NEWM 8f Good 78 4350

SALTY JACK 6 b g £33633

81a	1	LING	7f Aw	74	162*
67a	9	LING	7f Aw	79	337
82a	2	LING	7f Aw	79	423
86a	1	LING	8f Aw	81	485+
85a	3	LING	7f Aw		630
66	18	DONC	8f Good	91	733
77	13	NEWM	7f Gd/Sft	84	966
57	15	KEMP	8f Gd/Sft	84	1077
79	5	GOOD	7f Gd/Sft	80	1810
79	4	LING	8f Gd/Fm	79	2185
83	5	NEWM	8f Gd/Fm	79	2616
85	1	ASCO	8f Gd/Fm	79	3018*
85	3	ASCO	8f Gd/Fm	84	3338
60	9	EPSO	9f Good	85	3685
85	2	ASCO	8f Gd/Sft	84	4126
81	6	NEWM	8f Good	85	4348
0	19	NEWM	8f Soft	84	4545

SALUEM 3 b f £3810

76	3	YORK	10f Gd/Fm		1985
76	2	BATH	12f Gd/Fm		3517
76	2	KEMP	12f Soft		4040
73	5	NEWM	14f Gd/Fm	75	4213

SALVA 4 b f £0

49a	4	WOLV	8f Aw		920	
60	6	WARW	8f Soft		1062	
46	12	WIND	10f Gd/Fm		3045	t
0	17	GOOD	8f Good	60	3885	BL
47	7	GOOD	8f Soft	54	4066	

SALVAGE 5 b g £542

42	7	CATT	14f Gd/Fm	51	779
47	3	MUSS	14f Gd/Sft	47	903
39	7	NOTT	14f Gd/Sft	47	1087
24a	8	SOUT	16f Aw	47	1416
44	4	REDC	16f Good		1894
43	8	PONT	18f Firm	46	2176
32	5	MUSS	16f Gd/Sft		2536

SALVIANO 2 b g £0

35	12	YORK	8f Gd/Fm		3729
0	21	YORK	8f Soft		4281

SALVIATI 3 b c £2250

88	2	NEWB	6f Gd/Fm	85	1406
81	13	NEWM	6f Gd/Fm	88	1694

SALZGITTER 3 b f £1447

60	3	FOLK	7f Soft		961
72	3	SALI	10f Good		1343
64	7	KEMP	12f Gd/Fm		2751
69	6	SALI	12f Gd/Fm	76	3392
60	10	CHEP	10f Good	75	3870
64	3	BRIG	10f Heavy	72	4540

SAMADILLA 2 b f £9264

80	1	PONT	5f Good		2360*
78	4	DONC	5f Gd/Fm		2756
77	4	THIR	5f Gd/Fm	78	3145
80	1	**RIPO**	5f Gd/Fm	78	3712*
74	9	DONC	7f Gd/Fm	83	3860
76	4	HAYD	6f Soft	80	4090
75	3	YORK	6f Soft	75	4286

SAMARA MIDDLE EAST 2 b f £3542

86	6	ASCO	7f Good		4114
89	1	**AYR**	8f Heavy		4322*
96	6	SAIN	10f Soft		4556

SAMARA SONG 7 ch g £1440

49	10	WARW	8f Soft	64	817
30	7	WARW	11f Heavy	61	1003
56	5	BRIG	8f Firm	58	1330
59	2	YARM	7f Gd/Sft	56	1611

57	6	NEWM	8f Gd/Fm	56	1690
58	7	KEMP	8f Gd/Fm	59	1926
49	7	CARL	7f Gd/Fm	58	2241
47	4	CARL	8f Firm		2283
49	10	LEIC	7f Gd/Fm	56	2775
52	4	BATH	8f Firm	55	3623
51	10	LEIC	7f Firm	54	3839
39a	3	WOLV	8f Aw	47	4440

SAMARARDO 3 b c £5913

63a	2	WOLV	8f Aw		80
30a	11	SOUT	8f Aw	63	125
56a	3	WOLV	7f Aw		192
52	5	NOTT	10f Gd/Fm	58	2685
52	4	WARW	11f Gd/Fm	56	2842
50	6	NEWM	12f Gd/Fm	52	3167
47	4	EPSO	12f Gd/Fm	49	3417
54	2	FOLK	16f Gd/Fm	49	3588
58	1	**GOOD**	16f Soft	53	4075*
55	4	NOTT	16f Heavy	57	4508

SAMAWI 2 b c £0

65	8	DONC	7f Gd/Sft		4447

SAMEEAH 4 br f £0

3a	6	WOLV	9f Aw		378
18	7	FOLK	6f Gd/Fm		2291

SAMIYAH 4 b f £0

0a	14	SOUT	8f Aw		646

SAMMAL 4 b g £1240

25a	9	WOLV	5f Aw		639	BL
32a	10	SOUT	5f Aw	53	674	
49	5	SOUT	6f Good	53	802	
0	17	WARW	5f Heavy	51	1005	
0	12	CARL	6f Firm	49	1258	
49	4	CATT	6f Good		1664	
45	6	LEIC	6f Gd/Sft	46	1734	
47	2	CARL	6f Firm	45	2015	
0	14	NOTT	6f Aw	46	2192	
36	8	LEIC	6f Gd/Fm	46	2777	
25	6	CARL	6f Gd/Fm		3080	
34	9	YARM	6f Gd/Fm	43	3966	

SAMMIE DUROSE 3 b c £430

32a	5	WOLV	8f Aw	43	311	BL
41a	2	WOLV	9f Aw		382	
8a	11	SOUT	8f Aw	44	429	VIS
22a	8	SOUT	11f Aw	44	537	

SAMMYS SHUFFLE 5 b g £17530

54a	1	LING	10f Aw	50	22	bl
54a	3	LING	10f Aw	53	102	bl
56a	2	LING	10f Aw	53	161	bl
50a	5	LING	10f Aw	55	203	bl
58a	1	**LING**	10f Aw	55	220*	bl
56a	5	LING	10f Aw		268	bl
30a	8	LING	10f Aw	57	400	bl
36a	7	LING	12f Aw	57	441	bl
60a	1	**LING**	10f Aw	55	575*	bl
51a	5	LING	10f Aw	61	620	bl
59a	3	LING	10f Aw	59	632	bl
36a	7	LING	10f Aw	59	842	bl
40a	6	LING	10f Aw	59	880	bl
40	4	WIND	10f Gd/Sft	40	1100	bl
0	12	BRIG	12f Firm	40	1209	bl
39	2	BRIG	10f Gd/Sft	38	1509	bl
40	2	GOOD	9f Gd/Sft	40	1807	bl
35	3	WIND	10f Soft	41	2544	bl
43	2	BRIG	10f Gd/Fm	41	2727	bl
46	1	**EPSO**	10f Good	41	2790*	bl
48	2	SAND	8f Good	45	3227	bl
46	3	NEWM	10f Gd/Fm	45	3314	bl
41	5	WIND	10f Good	45	3356	bl
38	8	BRIG	10f Firm	48	3737	bl
37	12	GOOD	8f Good	48	3885	bl

SAMPOWER STAR 4 b c £141734

116	1	**LONG**	5f V		1320*

86	5	SAND	5f Soft		1566
115	2	ASCO	6f Good		2115
117	2	HAYD	6f Gd/Sft		3784
116	1	**ASCO**	6f Gd/Sft		4125+

SAMSAAM 3 b c £47644

74	1	**WIND**	12f Heavy	66	937*
81	1	**DONC**	15f Gd/Sft	73	1071*
93	1	**HAYD**	14f Soft	81	1821*
101	3	ASCO	16f Good		2068
103	2	NEWM	15f Gd/Fm		2594
109	1	**CHAN**	15f Soft		3065*
107	3	GOOD	14f Good		3645
84	7	NEWM	16f Good		4351

SAMUM 3 ch c £322581

122	1	**BADE**	12f V		3849*
119	6	LONG	12f Good		4262

SAMWAR 8 b g £14474

58a	8	WOLV	5f Aw	72	40	bl
74a	1	**SOUT**	5f Aw		71+	vis
76a	1	**WOLV**	5f Aw	69	139*	vis
71a	5	WOLV	5f Aw	75	146	vis
71a	7	WOLV	5f Aw	75	191	vis
74a	1	**SOUT**	5f Aw		214*	vis
71a	4	WOLV	5f Aw		272	vis
36a	9	WOLV	6f Aw		379	vis
51a	6	WOLV	6f Aw		465	vis
73a	2	WOLV	5f Aw	71	491	vis
72a	2	WOLV	6f Aw	69	518	vis
64a	6	WOLV	6f Aw	73	678	vis
26a	10	SOUT	6f Aw	73	697	vis
46a	6	WOLV	6f Aw		719	vis
58a	3	WOLV	5f Aw		753	vis
57a	2	WOLV	5f Aw		919	vis
34	9	DONC	6f Gd/Sft		1068	vis
54a	1	**WOLV**	5f Aw		1237*	vis
57a	2	WOLV	5f Aw		1392	vis
58a	2	SOUT	5f Aw	55	1806	vis
51a	5	WOLV	5f Aw	55	1976	vis
50a	6	WOLV	5f Aw	58	2078	vis
58a	3	LING	5f Aw		2650	vis
58a	2	WOLV	5f Aw	57	3271	vis
49a	6	SOUT	5f Aw	57	4156	vis
55a	3	WOLV	5f Aw	57	4223	vis
51a	5	WOLV	6f Aw	56	4358	vis
0a	P	WOLV	6f Aw	56	4442	vis

SAN DIMAS 3 gr c £0

69	9	LEIC	8f Good		789	
48	7	NOTT	10f Heavy	64	1022	
54	6	CARL	8f Firm	60	1255	
51	9	REDC	10f Firm	60	1299	BL
0	13	REDC	10f Good	56	1895	

SAN GLAMORE MELODY 6 b g £842

0a	12	WOLV	8f Aw		393
34a	3	WOLV	8f Aw		490
59a	3	WOLV	9f Aw		578

SAN MICHEL 8 b g £1006

0a	13	SOUT	7f Aw	50	69	bl
49a	6	WOLV	6f Aw		132	bl
41a	3	LING	6f Aw	44	148	
31a	7	SOUT	6f Aw		199	
34a	5	SOUT	6f Aw	44	218	VIS
8a	9	WOLV	6f Aw	41	432	
19a	7	SOUT	7f Aw		598	
10a	5	SOUT	7f Aw		693	
39a	4	WOLV	6f Aw		1139	vis
48	3	HAMI	6f Gd/Fm	46	1941	vis
0a	10	SOUT	7f Aw	34	2637	vis
37	3	CARL	6f Gd/Fm		3080	vis
0	17	HAMI	6f Gd/Sft	46	3377	vis

SAN SALVADOR 3 b c £46111

85	3	HAYD	6f Gd/Fm		808
92	2	NEWM	6f Good		956

83	1	**PONT**	6f Gd/Sft		1105*	
102	1	**LING**	6f Gd/Sft	83	1285*	
94	1	**NOTT**	6f Good		1409*	

SAN SEBASTIAN 6 ch g £85011
109	4	ASCO	16f Gd/Sft		1109	bl
103	6	SAND	16f Soft		1565	bl
116	4	ASCO	20f Good		2114	bl
117	3	GOOD	16f Good		3106	bl
101	6	DONC	16f Good		3877	bl
120	1	LONG	20f Good		4264*	bl
119	2	LONG	16f Heavy		4494	bl

SANAPTA 2 b f £0
40	10	WARW	15f Gd/Fm		3911
42a	7	WOLV	7f Aw		4385

SAND BANKES 2 ch c £7927
65a	2	SOUT	5f Aw		856	
39a	7	WOLV	5f Aw		1136	
48	6	BEVE	5f Good		1443	
70	1	**CHEP**	6f Heavy		1553*	VIS
68	2	CATT	6f Soft		1679	vis
74	1	**YARM**	7f Gd/Fm		1950*	vis
79	1	**MUSS**	7f Gd/Fm		2201*	vis
54	6	SALI	7f Gd/Sft	77	2468	vis
62	5	BRIG	7f Gd/Fm		2723	

SAND HAWK 5 ch g £21369
54a	1	**WOLV**	7f Aw		173*	bl
59a	2	WOLV	7f Aw	49	193	bl
56a	2	SOUT	6f Aw	54	246	bl
61a	1	**SOUT**	7f Aw	54	282*	VIS
67a	1	**WOLV**	7f Aw	60	323*	vis
65a	4	SOUT	7f Aw	64	368	vis
71a	2	SOUT	7f Aw	66	539	vis
66a	3	SOUT	7f Aw	64	587	vis
70a	5	SOUT	7f Aw	70	687	vis
0a	14	SOUT	6f Aw	69	2820	bl
34	7	CATT	7f Gd/Fm	41	3200	bl
40	4	HAMI	6f Gd/Sft	41	3377	bl
46	1	**CATT**	7f Good	41	3440*	bl
38	7	REDC	8f Gd/Fm	47	3634	bl
42	6	EPSO	7f Good	44	3765	bl
51	2	CHEP	7f Good	44	3871	bl
52	2	NEWC	7f Heavy	49	4428	bl
53	2	YARM	7f Soft	49	4513	bl

SAND PARTRIDGE 3 b f £7060
91	2	NAAS	7f Yldg		1751
95	2	LEOP	8f Gd/Fm		2570

SAND PEBBLES 3 b f £0
31	10	WIND	10f Good		3189

SANDABAR 7 b g £9357
46	10	NOTT	10f Good	60	786	t
45	9	BEVE	10f Heavy	60	975	t
60	3	MUSS	12f Gd/Fm	59	1432	t
60	2	MUSS	12f Firm	59	2048	t
65	1	**MUSS**	16f Gd/Fm	59	2203*	t
60	5	MUSS	14f Firm	66	2375	t
54	6	REDC	16f Gd/Fm	64	2866	t
49	3	CATT	12f Gd/Fm		3202	t
48	4	CARL	12f Firm		3570	
46	10	WARW	11f Gd/Fm	51	3915	t

SANDAL 2 b f £957
63	3	BRIG	5f Gd/Fm		1124	
70	4	CHES	5f Firm		1249	
68	5	DONC	6f Good		1513	
41	12	CHEP	6f Gd/Fm		2488	BL

SANDBAGGEDAGAIN 6 b g £1512
65	11	YORK	14f Firm	76	1329	
67	5	HAYD	14f Gd/Sft	74	1536	
65	5	YORK	12f Firm	71	2002	
70	2	HAYD	14f Gd/Fm	69	2455	
64	9	ASCO	16f Gd/Fm	70	2953	
61	4	BEVE	16f Good	70	3395	bl
57	7	CHES	16f Soft	69	4071	

SANDLES 2 b g £3402
77a	1	**WOLV**	5f Good		1236*	
76	5	BEVE	5f Gd/Fm		2483	
72	4	GOOD	6f Gd/Fm	74	3062	
72	4	BEVE	7f Gd/Fm	73	3411	
39	14	NEWC	8f Gd/Sft	72	3704	
67	7	WARW	7f Gd/Fm	72	3913	
66	5	LING	7f Soft	70	4191	
70	4	YARM	8f Soft	68	4393	

SANDMASON 3 ch c £11957
108	2	NEWM	10f Gd/Fm		1151
102	2	YORK	10f Firm		1340

SANDMOOR CHAMBRAY 9 ch g £0
0	14	WOLV	12f Gd/Fm	73	1307
51	7	DONC	12f Good	71	1518

SANDORRA 2 b f £669
67	7	YORK	6f Good		2692
51	6	NEWC	7f Gd/Fm		2985
66	4	YORK	7f Soft		4277
0	25	NEWM	6f Good		4345

SANDOWN CLANTINO 3 b f £0
6	9	LEIC	12f Gd/Fm		3218
31	8	BEVE	12f Gd/Fm		3671
0	14	THIR	8f Gd/Sft		3775
9a	9	WOLV	7f Aw		4384

SANDPOINT 4 b f £330
0	23	WIND	6f Gd/Fm	45	1196	
39	3	BATH	6f Firm	39	1994	
28	12	BATH	5f Gd/Sft	40	2555	
17	10	BATH	5f Firm		2788	
0	19	LING	6f Firm	39	3578	VIS

SANDROS BOY 3 b g £1064
55	3	RIPO	10f Gd/Fm		2105
53	2	CATT	14f Gd/Fm		2439
50	9	HAYD	11f Gd/Sft		3265
22	6	CATT	14f Soft		4002

SANGRA 3 b f £1812
55	4	AYR	9f Gd/Fm		1632	
63	2	NEWM	7f Firm	65	1855	
56	5	EPSO	9f Good	64	2795	
48	13	LING	7f Firm	62	3279	
59	2	BRIG	7f Firm		3739	BL
25	9	BATH	8f Soft	58	4435	bl

SANNAAN 2 b c £0
61	8	SAND	7f Gd/Fm		2494

SANS RIVALE 5 ch m £0
0a	13	SOUT	6f Aw	40	250
14a	7	SOUT	6f Aw	36	280
0a	12	SOUT	6f Aw	42	499

SANTA ISOBEL 2 ch f £1366
79	3	NEWB	5f Gd/Fm		1782
70	3	NEWB	6f Sft/Hvy		4471

SANTA LUCIA 4 b f £6032
21a	10	SOUT	14f Aw	57	37
0	15	PONT	10f Soft	63	871
58	2	CARL	12f Firm		1253
45	6	AYR	13f Gd/Fm		1657
0	13	PONT	17f Good	57	1867
50	1	**HAMI**	11f Firm		2393*
50	1	**HAMI**	11f Gd/Fm		2800*
44	4	NEWC	12f Good	46	3036
31	13	HAMI	12f Gd/Sft	44	3827

SANTANDRE 4 ch c £14580
70a	4	WOLV	5f Aw	73	40
71a	5	WOLV	7f Aw	72	143
70a	3	SOUT	6f Aw	70	218
41a	12	WOLV	6f Aw	70	258
55a	7	WOLV	9f Aw	70	349
62a	6	WOLV	6f Aw	68	435
67a	4	WOLV	8f Aw	66	521
69a	1	**WOLV**	7f Aw		623*
70a	1	**SOUT**	7f Aw	65	687*
69a	5	WOLV	7f Good	69	1235
0	13	DONC	7f Good	56	1559
51	7	CATT	7f Soft	54	1680
28	12	BEVE	7f Firm	52	1920
0	15	THIR	7f Gd/Fm	52	2063
47	5	CARL	7f Firm	47	2823
0	12	BEVE	7f Good	47	2882
41	6	BRIG	6f Gd/Fm	45	3243
48	3	CATT	7f Good	45	3440
17	14	EPSO	7f Good	47	3765
60a	8	WOLV	7f Aw		4224
0	14	DONC	7f Soft		4461

SANTIBURI GIRL 3 b f £18927
43	13	WARW	6f Heavy		888
60	6	NOTT	6f Gd/Fm	68	1273
66	1	**LING**	6f Good		1397*
53	7	YARM	8f Gd/Sft	69	1610
60	9	NEWB	7f Gd/Fm	69	1787
66	2	LEIC	6f Firm	66	2031
65	3	LING	7f Firm	67	2325
64	7	DONC	6f Gd/Fm	67	2577
60	9	LEIC	7f Firm	66	2918
69	1	**NEWB**	10f Gd/Fm	64	3178*
71	1	**REDC**	11f Firm	66	3329*
74	2	EPSO	10f Gd/Fm	72	3415
70	4	RIPO	12f Gd/Fm	72	3467
64	8	KEMP	10f Gd/Fm	72	3794
70	6	SAND	14f Gd/Fm	72	3948
64	6	GOOD	12f Soft		4061
61	6	BRIG	10f Gd/Sft	71	4118

SANTIBURI LAD 3 b g £4191
70	1	**RIPO**	5f Gd/Fm		3462*
75	2	PONT	6f Soft		4233
55	14	YORK	6f Soft		4287
54	11	DONC	7f Gd/Sft	69	4452

SANTISIMA TRINIDAD 2 b f £0
56	11	DONC	6f Good		1513
51	5	HAMI	8f Gd/Sft		3532
0	13	AYR	6f Soft		3958

SANTOLINA 2 b f £22564
87	1	LEIC	6f Firm		2029*
94	2	NEWM	6f Gd/Fm		2344
94	4	ASCO	6f Gd/Fm		2996
101	1	**KEMP**	6f Gd/Fm		3797+
100	7	NEWM	6f Good		4159

SAONE ET LOIRE 3 £0
0	11	LONG	8f V		1319

SAORSIE 2 b g £3575
0	13	NEWM	6f Gd/Fm		3162
0	11	SALI	6f Gd/Fm		3387
42	7	LING	6f Firm		3757
63	8	CHEP	8f Good		3867
58	1	**BRIG**	7f Soft	52	4416*
57	3	BRIG	8f Heavy	58	4538

SAPHIRE 4 ch f £5330
0	24	THIR	5f Soft	82	926
80	5	REDC	5f Gd/Sft	80	1133
90	6	NOTT	6f Good		1410
91	5	KEMP	5f Soft		1529
0	17	YORK	5f Gd/Fm	89	1980
86	2	HAYD	5f Gd/Fm	84	3322
86	4	SAND	5f Good	86	3473
73	8	HAYD	5f Gd/Sft	83	3788
86	6	NEWM	5f Good	86	4015
0	15	ASCO	5f Gd/Sft	90	4129
0	16	DONC	5f Soft	86	4466

SAPPHIRE MILL 3 gr f £0
36	6	SOUT	6f Soft		1605
0	11	LING	6f Gd/Fm		2183

SAPPHIRE SON 8 ch g £0
0	14	BRIG	12f Gd/Fm		893

SARA MOON CLASSIC 5 b g £0

15a 8 WOLV 9f Aw 259 bl

SARAFAN 3 b c £7200
115	5	ASCO	8f Good		2066	
99	3	CURR	9f Good		2410	
67	6	GOOD	8f Good		3647	

SARAH MADELINE 3 b f £0
48	5	DONC	7f Good		717	

SARATOV 2 b c £25710
77	3	HAYD	6f Gd/Fm		2454	
91	1	YORK	7f Gd/Fm		2649*	
98	1	ASCO	7f Gd/Fm		3015*	
96	3	YORK	7f Good		3537	
54	9	YORK	7f Soft	98	4279	

SARENA PRIDE 3 b f £5180
71	7	KEMP	9f Good		727	
73	5	WIND	6f Good	76	852	
60	9	BRIG	6f Gd/Fm	76	1126	
76	2	KEMP	6f Soft	74	1531	
76	4	EPSO	7f Gd/Sft	76	1826	
76	3	KEMP	8f Gd/Fm	76	2084	
71	8	GOOD	7f Gd/Fm	76	2128	
44	12	LEIC	7f Gd/Fm	76	2918	
60	10	EPSO	7f Good	76	3414	
0	14	LING	8f Firm	72	3831	

SARENA SPECIAL 3 b c £2050
74	2	KEMP	7f Soft		1018	
63	5	LING	7f Gd/Sft		1263	
73	7	KEMP	8f Soft		1532	
79	3	SAND	7f Good		1963	BL
0	18	GOOD	6f Good	74	2355	bl
70	4	FOLK	7f Good		2621	bl
39	12	WIND	8f Gd/Fm		3048	bl

SARI 4 b f £0
59a	9	LING	8f Aw	76	7	
46a	10	WOLV	7f Aw	73	79	BL

SARMATIAN 9 br g £0
15	11	HAMI	8f Good		847	t
0	13	HAMI	8f Gd/Fm	50	1190	t
0	13	HAMI	11f Gd/Fm	40	1361	t
0	14	MUSS	9f Firm	30	1689	t

SARPEDON 4 ch c £0
19a	9	SOUT	7f Aw		367	
29a	5	SOUT	6f Aw	34	425	
27a	9	SOUT	8f Aw		452	
18a	8	SOUT	12f Aw		498	BL
47a	5	SOUT	12f Aw		510	bl
37a	5	SOUT	12f Aw		556	bl
32a	6	SOUT	12f Aw		646	bl
33	7	CATT	7f Gd/Fm		778	

SARSON 4 b c £488
79	8	LING	6f Good	83	1676	
0	19	GOOD	6f Good	81	2355	
59	11	NEWM	6f Firm	79	3297	
69	7	NEWB	7f Soft	81	3481	
44	13	HAYD	7f Soft	75	3785	
60	7	CHES	6f Soft		4069	
71	4	SAND	7f Soft	70	4204	
65	6	YARM	7f Soft	70	4513	
66	8	NEWM	7f Soft	70	4547	

SARTEANO 6 ch m £224
19a	6	SOUT	8f Aw	30	340	
21a	3	SOUT	12f Aw	24	412	
14a	6	WOLV	16f Aw	20	494	
17a	5	WOLV	9f Aw	27	529	

SARTORIAL 4 b c £30080
99	1	HAYD	5f Gd/Sft		808*	
94	4	NEWB	5f Soft	95	914	
101	1	NEWM	6f Gd/Fm	95	1173*	
94	8	GOOD	6f Firm	100	3152	
91	7	SAND	5f Good	100	3473	
0	16	ASCO	5f Gd/Sft	100	4129	VIS

SARUM 14 b g £0

17a 9 SOUT 7f Aw 44 598 e

SASEEDO 10 ch g £0
24a	9	LING	10f Aw		3	
32a	11	LING	10f Aw	54	23	
1a	8	WOLV	12f Aw	47	408	bl
28a	9	LING	8f Aw		505	bl
32a	4	LING	12f Aw	37	620	bl
14a	10	LING	12f Aw		650	bl
14a	8	LING	12f Aw		775	bl
35	8	BRIG	10f Firm		1331	
21a	6	LING	12f Aw		2181	bl
0	12	SAND	10f Gd/Fm	46	2527	
40	8	LING	12f Firm		3281	
0a	15	LING	12f Aw		4101	bl

SASH 3 b f £420
57	5	LING	9f Firm		2322	
62	7	WIND	8f Soft		2548	
58	5	KEMP	8f Firm		2871	
51	9	WIND	8f Good	62	3643	
52	10	CHEP	7f Good	58	3871	
46a	7	LING	8f Aw	54	4330	
47a	3	LING	10f Aw	50	4482	

SASHA 3 ch c £539
61	4	BEVE	5f Gd/Fm		2519	
50	10	LEIC	5f Gd/Fm		2919	BL
41	8	DONC	5f Gd/Fm	50	3161	
48	4	THIR	5f Gd/Sft	47	3781	
50	10	REDC	5f Gd/Sft		4220	

SASHA STAR 2 b c £0
43	8	FOLK	7f Gd/Fm		2290	
46	6	EPSO	7f Good		2791	

SASHAY 2 b f £0
0	14	BATH	6f Soft		4138	

SATARRA 3 ch c £1171
70a	2	LING	10f Aw		2213	
76	4	KEMP	12f Gd/Fm		2751	
75	7	BATH	12f Gd/Sft		3818	

SATEEN 3 ch f £0
63	5	WARW	8f Soft		1062	

SATIRE 3 br f £854
42a	5	SOUT	8f Aw		1977	
37	10	WARW	8f Good		2464	
0	11	CATT	12f Gd/Fm	44	2746	
0a	12	SOUT	14f Aw	47	4370	
43	2	NOTT	10f Heavy	40	4509	

SATWA BOULEVARD 5 ch m £1206
42a	8	SOUT	8f Aw	50	326	
19a	7	SOUT	8f Aw	47	384	
25a	10	LING	10f Aw	44	618	
25	10	WIND	12f Gd/Fm	37	748	
21	12	RIPO	12f Soft	37	822	
27	11	BRIG	10f Firm		1210	
33	2	BRIG	8f Firm	32	2043	t
0	15	SALI	6f Gd/Fm	31	2230	t
0	14	WIND	8f Good	44	3355	t
30	7	BRIG	7f Firm		3559	t
35	3	BRIG	8f Firm		3738	t

SATYR 2 b c £0
0	14	LING	7f Soft		4268	

SATZUMA 3 ch c £0
0	14	YARM	8f Good		1771	
56	5	WARW	8f Good		2464	t
43	10	YARM	7f Good	64	3030	t
0	14	YARM	8f Good	57	3971	t

SAUCE TARTAR 2 ch f £5086
61	6	NEWM	6f Gd/Fm		2618	
72	1	FOLK	7f Gd/Fm		3039*	
50	9	NEWB	7f Gd/Fm	76	3068	
58	8	NEWC	8f Gd/Sft	76	3704	
73	3	YARM	7f Firm	72	3922	

SAUDIA 2 b f £3640
85	1	PONT	6f Soft		1700*	

SAVANNA MISS 2 b f £0
66	5	NOTT	5f Good		2009	
39	7	MUSS	5f Gd/Sft		2532	
17	9	LEIC	5f Gd/Fm		2772	
29	6	WIND	5f Good		3639	
25	9	BRIG	5f Soft		4171	
0	14	BATH	6f Soft		4431	

SAVANNAH QUEEN 3 b f £0
69	5	LEIC	7f Good		794	
48	8	PONT	6f Soft		877	
52	7	PONT	6f Gd/Sft		1105	
58	5	YARM	8f Gd/Sft	65	1610	
0	11	REDC	10f Good	62	1895	

SAVE THE PLANET 3 b f £0
59	9	LEIC	7f Good		794	
0	11	WIND	8f Heavy		934	
58	7	HAYD	11f Gd/Sft		1539	
0	15	WARW	11f Good	58	2463	
23a	7	SOUT	11f Aw	54	2945	BL

SAVE THE POUND 2 br c £0
37	5	NEWC	7f Gd/Fm		2271	
62	7	BEVE	7f Gd/Sft		3051	
43	7	REDC	7f Gd/Fm		3635	
46	6	AYR	8f Soft	60	3990	

SAVED BY THE BELLE 3 b f £0
26	5	BRIG	8f Soft		4175	

SAVING LIVES ATSEA 2 ch c £0
47	6	WIND	5f Gd/Fm		1426	
49	10	NEWM	6f Good		2854	
61	7	WIND	6f Good		3638	

SAVOIR FAIRE 4 b f £0
29	10	PONT	8f Firm	48	2180	
28	8	WARW	8f Good	38	2460	
17	9	RIPO	8f Gd/Fm		2834	VIS
20	9	NEWC	12f Good		3247	

SAVOIRE VIVRE 3 b c £20478
100	1	ASCO	10f Gd/Fm		2957*	
109	2	NEWB	13f Gd/Fm		3483	

SAWBO LAD 2 b c £2331
72	6	WARW	5f Soft		812	
73	8	ASCO	5f Gd/Sft		1107	
53	12	CHEP	6f Gd/Sft		1798	
0	16	LING	7f Gd/Fm		2182	
72	1	FOLK	7f Gd/Fm		3582*	
23	13	BATH	8f Gd/Fm	68	3817	
52a	4	SOUT	7f Aw		4369	

SAWLAJAN 9 ch g £0
0	17	SALI	14f Firm	57	1180	

SAWWAAH 3 b c £4615
85	6	NEWM	8f Firm		1188	
88	1	NOTT	8f Heavy		4505*	

SAYEDAH 2 b f £36029
92	2	GOOD	7f Good		3108	
92	2	NEWB	7f Firm		3985	
108	1	NEWM	7f Good		4356*	

SAYING GRACE 2 b f £6800
96	3	CURR	6f Gd/Sft		4060	
97	3	CORK	6f Gd/Fm		4315	

SCACHMATT 3 b c £6830
61	10	DONC	10f Gd/Sft		1054	
86	2	THIR	12f Good		1386	
81	4	GOOD	12f Gd/Sft		1808	
82	2	RIPO	10f Gd/Fm		3012	
84	1	YARM	10f Gd/Fm		3381*	
0	12	YARM	10f Firm	84	3941	

SCAFELL 3 b c £3675
51	8	DONC	10f Gd/Sft		731	
63a	2	LING	5f Aw		883	
51	12	NOTT	5f Firm		1266	VIS
69	5	DONC	5f Good		1516	vis
64	3	MUSS	5f Firm		1688	vis
64	1	HAMI	5f Firm		2096*	vis

SCAPAVIA — (top of column, partial entry)

35	10	SAND	5f Gd/Fm	64	2934	vis
60	8	LEIC	7f Firm	61	3839	
0	12	BEVE	7f Stt/Hvy	60	4044	vis
0	19	DONC	7f Gd/Sft	58	4452	BL

SCAPAVIA 2 b f £0

0	15	WIND	6f Gd/Sft		4289	

SCARLET LIVERY 4 b f £0

0	18	REDC	8f Firm	54	1296	
0	16	PONT	10f Good	54	1496	
31	9	HAMI	9f Gd/Fm	47	1939	
0	16	THIR	8f Gd/Fm	42	3344	
50	5	BEVE	10f Gd/Fm		3672	
25	8	THIR	8f Gd/Fm		3775	
0a	13	SOUT	11f Aw		4151	

SCARLET TANAGER 3 ch f £0

9a	10	SOUT	8f Aw		36	

SCARLET WOMAN 3 b f £0

0	17	NEWM	8f Firm		1188	
38a	8	SOUT	11f Aw		1502	

SCARLETT RIBBON 3 b f £5115

80	8	MAIS	6f Heavy		99	
96	2	LING	7f Gd/Sft		1283	
82	5	NEWM	8f Firm		2289	
81	9	NEWM	6f Good	95	4198	

SCARLETTA 3 b f £308

68	4	HAYD	11f Gd/Fm		1165	

SCARPE ROSSE 2 b f £0

80	5	NEWM	7f Gd/Fm		3459	
72	6	KEMP	7f Gd/Fm		3789	

SCARROTTOO 2 ch g £0

54	6	NEWM	7f Good		4344	
52	7	NEWM	8f Gd/Sft		4531	

SCARTEEN FOX 3 ch c £1650

110	4	NEWM	7f Good		950	
93	19	NEWM	8f Gd/Fm		1171	
109	5	CURR	8f Gd/Sft		1623	
97	11	ASCO	7f Good		2087	
98	8	NEWC	6f Firm		2335	

SCARTEEN SISTER 2 ch f £554

60	3	LING	6f Gd/Fm		2760	
54	8	KEMP	7f Gd/Fm		3074	

SCENE 5 b m £12356

38	16	DONC	8f Gd/Fm	76	715	
80	1	LEIC	8f Gd/Sft	76	831*	
61	7	THIR	8f Soft	79	931	
62	8	EPSO	10f Heavy	78	1031	
49	14	ASCO	8f Gd/Sft	78	1113	
69	7	HAYD	8f Soft	76	1490	
69	9	REDC	10f Gd/Sft	76	1561	
44	11	EPSO	9f Gd/Sft	74	1829	vis
65	11	YORK	8f Good	72	3810	
58	10	REDC	8f Gd/Sft	71	4217	
69	4	YORK	9f Heavy	69	4300	
79	1	NEWM	8f Good	69	4340*	
79	3	NEWB	10f Sft/Hv	78	4473	
77	6	NEWM	8f Soft	78	4545	

SCENIC LADY 4 b f £657

0	12	BRIG	10f Gd/Fm		1933	
0a	13	LING	12f Aw		2181	
23	2	BRIG	12f Firm	21	2904	BL
17	5	BRIG	12f Gd/Fm	28	3260	bl
34	4	BRIG	10f Firm		3526	
6	10	BRIG	12f Soft	30	4176	

SCENTED AIR 3 b f £0

48	8	WARW	8f Gd/Fm		3914	
59	5	NOTT	10f Heavy		4412	

SCHATZI 3 gr f £572

20	11	PONT	6f Soft		872	
56	2	NOTT	6f Gd/Sft		1081	
0	11	CARL	6f Gd/Sft		1723	
0	15	BEVE	5f Firm	55	1923	
37	9	AYR	7f Good		3364	

(continued)

47	5	CATT	6f Soft		4255	VIS
21	4	MUSS	8f Soft		4519	vis

SCHEHERAZADE 2 b f £0

0	19	DONC	8f Gd/Sft		4445	

SCHEMING 3 br g £9818

82	1	HAYD	12f Gd/Fm		3324*	
70	6	DONC	10f Gd/Fm		3865	
0	14	CHES	16f Soft	79	4071	
62	8	YORK	12f Soft	79	4280	
71	1	DONC	10f Gd/Sft	65	4448*	

SCHNITZEL 4 b f £0

49a	9	WOLV	7f Aw	75	79	

SCISSOR RIDGE 8 ch g £7245

58a	1	LING	7f Aw	52	29*	
57a	3	LING	7f Aw	58	59	
38a	10	LING	7f Aw	57	162	
55a	4	LING	7f Aw	56	239	
57a	3	LING	8f Aw	55	336	
57a	2	WOLV	8f Aw	55	411	
54a	4	LING	8f Aw	57	463	
57a	2	LING	8f Aw	56	594	
48a	6	LING	10f Aw	57	632	
55a	4	LING	8f Aw	57	776	
29a	10	WOLV	9f Aw	56	1037	
50	2	LING	7f Soft	44	1542	
51	3	NEWB	7f Gd/Sft	52	1590	
34	8	CHEP	7f Gd/Sft	47	1799	
40	6	GOOD	6f Gd/Fm	47	2124	
41	8	LING	8f Gd/Sft	52	2185	
42	5	GOOD	7f Good	48	2303	
31	9	SALI	7f Gd/Fm	46	3294	
43	5	NEWB	6f Firm	46	3455	
27	3	SALI	8f Firm	44	3753	
71	8	GOOD	7f Good		3884	
47a	8	LING	8f Aw	55	4330	

SCONCED 5 ch g £260

29a	3	WOLV	16f Aw	32	190	VIS
6a	7	WOLV	15f Aw	35	277	vis
12a	9	WOLV	16f Aw	35	482	vis

SCOTISH LAW 2 ch g £4349

74	2	CHEP	6f Gd/Fm		2972	
74	1	EPSO	6f Gd/Fm		3400*	
66	12	DONC	6f Firm		3888	
59	10	GOOD	8f Soft	76	4076	

SCOTLAND BAY 5 b m £0

7a	11	SOUT	7f Aw	52	75	
22a	11	LING	8f Aw		156	VIS
15a	8	WOLV	9f Aw	42	405	
0	13	LING	7f Gd/Sft		838	

SCOTTISH MEMORIES 4 ch g £3600

105	3	CURR	9f Gd/Sft		4059	

SCOTTISH SONG 7 b g £0

0	13	NOTT	16f Soft	40	3978	

SCOTTISH SPICE 3 b f £7190

77	6	NEWB	8f Soft	88	912	
74	13	NEWM	8f Firm	88	1183	
70	15	GOOD	9f Gd/Sft	86	1452	
83	5	GOOD	10f Gd/Fm	83	2358	
82	8	GOOD	9f Good	82	3658	
77	9	DONC	10f Firm	82	3899	
71	D	PONT	10f Soft	81	4085	
83	2	SAND	8f Soft	79	4206	
73	10	NEWM	8f Good	82	4340	
82	3	NOTT	8f Heavy	81	4506	

SCOTTY GUEST 3 b c £0

51	14	NEWM	10f Gd/Sft	80	979	
60	10	NEWB	8f Gd/Fm		1786	t

SCOTTYS FUTURE 2 b c £0

0	22	NEWM	6f Good		4341	
65	8	YARM	6f Heavy		4479	
68	9	DONC	6f Gd/Sft		4575	

SCRAMBLE 2 ch c £1435

73	3	NEWM	7f Good		4344	t

SCRATCH THE DOVE 3 ch f £0

0	14	LEIC	7f Good		794	
0	15	WARW	8f Heavy		884	
0	6	HAYD	11f Gd/Fm		1165	

SCREAMIN GEORGINA 2 b f £4637

59	7	THIR	5f Good		1381	
64	2	LEIC	5f Gd/Fm		2507	t
63	6	LEIC	5f Gd/Fm		2772*	t
66	1	FOLK	5f Gd/Fm		3038*	t
57	9	BEVE	5f Good	70	3394	t
66	5	MUSS	5f Gd/Fm	68	3743	t
56	10	LING	5f Good	65	4098	t

SCROOGE 4 b c £773

43a	3	WOLV	7f Aw		276	
58a	2	LING	8f Aw		316	
52a	5	LING	7f Aw		398	

SEA DANZIG 7 ch g £10774

57a	5	LING	12f Aw	65	245	
36a	7	LING	13f Aw	63	317	
66a	1	LING	14f Aw		335*	
31a	7	LING	14f Aw	64	374	
53a	4	LING	10f Aw	64	575	
67a	2	LING	14f Aw	64	618	BL
68a	2	WOLV	12f Aw		679	bl
71a	1	LING	14f Aw		772*	
49a	7	LING	10f Aw	70	880	bl
22	9	EPSO	12f Heavy	60	1030	bl
38	10	BRIG	12f Gd/Fm	57	1128	
0	24	NEWM	12f Firm	52	1852	
32	11	EPSO	12f Gd/Sft	49	2429	
46	4	BATH	10f Gd/Sft	49	2552	
0	16	BRIG	10f Gd/Fm	44	2727	
51	1	SALI	14f Gd/Fm	45	2982*	
40	10	SALI	14f Gd/Fm	53	3424	
48	5	BATH	17f Firm	53	3625	
37	10	KEMP	14f Gd/Fm	50	3800	
30	9	SAND	14f Gd/Fm	45	3948	
55a	7	LING	12f Aw		4101	
41a	8	LING	12f Aw	65	4271	bl

SEA DEER 11 ch g £0

61	8	YARM	6f Gd/Fm		1952	
71	11	NEWM	7f Gd/Fm	77	2133	
64	10	DONC	6f Gd/Fm		2580	
66	6	KEMP	8f Gd/Fm	75	2752	
54	9	YARM	7f Firm	72	2899	
59	9	YARM	7f Good	70	3238	
61	5	NEWM	6f Good	66	3613	

SEA DRIFT 3 gr f £6412

74	5	YARM	7f Gd/Fm		1951	
74	3	WARW	8f Good		2465	
74	1	NEWM	7f Gd/Fm		2860*	
64	3	REDC	7f Gd/Fm		2994	
43	13	NEWM	8f Gd/Fm	72	3317	
70	2	YARM	7f Good	70	3666	
63	7	LING	7f Soft	70	4192	

SEA EMPEROR 3 br g £1130

32	12	WARW	7f Heavy	58	887	
50	3	NOTT	8f Gd/Sft	55	1085	
0	16	REDC	10f Firm	51	1299	
46	4	HAYD	11f Gd/Fm	49	2453	
43	4	CARL	9f Firm	48	2825	
42	3	CARL	8f Gd/Fm	47	3082	VIS
0	15	HAYD	8f Gd/Fm	47	3288	vis
41	4	CHEP	7f Good	44	3873	vis

SEA GOD 9 ch g £0

0a	15	SOUT	11f Aw		178	
0a	12	SOUT	11f Aw		455	
0a	11	SOUT	16f Aw	28	502	
14a	10	SOUT	8f Aw		684	

SEA HAZE 3 ch c £1200

0	16	WIND	6f Firm	74	1289	

SEA ISLE (continued)

70	2	CHEP	5f Gd/Sft	71	1795	
64	8	BATH	6f Firm	72	1999	
61	8	SALI	5f Gd/Sft	72	2266	
0	12	SALI	6f Good	70	2690	
0	13	WIND	6f Gd/Fm	67	2885	
0	19	GOOD	5f Soft	63	4065	BL

SEA ISLE 4 ch f £0

40a	8	WOLV	8f Aw	64	3769
22a	10	WOLV	8f Aw	64	4021

SEA MARK 4 br c £7631

0	14	KEMP	7f Good	84	725
85	1	**NEWM**	8f Gd/Fm	80	4215*

SEA MINSTREL 4 b f £0

0a	10	SOUT	6f Aw	32	1421

SEA RAY 2 gr g £0

0	13	WIND	5f Gd/Fm	849
41	8	BRIG	5f Good	1124

SEA SPOUSE 9 ch g £0

49a	4	LING	10f Aw		375
18a	8	LING	8f Aw		574
30a	6	LING	10f Aw	44	620

SEA SQUIRT 3 b c £14570

67a	2	SOUT	8f Aw		198
77a	2	WOLV	9f Aw		720
80	3	THIR	12f Soft		906
0	11	WARW	12f Soft	78	1064
74	4	HAMI	11f Gd/Fm		1193
74	1	**CARL**	8f Firm		2018*
67	6	BEVE	10f Firm	76	2220
76	2	NEWC	9f Gd/Fm	75	2988
74	3	CARL	8f Gd/Fm		3081
71	1	**NEWM**	8f Gd/Fm		3456*
75	5	RIPO	8f Good	75	3699
75	2	HAMI	8f Gd/Sft	75	3826
58	11	CATT	12f Aw	74	4003
73	4	MUSS	8f Gd/Sft		4135

SEA STAR 2 b c £640

83	3	YARM	7f Soft	4514

SEA STORM 2 b g £0

59	9	MUSS	5f Gd/Sft	898
0	11	THIR	7f Gd/Fm	3776

SEA VIXEN 2 ch f £2785

80a	1	**SOUT**	6f Aw	1974*

SEA WAVE 5 b h £68931

118	3	SHA	12f Gd/Fm	185	
103	6	KRAN	10f Firm	657	
114	1	**NEWB**	13f Gd/Fm	1401*	t
105	5	NEWM	12f Good	2566	t

SEA YA MAITE 6 b g £6321

55a	1	**SOUT**	7f Aw	52	33*
47a	8	SOUT	7f Aw	58	69
0a	13	SOUT	11f Aw	55	126
29a	9	SOUT	8f Aw	54	176
48a	5	SOUT	7f Aw	53	282
52a	3	SOUT	8f Aw	53	326
59a	1	**SOUT**	8f Aw	52	345*
52a	5	SOUT	8f Aw	59	418
45a	5	WOLV	8f Aw	58	431
47a	5	SOUT	7f Aw	58	471
63a	2	SOUT	8f Aw	58	496
67a	1	**WOLV**	7f Aw	60	582*
26	6	BEVE	8f Aw	37	3407
54a	5	WOLV	9f Aw	66	4228
40a	13	SOUT	8f Aw	64	4365

SEAHORSE BOY 3 b g £527

45	11	THIR	6f Soft		909
0	14	DONC	7f Gd/Sft		1072
59	7	BEVE	5f Firm		1280
21	4	YORK	8f Firm		2006
49	9	BEVE	5f Firm	57	2223
0	12	DONC	6f Gd/Fm	57	2315
47	11	DONC	6f Gd/Fm	58	2577

SEAHORSE BOY (continued)

0	15	BEVE	5f Firm	52	2732
0	15	BEVE	8f Good		3393
0	13	BEVE	5f Good		3956 VIS

SEALED BY FATE 5 b g £896

49a	5	SOUT	6f Aw	51	697	vis
46	7	SAND	5f Gd/Fm	54	763	bl
42a	6	WOLV	6f Aw	50	923	vis
50	6	CARL	5f Firm		1256	vis
0	12	THIR	7f Gd/Sft		1351	vis
48	4	CARL	6f Firm	49	2015	vis
49	4	CARL	6f Gd/Fm		2240	vis
46	5	NEWC	5f Firm	48	2340	vis
40	7	BEVE	5f Gd/Fm	48	2517	vis
49	2	NOTT	6f Gd/Fm		2680	vis
44	7	BEVE	5f Firm	47	2732	vis
32	12	SAND	5f Gd/Fm	50	2925	vis
66	7	REDC	7f Gd/Sft		4218	
0	20	DONC	7f Soft		4461	

SEANS HONOR 2 b f £1024

68	5	WARW	5f Gd/Sft		1706	
66	4	NOTT	5f Good		2009	
65	4	HAMI	5f Gd/Fm		2639	
52	7	LEIC	5f Gd/Fm	66	2915	
52	6	HAYD	5f Gd/Sft	67	3264	
61	2	HAMI	5f Gd/Sft		3376	
61	5	REDC	5f Gd/Fm		3632	
52a	5	WOLV	5f Aw		4227	VIS

SEARCH AND DESTROY 2 b c £0

0	12	PONT	6f Soft	4082
0	11	LING	6f Soft	4189
60	10	YARM	6f Heavy	4479

SEASAME PARK 3 b f £273

30a	7	SOUT	8f Aw		36
18	11	SOUT	10f Good	806	BL
30a	3	WOLV	9f Aw		922
8a	9	WOLV	9f Aw		1141
0a	10	WOLV	9f Aw		1234
0	17	NOTT	8f Gd/Sft	46	1365

SEASON OF HOPE 4 ch f £308

28a	3	SOUT	11f Aw		248
6a	10	SOUT	11f Aw	33	324
10a	9	SOUT	11f Aw		455

SEASONAL 4 ch f £0

48	7	LEIC	12f Gd/Fm	76	2509

SEASONAL BLOSSOM 3 b f £0

35	10	GOOD	10f Soft	4081

SEASONS GREETINGS 2 b f £21134

100	2	CHAN	6f Good	3843
100	1	**CHAN**	5f Good	4051*

SEATTLE ART 6 b g £0

36	6	MUSS	16f Firm	55	1686
44	9	HAMI	13f Gd/Fm	50	1936
34	5	CARL	17f Gd/Fm	45	2244

SEATTLE BAY 3 b f £7685

104	2	SAIN	11f Heavy	1313

SEATTLE PRINCE 2 gr c £627

82	8	ASCO	6f Gd/Fm		3000
73	5	CHEP	6f Gd/Fm		3680
76	3	EPSO	9f Good		3853
70	6	BATH	10f Soft		4140
0	15	NEWM	8f Good	78	4350

SEAZUN 3 b f £32200

109	2	NEWM	7f Good	953
109	4	NEWM	8f Firm	1185
109	4	CURR	8f Gd/Sft	1626
86	8	ASCO	8f Good	2150
107	4	GOOD	8f Good	3647
93	7	NEWM	8f Gd/Fm	4211

SEBULBA 2 b g £3551

73a	2	WOLV	6f Aw	2077
77a	1	**SOUT**	6f Aw	2635*
65a	6	WOLV	6f Aw	3496

SEBULBA (continued)

0	17	DONC	7f Firm	77	3901
64	5	MUSS	8f Gd/Sft	72	4132
72a	3	SOUT	6f Aw	75	4367

SECOND AFFAIR 3 b f £4569

84	3	NOTT	8f Gd/Fm		1269
84	2	DONC	12f Gd/Fm		3157
68	4	CHES	12f Gd/Fm		3429
80	2	GOOD	10f Soft		4081
80	2	NOTT	10f Heavy		4408

SECOND GENERATION 3 ch g £0

58	9	SALI	6f Gd/Fm		2977
51	5	SAND	5f Good		3229
52	7	BATH	5f Gd/Fm		3820
43	13	GOOD	5f Soft	55	4065 BL
0	21	NEWM	6f Good	55	4185 bl
0	17	NEWM	7f Soft		4547

SECOND PAIGE 3 b c £8521

60	4	WIND	8f Gd/Fm	60	744
48	7	BRIG	8f Gd/Fm	58	892
60	2	WIND	10f Gd/Sft	56	1100
65	2	BEVE	12f Good	59	1446
72	1	**WIND**	12f Gd/Fm	62	2210*
74	1	**WIND**	12f Gd/Fm	69	2712*
57	5	WIND	11f Heavy	74	4529

SECOND STRIKE 2 b c £1182

73	5	YORK	6f Good	3812
77	3	GOOD	7f Soft	4063

SECOND VENTURE 2 b c £3156

52	7	AYR	7f Firm		2873
62	3	THIR	7f Gd/Sft		3776
74	2	AYR	6f Soft		3958
70	4	MUSS	6f Gd/Sft		4131
59	4	AYR	6f Heavy	70	4305
86	4	DONC	6f Gd/Sft		4449

SECOND WIND 5 ch g £17936

81	1	**LEIC**	7f Gd/Sft	70	834*	
79	5	KEMP	8f Soft	78	1015	
59	15	ASCO	7f Gd/Sft	78	1110	
55	13	GOOD	7f Gd/Sft	77	1483	
84	1	**NEWM**	7f Gd/Fm	75	2133+	t
82	2	NEWM	10f Gd/Fm	79	2287	t
88	4	NEWM	7f Gd/Fm	83	2616	t
77	9	GOOD	8f Good	83	3107	t
80	5	GOOD	6f Firm	83	3152	t
82	4	NEWM	7f Gd/Fm	83	3315	t

SECONDS AWAY 9 b g £3301

24	6	HAMI	9f Gd/Fm		1191
20	8	HAMI	11f Gd/Fm	30	1361
28	4	MUSS	9f Firm	28	1689
32	2	AYR	8f Good	29	2136
42	4	HAMI	9f Gd/Fm		2236
36	3	MUSS	14f Firm	37	2375
32	3	HAMI	11f Firm		2393
39	3	HAMI	9f Gd/Fm		2642
33	4	HAMI	9f Gd/Fm		2780
39	3	HAMI	11f Gd/Fm		2800
37	3	AYR	11f Firm		2875
27	3	MUSS	16f Good	32	3099
12	6	REDC	14f Firm		3311
0	11	MUSS	16f Gd/Fm	26	3742
23	6	HAMI	12f Soft		3804

SECRET AGENT 3 b c £18428

97	1	**WIND**	8f Good		851*
96	4	BATH	10f Good		1089
100	2	YORK	10f Gd/Fm	94	1310
100	3	GOOD	8f Gd/Sft	94	1452
79	15	SAND	10f Good	99	2475

SECRET CONQUEST 3 b f £367

0	20	NEWM	7f Gd/Fm	82	1153
66	13	YORK	7f Gd/Fm	79	1308
61	6	DONC	6f Good		1517
67	4	REDC	7f Firm	72	3328

66	5	MUSS	7f Gd/Fm	70	3593
46	12	RIPO	6f Good	70	3698
0	21	YORK	7f Good	67	3809
0	17	NOTT	6f Soft	65	3975
0	18	PONT	8f Soft	62	4232

SECRET DESTINY 3 b f £6286
90	5	NEWM	7f Gd/Sft		971
92	1	**SALI**	8f Firm		2024*
90	5	CHEP	10f Gd/Fm		2975
90	6	SALI	10f Gd/Fm		3389
90	3	NEWC	10f Good	90	3703

SECRET DROP 4 b f £941
43	8	BATH	12f Good	65	1091
66	7	NOTT	14f Gd/Sft		1369
0	14	CHEP	18f Gd/Sft	60	1800
55	7	WARW	16f Gd/Fm	60	2037
35	13	ASCO	16f Good	60	2173
48	4	BRIG	12f Firm	55	2893
53	3	HAYD	12f Good	50	3284 e
49	3	PONT	12f Soft	50	4229 e
45	6	NOTT	16f Heavy	50	4508 e

SECRET INDEX 2 b f £10513
86	1	**WIND**	5f Heavy		932*
90	1	**SALI**	5f Firm		1176*
92	5	ASCO	5f Good		2088
86	4	SALI	6f Gd/Sft		2469
97	4	NEWB	5f Gd/Fm		3482
85	6	KEMP	5f Gd/Fm		3797
86	8	CHAN	5f Good		4051
53	12	REDC	6f Gd/Fm		4219
79	13	NEWB	5f Gd/Sft		4454

SECRET PASSION 2 gr f £0
74	6	WARW	7f Gd/Fm		3910
57	6	BRIG	8f Gd/Sft		4116
43a	4	WOLV	8f Aw		4250

SECRET RENDEZVOUS 3 br f £0
39	14	THIR	6f Soft		909
0a	14	SOUT	6f Aw	55	1205
0a	14	SOUT	6f Aw	50	1421

SECRET SENTIMENT 2 b f £0
60	12	DONC	6f Heavy		4575

SECRET SPRING 8 b g £13452
84a	1	LING	8f Aw	80	7*
80a	7	SOUT	8f Aw	86	49
86a	2	LING	10f Aw		157
91a	1	**LING**	8f Aw	84	169*
86a	1	**LING**	8f Aw		208*
85a	4	LING	10f Aw	90	244
88a	7	LING	7f Aw	90	337
89a	7	LING	7f Aw	90	423
82a	5	LING	8f Aw	89	485
83a	5	LING	10f Aw	88	632
61	13	KEMP	10f Gd/Fm	80	3794
0	16	KEMP	8f Soft	78	4038

SECRET STYLE 5 b g £1344
73	3	DONC	11f Heavy	75	4579

SECRET VALLEY 2 b f £10020
92	2	SAN	8f Gd/Fm		2486

SECRETARIO 3 b f £0
46a	6	SOUT	8f Aw		328
44	6	SOUT	10f Good	54	807
0	14	NOTT	10f Soft	49	1644
16	10	BEVE	10f Gd/Fm	44	2484
0	16	BEVE	16f Good	39	2879
0	14	LEIC	8f Gd/Fm	45	3095 BL
24	8	PONT	8f Gd/Fm	40	3226 bl
3	11	AYR	7f Good		3364 bl
25	5	MUSS	8f Gd/Fm		3591 bl
5	10	HAMI	9f Gd/Sft		3823

SECRETE CONTRACT 2 b c £0
71	6	GOOD	8f Soft		4062

SECRETS OUT 4 b c £0
74	5	BEVE	7f Heavy		977
28	13	REDC	10f Gd/Sft	82	1561
0	16	YORK	9f Firm	76	2001 BL

SECURITY COUNCIL 2 b c £0
70	5	DONC	7f Heavy		4567

SECURON DANCER 2 b f £478
71	4	SALI	5f Firm		1176
66	8	GOOD	6f Gd/Fm		1957
58	6	WIND	6f Gd/Fm		3047
0	13	LING	5f Good	68	4098
51	9	NEWB	7f Gd/Sft	64	4453

SEDONA 3 b c £2289
46a	5	WOLV	7f Aw		493
0a	U	SOUT	8f Aw	50	555
48a	3	WOLV	6f Aw	50	706
28	11	NOTT	8f Heavy	50	1024
55	1	**NOTT**	8f Gd/Sft	47	1365*
51	7	MUSS	9f Firm	56	1689
34	9	REDC	9f Gd/Fm	56	2160
0	R	BEVE	10f Good	54	2883
0	R	RIPO	12f Gd/Fm	54	3181 BL

SEDUCTION 3 b f £0
0a	6	LING	12f Aw		1540
0	7	YARM	16f Gd/Sft		1613

SEDUCTIVE 2 b c £5385
55	8	BEVE	5f Gd/Fm		2480
78	2	EPSO	6f Gd/Sft		2628
79	3	AYR	7f Firm		2873
66	5	CHES	7f Gd/Fm		3508
80a	1	**WOLV**	8f Aw		4022*
69	6	MUSS	8f Gd/Sft	79	4132

SEE YOU LATER 3 b f £16600
92	6	NEWB	6f Good		1371
95	3	KEMP	5f Soft		1529
92	3	SAND	5f Gd/Fm		1987
74	15	ASCO	5f Good	96	2168
86	10	GOOD	5f Gd/Fm		3059
97	1	**SAND**	5f Good	93	3473*
103	2	DONC	5f Gd/Sft		3874
85	11	ASCO	5f Gd/Sft	96	4129
84	6	DONC	6f Heavy		4581

SEEK 4 br c £22067
86	2	PONT	10f Soft		874
86	5	YORK	14f Good	88	2695
92	1	**YORK**	12f Gd/Sft	86	3541*
0	11	ASCO	12f Gd/Sft	92	4128

SEEK THE LIGHT 3 b c £334
75	6	WIND	10f Gd/Fm		1200
79	4	SAND	10f Good		3232
4	7	BRIG	12f Gd/Sft		4119

SEEKER 3 ch f £2668
63	3	YARM	11f Firm		2897
63	2	NEWM	12f Gd/Sft		3313
67	3	CHEP	12f Good		3869

SEEKING SANCTUARY 3 ch f £278
44	7	YARM	6f Good		1773
37	10	YARM	7f Gd/Fm		1951
43	4	BATH	10f Firm	45	2789
42	5	SALI	12f Gd/Fm	44	3290

SEEKING SUCCESS 3 b f £8372
81	9	NEWM	7f Gd/Fm		971
60	7	WIND	8f Gd/Sft		1428
80	2	BATH	8f Gd/Sft		1669
90	2	SALI	8f Firm		2024
69	6	ASCO	8f Good		2679
80	1	**PONT**	8f Gd/Fm		3221*
77	3	PONT	8f Firm	85	3505
79	4	SAND	8f Gd/Fm	80	3944

SEEKING UTOPIA 3 b f £1775
75	5	KEMP	9f Good		727
66	8	NEWB	10f Gd/Fm	77	1785
70	4	SALI	12f Firm	73	2023

58	9	HAYD	12f Gd/Fm	71	2446
0	P	BATH	10f Firm	67	2789
36	12	LEIC	10f Gd/Fm	67	3217
60	3	RIPO	10f Gd/Fm	64	3465
60a	3	LING	8f Aw		3756
52	11	SAND	8f Gd/Fm	60	3944
42a	6	LING	10f Aw	58	4482

SEFTON BLAKE 6 b g £0
0a	11	SOUT	14f Aw	51	37

SEGAVIEW 4 b c £1120
56	4	WARW	15f Heavy	66	885
61	4	HAYD	14f Gd/Fm	62	1167
56	5	NOTT	14f Good	60	1411
57	4	RIPO	16f Good	58	1597
0	17	CATT	12f Soft	58	4003

SEL 2 b f £4938
51	3	YARM	7f Gd/Fm		1950
43	5	REDC	7f Gd/Fm		2155
62	1	**BRIG**	7f Gd/Sft		2424* BL
62	2	BRIG	7f Gd/Fm		2723 bl
55	5	SAND	7f Good	61	3468 bl
61	1	**BRIG**	7f Firm		3733* bl
0	13	GOOD	8f Soft	62	4076 bl
61	5	BRIG	7f Soft	62	4416 bl
49	6	BRIG	8f Heavy	62	4538 bl

SELHURSTPARK FLYER 9 b g £0
60	10	EPSO	6f Heavy	80	1028
0	20	THIR	6f Good	77	1383
65	6	EPSO	6f Gd/Sft	72	2432

SELIANA 4 b f £17600
63	2	LEIC	12f Gd/Fm		832
62	3	FOLK	12f Soft		964
69	4	NOTT	14f Good	70	1411
57	7	WARW	16f Gd/Sft	70	1711
79	2	ASCO	20f Good	68	2092
78	2	GOOD	20f Gd/Fm	76	3085
78	3	YARM	18f Gd/Fm	78	3967

SELKING 3 ch c £13035
97	3	NEWM	7f Good		955
103	2	HAYD	7f Gd/Fm		1163
92	4	EPSO	7f Gd/Sft		1830
101	7	ASCO	7f Good		2087
103	2	CHES	6f Firm		3172
80	8	ASCO	6f Gd/Fm		3303

SELLINGERS ROUND 4 ch g £0
32	10	LING	7f Good	55	4102
30a	8	WOLV	8f Aw	52	4437

SELTITUDE 4 b f £9606
112	3	LONG	5f V		1320
109	3	CHAN	5f Gd/Sft		1747
97	17	ASCO	5f Good		2065
102	6	LONG	5f Good		4261

SELTON HILL 3 b f £1190
62	3	RIPO	10f Soft	61	827
63	2	NOTT	10f Heavy	61	1022

SELVORINE 3 ch f £0
65	5	NEWB	9f Gd/Fm		3179
57	9	LEIC	10f Firm		3838
66	6	KEMP	12f Soft		4040
32	11	BATH	12f Soft	62	4433

SEMIRAMIS 3 b f £0
59a	4	LING	6f Aw	63	2
43a	8	LING	7f Aw	61	112

SENADOR 7 b g £0
0	22	ASCO	7f Gd/Fm	92	2997

SENATORS ALIBI 2 b c £0
46	14	DONC	7f Heavy		4567

SEND IT TO PENNY 3 b f £5559
40	13	RIPO	10f Soft	49	827
21	12	NOTT	8f Heavy	47	1024
54	2	RIPO	8f Good		1596
0	13	HAYD	7f Gd/Sft	44	1793 BL

54a	1	SOUT	8f Aw	44	1804*	bl
49	5	CARL	7f Firm	52	2017	bl
15	11	CARL	8f Firm	51	2281	bl
19a	9	SOUT	7f Aw	53	2637	bl
54	1	THIR	8f Gd/Fm	49	2964*	bl
0	13	CARL	8f Gd/Fm	55	3082	bl

SEND ME AN ANGEL 3 ch f £6235

72	4	THIR	12f Good		1157	
55	4	BRIG	12f Gd/Sft		1510	
62	2	BATH	12f Firm		1997	
63	2	YARM	14f Firm	61	2902	
57	6	NOTT	16f Gd/Fm	61	3112	
62	3	CATT	16f Good	64	3442	
70	1	YARM	14f Gd/Fm	62	3664*	
68	5	SAND	14f Gd/Fm	70	3948	
0	14	NEWM	14f Gd/Fm	70	4213	

SENDAWAR 4 b c £107641

125	1	LONG	9f Gd/Sft		1458*	
113	4	ASCO	10f Good		2089	
120	2	DEAU	8f Gd/Fm		3544	

SENIOR MINISTER 2 b c £10455

97	2	WIND	5f Gd/Fm		3044	
95	1	LING	5f Firm		3277*	
103	2	YORK	5f Gd/Fm		3567	

SENOR MIRO 2 b c £330

68	9	NEWM	7f Good		2563	
71	5	NEWM	6f Gd/Fm		2854	
70	4	GOOD	6f Good		3649	
58	9	NOTT	6f Soft	74	3976	

SENSE OF FREEDOM 3 ch f £10673

76	2	RIPO	10f Good		1599	
82	2	GOOD	12f Gd/Fm		1956	
79	2	PONT	12f Firm		2179	
78	3	HAYD	12f Gd/Fm	79	2446	
87	1	PONT	12f Gd/Fm	80	3224*	
80	5	MUSS	16f Gd/Sft	87	4134	

SENSIMELIA 2 b f £542

63	5	THIR	5f Good		1385	
67	3	HAYD	5f Gd/Sft		1835	
52	6	AYR	6f Good		2137	
61	5	MUSS	5f Good		3098	
50	10	HAYD	5f Gd/Sft	63	3475	

SEOMRA HOCHT 3 b g £236

45	8	AYR	9f Soft		3988	
67	4	MUSS	12f Gd/Sft		4133	
71	6	NOTT	10f Heavy		4408	

SEPTEMBER HARVEST 4 ch c £319

46a	6	WOLV	12f Aw	50	261	
42a	4	SOUT	8f Aw	48	601	
37a	4	SOUT	12f Aw	45	642	
0	19	DONC	10f Gd/Fm	50	705	
0	17	PONT	10f Soft	48	871	VIS
36a	7	SOUT	8f Aw	41	1207	
31	7	YARM	11f Gd/Fm	44	1614	vis
27	7	BEVE	8f Gd/Fm	39	3407	

SEQUOYAH 2 b f £107275

92	3	CURR	6f Good		2408	
100	2	CURR	7f Good		3555	
110	1	CURR	7f Gd/Fm		3845*	
106	5	NEWM	6f Good		4159	

SERAPHINA 3 ch f £10319

75	7	NEWB	7f Soft		913	
81	6	HAYD	5f Heavy		988	
103	2	BATH	5f Good		1090	
65	10	NOTT	6f Good		1410	
97	3	HAYD	6f Gd/Sft		1833	
99	15	ASCO	5f Good		2065	
0	18	ASCO	5f Gd/Fm	100	3016	BL
88	3	ASCO	5f Good	100	3301	
96	3	NEWM	5f Good		4182	

SEREN HILL 4 ch f £21494

87	7	SAIN	15f Heavy		140	

79	8	KEMP	16f Soft	85	997	
79	12	ASCO	12f Good	85	2674	
76	8	NEWB	13f Firm	83	2852	
84	2	HAYD	14f Gd/Fm	78	3323	
78	8	HAYD	14f Soft	82	3783	
74	9	ASCO	12f Good	82	4115	
86	1	YORK	12f Soft		4276*	
90	1	NEWM	12f Good	83	4342*	
95	3	DONC	12f Heavy	93	4580	

SEREN TEG 4 ch f £3058

61a	1	LING	5f Aw		440*	BL
66a	4	LING	5f Aw	69	506	bl
64a	4	WOLV	6f Aw	67	622	bl
0	16	SAND	5f Gd/Fm	57	763	bl
30	12	GOOD	6f Gd/Fm	52	2124	
32	11	SALI	6f Gd/Fm	52	2230	
43	1	BATH	5f Gd/Sft	47	2555	bl
41	4	BATH	6f Firm	44	2944	bl
37	6	WIND	6f Gd/Fm	45	3046	bl
32	8	LING	6f Firm	44	3493	bl
44a	7	WOLV	6f Aw	64	3774	bl

SERENGETI BRIDE 2 ch f £0

62	7	YARM	7f Soft		4514	

SERENUS 7 b g £0

75	5	KEMP	16f Soft	74	997	

SERGE LIFAR 2 b c £1097

82	3	KEMP	8f Soft		4036	
84	3	DONC	7f Gd/Sft		4446	

SERGEANT IMP 5 b g £1474

67a	7	LING	8f Aw		208	
48a	3	LING	8f Aw		316	
39a	3	LING	10f Aw	38	400	
39a	5	LING	12f Aw	48	486	
31a	4	LING	10f Aw	38	618	
41a	3	LING	10f Aw	40	880	
28a	7	LING	10f Aw	40	3828	

SERGEANT SLIPPER 3 ch c £6553

54a	8	SOUT	5f Aw		34	
63a	1	WOLV	5f Aw		145*	vis
61a	1	SOUT	5f Aw		217*	vis
45a	8	SOUT	6f Aw	62	365	vis
40	8	CATT	5f Aw		777	vis
67a	1	SOUT	5f Aw	60	870*	vis
42	7	BRIG	5f Firm	55	1334	vis
38	12	NEWC	5f Aw	53	2525	vis

SERGEANT YORK 4 b c £3954

91	11	NEWM	9f Gd/Sft		967	
101	5	WIND	8f Firm		1291	
78	3	BEVE	8f Good	80	1445	
78	3	HAYD	8f Gd/Sft		1489	
75	6	NOTT	8f Good		1872	
0	17	DONC	8f Gd/Fm	80	2349	
99	4	DONC	8f Good		2578	
77	5	DONC	8f Good		2757	VIS
77	3	LEIC	8f Gd/Fm	78	3334	vis
55	8	RIPO	8f Gd/Fm		3711	vis
58	7	NEWM	7f Good		4018	vis

SERIAL 6 bl g £0

0	13	MUSS	7f Firm		2046	

SERINGA 3 b f £4677

108	3	HANN	12f Good		3930	

SERPENT SYSTEMS 3 b f £319

0	12	NEWM	7f Good		3612	
23a	3	WOLV	7f Aw		4361	
10a	7	SOUT	6f Aw		4368	

SERRA NEGRA 3 b f £5073

80	1	WARW	8f Soft		1062*	
77	6	YORK	8f Firm	80	1341	
80	2	SAND	7f Soft	80	1564	

SERVICE STAR 3 b c £7775

80a	1	SOUT	8f Aw		86*	BL
73a	3	WOLV	8f Aw		171	bl

83a	2	LING	10f Aw	75	509	bl
89a	1	WOLV	9f Aw	80	625*	bl
77a	9	LING	10f Aw		690	bl

SERVICEABLE 2 ch f £3652

80	3	SAND	5f Gd/Fm		762	
82	1	WARW	5f Heavy		886*	
80	6	NEWB	5f Good		1372	
0	20	NEWM	6f Good	80	4338	
0	20	DONC	7f Heavy		4577	

SET AND MATCH 4 ch c £0

0a	17	SOUT	12f Aw	48	70	

SET THE FASHION 4 br c £25278

108	1	KRAN	10f Good		1230	bl

SEVEN 5 ch g £3853

60a	2	SOUT	6f Aw		30	bl
60a	2	WOLV	7f Aw		65	VIS
37a	3	SOUT	7f Aw		247	bl
62a	1	SOUT	6f Aw		414*	bl
62a	5	WOLV	6f Aw		465	bl
64a	4	SOUT	6f Aw		538	bl
34a	7	WOLV	7f Aw	61	711	bl
31	12	SOUT	7f Good	60	803	bl
52	4	DONC	6f Gd/Sft		1068	bl
43	9	NOTT	6f Firm	57	1273	bl
33	8	SOUT	7f Soft		1603	bl
55	3	THIR	8f Gd/Sft		3775	vis
49	5	CHEP	7f Good	50	3871	vis

SEVEN NO TRUMPS 3 ch c £1160

99	7	NEWM	7f Good		950	
46	7	ASCO	6f Gd/Sft		1111	
80	10	LING	6f Good		1674	BL
86	8	NEWM	5f Gd/Fm		2960	
90	3	DONC	6f Gd/Fm		3158	
62	8	LEIC	5f Good	98	3335	
81	8	SAND	5f Good	94	3473	
72	15	GOOD	5f Good	90	3646	
0	21	KEMP	6f Gd/Fm	85	3791	
70	15	AYR	5f Good	80	3960	

SEVEN O SEVEN 7 b g £0

9a	6	SOUT	8f Aw		500	
22a	7	SOUT	11f Aw	43	560	
11a	9	SOUT	8f Aw		686	

SEVEN OF NINE 2 b f £425

59	4	NEWM	8f Good		4019	

SEVEN OF SPADES 3 b c £0

57	10	REDC	5f Gd/Sft	68	1580	
55	5	RIPO	5f Good	64	1861	
44	13	DONC	5f Gd/Fm	62	3161	
30a	5	SOUT	4f Aw		4368	

SEVEN SING 2 b f £4481

90	3	NEWM	6f Gd/Fm		2618	
88	1	THIR	6f Gd/Fm		2968*	
85	10	NEWM	5f Good		3482	

SEVEN SPRINGS 4 b c £1178

33a	8	SOUT	6f Aw		32	
12a	12	WOLV	6f Aw		76	
15a	9	SOUT	8f Aw	40	647	
0a	11	WOLV	7f Aw	38	711	
39	6	NOTT	6f Good	45	787	
43	2	WARW	5f Heavy	43	1005	
0	13	NOTT	6f Firm	45	1273	
34a	3	SOUT	6f Aw	34	1422	
39	7	THIR	5f Gd/Sft	45	1714	
14a	12	SOUT	7f Aw	36	1806	
16	15	CARL	6f Firm	43	2015	
4a	14	SOUT	6f Aw	35	2385	
31	8	CATT	7f Gd/Fm	38	3200	
34	4	HAMI	5f Gd/Sft	33	3536	VIS
32	7	EPSO	7f Good	35	3765	

SEWARDS FOLLY 4 b f £0

0	18	WIND	12f Gd/Fm	56	748	
0	14	SOUT	10f Gd/Sft	49	859	

18 8 FOLK 10f Good 42 2625
0   9 BATH 10f Firm 42 2789

SEYOOLL 2 b f £919
84 4 CHEP 8f Gd/Fm   3678
82 3 SAND 8f Gd/Fm   3943

SHAAN MADARY 3 b f £5343
0   19 NEWB 10f Gd/Fm   1404
77 2   WARW 8f Good   2465
78 1   THIR 8f Good   2965*
76 4   THIR 8f Gd/Fm 77 3147
36 8   THIR 8f Gd/Fm 76 3345

SHAANARA 2 b f £3315
74 6   BEVE 7f Good   3953
0   19 NEWM 7f Good   4158
82 1   NEWC 7f Heavy   4403*

SHAANDAR 2 br c £0
62 12 DONC 7f Heavy   4567

SHAANXI ROMANCE 5 b g £13342
47   2   CATT 7f Gd/Fm   778 vis
36a 5   SOUT 8f Aw   869 vis
17a 9   WOLV 12f Aw   1039
0   20 REDC 8f Firm   49 1296 vis
47   5   SOUT 7f Soft   1603 tvi
43   5   THIR 7f Gd/Fm 47 2063 vis
44a 4   SOUT 8f Aw   44 2121 vis
45a 3   SOUT 8f Aw   45 2379 vis
29   6   BEVE 8f Aw   45 2481 vis
28a 6   SOUT 7f Aw   45 2637 vis
55a 1   SOUT 8f Aw   48 2817* vis
48   1   KEMP 8f Gd/Fm 43 3078* vis
54   2   CHES 8f Firm   52 3170 vis
51   3   BATH 8f Firm   49 3207 vis
51   4   BATH 8f Gd/Fm 52 3514 vis
10   12 GOOD 12f Good 52 3657 vis
37   6   YORK 12f Gd/Fm 52 3725 vis
0   14 YARM 8f Firm   50 3936 vis
0   17 LEIC 8f Gd/Sft   4032 vis
35a 7   WOLV 8f Aw   53 4363 vis
0   15 NOTT 8f Heavy 55 4506 vis

SHAARD 2 b c £24064
95   1 BATH 6f Gd/Sft   2550* BL
103 3 GOOD 7f Gd/Fm   3086 bl
97   4 RIPO 6f Good   3700 bl
108 1 DONC 6f Soft   4462* bl

SHABAASH 4 b c £207
42a 5   SOUT 8f Aw   50
47a 3   LING 10f Aw   111
12a 10 SOUT 8f Aw   43 177
33a 4   SOUT 11f Aw   40 325
20a 7   WOLV 12f Aw   37 410
13a 6   LING 13f Aw   34 458
20a 7   WOLV 9f Aw   517
9a   10 LING 10f Aw   34 620
0a   12 LING 12f Aw   650

SHABLAM 3 b c £3694
104 5 NEWM 7f Good   955
93   4 DONC 8f Gd/Sft   1069
103 4 CHES 10f Firm   1246
101 7 ASCO 10f Gd/Fm 105 2995
93   4 WIND 12f Good   3640 VIS

SHADALHI 2 ch f £0
46 7 BEVE 5f Firm   1918
59 5 THIR 6f Gd/Fm   2059

SHADED MEMOIR 2 ch f £0
69 6 HAYD 6f Gd/Fm   3320
71 7 KEMP 7f Soft   4035
62 8 DONC 7f Heavy   4567

SHADES OF JADE 12 gr m £0
0a 16 LING 7f Aw   43 28

SHADES OF LOVE 6 b g £0
41a 13 LING 7f Aw   4328

SHADIRWAN 9 b h £0

0   11 CHEP 18f Gd/Fm 40 2452

SHADOW PRINCE 3 ch c £12857
75 5 LING 7f Gd/Sft   839
53 7 KEMP 7f Soft   1018
79 1 KEMP 7f Firm   72 2261*
79 3 SAND 7f Gd/Fm 78 2922
80 3 GOOD 7f Gd/Fm 78 3130
71 7 SAND 8f Good   79 3435
69 5 GOOD 9f Good   79 3658
81 2 NEWB 8f Firm   78 3998

SHADOWBLASTER 3 b c £2706
87 5 NEWB 8f Good   1377
82 2 YARM 7f Firm   2770
78 2 SAND 10f Gd/Fm   2924
57 7 WIND 8f Good   3350
45 4 PONT 8f Soft   4234

SHADOWLESS 2 b c £10130
79   4 YARM 6f Good   1774
93   7 ASCO 6f Good   2067
101 2 NEWM 7f Gd/Fm   2613
99   3 ASCO 8f Gd/Fm   3304
80   7 NEWB 8f Firm   3983

SHADY DEAL 4 b c £4514
0a   14 LING 7f Aw   54 162
18a 7   WOLV 7f Aw   391
34a 4   LING 7f Aw   51 439
48a 7   LING 5f Aw   507
41a 7   LING 6f Aw   43 543
40a 3   LING 6f Aw   40 628
0a   11 LING 6f Aw   41 691
36   10 SAND 5f Gd/Fm 51 763
37   10 NEWB 6f Gd/Sft 48 1591
46   2   BATH 6f Firm   43 1994
46   2   BEVE 5f Firm   46 2223
51   1   BATH 5f Gd/Sft 47 2555*
51   3   WIND 5f Good   47 2716
51   4   SAND 5f Good   52 3436
42   8   SALI 5f Firm   52 3747
0   14 CHEP 5f Good   52 3872

SHADY POINT 3 b f £3696
62   7   NEWM 9f Gd/Sft   980
65   5   WARW 8f Soft   1063
68   6   NEWB 7f Firm   69 1405
73   2   YARM 8f Gd/Sft 67 1610
70a 1   SOUT 8f Aw   67 1803* VIS
63   7   PONT 8f Firm   70 2180 vis
100 6   NEWM 8f Gd/Fm   2597
76   10 NEWM 12f Gd/Fm   2857 vis
65   6   ASCO 8f Gd/Fm   3340 vis
65   9   CHEP 10f Good 77 3870 vis

SHAFAQ 3 b f £0
58 12 LING 6f Good   84 1676
77 6   YARM 7f Firm   80 2391
56 12 YARM 7f Firm   78 2768
0   14 WIND 6f Gd/Fm 77 3046 BL
49 8   FOLK 10f Gd/Fm 75 3585

SHAFFISHAYES 8 ch g £1193
43 11 PONT 10f Heavy 66 943
58 6   HAYD 14f Gd/Sft 65 1536
59 5   CATT 14f Soft   62 1683
55 4   RIPO 10f Good   60 1860
55 6   SAND 11f Good   57 2530
47 5   RIPO 12f Gd/Fm 56 2837
53 3   RIPO 12f Good   53 3013
31 9   HAYD 14f Gd/Fm 54 3323
48 6   HAYD 11f Gd/Sft 52 3480
49 7   CATT 12f Soft   52 4003
38 9   REDC 10f Gd/Sft 52 4221

SHAHED 3 ch c £662
56 6 KEMP 7f Soft   1018
79 3 KEMP 8f Firm   2871

SHAHIRAH 2 b f £4368

99 1 KEMP 7f Gd/Fm   3359*
81 9 ASCO 8f Good   4110
70 8 NEWB 7f Sft/Hvy   4467

SHAIBANI 3 b c £832
70 4 DONC 10f Good   1515

SHAIR 3 b g £8634
86 4 NEWM 10f Gd/Fm   2617
84 2 NEWM 12f Gd/Fm   2963
81 2 HAYD 12f Gd/Fm   3324
84 2 CHEP 12f Good   3869
86 1 GOOD 10f Soft   4081*

SHAKAKHAN 2 ch f £260
68 5 PONT 6f Soft   4083
68 3 PONT 6f Soft   4372

SHAKESPEARE 3 b c £8150
79   4 LEOP 10f Soft   949
109 1 CORK 10f Good   1898*
103 8 CURR 12f Good   2409

SHALARISE 3 ch f £687
0   16 HAMI 6f Gd/Fm 69 1192
0   20 NEWC 5f Gd/Sft 66 1479
0   12 CATT 5f Gd/Sft 62 1817 bl
55 5   AYR   5f Good   58 2165 bl
32 12 CARL 5f Firm   56 2280 bl
55 2   REDC 5f Gd/Sft 56 2864 bl
44 10 DONC 5f Gd/Fm 57 3161 VIS
0   18 HAMI 6f Gd/Sft 56 3377 vis
49 9   MUSS 8f Gd/Sft 56 3594 vis
0   17 HAMI 5f Gd/Sft 53 3825 bl
0   11 MUSS 5f Soft   50 4516 bl

SHALBEBLUE 3 b g £1488
64   3 REDC 7f Gd/Sft   1135
62   5 NEWC 8f Good   2337
54   9 DONC 8f Gd/Fm   2611
0   14 REDC 10f Firm 66 3310
0   13 RIPO 10f Good 60 3702
59   4 LEIC 10f Good 60 3842
30   7 HAYD 12f Soft 60 4092
29   4 LEIC 10f Heavy   4313 VIS
60a 3 WOLV 9f Aw   58 4382 vis

SHALIMAR 3 b f £11416
83 3 GOOD 7f Gd/Sft   1638
75 1 SALI 7f Gd/Fm   1886*
89 1 NEWM 8f Firm   82 2342*
73 8 NEWM 7f Good   88 2567

SHAM SHARIF 3 b f £2800
68   5 WARW 11f Soft   814
64   1 AYR   9f Gd/Fm   1632*
54   8 YARM 10f Gd/Fm 66 1955
55   8 WIND 10f Good   2372
55   8 CATT 12f Gd/Fm 62 2746
0   16 NEWM 12f Gd/Fm 60 3167 BL
16a 9 WOLV 9f Aw   55 4251

SHAMAH 3 ch f £5217
85 2 WIND 10f Good   850
90 1 WIND 8f Gd/Sft   1428*

SHAMAIEL 3 b f £11234
81   4 NEWM 10f Good   1857
96   4 ASCO 10f Good   2169
85   10 HAYD 12f Gd/Fm   2501
78   4 WIND 10f Gd/Fm   2889
102 3 ASCO 12f Gd/Fm   3305
90   9 YORK 12f Firm   3595
90   1 BATH 12f Good   3818*
78   12 YARM 10f Firm   3918
91   11 NEWM 12f Good   4343

SHAMAN 3 b c £8518
35a 10 LING 8f Aw   61 54
55a 4   LING 7f Aw   155
64a 1   LING 8f Aw   236*
65a 2   LING 10f Aw   286
66a 1   LING 10f Aw   882*

SHAWIN (continued)

54	8	WIND	12f Firm	60	1292	
63	1	**BRIG**	10f Firm		2041*	
64a	3	LING	12f Aw	69	2651	
63	2	BRIG	10f Firm	60	2908	
64	2	BRIG	10f Firm	63	3530	
41	7	BRIG	12f Firm	63	3560	
51	7	BRIG	8f Soft		4173	

SHAMEL 4 b c £0

0a	6	WOLV	12f Aw		679

SHAMO 2 b f £0

90	6	MAIS	6f V		3066
62	11	NEWM	7f Gd/Fm		4210

SHAMOKIN 8 b g £0

27a	5	SOUT	11f Aw		455
0	14	NEWC	12f Good		3247

SHAMPOOED 6 b m £1354

43	3	WARW	15f Heavy	50	885
50	2	NOTT	14f Gd/Sft	46	1087

SHAMROCK CITY 3 b c £13377

79	6	NEWM	8f Gd/Sft		981
80	23	NEWM	8f Gd/Fm		1171
112	4	YORK	10f Firm		1326
115	1	**NEWM**	10f Firm		1854*

SHAMSAN 3 ch c £8478

68a	4	LING	6f Aw		221	
68a	1	**LING**	8f Aw	63	266*	
5a	12	LING	10f Aw	69	315	
64a	3	LING	7f Aw	68	617	
66a	2	WOLV	9f Aw	66	709	
48	9	WARW	11f Heavy	67	1002	
59	5	THIR	8f Gd/Fm	62	2970	
65	2	LEIC	10f Gd/Fm	62	3093	
65	2	PONT	8f Gd/Fm	62	3226	
65	3	HAYD	11f Good	62	3285	
61	9	YORK	8f Good	65	3810	
64	3	BRIG	8f Soft		4173	BL
62a	4	WOLV	9f Aw	67	4382	bl

SHAMWARI SONG 5 b g £4053

45a	5	LING	10f Aw		163	
33a	7	LING	8f Aw		316	
19a	10	SOUT	7f Aw	40	368	t
0a	12	SOUT	8f Aw		452	
44a	2	LING	8f Aw		505	
8a	9	LING	8f Aw		574	
53a	3	LING	7f Aw		616	
41a	8	SOUT	7f Aw		667	
45	7	LEIC	7f Good		790	
39a	4	LING	10f Aw	43	842	
21	11	BRIG	8f Firm	43	1330	
42	3	AYR	8f Good	40	2136	
46	1	**CARL**	7f Firm	40	2282*	vis
37	8	HAYD	7f Gd/Fm	45	2442	vis

SHANGHAI LADY 4 b f £0

0	9	EPSO	9f Gd/Sft	70	2629	t
0	15	BRIG	7f Gd/Sft	65	4121	t

SHANGHAI LIL 8 b m £0

25a	7	SOUT	11f Aw	50	126	
0a	11	WOLV	12f Aw	48	170	
15a	11	WOLV	12f Aw	46	261	VIS

SHANNON DORE 3 b f £525

78	4	KEMP	6f Gd/Sft		1078
70	11	WIND	5f Gd/Sft	84	1427
65	8	NEWM	6f Good		2289
55	11	HAMI	6f Soft	78	3803

SHANNON FLYER 2 br c £0

0	12	YARM	6f Heavy		4479

SHANNONS DREAM 4 gr f £0

0	13	LEIC	10f Gd/Fm		2774
0	18	WIND	10f Gd/Fm		3045
0a	11	LING	7f Aw		4487

SHAPIRO 3 ch f £0

0	18	BEVE	5f Good		3956

SHAPOUR 3 b c £299

61	10	BATH	10f Good		1093
79	4	WIND	12f Good	76	2712
74	8	CHES	12f Firm	78	3173

SHARAF 7 b g £2840

0a	P	SOUT	16f Aw	46	737
43	4	NOTT	14f Gd/Sft	46	1087
51	2	LING	16f Gd/Fm	42	1394
50	3	WARW	16f Gd/Sft	51	1711
19	15	ASCO	16f Good	51	2173
49	4	CHEP	18f Gd/Fm	50	2452
48a	4	SOUT	16f Aw	50	2951
42	7	GOOD	16f Soft	48	4075
49	2	BATH	17f Soft	48	4139
29	6	PONT	17f Soft	43	4231

SHARAVAWN 3 b f £0

27a	9	LING	7f Aw		53	
34a	8	LING	7f Aw		94	BL
28a	9	LING	8f Aw		150	bl
11a	9	LING	10f Aw		204	bl
25	6	FOLK	12f Soft		964	
33	10	BRIG	12f Gd/Fm		1125	

SHARAZAN 7 b g £596

38	10	WARW	16f Gd/Sft	55	1711	
56	3	CHEP	18f Gd/Sft	55	1800	
32	16	ASCO	20f Good	63	2092	
32	12	ASCO	16f Good	55	2173	VIS

SHARED HARMONY 2 b c £0

58	6	GOOD	6f Good		3649
43	10	GOOD	6f Good		3881

SHAREEF 3 b c £3573

76a	1	**SOUT**	12f Aw		603*
95	5	NEWM	12f Gd/Fm		1168
95	7	LING	6f Good		1674
83	4	HAYD	12f Gd/Sft	93	1832

SHAREEF KHAN 3 b c £1034

70	11	WIND	10f Gd/Fm		1200	bl
74	3	WIND	10f Gd/Fm		2056	
70	3	BATH	12f Firm		2327	
38	6	THIR	12f Gd/Fm	72	2967	
0a	18	LING	12f Aw		4101	

SHARMY 4 b c £8742

101	1	**ASCO**	8f Gd/Sft		1112*
100	4	YORK	10f Firm	100	1342
101	5	SAND	8f Soft	100	1567

SHAROURA 4 ch f £2445

66	10	GOOD	7f Gd/Fm	80	2128
70	11	NEWC	5f Gd/Fm	80	2310
65	8	PONT	6f Good	78	2364
77	2	NOTT	5f Gd/Fm	74	2684
0	14	GOOD	6f Gd/Fm	77	3136
70	10	CARL	5f Firm	75	3572
70	9	AYR	5f Soft	74	3960
72	3	YORK	6f Soft		4287
33	9	NEWC	6f Heavy	71	4405
45	14	DONC	5f Heavy	69	4570

SHARP ACT 2 b c £0

65	12	NEWM	6f Gd/Fm		1691
64	12	KEMP	6f Gd/Fm		1924
73	5	WIND	5f Soft		2545
69	5	EPSO	6f Good		3852
53	10	NEWB	7f Gd/Sft	68	4453

SHARP BELLINE 3 b g £2716

67	4	NOTT	8f Gd/Fm		2188	
34	3	YARM	10f Firm		2765	
68	4	NEWM	10f Good		3021	
19	12	NEWM	10f Gd/Fm	59	3314	VIS
39	4	BEVE	10f Gd/Fm	52	3656	
52a	2	WOLV	8f Aw	51	4021	
23	6	BEVE	10f Sft/Hv	51	4046	
56a	2	WOLV	10f Gd/Fm	52	4386	

SHARP EDGE BOY 4 gr c £699

0a	13	SOUT	6f Aw	49	587	
39a	8	WOLV	6f Aw	49	622	
48	8	SOUT	7f Good	62	803	
46	7	THIR	6f Soft	60	908	
42	7	DONC	6f Gd/Sft		1073	
0	18	THIR	6f Gd/Sft	55	1356	
35	9	PONT	6f Good	52	1869	
51	2	CARL	6f Soft		2240	
34	10	HAMI	6f Gd/Sft	50	3377	
32	11	NEWC	5f Heavy	50	4407	
12	7	NEWC	6f Heavy	50	4425	
0	21	DONC	7f Soft		4461	

SHARP GOSSIP 4 b g £10946

0	15	PONT	6f Heavy	72	941	
50	15	DONC	6f Gd/Fm	70	1074	
0	15	BATH	6f Gd/Fm	67	1438	
43	11	LING	6f Good	63	1676	bl
44	7	YARM	8f Gd/Fm	58	2412	
57	2	MUSS	8f Gd/Fm	54	3745	
58	2	BATH	8f Soft	56	4143	
63a	1	**SOUT**	8f Aw	56	4365*	
62	1	**YARM**	7f Soft	56	4513*	

SHARP HAT 6 ch g £30932

62a	1	**LING**	5f Aw	57	91*	
59a	3	WOLV	5f Aw	60	146	
41a	11	LING	6f Aw	60	148	
37a	11	WOLV	6f Aw	59	232	
57a	3	SOUT	5f Aw	58	342	
58a	4	SOUT	6f Aw	58	386	
2	2	SOUT	6f Aw		414	
56a	4	SOUT	6f Aw	57	454	
59a	4	LING	5f Aw	59	543	
49	7	NOTT	6f Good	60	787	
58	2	HAYD	5f Gd/Sft	58	1792	
55	9	RIPO	5f Good	58	1861	
53	5	CARL	6f Firm	58	2015	
63a	2	SOUT	6f Aw		2118	
52	6	HAMI	5f Firm	57	2395	
67	1	**NEWC**	5f Good	57	2525*	
69	1	**AYR**	5f Gd/Fm	65	2721*	
53	6	NEWC	5f Good	58	2987	
68	3	HAYD	5f Good	68	3322	
0	17	GOOD	5f Good	70	3646	
72	5	EPSO	5f Good	70	3687	
74	2	HAYD	5f Gd/Sft	70	3788	
73	3	CHEP	5f Good	70	3872	
66	10	NEWM	5f Good	72	4015	
75	3	HAYD	5f Gd/Sft	72	4107	
61	12	YORK	6f Soft		4287	
63	8	DONC	5f Heavy	73	4570	

SHARP IMP 10 b g £0

0a	15	LING	7f Aw	45	29	bl
10a	10	LING	7f Aw	45	106	bl
22a	9	LING	7f Aw		159	bl

SHARP LIFE 3 b c £0

58	8	NEWM	6f Good		956
76	5	NEWM	10f Gd/Fm		2135
67	5	DONC	8f Gd/Fm		2611

SHARP MONKEY 5 b g £0

0	9	CATT	12f Gd/Fm		2742	bl

SHARP PEARL 7 ch g £0

0	22	NEWM	7f Soft	57	4547

SHARP PLAY 5 b g £44563

67	1	**PONT**	8f Good		1498*
84	10	EPSO	10f Good	95	1845
93	4	YORK	9f Firm	92	2001
96	2	ASCO	10f Good	92	2170
84	12	SAND	10f Good	92	2475
94	4	NEWM	10f Gd/Fm	96	2648
102	1	**GOOD**	10f Gd/Fm	96	3060*
93	13	GOOD	8f Good	103	3107
84	11	YORK	10f Gd/Fm	101	3563

101 6 NEWB 10f Firm 101 3997

SHARP REBUFF 9 b h £0
72 8 SAND 8f Heavy 84 1042
0 30 NEWM 8f Good 82 4340

SHARP RISK 3 ch c £1048
51a 5 LING 8f Aw 373
52a 3 LING 8f Aw 544
73 11 NEWM 10f Good 957
0 27 NEWM 8f Firm 75 1183
62a 2 SOUT 11f Aw 1502
28a 5 WOLV 9f Aw 2602

SHARP SCOTCH 7 b g £0
42 8 REDC 8f Gd/Sft 53 4217

SHARP SECRET 2 b f £7017
64a 5 SOUT 6f Aw 865
66 2 HAMI 6f Gd/Fm 2778
57 5 REDC 6f Gd/Fm 2990
75 1 WIND 6f Good 62 3354*
73 2 CATT 6f Good 68 3439
73 2 MUSS 7f Gd/Fm 68 3592
65 10 DONC 6f Firm 3888

SHARP SHUFFLE 7 ch g £8717
60a 1 WOLV 7f Aw 61*
59a 1 WOLV 8f Aw 138*
27a 11 SOUT 8f Aw 60 176
59a 2 WOLV 8f Aw 256
37a 7 WOLV 8f Aw 322
54a 2 WOLV 8f Aw 550
54a 4 WOLV 8f Aw 54 675
27a 11 WOLV 7f Aw 54 754
38 13 WARW 8f Heavy 60 1520
64 2 SALI 7f Gd/Fm 1884
63 3 KEMP 8f Gd/Fm 2747
47 2 RIPO 8f Gd/Fm 2834
60 1 CHEP 7f Gd/Fm 3253*
17 13 CHEP 8f Good 3868
8a 10 WOLV 8f Aw 54 4363

SHARP SMOKE 3 gr f £0
16a 6 SOUT 5f Aw 696
4 7 REDC 6f Gd/Sft 1562
0 14 MUSS 5f Firm 35 2374

SHARP SPICE 4 b f £9222
53 4 PONT 10f Heavy 62 943
61 4 NOTT 10f Gd/Sft 62 1086
39 4 CHEP 12f Heavy 62 1555
51 5 NEWB 10f Gd/Fm 60 1942
57 2 BRIG 10f Firm 2041
56 5 FOLK 10f Gd/Fm 58 2296 VIS
50 5 FOLK 10f Good 55 2625
54 3 BATH 10f Firm 55 2789
38 10 SALI 10f Firm 3390
57 3 LING 10f Firm 54 3581
62 1 EPSO 12f Good 53 3858*
58 4 HAYD 11f Gd/Sft 62 4108
30a 9 LING 12f Aw 61 4271
57 3 NEWM 12f Gd/Sft 60 4534

SHARP STEEL 5 ch g £4585
50a 2 SOUT 8f Aw 50
38a 5 SOUT 8f Aw 252
25a 6 WOLV 7f Aw 310 VIS
51a 2 SOUT 7f Aw 1305
63a 1 SOUT 8f Aw 1505*
59a 2 SOUT 7f Aw 56 1801
43a 5 SOUT 7f Aw 56 1979
60a 3 SOUT 8f Aw 58 2121
60a 2 SOUT 11f Aw 4151
30a 9 WOLV 9f Aw 58 4228

SHARP STEPPER 4 b f £24280
78a 1 SOUT 12f Aw 84*
78 3 NEWB 13f Gd/Fm 77 1784
79 6 ASCO 12f Good 78 2069
79 2 DONC 15f Gd/Fm 78 2319

86 1 YORK 14f Good 78 3811*
84 4 NEWM 12f Good 86 4162
67 13 NEWM 12f Good 85 4342

SHARP VISION 2 b f £0
18 8 LEIC 5f Gd/Fm 2507
32 10 BATH 6f Soft 4431

SHARPINCH 2 b c £0
69 6 LING 6f Soft 4188

SHARVIE 3 b g £0
52 12 WIND 10f Good 850
46 9 NOTT 14f Gd/Sft 1369
41 6 BEVE 16f Good 52 2879
36 10 NOTT 16f Gd/Fm 52 3112

SHARWAY LADY 5 b m £0
23a 4 WOLV 7f Aw 46 529
18a 6 WOLV 12f Aw 46 554 bl

SHATHER 3 b c £4709
83 9 NEWM 8f Gd/Sft 972
63a 3 SOUT 8f Aw 1204
65 4 LING 9f Firm 2322
67 3 NEWM 7f Gd/Fm 66 2855
75 2 NEWM 7f Gd/Fm 66 3163
77 2 NEWM 12f Good 72 3629
73 5 NEWB 7f Firm 75 3981
61 10 SAND 7f Soft 75 4204

SHATIN BEAUTY 3 b f £0
0 15 HAMI 6f Good 66 844
0 14 THIR 6f Gd/Fm 64 3349
45 14 CARL 5f Firm 64 3572
0 17 AYR 5f Soft 57 3960
0 23 NEWM 5f Good 55 4185
36 12 AYR 5f Heavy 51 4307
17 9 MUSS 5f Soft 46 4516

SHATIN DOLLYBIRD 2 ch f £6396
73 2 HAMI 5f Firm 1240
68 2 HAMI 5f Gd/Fm 1359
73 3 AYR 5f Good 2162
68 3 HAMI 5f Gd/Fm 2237
73 1 HAMI 5f Gd/Fm 2797*
55 8 MUSS 5f Good 76 3101
67 3 REDC 5f Gd/Fm 3632
73 4 MUSS 5f Gd/Fm 73 3743
0 13 NEWM 5f Good 72 4179

SHATIN LAW 2 b c £0
37 10 HAMI 5f Gd/Fm 1189

SHATIN PLAYBOY 2 ch c £1723
66 4 AYR 6f Gd/Fm 2717
63 4 HAMI 5f Gd/Sft 3533
61 7 AYR 7f Soft 3962
66 2 AYR 7f Heavy 4303
0 11 NEWC 5f Heavy 65 4423
72 5 MUSS 7f Soft 4517
66 7 MUSS 7f Soft 4562

SHATIN VENTURE 3 b c £10558
96 3 YORK 5f Firm 94 1308
85 10 YORK 6f Firm 95 2003
82 10 SAND 7f Gd/Fm 95 2495
84 12 ASCO 5f Gd/Fm 95 3016
81 5 CHES 6f Firm 92 3427
79 11 YORK 5f Gd/Fm 92 3569
85 1 HAYD 6f Heavy 3768*

SHATTERED SILENCE 3 b f £2806
67 7 NOTT 8f Gd/Fm 1269
78 3 SAND 10f Good 2531
78 3 KEMP 12f Gd/Fm 2751
75 3 HAYD 11f Gd/Sft 3265
75 3 BATH 12f Gd/Fm 3818
70 4 NOTT 10f Heavy 4408 VIS

SHAW VENTURE 3 ch c £327
35a 6 WOLV 6f Aw 67 638
17a 13 WOLV 5f Aw 1237
47 6 CHEP 7f Good 1972

38 7 CHEP 8f Gd/Fm 2448 bl
42 5 LEIC 8f Gd/Fm 2914
30 6 LING 10f Firm 3490
40 3 BATH 12f Firm 3624
0 15 LEIC 10f Heavy 4313

SHAYADI 3 £1650
94 4 LEOP 10f Gd/Fm 1314

SHAYZAN 3 b c £193
59a 4 WOLV 7f Aw 41
49a 6 LING 7f Aw 62 112
0 16 SALI 7f Good 1349
43a 7 LING 7f Aw 1745 t
33 12 CHEP 7f Good 1972 t

SHE ROCKS 2 b f £8256
82 1 LING 6f Good 1673*
92 4 ASCO 7f Good 2091
92 2 SALI 7f Gd/Fm 2267

SHE WADI WADI 2 b f £0
0 21 DONC 7f Gd/Sft 4447
62 7 DONC 7f Heavy 4567

SHEBEG 3 ch f £0
10a 10 LING 7f Aw 2759

SHEEP STEALER 12 gr g £0
4a 10 LING 16f Aw 42 285

SHEER FACE 6 b g £7089
51a 5 WOLV 9f Aw 65 270
58a 6 LING 8f Aw 62 336
40a 5 SOUT 11f Aw 59 474
36a 4 WOLV 8f Aw 612 bl
47 8 BRIG 8f Gd/Fm 62 1129
54 1 BRIG 10f Firm 1331*
59 3 BRIG 10f Firm 2041
57 3 BRIG 10f Gd/Sft 2423
52 5 BATH 10f Gd/Sft 57 2552
0 14 NEWM 10f Gd/Fm 55 2958
61 1 BRIG 10f Gd/Fm 53 3244*
61 2 NOTT 10f Good 3524
61 2 CHEP 10f Gd/Fm 60 3683
55 5 BATH 10f Soft 61 4436

SHEER FOCUS 2 b c £1932
46 9 HAYD 6f Soft 1823
63 5 AYR 6f Good 2137
56 7 BATH 6f Firm 2328
70 6 BATH 6f Firm 3620 t
66 7 LING 7f Firm 67 3830 t
71a 1 SOUT 7f Aw 4154* t

SHEER NATIVE 4 b f £1857
57a 1 SOUT 8f Aw 50*
72a 3 LING 10f Aw 76 90
19a 9 LING 12f Aw 72 245

SHEER PASSION 2 b c £0
73 8 NEWM 6f Gd/Fm 3162
61 10 NOTT 6f Good 3520
69 11 DONC 6f Firm 3888

SHEER SPIRIT 3 b f £5321
79 3 SALI 8f Firm 2024
80 1 NEWM 12f Gd/Fm 2963* t
87 4 SALI 14f Firm 3751 t
0 9 KEMP 12f Soft 4039

SHEER TENBY 3 b c £4803
71a 1 CAGN 10f Aw 606*
53 6 PONT 10f Gd/Sft 78 1104
73 7 LEIC 10f Gd/Fm 75 1735

SHEER VIKING 4 b c £16943
95 2 DONC 5f Gd/Fm 90 702
98 2 NEWM 6f Firm 95 1182
100 3 YORK 5f Firm 96 1324
101 2 HAYD 5f Gd/Sft 97 1533
81 16 ASCO 6f Good 99 2151
76 15 ASCO 5f Good 99 2676
92 10 ASCO 5f Gd/Fm 99 3016
93 5 HAYD 5f Gd/Fm 96 3322

89 8 DONC 6f Gd/Fm 96 3861
98 4 ASCO 5f Gd/Sft 95 4129
90 7 NEWM 5f Good 95 4339
88 5 NEWB 6f Gd/Sft 95 4456

SHEERNESS ESSITY 3 b f £0
28a 8 SOUT 7f Aw 88
25a 8 SOUT 8f Aw 303 BL
18a 7 WOLV 8f Aw 350

SHELTERED COVE 9 ch g £0
0a 10 LING 13f Aw 38 168

SHEPHERDS REST 8 b g £0
11a 10 SOUT 14f Aw 46 1301

SHEPPARDS WATCH 2 b f £11061
77 4 SAND 5f Gd/Fm 2526
92 1 **GOOD** 6f Gd/Fm 3090*
101 1 **HAYD** 6f Gd/Fm 3320*
90 9 NEWB 5f Gd/Fm 3482

SHERATON HEIGHTS 3 b f £0
31 8 CHEP 8f Gd/Fm 55 2661
44 7 SALI 7f Gd/Fm 54 3294
38 7 CHEP 10f Gd/Fm 49 3683
0 12 BATH 10f Soft 4141
3 10 LEIC 10f Heavy 4313

SHEREKIYA 2 b f £0
75 5 KEMP 7f Soft 4034
56 5 AYR 8f Heavy 4322

SHERGANZAR 5 b g £0
0a 13 SOUT 12f Aw 301 bl

SHERIFF 9 b g £13340
42 11 NOTT 14f Good 55 788
51 2 FOLK 15f Soft 50 963
46 8 BEVE 16f Firm 51 1276
46 2 RIPO 16f Good 44 1597
50 1 **BATH** 17f Firm 46 1996*
36 9 ASCO 16f Good 50 2173
47 3 BATH 17f Firm 49 2941
44 4 BATH 17f Firm 48 3625
51 1 **BATH** 17f Soft 47 4139*
58 1 **PONT** 18f Soft 51 4376*
11 13 NOTT 16f Heavy 57 4508

SHERIFF SONG 2 br c £0
0 14 NOTT 5f Gd/Sft 4503
0 17 DONC 6f Heavy 4575

SHERINGHAM 3 b f £1701
79a 1 **SOUT** 6f Aw 4364*
74 5 NEWM 6f Gd/Sft 4535

SHERVANA 4 b f £0
35 10 WIND 10f Gd/Fm 2056
0 13 SALI 10f Gd/Fm 2265
0 14 LEIC 10f Gd/Fm 2774

SHERZABAD 3 b c £0
39a 9 WOLV 9f Aw 1388 t
49 8 YARM 10f Gd/Fm 3383
35 15 GOOD 10f Good 55 3663
0 15 YORK 12f Soft 50 4280
29 13 NEWM 8f Gd/Sft 45 4536

SHES A GEM 5 b m £274
52a 3 SOUT 7f Aw 55 75 vis
34a 9 SOUT 6f Aw 54 212 vis

SHES GRAND 2 b f £0
49 6 CARL 5f Firm 2821

SHES MAGIC 3 b f £0
0 21 THIR 6f Soft 909
0a 12 WOLV 9f Aw 42 1040

SHES OUR MARE 7 b m £2240
94 2 CURR 8f Yldg 863

SHIBBOLETH 3 b c £33498
103 1 **NEWM** 7f Gd/Sft 983*
115 1 **NEWM** 7f Gd/Fm 1693+ t
116 4 ASCO 8f Good 2066 t

SHIBL 3 b c £22750
111 1 **CURR** 8f Gd/Fm 2740*

SHIBUNIS FALCON 3 b c £22772
95 1 **SAN** 10f Heavy 1228*

SHII TAKES GIRL 2 ch f £361
70 3 LING 8f Firm 3577
72 8 WARW 7f Gd/Fm 3910
70 5 WIND 8f Heavy 4524

SHIMLA 2 b f £984
59 8 SALI 6f Gd/Fm 1883
51 9 KEMP 7f Gd/Sft 2583
56 5 LEIC 7f Gd/Fm 2916
41 8 CHES 7f Soft 58 4070
56 2 PONT 8f Soft 53 4378

SHINBONE ALLEY 3 b c £4309
66 5 BEVE 5f Firm 1280
85 1 **DONC** 5f Gd/Fm 1843*
80 7 YARM 6f Gd/Fm 2197
72 14 YORK 5f Gd/Fm 90 3569
62 12 HAYD 6f Heavy 3768

SHINGHAAR 3 ch g £0
0 15 NEWM 8f Firm 1188
0 19 NEWM 10f Gd/Fm 1697
61 5 WIND 10f Gd/Fm 2056

SHINING OASIS 2 b f £5870
68 4 KEMP 6f Gd/Fm 2083
70 3 CHEP 5f Gd/Fm 2657
68 5 CHEP 6f Gd/Fm 2972
75 1 **FOLK** 7f Gd/Fm 70 3444*
72 2 EPSO 7f Good 73 3690

SHINING STAR 3 ch f £381
60 4 SOUT 7f Soft 65 1606
0 19 SALI 7f Gd/Fm 63 1889
57 5 HAYD 7f Gd/Sft 61 3269
34 12 FOLK 6f Gd/Fm 3587
57 4 NOTT 6f Soft 59 3975
60 3 WIND 6f Gd/Sft 58 4293
21 9 NEWC 6f Heavy 59 4425
55 5 YARM 6f Heavy 59 4480

SHINNER 2 b f £4517
59a 4 SOUT 5f Aw 865
75 2 REDC 5f Gd/Sft 1130
69 1 **PONT** 6f Good 1864*
55 4 WARW 7f Gd/Fm 2251
59a 9 SOUT 6f Aw 73 2948
53 9 PONT 8f Soft 69 4084

SHIRAZI 2 b c £452
69 5 HAYD 6f Gd/Fm 2454
66 6 CHEP 6f Gd/Fm 2972
74 3 SALI 7f Gd/Fm 3418
66 9 BATH 8f Gd/Fm 73 3817

SHIRLEY FONG 2 b f £0
71 7 WIND 5f Gd/Sft 1424
66 6 NEWM 6f Firm 1856
0 14 KEMP 7f Soft 4035
54 10 DONC 7f Soft 68 4460

SHIRLEY NOT 4 gr g £5787
0 16 PONT 6f Heavy 67 941
69 3 NEWC 5f Heavy 67 1008
73 1 **BEVE** 5f Firm 65 1278*
65 8 THIR 5f Gd/Sft 72 1714
71 4 HAYD 5f Gd/Sft 72 1792
72 7 YORK 5f Gd/Fm 72 1980 BL
70 5 RIPO 5f Gd/Fm 72 2107 bl
73 5 NEWC 5f Gd/Fm 74 2310 bl
54 10 BEVE 5f Gd/Fm 73 2517 VIS
59 9 PONT 5f Gd/Fm 72 2830 bl
0 18 BEVE 5f Good 70 3398

SHIRLEY OAKS 2 b f £0
0 14 WIND 5f Gd/Sft 1424
60 5 LING 7f Good 2653

SHIVA 5 ch m £65400
113 7 NEWM 9f Gd/Sft 967
123 1 **SAND** 10f Soft 1587+
118 3 SAND 10f Gd/Fm 2497
87 7 ASCO 12f Gd/Fm 2998
99 9 NEWM 10f Good 4355

SHOAL CREEK 3 b c £48500
100 9 CURR 12f Good 2409
114 4 YORK 10f Good 3539 VIS
109 1 **CURR** 9f Gd/Sft 4059* bl

SHOESHINE BOY 2 b g £19414
85 2 DONC 5f Gd/Fm 700
85 1 **WARW** 5f Soft 812*
94 1 **NEWM** 5f Soft 985*
98 1 **ASCO** 5f Gd/Sft 1107*
81 9 ASCO 5f Good 2113
86 11 NEWB 5f Firm 2849 BL
97 8 GOOD 5f Gd/Fm 3133

SHOLTO 2 b f £0
0 15 LEIC 6f Firm 2029
57 14 LING 5f Gd/Fm 2214
33 6 HAYD 6f Gd/Fm 2441 BL

SHONTAINE 7 b g £2699
21a 7 LING 7f Aw 40 58
30a 5 WOLV 8f Aw 38 255
40a 1 **SOUT** 8f Aw 38 297*
21a 6 SOUT 8f Aw 38 329
30a 6 SOUT 8f Aw 37 345
42a 3 WOLV 9f Aw 42 383
36a 3 WOLV 9f Aw 42 404
31a 3 WOLV 9f Aw 41 569
0 12 BEVE 8f Heavy 973
0 14 THIR 7f Gd/Sft 1351
0 18 YARM 8f Good 39 1772
39a 8 SOUT 8f Aw 2946
27 10 THIR 8f Gd/Fm 36 3344 bl
17 11 HAMI 8f Gd/Sft 36 3534 bl
30 4 BRIG 8f Firm 3738 bl
29a 5 LING 10f Aw 38 3828 bl

SHOOFHA 3 b f £0
31 10 BATH 12f Soft 4434

SHOOT AWAY 2 b f £0
35 11 MUSS 7f Soft 4517

SHORE VISION 2 b c £0
61 9 LING 6f Soft 4189

SHOTACROSS THE BOW 3 b c £2528
60 16 NEWM 8f Firm 77 1183
0 13 NEWM 8f Firm 76 1853
61 8 BATH 10f Gd/Sft 73 2552
68 3 WARW 11f Gd/Fm 68 2842
67 2 AYR 11f Gd/Fm 65 3140
67 3 RIPO 10f Good 67 3702
33 12 CHES 10f Soft 66 4074
65a 3 WOLV 9f Aw 65 4228
39a 11 LING 8f Aw 65 4330
0 12 BATH 10f Soft 65 4436

SHOTLEY MARIE 5 b m £0
34a 5 SOUT 8f Aw 45 bl
15a 6 SOUT 11f Aw 196 bl
15a 6 SOUT 11f Aw 248 bl
0a 8 SOUT 16f Aw 29 284 bl
0a P SOUT 12f Aw 344 bl

SHOUF AL BADOU 3 b c £3038
92a 6 NAD 9f Dirt 765
0 16 HAYD 8f Gd/Sft 97 1535
82 13 EPSO 7f Gd/Sft 94 1826
81 6 LING 8f Firm 2762
75 5 KEMP 7f Gd/Fm 83 3076
62 11 EPSO 7f Gd/Fm 80 3414
67 6 LING 7f Firm 76 3758
0 20 NEWM 7f Gd/Fm 72 4215
76a 1 **WOLV** 6f Aw 69 4380*

SHOULDHAVEGONEHOME 3 ch f £51
59a 2 WOLV 5f Aw 42 vis

35a	7	WOLV	6f Aw		228	BL
38a	5	SOUT	6f Aw		300	vis
25a	7	WOLV	6f Aw	54	397	bl
42a	5	LING	6f Aw		443	
46a	6	LING	6f Aw		527	bl
0	14	CATT	5f Gd/Sft	47	1817	

SHOW THE WAY 2 ch c £0
64	12	YARM	8f Soft		4512	

SHOWBOAT 6 b g £10319
104	5	KRAN	10f Firm		657	
107	6	NAD	9f Good		768	
111	3	WIND	8f Firm		1291	
84	10	ASCO	8f Good		2064	
108	3	NEWM	7f Firm		2343	
95	9	ASCO	8f Good		2675	
102	3	DONC	8f Gd/Fm		2757	
100	9	ASCO	8f Good	108	2993	
108	4	NEWB	7f Firm		3452	BL
90	3	CHEP	7f Gd/Fm		3682	bl
0	24	ASCO	7f Good	106	4112	

SHOWING 3 b c £0
64	8	LING	7f Gd/Sft		839	
41a	8	SOUT	6f Aw	60	1205	
55	6	NEWM	7f Gd/Fm	60	2855	t
44	13	NEWC	7f Good	60	3033	t
0	11	LING	8f Firm	57	3580	t
0	15	NEWM	7f Good		4018	t

SHRIVAR 3 b c £17509
44	13	DONC	7f Good	72	736	
61	5	BRIG	8f Gd/Sft		894	
60	5	WARW	11f Heavy	66	1002	
69	2	NOTT	14f Gd/Fm	62	1270	
66	4	LEIC	12f Gd/Sft	67	1571	
53	6	YARM	14f Gd/Fm	67	1949	
67	4	WIND	12f Gd/Fm	65	2210	
73	1	WARW	11f Good	65	2463*	
70	4	FOLK	12f Good	69	2624	
50	7	WARW	11f Gd/Fm	73	2842	
60	4	EPSO	10f Gd/Fm	71	3415	
70	2	CHEP	10f Good	69	3870	VIS
80	1	PONT	10f Soft		4088*	vis
81	1	NEWM	10f Good	75	4197*	vis
63	13	YARM	10f Soft	80	4392	vis
67	11	DONC	12f Heavy	80	4580	vis

SHUDDER 5 b g £3439
66	4	LING	7f Gd/Fm		838	
59	3	FOLK	5f Soft		960	
0	15	CHEP	7f Gd/Sft	65	1794	
60	3	SALI	7f Firm		1884	
58	1	FOLK	6f Gd/Fm		2292+	
58	6	PONT	6f Gd/Fm	60	2559	
60	3	SALI	6f Good	60	2690	
35	7	FOLK	6f Good	60	3041	

SHUFFLE 3 b c £0
0	12	SOUT	10f Gd/Sft		858	
19a	6	SOUT	8f Aw		1204	BL
51a	5	SOUT	11f Aw		1502	bl

SHUSH 2 b c £7273
84	1	KEMP	5f Soft		993*	
92	5	ASCO	5f Gd/Sft		1107	
83	6	EPSO	6f Good		1846	
73	12	ASCO	7f Good		2091	
92	1	LEIC	6f Gd/Fm	89	2773*	
73	13	GOOD	7f Firm	94	3149	
84	7	YORK	5f Gd/Fm		3567	
79	5	YARM	6f Soft		4390	

SHUWAIB 3 b c £30118
88	1	GOOD	12f Gd/Fm		1956*	
100	3	NEWM	15f Gd/Fm		2594	
104	1	DEAU	15f Gd/Fm		3545*	
102	4	LONG	15f Soft		3848	
104	3	DORT	14f Heavy		4265	

SHY PADDY 8 b g £0
0a	8	WOLV	12f Aw	38	437	
20a	10	WOLV	16f Aw	34	577	
33	9	LING	11f Good	43	1743	

SIAMO 3 gr c £12258
103	3	COLO	8f Good		1322	

SIAMO DISPERATI 2 ch c £1377
67	3	NEWC	5f Heavy		1764	
40	10	BEVE	5f Gd/Fm		2480	
39	12	YORK	8f Good		3812	
70	2	CATT	5f Soft		4252	
78	6	DONC	6f Gd/Sft		4449	
0	18	DONC	7f Heavy	71	4577	

SIBELIUS 3 b c £0
0	9	LEIC	12f Gd/Sft		832	
0	14	KEMP	8f Gd/Sft		1080	

SIBERTIGO 4 b g £0
0	12	LING	7f Gd/Sft		1261	
0	20	NEWM	8f Gd/Fm	55	1690	
32	7	NEWB	10f Gd/Fm	50	1942	
0	15	FOLK	12f Gd/Fm	45	3586	
0	16	SALI	8f Firm	45	3753	BL

SIBLA 2 b f £7185
80	5	NEWB	6f Gd/Fm		1403	
79	2	SALI	6f Gd/Fm		1882	
73	1	BATH	6f Firm		2328*	
82	2	SALI	6f Good		2687	
72	5	GOOD	6f Gd/Fm	80	3062	
89	1	BATH	6f Firm		3620*	
82	8	DONC	6f Gd/Sft		3862	

SICK AS A PARROT 5 ch g £2130
85a	6	LING	10f Aw	55		e
95a	5	WOLV	8f Aw	89	137	eBL
65a	7	LING	10f Aw		157	ebl

SIEGE 4 br c £4025
98a	8	NAD	8f Dirt		764	
108	3	NEWB	7f Firm		3452	

SIEGFRIED 4 ch g £0
22	7	BRIG	12f Gd/Sft	55	2425	

SIENA STAR 2 b g £10003
54	12	RIPO	5f Soft		821	
60	9	CARL	5f Firm		1252	
53a	4	SOUT	8f Aw		1503	
67	4	THIR	7f Gd/Fm		2057	
75	3	BEVE	5f Gd/Fm		2514	
76	2	CATT	7f Gd/Fm	72	2928	
78	2	BEVE	7f Gd/Fm	73	3411	
78	1	NEWM	8f Good	73	3609*	
56	7	AYR	8f Soft	78	3990	
70	4	MUSS	8f Gd/Sft	78	4132	

SIERRA STORM 5 gr m £0
44	6	THIR	8f Gd/Sft		1352	

SIFAT 5 b m £6089
51	5	WIND	12f Good	55	853	vis
61	1	YARM	10f Gd/Fm	54	1615*	vis
67	1	YARM	10f Good	60	1775*	vis
59	2	LING	9f Firm	56	1917	vis
65	3	NOTT	10f Good	66	3524	vis
34	13	NOTT	10f Soft		3979	vis

SIGN OF HOPE 3 ch c £18079
83	1	WIND	8f Gd/Fm	70	744*	
87	1	PONT	8f Gd/Fm	77	1495*	
96	2	ASCO	8f Good	86	2117	

SIGN OF NIKE 2 b c £13449
102	1	DEAU	6f Heavy		4488*	

SIGN OF THE DRAGON 3 b g £912
60	4	AYR	7f Good		2140	
44	5	PONT	8f Soft		4234	
45	3	AYR	10f Heavy		4326	

SIGN OF THE TIGER 3 b g £12588
57a	3	SOUT	8f Aw	56	125	

63a	1	SOUT	7f Aw	57	416*	
74a	1	WOLV	7f Aw	63	450*	
70a	4	LING	7f Aw	69	488	
65	4	DONC	7f Good	70	736	
69	2	CARL	8f Firm	68	1255	
69	3	THIR	8f Firm	68	1387	
72	1	NEWC	8f Gd/Sft	68	1477*	
60	14	CARL	8f Gd/Fm	73	2242	
54	12	NEWC	8f Good	73	2524	
0a	12	WOLV	9f Aw	73	3495	

SIGN THE TRUCE 2 ch c £0
64	7	NEWC	5f Heavy		1006	
52	6	PONT	8f Good		1497	

SIGNATORY 5 ch g £3097
98	2	DUSS	8f Gd/Sft		2910	

SIGNORINA CATTIVA 4 b f £20914
110	3	CAPA	10f Heavy		12	

SIGNS AND WONDERS 6 b m £388
60a	3	LING	12f Aw		772	

SIGY POINT 3 b f £0
0	14	CHEP	10f Gd/Fm		2448	
19	10	SALI	10f Gd/Fm		2981	
0	15	LEIC	10f Gd/Sft		4029	

SIHAFI 7 ch g £11381
0	17	BEVE	5f Firm	56	1278	
49	4	GOOD	5f Gd/Sft	54	1487	
55	3	AYR	5f Gd/Fm	54	1629	
39	10	GOOD	6f Gd/Fm	53	2124	
55	2	LING	5f Gd/Fm	53	2184	
55	3	WIND	6f Gd/Fm	53	2207	
50	6	NEWC	6f Gd/Fm	53	2275	
60	1	LING	5f Firm	56	2326+	
47	8	HAYD	5f Gd/Fm	59	2505	
63	4	DONC	5f Gd/Fm	59	2753	
51	3	BRIG	5f Firm		2905	
62	2	GOOD	5f Gd/Fm	59	3091	
58	4	CATT	5f Gd/Fm	59	3203	
58	5	PONT	5f Gd/Fm	59	3222	
54	8	CHES	6f Gd/Fm	61	3512	BL
71	1	MUSS	5f Gd/Fm	61	3594*	
54	12	BATH	6f Gd/Fm	68	3821	
61	15	DONC	5f Firm	68	3894	

SILCA BLANKA 8 b h £34412
54a	8	LING	7f Aw		104	
83	1	BRIG	8f Gd/Sft	75	895*	
88	1	CHES	8f Firm	81	1250*	
94	1	CHES	7f Gd/Sft	81	1778*	
67	13	EPSO	8f Good	89	1851	
92	3	YORK	8f Gd/Fm	93	2648	
104	2	CHES	7f Good		2670	
68	7	CHES	8f Gd/Fm	95	3427	
90	6	CHES	8f Firm	95	3510	
87	10	ASCO	8f Good	93	4112	
91	3	YORK	7f Soft	92	4278	

SILCA FANTASY 3 b f £653
56a	4	SOUT	7f Aw		278	
54a	4	WOLV	7f Aw		362	
36a	1	SOUT	8f Aw		415	
25a	6	WOLV	8f Aw		661	
36	10	LEIC	7f Firm	50	2026	
18	9	YARM	7f Gd/Fm		2413	

SILCA LEGEND 2 ch c £19081
85	2	KEMP	5f Gd/Sft		1079	
88	3	WIND	5f Firm		1290	
88	2	GOOD	5f Gd/Sft		1454	
89	4	SAND	5f Soft		1586	
91	2	CHEP	6f Good		1968	
88	2	RIPO	6f Gd/Fm		2106	
88	1	NEWC	6f Firm		2333*	
90	2	YORK	5f Good	87	2698	
94	6	LEOP	6f Good		3372	
97	1	CHES	6f Gd/Fm		3507*	

SILENT NIGHT 3 gr f £0

92	7	AYR	5f Soft			3959	
0	18	REDC	6f Gd/Sft			4219	
59	10	SALI	10f Firm	80		1177	
60	5	BATH	10f Gd/Fm			1439	
49	12	WIND	8f Good	70		3188	BL
48	8	SALI	8f Gd/Fm	70		3422	bl

SILENT SOUND 4 b c £1199

39	13	WIND	10f Gd/Sft	54	1100	
54	4	YARM	11f Gd/Sft	54	1614	
47	8	GOOD	9f Gd/Sft	53	1807	
38	10	YORK	12f Firm	56	2002	
53	2	YARM	10f Firm	52	2387	
52	5	SALI	12f Good	53	2689	
53	3	NEWM	10f Gd/Fm	53	2958	
51	4	YARM	14f Good	55	3233	
25a	10	LING	12f Aw		4186	

SILENT VALLEY 6 b m £0

0	14	NOTT	14f Good	32	788	
31	8	NOTT	14f Heavy	34	1023	
6a	7	SOUT	14f Aw	29	1501	
31	8	LEIC	12f Gd/Sft	37	1736	

SILENT VOICE 3 ch c £0

77	6	SALI	14f Firm		3751

SILENT WARNING 5 b g £3740

89	2	ASCO	16f Gd/Fm	82	2953	
76	6	GOOD	20f Gd/Fm	82	3085	
70	13	NEWM	18f Good	86	4353	

SILIC 5 b h £313253

123	1	GULF	8f Good		16*

SILK DAISY 4 b f £9863

60	4	WIND	8f Gd/Sft	64	1097	
45	5	CHEP	8f Heavy	63	1557	
63	1	GOOD	7f Gd/Fm	60	2128*	
59	5	NEWM	8f Firm	62	2342	
66	1	NOTT	8f Gd/Fm	62	3115*	
62	5	KEMP	8f Soft	66	4038	
0	18	NEWM	7f Soft	66	4547	

SILK GLOVE 3 b c £0

45	7	GOOD	9f Gd/Fm		2129

SILK LAW 2 ch f £10232

77	1	NOTT	6f Good		2010*	
80	1	WARW	7f Gd/Fm		2251*	
84	2	ASCO	8f Good	82	2678	
84	3	ASCO	7f Gd/Fm		3015	
0	19	DONC	7f Gd/Fm	85	3860	

SILK ON SONG 2 b c £0

17a	9	WOLV	7f Aw		4385

SILK SOUK 2 ch f £0

15	9	THIR	7f Gd/Fm		2059
0	9	BEVE	7f Gd/Fm		2513 VIS

SILK ST BRIDGET 3 b f £0

0	21	DONC	8f Gd/Sft	58	1053	
0	13	YARM	8f Gd/Sft	53	1610	
40	11	NEWB	7f Gd/Fm	53	1787	
32	11	LEIC	7f Firm	50	2026	
33	8	DONC	7f Gd/Fm	45	2320	BL
8		LEIC	8f Good	41	2512	bl
37	6	YARM	8f Firm	41	2767	bl
19	12	YARM	6f Gd/Fm	40	3966	
0	12	NEWC	7f Heavy	38	4428	

SILK ST JOHN 6 b g £18225

0	23	DONC	8f Good	90	733	
73	10	KEMP	8f Soft	88	1015	
84	6	SAND	8f Heavy	88	1042	
84	5	KEMP	8f Gd/Sft	88	1077	
90	1	HAYD	8f Soft	85	1490*	
90	3	GOOD	8f Gd/Sft		1635	
94	1	HAYD	8f Gd/Sft	88	1836*	
78	6	SALI	8f Gd/Fm	93	2229	
93	4	SAND	8f Gd/Fm	92	2528	
78	17	GOOD	8f Good	92	3107	

77	8	ASCO	8f Gd/Fm	91	3338	
74	9	ASCO	8f Gd/Sft	90	4126	
76	5	YORK	8f Soft	89	4284	
0	19	NEWM	8f Good	89	4348	
67	15	NEWM	8f Soft	86	4545	

SILK STOCKINGS 3 b f £1155

52	12	ASCO	8f Gd/Fm		1108	
72	3	WARW	11f Gd/Sft		1709	
67	9	ASCO	12f Good		2112	
36	7	YARM	11f Firm	73	2391	
54	8	YARM	10f Good	70	3031	
57	8	LING	10f Firm	65	3581	
47	11	WARW	16f Gd/Fm	60	3916	
0a	P	LING	16f Aw	60	4099	
0	17	LEIC	8f Sft/Hvy		4311	

SILKEN DALLIANCE 5 b m £2210

54a	8	SOUT	8f Aw	80	601	
50a	7	SOUT	8f Aw	76	669	
71	9	GOOD	8f Gd/Sft	80	1450	BL
81	2	HAYD	8f Gd/Sft	78	1836	
71	7	LING	8f Gd/Fm	81	2185	
45	11	GOOD	8f Gd/Fm	80	2356	

SILKEN FOX 3 b c £0

0	15	LING	7f Gd/Fm		1261	
0	15	SALI	7f Good		1349	VIS
31	7	NEWB	10f Gd/Sft		1593	BL
0	14	WIND	12f Gd/Fm		1880	bl

SILKEN LADY 4 br f £386

0	17	REDC	8f Firm	37	1300	
0	17	PONT	10f Good	37	1496	
0	17	YARM	8f Good	30	1772	
26	3	MUSS	12f Gd/Sft	25	2537	
34	6	YARM	11f Gd/Fm	37	2771	
22	7	WIND	12f Gd/Fm	25	2887	
17	5	YARM	10f Firm		3935	
14	8	BEVE	12f Sft/Hv		4041	
18	5	YARM	11f Soft	26	4391	
24	5	YARM	14f Soft		4510	

SILKEN TOUCH 2 b f £812

67	2	NOTT	5f Heavy		1020
25	6	LING	6f Good		1396

SILKEN WHISPER 3 b f £4248

90	1	SAND	10f Good		3232*
89	9	YARM	10f Soft		3918
58	9	ASCO	12f Gd/Sft		4130

SILKEN WINGS 2 b f £2204

72	3	GOOD	6f Good		2357
74	2	BATH	6f Firm		2784
71	2	CARL	5f Firm		3571
55	12	DONC	7f Gd/Fm	71	3860
49	11	LING	7f Soft	68	4191

SILKY DAWN 2 b f £785

90	3	NEWM	7f Good		4183	t
103	5	NEWM	7f Good		4356	t

SILKY FINISH 3 ch f £0

52	6	NOTT	10f Gd/Fm		3006

SILLA 2 b f £14047

64	9	BATH	6f Gd/Sft		1667	
82	3	SAND	5f Gd/Fm		1986	
86	1	SAND	5f Gd/Fm		2526*	
86	1	KEMP	5f Firm	81	2868*	
99	2	NEWB	5f Gd/Fm		3482	
81	7	KEMP	6f Gd/Fm		3797	
89	8	NEWB	5f Gd/Sft		4454	

SILLY GOOSE 2 b f £1370

82	6	NEWM	7f Good		3607
82	2	HAYD	8f Gd/Fm		4104

SILOGUE 3 b g £0

30	7	CATT	8f Good		2421
0	15	NOTT	6f Gd/Fm		2680
39	6	LEIC	8f Good		2914
17	9	PONT	8f Gd/Fm	40	3226

SILVAANI 2 gr c £273

60	4	LING	7f Soft		4483

SILVER ARROW 3 b f £0

75	12	NEWM	7f Gd/Sft		971	
55a	4	WOLV	7f Aw		1035	
39	9	LING	7f Good		1397	
40	11	WARW	7f Gd/Sft	65	1710	
39	10	WARW	12f Gd/Fm	60	2255	

SILVER AURIOLE 3 gr f £0

35	12	WARW	8f Heavy		884	
0	14	BATH	10f Good		1093	
27	7	BATH	8f Gd/Fm		1435	
0	15	WIND	6f Gd/Fm	50	1877	BL
0	14	LEIC	8f Gd/Fm	42	2506	bl

SILVER BULLET 4 gr g £0

0	22	REDC	7f Gd/Sft		1132	
37	9	REDC	7f Gd/Sft		1559	VIS
26	7	AYR	8f Good	29	2136	vis
0	18	RIPO	10f Soft		2538	vis
35	5	CARL	7f Firm		2824	BL

SILVER CHEVALIER 2 gr c £0

0	25	NEWM	8f Good		4349

SILVER CLOUD 2 gr f £0

0	19	WIND	5f Gd/Fm		1197	
37	10	REDC	6f Gd/Sft		1577	
0	18	WIND	8f Gd/Fm		1876	BL

SILVER COLOURS 3 b f £0

82	12	NEWM	7f Good		953

SILVER DAWN 3 gr f £0

35a	7	SOUT	6f Aw		4364

SILVER GREY LADY 2 gr f £850

73	3	NEWM	8f Good		4019
81	8	DONC	8f Gd/Sft		4445

SILVER GYRE 4 b f £545

32a	6	WOLV	16f Aw	56	66	
36a	6	WOLV	12f Aw	49	407	
45a	4	WOLV	16f Aw	48	482	
49a	2	SOUT	16f Aw	48	535	
40a	6	WOLV	16f Aw	42	577	BL

SILVER INFERNO 2 gr c £0

0	15	ASCO	7f Good		2091
58	7	WARW	7f Good		3692

SILVER JORDEN 2 gr f £23270

84	1	LING	6f Soft		1541*
89	1	YARM	6f Gd/Fm		1954*
84	7	NEWM	6f Firm		2344
98	1	SAND	7f Gd/Fm		2935*
100	4	DEAU	7f Gd/Sft		3722

SILVER PATRIARCH 6 gr g £

0	4	SHA	12f Gd/Fm		185

SILVER PRAIRIE 3 b f £0

57	9	NOTT	8f Soft		3977
40	7	HAYD	7f Soft		4093
0	13	LING	8f Soft		4274

SILVER PRINCE 5 gr g £0

0a	7	SOUT	7f Aw		427

SILVER QUEEN 3 ch f £844

45	10	WIND	12f Good	75	853	
48	8	BRIG	10f Good	72	1649	
58	8	REDC	8f Good	67	1892	
66	2	FOLK	10f Gd/Fm	63	2296	
61	4	FOLK	10f Good	65	2625	VIS
62	6	WIND	8f Gd/Fm	65	2890	vis
42	11	NEWM	8f Gd/Fm	63	3317	vis
30	8	BRIG	12f Firm	61	3560	
0	14	LEIC	8f Soft		4032	

SILVER ROBIN 4 b c £1012

88	2	NOTT	14f Gd/Sft		1369

SILVER SECRET 6 gr g £2023

0	19	REDC	8f Firm	40	1296
39	5	NEWM	8f Gd/Fm	38	1690

44	1	**HAYD**	11f Soft	38	1819*
40	6	YARM	10f Firm	47	2387
37	8	PONT	10f Gd/Fm	47	2556
44	6	NEWM	8f Gd/Fm	46	2802
38	8	NEWM	10f Gd/Fm	46	2958
39	5	NOTT	10f Gd/Fm	44	3111
37	5	WIND	12f Good	44	3186 BL
33	5	NEWM	10f Gd/Fm	43	3314 bl

SILVER SKY 4 gr f £0

0a	11	WOLV	7f Aw	47	121
10a	11	LING	8f Aw	40	147
0	13	BRIG	6f Firm	40	1211
0	15	BRIG	7f Firm	40	1336
0	14	WIND	6f Gd/Sft		1423
0	19	WARW	11f Gd/Sft	33	1707

SILVER SOCKS 3 gr c £639

0	20	RIPO	6f Good	53	1600
0	18	THIR	8f Gd/Fm	50	3124
40	6	BEVE	10f Good	44	3396
39	2	BEVE	8f Gd/Fm	39	3656

SILVER SPOON 3 b f £0

46	8	WARW	8f Soft		1063
0a	9	SOUT	8f Aw		1204
47	8	WIND	10f Firm		1293
0	13	REDC	14f Gd/Fm	45	1581

SILVER TONGUED 4 b c £318

35	7	BEVE	7f Firm	48	1275
22	10	NOTT	8f Good	44	1414
0	13	LING	7f Soft	40	1542
29	6	BRIG	7f Gd/Fm	35	1930
22	8	DONC	6f Gd/Fm	32	2315
22	4	THIR	6f Gd/Fm	30	3124
0	11	BEVE	10f Gd/Fm	28	3656
39a	10	LING	7f Aw		4331

SILVER TONIC 4 gr c £0

58	7	FOLK	7f Gd/Fm		2293
62	6	WARW	8f Good		2465

SILVERTOWN 5 b g £13513

59a	2	WOLV	9f Aw	53	60
0a	12	WOLV	12f Aw	55	170
65a	1	**WOLV**	9f Aw	55	569*
73a	1	**LING**	10f Aw	61	618*
14	4	WARW	11f Heavy	55	890
0	16	WIND	10f Gd/Sft	55	1100
60	2	WIND	8f Good	53	2367
68	1	**GOOD**	8f Good	58	3885*
72	1	**WIND**	10f Gd/Fm	65	4291*

SIMAND 8 b m £0

0	14	CARL	7f Firm	30	2282
0	12	RIPO	10f Soft		2538
17a	10	SOUT	8f Aw		2946 BL

SIMAS GOLD 2 b f £1827

60	6	WARW	5f Gd/Fm		2034
54a	1	**SOUT**	5f Aw		2384*

SIMBATU 3 b f £0

41a	8	LING	6f Aw	62	105
58	6	LEIC	6f Gd/Fm	62	2511
35	5	BRIG	5f Firm		2905
0	14	THIR	5f Gd/Sft	57	3781

SIMLA BIBI 2 b f £1624

75	3	LEIC	8f Firm		3836
71	3	YORK	8f Heavy		4297

SIMPATICH 2 ch c £15524

72	3	FOLK	7f Good		2620
58	6	BEVE	7f Gd/Fm		3057
89	3	BEVE	7f Good		3397
90	1	**SAN**	8f Heavy		4242*

SIMPLE IDEALS 6 b g £6492

0	19	BEVE	16f Firm	51	1276
44	2	REDC	14f Gd/Sft	46	1563
40	8	CATT	12f Gd/Fm	46	1816
41	5	REDC	14f Gd/Fm	42	2156

46	5	DONC	15f Gd/Fm	48	2319
40	6	HAMI	13f Gd/Fm	44	2643
41	5	DONC	12f Gd/Fm	44	2755
37	4	BEVE	12f Gd/Fm	40	3674
53	2	YORK	12f Gd/Fm	50	3725
46	5	CATT	12f Soft	48	4003
47	2	HAYD	14f Gd/Sft	48	4105
45	4	REDC	14f Gd/Sft	45	4222
43	6	YORK	14f Heavy	53	4299

SIMPLY BROKE 2 br g £0

43	9	RIPO	5f Good		1595
0	11	NEWC	6f Firm		2333

SIMPLY ERIC 2 b c £1705

71	2	HAMI	8f Gd/Sft		3532
62	4	YORK	8f Gd/Fm		3729
53	4	PONT	6f Soft		4372

SIMPLY NOBLE 4 b c £0

0	18	NEWM	10f Gd/Fm	75	1150
69	10	NEWB	10f Good	73	1375
58	8	NEWM	13f Gd/Sft	71	1594

SIMPLY REMY 2 ch g £0

42	11	NOTT	6f Good		1408
0	15	LING	6f Firm		3832
0	15	LING	6f Gd/Fm		4190

SIMPLY SENSATIONAL 3 ch c £1479

60	4	HAYD	8f Gd/Sft		3477
70	4	NEWC	8f Soft		3707
74	3	NOTT	8f Soft		3977
70	4	WIND	11f Heavy	73	4529

SIMULCASTING 3 ch c £505

51	11	DONC	7f Gd/Sft		1072
70	3	LING	7f Gd/Fm		1263
67	4	LEIC	8f Soft		1548

SINCERITY 3 b f £1758

63	7	YARM	8f Good		1771
78	2	WARW	8f Good		2464
65	3	YARM	7f Firm		2770
63	9	KEMP	8f Soft	77	4038
53	4	YARM	7f Soft		4387

SING A SONG 2 b f £4123

81	1	**WIND**	5f Soft		2545*
85	3	SALI	6f Gd/Sft		4164

SING AND DANCE 7 b m £2958

53	2	MUSS	12f Gd/Fm	50	1147
50	5	MUSS	12f Gd/Fm	52	1432
50	5	HAMI	13f Gd/Fm	52	2801
49	3	MUSS	12f Good	51	3102
54	2	CATT	14f Gd/Fm	51	3201
36	7	HAMI	13f Gd/Sft	49	3378
40	5	MUSS	14f Gd/Fm	53	3590

SING CHEONG 4 b c £1397

57a	2	LING	7f Aw		8
39a	4	LING	8f Aw	58	97
47a	3	LING	10f Aw		238
27a	8	WOLV	8f Aw		308 VIS
46a	4	LING	7f Aw	48	438
55	4	REDC	8f Firm	55	1296

SING FOR ME 5 br m £438

0a	12	SOUT	6f Aw		30
0a	11	SOUT	6f Aw		71
38a	7	WOLV	6f Aw		134
22a	10	SOUT	6f Aw		199
47a	8	WOLV	8f Aw		272
23a	9	WOLV	8f Aw		406
37a	4	SOUT	6f Aw		475
28a	8	WOLV	6f Aw	37	518
30a	4	SOUT	6f Aw		559
35a	2	SOUT	8f Aw	34	602
10a	4	SOUT	7f Aw		693
46a	5	WOLV	6f Aw		753
22a	9	WOLV	8f Aw		1139
31a	6	WOLV	6f Aw		1392

21	10	BEVE	5f Firm	37	1923
0a	13	SOUT	7f Aw	38	2122
32	6	WARW	5f Gd/Fm	35	2252
26a	5	SOUT	5f Aw	35	2632
24	7	BATH	5f Firm		2788

SINGLE CURRENCY 4 b c £0

25	7	LEIC	12f Gd/Sft		832
44	9	LING	10f Gd/Sft		1281
33	6	BRIG	12f Soft	55	4421

SINGLE HONOUR 2 b f £2257

79	5	BATH	7f Gd/Fm		1667
82	2	LEIC	7f Gd/Sft		3333
93	2	CHEP	8f Gd/Fm		3678
95	6	DONC	8f Gd/Fm		3876

SINGLE TRACK MIND 2 b c £1136

0	16	WIND	6f Gd/Fm		3047
69	5	LING	8f Good		4189
76	2	BRIG	6f Heavy		4537

SINGSONG 3 b g £6120

83	4	SAND	5f Heavy	90	1047
90	3	MUSS	5f Firm	88	1687
88	7	EPSO	5f Good	96	1849
92	3	DONC	5f Gd/Fm	89	2348
89	3	CHES	6f Good	91	2663
65	12	YORK	5f Gd/Fm	91	3569
79	5	EPSO	5f Good	91	3687
0	19	DONC	6f Gd/Fm	89	3861
85	6	DONC	5f Gd/Sft	86	4466

SINJAREE 2 b c £0

70	11	YARM	7f Firm		3940
75	5	BRIG	8f Soft		4417

SINNDAR 3 b c £1746694

116	2	LEOP	10f Soft		949 t
119	1	**LEOP**	10f Gd/Fm		1314* t
128	1	**EPSO**	12f Good		1848+ t
130	1	**CURR**	12f Good		2409* t
132	1	**LONG**	12f Good		3929*
134	1	**LONG**	12f Good		4262*

SINON 5 ch g £15070

109	1	**SAIN**	15f Heavy		140*
99	6	YORK	14f Firm		1339
102	5	CURR	14f Yldg		2405
98	7	YORK	14f Good	102	2695

SIONED LYN 3 b f £2191

80	2	WARW	11f Soft		814
0	12	BATH	10f Good		1093
48	10	SALI	10f Good		1344
53	3	CHEP	12f Heavy	63	1555
55	11	CHEP	10f Gd/Sft		1796
29	12	NOTT	10f Good		2012

SIOUX CHEF 3 b f £0

0	8	YARM	8f Heavy	72	4478

SIPOWITZ 6 b g £275

36a	5	SOUT	14f Aw		1975
13a	8	SOUT	12f Aw		2298
40a	3	WOLV	15f Gd/Fm	43	3276
29	11	FOLK	16f Gd/Fm	50	3448
0a	11	WOLV	15f Aw		4024

SIPSI FAWR 3 b f £5335

78	11	NEWM	7f Gd/Sft		971
82	1	**NOTT**	8f Gd/Sft		1084*
81	3	GOOD	10f Gd/Fm	76	1958
72	7	NEWM	8f Firm	78	2342

SIPTITZ HEIGHTS 2 b f £6119

53	5	CATT	5f Good		1813
73	14	ASCO	5f Good		2088
81	1	**PONT**	6f Good		2363*
75	9	ASCO	6f Gd/Fm		2996
90	5	AYR	5f Soft		3959
87	7	AYR	6f Gd/Sft		4009
85	5	CORK	6f Gd/Sft		4315
82	6	NEWB	7f Sft/Hvy		4467

SIR DESMOND 2 gr c £0

51	8	NEWM	6f Gd/Fm		3627	
34	8	NOTT	6f Soft		3973	

SIR ECHO 4 b c £0

71	12	NEWM	12f Good	85	4162	

SIR EDWARD BURROW 2 b c £799

61	7	HAMI	6f Good		1189	
52	4	CARL	6f Firm		2014	
25	11	NEWC	7f Good		2521	
39	8	NEWC	7f Good	56	3246	
49	10	AYR	7f Good		3363	
57	3	MUSS	8f Gd/Fm		3740	
41	6	PONT	10f Soft		4230	
0a	10	WOLV	8f Aw	59	4439	

SIR EFFENDI 4 ch c £8112

92	2	NEWB	9f Firm	90	2853	
89	7	GOOD	10f Gd/Fm	91	3060	
92	1	CHEP	7f Gd/Fm		3682+	
81	7	GOOD	7f Good		3884	

SIR FERBET 3 b c £13494

90a	2	WOLV	8f Aw		708	
90a	1	WOLV	8f Aw		920*	
50	10	SAND	8f Heavy	87	1055	
78	7	YORK	8f Firm	84	1341	
87	1	NEWM	8f Firm	83	1853*	
74	11	NEWM	8f Gd/Fm	87	2858	
81	9	NEWM	8f Good	86	3022	
81	4	CHEP	8f Gd/Fm	85	3254	
88	2	PONT	8f Firm	85	3505	
87	5	DONC	8f Firm	89	3897	
80	9	NEWM	8f Good	87	4348	
0	18	NEWM	8f Soft	87	4545	

SIR FRANCIS 2 b c £14965

78	5	DONC	5f Gd/Fm		700	
86	2	RIPO	5f Soft		821	
86	1	BRIG	5f Gd/Sft		891*	
42	10	NEWC	5f Heavy		1006	VIS
72	6	BATH	5f Firm		1995	
90	1	BRIG	6f Gd/Fm	82	3258*	
93	3	CATT	6f Good	88	3439	
91	2	WARW	15f Good	89	3693	
98	1	YARM	6f Soft		4390*	

SIR JACK 4 b c £1413

0	18	RIPO	6f Soft	80	824	
57	10	THIR	5f Soft		905	
25a	8	SOUT	7f Aw		1305	
57	2	BRIG	6f Gd/Sft		1508	
50	4	REDC	7f Gd/Sft		1559	
55	4	WIND	6f Gd/Fm	56	2054	
32	13	NOTT	6f Gd/Fm	56	2193	
36	6	NOTT	6f Gd/Fm		2680	
49	3	CATT	6f Gd/Fm		2744	bl
27	10	HAMI	6f Gd/Fm		2798	bl

SIR NICHOLAS 3 b c £11105

110	1	LEIC	6f Gd/Sft		829+	
112	2	ASCO	6f Gd/Sft		1111	
109	6	ASCO	6f Good		2115	
112	5	NEWM	6f Gd/Sft		2960	
106	7	DEAU	7f Good		3212	

SIR NINJA 3 b c £5207

83	5	THIR	8f Soft		925	
95	6	CHES	10f Good		1246	
100	2	KEMP	8f Soft		1530	
89	6	EPSO	7f Gd/Fm		1830	VIS
0	11	GOOD	12f Gd/Fm	102	3131	
0	32	NEWM	9f Gd/Fm	98	4212	

SIR SANDROVITCH 4 b g £3382

59	7	NEWC	5f Soft	71	758	
42	9	NEWC	5f Heavy	69	1008	
0	24	THIR	5f Good	66	1162	
65	4	BEVE	5f Firm	65	1278	
77	1	AYR	5f Gd/Fm	65	1629*	
65	8	MUSS	5f Firm	71	1687	
70	5	CATT	5f Gd/Fm	73	2418	

SIR WALTER 7 b g £0

21a	7	LING	10f Aw	38	102	BL
23a	7	WOLV	12f Aw		231	bl
25a	6	WOLV	9f Aw		292	bl

SIRENE 3 ch f £3598

54a	1	SOUT	7f Aw		88*	
10a	12	SOUT	8f Aw	56	128	
61a	2	SOUT	5f Aw	60	202	BL
48a	1	WOLV	8f Aw	60	275	bl
60a	2	SOUT	6f Aw		300	bl
0a	12	SOUT	10f Aw	60	1205	bl
47	8	WIND	6f Firm	60	1289	bl
0	15	NEWB	7f Gd/Fm	57	1787	
35	8	LEIC	6f Gd/Fm	52	2511	
51a	3	SOUT	5f Aw	58	2632	
44	5	NEWC	7f Good	48	3033	
23	7	LEIC	7f Gd/Fm		3218	bl
42	7	BATH	6f Gd/Fm	55	3516	bl
0a	11	SOUT	6f Aw	56	4156	bl

SIRINNDI 6 b g £3898

24a	10	SOUT	16f Aw	60	1416	
52	5	LING	11f Good	57	1743	
23	9	WARW	15f Good	52	2461	
19	9	LING	16f Firm	49	2763	
42	6	FOLK	16f Gd/Fm	46	3448	
48	2	FOLK	12f Gd/Fm	46	3586	
38	5	MUSS	16f Gd/Fm	44	3742	
43	6	NOTT	16f Soft	49	3978	
39	8	SALI	14f Gd/Sft	46	4166	
50	1	CATT	16f Soft	46	4258*	

SISAO 4 ch c £4403

45a	6	LING	6f Aw		25	bl
48a	3	WOLV	6f Aw		63	bl
60a	2	LING	6f Aw		95	bl
61a	1	WOLV	6f Aw		273*	bl
39a	8	SOUT	6f Aw	61	454	bl
32a	10	SOUT	6f Aw	59	499	bl
49a	4	LING	6f Aw	56	628	bl
0	14	FOLK	6f Soft	52	958	bl

SISTER CELESTINE 2 b f £4823

74	2	KEMP	6f Gd/Fm		3358	
69	4	WARW	7f Good		3692	
75	1	BEVE	7f Good		3952*	
75	4	NEWM	8f Good	74	4350	
68	6	DONC	8f Gd/Sft	74	4450	

SISTER KATE 3 b f £0

41	7	AYR	10f Gd/Fm		1655	
44	6	HAYD	8f Gd/Sft		1837	
42	7	BEVE	10f Gd/Fm	47	2484	
0	15	NEWC	7f Good	43	3033	

SITARA 2 ch f £0

68	8	REDC	6f Gd/Sft		4216	
71	8	LEIC	7f Stt/Hvy		4309	
0	13	WIND	8f Heavy		4524	

SITTING PRETTY 4 b f £0

0	P	THIR	12f Gd/Sft		1353	
0	13	PONT	10f Soft		1699	
23	5	MUSS	8f Gd/Sft	24	2533	
0	17	YARM	8f Good	24	3236	BL
0	14	HAMI	8f Gd/Sft	31	3380	bl
0	15	THIR	8f Gd/Sft		3775	
0	13	REDC	7f Gd/Fm		4218	

SIX FOR LUCK 8 b g £0

0	18	HAMI	6f Gd/Fm	54	1192	t
0	16	HAMI	6f Firm		1239	t
0	15	MUSS	5f Gd/Sft		1430	t
0	13	MUSS	5f Gd/Sft	38	2535	t
0	10	HAMI	6f Gd/Fm	37	2796	t

SIXTY SECONDS 2 b c £5653

94	2	NEWM	7f Good		2346	
96	1	LEIC	7f Firm		3840*	
80	12	NEWM	7f Good		4196	

SIZE DOESNT MATTER 2 b c £492

54	10	WARW	5f Soft		812	
47a	3	LING	5f Aw		878	
43	9	FOLK	7f Gd/Fm		3582	
25	11	LING	6f Firm		3757	

SKELTON MONARCH 3 ch c £1048

50a	6	WOLV	7f Aw		1035	
32a	6	WOLV	7f Aw		1141	
42	3	LEIC	8f Gd/Sft		1572	
18	8	NOTT	10f Soft	46	1644	
38	7	PONT	8f Good		1865	
0	13	CHES	10f Gd/Fm		2245	
46	3	BEVE	7f Firm		2731	
46	3	LEIC	8f Gd/Sft		2914	
20	13	HAYD	8f Gd/Sft		3266	t

SKI FREE 3 b f £0

21a	10	SOUT	5f Aw		217	t
31a	5	LING	5f Aw	46	234	
17a	6	LING	5f Aw		357	t
0a	8	SOUT	6f Aw	35	515	
9	8	CATT	6f Gd/Fm	46	2440	
0	12	YARM	8f Gd/Fm	38	3964	
0a	10	WOLV	7f Aw		4384	

SKI RUN 4 b f £25005

72	12	WIND	10f Good	77	1729	
85	1	ASCO	16f Gd/Fm	75	2953*	
110	3	YORK	16f Good		3538	
104	3	DONC	15f Gd/Fm		3863	
54	10	ASCO	12f Gd/Sft		4130	

SKI WELLS 2 b f £0

53	10	SALI	8f Gd/Sft		4163	
59	12	DONC	7f Heavy		4566	

SKIBO 3 b c £607

82	3	BATH	10f Good		1093	

SKIFFLE MAN 4 b g £0

0a	11	SOUT	12f Aw		84	

SKIMMER 2 b c £0

0	12	BRIG	7f Soft		4415	

SKIMMING 4 b c £3302

77a	1	WOLV	8f Aw		308*	
94a	4	WOLV	8f Aw		448	

SKIMRA 3 b f £2758

78	1	FOLK	12f Soft		964*	
91	5	CHAN	12f Gd/Sft		1748	

SKIP 6 b g £24194

117	1	BADE	6f Gd/Sft		1746*	

SKIPPING 3 b c £4611

108	2	DEAU	10f Good		3369	

SKITTLES 2 br f £0

65	7	DONC	5f Gd/Sft		1048	
49	8	NEWM	7f Gd/Fm		2599	
38	7	BRIG	7f Gd/Fm		2723	
0	P	YARM	7f Firm		2898	BL

SKUKUSA 2 b f £0

54	8	NOTT	6f Good		2010	

SKY CITY 4 b f £0

30a	8	LING	10f Aw		3	
0a	13	LING	10f Aw	47	100	
0a	10	LING	13f Aw	41	167	
27a	7	LING	10f Aw		238	
16a	5	LING	12f Aw		267	
44a	6	LING	10f Aw		314	
0a	11	LING	8f Aw		353	
0a	12	WOLV	12f Aw	32	408	
0	12	YARM	8f Gd/Fm		2411	
0	8	WIND	12f Good		2715	
0	11	YARM	14f Firm	34	2902	BL

SKY DOME 7 ch g £5772

52	11	NEWM	10f Gd/Fm	77	1150	

69	6	SALI	7f Good	75	1348
61	10	RIPO	8f Good	73	1598
78	2	KEMP	8f Gd/Fm	71	1926
73	3	GOOD	8f Gd/Fm	71	2126
73	9	CARL	8f Gd/Fm	75	2242
74	3	EPSO	9f Gd/Sft	73	2629
73	2	KEMP	8f Gd/Fm	72	3078
70	5	AYR	8f Good	72	3365
65	4	EPSO	9f Good	72	3685
64	5	WIND	8f Gd/Sft		4292
67	6	NEWM	8f Good	70	4340

SKY HOOK 3 ch c £0

51a	5	LING	6f Aw		153
47	5	LEIC	6f Gd/Fm	58	3095
35	10	LEIC	10f Gd/Fm	58	3217
14a	13	WOLV	8f Aw	52	3499 BL
40	8	BATH	8f Gd/Fm	52	3816 VIS
35a	8	SOUT	6f Aw	47	4156 vis
58	4	PONT	6f Soft		4233 bl

SKY QUEST 2 b c £1262

81	2	HAYD	7f Good		3287

SKY TO SEA 2 b c £355

76	3	MUSS	7f Soft		4562

SKYE 3 ch f £0

50a	9	SOUT	5f Aw		34

SKYE BLUE 3 b g £4347

33a	9	SOUT	6f Aw		46
72	5	WIND	10f Good		850
70	3	WARW	12f Soft	70	1064
53	12	WIND	12f Gd/Fm	70	1199
60	2	NEWB	10f Gd/Sft		1593
61	3	WIND	10f Good		2372
69	2	WIND	12f Good	65	2712
57	12	NEWM	12f Gd/Fm	68	3167
64	5	NOTT	14f Good	68	3522
61	6	BATH	13f Gd/Fm	65	3819
61	5	NOTT	10f Soft		3979
54	4	NEWM	12f Good		4178
57	2	AYR	11f Heavy		4304

SKYERS A KITE 5 b m £14354

46	2	RIPO	12f Soft	43	822
22	12	NOTT	14f Heavy	44	1023
42	6	PONT	12f Good	44	1499
40	5	LEIC	12f Gd/Sft	43	1736
43	3	CATT	12f Gd/Sft	43	1816
47	1	BEVE	12f Firm		2219*
43	5	BEVE	12f Good	47	2482
46	2	HAYD	12f Good	43	3284
51	1	HAMI	13f Gd/Sft	43	3378*
42	5	HAMI	12f Gd/Sft	44	3531
42	5	CATT	16f Soft	50	4006
68	1	YORK	10f Soft		4275*
22	7	NEWC	10f Heavy	44	4427

SKYERS FLYER 6 b m £524

16a	10	SOUT	6f Aw	46	1421
24	9	LEIC	6f Soft	46	1545
34	10	CATT	6f Gd/Sft	44	1815
28	9	BEVE	5f Firm	43	1923
27	8	NOTT	6f Gd/Fm	39	2193
10a	9	SOUT	6f Aw	42	2297
30	8	REDC	8f Gd/Fm	35	2861
26	6	BEVE	7f Good	35	2882
42	7	RIPO	8f Gd/Fm		3711
36	2	NEWC	7f Heavy	32	4426

SKYLARK 3 ch f £859

50a	7	SOUT	5f Aw		127
68	4	DONC	5f Good		1516
55	6	WARW	6f Gd/Sft		1712
58	5	SALI	6f Gd/Fm	67	2230
71	3	KEMP	7f Gd/Sft		2585
0	14	EPSO	7f Good	65	2794
49	10	SALI	6f Gd/Fm	65	3293

64	8	NEWM	8f Gd/Fm		3626

SLAM BID 3 b c £356

69	5	KEMP	7f Gd/Sft		2585
42a	6	SOUT	6f Aw		2947
52	3	HAYD	8f Gd/Sft		3266
34	8	NEWM	7f Good		3612 BL
13	14	YARM	8f Gd/Fm	53	3970
0	13	BATH	8f Soft	50	4435

SLANEYSIDE 3 ch g £2954

54	8	HAMI	11f Gd/Sft	67	3379
62	1	MUSS	12f Gd/Fm		3741*
0	7	AYR	15f Soft	65	3961 VIS
50a	7	WOLV	12f Aw	62	4226 vis
0	11	AYR	10f Heavy	60	4306
35a	6	WOLV	9f Aw	57	4382
46	8	MUSS	12f Soft	57	4521
18	13	MUSS	12f Gd/Sft	57	4560 BL

SLAPY DAM 8 b g £0

3a	10	WOLV	16f Aw	46	66
12	9	SALI	12f Gd/Fm	43	1888
0a	10	SOUT	11f Aw		2381
0	16	GOOD	11f Good	51	3887

SLASHER JACK 9 b g £0

41	9	MUSS	16f Gd/Sft	60	797

SLEAVE SILK 5 b m £3801

50a	2	LING	12f Aw	48	290
27a	8	LING	12f Aw	53	377
51a	1	LING	12f Aw	49	528*
35a	6	LING	16f Aw	55	548

SLEW THE RED 3 b c £11527

114	2	LONG	12f Soft		4394

SLICK WILLIE 3 b g £0

0	17	DONC	7f Good	76	736 bl
0	15	THIR	8f Good	75	1387
35	15	SAND	7f Soft	72	1569 bl
46	9	PONT	10f Good	68	1866

SLICKLY 4 gr c £49952

118	1	LONG	10f Good		2072*
120	1	LONG	10f Good		4238*
109	8	NEWM	10f Good		4355

SLIEVE BLOOM 3 b g £332

71	6	FOLK	7f Soft		962
55	10	LING	7f Gd/Sft		1261
64	5	NOTT	8f Soft		1643
0	12	CHEP	6f Gd/Fm	62	2489
0a	11	WOLV	8f Aw	60	3769
51	3	YARM	11f Firm		3917
24a	10	LING	12f Aw	49	4486

SLIGO BAY 2 b c £22122

101	3	LONG	9f Good		4237
103	2	CURR	8f Soft		4397
103	3	SAIN	10f Soft		4556

SLIP KILLICK 3 b f £0

74	6	CHES	7f Gd/Fm		1224
20	11	CARL	7f Firm	57	2017

SLIP STREAM 4 ch c £38710

80a	7	NAD	8f Dirt		764 VIS
90	15	ASCO	8f Good	111	2090
118	1	HOPP	8f Good		2573*

SLIPPER ROSE 2 ch f £722

56	4	DONC	5f Good		730
63	3	BEVE	5f Heavy		974
45	9	PONT	6f Good		1864
29	6	BEVE	7f Firm		2218
49	10	HAYD	6f Gd/Sft		2454
49	8	BEVE	5f Firm		2730
48	7	BEVE	5f Gd/Sft		3055
30	8	LEIC	6f Gd/Fm	52	3216
0	12	LEIC	8f Firm	48	3837
47a	5	WOLV	6f Aw		4244
36a	7	WOLV	8f Aw		4362
37	6	MUSS	5f Soft	45	4561

SLIPSTREAM KING 3 gr c £3842

110	3	LONG	8f Heavy		1025
107	1	LONG	8f V		1318

SLOANE 4 ch c £4842

78	2	NOTT	8f Good		784
70	1	NEWC	7f Firm		3604*

SLUMBERING 4 b c £12871

82	4	SAND	8f Heavy	82	1042
77	7	THIR	8f Good	81	1160
0	16	GOOD	8f Gd/Sft	80	1450
49	12	NEWB	7f Gd/Sft	80	1590 BL
49	11	WIND	10f Gd/Fm	76	1878
65	11	WIND	6f Gd/Fm	76	2054 bl
69	6	WIND	6f Good	70	2371 bl
69	3	EPSO	7f Good	70	2631 bl
69	4	NEWB	6f Firm	70	2813 bl
56	8	NEWM	6f Firm	70	3297 bl
47	8	EPSO	6f Good		3689 bl
59	5	LING	7f Good	67	4102
69	1	SAND	7f Soft	65	4204*
74	1	NOTT	6f Heavy	68	4411*
53	14	NEWM	7f Soft		4547

SMALL CHANGE 2 b f £12180

97	1	ASCO	7f Good		4114*
92	11	NEWM	7f Good		4356

SMALL FRY 2 b f £315

61a	3	SOUT	5f Aw		801

SMART DANCER 2 b c £4331

60	5	NEWC	5f Gd/Sft		1475
29	10	NEWC	5f Good		2521
69	4	CARL	5f Firm		2821
66	4	NEWC	6f Good		3032
79	1	THIR	4f Gd/Fm		3617*
47	10	DONC	8f Gd/Sft	78	4450

SMART PREDATOR 4 gr g £25351

34	12	LEIC	7f Gd/Sft	76	834
0	19	NEWC	7f Heavy	74	1011
72	3	THIR	8f Good	70	1158
57	9	THIR	6f Gd/Sft	70	1356
72	3	DONC	7f Good	70	1514
73	1	REDC	7f Gd/Fm		1579*
67	12	DONC	7f Gd/Fm	73	1840
73	5	YORK	6f Firm	72	2000
77	2	NEWC	6f Firm	72	2334
0	18	YORK	6f Good	76	2697
79	3	GOOD	6f Gd/Fm	76	3136
0	8	BEVE	5f Good	77	3398
87	1	YARM	5f Gd/Fm	77	3668*
85	3	DONC	6f Gd/Fm	84	3861
87	2	YARM	5f Firm	84	3920
86	5	HAYD	6f Gd/Fm	86	4107

SMART RIDGE 3 ch c £18635

99	5	SAND	8f Heavy	98	1055
97	7	HAYD	8f Gd/Sft	98	1535
99	2	EPSO	7f Gd/Sft		1830
57	19	ASCO	7f Good		2087
102	2	SAND	7f Gd/Fm	98	2495
101	3	GOOD	7f Firm		3155
106	4	SALI	8f Gd/Fm		3291
58	13	NEWB	8f Firm	100	3998
100	5	ASCO	7f Good	100	4112
83	7	YORK	7f Soft	99	4278

SMART SAVANNAH 4 b c £0

71	13	KEMP	8f Gd/Fm	93	1077

SMART SPIRIT 6 b m £0

36	5	LEIC	12f Good	47	791
31	9	SOUT	10f Gd/Sft	44	859

SMART SQUALL 5 b g £0

65	11	EPSO	10f Heavy	98	1031

SMARTER CHARTER 7 br g £7044

55	1	PONT	10f Soft	50	871*
57	2	NOTT	10f Gd/Fm	54	1272

59	3	YARM	10f Gd/Sft	55	1615	
59	2	PONT	10f Soft	55	1705	
58	2	YARM	10f Good	55	1775	
59	3	NOTT	10f Good		1875	
59	2	KEMP	12f Gd/Fm	57	2081	
48	5	PONT	10f Good	58	2366	
47	6	HAYD	11f Gd/Fm	58	2453	
55	3	BEVE	10f Gd/Sft	56	3052	
44	7	HAMI	12f Gd/Sft	56	3531	
43	6	YORK	10f Gd/Fm	56	3731	
54	4	SAND	10f Soft	54	4208	
52	4	PONT	12f Soft	54	4229	
43	5	NEWC	10f Heavy	51	4404	
40	7	MUSS	12f Soft	50	4560	

SMARTS MEGAN 4 b f £0

0	15	LEIC	10f Gd/Sft		833	
0	12	BRIG	7f Firm	34	1335	
6a	10	SOUT	7f Aw	34	1506	
18	7	NOTT	14f Gd/Fm	25	3002	
10	9	REDC	14f Gd/Fm		3633	

SMASHING TIME 2 b f £0

74	7	NEWM	7f Good	4184
68	8	YARM	8f Heavy	4475

SMILE ITS SHOWTIME 3 b g £0

31	10	NEWM	6f Good		956
54	8	NOTT	8f Gd/Sft		1084
45a	8	WOLV	9f Aw		1388
40	10	HAMI	8f Gd/Fm	49	1907

SMIRFYS PARTY 2 ch c £1957

68	6	CHES	5f Gd/Fm		2248
72	2	CHES	5f Gd/Fm		2668
76	5	PONT	5f Firm		3500
67	5	NOTT	6f Soft	71	3976
72a	3	WOLV	6f Aw		4225
65a	3	WOLV	5f Aw		4441

SMIRK 2 ch c £1570

79	6	NEWB	6f Firm		3980
74	11	NEWM	6f Good		4341
87	2	NEWB	6f Sft/Hvy		4471

SMITH AND WESTERN 2 b c £8548

68	5	WIND	5f Firm		1290
0	14	CHEP	6f Gd/Sft		1798
82	1	EPSO	7f Gd/Sft		2430*
87	2	ASCO	7f Good		2677
87	3	GOOD	6f Gd/Fm	85	3062
78	5	SALI	7f Gd/Fm		3391
77	13	DONC	6f Gd/Fm		3862
85	4	SALI	6f Gd/Fm		4164

SMOGAR 3 ch c £286

55a	3	LING	6f Aw		153

SMOKEY FROM CAPLAW 6 b g £0

0	20	AYR	6f Heavy	51	4327
43	5	MUSS	7f Soft	46	4522

SMOKIN BEAU 3 b g £23717

77a	3	SOUT	5f Aw	74	72	
81a	1	SOUT	5f Aw		127*	
75a	5	LING	6f Aw	77	222	
79a	3	WOLV	5f Aw	77	275	
80a	2	WOLV	5f Aw	78	361	
60a	10	WOLV	5f Aw	80	491	
65	9	WARW	8f Heavy		888	
77	2	KEMP	6f Soft	73	994	
60	8	LING	6f Gd/Sft	76	1285	VIS
64	10	WIND	10f Gd/Fm	76	1427	vis
60	10	ASCO	5f Good	75	2168	
72	3	SAND	5f Gd/Fm	72	2478	
63	6	SAND	5f Gd/Fm	71	2934	
81	1	GOOD	5f Gd/Fm	71	3135*	
84	1	NEWB	5f Gd/Fm	79	3485*	
70	13	GOOD	6f Good	83	3646	
80	7	AYR	5f Soft	83	3960	
79	9	AYR	6f Gd/Sft	83	4010	
76	10	WIND	5f Heavy	82	4527	

SMOOTH SAILING 5 gr g £7082

76	7	KEMP	8f Soft	85	1015	
84	4	KEMP	8f Gd/Sft	85	1077	
79	8	ASCO	7f Gd/Sft	85	1110	
53	10	LING	8f Gd/Fm	83	2185	
65	5	CHEP	8f Gd/Fm	80	2492	
82	1	NEWM	8f Gd/Fm	77	3118*	
72	8	NEWM	8f Gd/Fm	82	3325	
0	15	GOOD	9f Good	82	3883	
61	15	NEWM	8f Good	80	4340	

SMOOTH SAND 3 b c £7219

74	1	MUSS	8f Gd/Sft	67	800*	
77	1	BRIG	10f Gd/Sft	70	892*	
77	3	PONT	10f Gd/Sft	76	1104	
52	6	EPSO	10f Good		3857	
0	15	KEMP	8f Soft	78	4038	

SMOOTHIE 2 gr c £533

68	3	AYR	6f Gd/Fm		3137	
68	9	NEWB	7f Gd/Fm		3484	
59	5	HAYD	5f Soft		3767	
66	4	LING	5f Soft	68	4191	
24	10	PONT	8f Soft	66	4378	

SMUDGER SMITH 3 ch g £1532

55	8	REDC	10f Firm	63	1299	
67	3	BEVE	12f Good	63	1446	
52	4	REDC	14f Gd/Sft	60	1581	
52	6	RIPO	12f Good	63	1862	
47a	4	SOUT	12f Aw	59	2382	
53	6	BEVE	12f Gd/Fm	59	2482	VIS
49	2	AYR	15f Good	51	3367	vis
47	5	CATT	16f Good	51	3442	vis
43	5	CARL	17f Good	51	3575	vis

SMYSLOV 2 b c £5136

80	8	NEWM	7f Firm		2346	
80	4	NEWB	8f Firm		2708	
80	4	CHES	7f Firm		3169	
77	1	HAMI	8f Gd/Sft		3532*	
82	4	AYR	8f Soft	80	3990	

SNAKE GODDESS 2 b f £0

52	10	LING	7f Soft	4484

SNAP CRACKER 4 b f £768

19a	8	SOUT	6f Aw	66	183	
50a	7	LING	5f Aw	59	235	
0a	12	WOLV	6f Aw	51	352	
24a	11	WOLV	5f Aw	46	508	
44a	2	WOLV	7f Aw	42	751	
36	14	THIR	6f Soft	62	910	
0	18	NOTT	5f Gd/Sft	57	1082	
35	9	NEWC	5f Gd/Sft	52	1479	
26	11	LEIC	5f Gd/Sft	47	1734	
0a	y	SOUT	5f Aw	45	2632	
0	17	PONT	5f Gd/Fm	47	3222	
22	11	MUSS	5f Gd/Fm	42	3594	

SNATCH 3 b f £3066

30	6	RIPO	10f Gd/Fm		2105	
46	4	LEIC	10f Gd/Fm		2510	
29	9	LEIC	10f Good		2914	
16	12	YARM	8f Good	44	3236	
45	1	YARM	8f Gd/Fm	40	3970*	
47a	2	LING	10f Aw	45	4482	

SNETTERTON 3 £2305

104	4	LONG	12f Good	1380	BL

SNIZORT 3 £327

85	4	DONC	8f Good	3864
0	21	NEWM	8f Good	4349

SNOW BUNTING 2 ch c £704

92	3	NEWB	6f Gd/Fm	1403

SNOWEY MOUNTAIN 2 gr c £10313

64	6	YORK	6f Firm	2005
77	4	NEWC	7f Good	2521
72	4	WIND	6f Gd/Fm	3047

(SNOWEY MOUNTAIN cont.)

78	3	REDC	6f Firm	77	3327	
65	6	NEWM	8f Good	77	3609	
82	3	DONC	6f Firm		3888	
83	1	YARM	8f Gd/Fm	75	3968*	

SNOWSTORM 2 gr c £20532

84	2	AYR	6f Gd/Fm		1653	
94	6	ASCO	7f Good		2091	
89	1	AYR	7f Firm		2873*	
97	2	NOTT	8f Good		3523	
97	1	DONC	8f Gd/Fm	92	3879*	
92	10	DONC	8f Soft		4463	

SNUGFIT ROSIE 4 ch f £1457

57	5	CATT	16f Soft	60	4006
53	4	HAYD	14f Gd/Sft	58	4105
56	2	PONT	18f Soft	56	4376

SO DAINTY 3 b f £0

0	12	EPSO	9f Good	62	2795
0	17	WIND	8f Good	57	3188
0	17	LING	8f Firm	55	3580

SO DIVINE 2 br f £3053

69	4	CARL	5f Firm		2277
77	1	RIPO	5f Soft		2539*
76	5	DONC	5f Gd/Fm		2756

SO FOXY 2 b f £0

0	12	BATH	5f Firm		3204
0	15	YORK	5f Good		3812
44a	7	WOLV	7f Aw		4025
44a	4	WOLV	8f Aw		4362

SO PRECIOUS 3 b f £1151

92	4	ASCO	8f Gd/Sft		1108
91	7	LONG	10f Gd/Sft		1457
52	14	EPSO	12f Gd/Sft		1828
82	11	HAYD	12f Gd/Fm		2501
75	12	NEWM	8f Gd/Fm	89	2858
0	14	NOTT	8f Heavy	85	4506

SO SOBER 2 b c £2372

61	5	NOTT	6f Gd/Fm		1642
80	4	KEMP	5f Gd/Fm		2082
82	2	WIND	5f Soft		2545
54	7	YARM	5f Firm		2766
57	6	HAYD	5f Soft		3767
79	2	LING	5f Soft		4187
0	12	NOTT	5f Gd/Sft		4503

SO TEMPTING 2 b c £1121

59	3	NOTT	6f Heavy	4410
76	2	MUSS	7f Soft	4562

SO WILLING 4 gr g £278

31a	10	SOUT	7f Aw	65	33	
30a	7	SOUT	6f Aw	62	183	
37a	7	SOUT	6f Aw	62	218	VIS
18a	11	SOUT	6f Aw	55	250	vis
52a	6	WOLV	5f Aw	55	323	vis
15a	11	WOLV	6f Aw	49	351	vis
49a	6	WOLV	7f Aw	49	582	BL
15a	9	WOLV	7f Aw	48	711	bl
49	5	SOUT	7f Good	60	803	bl
48	6	MUSS	5f Gd/Sft	56	899	
30	8	REDC	7f Gd/Sft		1132	bl
33	11	THIR	7f Gd/Sft		1351	bl
0	16	REDC	7f Gd/Sft		1559	bl
0	19	LEIC	6f Gd/Sft	42	1734	vis

SOAKED 7 b g £10217

62a	10	WOLV	5f Aw	84	394	
63a	8	WOLV	5f Aw	80	491	
45a	8	WOLV	5f Aw	76	678	
0a	13	SOUT	6f Aw	73	1504	
56a	7	SOUT	5f Aw	68	1976	
42	8	CARL	5f Firm		2822	
0	R	CATT	5f Gd/Fm	56	2929	
72	2	BEVE	5f Gd/Sft		3056	bl
56	1	WIND	5f Good	50	3191*	bl
57	1	BATH	5f Firm	50	3209*	bl

56 3 BRIG 6f Gd/Fm 56 3243 bl
57 3 NEWM 6f Firm 56 3297 bl
59 4 PONT 5f Firm 61 3502 bl
0 13 BEVE 5f Gd/Fm 61 3653 bl
62 2 BRIG 5f Firm 61 3734 bl

SOARING PHOENIX 2 b c £0
41 11 LING 7f Soft 4483

SOARING SOFTLY 5 ch m £339754
120 1 GULF 11f Good 18*

SOBA JONES 3 b c £7552
46a 6 SOUT 6f Aw 558
40a 6 WOLV 5f Aw 624
38 10 SOUT 7f Gd/Sft 55 857
53 2 REDC 7f Gd/Fm 51 2145
52 3 CARL 8f Firm 51 2281
50 4 DONC 8f Gd/Fm 52 2612
50 3 RIPO 8f Gd/Fm 51 2839 BL
62 1 NEWC 5f Good 3035* bl
57 5 CARL 6f Firm 58 3194 bl
58 3 THIR 5f Gd/Fm 58 3349 bl
60 3 THIR 5f Gd/Fm 58 3619 bl
51 5 RIPO 6f Good 58 3698 bl
0 25 AYR 5f Soft 60 3960 bl

SOBER AS A JUDGE 3 b c £277
0 19 BRIG 10f Gd/Fm 45 892
35a 11 WOLV 7f Aw 1035
31 9 NEWM 8f Gd/Fm 2134
47 3 YARM 7f Gd/Fm 2413
34 10 LEIC 8f Gd/Fm 2914
0 14 YARM 8f Good 38 3236
26 8 NEWM 8f Gd/Fm 3456
45 7 YARM 7f Firm 3921
7 9 YARM 11f Soft 35 4391
0 17 NEWM 8f Gd/Sft 44 4536

SOBER HILL 2 b g £0
13a 8 WOLV 6f Aw 2077
41a 4 SOUT 7f Aw 2301

SOBIESKI 3 b c £39385
116 1 DEAU 10f V 2736*
116 3 LONG 12f Good 3929
111 4 LONG 10f Good 4238

SOBRIETY 3 b c £100980
100 1 DONC 8f Gd/Fm 1069*
98 9 HAYD 8f Gd/Sft 102 1535
101 6 ASCO 8f Good 100 2117
101 5 SAND 8f Gd/Fm 100 2528
109 1 YORK 10f Good 100 2696+
109 3 GOOD 12f Gd/Fm 3061

SOCIAL CONTRACT 3 b c £13163
65 7 SAND 7f Soft 77 1569
71 7 NEWB 8f Aw 1786
80 1 LEIC 7f Firm 75 2026*
79 3 GOOD 8f Gd/Fm 79 3063
76 4 NEWM 8f Gd/Fm 79 3118
75 9 KEMP 6f Gd/Fm 79 3791
84 1 NEWM 7f Good 78 4357* BL

SOCIAL HARMONY 6 b g £52250
109 2 CURR 6f Gd/Sft 1622
92 15 ASCO 6f Good 109 2151
113 1 FAIR 6f Firm 3548*
112 4 LEOP 5f Good 3923
113 1 CURR 7f Good 4056*

SOCIALIST 4 b c £318
26a 6 WOLV 12f Aw 581
42 3 BRIG 12f Gd/Sft 893
0a 12 SOUT 12f Aw 1203 BL
0 14 BRIG 12f Gd/Sft 34 1465
0 17 NOTT 14f Good 24 2008
44a 4 SOUT 11f Aw 4150

SOCIETY KING 5 b g £0
0 14 LEIC 8f Stt/Hvy 4311
32 7 BRIG 10f Soft 46 4419

SOCIETY TIMES 7 b g £0
28 5 HAMI 8f Gd/Fm 32 1907
10 11 AYR 11f Good 30 2139
12a 7 SOUT 8f Aw 35 2302

SODFAHH 2 ch f £0
61 6 FOLK 7f Gd/Fm 3583

SOFISIO 3 ch c £5571
73a 2 SOUT 8f Aw 48
74a 1 LING 7f Aw 94*
75a 4 LING 8f Aw 72 158
73a 4 WOLV 8f Aw 72 188
0 11 SALI 8f Firm 68 2025
70a 3 SOUT 7f Aw 73 2300
67 2 CHEP 8f Gd/Fm 63 2661
65 4 SALI 8f Gd/Fm 64 2980
59a 5 WOLV 8f Aw 72 3274
54 10 KEMP 8f Gd/Fm 64 3793
0 18 NEWM 7f Good 4018
51 6 BRIG 10f Soft 60 4174 BL
66a 2 LING 7f Aw 4331 bl

SOFT BREEZE 2 ch f £1180
79 3 YORK 7f Gd/Fm 1312

SOFTLY TREAD 2 b f £16250
102 1 CURR 7f Gd/Fm 3067*

SOHAPARA 5 ch m £0
0a 14 LING 12f Aw 267

SOLAIA 3 ch f £43455
98 4 KEMP 8f Soft 995
102 1 CHES 11f Gd/Fm 1223*
90 7 EPSO 12f Gd/Sft 1828
105 2 HAYD 12f Gd/Fm 2501
104 4 DEAU 10f Good 3211
102 4 DONC 15f Gd/Fm 3863
93 10 NEWM 12f Good 4343

SOLAR FLARE 2 b f £0
45 10 SALI 7f Firm 3748

SOLDIER ON 2 b c £23159
56 7 NEWM 5f Soft 984
76 2 WIND 5f Gd/Sft 1095
81 1 BRIG 5f Firm 1208*
67 5 WIND 5f Gd/Sft 1426
87 5 BEVE 5f Gd/Sft 1761
58 7 ASCO 6f Good 80 2678
79 1 GOOD 5f Good 73 3109*
79 3 SAND 5f Good 78 3431
77 5 NEWM 6f Gd/Fm 79 3630
87 2 EPSO 6f Good 79 3761
86 2 GOOD 6f Good 79 3886
88 1 AYR 6f Soft 84 3987*
83 6 NEWM 6f Gd/Fm 87 4214

SOLDIER POINT 2 ch c £1100
33 10 RIPO 6f Gd/Fm 2106
75 2 PONT 6f Gd/Fm 3223

SOLE SINGER 4 b c £879
53a 3 WOLV 12f Aw 50 170
52a 2 WOLV 12f Aw 50 261 BL
51a 5 SOUT 12f Aw 53 370

SOLITARY 3 b c £6971
97 2 NEWM 12f Good 951
94 2 THIR 12f Good 1157
88 1 RIPO 12f Good 3701* BL
75 11 NEWM 12f Good 82 4162 bl
83 5 NEWB 16f Gd/Sft 85 4458 bl

SOLLER BAY 3 b g £11618
64a 1 WOLV 9f Aw 395*
66a 3 LING 10f Aw 72 509
80 1 WIND 8f Heavy 72 933*
67 13 GOOD 9f Gd/Sft 79 1452
82 1 AYR 9f Good 76 2166*
75 9 SAND 10f Gd/Fm 82 2499

SOLLYS PAL 5 gr g £2898
15a 10 SOUT 7f Aw 57 75

44a 4 SOUT 8f Aw 52 176
35a 5 SOUT 7f Aw 50 304
45a 3 LING 7f Aw 47 439
49a 1 SOUT 7f Aw 45 1801* VIS
40 11 KEMP 7f Gd/Fm 52 3362 vis
47 3 WIND 6f Gd/Sft 48 4294 vis

SOLO BID 3 ch f £327
69 4 WIND 8f Soft 2548
45 8 CHEP 7f Gd/Fm 3256

SOLO DANCE 2 b f £502
58 4 DONC 7f Gd/Fm 2316
42 4 CATT 7f Gd/Fm 3198
59 8 BEVE 7f Good 3397
44 5 THIR 7f Gd/Fm 3615 BL
36 7 BEVE 7f Good 45 3950 bl
43 8 NEWM 7f Good 4336 bl

SOLO FLIGHT 3 gr c £3684
78 2 WIND 10f Gd/Fm 1293
82 1 BRIG 10f Soft 1466*
72 15 NEWM 10f Good 87 4197
71 12 NEWM 12f Good 85 4342
77 4 YARM 19f Soft 4515

SOLO PERFORMANCE 3 b f £4056
77 1 GOOD 12f Gd/Fm 2354*

SOLOIST 3 ch f £0
59 7 THIR 7f Good 1159
0 14 BEVE 12f Good 56 1446
0 15 RIPO 8f Good 1596
0 11 PONT 8f Good 1865
15 9 BEVE 7f Firm 2731

SOMALIA 3 b g £0
0a 12 LING 13f AW 4193 BL

SOME DUST 2 ch c £2883
0a U WOLV 6f Gd/Fm 1236
49 8 SALI 5f Good 1346
55a 2 LING 5f Aw 1916
61 1 YARM 5f Gd/Fm 2196*
61a 2 SOUT 5f Aw 2384

SOME MIGHT SAY 5 b g £0
22a 8 WOLV 12f Aw 231
0a 9 LING 13f Aw 44 317 BL

SOME WILL 2 b c £477
11 11 RIPO 6f Gd/Fm 2106
68 4 DONC 7f Gd/Fm 2576
56 8 PONT 5f Gd/Fm 3223

SOMERS HEATH 2 b f £7410
58 7 NOTT 6f Good 1408
60 9 NOTT 6f Gd/Sft 1641
68 1 YORK 6f Gd/Fm 1981*
39 9 ASCO 6f Good 69 2678
60 5 THIR 7f Gd/Fm 3128
60 6 BEVE 7f Gd/Fm 62 3411

SOMESESSION 3 b c £0
69 7 THIR 5f Gd/Fm 78 3349 bl
62 13 YORK 5f Gd/Fm 78 3569 bl
52a 11 WOLV 6f Aw 75 4380
0 19 DONC 7f Heavy 74 4574

SOMETHINGABOUTMARY 2 b f £405
29 9 BEVE 5f Heavy 974
39 7 REDC 6f Gd/Sft 1577
0 13 PONT 6f Good 1864
54 3 BEVE 7f Firm 2218

SON OF A GUN 6 b g £2083
84 4 NOTT 14f Gd/Sft 1369
80 2 HAYD 14f Soft 1824
71 3 RIPO 10f Good 3185

SON OF A PREACHER 2 ch c £0
44 13 DONC 5f Gd/Fm 1067
0 11 NOTT 6f Good 1413
0 12 SOUT 6f Soft 1602

SON OF SNURGE 4 b c £1544
61 15 CHES 19f Gd/Fm 86 1222

79 4 YORK 14f Firm 79 1329
68 14 ASCO 20f Good 79 2092
71 4 HAYD 14f Gd/Fm 78 2455 bl
74 3 SAND 14f Gd/Fm 75 2923 bl

SONATINA 2 b f £8212
88 1 FOLK 6f Gd/Fm   3443*
88 1 YARM 6f Gd/Fm   3965*

SONBELLE 3 b f £728
61a 4 LING 7f Aw 72 149
0a 7 WOLV 8f Aw 68 311
55 2 SALI 7f Good   1349
0 18 LEIC 6f Gd/Fm 65 2777
0 18 LING 6f Firm 59 3578
0 19 LEIC 6f Gd/Sft   4031

SONG N DANCE 2 br f £0
66 8 SAND 5f Gd/Fm   2526
60 5 BRIG 6f Firm   3525
38 6 LING 6f Firm   3757
52 10 LING 5f Good   4095
51a 4 LING 5f Aw   4333
35 7 BATH 6f Soft   4431

SONG OF SKYE 6 b m £6252
73a 2 WOLV 8f Aw 72 78
75a 2 LING 8f Aw 74 169
71a 8 LING 7f Aw 74 337
76a 3 LING 8f Aw 74 423
66a 6 LING 8f Aw 74 485
0 14 SALI 7f Good 72 1348
22 12 EPSO 9f Gd/Sft 70 1829
65 7 GOOD 7f Gd/Fm 68 2128
68 2 LING 8f Aw   2215
67 3 CATT 7f Gd/Fm 66 2420
61 6 DONC 7f Gd/Fm 67 2612

SONGS OF PRAISE 2 b g £0
0 12 BATH 8f Soft   4429

SONICOS 4 ch g £0
28a 10 SOUT 12f Aw   301
0a 8 WOLV 15f Aw   468
17 6 CARL 17f Gd/Fm 29 2244

SONIQUE 2 b f £0
10 10 NEWM 8f Gd/Sft   4531

SONTIME 3 b f £0
0 17 BATH 14f Gd/Fm 66 1438
55 8 WARW 7f Gd/Fm 62 2036
0 W FOLK 6f Gd/Fm   2291
44a 5 LING 7f Aw   2759
0 15 NOTT 6f Soft 58 3975
0 17 WIND 6f Gd/Sft 53 4294

SOONA 2 ch f £1729
48 10 WIND 5f Good   849
68 5 SAND 5f Heavy   1046
72 5 SAND 7f Gd/Fm   1988
55 5 FOLK 7f Good   2620
71 2 LEIC 7f Gd/Fm   2916
70 2 BRIG 7f Gd/Fm   3239
63 4 BRIG 6f Firm   3525

SOOTY TIME 2 ch g £1447
33a 6 SOUT 5f Aw   1206
58a 3 LING 5f Aw   1740
25a 7 LING 5f Aw   1916
41 6 YARM 6f Firm   2388
0a 6 WOLV 5f Aw   2605
58 2 LEIC 5f Gd/Fm   2772
47 3 FOLK 5f Gd/Fm   3038
56 4 BATH 5f Firm   3204
25 11 LING 5f Firm 57 3491
58 3 BATH 6f Soft   4431

SOPHALA 3 b f £4104
68 3 WIND 10f Good   3189
64 7 NEWM 8f Gd/Fm   3626
45 11 CHEP 10f Good 63 3870
65 1 BRIG 10f Soft 60 4174*

61 3 CATT 12f Soft 65 4256
63 4 PONT 10f Soft 67 4374
46 9 NEWM 12f Gd/Sft 67 4534

SOPHIELU 2 ch f £944
78 2 REDC 5f Gd/Sft   4496
82 4 DONC 6f Heavy   4576

SOPHOMORE 6 b g £3000
0a 9 SOUT 11f Aw 75 343
66a 3 SOUT 7f Aw 70 599
57 13 DONC 10f Gd/Fm 75 705
63a 6 SOUT 8f Aw 68 1207
49 9 BEVE 7f Firm 70 1275
66 1 LEIC 6f Gd/Fm   1731*
50 6 LEIC 8f Firm 65 2032
62 8 CARL 8f Gd/Fm 64 2242
0 14 BEVE 10f Gd/Fm 63 2518
37 10 NEWM 10f Gd/Fm 60 3314
50 2 RIPO 8f Gd/Fm   3711
46 9 LEIC 8f Gd/Sft   4033
53a 5 WOLV 8f Aw 60 4248
34 5 LEIC 8f Sft/Hvy   4311
50 5 REDC 8f Gd/Sft 52 4499

SOPRAN GLAUMIX 2 gr c £32104
103 1 SAN 8f Heavy   4243*
106 4 SAN 8f Heavy   4492

SOPRAN MONTANELLI 3 b c £3842
103 3 LONG 15f Soft   3848

SOPRAN ZANCHI 3 ch c £323
63 4 HAYD 7f Soft   4093

SORAYAS QUEST 2 b f £225
0 12 NEWC 6f Good   3245
57 4 THIR 7f Gd/Fm   3776
36 9 NEWC 7f Heavy   4403

SORBETT 3 b c £507
81 6 LEIC 6f Gd/Sft   829
71 8 DONC 8f Gd/Fm   1069
94 4 HAYD 6f Gd/Fm   1164
0 14 NEWM 8f Firm 92 1853
37 21 YORK 7f Good 87 2694

SORRENTO KING 3 ch c £1724
0 21 RIPO 10f Soft 53 827
0 11 BEVE 12f Gd/Sft 50 1758 bl
37 7 PONT 10f Firm 50 2175 bl
42 2 CATT 12f Gd/Fm 43 2746 bl
45 3 BEVE 10f Good 43 3396 bl
29 6 REDC 14f Gd/Fm 44 3637 bl

SOSSUS VLEI 4 b c £27381
110 2 SAIN 8f Heavy   10
107 5 SAND 10f Heavy   1057
106 1 CHES 10f Firm   1248*
106 3 SAND 10f Soft   1587

SOTONIAN 7 br g £4286
0a 11 LING 6f Aw 67 358
64a 5 WOLV 5f Aw 67 394
42a 11 WOLV 5f Aw 64 491
0a 11 SOUT 6f Aw 63 645
58a 3 LING 5f Aw 60 774
46a 7 WOLV 5f Aw 58 1140
61 6 BEVE 5f Firm 64 1278
56 6 CATT 5f Good 62 1662
59 3 CATT 6f Gd/Sft 62 1815
51a 4 WOLV 5f Aw 56 2078
56 5 BEVE 5f Gd/Fm 60 2517
58 3 CATT 5f Gd/Fm 58 2743
54 6 CATT 5f Gd/Fm 58 2929
52 5 WIND 5f Good 58 3191
59a 1 WOLV 5f Aw 54 3271*
49 9 CHES 5f Gd/Fm 58 3512
48 12 WIND 5f Gd/Sft 56 4295

SOUHAITE 4 b c £9038
46a 1 SOUT 12f Aw 40 68*
41a 3 SOUT 11f Aw 46 131

27a 7 WOLV 16f Aw 45 190
45a 3 SOUT 12f Aw 45 211
27a 7 WOLV 12f Aw 43 261
0 11 YARM 8f Good 42 1772
43 1 LEIC 8f Firm 40 2027*
41 7 BEVE 7f Firm 43 2221
0a 12 SOUT 8f Aw 42 2379
26 10 BATH 8f Firm 43 3623
49 1 CHEP 7f Good 41 3871*
0 17 NEWM 7f Good   4018
50a 1 WOLV 8f Aw 42 4440*

SOUND DOMINO 4 b g £1290
95 3 COLO 5f Soft   4146

SOUND THE TRUMPET 8 b g £3111
38a 4 LING 7f Aw 43 29 t
51a 4 WOLV 7f Aw   61 t
48a 1 LING 8f Aw 40 97* t
47a 5 LING 10f Aw 48 161 t
40a 8 LING 10f Aw 46 209 t
15a 7 SOUT 7f Aw 46 304 t
19a 6 WOLV 8f Aw 44 411 t
37a 8 LING 8f Aw 53 463 tvi
21a 8 LING 8f Aw 43 594 t
0 14 LEIC 7f Good   790 t
37 9 REDC 6f Firm   1298 t
24 6 SOUT 7f Soft   1601 t
32 8 CATT 6f Gd/Sft 40 1815 t
0 16 NOTT 6f Gd/Fm 38 2193 t
0 16 WARW 8f Good 38 2460 t

SOUNDS ACE 4 ch f £985
45 11 REDC 5f Gd/Sft 54 1133
49 6 NOTT 6f Gd/Fm 54 1412
0 18 DONC 5f Gd/Fm 51 1842
49 3 BEVE 5f Firm 51 1923 bl
46 7 WARW 6f Gd/Fm 49 2252 bl
49 3 CATT 5f Gd/Fm 49 2418 bl
45 8 NEWM 5f Good 51 2569 bl
38 7 DONC 5f Gd/Fm 48 2753 bl
37 14 GOOD 5f Gd/Fm 48 3091 bl
39 7 CATT 5f Gd/Fm 48 3203 bl
37 6 BRIG 5f Firm 49 3528 bl
0 17 YARM 5f Gd/Fm 43 3966 bl
0 16 NEWC 5f Heavy 43 4407 bl
39a 6 WOLV 6f Aw 43 4442 bl

SOUNDS COOL 4 b c £0
0a 16 SOUT 7f Aw 38 75
13a 10 SOUT 11f Aw   178
11a 6 SOUT 12f Aw 29 338
21a 5 WOLV 9f Aw 34 404
5a 11 WOLV 9f Aw   433
20a 4 SOUT 8f Aw 24 585
16a 9 SOUT 8f Aw   684
21 12 REDC 7f Gd/Sft   1132

SOUNDS CRAZY 3 b f £428
40a 10 SOUT 5f Aw   127
23a 9 SOUT 5f Aw   217 bl
41a 2 SOUT 5f Aw   283 bl
17a 10 SOUT 5f Aw   330 bl
0a 12 SOUT 8f Aw 41 429 bl

SOUNDS LUCKY 4 b c £1855
49a 6 LING 7f Aw   243
36a 10 WOLV 6f Aw 59 351
50a 4 WOLV 6f Aw   436
54a 4 WOLV 5f Aw   533
58a 1 WOLV 5f Aw 51 563* vis
43a 6 WOLV 5f Aw 57 609 vis
48 9 HAMI 5f Gd/Fm 56 1358 vis
37 11 NOTT 6f Gd/Fm 53 2192 vis
43 10 BRIG 5f Soft 53 2428 vis
0 16 LING 6f Firm 49 3578 vis
32a 10 WOLV 6f Aw 55 3774 BL

SOUNDS SOLO 4 b c £286

SOUNDS (cont.)

```
37a  6   SOUT   7f Aw         341  evi
60a  3   SOUT   6f Aw         389  cvi
38a  7   SOUT   8f Aw         452  cvi
31a  6   SOUT   7f Aw         501  cvi
17  10   WARW   7f Soft       816  vis
0a  11   SOUT   7f Aw      49 867  vis
```

SOUNDS SPECIAL 3 b f £0
```
0a  12   SOUT   8f Aw         328
0    1   NOTT   6f Gd/Sft  61 1082
0   15   DONC   6f Gd/Fm   56 2315
0   19   THIR   6f Gd/Fm   50 3124 BL
```

SOUNDS SWEET 4 ch f £0
```
19a  9   SOUT   8f Aw          45
0a  11   SOUT   6f Aw      31  87  bl
14a  8   WOLV   7f Aw         142
```

SOUPERFICIAL 9 gr g £847
```
27   9   DONC   6f Gd/Sft     1073
31  12   REDC   6f Firm       1298
47   2   NEWC   5f Heavy      1766
39   8   HAMI   6f Firm    50 2097
46   6   CARL   6f Gd/Fm      2240
46   4   HAMI   6f Gd/Fm   48 2641
45   6   HAMI   6f Gd/Fm      2798
0   18   THIR   6f Gd/Fm   47 3144
0   15   NEWC   6f Firm    46 3605
0   17   NEWC   6f Heavy   43 4425
```

SOUTH LANE 3 br g £0
```
50   5   REDC   7f Gd/Sft     1135
38   9   NEWC   8f Gd/Sft  48 1477
```

SOUTH SEA PEARL 3 b f £3000
```
80   2   RIPO   10f Gd/Fm     3185
78   2   EPSO   12f Gd/Fm     3416
78   3   RIPO   12f Good      3701
44   6   AYR    10f Soft   73 3989
0    1   NEWM   10f Good   69 4160
38a  9   LING   7f Aw         4487
```

SOUTHAMPTON 10 b g £0
```
0   13   CHEP   14f Gd/Fm  38 2490  vis
```

SOUTHBOUND TRAIN 4 ch g £0
```
0a  15   SOUT   8f Aw      50  83
```

SOUTHERN DANCER 2 b g £0
```
74   9   HAYD   8f Aw         3766
48  12   DONC   7f Gd/Fm      4447
```

SOUTHERN DOMINION 8 ch g £3453
```
59a  2   SOUT   5f Aw          71  bl
57a  2   WOLV   5f Aw      54 116  bl
41a  7   LING   5f Aw      57 166  bl
54a  4   SOUT   5f Aw         214  bl
56a  3   WOLV   5f Aw      55 291  bl
64a  1   LING   5f Aw      56 371* bl
```

SOVEREIGN ABBEY 4 b f £4003
```
40a  4   WOLV   6f Aw          63
49a  6   WOLV   7f Aw      60 121
62a  2   WOLV   8f Aw         308
57a  1   WOLV   9f Aw         378*
44a  4   WOLV   12f Aw     56 437
52a  3   SOUT   8f Aw      56 496
```

SOVEREIGN STATE 3 b c £5351
```
65  10   NEWM   8f Firm    74 1183
76   1   THIR   8f Good    73 1387*
52   7   EPSO   10f Gd/Sft 78 1831
73   5   BATH   8f Firm    78 2330
74   4   NEWM   8f Gd/Fm   76 2614
70   6   NOTT   8f Gd/Fm   76 3005
50  10   NEWB   6f Firm    75 3455
60  10   EPSO   9f Good    74 3856
0   13   NEWM   7f Good       4018
```

SOVEREIGNS COURT 7 ch g £4108
```
68   3   EPSO   9f Heavy      1033
58  15   NEWB   10f Good   70 1375
72   1   BATH   10f Gd/Sft 67 1666*
61   6   NOTT   10f Gd/Fm  73 3111
```
```
74   2   GOOD   12f Soft      4061
39  12   NEWB   10f Stt/Hv 73 4473
```

SOVIET FLASH 3 b c £3395
```
104  2   DONC   8f Firm       3893
104  4   NEWM   8f Gd/Fm      4180
97   6   NEWM   10f Gd/Sft    4532
```

SPA GULCH 2 ch g £0
```
56  15   NEWB   7f Firm       3999
0   16   LING   6f Soft       4190
```

SPA LANE 7 ch g £5823
```
38   5   NOTT   14f Heavy  37 1023
43   1   BEVE   16f Firm   40 1276*
45   4   PONT   12f Good   42 1499
43   3   RIPO   16f Good   42 1597
45   3   PONT   17f Good   43 1867
45   2   BEVE   12f Gd/Fm  43 2482
43   5   BEVE   16f Gd/Fm  43 2516
41   7   BEVE   16f Firm   44 2734
25   7   BEVE   12f Gd/Sft 43 3053
37   5   REDC   16f Firm   40 3331
32   8   BEVE   12f Gd/Fm  39 3674
28   8   NOTT   16f Soft   37 3978
21a  7   SOUT   16f Aw     33 4149
```

SPACE QUEST 3 b f £13449
```
98   1   LONG   12f Soft      4321*
```

SPACE RACE 6 b g £8972
```
77a  2   LING   10f Aw     75  22
62a 10   LING   10f Aw         55
77a  2   LING   12f Aw     76  151
82a  1   LING   12f Aw     76  245*
63a  6   LING   12f Aw     80  356
82a  2   LING   12f Aw     80  486
81a  2   LING   12f Aw     80  572
69a  5   LING   12f Aw     80  633
```

SPAIN 2 ch f £0
```
71   5   GOOD   7f Good       2306
53  12   CHEP   8f Good       3867
```

SPANISH SPUR 2 b c £1584
```
82   2   GOOD   8f Good       3906
72   5   SALI   8f Gd/Sft     4163
75   4   DONC   7f Gd/Sft     4447
```

SPANISH STAR 3 b c £4985
```
57a  5   LING   10f Aw         523
63a  1   WOLV   12f Aw         565*
60a  3   WOLV   12f Aw     67  640
46   6   WIND   10f Gd/Fm  74 2053
49   8   WIND   12f Good   69 2712
63   6   NEWM   10f Good      3021
40   9   YARM   8f Good    57 3236
68a  1   SOUT   11f Aw         4151*
31a 11   LING   12f Aw     67 4271
```

SPANKER 4 ch f £1240
```
63a  2   LING   10f Aw         56
61a  3   WOLV   12f Aw         144
13a  9   WOLV   9f Aw          189  BL
0a   7   LING   12f Aw         267  bl
```

SPARK OF LIFE 3 b f £7177
```
26  11   BRIG   10f Good   59 1649  bl
41   3   CHEP   7f Good       1972  bl
49   2   NEWM   8f Gd/Fm      2134  bl
42   3   LEIC   10f Gd/Fm     2510  bl
49   1   BRIG   8f Firm       2892* bl
58   1   KEMP   9f Gd/Fm   51 3357* bl
51   3   EPSO   9f Gd/Fm   51 3401  bl
51  11   SAND   10f Soft   57 4208  bl
```

SPARKLING DOVE 7 ch m £0
```
0a   8   WOLV   12f Aw         347  BL
0a   9   WOLV   12f Aw         710
0   18   LEIC   7f Good        790  bl
0   14   WARW   15f Heavy  46 885  bl
```

SPARKLING ISLE 3 ch f £0
```
0   15   LING   8f Firm     65 3580
```
```
0   16   GOOD   10f Soft    60 4067
0   17   LEIC   8f Stt/Hvy  54 4310
```

SPARKY 6 b g £2147
```
58   2   CARL   9f Firm    54 1254 bl
42   8   REDC   9f Gd/Sft  58 1583 bl
60   3   MUSS   9f Firm    57 2049 bl
60   2   CARL   8f Firm       2283 bl
```

SPARTAN HEARTBEAT 7 b g £0
```
0a   9   WOLV   12f Aw         144
0a   9   WOLV   16f Aw     56  194
```

SPARTAN ROYALE 6 b g £219
```
67   4   NEWC   16f Soft   67  760
```

SPARTAN SAILOR 2 b g £0
```
0   12   CHES   7f Soft        4068
```

SPECIAL 2 b f £0
```
52  10   WIND   6f Gd/Sft      4289
```

SPECIAL K 8 br m £711
```
45   2   PONT   8f Gd/Sft  42 1101
7    9   HAMI   9f Gd/Fm       2236
```

SPECIAL PERSON 5 ch m £0
```
25a 10   LING   7f Aw      49  59
```

SPECIAL PROMISE 3 ch g £11726
```
50a  5   WOLV   9f Aw      55  188
62a  1   LING   10f Aw     51  315*
69a  1   WOLV   9f Aw      58  392*
75a  1   SOUT   8f Aw      64  451*
79a  1   WOLV   8f Aw      73  495*
0   12   RIPO   10f Good   70 3702
46a  9   WOLV   12f Aw     74  4226
29  13   PONT   10f Soft   63 4315
```

SPECIAL RING 3 b c £3842
```
107  3   CHAN   9f Soft        2913
```

SPECIAL WEEK 5 br g £1071545
```
123  1   TOKY   12f Firm       123*
```

SPECIALIZE 8 b g £272
```
27a  9   SOUT   16f Aw     38 470 bl
34a  3   SOUT   16f Aw     33 535 bl
```

SPECIFIC SORCEROR 2 ch c £7406
```
76   5   SAND   7f Gd/Fm       2494
73   1   WARW   7f Gd/Fm       2841*
93   1   NEWC   8f Firm        3601*
91   3   DONC   8f Gd/Fm    88 3879
```

SPECKLED GEM 4 b f £0
```
0a  12   LING   6f Aw      36  154
41a  5   LING   6f Aw          313
38a  4   LING   6f Aw          354
```

SPECTINA 2 b f £0
```
34  11   LEIC   7f Stt/Hvy     4309
```

SPECTRE BROWN 10 b g £0
```
39   9   HAMI   11f Gd/Fm      1193
0   15   MUSS   12f Gd/Sft     4133
```

SPECTROMETER 3 ch c £7815
```
59   4   YARM   14f Gd/Fm  66 1949
74   1   BRIG   12f Gd/Sft 65 2425*
76   1   HAMI   13f Gd/Fm  71 2643*
77   2   CARL   12f Firm       3195
55  12   GOOD   12f Good    77 3887
```

SPEED OF LIGHT 2 b c £652
```
73   4   NEWM   7f Good        4344
```

SPEED ON 7 b g £1118
```
55  12   KEMP   5f Soft     82 1013
70   6   BATH   5f Gd/Fm       1441
80   3   NOTT   5f Good     77 1871
65  10   SALI   5f Gd/Fm    79 2266
73   5   EPSO   6f Gd/Sft   79 2432
65  11   BATH   5f Firm     78 3209
74   6   NEWB   5f Gd/Fm    76 3485
75   6   GOOD   6f Good     76 3904
68  11   NEWM   5f Good     76 4015
0   19   BATH   5f Soft     75 4432
```

SPEED VENTURE 3 b g £3430

SPEEDFIT (continued)

73	4	RIPO	8f Soft		826	
79	2	LING	10f Soft		1287	
76	2	GOOD	10f Gd/Sft		1640	
45a	5	LING	10f Aw		2213	
65	5	RIPO	10f Gd/Fm	74	2836	
66	7	ASCO	12f Gd/Fm	72	3014	
69	4	NEWM	12f Gd/Fm	70	3461	
53	9	PONT	10f Soft		4088	
64	4	BATH	12f Soft	66	4433	

SPEEDFIT FREE 3 b c £3055

0	16	RIPO	6f Good	70	1600
43	11	MUSS	5f Firm	65	2047
61	5	MUSS	8f Gd/Fm	65	2205
51	7	CARL	8f Firm	65	2281
46	4	BEVE	7f Firm		2731
43	4	LEIC	8f Gd/Fm		2914
57	1	**NOTT**	8f Gd/Fm		3004*
62	3	CARL	7f Firm		3196
55	6	BEVE	8f Good		3393
52	4	BEVE	7f Gd/Fm		3670
30	11	THIR	8f Gd/Sft		3775

SPEEDFIT TOO 5 b h £19529

100	7	ASCO	8f Good	98	2090	vis
105	1	**SALI**	8f Gd/Fm	98	2229*	vis
108	2	SAND	8f Gd/Fm	103	2528	vis
102	3	NEWB	7f Firm		2809	vis
98	7	ASCO	7f Gd/Fm	103	2997	vis
96	9	HAYD	11f Gd/Fm		3321	vis

SPEEDY CLASSIC 11 br g £0

28a	7	LING	8f Aw		93

SPEEDY GEE 2 b c £5784

67	3	WIND	5f Gd/Fm		743
74	6	WIND	5f Good		1727
83	1	**SAND**	5f Good		1962*
85	7	SAND	5f Gd/Fm		2529
85	5	NEWB	6f Firm		2808
98	6	GOOD	5f Gd/Fm		3133
0	9	LEOP	6f Good		3372
95	4	YORK	5f Gd/Fm		3567
95	6	CURR	6f Good		3844
79	3	BEVE	5f Sft/Hvy		4042

SPEEDY JAMES 4 ch c £169

50	6	THIR	6f Soft		927
0	19	HAYD	5f Gd/Sft	94	1533
0	19	YORK	5f Firm	88	1980
0	29	ASCO	6f Good	88	2151

SPEIRBHEAN 2 b f £1600

79	2	CURR	7f Good		2407

SPELLBINDER 4 b f £2180

69	3	FOLK	7f Soft		962
75	2	WARW	8f Firm		1062
70	2	WIND	10f Gd/Fm		2056
36	8	NEWM	8f Firm	72	2342

SPENCERS WOOD 3 b c £16752

98	1	NEWM	7f Firm		1186*
107	4	ASCO	8f Good		2675
105	3	DEAU	10f Good		3369
103	6	DONC	8f Firm		3893
110	5	NEWB	9f Firm		4000

SPENDENT 4 ch c £34961

106	3	SAIN	12f Soft		1461	bl
103	3	SAN	12f Gd/Fm		2074	bl

SPENDER 11 b g £206

36a	10	LING	5f Aw	75	91
37a	3	LING	7f Aw		159

SPETTRO 2 b c £33223

81	5	NEWM	5f Gd/Fm		1169
91	1	**CATT**	7f Gd/Fm		3198*
98	1	**NOTT**	8f Good		3523*
103	1	**HAYD**	8f Soft		3787*
110	3	SAN	8f Heavy		4492

SPICE ISLAND 2 b f £3591

SPICE ISLAND (continued)

52	5	NOTT	5f Firm		1267	
54	3	BEVE	5f Good		1443	
56	8	DONC	6f Gd/Fm		1838	
46	7	LEIC	6f Gd/Fm	54	4030	
65	1	**PONT**	6f Soft	53	4235*	
40	11	REDC	6f Gd/Sft	68	4502	

SPIN A YARN 3 b c £522

80	8	HAYD	8f Gd/Sft	86	810
63	14	YORK	8f Firm	85	1341
78	5	NEWM	8f Firm	82	1853
76	5	NEWM	8f Gd/Fm	81	2614
79	4	BATH	8f Firm	79	2942
73	5	RIPO	9f Gd/Fm	80	3182

SPINETAIL RUFOUS 2 b c £0

0	11	CHEP	5f Gd/Fm	3252
45	8	WIND	6f Good	3638
15	11	NOTT	6f Soft	3974
57a	4	WOLV	5f Aw	4227

SPINNER TOY 5 ch g £0

0	14	SALI	14f Good	2691

SPINNING STAR 4 ch f £2664

71a	1	LING	12f Aw	65	377*
61a	5	LING	12f Aw	70	528

SPINNING TOP 3 b f £9087

88	1	LING	10f Soft		1287*
106	2	GOOD	10f Gd/Sft		1469
0	7	CURR	10f Yldg		2404

SPIRIT HOUSE 2 b c £1336

77	2	BEVE	7f Gd/Fm	2514
81	7	ASCO	8f Good	3304

SPIRIT OF KHAMBANI 3 ch f £1276

50	10	THIR	7f Good		1159	
28	14	HAYD	6f Soft	56	1494	
37	8	AYR	11f Good	52	2139	
46	4	MUSS	12f Gd/Sft	46	2537	
48	2	BEVE	8f Firm	46	2735	
30	5	HAMI	11f Gd/Fm	46	2782	
38	8	AYR	9f Gd/Fm	47	3141	
11	11	HAMI	9f Gd/Fm	45	3380	BL
44	2	MUSS	8f Gd/Fm	42	3746	
42	4	YARM	8f Gd/Fm	43	3971	
0	12	SALI	10f Gd/Sft	45	4168	

SPIRIT OF LIGHT 3 b c £1896

63	7	WIND	8f Gd/Fm	70	744
57	8	BRIG	10f Gd/Sft	70	892
71	2	KEMP	9f Soft	67	999
71	3	MUSS	8f Gd/Fm		1144
34	10	NOTT	8f Good		1407
53	15	WIND	8f Good	69	1726
43	9	SALI	8f Good	68	2688
63	5	KEMP	9f Gd/Fm	66	3357
33	10	BRIG	8f Soft		4173

SPIRIT OF LOVE 5 ch h £26603

108	1	**MULH**	17f V		13*	
97	7	SAND	16f Soft		1565	
106	3	ASCO	22f Good		2153	
0	18	NEWC	16f Firm	108	2336	
106	3	NEWB	16f Firm	105	2705	BL
106	2	ASCO	16f Gd/Fm	105	3302	
108	4	YORK	16f Good		3538	
92	8	DONC	18f Gd/Fm		3877	
104	3	HAYD	14f Soft		4091	
0	18	NEWM	18f Good	107	4353	

SPIRIT OF PARK 3 b g £0

54	5	AYR	10f Good	2722
63	5	HAYD	12f Gd/Fm	3324
59	7	YORK	10f Good	3813

SPIRIT OF SONG 2 b f £756

75	4	NEWB	5f Good	1372
79	4	BATH	6f Firm	1667
0	6	CURR	6f Good	2400

SPIRIT OF TENBY 3 b c £7618

SPIRIT OF TENBY (continued)

62a	5	LING	8f Aw		26	
67	6	EPSO	9f Heavy		1032	
49	9	BRIG	7f Firm	67	1213	
66	3	SALI	8f Good	67	1345	
56	10	WIND	8f Good	65	1726	
66	3	SAND	8f Gd/Fm	65	1964	
65	3	SALI	8f Gd/Fm	64	2264	
40	10	SALI	8f Gd/Sft	64	2467	
57	4	EPSO	9f Good	64	2795	
58	7	WIND	10f Gd/Fm		3045	
62	2	BATH	12f Firm	63	3206	
68	1	**EPSO**	12f Gd/Fm	62	3417*	
61	4	BRIG	12f Firm	71	3560	
60	5	EPSO	12f Good	68	3686	
38	14	EPSO	12f Good	67	3858	
0	16	BATH	12f Soft	65	4433	

SPIRIT OF TEXAS 2 b c £1985

56	8	WIND	5f Heavy		932	
0	20	KEMP	6f Gd/Fm		1924	
59	8	EPSO	6f Gd/Sft		2628	
54	7	SALI	7f Gd/Fm		3418	BL
47	7	LEIC	8f Firm	56	3837	tbl
68	1	**NOTT**	8f Heavy		4507*	t

SPIRITO DI PUNTO 3 b f £700

66	3	CORK	10f Good	1898

SPLIT THE ACES 4 gr c £0

27	9	BATH	5f Good	44	1092	
0	16	BRIG	7f Firm	42	1336	
38	5	LEIC	6f Gd/Sft	38	1734	
5	5	SAND	5f Good		1966	
0	16	BATH	6f Firm	38	1994	
15	11	BATH	5f Good		2788	
21	10	BRIG	7f Firm		2907	
15	7	BATH	6f Firm		3208	bl

SPONTANEITY 4 ch f £1108

21	11	BRIG	12f Firm	60	1332	
36	6	BRIG	10f Gd/Fm		1933	
37	2	CHES	10f Gd/Fm		2245	
37	5	MUSS	12f Gd/Sft	42	2537	
32	10	CHES	10f Gd/Fm	48	2671	
43	5	YARM	10f Good		3234	VIS
29	6	BATH	12f Firm		3624	vis

SPORTING GESTURE 3 ch g £18102

0	12	BEVE	8f Firm	75	1279
0	13	BEVE	10f Good	73	1448
50	12	BEVE	7f Gd/Sft	69	1760
70	1	**YORK**	8f Gd/Fm	65	2645*
65	6	ASCO	10f Gd/Fm	70	2955
73	1	**CHES**	10f Gd/Fm	70	3426*
0	18	YORK	8f Good	74	3810
57	7	HAYD	8f Soft	73	4094
40	11	YORK	10f Soft		4282

SPORTING LAD 4 b c £0

97	7	WIND	8f Firm	1291

SPORTING LADDER 3 b f £268

78	4	NOTT	5f Good		1269
62	7	GOOD	9f Gd/Sft		1481
64a	4	SOUT	6f Aw		2299
49	13	CHEP	10f Good	75	3870

SPORTS EXPRESS 2 ch f £0

46	4	HAYD	6f Gd/Fm	2441
57	4	CATT	7f Gd/Fm	2927
51	5	THIR	7f Gd/Fm	3617

SPORTY MO 3 b c £7770

63a	4	WOLV	8f Aw	68	311	
60a	5	SOUT	6f Aw	68	365	
43a	9	SOUT	7f Aw	67	416	
67a	3	LING	7f Aw	64	488	VIS
75a	1	**LING**	10f Aw		545*	vis
81a	1	**LING**	8f Aw		595*	vis
74	3	WIND	8f Gd/Fm	70	744	bl
77	1	**BRIG**	8f Gd/Sft		894*	vis

0	18	CHES	8f Gd/Fm	77	1215	vis
56	12	BRIG	7f Gd/Sft	76	4121	vis
65	5	YARM	8f Heavy	74	4478	vis

SPOSA 4 b m £7443

48a	5	SOUT	12f Aw		301
60a	3	SOUT	12f Aw		556
60a	8	LING	10f Aw		593
62a	2	SOUT	16f Aw	60	644
56a	4	WOLV	16f Aw	60	664
7	12	DONC	18f Good	60	714
44	6	EPSO	12f Heavy	61	1030
61a	3	SOUT	14f Aw	62	1301
50	7	NEWC	17f Gd/Sft	57	1478
46	5	AYR	13f Gd/Fm		1657
0	P	ASCO	20f Good	59	2092
36	8	EPSO	12f Gd/Sft	47	2429
49a	1	SOUT	12f Aw		2636*
52	1	LEIC	12f Gd/Fm		2776*
46	4	PONT	12f Gd/Fm	49	2829
47	4	SAND	14f Gd/Fm	49	2923
49	3	NEWM	15f Good	53	3025
34	7	CATT	12f Gd/Fm	46	3201
26a	7	WOLV	15f Aw		4024
32	9	HAYD	14f Gd/Sft	48	4105

SPOT 3 gr f £777

43	12	WIND	10f Good		1725
66	3	SALI	7f Gd/Fm		2232
62a	4	WOLV	6f Aw		2604
52	7	BRIG	8f Firm	67	2906
44a	7	WOLV	8f Aw	63	3769
28a	10	LING	7f Aw		4487

SPREE LOVE 2 b f £1484

65a	2	SOUT	6f Aw		2635
85	4	GOOD	7f Good		3108
68	5	SALI	7f Gd/Fm		3420
43a	9	SOUT	6f Aw	73	4367

SPREE VISION 4 b c £7124

47	12	NEWC	10f Soft	64	757
45	10	HAMI	13f Good	60	845
38	7	HAMI	13f Gd/Fm	55	1363
51	4	AYR	13f Gd/Fm		1657
46	5	CATT	12f Gd/Sft	49	1816
55	1	HAMI	12f Gd/Fm	49	1908*
45	6	AYR	11f Good	53	2139
51	5	HAMI	13f Gd/Fm	54	2238
29	13	AYR	11f Soft	53	3963
0	14	REDC	14f Gd/Sft	51	4222
53	2	AYR	10f Heavy	49	4306
63	3	REDC	10f Soft		4501
29	11	MUSS	12f Soft	53	4560

SPRING ANCHOR 5 b g £0

7a	6	WOLV	12f Aw		626

SPRING BEACON 5 ch m £0

4a	6	SOUT	7f Aw		693
21a	7	SOUT	7f Aw		1305
15a	7	SOUT	11f Aw		1417
23a	9	SOUT	8f Aw		1505
19a	7	SOUT	8f Aw	28	2380

SPRING GIFT 3 b f £300

60	6	WIND	8f Gd/Fm		3048
66	4	SAND	8f Good		3474
54	6	YORK	10f Good		3813
44	10	WARW	8f Gd/Fm		3914

SPRING PURSUIT 4 b g £13298

67a	6	WOLV	9f Aw		662
47	13	DONC	8f Good	78	715
82	2	NOTT	10f Good	78	786
88	1	HAYD	12f Heavy	80	991*
89	3	KEMP	12f Gd/Sft	88	1076
82	7	NEWM	12f Firm	88	1187
0	16	YORK	12f Gd/Fm	88	1307
79	5	KEMP	10f Soft	86	1528
63	10	ASCO	10f Gd/Fm	84	3339
61	19	YORK	14f Gd/Fm	84	3565
64	12	DONC	12f Firm	80	3896
73	3	HAYD	12f Soft	78	4092
78	3	YORK	14f Heavy	78	4299
60	10	DONC	12f Soft	77	4464

SPRING SYMPHONY 2 b f £0

73	15	DONC	8f Gd/Sft		4445

SPRINGFIELDSUPREME 5 b g £0

0	15	BATH	12f Firm		2785

SPRINGS ETERNAL 3 b f £386

73a	3	SOUT	7f Aw	69	31
46a	8	SOUT	8f Aw	72	128

SPRINGS NOBLEQUEST 4 b f £0

34a	9	WOLV	6f Aw	54	466
34a	6	SOUT	7f Aw	49	588
40a	6	WOLV	6f Aw	49	622
28a	6	SOUT	6f Aw	44	698

SPRINGTIME LADY 4 ch f £3942

54a	5	LING	7f Aw	60	29	
62a	2	LING	8f Aw	59	96	
63a	2	LING	8f Aw	60	152	E
45a	8	LING	8f Aw	62	210	
58a	2	LING	10f Aw		314	
58a	2	LING	10f Aw		353	
43a	3	LING	12f Aw		457	
52	7	SALI	8f Gd/Sft	60	2467	
57	3	FOLK	10f Good	60	2625	
56	6	WIND	10f Gd/Fm	60	2888	

SPRINGWOOD JASMIN 2 b f £0

0	12	NOTT	6f Good		1408	t
57	5	LEIC	5f Soft		1550	t
42	6	NOTT	5f Good		1870	t
46	7	THIR	7f Gd/Fm		2057	t
35	10	NOTT	6f Soft		3974	t

SPUNKIE 7 ch g £0

90	5	DONC	15f Heavy		4568

SPUR OF GOLD 2 b f £0

59	6	REDC	5f Gd/Sft		1558
18	6	CARL	6f Firm		2014
24	7	REDC	7f Gd/Sft		4500

SPY KNOLL 6 b g £0

71	5	SALI	14f Firm	72	1180

SPY MASTER 2 b c £9079

76	7	NEWM	6f Gd/Fm		2598	
85	2	EPSO	7f Gd/Fm		3412	
83	3	EPSO	7f Good		3688	
81	4	WARW	7f Gd/Fm	83	3913	VIS
80	1	CATT	6f Soft		4001*	vis
79	3	NEWB	6f Sft/Hvy	81	4468	vis

SQUARE DANCER 4 b c £4491

51	8	PONT	6f Heavy	71	941
51	11	CARL	6f Firm	69	1257
0	20	THIR	6f Gd/Sft	69	1356
0	16	AYR	7f Gd/Fm	65	1631
59	5	HAMI	6f Firm	62	2097
45	4	HAMI	6f Firm		2396
50	10	DONC	7f Gd/Fm	60	2612
61	2	PONT	5f Firm	59	2830
51	6	BATH	8f Firm	58	2944
45	13	PONT	5f Gd/Fm	61	3222
55	5	PONT	5f Firm	60	3502
58	5	NEWC	6f Firm	60	3605
36	11	BEVE	5f Gd/Fm	58	3653
61	6	LEIC	7f Firm	60	3839
43	10	LEIC	8f Gd/Sft		4033
63	1	WIND	8f Gd/Sft	59	4294*
65a	3	WOLV	6f Aw	65	4358

SQUARE MILE MISS 7 b m £0

16a	9	LING	7f Aw	37	58
21a	7	LING	8f Aw	33	152

SQUIRE CORRIE 8 b g £0

0a	12	SOUT	6f Aw	51	602	
0a	12	SOUT	5f Aw	47	674	bl
0	P	MUSS	7f Gd/Fm	48	1149	

SQUIRE TAT 2 b c £0

66	5	NEWC	6f Firm		2333
63	12	YORK	6f Good		2692

SQUIRREL NUTKIN 2 br c £2235

76	2	DONC	5f Good		730
88	2	HAMI	5f Good		843
80	4	HAYD	5f Heavy		989

ST ANTIM 2 b f £3038

73	1	HAYD	6f Gd/Sft		3268*
76	5	GOOD	7f Soft		4063
0	P	LING	6f Soft	78	4269

ST EXPEDIT 3 b c £17645

84	2	LEIC	10f Gd/Sft		833
79	7	NEWM	10f Good		957
94	1	PONT	10f Gd/Sft		1103*
108	2	GOOD	10f Gd/Sft		1451
108	7	EPSO	12f Good		1848
108	3	HAYD	12f Gd/Fm		2503
97	8	GOOD	12f Good		3061
105	6	HAYD	11f Gd/Fm		3321

ST FLORENT 2 b f £1100

68	2	DONC	7f Gd/Fm		2316	
81	8	NEWM	7f Good		3020	
62	10	SALI	7f Gd/Fm		3292	
51	9	NEWM	8f Good	70	3609	VIS
60	7	BATH	8f Gd/Fm	66	3817	BL

ST GEORGES BOY 3 b c £675

0a	11	SOUT	8f Aw		86	
23a	6	SOUT	8f Aw	32	555	VIS
31a	9	WOLV	9f Aw		610	vis
0	16	LEIC	8f Good		789	
39	2	LING	11f Firm	36	1911	
29	4	MUSS	16f Firm	37	2373	
21a	5	LING	12f Aw	46	2651	
16	8	YARM	14f Firm	47	2902	

ST HELENSFIELD 5 ch g £21103

48	14	DONC	10f Gd/Sft	82	1070	
80	3	DONC	12f Good	79	1518	
65a	6	LING	12f Aw	79	1677	
80	3	RIPO	10f Good	79	1860	
81	2	LEIC	10f Firm		2030	VIS
83	2	ASCO	12f Good	79	2674	
68	10	KEMP	10f Gd/Fm	79	2750	
87	1	RIPO	12f Gd/Fm	81	2837*	
88	1	NEWC	14f Gd/Fm	85	2984*	
84	8	GOOD	14f Gd/Fm	86	3058	
89	2	NEWB	13f Firm	86	3454	

ST IVES 3 b c £0

0	16	SALI	6f Firm		1175	
36	6	BATH	8f Gd/Fm		1435	
28a	12	LING	6f Aw	47	1742	
0	16	CHEP	6f Gd/Fm	45	2489	
35	4	BRIG	7f Gd/Fm	43	3242	
9	10	YARM	8f Gd/Fm	40	3970	
0	8	BRIG	8f Soft		4175	VIS
34a	9	SOUT	6f Aw		4364	vis

ST LAWRENCE 6 gr g £6834

39a	6	SOUT	14f Aw	47	37
6a	7	SOUT	14f Aw		124
43a	2	LING	16f Aw	42	285
44a	3	SOUT	11f Aw	42	324
47a	1	SOUT	12f Aw	41	412*
47a	D	SOUT	16f Aw	42	470
49a	2	WOLV	12f Aw	42	489
49a	1	SOUT	16f Aw	42	542*
43a	3	WOLV	16f Aw	53	576
46a	3	SOUT	16f Aw	50	644
36	7	MUSS	16f Gd/Sft	42	797
24a	9	SOUT	14f Aw	48	1301

50a	2	SOUT	16f Aw	48	1416	
42a	4	SOUT	14f Aw	48	1501	
24	10	RIPO	12f Gd/Fm	40	3181	

ST MATTHEW 2 b c £0

55	8	NEWB	8f Gd/Sft		4457

ST NICHOLAS 2 b c £0

52	7	YARM	7f Good		3029
11a	9	WOLV	7f Aw		3497
13	15	YORK	8f Gd/Fm		3729
53	5	PONT	6f Soft		4373
59	14	DONC	6f Gd/Sft		4449

ST PACOKISE 3 b g £0

0	21	REDC	7f Gd/Fm		2994
30	7	REDC	9f Firm		3326
50	5	BEVE	7f Gd/Fm		3671
18	7	NEWC	7f Heavy	47	4428

STAFFORD KING 3 b c £1190

51	7	DONC	7f Good		717
60	4	WIND	8f Heavy	59	933
56	2	WARW	11f Heavy	52	1002
49	9	WIND	12f Gd/Fm	60	1199
41	13	WIND	12f Good	55	1730
58	7	HAMI	11f Gd/Fm		1909
43	6	BATH	12f Gd/Sft	51	2554
49	4	CHEP	12f Gd/Fm	51	2656
32	9	CHEP	12f Gd/Fm	51	3255
22	9	NOTT	10f Heavy	48	4509

STAFFORD PRINCE 3 br c £0

17a	8	WOLV	8f Aw	53	566
0a	9	WOLV	12f Aw	55	723
0	18	BATH	12f Gd/Sft	49	2554

STAGE DIRECTION 3 b c £5191

87	4	NEWB	10f Gd/Fm		1404	
89	4	NEWM	10f Gd/Fm		1697	
92	1	HAYD	11f Gd/Fm		2703*	t
73	4	NEWB	10f Firm	87	3453	t
73	5	DONC	10f Gd/Fm		3865	t

STAGE PASS 7 ch h £0

76	11	CHES	19f Gd/Fm	90	1222

STAGE PRESENCE 2 b f £0

0	9	CURR	7f Gd/Fm		3845
66	8	ASCO	7f Good		4114

STAGING POST 2 b c £2014

80	3	NEWC	7f Gd/Sft		3705
80	2	NOTT	8f Heavy		4504

STAKIS CASINOS BOY 6 ch g £0

0a	11	WOLV	12f Aw	49	4386

STALLONE 3 ch g £14667

74	4	WIND	10f Heavy		936
67	5	BEVE	7f Good		1444
64	5	WARW	7f Gd/Sft		1708
75	1	REDC	9f Gd/Fm	70	2160*
81	1	NEWC	8f Good	75	2524*
84	1	REDC	10f Gd/Fm	79	2992*
80	3	RIPO	9f Gd/Fm	83	3182

STAMFORD HILL 5 ch g £254

0	16	BEVE	8f Heavy		973
0	23	REDC	7f Gd/Sft		1132
0	14	THIR	12f Gd/Sft		1353
0	11	PONT	10f Soft	35	1705
12	5	CARL	14f Firm	33	2016
0	6	NEWC	12f Good		2523
31	9	REDC	9f Gd/Fm		2865
0	17	PONT	8f Firm		3506
13	5	THIR	8f Gd/Fm		3616
42	9	BEVE	12f Gd/Fm		3654
0	11	DONC	10f Gd/Fm		3865
0	14	REDC	7f Gd/Sft		4218
0	11	YORK	12f Soft		4276

STAND ASIDE 4 b c £295

45	5	BRIG	12f Gd/Fm		3241	
47	4	FOLK	16f Gd/Fm	50	3448	BL
0	16	LING	16f Firm	48	3755	bl
45	4	GOOD	16f Soft	46	4075	bl

STAND BY 3 b f £2779

62a	5	SOUT	5f Aw		179
59a	3	WOLV	7f Aw	56	257
54a	3	SOUT	6f Aw	56	331
28	10	LING	7f Aw	58	3758
0	14	GOOD	8f Good	58	3885
61a	1	SOUT	6f Aw		4368*
56a	3	LING	7f Aw		4487

STANDIFORD GIRL 3 b f £1336

24a	6	SOUT	8f Aw		869
47a	2	WOLV	9f Aw		1141
0	14	BEVE	10f Firm		1274
15	11	NOTT	10f Soft	45	1644
34a	7	WOLV	9f Aw	52	2080
40a	3	SOUT	8f Aw		2816
50a	2	SOUT	8f Aw		2946
43	4	HAYD	8f Gd/Sft		3266
26	9	MUSS	8f Gd/Fm	43	3746

STANDS TO REASON 2 gr g £392

73	4	NEWB	6f Sft/Hvy		4470

STAPLOY 2 b f £615

72	3	DONC	8f Heavy		4569

STAR ATTRACTION 3 b f £301

41	4	CHEP	10f Gd/Fm		2449
25	8	NOTT	10f Gd/Fm		3006
12	5	BRIG	10f Gd/Fm		3262
7	10	BATH	12f Firm		3624

STAR BRIEF 2 b c £265

52	10	NEWM	7f Gd/Fm		2599
58	4	NEWM	7f Firm		3296
35	10	FOLK	7f Gd/Fm		3582

STAR CAST 3 ch f £12975

76	1	WIND	12f Gd/Sft	68	1425*
79	1	GOOD	12f Gd/Fm	73	1637*
79	3	SALI	12f Gd/Sft	77	2470

STAR DYNASTY 3 b c £6201

87	3	LEIC	8f Good		789
90	2	PONT	10f Gd/Sft		1103
87	2	REDC	10f Gd/Sft	82	1561

STAR GLADE 2 b f £0

0	18	NEWB	7f Firm		3999
50	8	BRIG	8f Soft		4417

STAR MANAGER 10 b g £0

39	7	NOTT	16f Gd/Fm		2191
0a	16	LING	12f Aw		4101

STAR OF AKKAR 4 b f £15370

103	2	DEAU	10f Gd/Fm		3547

STAR OF WONDER 2 b f £0

50	9	SALI	8f Gd/Sft		4163
55	10	WIND	8f Heavy		4524

STAR PRINCESS 3 b f £6881

52	6	NOTT	5f Heavy		1021	
72	4	CHES	6f Gd/Fm	73	1220	
63	2	THIR	6f Gd/Sft		1354	
75	2	LING	6f Gd/Fm		2183	
75	4	YARM	6f Firm	75	2900	
66	2	SAND	5f Good		3229	
64	5	LING	6f Firm		3579	BL
75	3	GOOD	5f Good	73	3908	bl
74	3	YARM	5f Firm	73	3920	VIS
44	12	KEMP	6f Gd/Sft	74	4037	vis
67	5	YORK	6f Soft		4287	vis

STAR RAGE 10 b g £9929

81	6	DONC	18f Good	86	714
74	13	SALI	14f Firm	85	1180
0	F	CHES	19f Gd/Fm	85	1222
82	2	THIR	16f Gd/Sft	83	1355
82	2	MUSS	16f Firm	80	1686
78	5	AYR	15f Good	81	2164
80	5	NEWB	16f Firm	81	2812
78	4	REDC	16f Gd/Fm	80	2993
83	2	BEVE	16f Good	79	3395
82	1	THIR	16f Gd/Fm	79	3618*
81	7	GOOD	16f Good	84	3905

STAR SELECTION 9 b g £0

0	16	YORK	12f Firm	75	2002

STAR TURN 6 ch g £7826

61	1	NEWM	10f Gd/Fm	57	1150*
59	8	NEWB	10f Good	62	1375

STARBECK 2 b f £6908

68	4	THIR	6f Gd/Fm		3614
86	1	YORK	6f Soft		4283*
82	9	DONC	6f Soft		4462

STARBOARD TACK 4 b f £424

29a	11	SOUT	8f Aw	68	1303
35	8	SOUT	10f Soft	67	1608
67a	3	SOUT	8f Aw	67	1803
0	14	WARW	11f Good	63	2463
0	10	BATH	8f Firm	60	2942
0	16	SALI	14f Gd/Fm	60	3424

STARDARA 2 b f £0

69	6	CHEP	8f Gd/Fm		3678
39	5	NEWM	8f Good		4019

STARDREAMER 3 ch g £1260

0	13	DONC	8f Gd/Fm		2611
47	6	YARM	11f Firm		2897
52	2	BEVE	10f Gd/Fm		3677

STARFLEET 2 ch f £0

65	5	WIND	6f Gd/Fm		2886
74	7	NEWM	6f Gd/Fm		4209

STARLIGHT 3 b f £4450

65	1	THIR	7f Soft		929*
41	10	NOTT	8f Gd/Sft	64	1085
70	1	LING	7f Good	62	2592*
66	5	NEWM	7f Gd/Fm	70	3163
13	15	WIND	8f Good	70	3355
0	15	YARM	8f Firm	68	3936
0	13	LING	7f Soft	65	4192

STARLYTE GIRL 3 b f £24561

70	6	KEMP	9f Gd/Sft	88	1075
64	11	NEWB	10f Good		1374
84	1	SALI	10f Gd/Fm		1885*
87	2	GOOD	10f Gd/Fm	84	2358
90	1	WIND	8f Good	85	2713*
95	2	GOOD	10f Gd/Fm	90	3131

STARRY LADY 2 b f £1216

87	2	REDC	7f Gd/Sft		4216
80	4	YARM	8f Heavy		4477

STARRY MARY 2 b f £252

64	8	BATH	6f Gd/Sft		1667
68	4	NOTT	6f Good		2010
46	9	LING	7f Good		2653
28a	8	WOLV	6f Aw		3496
61	3	BRIG	8f Gd/Sft		4117

STATE APPROVAL 7 b g £2478

45a	6	WOLV	9f Aw	68	270
31a	8	SOUT	11f Aw	65	343
31a	10	SOUT	11f Aw	65	390
33a	10	SOUT	16f Aw	60	428
41a	7	WOLV	8f Aw		477
54a	2	SOUT	11f Aw	52	512
49a	3	SOUT	11f Aw	50	560
55a	3	SOUT	11f Aw	53	605
31a	6	SOUT	12f Aw	53	642
28a	8	SOUT	11f Aw	53	671
39a	5	SOUT	11f Aw	50	742
29a	9	SOUT	11f Aw	47	1306
33	6	LEIC	10f Soft	38	1546
33a	3	SOUT	11f Aw		1978
33a	3	SOUT	12f Aw		2298
8a	11	WOLV	16f Aw	33	2606
20a	8	SOUT	16f Aw	32	2951

STATE OPENING 3 ch f £0

0	20	BATH	12f Soft		4434	

STATE SHINTO 4 b c £11290

99	8	ASCO	12f Good		2149	VIS
117	3	MUNI	10f Soft		3071	vis

STATE WIND 4 ch g £0

0a	12	SOUT	8f Aw	52	585	bl
38a	6	WOLV	7f Aw	44	635	vis
0a	10	WOLV	8f Aw	41	676	vis
36	5	CATT	7f Gd/Fm		778	vis
38	8	PONT	6f Soft		872	vis
21	12	CARL	9f Firm	35	1254	vis
0	25	REDC	8f Firm	35	1300	vis

STATEROOM 2 ch c £0

78	7	ASCO	7f Gd/Sft		4124

STATO ONE 8 br h £43860

102	1	JAGE	9f Good		1323*

STATOSILVER 2 b c £0

43	5	CATT	5f Soft		4252
0	13	NEWC	6f Heavy		4402

STATOYORK 7 b g £14563

0	14	REDC	5f Gd/Sft	61	1580
38	11	RIPO	5f Gd/Fm	58	2107
57	5	NEWM	5f Good	58	2569
49	10	HAYD	5f Gd/Fm	58	2701
35	7	WARW	5f Gd/Fm	58	2845
35	18	GOOD	5f Gd/Fm	56	3091
0	15	GOOD	6f Gd/Fm	58	3136
52	7	PONT	5f Gd/Fm	56	3222
56	2	CHES	5f Gd/Fm	52	3512
62	1	CARL	5f Firm	52	3572*
57	4	BEVE	5f Good	62	3653
67	1	HAYD	5f Gd/Sft	59	3788*
62	5	DONC	5f Firm	65	3894
0	19	AYR	5f Soft	65	3960
54	13	WIND	5f Gd/Sft	64	4295
0	13	PONT	5f Soft	63	4377

STATUE GALLERY 2 ch c £4497

80	5	NEWM	6f Gd/Fm		3162
82	2	YARM	6f Gd/Fm		3385
71	1	BRIG	6f Firm		3732*
62	6	BRIG	6f Soft	83	4170

STAY BEHIND 2 ch f £669

86	3	KEMP	8f Gd/Fm		3799

STAYIN ALIVE 3 b c £3468

90a	1	LING	7f Aw		206*	t
81a	8	LING	10f Aw		690	t
48	16	NEWM	6f Gd/Sft	86	982	t

STEALTHY TIMES 3 ch f £312

80	11	NEWM	7f Good		955
58a	12	WOLV	6f Aw	83	1138
0	14	KEMP	6f Gd/Fm	83	1925
66	10	NEWM	8f Good	79	2564
73	5	LEIC	7f Gd/Fm	74	2918
59	5	DONC	7f Aw	73	3160
68	4	YARM	7f Aw	70	3666
0	20	YORK	8f Good	68	3810
44	9	NEWM	7f Good		4018
43	7	PONT	6f Soft		4233
44	12	DONC	7f Gd/Sft	60	4452

STEAMROLLER STANLY 7 b g £7615

71a	4	LING	12f Aw	72	151	
70a	3	SOUT	12f Aw	72	200	ebl
64a	3	LING	12f Aw	70	237	VIS
69a	3	LING	12f Aw	70	245	vis
53a	5	LING	13f Aw	69	317	vis
69a	2	SOUT	16f Aw		327	
64a	4	WOLV	16f Aw	69	380	
63a	6	SOUT	16f Aw	67	470	
42a	8	WOLV	12f Aw	67	489	
39	10	SOUT	11f Gd/Sft	57	855	bl
42a	7	SOUT	14f Aw	60	1301	
59a	4	SOUT	16f Aw		1802	
58a	1	SOUT	14f Aw		1975*	
43a	2	SOUT	12f Aw		2298	
58a	2	WOLV	16f Aw	55	2606	
30a	11	SOUT	16f Aw	56	2951	
28a	8	WOLV	15f Gd/Fm	55	3276	

STEEL BAND 2 b c £5425

86	3	NEWM	7f Firm		3298
84	1	CHEP	8f Gd/Fm		3680*
86	2	LEIC	7f Gd/Sft		4028

STEEL TRADER 3 b c £0

56	5	THIR	8f Gd/Sft		1717

STEINITZ 2 ch c £2240

81	2	SAND	7f Aw		2494
81	7	GOOD	7f Firm		3154

STELLISSIMA 5 ch m £542

45	3	MUSS	16f Gd/Sft	45	797	t

STEP ON DEGAS 7 b m £0

0	11	SAND	8f Heavy	53	1058
44	8	WARW	11f Gd/Fm	51	2033
0	15	EPSO	7f Aw	49	3765

STEPASTRAY 3 gr g £2166

0	12	REDC	10f Firm	54	1299
42	8	REDC	10f Good	50	1895
47	3	REDC	9f Gd/Fm	46	2160
80	6	HAYD	11f Gd/Fm		2703
53	3	REDC	11f Gd/Fm	52	2863
51	3	REDC	11f Gd/Fm	52	3310
44	8	REDC	11f Gd/Fm	52	3636
56	9	YORK	10f Good		3813

STEPPIN OUT 3 ch f £3575

73	1	SALI	6f Gd/Fm		2472*
66	7	GOOD	7f Good		3662
0	27	AYR	5f Soft	71	3960

STERLING GUARANTEE 2 b f £439

88	4	NEWM	8f Good		4161

STERLING HIGH 5 b g £360

47a	7	SOUT	8f Aw	58	251	
49a	4	SOUT	8f Aw	52	298	
38a	9	SOUT	8f Aw	58	340	t
53a	3	SOUT	8f Aw	51	418	t
40a	5	WOLV	8f Aw	49	447	t
41a	4	WOLV	9f Aw		553	t
18a	8	WOLV	8f Aw	51	569	t
0	14	SOUT	7f Good	52	803	t
0	14	WARW	11f Heavy	48	889	t
0	15	PONT	10f Heavy	48	943	tbl
0	17	PONT	10f Gd/Sft	42	1101	tbl
33	7	NOTT	10f Good	38	3524	t
12	6	NEWC	10f Heavy	41	4427	t

STEVAL 3 ch f £2941

47a	4	LING	5f Aw		883
14a	11	WOLV	5f Aw		1036
58	1	CATT	6f Soft		1678*

STICIBOOTS 3 b g £0

48a	5	WOLV	12f Aw		565
49a	5	SOUT	12f Aw		643
40a	7	WOLV	8f Aw		658
0	14	NOTT	14f Gd/Fm	52	1270

STICKS 2 ch f £390

56	3	NEWC	6f Gd/Fm		1476
0	P	REDC	7f Good		1890

STICKS AND STONES 8 b g £541

27a	7	WOLV	8f Aw		393
44a	2	WOLV	12f Aw		581
0	13	LEIC	10f Soft	43	1546
0	28	NEWM	12f Gd/Fm	38	1852
32	4	NOTT	14f Gd/Fm	34	3002
11	9	BRIG	12f Gd/Fm	34	3260

STILL IN LOVE 3 b f £1355

73	2	REDC	7f Gd/Sft		1135
46	5	BRIG	7f Firm		1333
73	3	LING	6f Gd/Fm		2183

STILL WATERS 5 b g £2587

16a	7	WOLV	9f Aw	65	172
0a	12	SOUT	8f Aw	62	251
35a	6	SOUT	8f Aw	57	601
0a	15	SOUT	8f Aw	57	647
0	14	BEVE	7f Firm	50	1275
48a	3	SOUT	7f Aw	45	1801
51a	1	SOUT	7f Aw	45	1979*
43a	3	SOUT	8f Aw	51	2637

STILMEMAITE 2 b f £1193

71	3	THIR	5f Soft		904
67	5	NEWC	5f Heavy		1006
64	7	THIR	5f Good		1161
56	7	AYR	6f Gd/Fm		1628
55	4	YORK	6f Gd/Fm		1981

STITCH IN TIME 4 ch g £4790

43	2	PONT	10f Soft	41	871	
47	2	BRIG	7f Gd/Sft	41	896	
43	3	BRIG	7f Firm	44	1336	
46	3	NOTT	8f Good	44	1414	
39	8	MUSS	9f Firm	45	1689	
52a	2	SOUT	8f Aw	44	2380	
14	11	WIND	8f Soft	44	2546	
32	5	BEVE	10f Good	40	2883	
27	4	CARL	8f Firm	36	3192	
35	3	BRIG	10f Gd/Fm	36	3244	VIS
49a	3	WOLV	8f Aw	49	3499	vis
37	3	CHEP	10f Gd/Fm	36	3683	vis
38	2	BRIG	12f Soft	36	4176	
44a	3	WOLV	12f Aw	49	4386	

STOCK PROOF 2 b c £0

69	12	NEWM	7f Good		4184

STOLEN MUSIC 7 b m £964

42	7	CATT	14f Good		1660
35	3	CATT	14f Gd/Sft		1814
35	2	REDC	16f Good		1894
11	8	REDC	14f Gd/Fm	35	2156

STOLI 2 ch c £0

72	8	HAYD	7f Soft		3786
78	6	NEWB	7f Firm		3999

STONE COLD 3 ch c £0

0	12	REDC	10f Gd/Sft	54	4221

STONE OF DESTINY 5 ch g £0

14a	10	WOLV	8f Aw	55	38
29a	9	WOLV	6f Aw		76

STONEY GARNETT 3 b f £3510

69	1	BRIG	5f Soft	65	1512*
69	2	BRIG	6f Good		1651
60	6	CHEP	5f Gd/Sft	68	1795
0	11	LING	6f Firm		3280
0	16	LING	6f Soft	67	4270

STOP BY 5 £15369

109	4	SAIN	12f Good		2406
91	4	LONG	12f Good		3927

STOP THE TRAFFIC 3 b f £4139

55a	4	LING	5f Aw		289	
64a	2	WOLV	6f Aw	58	397	
40a	5	SOUT	7f Aw		427	
64a	2	WOLV	6f Aw	61	479	
67a	2	WOLV	6f Aw	64	1138	
47a	8	WOLV	6f Aw	64	1233	
56a	5	WOLV	7f Aw	66	1390	
64	5	WARW	7f Gd/Sft	64	1710	
54	8	NOTT	8f Good	63	1873	
32	11	NEWM	8f Gd/Fm		2134	
0	8	FOLK	6f Gd/Fm		2292	VIS
6	11	WIND	6f Soft	52	2549	
40a	5	WOLV	6f Aw		2604	
37a	5	SOUT	6f Aw		2947	
43	6	NEWM	7f Gd/Fm		3318	t
22	7	YARM	6f Gd/Fm	46	3386	t

37 8 YARM 7f Firm 3921 t
37a 8 LING 7f Aw 4328 t
44a 2 WOLV 7f Aw 4384 t

STOPPES BROW 8 b g £3034
84a 4 WOLV 9f Aw 662
0 16 EPSO 10f Heavy 80 1031 bl
71 10 KEMP 8f Gd/Sft 80 1077 bl
74 6 GOOD 8f Gd/Sft 78 1450 bl
79 5 GOOD 8f Gd/Fm 78 2126 bl
76 2 EPSO 8f Gd/Sft 2433 bl
75 5 EPSO 8f Gd/Sft 77 2629 bl
72 6 GOOD 8f Gd/Fm 75 3063 bl
69 3 EPSO 9f Gd/Sft 3404 bl
70 4 GOOD 9f Good 70 3644 bl
70 4 GOOD 9f Good 70 3883 bl
60 7 WIND 9f Gd/Sft 4292 bl

STOPWATCH 5 b g £0
29a 7 LING 16f Aw 52 548

STORM BOY 2 b c c £8837
94 3 DEAU 7f Gd/Fm 3716
92 2 MAIS 7f Good 4049

STORM CRY 5 b g £0
52a 12 WOLV 7f Aw 68 323
0a 10 WOLV 8f Aw 63 381
0 17 SALI 9f Good 68 1348 t
0 16 KEMP 7f Gd/Fm 66 3362 t
0 15 CHEP 7f Good 63 3871 BL

STORM DREAM 3 b f £26650
105 2 LEOP 8f Gd/Fm 1315
109 3 CURR 8f Gd/Sft 1626

STORM FROM HEAVEN 2 b g £0
59a 4 WOLV 6f Aw 4244
56a 8 WOLV 6f Aw 4359

STORM HILL 4 b c £1160
0 16 NEWM 10f Gd/Fm 78 1150
74 8 SALI 12f Good 76 1350 t
75 2 SOUT 12f Soft 73 1604 t
0 U KEMP 12f Gd/Fm 73 1927 t

STORM KING 2 b c £0
63 8 DONC 6f Good 1513
27 9 NEWC 6f Firm 2333
68 5 HAYD 6f Gd/Fm 2700

STORM PRINCE 3 ch c £0
52a 6 WOLV 9f Aw 74 392
52a 8 WOLV 8f Aw 71 495
0 17 SALI 8f Good 70 1345
0 17 LEIC 8f Gd/Fm 68 3095
41 12 CHEP 10f Good 63 3870 VIS
0 13 BEVE 12f Good 63 3954

STORM SONG 3 ch c £0
33a 9 LING 7f Aw 155

STORM WIZARD 3 b c £3872
77 3 WIND 10f Heavy 936
73 4 EPSO 9f Heavy 1032
78 2 HAMI 11f Gd/Fm 1193
78 2 SAND 10f Soft 76 1585
0 12 EPSO 10f Gd/Sft 76 1831
0 12 KEMP 12f Soft 4040
58 6 NEWB 10f Sft/Hv 4474
25 6 WIND 11f Heavy 72 4529

STORMDANCER 3 ch c £0
27 9 WARW 12f Soft 63 1064

STORMING FOLEY 2 ch c £913
67 4 WIND 5f Gd/Fm 743
70 2 LEIC 5f Gd/Sft 828
59 5 BRIG 5f Firm 1208
46 8 SOUT 6f Soft 1602

STORMING HOME 2 b c £11151
60 9 NEWM 7f Firm 2867
100 1 NEWM 7f Gd/Fm 3121*
104 2 SAND 7f Good 3470
96 9 NEWM 7f Good 4196

STORMLESS 9 b g £0
40 7 NEWC 16f Soft 42 760

STORMSWELL 3 ch f £4658
38 9 NOTT 10f Heavy 57 1022
29 14 CARL 8f Firm 54 1255
49 3 CATT 7f Soft 1681
53 1 HAMI 8f Gd/Fm 49 1907*
45 5 REDC 9f Gd/Fm 51 2160
53 3 LEIC 8f Good 51 2512
0 15 BEVE 7f Good 52 2882
47 4 PONT 8f Gd/Fm 52 3226
43 8 HAYD 11f Gd/Sft 51 3480
49 4 CATT 7f Soft 50 4004
43 8 NOTT 8f Heavy 50 4414
37 7 MUSS 9f Soft 50 4523

STORMVILLE 3 b g £2300
66 6 DONC 7f Good 76 736
58 4 MUSS 9f Gd/Sft 902
32 10 PONT 10f Gd/Sft 69 1104
43 8 REDC 9f Aw 60 2160
61 2 BEVE 7f Firm 59 2733
43 6 THIR 8f Gd/Fm 62 3345
1 9 BEVE 8f Sft/Hvy 62 4045

STORMY CREST 2 b c £0
37 8 CATT 5f Soft 4253
46 8 MUSS 7f Soft 4562

STORMY RAINBOW 3 b c c £1510
70a 2 LING 8f Aw 591
63a 2 SOUT 8f Aw 694
67 5 SAND 7f Soft 69 4204
52a 8 LING 8f Aw 67 4335

STORMY SKYE 4 b c £2299
76 3 BRIG 12f Gd/Sft 1510 tbl
78 2 CHEP 18f Gd/Sft 76 1800 tbl
0 4 GOOD 14f Good 77 2305 tbl
39a 6 LING 13f AW 4193 t
64 12 NEWM 18f Good 79 4353 tbl

STORMY VOYAGE 2 b c £275
67 4 NOTT 6f Gd/Fm 2189
27 7 LING 6f Good 2652

STORNOWAY 2 b f £822
65 2 NOTT 6f Heavy 4410

STORYTELLER 6 b g £1735
0 18 THIR 5f Soft 86 926
77 7 THIR 5f Good 85 1162
0 15 THIR 6f Good 83 1383 vis
75 4 PONT 6f Soft 80 1702 vis
83 3 YORK 5f Gd/Fm 78 1980 vis
67 11 SAND 5f Gd/Fm 80 2473 vis
77 5 YORK 5f Gd/Fm 80 2644 vis

STRACHIN 6 b g £0
46 9 LEIC 8f Soft 78 1547

STRAHAN 3 b c £35884
92 1 NEWM 6f Gd/Sft 87 982*
98 2 NEWM 7f Gd/Fm 91 1153
100 2 GOOD 7f Gd/Sft 95 1470
102 3 ASCO 6f Good 99 2151
100 10 NEWM 7f Gd/Fm 101 2616
99 4 GOOD 7f Good 100 3648
89 14 ASCO 7f Good 100 4112
104 2 NEWM 7f Good 100 4195

STRAND OF GOLD 3 b c £582
77 5 SALI 6f Firm 1181
65 5 CHES 6f Gd/Fm 68 1220
54 8 SALI 7f Good 68 1348
74 5 HAYD 7f Gd/Sft 1537 BL
48 12 HAYD 7f Gd/Sft 65 1793 bl
56 7 HAYD 7f Gd/Sft 62 3269
42 7 BRIG 7f Soft 3739 bl
48 8 LING 7f Soft 57 4192 bl
55 3 DONC 7f Soft 4461 bl

STRANGE DESTINY 2 b f £19162

STRASBOURG 3 ch c £4300
0 17 GOOD 8f Good 97 1470
75 15 EPSO 7f Gd/Sft 93 1826
93 2 RIPO 8f Gd/Fm 88 2108
96 3 BATH 8f Firm 92 2330
73 10 ASCO 8f Gd/Fm 94 3338
56 15 YORK 8f Firm 94 3597
76 8 DONC 8f Firm 90 3897
52 12 NEWB 8f Firm 86 3998
67 6 YORK 8f Soft 82 4284
0 15 DONC 10f Gd/Sft 78 4448

STRATEGIC CHOICE 9 b h £0
89 10 HAYD 12f Gd/Fm 99 2502
93 7 YORK 12f Gd/Fm 99 2647 bl

STRATEGIC DANCER 3 b c £0
75 6 DONC 9f Gd/Fm 704
0 12 LEIC 10f Gd/Sft 833
24 11 WIND 10f Heavy 936
37 9 LEIC 12f Gd/Sft 64 1571

STRATH FILLAN 2 b f £0
46 10 PONT 6f Good 1864
43 9 WARW 7f Good 2459
64 9 NEWB 7f Firm 2810
52 5 YARM 8f Gd/Fm 56 3968

STRATS QUEST 6 b m £2520
37a 5 SOUT 6f Aw 44 87 vis
16a 6 SOUT 7f Aw 42 476 vis
33a 5 SOUT 7f Aw 38 602 vis
8a 8 WOLV 7f Aw 38 711 vis
32 11 LEIC 7f Good 790
54 1 WARW 7f Soft 816*
39 8 BRIG 7f Gd/Sft 54 896
37 9 WARW 5f Heavy 52 1005
43 5 NOTT 6f Gd/Sft 52 1082
5a 8 SOUT 8f Aw 36 1303
44 10 WIND 6f Gd/Sft 1423
44 5 LING 5f Soft 50 1543
29 7 CHEP 6f Heavy 50 1557
0 19 CHEP 7f Gd/Sft 46 1799 vis

STRATTON 3 b c £701
70 4 LING 5f Good 1399
47 9 NEWB 6f Gd/Fm 1783
61 3 PONT 8f Soft 4234
34 11 NOTT 8f Heavy 64 4414

STRAVINSKY 4 b c £0
109a 6 GULF 6f Fast 17 vis

STRAVSEA 5 b g £8926
23a 7 SOUT 7f Aw 45 75
49a 1 SOUT 8f Aw 43 176*
40a 11 SOUT 8f Aw 58 251
44a 3 SOUT 8f Aw 49 297
43a 5 SOUT 8f Aw 49 345
55a 1 SOUT 8f Aw 48 384*
60a 1 SOUT 8f Aw 54 430*
46a 6 SOUT 8f Aw 59 473
52a 3 SOUT 8f Aw 57 513
52a 5 SOUT 11f Aw 57 560
38a 7 SOUT 8f Aw 55 692
45a 4 SOUT 11f Aw 55 742
54a 2 SOUT 8f Aw 52 1303
41a 7 SOUT 8f Aw 52 1419
43a 9 SOUT 7f Aw 54 1801
0a 14 SOUT 8f Aw 53 2121

STRAWBERRY DAWN 2 gr f £280
60 4 LING 5f Firm 3576
6 5 BRIG 6f Firm 3732

STRAWMAN 3 b c £0

70	7	DONC	8f Gd/Fm		704	
0	13	KEMP	11f Soft		1017	
73	6	HAYD	11f Gd/Sft		1539	
56	5	BRIG	12f Gd/Sft		4119	
47	9	NOTT	10f Heavy		4408	

STREAK OF DAWN 3 b f £0
27	8	PONT	6f Good		1500	
24	10	BATH	10f Firm	35	2332	
18	9	FOLK	12f Good	41	2624	
0	15	BEVE	16f Good	35	2879	
26	9	CATT	16f Good	47	3442	
33	5	BRIG	12f Firm	46	3735	
18a	7	LING	12f Aw		3835	

STRECCIA 3 b f £287
50	6	BATH	10f Gd/Sft		1668	
49	4	CHEP	12f Good		1970	
0a	8	WOLV	9f Aw		2602	
0a	12	LING	16f Aw	45	4099	

STREET LIFE 2 ch g £256
0	19	NEWM	6f Good	4341
67	9	NEWM	6f Gd/Sft	4530
72	4	DONC	7f Heavy	4567

STREET WALKER 4 b f £302
50	4	WIND	12f Good	54	853	
0	14	NOTT	14f Heavy	54	1023	
35	11	BATH	13f Gd/Fm	51	1440	
36	6	WIND	12f Good	49	2370	VIS
40	4	NOTT	14f Good	44	2681	
24	8	CATT	16f Good	42	3442	

STREGONE 2 b g £21380
79	1	WIND	5f Gd/Fm		743*	
75	6	NEWC	5f Heavy		1006	
68	5	CHES	5f Gd/Fm		1214	BL
96	2	SAND	5f Soft		1586	
96	2	EPSO	6f Good		1846	
93	8	ASCO	6f Good		2067	
101	4	NEWM	7f Gd/Fm		2613	
102	2	NEWB	6f Firm		2850	
95	7	GOOD	6f Good		3105	
69	6	WIND	6f Good		3352	
90	7	DONC	6f Gd/Fm		3862	

STRENSALL 3 b c £0
0	15	REDC	7f Gd/Sft	4218

STRETFORD LASS 3 b f £3541
66a	3	WOLV	8f Aw		409	
67a	1	LING	8f Aw		544*	
58a	3	LING	10f Aw	68	597	

STRETTON 2 br c £1328
55	11	YORK	6f Firm	1328
81	3	RIPO	6f Good	2106
79	2	NEWC	6f Good	3245
66	9	YORK	7f Good	78 3542
25	10	YORK	6f Good	76 3807

STRICTLY PLEASURE 2 b g £0
58	6	DONC	6f Gd/Fm	1844
0	15	NEWC	6f Good	3245
44	7	YORK	7f Soft	4277

STRICTLY SPEAKING 3 b c £3072
55	10	WIND	8f Gd/Fm	67	744	
57	6	WIND	12f Heavy	64	937	BL
57	6	WARW	11f Heavy	64	1002	
43	8	BATH	8f Gd/Sft	58	1671	bl
64a	1	WOLV	12f Aw	54	3494*	
61	2	AYR	11f Soft	60	3963	
50	3	BRIG	12f Gd/Sft	60	4123	

STRIDHANA 4 ch f £0
0	17	CHEP	7f Gd/Fm	65	1799	
43	10	SALI	6f Gd/Fm	61	2230	
53	4	LING	6f Good	60	2654	
0	13	WIND	6f Gd/Fm	55	3046	
43	9	SALI	6f Gd/Fm	55	3293	VIS

STRIDING KING 5 ch g £0
0	20	WIND	6f Gd/Sft		1423	
0	17	SALI	7f Gd/Fm		1884	
0	F	FOLK	8f Gd/Fm		2292	VIS

STROMNESS 3 ch c £3458
101	3	DEAU	15f Gd/Fm	3545

STROMSHOLM 4 ch c £5151
47a	4	SOUT	6f Aw		685
56	8	LEIC	7f Gd/Sft	72	834
53	6	EPSO	9f Heavy		1033
68	3	NOTT	10f Gd/Sft	66	1370
69	2	BEVE	10f Firm	66	1921
65	4	YARM	10f Gd/Fm	67	2199
68	2	SAND	10f Gd/Fm	67	2527
67	3	WIND	10f Gd/Fm	67	2888
54	9	LEIC	8f Gd/Fm	67	3334

STRONG PRESENCE 3 b c £12332
82	1	NEWM	6f Gd/Fm		2807*
82	1	AYR	6f Good		3366
87	1	RIPO	8f Good	80	3699*

STRUMPET 2 bl f £7279
70	2	GOOD	5f Gd/Sft		1639
70	2	NEWB	6f Good		1943
79	1	SALI	5f Gd/Fm		2227*
56	6	GOOD	6f Gd/Fm	79	3062
78	3	NEWM	6f Gd/Fm	77	3630
75	3	DONC	7f Gd/Fm	78	3860
71	8	REDC	6f Good		4219
67	6	NEWB	7f Gd/Sft	76	4453
54	8	BRIG	8f Heavy	76	4538

STUNNING 2 b f £3842
88	3	SAIN	7f Gd/Sft	4314

STUTTER 2 ch c £0
89	5	ASCO	6f Gd/Fm	3000
84	5	NEWM	6f Good	4341

STUTTON GAL 4 b f £0
15a	11	SOUT	6f Aw	30		bl

STYLE DANCER 6 b g £31573
40a	10	LING	7f Aw	64	29	vis
60a	3	WOLV	7f Aw	60	79	
56a	3	LING	8f Aw	60	97	
48a	7	LING	8f Aw	59	169	vis
54	5	NEWC	8f Heavy	62	1007	
63	4	REDC	8f Firm	60	1300	
49	8	RIPO	8f Good	60	1598	
60	4	LEIC	8f Firm	59	2027	
60	7	CARL	8f Good	60	2242	
71	1	DONC	8f Gd/Fm	60	2349*	vis
72	1	BEVE	8f Gd/Fm	66	2481*	vis
69	7	YORK	7f Good	73	2645	vis
57	7	ASCO	8f Gd/Fm	70	3338	vis
69	3	REDC	8f Gd/Fm	69	3634	vis
72	1	YORK	7f Good	69	3809*	vis
68	10	AYR	7f Soft	72	3992	vis
74	2	AYR	8f Gd/Sft	72	4013	vis
53	13	ASCO	8f Gd/Sft	73	4126	vis

STYLISH FELLA 2 b c £0
58	9	NEWM	6f Gd/Fm		2598
44	13	WIND	6f Gd/Fm		3047
50	6	FOLK	6f Good		3582
44	6	LEIC	8f Firm	52	3837

STYLISH WAYS 8 b g £3027
50	12	DONC	6f Gd/Sft	66	1074
52	6	CARL	6f Firm	66	1258
67	2	WIND	6f Gd/Fm	63	2054
57	5	WIND	6f Gd/Fm	63	2207
70	3	WIND	6f Gd/Fm	66	2371
0	17	YORK	6f Good	70	2697
0	21	ASCO	7f Gd/Fm	68	2999
0	23	YORK	7f Good	68	3809

SUANCES 3 ch c £59559
116	1	LONG	9f Good	1379*
119	1	CHAN	9f V	1753*

SUAVE FRANKIE 4 ch c £0
30	10	PONT	10f Soft	48	1705	

SUAVE NATIVE 2 ch c £4225
96	1	YARM	6f Heavy	4479*

SUAVE PERFORMER 3 b g £1971
50a	7	WOLV	7f Aw		362
45a	4	WOLV	5f Aw		434
46a	5	WOLV	5f Aw		624
51	4	RIPO	10f Soft	51	827
52	2	LEIC	12f Gd/Sft	51	1571
51	4	BEVE	12f Gd/Sft	51	1758
45	4	NEWC	9f Gd/Fm	52	2276
49	5	FOLK	12f Good	50	2624

SUAVE SHOT 3 br f £0
0	13	SALI	6f Firm	1181

SUBADAR MAJOR 3 b g £0
24a	11	SOUT	8f Aw		198
0a	11	WOLV	8f Aw		362
21a	7	WOLV	8f Aw		409
26a	6	SOUT	12f Aw	35	2815

SUBSTANTIVE 3 ch f £0
33	8	YARM	7f Firm	2770

SUBTLE INFLUENCE 6 b h £2230
54	8	AYR	17f Soft	78	3993
73	2	AYR	13f Heavy	70	4325

SUBTLE POWER 3 b c £88899
92	1	NEWB	10f Gd/Fm	1404*
111	2	NEWM	10f Firm	1854
114	1	ASCO	12f Good	2148*
110	5	YORK	12f Good	3540

SUCH BOLDNESS 6 b g £414
13	10	PONT	10f Good	55	2366
0	15	WIND	10f Good	55	2544
22a	8	LING	10f Aw		2764
38	6	GOOD	9f Good	48	3110
47	3	LING	11f Firm	50	3282

SUCH FLAIR 3 b f £7428
65	3	NEWC	8f Heavy		1010
59	10	NOTT	8f Gd/Fm		1269
66a	4	WOLV	8f Aw	67	4021
71	1	PONT	10f Soft	66	4374*
75	1	BRIG	10f Heavy	72	4540*

SUDDEN FLIGHT 3 b c £16435
79	1	THIR	12f Soft		924*
78	3	PONT	12f Gd/Sft	80	1106
71	7	NOTT	14f Good	78	1411
79	2	RIPO	12f Good	76	2540
77	5	NEWM	12f Gd/Fm	78	3122
84	2	HAYD	12f Gd/Sft	78	3270
86	1	HAYD	14f Good	78	3323*
85	2	HAYD	14f Gd/Fm	84	3783
62	6	AYR	15f Soft	85	3961

SUDDEN SPIN 10 b g £0
0a	13	SOUT	14f Aw	55	37
31a	5	SOUT	14f Aw	48	182
15a	8	SOUT	16f Aw	43	253
19a	6	SOUT	16f Aw	36	737
33	5	MUSS	16f Gd/Fm		1145

SUDEST 6 b g £712
55a	9	SOUT	12f Aw	85	200	
0	13	NOTT	14f Good	65	1411	
62	3	BEVE	16f Gd/Fm	60	2516	BL

SUDRA 3 b c £0
82	10	HAYD	6f Gd/Sft	96	1534
60	8	YARM	6f Gd/Fm		2197
73	9	HAYD	6f Gd/Fm	88	3325
69	9	WIND	8f Good	83	3642

SUE ME 8 b g £2758
21a	10	SOUT	5f Aw		71	bl
39a	6	SOUT	6f Aw		199	
11a	10	SOUT	6f Aw	46	250	bl
53	7	MUSS	5f Gd/Fm	60	1143	bl

56	1	**MUSS**	5f Gd/Fm		1430*	bl
34	7	CATT	6f Good		1663	bl
58	6	AYR	5f Soft	56	3960	

SUEZ TORNADO 7 ch g £0
| 54 | 8 | WIND | 10f Gd/Fm | | 747 |
| 28 | 8 | KEMP | 12f Gd/Fm | 58 | 2081 |

SUGAR CUBE TREAT 4 b f £622
38	12	THIR	6f Soft	58	910
48	7	THIR	6f Gd/Sft	57	1356
45	12	AYR	7f Gd/Fm	55	1631
54	3	HAYD	5f Gd/Sft	55	1792
45	5	PONT	6f Good	53	1869
0	16	HAYD	6f Gd/Fm	54	2444
43	9	HAYD	5f Gd/Fm	52	2701
35	12	PONT	5f Gd/Fm	50	3222
17	15	AYR	6f Heavy	47	4327

SUGAR ROLO 2 b f £551
35	6	YARM	7f Firm		2898
49	5	NEWM	6f Good		3296
53	4	FOLK	5f Gd/Fm		3582
29	11	LEIC	8f Firm	55	3837
49a	3	SOUT	7f Aw		4154
36	11	NEWM	7f Good		4336
46	4	NEWM	8f Soft		4542

SUGARFOOT 6 ch g £71391
115	1	DONC	7f Gd/Sft		1049*
114	5	NEWB	8f Gd/Fm		1402
109	5	ASCO	8f Good		2064
115	1	**ASCO**	8f Good		2675+
101	13	ASCO	7f Gd/Fm	117	2997
110	7	DEAU	8f Soft		3544
116	5	LONG	8f Soft		3847
115	3	LONG	8f Good		4259
117	3	LONG	7f Soft		4395

SUGGEST 5 b g £0
| 15 | 7 | PONT | 17f Soft | 38 | 4231 |

SUHAIL 4 b c £0
| 0 | 18 | LING | 8f Soft | | 4273 |

SULTAN GAMAL 2 b c £2975
| 84 | 1 | **HAYD** | 5f Heavy | | 989* |

SULU 4 b g £4862
49	14	DONC	6f Good	75	716
59	7	RIPO	6f Soft	70	824
0	16	WARW	5f Heavy	67	1005
70	1	**THIR**	5f Good	63	1162*
51	13	PONT	5f Good	70	4087
47	12	REDC	5f Gd/Sft		4220
39	9	YORK	7f Heavy	66	4302
0	19	NEWC	6f Heavy	64	4405

SUMITAS 4 br c £107575
112	D	CAPA	10f Good		1321
117	2	ASCO	10f Good		2089
117	2	MUNI	10f Soft		3071
112	5	LEOP	10f Good		3925
116	2	SAN	8f Soft		4319

SUMITRA 4 b f £0
37	12	WARW	11f Good	51	2463
41	5	BATH	12f Firm		2785
29	7	FOLK	15f Gd/Fm	43	3040

SUMMER BOUNTY 4 b c £657
30a	11	WOLV	9f Aw	70	469
51a	6	WOLV	9f Aw	65	516
0a	11	WOLV	9f Aw	60	611
36a	7	WOLV	9f Aw	55	681
49a	2	WOLV	12f Aw	49	723
22a	10	LING	13f Aw	50	835
0	20	DONC	10f Gd/Sft	65	1050	t
52	12	CHES	9f Aw	65	1251

SUMMER CHERRY 3 b c £798
68	4	NEWB	10f Gd/Sft		1593
59	4	NOTT	10f Good	63	2011
42	6	BRIG	12f Gd/Sft	61	2425

63	3	KEMP	7f Gd/Fm	60	3362	t
53	6	EPSO	9f Good	60	3856	t
49	8	YARM	8f Gd/Fm	60	3971	t
0	24	NEWM	8f Gd/Sft	58	4536	

SUMMER DREAMS 3 b f £1960
81	2	SAND	10f Good		3432
74	3	GOOD	10f Good		3907
68	5	BATH	12f Soft		4434

SUMMER JAZZ 3 b f £892
| 61 | 5 | LING | 8f Soft | | 4273 |
| 65a | 2 | WOLV | 8f Aw | | 4551 |

SUMMER KEY 2 b f £0
0	16	WARW	7f Gd/Fm		3910
0	17	NEWM	8f Gd/Fm		4209
0	14	LING	7f Soft		4484

SUMMER SHADES 2 b f £760
67	3	LING	5f Firm		2324
46	6	WIND	6f Good		2714
69	4	LING	6f Firm		3492

SUMMER SONG 3 b f £32227
61	4	NEWC	8f Heavy		1010
71	5	NOTT	8f Gd/Fm		1268
73	3	HAYD	7f Gd/Sft		1537
73	1	**WIND**	10f Gd/Fm	68	2206*
76	1	**FOLK**	10f Good	70	2625*
77	1	**REDC**	9f Gd/Fm		2865*
80	3	NEWM	10f Good	76	3024
84	1	**RIPO**	10f Gd/Fm	76	3465*
87	1	**BEVE**	10f Gd/Fm	82	3676*
90	1	**THIR**	12f Gd/Sft	86	3778*
79	7	ASCO	12f Gd/Sft	90	4128
75	9	NEWM	10f Good		4337

SUMMER STOCK 2 b c £840
| 77 | 3 | GALW | 7f Good | | 3072 | BL |

SUMMER SYMPHONY 2 gr f £58364
97	1	**NEWM**	7f Good		3020*
103	2	GOOD	9f Good		3659
108	2	ASCO	8f Good		4110

SUMMER VIEW 3 b c £18363
90	1	**KEMP**	8f Firm		2871*
100	1	**SALI**	8f Gd/Fm		3421*
112	3	DONC	8f Good		3893
113	2	NEWM	9f Good		4347

SUMMERHILL PARKES 2 b f £552
| 67 | 3 | THIR | 6f Good | | 2968 |

SUMMONER 3 b c £21202
112	1	**DONC**	8f Good		735*
106	9	NEWM	8f Good		1171
101	4	SAND	8f Good		2476
115	1	**DONC**	8f Good		2757+
115	2	GOOD	8f Firm		3150

SUMTHINELSE 3 ch c £6882
62	5	DONC	6f Good		731
75	4	LING	6f Gd/Sft		837
57	12	NEWM	6f Gd/Sft	76	982	VIS
78	2	PONT	6f Firm		2177
75	1	**CHES**	7f Gd/Fm	73	2250*
75	4	NEWM	7f Gd/Sft	77	2855
72	6	NEWM	7f Firm	77	3163
71	10	NEWM	7f Gd/Fm	76	3629
73a	3	WOLV	7f Aw	74	3771
56	10	CHES	8f Soft		4069
49a	12	WOLV	6f Aw	73	4380

SUN BIRD 2 ch c £0
44a	5	SOUT	5f Aw		2818
45	12	WIND	6f Gd/Fm		3047
65	5	NEWC	6f Good		3245
33	8	PONT	6f Gd/Fm	62	4235	BL
7		WIND	10f Gd/Sft	62	4290
59	5	PONT	8f Soft	60	4378	bl

SUN CHARM 3 b c £2290
| 96 | 3 | KEMP | 8f Soft | | 1530 |

| 80 | 8 | SAND | 10f Gd/Fm | | 2497 | VIS |

SUN SILK 3 b f £0
52	8	SALI	7f Gd/Fm		2232
66	5	NOTT	10f Gd/Fm		3006
44	7	NEWC	8f Soft		3707
38a	5	LING	13f AW		4193

SUNDAY RAIN 3 b c £2591
71	4	DONC	10f Gd/Fm	68	701
71	2	CATT	12f Gd/Fm	68	782
70	2	THIR	12f Soft		924	bl
53	4	DONC	15f Gd/Sft	70	1071
69	5	NOTT	14f Gd/Fm	70	1270

SUNDERLAND 3 b c £3548
| 110 | 3 | MUNI | 7f Soft | | 4317 |

SUNDOWN 2 b f £449
| 40 | 15 | SALI | 7f Gd/Fm | | 3292 |
| 78 | 3 | WIND | 6f Gd/Sft | | 4288 |

SUNGIO 2 b c £1085
66	13	LING	7f Soft		4268
72	6	BRIG	8f Soft		4418
72	2	MUSS	8f Soft		4564

SUNLEY SCENT 2 ch f £0
| 58 | 8 | WIND | 6f Gd/Fm | | 4289 |
| 58 | 8 | NEWB | 6f Sft/Hvy | | 4470 |

SUNLEY SENSE 4 b c £17626
73	13	KEMP	6f Good	89	728
81	8	THIR	5f Soft	86	926
88	2	CHES	5f Firm	83	1245
88	4	YORK	5f Firm	83	1324
66	18	ASCO	6f Good	86	2151
77	10	DONC	5f Gd/Fm	85	2348
85	2	ASCO	5f Good	83	2676
72	14	ASCO	5f Good	83	3016
77	9	HAYD	5f Gd/Fm	84	3322
80	6	SAND	5f Good	86	3473
78	6	EPSO	5f Good	82	3687
80	4	HAYD	5f Gd/Sft	82	3788
75	9	YARM	5f Firm	79	3920
64	5	PONT	5f Soft	78	4377	VIS

SUNLEYS PICC 3 b f £0
0a	11	SOUT	6f Aw		685
61	6	KEMP	6f Good		729
19	7	THIR	7f Soft		929
55	5	LING	7f Good	60	2592
45	8	WIND	6f Gd/Fm	58	3046
0	13	BRIG	8f Soft	54	3561

SUNNY GLENN 2 ch c £3461
70	11	HAYD	7f Soft		3786
66	5	CHES	8f Soft		4072
81	1	**LING**	8f Good		4189*

SUNNY STROKA 2 b f £0
36	10	CHEP	5f Gd/Fm		3252
0	15	BATH	6f Soft		4138
0	16	BATH	6f Soft		4431

SUNRIDGE ROSE 2 b f £420
47	3	HAMI	5f Gd/Fm		1937
48a	6	WOLV	5f Aw		4227
41a	10	WOLV	6f Aw		4359

SUNRISE 3 b f £0
0	19	DONC	7f Good	61	736
0	11	LING	7f Gd/Sft	57	841
0a	9	WOLV	9f Aw		922

SUNRISE GIRL 3 ch f £0
0	9	LEIC	6f Gd/Sft		830
26a	6	WOLV	5f Aw		919
0a	10	WOLV	5f Aw		1392
0	13	BATH	5f Gd/Sft		1670
0	20	WARW	5f Gd/Fm	42	2252

SUNSET GLOW 3 gr c £528
| 55 | 3 | RIPO | 12f Gd/Fm | | 2103 |

SUNSET HARBOUR 7 br m £5039
| 42 | 2 | HAMI | 5f Firm | 39 | 1244 |

40	4	NOTT	5f Good	42	1412	
50	1	**BRIG**	5f Gd/Fm	42	1932*	
41	6	LING	5f Gd/Fm	47	2184	
48	3	WARW	5f Gd/Fm	47	2252	
41	6	BRIG	5f Soft	47	2428	
33	14	BATH	5f Gd/Sft	48	2555	
38	5	FOLK	5f Good	48	2623	
44	6	DONC	5f Gd/Fm	47	2753	
39	8	CHEP	5f Gd/Fm	46	2904	
41	6	RIPO	5f Gd/Fm	44	3180	
0	14	LING	6f Firm	43	3578	
0	19	CHEP	5f Good	42	3872	
40	10	LEIC	5f Gd/Sft	47	4027	
39	8	WIND	6f Gd/Sft	45	4293	
0	24	NEWB	5f Gd/Sft	43	4459	

SUNSET LADY 4 br f £434
29	11	THIR	8f Soft	60	931
44	9	NOTT	10f Gd/Sft	57	1086
48	3	CARL	12f Firm		1253
25	9	PONT	10f Good	49	1496

SUNSET SHORE 2 b f £0
0	P	REDC	6f Gd/Fm	2990

SUNSETTER 2 ch f £0
95	9	NEWM	6f Good	4159

SUNSHINE NSHOWERS 2 b f £557
80	3	NOTT	5f Gd/Fm	2683
74	5	HAYD	6f Gd/Fm	3320

SUNSTONE 2 b f £0
69	17	DONC	8f Gd/Sft	4445

SUPER DOMINION 3 ch c £1581
54	4	THIR	7f Gd/Fm		2058
66	3	HAYD	7f Gd/Fm		2443
59	3	CARL	7f Firm		2824
45	6	BRIG	7f Gd/Fm	57	3242
0	18	KEMP	12f Soft		4040
40	10	LING	7f Soft	54	4192
53a	5	SOUT	6f Aw		4364

SUPER GOLDLUCK 4 b c £49259
109	2	KRAN	10f Good	1230

SUPER KIM 3 b f £0
24	9	NOTT	10f Soft	52	1644
29	10	YARM	10f Gd/Fm	48	1955
42	6	NEWM	8f Firm		2345

SUPER LOVER 4 ch c £9677
116	2	BADE	6f Gd/Sft	1746

SUPER MONARCH 6 ch g £708
0	13	BRIG	8f Gd/Fm	65	1129	BL
53	9	LING	7f Soft	65	1542	
59a	4	LING	8f Aw	62	1915	
56	7	GOOD	9f Good	63	2304	
22	13	GOOD	8f Gd/Fm	63	2356	
45a	7	LING	7f Aw		2759	
16	11	WIND	8f Good	58	3355	
48	2	BRIG	8f Firm		3738	bl
45	11	CHEP	7f Good	53	3871	bl

SUPER SAINT 6 b g £0
22a	8	LING	8f Aw	92	t

SUPER STORY 3 b f £0
36	9	GOOD	10f Soft	4081
7	11	WIND	10f Heavy	4528

SUPER TASSA 4 ch f £29361
109	1	**SAIN**	11f Good	1378*
99	3	SAN	12f Gd/Fm	2073

SUPER VALUE 2 ch f £0
54	13	SALI	7f Gd/Fm	3292
58	8	LING	7f Firm	3829

SUPERAPPAROS 6 b g £0
37a	6	SOUT	6f Aw	32

SUPERBIT 8 b g £2052
31	14	BATH	5f Good	60	1092
55	6	NOTT	6f Gd/Fm		1368

54	1	**NOTT**	6f Gd/Fm		2680*
48a	8	WOLV	6f Aw		3275
40	10	PONT	5f Soft	57	4087

SUPERCHIEF 5 b g £8533
26a	10	WOLV	8f Aw		39	t
67a	3	LING	10f Aw		56	t
11a	9	LING	12f Aw	38	115	t
40a	3	LING	10f Aw	40	209	tBL
40a	4	LING	10f Aw	40	220	tvi
55a	4	LING	8f Aw		264	tvi
69a	2	LING	7f Aw		421	tbl
50a	1	**LING**	7f Aw	39	439*	tbl
52a	1	**LING**	7f Aw	44	504*	tbl
58a	1	**LING**	8f Aw	51	596*	tbl
53a	5	LING	8f Aw	58	776	tbl
29a	11	LING	8f Aw	58	1915	tbl
16	10	LING	6f Firm	45	2761	tbl
39	8	BATH	8f Firm	42	2942	tbl
34a	8	LING	8f Aw		3756	tvi
58a	2	LING	8f Aw		4272	tbl
58a	3	LING	7f Aw		4331	tbl
51a	5	LING	7f Aw		4487	tbl

SUPERFRILLS 7 b m £1676
23a	9	WOLV	6f Aw	41	923
37a	2	SOUT	6f Aw	37	1421
0	15	NEWC	6f Gd/Sft	40	1479
29a	8	SOUT	5f Aw	39	1806
37a	7	SOUT	8f Aw		2118
35a	4	SOUT	6f Aw	38	2385
0a	13	SOUT	6f Aw	37	2820
0	20	THIR	6f Gd/Fm	38	3144
32	5	HAMI	5f Gd/Sft	34	3536
0	21	REDC	6f Gd/Sft		4220
39	2	NEWC	6f Heavy	34	4425

SUPERIOR PREMIUM 6 br g £78148
95	8	NEWB	5f Soft	110	914	
96	9	NEWM	6f Good		952	
99	10	NEWM	5f Gd/Fm		1172	BL
111	1	**GOOD**	6f Gd/Sft		1453*	
82	6	SAND	5f Soft		1566	
121	1	**ASCO**	6f Good		2115*	

SUPERLAO 8 b m £0
30a	6	LING	6f Aw	33	154	
20a	7	LING	6f Aw	33	262	
29a	5	LING	6f Aw		354	
21a	8	LING	6f Aw		484	bl

SUPERSONIC 4 b f £1241
54a	4	WOLV	12f Aw		679	
45	6	SOUT	10f Soft	71	1608	
59	9	NEWB	10f Gd/Fm	71	1785	
65	4	WIND	10f Gd/Fm	66	2888	
0	11	YARM	10f Good	66	3031	
65	3	SALI	10f Gd/Fm	65	3390	t
0	18	KEMP	10f Gd/Fm	64	3794	
60a	3	LING	10f Aw		4100	t
36a	8	LING	12f Aw	59	4334	t
0	19	BATH	10f Soft	62	4436	t

SUPERSTAR LEO 2 b f £192713
86	2	WIND	5f Gd/Sft	1424
88	1	**CATT**	5f Good	1659*
100	1	**CATT**	5f Gd/Sft	1813*
107	1	**ASCO**	5f Good	2113*
109	1	**NEWB**	5f Firm	2849*
106	2	LEOP	5f Good	3372
112	1	**DONC**	5f Firm	3900*
117	2	LONG	5f Good	4261

SUPLIZI 9 b h £0
73	4	HAYD	12f Gd/Sft		1788
0	13	YORK	9f Firm	74	2001
0	17	NEWC	16f Firm	82	2336
54	10	SAND	11f Good	65	2530
58	6	KEMP	10f Gd/Fm	60	2750

0	11	KEMP	12f Firm	60	2872	
53	6	WIND	12f Gd/Fm	58	3049	
50	8	KEMP	12f Gd/Fm	58	3073	VIS
3	13	GOOD	12f Good	52	3657	
11	10	NOTT	16f Heavy	42	4508	

SUPPLY AND DEMAND 6 b g £35070
79	7	EPSO	10f Heavy	83	1031	
90	2	NEWM	10f Gd/Fm	86	1170	bl
93	2	KEMP	10f Soft	89	1528	bl
101	1	**EPSO**	10f Gd/Fm	90	1845*	bl

SUPREME ANGEL 5 b m £10649
59a	3	WOLV	5f Aw	59	614	bl
65a	1	**SOUT**	5f Aw	59	674*	bl
57	7	WIND	6f Gd/Fm	62	746	bl
58	4	FOLK	5f Soft		960	bl
48a	10	WOLV	5f Aw	65	1140	bl
68	1	**LING**	5f Gd/Sft	59	1264+	
68	3	LING	5f Good	66	1398	
64	5	NEWB	5f Gd/Sft	67	1591	
62	11	RIPO	5f Good	67	1861	
48	11	WIND	6f Good	66	2371	
61	7	SAND	5f Gd/Fm	66	2473	
0	15	SALI	6f Gd/Sft	77	4165	
62	7	WIND	5f Heavy	63	4527	

SUPREME MAIMOON 6 b h £274
50a	3	SOUT	12f Aw	49	68
0a	11	SOUT	11f Aw	49	126

SUPREME SALUTATION 4 ch g £6813
69	6	NEWC	11f Heavy	79	1011
60	12	THIR	8f Good	79	1160
75	6	CATT	7f Soft	77	1680
73	2	CARL	8f Firm		2018
49	7	BEVE	8f Gd/Fm	75	2481
68	6	YORK	7f Good	73	2694
69	7	AYR	7f Firm	72	2878
74	3	NEWC	7f Gd/Fm	72	2986
71	5	THIR	8f Gd/Fm	73	3147
67	5	REDC	7f Firm	73	3328
73	3	NEWC	7f Soft	72	3708
74	4	DONC	7f Gd/Fm	72	3880
77	2	AYR	7f Soft	72	3992
73	7	NEWM	7f Gd/Fm	72	4215

SUPREME SILENCE 3 b c £2320
0	11	NOTT	8f Gd/Fm		2188
59	9	SAND	10f Good		2531
41	7	KEMP	8f Firm		2871
40	8	LEIC	10f Gd/Fm	59	3217
52	7	FOLK	12f Gd/Fm	54	3586
41	9	NOTT	16f Soft	51	3978
56a	1	**LING**	16f Aw	47	4329*

SUPREME TRAVEL 2 b c £0
56	13	LING	5f Gd/Fm	2214
44	12	WARW	7f Good	2459
30	9	BRIG	8f Gd/Sft	4116

SUPREMELY DEVIOUS 3 ch f £1308
50a	6	LING	6f Aw		24	vis
49a	2	LING	7f Aw		155	vis
33a	6	WOLV	6f Aw		228	vis
47a	3	LING	7f Aw	48	287	vis
42a	3	WOLV	7f Aw	47	346	vis

SURE DANCER 5 b g £2409
104	6	ASCO	8f Good		2675	
104	2	SAND	9f Good		3230	
88	9	DONC	8f Firm	103	3897	BL

SURE FUTURE 4 b g £0
0	18	LING	16f Good	54	1394	bl
36	7	NOTT	10f Gd/Fm	49	3111	bl
40	5	LING	11f Aw	49	3282	bl
44	5	FOLK	12f Gd/Fm	48	3586	bl
41	8	EPSO	12f Good	44	3858	bl

SURE MARK 2 b c £9025
102	2	CURR	6f Good	2408

SURE QUEST 5 b m £20684

49a	2	WOLV	9f Aw	49	359	
48a	3	SOUT	11f Aw	49	474	
46a	4	WOLV	9f Aw	49	568	
50a	1	**WOLV**	12f Aw		710*	
52	1	**WIND**	12f Good	49	853*	
63	1	**BATH**	12f Good	52	1091*	
59	2	CHEP	12f Heavy	59	1555	
63	2	NEWB	10f Gd/Fm	59	1785	
61	3	WIND	12f Good	61	2370	
61	4	LEIC	12f Gd/Fm	61	2509	
59a	2	WOLV	12f Aw	58	4226	
58a	3	WOLV	12f Aw	58	4360	

SURE TO DREAM 7 b m £0

19a	8	SOUT	7f Aw	52	75	
42a	9	LING	6f Aw	50	154	bl
42a	4	LING	8f Aw		316	bl
0a	P	SOUT	7f Aw		501	bl

SURPRISE ENCOUNTER 4 ch c £5907

0	16	KEMP	8f Soft	83	1015
63	9	DONC	7f Good	82	1514
78	5	KEMP	8f Gd/Fm	78	1926
78	4	NEWM	7f Firm	78	2133
81	2	NEWB	7f Firm	78	2814
90	1	**LING**	7f Firm	79	3758+

SURPRISED 5 b g £30303

59	10	THIR	5f Gd/Sft	70	1357	
44	11	PONT	6f Good	69	1869	
69	1	**HAMI**	6f Gd/Fm		1905*	
64	5	HAMI	6f Gd/Fm	69	2796	
66	4	LEIC	5f Gd/Fm	69	3214	
71	6	BEVE	5f Good	69	3398	VIS
78	1	**GOOD**	6f Good	70	3646*	vis
78	3	GOOD	6f Good	76	3904	vis
80	4	AYR	5f Gd/Fm	77	4010	vis

SURVEYOR 5 ch g £0

52	16	EPSO	6f Good	88	1851
0	18	NEWM	7f Good	82	2133
67	8	DONC	6f Good		2580
58	7	YARM	5f Firm	70	2899
57	8	YARM	6f Heavy	68	4480

SUSANS DOWRY 4 b f £441

0	14	WIND	8f Good	62	2367
0	15	SALI	8f Gd/Sft	62	2467
0	12	HAYD	11f Gd/Sft	54	3480
42	4	HAMI	12f Gd/Sft	46	3827
0	15	YORK	10f Soft		4275
39	3	NEWC	10f Heavy	40	4404

SUSANS PRIDE 4 b g £6725

75	4	WIND	6f Gd/Fm	75	746
80	1	**CATT**	7f Gd/Fm	75	780+
59	9	LEIC	7f Gd/Sft	81	834
68	7	NEWC	7f Heavy	80	1011
76	3	WARW	7f Soft		1060
0	15	SALI	7f Good	78	1348
76	3	NEWB	7f Gd/Sft	77	1590
76	4	CHEP	7f Good	77	1969
71	7	LEIC	7f Gd/Fm	76	2775
67	5	NEWB	7f Firm	76	2814
76	4	EPSO	7f Gd/Fm	75	3414
71	5	GOOD	7f Good		3662
52	13	NEWB	7f Firm	75	3981

SUSIE THE FLOOSIE 2 b f £0

0	17	LING	6f Good		2588
53	7	THIR	7f Gd/Sft		3776
41	8	BRIG	8f Gd/Sft		4117
16a	10	WOLV	8f Aw		4362
27a	8	WOLV	8f Aw	44	4552

SUSIES FLYER 3 br f £0

82	5	HAYD	5f Heavy		988
65	9	NOTT	6f Good		1410
64	13	CHEP	5f Gd/Sft	84	1795

58	6	PONT	6f Firm		2177

SUSSEX LAD 3 b c £3029

65	7	NEWM	6f Good		956
77	4	SALI	6f Firm		1175
69	9	WIND	5f Gd/Sft	80	1427
72	6	GOOD	6f Gd/Fm	77	1961
73	4	FOLK	5f Gd/Fm		2294
69	6	LING	6f Gd/Fm	72	3280
77	1	**SALI**	6f Gd/Fm	72	3419+
75	6	WIND	5f Heavy	76	4527
66	12	DONC	7f Heavy	75	4574

SUSU 7 ch m £0

108	6	GULF	5f Good		16

SUSY WELLS 5 b m £0

25	11	REDC	7f Gd/Sft		1559
26	9	THIR	8f Gd/Sft	38	1718
23	5	CATT	14f Gd/Sft		1814
28	5	DONC	8f Gd/Fm	32	2315
0	13	RIPO	6f Gd/Fm	32	2839
0	11	BEVE	7f Good	35	2882

SUTTON COMMON 3 b c £5644

79	2	SOUT	7f Aw		804
0	23	NEWM	8f Gd/Fm	77	1183
77	2	BEVE	7f Good		1444
74	1	**BEVE**	7f Gd/Sft		1763*
49	19	RIPO	6f Gd/Fm	75	3464
30	12	NEWC	7f Soft	73	3708
50a	9	WOLV	7f Aw	73	3771

SWAGGER 4 ch g £9283

52a	1	**SOUT**	11f Aw	42	324*
60a	1	**SOUT**	12f Aw	49	370*
63a	1	**SOUT**	12f Aw	57	413*
63a	4	WOLV	16f Aw	63	552
61	1	**HAMI**	13f Gd/Fm	58	1363*

SWALDO 3 ch c £0

11a	7	SOUT	8f Aw		1204
40	8	LING	9f Firm		2322
35	8	LEIC	8f Gd/Fm		2914
26	8	WIND	12f Good		3351

SWALLOW FLIGHT 4 b c £81810

107	2	DONC	8f Gd/Fm		703
114	1	**WIND**	8f Gd/Fm		1291+
113	1	**SAND**	8f Soft	108	1567*
120	3	ASCO	8f Good		2064
119	1	**GOOD**	8f Gd/Fm		2359*
108	3	GOOD	7f Gd/Fm		3132
116	4	DONC	8f Gd/Fm		3875
107	5	NEWM	8f Good		4180

SWALLOW JAZ 3 b g £0

0	19	LEIC	8f Gd/Fm	54	3095

SWALLOW MAGIC 2 b c £0

0	16	NOTT	5f Gd/Sft		4503

SWAMPY 4 b c £0

39a	7	WOLV	9f Aw		189
34a	5	SOUT	9f Aw	45	297
36a	4	SOUT	8f Aw	45	340
0a	11	SOUT	7f Aw	42	471

SWAN HUNTER 7 b h £1093

55a	2	WOLV	15f Aw		174
32a	5	WOLV	12f Aw		231
51a	2	WOLV	15f Aw		363
17a	7	LING	16f Aw		402 BL

SWAN KNIGHT 4 b g £11498

95	2	YORK	8f Gd/Fm	90	2648
89	6	GOOD	7f Firm		3155
71	9	NEWM	10f Gd/Fm	94	3628
99	1	**BATH**	8f Soft		4142*
77	8	YORK	7f Soft	95	4278
96	3	NEWB	9f Sft/Hvy	95	4472
0	26	NEWM	8f Soft	95	4545

SWAN LAKE FR 4 b f £0

5a	10	LING	10f Aw		3

19a	9	LING	10f Aw		4100

SWAN PRINCE 3 b c £0

0	15	CHEP	8f Gd/Fm		2448

SWANDALE FLYER 8 ch g £2903

35	9	AYR	13f Gd/Fm		1657
0	10	RIPO	12f Gd/Fm	28	2109
19	5	CARL	14f Firm	31	2827
5	7	NEWC	12f Good	25	3036
17	2	BEVE	16f Gd/Fm	15	3406
23	1	**CARL**	17f Gd/Fm	20	3575*
15	7	MUSS	16f Gd/Fm	26	3742

SWANTON ABBOT 2 b c £0

68	8	LING	5f Firm		3277
49	9	HAYD	6f Gd/Sft		3478
70	5	LING	8f Firm		3577
48	15	DONC	8f Gd/Fm	74	3879

SWEET ANGELINE 3 b f £5587

52	9	BATH	10f Good	69	1094
53	7	SALI	8f Good	66	1345
58	5	YARM	10f Gd/Fm	63	1955
61	4	WIND	10f Gd/Fm	61	2206
61	3	YARM	11f Firm	60	2771
65	1	**THIR**	12f Gd/Fm	60	3125*
68	2	SALI	12f Gd/Fm	65	3392
68	3	REDC	11f Gd/Fm	38	3636
0	20	BATH	10f Soft	68	4436

SWEET AS A NUT 4 ch f £0

0a	1	SOUT	6f Aw	65	425
0a	13	SOUT	6f Aw	65	499
36	9	EPSO	6f Gd/Sft	55	2631
45	8	BRIG	7f Gd/Fm	55	2729

SWEET CICELY 3 b f £475

68	3	LING	10f Soft		1287
66	5	NEWB	10f Gd/Fm	68	1785
57	8	NEWB	10f Gd/Fm	66	3178
53	8	SALI	12f Gd/Fm	63	3392

SWEET DILEMMA 2 b f £38000

98	2	CURR	6f Yldg		3720

SWEET ENVIRONMENT 3 gr f £0

43	10	NOTT	8f Gd/Fm		2188

SWEET HAVEN 3 b f £720

0	14	WIND	8f Gd/Fm	60	744	
33	8	BEVE	7f Heavy	56	976	
0	12	NOTT	8f Gd/Sft	52	1085	
0	17	NOTT	8f Gd/Fm	47	2187	VIS
45	2	LEIC	8f Gd/Fm		3094	vis
25	8	YARM	8f Good	40	3236	vis
41a	10	WOLV	7f Aw		4224	vis
28	7	LEIC	8f Sft/Hvy	43	4310	vis

SWEET MAGIC 9 ch g £2199

40a	6	WOLV	5f Aw	60	146	t
35a	9	WOLV	5f Aw	57	291	t
36a	6	LING	5f Aw		440	t
52a	4	WOLV	5f Aw	53	445	t
40a	9	WOLV	5f Aw	51	518	t
45a	9	WOLV	5f Aw		533	tVI
58	4	NEWC	5f Soft	60	758	t
0	20	THIR	5f Good	59	1162	t
49a	4	WOLV	5f Aw		1237	t
54a	1	**WOLV**	5f Aw		1392*	t
54	4	MUSS	5f Gd/Fm		1430	t
27	7	NEWC	5f Heavy		1766	t
36a	7	WOLV	5f Aw	51	2078	t
36	7	HAMI	5f Gd/Fm	52	2233	t
38	7	WIND	5f Good	49	2716	t
33	13	RIPO	5f Gd/Fm	46	3180	t
19a	11	WOLV	5f Aw	50	3271	t
40	8	CATT	5f Good		3441	t

SWEET PATOOPIE 6 b m £0

13a	9	SOUT	16f Aw	70	51
0	14	NOTT	10f Heavy		4413

SWEET PROSPECT 2 b f £3874

SWEET (continued)

Pos	Fd	Course	Dist/Going	Rtg	Race	Notes
66	9	NEWM	6f Gd/Fm		1691	
82	1	**KEMP**	6f Gd/Fm		2748*	
85	4	HAYD	6f Gd/Fm		3320	
88	5	DONC	6f Gd/Fm		3862	
90	5	NEWM	7f Gd/Fm		4210	

SWEET REWARD 5 ch g £8859

Pos	Fd	Course	Dist/Going	Rtg	Race	Notes
63	1	NEWM	10f Gd/Fm	68	1150	
70	4	WIND	10f Good	68	1729	
41	7	GOOD	12f Gd/Fm	68	2127	
68	3	SAND	10f Gd/Fm	67	2527	
67	5	NEWM	10f Gd/Fm	67	3166	
66	3	SAND	10f Good	66	3471	
62	3	NOTT	10f Soft		3979	
68	1	KEMP	8f Soft	64	4038*	

SWEET ROSIE 5 b m £0

Pos	Fd	Course	Dist/Going	Rtg	Race	Notes
0a	10	LING	8f Aw	42	152	

SWEET SORROW 5 b m £4620

Pos	Fd	Course	Dist/Going	Rtg	Race	Notes
105	2	KEMP	10f Soft		1014	
83	6	YORK	10f Firm		1325	

SWEET TEDDY 3 b f £0

Pos	Fd	Course	Dist/Going	Rtg	Race	Notes
8a	10	WOLV	8f Aw		1234	
0	14	RIPO	8f Good		1596	
43	10	BATH	8f Firm	60	2331	t
23	10	THIR	8f Gd/Sft		3775	

SWEET VELETA 2 b f £262

Pos	Fd	Course	Dist/Going	Rtg	Race	Notes
50a	3	SOUT	6f Aw		1420	
46a	4	SOUT	6f Aw		1805	
45a	4	SOUT	7f Aw		2949	
0a	13	SOUT	7f Aw		4154	
35a	8	WOLV	8f Aw		4362	

SWEMBY 3 ch f £0

Pos	Fd	Course	Dist/Going	Rtg	Race	Notes
43	7	BATH	10f Gd/Sft		1668	
53	7	HAYD	11f Gd/Sft		3265	
0	11	BATH	12f Gd/Fm		3818	

SWIFT 6 ch g £0

Pos	Fd	Course	Dist/Going	Rtg	Race	Notes
0a	10	SOUT	14f Aw	79	37	
31a	9	SOUT	11f Aw	75	605	
48a	7	SOUT	12f Aw	69	671	
61a	6	SOUT	12f Aw	69	695	
0	15	NOTT	10f Soft		3979	
0	13	YORK	14f Heavy	58	4299	

SWIFT DISPERSAL 3 gr f £9986

Pos	Fd	Course	Dist/Going	Rtg	Race	Notes
30a	10	WOLV	7f Aw		362	
0a	12	SOUT	8f Aw		685	
75	1	**PONT**	6f Soft		877*	
55	8	KEMP	9f Gd/Sft	75	1075	
82	2	NEWB	7f Gd/Fm	74	1405	
82	3	GOOD	7f Gd/Sft	81	1470	

SWIFT MAIDEN 7 gr m £0

Pos	Fd	Course	Dist/Going	Rtg	Race	Notes
36a	8	WOLV	9f Aw	55	305	

SWIFTMAR 2 b f £545

Pos	Fd	Course	Dist/Going	Rtg	Race	Notes
65	3	AYR	8f Heavy		4322	
65	6	WIND	8f Heavy		4524	

SWIFTUR 3 b f £0

Pos	Fd	Course	Dist/Going	Rtg	Race	Notes
21a	8	WOLV	8f Aw		658	
0	13	WIND	8f Heavy		934	
0	14	BRIG	7f Gd/Fm	42	1930	BL
35	4	BATH	10f Firm	39	2332	

SWIFTWAY 6 ch g £2853

Pos	Fd	Course	Dist/Going	Rtg	Race	Notes
49	1	**NEWC**	16f Soft	44	760*	
38	5	BEVE	16f Good	48	3395	
0	11	AYR	17f Soft	47	3993	

SWING ALONG 5 ch m £5665

Pos	Fd	Course	Dist/Going	Rtg	Race	Notes
68a	1	**WOLV**	7f Aw	59	121*	
61a	6	LING	7f Aw	66	239	
0a	W	WOLV	8f Aw	66	254	
66a	2	SOUT	11f Aw	65	325	
61a	4	WOLV	9f Aw	65	359	
71a	1	**WOLV**	8f Aw	65	404*	
40a	9	WOLV	8f Aw	70	431	
0a	11	WOLV	12f Aw	70	489	
28a	5	LING	8f Aw		574	

Pos	Fd	Course	Dist/Going	Rtg	Race	Notes
65a	3	SOUT	7f Aw	68	598	
47a	3	SOUT	8f Aw		646	
50a	3	SOUT	11f Aw		672	
60	4	SOUT	10f Gd/Sft	59	859	
56a	8	SOUT	8f Aw	62	1207	
0a	12	SOUT	11f Aw	62	1306	
61	2	WARW	8f Heavy	59	1520	
40	17	NEWM	8f Gd/Fm	61	1690	
25	9	NEWB	10f Gd/Fm	61	1942	

SWING BAND 2 b c £10765

Pos	Fd	Course	Dist/Going	Rtg	Race	Notes
88	1	**NEWB**	7f Firm		2708*	
93	2	ASCO	7f Gd/Fm		3015	
93	4	NEWB	7f Firm		3450	
81	5	SAND	8f Soft		4203	

SWING BAR 7 b m £0

Pos	Fd	Course	Dist/Going	Rtg	Race	Notes
8	12	FOLK	10f Soft	48	965	
0	15	BEVE	10f Firm	46	1921	
26	7	FOLK	10f Good	41	2625	
35	7	YARM	8f Firm	41	2767	
25	7	BRIG	5f Gd/Sft	39	3557	
26	8	CHEP	10f Gd/Fm	39	3683	
30	4	SALI	10f Gd/Sft	35	4168	

SWING CITY 3 ch f £592

Pos	Fd	Course	Dist/Going	Rtg	Race	Notes
43	11	WIND	6f Good	62	852	
48	9	BRIG	6f Firm	59	1211	
53	3	SOUT	6f Soft		1605	
40	9	CATT	5f Gd/Sft	56	1817	
40	14	BEVE	5f Firm	56	2223	
0	15	CATT	7f Soft	53	4004	
38	10	YARM	7f Soft		4388	

SWING JOB 4 b f £590

Pos	Fd	Course	Dist/Going	Rtg	Race	Notes
0	16	LING	7f Firm	49	3279	
57	3	BRIG	7f Firm		3529	

SWINGING THE BLUES 6 b g £3671

Pos	Fd	Course	Dist/Going	Rtg	Race	Notes
36	17	REDC	10f Firm	56	1296	tvi
40	13	NEWM	12f Firm	56	1852	
55	1	**YARM**	10f Gd/Fm	54	2199*	vis
45	8	YARM	11f Firm	56	2771	vis
19	11	NEWM	10f Gd/Fm	56	3314	vis
0	16	NEWC	9f Firm	55	3603	BL
28a	7	WOLV	12f Aw	54	4386	vis
50	3	DONC	8f Heavy	52	4573	vis

SWINGING TRIO 3 b c £2782

Pos	Fd	Course	Dist/Going	Rtg	Race	Notes
0	13	LEIC	8f Good		789	t
63	9	WIND	10f Good		850	
59a	4	WOLV	9f Aw	62	2080	
76a	1	**LING**	10f Aw		2213*	
35	10	WIND	10f Good		2372	

SWINO 6 b g £2596

Pos	Fd	Course	Dist/Going	Rtg	Race	Notes
47a	4	SOUT	6f Aw	56	44	bl
26a	10	WOLV	6f Aw		76	vis
32a	8	SOUT	6f Aw	52	177	vis
56a	2	SOUT	6f Aw	52	212	vis
45a	4	SOUT	6f Aw	53	246	bl
41a	6	SOUT	7f Aw	53	299	bl
44	8	WARW	5f Heavy	56	1005	vis
49	11	WIND	6f Gd/Fm	55	1196	vis
54	4	CARL	9f Aw	55	1257	bl
52	4	WARW	8f Heavy	54	1520	
43	6	PONT	6f Good	53	1869	vis
33	9	CARL	7f Gd/Fm	51	2241	bl
42	7	NEWC	10f Firm	51	2275	vis
45	8	HAYD	6f Gd/Fm	51	2444	
27	10	SALI	6f Good	48	2690	vis
42	8	HAYD	6f Gd/Fm	48	2793	vis
47	2	BATH	6f Firm	46	2944	vis
41	7	CHEP	5f Gd/Fm	46	2976	vis
0	12	THIR	6f Gd/Fm	47	3123	vis
41	8	CHEP	8f Gd/Fm	48	3257	vis
27	12	LING	6f Firm	46	3493	vis
0	16	CHEP	7f Good	44	3873	vis

SWISS ALPS 3 b c £0

Pos	Fd	Course	Dist/Going	Rtg	Race	Notes
0	14	WIND	8f Gd/Sft		1099	
61	10	YARM	8f Good		1771	
33a	9	SOUT	6f Aw		2118	BL
9	10	YARM	8f Gd/Fm		2411	bl
14a	9	WOLV	9f Aw	49	4382	bl

SWOOSH 5 gr g £0

Pos	Fd	Course	Dist/Going	Rtg	Race	Notes
10	10	MUSS	7f Firm		1685	
0	8	NEWC	10f Heavy	50	1769	bl

SWYNFORD DREAM 7 b g £1743

Pos	Fd	Course	Dist/Going	Rtg	Race	Notes
50a	8	SOUT	5f Aw		71	
53	5	MUSS	5f Gd/Sft	60	798	
59	2	MUSS	5f Gd/Fm	58	1143	
48	9	THIR	5f Gd/Sft	59	1357	
58	4	AYR	5f Gd/Fm	59	1629	
59	2	CATT	5f Gd/Fm	58	2418	
53	6	AYR	5f Gd/Fm	58	2721	
48	7	CATT	5f Gd/Fm	58	2743	
46	9	CATT	5f Gd/Fm	56	3203	
40	10	PONT	5f Firm	54	3502	
52	5	THIR	5f Gd/Fm	54	3619	
39	10	EPSO	5f Good	52	3855	

SWYNFORD ELEGANCE 3 ch f £2156

Pos	Fd	Course	Dist/Going	Rtg	Race	Notes
40a	5	LING	6f Aw	49	2	
49a	8	SOUT	5f Aw		179	
30	8	REDC	6f Gd/Sft	44	1578	
47	2	HAYD	7f Gd/Fm	44	1793	
36	7	HAMI	8f Gd/Fm	42	1907	
0	11	REDC	8f Gd/Fm	46	2147	
23	11	THIR	7f Gd/Fm	44	3129	
0	16	HAYD	8f Good	44	3288	
44	2	YARM	8f Gd/Fm	40	3971	
41	4	PONT	8f Soft	51	4232	
0	17	NEWC	8f Heavy	44	4406	
30	12	NEWM	8f Gd/Sft	44	4536	

SWYNFORD PLEASURE 4 b f £10224

Pos	Fd	Course	Dist/Going	Rtg	Race	Notes
31a	8	WOLV	9f Aw	40	67	
41	4	MUSS	10f Aw	40	1149	
37	4	CARL	9f Firm	40	1254	
31	7	REDC	8f Good	39	1892	
44	1	HAMI	9f Gd/Fm	39	1939*	
45	3	HAMI	9f Firm	45	2094	
42	2	PONT	8f Firm	41	2180	
42	5	HAMI	9f Firm	45	2397	
47	3	BEVE	8f Gd/Fm	45	2481	
45	3	PONT	8f Gd/Fm	45	2561	
39	4	HAMI	9f Gd/Fm	45	2799	
51	3	RIPO	9f Gd/Fm	47	3011	
41	9	NEWM	8f Gd/Fm	51	3317	
37	10	LEIC	8f Gd/Fm	53	3334	
51	3	BEVE	7f Gd/Fm	50	3652	
30	10	YORK	10f Gd/Fm	50	3731	
49	4	BEVE	8f Good	50	3951	
41	4	MUSS	9f Soft	48	4520	

SWYNFORD WELCOME 4 b f £3276

Pos	Fd	Course	Dist/Going	Rtg	Race	Notes
29a	11	LING	7f Aw	56	29	
33a	10	SOUT	7f Aw	56	69	
19a	9	LING	8f Aw	50	152	
0a	12	WOLV	9f Aw	45	232	
0	18	NEWC	5f Gd/Sft	54	1479	
0	12	REDC	5f Gd/Sft	54	1580	BL
13	3	PONT	8f Good	49	1869	
0	18	RIPO	8f Gd/Fm	49	2099	bl
0	14	NEWM	8f Gd/Fm	49	2130	
46	1	**HAYD**	7f Gd/Fm	43	2442*	
0	12	CHES	8f Gd/Fm	46	2673	
23	8	NEWM	8f Gd/Fm	46	2804	
0	17	CATT	7f Good	46	3440	
0	19	LEIC	8f Sft/Hvy	44	4310	
0	10	NEWC	7f Heavy	44	4428	

SYCAMORE LODGE 9 ch g £590

Pos	Fd	Course	Dist/Going	Rtg	Race	Notes
37	9	PONT	6f Soft		872	
40	8	HAMI	6f Firm		1239	
0	18	DONC	7f Good	54	1519	

52	3	CATT	6f Good		1664	
48	4	CATT	7f Soft		1681	
41	9	HAMI	6f Gd/Fm	51	1941	
42	6	BEVE	7f Gd/Fm	48	2479	
43	8	CARL	7f Firm	47	2823	
46	3	CATT	7f Gd/Fm	47	2932	
39	10	THIR	6f Gd/Fm	45	3144	
37	9	CATT	7f Gd/Fm	45	3200	

SYLVA LEGEND 4 b c £1015

48a	5	LING	8f Aw		353	
42a	6	LING	10f Aw	68	374	
57a	7	SOUT	11f Aw	63	605	
68	3	NOTT	10f Gd/Sft	68	1364	t
68	3	NEWM	7f Firm	68	2347	tvi
60	9	NEWM	10f Gd/Fm	68	2958	tvi
54	11	NEWM	8f Gd/Fm	68	3118	tvi
55	10	BRIG	8f Firm	66	3527	tvi

SYLVA PARADISE 7 b g £7716

41	8	DONC	6f Good		1517	vis
70	4	NOTT	5f Good	74	1871	vis
66	5	WARW	6f Gd/Fm		2035	
59	9	LING	5f Firm	70	2326	vis
68	3	LEIC	6f Gd/Fm	68	2777	vis
42	11	NEWM	6f Gd/Fm	68	2961	vis
72	1	**BRIG**	5f Firm	68	3528*	vis
51	17	EPSO	5f Good	74	3687	vis
69	7	BRIG	5f Firm	74	3734	vis

SYLVA STORM 2 ch c £348

79	4	KEMP	7f Firm		2867	

SYLVAN GIRL 2 ch f £6509

67	3	YARM	6f Gd/Sft		1612	
67	2	YARM	6f Gd/Fm		1954	
33	5	PONT	6f Good		2363	
69	3	NEWM	6f Gd/Fm	67	3165	
58	8	REDC	6f Firm	68	3327	
66	4	NEWM	6f Gd/Fm	67	3630	
49	14	DONC	7f Gd/Fm	67	3860	
61	13	NEWM	7f Good	71	4157	
73a	5	LING	6f Aw		4332	
72a	2	WOLV	7f Aw		4385	

SYRAH 4 b f £516

37	6	WIND	12f Gd/Fm		1880	
15a	8	SOUT	11f Aw		2119	
29	9	HAYD	12f Gd/Fm		2457	
25	2	CATT	16f Gd/Fm		3199	

SYRINGA 2 b f £0

74	6	WIND	6f Gd/Sft		4288	
62	6	NOTT	5f Gd/Sft		4503	

T GS GIRL 3 gr f £0

0	14	WARW	7f Gd/Sft	60	1710	
44	6	RIPO	5f Gd/Fm		3462	
0	17	PONT	8f Soft	52	4232	

TAABEER 2 b c £2503

77	7	ASCO	7f Gd/Fm		2956	
83	2	NEWM	8f Gd/Fm		3458	
91	2	LEIC	7f Firm		3840	

TABBETINNA BLUE 3 b f £550

35a	7	LING	6f Aw		334	
20a	9	SOUT	6f Aw		685	
36	2	LING	7f Gd/Sft	35	841	
0	16	LING	6f Good		1399	
25a	6	SOUT	8f Aw	37	1804	
19	11	YARM	6f Gd/Fm	36	3966	

TABHEEJ 3 ch f £0

98	6	YORK	6f Firm		1338	
100	14	ASCO	5f Good		2065	
84	9	NEWB	6f Firm		2847	
93	6	NEWM	6f Gd/Fm		3120	
92	5	NEWM	6f Good	96	4198	

TABORITE 6 gr g £0

0a	8	SOUT	12f Aw	27	412	
0a	9	SOUT	16f Aw	22	535	

TACHOMETER 6 b m £630

65	4	EPSO	10f Gd/Sft		2627	
48	8	SAND	8f Gd/Fm		2938	
65	4	WIND	10f Good		3189	

TACTFUL REMARK 4 ch c £2032

85	11	KEMP	8f Soft	103	1015	
102	5	YORK	10f Firm	103	1342	
72	4	HAYD	8f Gd/Sft		1489	
52	23	ASCO	8f Good	100	2090	
93	3	ASCO	10f Gd/Fm		3017	
56	15	YORK	10f Gd/Fm	94	3563	
0	12	GOOD	9f Good	90	3883	
0	20	NEWM	8f Good	87	4348	

TADEO 7 ch g £1520

0	14	NEWC	5f Gd/Fm	102	2310	
97	3	HAYD	6f Gd/Fm		2458	
89	8	ASCO	5f Good	98	2676	
85	11	HAYD	5f Gd/Fm	96	3322	
62	22	RIPO	6f Gd/Fm	93	3464	
68	3	WARW	5f Good		3694	
64	5	SAND	5f Gd/Fm		3947	
70	9	SALI	6f Gd/Sft	78	4165	

TADORNE 3 gr f £4227

93	2	BORD	8f Good		2487	

TADREEJ 3 b c £0

65	7	WIND	8f Heavy	77	933	
31	10	WARW	12f Soft	75	1064	
0	17	BEVE	10f Good	72	1448	

TAFFETA 3 ch f £4152

77	5	GOOD	7f Gd/Sft		1638	
67	7	YARM	7f Gd/Fm		1951	
57	6	FOLK	7f Gd/Fm		2293	
66	4	LEIC	7f Gd/Fm	66	2918	
52	12	LING	7f Firm	65	3279	
69	1	**BRIG**	7f Firm		3529*	

TAFFRAIL 2 b g £0

0	14	LING	7f Soft		4267	
47	13	DONC	7f Gd/Sft		4447	

TAFFS WELL 7 b h £4084

73	4	DONC	8f Good	73	715	
69	7	KEMP	8f Gd/Sft	74	1077	
77	4	CHES	8f Firm	73	1250	
77	2	HAYD	8f Soft	73	1490	
68	6	NEWC	8f Gd/Fm	75	2311	
60	10	YORK	8f Gd/Fm	75	2645	
67	9	ASCO	8f Gd/Fm	73	3018	
58	12	CHES	8f Firm	73	3170	
63	14	YORK	8f Good	71	3810	
45	12	YARM	8f Firm	69	3936	
53	7	YORK	7f Heavy	66	4302	
49	15	REDC	7f Gd/Sft	64	4498	

TAJAR 8 b g £4648

38	6	DONC	10f Gd/Fm	43	705	
26	8	WARW	11f Heavy	43	889	
24	11	PONT	12f Good	40	1499	
25	8	HAYD	11f Soft	34	1819	
35	3	NEWM	12f Firm	34	1852	
38	1	**RIPO**	12f Gd/Fm	34	2109*	
33	7	YARM	10f Firm	41	2387	
38	3	PONT	10f Gd/Fm	37	2556	
24	8	CHEP	12f Gd/Fm	37	2971	
0	16	HAYD	12f Good	36	3284	
58a	2	LING	12f AW		4186	
39a	5	LING	12f Aw	43	4486	

TAJOUN 6 b g £11527

118	3	LONG	16f Gd/Sft		3851	
118	6	LONG	20f Good		4264	
118	3	LONG	16f Heavy		4494	

TAKALI 3 ch c £62800

112	4	CURR	10f Soft		1899	
113	5	CURR	12f Good		2409	
113	1	**CURR**	10f Gd/Fm		3068*	
113	1	**CURR**	10f Good		3556*	

TAKAMAKA BAY 3 ch c £6467

80	2	AYR	10f Gd/Fm		1655	
82	2	RIPO	9f Good		1863	
80	1	**AYR**	10f Heavy		4326*	

TAKAROA 2 b c £10077

72	3	ASCO	7f Good		2677	
86	3	GOOD	7f Firm		3154	
89	1	**THIR**	6f Gd/Fm		3614*	
74	14	DONC	6f Gd/Fm		3862	
88	1	**SALI**	7f Gd/Sft		4167*	
72	5	YORK	7f Soft		4277	
0	14	DONC	7f Soft	87	4460	

TAKE A TURN 5 br g £0

31	6	SAND	10f Soft	53	1570	
40	7	CHEP	10f Good	51	1973	

TAKE ACTION 3 b c £0

58a	5	WOLV	8f Aw		409	
34a	8	WOLV	9f Aw	52	1040	
15a	10	WOLV	12f Aw	52	1142	
0	13	NOTT	10f Soft	45	1644	
28	10	NOTT	14f Good	41	2008	BL

TAKE ANOTHER BOW 2 ch c £1063

85	3	NEWB	7f Gd/Fm		3484	
84	4	GOOD	6f Good		3881	

TAKE FLITE 3 b c £4698

82	2	DONC	7f Gd/Sft		1072	
72	8	GOOD	7f Gd/Sft	81	1470	
0	25	NEWM	6f Gd/Fm	79	1694	
75	3	AYR	7f Good		2140	
77	1	**FOLK**	7f Good		2621*	
74	6	SAND	7f Soft	77	4204	
61	11	NEWM	8f Good	75	4340	
46	7	YARM	8f Heavy	73	4478	

TAKE MANHATTAN 3 b c £11680

36a	7	SOUT	6f Aw		685	
50	9	DONC	6f Good		731	
51	6	WARW	7f Heavy	59	887	
53	6	NOTT	8f Heavy	57	1024	
66	1	**NOTT**	8f Gd/Sft	57	1085*	
75	1	**CARL**	8f Firm	62	1255*	
45	15	YORK	8f Firm	69	1341	
66	8	WIND	8f Good	72	1726	
59	9	NEWC	8f Good	70	2524	
23	10	SALI	8f Good	68	2688	
72	1	**BRIG**	8f Firm	65	2906*	
63	6	WIND	8f Good	70	3355	
60	6	GOOD	9f Good	70	3658	
70	4	KEMP	8f Gd/Fm	70	3793	
12	8	BEVE	8f Sft/Hvy	70	4045	
71	2	WIND	8f Gd/Sft		4292	
50	6	YARM	8f Heavy	69	4478	

TAKE NOTICE 7 b g £0

0	14	HAMI	8f Gd/Fm	31	1907	
11	6	HAMI	5f Gd/Fm	25	2233	
32	6	HAMI	6f Gd/Fm		2640	

TAKE TO TASK 2 b c £3778

80	2	AYR	7f Good		2161	
85	2	NEWC	7f Good		2521	
88	2	DONC	7f Gd/Sft		4447	

TAKER CHANCE 4 b g £862

0a	10	SOUT	7f Aw	48	476	
0a	13	WOLV	9f Aw	42	568	
35	8	THIR	8f Soft	50	907	
34	8	MUSS	7f Gd/Fm	47	1148	
37	7	HAMI	8f Gd/Fm	44	1360	vis
33	7	BEVE	7f Gd/Fm	41	2479	
39	6	MUSS	8f Gd/Sft	41	2533	
51	8	HAYD	7f Gd/Fm		2704	
34	6	REDC	9f Gd/Fm		2865	
40	2	THIR	8f Gd/Fm	39	2970	
47	9	REDC	7f Gd/Fm		2994	

27	11	AYR	7f Gd/Fm	39	3138
0	13	CHES	6f Soft		4069
56	7	PONT	10f Soft		4088
0	12	MUSS	8f Gd/Sft		4135
8	9	NEWC	10f Heavy	38	4404

TAKESMYBREATHAWAY 2 ch f £0

54	6	NEWM	6f Gd/Fm		2285
65	7	NEWB	6f Firm		3449

TAKHLID 9 b h £12581

85a	2	SOUT	7f Aw	80	35
85a	3	SOUT	8f Aw	80	49
86a	1	WOLV	6f Aw		132*
84a	1	WOLV	7f Aw		142*
50a	6	SOUT	8f Aw		195
61a	4	WOLV	8f Aw		256
58a	7	SOUT	6f Aw		279
69a	2	WOLV	6f Aw		406
70a	2	WOLV	6f Aw		465
61a	5	SOUT	7f Aw		511
68a	3	SOUT	6f Aw		538
53a	6	SOUT	8f Aw	70	598
56a	6	WOLV	7f Aw		677
58	5	THIR	8f Soft	62	907
28	10	NEWC	8f Heavy	60	1007
69a	1	WOLV	6f Aw		1137*
69a	3	SOUT	8f Aw	70	1207
55	3	SOUT	7f Soft		1603
62a	1	LING	7f Aw		1741*
65a	3	SOUT	8f Aw	67	2302

TAKING 4 gr g £0

0	16	BEVE	10f Firm	65	1921	t
35	8	PONT	10f Gd/Fm		2558	

TAKRIR 3 b c £4043

85	1	NEWB	8f Good		1376+

TAKWIN 3 b c £30672

61	13	NEWM	10f Good		957	t
66	3	PONT	10f Gd/Sft		1103	t
88	2	NEWM	12f Gd/Fm		1696	t
84	2	SAND	14f Good		2477	t
91	1	KEMP	12f Gd/Fm		2751*	t
91	1	SAND	14f Good	87	2936*	t
67	16	YORK	14f Firm	95	3599	t
97	1	DONC	12f Firm	92	3896+	
90	7	NEWM	12f Good	97	4162	

TAL Y LLYN 6 ch g £0

4	8	WARW	11f Heavy		1523

TALAASH 3 b c £17692

94	1	GOOD	12f Gd/Sft		1808*
97	3	DONC	10f Gd/Fm		2351
100	6	GOOD	12f Gd/Fm		3061
107	1	CLAI	12f Good		3718*
103	9	DONC	15f Firm		3898
106	6	LONG	15f Good		4239

TALAQI 3 b f £0

74	6	DONC	10f Gd/Sft		1051

TALARIA 4 ch f £7476

15	6	LEIC	8f Gd/Fm	72	831	
0	17	PONT	8f Heavy	67	941	
67	1	NOTT	6f Gd/Sft	62	1082+	
0	15	THIR	8f Gd/Sft	67	1356	t
0	21	DONC	6f Gd/Fm	67	1842	t
61	4	YARM	6f Gd/Fm	67	1953	t
33	10	LEIC	6f Firm	66	2031	t
58	5	LING	6f Good	40	2654	VIS
55	6	NOTT	6f Soft	62	3975	t
62	1	LEIC	6f Gd/Sft		4031*	t
64a	1	LING	7f Aw		4331*	
46a	8	LING	7f Aw		4487	

TALAT 2 b f £0

64	11	NEWM	7f Good		3020
46	6	LEIC	6f Gd/Fm		3215
52	9	FOLK	6f Gd/Fm		3583

TALBIYA 3 ch f £0

38	9	KEMP	7f Soft		1018

TALBOT AVENUE 2 b c £1117

69	4	CHES	5f Gd/Fm		2248
69	4	PONT	6f Gd/Fm		3223
77	3	WIND	6f Good		3638
0	18	NEWM	6f Good	75	4338

TALECA SON 5 b g £1338

7a	8	SOUT	12f Aw	38	70	
36a	4	WOLV	12f Aw		144	
44a	3	SOUT	11f Aw		196	
31a	4	SOUT	12f Aw	31	211	
37a	2	SOUT	11f Aw		248	
52a	2	WOLV	12f Aw		295	
21a	5	SOUT	12f Aw	29	338	
37a	4	SOUT	12f Aw		387	t
15a	10	WOLV	9f Aw		433	
0a	13	SOUT	8f Aw		869	
20	9	PONT	10f Heavy	42	943	VIS
24	6	HAMI	12f Firm	27	1241	
32a	5	SOUT	11f Aw		1415	
32	4	NOTT	10f Good	34	2007	
2a	7	SOUT	11f Aw		2381	
11a	5	SOUT	12f Aw		2636	vis

TALENT STAR 3 b g £330

46	9	NEWM	10f Gd/Fm		2135
53	4	WARW	8f Gd/Fm		2846
54	6	SALI	7f Gd/Fm		3423
47	8	BATH	6f Gd/Fm		3820

TALENTS LITTLE GEM 3 b f £0

32a	9	LING	6f Aw	57	105
0a	12	LING	7f Aw		155
49	4	BRIG	7f Firm	52	1336
43	5	BRIG	8f Soft	52	1511
4	8	BRIG	8f Gd/Fm		2040
39	5	CHEP	8f Gd/Fm		2448
36	13	REDC	8f Gd/Fm	44	2861
32	7	LEIC	8f Aw	45	3095

TALES OF BOUNTY 5 b g £0

56	8	SALI	14f Firm	60	1180
0	12	NEWB	13f Gd/Sft	59	1594

TALIB 6 b g £0

0a	12	WOLV	16f Aw	30	194	t
19a	4	WOLV	16f Aw	20	494	t
0a	8	SOUT	16f Aw	20	535	t
12a	6	WOLV	16f Aw	28	576	t

TALIBAN 4 b c £0

49	6	NOTT	8f Good		784
0	10	FOLK	7f Soft		961
0	10	THIR	8f Gd/Sft		1352

TALISKER BAY 2 b c £565

65	7	DONC	5f Gd/Fm		2318
64	5	YARM	5f Firm		2901
81	5	RIPO	5f Gd/Fm		3714
73	3	MUSS	5f Gd/Sft		4131
52	6	REDC	5f Gd/Sft		4496

TALK TO MOJO 3 ch c £4134

74	1	NEWB	12f Firm		2710*

TALLULAH BELLE 7 b m £8199

86a	3	LING	12f Aw		27
74a	6	WOLV	8f Aw	85	78
88a	1	WOLV	9f Aw	83	119+
73a	5	LING	10f Aw		157
16a	9	WOLV	9f Aw	87	172
64a	10	LING	10f Aw	86	244
69a	4	WOLV	8f Aw	84	551
82a	2	LING	10f Aw		593
71a	7	LING	10f Aw	82	632

TALLYWHACKER 3 b f £0

31a	9	WOLV	7f Aw		192
24a	6	LING	10f Aw		241

TAM OSHANTER 6 gr g £0

28a	6	WOLV	16f Aw	50	296

TAMASHAN 4 b c £0

43	8	LEIC	7f Good		790
0	13	BEVE	8f Heavy		973

TAMBOURINAIRE 3 gr c £4251

87	1	KEMP	6f Good		729*

TAMBURLAINE 2 b c £51697

93	2	GOOD	7f Firm		3154
108	2	NEWB	8f Firm		3983
106	1	NEWM	8f Good		4161*
111	2	DONC	8f Soft		4463

TAMIAMI TRAIL 2 b c £1051

0	15	NEWM	6f Gd/Fm		1691
72	11	SAND	7f Gd/Fm		2921
84	5	KEMP	8f Gd/Fm		3799
80	2	BATH	10f Soft		4140

TAMILIA 2 b f £0

50	14	SALI	7f Gd/Fm		3292
0	13	NOTT	6f Good		3520
0	15	WIND	8f Gd/Fm		4288
55	4	PONT	6f Soft		4373
31a	9	WOLV	8f Aw	54	4439

TAMING 4 ch c £1102

40a	9	LING	12f Aw	88	633	t
80	4	DONC	12f Gd/Fm	80	1839	
80	4	NEWB	16f Firm	79	3986	
62	16	NEWM	18f Good	79	4353	

TAMMAM 4 b c £2136

0	22	DONC	8f Good	91	733
87	7	NEWM	7f Gd/Sft	89	966
82	8	YORK	8f Firm	90	1327
85	5	GOOD	8f Gd/Sft	88	1450
89	3	LING	9f Good	86	1744
89	4	NOTT	8f Good		1872
82	4	SALI	8f Gd/Fm		2229
78	6	ASCO	8f Gd/Fm	86	3338
75	6	YARM	10f Gd/Fm		3669
66	8	KEMP	8f Good	80	4038
0	28	NEWM	9f Gd/Fm	83	4212

TANCRED ARMS 4 b f £3349

20a	9	SOUT	6f Aw	47	698	
48	2	NEWC	6f Soft		756	
47	2	PONT	6f Soft		872	
55	3	THIR	6f Soft	54	910	
33	12	NOTT	6f Gd/Sft	55	1082	
0	19	REDC	7f Firm	54	1297	
32	10	HAMI	6f Firm	53	2097	
44	3	CARL	6f Gd/Fm		2240	
35	11	CARL	7f Firm	48	2823	
54	2	CARL	6f Gd/Fm		3080	
0	14	CATT	7f Gd/Fm	46	3200	
49	3	REDC	6f Gd/Fm	47	3312	
42	7	NEWC	6f Firm	48	3605	
23	12	CATT	7f Soft	48	4004	
44	4	WIND	6f Gd/Sft	47	4294	vis
42	4	NEWC	6f Heavy	47	4425	vis

TANCRED TIMES 5 ch m £13210

42a	2	SOUT	6f Aw	39	87
34a	6	LING	6f Aw	42	148
18a	8	SOUT	6f Aw	42	250
22a	8	WOLV	6f Aw	41	351
41a	3	SOUT	6f Aw	41	697
30	5	NEWC	6f Soft		756
33	7	DONC	6f Gd/Sft		1068
37	5	HAMI	5f Firm	44	1244
47	3	REDC	6f Firm		1298
45	2	NEWC	5f Gd/Sft	40	1479
29	4	CATT	6f Good		1663
46	1	HAMI	5f Firm		2095*
53	1	HAMI	5f Firm	47	2395*
49	5	HAMI	6f Gd/Fm	52	2641
50	5	CATT	5f Gd/Fm	52	2929

53 | 2 | CATT | 5f Gd/Fm | 51 | 3203 |
46 | 6 | BEVE | 5f Good | 51 | 3398 |
50 | 7 | EPSO | 5f Good | 53 | 3855 |
43a | 6 | SOUT | 6f Aw | 47 | 4155 |
57 | 2 | WIND | 5f Gd/Sft | 53 | 4295 |
24 | 14 | NEWC | 5f Heavy | 57 | 4407 |
48 | 5 | MUSS | 5f Soft | 57 | 4516 |

TANCRED WALK 2 b f £0
47	7	REDC	6f Gd/Fm		2990	
44	6	CARL	5f Firm		3193	
0	13	YORK	6f Good		3814	

TANGERINE 3 ch f £0
0	22	THIR	6f Soft	72	910	
0	19	REDC	5f Gd/Sft	70	1133	
0	20	REDC	6f Firm		1298	
8	14	CATT	5f Gd/Fm	60	2418	
42	7	HAYD	8f Gd/Fm	55	2699	BL
0	16	NEWC	7f Good	52	3033	bl
45	5	BEVE	10f Good	47	3396	bl

TANGERINE FLYER 5 ch g £0
22a	9	WOLV	6f Aw		406
32a	6	WOLV	5f Aw		639
19	12	CATT	7f Gd/Fm		778
35	12	MUSS	5f Gd/Fm		1430

TANGO TWO THOUSAND 3 b f £5559
78	5	GOOD	8f Gd/Sft		1811
78	2	KEMP	9f Gd/Fm		2086
83	1	WIND	8f Soft		2548*
82	5	GOOD	9f Gd/Fm	85	3089

TANTALUS 3 ch c £15450
93	1	DONC	10f Good		713*	
102	3	CHES	12f Gd/Fm		1216	
99	4	GOOD	10f Gd/Sft		1451	
79	9	NEWM	15f Gd/Fm		2594	
91	6	GOOD	10f Gd/Fm	98	3131	t
95	3	DONC	12f Firm	95	3896	t
91	6	NEWM	14f Gd/Fm	95	4213	

TANTISPER 4 ch c £0
34a	5	SOUT	11f Aw		196	
25a	6	SOUT	12f Aw		498	VIS
0a	8	SOUT	14f Aw		668	

TANZILLA 3 b f £14330
93	1	NEWB	7f Soft		915*
100	2	KEMP	8f Soft		995
100	3	CHES	11f Gd/Fm		1223
97	7	SAN	11f Good		1459
0	9	CHAN	11f Gd/Sft		1901
86	12	ASCO	8f Good	100	4113
57	15	NEWM	12f Good		4343

TAP 3 b c £2646
87	1	FOLK	7f Soft		961*
73	6	LING	8f Gd/Sft		1262
58	15	SAND	8f Gd/Fm	87	2495
74a	5	WOLV	7f Aw	82	3771
72	6	HAYD	7f Gd/Sft	80	4106
61	7	YORK	10f Soft	76	4282
0	14	DONC	8f Heavy	72	4573

TAPAGE 4 b c £22130
48a	3	LING	10f Aw		3
23a	13	WOLV	9f Aw	53	67
50a	1	LING	8f Aw	46	1259*
57	1	BATH	8f Gd/Fm	51	1442*
53a	1	LING	8f Aw	48	1915*
62	1	BRIG	8f Gd/Fm	55	2726*
60	6	BATH	8f Firm	62	2942
64	2	BATH	8f Firm	61	3207
65	1	WIND	8f Good	60	3355*
51a	5	WOLV	8f Aw	64	3499
52	7	EPSO	9f Good	66	3685
64a	1	LING	8f Aw	59	4330*

TAPATCH 12 b g £0
0	17	PONT	10f Gd/Fm	44	2556

TAPAUA 4 b g £0
42a	7	SOUT	6f Aw	201	bl
29a	7	SOUT	7f Aw	249	bl
39a	6	WOLV	7f Aw	274	bl

TAR FIH 2 b f £1187
64	4	LING	6f Good	2652
66	3	BEVE	5f Gd/Fm	3408
87	4	WARW	7f Gd/Fm	3910

TARA GOLD 2 b f £1409
73	4	ASCO	6f Gd/Fm	3342
78	3	GOOD	7f Good	3650
80	4	LING	7f Firm	3829
82	13	NEWM	7f Good	4158

TARA HALL 3 b f £2769
0	7	DONC	15f Gd/Sft	53	1071
33	5	CHES	12f Gd/Fm	54	2246
59	1	AYR	11f Heavy		4304*

TARABAYA 3 b f £5509
77	6	GOOD	8f Gd/Sft		1811
83	1	KEMP	9f Gd/Fm		2086*
88	3	ASCO	10f Gd/Fm	85	2955
88	5	YARM	10f Gd/Fm		3669

TARABELA 3 b f £3458
95	3	LONG	12f Soft	4321

TARAS EMPEROR 2 b g £16380
78	4	RIPO	5f Soft		821
86	1	NEWC	5f Heavy		1006*
93	4	ASCO	5f Gd/Sft		1107
103	1	SAND	5f Soft		1586*
87	9	ASCO	6f Good		2067
103	5	GOOD	5f Gd/Fm		3133
85	8	YORK	5f Good		3566
87	9	DONC	5f Firm		3900
93	9	NEWB	5f Gd/Sft		4454

TARAS GIRL 3 b f £2530
95	3	HAYD	5f Heavy		988
96	5	BATH	5f Good		1090
74	11	HAYD	6f Gd/Sft	100	1534
0	22	YORK	6f Firm	97	2003
0	18	NEWC	5f Gd/Fm	93	2310
79	9	NEWM	6f Good	88	2568
0	12	CATT	5f Gd/Fm	84	2929
0	18	HAYD	5f Gd/Fm	80	3322
45	21	RIPO	6f Gd/Fm	75	3464
50	10	HAYD	5f Gd/Sft	70	3788

TARAS TIPPLE 2 b g £0
0	13	THIR	7f Gd/Sft	3776
44	7	REDC	5f Gd/Sft	4496

TARAWAN 4 ch c £0
41a	9	WOLV	8f Aw	87	580	vis
0	19	EPSO	10f Heavy	87	1031	vis
75	10	NEWM	10f Gd/Fm	86	1170	
0	16	WIND	10f Good	83	1729	
78	5	GOOD	8f Gd/Fm	79	2356	
54	12	YORK	8f Gd/Fm	79	2645	
0	16	GOOD	9f Good	76	3110	vis
54	7	EPSO	12f Good	73	3686	bl

TARAZA 2 b f £3250
77	2	LEOP	8f Heavy	4554

TARBOUSH 3 b c £4910
73	12	NEWM	10f Good	957
94	3	NEWM	10f Gd/Fm	1697
83	1	SAND	10f Gd/Fm	1992*

TARCOOLA 3 ch c £0
59	10	WIND	8f Gd/Sft		1099
0	F	BATH	8f Gd/Fm	65	1442
44	14	NEWB	8f Gd/Fm	65	1787
54	11	WIND	8f Gd/Fm		2211
0	16	GOOD	10f Good	56	3663

TARFSHI 2 b f £11314
85	1	DONC	7f Gd/Fm	3156*
92	3	KEMP	7f Gd/Fm	3789

93	1	SAND	8f Soft	4203*

TARRADALE 6 br g £0
0	24	REDC	8f Firm	48	1300
0	15	PONT	10f Soft		4088
0	21	REDC	8f Gd/Sft	53	4217
32	10	REDC	8f Gd/Sft	44	4499

TARRANAKI KNIGHT 2 b c £0
48	10	FOLK	6f Gd/Fm	3443
36	10	EPSO	7f Good	3760
0	16	WARW	15f Gd/Fm	3911

TARRIFA 3 ch f £0
0	14	WIND	10f Good	1725
37	8	NOTT	10f Heavy	4412

TARRY FLYNN 6 br g £14250
114	2	CURR	7f Yldg	862	bl
112	2	CURR	8f Good	4056	bl

TARSHEEH 3 b f £0
58	8	LING	7f Gd/Fm	840
54	7	WARW	8f Soft	1063

TARSKI 6 ch g £1545
37	7	LING	9f Good	52	1395	
43	3	GOOD	9f Gd/Sft	50	1807	
50	3	NEWB	10f Gd/Fm	50	1942	
48	3	BATH	10f Gd/Sft	48	2552	
46	5	WIND	10f Gd/Fm	48	2888	
43	4	WIND	12f Good	47	3186	
38	6	BATH	8f Firm	46	3623	VIS
0a	13	LING	12f Aw	44	4334	

TARTAN ISLAND 3 b c £1049
0	17	HAMI	5f Firm	53	1244	
0	18	REDC	6f Gd/Sft	48	1578	
52	2	MUSS	5f Gd/Fm		2204	VIS
42	5	MUSS	5f Gd/Fm	43	2374	vis
51	4	HAMI	6f Gd/Fm		2640	vis
38	7	HAMI	6f Gd/Fm		2798	BL
0	18	RIPO	5f Gd/Fm		3180	bl

TARTAN LASS 5 b m £0
0a	14	SOUT	6f Aw	75	129	t

TARWILA 3 ch f £2700
92	3	LEOP	10f Heavy	4558

TARXIEN 6 b g £0
60	8	KEMP	14f Good	83	726

TASSO DANCER 4 gr f £0
0	15	WIND	8f Gd/Sft		1428
43	7	CHEP	8f Heavy		1556
48	12	SALI	10f Gd/Fm		2265
35	5	BATH	10f Firm	47	2789
33	9	NOTT	14f Gd/Fm	42	3002

TATANTE 2 gr f £447
55	11	MUSS	5f Gd/Sft	4131
68	3	WIND	6f Gd/Sft	4289

TATE VENTURE 3 b g £2541
65	8	RIPO	8f Soft		826
65a	3	WOLV	7f Aw		1035
70a	1	SOUT	8f Aw		1204*
58	15	DONC	10f Firm	72	3899
52a	8	LING	12f Aw		4101
0	17	DONC	12f Soft	66	4464

TATTENHAM STAR 3 b c £1109
67a	3	LING	6f Aw	68	2
62a	5	LING	8f Aw	68	54
67a	7	LING	7f Aw		206
76	3	LING	6f Gd/Sft		837
67	6	SALI	6f Firm		1175
62	3	LING	7f Good		1397

TATTOO 5 b m £0
0a	11	WOLV	8f Aw	229
0a	8	LING	12f Aw	267
0a	12	SOUT	12f Aw	301

TATTY THE TANK 2 b c £567
22a	8	SOUT	7f Aw	4369

65 2 NOTT 8f Heavy 4507

TAUFAN BOY 7 b g £0
51 6 KEMP 14f Good 58 726 vis

TAUFANS MELODY 9 b g £6919
86 10 HAYD 12f Heavy 987
95 7 CHES 13f Firm 1247
103 2 GOOD 12f Gd/Sft 1474
102 3 CHES 13f Gd/Fm 102 3169
85 5 GOOD 14f Good 3645
76 7 NEWM 12f Good 4194 VIS

TAVERNER SOCIETY 5 b g £291
0 20 NEWB 10f Good 72 1375
60 4 CHEP 8f Heavy 1552
59a 4 LING 7f Aw 1739

TAW PARK 6 b g £0
81 5 HAYD 11f Gd/Fm 2703
63 6 ASCO 10f Gd/Fm 2957
60 6 CHEP 7f Gd/Fm 3256

TAWN AGAIN 4 b g £2172
31 10 THIR 6f Gd/Sft 1354
0 9 DONC 5f Gd/Fm 1843
0 15 NOTT 6f Gd/Fm 35 2192
21 9 DONC 6f Gd/Fm 35 2315
70 2 BEVE 5f Gd/Fm 2519
44 2 RIPO 6f Gd/Fm 42 2839

TAXI FOR ROBBO 3 b f £0
31 8 NOTT 8f Heavy 4505

TAXMERE 3 ch f £0
36 11 WARW 8f Heavy 884
34 9 HAYD 7f Gd/Fm 44 1793
0 17 BATH 12f Gd/Sft 49 2554
0 14 CHEP 12f Gd/Fm 43 3255

TAYAR 4 gr c £0
0a 9 WOLV 8f Aw 658 t

TAYEED 3 b c £0
26 6 BRIG 8f Soft 4177

TAYIF 4 gr c £0
0 19 NEWM 7f Gd/Sft 97 966 t
62 21 ASCO 7f Gd/Sft 96 1110
0 16 NEWM 7f Gd/Fm 95 2133
0 16 NEWM 7f Gd/Fm 92 2616
74 10 YARM 7f Firm 92 2768

TAYOVULLIN 6 ch m £2115
0a 12 SOUT 6f Aw 57 218
20a 8 WOLV 8f Aw 550
17a 10 SOUT 6f Aw 51 604 BL
0 15 THIR 8f Soft 47 931
34 6 MUSS 7f Gd/Fm 44 1148
40 5 CARL 8f Firm 44 1257
42 2 SOUT 7f Soft 41 1606
46 2 REDC 8f Good 43 1892
46 5 BEVE 7f Firm 46 2221
30 10 DONC 7f Gd/Fm 46 2320

TAYSEER 6 ch g £126430
61 19 DONC 8f Good 86 733
76 11 KEMP 8f Gd/Sft 86 1077
86 5 NEWM 6f Gd/Fm 86 1173
83 3 EPSO 9f Gd/Sft 86 1829
70 12 ASCO 6f Good 86 2151
90 3 NEWC 7f Firm 86 2338
97 1 NEWM 7f Gd/Fm 86 2616+
96 3 ASCO 7f Gd/Sft 93 2997
103 1 GOOD 6f Firm 93 3152+
99 7 YORK 7f Firm 3600
98 7 AYR 6f Gd/Sft 102 4012
113 2 ASCO 6f Gd/Sft 4125

TAZ MANIA 4 b g £0
36a 7 SOUT 6f Aw 30 tbl
15a 12 SOUT 5f Aw 214 tbl

TE ANAU 3 b f £0
31a 7 SOUT 6f Aw 300
23a 9 SOUT 8f Aw 49 429

12 10 NOTT 10f Soft 41 1644
10a 7 LING 12f Aw 44 2651
0 15 YARM 11f Soft 37 4391

TE DEUM 3 ch c £3107
0 14 SALI 8f Good 67 1345
59 5 SALI 12f Gd/Sft 63 2470
0 13 NEWM 12f Gd/Fm 59 3167
58 1 SALI 14f Gd/Sft 55 4166*
28 9 NOTT 16f Heavy 57 4508

TE QUIERO 2 gr c £0.
77 8 LING 7f Soft 4268

TEA FOR TEXAS 3 ch f £3578
48a 4 LING 6f Aw 153
54a 3 LING 5f Aw 289
51a 5 WOLV 7f Aw 362
49a 2 LING 7f Aw 527
46a 7 LING 7f Aw 51 654
53 1 BRIG 7f Firm 1212*
45 6 BRIG 8f Soft 54 1511
43 8 SALI 7f Gd/Fm 52 1889
39 9 LING 6f Good 50 2654
38 9 EPSO 7f Good 50 2794
41 4 BRIG 7f Firm 3559
44 3 LEIC 6f Gd/Sft 4031
0 12 NOTT 8f Heavy 49 4414

TEAM OF THREE 4 b g £0
0a 11 WOLV 15f Aw 39 277
0a 11 SOUT 8f Aw 30 345

TEAPOT ROW 5 b g £1727
103 5 NEWM 6f Good 952
90 10 YORK 7f Firm 1338
97 3 YARM 8f Gd/Fm 3667
99 6 NEWB 7f Firm 3995

TECHNICIAN 5 ch g £10377
21a 10 WOLV 7f Aw 52 582 bl
31a 12 WOLV 7f Aw 50 635
52 5 CATT 7f Gd/Fm 58 780 bl
66 2 THIR 7f Soft 929 bl
37 10 MUSS 7f Gd/Fm 56 1148 bl
0 17 DONC 7f Good 53 1519 bl
56 1 CARL 6f Firm 49 2015* bl
60 2 HAMI 7f Firm 2396 bl
56 3 HAYD 6f Gd/Fm 54 2444 bl
65 2 PONT 6f Firm 2833 bl
64 2 NEWC 6f Good 62 3037 bl
70 2 NEWM 6f Gd/Fm 65 3457 bl
0 13 GOOD 6f Good 69 3904 bl
0 18 YORK 6f Soft 4287
0 16 NEWC 6f Heavy 66 4405 bl
46a 5 WOLV 6f Aw 51 4553 bl

TEDBURROW 8 b g £40426
65 13 DONC 6f Good 734
105 7 NEWM 6f Good 952
101 13 NEWM 5f Gd/Fm 1172
103 8 YORK 6f Good 1338
116 1 NEWC 6f Firm 2335+
102 3 CHES 5f Gd/Fm 2669
99 7 CHES 6f Firm 3172
116 2 LEOP 5f Good 3923
113 4 ASCO 6f Gd/Sft 4125

TEDSTALE 2 ch c £1427
80 7 NEWM 7f Gd/Fm 3121
79 4 NEWM 8f Gd/Fm 3458
72 4 NEWC 7f Gd/Sft 3705
80 3 WARW 7f Gd/Fm 81 3913
64 5 BRIG 7f Soft 4172
0 18 NEWM 8f Good 80 4350

TEE CEE 3 b f £4209
70 5 NOTT 8f Gd/Sft 1084
71 3 SALI 7f Gd/Fm 1886
66 3 NOTT 8f Gd/Fm 2188
52 4 WARW 6f Good 2462

66 3 SALI 7f Gd/Fm 3423
70 1 CHEP 7f Good 65 3873*

TEEHEE 2 b c £1186
59 5 SALI 7f Gd/Fm 3418
74 5 CHEP 8f Good 3867
78 3 LEIC 7f Gd/Sft 4028
83 3 REDC 7f Gd/Fm 4500

TEEJAY N AITCH 8 b g £0
32 8 HAMI 9f Gd/Fm 1195 t

TEENAWON 2 ch f £808
43 3 YARM 6f Good 3028
56 2 LING 6f Firm 3278
0 13 FOLK 7f Gd/Fm 3582

TEEPLOY GIRL 5 b m £0
0a 6 WOLV 12f Aw 530
0a 11 WOLV 9f Aw 553

TEFI 2 ch c £2761
65 5 REDC 5f Gd/Sft 1558
69 3 CARL 6f Firm 2014
68 2 MUSS 7f Firm 2377
69 2 CARL 6f Gd/Fm 3079
65 3 THIR 7f Gd/Fm 3347
41 13 YORK 6f Good 3812
54 6 PONT 6f Soft 4372

TEGGIANO 3 b f £31050
108 2 ASCO 12f Good 2112
0 10 CURR 12f Gd/Fm 2739

TELECASTER 4 ch g £16370
40a 3 SOUT 7f Aw 40 299 BL
57a 1 WOLV 6f Aw 40 352* bl
63a 1 SOUT 6f Aw 48 386*
61a 2 SOUT 6f Aw 57 425 bl
65a 1 SOUT 6f Aw 59 587* bl
74a 1 WOLV 6f Aw 65 622* bl
57a 5 SOUT 6f Aw 69 645 bl
74a 2 WOLV 5f Aw 72 678 bl
66a 8 WOLV 6f Aw 74 4380 bl

TELLION 6 b g £258
47a 3 SOUT 12f Aw 48 339 vis
29a 7 SOUT 8f Aw 48 585 vis

TEMERAIRE 5 b g £10938
79a 5 LING 8f Aw 83 7
90a 1 LING 7f Aw 104*
79a 7 WOLV 7f Aw 90 143
63 9 KEMP 7f Good 83 725
83 2 LEIC 7f Gd/Sft 82 834
77 10 NEWM 7f Gd/Sft 83 966
62 11 RIPO 8f Good 82 1598
82 4 GOOD 8f Gd/Sft 82 1810
84 2 SAND 7f Gd/Fm 82 1989
82 3 KEMP 7f Good 83 2261
69 7 YARM 7f Firm 83 2768
56 12 ASCO 8f Gd/Fm 83 3338
0 21 NEWM 7f Good 82 4357
0 12 YARM 6f Heavy 80 4480

TEMESIDE TINA 4 ch f £189
24a 10 WOLV 9f Aw 43 60
26a 6 LING 8f Aw 114
41a 4 LING 8f Aw 265

TEMPER TANTRUM 2 b g £0
25a 8 WOLV 7f Aw 4385

TEMPEST 2 b c £30583
89 4 NEWM 7f Gd/Fm 3121
100 1 NEWB 7f Gd/Fm 3484*
100 2 DONC 7f Gd/Fm 3859
100 6 NEWM 7f Good 4196
114 3 NEWM 7f Good 4354

TEMPLE WAY 4 b g £65610
66 12 NEWM 12f Gd/Sft 75 968
78 2 SALI 14f Firm 74 1180
82 2 ASCO 16f Gd/Fm 79 2173
88 2 NEWC 16f Firm 82 2336

GOOD 2 b f (continued)

95	1	**GOOD**	14f Gd/Fm	88	3058*	VIS
83	15	YORK	14f Gd/Fm	95	3565	vis
93	5	DONC	15f Firm	93	3890	vis

TEMPLES TIME 2 b f £2793

76	4	NEWB	5f Gd/Fm		1589
71	3	NEWB	7f Firm		2810
48	6	HAYD	8f Gd/Sft		3268
78	1	**BRIG**	8f Gd/Sft		4116*
72	9	NEWM	8f Good	77	4350
70	5	BRIG	8f Heavy	74	4538

TEMPRAMENTAL 4 ch f £9809

41a	7	LING	7f Aw	47	28	bl
50a	5	LING	8f Aw		92	bl
39a	5	WOLV	8f Aw		136	
48a	3	SOUT	8f Aw		195	
24a	7	WOLV	8f Aw	41	227	bl
42a	2	SOUT	12f Aw	40	641	
46a	2	SOUT	12f Aw	40	683	
30a	5	SOUT	8f Aw	40	692	
47	3	SOUT	10f Gd/Fm	45	859	
46	3	NOTT	10f Gd/Sft	45	1086	
46	3	REDC	8f Firm	45	1296	
50	1	**PONT**	10f Good	45	1496*	
54	4	YARM	10f Gd/Sft	52	1615	
56	1	**REDC**	8f Good	51	1892*	
50	5	PONT	8f Good	55	2180	
44	7	PONT	8f Gd/Fm	55	2561	
20a	8	SOUT	8f Aw		2950	

TEMPTING FATE 2 b f £19024

91	2	GOOD	8f Gd/Fm		3090
95	1	**NEWB**	6f Firm		3449*
103	1	**SALI**	6f Firm		3749*
105	4	NEWM	7f Good		4356

TEN PAST SIX 8 ch g £0

0a	11	WOLV	12f Aw	60	407	
40a	5	SOUT	11f Aw		1417	vis
29a	6	SOUT	11f Aw		2119	bl
23	7	HAMI	13f Gd/Fm	47	2238	vis
19	9	HAMI	11f Gd/Fm	37	2638	vis
18	8	CATT	12f Gd/Fm		2742	vis
6	9	HAMI	13f Gd/Sft	38	3378	vis

TENACIOUS MELODY 4 b g £0

0	14	NOTT	8f Good		784
43	11	LING	10f Gd/Sft		1281
41	9	WIND	10f Gd/Fm		2056

TENBY HEIGHTS 4 b c £0

0	7	LEIC	12f Gd/Fm		3336	t
17	9	BATH	12f Firm		3624	tBL
0	16	WARW	16f Gd/Fm	41	3916	tbl

TENDER COVE 2 b c £0

97	6	CURR	6f Yldg		3720

TENDER TRAP 2 b c £0

72	5	NOTT	8f Heavy		4504

TENDERFOOT 2 b f £0

55	6	BRIG	8f Soft		4417

TENERIFE FLYER 2 ch f £236

51	6	BEVE	5f Heavy		974
0a	13	SOUT	5f Aw		1304
38	4	BEVE	7f Firm		2218
39	6	NEWC	7f Good	54	3246
44	7	HAMI	8f Gd/Sft		3532
52	4	NEWC	8f Soft		3706
56	4	PONT	8f Gd/Sft	55	4084
0	17	PONT	8f Soft	57	4378

TENNESSEE WALTZ 2 b f £0

46	11	LING	7f Firm		3829
0	24	DONC	8f Gd/Sft		4445
0	18	NEWM	7f Soft		4541

TENSILE 5 b g £4996

84	6	CHES	19f Gd/Fm	84	1222
82	8	GOOD	14f Gd/Sft	84	1484
91	7	ASCO	22f Good		2153
85	4	SAND	16f Gd/Fm	84	2498
86	3	CHES	19f Firm	88	3171
87	3	NEWM	15f Good	86	3611
85	5	ASCO	16f Good	87	4115
80	9	NEWM	18f Good	87	4353 VIS

TEODORA 3 b f £3599

83	5	KEMP	8f Soft		995	
85	10	GOOD	7f Gd/Sft	98	1470	
81	7	EPSO	7f Gd/Sft		1830	
74	6	YARM	6f Gd/Fm		2197	
88	2	NEWM	7f Good	87	2567	
70	7	LING	8f Firm		2762	
84	9	GOOD	7f Gd/Fm	86	3130	t
75	9	NEWM	7f Gd/Sft	85	3315	t
71	7	GOOD	7f Good	83	3648	t
0	21	ASCO	7f Good	84	4112	
0	18	NEWM	7f Gd/Sft	80	4215	

TEOFILIO 6 ch g £6998

67a	1	**LING**	8f Aw	62	594*	bl
69	6	KEMP	7f Gd/Fm	74	725	bl
59	11	GOOD	7f Gd/Sft	73	1810	bl
64	7	SAND	7f Gd/Fm	71	1989	bl
67	9	NEWM	7f Gd/Fm	71	2133	bl
62	10	KEMP	7f Gd/Fm	70	2261	bl
74	2	LEIC	7f Gd/Fm		2508	bl
69	3	NEWB	7f Firm	69	2814	bl
44	12	ASCO	8f Gd/Fm	69	3018	bl
40	9	WIND	8f Good	68	3355	bl
61a	4	WOLV	8f Aw	67	3499	bl
57a	5	LING	8f Aw		3756	bl
67	4	KEMP	7f Gd/Fm	66	3796	
50	12	NEWB	7f Firm	66	3981	
66a	2	WOLV	8f Aw	62	4248	bl
66a	2	WOLV	8f Aw	62	4358	bl
67a	2	WOLV	8f Aw	66	4550	bl

TEREED ELHAWA 2 b f £6253

64	6	YARM	6f Gd/Sft		1612
80	3	GOOD	8f Gd/Fm		1957
84	1	**NOTT**	6f Gd/Fm		3003*
80	4	CHES	6f Gd/Sft		3425
80	4	YARM	6f Soft		4390

TERIMONS DREAM 3 gr g £0

0	13	KEMP	12f Soft		4040

TERM OF ENDEARMENT 3 b f £4446

33	9	WARW	7f Heavy	55	887
0	18	DONC	8f Gd/Sft	52	1053
46a	5	LING	10f Aw	56	1265
41	6	BRIG	6f Gd/Sft	46	1464
31	11	REDC	6f Good	45	1891
31	5	BRIG	6f Firm	51	2042
43	2	YARM	7f Gd/Fm		2413
0a	13	SOUT	7f Aw		2633
26	8	THIR	8f Gd/Fm	43	2964
43	2	NEWM	8f Gd/Sft		3117
50	1	**LEIC**	7f Gd/Fm		3332*
42	3	BRIG	7f Firm		3559
22	13	BATH	8f Gd/Fm	49	3816
38	10	YARM	7f Firm		3921
0	18	LEIC	8f Sft/Hvy	46	4310

TERRA NOVA 3 ch f £1244

69	3	WARW	7f Gd/Sft		1708
51	10	LING	6f Gd/Fm	70	2216
46	3	KEMP	6f Gd/Sft		2582
39a	9	SOUT	7f Aw	65	4153

TERRAZZO 5 b g £0

26	7	CARL	8f Firm		2283

TERRE VIERGE 3 b f £13449

92	1	**LONG**	9f Heavy		4489*

TERRESTRIAL 2 ch c £7800

96	1	**NEWM**	8f Good		4349*

TERROIR 5 b g £5763

100	3	MAIS	6f Heavy		820
101	4	DEAU	6f V		2574	bl

TERTULLIAN 5 ch g £25807

115	3	BADE	6f Gd/Sft		1746
113	3	HAMB	6f Soft		2403
115	1	**MUNI**	7f Soft		4317*

TEST THE WATER 6 ch g £0

0a	11	LING	8f Aw	60	1259
38	8	LING	8f Aw	60	1395
0	12	LING	11f Good	56	1743
28a	7	LING	10f Aw	50	2186

TEXALINA 3 b f £7685

113	2	LONG	8f Heavy		1027

TEXANNIE 3 b f £0

7	12	CHEP	8f Good		3868
59	7	NEWM	10f Good		4017

TEYAAR 4 b g £14553

61a	5	WOLV	7f Aw		478	BL
69a	1	**SOUT**	6f Aw		558*	
52a	7	SOUT	6f Aw	70	645	
70a	1	**SOUT**	6f Aw		738*	
72a	1	**WOLV**	6f Aw	67	923*	
79	2	NEWC	5f Heavy	74	1008	
77	5	WIND	6f Gd/Fm	75	1196	
77	2	THIR	6f Gd/Fm	75	1383	
75a	2	SOUT	6f Aw	71	1504	
77a	2	WOLV	5f Aw	76	2078	
53	13	GOOD	6f Gd/Fm	76	3136	
0	18	YORK	6f Good	75	3543	

THAAYER 5 b g £2374

48a	7	WOLV	6f Aw	59	175
68a	1	**SOUT**	6f Aw	57	218*
62a	4	WOLV	6f Aw	64	232

THAILAND 2 ch f £0

60	10	NEWB	5f Gd/Fm		1782
38	10	BATH	6f Firm		2328
21	9	CATT	7f Gd/Fm		2417

THAMAN 3 b c £3776

58	10	LING	7f Gd/Sft		1263
73	1	**NEWM**	8f Gd/Fm		2134*

THAMES DANCER 4 ch c £7662

53a	7	SOUT	14f Aw	65	868
70	4	KEMP	12f Gd/Sft	70	1076
78	1	**LING**	16f Good	69	1394*
80	3	HAYD	14f Gd/Sft	78	1536
83	4	ASCO	20f Good	79	2092

THANKS MAX 2 b c £3094

32	10	THIR	7f Gd/Fm		3615
43	5	MUSS	8f Gd/Fm		3740
76	1	**HAMI**	5f Soft		3801*
31	10	AYR	6f Heavy	75	4305

THARI 3 b c £16883

90	7	CHES	10f Firm		1246	BL
94	6	ASCO	10f Gd/Fm	95	3339	
96	3	NEWB	13f Good	93	3994	
101	1	**NEWM**	14f Gd/Fm	95	4213*	
0	14	DONC	12f Heavy	102	4580	

THAT MAN AGAIN 8 ch g £12571

19	12	BRIG	5f Gd/Sft	75	897	bl
53	11	KEMP	5f Soft	75	1013	bl
51	12	LING	5f Gd/Sft	73	1264	bl
36	16	RIPO	5f Good	70	1861	bl
72	1	**SALI**	5f Firm	66	2022+	bl
61	9	LING	5f Gd/Fm	72	2184	bl
67	8	SAND	5f Gd/Fm	72	2473	bl
68	4	NEWM	5f Gd/Fm	71	2859	bl
67	3	BEVE	5f Gd/Sft		3056	bl
61	8	BATH	5f Firm	70	3209	bl
0	13	ASCO	5f Gd/Fm	69	3341	bl
59	5	BRIG	5f Firm	67	3528	bl
65	3	YARM	5f Gd/Fm	67	3668	bl
64	1	**SAND**	5f Gd/Fm		3947*	bl

THATCHAM 4 ch c £6134

49a 3 LING 8f Aw 50 776
52a 2 LING 10f Aw 50 880
39 11 WIND 10f Gd/Sft 50 1100
0a 13 WOLV 8f Aw 52 1393
41 4 YARM 7f Gd/Sft 47 1611 BL
59 1 **YARM** 6f Gd/Fm 46 1953* bl
61 2 WIND 6f Gd/Fm 58 2207 bl
60 3 YARM 6f Gd/Fm 58 2415 bl
46a 4 SOUT 6f Aw 52 4156 bl
0 18 DONC 7f Soft 4461 bl

THATCHED 10 b g £1631
41 5 CARL 9f Firm 45 1254
32 14 REDC 8f Firm 45 1296
39 6 MUSS 9f Firm 43 2049
53 7 CATT 7f Gd/Fm 2437
63 5 HAYD 7f Gd/Fm 2704
41 6 CARL 7f Firm 41 2823
58 3 REDC 9f Gd/Fm 2865
34 12 RIPO 9f Gd/Fm 47 3011
44 2 CATT 7f Gd/Fm 43 3200
52 4 REDC 8f Firm 3330
25 13 NEWC 7f Firm 44 3603
43 10 MUSS 8f Gd/Sft 4135

THATCHED COTTAGE 2 b f £0
69 6 BATH 5f Gd/Fm 3815

THATCHING LAD 7 gr g £0
28a 8 SOUT 6f Aw 199
0a 12 SOUT 8f Aw 252

THATCHMASTER 9 b g £1100
43 14 GOOD 9f Good 66 3110 t
49 9 SALI 10f Gd/Fm 64 3390 t
63 2 GOOD 9f Good 63 3644 t
49 7 GOOD 12f Good 63 3887 t
51 9 GOOD 8f Soft 62 4066 t

THATS ALL FOLKS 3 b c £5813
73a 3 LING 8f Aw 26
73a 3 WOLV 7f Aw 72 188
77a 1 **LING** 8f Aw 264*
77a 2 LING 10f Aw 420
61a 5 LING 10f Aw 73 509

THATS ALL JAZZ 2 b f £0
17 9 KEMP 5f Soft 993
56 11 NEWM 6f Gd/Fm 3162
33 6 ASCO 6f Gd/Fm 3342
36 9 RIPO 5f Gd/Fm 3710
49 8 YORK 6f Good 3812 VIS

THATS JAZZ 2 b f £3050
64 8 NOTT 5f Gd/Sft 1641
68 2 LING 6f Good 2588
73 2 NEWC 7f Gd/Fm 2985
58 10 NEWM 6f Gd/Fm 75 3165

THATS LIFE 5 b g £245
65a 3 WOLV 6f Aw 132
31a 9 WOLV 6f Aw 436

THE ANGEL GABRIEL 5 ch g £0
0 17 HAMI 6f Gd/Fm 54 1192
22 8 MUSS 5f Firm 1688

THE BARGATE FOX 4 b g £5216
55a 1 **WOLV** 9f Aw 47 60*
38a 7 SOUT 8f Aw 53 83
45a 4 SOUT 8f Aw 50 177
54a 1 **WOLV** 8f Aw 50 233*
57a 3 WOLV 12f Aw 56 260
54a 4 WOLV 9f Aw 56 349
40a 9 WOLV 9f Aw 56 383
55a 3 WOLV 9f Aw 55 568
0 14 NOTT 10f Gd/Fm 55 1272
0 25 NEWM 6f Gd/Fm 52 1690
31a 7 SOUT 8f Aw 55 2634
49 3 RIPO 12f Gd/Fm 48 3181
25 13 NOTT 10f Good 48 3524
0a 12 WOLV 12f Aw 54 4026

THE BARNSLEY BELLE 7 b m £1926
27a 4 SOUT 7f Aw 37 304
20a 5 SOUT 8f Aw 39 384
19a 7 SOUT 8f Aw 2816
54a 1 **SOUT** 8f Aw 2946*

THE BARNSLEY CHOP 2 b g £0
36 9 BEVE 7f Gd/Sft 3057
43 10 CATT 7f Good 3438

THE BIZZ 7 b m £0
0 18 BRIG 10f Firm 1210

THE BLUE BRAZIL 4 b g £0
22a 11 SOUT 6f Aw 201
0 15 YARM 11f Gd/Sft 27 1614
0 13 WIND 12f Gd/Fm 1880 VIS

THE BLUES ACADEMY 5 b g £0
0 13 RIPO 16f Good 62 1597

THE BOXER 4 b f £0
33 9 PONT 8f Firm 45 2180 t

THE BOY KING 8 ch g £0
0a 14 SOUT 16f Aw 36 4149 bl

THE BROKER 2 b c £0
0 13 CHEP 8f Good 3867

THE BULL MACABE 3 ch c £292
77a 3 LING 6f Aw 24

THE BUTTERWICK KID 7 ch g £355
53 6 CATT 12f Good 75 3437
70 4 CATT 12f Soft 72 4003
60 6 MUSS 16f Gd/Sft 70 4134
44 8 YORK 14f Heavy 69 4299

THE BYSTANDER 2 b f £11182
71 7 HAYD 8f Soft 3766
81 1 **YORK** 8f Soft 4281*
85 2 DONC 6f Gd/Sft 4449

THE CASTIGATOR 3 b c £0
33 6 HAMI 6f Gd/Fm 1905
19 10 REDC 8f Gd/Fm 61 2147
0 13 RIPO 8f Soft 53 2542
0 15 REDC 8f Firm 3330
22 10 BEVE 7f Gd/Fm 3671
0 18 YORK 9f Good 3808
34 10 MUSS 12f Gd/Sft 4133
0 12 REDC 7f Gd/Sft 4218
47 10 YORK 12f Soft 4276
65 5 AYR 8f Heavy 4308
25 12 DONC 7f Soft 4465
0 7 YARM 19f Gd/Sft 4515
45 8 NEWM 6f Gd/Sft 4535
18 9 DONC 15f Heavy 4568

THE CHOCOLATIER 2 b f £0
58 6 NOTT 6f Good 2010
51 5 NEWM 7f Gd/Fm 2599
72 8 NEWM 6f Gd/Fm 4209

THE COTTONWOOL KID 8 b g £1799
29a 1 **WOLV** 16f Aw 20 492* bl
15a 3 SOUT 16f Aw 21 542 bl

THE DARK LADY 2 b f £0
0 12 BATH 5f Good 1088
58 7 WARW 5f Heavy 1522

THE DIDDLER 3 b g £0
15a 7 SOUT 5f Aw 696
0a 10 SOUT 8f Aw 1204
44 7 SOUT 7f Soft 1607
0 16 LEIC 7f Firm 50 2026
0 15 LEIC 8f Gd/Fm 43 2506
0a 11 SOUT 8f Aw 2950

THE DOCTOR 2 b c £0
61 10 CHEP 7f Good 3866
55 7 BATH 10f Soft 4140
0 16 LING 7f Soft 4483

THE DOWNTOWN FOX 5 br g £7939
86a 1 **WOLV** 6f Aw 76 320+ vis

46a 11 WOLV 6f Aw 84 435 vis
0a 11 WOLV 6f Aw 84 532 vis
66 8 THIR 5f Soft 905 bl
64 6 WARW 7f Soft 1060 bl
72a 7 SOUT 6f Aw 83 1504 bl
59 10 NEWB 7f Gd/Sft 74 1590 vis
0 14 PONT 6f Gd/Fm 71 2559
70 2 HAYD 7f Gd/Fm 2704 bl
52 11 ASCO 8f Gd/Fm 70 3018 bl
69 4 WIND 8f Good 68 3188 bl
18 14 YORK 7f Heavy 67 4302 bl

THE EXHIBITION FOX 4 b c £1105
49 12 NOTT 10f Good 80 786
76 3 HAYD 8f Gd/Sft 76 1836
59 10 HAYD 7f Gd/Fm 86 2456
0 20 ASCO 8f Gd/Sft 76 2999
57 11 HAYD 8f Gd/Fm 78 3325
62 9 YORK 7f Good 73 3808
59 10 NEWB 7f Firm 72 3981
50 9 HAYD 8f Soft 72 4094

THE FAIRY FLAG 2 ch f £0
59 8 LING 7f Firm 3833
51 5 BRIG 8f Gd/Sft 4117
57a 6 WOLV 6f Aw 4359

THE FANCY MAN 2 ch c £2492
69 4 HAYD 6f Soft 1823
0 11 BEVE 6f Gd/Fm 2480
58 6 HAYD 6f Gd/Fm 2700
35 12 NEWC 7f Good 62 3246
65 1 **BEVE** 7f Good 57 3950* VIS
0 15 WIND 10f Gd/Sft 64 4290 vis
16 12 PONT 8f Soft 64 4378 vis

THE FINAL WORD 3 ch f £0
47a 5 WOLV 9f Aw 319
31a 7 WOLV 9f Aw 395
11a 8 WOLV 12f Aw 565
30 12 NOTT 8f Good 784
7 7 PONT 12f Heavy 939
0 15 BEVE 10f Firm 1274

THE FLYER 3 b c £705
50a 6 SOUT 12f Aw 643
0 12 KEMP 11f Soft 1017
64 2 LEIC 8f Gd/Sft 1572
39 9 LEIC 8f Gd/Sft 1731
32 8 BATH 12f Firm 3624
0 20 WARW 11f Gd/Fm 60 3915 BL

THE FOSSICK 4 ch g £0
30a 6 WOLV 12f Aw 519
0a 10 SOUT 12f Aw 643
7 9 REDC 8f Gd/Fm 29 2147
0 16 RIPO 10f Soft 2538

THE FROG QUEEN 3 b f £1476
43 9 WIND 12f Heavy 64 937
52 4 WIND 12f Gd/Sft 1096
48 12 WIND 12f Firm 57 1292
48 3 BRIG 10f Good 51 1649
41 7 BATH 10f Firm 50 2332
33 5 BRIG 10f Firm 50 3560
48 2 LEIC 10f Firm 48 3842
48 2 LEIC 10f Gd/Sft 4029

THE FUGATIVE 7 b m £2170
81 8 MAIS 6f Heavy 98
43a 8 WOLV 6f Aw 56 923
89 4 EPSO 6f Heavy 90 1028
95 5 LING 7f Gd/Sft 1283
79 6 EPSO 6f Good 89 1851
87 3 EPSO 8f Gd/Sft 88 2432
77 4 CHEP 6f Gd/Fm 2660
0 17 ASCO 6f Gd/Fm 84 2954

THE GAMBOLLER 5 b g £0
0 13 PONT 18f Firm 60 2176
30 6 CATT 16f Gd/Fm 53 2436 VIS

THE GAY FOX 6 gr g £17413

68	5	DONC	6f Gd/Sft	68	1074	t
68	3	NEWB	6f Gd/Sft	68	1591	tVI
58	7	NOTT	5f Good	68	1871	t
71	2	CHES	5f Soft	68	2247	tbl
68	4	HAYD	6f Gd/Fm	68	2444	tbl
75	1	**YORK**	6f Good	71	2697*	tbl
60	11	CHES	8f Firm	74	3170	tbl
0	19	YORK	6f Good	74	3543	tbl
72	4	CHES	5f Soft	73	4073	tbl
72	6	HAYD	5f Gd/Sft	73	4107	tbl
62	6	NOTT	6f Heavy	73	4411	tbl

THE GENERALS LADY 2 gr f £0

0	15	BEVE	5f Firm		2730
0	14	BEVE	5f Gd/Sft		3055

THE GIRLS FILLY 3 b f £2118

62a	2	LING	7f Aw		570	
54a	3	LING	8f Aw		615	
46	12	WIND	8f Gd/Fm	62	744	
0	14	BRIG	10f Gd/Sft	58	892	
22a	7	LING	10f Aw	58	1544	tBL
56a	2	LING	12f Aw	52	2217	
39a	6	LING	12f Aw	58	2593	
35	10	BRIG	10f Firm	51	2908	

THE GLEN 2 gr c £0

82	9	NEWM	8f Good		4349

THE GREEN GREY 6 gr g £22358

31	15	ASCO	8f Gd/Sft	64	1113	
57	9	NEWB	10f Good	61	1375	
59	6	WIND	10f Good	60	1729	
68	1	**WIND**	10f Gd/Fm	60	1878*	
41	11	KEMP	9f Gd/Fm	65	2085	
56	7	KEMP	8f Gd/Fm	65	2752	
70	1	**WIND**	10f Gd/Fm	66	2888*	
68	5	GOOD	9f Good	71	3110	
73	2	ASCO	10f Gd/Fm	69	3339	
67	5	GOOD	12f Good	71	3657	
72	4	EPSO	12f Good	71	3858	
72	3	SAND	14f Gd/Fm	71	3948	
71a	1	LING	12f Aw		4101*	
79a	1	**LING**	12f Aw	71	4271*	

THE GROOVER 4 ch g £0

7	10	WARW	11f Heavy		1523

THE IMPOSTER 5 ch g £2278

63a	1	**WOLV**	8f Aw		707*	
53a	8	WOLV	8f Aw	63	921	
0a	13	WOLV	8f Aw	62	1037	
42a	8	WOLV	8f Aw	60	1393	
29	7	WARW	11f Heavy		1523	
40	5	WARW	11f Gd/Fm	44	2033	
0	11	CHES	10f Gd/Fm		2245	VIS
35	7	WARW	8f Good	43	2460	
23	9	CATT	7f Gd/Fm	43	2932	

THE JAM SAHEB 3 b c £0

43	6	FOLK	7f Soft		961	
43	12	LING	6f Good		1399	t
0	14	SALI	8f Firm	50	2025	t
0	18	NEWM	8f Gd/Sft	45	4536	

THE JUDGE 2 b c £0

70	10	HAYD	7f Soft		3786

THE LAD 11 b g £0

27	9	BEVE	16f Gd/Fm	35	2516
18	6	CHEP	12f Gd/Fm	28	2971

THE LAMBTON WORM 6 b g £0

33a	4	SOUT	11f Aw	36	560
26a	6	SOUT	12f Aw	34	641
28a	5	SOUT	11f Aw		672

THE LAST RAMBO 3 b c £0

55	7	REDC	7f Gd/Sft		1134
44	8	NEWC	10f Gd/Sft		1480
0a	13	WOLV	9f Aw	42	2080
29	13	BEVE	16f Gd/Fm	54	2516

THE LONELY WIGEON 3 b c £0

43a	9	WOLV	7f Aw		1035	t
39a	5	SOUT	8f Aw		1204	t
29	9	BATH	8f Gd/Fm		1435	t
28	6	HAMI	8f Gd/Sft	40	3380	t
14	5	HAMI	9f Soft	40	3806	t
19	7	NOTT	10f Heavy	39	4509	

THE LOOSE SCREW 2 b g £0

61	6	HAYD	6f Soft		1823
50	7	REDC	5f Gd/Fm		2142
67	13	HAYD	7f Soft		3786
41a	7	WOLV	5f Aw		4247

THE MARSHALL 2 ch c £0

67	7	BATH	5f Good		1088	
47	9	SALI	5f Good		1346	
0	17	NEWB	5f Gd/Fm		1782	t
0a	14	SOUT	6f Aw	61	4367	BL

THE MERRY WIDOW 2 ch f £0

0	13	PONT	5f Gd/Fm		2828
45	8	THIR	7f Gd/Fm		3128
51	8	BEVE	7f Good		3952
35a	8	SOUT	7f Aw		4154
0a	9	WOLV	8f Aw		4249

THE NAMES BOND 2 b c £4939

85	3	DONC	5f Gd/Sft		1048
78	1	**CARL**	5f Firm		1252*
89	4	BEVE	5f Gd/Sft		1761
69	14	ASCO	7f Good		2091
0	12	REDC	6f Firm	79	3327
54	12	NEWC	8f Gd/Sft	75	3704
65	8	CATT	7f Soft	72	4007

THE NOBLEMAN 4 b g £536

35a	8	SOUT	12f Aw		301	
35a	5	SOUT	12f Aw		387	
29a	3	SOUT	11f Aw	32	561	
23a	3	SOUT	8f Aw	26	584	
0	28	REDC	8f Gd/Fm	32	1296	t

THE OLD SOLDIER 2 b c £0

58	7	YORK	8f Gd/Fm		3729
61	10	CHEP	8f Good		3867
40	8	PONT	6f Soft		4372

THE OMALLEY 3 b f £0

0a	7	SOUT	7f Aw		741

THE PRIEST 3 b g £0

21	8	CATT	6f Soft		4255

THE PRINCE 6 b g £32920

97a	1	**WOLV**	8f Aw	90	663*	t
79	8	KEMP	7f Good	90	725	t
89	5	YORK	8f Firm	90	1327	t
89	6	SAND	8f Soft	91	1567	
74	12	ASCO	8f Good	90	2090	tBL

THE PROOF 3 b c £0

29	12	NOTT	10f Good	50	3524
0	14	KEMP	12f Soft		4040

THE PROSECUTOR 3 b c £11564

74a	1	**WOLV**	8f Aw		118*
47a	6	WOLV	8f Aw	73	613
79a	1	**SOUT**	6f Aw	73	689*
63	5	LEIC	7f Good	70	792
55	9	SOUT	7f Gd/Sft	68	857
0	18	WARW	7f Soft	65	1061
64	1	**HAYD**	6f Soft	62	1494*
61	4	CATT	6f Good	62	1665
63	4	HAYD	7f Gd/Sft	66	3269
60a	7	WOLV	7f Aw	79	3771
51	7	GOOD	7f Soft	65	4080

THE PUZZLER 9 br g £1135

83	3	KEMP	5f Soft	83	1013
0	27	NEWM	6f Gd/Fm	83	1173
48	12	KEMP	6f Soft	82	1531
0	14	NOTT	5f Good	80	1871

THE REPUBLICAN 3 b g £0

0	9	NEWC	6f Soft		756	
14	9	HAMI	9f Gd/Fm		1195	
28	11	BEVE	10f Firm		1274	VIS
0	19	RIPO	8f Good		1858	
14	10	RIPO	8f Good		2834	vis

THE ROBSTER 3 ch c £1175

61	12	LEIC	8f Good		789	
60	2	BRIG	7f Firm		1333	
55	11	WIND	8f Good	65	1726	
0	20	NEWB	7f Gd/Fm	65	1787	BL
53	5	BRIG	7f Firm	60	2044	

THE ROXBURGH 3 b c £248

81	4	SALI	6f Firm		1181

THE SCAFFOLDER 2 b g £0

54	6	CATT	5f Gd/Sft		4253
68	5	NOTT	5f Gd/Sft		4503

THE SHADOW 4 br c £822

45	8	WIND	8f Good	60	854	
43	12	WIND	10f Gd/Sft	57	1100	
44	5	LEIC	10f Gd/Sft	54	1575	
43	7	BATH	10f Gd/Sft	50	2552	VIS
25	8	WIND	12f Gd/Fm	45	3049	vis
38	3	WIND	12f Good	40	3353	vis
68a	3	WOLV	12f Aw	65	4245	vis
47a	12	SOUT	14f Aw	66	4371	vis

THE SHEIKH 3 b c £675

58a	2	SOUT	8f Aw	56	555
40a	5	WOLV	8f Aw	56	613
33	9	YARM	11f Firm	56	2771

THE STAGER 8 b g £10179

28a	9	WOLV	8f Aw	59	38	t
59a	2	LING	10f Aw	57	203	t
68a	1	**SOUT**	8f Aw	58	329*	t
71a	1	**SOUT**	8f Aw	64	340*	t
69a	4	SOUT	8f Aw	70	418	t
61a	5	LING	10f Aw	74	575	t
76a	1	**SOUT**	8f Aw	70	669*	tvi
37a	12	WOLV	8f Aw	76	921	tvi
33a	11	SOUT	8f Aw	75	2634	tvi
60a	7	SOUT	8f Aw	75	2817	tvi

THE TATLING 3 b c £1744

88	18	NEWM	5f Gd/Fm		1172
102	3	NEWB	6f Good		1371
66	8	KEMP	5f Soft		1529
104	13	ASCO	5f Good		2065 t

THE THIRD CURATE 5 b g £3720

37a	9	LING	7f Aw	53	59	
28a	8	WOLV	7f Aw	48	187	
0	14	FOLK	10f Soft	51	965	
24a	7	SOUT	8f Aw	43	1421	bl
43a	1	**SOUT**	8f Aw	39	2379*	bl
49	1	**BRIG**	7f Gd/Fm	45	2729*	
37	9	BATH	8f Firm		3623	
31	13	YARM	7f Soft	48	4513	

THE TRADER 2 ch c £13460

71	3	KEMP	5f Soft		993
76	3	BATH	6f Gd/Sft		2550
77	2	LING	6f Firm		2760
85	2	BATH	5f Firm		2940
84	1	**NOTT**	5f Gd/Fm		3114*
92	1	**FOLK**	5f Gd/Fm		3446*
100	3	RIPO	5f Gd/Fm		3714
104	4	DONC	5f Firm		3900
86	11	NEWB	5f Gd/Sft		4454

THE TUBE 2 b f £0

15a	9	WOLV	6f Aw		4381

THE WALL 2 b f £0

20	8	WIND	5f Gd/Sft		1095
50a	5	LING	5f Aw		1740
35a	8	SOUT	5f Aw		2120
41	11	ASCO	7f Gd/Fm		3015
17	9	WIND	5f Good		3639

(continued)

62	8	BATH	5f Gd/Fm		3815
30	9	LING	6f Good		4097
0	20	NEWM	7f Good		4336
17	13	NEWM	8f Soft		4542

THE WALRUS 3 b g £1237

31a	10	WOLV	9f Aw		610
51	3	SOUT	10f Good		806
70	3	HAMI	11f Good		848
0	14	REDC	10f Firm	59	1299
48	7	CATT	12f Good		1661
50	5	LING	11f Firm	49	1911
35a	5	WOLV	9f Aw	49	2080
37a	2	SOUT	11f Aw		2381

THE WHISTLING TEAL 4 b c £1145

82a	7	WOLV	8f Aw	89	663
78	11	DONC	8f Good	84	733
85	3	PONT	8f Soft	83	875
74	7	SAND	8f Heavy	83	1042
0	16	SAND	8f Gd/Fm	82	2528
0	34	NEWM	9f Gd/Fm	80	4212

THE WIFE 3 b f £1305

66	10	YORK	8f Firm	81	1341
0	13	RIPO	8f Good	80	1598
80	3	YORK	9f Firm	78	2001
77	5	REDC	10f Gd/Fm	80	2157
77	5	YORK	8f Gd/Fm	80	2645

THE WILD WIDOW 6 gr m £17278

31a	7	LING	10f Aw		111	bl
0a	14	SOUT	8f Aw		869	bl
40a	2	WOLV	9f Aw		922	bl
47	2	WARW	11f Heavy		1523	bl
52	2	LEIC	8f Gd/Sft		1731	VIS
71	1	NEWB	10f Gd/Fm	50	1942*	vis
67	1	LEIC	8f Firm	56	2032*	vis
63	1	KEMP	9f Gd/Fm	56	2085*	vis
79	1	CHEP	10f Gd/Fm	68	2493*	vis
65	8	KEMP	8f Gd/Sft	74	2581	vis
75	5	GOOD	12f Good	80	3887	vis

THE WOODSTOCK LADY 3 ch f £4023

88	9	ASCO	8f Gd/Sft		1108
85	7	NEWB	10f Good		1374
91	2	HAYD	12f Gd/Sft	87	1832
87	4	NEWM	16f Gd/Fm	91	2600
81	8	GOOD	14f Firm	90	3153
76	10	NEWM	12f Good	87	4162
0	14	DONC	15f Gd/Sft	84	4451

THEATRE KING 6 b g £4035

103	3	MAIS	15f Soft		1897

THEATRE LADY 2 b f £782

62	4	AYR	8f Heavy		4322
76	3	NEWC	7f Heavy		4403

THEATRE SCRIPT 2 ch c £4251

98	1	DONC	8f Gd/Fm		3864*

THEATRELAND 3 b c £0

66	9	SALI	10f Firm	75	1177
73	6	LEIC	10f Gd/Sft	74	1735 VIS

THEATRO DANIELLI 3 b f £0

0	8	WARW	11f Soft		814 t

THEBAN 2 b g £678

72	5	THIR	5f Good		1161
65	4	AYR	7f Good		2161
71	3	CATT	7f Gd/Fm		2417
67a	4	SOUT	6f Aw	69	2948

THEORETICALLY 3 b f £3150

106	3	LEOP	8f Gd/Fm		1315
102	6	CURR	8f Gd/Sft		1626
0	8	CURR	12f Gd/Fm		2739

THEOS LAD 3 b c £3449

27	5	MUSS	7f Firm		2046
48	7	MUSS	5f Firm	52	2374
54	1	HAMI	6f Gd/Fm		2798*
53	7	AYR	7f Good		3364

54	3	MUSS	7f Gd/Fm	54	3593
0	16	PONT	6f Soft		4233

THERE WITH ME 3 b f £906

68	3	YARM	7f Soft		4387
51	3	MUSS	8f Soft		4519

THERES TWO 2 b f £4977

80	3	NEWB	6f Firm		3449
89	1	GOOD	6f Good		3661*
88	10	DONC	8f Gd/Fm		3876
77	5	SALI	6f Gd/Sft		4164

THERESA GREEN 2 b f £4967

39	7	SAND	5f Heavy		1046
0	13	BATH	6f Gd/Sft		1667
66	3	SALI	6f Good		1883
41	8	SALI	7f Gd/Sft	69	2468
71	1	KEMP	6f Gd/Fm	64	3075*
68	4	SAND	5f Good	70	3228
60	10	DONC	7f Gd/Fm	69	3860

THERMAL SPRING 3 ch f £1860

79	2	THIR	7f Good		1159
77	4	BATH	8f Gd/Sft		1669
61	9	CHEP	10f Gd/Fm	78	2450

THEWAYSHEWALKS 3 b f £0

15a	1	SOUT	8f Aw		1977	
0a	11	SOUT	11f Aw		2381	
0	13	WIND	8f Soft		2548	t
0	18	WIND	12f Gd/Fm	36	2887	t

THEWHIRLINGDERVISH 2 ch c £2220

58	10	REDC	6f Good		1893
58	9	CARL	6f Gd/Fm		2239
78	3	NEWC	7f Good		2521
72	2	REDC	7f Gd/Fm	70	2991
50	13	NEWC	8f Gd/Sft	71	3704
29	10	AYR	8f Soft	71	3990

THIEVES WELCOME 3 b f £0

58	9	RIPO	8f Soft		826
51	7	NOTT	8f Good	63	1414
0a	16	SOUT	12f Aw		4366
0	17	REDC	8f Gd/Sft	60	4499

THIHN 5 ch g £9104

54	2	LING	9f Good	53	1395
45	8	LING	11f Good	54	1743
54	3	LEIC	8f Firm	53	2032
48	9	WIND	8f Good	53	2367
25	8	WIND	10f Gd/Fm	52	2888
40	9	GOOD	10f Good	53	3663
53	2	SALI	8f Firm	50	3753
50	3	GOOD	8f Good	47	3885
62	1	BEVE	8f Good	53	3951*
65	2	BEVE	8f Stt/Hvy	59	4044
66	2	WIND	10f Gd/Sft	62	4291
53	8	BATH	10f Soft	64	4436
59	5	NOTT	8f Heavy	64	4506
66	2	MUSS	8f Soft	64	4565

THIRTY SIX CEE 3 b f £0

48a	8	WOLV	8f Aw		171
0	17	NOTT	6f Gd/Sft	60	1082
57	5	WIND	10f Firm		1293
32	13	BRIG	10f Gd/Sft	55	1509
38a	5	SOUT	8f Aw	52	1803
37	9	LEIC	10f Gd/Fm		2510
8a	10	WOLV	9f Aw		3498
26	12	WARW	11f Good		3691

THOMAS HENRY 4 br c £4396

65a	1	LING	10f Aw		110*
45a	6	LING	10f Aw		163
0a	12	LING	10f Aw	65	244
0a	11	WOLV	8f Aw		393
44a	6	LING	8f Aw		505
41a	6	LING	12f Aw	50	621
36a	8	LING	12f Aw		650
56	5	DONC	10f Gd/Fm	57	705

56	5	NOTT	10f Good	57	786	
41	10	BRIG	10f Firm		1210	
35	12	WARW	8f Heavy	54	1520	vis
48	3	LEIC	8f Gd/Sft		1731	
23a	5	LING	10f Aw	41	2212	
36	8	SALI	8f Gd/Sft	49	2467	
30a	3	LING	10f Aw		2587	
44	4	WIND	12f Gd/Fm	45	2887	
30	6	BEVE	10f Gd/Sft	41	3052	
34a	3	LING	10f Aw	36	3828	
37	5	SAND	10f Soft	39	4208	
44	1	YARM	11f Soft	39	4391*	
0a	13	LING	12f Aw	42	4486	

THOMAS SMYTHE 2 ch c £4079

42	7	KEMP	5f Soft		993
68	2	BRIG	6f Gd/Sft		1507
73	2	BRIG	6f Good		1648
68a	6	SOUT	6f Aw	74	2948
68	3	BRIG	6f Soft	73	4170
73	2	PONT	6f Soft	73	4235
74a	2	WOLV	8f Aw	74	4439

THORNCLIFF FOX 3 ch c £1627

47	11	WARW	7f Soft	77	1061	
64	4	THIR	6f Gd/Sft		1354	VIS
51	8	REDC	7f Gd/Sft		1579	bl
54	3	DONC	5f Gd/Fm		1843	vis
55	6	CARL	5f Firm	61	2280	vis
50	9	BEVE	5f Firm	58	2732	vis
57	3	REDC	5f Gd/Fm	58	2864	vis
58	3	RIPO	5f Gd/Fm	59	3180	vis
45	11	CATT	5f Gd/Fm	59	3203	vis
33	12	BEVE	5f Good		3956	vis

THORNTOUN DANCER 2 b f £2217

58	7	HAMI	5f Good		843
46	11	CARL	5f Gd/Fm		1252
54	5	AYR	6f Gd/Fm		2717
57	6	AYR	7f Good		2873
62	3	HAMI	8f Gd/Sft		3532
32	8	AYR	8f Soft		3990
62	2	AYR	8f Heavy		4323
62	3	PONT	8f Soft	60	4378

THORNTOUN DIVA 2 ch f £1574

69	3	NEWC	5f Soft		755	
44	10	HAMI	5f Good		843	
77	2	NEWC	5f Heavy		1006	
0	20	DONC	6f Firm		3888	VIS
65	8	AYR	6f Soft	79	3987	
56	6	AYR	6f Heavy	71	4305	t
0	12	NEWC	5f Heavy	71	4423	t

THORNTOUN GOLD 4 ch f £6560

45	4	AYR	8f Gd/Fm	45	1658	
37	9	REDC	8f Good	45	1892	
46	1	PONT	8f Firm	44	2180*	
0	9	HAMI	9f Good	49	2397	
29	11	PONT	8f Gd/Fm	49	2561	
43	2	AYR	11f Firm		2875	
48	3	THIR	8f Gd/Fm	49	2970	
46	5	AYR	9f Gd/Fm	49	3141	
44	5	HAYD	11f Good	46	3285	
47	2	AYR	10f Good	46	3368	BL
38	9	REDC	11f Gd/Fm	46	3636	bl
0	23	YORK	9f Good		3808	
31	8	AYR	9f Soft		3988	bl

THORNTOUN HOUSE 7 b g £0

11	6	NEWC	16f Heavy	31	4424	vis

THREAT 4 br c £6802

84	10	DONC	5f Gd/Fm	98	702	
0	28	NEWM	6f Gd/Fm	95	1173	
0	15	YORK	6f Firm	91	1337	
60	11	DONC	7f Good	86	1514	t
69	9	GOOD	7f Gd/Sft	80	1810	

THREE ... (continued)

69	6	SAND	7f Gd/Fm	75	1989	
48	13	KEMP	7f Firm	72	2261	
63	7	HAYD	5f Gd/Fm	67	3322	t
36	12	CHES	5f Firm	67	3512	t
62	5	HAYD	5f Gd/Sft	64	3788	t
71	1	**DONC**	5f Firm	64	3894*	t
75	3	NEWM	5f Good	71	4015	t
63	5	CHES	5f Firm	71	4073	t
70	7	YORK	5f Soft	73	4285	t
71	3	BATH	5f Soft	72	4432	t

THREE ANGELS 5 b g £924
72	2	MUSS	7f Gd/Fm	68	1431
62	5	YARM	7f Gd/Sft	68	1611
0	15	NEWM	7f Gd/Fm	70	2133
60	8	CARL	9f Good	70	2241
0	15	NEWM	6f Good	67	3613

THREE CHEERS 6 br g £26913
110	1	**MAIS**	15f Soft	1897*	
108	2	ASCO	22f Good	2153	vis
107	7	GOOD	16f Good	3106	vis
109	3	DEAU	15f Gd/Sft	3552	bl
105	5	DONC	18f Gd/Fm	3877	vis
114	8	LONG	20f Good	4264	bl

THREE CHERRIES 4 ch f £416
25	4	HAMI	9f Gd/Fm		1191
34	11	HAMI	11f Gd/Fm	47	1361
37	8	THIR	8f Gd/Sft	44	1718
0	14	REDC	8f Good	44	1892
0	19	RIPO	8f Good	41	2099
25	10	BEVE	7f Gd/Fm	40	2479
22	8	PONT	8f Gd/Fm	40	2561
30	4	CATT	12f Gd/Fm		2742
38	5	CARL	12f Firm		2826
26	5	NEWC	12f Good		3247
65	4	REDC	9f Firm		3326
29	5	BEVE	10f Gd/Fm	34	3656
22	14	YORK	9f Good		3808
24	7	REDC	11f Soft		4497

THREE CLOUDS 3 b c £560
95	3	GOWR	9f Gd/Sft	818

THREE GREEN LEAVES 4 ch f £11197
60	9	HAYD	12f Heavy	97	991
85	8	NEWM	10f Gd/Fm	95	1170
90	8	YORK	12f Gd/Fm	92	1307
90	1	**NEWM**	12f Gd/Fm		1695*
85	9	EPSO	12f Good	90	1850
89	3	YORK	12f Gd/Fm	89	2647
87	6	NEWB	13f Firm	89	2852
87	6	GOOD	14f Gd/Fm	89	3058
84	2	PONT	12f Good	86	3504
22	22	YORK	14f Gd/Fm	86	3565
55	15	DONC	12f Firm	86	3896

THREE LEADERS 4 ch g £277
0a	11	WOLV	7f Aw	47	583	
17a	6	SOUT	8f Aw	42	648	
26	11	NOTT	6f Good	51	787	
27	12	CARL	6f Firm	48	1257	bl
27	13	HAMI	5f Gd/Fm	48	1358	bl
40	4	PONT	8f Good		1498	
24	8	DONC	7f Good	43	1519	
35	9	CHES	10f Gd/Fm		2245	
39	4	HAMI	9f Firm		2397	
26	9	PONT	10f Gd/Fm	38	2556	
40	5	HAMI	9f Gd/Fm		2780	

THREE LIONS 3 ch c £11685
57	11	SAND	10f Gd/Fm	68	2499
67	1	**BEVE**	10f Good		2884*
66	6	NEWM	10f Gd/Fm	68	3166
67	4	NOTT	14f Good	67	3522
75	1	**KEMP**	14f Gd/Fm	67	3800*
68	9	NEWM	14f Gd/Fm	74	4213
83	1	**WIND**	11f Heavy	72	4529*

THREE OWLS 3 b f £3932
52	3	WARW	7f Good	3696
80	1	**BRIG**	8f Soft	4177*
73	5	BRIG	8f Soft	4420

THREE POINTS 3 b c £61763
107	3	NEWM	9f Gd/Sft	980
105	2	CHES	10f Firm	1246
104	4	CHAN	9f V	1753
108	4	ASCO	8f Good	2087
113	1	**NEWB**	7f Firm	2809+
114	2	GOOD	7f Gd/Fm	3132
114	1	**DEAU**	6f Gd/Sft	3724*

THREE WHITE SOX 3 ch f £4981
55	8	SALI	10f Good		1344
64	3	GOOD	10f Gd/Sft		1640
64	2	SAND	11f Good	62	1967
64	5	YARM	14f Gd/Fm	65	2195
65	5	KEMP	12f Firm	64	2872
66	1	**LEIC**	12f Gd/Fm		3219*

THREE WISHES 3 b f £980
94	3	CURR	8f Yldg	863

THREEFORTYCASH 3 b c £0
46a	4	SOUT	7f Aw		427
33a	5	SOUT	8f Aw		500
0	15	NOTT	8f Heavy	51	1024
0	12	MUSS	7f Gd/Fm	51	1148
43	6	BEVE	10f Firm		1274
22	10	PONT	8f Good		1865
34	7	BEVE	7f Firm		2731
25	8	THIR	8f Gd/Fm	42	2964
32	5	NEWC	12f Good		3247
17	7	BEVE	16f Gd/Fm	39	3406

THREEZEDZZ 2 ch c £18883
78	1	**WIND**	5f Good		849*
91	2	WIND	5f Firm		1290
99	6	ASCO	5f Good		2113
95	3	NEWB	5f Firm		2849
83	4	WIND	8f Good		3352
0	19	DONC	6f Gd/Fm		3862
93	2	NEWM	6f Gd/Fm	90	4214

THROUGH THE RYE 4 ch c £0
66	7	HAYD	11f Gd/Sft	93	1790 t

THROWER 9 b g £3479
56a	1	**SOUT**	16f Aw	50	470*
55a	4	SOUT	16f Aw	56	535
41a	5	WOLV	12f Aw	53	608
42	8	DONC	10f Gd/Fm	53	705
34	11	AYR	11f Soft	51	3963
50	3	CHES	16f Soft	51	4071

THUNDER SKY 4 b c £3303
75a	8	NAD	8f Dirt		764	
75	4	YARM	8f Good		1771	
68	5	YORK	10f Good		1985	
75	1	**FOLK**	7f Gd/Fm		2293*	VIS
0	19	NEWM	7f Gd/Fm	80	2616	vis
77	8	KEMP	8f Firm	80	2870	vis
75	5	YARM	7f Good	77	3238	vis
67	7	YARM	8f Firm	75	3936	vis

THUNDERED 2 gr c £0
57	7	EPSO	7f Good	3412
27	10	KEMP	8f Soft	4036

THUNDERING PAPOOSE 5 b m £0
18	11	NOTT	10f Good	38	3524

THUNDERING SURF 3 b c £12596
74	7	LEIC	8f Good		789
81	8	NEWM	10f Gd/Fm		1697
84	1	**SAND**	10f Gd/Fm	75	2499*
79	3	NEWB	10f Firm		3453
80	5	KEMP	10f Gd/Fm	83	3794
86	4	NEWM	10f Good	82	4197
81	3	YARM	10f Soft	83	4392
83	2	YARM	19f Good		4515

THUNDERMILL 2 ch c £697
67	5	SAND	7f Good		2474
79	3	KEMP	7f Firm		2867
82	6	DONC	8f Gd/Fm		3864
73	8	GOOD	8f Soft	81	4076

THWAAB 8 b g £10473
34	10	HAMI	6f Firm		1239	
28	6	CARL	7f Firm	45	2282	bl
49	1	**CARL**	7f Firm	41	2823*	
48	1	**REDC**	8f Gd/Fm	41	2861*	bl
58	1	**REDC**	8f Firm	54	3309*	bl
43	7	REDC	7f Firm	54	3328	bl

TIBBIE 2 b f £0
58	11	NEWM	6f Gd/Fm		4209
64	5	BATH	8f Soft		4429

TIC TAC MAC 3 b c £0
0a	11	LING	7f Aw		164
6a	10	LING	10f Aw		204
0	11	LING	11f Firm	35	1914

TICCATOO 2 br f £3461
75a	1	**SOUT**	5f Aw		865*
67	9	DONC	5f Gd/Sft		1067
59	10	NOTT	5f Gd/Fm		1641
43	8	CHES	5f Good	70	2665
62	2	LEIC	5f Gd/Fm	64	2915
39	7	NOTT	5f Good	62	3519
51	9	LEIC	6f Gd/Sft	60	4030
34	10	NOTT	6f Heavy		4410

TICK TOCK 3 ch c £2115
47	7	CARL	5f Firm		1256	
44	7	NOTT	5f Gd/Sft		1368	
55	2	BRIG	5f Soft	55	1512	
54	2	AYR	5f Gd/Fm	51	1629	
38	11	HAMI	5f Gd/Fm	55	1910	
49	9	WARW	5f Gd/Fm	54	2252	
0	14	HAYD	5f Gd/Fm	52	2505	
61	4	CATT	5f Good		3441	VIS
35	12	THIR	5f Gd/Sft	49	3781	vis
41	8	CHEP	5f Good	49	3872	
56	6	REDC	5f Gd/Fm	49	4220	vis
47	3	AYR	5f Heavy	46	4307	vis
40	8	NEWB	5f Gd/Sft	46	4459	vis

TICKER 2 b c £402
76	3	MUSS	5f Gd/Fm	1146
70	6	AYR	5f Gd/Fm	1653

TICKLE 2 b f £11698
47	9	LING	6f Good		2588
73	2	WIND	6f Good		3187
70	2	BATH	5f Gd/Fm		3513
72	1	**YORK**	6f Good		3812*
79	1	**LING**	6f Soft	73	4269*

TICKLISH 4 b f £465
64	3	LING	7f Gd/Sft		838
62	7	EPSO	6f Heavy	68	1028

TIERRA DEL FUEGO 6 b m £0
2a	11	SOUT	8f Aw	38	326
11a	7	SOUT	11f Aw		670

TIGER GRASS 4 gr c £0
8	10	SOUT	10f Soft	58	1608
43	6	WARW	12f Gd/Fm	56	2254

TIGER IMP 4 b g £2772
56	10	LING	5f Gd/Sft	72	1264	
61	6	NEWB	5f Gd/Fm	70	3176	
0	12	ASCO	5f Good	67	3341	
70	1	**FOLK**	5f Gd/Fm		3584*	t
56	11	CHEP	5f Good	68	3872	t

TIGER PRINCESS 3 b m £0
0a	14	SOUT	7f Aw	278

TIGER ROYAL 4 gr g £8400
107	3	CURR	6f Soft		4398 bl
105	2	LEOP	6f Heavy	102	4555 bl

TIGER TALK 4 ch c £0

0	15	GOOD	7f Gd/Sft	80	1483	BL
0	11	LING	11f Good	75	1743	
0	12	WIND	8f Gd/Fm	72	2051	
13	14	HAYD	11f Gd/Fm	65	2453	VIS
0	16	WIND	10f Soft	65	2544	vis
41	5	BEVE	12f Gd/Sft	57	3053	
46	8	BEVE	12f Gd/Fm		3654	

TIGHTROPE 5 b g £11786

59a	2	LING	10f Aw		1	
43a	8	SOUT	11f Aw	60	131	
63a	2	WOLV	9f Aw	58	172	
63a	4	WOLV	9f Aw	65	230	
48a	6	LING	10f Aw	64	244	
63a	3	WOLV	9f Aw	64	271	
36a	8	WOLV	9f Aw	64	309	VIS
0a	12	WOLV	9f Aw	62	611	
70a	1	LING	10f Aw	62	632*	
0	18	NEWC	10f Soft	64	757	
0	14	HAMI	9f Good	57	846	
0a	11	WOLV	9f Aw		922	

TIGONTIME 3 b f £0

0	9	BEVE	10f Gd/Fm		3672
29	8	CATT	7f Soft		4005

TIGRE 3 b c £6190

80	4	THIR	7f Good		1159
0	19	GOOD	9f Gd/Sft	85	1452
53	8	EPSO	10f Gd/Sft	82	1831
83	2	AYR	10f Gd/Fm		2722
83	1	RIPO	10f Gd/Fm		3012*
81	3	REDC	11f Firm	82	3329

TIHEROS GLENN 4 ch g £0

0	15	PONT	8f Heavy		942

TIJIYR 4 gr c £7685

113	2	DEAU	10f Good		3370

TIKRAM 3 ch c £4124

82	7	NEWM	10f Gd/Fm		1697
83	3	GOOD	10f Soft		4081
90	1	NOTT	10f Heavy		4408*

TILER 8 br g £0

0	P	MUSS	7f Firm		2046

TILIA 4 b f £0

0	13	SALI	6f Gd/Fm	49	2230
32	11	BRIG	5f Soft	49	2428

TILLERMAN 4 b c £88366

100	3	ASCO	8f Gd/Sft		1112
106	5	ASCO	8f Good	100	2090
101	11	NEWM	7f Gd/Fm	103	2616
112	1	ASCO	7f Gd/Fm	103	2997*
104	6	NEWB	7f Firm		3452

TIMAHS 4 b c £166667

112	1	KRAN	10f Good		656*

TIMBOROA 4 b c £192261

115	1	CAPA	10f Good		1321*
112	5	DEAU	8f Gd/Fm		3544

TIME 3 b g £0

24a	9	LING	6f Aw		221

TIME AND AGAIN 4 ch f £0

0a	12	SOUT	6f Aw		199
20a	8	SOUT	7f Aw		249
0	13	MUSS	8f Gd/Fm	28	3746

TIME AWAY 2 b f £5731

91	2	NEWM	7f Good		3607
92	1	SAND	8f Gd/Fm		3943*

TIME BOMB 3 b g £1218

62	4	WARW	7f Heavy		1525
51	9	SALI	7f Gd/Fm		1886
0	15	WARW	5f Gd/Fm	56	2252
47	6	CHEP	6f Gd/Fm	53	2489
37	11	EPSO	7f Good	52	2794
0	18	LEIC	8f Gd/Fm	49	3095

25	10	EPSO	6f Gd/Fm	47	3405
34	10	LING	6f Firm	46	3759
52	9	LING	8f Soft		4273
47	2	WIND	6f Heavy		4526

TIME CAN TELL 6 ch g £3701

41a	4	WOLV	16f Aw	58	66	
22a	5	SOUT	14f Aw		124	
13a	10	WOLV	16f Aw	55	141	bl
25a	5	WOLV	16f Aw	50	348	
34a	5	SOUT	16f Aw	43	644	
48a	1	**SOUT**	16f Aw	40	737*	
49a	3	WOLV	16f Aw	47	918	
44a	4	SOUT	16f Aw	47	1416	
49a	2	SOUT	14f Aw	47	1501	
33	10	NEWM	12f Firm	45	1852	
49a	3	WOLV	16f Aw	47	2606	
27a	10	SOUT	16f Aw	47	2951	

TIME FOR MUSIC 3 b c £0

69	10	GOOD	5f Gd/Fm	82	3135
66	10	RIPO	6f Good	80	3698
61	11	YARM	8f Firm	78	3936
0	18	KEMP	8f Soft	78	4038

TIME FOR THE CLAN 3 ch g £0

0	16	HAMI	6f Gd/Fm	51	1941	
20	9	HAMI	6f Gd/Fm	46	2233	
0	12	REDC	5f Gd/Fm	41	2864	VIS
0	17	THIR	6f Gd/Fm	36	3144	
0	13	REDC	8f Firm		3330	
0	16	PONT	8f Firm		3506	
44	6	BEVE	7f Gd/Fm		3670	
22	10	THIR	5f Gd/Sft	30	3781	vis
43	5	YORK	9f Good		3808	
0	18	PONT	10f Soft		4088	
0	13	MUSS	8f Gd/Sft		4135	
0	18	REDC	5f Gd/Sft		4220	
55	8	AYR	8f Heavy		4308	
35	11	DONC	7f Soft		4465	
0	8	YARM	19f Soft		4515	
43	9	NEWM	6f Gd/Sft		4535	

TIME IS MONEY 8 br g £0

0a	3	SOUT	7f Aw	36	1979
5	11	HAMI	10f Aw	42	2233
0	22	REDC	7f Gd/Fm		2994

TIME LOSS 5 ch g £0

39	11	CATT	14f Gd/Fm	58	779	
51	5	WIND	10f Gd/Sft	52	1100	
46	4	NOTT	10f Gd/Fm	52	1272	
37	9	MUSS	12f Gd/Fm	50	1432	
1	12	PONT	10f Soft	47	1705	
0	14	HAYD	11f Soft	47	1819	
21	11	HAMI	9f Gd/Sft		3375	VIS

TIME MAITE 2 b g £12078

66	4	BEVE	5f Heavy		974
63a	3	SOUT	5f Aw		1302
64	1	**NEWC**	6f Gd/Sft		1476*
66	3	LEIC	5f Soft		1549
57	5	YORK	5f Gd/Fm		1981
65	3	YORK	5f Good	65	2698
70	1	**HAYD**	5f Gd/Sft	63	3475*
68	3	HAMI	5f Soft	67	3802
58	13	NEWM	6f Good	68	4338
76	1	**NEWC**	5f Heavy	68	4423*

TIME MARCHES ON 2 b g £0

0	12	REDC	5f Gd/Sft		4496

TIME N TIME AGAIN 2 b g £3558

89	1	**HAMI**	5f Good		843*
77	10	ASCO	5f Gd/Sft		1107
91	8	ASCO	5f Gd/Fm		2113
71	7	CHES	5f Gd/Fm		2248
77	10	AYR	5f Soft		3959

TIME OF NIGHT 7 gr m £0

13a	12	SOUT	7f Aw	54	33

TIME ON MY HANDS 4 b g £554

30a	8	SOUT	8f Aw		45	t
0a	P	SOUT	11f Aw	49	131	tBL
0a	15	SOUT	8f Aw	49	177	tbl
45a	2	WOLV	12f Aw	43	260	t
0a	n	SOUT	12f Aw	44	370	t
0a	9	WOLV	12f Aw	44	408	t
0a	11	SOUT	8f Aw	42	497	tbl
19	13	RIPO	12f Soft	34	822	t
36	6	BEVE	8f Heavy		973	bl
0	18	REDC	7f Gd/Sft		1132	tbl

TIME PROOF 2 b g £0

54	7	THIR	7f Gd/Fm		3347
44	11	THIR	7f Gd/Fm		3617
0	11	PONT	6f Soft		4082

TIME TEMPTRESS 4 b f £1298

4a	11	SOUT	8f Aw	60	648
27a	7	SOUT	8f Aw	55	1303
50	8	THIR	8f Gd/Fm	60	2062
43	2	RIPO	10f Soft		2538
48	2	CATT	12f Gd/Fm		2742

TIME TO FLY 7 b g £231

0	19	NOTT	6f Good	44	787	bl
0	14	NEWC	7f Firm	44	2340	bl
39	5	NEWC	10f Good	41	2525	bl
14	12	DONC	5f Gd/Fm	42	2753	bl
62	4	BEVE	5f Gd/Sft		3056	bl
33	10	REDC	6f Firm	42	3312	bl
0	16	THIR	5f Gd/Fm	40	3619	bl
34	6	BEVE	5f Gd/Fm	43	3653	bl
46	9	BEVE	5f Sft/Hvy		4043	bl
0	11	CHES	6f Soft		4069	bl
0	14	REDC	5f Gd/Fm		4220	bl
66	8	DONC	7f Soft		4465	bl

TIME TO REMEMBER 2 b c £5628

66	3	PONT	6f Good		2363
78	1	**PONT**	6f Gd/Fm		3223*
80	4	YORK	7f Good	78	3542
62	6	YORK	6f Good	80	3807

TIME TO SKIP 3 b f £0

0	14	LEIC	8f Gd/Fm		3094
0	17	WARW	11f Gd/Fm		3691

TIME TO WYN 4 b c £508

0a	15	SOUT	8f Aw	48	2380
30	9	HAYD	8f Good	46	3288
40	5	HAYD	11f Gd/Sft	42	3480
21	6	NEWC	8f Heavy	40	4406
41	2	MUSS	9f Soft	40	4523

TIME VALLY 3 ch f £7554

65	7	NEWB	7f Gd/Fm	66	1405
72	1	**NEWM**	7f Firm	64	1855*
53	9	KEMP	8f Gd/Fm	71	2084
67	5	DONC	7f Gd/Fm	71	2612
67	5	NEWM	7f Gd/Fm	70	2855
70	4	NEWM	8f Gd/Fm	70	3317
51	9	GOOD	9f Good	70	3658
0	13	NOTT	8f Heavy	69	4414

TIMELESS CHICK 3 ch f £2426

35a	9	SOUT	8f Aw	55	555	
28a	9	WOLV	9f Aw	51	709	
44	4	SOUT	10f Good		806	VIS
47	3	NOTT	8f Gd/Sft	48	1365	bl
36	7	YARM	8f Good	48	1772	bl
43	5	NOTT	8f Gd/Fm	47	2187	bl
57	1	**WARW**	8f Good	47	2460*	vis
50	10	LEIC	7f Gd/Fm	57	2918	vis
47	6	PONT	8f Gd/Fm	57	3226	vis
34	10	BRIG	8f Firm	55	3561	vis

TIMELESS FARRIER 2 b c £0

56	6	BRIG	5f Firm		2039
70	6	LING	5f Gd/Fm		2214
62	7	SAND	5f Gd/Fm		2933

TIMELESS QUEST 3 ch f £0 — and preceding entry

48	7	RIPO	5f Gd/Fm		3710	t
74a	4	WOLV	6f Aw		4379	

TIMELESS QUEST 3 ch f £0

0a	15	SOUT	7f Aw	60	1202	
0	15	NOTT	8f Gd/Sft	50	1365	
0	19	REDC	6f Gd/Sft	45	1578	

TIMES SQUARE 2 b c £10800

79	4	WIND	5f Heavy		932	
81	3	DONC	6f Gd/Sft		1067	
82	1	CATT	6f Gd/Fm		2926*	
62	7	NEWC	7f Good	78	3246	
87	1	NEWB	7f Gd/Fm	78	3486*	
80	8	NEWM	6f Gd/Fm	86	3630	BL
80	8	WARW	7f Good	86	3913	

TIMI 3 b f £118533

107	2	CAPA	8f Heavy		1117	
107	1	SAN	11f Good		1459*	

TIMIDJAR 7 b g £0

24a	10	WOLV	12f Aw	60	260	VIS

TINAS ROYALE 4 b f £0

38	5	BRIG	5f Gd/Sft	50	897	
33	12	MUSS	5f Gd/Fm	50	1143	
0	15	HAMI	6f Firm		1239	
0	14	REDC	6f Gd/Sft	43	1578	
0	17	BATH	6f Firm	39	1994	
0	16	WARW	5f Gd/Sft	35	2252	
0	17	NOTT	6f Gd/Fm		2680	
21a	6	SOUT	6f Aw		2819	
0	16	YARM	6f Gd/Fm	28	3966	

TING 3 b g £250

58a	5	SOUT	5f Aw	62	202	
52a	4	WOLV	7f Aw	59	294	
33a	6	LING	8f Aw	56	355	
32a	11	SOUT	8f Aw	54	555	
48a	5	WOLV	8f Aw	51	4021	

TINKERS CLOUGH 3 b g £0

0	8	PONT	10f Gd/Sft		1103	
9a	10	SOUT	6f Aw		2299	
0a	9	WOLV	8f Aw		2602	

TINKERS SURPRISE 6 b g £275

41a	9	SOUT	5f Aw		71	
40a	6	WOLV	5f Aw	46	116	bl
34a	5	WOLV	5f Aw	43	291	bl
36a	3	WOLV	5f Aw	40	351	bl
44a	6	WOLV	5f Aw		379	bl
52a	5	WOLV	6f Aw		533	bl
29a	6	WOLV	5f Aw	40	563	bl
40a	4	WOLV	5f Aw		639	bl

TINSEL WHISTLE 3 b c £0

0	14	WIND	6f Firm	76	1289	
65	6	KEMP	6f Gd/Fm	74	1925	
48	6	BRIG	6f Firm	74	2042	
39	7	KEMP	6f Gd/Fm		2747	

TINY MIND 2 b c £0

0a	9	SOUT	5f Aw		1302	
8a	7	SOUT	6f Aw		1420	
12	11	CATT	6f Soft		1679	
0	8	REDC	6f Firm		3307	
0	11	NEWC	8f Soft		3706	VIS

TINY TIM 2 b g £0

54	6	BATH	6f Firm		2784	
62	4	SALI	7f Gd/Fm		3388	
63	8	EPSO	7f Good		3760	
0	17	LING	7f Firm	64	4191	

TIP THE SCALES 2 b c £1060

62	10	DONC	6f Good		1513	
61	5	AYR	7f Good		2161	
52	7	THIR	7f Gd/Fm		3128	VIS
65	2	NEWM	7f Firm		3296	vis

TIPPERARY SUNSET 6 gr g £9438

32	9	NEWC	8f Heavy	63	1007	
51	7	BEVE	8f Firm	62	1279	
60	2	LEIC	8f Soft	60	1547	
59	3	BEVE	9f Gd/Sft	60	1762	
52	6	BEVE	7f Firm	60	1920	
61	6	CARL	8f Gd/Fm	60	2242	
61	4	NEWM	8f Good	60	2564	
59	4	BEVE	8f Gd/Sft	60	3054	
64	1	BEVE	7f Gd/Fm	59	3652*	BL
65	4	LEIC	7f Firm	63	3839	bl
54	12	AYR	7f Soft	63	3992	bl
43	16	REDC	7f Gd/Sft	63	4498	bl

TIRANA 2 b c £0

50	12	DONC	5f Gd/Sft		1067	
46	9	NOTT	6f Good		1408	
50	7	SOUT	6f Soft		1602	
48a	4	WOLV	8f Aw	49	4439	

TISSALY 2 b f £2726

86	2	YARM	7f Good		3027	
80	3	YARM	7f Good		3237	
80	6	YARM	6f Firm		3938	

TISSIFER 4 b c £9998

96	2	LEIC	7f Gd/Sft		1574	
104	2	DONC	10f Gd/Fm		1841	
51	28	ASCO	8f Good	108	2090	
98	9	YORK	10f Good	107	2696	
98	4	NEWB	11f Firm		2851	
98	3	DONC	10f Firm		3889	bl
94	3	AYR	8f Gd/Sft	98	4013	
89	9	NEWM	12f Good	97	4162	

TITAN 5 b g £0

37a	6	LING	8f Aw		92	
12a	10	WOLV	8f Aw	40	227	
35a	7	LING	8f Aw		505	
28a	9	LING	7f Aw		547	
12a	10	LING	8f Aw	43	594	
41	5	WARW	8f Soft	46	817	
0	15	BRIG	7f Gd/Sft	44	896	
0	18	WARW	8f Good	41	2460	
43	5	CHEP	7f Gd/Fm		3253	

TITAN LAD 3 b c £0

0	15	BATH	10f Good	50	1094	
0	16	CHEP	7f Good		1972	
1	7	WIND	12f Good		2715	
0	12	BATH	12f Firm		3624	

TITIAN ANGEL 3 ch f £293

81	6	SAND	10f Heavy		1045	
89	7	NEWM	10f Good		1184	
75	4	HAYD	12f Soft		1493	

TITUS BRAMBLE 3 b c £3987

49	9	WIND	12f Gd/Fm	60	748	
0	13	WIND	12f Heavy	56	937	
39	9	BATH	8f Gd/Sft	54	1671	
42	6	BATH	10f Firm	50	2332	
12a	8	LING	12f Aw	47	2651	
40	1	YARM	10f Firm		2765*	
37	4	RIPO	10f Gd/Fm	41	3008	
52	1	WIND	12f Good		3351*	
43	5	BATH	12f Firm		3624	

TIYE 5 b m £0

27	9	NOTT	10f Gd/Fm	50	3111	vis
14a	8	WOLV	12f Aw	45	3494	

TIYOUN 2 b g £6021

70	3	NEWC	8f Firm		3601	
83	2	NOTT	8f Soft		3972	
84	1	PONT	8f Soft		4086*	
83	4	YORK	7f Soft	83	4279	

TO THE LAST MAN 4 b c £0

39	7	BEVE	10f Gd/Fm	58	3410	
35	11	REDC	8f Gd/Fm	57	3634	
36	9	YORK	10f Soft		4275	BL
29	8	NEWC	8f Heavy	50	4406	

TO THE ROOF 8 b g £0

61	8	CHES	5f Gd/Fm		2669	

TO THE STARS 3 b f £0

0	18	SALI	6f Firm		1181	
0	12	SALI	10f Good		1343	
21	10	SALI	8f Firm		2024	

TOBARANAMA 3 £3250

92	5	LEOP	14f Good		2909	
100	3	CURR	10f Gd/Sft		4241	

TOBLERSONG 5 b g £1581

43	4	FOLK	6f Soft	53	958	t
0	13	WARW	8f Soft	52	1066	t
36	9	MUSS	7f Gd/Fm	52	1148	t
39	6	DONC	7f Good	49	1519	t
43	4	NEWM	8f Gd/Fm	46	2130	t
46	4	GOOD	7f Good	48	2303	t
44	2	YARM	8f Gd/Fm		2411	tvi
31	9	CHES	8f Good	45	2673	t
36	4	BRIG	7f Gd/Fm	45	2728	tvi
33	15	REDC	8f Gd/Fm	45	2861	t
42	3	NEWB	8f Firm	42	3455	vis
0	18	NEWC	6f Firm	42	3605	vis
0	14	YARM	7f Firm	42	3939	vis

TOBOUGG 2 b c £169618

105	1	YORK	7f Gd/Fm		3730*	
119	1	LONG	7f Gd/Sft		4054*	
119	1	NEWM	7f Good		4354*	

TOBY GRIMES 3 ch g £0

0	15	WARW	11f Good		3691	
19a	10	LING	10f Aw		4100	

TOBYTOO 2 b c £0

0a	15	SOUT	5f Aw		1418	
0	10	RIPO	6f Good		1859	
0	12	NEWC	7f Good		2521	BL
34	9	HAYD	6f Gd/Fm		2700	
42	9	REDC	7f Gd/Fm		2862	
0	11	LEIC	6f Gd/Fm		3333	
0	12	BEVE	8f Aw		3675	
0	11	NEWM	6f Gd/Sft		4535	

TODAYS MAN 3 b g £0

0	5	CATT	14f Gd/Fm		2930	

TOEJAM 7 ch g £2196

26	7	PONT	10f Soft		1699	
0	15	RIPO	8f Good		1858	
39	1	REDC	8f Gd/Fm	30	2147*	VIS
33	5	NEWC	10f Gd/Fm	36	2309	
28	10	PONT	10f Gd/Fm	42	2556	vis
38	4	BEVE	7f Good	40	2882	
54	6	REDC	7f Gd/Fm		2994	
38	9	BEVE	8f Good		3393	vis

TOFFEE NOSED 2 ch f £1887

80	4	NEWM	7f Good		4184	
84	2	NEWM	7f Soft		4541	

TOKEN 2 b c £826

67	8	LEIC	7f Gd/Fm		3333	
70	4	KEMP	8f Soft		4036	
85	3	LING	7f Soft		4267	
51	10	BRIG	8f Heavy	80	4538	

TOLDYA 3 b f £10519

50a	2	LING	6f Aw		153	
56a	2	LING	6f Aw	50	242	
46a	4	LING	7f Aw	52	287	BL
56a	3	LING	6f Aw		334	bl
58a	2	LING	5f Aw		507	bl
62a	1	LING	5f Aw	55	526*	bl
58a	3	WOLV	5f Aw	61	563	bl
64	2	LING	6f Firm		3759	
62	4	GOOD	5f Good	62	3908	
67	1	LING	6f Soft	62	4270+	
62	6	DONC	5f Heavy	68	4570	

TOLERATION 3 b f £0

76	9	NEWB	6f Good		1371	
0	19	SALI	6f Gd/Fm	84	1887	
48	12	BATH	5f Firm	81	3209	

TOLSTOY 3 b c £7781

84	5	BRIG	10f Gd/Fm		1127
85	2	NEWC	8f Firm		2337
83	2	FOLK	10f Gd/Fm		3042
83	2	YARM	10f Gd/Fm		3381
86	2	LEIC	10f Firm		3838
83	2	MUSS	12f Gd/Sft		4133

TOM DOUGAL 5 b g £0

39	17	DONC	8f Good	80	715
69	8	HAYD	8f Soft	78	1490
71	5	AYR	8f Good		2138
64	12	DONC	8f Gd/Fm	74	2349
46	12	REDC	8f Gd/Fm	71	3634
66	7	MUSS	8f Gd/Sft		4135

TOM TAILOR 6 b g £0

44	10	SALI	14f Gd/Sft	57	4166

TOM TUN 5 b g £10922

76a	2	SOUT	6f Aw	74	47	
71a	6	SOUT	6f Aw	76	129	
75a	5	WOLV	6f Aw	76	435	
76a	2	WOLV	5f Aw	75	579	
81	3	DONC	6f Good	80	716	
30	11	NEWC	5f Heavy	80	1008	
71	5	YORK	5f Firm	78	1324	
76	5	CATT	5f Good	77	1662	
61	15	YORK	6f Firm	75	2000	
65	9	DONC	6f Gd/Fm		2580	
71	1	LEIC	6f Gd/Fm		3097*	t
75	1	HAMI	6f Gd/Sft	70	3377*	t
0	17	YORK	7f Good	73	3809	t
64	11	AYR	6f Gd/Fm	74	4010	t

TOMAMIE 2 b f £0

48	8	HAYD	5f Heavy		989
43	7	THIR	5f Good		1385
35	9	WARW	5f Gd/Sft		1706
19a	12	SOUT	5f Aw		2120
0	11	THIR	7f Gd/Fm		3127
33	9	THIR	7f Gd/Fm		3347

TOMASINO 2 br c £3757

79	4	AYR	8f Gd/Sft		4008
68	6	YORK	8f Soft		4281
83	1	NEWC	8f Heavy		4422*

TOMASZEWSKI 5 b g £0

52	7	NOTT	10f Gd/Sft	62	1364
50	6	LING	11f Firm	60	3282
54	5	YARM	14f Gd/Fm	55	3664
0	15	BATH	13f Gd/Fm	54	3819

TOMBA 6 ch g £27477

111	2	GOOD	6f Gd/Sft		1453	
104	7	BADE	6f Gd/Sft		1746	
105	3	DEAU	6f V		2574	
101	5	YARM	6f Good		3235	BL
93	9	YORK	7f Firm		3600	bl
115	3	HAYD	6f Gd/Sft		3784	
102	8	ASCO	6f Gd/Fm		4125	
113	7	LONG	7f Soft		4395	

TOMENOSO 2 b c £0

58	7	BRIG	7f Gd/Fm	3239
8a	10	WOLV	6f Aw	3496

TOMMY CARSON 5 b g £854

52	6	SALI	12f Good	52	1350	bl
52	2	SALI	12f Gd/Fm	52	1888	bl
41	5	KEMP	12f Gd/Fm	52	2081	bl
28	10	EPSO	12f Good	53	2793	bl
47	4	LING	11f Firm	50	3282	bl
35	11	SALI	14f Gd/Fm	50	3424	bl
48	6	FOLK	12f Gd/Fm	50	3586	bl
38	8	BATH	13f Gd/Fm	46	3819	bl
0	14	GOOD	12f Good	48	3887	bl

TOMMY LORNE 2 b c £600

74	6	NEWM	7f Good	3608
77	3	NOTT	8f Soft	3972

68	7	DONC	8f Heavy		4569

TOMMY SMITH 2 ch g £4767

47	7	BEVE	5f Good		1443	
60	8	BEVE	5f Gd/Sft		1761	
62	4	BEVE	5f Firm		1918	
68	1	MUSS	5f Gd/Fm		2200*	
70	1	HAMI	6f Firm		2394*	
59	6	DONC	5f Gd/Fm	71	2575	
59	5	DONC	6f Gd/Fm		2754	
31	12	BEVE	5f Good	63	3673	
39	11	HAMI	5f Soft	60	3802	VIS

TOMS DEAL 6 ch m £0

0	4	LING	11f Firm	3754

TOMTHEVIC 2 ch g £8931

68	4	PONT	5f Soft		1698	
62	7	PONT	5f Good		2360	
82	3	HAYD	6f Gd/Fm		2700	
81	2	CATT	6f Gd/Fm		2926	t
79	1	THIR	5f Gd/Fm		3143*	t
0	13	REDC	6f Firm	80	3327	t
83	1	REDC	5f Gd/Sft		3632*	t

TONDYNE 3 b c £3062

21a	7	WOLV	8f Aw		661
55	1	NOTT	6f Good	45	785*
41	6	CATT	6f Good	57	1665

TONG ROAD 4 gr g £985

20a	8	WOLV	6f Aw		63	
0a	14	SOUT	5f Aw	40	1806	
0a	12	SOUT	7f Aw	35	2637	
30	12	THIR	6f Gd/Fm	37	3144	
0	15	HAMI	5f Gd/Sft	34	3536	BL
36	2	THIR	5f Gd/Sft	34	3781	
8	14	AYR	6f Heavy	37	4327	

TONGA 3 gr f £0

14a	10	SOUT	7f Aw	88

TONIC 4 b c £3062

65	9	NEWC	7f Heavy	82	1011
65	7	NEWM	10f Gd/Fm	82	1150
76	4	SOUT	12f Soft	78	1604
75	3	HAYD	12f Gd/Sft	78	1788
72	1	WIND	12f Gd/Fm		1880*
79	6	ASCO	20f Good	77	2092

TONIGHTS PRIZE 6 b g £4501

79	1	WIND	10f Firm		1288*
73	4	NOTT	10f Gd/Fm	78	2190
72	6	YORK	10f Good	78	2696
62	7	SAND	10f Gd/Fm	77	3471
0	17	KEMP	10f Gd/Fm	75	3794

TONTO OREILLY 2 gr c £0

58	7	YORK	6f Soft	4283
62	9	YARM	6f Heavy	4479
68	11	DONC	6f Heavy	4575

TONY 2 b c £0

54	11	HAYD	6f Gd/Fm		2454
39	10	HAYD	6f Gd/Sft		3478
38	9	REDC	5f Gd/Sft		3632
0	20	PONT	8f Soft	53	4378

TONY DANCER 2 ch c £0

20a	11	SOUT	6f Aw	2635
0	10	CHEP	6f Gd/Fm	2972
47	4	NOTT	8f Heavy	4507

TONY TIE 4 b c £44676

50a	9	WOLV	8f Aw	74	137	
71	6	DONC	8f Good	74	715	
76	2	HAMI	9f Good	74	846	
82	2	THIR	8f Good	77	1160	
85	3	HAYD	8f Soft	81	1490	
86	1	AYR	10f Gd/Fm	81	1656+	
81	8	YORK	9f Firm	85	2001	
86	2	NEWC	8f Gd/Fm	85	2311	
65	15	YORK	10f Good	85	2696	
89	2	AYR	7f Firm	85	2878	
88	1	NEWC	7f Gd/Fm	85	2986*	
90	2	HAYD	8f Gd/Fm	87	3325	
92	2	AYR	8f Good	87	3365	
92	2	YORK	8f Firm	91	3597	
83	8	HAYD	7f Soft	93	3785	
0	26	AYR	6f Gd/Sft	90	4012	VIS
0	22	ASCO	7f Good	93	4112	
86	3	YORK	8f Soft	90	4284	
0	23	NEWM	8f Soft	90	4545	
0	16	DONC	7f Heavy	88	4574	

TOORAK 3 b c £0

66	7	WIND	8f Gd/Fm		1099
74	8	NEWB	10f Gd/Fm		1404
52	8	SALI	12f Gd/Sft	75	2470

TOOTORIAL 3 b c £0

41a	4	SOUT	6f Aw	4368

TOP BANANA 9 ch g £0

36	10	BRIG	7f Gd/Sft	61	896
35a	8	SOUT	7f Aw	59	1979
48	10	CHEP	7f Good	59	3873

TOP CEES 10 b g £0

0	P	CHES	10f Gd/Fm	99	1222

TOP HAND 3 ch f £355

68	4	KEMP	9f Soft	75	999
63	9	BEVE	10f Good	75	1448
39	10	PONT	10f Good	72	1866
51	8	CHEP	10f Gd/Fm	67	2450
45	8	THIR	12f Gd/Fm	63	3125
47	8	BEVE	12f Good	58	3954

TOP NOLANS 2 ch c £1721

77	7	NEWM	6f Gd/Fm		2132	
71	5	MUSS	5f Gd/Sft		2532	
73	3	BRIG	6f Gd/Fm		2724	
68	3	CARL	6f Gd/Fm		3079	
68	8	NEWM	6f Gd/Fm	79	3165	VIS
69	4	EPSO	6f Gd/Fm		3400	
45	9	EPSO	7f Good	71	3690	

TOP OF THE CHARTS 4 b c £3103

33	5	NOTT	14f Good	37	2008	
20	8	CARL	17f Gd/Fm	35	2244	
39	1	MUSS	16f Good	32	3099*	bl
34	7	THIR	16f Gd/Fm	40	3348	bl
36	4	CATT	16f Soft	38	4258	bl
0	9	NEWC	16f Heavy	38	4424	bl

TOP OF THE CLASS 3 b f £492

0	25	NEWM	8f Firm	68	1183	
0	16	NEWC	8f Gd/Sft	66	1477	
0	19	RIPO	6f Good	66	1600	VIS
0	3	WARW	7f Gd/Sft	62	1710	
0	16	REDC	6f Good	62	1891	
26	11	CARL	8f Firm	62	3574	
0	14	NEWC	7f Heavy	59	4428	
0	8	MUSS	9f Soft	59	4520	BL

TOP OF THE PARKES 3 b f £2513

64a	3	WOLV	6f Aw		2604
34a	7	SOUT	6f Aw		2947
61	2	FOLK	5f Gd/Fm		3584
36	8	THIR	6f Gd/Fm		3780
58	0	BEVE	5f Good		3956
44a	10	WOLV	6f Aw	63	4358

TOP OF THE POPS 4 b g £640

57a	2	WOLV	7f Aw	1038

TOP QUALITY 2 b f £0

54	5	REDC	7f Firm	3308
0	14	YORK	8f Soft	4281
21	10	NEWC	7f Heavy	4403

TOPAZ 5 b g £517

0a	12	SOUT	12f Aw	38	370
35	4	SOUT	10f Soft	41	1608
0	15	NOTT	14f Good	37	1874
26a	8	WOLV	16f Aw	34	2606
26a	2	WOLV	12f Aw	26	3494

TOPLESS IN TUSCANY 3 b f £845 (continued)

```
35a 6   WOLV 15f Aw        4024
42a 7   LING 12f AW        4186
```

TOPLESS IN TUSCANY 3 b f £845

```
0   18  CHEP 7f Good           1972
66  3   SALI 6f Gd/Fm          2472
36a 6   WOLV 6f Aw             2604
0   13  BEVE 5f Gd/Sft         3056
20  13  SALI 6f Gd/Fm      65  3293
48  4   BRIG 7f Firm           3529
36  9   WARW 7f Good           3696
0   14  WARW 8f Gd/Fm          3914
35a 7   LING 7f Aw             4331
```

TOPMAN 3 ch c £0

```
0   10  BATH 12f Gd/Fm         3517
0   5   LING 11f Firm          3754
0a  14  LING 16f Aw        40  4099
0   16  BATH 12f Soft          4434
```

TOPOS GUEST 2 b f £403

```
65  5   LEIC 6f Gd/Fm          3096
57  4   YORK 6f Good           3814
62  11  DONC 6f Gd/Sft         4449
```

TOPOSHEES 3 b c £0

```
53  6   LING 5f Good           2590
```

TOPSY MORNING 3 b f £2700

```
94  3   LEOP 8f Gd/Fm          2570
```

TOPTON 6 b g £24338

```
66a 10  LING 8f Aw     84      7  bl
84a 2   LING 7f Aw            104  bl
85a 3   LING 8f Aw     84    169  bl
86a 2   SOUT 7f Aw     84    216  bl
81a 4   SOUT 7f Aw     85    282  bl
87a 2   LING 7f Aw     84    337  bl
85a 6   LING 7f Aw     85    423  bl
93a 1   LING 8f Aw     85    463* bl
92a 3   LING 8f Aw     91    485  bl
71a 7   LING 10f Aw          593  bl
68a 11  WOLV 8f Aw     93    663  bl
76  2   DONC 8f Good   74    715  bl
0   15  PONT 8f Soft   76    875  bl
61  11  CHES 8f Firm   76   1250  bl
73  5   DONC 8f Aw     74   1840  bl
66  10  KEMP 8f Gd/Fm  74   1926  bl
70  8   NEWM 8f Gd/Fm  74   2133  bl
71  2   YARM 8f Gd/Fm  70   2412  bl
71  3   NEWM 8f Good   70   2564  bl
68  5   YARM 7f Firm   72   2768  bl
75  1   YARM 7f Firm   72   2899* bl
63  8   YARM 7f Gd/Fm  75   3384  bl
75  6   DONC 7f Gd/Fm  75   3880  bl
63  9   YARM 8f Firm   75   3936  bl
0   26  NEWM 7f Gd/Fm  74   4215  bl
72  4   NEWM 8f Good   73   4340  bl
52  16  NEWM 8f Soft   73   4545  bl
74  2   DONC 7f Heavy  72   4574  bl
```

TORGAU 3 b f £0

```
105 7   NEWM 8f Firm           1185
```

TORMENTOSO 3 b c £215

```
57a 4   WOLV 9f Aw             319
41a 6   WOLV 9f Aw             395
0   15  WIND 12f Firm      68  1292
37  5   YARM 16f Gd/Sft        1613
28  10  BATH 13f Gd/Fm     59  3518
68  5   CHEP 7f Gd/Fm          3682
25  8   BATH 8f Soft       51  4143
```

TORNADO PRINCE 5 ch g £36436

```
56  10  REDC 8f Firm       61  1296
65  1   THIR 7f Gd/Fm      60  2063*
66  4   CARL 8f Gd/Fm      65  2242
65  D   NEWM 8f Good       65  2564
71  2   ASCO 7f Gd/Fm      65  2999
63  7   CHES 8f Firm       70  3170
84  1   ASCO 8f Gd/Sft     70  4126*
```

TOROCA 2 ch f £28600

```
69  16  NEWM 8f Good   85   4348
67  14  NEWM 8f Soft   85   4545
109 2   NEWM 6f Good        4159
```

TORRENT 5 ch g £18645

```
60a 2   WOLV 5f Aw     58     40  bl
57a 3   WOLV 6f Aw            82  bl
64a 2   WOLV 5f Aw     60    139  bl
71a 1   LING 6f Aw     60    154* bl
73a 1   LING 5f Aw     67    205* bl
70a 3   LING 5f Aw     73    235  bl
71a 3   LING 5f Aw     73    312  bl
66a 6   LING 5f Aw     73    403  bl
69a 5   WOLV 5f Aw     72    491
67a 5   LING 5f Aw     71    573  bl
60  3   THIR 5f Good   60   1162  bl
48  11  THIR 6f Gd/Sft 61   1357  bl
59  4   CATT 5f Good   60   1662  bl
58  4   THIR 5f Gd/Sft 60   1714  bl
61  4   RIPO 5f Good   59   1861  bl
60  2   RIPO 5f Gd/Fm  60   2107  bl
59  4   CATT 5f Good   60   2418  bl
57  6   NEWC 5f Good   60   2525  bl
62  3   DONC 5f Good   58   2753  bl
60  3   CATT 5f Gd/Fm  58   3203  bl
61  3   BEVE 5f Good   58   3398  bl
62  1   BRIG 5f Firm        3562* bl
62  3   FOLK 6f Gd/Fm       3587  bl
66  3   SALI 5f Firm   66   3747  bl
65  5   YARM 5f Firm   67   3920  bl
72  1   PONT 5f Soft   67   4087* bl
66  8   HAYD 5f Gd/Sft 73   4107  bl
72  3   REDC 5f Gd/Sft      4220  bl
67  9   YORK 5f Soft   73   4285  bl
48  11  PONT 5f Soft   72   4377  bl
57  9   DONC 5f Heavy  70   4570  bl
```

TORRID KENTAVR 3 b c £9452

```
88  3   BRIG 10f Gd/Fm        1127
87  3   NEWM 10f Gd/Fm        2135
84  1   BATH 12f Firm         2327*
86  8   ASCO 12f Good  87     2674
82  9   GOOD 12f Gd/Fm 87     3088
68  5   EPSO 10f Gd/Fm 85     3415
89a 1   WOLV 12f Aw    83    4226*
```

TORROS STRAITS 3 b f £0

```
58  11  LEIC 7f Good          794
```

TORTUGUERO 2 b c £40655

```
65  11  NEWM 6f Good          1691
78  6   NEWB 6f Gd/Fm         1943
82  1   AYR 7f Good           2161*
85  1   SALI 7f Gd/Sft 81     2468*
98  2   AYR 7f Good    86     2718
100 4   GOOD 7f Gd/Fm         3086
99  7   DONC 7f Firm          3891
101 4   NEWM 7f Good          4158
```

TORY BOY 5 b g £547

```
48a 4   SOUT 16f Aw    49     51
48a 3   WOLV 16f Aw    51    135  bl
40a 4   SOUT 16f Aw    47    542
```

TOSHIBA TIMES 4 b g £0

```
0   17  RIPO 8f Good   50   1598
0   16  AYR 8f Gd/Fm   40   1658
0   12  HAMI 8f Gd/Fm  34   1907  VIS
```

TOTAL CARE 3 br c £8410

```
88  2   NEWB 11f Soft         916
89  2   WIND 10f Good         1200
89  2   GOOD 10f Gd/Fm        1455
87  1   KEMP 12f Gd/Fm        1929*
64  14  HAYD 12f Gd/Fm 89     2502
```

TOTAL DELIGHT 4 b c £11010

```
80  1   LEIC 10f Good  74    793* t
0   15  EPSO 10f Heavy 82   1031  t
66  11  YORK 12f Gd/Fm 82   1307  t
78a 4   LING 12f Aw    80   1677
83  1   SAND 14f Gd/Fm 80   1991* t
82  2   GOOD 14f Good  82   2305  t
0   12  SAND 16f Gd/Fm 85   2498  t
54  8   ASCO 12f Gd/Fm 82   3001  VIS
35  9   SAND 14f Good  80   3472  vis
75  4   BEVE 12f Gd/Fm       3654  t
56  11  GOOD 12f Good  75   3887  t
```

TOTAL LOVE 3 ch f £6738

```
60  8   NEWB 7f Soft          913
99  2   LEIC 7f Gd/Sft        1733
100 5   ASCO 8f Good          2150
89  3   NEWC 7f Gd/Fm         2274
90  4   ASCO 8f Gd/Fm         3340
80  11  NEWC 10f Good  97     3703
79  16  NEWM 7f Good   94     4195
```

TOTAL MAGIC 2 ch c £0

```
59  8   BATH 5f Good          1088
```

TOTAL TROPIX 5 b m £0

```
0a  10  SOUT 8f Aw     40    513  VIS
22  7   MUSS 16f Gd/Fm        1145
```

TOTALLY COMMITTED 2 b c £3262

```
0   12  HAYD 5f Gd/Sft        1488
76  3   KEMP 6f Gd/Fm         1924
77  2   HAYD 6f Gd/Fm         2454
73  3   EPSO 7f Good          2791
59  6   NEWM 8f Gd/Fm  80     2962
75  8   HAYD 8f Soft          3766
76  4   DONC 8f Gd/Fm  74     3879
```

TOTALLY SCOTTISH 4 b g £0

```
26  8   LEIC 10f Gd/Sft 54   1575
43  5   AYR 13f Good   49    2141
43  6   BEVE 16f Firm  44    2734
38  5   AYR 13f Good   43    3367
29  7   CARL 17f Good  43    3575
25  10  NOTT 16f Soft  39    3978  tBL
```

TOTEM DANCER 7 b m £8938

```
29a 9   WOLV 12f Aw    54    261
0a  10  LING 12f Aw    54    377  vis
0   18  DONC 12f Gd/Fm 60    699  vis
49  9   SOUT 16f Gd/Sft 57   860
62  1   NOTT 14f Gd/Sft 51  1087*
56  9   YORK 14f Good  59   1329
59  2   MUSS 14f Good         1433
60  4   MUSS 16f Gd/Fm 61    1686
60  2   CARL 14f Firm  60    2016
32  8   WARW 15f Good  60    2461
55  6   HAMI 13f Gd/Sft 58   3378
56  3   HAYD 14f Soft  56    3783
0   13  CHES 16f Soft  57    4071
0   10  YORK 14f Heavy 56    4299
48  3   MUSS 13f Soft  51    4521
```

TOTOM 5 b m £2070

```
73  4   WIND 10f Firm         1288
75a 3   LING 12f Aw    73    1677
69  4   KEMP 14f Gd/Fm 73    1928
70  4   SALI 14f Gd/Fm 73    2268
72  5   NEWB 13f Firm  73    2852
66  4   EPSO 12f Gd/Fm 71    3402
63  7   KEMP 10f Gd/Fm 69    3794
43  9   BRIG 10f Gd/Sft 68   4118
```

TOUCH FOR GOLD 3 br f £3770

```
56  7   GOOD 8f Gd/Sft        1449
66  1   NEWC 9f Good          3248*
48  8   BEVE 10f Gd/Fm 73    3676
```

TOUCH OF FAIRY 4 b c £253

```
91  10  DONC 6f Good          734
85  4   HAYD 5f Gd/Sft        808
59  12  WIND 6f Heavy         935
0   27  NEWM 7f Gd/Fm  84    4215  t
```

TOUCH OF THE BLUES 3 b c £37675

114	1	MAIS	7f Heavy		9*	

TOUCH THE SKY 3 b f £0
0	P	SALI	6f Firm	1175	

TOUCHY FEELINGS 2 b f £657
74	3	KEMP	7f Firm	2259	
64	8	SALI	7f Gd/Fm	3292	

TOUGH GUY 4 b c £5848
99	3	JAGE	9f Good	1323	

TOUGH MEN 3 b c £5549
76	5	GOOD	8f Gd/Sft	1449	
87	2	LING	9f Firm	1912	
95	1	DONC	10f Gd/Fm	2317+	

TOUGH SPEED 3 b c £630
101	5	NEWM	7f Gd/Fm	1693	

TOUGH TIMES 3 b g £1160
70	5	NEWC	7f Soft		759
70	6	RIPO	8f Soft		826
49	12	DONC	7f Gd/Sft		1072
70	2	NEWC	9f Good		3248
59	5	RIPO	10f Good	69	3702
0	12	YORK	10f Good		3813
36	10	AYR	9f Soft		3988 BL

TOUJOURS RIVIERA 10 ch g £8138
0	15	NEWM	7f Firm	65	2347
0	11	NEWM	8f Gd/Fm	62	2802
52	1	NEWM	8f Gd/Fm		3117*
55	5	BEVE	8f Good		3393
60	1	THIR	8f Gd/Sft		3775*
57	2	BRIG	8f Gd/Sft		4122
59a	6	WOLV	12f Aw	65	4226
56a	2	WOLV	12f Aw		4549

TOUS LES JOURS 4 b f £2370
63	2	REDC	7f Firm	60	1297
58	8	AYR	7f Gd/Fm	62	1631
0	12	REDC	8f Good	62	1892

TOWER OF SONG 3 ch c £4540
71a	1	SOUT	8f Aw		36*
60a	4	LING	7f Aw	67	112
69a	2	SOUT	8f Aw	67	125
42a	9	SOUT	8f Aw	69	213
50a	5	WOLV	9f Aw	69	392
59a	4	WOLV	8f Aw	67	495
66a	2	WOLV	8f Aw	65	566
57a	3	SOUT	11f Aw		586
42a	5	WOLV	12f Aw	66	640
0a	9	SOUT	11f Aw		670
41a	4	SOUT	7f Aw		741
34	9	SOUT	10f Good		806
0	16	BEVE	7f Heavy	57	976 BL
0a	12	SOUT	8f Aw		1505 bl
29	7	SOUT	7f Soft		1601

TOWN GIRL 3 ch f £0
69	7	NEWM	10f Firm	1857 t	

TOWN GOSSIP 3 ch f £3055
66	7	BATH	8f Gd/Sft		1669
65	5	SALI	8f Firm		2024
0	18	WARW	11f Good	65	2463
49	7	CHEP	12f Gd/Fm	60	3255
48a	3	WOLV	15f Aw		4024
54a	1	WOLV	12f Aw	49	4360*

TOY STORY 4 b c £1282
46a	2	SOUT	11f Aw		196
40a	6	SOUT	16f Aw	49	284
37a	3	LING	13f Aw		483 VIS
57a	3	WOLV	16f Aw		519 vis
0a	11	SOUT	14f Aw		668 bl
0a	8	WOLV	12f Aw		752

TOYON 3 b g £2302
59	6	PONT	6f Gd/Sft		1105
52	12	BEVE	5f Firm		1280
66	6	LING	6f Good		1399
63a	5	SOUT	7f Aw	67	2300

67	2	LING	7f Good	65	2591
66a	2	SOUT	8f Aw	63	2817
58a	3	SOUT	6f Aw		2947
60a	4	WOLV	8f Aw	65	3274
48a	9	WOLV	8f Aw	64	3499
56	7	LING	7f Good	68	4102
65	5	LING	7f Soft	68	4192
50	8	WIND	8f Gd/Sft		4292

TRACK THE CAT 2 b c £868
76	2	HAYD	6f Gd/Sft		3268

TRAGIC DANCER 4 b c £0
47a	8	LING	12f Aw	73	151

TRAGIC LADY 4 b f £0
0	12	AYR	8f Good	40	2136

TRAHERN 3 b c £12078
92	4	NEWM	8f Good		972
86	2	BATH	10f Good		1093
88	1	REDC	10f Gd/Sft		1582*
105	4	ASCO	12f Good		2148
65	18	SAND	10f Good	92	2475
63	17	YORK	10f Gd/Fm	105	3563
93	16	NEWB	10f Firm	105	3997 BL

TRAIKEY 8 b h £0
32	8	BEVE	8f Gd/Fm	51	3407
15	9	BEVE	7f Stt/Hvy	44	4044

TRAJAN 3 b c £2204
58a	4	LING	7f Aw		651
74	7	AYR	7f Gd/Fm	77	1631
51	6	NEWB	7f Firm	75	2814
49	7	BRIG	8f Gd/Fm	70	3261 VIS
69	2	EPSO	8f Gd/Fm	70	3405
60	4	LING	8f Firm	66	3580
70	4	EPSO	7f Good	70	3765
44	11	NEWM	7f Good		4018
58	9	BRIG	8f Gd/Sft	68	4120
26a	6	SOUT	6f Aw		4368

TRAMLINE 7 b h £0
33	9	WARW	15f Heavy	62	885

TRAMWAY 2 ch c £1070
85	2	DONC	7f Gd/Sft		4446

TRANS ISLAND 5 b g £77155
118	2	SAND	8f Heavy		1043
117	2	NEWB	8f Gd/Fm		1402
117	1	EPSO	9f Good		1847*
116	4	DEAU	8f V		2571
0	7	LONG	7f Soft		4395

TRAPPER NORMAN 8 b g £0
28	10	DONC	6f Gd/Sft		1073
0	14	BEVE	8f Good		3393
0	14	YARM	7f Firm		3921

TRAVEL TARDIA 2 br c £2781
73	11	LING	7f Soft		4268
83	2	PONT	6f Soft		4372
85a	1	WOLV	6f Aw		4548*

TRAVELLERS DREAM 2 b c £624
44	10	NOTT	6f Gd/Fm		1408
68	3	GOOD	7f Gd/Fm		2125
60	6	FOLK	7f Good		2620
58	10	BATH	8f Gd/Fm	66	3817
0	16	WIND	10f Gd/Fm		4290

TRAVELLERS REST 3 b g £0
0	12	SAND	10f Good		2531
78	5	WIND	10f Good		2889
0	10	HAYD	11f Gd/Fm		3265
0	19	SALI	14f Gd/Sft	69	4166

TRAVELLING BAND 2 b c £0
77	5	DONC	5f Gd/Sft		1067

TRAVELLING LITE 3 b c £4346
82	3	KEMP	9f Good		727
80	4	SALI	10f Firm	80	1177
84	2	NEWB	8f Gd/Fm		1786
0	28	ASCO	8f Good	80	2117

82	3	ASCO	8f Gd/Fm	80	3018
77	4	SAND	8f Good	82	3435
72	9	KEMP	8f Gd/Fm	81	3793
61	11	SAND	8f Soft	79	4206 VIS

TRAVELMATE 6 b g £0
79	7	ASCO	16f Gd/Sft		1109

TRAVESTY OF LAW 3 ch c £4089
73	12	EPSO	5f Good	103	1849
0	23	ASCO	5f Good		2065
80	13	ASCO	5f Good	100	2168
78	13	SAND	5f Gd/Fm	93	2473
70	12	ASCO	5f Good	85	2676 BL
79	3	SAND	5f Gd/Fm	79	2934 bl
85	2	GOOD	5f Gd/Fm	79	3135 bl
84	5	YORK	5f Gd/Fm	84	3569 bl
103	5	DONC	5f Gd/Fm		3874
83	4	YARM	5f Firm	84	3920
60	7	NEWB	6f Gd/Sft	84	4456
71	13	WIND	5f Heavy	84	4527

TRAWLING 4 b f £0
39a	8	LING	8f Aw	65	147
43a	8	LING	7f Aw		243
34a	10	LING	8f Aw	55	336

TREASURE CHEST 5 b g £298
0	9	NEWB	16f Soft	73	917 vis
64	8	LING	16f Good	68	1394 vis
61	8	WARW	15f Heavy	66	1524 vis
65	4	CHEP	18f Gd/Fm	64	1800 vis
61	9	ASCO	20f Good	63	2092 vis
57	5	ASCO	16f Gd/Fm	63	2173 vis
51	8	CHEP	18f Gd/Fm	60	2490 vis
53	6	ASCO	16f Gd/Fm	56	2953 vis
44	9	FOLK	16f Gd/Fm	52	3448 vis
0a	P	LING	16f Aw	48	4329 vis

TREASURE TOUCH 6 b g £23538
40a	7	SOUT	5f Aw	59	673
49	8	CARL	5f Firm		1256
0	15	THIR	5f Gd/Sft	59	1357 BL
61	1	CATT	6f Good		1664*
67	1	CATT	6f Gd/Sft	60	1815+
60	3	YARM	6f Good	81	1953
35a	9	WOLV	5f Aw	55	2078
60	1	CARL	5f Aw		2240*
62	3	CHES	8f Gd/Fm	64	2673
70	1	LEIC	6f Gd/Fm	64	2777*
72	3	WARW	6f Gd/Fm	70	2845
63	7	CATT	5f Gd/Fm	70	2929
72	1	CARL	5f Aw		3080*
74	2	HAMI	6f Gd/Sft	70	3377
70	4	CATT	7f Good	70	3440
59	15	YORK	6f Good	70	3543
67	6	NEWM	6f Good	70	3613
51	9	LING	7f Good	70	4102
36a	9	SOUT	6f Aw	52	4156
64	5	BATH	5f Soft	70	4432
72	1	REDC	7f Gd/Sft	68	4498*
71	3	DONC	7f Heavy	71	4574

TREBLE RED 2 b f £0
56	6	HAYD	8f Gd/Sft		4104
0	16	NEWM	7f Good		4336
0	16	NEWM	8f Soft		4542

TREMEZZO 2 b c £644
64	3	GOOD	6f Good		4079
40	11	BATH	6f Soft		4137

TREMOR 2 ch c £0
23	12	NEWM	8f Soft		4542

TRES RAVI 3 br f £7685
108	2	DEAU	10f Gd/Fm		3546

TRESS 2 ch f £224
58	7	LING	6f Good		3832
77	4	WIND	6f Gd/Sft		4288

TREVERRICK 5 b g £0

48	5	BRIG	10f Soft	55	4419	t
15	12	REDC	11f Soft		4497	t

TREWORNAN 3 b f £0

0	17	NEWB	7f Gd/Fm	77	1405
40	10	NOTT	8f Good	75	1873

TRIBAL PEACE 8 ch g £0

27a	10	LING	10f Aw		157	
27a	11	LING	10f Aw	49	224	
16a	9	LING	10f Aw	44	2186	
0a	12	LING	10f Aw	44	2212	BL

TRIBAL PRINCE 3 b c £6619

55	11	SAND	7f Soft	74	1569
65	8	LEIC	7f Firm	72	2026
76	1	**FOLK**	7f Gd/Fm	70	3445*
78	3	NEWM	7f Gd/Fm	74	3629
77	4	YORK	7f Good	77	3809
78	2	YARM	8f Firm	77	3936
50	11	HAYD	8f Soft	77	4094
72	8	NEWM	8f Good	77	4340

TRICCOLO 3 b c £18818

55	8	THIR	6f Soft		909
78	1	**SALI**	8f Good	66	1345*
59	5	PONT	8f Good	72	1495
81	1	**SAND**	8f Good	74	1964*
75	3	YARM	8f Gd/Fm	77	2412
82	1	**NOTT**	8f Good	77	3005*
77	5	SAND	8f Good	83	3435
82	6	NEWM	10f Good	82	4197

TRICKS 4 b f £0

52	5	WIND	8f Gd/Fm	55	1201

TRICKSY 2 b f £0

41	9	LEIC	7f Gd/Fm	2916

TRILLIE 2 b f £9550

76	1	**SALI**	6f Gd/Fm		2979*
87	1	**SALI**	7f Gd/Fm		3391*
80	6	GOOD	7f Good		3659
0	21	NEWM	8f Gd/Fm	91	4157
88	2	YARM	6f Soft		4390
72	7	NEWM	6f Gd/Sft		4535

TRILLIONAIRE 2 ch g £330

56	12	NEWB	7f Firm		2708
66	6	LING	8f Firm		3577
76	4	EPSO	7f Good		3760
60	11	NEWB	7f Gd/Sft	76	4453

TRINCULO 3 b c £17095

67a	8	NAD	9f Dirt		765
95	7	NEWM	7f Gd/Sft	108	969
108	3	ASCO	6f Gd/Sft		1111
106	4	LING	6f Good		1674
102	16	SCOT	6f Good		2065
103	4	NEWC	6f Firm		2335
101	8	NEWM	6f Gd/Fm		2615
0	21	GOOD	6f Firm	108	3152
89	7	ASCO	6f Gd/Fm		3303 BL
113	3	ASCO	6f Gd/Sft		4125

TRINIDAD 3 ch f £6452

101	1	**COLO**	5f Soft	4146*

TRINITY 4 b c £296

49	16	DONC	6f Gd/Fm	73	1074
63	12	HAYD	5f Gd/Fm	72	2701
55	6	WARW	6f Good	69	2845
65	4	NEWC	6f Good	66	3037
0	16	BEVE	5f Good	66	3398
55	14	AYR	5f Soft		3960
0	27	AYR	6f Gd/Sft	65	4010

TRINITY BAY 3 b f £0

6	10	RIPO	5f Gd/Fm	3462

TRIPLE BLUE 2 ch c £23842

88	1	**LING**	5f Gd/Sft	1260*
94	1	**KEMP**	6f Soft	1526*
94	3	EPSO	6f Good	1846
96	5	ASCO	6f Good	2067

100	2	SAND	5f Gd/Fm	2529
98	4	NEWB	6f Firm	2850
99	5	GOOD	6f Good	3105
98	3	KEMP	6f Firm	3797
103	4	NEWB	6f Firm	3996
86	11	NEWM	7f Good	4196
98	6	NEWB	7f Gd/Sft	4455

TRIPLE DASH 4 ch c £7060

85	5	ASCO	8f Gd/Fm		1112	
75	7	LING	7f Soft	100	1286	
80	13	GOOD	8f Gd/Sft	97	1450	
67	9	HAYD	8f Gd/Sft	93	1836	
68	10	SAND	7f Gd/Fm	89	1989	
87	7	SAND	10f Good	89	2475	
88	4	YORK	10f Good	84	2696	
80	11	GOOD	8f Good	87	3107	
86	5	NEWM	9f Gd/Fm	88	4212	BL

TRIPLE SHARP 3 ch f £4294

72	4	WIND	8f Gd/Sft		1428
80	1	**CHEP**	10f Gd/Sft		1796*
0	14	SAND	8f Soft	82	4206
73	6	DONC	10f Gd/Sft	78	4448

TRIPLE WOOD 3 b f £5002

76	5	CHES	7f Gd/Fm		1224
77	4	PONT	10f Good		2365
74	3	WIND	8f Soft		2548
71	1	**CARL**	7f Firm		2824*
65	11	NEWM	8f Good	75	3022
62	8	NEWM	8f Gd/Fm	72	3317
58	10	BEVE	7f Gd/Fm	69	3652

TRIPPITAKA 3 b f £673

59	7	NEWM	10f Gd/Fm		2135
52	8	YORK	10f Good		3813
59	3	HAYD	11f Soft		4089

TRISTACENTURY 7 b g £1089

78	4	SAND	9f Good		3230
76	4	HAYD	12f Gd/Sft		3479
75	5	SALI	14f Firm		3751
39	9	MUSS	16f Gd/Sft	65	4134

TROILUS 3 ch c £7655

75	8	NEWM	10f Good		957	
83	3	GOOD	12f Gd/Fm		1956	
80	2	DONC	12f Gd/Fm		2609	
80	2	YARM	11f Firm		2897	VIS
80	1	**NEWM**	12f Gd/Fm		3313*	BL
63	10	DONC	15f Gd/Sft	80	4451	

TROIS 4 b c £12226

67a	1	**WOLV**	9f Aw		189*
72a	1	**WOLV**	9f Aw	67	271*
14a	10	WOLV	9f Aw	73	309
72a	3	WOLV	9f Aw	71	611
54	13	NEWC	10f Soft	71	757
0	12	PONT	10f Heavy	66	943
60	5	BEVE	8f Firm	62	1279
40	9	CHES	10f Firm	61	1777
58	4	MUSS	9f Firm	59	2049
49	5	MUSS	12f Good	58	3102
59	2	LEIC	10f Gd/Fm	55	3337
75a	1	**WOLV**	10f Aw	70	3495*
0	16	YORK	10f Gd/Fm	58	3731
0	14	YARM	10f Firm	58	3941
51	7	LEIC	8f Gd/Fm		4033

TROIS ELLES 4 b c £325

0a	10	WOLV	8f Aw	37	431
31a	3	LING	8f Aw	40	596
25	6	FOLK	10f Soft	45	965
27	10	REDC	8f Firm	43	1300
26	5	SOUT	10f Soft	43	1608

TROJAN HERO 9 ch g £2370

48a	6	WOLV	7f Aw		61
60a	2	WOLV	8f Aw		82
60a	1	**SOUT**	6f Aw		201*

43a	8	SOUT	5f Aw		214	
25a	9	WOLV	6f Aw	59	226	
56a	4	WOLV	6f Aw	57	352	
60a	5	SOUT	6f Aw		389	
58a	3	WOLV	6f Aw		436	
42a	7	WOLV	6f Aw		465	
31a	11	WOLV	6f Aw	54	923	
34a	6	WOLV	6f Aw		1139	VIS
29	8	BRIG	6f Gd/Sft		1508	t
31a	6	LING	6f Aw		1913	t
13	12	NOTT	6f Gd/Fm	35	2193	
0a	15	SOUT	6f Aw	44	2385	t
0	13	WIND	5f Good	38	2716	vis

TROJAN PRINCE 2 b c £1437

43	13	DONC	5f Good		730
63	7	NOTT	6f Gd/Fm		1413
80	2	DONC	6f Good		1513
70	5	DONC	6f Gd/Fm		1838
61	6	SAND	5f Good	74	3228
49	11	YORK	7f Good	70	3542
59	4	GOOD	6f Good	63	3886

TROJAN WOLF 5 ch g £8269

70a	1	**SOUT**	8f Aw	57	85*
75a	1	**SOUT**	11f Aw	63	126*
76a	1	**WOLV**	8f Aw	70	255*
61a	4	LING	12f Aw	77	332
61a	5	SOUT	7f Aw	75	598
68a	3	SOUT	8f Aw	73	669
0	14	DONC	10f Gd/Fm	62	705
48a	10	WOLV	8f Aw	71	921
0a	13	SOUT	8f Aw	69	1207
43	8	LING	7f Good	57	1672
0	16	GOOD	9f Gd/Sft	57	1807
47a	12	SOUT	8f Aw	67	2121
50a	6	SOUT	8f Aw	67	2302
69a	1	**SOUT**	11f Aw		2816*
55a	5	SOUT	8f Aw		2950
17	12	YARM	7f Good	56	3238

TROOPER 6 b g £0

36	9	CATT	12f Good	60	3437

TROPICAL BEACH 7 b g £0

37	13	REDC	8f Firm	50	1296	vis
40	6	BRIG	8f Gd/Sft	50	1462	vis
39	6	BEVE	7f Gd/Sft	47	1760	vis
37	9	WARW	11f Gd/Fm	45	2033	vis
33	8	RIPO	8f Soft	42	2542	vis
0	14	BRIG	8f Gd/Fm	42	2729	vis

TROPICAL KING 3 b c £5545

58a	4	SOUT	6f Aw	64	365
58a	2	WOLV	6f Aw		434
58a	5	WOLV	6f Aw		549
55a	2	WOLV	6f Aw		624
62a	1	**WOLV**	5f Aw		659*
56a	1	**SOUT**	5f Aw		696*
49a	6	WOLV	6f Aw		706

TROPICAL RIVER 2 b c £0

50	6	KEMP	5f Gd/Sft	1079
0	16	NEWB	6f Firm	3980
0	18	NEWB	6f Stt/Hvy	4471

TROTTERS FUTURE 2 b c £0

63	12	YARM	7f Soft	4514
0	20	DONC	8f Heavy	4569

TROUBADOUR GIRL 2 b f £260

48	13	KEMP	6f Gd/Fm	1924
43	8	BATH	6f Firm	2328
28a	7	SOUT	5f Aw	2818
50	3	LING	6f Firm	3757
75	8	NEWM	6f Good	4345
45a	6	WOLV	5f Aw	4441

TROUBLE 4 b c £0

0	19	WARW	11f Gd/Fm	55	3915
0a	13	SOUT	11f Aw		4150

TROUBLE MOUNTAIN 3 br c £0
101	6	NEWM	7f Gd/Sft	110	969	
89	5	YARM	7f Firm		2389	
93	9	NEWB	7f Firm		2809	
0	16	NEWM	7f Gd/Fm	103	3315	
90	8	NEWB	8f Firm	97	3998	
86	6	NEWB	9f Sft/Hvy	95	4472	

TROUBLE NEXT DOOR 2 b c £0
| 25 | 9 | NEWM | 8f Gd/Sft | | 4531 | |

TROUBLESHOOTER 2 b c £3743
84	6	NEWB	6f Gd/Fm		1403	
66	9	NEWB	5f Gd/Fm		1782	
74	2	NOTT	5f Good		2009	
65	8	LING	6f Good	72	2589	
70	2	LEIC	6f Gd/Fm	72	2773	
61	7	NEWB	7f Firm	71	3175	
62	6	WARW	15f Good	68	3693	BL
72	2	YORK	6f Good		3814	bl
65	6	SAND	5f Good		3942	bl
72	3	LING	5f Good		4095	bl
0	15	LING	6f Soft	72	4269	bl

TROYS GUEST 2 gr f £1089
68	5	HAYD	6f Gd/Fm		2500	
68	3	PONT	5f Good		3223	
68	3	CHES	7f Gd/Fm		3508	
66	6	HAMI	6f Gd/Sft	74	3824	
31	8	HAYD	8f Good	72	4090	

TRUDIE 2 b f £420
51a	6	SOUT	5f Aw		1418	
0	14	BEVE	5f Good		3955	
59	3	CATT	5f Soft		4252	
0	15	NEWC	5f Heavy	59	4423	

TRUE CRYSTAL 3 b f £4865
85	1	KEMP	10f Firm		2258*	
85	9	NEWM	12f Gd/Fm		2857	
88	3	NEWB	12f Gd/Fm		3487	
77	11	DONC	15f Gd/Fm		3863	

TRUE NIGHT 3 b c £3303
| 79 | 4 | SALI | 6f Gd/Fm | | 2977 | |
| 79 | 1 | LING | 6f Firm | | 3579* | |

TRUE NOTE 2 b c £0
| 0 | 16 | NEWB | 6f Sft/Hvy | | 4471 | |

TRUE OBSESSION 3 br c £0
35	13	HAYD	8f Gd/Sft	76	810	
63	5	CHES	10f Gd/Sft		1779	
0a	8	SOUT	12f Aw	65	2123	

TRUE ROMANCE 4 b g £0
0a	11	LING	12f Aw		457	
20a	7	WOLV	12f Aw		519	
23a	10	WOLV	7f Aw		567	
0	11	NOTT	14f Gd/Sft		1369	BL
45	5	YARM	14f Gd/Fm		2194	

TRUE THUNDER 3 b c £6743
| 88 | 1 | NEWC | 8f Firm | | 2337* | |

TRUFFLE 4 b f £0
| 39a | 12 | LING | 7f Aw | 65 | 107 | |

TRUMP STREET 4 b f £5207
24a	7	WOLV	7f Aw	53	614	
0a	12	WOLV	7f Aw	48	711	
50	2	WARW	8f Soft	46	817	
29	5	WIND	8f Gd/Sft	48	1097	
0	14	LING	7f Soft	48	1542	
53	1	CHEP	6f Heavy	48	1557*	
0	14	CHEP	5f Gd/Fm	52	1794	
42	9	CHEP	6f Gd/Fm	53	3257	
28	9	BATH	6f Gd/Fm	52	3516	
37	7	BRIG	6f Firm	52	3528	BL
0	18	BATH	8f Gd/Fm	49	3821	bl
0	16	SAND	5f Soft		4207	
0	22	WIND	6f Gd/Sft	46	4294	

TRUMPET BLUES 4 br c £416
| 47a | 9 | SOUT | 6f Aw | | 389 | |

51a	3	WOLV	7f Aw		531	
0	15	NOTT	6f Good	55	787	
22	11	DONC	6f Gd/Sft		1068	
36	11	REDC	6f Firm		1298	
0	12	THIR	6f Gd/Sft		3780	

TRUMPET SOUND 3 b c £10188
94	1	BRIG	10f Gd/Fm		1127*	
85	7	LING	11f Gd/Fm		1284	
106	4	NEWM	10f Firm		1854	
107	2	NEWB	10f Firm		2851	
99	6	NEWM	8f Good		4180	t
93	10	NEWM	9f Good		4347	t

TRUMPINGTON 2 ch f £8005
61	8	WIND	6f Gd/Fm		1876	
65	3	WARW	7f Good		2459	
76	1	NEWB	7f Firm		2810*	
59	10	NEWB	7f Gd/Fm	77	3175	
63	4	BEVE	6f Good		3491	
61	7	NEWM	8f Good	75	3609	
75	1	WIND	10f Gd/Sft	69	4290*	

TRUST IN PAULA 2 b f £0
73	7	SALI	7f Firm		3748	
66	12	WARW	6f Gd/Fm		3910	
69	8	WIND	6f Gd/Sft		4288	

TRUSTED MOLE 2 b c £1001
65	6	HAMI	5f Gd/Fm		1189	
67	6	NOTT	6f Good		1413	
65	3	BRIG	6f Good		1648	BL
32a	7	SOUT	6f Aw		1974	bl
67	4	SALI	7f Gd/Sft	67	2468	
67	4	NEWB	6f Gd/Fm	69	3175	
43a	8	WOLV	7f Aw	69	3273	
52	12	BATH	8f Gd/Fm	67	3817	

TRUSTTHUNDER 2 ch f £5817
71	7	NEWM	7f Gd/Fm		1691	
80	2	LING	7f Gd/Fm		2182	
75	2	NEWB	7f Firm		2810	
66	11	SAND	7f Gd/Fm		2935	
87	1	LING	6f Soft		4188*	
79	7	NEWM	6f Good		4345	

TRUTH BE KNOWN 2 gr c £0
| 0 | 13 | BATH | 5f Gd/Sft | | 2550 | |
| 0 | 11 | WIND | 5f Good | | 3639 | BL |

TRY PARIS 4 b c £0
14a	9	WOLV	9f Aw	44	568	vis
0	20	DONC	12f Gd/Fm	50	699	
0	15	PONT	8f Gd/Sft	44	1101	vis
43	4	BRIG	10f Firm		1331	vis
35	4	YARM	10f Good	35	1775	vis
19	8	WARW	12f Gd/Fm	35	2255	vis

TRYPHAENA 5 b m £6000
| 83 | 4 | NEWM | 18f Good | 79 | 4353 | t |

TRYSOR 4 b c £3483
0	13	LING	7f Gd/Sft		1263	
62	7	WARW	7f Heavy		1525	
40	7	DONC	5f Gd/Fm		1843	
29	11	RIPO	8f Soft	54	2542	
30	12	NEWM	8f Gd/Fm	52	3118	
51	2	THIR	8f Gd/Fm	47	3344	VIS
57	1	HAMI	8f Gd/Sft	47	3534*	vis

TSUNAMI 4 b f £433
0a	11	LING	10f Aw		268	
30a	6	WOLV	9f Aw		433	
31	6	CATT	7f Gd/Fm		778	
20a	8	SOUT	8f Aw		869	
36a	3	SOUT	8f Aw	38	1419	

TSWALU 3 b f £0
| 0 | 18 | AYR | 11f Soft | 58 | 3963 | |

TUCSON 3 ch c £0
| 28a | 6 | LING | 11f Aw | | 1741 | |
| 0a | 14 | LING | 10f Aw | | 2587 | |

TUDOR REEF 2 b c £9538

74	9	NEWB	6f Gd/Fm		1943	
81	4	SALI	7f Gd/Fm		2269	
68	6	CHES	7f Firm		3169	
81	4	YARM	7f Firm		3940	
91	1	BRIG	8f Soft		4417*	
101	1	DONC	8f Heavy		4572*	

TUDOR ROMANCE 15 b g £0
| 0 | 15 | SAND | 10f Gd/Fm | 46 | 2527 | t |
| 0a | 15 | LING | 12f AW | | 4186 | |

TUFAMORE 4 ch g £4211
26a	4	LING	12f Aw		267	
63a	2	WOLV	9f Aw		360	vis
51a	1	WOLV	8f Aw	46	411*	vis
0a	12	SOUT	8f Aw	46	418	vis
50a	5	WOLV	9f Aw	57	516	vis
51a	3	WOLV	8f Aw		550	BL
52a	3	SOUT	8f Aw		684	bl
39	5	CHES	10f Gd/Fm		2245	vis
32	8	RIPO	10f Soft		2538	bl

TUFTY HOPPER 3 b g £9504
52a	6	WOLV	9f Aw		610	
51a	4	SOUT	12f Aw		643	
63	4	LEIC	12f Gd/Sft		832	
58a	2	WOLV	12f Aw	56	1142	
56a	2	WOLV	12f Good	56	1238	
67	4	YARM	11f Good	65	1770	
62	3	YARM	14f Gd/Fm	65	1949	
74	3	YARM	14f Gd/Fm		2194	
63	2	YARM	11f Firm		2386	
67	2	YARM	14f Gd/Fm	63	2416	
72	2	NEWB	12f Firm		2710	
59	7	YARM	11f Gd/Fm	65	2771	
61	4	YARM	11f Firm		2897	
69	5	NEWM	15f Good		3023	BL
65	3	LING	14f Firm		3489	
67	3	BATH	13f Gd/Fm	65	3819	
67	2	BEVE	12f Good		3954	
58	6	CATT	12f Soft	69	4256	
54a	6	LING	16f Aw	65	4329	
62a	2	WOLV	12f Aw	63	4443	VIS

TUI 5 b m £3449
26	5	SOUT	11f Gd/Sft	36	855	
37	1	BRIG	12f Firm	32	1332*	
39	5	WARW	15f Heavy	40	1524	
37	4	LEIC	12f Gd/Sft	39	1736	
12	20	NEWM	12f Firm	39	1852	
37	3	WARW	16f Gd/Fm	38	2037	

TUIGAMALA 9 b g £0
| 0a | 14 | LING | 12f Aw | | 4101 | |

TULSA 6 b g £714
35	5	EPSO	12f Good	39	2793	
36	5	WIND	12f Gd/Fm	37	3049	bl
36	2	CHEP	12f Gd/Fm	35	3255	bl
31	7	FOLK	16f Gd/Fm	37	3448	bl
26	11	EPSO	12f Good	44	3858	bl
0a	12	LING	12f Aw	38	4486	bl

TUMBLEWEED GLEN 4 ch g £0
| 0 | 13 | GOOD | 16f Soft | 65 | 4075 | bl |

TUMBLEWEED QUARTET 4 b c £0
77	5	DONC	8f Good	79	715	t
72	6	BRIG	8f Gd/Fm	79	895	t
0	19	ASCO	8f Gd/Sft	77	1113	t
70	11	NEWB	10f Good	75	1375	tbl

TUMBLEWEED RIDGE 7 ch b £40884
114	2	DONC	7f Gd/Sft		1049	tbl
108	3	LONG	7f Good		1617	bl
116	1	LEOP	7f Good		2070*	t
116	3	LONG	7f Good		2226	
105	7	NEWM	7f Firm		2343	tbl
107	4	GOOD	7f Gd/Fm		3132	tbl
0	P	NEWB	7f Firm		3452	t

TUMBLEWEED RIVER 4 ch c £1952

66 16 ASCO 7f Gd/Sft 85 1110
45 10 HAYD 8f Gd/Sft 83 1836 BL
52 15 NEWB 7f Firm 78 3981
77 2 SAND 7f Soft 74 4204
32 12 YORK 7f Heavy 76 4302
49 7 DONC 7f Soft 4461

TUMBLEWEED TENOR 2 b g £3194
77 5 DONC 5f Gd/Sft 1048
73 2 BRIG 5f Firm 1208
51 8 WIND 5f Good 2368
73 3 LING 7f Firm 70 3830
75a 1 **WOLV** 6f Aw 4381*

TUMBLEWEED TOR 3 b c £13978
63 8 KEMP 9f Soft 85 999
89 3 SAND 8f Heavy 83 1055
90 1 **NOTT** 8f Gd/Sft 1366*
88 14 ASCO 8f Good 94 2117
91 6 GOOD 10f Gd/Fm 92 2358
91 3 NEWM 8f Gd/Fm 91 2614
90 6 NEWM 8f Gd/Fm 92 2858
90 3 SAND 8f Good 91 3435
89 3 DONC 8f Firm 90 3897
70 10 NEWB 8f Firm 90 3998

TUMBLEWEED WIZARD 3 ch g £0
44 7 CATT 12f Gd/Fm 68 782
58 6 SAND 14f Good 2477
15 15 BATH 12f Gd/Sft 65 2554 BL

TUNEFUL MELODY 2 b f £0
42a 8 WOLV 5f Aw 4441

TUPGILL CENTURION 2 b g £263
47 4 MUSS 8f Gd/Fm 3740
56 5 BEVE 7f Good 3949
0a 8 SOUT 8f Aw 4152

TUPGILL FLIGHT 2 b f £0
49 8 PONT 5f Heavy 938
38 9 REDC 6f Gd/Sft 1577
0 12 THIR 7f Gd/Sft 3776
32 10 BEVE 7f Good 3953
26a 5 SOUT 8f Aw 4152

TUPGILL TANGO 2 ch g £6669
54 10 BEVE 7f Good 3952
80 1 **YORK** 8f Heavy 4297*
74 6 PONT 8f Soft 4375

TUPGILL TIPPLE 2 b f £998
62a 2 SOUT 5f Aw 2120
52 3 HAYD 6f Gd/Sft 2441
45a 4 SOUT 5f Aw 2818
0 13 BEVE 5f Gd/Sft 3055
28 11 BEVE 5f Good 53 3394 VIS
49a 5 WOLV 6f Aw 4359
30 9 MUSS 5f Soft 48 4561

TUPGILL TURBO 2 ch g £1740
32 3 YORK 7f Good 2693
59 5 NEWC 6f Good 3032

TURAATH 4 b c £3209
63 7 DONC 12f Good 732
88 7 KEMP 10f Soft 1014
88 2 SALI 10f Gd/Sft 2471
0 14 NEWB 10f Sft/Hv 90 4473

TURBO BLUE 2 ch f £0
53 8 SALI 5f Gd/Fm 2227
56 8 BATH 6f Firm 3205
46 9 FOLK 6f Gd/Fm 3443
0 12 BATH 6f Soft 4431
0 12 NOTT 8f Heavy 4507

TURBOTIERE 5 br m £7684
88 3 LONG 12f Heavy 1034
107 3 SAIN 11f Good 1378

TURGENEV 11 b g £882
0a 10 SOUT 14f Aw 124
0a 11 WOLV 16f Aw 34 576
0a 14 SOUT 14f Aw 668

---

0 15 BEVE 16f Firm 37 1276
42 5 NEWC 17f Gd/Sft 46 1478
21 9 RIPO 16f Good 31 1597
49 6 CATT 14f Good 1660
19 6 REDC 16f Good 1894
37 4 HAMI 13f Gd/Sft 38 3378
30 11 HAYD 14f Gd/Sft 48 4105
34 9 YORK 12f Soft 43 4280
34 2 YARM 14f Soft 4510

TURKU 2 b c £7649
89 1 **HAYD** 7f Gd/Sft 4103*
76 3 YORK 7f Soft 4277
90 2 NEWM 8f Gd/Sft 4531

TURN TO STONE 6 b g £0
14a 9 WOLV 9f Aw 35 637
6a 5 SOUT 12f Aw 38 682 bl

TURNBERRY ISLE 2 ch c £85100
104 1 **ASCO** 8f Gd/Fm 3304*
110 2 ASCO 8f Gd/Sft 4127
114 1 **CURR** 8f Soft 4397*

TURNED OUT WELL 3 b g £3509
32a 5 WOLV 7f Aw 45 450
34a 5 SOUT 11f Aw 40 536
41 1 BEVE 16f Good 40 2879*
47 3 NOTT 16f Gd/Sft 45 3112
45 4 HAYD 16f Gd/Sft 46 3476

TURNING LEAF 3 b f £7742
100 3 DUSS 8f Good 1229

TURNPOLE 9 br g £8658
75 8 DONC 17f Gd/Sft 84 1052
74 6 HAYD 16f Gd/Sft 80 1791
73 4 AYR 15f Good 75 2164
78 1 **NEWM** 16f Gd/Sft 74 2600*
76 4 ASCO 16f Good 77 4115
60 15 NEWM 18f Good 79 4353
35 10 DONC 17f Heavy 75 4579

TURQUOISE GEM 3 b f £0
53 7 SALI 7f Gd/Fm 2232

TURTLE 4 b g £0
0 15 NEWC 9f Firm 46 3603
6 10 NEWC 10f Heavy 41 4404

TURTLE SOUP 4 b c £3071
77 1 **NEWB** 13f Gd/Sft 74 1594*
71 5 GOOD 14f Gd/Fm 77 1959

TURTLE VALLEY 4 b c £3315
81a 7 SOUT 12f Aw 95 695
92 7 KEMP 16f Soft 95 997
79 10 GOOD 14f Gd/Sft 90 1484
94 2 KEMP 16f Soft 90 1527
92 3 HAYD 16f Gd/Sft 93 1791

TURTLES RISING 4 b f £654
0 19 DONC 6f Gd/Fm 66 1842
63 3 PONT 6f Good 64 2180
0 15 HAYD 7f Gd/Sft 65 2442
39 10 LEIC 7f Gd/Fm 2508 bl

TUSCAN 2 b f £981
65 4 GOOD 6f Good 2357
64 6 KEMP 6f Gd/Fm 2748
34 12 ASCO 7f Gd/Fm 3015
61 2 BATH 7f Firm 3204
63 4 WARW 5f Gd/Fm 3912
2a 11 WOLV 6f Aw 4246

TUSCAN DREAM 5 b g £7109
57a 9 WOLV 5f Aw 73 1140
57 13 MUSS 5f Firm 73 1687
64 5 CHES 5f Gd/Sft 73 1781
76 1 **RIPO** 5f Gd/Fm 70 2107*
76 2 LING 5f Firm 73 2326
75 4 CATT 5f Gd/Fm 75 2743
61 15 GOOD 5f Gd/Fm 75 3091
75 3 BRIG 5f Good 75 3528
72 5 EPSO 5f Good 75 3687

---

78 3 EPSO 5f Good 76 3855

TUSCAN FLYER 2 b c £0
61 8 LING 5f Gd/Sft 1260
58 5 CHES 5f Gd/Sft 1776
66 8 CARL 5f Firm 2277
39 9 REDC 8f Gd/Sft 4496

TUSSLE 5 b g £22000
0 17 HAYD 5f Gd/Sft 92 1533
95 2 ASCO 6f Good 89 2151
0 21 ASCO 7f Gd/Fm 94 2997

TUZLA 6 b m £120482
119 2 GULF 8f Good 16

TWEED 3 ch c £1304
49 13 WIND 8f Gd/Fm 66 744
53 7 WARW 11f Heavy 63 1002
54a 4 WOLV 12f Good 57 1238 VIS
55 3 MUSS 12f Soft 55 4560

TWEED MILL 3 b f £5126
85 2 WIND 8f Gd/Fm 745
82 1 **EPSO** 9f Heavy 1032*
78 12 HAYD 8f Gd/Sft 88 1535
64 10 ASCO 8f Good 86 2167
45 8 SAND 8f Good 3945
26 11 HAYD 7f Gd/Sft 80 4106

TWENTY FIRST 4 ch f £2982
51 8 NOTT 10f Gd/Sft 63 1086
67 6 WIND 10f Firm 1288
27 12 PONT 10f Good 63 1496
62 1 **BRIG** 8f Firm 60 2043*

TWICE 4 b c £412
55 8 LING 10f Soft 1287
0 16 BATH 10f Gd/Sft 67 1666 t
39 5 BRIG 12f Gd/Fm 1934 t
55a 3 LING 12f Aw 53 4486 t

TWICE AS SHARP 8 ch h £0
69 14 KEMP 6f Good 88 728

TWICE BLESSED 3 ch c £3571
71a 2 WOLV 6f Aw 118
72a 1 **LING** 7f Aw 164*
0 11 SAND 8f Heavy 73 1055

TWICKERS 4 b f £0
23a 9 WOLV 5f Aw 1036
60 6 REDC 5f Gd/Sft 62 1133
50 13 BEVE 5f Firm 61 1278
0 14 NEWC 5f Gd/Sft 60 1479
0 13 REDC 5f Gd/Sft 60 1580 BL
45 12 MUSS 5f Firm 58 1687 bl
0 13 BEVE 5f Firm 53 1923
45 6 BEVE 5f Firm 49 2223 bl
42 8 CATT 5f Gd/Fm 59 2418 VIS
40a 9 SOUT 5f Aw 57 2632 bl

TWILIGHT DANCER 2 b f £0
63 6 CHEP 8f Good 3867
45a 1 WOLV 8f Aw 4249
53 10 NOTT 8f Heavy 4504

TWILIGHT HAZE 2 b c £0
0 29 NEWM 8f Good 4349

TWILIGHT MISTRESS 2 b f £631
56 9 NOTT 6f Gd/Fm 2683
49 8 WIND 6f Gd/Fm 2886
72 4 CHEP 5f Gd/Fm 3252
71 3 BATH 5f Gd/Fm 3513
57 10 NOTT 5f Gd/Sft 4503

TWILIGHT WORLD 3 b g £5498
52 1 **MUSS** 9f Gd/Sft 47 2534*
48 3 CARL 9f Firm 55 2825
58 2 BRIG 10f Soft 55 4174
23a 7 WOLV 9f Aw 55 4251

TWIN LOGIC 3 ch f £6174
83 5 NEWB 7f Soft 915
66 4 WARW 8f Soft 1063
83 3 BEVE 10f Good 1447

79	2	CHEP	10f Gd/Sft		1796	
83	1	**EPSO**	10f Gd/Sft		2627*	
88	7	SALI	10f Gd/Fm		3389	

TWIN TIME 6 b m £8108

47	4	SAND	8f Heavy	61	1058	
65	4	BATH	8f Gd/Fm	61	1442	
66	3	KEMP	8f Gd/Fm	64	1926	
69	1	**GOOD**	7f Good	64	2303*	
63	4	BRIG	7f Soft	64	2427	
66	3	BATH	8f Firm	65	2942	
61	4	BATH	8f Firm	67	3207	

TWIST 3 b c £1198

60	8	BRIG	7f Gd/Fm		1125	
64	8	SAND	9f Gd/Fm	70	1990	
57	8	BATH	8f Firm	66	2330	
63	5	LEIC	8f Gd/Fm	63	2512	
50	8	KEMP	8f Gd/Fm	62	2752	BL
61	2	THIR	12f Gd/Fm	62	2967	
60	5	BATH	12f Firm	63	3206	
47	8	LING	11f Firm	60	3282	

TWO CLUBS 4 br f £18669

103	1	**MAIS**	6f Heavy		98*

TWO JACKS 3 b c £0

51	10	THIR	6f Soft		909	
0	13	DONC	6f Gd/Fm	60	2315	
39	8	MUSS	5f Gd/Sft	52	2535	
0	17	THIR	5f Gd/Sft	47	3781	t

TWO PACK 4 b c £0

20a	9	LING	6f Aw	95	bl
8a	11	LING	7f Aw	159	e

TWO SOCKS 7 ch g £8227

49	6	BRIG	12f Gd/Fm	57	1128
63	1	**BRIG**	12f Firm	57	1209*
63	4	SALI	12f Good	61	1350
64	1	**KEMP**	12f Gd/Fm	60	1927*
0	19	EPSO	12f Good	62	3858
63	2	SALI	10f Gd/Sft	61	4169
47	12	YORK	12f Soft	61	4280
0	15	BATH	12f Soft	60	4433

TWO STEP 4 b f £3431

30a	7	WOLV	8f Aw		39	
35a	6	WOLV	8f Aw		133	
0a	13	WOLV	9f Aw		189	
17	11	BRIG	7f Firm	34	1336	t
0	13	BRIG	6f Gd/Sft	34	1464	t
34a	1	**SOUT**	5f Aw	30	2632+	t
0a	12	SOUT	8f Aw	37	2820	t
38	5	WIND	6f Gd/Fm	45	3046	t
28	7	LEIC	5f Gd/Fm	41	3214	t
41	3	NEWM	6f Good	43	3613	t
44	2	YARM	6f Gd/Fm	42	3966	t
43a	5	WOLV	9f Aw	43	4442	t

TWOFORTEN 5 b g £1027

40a	7	LING	10f Aw	43	23	bl
35a	5	LING	12f Aw	38	115	
14a	7	LING	13f Aw		524	bl
19a	6	LING	10f Aw		775	bl
30	6	BRIG	12f Gd/Sft		893	
49	7	BRIG	10f Firm		1210	bl
35	10	BRIG	10f Firm		1331	bl
26	10	GOOD	9f Gd/Sft	36	1807	vis
48	3	BRIG	10f Gd/Fm		1933	vis
31	6	NEWM	7f Firm	40	2347	vis
36	5	WARW	12f Good	41	2466	
0	20	SALI	12f Good	43	2689	vis
0	14	BRIG	10f Gd/Fm	38	2727	vis
39	7	NEWM	8f Gd/Fm	42	2802	
30	6	WIND	12f Good	38	3186	
35	9	GOOD	9f Good	47	3644	vis
37	3	GOOD	10f Good	36	3663	
18	10	BRIG	10f Firm	32	3737	
0	11	GOOD	12f Soft		4061	

25	5	BRIG	12f Soft	36	4176	

TWOS BETTER 3 br g £336

47	9	BRIG	10f Gd/Sft	64	892
57	3	WIND	12f Gd/Sft		1096
56	6	WIND	12f Firm	60	1292
42	15	WIND	12f Good	58	1730
44	7	LING	11f Gd/Fm	55	2321

TYCANDO 3 ch c £1500

77a	2	LING	7f Aw	70	112	
80a	2	LING	6f Aw	76	222	
34a	11	WOLV	6f Aw	78	275	
58a	5	LING	6f Aw		376	VIS
57a	8	WOLV	7f Aw	76	534	
24	11	LING	7f Firm	72	2325	
55a	6	LING	7f Aw		2759	

TYCOON TINA 6 b m £422

22a	3	WOLV	9f Aw	28	529
17a	6	SOUT	11f Aw	29	561

TYCOONS LAST 3 b f £12829

40	3	MUSS	12f Gd/Sft		799	
41	5	BEVE	12f Heavy	53	978	
32a	7	WOLV	12f Aw	49	1142	
31	7	REDC	14f Gd/Sft	46	1581	
34	4	BRIG	12f Gd/Fm	41	1935	
70	3	CHES	13f Gd/Fm		2249	
31	5	BATH	10f Firm	36	2332	
36	3	CATT	12f Gd/Fm	37	2746	
16	10	BEVE	16f Good	35	2879	
67	4	HAYD	12f Gd/Fm		3324	
61	1	**HAYD**	11f Gd/Sft	58	4108*	
0	16	DONC	10f Gd/Sft	61	4448	
47	6	NOTT	10f Heavy	61	4509	

TYLERS TOAST 4 ch c £8855

60a	2	WOLV	9f Aw		433
63a	1	**WOLV**	9f Aw		490*
68a	1	**WOLV**	9f Aw	62	516*
72a	1	**WOLV**	9f Aw	67	637*
0	11	KEMP	10f Soft	65	1528
62	5	LING	9f Good	65	1744
39	10	WIND	10f Gd/Fm	65	1878

TYPE ONE 2 b c £547

0	13	LING	6f Good		2588
75	3	SAND	5f Gd/Fm		2933
73	4	CARL	5f Firm		3193

TYPHOON GINGER 5 ch m £2246

52	6	DONC	10f Gd/Sft	61	1070
57	6	REDC	7f Firm	60	1297
58	2	HAMI	8f Gd/Fm		1940
0	17	YORK	10f Gd/Sft	58	3731
54	5	BEVE	8f Good	57	3951
57	3	NOTT	10f Heavy		4413
44	6	NEWM	12f Gd/Sft	55	4534
79	3	DONC	10f Heavy		4571

TYPHOON TILLY 3 b c £11504

52	3	BEVE	12f Gd/Fm	50	1758
61	1	**YARM**	14f Gd/Fm	51	2195*
65	1	**YARM**	14f Gd/Fm	57	2416*
72	1	**NOTT**	14f Gd/Fm	63	2681*
71	2	SAND	14f Gd/Fm	72	2936
67	6	HAYD	14f Gd/Fm	72	3323

TYRA 4 b f £0

40	8	NOTT	8f Good		784	
14	7	BRIG	12f Gd/Sft		893	
0	16	NOTT	10f Gd/Fm	58	1272	
0	16	WARW	8f Heavy	50	1520	BL

TYROLEAN LOVE 4 b f £0

32	7	BRIG	12f Gd/Fm	47	1128
35	6	BATH	13f Gd/Fm	44	1440
0	12	LEIC	12f Gd/Sft	39	1736

UBITOO 3 b c £269

26a	9	LING	8f Aw		26
40a	7	LING	7f Aw		94

0a	12	LING	7f Aw		164	
0	15	SALI	7f Gd/Fm		1884	
0	12	BRIG	8f Firm		2040	
39	5	FOLK	8f Gd/Fm		2291	BL
37	3	LING	7f Good	37	2592	bl
9	9	BRIG	7f Gd/Fm	35	2728	bl
26	7	BRIG	6f Firm	36	2896	bl
19	9	BRIG	7f Gd/Fm	34	3242	bl
18	8	BRIG	8f Firm		3736	bl
0	9	YARM	11f Firm		3917	
0	11	YARM	10f Firm		3935	bl

UHOOMAGOO 2 b c £12376

76	2	DONC	5f Good		712	
76	1	**THIR**	5f Soft		928*	
76a	1	**SOUT**	5f Aw		1302*	
75	3	CHES	6f Firm	74	3168	
86	1	**CATT**	6f Good	74	3439*	
79	3	MUSS	7f Gd/Fm	80	3592	
80	4	YORK	6f Good	82	3807	
76	5	DONC	7f Firm	81	3901	

ULSHAW 3 ch c £633

51	9	THIR	12f Good		1386	
54	3	REDC	14f Gd/Fm		2144	
42	7	HAYD	14f Gd/Fm	56	2445	
0	13	BEVE	16f Good	46	2879	
24	7	CARL	14f Gd/Fm	46	3084	VIS
37	4	REDC	14f Firm		3311	vis
29	4	CARL	17f Firm	39	3575	vis

ULTIMAJUR 2 br c £0

40	10	NEWM	5f Soft		984

ULTIMATE CHOICE 2 b c £0

67	7	BRIG	7f Soft	4415
57a	5	WOLV	6f Aw	4548

ULTRA CALM 4 ch g £1647

52a	9	LING	10f Aw	62	23	
62a	3	WOLV	9f Aw	59	349	
44a	8	WOLV	9f Aw	59	383	
0a	11	WOLV	8f Aw		477	vis
45a	6	WOLV	9f Aw		517	
0	16	HAMI	9f Good	60	846	t
0	18	PONT	8f Gd/Sft	57	1101	tbl
57a	2	SOUT	11f Aw		1417	
51a	2	SOUT	11f Aw		1978	
27	9	WIND	10f Soft	47	2544	

ULUNDI 5 b g £24989

65a	1	**WOLV**	8f Aw		661*
90	1	**WIND**	10f Gd/Fm		747*
91	3	PONT	10f Soft		874
91	3	YORK	10f Firm	90	1342
81	13	ASCO	12f Good	90	2069
88	8	SAND	10f Good	90	2475
90	2	SAND	10f Gd/Fm	90	2937
89	5	GOOD	10f Gd/Fm	90	3060
96	2	SAND	10f Good	90	3471
97	1	**KEMP**	12f Gd/Fm	92	3798*
66	10	ASCO	12f Gd/Sft	96	4128

ULYSSES DAUGHTER 3 ch f £6765

71	4	NEWB	6f Gd/Fm		1783	t
72	2	SALI	6f Gd/Sft		2472	t
72	1	**BATH**	6f Gd/Fm		3820*	t
64	5	KEMP	6f Gd/Sft	72	4037	t
73	4	NEWM	5f Good	72	4185	t
76	2	BATH	5f Soft	72	4432	t
0	16	DONC	5f Heavy	76	4570	

UMBOPA 2 b c £0

45	10	PONT	8f Soft	4086
7	9	PONT	10f Soft	4230

UMBRIAN GOLD 4 b f £1220

78	2	WIND	8f Gd/Fm	76	1097
0	18	NEWB	10f Good	77	1375
64	8	LEIC	8f Soft	77	1547
48	11	KEMP	9f Gd/Sft	76	2581

UMISTIM 3 ch c £56363
116	1	NEWM	8f Gd/Sft		981*	
112	6	NEWM	8f Gd/Fm		1171	
90	5	KEMP	8f Soft		1530	
116	2	ASCO	7f Good		2087	
97	7	NEWB	7f Firm		3452	
112	2	NEWB	7f Firm		3995	
106	7	NEWM	9f Good		4347	
115	1	DONC	7f Soft		4465*	

UNAWARE 3 b c £4356
56	5	HAYD	11f Heavy	92	990	
90	3	CHES	12f Gd/Fm	90	1225	
91	4	HAYD	12f Gd/Fm	92	2702	
86	8	GOOD	12f Gd/Fm	90	3088	
88	3	NEWB	12f Gd/Fm		3487	
83	4	NEWM	14f Good	87	4016	

UNCHAIN MY HEART 4 b f £14575
58a	1	LING	8f Aw		114*	bl
62a	3	LING	8f Aw	62	152	bl
20a	11	LING	8f Aw	62	210	bl
61a	1	LING	7f Aw		616*	bl
49a	6	LING	8f Aw	60	776	bl
49a	3	LING	7f Aw	58	879	bl
38	10	BRIG	7f Firm	56	1213	
37	8	THIR	7f Gd/Fm	53	2063	bl
55	1	DONC	7f Gd/Fm	50	2320*	bl
49	4	YARM	7f Firm	50	2899	bl
61	1	KEMP	7f Gd/Fm	53	3362*	VIS
63	1	LEIC	7f Aw	57	3839*	vis
37a	10	LING	8f Aw	57	4335	vis

UNCLE DOUG 9 b g £0
0	13	CATT	16f Soft	46	4006

UNCLE EXACT 3 b c £0
0	17	THIR	5f Soft	81	926
0	20	DONC	6f Gd/Sft	77	1074
48a	12	WOLV	5f Aw	77	1140
37	9	MUSS	6f Gd/Fm		1430
59	5	RIPO	6f Gd/Fm	69	2101
52	9	CARL	5f Firm	68	2280

UNCLE FOLDING 2 b c £0
67	6	GOOD	6f Gd/Sft		1809
40	9	BEVE	7f Gd/Sft		3051
0	13	LEIC	6f Gd/Fm		3333
42	8	YARM	8f Gd/Fm		3968 tBL

UNCLE OBERON 4 b c £0
5a	6	WOLV	9f Aw		446	
47a	7	WOLV	7f Aw		478	
45	4	SOUT	7f Good	52	803	
0	18	BRIG	7f Gd/Sft	50	896	
0	17	NOTT	6f Firm	44	1273	VIS

UNDENIABLE 2 b g £0
63	7	NOTT	8f Heavy		4504
63	9	DONC	7f Heavy		4566

UNDER THE SAND 3 b c £5072
0	17	NEWM	7f Gd/Sft		983
69	7	DONC	10f Gd/Sft		1054
62	7	LING	7f Gd/Sft		1261
69	4	SAND	10f Soft	68	1585
67	2	RIPO	12f Good	68	1862
56	9	WIND	12f Good	68	3353
77	1	HAYD	11f Gd/Sft	83	3480*
75	6	CATT	12f Soft	78	4003
62	10	REDC	10f Gd/Fm		4221

UNDERCOVER GIRL 2 b f £0
53	5	GOOD	7f Gd/Fm		2125
36	12	KEMP	7f Gd/Sft		2583
64	8	KEMP	7f Soft		4034
55	7	BRIG	7f Soft	57	4416

UNDERWOOD FERN 2 b c £0
62	14	DONC	6f Gd/Fm		4575

UNDETERRED 4 ch c £9822
0	20	NEWM	7f Gd/Sft	96	966
92	3	LING	7f Soft	93	1286
84	6	DONC	7f Good	93	1514
89	4	YORK	6f Gd/Fm	91	1983
88	1	CHEP	6f Gd/Fm		2660*
73	14	ASCO	6f Gd/Fm	90	2954
0	22	KEMP	6f Gd/Fm	89	3791

UNFORTUNATE 3 ch f £5277
18a	7	SOUT	6f Aw		74	BL
51a	2	WOLV	5f Aw		145	
53a	1	SOUT	6f Aw		181*	
46a	4	LING	6f Aw		207	
50a	6	WOLV	7f Aw	53	257	
44a	5	SOUT	6f Aw	53	331	
46a	3	SOUT	7f Aw		589	
31a	7	WOLV	5f Aw		659	
47	6	LEIC	6f Gd/Sft		830	
27a	9	SOUT	6f Aw	50	1205	
0	17	REDC	7f Gd/Sft		1559	
51	1	LEIC	6f Gd/Sft	46	1734*	bl
50	4	THIR	6f Gd/Fm	51	2060	bl
44	4	CARL	6f Gd/Fm	51	2243	bl
22	12	LEIC	6f Gd/Fm	52	2511	bl

UNICORN STAR 3 b g £1992
32a	8	SOUT	8f Aw		86	
38	4	MUSS	12f Gd/Sft		799	
49	3	BEVE	10f Firm		1274	
47	6	BEVE	12f Gd/Fm	50	1758	
49	2	PONT	12f Good	48	2362	
44	5	CATT	12f Gd/Fm	50	2746	VIS
45	2	BEVE	12f Gd/Sft	48	3050	
45	3	BEVE	16f Gd/Fm	46	3406	
28	8	CARL	17f Firm	46	3575	

UNIMPEACHABLE 3 b f £2209
0	16	WIND	8f Gd/Fm	64	744
0	16	BRIG	10f Gd/Sft	62	892
46	8	WARW	11f Heavy	57	1002
47	5	BRIG	12f Gd/Sft	51	1465
52	2	NOTT	10f Soft	51	1644
38	6	WARW	11f Gd/Sft	47	1707
53	4	WARW	11f Gd/Fm	54	2033
40	4	CHES	12f Gd/Fm	54	2246
47	2	LEIC	10f Gd/Fm		2510
47	2	LEIC	12f Gd/Fm		2776
50	5	NOTT	16f Gd/Sft	51	3112
4a	12	WOLV	15f Gd/Fm	51	3276

UNITED FRONT 8 br g £0
0	14	SALI	14f Firm	57	1180	t
0	20	LING	16f Good	48	1394	VIS
0	14	WARW	16f Gd/Sft	38	1711	t

UNITED PASSION 3 b f £1235
50a	2	SOUT	5f Aw		740	
46	7	NOTT	5f Heavy		1021	
31a	7	WOLV	7f Aw		1036	
53a	3	SOUT	5f Aw	54	1976	
44a	5	SOUT	5f Aw	54	2632	t

UNLIKELY 2 ch c £1140
69	3	YORK	6f Gd/Fm		1981
0	12	LING	6f Good		2588
61	7	LING	5f Good		4096
41	9	SAND	5f Soft	64	4202

UNLIKELY LADY 4 b f £0
0a	14	SOUT	6f Aw		30
3a	11	WOLV	6f Aw		134

UNMASKED 4 ch f £1160
24	7	MUSS	5f Gd/Sft	38	798
17	8	MUSS	5f Gd/Sft	34	901
0	14	MUSS	5f Gd/Sft	33	1143
0	13	THIR	7f Gd/Sft		1351
33	8	REDC	7f Gd/Sft		1559
24	11	CARL	5f Gd/Sft	30	1724
24	3	MUSS	7f Firm		2046
38	3	HAMI	9f Gd/Fm		2236
27	3	MUSS	8f Gd/Sft	27	2533
29	12	HAMI	9f Gd/Fm		2642
10	7	HAMI	9f Gd/Fm		2780
0	12	AYR	7f Gd/Fm	27	3138 BL

UNPARALLELED 2 b f £2366
71	2	WIND	6f Gd/Fm		3047	
68	2	LING	5f Firm		3576	
67	7	GOOD	6f Good		3881	
0	12	CATT	7f Soft	71	4254	BL

UNSEEDED 3 ch f £3874
87	1	DONC	10f Gd/Sft		1051*
70	10	NEWB	10f Good		1374
97	6	ASCO	12f Good		2112
64	13	YORK	12f Firm		3595
0	20	NEWM	12f Good	95	4342

UNSHAKEN 6 b g £5049
66	9	DONC	6f Good	75	716
74	2	HAMI	6f Good	73	844
73	4	NEWC	5f Heavy	74	1008
59	11	HAMI	6f Gd/Fm	74	1192
73	7	HAYD	5f Gd/Sft	73	1533
57	15	RIPO	5f Good	71	1861
54	12	NEWC	6f Firm	69	2334
65	7	HAYD	6f Gd/Fm	69	2444
56	10	PONT	5f Gd/Fm	68	3222
0	17	HAYD	5f Gd/Sft	68	3322
69	1	CARL	7f Firm		3573*
65	9	LEIC	7f Firm	67	3839
69	5	AYR	7f Soft	67	3992
0	19	YORK	6f Heavy	66	4302
0	20	NEWC	6f Heavy	65	4405

UNSIGNED 2 b c £1083
82	7	KEMP	8f Gd/Fm		3799
83	4	GOOD	7f Soft		4063
62	3	LING	7f Soft		4483

UNTOLD STORY 5 b g £210
4a	9	LING	6f Aw	38	263	
21a	6	WOLV	5f Aw	38	306	
14a	6	SOUT	12f Aw	32	339	
29a	4	WOLV	9f Aw		446	
13a	6	WOLV	12f Aw	26	520	
0a	11	WOLV	9f Aw	28	569	bl
0	18	WARW	11f Good		3691	

UNVEIL 2 b f £340
55a	4	WOLV	5f Aw		1136
59a	4	WOLV	5f Good		1236
56	6	BRIG	5f Gd/Sft		1463
47	6	LEIC	6f Gd/Fm	64	2773
28	5	YARM	6f Good		3028
44	10	BATH	5f Firm		3204
50	3	WIND	5f Good		3639
44	4	LEIC	8f Firm	49	3837
36a	11	WOLV	7f Aw		4025
45	4	LING	6f Soft		4190

UP AND AWAY 6 b g £12903
109	2	HOPP	8f Good		2573

UP IN FLAMES 9 br g £1478
33a	8	WOLV	9f Aw		292	
0a	12	WOLV	9f Aw	38	305	
8a	7	WOLV	9f Aw	33	405	
4a	9	WOLV	12f Aw	29	520	t
48	2	REDC	7f Gd/Fm		1132	t
11	15	REDC	8f Firm	38	1300	t
38	3	LEIC	10f Soft	37	1546	t
39	5	AYR	8f Good	40	2136	t
29	6	PONT	10f Good	40	2366	t
30	3	NEWC	8f Heavy	38	4406	t

UP ON POINTS 2 ch f £5924
80	2	SALI	7f Gd/Fm		3420
91	1	SALI	7f Gd/Fm		3752*

UP TEMPO 2 b c £19360
86	2	BEVE	5f Heavy		974

80	1	**MUSS**	5f Gd/Fm		1146*	
94	3	BEVE	5f Gd/Sft		1761	
89	2	DONC	5f Gd/Fm		2318	
87	2	BEVE	5f Gd/Fm		2483	
98	3	NEWB	5f Gd/Fm		2849	
88	2	RIPO	6f Gd/Fm		3184	

UP THE KYBER 3 b c £607

75	3	WARW	8f Heavy		884
61	8	WARW	7f Soft	76	1061
66	8	NEWB	7f Gd/Fm	74	1787

UPLIFTING 5 b m £0

57	8	BRIG	6f Gd/Fm	69	1126
49	9	GOOD	6f Gd/Sft	67	1471
0	15	KEMP	7f Gd/Fm	63	3796
0	15	BRIG	6f Gd/Sft	62	4120

UPPER BULLENS 3 ch c £0

42a	7	WOLV	9f Aw		319
0	18	LEIC	10f Firm	65	3842
0	17	AYR	11f Soft	65	3963

UPPER CHAMBER 4 b g £3201

0	20	NOTT	6f Gd/Fm	43	2193
0	16	BEVE	5f Firm	43	2223
33	7	THIR	6f Gd/Fm	37	3144
30	8	RIPO	5f Gd/Fm	37	3180
50	5	CATT	5f Good		3441
37	1	**THIR**	5f Gd/Sft	35	3781*
22	7	MUSS	5f Soft	42	4516

UPSTREAM 2 b f £1047

75	4	WIND	5f Gd/Fm		1424
75	4	SAND	5f Gd/Fm		1986
73	3	CHEP	6f Gd/Fm		2488
0	23	REDC	6f Gd/Sft		4219

URBAN MYTH 2 b c £0

66	11	BATH	8f Soft		4430

URBAN OCEAN 4 ch c £19500

114	1	**CURR**	10f Soft		1121*
113	5	CURR	11f Gd/Sft		1625
95	9	ASCO	12f Good		2149
0	6	CURR	10f Good		3068

URGENT REPLY 7 b g £627

0	15	NOTT	14f Good	40	788	t
23	8	YARM	11f Gd/Fm	36	1614	
0	12	WARW	16f Gd/Sft	37	1711	t
24	6	WARW	16f Gd/Fm	28	2037	
17	6	MUSS	16f Gd/Fm	27	2203	
24	2	MUSS	16f Firm	24	2373	
12	6	MUSS	16f Gd/Sft		2536	
13	8	FOLK	15f Gd/Fm	28	3040	

URGENT SWIFT 7 ch g £12189

61a	3	SOUT	14f Aw	67	182
60a	5	SOUT	16f Aw	62	470
65a	1	**SOUT**	12f Aw	60	590*
62a	4	SOUT	12f Aw	63	641
65	4	DONC	12f Gd/Fm	67	699
57	11	HAYD	14f Gd/Fm	66	1167
69a	1	**SOUT**	14f Aw	63	1301*
58	7	NEWB	13f Gd/Fm	65	1784
68	1	**GOOD**	14f Gd/Fm	61	1959*
68	2	AYR	15f Good	68	2164
60	4	KEMP	14f Gd/Sft	68	2584
59	7	NEWB	16f Firm	68	2812
65	5	SAND	14f Gd/Fm	67	2923
56	8	SALI	14f Gd/Fm	65	3424
50	10	YARM	14f Gd/Fm	67	3664

URSA MAJOR 6 b g £24742

0a	16	LING	7f Aw	70	162	
58a	4	LING	8f Aw	64	210	bl
53a	8	LING	7f Aw	62	239	bl
65a	2	LING	8f Aw	60	336	
67a	1	**LING**	10f Aw	62	374*	
69a	2	LING	10f Aw	67	442	
78a	1	**LING**	12f Aw	67	508*	

85a	1	**LING**	12f Aw	78	572*
69a	6	LING	12f Aw	85	633
0a	12	LING	10f Aw		690

US AND THEM 3 ch f £0

0	12	NOTT	8f Gd/Fm		1269	BL

USTIMONA 3 b f £38667

103	2	CAPA	10f Heavy		4396

UTAH 6 b g £826

27a	9	LING	10f Aw	51	220	
28a	7	WOLV	9f Aw	48	306	
41a	4	WOLV	7f Aw		396	bl
44a	3	LING	7f Aw	43	438	bl
41a	2	SOUT	7f Aw	40	471	bl
34a	8	LING	8f Aw		505	bl
19a	9	SOUT	8f Aw	43	584	bl
30a	7	WOLV	12f Aw		752	

UTMOST 2 ch f £0

44	9	WARW	5f Gd/Fm		2034
33	10	CARL	6f Gd/Fm		2239
0	11	CATT	7f Good		3438

UZY 4 ch c £0

0	18	NEWM	8f Gd/Fm	49	2130	
0	13	CHEP	5f Gd/Fm	43	2976	t
0	13	FOLK	7f Gd/Fm	38	3445	bl
0	12	YARM	10f Firm		3935	

VACAMONTE 2 ch c £12818

113	1	**NEWM**	7f Gd/Fm		2613*
94	5	SAND	7f Good		3470
109	6	NEWM	7f Gd/Fm		4354

VAHORIMIX 2 gr c £7685

97	2	CHAN	8f Soft		4144

VAIL PEAK 2 b c £0

67	5	HAYD	5f Gd/Sft		1835
36	11	NEWC	7f Gd/Sft		3705
59	5	NOTT	6f Aw		3974

VALDERO 3 ch c £348

77	16	NEWM	8f Gd/Sft		972
69	4	WIND	8f Gd/Fm		1099
44	9	CHEP	8f Heavy		1556
0	17	GOOD	10f Good	70	3663
0	11	BEVE	12f Good	67	3954

VALDESCO 2 ch c £4355

76	3	SAND	5f Good		1962
73	4	WIND	5f Soft		2545
76	1	**BRIG**	6f Gd/Fm		2724*
76	9	GOOD	7f Firm	82	3149
73	4	NOTT	6f Gd/Fm	76	3519

VALENTINE BAND 3 b f £3542

96	1	**PONT**	10f Good		2365*

VALENTINES VISION 3 b c £2252

19a	9	WOLV	9f Aw		3498
51	3	YARM	7f Firm		3921
46a	4	LING	8f Aw		4272
50a	1	**WOLV**	7f Aw		4384*

VALENTINO 3 ch c £86662

115	3	LONG	8f V		1318
119	2	ASCO	8f Gd/Fm		2066 t
114	7	GOOD	8f Gd/Fm		3087 t
119	2	DONC	8f Gd/Fm		3875 t
93	10	ASCO	8f Good		4111 t

VALEUREUX 2 ch c £0

0	16	NEWB	6f Stt/Hvy		4470

VALHALLA GOLD 6 ch g £0

0	14	PONT	8f Good		1498

VALLEY CHAPEL 4 ch c £43860

111	1	**TABY**	12f Good		3931*

VALLEY OF DREAMS 2 b f £0

63	12	NEWB	7f Firm		3999

VALS RING 2 ch c £0

0a	12	LING	6f Aw		4332

VANADIUM ORE 7 b g £0

24	6	NEWC	12f Good	41	3036	

VANBOROUGH LAD 11 b g £2940

29	5	WARW	11f Heavy	38	889	
0	14	SALI	12f Good	48	1350	
15	10	BRIG	12f Gd/Sft	35	1465	
36	2	BATH	10f Gd/Fm	36	1666	
35	1	**WARW**	11f Gd/Sft	31	1707*	
27	7	HAYD	11f Soft	36	1819	
27	10	CHES	10f Gd/Fm		2245	
18	8	LING	10f Good	38	2655	
0	P	HAMI	9f Gd/Sft		3375	

VANISHING DANCER 3 ch c £5276

59a	3	LING	10f Aw		523	
0	W	MUSS	12f Gd/Sft		799	
36	10	WIND	12f Heavy	60	937	VIS
59a	3	WOLV	12f Good	59	1238	
64	3	NEWB	10f Gd/Fm		1593	
71a	1	**LING**	12f Aw	59	2651*	
71	2	REDC	14f Gd/Fm	65	3637	
0	8	AYR	15f Soft	49	3961	
54	8	MUSS	16f Soft	68	4563	

VANITY 3 b f £0

26	6	WIND	6f Heavy		4526

VANNUCCI 3 b g £0

59	9	WIND	8f Gd/Fm		1099

VANTAGE POINT 4 b c £1776

52a	3	LING	12f Aw	48	115
51a	3	WOLV	16f Aw	49	141
52a	2	LING	13f Aw	49	167
53a	2	SOUT	12f Aw	49	211
0	17	NOTT	16f Heavy	49	4508

VARIEGATION 2 ch g £0

0	17	LING	7f Soft		4483
0	15	DONC	7f Heavy		4567

VARIETY 3 ch f £2339

0	17	NEWB	10f Gd/Fm		1404
69	3	NEWM	12f Gd/Fm		2963
65	6	YARM	10f Gd/Fm		3381
62	3	HAYD	11f Gd/Sft	65	4108
0	12	BATH	12f Soft	65	4433

VARIETY SHOP 4 b f £3912

85	1	**RIPO**	8f Soft		2543*
90	4	GOOD	7f Good		3884

VASARI 6 ch g £0

45a	10	LING	7f Aw	70	107
47a	6	LING	7f Aw		4487

VEGAS 4 ch f £0

3a	8	LING	8f Aw		264
9	8	BRIG	12f Gd/Sft		893
0	17	BRIG	12f Firm	38	1209

VEIL OF AVALON 3 b f £20502

90	6	DONC	8f Gd/Sft		1069
93	2	WARW	7f Gd/Fm		2769
96	1	**GOOD**	7f Firm		3155*
102	3	EPSO	7f Good		3763
101	2	DONC	7f Gd/Fm		3878

VELMEZ 7 ch g £0

0	12	PONT	18f Firm	60	2176	bl

VELVET GLADE 2 b f £4286

90	3	ASCO	6f Gd/Fm		2952
90	1	**LING**	7f Gd/Fm		3833*
88	6	ASCO	8f Good		4110

VELVET JONES 7 b g £0

0	14	CHEP	9f Gd/Fm	36	2658

VELVET LADY 3 b f £8351

92	2	NEWB	7f Soft		915
107	6	NEWM	8f Firm		1185
87	5	NEWB	10f Good		1374
106	1	**ASCO**	8f Gd/Fm		3019*

VENDOME 2 b c £12948

54	12	MUSS	5f Gd/Fm		1429

0	15	KEMP	6f Gd/Fm		1924	
61	11	LING	5f Gd/Fm		2214	
77	3	THIR	5f Gd/Fm		3143	
77	3	HAYD	5f Gd/Sft	73	3475	
81	1	**BEVE**	5f Gd/Fm	74	3673*	
83	2	MUSS	5f Gd/Fm	80	3743	
85	2	LING	5f Good	81	4098	
83	3	NEWM	5f Good	81	4179	
0	15	NEWB	6f Sft/Hvy	83	4468	

VENIKA VITESSE 4 b g £0

0	22	THIR	5f Soft	71	926	
65	8	DONC	6f Gd/Sft	70	1074	
54	14	BEVE	5f Firm	69	1278	
0	13	CATT	6f Gd/Sft	67	1815	
0	22	YORK	6f Firm	64	2000	
0	12	REDC	6f Gd/Fm	61	2158	
41	9	NEWC	6f Good	58	3037	
53	5	REDC	6f Firm	54	3312	

VENTO DEL ORENO 3 ch f £819

70	5	SALI	10f Good		1344	
61	6	RIPO	10f Good		1599	
45	11	DONC	8f Gd/Fm		2611	
0	13	YARM	10f Good	68	3031	
64	4	WARW	8f Gd/Fm		3914	
63	2	BRIG	8f Soft		4173	
56	5	LEIC	8f Sft/Hvy	62	4310	
53	7	MUSS	8f Soft	62	4565	

VENTURA 2 b f £1600

75	2	CURR	6f Gd/Sft	1624	

VENTURE CAPITALIST 11 ch g £0

0	12	PONT	6f Soft		872	
4	14	CARL	6f Firm	66	1258	
0	W	REDC	6f Firm		1298	

VERBOSE 3 b f £7386

92	1	**WIND**	8f Gd/Fm	745*	
100	2	ASCO	8f Gd/Sft	1108	
93	5	EPSO	9f Gd/Fm	1825	
94	9	GOOD	7f Good	3104	
82	10	DONC	7f Gd/Fm	3878	

VERDURA 3 b f £1094

70	6	KEMP	9f Gd/Fm		2086	
70	4	BRIG	8f Soft		2426	
56	7	NEWB	10f Firm	70	2811	
50	12	HAYD	7f Gd/Sft	67	3269	BL
62a	2	LING	8f Aw		3756	t
19a	12	WOLV	9f Aw	62	4251	

VERIDIAN 7 b g £18367

84	1	**CHES**	12f Firm	76	1251*	
85	3	ASCO	12f Good	81	2069	
79	4	ASCO	12f Gd/Fm	82	3001	
83	2	GOOD	12f Good	82	3657	

VERSATILITY 7 b m £4061

45	5	NOTT	14f Good	50	788	
48	3	SOUT	16f Gd/Sft	47	860	
54	1	**FOLK**	15f Soft	47	963*	
36	13	NOTT	14f Gd/Sft	57	1087	
42	5	WARW	16f Gd/Fm	53	1711	
47	6	BATH	17f Firm	50	1996	
47	3	WARW	16f Gd/Fm	48	2256	
32	9	CHEP	18f Gd/Fm	48	2452	

VETORITY 3 b f £1321

69	3	SAND	10f Gd/Fm		1992	
60	5	GOOD	12f Gd/Fm		2354	
66	3	LEIC	10f Good		2774	
57	10	NEWB	10f Gd/Fm	73	3178	
66	4	BATH	10f Soft		4141	
0	11	BATH	12f Soft		4434	

VIA CAMP 3 b f £3399

83	4	ASCO	8f Good		2171	
83	6	NEWM	7f Good	90	2567	
87	2	YARM	10f Good		3669	
55	9	DONC	10f Gd/Fm		3865	

VICE PRESIDENTIAL 5 ch g £2345

61a	1	**SOUT**	6f Aw		32*	
22a	10	WOLV	6f Aw		134	
58a	2	SOUT	7f Aw		249	
56a	5	SOUT	6f Aw	58	388	
29a	9	SOUT	6f Aw		414	
37a	8	SOUT	6f Aw		538	
50a	4	SOUT	6f Aw	54	604	
43a	5	WOLV	6f Aw		719	
33a	8	SOUT	6f Aw	50	1422	
34	4	SOUT	7f Soft		1601	
24	12	LEIC	6f Gd/Sft	46	1734	
4	8	NEWC	6f Heavy	41	4425	

VICIOUS CIRCLE 6 b g £5000

108	4	GOOD	12f Gd/Fm	109	3134	
107	4	NEWM	16f Good		4351	

VICIOUS DANCER 2 b g £16723

40	7	RIPO	6f Gd/Fm	3009	
91	6	YORK	6f Gd/Fm	3568	
92	1	**YORK**	6f Good	3814*	
99	1	**AYR**	5f Soft	3959*	
80	15	NEWB	5f Gd/Sft	4454	

VICIOUS KNIGHT 2 b c £13134

85	6	NEWM	7f Firm	2346	
86	1	**BEVE**	7f Good	2881*	
103	2	ASCO	8f Gd/Fm	3304	
93	6	GOOD	8f Good	3882	

VICKY SCARLETT 3 gr f £0

21	10	HAYD	6f Gd/Fm	3266	
14	11	BEVE	7f Gd/Fm	3671	

VICKY VETTORI 3 b f £0

18a	10	LING	8f Aw		150	
23a	5	SOUT	8f Aw	31	555	
0a	10	LING	7f Aw	35	654	
0	13	WARW	7f Soft		816	

VICTEDDU 2 b f £0

70	6	NOTT	5f Gd/Sft	1641	
54	7	NOTT	6f Good	2010	

VICTOIRE 4 b f £0

28a	8	SOUT	7f Aw	64	588	
0a	12	SOUT	8f Aw	58	648	
0	17	RIPO	8f Gd/Fm	60	2099	
0	12	WARW	8f Good	54	2460	VIS
0	13	YARM	8f Aw	48	2767	vis

VICTOR LASZLO 8 b g £955

31	2	MUSS	16f Good	31	3099	

VICTOR POWER 5 ro g £0

0	14	DONC	8f Gd/Fm	2611	
0	13	BATH	12f Firm	2785	
0	15	CHEP	8f Good	3868	

VICTORIA CROSS 2 b f £0

76	8	NEWM	6f Good	4341	

VICTORIAN LADY 3 b f £296

51	7	WIND	10f Firm		1293	
32	7	BRIG	10f Soft		1466	
21	4	YARM	11f Firm		2386	
0	16	NOTT	16f Gd/Fm	42	3112	

VICTORIET 3 ch f £1264

51	5	BATH	8f Gd/Fm		1435	
48	5	SALI	7f Gd/Fm	52	1889	
46	7	LEIC	8f Gd/Fm	50	2512	
48	4	HAYD	8f Gd/Fm	50	2699	
68	4	WARW	8f Gd/Fm		2844	
48	4	HAYD	8f Good	48	3288	
56	4	EPSO	9f Good		3413	
41	7	EPSO	9f Good	49	3856	
35a	4	WOLV	8f Aw	47	4440	

VICTORIOUS 4 ch c £7196

65a	1	**WOLV**	7f Aw	58	711*	
61	1	**THIR**	7f Soft	58	908*	
0	15	NEWC	7f Heavy	62	1011	
39	11	DONC	7f Good	62	1519	
60	5	AYR	7f Gd/Fm	62	1631	t
47	10	BEVE	7f Gd/Sft	61	1760	t
0	14	NEWC	7f Heavy	60	4426	
64a	3	WOLV	7f Aw	63	4550	

VICTORS CROWN 3 b c £0

43	10	YARM	7f Gd/Fm	68	3384	
66	6	LING	6f Firm		3579	
0	16	RIPO	6f Good	63	3698	
33	11	THIR	6f Gd/Sft		3780	
29	9	YARM	8f Gd/Fm	58	3970	

VICTORY DAY 3 b c £0

67	21	NEWM	5f Gd/Fm		1172	

VICTORY ROLL 4 b c £1344

63	9	DONC	10f Gd/Sft	1054	
69	2	SAND	10f Soft	1588	
0	6	DONC	12f Gd/Fm	2609	
0	17	PONT	10f Soft	4088	
46	6	NOTT	10f Heavy	4413	

VICTORY STAR 5 ch g £0

38a	5	WOLV	12f Aw	44	410	bl

VIE INDIENNE 4 ch f £0

0a	12	WOLV	6f Aw		82	BL

VIEWFORTH 2 b c £713

72	4	CARL	5f Firm		3571	
76	3	HAYD	5f Soft		3767	
0	11	AYR	6f Soft		3958	
19	11	AYR	6f Heavy	75	4305	

VIKING PRINCE 3 b g £0

0a	8	LING	6f Aw		334	
66	8	LING	6f Gd/Sft		837	
70	9	SALI	6f Firm		1181	
0	17	SALI	7f Gd/Fm	55	1889	
2	11	BRIG	8f Firm		2040	

VILLA CARLOTTA 2 ch f £1608

76	3	NEWM	7f Good	4020	
71	9	LING	7f Soft	4268	
82	3	NEWM	7f Soft	4541	

VILLA ROMANA 3 b f £277

24a	13	SOUT	8f Aw	73	125	
43	7	CARL	8f Gd/Fm		3081	
26	6	LEIC	7f Gd/Fm		3218	
57a	5	WOLV	6f Aw	60	4023	
47a	8	WOLV	6f Aw	58	4223	
37a	3	WOLV	7f Aw		4384	

VILLA VIA 3 b f £6563

67	5	NEWM	6f Good		956	
72	3	SALI	6f Firm		1175	
75	2	LING	6f Good		1399	
73	2	YARM	5f Gd/Sft		1609	
70	1	**BEVE**	5f Gd/Fm		3651*	
0	18	KEMP	6f Gd/Fm	72	3791	
0	14	NEWM	5f Good	70	4015	
62	12	NEWM	5f Good		4185	

VILLAGE NATIVE 7 ch g £834

43a	8	WOLV	6f Aw	59	352	bl
17a	7	WOLV	9f Aw	57	447	bl
41a	10	LING	6f Aw	52	543	bl
0a	12	WOLV	7f Aw	52	583	bl
25a	9	WOLV	8f Aw	52	707	bl
41	7	BRIG	7f Firm	54	1213	bl
54	9	WIND	6f Gd/Sft		1423	bl
36a	7	LING	7f Aw		1739	bl
46	6	BATH	6f Firm	51	1994	bl
50	2	BATH	8f Firm	49	2331	bl
40	9	LING	6f Firm		3578	bl
34	10	SALI	8f Firm	51	3753	bl
0a	17	LING	12f Aw		4101	bl

VILLEGGIATURA / b g £0

34	8	BATH	12f Firm		2785	
8	11	BATH	17f Firm	60	2941	

VILLIAN 5 b m £964

72	3	DONC	12f Gd/Fm	3157	

65 4 EPSO 12f Gd/Fm 3416
71 6 BATH 12f Gd/Fm 3818

VINCENT 5 b g £10486
51a	1	SOUT	16f Aw	46	1416*
0	18	WARW	16f Gd/Sft	47	1711
56a	1	WOLV	16f Aw	51	2606*
56a	3	SOUT	16f Aw	53	2951
40	4	PONT	17f Firm	41	3501
37	4	RIPO	16f Gd/Fm	41	3715
61a	1	WOLV	15f Aw		4024*
59a	1	SOUT	16f Aw	55	4149*
33	5	PONT	17f Soft	44	4231
59a	2	SOUT	14f Aw	58	4370

VINCENTIA 2 ch f £933
0	11	PONT	6f Firm		2174
71	4	NEWM	7f Gd/Fm		2806
79	4	LEIC	7f Sft/Hvy		4309
75	3	MUSS	7f Soft		4559

VINE COURT 2 b f £0
59	7	SALI	5f Good		1346
65	6	GOOD	6f Gd/Fm		1486
63	7	WIND	5f Soft		2545
36	5	BRIG	5f Soft		4171
0	17	BRIG	7f Soft	55	4416

VINNIE ROE 2 b c £4500
103	3	CURR	8f Soft		4397

VINTAGE PREMIUM 3 b c £43173
88	2	HAYD	8f Gd/Sft	84	810
95	1	NEWB	8f Soft	86	912*
97	4	SAND	8f Heavy	94	1055
80	9	YORK	10f Gd/Fm	94	1310
100	2	HAYD	8f Gd/Sft	94	1535
101	2	YORK	10f Firm	97	2004
101	1	DONC	10f Gd/Fm		2351*
103	6	NEWM	10f Gd/Fm	100	2596
88	9	YORK	10f Gd/Fm	100	3563
101	2	HAYD	11f Soft	100	3782
100	3	AYR	11f Gd/Sft		4011
0	29	NEWM	9f Gd/Fm	100	4212

VIOLENT 2 b f £4888
45	9	CATT	5f Good		1659	
53	7	SALI	5f Soft		1882	
0	18	LING	5f Gd/Fm		2214	
65	2	NEWM	7f Gd/Fm		2599	VIS
62	1	BRIG	7f Gd/Fm		2723*	vis
65	2	BRIG	7f Firm	64	2894	vis
56	10	ASCO	7f Gd/Fm		3015	vis
47a	4	WOLV	8f Aw		3772	vis
0	13	YARM	7f Gd/Fm	63	3922	vis

VIOLET 4 b f £4426
0a	14	LING	7f Aw	70	29	VIS
37a	8	WOLV	8f Aw	65	78	
26a	10	LING	10f Aw	60	160	
0	14	SOUT	7f Soft	60	1606	
40	7	LEIC	6f Firm	53	2031	vis
27	6	WARW	8f Gd/Fm	48	2257	vis
39	11	DONC	8f Gd/Sft	48	2349	BL
50	1	EPSO	8f Gd/Sft	48	2631*	bl
43	7	KEMP	7f Gd/Fm	50	2749	bl
48	5	PONT	5f Gd/Fm	51	2830	bl
31	14	ASCO	7f Gd/Fm	53	2999	bl
47	6	ASCO	5f Gd/Fm	51	3341	bl
0	17	BEVE	5f Good	51	3398	bl
0	21	ASCO	8f Gd/Sft	70	4126	
24	10	WIND	6f Gd/Sft	48	4294	

VIRGIN SOLDIER 4 ch g £52841
62a	1	LING	16f Aw	55	6*
73a	1	SOUT	14f Aw	55	37*
78a	1	WOLV	16f Aw	66	66*
84a	1	SOUT	14f Aw	71	89*
77a	2	LING	12f Aw	71	115
86	1	NEWC	17f Gd/Sft	78	1478*

82	8	NEWC	16f Firm	84	2336
87	2	SAND	16f Gd/Fm	83	2498
85	4	GOOD	20f Gd/Fm	85	3085
87	2	CHES	19f Firm	88	3171
93	1	NEWM	16f Firm	85	3295*
96	3	YORK	14f Gd/Fm	89	3565
96	3	YORK	14f Good	95	3811
90	10	DONC	15f Gd/Fm	95	3890

VIRTUAL REALITY 9 b g £2301
75	10	THIR	8f Good	87	1160
73	5	SALI	8f Gd/Fm	86	2229
60	5	EPSO	9f Gd/Fm		3404
76	1	BRIG	8f Gd/Fm		3738*

VISCOUNT BANKES 2 ch c £438
80	4	DONC	5f Gd/Fm		700
51	9	HAMI	5f Good		843
45	13	LING	7f Good		2653

VISION OF NIGHT 4 b c £19348
107	1	YARM	6f Good		3235*
115	1	NEWM	6f Good		3610+
92	10	HAYD	6f Gd/Sft		3784

VISITATION 2 b f £2597
46	11	CHEP	6f Gd/Fm		2488
53a	1	SOUT	7f Aw		2949*
62	2	THIR	6f Gd/Fm		3127
60	7	YORK	7f Good	70	3542
43	13	DONC	8f Gd/Fm	67	3879

VISLINK 2 br c £1090
0	15	CHEP	6f Gd/Sft		1798
53	7	EPSO	6f Gd/Fm		2430
49	9	WARW	7f Gd/Fm		2841
13	10	NEWC	6f Gd/Fm		2983
72	2	EPSO	6f Gd/Fm		3400
0a	12	SOUT	6f Aw	70	4367

VITA SPERICOLATA 3 b f £22502
100	2	KEMP	5f Soft		1529	
98	4	EPSO	5f Good	102	1849	
81	8	SAND	5f Gd/Fm		2496	
100	3	NEWM	5f Gd/Fm		2960	
104	3	ASCO	6f Gd/Fm		3303	
93	8	YORK	7f Firm		3600	
100	4	NEWB	5f Firm		3982	
100	2	BEVE	5f Sft/Hvy		4043	
95	5	NEWM	5f Good		4182	VIS
95	8	NEWM	6f Good		4346	vis

VITESSE 2 b f £0
0	15	WIND	6f Good		3187
65	7	NEWM	6f Gd/Sft		4530

VITUS BERING 3 b g £0
44	8	PONT	8f Firm		3506	t

VODKA 2 b g £0
41	5	NEWC	6f Gd/Sft		1476
60	6	BEVE	5f Good		1918
45	10	HAYD	6f Gd/Fm		3268

VOLATA 2 b c £5252
92	1	NEWM	6f Gd/Fm		1691*
92	9	NEWM	7f Good		4354

VOLONTIERS 5 b g £22523
81a	2	LING	8f Aw	79	7
64a	5	LING	7f Aw		104
57	10	KEMP	7f Good	79	725
76	4	BRIG	8f Gd/Sft	77	895
85	1	THIR	8f Good	76	1160*
79	6	HAYD	8f Soft	83	1490
73	8	SAND	7f Gd/Fm	83	1989
85	2	GOOD	8f Gd/Fm	82	2356
84	2	DONC	8f Gd/Fm	82	2758
81	7	GOOD	8f Gd/Fm	85	3063
71	14	GOOD	8f Good	82	3107
87	2	LING	7f Firm	84	3758
83	7	DONC	7f Gd/Fm	84	3880
87	3	NEWB	7f Firm	86	3981

87	4	NEWM	7f Good	87	4195

VOLTE FACE 2 ch f £0
0	21	NEWM	6f Good		4341

VOLVORETA 3 ch f £267001
118	1	SAIN	11f V		944*
118	2	CHAN	11f Gd/Sft		1901
122	1	LONG	12f Good		3928*
122	3	LONG	12f Good		4262

VOSBURGH 4 br g £0
36a	9	SOUT	6f Aw	201	bl
0a	P	SOUT	7f Aw	249	bl

VRIN 5 b g £281
71	13	ASCO	12f Good	80	2674
64	4	NEWC	14f Soft	78	3709

WA NAAM 2 ch c £0
0	15	NEWM	6f Gd/Sft		4530

WADENHOE 3 b f £0
51	6	NOTT	12f Heavy	63	1022
54	7	WIND	12f Firm	60	1292
42	8	BEVE	12f Good	60	1446
0	8	HAYD	16f Gd/Sft	53	3476
9	10	BATH	8f Soft	48	4435
0	23	NEWM	8f Gd/Fm	48	4536

WADI 5 b g £7067
0	22	NEWB	10f Good	62	1375
53	6	WIND	12f Good	58	1730
52	7	KEMP	12f Gd/Fm	58	1927
50	4	SALI	10f Gd/Fm	52	2270
61	1	FOLK	12f Gd/Fm	52	2295*
55	7	SAND	11f Good	59	2530
66	1	HAMI	11f Gd/Fm	58	2782*
66	4	WIND	12f Gd/Fm	65	3049
65	3	HAMI	11f Gd/Sft	65	3379

WAFFIGG 3 b c £4872
85	5	KEMP	11f Soft		1017
86	1	CHEP	12f Heavy		1554*
89	10	ASCO	16f Good		2068
87	3	WIND	12f Soft		2547
57	5	LEIC	12f Gd/Fm	90	2917

WAFFLES OF AMIN 3 b c £3083
82a	1	WOLV	5f Aw		77*
73a	6	LING	6f Aw	86	105
69	7	SALI	6f Firm	79	1178
57	8	KEMP	6f Soft	76	1531
74	4	BRIG	7f Good	76	1652
65	8	SALI	6f Gd/Fm	74	1887
63	7	LING	6f Gd/Fm	73	2216
63	5	LING	8f Firm	71	3580
0	18	LEIC	7f Firm	69	3839

WAFFS FOLLY 5 b m £2076
41	7	NOTT	6f Gd/Sft	56	1082
29	12	LEIC	6f Soft	55	1545
48	3	SALI	6f Gd/Fm	53	2230
50	5	CHEP	5f Gd/Fm	52	2976
52	3	SALI	5f Gd/Fm		3293
54	2	SALI	5f Firm	51	3747
54	4	WIND	5f Gd/Sft	54	4295
54	4	NEWB	5f Gd/Sft	54	4459

WAFIR 8 b h £4449
57	4	RIPO	12f Soft	56	822	
44	3	MUSS	16f Gd/Fm		1145	
56a	2	SOUT	12f Aw		1203	VIS
41a	6	SOUT	14f Aw	54	1301	vis
52	4	CATT	14f Good		1660	bl
48	2	CARL	12f Gd/Sft		1720	
49	1	HAMI	11f Gd/Fm	43	2638*	
47	3	CARL	14f Firm	48	2827	
36	5	CATT	12f Good	48	3437	

WAHJ 5 ch g £22613
84	9	DONC	8f Good	90	733
92	1	HAYD	7f Soft		1820*
96	1	HAYD	7f Gd/Fm	88	2456+

<table>
<tr><td>96</td><td>2</td><td>YARM</td><td>7f Firm</td><td>92</td><td>2768</td></tr>
<tr><td>0</td><td>24</td><td>ASCO</td><td>7f Gd/Fm</td><td>90</td><td>2997</td></tr>
<tr><td>98</td><td>1</td><td>**NEWB**</td><td>7f Gd/Fm</td><td>95</td><td>3481+</td></tr>
<tr><td>96</td><td>7</td><td>YARM</td><td>6f Firm</td><td></td><td>3937</td></tr>
</table>

WAIKIKI BEACH 9 ch g £2488

54a	4	SOUT	8f Aw		45	bl
29a	9	SOUT	8f Aw	56	83	bl
55a	1	**WOLV**	8f Aw		136*	bl
0a	11	WOLV	8f Aw	55	255	bl
32a	8	WOLV	8f Aw	54	431	bl
26a	8	SOUT	7f Aw	52	598	bl
42a	4	SOUT	8f Aw		686	bl
25	7	BRIG	8f Gd/Sft	37	1462	bl
0	17	GOOD	9f Gd/Sft	36	1807	
36a	6	LING	10f Aw		2764	bl
44	2	LING	10f Firm		3490	bl
0	16	BRIG	10f Firm	43	3737	bl
39a	6	LING	8f Aw		4272	bl
1a	12	LING	12f Aw	44	4334	bl
42	3	BRIG	10f Soft	42	4419	bl

WAIKIKI DANCER 2 br f £0

0	12	LING	8f Firm		3577
53	10	LING	6f Firm		3832
36	10	LEIC	7f Sft/Hvy		4309
55a	6	WOLV	6f Aw		4379

WAINAK 2 b c £4075

63	9	SALI	7f Gd/Fm		2269
84	2	SALI	7f Good		2686
84	2	BEVE	7f Gd/Sft		3051
84	3	EPSO	7f Gd/Fm		3412
79	2	THIR	8f Gd/Fm		3779

WAIT FOR THE WILL 4 ch c £22519

0	17	NEWM	12f Gd/Sft	79	968
70	11	KEMP	12f Gd/Sft	77	1076
78	1	**SALI**	12f Good	73	1350*
78	2	NEWB	12f Gd/Fm	75	1784
78	2	KEMP	14f Gd/Fm		1928
85	3	GOOD	12f Gd/Fm	77	2127
86	1	**ASCO**	12f Gd/Fm	80	3001* bl
86	3	GOOD	14f Gd/Fm	83	3058 bl
71	14	YORK	12f Good	85	3541 bl

WAITING KNIGHT 5 br g £2039

19a	9	SOUT	11f Aw		178	vis
0a	11	WOLV	8f Aw	56	227	vis
39a	4	SOUT	8f Aw		252	vis
21a	9	SOUT	8f Aw	52	297	vis
0a	12	SOUT	8f Aw		600	vis
47a	2	SOUT	8f Aw		646	vis
45a	4	SOUT	7f Aw		693	vis
44a	2	SOUT	8f Aw		869	vis
46a	3	SOUT	7f Aw		1305	vis
44a	4	SOUT	8f Aw		1505	vis

WAJINA 4 b f £22670

100	3	CHAN	15f Good		2402
107	2	DEAU	15f Gd/Sft		3552
108	2	LONG	16f Gd/Sft		3851

WAKI MUSIC 2 b f £9124

95	1	**KEMP**	7f Gd/Fm		3074*
98	3	GOOD	7f Good		3659
98	5	DONC	8f Gd/Fm		3876

WALDOR 2 b c £0

54	8	NEWM	5f Soft		984
77	9	NEWM	7f Firm		2346

WALLACE 4 b c £0

0	5	SHA	8f Aw		184

WALLY MCARTHUR 2 b c £25726

61	8	CARL	5f Firm		1252
71	3	RIPO	5f Good		1595
76	2	HAMI	5f Gd/Fm		2234
80	1	BEVE	5f Gd/Fm		2480*
87	1	**DONC**	6f Gd/Fm		2754*
56	8	GOOD	6f Gd/Fm	88	3062
61	4	CHES	6f Gd/Fm		3507
83	2	YORK	6f Good	81	3807
86	3	REDC	6f Gd/Sft		4219
80	11	NEWM	6f Good	86	4338

WALNUT LADY 3 ch f £3599

92	2	MAIS	6f Heavy		99

WALNUT WONDER 3 b f £0

0	18	LING	6f Gd/Sft		837

WALTER THE WHISTLE 3 b c £0

48	5	SALI	7f Good		1349	
42	4	LEIC	8f Gd/Sft		1572	
25	9	LING	11f Firm	46	1914	BL
0	15	NOTT	8f Gd/Fm	44	2187	
0	12	CHEP	8f Gd/Fm		2448	bl

WANNA SHOUT 2 b f £660

68	5	WARW	5f Soft		812
64	5	WARW	5f Heavy		886
73	2	CATT	5f Good		1659

WANNABE AROUND 2 b c £1925

79	6	ASCO	7f Gd/Fm		2956
82	3	YARM	7f Firm		3940
84	2	LING	7f Soft		4483
84	4	DONC	7f Heavy		4566

WANNABE BOLD 2 b f £0

45	9	PONT	5f Heavy		938
0	11	NEWC	6f Gd/Fm		2312
0a	10	SOUT	7f Aw		2949

WAR BABY 4 b f £0

44a	7	LING	10f Aw		314	
7a	11	LING	13f Aw	36	835	
0	14	BRIG	12f Firm	38	1209	VIS
12	9	FOLK	12f Gd/Fm	30	2295	

WAR GAME 4 b f £36503

108	2	SAIN	11f Good		1378
111	1	**MAIS**	13f Soft		2737*

WARDAT ALLAYL 3 b f £0

71	7	NEWB	10f Gd/Fm		1945

WARDEN WARREN 2 b c £6904

62	13	NEWM	6f Gd/Fm		1691
94	1	**NEWM**	6f Gd/Fm		2132*
89	2	WIND	6f Good		3352
85	6	NEWM	6f Gd/Fm	89	3630
87	5	NEWM	8f Gd/Fm	89	4214

WARLINGHAM 2 b c £7463

77	4	LING	5f Gd/Sft		1260
67	6	GOOD	5f Gd/Sft		1639
72	3	NOTT	5f Good		1870
78	6	KEMP	5f Gd/Fm		2082
77	2	LING	5f Firm		2324
80	1	**YARM**	5f Firm		2766*
69a	4	WOLV	6f Aw		3496
76	3	CHEP	5f Gd/Fm	78	3679
40	12	GOOD	6f Good	78	3886

WARNING NOTE 3 b c £876

86a	2	LING	8f Aw		103

WARNING REEF 7 b g £28409

61	4	CHES	10f Gd/Fm	62	1217
65	5	CHES	12f Firm	62	1251
54	6	DONC	12f Good	61	1518
56	5	CHES	10f Gd/Sft	59	1777
55	3	MUSS	12f Firm	57	2048
56	2	CARL	12f Firm	57	2279
56	3	CHES	10f Gd/Fm	55	2671
60	1	**KEMP**	12f Firm	55	2872*
60	2	DONC	10f Gd/Fm	58	3159
67	1	**NEWM**	12f Gd/Fm	59	3461*
63	4	YORK	12f Good	63	3541
67	2	THIR	12f Gd/Sft	65	3778
57	4	HAYD	12f Soft	67	4092
0	14	DONC	12f Firm	67	4464
0	17	DONC	12f Heavy	68	4580

WARNINGFORD 6 b g £44440

113	2	NEWM	6f Good		952	
110	4	SAND	8f Heavy		1043	
111	2	LONG	7f Good		1617	
102	6	HAYD	7f Gd/Fm		1834	
103	3	EPSO	7f Good		3763	
114	1	**NEWM**	7f Firm		3995*	
112	5	ASCO	6f Gd/Sft		4125	
88	8	NEWM	7f Good		4352	
109	3	NEWM	8f Soft		4544	

WARRING 6 b g £5742

43	5	WARW	8f Soft	50	1066
28	11	BATH	8f Gd/Fm	49	1442
33	3	CARL	8f Gd/Sft	46	1721
0	16	CHEP	7f Gd/Sft	46	1794
13	11	BATH	8f Firm	43	1998
40	3	WIND	8f Good	39	3188
40	4	WIND	8f Good	46	3355
45	1	**BATH**	8f Gd/Fm	42	3514*
43	3	BATH	8f Firm	44	3623
23	8	MUSS	8f Soft	44	3745
0	17	GOOD	8f Soft	44	4066

WARRIOR KING 6 b g £0

31a	8	WOLV	8f Aw		138	
25a	9	SOUT	8f Aw		197	
25a	7	WOLV	8f Aw	43	254	
40a	5	WOLV	12f Aw		295	
0a	12	SOUT	11f Aw	33	325	
4a	10	WOLV	9f Aw	34	404	
0a	8	SOUT	11f Aw	38	474	vis
20a	6	SOUT	7f Aw		511	vis

WARRIOR QUEEN 3 b f £0

108	7	ASCO	5f Good		2065	
65	13	GOOD	5f Gd/Fm		3059	VIS

WASEEM 3 ch c £16487

68a	1	**WOLV**	7f Aw		493*
50	8	BRIG	8f Gd/Sft		894
59	8	CARL	8f Firm	70	1255
72	2	REDC	11f Gd/Sft	67	1560
76	1	**PONT**	10f Good	70	1866*
60	10	CARL	12f Firm	75	2279
76	3	REDC	10f Gd/Fm	75	2992
78	1	**THIR**	10f Gd/Fm	75	3148*
55	10	RIPO	10f Gd/Fm	77	3713

WASEYLA 3 b f £0

67	7	WIND	12f Gd/Fm	75	1199
0	13	YARM	11f Heavy		4481

WASP RANGER 6 b g £14634

68	7	KEMP	12f Gd/Sft	72	1076
77	2	LING	11f Good	72	1743
73	2	NEWB	10f Gd/Fm	72	1942
77	3	NEWM	10f Gd/Fm	75	2287
80	1	**SAND**	11f Good	75	2530* bl
79	6	KEMP	12f Firm	79	2872 bl
81	2	BATH	12f Firm	79	2943 bl
80	2	EPSO	12f Good	79	3686
70	9	DONC	12f Firm	79	3896 bl

WASSL STREET 8 b g £0

39	5	FOLK	15f Soft	48	963

WATCHING 3 ch c £69063

107	2	LEIC	6f Gd/Sft		829
115	1	**HAYD**	5f Heavy		988*
115	2	LONG	5f V		1320
115	2	CHAN	5f Gd/Sft		1747
107	11	ASCO	5f Good		2065
114	1	**SAND**	5f Gd/Fm		2496*
105	4	GOOD	5f Gd/Fm		3059
114	4	YORK	5f Firm		3598
106	5	LEOP	5f Good		3923
93	10	LONG	5f Good		4261

WATCHKEEPER 2 b f £233

74	4	LING	7f Firm		3833

WATER BABE 3 b f £7604

52	4	WIND	6f Gd/Fm	60	1877
64	1	**LEIC**	6f Gd/Fm	59	2511*
61	7	WIND	6f Gd/Fm	65	2885
68	1	**YARM**	6f Gd/Fm	64	3386*
44	11	FOLK	6f Gd/Fm		3587

WATER FLOWER 6 b m £4173

49	7	BATH	12f Good	68	1091	
71	1	**SALI**	12f Firm	68	2023*	
57	8	HAYD	12f Gd/Fm	70	2446	
0	12	SALI	12f Good	70	2689	
58	9	SALI	12f Gd/Fm	69	3392	vis
54	9	GOOD	12f Good	66	3657	
49	8	SAND	14f Gd/Fm	62	3948	
0	31	NEWM	18f Good	79	4353	

WATER JUMP 3 b c £22890

96	1	**SALI**	10f Firm	85	1177*
98	2	ASCO	12f Good	90	2116
95	3	GOOD	12f Good	95	3131

WATER LOUP 4 b f £2228

30a	6	SOUT	8f Aw	46	692	
34	7	SOUT	10f Gd/Sft	46	859	
25	8	PONT	8f Gd/Fm	43	1101	
0	12	YARM	8f Good	40	1772	
17	7	LEIC	8f Firm	35	2032	
23	6	EPSO	9f Gd/Sft		2433	VIS
31a	2	SOUT	12f Aw		2636	
31	2	WARW	13f Gd/Fm	29	2843	
32	2	CARL	14f Gd/Fm	30	3084	
24	6	CHEP	12f Gd/Fm	34	3255	
35	3	REDC	14f Gd/Fm		3633	

WATERFORD SPIRIT 4 ch c £0

45	13	NEWC	5f Soft	75	758	
0	19	THIR	5f Soft	74	926	
0	W	NEWC	5f Heavy	72	1008	
57	14	THIR	5f Good	72	1162	
0	13	NOTT	5f Good	70	1412	
53	11	REDC	5f Gd/Sft	67	1580	
51	11	CATT	5f Good	67	1662	
0	12	THIR	5f Gd/Sft	67	1714	BL
52	7	RIPO	5f Gd/Fm	62	2107	t
51	13	DONC	5f Firm	58	3894	
35	9	PONT	5f Soft	54	4377	

WATERFRONT 4 b c £0

10a	9	SOUT	8f Aw	47	648
0a	9	SOUT	11f Aw		672

WATERGOLD 3 ch c £0

60	5	PONT	6f Gd/Fm		1105	
24	14	NEWC	8f Gd/Sft	50	1477	
0	12	CARL	8f Aw		1723	VIS
31	11	HAMI	8f Gd/Fm	48	1907	vis
33	10	AYR	8f Good	46	2136	vis
49	6	AYR	7f Good		3364	BL
34	9	BEVE	8f Gd/Fm		3671	bl
17a	8	WOLV	7f Aw		4361	bl

WATERGRASSHILL 3 b f £3039

57a	2	LING	6f Aw	56	105
55a	5	LING	8f Aw	58	158
57a	4	LING	8f Aw	58	222
42	5	NOTT	6f Good	57	785
57	2	WIND	6f Good	55	852
43	8	KEMP	6f Soft	60	994
49	5	WIND	6f Firm	57	1289

WATERPARK 2 b f £7253

40a	6	SOUT	5f Aw		801
58	3	THIR	5f Soft		928
66	2	THIR	5f Good		1381
68	1	**HAYD**	5f Gd/Fm		1492*
80	1	**AYR**	6f Gd/Fm		1628*
61	10	PONT	6f Gd/Fm	77	2557

WATHBAT MUJTAHID 3 ch c £0

79	5	THIR	7f Good		1159
52	6	CHEP	8f Heavy		1556

WATTNO ELJOHN 2 b c £4000

22	10	WIND	5f Heavy		932
73	9	CHEP	6f Gd/Fm		1798
67	9	LING	5f Gd/Fm		2214
65	1	**BATH**	5f Gd/Sft		2551*
61	6	BRIG	7f Firm	69	2894
62	3	BRIG	6f Gd/Fm	64	3258
57	5	LING	6f Soft		4190
66	3	NEWM	7f Good		4336
64	4	DONC	7f Heavy	65	4577

WATTREY 2 b f £342

67	4	HAYD	8f Gd/Sft		4104

WAVE OF OPTIMISM 5 ch g £38053

0	20	NEWM	12f Gd/Sft	76	968
78	1	**DONC**	17f Gd/Sft	74	1052*
84	1	**KEMP**	16f Soft	79	1527*
72	9	HAYD	16f Gd/Sft	83	1791
54	11	YORK	14f Good	83	3811
65	11	ASCO	16f Good	80	4115
89	2	NEWM	16f Good	82	4353
84	6	MUSS	16f Soft	90	4563

WAVERLEY ROAD 3 ch c £1605

76	5	DONC	8f Gd/Fm		704
50	13	WIND	10f Good		850
57	6	NOTT	10f Gd/Sft	65	1364
62	5	LEIC	10f Gd/Sft	63	1735
53	8	WIND	10f Gd/Fm		3045
60	2	KEMP	9f Gd/Fm	59	3357
38	6	BRIG	10f Firm	69	3557
58	2	LEIC	8f Gd/Sft		4033

WAX LYRICAL 4 b f £0

71	7	SAND	7f Soft	85	1564	
50	15	EPSO	6f Good	82	1851	
0	15	WIND	10f Good	78	2207	
53	7	NEWM	6f Gd/Fm	74	2804	
30	7	LEIC	8f Gd/Sft		3097	BL

WAY OUT WEST 3 b f £0

41	9	SOUT	7f Good		804
2a	8	SOUT	8f Aw		1204
0	12	BEVE	7f Good		1444
0	13	HAMI	8f Gd/Fm	42	1907
9	11	PONT	12f Good	37	2362

WAYFARER 2 b c £700

76	3	CURR	6f Gd/Sft		1624

WEALTHY STAR 5 b g £0

0	16	KEMP	7f Good	91	725	t
84	5	BRIG	8f Gd/Sft	88	895	t
89	5	NEWM	7f Gd/Sft	88	966	t
75	12	KEMP	8f Gd/Fm	86	1077	t

WEE BARNEY 3 b g £0

0	13	NOTT	8f Gd/Sft	43	1365	
26	11	MUSS	8f Gd/Fm	43	1434	
0	14	LEIC	8f Gd/Fm		2914	
0	15	THIR	8f Gd/Fm	36	2964	
0	11	MUSS	7f Good	36	3103	BL

WEE JIMMY 4 b c £0

1a	7	WOLV	9f Aw		490	
0	15	NOTT	14f Gd/Fm	35	3002	BL

WEET A MINUTE 7 ro h £18136

76a	8	WOLV	9f Aw	98	137	
103ε	1	**WOLV**	9f Aw	96	230*	
102ε	2	WOLV	8f Aw		321	
100ε	2	WOLV	8f Aw		448	
100ε	2	WOLV	9f Aw		480	
91a	2	WOLV	9f Aw		662	
104	5	DONC	8f Gd/Fm		703	
91	6	YORK	10f Firm	93	1342	
0	14	YORK	9f Firm	92	2001	
0	17	SAND	8f Gd/Fm	89	2528	BL
81	5	NEWB	9f Firm	86	2853	
83	4	DONC	10f Gd/Fm	83	3159	
89	3	YARM	10f Gd/Fm		3669	

61	8	DONC	10f Gd/Fm		3865
57	25	NEWM	9f Gd/Fm	83	4212
0	18	DONC	12f Soft	80	4464

WEET A WHILE 2 b c £0

57	10	DONC	6f Gd/Fm		2608
56	7	HAYD	6f Gd/Fm		3268
68	5	NOTT	6f Good		3520
56	7	WARW	15f Gd/Fm		3911
37	7	PONT	6f Soft	62	4235
14	10	DONC	7f Heavy		4567

WEET AND SEE 6 b g £0

0a	11	WOLV	9f Aw	52	568

WEET FOR ME 4 b c £6035

68	7	DONC	18f Good	76	714
24	13	WARW	15f Heavy	76	885
76	3	YORK	14f Firm	75	1329
58	8	HAYD	14f Gd/Sft	76	1536
78	1	**DONC**	15f Gd/Fm	75	2319*
68	6	NEWM	16f Gd/Fm	77	2600
79	3	HAYD	16f Gd/Fm	77	3323
0	33	NEWM	18f Good	79	4353
65	7	DONC	17f Heavy	79	4579

WEETMANS WEIGH 7 b h £9092

99a	2	SOUT	8f Aw	94	49
92a	4	WOLV	8f Aw		321
92a	6	SOUT	7f Aw	97	539
81a	4	WOLV	8f Aw	97	580
82a	8	WOLV	8f Aw	94	663
60	10	DONC	8f Good	78	715
72	8	THIR	8f Good	76	1160
60	12	CHES	8f Firm	76	1250
71	4	HAYD	8f Soft	74	1490
70	6	DONC	7f Gd/Fm	72	1840
71	4	CARL	8f Firm		2018
63	8	DONC	8f Gd/Fm	70	2349
61	6	LEIC	7f Gd/Fm		2508
61	5	HAYD	8f Good	66	3288
63	8	AYR	7f Soft	64	3992
67	1	**NEWM**	7f Soft	62	4547*

WEETRAIN 4 b f £0

0a	13	WOLV	6f Aw	48	226
32a	6	WOLV	5f Aw	44	291
0a	12	SOUT	6f Aw		389
30a	8	WOLV	5f Aw		624

WELCHS DREAM 3 b f £615

63a	4	LING	6f Aw		24	
72a	2	WOLV	6f Aw		62	
50a	4	WOLV	6f Aw		228	
43a	5	WOLV	5f Aw	70	361	
66	6	CHES	5f Gd/Fm	73	1219	
61	10	REDC	6f Good	70	1891	
59	7	CARL	5f Firm	67	2280	
54	6	CHES	5f Good	66	2663	
33	10	HAYD	6f Gd/Fm		3283	
0	13	PONT	5f Firm	59	3502	BL

WELCOME ABOARD 3 ch f £3163

58	3	HAYD	7f Heavy		992
59	9	NOTT	8f Gd/Fm		1269
75	1	**LEIC**	8f Soft		1548*
61	7	PONT	10f Good	72	1866

WELCOME BACK 3 ch g £928

43	7	MUSS	8f Gd/Sft	47	800
0	14	HAMI	11f Gd/Fm	44	1361
35	5	REDC	14f Gd/Sft	44	1581
38	5	BEVE	8f Firm	40	2735
37	3	THIR	8f Gd/Fm	40	2964
33	6	BEVE	12f Gd/Fm	40	3050
32	3	REDC	14f Gd/Fm	40	3637
17a	10	WOLV	12f Aw	35	3773

WELCOME FRIEND 3 b c £7919

91	1	**SALI**	6f Firm		1181*
92	2	CHEP	7f Gd/Fm		3682

WELCOME GIFT / table data (UK horse racing form guide)

100	2	GOOD	7f Good			3884	

WELCOME GIFT 4 b g £4857
40a	2	WOLV	7f Aw			173	
59a	2	WOLV	7f Aw			293	
59a	2	SOUT	7f Aw			367	
68a	1	**WOLV**	6f Aw			434*	
65	6	GOOD	7f Gd/Sft	69		1483	
59	9	NEWB	6f Gd/Sft	69		1591	

WELCOME HEIGHTS 6 b g £0
| 0a | 16 | SOUT | 11f Aw | 53 | | 126 | |
| 0 | 16 | PONT | 10f Soft | | | 4088 | |

WELCOME SHADE 3 gr g £2942
70a	1	LING	6f Aw	63		2*	
67a	4	LING	6f Aw	69		165	
58	2	BRIG	7f Firm			1212	
48a	9	WOLV	7f Aw	68		1390	
56	7	WIND	8f Good	61		1726	
0	8	BATH	12f Firm			1997	
20	7	WARW	11f Gd/Fm			2253	
0a	7	WOLV	9f Aw			2602	BL

WELCOME TO UNOS 3 ch g £1695
47	8	NEWC	6f Heavy	72		1768	
55	6	THIR	6f Gd/Fm	69		2060	
66	3	CATT	6f Gd/Fm	66		2440	
57	10	AYR	7f Gd/Fm	66		2719	
64	2	NEWC	7f Good	64		3250	
57	7	CATT	7f Good	64		3440	
59	6	CARL	7f Firm			3573	
50a	5	WOLV	8f Aw	62		3769	
30	5	BEVE	8f Sft/Hvy	62		4045	

WELDUNFRANK 7 b g £0
54	9	HAMI	11f Good			848	
61	8	NOTT	14f Gd/Sft			1369	
60	5	REDC	10f Gd/Sft			1582	
38	6	BRIG	12f Gd/Fm			1934	
45	9	WARW	12f Gd/Fm	60		2254	
38	8	HAMI	11f Gd/Fm	55		2638	

WELL MAKE IT 2 b c £0
62	6	LING	6f Firm			2760	
76	9	GOOD	7f Good			3154	
75	9	KEMP	8f Gd/Fm			3799	
52	12	GOOD	8f Soft	72		4076	

WELL MINDED 3 br f £38634
| 105 | 3 | SAN | 11f Good | | | 1459 | |
| 110 | 2 | HANN | 12f Good | | | 3930 | |

WELLBEING 3 b c £48061
99	1	NEWM	12f Gd/Fm			951*	
106	1	NEWM	12f Gd/Fm			1168*	
110	5	EPSO	12f Good			1848	
117	1	NEWM	12f Good			4194+	
115	1	NEWB	12f Sft/Hv			4469*	

WELLCOME INN 6 ch g £4119
19a	7	SOUT	12f Aw	27		211	t
0a	9	SOUT	16f Aw	45		253	t
60a	2	SOUT	11f Aw			369	t
26a	2	SOUT	12f Aw	23		413	t
43a	3	SOUT	12f Aw			498	t
48a	3	WOLV	9f Aw			553	t
29a	4	WOLV	12f Aw	37		608	t
40a	1	**WOLV**	9f Aw	35		749*	t
22	4	CARL	8f Gd/Sft	36		1721	t
0a	10	SOUT	9f Aw			2816	t

WELLOW 4 b g £0
| 0a | 15 | SOUT | 6f Aw | | | 30 | tBL |

WELODY 4 ch c £3959
61a	4	WOLV	7f Aw			478	
66a	2	WOLV	9f Aw			578	BL
73a	1	**WOLV**	8f Aw			658*	bl
0	10	DONC	12f Good			732	bl
3	13	GOOD	8f Gd/Sft	69		1473	bl
51	4	WARW	8f Gd/Fm	64		2257	bl
49	13	DONC	8f Gd/Fm	64		2349	vis
35	10	YARM	8f Gd/Fm	64		2412	bl
53	8	BEVE	10f Gd/Fm	60		2518	
43a	8	SOUT	8f Aw	69		2634	
48	8	SAND	8f Gd/Fm			2920	bl
0	15	WIND	10f Gd/Fm			3045	
0	11	NEWM	7f Gd/Fm			3318	
37a	11	WOLV	8f Aw	65		3499	bl
59a	3	WOLV	8f Aw	60		4248	bl

WELSH BORDER 2 ch c £9607
| 88 | 1 | NOTT | 8f Soft | | | 3972* | |
| 91 | 1 | NEWM | 8f Gd/Sft | | | 4531* | |

WELSH DREAM 3 b c £9074
61	1	NEWM	12f Gd/Fm	53		3167*	
67	1	BRIG	12f Firm	61		3560*	
69	2	BRIG	12f Gd/Sft	69		4123	

WELSH MAIN 3 br c £11006
| 92 | 1 | WIND | 10f Gd/Fm | | | 2889* | |
| 97 | 1 | YARM | 10f Gd/Fm | | | 3669+ | |

WELSH PLOY 3 b f £3388
79a	1	**LING**	8f Aw	73		158*	
77a	2	SOUT	8f Aw	76		213	
0	14	GOOD	10f Soft	78		4067	
0	19	YORK	9f Heavy	74		4300	
0	20	NEWM	8f Gd/Sft	69		4536	

WELSH VALLEY 3 b f £876
69a	2	SOUT	6f Aw			685	
43a	7	SOUT	5f Aw			740	
58	4	LING	7f Good			1397	
49	8	WARW	7f Gd/Sft	66		1710	

WELSH WIND 4 b g £12406
93	2	WIND	8f Good			851	
90	2	LING	8f Gd/Sft			1262	
29	2	ASCO	8f Good	90		2090	
87	4	HAYD	8f Gd/Fm	90		3325	
90	2	WIND	8f Good	88		3642	
93	2	GOOD	8f Good	90		3883	
93	3	NEWM	10f Good			4017	
0	8	PONT	10f Soft	92		4085	t

WELVILLE 7 b g £5860
| 104±1 | | WOLV | 8f Aw | | | 321* | t |

WENDS DAY 5 br g £236
| 65 | 4 | NEWB | 13f Gd/Sft | 65 | | 1594 | |

WENSUM DANCER 3 b f £1545
0	13	WIND	10f Firm			1293	
45	4	BRIG	10f Soft			1466	
56	12	NEWM	10f Gd/Fm			1697	
30	6	BRIG	12f Gd/Fm	49		1935	
36	4	YARM	8f Gd/Fm			2411	
39	7	HAYD	8f Gd/Sft			3266	
44	4	YARM	10f Gd/Fm			3382	
52	2	NEWM	12f Good			4178	
31	5	AYR	11f Heavy			4304	

WERE NOT JOKEN 3 b f £0
35	8	LING	7f Good	55		2592	
41	10	REDC	10f Gd/Fm	52		2864	
53	8	LEIC	5f Gd/Fm			2919	
0	14	CARL	6f Firm	49		3194	VIS

WERE NOT STOPPIN 5 b g £13066
0a	14	SOUT	8f Aw			252	
0a	14	SOUT	11f Aw	24		324	
22a	5	WOLV	8f Aw	35		432	
3a	7	SOUT	8f Aw	25		584	
33a	5	SOUT	11f Aw			670	
38	1	BEVE	8f Heavy			973*	
50	1	**REDC**	8f Firm	40		1300+	
55	1	**REDC**	9f Gd/Sft	47		1583*	
51	4	GOOD	9f Gd/Sft	53		1807	
61	1	**PONT**	10f Gd/Fm	53		2556*	
59	3	BEVE	10f Gd/Fm	60		3410	
45	7	YORK	9f Gd/Fm	59		3731	
27	12	YORK	9f Heavy	58		4300	

WESLEYS LAD 6 b g £0

| 38a | 5 | WOLV | 12f Aw | 49 | | 489 | |

WEST END DANCER 3 b f £544
51a	5	SOUT	8f Aw			48	
38a	9	WOLV	8f Aw			171	
32a	10	LING	10f Aw			240	
0a	10	LING	12f Aw			457	BL
39	5	BEVE	10f Firm			1274	
29	7	WARW	11f Gd/Sft	40		1707	
38	3	WIND	12f Good			2715	
37	3	REDC	11f Gd/Fm			2989	
22	8	NEWC	12f Good			3247	
40	9	YARM	14f Gd/Fm	48		3664	
31	4	NOTT	14f Heavy	34		4409	VIS
16	10	NEWM	12f Gd/Sft	44		4534	

WEST ORDER 2 ch g £12983
| 90 | 1 | NEWB | 7f Firm | | | 3999* | |
| 100 | 1 | NEWM | 7f Good | | | 4344* | |

WESTBROOK 4 b g £0
| 33a | 8 | LING | 10f Aw | | | 629 | VIS |

WESTCOURT MAGIC 7 b g £0
73	9	YORK	5f Gd/Fm	77		1980	
59	11	YORK	5f Gd/Fm	75		2644	
57	10	CATT	5f Gd/Fm	73		2929	
51	14	PONT	5f Gd/Fm	70		3222	
32	13	CHES	5f Gd/Fm	67		3512	
47	6	CHES	5f Soft	63		4073	

WESTENDER 4 b g £20990
92	2	YORK	10f Firm	87		1342	
92	2	NEWM	12f Gd/Fm			1695	
94	5	ASCO	12f Good	91		2069	
84	7	YORK	10f Good	91		2696	
95	2	ASCO	10f Gd/Fm	92		2995	
98	1	**NEWB**	11f Firm	93		3451*	
58	16	YORK	10f Gd/Fm	96		3563	

WESTERN BAY 4 b c £0
56	6	WIND	10f Gd/Fm			2056	
68	8	SALI	10f Gd/Fm			2265	
52	7	WARW	8f Good			2464	
0	10	YARM	14f Firm	64		2902	
0a	11	WOLV	12f Aw	54		4245	

WESTERN COMMAND 4 b g £11968
49a	6	WOLV	12f Aw	60		43	
61a	2	SOUT	12f Aw	60		70	
61a	2	SOUT	11f Aw	59		131	
69a	1	**WOLV**	12f Aw	63		170*	
59a	4	SOUT	11f Aw	67		302	
55a	5	SOUT	11f Aw	69		343	vis
62a	7	SOUT	12f Aw	69		370	
62a	3	WOLV	12f Aw	67		407	
60a	3	WOLV	12f Aw	65		437	
37a	6	WOLV	12f Aw	65		456	bl
64a	2	SOUT	12f Aw			510	
67a	1	**SOUT**	11f Aw	62		560*	
48a	6	WOLV	12f Aw	68		590	
52a	8	SOUT	11f Aw	66		605	
63a	3	SOUT	12f Aw	65		642	
53a	4	WOLV	12f Aw	63		723	
42a	6	SOUT	11f Aw	63		742	
62a	4	WOLV	16f Aw	61		918	
56a	5	SOUT	14f Aw	59		1301	
62a	1	SOUT	14f Aw	59		1501*	
21	8	SOUT	12f Soft	49		1604	
54a	6	LING	12f Aw	60		1677	
46	2	REDC	14f Gd/Fm	64		2156	
31	8	LING	16f Firm	46		2763	
43	6	HAYD	12f Good	46		3284	
23a	8	WOLV	15f Aw			4024	
58a	3	WOLV	12f Aw	58		4226	
48a	5	WOLV	12f Aw	58		4245	
56a	3	SOUT	12f Aw			4366	

WESTERN EDGE 2 b f £497
| 71 | 5 | SAND | 8f Gd/Fm | | | 3943 | |

74	6	LEIC	7f Sft/Hvy		4309
80	3	YARM	8f Heavy		4477
0	17	DONC	7f Heavy	75	4577

WESTERN FLAME 2 b f £944

64	5	GOOD	6f Good		2357
72	2	CATT	6f Soft		4001
47	12	BRIG	7f Soft		4172
0	22	NEWM	6f Good	72	4338

WESTERN GENERAL 9 ch g £0

31	11	HAMI	9f Good	·60	846
40	5	HAMI	9f Gd/Fm		2236
19	5	HAMI	11f Firm		2393

WESTERN HERO 2 ch c £5068

69	3	WIND	5f Firm		1095
64	3	BRIG	5f Firm		1208
83	2	BATH	6f Gd/Sft		2550
79	1	WIND	5f Good		2711*
77	5	NEWM	6f Good	81	3165
61	7	SAND	5f Soft	79	4202

WESTERN RAINBOW 4 b c £5626

53a	2	SOUT	8f Aw	46	85	
46a	4	SOUT	8f Aw	45	176	
50a	2	WOLV	9f Aw	48	271	
57a	2	SOUT	12f Aw	51	338	
51a	4	SOUT	12f Aw	51	370	BL
58a	1	LING	13f Aw		483*	
58a	2	WOLV	12f Aw	53	554	
42a	6	WOLV	16f Aw	60	664	VIS

WESTERN RIDGE 3 b c £0

| 0 | 11 | YARM | 11f Heavy | | 4481 |

WESTERN SUMMER 3 ch c £1188

| 100 | 4 | NEWM | 9f Gd/Sft | | 980 |
| 101 | 13 | NEWM | 8f Gd/Fm | | 1171 |

WESTERN VENTURE 7 ch g £0

| 36 | 6 | HAMI | 9f Gd/Fm | | 1195 |

WESTERNMOST 2 b g £0

54	9	PONT	5f Good		2360
47	11	PONT	6f Gd/Fm		2828
52	6	HAMI	8f Gd/Sft		3532

WESTGATE RUN 3 b f £17632

41	7	CARL	6f Firm	58	1258
58	1	WARW	11f Gd/Fm	54	2033*
58	1	HAMI	8f Firm	54	2094*
55	3	PONT	10f Good	59	2366
59	3	HAMI	12f Firm	59	2392
65	1	BRIG	12f Gd/Fm		2725*
69	1	NOTT	10f Gd/Fm	61	3007*
70	2	RIPO	10f Good		3013
70	1	AYR	11f Gd/Fm	67	3140*
67	9	YORK	12f Good	71	3541
59	13	DONC	10f Firm	71	3899

WESTLIFE 2 b f £0

| 50 | 7 | WARW | 5f Gd/Sft | | 1706 |
| 40a | 6 | SOUT | 5f Aw | | 2120 |

WESTMINSTER 8 ch g £0

| 0a | 14 | SOUT | 14f Aw | 60 | 37 |

WESTMINSTER CITY 4 b c £4185

53a	5	WOLV	9f Aw	53	60	vis
31a	8	LING	12f Aw		101	vis
0a	12	WOLV	16f Aw	47	141	vis
34a	3	WOLV	9f Aw		259	vis
58a	2	WOLV	9f Aw		292	vis
54a	1	WOLV	8f Aw		322*	vis
54	2	WIND	12f Gd/Sft	53	748	
0	U	EPSO	12f Heavy	61	1030	
49	10	KEMP	12f Gd/Sft	56	1076	
50	4	LING	9f Good	53	1395	
47	4	SAND	10f Soft	53	1570	BL
35	9	WIND	10f Good		1880	bl
52	4	BRIG	10f Gd/Fm		1933	bl
46	9	LING	8f Gd/Fm		2215	bl
41	5	CHEP	8f Gd/Fm	49	2658	bl

WESTON HILLS 2 b c £0

35	7	WIND	5f Gd/Sft		1095
55	8	YORK	8f Gd/Fm		3729
71	10	WARW	7f Gd/Fm		3909

WESTSIDE FLYER 4 ch f £0

| 20a | 8 | SOUT | 6f Aw | 43 | 280 |

WESTWOOD VIEW 4 b f £0

0a	12	SOUT	7f Aw	40	69
36a	4	SOUT	11f Aw		196
22a	5	SOUT	11f Aw		248
34a	7	SOUT	12f Aw		301

WETHAAB 3 b c £2960

49	8	DONC	7f Good		717	
55	4	PONT	10f Gd/Sft		1103	
44	7	BEVE	12f Gd/Sft	55	1758	
58	1	WARW	12f Gd/Fm	50	2254*	BL
44	6	CATT	12f Gd/Fm	56	2422	bl
35	11	RIPO	12f Gd/Fm	59	3181	bl
39	7	REDC	14f Gd/Fm	55	3637	bl

WHALAH 2 ch f £0

| 71 | 10 | NEWM | 7f Good | | 3607 |

WHALE BEACH 2 b c £6973

76	7	NEWM	6f Gd/Fm		3162
81	1	WIND	6f Good		3638*
88	2	DONC	7f Firm	83	3901
90	3	NEWM	8f Gd/Fm	88	4350

WHARFEDALE CYGNET 2 b f £215

46	6	RIPO	5f Good		1595
49	4	MUSS	5f Firm		2045
45	7	MUSS	5f Good		3098

WHARFEDALE GHOST 2 gr c £0

14a	9	SOUT	5f Aw		1206
0	13	MUSS	5f Gd/Fm		1429
20	5	MUSS	7f Gd/Fm		2201

WHARFEDALE LADY 2 b f £0

67	7	RIPO	5f Soft		821
57	7	CARL	5f Firm		1252
0	11	REDC	6f Gd/Sft		1577
30	8	CATT	7f Gd/Fm		2927
46	6	RIPO	6f Gd/Fm		3184
0	13	AYR	8f Soft		3957

WHAT A CRACKER 3 b f £0

36	6	THIR	12f Gd/Fm	47	3125
0	13	FOLK	16f Gd/Fm	47	3448
0	10	REDC	14f Gd/Fm	42	3637
7a	9	LING	12f Aw		3835

WHAT A DANCER 3 b g £912

55	7	RIPO	10f Gd/Fm		3012
70	2	REDC	9f Gd/Fm		3326
35	6	NEWC	7f Gd/Fm		3604

WHAT A FUSS 7 b g £0

| 0 | 13 | PONT | 10f Soft | 46 | 871 |

WHATSITSNAME 4 br g £0

28a	8	SOUT	7f Aw		73
45a	5	WOLV	8f Aw		133
0a	14	SOUT	12f Aw	44	215
19a	9	WOLV	9f Aw	40	404
0a	13	LING	10f Aw	35	618

WHATTA MADAM 4 gr f £0

44a	6	LING	5f Aw	49	57	t
45a	4	LING	6f Aw	47	154	t
37a	4	LING	6f Aw	45	263	t
30a	10	WOLV	6f Aw		1137	t
52	5	BRIG	6f Firm	56	1211	t
32	7	BRIG	6f Gd/Sft		1508	t

WHEN IN ROME 2 b c £427

73	6	NEWM	8f Gd/Fm		3458
92	3	CHEP	8f Good		3867
101	6	ASCO	8f Gd/Sft		4127

WHENWILLIEMETHARRY 3 b f £0

| 64 | 6 | BATH | 10f Good | 68 | 1094 |

| 36 | 13 | BRIG | 8f Firm | 67 | 1330 |

WHERE THE HEART IS 2 ch c £880

71	3	YARM	6f Gd/Fm		2414
95	5	YORK	7f Gd/Fm		3730
71	4	AYR	7f Soft		3962
0	19	NEWM	8f Good	81	4350

WHERES CHARLOTTE 3 b f £310

49a	3	LING	6f Aw	49	4
27a	10	LING	6f Aw	55	105
0a	11	LING	7f Aw		155
32a	6	LING	6f Aw	47	242

WHERES JASPER 2 ch g £13518

83	2	HAYD	5f Gd/Sft		1488
85	1	HAYD	6f Soft		1823*
94	2	GOOD	6f Good		2307
91	10	NEWB	5f Firm		2849
94	1	HAYD	6f Good		3286*
76	15	DONC	6f Gd/Fm		3862
92	5	REDC	6f Gd/Sft		4219

WHISKY NINE 2 b c £0

| 57 | 7 | LING | 6f Gd/Fm | | 4188 |

WHISTLER 3 ch c £13526

70	2	KEMP	6f Gd/Sft		2582
78	4	NEWM	6f Gd/Fm		2807
83	1	SALI	6f Good		2977*
80	2	BATH	5f Firm		3622
85	1	NEWM	5f Good	79	4185*
89	5	NEWM	5f Good	90	4339
91	3	DONC	5f Soft	88	4466

WHISTLING DIXIE 4 ch g £6496

38a	2	SOUT	11f Aw	36	1306	
23a	6	SOUT	14f Aw	36	1501	
0	25	NEWM	12f Firm	43	1852	
46	1	PONT	10f Good	40	2366*	
39	4	PONT	10f Gd/Fm	40	2556	
47	1	LING	10f Good	40	2655*	
42	5	BRIG	10f Gd/Fm	47	3244	
47	3	WIND	10f Good	47	3356	
24	13	YORK	10f Gd/Fm	49	3731	bl
38	6	PONT	12f Soft	48	4229	

WHISTLING JACK 4 b g £0

| 0 | 18 | RIPO | 12f Soft | 60 | 822 | tbl |

WHITE AMIT 2 b f £0

| 52 | 8 | KEMP | 7f Gd/Fm | | 3789 | |
| 20a | 10 | WOLV | 8f Aw | | 4022 | T |

WHITE EMIR 7 b g £11301

53a	8	WOLV	6f Aw		132
57	3	CHEP	7f Gd/Sft	56	1794
60	2	WARW	8f Gd/Fm	57	2257
64	1	KEMP	7f Gd/Fm	59	2749*
64	4	KEMP	7f Gd/Fm	62	3362
53	9	KEMP	7f Gd/Fm	62	3796
66	1	BRIG	7f Gd/Sft	61	4121*

WHITE HOUSE 3 b f £5494

84	4	SAND	10f Heavy		1045
51	4	HAMI	9f Firm		1242
85	3	NEWM	10f Gd/Fm		2617
80	1	AYR	10f Gd/Fm		3142*
78	9	YORK	14f Firm	81	3599
0	20	DONC	12f Heavy	79	4580

WHITE MAGIC 3 b f £0

| 0 | 13 | WIND | 8f Gd/Fm | | 3048 |
| 18 | 9 | WIND | 12f Good | | 3351 |

WHITE MARVEL 2 b f £318

65	6	CARL	5f Firm		2277
72	3	CHEP	6f Gd/Fm		2447
52	7	WIND	6f Gd/Fm		2886

WHITE PLAINS 7 b g £23300

69a	4	LING	7f Aw		104	
75a	3	WOLV	8f Aw	80	172	t
78a	3	WOLV	9f Aw	79	230	t
84a	1	LING	12f Aw	79	237*	t

89a 1 **LING** 10f Aw 85 244* t
76a 4 LING 10f Aw 89 374 t
49a 8 LING 12f Aw 89 422 t
87a 3 LING 10f Aw 87 546 t
88a 3 LING 12f Aw 87 572 t
83a 3 LING 12f Aw 87 633 tE
82a 5 WOLV 9f Aw 662 t
0a 13 LING 10f Aw 690 et
34a 11 LING 12f Aw 83 4226

WHITE SANDS 3 b f £0
40 11 THIR 7f Good 1159
0 14 WIND 8f Gd/Sft 1428
32a 11 LING 6f Aw 50 1742
8a 6 LING 12f Aw 45 2217
19a 9 SOUT 8f Aw 45 2379
20 10 BEVE 8f Firm 43 2735
24a 8 LING 10f Aw 38 3828

WHITE SETTLER 7 b g £2520
53 3 CHEP 7f Gd/Fm 3253
54 1 **YARM** 7f Firm 3921*
43 13 LEIC 8f Gd/Sft 4033
22 10 LEIC 8f Sft/Hvy 4311

WHITE STAR LADY 2 ch f £3176
58a 5 SOUT 5f Aw 1304
61 8 RIPO 5f Soft 2539
54 5 CARL 5f Firm 2821
56 9 THIR 5f Gd/Fm 3346
59 1 **MUSS** 5f Gd/Fm 3589*
60 3 LEIC 6f Gd/Sft 59 4030
0 16 DONC 6f Gd/Sft 4449

WHITE SUMMIT 3 b c £0
0 18 CHEP 6f Gd/Fm 53 2489
54 9 LEIC 5f Gd/Fm 2919
0 16 LING 6f Firm 50 3493
48 6 WARW 5f Good 3694
53 7 SAND 5f Gd/Fm 3947
0 22 WIND 5f Gd/Sft 49 4295
0 21 NEWB 5f Gd/Sft 46 4459

WHITE WATERS 4 b g £0
43a 6 LING 7f Aw 651
0 18 WARW 11f Heavy 51 889

WHITE WILLOW 11 br g £0
54a 4 WOLV 16f Aw 2076 bl
0 9 NOTT 14f Gd/Fm 40 2681 bl

WHITEFOOT 3 b f £18575
101 4 SAND 10f Heavy 1056
102 1 **NEWB** 10f Good 1374*
74 13 EPSO 12f Gd/Sft 1828
98 5 ASCO 12f Good 2112

WHITEGATE WAY 3 b f £315
57 8 BEVE 7f Good 1444
57 10 BATH 8f Gd/Sft 1669
58 4 HAYD 7f Gd/Fm 2443
40 7 CATT 7f Gd/Fm 52 2932
34 10 THIR 8f Gd/Fm 52 2964
28 11 BATH 8f Gd/Fm 49 3816

WHITGREY ROSE 3 b f £1658
70 8 GOOD 8f Gd/Sft 1811
75 4 KEMP 10f Firm 2258
74 2 KEMP 8f Gd/Fm 2871

WHITLEYGRANGE GIRL 3 b f £0
21a 6 SOUT 8f Aw 415
20a 7 WOLV 7f Aw 493
32a 5 LING 7f Aw 570
31 7 CATT 7f Soft 4005
32 6 CATT 6f Soft 4255

WHIZZ 3 b f £0
37 6 DONC 10f Heavy 4571

WHIZZ KID 6 b m £16489
20a 7 WOLV 5f Aw 44 678
40 13 SAND 5f Gd/Fm 59 763
49 5 THIR 6f Soft 58 910

66 1 **WARW** 5f Heavy 56 1005*
67 2 REDC 5f Gd/Sft 62 1133
66 3 BEVE 5f Firm 66 1278
42a 1 **WOLV** 6f Aw 37 1391*
68 2 LING 5f Soft 66 1543
33a 6 SOUT 5f Aw 41 1806
63 10 RIPO 5f Good 67 1861
75 1 **CHEP** 5f Gd/Fm 67 2451*
59 15 HAYD 5f Gd/Fm 73 2701
56 10 WIND 6f Gd/Fm 73 3046
64 8 NEWB 5f Gd/Fm 73 3176
48 9 BRIG 5f Firm 71 3528
0 18 BEVE 5f Gd/Fm 71 3653
57 10 CHEP 5f Good 68 3872
68 5 AYR 5f Soft 68 3960
62 7 HAYD 5f Gd/Sft 68 4107
2 REDC 5f Gd/Sft 4220
64 6 YORK 5f Soft 67 4285
0 13 BATH 5f Soft 66 4432

WHO CARES WINS 4 ch c £1213
68 15 NEWM 12f Gd/Sft 80 968
73 10 YORK 14f Firm 79 1329
0 13 NEWB 13f Gd/Fm 76 1784 vis
76 3 SAND 14f Gd/Fm 75 1991
74 4 SAND 11f Good 75 2530
55 14 ASCO 12f Good 74 2674 BL

WHO DA LEADER 3 b c £0
0 15 NOTT 8f Good 69 1414
58 5 SALI 8f Firm 64 2025
0 15 NEWM 8f Gd/Fm 2134
45 6 NEWM 10f Gd/Fm 2284
36 8 CHEP 8f Gd/Fm 53 2448
0 15 CHEP 8f Gd/Fm 53 2658
0 16 BRIG 7f Gd/Fm 49 3242

WHO GOES THERE 4 ch f £6895
41a 5 LING 8f Aw 265
8a 9 LING 10f Aw 33 620
0 20 WIND 10f Gd/Sft 46 1100
0 16 YARM 7f Gd/Sft 42 1611
44 2 CHEP 7f Gd/Sft 42 1794
15 9 LEIC 6f Firm 44 2031
36 9 BRIG 7f Soft 44 2427
46 3 CHEP 8f Gd/Fm 44 2658
34 8 KEMP 7f Gd/Fm 42 2749
52 1 **CHEP** 7f Gd/Fm 46 2974*
47 6 WIND 8f Good 52 3188
56 1 **LING** 7f Firm 52 3279*
42 7 FOLK 7f Gd/Fm 58 3445
16 12 KEMP 7f Gd/Fm 56 3796

WHY WORRY NOW 4 ch f £0
46a 5 LING 7f Aw 8 BL
37a 7 WOLV 8f Aw 58 78
42a 8 WOLV 7f Aw 56 121 bl

WHYOME 3 b c £2761
104 3 THIR 8f Soft 925

WICKED 3 ch f £0
46a 6 LING 7f Aw 155 VIS

WICKHAM 4 b f £0
0 15 LING 7f Gd/Sft 1263
0 13 WIND 8f Gd/Sft 1428
0 20 WIND 12f Good 50 1730
0 11 YARM 8f Firm 43 2767
0a 10 SOUT 8f Aw 2950 BL

WIDAR 6 b h £6050
102a 3 LING 10f Aw 690

WIGMAN LADY 3 b f £0
55 5 REDC 7f Gd/Sft 1134
55 8 BEVE 10f Good 1447

WILBY WILLIE 4 bl g £0
0 15 LEIC 10f Gd/Fm 2774

WILCOY WARRIER 4 ch g £0
0a 10 WOLV 9f Aw 378

0a P WOLV 8f Aw 920

WILCUMA 9 b g £5451
46a 9 SOUT 11f Aw 85 302
85a 1 **WOLV** 16f Aw 80 380*
67a 5 WOLV 16f Aw 84 664
83 5 KEMP 14f Good 84 726
84 3 HAMI 13f Good 83 845
50 8 HAYD 12f Heavy 84 991
84 3 NEWB 12f Aw 83 3454
68 8 DONC 12f Soft 82 4464

WILD COLONIAL BOY 5 b g £289
42a 4 LING 16f Aw 46 548
35a 4 LING 16f Aw 42 649
31 7 KEMP 14f Good 52 726
25 13 LING 16f Good 40 1394
19 17 ASCO 20f Good 57 2092
26 6 CHEP 18f Gd/Fm 35 2452
0 17 LING 16f Firm 33 3755

WILD FLIGHT 3 b g £0
25a 9 SOUT 8f Aw 86
21 9 REDC 10f Gd/Sft 1582

WILD IMAGINATION 6 b g £3957
95a 3 BELM 9f Dirt 1616

WILD MAGIC 3 ch f £0
0 14 BATH 8f Gd/Sft 1670

WILD NETTLE 6 ch m £884
26a 10 LING 7f Aw 225
0a 12 WOLV 9f Aw 30 306
1a 9 LING 8f Aw 544 BL
20a 8 LING 10f Aw 38 1265
56 7 SALI 10f Good 1344
59 4 CHEP 8f Heavy 1556
33 2 LEIC 8f Gd/Sft 1732
0 12 LEIC 8f Firm 35 2032

WILD RICE 8 b g £0
53a 4 LING 10f Aw 110
32a 8 LING 7f Aw 159
45a 6 LING 10f Aw 333
0a 11 WOLV 12f Aw 40 410 bl
46a 8 SOUT 8f Aw 600 bl
0a 13 SOUT 8f Aw 646 bl

WILD RIVER 3 b c £259
40 8 NEWM 12f Good 951
53 4 NEWC 12f Good 3034
47 5 NEWC 9f Good 3248

WILD SKY 6 b g £0
31 19 DONC 8f Good 81 715 t
59 9 NEWM 10f Gd/Fm 80 1150 tvi
70 10 NEWM 7f Gd/Fm 76 2133 tvi
68 5 NEWB 8f Firm 74 2707 tvi

WILD SPIRIT 2 b g £0
59 5 LING 6f Firm 3492
1 6 BRIG 6f Firm 3732
28 9 NOTT 6f Soft 3973

WILD THING 4 b c £879
62a 2 SOUT 6f Aw 32
41a 9 LING 7f Aw 63 106
36a 12 LING 7f Aw 61 162 BL
59a 3 LING 5f Aw 59 205 bl
0a F LING 6f Aw 288 bl

WILDERNESS 3 b f £0
53 9 SALI 14f Good 2691
40 7 SALI 14f Firm 3751

WILDFLOWER 3 b f £9967
73 1 KEMP 7f Soft 1012*
69 7 BATH 5f Gd/Fm 1441
68 9 DONC 6f Gd/Fm 74 2577
55 10 KEMP 7f Gd/Fm 72 3076
69 4 NEWM 7f Gd/Fm 69 3460
77 1 **GOOD** 7f Soft 68 4080*
79 3 SAND 7f Soft 77 4204

WILEMMGEO 3 b f £24760

38a	8	SOUT	7f Aw	60	31	
55a	1	WOLV	8f Aw		80*	
33a	8	LING	8f Aw	54	158	
54a	2	WOLV	8f Aw		350	
54a	1	WOLV	9f Aw		382*	VIS
54a	2	WOLV	9f Aw		481	vis
55a	1	SOUT	8f Aw		514*	vis
47	8	DONC	10f Gd/Fm	60	701	
56	5	SOUT	10f Good	59	807	
0	12	YARM	8f Gd/Sft	56	1610	
43a	5	SOUT	8f Aw	54	1804	
44	9	REDC	6f Good	53	1891	
36	8	WIND	8f Gd/Fm	53	2051	
36	9	WIND	10f Gd/Fm	50	2206	
49	1	BEVE	8f Firm	45	2735*	
52	1	BEVE	7f Good	45	2882*	
53	4	CHEP	7f Good	53	3871	
57	1	SAND	10f Soft	51	4208*	
58	1	PONT	8f Soft	51	4232+	
23	14	PONT	10f Soft	58	4374	
61	2	BATH	10f Soft	58	4436	

WILFRAM 3 b g £8748

0	13	WARW	7f Soft	68	1061
33	8	BRIG	7f Soft		1467
0	14	SALI	7f Gd/Fm	58	1889
53	3	DONC	6f Gd/Fm	53	2315
60	1	CHEP	6f Gd/Fm	53	2489*
54	6	BEVE	7f Firm	60	2733
60	3	NOTT	8f Gd/Fm	60	3005
61	2	RIPO	9f Gd/Fm	60	3182
57	4	CHEP	10f Gd/Fm	61	3683
60	5	CHEP	10f Good	61	3870
62	1	LEIC	8f Gd/Sft		4033*

WILL IVESON 3 b c £8066

58a	8	SOUT	7f Aw	64	31	
46a	5	SOUT	8f Aw	61	128	
48a	5	SOUT	8f Aw	57	213	
59a	1	WOLV	8f Aw	53	311*	
58a	2	LING	8f Aw	58	401	VIS
65a	1	LING	8f Aw	58	419*	vis
55	11	RIPO	10f Soft	64	827	
47	1	HAMI	9f Gd/Fm		1191*	
40a	4	WOLV	8f Aw		1234	vis

WILLIAM THE LION 3 b c £1078

58	9	THIR	7f Good		1159
47	5	LEIC	8f Gd/Sft		1572
53	5	CARL	9f Gd/Sft	55	1722
52	2	AYR	13f Good	52	2141
42	7	LEIC	10f Gd/Fm		2510
49	4	CATT	12f Gd/Fm	52	2746
11	11	CATT	14f Gd/Fm	49	3201
6	10	BEVE	16f Gd/Fm	50	3406

WILLIAMS NEWS 5 b g £126582

121	2	WOOD	12f Firm		4400

WILLIAMS WELL 6 ch g £36225

47	7	NEWC	5f Heavy	66	1008	bl
58	6	THIR	5f Good	64	1162	bl
56	9	BEVE	5f Firm	62	1278	bl
68	1	NOTT	5f Good	60	1412*	bl
68	4	REDC	5f Gd/Sft	66	1580	bl
68	3	THIR	5f Good	66	1714	bl
67	6	YORK	6f Firm	68	2000	bl
63	5	CHES	5f Good	68	2247	bl
64	5	NEWC	6f Firm	68	2334	bl
68	2	CATT	5f Gd/Fm	67	2743	bl
71	2	CATT	5f Gd/Fm	67	2929	bl
70	2	THIR	6f Gd/Fm	67	3123	bl
77	1	PONT	5f Gd/Fm	70	3222*	bl
82	1	RIPO	6f Gd/Fm	75	3464*	bl
78	6	GOOD	6f Good	80	3646	bl
63	15	AYR	5f Good	80	4010	bl
70	9	HAYD	5f Gd/Sft	80	4107	bl
65	13	YORK	5f Soft	79	4285	bl

WILLIAMSHAKESPEARE 4 b c £0

73	11	NEWM	12f Gd/Sft	80	968
0	15	YARM	10f Soft	78	4392

WILLIE CONQUER 8 ch g £15539

63	1	BRIG	10f Firm		1210*
71	9	SAND	10f Good	84	1965
0	19	ASCO	12f Good	84	2069
64	1	BRIG	10f Gd/Sft		2423*
59	7	NEWM	10f Gd/Fm	75	2805
71	1	SALI	10f Good		2981*
71	1	YARM	10f Good		3234*
72	1	BRIG	10f Firm		3526*
62	2	YORK	9f Good		3808
72	3	YARM	10f Gd/Fm	70	3941
68a	4	LING	12f Aw	71	4271

WILLOUGHBYS BOY 3 b c £20373

59	9	LING	7f Gd/Fm		839
81	3	THIR	7f Good		1159
84	1	BEVE	7f Good		1444*
68	6	BEVE	8f Gd/Fm	80	2515
84	1	YARM	7f Firm	78	2768*
82	6	SAND	7f Gd/Fm	84	2922
85	2	EPSO	7f Gd/Fm	84	3414
69	13	NEWM	7f Gd/Fm	84	3629
89	1	SAND	8f Gd/Fm		3945*
73	10	NEWM	8f Good		4199

WILLOW MAGIC 3 b f £2289

65a	2	LING	5f Aw	62	234
53a	5	LING	5f Aw	62	269
17a	8	LING	6f Aw		399
61	4	BRIG	5f Firm	62	1334
61	3	BRIG	5f Soft	62	1512
51	8	BRIG	5f Gd/Fm	61	1932
61	3	BRIG	6f Firm	61	2042
60	4	BRIG	5f Soft	60	2428
60	3	FOLK	5f Good	60	2623
53	4	BRIG	5f Firm	59	2896
57	4	EPSO	5f Gd/Fm	58	3405
41	5	BRIG	7f Firm		3739
41	9	EPSO	5f Gd/Fm	58	3854
40	10	BRIG	6f Gd/Sft	56	4120

WILLRACK TIMES 3 b f £0

51a	5	WOLV	6f Aw	60	706
13	13	NOTT	6f Good	60	785
16a	10	WOLV	5f Aw		1036
0	14	BATH	6f Firm	58	1994
19	9	BATH	6f Firm		2788
27	14	DONC	5f Gd/Fm	47	3161
44	4	BRIG	5f Good		3562
41	5	WARW	5f Good		3694
0	15	BEVE	5f Good		3956

WILLY BANG BANG 3 b c £0

40	8	HAMI	11f Gd/Fm		1193
7	9	THIR	8f Gd/Sft		1352
44	7	RIPO	10f Good		1599

WILLYEVER 6 b g £0

24a	11	SOUT	7f Aw		667	VIS

WILMORE 4 gr g £0

34a	7	LING	10f Aw	3

WILOMENO 4 b f £0

0a	1	LING	8f Aw	114
0a	13	SOUT	11f Aw	455

WILSON BLYTH 2 b c £6746

69	2	REDC	5f Gd/Sft		1131
76	2	PONT	6f Good		1497
83	1	HAMI	6f Gd/Fm		2237*
82	4	BEVE	5f Gd/Fm		2483
77	3	HAMI	5f Gd/Fm		2797
74	4	CATT	6f Good	79	3439
76	2	NEWC	5f Firm		3602
55	6	YORK	6f Soft	75	4286

WILTON 5 ch g £9818

61a	3	SOUT	8f Aw		600	t
23a	9	SOUT	8f Aw	66	669	t
68	1	HAMI	8f Good		847*	
68	1	PONT	10f Heavy	67	943*	t
58	8	DONC	10f Gd/Sft	71	1070	
60a	1	SOUT	12f Aw		1203*	
54	7	GOOD	8f Gd/Sft	70	1473	
0	15	CATT	12f Soft	70	4003	
54	5	PONT	10f Soft	65	4374	
60	4	REDC	10f Soft		4501	

WIND CHIME 3 ch c £3465

80	2	LING	7f Gd/Sft		839
69	12	GOOD	7f Gd/Fm	78	3130
70	11	NEWM	7f Gd/Fm	76	3629
74	2	LING	7f Firm		3834
72	2	YARM	6f Gd/Fm		3919
59	10	KEMP	8f Soft	74	4038

WINDCHILL 2 ch f £11806

50	11	RIPO	5f Soft		821
46	7	THIR	5f Soft		928
56	2	BEVE	5f Good		1443
56	2	THIR	6f Gd/Fm		1713
63	1	REDC	7f Good		1890*
61	1	NEWC	6f Gd/Fm		2312*
63	3	CATT	7f Gd/Fm	60	2928
59	4	REDC	6f Firm	60	3327

WINDFALL 3 b c £581

54	8	THIR	12f Good		1157	
77	3	LING	9f Firm		1912	
51	8	LING	7f Firm	75	2325	
37	10	EPSO	9f Good	70	2795	
38	8	WARW	11f Gd/Fm	70	2842	
14	11	NEWM	8f Gd/Fm		3456	VIS
40	6	FOLK	10f Gd/Fm	62	3585	

WINDMILL 3 b f £3294

82	4	BEVE	10f Good		1447	
53	1	CATT	14f Gd/Fm		2439*	
66	4	RIPO	12f Gd/Fm	75	2837	
67	4	THIR	12f Gd/Fm	70	3125	
42	7	BEVE	16f Good		3395	
0	12	BEVE	12f Good	65	3954	BL

WINDMILL LANE 3 b f £6282

60	2	BEVE	12f Heavy	60	978	
50	6	PONT	12f Gd/Sft	60	1106	
51a	3	SOUT	11f Aw		1502	
35	7	RIPO	12f Good	58	1862	VIS
56a	2	SOUT	12f Aw	52	2123	
57	1	CARL	17f Gd/Fm	53	2244*	
58	7	BEVE	16f Gd/Fm	60	2516	
66	3	CHES	16f Gd/Fm	64	2672	
52a	5	SOUT	12f Aw	56	2815	
44	9	LEIC	12f Gd/Fm		3219	
44	5	HAYD	16f Gd/Fm	80	3476	
29	11	CATT	16f Soft	56	4006	

WINDRUSH BOY 10 br g £0

0	17	LING	5f Gd/Fm	41	2184
32	8	BATH	5f Gd/Sft	38	2555
25	7	FOLK	5f Good	38	2623
41	4	BATH	5f Firm		2788
42	4	BRIG	5f Firm		2905
36	4	RIPO	5f Gd/Fm	38	3180
41	6	BRIG	5f Firm		3562
39	7	WARW	5f Good		3694
0	16	CHEP	5f Good	38	3872

WINDSHIFT 4 b g £4191

60a	11	SOUT	7f Aw	78	216	vis
73a	5	SOUT	8f Aw	76	251	vis
75a	4	WOLV	8f Aw	76	309	vis
80a	1	WOLV	8f Aw	74	381*	vis
57a	6	WOLV	8f Aw	78	580	BL
0	16	PONT	10f Heavy	70	943	vis
28	9	EPSO	9f Heavy		1033	vis

WINDSOR BOY 3 b c £131169 (preceding entries)

0	23	ASCO	8f Gd/Sft	67	1113	vis
0	13	PONT	8f Good		1498	
0	23	REDC	8f Gd/Sft	57	4217	bl

WINDSOR BOY 3 b c £131169

103	2	CHES	12f Gd/Fm		1216
104	2	CAPA	12f Gd/Fm		1618

WINFIELD 2 ch c £0

47	9	BATH	6f Gd/Sft		2550	
70	4	CHEP	6f Gd/Fm		2972	
47	9	GOOD	6f Good		3649	
22	10	HAYD	6f Soft	71	4090	
0	22	REDC	6f Gd/Sft		4219	BL

WINGED ANGEL 3 ch g £7438

66	4	SOUT	7f Good		804	
51	9	THIR	6f Soft		909	
45a	8	WOLV	7f Aw		1035	
0	13	THIR	8f Good	62	1387	
44	10	NEWC	8f Good	59	2524	
58	1	REDC	11f Gd/Fm	55	2863*	
53	5	AYR	11f Gd/Fm	58	3140	
41	11	REDC	11f Gd/Fm	57	3636	
0	13	BEVE	10f Sft/Hv	55	4046	VIS

WINGED GREYBIRD 6 gr m £0

0a	14	LING	16f Aw	40	4329	t

WINGED HUSSAR 7 b g £750

100	5	ASCO	22f Good		2153
100	4	LEOP	12f Good		3371

WINGS AS EAGLES 3 gr c £0

72	7	KEMP	9f Gd/Fm		2086
45	7	NEWB	12f Firm		2710

WINGS OF SOUL 2 b c £1254

87	3	NEWB	8f Gd/Sft		4457

WINLEAH 4 gr c £0

4a	10	WOLV	8f Aw		138
0a	13	SOUT	11f Aw	27	324

WINNING PLEASURE 2 b c £0

0	16	NEWM	7f Good		4183
0	15	YARM	7f Soft		4514
77	7	DONC	7f Heavy		4566

WINNING VENTURE 3 b c £9920

112	3	NEWM	7f Good		950	
87	21	NEWM	8f Gd/Fm		1171	
107	2	NEWB	6f Good		1371	
106	3	LING	6f Good		1674	
92	9	NEWC	6f Firm		2335	
106	7	NEWM	6f Gd/Fm		2615	
98	9	DEAU	6f Good		3212	
95	9	HAYD	6f Gd/Sft		3784	BL
102	5	GOOD	7f Soft		4078	

WINNIPEG 4 ch f £0

28a	8	LING	6f Aw		95
0a	12	LING	7f Aw		156
0	8	BRIG	8f Soft		4177

WINSOME GEORGE 5 b g £4882

47a	2	SOUT	12f Aw	47	682	
47	3	SOUT	12f Good	47	805	
48a	3	SOUT	14f Aw	51	868	
14a	10	SOUT	14f Aw	47	1501	
44	7	AYR	13f Gd/Fm		1657	BL
40	4	MUSS	14f Firm	43	2050	vis
27	7	REDC	14f Gd/Fm	43	2156	vis
32	5	CATT	12f Gd/Fm		2742	vis
25	9	CHEP	12f Gd/Fm	40	2971	
17	6	BRIG	12f Gd/Fm	32	3260	vis
34	8	FOLK	12f Gd/Fm		3447	vis
12	6	BATH	17f Firm	30	3625	vis
28	4	HAMI	11f Soft	28	3805	vis
27	1	HAMI	12f Gd/Sft	21	3827*	
15	10	NEWM	12f Good		4178	
30	11	YORK	12f Soft	43	4280	
0a	14	SOUT	14f Aw	38	4371	

WINSTON 7 b g £0

WINTER DOLPHIN 2 b f £0 (preceding entries)

5a	8	SOUT	7f Aw	35	496	
0a	8	SOUT	12f Aw	32	642	
0	22	REDC	8f Firm	37	1300	

WINTER DOLPHIN 2 b f £0

38	9	CHEP	5f Gd/Fm		3252
59	6	BATH	5f Gd/Fm		3513
60	6	LING	5f Good		4096
52	9	LING	6f Soft	62	4269
59a	4	WOLV	5f Aw		4441

WINTER JASMINE 2 b f £385

65	9	WIND	5f Gd/Fm		1197
77	4	WIND	5f Good		1727
63	7	KEMP	6f Gd/Fm		1924

WINTER SOLSTICE 2 b f £7685

102	2	CHAN	8f Good		3934
102	7	LONG	8f Good		4260
96	7	SAIN	10f Soft		4556

WINTZIG 3 b f £2547

0	15	DONC	10f Gd/Fm	71	701
53	5	THIR	12f Soft		924
69	2	PONT	8f Good	65	1495
59	5	BATH	8f Gd/Sft	65	1671
0	11	YARM	10f Gd/Fm	67	1955
37	3	NEWM	8f Firm		2345
46a	3	WOLV	9f Aw		2602
34	11	PONT	8f Gd/Fm	62	2831
58	4	CARL	8f Firm	58	3574
54	4	LEIC	8f Gd/Sft		4032

WISHBONE ALLEY 5 b g £8132

35a	7	SOUT	7f Aw	45	69	bl
45a	2	LING	6f Aw	41	154	vis
47a	2	LING	6f Aw	43	235	vis
48a	2	WOLV	5f Aw	45	291	vis
51a	1	LING	5f Aw	45	312*	vis
52a	3	LING	6f Aw	53	358	vis
52a	2	LING	6f Aw	50	371	vis
0a	11	WOLV	5f Aw	51	445	vis
48a	4	LING	5f Aw	51	573	vis
53a	2	LING	6f Aw	50	634	vis
0	11	SOUT	6f Good	53	802	vis
51a	3	LING	6f Aw	52	881	vis
46	9	CARL	5f Firm		1256	vis
41	8	THIR	6f Gd/Sft	52	1356	vis
42	12	MUSS	7f Gd/Fm	51	1431	
0	12	YARM	6f Gd/Fm	48	1953	vis
35	7	NOTT	6f Gd/Fm	45	2193	bl
47	3	NEWC	6f Gd/Fm	45	2275	
39	14	REDC	8f Gd/Fm	47	2861	
46	5	NEWC	6f Good	47	3037	
0	14	REDC	6f Firm	46	3312	vis
39	8	NEWC	6f Firm	45	3605	

WISHEDHADGONEHOME 3 b f £858

41a	8	LING	7f Aw		53	
35a	10	LING	7f Aw		155	
52a	2	WOLV	7f Aw		192	VIS
42a	6	LING	8f Aw		236	BL
42a	3	LING	8f Aw		241	vis
33a	10	WOLV	7f Aw	54	257	vis
37a	5	WOLV	8f Aw		350	vis
30a	6	SOUT	8f Aw		514	vis
28	10	LEIC	6f Gd/Fm	51	2511	vis
26	10	PONT	8f Gd/Fm	44	2831	vis
36	4	THIR	8f Gd/Fm	44	2964	vis
31	4	LEIC	7f Gd/Fm		3332	vis
35	9	BEVE	7f Gd/Fm		3670	vis

WISHFUL THINKER 3 b g £3352

51	8	NOTT	8f Gd/Fm	70	1085
37	11	NOTT	8f Good	67	1414
56	10	LEIC	10f Gd/Sft	63	1735
55	3	HAMI	8f Firm		2093
49	8	NEWM	8f Firm		2345
47	1	REDC	11f Gd/Fm		2989*

WISHFUL THINKER continued (column 3 preceding)

49	2	MUSS	9f Gd/Fm		3591
0	13	WARW	11f Gd/Fm	47	3915
51	4	WIND	10f Heavy		4528

WITCHS BREW 3 b f £0

49	7	PONT	12f Gd/Sft	60	1106

WITH A WILL 6 b g £9863

54	3	LING	9f Good	54	1395
47	3	NOTT	8f Soft	55	1646
64	1	WIND	10f Good		2372*
51	4	WIND	10f Soft	60	2544
68	1	WIND	8f Good	61	3188*
70	1	SALI	8f Firm	66	3753*
56	12	NEWM	8f Good	70	4340

WITH RESPECT 3 b f £322

57	10	NOTT	8f Gd/Fm		1268
42	10	HAMI	8f Gd/Fm	58	1939
29a	5	SOUT	12f Aw	53	2382
39	4	NOTT	10f Gd/Fm	49	3007
10a	9	WOLV	12f Aw	46	3494
0	16	YARM	8f Gd/Fm	39	3970

WITHIN THE LAW 2 b f £290

26	12	CATT	5f Soft		4252
41	4	AYR	7f Heavy		4303

WITHOUT FRIENDS 6 b g £0

27a	7	LING	8f Aw		101	vis
44a	6	SOUT	8f Aw		197	
26a	8	SOUT	8f Aw		252	
53a	4	LING	10f Aw		333	
18a	4	WOLV	12f Aw	35	408	
0a	12	LING	8f Aw	33	620	vis

WITNEY ROYALE 2 ch g £3470

74	1	DONC	6f Gd/Fm		1838*
74	4	BEVE	7f Gd/Fm		2514
0	10	CURR	6f Yldg		3720
0	21	DONC	7f Firm	82	3901

WITTON WOOD 3 b c £313

47a	3	LING	10f Aw		286
31a	6	WOLV	8f Aw		350

WODHILL FOLLY 3 ch f £0

65	6	NEWM	8f Gd/Fm		3626
59	9	YARM	11f Heavy		4481

WOLF VENTURE 2 ch c £874

58a	4	SOUT	8f Aw		1974
80	8	EPSO	7f Good		3760
78	5	WARW	7f Gd/Fm		3909
54	8	BRIG	6f Soft	79	4170
63	15	NEWM	6f Good	77	4338

WONDERFUL MAN 4 ch c £0

53	6	REDC	8f Firm	53	1296
0	13	HAYD	11f Gd/Sft	53	3480
0	14	BEVE	10f Gd/Fm	49	3652

WONDERGREEN 2 b g £4081

61	6	PONT	5f Good		2360
53	10	BEVE	5f Firm		2730
54	10	RIPO	8f Good		3466
75	3	YORK	8f Gd/Fm		3729
73	1	BEVE	7f Good		3949*
60	7	YORK	7f Soft	74	4279

WONDERLAND 3 b f £0

24	15	WARW	7f Heavy	58	887	
24	7	HAMI	8f Gd/Fm		1191	
45	5	NOTT	8f Gd/Sft	48	1365	VIS
0	12	NOTT	10f Soft	46	1644	
15	12	AYR	11f Good	44	2139	

WONTCOSTALOTBUT 6 b m £2190

54	2	SAND	16f Heavy	51	1044
51	9	LING	16f Good	56	1394
45	11	CHEP	18f Gd/Sft	56	1800

WOOD POUND 4 b c £4106

87a	1	SOUT	12f Aw		301*
90a	2	SOUT	11f Aw	85	343
68a	5	LING	12f Aw	87	422

WOODBASTWICK CHARM 3 b c £0

59	11	WIND	10f Good			850
0	12	DONC	10f Gd/Sft			1054
0	20	WIND	12f Firm	54		1292
41	7	LEIC	8f Gd/Fm	49		2506
27	9	MUSS	7f Good	44		3103
46	5	YARM	10f Good			3382
30	6	BEVE	10f Gd/Fm	39		3656

WOODCUT 4 ch g £0

38a	7	WOLV	6f Aw		406
0a	11	SOUT	7f Aw	29	476
1a	9	SOUT	6f Aw	26	604

WOODEN DOLL 2 ch f £15370

103	2	DEAU	7f Gd/Sft	3722
103	3	LONG	7f Gd/Sft	4054

WOODFIELD 2 b c £1050

76	8	NEWM	7f Good	2563
85	3	ASCO	7f Gd/Fm	2956
71	7	NEWM	7f Good	3608
0	20	NEWM	7f Good	4158

WOODLAND RIVER 3 ch c £4054

0	12	LING	7f Gd/Sft		840
0	18	NEWM	7f Gd/Sft		983
84	2	RIPO	8f Gd/Fm		2104
90	1	**WARW**	8f Good		2465*
78	10	NEWM	8f Good	86	3022

WOODLANDS 3 b c £378

52	3	CATT	7f Soft		1682
0	14	NEWM	6f Firm	85	3297
55	8	LING	6f Firm		3579
0	15	YARM	7f Firm	70	3939

WOODLANDS LAD TOO 8 b g £0

0	13	WARW	8f Good		2464
0	13	CHEP	12f Gd/Fm	36	2656
0	16	WIND	12f Gd/Fm	26	2887

WOODWIND DOWN 3 b f £2079

62a	2	LING	7f Aw		651
56	9	WIND	8f Gd/Fm	65	744
11	7	WARW	7f Soft		813
40	9	YARM	8f Gd/Sft	58	1610
44	7	SALI	7f Good		1884
48	3	NOTT	8f Gd/Fm	48	2187
48	2	CARL	9f Firm	48	2825
41	5	CARL	8f Gd/Fm	48	3082

WOODYATES 3 b f f £1907

0	12	SALI	7f Good			1349
53	6	NEWB	8f Aw			3179
40	8	SALI	7f Gd/Fm			3423
53	5	GOOD	10f Good	55		3663
47	8	BATH	10f Soft			4141
0	14	NEWM	12f Good			4178 t
45	1	**WIND**	10f Heavy			4528*

WOODYS BOY 6 gr g £0

61	5	NEWM	12f Gd/Fm	65	2131
58	6	NEWB	16f Firm	63	2812
0	P	NEWM	16f Firm	60	3295

WOOLFE 3 ch f £2831

75	3	SAND	8f Gd/Fm		2938
72	3	WIND	8f Good		3190
70	2	SAND	8f Good		3474
0	13	BRIG	10f Gd/Sft	72	4118
59	4	NOTT	8f Heavy		4505 VIS

WOOLLY WINSOME 4 br g £316

16a	11	WOLV	8f Aw			39
49a	6	LING	8f Aw			109 VIS
50a	5	LING	7f Aw			225 vis
47a	3	SOUT	7f Aw			367
16a	8	WOLV	8f Aw			409
0a	13	SOUT	8f Aw	46		496 bl
0	15	WARW	11f Heavy	46		889
37	6	SALI	6f Good	43		2690
16	7	RIPO	6f Gd/Fm	40		2839

33	5	BRIG	8f Gd/Sft		4122
30	12	SAND	10f Soft	38	4208
41a	5	LING	7f Aw		4331

WOORE LASS 4 ch f £1188

0	21	REDC	7f Firm	53	1297
44	10	AYR	8f Gd/Fm	50	1658
0	17	REDC	8f Good	47	1892
56	2	MUSS	9f Firm		2376
38	4	PONT	8f Gd/Fm	44	2561
45	5	DONC	8f Gd/Fm	50	2758
34	9	NEWC	9f Firm	47	3603
0	18	NEWC	8f Heavy	45	4406

WORK OF FICTION 3 b c £321

0	21	NEWM	8f Gd/Sft		972
64	4	BATH	8f Gd/Fm		1436
57	4	HAYD	7f Gd/Fm		1789
57	4	BRIG	7f Firm	63	2044
43	10	KEMP	7f Gd/Fm	61	2749

WORLD CLEEK 5 gr h £0

109a	6	NAD	10f Dirt	769

WORLDLY MANNER 4 b c £1158

88a	10	NAD	10f Dirt	769	vis
89	7	NEWB	8f Gd/Fm	1402	vis
92	3	NOTT	8f Good	1872	vis

WORSTED 3 ch f £1647

56	3	LING	5f Good		2590
58	5	SAND	5f Gd/Fm	60	2934
63	2	SAND	5f Good	59	3436

WORTH A GAMBLE 2 ch c £0

0	20	NEWB	6f Firm	3980
54	10	LING	6f Soft	4188
50	12	NEWB	6f Sft/Hvy	4471

WORTH A RING 2 b f £0

0a	11	SOUT	5f Aw	1304
43a	5	SOUT	7f Aw	4154
34a	8	WOLV	6f Aw	4246
0	21	NEWM	7f Good	4336

WORTH THE RISK 3 b f £1076

53	3	BEVE	8f Firm		2222
40	5	BEVE	10f Gd/Fm	41	2484
23	7	CARL	9f Firm	40	2825
12	8	REDC	14f Gd/Fm	40	3637
30	2	CATT	14f Soft		4002
11	8	AYR	11f Heavy		4304

WORTHILY 2 b c £31121

0	13	NEWC	7f Good	2521
78	5	HAYD	7f Soft	3786
93	1	**KEMP**	8f Soft	4036*
96	2	SAND	8f Soft	4203
103	1	**PONT**	8f Soft	4375*
98	1	**NEWM**	10f Soft	4543*

WOVEN ROVING 4 b c £0

0	23	ASCO	7f Gd/Fm	97	2997

WRANGEL 6 ch g £2383

49	7	THIR	12f Gd/Sft		1353
0	13	RIPO	10f Soft		2538
48	1	**CATT**	12f Gd/Fm		3202*
38a	6	SOUT	16f Aw	48	4149

WRAY 8 ch g £8500

106	2	LEOP	7f Sft/Hvy	15
108	4	CURR	7f Yldg	862
96	3	CURR	10f Soft	1121

WROTHAM ARMS 3 b f £0

0	18	NEWM	7f Gd/Sft	971
6a	8	WOLV	9f Aw	1141
12	8	NEWM	10f Gd/Fm	2284 BL

WRY ARDOUR 4 b g £0

14a	12	SOUT	8f Aw	38	85
0a	16	SOUT	12f Aw	33	215
0a	12	SOUT	8f Aw	33	496

WURZEL 3 ch c £0

65	8	NEWB	8f Soft	85	912

WUXI VENTURE 5 b g £0

54a	7	SOUT	8f Aw	79	601
42a	8	SOUT	8f Aw	76	669
64a	8	SOUT	7f Aw	76	687
0	21	DONC	8f Good	79	715
66	8	PONT	8f Soft	77	875
67	8	BEVE	10f Heavy	77	975
45	11	DONC	10f Gd/Sft	73	1070
39	11	BEVE	8f Firm	69	1279

WYCHWOOD CHARMER 3 b f £0

0a	13	WOLV	6f Aw	118

WYN 5 b m £0

26	6	CHEP	6f Heavy	47	1557

XALOC BAY 2 br c £2081

82	2	AYR	6f Good		2137
87	2	HAYD	6f Gd/Fm		2700
64	12	AYR	5f Soft		3959
69	11	NEWM	6f Gd/Fm	80	4214
61	7	YARM	5f Soft	77	4511

XANADU 4 ch g £35894

26	11	MUSS	5f Gd/Fm	56	798
18	11	HAMI	6f Good	55	844
63	1	**HAMI**	6f Gd/Fm	54	1192+
69	1	**HAMI**	6f Firm		1239*
69	2	CARL	5f Firm		1256
42	13	THIR	6f Good	64	1383
69	1	**MUSS**	5f Firm	64	1687*
60	10	HAYD	6f Gd/Fm	68	2444
77	1	**HAYD**	5f Gd/Fm	68	2505*
78	2	AYR	5f Gd/Fm	75	2721
75	4	PONT	5f Gd/Fm	75	2830
79	3	NEWC	5f Gd/Fm	77	2987
75	6	HAYD	5f Gd/Fm	78	3322
60	14	RIPO	6f Gd/Fm	78	3464
79	2	DONC	5f Firm	77	3894
0	23	AYR	6f Gd/Sft	77	4010

XANIA 3 b f £0

35a	8	WOLV	6f Aw		118
19a	12	WOLV	7f Aw	51	257

XATIVA 3 b f £0

18a	11	SOUT	8f Aw		328
18a	8	WOLV	6f Aw	54	397
43a	4	LING	7f Aw	48	773
0	17	WARW	7f Heavy	55	887

XELLANCE 3 b c £28010

42a	1	**SOUT**	11f Aw	35	536*
24a	5	LING	10f Aw	43	597
46a	1	**WOLV**	12f Aw	42	1142*
0	U	LEIC	12f Gd/Sft	45	1571
27	7	YARM	14f Gd/Fm	45	1949
52	1	**MUSS**	14f Firm	45	2050*
53a	1	**SOUT**	12f Aw	48	2123*
52	1	**REDC**	14f Gd/Fm	46	2156*
52	2	MUSS	16f Gd/Fm	47	2203
53	2	FOLK	12f Gd/Fm	46	2295
66	1	**CHEP**	18f Gd/Fm	52	2452*
60	4	BEVE	16f Gd/Fm	58	2516
66	1	**REDC**	16f Gd/Fm	62	2866*
66	2	YARM	16f Good	66	3026
69	3	REDC	16f Soft	68	3331
74	1	**WARW**	16f Good	70	3695*
73	4	YARM	18f Gd/Fm	75	3967

XENOS 3 b c £260

35a	8	SOUT	5f Aw		217
32a	7	LING	6f Aw	49	242
42a	5	SOUT	7f Aw		283
37a	6	SOUT	8f Aw		303
44a	1	**WOLV**	9f Aw		481
20a	9	SOUT	11f Aw	45	537
42a	4	LING	8f Aw		595 BL

XIBALBA 3 b c £2533

71	1	**NOTT**	8f Good	67	1414*

71 4 LEIC 10f Gd/Sft 70 1735
0 12 BEVE 10f Gd/Fm 69 2518
0 14 NEWM 12f Gd/Fm 69 3167
0 U KEMP 9f Gd/Fm 68 3357 VIS

XIPE TOTEC 2 ch c £4289
53 10 LEIC 6f Firm 2029
87 1 **HAYD** 6f Gd/Fm 2700*
90 3 RIPO 6f Gd/Fm 3184
79 6 REDC 6f Firm 81 3327

XSYNNA 4 b c £766
54a 5 SOUT 6f Aw 63 212
53a 4 LING 7f Aw 243
60a 2 WOLV 6f Aw 59 351
38a 6 SOUT 6f Aw 414
35a 7 WOLV 6f Aw 1139
0 26 NEWM 8f Gd/Fm 54 1690
0 18 LEIC 6f Gd/Sft 54 1734 bl
37a 10 WOLV 6f Aw 56 4023 bl

XTRA 2 b c £1082
70 17 NEWM 8f Good 4349
85 3 NEWM 8f Gd/Sft 4531

XUA 3 b f £57630
108 1 **CAPA** 8f Heavy 1117*
103 10 LONG 8f V 1319
109 8 CHAN 11f Gd/Sft 1901

XYLEM 9 ch g £2046
38a 3 WOLV 12f Aw 347
40a 2 WOLV 12f Aw 36 410
39a 3 LING 13f Aw 38 460 vis
23a 7 WOLV 12f Aw 38 520 vis
39a 2 WOLV 16f Aw 38 577 vis
39a 3 SOUT 14f Aw 668 vis
16 9 RIPO 12f Soft 30 822 vis
33a 5 WOLV 16f Aw 37 918 vis
42 4 MUSS 16f Gd/Fm 1145 vis
0 12 NOTT 14f Good 25 2008 vis
0 14 WIND 12f Gd/Fm 24 2887 bl

Y TO KMAN 2 b c £9965
80 1 **KEMP** 5f Good 724*
87 2 NEWB 5f Soft 911
80 4 CHES 5f Gd/Fm 1214
0 17 NEWM 6f Gd/Fm 88 4214
85 6 NEWM 6f Good 85 4338
92 1 **YARM** 5f Soft 85 4511*

YA TARRA 3 ch f £2690
78 3 NOTT 10f Heavy 4408
82 2 DONC 10f Heavy 4571

YABINT EL SHAM 4 b f £6622
33a 11 SOUT 6f Aw 66 44 t
66a 1 **WOLV** 5f Aw 60 191* t
59a 5 SOUT 5f Aw 64 342
67a 2 WOLV 5f Aw 64 394
70a 3 WOLV 6f Aw 69 466
52a 9 WOLV 6f Aw 69 491
62a 7 WOLV 5f Aw 70 579
45a 11 WOLV 6f Aw 69 1391
0 20 DONC 6f Gd/Fm 66 1842
0a 12 WOLV 6f Aw 66 2078
48a 8 SOUT 5f Aw 62 2632 t
46 7 WIND 5f Good 60 3191 t
49a 7 WOLV 6f Aw 58 3271
0 14 BEVE 5f Gd/Fm 55 3653 t
45 7 LEIC 6f Gd/Fm 4031
43a 5 WOLV 6f Aw 54 4363

YAFA 4 ch g £0
46 9 EPSO 9f Heavy 1032
34 10 LING 10f Soft 1287
0 15 YARM 8f Good 1771
17a 8 SOUT 7f Aw 40 2122 BL

YAHESKA 3 b f £0
13a 5 LING 10f Aw 40 1544
28 8 WIND 12f Gd/Fm 1880

44 8 YARM 10f Firm 52 2387 BL
0a 11 SOUT 7f Aw 2633 bl

YAKAREEM 4 b c £2750
51a 12 WOLV 8f Aw 98 137
94 4 EPSO 9f Good 1847
75 5 DONC 10f Gd/Fm 2351
72 8 GOOD 7f Gd/Fm 3132
84 8 WIND 10f Good 3641
83 9 YORK 9f Gd/Fm 3726

YALAIL 4 b c £0
0a 12 LING 10f Aw 1
24a 7 WOLV 16f Aw 60 66
24a 11 LING 12f Aw 53 115
30 8 NEWM 7f Gd/Fm 3318
36a 4 WOLV 12f Aw 46 3494
11a 10 LING 12f Aw 3835

YANKEE DANCER 5 b m £0
23 11 PONT 10f Good 55 1496
0 14 CATT 14f Soft 52 1683
25 10 HAYD 12f Gd/Sft 45 2446
17a 9 WOLV 8f Aw 45 2601
11 9 BEVE 12f Gd/Fm 36 3053
28 8 RIPO 12f Gd/Fm 38 3181
15a 7 WOLV 15f Gd/Fm 36 3276
0a 14 SOUT 14f Aw 38 4370

YANUS 2 b c £0
0 12 NOTT 6f Good 3520
0 15 LEIC 7f Firm 3840
0 13 LING 6f Soft 4189

YAQOOTAH 2 ch f £0
76 7 YARM 6f Firm 3938

YARA 3 b f £12350
95 2 CURR 7f Soft 1122
0 7 CURR 8f Gd/Sft 1626
99 6 CURR 10f Yldg 2404
109 2 CURR 10f Gd/Fm 3068

YAROB 7 ch h £18555
69 7 CATT 7f Gd/Fm 78 780
84 1 **PONT** 8f Soft 77 875*
70 9 KEMP 8f Soft 82 1015
95 1 **DONC** 10f Gd/Sft 82 1070*
65 15 THIR 8f Good 88 1160
93 2 CHES 10f Gd/Fm 88 1217
82 6 EPSO 10f Good 91 1845
28 31 ASCO 8f Good 91 2090
72 6 NEWC 10f Good 90 2522
49 14 ASCO 8f Gd/Fm 88 3018
63 6 NEWM 12f Good 4178
55 9 YORK 10f Soft 4275

YATTARNA 4 b c £298
32a 5 WOLV 12f Aw 59 554
55 4 NOTT 14f Good 54 1874
50 4 WARW 16f Gd/Fm 53 2256

YAVANAS PACE 8 ch g £146574
93 7 NAD 12f Good 767
114 1 **HAYD** 12f Heavy 987*
93 8 NEWM 8f Gd/Fm 1152
108 4 CHES 13f Firm 1247
108 3 LONG 16f Gd/Sft 1456
114 2 ASCO 12f Good 2149
114 2 NEWM 12f Good 2566
112 6 DUSS 12f Good 2911
116 2 CURR 12f Good 4055
116 2 COLO 12f Soft 4147

YAZAIN 4 b c £428
68 3 FOLK 7f Gd/Fm 2293
0 11 WARW 8f Good 2464
56 10 LING 7f Firm 3834
0 16 BRIG 6f Gd/Sft 65 4120

YAZMIN 3 b f £0
77 6 NEWB 7f Soft 913
85 10 LING 7f Gd/Sft 1283

YEAST 8 b g £8444
37 9 LING 7f Soft 83 1286
61 2 PONT 8f Good 1498
58 12 KEMP 8f Gd/Fm 72 1926
75 1 **LING** 8f Gd/Fm 2215*
79 1 **LEIC** 7f Gd/Fm 2508*
77 2 NEWM 8f Gd/Fm 74 2802

YELLOW TRUMPET 2 b f £2879
75 1 **CARL** 5f Firm 3571*

YENALED 3 gr c £11645
63 3 REDC 10f Firm 59 1299
67 1 **MUSS** 8f Gd/Fm 59 1434*
55 6 REDC 11f Gd/Sft 65 1560
65 2 AYR 9f Good 65 2166
59 4 MUSS 8f Firm 65 2378
52 6 REDC 11f Gd/Fm 64 2863
61 2 HAYD 8f Good 64 3288
59 2 THIR 8f Gd/Fm 54 3345
58 5 REDC 8f Gd/Fm 59 3634
64 1 **MUSS** 7f Gd/Sft 59 4136*
54 9 DONC 7f Gd/Sft 64 4452
63 3 MUSS 8f Soft 64 4565

YERTLE 3 b c £268
85 8 NEWM 8f Gd/Sft 972
61 8 LING 7f Gd/Fm 1263
59 3 BATH 8f Gd/Fm 1435
52 6 SAND 8f Good 69 1964
0 11 BEVE 8f Sft/Hvy 65 4045
50 9 WIND 10f Gd/Sft 60 4291

YES COLONEL 3 gr c £0
34a 8 LING 8f Aw 26

YES KEEMO SABEE 5 b g £4634
0a 6 WOLV 16f Aw 66 627
4a 10 SOUT 12f Aw 62 671
0 15 HAYD 14f Gd/Fm 68 1167
56 11 BEVE 16f Firm 68 1276
53 8 NEWC 17f Gd/Sft 60 1478
25 7 PONT 17f Soft 56 1701 VIS
49 8 PONT 17f Good 54 1867
50 2 WARW 15f Good 50 2461
46 5 CHES 16f Gd/Fm 50 2672
46 3 BEVE 12f Gd/Sft 47 3053
46 3 THIR 16f Gd/Fm 45 3348
22 9 CHES 16f Gd/Fm 45 3511
47 2 BEVE 12f Gd/Fm 45 3674 BL
45 9 HAYD 14f Soft 50 3783 bl
41 8 GOOD 16f Good 52 3905 bl
47 2 CATT 12f Soft 46 4003 bl

YETTI 2 ch f £2109
71 2 NOTT 6f Good 2010
70 2 BATH 6f Firm 2328
58 5 BEVE 5f Firm 2730
69 3 LING 5f Firm 69 3491
63 6 LEIC 6f Gd/Sft 70 4030
66 5 LING 6f Soft 70 4269

YNYSMON 2 b c £4136
63 5 BATH 6f Firm 2784
62 7 CHEP 5f Gd/Fm 3252
80 4 PONT 5f Firm 3500
62 15 DONC 6f Firm 3888
79 1 **MUSS** 5f Gd/Sft 4131*
64 11 NEWB 6f Sft/Hvy 77 4468

YORBA LINDA 5 ch m £8282
85 8 BEVE 5f Firm 1277
70 7 KEMP 5f Soft 1529
85 5 MUSS 5f Firm 86 1687
74 8 SAND 5f Gd/Fm 1987
89 7 NEWC 10f Firm 2339
90 1 **DUSS** 8f Good 2910*

YORK CLIFF 2 b c £605
91 3 YARM 8f Soft 4512

YORK WHINE 2 ch f £0

0 18 NEWM 6f Gd/Sft 4530

YORKER 2 b c £0
67	10	PONT	5f Firm			3500	
0	16	BEVE	5f Good			3955	
65	8	NOTT	5f Gd/Sft			4503	

YORKIE TOO 4 b g £0
0a	12	SOUT	7f Aw	48	867	VIS
28a	8	WOLV	6f Aw		1139	bl
38	5	REDC	6f Gd/Sft	46	1578	bl
23	14	LEIC	6f Gd/Sft	46	1734	
0	16	BRIG	7f Gd/Fm	44	1930	bl

YORKIES BOY 5 ro g £26068
84	9	NEWB	5f Soft	102	914	
87	5	KEMP	6f Soft		1016	
87	2	HAYD	6f Gd/Fm		1164	
91	2	BEVE	5f Firm		1277	
78	16	HAYD	5f Gd/Sft	90	1533	
97	4	SAND	5f Gd/Fm		1987	
105	1	HAYD	6f Gd/Fm		2458*	
96	6	NEWB	6f Aw	105	2706	
103	7	NEWM	5f Gd/Fm		2960	
108	1	CHES	6f Firm		3172*	
85	11	YORK	7f Aw		3600	
105	4	EPSO	7f Good		3763	
0	14	NEWM	5f Good		4182	
100	7	NEWM	6f Good		4346	
92	6	NEWB	6f Gd/Sft	106	4456	bl
68	10	DONC	6f Heavy		4581	bl

YORKSHIRE 6 ch g £8080
102	5	CHES	19f Firm	105	3171
104	3	NEWB	13f Gd/Fm		3483
80	20	YORK	14f Gd/Fm	105	3565
99	4	DONC	15f Heavy		4568

YORKSHIRE ROSE 2 b f £1090
82	2	LING	7f Soft	4268

YOU ARE THE ONE 3 b f £4992
81	1	NEWM	8f Gd/Fm	3626*
87	10	YARM	10f Firm	3918
87	8	NEWM	10f Good	4337

YOU DA MAN 3 b c £11855
61a	4	LING	7f Aw		421	
78a	2	WOLV	9f Aw		467	
60a	2	LING	10f Aw		523	
45a	4	SOUT	12f Aw		603	BL
75a	1	LING	10f Aw		629*	
78	2	WIND	8f Gd/Fm	70	744	
60	5	KEMP	9f Soft	73	999	
76	1	NEWM	12f Gd/Fm	73	2131*	
62	7	SALI	12f Gd/Sft	75	2470	
68	6	WIND	10f Good	75	3356	
77	3	EPSO	10f Gd/Fm		3403	

YOUHADYOURWARNING 3 br f £1610
75	3	WIND	9f Gd/Sft	1428
75	2	YARM	11f Heavy	4481

YOUNG ALEX 2 ch c £4743
40	12	DONC	5f Good		730
70	1	BRIG	5f Gd/Fm		1931*
74	1	CHEP	6f Gd/Fm		2447*
70	4	CATT	7f Gd/Fm	73	2928
55a	5	SOUT	6f Aw		4367

YOUNG BEN 8 ch g £0
28	10	CATT	7f Gd/Fm		778
34a	5	WOLV	6f Aw	1139	vis
0	12	HAMI	6f Firm	1239	vis
41	9	CARL	5f Firm	2822	vis

YOUNG BIGWIG 6 b g £2224
42a	10	SOUT	6f Aw	74	44
59a	9	LING	6f Aw	74	113
27a	11	SOUT	6f Aw	71	218
0a	12	LING	6f Aw	68	358
53a	6	SOUT	6f Aw	65	425
0a	16	SOUT	6f Aw	62	645
54	3	HAMI	6f Firm		1239
48a	4	SOUT	7f Aw	58	1979
52	5	REDC	6f Gd/Fm	55	2158
55	3	NOTT	6f Gd/Sft	55	2192
55	3	HAMI	6f Gd/Fm	55	2796
52	4	AYR	6f Firm	55	2877
47	9	REDC	6f Firm	55	3312
54a	3	WOLV	6f Aw	56	3774
45a	10	WOLV	6f Aw	56	4223
0	16	AYR	6f Heavy	53	4327
46a	4	WOLV	6f Aw	55	4444
46a	6	WOLV	6f Aw	53	4553

YOUNG BUTT 7 ch g £0
0a	P	WOLV	12f Aw	33	723
0	13	BRIG	12f Gd/Sft		893

YOUNG IBNR 5 b g £5100
40a	5	WOLV	5f Aw		76
47a	3	WOLV	5f Aw	46	116
45a	3	LING	5f Aw	47	166
34a	7	WOLV	5f Aw	46	352
52a	5	WOLV	5f Aw		379
41a	6	WOLV	5f Aw	46	445
46a	8	WOLV	5f Aw		533
49a	1	WOLV	5f Aw		639*
56a	4	WOLV	5f Aw		753
44a	4	WOLV	5f Aw		919
55a	3	WOLV	5f Aw		1237
35a	8	WOLV	5f Aw		1392
0a	15	SOUT	5f Aw	48	1806
50	1	RIPO	5f Gd/Fm	47	3180*
51a	5	WOLV	5f Aw	53	3271
39	9	PONT	5f Soft	53	4087
36a	11	WOLV	6f Aw	50	4442

YOUNG JACK 2 b c £1546
69	5	NOTT	6f Good		1408
72	2	SOUT	6f Soft		1602
68	3	THIR	7f Gd/Fm		2057
64	5	SALI	7f Gd/Sft	72	2468
55	6	WIND	6f Heavy	68	4525

YOUNG MONASH 2 b g £0
46a	4	SOUT	5f Aw	1206

YOUNG PRECEDENT 6 b g £0
0	18	PONT	8f Soft	81	875
0	18	KEMP	8f Gd/Fm	79	1926

YOUNG ROOSTER 3 b c £0
44	6	HAYD	7f Gd/Fm	2443

YOUNG ROSEIN 4 b f £7505
44	9	HAMI	8f Gd/Fm	56	1243
43	13	MUSS	7f Gd/Fm	55	1431
53	3	RIPO	8f Soft	53	2542
41	8	PONT	8f Gd/Fm	53	2831
37	13	RIPO	8f Gd/Fm	53	3011
38	6	CARL	8f Firm	51	3192
59	1	HAYD	8f Good	51	3288*
61	1	CARL	8f Firm	57	3574*
56	3	LEIC	8f Gd/Sft		4033
0	19	REDC	8f Gd/Sft	59	4217
55	3	LEIC	8f Sft/Hvy	58	4310
41	10	MUSS	8f Soft	58	4565

YOUNG TERN 2 b c £0
61	9	HAYD	6f Gd/Fm		2454
45	11	HAYD	6f Gd/Sft		3268
58	8	BATH	6f Soft		4137
74	8	DONC	6f Gd/Sft		4449
0	19	DONC	7f Heavy	66	4577

YOUNG UN 5 b g £5446
57	7	NOTT	10f Good	65	786
62	6	DONC	10f Gd/Sft	64	1050
51	11	WIND	8f Gd/Fm	63	1201
63	4	NOTT	10f Gd/Fm		1370
66	2	LING	9f Good	62	1744
54	7	BEVE	10f Gd/Fm	62	1921
63	2	NOTT	10f Gd/Fm	63	2190
62	5	SAND	10f Gd/Fm	64	2527
56	5	LING	10f Good	64	2655
58	7	WIND	10f Gd/Fm	63	2888
47	10	DONC	10f Gd/Fm	62	3159
52	7	YARM	10f Gd/Fm		3383
54	3	YORK	9f Good		3808
27	11	CHES	10f Soft	59	4074
47	14	SAND	10f Soft	58	4208
46	10	WIND	10f Gd/Sft	58	4291

YOUR THE LADY 3 b f £7778
70	5	KEMP	8f Gd/Fm	72	2084
77	1	CHEP	8f Gd/Fm	70	2661*
68	1	BRIG	8f Firm		2895*
68	7	NEWB	8f Gd/Fm	74	3178
76	2	FOLK	10f Gd/Fm	74	3585

YOURE SPECIAL 3 b c £22608
75a	2	WOLV	8f Aw		171	
82a	1	WOLV	9f Aw		319*	
58	11	DONC	10f Gd/Fm	77	701	
57	13	DONC	8f Gd/Sft	75	1053	
56	7	RIPO	8f Gd/Fm	72	3713	
59	6	BEVE	12f Good	87	3954	
49a	8	WOLV	12f Aw	74	4245	
64	1	NEWC	16f Heavy	58	4424*	VIS
71	1	NOTT	16f Gd/Fm	64	4508*	
79	1	MUSS	16f Soft	68	4563*	

YUKA SAN 2 ch f £0
47	6	NOTT	5f Firm	1267
44	11	RIPO	5f Soft	2539
54	4	BATH	6f Firm	2939
56	7	BATH	5f Firm	3621
57	5	WARW	15f Gd/Fm	3912

YURA MADAM 2 b f £0
0	12	FOLK	7f Gd/Fm	3582
8	5	BRIG	7f Firm	3733
0	29	NEWM	7f Good	4336

ZAAJER 4 ch c £23959
108	5	KEMP	10f Soft	1014
109	3	NEWB	13f Gd/Fm	1401
111	1	CHES	13f Gd/Fm	1093509*
89	5	AYR	11f Gd/Sft	4011

ZABIONIC 3 ch c £325
56	4	DONC	7f Good		717	
61a	7	WOLV	8f Aw	69	921	
48	13	CARL	8f Firm	67	1255	
52	7	WARW	11f Heavy	63	1521	BL
44	9	NOTT	10f Good		2012	bl
65	6	NOTT	8f Gd/Fm		2188	
42	7	BEVE	10f Gd/Sft	54	3052	

ZAFARELLI 6 gr g £0
27	9	FOLK	15f Soft	48	963	vis

ZAFFIA 3 b f £0
78	8	NEWB	8f Good		1377
65	10	NEWB	7f Gd/Fm	75	1787

ZAFILLY 2 ch f £0
42	9	KEMP	10f Gd/Fm	3789
69	7	GOOD	7f Soft	4063
34	13	NEWM	7f Good	4336

ZAFONICS SONG 3 br c £18656
87	3	NEWM	10f Good		957
102	5	SAND	10f Heavy		1056
78	1	YARM	11f Firm		2386*
101	2	GOOD	12f Gd/Fm	96	3088
103	7	NEWB	11f Firm		3984

ZAFONIUM 3 ch c £32955
108	2	ASCO	12f Good		2148	
98	4	HAYD	12f Gd/Fm		2503	
0	7	KEMP	12f Gd/Fm		3792	
105	6	NEWB	11f Firm		3984	BL
86	6	NEWM	12f Good		4194	

ZAGALETA 3 b f £7222

```
47  10  THIR  8f Soft       76  931
0   18  YORK  8f Firm       76  1341
34  10  PONT  6f Good       72  2364  t
63  2   BEVE  10f Good          2884
68  1   AYR   10f Good      63  3368*
74  2   LING  10f Firm      69  3581
70  3   CHEP  10f Good      69  3870
71  2   PONT  10f Soft          4088
```

ZAHA 5 b g £3422
```
49a 6   WOLV  12f Aw        64  437
38  12  DONC  12f Gd/Fm     57  699
22  9   WARW  11f Heavy     55  889
63  1   NOTT  10f Gd/Sft    52  1370*
62  4   BEVE  10f Firm      61  1921
40  10  YARM  10f Good      61  2199
35  11  WIND  10f Good      61  2544
58  7   EPSO  10f Good      61  2790
41a 8   SOUT  12f Aw            4366
```

ZAHEEMAH 2 b f £4588
```
63  6   ASCO  6f Good           2172
95  4   NEWM  6f Good           2565
92  5   ASCO  6f Gd/Fm          2996
92  2   SAND  8f Good           3433
```

ZALAL 5 b g £0
```
77  15  ASCO  12f Good      95  2069
```

ZAMAT 4 b g £547
```
34  10  THIR  6f Gd/Sft         3780
84  4   REDC  7f Gd/Sft         4218
13  8   AYR   10f Heavy     47  4306
29  7   NEWC  10f Heavy     47  4404
```

ZANAY 4 b c £52820
```
81a 4   SOUT  8f Aw         82  49
97a 1   LING  10f Aw            157*
107a 1  LING  10f Aw        95  442*
100a 1  LING  10f Aw            593+
107a 1  LING  10f Aw            690*
68  17  DONC  8f Good       90  733
76  4   CHEP  10f Gd/Sft        1797
82  9   ASCO  8f Good       90  2090  BL
```

ZANDEED 2 b c £0
```
73  5   YORK  6f Firm           1328
63  9   LEIC  6f Firm           2029
```

ZANDOS CHARM 2 b f £3337
```
52  5   BATH  6f Firm           2939
0   16  WIND  6f Good           3187
67  1   SALI  7f Gd/Fm          3388*
63  3   EPSO  7f Good       66  3690
0   12  YARM  7f Firm       66  3922
0   17  NEWM  7f Good           4336
```

ZANGOOEY 2 ch g £0
```
40  8   YORK  7f Soft           4277
37  10  YARM  6f Soft           4390
0   6   DONC  8f Heavy          4572
```

ZANZIBAR 2 b f £1926
```
84  5   GOOD  7f Good           3108
74  2   EPSO  9f Good           3853
85  3   DONC  8f Gd/Sft         4445
```

ZAOLA 4 b f £0
```
0   14  NEWM  7f Aw         67  2347
```

ZARAGOSSA 4 gr f £0
```
61  5   THIR  5f Good       65  1162
54  9   NOTT  5f Good       64  1412
58  7   MUSS  5f Firm       62  1687
59  5   WARW  5f Gd/Fm      60  2252
30  12  CATT  5f Gd/Fm      60  2418
48  7   NOTT  5f Good       58  2684
55  6   EPSO  5f Good       56  3855
41a 12  WOLV  6f Aw         56  4223
26a 10  WOLV  6f Aw         52  4444
```

ZARKIYA 3 b f £44240
```
110 4   LONG  8f V              1319
112 1   CHAN  8f V              1754*
```

```
105 4   ASCO  8f Good           2150
```

ZATOPEK 8 b g £0
```
23a 5   WOLV  12f Aw            1389
```

ZAZA TOP 2 ch f £20942
```
100 2   SAN   8f Soft           4318
```

ZECHARIAH 4 b c £664
```
48  4   THIR  8f Soft       50  907
39  6   PONT  8f Gd/Sft     49  1101
39  5   DONC  7f Good       47  1519
40  6   THIR  8f Gd/Sft     45  1718
41  4   BEVE  7f Gd/Sft     45  1760
9   15  BEVE  7f Aw         45  1920
28  9   BEVE  7f Gd/Fm      41  2479
30  4   NEWC  8f Heavy      38  4406
```

ZEITING 3 b f f £15070
```
99  1   MAIS  6f Heavy          99*
108 6   LONG  8f V              1319
```

ZELBECK 4 b f £0
```
24a 8   LING  6f Aw         46  262
0a  13  WOLV  6f Aw         41  352
0a  12  LING  7f Aw         35  438  VIS
```

ZELOSO 2 b c £7498
```
77  10  NEWB  6f Gd/Fm          1403
84  3   NEWM  6f Gd/Fm          1691
78  10  ASCO  7f Good           2091
87  2   SALI  7f Gd/Sft     84  2468
85  1   HAYD  7f Good           3287*
89  4   HAYD  8f Soft           3787
92  3   CHES  8f Soft           4072  VIS
73  7   PONT  8f Soft           4375  vis
```

ZENDIUM 2 b g £0
```
67  9   YORK  6f Good           2692
```

ZEPPO 5 ch g £3809
```
56  8   WIND  6f Gd/Fm      57  1196
58  4   BATH  6f Gd/Fm      57  1438
50  9   CHEP  7f Gd/Sft     58  1794
55  6   SALI  6f Gd/Fm      58  1887
56  4   NOTT  6f Gd/Sft     57  2192
50  4   LEIC  5f Good       57  2623
54  5   LEIC  6f Gd/Fm      57  2777  bl
56  2   CHEP  7f Gd/Fm          3253
61  1   LING  6f Firm       56  3578*
62  3   EPSO  7f Good       62  3765
51  9   BATH  6f Gd/Fm      61  3821
```

ZERO GRAVITY 3 b g £636
```
57  6   WIND  10f Firm          1293
83  3   GOOD  12f Gd/Sft        1808
57  6   NEWB  12f Firm          2710
```

ZESTRIL 3 ch f £0
```
57  11  CHES  8f Gd/Fm      81  1215
69  10  AYR   6f Gd/Fm      80  1654
66  6   RIPO  6f Gd/Fm      77  2101
68  6   CATT  7f Gd/Fm      72  2438
40  10  HAMI  6f Gd/Fm      69  2779
57  8   NEWC  6f Good       66  3037  VIS
59  5   THIR  5f Gd/Fm      63  3349  vis
```

ZETAGALOPON 2 b f £0
```
0   14  LING  6f Good           4097
```

ZEYAARAH 3 ch f £3496
```
74  3   HAYD  12f Gd/Fm         3324
82  1   LING  11f Firm          3754*
59  12  SAND  14f Gd/Fm     80  3948
```

ZHITOMIR 2 ch c £7273
```
58  6   KEMP  5f Soft           993
72  4   NEWM  6f Gd/Fm          2854
60  8   WIND  6f Gd/Fm          3047
61  6   GOOD  7f Good       70  3660
86  1   EPSO  6f Good           3852*
82  2   GOOD  6f Soft           4079
86  3   NEWM  6f Gd/Fm      85  4214
70  13  NEWB  6f Sft/Hvy    86  4468
```

ZIBAK 6 b g £0

```
0   13  CARL  6f Firm       40  1258
34  6   MUSS  7f Firm           1685
33  5   HAMI  6f Gd/Fm      36  1941
25  4   CARL  7f Firm       35  2282
24  7   MUSS  5f Gd/Sft     33  2535
30  6   HAMI  6f Gd/Fm      37  2796
24  8   AYR   7f Gd/Fm      31  3138
22  11  RIPO  6f Gd/Fm      31  3180
```

ZIBELINE 3 b c £12569
```
75  7   NEWM  7f Gd/Fm      74  1153
75  2   YORK  8f Firm       73  1341
72  4   HAYD  11f Soft      73  1491
82  4   YORK  10f Firm      80  2004
82  1   CHEP  10f Gd/Fm     78  2450*
86  5   NEWM  10f Gd/Fm     84  2596
87  2   ASCO  12f Gd/Fm     83  3014
79  3   YORK  12f Gd/Fm     87  3728
0   21  NEWM  10f Good      85  4197
```

ZIBET 2 b f £706
```
80  3   NEWM  6f Gd/Sft         4530
```

ZIBILENE 3 b f £8324
```
84  2   NEWM  10f Firm          1857
74  1   PONT  12f Gd/Fm         2560*
97  5   NEWB  12f Gd/Fm         3177
99  3   NEWM  10f Good          4337
```

ZIDAC 8 br g £2172
```
49  10  BRIG  10f Gd/Sft    65  1509
48  11  SALI  10f Gd/Fm     65  3390
58  2   WARW  11f Good          3691
49a 6   LING  10f Aw        60  3828
62  2   SAND  10f Soft      59  4208
62  2   BRIG  10f Soft      60  4419
```

ZIETING 2 b c £283
```
29  9   RIPO  7f Good           3009
63  5   LING  5f Firm           3576
47  4   BEVE  5f Sft/Hvy        4042
```

ZIETUNZEEN 2 b f £53491
```
76  2   HAYD  5f Gd/Fm          1166
76  3   HAYD  5f Gd/Sft         1538
86  3   ASCO  5f Good           2152
90  5   NEWB  5f Firm           2849
89  5   GOOD  6f Gd/Fm          3090
81  1   NOTT  6f Good           3520*
85  4   AYR   6f Gd/Fm          4009
98  2   REDC  6f Gd/Sft         4219
86  1   DONC  6f Gd/Sft         4449*
```

ZIETZIG 3 b c £29830
```
37a 7   SOUT  6f Aw         82  689
82  5   NEWM  7f Gd/Fm      80  1153
77  5   LING  10f Firm      80  1285
73  7   GOOD  7f Gd/Sft     81  1470
72  16  NEWM  6f Gd/Fm      79  1694
76  6   EPSO  7f Gd/Sft     78  1826
74  4   LING  6f Gd/Fm      76  2216
68  8   YORK  8f Gd/Fm      76  2645
81  1   GOOD  7f Gd/Fm      75  3130*
58  13  CHES  8f Gd/Fm      80  3510
77  7   GOOD  6f Good       80  3646
0   20  KEMP  6f Gd/Fm      79  3791
35  11  YORK  7f Heavy      78  4302
```

ZIG ZIG 3 b c £3420
```
73  3   BEVE  7f Firm           1922
74a 1   SOUT  6f Aw             2299*
0   13  REDC  7f Firm       72  3328
```

ZIGGY STARDUST 5 b g £2103
```
36  3   BRIG  12f Good          1647
33  4   NEWM  12f Firm      34  1852
33  3   CHEP  18f Gd/Fm     33  2452
35  2   FOLK  16f Gd-ad     33  2622
32  4   BATH  17f Firm      37  2941
```

ZIGGYS DANCER 9 b h £1717
```
60a 7   LING  6f Aw         75  223
```

64a	8	WOLV	5f Aw	70	394
65a	4	WOLV	6f Aw		465
66a	3	WOLV	5f Aw	65	518
68a	3	WOLV	5f Aw	67	609
78	4	THIR	5f Soft	78	926
65	9	CHES	5f Firm	82	1245
76	4	THIR	5f Gd/Sft	77	1357
21	10	CHES	5f Gd/Sft	77	1781
58	13	CHES	5f Gd/Fm	77	2247
77	8	DONC	5f Gd/Fm	82	2348
0	16	THIR	6f Gd/Fm	78	3123
44	11	HAYD	6f Gd/Fm		3283
68	6	CHES	5f Gd/Fm	72	3512
63	12	DONC	5f Firm	70	3894 VIS
60	11	YORK	5f Soft	68	4285

ZILARATOR 4 b g £22211

73	6	PONT	10f Soft		874
91	1	EPSO	12f Heavy	85	1030*
90	6	GOOD	14f Gd/Sft	90	1484
97	1	KEMP	12f Soft		4039*
90	5	NEWM	12f Good	93	4162
97	2	DONC	12f Heavy		4578

ZILCH 2 ch c £38729

93	2	NEWB	5f Gd/Fm		1782
88	4	GOOD	6f Gd/Fm		3064
106	2	YORK	6f Gd/Fm		3566
105	3	DONC	5f Firm		3900
96	4	DONC	6f Soft		4462
103	1	DONC	6f Heavy		4575*

ZILINA 5 £1050

96	4	LEOP	5f Yldg		1757

ZILKHA 2 gr f £0

45	12	SAND	5f Gd/Fm		3942
0	11	LING	5f Good		4095
0	16	WIND	6f Gd/Sft		4289

ZILUTTE 3 b g £256

29	4	NEWC	5f Good		3035
58	5	RIPO	6f Gd/Fm		3462
50	6	THIR	6f Gd/Sft		3780

ZINCALO 4 gr c £1801

25a	13	LING	13f Aw	65	835
59	4	NOTT	14f Heavy	60	1023 t
49	8	NOTT	14f Good	58	1411 t
60	1	NOTT	14f Good	56	1874* t
60	3	REDC	14f Gd/Fm	59	2156 t
54	3	YARM	14f Gd/Fm	60	2416 t
46	6	NEWM	15f Gd/Fm	59	2856 t
47	9	SAND	16f Good	57	3434 t
0	11	LING	16f Firm	54	3755
0	11	YARM	14f Heavy	50	4476

ZINDABAD 4 b c £4645

110	3	LEIC	12f Firm		2028
112	3	KEMP	10f Firm		2260

ZIRCONI 4 b c £1677

72	4	DONC	6f Good		1517
0	17	YORK	6f Firm	77	2000
77	3	DONC	6f Gd/Fm		2580
68	3	HAYD	7f Gd/Fm		2704
66	8	NEWC	7f Gd/Fm	76	2986
66	11	AYR	7f Soft	75	3992 VIS
47	9	DONC	7f Soft		4461

ZOENA 3 ch f £1156

43a	7	LING	6f Aw	63	4
0	17	WIND	6f Gd/Fm	63	1877
57	4	WARW	5f Gd/Fm	58	2252
55	5	SAND	5f Gd/Fm	58	2478
46	6	FOLK	5f Good	57	2623
51	3	DONC	5f Gd/Fm	55	3161
47	7	SALI	6f Gd/Fm	55	3293
39	5	BRIG	5f Firm		3562
64	3	BATH	6f Gd/Fm		3820
56	11	SAND	5f Gd/Fm		3947

ZOES NEWSBOX 6 b m £0

21a	10	LING	6f Aw		25
20a	9	WOLV	6f Aw		134
23a	10	SOUT	6f Aw		279
12a	7	LING	5f Aw	28	372

ZOLA 4 ch c £0

5a	9	LING	16f Aw	46	649
45a	5	SOUT	16f Aw		1802
0	11	BATH	17f Firm	41	1996 BL
5	9	REDC	14f Gd/Fm	30	2156 bl
0	12	CHEP	18f Gd/Fm	28	2452
7	10	BATH	17f Firm	39	2941
0a	13	LING	12f Aw		4101 VIS
0a	15	SOUT	14f Aw	38	4370

ZOMARADAH 5 b m £79775

118	3	GULF	11f Good		18
104	4	GOOD	10f Soft		4064

ZONING 3 b c £15000

113	4	NEWM	8f Gd/Fm		1171

ZORBA 6 b g £0

28	6	WARW	11f Heavy	58	1003 bl

ZORRO 6 gr g £5363

57a	1	LING	13f Aw	50	167*
55	1	WIND	12f Gd/Fm	52	748*

ZOUDIE 2 b f £0

78	5	NEWM	7f Soft		4541

ZOZARHARRY 2 b c £0

51	9	LEIC	6f Gd/Fm		3215
0	13	YARM	7f Firm		3940
74	5	YARM	6f Heavy		4479

ZSARABAK 3 br g £0

0	18	HAYD	12f Good	56	3284
0	12	PONT	12f Soft	52	4229 t

ZUCCHERO 4 br c £12890

67	6	NEWB	8f Firm	76	2707 VIS
82	1	NEWB	7f Firm	76	2814* bl
77	6	ASCO	6f Gd/Fm	80	2954 bl
74	5	LING	7f Firm	80	3758 bl
81	5	DONC	7f Gd/Fm	80	3880
78	4	NEWB	7f Firm	79	3981
84	3	ASCO	7f Good	80	4112
81	6	NEWM	7f Good	83	4195

ZUHAIR 7 ch g £26824

79	7	DONC	6f Good	86	716
0	20	THIR	5f Soft	84	926
0	18	THIR	5f Good	82	1162
61	11	CHES	5f Firm	82	1245
64	13	THIR	5f Gd/Sft	80	1357
68	9	REDC	5f Gd/Sft	77	1580
0	19	YORK	6f Firm	74	2000
72	3	PONT	6f Gd/Fm	71	2559
74	3	YORK	5f Gd/Fm	71	2644
83	1	GOOD	5f Gd/Fm	72	3091*
70	5	GOOD	6f Good	79	3136
76	9	RIPO	6f Good	79	3464
79	5	GOOD	6f Good	79	3646
78	7	KEMP	6f Gd/Fm	79	3791
87	1	GOOD	6f Good	79	3904*
82	8	AYR	6f Gd/Sft	86	4012
63	11	YORK	6f Heavy	84	4301

ZULFAA 2 b f £4217

89	4	NEWM	7f Good		3020
90	1	LING	8f Firm		3577*
84	2	AYR	8f Gd/Sft		4008

ZULU DAWN 4 b c £1154

81	3	WIND	8f Good		1879
78	3	AYR	8f Good		2138
63	12	SAND	8f Firm	78	2528
55	8	NEWB	8f Firm	76	2707
72	5	KEMP	8f Gd/Fm	74	3078
67	7	RIPO	8f Good	72	3699
51	14	ASCO	8f Gd/Sft	71	4126
0	14	BATH	12f Soft	69	4433

ZURS 7 b g £0

0	16	SAND	10f Soft	68	4208
32	9	BRIG	12f Soft	61	4421

ZYDECO 5 b g £552

82	4	NEWB	10f Sft/Hv	83	4473

ZYZ 3 b c £9075

104	2	DONC	8f Good		735
104	3	KEMP	8f Soft		996
104	3	CHES	10f Firm		1246
102	9	EPSO	12f Good		1848
89	5	EPSO	10f Good		3684
99	9	NEWM	9f Gd/Fm	105	4212

Notes

Notes

STATISTICS
2000 Flat Season

1. TRAINERS RECORD

All trainers with two runners or more in 2000 are listed alphabetically. For each trainer we show the number of winners, runners and win percentage. The section at the end "Highest Win Percent", includes all trainers with 20 runners or more and a win percentage of 14 or greater.

2. OWNERS/TRAINERS/JOCKEYS/SIRES

The end of season tables for the top owners, trainers, jockeys and sires, arranged by number of winners.

TRAINERS' RECORD - Winners/Runners - Nov 8 1999 - Nov 4 2000

Trainer	W	R	%	Trainer	W	R	%	Trainer	W	R	%
Akbary H	3	41	7%	Charlton R	34	199	17%	Haggas W J	48	230	21%
Akehurst J	8	112	7%	Chung G H	5	66	8%	Haigh W W	4	73	5%
Allan R	1	22	5%	Clay W	0	19	0%	Haine Mrs D	1	9	11%
Allen M A	0	2	0%	Clinton P L	0	20	0%	Hall Miss E	0	18	0%
Allen C N	15	205	7%	Coakley D J	2	44	5%	Hall L Montague	8	79	10%
Alston E J	26	374	7%	Cole P I	54	331	16%	Ham G A	0	30	0%
Arbuthnot D P	11	195	6%	Collingridge H J	11	147	7%	Hamilton N	6	54	11%
Armstrong R W	7	121	6%	Comerford K C	2	54	4%	Hammond M D	2	70	3%
Arnold T J	0	13	0%	Cosgrove D S	16	115	14%	Hanbury B	20	193	10%
Arnold J R	1	33	3%	Cottrell L G	7	76	9%	Hannon R	135	1128	12%
Babbage N M	1	18	6%	Cowell R H	9	89	10%	Harris John A	0	2	0%
Bailey A	16	233	7%	Cox C G	3	146	2%	Harris J L	14	121	12%
Bailey K C	0	4	0%	Craze Miss F	6	102	6%	Harris P W	36	401	9%
Baker R J	4	56	7%	Crowley Miss M	0	2	0%	Haslam P C	38	235	16%
Balding I A	50	448	11%	Cullinan J	8	80	10%	Hawke N J	0	2	0%
Balding G B	12	123	10%	Cumani L M	31	222	14%	Haynes H E	0	19	0%
Balding J	7	127	6%	Cundell P D	4	37	11%	Haynes M J	1	37	3%
Barker D W	9	176	5%	Cunningham W S	2	19	11%	Hayward P	0	5	0%
Barnett G	2	38	5%	Curley B J	10	69	14%	Hedger P R	0	19	0%
Barratt L J	0	12	0%	Curtis R	3	19	16%	Henderson N J	3	13	23%
Barr R E	2	80	3%	Cuthbert T K	2	9	22%	Herries Lady	8	136	6%
Barron T D	46	314	15%	Cyzer C A	4	112	4%	Hetherton J	15	198	8%
Barrow A	0	3	0%	D'Arcy P W	2	42	5%	Hiatt P W	8	89	9%
Bastiman R	7	140	5%	Dace L A	0	63	0%	Hills B W	73	669	11%
Baugh B J	2	67	3%	Dalton P T	1	19	5%	Hills J W	26	276	9%
Baxter Miss E	0	8	0%	Davis D	2	54	4%	Hoad R C	0	6	0%
Beckett R M	5	57	9%	Davison Miss C	0	6	0%	Hobbs A G	0	10	0%
Bell K	2	46	4%	Dicken A R	0	17	0%	Hobbs P J	0	10	0%
Bell M W	50	408	12%	Dickin R	0	16	0%	Hodges R J	6	113	5%
Berry A	72	792	9%	Dickman A	1	33	3%	Hogg K W	1	44	2%
Berry N E	0	32	0%	Dods M	21	292	7%	Hollinshead R	34	450	8%
Berry J	2	21	10%	Dondi C	0	2	0%	Holmes G	0	14	0%
Berry John	7	110	6%	Doran B N	0	14	0%	Horgan C A	3	53	6%
Best J R	6	59	10%	Dow S	18	350	5%	Houghton R Johnson	20	195	10%
Bethell J D	8	122	7%	Doyle Miss S	5	44	11%	Howe H S	2	25	8%
Bishop K	0	10	0%	Drew C	0	8	0%	Howling P	16	277	6%
Blanshard M	17	210	8%	Duffield Mrs A	5	91	5%	Incisa Don Enrico	4	153	3%
Booth C B	0	60	0%	Dunlop E L	51	348	15%	Ingram R	8	92	9%
Bosley M R	2	40	5%	Dunlop J L	108	599	18%	Ivory K T	21	210	10%
Bowen P	2	40	5%	Dutfield Mrs N	11	153	7%	James E L	3	35	9%
Bowlby Mrs J	0	33	0%	Dwyer C A	18	215	8%	James L Lloyd	1	40	3%
Bowring S R	17	255	7%	Easterby T D	58	669	9%	James A P	0	8	0%
Bradburne Mrs C	0	3	0%	Easterby M W	31	392	8%	Jarvis M A	44	285	15%
Bradley J M	42	582	7%	Eccles P	0	14	0%	Jarvis A P	24	260	9%
Bravery G C	15	108	14%	Eddy D	2	36	6%	Jarvis W	29	204	14%
Brennan O	0	4	0%	Egerton C R	5	40	13%	Jefferson J M	1	23	4%
Bridger J J	5	249	2%	Ellison B	3	93	3%	Jenkins J R	12	130	9%
Bridgwater D G	2	11	18%	Elsworth D C	33	353	9%	Jewell Mrs C	0	29	0%
Bridgwater Mrs M	0	10	0%	Enright G P	0	30	0%	Johnson Mrs E	1	38	3%
Brisbourne W M	31	210	15%	Etherington T J	6	62	10%	Johnson B R	8	62	13%
Brittain C E	31	401	8%	Eustace J P	12	115	10%	Johnston M	145	877	17%
Brittain M	10	221	5%	Evans P D	25	441	6%	Jones Bob	2	34	6%
Brookshaw S A	1	8	13%	Eyre J L	24	416	6%	Jones G	0	6	0%
Brotherton R	13	153	8%	Fahey R A	41	337	12%	Jones D Haydn	9	115	8%
Brown K Cunningham	5	72	7%	Fairhurst C W	14	165	8%	Jones Mrs Merrita	1	9	11%
Brown G	0	17	0%	Fanshawe J R	41	300	14%	Jones T M	3	66	5%
Buckley M A	6	106	6%	Felgate P S	7	112	6%	Jones A P	0	4	0%
Burchell D	0	61	0%	Fierro G	0	2	0%	Jordan F	1	54	2%
Burgoyne P	0	66	0%	Fisher R F	0	12	0%	Juckes A G	1	29	3%
Burke K R	49	475	10%	FitzGerald J G	6	75	8%	Keddy T	2	29	7%
Butler G A	26	197	13%	Flower R M	3	117	3%	Kellett C N	4	117	3%
Butler P	0	40	0%	Forbes A L	0	4	0%	Kelleway A	2	9	22%
Bycroft N	2	98	2%	Ford Mrs P	0	5	0%	Kelleway Miss Gay	17	224	8%
Caldwell T H	1	28	4%	Ford R	0	10	0%	Kelly G P	0	43	0%
Callaghan N A	19	195	10%	Foustok Miss I	0	17	0%	Kemp W T	0	39	0%
Camacho Miss A	11	61	18%	Fox J C	5	59	8%	Kettle M	6	75	8%
Campion Mark	0	6	0%	Frost R G	0	2	0%	Kettlewell S E	5	96	5%
Candy H	15	138	11%	Gallagher J	0	3	0%	Kinane C M	0	9	0%
Cantillon D E	2	12	17%	George Miss M	2	24	8%	King Mrs	6	48	13%
Carroll D	6	126	5%	Gilbert J A	0	29	0%	King J S	9	56	16%
Carroll A W	1	92	1%	Gilligan P L	6	45	13%	Knight Miss C	0	5	0%
Case B I	0	20	0%	Given J G	22	253	9%	Knight S G	2	30	7%
Cecil H A	62	257	24%	Glover J A	17	157	11%	Lamyman Mrs S	2	105	2%
Chamberlain A J	0	2	0%	Goldie J S	28	355	8%	Lavelle Miss C	1	22	5%
Chamings P R	3	47	6%	Gollings S	4	79	5%	Leavy B D	0	32	0%
Chance Noel T	0	12	0%	Gosden J M	83	452	18%	Leigh J P	2	7	29%
Channon M R	103	850	12%	Graham N A	13	117	11%	Littmoden N P	60	586	10%
Chapman M C	8	154	5%	Grant C	2	38	5%	Llewellyn B J	1	18	6%
Chapman D W	32	450	7%	Gubby B	1	30	3%	Lockwood A J	2	16	13%
Chappell Major N	4	63	6%	Guest R	13	172	8%	Long J E	0	14	0%

Trainer	W	R	%
Lungo L	1	12	8%
Macauley Mrs N	19	312	6%
Mackie J	1	22	5%
Mactaggart B	0	9	0%
Madgwick M	1	52	2%
Mahdi K	9	199	5%
Makin P J	33	185	18%
Manners H J	1	6	17%
Mann C J	0	3	0%
Margarson G G	5	124	4%
Marks D	4	30	13%
Marvin R F	0	81	0%
McAuliffe K	5	129	4%
McCain D	0	9	0%
McCarthy T D	1	25	4%
McCourt G M	5	86	6%
McEntee P S	7	72	10%
McGhin R	1	5	20%
McGovern T P	2	20	10%
McHale Miss A	4	45	9%
McKeown W	0	9	0%
McMahon B A	33	363	9%
McNae A J	5	113	4%
Meehan B J	43	470	9%
Mellor S	1	39	3%
Milligan Miss Kate	0	11	0%
Millman B R	30	231	13%
Mills T G	23	154	15%
Mitchell P	10	122	8%
Mitchell Pat	1	41	2%
Moffatt D	0	64	0%
Monteith P	5	81	6%
Moore G L	47	417	11%
Moore G M	6	66	9%
Moore J S	8	172	5%
Morgan K A	1	36	3%
Morgan B C	2	60	3%
Morgan Mrs J	2	12	17%
Morris D	12	115	10%
Morris Derrick	5	49	10%
Morrison H	7	82	9%
Muggeridge M P	2	45	4%
Muir W R	30	428	7%
Mulholland A B	2	40	5%
Mullineaux M	3	68	4%
Mullins J W	0	9	0%
Murphy F	3	25	12%
Murphy P G	0	38	0%
Murphy D J	0	15	0%
Murphy A T	0	55	0%
Murray B W	0	44	0%
Musson W J	16	179	9%
Naughton T J	1	68	1%
Naughton Mrs M	0	6	0%
Naylor Dr	7	81	9%
Neville J	4	49	8%
Newcombe A G	12	190	6%
Nicholls D	76	739	10%
Nolan D A	2	48	4%
Norton J	5	78	6%
Noseda J	42	176	24%
O'Brien D C	0	7	0%
O'Gorman W A	1	9	11%
O'Keeffe Jedd	0	13	0%
O'Neill E J	5	78	6%
O'Neill J J	1	60	2%
O'Neill O	0	6	0%
O'Shea J M	0	23	0%
O'Sullivan R J	4	134	3%
Old J B	0	8	0%
Osborne J A	8	228	4%
Osbourne J Smyth	6	78	8%
Palling B	13	220	6%
Parker C	0	2	0%
Parkes J	1	45	2%
Payne J W	6	83	7%
Peacock R E	0	13	0%
Pearce B A	5	65	8%
Pearce J	32	383	8%
Peill M A	1	15	7%
Perratt Miss A	20	335	6%
Perrett Mrs J	29	198	15%
Phillips R T	1	19	5%
Pipe M C	10	100	10%
Pitman M	0	8	0%
Polglase M J	23	276	8%
Popham C L	0	8	0%
Portman J G	5	94	5%
Poulton Jamie	11	158	7%
Poulton Julian	4	64	6%
Powell T E	1	15	7%
Powell B G	0	2	0%
Prescott Sir Mark	60	258	23%
Price C J	0	11	0%
Price R J	5	60	8%
Pritchard P A	0	7	0%
Prodromou G	0	2	0%
Purdy P D	0	22	0%
Quinlan M G	4	41	10%
Quinn J J	17	189	9%
Quinn M	12	233	5%
Rees Mrs S	9	143	6%
Reid Andrew	24	160	15%
Reveley Mrs M	25	266	9%
Richards Mrs L	5	34	15%
Richardson D	1	2	50%
Rich P M	0	3	0%
Ritchens P C	0	4	0%
Rothwell B S	11	213	5%
Rowe R	1	15	7%
Rowland Miss E	0	2	0%
Russell Miss V	0	5	0%
Ryan K A	29	299	10%
Ryan M J	10	199	5%
Salaman M	2	33	6%
Sanders Miss B	6	61	10%
Sasse D	1	24	4%
Saunders M S	5	93	5%
Scargill Dr D	2	40	5%
Scott A	0	14	0%
Semple I	9	136	7%
Senior A	0	14	0%
Shaw D	17	351	5%
Sheehan J J	0	29	0%
Sherwood S H	0	2	0%
Siddall Miss C	1	43	2%
Simpson R	0	5	0%
Sly Mrs P	0	18	0%
Smart B	9	185	5%
Smith A	2	33	6%
Smith N A	0	3	0%
Smith C	12	136	9%
Smith A D	0	22	0%
Smith Denys	2	59	3%
Smith Mrs J	0	7	0%
Smith D	4	43	9%
Smith Miss	0	16	0%
Smith Mrs N	1	3	33%
Smith Paul	0	4	0%
Soane V	8	138	6%
Southcombe Jane	1	9	11%
Sowersby M E	0	23	0%
Spearing J L	2	79	3%
Spicer R C	2	51	4%
Stanners E	0	11	0%
Stewart A C	22	144	15%
Stokell Miss A	0	21	0%
Storey W	7	103	7%
Stoute Sir Michael	96	491	20%
Streeter A	2	50	4%
Stubbs Mrs L	6	125	5%
Suroor Saeed bin	41	187	22%
Tate T P	2	15	13%
Thompson Ronald	8	71	11%
Thomson Mrs D	0	17	0%
Thom D T	1	7	14%
Thornton C W	5	84	6%
Tinkler N	18	291	6%
Tinning W H	2	19	11%
Todhunter M	0	28	0%
Toller J R	19	145	13%
Tompkins M H	9	271	3%
Townsley Mrs P	0	4	0%
Tregoning M P	19	131	15%
Tuck J C	0	20	0%
Tuer E W	0	7	0%
Turnell Andrew	8	108	7%
Turner W Best	0	28	0%
Turner W M	18	167	11%
Turner J R	0	14	0%
Usher M I	12	146	8%
Wainwright J S	5	172	3%
Wall C F	30	197	15%
Wall T	0	16	0%
Walton Mrs L	0	8	0%
Wane Martyn	0	85	0%
Ward Mrs C	1	17	6%
Waring Mrs Barbara	1	20	5%
Watson F	3	15	20%
Watson T R	3	28	11%
Weeden M J	0	30	0%
Weedon C	1	13	8%
Weymes E	0	4	0%
Weymes J R	1	69	1%
Wharton J	0	21	0%
Wheeler E A	16	148	11%
Whillans A C	0	2	0%
Whitaker R M	10	148	7%
Wigham M	11	76	14%
Wilkinson M J	0	5	0%
Williams S C	17	180	9%
Williams Ian	4	62	6%
Williams D L	0	8	0%
Williamson Mrs L	0	4	0%
Williams Miss Veneti	0	3	0%
Wilson N	0	36	0%
Wilton Miss J	15	147	10%
Winkworth P	0	4	0%
Wintle D J	2	37	5%
Wood I A	6	51	12%
Woodhouse R E	0	4	0%
Woodman S	2	47	4%
Woods S C	31	263	12%
Woods Lindsay	0	2	0%
Woodward G	7	111	6%
Wragg G	27	151	18%
Wylie R D	0	9	0%
Yardley G H	0	9	0%

Highest Win Percent

Cecil H A	62	257	24%
Noseda J	42	176	24%
Prescott Sir Mark	60	258	23%
Suroor Saeed bin	41	187	22%
Haggas W J	48	230	21%
Stoute Sir Michael	96	491	20%
Wragg G	27	151	18%
Gosden J M	83	452	18%
Dunlop J L	108	596	18%
Makin P J	33	185	18%
Camacho Miss A	11	61	18%
Johnston M	145	877	17%
Charlton R	34	199	17%
King J S	9	56	16%
Cole P I	54	331	16%
Haslam P C	38	235	16%
Dunlop E L	51	348	15%
Brisbourne W M	31	210	15%
Jarvis M A	44	285	15%
Stewart A C	22	144	15%
Mills T G	23	154	15%
Perrett Mrs J	29	198	15%
Barron T D	46	314	15%
Reid Andrew	24	160	15%
Richards Mrs L	5	34	15%
Tregoning M P	19	131	15%
Wall C F	30	197	15%
Jarvis W	29	204	14%
Curley B J	10	69	14%
Cosgrove D S	16	115	14%
Fanshawe J R	41	300	14%
Cumani L M	31	222	14%
Bravery G C	15	108	14%
Wigham M	11	76	14%
King Mrs	6	48	13%
Egerton C R	5	40	13%
Millman B R	30	231	13%
Marks D	4	30	13%
Butler G A	26	197	13%
Toller J R	19	145	13%
Johnson B R	8	62	13%
Gilligan P L	6	45	13%
Bell M W	50	408	12%
Fahey R A	41	337	12%
Harris J L	14	121	12%
Channon M R	103	850	12%
Murphy F	3	25	12%
Wood I A	6	51	12%
Woods S C	31	263	12%
Hannon R	135	1128	12%

Top Owners Nov 8 '99 - Nov 4 '00 by Races Won

Name	Best Horse	Races Won	Win Money
Hamdan Al Maktoum	Lahan	86	1054740
K Abdulla	Observatory	82	1082683
Maktoum Al Maktoum	Fantastic Light	49	1162229
Godolphin	Dubai Millennium	41	5308005
Cheveley Park Stud	Regal Rose	40	356775
H H Aga Khan	Sinndar	37	2688183
M Tabor	Montjeu	35	2283150
Sheikh Ahmed Al Maktoum	Tobougg	28	363289
A S Reid	Tapage	25	102785
HRH Prince Fahd Salman	Sailing	21	256717
J David Abell	Saratov	21	99754
P D Savill	Royal Rebel	19	187475
Highclere Thor'bred Ltd	Petrushka	17	433050
Lucayan Stud	Atlantis Prince	17	187820
Mrs John Magnier	Giants Causeway	17	950752
Sheikh Mohammed	Sobieski	17	160182
J C Smith	Persian Punch	16	126299
John Pointon & Sons	Over The Moon	16	38251
Hesmonds Stud	Claxon	15	185237
Nigel Shields	Zietzig	15	80827
David W Chapman	Redoubtable	14	41693
Richard Green	John Ferneley	14	120307
J M Bradley	Juwwi	13	77193
Paul J Dixon	Safarando	13	54933
The Queen	Blueprint	13	158882
Exors Of Lord Howard	Wellbeing	12	124780
Mr & Mrs G Middlebrook	Riberac	12	91042
R E Sangster	Branicki	12	49111
Robert Hitchins	Nicobar	12	99627
Andy Peake	Keen Hands	11	29458
Guy Reed	Flossy	11	51750
J E Abbey	Noukari	11	49705
J R Good	Holding Court	11	300867
Mrs J Hazell	Entity	11	33749
Christopher Wright	Captains Log	10	44867
Frank Brady	Indian Spark	10	77722
George Strawbridge	Limelighting	10	83826
Niarchos Family	Enthused	10	137765
Tommy Staunton	Inch Perfect	10	43547
Wafic Said	Eminence Grise	10	64358
A Al-Rostamani	Murghem	9	138967

Top Owners Nov 8 '99 - Nov 4 '00 by Prize Money

Name	Best Horse	Races Won	Win Money
Godolphin	Dubai Millennium	41	5308005
H H Aga Khan	Sinndar	37	2688183
M Tabor	Montjeu	35	2283150
Maktoum Al Maktoum	Fantastic Light	49	1162229
K Abdulla	Observatory	82	1082683
Hamdan Al Maktoum	Lahan	86	1054740
Mrs John Magnier	Giants Causeway	17	950752
Sheikh Marwan Al Maktoum	Conflict	8	451743
The Thoroughbred Corp	Anees	6	437159
Highclere T'bred Racing	Petrushka	17	433050
Gary A Tanaka	Docksider	5	413479
Sheikh Ahmed Al Maktoum	Tobougg	28	363289
Cheveley Park Stud	Regal Rose	40	356775
Wertheimer Et Frere	Egyptband	7	343901
J R Good	Holding Court	11	300867
L Neil Jones	Millenary	4	292200
Saeed Suhail	Kings Best	3	286203
HRH Prince Fahd Salman	Sailing	21	256717
Lordship Stud	Love Divine	4	216582
J R Chester	Nuclear Debate	3	211318
The National Stud	Golden Snake	2	202827
Baron E de Rothschild	Indian Danehill	6	195966
Lucayan Stud	Atlantis Prince	17	187820
P D Savill	Royal Rebel	19	187475
Hesmonds Stud	Claxon	15	185237
Lord Weinstock	Air Marshall	7	171786
Mrs J K Powell	Goggles	2	163132
Sheikh Mohammed	Sobieski	17	160182
The Queen	Blueprint	13	158882
The Owl Society	Arctic Owl	2	157800
S Cohen & Sir Eric Parker	Indian Lodge	3	154796
John E Bodie	Give The Slip	3	152755
T H Bennett	Pipalong	7	144855
Bloomsbury Stud	Bay Of Islands	5	141554
J-L Lagardere	Amilynx	5	140251
A Al-Rostamani	Murghem	9	138967
Niarchos Family	Enthused	10	137765
Lord Lloyd-Webber	Crystal Music	4	128799
Lady Clague	Namid	5	128156
J C Smith	Persian Punch	16	126299
Exors of Lord Howard	Wellbeing	12	124780

Top Flat Trainers Nov 8 '99 - Nov 4 '00

Name	Wins	Plce	Runs	Win%	Win + Plce%	Win Money
M Johnston	145	242	877	17 %	44 %	1,211,734
R Hannon	135	272	1128	12 %	36 %	1,071,615
J L Dunlop	108	144	596	18 %	42 %	1,495,002
M R Channon	103	201	850	12 %	36 %	1,009,015
Sir Michael Stoute	96	141	491	20 %	48 %	2,921,953
J H M Gosden	83	135	452	18 %	48 %	1,136,957
D Nicholls	76	124	739	10 %	27 %	520,895
B W Hills	73	141	669	11 %	32 %	496,121
A Berry	72	165	792	9 %	30 %	290,251
H R A Cecil	62	73	257	24 %	53 %	801,713
N P Littmoden	60	115	586	10 %	30 %	256,254
Sir Mark Prescott	60	50	258	23 %	43 %	278,051
T D Easterby	58	117	669	9 %	26 %	416,370
P F I Cole	54	68	331	16 %	37 %	796,328
E A L Dunlop	51	78	348	15 %	37 %	332,373
I A Balding	50	90	448	11 %	31 %	337,926
M L W Bell	50	98	408	12 %	36 %	293,893
K R Burke	49	118	475	10 %	35 %	222,376
W J Haggas	48	67	230	21 %	50 %	466,599
G L Moore	47	92	417	11 %	33 %	171,153
T D Barron	46	49	314	15 %	30 %	221,066
M A Jarvis	44	72	285	15 %	41 %	572,089
B J Meehan	43	99	470	9 %	30 %	321,743
A P O'Brien	43	51	172	25 %	55 %	2,750,039
J M Bradley	42	83	582	7 %	21 %	185,306
J Noseda	42	44	176	24 %	49 %	232,410
R A Fahey	41	56	337	12 %	29 %	282,527
J R Fanshawe	41	75	300	14 %	39 %	515,353
Saeed bin Suroor	41	54	187	22 %	51 %	6,014,346
P C Haslam	38	52	235	16 %	38 %	133,791
P W Harris	36	67	401	9 %	26 %	537,961
R Charlton	34	52	199	17 %	43 %	265,364
R Hollinshead	34	70	450	8 %	23 %	108,784
D R C Elsworth	33	69	353	9 %	29 %	287,335
P J Makin	33	51	185	18 %	45 %	147,953
B A McMahon	33	67	363	9 %	28 %	125,463
D W Chapman	32	82	450	7 %	25 %	96,911
J Pearce	32	58	383	8 %	23 %	101,821
W M Brisbourne	31	39	210	15 %	33 %	137,547
C E Brittain	31	72	401	8 %	26 %	496,880

2YO Trainers Record - Mar 23 - Nov 4

Name	Wins	Plcd	Runs	Win%	Win + Plce%	Win Money
R Hannon	67	117	430	16%	43%	514995
M R Channon	53	113	363	15%	46%	583680
A Berry	39	82	299	13%	40%	164139
J L Dunlop	29	57	217	13%	40%	143051
M Johnston	29	51	170	17%	47%	180869
T D Easterby	27	52	284	10%	28%	136495
P F I Cole	26	21	98	27%	48%	187651
Sir Mark Prescott	26	23	110	24%	45%	144804
B W Hills	23	51	199	12%	37%	105103
A P O'Brien	22	33	82	27%	67%	942657
Sir Michael Stoute	21	32	115	18%	46%	395669
J H M Gosden	20	33	112	18%	47%	250351
B J Meehan	19	48	200	10%	34%	205902
M L W Bell	17	39	146	12%	38%	84296
J Noseda	16	11	50	32%	54%	75571
W G M Turner	15	20	102	15%	34%	44495
I A Balding	13	26	125	10%	31%	56786
E A L Dunlop	13	21	119	11%	29%	74281
A P Jarvis	13	23	104	13%	35%	45924
K R Burke	12	25	135	9%	27%	35723
H R A Cecil	12	11	36	33%	64%	57655
M A Jarvis	12	19	74	16%	42%	68039
N A Callaghan	11	8	71	15%	27%	42194
Mrs P N Dutfield	11	15	82	13%	32%	76338
S P C Woods	11	17	57	19%	49%	116636
T D Barron	10	11	49	20%	43%	107753
R Charlton	10	15	62	16%	40%	47017
J G Given	9	10	71	13%	27%	23209
W J Haggas	9	17	55	16%	47%	212353
P W Harris	9	13	98	9%	22%	63772
L M Cumani	7	19	59	12%	44%	35204
N P Littmoden	7	20	85	8%	32%	48613
B R Millman	7	21	61	11%	46%	20030
J A Osborne	7	14	113	6%	19%	27502
M P Tregoning	7	10	46	15%	37%	74422
M W Easterby	6	18	92	7%	26%	20187
J R Fanshawe	6	14	39	15%	51%	46198
P J Makin	6	12	31	19%	58%	24237
K A Ryan	6	21	81	7%	33%	17901
J D Bethell	5	5	34	15%	29%	24245

Top Flat Jockeys - Nov 8 '99 - Nov 4 '00

Name	Wins	Plcd	Runs	Win%	Win+Place%
K Darley	154	257	1008	15%	41%
T Quinn	142	213	795	18%	45%
Pat Eddery	140	180	873	16%	37%
R Hughes	106	180	800	13%	36%
J Fortune	93	149	704	13%	34%
A Culhane	87	196	920	9%	31%
S Sanders	84	156	746	11%	32%
R Hills	83	109	469	18%	41%
F Norton	83	170	841	10%	30%
J P Spencer	81	107	586	14%	32%
M Hills	80	146	613	13%	37%
D Holland	80	143	576	14%	39%
L Newman	77	122	671	11%	30%
N Callan	75	156	716	10%	32%
J Reid	71	165	742	10%	32%
G Duffield	70	124	725	10%	27%
G Carter	68	111	562	12%	32%
J Fanning	65	121	656	10%	28%
L Dettori	62	83	314	20%	46%
P Robinson	61	72	456	13%	29%
K Fallon	60	89	333	18%	45%
J Weaver	59	116	540	11%	32%
M J Kinane	57	51	207	28%	52%
F Lynch	56	101	522	11%	30%
J Carroll	55	123	600	9%	30%
Martin Dwyer	55	96	514	11%	29%
W Supple	50	109	578	9%	28%
R Mullen	47	70	430	11%	27%
M Roberts	47	80	405	12%	31%
M Tebbutt	47	95	482	10%	29%
Craig Williams	46	83	366	13%	35%
K Dalgleish	45	85	459	10%	28%
A Clark	44	70	447	10%	26%
J Mackay	44	80	426	10%	29%
T G McLaughlin	44	85	519	8%	25%
P M Quinn	44	82	479	9%	26%
R Winston	43	103	604	7%	24%
P Doe	42	122	649	6%	25%
J F Egan	42	91	392	11%	34%
D Sweeney	42	99	472	9%	30%

Top Flat Sires - Nov 8 '99 to Nov 4 '00

Name	Wins	Plcd	Runs	Win%	Win + Plce%	Win Money
Sadler's Wells	63	92	340	19%	46%	1961250
Efisio	62	122	609	10%	30%	331479
Mujadil	62	94	448	14%	35%	331415
Common Grounds	59	84	541	11%	26%	592442
Beveled	58	111	579	10%	29%	261151
Indian Ridge	58	117	510	11%	34%	455488
Night Shift	50	82	453	11%	29%	342327
Cadeaux Genereux	49	76	442	11%	28%	288531
Warning	49	92	419	12%	34%	493224
Green Desert	46	53	290	16%	34%	252310
Polar Falcon	46	99	402	11%	36%	296446
Komaite	42	89	457	9%	29%	293545
Danehill	41	56	271	15%	36%	1407635
Caerleon	39	72	253	15%	44%	395265
Emarati	39	76	449	9%	26%	170851
Inchinor	39	76	386	10%	30%	309073
Darshaan	38	40	198	19%	39%	464917
First Trump	37	70	372	10%	29%	152925
Namaqualand	37	45	268	14%	31%	208365
Prince Sabo	37	69	419	9%	25%	130741
Barathea	36	57	275	13%	34%	372614
Grand Lodge	36	42	193	19%	40%	2088089
Salse	36	57	270	13%	34%	403993
Pursuit Of Love	35	79	396	9%	29%	178553
Rainbow Quest	35	64	229	15%	43%	524546
Selkirk	35	77	267	13%	42%	280467
College Chapel	34	71	372	9%	28%	265262
Machiavellian	34	57	234	15%	39%	312791
Zafonic	34	36	199	17%	35%	389759
Unfuwain	33	64	283	12%	34%	688021
Wolfhound	33	68	338	10%	30%	122331
Clantime	32	64	440	7%	22%	137105
Royal Academy	31	71	334	9%	31%	177418
Persian Bold	30	47	304	10%	25%	154133
Thatching	30	60	342	9%	26%	185492
Mujtahid	29	51	299	10%	27%	158910
Piccolo	29	57	317	9%	27%	162281
Pips Pride	29	53	312	9%	26%	252249
Alzao	28	66	298	9%	32%	323130
Deploy	28	60	305	9%	29%	119952

Using The Ratings

The ratings in this book are expressed in pounds on a scale of 0-140. To assess any race where the horses are all of the same age, simply subtract the weight each horse is set to carry from 10-0 and add the result to the Superform rating.

E.G. Dunan 4-9-2 rated 61   10-0 minus 9-2 = 12   12 + 61 = 73

Make these calculations for each horse in turn. The horse with the highest adjusted rating is most favoured by the weights.

To assess a race in which there are horses of different ages, consult the scale of age, weight and distance found on the last 3 pages at the back of the book. On consulting the scale, according to the distance of the race, the month in which it is taking place (and time within the month) and the age of the horse, subtract the weight the horse is set to carry from the weight now pin-pointed in the table. Then add the result to the horse's Superform rating.

E.G.   **7 furlong race on 11th April**

Dunan 4-9-2 rated 61 Table weight 10-0 minus 9-2 =12   12 plus 61=73
Grady 3-8-1   rated 61 Table weight 9-0 minus 8-1 =13   13 plus 61=74
Budge 3-7-10 rated 60 Table weight 9-0 minus 7-10=18 18 plus 60=78
                  Budge has the best chance at the weights

USING THE RATINGS
A considerable time saving method for rating any race meeting is to make calculations only for those horses mentioned in the betting forecast. This applies to the majority of bread and butter racing but valuable handicaps need more detailed treatment. Concentrating only on horses mentioned in the betting forecast should take about twenty minutes per meeting - with practice. Another advantage of working this way is that you can compare the odds on offer with the ratings calculated. It should not take long before you become adept at spotting value for money.

VALUE OF RECENT FORM
Please remember that ratings are not magic figures. Above all, you must take into account whether or not the horse is racefit. Unless you have a direct stable link the only way to be sure of fitness is to have printed evidence of a good recent run. By recent we mean no more than 40 days ago. Also try to ensure that the rating which you are using was achieved recently. As a general rule form more than 40 days old must be treated with caution. However horses from top stables such as Gosden, Cecil or Stoute can usually be relied upon to be fit whenever they run.

PATTERN OF EVENTS
Don't become so tied up with figures that you miss the broad pattern of events in racehorse performances. Most horses, especially handicappers, need a set of conditions before they are able to produce their best. The distance must be right: their going requirements must be met and for many horses, particularly front running types, the course must be suitable.

Time/Pace/Going Figures

We do use race times to calculate the prevailing going on the day, and also to give an idea of the relative pace at which each race was run.

Firstly we compare the race time with the standard time for the track. When this is calculated on a per furlong basis over 6 races, a fairly accurate picture of the prevailing going emerges.

Take for example a race over 5f that returns a time of 63 secs. The standard time for the track is 59 secs. Thus the race was run in 4 seconds slower than standard time. Divide 4 (seconds) by 5 (furlongs) which equals 0.80. Do this for all six races which would typically give figures of .80, 1.00, .65, 1.10, 1.15, 1.05. Add the figures together - total 5.75 for 6 races. Divide 5.75 by 6 (races) and we have an average per furlong figure of .96 (.9583 rounded up).

This would indicate that the going was on the soft side or good since we use the following table as a guide:

1.30 and upwards	HEAVY
0.90 to 1.30	SOFT
0.60 to 0.90	GOOD/SOFT
0.40 to 0.60	GOOD
0.20 to 0.40	GOOD/FIRM
Below 0.20	FIRM

The average figure for each meeting is printed after the going in each race - usually without the decimal point. Thus - Good 60.

The official going report is also printed at the start of each meeting.

Please note that we may omit races from the calculations should these races have been very slow run. There are also days when small fields and/or a succession of slow run races make it impossible to produce any meaningful figure.

PACE FIGURES

We also find this going figure useful in determining the relative **pace** of each race. In the above example the average per furlong figure for the meeting was .96. The third race produced a figure of only .65 and was therefore run at a relatively fast pace. Conversely the fifth race with a figure of 1.15 was a fairly slow run affair.

We indicate in the results whether the race was fast or slow run. This figure is calculated by comparing the figure for each race with the average for the meeting. Thus the first race would be +16 Fast (.96 minus .80) Race five would be -19 slow (.96 - 1.15).

The general conclusions to be drawn from the pace figures are:

Slow pace - Form might be suspect particularly with regard to placed horses (especially in non handicaps).

Fast Pace - Form can be relied on and the form of close up, placed horses should work out well. Easy winners can be followed with some confidence.

Compiling The Ratings

COMPILING THE RATINGS

The ratings published in this book are expressions of opinion, based wherever possible on collateral form. Superform ratings are presented on the same 0-140 scale as used by the official BHB Handicappers and Superform ratings may be compared directly with the official figures.

In studying form and assessing racehorse performance, we are trying to complete a complex jigsaw puzzle. The picture is not complete until the end of the season and sometimes not even then. Many of the "pieces" are definitely shaped and slot into obvious places (the older handicappers), but so many of the pieces have no precise shape and we can only place them tentatively until more of the picture is revealed - and some of the pieces are changing shape as we study them! These non-precise and changing pieces are represented by the late season 2yo's and those 3yo maidens that did not run or were lightly raced in their first season.

However experience helps greatly in rating these animals. Collateral form is the basis for our ratings but of course none exists with the early 2yo's. Experience shows that the early two year old maiden races are won by the same standard of animal each year. Thus we start by giving the early winners "average figures" that one expects for these races and soon the winners or placed horses begin to race against one another and we have the beginnings of collateral form. As results unfold and our handicappers discover that a race has been underrated or overrated, the ratings for the race are revised.
The revision is done on a daily basis throughout the season and all adjustments to the ratings have been incorporated in this annual.

OFFICIAL RATINGS

At the start of each handicap race, in the right hand margin, the figure in brackets [] represents the official rating of a horse set to carry 10-0 in that race. If the figure is 100, a horse carrying 10-0 is running off an official mark of 100 in that race. A horse carrying 8-8 is rated 80 since it carries 20lb less than 10-0. This has been a feature of Superform since 1985. **However since March 21st 1994, in handicaps this official figure is now printed after the horse's weight and this should save much mental arithmetic.**

GUIDE TO CLASS

The following is a fair guide to class:

130 plus	Top class, cream of the crop, multiple Group 1 winner.
125 - 129	Very high class: a good Group 1 winner
120 - 125	High class: capable of Group 1/2 success.
115 - 120	Very smart: capable of winning Group 2/3 events.
110 - 115	Smart: capable of Listed/Group 3 success.
100 - 110	Very useful handicapper/ potential Listed/Group 3 winner.
90 - 100	Useful handicapper.
80 - 90	Fair handicapper.
70 - 80	Average handicapper.
60 - 70	Moderate handicapper/Selling class.
50 and below	Moderate/Selling handicapper.

Racecourse Guide

ASCOT A right handed triangular track: quite a stiff course with an uphill finish: 5,6,7f tracks and the straight mile over which the Royal Hunt Cup is run, are undulating with a stiff uphill climb in the last two furlongs. **Round mile**, 10, 12 furlongs and upwards are undulating, the run in is short, only 2 and a half furlongs, and it is not a good track for coming with a late run: particularly testing track when the ground is soft: in big fields on the straight course, low numbers have an advantage: on the round course there is little advantage but on soft ground high numbers may have a slight edge.

AYR A left handed, flat galloping track: a very fair course which favours the big and strong galloping types: 5 and 6f tracks are straight and easy and in big fields on soft ground, low numbers are favoured but on fast ground, high numbers have the advantage: races run over 7f and upwards are on the turn, left handed, and low numbers hold an advantage: there is a good run in of four and a half furlongs.

BATH A left handed, galloping, oval track with quite a steep uphill finish: 5f and 5f 170 yds tracks bend to the left and are stiff: low numbers are slightly favoured in races up to 1 mile: the run in for races over 7f upwards is a good half mile.

BEVERLEY A right handed oval course with a stiff uphill finish: the 5f course has a slight bend to the right and is a particularly tough test for two year olds: high numbers are favoured over 5f and have an advantage in races up to 1m1f: the run in is a short two and a half furlongs.

BRIGHTON A left handed, very undulating track which is against the big long striding animal and favours handy types, front runners, and those who might have lost some of their zest for the game: 5 and 6f tracks are sharp and easy and on the turn, so that a low number and speed from the gate give an advantage: on soft ground, runners tack to the stands side which gives high numbers a slight edge: the run in is three and a half furlongs: course stands on chalk and the going is rarely very soft but often firm: a course for specialists.

CARLISLE A right handed, undulating, pear shaped course with a stiff uphill run in of three and a half furlongs: the undulations are pronounced and the track is a testing one: the subsoil is clay and the going tends to extremes: 5 and 6f tracks are on the turn and high numbers are favoured except on soft ground when low numbers have an edge.

CATTERICK A very sharp, left handed, oval track, only 9f round, and the 5f track is downhill all the way: front runners are at home here with the accent on speed: on fast ground low numbers hold the advantage in sprints but on soft ground high numbers do best: a course for specialists.

CHEPSTOW A left handed oval circuit of 2 miles with undulations but the course is generally galloping: all races up to 1 mile are run on a straight track which provides quite a stiff test and the accent is on stamina: seems little draw advantage at present: the run in is 5f and this is not a front runners track.

CHESTER An extremely sharp, left handed track, only 1 mile round: this is a front runner's track where all the racing is done on the turn: it suits those animals who need a bit of kidding and is most definitely a course for specialists: unfortunately form shown here is so often not repeated elsewhere: low numbers have a big advantage in all races up to 7f 122yds on fast and soft ground: a course for specialists.

DONCASTER A left handed flat galloping track: ideal for the big, long striding horse, and the powerful galloper: the run in is 5f and the accent is on stamina and courage: there is a round mile track where low numbers are slightly favoured: on the straight course there now appears no draw advantage but in big fields when the ground is soft, recently low numbers have done best.

EPSOM A left handed track with pronounced undulations and a fairly short run in of three and a half furlongs: it is all against the long striding horse: front runners have a good record here and the gradients seem to rekindle enthusiasm in those horses who may have lost some zest: the sprint tracks are fast, downhill nearly all the way: over 5f speed from the gate is essential, high numbers are best: low numbers are favoured from 6f to 1 mile: not a track for the inexperienced 2 year old: the course stands on chalk, rarely rides very soft, but despite the watering system, it can be firm: a course for specialists.

FOLKESTONE A right handed, undulating track with a fairly short run-in of just over two and a half furlongs: easy track, no great demand made on stamina: high numbers have held a significant advantage over 5-6f on soft or heavy but on firm ground low numbers have a slight edge.

GOODWOOD A right handed track with severe undulations: totally unsuited to the big long striding animal: small, handy types who can keep good balance galloping downhill, have the advantage: the 5f track is very fast and speed from the gate is essential: a high draw is generally an advantage on fast ground: the track suits front runners: a course for specialists.

HAMILTON A right handed, undulating course with a run in of 5f: the run in contains a dip 3f from the winning post and a fairly stiff uphill finish: the course stands on clay and in wet weather it rides very heavy: the 5 and 6f tracks are straight and on the stiff side: on soft ground, high numbers have an definite advantage in the sprints.

HAYDOCK A left handed, flat galloping track, with a run-in of some four and a half furlongs: the home stretch is on the rise and the accent is on stamina and courage: in races up to 1 mile, low numbers have the advantage: however when the going rides soft, and especially when the stalls are on the stands side, high numbers are favoured over 5-6f.

KEMPTON A right handed track with a three and a half furlong run in: the bends are quite sharp: a good track for front runners: the separate 5 and 6f track is straight and low numbers have an advantage when the stalls are on the stands' side, especially on soft ground: when the stalls are on the far side, high numbers have the edge: on the round course, in races of 7 - 10f, high numbers are favoured.

LEICESTER A right handed, oval, a stiff galloping track with a run in of 5f: all races up to and including one mile are run on a straight track: a low draw has some advantage on the straight course and this increases on soft ground: the track stands on clay and limestone and in wet weather it rides very soft.

LINGFIELD Turf A left handed, undulating track with a short run in of three and a half furlongs: the gradients and the uphill turn into the straight are similar to Epsom: the track is not for a long striding horse: races from 5f to 7f 140yds are run on a straight track which is mainly downhill and is therefore, fast and easy: fast starters and front runners do well here: on the straight track, high numbers hold an advantage but on soft or heavy ground, very low numbers are favoured, especially over 7f 140ys.

LINGFIELD All Weather Left handed, turning track, 10f round, with a run in of less than 2f. However, note that the 5f track is not straight but turns left throughout the first 3f: the surface is equitrack which seems to provide a much faster surface than the fibresand used at Southwell: horses running well here on equitrack are not certain to reproduce the form on fibresand, and vice versa: a front running type, with a low, inside draw fits the bill here: a course for specialists.

MUSSELBURGH A right handed, oval track, 10f in circumference: an easy course, on the sharp side and front runners do well here: over the 5f straight track, when the stalls are on the stands side, low numbers are best (especially on soft ground) but high numbers are favoured when the stalls are on the far side: high numbers are best over the round 7f/1m track: the course drains well and has a watering system so that the going is rarely extreme.

NEWBURY A left handed, oval, galloping track with a long run in of 5f: the sprint course is quite straight and there are also straight 7f and mile tracks: on the straight course the draw has little advantage, but in big fields and especially on soft going, high numbers are favoured: the course stands on gravel and drains well: the accent is on stamina.

NEWCASTLE A left handed, oval galloping course with a good 4f run in which rises steadily: the 5, 6 and 7f tracks are straight and quite stiff: on good or fast going, high numbers hold a slight advantage but on soft ground, low numbers have a considerable edge: a fair course where stamina is needed.

NEWMARKET (Rowley Mile Course:) All races from 5 - 10f are run on the straight track with an uphill finish: courage and stamina are needed: races over 12f and upwards are run right handed and the course is stiff and galloping: all meetings, except the summer meetings in June, July and August are held on this course: low numbers are favoured especially on soft ground with runners on the stands side often benefiting from fresh ground.

NEWMARKET (July Course:) All races up to, and including, one mile are run on a straight track, with the final furlong being uphill: races over 10f turn right into the straight: a stiff galloping track: the meetings of June, July and August are held here: draw has little advantage.

NOTTINGHAM A left handed, flat, oval track with a long run in of 5f: a very fair course: when the stalls are on the far side, low numbers have an advantage but when the stalls are on the stands' side high numbers are preferred, especially on soft ground.

PONTEFRACT A left handed, sharp and undulating track, with a short run in of 2f and a stiff uphill finish: the 5 and 6f tracks turn left handed into the straight and low numbers have the advantage on fast ground but on soft ground, high numbers are favoured: however the sprint course is stiff, and stamina is important: the going tends to extremes, getting firm or very heavy.

REDCAR A left handed, flat, galloping track with a long run in of 5f: a fair course and is ideal for the big, long striding horse: all races up to and including 9f, are run on a straight track: high numbers are best in sprints no matter where the stalls are placed since the field usually comes across to the stands rail.

RIPON A right handed, oval track with a long run in of 5f which is slightly on the ascent: the bends are just on the sharp side: the undulations in the straight are not nearly as severe as they appear to the eye: the drainage is good and going is rarely extreme: high numbers are favoured on the round course but low numbers are best on the straight course on good or fast ground.

SALISBURY A right handed track, but little racing is done on the turn and there is a long run in of 7f: the last 4f of the home straight are uphill: the course is a stiff galloping track where stamina is important: all races up to and including 1 mile are straight and the uphill finish is a stiff test for 2 year olds: the ground seems slightly better on the stands side and most riders tack over to that side which gives low numbers an advantage on soft ground: it takes a genuine sort to win here.

SANDOWN A right handed, oval, galloping track with an uphill run in of 4f - stamina is all important: the 5f track is quite separate, uphill all the way and provides a real test of stamina for a two year old: when the stalls are on the stands side, low numbers are best but high numbers have a big advantage when the stalls are placed on the far side, especially on soft ground.

SOUTHWELL All Weather A left hand, oval track, 10f around with a run-in of just over 2f. The 5f track is straight. The surface is fibresand which appears to provide a slower surface than the equitrack used at Lingfield and makes more demands on stamina: the 1m4f standard time here is 2m 34.2 secs but at Lingfield it is 2m 30 secs: form on fibresand is often not reproduced on equitrack and vice versa: a handy, front running type of horse, with a low, inside draw fits the bill here in races of 6f to 1m.

THIRSK A left handed, flat, oval track, 10f round with fairly easy turns: the run in is 4f: an easy track with the emphasis on speed: the 5 and 6f track is straight with slight undulations and high numbers have a significant advantage in large fields on good or fast ground: but on soft ground low numbers are favoured: over 7f/1m low numbers are favoured.

WARWICK A left handed, circular track with a short run in of 3f: there are undulations on the back straight but all races up to 1 mile are run on flat ground: the 5 and 6f tracks bend left into the short straight: not a course to delay making a challenge and it does suit front runners: low numbers are preferred on good or fast ground but on soft or heavy, high numbers hold an advantage up to 1m.

WINDSOR The track is in the form of a figure of eight: only in races over 12f and upwards do they gallop both right and left handed: only right handed turns are encountered in races up to 1 mile: the 5 and 6f tracks are nearly straight, flat and quite easy: high numbers have a slight advantage on fast ground but on soft, low number do best: the 5f run in makes this a fair track despite the turns.

WOLVERHAMPTON The all weather track is a left handed oval course of only one mile, with a 380yds run-in and tight bends: the fibresand is a slower surface with more demand on stamina than the equitrack used at Lingfield: form on fibresand is often not repeated on equitrack and vice versa: high numbers have the advantage.

YARMOUTH A left handed course with a 5f run in: races up to and including 1 mile are run on a straight track: suitable course for delivering a late challenge: high numbers are favoured on the straight course except when stalls are on the far side (low).

YORK A left handed, flat, galloping course: ideal for the big, powerful galloper and stamina and courage are required to win here: the 5 and 6f track is quite straight: over 5/6f low numbers have an advantage on soft ground especially when the stalls are placed on the far side otherwise the draw seems unpredictable.

Abbreviations

abs	= absent or absence	ldrs	= leaders
al	= always	lkd	= looked
appr	= approaching	mdn	= maiden
bhnd	= behind	mid-div	= mid-division
bckd	= backed	mkt	= market (betting)
bl	= blinkers	mod	= 1. moderate
BL	= blinkered first time		= 2. modest
blnd	= blundered	mstk	= mistake
blnks	= blinkers	ndd	= needed
btn	= beaten	nrr	= nearer
btr	= better	nrst	= nearest
C/D	= course & distance	nvr	= never
ch	= chance	oh	= see under weights page 8
chall	= challenge	op	= opened
clr	= clear	ow	= see under weights page 8
chse	= chase	plcd	= placed
chsd	= chased	poss	= possibly
cmftbly	= comfortably	press	= pressure
disapp	= disappointing	prev	= previously
dist	= distance i.e 240yds	prog	= progress
	from winning post	prom	= prominent
drvn	= driven	p.u.	= pulled up
dsptd	= disputed	qcknd	= quickened
eff	= 1. effort	rcd	= raced
	= 2. effective	rdn	= ridden
ent	= entering	rem	= reminder
ev	= every	rnr-up	= runner-up
ex	= penalty for recent win	sev	= several
fav	= 1. After SP = favourite	soft	= soft
	= 2. In text = favoured	sh	= short
fdd	= faded	shld	= should
fin	= finished	shrp	= sharp
fm	= firm going	sn	= soon
gall	= galloping	styd	= stayed
gd	= good	str	= straight
Gr	= Group	swtg	= sweating
hcap	= handicap	t.o.	= tailed off
hd	= head	trk	= track
hdd	= headed	unbtn	= unbeaten
hdle	= hurdle	undul	= undulating
hdwy	= headway	unpl	= unplaced
hmpd	= hampered	vis	= visor
hvy	= heavy	VIS	= visor for first time
impr	= impression/improve	wnr	= winner
ins	= inside	wknd	= weakened
juv	= juvenile	wl	= well
ld	= lead	$	= rating is prob unreliable

SUPERFORM DAILY HANDICAP

Superform Daily Handicap analyses all races to come. The horses are printed in-order-of-merit so that the relative chance of any horse can be seen at a glance. The cards are despatched 3 or 4 days in advance of racing so that you can study form at leisure the day or evening before racing. The Daily Handicap makes all the ratings calculations and provides much extra information which greatly speeds up form study - as you can see from the key printed below.

A FREE SAMPLE is available from Furlong Press, High St., Shoreham By Sea, West Sussex. BN43 5DB

Usual subscription rates - Daily for 4 weeks £36   6 Fri/Saturdays only £25

Send cheque or postal order or order by credit card.   Access/Visa etc telephone 01273 452441   (24 hours)

Adjusted Rating in-order-of-merit	Last 3 race references	Last 7 Form Figures	Number days since last run	Trainer	Three latest ratings plus distance and going.	Official rise or fall in weights since last run.
129	1500- 1835* 2347*	402-1211	IN SUPERFORM 21	A Trainer 3-9-0	105 10sft 109 12gd 115 11fg	+7

3.10 GR 1 INTERNATIONAL STKS 3YO+ (A)   1m2f85y .. 3 yo rec8 lb..   6 Decs

10/11F   5/4

1 —135	2066* 2497+ 3087+ 122111	Giants Causeway 20	A P O'Brien	3- 8-11	120 8gd	126 10g/f	126 8g/f		M J Kinane
2 —134	1291- 2064+ 2497- 11- 212	Kalanisi 45	Sir Michael St	4- 9- 5	117 8.3fm	122 8gd	125 10g/f		Pat Eddery
127	186 655 769 103-20	Lear Spear 150	D R C Elsworth	5- 9- 5	118 10g/f	118a 10aw	103a 10aw		T Quinn
125	1623 1848 3071 - 13405	Barathea Guest 23	M R Channon	3- 8-11	116 8gd	106 12gd	112 10sft		L Dettori
123	1043 1402 3087 20- 360	Almushtarak 20	K Mahdi	7- 9- 5	114 8hvy	109 8g/f	108 8g/f		R Cochrane
* 109	2409 2- 5310	Shoal Creek 51	A P O'Brien	3- 8-11			100 12gd	v/s	

Scale Of Age, Weight And Distance

Dist	Age	JAN 1-15	JAN 16-31	FEB 1-15	FEB 16-28	MAR 1-15	MAR 16-31	APR 1-15	APR 16-30
5f	2						6-9	6-12	7-1
	3	8-13	8-13	9-0	9-0	9-1	9-2	9-3	9-4
	4	10-0	10-0	10-0	10-0	10-0	10-0	10-0	10-0
6f	3	8-12	8-12	8-13	8-13	9-0	9-1	9-2	9-3
	4	10-0	10-0	10-0	10-0	10-0	10-0	10-0	10-0
7f	3	8-10	8-10	8-11	8-11	8-12	8-13	9-0	9-1
	4	10-0	10-0	10-0	10-0	10-0	10-0	10-0	10-0
8f	3	8-8	8-8	8-9	8-9	8-10	8-11	8-13	9-0
	4	9-13	9-13	10-0	10-0	10-0	10-0	10-0	10-0
9f	3	8-6	8-6	8-7	8-7	8-8	8-9	8-11	8-13
	4	9-13	9-13	10-0	10-0	10-0	10-0	10-0	10-0
10f	3	8-5	8-5	8-6	8-6	8-7	8-8	8-9	8-11
	4	9-12	9-12	9-13	9-13	10-0	10-0	10-0	10-0
11f	3	8-4	8-4	8-5	8-5	8-6	8-7	8-8	8-9
	4	9-11	9-11	9-12	9-12	9-13	9-13	10-0	10-0
12f	3	8-3	8-3	8-4	8-4	8-5	8-6	8-7	8-8
	4	9-10	9-10	9-11	9-11	9-12	9-12	9-13	9-13
13f	3	8-2	8-2	8-3	8-3	8-4	8-5	8-6	8-7
	4	9-9	9-9	9-10	9-10	9-11	9-11	9-12	9-13
14f	3	8-1	8-1	8-2	8-2	8-3	8-4	8-5	8-6
	4	9-8	9-8	9-9	9-9	9-10	9-10	9-11	9-12
15f	3	8-0	8-0	8-1	8-1	8-2	8-3	8-4	8-5
	4	9-8	9-8	9-9	9-9	9-10	9-10	9-11	9-11
16f	3	7-13	7-13	8-0	8-0	8-1	8-2	8-3	8-4
	4	9-7	9-7	9-8	9-8	9-9	9-9	9-10	9-10
18f	3	7-11	7-11	7-12	7-12	7-13	8-0	8-1	8-2
	4	9-6	9-6	9-7	9-7	9-8	9-8	9-9	9-9
20f	3	7-9	7-9	7-10	7-10	7-11	7-12	7-13	8-0
	4	9-5	9-5	9-6	9-6	9-7	9-7	9-8	9-8

Scale Of Age, Weight And Distance

Dist	Age	MAY 1-15	MAY 16-31	JUNE 1-15	JUNE 16-30	JULY 1-15	JULY 16-31	AUG 1-15	AUG 16-31
5f	2	7-4	7-6	7-8	7-10	7-12	8-0	8-2	8-4
	3	9-5	9-6	9-7	9-8	9-9	9-10	9-11	9-12
	4	10-0	10-0	10-0	10-0	10-0	10-0	10-0	10-0
6f	2	6-12	7-1	7-4	7-6	7-9	7-11	8-0	8-2
	3	9-4	9-5	9-6	9-7	9-8	9-9	9-10	9-11
	4	10-0	10-0	10-0	10-0	10-0	10-0	10-0	10-0
7f	2					7-4	7-7	7-10	7-12
	3	9-2	9-3	9-4	9-5	9-6	9-7	9-8	9-9
	4	10-0	10-0	10-0	10-0	10-0	10-0	10-0	10-0
8f	2							7-5	7-8
	3	9-1	9-2	9-3	9-4	9-5	9-6	9-7	9-8
	4	9-13	9-13	10-0	10-0	10-0	10-0	10-0	10-0
9f	3	9-0	9-1	9-2	9-3	9-4	9-5	9-6	9-7
	4	10-0	10-0	10-0	10-0	10-0	10-0	10-0	10-0
10f	3	8-13	9-0	9-1	9-2	9-3	9-4	9-5	9-6
	4	10-0	10-0	10-0	10-0	10-0	10-0	10-0	10-0
11f	3	8-11	8-13	9-0	9-1	9-2	9-3	9-4	9-5
	4	10-0	10-0	10-0	10-0	10-0	10-0	10-0	10-0
12f	3	8-9	8-11	8-13	9-0	9-1	9-2	9-3	9-10
	4	10-0	10-0	10-0	10-0	10-0	10-0	10-0	10-0
13f	3	8-8	8-9	8-11	8-13	9-0	9-1	9-2	9-3
	4	10-0	10-0	10-0	10-0	10-0	10-0	10-0	10-0
14f	3	8-7	8-8	8-9	8-11	8-13	9-0	9-1	9-2
	4	9-13	10-0	10-0	10-0	10-0	10-0	10-0	10-0
15f	3	8-6	8-7	8-8	8-9	8-11	8-13	9-0	9-1
	4	9-12	9-13	10-0	10-0	10-0	10-0	10-0	10-0
16f	3	8-5	8-6	8-7	8-8	8-9	8-11	8-13	9-0
	4	9-11	9-12	9-13	10-0	10-0	10-0	10-0	10-0
18f	3	8-3	8-4	8-5	8-6	8-7	8-8	8-10	8-12
	4	9-10	9-11	9-12	9-13	10-0	10-0	10-0	10-0
20f	3	7-13	8-2	8-3	8-4	8-5	8-6	8-8	8-10
	4	9-9	9-10	9-11	9-12	9-13	10-0	10-0	10-0

Scale Of Age, Weight And Distance

Dist	Age	SEPT 1-15	SEPT 16-30	OCT 1-15	OCT 16-30	NOV 1-15	NOV 16-30	DEC 1-15	DEC 16-31
5f	2	8-6	8-8	8-9	8-10	8-11	8-11	8-12	8-12
	3	9-13	9-13	10-0	10-0	10-0	10-0	10-0	10-0
	4	10-0	10-0	10-0	10-0	10-0	10-0	10-0	10-0
6f	2	8-4	8-6	8-7	8-8	8-9	8-10	8-11	8-11
	3	9-12	9-12	9-13	9-13	10-0	10-0	10-0	10-0
	4	10-0	10-0	10-0	10-0	10-0	10-0	10-0	10-0
7f	2	8-1	8-2	8-5	8-6	8-7	8-8	8-9	8-9
	3	9-10	9-11	9-12	9-12	9-13	9-13	10-0	10-0
	4	10-0	10-0	10-0	10-0	10-0	10-0	10-0	10-0
8f	2	7-11	8-0	8-2	8-4	8-5	8-6	8-7	8-8
	3	9-9	9-10	9-11	9-11	9-12	9-12	9-13	9-13
	4	9-13	9-13	10-0	10-0	10-0	10-0	10-0	10-0
9f	3	9-8	9-9	9-10	9-10	9-11	9-11	9-12	9-12
	4	10-0	10-0	10-0	10-0	10-0	10-0	10-0	10-0
10f	3	9-7	9-8	9-9	9-9	9-10	9-10	9-11	9-11
	4	10-0	10-0	10-0	10-0	10-0	10-0	10-0	10-0
11f	3	9-6	9-7	9-8	9-8	9-9	9-9	9-10	9-10
	4	10-0	10-0	10-0	10-0	10-0	10-0	10-0	10-0
12f	3	9-5	9-6	9-7	9-7	9-8	9-8	9-9	9-9
	4	10-0	10-0	10-0	10-0	10-0	10-0	10-0	10-0
13f	3	9-4	9-5	9-6	9-6	9-7	9-7	9-8	9-8
	4	10-0	10-0	10-0	10-0	10-0	10-0	10-0	10-0
14f	3	9-3	9-4	9-5	9-5	9-6	9-6	9-7	9-7
	4	10-0	10-0	10-0	10-0	10-0	10-0	10-0	10-0
15f	3	9-2	9-3	9-4	9-5	9-6	9-6	9-7	9-7
	4	10-0	10-0	10-0	10-0	10-0	10-0	10-0	10-0
16f	3	9-1	9-2	9-3	9-4	9-5	9-5	9-6	9-6
	4	10-0	10-0	10-0	10-0	10-0	10-0	10-0	10-0
18f	3	9-0	9-1	9-2	9-3	9-4	9-4	9-5	9-5
	4	10-0	10-0	10-0	10-0	10-0	10-0	10-0	10-0
20f	3	8-12	9-0	9-1	9-2	9-3	9-3	9-4	9-4
	4	10-0	10-0	10-0	10-0	10-0	10-0	10-0	10-0

A To Z Index

With the A To Z Index, you can see at a glance where each horse performed best, and pinpoint it's optimum distance, going and track preferences.

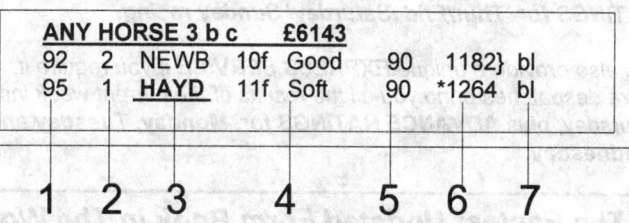

ANY HORSE 3 b c			**£6143**			
92	2	NEWB	10f	Good	90	1182} bl
95	1	**HAYD**	11f	Soft	90	*1264 bl

1 2 3 4 5 6 7

*The first line in **bold type and underlined** provides the horse's name, age, sex and total prize money won last season (win and place).*

1 — Superform performance rating in that race.
a = all weather rating
Each time a horse runs, Superform's experienced handicappers award a rating which indicates the "worth" of the performance.
The Scale used is 0-140, as used by the official handicappers.

2 — Finishing position.   F=fell   U=unseated   R=refused.
B=brought down   P=pulled up

3 — Track name. **Bold underlined** type indicates a win

4 — Distance of the race and state of the ground on the day.

5 — If the race is a handicap, the official rating going into the race (the rating the horse ran off) is shown here.   This figure also includes any pounds out of the handicap.   For example a horse rated officially 80 may be allotted 7-3 in a handicap.   However the race conditions state that the minimum weight to be carried is 7-10. Thus the horse is said to be 7lbs out of the handicap and in effect runs off an official mark of 87.

6 — The race reference number * indicates a win } indicates last season.

7 — Any headgear worn.   bl=blinkers BL=blinkers worn for first time
vis=visor   VIS=visor worn for first time t=tongue strap